SportingNews
BOOKS

The BASEBALL REGISTER & FANTASY HANDBOOK

2006 EDITION

EDITED BY: Tom Gatto.
CONTRIBUTING EDITORS: Ryan Fagan, Zach Bodendieck, Erin Farrell, Shawn Reid, Steve Gietschier
CONTRIBUTING WRITERS: Tom Gatto, Shawn Reid, Lewis Shaw.

COVER DESIGN BY: Chad Painter.
PAGE LAYOUT BY: Chad Painter, Bob Parajon, Ryan Fagan

Major league statistics compiled by STATS, Inc., a News Corporation company, 8130 Lehigh Avenue, Morton Grove, IL 60053. STATS is a trademark of Sports Team Analysis and Tracking Systems, Inc.

Minor league statistics provided by SportsTicker; MLB.com also contributed/delivered stats; Hitting/pitching zones provided by Baseball Info Solutions.

ISBN: 0-89204-801-8

10 9 8 7 6 5 4 3 2 1

CONTENTS

EXPLANATION OF FOOTNOTES AND ABBREVIATIONS

INSIDE THE HITTING/PITCHING ZONES

The chart that accompanies the players' biographies represents batting averages (for position players) and opponents' batting average (for pitchers) on pitches that were thrown into one of nine parts of the strike zone, as defined by Baseball Info Solutions.

Consider each zone as if you were viewing it from the pitcher's mound. Zones 1,2 and 3 represent the area from above the belt to below the belt. Zones 4, 5 and 6 represent from below the belt to above the knee. Zones 7, 8 and 9 represent from above the knee to below the knee. The zone numbers and placements do not change based on the handedness of the batter. Players received charts if they compiled 50 or more at-bats; pitchers received charts if they had 50 or more opponents' at-bats. Shaded areas indicate the highest averages for hitters and the lowest averages for pitchers.

INSIDE THE SCOUTING REPORTS

A major league scout with more than 30 years of experience provided the expertise and wrote the majority of the reports in this book. Grades were assigned using several factors:

On a scale of 1 to 10. A 10 is best, obviously, but not necessarily perfect. Barry Bonds, for example, is not a 10 defensively, but his offense is so dominant that his overall score is a 10.

The future is now. These grades are based on a combination of how a player performed last year and how he is expected to perform in 2006. A player who missed significant time because of injury will be graded lower because of uncertainty about his recovery. Pitchers are affected the most.

Offense matters. Grades are tilted toward a player's production with the bat much as today's game is driven by offense. In other words, the more power, the better.

It's the job. Generally, a situational reliever is a situational reliever because he's not good enough to set up or close. His shortcomings, however, might not show up in his grade, which is based on how well he does his job as a situational reliever. He is not docked because he lacks the ability to be a closer.

EXPLANATION OF FOOTNOTES AND ABBREVIATIONS cont.

Eyes of the beholder. These are our grades, and you probably will disagree with some of them. That's OK. One scout's top prospect can be another scout's most overrated prospect. Scouting is subjective and always will be, no matter how much the number crunchers believe otherwise.

NOTE FOR STATISTICAL COMPARISONS: Player strikes forced the cancellation of games in the 1972 season (10 days missed), the 1981 season (50 days missed), the 1994 season (52 days missed) and the 1995 season (18 games missed). Positions are listed in descending order of games played; because of limited space, pinch hitter and pinch runner are listed in the regular-season section only if a player did not play a defensive position.

*   Led league. For fielding statistics, the player led the league at the position shown.

•   Tied for league lead. For fielding statistics, the player tied for the league lead at the position shown.

†   Led league, but number indicated is total figure for two or more positions.

‡   Tied for league lead, but number indicated is total figure for two or more positions.

§   Led or tied for league lead, but total figure is divided between two different teams.

...   Statistic unavailable, inapplicable, unofficial or mathematically impossible to calculate.

—   Manager statistic inapplicable.

LEAGUES: A.A.—American Association. **A.L.**—American. **App., Appal.**—Appalachian. **AZL**—Arizona Rookie League. **Atl.**—Atlantic. **Cal., Calif.**—California. **Can-Am.**—Canadian-American. **Car., Caro., Carol.**—Carolina. **Cent.**—Central. **DSL**—Dominican Summer. **East.**—Eastern. **Fla. St., FSL**—Florida State. **GCL**—Gulf Coast. **I.L., Int'l.**—International. **Jp. Cen.**—Japan Central. **Jp. East.**—Japan Eastern. **Jp. Pac.**—Japan Pacific. **Jp. West.**—Japan Western. **Kor.**—Korean. **Mex.**—Mexican. **Mid., Midw.**—Midwest. **N.L.**—National. **Nor., North.**—Northern. **N'west, N'West, NW**—Northwest. **NY-Penn.**, **N.Y.-Penn., N.Y.-Penn, NY-P, NYP**—New York-Pennsylvania. **PCL**—Pacific Coast. **Pio., Pion.**—Pioneer. **S. Atl., SAL**—South Atlantic. **Sou., South.**—Southern. **Tai.**—Taiwan. **Tex.**—Texas. **Tex.-La.**—Texas-Louisiana. **VSL**—Venezuelan Summer. **West.**—Western.

TEAMS: Aguas.—Aguascalientes. **Alb./Colon., Alb./Colonie**—Albany/Colonie. **Ariz.**—Arizona. **Ariz. D-backs**—Arizona League Diamondbacks. **Belling.**—Bellingham. **Birm.**—Birmingham. **Brevard Co.**—Brevard County. **Cant./Akr.**—Canton/Akron. **Ced. Rap., Cedar Rap.**—Cedar Rapids. **Cent. Ore.**—Central Oregon. **Central Vall.**—Central Valley. **Char., Charl.**—Charleston. **Chatt.**—Chattanooga. **Chiba Lot.**—Chiba Lotte. **Ciu. Juarez**—Ciudad Juarez. **Colo. Spr., Colo. Springs**—Colorado Springs. **Dall./Fort W.**—Dallas/Fort Worth. **Day. Beach.**—Daytona Beach. **Dom.**—Dominican. **Dom. Inds.**—Dominican Indians. **Dom. B. Jays**—Dominican Blue Jays. **Dom. Orioles/WS**—Dominican Orioles/White Sox. **Elizabeth.**—Elizabethton. **Fort Lauder., Fort Laud.**—Fort Lauderdale. **GC**—Gulf Coast. **GC Whi. Sox**—Gulf Coast White Sox. **Greens.**—Greensboro. **Jacksonv.**—Jacksonville. **Johns. City**—Johnson City. **Kane Co.**—Kane County. **M.C., Mex. City**—Mexico City. **M.C. R. Dev.**—Mexico City Red Devils. **Monc.**—Monclova. **Montgom.**— Montgomery. **Niag. F., Niag. Falls**—Niagara Falls. **Okla. City**—Oklahoma City. **Prince Will., Prin. Will., Prin. William**—Prince William. **Ral./Dur.**—Raleigh/Durham. **Rancho Cuca.**—Rancho Cucamonga. **Salt.**—Saltillo. **Salt.-Monc.**—Saltillo-Monclova. **San. Dom., San. Domingo**—Santo Domingo. **San Bern.**—San Bernardino. **San Fran.**—San Francisco. **Scran./W.B.**—Scranton/Wilkes-Barre. **S.C.**—South Carolina. **S. Oregon**—Southern Oregon. **Spartan.**—Spartanburg. **St. Cath., St. Cathar.**—St. Catharines. **St. Pete.**—St. Petersburg. **Stock.**—Stockton. **Ven.**—Venezuelan. **W. Mich.**—West Michigan. **Will.**—Williamsport. **Win.-Salem**—Winston-Salem. **Wis. Rap., Wis. Rapids**—Wisconsin Rapids. **W.P. Beach**—West Palm Beach. **W.Va.**—West Virginia. **Yo. Bay, Yoko. Bay**—Yokohama Bay.

STATISTICS: A—assists. **AB**—at-bats. **Avg.**—average (average allowed for pitchers). **BB**—bases on balls. **CG**—complete games. **CS**—caught stealing. **E**—errors. **ER**—earned runs. **ERA**—earned run average. **G**—games. **GDP**—grounded into double play. **GS**—games started. **H**—hits. **HBP**—hit by pitch. **Hld.**—holds. **HR**—home runs. **IBB**—intentional bases on balls. **IP**—innings pitched. **L**—losses. **OBP**—on-base percentage. **OPS**—on-base plus slugging percentage. **Pct.**—winning percentage. **PO**—putouts. **Pos.**—position. **R**—runs. **RBI**—runs batted in. **SB**—stolen bases. **ShO**—shutouts. **SLG**—slugging percentage. **SO**—strikeouts. **Sv.**—saves. **Sv.Opp.**—save opportunities. **W**—wins. **WHIP**—walks plus hits divided by innings pitched. **2B**—doubles. **3B**—triples.

2005 PLAYERS LIST

Year-by-year major and minor league statistics for every player who played in at least one major league game in 2005

Career transactions and biographical information

Strike zone charts and lefty-righty splits for every batter with at least 50 at-bats and pitcher with at least 50 batters faced

A

ABERNATHY, BRENT — 2B

PERSONAL: Born September 23, 1977, in Atlanta. ... 6-1/191. ... Bats right, throws right. ... Full name: Michael Brent Abernathy. ... High school: Lovett School (Atlanta).

TRANSACTIONS/CAREER NOTES: Selected by Toronto Blue Jays organization in second round of 1996 free-agent draft; pick received as part of compensation from Florida Marlins for signing of Type-B free agent OF Devon White. ... Traded by Blue Jays with cash to Tampa Bay Devil Rays for Ps Steve Trachsel and Mark Guthrie (July 31, 2000). ... Claimed on waivers by Kansas City Royals (April 4, 2003). ... Released by Royals (November 7, 2003). ... Signed by Detroit Tigers (January 6, 2004). ... Traded by Tigers to Cleveland Indians for cash (March 25, 2004). ... Signed as a free agent by Minnesota Twins organization (January 3, 2005). ... On disabled list (June 15-July 1, 2005).

2005 GAMES PLAYED BY POSITION (MLB): 2B—17, OF—5, DH—2.

BRENT ABERNATHY'S HITTING ZONE

.200	.000	.000
.636	.500	.250
.333	.000	.000

LEFTY-RIGHTY SPLITS

vs.	Avg.	AB	H	2B	3B	HR	RBI	BB	SO	OBP	Slg.
L	.227	22	5	1	0	0	1	3	5	.346	.273
R	.244	45	11	0	0	1	5	4	4	.300	.311

									BATTING										FIELDING	
Year	Team (League)	Pos.	G	AB	R	H	2B	3B	HR	RBI	BB	SO	HBP	GDP	SB-CS	Avg.	OBP	SLG	OPS	E	Avg.
1997—	Hagerstown (S. Atl.)	2B	99	379	69	117	27	2	1	26	30	32	6	6	22-13	.309	.367	.398	.765	12	.973
1998—	Dunedin (Fla. St.)	2B	124	485	85	159	36	1	3	65	44	38	1	11	35-13	.328	.381	.425	.806	16	.973
1999—	Knoxville (Sou.)	2B	136	577	108	168	42	1	13	62	55	47	6	11	34-15	.291	.355	.435	.790	16	.976
2000—	Syracuse (Int'l)	2B	92	358	47	106	21	2	4	35	26	32	1	7	14-13	.296	.343	.399	.742	11	.973
—	Durham (Int'l)	2B	27	91	14	24	6	0	1	15	11	11	4	0	9-2	.264	.351	.363	.714	3	.973
2001—	Durham (Int'l)	2B	61	252	45	76	20	0	4	23	16	23	2	3	11-4	.302	.346	.429	.775	9	.969
—	Tampa Bay (A.L.)	2B	79	304	43	82	17	1	5	33	27	35	0	3	8-3	.270	.328	.382	.710	7	.981
2002—	Tampa Bay (A.L.)	2B-DH	117	463	46	112	18	4	2	40	25	46	8	10	8-4	.242	.288	.311	.599	12	.979
2003—	Tampa Bay (A.L.)	2B	2	7	1	0	0	0	0	0	0	0	0	0	1-0	.000	.000	.000	.000	1	.900
—	Durham (Int'l)	2B	1	5	0	3	0	0	0	1	0	0	0	0	0-0	.600	.600	.600	1.200	0	...
—	Kansas City (A.L.)	2B	10	27	2	2	0	0	0	0	1	3	0	2	0-0	.074	.107	.074	.181	0	1.000
—	Omaha (PCL)	2B-3B																			
	SS	92	368	60	107	22	0	7	40	34	38	4	9	13-7	.291	.354	.408	.762	12	.973
2004—	Buffalo (Int'l)	2B-3B-OF	103	354	68	104	24	3	10	56	33	29	3	12	27-5	.294	.357	.463	.820	14	.763
2005—	Rochester (Int'l)	2B-OF-DH																			
	3B	57	215	35	70	13	0	6	25	21	20	3	7	7-3	.326	.388	.470	.858	6	.962
—	Minnesota (A.L.)	2B-OF-DH	24	67	5	16	1	0	1	6	7	4	1	2	2-0	.239	.316	.299	.614	2	.971
	Major League totals (4 years)		232	868	97	212	36	5	8	79	60	93	9	15	21-7	.244	.297	.325	.622	22	.979

ABREU, BOBBY — OF

PERSONAL: Born March 11, 1974, in Aragua, Venezuela. ... 6-0/211. ... Bats left, throws right. ... Full name: Bob Kelly Abreu. ... Name pronounced: ah-BRAY-you.

TRANSACTIONS/CAREER NOTES: Signed as a non-drafted free agent by Houston Astros organization (August 21, 1990). ... On disabled list (May 25-July 1, 1997); included rehabilitation assignments to Jackson and New Orleans. ... Selected by Tampa Bay Devil Rays in first round (sixth pick overall) of expansion draft (November 18, 1997). ... Traded by Devil Rays to Philadelphia Phillies for SS Kevin Stocker (November 18, 1997).

HONORS: Won N.L. Gold Glove as outfielder (2005).

2005 GAMES PLAYED BY POSITION (MLB): OF—158, DH—3.

BOBBY ABREU'S HITTING ZONE

.435	.526	.351
.354	.476	.233
.241	.208	.200

LEFTY-RIGHTY SPLITS

vs.	Avg.	AB	H	2B	3B	HR	RBI	BB	SO	OBP	Slg.
L	.275	207	57	12	0	5	28	23	45	.353	.406
R	.291	381	111	25	1	19	74	94	89	.430	.512

SCOUTING REPORT *Offense:* Abreu has an outstanding swing with good bat speed and control. Can use the whole field and is a good breaking-ball hitter. Power numbers will continue to increase. Gets into problems when he chases too many high fastballs out of the zone. *Defense:* He has a solid, accurate arm with a quick over-the-top release. Gets better jumps to the line than to the alley and is a little apprehensive near the wall. Gets very good jumps coming in on the ball. *Outlook:* An underrated player, Abreu has the ability to lead the league in hitting. Hit the skids after the Home Run Derby and struggled the second half last season but still is one of the game's best hitters. **Grade 9**

									BATTING										FIELDING	
Year	Team (League)	Pos.	G	AB	R	H	2B	3B	HR	RBI	BB	SO	HBP	GDP	SB-CS	Avg.	OBP	SLG	OPS	E	Avg.
1991—	GC Astros (GCL)	OF-SS	56	183	21	55	7	3	0	20	17	27	1	3	10-6	.301	.358	.372	.729	5	.943
1992—	Asheville (S. Atl.)	OF	135	480	81	140	21	4	8	48	63	79	3	5	15-11	.292	.375	.402	.777	11	.943
1993—	Osceola (Fla. St.)	OF	129	474	62	134	21	17	5	55	51	90	1	8	10-14	.283	.352	.430	.782	8	.961
1994—	Jackson (Texas)	OF	118	400	61	121	25	9	16	73	42	81	3	2	12-10	.303	.368	.530	.898	4	.967
1995—	Tucson (PCL)	OF-2B	114	415	72	126	24	17	10	75	67	120	1	6	16-14	.304	.395	.516	.911	7	.970
1996—	Tucson (PCL)	OF-DH	132	484	86	137	14	16	13	68	83	111	2	5	24-18	.283	.389	.459	.847	7	.969
—	Houston (N.L.)	OF	15	22	1	5	1	0	0	1	2	3	0	1	0-0	.227	.292	.273	.564	0	1.000
1997—	Houston (N.L.)	OF	59	188	22	47	10	2	3	26	21	48	1	0	7-2	.250	.329	.372	.701	2	.978
—	Jackson (Texas)	OF	3	12	2	2	1	0	0	0	1	5	0	0	0-0	.167	.231	.250	.481	0	1.000
—	New Orleans (A.A.)	OF	47	194	25	52	9	4	2	22	21	49	0	4	7-4	.268	.335	.387	.721	1	.990
1998—	Philadelphia (N.L.)	OF	151	497	68	155	29	6	17	74	84	133	0	6	19-10	.312	.409	.497	.906	8	.989
1999—	Philadelphia (N.L.)	OF-DH	152	546	118	183	35	•11	20	93	109	113	3	13	27-9	.335	.446	.549	.995	8	.989
2000—	Philadelphia (N.L.)	OF	154	576	103	182	42	10	25	79	100	116	1	12	28-8	.316	.416	.554	.970	4	.989
2001—	Philadelphia (N.L.)	OF	•162	588	118	170	48	4	31	110	106	137	1	13	36-14	.289	.393	.543	.936	8	.976
2002—	Philadelphia (N.L.)	OF	157	572	102	176	*50	6	20	85	104	117	3	11	31-12	.308	.413	.521	.934	5	.983
2003—	Philadelphia (N.L.)	OF	158	577	99	173	35	1	20	101	109	126	4	13	22-9	.300	.409	.468	.877	6	.986
2004—	Philadelphia (N.L.)	OF	159	574	118	173	47	1	30	105	127	116	5	5	40-5	.301	.428	.544	.971	6	.982
2005—	Philadelphia (N.L.)	OF-DH	•162	588	104	168	37	1	24	102	117	134	6	7	31-9	.286	.405	.474	.879	4	.986
	Major League totals (10 years)		1329	4728	853	1432	334	42	190	776	879	1043	22	81	241-78	.303	.411	.512	.923	46	.982

DIVISION SERIES RECORD

Year—Team (League)	Pos.	G	AB	R	H	2B	3B	HR	RBI	BB	SO	HBP	GDP	SB-CS	Avg.	OBP	SLG	OPS	E	Avg.
1997—Houston (N.L.)		3	3	0	1	0	0	0	0	0	2	0	0	1-0	.333	.333	.333	.667	...	...

ALL-STAR GAME RECORD

		G	AB	R	H	2B	3B	HR	RBI	BB	SO	HBP	GDP	SB-CS	Avg.	OBP	SLG	OPS	E	Avg.
All-Star Game totals (2 years)		2	3	0	1	0	0	0	0	1	1	0	0	0-0	.333	.500	.333	.833	0	...

ACCARDO, JEREMY   P

PERSONAL: Born December 18, 1981, in Phoenix. ... 6-2/190. ... Throws right, bats right. ... Full name: Jeremy Lee Accardo. ... High school: Mesa (Arizona). ... College: Illinois State.
TRANSACTIONS/CAREER NOTES: Signed as a non-drafted free agent by San Francisco Giants organization (August 12, 2003).
CAREER HITTING: 1-for-2 (.500), 0 R, 0 2B, 0 3B, 0 HR, 0 RBI.

JEREMY ACCARDO'S PITCHING ZONE

.429	.000	.250
.280	.222	.333
.000	.667	.333

LEFTY-RIGHTY SPLITS

vs.	Avg.	AB	H	2B	3B	HR	RBI	BB	SO	OBP	Slg.
L	.182	44	8	0	0	0	2	3	8	.245	.182
R	.265	68	18	2	0	2	7	6	8	.324	.382

Year—Team (League)	W	L	Pct.	ERA	WHIP	G	GS	CG	ShO	Hld.	Sv.-Opp.	IP	H	R	ER	HR	BB-IBB	SO	Avg.
2004—San Jose (Calif.)	1	2	.333	4.25	1.31	50	0	0	0	...	27-...	55.0	57	28	26	3	15-1	43	.257
—Norwich (East.)	2	1	.667	5.40	1.32	7	0	0	0	...	1-...	8.1	9	5	5	1	2-1	5	.265
2005—Norwich (East.)	1	0	1.000	0.93	0.93	8	0	0	0	0	4-5	9.2	8	3	1	0	1-0	15	.211
—San Jose (Calif.)	0	0	...	0.00	1.00	2	0	0	0	0	1-1	2.0	1	0	0	0	1-0	3	.143
—Fresno (PCL)	2	0	1.000	1.95	1.08	25	0	0	0	5	3-3	32.1	25	7	7	0	10-1	30	.214
—San Francisco (N.L.)	1	5	.167	3.94	1.18	28	0	0	0	4	0-1	29.2	26	13	13	2	9-1	16	.232
Major League totals (1 year)	1	5	.167	3.94	1.18	28	0	0	0	4	0-1	29.2	26	13	13	2	9-1	16	.232

ACEVEDO, JOSE   P

PERSONAL: Born December 18, 1977, in Santo Domingo, Dominican Republic. ... 6-0/185. ... Throws right, bats right. ... Full name: Jose Omar Acevedo. ... Name pronounced: AH-ceh-vedo. ... Cousin of Juan Marichal, pitcher with three major league teams (1960-75).
TRANSACTIONS/CAREER NOTES: Signed as a non-drafted free agent by Cincinnati Reds organization (December 7, 1996). ... On disabled list (August 7, 2003-remainder of season). ... Traded by Reds to Colorado Rockies for P Allan Simpson (April 9, 2005). ... On disabled list (May 30-July 18, 2005); included rehabilitation assignment to Colorado Springs.
CAREER HITTING: 8-for-101 (.079), 2 R, 2 2B, 0 3B, 0 HR, 4 RBI.

JOSE ACEVEDO'S PITCHING ZONE

.357	.353	.450
.458	.278	.209
.192	.357	.467

LEFTY-RIGHTY SPLITS

vs.	Avg.	AB	H	2B	3B	HR	RBI	BB	SO	OBP	Slg.
L	.348	135	47	11	3	7	28	11	10	.389	.630
R	.293	133	39	8	0	6	18	5	21	.319	.489

Year—Team (League)	W	L	Pct.	ERA	WHIP	G	GS	CG	ShO	Hld.	Sv.-Opp.	IP	H	R	ER	HR	BB-IBB	SO	Avg.
1997—Char., W.Va. (SAL)	3	3	.500	3.92	1.22	15	8	0	0	...	0-...	57.1	61	29	25	8	9-0	34	.268
1998—Char., W.Va. (SAL)	9	9	.500	3.91	1.32	25	25	2	0	...	0-...	158.2	169	74	69	9	40-0	132	.275
1999—Clinton (Midw.)	8	6	.571	3.77	1.21	24	24	1	1	...	0-...	133.2	119	65	56	14	43-0	136	.236
2000—Dayton (Midw.)	11	5	.688	3.89	1.33	25	23	0	0	...	0-...	141.0	135	74	61	16	53-0	123	.247
2001—Chattanooga (Sou.)	4	4	.500	3.69	1.19	16	11	0	0	...	0-...	78.0	68	34	32	6	25-1	82	.239
—Cincinnati (N.L.)	5	7	.417	5.44	1.41	18	18	0	0	...	0-...	96.0	101	61	58	17	34-2	68	.272
2002—Cincinnati (N.L.)	4	2	.667	7.23	1.69	6	5	0	0	...	0-0	23.2	28	21	19	8	12-0	14	.292
—Louisville (Int'l.)	12	7	.632	3.20	1.16	23	23	0	0	...	0-0	154.2	146	61	55	16	34-0	128	.250
2003—Louisville (Int'l.)	6	2	.750	3.43	1.30	29	3	0	0	...	0-0	60.1	56	26	23	5	20-1	57	.246
—Cincinnati (N.L.)	2	0	1.000	2.67	0.85	5	4	1	0	0	0-0	27.0	17	8	8	3	6-1	23	.183
2004—Cincinnati (N.L.)	5	12	.294	5.94	1.48	39	27	0	0	2	0-0	157.2	188	108	104	30	45-8	117	.292
2005—Louisville (Int'l.)	0	0	...	0.00	0.50	1	1	0	0	0	0-0	4.0	2	0	0	0	0-0	3	.167
—Colo. Springs (PCL)	1	2	.333	3.29	1.39	4	4	0	0	0	0-0	13.2	17	5	5	3	2-0	11	.309
—Colorado (N.L.)	2	4	.333	6.47	1.59	36	5	0	0	6	1-2	64.0	86	48	46	13	16-3	31	.321
Major League totals (5 years)	18	25	.419	5.74	1.45	104	59	1	0	8	1-2	368.1	420	246	235	71	113-14	253	.285

ADAMS, MIKE   P

PERSONAL: Born July 29, 1978, in Corpus Christi, Texas. ... 6-5/190. ... Throws right, bats right. ... Full name: Jon Michael Adams. ... High school: Sinton (Texas). ... College: Texas A&M-Kingsville.
TRANSACTIONS/CAREER NOTES: Signed as a non-drafted free agent by Milwaukee Brewers organization (May 15, 2001).
CAREER HITTING: 0-for-0 (.000), 0 R, 0 2B, 0 3B, 0 HR, 0 RBI.

MIKE ADAMS' PITCHING ZONE

.400	.500	.500
.000	.000	.250
.000	.000	.500

LEFTY-RIGHTY SPLITS

vs.	Avg.	AB	H	2B	3B	HR	RBI	BB	SO	OBP	Slg.
L	.200	20	4	1	0	0	1	4	7	.333	.250
R	.258	31	8	0	0	2	4	6	7	.378	.452

Year—Team (League)	W	L	Pct.	ERA	WHIP	G	GS	CG	ShO	Hld.	Sv.-Opp.	IP	H	R	ER	HR	BB-IBB	SO	Avg.
2001—Ogden (Pion.)	2	2	.500	2.81	1.00	23	0	0	0	...	12-...	32.0	26	10	10	4	6-1	44	.220
2002—Beloit (Midw.)	0	0	...	2.93	0.98	11	0	0	0	...	5-...	15.1	13	6	5	1	2-0	21	.228
—High Desert (Calif.)	2	1	.667	2.57	1.14	10	0	0	0	...	5-...	14.0	9	6	4	2	7-0	23	.173
—Huntsville (Sou.)	1	0	1.000	3.38	1.39	13	0	0	0	...	1-...	18.2	14	11	7	3	12-0	17	.209

Year	Team (League)	W	L	Pct.	ERA	WHIP	G	GS	CG	ShO	Hld.	Sv.-Opp.	IP	H	R	ER	HR	BB-IBB	SO	Avg.
2003—Huntsville (Sou.)		3	7	.300	3.15	1.22	45	2	0	0	...	14-...	74.1	58	30	26	6	33-1	83	.208
2004—Indianapolis (Int'l)		2	0	1.000	2.61	0.87	10	2	0	0	...	0-...	31.0	23	10	9	3	4-0	37	.209
—Milwaukee (N.L.)		2	3	.400	3.40	1.21	46	0	0	0	12	0-5	53.0	50	21	20	5	14-2	39	.248
2005—Milwaukee (N.L.)		0	1	.000	2.70	1.65	13	0	0	0	2	1-2	13.1	12	4	4	2	10-1	14	.235
—Nashville (PCL)		3	4	.429	5.75	1.31	26	0	0	0	4	2-5	36.0	35	23	23	3	12-0	45	.263
Major League totals (2 years)		2	4	.333	3.26	1.30	59	0	0	0	14	1-7	66.1	62	25	24	7	24-3	53	.245

A

ADAMS, RUSS   SS

PERSONAL: Born August 30, 1980, in Laurinburg, N.C. ... 6-1/180. ... Bats left, throws right. ... Full name: Russ Moore Adams. ... High school: Scotland (Laurinburg, N.C.). ... College: North Carolina.

TRANSACTIONS/CAREER NOTES: Selected by Toronto Blue Jays organization in first round (14th pick overall) of 2002 free-agent draft.

2005 GAMES PLAYED BY POSITION (MLB): SS—132.

SCOUTING REPORT *Offense:* Adams is a very disciplined hitter, with good bat control and a compact swing. Doesn't have a lot of power but is good from gap to gap. Runs well and can steal bases, but doesn't need to with the Jays. *Defense:* His hands are stiff and his balance isn't very good. Sets up way too early and doesn't appear to have much give in his body; ball will frequently roll up his arm. Has a lot of trouble fielding slowly hit balls. Relies on a quick release to throw out runners because his arm is average. Doesn't have really quick feet and range is below average. *Outlook:* Adams needs to tighten up on defense so that he doesn't become a liability in the field. Might eventually have to move from the middle infield. *Grade 5.9*

RUSS ADAMS'S HITTING ZONE

.125	.476	.375
.360	.391	.239
.167	.250	.210

LEFTY-RIGHTY SPLITS

vs.	Avg.	AB	H	2B	3B	HR	RBI	BB	SO	OBP	Slg.
L	.195	87	17	5	1	1	8	13	18	.307	.310
R	.269	394	106	22	4	7	55	37	39	.329	.398

Year	Team (League)	Pos.	G	AB	R	H	2B	3B	HR	RBI	BB	SO	HBP	GDP	SB-CS	Avg.	OBP	SLG	OPS	E	Avg.
2002—Auburn (NY-Penn)		SS	30	113	25	40	7	3	0	16	24	11	1	1	13-1	.354	.464	.469	.933	4	.963
—Dunedin (Fla. St.)		SS	37	147	23	34	4	2	1	12	18	17	2	1	5-2	.231	.321	.306	.628	9	.947
2003—Dunedin (Fla. St.)		SS	68	258	50	72	9	5	3	16	38	27	6	5	9-2	.279	.380	.388	.768	19	.941
—New Haven (East.)		SS	65	271	42	75	10	4	4	26	30	37	0	5	8-1	.277	.349	.387	.736	16	.944
2004—Syracuse (Int'l)		SS-DH	122	483	58	139	37	3	5	54	45	62	5	9	6-2	.288	.351	.408	.753	33	.939
—Toronto (A.L.)		SS	22	72	10	22	2	1	4	10	5	5	1	0	1-0	.306	.359	.528	.887	5	.936
2005—Toronto (A.L.)		SS	139	481	68	123	27	5	8	63	50	57	3	5	11-2	.256	.325	.383	.707	26	.952
Major League totals (2 years)			161	553	78	145	29	6	12	73	55	62	4	8	12-2	.262	.329	.401	.730	31	.950

ADAMS, TERRY   P

PERSONAL: Born March 6, 1973, in Mobile, Ala. ... 6-3/220. ... Throws right, bats right. ... Full name: Terry Wayne Adams. ... High school: Mary G. Montgomery (Semmes, Ala.).

TRANSACTIONS/CAREER NOTES: Selected by Chicago Cubs organization in fourth round of 1991 free-agent draft. ... On disabled list (June 21-September 21, 1993). ... On disabled list (March 26-May 8 and June 19-July 4, 1999) ... Traded by Cubs with P Chad Ricketts and a player to be named to Los Angeles Dodgers for P Ismael Valdes and 2B Eric Young (December 12, 1999); Dodgers acquired P Brian Stephenson to complete deal. ... Signed as a free agent by Philadelphia Phillies (January 17, 2002). ... On restricted list (May 26-27, 2003). ... On disabled list (August 27-September 11, 2003). ... Signed as a free agent by Toronto Blue Jays (January 7, 2004). ... Traded by Blue Jays to Boston Red Sox for 3B John Hattig (July 24, 2004). ... Signed as a free agent by Philadelphia Phillies (January 11, 2005). ... On restricted list (August 2, 2005-remainder of season).

CAREER HITTING: 4-for-78 (.051), 2 R, 1 2B, 0 3B, 0 HR, 2 RBI.

SCOUTING REPORT *Throws:* He throws a two-seam fastball up to 91 mph, but his four-seam fastball touches 90. Also shows a slider. *Tendencies:* He is a sinkerballer who relies on his experience and savvy. No longer has a true out pitch. Once was an aggressive ground-ball pitcher, but unless he recovers command of the low zone, his career might be at an end. Now struggles to get his slider over for strikes. Four-seamer is flat. *Outlook:* Adams will get a look this spring because of his experience. Has lost velocity and command, making his future questionable. *Grade 5.6*

TERRY ADAMS'S PITCHING ZONE

.250	.571	.000
.375	.333	.625
.333	.333	.667

LEFTY-RIGHTY SPLITS

vs.	Avg.	AB	H	2B	3B	HR	RBI	BB	SO	OBP	Slg.
L	.385	26	10	1	0	2	5	7	2	.529	.654
R	.417	36	15	7	0	1	10	3	2	.500	.694

Year	Team (League)	W	L	Pct.	ERA	WHIP	G	GS	CG	ShO	Hld.	Sv.-Opp.	IP	H	R	ER	HR	BB-IBB	SO	Avg.
1991—Huntington (Appal.)		0	9	.000	5.77	2.24	14	13	0	0	...	0-...	57.2	67	56	37	1	62-0	52	.293
1992—Peoria (Midw.)		7	12	.368	4.41	1.46	25	25	3	1	...	0-...	157.0	144	95	77	7	86-0	96	.251
1993—Daytona (Fla. St.)		3	5	.375	4.97	1.71	13	13	0	0	...	0-...	70.2	78	47	39	2	43-0	35	.288
1994—Daytona (Fla. St.)		9	10	.474	4.38	1.58	39	7	0	0	...	7-...	84.1	87	47	41	5	46-3	64	.266
1995—Orlando (South.)		2	3	.400	1.43	1.04	37	0	0	0	...	19-...	37.2	23	9	6	2	16-1	26	.177
—Iowa (Am. Assoc.)		0	0	...	0.00	0.79	7	0	0	0	...	5-...	6.1	3	0	0	0	2-0	10	.130
—Chicago (N.L.)		1	1	.500	6.50	1.78	18	0	0	0	...	1-1	18.0	22	15	13	0	10-1	15	.289
1996—Chicago (N.L.)		3	6	.333	2.94	1.32	69	0	0	0	11	4-8	101.0	84	36	33	6	49-6	78	.231
1997—Chicago (N.L.)		2	9	.182	4.62	1.77	74	0	0	0	11	18-22	74.0	91	43	38	3	40-6	64	.306
1998—Chicago (N.L.)		7	7	.500	4.33	1.56	63	0	0	0	13	1-7	72.2	72	39	35	7	41-3	73	.255
—Iowa (PCL)		0	0	...	0.00	1.00	3	0	0	0	...	0-...	4.0	1	1	0	0	3-0	5	.077
1999—West Tenn (Sou.)		0	0	...	16.88	2.63	2	1	0	0	...	0-...	2.2	6	5	5	0	2-0	2	.417
—Chicago (N.L.)		6	3	.667	4.02	1.35	52	0	0	0	3	13-18	65.0	60	33	29	8	28-2	57	.245
2000—Los Angeles (N.L.)		6	9	.400	3.52	1.41	66	0	0	0	15	2-7	84.1	80	42	33	6	39-0	56	.245
2001—Los Angeles (N.L.)		12	8	.600	4.33	1.36	43	22	0	0	9	0-1	166.1	172	84	80	9	54-1	141	.267
2002—Philadelphia (N.L.)		7	9	.438	4.35	1.39	46	19	0	0	12	0-1	136.2	132	76	66	9	58-5	96	.255
2003—Philadelphia (N.L.)		1	4	.200	2.65	1.34	66	0	0	0	16	0-0	68.0	68	22	20	1	23-4	51	.268

Year Team (League)	W	L	Pct.	ERA	WHIP	G	GS	CG	ShO	Hld.	Sv.-Opp.	IP	H	R	ER	HR	BB-IBB	SO	Avg.
2004— Toronto (A.L.)	4	4	.500	3.98	1.65	42	0	0	0	2	3-6	43.0	49	20	19	4	22-2	35	.290
— Boston (A.L.)	2	0	1.000	6.00	1.52	19	0	0	0	1	0-0	27.0	35	19	18	6	6-1	21	.321
2005— Philadelphia (N.L.)	0	2	.000	12.83	2.63	16	0	0	0	2	0-1	13.1	25	19	19	3	10-2	4	.403
— Scran./W.B. (I.L.)	1	2	.333	4.41	1.84	14	0	0	0	0	0-0	16.1	22	14	8	1	8-1	14	.306
American League totals (1 year)	6	4	.600	4.76	1.60	61	0	0	0	3	3-6	70.0	84	39	37	10	28-3	56	.302
National League totals (10 years)	45	58	.437	4.12	1.45	513	41	0	0	87	39-66	799.1	806	409	366	53	352-30	635	.263
Major League totals (11 years)	51	62	.451	4.17	1.46	574	41	0	0	90	42-72	869.1	890	448	403	63	380-33	691	.266

ADKINS, JON — P

PERSONAL: Born August 30, 1977, in Huntington, W.Va. ... 5-11/210. ... Throws right, bats left. ... Full name: Jonathan Scott Adkins. ... High school: Wayne (W.Va.). ... College: Oklahoma State.

TRANSACTIONS/CAREER NOTES: Selected by Oakland Athletics organization in ninth round of 1998 free-agent draft. ... Traded by A's to Chicago White Sox for 2B Ray Durham and cash (July 25, 2002).

CAREER HITTING: 0-for-0 (.000), 0 R, 0 2B, 0 3B, 0 HR, 0 RBI.

LEFTY-RIGHTY SPLITS

vs.	Avg.	AB	H	2B	3B	HR	RBI	BB	SO	OBP	Slg.
L	.389	18	7	3	0	0	4	2	0	.476	.556
R	.316	19	6	1	0	0	5	2	1	.381	.368

Year Team (League)	W	L	Pct.	ERA	WHIP	G	GS	CG	ShO	Hld.	Sv.-Opp.	IP	H	R	ER	HR	BB-IBB	SO	Avg.
1998—					Did not play.														
1999— Modesto (California)	9	5	.643	4.76	1.40	26	15	0	0	...	1-...	102.0	113	65	54	6	30-1	93	.276
2000— Ariz. A's (Ariz.)	1	1	.500	3.00	1.20	4	2	0	0	...	0-...	15.0	15	6	5	1	3-0	17	.234
— Sacramento (PCL)	0	1	.000	9.00	1.75	1	1	0	0	...	0-...	4.0	6	4	4	2	1-0	2	.333
— Modesto (California)	5	2	.714	1.81	1.17	9	7	1	0	...	0-...	49.2	41	17	10	1	17-0	38	.225
2001— Midland (Texas)	8	8	.500	4.46	1.33	24	24	1	1	...	0-...	137.1	147	71	68	9	36-1	74	.273
— Sacramento (PCL)	1	0	1.000	4.26	1.97	3	2	0	0	...	0-...	12.2	17	9	6	1	8-0	7	.333
2002— Modesto (California)	0	1	.000	8.10	1.80	1	1	0	0	...	0-...	6.2	11	7	6	0	1-0	4	.379
— Sacramento (PCL)	7	6	.538	6.03	1.77	20	20	0	0	...	0-...	97.0	139	74	65	9	33-0	76	.338
— Charlotte (Int'l)	4	2	.667	3.69	1.27	8	7	1	0	...	0-...	46.1	47	20	19	4	12-0	31	.260
2003— Charlotte (Int'l)	7	8	.467	3.96	1.25	26	19	1	1	...	1-...	122.2	119	65	54	11	34-1	59	.254
— Chicago (A.L.)	0	0	...	4.82	1.61	4	0	0	0	0	0-0	9.1	8	5	5	1	7-0	3	.250
2004— Chicago (A.L.)	2	3	.400	4.65	1.53	50	0	0	0	5	0-0	62.0	75	35	32	13	20-3	44	.305
2005— Chicago (A.L.)	0	1	.000	8.64	2.04	5	0	0	0	0	0-0	8.1	13	8	8	0	4-2	1	.351
— Charlotte (Int'l)	4	9	.308	5.37	1.50	23	21	0	0	...	0-...	127.1	148	81	76	20	43-1	92	.295
Major League totals (3 years)	2	4	.333	5.08	1.59	59	0	0	0	5	0-0	79.2	96	48	45	14	31-5	48	.305

AFFELDT, JEREMY — P

PERSONAL: Born June 6, 1979, in Phoenix, Ariz. ... 6-4/215. ... Throws left, bats left. ... Full name: Jeremy David Affeldt. ... Name pronounced: AFF-felt. ... High school: Northwest Christian (Spokane, Wash.).

TRANSACTIONS/CAREER NOTES: Selected by Kansas City Royals organization in third round of 1997 free-agent draft. ... On disabled list (June 9-August 1, 2002); included rehabilitation assignment to Wichita. ... On disabled list (April 20-May 6, 2003; and June 27-August 21, 2004); included rehabilitation assignment to Omaha. ... On disabled list (April 16-June 4; and June 20-July 7, 2005); included rehabilitation assignments to Omaha.

CAREER HITTING: 2-for-6 (.333), 0 R, 0 2B, 0 3B, 0 HR, 2 RBI.

SCOUTING REPORT *Throws:* Affeldt features a fastball at 93-96 mph and a curve at 75-80. *Tendencies:* His four-seam fastball has good riding action up in the zone. Curveball is extremely tight with excellent rotation and downward bite; can command it even though it has a sizable break. Deception in his delivery makes his fastball jump. Still needs to work on his command. *Outlook:* Affeldt probably will move back into the rotation in 2006. Became a reliever due to persistent blister problems and may have to change the grip on his curveball. *Grade 7.3*

JEREMY AFFELDT'S PITCHING ZONE

.313	.133	.500
.267	.421	.345
.111	.529	.091

LEFTY-RIGHTY SPLITS

vs.	Avg.	AB	H	2B	3B	HR	RBI	BB	SO	OBP	Slg.
L	.263	57	15	1	0	0	7	13	14	.400	.281
R	.283	145	41	8	2	3	20	16	25	.352	.428

Year Team (League)	W	L	Pct.	ERA	WHIP	G	GS	CG	ShO	Hld.	Sv.-Opp.	IP	H	R	ER	HR	BB-IBB	SO	Avg.
1997— GC Royals (GCL)	2	0	1.000	4.50	1.38	10	9	0	0	...	0-...	40.0	34	24	20	3	21-0	36	.243
1998— Lansing (Midw.)	0	3	.000	9.53	2.29	6	3	0	0	...	0-...	17.0	27	21	18	1	12-0	8	.355
— GC Royals (GCL)	4	3	.571	2.89	1.32	12	9	0	0	...	0-...	56.0	50	24	18	1	24-0	67	.243
1999— Char., W.Va. (SAL)	7	7	.500	3.83	1.53	27	24	2	1	...	0-...	143.1	140	78	61	4	80-0	111	.261
2000— Wilmington (Caro.)	5	15	.250	4.09	1.47	27	26	0	0	...	0-...	147.1	158	87	67	7	59-0	92	.275
2001— Wichita (Texas)	10	6	.625	3.90	1.37	25	25	0	0	...	0-...	145.1	153	74	63	9	46-0	128	.276
2002— Kansas City (A.L.)	3	4	.429	4.64	1.57	34	7	0	0	1	0-1	77.2	85	41	40	8	37-4	67	.274
— Wichita (Texas)	0	0	...	1.50	0.67	3	3	0	0	...	0-...	6.0	1	1	1	0	3-0	3	.059
2003— Kansas City (A.L.)	7	6	.538	3.93	1.30	36	18	0	3	3	4-4	126.0	126	58	55	12	38-1	98	.261
2004— Omaha (PCL)	0	0	...	0.00	0.50	4	0	0	0	...	3-...	4.0	2	0	0	0	0-0	5	.154
— Kansas City (A.L.)	3	4	.429	4.95	1.61	38	8	0	0	0	13-17	76.1	91	49	42	6	32-2	49	.302
2005— Omaha (PCL)	0	1	.000	6.48	1.80	9	0	0	0	1	0-0	8.1	9	7	6	1	6-0	9	.290
— Kansas City (A.L.)	0	2	.000	5.26	1.71	49	0	0	0	12	0-0	49.2	56	35	29	3	29-2	39	.277
Major League totals (4 years)	13	16	.448	4.53	1.50	157	33	0	0	16	17-22	329.2	358	183	166	29	136-9	253	.276

AGUILA, CHRIS — OF

PERSONAL: Born February 23, 1979, in Redwood City, Calif. ... 5-11/180. ... Bats right, throws right. ... Full name: Christopher Louis Aguila. ... High school: McQueen (Reno, Nev.).

TRANSACTIONS/CAREER NOTES: Selected by Florida Marlins organization in third round of 1997 free-agent draft.

2005 GAMES PLAYED BY POSITION (MLB): OF—42.

CHRIS AGUILA'S HITTING ZONE

.000	.000	.000
.292	.000	.167
.700	.100	.000

LEFTY-RIGHTY SPLITS

vs.	Avg.	AB	H	2B	3B	HR	RBI	BB	SO	OBP	Slg.
L	.240	25	6	1	0	0	1	1	5	.269	.280
R	.245	53	13	2	0	0	3	2	14	.273	.283

Year	Team (League)	Pos.	G	AB	R	H	2B	3B	HR	RBI	BB	SO	HBP	GDP	SB-CS	Avg.	OBP	SLG	OPS	E	Avg.
1997—	GC Marlins (GCL)	3B	46	157	12	34	7	0	1	17	21	49		3	2-1	.217	.309	.280	.590	22	.843
1998—	GC Marlins (GCL)	3B	51	171	29	46	12	3	4	29	19	49	2	4	6-2	.269	.349	.444	.793	15	.850
1999—	Kane Co. (Midw.)	OF	122	430	74	105	21	7	15	78	40	127	9	9	14-4	.244	.320	.430	.750	5	.977
2000—	Brevard County (FSL)	OF	136	518	68	125	27	3	9	56	37	105	1	11	8-8	.241	.292	.357	.649	5	.985
2001—	Brevard County (FSL)	OF	73	272	44	75	15	3	10	34	21	54	2	7	8-4	.276	.328	.463	.791	3	.984
—	Portland (East.)	OF	64	241	25	62	16	1	4	29	18	50	3	4	5-7	.257	.312	.382	.694	3	.969
2002—	Portland (East.)	OF	130	429	62	126	28	4	6	46	48	101	4	8	14-8	.294	.369	.420	.788	3	.988
2003—	GC Marlins (GCL)	OF	1	4	1	3	0	0	1	2	0	1	0	0	0-0	.750	.750	1.500	2.250	0	...
—	Carolina (Southern)	OF	93	337	58	108	21	3	11	55	36	67	2	6	6-2	.320	.384	.499	.883	2	.989
2004—	Albuquerque (PCL)	OF-DH	97	330	61	103	23	2	11	56	37	82	2	8	8-3	.312	.380	.494	.870	5	.984
—	Florida (N.L.)	OF	29	45	10	10	2	1	3	5	2	12	0	0	0-0	.222	.255	.511	.766	2	1.000
2005—	Albuquerque (PCL)	OF	38	138	27	49	13	2	7	25	14	21	0	3	8-2	.355	.412	.630	1.042	0	1.000
—	Florida (N.L.)	OF	65	78	11	19	3	0	0	4	3	19	0	0	0-1	.244	.272	.282	.554	0	1.000
Major League totals (2 years)			94	123	21	29	5	1	3	9	5	31	0	0	0-1	.236	.266	.366	.631	2	.968

ALEXANDER, MANNY — 2B/SS

PERSONAL: Born March 20, 1971, in San Pedro de Macoris, Dominican Republic. ... 5-10/180. ... Bats right, throws right. ... Full name: Manuel Alexander.

TRANSACTIONS/CAREER NOTES: Signed as a non-drafted free agent by Baltimore Orioles organization (February 4, 1988). ... On disabled list (March 25-May 2, 1995). ... Traded by Orioles with IF Scott McClain to New York Mets for P Hector Ramirez (March 22, 1997). ... On disabled list (June 13-July 10 and August 1-11, 1997). ... Traded by Mets to Chicago Cubs (August 14, 1997), completing deal in which Mets traded OF Lance Johnson and two players to be named to Cubs for OF Brian McRae and Ps Mel Rojas and Turk Wendell (August 8, 1997); Mets traded P Mark Clark to Cubs as part of deal (August 11, 1997). ... Traded by Cubs to Boston Red Sox for OF Damon Buford (December 10, 1999). ... On disabled list (September 29, 2000-remainder of season). ... Signed as a free agent by Seattle Mariners organization (February 16, 2001). ... Signed as a free agent by New York Yankees organization (February 4, 2002). ... Released by Yankees (March 13, 2002). ... Acquired by Milwaukee Brewers organization from Cordoba of the Mexican League (August 10, 2002). ... Traded by Brewers to Texas Rangers for cash (March 25, 2003). ... Traded by Rangers to San Diego Padres for P Juan Jiminez (August 31, 2005). ... Released by Padres (October 13, 2005).

CAREER PITCHING: 0-0, 67.50 ERA, 1 G, 0.2 IP, 1 H, 5 R, 5 ER, 4 BB,) SO

2005 GAMES PLAYED BY POSITION (MLB): 2B—5, SS—4, 3B—1, 1B—1.

LEFTY-RIGHTY SPLITS

vs.	Avg.	AB	H	2B	3B	HR	RBI	BB	SO	OBP	Slg.
L	.250	4	1	0	0	0	0	0	1	.250	.250
R	.071	14	1	1	0	0	0	2	4	.235	.143

Year	Team (League)	Pos.	G	AB	R	H	2B	3B	HR	RBI	BB	SO	HBP	GDP	SB-CS	Avg.	OBP	SLG	OPS	E	Avg.
1989—	Bluefield (Appal.)	SS	65	274	49	85	13	2	2	34	20	49	3	2	19-8	.310	.361	.394	.755	*32	.908
1990—	Wausau (Midw.)	SS	44	152	16	27	3	1	0	11	12	41	1	2	8-3	.178	.238	.211	.449	11	.938
1991—	Hagerstown (East.)	SS	3	9	3	3	1	0	0	2	1	3	1	0	0-0	.333	.417	.444	.861	0	1.000
—	Frederick (Carolina)	SS	134	548	81	143	17	3	3	42	44	68	2	4	47-14	.261	.318	.319	.637	32	.951
1992—	Hagerstown (East.)	SS	127	499	69	129	23	8	2	41	25	62	6	10	43-12	.258	.300	.349	.648	36	.929
—	Rochester (Int'l)	SS	6	24	3	7	1	0	0	3	1	3	0	0	2-2	.292	.320	.333	.653	1	.974
—	Baltimore (A.L.)	SS	4	5	1	1	0	0	0	0	0	3	0	0	0-0	.200	.200	.200	.400	0	1.000
1993—	Rochester (Int'l)	SS	120	471	55	115	23	8	6	51	22	60	4	11	19-7	.244	.283	.365	.648	18	.966
—	Baltimore (A.L.)	DH	3	0	1	0	0	0	0	0	0	0	0	0	0-0	...	...	...	...	0	...
1994—	Rochester (Int'l)	SS-2B	111	426	63	106	23	6	6	39	16	67	3	7	30-8	.249	.278	.373	.651	33	.939
1995—	Baltimore (A.L.)	2B-SS-3B-DH	94	242	35	57	9	1	3	23	20	30	2	2	11-4	.236	.294	.318	.612	10	.969
1996—	Baltimore (A.L.)	OF-DH-P-SS-2B-3B	54	68	6	7	0	0	0	4	3	27	0	2	3-3	.103	.141	.103	.244	5	.936
1997—	New York (N.L.)	2B-SS-3B	54	149	26	37	9	3	2	15	9	38	1	3	11-0	.248	.291	.389	.680	4	.979
—	St. Lucie (Fla. St.)	SS	1	4	0	1	0	0	0	0	0	1	0	0	0-0	.250	.250	.250	.500	0	1.000
—	Chicago (N.L.)	SS-2B	33	99	11	29	3	1	1	7	8	16	2	3	2-1	.293	.346	.374	.720	7	.949
1998—	Chicago (N.L.)	SS-2B-3B-DH-OF	108	264	34	60	10	1	5	25	18	66	1	6	4-1	.227	.277	.330	.606	7	.970
1999—	Chicago (N.L.)	SS-3B-2B-OF	90	177	17	48	11	2	0	15	10	38	0	1	4-0	.271	.309	.356	.664	7	.954
2000—	Boston (A.L.)	3B-SS-2B-DH	101	194	30	41	4	3	4	19	13	41	0	0	2-0	.211	.261	.325	.586	7	.962
2001—	Tacoma (PCL)	2B-SS-3B-OF	97	344	46	97	26	2	8	51	14	55	2	6	5-9	.282	.311	.439	.750	13	.961
2002—	Indianapolis (Int'l)	3B-SS	22	85	11	25	6	1	1	7	4	17	0	2	5-3	.294	.326	.424	.749	3	.944
—	Cordoba (Mex.)	IF	54	217	31	64	10	2	1	16	26	21	1	4	14-4	.295	.345	.373	.718	...	...
2003—	Oklahoma (PCL)	SS-2B-3B-DH	120	450	52	116	17	6	4	48	30	75	4	11	27-10	.258	.309	.349	.658	15	.973
2004—	Oklahoma (PCL)	SS	93	361	65	104	29	4	10	49	27	45	1	6	8-4	.288	.338	.474	.811	18	.965
—	Texas (A.L.)	2B-SS-3B	21	21	3	5	2	0	0	3	1	7	0	0	0-0	.238	.273	.333	.606	3	.914
2005—	Oklahoma (PCL)	SS-3B-1B-DH-OF-2B	108	417	64	129	23	6	12	67	38	66	0	8	27-9	.309	.368	.480	.847	23	.955
—	Portland (PCL)	SS	4	16	0	4	2	0	0	1	1	4	0	0	0-1	.250	.294	.375	.669	1	.933
—	San Diego (N.L.)	2B-SS-1B-3B	10	18	0	2	1	0	0	2	5	1	0	0	0-0	.111	.238	.167	.405	1	.950
American League totals (6 years)			277	530	76	115	15	4	7	49	37	108	2	4	16-7	.209	.264	.292	.556	25	.960
National League totals (4 years)			295	707	88	176	34	7	8	62	47	163	5	13	21-2	.249	.299	.351	.650	26	.965
Major League totals (10 years)			572	1237	164	287	49	11	15	111	84	271	7	17	37-9	.232	.284	.326	.610	51	.963

DIVISION SERIES RECORD

Year — Team (League)	Pos.	G	AB	R	H	2B	3B	HR	RBI	BB	SO	HBP	GDP	SB-CS	Avg.	OBP	SLG	OPS	E	Avg.
1996— Baltimore (A.L.)	DH	3	0	2	0	0	0	0	0	0	0	0	0	0-0	...	...	...	...	...	...
1998— Chicago (N.L.)	SS	2	5	0	0	0	0	0	0	1	0	0	0	0-0	.000	.000	.000	.000	0	1.000
Division series totals (2 years)		5	5	2	0	0	0	0	0	1	0	0	0	0-0	.000	.000	.000	.000	0	1.000

ALFONSECA, ANTONIO   P

PERSONAL: Born April 16, 1972, in La Romana, Dominican Republic. ... 6-5/250. ... Throws right, bats right. ... Name pronounced: al-fon-SAY-kah.

TRANSACTIONS/CAREER NOTES: Signed as a non-drafted free agent by Montreal Expos organization (July 3, 1989). ... Selected by Florida Marlins organization from Expos organization in Rule 5 minor league draft (December 13, 1993). ... On disabled list (May 15-June 15, 1995; and July 12-September 3, 1996; and May 14-31, 1998). ... Traded by Marlins with P Matt Clement to Chicago Cubs for Ps Julian Tavarez, Jose Cueto and Dontrelle Willis and C Ryan Jorgensen (March 27, 2002). ... On disabled list (March 21-May 5, 2003); included rehabilitation assignment to Iowa. ... On suspended list (September 5-12, 2003). ... Signed as a free agent by Atlanta Braves (December 23, 2003). ... Signed as a free agent by Marlins (December 17, 2004). ... On disabled list (April 22-July 26, 2005); included rehabilitation assignment to Jupiter.

HONORS: Named N.L. Fireman of the Year by THE SPORTING NEWS (2000).

CAREER HITTING: 2-for-13 (.154), 0 R, 0 2B, 0 3B, 0 HR, 2 RBI.

SCOUTING REPORT **Throws:** Alfonseca's main pitches are a fastball that ranges from 93-95 mph, a slider from 83-86 and a split-finger fastball from 86-87. ***Tendencies:*** He throws a very heavy sinking fastball. Slider is quick but occasionally flat. Is effective at keeping his pitches down but will revert to being a thrower at times. Works behind in the count too much. ***Outlook:*** Alfonseca never really pitched well in 2005 after missing the first part of the year with elbow problems and never really pitched well. Needs a productive spring to shed doubts about his arm. ***Grade 6***

ANTONIO ALFONSECA'S PITCHING ZONE

...	.000	.444
.364	.167	.348
.857	.167	.250

LEFTY-RIGHTY SPLITS

vs.	Avg.	AB	H	2B	3B	HR	RBI	BB	SO	OBP	Slg.
L	.244	45	11	3	1	0	8	5	3	.308	.356
R	.346	52	18	2	0	2	11	9	13	.460	.500

Year — Team (League)	W	L	Pct.	ERA	WHIP	G	GS	CG	ShO	Hld.	Sv.-Opp.	IP	H	R	ER	HR	BB-IBB	SO	Avg.
1990— Dom. Expos (DSL)	3	5	.375	3.60	1.53	13	13	1	0	...	0-...	60.0	60	29	24		32-...	19	...
1991— GC Expos (GCL)	3	3	.500	3.88	1.39	11	10	0	0	...	0-...	51.0	46	33	22	2	25-0	38	.240
1992— GC Expos (GCL)	3	4	.429	3.68	1.36	12	10	1	1	...	0-...	66.0	55	31	27	0	35-0	62	.233
1993— Jamestown (NYP)	2	2	.500	6.15	1.57	15	4	0	0	...	1-...	33.2	31	26	23	3	22-1	29	.250
1994— Kane Co. (Midw.)	6	5	.545	4.07	1.15	32	9	0	0	...	0-...	86.1	78	41	39	5	21-1	74	.234
1995— Portland (East.)	9	3	.750	3.64	1.28	19	17	1	0	...	0-...	96.1	81	43	39	6	42-1	75	.229
1996— Charlotte (Int'l)	4	4	.500	5.53	1.51	14	13	0	0	...	1-...	71.2	86	47	44	8	22-0	51	.296
1997— Charlotte (Int'l)	7	2	.778	4.32	1.34	46	0	0	0	...	7-...	58.1	58	34	28	8	20-3	45	.264
— Florida (N.L.)	1	3	.250	4.91	1.79	17	0	0	0	0	0-0	25.2	36	16	14	3	10-3	19	.324
1998— Florida (N.L.)	4	6	.400	4.08	1.53	58	0	0	0	9	8-14	70.2	75	36	32	10	33-9	46	.281
1999— Florida (N.L.)	4	5	.444	3.24	1.39	73	0	0	0	5	21-25	77.2	79	28	28	4	29-6	46	.274
2000— Florida (N.L.)	5	6	.455	4.24	1.51	68	0	0	0	*	45-49	70.0	82	35	33	7	24-3	47	.291
2001— Florida (N.L.)	4	4	.500	3.06	1.35	58	0	0	0	0	28-34	61.2	68	24	21	6	15-3	40	.281
2002— Chicago (N.L.)	2	5	.286	4.00	1.47	66	0	0	0	0	19-28	74.1	73	34	33	7	36-3	61	.257
2003— Iowa (PCL)	0	1	.000	4.91	1.90	3	0	0	0	...	0-...	3.2	6	2	2	0	1-0	5	.353
— Chicago (N.L.)	3	1	.750	5.83	1.55	60	0	0	0	0	0-4	66.1	76	43	43	7	27-3	51	.290
2004— Atlanta (N.L.)	6	4	.600	2.57	1.34	79	0	0	0	13	0-1	73.2	71	24	21	5	28-5	45	.255
2005— Jupiter (Fla. St.)	0	0	...	3.00	1.00	3	1	0	0	...	0-0	3.0	3	1	1	1	0-0	4	.300
— Florida (N.L.)	1	1	.500	4.94	1.57	33	0	0	0	8	0-2	27.1	29	15	15	2	14-4	16	.299
Major League totals (9 years)	30	35	.462	3.95	1.47	512	0	0	0	44	121-159	547.1	589	255	240	49	216-39	371	.279

DIVISION SERIES RECORD

Year — Team (League)	W	L	Pct.	ERA	WHIP	G	GS	CG	ShO	Hld.	Sv.-Opp.	IP	H	R	ER	HR	BB-IBB	SO	Avg.
1997— Florida (N.L.)			Did not play.																
2003— Chicago (N.L.)	0	0	...	0.00	1.00	1	0	0	0	0	0-0	1.0	1	0	0	0	0-0	0	.250
2004— Atlanta (N.L.)	1	0	1.000	4.91	1.09	4	0	0	0	0	0-0	3.2	2	2	2	0	2-0	0	.154
Division series totals (2 years)	1	0	1.000	3.86	1.07	5	0	0	0	0	0-0	4.2	3	2	2	0	2-0	0	.176

CHAMPIONSHIP SERIES RECORD

Year — Team (League)	W	L	Pct.	ERA	WHIP	G	GS	CG	ShO	Hld.	Sv.-Opp.	IP	H	R	ER	HR	BB-IBB	SO	Avg.
1997— Florida (N.L.)			Did not play.																
2003— Chicago (N.L.)	0	0	...	0.00	1.71	3	0	0	0	0	0-0	2.1	2	0	0	0	2-1	0	.333

WORLD SERIES RECORD

Year — Team (League)	W	L	Pct.	ERA	WHIP	G	GS	CG	ShO	Hld.	Sv.-Opp.	IP	H	R	ER	HR	BB-IBB	SO	Avg.
1997— Florida (N.L.)	0	0	...	0.00	1.11	3	0	0	0	0	0-0	6.1	6	0	0	0	1-0	5	.250

ALFONZO, EDGARDO   3B

PERSONAL: Born November 8, 1973, in Soapire, Venezuela. ... 5-11/226. ... Bats right, throws right. ... Full name: Edgardo Antonio Alfonzo. ... High school: Cecilio Acosto (Venezuela).

TRANSACTIONS/CAREER NOTES: Signed as non-drafted free agent by New York Mets organization (February 19, 1991). ... On disabled list (August 11, 1995-remainder of season; and May 4-19, 1998). ... On disabled list (June 14-July 3, 2001); included rehabilitation assignment to Norfolk. ... On disabled list (August 4-24, 2002). ... Signed as a free agent by San Francisco Giants (December 15, 2002). ... On disabled list (June 14-July 22, 2005); included rehabilitation assignment to Fresno.

RECORDS: Shares major league record for runs scored, 9-inning game (6, August 30, 1999).

2005 GAMES PLAYED BY POSITION (MLB): 3B—97, 2B—2.

SCOUTING REPORT **Offense:** He's a good contact hitter, but his run production and power continue to decline. Has lost bat speed and his swing has gotten longer. Has become a line-drive

EDGARDO ALFONZO'S HITTING ZONE

.269	.400	.241
.286	.422	.273
.298	.417	.222

LEFTY-RIGHTY SPLITS

vs.	Avg.	AB	H	2B	3B	HR	RBI	BB	SO	OBP	Slg.
L	.267	90	24	3	0	1	10	6	8	.313	.333
R	.281	278	78	14	1	1	33	21	26	.331	.349

hitter who takes the ball through the middle instead of pulling it for power. Has not made adjustments to his home park. Is not a good runner. ***Defense:*** Alfonzo has good hands, but his range is limited on both sides. Was converted from second base because of his decrease in range. Has an accurate arm. ***Outlook:*** He no longer provides consistent offense for his club. ***Grade 6.3***

A

Year	Team (League)	Pos.	G	AB	R	H	2B	3B	HR	RBI	BB	SO	HBP	GDP	SB-CS	Avg.	OBP	SLG	OPS	E	Avg.
1991— GC Mets (GCL)		2B-3B-SS	54	175	29	58	8	4	0	27	34	12	2	1	6-4	.331	.433	.423	.856	9	.958
1992— St. Lucie (Fla. St.)		2B	4	5	0	0	0	0	0	0	0	0	0	0	0-0	.000	.000	.000	.000	0	1.000
— Pittsfield (NYP)		SS	74	298	44	106	13	5	1	44	18	31	0	6	7-5	.356	.388	.443	.830	26	.933
1993— St. Lucie (Fla. St.)		SS	128	494	75	145	18	3	11	86	57	51	5	13	26-16	.294	.366	.409	.775	29	.954
1994— Binghamton (East.)		1B-2B-SS	127	498	89	146	34	2	15	75	64	55	0	9	14-11	.293	.369	.460	.829	27	.958
1995— New York (N.L.)		3B-2B-SS	101	335	26	93	13	5	4	41	12	37	1	7	1-1	.278	.301	.382	.683	7	.973
1996— New York (N.L.)		2B	123	368	36	96	15	2	4	40	25	56	0	8	2-0	.261	.304	.345	.649	11	.973
1997— New York (N.L.)		3B-SS-2B	151	518	84	163	27	2	10	72	63	56	5	4	11-6	.315	.391	.432	.823	12	.970
1998— New York (N.L.)		3B-SS	144	557	94	155	28	2	17	78	65	77	3	11	8-3	.278	.355	.427	.782	9	.976
1999— New York (N.L.)		2B	158	628	123	191	41	2	27	108	85	85	3	14	9-2	.304	.385	.502	.886	5	.993
2000— New York (N.L.)		2B-DH	150	544	109	176	40	2	25	94	95	70	5	12	3-2	.324	.425	.542	.967	10	.985
2001— New York (N.L.)		2B	124	457	64	111	22	0	17	49	51	62	5	7	5-0	.243	.322	.403	.725	7	.987
— Norfolk (Int'l)		2B	2	8	0	0	0	0	0	0	0	0	0	1	0-0	.000	.000	.000	.000	0	1.000
2002— New York (N.L.)		3B	135	490	78	151	26	0	16	56	62	55	7	5	6-0	.308	.391	.459	.851	12	.969
2003— San Francisco (N.L.)		3B-2B	142	514	56	133	25	2	13	81	58	41	4	14	5-2	.259	.334	.391	.726	11	.968
2004— San Francisco (N.L.)		3B-2B	139	519	66	150	26	1	11	77	46	40	5	15	1-1	.289	.350	.407	.757	14	.961
2005— Fresno (PCL)		3B-DH	4	15	2	7	2	0	0	1	0	0	0	0	0-0	.467	.467	.600	1.067	0	1.000
— San Francisco (N.L.)		3B-2B	109	368	36	102	17	1	2	43	27	34	2	11	2-0	.277	.327	.345	.672	8	.968
Major League totals (11 years)			1476	5298	772	1521	280	18	146	739	589	613	40	108	53-17	.287	.359	.429	.789	106	.977

DIVISION SERIES RECORD

Year	Team (League)	Pos.	G	AB	R	H	2B	3B	HR	RBI	BB	SO	HBP	GDP	SB-CS	Avg.	OBP	SLG	OPS	E	Avg.
1999— New York (N.L.)		2B	4	16	6	4	1	0	3	6	3	2	0	0	0-0	.250	.368	.875	1.243	0	1.000
2000— New York (N.L.)		2B	4	18	1	5	2	0	1	5	1	2	0	0	0-1	.278	.316	.556	.871	0	1.000
2003— San Francisco (N.L.)		3B	4	17	3	9	4	0	0	5	1	1	0	0	0-0	.529	.556	.765	1.320	0	1.000
Division series totals (3 years)			12	51	10	18	7	0	4	16	5	5	0	0	0-1	.353	.411	.725	1.136	0	1.000

CHAMPIONSHIP SERIES RECORD

Year	Team (League)	Pos.	G	AB	R	H	2B	3B	HR	RBI	BB	SO	HBP	GDP	SB-CS	Avg.	OBP	SLG	OPS	E	Avg.
1999— New York (N.L.)		2B	6	27	2	6	4	0	0	1	1	9	0	0	0-0	.222	.250	.370	.620	1	.971
2000— New York (N.L.)		2B	5	18	5	8	1	1	0	4	4	1	0	0	0-0	.444	.565	.611	1.176	0	1.000
Champ. series totals (2 years)			11	45	7	14	5	1	0	5	5	10	1	0	0-0	.311	.392	.467	.859	1	.979

WORLD SERIES RECORD

Year	Team (League)	Pos.	G	AB	R	H	2B	3B	HR	RBI	BB	SO	HBP	GDP	SB-CS	Avg.	OBP	SLG	OPS	E	Avg.
2000— New York (N.L.)		2B	5	21	1	3	0	0	0	1	1	5	1	0	0-0	.143	.217	.143	.360	0	1.000

ALL-STAR GAME RECORD

	G	AB	R	H	2B	3B	HR	RBI	BB	SO	HBP	GDP	SB-CS	Avg.	OBP	SLG	OPS	E	Avg.
All-Star Game totals (1 year)	1	2	0	0	0	0	0	0	0	1	0	0	0-0	.000	.000	.000	.000	0	1.000

ALLEN, CHAD   OF

PERSONAL: Born February 6, 1975, in Dallas. ... 6-1/200. ... Bats right, throws right. ... Full name: John Chad Allen. ... High school: Duncanville (Texas). ... College: Texas A&M.

TRANSACTIONS/CAREER NOTES: Selected by Cincinnati Reds organization in 38th round of 1993 free-agent draft; did not sign. ... Selected by Minnesota Twins organization in fourth round of 1996 free-agent draft. ... On disabled list (June 4-19 and August 15, 2001-remainder of season). ... Signed as a free agent by Baltimore Orioles organization (March 27, 2002). ... Released by Orioles (April 16, 2002). ... Signed by Cleveland Indians organization (May 13, 2002). ... Released by Indians (September 30, 2002). ... Signed by Florida Marlins organization (November 25, 2002). ... Signed as a free agent by Texas Rangers organization (November 26, 2003). ... Released by Rangers (August 7, 2005). ... Signed as free agent by St. Louis Cardinals organization (August 12, 2005).

2005 GAMES PLAYED BY POSITION (MLB): DH—18, OF—2.

CHAD ALLEN'S HITTING ZONE

.250	1.000	.000
.417	.600	.500
.250	.200	.000

LEFTY-RIGHTY SPLITS

vs.	Avg.	AB	H	2B	3B	HR	RBI	BB	SO	OBP	Slg.
L	.351	37	13	0	1	0	4	1	6	.368	.405
R	.125	16	2	1	0	0	1	1	7	.176	.188

Year	Team (League)	Pos.	G	AB	R	H	2B	3B	HR	RBI	BB	SO	HBP	GDP	SB-CS	Avg.	OBP	SLG	OPS	E	Avg.
1996— Fort Wayne (Midw.)		OF	7	21	2	9	0	0	0	2	3	2	0	0	1-1	.429	.480	.429	.909	0	1.000
1997— Fort Myers (FSL)		OF	105	401	66	124	18	4	3	45	40	51	2	9	27-15	.309	.373	.397	.770	5	.977
— New Britain (East.)		OF	30	115	20	29	9	1	4	18	9	21	0	3	2-0	.252	.304	.452	.756	1	.977
1998— New Britain (East.)		OF	137	504	70	132	31	7	8	82	51	78	6	19	21-9	.262	.334	.399	.733	4	.980
1999— Minnesota (A.L.)		OF-DH	137	481	69	133	21	3	10	46	37	89	2	10	14-7	.277	.330	.395	.725	7	.975
2000— Salt Lake (PCL)		OF	96	389	71	121	21	5	9	67	31	72	1	13	10-2	.311	.363	.460	.823	1	.993
— Minnesota (A.L.)		OF	15	50	2	15	3	0	0	7	3	14	1	1	0-2	.300	.345	.360	.705	0	1.000
2001— Minnesota (A.L.)		OF-DH	57	175	20	46	13	2	4	20	19	37	0	7	1-2	.263	.333	.429	.762	2	.968
— Edmonton (PCL)		OF	6	22	4	8	2	0	1	1	4	1	1	0	2-0	.364	.481	.591	1.072	0	1.000
2002— Rochester (Int'l)		OF	8	32	1	7	2	1	0	1	0	6	0	...	0-0	.219	.219	.344	.563	0	1.000
— Buffalo (Int'l)		OF	70	279	45	84	20	1	10	62	15	34	2	1	0-1	.301	.340	.487	.828	0	1.000
— Cleveland (A.L.)		OF	5	10	0	1	1	0	0	0	0	3	0	1	0-0	.100	.100	.200	.300	0	1.000
2003— Florida (N.L.)		OF-DH	12	24	2	5	1	1	0	0	0	5	1	1	0-0	.208	.240	.333	.573	0	1.000
— Albuquerque (PCL)		OF-DH	91	337	45	109	30	2	6	53	18	48	6	10	11-10	.323	.364	.496	.860	3	.993
2004— Oklahoma (PCL)		OF-DH-1B	93	386	75	138	28	3	7	70	31	72	5	9	18-2	.358	.407	.500	.907	1	.993
— Texas (A.L.)		OF	20	58	4	14	4	1	0	6	2	13	0	1	0-1	.241	.262	.345	.607	0	1.000
2005— Texas (A.L.)		DH-OF	21	53	5	15	1	1	0	5	2	13	0	2	0-1	.283	.309	.340	.649	0	1.000
— Oklahoma (PCL)		OF-DH	45	200	34	69	12	0	8	33	10	31	0	8	9-2	.345	.374	.525	.899	2	.985
— Memphis (PCL)		OF	25	86	11	25	6	0	3	13	7	14	0	1	1-2	.291	.337	.465	.802	0	1.000
American League totals (6 years)			255	827	100	224	43	7	14	84	63	168	3	22	15-13	.271	.323	.391	.714	9	.977
National League totals (1 year)			12	24	2	5	1	1	0	0	0	5	1	1	0-0	.208	.240	.333	.573	0	1.000
Major League totals (7 years)			267	851	102	229	44	8	14	84	63	173	4	23	15-13	.269	.321	.389	.710	9	.978

ALMANZA, ARMANDO   P

PERSONAL: Born October 26, 1972, in El Paso, Texas. ... 6-3/240. ... Throws left, bats left. ... Full name: Armando N. Almanza. ... High school: Bel Air (El Paso, Texas). ... Junior college: New Mexico JC.

TRANSACTIONS/CAREER NOTES: Selected by St. Louis Cardinals organization in 21st round of 1993 free-agent draft. ... Traded by Cardinals with P Braden Looper and SS Pablo Ozuna to Florida Marlins for SS Edgar Renteria (December 14, 1998). ... On disabled list (March 30-May 21, 2002); included rehabilitation assignment to Jupiter. ... On disabled list (August 21, 2003-remainder of season). ... Signed as a free agent by Atlanta Braves (December 22, 2003). ... On disabled list (March 31-May 11, 2004); included rehabilitation assignments to Greenville and Richmond. ... Signed as a free agent by San Francisco Giants organization (December 10, 2004). ... Signed as free agent by Arizona Diamondbacks organization (April 18, 2005). ... Signed as free agent by Cardinals organization (August 3, 2005).

CAREER HITTING: 0-for-4 (.000), 0 R, 0 2B, 0 3B, 0 HR, 0 RBI.

LEFTY-RIGHTY SPLITS

vs.	Avg.	AB	H	2B	3B	HR	RBI	BB	SO	OBP	Slg.
L	.286	7	2	0	0	1	3	1	2	.375	.714
R	.333	9	3	2	0	0	0	2	0	.455	.556

Year	Team (League)	W	L	Pct.	ERA	WHIP	G	GS	CG	ShO	Hld.	Sv.-Opp.	IP	H	R	ER	HR	BB-IBB	SO	Avg.
1993— Ariz. Cardinals (Ariz.)		4	1	.800	3.21	1.24	20	4	0	0	...	0-...	42.0	38	19	15	2	14-0	56	.236
— Johnson City (App.)		1	1	.500	4.15	2.08	3	3	0	0	...	0-...	4.1	6	2	2	1	3-0	4	.333
1994— Madison (Midw.)		Did not play.																		
1995— Savannah (S. Atl.)		3	9	.250	3.92	1.37	20	20	0	0	...	0-...	108.0	108	62	47	13	40-1	72	.255
1996— Peoria (Midw.)		8	6	.571	2.76	1.32	52	1	0	0	...	0-...	62.0	50	27	19	2	32-5	67	.216
1997— Prince Will. (Car.)		2	3	.400	1.67	1.08	58	0	0	0	...	36-...	64.2	38	18	12	3	32-1	83	.172
1998— Arkansas (Texas)		4	1	.800	3.31	1.38	28	0	0	0	...	8-...	32.2	27	13	12	2	18-0	46	.225
— Memphis (PCL)		3	1	.750	3.03	1.51	31	0	0	0	...	1-...	35.2	35	18	12	1	19-1	45	.246
1999— Calgary (PCL)		2	2	.500	10.90	2.71	15	0	0	0	...	0-...	17.1	29	27	21	3	18-0	20	.363
— Portland (East.)		0	1	.000	3.97	0.79	10	0	0	0	...	3-...	11.1	5	5	5	1	4-0	20	.139
— Florida (N.L.)		0	1	.000	1.72	1.09	14	0	0	0	3	0-0	15.2	8	4	3	1	9-1	20	.154
2000— Florida (N.L.)		4	2	.667	4.86	1.75	67	0	0	0	13	0-4	46.1	38	27	25	3	43-6	46	.228
2001— Florida (N.L.)		2	2	.500	4.83	1.46	52	0	0	0	12	0-2	41.0	34	24	22	8	26-1	45	.230
2002— Jupiter (Fla. St.)		0	0	...	0.00	0.60	6	5	0	0	...	0-...	6.2	1	0	0	0	3-0	6	.050
— Florida (N.L.)		3	2	.600	4.34	1.29	51	0	0	0	12	2-4	45.2	36	22	22	8	23-1	57	.224
2003— Florida (N.L.)		4	5	.444	6.08	1.67	51	0	0	0	6	0-2	50.1	59	37	34	10	25-2	49	.296
2004— Greenville (Sou.)		0	3	.000	8.10	2.25	5	2	0	0	...	0-...	6.2	12	6	6	0	3-0	5	.429
— Atlanta (N.L.)		1	1	.500	6.17	1.37	13	0	0	0	0	0-0	11.2	9	8	8	3	7-2	13	.200
— Richmond (Int'l)		1	1	.500	3.55	1.62	20	0	0	0	...	1-...	25.1	26	13	10	1	15-0	20	.255
2005— Fresno (PCL)		0	1	.000	13.50	2.10	2	0	0	0	...	0-0	3.1	5	5	5	1	2-0	3	.385
— Tennessee (Sou.)		1	0	1.000	4.91	1.77	6	0	0	0	1	1-1	7.1	9	5	4	1	4-0	7	.290
— Tucson (PCL)		1	0	1.000	1.80	1.27	15	0	0	0	2	1-1	15.0	12	6	3	2	7-0	19	.218
— Arizona (N.L.)		0	0	...	2.25	2.00	6	0	0	0	2	0-1	4.0	5	1	1	1	3-0	2	.313
— Memphis (PCL)		0	0	...	6.30	1.50	10	0	0	0	...	0-0	10.0	13	7	7	2	2-0	9	.317
Major League totals (7 years)		14	13	.519	4.82	1.51	254	0	0	0	48	2-13	214.2	189	123	115	34	136-13	232	.240

ALMANZAR, CARLOS   P

PERSONAL: Born November 6, 1973, in Santiago, Dominican Republic. ... 6-2/200. ... Throws right, bats right. ... Full name: Carlos Manuel Almanzar. ... Name pronounced: al-MAN-sar.

TRANSACTIONS/CAREER NOTES: Signed as a non-drafted free agent by Toronto Blue Jays organization (December 10, 1990). ... Traded by Blue Jays with P Woody Williams and OF Peter Tucci to San Diego Padres for P Joey Hamilton (December 13, 1998). ... On disabled list (April 24-May 27, 1999); included rehabilitation assignment to Las Vegas. ... Traded by Padres to New York Yankees for P David Lee (March 25, 2001). ... Signed as a free agent by Colorado Rockies organization (January 20, 2002). ... Claimed on waivers by Cincinnati Reds (March 30, 2002). ... On disabled list (June 11, 2002-remainder of season); included rehabilitation assignment to Louisville. ... Signed as a free agent by Texas Rangers organization (October 30, 2003). ... On suspended list (September 22-26, 2004). ... On disabled list (May 1, 2005-remainder of season).

CAREER HITTING: 0-for-4 (.000), 0 R, 0 2B, 0 3B, 0 HR, 0 RBI.

LEFTY-RIGHTY SPLITS

vs.	Avg.	AB	H	2B	3B	HR	RBI	BB	SO	OBP	Slg.
L	.556	9	5	1	0	1	6	5	0	.667	1.000
R	.357	14	5	1	0	1	4	2	3	.444	.643

Year	Team (League)	W	L	Pct.	ERA	WHIP	G	GS	CG	ShO	Hld.	Sv.-Opp.	IP	H	R	ER	HR	BB-IBB	SO	Avg.
1991— Dom. B. Jays (DSL)		3	1	.750	2.83	1.34	6	6	1	0	...	0-...	35.0	36	17	11	...	11-...	20	...
1992— Dom. B. Jays (DSL)		10	0	1.000	2.01	1.13	13	11	2	1	...	1-...	67.0	45	26	15	...	31-...	60	...
1993— Dom. B. Jays (DSL)		5	2	.714	3.38	1.33	16	9	0	0	...	0-...	69.1	60	35	26	...	32-...	59	...
1994— Medicine Hat (Pio.)		7	4	.636	2.87	1.19	14	14	0	0	...	0-...	84.2	82	38	27	2	19-0	77	.255
1995— Knoxville (Southern)		3	12	.200	3.99	1.39	35	19	0	0	...	2-...	126.1	144	77	56	10	32-1	93	.287
1996— Knoxville (Southern)		7	8	.467	4.85	1.47	54	0	0	0	...	9-...	94.2	106	58	51	13	33-6	105	.280
1997— Knoxville (Southern)		1	1	.500	4.91	1.36	21	0	0	0	...	8-...	25.2	30	14	14	2	5-1	25	.300
— Syracuse (Int'l)		5	1	.833	1.41	0.75	32	0	0	0	...	3-...	51.0	30	9	8	2	8-0	47	.170
— Toronto (A.L.)		0	1	.000	2.70	0.60	4	0	0	0	0	0-0	3.1	1	1	1	1	1-0	4	.091
1998— Toronto (A.L.)		2	2	.500	5.34	1.47	25	0	0	0	1	0-3	28.2	34	18	17	4	8-2	20	.286
— Syracuse (Int'l)		3	6	.333	2.31	1.13	30	0	0	0	...	3-...	50.2	44	21	13	7	13-2	53	.229
1999— San Diego (N.L.)		0	0	...	7.47	1.69	28	0	0	0	0	0-3	37.1	48	32	31	6	15-2	30	.316
— Las Vegas (PCL)		1	3	.250	9.53	1.76	11	0	0	0	...	0-...	22.2	32	25	24	11	8-1	18	.337
2000— San Diego (N.L.)		4	5	.444	4.39	1.41	62	0	0	0	8	0-3	69.2	73	35	34	12	25-2	56	.266
— Las Vegas (PCL)		0	0	...	4.50	1.50	4	0	0	0	...	0-...	6.0	9	4	3	1	0-0	7	.321
2001— New York (A.L.)		0	1	.000	3.38	1.50	10	0	0	0	4	0-2	10.2	14	4	4	2	2-1	6	.333
— Columbus (Int'l)		2	1	.667	2.43	1.26	35	0	0	0	...	18-...	33.1	36	10	9	2	6-2	26	.279
2002— Louisville (Int'l)		1	0	1.000	2.74	1.13	21	0	0	0	...	11-...	23.0	21	7	7	0	5-0	19	.247
— Cincinnati (N.L.)		0	1	.000	2.31	0.94	8	1	0	0	0	0-0	11.2	6	4	3	0	5-1	7	.158
2003— Louisville (Int'l)		2	2	.500	3.50	1.08	42	0	0	0	...	23-...	46.1	47	19	18	2	3-0	54	.251
2004— Texas (A.L.)		7	3	.700	3.72	1.17	67	0	0	0	20	0-2	72.2	66	32	30	8	19-4	44	.244
2005— Texas (A.L.)		0	0	...	14.40	3.40	6	0	0	0	0	0-0	5.0	10	8	8	2	7-0	3	.435
American League totals (5 years)		9	7	.563	4.49	1.35	112	0	0	0	21	0-7	120.1	125	63	60	17	37-7	77	.269
National League totals (3 years)		4	6	.400	5.16	1.45	98	1	0	0	8	0-3	118.2	127	71	68	18	45-5	93	.274
Major League totals (8 years)		13	13	.500	4.82	1.40	210	1	0	0	29	0-10	239.0	252	134	128	35	82-12	170	.271

ALOMAR, SANDY   C

PERSONAL: Born June 18, 1966, in Salinas, Puerto Rico. ... 6-5/235. ... Bats right, throws right. ... Full name: Santos Alomar Jr.. ... Name pronounced: AL-uh-mar. ... High school: Luis Munoz Rivera (Salinas, Puerto Rico). ... Son of Sandy Alomar, coach, New York Mets, and infielder with six major league teams (1964-78); brother of Roberto Alomar, second baseman with seven major-league teams (1989-2004).

TRANSACTIONS/CAREER NOTES: Signed as a non-drafted free agent by San Diego Padres organization (October 21, 1983). ... Traded by Padres with OF Chris James and 3B Carlos Baerga to Cleveland Indians for OF Joe Carter (December 6, 1989). ... On disabled list (May 15-June 17 and July 29, 1991-remainder of season); included rehabilitation assignments to Colorado Springs. ... On disabled list (May 2-18, 1992). ... On suspended list (July 29-August 2, 1992). ... On disabled list (May 1-August 7, 1993); included rehabilitation assignment to Charlotte. ... On disabled list (April 24-May 11, 1994). ... On disabled list (April 19-June 29, 1995); included rehabilitation assignment to Canton/Akron. ... On disabled list (May 11-September 6, 1999); included rehabilitation assignments to Akron and Buffalo. ... On disabled list (April 19-May 8, 2000). ... Signed as a free agent by Chicago White Sox (December 18, 2000). ... On disabled list (August 8-September 18, 2001). ... On disabled list (June 13-July 1, 2002); included rehabilitation assignment to Charlotte. ... Traded by White Sox to Colorado Rockies for P Enemencio Pacheco (July 29, 2002). ... Signed as a free agent by White Sox (December 20, 2002). ... On disabled list (May 31-June 23, 2003); included rehabilitation assignment to Charlotte. ... On disabled list (August 16-September 1, 2004). ... Signed as a free agent by Texas Rangers (December 8, 2004).

RECORDS: Shares major league record for most doubles, game (4, June 6, 1997).

HONORS: Named Minor League co-Player of the Year by THE SPORTING NEWS (1988). ... Named Minor League Player of the Year by THE SPORTING NEWS (1989). ... Named A.L. Rookie Player of the Year by THE SPORTING NEWS (1990). ... Named A.L. Rookie of the Year by Baseball Writers' Association of America (1990). ... Won A.L. Gold Glove at catcher (1990).

2005 GAMES PLAYED BY POSITION (MLB): C—46.

SCOUTING REPORT Alomar is nearing the end of his career and is having problems with his knees. Bat is really slow; looks for the ball out over the plate to take it the opposite way. No longer drives the ball with authority. Reflexes have slowed considerably behind the plate, but still calls a good game because of his experience. No longer throws well and doesn't have quick footwork with his setup. Can only catch once a week now. *Grade 4.5*

SANDY ALOMAR JR.'S HITTING ZONE

.300	.400	.333
.143	.636	.333
.300	.250	.000

LEFTY-RIGHTY SPLITS

vs.	Avg.	AB	H	2B	3B	HR	RBI	BB	SO	OBP	Slg.
L	.385	26	10	4	0	0	5	0	2	.407	.538
R	.245	102	25	3	0	0	9	5	10	.280	.275

BATTING / FIELDING

Year Team (League)	Pos.	G	AB	R	H	2B	3B	HR	RBI	BB	SO	HBP	GDP	SB-CS	Avg.	OBP	SLG	OPS	E	Avg.
1984— Spokane (N'west)	1B-C	59	219	13	47	5	0	0	21	13	20	1	7	3-0	.215	.260	.237	.497	8	.985
1985— Char., S.C. (SAL)	C-OF	100	352	38	73	7	0	3	43	31	30	3	9	3-1	.207	.276	.253	.529	18	.979
1986— Beaumont (Texas)	C	100	346	36	83	15	1	4	27	15	35	1	16	2-6	.240	.271	.324	.595	18	.969
1987— Wichita (Texas)	C	103	375	50	115	19	1	8	65	21	37	5	12	1-5	.307	.346	.427	.772	15	.978
1988— Las Vegas (PCL)	C-OF	93	337	59	100	9	5	16	71	28	35	4	11	1-1	.297	.354	.496	.849	14	.978
— San Diego (N.L.)		1	1	0	0	0	0	0	0	0	1	0	0	0-0	.000	.000	.000	.000	...	...
1989— Las Vegas (PCL)	C-OF	131	523	88	160	33	8	13	101	42	58	2	23	3-1	.306	.358	.474	.832	12	.984
— San Diego (N.L.)	C	7	19	1	4	1	0	1	6	3	3	0	1	0-0	.211	.318	.421	.739	0	1.000
1990— Cleveland (A.L.)	C	132	445	60	129	26	2	9	66	25	46	2	10	4-1	.290	.326	.418	.744	14	.981
1991— Cleveland (A.L.)	C-DH	51	184	10	40	9	0	0	7	8	24	4	4	0-0	.217	.264	.266	.530	4	.987
— Colo. Springs (PCL)	C	12	35	5	14	2	0	1	10	5	0	0	0	0-0	.400	.463	.543	1.006	1	.833
1992— Cleveland (A.L.)	C-DH	89	299	22	75	16	0	2	26	13	32	5	7	3-3	.251	.293	.324	.618	2	.996
1993— Cleveland (A.L.)	C	64	215	24	58	7	1	6	32	11	28	6	3	3-1	.270	.318	.395	.713	6	.984
— Charlotte (Int'l)	C	12	44	8	16	5	0	1	8	5	1	1	1	0-0	.364	.440	.545	.985	0	1.000
1994— Cleveland (A.L.)	C	80	292	44	84	15	1	14	43	25	31	2	7	8-4	.288	.347	.490	.837	2	.996
1995— Cant./Akr. (Eastern)	C-DH	6	15	3	6	1	0	0	1	1	1	0	1	0-0	.400	.438	.467	.904	1	.958
— Cleveland (A.L.)	C	66	203	32	61	6	0	10	35	7	26	3	8	3-1	.300	.332	.478	.810	1	.995
1996— Cleveland (A.L.)	C-1B	127	418	53	110	23	0	11	50	19	42	3	20	1-0	.263	.299	.397	.696	9	.988
1997— Cleveland (A.L.)	C-DH	125	451	63	146	37	0	21	83	19	48	3	16	0-2	.324	.354	.545	.900	* 12	.985
1998— Cleveland (A.L.)	C-DH	117	409	45	96	26	2	6	44	18	45	3	15	0-3	.235	.270	.352	.622	6	.992
1999— Cleveland (A.L.)	C-DH	37	137	19	42	13	0	6	25	4	23	0	1	0-1	.307	.322	.533	.855	7	.974
— Akron (East.)	C-DH	10	29	8	9	0	0	1	6	3	2	0	0	1-0	.310	.353	.414	.767	1	.929
— Buffalo (Int'l)	C-DH	10	33	9	9	2	1	2	10	6	3	1	1	0-0	.273	.400	.576	.976	3	.921
2000— Cleveland (A.L.)	C-DH	97	356	44	103	16	2	7	42	16	41	4	9	2-2	.289	.324	.404	.728	8	.989
2001— Chicago (A.L.)	C	70	220	17	54	8	1	4	21	12	17	2	6	1-2	.245	.288	.345	.634	4	.990
2002— Chicago (A.L.)	C	51	167	21	48	10	1	7	25	5	14	1	5	0-0	.287	.309	.485	.794	2	.994
— Charlotte (Int'l)	C	3	8	0	1	0	0	0	0	0	0	0	0	0-0	.125	.125	.125	.250	0	1.000
— Colorado (N.L.)	C	38	116	8	31	4	0	0	12	4	19	0	6	0-0	.267	.292	.302	.593	0	1.000
2003— Charlotte (Int'l)	C-DH	5	15	2	4	0	0	0	1	1	1	0	2	0-0	.267	.313	.267	.579	0	1.000
— Chicago (A.L.)	C	75	194	22	52	12	0	5	26	4	17	0	4	0-0	.268	.281	.407	.689	1	.997
2004— Chicago (A.L.)	C-DH	50	146	15	35	4	0	2	14	11	13	2	4	0-0	.240	.298	.308	.606	3	.990
2005— Texas (A.L.)	C	46	128	11	35	7	0	0	14	5	12	1	3	0-0	.273	.306	.328	.634	2	.989
American League totals (16 years)		1277	4264	502	1168	235	10	110	553	202	459	41	122	25-24	.274	.311	.411	.722	84	.989
National League totals (3 years)		46	136	9	35	5	0	1	18	7	23	0	7	0-0	.257	.294	.316	.610	0	1.000
Major League totals (18 years)		1323	4400	511	1203	240	10	111	571	209	482	41	129	25-24	.273	.310	.408	.719	84	.989

DIVISION SERIES RECORD

Year Team (League)	Pos.	G	AB	R	H	2B	3B	HR	RBI	BB	SO	HBP	GDP	SB-CS	Avg.	OBP	SLG	OPS	E	Avg.
1995— Cleveland (A.L.)	C	3	11	1	2	1	0	0	1	0	1	0	0	0-0	.182	.182	.273	.455	0	1.000
1996— Cleveland (A.L.)	C	4	16	0	2	0	0	0	3	0	2	0	0	0-1	.125	.125	.125	.250	1	.967
1997— Cleveland (A.L.)	C	5	19	4	6	1	0	2	5	0	2	0	0	0-0	.316	.316	.684	1.000	1	.967
1998— Cleveland (A.L.)	C	4	13	2	3	3	0	0	2	1	4	0	3	0-0	.231	.286	.462	.747	1	.967
1999— Cleveland (A.L.)	C	5	14	1	2	0	0	1	1	2	6	0	0	0-0	.143	.235	.143	.378	1	.971
Division series totals (5 years)		21	73	8	15	5	0	3	12	3	15	0	3	0-1	.205	.234	.356	.590	4	.975

CHAMPIONSHIP SERIES RECORD

Year Team (League)	Pos.	G	AB	R	H	2B	3B	HR	RBI	BB	SO	HBP	GDP	SB-CS	Avg.	OBP	SLG	OPS	E	Avg.
1995— Cleveland (A.L.)	C	5	15	0	4	1	1	0	1	1	1	0	0	0-0	.267	.313	.467	.779	1	.971
1997— Cleveland (A.L.)	C	6	24	3	3	0	0	1	4	1	3	0	1	0-0	.125	.160	.250	.410	0	1.000
1998— Cleveland (A.L.)	C	5	16	1	1	0	0	0	0	0	2	0	0	0-0	.063	.118	.063	.180	2	.938
Champ. series totals (3 years)		16	55	4	8	1	1	1	5	2	6	0	1	0-0	.145	.190	.255	.444	3	.974

WORLD SERIES RECORD

Year Team (League)	Pos.	G	AB	R	H	2B	3B	HR	RBI	BB	SO	HBP	GDP	SB-CS	Avg.	OBP	SLG	OPS	E	Avg.
1995—Cleveland (A.L.)	C	5	15	0	3	2	0	0	0	0	2	0	0	0-0	.200	.200	.333	.533	0	1.000
1997—Cleveland (A.L.)	C	7	30	5	11	1	0	2	10	2	3	0	2	0-0	.367	.406	.600	1.006	0	1.000
World Series totals (2 years)		12	45	5	14	3	0	2	11	2	5	0	2	0-0	.311	.340	.511	.852	0	1.000

ALL-STAR GAME RECORD

	G	AB	R	H	2B	3B	HR	RBI	BB	SO	HBP	GDP	SB-CS	Avg.	OBP	SLG	OPS	E	Avg.
All-Star Game totals (6 years)	6	12	2	5	0	0	1	3	0	0	1	0	0-0	.417	.417	.667	1.083	0	1.000

ALOU, MOISES   OF

PERSONAL: Born July 3, 1966, in Atlanta, Ga. ... 6-3/220. ... Bats right, throws right. ... Full name: Moises Rojas Alou. ... Name pronounced: MOY-zes ah-LOO. ... High school: C.E.E. (Santo Domingo, Dominican Republic). ... Junior college: Canada College (Calif.). ... College: Canada College (CA). ... Son of Felipe Alou, manager, San Francisco Giants, and outfielder with six major league teams (1958-1974); nephew of Jesus Alou, outfielder with four major league teams (1963-75 and 1978-79); nephew of Matty Alou, outfielder with six major league teams (1960-74).

TRANSACTIONS/CAREER NOTES: Selected by Pittsburgh Pirates organization in first round (second pick overall) of January 1986 free-agent draft. ... Traded by Pirates to Montreal Expos (August 16, 1990), completing deal in which Expos traded P Zane Smith to Pirates for P Scott Ruskin, SS Willie Greene and a player to be named (August 8, 1990). ... On disabled list (March 19, 1991-entire season; July 7-27, 1992; September 18, 1993-remainder of season; August 18-September 5 and September 11, 1995-remainder of season; and July 8-23, 1996). ... On suspended list (August 23-27, 1996). ... Signed as a free agent by Florida Marlins (December 12, 1996). ... Traded by Marlins to Houston Astros for Ps Oscar Henriquez and P Manuel Barrios and a player to be named (November 11, 1997); Marlins acquired P Mark Johnson to complete deal (December 16, 1997). ... On disabled list (April 3, 1999-entire season; April 27-May 14, 2000; and March 29-April 16, 2001). ... Signed as a free agent by Chicago Cubs (December 19, 2001). ... On disabled list (March 31-April 15, 2002); included rehabilitation assignment to Daytona. ... Signed as a free agent by San Francisco Giants (January 5, 2005). ... On disabled list (April 7-22; and August 3-19, 2005).

2005 GAMES PLAYED BY POSITION (MLB): OF—117, DH—3.

SCOUTING REPORT

Offense: Alou is an excellent fastball hitter with a short but sweeping swing. Has one of the most unusual approaches: Hits from a dead start and has a slight lift, forcing him to hit off his back foot. Has good bat speed with plus power. Pitchers attempt to come hard inside on him, but he is very quick there. Pitchers can change speeds and get him out on his front foot. Doesn't run well as he's prone to leg problems. **Defense:** He has lost a step and doesn't get good jumps. Hands are a little stiff. Has arm strength but a slow release. Is accurate. **Outlook:** Still a good offensive player with power to all fields, Alou is a consistent run producer. Defense has declined and he no longer runs well but when healthy is valuable. **Grade 8**

MOISES ALOU'S HITTING ZONE

.259	.435	.389
.302	.392	.310
.351	.333	.385

LEFTY-RIGHTY SPLITS

vs.	Avg.	AB	H	2B	3B	HR	RBI	BB	SO	OBP	Slg.
L	.372	94	35	8	1	7	21	15	7	.455	.702
R	.306	333	102	13	2	12	42	41	36	.384	.465

Year Team (League)	Pos.	G	AB	R	H	2B	3B	HR	RBI	BB	SO	HBP	GDP	SB-CS	Avg.	OBP	SLG	OPS	E	Avg.
1986—Watertown (NYP)	OF	69	254	30	60	9	8	6	35	22	72	1	5	14-8	.236	.300	.406	.705	7	.952
1987—Macon (S. Atl.)	OF	4	8	1	1	0	0	0	0	2	4	0	0	0-0	.125	.300	.125	.425	0	1.000
—Watertown (NYP)	OF	39	117	20	25	6	2	4	8	16	36	4	0	6-3	.214	.324	.402	.725	2	.957
1988—Augusta (S. Atl.)	OF	105	358	58	112	23	5	7	62	51	84	5	5	24-12	.313	.399	.464	.863	9	.962
1989—Salem (Carol.)	OF	86	321	50	97	29	2	14	53	35	69	3	6	12-5	.302	.374	.536	.910	10	.947
—Harrisburg (East.)	OF	54	205	36	60	5	2	3	19	17	38	0	1	8-4	.293	.344	.380	.724	2	.978
1990—Harrisburg (East.)	OF	36	132	19	39	12	2	3	22	16	21	1	5	7-4	.295	.373	.485	.858	1	.990
—Buffalo (A.A.)	OF	75	271	38	74	4	6	5	31	30	43	2	...	9-4	.273	.345	.387	.733	8	.957
—Pittsburgh (N.L.)	OF	2	5	0	1	0	0	0	0	0	0	1	1	0-0	.200	.200	.200	.400	0	1.000
—Indianapolis (A.A.)	OF	15	55	6	12	1	0	0	6	3	7	0		4-3	.218	.254	.236	.491	0	1.000
—Montreal (N.L.)	OF	14	15	4	3	0	1	0	0	0	3	0	0	0-0	.200	.200	.333	.533	0	1.000
1991—Montreal (N.L.)						Did not play.														
1992—Montreal (N.L.)	OF	115	341	53	96	28	2	9	56	25	46	1	5	16-2	.282	.328	.455	.783	4	.978
1993—Montreal (N.L.)	OF	136	482	70	138	29	6	18	85	38	53	5	9	17-6	.286	.340	.483	.824	4	.985
1994—Montreal (N.L.)	OF	107	422	81	143	31	5	22	78	42	63	2	7	7-6	.339	.397	.592	.989	3	.986
1995—Montreal (N.L.)	OF	93	344	48	94	22	0	14	58	29	56	9	9	4-3	.273	.342	.459	.801	3	.981
1996—Montreal (N.L.)	OF	143	540	87	152	28	2	21	96	49	83	2	15	9-4	.281	.339	.457	.797	3	.989
1997—Florida (N.L.)	OF	150	538	88	157	29	5	23	115	70	85	4	13	9-5	.292	.373	.493	.866	3	.988
1998—Houston (N.L.)	OF-DH	159	584	104	182	34	5	38	124	84	87	5	14	11-3	.312	.399	.582	.981	5	.980
1999—Houston (N.L.)						Did not play.														
2000—Houston (N.L.)	OF-DH	126	454	82	161	28	2	30	114	52	45	2	* 21	3-3	.355	.416	.623	1.039	6	.970
2001—Houston (N.L.)	OF-DH	136	513	79	170	31	1	27	108	57	57	3	18	5-1	.331	.396	.554	.949	2	.991
2002—Daytona (Fla. St.)	OF	2	8	0	5	1	0	0	2	1	1	0	0	0-0	.625	.667	.750	1.417	0	1.000
—Chicago (N.L.)	OF-DH	132	484	50	133	23	1	15	61	47	61	0	15	8-0	.275	.337	.419	.757	2	.991
2003—Chicago (N.L.)	OF-DH	151	565	83	158	35	1	22	91	63	67	7	16	3-1	.280	.357	.462	.819	6	.972
2004—Chicago (N.L.)	OF-DH	155	601	106	176	36	3	39	106	68	80	0	12	3-0	.293	.361	.557	.919	8	.969
2005—San Francisco (N.L.)	OF-DH	123	427	67	137	21	3	19	63	56	43	3	11	5-1	.321	.400	.518	.918	8	.966
Major League totals (14 years)		1742	6315	1002	1901	375	37	297	1155	680	829	43	166	100-35	.301	.369	.513	.882	57	.981

DIVISION SERIES RECORD

Year Team (League)	Pos.	G	AB	R	H	2B	3B	HR	RBI	BB	SO	HBP	GDP	SB-CS	Avg.	OBP	SLG	OPS	E	Avg.
1997—Florida (N.L.)	OF	3	14	1	3	1	0	0	3	0	3	0	1	0-0	.214	.214	.286	.500	0	1.000
1998—Houston (N.L.)	OF	4	16	0	3	0	0	0	0	2	0	1	0	0-0	.188	.188	.188	.375	0	1.000
2001—Houston (N.L.)	OF	3	12	0	2	1	0	0	0	0	3	0	1	0-0	.167	.167	.250	.417	0	1.000
2003—Chicago (N.L.)	OF	5	20	3	10	1	0	0	3	1	4	0	1	1-0	.500	.524	.550	1.074	0	1.000
Division series totals (4 years)		15	62	4	18	3	0	0	5	3	10	0	3	1-0	.290	.302	.339	.640	0	1.000

CHAMPIONSHIP SERIES RECORD

Year Team (League)	Pos.	G	AB	R	H	2B	3B	HR	RBI	BB	SO	HBP	GDP	SB-CS	Avg.	OBP	SLG	OPS	E	Avg.
1997—Florida (N.L.)	OF	5	15	0	1	0	0	0	1	1	2	0	0	0-0	.067	.125	.133	.258	1	1.000
2003—Chicago (N.L.)	OF	7	29	4	9	1	0	2	5	2	1	0	2	0-0	.310	.355	.552	.907	1	1.000
Champ. series totals (2 years)		12	44	4	10	2	0	2	10	3	4	0	3	0-0	.227	.277	.409	.686	0	1.000

Year	Team (League)	Pos.	G	AB	R	H	2B	3B	HR	RBI	BB	SO	HBP	GDP	SB-CS	Avg.	OBP	SLG	OPS	E	Avg.
1997— Florida (N.L.)		OF	7	28	6	9	2	0	3	6	3	6	0	0	1-0	.321	.387	.714	1.101	0	1.000

ALL-STAR GAME RECORD

	G	AB	R	H	2B	3B	HR	RBI	BB	SO	HBP	GDP	SB-CS	Avg.	OBP	SLG	OPS	E	Avg.
All-Star Game totals (6 years)	6	10	2	5	2	0	0	1	1	3	0	0	0-0	.500	.545	.700	1.245	0	1.000

ALVAREZ, ABE — P

PERSONAL: Born October 17, 1982, in Los Angeles. ... 6-2/190. ... Throws left, bats left. ... Full name: Abraham Alvarez. ... High school: Fontana (Calif.). ... College: Long Beach State.

TRANSACTIONS/CAREER NOTES: Selected by Boston Red Sox organization in second round of 2003 free-agent draft.

CAREER HITTING: 0-for-0 (.000), 0 R, 0 2B, 0 3B, 0 HR, 0 RBI.

LEFTY-RIGHTY SPLITS

vs.	Avg.	AB	H	2B	3B	HR	RBI	BB	SO	OBP	Slg.
L	.750	4	3	0	0	0	2	0	1	.750	.750
R	.333	9	3	1	0	1	1	0	0	.333	.778

Year	Team (League)	W	L	Pct.	ERA	WHIP	G	GS	CG	ShO	Hld.	Sv.-Opp.	IP	H	R	ER	HR	BB-IBB	SO	Avg.
2003— Lowell (NY-Penn)		0	0	...	0.00	0.58	9	9	0	0	...	0-...	19.0	9	2	0	0	2-1	19	.138
2004— Boston (A.L.)		0	1	.000	9.00	2.60	1	1	0	0	0	0-0	5.0	8	5	5	2	5-0	2	.400
— Portland (East.)		10	9	.526	3.59	1.21	26	26	0	0	...	0-...	135.1	132	65	54	13	32-0	108	.252
2005— Boston (A.L.)		0	0	...	15.43	2.57	2	0	0	0	0	0-0	2.1	6	4	4	1	0-0	1	.462
— Pawtucket (Int'l)		11	6	.647	4.85	1.20	26	26	0	0	0	0-0	144.2	143	84	78	17	31-0	109	.255
Major League totals (2 years)		0	1	.000	11.05	2.59	3	1	0	0	0	0-0	7.1	14	9	9	3	5-0	3	.424

ALVAREZ, WILSON — P

PERSONAL: Born March 24, 1970, in Maracaibo, Venezuela. ... 6-1/255. ... Throws left, bats left. ... Full name: Wilson Eduardo Alvarez.

TRANSACTIONS/CAREER NOTES: Signed as a non-drafted free agent by Texas Rangers organization (September 23, 1986). ... Traded by Rangers with IF Scott Fletcher and OF Sammy Sosa to Chicago White Sox for OF Harold Baines and IF Fred Manrique (July 29, 1989). ... Traded by White Sox with P Danny Darwin and P Roberto Hernandez to San Francisco Giants for SS Michael Caruso, OF Brian Manning, P Lorenzo Barcelo, P Keith Foulke, P Bobby Howry and P Ken Vining (July 31, 1997). ... Signed as a free agent by Tampa Bay Devil Rays (December 3, 1997). ... On disabled list (May 21-July 6, 1998; April 12-29 and July 24-August 8, 1999; March 25, 2000-entire season; March 23, 2001-entire season; April 15-May 31 and July 15-August 5, 2002). ... Released by Devil Rays (September 30, 2002). ... Signed by Los Angeles Dodgers organization (January 16, 2003). ... On disabled list (March 25-May 3; May 31-July 19 and August 11-September 20, 2005); included rehabilitation assignment to Las Vegas. ... Announced retirement (October 19, 2005).

CAREER HITTING: 13-for-95 (.137), 6 R, 0 2B, 0 3B, 0 HR, 1 RBI.

WILSON ALVAREZ'S PITCHING ZONE

.500	.400	.400
.286	.273	.368
.200	.250	.000

LEFTY-RIGHTY SPLITS

vs.	Avg.	AB	H	2B	3B	HR	RBI	BB	SO	OBP	Slg.
L	.387	31	12	3	0	1	5	1	4	.406	.581
R	.284	67	19	3	0	6	16	6	12	.333	.597

Year	Team (League)	W	L	Pct.	ERA	WHIP	G	GS	CG	ShO	Hld.	Sv.-Opp.	IP	H	R	ER	HR	BB-IBB	SO	Avg.
1987— Gastonia (S. Atl.)		1	5	.167	6.47	1.94	8	6	0	0	...	0-...	32.0	39	24	23	5	23-0	19	.312
— GC Rangers (GCL)		2	5	.286	5.24	1.39	10	10	0	0	...	0-...	44.2	41	29	26	6	21-0	46	.246
1988— Gastonia (S. Atl.)		4	11	.267	2.98	1.28	23	23	1	0	...	0-...	127.0	113	63	42	5	49-1	134	.233
— Okla. City (A.A.)		1	1	.500	3.78	1.38	5	3	0	0	...	0-...	16.2	17	8	7	2	6-0	9	.274
1989— Charlotte (Fla. St.)		7	4	.636	2.11	1.10	13	13	3	2	...	0-...	81.0	68	29	19	2	21-0	51	.227
— Tulsa (Texas)		2	2	.500	2.06	1.17	7	7	1	1	...	0-...	48.0	40	14	11	1	16-3	29	.227
— Texas (A.L.)		0	1	.000	...	...	1	1	0	0	0	0-0	0.0	3	3	3	2	2-0	0	1.000
— Birmingham (Sou.)		2	1	.667	3.03	1.35	6	6	0	0	...	0-...	35.2	32	12	12	2	16-0	18	.246
1990— Vancouver (PCL)		7	7	.500	6.00	1.89	17	15	1	0	...	0-...	75.0	91	54	50	7	51-0	35	.314
— Birmingham (Sou.)		5	1	.833	4.27	1.49	7	7	1	0	...	0-...	46.1	44	24	22	4	25-0	36	.246
1991— Birmingham (Sou.)		10	6	.625	1.83	1.20	23	23	3	2	...	0-...	152.1	109	46	31	6	74-0	165	.200
— Chicago (A.L.)		3	2	.600	3.51	1.35	10	9	2	1	0	0-0	56.1	47	26	22	9	29-0	32	.230
1992— Chicago (A.L.)		5	3	.625	5.20	1.67	34	9	0	0	3	1-1	100.1	103	64	58	12	65-2	66	.272
1993— Chicago (A.L.)		15	8	.652	2.95	1.40	31	31	1	1	0	0-0	207.2	168	78	68	14	* 122-8	155	.230
— Nashville (A.A.)		0	1	.000	2.84	1.42	1	1	0	0	...	0-...	6.1	7	2	2	0	2-0	8	.304
1994— Chicago (A.L.)		12	8	.600	3.45	1.29	24	24	2	1	0	0-0	161.2	147	72	62	16	62-1	108	.241
1995— Chicago (A.L.)		8	11	.421	4.32	1.51	29	29	3	0	0	0-0	175.0	171	96	84	21	93-4	118	.258
1996— Chicago (A.L.)		15	10	.600	4.22	1.44	35	35	0	0	0	0-0	217.1	216	106	102	21	97-3	181	.258
1997— Chicago (A.L.)		9	8	.529	3.03	1.24	22	22	2	1	0	0-0	145.2	126	61	49	17	55-1	110	.232
— San Francisco (N.L.)		4	3	.571	4.48	1.36	11	11	0	0	0	0-0	66.1	54	36	33	9	36-3	69	.224
1998— Tampa Bay (A.L.)		6	14	.300	4.73	1.39	25	25	0	0	0	0-0	142.2	130	78	75	18	68-0	107	.245
— GC Devil Rays (GCL)		0	0	...	0.00	1.00	1	1	0	0	...	0-...	3.0	2	0	0	0	1-0	4	.200
— St. Pete. (FSL)		0	1	.000	27.00	4.20	1	1	0	0	...	0-...	1.2	5	5	5	1	2-0	2	.500
— Durham (Int'l)		0	0	...	3.86	1.29	1	1	0	0	...	0-...	4.2	4	2	2	0	2-0	6	.235
1999— Tampa Bay (A.L.)		9	9	.500	4.22	1.49	28	28	1	0	0	0-0	160.0	159	92	75	22	79-1	128	.260
2000— St. Pete. (FSL)		0	0	...	0.00	0.00	1	1	0	0	...	0-...	4.0	0	0	0	0	0-0	2	.000
2001— Orlando (South.)		1	3	.250	4.43	1.48	5	5	0	0	...	0-...	20.1	24	10	10	2	6-0	18	.286
— Durham (Int'l)		1	1	.500	3.00	1.44	4	4	0	0	...	0-...	18.0	20	8	6	1	7-0	16	.282
2002— Tampa Bay (A.L.)		2	3	.400	5.28	1.55	23	10	0	0	2	1-1	75.0	80	47	44	13	36-3	56	.272
— Orlando (South.)		1	0	1.000	1.13	1.00	2	2	0	0	...	0-...	8.0	6	1	1	0	2-0	7	.222
2003— Las Vegas (PCL)		5	1	.833	3.44	0.90	8	8	0	0	...	0-...	47.0	36	9	7	1	6-0	33	.216
— Los Angeles (N.L.)		6	2	.750	2.37	1.08	21	12	1	1	1	1-1	95.0	80	27	25	5	23-1	82	.230
2004— Los Angeles (N.L.)		7	6	.538	4.03	1.16	40	15	0	0	2	1-2	120.2	109	56	54	14	31-2	102	.244
2005— Las Vegas (PCL)		0	1	.000	2.35	0.78	4	4	0	0	...	0-...	7.2	4	2	2	1	2-0	9	.154
— Los Angeles (N.L.)		1	4	.200	5.63	1.58	21	2	0	0	2	0-0	24.0	31	15	15	7	7-0	16	.316
American League totals (11 years)		84	77	.522	4.01	1.43	262	223	11	4	5	2-2	1441.2	1350	723	642	157	708-23	1061	.249
National League totals (4 years)		18	15	.545	3.74	1.21	93	40	1	1	5	2-3	306.0	274	134	127	33	97-6	269	.242
Major League totals (14 years)		102	92	.526	3.96	1.39	355	263	12	5	10	4-5	1747.2	1624	857	769	190	805-29	1330	.248

DIVISION SERIES RECORD

Year	Team (League)	W	L	Pct.	ERA	WHIP	G	GS	CG	ShO	Hld.	Sv.-Opp.	IP	H	R	ER	HR	BB-IBB	SO	Avg.
1997— San Francisco (N.L.)		0	1	.000	6.00	1.67	1	1	0	0	0	0-0	6.0	6	4	4	1	4-0	4	.261
2004— Los Angeles (N.L.)		0	1	.000	10.80	1.20	2	0	0	0	0	0-0	3.1	4	4	4	1	0-0	4	.286
Division series totals (2 years)		0	2	.000	7.71	1.50	3	1	0	0	0	0-0	9.1	10	8	8	2	4-0	8	.270

CHAMPIONSHIP SERIES RECORD

Year	Team (League)	W	L	Pct.	ERA	WHIP	G	GS	CG	ShO	Hld.	Sv.-Opp.	IP	H	R	ER	HR	BB-IBB	SO	Avg.
1993—Chicago (A.L.)		1	0	1.000	1.00	1.00	1	1	0	0	0	0-0	9.0	7	1	1	0	2-0	6	.226

ALL-STAR GAME RECORD

		W	L	Pct.	ERA	WHIP	G	GS	CG	ShO	Hld.	Sv.-Opp.	IP	H	R	ER	HR	BB-IBB	SO	Avg.
All-Star Game totals (1 year)		0	0	...	0.00	0.00	1	0	0	0	1	0-0	1.0	0	0	0	0	0-0	0	.000

AMBRES, CHIP — OF

PERSONAL: Born December 19, 1979, in Beaumont, Texas. ... 6-1/190. ... Bats right, throws right. ... Full name: Raymond Payne Ambres. ... High school: Westbrook (Beaumont, Texas). ... College: None.
TRANSACTIONS/CAREER NOTES: Selected by Florida Marlins organization in first round (27th pick overall) of free-agent draft (June 2, 1998). ... Signed as a free agent by Boston Red Sox organization (November 19, 2004). ... Traded by Red Sox with P Juan Cedeno to Kansas City Royals for IF Tony Graffanino (July 19, 2005).
2005 GAMES PLAYED BY POSITION (MLB): OF—47, DH—2.

SCOUTING REPORT Ambres is an athletic player with a football background. Has a quick bat but a slightly long stroke. Has problems with breaking pitches. Is only an average runner and is slow getting out of the box. Can play center field and left field but doesn't get consistent jumps and takes erratic routes. Has stiff hands. Will get a chance to make the team next spring because of his bat. *Grade 5.2*

CHIP AMBRES' HITTING ZONE

.333	.375	.133
.172	.500	.300
.500	.300	.000

LEFTY-RIGHTY SPLITS

vs.	Avg.	AB	H	2B	3B	HR	RBI	BB	SO	OBP	Slg.
L	.239	88	21	6	0	3	6	7	14	.295	.409
R	.246	57	14	2	0	1	3	9	18	.362	.333

									BATTING								FIELDING	
Year	Team (League)	Pos.	G	AB	R	H	2B	3B	HR	RBI	BB	SO	HBP	GDP	SB-CS	Avg.	OBP	SLG	OPS	E	Avg.
1999—GC Marlins (GCL)		OF	37	139	29	49	13	3	1	15	25	19	2	0	22-3	.353	.452	.511	.963	4	.939
—Utica (N.Y.-Penn)		OF	28	105	24	28	3	6	5	15	21	25	1	1	11-4	.267	.388	.552	.940	2	.956
2000—Kane Co. (Midw.)		OF	84	320	46	74	16	3	7	28	52	72	3	3	26-8	.231	.342	.366	.708	2	.989
2001—Kane Co. (Midw.)		OF	96	377	79	100	26	8	5	41	53	81	11	7	19-15	.265	.369	.416	.785	5	.977
2002—Jupiter (Fla. St.)		OF	123	509	88	120	25	7	9	37	57	98	9	6	23-8	.236	.323	.365	.688	4	.987
2003—Carolina (Southern)		OF	127	380	75	98	23	8	10	55	72	81	2	3	9-6	.258	.376	.439	.815	0	1.000
2004—Carolina (Southern)		OF	137	452	81	109	28	3	20	62	76	117	6	7	26-9	.241	.352	.449	.801	5	.857
2005—Pawtucket (Int'l)		OF-DH	84	279	47	82	20	3	10	50	47	64	4	8	19-5	.294	.401	.495	.895	8	.973
—Kansas City (A.L.)		OF-DH	53	145	25	35	8	0	4	9	16	32	2	5	3-2	.241	.323	.379	.702	1	.988
Major League totals (1 year)			53	145	25	35	8	0	4	9	16	32	2	5	3-2	.241	.323	.379	.702	1	.988

AMEZAGA, ALFREDO — SS/3B

PERSONAL: Born January 16, 1978, in Obregon, Mexico. ... 5-10/165. ... Bats both, throws right. ... Name pronounced: ah-MEZZ-ah-guh. ... High school: Miami Senior (Miami). ... Junior college: St. Petersburg (Fla.).
TRANSACTIONS/CAREER NOTES: Selected by Colorado Rockies organization in 36th round of 1997 free-agent draft; did not sign. ... Selected by Colorado Rockies organization in 44th round of 1998 free-agent draft; did not sign. ... Selected by Anaheim Angels organization in 13th round of 1999 free-agent draft. ... Claimed on waivers by Colorado Rockies (December 17, 2004). ... Claimed on waivers by Pittsburgh Pirates (April 20, 2005).
2005 GAMES PLAYED BY POSITION (MLB): 3B—1, SS—1.

LEFTY-RIGHTY SPLITS

vs.	Avg.	AB	H	2B	3B	HR	RBI	BB	SO	OBP	Slg.
L	.000	4	0	0	0	0	0	1	0	.200	.000
R	.500	2	1	0	0	0	0	0	0	.500	.500

									BATTING								FIELDING	
Year	Team (League)	Pos.	G	AB	R	H	2B	3B	HR	RBI	BB	SO	HBP	GDP	SB-CS	Avg.	OBP	SLG	OPS	E	Avg.
1999—Butte (Pion.)		2B-SS	8	34	11	10	2	0	0	5	5	5	1	0	6-2	.294	.400	.353	.753	0	1.000
—Boise (N'west)		2B-SS	48	205	52	66	6	4	2	29	23	29	5	7	14-3	.322	.402	.420	.821	12	.953
2000—Lake Elsinore (Calif.)		2B-SS	108	420	90	117	13	4	4	44	63	70	4	4	73-21	.279	.374	.357	.731	22	.961
2001—Arkansas (Texas)		SS	70	285	50	89	10	5	4	21	22	55	4	0	24-15	.312	.370	.425	.794	13	.964
—Salt Lake (PCL)		SS	49	200	28	50	5	4	1	16	14	45	3	2	9-6	.250	.307	.330	.637	11	.954
2002—Salt Lake (PCL)		SS-2B	128	518	77	130	25	7	6	51	45	100	8	15	23-14	.251	.317	.361	.678	24	.962
—Anaheim (A.L.)		SS-DH	12	13	3	7	2	0	0	2	0	1	0	1	1-0	.538	.538	.692	1.231	0	1.000
2003—Salt Lake (PCL)		SS-2B-DH	75	317	55	110	20	5	3	45	20	39	4	3	14-8	.347	.391	.470	.861	7	.982
—Anaheim (A.L.)		SS-3B	37	105	15	22	3	2	0	7	9	23	1	2	2-2	.210	.278	.333	.612	5	.962
2004—Salt Lake (PCL)		SS-3B-2B	32	135	15	35	5	2	2	14	13	18	1	1	7-0	.259	.329	.370	.699	7	.961
—Anaheim (A.L.)	DH	73	93	12	15	2	0	2	11	3	24	3	2	3-2	.161	.212	.247	.459	3	.978
2005—Colorado (N.L.)		3B	2	3	1	1	0	0	0	0	0	0	0	0	0-0	.333	.333	.333	.667	0	...
—Pittsburgh (N.L.)		SS	3	3	1	0	0	0	0	0	1	0	0	0	1-0	.000	.250	.000	.250	0	1.000
—Indianapolis (Int'l)		SS	64	185	28	63	12	2	1	12	17	27	2	1	14-7	.341	.398	.443	.841	8	...
American League totals (3 years)			122	211	30	44	7	2	4	20	12	48	4	5	6-4	.209	.264	.318	.582	8	.972
National League totals (1 year)			5	6	2	1	0	0	0	0	1	0	0	0	1-0	.167	.286	.167	.452	0	1.000
Major League totals (4 years)			127	217	32	45	7	2	4	20	13	48	4	5	7-4	.207	.265	.313	.578	8	.972

DIVISION SERIES RECORD

									BATTING								FIELDING	
Year	Team (League)	Pos.	G	AB	R	H	2B	3B	HR	RBI	BB	SO	HBP	GDP	SB-CS	Avg.	OBP	SLG	OPS	E	Avg.
2004—Anaheim (A.L.)		2B	2	2	0	0	0	0	0	0	0	2	0	0	0-0	.000	.000	.000	.000	0	1.000

ANDERSON, BRIAN J.　　　　　　　　　　P

PERSONAL: Born April 26, 1972, in Portsmouth, Va. ... 6-1/185. ... Throws left, bats right. ... Full name: Brian James Anderson. ... High school: Geneva (Ohio). ... College: Wright State.

TRANSACTIONS/CAREER NOTES: Selected by California Angels organization in first round (third pick overall) of 1993 free-agent draft. ... On disabled list (May 7-June 7, 1994); included rehabilitation assignment to Lake Elsinore. ... On disabled list (May 6-June 20, 1995); included rehabilitation assignment to Lake Elsinore. ... Traded by Angels to Cleveland Indians for Ps Jason Grimsley and Pep Harris (February 15, 1996). ... On disabled list (July 5-August 12, 1997); included rehabilitation assignment to Buffalo. ... Selected by Arizona Diamondbacks in first round (second pick overall) of expansion draft (November 18, 1997). ... On disabled list (April 12-May 2 and June 3-July 1, 2001); included rehabilitation assignments to Tucson. ... Signed as a free agent by Indians (December 23, 2002). ... Traded by Indians with a player to be named and cash to Kansas City Royals for OF Trey Dyson and P Kieran Mattison (August 25, 2003). ... Royals acquired Chris White to complete the deal (November 6, 2003). ... On disabled list (May 9, 2005-remainder of season); included rehabilitation assignments to Omaha and Wichita.

HONORS: Named A.L. Rookie Pitcher of the Year by THE SPORTING NEWS (1994).

CAREER HITTING: 35-for-255 (.137), 15 R, 5 2B, 3 3B, 1 HR, 10 RBI.

SCOUTING REPORT **_Throws:_** His fastball tops out at 89 mph, and he also has a curveball, slider and changeup. **_Tendencies:_** Anderson is a finesse guy who must be in command with his control. Must keep his fastball down because he can't win when he throws it upstairs. Expands the plate with his fastball and likes to use his curve early in counts against righthanders. Throws a slider any time to lefthanders. Change is his best pitch; he turns it over with excellent movement. Has one of the best pickoff moves in the game. **_Outlook:_** Anderson, coming off elbow surgery, is a back-of-the-rotation starter who must prove he is healthy in the spring to win a spot. **_Grade 5.8_**

BRIAN ANDERSON'S PITCHING ZONE

.333	.500	.000
.360	.250	.308
.321	.250	.167

LEFTY-RIGHTY SPLITS

vs.	Avg.	AB	H	2B	3B	HR	RBI	BB	SO	OBP	Slg.
L	.080	25	2	0	0	0	0	1	5	.115	.080
R	.359	103	37	7	2	7	21	3	12	.374	.670

Year — Team (League)	W	L	Pct.	ERA	WHIP	G	GS	CG	ShO	Hld.	Sv.-Opp.	IP	H	R	ER	HR	BB-IBB	SO	Avg.
1993— Midland (Texas)	0	1	.000	3.38	1.50	2	2	0	0	...	0-...	10.2	16	5	4	2	0-0	9	.340
— Vancouver (PCL)	0	1	.000	12.38	2.38	2	2	0	0	...	0-...	8.0	13	12	11	3	6-0	2	.394
— California (A.L.)	0	0	...	3.97	1.15	4	1	0	0	0	0-0	11.1	11	5	5	1	2-0	4	.256
1994— California (A.L.)	7	5	.583	5.22	1.45	18	18	0	0	0	0-0	101.2	120	63	59	13	27-0	47	.300
— Lake Elsinore (Calif.)	0	1	.000	3.00	0.50	2	2	0	0	0	0-...	12.0	6	4	4	1	0-0	9	.146
1995— California (A.L.)	6	8	.429	5.87	1.40	18	17	1	0	0	0-0	99.2	110	66	65	24	30-2	45	.282
— Lake Elsinore (Calif.)	1	1	.500	1.93	0.79	3	3	0	0	0	0-0	14.0	10	3	3	0	1-0	13	.204
1996— Buffalo (A.A.)	11	5	.688	3.59	1.20	19	19	2	0	0	0-...	128.0	125	57	51	14	28-0	85	.253
— Cleveland (A.L.)	3	1	.750	4.91	1.40	10	9	0	0	1	0-0	51.1	58	29	28	9	14-1	21	.296
1997— Buffalo (A.A.)	7	1	.875	3.05	1.09	15	15	1	1	0	0-...	85.2	78	33	29	13	15-0	60	.238
— Cleveland (A.L.)	4	2	.667	4.69	1.38	8	8	0	0	0	0-0	48.0	55	28	25	7	11-0	22	.301
1998— Arizona (N.L.)	12	13	.480	4.33	1.18	32	32	2	1	0	0-0	208.0	221	109	100	* 39	24-2	95	.274
1999— Arizona (N.L.)	8	2	.800	4.57	1.32	31	19	2	1	1	1-2	130.0	144	69	66	18	28-3	75	.279
— Tucson (PCL)	0	1	.000	5.40	1.50	2	2	0	0	0	0-...	6.2	9	5	4	1	1-0	8	.333
2000— Arizona (N.L.)	11	7	.611	4.05	1.24	33	32	2	0	0	0-0	213.1	226	101	96	38	39-7	104	.275
2001— Arizona (N.L.)	4	9	.308	5.20	1.40	29	22	1	0	0	0-1	133.1	156	93	77	25	30-2	55	.295
— Tucson (PCL)	1	0	1.000	1.50	0.75	2	2	0	0	0	0-...	12.0	7	2	2	0	2-0	8	.167
2002— Arizona (N.L.)	6	11	.353	4.79	1.32	35	24	0	0	1	0-0	156.0	174	86	83	23	32-3	81	.284
2003— Arizona (N.L.)	9	10	.474	3.71	1.31	25	24	0	0	0	0-0	148.0	162	88	61	21	32-3	72	.282
— Kansas City (A.L.)	5	1	.833	3.99	1.23	7	7	2	1	0	0-0	49.2	50	22	22	6	11-0	15	.272
2004— Kansas City (A.L.)	6	12	.333	5.64	1.63	35	26	2	1	2	0-0	166.0	217	123	104	33	53-4	70	.320
2005— Kansas City (A.L.)	1	2	.333	6.75	1.40	6	6	0	0	0	0-0	30.2	39	24	23	7	4-1	17	.305
— Wichita (Texas)	0	0	...	13.50	3.75	1	1	0	0	0	0-0	1.1	5	3	2	1	0-0	2	.500
— Omaha (PCL)	0	0	...	6.23	0.92	1	1	0	0	0	0-0	4.1	3	3	3	1	1-0	2	.188
American League totals (8 years)	41	41	.500	4.99	1.42	131	116	5	2	3	0-0	706.1	822	448	392	121	184-11	313	.296
National League totals (5 years)	41	42	.494	4.52	1.28	160	129	7	2	2	1-3	840.2	921	458	422	143	153-17	410	.280
Major League totals (13 years)	82	83	.497	4.74	1.34	291	245	12	4	5	1-3	1547.0	1743	906	814	264	337-28	723	.287

DIVISION SERIES RECORD

Year — Team (League)	W	L	Pct.	ERA	WHIP	G	GS	CG	ShO	Hld.	Sv.-Opp.	IP	H	R	ER	HR	BB-IBB	SO	Avg.
1999— Arizona (N.L.)	0	0	...	2.57	1.00	1	1	0	0	0	0-0	7.0	7	2	2	1	0-0	4	.250
2001— Arizona (N.L.)	0	0	...	2.25	0.75	2	0	0	0	1	0-0	4.0	3	1	1	1	0-0	3	.214
Division series totals (2 years)	0	0	...	2.45	0.91	3	1	0	0	1	0-0	11.0	10	3	3	2	0-0	7	.238

CHAMPIONSHIP SERIES RECORD

Year — Team (League)	W	L	Pct.	ERA	WHIP	G	GS	CG	ShO	Hld.	Sv.-Opp.	IP	H	R	ER	HR	BB-IBB	SO	Avg.
1997— Cleveland (A.L.)	1	0	1.000	1.42	0.63	3	0	0	0	0	0-0	6.1	1	1	1	0	3-1	7	.048
2001— Arizona (N.L.)	1	0	1.000	2.70	1.50	1	0	0	0	0	0-0	3.1	4	1	1	0	1-0	0	.308
Champ. series totals (2 years)	2	0	1.000	1.86	0.93	4	0	0	0	0	0-0	9.2	5	2	2	0	4-1	7	.147

WORLD SERIES RECORD

Year — Team (League)	W	L	Pct.	ERA	WHIP	G	GS	CG	ShO	Hld.	Sv.-Opp.	IP	H	R	ER	HR	BB-IBB	SO	Avg.
1997— Cleveland (A.L.)	0	0	...	2.45	0.55	3	0	0	0	2	1-1	3.2	2	1	1	0	0-0	2	.154
2001— Arizona (N.L.)	0	1	.000	3.38	1.50	1	1	0	0	0	0-0	5.1	5	2	2	1	3-0	1	.238
World Series totals (2 years)	0	1	.000	3.00	1.11	4	1	0	0	2	1-1	9.0	7	3	3	1	3-0	3	.206

ANDERSON, BRIAN N.　　　　　　　　　OF

PERSONAL: Born March 11, 1982, in Tucson, Ariz. ... 6-2/205. ... Bats right, throws right. ... Full name: Brian Nikola Anderson. ...High school: Canyon Del Oro ... College: Arizona.

TRANSACTIONS/CAREER NOTES: Selected by Chicago White organization in first round (15th pick overall) of 2003 free-agent draft.

2005 GAMES PLAYED BY POSITION (MLB): OF—12.

SCOUTING REPORT **_Offense:_** He is a power hitter who likes to use the whole field. Has the ability to walk, make steady contact and pound mistakes. Needs reps to make his power swing consistent. Looks for average fastballs up and over the outer third of the plate, which he can drive. Is a slightly above-average runner. **_Defense:_** He still might not have the speed or instincts to play center field. Seems to get better jumps on the ball when playing in the corners. Plus arm gives him a good chance of playing every day. **_Outlook:_** He projects

LEFTY-RIGHTY SPLITS

vs.	Avg.	AB	H	2B	3B	HR	RBI	BB	SO	OBP	Slg.
L	.083	12	1	0	0	0	0	0	5	.083	.083
R	.227	22	5	1	0	2	3	0	7	.227	.545

as an above-average starting corner outfielder, alhough that is not likely to happen with the White Sox anytime soon. Injury history could limit his potential. *Grade 7*

Year Team (League)	Pos.	G	AB	R	H	2B	3B	HR	RBI	BB	SO	HBP	GDP	SB-CS	Avg.	OBP	SLG	OPS	E	Avg.
2003—Great Falls (Pio.)	OF	13	49	6	19	2	1	2	13	9	10	1	1	3-1	.388	.492	.592	1.084	0	1.000
2004—Win.-Salem (Car.)	OF	69	254	43	81	22	4	8	46	29	44	3	3	10-1	.319	.394	.531	.925	1	.933
—Birmingham (Sou.)	OF	48	185	26	50	9	3	4	27	19	30	3	3	3-2	.270	.346	.416	.762	1	.000
2005—Charlotte (Int'l)	OF-DH	118	448	71	132	24	3	16	57	44	115	4	11	4-2	.295	.360	.469	.829	8	.986
—Chicago (A.L.)	OF	13	34	3	6	1	0	2	3	0	12	0	2	1-0	.176	.176	.382	.559	0	1.000
Major League totals (1 year)		13	34	3	6	1	0	2	3	0	12	0	2	1-0	.176	.176	.382	.559	0	1.000

ANDERSON, GARRET — OF

PERSONAL: Born June 30, 1972, in Los Angeles. ... 6-3/225. ... Bats left, throws left. ... Full name: Garret Joseph Anderson. ... High school: John F. Kennedy (Granada Hills, Calif.).

TRANSACTIONS/CAREER NOTES: Selected by California Angels organization in fourth round of 1990 free-agent draft. ... Angels franchise renamed Anaheim Angels for 1997 season. ... On disabled list (April 22-June 10, 2004); included rehabilitation assignment to Rancho Cucamonga. ... Angels franchise renamed Los Angeles Angels of Anaheim for 2005 season.

HONORS: Named A.L. Rookie Player of the Year by THE SPORTING NEWS (1995).

2005 GAMES PLAYED BY POSITION (MLB): OF—106, DH—36.

SCOUTING REPORT **Offense:** Anderson has an outstanding stroke that is slightly long but very fluid and generates good power and bat speed. Covers the plate well.Keeps his hands back to hit the breaking ball. Uses the entire field. Adjusts quickly to lefthanders. At times last year tried to pull the ball too much. Is a good baserunner but slow out of the box. **Defense:** He is a natural left fielder because of his lack of arm strength and slow release. Has improved his jumps coming in and going back after being exposed to center field. His deceptive running stride eats up a lot of ground. Has above-average lateral range. **Outlook:** Anderson has been criticized for his demeanor on the field but is a very good offensive player. Has been prone to injuries the past two seasons. *Grade 8.5*

GARRET ANDERSON'S HITTING ZONE

.389	.391	.222
.356	.392	.252
.308	.276	.259

LEFTY-RIGHTY SPLITS

vs.	Avg.	AB	H	2B	3B	HR	RBI	BB	SO	OBP	Slg.
L	.330	188	62	7	0	5	37	6	32	.347	.447
R	.261	387	101	27	1	12	59	17	52	.290	.429

Year Team (League)	Pos.	G	AB	R	H	2B	3B	HR	RBI	BB	SO	HBP	GDP	SB-CS	Avg.	OBP	SLG	OPS	E	Avg.
1990—Ariz. Angels (Ariz.)	OF	32	127	5	27	2	0	0	14	2	24	2	3	3-0	.213	.231	.228	.460	2	.965
—Boise (N'west)	OF	25	83	11	21	3	1	1	8	4	18	0	3	0-1	.253	.284	.349	.633	2	.950
1991—Quad City (Midw.)	OF	105	392	40	102	22	2	2	42	20	89	0	16	5-6	.260	.295	.342	.637	10	.943
1992—Palm Springs (Calif.)	OF	81	322	46	104	15	2	1	62	21	61	1	9	1-1	.323	.366	.391	.758	6	.959
—Midland (Texas)	OF	39	146	16	40	5	0	2	19	9	30	0	8	2-1	.274	.316	.349	.665	1	.986
1993—Vancouver (PCL)	OF-1B	124	467	57	137	34	4	4	71	31	95	0	15	3-4	.293	.334	.409	.743	2	.991
1994—Vancouver (PCL)	OF-DH-1B	123	505	75	162	42	6	12	102	28	93	1	7	3-3	.321	.356	.499	.855	2	.990
—California (A.L.)	OF	5	13	0	5	0	0	0	1	0	2	0	0	0-0	.385	.385	.385	.769	0	1.000
1995—California (A.L.)	OF-DH	106	374	50	120	19	1	16	69	19	65	1	8	6-2	.321	.352	.505	.857	5	.978
—Vancouver (PCL)	OF-DH	14	61	9	19	7	0	0	12	5	14	0	3	0-0	.311	.364	.426	.790	1	.957
1996—California (A.L.)	OF-DH	150	607	79	173	33	2	12	72	27	84	0	22	7-9	.285	.314	.405	.719	7	.979
1997—Anaheim (A.L.)	OF-DH	154	624	76	189	36	3	8	92	30	70	2	20	10-4	.303	.334	.409	.743	3	.992
1998—Anaheim (A.L.)	OF	156	622	62	183	41	7	15	79	29	80	1	13	8-3	.294	.325	.455	.780	6	.983
1999—Anaheim (A.L.)	OF-DH	157	620	88	188	36	2	21	80	34	81	0	15	3-4	.303	.336	.469	.806	3	.993
2000—Anaheim (A.L.)	OF-DH-1B	159	647	92	185	40	3	35	117	24	87	0	21	7-6	.286	.307	.519	.827	4	.990
2001—Anaheim (A.L.)	OF-DH	161	672	83	194	39	2	28	123	27	100	0	12	13-6	.289	.314	.478	.792	2	.994
2002—Anaheim (A.L.)	OF-DH	158	638	93	195	•56	3	29	123	30	80	0	11	6-4	.306	.332	.539	.871	2	.994
2003—Anaheim (A.L.)	OF-DH	159	638	80	201	•49	4	29	116	31	83	0	15	6-3	.315	.345	.541	.885	1	.997
2004—Rancho Cuca. (Calif.)	OF	3	9	1	4	0	0	1	1	1	1	0	0	0-0	.444	.500	.778	1.278	0	1.000
—Anaheim (A.L.)	OF-DH	112	442	57	133	20	1	14	75	29	75	1	3	2-1	.301	.343	.446	.789	2	.991
2005—Los Angeles (A.L.)	OF-DH	142	575	68	163	34	1	17	96	23	84	0	13	1-1	.283	.308	.435	.743	5	.976
Major League totals (12 years)		1619	6472	828	1929	403	29	224	1043	303	891	5	153	69-43	.298	.327	.473	.800	40	.988

DIVISION SERIES RECORD

Year Team (League)	Pos.	G	AB	R	H	2B	3B	HR	RBI	BB	SO	HBP	GDP	SB-CS	Avg.	OBP	SLG	OPS	E	Avg.
2002—Anaheim (A.L.)	OF	4	18	5	7	2	0	1	4	1	3	0	1	0-0	.389	.421	.667	1.088	0	1.000
2004—Anaheim (A.L.)	OF	3	13	1	2	0	0	0	0	0	3	0	0	0-0	.154	.154	.154	.308	0	1.000
2005—Los Angeles (A.L.)	OF	5	19	2	5	0	1	2	7	0	0	0	0	0-0	.263	.250	.684	.934	0	1.000
Division series totals (3 years)		12	50	8	14	2	1	3	11	1	6	0	1	0-0	.280	.288	.540	.828	0	1.000

CHAMPIONSHIP SERIES RECORD

Year Team (League)	Pos.	G	AB	R	H	2B	3B	HR	RBI	BB	SO	HBP	GDP	SB-CS	Avg.	OBP	SLG	OPS	E	Avg.
2002—Anaheim (A.L.)	OF	5	20	3	5	1	0	1	3	1	4	0	0	0-1	.250	.286	.450	.736	0	1.000
2005—Los Angeles (A.L.)	OF	5	17	2	3	0	0	1	2	1	5	0	0	0-0	.176	.211	.353	.563	0	1.000
Champ. series totals (2 years)		10	37	5	8	1	0	2	5	2	9	0	0	0-1	.216	.250	.405	.655	0	1.000

WORLD SERIES RECORD

Year Team (League)	Pos.	G	AB	R	H	2B	3B	HR	RBI	BB	SO	HBP	GDP	SB-CS	Avg.	OBP	SLG	OPS	E	Avg.
2002—Anaheim (A.L.)	OF	7	32	3	9	1	0	0	6	0	3	0	1	0-0	.281	.281	.313	.594	1	.947

ALL-STAR GAME RECORD

	G	AB	R	H	2B	3B	HR	RBI	BB	SO	HBP	GDP	SB-CS	Avg.	OBP	SLG	OPS	E	Avg.
All-Star Game totals (3 years)	3	10	1	3	1	0	1	3	0	2	0	0	0-0	.300	.300	.700	1.000	0	...

ANDERSON, JASON — P

PERSONAL: Born June 9, 1979, in Danville, Ill. ... 6-0/188. ... Throws right, bats left. ... Full name: Jason Roger Anderson. ... High school: Danville (Ill.). ... College: Illinois.

TRANSACTIONS/CAREER NOTES: Selected by Kansas City Royals organization in sixth round of 1997 free-agent draft; did not sign. ... Selected by New York Yankees organization in 10th round of 2000 free-agent draft. ... Traded by Yankees with Ps Ryan Bicondoa and Anderson Garcia to New York Mets for P Armando Benitez (July 18, 2003). ... Claimed on waivers by Cleveland Indians (April 8, 2004). ... Claimed on waivers by New York Yankees (June 1, 2004).

CAREER HITTING: 0-for-0 (.000), 0 R, 0 2B, 0 3B, 0 HR, 0 RBI.

LEFTY-RIGHTY SPLITS

vs.	Avg.	AB	H	2B	3B	HR	RBI	BB	SO	OBP	Slg.
L	.125	8	1	0	0	0	0	3	1	.364	.125
R	.250	12	3	2	1	0	3	4	1	.438	.583

Year	Team (League)	W	L	Pct.	ERA	WHIP	G	GS	CG	ShO	Hld.	Sv.-Opp.	IP	H	R	ER	HR	BB-IBB	SO	Avg.
2000—	Staten Island (N.Y.-Penn.) .	6	5	.545	4.03	1.36	15	15	0	0	...	0-...	80.1	84	41	36	1	25-0	73	.273
2001—	Greensboro (S. Atl.)	7	9	.438	3.76	1.34	23	19	1	0	...	1-...	124.1	127	68	52	9	40-1	101	.267
—	Staten Island (N.Y.-Penn.) .	5	1	.833	1.70	0.92	7	7	0	0	...	0-...	47.2	32	9	9	2	12-0	56	.190
2002—	Tampa (Fla. St.)	4	2	.667	4.07	1.23	12	3	0	0	...	1-...	24.1	27	13	11	2	3-0	22	.281
—	Norwich (East.)	1	1	.500	0.93	0.98	16	0	0	0	...	2-...	19.1	14	2	2	1	5-1	21	.212
—	Columbus (Int'l)	5	1	.833	3.15	1.08	26	0	0	0	...	7-...	34.1	26	13	12	3	11-0	28	.211
2003—	Columbus (Int'l)	0	0	...	0.00	0.65	6	0	0	0	...	3-...	7.2	3	0	0	0	2-0	13	.115
—	New York (A.L.)	1	0	1.000	4.79	1.79	22	0	0	0	0	0-0	20.2	23	13	11	3	14-4	9	.280
—	Norfolk (Int'l)	1	3	.250	2.70	1.07	10	5	0	0	0	4-...	23.1	18	8	7	3	7-0	9	.214
—	New York (N.L.)	0	0	...	5.06	1.41	6	0	0	0	0	0-0	10.2	10	6	6	2	5-1	7	.256
2004—	Cleveland (A.L.)	0	0	...	45.00	5.00	1	0	0	0	0	0-0	1.0	1	5	5	1	4-1	1	.250
—	Buffalo (Int'l)	2	1	.667	2.76	1.04	9	0	0	0	0	1-...	16.1	15	5	5	1	2-1	11	.254
—	Columbus (Int'l)	1	3	.250	4.63	1.34	36	0	0	0	0	1-...	44.2	48	24	23	4	12-0	38	.264
2005—	New York (A.L.)	1	0	1.000	7.94	1.94	3	0	0	0	0	0-0	5.2	5	5	5	0	7-1	2	.200
—	Columbus (Int'l)	4	1	.800	2.66	0.92	55	0	0	0	6	10-13	67.2	44	21	20	4	18-1	60	.190
	American League totals (3 years)	2	0	1.000	6.91	1.94	26	0	0	0	0	0-0	27.1	28	23	21	4	25-6	12	.264
	National League totals (1 year)	0	0	...	5.06	1.41	6	0	0	0	0	0-0	10.2	10	6	6	2	5-1	7	.256
	Major League totals (3 years)	2	0	1.000	6.39	1.79	32	0	0	0	0	0-0	38.0	38	29	27	6	30-7	19	.262

ANDERSON, MARLON — 2B/OF

PERSONAL: Born January 6, 1974, in Montgomery, Ala. ... 5-11/200. ... Bats left, throws right. ... Full name: Marlon Ordell Anderson. ... High school: Prattville (Ala.). ... College: South Alabama.

TRANSACTIONS/CAREER NOTES: Selected by Philadelphia Phillies organization in second round of 1995 free-agent draft; choice received from St. Louis Cardinals as part of compensation for Cardinals signing Type A free-agent P Danny Jackson. ... Signed as a free agent by Tampa Bay Devil Rays (January 16, 2003). ... On suspended list (July 29-August 1, 2003). ... Signed as a free agent by St. Louis Cardinals (January 9, 2004). ... Released by Cardinals (November 19, 2004). ... Signed by New York Mets organization (December 23, 2004).

2005 GAMES PLAYED BY POSITION (MLB): 1B—23, OF—23, 2B—20, DH—2.

SCOUTING REPORT *Offense:* Anderson crowds the plate, daring pitchers to try to throw fastballs past him. Will dive over the plate. Has a quick bat and some power on balls down in the zone. Is susceptible to off-speed pitches because his swing has a lot of moving parts. Has become a good pinch hitter because he can hit good fastballs. Is a good runner but doesn't try to steal bases. *Defense:* His hands are stiff, and his arm is below average. Moves to his backhand well but has limited range. *Outlook:* Anderson's defense prevents him from playing regularly, but his bat makes him a valuable asset off the bench. *Grade 5.7*

MARLON ANDERSON'S HITTING ZONE

.250	.143	.308
.294	.474	.250
.222	.500	.297

LEFTY-RIGHTY SPLITS

vs.	Avg.	AB	H	2B	3B	HR	RBI	BB	SO	OBP	Slg.
L	.267	15	4	1	0	0	2	0	4	.313	.333
R	.264	220	58	8	0	7	17	18	41	.317	.395

Year	Team (League)	Pos.	G	AB	R	H	2B	3B	HR	RBI	BB	SO	HBP	GDP	SB-CS	Avg.	OBP	SLG	OPS	FIELDING E	Avg.
1995—	Batavia (NY-Penn)	2B	74	312	52	92	13	4	3	40	15	20	4	2	22-8	.295	.331	.391	.722	14	.965
1996—	Clearwater (FSL)	2B	60	257	37	70	10	3	2	22	14	18	2	4	26-1	.272	.315	.358	.673	16	.958
—	Reading (East.)	2B	75	314	38	86	14	3	3	28	26	44	1	5	17-9	.274	.330	.366	.697	18	.957
1997—	Reading (East.)	2B	137	553	88	147	18	6	10	62	42	77	10	8	27-15	.266	.328	.374	.703	29	.961
1998—	Scran./W.B. (I.L.)	2B	136	575	104	176	32	14	16	86	28	77	7	11	24-12	.306	.343	.494	.837	28	.959
—	Philadelphia (N.L.)	2B	17	43	4	14	3	0	1	4	1	6	0	0	2-0	.326	.333	.465	.798	1	.978
1999—	Philadelphia (N.L.)	2B	129	452	48	114	26	4	5	54	24	61	2	6	13-2	.252	.292	.361	.652	11	.978
2000—	Scran./W.B. (I.L.)	2B	103	397	57	121	18	8	8	53	39	43	5	2	24-10	.305	.370	.451	.821	14	.969
—	Philadelphia (N.L.)	2B	41	162	10	37	8	1	1	15	12	22	0	5	2-2	.228	.282	.309	.591	2	.989
2001—	Philadelphia (N.L.)	2B	147	522	69	153	30	2	11	61	35	74	2	12	8-5	.293	.337	.420	.758	12	.970
2002—	Philadelphia (N.L.)	2B	145	539	64	139	30	6	8	48	42	71	5	16	5-1	.258	.315	.380	.696 *	20	.970
2003—	Tampa Bay (A.L.) 2B-DH-OF		145	482	59	130	27	3	6	67	41	60	3	6	19-3	.270	.328	.376	.703	15	.973
2004—	St. Louis (N.L.) 2B-OF-1B																				
		DH	113	253	31	60	12	0	8	31	18	56	3	1	6-2	.237	.269	.379	.649	7	.961
2005—	New York (N.L.) 1B-OF-2B																				
		DH	123	235	31	62	9	0	7	19	18	45	1	4	6-2	.264	.316	.391	.708	3	.990
	American League totals (1 year)		145	482	59	130	27	3	6	67	41	60	3	6	19-3	.270	.328	.376	.703	15	.973
	National League totals (7 years)		715	2206	257	579	118	13	41	229	144	317	11	46	42-13	.262	.308	.383	.692	56	.978
	Major League totals (8 years)		860	2688	316	709	145	16	47	296	185	377	14	52	61-16	.264	.312	.382	.694	71	.977

DIVISION SERIES RECORD

Year	Team (League)	Pos.	G	AB	R	H	2B	3B	HR	RBI	BB	SO	HBP	GDP	SB-CS	Avg.	OBP	SLG	OPS	E	Avg.
2004—	St. Louis (N.L.)		3	3	0	0	0	0	0	0	0	1	0	0	0-0	.000	.000	.000	.000	0	...

CHAMPIONSHIP SERIES RECORD

Year	Team (League)	Pos.	G	AB	R	H	2B	3B	HR	RBI	BB	SO	HBP	GDP	SB-CS	Avg.	OBP	SLG	OPS	E	Avg.
2004—	St. Louis (N.L.)	2B	5	3	1	1	1	0	0	0	1	0	1	0	0-0	.333	.600	.667	1.267	0	...

WORLD SERIES RECORD

Year	Team (League)	Pos.	G	AB	R	H	2B	3B	HR	RBI	BB	SO	HBP	GDP	SB-CS	Avg.	OBP	SLG	OPS	E	Avg.
2004—	St. Louis (N.L.)	2B-DH	4	6	0	1	0	0	0	0	0	0	0	0	0-0	.167	.167	.333	.500	0	1.000

ANDERSON, MATT   P

PERSONAL: Born August 17, 1976, in Louisville. ... 6-4/200. ... Throws right, bats right. ... Full name: Matthew Jason Anderson. ... High school: St. Xavier (Louisville). ... College: Rice.
TRANSACTIONS/CAREER NOTES: Selected by Detroit Tigers organization in first round (first pick overall) of free-agent draft (June 3, 1997). ... On disabled list (April 27-May 18 and May 19-September 20, 2002). ... Signed as a free agent by Colorado Rockies organization (February 24, 2005).
CAREER HITTING: 0-for-0 (.000), 0 R, 0 2B, 0 3B, 0 HR, 0 RBI.

LEFTY-RIGHTY SPLITS

vs.	Avg.	AB	H	2B	3B	HR	RBI	BB	SO	OBP	Slg.
L	.611	18	11	1	0	2	5	5	1	.696	1.000
R	.276	29	8	0	0	1	8	6	3	.421	.379

Year Team (League)	W	L	Pct.	ERA	WHIP	G	GS	CG	ShO	Hld.	Sv.-Opp.	IP	H	R	ER	HR	BB-IBB	SO	Avg.
1998—Lakeland (Fla. St.)	1	0	1.000	0.69	1.00	17	0	0	0	...	3-...	26.0	18	4	2	0	8-0	34	.186
—Jacksonville (Sou.)	1	0	1.000	0.60	0.80	13	0	0	0	...	10-...	15.0	7	1	1	1	5-0	11	.143
—Detroit (A.L.)	5	1	.833	3.27	1.57	42	0	0	0	6	0-4	44.0	38	16	16	3	31-4	44	.250
1999—Detroit (A.L.)	2	1	.667	5.68	1.79	37	0	0	0	3	0-2	38.0	33	27	24	8	35-1	32	.232
—Toledo (Int'l)	0	4	.000	6.39	1.66	24	4	0	0	...	5-...	38.0	32	27	27	9	31-0	35	.229
2000—Detroit (A.L.)	3	2	.600	4.72	1.43	69	0	0	0	9	1-1	74.1	61	44	39	8	45-4	71	.228
2001—Detroit (A.L.)	3	1	.750	4.82	1.32	62	0	0	0	9	22-24	56.0	56	33	30	2	18-4	52	.257
2002—Detroit (A.L.)	2	1	.667	9.00	2.27	12	0	0	0	0	0-2	11.0	17	13	11	1	8-1	8	.378
2003—Toledo (Int'l)	1	3	.250	3.79	1.53	23	5	0	0	...	3-...	38.0	50	23	16	4	8-1	31	.314
—Detroit (A.L.)	0	1	.000	5.40	1.46	23	0	0	0	4	3-4	23.1	25	17	14	5	9-1	13	.272
2004—Toledo (Int'l)	0	5	.000	5.82	1.88	34	0	0	0	...	1-...	34.0	41	26	22	5	23-3	25	.289
2005—Colorado (N.L.)	0	0	...	12.60	3.00	12	0	0	0	2	0-0	10.0	19	17	14	3	11-0	4	.404
—Colo. Springs (PCL)	3	3	.500	4.21	1.21	46	0	0	0	2	9-12	47.0	36	23	22	5	21-0	46	.212
American League totals (6 years)	**15**	**7**	**.682**	**4.89**	**1.52**	**245**	**0**	**0**	**0**	**31**	**26-37**	**246.2**	**230**	**150**	**134**	**27**	**146-15**	**220**	**.251**
National League totals (1 year)	**0**	**0**	**...**	**12.60**	**3.00**	**12**	**0**	**0**	**0**	**2**	**0-0**	**10.0**	**19**	**17**	**14**	**3**	**11-0**	**4**	**.404**
Major League totals (7 years)	**15**	**7**	**.682**	**5.19**	**1.58**	**257**	**0**	**0**	**0**	**33**	**26-37**	**256.2**	**249**	**167**	**148**	**30**	**157-15**	**224**	**.258**

ANDINO, ROBERT   SS

PERSONAL: Born April 25, 1984, in Miami. ... 6-0/170. ... Bats right, throws right. ... Full name: Robert Lazaro Andino. ... High school: Southridge (Miami).
TRANSACTIONS/CAREER NOTES: Selected by Florida Marlins organization in second round of 2002 free-agent draft.
2005 GAMES PLAYED BY POSITION (MLB): SS—17.

LEFTY-RIGHTY SPLITS

vs.	Avg.	AB	H	2B	3B	HR	RBI	BB	SO	OBP	Slg.
L	.111	9	1	1	0	0	0	0	4	.111	.222
R	.171	35	6	3	0	1	5	4	.275	.257

Year Team (League)	Pos.	G	AB	R	H	2B	3B	HR	RBI	BB	SO	HBP	GDP	SB-CS	Avg.	OBP	SLG	OPS	E	Avg.
2002—GC Marlins (GCL)	SS	9	27	2	7	0	0	0	2	5	6	0	1	3-0	.259	.364	.259	.623	1	.974
—Jamestown (NYP)	SS	9	36	2	6	1	1	0	3	1	9	0	2	1-0	.167	.189	.250	.439	1	.976
2003—Greensboro (S. Atl.)	SS	119	416	45	78	17	2	2	27	46	128	0	6	6-5	.188	.266	.252	.518	28	.945
2004—Greensboro (S. Atl.)	SS	76	295	27	83	10	1	8	46	18	83	1	5	9-2	.281	.321	.403	.724	21	.475
—Jupiter (Fla. St.)	SS-2B	49	196	18	55	7	2	0	15	7	43	0	3	6-2	.281	.304	.337	.641	7	.000
2005—Carolina (Southern)	SS-2B	127	516	63	139	30	0	5	48	37	111	6	11	22-7	.269	.324	.324	.680	27	.952
—Florida (N.L.)	SS	17	44	4	7	4	0	0	1	5	8	0	2	1-0	.159	.245	.250	.495	2	.956
Major League totals (1 year)		**17**	**44**	**4**	**7**	**4**	**0**	**0**	**1**	**5**	**8**	**0**	**2**	**1-0**	**.159**	**.245**	**.250**	**.495**	**2**	**.956**

AQUINO, GREG   P

PERSONAL: Born January 11, 1978, in Palenque, Dominican Republic. ... 6-1/188. ... Throws right, bats right. ... Full name: Gregori Emilio Aquino. ... Name pronounced: uh-KEE-no. ... High school: Americo Lugo (Santo Domingo, D.R.).
TRANSACTIONS/CAREER NOTES: Signed as a non-drafted free agent by Arizona Diamondbacks organization (November 8, 1995). ... An infielder in the Diamondbacks organization (1996-1999). ... On disabled list (April 9-June 12, 2005); included rehabilitation assignment to Tucson.
CAREER HITTING: 0-for-1 (.000), 0 R, 0 2B, 0 3B, 0 HR, 0 RBI.

SCOUTING REPORT ***Throws:*** Aquino relies on a 94-97 mph fastball, a slider in the mid-80s and a changeup. ***Tendencies:*** When healthy, he has an exceptionally live fastball as his out pitch; it has good movement down and in to righthanded hitters. Slider has a short, sweeping action, but it needs to be more consistent. Is tough on lefthanders and righthanders. Does not use the change very much because arm speed on it is slower than for other pitches. Will overthrow at times. ***Outlook:*** Aquino's role for 2006 is in question. Has an elbow problem that could require surgery. ***Grade 6.2***

GREG AQUINO'S PITCHING ZONE

.250	.286	.600
.375	.417	.200
.400	.500	.125

LEFTY-RIGHTY SPLITS

vs.	Avg.	AB	H	2B	3B	HR	RBI	BB	SO	OBP	Slg.
L	.304	56	17	4	0	1	9	7	13	.391	.429
R	.329	76	25	8	0	6	19	10	21	.422	.671

Year Team (League)	W	L	Pct.	ERA	WHIP	G	GS	CG	ShO	Hld.	Sv.-Opp.	IP	H	R	ER	HR	BB-IBB	SO	Avg.
1999—Ariz. D'backs (Ariz.)	1	2	.333	3.79	1.58	13	2	0	0	...	0-...	19.0	17	11	8	0	13-0	20	.246
2000—South Bend (Mid.)	5	7	.417	4.46	1.47	29	18	0	0	...	0-...	119.0	119	67	59	9	56-0	93	.260
2001—Lancaster (Calif.)	2	5	.286	8.14	1.98	25	4	0	0	...	0-...	42.0	59	40	38	7	24-0	39	.331
—Yakima (N'west)	4	2	.667	3.30	1.14	8	8	0	0	...	0-...	46.1	39	18	17	2	14-1	39	.229
2002—Yakima (N'west)	1	1	.500	2.06	1.23	6	6	0	0	...	0-...	35.0	26	9	8	0	17-0	34	.213
—Lancaster (Calif.)	4	1	.800	3.67	1.39	8	8	0	0	...	0-...	49.0	50	20	20	3	18-0	50	.267
2003—El Paso (Texas)	7	3	.700	3.46	1.43	20	20	0	0	...	0-...	106.2	115	43	41	5	38-1	91	.278
2004—Tucson (PCL)	1	3	.250	6.37	1.72	21	2	0	0	...	1-...	29.2	33	25	21	2	18-0	19	.270
—Arizona (N.L.)	0	2	.000	3.06	1.16	34	0	0	0	1	16-19	35.1	24	15	12	4	17-2	26	.194
2005—Tucson (PCL)	1	0	1.000	1.04	0.46	6	0	0	0	...	0-0	8.2	1	1	1	0	7-0	9	.034
—Arizona (N.L.)	0	1	.000	7.76	1.88	35	0	0	0	3	1-3	31.1	42	29	27	7	17-1	34	.318
Major League totals (2 years)	**0**	**3**	**.000**	**5.27**	**1.50**	**69**	**0**	**0**	**0**	**4**	**17-22**	**66.2**	**66**	**44**	**39**	**11**	**34-3**	**60**	**.258**

ARDOIN, DANNY   C

PERSONAL: Born July 8, 1974, in Ville Platte, La. ... 6-0/218. ... Bats right, throws right. ... Full name: Daniel Wayne Ardoin. ... Name pronounced: ar-DWAH. ... High school: Sacred Heart (Ville Platte, La.). ... Junior college: Texarkana (Texas) C.C. ... College: McNeese State.

TRANSACTIONS/CAREER NOTES: Selected by Boston Red Sox organization in 41st round of 1993 free-agent draft; did not sign. ... Selected by Cleveland Indians organization in 39th round of 1994 free-agent draft; did not sign. ... Selected by Oakland Athletics organization in fifth round of 1995 free-agent draft. ... Traded by A's to Minnesota Twins for 1B/OF Mario Valdez (July 31, 2000). ... Signed as a free agent by Kansas City Royals organization (December 22, 2001). ... Released by Royals (May 16, 2002). ... Signed as a free agent by Texas Rangers organization (May 17, 2002). ... Signed as a free agent by Colorado Rockies organization (December 14, 2004).

2005 GAMES PLAYED BY POSITION (MLB): C—80.

SCOUTING REPORT Ardoin was Colorado's best defensive catcher last year and took over the No. 1 job in the second half. Has an above-average, accurate, arm and a quick release. Is adept at blocking balls in the dirt and is active behind the plate. Works well with pitchers. Bat speed is slow. Tends to push the bat and does not generate a lot of power. Is a dead-red hitter who has a lot of trouble handling breaking stuff. Is better suited as a backup. **Grade 4.9**

DANNY ARDOIN'S HITTING ZONE

.182	.125	.077
.333	.545	.235
.292	.286	.250

LEFTY-RIGHTY SPLITS

vs.	Avg.	AB	H	2B	3B	HR	RBI	BB	SO	OBP	Slg.
L	.277	47	13	3	0	1	5	6	12	.370	.404
R	.215	163	35	7	0	5	17	14	57	.305	.350

Year	Team (League)	Pos.	G	AB	R	H	2B	3B	HR	RBI	BB	SO	HBP	GDP	SB-CS	Avg.	OBP	SLG	OPS	E	Avg.
1995—S. Oregon (N'west)		C	58	175	28	41	9	1	2	23	31	50	9	2	2-1	.234	.370	.331	.701	* 14	.971
1996—Modesto (California)		1B-3B-C	91	317	55	83	13	3	6	34	47	81	9	9	5-7	.262	.371	.379	.749	21	.980
1997—Visalia (Calif.)		1B-3B-C																			
		OF	43	145	16	34	7	1	3	19	21	39	4	3	0-1	.234	.347	.359	.706	5	.987
—Huntsville (Sou.)		3B-C	57	208	26	48	10	1	4	23	17	38	3	7	2-3	.231	.296	.346	.642	10	.972
1998—Huntsville (Sou.)		1B-C-OF	109	363	67	90	21	0	16	62	62	87	7	10	8-4	.248	.367	.438	.805	12	.982
1999—Vancouver (PCL)		C-3B-1B	109	336	53	85	13	2	6	34	50	78	9	12	3-3	.253	.364	.375	.739	10	.984
2000—Sacramento (PCL)		C-1B-3B	67	234	42	65	16	1	6	34	34	72	8	5	6-0	.278	.385	.432	.817	8	.980
—Modesto (California)		C	4	10	1	3	1	0	0	2	0	4	1	0	0-0	.300	.364	.400	.764	1	.960
—Salt Lake (PCL)		C	3	9	1	2	0	0	0	0	3	4	0	0	0-0	.222	.417	.222	.639	0	1.000
—Minnesota (A.L.)		C	15	32	4	4	1	0	1	5	8	10	0	0	0-0	.125	.300	.250	.550	1	.989
2001—Edmonton (PCL)		C-OF	88	302	37	77	18	1	5	37	22	81	1	8	2-6	.255	.304	.371	.675	6	.989
2002—Omaha (PCL)		C-1B	25	77	10	16	3	0	3	10	11	25	0	1	1-0	.208	.297	.364	.660	3	.984
—Tulsa (Texas)		C	8	21	1	3	0	0	0	0	4	9	0	1	0-0	.143	.280	.143	.423	0	1.000
—Oklahoma (PCL)		C-OF	33	106	10	24	5	0	2	11	10	31	2	2	0-0	.226	.303	.330	.633	4	.984
2003—Oklahoma (PCL)		C-3B-DH	74	239	35	58	11	2	7	35	21	58	3	9	0-2	.243	.311	.393	.704	10	.973
2004—Texas (A.L.)		C	6	8	1	1	0	0	0	1	3	2	0	0	0-0	.125	.364	.125	.489	1	.958
—Oklahoma (PCL)		C	68	237	50	73	12	0	10	44	41	66	8	9	1-1	.308	.422	.485	.907	11	.976
2005—Colo. Springs (PCL)		C-1B-DH	44	142	27	48	12	2	6	24	20	38	6	7	3-1	.338	.438	.577	1.015	2	.994
—Colorado (N.L.)		C	80	210	28	48	10	0	6	22	20	69	9	8	1-1	.229	.320	.362	.681	6	.988
American League totals (2 years)			21	40	5	5	1	0	1	6	11	12	0	0	0-0	.125	.314	.225	.539	2	.982
National League totals (1 year)			80	210	28	48	10	0	6	22	20	69	9	8	1-1	.229	.320	.362	.681	6	.988
Major League totals (3 years)			101	250	33	53	11	0	7	28	31	81	9	8	1-1	.212	.318	.340	.658	8	.987

ARMAS, TONY   P

PERSONAL: Born April 29, 1978, in Puerto Piritu, Venezuela. ... 6-3/225. ... Throws right, bats right. ... Full name: Antonio Jose Armas. ... Name pronounced: AR-mus. ... Son of Tony Armas, outfielder with four major league teams (1976-89); nephew of Marcos Armas, outfielder with Oakland Athletics (1993).

TRANSACTIONS/CAREER NOTES: Signed as a non-drafted free agent by New York Yankees organization (August 16, 1994). ... Traded by Yankees with a player to be named to Boston Red Sox for C Mike Stanley and SS Randy Brown (August 13, 1997); Red Sox acquired P Jim Mecir to complete deal (September 29, 1997). ... Traded by Red Sox to Montreal Expos (December 18, 1997), completing deal in which Red Sox traded P Carl Pavano and a player to be named to Expos for P Pedro Martinez (November 18, 1997). ... On disabled list (April 1-28 and July 19-September 6, 2000); included rehabilitation assignments to Jupiter and Ottawa. ... On disabled list (July 27-August 19, 2002; and April 21, 2003-remainder of season). ... On disabled list (March 26-May 31, 2004); included rehabilitation assignments to Brevard County and Edmonton. ... Expos franchise transferred to Washington, D.C., and renamed Washington Nationals for 2005 season (December 3, 2004). ... On disabled list (March 28-May 9; and September 17, 2005-remainder of season).

CAREER HITTING: 20-for-189 (.106), 5 R, 1 2B, 1 3B, 0 HR, 7 RBI.

TONY ARMAS'S PITCHING ZONE

.289	.462	.226
.278	.314	.295
.222	.158	.353

LEFTY-RIGHTY SPLITS

vs.	Avg.	AB	H	2B	3B	HR	RBI	BB	SO	OBP	Slg.
L	.276	185	51	9	1	10	28	32	24	.385	.497
R	.241	203	49	11	2	6	25	22	35	.326	.404

Year	Team (League)	W	L	Pct.	ERA	WHIP	G	GS	CG	ShO	Hld.	Sv.-Opp.	IP	H	R	ER	HR	BB-IBB	SO	Avg.
1995—GC Yankees (GCL)		0	1	.000	0.64	1.29	5	4	0	0	...	0-...	14.0	12	9	1	1	6-0	13	.226
1996—Oneonta (NYP)		1	1	.500	5.74	1.60	3	3	0	0	...	0-...	15.2	14	12	10	1	11-0	14	.230
—GC Yankees (GCL)		4	1	.800	3.15	1.18	8	7	0	0	...	1-...	45.2	41	18	16	1	13-0	45	.236
1997—Greensboro (S. Atl.)		5	2	.714	1.05	0.95	9	9	2	1	...	0-...	51.2	36	13	6	3	13-0	64	.190
—Tampa (Fla. St.)		3	1	.750	3.33	1.28	9	9	0	0	...	0-...	46.0	43	23	17	1	16-3	26	.251
—Sarasota (Fla. St.)		2	1	.667	6.62	1.70	3	3	0	0	...	0-...	17.2	18	13	13	2	12-0	9	.281
1998—Jupiter (Fla. St.)		12	8	.600	2.88	1.30	27	27	1	1	...	0-...	153.1	140	63	49	11	59-0	136	.244
1999—Harrisburg (East.)		9	7	.563	2.89	1.19	24	24	1	1	...	0-...	149.2	123	62	48	10	55-0	106	.221
—Montreal (N.L.)		0	1	.000	1.50	1.67	1	1	0	0	0	0-0	6.0	8	4	1	0	2-1	2	.320
2000—Jupiter (Fla. St.)		0	0	...	0.00	0.86	1	1	0	0	0	0-0	4.2	4	0	0	0	0-0	8	.222
—Ottawa (Int'l)		1	2	.333	3.79	1.37	4	4	0	0	0	0-0	19.0	22	11	8	3	4-0	12	.275
—Montreal (N.L.)		7	9	.438	4.36	1.31	17	17	0	0	0	0-0	95.0	74	49	46	10	50-2	59	.218
2001—Montreal (N.L.)		9	14	.391	4.03	1.38	34	34	0	0	0	0-0	196.2	180	101	88	18	91-6	176	.247
2002—Montreal (N.L.)		12	12	.500	4.44	1.38	29	29	0	0	0	0-0	164.1	149	87	81	22	78-12	131	.243
2003—Montreal (N.L.)		2	1	.667	2.61	1.06	5	5	0	0	0	0-0	31.0	25	9	9	4	8-0	23	.225
2004—Brevard County (FSL)		0	1	.000	6.75	1.39	2	2	0	0	0	0-0	9.1	5	7	7	1	7-0	7	.179
—Edmonton (PCL)		0	0	...	1.80	1.20	2	2	0	0	0	0-...	10.0	11	4	2	0	1-0	5	.268

Year	Team (League)	W	L	Pct.	ERA	WHIP	G	GS	CG	ShO	Hld.	Sv.-Opp.	IP	H	R	ER	HR	BB-IBB	SO	Avg.
	—Montreal (N.L.)	2	4	.333	4.88	1.54	16	16	0	0	0	0-0	72.0	66	41	39	13	45-6	54	.247
2005	—New Orleans (PCL)	1	2	.333	4.38	1.46	5	5	0	0	0	0-0	24.2	26	13	12	3	10-3	21	.268
	—Washington (N.L.)	7	7	.500	4.97	1.52	19	19	0	0	0	0-0	101.1	100	57	56	16	54-4	59	.258
	Major League totals (7 years)	39	48	.448	4.32	1.40	121	121	0	0	0	0-0	666.1	602	348	320	83	328-31	504	.244

ARROYO, BRONSON   P

PERSONAL: Born February 24, 1977, in Key West, Fla. ... 6-5/190. ... Throws right, bats right. ... Full name: Bronson Anthony Arroyo. ... Name pronounced: ah-ROY-yoh. ... High school: Hernando (Fla.).

TRANSACTIONS/CAREER NOTES: Selected by Pittsburgh Pirates organization in third round of 1995 free-agent draft. ... Claimed on waivers by Boston Red Sox (February 4, 2003). ... On suspended list (May 17-25, 2005).

CAREER HITTING: 4-for-55 (.073), 2 R, 2 2B, 0 3B, 0 HR, 1 RBI.

SCOUTING REPORT **Throws:** His fastball reaches 88-91 mph. Also has a 73-76 mph curveball, which is more of a slurve, and a changeup. **Tendencies:** : He has a deceptive delivery and throws easily to create a very sneaky fastball that moves late. Has good command to both sides of the plate with his fastball, a pitch he has improved by keeping it down. Breaking ball is a slurve with the speed of a curve that helps expand the plate laterally. Throws change to lefthanders. **Outlook:** Arroyo is a very versatile pitcher who can be a fifth starter or long man out of the bullpen. Has a very resilient arm. Deceptiveness allows him to pitch with his fastball, even though its velocity is marginal. **Grade 7.3**

BRONSON ARROYO'S PITCHING ZONE

.228	.200	.288
.329	.400	.331
.226	.302	.283

LEFTY-RIGHTY SPLITS

vs.	Avg.	AB	H	2B	3B	HR	RBI	BB	SO	OBP	Slg.
L	.288	469	135	35	4	17	58	30	50	.343	.488
R	.234	333	78	21	4	5	35	24	50	.291	.366

Year	Team (League)	W	L	Pct.	ERA	WHIP	G	GS	CG	ShO	Hld.	Sv.-Opp.	IP	H	R	ER	HR	BB-IBB	SO	Avg.
1995	—GC Pirates (GCL)	5	4	.556	4.26	1.32	13	9	0	0	...	1-...	61.1	72	39	29	4	9-0	48	.277
1996	—Augusta (S. Atl.)	8	6	.571	3.52	1.17	26	26	0	0	...	0-...	135.2	123	64	53	11	36-0	107	.242
1997	—Lynchburg (Caro.)	12	4	.750	3.31	1.17	24	24	3	1	...	0-...	160.1	154	69	59	17	33-0	121	.250
1998	—Carolina (Southern)	9	8	.529	5.46	1.65	23	22	1	0	...	0-...	127.0	158	91	77	18	51-0	93	.310
1999	—Altoona (East.)	15	4	.789	3.65	1.47	25	25	2	1	...	0-...	153.0	167	73	62	15	58-1	100	.280
	—Nashville (PCL)	0	2	.000	10.38	2.46	3	3	0	0	...	0-...	13.0	22	15	15	1	10-0	11	.367
2000	—Nashville (PCL)	8	2	.800	3.65	1.21	13	13	1	0	...	0-...	88.2	82	43	36	7	25-3	52	.251
	—Pittsburgh (N.L.)	2	6	.250	6.40	1.73	20	12	0	0	0	0-0	71.2	88	61	51	10	36-6	50	.302
	—Lynchburg (Caro.)	0	0	...	3.86	1.43	1	1	0	0	0	0-0	7.0	8	3	3	0	2-0	3	.267
2001	—Pittsburgh (N.L.)	5	7	.417	5.09	1.51	24	13	1	0	2	0-0	88.1	99	54	50	12	34-6	39	.289
	—Nashville (PCL)	6	2	.750	3.93	1.18	9	9	2	1	...	0-...	66.1	63	32	29	6	15-1	49	.247
2002	—Nashville (PCL)	8	6	.571	2.96	1.08	22	21	3	2	...	0-...	143.0	126	57	47	10	28-1	116	.236
	—Pittsburgh (N.L.)	2	1	.667	4.00	1.67	9	4	0	0	1	0-0	27.0	30	14	12	1	15-3	22	.283
2003	—Pawtucket (Int'l)	12	6	.667	3.43	1.10	24	24	1	1	...	0-...	149.2	148	66	57	9	23-0	155	.252
	—Boston (A.L.)	0	0	...	2.08	0.81	6	0	0	0	0	1-1	17.1	10	5	4	2	4-2	14	.164
2004	—Boston (A.L.)	10	9	.526	4.03	1.22	32	29	0	0	0	0-0	178.2	171	99	80	17	47-3	142	.249
2005	—Boston (A.L.)	14	10	.583	4.51	1.30	35	32	0	0	0	0-0	205.1	213	116	103	22	54-3	100	.266
	American League totals (3 years)	24	19	.558	4.19	1.24	73	61	0	0	0	1-1	401.1	394	220	187	39	105-8	256	.254
	National League totals (3 years)	9	14	.391	5.44	1.61	53	29	1	0	3	0-0	187.0	217	129	113	23	85-15	111	.294
	Major League totals (6 years)	33	33	.500	4.59	1.36	126	90	1	0	3	1-1	588.1	611	349	300	62	190-23	367	.267

DIVISION SERIES RECORD

Year	Team (League)	W	L	Pct.	ERA	WHIP	G	GS	CG	ShO	Hld.	Sv.-Opp.	IP	H	R	ER	HR	BB-IBB	SO	Avg.
2004	—Boston (A.L.)	0	0	...	3.00	0.83	1	1	0	0	0	0-0	6.0	3	2	2	1	2-0	7	.143
2005	—Boston (A.L.)	0	0	...	18.00	4.00	1	0	0	0	0	0-0	1.0	2	2	2	1	2-0	1	.400
	Division series totals (2 years)	0	0	...	5.14	1.29	2	1	0	0	0	0-0	7.0	5	4	4	2	4-0	8	.192

CHAMPIONSHIP SERIES RECORD

Year	Team (League)	W	L	Pct.	ERA	WHIP	G	GS	CG	ShO	Hld.	Sv.-Opp.	IP	H	R	ER	HR	BB-IBB	SO	Avg.
2003	—Boston (A.L.)	0	0	...	2.70	1.20	3	0	0	0	0	0-0	3.1	2	1	1	1	2-0	5	.167
2004	—Boston (A.L.)	0	0	...	15.75	2.50	3	1	0	0	1	0-0	4.0	8	7	7	2	2-0	3	.421
	Champ. series totals (2 years)	0	0	...	9.82	1.91	6	1	0	0	1	0-0	7.1	10	8	8	3	4-0	8	.323

WORLD SERIES RECORD

Year	Team (League)	W	L	Pct.	ERA	WHIP	G	GS	CG	ShO	Hld.	Sv.-Opp.	IP	H	R	ER	HR	BB-IBB	SO	Avg.
2004	—Boston (A.L.)	0	0	...	6.75	1.88	1	0	0	0	1	0-0	2.2	4	2	2	0	1-0	4	.333

ASTACIO, EZEQUIEL   P

PERSONAL: Born November 4, 1979, in Hato Mayor, Dominican Republic. ... 6-3/150. ... Throws right, bats right. ... Full name: Ezequiel F. Astacio. ... Name pronounced: ah-STAH-see-oh.

TRANSACTIONS/CAREER NOTES: Signed as a non-drafted free agent by Philadelphia Phillies organization (February 22, 1998). ... Traded by Phillies with Ps Brandon Duckworth and Taylor Buchholz to Houston Astros for P Billy Wagner (November 3, 2003).

CAREER HITTING: 3-for-21 (.143), 0 R, 0 2B, 0 3B, 0 HR, 0 RBI.

EZEQUIEL ASTACIO'S PITCHING ZONE

.500	.526	.154
.392	.533	.271
.304	.313	.100

LEFTY-RIGHTY SPLITS

vs.	Avg.	AB	H	2B	3B	HR	RBI	BB	SO	OBP	Slg.
L	.313	163	51	10	2	12	32	14	30	.363	.620
R	.290	169	49	11	0	11	21	11	36	.330	.550

Year	Team (League)	W	L	Pct.	ERA	WHIP	G	GS	CG	ShO	Hld.	Sv.-Opp.	IP	H	R	ER	HR	BB-IBB	SO	Avg.
1998	—DSL Phillies	0	3	.000	7.71	2.29	15	4	0	0	...	0-...	21.0	26	29	18	3	22-1	16	.283
1999	—DSL Phillies	5	2	.714	2.67	1.20	12	12	0	0	...	0-...	64.0	50	24	19	4	27-0	42	.221

Year	Team (League)	W	L	Pct.	ERA	WHIP	G	GS	CG	ShO	Hld.	Sv.-Opp.	IP	H	R	ER	HR	BB-IBB	SO	Avg.
2000— DSL Phillies	7	5	.583	2.20	1.00	15	15	0	0	...	0-...	90.0	70	40	22	1	20-0	97	.207
2001— GC Phillies (GCL)	4	2	.667	2.30	1.23	9	9	0	0	...	0-...	47.0	48	16	12	2	10-0	42	.268
2002— Lakewood (S. Atl.)	10	7	.588	3.31	1.35	25	25	1	0	...	0-...	152.1	159	61	56	9	46-1	100	.275
2003— Clearwater (FSL)	15	5	.750	3.29	1.14	25	22	2	1	...	0-...	147.2	140	60	54	9	29-0	83	.247
2004— Round Rock (Texas)	13	10	.565	3.89	1.20	28	28	1	0	...	0-...	176.0	155	89	76	12	56-1	185	.240
2005— Round Rock (PCL)	4	4	.500	3.02	0.99	13	12	0	0	0	1-1	65.2	53	25	22	6	12-0	57	.220
— Houston (N.L.)	3	6	.333	5.67	1.54	22	14	0	0	0	0-0	81.0	100	56	51	23	25-2	66	.301
Major League totals (1 year)	3	6	.333	5.67	1.54	22	14	0	0	0	0-0	81.0	100	56	51	23	25-2	66	.301

CHAMPIONSHIP SERIES RECORD

Year	Team (League)	W	L	Pct.	ERA	WHIP	G	GS	CG	ShO	Hld.	Sv.-Opp.	IP	H	R	ER	HR	BB-IBB	SO	Avg.
2005— Houston (N.L.)	0	0	...	0.00	0.00	1	0	0	0	0	0-0	1.0	0	0	0	0	0-0	2	.000

WORLD SERIES RECORD

Year	Team (League)	W	L	Pct.	ERA	WHIP	G	GS	CG	ShO	Hld.	Sv.-Opp.	IP	H	R	ER	HR	BB-IBB	SO	Avg.
2005— Houston (N.L.)	0	1	.000	27.00	9.00	1	0	0	0	0	0-0	0.2	4	2	2	1	2-0	0	.800

ASTACIO, PEDRO P

PERSONAL: Born November 28, 1969, in Hato Mayor, Dominican Republic. ... 6-2/210. ... Throws right, bats right. ... Full name: Pedro Julio Astacio. ... Name pronounced: ah-STAH-see-oh. ... High school: Pilar Rondon (Dominican Republic).

TRANSACTIONS/CAREER NOTES: Signed as a non-drafted free agent by Los Angeles Dodgers organization (November 21, 1987). ... Traded by Dodgers to Colorado Rockies for 2B Eric Young (August 19, 1997). ... Traded by Rockies to Houston Astros for P Scott Elarton and a player to be named (July 31, 2001); Rockies acquired P Garrett Gentry to complete deal (September 27, 2001). ... On disabled list (August 29, 2001-remainder of season). ... Signed as a free agent by New York Mets (January 16, 2002). ... On disabled list (March 21-April 24 and May 22, 2003-remainder of season); included rehabilitation assignment to St. Lucie. ... Signed as a free agent by Boston Red Sox organization (June 30, 2004). ... On suspended list (September 29-October 2, 2004). ... Signed as free agent by Texas Rangers organization (February 4, 2005). ... On disabled list (March 25-April 10, 2005). ... Released by Rangers (June 21, 2005). ... Signed by San Diego Padres organization (June 30, 2005). ... On disabled list (August 29-September 13, 2005).

CAREER HITTING: 85-for-652 (.130), 29 R, 8 2B, 1 3B, 0 HR, 28 RBI.

SCOUTING REPORT **Throws:** Astacio has an upper-80s fastball, a slurve and a changeup. **Tendencies:** He can run his fastball, which has occasional sinking action, to the inside part of the plate against righthanded and lefthanded hitters. Changes speeds with his slurve; can throw it slower, with a big break, or harder with a flat break. Relies too much on his breaking ball when he gets in trouble and starts to nibble. Must have good command to win. **Outlook:** Though he knows how to keep hitters off balance, Astacio's motion puts extra stress on his shoulder; he is an injury waiting to happen. **Grade 6.8**

PEDRO ASTACIO'S PITCHING ZONE

.286	.250	.273
.268	.442	.323
.310	.258	.183

LEFTY-RIGHTY SPLITS

vs.	Avg.	AB	H	2B	3B	HR	RBI	BB	SO	OBP	Slg.
L	.244	271	66	18	1	11	32	25	51	.308	.439
R	.306	219	67	11	2	6	34	12	27	.342	.457

Year	Team (League)	W	L	Pct.	ERA	WHIP	G	GS	CG	ShO	Hld.	Sv.-Opp.	IP	H	R	ER	HR	BB-IBB	SO	Avg.
1988— Dom. Dodgers (DSL)	4	2	.667	2.08	1.28	8	7	1			0-...	47.2	43	21	11	...	18-...	20	...
1989— GC Dodgers (GCL)	7	3	.700	3.17	1.16	12	12	1	1		0-...	76.2	77	30	27	3	12-0	52	.258
1990— Vero Beach (FSL)	1	5	.167	6.32	1.64	8	8	0	0		0-...	47.0	54	39	33	3	23-0	41	.286
— Yakima (N'west)	2	0	1.000	1.74	0.63	3	3	0	0		0-...	20.2	9	8	4	0	4-0	22	.123
— Bakersfield (Calif.)	5	2	.714	2.77	1.17	10	7	1	0		0-...	52.0	46	22	16	3	15-1	34	.238
1991— Vero Beach (FSL)	5	3	.625	1.67	0.88	9	9	3	1		0-...	59.1	44	19	11	0	8-0	45	.209
— San Antonio (Texas)	4	11	.267	4.78	1.60	19	19	2	1		0-...	113.0	142	67	60	9	39-3	62	.318
1992— Albuquerque (PCL)	6	6	.500	5.47	1.61	24	15	1	0		0-...	98.2	115	68	60	8	44-1	66	.293
— Los Angeles (N.L.)	5	5	.500	1.98	1.22	11	11	4	4	0	0-0	82.0	80	23	18	1	20-4	43	.255
1993— Los Angeles (N.L.)	14	9	.609	3.57	1.25	31	31	3	2	0	0-0	186.1	165	80	74	14	68-5	122	.239
1994— Los Angeles (N.L.)	6	8	.429	4.29	1.27	23	23	3	1	0	0-0	149.0	142	77	71	18	47-4	108	.252
1995— Los Angeles (N.L.)	7	8	.467	4.24	1.27	48	11	1	1	2	0-1	104.0	103	53	49	12	29-5	80	.261
1996— Los Angeles (N.L.)	9	8	.529	3.44	1.29	35	32	0	0	0	0-0	211.2	207	86	81	18	67-9	130	.261
1997— Los Angeles (N.L.)	7	9	.438	4.10	1.29	29	26	2	1	0	0-0	153.2	151	75	70	15	47-0	115	.256
— Colorado (N.L.)	5	1	.833	4.25	1.29	7	7	0	0	0	0-0	48.2	49	23	23	7	14-0	51	.262
1998— Colorado (N.L.)	13	14	.481	6.23	1.52	35	34	0	0	0	0-0	209.1	245	* 160	* 145	* 39	74-0	170	.294
1999— Colorado (N.L.)	17	11	.607	5.04	1.44	34	34	7	0	0	0-0	232.0	258	140	130	* 38	75-6	210	.285
2000— Colorado (N.L.)	12	9	.571	5.27	1.50	32	32	3	0	0	0-0	196.1	217	119	115	32	77-5	193	.281
2001— Colorado (N.L.)	6	13	.316	5.49	1.43	22	22	4	1	0	0-0	141.0	151	91	86	21	50-3	125	.276
— Houston (N.L.)	2	1	.667	3.14	1.19	4	4	0	0	0	0-0	28.2	30	10	10	1	4-0	19	.267
2002— New York (N.L.)	12	11	.522	4.79	1.33	31	31	3	1	0	0-0	191.2	192	106	102	* 32	63-5	152	.262
2003— St. Lucie (Fla. St.)	0	2	.000	2.08	1.00	4	4	0	0		0-...	17.1	15	6	4	0	3-0	15	.231
— New York (N.L.)	3	2	.600	7.36	1.77	7	7	0	0	0	0-0	36.2	47	30	30	8	18-1	20	.311
2004— GC Red Sox (GCL)	1	0	1.000	0.00	0.90	2	1	0	0		0-...	4.2	4	3	0	0	0-0	6	.211
— Portland (East.)	0	0	...	0.00	1.00	1	0	0	0		0-...	4.0	3	0	0	0	1-0	4	.214
— Pawtucket (Int'l)	0	1	.000	2.89	1.07	2	2	0	0		0-...	9.1	9	4	3	1	1-0	7	.250
— Boston (A.L.)	0	0	...	10.38	2.08	5	1	0	0	0	0-0	8.2	13	10	10	2	5-0	6	.342
2005— Texas (A.L.)	2	8	.200	6.04	1.34	12	12	0	0	0	0-0	67.0	79	45	45	13	11-1	45	.292
— Portland (PCL)	0	1	.000	15.75	2.50	1	1	0	0		0-...	4.0	10	7	7	0	0-0	1	.500
— San Diego (N.L.)	4	2	.667	3.17	1.34	12	10	0	0	0	0-0	59.2	54	21	21	4	26-3	33	.247
American League totals (2 years)	2	8	.200	6.54	1.43	17	13	0	0	0	0-0	75.2	92	55	55	15	16-1	51	.298
National League totals (13 years)	122	111	.524	4.54	1.36	358	313	30	11	2	0-1	2030.2	2091	1094	1025	262	679-50	1571	.268
Major League totals (14 years)	124	119	.510	4.61	1.37	375	326	30	11	2	0-1	2106.1	2183	1149	1080	277	695-51	1622	.269

DIVISION SERIES RECORD

Year	Team (League)	W	L	Pct.	ERA	WHIP	G	GS	CG	ShO	Hld.	Sv.-Opp.	IP	H	R	ER	HR	BB-IBB	SO	Avg.
1995— Los Angeles (N.L.)	0	0	...	0.00	0.30	3	0	0	0	0	0-0	3.1	1	0	0	0	0-0	5	.091
1996— Los Angeles (N.L.)	0	0	...	0.00	0.00	1	0	0	0	0	0-0	1.2	0	0	0	0	0-0	1	.000
2005— San Diego (N.L.)	0	1	.000	4.50	1.50	1	1	0	0	0	0-0	4.0	3	4	2	0	3-0	4	.200
Division series totals (3 years)	0	1	.000	2.00	0.78	5	1	0	0	0	0-0	9.0	4	4	2	0	3-0	10	.129

ATCHISON, SCOTT — P

PERSONAL: Born March 29, 1976, in Denton, Texas. ... 6-2/180. ... Throws right, bats right. ... Full name: Scott Barhan Atchison. ... High school: McCullough (Granbury, Texas). ... College: Texas Christian.
TRANSACTIONS/CAREER NOTES: Selected by Seattle Mariners organization in 36th round of 1994 free-agent draft; did not sign. ... Selected by Mariners organization in 49th round of 1998 free-agent draft. ... On disabled list (April 2-September 3, 2005); included rehabilitation assignments to AZL Mariners, San Antonio and Tacoma.
CAREER HITTING: 0-for-0 (.000), 0 R, 0 2B, 0 3B, 0 HR, 0 RBI.

LEFTY-RIGHTY SPLITS

vs.	Avg.	AB	H	2B	3B	HR	RBI	BB	SO	OBP	Slg.
L	.091	11	1	0	0	1	2	0	4	.091	.364
R	.400	15	6	2	0	0	2	1	5	.438	.533

Year — Team (League)	W	L	Pct.	ERA	WHIP	G	GS	CG	ShO	Hld.	Sv.-Opp.	IP	H	R	ER	HR	BB-IBB	SO	Avg.
1998—					Did not play.														
1999—Wisconsin (Midw.)	4	5	.444	3.42	1.13	15	13	0	0	...	0-...	81.2	67	34	31	4	25-1	85	.228
2000—Tacoma (PCL)	1	1	.500	3.81	1.08	5	5	0	0	...	0-...	26.0	22	11	11	3	6-0	18	.227
—Lancaster (Calif.)	5	5	.500	3.69	1.41	18	18	1	0	...	0-...	97.2	117	58	40	10	21-0	77	.289
2001—San Antonio (Texas)	9	10	.474	4.24	1.46	24	24	1	0	...	0-...	136.0	171	84	64	11	28-0	83	.315
2002—Tacoma (PCL)	5	10	.333	4.63	1.24	27	21	1	1	...	2-...	124.1	123	68	64	13	31-0	112	.256
2003—Tacoma (PCL)	6	9	.400	4.31	1.39	39	7	0	0	...	1-...	108.2	114	57	52	8	37-2	83	.269
2004—Tacoma (PCL)	5	3	.625	4.15	1.40	40	1	0	0	...	7-...	69.1	71	35	32	8	26-2	76	.266
—Seattle (A.L.)	2	3	.400	3.52	1.40	25	0	0	0	2	0-0	30.2	29	12	12	4	14-2	36	.250
2005—Ariz. Mariners (AZL)	0	0	...	5.40	1.60	4	3	0	0	0	0-0	5.0	7	3	3	0	1-0	9	.333
—San Antonio (Texas)	0	0	...	0.00	0.83	5	0	0	0	2	0-0	6.0	3	0	0	0	2-0	8	.143
—Tacoma (PCL)	0	0	...	4.15	1.38	10	0	0	0	1	0-0	13.0	13	6	6	0	5-0	17	.255
—Seattle (A.L.)	0	0	...	6.75	1.20	6	0	0	0	0	0-0	6.2	7	5	5	1	1-0	9	.269
Major League totals (2 years)	2	3	.400	4.10	1.37	31	0	0	0	2	0-0	37.1	36	17	17	5	15-2	45	.254

ATKINS, GARRETT — 3B

PERSONAL: Born December 12, 1979, in Orange, Calif. ... 6-3/210. ... Bats right, throws right. ... Full name: Garrett Bernard Atkins. ... High school: University (Irvine, Calif.). ... College: UCLA.
TRANSACTIONS/CAREER NOTES: Selected by New York Mets organization in 10th round of 1997 free-agent draft; did not sign. ... Selected by Colorado Rockies organization in fifth round of 2000 free-agent draft. ... On disabled list (April 3-26, 2005); included rehabilitation assignment to Colorado Springs.
2005 GAMES PLAYED BY POSITION (MLB): 3B—136.

SCOUTING REPORT

Offense: In his first full year in the majors, Atkins adjusted well to major league pitching. Has a good stroke and goes with the pitch. Is patient, makes good contact and is productive against lefthanded pitchers. Should hit for more power as he gains experience. **Defense:** Atkins worked on his agility before the 2005 season, and it paid off with improved flexibility and steadier hands. Will have to keep his weight down to retain his quickness. Can be erratic with his throws because of bad footwork but should improve. **Outlook:** Atkins will be steady offensively, and his improved defense should make him a fixture with the Rockies for several years. **Grade 7.3**

GARRETT ATKINS' HITTING ZONE

.345	.409	.321
.336	.345	.242
.229	.346	.231

LEFTY-RIGHTY SPLITS

vs.	Avg.	AB	H	2B	3B	HR	RBI	BB	SO	OBP	Slg.
L	.291	110	32	7	0	3	17	11	11	.358	.436
R	.286	409	117	24	1	10	72	34	61	.344	.423

Year — Team (League)	Pos.	G	AB	R	H	2B	3B	HR	RBI	BB	SO	HBP	GDP	SB-CS	Avg.	OBP	SLG	OPS	E	Avg.
2000—Portland (N'west)	1B-3B	69	251	34	76	12	0	7	47	45	48	2	3	2-0	.303	.411	.434	.846	6	.983
2001—Salem (Carol.)	1B-3B	135	465	70	151	43	5	5	67	54	98	8	8	6-4	.325	.421	.471	.892	7	.995
2002—Carolina (Southern)	3B-1B	128	510	71	138	27	3	12	61	59	77	2	12	6-6	.271	.345	.406	.751	19	.951
2003—Colo. Springs (PCL)	3B-DH-1B	118	439	80	140	30	1	13	67	45	52	3	9	2-4	.319	.382	.481	.863	20	.942
—Colorado (N.L.)	3B	25	69	6	11	2	0	0	4	3	14	1	1	0-0	.159	.205	.188	.394	6	.850
2004—Colo. Springs (PCL)	3B-1B-DH	122	445	88	163	43	3	15	94	57	45	4	20	0-0	.366	.434	.578	1.012	21	.933
—Colorado (N.L.)	3B-1B-OF	15	28	3	10	2	0	1	8	4	3	0	0	0-0	.357	.424	.536	.960	0	1.000
2005—Colo. Springs (PCL)	3B	5	21	4	7	1	0	1	3	2	4	0	0	0-0	.333	.391	.524	.915	1	.917
—Colorado (N.L.)	3B	138	519	62	149	31	1	13	89	45	72	5	18	0-2	.287	.347	.426	.773	18	.950
Major League totals (3 years)		178	616	71	170	35	1	14	101	52	89	6	19	0-2	.276	.336	.404	.740	24	.944

AURILIA, RICH — SS/2B

PERSONAL: Born September 2, 1971, in Brooklyn, N.Y. ... 6-1/189. ... Bats right, throws right. ... Full name: Richard Santo Aurilia. ... Name pronounced: uh-REEL-yuh. ... High school: Xaverian (Brooklyn, N.Y.). ... College: St. John's.
TRANSACTIONS/CAREER NOTES: Selected by Texas Rangers organization in 24th round of 1992 free-agent draft. ... Traded by Rangers with IF/OF Desi Wilson to San Francisco Giants for P John Burkett (December 24, 1994). ... On disabled list (September 24, 1996-remainder of season; July 4-20, 1998; May 20-June 4, 2002; and August 4-19, 2003). ... Signed as a free agent by Seattle Mariners (January 9, 2004). ... Traded by Mariners to San Diego Padres for a player to be named or cash (July 19, 2004). ... Signed as a free agent by Cincinnati Reds organization (January 24, 2005). ... On disabled list (May 11-29, 2005); included rehabilitation assignment to Louisville.
2005 GAMES PLAYED BY POSITION (MLB): 2B—68, SS—30, 3B—18.

SCOUTING REPORT

Offense: Aurilia has a compact stroke that allows him to make good contact. Will take the ball to the opposite field. Is a better high-ball hitter. Is a good situational hitter. Is not a good runner or a threat to steal bases. **Defense:** Aurilia has good hands and charges the ball well. Doesn't have the range to play shortstop anymore, which is why he played second base for the Reds. Moves better to his left. Has an accurate, quick release. **Outlook:** Aurilia proved he could be a regular again, but his numbers were inflated by his home park (Cincinnati's Great American Ball Park) in 2005. **Grade 6.1**

RICH AURILIA'S HITTING ZONE

.182	.353	.417
.299	.269	.200
.246	.290	.476

LEFTY-RIGHTY SPLITS

vs.	Avg.	AB	H	2B	3B	HR	RBI	BB	SO	OBP	Slg.
L	.272	125	34	6	0	4	18	15	16	.350	.416
R	.286	301	86	17	2	10	50	22	51	.333	.455

Year	Team (League)	Pos.	G	AB	R	H	2B	3B	HR	RBI	BB	SO	HBP	GDP	SB-CS	Avg.	OBP	SLG	OPS	E	Avg.
														BATTING						FIELDING	
1992—Butte (Pion.)	SS	59	202	37	68	11	3	3	30	42	18	0	2	13-9	.337	.447	.465	.913	14	.943	
1993—Charlotte (Fla. St.)	SS	122	440	80	136	16	5	5	56	75	57	3	9	15-18	.309	.408	.402	.810	24	.964	
1994—Tulsa (Texas)	SS	129	458	67	107	18	6	12	57	53	74	4	8	10-13	.234	.315	.378	.693	24	.962	
1995—Shreveport (Texas)	SS	64	226	29	74	17	1	4	42	27	26	1	8	10-3	.327	.398	.465	.863	14	.962	
—Phoenix (PCL)	SS	71	258	42	72	12	0	5	34	35	29	0	4	2-2	.279	.361	.384	.745	9	.975	
—San Francisco (N.L.)	SS	9	19	4	9	3	0	2	4	1	2	0	1	1-0	.474	.476	.947	1.424	0	1.000	
1996—Phoenix (PCL)	SS-2B	7	30	9	13	7	0	0	4	2	3	0	1	1-1	.433	.469	.667	1.135	1	.972	
—San Francisco (N.L.)	SS-2B	105	318	27	76	7	1	3	26	25	52	1	1	4-1	.239	.295	.296	.590	10	.975	
1997—San Francisco (N.L.)	SS	46	102	16	28	8	0	5	19	8	15	0	3	1-1	.275	.321	.500	.821	3	.979	
—Phoenix (PCL)	SS	8	34	9	10	2	0	1	5	5	4	0	1	2-1	.294	.385	.441	.826	0	1.000	
1998—San Francisco (N.L.)	SS	122	413	54	110	27	2	9	49	31	62	2	3	3-3	.266	.319	.407	.726	10	.979	
1999—San Francisco (N.L.)	SS	152	558	68	157	23	1	22	80	43	71	5	16	2-3	.281	.336	.444	.780	* 28	.957	
2000—San Francisco (N.L.)	SS	141	509	67	138	24	2	20	79	54	90	0	15	1-2	.271	.339	.444	.783	21	.967	
2001—San Francisco (N.L.)	SS	156	636	114	* 206	37	5	37	97	47	83	0	14	1-3	.324	.369	.572	.941	17	.975	
2002—San Francisco (N.L.)	SS	133	538	76	138	35	2	15	61	37	90	4	15	1-2	.257	.305	.413	.718	11	.980	
2003—San Francisco (N.L.)	SS-DH	129	505	65	140	26	1	13	58	36	82	1	18	2-2	.277	.325	.410	.735	13	.974	
2004—Seattle (A.L.)	SS	73	261	27	63	13	0	4	28	22	43	2	10	1-0	.241	.304	.337	.641	3	.990	
—San Diego (N.L.)	3B-2B-SS-1B	51	138	22	35	8	2	2	16	15	28	2	2	0-0	.254	.331	.384	.715	7	.937	
2005—Louisville (Int'l)	SS	1	3	2	1	1	0	0	1	2	1	0	0	0-0	.333	.600	.667	1.267	0	1.000	
—Cincinnati (N.L.)	2B-SS-3B	114	426	61	120	23	2	14	68	37	67	1	8	2-0	.282	.338	.444	.782	10	.979	
American League totals (1 year)		73	261	27	63	13	0	4	28	22	43	2	10	1-0	.241	.304	.337	.641	3	.990	
National League totals (11 years)		1158	4162	574	1157	221	18	142	557	334	642	16	96	18-17	.278	.332	.442	.774	130	.972	
Major League totals (11 years)		1231	4423	601	1220	234	18	146	585	356	685	18	106	19-17	.276	.330	.436	.766	133	.973	

DIVISION SERIES RECORD

Year	Team (League)	Pos.	G	AB	R	H	2B	3B	HR	RBI	BB	SO	HBP	GDP	SB-CS	Avg.	OBP	SLG	OPS	E	Avg.
2000—San Francisco (N.L.)	SS	4	15	0	2	1	0	0	0	0	3	0	0	0-0	.133	.133	.200	.333	1	.955	
2002—San Francisco (N.L.)	SS	5	21	4	5	1	0	2	7	1	5	0	0	0-0	.238	.273	.571	.844	0	1.000	
2003—San Francisco (N.L.)	SS	4	15	4	2	1	0	0	1	3	3	0	0	0-0	.133	.278	.200	.478	2	.926	
Division series totals (3 years)		13	51	8	9	3	0	2	8	4	11	0	0	0-0	.176	.236	.353	.589	3	.958	

CHAMPIONSHIP SERIES RECORD

Year	Team (League)	Pos.	G	AB	R	H	2B	3B	HR	RBI	BB	SO	HBP	GDP	SB-CS	Avg.	OBP	SLG	OPS	E	Avg.
2002—San Francisco (N.L.)	SS	5	15	4	5	1	0	2	5	2	2	1	0	0-0	.333	.421	.800	1.221	1	.955	

WORLD SERIES RECORD

Year	Team (League)	Pos.	G	AB	R	H	2B	3B	HR	RBI	BB	SO	HBP	GDP	SB-CS	Avg.	OBP	SLG	OPS	E	Avg.
2002—San Francisco (N.L.)	SS	7	32	5	8	2	2	1	5	1	9	0	0	0-0	.250	.273	.500	.773	0	1.000	

ALL-STAR GAME RECORD

		G	AB	R	H	2B	3B	HR	RBI	BB	SO	HBP	GDP	SB-CS	Avg.	OBP	SLG	OPS	E	Avg.
All-Star Game totals (1 year)		1	2	0	0	0	0	0	0	0	0	0	0	0-0	.000	.000	.000	.000	0	1.000

AUSMUS, BRAD   C

PERSONAL: Born April 14, 1969, in New Haven, Conn. ... 5-11/190. ... Bats right, throws right. ... Full name: Bradley David Ausmus. ... Name pronounced: AHHS-muss. ... High school: Cheshire (Conn.). ... College: Dartmouth.

TRANSACTIONS/CAREER NOTES: Selected by New York Yankees organization in 48th round of 1987 free-agent draft. ... Selected by Colorado Rockies in third round (54th pick overall) of expansion draft (November 17, 1992). ... Traded by Rockies with P Doug Bochtler and a player to be named to San Diego Padres for Ps Bruce Hurst and Greg W. Harris (July 26, 1993); Padres acquired P Andy Ashby to complete deal (July 27, 1993). ... Traded by Padres with SS Andujar Cedeno and P Russ Spear to Detroit Tigers for C John Flaherty and SS Chris Gomez (June 18, 1996). ... On suspended list (September 4-5, 1996). ... Traded by Tigers with Ps Jose Lima, C.J. Nitkowski and Trever Miller and IF Daryle Ward to Houston Astros for OF Brian L. Hunter, IF Orlando Miller, Ps Doug Brocail and Todd Jones and cash (December 10, 1996). ... Traded by Astros with P C.J. Nitkowski to Tigers for C Paul Bako, Ps Dean Crow, Mark Persails and Brian Powell and 3B Carlos Villalobos (January 14, 1999). ... Traded by Tigers with Ps Doug Brocail and Nelson Cruz to Astros for C Mitch Meluskey, P Chris Holt and OF Roger Cedeno (December 11, 2000).

HONORS: Won N.L. Gold Glove at catcher (2001 and 2002).

2005 GAMES PLAYED BY POSITION (MLB): C—134, 2B—1, SS—1.

SCOUTING REPORT *Offense:* A contact hitter with a short stroke, Ausmus has changed his approach by spreading out his stance and using his hands more. Hits with a slight hand hitch and must have excellent timing. Is a high-ball hitter without a lot of power. Has cut down his swing to take the ball back through the middle. Stays on the breaking ball. Is a good bunter. Is a good runner for a catcher. *Defense:* He is one of the more astute catchers in terms of calling a game. Has good hands with range to either side. Gets the ball up and out of his glove quickly to compensate for lack of velocity on his throws. Adjusts quickly to the type of pitching staff he has. *Outlook:* Ausmus is one of the best at handling a pitching staff; whatever he hits is a bonus. ***Grade 7.9***

BRAD AUSMUS' HITTING ZONE

.375	.455	.182
.284	.291	.218
.314	.240	.000

LEFTY-RIGHTY SPLITS

vs.	Avg.	AB	H	2B	3B	HR	RBI	BB	SO	OBP	Slg.
L	.293	92	27	6	0	2	19	18	3	.409	.424
R	.247	295	73	13	0	1	28	33	45	.332	.302

Year	Team (League)	Pos.	G	AB	R	H	2B	3B	HR	RBI	BB	SO	HBP	GDP	SB-CS	Avg.	OBP	SLG	OPS	E	Avg.
														BATTING						FIELDING	
1988—GC Yankees (GCL)	C	43	133	22	34	2	0	0	15	11	25	2	4	5-2	.256	.320	.271	.590	9	.979	
—Oneonta (NYP)	C	2	4	0	1	0	0	0	0	0	2	0	1	0-0	.250	.250	.250	.500	0	...	
1989—Oneonta (NYP)	3B-C	52	165	29	43	6	0	1	18	22	28	0	2	6-4	.261	.348	.315	.663	7	.984	
1990—Prince Will. (Car.)	C	107	364	46	86	12	2	0	27	32	73	3	7	2-8	.236	.303	.280	.583	5	.993	
1991—Prince Will. (Car.)	C	63	230	28	70	14	3	2	30	24	37	0	2	17-6	.304	.366	.417	.783	5	.990	
—Alb./Colon. (East.)	C	67	229	36	61	9	2	1	29	27	36	1	8	14-3	.266	.345	.336	.681	4	.992	
1992—Alb./Colon. (East.)	C	5	18	0	3	0	1	0	1	2	3	0	1	2-1	.167	.250	.278	.528	1	.970	
—Columbus (Int'l)	C-OF	111	364	48	88	14	2	4	35	40	56	1	14	19-5	.242	.317	.313	.630	9	.988	
1993—Colo. Springs (PCL)	C	76	241	31	65	10	4	2	33	27	41	1	6	10-6	.270	.342	.369	.711	6	.987	
—San Diego (N.L.)	C	49	160	18	41	8	1	5	12	16	28	0	2	2-0	.256	.283	.413	.696	8	.975	

Year Team (League)	Pos.	G	AB	R	H	2B	3B	HR	RBI	BB	SO	HBP	GDP	SB-CS	Avg.	OBP	SLG	OPS	E	Avg.
1994— San Diego (N.L.)	C-1B	101	327	45	82	12	1	7	24	30	63	1	8	5-1	.251	.314	.358	.672	7	.991
1995— San Diego (N.L.)	C-1B	103	328	44	96	16	4	5	34	31	56	2	6	16-5	.293	.353	.412	.765	6	.992
1996— San Diego (N.L.)	C	50	149	16	27	4	0	1	13	13	27	3	4	1-4	.181	.261	.228	.489	6	.982
— Detroit (A.L.)	C	75	226	30	56	12	0	4	22	26	45	2	4	3-4	.248	.328	.354	.682	4	.992
1997— Houston (N.L.)	C	130	425	45	113	25	1	4	44	38	78	3	8	14-6	.266	.326	.358	.684	7	.992
1998— Houston (N.L.)	C	128	412	62	111	10	4	6	45	53	60	3	18	10-3	.269	.356	.357	.713	7	.992
1999— Detroit (A.L.)	C	127	458	62	126	25	6	9	54	51	71	14	11	12-9	.275	.365	.415	.779	2	.998
2000— Detroit (A.L.)	C-1B-2B																			
	3B	150	523	75	139	25	3	7	51	69	79	6	19	11-5	.266	.357	.365	.722	8	.992
2001— Houston (N.L.)	C	128	422	45	98	23	4	5	34	30	64	1	13	4-1	.232	.284	.341	.625	3	.997
2002— Houston (N.L.)	C	130	447	57	115	19	3	6	50	38	71	6	* 30	2-3	.257	.322	.353	.675	3	.997
2003— Houston (N.L.)	C	143	450	43	103	12	2	4	47	46	66	4	8	5-3	.229	.303	.291	.594	3	.997
2004— Houston (N.L.)	C	129	403	38	100	14	1	5	31	33	54	2	13	2-2	.248	.306	.325	.631	5	.995
2005— Houston (N.L.)	C-2B-SS	134	387	35	100	19	0	3	47	51	48	5	17	5-3	.258	.351	.331	.682	1	.999
American League totals (3 years)		352	1207	167	321	62	9	20	127	146	195	22	34	26-18	.266	.354	.382	.736	14	.994
National League totals (11 years)		1225	3910	448	986	162	21	51	381	369	617	30	127	66-31	.252	.319	.343	.663	56	.994
Major League totals (13 years)		1577	5117	615	1307	224	30	71	508	515	812	52	161	92-49	.255	.328	.353	.680	70	.994

DIVISION SERIES RECORD

Year Team (League)	Pos.	G	AB	R	H	2B	3B	HR	RBI	BB	SO	HBP	GDP	SB-CS	Avg.	OBP	SLG	OPS	E	Avg.
1997— Houston (N.L.)	C	2	5	1	2	1	0	0	2	0	1	0	1	0-0	.400	.400	.600	1.000	0	1.000
1998— Houston (N.L.)	C	4	9	0	2	0	0	0	0	0	4	0	0	0-0	.222	.222	.222	.444	0	1.000
2001— Houston (N.L.)	C	3	8	1	2	0	0	1	2	0	0	0	1	0-0	.250	.250	.625	.875	0	1.000
2004— Houston (N.L.)	C	5	9	3	3	0	0	1	1	3	3	0	0	0-0	.333	.500	.667	1.167	0	1.000
2005— Houston (N.L.)	C-1B	4	18	3	4	1	0	1	1	2	4	0	2	0-0	.222	.300	.444	.744	0	1.000
Division series totals (5 years)		18	49	8	13	2	0	3	6	5	12	0	4	0-0	.265	.333	.490	.823	0	1.000

CHAMPIONSHIP SERIES RECORD

Year Team (League)	Pos.	G	AB	R	H	2B	3B	HR	RBI	BB	SO	HBP	GDP	SB-CS	Avg.	OBP	SLG	OPS	E	Avg.
2004— Houston (N.L.)	C	7	19	0	2	0	0	0	0	2	8	0	0	0-0	.105	.190	.105	.296	0	1.000
2005— Houston (N.L.)	C	6	22	3	7	2	0	0	1	1	6	0	0	1-0	.318	.333	.409	.742	0	1.000
Champ. series totals (2 years)		13	41	3	9	2	0	0	1	3	14	0	0	1-0	.220	.267	.268	.535	0	1.000

WORLD SERIES RECORD

Year Team (League)	Pos.	G	AB	R	H	2B	3B	HR	RBI	BB	SO	HBP	GDP	SB-CS	Avg.	OBP	SLG	OPS	E	Avg.
2005— Houston (N.L.)	C	4	16	1	4	1	0	0	1	1	3	1	1	0-0	.250	.333	.313	.646	0	1.000

ALL-STAR GAME RECORD

	G	AB	R	H	2B	3B	HR	RBI	BB	SO	HBP	GDP	SB-CS	Avg.	OBP	SLG	OPS	E	Avg.
All-Star Game totals (1 year)	1	1	0	0	0	0	0	0	0	0	0	0	0-0	.000	.000	.000	.000	0	1.000

AYALA, LUIS   P

PERSONAL: Born January 12, 1978, in Los Mochis, Mexico. ... 6-2/186. ... Throws right, bats right. ... Full name: Luis Ignacio Ayala. ... Name pronounced: eye-YA-lah.

TRANSACTIONS/CAREER NOTES: Contract purchased by Colorado Rockies organization from Saltillo of the Mexican League (October 14, 1999). ... Loaned by Rockies organization to Saltillo (April 13, 2000-entire season). ... Contract sold by Rockies to Saltillo (May 15, 2001). ... Contract purchased by Montreal Expos from Saltillo (August 13, 2002). ... Signed as a free agent by Arizona Diamondbacks organization (October 23, 2002). ... Selected by Montreal Expos from Diamondbacks organization in Rule 5 major league draft (December 16, 2002). ... On disabled list (June 22-July 21, 2003); included rehabilitation assignment to GCL Expos. ... Expos franchise transferred to Washington, D.C., and renamed Washington Nationals for 2005 season (December 3, 2004).

CAREER HITTING: 4-for-13 (.308), 0 R, 1 2B, 0 3B, 0 HR, 0 RBI.

SCOUTING REPORT *Throws:* His fastball ranges from 90-93 mph. Also throws a slider at 84. *Tendencies:* Ayala is a two-pitch pitcher with a very herky-jerky delivery. Has excellent arm speed. Heavy, sinking fastball has excellent life down in the zone. Slider is very quick and is thrown from the same release point as his fastball. Is far more effective against righthanded hitters than lefthanders; he doesn't have a pitch to get lefties out consistently and his release point allows them to quickly pick up the ball. Can become one-dimensional with the sinker. *Outlook:* Ayala's command has gone below average to above average. Could be a candidate to close if he were more consistent against lefthanders. *Grade 7.7*

LUIS AYALA'S PITCHING ZONE

.364	.250	.214
.217	.405	.438
.333	.278	.174

LEFTY-RIGHTY SPLITS

vs.	Avg.	AB	H	2B	3B	HR	RBI	BB	SO	OBP	Slg.
L	.350	123	43	12	0	5	19	7	18	.379	.569
R	.230	139	32	3	0	2	10	7	22	.294	.295

Year Team (League)	W	L	Pct.	ERA	WHIP	G	GS	CG	ShO	Hld.	Sv.-Opp.	IP	H	R	ER	HR	BB-IBB	SO	Avg.
1997— Saltillo (Mex.)	7	5	.583	4.62	1.56	37	2	0	0	...	0-...	62.1	76	37	32	3	21-4	30	...
1998— Saltillo (Mex.)	7	8	.467	5.62	1.80	47	4	0	0	...	7-...	83.1	105	52	52	2	45-13	29	...
1999— Saltillo (Mex.)	7	3	.700	1.71	0.96	61	0	0	0	...	41-...	79.0	54	17	15	1	22-5	28	...
2000— Saltillo (Mex.)	5	3	.625	2.76	1.26	55	0	0	0	...	25-...	65.1	69	22	20	4	13-1	38	...
2001— Saltillo (Mex.)	1	2	.333	2.03	1.13	33	0	0	0	...	21-...	40.0	34	11	9	2	11-0	34	...
— Salem (Carol.)	0	1	.000	4.05	1.80	13	0	0	0	...	7-...	13.1	19	10	6	0	5-0	10	.358
2002— Saltillo (Mex.)	3	5	.375	1.68	1.08	49	0	0	0	...	23-...	53.2	43	16	10	2	15-0	43	...
— Ottawa (Int'l)	0	0	...	3.52	1.43	6	0	0	0	...	0-...	7.2	7	3	3	1	4-0	6	.250
2003— GC Expos (GCL)	0	0	...	0.00	1.09	2	2	0	0	...	0-...	3.2	3	2	0	0	2-0	2	.154
— Montreal (N.L.)	10	3	.769	2.92	1.10	65	0	0	0	19	5-8	71.0	65	27	23	8	13-3	46	.244
2004— Montreal (N.L.)	6	12	.333	2.69	1.18	81	0	0	0	21	2-7	90.1	92	30	27	6	15-2	63	.268
2005— Washington (N.L.)	8	7	.533	2.66	1.25	68	0	0	0	22	1-3	71.0	75	23	21	7	14-4	40	.286
Major League totals (3 years)	24	22	.522	2.75	1.18	214	0	0	0	62	8-18	232.1	232	80	71	21	42-9	149	.266

AYBAR, MANNY — P

PERSONAL: Born May 4, 1972, in Bani, Dominican Republic. ... 6-1/177. ... Throws right, bats right. ... Full name: Manuel Antonio Aybar. ... Name pronounced: EYE-bar.

TRANSACTIONS/CAREER NOTES: Signed as a non-drafted free agent by St. Louis Cardinals organization (October 21, 1991). ... Traded by Cardinals with Ps Jose Jimenez and Rick Croushore and IF Brent Butler to Colorado Rockies for Ps Darryl Kile, Dave Veres and Luther Hackman (November 16, 1999). ... Traded by Rockies to Cincinnati Reds for P Gabe White (April 7, 2000). ... On disabled list (July 2-24, 2000); included rehabilitation assignment to Louisville. ... Traded by Reds to Florida Marlins for P Jorge Cordova (July 26, 2000). ... Traded by Marlins to Chicago Cubs for P Oswaldo Mairena (March 30, 2001). ... Traded by Cubs with a player to be named to Tampa Bay Devil Rays for 1B Fred McGriff (July 27, 2001); Devil Rays acquired SS Jason Smith to complete deal (August 5, 2001). ... Signed as a free agent by San Francisco Giants (February 2, 2002). ... On disabled list (August 15-September 1, 2002); included rehabilitation assignment to Fresno. ... Signed as a free agent by Arizona Diamondbacks organization (January 24, 2003). ... Released by Diamondbacks (March 2003). ... Signed by Giants organization (March 31, 2003). ... Signed as a free agent by Puebla of the Mexican League (January 2004). ... Signed as a free agent by New York Mets organization (December 28, 2004).

CAREER HITTING: 13-for-70 (.186), 6 R, 0 2B, 0 3B, 1 HR, 5 RBI.

MANNY AYBAR'S PITCHING ZONE

.273	.600	.125
.393	.250	.400
.214	.400	.000

LEFTY-RIGHTY SPLITS

vs.	Avg.	AB	H	2B	3B	HR	RBI	BB	SO	OBP	Slg.
L	.270	37	10	3	1	3	8	5	10	.349	.649
R	.318	66	21	7	1	1	10	2	17	.343	.500

Year	Team (League)	W	L	Pct.	ERA	WHIP	G	GS	CG	ShO	Hld.	Sv.-Opp.	IP	H	R	ER	HR	BB-IBB	SO	Avg.
1992—	Dom. Cardinals (DSL)	1	0	1.000	0.00	1.33	55	0	0	0	...	0-...	3.0	1	0	0	...	3-...	1	...
1993—	Dom. Cardinals (DSL)	4	4	.500	3.15	1.22	13	11	1	0	...	0-...	71.1	54	33	25	...	33-...	66	...
1994—	Ariz. Cardinals (Ariz.)	6	1	.857	2.12	1.07	13	13	1	0	...	0-...	73.0	69	25	17	0	9-0	79	.250
1995—	Savannah (S. Atl.)	3	8	.273	3.04	1.05	18	18	2	1	...	0-...	112.2	82	46	38	8	36-0	99	.199
—	St. Pete. (FSL)	2	5	.286	3.35	1.18	9	9	0	0	...	0-...	49.0	42	27	18	4	16-0	43	.228
1996—	Arkansas (Texas)	8	6	.571	3.05	1.27	20	20	0	0	...	0-...	121.0	120	53	41	10	34-0	83	.259
—	Louisville (A.A.)	2	2	.500	3.23	1.08	5	5	0	0	...	0-...	30.2	26	12	11	1	7-0	25	.226
1997—	Louisville (A.A.)	5	8	.385	3.48	1.28	22	22	3	2	...	0-...	137.0	131	60	53	10	45-2	114	.250
—	St. Louis (N.L.)	2	4	.333	4.24	1.40	12	12	0	0	0	0-0	68.0	66	33	32	8	29-0	41	.259
1998—	St. Louis (N.L.)	6	6	.500	5.98	1.62	20	14	0	0	0	0-0	81.1	90	58	54	6	42-1	57	.281
—	Memphis (PCL)	10	0	1.000	2.60	0.95	13	13	0	0	...	0-...	83.0	62	24	24	7	17-0	63	.207
1999—	St. Louis (N.L.)	4	5	.444	5.47	1.44	65	1	0	0	12	3-5	97.0	104	67	59	13	36-3	74	.272
2000—	Colorado (N.L.)	0	1	.000	16.20	3.00	1	0	0	0	0	0-0	1.2	5	3	3	1	0-0	0	.500
—	Cincinnati (N.L.)	1	1	.500	4.83	1.45	32	0	0	0	1	0-0	50.1	51	31	27	7	22-2	31	.262
—	Louisville (Int'l)	0	2	.000	13.50	3.00	3	2	0	0	...	0-...	6.2	10	10	10	0	10-0	1	.345
—	Florida (N.L.)	1	0	1.000	2.63	1.13	21	0	0	0	0	0-1	27.1	18	8	8	1	13-1	14	.184
2001—	Chicago (N.L.)	2	1	.667	6.35	1.99	17	1	0	0	2	0-0	22.2	28	19	16	5	17-0	16	.304
—	Iowa (PCL)	1	2	.333	5.02	1.35	8	7	1	1	...	0-...	43.0	42	26	24	8	16-1	32	.251
—	Durham (Int'l)	1	3	.250	5.68	1.55	11	3	0	0	...	0-...	31.2	40	25	20	5	9-0	29	.307
2002—	Fresno (PCL)	1	4	.200	3.75	1.25	45	0	0	0	...	24-...	51.0	46	24	21	6	18-1	53	.243
—	San Francisco (N.L.)	1	0	1.000	2.51	1.33	15	0	0	0	1	0-0	14.1	16	6	4	1	3-2	11	.271
2003—	San Francisco (N.L.)	0	0	...	6.00	2.33	3	0	0	0	0	0-0	3.0	4	2	2	1	3-0	2	.333
—	Fresno (PCL)	2	4	.333	4.08	1.34	52	0	0	0	...	17-...	58.0	55	27	26	7	23-0	45	.253
2004—	Puebla (Mex.)	2	2	.500	4.64	1.36	18	0	0	0	...	7-...	22.0	25	12	11	5	5-2	21	.281
2005—	New York (N.L.)	0	0	...	6.04	1.50	22	0	0	0	2	0-1	25.1	31	17	17	4	7-1	27	.301
—	Norfolk (Int'l)	3	0	1.000	1.41	1.06	24	0	0	0	3	4-4	32.0	26	7	5	1	8-0	27	.224
Major League totals (8 years)		**17**	**18**	**.486**	**5.11**	**1.50**	**208**	**28**	**0**	**0**	**18**	**3-7**	**391.0**	**413**	**244**	**222**	**49**	**172-10**	**273**	**.271**

DIVISION SERIES RECORD

Year	Team (League)	W	L	Pct.	ERA	WHIP	G	GS	CG	ShO	Hld.	Sv.-Opp.	IP	H	R	ER	HR	BB-IBB	SO	Avg.
2002—	San Francisco (N.L.)	0	0	...	6.75	1.13	2	0	0	0	0	0-0	2.2	2	2	2	1	1-0	3	.200

AYBAR, WILLY — 3B

PERSONAL: Born March 9, 1983, in Bani, Dominican Republic. ... 6-0/175. ... Bats both, throws right. ... Full name: Willy Del Jesus Aybar. ... Name pronounced: EYE-bar.

TRANSACTIONS/CAREER NOTES: Signed as a non-drafted free agent by Los Angeles Dodgers organization (January 31, 2000).

2005 GAMES PLAYED BY POSITION (MLB): 3B—20, 2B—6.

SCOUTING REPORT *Offense:* Aybar had a strong showing in his first taste of the majors late last season. Is a much better hitter from the left side, where he displays excellent discipline. From the right side, he is more of a pull hitter and, as a result, tends to overswing. Has plus speed and good basestealing ability. *Defense:* He has below-average range but good hands and an accurate arm. Third base might be his best position. *Outlook:* Aybar should be a productive utility infielder as well as a pinch hitter from the left side. *Grade 6.6*

WILLY AYBAR'S HITTING ZONE

.000	.000	.000
.364	.417	.429
.250	.250	.333

LEFTY-RIGHTY SPLITS

vs.	Avg.	AB	H	2B	3B	HR	RBI	BB	SO	OBP	Slg.
L	.241	29	7	4	0	0	3	4	3	.353	.379
R	.368	57	21	4	0	1	7	14	8	.493	.491

Year	Team (League)	Pos.	G	AB	R	H	2B	3B	HR	RBI	BB	SO	HBP	GDP	SB-CS	Avg.	OBP	SLG	OPS	E	Avg.
2000—	Great Falls (Pio.)	3B	70	266	39	70	15	1	4	49	36	45	0	3	5-5	.263	.349	.372	.721	18	.908
2001—	Wilmington (S. Atl.)	3B	120	431	45	102	25	2	4	48	43	64	3	4	7-9	.237	.307	.332	.639	18	.948
—	Vero Beach (FSL)	3B	2	7	0	2	0	0	0	0	1	2	0	0	0-0	.286	.375	.286	.661	0	1.000
2002—	Vero Beach (FSL)	3B	108	372	56	80	18	2	11	65	69	54	3	7	15-8	.215	.339	.363	.702	15	.943
2003—	Vero Beach (FSL)	3B	119	445	47	122	29	3	11	74	41	70	3	3	9-9	.274	.336	.427	.763	17	.947
2004—	Jacksonville (Sou.)	2B	126	482	56	133	27	0	15	77	50	77	3	11	8-10	.276	.346	.425	.771	15	.867
2005—	Las Vegas (PCL)	3B-2B-DH	108	401	47	119	26	4	5	60	40	56	1	8	1-6	.297	.356	.419	.775	10	.967
—	Los Angeles (N.L.)	3B-2B	26	86	12	28	8	0	1	10	18	11	1	0	3-1	.326	.448	.453	.901	2	.967
Major League totals (1 year)			**26**	**86**	**12**	**28**	**8**	**0**	**1**	**10**	**18**	**11**	**1**	**0**	**3-1**	**.326**	**.448**	**.453**	**.901**	**2**	**.967**

BACKE, BRANDON   P

PERSONAL: Born April 5, 1978, in Galveston, Texas. ... 6-0/180. ... Throws right, bats right. ... Full name: Brandon Allen Backe. ... Name pronounced: BACK-ee. ... High school: Ball (Galveston, Texas). ... Junior college: Galveston (Texas) Community College.
TRANSACTIONS/CAREER NOTES: Selected by Milwaukee Brewers organization in 36th round of 1996 free-agent draft; did not sign. ... Selected by Tampa Bay Devil Rays organization in 18th round of 1998 free-agent draft. ... Played three seasons as an outfielder in Devil Rays organization (1998-2000). ... Traded by Devil Rays to Houston Astros for IF Geoff Blum (December 14, 2003). ... On disabled list (July 27-September 3, 2005); included rehabilitation assignment to Corpus Christi.
CAREER HITTING: 15-for-61 (.246), 9 R, 2 2B, 2 3B, 1 HR, 12 RBI.

SCOUTING REPORT **Throws:** He throws a 91-94 mph fastball, a low-80s slider, a curveball at 73-75 and a changeup. **Tendencies:** Backe continues to move up in the rotation. Is pitching more at the upper range of his velocity with good command, but must keep the ball down to keep it in the park. Throws a curveball with good rotation to lefthanders but his slider—with a very late, sharp break—has become his best pitch. Can change speeds with his fastball and curve. Will pitch inside. **Outlook:** Backe has proved he can pitch in big games. Has outstanding makeup and has improved his overall stuff. Is hyper on the mound, so if he can get through the first few innings he can be tough. *Grade 7.3*

BRANDON BACKE'S PITCHING ZONE

.194	.550	.435
.303	.365	.270
.102	.350	.280

LEFTY-RIGHTY SPLITS

vs.	Avg.	AB	H	2B	3B	HR	RBI	BB	SO	OBP	Slg.
L	.260	273	71	13	0	8	34	31	45	.334	.396
R	.266	301	80	21	3	11	37	36	52	.352	.465

Year Team (League)	W	L	Pct.	ERA	WHIP	G	GS	CG	ShO	Hld.	Sv.-Opp.	IP	H	R	ER	HR	BB-IBB	SO	Avg.
2001—Char., S.C. (SAL)	2	1	.667	2.92	0.97	16	0	0	0	...	7-...	24.2	17	8	8	2	7-1	20	.200
—Bakersfield (Calif.)	1	0	1.000	1.09	0.85	17	0	0	0	...	3-...	24.2	13	7	3	1	8-0	13	.149
—Orlando (South.)	1	0	1.000	5.73	1.41	14	0	0	0	...	0-...	22.0	20	14	14	1	11-0	20	.253
2002—Orlando (South.)	4	6	.400	4.68	1.39	20	14	3	1	...	2-...	92.1	91	58	48	9	37-1	45	.256
—Tampa Bay (A.L.)	0	0	...	6.92	1.69	9	2	0	0	0	0-0	13.0	15	10	10	3	7-0	6	.288
2003—Durham (Int'l)	2	1	.667	4.64	1.40	16	2	0	0	0	0-0	33.0	33	21	17	1	13-0	27	.250
—Tampa Bay (A.L.)	1	1	.500	5.44	1.46	28	0	0	0	5	0-0	44.2	40	28	27	6	25-1	36	.247
2004—New Orleans (PCL)	6	5	.545	2.80	1.29	19	9	0	0	0	0-0	64.1	57	26	20	7	26-1	74	.241
—Houston (N.L.)	5	3	.625	4.30	1.52	33	9	0	0	3	0-0	67.0	75	33	32	10	27-4	54	.290
2005—Corpus Christi (Texas)	0	1	.000	2.25	0.63	2	2	0	0	0	0-0	8.0	4	2	2	1	0-0	11	.143
—Houston (N.L.)	10	8	.556	4.76	1.46	26	25	1	1	0	0-0	149.1	151	82	79	19	67-1	97	.263
American League totals (2 years)	1	1	.500	5.77	1.51	37	2	0	0	5	0-0	57.2	55	38	37	9	32-1	42	.257
National League totals (2 years)	15	11	.577	4.62	1.48	59	34	1	1	3	0-0	216.1	226	115	111	29	94-5	151	.271
Major League totals (4 years)	16	12	.571	4.86	1.49	96	34	1	1	8	0-0	274.0	281	153	148	38	126-6	193	.268

DIVISION SERIES RECORD

Year Team (League)	W	L	Pct.	ERA	WHIP	G	GS	CG	ShO	Hld.	Sv.-Opp.	IP	H	R	ER	HR	BB-IBB	SO	Avg.
2004—Houston (N.L.)	1	0	1.000	3.00	1.17	1	1	0	0	0	0-0	6.0	5	2	2	1	2-1	5	.227
2005—Houston (N.L.)	0	0	...	8.44	1.69	2	1	0	0	0	0-0	5.1	6	5	5	1	3-0	3	.300
Division series totals (2 years)	1	0	1.000	5.56	1.41	3	2	0	0	0	0-0	11.1	11	7	7	2	5-1	8	.262

CHAMPIONSHIP SERIES RECORD

Year Team (League)	W	L	Pct.	ERA	WHIP	G	GS	CG	ShO	Hld.	Sv.-Opp.	IP	H	R	ER	HR	BB-IBB	SO	Avg.
2004—Houston (N.L.)	0	0	...	2.84	0.79	2	2	0	0	0	0-0	12.2	6	4	4	1	4-0	10	.140
2005—Houston (N.L.)	0	0	...	1.59	0.88	1	1	0	0	0	0-0	5.2	2	1	1	0	3-0	7	.118
Champ. series totals (2 years)	0	0	...	2.45	0.82	3	3	0	0	0	0-0	18.1	8	5	5	1	7-0	17	.133

WORLD SERIES RECORD

Year Team (League)	W	L	Pct.	ERA	WHIP	G	GS	CG	ShO	Hld.	Sv.-Opp.	IP	H	R	ER	HR	BB-IBB	SO	Avg.
2005—Houston (N.L.)	0	0	...	0.00	0.71	1	1	0	0	0	0-0	7.0	5	0	0	0	0-0	7	.192

BAERGA, CARLOS   1B/3B

PERSONAL: Born November 4, 1968, in San Juan, Puerto Rico. ... 5-11/215. ... Bats both, throws right. ... Full name: Carlos Obed Baerga. ... Name pronounced: by-AIR-ga. ... High school: Barbara Ann Rooshart (Rio Piedras, Puerto Rico).
TRANSACTIONS/CAREER NOTES: Signed as a non-drafted free agent by San Diego Padres organization (November 4, 1985). ... Traded by Padres with C Sandy Alomar and OF Chris James to Cleveland Indians for OF Joe Carter (December 6, 1989). ... Traded by Indians with IF Alvaro Espinoza to New York Mets for IFs Jose Vizcaino and Jeff Kent (July 29, 1996). ... Signed as a free agent by St. Louis Cardinals (January 27, 1999). ... Released by Cardinals (March 17, 1999). ... Signed by Cincinnati Reds organization (March 23, 1999). ... Released by Reds (June 4, 1999). ... Signed by San Diego Padres organization (June 6, 1999). ... Traded by Padres to Indians for cash considerations (August 16, 1999). ... Signed as a free agent by Tampa Bay Devil Rays organization (February 24, 2000). ... Contract voided (March 21, 2000). ... Signed by Seattle Mariners organization (January 19, 2001). ... Released by Mariners (March 30, 2001). ... Signed by Boston Red Sox organization (December 18, 2001). ... On disabled list (July 2-26, 2002). ... Signed as a free agent by Arizona Diamondbacks organization (January 31, 2003). ... On disabled list (June 10-July 19, 2004); included rehabilitation assignment to Tucson. ... Signed as a free agent by Washington Nationals organization (February 2, 2005).
2005 GAMES PLAYED BY POSITION (MLB): 3B—20, 1B—11, 2B—7, DH—1.

CARLOS BAERGA'S HITTING ZONE

.273	.222	.143
.385	.333	.235
.100	.333	.333

LEFTY-RIGHTY SPLITS

vs.	Avg.	AB	H	2B	3B	HR	RBI	BB	SO	OBP	Slg.
L	.261	23	6	1	0	1	3	4	1	.414	.435
R	.252	135	34	6	0	1	16	3	16	.299	.319

									BATTING									FIELDING	
Year Team (League)	Pos.	G	AB	R	H	2B	3B	HR	RBI	BB	SO	HBP	GDP	SB-CS	Avg.	OBP	SLG	OPS	E	Avg.
1986—Char., S.C. (SAL)	2B-SS	111	378	57	102	14	4	7	41	26	60	5	4	6-1	.270	.321	.384	.705	27	.943
1987—Char., S.C. (SAL)	2B-SS	134	515	83	157	23	9	7	50	38	107	12	10	26-21	.305	.365	.425	.790	† 36	.943
1988—Wichita (Texas)	2B-SS	122	444	67	121	28	1	12	65	31	83	9	8	4-4	.273	.331	.421	.752	33	.943
1989—Las Vegas (PCL)	3B	132	520	63	143	28	2	10	74	30	98	6	6	6-6	.275	.319	.394	.713	* 32	.916
1990—Cleveland (A.L.)	2B-3B-SS	108	312	46	81	17	2	7	47	16	57	4	4	0-2	.260	.300	.394	.694	17	.935
—Colo. Springs (PCL)	3B	12	50	11	19	2	1	1	11	5	4	0	4	1-0	.380	.436	.520	.956	4	.925
1991—Cleveland (A.L.)	2B-3B-SS	158	593	80	171	28	2	11	69	48	74	6	12	3-2	.288	.346	.398	.744	21	.959
1992—Cleveland (A.L.)	2B-DH	161	657	92	205	32	1	20	105	35	76	13	15	10-2	.312	.354	.455	.809	19	.979
1993—Cleveland (A.L.)	2B-DH	154	624	105	200	28	6	21	114	34	68	6	17	15-4	.321	.355	.486	.840	17	.979
1994—Cleveland (A.L.)	2B-DH	103	442	81	139	32	2	19	80	10	45	6	10	8-3	.314	.333	.525	.858	* 15	.973

Year	Team (League)	Pos.	G	AB	R	H	2B	3B	HR	RBI	BB	SO	HBP	GDP	SB-CS	Avg.	OBP	SLG	OPS	E	Avg.
1995— Cleveland (A.L.)		2B-DH	135	557	87	175	28	2	15	90	35	31	3	15	11-2	.314	.355	.452	.807	19	.973
1996— Cleveland (A.L.)		2B	100	424	54	113	25	0	10	55	16	25	7	15	1-1	.267	.302	.396	.698	15	.971
— New York (N.L.)		1B-3B-2B	26	83	5	16	3	0	2	11	5	2	2	8	0-0	.193	.253	.301	.554	4	.966
1997— New York (N.L.)		2B	133	467	53	131	25	1	9	52	20	54	3	13	2-6	.281	.311	.396	.707	14	.978
1998— New York (N.L.)		2B	147	511	46	136	27	1	7	53	24	55	6	21	0-1	.266	.303	.364	.667	9	.986
1999— Indianapolis (Int'l)		3B-2B-1B																			
		DH	52	221	32	64	10	0	3	27	10	18	1	11	2-1	.290	.321	.376	.696	6	.975
— Las Vegas (PCL)		3B-2B	21	91	15	26	7	0	2	9	9	5	1	2	0-0	.286	.356	.429	.785	5	.919
— San Diego (N.L.)		2B-3B-1B																			
		DH	33	80	6	20	1	0	2	5	6	14	2	2	1-0	.250	.318	.338	.656	2	.962
— Cleveland (A.L.)		3B-2B-DH	22	57	4	13	0	0	1	5	4	10	0	3	1-1	.228	.274	.281	.555	1	.976
2000—			Did not play.																		
2001— Samsung (Kor.)				120	18	33	...	0	4	17	10	12	...	...	...-...	.275	...	.375	...	...	...
— Long Island (Atl.)			53	203	38	64	9	3	9	44	19	24	...	...	3-...	.315	...	.522	...	...	...
2002— Boston (A.L.)		DH-2B-3B	73	182	17	52	11	0	2	19	7	20	2	6	6-0	.286	.316	.379	.695	1	.983
2003— Arizona (N.L.)		1B-2B-DH																			
		3B	105	207	31	71	13	0	4	39	18	20	6	1-1		.343	.396	.464	.859	3	.986
2004— Tucson (PCL)		DH	1	4	1	1	1	0	0	0	0	0	0	0	0-0	.250	.250	.500	.750	0	...
— Arizona (N.L.)		1B-DH	79	85	6	20	2	0	2	11	6	12	3	7	0-0	.235	.309	.329	.638	0	1.000
2005— Washington (N.L.)		3B-1B-2B																			
		DH	93	158	18	40	7	0	2	19	7	17	8	4	0-0	.253	.318	.335	.653	6	.954
American League totals (9 years)			1014	3848	566	1149	201	15	106	584	205	406	47	97	55-16	.299	.338	.441	.779	131	.971
National League totals (7 years)			616	1591	165	434	78	2	28	190	86	174	26	61	4-8	.273	.318	.377	.695	38	.979
Major League totals (14 years)			1630	5439	731	1583	279	17	134	774	291	580	73	158	59-24	.291	.332	.423	.754	169	.973

DIVISION SERIES RECORD

Year	Team (League)	Pos.	G	AB	R	H	2B	3B	HR	RBI	BB	SO	HBP	GDP	SB-CS	Avg.	OBP	SLG	OPS	E	Avg.
1995— Cleveland (A.L.)		2B	3	14	2	4	1	0	0	1	0	1	0	0	0-0	.286	.333	.357	.690	1	.929

CHAMPIONSHIP SERIES RECORD

Year	Team (League)	Pos.	G	AB	R	H	2B	3B	HR	RBI	BB	SO	HBP	GDP	SB-CS	Avg.	OBP	SLG	OPS	E	Avg.
1995— Cleveland (A.L.)		2B	6	25	3	10	0	0	1	4	2	3	0	0	0-0	.400	.444	.520	.964	0	1.000

WORLD SERIES RECORD

Year	Team (League)	Pos.	G	AB	R	H	2B	3B	HR	RBI	BB	SO	HBP	GDP	SB-CS	Avg.	OBP	SLG	OPS	E	Avg.
1995— Cleveland (A.L.)		2B	6	26	1	5	2	0	0	4	1	1	0	1	0-0	.192	.222	.269	.491	1	.975

ALL-STAR GAME RECORD

			G	AB	R	H	2B	3B	HR	RBI	BB	SO	HBP	GDP	SB-CS	Avg.	OBP	SLG	OPS	E	Avg.
All-Star Game totals (3 years)			3	6	3	4	2	0	1	0	1	0	1	0	0-1	.667	.667	1.000	1.667	0	1.000

BAEZ, DANYS · P

PERSONAL: Born September 10, 1977, in Pinar del Rio, Cuba. ... 6-3/225. ... Throws right, bats right. ... Name pronounced: DAN-ees BUY-ez.

TRANSACTIONS/CAREER NOTES: Signed as a non-drafted free agent by Cleveland Indians organization (November 5, 1999). ... Signed as a free agent by Tampa Bay Devil Rays (January 6, 2004).

CAREER HITTING: 0-for-3 (.000), 0 R, 0 2B, 0 3B, 0 HR, 0 RBI.

SCOUTING REPORT Throws: Baez's three main pitches are a fastball at 92-96 mph, a slider at 87-90 and a split-finger fastball at 84-87. *Tendencies:* He is a power pitcher who doesn't change speeds well but can create deception by altering hitters' planes of vision. Rides his four-seamer that is difficult for hitters to center. Runs his slider away from righthanders. Puts lefthanded and righthanders away with a late-biting splitter. Tends to have a high pitch count. *Outlook:* There are concerns about Baez's long-term health because of his delivery, but there are no questions about his arm, aptitude or makeup. Is a closer on a second-division club but has the stuff to pitch for contenders. *Grade 8*

DANYS BAEZ'S PITCHING ZONE

.364	.214	.185
.381	.261	.231
.462	.273	.185

LEFTY-RIGHTY SPLITS

vs.	Avg.	AB	H	2B	3B	HR	RBI	BB	SO	OBP	Slg.
L	.268	149	40	6	1	4	21	17	26	.341	.403
R	.215	121	26	1	0	3	11	13	25	.299	.298

Year	Team (League)	W	L	Pct.	ERA	WHIP	G	GS	CG	ShO	Hld.	Sv.-Opp.	IP	H	R	ER	HR	BB-IBB	SO	Avg.
2000— Kinston (Carol.)		2	2	.500	4.71	1.31	9	9	0	0	...	0-...	49.2	45	29	26	5	20-0	56	.236
— Akron (East.)		4	9	.308	3.68	1.27	18	18	0	0	...	0-...	102.2	98	46	42	6	32-0	77	.259
2001— Buffalo (Int'l)		2	0	1.000	3.20	1.07	16	0	0	0	...	3-...	25.1	18	9	9	2	9-0	30	.200
— Akron (East.)		0	0	...	0.00	0.50	1	0	0	0	...	0-...	2.0	1	0	0	0	0-0	2	.143
— Cleveland (A.L.)		5	3	.625	2.50	1.07	43	0	0	0	14	0-1	50.1	34	22	14	5	20-4	52	.191
2002— Cleveland (A.L.)		10	11	.476	4.41	1.46	39	26	1	0	...	6-8	165.1	160	84	81	14	82-5	130	.256
2003— Cleveland (A.L.)		2	9	.182	3.81	1.16	73	0	0	0	5	25-35	75.2	65	36	32	9	23-0	66	.229
2004— Tampa Bay (A.L.)		4	4	.500	3.57	1.31	62	0	0	0	1	30-33	68.0	60	31	27	6	29-4	52	.237
2005— Tampa Bay (A.L.)		5	4	.556	2.86	1.33	67	0	0	0	0	41-49	72.1	66	27	23	7	30-0	51	.244
Major League totals (5 years)		26	31	.456	3.69	1.32	284	26	1	0	20	102-126	431.2	385	200	177	41	184-13	351	.239

DIVISION SERIES RECORD

Year	Team (League)	W	L	Pct.	ERA	WHIP	G	GS	CG	ShO	Hld.	Sv.-Opp.	IP	H	R	ER	HR	BB-IBB	SO	Avg.
2001— Cleveland (A.L.)		0	0	...	2.45	1.09	3	0	0	0	0	0-0	3.2	4	1	1	0	0-0	6	.267

BAGWELL, JEFF · 1B

PERSONAL: Born May 27, 1968, in Boston, Mass. ... 6-0/215. ... Bats right, throws right. ... Full name: Jeffrey Robert Bagwell. ... Name pronounced: BAG-well. ... High school: Xavier (Middletown, Conn.). ... College: Hartford.

TRANSACTIONS/CAREER NOTES: Selected by Boston Red Sox organization in fourth round of 1989 free-agent draft. ... Traded by Red Sox to Houston Astros for P Larry Andersen (August 31, 1990). ... On disabled list (July 31-September 1, 1995); included rehabilitation assignment to Jackson. ... On disabled list (May 13-28, 1998). ... On disabled list (May 10-September 9, 2005); included rehabilitation assignment to Corpus Christi.

RECORDS: Shares major league records for most doubles, game (4, June 14, 1996), and most bases on balls, game (6, August 20, 1999, 16 innings).
HONORS: Named N.L. Rookie Player of the Year by THE SPORTING NEWS (1991). ... Named N.L. Rookie of the Year by Baseball Writers' Association of America (1991). ... Named Major League Player of the Year by THE SPORTING NEWS (1994). ... Named N.L. Most Valuable Player by Baseball Writers' Association of America (1994). ... Won N.L. Gold Glove at first base (1994).
2005 GAMES PLAYED BY POSITION (MLB): 1B—24.

SCOUTING REPORT
Offense: Chronic shoulder problems have finally caught up to him. Showed obvious declines in strength and bat speed after returning from surgery, but still wasn't 100 percent. Likely won't regain his stroke and power, though. Is not able to get to the ball upstairs. Can't run but has good instincts. **Defense:** Prior to the surgery, Bagwell couldn't throw well enough to get the ball to second base and became a defensive liability. Has good hands but very limited range. **Outlook:** It is very questionable if he can play next season, but he surprised many by being available for the playoffs. **Grade 7**

JEFF BAGWELL'S HITTING ZONE

.375	.000	.000
.375	.350	.273
.091	.500	.000

LEFTY-RIGHTY SPLITS

vs.	Avg.	AB	H	2B	3B	HR	RBI	BB	SO	OBP	Slg.
L	.300	20	6	0	0	1	4	5	7	.423	.450
R	.238	80	19	4	0	2	15	13	14	.340	.363

B

										BATTING									FIELDING	
Year	Team (League)	Pos.	G	AB	R	H	2B	3B	HR	RBI	BB	SO	HBP	GDP	SB-CS	Avg.	OBP	SLG	OPS	E	Avg.
1989—	GC Red Sox (GCL)	2B-3B	5	19	3	6	1	0	0	3	3	0	0	1	0-0	.316	.409	.368	.778	2	.875
—	Winter Haven (FSL)	1B-2B-3B	64	210	27	65	13	2	2	19	23	25	3	7	1-1	.310	.384	.419	.803	12	.931
1990—	New Britain (East.)	3B	136	481	63	160	34	7	4	61	73	57	7	15	5-7	.333	.423	.457	.881	34	.914
1991—	Houston (N.L.)	1B	156	554	79	163	26	4	15	82	75	116	* 13	12	7-4	.294	.387	.437	.824	12	.991
1992—	Houston (N.L.)	1B	• 162	586	87	160	34	6	18	96	84	97	12	17	10-6	.273	.368	.444	.812	7	.995
1993—	Houston (N.L.)	1B	142	535	76	171	37	4	20	88	62	73	3	20	13-4	.320	.388	.516	.903	9	.993
1994—	Houston (N.L.)	1B-OF	110	400	* 104	147	32	2	39	* 116	65	65	4	12	15-4	.368	.451	* .750	1.201	† 9	.991
1995—	Houston (N.L.)	1B	114	448	88	130	29	0	21	87	79	102	6	9	12-5	.290	.399	.496	.894	5	.994
—	Jackson (Texas)	1B-DH	4	12	0	2	0	0	0	3	2	1	0	0	0-0	.167	.375	.167	.542	0	1.000
1996—	Houston (N.L.)	1B	* 162	568	111	179	* 48	2	31	120	135	114	10	15	21-7	.315	.451	.570	1.021	* 16	.989
1997—	Houston (N.L.)	1B-DH	* 162	566	109	162	40	2	43	135	127	122	16	10	31-10	.286	.425	.592	1.017	11	.993
1998—	Houston (N.L.)	1B	147	540	124	164	33	1	34	111	109	90	7	14	19-7	.304	.424	.557	.981	7	.995
1999—	Houston (N.L.)	1B-DH	* 162	562	* 143	171	35	0	42	126	* 149	127	11	18	30-11	.304	.454	.591	1.045	8	.994
2000—	Houston (N.L.)	1B-DH	159	590	* 152	183	37	1	47	132	107	116	15	19	9-6	.310	.424	.615	1.039	9	.994
2001—	Houston (N.L.)	1B	161	600	126	173	43	4	39	130	106	135	6	20	11-3	.288	.397	.568	.966	12	.992
2002—	Houston (N.L.)	1B-DH	158	571	94	166	33	2	31	98	101	130	10	16	7-3	.291	.401	.518	.919	7	.995
2003—	Houston (N.L.)	1B	160	605	109	168	28	2	39	100	88	119	6	25	11-4	.278	.373	.524	.897	9	.994
2004—	Houston (N.L.)	1B-DH	156	572	104	152	29	2	27	89	96	131	8	12	6-4	.266	.377	.465	.842	6	.995
2005—	Corpus Christi (Texas)	DH	3	9	1	2	0	0	0	1	3	3	0	1	0-0	.222	.417	.222	.639	0	...
—	Houston (N.L.)	1B	39	100	11	25	4	0	3	19	18	21	1	2	0-0	.250	.358	.380	.738	0	1.000
Major League totals (15 years)				2150	7797	1517	2314	488	32	449	1529	1401	1558	128	221	202-78	.297	.408	.540	.948	129	.993

DIVISION SERIES RECORD

Year	Team (League)	Pos.	G	AB	R	H	2B	3B	HR	RBI	BB	SO	HBP	GDP	SB-CS	Avg.	OBP	SLG	OPS	E	Avg.
1997—	Houston (N.L.)	1B	3	12	0	1	0	0	0	0	1	5	0	0	0-0	.083	.154	.083	.237	2	.920
1998—	Houston (N.L.)	1B	4	14	0	2	0	0	0	4	1	6	1	0	0-0	.143	.250	.143	.393	0	1.000
1999—	Houston (N.L.)	1B	4	13	3	2	0	0	0	0	5	4	1	0	0-0	.154	.421	.154	.575	0	1.000
2001—	Houston (N.L.)	1B	3	7	0	3	0	0	0	0	5	1	0	0	0-1	.429	.667	.429	1.095	0	1.000
2004—	Houston (N.L.)	1B	5	22	5	7	2	0	2	5	3	3	0	1	0-0	.318	.400	.682	1.082	1	.981
2005—	Houston (N.L.)	PH	2	2	1	1	0	0	0	1	0	0	0	0	0-0	.500	.500	.500	1.000	0	...
Division series totals (6 years)			21	70	9	16	2	0	2	10	15	19	2	1	0-1	.229	.379	.343	.722	3	.983

CHAMPIONSHIP SERIES RECORD

Year	Team (League)	Pos.	G	AB	R	H	2B	3B	HR	RBI	BB	SO	HBP	GDP	SB-CS	Avg.	OBP	SLG	OPS	E	Avg.
2004—	Houston (N.L.)	1B	7	27	1	7	2	0	0	3	4	5	0	1	1-1	.259	.355	.333	.688	0	1.000
2005—	Houston (N.L.)	PH	1	1	0	0	0	0	0	0	0	0	0	0	0-0	.000	.000	.000	.000	0	...
Champ. series totals (2 years)			8	28	1	7	2	0	0	3	4	5	0	1	1-1	.250	.344	.321	.665	0	1.000

WORLD SERIES RECORD

Year	Team (League)	Pos.	G	AB	R	H	2B	3B	HR	RBI	BB	SO	HBP	GDP	SB-CS	Avg.	OBP	SLG	OPS	E	Avg.
2005—	Houston (N.L.)	DH	4	8	1	1	0	0	0	0	0	1	0	0	0-0	.125	.300	.125	.425	0	...

ALL-STAR GAME RECORD

			G	AB	R	H	2B	3B	HR	RBI	BB	SO	HBP	GDP	SB-CS	Avg.	OBP	SLG	OPS	E	Avg.
All-Star Game totals (4 years)			4	12	1	3	0	0	0	0	0	4	0	0	0-0	.250	.250	.250	.500	0	1.000

BAJENARU, JEFF   P

PERSONAL: Born March 21, 1978, in Pomona, Calif. ... 6-1/190. ... Throws right, bats right. ... Full name: Jeffrey Michael Bajenaru. ... Name pronounced: Bah-juh-NAIR-oh. ... High school: Ayala (Chino Hills, Calif.). ... Junior college: Riverside (Calif.) Community College. ... College: Oklahoma.
TRANSACTIONS/CAREER NOTES: Selected by Oakland Athletics organization in 13th round of 1998 free-agent draft; did not sign. ... Selected by Chicago White Sox organization in 36th round of 1999 free-agent draft.
CAREER HITTING: 0-for-0 (.000), 0 R, 0 2B, 0 3B, 0 HR, 0 RBI.

LEFTY-RIGHTY SPLITS

vs.	Avg.	AB	H	2B	3B	HR	RBI	BB	SO	OBP	Slg.
L	.300	10	3	0	0	2	3	0	2	.300	.900
R	.125	8	1	0	0	0	0	0	1	.125	.125

Year	Team (League)	W	L	Pct.	ERA	WHIP	G	GS	CG	ShO	Hld.	Sv.-Opp.	IP	H	R	ER	HR	BB-IBB	SO	Avg.
2000—	Bristol (Appal.)	1	1	.500	3.77	1.05	12	0	0	0	...	5-...	14.1	10	6	6	2	5-0	31	.179
—	Win.-Salem (Car.)	2	0	1.000	4.38	0.97	10	0	0	0	...	2-...	12.1	7	6	6	1	5-0	15	.167
2001—	Birmingham (Sou.)	0	0	...	0.00	1.62	2	0	0	0	...	0-...	4.1	4	0	0	0	3-0	5	.222
—	Win.-Salem (Car.)	2	4	.333	3.35	1.31	35	0	0	0	...	10-...	40.1	32	16	15	3	21-2	51	.216
2002—				Did not play.																
2003—	Birmingham (Sou.)	4	2	.667	3.20	1.25	50	0	0	0	...	14-...	64.2	53	29	23	2	28-3	62	.225
2004—	Birmingham (Sou.)	2	0	1.000	1.34	0.89	32	0	0	0	...	12-...	33.2	19	9	5	3	11-0	51	.158
—	Charlotte (Int'l)	1	2	.333	1.80	0.75	16	0	0	0	...	10-...	20.0	12	6	4	2	3-0	16	.171

Year	Team (League)	W	L	Pct.	ERA	WHIP	G	GS	CG	ShO	Hld.	Sv.-Opp.	IP	H	R	ER	HR	BB-IBB	SO	Avg.
	—Chicago (A.L.)	0	1	.000	10.80	2.52	9	0	0	0	0	0-0	8.1	15	10	10	0	6-1	8	.405
2005	—Charlotte (Int'l)	4	6	.400	1.41	1.05	61	0	0	0	3	19-23	70.1	45	14	11	4	29-5	83	.185
	—Chicago (A.L.)	0	0	...	6.23	0.92	4	0	0	0	0	0-0	4.1	4	3	3	2	0-0	3	.222
Major League totals (2 years)		0	1	.000	9.24	1.97	13	0	0	0	0	0-0	12.2	19	13	13	2	6-1	11	.345

BAKER, JEFF 3B

PERSONAL: Born June 21, 1981, in Badkissagen, West Germany. ... 6-2/210. ... Bats right, throws right. ... Full name: Jeffrey Glen Baker. ... High school: Gar-Field (Va.). ... College: Clemson.
TRANSACTIONS/CAREER NOTES: Selected by Colorado Rockies organization in fourth round of 2002 free-agent draft.
2005 GAMES PLAYED BY POSITION (MLB): 3B—10.

LEFTY-RIGHTY SPLITS

vs.	Avg.	AB	H	2B	3B	HR	RBI	BB	SO	OBP	Slg.
L	.278	18	5	3	0	0	2	4	6	.409	.444
R	.150	20	3	1	0	1	2	1	6	.190	.350

			BATTING																	FIELDING	
Year	Team (League)	Pos.	G	AB	R	H	2B	3B	HR	RBI	BB	SO	HBP	GDP	SB-CS	Avg.	OBP	SLG	OPS	E	Avg.
2003	—Asheville (S. Atl.)	3B	70	263	44	76	17	0	11	44	30	79	9	2	4-2	.289	.377	.479	.856	16	.902
2004	—Visalia (Calif.)	3B	72	267	60	88	23	1	11	64	47	70	6	5	1-0	.330	.439	.547	.986	20	.900
	—Tulsa (Texas)	3B	24	91	10	27	5	1	4	20	7	22	0	3	1-0	.297	.343	.505	.848	5	.000
2005	—Colorado (N.L.)	3B	12	38	6	8	4	0	1	4	5	12	0	1	0-0	.211	.302	.395	.697	1	.958
Major League totals (1 year)			12	38	6	8	4	0	1	4	5	12	0	1	0-0	.211	.302	.395	.697	1	.958

BAKER, SCOTT P

PERSONAL: Born September 19, 1981, in Shreveport, La. ... 6-4/221. ... Throws right, bats right. ... Full name: Timothy Scott Baker. ... High school: Captain Shreve (La.). ... College: Oklahoma State.
TRANSACTIONS/CAREER NOTES: Selected by Minnesota Twins organization in second round of 2003 free-agent draft.
CAREER HITTING: 0-for-0 (.000), 0 R, 0 2B, 0 3B, 0 HR, 0 RBI.

SCOUTING REPORT ***Throws:*** His fastball tops out at 95 mph but he throws mostly in the low 90s. Has a slider, curve and changeup. ***Tendencies:*** Baker relies on his fastball and changeup and a strong sense of how to pitch. Doesn't overpower but has good command of all his pitches. Does a good job of keeping the ball low in the zone. Smooth delivery bodes well for the health of his arm. ***Outlook:*** Baker did enough during his first 10 starts in the majors to enter spring training with a chance of making the rotation, but likely will need more experience before he sticks. Should become a reliable innings-eater down the road. ***Grade 7.2***

SCOTT BAKER'S PITCHING ZONE

.200	.222	.105
.333	.091	.304
.250	.500	.364

LEFTY-RIGHTY SPLITS

vs.	Avg.	AB	H	2B	3B	HR	RBI	BB	SO	OBP	Slg.
L	.221	86	19	2	0	2	5	7	16	.274	.314
R	.257	113	29	7	0	3	13	7	16	.300	.398

Year	Team (League)	W	L	Pct.	ERA	WHIP	G	GS	CG	ShO	Hld.	Sv.-Opp.	IP	H	R	ER	HR	BB-IBB	SO	Avg.
2003	—Quad City (Midw.)	3	1	.750	2.49	1.05	11	11	0	0	...	0-...	50.2	45	16	14	4	8-0	47	.234
2004	—Fort Myers (FSL)	4	2	.667	2.40	1.02	7	7	0	0	...	0-...	45.0	40	13	12	1	6-0	37	.234
	—New Britain (East.)	5	3	.625	2.43	0.81	10	10	2	2	...	0-...	70.1	44	23	19	2	13-2	72	.174
	—Rochester (Int'l)	1	3	.250	4.97	1.47	9	9	0	0	...	0-...	54.1	65	31	30	3	15-1	36	.295
2005	—Rochester (Int'l)	5	8	.385	3.01	1.11	22	22	1	1	0	0-0	134.2	123	50	45	15	26-1	107	.242
	—Minnesota (A.L.)	3	3	.500	3.35	1.16	10	9	0	0	1	0-0	53.2	48	21	20	5	14-0	32	.241
Major League totals (1 year)		3	3	.500	3.35	1.16	10	9	0	0	1	0-0	53.2	48	21	20	5	14-0	32	.241

BAKO, PAUL C

PERSONAL: Born June 20, 1972, in Lafayette, La. ... 6-2/215. ... Bats left, throws right. ... Full name: Gabor Paul Bako II. ... Name pronounced: BAH-koh. ... High school: Lafayette (La.). ... College: Southwestern Louisiana.
TRANSACTIONS/CAREER NOTES: Selected by Cincinnati Reds organization in fifth round of 1993 free-agent draft. ... Traded by Reds with P Donne Wall to Detroit Tigers for OF Melvin Nieves (November 11, 1997). ... Traded by Tigers with Ps Dean Crow, Mark Persails and Brian Powell and 3B Carlos Villalobos to Houston Astros for C Brad Ausmus and P C.J. Nitkowski (January 14, 1999). ... Traded by Astros to Florida Marlins for cash (April 11, 2000). ... Claimed on waivers by Atlanta Braves (July 21, 2000). ... Traded by Braves with P Jose Cabrera to Milwaukee Brewers for C Henry Blanco (March 20, 2002). ... On disabled list (June 9-24, 2002). ... Traded by Brewers to Chicago Cubs for a player to be named (November 26, 2002); Brewers acquired IF Ryan Gripp to complete deal (December 16, 2002). ... Signed as a free agent by Los Angeles Dodgers (January 13, 2005). ... On disabled list (May 27, 2005-remainder of season).
2005 GAMES PLAYED BY POSITION (MLB): C—13.

SCOUTING REPORT Bako missed much of the season after undergoing knee surgery. Is respected for his strength calling a game. Has good footwork but relies on a quick release as his arm strength is just average. Is a solid defender with good hands. Offers a good target and frames pitches well. Blocks pitches in the dirt. Has a long stroke without a lot of bat speed. Can't get to high fastballs but is a decent low-ball hitter. Is a solid backup with excellent aptitude but his bat won't allow him to play enough to be overexposed. ***Grade 4.6***

LEFTY-RIGHTY SPLITS

vs.	Avg.	AB	H	2B	3B	HR	RBI	BB	SO	OBP	Slg.
L	.250	4	1	0	0	0	1	0	1	.250	.250
R	.250	36	9	2	0	0	3	7	11	.372	.306

			BATTING																	FIELDING	
Year	Team (League)	Pos.	G	AB	R	H	2B	3B	HR	RBI	BB	SO	HBP	GDP	SB-CS	Avg.	OBP	SLG	OPS	E	Avg.
1993	—Billings (Pion.)	1B-C	57	194	34	61	11	0	4	30	22	37	1	5	5-1	.314	.382	.433	.815	6	.984
1994	—Win.-Salem (Car.)	C	90	289	29	59	9	1	3	26	35	81	4	6	2-2	.204	.299	.273	.572	15	.977
1995	—Win.-Salem (Car.)	C	82	249	29	71	11	2	7	27	42	66	1	6	3-1	.285	.389	.430	.819	6	.989
1996	—Chattanooga (Sou.)	C	110	360	53	106	27	0	8	48	48	93	5	5	1-0	.294	.381	.436	.817	13	.984
1997	—Indianapolis (A.A.)	C	104	321	34	78	14	1	8	43	34	81	2	7	0-5	.243	.316	.368	.683	6	.991
1998	—Toledo (Int'l)	C	13	48	5	14	3	1	1	6	1	13	0	1	0-0	.292	.300	.458	.758	1	.988
	—Detroit (A.L.)	C	96	305	23	83	12	1	3	30	23	82	0	3	1-1	.272	.319	.348	.667	6	.989
1999	—New Orleans (PCL)	C	12	47	2	9	3	1	1	4	1	11	0	1	0-0	.191	.208	.362	.570	1	.984
	—Houston (N.L.)	C	73	215	16	55	14	1	2	17	26	57	0	4	1-1	.256	.332	.358	.690	6	.988
2000	—Houston (N.L.)	C	1	2	0	0	0	0	0	0	0	1	0	0	0-0	.000	.000	.000	.000	0	1.000

Year Team (League)	Pos.	G	AB	R	H	2B	3B	HR	RBI	BB	SO	HBP	GDP	SB-CS	Avg.	OBP	SLG	OPS	E	Avg.
—Florida (N.L.)	C	56	161	10	39	6	1	0	14	22	48	1	4	0-0	.242	.335	.292	.627	3	.991
—Atlanta (N.L.)	C-1B	24	58	8	11	4	0	2	6	5	15	0	2	0-0	.190	.254	.362	.616	1	.992
2001—Atlanta (N.L.)	C	61	137	19	29	10	1	2	15	20	34	0	3	1-0	.212	.312	.343	.655	3	.991
2002—Milwaukee (N.L.)	C	87	234	24	55	8	1	4	20	20	46	0	4	0-2	.235	.295	.329	.624	4	.991
2003—Chicago (N.L.)	C	70	188	19	43	13	3	0	17	22	47	1	2	0-1	.229	.311	.330	.641	6	.987
2004—Chicago (N.L.)	C	49	138	13	28	8	0	1	10	15	29	2	4	1-0	.203	.288	.283	.571	4	.989
2005—Los Angeles (N.L.)	C	13	40	1	10	2	0	0	4	7	12	0	0	0-0	.250	.362	.300	.662	1	.985
American League totals (1 year)		96	305	23	83	12	1	3	30	23	82	0	3	1-1	.272	.319	.348	.667	6	.989
National League totals (7 years)		434	1173	110	270	77	8	14	133	103	289	4	23	3-4	.230	.311	.326	.637	28	.990
Major League totals (8 years)		530	1478	133	353	77	8	14	133	160	371	4	26	4-5	.239	.313	.330	.643	34	.990

DIVISION SERIES RECORD

Year Team (League)	Pos.	G	AB	R	H	2B	3B	HR	RBI	BB	SO	HBP	GDP	SB-CS	Avg.	OBP	SLG	OPS	E	Avg.
2000—Atlanta (N.L.)	C	2	1	0	0	0	0	0	0	1	0	0	0	0-0	.000	.000	.000	.000	1	.800
2001—Atlanta (N.L.)	C	3	7	1	2	1	0	1	3	1	0	0	0	0-0	.286	.375	.857	1.232	0	1.000
2003—Chicago (N.L.)	C	3	4	0	0	0	0	0	1	2	2	0	0	0-0	.000	.333	.000	.333	0	1.000
Division series totals (3 years)		8	12	1	2	1	0	1	4	3	3	0	0	0-0	.167	.333	.500	.833	1	.976

CHAMPIONSHIP SERIES RECORD

Year Team (League)	Pos.	G	AB	R	H	2B	3B	HR	RBI	BB	SO	HBP	GDP	SB-CS	Avg.	OBP	SLG	OPS	E	Avg.
2001—Atlanta (N.L.)	C	3	3	0	0	0	0	0	0	0	0	0	0	0-0	.000	.000	.000	.000	0	1.000
2003—Chicago (N.L.)	C	6	16	4	4	1	0	0	1	1	7	0	0	0-0	.250	.294	.313	.607	0	1.000
Champ. series totals (2 years)		9	19	4	4	1	0	0	1	1	7	0	0	0-0	.211	.250	.263	.513	0	1.000

BALDWIN, JAMES   P

B

PERSONAL: Born July 15, 1971, in Southern Pines, N.C. ... 6-3/235. ... Throws right, bats right. ... Full name: James J. Baldwin Jr. ... High school: Pinecrest (Southern Pines, N.C.).

TRANSACTIONS/CAREER NOTES: Selected by Chicago White Sox organization in fourth round of 1990 free-agent draft. ... On disabled list (August 3-19, 1994). ... On disabled list (March 23-April 21, 2001); included rehabilitation assignment to Charlotte. ... Traded by White Sox to Los Angeles Dodgers for Ps Onan Masaoka and Gary Majewski and OF Jeff Barry (July 26, 2001). ... Signed as a free agent by Seattle Mariners (February 1, 2002). ... Signed as a free agent by Kansas City Royals organization (January 23, 2003). ... Signed as a free agent by Minnesota Twins organization (June 10, 2003). ... Signed as a free agent by New York Mets organization (February 9, 2004). ... Signed as a free agent by Detroit Tigers organization (June 6, 2004). ... Signed as a free agent by Baltimore Orioles (January 14, 2005). ... Claimed on waivers by Texas Rangers (July 21, 2005). ... Claimed on waivers by Baltimore Orioles (August 22, 2005).

HONORS: Named A.L. Rookie Pitcher of the Year by THE SPORTING NEWS (1996).

CAREER HITTING: 4-for-44 (.091), 1 R, 1 2B, 1 3B, 0 HR, 2 RBI.

JAMES BALDWIN'S PITCHING ZONE

.286	.273	.214
.343	.478	.097
.238	.100	.320

LEFTY-RIGHTY SPLITS

vs.	Avg.	AB	H	2B	3B	HR	RBI	BB	SO	OBP	Slg.
L	.209	110	23	8	1	2	14	13	17	.299	.355
R	.301	103	31	2	1	6	18	3	12	.318	.515

Year Team (League)	W	L	Pct.	ERA	WHIP	G	GS	CG	ShO	Hld.	Sv.-Opp.	IP	H	R	ER	HR	BB-IBB	SO	Avg.
1990—GC Whi. Sox (GCL)	1	6	.143	4.10	1.34	9	7	0	0	...	0-...	37.1	32	29	17	1	18-0	32	.225
1991—GC Whi. Sox (GCL)	3	1	.750	2.12	0.94	6	6	0	0	...	0-...	34.0	16	8	8	0	16-0	48	.140
—Utica (N.Y.-Penn)	1	4	.200	5.30	1.79	7	7	1	0	...	0-...	37.1	40	26	22	0	27-0	23	.267
1992—South Bend (Mid.)	9	5	.643	2.42	1.18	21	21	1	1	...	0-...	137.2	118	53	37	6	45-0	137	.228
—Sarasota (Fla. St.)	1	2	.333	2.87	1.01	6	6	1	0	...	0-...	37.2	31	13	12	2	7-0	39	.225
1993—Birmingham (Sou.)	8	5	.615	2.25	1.14	17	17	4	0	...	0-...	120.0	94	48	30	6	43-0	107	.219
—Nashville (A.A.)	5	4	.556	2.61	1.14	10	10	1	0	...	0-...	69.0	43	21	20	5	36-0	61	.180
1994—Nashville (A.A.)	12	6	.667	3.72	1.40	26	26	2	0	...	0-...	162.0	144	75	67	14	83-1	156	.237
1995—Chicago (A.L.)	0	1	.000	12.89	2.80	6	4	0	0	0	0-0	14.2	32	22	21	6	9-1	10	.444
—Nashville (A.A.)	5	9	.357	5.85	1.72	18	18	0	0	...	0-...	95.1	120	76	62	27	44-1	89	.302
1996—Nashville (A.A.)	1	1	.500	0.64	0.64	2	2	1	0	...	0-...	14.0	5	1	1	0	4-0	15	.116
—Chicago (A.L.)	11	6	.647	4.42	1.33	28	28	0	0	0	0-0	169.0	168	88	83	24	57-3	127	.257
1997—Chicago (A.L.)	12	•15	.444	5.27	1.44	32	32	1	0	0	0-0	200.0	205	128	117	19	83-3	140	.262
1998—Chicago (A.L.)	13	6	.684	5.32	1.48	37	24	0	0	0	0-1	159.0	176	103	94	18	60-2	108	.278
1999—Chicago (A.L.)	12	13	.480	5.10	1.51	35	33	1	0	0	0-0	199.1	219	119	113	34	81-1	123	.278
2000—Chicago (A.L.)	14	7	.667	4.65	1.37	29	28	2	1	0	0-0	178.0	185	96	92	34	59-3	116	.272
2001—Charlotte (Int'l)	1	0	1.000	5.25	1.17	2	2	0	0	...	0-...	12.0	12	7	7	2	2-0	11	.273
—Chicago (A.L.)	7	5	.583	4.61	1.54	17	16	2	1	0	0-0	95.2	109	56	49	15	38-0	42	.286
—Los Angeles (N.L.)	3	6	.333	4.20	1.35	12	12	0	0	0	0-0	79.1	82	39	37	10	25-1	53	.274
2002—Seattle (A.L.)	7	10	.412	5.28	1.52	30	23	0	0	0	0-0	150.0	179	95	88	26	49-2	88	.298
2003—Omaha (PCL)	3	2	.600	4.08	1.30	8	8	0	0	...	0-...	46.1	48	25	21	3	13-0	24	.265
—Rochester (Int'l)	0	2	.000	2.43	0.90	5	5	0	0	...	0-...	29.2	25	11	8	2	3-0	18	.225
—Minnesota (A.L.)	0	1	.000	5.40	1.67	10	0	0	0	6	1-2	15.0	21	10	9	6	4-1	7	.333
2004—Norfolk (Int'l)	3	2	.600	2.90	1.26	5	5	0	0	...	0-...	31.0	34	11	10	3	5-0	24	.281
—New York (N.L.)	0	2	.000	15.00	3.00	2	2	0	0	0	0-0	6.0	13	10	10	3	5-1	1	.448
—Toledo (Int'l)	5	7	.417	3.74	1.12	18	16	3	0	...	1-...	115.2	110	52	48	12	20-3	61	.255
2005—Ottawa (Int'l)	3	2	.600	4.60	1.19	8	8	0	0	...	0-...	47.0	52	25	24	6	4-0	25	.272
—Texas (A.L.)	0	2	.000	5.19	1.44	8	0	0	0	0	1-1	17.1	18	10	10	3	7-1	9	.273
—Baltimore (A.L.)	0	0	...	3.20	1.14	20	0	0	0	5	0-0	39.1	36	18	14	5	9-0	20	.245
American League totals (10 years)	76	66	.535	5.02	1.46	252	188	7	2	1	2-4	1237.1	1348	745	690	190	456-17	790	.277
National League totals (2 years)	3	8	.273	4.96	1.46	14	14	0	0	0	0-0	85.1	95	49	47	13	30-2	54	.290
Major League totals (11 years)	79	74	.516	5.01	1.46	266	202	7	2	1	2-4	1322.2	1443	794	737	203	486-19	844	.278

DIVISION SERIES RECORD

Year Team (League)	W	L	Pct.	ERA	WHIP	G	GS	CG	ShO	Hld.	Sv.-Opp.	IP	H	R	ER	HR	BB-IBB	SO	Avg.
2000—Chicago (A.L.)	0	0	...	1.50	1.00	1	1	0	0	0	0-0	6.0	3	1	1	0	3-0	2	.150

ALL-STAR GAME RECORD

Year Team (League)	W	L	Pct.	ERA	WHIP	G	GS	CG	ShO	Hld.	Sv.-Opp.	IP	H	R	ER	HR	BB-IBB	SO	Avg.
All-Star Game totals (1 year)	1	0	1.000	9.00	2.00	1	0	0	0	0	0-0	1.0	2	1	1	1	0-0	0	.400

BARAJAS, ROD   C

PERSONAL: Born September 5, 1975, in Ontario, Calif. ... 6-2/220. ... Bats right, throws right. ... Full name: Rodrigo Richard Barajas. ... Name pronounced: bar-AH-hoss. ... High school: Sante Fe Springs (Calif.). ... Junior college: Cerritos (Calif.). ... College: Cerritos (CA) JC.

TRANSACTIONS/CAREER NOTES: Signed as a non-drafted free agent by Arizona Diamondbacks organization (January 23, 1996). ... Loaned by Diamondbacks organization to Oakland Athletics organization (April 5-June 16, 1996). ... On disabled list (April 7-28 and July 5-23, 2003); included rehabilitation assignments to Tucson and Lancaster. ... Signed as a free agent by Texas Rangers organization (January 15, 2004).

2005 GAMES PLAYED BY POSITION (MLB): C—119, 1B—1.

SCOUTING REPORT *Offense:* Barajas has a long, but strong, stroke. Has problems with breaking stuff. Likes the ball out over the plate and has very good alley power. Is not a very selective hitter but has become a legitimate power threat. *Defense:* He is a durable receiver with a strong arm and good footwork. Is one of the more aggressive catchers in the league, blocking and shifting with balls in the dirt and is not afraid to block the plate. Demands a lot out of his pitching staff and fights to get calls. *Outlook:* Barajas is an underrated player who has improved in all aspects of the game. Club really likes his toughness. Should continue to improve at the plate. *Grade 7.7*

ROD BARAJAS'S HITTING ZONE

.074	.313	.185
.423	.231	.333
.160	.111	.533

LEFTY-RIGHTY SPLITS

vs.	Avg.	AB	H	2B	3B	HR	RBI	BB	SO	OBP	Slg.
L	.272	92	25	5	0	5	12	4	14	.309	.489
R	.248	318	79	19	0	16	48	22	56	.305	.459

Year Team (League)	Pos.	G	AB	R	H	2B	3B	HR	RBI	BB	SO	HBP	GDP	SB-CS	Avg.	OBP	SLG	OPS	E	Avg.
1996—Visalia (Calif.)	C	27	74	6	12	3	0	0	8	7	21	1	3	0-0	.162	.244	.203	.447	0	1.000
—Lethbridge (Pion.)	1B-C	51	175	47	59	9	3	10	50	12	24	2	6	2-1	.337	.378	.594	.973	5	.986
1997—High Desert (Calif.)	1B-C	57	199	24	53	11	0	7	30	8	41	1	7	0-2	.266	.297	.427	.724	3	.993
1998—High Desert (Calif.)	C	113	442	67	134	26	0	23	81	25	81	7	13	1-1	.303	.345	.518	.863	14	.983
1999—El Paso (Texas)	C-DH-1B	127	510	77	162	41	2	14	95	24	73	8	8	2-0	.318	.354	.488	.842	14	.985
—Arizona (N.L.)	C	5	16	3	4	1	0	1	3	1	1	0	0	0-0	.250	.294	.500	.794	0	1.000
2000—Tucson (PCL)	C-1B-3B	110	416	43	94	25	0	13	75	14	65	5	13	4-3	.226	.253	.380	.633	14	.980
—Arizona (N.L.)	C	5	13	1	3	0	0	1	3	0	4	0	0	0-0	.231	.231	.462	.692	0	1.000
2001—Arizona (N.L.)	C	51	106	9	17	3	0	3	9	4	26	0	0	0-0	.160	.191	.274	.464	1	.995
—Tucson (PCL)	1B-C-3B	45	162	23	52	13	0	9	32	9	23	3	2	3-1	.321	.366	.568	.934	3	.990
2002—Tucson (PCL)	C-1B	70	154	12	36	10	0	3	23	10	25	3	4	1-0	.234	.288	.357	.645	1	.997
—Tucson (PCL)	C-1B	5	16	2	7	1	0	1	1	1	2	0	0	0-0	.438	.471	.688	1.158	0	1.000
2003—Tucson (PCL)	C-DH	4	16	3	7	1	0	1	4	1	1	0	0	0-0	.438	.471	.688	1.158	0	1.000
—Lancaster (Calif.)	C-DH	3	12	2	5	0	0	0	3	1	2	0	0	0-0	.417	.462	.417	.878	0	1.000
—Arizona (N.L.)	C	80	220	19	48	15	0	3	28	14	43	1	6	0-0	.218	.265	.327	.592	0	1.000
2004—Texas (A.L.)	C-1B	108	358	50	89	26	1	16	58	13	63	3	3	0-1	.249	.276	.453	.728	7	.990
2005—Texas (A.L.)	C-1B	120	410	53	104	24	0	21	60	26	70	6	6	0-0	.254	.306	.466	.771	9	.988
American League totals (2 years)		228	768	103	193	50	1	36	118	39	133	9	9	0-1	.251	.292	.460	.751	16	.989
National League totals (5 years)		211	509	44	108	29	0	11	66	29	99	4	10	1-0	.212	.257	.334	.591	2	.998
Major League totals (7 years)		439	1277	147	301	79	1	47	184	68	232	13	19	1-1	.236	.278	.410	.688	18	.993

DIVISION SERIES RECORD

Year Team (League)	Pos.	G	AB	R	H	2B	3B	HR	RBI	BB	SO	HBP	GDP	SB-CS	Avg.	OBP	SLG	OPS	E	Avg.
2001—Arizona (N.L.)	C	1	0	0	0	0	0	0	0	0	0	0	0	0-0	...	...	...	...	0	...
2002—Arizona (N.L.)	C	2	4	1	1	0	0	1	1	0	1	0	0	0-0	.250	.250	1.000	1.250	0	1.000
Division series totals (2 years)		3	4	1	1	0	0	1	1	0	1	0	0	0-0	.250	.250	1.000	1.250	0	1.000

CHAMPIONSHIP SERIES RECORD

Year Team (League)	Pos.	G	AB	R	H	2B	3B	HR	RBI	BB	SO	HBP	GDP	SB-CS	Avg.	OBP	SLG	OPS	E	Avg.
2001—Arizona (N.L.)	C	Did not play.																		

WORLD SERIES RECORD

Year Team (League)	Pos.	G	AB	R	H	2B	3B	HR	RBI	BB	SO	HBP	GDP	SB-CS	Avg.	OBP	SLG	OPS	E	Avg.
2001—Arizona (N.L.)	C	2	5	1	2	0	0	1	1	0	0	0	0	0-0	.400	.400	1.000	1.400	0	1.000

BARD, JOSH   C

PERSONAL: Born March 30, 1978, in Ithaca, N.Y. ... 6-3/215. ... Bats both, throws right. ... Full name: Joshua David Bard. ... High school: Cherry Creek (Englewood, Colo.). ... College: Texas Tech.

TRANSACTIONS/CAREER NOTES: Selected by Minnesota Twins organization in 35th round of 1996 free-agent draft; did not sign. ... Selected by Colorado Rockies organization in third round of 1999 free-agent draft. ... Traded by Rockies with OF Jody Gerut to Cleveland Indians for OF Jacob Cruz (June 2, 2001). ... On disabled list (March 28-July 5, 2004); included rehabilitation assignments to Akron and Buffalo.

2005 GAMES PLAYED BY POSITION (MLB): C—31.

SCOUTING REPORT With the emergence of Victor Martinez as the everyday catcher, Bard doesn't see a lot of playing time. Relies on a short, quick release to compensate for a short arm that can be erratic, especially when he rushes. Is agile defensively but drops too many pitches. Has a long stroke from both sides of the plate, with slightly more power from the left. Must commit early when hitting and has problems adjusting to and picking up the spin on breaking balls. *Grade 4.5*

JOSH BARD'S HITTING ZONE

.333	.000	.500
.100	.000	.250
.125	.167	.200

LEFTY-RIGHTY SPLITS

vs.	Avg.	AB	H	2B	3B	HR	RBI	BB	SO	OBP	Slg.
L	.148	27	4	1	0	1	2	3	4	.233	.296
R	.214	56	12	3	0	0	7	6	7	.281	.268

Year	Team (League)	Pos.	G	AB	R	H	2B	3B	HR	RBI	BB	SO	HBP	GDP	SB-CS	Avg.	OBP	SLG	OPS	E	Avg.
1999—			Did not play.																		
2000—Salem (Carol.)		C	93	309	40	88	17	0	2	25	32	33	1	6	3-1	.285	.352	.359	.711	10	.987
—Colo. Springs (PCL)		C	4	17	0	4	0	0	0	1	0	2	0	0	0-0	.235	.235	.235	.471	1	.923
2001—Carolina (Southern)		C	35	124	14	32	13	0	1	24	19	23	1	1	0-1	.258	.359	.387	.746	2	.993
—Akron (East.)		C	51	194	26	54	11	0	4	25	16	27	2	4	0-0	.278	.338	.397	.735	4	.986
—Mahoning Valley (N.Y.-Penn.)		C	13	44	7	12	4	0	2	8	6	2	1	1	0-1	.273	.373	.500	.873	3	.769
—Buffalo (Int'l)		DH	1	4	0	0	0	0	0	0	0	1	0	0	0-0	.000	.000	.000	.000	...	...
2002—Buffalo (Int'l)		C	94	344	36	102	26	2	6	53	20	45	0	13	0-0	.297	.332	.436	.768	11	.984
—Cleveland (A.L.)		C	24	90	9	20	5	0	3	12	4	13	0	6	0-0	.222	.255	.378	.633	2	.988
2003—Buffalo (Int'l)		C-DH	35	115	14	38	7	0	5	21	14	17	1	5	1-2	.330	.408	.522	.929	1	.995
—Cleveland (A.L.)		C-DH	91	303	25	74	13	1	8	36	22	53	0	9	0-2	.244	.293	.373	.666	5	.991
2004—Akron (East.)		DH-C	10	30	5	5	1	0	0	5	7	5	0	2	0-0	.167	.324	.200	.524	0	1.000
—Buffalo (Int'l)		C-DH	40	156	25	41	10	0	4	18	11	23	0	7	0-0	.263	.310	.404	.713	3	.988
—Cleveland (A.L.)		C	7	19	5	8	2	0	1	4	3	0	0	0	0-0	.421	.478	.684	1.162	0	1.000
2005—Cleveland (A.L.)		C	34	83	6	16	4	0	1	9	9	11	0	2	0-0	.193	.266	.277	.543	3	.983
Major League totals (4 years)			156	495	45	118	24	1	13	61	38	77	0	17	0-2	.238	.289	.370	.659	10	.989

BARMES, CLINT — SS

PERSONAL: Born March 6, 1979, in Vincennes, Ind. ... 6-0/175. ... Bats right, throws right. ... Full name: Clint Harold Barmes. ... Name pronounced: BAR-muss. ... High school: Lincoln (Vincennes, Ind.). ... College: Indiana State.
TRANSACTIONS/CAREER NOTES: Selected by Colorado Rockies organization in 10th round of 2000 free-agent draft. ... On disabled list (June 6-September 2, 2005); included rehabilitation assignment to Tulsa.
2005 GAMES PLAYED BY POSITION (MLB): SS—80.

SCOUTING REPORT **Offense:** Prior to suffering a broken collarbone last season, Barmes had good bat speed and could hit the ball to all fields. Struggled to regain his stroke and bat speed after returning from the D.L. Will develop enough power to hit 20 homers a year while playing in Coors Field. Is a good situational hitter. Is an average runner. **Defense:** Barmes has a rangy build, though he still needs to improve his agility in the field. Has soft hands and moves better to his left than to his right. **Outlook:** The Rockies are considering him as their leadoff hitter for 2006 because of his patience at the plate. Should regain his bat speed, barring complications from the injury, and hit between .280 and .290. **Grade 6.4**

CLINT BARMES' HITTING ZONE

.200	.300	.478
.327	.306	.341
.359	.125	.357

LEFTY-RIGHTY SPLITS

vs.	Avg.	AB	H	2B	3B	HR	RBI	BB	SO	OBP	Slg.
L	.289	90	26	3	0	4	10	2	10	.312	.456
R	.288	260	75	16	1	6	36	14	26	.336	.427

Year	Team (League)	Pos.	G	AB	R	H	2B	3B	HR	RBI	BB	SO	HBP	GDP	SB-CS	Avg.	OBP	SLG	OPS	E	Avg.
2000— Portland (N'west)		SS-OF	45	181	37	51	6	4	2	16	18	28	5	1	12-9	.282	.361	.392	.753	12	.934
—Asheville (S. Atl.)		2B-SS-3B																			
		OF	19	81	11	14	4	0	0	4	10	13	1	3	4-1	.173	.269	.222	.491	2	.977
2001—Asheville (S. Atl.)		SS	74	285	40	74	14	1	5	24	17	37	7	6	21-7	.260	.314	.368	.683	22	.943
—Salem (Carol.)		SS	38	121	17	30	3	3	0	9	15	20	4	5	4-1	.248	.350	.322	.672	13	.934
2002—Carolina (Southern)		SS	103	438	62	119	23	2	15	60	31	72	9	3	15-11	.272	.329	.436	.765	33	.940
2003—Colo. Springs (PCL)		SS-2B	136	493	63	136	35	1	7	54	22	63	9	9	12-7	.276	.316	.394	.709	29	.951
—Colorado (N.L.)		SS	12	25	2	8	2	0	0	2	0	10	2	0	0-0	.320	.357	.400	.757	2	.958
2004—Colo. Springs (PCL) SS-2B-DH			125	533	104	175	42	2	16	51	28	61	15	5	20-8	.328	.376	.505	.881	20	.964
—Colorado (N.L.)		2B-SS	20	71	14	20	3	1	2	10	3	10	1	2	0-1	.282	.320	.437	.757	2	.980
2005—Tulsa (Texas)		SS-DH	8	34	6	11	1	0	0	0	1	3	0	2	1-0	.324	.343	.353	.696	1	.957
—Colorado (N.L.)		SS	81	350	55	101	19	1	10	46	16	36	6	4	6-4	.289	.330	.434	.764	17	.958
Major League totals (3 years)			113	446	71	129	24	2	12	58	19	56	9	6	6-5	.289	.330	.433	.763	21	.962

BARRETT, MICHAEL — C

PERSONAL: Born October 22, 1976, in Atlanta. ... 6-3/210. ... Bats right, throws right. ... Full name: Michael Patrick Barrett. ... High school: Pace Academy (Atlanta).
TRANSACTIONS/CAREER NOTES: Selected by Montreal Expos organization in first round (28th pick overall) of 1995 free-agent draft. ... On disabled list (June 24-July 11, 1999); included rehabilitation assignment to Ottawa. ... On disabled list (July 27-September 10, 2003); included rehabilitation assignment to Edmonton. ... Traded by Expos to Oakland Athletics for P Brett Price (December 15, 2003). ... Traded by Athletics to Chicago Cubs for C Damian Miller (December 16, 2003).
2005 GAMES PLAYED BY POSITION (MLB): C—122, DH—1.

SCOUTING REPORT **Offense:** Barrett, slowed by an injury last season, has a slightly long swing but his bat speed has improved. Likes the ball up out over the plate. Has improved at picking up breaking pitches and using the whole field. Is a better hitter against lefthanders. Doesn't run well. **Defense:** He is tall for a catcher and doesn't have much natural quickness. Has arm strength but his release is inconsistent; throws that are rushed tend to tail. Still drops too many pitches while reaching for balls in the dirt. Intelligent and works well with his pitching staff. **Outlook:** Barrett, who will handle one of the top pitching staffs in the game, should continue to increase his offensive production, but he is only average behind the plate. **Grade 7.2**

MICHAEL BARRETT'S HITTING ZONE

.414	.235	.350
.222	.442	.294
.294	.304	.136

LEFTY-RIGHTY SPLITS

vs.	Avg.	AB	H	2B	3B	HR	RBI	BB	SO	OBP	Slg.
L	.320	125	40	13	2	7	24	20	12	.415	.624
R	.258	299	77	19	1	9	37	20	49	.314	.418

Year	Team (League)	Pos.	G	AB	R	H	2B	3B	HR	RBI	BB	SO	HBP	GDP	SB-CS	Avg.	OBP	SLG	OPS	E	Avg.
1995—GC Expos (GCL)		3B-SS	50	183	22	57	13	4	0	19	15	19	0	1	7-6	.311	.362	.426	.788	25	.893
—Vermont (NYP)		SS	3	10	0	1	0	0	0	1	1	1	0	0	0-0	.100	.167	.100	.267	0	1.000

Year	Team (League)	Pos.	G	AB	R	H	2B	3B	HR	RBI	BB	SO	HBP	GDP	SB-CS	Avg.	OBP	SLG	OPS	E	Avg.
																BATTING				FIELDING	
1996— Delmarva (S. Atl.)		C-DH-3B	129	474	57	113	29	4	4	62	18	42	9	9	5-11	.238	.277	.342	.618	15	.978
1997— W.P. Beach (FSL)		C-DH	119	423	52	120	30	0	8	61	36	49	5	11	7-4	.284	.340	.411	.751	13	.982
1998— Harrisburg (East.)		C-3B-DH	120	453	78	145	32	2	19	87	27	43	2	16	7-6	.320	.358	.525	.883	12	.981
— Montreal (N.L.)		3B-C	8	23	3	7	2	0	1	2	3	6	1	0	0-0	.304	.407	.522	.929	3	.912
1999— Harrisburg (East.)		3B-C-SS	126	433	53	127	32	3	8	52	32	39	3	18	0-2	.293	.345	.436	.782	14	.973
— Ottawa (Int'l)		3B	2	7	1	3	0	0	0	2	1	0	0	0	0-1	.429	.500	.429	.929	1	.800
2000— Ottawa (Int'l)		3B-C	31	120	21	43	7	0	2	19	13	10	2	5	1-0	.358	.430	.467	.896	5	.945
— Montreal (N.L.)		3B-C	89	271	28	58	15	1	1	22	23	35	1	7	0-1	.214	.277	.288	.565	15	.949
2001— Montreal (N.L.)		C	132	472	42	118	33	2	6	38	25	54	2	14	2-1	.250	.289	.367	.655	7	.993
2002— Montreal (N.L.)		C-1B	117	376	41	99	20	1	12	49	40	65	1	14	6-3	.263	.332	.418	.749	6	.989
2003— Edmonton (PCL)		C	2	6	2	2	1	0	0	0	0	2	0	0	1-0	.333	.333	.500	.833	0	1.000
— Montreal (N.L.)		C	70	226	33	47	9	2	10	30	21	37	2	6	0-0	.208	.280	.398	.678	1	.998
2004— Chicago (N.L.)		C	134	455	51	131	32	6	16	65	33	64	5	13	1-4	.287	.337	.489	.826	6	.994
2005— Chicago (N.L.)		C-DH	133	424	48	117	32	3	16	61	40	61	7	7	0-3	.276	.345	.479	.824	6	.994
Major League totals (8 years)			809	2681	303	704	175	18	70	319	217	361	22	79	9-14	.263	.320	.420	.740	61	.988

BARTLETT, JASON — SS

PERSONAL: Born October 30, 1979, in Mountain View, Calif. ... 6-0/180. ... Bats right, throws right. ... Full name: Jason Alan Bartlett. ... High school: St. Mary's (Lodi, Calif.). ... College: Oklahoma.

TRANSACTIONS/CAREER NOTES: Selected by San Diego Padres organization in 13th round of 2001 free-agent draft. ... Traded by Padres to Minnesota Twins for OF Brian Buchanan (July 12, 2002).

2005 GAMES PLAYED BY POSITION (MLB): SS—68, DH—5.

SCOUTING REPORT Bartlett compounded his problems at the plate lat season by chasing a lot of bad pitches. Has good bat speed and a line-drive stroke but not a lot of power. Is a good runner. Infield actions are fluid. Became erratic when he appeared to lose confidence early in the season. Settled down after a minor league stint and showed above-average and a qukck first step to his left. Job will be his to lose in the spring. *Grade 5.5*

JASON BARTLETT'S HITTING ZONE

.214	.300	.316
.265	.286	.129
.250	.200	.200

LEFTY-RIGHTY SPLITS

vs.	Avg.	AB	H	2B	3B	HR	RBI	BB	SO	OBP	Slg.
L	.277	65	18	3	0	3	8	3	9	.304	.462
R	.226	159	36	7	1	0	8	18	28	.320	.283

Year	Team (League)	Pos.	G	AB	R	H	2B	3B	HR	RBI	BB	SO	HBP	GDP	SB-CS	Avg.	OBP	SLG	OPS	E	Avg.
																BATTING				FIELDING	
2001— Eugene (Northwest)		SS	68	267	49	80	12	4	3	37	28	47	4	6	12-4	.300	.371	.408	.779	17	.946
2002— Lake Elsinore (Calif.)		SS	75	308	57	77	14	4	1	33	32	53	5	7	24-5	.250	.329	.331	.660	22	.929
— Fort Myers (FSL)		SS-3B-2B	39	145	24	38	7	0	2	9	17	24	2	1	11-2	.262	.341	.352	.693	7	.949
2003— New Britain (East.)		SS	139	548	96	162	31	8	8	48	58	67	20	7	41-24	.296	.380	.425	.805	20	.969
2004— GC Twins (GCL)		SS	5	14	1	5	1	0	0	1	0	3	1	0	0-0	.357	.400	.429	.829	2	.846
— Rochester (Int'l)		SS-2B-DH	67	269	54	89	15	7	3	29	33	37	7	1	7-3	.331	.415	.472	.873	19	.946
— Minnesota (A.L.)		SS-2B-DH	8	12	2	1	0	0	0	1	1	1	0	0	2-0	.083	.154	.083	.237	2	.895
2005— Rochester (Int'l)		SS-DH	61	229	41	76	10	2	5	33	29	34	4	3	7-3	.332	.405	.459	.864	12	.956
— Minnesota (A.L.)		SS-DH	74	224	33	54	10	1	3	16	21	37	4	6	4-0	.241	.316	.335	.651	7	.979
Major League totals (2 years)			82	236	35	55	10	1	3	17	22	38	4	6	6-0	.233	.308	.322	.630	9	.974

BARTOSH, CLIFF — P

PERSONAL: Born September 5, 1979, in West, Texas. ... 6-2/180. ... Throws left, bats left. ... Full name: Clifford Paul Bartosh. ... High school: Duncanville (Texas).

TRANSACTIONS/CAREER NOTES: Selected by San Diego Padres organization in 29th round of 1998 free-agent draft. ... Claimed on waivers by Detroit Tigers (October 31, 2003). ... Claimed on waivers by Cleveland Indians (December 8, 2003). ... Traded by Indians to Chicago Cubs for P Ronald Bay (March 29, 2005).

CAREER HITTING: 1-for-1 (1.000), 0 R, 0 2B, 0 3B, 0 HR, 0 RBI.

CLIFF BARTOSH'S PITCHING ZONE

.250	.500	.500
.273	.556	.273
.143	.571	.083

LEFTY-RIGHTY SPLITS

vs.	Avg.	AB	H	2B	3B	HR	RBI	BB	SO	OBP	Slg.
L	.269	26	7	0	0	1	4	7	3	.412	.385
R	.327	49	16	5	0	6	9	4	12	.400	.796

Year	Team (League)	W	L	Pct.	ERA	WHIP	G	GS	CG	ShO	Hld.	Sv.-Opp.	IP	H	R	ER	HR	BB-IBB	SO	Avg.
1998— Ariz. Padres (Ariz.)		3	2	.600	3.48	1.34	13	5	0	0	...	0-...	44.0	43	23	17	2	16-0	43	.257
1999— Fort Wayne (Midw.)		5	12	.294	4.44	1.43	35	20	1	1	...	0-...	129.2	136	76	64	14	49-0	100	.270
2000— Fort Wayne (Midw.)		8	4	.667	3.04	1.22	50	4	0	0	...	1-...	77.0	50	40	26	6	44-3	94	.178
2001— Lake Elsinore (Calif.)		6	2	.750	1.58	1.18	38	0	0	0	...	10-...	45.2	42	17	8	2	12-5	66	.237
— Mobile (Sou.)		1	2	.333	3.97	1.46	20	0	0	0	...	2-...	22.2	20	12	10	5	13-1	20	.233
2002— Mobile (Sou.)		2	4	.333	3.18	1.22	62	0	0	0	...	25-...	70.2	54	28	25	4	32-5	70	.211
2003— Portland (PCL)		2	5	.286	4.29	1.25	64	0	0	0	...	10-...	71.1	67	36	34	4	22-1	51	.249
2004— Buffalo (Int'l)		0	3	.000	2.80	0.96	28	0	0	0	...	3-...	35.1	26	11	11	3	8-2	46	.202
— Cleveland (A.L.)		1	0	1.000	4.66	1.71	34	0	0	0	3	0-2	19.1	22	10	10	4	11-0	25	.275
2005— Chicago (N.L.)		0	2	.000	5.49	1.73	19	0	0	0	4	0-0	19.2	23	13	12	7	11-0	15	.307
— Iowa (PCL)		1	2	.333	5.08	1.98	22	0	0	0	4	1-2	28.1	40	18	16	3	16-2	26	.341
American League totals (1 year)		1	0	1.000	4.66	1.71	34	0	0	0	3	0-2	19.1	22	10	10	4	11-0	25	.275
National League totals (1 year)		0	2	.000	5.49	1.73	19	0	0	0	4	0-0	19.2	23	13	12	7	11-0	15	.307
Major League totals (2 years)		1	2	.333	5.08	1.72	53	0	0	0	4	0-2	39.0	45	23	22	11	22-0	40	.290

BATISTA, MIGUEL   P

PERSONAL: Born February 19, 1971, in Santo Domingo, Dominican Republic. ... 6-1/197. ... Throws right, bats right. ... Full name: Miguel Jerez Batista. ... Name pronounced: bah-TEESE-tah. ... High school: Nuevo Horizondes (San Pedro de Macoris, D.R.) .

TRANSACTIONS/CAREER NOTES: Signed as a non-drafted free agent by Montreal Expos organization (February 29, 1988). ... Selected by Pittsburgh Pirates from Expos organization in Rule 5 major league draft (December 9, 1991). ... Returned to Expos organization (April 23, 1992). ... Released by Expos (November 18, 1994). ... Signed by Florida Marlins organization (December 9, 1994). ... Claimed on waivers by Chicago Cubs (December 17, 1996). ... Traded by Cubs to Expos for OF Henry Rodriguez (December 12, 1997). ... On disabled list (July 16-August 10, 1999); included rehabilitation assignment to Ottawa. ... Traded by Expos to Kansas City Royals for P Brad Rigby (April 25, 2000). ... Signed as a free agent by Arizona Diamondbacks organization (November 3, 2000). ... On suspended list (May 23-June 2, 2003). ... Signed as a free agent by Toronto Blue Jays (December 18, 2003).

CAREER HITTING: 21-for-224 (.094), 16 R, 4 2B, 0 3B, 2 HR, 5 RBI.

SCOUTING REPORT **Throws:** Batista has refined his approach since becoming a closer; he throws only his mid- to upper-90s fastball and a split-finger fastball. **Tendencies:** Batista has an overpowering riding fastball that is sneaky because of the deceptiveness of his delivery. Is not afraid to knock a hitter off the plate with his fastball. Splitter is extremely quick and late-biting. Has good command of both pitches and forces hitters to change their focus up and down in the zone. Is throwing harder in relief because he doesn't have to pace himself. Is an extremely intelligent player. **Outlook:** He will remain the Blue Jays' closer after registering 31 saves in 2005, and he will build on that success. **Grade 7.8**

MIGUEL BATISTA'S PITCHING ZONE

.286	.214	.000
.315	.353	.255
.481	.333	.259

LEFTY-RIGHTY SPLITS

vs.	Avg.	AB	H	2B	3B	HR	RBI	BB	SO	OBP	Slg.
L	.256	156	40	6	0	3	19	15	29	.326	.353
R	.282	142	40	6	0	6	29	12	25	.338	.451

Year	Team (League)	W	L	Pct.	ERA	WHIP	G	GS	CG	ShO	Hld.	Sv.-Opp.	IP	H	R	ER	HR	BB-IBB	SO	Avg.
1989—	Dom. Expos (DSL)	1	7	.125	4.24	1.56	13	11	0	0		0-...	68.0	56	46	32	...	50-...	60	...
1990—	GC Expos (GCL)	4	3	.571	2.06	1.27	9	6	0	0		0-...	39.1	33	16	9	0	17-0	21	.226
—	Rockford (Midwest)	0	1	.000	8.76	1.70	3	2	0	0		0-...	12.1	16	13	12	2	5-0	7	.302
1991—	Rockford (Midwest)	11	5	.688	4.04	1.37	23	23	2	1		0-...	133.2	126	74	60	1	57-0	90	.245
1992—	Pittsburgh (N.L.)	0	0	...	9.00	3.50	1	0	0	0	0	0-0	2.0	4	2	2	1	3-0	1	.400
—	W.P. Beach (FSL)	7	7	.500	3.79	1.36	24	24	1	0		0-...	135.1	130	69	57	3	54-1	92	.251
1993—	Harrisburg (East.)	13	5	.722	4.34	1.60	26	26	0	0		0-...	141.0	139	79	68	11	86-0	91	.263
1994—	Harrisburg (East.)	0	1	.000	2.38	1.50	3	3	0	0		0-...	11.1	8	3	3	0	9-0	5	.200
1995—	Charlotte (Int'l)	6	12	.333	4.80	1.53	34	18	0	0		0-...	116.1	118	79	62	11	60-2	58	.260
1996—	Charlotte (Int'l)	4	3	.571	5.38	1.71	47	2	0	0		4-...	77.0	93	57	46	4	39-0	56	.303
—	Florida (N.L.)	0	0	...	5.56	1.41	9	0	0	0	0	0-0	11.1	9	8	7	0	7-2	6	.231
1997—	Iowa (Am. Assoc.)	9	4	.692	4.20	1.27	31	14	2	2		0-...	122.0	117	60	57	19	38-1	95	.252
—	Chicago (N.L.)	0	5	.000	5.70	1.65	11	6	0	0	0	0-0	36.1	36	24	23	4	24-2	27	.267
1998—	Montreal (N.L.)	3	5	.375	3.80	1.53	56	13	0	0	3	0-...	135.0	141	66	57	12	65-7	92	.274
1999—	Montreal (N.L.)	8	7	.533	4.88	1.51	39	17	2	1	0	1-1	134.2	146	88	73	10	58-2	95	.280
—	Ottawa (Int'l)	0	1	.000	2.25	0.88	3	3	0	0		0-...	8.0	3	2	2	1	4-0	7	.115
2000—	Montreal (N.L.)	0	1	.000	14.04	2.64	4	0	0	0	0	0-2	8.1	19	14	13	2	3-0	7	.452
—	Kansas City (A.L.)	2	6	.250	7.74	1.75	14	9	0	0	0	0-0	57.0	66	54	49	17	34-2	30	.292
—	Omaha (PCL)	2	2	.500	6.04	1.48	18	1	0	0		3-...	28.1	35	20	19	6	7-0	27	.302
2001—	Arizona (N.L.)	11	8	.579	3.36	1.24	48	18	0	0	0	0-0	139.1	113	57	52	13	60-2	90	.226
2002—	Arizona (N.L.)	8	9	.471	4.29	1.31	36	29	1	0	2	0-0	184.2	172	99	88	12	70-3	112	.245
2003—	Arizona (N.L.)	10	9	.526	3.54	1.33	36	29	2	1	0	0-0	193.1	197	85	76	13	60-3	142	.267
2004—	Toronto (A.L.)	10	13	.435	4.80	1.52	38	31	2	1	0	5-5	198.2	206	115	106	22	• 96-1	104	.273
2005—	Toronto (A.L.)	5	8	.385	4.10	1.43	71	0	0	0	0	31-39	74.2	80	39	34	9	27-5	54	.268
	American League totals (3 years)	17	27	.386	5.15	1.54	123	40	2	1	0	36-44	330.1	352	208	189	48	157-8	188	.275
	National League totals (9 years)	40	44	.476	4.16	1.40	240	112	5	2	9	1-3	845.0	837	443	391	67	350-21	572	.262
	Major League totals (11 years)	57	71	.445	4.44	1.44	363	152	7	3	9	37-47	1175.1	1189	651	580	115	507-29	760	.265

DIVISION SERIES RECORD

Year	Team (League)	W	L	Pct.	ERA	WHIP	G	GS	CG	ShO	Hld.	Sv.-Opp.	IP	H	R	ER	HR	BB-IBB	SO	Avg.
2001—	Arizona (N.L.)	1	0	1.000	2.70	0.60	2	1	0	0	0	0-0	6.2	3	2	2	1	1-0	4	.136
2002—	Arizona (N.L.)	0	1	.000	9.82	2.18	1	1	0	0	0	0-0	3.2	5	4	4	0	3-0	1	.357
	Division series totals (2 years)	1	1	.500	5.23	1.16	3	2	0	0	0	0-0	10.1	8	6	6	1	4-0	5	.222

CHAMPIONSHIP SERIES RECORD

Year	Team (League)	W	L	Pct.	ERA	WHIP	G	GS	CG	ShO	Hld.	Sv.-Opp.	IP	H	R	ER	HR	BB-IBB	SO	Avg.
2001—	Arizona (N.L.)	0	1	.000	5.14	1.00	2	1	0	0	0	0-0	7.0	5	4	4	2	2-0	3	.185

WORLD SERIES RECORD

Year	Team (League)	W	L	Pct.	ERA	WHIP	G	GS	CG	ShO	Hld.	Sv.-Opp.	IP	H	R	ER	HR	BB-IBB	SO	Avg.
2001—	Arizona (N.L.)	0	0	...	0.00	1.25	2	1	0	0	0	0-0	8.0	5	0	0	0	5-0	6	.192

BAUER, RICK   P

PERSONAL: Born January 10, 1977, in Garden Grove, Calif. ... 6-6/223. ... Throws right, bats right. ... Full name: Richard Edward Bauer. ... Name pronounced: BOW-er. ... High school: Centennial (Meridian, Idaho). ... Junior college: Treasure Valley (Ore.) Community College.

TRANSACTIONS/CAREER NOTES: Selected by Baltimore Orioles organization in fifth round of 1997 free-agent draft. ... On disabled list (June 15-July 3, 2004); included rehabilitation assignments to Bowie and Ottawa. ... Signed as a free agent by Texas Rangers organization (November 9, 2005).

CAREER HITTING: 0-for-0 (.000), 0 R, 0 2B, 0 3B, 0 HR, 0 RBI.

LEFTY-RIGHTY SPLITS

vs.	Avg.	AB	H	2B	3B	HR	RBI	BB	SO	OBP	Slg.
L	.412	17	7	3	0	2	4	2	1	.474	.941
R	.316	19	6	1	0	0	7	2	4	.381	.368

Year	Team (League)	W	L	Pct.	ERA	WHIP	G	GS	CG	ShO	Hld.	Sv.-Opp.	IP	H	R	ER	HR	BB-IBB	SO	Avg.
1997—	Bluefield (Appal.)	8	3	.727	2.86	1.08	13	13	0	0	...	0-...	72.1	58	31	23	1	20-0	67	.218
—	Delmarva (S. Atl.)	0	0	...	0.00	0.50	1	0	0	0	...	1-...	2.0	0	0	0	0	1-0	2	.000
1998—	Delmarva (S. Atl.)	5	8	.385	4.73	1.45	22	22	1	1	...	0-...	118.0	127	69	62	11	44-0	81	.285
1999—	Frederick (Carolina)	10	9	.526	4.56	1.40	26	26	4	0	...	0-...	152.0	159	85	77	17	54-2	123	.273
2000—	Bowie (East.)	6	8	.429	5.30	1.50	26	23	1	0	...	1-...	129.0	154	89	76	16	39-1	87	.293
—	Frederick (Carolina)	0	1	.000	5.21	1.37	3	3	0	0	...	0-...	19.0	20	13	11	1	6-0	15	.278

Year Team (League)	W	L	Pct.	ERA	WHIP	G	GS	CG	ShO	Hld.	Sv.-Opp.	IP	H	R	ER	HR	BB-IBB	SO	Avg.
2001— Bowie (East.)	2	6	.250	3.54	1.02	9	9	2	0		0-...	61.0	52	27	24	8	10-0	34	.227
— Rochester (Int'l)	10	4	.714	3.89	1.30	19	18	1	1		0-...	113.1	119	63	49	10	28-0	89	.263
— Baltimore (A.L.)	0	5	.000	4.64	1.33	6	6	0	0	0	0-0	33.0	35	22	17	7	9-0	16	.265
2002— Baltimore (A.L.)	6	7	.462	3.98	1.43	56	1	0	0	12	1-5	83.2	84	41	37	12	36-4	45	.268
— Rochester (Int'l)	0	1	.000	6.75	1.50	1	1	0	0		0-...	4.0	4	4	3	2	2-0	1	.267
2003— Ottawa (Int'l)	3	1	.750	2.45	1.20	7	7	0	0		0-...	36.2	31	10	10	1	13-0	21	.235
— Baltimore (A.L.)	0	0	...	4.55	1.34	35	0	0	0	3	0-1	61.1	58	36	31	5	24-3	43	.256
2004— Bowie (East.)	0	0	...	0.00	0.67	1	1	0	0		0-...	3.0	2	0	0	0	0-0	1	.200
— Ottawa (Int'l)	3	5	.375	4.00	1.40	11	11	0	0		0-...	63.0	69	28	28	3	19-0	42	.285
— Baltimore (A.L.)	2	1	.667	4.70	1.29	23	2	0	0	0	0-1	53.2	49	31	28	4	20-0	37	.238
2005— Baltimore (A.L.)	0	0	...	9.72	2.04	5	0	0	0	0	0-0	8.1	13	9	9	2	4-0	5	.361
— Ottawa (Int'l)	3	8	.273	4.00	1.60	30	10	0	0	7	1-2	74.1	84	38	33	12	35-3	43	.294
Major League totals (5 years)	8	13	.381	4.58	1.38	125	9	0	0	15	1-7	240.0	239	139	122	30	93-7	146	.261

B

BAUTISTA, DENNY   P

PERSONAL: Born August 23, 1980, in Sanchez, Dominican Republic. ... 6-5/170. ... Throws right, bats right. ... Full name: Denny M. Bautista.

TRANSACTIONS/CAREER NOTES: Signed as a non-drafted free agent by Florida Marlins organization (April 11, 2000). ... Traded by Marlins with P Don Levinski to Baltimore Orioles for OF/1B Jeff Conine (August 31, 2003). ... Traded by Orioles to Kansas City Royals for P Jason Grimsley (June 21, 2004). ... On disabled list (May 12, 2005-remainder of season).

CAREER HITTING: 0-for-0 (.000), 0 R, 0 2B, 0 3B, 0 HR, 0 RBI.

SCOUTING REPORT **Throws:** His fastball reaches 98 mph, and he throws a curve, slurve and changeup. **Tendencies:** He has a live arm with plus stuff but throws too much over the middle of the plate. Inconsistent mechanics lead to a lack of command. Has good ability to change speeds but hasn't learned how to set hitters up. **Outlook:** He did not pitch last season after May 11, so his role for this season is difficult to determine. Makes sense to send him to the bullpen until the team can really see how he's pitching. *Grade 7.3*

DENNY BAUTISTA'S PITCHING ZONE

.250	.167	.125
.182	.231	.333
.000	.333	.333

LEFTY-RIGHTY SPLITS

vs.	Avg.	AB	H	2B	3B	HR	RBI	BB	SO	OBP	Slg.
L	.288	80	23	6	0	1	11	10	11	.363	.400
R	.220	59	13	2	0	1	9	7	12	.324	.305

Year Team (League)	W	L	Pct.	ERA	WHIP	G	GS	CG	ShO	Hld.	Sv.-Opp.	IP	H	R	ER	HR	BB-IBB	SO	Avg.
2000— GC Marlins (GCL)	6	2	.750	2.43	1.05	11	11	2	0	...	0-...	63.0	49	24	17	1	17-1	58	.209
— Utica (N.Y.-Penn)	0	0	...	3.60	1.20	1	1	0	0	...	0-...	5.0	4	3	2	0	2-0	5	.222
2001— Utica (N.Y.-Penn)	3	1	.750	2.08	0.79	7	7	0	0	...	0-...	39.0	25	16	9	0	6-0	31	.174
— Kane Co. (Midw.)	3	1	.750	4.35	1.45	8	7	0	0	...	0-...	39.1	43	21	19	2	14-0	20	.281
2002— Jupiter (Fla. St.)	4	6	.400	4.99	1.36	19	15	0	0	...	0-...	88.1	80	52	49	6	40-0	79	.242
2003— Jupiter (Fla. St.)	8	4	.667	3.21	1.23	14	14	0	0	...	0-...	84.0	68	32	30	2	35-0	77	.219
— Carolina (Southern)	4	5	.444	3.71	1.50	11	11	0	0	...	0-...	53.1	45	33	22	5	35-0	61	.226
2004— Baltimore (A.L.)	0	0	...	36.00	4.00	2	0	0	0	0	0-0	2.0	6	8	8	1	2-0	2	.545
— Bowie (East.)	3	5	.375	4.74	1.45	14	13	0	0	...	0-...	62.2	58	37	33	5	33-1	72	.243
— Wichita (Texas)	4	3	.571	2.54	1.22	12	12	0	0	...	0-...	81.2	68	32	23	3	32-0	73	.227
— Kansas City (A.L.)	0	4	.000	6.51	1.77	5	5	0	0	0	0-0	27.2	38	20	20	2	11-1	18	.333
2005— Kansas City (A.L.)	2	2	.500	5.80	1.49	7	7	0	0	0	0-0	35.2	36	23	23	2	17-0	23	.259
— Omaha (PCL)	0	1	.000	2.77	1.08	6	6	0	0	...	0-...	13.0	8	4	4	0	6-0	12	.174
Major League totals (2 years)	2	6	.250	7.03	1.68	14	12	0	0	0	0-0	65.1	80	51	51	5	30-1	42	.303

BAUTISTA, JOSE   OF/3B

PERSONAL: Born October 19, 1980, in Santo Domingo, Dominican Republic. ... 6-0/192. ... Bats right, throws right. ... Full name: Jose Antonio Bautista. ... High school: Instituto San Juan Bautista (Santo Domingo, D.R.). ... Junior college: Chipola (Fla.) .

TRANSACTIONS/CAREER NOTES: Selected by Pittsburgh Pirates organization in 20th round of 2000 free-agent draft. ... Selected by Baltimore Orioles from Pirates organization in Rule 5 major league draft (December 15, 2003). ... Claimed on waivers by Tampa Bay Devil Rays (June 3, 2004). ... Traded by Devil Rays to Kansas City Royals for cash (June 28, 2004). ... Traded by Royals to New York Mets for C Justin Huber (July 30, 2004). ... Traded by Mets with IF Ty Wigginton and P Matt Peterson to Pittsburgh Pirates for P Kris Benson and IF Jeff Keppinger (July 30, 2004).

2005 GAMES PLAYED BY POSITION (MLB): 3B—8.

LEFTY-RIGHTY SPLITS

vs.	Avg.	AB	H	2B	3B	HR	RBI	BB	SO	OBP	Slg.
L	.273	11	3	1	0	0	1	2	2	.385	.364
R	.059	17	1	0	0	0	0	1	5	.111	.059

Year Team (League)	Pos.	G	AB	R	H	2B	3B	HR	RBI	BB	SO	HBP	GDP	SB-CS	Avg.	OBP	SLG	OPS	E	Avg. (Fielding)
2001— Will. (NYP)	3B-OF	62	220	43	63	10	3	5	30	21	41	6	5	8-1	.286	.364	.427	.792	8	.927
2002— Hickory (S. Atl.)	3B-SS	129	438	72	132	26	3	14	57	67	104	8	12	3-2	.301	.402	.470	.872	24	.918
2003— GC Pirates (GCL)	3B	7	23	5	8	1	0	1	3	4	7	0	0	0-0	.348	.429	.522	.950	1	.929
— Lynchburg (Caro.)	3B-2B	51	165	28	40	14	2	4	20	27	48	3	1	1-5	.242	.359	.424	.783	10	.936
2004— Baltimore (A.L.) OF-3B-DH	16	11	3	3	0	0	0	1	3	1	0	0	0-0	.273	.333	.273	.606	0	1.000
— Tampa Bay (A.L.) OF-3B-DH	12	12	1	2	0	0	1	1	3	7	0	0	0-1	.167	.333	.167	.500	1	1.000
— Kansas City (A.L.)	3B-OF	13	25	1	5	1	0	0	1	2	3	0	0	0-0	.200	.231	.240	.471	2	.957
— Pittsburgh (N.L.)	OF	23	40	1	8	2	0	0	0	2	18	0	0	0-0	.200	.238	.250	.488	3	.864
2005— Altoona (East.)	3B-DH	117	445	63	126	27	1	23	90	48	101	10	9	7-3	.283	.364	.503	.868	24	.924
— Indianapolis (Int'l)	3B	13	51	6	13	3	0	1	4	4	10	0	2	1-1	.255	.309	.373	.682	0	1.000
— Pittsburgh (N.L.)	3B	11	28	3	4	1	0	0	1	3	7	0	1	1-0	.143	.226	.179	.404	1	.952
American League totals (1 year)		41	48	5	10	1	0	1	2	7	11	0	0	0-1	.208	.283	.229	.512	5	.971
National League totals (2 years)		34	68	4	12	3	0	0	1	5	25	0	1	1-0	.176	.233	.221	.453	4	.907
Major League totals (2 years)		75	116	9	22	4	0	1	3	10	47	0	3	1-1	.190	.254	.224	.478	5	.935

BAY, JASON — OF

PERSONAL: Born September 20, 1978, in Trail, British Columbia. ... 6-2/200. ... Bats right, throws right. ... Full name: Jason Raymond Bay. ... High school: J. Lloyd Crowe Secondary (Trail, B.C.). ... College: Gonzaga.
TRANSACTIONS/CAREER NOTES: Selected by Montreal Expos organization in 22nd round of 2000 free-agent draft. ... Traded by Expos with P Jim Serrano to New York Mets for SS Lou Collier (March 27, 2002). ... Traded by Mets with Ps Bobby M. Jones and Josh Reynolds to San Diego Padres for Ps Steve Reed and Jason Middlebrook (July 31, 2002). ... Traded by Padres with P Oliver Perez and a player to be named to Pittsburgh Pirates for OF Brian Giles (August 27, 2003); Pirates obtained P Cory Stewart to complete deal (October 2, 2003). ... On disabled list (March 26-May 7, 2004); included rehabilitation assignment to Nashville.
HONORS: Named N.L. Rookie of the Year by THE SPORTING NEWS (2004). ... Named N.L. Rookie of the Year by Baseball Writers' Association of America (2004).
2005 GAMES PLAYED BY POSITION (MLB): OF—162.

SCOUTING REPORT *Offense:* Bay has a sound hitting approach and good bat speed. Two years removed from shoulder problems, is now able to get full extension, meaning power numbers should continue to escalate. Plate discipline is improving. Is a good runner, but doesn't display basestealing instincts. *Defense:* Bay can play both left and center. Showed improvement in his arm strength; is accurate but still not average. Improved his reads and jumps in left after his exposure in center. Still a little cautious to dive for balls but has good range; will improve as he gains more confidence in his shoulder. *Outlook:* He is a complete offensive player and will be a perennial All-Star as his numbers continue to grow. *Grade 8.3*

JASON BAY'S HITTING ZONE

.433	.333	.267
.296	.517	.339
.299	.375	.292

LEFTY-RIGHTY SPLITS

vs.	Avg.	AB	H	2B	3B	HR	RBI	BB	SO	OBP	Slg.
L	.347	150	52	14	3	7	26	27	28	.444	.620
R	.292	449	131	30	3	25	75	68	114	.388	.539

Year Team (League)	Pos.	G	AB	R	H	2B	3B	HR	RBI	BB	SO	HBP	GDP	SB-CS	Avg.	OBP	SLG	OPS	E	Avg.
2000—Vermont (NYP)	OF	35	135	17	41	5	0	2	12	11	25	1	2	17-4	.304	.358	.385	.743	0	1.000
2001—Jupiter (Fla. St.)	OF-2B	38	123	12	24	4	1	1	10	18	26	2	4	10-3	.195	.306	.268	.574	3	.963
—Clinton (Midw.)	OF	87	318	67	115	20	4	13	61	48	62	4	4	15-2	.362	.449	.572	1.021	3	.984
2002—St. Lucie (Fla. St.)	OF	69	261	48	71	12	2	9	54	34	54	5	4	22-2	.272	.363	.437	.800	6	.950
—Binghamton (East.)	OF	34	107	17	31	4	2	4	19	15	23	3	2	13-3	.290	.383	.477	.859	2	.956
—Mobile (Sou.)	OF	23	81	16	25	5	2	4	12	13	22	1	0	4-2	.309	.411	.568	.978	0	1.000
2003—San Diego (N.L.)	OF	3	8	2	2	1	0	1	2	1	1	1	0	0-0	.250	.400	.750	1.150	0	1.000
—Portland (PCL)	OF	91	307	64	93	11	1	20	59	55	71	5	3	23-4	.303	.410	.541	.951	1	.995
—Pittsburgh (N.L.)	OF	27	79	13	23	6	1	3	12	18	28	0	0	3-1	.291	.423	.506	.929	1	.976
2004—Nashville (PCL)	OF	10	3	4	3	2	0	1	3	3	5	0	0	0-0	.400	.538	.900	1.438	0	1.000
—Pittsburgh (N.L.)	OF	120	411	61	116	24	4	26	82	41	129	10	9	4-6	.282	.358	.550	.907	2	.991
2005—Pittsburgh (N.L.)	OF	•162	599	110	183	44	6	32	101	95	142	6	12	21-1	.306	.402	.559	.961	4	.988
Major League totals (3 years)		312	1097	186	324	75	11	62	197	155	300	17	21	28-8	.295	.387	.553	.941	7	.988

BAYLISS, JONAH — P

PERSONAL: Born August 13, 1980, in North Adams, Mass. ... 6-2/210. ... Throws right, bats right. ... Full name: Jonah James Bayliss. ... High school: Lawrence Academy (Growton, Mass.) ... College: Trinity College.
TRANSACTIONS/CAREER NOTES: Selected by Kansas City Royals organization in seventh round of 2002 free-agent draft.
CAREER HITTING: 0-for-0 (.000), 0 R, 0 2B, 0 3B, 0 HR, 0 RBI.

LEFTY-RIGHTY SPLITS

vs.	Avg.	AB	H	2B	3B	HR	RBI	BB	SO	OBP	Slg.
L	.200	20	4	0	0	2	5	2	5	.304	.500
R	.136	22	3	1	0	0	2	2	5	.240	.182

Year Team (League)	W	L	Pct.	ERA	WHIP	G	GS	CG	ShO	Hld.	Sv.-Opp.	IP	H	R	ER	HR	BB-IBB	SO	Avg.
2002—Spokane (N'west)	4	8	.333	5.35	1.40	15	15	0	0	...	0-...	70.2	70	46	42	9	29-0	81	.264
2003—Burlington (Midw.)	7	12	.368	3.86	1.41	26	26	2	1	...	0-...	140.0	129	78	60	11	69-0	133	.242
2004—Wilmington (Caro.)	6	6	.500	4.93	1.46	24	24	0	0	...	0-...	111.1	119	70	61	11	44-0	79	.287
2005—Kansas City (A.L.)	0	0	...	4.63	0.94	11	0	0	0	0	0-0	11.2	7	6	6	2	4-0	10	.167
—Wichita (Texas)	1	2	.333	2.84	1.21	30	0	0	0	1	8-9	57.0	43	19	18	5	26-0	63	.208
Major League totals (1 year)	0	0	...	4.63	0.94	11	0	0	0	0	0-0	11.2	7	6	6	2	4-0	10	.167

BAZARDO, YORMAN — P

PERSONAL: Born July 11, 1984, in Maracay, Venezuela. ... 6-2/202. ... Throws right, bats right. ... Full name: Yorman Osorio Bazardo. ... College: None.
TRANSACTIONS/CAREER NOTES: Signed as a non-drafted free agent by Florida Marlins organization (July 19, 2000). ... Traded by Marlins with P Mike Flannery to Seattle Mariners for P Ron Villone (July 31, 2005).
CAREER HITTING: 0-for-1 (.000), 0 R, 0 2B, 0 3B, 0 HR, 0 RBI.

LEFTY-RIGHTY SPLITS

vs.	Avg.	AB	H	2B	3B	HR	RBI	BB	SO	OBP	Slg.
L	.250	4	1	1	0	0	2	1	0	.400	.500
R	.667	6	4	1	0	0	4	1	2	.714	.833

Year Team (League)	W	L	Pct.	ERA	WHIP	G	GS	CG	ShO	Hld.	Sv.-Opp.	IP	H	R	ER	HR	BB-IBB	SO	Avg.
2001—Ciu.Alianza (VSL)	7	2	.778	2.43	1.09	12	12	1	0	...	0-...	70.1	59	26	19	0	18-0	62	...
2002—Jamestown (NYP)	5	0	1.000	2.72	1.24	25	0	0	0	...	6-...	36.1	39	11	11	0	6-0	26	.275
2003—Greensboro (S. Atl.)	9	8	.529	3.12	1.22	21	21	4	2	...	0-...	130.0	132	56	45	8	26-0	70	.261
2004—Jupiter (Fla. St.)	5	9	.357	3.27	1.24	25	25	2	2	...	0-...	154.1	161	78	56	3	30-0	95	.274
2005—Florida (N.L.)	0	0	...	21.60	4.20	1	0	0	0	0	0-0	1.2	5	4	4	0	2-0	2	.500
—Carolina (Southern)	8	7	.533	3.99	1.33	19	19	0	0	...	0-0	108.1	108	60	48	12	36-3	73	.263
—San Antonio (Texas)	3	1	.750	4.28	1.46	6	6	0	0	...	0-0	33.2	38	16	16	4	11-0	26	.295
Major League totals (1 year)	0	0	...	21.60	4.20	1	0	0	0	0	0-0	1.2	5	4	4	0	2-0	2	.500

BEAN, COLTER — P

PERSONAL: Born January 16, 1977, in Anniston, Ala. ... 6-6/255. ... Throws right, bats left. ... Full name: Randall Colter Bean. ... High school: Vestavia Hills (Birmingham, Ala.). ... College: Auburn.
TRANSACTIONS/CAREER NOTES: Signed as a non-drafted free agent by New York Yankees organization (May 31, 2000). ... Selected by Boston Red Sox from Yankees organization in Rule 5 major league draft (December 15, 2003); returned to Yankees organization (March 18, 2004).
CAREER HITTING: 0-for-0 (.000), 0 R, 0 2B, 0 3B, 0 HR, 0 RBI.

LEFTY-RIGHTY SPLITS

vs.	Avg.	AB	H	2B	3B	HR	RBI	BB	SO	OBP	Slg.
L	.500	2	1	0	0	0	1	1	0	.667	.500
R	.000	5	0	0	0	0	0	1	2	.167	.000

B

Year	Team (League)	W	L	Pct.	ERA	WHIP	G	GS	CG	ShO	Hld.	Sv.-Opp.	IP	H	R	ER	HR	BB-IBB	SO	Avg.
2000—	Staten Island (N.Y.-Penn.) .	0	0	—	4.50	3.00	3	0	0	0	...	0-...	2.0	3	3	1	0	3-1	2	.273
	—Greensboro (S. Atl.)	1	0	1.000	4.91	1.25	18	0	0	0	...	0-...	25.2	21	16	14	1	11-0	35	.214
2001—	Tampa (Fla. St.)	7	1	.875	1.46	0.91	32	0	0	0	...	2-...	49.1	27	9	8	0	18-2	77	.155
	—Norwich (East.)	0	1	.000	9.00	2.00	1	0	0	0	...	0-...	1.0	1	1	1	1	1-0	0	.250
2002—	Norwich (East.)	0	2	.000	6.75	1.88	12	0	0	0	...	0-...	10.2	14	8	8	1	6-0	9	.318
	—Tampa (Fla. St.)	2	2	.500	1.98	1.01	46	0	0	0	...	9-...	54.2	34	17	12	2	21-2	78	.174
2003—	Trenton (East.)	0	0	—	0.00	0.86	3	0	0	0	...	0-...	4.2	2	0	0	0	2-0	9	.125
	—Columbus (Int'l)	4	2	.667	2.87	1.16	50	0	0	0	...	4-...	69.0	53	33	22	5	27-2	70	.210
2004—	Columbus (Int'l)	9	3	.750	2.29	1.02	53	0	0	0	...	1-...	82.2	61	24	21	3	23-0	109	.198
2005—	New York (A.L.)	0	0	—	4.50	1.50	1	0	0	0	0	0-0	2.0	1	1	1	0	2-0	2	.143
	—Columbus (Int'l)	4	7	.364	3.01	1.38	65	0	0	0	18	0-2	71.2	60	33	24	5	39-7	82	.226
Major League totals (1 year)		0	0	—	4.50	1.50	1	0	0	0	0	0-0	2.0	1	1	1	0	2-0	2	.143

B

BECKETT, JOSH — P

PERSONAL: Born May 15, 1980, in Spring, Texas. ... 6-5/222. ... Throws right, bats right. ... Full name: Joshua Patrick Beckett. ... High school: Spring (Texas).
TRANSACTIONS/CAREER NOTES: Selected by Florida Marlins organization in first round (second pick overall) of 1999 free-agent draft. ... On disabled list (April 29-May 14, June 5-July 16 and August 23-September 11, 2002); included rehabilitation assignments to GCL Marlins and Jupiter. ... On disabled list (May 8-July 1, 2003); included rehabilitation assignments to Jupiter and Carolina. ... On disabled list (May 31-June 17, June 18-July 5 and July 6-30, 2004). ... On disabled list (June 15-30 and July 8-23, 2005).
HONORS: Named Minor League Player of the Year by THE SPORTING NEWS (2001).
CAREER HITTING: 26-for-187 (.139), 11 R, 8 2B, 0 3B, 1 HR, 11 RBI.

SCOUTING REPORT *Throws:* Beckett is a power pitcher with a fastball that ranges from 92-96 mph, a hard, downward-breaking curveball and an improving straight changeup. *Tendencies:* He is a strikeout pitcher who can work up in the zone with a riding four-seam fastball or down with a two-seam fastball. Lacks maturity and tends to lose focus, negating his great stuff. Doesn't make adjustments in his game plan quickly enough. Has been successful thus far with pure stuff. *Outlook:* Beckett is a high-maintenance pitcher with superior stuff, but until he matures, he isn't going to live up to his expectations. Has No. 1 stuff and one day could win a Cy Young if he stays healthy. **Grade 7.9**

JOSH BECKETT'S PITCHING ZONE

.179	.324	.261
.226	.317	.288
.178	.429	.212

LEFTY-RIGHTY SPLITS

vs.	Avg.	AB	H	2B	3B	HR	RBI	BB	SO	OBP	Slg.
L	.217	332	72	17	3	7	26	40	87	.303	.349
R	.252	321	81	17	3	7	37	18	79	.303	.389

Year	Team (League)	W	L	Pct.	ERA	WHIP	G	GS	CG	ShO	Hld.	Sv.-Opp.	IP	H	R	ER	HR	BB-IBB	SO	Avg.
2000—	Kane Co. (Midw.)	2	3	.400	2.12	1.01	13	12	0	0	...	0-...	59.1	45	18	14	4	15-0	61	.214
2001—	Brevard County (FSL)	6	0	1.000	1.23	0.72	13	12	0	0	...	0-...	65.2	32	13	9	0	15-0	101	.145
	—Portland (East.)	8	1	.889	1.82	0.93	13	13	0	0	...	0-...	74.1	50	16	15	8	19-0	102	.191
	—Florida (N.L.)	2	2	.500	1.50	1.04	4	4	0	0	0	0-0	24.0	14	9	4	3	11-0	24	.161
2002—	Florida (N.L.)	6	7	.462	4.10	1.27	23	21	0	0	0	0-0	107.2	93	56	49	13	44-2	113	.232
	—GC Marlins (GCL)	0	0	—	4.50	1.50	1	1	0	0	0	0-0	4.0	5	2	2	0	1-0	7	.294
	—Jupiter (Fla. St.)	1	0	1.000	0.00	0.83	1	1	0	0	0	0-0	6.0	4	0	0	0	1-0	12	.174
2003—	Jupiter (Fla. St.)	0	0	—	0.00	0.70	1	1	0	0	0	0-0	3.0	2	0	0	0	0-0	5	.182
	—Carolina (Southern)	0	0	—	4.50	1.00	1	1	0	0	0	0-0	4.0	4	2	2	1	0-0	7	.267
	—Florida (N.L.)	9	8	.529	3.04	1.32	24	23	0	0	0	0-0	142.0	132	54	48	9	56-4	152	.246
2004—	Florida (N.L.)	9	9	.500	3.79	1.22	26	26	1	1	0	0-0	156.2	137	72	66	16	54-3	152	.235
2005—	Florida (N.L.)	15	8	.652	3.38	1.18	29	29	2	1	0	0-0	178.2	153	75	67	14	58-2	166	.234
Major League totals (5 years)		41	34	.547	3.46	1.23	106	103	3	2	0	0-0	609.0	529	266	234	55	223-11	607	.234

DIVISION SERIES RECORD

Year	Team (League)	W	L	Pct.	ERA	WHIP	G	GS	CG	ShO	Hld.	Sv.-Opp.	IP	H	R	ER	HR	BB-IBB	SO	Avg.
2003—	Florida (N.L.)	0	1	.000	1.29	1.00	1	1	0	0		0-0	7.0	2	1	1	0	5-1	9	.087

CHAMPIONSHIP SERIES RECORD

Year	Team (League)	W	L	Pct.	ERA	WHIP	G	GS	CG	ShO	Hld.	Sv.-Opp.	IP	H	R	ER	HR	BB-IBB	SO	Avg.
2003—	Florida (N.L.)	1	0	1.000	3.26	0.67	3	2	1	1	0	0-0	19.1	11	7	7	3	2-0	19	.162

WORLD SERIES RECORD

Year	Team (League)	W	L	Pct.	ERA	WHIP	G	GS	CG	ShO	Hld.	Sv.-Opp.	IP	H	R	ER	HR	BB-IBB	SO	Avg.
2003—	Florida (N.L.)	1	1	.500	1.10	0.80	2	2	1	1	0	0-0	16.1	8	2	2	0	5-0	19	.148

BEDARD, ERIK — P

PERSONAL: Born March 6, 1979, in Navan, Ontario. ... 6-1/189. ... Throws left, bats left. ... Full name: Erik Joseph Bedard. ... High school: Garneau (Navan, Ontario). ... Junior college: Norwalk (Conn.) Community College.
TRANSACTIONS/CAREER NOTES: Selected by Baltimore Orioles organization in sixth round of 1999 free-agent draft. ... On disabled list (March 28-September 1, 2003); included rehabilitation assignment to GCL Orioles. ... On disabled list (May 26-July 18, 2005); included rehabilitation assignments to Bowie and Delmarva.
CAREER HITTING: 0-for-4 (.000), 0 R, 0 2B, 0 3B, 0 HR, 0 RBI.

SCOUTING REPORT *Throws:* Bedard's fastball reaches 93 mph and has late movement. Also throws a change and a curveball. *Tendencies:* Bedard is a high-count pitcher who doesn't trust his stuff. Is too deliberate on the mound and inconsistent with his push off the rubber. Labors with his control. Needs to realize he has a good arm. Curve is rolling more now. Inconsistent with the arm speed and location of his change. *Outlook:* He needs to speed himself up on the mound and challenge hitters by pitching off his fastball. A difficult pitcher to play behind, as he's frequently in 3-2 counts and often reaches pitch-count limits by fifth or sixth inning. There is a lot more to this arm than he shows. **Grade 5.3**

ERIK BEDARD'S PITCHING ZONE

.235	.364	.333
.187	.403	.277
.226	.278	.261

LEFTY-RIGHTY SPLITS

vs.	Avg.	AB	H	2B	3B	HR	RBI	BB	SO	OBP	Slg.
L	.252	135	34	3	0	2	12	11	36	.318	.319
R	.263	400	105	20	1	8	43	46	89	.338	.378

Year Team (League)	W	L	Pct.	ERA	WHIP	G	GS	CG	ShO	Hld.	Sv.-Opp.	IP	H	R	ER	HR	BB-IBB	SO	Avg.
1999— GC Orioles (GCL)	2	1	.667	1.86	1.14	8	6	0	0	...	0-...	29.0	20	7	6	1	13-0	41	.192
2000— Delmarva (S. Atl.)	9	4	.692	3.57	1.20	29	22	1	1	...	2-...	111.0	98	48	44	2	35-0	131	.233
2001— Frederick (Carolina)	9	2	.818	2.15	0.98	17	17	0	0	...	0-...	96.1	68	27	23	4	26-0	130	.198
— GC Orioles (GCL)	0	1	.000	3.00	1.17	2	2	0	0	...	0-...	6.0	4	2	2	0	3-0	7	.200
2002— Bowie (East.)	6	3	.667	1.97	1.06	13	12	0	0	...	0-...	68.2	43	18	15	0	30-0	66	.176
— Baltimore (A.L.)	0	0	...	13.50	3.00	2	0	0	0	0	0-0	0.2	2	1	1	0	0-0	1	.500
2003— GC Orioles (GCL)	0	0	...	1.13	0.80	3	3	0	0	...	0-...	8.0	4	1	1	0	2-0	11	.154
— Aberdeen (N.Y.-Penn.)	0	0	...	2.35	1.00	2	2	0	0	...	0-...	7.2	7	2	2	0	1-0	13	.233
— Frederick (Carolina)	0	1	.000	7.36	1.60	1	1	0	0	...	0-...	3.2	5	3	3	1	1-0	2	.357
2004— Ottawa (Int'l)	0	1	.000	7.20	2.20	2	2	0	0	...	0-...	5.0	8	4	4	1	3-0	3	.348
— Baltimore (A.L.)	6	10	.375	4.59	1.60	27	26	0	0	0	0-0	137.1	149	83	70	13	71-1	121	.270
2005— Bowie (East.)	0	1	.000	9.00	1.50	1	1	0	0	...	0-0	2.0	2	2	2	0	1-0	4	.250
— Delmarva (S. Atl.)	1	0	1.000	0.00	0.80	1	1	0	0	...	0-0	5.0	3	0	0	0	1-0	9	.176
— Baltimore (A.L.)	6	8	.429	4.00	1.38	24	24	0	0	0	0-0	141.2	139	66	63	10	57-1	125	.260
Major League totals (3 years)	12	18	.400	4.31	1.49	53	50	0	0	0	0-0	279.2	290	150	134	23	128-2	247	.266

B

BEIMEL, JOE   P

PERSONAL: Born April 19, 1977, in St. Marys, Pa. ... 6-3/217. ... Throws left, bats left. ... Full name: Joseph Ronald Beimel. ... Name pronounced: BYE-muhl. ... High school: St. Marys Area (Pa.). ... College: Duquesne.

TRANSACTIONS/CAREER NOTES: Selected by Texas Rangers organization in 26th round of 1996 free-agent draft; did not sign. ... Selected by Pittsburgh Pirates organization in 18th round of 1998 free-agent draft. ... Released by Pirates (March 31, 2004). ... Signed by Minnesota Twins organization (April 11, 2004). ... Signed as a free agent by Tampa Bay Devil Rays organization (November 12, 2004).

CAREER HITTING: 10-for-41 (.244), 3 R, 1 2B, 0 3B, 0 HR, 1 RBI.

LEFTY-RIGHTY SPLITS

vs.	Avg.	AB	H	2B	3B	HR	RBI	BB	SO	OBP	Slg.
L	.429	21	9	0	1	0	1	2	2	.478	.524
R	.231	26	6	1	2	1	4	2	1	.286	.538

Year Team (League)	W	L	Pct.	ERA	WHIP	G	GS	CG	ShO	Hld.	Sv.-Opp.	IP	H	R	ER	HR	BB-IBB	SO	Avg.
1998— Erie (N.Y.-Penn)	1	4	.200	6.32	1.66	17	6	0	0	...	0-...	47.0	56	39	33	6	22-0	37	.296
1999— Hickory (S. Atl.)	5	11	.313	4.43	1.45	29	22	0	0	...	0-...	130.0	146	81	64	12	43-0	102	.289
2000— Lynchburg (Caro.)	10	6	.625	3.36	1.28	18	18	2	1	...	0-...	120.2	111	49	45	6	44-1	82	.247
— Altoona (East.)	1	6	.143	4.16	1.48	10	10	1	0	...	0-...	62.2	72	38	29	8	21-0	28	.288
2001— Pittsburgh (N.L.)	7	11	.389	5.23	1.56	42	15	0	0	...	0-0	115.1	131	72	67	12	49-4	58	.290
2002— Pittsburgh (N.L.)	2	5	.286	4.64	1.56	53	8	0	0	5	0-1	85.1	88	49	44	9	45-12	53	.267
2003— Pittsburgh (N.L.)	1	3	.250	5.05	1.64	69	0	0	0	12	0-5	62.1	69	35	35	7	33-6	42	.299
2004— Rochester (Int'l)	2	4	.333	6.97	1.73	49	1	0	0	...	2-...	62.0	83	54	48	7	24-1	44	.322
— Minnesota (A.L.)	0	0	...	43.20	6.00	3	0	0	0	0	0-0	1.2	8	8	8	1	2-0	2	.615
2005— Durham (Int'l)	1	2	.333	3.93	1.50	48	0	0	0	9	0-2	52.2	58	28	23	3	21-1	36	.276
— Tampa Bay (A.L.)	0	0	...	3.27	1.73	7	0	0	0	0	0-0	11.0	15	4	4	1	4-1	3	.319
American League totals (2 years)	0	0	...	8.53	2.29	10	0	0	0	0	0-0	12.2	23	12	12	2	6-1	5	.383
National League totals (3 years)	10	19	.345	5.00	1.58	164	23	0	0	17	0-6	263.0	288	156	146	28	127-22	153	.284
Major League totals (5 years)	10	19	.345	5.16	1.61	174	23	0	0	17	0-6	275.2	311	168	158	30	133-23	158	.290

BELISLE, MATT   P

PERSONAL: Born June 6, 1980, in Austin, Texas. ... 6-3/195. ... Throws right, bats both. ... Full name: Matthew Thomas Belisle. ... Name pronounced: be-LYLE: ... High school: McCallum (Austin, Texas).

TRANSACTIONS/CAREER NOTES: Selected by Atlanta Braves organization in second round of 1998 free-agent draft. ... Traded by Braves to Cincinnati Reds (August 14, 2003), completing deal in which Braves acquired P Kent Mercker for a player to be named (August 12, 2003).

CAREER HITTING: 1-for-8 (.125), 0 R, 0 2B, 0 3B, 0 HR, 0 RBI.

MATT BELISLE'S PITCHING ZONE

.353	.538	.250
.289	.313	.443
.290	.150	.222

LEFTY-RIGHTY SPLITS

vs.	Avg.	AB	H	2B	3B	HR	RBI	BB	SO	OBP	Slg.
L	.331	127	42	7	0	4	16	14	21	.414	.480
R	.273	216	59	10	1	7	35	12	38	.315	.426

Year Team (League)	W	L	Pct.	ERA	WHIP	G	GS	CG	ShO	Hld.	Sv.-Opp.	IP	H	R	ER	HR	BB-IBB	SO	Avg.
1999— Danville (Appal.)	2	5	.286	4.67	1.53	14	14	0	0	...	0-...	71.1	86	50	37	3	23-0	60	.291
2000— Myrtle Beach (Carol.)	3	4	.429	3.43	1.06	12	12	0	0	...	0-...	78.2	72	32	30	5	11-0	71	.246
— Macon (S. Atl.)	9	5	.643	2.37	0.95	15	15	1	0	...	0-...	102.1	79	37	27	7	18-0	97	.216
2001—					Did not play.														
2002— Greenville (Sou.)	5	9	.357	4.35	1.26	26	26	1	0	...	0-...	159.1	162	91	77	18	39-1	123	.261
2003— Greenville (Sou.)	6	8	.429	3.52	1.36	21	21	1	0	...	0-...	125.1	128	59	49	5	42-2	94	.272
— Richmond (Int'l)	1	1	.500	2.25	0.85	3	3	0	0	...	0-...	20.0	17	6	5	1	0-0	10	.230
— Louisville (Int'l)	1	3	.250	3.81	1.38	4	4	0	0	...	0-...	26.0	31	15	11	2	5-0	15	.304
— Cincinnati (N.L.)	1	1	.500	5.19	1.38	6	0	0	0	0	0-1	8.2	10	5	5	1	2-0	6	.303
2004— Louisville (Int'l)	9	11	.450	5.26	1.49	28	28	2	1	...	0-...	162.2	192	104	95	16	51-4	106	.303
2005— Cincinnati (N.L.)	4	8	.333	4.41	1.48	60	5	0	0	8	1-4	85.2	101	49	42	11	26-6	59	.294
Major League totals (2 years)	5	9	.357	4.48	1.47	66	5	0	0	8	1-5	94.1	111	54	47	12	28-6	65	.295

BELL, DAVID   3B

PERSONAL: Born September 14, 1972, in Cincinnati. ... 5-10/181. ... Bats right, throws right. ... Full name: David Michael Bell. ... High school: Moeller (Cincinnati). ... Son of Buddy Bell, manager, Kansas City Royals and third baseman with four major league teams (1972-89); brother of Mike Bell, third baseman with Cincinnati Reds (2000); and grandson of Gus Bell, outfielder with four major league teams (1950-64).

TRANSACTIONS/CAREER NOTES: Selected by Cleveland Indians organization in seventh round of 1990 free-agent draft. ... Traded by Indians with C Pepe McNeal and P Rick Heiserman to St. Louis Cardinals for P Ken Hill (July 27, 1995). ... On disabled list (April 29-June 30, 1997); included rehabilitation assignments to Arkansas and Louisville. ... Claimed on waivers by Indians (April 14, 1998). ... Traded by Indians to Seattle Mariners for 2B Joey Cora (August 31, 1998). ... Traded by Mariners to San Francisco Giants for SS Desi Relaford and cash (January 25, 2002). ... Signed as a free agent by Philadelphia Phillies (November 24, 2002). ... On disabled list (July 11-September 23, 2003).

2005 GAMES PLAYED BY POSITION (MLB): 3B—150.

B

SCOUTING REPORT *Offense:* His short, compact stroke is an asset, but his bat speed is declining. Is very good against lefthanders. Has become more of a streak hitter who likes the ball up so he can pull it. Can still cheat on a fastball, especially on the inner half of the plate, and pull it for power. *Defense:* Bell is an underrated fielder. Excellent instincts and positioning compensate for declining range. Has very soft, quick hands and surprising agility. Has a quick first step to the line. Arm strength is just average and can be erratic. *Outlook:* A true professional player, Bell likely can't hit more than 15 home runs a year or hit much above .250. Is a good complementary player on a club with power at other positions. *Grade 7.3*

DAVID BELL'S HITTING ZONE

.190	.208	.176
.377	.253	.150
.140	.467	.238

LEFTY-RIGHTY SPLITS

vs.	Avg.	AB	H	2B	3B	HR	RBI	BB	SO	OBP	Slg.
L	.400	135	54	14	0	4	27	16	16	.461	.593
R	.199	422	84	17	1	6	34	31	53	.260	.287

Year Team (League)	Pos.	G	AB	R	H	2B	3B	HR	RBI	BB	SO	HBP	GDP	SB-CS	Avg.	OBP	SLG	OPS	E	Avg.
1990—GC Indians (GCL)	3B	30	111	18	29	5	1	0	13	10	8	4	5	1-1	.261	.341	.324	.666	7	.919
—Burlington (Appal.)	3B	12	42	4	7	1	1	0	2	2	5	1	1	2-1	.167	.217	.238	.455	3	.921
1991—Columbus (S. Atl.)	3B	136	491	47	113	24	1	5	63	37	50	5	22	3-2	.230	.287	.314	.601	31	.920
1992—Kinston (Carol.)	3B	123	464	52	117	17	2	6	47	54	66	1	13	2-4	.252	.327	.336	.663	20	.946
1993—Cant./Akr. (Eastern)	3B-2B-SS	129	483	69	141	20	2	9	60	43	54	3	12	3-4	.292	.350	.398	.747	21	.950
1994—Charlotte (Int'l)	3B-SS-2B	134	481	66	141	17	4	18	88	41	54	9	...	2-5	.293	.355	.457	.812	20	.956
1995—Buffalo (A.A.)	3B-SS-2B	70	254	34	69	11	1	8	34	22	37	4	...	0-3	.272	.336	.417	.753	11	.952
—Cleveland (A.L.)	3B	2	2	0	0	0	0	0	0	0	0	0	0	0-0	.000	.000	.000	.000	0	1.000
—Louisville (A.A.)	2B	18	76	9	21	3	1	1	9	2	10	3		4-0	.276	.321	.382	.703	1	.989
—St. Louis (N.L.)	2B-3B	39	144	13	36	7	2	2	19	4	25	2	0	1-2	.250	.278	.368	.646	7	.964
1996—St. Louis (N.L.)	3B-2B-SS	62	145	12	31	6	0	1	9	10	22	1	3	1-1	.214	.268	.276	.543	5	.969
—Louisville (A.A.)	2B-3B-SS	42	136	9	24	5	1	0	7	7	15	0	4	1-2	.176	.217	.228	.445	5	.973
1997—St. Louis (N.L.)	3B-2B-SS	66	142	9	30	7	2	1	12	10	28	0	2	1-0	.211	.261	.310	.571	8	.949
—Arkansas (Texas)	3B-2B	9	32	3	7	2	0	1	3	2	2	0	1	1-0	.219	.265	.375	.640	1	.947
—Louisville (A.A.)	2B-3B-DH																			
	SS	6	22	3	5	0	0	1	4	0	6	1	0	0-0	.227	.250	.364	.614	1	.941
1998—St. Louis (N.L.)	3B-2B	4	9	0	2	1	0	0	0	0	3	0	0	0-0	.222	.222	.333	.556	0	1.000
—Cleveland (A.L.)	2B-3B-1B																			
	SS	107	340	37	89	21	2	10	41	22	54	2	8	0-4	.262	.306	.424	.730	9	.983
—Seattle (A.L.)	OF	21	80	11	26	8	0	3	8	5	8	0	3	0-0	.325	.365	.425	.790	1	.991
1999—Seattle (A.L.)	2B-1B-SS	157	597	92	160	31	2	21	78	58	90	2	7	7-4	.268	.331	.432	.763	17	.978
2000—Seattle (A.L.)	3B-2B-SS																			
	DH-SS	133	454	57	112	24	2	11	47	42	66	6	11	2-3	.247	.316	.381	.697	15	.963
2001—Seattle (A.L.)	3B-1B	135	470	62	122	28	0	15	64	28	59	3	8	2-1	.260	.303	.415	.718	14	.962
2002—San Francisco (N.L.)	3B-2B-SS																			
	1B	154	552	82	144	29	2	20	73	54	80	9	18	1-2	.261	.333	.429	.762	12	.971
2003—Philadelphia (N.L.)	3B-2B	85	297	32	58	14	0	4	37	41	40	4	7	0-0	.195	.296	.283	.579	8	.968
2004—Philadelphia (N.L.)	3B	143	533	67	155	33	1	18	77	57	75	6	14	1-1	.291	.363	.458	.821	24	.943
2005—Philadelphia (N.L.)	3B	150	557	53	138	31	1	10	61	47	69	5	24	0-1	.248	.310	.361	.671	21	.951
American League totals (5 years)		555	1943	259	509	112	6	57	238	155	277	13	37	11-12	.262	.318	.414	.731	56	.974
National League totals (8 years)		703	2379	268	594	128	8	56	288	223	342	27	68	5-7	.250	.318	.381	.699	85	.958
Major League totals (11 years)		1258	4322	527	1103	240	14	113	526	378	619	40	105	16-19	.255	.318	.396	.714	141	.966

DIVISION SERIES RECORD

Year Team (League)	Pos.	G	AB	R	H	2B	3B	HR	RBI	BB	SO	HBP	GDP	SB-CS	Avg.	OBP	SLG	OPS	E	Avg.
2000—Seattle (A.L.)	3B	3	11	0	4	1	0	0	1	2	2	0	0	0-0	.364	.462	.455	.916	0	1.000
2001—Seattle (A.L.)	3B	5	16	2	5	1	0	1	2	1	6	0	0	0-0	.313	.333	.563	.896	0	1.000
2002—San Francisco (N.L.)	3B	5	16	3	3	0	0	0	1	3	4	0	0	0-0	.188	.316	.188	.503	1	.944
Division series totals (3 years)		13	43	5	12	2	0	1	4	6	12	0	0	0-0	.279	.360	.395	.755	1	.969

CHAMPIONSHIP SERIES RECORD

Year Team (League)	Pos.	G	AB	R	H	2B	3B	HR	RBI	BB	SO	HBP	GDP	SB-CS	Avg.	OBP	SLG	OPS	E	Avg.
2000—Seattle (A.L.)	3B	5	18	0	4	0	0	0	0	0	0	0	0	0-0	.222	.222	.222	.444	0	1.000
2001—Seattle (A.L.)	3B	5	16	1	3	0	0	0	0	0	3	0	0	0-0	.188	.188	.188	.375	1	.923
2002—San Francisco (N.L.)	3B	5	17	4	7	1	0	1	1	2	3	0	0	0-0	.412	.474	.647	1.121	0	1.000
Champ. series totals (3 years)		15	51	5	14	1	0	1	5	2	6	0	0	0-0	.275	.302	.353	.655	1	.974

WORLD SERIES RECORD

Year Team (League)	Pos.	G	AB	R	H	2B	3B	HR	RBI	BB	SO	HBP	GDP	SB-CS	Avg.	OBP	SLG	OPS	E	Avg.
2002—San Francisco (N.L.)	3B	7	23	4	7	0	0	1	4	5	4	1	1	0-1	.304	.448	.435	.883	2	.889

BELL, HEATH   P

PERSONAL: Born September 29, 1977, in Oceanside, Calif. ... 6-2/244. ... Throws right, bats right. ... Full name: Heath Justin Bell. ... High school: Rancho Santiago (Calif.). ... Junior college: Santa Ana (Calif.). ...
TRANSACTIONS/CAREER NOTES: Selected by Tampa Bay Devil Rays organization in 69th round of 1997 free-agent draft; did not sign. ... Signed as a non-drafted free agent by New York Mets organization (June 16, 1998).
CAREER HITTING: 0-for-4 (.000). 0 R, 0 2B, 0 3B, 0 HR, 0 RBI.

HEATH BELL'S PITCHING ZONE

.455	.333	.231
.447	.292	.212
.261	.333	.429

LEFTY-RIGHTY SPLITS

vs.	Avg.	AB	H	2B	3B	HR	RBI	BB	SO	OBP	Slg.
L	.312	77	24	2	0	1	7	7	13	.369	.377
R	.288	111	32	5	0	2	17	6	30	.331	.387

Year Team (League)	W	L	Pct.	ERA	WHIP	G	GS	CG	ShO	Hld.	Sv.-Opp.	IP	H	R	ER	HR	BB-IBB	SO	Avg.
1998—Kingsport (Appalachian)	1	0	1.000	2.54	1.11	22	0	0	0	...	8-...	46.0	40	15	13	5	11-0	61	.231
1999—Capital City (SAL)	1	7	.125	2.60	1.03	55	0	0	0	...	25-...	62.1	47	23	18	5	17-0	68	.203

Year Team (League)	W	L	Pct.	ERA	WHIP	G	GS	CG	ShO	Hld.	Sv.-Opp.	IP	H	R	ER	HR	BB-IBB	SO	Avg.
2000— St. Lucie (Fla. St.)	5	1	.833	2.55	1.07	48	0	0	0	...	23-...	60.0	43	19	17	4	21-2	75	.201
2001— Binghamton (East.)	3	1	.750	6.02	1.65	43	0	0	0	...	4-...	61.1	82	44	41	13	19-3	55	.320
2002— Norfolk (Int'l)	3	4	.429	4.26	1.48	22	0	0	0	...	5-...	31.2	38	15	15	2	9-1	28	.302
— Binghamton (East.)	1	0	1.000	1.18	0.74	24	0	0	0	...	6-...	38.0	22	6	5	0	6-0	49	.168
2003— Norfolk (Int'l)	2	3	.400	4.71	1.25	40	0	0	0	...	3-...	49.2	54	26	26	4	8-0	54	.284
2004— Binghamton (East.)	0	0	...	0.00	1.00	1	0	0	0	...	0-...	2.0	2	0	0	0	0-0	0	.250
— Norfolk (Int'l)	3	1	.750	3.23	1.19	45	0	0	0	...	16-...	55.2	42	21	20	4	24-2	69	.210
— New York (N.L.)	0	2	.000	3.33	1.15	17	0	0	0	1	0-1	24.1	22	9	9	5	6-0	27	.253
2005— Norfolk (Int'l)	1	0	1.000	1.69	0.75	13	2	0	0	0	6-6	26.2	15	5	5	1	5-0	29	.167
— New York (N.L.)	1	3	.250	5.59	1.48	42	0	0	0	4	0-0	46.2	56	30	29	3	13-3	43	.298
Major League totals (2 years)	1	5	.167	4.82	1.37	59	0	0	0	5	0-1	71.0	78	39	38	8	19-3	70	.284

BELL, ROB   P

PERSONAL: Born January 17, 1977, in Newburgh, N.Y. ... 6-5/225. ... Throws right, bats right. ... Full name: Robert Allen Bell. ... High school: Marlboro (N.Y.) Central.
TRANSACTIONS/CAREER NOTES: Selected by Atlanta Braves organization in third round of 1995 free-agent draft. ... Traded by Braves with OF Michael Tucker and P Denny Neagle to Cincinnati Reds for 2B Bret Boone and P Mike Remlinger (November 10, 1998). ... Traded by Reds to Texas Rangers for OF Ruben Mateo and 3B Edwin Encarnacion (June 15, 2001). ... Released by Rangers (March 12, 2003). ... Signed by Tampa Bay Devil Rays organization (March 17, 2003). ... On disabled list (May 15-July 9, 2005); included rehabilitation assignment to Durham.
CAREER HITTING: 5-for-60 (.083), 2 R, 2 2B, 0 3B, 0 HR, 0 RBI.

ROB BELL'S PITCHING ZONE

.143	.500	.333
.429	.500	.321
.222	.429	.500

LEFTY-RIGHTY SPLITS

vs.	Avg.	AB	H	2B	3B	HR	RBI	BB	SO	OBP	Slg.
L	.383	60	23	3	1	2	8	7	7	.448	.567
R	.333	54	18	4	0	5	20	5	6	.403	.685

Year Team (League)	W	L	Pct.	ERA	WHIP	G	GS	CG	ShO	Hld.	Sv.-Opp.	IP	H	R	ER	HR	BB-IBB	SO	Avg.
1995— GC Braves (GCL)	1	6	.143	6.88	1.53	10	8	0	0	...	0-...	34.0	38	29	26	2	14-0	33	.279
1996— Eugene (Northwest)	5	6	.455	5.11	1.46	16	16	0	0	...	0-...	81.0	89	49	46	5	29-1	74	.282
1997— Macon (S. Atl.)	14	7	.667	3.68	1.26	27	27	1	0	...	0-...	146.2	144	72	60	15	41-1	140	.258
1998— Danville (Carol.)	7	9	.438	3.28	1.21	28	28	2	0	...	0-...	178.1	169	79	65	8	46-0	197	.252
1999— Chattanooga (Sou.)	3	6	.333	3.13	1.28	12	12	2	1	...	0-...	72.0	75	30	25	7	17-0	68	.276
— GC Reds (GCL)	0	0	...	1.13	0.38	2	2	0	0	...	0-...	8.0	3	1	1	0	0-0	11	.120
2000— Cincinnati (N.L.)	7	8	.467	5.00	1.45	26	26	1	0	0	0-...	140.1	130	84	78	32	73-6	112	.243
— Louisville (Int'l)	4	0	1.000	3.73	1.17	6	6	0	0	...	0-...	41.0	35	18	17	6	13-0	47	.224
2001— Cincinnati (N.L.)	0	5	.000	5.48	1.42	9	9	0	0	0	0-...	44.1	46	28	27	9	17-1	33	.275
— Louisville (Int'l)	2	2	.500	3.33	1.33	5	4	0	0	...	0-...	27.0	32	10	10	4	4-0	26	.288
— Texas (A.L.)	5	5	.500	7.18	1.68	18	18	0	0	0	0-...	105.1	130	87	84	23	47-0	64	.310
2002— Oklahoma (PCL)	5	0	1.000	4.06	1.26	12	11	2	2	...	0-...	75.1	70	36	34	10	25-0	55	.247
— Texas (A.L.)	4	3	.571	6.22	1.57	17	15	0	0	0	0-...	94.0	113	69	65	14	35-0	70	.296
— Tulsa (Texas)	1	0	1.000	0.00	0.50	1	1	0	0	...	0-...	8.0	4	0	0	0	0-5	6	.154
2003— Durham (Int'l)	6	4	.600	4.02	1.20	12	12	0	0	...	0-...	71.2	72	33	32	10	15-1	48	.260
— Tampa Bay (A.L.)	5	4	.556	5.52	1.41	19	18	0	0	0	0-...	101.0	103	64	62	15	39-1	44	.263
2004— Durham (Int'l)	5	0	1.000	1.69	0.96	7	7	0	0	...	0-...	37.1	28	7	7	3	8-0	35	.209
— Tampa Bay (A.L.)	8	8	.500	4.46	1.32	24	19	1	0	0	0-...	123.0	121	71	61	16	41-0	57	.253
2005— Tampa Bay (A.L.)	1	1	.500	8.28	2.12	18	3	0	0	0	0-0	25.0	41	25	23	7	12-0	13	.360
— Durham (Int'l)	1	3	.250	7.71	1.89	22	2	0	0	0	0-1	44.1	64	39	38	12	20-2	26	.344
American League totals (5 years)	23	21	.523	5.92	1.52	86	73	1	0	0	0-0	448.1	508	316	295	77	174-1	248	.284
National League totals (2 years)	7	13	.350	5.12	1.44	35	35	1	0	0	0-0	184.2	176	112	105	41	90-7	145	.251
Major League totals (6 years)	30	34	.469	5.69	1.50	121	108	2	0	0	0-0	633.0	684	428	400	118	264-8	393	.275

BELLHORN, MARK   2B/3B

PERSONAL: Born August 23, 1974, in Boston. ... 6-1/205. ... Bats both, throws right. ... Full name: Mark Christian Bellhorn. ... High school: Oviedo (Fla.). ... College: Auburn.
TRANSACTIONS/CAREER NOTES: Drafted by San Diego Padres organization in 37th round of 1992 free-agent draft; did not sign. ... Selected by Oakland Athletics organization in second round of 1993 free-agent draft. ... Traded by A's to Chicago Cubs for IF Adam Morrissey (November 2, 2001). ... Traded by Cubs to to Colorado Rockies for IF Jose Hernandez (June 20, 2003). ... On disabled list (August 1-23, 2003); included rehabilitation assignment to Colorado Springs. ... Traded by Rockies to Boston Red Sox for a player to be named (December 15, 2003). ... On disabled list (August 2-20, 2004); included rehabilitation assignment to Pawtucket. ... On disabled list (July 18-August 19, 2005); included rehabilitation assignment to Pawtucket. ... Released by Red Sox (August 26, 2005). ... Signed by New York Yankees (August 30, 2005).
2005 GAMES PLAYED BY POSITION (MLB): 2B—85, 3B—4, SS—3.

SCOUTING REPORT *Offense:* Bellhorn bottomed out in 2005. Lost bat speed and continued to strike out at an alarming rate. Is too patient and consistently is hitting in pitcher's counts. Will expand the zone up late in the count. *Defense:* Bellhorn can be overexposed on defense. Has stiff hands. Plays deep to compensate for his lack of range. Doesn't have good lower-body agility and lays back on the ball. Is not fluid making the pivot on the double play. *Outlook:* His value has dropped rapidly. *Grade 4.8*

MARK BELLHORN'S HITTING ZONE

.133	.300	.263
.240	.316	.222
.207	.067	.277

LEFTY-RIGHTY SPLITS

vs.	Avg.	AB	H	2B	3B	HR	RBI	BB	SO	OBP	Slg.
L	.228	101	23	9	0	3	7	15	41	.325	.406
R	.201	199	40	11	0	5	23	37	71	.324	.332

Year Team (League)	Pos.	G	AB	R	H	2B	3B	HR	RBI	BATTING BB	SO	HBP	GDP	SB-CS	Avg.	OBP	SLG	OPS	FIELDING E	Avg.
1995— Modesto (California)	SS	56	229	35	59	12	0	6	31	27	52	4	9	5-2	.258	.346	.389	.735	21	.927
1996— Huntsville (Sou.)	IF	131	468	84	117	24	5	10	71	73	124	4	7	19-2	.250	.353	.387	.740	32	.945
1997— Edmonton (PCL)	2B-SS-3B-DH	70	241	54	79	18	3	11	46	64	59	2	4	6-6	.328	.472	.564	1.037	13	.957

Year	Team (League)	Pos.	G	AB	R	H	2B	3B	HR	RBI	BB	SO	HBP	GDP	SB-CS	Avg.	OBP	SLG	OPS	E	Avg.
																BATTING				FIELDING	
	— Oakland (A.L.) 3B-2B-DH	SS	68	224	33	51	9	1	6	19	32	70	0	1	7-1	.228	.324	.357	.681	9	.956
1998	—Edmonton (PCL) 3B-2B-DH	SS-1B	87	309	57	77	20	4	10	44	62	90	6	8	6-2	.249	.384	.437	.820	11	.965
	— Oakland (A.L.) 3B-DH-SS	2B	11	12	1	1	1	0	0	1	3	4	1	0	2-0	.083	.313	.167	.479	0	1.000
1999	—Ariz. A's (Ariz.)	2B-DH	12	43	11	10	3	0	0	5	11	9	0	1	0-0	.233	.389	.302	.691	0	1.000
	— Midland (Texas)	2B	17	57	12	17	3	0	2	8	11	13	0	2	1-0	.298	.412	.456	.868	2	.973
2000	—Sacramento (PCL) 3B-2B-SS	1B	117	436	111	116	17	11	24	73	94	121	5	5	20-5	.266	.399	.521	.920	15	.956
	— Oakland (A.L.) 2B-3B-SS		9	13	2	2	0	0	0	0	2	6	0	0	0-0	.154	.267	.154	.421	0	1.000
2001	—Sacramento (PCL) OF-2B-SS	3B	43	156	30	42	8	0	12	36	22	60	4	0	3-0	.269	.370	.538	.908	2	.985
	— Oakland (A.L.) 2B-3B-SS	DH-OF	38	74	11	10	1	2	1	4	7	37	0	1	0-0	.135	.210	.243	.453	5	.932
2002	—Chicago (N.L.) 3B-1B	SS-OF	146	445	86	115	24	4	27	56	76	144	6	6	7-5	.258	.374	.512	.886	11	.977
2003	—Chicago (N.L.)	3B	51	139	15	29	7	1	2	22	29	46	1	2	3-3	.209	.341	.317	.658	6	.938
	— Colo. Springs (PCL)	3B-2B	16	54	11	21	5	1	4	16	11	10	0	0	2-0	.389	.485	.741	1.226	1	.981
	— Colorado (N.L.) 2B-3B-SS	OF-1B	48	110	12	26	3	0	0	4	21	32	2	1	2-3	.236	.368	.264	.632	3	.974
2004	—Pawtucket (Int'l)	2B	2	6	1	1	1	0	0	0	0	2	0	0	0-0	.167	.167	.333	.500	1	1.000
	— Boston (A.L.) 2B-3B-DH	SS	138	523	93	138	37	3	17	82	88	*177	5	8	6-1	.264	.373	.444	.817	14	.977
2005	—Boston (A.L.)	2B-SS	85	283	41	61	20	0	7	28	49	109	0	4	3-0	.216	.328	.360	.689	7	.983
	— Pawtucket (Int'l)	2B-DH	16	68	9	12	4	0	2	9	4	24	2	1	0-0	.176	.243	.324	.567	3	.914
	— New York (A.L.) 3B-2B-SS		9	17	2	2	0	0	1	2	3	3	0	0	0-0	.118	.250	.294	.544	1	.958
	American League totals (6 years)		358	1146	183	265	68	6	32	136	184	406	6	14	18-2	.231	.339	.385	.724	36	.973
	National League totals (2 years)		245	694	113	170	34	5	29	82	126	222	8	9	12-11	.245	.366	.434	.800	20	.971
	Major League totals (8 years)		603	1840	296	435	102	11	61	218	310	628	15	23	30-13	.236	.349	.403	.753	56	.972

DIVISION SERIES RECORD

Year	Team (League)	Pos.	G	AB	R	H	2B	3B	HR	RBI	BB	SO	HBP	GDP	SB-CS	Avg.	OBP	SLG	OPS	E	Avg.
2004	—Boston (A.L.)	2B	3	11	2	1	0	0	0	0	5	4	0	0	0-0	.091	.375	.091	.466	0	1.000
2005	—New York (A.L.)		1	0	0	0	0	0	0	0	0	0	0	0	0-0	...	...	...	...	0	...
	Division series totals (2 years)		4	11	2	1	0	0	0	0	5	4	0	0	0-0	.091	.375	.091	.466	0	1.000

CHAMPIONSHIP SERIES RECORD

Year	Team (League)	Pos.	G	AB	R	H	2B	3B	HR	RBI	BB	SO	HBP	GDP	SB-CS	Avg.	OBP	SLG	OPS	E	Avg.
2004	—Boston (A.L.)	2B	7	26	3	5	2	0	2	4	5	11	0	1	0-0	.192	.323	.500	.823	0	1.000

WORLD SERIES RECORD

Year	Team (League)	Pos.	G	AB	R	H	2B	3B	HR	RBI	BB	SO	HBP	GDP	SB-CS	Avg.	OBP	SLG	OPS	E	Avg.
2004	—Boston (A.L.)	2B	4	10	3	3	1	0	1	4	5	2	1	1	0-0	.300	.563	.700	1.263	1	.938

BELLIARD, RONNIE — 2B/3B

PERSONAL: Born April 7, 1975, in Bronx, N.Y. ... 5-8/197. ... Bats right, throws right. ... Full name: Ronald Belliard. ... Name pronounced: BELL-ee-yard. ... High school: Central (Miami). ... Cousin of Rafael Belliard, infielder with two major league teams (1982-98).

TRANSACTIONS/CAREER NOTES: Selected by Milwaukee Brewers organization in eighth round of 1994 free-agent draft. ... On disabled list (August 8-September 30, 2001). ... Signed as a free agent by Colorado Rockies organization (January 19, 2003). ... On disabled list (June 2-23, 2003); included rehabilitation assignment to Colorado Springs. ... Released by Rockies (November 20, 2003). ... Signed by Cleveland Indians (December 26, 2003).

2005 GAMES PLAYED BY POSITION (MLB): 2B—141.

SCOUTING REPORT **Offense:** Belliard is an aggressive fastball hitter. Has a long swing and likes to pull the ball. Will chase bad breaking balls but has a quick bat. Likes the ball up. Is not a good situational hitter and not a good baserunner. **Defense:** Belliard has good agility despite not having a typical middle infielder's body. Plays deeper than any other second baseman but has improved his range. Has quick feet and a strong arm, making him one of the best at turning double plays. Has good instincts. **Outlook:** Belliard is coming off his best offensive year, and he is a very good defensive second baseman. Has increased his value and is looking for a continued offensive improvement in 2006. *Grade 7.7*

RONNIE BELLIARD'S HITTING ZONE

.250	.333	.333
.396	.319	.210
.207	.448	.375

LEFTY-RIGHTY SPLITS

vs.	Avg.	AB	H	2B	3B	HR	RBI	BB	SO	OBP	Slg.
L	.287	150	43	13	0	4	22	14	29	.345	.453
R	.282	386	109	23	1	13	56	21	43	.316	.448

Year	Team (League)	Pos.	G	AB	R	H	2B	3B	HR	RBI	BB	SO	HBP	GDP	SB-CS	Avg.	OBP	SLG	OPS	E	Avg.
																BATTING				FIELDING	
1994	—Ariz. Brewers (Ariz.) 2B-3B-SS		39	143	32	42	7	3	0	27	14	25	3	3	7-0	.294	.366	.385	.751	12	.935
1995	—Beloit (Midw.)	2B-3B	130	461	76	137	28	5	13	76	36	67	7	10	16-12	.297	.356	.464	.821	26	.956
1996	—El Paso (Texas)	2B-DH	109	416	73	116	20	8	3	57	60	51	4	11	26-10	.279	.373	.387	.760	16	.959
1997	—Tucson (PCL)	2B-SS	118	443	80	125	35	4	4	55	61	69	11	13	10-7	.282	.379	.406	.785	26	.959
1998	—Louisville (Int'l)	2B-SS	133	507	114	163	36	7	14	73	69	77	8	17	33-12	.322	.408	.503	.911	14	.979
	— Milwaukee (N.L.)	2B	8	5	1	1	0	0	0	0	0	0	0	0	0-0	.200	.200	.200	.400	1	...
1999	—Louisville (Int'l)	2B	29	108	14	26	4	0	1	8	14	13	1	3	12-2	.241	.331	.306	.636	3	.975
	— Milwaukee (N.L.)	2B-3B-SS	124	457	60	135	29	4	8	58	64	59	0	16	4-5	.295	.379	.429	.808	13	.978
2000	—Milwaukee (N.L.)	2B	152	571	83	150	30	9	8	54	82	84	3	12	7-5	.263	.354	.389	.743	*19	.990
2001	—Milwaukee (N.L.)	2B	101	364	69	96	30	3	11	36	35	65	5	5	5-2	.264	.335	.453	.788	5	.990
2002	—Milwaukee (N.L.)	2B-3B	104	289	30	61	13	0	3	26	18	46	1	9	2-3	.211	.257	.287	.544	10	.963
2003	—Colo. Springs (PCL)	2B	6	19	2	5	1	0	0	0	0	4	0	0	0-0	.263	.263	.316	.579	0	1.000
	— Colorado (N.L.)	2B	116	447	73	124	31	2	8	50	49	71	2	7	7-2	.277	.351	.409	.760	15	.973
2004	—Cleveland (A.L.)	2B-DH	152	599	78	169	48	1	12	70	60	98	2	18	3-2	.282	.348	.426	.774	14	.981

Year Team (League)	Pos.	G	AB	R	H	2B	3B	HR	RBI	BB	SO	HBP	GDP	SB-CS	Avg.	OBP	SLG	OPS	FIELDING E	Avg.
2005—Cleveland (A.L.)	2B	145	536	71	152	36	1	17	78	35	72	1	17	2-2	.284	.325	.450	.774	13	.981
American League totals (2 years)		297	1135	149	321	84	2	29	148	95	170	3	35	5-4	.283	.337	.437	.774	27	.981
National League totals (6 years)		605	2133	316	567	133	18	38	224	248	325	11	49	25-17	.266	.343	.398	.741	62	.977
Major League totals (8 years)		902	3268	465	888	217	20	67	372	343	495	14	84	30-21	.272	.341	.412	.753	89	.978

ALL-STAR GAME RECORD

	G	AB	R	H	2B	3B	HR	RBI	BB	SO	HBP	GDP	SB-CS	Avg.	OBP	SLG	OPS	E	Avg.
All-Star Game totals (1 year)	1	1	0	0	0	0	0	0	0	1	0	0	0-0	.000	.000	.000	.000	0	1.000

BELTRAN, CARLOS   OF

PERSONAL: Born April 24, 1977, in Manati, Puerto Rico. ... 6-1/190. ... Bats both, throws right. ... Full name: Carlos Ivan Beltran. ... Name pronounced: BELL-tron. ... High school: Fernando Callejas (Manati, Puerto Rico).

TRANSACTIONS/CAREER NOTES: Selected by Kansas City Royals organization in second round of 1995 free-agent draft. ... On disabled list (July 4-September 4, 2000); included rehabilitation assignments to GCL Royals, Wilmington and Omaha. ... On disabled list (March 21-April 18, 2003); included rehabilitation assignment to Wichita. ... Traded by Royals to Houston Astros as part of three-team deal in which Royals acquired C John Buck and cash from Astros and P Mike Wood and 3B Mark Teahen from Oakland Athletics and A's acquired P Octavio Dotel from Astros (June 24, 2003). ... Signed as a free agent by New York Mets (January 10, 2005).

HONORS: Named A.L. Rookie Player of the Year by THE SPORTING NEWS (1999). ... Named A.L. Rookie of the Year by Baseball Writers' Association of America (1999).

2005 GAMES PLAYED BY POSITION (MLB): OF—150.

SCOUTING REPORT **Offense:** Beltran didn't live up to expectations as he couldn't duplicate his performance with the Astros in 2004. Has a long stroke but good bat speed, with better power from the left side. Appeared to put too much pressure on himself with runners in scoring position after signing his big contract. Has superior base-stealing instincts and ability. ***Defense:*** Still an elite center fielder, Beltran gets an outstanding jump and has excellent closing speed. Has exceptional agility and outstanding instincts. Knows when to leave his feet. Charges the ball well and is accurate with a quick release. ***Outlook:*** A five-tool player, Beltran often appeared over-anxious at the plate last season but should settle down and produce more favorable numbers in 2006. ***Grade 8.5***

CARLOS BELTRAN'S HITTING ZONE

.194	.344	.367
.338	.303	.303
.273	.231	.180

LEFTY-RIGHTY SPLITS

vs.	Avg.	AB	H	2B	3B	HR	RBI	BB	SO	OBP	Slg.
L	.308	130	40	9	0	2	14	12	26	.364	.423
R	.254	452	115	25	2	14	64	44	70	.320	.412

Year Team (League)	Pos.	G	AB	R	H	2B	3B	HR	RBI	BB	SO	HBP	GDP	SB-CS	Avg.	OBP	SLG	OPS	FIELDING E	Avg.
1995—GC Royals (GCL)	OF	52	180	29	50	9	0	0	23	13	30	3	1	5-3	.278	.332	.328	.659	2	.977
1996—Lansing (Midw.)	OF	11	42	3	6	2	0	0	1	1	11	0	0	1-0	.143	.163	.190	.353	2	.938
—Spokane (N'west)	OF	59	215	29	58	8	3	7	29	31	65	0	4	10-2	.270	.359	.433	.791	7	.938
1997—Wilmington (Caro.)	OF	120	419	57	96	15	4	11	46	46	96	4	10	17-7	.229	.311	.363	.673	8	.968
1998—Wilmington (Caro.)	OF	52	192	32	53	14	0	5	32	25	39	2	2	11-7	.276	.364	.427	.791	2	.983
—Wichita (Texas)	OF	47	182	50	64	13	3	14	44	23	30	1	4	7-1	.352	.427	.687	1.114	4	.960
—Kansas City (A.L.)	OF	14	58	10	16	5	3	0	7	3	12	1	2	3-0	.276	.317	.466	.783	1	.978
1999—Kansas City (A.L.)	OF-DH	156	663	112	194	27	7	22	108	46	123	4	17	27-8	.293	.337	.454	.791	* 12	.972
2000—Kansas City (A.L.)	OF-DH	98	372	49	92	15	4	7	44	35	69	0	12	13-0	.247	.309	.366	.675	6	.975
—GC Royals (GCL)	DH	1	4	3	2	1	0	1	1	1	0	0	0	0-0	.500	.600	1.500	2.100	...	...
—Wilmington (Caro.)	OF	3	13	2	4	0	1	2	6	0	5	0	0	0-0	.308	.308	.923	1.231	0	1.000
—Omaha (PCL)	OF	5	18	4	6	1	0	2	2	3	3	1	0	1-0	.333	.455	.722	1.177	0	1.000
2001—Kansas City (A.L.)	OF-DH	156	617	106	189	32	12	24	101	52	120	5	7	31-1	.306	.362	.514	.876	5	.988
2002—Kansas City (A.L.)	OF-DH	•162	637	114	174	44	7	29	105	71	135	4	12	35-7	.273	.346	.501	.847	7	.983
2003—Wichita (Texas)	OF-DH	3	9	3	3	2	0	0	1	2	3	0	0	1-0	.333	.455	.556	1.010	0	1.000
—Kansas City (A.L.)	OF-DH	141	521	102	160	14	10	26	100	72	81	2	4	41-4	.307	.389	.522	.911	5	.987
2004—Kansas City (A.L.)	OF	69	266	51	74	19	2	15	51	37	44	2	4	14-3	.278	.367	.534	.901	3	.985
—Houston (N.L.)	OF	90	333	70	86	17	7	23	53	55	57	5	4	28-0	.258	.368	.559	.926	5	.977
2005—New York (N.L.)	OF	151	582	83	155	34	2	16	78	56	96	2	9	17-6	.266	.330	.414	.744	4	.990
American League totals (7 years)		795	3134	546	899	156	45	123	516	316	584	18	62	164-23	.287	.352	.483	.835	39	.982
National League totals (2 years)		241	915	153	241	51	9	39	131	111	153	7	13	45-6	.263	.344	.467	.811	9	.985
Major League totals (8 years)		1036	4049	699	1140	207	54	162	647	427	737	25	75	209-29	.282	.350	.479	.829	48	.982

DIVISION SERIES RECORD

Year Team (League)	Pos.	G	AB	R	H	2B	3B	HR	RBI	BB	SO	HBP	GDP	SB-CS	Avg.	OBP	SLG	OPS	E	Avg.
2004—Houston (N.L.)	OF	5	22	9	10	2	0	4	9	1	4	1	0	2-0	.455	.500	1.091	1.591	0	1.000

CHAMPIONSHIP SERIES RECORD

Year Team (League)	Pos.	G	AB	R	H	2B	3B	HR	RBI	BB	SO	HBP	GDP	SB-CS	Avg.	OBP	SLG	OPS	E	Avg.
2004—Houston (N.L.)	OF	7	24	12	10	1	0	4	5	8	4	0	0	4-0	.417	.563	.958	1.521	0	1.000

ALL-STAR GAME RECORD

	G	AB	R	H	2B	3B	HR	RBI	BB	SO	HBP	GDP	SB-CS	Avg.	OBP	SLG	OPS	E	Avg.
All-Star Game totals (2 years)	2	5	1	2	0	0	0	0	0	1	0	1	0-0	.400	.400	.400	.800	0	1.000

BELTRE, ADRIAN   3B

PERSONAL: Born April 7, 1979, in Santo Domingo, Dominican Republic. ... 5-11/220. ... Bats right, throws right. ... Full name: Adrian Perez Beltre. ... Name pronounced: BELL-tray. ... High school: Liceo Maximo Gomez (Santo Domingo, D.R.).

TRANSACTIONS/CAREER NOTES: Signed as a non-drafted free agent by Los Angeles Dodgers organization (July 7, 1994). ... On disabled list (May 28-June 17, 2000). ... On disabled list (March 23-May 12, 2001); included rehabilitation assignments to Vero Beach and Las Vegas. ... Signed as a free agent by Seattle Mariners (December 17, 2004).

2005 GAMES PLAYED BY POSITION (MLB): 3B—155, DH—1.

SCOUTING REPORT *Offense:* Changing leagues really caused Beltre to struggle. Did not pull the ball as much or handle the inside fastball as well. Has good bat speed but saw more breaking balls than in the N.L. Was too quick on breaking balls and too slow on fastballs. Has natural bat speed, however, and is extremely strong; can drive the ball to all fields. Hits off his back foot and has a slight lift to his swing. *Defense:* Beltre's offense may have declined, but his defense did not. Has quick feet, soft hands and good range to his left and right. Is very agile and has a plus arm with excellent accuracy. *Outlook:* Beltre's offense leveled out in 2005, but he should be better in his second year in the A.L. Is capable of 30-plus home runs and 100 RBIs. *Grade 9.0*

ADRIAN BELTRE'S HITTING ZONE

.263	.143	.379
.298	.426	.288
.280	.174	.276

LEFTY-RIGHTY SPLITS

vs.	Avg.	AB	H	2B	3B	HR	RBI	BB	SO	OBP	Slg.
L	.275	149	41	9	0	7	24	8	19	.325	.477
R	.249	454	113	27	1	12	63	30	89	.296	.392

Year	Team (League)	Pos.	G	AB	R	H	2B	3B	HR	RBI	BB	SO	HBP	GDP	SB-CS	Avg.	OBP	SLG	OPS	E	Avg.
1995— Dom. Dodgers (DSL)		3B	62	218	56	67	15	3	8	40	54	26	...	...	2-1	.307	...	.514	...	19	.920
1996— Savannah (S. Atl.)		3B-2B	68	244	48	75	14	3	16	59	35	46	7	7	4-3	.307	.406	.586	.992	19	.912
— San Bern. (Calif.)		3B-DH	63	238	40	62	13	1	10	40	19	44	5	3	3-4	.261	.322	.450	.772	7	.953
1997— Vero Beach (FSL)		3B-OF	123	435	95	138	24	2	26	104	67	66	6	9	25-9	.317	.407	.561	.967	37	.895
1998— San Antonio (Texas)		3B-DH	64	246	49	79	21	2	13	56	39	37	2	3	20-4	.321	.411	.581	.992	17	.910
— Los Angeles (N.L.)		3B-SS	77	195	18	42	9	0	7	22	14	37	3	4	3-1	.215	.278	.369	.648	13	.926
1999— Los Angeles (N.L.)		3B	152	538	84	148	27	5	15	67	61	105	6	4	18-7	.275	.352	.428	.780	• 29	.932
2000— Los Angeles (N.L.)		3B-SS	138	510	71	148	30	5	20	85	56	80	2	13	12-5	.290	.360	.475	.835	23	.944
2001— Vero Beach (FSL)		3B	3	9	0	4	1	0	0	1	2	1	1	0	0-0	.444	.583	.556	1.139	0	1.000
— Las Vegas (PCL)		3B	2	5	2	3	1	0	1	2	2	0	0	0	0-0	.600	.714	1.400	2.114	1	.833
— Los Angeles (N.L.)		3B-SS	126	475	59	126	22	4	13	60	28	82	5	9	13-4	.265	.310	.411	.720	16	.953
2002— Los Angeles (N.L.)		3B	159	587	70	151	26	5	21	75	37	96	4	17	7-5	.257	.303	.426	.729	20	.954
2003— Los Angeles (N.L.)		3B-SS	158	559	50	134	30	2	23	80	37	103	5	13	2-2	.240	.290	.424	.714	19	.967
2004— Los Angeles (N.L.)		3B-SS	156	598	104	200	32	0	* 48	121	53	87	2	15	7-2	.334	.388	.629	1.017	10	.978
2005— Seattle (A.L.)		3B-DH	156	603	69	154	36	1	19	87	38	108	5	15	3-1	.255	.303	.413	.716	14	.967
American League totals (1 year)			156	603	69	154	36	1	19	87	38	108	5	15	3-1	.255	.303	.413	.716	14	.967
National League totals (7 years)			966	3462	456	949	176	18	147	510	286	590	27	75	62-26	.274	.332	.463	.794	130	.951
Major League totals (8 years)			1122	4065	525	1103	212	19	166	597	324	698	32	90	65-27	.271	.327	.455	.783	144	.954

DIVISION SERIES RECORD

Year	Team (League)	Pos.	G	AB	R	H	2B	3B	HR	RBI	BB	SO	HBP	GDP	SB-CS	Avg.	OBP	SLG	OPS	E	Avg.
2004— Los Angeles (N.L.)		3B	4	15	1	4	0	0	0	1	0	3	0	0	0-0	.267	.250	.267	.517	0	1.000

BENITEZ, ARMANDO   P

PERSONAL: Born November 3, 1972, in Ramon Santana, Dominican Republic. ... 6-4/229. ... Throws right, bats right. ... Full name: Armando German Benitez. ... Name pronounced: buh-NEE-tezz.

TRANSACTIONS/CAREER NOTES: Signed as a non-drafted free agent by Baltimore Orioles organization (April 1, 1990). ... On disabled list (April 20-August 26, 1996); included rehabilitation assignments to Bowie and GCL Orioles. ... On suspended list (May 20-28, 1998). ... Traded by Orioles to New York Mets for C Charles Johnson (December 1, 1998). ... Traded by Mets to New York Yankees for Ps Jason Anderson, Ryan Bicondoa and Anderson Garcia (July 18, 2003). ... Traded by Yankees to Seattle Mariners for P Jeff Nelson (August 6, 2003). ... Signed as a free agent by Florida Marlins (January 6, 2004). ... On disabled list (July 23-August 12, 2004). ... Signed as a free agent by San Francisco Giants (November 30, 2004). ... On disabled list (April 27-August 15, 2005); included rehabilitaion assignment to San Jose.

HONORS: Named N.L. co-Reliever of the Year by THE SPORTING NEWS (2001).

CAREER HITTING: 0-for-8 (.000), 0 R, 0 2B, 0 3B, 0 HR, 2 RBI.

SCOUTING REPORT *Throws:* Benitez has three pitches—a fastball at 90-95 mph, a slider at 85-88 and a split-finger fastball at 87-90. *Tendencies:* He throws a heavy fastball that bores in on hitters. Is not afraid to challenge hitters on the inner half of the plate. Power slider runs sharply away from righthanders and jams lefthanders. Splitter is an out pitch and has improved. *Outlook:* Barring offseason complications from the hamstring injuries he suffered early last season, Benitez should again be one of the better closers in the league in 2006. *Grade 9*

ARMANDO BENITEZ'S PITCHING ZONE

.500	.333	.250
.150	.333	.316
.154	.333	.083

LEFTY-RIGHTY SPLITS

vs.	Avg.	AB	H	2B	3B	HR	RBI	BB	SO	OBP	Slg.
L	.212	52	11	2	0	4	9	10	8	.339	.481
R	.246	57	14	5	0	1	7	6	15	.308	.386

Year	Team (League)	W	L	Pct.	ERA	WHIP	G	GS	CG	ShO	Hld.	Sv.-Opp.	IP	H	R	ER	HR	BB-IBB	SO	Avg.
1990— Dominican Orioles/W.S. (DSL)		3	1	.750	2.72	1.37	19	0	0	0	...	8-...	43.0	39	23	13	...	20-...	34	...
1991— GC Orioles (GCL)		3	2	.600	2.72	1.27	14	3	0	0	...	0-...	36.1	35	16	11	2	11-0	33	.252
1992— Bluefield (Appal.)		1	2	.333	4.31	1.85	25	0	0	0	...	5-...	31.1	35	31	15	1	23-0	37	.276
1993— Albany (S. Atl.)		5	1	.833	1.52	0.94	40	0	0	0	...	14-...	53.1	31	10	9	2	19-0	83	.168
— Frederick (Carolina)		3	0	1.000	0.66	0.80	12	0	0	0	...	4-...	13.2	7	1	1	0	4-0	29	.149
1994— Bowie (East.)		8	4	.667	3.14	1.12	53	0	0	0	...	16-...	71.2	41	29	25	6	39-0	106	.160
— Baltimore (A.L.)		0	0	...	0.90	1.20	3	0	0	0	0	0-0	10.0	8	1	1	0	4-0	14	.216
1995— Baltimore (A.L.)		1	5	.167	5.66	1.55	44	0	0	0	6	2-5	47.2	37	33	30	8	37-2	56	.213
— Rochester (Int'l)		2	2	.500	1.25	0.78	17	0	0	0	...	8-...	21.2	10	4	3	2	7-0	37	.135
1996— Baltimore (A.L.)		1	0	1.000	3.77	0.91	18	0	0	0	1	4-5	14.1	7	6	6	2	6-0	20	.143
— Bowie (East.)		0	0	...	4.50	1.17	4	4	0	0	...	0-...	6.0	7	3	3	0	4-0	8	.292
— GC Orioles (GCL)		1	0	1.000	0.00	0.50	2	2	0	0	...	0-...	2.0	1	0	0	0	0-0	5	.143
— Rochester (Int'l)		0	0	...	2.25	1.00	2	0	0	0	...	1-...	4.0	3	1	1	0	1-0	5	.188
1997— Baltimore (A.L.)		4	5	.444	2.45	1.25	71	0	0	0	20	9-10	73.1	49	22	20	7	43-5	106	.191
1998— Baltimore (A.L.)		5	6	.455	3.82	1.27	71	0	0	0	3	22-26	68.1	48	29	29	10	39-2	87	.195
1999— New York (N.L.)		4	3	.571	1.85	1.04	77	0	0	0	17	22-28	78.0	40	17	16	4	41-4	128	.148
2000— New York (N.L.)		4	4	.500	2.61	1.01	76	0	0	0	...	41-46	76.0	39	24	22	9	38-2	106	.148
2001— New York (N.L.)		6	4	.600	3.77	1.30	73	0	0	0	...	43-46	76.1	59	32	32	12	40-6	93	.214

Year Team (League)	W	L	Pct.	ERA	WHIP	G	GS	CG	ShO	Hld.	Sv.-Opp.	IP	H	R	ER	HR	BB-IBB	SO	Avg.
2002—New York (N.L.)	1	0	1.000	2.27	1.05	62	0	0	0	0	33-37	67.1	46	20	17	8	25-0	79	.190
2003—New York (N.L.)	3	3	.500	3.10	1.32	45	0	0	0	0	21-28	49.1	41	18	17	5	24-1	50	.223
—New York (A.L.)	1	1	.500	1.93	1.50	9	0	0	0	4	0-0	9.1	8	4	2	0	6-1	10	.235
—Seattle (A.L.)	0	0	...	3.14	1.47	15	0	0	0	1	0-1	14.1	10	5	5	1	11-1	15	.189
2004—Florida (N.L.)	2	2	.500	1.29	0.82	64	0	0	0	0	• 47-51	69.2	36	11	10	6	21-4	62	.152
2005—San Jose (Calif.)	0	0	...	0.00	0.50	2	2	0	0	0	0-0	2.0	0	0	0	0	1-0	0	.000
—San Francisco (N.L.)	2	3	.400	4.50	1.37	30	0	0	0	0	19-23	30.0	25	17	15	5	16-0	23	.229
American League totals (6 years)	12	17	.414	3.53	1.32	231	0	0	0	35	37-47	237.1	167	100	93	28	146-11	308	.198
National League totals (7 years)	22	19	.537	2.60	1.10	427	0	0	0	17	226-259	446.2	286	139	129	50	205-17	541	.181
Major League totals (12 years)	34	36	.486	2.92	1.18	658	0	0	0	52	263-306	684.0	453	239	222	78	351-28	849	.187

DIVISION SERIES RECORD

Year Team (League)	W	L	Pct.	ERA	WHIP	G	GS	CG	ShO	Hld.	Sv.-Opp.	IP	H	R	ER	HR	BB-IBB	SO	Avg.
1996—Baltimore (A.L.)	2	0	1.000	2.25	0.75	3	0	0	0	0	0-1	4.0	1	1	1	1	2-0	6	.083
1997—Baltimore (A.L.)	0	0	...	3.00	1.67	3	0	0	0	2	0-0	3.0	3	1	1	1	2-0	4	.250
1999—New York (N.L.)	0	0	...	0.00	1.29	2	0	0	0	0	0-1	2.1	2	0	0	0	1-1	2	.250
2000—New York (N.L.)	1	0	1.000	6.00	1.67	2	0	0	0	0	0-1	3.0	4	2	2	1	1-1	3	.308
Division series totals (4 years)	3	0	1.000	2.92	1.30	10	0	0	0	2	0-3	12.1	10	4	4	3	6-2	15	.222

CHAMPIONSHIP SERIES RECORD

Year Team (League)	W	L	Pct.	ERA	WHIP	G	GS	CG	ShO	Hld.	Sv.-Opp.	IP	H	R	ER	HR	BB-IBB	SO	Avg.
1996—Baltimore (A.L.)	0	0	...	7.71	2.57	3	0	0	0	0	1-2	2.1	3	2	2	2	3-1	2	.300
1997—Baltimore (A.L.)	0	2	.000	12.00	2.33	4	0	0	0	0	0-1	3.0	3	4	4	2	4-0	6	.250
1999—New York (N.L.)	0	0	...	1.35	0.75	5	0	0	0	0	1-1	6.2	3	1	1	0	2-0	9	.136
2000—New York (N.L.)	0	0	...	0.00	1.67	3	0	0	0	0	1-1	3.0	3	2	0	0	2-0	2	.231
Champ. series totals (4 years)	0	2	.000	4.20	1.53	15	0	0	0	0	3-5	15.0	12	9	7	4	11-1	19	.211

WORLD SERIES RECORD

Year Team (League)	W	L	Pct.	ERA	WHIP	G	GS	CG	ShO	Hld.	Sv.-Opp.	IP	H	R	ER	HR	BB-IBB	SO	Avg.
2000—New York (N.L.)	0	0	...	3.00	1.67	3	0	0	0	0	1-2	3.0	3	1	1	0	2-0	2	.250

BENNETT, GARY   C

PERSONAL: Born April 17, 1972, in Waukegan, Ill. ... 6-0/208. ... Bats right, throws right. ... Full name: Gary David Bennett. ... High school: Waukegan East (Ill.).
TRANSACTIONS/CAREER NOTES: Selected by Philadelphia Phillies organization in 11th round of 1990 free-agent draft. ... Signed as a free agent by Boston Red Sox organization (February 10, 1997). ... Signed as a free agent by Phillies organization (December 27, 1997). ... Traded by Phillies to New York Mets for C Todd Pratt (July 23, 2001). ... Traded by Mets to Colorado Rockies for a player to be named (August 24, 2001); Mets acquired OF Endy Chavez to complete deal (December 27, 2001). ... Signed as a free agent by San Diego Padres (December 23, 2002). ... On disabled list (April 17-May 23, 2003). ... Signed as a free agent by Milwaukee Brewers organization (December 22, 2003). ... Signed as a free agent by Montreal Expos (November 29, 2004). ... Expos franchise transferred to Washington, D.C., and renamed Washington Nationals for 2005 season (December 3, 2004).
2005 GAMES PLAYED BY POSITION (MLB): C—64.

SCOUTING REPORT Bennett is a solid backup. Has never hit much; has a slow bat and is not a good breaking-ball hitter. Sits on the fastball and likes the ball up to take it the other way. Has arm strength but is a little too deliberate with his throws sometimes. Drops more pitches than he should. Best asset is his makeup and willingness to block the plate. He's not afraid of contact.
Grade 4.8

GARY BENNETT'S HITTING ZONE

.000	.167	.000
.238	.476	.185
.276	.182	.455

LEFTY-RIGHTY SPLITS

vs.	Avg.	AB	H	2B	3B	HR	RBI	BB	SO	OBP	Slg.
L	.198	81	16	3	0	1	7	8	10	.261	.272
R	.237	118	28	4	0	0	14	13	27	.323	.271

Year Team (League)	Pos.	G	AB	R	H	2B	3B	HR	RBI	BB	SO	HBP	GDP	SB-CS	Avg.	OBP	SLG	OPS	E	Avg.
1990—Martinsville (App.)	C	16	52	3	14	2	1	0	10	4	15	0	0	0-1	.269	.316	.346	.662	3	.965
1991—Martinsville (App.)	C	41	136	15	32	7	0	1	16	17	26	5	5	0-1	.235	.340	.309	.648	2	.994
1992—Batavia (NY-Penn)	C	47	146	22	30	2	0	0	12	15	27	2	1	2-1	.205	.288	.219	.508	2	.994
1993—Spartanburg (SAL)	C	42	126	18	32	4	1	0	15	12	22	1	2	0-2	.254	.321	.302	.623	2	.992
—Clearwater (FSL)	C	17	55	5	18	0	0	1	6	3	10	1	0	0-1	.327	.373	.382	.755	0	1.000
1994—Clearwater (FSL)	C	19	55	6	13	3	0	0	10	8	6	0	1	0-0	.236	.328	.291	.619	1	.991
—Reading (East.)	C	63	208	13	48	9	0	3	22	14	26	0	6	0-1	.231	.276	.317	.593	2	.995
1995—Reading (East.)	C-DH	86	271	27	64	11	0	4	40	22	36	3	12	0-0	.236	.299	.321	.620	4	.994
—Scran./W.B. (I.L.)	C	7	20	1	3	0	0	0	1	2	2	0	0	0-0	.150	.227	.150	.377	0	1.000
—Philadelphia (N.L.)		1	1	0	0	0	0	0	0	0	1	0	0	0-0	.000	.000	.000	.000	...	...
1996—Scran./W.B. (I.L.)	C	91	286	37	71	15	1	8	37	24	43	3	10	1-0	.248	.310	.392	.702	7	.988
—Philadelphia (N.L.)	C	6	16	0	4	0	0	0	1	2	6	0	0	0-0	.250	.333	.250	.583	0	1.000
1997—Pawtucket (Int'l)	C-1B	71	224	16	48	7	1	4	22	18	39	2	10	1-1	.214	.278	.308	.586	8	.986
1998—Scran./W.B. (I.L.)	C-DH-1B	86	282	33	72	18	0	10	40	25	46	2	6	0-0	.255	.316	.426	.742	1	.998
—Philadelphia (N.L.)	C	9	31	4	9	0	0	0	3	5	5	0	1	0-0	.290	.378	.290	.669	0	1.000
1999—Philadelphia (N.L.)	C	36	88	7	24	4	0	1	21	4	11	0	7	0-0	.273	.298	.352	.650	4	.971
2000—Scran./W.B. (I.L.)	C	92	317	47	97	24	0	12	52	40	44	7	9	1-0	.306	.393	.495	.889	2	.996
—Philadelphia (N.L.)	C	31	74	8	18	5	0	2	5	13	15	2	2	0-0	.243	.371	.392	.763	1	.995
2001—Philadelphia (N.L.)	C	26	75	8	16	3	1	1	6	9	10	0	0	0-0	.213	.294	.320	.614	2	.987
—New York (N.L.)		1	1	0	1	0	0	0	0	0	0	0	0	0-0	1.000	1.000	1.000	2.000	...	...
—Norfolk (Int'l)	C-3B	20	67	7	20	5	0	2	14	4	12	1	0	0-0	.299	.342	.463	.805	0	1.000
—Colorado (N.L.)	C	19	55	7	15	3	0	1	4	3	5	1	0	0-0	.273	.317	.382	.698	0	1.000
2002—Colorado (N.L.)	C	90	291	26	77	10	2	4	26	15	45	6	10	1-3	.265	.314	.354	.668	4	.992
2003—San Diego (N.L.)	C	96	307	26	73	15	0	2	42	24	48	2	3	3-0	.238	.296	.306	.602	2	.993
2004—Milwaukee (N.L.)	C	75	219	18	49	14	0	3	20	22	32	2	1	0-1	.224	.297	.329	.626	3	.993
2005—Washington (N.L.)	C	68	199	11	44	7	0	1	21	21	37	1	7	0-0	.221	.298	.271	.569	6	.986
Major League totals (10 years)		458	1357	115	330	61	3	15	149	118	224	15	43	5-4	.243	.308	.326	.634	22	.991

BENOIT, JOAQUIN   P

PERSONAL: Born July 26, 1977, in Santiago, Dominican Republic. ... 6-3/220. ... Throws right, bats right. ... Full name: Joaquin Antonio Benoit. ... Name pronounced: ben-WUH.

TRANSACTIONS/CAREER NOTES: Signed as a non-drafted free agent by Texas Rangers organization (May 20, 1996). ... On disabled list (June 1-22, 2003); included rehabilitation assignment to Oklahoma. ... On disabled list (August 23-September 7, 2004); included rehabilitation assignment to Frisco. ... On disabled list (March 25-May 2 and June 12-28, 2005); included rehabilitation assignments to Okalahoma and AZL Rangers.

CAREER HITTING: 0-for-9 (.000), 1 R, 0 2B, 0 3B, 0 HR, 0 RBI.

SCOUTING REPORT
Throws: He attacks hitters with a 90-95 mph fastball, an 83-86 slider and a changeup. Also throws an occasional curveball. *Tendencies:* Benoit is a strikeout pitcher with a deceptive motion. Best pitch is the fastball, which comes in heavy and with a good sinking action. Has problems staying on top of the ball at times and his stuff flattens out. Slider has improved. Has excellent motion and movement with a circle change that is a good complement to his above-average fastball. Has some problems with righthanders but his changeup tends to nullify lefties. Should think about abandoning his curve. *Outlook:* Benoit has more value as a starter, but he pitches better in relief. **Grade 6.4**

JOAQUIN BENOIT'S PITCHING ZONE

.167	.409	.200
.224	.227	.205
.235	.286	.263

LEFTY-RIGHTY SPLITS

vs.	Avg.	AB	H	2B	3B	HR	RBI	BB	SO	OBP	Slg.
L	.227	163	37	3	0	7	17	24	39	.326	.374
R	.196	163	32	6	1	2	17	14	39	.267	.282

Year	Team (League)	W	L	Pct.	ERA	WHIP	G	GS	CG	ShO	Hld.	Sv.-Opp.	IP	H	R	ER	HR	BB-IBB	SO	Avg.
1996—	Dom. Rangers (DSL)	6	5	.545	2.28	1.15	14	13	2	1	...	0-...	75.0	63	26	19	...	23-...	63	...
1997—	GC Rangers (GCL)	3	3	.500	2.05	1.16	10	10	1	0	...	0-...	44.0	40	14	10	0	11-0	38	.244
1998—	Savannah (S. Atl.)	4	3	.571	3.83	1.21	15	1	0	0	...	0-...	80.0	79	41	34	8	18-0	68	.252
1999—	Charlotte (Fla. St.)	7	4	.636	5.31	1.59	22	22	0	0	...	0-...	105.0	117	67	62	5	50-0	83	.283
2000—	Tulsa (Texas)	4	4	.500	3.83	1.25	16	16	0	0	...	0-...	82.1	73	40	35	6	30-0	72	.237
2001—	Tulsa (Texas)	1	0	1.000	3.32	1.34	4	4	0	0	...	0-...	21.2	23	8	8	1	6-0	23	.264
	—Oklahoma (PCL)	9	5	.643	4.19	1.42	24	24	1	1	...	0-...	131.0	113	63	61	14	73-0	142	.234
	—Texas (A.L.)	0	0	...	10.80	2.20	1	1	0	0	0	0-0	5.0	6	6	6	3	3-0	4	.364
2002—	Oklahoma (PCL)	8	4	.667	3.56	1.13	16	16	0	0	...	0-...	98.2	74	42	39	8	37-0	103	.204
	—Texas (A.L.)	4	5	.444	5.31	1.76	17	13	0	0	0	1-1	84.2	91	51	50	6	58-2	59	.277
	—Charlotte (Fla. St.)	0	0	...	0.00	0.80	1	1	0	0	...	0-...	5.0	1	0	0	0	3-0	8	.059
2003—	Oklahoma (PCL)	2	1	.667	3.82	1.20	6	6	0	0	...	0-...	33.0	28	17	14	3	11-0	31	.231
	—Texas (A.L.)	8	5	.615	5.49	1.43	25	17	0	0	0	0-0	105.0	99	67	64	23	51-0	87	.246
2004—	Frisco (Texas)	0	0	...	0.00	0.00	1	1	0	0	...	0-...	2.0	0	0	0	0	0-0	6	.000
	—Texas (A.L.)	3	5	.375	5.68	1.40	28	15	0	0	0	0-0	103.0	113	67	65	19	31-0	95	.279
2005—	Oklahoma (PCL)	0	0	.000	5.40	1.60	3	1	0	0	0	0-0	5.0	4	3	3	1	4-0	2	.235
	—Arizona Rangers (AZL)	0	0	...	0.00	0.50	1	1	0	0	...	0-...	2.0	0	0	0	0	1-0	4	.000
	—Texas (A.L.)	4	4	.500	3.72	1.23	32	9	0	0	0	5	0-0	87.0	69	39	36	9	38-0	78	.212
Major League totals (5 years)		**19**	**19**	**.500**	**5.17**	**1.46**	**103**	**55**	**0**	**0**	**5**	**1-1**	**384.2**	**380**	**230**	**221**	**60**	**181-2**	**323**	**.255**

BENSON, KRIS   P

PERSONAL: Born November 7, 1974, in Superior, Wis. ... 6-4/195. ... Throws right, bats right. ... Full name: Kristin James Benson. ... High school: Spayberry (Marietta, Ga.). ... College: Clemson.

TRANSACTIONS/CAREER NOTES: Selected by Pittsburgh Pirates organization in first round (first pick overall) of 1996 free-agent draft. ... On disabled list (March 31, 2001-entire season). ... On disabled list (March 22-May 13, 2002); included rehabilitation assignments to Nashville and Altoona. ... On disabled list (July 28, 2003-remainder of season). ... Traded by Pirates with IF Jeff Keppinger to New York Mets for 3B Ty Wigginton, IF Jose Bautista and P Matt Peterson (July 30, 2004). ... On disabled list (April 4-May 5, 2005); included rehabilitation assignment to St. Lucie.

CAREER HITTING: 40-for-307 (.130), 22 R, 7 2B, 0 3B, 0 HR, 20 RBI.

SCOUTING REPORT
Throws: He hits 90-92 mph with his fastball. Also throws a slider and changeup. *Tendencies:* Benson has good sinking action on his fastball, but he isn't throwing as hard as he used to. Has a loose arm and a good delivery. Has a quick-breaking slider and can turn his changeup over and sink it. Throws strikes. *Outlook:* Benson last season proved he was healthy, but his stuff has declined and New York might not suit his makeup. Might never be as good as he was in Pittsburgh. **Grade 7.2**

KRIS BENSON'S PITCHING ZONE

.360	.150	.156
.305	.233	.290
.197	.303	.294

LEFTY-RIGHTY SPLITS

vs.	Avg.	AB	H	2B	3B	HR	RBI	BB	SO	OBP	Slg.
L	.268	313	84	20	1	12	39	31	35	.334	.454
R	.240	363	87	13	0	12	37	18	60	.281	.375

Year	Team (League)	W	L	Pct.	ERA	WHIP	G	GS	CG	ShO	Hld.	Sv.-Opp.	IP	H	R	ER	HR	BB-IBB	SO	Avg.
1997—	Lynchburg (Caro.)	5	2	.714	2.58	1.04	10	10	0	0	...	0-...	59.1	49	20	17	1	13-0	72	.221
	—Carolina (Southern)	3	5	.375	4.98	1.65	14	14	0	0	...	0-...	68.2	81	49	38	11	32-1	66	.289
1998—	Nashville (PCL)	8	10	.444	5.37	1.36	28	28	1	1	...	0-...	156.0	162	102	93	26	50-5	129	.269
1999—	Pittsburgh (N.L.)	11	14	.440	4.07	1.36	31	31	2	0	0	0-0	196.2	184	105	89	16	83-5	139	.249
2000—	Pittsburgh (N.L.)	10	12	.455	3.85	1.34	32	32	2	1	0	0-0	217.2	206	104	93	24	86-5	184	.249
2001—	Pittsburgh (N.L.)				Did not play.															
2002—	Nashville (PCL)	0	2	.000	1.53	0.91	4	4	0	0	...	0-...	17.2	8	4	3	1	8-0	25	.133
	—Altoona (East.)	1	0	1.000	1.29	0.71	1	1	0	0	...	0-...	7.0	5	1	1	1	0-0	7	.208
	—Pittsburgh (N.L.)	9	6	.600	4.70	1.55	25	25	0	0	0	0-0	130.1	152	76	68	18	50-8	79	.295
2003—	Pittsburgh (N.L.)	5	9	.357	4.97	1.55	18	18	0	0	0	0-0	105.0	127	67	58	14	36-4	83	.295
2004—	Pittsburgh (N.L.)	8	8	.500	4.22	1.37	20	20	0	0	0	0-0	132.1	137	69	62	7	44-5	83	.272
	—New York (N.L.)	4	4	.500	4.50	1.21	11	11	0	0	0	0-0	68.0	65	37	34	8	17-3	51	.244
2005—	St. Lucie (Fla. St.)	0	0	.000	0.00	0.00	1	1	0	0	0	0-0	3.0	0	0	0	0	0-0	4	.000
	—New York (N.L.)	10	8	.556	4.13	1.26	28	28	0	0	0	0-0	174.1	171	86	80	24	49-5	95	.253
Major League totals (6 years)		**57**	**61**	**.483**	**4.25**	**1.37**	**165**	**165**	**5**	**2**	**0**	**0-0**	**1024.1**	**1042**	**544**	**484**	**111**	**365-35**	**699**	**.263**

BENTZ, CHAD   P

PERSONAL: Born May 5, 1980, in Seward, Alaska. ... 6-2/215. ... Throws left, bats right. ... Full name: Chad Robert Bentz. ... High school: Juneau-Douglas (Alaska). ... College: Long Beach State.

TRANSACTIONS/CAREER NOTES: Selected by New York Yankees organization in 34th round of 1999 free-agent draft; did not sign. ... Selected by Montreal Expos organization in seventh round of 2001 free-agent draft. ... Expos franchise transferred to Washington, D.C., for 2005 season and renamed Washington Nationals (December 3, 2004). ... Released by Nationals (December 13, 2004). ... Signed by Florida Marlins organization (December 18, 2004).

CAREER HITTING: 1-for-2 (.500), 0 R, 0 2B, 0 3B, 0 HR, 0 RBI.

LEFTY-RIGHTY SPLITS

vs.	Avg.	AB	H	2B	3B	HR	RBI	BB	SO	OBP	Slg.
L	.333	6	2	0	0	0	0	0	0	.333	.333
R	.750	8	6	1	1	2	7	0	0	.750	1.875

Year Team (League)	W	L	Pct.	ERA	WHIP	G	GS	CG	ShO	Hld.	Sv.-Opp.	IP	H	R	ER	HR	BB-IBB	SO	Avg.
2001— Vermont (NYP)	1	3	.250	4.91	1.36	8	8	0	0	...	0-...	36.2	39	23	20	2	11-0	38	.264
2002— Brevard County (FSL)	0	1	.000	3.64	1.48	23	0	0	0	...	5-...	29.2	30	14	12	1	14-2	34	.259
2003— Harrisburg (East.)	1	4	.200	2.55	1.31	52	0	0	0	...	16-...	84.2	72	31	24	4	39-2	56	.241
2004— Montreal (N.L.)	0	3	.000	5.86	1.66	36	0	0	0	5	0-0	27.2	23	19	18	5	23-3	18	.228
— Edmonton (PCL)	0	0	...	3.60	1.60	5	0	0	0	...	0-...	5.0	5	2	2	1	3-0	2	.278
— Harrisburg (East.)	0	1	.000	8.59	1.77	5	1	0	0	...	1-...	7.1	5	7	7	2	8-0	2	.200
2005— Carolina (Southern)	1	0	1.000	1.29	1.43	7	0	0	0	2	0-0	7.0	6	3	1	0	4-0	5	.222
— Florida (N.L.)	0	0	...	31.50	4.00	4	0	0	0	2	0-0	2.0	8	7	7	2	0-0	0	.571
— Albuquerque (PCL)	0	1	.000	4.01	1.49	31	0	0	0	8	1-2	33.2	36	20	15	4	14-0	32	.273
Major League totals (2 years)	0	3	.000	7.58	1.82	40	0	0	0	7	0-0	29.2	31	26	25	7	23-3	18	.270

BERGMANN, JAY   P

PERSONAL: Born September 25, 1981, in Neptune, N.J. ... 6-4/190. ... Throws right, bats right. ... Full name: Jason Chris Bergmann. ... College: Rutgers.

TRANSACTIONS/CAREER NOTES: Selected by Montreal Expos organization in 11th round of 2002 free-agent draft. ... Expos franchise transferred to Washington, D.C., and renamed Washington Nationals for 2005 season (December 3, 2004).

CAREER HITTING: 1-for-3 (.333), 2 R, 0 2B, 0 3B, 0 HR, 0 RBI.

JAY BERGMANN'S PITCHING ZONE

.000	.000	.100
.429	.167	.364
.000	.250	.000

LEFTY-RIGHTY SPLITS

vs.	Avg.	AB	H	2B	3B	HR	RBI	BB	SO	OBP	Slg.
L	.355	31	11	4	0	0	4	6	7	.447	.484
R	.077	39	3	0	0	1	2	5	14	.217	.154

Year Team (League)	W	L	Pct.	ERA	WHIP	G	GS	CG	ShO	Hld.	Sv.-Opp.	IP	H	R	ER	HR	BB-IBB	SO	Avg.
2002— Vermont (NYP)	7	4	.636	2.89	1.13	14	14	0	0	...	0-...	71.2	48	27	23	4	33-0	57	.194
2003— Savannah (S. Atl.)	6	11	.353	4.29	1.48	23	22	1	1	...	0-...	109.0	108	57	52	8	53-0	82	.264
2004— Savannah (S. Atl.)	3	7	.300	4.85	1.55	13	13	0	0	...	0-...	65.0	67	43	35	6	34-0	58	.269
— Brevard County (FSL)	3	2	.600	1.14	1.20	24	0	0	0	...	8-...	31.2	20	7	4	0	18-3	28	.177
— Harrisburg (East.)	0	2	.000	9.00	2.25	2	0	0	0	...	0-...	4.0	7	5	4	3	2-1	3	.368
2005— Harrisburg (East.)	2	0	1.000	1.22	1.16	21	0	0	0	...	5-6	37.0	27	7	5	3	16-1	37	.201
— New Orleans (PCL)	3	2	.600	3.16	1.05	20	0	0	0	...	2-5	37.0	26	15	13	5	13-1	39	.203
— Washington (N.L.)	2	0	1.000	2.75	1.27	15	1	0	0	...	0-0	19.2	14	6	6	1	11-1	21	.200
Major League totals (1 year)	2	0	1.000	2.75	1.27	15	1	0	0	...	0-0	19.2	14	6	6	1	11-1	21	.200

BERGOLLA, WILLIAM   2B

PERSONAL: Born February 4, 1983, in Carabobo, Venezuela. ... 6-0/175. ... Bats right, throws right. ... Full name: William Jose Bergolla. ... Name pronounced: ber-GOAL-ah

TRANSACTIONS/CAREER NOTES: Signed as a non-drafted free agent by Cincinnati Reds organization (November 15, 1999).

2005 GAMES PLAYED BY POSITION (MLB): 2B—9, SS—1.

LEFTY-RIGHTY SPLITS

vs.	Avg.	AB	H	2B	3B	HR	RBI	BB	SO	OBP	Slg.
L	.214	14	3	0	0	0	0	0	4	.214	.214
R	.083	24	2	0	0	0	1	0	6	.083	.083

Year Team (League)	Pos.	G	AB	R	H	2B	3B	HR	RBI	BB	SO	HBP	GDP	SB-CS	Avg.	OBP	SLG	OPS	E	Avg.
2000— Cagua (VSL)		13	43	6	16	3	2	0	5	8	3	1	1	1-1	.372	.481	.535	1.016	...	...
— GC Reds (GCL)	2B-3B-SS	8	22	2	4	0	0	0	4	4	2	0	0	3-1	.182	.308	.182	.490	1	.964
2001— Billings (Pion.)	2B-SS	57	232	47	75	5	3	4	24	24	21	2	1	22-7	.323	.387	.422	.809	21	.924
2002— Dayton (Midw.)	2B-SS	68	274	38	68	13	1	3	23	16	36	1	6	13-2	.248	.291	.336	.627	12	.959
— Billings (Pion.)	2B-SS	53	210	35	74	9	1	3	29	24	26	0	2	16-5	.352	.408	.448	.856	17	.935
2003— Potomac (Carol.)	2B-SS	128	523	77	142	25	3	2	31	29	59	1	13	52-18	.272	.309	.342	.651	27	.959
2004— Chattanooga (Sou.)	2B-SS	116	466	79	132	26	1	4	38	40	63	3	14	36-6	.283	.342	.369	.711	19	.800
2005— Cincinnati (N.L.)	2B-SS	17	38	3	5	0	0	0	1	0	10	0	1	0-0	.132	.132	.132	.263	0	1.000
— Louisville (Int'l)	2B-SS-DH	98	400	59	117	23	5	2	38	19	39	1	12	16-3	.293	.325	.390	.715	13	.970
Major League totals (1 year)		17	38	3	5	0	0	0	1	0	10	0	1	0-0	.132	.132	.132	.263	0	1.000

BERKMAN, LANCE   OF/1B

PERSONAL: Born February 10, 1976, in Waco, Texas. ... 6-1/220. ... Bats both, throws left. ... Full name: William Lance Berkman. ... High school: Canyon (New Braunfels, Texas). ... College: Rice.

TRANSACTIONS/CAREER NOTES: Selected by Houston Astros organization in first round (16th pick overall) of 1997 free-agent draft. ... On disabled list (March 30-May 6, 2005); included rehabilitation assignment to Round Rock.

2005 GAMES PLAYED BY POSITION (MLB): 1B—96, OF—49, DH—3.

SCOUTING REPORT Offense: Berkman has good power from both sides of the plate. Tends to hit down on the ball and has become very efficient slapping the ball over the short left field porch in Houston. Has better bat speed and is a better overall hitter from his unnatural left side. Handles the breaking ball well and keeps his hands back so he is rarely fooled. Is not a very good runner. **Defense:** He gets deceptive jumps on the ball, but doesn't have good closing speed or range laterally. Can make unexpected plays, considering his body type. Below-average arm strength and slow release make him a better fit for left than right field. **Outlook:** Berkman is a good situational hitter who uses the entire field. Could play first base in 2006 but needs a lot of work there. **Grade 9.1**

LANCE BERKMAN'S HITTING ZONE

.259	.348	.250
.329	.451	.330
.262	.242	.303

LEFTY-RIGHTY SPLITS

vs.	Avg.	AB	H	2B	3B	HR	RBI	BB	SO	OBP	Slg.
L	.294	126	37	8	0	3	16	26	16	.416	.429
R	.292	342	100	26	1	21	66	65	56	.409	.558

Year Team (League)	Pos.	G	AB	R	H	2B	3B	HR	RBI	BB	SO	HBP	GDP	SB-CS	Avg.	OBP	SLG	OPS	E	Avg.
1997—Kissimmee (Fla. St.)	OF-DH	53	184	31	54	10	0	12	35	37	38	2	2	2-1	.293	.417	.543	.961	0	1.000
1998—Jackson (Texas)	OF-DH	122	425	82	130	34	0	24	89	85	82	4	12	6-4	.306	.424	.555	.979	4	.980
—New Orleans (PCL)	OF	17	59	14	16	4	0	6	13	12	16	2	1	0-0	.271	.411	.644	1.055	0	1.000
1999—New Orleans (PCL)	OF-1B	64	226	42	73	20	0	8	49	39	47	0	10	7-1	.323	.419	.518	.937	4	.972
—Houston (N.L.)	OF-1B	34	93	10	22	2	0	4	15	12	21	0	2	5-1	.237	.321	.387	.708	2	.956
2000—New Orleans (PCL)	OF	31	112	18	37	4	2	6	27	31	20	1	7	4-4	.330	.479	.563	1.042	2	.982
—Houston (N.L.)	OF-1B	114	353	76	105	28	1	21	67	56	73	1	6	6-2	.297	.388	.561	.949	6	.968
2001—Houston (N.L.)	OF	156	577	110	191	* 55	5	34	126	92	121	13	8	7-9	.331	.430	.620	1.051	6	.981
2002—Houston (N.L.)	OF	158	578	106	169	35	2	42	* 128	107	118	4	10	8-4	.292	.405	.578	.982	7	.977
2003—Houston (N.L.)	OF	153	538	110	155	35	6	25	93	107	108	9	10	5-3	.288	.412	.515	.927	3	.989
2004—Houston (N.L.)	OF-1B	160	544	104	172	40	3	30	106	127	101	10	10	9-7	.316	.450	.566	1.016	2	.992
2005—Round Rock (PCL)	OF	4	14	2	4	1	0	0	1	3	4	0	0	0-0	.286	.412	.357	.769	0	1.000
—Houston (N.L.) 1B-OF-DH		132	468	76	137	34	1	24	82	91	72	4	18	4-1	.293	.411	.524	.934	8	.991
Major League totals (7 years)		907	3151	592	951	229	18	180	617	592	614	41	64	44-27	.302	.416	.557	.973	34	.985

DIVISION SERIES RECORD

Year Team (League)	Pos.	G	AB	R	H	2B	3B	HR	RBI	BB	SO	HBP	GDP	SB-CS	Avg.	OBP	SLG	OPS	E	Avg.
2001—Houston (N.L.)	OF	3	12	0	2	0	0	0	0	0	4	0	2	0-0	.167	.167	.167	.333	0	1.000
2004—Houston (N.L.)	OF	5	22	5	9	1	0	1	3	3	6	0	0	0-1	.409	.480	.591	1.071	1	.800
2005—Houston (N.L.)	1B-OF	4	14	4	5	1	0	1	5	3	4	1	1	0-0	.357	.500	.643	1.143	0	1.000
Division series totals (3 years)		12	48	9	16	2	0	2	8	6	14	1	3	0-1	.333	.418	.500	.918	1	.977

CHAMPIONSHIP SERIES RECORD

Year Team (League)	Pos.	G	AB	R	H	2B	3B	HR	RBI	BB	SO	HBP	GDP	SB-CS	Avg.	OBP	SLG	OPS	E	Avg.
2004—Houston (N.L.)	OF	7	24	7	7	2	0	3	9	5	4	0	0	1-0	.292	.400	.750	1.150	0	1.000
2005—Houston (N.L.)	1B-OF	6	21	2	6	2	0	1	3	4	3	0	1	0-0	.286	.400	.524	.924	0	1.000
Champ. series totals (2 years)		13	45	9	13	4	0	4	12	9	7	0	1	1-0	.289	.400	.644	1.044	0	1.000

WORLD SERIES RECORD

Year Team (League)	Pos.	G	AB	R	H	2B	3B	HR	RBI	BB	SO	HBP	GDP	SB-CS	Avg.	OBP	SLG	OPS	E	Avg.
2005—Houston (N.L.)	OF-1B	4	13	0	5	2	0	0	6	5	5	0	0	0-0	.385	.526	.538	1.065	0	1.000

ALL-STAR GAME RECORD

		G	AB	R	H	2B	3B	HR	RBI	BB	SO	HBP	GDP	SB-CS	Avg.	OBP	SLG	OPS	E	Avg.
All-Star Game totals (3 years)		3	7	0	2	0	0	0	0	0	0	0	0	1-0	.286	.286	.286	.571	0	1.000

BERNERO, ADAM   P

PERSONAL: Born November 28, 1976, in Los Gatos, Calif. ... 6-4/210. ... Throws right, bats right. ... Full name: Adam Gino Bernero. ... Name pronounced: bur-NAIR-o. ... High school: John F. Kennedy (Sacramento, Calif.). ... College: Armstrong Atlantic State (Savannah, Ga.).

TRANSACTIONS/CAREER NOTES: Selected by Chicago White Sox organization in 24th round of 1994 free-agent draft; did not sign. ... Selected by Colorado Rockies organization in 38th round of 1996 free-agent draft; did not sign. ... Signed as a non-drafted free agent by Detroit Tigers organization (May 21, 1999). ... Traded by Tigers to Colorado Rockies for C Ben Petrick (July 13, 2003). ... On disabled list (April 3-June 30, 2004); included rehabilitation assignments to Tulsa and Colorado Springs. ... Signed as a free agent by Atlanta Braves organization (January 19, 2005).

CAREER HITTING: 1-for-16 (.063), 2 R, 0 2B, 0 3B, 0 HR, 0 RBI.

ADAM BERNERO'S PITCHING ZONE

.417	.400	.455
.333	.421	.313
.273	.429	.286

LEFTY-RIGHTY SPLITS

vs.	Avg.	AB	H	2B	3B	HR	RBI	BB	SO	OBP	Slg.
L	.263	99	26	4	1	4	14	6	18	.327	.444
R	.365	96	35	4	0	1	19	6	19	.394	.438

Year Team (League)	W	L	Pct.	ERA	WHIP	G	GS	CG	ShO	Hld.	Sv.-Opp.	IP	H	R	ER	HR	BB-IBB	SO	Avg.
1999—W. Mich. (Mid.)	8	4	.667	2.54	1.02	15	15	2	1	...	0-...	95.2	75	36	27	8	23-0	80	.210
2000—Jacksonville (Sou.)	2	5	.286	2.79	1.27	10	10	0	0	...	0-...	61.1	54	26	19	6	24-0	46	.237
—Toledo (Int'l)	3	1	.750	2.47	0.93	7	7	1	1	...	0-...	47.1	34	16	13	5	10-0	37	.201
—Detroit (A.L.)	0	1	.000	4.19	1.34	12	4	0	0	1	0-0	34.1	33	18	16	3	13-1	20	.270
2001—Toledo (Int'l)	6	11	.353	5.13	1.61	26	25	1	0	...	0-...	140.1	172	90	80	13	54-0	99	.303
—Detroit (A.L.)	0	0	...	7.30	1.38	5	0	0	0	0	0-0	12.1	13	13	10	4	4-0	8	.260
2002—Toledo (Int'l)	2	2	.500	1.58	1.04	9	9	2	1	...	0-...	57.0	46	13	10	2	13-0	49	.223
—Detroit (A.L.)	4	7	.364	6.20	1.56	28	11	0	0	0	0-0	101.2	128	74	70	17	31-1	69	.309
2003—Detroit (A.L.)	1	12	.077	6.08	1.44	18	17	0	0	0	0-0	100.2	104	68	68	14	41-0	54	.267
—Colorado (N.L.)	0	2	.000	5.23	1.41	31	0	0	0	5	0-0	32.2	33	22	19	5	13-1	26	.266
2004—Tulsa (Texas)	1	0	1.000	0.00	0.50	1	1	0	0	...	0-...	6.0	2	1	0	1	1-0	3	.105
—Colo. Springs (PCL)	3	2	.600	3.17	1.39	9	8	0	0	...	0-...	48.1	57	23	17	0	10-0	48	.294
—Colorado (N.L.)	1	1	.500	5.57	1.64	16	2	0	0	1	0-1	32.1	36	20	20	7	17-2	21	.283
2005—Atlanta (N.L.)	4	3	.571	6.51	1.55	36	0	0	0	4	0-1	47.0	61	35	34	5	12-3	37	.313
—Richmond (Int'l)	5	5	.500	3.40	1.36	10	9	0	0	...	0-...	53.0	57	27	20	6	15-0	41	.274
American League totals (4 years)	5	20	.200	5.93	1.47	63	32	0	0	1	0-0	249.0	278	173	164	38	89-2	151	.285
National League totals (3 years)	5	6	.455	5.87	1.54	83	2	0	0	10	0-4	112.0	130	77	73	17	42-6	84	.291
Major League totals (6 years)	10	26	.278	5.91	1.49	146	34	0	0	11	0-4	361.0	408	250	237	55	131-8	235	.287

PERSONAL: Born January 27, 1978, in Santo Domingo, Dominican Republic. ... 6-0/175. ... Bats right, throws right. ... Full name: Angel Maria Berroa.
TRANSACTIONS/CAREER NOTES: Signed as a non-drafted free agent by Oakland Athletics organization (August 14, 1997). ... Traded by A's with C A.J. Hinch and cash to Kansas City Royals as part of three-team deal in which Royals acquired P Roberto Hernandez from Tampa Devil Rays, A's acquired P Cory Lidle from Devil Rays and OF Johnny Damon, IF Mark Ellis and cash from Royals and Devil Rays received OF Ben Grieve and acquired cash from A's (January 8, 2001). ... On disabled list (April 16-May 1, 2004); included rehabilitation assignment to Wichita.
HONORS: Named A.L. Rookie of the Year by Baseball Writers' Association of America (2003).
2005 GAMES PLAYED BY POSITION (MLB): SS—159.

SCOUTING REPORT **Offense:** Pitchers should never throw the undisciplined Berroa a strike; he constantly chases breaking balls in the dirt and fastballs up. Has some bat speed. Is beginning to hit the ball the other way and stop being a dead pull hitter. Doesn't make a lot of adjustments. Is better on balls on the inner half of the plate. Runs well but doesn't have good instincts. **Defense:** Berroa has outstanding arm strength from the hole but can be erratic on routine plays. Has good range and hands. Loses concentration and takes his offensive frustrations out to the field. **Outlook:** Until he learns the strike zone, Berroa will continue to struggle at the plate. Can be a good player but needs to be under control more. *Grade 6.3*

ANGEL BERROA'S HITTING ZONE

.387	.235	.231
.372	.375	.262
.254	.259	.333

LEFTY-RIGHTY SPLITS

vs.	Avg.	AB	H	2B	3B	HR	RBI	BB	SO	OBP	Slg.
L	.278	176	49	6	1	5	11	7	32	.308	.409
R	.266	432	115	15	4	6	44	11	76	.304	.361

							BATTING												FIELDING	
Year Team (League)	Pos.	G	AB	R	H	2B	3B	HR	RBI	BB	SO	HBP	GDP	SB-CS	Avg.	OBP	SLG	OPS	E	Avg.
1998—Dom. Athletics (DSL)		58	196	51	48	7	4	8	37	25	37	...	...	4-...	.245	...	.444	...	...	...
1999—Ariz. A's (Ariz.)	2B-3B-OF																			
	SS	46	169	42	49	11	4	2	24	16	26	7	1	11-4	.290	.371	.438	.809	18	.925
—Midland (Texas)	SS	4	17	3	1	1	0	0	0	0	2	0	0	0-0	.059	.059	.118	.176	2	.889
2000—Visalia (Calif.)	SS	129	429	61	119	25	6	10	63	30	70	10	10	11-9	.277	.337	.434	.770	54	.909
2001—Wilmington (Caro.)	SS	51	199	43	63	18	4	6	25	9	41	14	7	10-6	.317	.382	.538	.920	17	.933
—Wichita (Texas)	SS	80	304	63	90	20	4	8	42	17	55	22	6	15-6	.296	.373	.467	.840	13	.965
—Kansas City (A.L.)	SS	15	53	8	16	2	0	0	4	3	10	0	2	2-0	.302	.339	.340	.679	3	.953
2002—Omaha (PCL)	SS	77	297	37	64	11	4	8	35	15	84	11	5	6-4	.215	.277	.360	.637	16	.956
—Kansas City (A.L.)	SS	20	75	8	17	7	1	0	5	7	10	1	1	3-0	.227	.301	.347	.648	4	.964
2003—Kansas City (A.L.)	SS	158	567	92	163	28	7	17	73	29	100	18	13	21-5	.287	.338	.452	.789	24	.968
2004—Wichita (Texas)	SS	11	51	8	16	1	0	3	10	2	8	0	0	3-2	.314	.340	.510	.849	0	1.000
—Kansas City (A.L.)	SS	134	512	72	134	27	6	8	45	23	87	12	10	14-8	.262	.308	.385	.693	28	.955
2005—Kansas City (A.L.)	SS	159	608	68	164	21	5	11	55	14	108	14	13	7-5	.270	.305	.375	.680	25	.965
Major League totals (5 years)		486	1815	248	494	85	19	36	180	80	315	45	39	47-18	.272	.317	.399	.717	84	.963

PERSONAL: Born April 29, 1975, in Cumana, Venezuela. ... 6-2/200. ... Throws right, bats right. ... Full name: Rafael Jose Betancourt. ... High school: A.J.S. (Cumana, Venezuela). ... College: Isaac Newton College (Venezuela).
TRANSACTIONS/CAREER NOTES: Signed as a non-drafted free agent by Boston Red Sox organization (September 6, 1993). ... Played three seasons as an infielder in Red Sox organization (1994-96). ... Contract purchased from Red Sox organization by Yokohama of the Japan Central League (November 18, 1999). ... Signed as a free agent by Red Sox organization (December 13, 2000). ... Signed as a free agent by Cleveland Indians organization (February 6, 2003). ... On disabled list (June 26-July 11, 2004); included rehabilitation assignment to Akron. ... On disabled list (July 3-18, 2005). ... On restricted list (July 8-18, 2005).
CAREER HITTING: 0-for-0 (.000), 0 R, 0 2B, 0 3B, 0 HR, 0 RBI.

SCOUTING REPORT **Throws:** He relies on a fastball that hits 90-94 mph and a slider. **Tendencies:** Betancourt has a short overhand arm action with some deception from the stretch. Has a good arm angle and hides the ball well. Occasionally will cut his fastball to run from righthanders. Slider has a quick break and good depth. **Outlook:** Betancourt is a good setup reliever, but is versatile enough to be move into a middle role. *Grade 6.6*

RAFAEL BETANCOURT'S PITCHING ZONE

.211	.190	.000
.234	.273	.294
.267	.182	.333

LEFTY-RIGHTY SPLITS

vs.	Avg.	AB	H	2B	3B	HR	RBI	BB	SO	OBP	Slg.
L	.264	87	23	4	0	2	9	11	15	.347	.379
R	.204	167	34	10	0	3	19	6	58	.231	.317

Year Team (League)	W	L	Pct.	ERA	WHIP	G	GS	CG	ShO	Hld.	Sv.-Opp.	IP	H	R	ER	HR	BB-IBB	SO	Avg.
1997—Michigan (Midw.)	0	3	.000	1.95	0.87	27	0	0	0	...	11-...	32.1	26	9	7	2	2-0	52	.213
1998—GC Red Sox (GCL)	0	2	.000	7.20	1.40	4	3	0	0	...	0-...	5.0	6	5	4	1	1-0	4	.300
—Sarasota (Fla. St.)	3	1	.750	3.54	1.00	20	0	0	0	...	2-...	28.0	22	12	11	2	6-0	33	.212
—Trenton (East.)	0	0	...	6.75	1.29	7	0	0	0	...	0-...	9.1	7	7	7	0	3-0	9	.237
1999—Sarasota (Fla. St.)	0	0	...	0.00	0.86	7	0	0	0	...	4-...	7.0	5	0	0	0	1-0	8	.208
—Trenton (East.)	6	2	.750	3.62	1.10	39	0	0	0	...	13-...	54.2	50	24	22	7	10-0	57	.248
2000—Yo. Bay. (Jp. Cn.)	1	2	.333	4.08	1.43	11	4	0	0	...	0-...	28.2	30	16	13	5	11-...	16	...
—Samsung (Kor.)	1	0	1.000	1.17	1.00	20	0	0	0	...	6-...	23.0	17	3	3	0	6-...	29	...
2001—Trenton (East.)	0	1	.000	5.63	1.29	16	0	0	0	...	4-...	24.0	28	16	15	0	3-0	27	.295
2002—	Did not play.																		
2003—Akron (East.)	0	0	...	1.39	1.01	31	0	0	0	...	16-...	45.1	33	10	7	0	13-2	75	.195
—Buffalo (Int'l)	0	0	...	4.05	1.20	4	0	0	0	...	1-...	6.2	6	3	3	1	2-0	6	.240
—Cleveland (A.L.)	2	2	.500	2.13	1.05	33	0	0	0	4	1-3	38.0	27	11	9	5	13-2	46	.196
2004—Akron (East.)	0	0	...	0.00	1.00	1	0	0	0	...	0-...	1.0	0	0	0	0	1-0	2	.000
—Cleveland (A.L.)	5	6	.455	3.92	1.34	68	0	0	0	12	4-11	66.2	71	32	29	7	18-6	76	.268
2005—Cleveland (A.L.)	4	3	.571	2.79	1.09	54	0	0	0	10	1-3	67.2	57	23	21	5	17-2	73	.224
Major League totals (3 years)	11	11	.500	3.08	1.18	155	0	0	0	26	6-17	172.1	155	66	59	17	48-10	185	.236

BETANCOURT, YUNIESKY — 2B

PERSONAL: Born January 31, 1982, in Santa Clara, Cuba. ... 5-10/190. ... Bats right, throws right. ... Full name: Yuniesky Betancourt.
TRANSACTIONS/CAREER NOTES: Signed as a non-drafted free agent by Seattle Mariners organization (January 25, 2005).
2005 GAMES PLAYED BY POSITION (MLB): SS—53, 2B—9.

SCOUTING REPORT In his first year in professional baseball, Betancourt showed a short, quick stroke and bat speed that continued to improve week to week. Is a good high-ball hitter with an idea of the strike zone. Has some gap power now but will hit some home runs when he gets stronger. Can run and will be a good base stealer. Could become one of the game's best fielding shortstops. Has outstanding agility with exceptional range to the hole. Has extremely soft, quick hands and fluid actions. Has arm strength and is very accurate throwing off balance. Will come along very quickly. **Grade 6.2**

YUNIESKY BETANCOURT'S HITTING ZONE

.304	.357	.125
.273	.222	.500
.227	.200	.200

LEFTY-RIGHTY SPLITS

vs.	Avg.	AB	H	2B	3B	HR	RBI	BB	SO	OBP	Slg.
L	.286	49	14	5	2	0	3	4	6	.340	.469
R	.247	162	40	6	3	1	12	7	18	.283	.340

Year Team (League)	Pos.	G	AB	R	H	2B	3B	HR	RBI	BB	SO	HBP	GDP	SB-CS	Avg.	OBP	SLG	OPS	E	Avg.
2005— San Antonio (Texas)	SS-2B	52	227	25	62	10	3	5	20	9	18	1	2	12-7	.273	.301	.410	.711	5	.980
— Tacoma (PCL)	SS-2B	49	183	13	54	9	6	2	30	6	14	2	3	7-5	.295	.323	.443	.766	3	.989
— Seattle (A.L.)	SS-2B	60	211	24	54	11	5	1	15	11	24	2	2	1-3	.256	.296	.370	.666	5	.981
Major League totals (1 year)		60	211	24	54	11	5	1	15	11	24	2	2	1-3	.256	.296	.370	.666	5	.981

BETEMIT, WILSON — SS/3B

PERSONAL: Born July 28, 1980, in Santo Domingo, Dominican Republic. ... 6-3/190. ... Bats both, throws right. ... Name pronounced: BET-a-mitt. ... High school: Juan Bautista Safra (Santo Domingo, D.R.).
TRANSACTIONS/CAREER NOTES: Signed as a non-drafted free agent by Atlanta Braves organization (July 28, 1996).
2005 GAMES PLAYED BY POSITION (MLB): 3B—63, SS—25, 2B—1.

SCOUTING REPORT His arm is extremely strong and he gets rid of the ball quickly from the hole. Has very good hands and agility but appears to lose concentration at times. Doesn't run as well as most middle infielders. Has a longer, stronger stroke righthanded; uses his hands more in a much shorter swing lefthanded. Has better bat control from the left side. Doesn't pull the ball much and will not have much power. Has more value as a utility player. **Grade 4.8**

WILSON BETEMIT'S HITTING ZONE

.333	.400	.308
.393	.250	.355
.500	.348	.346

LEFTY-RIGHTY SPLITS

vs.	Avg.	AB	H	2B	3B	HR	RBI	BB	SO	OBP	Slg.
L	.256	78	20	4	1	1	6	4	16	.289	.372
R	.327	168	55	8	3	3	14	18	39	.390	.464

Year Team (League)	Pos.	G	AB	R	H	2B	3B	HR	RBI	BB	SO	HBP	GDP	SB-CS	Avg.	OBP	SLG	OPS	E	Avg.
1997— GC Braves (GCL)	SS	32	113	12	24	6	1	0	15	9	32	0	3	0-0	.212	.270	.283	.554	20	.856
1998— GC Braves (GCL)	SS	51	173	23	38	8	4	5	16	20	49	0	1	6-5	.220	.301	.399	.699	20	.908
1999— Danville (Appal.)	SS	67	259	39	83	18	2	5	53	27	63	1	4	3-4	.320	.383	.463	.846	33	.899
2000— Jamestown (NYP)	SS	69	269	54	89	15	2	5	37	30	37	1	4	3-4	.331	.393	.457	.851	29	.910
2001— Myrtle Beach (Carol.)	SS	84	318	38	88	20	1	7	43	23	71	1	8	8-5	.277	.324	.412	.736	23	.944
— Greenville (Sou.)	SS	47	183	22	65	14	0	5	19	12	36	1	4	6-2	.355	.394	.514	.908	9	.954
— Atlanta (N.L.)	SS	8	3	1	0	0	0	0	0	2	3	0	0	1-0	.000	.400	.000	.400	0	...
2002— GC Braves (GCL)	SS	7	19	2	5	4	0	0	2	5	2	0	0	1-0	.263	.417	.474	.890	2	.867
— Richmond (Int'l)	SS	93	343	43	84	17	1	8	34	34	82	1	7	8-5	.245	.312	.370	.683	21	.946
2003— Richmond (Int'l)	3B-DH-SS	127	478	55	125	23	13	8	65	38	115	0	8	8-5	.262	.315	.414	.729	28	.902
2004— Richmond (Int'l)	3B-SS	105	356	48	99	24	2	13	59	32	99	0	17	3-3	.278	.336	.466	.802	16	.944
— Atlanta (N.L.)	SS-3B	22	47	2	8	0	0	0	3	4	16	0	0	0-1	.170	.231	.170	.401	3	.943
2005— Atlanta (N.L.)	3B-SS-2B	115	246	36	75	12	4	4	20	22	55	0	5	1-3	.305	.359	.435	.794	7	.964
Major League totals (3 years)		145	296	39	83	12	4	4	23	28	74	0	5	2-4	.280	.339	.389	.728	10	.960

DIVISION SERIES RECORD

Year Team (League)	Pos.	G	AB	R	H	2B	3B	HR	RBI	BB	SO	HBP	GDP	SB-CS	Avg.	OBP	SLG	OPS	E	Avg.
2004— Atlanta (N.L.)		1	0	0	0	0	0	0	0	0	0	0	0	0-0	...	...	...	...	0	...
2005— Atlanta (N.L.)		2	2	0	1	0	0	0	0	0	1	0	0	0-0	.500	.500	.500	1.000	0	...
Division series totals (2 years)		3	2	0	1	0	0	0	0	0	1	0	0	0-0	.500	.500	.500	1.000	0	...

BIGBIE, LARRY — OF

PERSONAL: Born November 4, 1977, in Hobart, Ind. ... 6-4/207. ... Bats left, throws right. ... Full name: Larry Robert Bigbie. ... Name pronounced: BIGG-bee. ... High school: Hobart (Ind.). ... College: Ball State.
TRANSACTIONS/CAREER NOTES: Selected by Baltimore Orioles organization in first round (21st pick overall) of 1999 free-agent draft; pick received from Texas Rangers as part of compensation for signing of Type A free-agent 1B Rafael Palmeiro. ... On disabled list (May 22-July 27, 2003); included rehabilitation assignments to Ottawa and GCL Orioles. ... On disabled list (August 16-September 1, 2004); included rehabilitation assignment to Frederick. ... On disabled list (May 28-June 13, 2005); included rehabilitation assignment to Ottawa. ... Traded by Orioles to Colorado Rockies for OF Eric Byrnes (July 29, 2005). ... On disabled list (August 23-September 6, 2005); included rehabilitation assignment to Colorado Springs.
2005 GAMES PLAYED BY POSITION (MLB): OF—77.

SCOUTING REPORT *Offense:* Bigbie is a good athlete but has not progressed as quickly as his tools would indicate. Has a fluid but slightly long stroke and average bat speed. Is a better low-ball hitter whose power will increase when he begins to pull the ball more; in fact, has potential for plus power. Has speed but should be a better baserunner. *Defense:* Bigbie doesn't get great jumps or reads, but his speed allows him to run down balls. Has a tendency to trail the ball to the alley. Has an average arm but is accurate. *Outlook:* He has good physical tools but needs to speed up his bat. Might stay in center field for the Rockies. *Grade 6.3*

B

LARRY BIGBIE'S HITTING ZONE

.143	.286	.235
.280	.250	.303
.143	.077	.394

LEFTY-RIGHTY SPLITS

vs.	Avg.	AB	H	2B	3B	HR	RBI	BB	SO	OBP	Slg.
L	.247	73	18	2	0	0	9	5	22	.295	.274
R	.236	199	47	8	2	5	14	19	45	.303	.372

Year — Team (League)	Pos.	G	AB	R	H	2B	3B	HR	RBI	BB	SO	HBP	GDP	SB-CS	Avg.	OBP	SLG	OPS	E	Avg.
1999— Bluefield (Appal.)	OF	8	30	3	8	0	0	0	4	3	8	1	1	1-3	.267	.343	.267	.610	0	1.000
— Delmarva (S. Atl.)	OF	43	165	18	46	7	3	2	27	29	42	0	4	3-1	.279	.381	.394	.775	3	.950
2000— Frederick (Carolina)	OF	55	201	33	59	11	0	2	28	23	34	0	3	7-3	.294	.360	.378	.738	3	.975
— Bowie (East.)	OF	31	112	11	27	6	0	0	5	11	28	0	3	0-0	.241	.309	.295	.604	0	1.000
2001— Bowie (East.)	OF	71	262	41	77	13	3	8	33	40	54	0	5	10-7	.294	.386	.458	.844	4	.972
— Baltimore (A.L.)	OF	47	131	15	30	4	0	2	11	17	42	0	2	4-1	.229	.318	.321	.638	0	1.000
— Rochester (Int'l)	OF	10	42	5	13	4	0	1	2	3	8	0	0	1-1	.310	.356	.476	.832	0	1.000
2002— Rochester (Int'l)	OF	98	348	42	105	23	2	2	35	35	79	1	9	7-3	.302	.363	.397	.760	2	.990
— Baltimore (A.L.)	OF	16	34	1	6	1	0	0	3	1	11	0	1	1-0	.176	.194	.206	.400	0	1.000
2003— GC Orioles (GCL)	OF	2	6	1	2	1	0	0	0	0	1	0	0	0-0	.333	.333	.500	.833	0	1.000
— Ottawa (Int'l)	OF-DH	30	117	23	41	14	4	3	21	14	31	1	1	0-0	.350	.421	.615	1.036	1	.974
— Baltimore (A.L.)	OF	83	287	43	87	15	1	9	31	29	60	0	2	7-1	.303	.365	.456	.821	1	.994
2004— Frederick (Carolina)	OF	1	5	2	2	0	0	2	2	0	1	0	0	0-0	.400	.400	1.600	2.000	0	...
— Baltimore (A.L.)	OF-DH	139	478	76	134	23	1	15	68	45	113	1	7	8-3	.280	.341	.427	.768	2	.993
2005— Ottawa (Int'l)	OF-DH	4	17	3	5	2	0	1	2	0	6	1	0	0-0	.294	.294	.588	.882	0	...
— Baltimore (A.L.)	OF	67	206	22	51	9	1	5	21	21	49	0	2	3-3	.248	.314	.374	.688	0	1.000
— Colo. Springs (PCL)	OF	3	8	4	3	2	1	0	2	2	3	0	0	0-0	.375	.500	.875	1.375	0	1.000
— Colorado (N.L.)	OF	23	66	5	14	1	1	0	2	3	18	1	0	2-0	.212	.257	.258	.515	0	1.000
American League totals (5 years)		352	1136	157	308	54	3	31	134	113	275	1	14	23-8	.271	.335	.406	.741	3	.996
National League totals (1 year)		23	66	5	14	1	1	0	2	3	18	1	0	2-0	.212	.257	.258	.515	0	1.000
Major League totals (5 years)		375	1202	162	322	55	4	31	136	116	293	2	14	25-8	.268	.331	.398	.729	3	.996

BIGGIO, CRAIG — 2B

PERSONAL: Born December 14, 1965, in Smithtown, N.Y. ... 5-11/185. ... Bats right, throws right. ... Full name: Craig Alan Biggio. ... Name pronounced: BIDG-ee-oh. ... High school: Kings Park (N.Y.). ... College: Seton Hall.

TRANSACTIONS/CAREER NOTES: Selected by Houston Astros organization in first round (22nd pick overall) of 1987 free-agent draft. ... On disabled list (August 2, 2000-remainder of season).

RECORDS: Shares major league record for grounding into fewest double plays; minimum 150 games played (0, 1997). ... Holds major league record for most times hit by pitch, career (273).

HONORS: Won N.L. Gold Glove at second base (1994-97).

2005 GAMES PLAYED BY POSITION (MLB): 2B—141, DH—5.

SCOUTING REPORT *Offense:* He changed his approach and cut down his leg lift to compensate for a decrease in bat speed. Has shortened his swing and is quicker to the ball on the inner half. Has become more of a dead-pull hitter and home run production is up. Has problems with the ball away, especially breaking stuff. Still an above-average runner who picks his spots well. *Defense:* Biggio moved back to second base last season. Is not a fluid infielder but is getting better jumps to his left. Tends to field the ball deep and doesn't have real soft hands. Arm strength is lacking and must have a quick release on the pivot to throw out runners. *Outlook:* He continues to make adjustments at 40 and still is a productive player. Showing new signs of power in cozy Minute Maid Park. *Grade 8*

CRAIG BIGGIO'S HITTING ZONE

.257	.379	.250
.310	.348	.321
.206	.269	.200

LEFTY-RIGHTY SPLITS

vs.	Avg.	AB	H	2B	3B	HR	RBI	BB	SO	OBP	Slg.
L	.243	148	36	8	1	6	16	11	18	.307	.432
R	.271	442	120	32	0	20	53	26	72	.331	.480

Year — Team (League)	Pos.	G	AB	R	H	2B	3B	HR	RBI	BB	SO	HBP	GDP	SB-CS	Avg.	OBP	SLG	OPS	E	Avg.
1987— Asheville (S. Atl.)	C-OF	64	216	59	81	17	2	9	49	39	33	2	5	31-10	.375	.471	.597	1.068	2	.995
1988— Tucson (PCL)	C-OF	77	281	60	90	21	4	3	41	40	39	3	2	19-4	.320	.408	.456	.863	6	.983
— Houston (N.L.)	C	50	123	14	26	6	1	3	5	7	29	0	1	6-1	.211	.254	.350	.603	3	.991
1989— Houston (N.L.)	C-OF	134	443	64	114	21	2	13	60	49	64	6	7	21-3	.257	.336	.402	.738	9	.989
1990— Houston (N.L.)	C-OF	150	555	53	153	24	2	4	42	53	79	3	11	25-11	.276	.342	.348	.689	13	.982
1991— Houston (N.L.)	2B-C-OF	149	546	79	161	23	4	4	46	53	71	2	2	19-6	.295	.358	.374	.731	11	.989
1992— Houston (N.L.)	2B	•162	613	96	170	32	3	6	39	94	95	7	5	38-15	.277	.378	.369	.747	12	.984
1993— Houston (N.L.)	2B	155	610	98	175	41	5	21	64	77	93	10	10	15-17	.287	.373	.474	.847	14	.982
1994— Houston (N.L.)	2B	114	437	88	139	* 44	5	6	56	62	58	8	5	* 39-4	.318	.411	.483	.893	7	.988
1995— Houston (N.L.)	2B	141	553	123	167	30	2	22	77	80	85	* 22	14	33-8	.302	.406	.483	.889	10	.986
1996— Houston (N.L.)	2B	•162	605	113	174	24	4	15	75	75	72	* 27	10	25-7	.288	.386	.415	.801	10	.988
1997— Houston (N.L.)	2B	•162	619	* 146	191	37	8	22	81	84	107	* 34	0	47-10	.309	.415	.501	.916	18	.979
1998— Houston (N.L.)	2B-DH	160	646	123	210	* 51	2	20	88	64	113	23	10	50-8	.325	.403	.503	.906	15	.980
1999— Houston (N.L.)	2B-OF-DH	160	639	123	188	* 56	0	16	73	88	107	11	5	28-14	.294	.386	.457	.843	12	.985
2000— Houston (N.L.)	2B	101	377	67	101	13	5	8	35	61	73	16	5	10-12	.268	.388	.393	.780	6	.987
2001— Houston (N.L.)	2B-DH	155	617	118	180	35	3	20	70	66	100	* 28	11	7-4	.292	.382	.455	.838	11	.984
2002— Houston (N.L.)	2B-OF	145	577	96	146	36	3	15	58	50	111	17	15	16-2	.253	.330	.404	.734	8	.988
2003— Houston (N.L.)	OF	153	628	102	166	44	2	15	62	57	116	* 27	8	8-4	.264	.350	.412	.763	1	.997
2004— Houston (N.L.)	OF-DH	156	633	100	178	47	0	24	63	40	94	15	8	7-2	.281	.337	.469	.806	9	.966
2005— Houston (N.L.)	2B-DH	155	590	94	156	40	1	26	69	37	90	17	10	11-1	.264	.325	.468	.792	16	.976
Major League totals (18 years)		2564	9811	1697	2795	604	52	260	1063	1097	1557	273	130	407-119	.285	.370	.437	.807	185	.985

DIVISION SERIES RECORD

Year	Team (League)	Pos.	G	AB	R	H	2B	3B	HR	RBI	BB	SO	HBP	GDP	SB-CS	Avg.	OBP	SLG	OPS	E	Avg.
1997—Houston (N.L.)		2B	3	12	0	1	0	0	0	0	1	0	0	0	0-0	.083	.154	.083	.237	1	.923
1998—Houston (N.L.)		2B	4	11	3	2	1	0	0	1	4	4	2	0	0-0	.182	.471	.273	.743	1	.950
1999—Houston (N.L.)		2B	4	19	1	2	0	0	0	0	1	5	0	0	0-0	.105	.150	.105	.255	0	1.000
2001—Houston (N.L.)		2B	3	12	0	2	0	0	0	0	0	1	0	0	0-0	.167	.167	.167	.333	0	1.000
2004—Houston (N.L.)		OF	5	20	5	8	2	0	1	4	2	4	0	1	1-0	.400	.455	.650	1.105	0	1.000
2005—Houston (N.L.)		2B	4	19	6	6	4	0	0	1	2	5	0	0	1-0	.316	.364	.526	.890	0	1.000
Division series totals (6 years)			23	93	15	21	7	0	1	6	10	19	2	1	2-0	.226	.311	.333	.645	2	.980

CHAMPIONSHIP SERIES RECORD

Year	Team (League)	Pos.	G	AB	R	H	2B	3B	HR	RBI	BB	SO	HBP	GDP	SB-CS	Avg.	OBP	SLG	OPS	E	Avg.
2004—Houston (N.L.)		OF	7	32	3	6	1	0	1	1	0	4	0	0	0-1	.188	.188	.313	.500	1	1.000
2005—Houston (N.L.)		2B	6	24	2	8	0	0	0	3	2	3	0	0	0-0	.333	.385	.333	.718	0	1.000
Champ. series totals (2 years)			13	56	5	14	1	0	1	4	2	7	0	0	0-1	.250	.276	.321	.597	0	1.000

WORLD SERIES RECORD

Year	Team (League)	Pos.	G	AB	R	H	2B	3B	HR	RBI	BB	SO	HBP	GDP	SB-CS	Avg.	OBP	SLG	OPS	E	Avg.
2005—Houston (N.L.)		2B	4	18	3	4	1	0	0	1	1	4	0	0	0-0	.222	.263	.278	.541	0	1.000

ALL-STAR GAME RECORD

			G	AB	R	H	2B	3B	HR	RBI	BB	SO	HBP	GDP	SB-CS	Avg.	OBP	SLG	OPS	E	Avg.
All-Star Game totals (7 years)			7	15	2	1	0	0	1	2	0	5	1		0-0	.067	.125	.267	.392	1	.957

BLAKE, CASEY   OF

PERSONAL: Born August 23, 1973, in Des Moines, Iowa. ... 6-2/210. ... Bats right, throws right. ... Full name: William Casey Blake. ... High school: Indianola (Iowa). ... College: Wichita State.

TRANSACTIONS/CAREER NOTES: Selected by Philadelphia Phillies organization in 11th round of 1992 free-agent draft; did not sign. ... Selected by New York Yankees organization in 45th round of 1995 free-agent draft; did not sign. ... Selected by Toronto Blue Jays organization in seventh round of 1996 free-agent draft. ... Claimed on waivers by Minnesota Twins (May 23, 2000). ... Claimed on waivers by Baltimore Orioles (September 21, 2001). ... Claimed on waivers by Twins (October 12, 2001). ... Released by Twins (October 14, 2002). ... Signed by Cleveland Indians organization (December 18, 2002).

2005 GAMES PLAYED BY POSITION (MLB): OF—138, 3B—6, 1B—4.

SCOUTING REPORT **Offense:** Blake's production dropped last season. Lost some bat speed and had trouble with breaking stuff. Didn't hit well runners on base as his impatience grew. A streaky hitter, he can drive the ball to the opposite field. Power is an asset. Is an average runner and not a basestealing threat. **Defense:** Blake's glove kept in the lineup despite his early struggles. Adapted well to his move to the outfield, getting better lateral jumps in the second half. Was better at coming in than going back. Has enough arm to play right field though he often overthrows his cutoff man. **Outlook:** He could develop into a role player with his ability to play multiple positions, unless he can hit enough to play every day. **Grade 7.5**

CASEY BLAKE'S HITTING ZONE

.325	.200	.083
.250	.367	.241
.205	.371	.292

LEFTY-RIGHTY SPLITS

vs.	Avg.	AB	H	2B	3B	HR	RBI	BB	SO	OBP	Slg.
L	.241	137	33	6	0	11	17	11	34	.302	.526
R	.241	386	93	26	1	12	41	32	82	.310	.407

Year	Team (League)	Pos.	G	AB	R	H	2B	3B	HR	RBI	BB	SO	HBP	GDP	SB-CS	Avg.	OBP	SLG	OPS	E	Avg.
1996—Hagerstown (SAL)	1B-3B-OF	48	172	29	43	13	1	2	18	11	40	7	3	5-3	.250	.318	.372	.690	12	.906
1997—Dunedin (Fla. St.)	3B-SS	129	449	56	107	21	0	7	39	48	91	6	5	19-9	.238	.319	.332	.651	39	.895
1998—Dunedin (Fla. St.)	3B	88	340	62	119	28	3	11	65	30	81	9	5	9-6	.350	.409	.547	.956	16	.939
—Knoxville (Southern)	3B	45	172	41	64	15	4	7	38	22	25	2	6	10-0	.372	.442	.628	1.070	11	.913
1999—Syracuse (Int'l)	3B-DH-SS	110	387	69	95	16	2	22	75	61	82	7	10	9-5	.245	.357	.468	.824	10	.963
—Toronto (A.L.)	3B	14	39	6	10	2	0	1	1	2	7	0	1	0-0	.256	.293	.385	.677	0	1.000
—St. Catharines (NYP)	3B	1	3	0	2	0	0	0	0	1	0	0	0	0-0	.667	.750	.667	1.417	0	1.000
2000—Syracuse (Int'l)	3B-SS	30	106	10	23	6	1	2	7	8	23	3	2	0-3	.217	.291	.349	.640	2	.971
—Salt Lake (PCL)	3B-SS-1B	80	293	59	93	22	2	12	52	39	59	6	4	7-2	.317	.406	.529	.935	14	.934
—Minnesota (A.L.)	3B-1B-DH	7	16	1	3	2	0	0	1	3	7	1	1	0-0	.188	.333	.313	.646	0	1.000
2001—Edmonton (PCL)	3B-1B-2B																			
	SS-OF	94	375	64	116	24	6	10	49	34	66	6	11	14-3	.309	.376	.485	.861	11	.961
—Minnesota (A.L.)	3B-DH-1B	13	22	1	7	1	0	0	2	3	8	0	0	1-0	.318	.400	.364	.764	1	.955
—Baltimore (A.L.)	1B-DH	6	15	2	2	0	0	1	2	1	4	0	0	2-0	.133	.188	.333	.521	1	.967
2002—Edmonton (PCL)	3B-2B-1B																			
	OF	126	482	87	149	25	3	19	58	54	78	6	11	24-9	.309	.383	.492	.874	12	.969
—Minnesota (A.L.)	3B-1B-DH	9	20	2	4	1	0	0	1	2	7	0	0	0-0	.200	.273	.250	.523	2	.920
2003—Cleveland (A.L.)	3B-1B	152	557	80	143	35	0	17	67	38	109	10	11	7-9	.257	.312	.411	.723	19	.965
2004—Cleveland (A.L.)	3B	152	587	93	159	36	3	28	88	68	139	9	19	5-8	.271	.354	.486	.839	26	.940
2005—Cleveland (A.L.)	OF-3B-1B	147	523	72	126	32	1	23	58	43	116	10	9	4-5	.241	.308	.438	.746	10	.971
Major League totals (7 years)		500	1779	257	454	109	4	70	220	160	397	30	41	19-22	.255	.324	.439	.763	59	.959

BLALOCK, HANK   3B

PERSONAL: Born November 21, 1980, in San Diego, Calif. ... 6-1/200. ... Bats left, throws right. ... Full name: Hank Joe Blalock. ... Name pronounced: BLAY-lock. ... High school: Rancho Bernardo (San Diego).

TRANSACTIONS/CAREER NOTES: Selected by Texas Rangers organization in third round of 1999 free-agent draft.

2005 GAMES PLAYED BY POSITION (MLB): 3B—158, DH—2.

SCOUTING REPORT *Offense:* Blalock is one of the most aggressive hitters in the majors. Hits with a short stride and likes to lift the ball. Has good power when pulling the ball but sometimes swings too hard. Will chase pitches out of the zone. Is vulnerable to off-speed pitches and continues to drop off in the second half as he tires and presses. Has a lot of holes in his swing, especially up. Is not selective and has trouble with lefthanded pitching. Is not a good runner. *Defense:* Blalock has improved his first step, quickness, agility and body control. Has quick hands and range to both sides. Has good arm strength and accuracy but a slow release. *Outlook:* Blalock has the potential to hit 35 or more home runs, but he needs to put two halves together to do so. Must improve his plate discipline and cut down his strikeouts. *Grade 7.9*

HANK BLALOCK'S HITTING ZONE

.333	.304	.205
.410	.333	.307
.250	.241	.179

LEFTY-RIGHTY SPLITS

vs.	Avg.	AB	H	2B	3B	HR	RBI	BB	SO	OBP	Slg.
L	.196	194	38	7	0	8	19	7	53	.228	.356
R	.291	453	132	27	0	17	73	44	79	.354	.464

Year Team (League)	Pos.	G	AB	R	H	2B	3B	HR	RBI	BB	SO	HBP	GDP	SB-CS	Avg.	OBP	SLG	OPS	E	Avg.
1999—GC Rangers (GCL)	3B	51	191	34	69	17	6	3	38	25	23	1	7	3-2	.361	.428	.560	.988	12	.914
—Savannah (S. Atl.)	3B	7	25	3	6	1	0	1	2	1	3	1	0	0-0	.240	.286	.400	.686	5	.762
2000—Savannah (S. Atl.)	3B	139	512	66	153	32	2	10	77	62	53	5	13	31-8	.299	.373	.428	.801	20	.942
2001—Tulsa (Texas)	3B	68	272	50	89	18	4	11	61	39	38	2	5	3-3	.327	.413	.544	.957	8	.953
—Charlotte (Fla. St.)	3B	63	237	46	90	19	1	7	47	26	31	1	6	7-4	.380	.437	.557	.994	7	.963
2002—Texas (A.L.)	3B	49	147	16	31	8	0	3	17	20	43	1	2	0-0	.211	.306	.327	.632	6	.943
—Oklahoma (PCL)	3B-2B	95	387	63	119	32	1	8	62	34	61	1	9	2-1	.307	.363	.457	.821	16	.938
2003—Texas (A.L.)	3B-2B	143	567	89	170	33	3	29	90	44	97	1	16	2-3	.300	.350	.522	.872	16	.957
2004—Texas (A.L.)	3B	159	624	107	172	38	3	32	110	75	149	6	13	2-2	.276	.355	.500	.855	17	.957
2005—Texas (A.L.)	3B-DH	161	647	80	170	34	0	25	92	51	132	3	16	1-0	.263	.318	.431	.749	11	.973
Major League totals (4 years)		512	1985	292	543	113	6	89	309	190	421	11	47	5-5	.274	.338	.471	.809	50	.961

ALL-STAR GAME RECORD

	G	AB	R	H	2B	3B	HR	RBI	BB	SO	HBP	GDP	SB-CS	Avg.	OBP	SLG	OPS	E	Avg.
All-Star Game totals (2 years)	2	3	1	1	0	0	1	2	0	0	0	0	0-0	.333	.333	1.333	1.667	0	...

BLANCO, ANDRES — SS/2B

PERSONAL: Born April 11, 1984, in Carabobo, Venezuela. ... 5-10/155. ... Bats both, throws right. ... Full name: Andres Eloy Blanco. ... Name pronounced: BLAHN-ko. ... High school: El Carmen (Venezuela).
TRANSACTIONS/CAREER NOTES: Signed as a non-drafted free agent by Kansas City Royals organization (August 2, 2000).
2005 GAMES PLAYED BY POSITION (MLB): 2B—24, SS—7.

ANDRES BLANCO'S HITTING ZONE

.000	.667	.000
.143	.000	.273
.000	.333	.375

LEFTY-RIGHTY SPLITS

vs.	Avg.	AB	H	2B	3B	HR	RBI	BB	SO	OBP	Slg.
L	.111	27	3	0	0	0	1	0	0	.138	.111
R	.269	52	14	0	1	0	4	0	5	.264	.308

Year Team (League)	Pos.	G	AB	R	H	2B	3B	HR	RBI	BB	SO	HBP	GDP	SB-CS	Avg.	OBP	SLG	OPS	E	Avg.
2001—Guacara 1 (VSL)		54	188	38	56	0	3	0	16	28	23	...		9-12	.298		.330	...	22	...
2002—GC Royals (GCL)	SS	52	193	27	48	8	0	0	14	15	29	4	2	16-4	.249	.315	.290	.605	13	.945
—Wilmington (Caro.)	SS	5	13	2	4	1	0	0	0	1	4	0	0	0-0	.308	.357	.385	.742	2	.926
2003—Wilmington (Caro.)	SS	113	394	61	96	11	3	0	25	44	50	8	9	13-7	.244	.330	.287	.617	26	.947
2004—Kansas City (A.L.)	SS	19	60	9	19	2	2	0	5	5	6	1	0	1-2	.317	.379	.417	.795	4	.959
—Wichita (Texas)	SS	93	324	34	80	10	2	0	21	18	44	7	14	7-6	.247	.299	.290	.575	14	.951
2005—High Desert (Calif.)	2B	3	10	0	5	1	0	0	3	0	1	0	0	1-2	.500	.500	.600	1.100	0	1.000
—Arizona Royals (AZL)	SS-DH	7	25	6	8	1	0	2	9	1	7	1	0	1-2	.320	.370	.400	.970	3	.889
—Wichita (Texas)	SS	9	37	5	7	0	0	1	5	3	7	0	0	0-0	.189	.250	.270	.520	0	1.000
—Omaha (PCL)	SS	35	114	13	29	4	2	1	9	10	23	3	3	2-0	.254	.331	.351	.682	10	.944
—Kansas City (A.L.)	2B-SS	26	79	6	17	0	1	0	5	0	5	1	3	0-1	.215	.220	.241	.460	3	.979
Major League totals (2 years)		45	139	15	36	2	3	0	10	5	11	2	3	1-3	.259	.291	.317	.607	7	.971

BLANCO, HENRY — C

PERSONAL: Born August 29, 1971, in Caracas, Venezuela. ... 5-11/224. ... Bats right, throws right. ... Full name: Henry Ramon Blanco. ... Name pronounced: BLAHN-ko. ... High school: Antonio Jose de Sucre (Venezuela).
TRANSACTIONS/CAREER NOTES: Signed as a non-drafted free agent by Los Angeles Dodgers organization (November 12, 1989). ... On disabled list (March 22-July 29, 1998); included rehabilitation assignment to San Bernardino. ... Signed as a free agent by Colorado Rockies organization (December 18, 1998). ... Traded by Rockies with P Jamey Wright to Milwaukee Brewers as part of three-way deal in which Rockies acquired 3B Jeff Cirillo, P Scott Karl and cash from Brewers, Oakland Athletics acquired P Justin Miller and cash from Rockies and Brewers acquired P Jimmy Haynes from A's (December 13, 1999). ... On disabled list (April 14-May 2, 2000); included rehabilitation assignment to Indianapolis. ... Traded by Brewers to Atlanta Braves for C Paul Bako and P Jose Cabrera (March 20, 2002). ... On disabled list (August 12-27, 2002). ... Signed as a free agent by Minnesota Twins (December 18, 2003). ... Signed as a free agent by Chicago Cubs (December 7, 2004).
2005 GAMES PLAYED BY POSITION (MLB): C—54.

SCOUTING REPORT Blanco is in the major leagues because of his defense. Works exceptionally well with pitchers, has good hands and frames pitches well. Is mobile and helps pitchers by blocking balls in the dirt but must continually watch his weight to retain his quickness. Has an accurate, above-average arm and has worked to improve his release. Doesn't have a quick bat, but will flash occasional power, especially on balls away. Has problems handling pitches on the inner half of the plate and is not a good breaking-ball hitter. *Grade 6*

HENRY BLANCO'S HITTING ZONE

.273	.600	.000
.194	.200	.400
.192	.333	.000

LEFTY-RIGHTY SPLITS

vs.	Avg.	AB	H	2B	3B	HR	RBI	BB	SO	OBP	Slg.
L	.194	31	6	3	0	2	4	3	4	.265	.484
R	.254	130	33	3	0	4	21	8	20	.293	.369

Year Team (League)	Pos.	G	AB	R	H	2B	3B	HR	RBI	BB	SO	HBP	GDP	SB-CS	Avg.	OBP	SLG	OPS	E	Avg.
1990—GC Dodgers (GCL)	3B	60	178	23	39	8	0	1	19	26	41	1	6	7-2	.219	.316	.281	.597	11	.941
1991—Vero Beach (FSL)	3B-SS	5	7	0	1	0	0	0	0	2	0	0	0	0-0	.143	.333	.143	.476	0	1.000
—Great Falls (Pio.)	1B-3B	62	216	35	55	7	1	5	28	27	39	1	5	3-6	.255	.336	.366	.702	8	.960
1992—Bakersfield (Calif.)	3B	124	401	42	94	21	2	5	52	51	91	9	10	10-6	.234	.328	.334	.662	14	.959
1993—San Antonio (Texas)	3B-1B-SS	117	374	33	73	19	1	10	42	29	80	4	7	3-3	.195	.260	.332	.591	16	.952
1994—San Antonio (Texas)	3B-1B-P	132	405	36	93	23	2	6	38	53	67	2	12	6-6	.230	.320	.341	.660	21	.924
1995—San Antonio (Texas)	3B-C	88	302	37	77	18	4	12	48	29	52	4	4	1-1	.255	.328	.460	.789	11	.964
—Albuquerque (PCL)	3B-1B-OF	29	97	11	22	4	1	2	13	10	23	0	3	0-0	.227	.294	.351	.644	2	.988
1996—San Antonio (Texas)	C-3B	92	307	39	82	14	1	5	40	28	38	0	5	2-3	.267	.324	.368	.692	13	.979
—Albuquerque (PCL)	C	2	6	1	1	0	0	0	0	0	3	0	0	0-0	.167	.167	.167	.333	1	1.000
1997—Albuquerque (PCL)	C-1B-DH OF	91	294	38	92	20	1	6	47	37	63	1	7	7-4	.313	.388	.449	.837	3	.996
—Los Angeles (N.L.)	1B-3B	3	5	1	2	0	0	1	1	0	1	0	0	0-0	.400	.400	1.000	1.400	0	1.000
1998—San Bern. (Calif.)	C-DH	7	19	5	6	1	0	2	3	4	6	0	2	1-0	.316	.435	.684	1.119	0	1.000
—Albuquerque (PCL)	C-DH	48	134	19	36	11	0	4	23	22	27	0	5	2-0	.269	.367	.440	.807	4	.985
1999—Colo. Springs (PCL)	C	15	57	8	19	4	0	3	12	1	12	0	1	0-1	.333	.339	.561	.900	1	.990
—Colorado (N.L.)	C-OF	88	263	30	61	12	3	6	28	34	38	1	4	1-1	.232	.320	.369	.689	5	.992
2000—Milwaukee (N.L.)	C	93	284	29	67	24	0	7	31	36	60	0	9	0-3	.236	.318	.394	.712	5	.991
—Indianapolis (Int'l)	DH	1	3	1	1	1	0	0	0	1	0	0	1	0-0	.333	.500	.667	1.167	...	...
2001—Milwaukee (N.L.)	C	104	314	33	66	18	3	6	31	34	72	2	10	3-1	.210	.290	.344	.634	6	.992
2002—Atlanta (N.L.)	C	81	221	17	45	9	1	6	22	20	51	1	5	0-2	.204	.267	.335	.602	3	.993
2003—Atlanta (N.L.)	C	55	151	11	30	8	0	1	13	10	21	1	3	0-0	.199	.252	.272	.523	1	.996
2004—Minnesota (A.L.)	C	114	315	36	65	19	1	10	37	21	56	3	8	0-3	.206	.260	.368	.628	7	.991
2005—Chicago (N.L.)	C	54	161	16	39	6	0	6	25	11	24	0	6	0-0	.242	.287	.391	.679	1	.998
American League totals (1 year)		114	315	36	65	19	1	10	37	21	56	3	8	0-3	.206	.260	.368	.628	7	.991
National League totals (7 years)		478	1399	137	310	77	7	33	151	145	267	5	37	4-7	.222	.294	.357	.651	21	.993
Major League totals (8 years)		592	1714	173	375	96	8	43	188	166	323	8	45	4-10	.219	.288	.359	.647	28	.993

DIVISION SERIES RECORD

Year Team (League)	Pos.	G	AB	R	H	2B	3B	HR	RBI	BB	SO	HBP	GDP	SB-CS	Avg.	OBP	SLG	OPS	E	Avg.
2002—Atlanta (N.L.)	C	2	6	0	1	0	0	0	0	2	0	0	0	0-0	.167	.167	.167	.333	0	1.000
2004—Minnesota (A.L.)	C	4	8	1	2	0	0	1	2	0	2	0	1	0-0	.250	.222	.625	.847	1	.957
Division series totals (2 years)		6	14	1	3	0	0	1	2	2	4	0	1	0-0	.214	.200	.429	.629	1	.970

BLANCO, TONY — 3B/OF

PERSONAL: Born November 10, 1981, in San Juan de la Maguana, Dominican Republic. ... 6-1/175. ... Bats right, throws right. ... Full name: Tony Enrique Blanco.

TRANSACTIONS/CAREER NOTES: Signed as a nondrafted free agent by Boston Red Sox organization (July 2, 1998) ... Traded by Red Sox with P Josh Thigpen to Cincinnati Reds (December 16, 2002), completing deal in which Reds traded 2B Todd Walker to Red Sox for two players to be named (December 12, 2002). ... Selected by Washington Nationals from Reds organization in Rule 5 major league draft (December 13, 2004). ... On disabled list (July 13-August 5, 2005).

2005 GAMES PLAYED BY POSITION (MLB): OF—11, 3B—5, 1B—3, DH—1.

TONY BLANCO'S HITTING ZONE

.000	.250	.000
.176	.400	.125
.111	.500	.200

LEFTY-RIGHTY SPLITS

vs.	Avg.	AB	H	2B	3B	HR	RBI	BB	SO	OBP	Slg.
L	.172	29	5	0	0	1	1	1	11	.200	.241
R	.182	33	6	1	0	1	6	1	8	.229	.303

Year Team (League)	Pos.	G	AB	R	H	2B	3B	HR	RBI	BB	SO	HBP	GDP	SB-CS	Avg.	OBP	SLG	OPS	E	Avg.
1999—Boston SP (DSL)		67	249	36	69	12	5	8	41	29	65	6	8	12-5	.277	.366	.462	.828	...	...
2000—GC Red Sox (GCL)	3B	52	190	32	73	13	1	13	50	18	38	4	3	6-4	.384	.442	.668	1.110	20	.864
—Lowell (NY-Penn)	3B	9	28	1	4	1	0	0	0	2	12	1	0	1-0	.143	.226	.179	.405	4	.818
2001—Augusta (S. Atl.)	3B	96	370	44	98	23	2	17	69	17	78	7	17	1-0	.265	.308	.476	.784	21	.841
2002—Sarasota (Fla. St.)	3B	65	244	22	54	13	2	6	32	6	70	4	3	2-0	.221	.250	.365	.615	30	.828
2003—Potomac (Carol.)	1B	69	241	33	64	17	2	10	49	26	62	4	5	0-0	.266	.338	.477	.815	4	.971
2004—Potomac (Carol.)	1B	62	216	42	66	10	0	17	47	27	66	11	4	2-0	.306	.403	.588	.991	9	.985
—Chattanooga (Sou.)	OF	58	220	25	54	8	1	12	31	15	53	2	8	0-0	.245	.300	.455	.755	3	.000
2005—New Orleans (PCL)	3B-OF	16	64	7	18	4	0	2	14	2	13	0	6	1-0	.281	.294	.438	.732	5	.909
—Washington (N.L.)	OF-3B-1B DH	56	62	7	11	3	0	1	7	2	19	1	0	1-0	.177	.215	.274	.490	2	.929
Major League totals (1 year)		56	62	7	11	3	0	1	7	2	19	1	0	1-0	.177	.215	.274	.490	2	.929

BLANTON, JOE — P

PERSONAL: Born December 11, 1980, in Bowling Green, Ky. ... 6-3/225. ... Throws right, bats right. ... Full name: Joseph Matthew Blanton. ... High school: Franklin-Simpson (Franklin, Ky.). ... College: Kentucky.

TRANSACTIONS/CAREER NOTES: Selected by Oakland Athletics organization in first round (24th pick overall) of 2002 free-agent draft; pick received as compensation for New York Yankees signing Type A free-agent 1B Jason Giambi.

CAREER HITTING: 1-for-3 (.333), 0 R, 0 2B, 0 3B, 0 HR, 0 RBI.

SCOUTING REPORT **Throws:** Blanton throws an 86-93 mph fastball, a curveball, slider and changeup. **Tendencies:** He is a deceptive control pitcher who doesn't often pitch at his top velocity. Prefers to throw around 90 and keep the ball down. Curve has a big, quick break, but the slider is a more consistent breaking ball. Has good motion and movement on his straight changeup, which he throws to lefthanders. Has a good idea of how to approach hitters. **Outlook:** Blanton is a pitcher who grows on you the more he pitches. Is poised and has command of all his pitches. Will consistently work deep into games and provide 200 innings a year with at least 15 wins. *Grade 7.4*

JOE BLANTON'S PITCHING ZONE

.282	.304	.291
.280	.349	.191
.224	.211	.282

LEFTY-RIGHTY SPLITS

vs.	Avg.	AB	H	2B	3B	HR	RBI	BB	SO	OBP	Slg.
L	.228	404	92	24	2	8	33	33	56	.286	.356
R	.246	350	86	18	2	15	47	34	60	.316	.437

B

Year Team (League)	W	L	Pct.	ERA	WHIP	G	GS	CG	ShO	Hld.	Sv.-Opp.	IP	H	R	ER	HR	BB-IBB	SO	Avg.
2002— Vancouver (N'west)	1	1	.500	3.14	0.91	4	2	0	0	...	0-...	14.1	11	5	5	0	2-0	15	.216
— Modesto (California)	0	1	.000	7.50	2.33	2	1	0	0	...	0-...	6.0	8	6	5	1	6-0	6	.296
2003— Kane Co. (Midw.)	8	7	.533	2.57	0.97	21	21	2	2	...	0-...	133.0	110	47	38	6	19-0	144	.219
— Midland (Texas)	3	1	.750	1.26	0.79	7	5	1	0	...	1-...	35.2	21	6	5	1	7-0	30	.174
2004— Sacramento (PCL)	11	8	.579	4.19	1.32	28	26	1	0	...	0-...	176.1	199	101	82	13	34-2	143	.284
— Oakland (A.L.)	0	0	...	5.63	1.00	3	0	0	0	0	0-0	8.0	6	5	5	1	2-0	6	.214
2005— Oakland (A.L.)	12	12	.500	3.53	1.22	33	33	2	0	0	0-0	201.1	178	86	79	23	67-3	116	.236
Major League totals (2 years)	12	12	.500	3.61	1.21	36	33	2	0	0	0-0	209.1	184	91	84	24	69-3	122	.235

BLOOMQUIST, WILLIE   3B/SS

PERSONAL: Born November 27, 1977, in Bremerton, Wash. ... 5-11/185. ... Bats right, throws right. ... Full name: William Paul Bloomquist. ... High school: South Kitsap (Port Orchard, Wash.). ... College: Arizona State.
TRANSACTIONS/CAREER NOTES: Selected by Seattle Mariners organization in eighth round of 1996 free-agent draft; did not sign. ... Selected by Mariners organization in third round of 1999 free-agent draft. ... On disabled list (May 2-21, 2004); included rehabilitation assignment to Tacoma. ... On disabled list (August 30, 2005-remainder of season).
2005 GAMES PLAYED BY POSITION (MLB): 2B—32, SS—24, OF—15, 3B—6, DH—1, 1B—1.

SCOUTING REPORT Bloomquist posted career highs in all offensive categories in 2005 but still must prove he can hit well enough to play every day. Has shortened his stroke but has too much movement at the plate. Uses a leg kick and can lose his timing quickly. Has little power. Is a good runner who can steal bases. Has quick, soft hands and good range to both sides. Is quick and agile and has a strong arm. Is aggressive and has good overall makeup. **Grade 5.4**

WILLIE BLOOMQUIST'S HITTING ZONE

.107	.333	.286
.378	.333	.273
.294	.364	.235

LEFTY-RIGHTY SPLITS

vs.	Avg.	AB	H	2B	3B	HR	RBI	BB	SO	OBP	Slg.
L	.247	77	19	3	0	0	4	3	5	.280	.286
R	.262	172	45	12	2	0	18	8	33	.293	.355

								BATTING							FIELDING	
Year Team (League)	Pos.	G	AB	R	H	2B	3B	HR	RBI	BB	SO	HBP	GDP	SB-CS	Avg.	OBP	SLG	OPS	E	Avg.
1999— Everett (N'west)	2B-OF	42	178	35	51	10	3	2	27	22	25	1	1	17-5	.287	.366	.410	.776	7	.954
2000— Lancaster (Calif.)	2B-SS	64	256	63	97	19	6	2	51	37	27	0	3	22-12	.379	.456	.523	.979	12	.961
— Tacoma (PCL)	2B	51	191	17	43	5	1	1	23	7	28	0	1	5-0	.225	.249	.277	.526	3	.987
2001— San Antonio (Texas)	2B-SS	123	491	59	125	23	2	0	28	28	55	1	11	34-9	.255	.294	.310	.603	24	.959
2002— Tacoma (PCL)	OF-2B-3B																			
	SS	104	337	47	91	14	3	6	47	29	44	3	5	20-10	.270	.331	.383	.713	12	.961
— Seattle (A.L.) OF-2B-DH		12	33	11	15	4	0	0	7	5	2	0	0	3-1	.455	.526	.576	1.102	0	1.000
2003— Seattle (A.L.) 3B-SS-DH																				
	OF-2B-1B	89	196	30	49	7	2	1	14	19	39	1	6	4-1	.250	.317	.321	.638	4	.975
2004— Tacoma (PCL)	SS-OF	3	12	2	5	0	0	1	3	0	2	0	1	1-0	.417	.417	.667	1.083	0	1.000
— Seattle (A.L.) 3B-SS-1B																				
	OF-DH-2B	93	188	27	46	10	0	2	18	10	48	0	2	13-2	.245	.283	.330	.613	10	.956
2005— Seattle (A.L.) 2B-SS-OF																				
	3B-1B-DH	82	249	27	64	15	2	0	22	11	38	1	5	14-1	.257	.289	.333	.622	6	.977
Major League totals (4 years)		276	666	95	174	36	4	3	61	45	127	2	13	34-5	.261	.308	.341	.649	20	.970

BLUM, GEOFF   2B/3B

PERSONAL: Born April 26, 1973, in Redwood City, Calif. ... 6-3/200. ... Bats both, throws right. ... Full name: Geoffrey Edward Blum. ... Name pronounced: bluhm. ... High school: Chino (Calif.). ... College: California.
TRANSACTIONS/CAREER NOTES: Selected by Montreal Expos organization in seventh round of 1994 free-agent draft. ... Traded by Expos to Houston Astros for 3B Chris Truby (March 12, 2002). ... Traded by Astros to Tampa Bay Devil Rays for P Brandon Backe (December 14, 2003). ... Released by Devil Rays (November 19, 2004). ... Signed by San Diego Padres (December 8, 2004). ... On disabled list (April 30-May 18, 2005); included rehabilitation assignment to Lake Elsinore. ... Traded by Padres to Chicago White Sox for P Ryan Meaux (July 31, 2005). ... Signed as a free agent by Padres (November 16, 2005).
2005 GAMES PLAYED BY POSITION (MLB): 3B—46, 2B—21, SS—20, 1B—14.

SCOUTING REPORT Blum is a role player who can play all four infield positions. Has more power and hits better from the left side. Has to guess fastball to drive the ball. Has good hands, a plus arm and good range to his left. Is a smart player with good instincts but is not a good enough hitter to play every day. **Grade 5.3**

GEOFF BLUM'S HITTING ZONE

.143	.400	.267
.220	.290	.230
.286	.111	.152

LEFTY-RIGHTY SPLITS

vs.	Avg.	AB	H	2B	3B	HR	RBI	BB	SO	OBP	Slg.
L	.213	94	20	2	0	3	6	6	15	.260	.330
R	.236	225	53	13	2	3	19	22	28	.311	.351

								BATTING							FIELDING	
Year Team (League)	Pos.	G	AB	R	H	2B	3B	HR	RBI	BB	SO	HBP	GDP	SB-CS	Avg.	OBP	SLG	OPS	E	Avg.
1994— Vermont (NYP)	SS	63	241	48	83	15	1	3	38	33	21	3	4	5-5	.344	.428	.452	.880	15	.948
1995— W.P. Beach (FSL)	2B-3B-SS	125	457	54	120	20	2	1	62	34	61	3	12	6-5	.263	.313	.322	.635	18	.963
1996— Harrisburg (East.)		120	396	47	95	22	2	1	41	59	51	3	11	6-7	.240	.341	.313	.654	9	.984
1997— Ottawa (Int'l)	2B-3B-SS	118	407	59	101	21	2	3	35	52	73	3	6	14-6	.248	.333	.332	.665	17	.969
1998— Ottawa (Int'l)	2B	8	23	1	4	0	0	0	1	3	6	0	0	0-0	.174	.269	.174	.443	0	1.000
— GC Expos (GCL)	2B	5	18	0	3	1	1	0	1	0	4	0	0	0-0	.167	.211	.333	.544	0	1.000
— Jupiter (Fla. St.) 2B-3B-SS		17	58	13	16	6	0	0	5	13	14	1	0	1-0	.276	.411	.379	.790	2	.976
— Harrisburg (East.) 1B-2B-3B																				
	SS	39	139	25	43	12	3	6	21	17	24	4	3	2-1	.309	.400	.568	.968	2	.986

Year	Team (League)	Pos.	G	AB	R	H	2B	3B	HR	RBI	BB	SO	HBP	GDP	SB-CS	Avg.	OBP	SLG	OPS	E	Avg.
																BATTING				FIELDING	
1999—Ottawa (Int'l)		SS-1B-2B																			
		3B-DH	77	268	43	71	14	1	10	37	37	39	2	5	6-1	.265	.350	.437	.787	12	.965
—Montreal (N.L.)		SS-2B	45	133	21	32	7	2	8	18	17	25	0	3	1-0	.241	.327	.504	.830	10	.929
2000—Montreal (N.L.)		3B-SS-2B																			
		1B	124	343	40	97	20	2	11	45	26	60	3	4	1-4	.283	.335	.449	.784	9	.974
2001—Montreal (N.L.)		3B-OF-2B																			
		1B-SS	148	453	57	107	25	0	9	50	43	94	10	12	9-5	.236	.313	.351	.664	8	.980
2002—Houston (N.L.)		3B-OF-SS																			
		1B-2B	130	368	45	104	20	4	10	52	49	70	1	8	2-0	.283	.367	.440	.807	8	.972
2003—Houston (N.L.)		3B-2B-SS																			
		1B-OF	123	420	51	110	19	0	10	52	20	50	2	15	0-0	.262	.295	.379	.674	7	.975
2004—Tampa Bay (A.L.)		3B-2B-OF																			
		1B-DH-SS	112	339	38	73	21	0	8	35	24	58	0	4	2-3	.215	.266	.348	.614	10	.970
2005—Lake Elsinore (Calif.)		2B-SS	2	8	3	2	0	0	2	5	1	2	0	0	0-0	.250	.333	1.000	1.333	1	.944
—San Diego (N.L.)		3B-2B-SS																			
		1B	78	224	26	54	13	1	5	22	24	28	3	5	3-2	.241	.321	.375	.696	3	.985
—Chicago (A.L.)		1B-3B-SS																			
		2B	31	95	6	19	2	1	1	3	4	15	0	1	0-1	.200	.232	.274	.506	3	.981
American League totals (2 years)			143	434	44	92	23	1	9	38	28	73	0	5	2-4	.212	.259	.332	.590	13	.973
National League totals (6 years)			648	1941	240	504	104	9	53	239	179	327	19	47	16-11	.260	.326	.404	.730	45	.973
Major League totals (7 years)			791	2375	284	596	127	10	62	277	207	400	19	52	18-15	.251	.314	.391	.705	58	.973

DIVISION SERIES RECORD

Year	Team (League)	Pos.	G	AB	R	H	2B	3B	HR	RBI	BB	SO	HBP	GDP	SB-CS	Avg.	OBP	SLG	OPS	E	Avg.
2005—Chicago (A.L.)		1B	1	1	0	0	0	0	0	0	0	0	0	0	0-0	.000	.000	.000	.000	0	.000

WORLD SERIES RECORD

Year	Team (League)	Pos.	G	AB	R	H	2B	3B	HR	RBI	BB	SO	HBP	GDP	SB-CS	Avg.	OBP	SLG	OPS	E	Avg.
2005—Chicago (A.L.)		2B	1	1	1	1	0	0	1	1	0	0	0	0	0-0	1.000	1.000	4.000	5.000	0	1.000

BOCACHICA, HIRAM — OF

PERSONAL: Born March 4, 1976, in Ponce, Puerto Rico. ... 5-11/180. ... Bats right, throws right. ... Full name: Hiram Colon Bocachica. ... Name pronounced: hear-ram bow-ka-CHEE-ka. ... High school: Rexville (Bayamon, Puerto Rico).

TRANSACTIONS/CAREER NOTES: Selected by Montreal Expos organization in first round (21st pick overall) of 1994 free-agent draft. ... Traded by Expos with P Carlos Perez and SS Mark Grudzielanek to Los Angeles Dodgers for 2B Wilton Guerrero, P Ted Lilly, OF Peter Bergeron and 1B Jonathan Tucker (July 31, 1998). ... On disabled list (July 9-26, 2001). ... Traded by Dodgers to Detroit Tigers for P Tom Farmer and a player to be named (July 25, 2002); Dodgers acquired P Jason Frasor to complete deal (September 18, 2002). ... Signed as a free agent by Seattle Mariners organization (January 16, 2004). ... Signed as a free agent by Oakland Athletics organization (November 19, 2004).

2005 GAMES PLAYED BY POSITION (MLB): OF—6, 3B—2, DH—1.

LEFTY-RIGHTY SPLITS

vs.	Avg.	AB	H	2B	3B	HR	RBI	BB	SO	OBP	Slg.
L	.286	7	2	0	0	0	0	0	2	.286	.286
R	.000	12	0	0	0	0	0	0	5	.000	.000

Year	Team (League)	Pos.	G	AB	R	H	2B	3B	HR	RBI	BB	SO	HBP	GDP	SB-CS	Avg.	OBP	SLG	OPS	E	Avg.
																BATTING				FIELDING	
1994—GC Expos (GCL)		SS	43	168	31	47	9	0	5	16	15	42	2	1	11-4	.280	.346	.423	.769	23	.896
1995—Albany (S. Atl.)		2B-SS	96	380	65	108	20	0	2	30	52	78	8	4	47-17	.284	.381	.405	.786	58	.881
1996—W.P. Beach (FSL)		DH-SS	71	267	50	90	17	5	2	26	34	47	6	6	21-3	.337	.419	.461	.880	24	.833
—GC Expos (GCL)		DH	9	32	11	8	3	0	0	2	5	3	1	0	2-1	.250	.368	.344	.712	...	...
1997—Harrisburg (East.)		SS-2B-DH	119	443	82	123	19	3	11	35	41	98	13	3	29-12	.278	.354	.409	.763	32	.909
1998—Harrisburg (East.)		OF-DH	80	296	39	78	18	4	4	27	21	61	11	1	20-8	.264	.334	.392	.726	10	.946
—Ottawa (Int'l)		OF	12	41	5	8	3	1	0	5	6	14	1	1	2-0	.195	.313	.317	.630	0	1.000
—Albuquerque (PCL)		OF	26	101	16	24	7	1	4	16	13	24	6	1	5-3	.238	.358	.446	.804	2	.976
1999—San Antonio (Texas)		2B-DH	123	477	84	139	22	10	11	60	60	71	13	6	30-15	.291	.382	.449	.831	31	.946
2000—Albuquerque (PCL)		2B	124	482	99	155	38	4	23	84	40	100	15	7	10-14	.322	.390	.560	.950	23	.963
—Los Angeles (N.L.)		2B	8	10	2	3	0	0	0	0	0	2	0	0	0-0	.300	.300	.300	.600	0	1.000
2001—Los Angeles (N.L.)		2B-OF-3B	75	133	15	31	11	1	2	9	9	33	1	1	4-1	.233	.287	.376	.663	7	.919
2002—Los Angeles (N.L.)		OF-DH	49	65	12	14	3	0	4	9	5	19	0	1	1-1	.215	.271	.446	.718	2	.960
—Detroit (A.L.)		OF-2B-DH	34	103	14	23	4	0	4	8	5	22	0	2	2-2	.223	.259	.379	.638	2	.969
2003—Detroit (A.L.)		OF	6	22	1	1	1	0	0	0	0	7	0	0	0-0	.045	.045	.091	.136	0	1.000
—Toledo (Int'l)		OF-2B-3B																			
		DH	95	322	48	78	19	3	12	37	24	57	10	5	11-6	.242	.313	.432	.745	11	.954
2004—Tacoma (PCL)		OF-1B-DH	40	136	22	39	5	1	10	25	17	36	8	2	12-3	.287	.393	.559	.951	4	.957
—Seattle (A.L.)		OF-DH	50	90	9	22	5	0	3	6	12	27	1	1	5-4	.244	.337	.400	.737	0	1.000
2005—Ariz. A's (Ariz.)		OF-DH	4	12	1	1	1	0	0	1	0	3	0	0	0-0	.083	.083	.167	.250	0	...
—Sacramento (PCL)		3B-DH	4	17	2	7	2	0	2	6	1	4	0	0	0-0	.412	.444	.882	1.327	0	1.000
—Oakland (A.L.)		OF-3B-DH	9	19	2	2	0	0	0	0	0	7	0	0	0-0	.105	.105	.105	.211	0	...
American League totals (4 years)			99	234	26	48	10	0	7	14	17	63	1	3	7-6	.205	.261	.338	.598	2	.987
National League totals (3 years)			132	208	29	48	14	1	6	18	14	54	1	2	5-2	.231	.283	.394	.677	9	.935
Major League totals (6 years)			231	442	55	96	24	1	13	32	31	117	2	5	12-8	.217	.271	.364	.635	10	.964

BONDERMAN, JEREMY — P

PERSONAL: Born October 28, 1982, in Kennewick, Wash. ... 6-2/210. ... Throws right, bats right. ... Full name: Jeremy Allen Bonderman. ... High school: Pasco (Wash.).

TRANSACTIONS/CAREER NOTES: Selected by Oakland Athletics in first round (26th pick overall) of 2001 free-agent draft; pick received as compensation for New York Mets signing free-agent P Kevin Appier. ... Traded by A's to Detroit Tigers (August 22, 2002), completing three-team deal in which Tigers acquired 1B Carlos Pena, P Franklyn German and a player to be named from A's; A's acquired P Ted Lilly, OF John-Ford Griffin and P Jason Arnold from New York Yankees and Yankees acquired P Jeff Weaver from Tigers (July 6, 2002). ... On suspended list (July 25-31, 2005).

CAREER HITTING: 0-for-15 (.000), 0 R, 0 2B, 0 3B, 0 HR, 0 RBI.

SCOUTING REPORT

Throws: Bonderman has overpowering stuff, throwing a 92-97 mph fastball, a power slider in the upper 80s and an improved changeup. **Tendencies:** He is a strike-out pitcher with late life on his fastball. Has good velocity and tilt on his slider, which could be a devastating pitch. Has improved his changeup and can be dominating at times. No longer is a one-speed pitcher. **Outlook:** He is a No. 1 starter who will just get better. Has an aggressive makeup and will be an All-Star for many years. **Grade 8.5**

JEREMY BONDERMAN'S PITCHING ZONE

.143	.308	.321
.234	.386	.338
.268	.368	.304

LEFTY-RIGHTY SPLITS

vs.	Avg.	AB	H	2B	3B	HR	RBI	BB	SO	OBP	Slg.
L	.287	425	122	34	5	12	53	32	83	.338	.475
R	.249	309	77	10	2	9	39	25	62	.310	.382

B

Year	Team (League)	W	L	Pct.	ERA	WHIP	G	GS	CG	ShO	Hld.	Sv.-Opp.	IP	H	R	ER	HR	BB-IBB	SO	Avg.
2002—	Modesto (California)	9	8	.529	3.61	1.27	25	25	1	0	...	0-...	144.2	129	77	58	15	55-1	160	.233
—	Lakeland (Fla. St.)	0	1	.000	6.00	1.25	2	2	1	0	...	0-...	12.0	11	8	8	3	4-0	10	.262
2003—	Detroit (A.L.)	6	19	.240	5.56	1.55	33	28	0	0	0	0-0	162.0	193	118	100	23	58-2	108	.294
2004—	Detroit (A.L.)	11	13	.458	4.89	1.31	33	32	2	• 2	0	0-0	184.0	168	101	100	24	73-5	168	.242
2005—	Detroit (A.L.)	14	13	.519	4.57	1.35	29	29	4	0	0	0-0	189.0	199	101	96	21	57-0	145	.271
Major League totals (3 years)		31	45	.408	4.98	1.40	95	89	6	2	0	0-0	535.0	560	320	296	68	188-7	421	.269

BONDS, BARRY — OF

PERSONAL: Born July 24, 1964, in Riverside, Calif. ... 6-2/228. ... Bats left, throws left. ... Full name: Barry Lamar Bonds. ... High school: Serra (San Mateo, Calif.). ... College: Arizona State. ... Son of Bobby Bonds, outfielder with eight major league teams (1968-81).

TRANSACTIONS/CAREER NOTES: Selected by San Francisco Giants organization in second round of June 1982 free-agent draft; did not sign. ... Selected by Pittsburgh Pirates organization in first round (sixth pick overall) of June 1985 free-agent draft. ... On disabled list (June 15-July 4, 1992). ... Signed as a free agent by Giants (December 8, 1992). ... On suspended list (August 14-16, 1998). ... On disabled list (April 18-June 9, 1999). ... On disabled list (April 2-September 12, 2005).

RECORDS: Holds major league records for most home runs, season (73, 2001); highest slugging percentage, season (.863, 2001); highest on-base percentage, season (.609, 2004); most bases on balls, season (232, 2004); and most intentional bases on balls, season (120, 2004). ... Holds major league record for most bases on balls, career (2,311), and most intentional bases on balls, career (607).

HONORS: Named Major League Player of the Year by THE SPORTING NEWS (1990, 2001 and 2004). ... Named N.L. Player of the Year by THE SPORTING NEWS (1990 and 1991). ... Named N.L. Most Valuable Player by Baseball Writers' Association of America (1990, 1992-93 and 2001-04). ... Won N.L. Gold Glove as outfielder (1990-94 and 1996-98).

2005 GAMES PLAYED BY POSITION (MLB): OF—13.

SCOUTING REPORT

Offense: Bonds missed five months with three knee surgeries, but showed in his September return he had not lost any bat speed or power. Has one of the shortest, most compact strokes ever used by a power hitter. Stays inside the ball with a slight lift to his swing and power to all fields. Continues to be pitched around. No longer runs well but has good instincts on the bases. **Defense:** Bonds has become very apprehensive in the field. Plays ball in front and doesn't change direction well as he protects his knee. Range has declined, but uses good jumps and proper angles to compensate. Arm is short but accurate with a quick release. **Outlook:** There are concerns with his knee but Bonds at 75 percent is better than 95 percent of the players in the major leagues. **Grade 10**

LEFTY-RIGHTY SPLITS

vs.	Avg.	AB	H	2B	3B	HR	RBI	BB	SO	OBP	Slg.
L	.600	5	3	0	0	1	2	0	0	.600	1.200
R	.243	37	9	1	0	4	8	9	6	.383	.595

Year	Team (League)	Pos.	G	AB	R	H	2B	3B	HR	RBI	BB	SO	HBP	GDP	SB-CS	Avg.	OBP	SLG	OPS	E	Avg.
1985—	Prince Will. (Car.)	OF	71	254	49	76	16	4	13	37	37	52	0	3	15-3	.299	.383	.547	.930	5	.976
1986—	Hawaii (PCL)	OF	44	148	30	46	7	2	7	37	33	31	2	1	16-5	.311	.435	.527	.963	2	.983
—	Pittsburgh (N.L.)	OF	113	413	72	92	26	3	16	48	65	102	2	4	36-7	.223	.330	.416	.746	5	.983
1987—	Pittsburgh (N.L.)	OF	150	551	99	144	34	9	25	59	54	88	3	4	32-10	.261	.329	.492	.821	5	.986
1988—	Pittsburgh (N.L.)	OF	144	538	97	152	30	5	24	58	72	82	2	3	17-11	.283	.368	.491	.859	6	.980
1989—	Pittsburgh (N.L.)	OF	159	580	96	144	34	6	19	58	93	93	1	9	32-10	.248	.351	.426	.777	6	.984
1990—	Pittsburgh (N.L.)		151	519	104	156	32	3	33	114	93	83	3	8	52-13	.301	.406 *	.565	.970	6	.983
1991—	Pittsburgh (N.L.)	OF	153	510	95	149	28	5	25	116	107	73	4	8	43-13	.292 *	.410	.514	.924	3	.991
1992—	Pittsburgh (N.L.)	OF	140	473	* 109	147	36	5	34	103	* 127	69	5	9	39-8	.311 *	.456 *	.624	1.080	3	.991
1993—	San Francisco (N.L.)	OF	159	539	129	181	38	4	* 46	* 123	126	79	2	11	29-12	.336 *	.458 *	.677	1.136	5	.984
1994—	San Francisco (N.L.)	OF	112	391	89	122	18	1	37	81	* 74	43	6	4	29-9	.312	.426	.647	1.073	3	.986
1995—	San Francisco (N.L.)	OF	• 144	506	109	149	30	7	33	104	* 120	83	5	12	31-10	.294 *	.432	.577	1.009	6	.980
1996—	San Francisco (N.L.)	OF	158	517	122	159	27	3	42	129	* 151	76	1	11	40-7	.308	.461	.615	1.076	6	.980
1997—	San Francisco (N.L.)	OF	159	532	123	155	26	5	40	101	* 145	87	8	13	37-8	.291	.446	.585	1.031	5	.984
1998—	San Francisco (N.L.)	OF	156	552	120	167	44	7	37	122	130	92	8	15	28-12	.303	.438	.609	1.047	5	.984
1999—	San Francisco (N.L.)	OF-DH	102	355	91	93	20	2	34	83	73	62	3	6	15-2	.262	.389	.617	1.006	3	.984
2000—	San Francisco (N.L.)	OF	143	480	129	147	28	4	49	106	* 117	77	3	6	11-3	.306	.440	.688	1.127	3	.989
2001—	San Francisco (N.L.)	OF-DH	153	476	129	156	32	2	* 73	137	* 177	93	9	5	13-3	.328 *	.515 *	.863	1.379	6	.977
2002—	San Francisco (N.L.)	OF-DH	143	403	117	149	31	2	46	110	* 198	47	9	4	9-2	.370 *	.582 *	.799	1.381	4	.968
2003—	San Francisco (N.L.)	OF-DH	130	390	111	133	22	1	45	90	* 148	58	10	7	7-0	.341 *	.529 *	.749	1.278	2	.992
2004—	San Francisco (N.L.)	OF-DH	147	373	129	135	27	3	45	101	* 232	41	9	5	6-1	* .362 *	.609 *	.812	1.422	4	.983
2005—	San Francisco (N.L.)	OF	14	42	8	12	1	0	5	10	9	6	0	0	0-0	.286	.404	.667	1.071	0	1.000
Major League totals (20 years)			2730	9140	2078	2742	564	77	708	1853	2311	1434	93	143	506-141	.300	.442	.611	1.053	90	.984

DIVISION SERIES RECORD

Year	Team (League)	Pos.	G	AB	R	H	2B	3B	HR	RBI	BB	SO	HBP	GDP	SB-CS	Avg.	OBP	SLG	OPS	E	Avg.
1997—	San Francisco (N.L.)	OF	3	12	0	3	2	0	0	2	0	3	0	0	1-0	.250	.231	.417	.647	0	1.000
2000—	San Francisco (N.L.)	OF	4	17	2	3	1	1	0	1	3	4	0	0	1-0	.176	.300	.353	.653	0	1.000
2002—	San Francisco (N.L.)	OF	5	17	5	5	0	0	3	4	4	1	0	0	0-1	.294	.409	.824	1.233	1	.909
2003—	San Francisco (N.L.)	OF	4	9	3	2	1	0	0	2	8	0	0	0	1-0	.222	.556	.333	.889	0	1.000
Division series totals (4 years)			16	55	10	13	4	1	3	9	15	8	0	0	3-1	.236	.384	.509	.893	1	.968

CHAMPIONSHIP SERIES RECORD

Year	Team (League)	Pos.	G	AB	R	H	2B	3B	HR	RBI	BB	SO	HBP	GDP	SB-CS	Avg.	OBP	SLG	OPS	E	Avg.
1990— Pittsburgh (N.L.)	OF	6	18	4	3	0	0	0	1	6	5	0	0	2-0	.167	.375	.167	.542	0	1.000
1991— Pittsburgh (N.L.)	OF	7	27	1	4	1	0	0	0	2	4	0	1	3-0	.148	.207	.185	.392	1	.938
1992— Pittsburgh (N.L.)	OF	7	23	5	6	1	0	1	2	6	4	1	0	1-0	.261	.433	.435	.868	0	1.000
2002— San Francisco (N.L.)	OF	5	11	5	3	0	1	1	6	10	2	0	0	0-0	.273	.591	.727	1.318	0	1.000
Champ. series totals (4 years)		25	79	15	16	2	1	2	9	24	15	1	1	6-0	.203	.390	.329	.720	1	.982

WORLD SERIES RECORD

Year	Team (League)	Pos.	G	AB	R	H	2B	3B	HR	RBI	BB	SO	HBP	GDP	SB-CS	Avg.	OBP	SLG	OPS	E	Avg.
2002— San Francisco (N.L.)	OF	7	17	8	8	2	0	4	6	13	3	0	0	0-0	.471	.700	1.294	1.994	1	.909

ALL-STAR GAME RECORD

			G	AB	R	H	2B	3B	HR	RBI	BB	SO	HBP	GDP	SB-CS	Avg.	OBP	SLG	OPS	E	Avg.
All-Star Game totals (12 years)			12	29	5	6	1	0	2	7	4	5	0		1-1	.207	.294	.517	.811	0	1.000

B

BOOKER, CHRIS   P

PERSONAL: Born December 9, 1976, in Monroeville, Ala. ... 6-3/230. ... Throws right, bats right. ... Full name: Christopher Scott Booker. ... High school: Monroe County (Monroeville, Ala.). ... College: None.
TRANSACTIONS/CAREER NOTES: Selected by Chicago Cubs organization in 20th round of free-agent draft (June 1, 1995). ... Traded by Cubs with P Ben Shaffar to Cincinnati Reds for OF Michael Tucker (July 20, 2001).
CAREER HITTING: 0-for-0 (.000), 0 R, 0 2B, 0 3B, 0 HR, 0 RBI.

LEFTY-RIGHTY SPLITS

vs.	Avg.	AB	H	2B	3B	HR	RBI	BB	SO	OBP	Slg.
L	.667	3	2	0	0	1	2	2	0	.800	1.667
R	.500	8	4	1	0	1	5	2	2	.600	1.000

Year	Team (League)	W	L	Pct.	ERA	WHIP	G	GS	CG	ShO	Hld.	Sv.-Opp.	IP	H	R	ER	HR	BB-IBB	SO	Avg.
1995— GC Cubs (GCL)	3	2	.600	2.76	1.21	13	7	0	0	...	1-...	43.0	36	22	13	0	16-0	43	.232
1996— Daytona (Fla. St.)	0	0	...	0.00	1.33	1	1	0	0	...	0-...	3.0	1	1	0	0	3-0	2	.125
— Will. (NYP)	4	6	.400	5.31	1.77	14	14	0	0	...	0-...	61.0	57	51	36	2	51-1	52	.246
1997— Will. (NYP)	1	5	.167	3.35	1.40	24	3	0	0	...	1-...	45.2	39	20	17	2	25-0	60	.234
1998— Rockford (Midwest)	1	2	.333	3.36	1.54	44	1	0	0	...	4-...	65.0	47	32	24	2	53-4	78	.212
1999— Daytona (Fla. St.)	2	5	.286	3.95	1.49	42	0	0	0	...	6-...	73.0	72	45	32	6	37-1	68	.254
2000— Daytona (Fla. St.)	0	2	.000	2.28	1.41	31	0	0	0	...	10-...	27.2	25	12	7	0	14-1	34	.238
— West Tenn (Sou.)	1	0	1.000	3.68	1.50	12	0	0	0	...	1-...	14.2	10	8	6	1	12-0	21	.189
2001— West Tenn (Sou.)	2	6	.250	4.33	1.44	45	0	0	0	...	1-...	52.0	39	29	25	7	36-2	76	.205
— Chattanooga (Sou.)	2	0	1.000	3.94	1.50	16	0	0	0	...	1-...	16.0	13	7	7	1	11-0	25	.217
2003— Dayton (Midw.)	0	0	...	9.00	1.60	5	0	0	0	...	1-...	5.0	4	5	5	3	4-0	6	.211
— GC Reds (GCL)	0	2	.000	8.49	2.14	12	0	0	0	...	2-...	11.2	17	11	11	1	8-0	11	.327
2004— Chattanooga (Sou.)	2	0	1.000	1.38	1.31	28	0	0	0	...	5-...	39.0	26	6	6	0	25-4	57	.182
— Louisville (Int'l)	0	1	.000	4.50	1.67	7	0	0	0	...	2-...	12.0	10	6	6	2	10-0	9	.213
2005— Cincinnati (N.L.)	0	0	...	31.50	5.00	3	0	0	0	0	0-0	2.0	6	8	7	2	4-0	2	.545
— Louisville (Int'l)	8	4	.667	2.49	1.12	59	0	0	0	0	20-24	65.0	45	20	18	2	28-1	91	.195
Major League totals (1 year)	0	0	...	31.50	5.00	3	0	0	0	0	0-0	.	2.0	6	8	7	2	4-0	2	.545

BOONE, AARON   3B

PERSONAL: Born March 9, 1973, in La Mesa, Calif. ... 6-2/200. ... Bats right, throws right. ... Full name: Aaron John Boone. ... High school: Villa Park (Calif.). ... College: Southern California. ... Son of Bob Boone, catcher with three major league teams (1972-90) and manager of Kansas City Royals (1995-97) and Cincinnati Reds (2001-03); brother of Bret Boone, second baseman, Seattle Mariners and Minnesota Twins in 2005; grandson of Ray Boone, infielder with six major league teams (1948-60).
TRANSACTIONS/CAREER NOTES: Selected by California Angels organization in 43rd round of 1991 free-agent draft; did not sign. ... Selected by Cincinnati Reds organization in third round of 1994 free-agent draft. ... On disabled list (July 10, 2000-remainder of season). ... On disabled list (May 15-June 15, August 15-September 1 and September 24, 2001-remainder of season); included rehabilitation assignment to Louisville. ... Traded by Reds to New York Yankees for Ps Brandon Claussen and Charlie Manning and cash (July 31, 2003). ... Released by Yankees (February 26, 2004). ... Signed by Cleveland Indians (June 26, 2004). ... On disabled list (June 26, 2004-remainder of season).
2005 GAMES PLAYED BY POSITION (MLB): 3B—142, DH—1.

SCOUTING REPORT *Offense:* Boone became more patient at the plate last season as he gained the confidence to hit late in the count. Has the ability to hit 20-plus home runs a year. Gets in trouble when he pulls the ball too much. Needs to stay on the breaking ball better and use the whole field. Is a very good baserunner. *Defense:* He is outstanding defensively, with exceptionally quick feet and an excellent first step. Is very adept at fielding bad hops because he stays down on the ball. Has a strong arm and his accuracy has improved. *Outlook:* He should continue where he left off in the second half of 2005. Has outstanding instincts and is a professional player who should get better. *Grade 7.7*

AARON BOONE'S HITTING ZONE

.294	.182	.292
.250	.319	.262
.216	.313	.308

LEFTY-RIGHTY SPLITS

vs.	Avg.	AB	H	2B	3B	HR	RBI	BB	SO	OBP	Slg.
L	.229	118	27	4	0	7	14	17	22	.336	.441
R	.247	393	97	15	1	9	46	18	70	.288	.359

Year	Team (League)	Pos.	G	AB	R	H	2B	3B	HR	RBI	BB	SO	HBP	GDP	SB-CS	Avg.	OBP	SLG	OPS	E	Avg.
1994— Billings (Pion.)	1B-3B	67	256	48	70	15	5	7	55	36	35	3	7	6-3	.273	.362	.453	.815	18	.924
1995— Chattanooga (Sou.)	3B	23	66	6	15	3	0	0	3	5	12	0	5	2-0	.227	.274	.273	.547	6	.875
— Win.-Salem (Car.)	3B	108	395	61	103	19	1	14	50	43	77	9	4	11-7	.261	.345	.420	.765	21	.940
1996— Chattanooga (Sou.) 3B-SS-DH	136	548	86	158	44	7	17	95	38	77	5	5	21-10	.288	.338	.487	.825	22	.945
1997— Indianapolis (A.A.) 3B-SS-2B	131	476	79	138	30	4	22	75	40	81	1	11	12-4	.290	.344	.508	.853	24	.941
— Cincinnati (N.L.)	3B-2B	16	49	5	12	1	0	0	5	2	5	0	1	1-0	.245	.275	.265	.540	3	.917
1998— Cincinnati (N.L.)	3B-2B-SS	58	181	24	51	13	2	2	28	15	36	1	3	6-1	.282	.350	.409	.759	8	.944
— Indianapolis (Int'l) 3B-2B-SS	87	332	56	80	18	1	7	38	31	71	8	6	17-5	.241	.316	.364	.680	19	.943
1999— Cincinnati (N.L.)	3B-SS	139	472	56	132	26	5	14	72	30	79	8	6	17-6	.280	.330	.445	.775	15	.936
— Indianapolis (Int'l) 3B-2B-SS	11	41	6	14	2	1	0	7	3	4	2	1	0-0	.341	.388	.439	.827	3	.930
2000— Cincinnati (N.L.)	3B-SS	84	291	44	83	18	0	12	43	24	52	10	5	6-1	.285	.356	.471	.826	8	.936
2001— Cincinnati (N.L.)	3B	103	381	54	112	26	4	14	62	29	71	8	6	6-3	.294	.351	.483	.834	19	.936
— Louisville (Int'l)	3B	1	4	0	1	0	0	0	0	0	5	0	0	0-0	.250	.250	.250	.500	0	1.000
2002— Cincinnati (N.L.)	3B-SS	•162	606	83	146	38	4	26	87	56	111	10		32-8	.241	.314	.439	.753	22	.956

Year Team (League)	Pos.	G	AB	R	H	2B	3B	HR	RBI	BB	SO	HBP	GDP	SB-CS	Avg.	OBP	SLG	OPS	E	Avg.
																		FIELDING		
																BATTING				
2003— Cincinnati (N.L.) 3B-2B-SS		106	403	61	110	19	3	18	65	35	74	5	6	15-3	.273	.339	.469	.808	17	.956
—New York (A.L.)	3B	54	189	31	48	13	0	6	31	11	30	3	7	8-0	.254	.302	.418	.720	6	.961
2004— Cleveland (A.L.)			Did not play.																	
2005— Cleveland (A.L.)	3B-DH	143	511	61	124	19	1	16	60	35	92	9	16	9-3	.243	.299	.378	.677	18	.955
American League totals (2 years)		197	700	92	172	32	1	22	91	46	122	12	23	17-3	.246	.300	.389	.689	24	.956
National League totals (7 years)		668	2383	327	646	141	14	86	362	191	428	46	39	83-22	.271	.334	.450	.785	92	.953
Major League totals (8 years)		865	3083	419	818	173	15	108	453	237	550	58	62	100-25	.265	.327	.436	.763	116	.953

DIVISION SERIES RECORD

Year Team (League)	Pos.	G	AB	R	H	2B	3B	HR	RBI	BB	SO	HBP	GDP	SB-CS	Avg.	OBP	SLG	OPS	E	Avg.
2003— New York (A.L.)	3B	4	15	1	3	1	0	1	3	0	3	0	0	1-0	.200	.200	.267	.467	0	1.000

CHAMPIONSHIP SERIES RECORD

Year Team (League)	Pos.	G	AB	R	H	2B	3B	HR	RBI	BB	SO	HBP	GDP	SB-CS	Avg.	OBP	SLG	OPS	E	Avg.
2003— New York (A.L.)	3B	7	17	2	3	0	0	1	2	1	6	1	0	1-1	.176	.263	.353	.616	2	.857

WORLD SERIES RECORD

Year Team (League)	Pos.	G	AB	R	H	2B	3B	HR	RBI	BB	SO	HBP	GDP	SB-CS	Avg.	OBP	SLG	OPS	E	Avg.
2003— New York (A.L.)	3B	6	21	1	3	0	0	1	2	0	6	0	0	0-0	.143	.136	.286	.422	3	.850

ALL-STAR GAME RECORD

		G	AB	R	H	2B	3B	HR	RBI	BB	SO	HBP	GDP	SB-CS	Avg.	OBP	SLG	OPS	E	Avg.
All-Star Game totals (1 year)		1	1	0	0	0	0	0	0	0	0	0	0	0-0	.000	.000	.000	.000	0	—

BOONE, BRET — 2B

PERSONAL: Born April 6, 1969, in El Cajon, Calif. ... 5-10/190. ... Bats right, throws right. ... Full name: Bret Robert Boone. ... High school: El Dorado (Yorba Linda, Calif.). ... College: Southern California. ... Son of Bob Boone, catcher with three major league teams (1972-90) and manager of Kansas City Royals (1995-97) and Cincinnati Reds (2001-03); brother of Aaron Boone, third baseman, Cleveland Indians; grandson of Ray Boone, infielder with six major league teams (1948-60).

TRANSACTIONS/CAREER NOTES: Selected by Minnesota Twins organization in 28th round of 1987 free-agent draft; did not sign. ... Selected by Seattle Mariners organization in fifth round of 1990 free-agent draft. ... Traded by Mariners with P Erik Hanson to Cincinnati Reds for P Bobby Ayala and C Dan Wilson (November 2, 1993). ... On disabled list (April 1-16, 1996). ... Traded by Reds with P Mike Remlinger to Atlanta Braves for Ps Denny Neagle and Rob Bell and OF Michael Tucker (November 10, 1998). ... Traded by Braves with OF/1B Ryan Klesko and P Jason Shiell to San Diego Padres for 2B Quilvio Veras, 1B Wally Joyner and OF Reggie Sanders (December 22, 1999). ... On disabled list (August 27, 2000-remainder of season). ... Signed as a free agent by Mariners (December 22, 2000). ... Traded by Mariners with cash to Minnesota Twins for player to be named (July 11, 2005). ... Released by Twins (July 31, 2005).

HONORS: Won N.L. Gold Glove at second base (1998). ... Won A.L. Gold Glove at second base (2002-04).

2005 GAMES PLAYED BY POSITION (MLB): 2B—88.

SCOUTING REPORT Offense: Boone probably regressed as much as any player in baseball last season, when he lost bat speed and let his frustration get the best of him. Is not selective. Can hit the fastball but is unable to lay off high heat. Has opposite-field power, though his power declined severely last season. Will adjust his approach at the plate with the count. *Defense:* Boone has quick, soft hands, but his range declined last season. Doesn't read the ball off the bat as quickly as he once did. Is adept making the pivot on double plays and avoiding contact. *Outlook:* He is working hard this winter to regain his stroke—if he can be 75 percent of what he was, Boone is a good gamble. *Grade 6.5*

BRET BOONE'S HITTING ZONE

.235	.200	.333
.220	.270	.222
.211	.267	.235

LEFTY-RIGHTY SPLITS

vs.	Avg.	AB	H	2B	3B	HR	RBI	BB	SO	OBP	Slg.
L	.203	79	16	4	1	2	8	11	15	.300	.354
R	.227	247	56	11	2	5	29	17	50	.286	.348

Year Team (League)	Pos.	G	AB	R	H	2B	3B	HR	RBI	BB	SO	HBP	GDP	SB-CS	Avg.	OBP	SLG	OPS	E	Avg.
																BATTING			**FIELDING**	
1990— Peninsula (Caro.)	2B	74	255	42	68	13	2	8	38	47	57	1	1	5-2	.267	.383	.427	.810	19	.951
1991— Jacksonville (Sou.)	2B-3B	139	475	64	121	18	1	19	75	72	123	5	21	9-9	.255	.357	.417	.774	21	.970
1992— Calgary (PCL)	2B-SS	118	439	73	138	26	5	13	73	60	88	5	12	17-12	.314	.398	.485	.883	10	.984
—Seattle (A.L.)	2B-3B	33	129	15	25	4	0	4	15	4	34	1	4	1-1	.194	.224	.318	.542	6	.966
1993— Calgary (PCL)	2B	71	274	48	91	18	3	8	56	28	58	1	7	3-8	.332	.388	.507	.896	8	.976
—Seattle (A.L.)	2B-DH	76	271	31	68	12	2	12	38	17	52	4	6	2-3	.251	.301	.443	.743	3	.991
1994— Cincinnati (N.L.)	2B-3B	108	381	59	122	25	2	12	68	24	74	8	10	3-4	.320	.368	.491	.858	12	.975
1995— Cincinnati (N.L.)	2B	138	513	63	137	34	2	15	68	41	84	6	14	5-1	.267	.326	.429	.755	4	.994
1996— Cincinnati (N.L.)	2B	142	520	56	121	21	3	12	69	31	100	3	9	3-2	.233	.275	.354	.629	6	.991
1997— Cincinnati (N.L.)	2B	139	443	40	99	25	1	7	46	45	101	4	11	5-5	.223	.298	.332	.630	2	.997
—Indianapolis (A.A.)	2B	3	7	1	2	1	0	0	1	2	2	0	0	1-0	.286	.444	.429	.873	0	1.000
1998— Cincinnati (N.L.)	2B	157	583	76	155	38	1	24	95	48	104	4	23	6-4	.266	.324	.458	.782	9	.988
1999— Atlanta (N.L.)	2B	152	608	102	153	38	1	20	63	47	112	5	11	14-9	.252	.310	.416	.726	13	.982
2000— San Diego (N.L.)	2B	127	463	61	116	18	2	19	74	50	97	5	11	8-4	.251	.326	.421	.747	15	.977
2001— Seattle (A.L.)	2B-DH	158	623	118	206	37	3	37	* 141	40	110	9	11	5-5	.331	.372	.578	.950	10	.986
2002— Seattle (A.L.)	2B-DH	155	608	88	169	34	3	24	107	53	102	6	11	12-5	.278	.339	.462	.801	7	.989
2003— Seattle (A.L.)	2B	159	622	111	183	35	5	35	117	68	125	7	17	16-3	.294	.366	.535	.902	7	.990
2004— Seattle (A.L.)	2B	148	593	74	149	30	0	24	83	56	135	3	18	10-5	.251	.317	.423	.740	14	.978
2005— Seattle (A.L.)	2B	74	273	30	63	15	3	7	34	24	52	3	9	4-2	.231	.299	.385	.684	7	.979
—Minnesota (A.L.)	2B	14	53	3	9	0	0	0	3	4	13	1	3	0-0	.170	.241	.170	.411	2	.974
American League totals (7 years)		817	3172	470	872	167	16	143	538	266	623	34	79	50-24	.275	.334	.473	.807	56	.984
National League totals (7 years)		963	3511	457	903	199	12	109	483	286	672	35	89	44-29	.257	.316	.414	.730	61	.987
Major League totals (14 years)		1780	6683	927	1775	366	28	252	1021	552	1295	69	168	94-53	.266	.325	.442	.767	117	.986

DIVISION SERIES RECORD

Year Team (League)	Pos.	G	AB	R	H	2B	3B	HR	RBI	BB	SO	HBP	GDP	SB-CS	Avg.	OBP	SLG	OPS	E	Avg.
1995— Cincinnati (N.L.)	2B	3	10	4	3	1	0	1	1	1	3	0	0	1-0	.300	.364	.700	1.064	0	1.000
1999— Atlanta (N.L.)	2B	4	19	3	9	1	0	0	1	0	4	0	1	1-0	.474	.474	.526	1.000	0	1.000
2001— Seattle (A.L.)	2B	5	21	1	2	0	0	0	0	1	11	0	1	1-0	.095	.136	.095	.232	1	.960
Division series totals (3 years)		12	50	8	14	2	0	1	2	2	18	0	2	3-0	.280	.308	.380	.688	1	.984

CHAMPIONSHIP SERIES RECORD

Year Team (League)	Pos.	G	AB	R	H	2B	3B	HR	RBI	BB	SO	HBP	GDP	SB-CS	Avg.	OBP	SLG	OPS	E	Avg.
1995—Cincinnati (N.L.)	2B	4	14	1	3	0	0	0	1	2	0	1	2	0-0	.214	.267	.214	.481	0	1.000
1999—Atlanta (N.L.)	2B	6	22	2	4	1	0	0	1	1	7	1	0	2-1	.182	.250	.227	.477	0	1.000
2001—Seattle (A.L.)	2B	5	19	2	6	0	0	2	6	2	2	0	0	0-0	.316	.381	.632	1.013	0	1.000
Champ. series totals (3 years)		15	55	5	13	1	0	2	7	4	11	1	2	2-1	.236	.300	.364	.664	0	1.000

WORLD SERIES RECORD

Year Team (League)	Pos.	G	AB	R	H	2B	3B	HR	RBI	BB	SO	HBP	GDP	SB-CS	Avg.	OBP	SLG	OPS	E	Avg.
1999—Atlanta (N.L.)	2B	4	13	1	7	4	0	0	3	1	3	0	0	0-1	.538	.571	.846	1.418	0	1.000

ALL-STAR GAME RECORD

		G	AB	R	H	2B	3B	HR	RBI	BB	SO	HBP	GDP	SB-CS	Avg.	OBP	SLG	OPS	E	Avg.
All-Star Game totals (2 years)		2	4	0	0	0	0	0	0	0	1	0	0	0-0	.000	.000	.000	.000	0	1.000

B

BOOTCHECK, CHRIS   P

PERSONAL: Born October 24, 1978, in La Porte, Ind. ... 6-5/200. ... Throws right, bats right. ... Full name: Christopher Brandon Bootcheck. ... High school: La Porte (Ind.). ... College: Auburn.
TRANSACTIONS/CAREER NOTES: Selected by Anaheim Angels in first round (20th pick overall) of 2000 free-agent draft. ... Angels franchise renamed Los Angeles Angels of Anaheim for 2005 season.
CAREER HITTING: 0-for-0 (.000), 0 R, 0 2B, 0 3B, 0 HR, 0 RBI.

CHRIS BOOTCHECK'S PITCHING ZONE

.286	.000	.143
.100	.556	.333
.000	.667	.250

LEFTY-RIGHTY SPLITS

vs.	Avg.	AB	H	2B	3B	HR	RBI	BB	SO	OBP	Slg.
L	.273	33	9	3	1	1	4	3	2	.324	.515
R	.244	41	10	1	0	0	2	1	6	.262	.268

Year Team (League)	W	L	Pct.	ERA	WHIP	G	GS	CG	ShO	Hld.	Sv.-Opp.	IP	H	R	ER	HR	BB-IBB	SO	Avg.
2001—Rancho Cuca. (Calif.)	8	4	.667	3.93	1.23	15	14	1	0	...	0-...	87.0	84	45	38	11	23-0	86	.251
—Arkansas (Texas)	3	3	.500	5.45	1.38	6	6	1	0	...	0-...	36.1	39	25	22	3	11-0	22	.265
2002—Arkansas (Texas)	8	7	.533	4.81	1.42	19	19	3	0	...	0-...	116.0	130	68	62	11	35-0	90	.277
—Salt Lake (PCL)	4	3	.571	3.88	1.38	9	9	1	1	...	0-...	58.0	64	29	25	8	16-0	38	.283
2003—Salt Lake (PCL)	8	9	.471	4.25	1.38	28	26	3	0	...	0-...	171.1	194	103	81	19	43-1	82	.290
—Anaheim (A.L.)	0	1	.000	9.58	2.13	4	1	0	0	0	0-0	10.1	16	13	11	5	6-0	7	.340
2004—Salt Lake (PCL)	11	9	.550	5.12	1.60	28	28	3	1	...	0-...	163.1	202	109	93	22	60-2	105	.306
2005—Los Angeles (A.L.)	0	1	.000	3.38	1.23	5	2	0	0	0	1-1	18.2	19	7	7	1	4-1	8	.257
—Salt Lake (PCL)	7	4	.636	5.42	1.67	21	21	0	0	...	0-...	116.1	144	75	70	13	50-0	90	.312
Major League totals (2 years)	0	2	.000	5.59	1.55	9	3	0	0	0	1-1	29.0	35	20	18	6	10-1	15	.289

BORCHARD, JOE   OF

PERSONAL: Born November 25, 1978, in Panorama City, Calif. ... 6-5/220. ... Bats both, throws right. ... Full name: Joseph Edward Borchard. ... Name pronounced: BORE-churd. ... High school: Camarillo (Calif.). ... College: Stanford.
TRANSACTIONS/CAREER NOTES: Selected by Baltimore Orioles organization in 20th round of 1997 free-agent draft; did not sign. ... Selected by Chicago White Sox organization in first round (12th pick overall) of 2000 free-agent draft.
2005 GAMES PLAYED BY POSITION (MLB): DH—3, OF—2.

Year Team (League)	Pos.	G	AB	R	H	2B	3B	HR	RBI	BB	SO	HBP	GDP	SB-CS	Avg.	OBP	SLG	OPS	E	Avg.
2000—Ariz. White Sox (Ariz.)	OF	7	29	3	12	4	0	0	8	4	4	0	0	0-0	.414	.485	.552	1.037	0	1.000
—Win.-Salem (Car.)	OF	14	52	7	15	3	0	2	7	6	9	2	0	0-0	.288	.377	.462	.839	0	1.000
—Birmingham (Sou.)	OF	6	22	3	5	0	1	0	3	3	8	0	1	0-0	.227	.308	.318	.626	1	.875
2001—Birmingham (Sou.)	OF	133	515	95	152	27	1	27	98	67	158	10	13	5-4	.295	.384	.509	.892	12	.965
2002—Win.-Salem (Car.)	OF	2	3	1	0	0	0	0	0	0	6	0	0	0-0	.000	.000	.000	.000	0	1.000
—Charlotte (Int'l)	OF	117	438	62	119	35	2	20	59	49	139	4	11	2-4	.272	.349	.498	.847	3	.990
—Chicago (A.L.)	OF	16	36	5	8	0	0	2	5	1	14	0	0	0-0	.222	.243	.389	.632	0	1.000
2003—Charlotte (Int'l)	OF	16	49	5	9	1	0	1	5	5	18	0	0	0-1	.184	.246	.265	.511	0	1.000
—Chicago (A.L.)	OF	114	435	62	110	20	2	13	53	27	103	8	14	2-4	.253	.307	.398	.705	5	.985
2004—Charlotte (Int'l)	OF-DH	82	301	44	80	21	0	16	48	30	68	2	7	4-3	.266	.333	.495	.828	4	.980
—Chicago (A.L.)	OF-DH	63	201	26	35	4	1	9	20	19	57	1	4	1-0	.174	.249	.338	.587	3	.972
2005—Charlotte (Int'l)	OF-DH	134	494	69	130	20	0	29	67	50	143	4	19	6-4	.263	.335	.480	.815	6	.989
—Chicago (A.L.)	DH-OF	7	12	0	5	2	0	0	0	0	4	0	0	0-1	.417	.417	.583	1.000	0	1.000
Major League totals (4 years)		102	298	36	57	7	1	12	30	25	93	1	4	1-2	.191	.254	.342	.596	3	.982

BORDERS, PAT   C

PERSONAL: Born May 14, 1963, in Columbus, Ohio. ... 6-2/200. ... Bats right, throws right. ... Full name: Patrick Lance Borders. ... High school: Lake Wales (Fla.).
TRANSACTIONS/CAREER NOTES: Selected by Toronto Blue Jays organization in sixth round of June 1982 free-agent draft. ... On disabled list (July 5-August 19, 1988); included rehabilitation assignment to Syracuse. ... Signed as a free agent by Kansas City Royals (April 10, 1995). ... Traded by Royals to Houston Astros for a player to be named (August 12, 1995); Royals acquired P Rick Huisman to complete deal (August 17, 1995). ... On suspended list (September 8-14, 1995). ... Signed as a free agent by St. Louis Cardinals organization (January 10, 1996). ... Traded by Cardinals to California Angels for P Ben VanRyn (June 15, 1996). ... Traded by Angels to Chicago White Sox for P Robert Ellis (July 27, 1996). ... Signed as a free agent by Cleveland Indians organization (December 13, 1996). ... Released by Indians (August 30, 1999). ... Signed by Blue Jays (August 31, 1999). ... Signed as a free agent by Tampa Bay Devil Rays (January 27, 2000). ... Traded by Devil Rays to Seattle Mariners for cash (August 27, 2001). ... Signed as a free agent by Texas Rangers organization (February 2, 2002). ... Released by Rangers (April 2, 2002). ... Signed by Mariners organization (April 8, 2002). ... Traded by Mariners to Minnesota Twins for OF B.J. Garbe (August 31, 2004). ...Signed as a free agent by Milwaukee Brewers organization (November 17, 2004). ... Traded by Brewers to Seattle Mariners organization for cash (May 19, 2005). ... Released by Mariners (August 8, 2005).

PAT BORDERS'S HITTING ZONE

.333	.200	.143
.320	.250	.000
.300	.375	.000

LEFTY-RIGHTY SPLITS

vs.	Avg.	AB	H	2B	3B	HR	RBI	BB	SO	OBP	Slg.
L	.324	37	12	3	0	1	4	2	6	.359	.486
R	.138	80	11	2	0	0	3	2	16	.167	.163

2005 GAMES PLAYED BY POSITION (MLB): C—39.

										BATTING										FIELDING	
Year	Team (League)	Pos.	G	AB	R	H	2B	3B	HR	RBI	BB	SO	HBP	GDP	SB-CS	Avg.	OBP	SLG	OPS	E	Avg.
1982— Medicine Hat (Pio.)		3B	61	217	30	66	12	2	5	33	24	52	2	...	1-2	.304	.377	.447	.824	25	.826
1983— Florence (S. Atl.)		3B	131	457	62	125	31	4	5	54	46	116	1	...	4-1	.274	.341	.392	.732	41	.881
1984— Florence (S. Atl.)	1B-3B-OF		131	467	69	129	32	5	12	85	56	109	1	6	3-4	.276	.353	.443	.796	15	.967
1985— Kinston (Carol.)		1B	127	460	43	120	16	1	10	60	45	116	1	11	6-5	.261	.327	.365	.692	20	.978
1986— Florence (S. Atl.)		C-OF	16	40	8	15	7	0	3	9	2	9	0	0	0-0	.375	.405	.775	1.180	0	1.000
— Knoxville (Southern)		1B-C	12	34	3	12	1	0	2	5	1	6	0	2	0-3	.353	.371	.559	.930	3	.943
— Kinston (Carol.)	1B-C-OF		49	174	24	57	10	0	6	26	10	42	1	5	0-0	.328	.366	.489	.854	7	.971
1987— Dunedin (Fla. St.)		1B	3	11	0	4	0	0	0	1	0	3	0	0	0-0	.364	.364	.364	.727	0	1.000
— Knoxville (Southern)		3B-C	94	349	44	102	14	1	11	51	20	56	2	13	2-5	.292	.332	.433	.764	12	.976
1988— Toronto (A.L.)	2B-3B-C																				
		DH	56	154	15	42	6	3	5	21	3	24	0	5	0-0	.273	.285	.448	.733	7	.970
— Syracuse (Int'l)		C	35	120	11	29	8	0	3	14	16	22	0	1	0-0	.242	.326	.383	.709	2	.991
1989— Toronto (A.L.)		C-DH	94	241	22	62	11	1	3	29	11	45	1	7	2-1	.257	.290	.349	.639	6	.980
1990— Toronto (A.L.)		C-DH	125	346	36	99	24	2	15	49	18	57	0	17	0-1	.286	.319	.497	.816	4	.993
1991— Toronto (A.L.)		C	105	291	22	71	17	0	5	36	11	45	1	8	0-0	.244	.271	.354	.625	4	.993
1992— Toronto (A.L.)		C	138	480	47	116	26	2	13	53	33	75	2	11	1-1	.242	.290	.385	.676	8	.991
1993— Toronto (A.L.)		C	138	488	38	124	30	0	9	55	20	66	2	18	2-2	.254	.285	.371	.656	* 13	.986
1994— Toronto (A.L.)		C	85	295	24	73	13	1	3	26	15	50	0	7	1-1	.247	.284	.329	.613	8	.988
1995— Kansas City (A.L.)		C-DH	52	143	14	33	8	1	4	13	7	22	0	1	0-0	.231	.267	.385	.651	0	1.000
— Houston (N.L.)		C	11	35	1	4	0	0	0	0	2	7	0	2	0-0	.114	.162	.114	.276	1	.987
1996— St. Louis (N.L.)		C-1B	26	69	3	22	3	0	0	4	1	14	0	1	0-1	.319	.329	.362	.691	3	.977
— California (A.L.)		C	19	57	6	13	3	0	2	8	3	11	0	1	0-1	.228	.267	.386	.653	2	.984
— Chicago (A.L.)		C-DH	31	94	6	26	1	0	3	6	5	18	0	2	0-0	.277	.313	.383	.696	3	.982
1997— Cleveland (A.L.)		C	55	159	17	47	7	1	4	15	9	27	2	5	0-2	.296	.341	.428	.769	0	1.000
1998— Cleveland (A.L.)		C-3B	54	160	12	38	6	0	6	16	6	40	2	3	0-1	.238	.289	.275	.564	8	.974
1999— Buffalo (Int'l)		C-DH	55	198	17	47	7	0	5	23	12	31	3	5	0-1	.237	.290	.348	.638	5	.986
— Cleveland (A.L.)		C-3B	6	20	2	6	0	1	0	3	0	3	0	0	0-1	.300	.300	.400	.700	2	.943
— Cleveland (A.L.)		C-DH	14	1	3	0	0	1	3	1	2	0	0	0-0	.214	.267	.429	.695	0	1.000
2000— Durham (Int'l)		C-1B	96	348	44	95	16	0	12	55	20	66	1	8	7-2	.273	.311	.422	.733	3	.995
2001— Durham (Int'l)		C-1B	87	313	26	74	15	1	2	28	16	61	2	14	3-2	.236	.278	.310	.588	4	.989
— Tacoma (PCL)		C	3	11	2	3	0	0	1	2	1	1	1	1	0-0	.273	.385	.545	.930	0	1.000
— Seattle (A.L.)		C	5	6	1	3	0	0	0	0	0	2	0	0	0-0	.500	.500	.500	1.000	1	.923
2002— Tacoma (PCL)	C-3B-1B		92	317	42	84	16	1	12	27	11	47	0	6	3-2	.265	.289	.435	.724	5	.992
— Seattle (A.L.)		C-DH	4	4	0	2	1	0	0	1	0	1	0	0	0-0	.500	.500	.750	1.250	0	1.000
2003— Tacoma (PCL)	C-DH-1B		79	293	36	92	27	1	12	51	20	54	4	12	1-2	.314	.363	.536	.898	6	.987
— Seattle (A.L.)	C-3B-DH		12	14	1	2	1	0	0	1	1	5	0	0	0-0	.143	.200	.214	.414	0	1.000
2004— Seattle (A.L.)		C	19	53	6	10	2	0	1	5	1	12	0	2	1-1	.189	.204	.283	.487	1	.992
— Tacoma (PCL)		C	36	137	16	35	5	1	5	13	3	28	3	4	0-1	.255	.287	.416	.703	1	.996
— Minnesota (A.L.)		C	19	42	3	12	4	0	0	5	0	10	1	0	2-0	.286	.302	.381	.683	3	.968
2005— Nashville (PCL)		C	26	98	8	24	2	0	3	8	6	16	1	6	1-2	.245	.265	.357	.622	5	.976
— Seattle (A.L.)		C	39	117	12	23	5	0	1	7	4	22	1	4	0-0	.197	.228	.265	.493	2	.990
American League totals (17 years)			1062	3178	285	805	165	12	69	342	152	536	12	91	9-13	.253	.288	.378	.666	72	.988
National League totals (2 years)			37	104	4	26	3	0	0	4	3	21	0	3	0-1	.250	.271	.279	.550	4	.980
Major League totals (17 years)			1099	3282	289	831	168	12	69	346	155	557	12	94	9-14	.253	.288	.375	.663	76	.987

DIVISION SERIES RECORD

Year	Team (League)	Pos.	G	AB	R	H	2B	3B	HR	RBI	BB	SO	HBP	GDP	SB-CS	Avg.	OBP	SLG	OPS	E	Avg.
2004— Minnesota (A.L.)		C	2	2	0	0	0	0	0	0	0	1	0	0	0-0	.000	.000	.000	.000	0	1.000

CHAMPIONSHIP SERIES RECORD

Year	Team (League)	Pos.	G	AB	R	H	2B	3B	HR	RBI	BB	SO	HBP	GDP	SB-CS	Avg.	OBP	SLG	OPS	E	Avg.
1989— Toronto (A.L.)		C	1	1	0	1	0	0	0	0	0	0	0	0	0-0	1.000	1.000	1.000	2.000	0	1.000
1991— Toronto (A.L.)		C	5	19	0	5	1	0	0	2	0	0	0	2	0-0	.263	.263	.316	.579	2	.955
1992— Toronto (A.L.)		C	6	22	3	7	0	0	1	3	1	1	0	0	0-0	.318	.320	.455	.775	1	.976
1993— Toronto (A.L.)		C	6	24	1	6	1	0	0	3	0	6	0	0	1-0	.250	.250	.292	.542	0	1.000
Champ. series totals (4 years)			18	66	4	19	2	0	1	8	1	7	0	2	1-0	.288	.290	.364	.653	3	.977

WORLD SERIES RECORD

Year	Team (League)	Pos.	G	AB	R	H	2B	3B	HR	RBI	BB	SO	HBP	GDP	SB-CS	Avg.	OBP	SLG	OPS	E	Avg.
1992— Toronto (A.L.)		C	6	20	2	9	3	0	1	3	2	1	0	0	0-0	.450	.500	.750	1.250	1	.981
1993— Toronto (A.L.)		C	6	23	2	7	0	0	1	1	2	1	0	1	0-0	.304	.360	.304	.664	1	.981
World Series totals (2 years)			12	43	4	16	3	0	1	4	4	2	0	1	0-0	.372	.426	.512	.937	2	.981

BOROWSKI, JOE   P

PERSONAL: Born May 4, 1971, in Bayonne, N.J. ... 6-2/225. ... Throws right, bats right. ... Full name: Joseph Thomas Borowski. ... Name pronounced: bor-OW-ski. ... High school: Marist (Bayonne, N.J.). ... College: Rutgers.
TRANSACTIONS/CAREER NOTES: Selected by Chicago White Sox organization in 32nd round of 1989 free-agent draft. ... Traded by White Sox to Baltimore Orioles for IF Pete Rose II (March 21, 1991). ... Traded by Orioles with P Rachaad Stewart to Atlanta Braves for P Kent Mercker (December 17, 1995). ... Claimed on waivers by New York Yankees (September 15, 1997). ... On disabled list (August 24-September 8, 1998). ... Claimed on waivers by Milwaukee Brewers (December 4, 1998). ... Signed as a free agent by Cincinnati Reds organization (November 9, 1999). ... Released by Reds (April 14, 2000). ... Signed by Chicago Cubs organization (December 11, 2000). ... On disabled list (June 5, 2004-remainder of season); included rehabilitation assignment to Iowa. ... On disabled list (March 25-May 20, 2005); included rehabilitation assignment to Iowa. ... Released by Cubs (July 7, 2005). ... Signed by Tampa Bay Devil Rays (July 14, 2005).
CAREER HITTING: 2-for-9 (.222), 1 R, 0 2B, 0 3B, 0 HR, 0 RBI.

SCOUTING REPORT **Throws:** Borowski's fastball range now is in the upper 80s after a series of arm problems. Also has a slider in the low 80s and a split-finger fastball. *Tendencies:* Borowski has good location and his slider is quick. Relies on his splitter late in the count, making him far more effective against lefthanders than righthanders. *Outlook:* Borowski's outstanding makeup allowed him to come back from his injuries. May never have the same velocity he had as the Cubs' closer, but still can be effective as a setup man. *Grade 7*

JOE BOROWSKI'S PITCHING ZONE

.389	.200	.091
.205	.263	.429
.182	.250	.091

LEFTY-RIGHTY SPLITS

vs.	Avg.	AB	H	2B	3B	HR	RBI	BB	SO	OBP	Slg.
L	.198	81	16	2	1	2	13	7	14	.261	.321
R	.244	90	22	5	0	6	17	5	13	.284	.500

Year	Team (League)	W	L	Pct.	ERA	WHIP	G	GS	CG	ShO	Hld.	Sv.-Opp.	IP	H	R	ER	HR	BB-IBB	SO	Avg.
1990— GC Whi. Sox (GCL)		2	8	.200	5.58	1.61	12	11	0	0	...	0-...	61.1	74	47	38	3	25-0	67	.289

B

Year Team (League)	W	L	Pct.	ERA	WHIP	G	GS	CG	ShO	Hld.	Sv.-Opp.	IP	H	R	ER	HR	BB-IBB	SO	Avg.
1991—Kane Co. (Midw.)	7	2	.778	2.56	1.27	49	0	0	0	...	13-...	81.0	60	26	23	2	43-2	76	.207
1992—Frederick (Carolina)	5	6	.455	3.70	1.51	48	0	0	0	...	10-...	80.1	71	40	33	3	50-3	85	.238
1993—Frederick (Carolina)	1	1	.500	3.61	1.57	42	2	0	0	...	11-...	62.1	61	30	25	5	37-0	70	.258
—Bowie (East.)	3	0	1.000	0.00	1.25	9	0	0	0	...	0-...	17.2	11	0	0	0	11-3	17	.180
1994—Bowie (East.)	3	4	.429	1.91	1.21	49	0	0	0	...	14-...	66.0	52	14	14	3	28-3	73	.213
1995—Rochester (Int'l)	1	3	.250	4.04	1.40	28	0	0	0	...	6-...	35.2	32	16	16	3	18-2	32	.256
—Bowie (East.)	2	2	.500	3.92	1.11	16	0	0	0	...	7-...	20.2	16	9	9	2	7-1	32	.211
—Baltimore (A.L.)	0	0	...	1.23	1.23	6	0	0	0	...	0-0	7.1	5	1	1	0	4-0	3	.192
1996—Richmond (Int'l)	1	5	.167	3.71	1.35	34	0	0	0	...	7-...	53.1	42	25	22	4	30-1	40	.226
—Atlanta (N.L.)	2	4	.333	4.85	1.77	22	0	0	0	1	0-0	26.0	33	15	14	4	13-4	15	.324
1997—Atlanta (N.L.)	2	2	.500	3.75	1.79	20	0	0	0	2	0-0	24.0	27	11	10	2	16-4	6	.287
—Richmond (Int'l)	1	2	.333	3.58	1.35	21	0	0	0	...	2-...	37.2	32	16	15	3	19-2	34	.234
—New York (A.L.)	0	1	.000	9.00	3.00	1	0	0	0	0	0-0	2.0	2	2	2	0	4-1	2	.250
1998—Columbus (Int'l)	3	3	.500	2.93	1.43	45	0	0	0	...	4-...	73.2	66	25	24	6	39-1	67	.243
—New York (A.L.)	1	0	1.000	6.52	1.55	8	0	0	0	0	0-0	9.2	11	7	7	0	4-0	7	.289
1999—Louisville (Int'l)	6	2	.750	5.46	1.55	56	0	0	0	...	4-...	89.0	94	59	54	7	44-3	70	.275
2000—Newark (Atl.)	6	3	.667	5.50	1.62	28	0	0	0	...	6-...	37.2	44	23	23	5	17-...	39	
—Monterrey (Mex.)	4	2	.667	3.19	1.16	12	5	0	0	...	1-...	42.1	31	15	15	5	18-...	44	...
2001—Iowa (PCL)	8	7	.533	2.62	1.03	39	12	1	1	...	1-...	110.0	87	35	32	10	26-3	131	.216
—Chicago (N.L.)	0	1	.000	32.40	5.40	1	1	0	0	0	0-0	1.2	6	6	6	1	3-0	1	.667
2002—Chicago (N.L.)	4	4	.500	2.73	1.18	73	0	0	0	12	2-6	95.2	84	31	29	10	29-6	97	.239
2003—Chicago (N.L.)	2	2	.500	2.63	1.05	68	0	0	0	1	33-37	68.1	53	23	20	5	19-1	66	.207
2004—Chicago (N.L.)	2	4	.333	8.02	1.97	22	0	0	0	0	9-11	21.1	27	19	19	3	15-2	17	.303
—Iowa (PCL)	0	3	.000	8.22	1.70	7	3	0	0	...	0-...	7.2	9	8	7	1	4-0	2	.290
2005—Iowa (PCL)	0	0	...	2.25	0.75	7	0	0	0	0	0-0	8.0	3	4	2	2	3-0	4	.107
—Chicago (N.L.)	0	0	...	6.55	1.18	11	0	0	0	1	0-0	11.0	12	8	8	5	1-0	11	.261
—Tampa Bay (A.L.)	1	5	.167	3.82	1.05	32	0	0	0	19	0-4	35.1	26	15	15	3	11-1	16	.208
American League totals (4 years)	2	6	.250	4.14	1.23	47	0	0	0	19	0-4	54.1	44	25	25	3	23-2	28	.223
National League totals (7 years)	12	17	.414	3.85	1.36	217	1	0	0	17	44-54	248.0	242	113	106	30	96-17	213	.255
Major League totals (9 years)	14	23	.378	3.90	1.34	264	1	0	0	36	44-58	302.1	286	138	131	33	119-19	241	.250

DIVISION SERIES RECORD

Year Team (League)	W	L	Pct.	ERA	WHIP	G	GS	CG	ShO	Hld.	Sv.-Opp.	IP	H	R	ER	HR	BB-IBB	SO	Avg.
2003—Chicago (N.L.)	0	0	...	0.00	0.50	2	0	0	0	0	1-1	2.0	1	0	0	0	0-0	5	.143

CHAMPIONSHIP SERIES RECORD

Year Team (League)	W	L	Pct.	ERA	WHIP	G	GS	CG	ShO	Hld.	Sv.-Opp.	IP	H	R	ER	HR	BB-IBB	SO	Avg.
2003—Chicago (N.L.)	1	0	1.000	1.59	1.41	3	0	0	0	0	0-1	5.2	5	2	1	0	3-1	1	.227

BOTTALICO, RICKY   P

PERSONAL: Born August 26, 1969, in New Britain, Conn. ... 6-0/215. ... Throws right, bats left. ... Full name: Richard Paul Bottalico. ... Name pronounced: bo-TAL-e-koh. ... High school: South Catholic (Hartford, Conn.). ... College: Central Connecticut State.

TRANSACTIONS/CAREER NOTES: Signed as a non-drafted free agent by Philadelphia Phillies organization (July 21, 1991). ... On disabled list (April 24-July 1, 1998); included rehabilitation assignment to Scranton/Wilkes-Barre. ... On suspended list (August 25-28, 1998). ... Traded by Phillies with P Garrett Stephenson to St. Louis Cardinals for OF Ron Gant and Ps Jeff Brantley and Cliff Politte (November 19, 1998). ... Signed as a free agent by Kansas City Royals (January 27, 2000). ... Signed as a free agent by Phillies (December 15, 2000). ... On disabled list (June 29-July 20, 2001); included rehabilitation assignment to Reading. ... On disabled list (June 23, 2002-remainder of season). ... Signed as a free agent by Arizona Diamondbacks organization (January 30, 2003). ... Signed as a free agent by New York Mets organization (February 9, 2004). ... Signed as a free agent by Milwaukee Brewers (January 21, 2005). ... Released by Brewers (July 29, 2005). ... Signed by Boston Red Sox organization (August 8, 2005).

CAREER HITTING: 2-for-17 (.118), 1 R, 2 2B, 0 3B, 0 HR, 1 RBI.

RICKY BOTTALICO'S PITCHING ZONE

.375	.429	.333
.375	.375	.158
.250	.000	.263

LEFTY-RIGHTY SPLITS

vs.	Avg.	AB	H	2B	3B	HR	RBI	BB	SO	OBP	Slg.
L	.260	77	20	1	0	5	19	10	13	.341	.468
R	.271	85	23	3	0	2	11	9	16	.357	.376

Year Team (League)	W	L	Pct.	ERA	WHIP	G	GS	CG	ShO	Hld.	Sv.-Opp.	IP	H	R	ER	HR	BB-IBB	SO	Avg.
1991—Martinsville (App.)	3	2	.600	4.09	1.36	7	6	2	1	...	0-...	33.0	32	20	15	2	13-0	38	.248
—Spartanburg (SAL)	2	0	1.000	0.00	0.40	2	2	0	0	...	0-...	15.0	4	0	0	0	2-0	11	.082
1992—Spartanburg (SAL)	5	10	.333	2.41	1.25	42	11	1	0	...	13-...	119.2	94	41	32	6	56-0	118	.216
1993—Clearwater (FSL)	1	0	1.000	2.75	1.22	13	0	0	0	...	4-...	19.2	19	6	6	0	5-0	19	.257
—Reading (East.)	3	3	.500	2.25	1.24	49	0	0	0	...	20-...	72.0	63	22	18	4	26-3	65	.236
1994—Scran./W.B. (I.L.)	3	1	.750	8.87	2.42	19	0	0	0	...	3-...	22.1	32	27	22	4	22-2	22	.327
—Reading (East.)	2	2	.500	2.53	0.91	38	0	0	0	...	22-...	42.2	29	13	12	6	10-0	51	.190
—Philadelphia (N.L.)	0	0	...	0.00	1.33	3	0	0	0	0	0-0	3.0	3	0	0	0	1-0	3	.250
1995—Philadelphia (N.L.)	5	3	.625	2.46	1.05	62	0	0	0	* 20	1-5	87.2	50	25	24	7	42-3	87	.167
1996—Philadelphia (N.L.)	4	5	.444	3.19	1.03	61	0	0	0	0	34-38	67.2	47	24	24	6	23-2	74	.197
1997—Philadelphia (N.L.)	2	5	.286	3.65	1.49	69	0	0	0	0	34-41	74.0	68	31	30	7	42-4	89	.245
1998—Philadelphia (N.L.)	1	5	.167	6.44	1.82	39	0	0	0	3	6-7	43.1	54	31	31	7	25-5	27	.305
—Scran./W.B. (I.L.)	0	1	.000	2.92	1.38	10	5	0	0	...	1-...	12.1	8	4	4	1	4-0	4	.190
1999—St. Louis (N.L.)	3	7	.300	4.91	1.80	68	0	0	0	8	20-28	73.1	83	45	40	9	49-1	66	.284
2000—Kansas City (A.L.)	9	6	.600	4.83	1.46	62	0	0	0	1	16-23	72.2	65	40	39	12	41-3	56	.239
2001—Philadelphia (N.L.)	3	4	.429	3.90	1.24	66	0	0	0	22	3-7	67.0	58	31	29	11	25-2	57	.241
—Reading (East.)	0	1	.000	1.80	0.80	3	3	0	0	...	0-...	5.0	3	2	1	1	1-0	5	.167
2002—Philadelphia (N.L.)	0	3	.000	4.61	1.68	30	0	0	0	15	0-1	27.1	33	16	14	3	13-2	24	.300
2003—Arizona (N.L.)	1	0	1.000	5.40	3.00	2	0	0	0	1	0-0	1.2	3	1	1	0	2-1	2	.375
—Tucson (PCL)	2	2	.500	3.66	1.40	31	0	0	0	...	9-...	39.1	39	24	16	4	16-1	28	.258
2004—Norfolk (Int'l)	0	0	...	0.00	1.50	5	0	0	0	...	0-...	7.1	7	1	0	0	4-0	8	.233
—New York (N.L.)	3	2	.600	3.38	1.27	60	0	0	0	12	0-4	69.1	54	30	26	8	34-7	61	.215
2005—Milwaukee (N.L.)	2	2	.500	4.54	1.49	40	0	0	0	9	2-6	41.2	43	24	21	7	19-0	29	.265
—Pawtucket (Int'l)	0	0	...	4.32	1.08	6	0	0	0	...	0-...	8.1	5	4	4	1	4-0	6	.200
American League totals (1 year)	9	6	.600	4.83	1.46	62	0	0	0	1	16-23	72.2	65	40	39	12	41-3	56	.239
National League totals (11 years)	24	36	.400	3.88	1.39	500	0	0	0	90	100-137	556.0	496	258	240	59	275-27	519	.240
Major League totals (12 years)	33	42	.440	3.99	1.40	562	0	0	0	91	116-160	628.2	561	298	279	71	316-30	575	.240

	W	L	Pct.	ERA	WHIP	G	GS	CG	ShO	Hld.	Sv.-Opp.	IP	H	R	ER	HR	BB-IBB	SO	Avg.
All-Star Game totals (1 year)	0	0	...	0.00	0.00	1	0	0	0	0	0-0	1.0	0	0	0	0	0-0	1	.000

BOTTS, JASON — 1B

PERSONAL: Born July 26, 1980, in Paso Robles, Calif. ... 6-5/250. ... Bats both, throws right. ... Full name: Jason Carl Botts. ... High school: Paso Robles (Calif.). ... Junior college: Glendale (Calif.) Community College.

TRANSACTIONS/CAREER NOTES: Selected by Texas Rangers organization in 46th round of 1999 free-agent draft.

2005 GAMES PLAYED BY POSITION (MLB): OF—7, DH—3.

LEFTY-RIGHTY SPLITS

vs.	Avg.	AB	H	2B	3B	HR	RBI	BB	SO	OBP	Slg.
L	.000	1	0	0	0	0	0	1	0	.500	.000
R	.308	26	8	0	0	0	3	2	13	.357	.308

							BATTING											FIELDING	
Year Team (League)	Pos.	G	AB	R	H	2B	3B	HR	RBI	BB	SO	HBP	GDP	SB-CS	Avg.	OBP	SLG	OPS	E	Avg.
2000—GC Rangers (GCL)	1B	48	163	36	52	12	0	6	34	26	29	10	5	4-1	.319	.440	.503	.943	4	.991
2001—Savannah (S. Atl.)	1B-OF	114	392	63	121	24	2	9	50	53	88	20	10	13-7	.309	.416	.449	.865	8	.985
—Charlotte (Fla. St.)	OF	4	12	1	2	1	0	0	0	4	4	0	0	0-0	.167	.375	.250	.625	0	1.000
2002—Charlotte (Fla. St.)	OF	116	401	67	102	22	5	9	54	75	99	14	4	7-2	.254	.387	.401	.788	4	.983
2003—Stockton (Calif.)	1B	76	283	58	89	14	2	9	61	45	59	1	8	12-3	.314	.409	.473	.882	16	.977
—Frisco (Texas)	OF-1B	55	194	26	51	11	1	4	27	21	45	3	6	6-1	.263	.341	.392	.733	5	.972
2004—Frisco (Texas)	OF-1B	133	481	85	141	25	3	24	92	77	126	10	18	7-4	.293	.399	.507	.906	19	.992
2005—Oklahoma (PCL)	OF-DH	133	510	93	146	31	7	25	102	67	152	8	13	2-4	.286	.375	.522	.897	14	.948
—Texas (A.L.)	OF-DH	10	27	4	8	0	0	0	3	3	13	0	1	0-0	.296	.367	.296	.663	1	.900
Major League totals (1 year)		10	27	4	8	0	0	0	3	3	13	0	1	0-0	.296	.367	.296	.663	1	.900

BOWYER, TRAVIS — P

PERSONAL: Born August 3, 1981, in Lynchburg, Va. ... 6-3/200. ... Throws right, bats right. ... Full name: Travis Charlton Bowyer. ... High school: Liberty (Bedford, Va.). ... College: None.

TRANSACTIONS/CAREER NOTES: Selected by Minnesota Twins organization in 20th round of 1999 free-agent draft.

CAREER HITTING: 0-for-0 (.000), 0 R, 0 2B, 0 3B, 0 HR, 0 RBI.

LEFTY-RIGHTY SPLITS

vs.	Avg.	AB	H	2B	3B	HR	RBI	BB	SO	OBP	Slg.
L	.286	21	6	0	0	1	2	1	7	.318	.429
R	.250	16	4	1	0	2	6	2	5	.350	.625

Year Team (League)	W	L	Pct.	ERA	WHIP	G	GS	CG	ShO	Hld.	Sv.-Opp.	IP	H	R	ER	HR	BB-IBB	SO	Avg.
1999—GC Twins (GCL)	1	0	1.000	0.00	0.00	1	0	0	0		0-...	1.0	0	0	0	0	0-0	1	.000
2000—GC Twins (GCL)	3	5	.375	4.07	1.39	12	12	1	0		0-...	55.1	55	31	25	2	22-0	36	.255
2001—Elizabethton (App.)	2	5	.286	6.10	1.51	9	8	0	0		0-...	38.1	38	30	26	3	20-0	34	.266
2002—Quad City (Midw.)	4	4	.500	2.16	1.31	39	9	0	0		3-...	91.2	74	28	22	2	46-0	90	.224
2003—Fort Myers (FSL)	5	2	.714	3.83	1.55	45	0	0	0		1-...	80.0	68	43	34	1	56-2	70	.244
2004—Fort Myers (FSL)	3	0	1.000	0.30	1.18	17	0	0	0		2-...	29.2	18	6	1	0	17-2	32	.168
—New Britain (East.)	6	3	.667	1.76	1.30	31	0	0	0		1-...	61.1	42	17	12	3	38-1	65	.188
2005—Rochester (Int'l)	4	2	.667	2.78	1.22	59	0	0	0	2	23-23	74.1	51	23	23	4	40-0	96	.195
—Minnesota (A.L.)	0	1	.000	5.59	1.34	8	0	0	0	0	0-1	9.2	10	6	6	3	3-0	12	.270
Major League totals (1 year)	0	1	.000	5.59	1.34	8	0	0	0	0	0-1	9.2	10	6	6	3	3-0	12	.270

BOYER, BLAINE — P

PERSONAL: Born July 11, 1981, in Atlanta. ... 6-3/215. ... Throws right, bats right. ... Full name: Blaine Thomas Boyer. ... High school: Walton (Marietta, Ga.).

TRANSACTIONS/CAREER NOTES: Selected by Atlanta Braves organization in third round of 2000 free-agent draft.

CAREER HITTING: 0-for-0 (.000), 0 R, 0 2B, 0 3B, 0 HR, 0 RBI.

BLAINE BOYER'S PITCHING ZONE

.385	.375	.091
.214	.235	.188
.182	.333	.100

LEFTY-RIGHTY SPLITS

vs.	Avg.	AB	H	2B	3B	HR	RBI	BB	SO	OBP	Slg.
L	.298	47	14	3	0	0	3	9	9	.411	.362
R	.200	90	18	4	0	1	7	8	24	.277	.278

Year Team (League)	W	L	Pct.	ERA	WHIP	G	GS	CG	ShO	Hld.	Sv.-Opp.	IP	H	R	ER	HR	BB-IBB	SO	Avg.
2000—GC Braves (GCL)	1	3	.250	2.51	1.33	11	5	0	0	...	1-...	32.1	24	16	9	0	19-0	27	.200
2001—Danville (Appal.)	4	5	.444	4.32	1.34	13	12	0	0	...	0-...	50.0	48	35	24	4	19-0	57	.250
2002—Macon (S. Atl.)	5	9	.357	3.07	1.29	43	0	0	0	...	1-...	70.1	52	30	24	0	39-3	73	.207
2003—Rome (S. Atl.)	12	8	.600	3.69	1.49	30	26	1	0	...	0-...	136.2	146	70	56	5	58-0	115	.271
2004—Myrtle Beach (Carol.)	10	10	.500	2.98	1.21	28	28	0	0	...	0-...	154.0	138	63	51	4	49-0	95	.250
2005—Mississippi (Sou.)	2	4	.333	5.03	1.66	14	8	0	0	2	0-0	48.1	62	28	27	4	18-3	40	.321
—Atlanta (N.L.)	4	2	.667	3.11	1.30	43	0	0	0	9	0-2	37.2	32	13	13	1	17-0	33	.234
Major League totals (1 year)	4	2	.667	3.11	1.30	43	0	0	0	9	0-2	37.2	32	13	13	1	17-0	33	.234

BRADFORD, CHAD — P

PERSONAL: Born September 14, 1974, in Jackson, Miss. ... 6-5/203. ... Throws right, bats right. ... Full name: Chadwick Lee Bradford. ... High school: Byram (Jackson, Miss.). ... College: Southern Mississippi.

TRANSACTIONS/CAREER NOTES: Selected by Chicago White Sox organization in 34th round of 1994 free-agent draft; did not sign. ... Selected by White Sox organization in 13th round of 1996 free-agent draft. ... Traded by White Sox to Oakland Athletics for a player to be named (December 7, 2000); White Sox acquired C Miguel Olivo to complete deal (December 13, 2000). ... On disabled list (August 8-23, 2004); included rehabilitation assignment to Sacramento. ... On disabled list (March 30-July 13, 2005); included rehabilitation assignments to AZL Athletics, Sacramento and Stockton. ... Traded by Athletics to Boston Red Sox for OF Jay Payton (July 14, 2005).

CAREER HITTING: 0-for-0 (.000), 0 R, 0 2B, 0 3B, 0 HR, 0 RBI.

B

SCOUTING REPORT *Throws:* Bradford checks in with a mid-80s sinker and a slider that has been clocked at 69 mph. *Tendencies:* This submariner has one of the most unusual deliveries in the game—definitely the lowest release point. His pitches are difficult to pick up, which more than compensates for the low velocity on his fastball. Is a ground-ball pitcher with good movement on his sinker. Slider spins like a Frisbee and tends to rise; it's less effective against lefthanders. Made too many mistakes up in the zone last season. *Outlook:* Bradford continues to have back problems, which makes life difficult for a guy who throws from down under. Better now in a middle role rather than in a critical setup spot. *Grade 7.4*

CHAD BRADFORD'S PITCHING ZONE

.000	...	.250
.333	.333	.278
.333	.222	.500

LEFTY-RIGHTY SPLITS

vs.	Avg.	AB	H	2B	3B	HR	RBI	BB	SO	OBP	Slg.
L	.409	22	9	0	0	1	8	2	1	.480	.545
R	.282	71	20	2	0	0	14	2	9	.316	.310

Year Team (League)	W	L	Pct.	ERA	WHIP	G	GS	CG	ShO	Hld.	Sv.-Opp.	IP	H	R	ER	HR	BB-IBB	SO	Avg.
1996— Hickory (S. Atl.)	0	2	.000	0.90	0.93	28	0	0	0	...	18-...	30.0	21	7	3	1	7-1	27	.194
1997— Win.-Salem (Car.)	3	7	.300	3.95	1.39	46	0	0	0	...	15-...	54.2	51	30	24	2	25-5	43	.239
1998— Birmingham (Sou.)	1	1	.500	2.60	1.21	10	0	0	0	...	1-...	17.1	13	6	5	2	8-0	14	.203
—Calgary (PCL)	4	1	.800	1.94	1.20	29	0	0	0	...	0-...	51.0	50	12	11	3	11-2	27	.260
—Chicago (A.L.)	2	1	.667	3.23	1.11	29	0	0	0	9	1-3	30.2	27	16	11	0	7-0	11	.229
1999— Charlotte (Int'l)	9	3	.750	1.94	1.05	47	0	0	0	...	5-...	74.1	63	19	16	2	15-0	56	.231
—Chicago (A.L.)	0	0	...	19.64	3.82	3	0	0	0	0	0-0	3.2	9	8	8	1	5-0	0	.474
2000— Charlotte (Int'l)	2	4	.333	1.51	0.93	55	0	0	0	...	10-...	53.2	38	18	9	2	12-1	42	.200
—Chicago (A.L.)	1	0	1.000	1.98	1.02	12	0	0	0	2	0-0	13.2	13	4	3	0	1-1	9	.255
2001— Sacramento (PCL)	0	0	...	0.38	0.72	12	0	0	0	...	2-...	23.2	15	2	1	0	2-0	24	.181
—Oakland (A.L.)	2	1	.667	2.70	1.28	35	0	0	0	4	1-4	36.2	41	12	11	6	6-0	34	.281
2002— Oakland (A.L.)	4	2	.667	3.11	1.15	75	0	0	0	24	2-5	75.1	73	29	26	2	14-5	56	.253
2003— Oakland (A.L.)	7	4	.636	3.04	1.26	72	0	0	0	23	2-5	77.0	67	28	26	7	30-9	62	.234
2004— Sacramento (PCL)	0	0	...	0.00	0.50	2	0	0	0	...	0-...	2.0	1	0	0	0	0-0	3	.143
—Oakland (A.L.)	5	7	.417	4.42	1.40	68	0	0	0	14	1-4	59.0	51	32	29	5	24-9	34	.234
2005— Ariz. A's (Ariz.)	0	0	...	0.00	1.00	3	3	0	0	...	0-0	3.0	3	0	0	0	0-0	2	.273
—Sacramento (PCL)	0	0	...	6.00	1.33	3	1	0	0	...	0-0	3.0	4	2	2	1	0-0	1	.333
—Stockton (Calif.)	0	0	...	3.86	1.71	3	0	0	0	1	0-0	2.1	3	1	1	0	1-0	1	.300
—Boston (A.L.)	2	1	.667	3.86	1.41	31	0	0	0	8	0-1	23.1	29	10	10	1	4-1	10	.312
Major League totals (8 years)	**23**	**16**	**.590**	**3.49**	**1.26**	**325**	**0**	**0**	**0**	**84**	**7-22**	**319.1**	**310**	**139**	**124**	**22**	**91-25**	**216**	**.255**

DIVISION SERIES RECORD

Year Team (League)	W	L	Pct.	ERA	WHIP	G	GS	CG	ShO	Hld.	Sv.-Opp.	IP	H	R	ER	HR	BB-IBB	SO	Avg.
2000— Chicago (A.L.)	0	0	...	0.00	3.00	1	0	0	0	0	0-1	0.2	2	0	0	0	0-0	0	.667
2001— Oakland (A.L.)	0	0	...	0.00	0.00	1	0	0	0	0	0-0	1.0	0	0	0	0	0-0	1	.000
2002— Oakland (A.L.)	0	0	...	0.00	0.33	2	0	0	0	0	0-0	3.0	1	0	0	0	0-0	1	.111
2003— Oakland (A.L.)	0	0	...	0.00	1.64	4	0	0	0	0	0-0	3.2	4	0	0	0	2-2	5	.286
2005— Boston (A.L.)	0	0	...	0.00	0.75	2	0	0	0	0	0-0	1.1	1	0	0	0	0-0	1	.200
Division series totals (5 years)	**0**	**0**	**...**	**0.00**	**1.03**	**10**	**0**	**0**	**0**	**0**	**0-1**	**9.2**	**8**	**0**	**0**	**0**	**2-2**	**8**	**.235**

BRADLEY, MILTON   OF

PERSONAL: Born April 15, 1978, in Harbor City, Calif. ... 6-0/205. ... Bats both, throws right. ... Full name: Milton Obelle Bradley. ... High school: Polytechnic (Long Beach, Calif.).

TRANSACTIONS/CAREER NOTES: Selected by Montreal Expos organization in second round of 1996 free-agent draft. ... Traded by Expos to Cleveland Indians for P Zach Day (July 31, 2001). ... On disabled list (May 2-June 4 and August 14-30, 2002); included rehabilitation assignments to Buffalo and Akron. ... On disabled list (April 23-May 8 and August 15, 2003-remainder of season). ... Traded by Indians to Los Angeles Dodgers for OF Franklin Gutierrez and a player to be named (April 3, 2004); Indians received P Andrew Brown to complete deal (May 19, 2004). ... On suspended list (September 29, 2004-remainder of season). ... On disabled list (June 3-July 23; and August 25, 2005-remainder of season) included rehabilitation assignments to Las Vegas.
2005 GAMES PLAYED BY POSITION (MLB): OF—72.

SCOUTING REPORT *Offense:* He has an extremely quick bat from the left side with a short stroke. Has above-average power, especially on the ball down. Strikes out too much because he has problems avoiding the high fastball. Is a good runner but needs to make better reads. *Defense:* Bradley is a good defensive player when he makes the effort. Is very athletic and fast. Reads the ball off the bat well. Has plus lateral range and runs to the ball well. Arm is average, and occasionally is slow on his release. *Outlook:* Immensely talented but a lightning rod for trouble, Bradley has most clubs concerned about his temper to the point he may have trouble getting a job. *Grade 6*

MILTON BRADLEY'S HITTING ZONE

.167	.364	.429
.298	.405	.368
.143	.476	.194

LEFTY-RIGHTY SPLITS

vs.	Avg.	AB	H	2B	3B	HR	RBI	BB	SO	OBP	Slg.
L	.278	79	22	4	0	4	7	1	12	.293	.481
R	.294	204	60	10	1	9	31	24	35	.371	.485

							BATTING										FIELDING	
Year Team (League)	Pos.	G	AB	R	H	2B	3B	HR	RBI	BB	SO	HBP	GDP	SB-CS	Avg.	OBP	SLG	OPS	E	Avg.
1996— GC Expos (GCL)	OF	32	112	18	27	7	1	1	12	13	15	1	2	7-4	.241	.320	.348	.669	3	.949
1997— Vermont (NYP)	OF	50	200	29	60	7	5	3	30	17	34	0	6	7-7	.300	.352	.430	.782	4	.967
—GC Expos (GCL)	OF	9	25	6	5	2	0	1	2	4	4	1	0	2-2	.200	.333	.400	.733	1	.938
1998— Cape Fear (S. Atl.)	OF	75	281	54	85	21	4	6	50	23	57	4	7	13-8	.302	.360	.470	.830	3	.968
—Jupiter (Fla. St.)	OF	67	261	55	75	14	1	5	34	30	42	5	3	17-9	.287	.369	.406	.775	1	.993
1999— Harrisburg (East.)	OF	87	346	62	114	22	5	12	50	33	61	3	5	14-10	.329	.391	.526	.917	5	.971
2000— Ottawa (Int'l)	OF	88	342	58	104	20	1	6	29	45	56	1	5	10-15	.304	.385	.421	.806	3	.987
—Montreal (N.L.)	OF	42	154	20	34	8	1	2	15	14	32	1	3	2-1	.221	.288	.325	.613	2	.979
2001— Montreal (N.L.)	OF	67	220	19	49	16	3	1	19	19	62	1	6	7-4	.223	.288	.336	.624	2	.988
—Ottawa (Int'l)	OF	35	136	21	37	7	2	2	13	23	30	2	...	14-1	.272	.383	.397	.780	1	.986
—Buffalo (Int'l)	OF	30	114	18	29	3	0	5	15	19	31	0	...	9-2	.254	.361	.412	.773	0	1.000
—Cleveland (A.L.)	OF-DH	10	8	3	4	1	0	0	0	2	3	0	1	1-1	.222	.300	.278	.578	1	.929
2002— Cleveland (A.L.)	OF-DH	98	325	48	81	18	3	9	38	32	58	0	12	6-3	.249	.317	.406	.723	4	.982

Year	Team (League)	Pos.	G	AB	R	H	2B	3B	HR	RBI	BB	SO	HBP	GDP	SB-CS	Avg.	OBP	SLG	OPS	E	Avg.
	— Buffalo (Int'l)	OF	6	23	3	6	0	0	0	3	3	5	0	0	2-1	.261	.321	.261	.582	0	1.000
	— Akron (East.)	OF	3	11	1	3	1	0	0	1	1	1	0	0	0-1	.273	.333	.364	.697	0	1.000
2003— Cleveland (A.L.)	OF-DH	101	377	61	121	34	2	10	56	64	73	5	10	17-7	.321	.421	.501	.923	2	.992
2004— Los Angeles (N.L.)	OF	141	516	72	138	24	0	19	67	71	123	6	12	15-11	.267	.362	.424	.786	8	.977
2005— Las Vegas (PCL)	OF	5	13	2	4	0	0	0	1	1	2	0	0	1-1	.308	.357	.308	.665	0	1.000
	— Los Angeles (N.L.)	OF	75	283	49	82	14	1	13	38	25	47	2	6	6-1	.290	.350	.484	.835	2	.989
American League totals (3 years)			209	720	112	206	53	5	19	94	98	134	5	23	24-11	.286	.373	.453	.826	7	.986
National League totals (4 years)			325	1173	160	303	62	5	35	139	129	264	10	27	30-17	.258	.336	.409	.745	14	.982
Major League totals (6 years)			534	1893	272	509	115	10	54	233	227	398	15	50	54-28	.269	.350	.426	.776	21	.984

DIVISION SERIES RECORD

Year	Team (League)	Pos.	G	AB	R	H	2B	3B	HR	RBI	BB	SO	HBP	GDP	SB-CS	Avg.	OBP	SLG	OPS	E	Avg.
2004— Los Angeles (N.L.)	OF	4	11	1	3	1	0	1	1	5	2	0	1	2-0	.273	.500	.636	1.136	0	1.000

BRANYAN, RUSSELL — 3B/1B

PERSONAL: Born December 19, 1975, in Warner Robins, Ga. ... 6-3/195. ... Bats left, throws right. ... Full name: Russell Oles Branyan. ... Name pronounced: BRAN-yen. ... High school: Stratford Academy (Warner Robins, Ga.).

TRANSACTIONS/CAREER NOTES: Selected by Cleveland Indians organization in seventh round of 1994 free-agent draft. ... Traded by Indians to Cincinnati Reds for OF Ben Broussard (June 7, 2002). ... On disabled list (March 18-May 29 and August 13-28, 2003); included rehabilitation assignments to Louisville. ... Signed as a free agent by Atlanta Braves organization (January 21, 2004). ... Traded by Braves to Indians for P Scott Sturkie (April 25, 2004). ... Traded by Indians to Milwaukee Brewers for future considerations (July 25, 2004). ... On disabled list (June 2-July 4, 2005); included rehabilitation assignment to Nashville.

2005 GAMES PLAYED BY POSITION (MLB): 3B—59, 1B—5, OF—3, DH—1.

SCOUTING REPORT Offense: Branyan has as much raw power as anyone, but he always is going to strike out a lot. Has good power to all fields but is streaky. Has holes at the plate and consistently swings through pitches. Is slow to make adjustments and can be fooled by off-speed pitches. **Defense:** He showed improvement on defense, especially fielding the ball, but he still doesn't have good footwork. Has limited range. Is better moving to his left and is an erratic thrower. **Outlook:** Branyan never has made enough contact to realize his power potential and become an everyday player. Has struggled to make the necessary adjustments to be a successful hitter. **Grade 5.7**

RUSSELL BRANYAN'S HITTING ZONE

.250	.143	.167
.167	.429	.275
.200	.500	.375

LEFTY-RIGHTY SPLITS

vs.	Avg.	AB	H	2B	3B	HR	RBI	BB	SO	OBP	Slg.
L	.050	20	1	0	0	0	1	1	13	.095	.050
R	.280	182	51	11	0	12	30	38	67	.405	.538

Year	Team (League)	Pos.	G	AB	R	H	2B	3B	HR	RBI	BB	SO	HBP	GDP	SB-CS	Avg.	OBP	SLG	OPS	E	Avg.
1994— Burlington (Appal.)	3B	55	171	21	36	10	0	5	13	25	64	4	3	4-2	.211	.323	.357	.680	21	.851
1995— Columbus (S. Atl.)	3B	76	277	46	71	8	6	19	55	27	120	3	6	1-1	.256	.326	.534	.860	26	.856
1996— Columbus (S. Atl.)	3B-DH	130	482	102	129	20	4	40	106	62	166	5	4	7-4	.268	.355	.575	.930	44	.885
1997— Kinston (Carol.)	3B-DH	83	297	59	86	26	2	27	75	52	94	5	9	3-1	.290	.398	.663	1.062	21	.897
	— Akron (East.)	3B-DH	41	137	26	32	4	0	12	30	28	56	2	1	0-0	.234	.369	.526	.895	11	.921
1998— Akron (East.)	3B-DH	43	163	35	48	11	3	16	46	35	58	0	1	1-1	.294	.417	.693	1.110	7	.932
	— Cleveland (A.L.)	3B	1	4	0	0	0	0	0	0	0	2	0	0	0-0	.000	.000	.000	.000	0	1.000
1999— Buffalo (Int'l)	3B	109	395	51	82	11	1	30	67	52	187	4	5	8-3	.208	.305	.468	.773	23	.921
	— Cleveland (A.L.)	3B-DH	11	38	4	8	2	0	1	6	3	19	1	0	0-0	.211	.286	.342	.628	1	.960
2000— Buffalo (Int'l)	3B-OF	64	229	46	56	9	2	21	60	28	93	2	2	1-1	.245	.330	.576	.906	9	.942
	— Cleveland (A.L.) .. OF-DH-3B	67	193	32	46	7	2	16	38	22	76	4	2	0-0	.238	.327	.544	.871	3	.954
2001— Cleveland (A.L.) ..3B-OF-DH	113	315	48	73	16	2	20	54	38	132	3	1	1-1	.232	.316	.486	.802	14	.931
2002— Cleveland (A.L.) .. OF-3B-DH	50	161	16	33	4	0	8	17	17	65	0	3	1-2	.205	.278	.379	.657	2	.976
	— Cincinnati (N.L.) .. OF-1B-3B DH	84	217	34	53	9	1	16	39	34	86	2	2	3-1	.244	.349	.516	.865	6	.977
2003— Louisville (Int'l) DH-OF-1B	3B	14	49	5	16	5	0	1	3	9	15	1	0	0-0	.327	.441	.490	.930	1	.968
	— Cincinnati (N.L.) ... 3B-OF-1B DH	74	176	22	38	12	0	9	26	27	69	1	1	0-0	.216	.322	.438	.759	3	.985
2004— Richmond (Int'l)	OF	11	28	5	5	0	0	1	4	13	11	1	0	0-0	.179	.452	.286	.738	0	1.000
	— Buffalo (Int'l) .... 1B-3B-OF DH	82	313	58	90	16	2	25	75	42	102	5	5	5-2	.288	.374	.591	.965	6	.987
	— Milwaukee (N.L.) .. 3B-1B-OF	51	158	21	37	11	1	11	27	20	68	2	1	1-0	.234	.324	.525	.849	5	.964
2005— Nashville (PCL) .. OF-3B-1B-OF	6	17	4	5	4	0	1	3	3	8	0	0	0-0	.294	.400	.706	1.106	0	1.000
	— Milwaukee (N.L.) .. 3B-1B-OF DH	85	202	23	52	11	0	12	31	39	80	0	3	1-0	.257	.378	.490	.868	7	.956
American League totals (5 years)			242	711	100	160	29	4	45	115	80	294	8	7	2-3	.225	.307	.467	.774	20	.947
National League totals (4 years)			294	753	100	180	43	2	48	123	120	303	5	7	5-1	.239	.345	.493	.838	21	.972
Major League totals (8 years)			536	1464	200	340	72	6	93	238	200	597	13	14	7-4	.232	.327	.480	.807	41	.964

DIVISION SERIES RECORD

Year	Team (League)	Pos.	G	AB	R	H	2B	3B	HR	RBI	BB	SO	HBP	GDP	SB-CS	Avg.	OBP	SLG	OPS	E	Avg.
2001— Cleveland (A.L.)	OF	2	3	1	1	0	0	0	0	0	1	0	0	0-0	.333	.333	.333	.667	0	...

BRAZELTON, DEWON — P

PERSONAL: Born June 16, 1980, in Tullahoma, Tenn. ... 6-4/214. ... Throws right, bats right. ... Full name: Dewon Cortez Brazelton. ... Name pronounced: de-wan bra-zel-ton. ... High school: Tullahoma (Tenn.). ... College: Middle Tennessee State.

TRANSACTIONS/CAREER NOTES: Selected by Tampa Bay Devil Rays organization in first round (third pick overall) of 2001 free-agent draft. ... On suspended list (September 8-11, 2005).

CAREER HITTING: 0-for-2 (.000), 0 R, 0 2B, 0 3B, 0 HR, 0 RBI.

SCOUTING REPORT *Throws:* He throws a fastball 89-94 mph, a slider at 83-87 and a curveball at 72-75. *Tendencies:* He is all over the place with his plus fastball because of his complicated delivery. Slider is a good breaking pitch, but his curve is just a looping one. Has outstanding motion and movement with a changeup he turns over, which has made him effective against left-handers. *Outlook:* He is a frustrating pitcher because he has great athletic ability but is unable to channel that into a consistent delivery. Is running out of time to contribute. *Grade 5.7*

DEWON BRAZELTON'S PITCHING ZONE

.294	.250	.375
.293	.429	.429
.400	.294	.308

LEFTY-RIGHTY SPLITS

vs.	Avg.	AB	H	2B	3B	HR	RBI	BB	SO	OBP	Slg.
L	.303	142	43	10	2	5	30	28	26	.423	.507
R	.312	141	44	8	0	7	27	32	17	.440	.518

Year Team (League)	W	L	Pct.	ERA	WHIP	G	GS	CG	ShO	Hld.	Sv.-Opp.	IP	H	R	ER	HR	BB-IBB	SO	Avg.
2002—Orlando (South.)	5	9	.357	3.33	1.34	26	26	1	0	...	0-...	146.0	129	69	54	7	67-1	109	.241
—Durham (Int'l)	1	0	1.000	0.00	1.20	1	1	0	0	...	0-...	5.0	5	0	0	0	1-0	6	.263
—Tampa Bay (A.L.)	0	1	.000	4.85	1.38	2	2	0	0	...	0-0	13.0	12	7	7	3	6-0	5	.279
2003—Durham (Int'l)	2	2	.500	4.21	1.30	5	5	0	0	...	0-...	25.2	23	14	12	1	11-0	18	.235
—Tampa Bay (A.L.)	1	6	.143	6.89	1.66	10	10	0	0	0	0-0	48.1	57	49	37	9	23-1	24	.292
—Bakersfield (Calif.)	1	5	.167	5.26	1.60	9	9	0	0	...	0-...	49.2	62	33	29	4	19-0	42	.298
—Orlando (South.)	2	0	1.000	2.53	1.50	2	2	0	0	...	0-...	10.2	8	6	3	0	8-0	5	.200
2004—Durham (Int'l)	4	4	.500	4.71	1.53	10	10	0	0	...	0-...	49.2	61	35	26	0	15-0	38	.299
—Tampa Bay (A.L.)	6	8	.429	4.77	1.44	22	21	0	0	...	0-0	120.2	121	71	64	12	53-2	64	.260
2005—Montgom. (Sou.)	0	0	...	0.00	0.67	1	1	0	0	...	0-0	3.0	2	0	0	0	0-0	6	.182
—Durham (Int'l)	2	2	.500	3.72	1.48	5	5	0	0	...	0-0	29.0	29	17	12	3	14-0	26	.252
—Tampa Bay (A.L.)	1	8	.111	7.61	2.07	20	8	0	0	...	0-1	71.0	87	65	60	12	60-3	43	.307
Major League totals (4 years)	8	23	.258	5.98	1.66	54	41	0	0	1	0-1	253.0	277	192	168	36	142-6	136	.281

BRAZOBAN, YHENCY   P

PERSONAL: Born June 11, 1980, in Santo Domingo, Dominican Republic. ... 6-1/170. ... Throws right, bats right. ... Full name: Yhency Jose Brazoban.
TRANSACTIONS/CAREER NOTES: Signed as a non-drafted free agent by New York Yankees organization (July 10, 1997). ... Played five seasons as an outfielder in Yankees organization (1998-2002). ... Traded by Yankees with Ps Jeff Weaver and Brandon Wheedon and cash to Los Angeles Dodgers for P Kevin Brown (December 13, 2003).
CAREER HITTING: 0-for-3 (.000), 0 R, 0 2B, 0 3B, 0 HR, 0 RBI.

YHENCY BRAZOBAN'S PITCHING ZONE

.158	.273	.129
.333	.265	.366
.238	.500	.375

LEFTY-RIGHTY SPLITS

vs.	Avg.	AB	H	2B	3B	HR	RBI	BB	SO	OBP	Slg.
L	.267	135	36	7	1	9	30	22	29	.377	.533
R	.250	136	34	15	1	2	20	10	32	.311	.419

Year Team (League)	W	L	Pct.	ERA	WHIP	G	GS	CG	ShO	Hld.	Sv.-Opp.	IP	H	R	ER	HR	BB-IBB	SO	Avg.
2002—GC Yankees (GCL)	0	0	...	4.50	1.17	6	0	0	0	...	0-...	6.0	3	3	3	0	4-0	11	.136
2003—Trenton (East.)	2	2	.500	7.81	1.70	20	0	0	0	...	3-...	27.2	33	25	24	5	14-1	19	.314
—GC Yankees (GCL)	0	0	...	6.00	2.00	3	0	0	0	...	0-...	3.0	5	3	2	0	1-1	5	.385
—Tampa (Fla. St.)	0	2	.000	2.83	1.36	24	0	0	0	...	15-...	28.2	27	13	9	0	12-2	34	.245
2004—Jacksonville (Sou.)	4	4	.500	2.65	1.18	37	0	0	0	...	13-...	51.0	38	18	15	4	22-1	61	.210
—Las Vegas (PCL)	2	0	1.000	2.19	1.22	10	0	0	0	...	1-...	12.1	14	3	3	1	1-0	17	.286
—Los Angeles (N.L.)	6	2	.750	2.48	1.22	31	0	0	0	5	0-0	32.2	25	9	9	2	15-2	21	.219
2005—Los Angeles (N.L.)	4	10	.286	5.33	1.40	74	0	0	0	8	21-27	72.2	70	46	43	11	32-4	61	.258
Major League totals (2 years)	10	12	.455	4.44	1.35	105	0	0	0	13	21-27	105.1	95	55	52	13	47-6	88	.247

DIVISION SERIES RECORD

Year Team (League)	W	L	Pct.	ERA	WHIP	G	GS	CG	ShO	Hld.	Sv.-Opp.	IP	H	R	ER	HR	BB-IBB	SO	Avg.
2004—Los Angeles (N.L.)	0	0	...	3.00	1.00	2	0	0	0	0	0-0	3.0	1	1	1	0	2-0	2	.100

BRESLOW, CRAIG   P

PERSONAL: Born August 8, 1980, in New Haven, Conn. ... 6-1/180. ... Throws left, bats left. ... Full name: Craig Andrew Breslow. ... High school: Trumbull (Conn.). ... College: Yale.
TRANSACTIONS/CAREER NOTES: Selected by Milwaukee Brewers organization in 26th round of 2002 free-agent draft. ... Released by Brewers (July 16, 2004). ... Signed by New Jersey of the independent Northeast League (July 2004). ... Signed as free agent by San Diego Padres organization (February 2005).
CAREER HITTING: 0-for-1 (.000), 0 R, 0 2B, 0 3B, 0 HR, 0 RBI.

CRAIG BRESLOW'S PITCHING ZONE

.200	.333	.333
.545	1.000	.111
.100	.000	.000

LEFTY-RIGHTY SPLITS

vs.	Avg.	AB	H	2B	3B	HR	RBI	BB	SO	OBP	Slg.
L	.063	16	1	1	0	0	0	5	5	.286	.125
R	.298	47	14	1	0	1	3	8	9	.404	.383

Year Team (League)	W	L	Pct.	ERA	WHIP	G	GS	CG	ShO	Hld.	Sv.-Opp.	IP	H	R	ER	HR	BB-IBB	SO	Avg.
2002—Ogden (Pion.)	6	2	.750	1.82	1.21	23	0	0	0	...	2-...	54.1	42	15	11	2	24-0	56	.218
2003—Beloit (Midw.)	3	4	.429	5.12	1.40	33	0	0	0	...	2-...	65.0	64	43	37	4	27-0	80	.254
2004—High Desert (Calif.)	1	3	.250	7.19	1.89	23	0	0	0	...	0-...	41.1	54	39	33	5	24-0	41	.305
—New Jersey (Northeast)	3	1	.750	4.10	1.22	19	0	0	0	...	1-...	26.1	19	13	12	2	13-1	37	.204
2005—Mobile (Sou.)	2	1	.667	2.75	1.05	40	0	0	0	9	0-0	52.1	38	16	16	3	17-2	47	.212
—Portland (PCL)	0	1	.000	4.00	1.33	7	0	0	0	1	0-0	9.0	11	4	4	1	6-0	9	.314
—San Diego (N.L.)	0	0	...	2.20	1.71	14	0	0	0	1	0-0	16.1	15	6	4	1	13-0	14	.238
Major League totals (1 year)	0	0	...	2.20	1.71	14	0	0	0	1	0-0	16.1	15	6	4	1	13-0	14	.238

B

BRITO, EUDE — P

PERSONAL: Born August 19, 1978, in Sabana de la Mar, Dominican Republic. ... 5-11/160. ... Throws left, bats left. ... Full name: Eude Ezequiel Brito. ... High school: Liceo Virginia Pou (Dominican Republic).
TRANSACTIONS/CAREER NOTES: Signed as a non-drafted free agent by Philadelphia Phillies organization (July 3, 1998).
CAREER HITTING: 1-for-7 (.143), 1 R, 0 2B, 0 3B, 0 HR, 0 RBI.

EUDE BRITO'S PITCHING ZONE

.200	.000	.000
.286	.667	.000
.375	.500	.100

LEFTY-RIGHTY SPLITS

vs.	Avg.	AB	H	2B	3B	HR	RBI	BB	SO	OBP	Slg.
L	.231	13	3	0	0	1	2	2	1	.375	.462
R	.254	67	17	6	1	1	6	9	14	.346	.418

Year Team (League)	W	L	Pct.	ERA	WHIP	G	GS	CG	ShO	Hld.	Sv.-Opp.	IP	H	R	ER	HR	BB-IBB	SO	Avg.
1999— GC Phillies (GCL)	0	1	.000	5.02	2.02	12	3	0	0	...	0-...	28.2	39	22	16	0	19-0	23	.336
2000— GC Phillies (GCL)	3	5	.375	2.54	1.15	9	7	0	0	...	0-...	49.2	38	20	14	1	19-0	42	.210
— Batavia (NY-Penn)	1	1	.500	5.40	1.04	4	3	0	0	...	0-...	18.1	16	14	11	0	3-0	11	.225
2001— Lakewood (S. Atl.)	4	3	.571	2.73	0.97	44	0	0	0	...	6-...	69.1	53	28	21	7	14-2	58	.210
2002— Lakewood (S. Atl.)	1	1	.500	2.55	1.13	11	0	0	0	...	1-...	17.2	14	5	5	1	6-0	11	.226
— Clearwater (FSL)	3	3	.500	5.71	1.56	20	0	0	0	...	0-...	34.2	40	22	22	5	14-1	27	.292
2003— Clearwater (FSL)	4	3	.571	3.09	1.32	36	0	0	0	...	6-...	58.1	50	21	20	3	27-1	54	.231
2004— Reading (East.)	8	6	.571	4.42	1.40	43	7	1	0	...	4-...	97.2	95	56	48	10	42-2	84	.256
2005— Scran./W.B. (I.L.)	6	2	.750	4.85	1.38	28	15	0	0	1	0-1	98.1	97	59	53	13	39-0	76	.266
— Philadelphia (N.L.)	1	2	.333	3.68	1.41	6	5	0	0	...	0-0	22.0	20	9	9	2	11-1	15	.250
Major League totals (1 year)	1	2	.333	3.68	1.41	6	5	0	0	...	0-0	22.0	20	9	9	2	11-1	15	.250

BROCAIL, DOUG — P

PERSONAL: Born May 16, 1967, in Clearfield, Pa. ... 6-5/235. ... Throws right, bats left. ... Full name: Douglas Keith Brocail. ... Name pronounced: broh-KALE. ... High school: Lamar (Colo.). ... Junior college: Lamar (Colo.) Community College. ...
TRANSACTIONS/CAREER NOTES: Selected by San Diego Padres organization in first round (12th pick overall) of January 1986 free-agent draft. ... On disabled list (April 2-June 28, 1994); included rehabilitation assignments to Wichita and Las Vegas. ... Traded by Padres with OFs Phil Plantier and Derek Bell, P Pedro Martinez and IF Craig Shipley and SS Ricky Gutierrez to Houston Astros for 3B Ken Caminiti, OF Steve Finley, SS Andujar Cedeno, 1B Roberto Petagine, P Brian Williams and a player to be named (December 28, 1994); Padres acquired P Sean Fesh to complete deal (May 1, 1995). ... On disabled list (May 11-August 15, 1996); included rehabilitation assignments to Jackson and Tucson. ... Traded by Astros with OF Brian L. Hunter, IF Orlando Miller, P Todd Jones and cash to Detroit Tigers for C Brad Ausmus, Ps Jose Lima, C.J. Nitkowski and Trever Miller and 1B Daryle Ward (December 10, 1996). ... On suspended list (June 10-13, 1998). ... On disabled list (August 9-24, 1998). ... On suspended list (April 28-May 1, 2000). ... On disabled list (August 14-September 1 and September 29, 2000-remainder of season). ... Traded by Tigers with C Brad Ausmus and P Nelson Cruz to Astros for C Mitch Meluskey, P Chris Holt and OF of Roger Cedeno (December 11, 2000). ... On disabled list (March 31, 2001-entire season); included rehabilitation assignments to New Orleans and Round Rock. ... On disabled list (March 22, 2002-entire season). ... Signed as a free agent by Texas Rangers organization (February 18, 2004). ... On disabled list (May 9-June 7 and July 25-August 9, 2004); included rehabilitation assignments to Oklahoma and Frisco. ... On suspended list (September 26-October 2, 2004).
CAREER HITTING: 11-for-67 (.164), 9 R, 0 2B, 1 3B, 0 HR, 1 RBI.

SCOUTING REPORT **Throws:** His fastball is in the low- to mid-90s. Also throws a curveball and slider. **Tendencies:** Brocail threw surprisingly well last season after years of arm problems. Fastball is very heavy and bores in on righthanders. Wraps his curve but has very tight downward biting rotation and will change speeds off of it. Slider is quick with good tilt. Is more effective pitching to righthanders than lefthanders. Has exceptional makeup and is fearless. **Outlook:** This setup reliever's arm has bounced back and he is throwing harder than recent years, but a lack of command keeps him in too many hitters' counts. ***Grade 6.3***

DOUG BROCAIL'S PITCHING ZONE

.222	.200	.227
.314	.324	.436
.192	.286	.500

LEFTY-RIGHTY SPLITS

vs.	Avg.	AB	H	2B	3B	HR	RBI	BB	SO	OBP	Slg.
L	.346	127	44	11	2	1	20	19	16	.430	.488
R	.267	172	46	9	1	1	24	15	45	.333	.349

Year Team (League)	W	L	Pct.	ERA	WHIP	G	GS	CG	ShO	Hld.	Sv.-Opp.	IP	H	R	ER	HR	BB-IBB	SO	Avg.
1986— Spokane (N'west)	5	4	.556	3.81	1.62	16	15	0	0	...	0-...	85.0	85	52	36	4	53-1	77	...
1987— Char., S.C. (SAL)	2	6	.250	4.09	1.32	19	18	0	0	...	0-...	92.1	94	51	42	6	28-0	68	.263
1988— Char., S.C. (SAL)	8	6	.571	2.69	1.23	22	13	5	0	...	2-...	107.0	107	40	32	3	25-0	107	.257
1989— Wichita (Texas)	5	9	.357	5.21	1.54	23	22	1	1	...	0-...	134.2	158	88	78	11	50-4	95	.292
1990— Wichita (Texas)	2	2	.500	4.33	1.48	12	9	0	0	...	0-...	52.0	53	30	25	7	24-0	27	.265
1991— Wichita (Texas)	10	7	.588	3.87	1.30	34	16	3	3	...	6-...	146.1	147	76	63	15	43-3	108	.259
1992— Las Vegas (PCL)	10	10	.500	3.97	1.45	29	25	4	0	...	0-...	172.1	187	82	76	7	63-5	103	.285
— San Diego (N.L.)	0	0	...	6.43	1.57	3	3	0	0	...	0-0	14.0	17	10	10	2	5-0	15	.298
1993— Las Vegas (PCL)	4	2	.667	3.68	1.27	10	8	0	0	...	1-...	51.1	51	26	21	4	14-0	32	.254
— San Diego (N.L.)	4	13	.235	4.56	1.44	24	24	0	0	...	0-0	128.1	143	75	65	16	42-4	70	.283
1994— Wichita (Texas)	0	0	...	0.00	1.00	2	0	0	0	...	0-...	4.0	3	1	0	0	1-0	2	.200
— Las Vegas (PCL)	0	0	...	7.11	1.82	7	3	0	0	...	0-...	12.2	21	12	10	1	2-0	8	.375
— San Diego (N.L.)	0	0	...	5.82	1.53	12	0	0	0	...	0-1	17.0	21	13	11	1	5-3	11	.304
1995— Houston (N.L.)	6	4	.600	4.19	1.41	36	7	0	0	...	1-1	77.1	87	40	36	10	22-2	39	.280
— Tucson (PCL)	1	0	1.000	3.86	1.35	3	3	0	0	...	0-...	16.1	18	9	7	1	4-0	16	.269
1996— Houston (N.L.)	1	5	.167	4.58	1.53	23	4	0	0	1	0-0	53.0	58	31	27	7	23-1	34	.289
— Jackson (Texas)	0	0	...	0.00	0.50	2	2	0	0	...	0-...	4.0	1	0	0	0	1-0	5	.077
— Tucson (PCL)	0	1	.000	7.36	1.77	5	1	0	0	...	0-...	7.1	12	6	6	1	1-0	4	.375
1997— Detroit (A.L.)	3	4	.429	3.23	1.41	61	4	0	0	16	2-9	78.0	74	31	28	10	36-4	60	.256
1998— Detroit (A.L.)	5	2	.714	2.73	1.04	60	0	0	0	11	0-1	62.2	47	23	19	2	18-3	55	.211
1999— Detroit (A.L.)	4	4	.500	2.52	1.04	70	0	0	0	23	2-4	82.0	60	23	23	7	25-1	78	.206
2000— Detroit (A.L.)	5	4	.556	4.09	1.40	49	0	0	0	19	0-5	50.2	57	25	23	5	14-2	41	.285
2001— New Orleans (PCL)	0	0	...	0.00	1.29	2	0	0	0	...	0-...	2.1	2	0	0	0	1-0	2	.222

B

Year	Team (League)	W	L	Pct.	ERA	WHIP	G	GS	CG	ShO	Hld.	Sv.-Opp.	IP	H	R	ER	HR	BB-IBB	SO	Avg.
	— Round Rock (Texas)	0	0	...	0.00	0.00	1	1	0	0	...	0-...	1.0	0	0	0	0	0-0	1	.000
2002— Houston (N.L.)			Did not play.																	
2003— Houston (N.L.)			Did not play.																	
2004— Oklahoma (PCL)	2	0	1.000	4.19	1.14	12	0	0	0		0-...	19.1	20	9	9	1	2-0	19	.263
— Frisco (Texas)	0	0	...	2.08	0.46	1	1	0	0		0-...	4.1	2	1	1	1	0-0	6	.143
— Texas (A.L.)	4	1	.800	4.13	1.41	43	0	0	0	4	1-1	52.1	54	29	24	2	20-1	43	.269
2005— Texas (A.L.)	5	3	.625	5.52	1.69	61	0	0	0	5	1-4	73.1	90	48	45	2	34-3	61	.301
American League totals (6 years)	26	18	.591	3.65	1.33	344	4	0	0	78	6-24	399.0	382	179	162	28	147-14	338	.254
National League totals (5 years)	11	22	.333	4.63	1.46	98	38	0	0	1	1-2	289.2	326	169	149	36	97-10	169	.285
Major League totals (11 years)	37	40	.481	4.06	1.38	442	42	0	0	79	7-26	688.2	708	348	311	64	244-24	507	.267

BROOKS, FRANK   P

PERSONAL: Born September 6, 1978, in Brooklyn, N.Y. ... 6-1/200. ... Throws left, bats left. ... Full name: Frank J. Brooks. ... High school: Sheepshead Bay (Brooklyn, N.Y.). ... College: St. Peter's.

TRANSACTIONS/CAREER NOTES: Selected by Philadelphia Phillies organization in 13th round of 1999 free-agent draft. ... Traded by Phillies to Pittsburgh Pirates for P Mike Williams and cash (July 20, 2003). ... Selected by New York Mets from Pirates organization in Rule 5 major league draft (December 15, 2003). ... Traded by Mets to Oakland Athletics for a player to be named (December 15, 2003). ... Claimed on waivers by Boston Red Sox (March 18, 2004). ... Returned to Pirates organization (March 31, 2004). ... Claimed on waivers by Los Angeles Dodgers (December 11, 2004). ... Claimed on waivers by Atlanta Braves (April 13, 2005).

CAREER HITTING: 0-for-1 (.000), 0 R, 0 2B, 0 3B, 0 HR, 0 RBI.

LEFTY-RIGHTY SPLITS

vs.	Avg.	AB	H	2B	3B	HR	RBI	BB	SO	OBP	Slg.
L	1.000	1	1	0	0	0	1	0	0	1.000	1.000
R	.000	0	0	0	0	0	0	0	0	.000	.000

Year	Team (League)	W	L	Pct.	ERA	WHIP	G	GS	CG	ShO	Hld.	Sv.-Opp.	IP	H	R	ER	HR	BB-IBB	SO	Avg.
1999— Batavia (NY-Penn)	7	3	.700	2.91	1.25	16	12	1	1	...	0-...	77.1	64	26	25	2	33-0	58	.232
2000— Piedmont (S. Atl.)	14	8	.636	3.44	1.19	29	27	3	2	...	0-...	177.2	152	78	68	17	60-0	138	.236
2001— Clearwater (FSL)	5	10	.333	4.71	1.52	37	15	0	0	...	1-...	112.2	113	70	59	18	58-2	92	.262
2002— Clearwater (FSL)	3	5	.375	3.46	1.56	35	0	0	0	...	7-...	39.0	34	18	15	2	27-3	33	.233
— Reading (East.)	1	1	.500	3.10	1.41	17	1	0	0	...	2-...	29.0	29	11	10	1	12-0	23	.266
2003— Reading (East.)	3	4	.429	2.30	0.90	34	0	0	0	...	9-...	58.2	40	16	15	5	13-1	71	.194
— Altoona (East.)	0	0	...	7.71	1.29	4	0	0	0	...	0-...	2.1	3	2	2	1	0-0	4	.300
— Nashville (PCL)	2	0	1.000	2.54	1.16	16	0	0	0	...	2-...	28.1	22	9	8	2	11-2	22	.218
2004— Nashville (PCL)	6	3	.667	4.10	1.24	42	8	0	0	...	2-...	83.1	81	42	38	13	22-0	55	.255
— Pittsburgh (N.L.)	0	1	.000	4.67	1.27	11	1	0	0	...	0-0	17.1	13	10	9	5	9-2	18	.203
2005— Las Vegas (PCL)	0	0	...	0.00	1.80	1	0	0	0	...	0-0	1.2	2	2	0	0	1-0	0	.250
— Atlanta (N.L.)	0	0	...	0.00	3.00	1	0	0	0	...	0-0	0.1	1	0	0	0	0-0	0	1.000
— Richmond (Int'l)	3	4	.429	2.73	1.25	54	0	0	0	6	0-3	56.0	46	27	17	4	24-2	49	.222
Major League totals (2 years)	0	1	.000	4.58	1.30	12	1	0	0	...	0-0	17.2	14	10	9	5	9-2	18	.215

BROUSSARD, BEN   1B/OF

PERSONAL: Born September 24, 1976, in Beaumont, Texas. ... 6-2/220. ... Bats left, throws left. ... Full name: Benjamin Isaac Broussard. ... Name pronounced: brew-SARD. ... High school: Hardin-Jefferson (Sour Lake, Texas). ... College: McNeese State.

TRANSACTIONS/CAREER NOTES: Selected by Cincinnati Reds organization in second round of 1999 free-agent draft. ... Traded by Reds to Cleveland Indians for 3B Russell Branyan (June 7, 2002). ... On disabled list (March 21-April 6, 2003); included rehabilitation assignment to Buffalo.

2005 GAMES PLAYED BY POSITION (MLB): 1B—138, DH—2.

SCOUTING REPORT **Offense:** Broussard is an extremely streaky hitter. Swing has gotten a little longer and now has a slight uppercut approach. Is starting to use more of the field but still pulls for power. Has been turning on inside pitches. Has a lot of trouble with lefthanders. **Defense:** He is an underrated defensive first baseman with good agility and good hands. Gets good jumps on the ball to either side and has quick hands fielding bad hops and errant throws. Starts the double play well and his arm is accurate. Has played some in left field but doesn't have the range or arm strength for regular duty there. **Outlook:** Broussard is more of a platoon player and better suited to hitting lower in the order. **Grade 7.7**

BEN BROUSSARD'S HITTING ZONE

.133	.167	.294
.367	.380	.280
.231	.167	.339

LEFTY-RIGHTY SPLITS

vs.	Avg.	AB	H	2B	3B	HR	RBI	BB	SO	OBP	Slg.
L	.225	80	18	4	1	3	11	2	26	.250	.413
R	.262	386	101	26	4	16	57	30	72	.318	.474

Year	Team (League)	Pos.	G	AB	R	H	2B	3B	HR	RBI	BB	SO	HBP	GDP	SB-CS	Avg.	OBP	SLG	OPS	E	Avg.
1999— Billings (Pion.)	1B-OF	38	145	39	59	11	2	14	48	34	30	4	0	1-0	.407	.527	.800	1.327	5	.963
— Clinton (Midw.)	1B-OF	5	20	8	11	4	1	2	6	3	4	0	0	0-0	.550	.609	1.150	1.759	2	.926
— Chattanooga (Sou.)	1B-OF	35	127	26	27	5	0	8	21	11	41	3	0	1-0	.213	.291	.441	.732	2	.987
2000— Chattanooga (Sou.)	1B-OF	87	286	64	73	8	4	14	51	72	78	6	6	15-2	.255	.413	.458	.871	10	.958
2001— Mudville California (Calif.) .	1B	30	102	14	25	5	0	5	21	16	31	4	2	0-0	.245	.360	.441	.801	2	.992
— Chattanooga (Sou.)	1B-OF	100	353	81	113	27	0	23	69	61	69	8	5	10-3	.320	.428	.592	1.020	8	.990
2002— Louisville (Int'l)	1B	57	187	31	51	14	1	11	30	31	50	9	...	4-1	.273	.396	.535	.930	2	.995
— Buffalo (Int'l)	OF-1B	42	153	30	37	8	0	5	21	24	30	3	...	0-0	.242	.354	.392	.746	3	.975
— Cleveland (A.L.)	OF-1B-DH	39	112	10	27	4	0	4	9	7	25	1	3	0-0	.241	.292	.384	.676	1	.974
2003— Buffalo (Int'l)	1B-DH	32	120	17	30	2	1	3	15	9	29	1	1	3-0	.250	.303	.358	.661	2	.990
— Cleveland (A.L.)	1B	116	386	53	96	21	3	16	55	32	75	5	6	5-2	.249	.312	.443	.755	9	.991
2004— Cleveland (A.L.)	1B	139	418	57	115	28	5	17	82	52	64	12	7	4-2	.275	.370	.488	.858	6	.994
2005— Cleveland (A.L.)	1B-DH	142	466	59	119	30	5	19	68	32	98	4	4	2-2	.255	.307	.464	.770	5	.992
Major League totals (4 years)		436	1382	179	357	83	13	56	214	123	293	22	20	11-6	.258	.327	.459	.786	26	.992

BROWER, JIM   P

PERSONAL: Born December 29, 1972, in Edina, Minn. ... 6-3/215. ... Throws right, bats right. ... Full name: James Robert Brower. ... Name pronounced: BROW-er. ... High school: Minnetonka (Minn.). ... College: Minnesota.

TRANSACTIONS/CAREER NOTES: Selected by Texas Rangers organization in sixth round of 1994 free-agent draft. ... Released by Rangers (April 15, 1998). ... Signed by Cleveland Indians organization (April 18, 1998). ... Traded by Indians with P Robert Pugmire to Cincinnati Reds for C Eddie Taubensee (November 16, 2000). ... Traded by

Reds to Montreal Expos for P Bruce Chen (June 14, 2002). ... Traded by Expos with a player to be named to San Francisco Giants for P Livan Hernandez, 3B/C Edwards Guzman and cash (March 24, 2003); Giants acquired P Matt Blank to complete deal (April 30, 2003). ... Released by Giants (June 12, 2005). ... Signed by Atlanta Braves (June 16, 2005).
CAREER HITTING: 12-for-59 (.203), 9 R, 1 2B, 0 3B, 0 HR, 4 RBI.

SCOUTING REPORT **Throws:** Brower's fastball is 88-92 mph and his slider is around 83. Also throws a changeup. **Tendencies:** Brower's velocity is really down, a product of appearing in 89 games for the Giants in 2004. Fastball will sink but not as sharply, when he's up in the zone now, he's in trouble. Likes to run his slider away from righthanders but the pitch occasionally is flat. Has good motion with movement on his straight change. Sinker could abandon him at any time. **Outlook:** No longer is he a setup reliever; he's more a middle man. Could bounce back next year with a decrease in workload, but has a very fine line between being overworked and underworked. **Grade 6.5**

JIM BROWER'S PITCHING ZONE

.111	.167	.286
.256	.529	.324
.273	.438	.360

LEFTY-RIGHTY SPLITS

vs.	Avg.	AB	H	2B	3B	HR	RBI	BB	SO	OBP	Slg.
L	.303	99	30	6	1	4	13	11	15	.375	.505
R	.301	143	43	5	0	7	25	21	38	.405	.483

Year	Team (League)	W	L	Pct.	ERA	WHIP	G	GS	CG	ShO	Hld.	Sv.-Opp.	IP	H	R	ER	HR	BB-IBB	SO	Avg.
1994—	Hudson Valley (NYP)	2	1	.667	3.20	1.02	4	4	1	0	...	0-...	19.2	14	10	7	0	6-0	15	.189
—	Char., S.C. (SAL)	7	3	.700	1.72	0.99	12	12	3	2	...	0-...	78.2	52	18	15	2	26-1	84	.186
1995—	Charlotte (Fla. St.)	7	10	.412	3.89	1.34	27	27	2	1	...	0-...	173.2	170	93	75	16	62-1	110	.256
1996—	Charlotte (Fla. St.)	9	8	.529	3.79	1.30	23	21	2	0	...	0-...	145.0	148	67	61	11	40-0	86	.267
—	Tulsa (Texas)	3	2	.600	3.78	1.35	5	5	1	1	...	0-...	33.1	35	16	14	4	10-0	16	.273
1997—	Tulsa (Texas)	5	12	.294	5.21	1.41	23	23	1	0	...	0-...	140.0	156	99	81	13	42-1	103	.286
—	Okla. City (A.A.)	2	1	.667	7.23	2.04	4	3	0	0	...	0-...	18.2	30	17	15	3	8-0	7	.370
1998—	Akron (East.)	13	5	.722	3.01	1.16	23	23	2	2	...	0-...	155.2	142	60	52	9	38-0	91	.246
1999—	Buffalo (Int'l)	11	11	.500	4.73	1.39	27	27	0	0	...	0-...	160.0	164	101	84	23	59-6	76	.270
—	Cleveland (A.L.)	3	1	.750	4.56	1.44	9	2	0	0	0	0-0	25.2	27	13	13	8	10-1	18	.270
2000—	Buffalo (Int'l)	9	4	.692	3.11	1.21	16	15	1	0	...	0-...	101.1	99	41	35	7	24-1	68	.253
—	Cleveland (A.L.)	2	3	.400	6.24	1.79	17	11	0	0	0	0-0	62.0	80	45	43	11	31-1	32	.309
2001—	Louisville (Int'l)	1	0	1.000	4.09	1.27	2	2	0	0	...	0-...	11.0	12	5	5	1	2-0	11	.273
—	Cincinnati (N.L.)	7	10	.412	3.97	1.38	46	10	0	0	2	1-2	129.1	119	65	57	17	60-5	94	.247
2002—	Cincinnati (N.L.)	2	0	1.000	3.89	1.22	22	0	0	0	0	0-0	39.1	38	18	17	2	10-1	24	.260
—	Montreal (N.L.)	1	2	.333	4.83	1.49	30	0	0	0	0	0-1	41.0	39	22	22	5	22-1	33	.245
2003—	San Francisco (N.L.)	8	5	.615	3.96	1.29	51	5	0	0	2	2-3	100.0	90	48	44	8	39-2	65	.249
2004—	San Francisco (N.L.)	7	7	.500	3.29	1.35	* 89	0	0	0	24	1-5	93.0	90	42	34	6	36-2	63	.259
2005—	San Francisco (N.L.)	2	1	.667	6.53	1.81	32	0	0	0	5	1-3	30.1	40	22	22	5	15-0	25	.320
—	Richmond (Int'l)	0	1	.000	2.25	0.75	4	0	0	0	0	1-1	4.0	1	1	1	0	2-0	1	.091
—	Atlanta (N.L.)	1	2	.333	4.20	1.67	37	0	0	0	7	0-0	30.0	33	14	14	6	17-3	28	.282
American League totals (2 years)		5	4	.556	5.75	1.69	26	13	0	0	0	0-0	87.2	107	58	56	19	41-2	50	.298
National League totals (5 years)		28	27	.509	4.08	1.40	307	15	0	0	46	5-14	463.0	449	231	210	49	199-14	332	.258
Major League totals (7 years)		33	31	.516	4.35	1.45	333	28	0	0	46	5-14	550.2	556	289	266	68	240-16	382	.265

DIVISION SERIES RECORD

Year	Team (League)	W	L	Pct.	ERA	WHIP	G	GS	CG	ShO	Hld.	Sv.-Opp.	IP	H	R	ER	HR	BB-IBB	SO	Avg.
2003—	San Francisco (N.L.)	0	0	...	6.00	2.67	2	0	0	0	0	0-0	3.0	5	3	2	0	3-1	3	.357
2005—	Atlanta (N.L.)	0	0	...	0.00	0.56	3	0	0	0	0	0-0	5.1	0	0	0	0	3-0	2	.000
Division series totals (2 years)		0	0	...	2.16	1.32	5	0	0	0	0	0-0	8.1	5	3	2	0	6-1	5	.192

BROWN, EMIL   OF

PERSONAL: Born December 29, 1974, in Chicago. ... 6-2/193. ... Bats right, throws right. ... Full name: Emil Quincy Brown. ... High school: Harlan (Chicago). ... Junior college: Indian River Community College (Fla.).
TRANSACTIONS/CAREER NOTES: Selected by Oakland Athletics organization in sixth round of 1994 free-agent draft. ... Selected by Pittsburgh Pirates from A's organization in Rule 5 major league draft (December 9, 1996). ... On disabled list (June 19-July 4, 2000); included rehabilitation assignment to Nashville. ... Traded by Pirates to San Diego Padres for P Shawn Camp and OF Shawn Garrett (July 10, 2001). ... Signed as a free agent by Tampa Bay Devil Rays organization (January 28, 2002). ... Signed as a free agent by Cincinnati Reds organization (November 19, 2002). ... Signed as a free agent by St. Louis Cardinals organization (January 9, 2004) ... Released by Cardinals (May 3, 2004) ... Signed by Campeche of the Mexican League (2004). ... Signed as a free agent by Houston Astros organization (August 12, 2004). ... Signed as a free agent by Kansas City Royals organization (December 16, 2004).
2005 GAMES PLAYED BY POSITION (MLB): OF—139, DH—10.

SCOUTING REPORT Brown had his best year at the plate in his first year as a regular. Showed consistency. Has improved his bat speed and has good power when pulling the ball. Hits well with runners on and can use the whole field. Still has problems with breaking pitches. Is a good runner and has good basestealing instincts. Will move to left field after having problems tracking the ball in right field. Has good arm strength but lacks accuracy. Is not likely to duplicate 2005 numbers. **Grade 7.3**

EMIL BROWN'S HITTING ZONE

.286	.263	.167
.303	.403	.294
.226	.324	.400

LEFTY-RIGHTY SPLITS

vs.	Avg.	AB	H	2B	3B	HR	RBI	BB	SO	OBP	Slg.
L	.313	182	57	10	2	9	32	17	32	.368	.538
R	.273	363	99	21	3	8	54	31	76	.339	.413

Year	Team (League)	Pos.	G	AB	R	H	2B	3B	HR	RBI	BB	SO	HBP	GDP	SB-CS	Avg.	OBP	SLG	OPS	E	Avg.
1994—	Ariz. A's (Ariz.)	OF-OF	32	86	13	19	1	1	3	12	13	12	4	2	5-1	.221	.350	.360	.710	1	.979
1995—	W. Mich. (Mid.)	OF-OF	124	459	63	115	17	3	3	67	52	77	11	17	35-19	.251	.337	.320	.657	8	.957
1996—	Modesto (California)	OF-OF	57	211	50	64	10	1	10	47	32	51	6	5	13-5	.303	.406	.502	.908	4	.962
—	Scottsdale (Ariz.)	OF	4	15	5	4	3	0	0	2	3	2	...	...	1-1	.267	...	.467	...	0	1.000
—	Ariz. A's (Ariz.)	OF	4	15	5	4	3	0	0	2	3	1	2	1	1-1	.267	.421	.467	.888	0	1.000

B

B

Year Team (League)	Pos.	G	AB	R	H	2B	3B	HR	RBI	BB	SO	HBP	GDP	SB-CS	Avg.	OBP	SLG	OPS	E	Avg.
1997— Pittsburgh (N.L.)	OF	66	95	16	17	2	1	2	6	10	32			5-1	.179	.257	.284	.541	3	.948
1998— Carolina (Southern) ....OF-OF-DH		123	466	89	154	31	2	14	67	50	71	11	12	24-7	.330	.401	.496	.897	6	.972
— Pittsburgh (N.L.)	OF	13	39	2	10	1	0	0	3	1	11			0-0	.256	.275	.282	.557	0	1.000
1999— Nashville (PCL) ....OF-OF-DH		110	430	97	132	20	5	18	60	35	80	7	7	16-5	.307	.366	.502	.868	10	.948
— Pittsburgh (N.L.)	OF	6	14	0	2	1	0	0	0	0	3	0		0-0	.143	.143	.214	.357	0	1.000
2000— Nashville (PCL)	OF-OF	70	237	44	74	20	1	5	25	40	44	6	8	26-4	.312	.423	.468	.891	3	.978
— Pittsburgh (N.L.)	OF	50	119	13	26	5	0	3	16	11	34	3		3-1	.218	.299	.336	.635	0	1.000
2001— Pittsburgh (N.L.)	OF	61	123	18	25	4	1	3	13	15	42	2		10-4	.203	.300	.325	.625	1	.988
— San Diego (N.L.)	OF	13	14	3	1	0	0	0	1	1	7	0		2-0	.071	.133	.071	.205	0	1.000
— Portland (PCL)	OF-OF	22	78	10	25	8	2	3	8	6	17	2	2	3-1	.321	.384	.590	.974	0	1.000
2002— Durham (Int'l) ....OF-OF		116	422	58	120	24	3	12	58	34	81	10	7	10-2	.284	.347	.441	.788	9	.963
2003— Louisville (Int'l)	OF	97	369	58	109	20	3	12	63	27	76	4	7	18-3	.295	.343	.463	.806	5	.979
2004— Memphis (PCL)	OF	19	57	7	16	3	0	0	4	5	9	1	2	1-1	.281	.349	.333	.682	0	1.000
— Campeche (Mex.)	OF	28	101	23	32	8	0	8	24	15	16	1	1	0-0	.317	.403	.634	1.037	2	.000
— New Orleans (PCL)	OF	26	92	12	31	10	1	2	17	4	20	4	3	4-2	.337	.386	.533	.919	1	.000
2005— Kansas City (A.L.) ....OF-DH		150	545	75	156	31	5	17	86	48	108	8	14	10-1	.286	.349	.455	.804	12	.958
American League totals (1 year)		150	545	75	156	31	5	17	86	48	108	8	14	10-1	.286	.349	.455	.804	12	.958
National League totals (5 years)		209	404	52	81	13	2	8	38	38	129	5	...	20-6	.200	.277	.302	.579	4	.983
Major League totals (6 years)		359	949	127	237	44	7	25	124	86	237	13	14	30-7	.250	.318	.390	.708	16	.969

BROWN, KEVIN — P

PERSONAL: Born March 14, 1965, in McIntyre, Ga. ... 6-4/220. ... Throws right, bats right. ... Full name: James Kevin Brown. ... High school: Wilkinson County (Irwinton, Ga.). ... College: Georgia Tech.

TRANSACTIONS/CAREER NOTES: Selected by Texas Rangers organization in first round (fourth pick overall) of June 1986 free-agent draft. ... On disabled list (August 14-29, 1990 and March 27-April 11, 1993). ... Signed as a free agent by Baltimore Orioles (April 9, 1995). ... On disabled list (June 23-July 17, 1995). ... Signed as a free agent by Florida Marlins (December 22, 1995). ... On disabled list (May 13-28, 1996). ... Traded by Marlins to San Diego Padres for Ps Rafael Medina and Steve Hoff and 1B Derrek Lee (December 15, 1997). ... Signed as a free agent by Los Angeles Dodgers (December 12, 1998). ... On disabled list (April 9-25, 2000; March 24-April 10, May 30-June 24 and July 16-August 28, 2001). ... On disabled list (April 14-30 and May 27-August 15, 2002); included rehabilitation assignment to Las Vegas. ... On disabled list (July 4-19, 2003). ... Traded by Dodgers to New York Yankees for Ps Jeff Weaver, Yhency Brazoban and Brandon Wheedon and cash (December 13, 2003). ... On disabled list (June 10-July 30, 2004); included rehabilitation assignments to Trenton, Columbus and Staten Island. ... On disabled list (April 2-17, June 19-July 18 and July 24, 2005-remainder of season).

HONORS: Named N.L. Pitcher of the Year by THE SPORTING NEWS (1998).

CAREER HITTING: 64-for-495 (.129), 20 R, 10 2B, 0 3B, 2 HR, 29 RBI.

KEVIN BROWN'S PITCHING ZONE

.154	.167	.231
.364	.524	.474
.406	.231	.341

LEFTY-RIGHTY SPLITS

vs.	Avg.	AB	H	2B	3B	HR	RBI	BB	SO	OBP	Slg.
L	.335	167	56	12	1	0	21	11	24	.383	.419
R	.347	147	51	7	0	5	28	8	26	.394	.497

Year Team (League)	W	L	Pct.	ERA	WHIP	G	GS	CG	ShO	Hld.	Sv.-Opp.	IP	H	R	ER	HR	BB-IBB	SO	Avg.
1986— GC Rangers (GCL)	0	0	...	6.00	1.50	3	0	0	0		0-...	6.0	7	4	4	0	2-0	1	.292
— Tulsa (Texas)	0	0	...	4.50	1.40	3	2	0	0	...	0-...	10.0	9	7	5	0	5-0	10	.220
— Texas (A.L.)	1	0	1.000	3.60	1.20	1	1	0	0	0	0-...	5.0	6	2	2	0	0-0	4	.316
1987— Tulsa (Texas)	1	4	.200	7.29	1.69	8	8	0	0	...	0-...	42.0	53	36	34	3	18-1	26	.308
— Okla. City (A.A.)	0	5	.000	10.73	2.01	5	5	0	0	...	0-...	24.1	32	32	29	2	17-0	9	.311
— Charlotte (Fla. St.)	0	2	.000	2.72	1.38	6	6	1	0	...	0-...	36.1	33	14	11	1	17-0	21	.248
1988— Tulsa (Texas)	12	10	.545	3.51	1.35	26	26	5	0	...	0-...	174.1	174	94	68	5	61-1	118	.261
— Texas (A.L.)	1	1	.500	4.24	1.76	4	4	1	0	0	0-0	23.1	33	15	11	2	8-0	12	.330
1989— Texas (A.L.)	12	9	.571	3.35	1.24	28	28	7	0	0	0-0	191.0	167	81	71	10	70-2	104	.234
1990— Texas (A.L.)	12	10	.545	3.60	1.31	26	26	6	2	0	0-0	180.0	175	84	72	13	60-3	88	.255
1991— Texas (A.L.)	9	12	.429	4.40	1.53	33	33	0	0	0	0-0	210.2	233	116	103	17	90-5	96	.284
1992— Texas (A.L.)	• 21	11	.656	3.32	1.27	35	35	11	1	0	0-0	* 265.2	* 262	117	98	11	76-2	173	.260
1993— Texas (A.L.)	15	12	.556	3.59	1.30	34	34	12	3	0	0-0	233.0	228	105	93	14	74-5	142	.252
1994— Texas (A.L.)	7	9	.438	4.82	1.58	26	• 25	3	0	0	0-0	170.0	* 218	109	91	18	50-3	123	.314
1995— Baltimore (A.L.)	10	9	.526	3.60	1.18	26	26	3	1	0	0-0	172.1	155	73	69	10	48-1	117	.241
1996— Florida (N.L.)	17	11	.607	* 1.89	0.94	32	32	5	* 3	0	0-0	233.0	187	60	49	8	33-2	159	.220
1997— Florida (N.L.)	16	8	.667	2.69	1.18	33	33	6	2	0	0-0	237.1	214	77	71	10	66-7	205	.240
1998— San Diego (N.L.)	18	7	.720	2.38	1.07	36	* 35	7	3	1	0-0	257.0	225	77	68	8	49-4	257	.235
1999— Los Angeles (N.L.)	18	9	.667	3.00	1.07	35	* 35	5	1	0	0-0	252.1	210	99	84	19	59-1	221	.222
2000— Los Angeles (N.L.)	13	6	.684	* 2.58	0.99	33	33	5	1	0	0-0	230.0	181	76	66	21	47-1	216	* .213
2001— Los Angeles (N.L.)	10	4	.714	2.65	1.14	20	19	1	0	0	0-0	115.2	94	41	34	8	38-2	104	.224
2002— Los Angeles (N.L.)	3	4	.429	4.81	1.43	17	10	0	0	1	0-0	63.2	68	36	34	9	23-1	58	.274
— Las Vegas (PCL)	1	0	1.000	1.86	0.93	2	2	0	0	0	0-...	9.2	6	2	2	0	3-0	7	.182
2003— Los Angeles (N.L.)	14	9	.609	2.39	1.14	32	32	0	0	0	0-0	211.0	184	67	56	11	56-2	185	.236
2004— Trenton (East.)	0	1	.000	13.50	3.50	1	1	0	0	0	0-...	2.0	7	5	3	0	0-0	0	.500
— Columbus (Int'l)	0	0	...	4.50	1.50	1	1	0	0	0	0-...	4.0	5	2	2	1	1-0	3	.313
— Staten Island (N.Y.-Penn.) .	0	1	.000	3.00	1.17	1	1	0	0	0	0-...	6.0	6	4	2	0	1-0	6	.240
— New York (A.L.)	10	6	.625	4.09	1.27	22	22	0	0	0	0-0	132.0	132	65	60	14	35-0	83	.262
2005— New York (A.L.)	4	7	.364	6.50	1.72	13	13	0	0	0	0-0	73.1	107	57	53	5	19-1	50	.341
American League totals (11 years)	102	86	.543	3.93	1.36	248	247	43	7	0	0-0	1656.1	1716	824	723	114	530-22	992	.268
National League totals (8 years)	109	58	.653	2.60	1.08	238	229	29	10	2	0-0	1600.0	1363	533	462	94	371-20	1405	.230
Major League totals (19 years)	211	144	.594	3.28	1.22	486	476	72	17	2	0-0	3256.1	3079	1357	1185	208	901-42	2397	.249

DIVISION SERIES RECORD

Year Team (League)	W	L	Pct.	ERA	WHIP	G	GS	CG	ShO	Hld.	Sv.-Opp.	IP	H	R	ER	HR	BB-IBB	SO	Avg.
1997— Florida (N.L.)	0	0	...	1.29	0.57	1	1	0	0	0	0-0	7.0	4	1	1	0	0-0	5	.167
1998— San Diego (N.L.)	1	0	1.000	0.61	0.82	2	2	0	0	0	0-0	14.2	5	1	1	0	7-0	21	.109
2004— New York (A.L.)	1	0	1.000	1.50	1.33	1	1	0	0	0	0-0	6.0	8	1	1	0	0-0	1	.348
Division series totals (3 years)	2	0	1.000	0.98	0.87	4	4	0	0	0	0-0	27.2	17	3	3	0	7-0	27	.183

CHAMPIONSHIP SERIES RECORD

Year Team (League)	W	L	Pct.	ERA	WHIP	G	GS	CG	ShO	Hld.	Sv.-Opp.	IP	H	R	ER	HR	BB-IBB	SO	Avg.
1997— Florida (N.L.)	2	0	1.000	4.20	1.40	2	2	1	0	0	0-0	15.0	16	7	7	2	5-0	11	.276
1998— San Diego (N.L.)	1	1	.500	2.61	0.87	2	1	1	0	0	0-1	10.1	5	3	3	1	4-0	12	.143
2004— New York (A.L.)	0	1	.000	21.60	3.90	2	2	0	0	0	0-0	3.1	9	9	8	2	4-0	2	.500
Champ. series totals (3 years)	3	2	.600	5.65	1.50	6	5	2	1	0	0-1	28.2	30	19	18	5	13-0	25	.270

Year Team (League)	W	L	Pct.	ERA	WHIP	G	GS	CG	ShO	Hld.	Sv.-Opp.	IP	H	R	ER	HR	BB-IBB	SO	Avg.
						WORLD SERIES RECORD													
1997—Florida (N.L.)	0	2	.000	8.18	1.82	2	2	0	0	0	0-0	11.0	15	10	10	1	5-0	6	.375
1998—San Diego (N.L.)	0	1	.000	4.40	1.40	2	2	0	0	0	0-0	14.1	14	7	7	0	6-2	13	.259
World Series totals (2 years)	0	3	.000	6.04	1.58	4	4	0	0	0	0-0	25.1	29	17	17	1	11-2	19	.309
						ALL-STAR GAME RECORD													
All-Star Game totals (5 years)	1	0	1.000	1.93	1.07	5	1	0	0	0	0-0	4.2	2	1	1	0	3-0	2	.133

BROXTON, JONATHAN — P

PERSONAL: Born June 16, 1984, in Augusta, Ga. ... 6-4/240. ... Throws right, bats right. ... Full name: Jonathan Roy Broxton. ... High school: Burke County (Waynesboro, Ga.). ... College: None.
TRANSACTIONS/CAREER NOTES: Selected by Los Angeles Dodgers organization in second round of 2002 free-agent draft.
CAREER HITTING: 0-for-0 (.000), 0 R, 0 2B, 0 3B, 0 HR, 0 RBI.

B

JONATHAN BROXTON'S PITCHING ZONE

.200	.000	.250
.125	.250	.429
.250	.750	.250

LEFTY-RIGHTY SPLITS

vs.	Avg.	AB	H	2B	3B	HR	RBI	BB	SO	OBP	Slg.
L	.304	23	7	1	0	0	4	10	5	.486	.348
R	.200	30	6	2	0	0	4	2	17	.273	.267

Year Team (League)	W	L	Pct.	ERA	WHIP	G	GS	CG	ShO	Hld.	Sv.-Opp.	IP	H	R	ER	HR	BB-IBB	SO	Avg.
2002—Great Falls (Pio.)	2	0	1.000	2.76	1.30	11	6	0	0		2-...	29.1	22	9	9	0	16-0	33	.212
2003—South Georgia (S. Atl.)	4	2	.667	3.13	1.31	9	8	0	0		0-...	37.1	27	15	13	1	22-0	30	.208
2004—Vero Beach (FSL)	11	6	.647	3.23	1.19	23	23	1	1		0-...	128.1	110	49	46	7	43-0	144	.237
2005—Jacksonville (Sou.)	5	3	.625	3.17	1.14	33	13	0	0	2	5-5	96.2	79	36	34	4	31-0	107	.223
—Los Angeles (N.L.)	1	0	1.000	5.93	1.83	14	0	0	0	1	0-1	13.2	13	11	9	0	12-2	22	.245
Major League totals (1 year)	1	0	1.000	5.93	1.83	14	0	0	0	1	0-1	13.2	13	11	9	0	12-2	22	.245

BRUNEY, BRIAN — P

PERSONAL: Born February 17, 1982, in Astoria, Ore. ... 6-3/226. ... Throws right, bats right. ... Full name: Brian Anthony Bruney. ... Name pronounced: BREW-nee. ... High school: Warrenton (Ore.).
TRANSACTIONS/CAREER NOTES: Selected by Arizona Diamondbacks organization in 12th round of 2000 free-agent draft. ... On disabled list (May 27-July 6, 2004); included rehabilitation assignment to Tucson.
CAREER HITTING: 0-for-1 (.000), 0 R, 0 2B, 0 3B, 0 HR, 0 RBI.

BRIAN BRUNEY'S PITCHING ZONE

.143	.667	.400
.316	.478	.345
.353	.143	.182

LEFTY-RIGHTY SPLITS

vs.	Avg.	AB	H	2B	3B	HR	RBI	BB	SO	OBP	Slg.
L	.280	82	23	4	1	3	18	19	22	.422	.463
R	.314	105	33	6	2	3	20	16	29	.421	.495

Year Team (League)	W	L	Pct.	ERA	WHIP	G	GS	CG	ShO	Hld.	Sv.-Opp.	IP	H	R	ER	HR	BB-IBB	SO	Avg.
2000—Ariz. D'backs (Ariz.)	4	1	.800	6.48	2.00	20	2	0	0	...	2-...	25.0	21	23	18	2	29-0	24	.221
2001—South Bend (Mid.)	1	4	.200	4.13	1.32	26	0	0	0	...	8-...	32.2	24	19	15	1	19-2	40	.205
—Yakima (N'west)	1	2	.333	5.14	1.43	15	0	0	0	...	2-...	21.0	19	14	12	2	11-0	28	.226
2002—South Bend (Mid.)	4	3	.571	1.68	1.12	37	0	0	0	...	10-...	48.1	37	15	9	1	17-4	54	.210
—El Paso (Texas)	0	2	.000	2.92	1.22	10	0	0	0	...	0-...	12.1	11	5	4	1	4-1	14	.268
2003—El Paso (Texas)	0	2	.000	2.59	1.34	28	0	0	0	...	14-...	31.1	29	17	9	1	13-2	26	.234
—Tucson (PCL)	3	1	.750	2.81	1.31	32	0	0	0	...	12-...	32.0	24	12	10	0	18-0	32	.207
2004—Tucson (PCL)	2	0	1.000	1.18	1.00	31	0	0	0	...	5-...	38.0	18	8	5	1	20-1	42	.141
—Arizona (N.L.)	3	4	.429	4.31	1.50	30	0	0	0	3	0-1	31.1	20	16	15	2	27-5	34	.189
2005—Tucson (PCL)	1	0	1.000	1.93	1.71	4	0	0	0	0	0-0	4.2	3	3	1	0	5-0	3	.188
—Arizona (N.L.)	1	3	.250	7.43	1.98	47	0	0	0	4	12-16	46.0	56	39	38	6	35-2	51	.299
Major League totals (2 years)	4	7	.364	6.17	1.78	77	0	0	0	7	12-17	77.1	76	55	53	8	62-7	85	.259

BRUNTLETT, ERIC — SS/OF

PERSONAL: Born March 29, 1978, in Lafayette, Ind. ... 6-0/190. ... Bats right, throws right. ... Full name: Eric Kevin Bruntlett. ... High school: William Henry Harrison (West Lafayette, Ind.). ... College: Stanford.
TRANSACTIONS/CAREER NOTES: Selected by Los Angeles Dodgers organization in 72nd round of 1996 free-agent draft; did not sign. ... Selected by Houston Astros in ninth round of 2000 free-agent draft.
2005 GAMES PLAYED BY POSITION (MLB): 2B—28, OF—26, SS—10, 3B—8, 1B—1.

SCOUTING REPORT A dead fastball hitter, Bruntlett is very aggressive and likes the ball up. Has a short stroke and has improved his bat speed. Can drive the ball to the deeper parts of the park. Is a very good base runner with good instincts. Can play anywhere in the field. Has very good hands with range to his right and the arm strength to throw accurately from the hole. Has improved at getting jumps in the outfield. Is one of the most versatile players in the league and accepts his role. *Grade 5.7*

ERIC BRUNTLETT'S HITTING ZONE

.000	.333	.000
.360	.400	.333
.071	.000	.333

LEFTY-RIGHTY SPLITS

vs.	Avg.	AB	H	2B	3B	HR	RBI	BB	SO	OBP	Slg.
L	.295	61	18	4	2	2	8	7	14	.377	.525
R	.125	48	6	1	0	2	6	3	11	.176	.271

B

Year Team (League)	Pos.	G	AB	R	H	2B	3B	HR	RBI	BB	SO	HBP	GDP	SB-CS	Avg.	OBP	SLG	OPS	E	Avg.
2000—Martinsville (App.)	SS-OF	50	172	40	47	11	4	1	21	30	22	11	2	14-1	.273	.413	.401	.814	12	.944
2001—Round Rock (Texas)	SS	123	503	84	134	23	3	3	40	50	76	8	7	23-7	.266	.340	.342	.682	23	.956
—New Orleans (PCL)	SS	5	16	3	2	0	0	0	1	2	1	0	1	0-0	.125	.222	.125	.347	0	1.000
2002—Round Rock (Texas)	SS-2B	116	464	81	123	21	2	2	48	56	61	10	17	35-12	.265	.351	.332	.683	19	.966
—New Orleans (PCL)	SS-2B	18	68	9	14	3	0	0	1	10	10	0	3	1-1	.206	.308	.250	.558	6	.941
2003—New Orleans (PCL)	SS-2B-OF	84	324	48	84	10	0	2	27	35	51	3	3	9-4	.259	.332	.309	.641	13	.967
—Houston (N.L.)	SS-2B-OF-3B	31	54	3	14	3	0	1	4	0	0	0	1	0-0	.259	.255	.370	.625	1	.981
2004—New Orleans (PCL)	SS-OF-2B	86	332	50	83	12	4	6	37	35	72	7	10	14-4	.250	.331	.364	.695	12	.970
—Houston (N.L.)	SS-2B-OF	45	52	14	13	2	0	4	8	7	13	0	0	4-0	.250	.328	.519	.847	3	.947
2005—Houston (N.L.)	2B-OF-SS-3B-1B	91	109	19	24	5	2	4	14	10	25	1	4	7-2	.220	.292	.413	.705	2	.982
Major League totals (3 years)		167	215	36	51	10	2	9	26	17	48	1	5	11-2	.237	.292	.428	.720	6	.973

DIVISION SERIES RECORD

Year Team (League)	Pos.	G	AB	R	H	2B	3B	HR	RBI	BB	SO	HBP	GDP	SB-CS	Avg.	OBP	SLG	OPS	E	Avg.
2004—Houston (N.L.)	SS	2	1	0	0	0	0	0	0	1	0	0	0	0-0	.000	.500	.000	.500	0	1.000
2005—Houston (N.L.)	OF-2B-SS	3	6	1	1	0	0	0	0	0	4	0	0	0-0	.167	.167	.167	.333	0	1.000
Division series totals (2 years)		5	7	1	1	0	0	0	0	1	4	0	0	1-0	.143	.250	.143	.393	0	1.000

CHAMPIONSHIP SERIES RECORD

Year Team (League)	Pos.	G	AB	R	H	2B	3B	HR	RBI	BB	SO	HBP	GDP	SB-CS	Avg.	OBP	SLG	OPS	E	Avg.
2004—Houston (N.L.)	SS	4	2	0	0	0	0	0	0	0	0	0	0	0-0	.000	.000	.000	.000	0	...
2005—Houston (N.L.)	2B-SS	5	1	0	0	0	0	0	0	0	1	0	0	0-0	.000	.000	.000	.000	0	1.000
Champ. series totals (2 years)		9	3	0	0	0	0	0	0	0	1	0	0	0-0	.000	.000	.000	.000	0	1.000

WORLD SERIES RECORD

Year Team (League)	Pos.	G	AB	R	H	2B	3B	HR	RBI	BB	SO	HBP	GDP	SB-CS	Avg.	OBP	SLG	OPS	E	Avg.
2005—Houston (N.L.)	2B-OF	2	0	0	0	0	0	0	0	0	0	0	0	0-0	...	...	...	...	0	1.000

BUBELA, JAIME — OF

PERSONAL: Born June 6, 1978, in Houston. ... 6-1/200. ... Bats left, throws right. ... Full name: Jaime L. Bubela. ... College: Baylor.
TRANSACTIONS/CAREER NOTES: Selected by Seattle Mariners organization in seventh round of 2000 free-agent draft.
2005 GAMES PLAYED BY POSITION (MLB): OF—7, DH—1.

LEFTY-RIGHTY SPLITS

vs.	Avg.	AB	H	2B	3B	HR	RBI	BB	SO	OBP	Slg.
L	.167	6	1	0	0	0	0	0	2	.167	.167
R	.077	13	1	0	0	0	0	1	2	.143	.077

Year Team (League)	Pos.	G	AB	R	H	2B	3B	HR	RBI	BB	SO	HBP	GDP	SB-CS	Avg.	OBP	SLG	OPS	E	Avg.
2000—Everett (N'west)	OF	30	113	11	26	1	3	1	13	14	25	3	0	13-3	.230	.331	.319	.650	3	.940
—Lancaster (Calif.)	OF	9	29	6	4	1	0	0	2	5	12	1	1	4-0	.138	.286	.172	.458	0	1.000
2001—Wisconsin (Midw.)	OF	132	530	96	161	27	12	6	68	44	116	1	1	34-13	.304	.357	.434	.791	9	.954
2002—San Bern. (Calif.)	OF	118	462	69	134	25	10	7	67	40	129	4	7	30-7	.290	.351	.433	.784	4	.981
2003—San Antonio (Texas)	OF	128	473	60	131	29	7	4	61	31	108	3	4	26-11	.277	.323	.393	.716	7	.971
2004—Ariz. Mariners (Ariz.)	OF	16	67	12	23	3	1	2	12	4	9	0	2	2-1	.343	.375	.507	.882	0	1.000
—San Antonio (Texas)	OF	46	166	13	37	3	0	2	15	8	42	2	2	2-2	.223	.267	.277	.544	2	.000
2005—San Antonio (Texas)	OF-DH	130	520	84	152	20	5	9	57	34	118	5	12	40-6	.292	.340	.402	.742	16	.969
—Seattle (A.L.)	OF-DH	11	19	3	2	0	0	0	0	1	4	0	1	1-0	.105	.150	.105	.255	0	1.000
Major League totals (1 year)		11	19	3	2	0	0	0	0	1	4	0	1	1-0	.105	.150	.105	.255	0	1.000

BUCK, JOHN — C

PERSONAL: Born July 7, 1980, in Kemmerer, Wyo. ... 6-3/210. ... Bats right, throws right. ... Full name: Johnathan R. Buck. ... High school: Taylorsville (Utah).
TRANSACTIONS/CAREER NOTES: Selected by Houston Astros organization in seventh round of 1998 free-agent draft. ... Traded by Astros with cash to Kansas City Royals as part of three-team deal in which Astros acquired OF Carlos Beltran from Royals, Royals acquired P Mike Wood and 3B Mark Teahen from Oakland Athletics and Athletics acquired P Octavio Dotel from Astros (June 24, 2004).
2005 GAMES PLAYED BY POSITION (MLB): C—117.

SCOUTING REPORT *Offense:* Buck has not been consistent since coming up to the majors. Has a long stroke with a slider-speed bat. Likes the ball out over the plate but still has a lot of holes, especially inside. Has power but numbers won't show it until he pulls the ball more. Is prone to prolonged slumps. *Defense:* Buck is very aggressive and active behind the plate and has an excellent work ethic. Loves to block balls in the dirt and is very mobile for a tall catcher. Sets a good target and is willing to take charge of the pitchers. Will develop better hands. *Outlook:* The youngster could be slow to develop, but he has good tools and will be a good defensive catcher when he smooths out his footwork. Needs to be more aggressive at the plate. *Grade 6.1*

JOHN BUCK'S HITTING ZONE

.273	.286	.095
.277	.281	.327
.261	.316	.000

LEFTY-RIGHTY SPLITS

vs.	Avg.	AB	H	2B	3B	HR	RBI	BB	SO	OBP	Slg.
L	.310	116	36	7	0	2	11	12	27	.372	.422
R	.214	285	61	14	1	10	36	11	67	.250	.375

Year Team (League)	Pos.	G	AB	R	H	2B	3B	HR	RBI	BB	SO	HBP	GDP	SB-CS	Avg.	OBP	SLG	OPS	E	Avg.
1998—GC Astros (GCL)	C	36	126	24	36	9	0	3	15	13	22	2	0	2-2	.286	.362	.429	.790	4	.983
1999—Auburn (NY-Penn)	C	63	233	36	57	17	0	3	29	25	48	5	7	7-1	.245	.328	.356	.685	16	.974
—Michigan (Midw.)	C	4	10	1	1	1	0	0	0	2	3	0	0	0-0	.100	.250	.200	.450	0	1.000
2000—Michigan (Midw.)	C	109	390	57	110	33	0	10	71	55	81	5	8	2-4	.282	.374	.444	.817	15	.982
2001—Lexington (S. Atl.)	C	122	443	72	122	24	1	22	89	37	84	12	8	4-9	.275	.345	.483	.828	6	.995
2002—Round Rock (Texas)	C	120	448	48	118	29	3	12	89	31	93	6	11	2-3	.263	.314	.422	.736	8	.993
2003—New Orleans (PCL)	C	78	274	32	70	18	2	2	39	14	53	4	11	1-0	.255	.301	.358	.659	3	.993
2004—New Orleans (PCL)	C-DH	65	227	31	68	11	0	13	35	21	39	4	13	0-1	.300	.368	.507	.864	11	.993
—Kansas City (A.L.)	C-DH	71	238	36	56	9	0	12	30	15	79	0	6	1-1	.235	.280	.424	.704	3	.992
2005—Kansas City (A.L.)	C	118	401	40	97	21	1	12	47	23	94	3	9	2-2	.242	.287	.389	.676	5	.996
Major League totals (2 years)		189	639	76	153	30	1	24	77	38	173	3	15	3-3	.239	.284	.402	.686	8	.995

BUEHRLE, MARK   P

PERSONAL: Born March 23, 1979, in St. Charles, Mo. ... 6-2/220. ... Throws left, bats left. ... Full name: Mark Anthony Buehrle. ... Name pronounced: BURR-lee. ... High school: Francis Howell North (St. Charles, Mo.). ... Junior college: Jefferson (Hillsboro, Mo.).
TRANSACTIONS/CAREER NOTES: Selected by Chicago White Sox organization in 38th round of 1998 free-agent draft.
CAREER HITTING: 2-for-21 (.095), 1 R, 0 2B, 0 3B, 0 HR, 1 RBI.

SCOUTING REPORT** **Throws:** Buehrle throws a fastball from 88-91 mph, a slider/cut fastball from 83-85, a curve from 73-76 and a circle change. **Tendencies:** He has command of all his pitches, and his ability to hide his average fastball makes up for a lack of velocity. Has excellent tailing action on the fastball and can run his cut fastball in on righthanders. Pitches to both sides of the plate and works as quickly as anyone. Is a ground-ball pitcher with good mound presence. **Outlook:** Buehrle is durable and dictates the tempo to hitters. Is going to be among the leaders in wins every year. **Grade 9

MARK BUEHRLE'S PITCHING ZONE

.260	.314	.176
.297	.342	.278
.223	.423	.275

LEFTY-RIGHTY SPLITS

vs.	Avg.	AB	H	2B	3B	HR	RBI	BB	SO	OBP	Slg.
L	.271	207	56	12	1	4	25	4	35	.290	.396
R	.260	709	184	32	1	16	60	36	114	.296	.375

Year Team (League)	W	L	Pct.	ERA	WHIP	G	GS	CG	ShO	Hld.	Sv.-Opp.	IP	H	R	ER	HR	BB-IBB	SO	Avg.
1999—Burlington (Midw.)	7	4	.636	4.10	1.23	20	14	1	1	...	3-...	98.2	105	49	45	8	16-1	91	.271
2000—Birmingham (Sou.)	8	4	.667	2.28	0.94	16	16	1	1	...	0-...	118.2	95	37	30	8	17-0	68	.222
—Chicago (A.L.)	4	1	.800	4.21	1.44	28	3	0	0	3	0-2	51.1	55	27	24	5	19-1	37	.272
2001—Chicago (A.L.)	16	8	.667	3.29	1.07	32	32	4	2	0	0-0	221.1	188	89	81	24	48-2	126	.230
2002—Chicago (A.L.)	19	12	.613	3.58	1.24	34	34	5	2	0	0-0	239.0	236	102	95	25	61-7	134	.260
2003—Chicago (A.L.)	14	14	.500	4.14	1.35	35	35	2	0	0	0-0	230.1	250	124	106	22	61-2	119	.278
2004—Chicago (A.L.)	16	10	.615	3.89	1.26	35	•35	4	1	0	0-0	*245.1	257	119	106	33	51-2	165	.271
2005—Chicago (A.L.)	16	8	.667	3.12	1.18	33	33	3	1	0	0-0	*236.2	•240	99	82	20	40-4	149	.262
Major League totals (6 years)	85	53	.616	3.63	1.23	197	172	18	6	3	0-2	1224.0	1226	560	494	129	280-18	730	.262

DIVISION SERIES RECORD

Year Team (League)	W	L	Pct.	ERA	WHIP	G	GS	CG	ShO	Hld.	Sv.-Opp.	IP	H	R	ER	HR	BB-IBB	SO	Avg.
2000—Chicago (A.L.)	0	0	...	0.00	6.00	1	0	0	0	0	0-0	0.1	2	0	0	0	0-0	1	.667
2005—Chicago (A.L.)	1	0	1.000	5.14	1.29	1	1	0	0	0	0-0	7.0	8	4	4	0	1-1	2	.276
Division series totals (2 years)	1	0	1.000	4.91	1.50	2	1	0	0	0	0-0	7.1	10	4	4	0	1-1	3	.313

CHAMPIONSHIP SERIES RECORD

Year Team (League)	W	L	Pct.	ERA	WHIP	G	GS	CG	ShO	Hld.	Sv.-Opp.	IP	H	R	ER	HR	BB-IBB	SO	Avg.
2005—Chicago (A.L.)	1	0	1.000	1.00	0.56	1	1	1	0	0	0-0	9.0	5	1	1	1	0-0	4	.167

WORLD SERIES RECORD

Year Team (League)	W	L	Pct.	ERA	WHIP	G	GS	CG	ShO	Hld.	Sv.-Opp.	IP	H	R	ER	HR	BB-IBB	SO	Avg.
2005—Chicago (A.L.)	0	0	...	4.91	0.95	1	0	0	0	0	1-1	7.1	7	4	4	1	0-0	6	.250

ALL-STAR GAME RECORD

Year Team (League)	W	L	Pct.	ERA	WHIP	G	GS	CG	ShO	Hld.	Sv.-Opp.	IP	H	R	ER	HR	BB-IBB	SO	Avg.
All-Star Game totals (2 years)	1	0	1.000	2.25	1.25	2	1	0	0	0	0-0	4.0	5	1	1	0	0-0	5	.313

BUKVICH, RYAN   P

PERSONAL: Born May 13, 1978, in Naperville, Ill. ... 6-2/250. ... Throws right, bats right. ... Full name: Ryan Adrien Bukvich. ... Name pronounced: BUCK-vich. ... High school: Northwest Rankin (Brandon, Miss.). ... College: Mississippi.
TRANSACTIONS/CAREER NOTES: Selected by Kansas City Royals organization in 11th round of 2000 free-agent draft. ... Traded by Royals with P Darrell May to San Diego Padres for OF Terrence Long, P Dennis Tankersley and cash (November 8, 2004). ... Claimed on waivers by Texas Rangers (February 4, 2005). ... On disabled list (April 18, 2005-remainder of season).
CAREER HITTING: 0-for-0 (.000), 0 R, 0 2B, 0 3B, 0 HR, 0 RBI.

LEFTY-RIGHTY SPLITS

vs.	Avg.	AB	H	2B	3B	HR	RBI	BB	SO	OBP	Slg.
L	.500	4	2	0	0	0	0	3	1	.714	.500
R	.000	8	0	0	0	0	0	3	3	.273	.000

Year Team (League)	W	L	Pct.	ERA	WHIP	G	GS	CG	ShO	Hld.	Sv.-Opp.	IP	H	R	ER	HR	BB-IBB	SO	Avg.
2000—Spokane (N'west)	2	0	1.000	0.64	1.00	10	0	0	0	...	2-...	14.0	5	1	1	0	9-0	15	.111
—Char., W.Va. (SAL)	0	0	...	1.88	0.91	11	0	0	0	...	4-...	14.1	6	3	3	0	7-0	17	.128
—Wilmington (Caro.)	0	1	.000	18.00	4.00	2	0	0	0	...	1-...	2.0	3	4	4	0	5-2	3	.375
2001—Wilmington (Caro.)	0	1	.000	1.72	1.25	37	0	0	0	...	13-...	57.2	41	16	11	1	31-0	80	.194
—Wichita (Texas)	0	0	...	3.75	0.92	7	0	0	0	...	0-...	12.0	9	6	5	2	2-0	14	.200
2002—Wichita (Texas)	1	1	.500	1.31	0.93	23	0	0	0	...	8-...	34.1	17	8	5	0	15-1	47	.145
—Omaha (PCL)	1	0	1.000	0.00	0.80	12	0	0	0	...	8-...	13.2	4	0	0	0	7-0	17	.093
—Kansas City (A.L.)	1	1	.500	6.12	1.80	26	0	0	0	5	0-1	25.0	26	19	17	2	19-3	20	.277
2003—Kansas City (A.L.)	1	0	1.000	9.58	2.03	9	0	0	0	0	0-0	10.1	12	11	11	2	9-0	8	.293
—Omaha (PCL)	1	2	.333	4.91	1.70	34	0	0	0	...	5-...	36.2	39	21	20	2	25-0	44	.273
2004—Kansas City (A.L.)	0	0	...	3.68	1.50	9	0	0	0	1	1-1	7.1	4	3	3	0	7-0	7	.182
—Omaha (PCL)	3	4	.429	4.37	1.33	38	0	0	0	...	7-...	47.1	33	25	23	4	30-0	60	.193
2005—Texas (A.L.)	0	0	...	11.25	2.00	4	0	0	0	0	0-0	4.0	2	5	5	0	6-0	4	.167
Major League totals (4 years)	2	0	1.000	6.94	1.82	48	0	0	0	7	1-2	46.2	44	38	36	4	41-3	39	.260

BULGER, JASON   P

PERSONAL: Born December 6, 1978, in Lawrenceville, Ga. ... 6-4/215. ... Throws right, bats right. ... Full name: Jason Patrick Bulger. ... High school: Snellville (Ga.) Brookwood. ... College: Valdosta State.
TRANSACTIONS/CAREER NOTES: Selected by Arizona Diamondbacks organization in first round (22nd pick overall) of 2001 free-agent draft.
CAREER HITTING: 0-for-0 (.000), 0 R, 0 2B, 0 3B, 0 HR, 0 RBI.

LEFTY-RIGHTY SPLITS

vs.	Avg.	AB	H	2B	3B	HR	RBI	BB	SO	OBP	Slg.
L	.294	17	5	1	2	0	4	4	2	.429	.588
R	.360	25	9	2	0	1	2	1	7	.385	.560

Year Team (League)	W	L	Pct.	ERA	WHIP	G	GS	CG	ShO	Hld.	Sv.-Opp.	IP	H	R	ER	HR	BB-IBB	SO	Avg.
2002—South Bend (Mid.)	4	9	.308	4.94	1.58	20	20	1	0	...	0-...	94.2	111	65	52	5	39-0	84	.291

Year	Team (League)	W	L	Pct.	ERA	WHIP	G	GS	CG	ShO	Hld.	Sv.-Opp.	IP	H	R	ER	HR	BB-IBB	SO	Avg.
—Lancaster (Calif.)		1	1	.500	5.40	1.40	2	2	0	0	...	0-...	10.0	11	7	6	0	3-0	12	.289
2003—Lancaster (Calif.)		2	1	.667	6.75	1.62	4	4	0	0	...	0-...	17.1	23	13	13	3	5-0	20	.311
2004—Lancaster (Calif.)		0	1	.000	1.52	1.01	21	0	0	0	...	11-...	23.2	14	4	4	0	10-1	31	.165
—El Paso (Texas)		0	3	.000	3.91	1.70	24	0	0	0	...	8-...	25.1	24	12	11	0	19-2	26	.240
2005—Tucson (PCL)		3	6	.333	3.54	1.38	56	0	0	0	9	4-7	56.0	50	28	22	3	27-1	55	.244
—Arizona (N.L.)		1	0	1.000	5.40	1.90	9	0	0	0	0	0-0	10.0	14	6	6	1	5-1	9	.333
Major League totals (1 year)		1	0	1.000	5.40	1.90	9	0	0	0	0	0-0	10.0	14	6	6	1	5-1	9	.333

BULLINGTON, BRYAN   P

PERSONAL: Born September 30, 1980, in Indianapolis, Ind. ... 6-4/222. ... Throws right, bats right. ... Full name: Bryan Paul Bullington. ... College: Ball State.
TRANSACTIONS/CAREER NOTES: Selected by Pittsburgh Pirates organization in first round (first pick overall) of 2002 free-agent draft.
CAREER HITTING: 0-for-0 (.000), 0 R, 0 2B, 0 3B, 0 HR, 0 RBI.

LEFTY-RIGHTY SPLITS

vs.	Avg.	AB	H	2B	3B	HR	RBI	BB	SO	OBP	Slg.
L	1.000	1	1	1	0	0	0	0	0	1.000	2.000
R	.000	3	0	0	0	0	2	1	1	.333	.000

Year	Team (League)	W	L	Pct.	ERA	WHIP	G	GS	CG	ShO	Hld.	Sv.-Opp.	IP	H	R	ER	HR	BB-IBB	SO	Avg.
2003—Hickory (S. Atl.)		5	1	.833	1.39	0.79	8	7	0	0	...	0-...	45.1	25	10	7	3	11-0	46	.155
—Lynchburg (Caro.)		8	4	.667	3.05	1.32	17	17	2	1	...	0-...	97.1	101	39	33	5	27-0	67	.270
2004—Altoona (East.)		12	7	.632	4.10	1.43	26	26	0	0	...	0-...	145.0	160	77	66	18	47-1	100	.289
2005—Indianapolis (Int'l)		9	5	.643	3.38	1.19	18	18	1	0	0	0-0	109.1	104	48	41	11	26-1	82	.251
—Pittsburgh (N.L.)		0	0	...	13.50	1.50	1	0	0	0	0	0-0	1.1	1	2	2	0	1-0	1	.250
Major League totals (1 year)		0	0	...	13.50	1.50	1	0	0	0	0	0-0	1.1	1	2	2	0	1-0	1	.250

BUMP, NATE   P

PERSONAL: Born July 24, 1976, in Towanda, Pa. ... 6-2/196. ... Throws right, bats left. ... Full name: Nathan Louis Bump. ... High school: Towanda (Pa.) . ... College: Penn State.
TRANSACTIONS/CAREER NOTES: Selected by Boston Red Sox organization in 23rd round of 1997 free-agent draft; did not sign. ... Selected by San Francisco Giants organization in first round (25th overall) of 1998 free-agent draft. ... Traded by Giants with P Jason Grilli to Florida Marlins for P Livan Hernandez (July 24, 1999). ... On disabled list (July 19, 2005-remainder of season).
CAREER HITTING: 1-for-10 (.100), 1 R, 0 2B, 0 3B, 0 HR, 0 RBI.

NATE BUMP'S PITCHING ZONE

.556	.222	.400
.138	.438	.314
.143	.000	.400

LEFTY-RIGHTY SPLITS

vs.	Avg.	AB	H	2B	3B	HR	RBI	BB	SO	OBP	Slg.
L	.265	68	18	4	0	3	9	8	10	.342	.456
R	.309	81	25	1	0	2	8	4	8	.356	.395

Year	Team (League)	W	L	Pct.	ERA	WHIP	G	GS	CG	ShO	Hld.	Sv.-Opp.	IP	H	R	ER	HR	BB-IBB	SO	Avg.
1998—Salem-Keizer (N'west)		0	0	...	0.00	1.00	2	2	0	0	...	0-...	8.0	5	0	0	0	3-0	8	.192
—San Jose (Calif.)		6	1	.857	1.75	0.99	11	11	0	0	...	0-...	61.2	37	13	12	2	24-0	61	.175
1999—Shreveport (Texas)		4	10	.286	3.31	1.27	17	17	1	1	...	0-...	92.1	85	40	34	9	32-0	59	.242
—Portland (East.)		2	6	.250	6.07	1.60	8	8	0	0	...	0-...	43.0	57	38	29	3	12-0	33	.311
2000—Portland (East.)		8	9	.471	4.57	1.46	26	26	3	1	...	0-...	149.2	169	85	76	16	49-1	98	.287
2001—Portland (East.)		4	5	.444	5.27	1.19	11	8	0	0	...	0-...	54.2	55	41	32	10	10-0	41	.259
2002—Portland (East.)		7	6	.538	3.38	1.09	20	20	3	0	...	0-...	127.2	110	56	48	5	29-0	81	.227
2003—Albuquerque (PCL)		6	5	.545	4.43	1.32	15	15	0	0	...	0-...	85.1	89	48	42	4	24-1	52	.267
—Florida (N.L.)		4	0	1.000	4.71	1.49	32	0	0	0	6	0-0	36.1	34	21	19	3	20-0	17	.250
2004—Albuquerque (PCL)		0	0	...	1.39	0.62	3	2	0	0	...	0-...	13.0	7	2	2	0	1-0	12	.159
—Florida (N.L.)		2	4	.333	5.01	1.60	50	2	0	0	5	1-4	73.2	86	46	41	7	32-8	44	.297
2005—Albuquerque (PCL)		1	0	1.000	1.80	0.80	1	1	0	0	0	0-0	5.0	4	1	1	0	0-0	6	.211
—Florida (N.L.)		0	3	.000	4.03	1.45	31	0	0	0	2	0-1	38.0	43	18	17	5	12-1	18	.289
Major League totals (3 years)		6	7	.462	4.68	1.53	113	2	0	0	13	1-5	148.0	163	85	77	15	64-9	79	.283

CHAMPIONSHIP SERIES RECORD

Year	Team (League)	W	L	Pct.	ERA	WHIP	G	GS	CG	ShO	Hld.	Sv.-Opp.	IP	H	R	ER	HR	BB-IBB	SO	Avg.
2003—Florida (N.L.)		0	0	...	6.00	1.00	2	0	0	0	0	0-0	3.0	3	2	2	1	0-0	3	.250

BURGOS, AMBIORIX   P

PERSONAL: Born April 19, 1984, in Nagua, Dominican Republic. ... 6-3/235. ... Throws right, bats right. ... Full name: Ambiorix Burgos. ... High school: San Jose de Villa (Nagua, D.R.).
TRANSACTIONS/CAREER NOTES: Signed as a non-drafted free agent by Kansas City Royals organization (November 14, 2000). ... On disabled list (June 20-July 14, 2005).
CAREER HITTING: 0-for-0 (.000), 0 R, 0 2B, 0 3B, 0 HR, 0 RBI.

AMBIORIX BURGOS'S PITCHING ZONE

.300	.111	.222
.265	.632	.171
.286	.308	.333

LEFTY-RIGHTY SPLITS

vs.	Avg.	AB	H	2B	3B	HR	RBI	BB	SO	OBP	Slg.
L	.300	100	30	6	0	2	16	17	35	.403	.420
R	.216	139	30	5	1	4	13	14	30	.306	.353

Year	Team (League)	W	L	Pct.	ERA	WHIP	G	GS	CG	ShO	Hld.	Sv.-Opp.	IP	H	R	ER	HR	BB-IBB	SO	Avg.
2001—Dom. Royals (DSL)		2	5	.286	4.97	1.70	13	11	0	0	...	0-...	50.2	51	36	28	1	35-0	38	.262
2002—Dom. Royals (DSL)		0	9	.000	5.47	1.47	13	12	0	0	...	0-...	51.0	47	42	31	1	28-0	33	.241
2003—Arizona Royals 1 (AZL)		3	2	.600	4.00	1.47	9	7	0	0	...	0-...	36.0	37	22	16	1	16-0	43	.269
—Burlington (Midw.)		0	1	.000	5.40	1.80	2	2	0	0	...	0-...	5.0	3	3	3	1	6-0	4	.200
2004—Burlington (Midw.)		7	11	.389	4.38	1.38	27	26	0	0	...	0-...	133.2	109	70	65	13	75-1	172	.228
2005—Wichita (Texas)		1	1	.500	4.97	1.26	12	0	0	0	2	1-2	12.2	8	7	7	1	8-0	19	.170
—Kansas City (A.L.)		3	5	.375	3.98	1.44	59	0	0	0	11	2-6	63.1	60	29	28	6	31-1	65	.251
Major League totals (1 year)		3	5	.375	3.98	1.44	59	0	0	0	11	2-6	63.1	60	29	28	6	31-1	65	.251

PERSONAL: Born March 11, 1980, in Louisville, Ky. ... 5-11/180. ... Bats right, throws right. ... Full name: Christopher Allan Burke. ... High school: St.Xavier (Louisville). ... College: Tennessee.
TRANSACTIONS/CAREER NOTES: Selected by Houston Astros organization in first round (10th pick overall) of 2001 free-agent draft.
2005 GAMES PLAYED BY POSITION (MLB): OF—84, 2B—18.

SCOUTING REPORT **Offense:** Burke is an aggressive hitter with a short stroke. Is a good fastball hitter with deceptive power. Can take the ball the other way and is not afraid to go deep in the count. Is fairly advanced for his lack of experience. Is a good runner who will steal bases. **Defense:** He is out of position in the outfield, where he still is learning how to get jumps on the ball after moving from second base. Trails the ball going back and gets better jumps—and has better range—coming in. Still throws like an infielder. Is accurate but has not stretched out his arm. **Outlook:** Burke, whose playoff run propelled him into the spotlight, is going to hit and could contribute 15 home runs a year. Won't play second base as long as Craig Biggio is around. ***Grade 6.2***

CHRIS BURKE'S HITTING ZONE

.308	.500	.158
.247	.351	.280
.333	.200	.000

LEFTY-RIGHTY SPLITS

vs.	Avg.	AB	H	2B	3B	HR	RBI	BB	SO	OBP	Slg.
L	.265	117	31	7	1	2	8	8	18	.310	.393
R	.239	201	48	12	1	3	18	15	44	.308	.353

Year	Team (League)	Pos.	G	AB	R	H	2B	3B	HR	RBI	BB	SO	HBP	GDP	SB-CS	Avg.	OBP	SLG	OPS	E	Fielding Avg.
2001—	Michigan (Midw.)	SS	56	233	47	70	11	6	3	17	26	31	3	3	21-8	.300	.376	.438	.814	17	.931
2002—	Round Rock (Texas)	2B-SS	136	481	66	127	19	8	3	37	39	61	10	8	16-15	.264	.330	.356	.686	23	.965
2003—	Round Rock (Texas)	2B-SS-OF	137	549	88	165	23	8	3	41	57	57	14	8	34-10	.301	.379	.388	.767	21	.969
2004—	New Orleans (PCL)	2B	123	483	93	152	33	6	16	52	55	76	13	7	37-14	.315	.396	.507	.888	11	.983
—	Houston (N.L.)	2B	17	17	2	1	0	0	0	0	3	3	0	0	0-0	.059	.200	.059	.259	0	1.000
2005—	Round Rock (PCL)	2B-OF	22	90	15	28	6	2	2	11	8	13	2	2	9-0	.311	.380	.489	.869	1	.991
—	Houston (N.L.)	OF-2B	108	318	49	79	19	2	5	26	23	62	6	7	11-6	.248	.309	.368	.676	1	.994
	Major League totals (2 years)		125	335	51	80	19	2	5	26	26	65	6	7	11-6	.239	.303	.352	.655	1	.995

DIVISION SERIES RECORD

Year	Team (League)	Pos.	G	AB	R	H	2B	3B	HR	RBI	BB	SO	HBP	GDP	SB-CS	Avg.	OBP	SLG	OPS	E	Avg.
2005— Houston (N.L.)		OF	3	3	1	2	1	0	1	1	1	0	0	0	0-0	.667	.750	2.000	2.750	0	1.000

CHAMPIONSHIP SERIES RECORD

Year	Team (League)	Pos.	G	AB	R	H	2B	3B	HR	RBI	BB	SO	HBP	GDP	SB-CS	Avg.	OBP	SLG	OPS	E	Avg.
2005— Houston (N.L.)		OF	6	20	5	6	0	1	1	3	1	3	0	0	0-0	.300	.333	.550	.883	0	1.000

WORLD SERIES RECORD

Year	Team (League)	Pos.	G	AB	R	H	2B	3B	HR	RBI	BB	SO	HBP	GDP	SB-CS	Avg.	OBP	SLG	OPS	E	Avg.
2005— Houston (N.L.)		OF-2B	4	5	1	0	0	0	0	0	2	0	0	0	2-0	.000	.286	.000	.286	0	1.000

PERSONAL: Born September 24, 1971, in Roseburg, Ore. ... 6-0/220. ... Bats right, throws right. ... Full name: James Eugene Burke. ... High school: Roseburg (Ore.). ... College: Oregon State.
TRANSACTIONS/CAREER NOTES: Selected by California Angels organization in ninth round of 1993 free-agent draft. ... Angels franchise renamed Anaheim Angels for 1997 season. ... Signed as a free agent by Chicago White Sox organization (January 27, 2003). ... Signed as a free agent by Texas Rangers organization (November 3, 2005).
2005 GAMES PLAYED BY POSITION (MLB): 1B—1.

LEFTY-RIGHTY SPLITS

vs.	Avg.	AB	H	2B	3B	HR	RBI	BB	SO	OBP	Slg.
L	.000	1	0	0	0	0	0	0	0	.000	.000
R	.000	0	0	0	0	0	0	0	0	.000	.000

Year	Team (League)	Pos.	G	AB	R	H	2B	3B	HR	RBI	BB	SO	HBP	GDP	SB-CS	Avg.	OBP	SLG	OPS	E	Fielding Avg.
1993—	Boise (N'west)	3B	66	226	32	68	11	1	1	30	39	28	5	4	2-3	.301	.412	.372	.783	18	.873
1994—	Cedar Rap. (Midw.)	1B-3B	127	469	57	124	24	1	1	47	40	64	12	15	6-8	.264	.333	.326	.659	22	.973
1995—	Lake Elsinore (Calif.)	1B-3B	106	365	47	100	15	6	2	56	32	53	9	12	6-4	.274	.344	.364	.708	22	.949
1996—	Midland (Texas)	1B-3B-C																			
		OF	45	144	24	46	8	2	2	16	20	22	2	1	1-1	.319	.410	.444	.854	5	.968
—	Vancouver (PCL)	3B-C-OF	41	156	12	39	5	0	1	14	7	18	1	5	2-1	.250	.283	.301	.584	5	.952
1997—	Midland (Texas)	1B-3B-C																			
		OF	116	428	77	141	44	3	6	72	40	46	8	12	2-3	.329	.395	.488	.883	27	.956
—	Vancouver (PCL)	3B-C	8	27	4	8	1	0	0	3	3	2	1	1	0-0	.296	.387	.333	.720	3	.923
1998—	Vancouver (PCL)	1B-3B-C	61	162	16	35	6	0	2	14	13	25	6	7	0-1	.216	.295	.290	.585	5	.985
—	Midland (Texas)	3B	12	41	7	10	1	0	0	4	7	4	0	4	0-0	.244	.354	.268	.622	3	.870
1999—	Edmonton (PCL)	1B-2B-3B																			
		C-P	46	149	29	50	9	0	3	16	23	18	3	2	0-1	.336	.434	.456	.891	5	.958
2000—	Edmonton (PCL)	2B-3B-C	75	263	25	63	12	0	0	17	19	42	5	5	1-1	.240	.301	.285	.586	6	.980
2001—	Salt Lake (PCL)	C-3B-1B																			
		OF	61	215	25	47	10	3	0	27	19	28	5		1-0	.219	.292	.293	.585	5	.988
—	Anaheim (A.L.)	C-1B-3B	9	5	1	1	0	0	0	0	0	2	0	0	0-0	.200	.200	.200	.400	0	1.000
2002—	Salt Lake (PCL)	C-3B-1B	88	316	47	96	12	4	4	44	20	37	4	9	1-3	.304	.350	.443	.793	13	.974
2003—	Charlotte (Int'l)	C-DH-1B																			
		3B	94	323	47	104	13	0	6	50	20	39	4	9	1-1	.322	.363	.418	.781	6	.990
—	Chicago (A.L.)	C-1B-DH	6	8	0	3	0	0	0	2	0	0	0	0	0-0	.375	.375	.375	.750	0	1.000
2004—	Charlotte (Int'l)	C-DH	37	134	12	31	8	0	2	12	9	15	2		0-0	.231	.286	.321	.607	2	.993
—	Chicago (A.L.)	C-1B-DH																			
		3B-OF	57	120	22	40	5	0	0	15	10	13	1	3	0-0	.333	.386	.408	.795	3	.987
2005—	Chicago (A.L.)	1B	1	1	0	0	0	0	0	0	0	0	0	0	0-0	.000	.000	.000	.000	0	...
—	Charlotte (Int'l)	C-3B-2B																			
		1B-DH	102	358	50	95	22	1	0	53	36	53	13	12	1-3	.265	.350	.416	.767	6	.988
	Major League totals (4 years)		73	134	23	44	9	0	0	17	10	15	1	3	0-0	.328	.377	.396	.772	3	.988

BURNETT, A.J.   P

PERSONAL: Born January 3, 1977, in North Little Rock, Ark. ... 6-4/230. ... Throws right, bats right. ... Full name: Allan James Burnett. ... High school: Central Arkansas Christian (North Little Rock).
TRANSACTIONS/CAREER NOTES: Selected by New York Mets organization in eighth round of 1995 free-agent draft. ... Traded by Mets with P Jesus Sanchez and OF Robert Stratton to Florida Marlins for P Al Leiter and 2B Ralph Milliard (February 6, 1998). ... On disabled list (March 17-July 20, 2000); included rehabilitation assignments to Brevard County and Calgary. ... On disabled list (March 23-May 7, 2001); included rehabilitation assignment to Brevard County. ... On disabled list (August 19-September 14, 2002; and March 21-April 9 and April 26, 2003-remainder of season). ... On disabled list (March 26-June 3, 2004); included rehabilitation assignments to Jupiter and Albuquerque.
CAREER HITTING: 34-for-253 (.134), 12 R, 6 2B, 3 3B, 3 HR, 9 RBI.

SCOUTING REPORT *Throws:* Burnett has an overpowering fastball that hits 94-98 mph, a sharp curveball and a changeup. *Tendencies:* He has overpowering velocity, especially up in the zone, and one of the best curveballs in the National League. Has good arm speed on his changeup. Needs to focus better and learn to control his emotions. Pitches behind in the count too much and has high pitch counts. *Outlook:* Burnett is immature and has a history of arm problems. Change of scenery might allow him to reach his potential. *Grade 7.9*

A.J. BURNETT'S PITCHING ZONE

.378	.333	.296
.246	.325	.224
.302	.234	.160

LEFTY-RIGHTY SPLITS

vs.	Avg.	AB	H	2B	3B	HR	RBI	BB	SO	OBP	Slg.
L	.226	402	91	13	3	6	31	44	107	.305	.318
R	.249	373	93	14	3	6	45	35	91	.319	.351

Year	Team (League)	W	L	Pct.	ERA	WHIP	G	GS	CG	ShO	Hld.	Sv.-Opp.	IP	H	R	ER	HR	BB-IBB	SO	Avg.
1995—GC Mets (GCL)		2	3	.400	4.28	1.49	9	8	0	0	...	0-...	33.2	27	16	16	2	23-0	26	.231
1996—Kingsport (Appalachian)		4	0	1.000	3.88	1.47	12	12	0	0	...	0-...	58.0	31	26	25	0	54-0	68	.171
1997—GC Mets (GCL)		0	1	.000	3.18	1.41	3	2	0	0	...	0-...	11.1	8	8	4	0	8-0	15	.182
—Pittsfield (NYP)		3	1	.750	4.70	1.43	20	9	0	0	...	0-...	44.0	28	26	23	3	35-0	48	.188
1998—Kane Co. (Midw.)		10	4	.714	1.97	1.00	20	20	0	0	...	0-...	119.0	74	27	26	3	45-0	186	.179
1999—Portland (East.)		6	12	.333	5.52	1.68	26	23	0	0	...	0-...	120.2	132	91	74	15	71-0	121	.281
—Florida (N.L.)		4	2	.667	3.48	1.50	7	7	0	0	0	0-0	41.1	37	23	16	3	25-2	33	.242
2000—Brevard County (FSL)		0	0	...	3.68	1.36	2	2	0	0	0	0-...	7.1	4	3	3	0	6-0	6	.160
—Calgary (PCL)		0	0	...	0.00	0.60	1	1	0	0	0	0-...	5.0	0	0	0	0	3-0	6	.000
—Florida (N.L.)		3	7	.300	4.79	1.50	13	13	0	0	0	0-0	82.2	80	46	44	8	44-3	57	.259
2001—Brevard County (FSL)		0	0	...	1.93	0.86	2	2	0	0	0	0-...	9.1	4	2	2	0	3-0	10	.129
—Florida (N.L.)		11	12	.478	4.05	1.32	27	27	2	1	0	0-0	173.1	145	82	78	20	83-3	128	.231
2002—Florida (N.L.)		12	9	.571	3.30	1.19	31	29	7	* 5	0	0-1	204.1	153	84	75	12	90-5	203	.209
2003—Florida (N.L.)		0	2	.000	4.70	1.57	4	4	0	0	0	0-0	23.0	18	13	12	2	18-2	21	.217
2004—Jupiter (Fla. St.)		0	0	...	0.00	1.00	1	1	0	0	0	0-...	4.0	2	1	0	0	2-0	4	.133
—Albuquerque (PCL)		0	0	...	10.80	2.70	1	1	0	0	0	0-...	3.1	7	4	4	1	2-0	6	.412
—Florida (N.L.)		7	6	.538	3.68	1.17	20	19	1	0	0	0-0	120.0	102	50	49	9	38-0	113	.231
2005—Florida (N.L.)		12	12	.500	3.44	1.26	32	32	4	2	0	0-0	209.0	184	97	80	12	79-1	198	.237
Major League totals (7 years)		**49**	**50**	**.495**	**3.73**	**1.28**	**134**	**131**	**14**	**8**	**0**	**0-1**	**853.2**	**719**	**395**	**354**	**66**	**377-16**	**753**	**.230**

BURNITZ, JEROMY   OF

PERSONAL: Born April 15, 1969, in Westminster, Calif. ... 6-0/213. ... Bats left, throws right. ... Full name: Jeromy Neal Burnitz. ... Name pronounced: ber-NITS. ... High school: Conroe (Texas). ... College: Oklahoma State.
TRANSACTIONS/CAREER NOTES: Selected by Milwaukee Brewers organization in 24th round of 1987 free-agent draft; did not sign. ... Selected by New York Mets organization in first round (17th pick overall) of 1990 free-agent draft. ... Traded by Mets with P Joe Roa to Cleveland Indians for Ps Paul Byrd, Jerry DiPoto and Dave Mlicki and a player to be named (November 18, 1994); Mets acquired 2B Jesus Azuaje to complete deal (December 6, 1994). ... Traded by Indians to Milwaukee Brewers for 3B/1B Kevin Seitzer (August 31, 1996). ... On disabled list (July 18-August 20, 1999). ... Traded by Brewers with P Jeff D'Amico, IF Lou Collier and OF/1B Mark Sweeney to Mets as part of three-team deal in which Brewers acquired P Glendon Rusch and IF Lenny Harris from Mets and OF Alex Ochoa from Rockies, Rockies acquired IFs Todd Zeile, OF Benny Agbayani and cash from Rockies, and Mets acquired 1B/OF Ross Gload and Craig House from Rockies (January 21, 2002). ... On disabled list (April 23-May 23, 2003); included rehabilitation assignment to Binghamton. ... Traded by Mets to Los Angeles Dodgers for IF Victor Diaz and Ps Joselo Diaz and Kole Strayhorn (July 14, 2003). ... Signed as a free agent by Colorado Rockies (January 9, 2004). ... Signed as a free agent by Chicago Cubs (February 2, 2005).
2005 GAMES PLAYED BY POSITION (MLB): OF—160.

SCOUTING REPORT *Offense:* This fastball hitter has a very big swing and an aggressive uppercut and good bat speed. Has some holes in his swing, has an especially difficult time laying off high pitches. Will chase breaking balls. Has very good power and can drive the ball to the opposite field. Stays in against lefthanded pitching and has shown the ability to become more patient with runners on. Is not a good baserunner. *Defense:* He has improved his jumps coming in on the ball. Has average range and a good throwing arm but can be erratic. *Outlook:* Burnitz is a high-strikeout, high-production player with exceptional makeup. Can hit the ball out of any part of the park and is one of the most aggressive hitters in the league. *Grade 7.8*

JEROMY BURNITZ'S HITTING ZONE

.296	.333	.370
.275	.400	.250
.414	.200	.200

LEFTY-RIGHTY SPLITS

vs.	Avg.	AB	H	2B	3B	HR	RBI	BB	SO	OBP	Slg.
L	.236	182	43	9	1	9	35	7	39	.268	.445
R	.267	423	113	22	1	15	52	50	70	.345	.430

Year	Team (League)	Pos.	G	AB	R	H	2B	3B	HR	RBI	BB	SO	HBP	GDP	SB-CS	Avg.	OBP	SLG	OPS	E	Avg.
1990—Pittsfield (NYP)		OF	51	173	37	52	6	5	6	22	45	39	3	3	12-5	.301	.444	.497	.942	0	1.000
—St. Lucie (Fla. St.)		OF	11	32	6	5	1	0	0	3	7	12	4	0	1-0	.156	.372	.188	.560	0	1.000
1991—Williamsport (East.)		OF	135	457	80	103	16	10	31	85	104	127	4	7	31-13	.225	.368	.508	.876	11	.958
1992—Tidewater (Int'l)		OF	121	445	56	108	21	3	8	40	33	84	3	7	30-7	.243	.298	.357	.655	6	.967
1993—Norfolk (Int'l)		OF	65	255	33	58	15	3	8	44	25	53	2	6	10-7	.227	.298	.404	.702	1	.993
—New York (N.L.)		OF	86	263	49	64	10	6	13	38	38	66	1	2	3-6	.243	.339	.475	.814	4	.977
1994—New York (N.L.)		OF	45	143	26	34	4	0	3	15	23	45	1	2	1-1	.238	.347	.329	.676	2	.970
—Norfolk (Int'l)		OF-DH	85	314	58	75	15	5	14	49	49	82	1	9	18-6	.239	.340	.452	.792	4	.979
1995—Buffalo (A.A.)		OF	128	443	72	126	26	7	19	85	50	83	3	6	13-5	.284	.359	.503	.862	5	.981

Year	Team (League)	Pos.	G	AB	R	H	2B	3B	HR	RBI	BB	SO	HBP	GDP	SB-CS	Avg.	OBP	SLG	OPS	E	Avg.
	—Cleveland (A.L.)	OF-DH	9	7	4	4	1	0	0	0	0	0	0	0	0-0	.571	.571	.714	1.286	0	1.000
1996—	Cleveland (A.L.)	OF-DH	71	128	30	36	10	0	7	26	25	31	2	3	2-1	.281	.406	.523	.930	0	1.000
	—Milwaukee (A.L.)	OF	23	72	8	17	4	0	2	14	8	16	2	1	2-0	.236	.321	.375	.696	1	.975
1997—	Milwaukee (A.L.)	OF	153	494	85	139	37	8	27	85	75	111	5	8	20-13	.281	.382	.553	.934	7	.975
1998—	Milwaukee (N.L.)	OF	161	609	92	160	28	1	38	125	70	158	4	9	7-4	.263	.339	.499	.838	9	.972
1999—	Milwaukee (N.L.)	OF-DH	130	467	87	126	33	2	33	103	91	124	16	11	7-3	.270	.402	.561	.963	5	.982
2000—	Milwaukee (N.L.)	OF-DH	161	564	91	131	29	2	31	98	99	121	14	12	6-4	.232	.356	.456	.811	7	.979
2001—	Milwaukee (N.L.)	OF	154	562	104	141	32	4	34	100	80	150	5	8	0-4	.251	.347	.504	.851	6	.981
2002—	New York (N.L.)	OF-DH	154	479	65	103	15	0	19	54	58	135	10	11	10-7	.215	.311	.365	.677	9	.966
2003—	Binghamton (East.)	OF	3	13	1	3	0	0	1	3	0	4	0	0	1-0	.231	.231	.462	.692	0	1.000
	—New York (N.L.)	OF	65	234	38	64	18	0	18	45	21	55	4	4	1-4	.274	.344	.581	.925	2	.986
	—Los Angeles (N.L.)	OF	61	230	25	47	4	0	13	32	14	57	1	4	4-0	.204	.252	.391	.643	5	.946
2004—	Colorado (N.L.)	OF-DH	150	540	94	153	30	4	37	110	58	124	5	7	5-6	.283	.356	.559	.916	7	.974
2005—	Chicago (N.L.)	OF	160	605	84	156	31	2	24	87	57	109	3	12	5-4	.258	.322	.435	.757	5	.984
	American League totals (3 years)		256	701	127	196	52	8	36	125	108	158	9	12	24-14	.280	.382	.531	.912	8	.978
	National League totals (10 years)		1327	4696	755	1179	234	21	263	807	609	1144	64	79	49-43	.251	.342	.478	.820	61	.976
	Major League totals (13 years)		1583	5397	882	1375	286	29	299	932	717	1302	73	91	73-57	.255	.348	.485	.832	69	.977

ALL-STAR GAME RECORD

	G	AB	R	H	2B	3B	HR	RBI	BB	SO	HBP	GDP	SB-CS	Avg.	OBP	SLG	OPS	E	Avg.
All-Star Game totals (1 year)	1	2	1	1	1	0	0	0	0	0	0	0	0-0	.500	.500	1.000	1.500	0	...

BURNS, MIKE   P

PERSONAL: Born July 14, 1978, in Westminster, Calif. ... 6-1/205. ... Throws right, bats right. ... Full name: Michael John Burns. ... College: UCLA.
TRANSACTIONS/CAREER NOTES: Selected by Houston Astros organization in 30th round of 2000 free-agent draft. ... Claimed off of waivers by Cincinnati Reds (November 16, 2005).
CAREER HITTING: 0-for-0 (.000), 0 R, 0 2B, 0 3B, 0 HR, 0 RBI.

MIKE BURNS' PITCHING ZONE

.111	.231	.333
.167	.400	.316
.083	.250	.625

LEFTY-RIGHTY SPLITS

vs.	Avg.	AB	H	2B	3B	HR	RBI	BB	SO	OBP	Slg.
L	.328	58	19	4	1	1	5	1	8	.361	.483
R	.156	64	10	3	0	5	11	7	12	.270	.438

Year	Team (League)	W	L	Pct.	ERA	WHIP	G	GS	CG	ShO	Hld.	Sv.-Opp.	IP	H	R	ER	HR	BB-IBB	SO	Avg.
2000—	Martinsville (App.)	2	7	.222	4.52	1.28	12	12	0	0	...	0-...	65.2	75	52	33	12	9-0	51	.281
2001—	Michigan (Midw.)	7	7	.500	3.95	1.20	29	21	1	0	...	1-...	132.0	131	67	58	10	27-0	108	.260
2002—	Michigan (Midw.)	14	9	.609	2.49	0.97	28	28	3	2	...	0-...	181.0	146	59	50	12	29-1	126	.218
2003—	Round Rock (Texas)	2	13	.133	6.13	1.50	38	14	0	0	...	0-...	105.2	129	80	72	15	30-3	89	.297
2004—	Round Rock (Texas)	11	3	.786	1.67	0.97	56	0	0	0	...	9-...	80.2	63	18	15	1	15-3	94	.209
2005—	Round Rock (PCL)	2	1	.667	2.10	0.87	25	0	0	0	0	13-15	30.0	22	7	7	4	4-0	34	.200
	—Houston (N.L.)	0	0	...	4.94	1.19	27	0	0	0	1	0-0	31.0	29	18	17	6	8-1	20	.238
	Major League totals (1 year)	0	0	...	4.94	1.19	27	0	0	0	1	0-0	31.0	29	18	17	6	8-1	20	.238

BURRELL, PAT   OF

PERSONAL: Born October 10, 1976, in Eureka Springs, Ark. ... 6-4/223. ... Bats right, throws right. ... Full name: Patrick Brian Burrell. ... Name pronounced: BURL. ... High school: Bellarmine Prep (San Jose). ... College: Miami.
TRANSACTIONS/CAREER NOTES: Selected by Boston Red Sox organization in 43rd round of 1995 free-agent draft; did not sign. ... Selected by Philadelphia Phillies organization in first round (first pick overall) of 1998 free-agent draft. ... On disabled list (August 4-September 3, 2004); included rehabilitation assignment to Reading.
2005 GAMES PLAYED BY POSITION (MLB): OF—153.

SCOUTING REPORT *Offense:* Made adjustments in 2005 by quieting down his front side and keeping his hands back while driving them through the ball. Doesn't fly open as much. Has good bat speed in spite of his long stroke. Has become a more patient hitter but still has a propensity to strike out in streaks. Has exceptional power to all fields but remains cognizant of not being too pull-conscious. Not a good runner yet is aggressive on bases. *Defense:* He's underrated in the outfield and has improved his lateral jumps and reads. Still has problems reading balls hit directly at him. Is an accurate thrower with average arm strength and a quick release. *Outlook:* Burrell had his best year in 2005 and should continue to put up big numbers in homer-friendly Citizens Bank Park. *Grade 8.3*

PAT BURRELL'S HITTING ZONE

.306	.348	.194
.267	.435	.333
.246	.375	.308

LEFTY-RIGHTY SPLITS

vs.	Avg.	AB	H	2B	3B	HR	RBI	BB	SO	OBP	Slg.
L	.318	154	49	6	0	10	29	35	38	.442	.552
R	.267	408	109	21	1	22	88	64	122	.367	.485

Year	Team (League)	Pos.	G	AB	R	H	2B	3B	HR	RBI	BB	SO	HBP	GDP	SB-CS	Avg.	OBP	SLG	OPS	E	Avg.
1998—	Clearwater (FSL)	1B	37	132	29	40	7	1	7	30	27	22	0	3	2-0	.303	.416	.530	.946	1	.995
1999—	Reading (East.)	1B-OF	117	417	84	139	28	6	28	90	79	103	0	13	3-1	.333	.438	.631	1.068	12	.985
	—Scran./W.B. (I.L.)	1B-OF	10	33	4	5	0	0	1	4	4	8	1	0	0-1	.152	.263	.242	.506	0	1.000
2000—	Scran./W.B. (I.L.)	OF-1B	40	143	31	42	15	1	4	25	32	36	0	1	1-1	.294	.420	.497	.917	2	.987
	—Philadelphia (N.L.)	1B-OF-DH	111	408	57	106	27	1	18	79	63	139	1	5	0-0	.260	.359	.463	.822	8	.986
2001—	Philadelphia (N.L.)	OF-DH	155	539	70	139	29	2	27	89	70	162	5	12	2-1	.258	.346	.469	.816	7	.972
2002—	Philadelphia (N.L.)	OF	157	586	96	165	39	2	37	116	89	153	3	16	1-0	.282	.376	.544	.920	6	.979
2003—	Philadelphia (N.L.)	OF-DH	146	522	57	109	31	4	21	64	72	142	4	18	0-0	.209	.309	.404	.713	6	.976
2004—	Reading (East.)	OF	4	15	2	3	0	0	2	4	3	7	0	0	0-0	.200	.333	.600	.933	1	.875
	—Philadelphia (N.L.)	OF	127	448	66	115	17	0	24	84	78	130	2	10	2-0	.257	.365	.455	.821	4	.983
2005—	Philadelphia (N.L.)	OF	154	562	78	158	27	1	32	117	99	160	3	12	0-0	.281	.389	.504	.892	7	.972
	Major League totals (6 years)		850	3065	424	792	170	10	159	549	471	886	18	73	5-1	.258	.358	.476	.834	38	.979

BURROUGHS, SEAN — 3B

PERSONAL: Born September 12, 1980, in Atlanta. ... 6-2/200. ... Bats left, throws right. ... Full name: Sean Patrick Burroughs. ... High school: Wilson (Long Beach, Calif.). ... Son of Jeff Burroughs, outfielder with five major league teams (1970-85).

TRANSACTIONS/CAREER NOTES: Selected by San Diego Padres organization in first round (ninth pick overall) of 1998 free-agent draft. ... On disabled list (May 29-July 15, 2002); included rehabilitation assignment to Portland. ...Career major league pitching: 0-0, 27.00 ERA, 1 G, 1.0 IP, 4 H, 3 R, 3 ER, 0 BB, 0 SO.

2005 GAMES PLAYED BY POSITION (MLB): 3B—78, SS—1, P—1.

SCOUTING REPORT *Offense:* Burroughs regressed as much as any hitter in the league last season. Showed no power. Is a pronounced inside-out hitter and rarely pulls the ball. Showed a decline in bat speed. Slightly uppercut swing makes it difficult to develop power. Makes good contact and rarely strikes out, but can't drive the ball through the gaps with authority. Is rigid at the plate. *Defense:* His good hands don't make up for his limited range. Is better at charging than moving laterally. Has good arm strength but is slowed by a deliberate setup. *Outlook:* With Vinny Castilla on board in San Diego, Burroughs might need a very big spring just to win a job somewhere. *Grade 6*

SEAN BURROUGHS'S HITTING ZONE

.250	.364	.333
.308	.367	.262
.320	.150	.194

LEFTY-RIGHTY SPLITS

vs.	Avg.	AB	H	2B	3B	HR	RBI	BB	SO	OBP	Slg.
L	.172	58	10	0	0	1	5	1	9	.222	.224
R	.270	226	61	7	2	0	12	23	32	.343	.319

Year	Team (League)	Pos.	G	AB	R	H	2B	3B	HR	RBI	BB	SO	HBP	GDP	SB-CS	Avg.	OBP	SLG	OPS	E	Avg.
1999— Rancho Cuca. (Calif.)		3B	6	23	3	10	3	0	1	5	3	3	1	1	0-1	.435	.519	.696	1.214	0	1.000
— Fort Wayne (Midw.)		3B	122	426	65	153	30	3	5	80	74	59	14	10	17-15	.359	.464	.479	.943	37	.898
2000— Mobile (Sou.)		3B	108	392	46	114	29	4	2	42	58	45	3	10	6-8	.291	.383	.401	.783	16	.947
2001— Portland (PCL)		3B	104	394	60	127	28	1	9	55	37	54	4	13	9-2	.322	.386	.467	.853	10	.949
2002— San Diego (N.L.)		3B-2B	63	192	18	52	5	1	1	11	12	30	1	6	2-0	.271	.317	.323	.640	8	.949
— Portland (PCL)		2B-3B	50	179	29	54	16	2	2	23	21	16	3	5	1-0	.302	.380	.447	.827	6	.969
2003— San Diego (N.L.)		3B	146	517	62	148	27	6	7	58	44	75	11	13	7-2	.286	.352	.402	.755	12	.966
2004— San Diego (N.L.)		3B	130	523	76	156	23	3	2	47	31	52	9	6	5-4	.298	.348	.365	.713	14	.957
2005— Portland (PCL)		3B	32	124	21	36	8	0	3	14	9	15	5	0	0-0	.290	.362	.427	.790	4	.949
— San Diego (N.L.)		3B-P-SS	93	284	20	71	7	2	1	17	24	41	5	7	4-0	.250	.318	.299	.618	8	.962
Major League totals (4 years)			432	1516	176	427	62	12	11	133	111	198	26	32	18-6	.282	.340	.360	.700	42	.960

DIVISION SERIES RECORD

Year	Team (League)	Pos.	G	AB	R	H	2B	3B	HR	RBI	BB	SO	HBP	GDP	SB-CS	Avg.	OBP	SLG	OPS	E	Avg.
2005— San Diego (N.L.)		PH	2	1	0	0	0	0	0	0	0	0	0	0	0-0	.000	.000	.000	.000	0	...

BUSH, DAVID — P

PERSONAL: Born November 9, 1979, in Pittsburgh. ... 6-2/212. ... Throws right, bats right. ... Full name: David T. Bush. ... High school: Conestoga (Berwyn, Pa.). ... College: Wake Forest.

TRANSACTIONS/CAREER NOTES: Selected by Tampa Bay Devil Rays organization in fourth round of 2001 free-agent draft; did not sign. ... Selected by Toronto Blue Jays organization in second round of 2002 free-agent draft.

CAREER HITTING: 0-for-2 (.000), 0 R, 0 2B, 0 3B, 0 HR, 0 RBI.

SCOUTING REPORT *Throws:* His fastball hits 93 mph and his two-seamer touches 90. Also has overhand curve and changeup. *Tendencies:* Bush is a control pitcher who uses his fastball to set up his off-speed pitches. Has an aggressive approach. Pounds the strike zone so consistently he sometimes runs into trouble when he is over the plate too much. Has good mechanics and mixes his pitches intelligently. Tends to leave pitches up when throwing from the stretch. Is a good fielder. *Outlook:* Bush never stops coming at hitters, even when he's hit hard. That should make him a valuable innings-eater type at the back of the rotation. *Grade 7.3*

DAVID BUSH'S PITCHING ZONE

.333	.278	.281
.272	.389	.278
.245	.182	.295

LEFTY-RIGHTY SPLITS

vs.	Avg.	AB	H	2B	3B	HR	RBI	BB	SO	OBP	Slg.
L	.269	268	72	16	0	12	32	15	36	.312	.463
R	.269	260	70	21	2	8	34	14	39	.331	.458

Year	Team (League)	W	L	Pct.	ERA	WHIP	G	GS	CG	ShO	Hld.	Sv.-Opp.	IP	H	R	ER	HR	BB-IBB	SO	Avg.
2002— Auburn (NY-Penn)	1	1	.500	2.82	0.90	18	0	0	0	...	10-...	22.1	13	9	7	1	7-2	39	.159
— Dunedin (Fla. St.)	0	1	.000	2.03	0.90	7	0	0	0	...	0-...	13.1	10	3	3	1	2-0	9	.222
2003— Dunedin (Fla. St.)	7	3	.700	2.81	0.95	14	14	0	0	...	0-...	77.0	64	29	24	6	9-0	75	.223
— New Haven (East.)	7	3	.700	2.78	1.14	14	14	1	0	...	0-...	81.0	73	26	25	4	19-1	73	.239
2004— Syracuse (Int'l)	6	6	.500	4.06	1.28	16	16	2	0	...	0-...	99.2	108	52	45	7	20-1	88	.276
— Toronto (A.L.)	5	4	.556	3.69	1.23	16	16	1	0	0	0-0	97.2	95	47	40	11	25-2	64	.255
2005— Syracuse (Int'l)	2	2	.500	4.42	1.35	9	9	0	0	0	0-0	55.0	65	28	27	6	9-0	40	.294
— Toronto (A.L.)	5	11	.313	4.49	1.25	25	24	2	0	0	0-0	136.1	142	73	68	20	29-3	75	.269
Major League totals (2 years)	10	15	.400	4.15	1.24	41	40	3	1	0	0-0	234.0	237	120	108	31	54-5	139	.263

BYNUM, FREDDIE — 2B

PERSONAL: Born March 15, 1980, in Wilson, N.C. ... 6-1/180. ... Bats left, throws right. ... Full name: Freddie Lee Bynum Jr. ... High school: Beddingfield (Wilson, N.C.). ... Junior college: Pitt Community College (Greenville, N.C.).

TRANSACTIONS/CAREER NOTES: Selected by Oakland Athletics organization in second round of 2000 free-agent draft.

2005 GAMES PLAYED BY POSITION (MLB): 2B—3, OF—2.

LEFTY-RIGHTY SPLITS

vs.	Avg.	AB	H	2B	3B	HR	RBI	BB	SO	OBP	Slg.
L	.000	1	0	0	0	0	0	0	1	.000	.000
R	.333	6	2	1	0	0	1	0	2	.333	.500

Year	Team (League)	Pos.	G	AB	R	H	2B	3B	HR	RBI	BB	SO	HBP	GDP	SB-CS	Avg.	OBP	SLG	OPS	E	Avg.
2000— Vancouver (N'west)		SS	72	281	52	72	10	1	1	26	31	58	5	3	22-12	.256	.341	.310	.651	29	.917

Year Team (League)	Pos.	G	AB	R	H	2B	3B	HR	RBI	BB	SO	HBP	GDP	SB-CS	Avg.	OBP	SLG	OPS	E	Avg.
2001—Modesto (California)	SS-2B-3B	120	440	59	115	19	7	2	46	41	95	1	8	28-11	.261	.325	.350	.675	41	.922
2002—Visalia (Calif.)	2B-2B	135	539	83	165	26	5	3	56	64	116	7	9	41-21	.306	.385	.390	.775	*36	.948
2003—Midland (Texas)	OF-2B	132	510	84	134	18	9	5	58	56	135	8	6	22-8	.263	.344	.363	.707	33	.952
2004—Midland (Texas)	OF-2B	65	265	38	71	13	4	1	22	24	56	2	1	18-7	.268	.332	.358	.690	2	.950
—Sacramento (PCL)	OF-SS-2B	66	258	42	73	11	2	2	26	19	61	3	8	21-4	.283	.339	.364	.703	8	.000
2005—Sacramento (PCL)	OF-SS-2B	102	378	56	105	16	9	2	40	38	83	3	3	23-7	.278	.347	.384	.730	14	.968
—Oakland (A.L.)	2B-OF	7	7	0	2	1	0	0	1	0	3	0	0	0-0	.286	.286	.429	.714	0	1.000
Major League totals (1 year)		7	7	0	2	1	0	0	1	0	3	0	0	0-0	.286	.286	.429	.714	0	1.000

BYRD, MARLON — OF

PERSONAL: Born August 30, 1977, in Boynton Beach, Fla. ... 6-0/229. ... Bats right, throws right. ... Full name: Marlon Jerrard Byrd. ... High school: Sprayberry (Marietta, Ga.). ... Junior college: Georgia Perimeter.

TRANSACTIONS/CAREER NOTES: Selected by Philadelphia Phillies organization in 10th round of 1999 free-agent draft. ... On disabled list (April 14-29, 2003); included rehabilitation assignment to Reading. ... On disabled list (April 8-May 3, 2005); included rehabilitation assignment to Scranton. ... Traded by Phillies to Washington Nationals for OF Endy Chavez (May 14, 2005).

2005 GAMES PLAYED BY POSITION (MLB): OF—70, DH—2.

SCOUTING REPORT *Offense:* He is a stiff hitter who is slow to make adjustments. Doesn't take advantage of his strength because he has a two-part swing. Likes the ball out over the plate but has problems with breaking balls. Power numbers don't indicate his strength. *Defense:* He's not consistent with his reads and jumps, but his speed allows him to outrun mistakes. Has average arm strength but below-average instincts. *Outlook:* Byrd is a former football player who has been slow to learn the game. Has some tools but might need more time to develop. *Grade 5.9*

MARLON BYRD'S HITTING ZONE

.364	.200	.077
.308	.382	.292
.188	.400	.375

LEFTY-RIGHTY SPLITS

vs.	Avg.	AB	H	2B	3B	HR	RBI	BB	SO	OBP	Slg.
L	.323	93	30	8	1	1	15	8	19	.369	.462
R	.228	136	31	7	1	1	11	11	31	.291	.316

Year Team (League)	Pos.	G	AB	R	H	2B	3B	HR	RBI	BB	SO	HBP	GDP	SB-CS	Avg.	OBP	SLG	OPS	E	Avg.
1999—Batavia (NY-Penn)	OF	65	243	40	72	7	6	13	50	28	70	5	3	8-2	.296	.376	.535	.911	7	.926
2000—Piedmont (S. Atl.)	OF	133	515	104	159	29	13	17	93	51	110	10	7	41-5	.309	.379	.515	.893	4	.980
2001—Reading (East.)	OF	137	510	108	161	22	8	28	89	52	93	11	7	32-5	.316	.386	.555	.941	3	.994
2002—Scran./W.B. (I.L.)	OF	136	538	103	160	37	7	15	63	46	98	11	5	15-1	.297	.362	.476	.838	8	.975
—Philadelphia (N.L.)	OF	10	35	2	8	2	0	1	1	1	8	0	0	0-2	.229	.250	.371	.621	0	1.000
2003—Scran./W.B. (I.L.)	OF	1	4	1	3	1	0	0	0	0	1	0	0	0-0	.750	.750	1.000	1.750	0	1.000
—Reading (East.)	OF	3	16	3	5	0	0	1	3	0	3	0	0	0-0	.313	.313	.500	.813	1	.800
—Philadelphia (N.L.)	OF	135	495	86	150	28	4	7	45	44	94	7	8	11-1	.303	.366	.418	.784	5	.984
2004—Scran./W.B. (I.L.)	OF	37	152	13	40	11	1	2	17	10	18	4	5	2-3	.263	.323	.388	.712	2	.980
—Philadelphia (N.L.)	OF	106	346	48	79	13	2	5	33	22	68	7	10	2-2	.228	.287	.321	.608	2	.990
2005—Scran./W.B. (I.L.)	OF	5	19	4	7	1	0	3	5	0	3	0	0	0-0	.368	.368	.895	1.263	6	.824
—Philadelphia (N.L.)	OF	5	13	0	4	0	0	0	0	1	3	1	0	0-0	.308	.400	.308	.708	0	1.000
—New Orleans (PCL)	OF-DH	21	81	19	33	6	0	5	11	9	7	2	6	4-1	.407	.478	.667	1.145	0	1.000
—Was. (N.L.)	OF-DH	74	216	20	57	15	2	2	26	18	47	1	5	5-1	.264	.318	.380	.698	2	.985
Major League totals (4 years)		330	1105	156	298	58	8	15	105	86	220	16	23	18-6	.270	.329	.377	.707	9	.986

BYRD, PAUL — P

PERSONAL: Born December 3, 1970, in Louisville, Ky. ... 6-1/190. ... Throws right, bats right. ... Full name: Paul Gregory Byrd. ... High school: St. Xavier (Louisville, Ky.). ... College: Louisiana State.

TRANSACTIONS/CAREER NOTES: Selected by Cincinnati Reds organization in 13th round of 1988 free-agent draft; did not sign. ... Selected by Cleveland Indians organization in fourth round of 1991 free-agent draft. ... Traded by Indians with Ps Dave Mlicki and Jerry DiPoto and a player to be named to New York Mets for OF Jeromy Burnitz and P Joe Roa (November 18, 1994); Mets acquired 2B Jesus Azuaje to complete deal (December 6, 1994). ... On disabled list (March 22-June 9, 1996); included rehabilitation assignment to Norfolk. ... Traded by Mets with a player to be named to Atlanta Braves for P Greg McMichael (November 25, 1996); Braves acquired P Andy Zwirchitz to complete deal (May 25, 1997). ... Claimed on waivers by Philadelphia Phillies (August 14, 1998). ... On disabled list (July 27, 2000-remainder of season). ... Traded by Phillies to Kansas City Royals for P Jose Santiago (June 5, 2001). ... On disabled list (September 22, 2001-remainder of season). ... Signed as a free agent by Braves (December 17, 2002). ... On disabled list (March 21, 2003-entire season); included rehabilitation assignment to Greenville. ... On disabled list (March 26-June 19, 2004); included rehabilitation assignments to Greenville and Richmond. ... Signed as a free agent by Anaheim Angels (December 14, 2004). ... Angels franchise renamed Los Angeles Angels of Anaheim for 2005 season.

CAREER HITTING: 23-for-145 (.159), 11 R, 0 2B, 0 3B, 0 HR, 10 RBI.

SCOUTING REPORT *Throws:* His repertoire includes an 84-89 mph fastball, a curveball, a slider and a changeup. *Tendencies:* He relies on deception, control and feel. Is very aggressive, especially considering his average-at-best stuff. Gets good movement with his fastball down in the zone. Is effective to both sides of the plate. Throws a looping curve to lefthanders and runs his slider away from righthanders. Changes speeds and angles with all his pitches, which keeps hitters off-balance. *Outlook:* He never seems to throw the same pitch twice. Has excellent makeup and could provide a nice complement to the power pitchers in the Angels' rotation. *Grade 7.2*

PAUL BYRD'S PITCHING ZONE

.250	.378	.250
.269	.422	.270
.259	.344	.290

LEFTY-RIGHTY SPLITS

vs.	Avg.	AB	H	2B	3B	HR	RBI	BB	SO	OBP	Slg.
L	.306	421	129	23	4	13	40	21	33	.339	.473
R	.234	372	87	24	2	9	48	7	69	.257	.382

Year Team (League)	W	L	Pct.	ERA	WHIP	G	GS	CG	ShO	Hld.	Sv.-Opp.	IP	H	R	ER	HR	BB-IBB	SO	Avg.
1991—Kinston (Carol.)	4	3	.571	3.16	1.21	14	11	0	0		0-...	62.2	40	27	22	7	36-0	62	.181
1992—Cant./Akr. (Eastern)	14	6	.700	3.01	1.29	24	24	4	0		0-...	152.1	122	68	51	4	75-2	118	.216

B

Year	Team (League)	W	L	Pct.	ERA	WHIP	G	GS	CG	ShO	Hld.	Sv.-Opp.	IP	H	R	ER	HR	BB-IBB	SO	Avg.
1993—	Charlotte (Int'l)	7	4	.636	3.89	1.36	14	14	1	1	...	0-...	81.0	80	43	35	9	30-0	54	.257
—	Cant./Akr. (Eastern)	0	0	...	3.60	1.00	2	1	0	0	...	0-...	10.0	7	4	4	1	3-0	8	.189
1994—	Cant./Akr. (Eastern)	5	9	.357	3.81	1.34	21	20	4	1	...	0-...	139.1	135	70	59	10	52-3	106	.255
—	Charlotte (Int'l)	2	2	.500	3.93	1.20	9	4	0	0	...	1-...	36.2	33	19	16	5	11-1	15	.250
1995—	Norfolk (Int'l)	3	5	.375	2.79	1.06	22	10	1	0	...	6-...	87.0	71	29	27	6	21-0	61	.227
—	New York (N.L.)	2	0	1.000	2.05	1.14	17	0	0	0	3	0-0	22.0	18	6	5	1	7-1	26	.222
1996—	Norfolk (Int'l)	2	0	1.000	3.52	1.04	5	0	0	0	...	1-...	7.2	4	3	3	0	4-1	8	.148
—	New York (N.L.)	1	2	.333	4.24	1.48	38	0	0	0	3	0-2	46.2	48	22	22	7	21-4	31	.265
1997—	Atlanta (N.L.)	4	4	.500	5.26	1.42	31	4	0	0	1	0-0	53.0	47	34	31	6	28-4	37	.235
—	Richmond (Int'l)	2	1	.667	3.18	0.88	3	3	0	0	...	0-...	17.0	14	6	6	2	1-0	14	.230
1998—	Richmond (Int'l)	5	5	.500	3.69	1.25	17	17	2	0	...	0-...	102.1	92	44	42	9	36-2	84	.241
—	Atlanta (N.L.)	0	0	...	13.50	2.50	1	0	0	0	0	0-0	2.0	4	3	3	0	1-0	1	.400
—	Philadelphia (N.L.)	5	2	.714	2.29	1.05	8	8	2	1	0	0-0	55.0	41	16	14	6	17-1	38	.204
1999—	Philadelphia (N.L.)	15	11	.577	4.60	1.38	32	32	1	0	0	0-0	199.2	205	119	102	34	70-2	106	.265
2000—	Philadelphia (N.L.)	2	9	.182	6.51	1.49	17	15	0	0	0	0-0	83.0	89	67	60	17	35-2	53	.271
—	Scran./W.B. (I.L.)	2	0	1.000	1.73	1.00	3	3	2	0	...	0-...	26.0	20	6	5	2	6-0	10	.215
2001—	Clearwater (FSL)	0	3	.000	3.42	1.23	4	4	0	0	...	0-...	23.2	24	10	9	4	5-0	17	.267
—	Scran./W.B. (I.L.)	1	3	.250	3.65	1.11	5	5	0	0	...	0-...	37.0	34	18	15	4	7-0	35	.239
—	Philadelphia (N.L.)	0	1	.000	8.10	1.40	3	1	0	0	0	0-0	10.0	10	9	9	1	4-0	3	.278
—	Kansas City (A.L.)	6	6	.500	4.05	1.41	16	15	1	0	0	0-0	93.1	110	45	42	11	22-1	49	.298
2002—	Kansas City (A.L.)	17	11	.607	3.90	1.15	33	33	* 7	2	0	0-0	228.1	224	111	99	36	38-1	129	.256
2003—	Greenville (Sou.)	0	0	...	8.31	2.10	1	1	0	0	...	0-...	4.1	8	6	4	1	1-0	3	.364
2004—	Greenville (Sou.)	1	1	.500	7.11	1.42	3	3	0	0	...	0-...	12.2	13	10	10	2	5-0	8	.271
—	Richmond (Int'l)	0	1	.000	7.71	1.07	1	1	0	0	...	0-...	4.2	3	4	4	0	2-0	5	.167
—	Atlanta (N.L.)	8	7	.533	3.94	1.24	19	19	0	0	0	0-0	114.1	123	57	50	18	19-0	79	.270
2005—	Los Angeles (A.L.)	12	11	.522	3.74	1.19	31	31	2	1	0	0-0	204.1	216	95	85	22	28-1	102	.272
American League totals (3 years)		**35**	**28**	**.556**	**3.87**	**1.21**	**80**	**79**	**10**	**3**	**0**	**0-0**	**526.0**	**550**	**251**	**226**	**69**	**88-3**	**280**	**.270**
National League totals (8 years)		**37**	**36**	**.507**	**4.55**	**1.34**	**166**	**79**	**3**	**1**	**7**	**0-2**	**585.2**	**585**	**333**	**296**	**90**	**202-14**	**374**	**.258**
Major League totals (10 years)		**72**	**64**	**.529**	**4.23**	**1.28**	**246**	**158**	**13**	**4**	**7**	**0-2**	**1111.2**	**1135**	**584**	**522**	**159**	**290-17**	**654**	**.264**

DIVISION SERIES RECORD

Year	Team (League)	W	L	Pct.	ERA	WHIP	G	GS	CG	ShO	Hld.	Sv.-Opp.	IP	H	R	ER	HR	BB-IBB	SO	Avg.
2004—	Atlanta (N.L.)	0	1	.000	6.35	1.94	2	0	0	0	0	0-0	5.2	8	4	4	1	3-1	3	.364
2005—	Los Angeles (A.L.)	0	0	...	9.82	2.45	1	1	0	0	0	0-0	3.2	7	4	4	1	2-0	2	.389
Division series totals (2 years)		**0**	**1**	**.000**	**7.71**	**2.14**	**3**	**1**	**0**	**0**	**0**	**0-0**	**9.1**	**15**	**8**	**8**	**2**	**5-1**	**5**	**.375**

CHAMPIONSHIP SERIES RECORD

Year	Team (League)	W	L	Pct.	ERA	WHIP	G	GS	CG	ShO	Hld.	Sv.-Opp.	IP	H	R	ER	HR	BB-IBB	SO	Avg.
2005—	Los Angeles (A.L.)	1	0	1.000	3.38	1.13	2	2	0	0	0	0-0	10.2	10	4	4	1	2-0	2	.256

BYRDAK, TIM — P

PERSONAL: Born October 31, 1973, in Oak Lawn, Ill. ... 5-11/180. ... Throws left, bats left. ... Full name: Timothy Christopher Byrdak. ... Name pronounced: BIRD-ek. ... High school: Oak Forest (Ill.). ... Junior college: South Suburban College (Ill.). ... College: Rice.

TRANSACTIONS/CAREER NOTES: Selected by Kansas City Royals organization in fifth round of 1994 free-agent draft. ... On disabled list (June 27-August 19, 1996). ... Signed by Cleveland Indians organization (December 23, 2000). ... On disabled list (April 29, 2001-remainder of season). ... Signed as a free agent by San Diego Padres organization (February 1, 2004). ... Signed as a free agent by Baltimore Orioles organization (June 22, 2004).

CAREER HITTING: 1-for-2 (.500), 1 R, 1 2B, 0 3B, 0 HR, 0 RBI.

TIM BYRDAK'S PITCHING ZONE

.200	.333	.833
.250	.143	.308
.286	.429	.143

LEFTY-RIGHTY SPLITS

vs.	Avg.	AB	H	2B	3B	HR	RBI	BB	SO	OBP	Slg.
L	.214	56	12	4	0	0	6	9	16	.323	.286
R	.300	50	15	0	0	1	8	12	15	.438	.360

Year	Team (League)	W	L	Pct.	ERA	WHIP	G	GS	CG	ShO	Hld.	Sv.-Opp.	IP	H	R	ER	HR	BB-IBB	SO	Avg.
1994—	Eugene (Northwest)	4	5	.444	3.07	1.09	15	15	0	0	...	0-...	73.1	60	33	25	6	20-0	77	.220
1995—	Wilmington (Caro.)	11	5	.688	2.16	0.98	27	26	0	0	...	0-...	166.1	118	46	40	7	45-2	127	.198
1996—	Wichita (Texas)	5	7	.417	6.91	1.84	15	15	0	0	...	0-...	84.2	112	73	65	15	44-0	47	.331
1997—	Wilmington (Caro.)	4	3	.571	3.51	1.12	22	2	0	0	...	3-...	41.0	34	17	16	3	12-4	47	.225
1998—	Wichita (Texas)	3	5	.375	4.15	1.65	34	0	0	0	...	2-...	52.0	58	29	24	3	28-1	37	.284
—	Omaha (PCL)	2	1	.667	2.45	1.39	26	0	0	0	...	1-...	36.2	31	13	10	3	20-0	32	.230
—	Kansas City (A.L.)	0	0	...	5.40	3.00	3	0	0	0	...	0-...	1.2	5	1	1	1	0-...	1	.556
1999—	Omaha (PCL)	3	1	.750	1.81	1.35	33	0	0	0	...	4-...	49.2	39	19	10	0	28-2	51	.219
—	Kansas City (A.L.)	0	3	.000	7.66	2.11	33	0	0	0	10	0-...	24.2	32	24	21	5	20-...	17	.308
2000—	Omaha (PCL)	6	2	.750	4.44	1.67	34	1	0	0	...	4-...	52.2	59	27	26	5	29-3	47	.286
—	Kansas City (A.L.)	0	1	.000	11.37	2.37	12	0	0	0	3	0-...	6.1	11	8	8	3	4-...	8	.367
—	Wichita (Texas)	0	0	...	5.40	1.80	4	0	0	0	...	0-...	6.2	9	4	4	1	3-0	1	.346
2001—	Buffalo (Int'l)	2	0	1.000	4.67	1.33	4	3	0	0	...	0-...	17.1	18	10	9	1	5-0	17	.265
2002—	Kinston (Carol.)	1	0	1.000	4.50	1.75	2	0	0	0	...	0-...	4.0	3	2	2	0	4-0	3	.214
—	Akron (East.)	0	0	...	6.23	2.08	9	0	0	0	...	1-...	13.0	16	12	9	0	11-0	8	.308
2003—	Joliet (North.)	2	1	.667	2.67	1.22	5	5	0	0	...	0-...	33.2	31	17	10	3	10-0	18	.238
—	Gary (North.)	2	4	.333	4.34	1.28	10	10	1	0	...	0-...	66.1	60	33	32	7	25-0	58	.248
2004—	Portland (PCL)	3	0	1.000	5.45	1.68	20	2	0	0	...	0-...	38.0	47	28	23	3	17-0	25	.307
—	Ottawa (Int'l)	2	1	.667	4.19	1.69	33	1	0	0	...	2-...	34.1	46	20	16	4	12-1	43	.309
2005—	Ottawa (Int'l)	3	2	.600	2.09	0.98	37	0	0	0	2	11-14	38.2	32	12	9	4	15-1	44	.170
—	Baltimore (A.L.)	0	1	.000	4.05	1.80	41	0	0	0	11	1-1	26.2	27	14	12	1	21-1	31	.255
Major League totals (4 years)		**0**	**5**	**.000**	**6.37**	**2.02**	**89**	**0**	**0**	**0**	**24**	**2-1**	**59.1**	**75**	**47**	**42**	**10**	**45-1**	**57**	**.313**

BYRNES, ERIC — OF

PERSONAL: Born February 16, 1976, in Redwood City, Calif. ... 6-2/210. ... Bats right, throws right. ... Full name: Eric James Byrnes. ... High school: St. Francis (Mountain View, Calif.). ... College: UCLA.

TRANSACTIONS/CAREER NOTES: Selected by Los Angeles Dodgers organization in 38th round of 1994 free-agent draft; did not sign. ... Selected by Houston Astros organization in fourth round of 1997 free-agent draft; did not sign. ... Selected by Oakland Athletics organization in eighth round of 1998 free-agent draft. ... Traded by Athletics with SS Omar Quintanilla to Colorado Rockies for Ps Joe Kennedy and Jay Witasick (July 13, 2005). ... Traded by Rockies to Baltimore Orioles for OF Larry Bigbie (July 29, 2005).

2005 GAMES PLAYED BY POSITION (MLB): OF—119, DH—4.

SCOUTING REPORT **Offense:** Byrnes is the most energetic player in the game. Is hyper to the point it interferes with instincts. Has a complex approach at the plate, with various starts and stops; his momentum and timing can be thrown off. Is a streaky hitter with some power, prone to severe slumps. Bat speed has declined and has problems with the ball inside. Lacks patience to wait for good pitch. Is a plus runner. **Defense:** Byrnes is a fearless outfielder who can play all three positions. Plays on sheer aggressiveness. Actually speeds up as he gets closer to the wall. Arm strength is slightly below average. **Outlook:** Byrnes' makeup is off the charts. He can be the best player one week and the worst the next. Has too many ups and downs. Will eventually be a fourth outfielder. **Grade 6.9**

ERIC BYRNES' HITTING ZONE

.297	.150	.143
.302	.364	.107
.246	.235	.111

LEFTY-RIGHTY SPLITS

vs.	Avg.	AB	H	2B	3B	HR	RBI	BB	SO	OBP	Slg.
L	.263	156	41	10	2	5	20	15	20	.335	.449
R	.203	256	52	14	1	5	20	17	51	.268	.324

								BATTING								FIELDING	
Year Team (League)	Pos.	G	AB	R	H	2B	3B	HR	RBI	BB	SO	HBP	GDP	SB-CS	Avg.	OBP	SLG	OPS	E	Avg.
1998—S. Oregon (N'west)	PH	42	169	36	53	10	2	7	31	16	16	2	3	6-1	.314	.378	.521	.898	1	.986
—Visalia (Calif.)	OF	29	108	26	46	9	2	4	21	18	15	1	2	11-1	.426	.504	.657	1.161	3	.952
1999—Modesto (California)	OF	96	365	86	123	28	1	6	66	58	37	9	14	28-8	.337	.433	.468	.901	6	.960
—Midland (Texas)	OF	43	164	25	39	14	0	1	22	17	32	3	5	6-3	.238	.316	.341	.657	5	.923
2000—Midland (Texas)	OF	67	259	49	78	25	2	5	37	43	38	1	5	21-11	.301	.395	.471	.866	2	.983
—Sacramento (PCL)	OF	67	243	55	81	23	1	9	47	31	30	2	3	12-5	.333	.410	.547	.957	2	.980
—Oakland (A.L.)	OF-DH	10	10	5	3	0	0	0	0	0	1	1	0	2-1	.300	.364	.300	.664	0	1.000
2001—Sacramento (PCL)	OF	100	415	81	120	23	2	20	51	33	66	5	10	25-3	.289	.343	.499	.842	5	.973
—Oakland (A.L.)	OF-DH	19	38	9	9	1	0	3	5	4	6	1	0	1-0	.237	.326	.500	.826	1	.933
2002—Sacramento (PCL)	OF	31	119	16	31	7	0	4	16	7	15	0	2	5-1	.261	.302	.420	.722	2	.971
—Oakland (A.L.)	OF-DH	90	94	24	23	4	2	3	11	4	17	3	3	3-0	.245	.291	.426	.717	1	.982
2003—Oakland (A.L.)	OF-DH	121	414	64	109	27	9	12	51	42	71	2	3	10-2	.263	.333	.459	.792	2	.991
2004—Oakland (A.L.)	OF-DH	143	569	91	161	39	3	20	73	46	111	12	11	17-1	.283	.347	.467	.814	3	.989
2005—Oakland (A.L.)	OF-DH	59	192	30	51	15	2	7	24	14	27	7	1	2-2	.266	.336	.474	.810	2	.984
—Colorado (N.L.)	OF	15	53	2	10	2	0	0	5	7	11	0	1	2-0	.189	.283	.226	.510	1	.976
—Baltimore (A.L.)	OF	52	167	17	32	7	1	3	11	11	33	1	5	3-0	.192	.246	.299	.545	3	.969
American League totals (6 years)		494	1484	240	388	93	17	48	175	121	266	27	23	38-6	.261	.326	.444	.771	12	.985
National League totals (1 year)		15	53	2	10	2	0	0	5	7	11	0	1	2-0	.189	.283	.226	.510	1	.976
Major League totals (6 years)		509	1537	242	398	95	17	48	180	128	277	27	24	40-6	.259	.325	.437	.761	13	.984

DIVISION SERIES RECORD

Year Team (League)	Pos.	G	AB	R	H	2B	3B	HR	RBI	BB	SO	HBP	GDP	SB-CS	Avg.	OBP	SLG	OPS	E	Avg.
2001—Oakland (A.L.)		2	2	0	0	0	0	0	0	0	1	0	0	0-0	.000	.000	.000	.000	...	...
2002—Oakland (A.L.)	OF	2	1	0	0	0	0	0	0	0	1	0	0	0-0	.000	.000	.000	.000	0	1.000
2003—Oakland (A.L.)	OF	5	13	2	6	1	0	0	2	0	5	0	0	1-0	.462	.462	.538	1.000	0	1.000
Division series totals (3 years)		9	16	2	6	1	0	0	2	0	7	0	0	1-0	.375	.375	.438	.813	0	1.000

CABRERA, DANIEL — P

PERSONAL: Born May 28, 1981, in San Pedro de Macoris, Dominican Republic. ... 6-7/230. ... Throws right, bats right. ... Full name: Daniel Alberto Cabrera.

TRANSACTIONS/CAREER NOTES: Signed as a non-drafted free agent by Baltimore Orioles organization (March 15, 1999). ... On disabled list (August 23-September 6, 2005); included rehabilitation assignment to Bowie.

CAREER HITTING: 0-for-5 (.000), 0 R, 0 2B, 0 3B, 0 HR, 0 RBI.

SCOUTING REPORT **Throws:** Cabrera has an overpowering fastball that is near 100 mph. Also has a two-seam fastball, a curve, a slider and a changeup. **Tendencies:** Cabrera easily throws heat from a high three-quarters arm angle. Has gained velocity since 2004 and can simply overpower hitters up in the zone. Has very good life on his two-seamer, which he can run back over the plate from lefthanders. Doesn't have good rotation with his curve but has a much better slider. Doesn't have a good feel for his changeup. **Outlook:** If he can gain command, he could become one of the most dominant starters in the league. Mechanics aren't consistent, and he becomes inventive on the mound at times. **Grade 8.2**

DANIEL CABRERA'S PITCHING ZONE

.239	.273	.351
.223	.413	.278
.240	.294	.206

LEFTY-RIGHTY SPLITS

vs.	Avg.	AB	H	2B	3B	HR	RBI	BB	SO	OBP	Slg.
L	.285	337	96	22	4	12	55	60	77	.400	.481
R	.174	276	48	7	0	2	25	27	80	.257	.221

Year Team (League)	W	L	Pct.	ERA	WHIP	G	GS	CG	ShO	Hld.	Sv.-Opp.	IP	H	R	ER	HR	BB-IBB	SO	Avg.
1999—Dom. Orioles (DSL)	2	4	.333	4.71	1.77	14	10	1	...	...	0-...	57.1	60	42	30	3	42-...	74	.260
2000—Dom. Orioles (DSL)	8	1	.889	2.52	1.16	12	10	2	...	...	0-...	71.1	45	26	20	3	38-...	44	.167
—Dom. Orioles (DSL)	2	4	.333	4.71	1.78	14	10	1	...	...	0-...	0.0	60	42	30	3	42-...	74	.260
2001—GC Orioles (GCL)	2	3	.400	5.53	1.72	12	7	0	0	...	0-...	40.2	31	29	25	1	39-2	36	.215
2002—Bluefield (Appal.)	5	2	.714	3.28	1.28	12	12	0	0	...	0-...	60.1	52	25	22	0	25-0	69	.234
2003—Delmarva (S. Atl.)	5	9	.357	4.24	1.46	26	26	1	0	...	0-...	125.1	105	74	59	6	78-0	120	.225
2004—Bowie (East.)	0	1	.000	2.63	0.84	5	5	0	0	...	0-...	27.1	11	10	8	1	10-0	35	.125
—Baltimore (A.L.)	12	8	.600	5.00	1.58	28	27	1	1	0	1-1	147.2	145	85	82	14	89-2	76	.259
2005—Bowie (East.)	1	0	1.000	3.00	1.67	1	1	0	0	0	0-0	6.0	8	3	2	1	2-0	7	.320
—Baltimore (A.L.)	10	13	.435	4.52	1.43	29	29	0	0	0	0-0	161.1	144	92	81	14	87-2	157	.235
Major League totals (2 years)	22	21	.512	4.75	1.50	57	56	1	1	0	1-1	309.0	289	177	163	28	176-4	233	.246

C

CABRERA, FERNANDO — P

PERSONAL: Born November 16, 1981, in Toja Baja, Puerto Rico. ... 6-4/170. ... Throws right, bats right. ... Full name: Fernando Jose Cabrera. ... High school: Discipulous de Cristo (Toja Baja).
TRANSACTIONS/CAREER NOTES: Selected by Cleveland Indians organization in 10th round of 1999 free-agent draft.
CAREER HITTING: 0-for-0 (.000), 0 R, 0 2B, 0 3B, 0 HR, 0 RBI.

FERNANDO CABRERA'S PITCHING ZONE

.500	.100	.400
.214	.357	.278
.000	.000	.429

LEFTY-RIGHTY SPLITS

vs.	Avg.	AB	H	2B	3B	HR	RBI	BB	SO	OBP	Slg.
L	.196	46	9	2	1	0	5	7	7	.302	.283
R	.224	67	15	4	0	1	2	4	22	.268	.328

Year Team (League)	W	L	Pct.	ERA	WHIP	G	GS	CG	ShO	Hld.	Sv.-Opp.	IP	H	R	ER	HR	BB-IBB	SO	Avg.
2000— Burlington (Appal.)	3	7	.300	4.61	1.23	13	13	0	0	...	0-...	68.1	64	42	35	4	20-0	50	.252
2001— Columbus (S. Atl.)	5	6	.455	3.61	1.33	20	20	0	0	...	0-...	94.2	89	49	38	7	37-1	96	.242
2002— Kinston (Carol.)	6	8	.429	3.52	1.12	21	21	0	0	...	0-...	110.0	83	48	43	7	40-2	107	.206
— Akron (East.)	1	2	.333	5.33	1.41	7	4	0	0	...	1-...	27.0	26	16	16	1	12-0	29	.252
2003— Akron (East.)	9	4	.692	2.97	1.25	36	15	0	0	...	5-...	109.0	96	41	36	8	40-0	115	.237
2004— Buffalo (Int'l)	4	3	.571	3.79	1.32	45	0	0	0	...	5-...	76.0	57	37	32	9	43-3	93	.208
— Cleveland (A.L.)	0	0	...	3.38	0.75	4	0	0	0	0	0-0	5.1	3	3	2	0	1-0	6	.167
2005— Buffalo (Int'l)	6	1	.857	1.23	0.92	30	0	0	0	3	3-3	51.1	36	8	7	3	11-2	68	.196
— Cleveland (A.L.)	2	1	.667	1.47	1.14	15	0	0	0	1	0-0	30.2	24	7	5	1	11-1	29	.212
Major League totals (2 years)	2	1	.667	1.75	1.08	19	0	0	0	1	0-0	36.0	27	10	7	1	12-1	35	.206

CABRERA, MELKY — OF

PERSONAL: Born August 11, 1984, in Santo Domingo, Dominican Republic. ... 5-11/170. ... Bats both, throws left. ... Full name: Melky Cabrera. ... College: None.
TRANSACTIONS/CAREER NOTES: Signed as a nondrafted free agent by New York Yankees organization (November 13, 2001).
2005 GAMES PLAYED BY POSITION (MLB): OF—6.

LEFTY-RIGHTY SPLITS

vs.	Avg.	AB	H	2B	3B	HR	RBI	BB	SO	OBP	Slg.
L	.333	6	2	0	0	0	0	0	0	.333	.333
R	.154	13	2	0	0	0	0	0	2	.154	.154

Year Team (League)	Pos.	G	AB	R	H	2B	3B	HR	RBI	BB	SO	HBP	GDP	SB-CS	Avg.	OBP	SLG	OPS	E	Avg.
2002— Dom. Yankees (DSL)	OF	60	218	37	73	19	3	3	29	18	23	3	3	7-2	.335	.388	.491	.879	...	...
2003— Staten Island (N.Y.-Penn.) .	OF	67	279	34	79	10	2	2	31	23	36	4	6	13-5	.283	.345	.355	.700	3	.979
2004— Battle Creek (Midw.)	OF	42	171	35	57	16	3	0	16	15	23	0	2	7-2	.333	.383	.462	.845	1	.952
— Tampa (Fla. St.)	OF	85	333	48	96	20	3	8	.51	23	59	5	8	3-1	.288	.341	.438	.779	3	.000
2005— New York (A.L.)	OF	6	19	1	4	0	0	0	0	0	2	0	0	0-0	.211	.211	.211	.421	0	1.000
— Columbus (Int'l)	OF-DH	26	101	15	25	3	0	3	17	9	15	0	0	2-0	.248	.309	.366	.675	0	1.000
— Trenton (East.)	OF-DH	106	426	57	117	22	3	10	60	28	72	4	11	11-2	.275	.322	.411	.733	8	.985
Major League totals (1 year)		6	19	1	4	0	0	0	0	0	2	0	0	0-0	.211	.211	.211	.421	0	1.000

CABRERA, MIGUEL — OF

PERSONAL: Born April 18, 1983, in Maracay, Venezuela. ... 6-2/210. ... Bats right, throws right. ... Full name: Jose Miguel Torres Cabrera.
TRANSACTIONS/CAREER NOTES: Signed as a non-drafted free agent by Florida Marlins organization (July 2, 1999).
2005 GAMES PLAYED BY POSITION (MLB): OF—134, 3B—29.

SCOUTING REPORT *Offense:* Cabrera has the swing and aptitude to produce well beyond his years. Nothing seems to faze him at the plate. Has a fluid stroke with exceptional bat speed and power to all fields. Has the ability to adjust to tough pitches on the inner half of the plate. Can run but is not a basestealer. *Defense:* He has issues on defense, especially going back. Is better going to the alley. Has an average arm and is accurate. Could be ticketed for third base, where he has shown agility and a good arm. *Outlook:* Cabrera is an extraordinary talent and one of the game's rising offensive stars. Will be one of the game's premier power hitters and run producers in a very short time. Appeared to be moody and indifferent at times in '05. Could become a high-maintenance player. *Grade 9.4*

MIGUEL CABRERA'S HITTING ZONE

.353	.320	.348
.333	.492	.438
.355	.438	.341

LEFTY-RIGHTY SPLITS

vs.	Avg.	AB	H	2B	3B	HR	RBI	BB	SO	OBP	Slg.
L	.299	117	35	9	1	6	27	23	24	.408	.547
R	.329	496	163	34	1	27	89	41	101	.379	.565

Year Team (League)	Pos.	G	AB	R	H	2B	3B	HR	RBI	BB	SO	HBP	GDP	SB-CS	Avg.	OBP	SLG	OPS	E	Avg.
2000— GC Marlins (GCL)	SS	57	219	38	57	10	2	2	22	23	46	6	7	1-0	.260	.344	.352	.696	13	.950
— Utica (N.Y.-Penn)	SS-2B-3B	8	32	3	8	2	0	0	6	2	6	0	0	0-0	.250	.294	.313	.607	4	.902
2001— Kane Co. (Midw.)	SS-3B	110	422	61	113	19	4	7	66	37	76	2	10	3-0	.268	.328	.382	.709	32	.931
2002— Jupiter (Fla. St.)	3B-SS	124	489	77	134	43	1	9	75	38	85	9	19	10-1	.274	.333	.421	.754	17	.941
2003— Carolina (Southern)	3B-OF-DH	69	266	46	97	29	3	10	59	31	49	2	8	9-4	.365	.429	.609	1.038	15	.926
— Florida (N.L.)	OF-3B	87	314	39	84	21	3	12	62	25	84	2	12	0-2	.268	.325	.468	.794	4	.978
2004— Florida (N.L.)	OF-DH	160	603	101	177	31	1	33	112	68	148	6	20	5-2	.294	.366	.512	.879	9	.968
2005— Florida (N.L.)	OF-3B	158	613	106	198	43	2	33	116	64	125	2	20	1-0	.323	.385	.561	.947	7	.975
Major League totals (3 years)		405	1530	246	459	95	6	78	290	157	357	10	52	6-4	.300	.366	.523	.889	20	.973

DIVISION SERIES RECORD

Year Team (League)	Pos.	G	AB	R	H	2B	3B	HR	RBI	BB	SO	HBP	GDP	SB-CS	Avg.	OBP	SLG	OPS	E	Avg.
2003— Florida (N.L.)	3B	4	14	1	4	2	0	0	3	1	6	0	0	0-0	.286	.333	.429	.762	1	.900

CHAMPIONSHIP SERIES RECORD

Year Team (League)	Pos.	G	AB	R	H	2B	3B	HR	RBI	BB	SO	HBP	GDP	SB-CS	Avg.	OBP	SLG	OPS	E	Avg.
2003— Florida (N.L.)	OF-3B-SS	7	30	9	10	0	0	3	6	2	6	1	1	0-0	.333	.394	.633	1.027	0	1.000

C

Year Team (League)	Pos.	G	AB	R	H	2B	3B	HR	RBI	BB	SO	HBP	GDP	SB-CS	Avg.	OBP	SLG	OPS	E	Avg.
WORLD SERIES RECORD																				
2003— Florida (N.L.)	OF	6	24	1	4	0	0	1	3	1	7	0	1	0-0	.167	.200	.292	.492	1	.938

	G	AB	R	H	2B	3B	HR	RBI	BB	SO	HBP	GDP	SB-CS	Avg.	OBP	SLG	OPS	E	Avg.
ALL-STAR GAME RECORD																			
All-Star Game totals (2 years)	2	4	0	0	0	0	0	1	0	1	0	0	0-0	.000	.000	.000	.000	0	1.000

CABRERA, ORLANDO — SS

PERSONAL: Born November 2, 1974, in Cartagena, Colombia. ... 5-10/190. ... Bats right, throws right. ... Full name: Orlando Luis Cabrera. ... Brother of Jolbert Cabrera, infielder/outfielder, for three major league teams (1998-2004).

TRANSACTIONS/CAREER NOTES: Signed as a non-drafted free agent by Montreal Expos organization (June 1, 1993). ... On disabled list (August 9, 1999-remainder of season). ... On disabled list (July 15-August 15, 2000); included rehabilitation assignment to Ottawa. ... Traded by Expos to Boston Red Sox as part of four-team deal in which Expos acquired SS Alex S. Gonzalez, P Francis Beltran and IF Brendan Harris from Cubs, Cubs acquired SS Nomar Garciaparra and OF Matt Murton from Red Sox, Red Sox acquired 1B Doug Mientkiewicz from Twins and Twins acquired P Justin Jones from Cubs (July 31, 2004). ... Signed as a free agent by Anaheim Angels (January 12, 2005). ... Angels franchise renamed Los Angeles Angels of Anaheim for 2005 season. ... On disabled list (July 1-16, 2005).

HONORS: Won N.L. Gold Glove at shortstop (2001).

2005 GAMES PLAYED BY POSITION (MLB): SS—140.

SCOUTING REPORT **Offense:** Cabrera never will hit for a high average because he never shortens up; he'll overswing and pull off the ball instead. Has a very long stroke but still has good bat speed. Is a dead high-ball hitter who looks fastball. Rarely strikes out despite the lack of patience. Has occasional power. Is better going first to third than home to first because his swing makes him slow out of the box. **Defense:** This top-flight defender saves countless runs with his range, quickness and agility. Reads the ball off the bat well. Gets good jumps in either direction. Has very quick hands. Throws well from the hole. **Outlook:** He would be a better player if he weren't so overly aggressive at the plate. Is a better second-half player than first-half player. **Grade 7.9**

ORLANDO CABRERA'S HITTING ZONE

.300	.200	.206
.284	.338	.310
.246	.093	.150

LEFTY-RIGHTY SPLITS

vs.	Avg.	AB	H	2B	3B	HR	RBI	BB	SO	OBP	Slg.
L	.242	157	38	8	2	1	19	16	11	.314	.338
R	.264	383	101	20	1	7	38	22	39	.306	.376

Year Team (League)	Pos.	G	AB	R	H	2B	3B	HR	RBI	BB	SO	HBP	GDP	SB-CS	Avg.	OBP	SLG	OPS	E	Avg.
1993— Dom. Expos (DSL)	IF	38	122	24	42	6	1	1	17	18	11	...	...	14-...	.344		.434	...	3	.982
1994— GC Expos (GCL)	2B-OF-SS	22	73	13	23	4	1	0	11	5	8	0	2	6-0	.315	.359	.397	.756	4	.941
1995— Vermont (NYP)	2B-SS	65	248	37	70	12	5	3	33	16	28	1	3	15-8	.282	.323	.407	.731	17	.950
— W.P. Beach (FSL)	SS	3	5	0	1	0	0	0	0	0	1	0	0	0-0	.200	.200	.200	.400	1	.833
1996— Delmarva (S. Atl.)	2B-SS	134	512	86	129	28	4	14	65	54	65	5	4	51-18	.252	.327	.404	.731	27	.953
1997— W.P. Beach (FSL)	SS-DH-2B	69	279	56	77	19	2	5	26	27	33	0	1	32-12	.276	.340	.412	.752	20	.927
— Harrisburg (East.)	SS-2B	35	133	34	41	13	2	5	20	15	18	0	1	7-2	.308	.378	.549	.927	5	.966
— Ottawa (Int'l)	SS-2B	31	122	17	32	5	2	2	14	7	16	2	0	8-1	.262	.306	.385	.691	3	.979
— Montreal (N.L.)	SS-2B	16	18	4	4	0	0	0	2	1	3	0	1	1-2	.222	.263	.222	.485	1	.963
1998— Ottawa (Int'l)	SS-2B	66	272	31	63	9	4	0	26	28	27	0	4	19-9	.232	.298	.294	.592	12	.963
— Montreal (N.L.)	SS-2B	79	261	44	73	16	5	3	22	18	27	0	6	6-2	.280	.325	.414	.739	7	.978
1999— Montreal (N.L.)	SS	104	382	48	97	23	5	8	39	18	38	3	9	2-2	.254	.293	.403	.696	10	.979
2000— Montreal (N.L.)	SS-2B	125	422	47	100	25	1	13	55	25	28	1	12	4-4	.237	.279	.393	.673	10	.981
— Ottawa (Int'l)	SS	2	6	1	4	0	0	0	0	1	0	1	0	0-0	.667	.750	.667	1.417	0	1.000
2001— Montreal (N.L.)	SS	•162	626	64	173	41	6	14	96	43	54	4	15	19-7	.276	.324	.428	.752	11	.986
2002— Montreal (N.L.)	SS	153	563	64	148	43	1	7	56	48	53	2	16	25-7	.263	.321	.380	.701	* 29	.962
2003— Montreal (N.L.)	SS	162	626	95	186	47	2	17	80	52	64	1	18	24-2	.297	.347	.460	.807	18	.975
2004— Montreal (N.L.)	SS	103	390	41	96	19	2	4	31	28	31	2	12	12-3	.246	.298	.336	.634	7	.984
— Boston (A.L.)	SS	58	228	33	67	19	1	6	31	11	23	1	4	4-1	.294	.320	.465	.785	8	.966
2005— Los Angeles (A.L.)	SS	141	540	70	139	28	3	8	57	38	50	3	10	21-2	.257	.309	.365	.674	7	.988
American League totals (2 years)		199	768	103	206	47	4	14	88	49	73	4	14	25-3	.268	.312	.405	.707	15	.982
National League totals (8 years)		904	3288	407	877	214	22	66	381	233	298	13	89	93-29	.267	.315	.405	.721	93	.977
Major League totals (9 years)		1103	4056	510	1083	261	26	80	469	282	371	17	103	118-32	.267	.315	.403	.718	108	.978

Year Team (League)	Pos.	G	AB	R	H	2B	3B	HR	RBI	BB	SO	HBP	GDP	SB-CS	Avg.	OBP	SLG	OPS	E	Avg.
DIVISION SERIES RECORD																				
2004— Boston (A.L.)	SS	3	13	1	2	1	0	0	3	2	1	0	0	0-0	.154	.267	.231	.497	0	1.000
2005— Los Angeles (A.L.)	SS	5	21	3	5	2	0	0	3	0	1	0	0	0-0	.238	.238	.333	.571	1	.950
Division series totals (2 years)		8	34	4	7	3	0	0	6	2	3	0	0	0-0	.206	.250	.294	.544	1	.964

Year Team (League)	Pos.	G	AB	R	H	2B	3B	HR	RBI	BB	SO	HBP	GDP	SB-CS	Avg.	OBP	SLG	OPS	E	Avg.
CHAMPIONSHIP SERIES RECORD																				
2004— Boston (A.L.)	SS	7	29	5	11	2	0	0	5	3	5	0	1	1-0	.379	.424	.448	.873	0	1.000
2005— Los Angeles (A.L.)	SS	5	20	1	4	1	0	1	3	0	2	0	0	0-0	.200	.200	.400	.600	1	.955
Champ. series totals (2 years)		12	49	6	15	3	0	1	8	3	7	0	1	1-0	.306	.340	.429	.768	1	.982

Year Team (League)	Pos.	G	AB	R	H	2B	3B	HR	RBI	BB	SO	HBP	GDP	SB-CS	Avg.	OBP	SLG	OPS	E	Avg.
WORLD SERIES RECORD																				
2004— Boston (A.L.)	SS	4	17	3	4	1	0	0	3	3	1	1	0	0-0	.235	.381	.294	.675	0	1.000

CAIN, MATT — P

PERSONAL: Born October 1, 1984, in Dothan, Ala. ... 6-3/231. ... Throws right, bats right. ... Full name: Matthew Thomas Cain. ... High school: Houston (Germantown, Tenn.).

TRANSACTIONS/CAREER NOTES: Selected by San Francisco Giants organization in first round (25th pick overall) of 2002 free-agent draft.

CAREER HITTING: 1-for-15 (.067), 1 R, 1 2B, 0 3B, 0 HR, 0 RBI.

SCOUTING REPORT *Throws:* Cain has a 91-94 mph fastball, a curveball, slider and changeup. *Tendencies:* He has an inconsistent release point and labors with his command, but his arm is lively. Is not as effective up when he starts to overthrow. Pitches are easy to follow despite good velocity. Curveball is often too hard and lacks spin and straight changeup lacks much action. *Outlook:* Once Cain improves his command and his breaking ball, he should climb a team's rotation and possibly become a No. 1 starter. *Grade 7.5*

MATT CAIN'S PITCHING ZONE

.167	.167	.100
.208	.190	.222
.200	.000	.091

LEFTY-RIGHTY SPLITS

vs.	Avg.	AB	H	2B	3B	HR	RBI	BB	SO	OBP	Slg.
L	.160	75	12	0	1	2	7	12	10	.276	.267
R	.143	84	12	0	0	2	3	7	20	.207	.214

Year	Team (League)	W	L	Pct.	ERA	WHIP	G	GS	CG	ShO	Hld.	Sv.-Opp.	IP	H	R	ER	HR	BB-IBB	SO	Avg.
2002—	Ariz. Giants (Ariz.)	0	1	.000	3.72	1.24	8	7	0	0	...	0-...	19.1	13	10	8	1	11-0	20	.197
2003—	Hagerstown (SAL)	4	4	.500	2.55	1.09	14	14	0	0	...	0-...	74.0	57	24	21	5	24-0	90	.209
2004—	San Jose (Calif.)	7	1	.875	1.86	1.03	13	13	0	0	...	0-...	72.2	58	25	15	5	17-0	89	.216
—Norwich (East.)		6	4	.600	3.35	1.31	15	15	0	0	...	0-...	86.0	73	44	32	7	40-0	72	.236
2005—	Fresno (PCL)	10	5	.667	4.39	1.31	26	26	1	0	0	0-0	145.2	118	77	71	22	73-0	176	.218
—San Francisco (N.L.)		2	1	.667	2.33	0.93	7	7	1	0	0	0-0	46.1	24	12	12	4	19-1	30	.151
Major League totals (1 year)		2	1	.667	2.33	0.93	7	7	1	0	0	0-0	46.1	24	12	12	4	19-1	30	.151

CAIRO, MIGUEL — 2B/1B

PERSONAL: Born May 4, 1974, in Anaco, Venezuela. ... 6-1/208. ... Bats right, throws right. ... Full name: Miguel Jesus Cairo. ... Name pronounced: KYE-row. ... High school: Escuela Anaco (Venezuela).

TRANSACTIONS/CAREER NOTES: Signed as a non-drafted free agent by Los Angeles Dodgers organization (September 20, 1990). ... Traded by Dodgers with 3B Willis Otanez to Seattle Mariners for 3B Mike Blowers (November 29, 1995). ... Traded by Mariners with P Bill Risley to Toronto Blue Jays for Ps Edwin Hurtado and Paul Menhart (December 18, 1995). ... Traded by Blue Jays to Chicago Cubs for P Jason Stevenson (November 20, 1996). ... Selected by Tampa Bay Devil Rays in first round (eighth pick overall) of expansion draft (November 18, 1997). ... On disabled list (April 24-May 17 and July 26-August 11, 1999; included rehabilitation assignments to Orlando and St. Petersburg. ... Released by Devil Rays (November 27, 2000). ... Signed by Oakland Athletics organization (January 7, 2001). ... Traded by A's to Chicago Cubs for 3B/1B Eric Hinske (March 28, 2001). ... Claimed on waivers by St. Louis Cardinals (August 10, 2001). ... On disabled list (June 19-July 29, 2003; included rehabilitation assignment to Memphis. ... Signed as a free agent by New York Yankees (December 19, 2003). ... Signed as a free agent by New York Mets (January 10, 2005). ... On disabled list (June 15-July 2, 2005); included rehabilitation assignments to GCL Mets and St. Lucie.

2005 GAMES PLAYED BY POSITION (MLB): 2B—82, 1B—8, 3B—3, OF—3.

SCOUTING REPORT *Offense:* Cairo has a quick inside-out stroke and hits off his front foot. Is a better fastball hitter than a breaking-ball hitter. Stays inside the ball and takes it to the opposite field. Is a good contact hitter with little power. Can run and has good instincts. *Defense:* Cairo's versatility is an asset—he can play anywhere on the infield or outfield. Is not a fluid infielder and has rigid hands though. Gets good jumps on the ball and makes good pivots. Is better suited for second base than shortstop. *Outlook:* Cairo doesn't have much natural ability, but his willingness to play multiple positions and chip in offensively earns him a spot in the lineup. *Grade 6.4*

MIGUEL CAIRO'S HITTING ZONE

.200	.278	.227
.233	.342	.289
.324	.125	.313

LEFTY-RIGHTY SPLITS

vs.	Avg.	AB	H	2B	3B	HR	RBI	BB	SO	OBP	Slg.
L	.191	89	17	4	0	1	4	4	8	.234	.270
R	.273	238	65	14	0	1	15	15	23	.318	.345

Year	Team (League)	Pos.	G	AB	R	H	2B	3B	HR	RBI	BB	SO	HBP	GDP	SB-CS	Avg.	OBP	SLG	OPS	E	Avg.
1991—	Dom. Dodgers (DSL)	IF	57	203	16	45	5	1	0	17	0	17			8-...	.222		.256		...	...
1992—	GC Dodgers (GCL)	3B-SS	21	76	10	23	5	2	0	9	2	6	2	1	1-0	.303	.333	.421	.754	4	.953
—Vero Beach (FSL)	2B-3B	36	125	7	28	0	0	0	7	11	12	0	3	5-3	.224	.285	.224	.509	10	.935
1993—	Vero Beach (FSL)	2B-3B-SS	90	346	50	109	10	1	1	23	28	22	7	2	23-16	.315	.378	.358	.736	18	.959
1994—	Bakersfield (Calif.)	3B-SS	133	533	76	155	23	4	2	48	34	37	6	9	44-23	.291	.338	.360	.698	28	.958
1995—	San Antonio (Texas)	2B-SS-DH	107	435	53	121	20	1	1	41	26	31	5	6	33-16	.278	.323	.336	.659	23	.958
1996—	Syracuse (Int'l)	2B-3B-SS	120	465	71	129	14	4	3	48	26	44	8	5	27-9	.277	.323	.344	.667	23	.955
—Toronto (A.L.)	2B	9	27	5	6	2	0	0	1	1	7	1	1	0-0	.222	.300	.296	.596	0	1.000
1997—	Iowa (Am. Assoc.)	2B-3B-SS	135	569	82	159	35	4	5	46	24	54	6	9	40-15	.279	.314	.381	.695	20	.969
—Chicago (N.L.)	2B-SS	16	29	7	7	1	0	0	1	2	3	1	0	0-0	.241	.313	.276	.588	0	1.000
1998—	Tampa Bay (A.L.)	2B-DH	150	515	49	138	26	5	5	46	24	44	6	9	19-8	.268	.307	.367	.674	16	.978
1999—	Tampa Bay (A.L.)	2B-DH	120	465	61	137	15	5	3	36	24	46	7	13	22-7	.295	.335	.368	.703	9	.983
—Orlando (South.)	2B	3	13	1	5	2	0	0	1	0	1	0	0	0-1	.385	.385	.538	.923	0	1.000
—St. Pete. (FSL)	2B	3	13	2	5	0	0	0	1	2	0	0	0	1-1	.385	.429	.385	.813	1	1.000
2000—	Tampa Bay (A.L.)	2B-DH	119	375	49	98	18	2	1	34	29	34	2	7	28-7	.261	.314	.328	.642	9	.983
2001—	Iowa (PCL)	2B-SS-3B	34	123	22	37	7	1	3	14	8	11	1	3	9-4	.301	.348	.447	.796	3	.978
—Chicago (N.L.)	3B-2B-SS	66	123	20	35	3	1	2	9	16	21	0	3	2-1	.285	.364	.374	.738	7	.917
—St. Louis (N.L.)	OF-2B-3B																			
	1B-SS	27	33	5	11	5	0	1	7	2	2	0	1	0-0	.333	.371	.576	.947	1	.929
2002—	St. Louis (N.L.)	OF-2B-3B																			
	SS-1B-DH	108	184	28	46	9	2	2	23	13	36	3	5	1-1	.250	.307	.353	.660	4	.963
2003—	Memphis (PCL)	2B-DH	3	13	2	3	1	0	0	0	0	3	0	0	0-0	.231	.231	.308	.538	0	1.000
—St. Louis (N.L.)	2B-OF-3B																			
	SS-1B	92	261	41	64	15	2	5	32	13	30	6	6	4-1	.245	.289	.375	.665	6	.972
2004—	New York (A.L.)	2B-3B-SS																			
	1B	122	360	48	105	17	5	6	42	18	49	14	7	11-3	.292	.346	.417	.763	8	.984
2005—	St. Lucie (Fla. St.)	DH	1	4	0	1	0	0	0	0	0	1	0	0	0-0	.250	.250	.250	.500	0	
—GC Mets (GCL)	2B-DH	3	13	3	4	1	0	0	0	0	0	0	0	0-0	.308	.308	.385	.692	0	1.000
—New York (N.L.)	2B-1B-3B																			
	OF	100	327	31	82	18	0	2	19	19	31	4	5	13-3	.251	.296	.324	.620	7	.983
American League totals (5 years)			520	1742	212	484	78	17	15	159	97	182	30	37	80-25	.278	.324	.368	.692	42	.983
National League totals (5 years)			409	957	132	245	51	5	12	91	65	123	14	20	20-6	.256	.308	.357	.666	25	.972
Major League totals (10 years)			929	2699	344	729	129	22	27	250	162	305	44	57	100-31	.270	.318	.364	.683	67	.980

DIVISION SERIES RECORD

Year Team (League)	Pos.	G	AB	R	H	2B	3B	HR	RBI	BB	SO	HBP	GDP	SB-CS	Avg.	OBP	SLG	OPS	E	Avg.
2001— St. Louis (N.L.)	OF	3	5	0	1	0	0	0	0	0	1	0	0	1-0	.200	.200	.200	.400	0	1.000
2002— St. Louis (N.L.)	3B	2	4	2	4	1	0	0	3	0	0	1	0	0-1	1.000	1.000	1.250	2.250	0	1.000
2004— New York (A.L.)	2B	4	14	3	3	1	0	0	1	2	5	0	0	0-0	.214	.313	.286	.598	0	1.000
Division series totals (3 years)		9	23	5	8	2	0	0	4	2	6	1	0	1-1	.348	.423	.435	.858	0	1.000

CHAMPIONSHIP SERIES RECORD

Year Team (League)	Pos.	G	AB	R	H	2B	3B	HR	RBI	BB	SO	HBP	GDP	SB-CS	Avg.	OBP	SLG	OPS	E	Avg.
2002— St. Louis (N.L.)	3B	3	13	2	5	0	0	1	2	0	2	0	0	0-0	.385	.385	.615	1.000	0	1.000
2004— New York (A.L.)	2B	7	25	4	7	3	0	0	0	2	4	0	0	1-0	.280	.419	.400	.819	0	1.000
Champ. series totals (2 years)		10	38	6	12	3	0	1	2	2	6	0	0	1-0	.316	.409	.474	.883	0	1.000

CALERO, KIKO   P

PERSONAL: Born January 9, 1975, in Santurce, Puerto Rico. ... 6-1/180. ... Throws right, bats right. ... Full name: Enrique Nomar Calero. ... High school: University Gardens (Puerto Rico). ... College: St. Thomas (Fla.).

TRANSACTIONS/CAREER NOTES: Selected by Kansas City Royals organization in 27th round of 1996 free-agent draft. ... Signed as a free agent by St. Louis Cardinals organization (December 3, 2002). ... On disabled list (August 7-September 4, 2004); included rehabilitation assignment to Memphis. ... Traded by Cardinals with P Danny Haren and C Daric Barton to Oakland Athletics for P Mark Mulder (December 19, 2004). ... On disabled list (May 10-June 5, 2005); included rehabilitation assignment to Sacramento.

CAREER HITTING: 1-for-6 (.167), 1 R, 0 2B, 0 3B, 0 HR, 1 RBI.

SCOUTING REPORT **Throws:** Calero basically is a two-pitch pitcher, with a sinking fastball in the upper 80s and a slider in the upper 70s. **Tendencies:** When he's healthy (he had elbow problems last season), Calero tends to rely too much on his slider. Will change the size of the break on the pitch depending on the situation and the count. Fastball will sink but doesn't have the late life it had before the injury. Throws strikes and is extremely effective to righthanders but doesn't have a quality pitch to get out lefthanders. Needs to trust his fastball more to build up arm strength and regain his sinker. **Outlook:** Calero developed elbow problems by throwing too many sliders. Will go into the spring in a middle-relief role and will need to earn an opportunity to set up. *Grade 6.1*

KIKO CALERO'S PITCHING ZONE

.143	.125	.222
.263	.333	.313
.263	.500	.000

LEFTY-RIGHTY SPLITS

vs.	Avg.	AB	H	2B	3B	HR	RBI	BB	SO	OBP	Slg.
L	.319	72	23	2	0	4	9	10	14	.398	.514
R	.162	136	22	3	0	2	13	8	38	.214	.228

Year Team (League)	W	L	Pct.	ERA	WHIP	G	GS	CG	ShO	Hld.	Sv.-Opp.	IP	H	R	ER	HR	BB-IBB	SO	Avg.
1996— Spokane (N'west)	4	2	.667	2.52	1.27	17	11	0	0	...	1-...	75.0	77	34	21	5	18-0	61	.265
1997— Wichita (Texas)	11	9	.550	4.44	1.28	23	22	2	0	...	0-...	127.2	120	78	63	15	44-0	100	.248
1998— Lansing (Midw.)	1	0	1.000	3.78	1.56	4	4	0	0	...	0-...	16.2	19	7	7	1	7-0	10	.284
— Wichita (Texas)	1	0	1.000	9.64	2.07	3	3	0	0	...	0-...	14.0	23	16	15	2	6-0	5	.359
— Wilmington (Caro.)	7	3	.700	2.86	1.28	17	17	0	0	...	0-...	97.2	74	33	31	7	51-1	90	.213
1999— Wichita (Texas)	9	3	.750	4.11	1.55	26	23	1	1	...	1-...	129.1	143	67	59	14	57-3	92	.279
2000— Wichita (Texas)	10	7	.588	3.63	1.35	28	25	0	0	...	0-...	153.2	141	74	62	16	66-0	130	.251
2001— Wichita (Texas)	14	5	.737	3.33	1.29	27	19	0	0	...	0-...	124.1	110	57	46	10	51-1	94	.237
2002— Wichita (Texas)	1	0	1.000	2.25	0.94	5	2	0	0	...	0-...	16.0	10	5	4	2	5-0	15	.172
— Omaha (PCL)	7	7	.500	3.44	1.17	20	18	0	0	...	0-...	125.2	112	52	48	11	35-1	109	.244
2003— St. Louis (N.L.)	1	1	.500	2.82	1.28	26	1	0	0	1	1-4	38.1	29	12	12	5	20-2	51	.212
2004— Memphis (PCL)	0	0	...	2.49	1.22	12	3	0	0	...	1-...	25.1	20	8	7	3	11-2	33	.222
— St. Louis (N.L.)	3	1	.750	2.78	0.82	41	0	0	0	12	2-3	45.1	27	14	14	5	10-1	47	.176
2005— Sacramento (PCL)	0	0	...	9.00	2.00	2	0	0	0	0	0-0	2.0	4	2	2	0	0-0	2	.400
— Oakland (A.L.)	4	1	.800	3.23	1.13	58	0	0	0	12	1-2	55.2	45	20	20	6	18-2	52	.216
American League totals (1 year)	4	1	.800	3.23	1.13	58	0	0	0	12	1-2	55.2	45	20	20	6	18-2	52	.216
National League totals (2 years)	4	2	.667	2.80	1.03	67	1	0	0	13	3-7	83.2	56	26	26	10	30-3	98	.193
Major League totals (3 years)	8	3	.727	2.97	1.07	125	1	0	0	25	4-9	139.1	101	46	46	16	48-5	150	.203

DIVISION SERIES RECORD

Year Team (League)	W	L	Pct.	ERA	WHIP	G	GS	CG	ShO	Hld.	Sv.-Opp.	IP	H	R	ER	HR	BB-IBB	SO	Avg.
2004— St. Louis (N.L.)	0	0	...	0.00	0.00	1	0	0	0	0	0-0	1.0	0	0	0	0	0-0	2	.000

CHAMPIONSHIP SERIES RECORD

Year Team (League)	W	L	Pct.	ERA	WHIP	G	GS	CG	ShO	Hld.	Sv.-Opp.	IP	H	R	ER	HR	BB-IBB	SO	Avg.
2004— St. Louis (N.L.)	0	0	...	3.86	1.29	5	0	0	0	2	0-1	7.0	8	3	3	1	1-0	7	.296

WORLD SERIES RECORD

Year Team (League)	W	L	Pct.	ERA	WHIP	G	GS	CG	ShO	Hld.	Sv.-Opp.	IP	H	R	ER	HR	BB-IBB	SO	Avg.
2004— St. Louis (N.L.)	0	0	...	13.50	4.50	2	0	0	0	0	0-0	1.1	2	2	2	0	4-0	0	.400

CALI, CARMEN   P

PERSONAL: Born November 2, 1978, in Cleveland, Ohio. ... 5-10/185. ... Throws left, bats left. ... Full name: Carmen Salvatore Cali. ... Name pronounced: CAL-ee. ...High school: Naples (Fla.). ... College: Florida Atlantic.

TRANSACTIONS/CAREER NOTES: Selected by St. Louis Cardinals organization in 10th round of 2000 free-agent draft.

CAREER HITTING: 0-for-0 (.000), 0 R, 0 2B, 0 3B, 0 HR, 0 RBI.

LEFTY-RIGHTY SPLITS

vs.	Avg.	AB	H	2B	3B	HR	RBI	BB	SO	OBP	Slg.
L	.333	9	3	0	0	2	3	2	2	.417	1.000
R	.412	17	7	3	0	1	4	4	3	.524	.765

Year Team (League)	W	L	Pct.	ERA	WHIP	G	GS	CG	ShO	Hld.	Sv.-Opp.	IP	H	R	ER	HR	BB-IBB	SO	Avg.
2000— New Jersey (NYP)	2	7	.222	4.89	1.40	14	14	0	0	...	0-...	70.0	68	45	38	3	30-0	55	.261
2001— Peoria (Midw.)	7	3	.700	6.00	1.71	39	0	0	0	...	1-...	48.0	53	40	32	4	29-0	47	.275
— Potomac (Carol.)	1	0	1.000	2.19	1.46	12	0	0	0	...	0-...	12.1	12	4	3	1	6-1	9	.279
2002— Potomac (Carol.)	2	2	.500	4.11	1.49	29	0	0	0	...	0-...	35.0	31	18	16	1	21-2	24	.248
— Peoria (Midw.)	1	1	.500	1.78	1.42	24	0	0	0	...	2-...	35.1	36	17	7	0	14-0	27	.259
2003— Palm Beach (FSL)	2	1	.667	4.99	1.48	62	0	0	0	...	3-...	70.1	72	49	39	2	32-6	70	.265
2004— Tennessee (Sou.)	1	2	.333	2.91	1.34	38	0	0	0	...	14-...	46.1	43	19	15	3	19-3	47	.246
— Memphis (PCL)	1	1	.500	2.70	1.05	17	0	0	0	...	3-...	20.0	17	6	6	4	4-0	20	.227
— St. Louis (N.L.)	0	0	...	8.59	2.59	10	0	0	0	0	0-0	7.1	13	7	7	1	6-1	8	.394
2005— St. Louis (N.L.)	0	0	...	10.50	2.67	6	0	0	0	0	0-0	6.0	10	8	7	3	6-1	5	.385
Major League totals (2 years)	0	0	...	9.45	2.63	16	0	0	0	0	0-0	13.1	23	15	14	4	12-2	13	.390

C

CALZADO, NAPOLEON — 3B

PERSONAL: Born February 9, 1977, in Santo Domingo, Dominican Republic. ... 6-3/201. ... Bats right, throws right.

TRANSACTIONS/CAREER NOTES: Signed as a non-drafted free agent by Baltimore Orioles organization (September 11, 1996). ... Traded by Orioles to Atlanta Braves for player to be named (April 14, 2004). ... Signed as a free agent by Orioles organization (December 16, 2004).

2005 GAMES PLAYED BY POSITION (MLB): OF—2.

LEFTY-RIGHTY SPLITS

vs.	Avg.	AB	H	2B	3B	HR	RBI	BB	SO	OBP	Slg.
L	.200	5	1	0	0	0	0	0	1	.200	.200
R	.000	0	0	0	0	0	0	0	0	.000	.000

Year	Team (League)	Pos.	G	AB	R	H	2B	3B	HR	RBI	BB	SO	HBP	GDP	SB-CS	Avg.	OBP	SLG	OPS	E	Avg.
1997—Dom. Orioles (DSL)			64	234	41	75	7	3	0	26	23	36	1	4	18-9	.321	.379	.376	.755	...	...
1998—Dom. Orioles (DSL)			25	88	15	22	3	2	0	10	10	9	1	3	12-2	.250	.320	.330	.650	...	...
—GC Orioles (GCL)		3B-SS-1B	31	113	15	26	6	1	1	18	10	17	1	2	1-1	.230	.296	.381	.677	8	.935
1999—Bluefield (Appal.)		SS-3B	52	199	46	58	11	2	6	31	20	32	3	3	9-1	.291	.363	.457	.820	22	.899
—Delmarva (S. Atl.)		3B	6	18	2	5	1	0	0	1	0	4	0	1	0-0	.278	.263	.333	.596	2	.800
2000—Delmarva (S. Atl.)		3B-1B	131	503	81	140	20	6	7	83	31	68	11	11	29-11	.278	.329	.384	.713	31	.918
2001—Frederick (Carolina)		3B-SS	121	464	50	133	20	2	5	41	16	52	6	9	34-14	.287	.316	.371	.687	25	.925
2002—Bowie (East.)		3B	130	482	71	133	20	3	3	42	34	50	7	12	42-11	.276	.332	.349	.681	24	.938
2003—Bowie (East.)		3B-OF-SS	40	166	16	44	6	1	1	11	5	14	2	4	11-3	.265	.293	.331	.624	6	.946
—Ottawa (Int'l)		3B-OF-SS	51	196	30	61	7	4	0	15	14	30	2	1	9-3	.311	.363	.388	.751	11	.924
—Aberdeen (N.Y.-Penn.)		OF	4	16	5	3	0	0	0	0	2	0	0	0	3-0	.188	.278	.188	.466	0	1.000
2004—Bowie (East.)		OF	4	15	2	4	1	0	0	0	1	1	0	0	2-0	.267	.313	.333	.646	1	.750
—Greenville (Sou.)		OF-1B-3B																			
		2B	119	449	68	161	28	4	8	59	22	59	8	10	18-8	.359	.395	.506	.901	11	.978
—Richmond (Int'l)		OF-3B	5	19	2	4	1	0	0	2	0	2	0	0	0-0	.211	.211	.263	.474	1	1.000
2005—Baltimore (A.L.)		OF	4	5	0	1	0	0	0	0	0	1	0	0	0-0	.200	.200	.200	.400	0	1.000
—Ottawa (Int'l)		3B-OF-1B																			
		C	120	447	54	137	22	1	11	61	21	46	6	13	10-6	.306	.344	.434	.778	18	.954
Major League totals (1 year)			4	5	0	1	0	0	0	0	0	1	0	0	0-0	.200	.200	.200	.400	0	1.000

CAMERON, MIKE — OF

PERSONAL: Born January 8, 1973, in LaGrange, Ga. ... 6-2/200. ... Bats right, throws right. ... Full name: Michael Terrance Cameron. ... High school: La Grange (Ga.).

TRANSACTIONS/CAREER NOTES: Selected by Chicago White Sox organization in 18th round of 1991 free-agent draft. ... Traded by White Sox to Cincinnati Reds for 1B/3B Paul Konerko (November 11, 1998). ... Traded by Reds with Ps Brett Tomko and Jake Meyer and IF Antonio Perez to Seattle Mariners for OF Ken Griffey Jr. (February 10, 2000). ... Signed as a free agent by New York Mets (December 23, 2003). ... On disabled list (April 8-May 5 and August 12, 2005-remainder of season); included rehabilitation assignments to Norfolk and St. Lucie.

RECORDS: Shares major league record for most home runs, game (4, May 2, 2002).

HONORS: Won A.L. Gold Glove as outfielder (2001 and 2003).

2005 GAMES PLAYED BY POSITION (MLB): OF—76.

SCOUTING REPORT **Offense:** Cameron can generate bat speed despite having a very long stroke. Likes the ball out over the plate and is a better fastball hitter than breaking-ball hitter. Will cut down on his stroke and use the whole field with runners in scoring position. Gets into trouble when he starts to hook the ball and tries to pull outside pitches. Is a good runner with strong basestealing instincts. **Defense:** Cameron is a pure athlete, as shown by a successful move from center field to right. Has good range to the alley and the line and goes back well. Has an accurate arm with a quick release. **Outlook:** The severe facial injuries Cameron suffered in an outfield collision with Carlos Beltran raises questions about Cameron's future performance. ***Grade 7***

MIKE CAMERON'S HITTING ZONE

.400	.375	.583
.277	.381	.255
.075	.357	.294

LEFTY-RIGHTY SPLITS

vs.	Avg.	AB	H	2B	3B	HR	RBI	BB	SO	OBP	Slg.
L	.311	74	23	4	0	6	14	6	15	.370	.608
R	.261	234	61	19	2	6	25	23	70	.333	.436

Year	Team (League)	Pos.	G	AB	R	H	2B	3B	HR	RBI	BB	SO	HBP	GDP	SB-CS	Avg.	OBP	SLG	OPS	E	Avg.
1991—GC Whi. Sox (GCL)		OF	44	136	20	30	3	0	0	11	17	29	4	3	13-2	.221	.325	.243	.567	3	.951
1992—Utica (N.Y.-Penn)		OF	26	87	15	24	1	4	2	12	11	26	0	0	3-7	.276	.354	.448	.802	0	1.000
—South Bend (Mid.)		OF	35	114	19	26	8	1	1	9	10	37	4	0	2-3	.228	.310	.342	.652	3	.957
1993—South Bend (Mid.)		OF	122	411	52	98	14	5	0	30	27	101	6	8	19-10	.238	.292	.297	.589	4	.985
1994—Prince Will. (Car.)		OF	131	468	86	116	15	17	6	48	60	101	8	6	22-10	.248	.343	.391	.734	6	.979
1995—Birmingham (Sou.)		OF	107	350	64	87	20	5	11	60	54	104	6	9	21-12	.249	.355	.429	.784	4	.985
—Chicago (A.L.)		OF	28	38	4	7	2	0	1	2	3	15	0	0	0-0	.184	.244	.316	.560	0	1.000
1996—Birmingham (Sou.)		OF-DH	123	473	120	142	34	12	28	77	71	117	12	5	39-15	.300	.402	.600	1.002	7	.973
—Chicago (A.L.)		OF-DH	11	11	1	1	0	0	0	0	1	3	0	0	0-1	.091	.167	.091	.258	0	1.000
1997—Nashville (A.A.)		OF-DH	30	120	21	33	7	3	6	17	18	31	3	1	4-2	.275	.378	.533	.911	1	.985
—Chicago (A.L.)		OF-DH	116	379	63	98	18	3	14	55	55	105	5	8	23-2	.259	.356	.433	.789	5	.985
1998—Chicago (A.L.)		OF	141	396	53	83	16	5	8	43	37	101	6	6	27-11	.210	.285	.336	.621	4	.988
1999—Cincinnati (N.L.)		OF	146	542	93	139	34	9	21	66	80	145	6	4	38-12	.256	.357	.469	.825	8	.979
2000—Seattle (A.L.)		OF	155	543	96	145	28	4	19	78	78	133	6	10	24-7	.267	.365	.438	.803	5	.985
2001—Seattle (A.L.)		OF-DH	150	540	99	144	30	5	25	110	69	155	10	13	34-5	.267	.353	.480	.832	6	.986
2002—Seattle (A.L.)		OF-DH	158	545	84	130	26	5	25	80	79	176	7	8	31-8	.239	.340	.442	.782	5	.985
2003—Seattle (A.L.)		OF	147	534	74	135	31	5	18	76	70	137	6	13	17-7	.253	.344	.431	.774	4	.992
2004—New York (N.L.)		OF	140	493	76	114	30	1	30	76	57	143	8	5	22-6	.231	.319	.479	.798	8	.978
2005—St. Lucie (Fla. St.)		OF	4	10	3	3	2	0	0	3	3	2	0	0	0-0	.300	.533	.500	1.033	0	1.000
—Norfolk (Int'l)		OF	2	7	2	2	0	1	0	2	3	3	0	0	0-0	.286	.500	.571	1.071	0	1.000
—New York (N.L.)		OF	76	308	47	84	23	2	12	39	29	85	4	5	13-1	.273	.342	.477	.819	6	.963
American League totals (8 years)			906	2986	474	743	151	27	110	444	392	825	42	58	156-41	.249	.340	.428	.769	30	.988
National League totals (3 years)			362	1343	216	337	87	12	63	181	166	373	18	14	73-19	.251	.340	.474	.814	22	.976
Major League totals (11 years)			1268	4329	690	1080	238	39	173	625	558	1198	60	72	229-60	.249	.340	.442	.783	52	.985

C

DIVISION SERIES RECORD

Year Team (League)	Pos.	G	AB	R	H	2B	3B	HR	RBI	BB	SO	HBP	GDP	SB-CS	Avg.	OBP	SLG	OPS	E	Avg.
2000— Seattle (A.L.)	OF	3	12	2	3	0	0	0	2	0	0	1	1	1-0	.250	.308	.250	.558	0	1.000
2001— Seattle (A.L.)	OF	5	18	2	4	3	0	1	3	2	7	1	0	0-1	.222	.333	.556	.889	0	1.000
Division series totals (2 years)		8	30	4	7	3	0	1	5	2	7	2	1	1-1	.233	.324	.433	.757	0	1.000

CHAMPIONSHIP SERIES RECORD

Year Team (League)	Pos.	G	AB	R	H	2B	3B	HR	RBI	BB	SO	HBP	GDP	SB-CS	Avg.	OBP	SLG	OPS	E	Avg.
2000— Seattle (A.L.)	OF	6	18	3	2	0	0	0	1	2	7	0	0	1-0	.111	.200	.111	.311	0	1.000
2001— Seattle (A.L.)	OF	5	17	3	3	2	0	0	4	4	1	1	1	0-0	.176	.364	.294	.658	0	1.000
Champ. series totals (2 years)		11	35	6	5	2	0	0	1	6	11	1	1	1-0	.143	.286	.200	.486	0	1.000

ALL-STAR GAME RECORD

	G	AB	R	H	2B	3B	HR	RBI	BB	SO	HBP	GDP	SB-CS	Avg.	OBP	SLG	OPS	E	Avg.
All-Star Game totals (1 year)	1	3	0	1	0	0	0	0	0	1	0	0	0-0	.333	.333	.667	1.000	0	1.000

CAMP, SHAWN — P

PERSONAL: Born November 18, 1975, in Fairfax, Va. ... 6-1/200. ... Throws right, bats right. ... Full name: Shawn Anthony Camp. ... High school: James W. Robinson Jr. Secondary School (Fairfax, Va.) ... College: George Mason.

TRANSACTIONS/CAREER NOTES: Selected by San Diego Padres organization in 16th round of 1997 free-agent draft. ... Traded by Padres with OF Shawn Gilbert to Pittsburgh Pirates for OF Emil Brown (July 10, 2001). ... Signed as a free agent by Kansas City Royals organization (October 29, 2003).

CAREER HITTING: 0-for-0 (.000), 0 R, 0 2B, 0 3B, 0 HR, 0 RBI.

SHAWN CAMP'S PITCHING ZONE

.250	.200	.286
.435	.360	.441
.200	.429	.389

LEFTY-RIGHTY SPLITS

vs.	Avg.	AB	H	2B	3B	HR	RBI	BB	SO	OBP	Slg.
L	.407	91	37	9	0	0	21	7	12	.446	.505
R	.274	117	32	6	1	4	21	6	16	.323	.444

Year Team (League)	W	L	Pct.	ERA	WHIP	G	GS	CG	ShO	Hld.	Sv.-Opp.	IP	H	R	ER	HR	BB-IBB	SO	Avg.
1997— Idaho Falls (Pio.)	2	1	.667	5.51	1.68	30	0	0	0	...	12-...	32.2	41	22	20	3	14-0	41	.311
1998— Clinton (Midw.)	3	5	.375	2.62	1.24	47	0	0	0	...	13-...	55.0	48	19	16	0	20-4	62	.232
1999— Rancho Cuca. (Calif.)	1	5	.167	3.95	1.41	53	0	0	0	...	6-...	66.0	68	37	29	4	25-3	78	.271
2000— Rancho Cuca. (Calif.)	1	0	1.000	1.45	0.80	14	0	0	0	...	6-...	18.2	10	3	3	0	5-0	18	.154
— Mobile (Sou.)	3	3	.500	2.43	1.30	45	0	0	0	...	1-...	59.1	47	23	16	4	30-2	53	.217
2001— Portland (PCL)	1	0	1.000	0.00	0.43	4	1	0	0	...	0-...	7.0	2	0	0	0	1-0	6	.095
— Mobile (Sou.)	6	2	.750	4.44	1.25	35	1	0	0	...	0-...	48.2	46	24	24	2	15-1	55	.261
— Altoona (East.)	4	0	1.000	4.24	1.41	8	3	0	0	...	0-...	23.1	25	14	11	3	8-1	19	.278
— Nashville (PCL)	0	0	...	2.12	1.12	11	0	0	0	...	0-...	17.0	11	4	4	1	8-1	15	.190
2002— Nashville (PCL)	4	1	.800	3.24	1.11	39	0	0	0	...	2-...	58.1	50	22	21	5	15-3	59	.239
2003— Nashville (PCL)	0	1	.000	4.98	1.50	33	1	0	0	...	0-...	43.1	50	26	24	2	15-2	36	.289
— Altoona (East.)	0	2	.000	4.34	1.28	18	0	0	0	...	0-...	29.0	26	14	14	2	11-0	35	.236
2004— Omaha (PCL)	1	1	.500	5.32	1.45	15	0	0	0	...	1-...	22.0	26	14	13	2	6-0	21	.289
— Kansas City (A.L.)	2	2	.500	3.92	1.35	42	0	0	0	5	2-3	66.2	74	37	29	10	16-1	51	.285
2005— Omaha (PCL)	3	6	.333	3.86	1.37	21	7	0	0	1	1-1	67.2	71	36	29	9	22-1	42	.275
— Kansas City (A.L.)	1	4	.200	6.43	1.67	29	0	0	0	0	0-2	49.0	69	40	35	4	13-3	28	.332
Major League totals (2 years)	3	6	.333	4.98	1.49	71	0	0	0	5	2-5	115.2	143	77	64	14	29-4	79	.306

CAMPILLO, JORGE — P

PERSONAL: Born August 10, 1978, in Tijuana, Mexico. ... 6-1/190. ... Throws right, bats right. ... Full name: Jorge Hidalgo Campillo. ... Name pronounced: cam-PEA-oh.

TRANSACTIONS/CAREER NOTES: Signed as a free agent by Seattle Mariners organization (March 3, 2005). ... On disabled list (August 3, 2005-remainder of season).

CAREER HITTING: 0-for-0 (.000), 0 R, 0 2B, 0 3B, 0 HR, 0 RBI.

LEFTY-RIGHTY SPLITS

vs.	Avg.	AB	H	2B	3B	HR	RBI	BB	SO	OBP	Slg.
L	.000	4	0	0	0	0	0	0	1	.000	.000
R	.250	4	1	0	0	0	1	0	0	.400	.500

Year Team (League)	W	L	Pct.	ERA	WHIP	G	GS	CG	ShO	Hld.	Sv.-Opp.	IP	H	R	ER	HR	BB-IBB	SO	Avg.
1997— Tigres (Mex.)	1	0	1.000	4.50	1.75	2	0	0	0	...	0-...	4.0	2	2	2	0	5-0	4	.143
1998— Tigres (Mex.)	6	2	.750	5.11	1.91	24	7	1	0	...	0-...	68.2	76	43	39	6	55-3	42	.297
1999— Tigres (Mex.)	1	2	.333	2.90	1.35	32	0	0	0	...	1-...	71.1	50	29	23	3	46-2	41	.200
2000— Tigres (Mex.)	9	7	.563	6.84	1.72	25	17	1	0	...	0-...	98.2	128	79	75	22	42-2	58	.313
2001— Tigres (Mex.)	6	3	.667	3.53	1.52	30	9	0	0	...	2-...	86.2	95	43	34	12	37-4	64	.280
2002— Tigres (Mex.)	5	5	.500	5.53	1.57	25	15	0	0	...	0-...	94.1	111	62	58	14	37-2	64	.292
2003— Tigres (Mex.)	12	5	.706	2.79	1.22	21	21	2	1	...	0-...	119.1	116	47	37	7	30-1	63	.258
2004— Tigres (Mex.)	5	5	.500	5.38	1.50	17	16	1	0	...	0-...	98.2	120	67	59	14	28-2	66	.306
2005— Ariz. Mariners (Ariz.)	0	2	.000	5.73	1.82	4	4	0	0	0	0-0	11.0	18	11	7	0	2-0	10	.367
— Tacoma (PCL)	4	1	.800	2.71	1.22	12	12	0	0	0	0-0	66.1	63	21	20	5	18-0	43	.259
— Seattle (A.L.)	0	0	...	0.00	1.00	2	1	0	0	0	0-0	2.0	1	0	0	0	1-0	1	.125
Major League totals (1 year)	0	0	...	0.00	1.00	2	1	0	0	0	0-0	2.0	1	0	0	0	1-0	1	.125

CANO, ROBINSON — 2B

PERSONAL: Born October 22, 1982, in San Pedro de Macoris, Dominican Republic. ... 6-0/170. ... Bats left, throws right. ... Full name: Robinson Jose Cano. ... Son of Jose Cano, pitcher for Houston Astros (1989).

TRANSACTIONS/CAREER NOTES: Signed as a non-drafted free agent by New York Yankees organization (January 5, 2001).

2005 GAMES PLAYED BY POSITION (MLB): 2B—131.

C

SCOUTING REPORT *Offense:* Cano could be an excellent hitter once he becomes more disciplined. Hits with an inside-out swing but has good bat speed, especially on the inner half. Will chases pitches. Has good power for his size and can run. Will steal 15-20 bases per year. Makes good contact for a young player. *Defense:* He has good hands but tries to be flashy and becomes careless at times. Gets good jumps on the ball and has above-average range to his right. Has good footwork and makes a quick transfer on the pivot. Tends to have mental lapses. *Outlook:* Cano needs to settle down defensively, but his bat speed and ability to put the ball in play and hit for power give him a chance to be a very good offensive player. *Grade 7.2*

ROBINSON CANO'S HITTING ZONE

.296	.393	.351
.298	.387	.359
.296	.263	.219

LEFTY-RIGHTY SPLITS

vs.	Avg.	AB	H	2B	3B	HR	RBI	BB	SO	OBP	Slg.
L	.270	148	40	7	0	2	17	7	25	.304	.358
R	.307	374	115	27	4	12	45	9	43	.326	.497

Year	Team (League)	Pos.	G	AB	R	H	2B	3B	HR	RBI	BB	SO	HBP	GDP	SB-CS	Avg.	OBP	SLG	OPS	E	Avg.
2001—GC Yankees (GCL)		2B-SS-3B	57	200	37	46	14	2	3	34	28	27	3	4	11-2	.230	.330	.365	.695	11	.959
— Staten Island (N.Y.-Penn.)		3B-SS	2	8	0	2	0	0	0	2	0	2	0	0	0-0	.250	.250	.250	.500	1	.833
2002—Greensboro (S. Atl.)		SS-2B	113	474	67	131	20	9	14	66	29	78	3	8	2-1	.276	.321	.445	.766	37	.935
— Staten Island (N.Y.-Penn.)		3B-SS	22	87	11	24	5	1	1	15	4	8	0	1	6-1	.276	.308	.391	.699	3	.971
2003—Tampa (Fla. St.)		2B	90	366	50	101	16	3	5	50	17	49	4	5	1-1	.276	.313	.377	.690	13	.970
— Trenton (East.)		2B-3B	46	164	21	46	9	1	1	13	9	16	6	6	0-0	.280	.341	.366	.707	5	.977
2004—Trenton (East.)		2B-3B	74	292	43	88	20	8	7	44	24	40	3	6	2-4	.301	.356	.497	.853	12	.864
— Columbus (Int'l)		2B-SS	61	216	22	56	9	2	6	30	18	27	1	7	0-1	.259	.316	.403	.719	4	.000
2005—Columbus (Int'l)		2B-3B-3B-DH	24	108	19	36	8	3	4	24	6	13	0	2	0-0	.333	.368	.574	.942	4	.967
— New York (A.L.)		2B	132	522	78	155	34	4	14	62	16	68	3	16	1-3	.297	.320	.458	.778	17	.974
Major League totals (1 year)			132	522	78	155	34	4	14	62	16	68	3	16	1-3	.297	.320	.458	.778	17	.974

DIVISION SERIES RECORD

Year	Team (League)	Pos.	G	AB	R	H	2B	3B	HR	RBI	BB	SO	HBP	GDP	SB-CS	Avg.	OBP	SLG	OPS	E	Avg.
2005—New York (A.L.)		2B	5	19	3	5	3	0	0	5	2	4	0	0	0-1	.263	.333	.421	.754	2	.941

CANTU, JORGE   2B/3B

PERSONAL: Born January 30, 1982, in Reynosa, Mexico. ... 6-1/184. ... Bats right, throws right. ... Full name: Jorge Luis Cantu. ... High school: Sharyland (McAllen, Texas).
TRANSACTIONS/CAREER NOTES: Signed as a non-drafted free agent by Tampa Bay Devil Rays organization (July 2, 1998).
2005 GAMES PLAYED BY POSITION (MLB): 2B—80, 3B—62, DH—13.

SCOUTING REPORT *Offense:* Cantu is a free swinger with a live bat. Can handle the fastball up in the zone and is a good mistake hitter. Will take the ball to the opposite field. Has good bat speed and power to all fields. Has become a good situational hitter. Doesn't run well. *Defense:* Cantu can be erratic whether he's at second or third base. Doesn't have quick feet. Has stiff hands and slow reactions. Has a strong arm but can be very careless. *Outlook:* Cantu was one of the league's biggest surprises, showing more power and run production than expected. Will have to find a defensive position, possibly first base. Is capable of duplicating his 2005 numbers. *Grade 8.0*

JORGE CANTU'S HITTING ZONE

.300	.355	.179
.361	.488	.320
.294	.167	.346

LEFTY-RIGHTY SPLITS

vs.	Avg.	AB	H	2B	3B	HR	RBI	BB	SO	OBP	Slg.
L	.256	156	40	11	1	6	26	4	29	.282	.455
R	.296	442	131	29	0	22	91	15	54	.321	.511

Year	Team (League)	Pos.	G	AB	R	H	2B	3B	HR	RBI	BB	SO	HBP	GDP	SB-CS	Avg.	OBP	SLG	OPS	E	Avg.
1999—Hudson Valley (NYP)		SS	72	281	33	73	17	2	1	33	20	59	2	8	3-4	.260	.313	.345	.658	25	.928
2000—Char., S.C. (SAL)		SS-2B	46	186	25	56	13	2	2	24	10	39	3	3	3-3	.301	.345	.425	.770	17	.944
— St. Pete. (FSL)		SS	36	130	18	38	5	2	1	14	3	13	1	3	4-2	.292	.313	.385	.698	8	.944
2001—Orlando (South.)		SS	130	512	58	131	26	3	4	45	17	93	8	13	4-9	.256	.287	.342	.629	26	.948
2002—Orlando (South.)		SS-3B-2B	131	512	50	124	31	1	3	43	23	74	4	13	2-6	.242	.278	.324	.602	41	.931
2003—Orlando (South.)		3B-SS-2B	43	158	15	34	10	0	3	17	9	27	1	3	0-3	.215	.259	.335	.594	6	.940
— Durham (Int'l)		SS-3B	60	200	26	59	16	1	4	30	8	21	2	5	2-1	.295	.319	.445	.764	12	.949
2004—Durham (Int'l)		2B-SS-3B																			
		DH	95	368	57	111	33	4	22	80	16	64	4	11	3-0	.302	.335	.576	.904	15	.964
— Tampa Bay (A.L.)		2B-3B-DH																			
			50	173	25	52	20	1	2	17	9	44	2	5	0-0	.301	.341	.462	.803	8	.956
2005—Tampa Bay (A.L.)		2B-3B-DH	150	598	73	171	40	1	28	117	19	83	6	24	1-0	.286	.311	.497	.808	21	.953
Major League totals (2 years)			200	771	98	223	60	2	30	134	28	127	8	29	1-0	.289	.318	.489	.807	29	.954

CAPELLAN, JOSE   P

PERSONAL: Born January 13, 1981, in Cotui, Dominican Republic. ... 6-4/235. ... Throws right, bats right. ... Full name: Jose Francisco Capellan. ... Name pronounced: cap-AY-ahn
TRANSACTIONS/CAREER NOTES: Signed as a non-drafted free agent by Atlanta Braves organization (August 6, 1998). ... Traded by Braves with a player to be named to Milwaukee Brewers for P Dan Kolb (December 11, 2004); Brewers acquired P Alec Zumwalt to complete deal (December 13, 2004).
CAREER HITTING: 0-for-2 (.000), 0 R, 0 2B, 0 3B, 0 HR, 0 RBI.

SCOUTING REPORT *Throws:* Capellan's fastball has been clocked at 94-97 mph, and he has the potential to keep it consistently in the high 90s. Also throws a slider and changeup. *Tendencies:* Capellan has tremendous raw arm strength but has not yet learned how to pitch. Does not always repeat his arm slot. Curveball can be flat and his changeup is inconsistent. Lacks great movement on his power fastball. *Outlook:* He pitches in a setup role now and is better suited to relief in general. Fastball gives him a lot of potential. Should be a closer in the future. *Grade 6.6*

JOSE CAPELLAN'S PITCHING ZONE

.000	.500	.000
.250	.143	.667
.500	.000	.000

LEFTY-RIGHTY SPLITS

vs.	Avg.	AB	H	2B	3B	HR	RBI	BB	SO	OBP	Slg.
L	.235	17	4	0	0	0	4	4	2	.348	.235
R	.317	41	13	3	1	1	4	1	12	.333	.512

Year	Team (League)	W	L	Pct.	ERA	WHIP	G	GS	CG	ShO	Hld.	Sv.-Opp.	IP	H	R	ER	HR	BB-IBB	SO	Avg.
1999—Dominican Braves (DSL)	3	3	.500	3.58	1.36	14	10	0	0	...	2-...	60.1	54	31	24	1	28-...	46	.242

C

Year Team (League)	W	L	Pct.	ERA	WHIP	G	GS	CG	ShO	Hld.	Sv.-Opp.	IP	H	R	ER	HR	BB-IBB	SO	Avg.
2000— Dominican Braves (DSL) ...	3	8	.273	3.69	1.38	14	14	0	0		0-0	68.1	58	45	28	0	36-...	68	.221
2001— Danville (Appal.)	0	0		1.72	1.02	3	3	0	0	...	0-...	15.2	12	7	3	1	4-0	25	.200
2002—	Did not play.																		
2003— GC Braves (GCL)	0	1	.000	2.65	1.53	5	5	0	0		0-...	17.0	18	7	5	0	8-0	17	.277
— Rome (S. Atl.)	1	2	.333	3.80	1.31	14	12	1	0		0-...	47.1	43	23	20	2	19-0	32	.253
2004— Myrtle Beach (Carol.)	5	1	.833	1.94	0.82	8	8	1	1		0-...	46.1	27	11	10	0	11-0	62	.168
— Greenville (Sou.)	5	1	.833	2.50	1.43	9	8	0	0		0-...	50.1	53	15	14	1	19-0	53	.270
— Richmond (Int'l)	4	2	.667	2.51	1.12	7	7	0	0		0-...	43.0	33	13	12	0	15-1	37	.214
— Atlanta (N.L.)	0	1	.000	11.25	2.38	3	2	0	0	0	0-0	8.0	14	10	10	2	5-0	4	.400
2005— Nashville (PCL)	5	3	.625	3.87	1.43	36	12	0	0		6-8	90.2	88	42	39	4	42-2	76	.257
— Milwaukee (N.L.)	1	1	.500	2.87	1.40	17	0	0	0	3	0-0	15.2	17	6	5	1	5-0	14	.293
Major League totals (2 years)	1	2	.333	5.70	1.73	20	2	0	0	3	0-0	23.2	31	16	15	3	10-0	18	.333

CAPPS, MATT — P

PERSONAL: Born September 3, 1983, in Douglasville, Ga. ... 6-3/238. ... Throws right, bats right. ... Full name: Matthew Dicus Capps. ... College: None.

TRANSACTIONS/CAREER NOTES: Selected by Pittsburgh Pirates organization in seventh round of 2002 free-agent draft.

CAREER HITTING: 0-for-0 (.000), 0 R, 0 2B, 0 3B, 0 HR, 0 RBI.

LEFTY-RIGHTY SPLITS

vs.	Avg.	AB	H	2B	3B	HR	RBI	BB	SO	OBP	Slg.
L	.250	4	1	1	0	0	1	0	1	.250	.500
R	.364	11	4	0	0	0	2		2	.417	.364

Year Team (League)	W	L	Pct.	ERA	WHIP	G	GS	CG	ShO	Hld.	Sv.-Opp.	IP	H	R	ER	HR	BB-IBB	SO	Avg.
2002— GC Pirates (GCL)	1	0	1.000	0.69	1.46	7	0	0	0		1-...	13.0	13	2	1	0	6-0	8	.271
2003— GC Pirates (GCL)	5	1	.833	1.87	0.78	10	10	1	0		0-...	62.2	40	16	13	1	9-0	54	.178
— Lynchburg (Caro.)	0	0		5.40	1.40	1	1	0	0		0-...	5.0	3	3	3	0	4-0	5	.167
2004— Hickory (S. Atl.)	2	3	.400	10.07	2.33	12	8	0	0		0-...	42.0	82	55	47	8	16-0	27	.400
— Will. (NYP)	3	5	.375	4.85	1.35	11	11	0	0		0-...	65.0	84	43	35	7	4-1	33	.312
2005— Hickory (S. Atl.)	3	4	.429	2.52	0.97	35	0	0	0	1	14-20	53.2	47	15	15	0	5-2	39	.239
— Altoona (East.)	0	2	.000	2.70	1.10	17	0	0	0	2	7-9	20.0	21	8	6	2	1-0	26	.250
— Pittsburgh (N.L.)	0	0		4.50	1.25	4	0	0	0	0	0-0	4.0	5	2	2	0	0-0	3	.333
Major League totals (1 year)	0	0		4.50	1.25	4	0	0	0	0	0-0	4.0	5	2	2	0	0-0	3	.333

CAPUANO, CHRIS — P

PERSONAL: Born August 19, 1978, in Springfield, Mass. ... 6-3/210. ... Throws left, bats left. ... Full name: Christopher Frank Capuano. ... Name pronounced: cap-u-ON-o. ... High school: Cathedral (West Springfield, Mass.). ... High school: Alexander (La.). ... College: Duke.

TRANSACTIONS/CAREER NOTES: Selected by Pittsburgh Pirates organization in 45th round of 1996 free-agent draft; did not sign. ... Selected by Arizona Diamondbacks organization in eighth round of 1999 free-agent draft. ... Traded by Diamondbacks with SS Craig Counsell, 2B Junior Spivey, 1B Lyle Overbay, C Chad Moeller and P Jorge de la Rosa to Milwaukee Brewers for 1B Richie Sexson, P Shane Nance and a player to be named (December 1, 2003); Diamondbacks acquired OF Noochie Varner to complete deal (December 15, 2003). ... On disabled list (April 19-May 26, May 27-June 12 and August 25, 2004-remainder of season); included rehabilitation assignments to Beloit, High Desert and Indianapolis.

CAREER HITTING: 18-for-109 (.165), 5 R, 5 2B, 0 3B, 0 HR, 11 RBI.

SCOUTING REPORT Throws: Capuano's fastball ranges from 83-87 mph and complements a slurve-type slider in the upper 70s and a changeup. ***Tendencies:*** Capuano was one of the most improved pitchers in the league in 2005. Has an exceptional feel for changing speeds and locating his below-average fastball, which has deception and good late life. Slider has an in-between break with the speed of a curve and break of a slider. Has a good change with arm speed and movement. ***Outlook:*** A pitcher in the Jamie Moyer mode, Capuano has better overall stuff to go with that type of feel and command. Could top the 20-win mark in 2006 with improved run support. ***Grade 9***

CHRIS CAPUANO'S PITCHING ZONE

.193	.242	.200
.355	.379	.186
.247	.194	.250

LEFTY-RIGHTY SPLITS

vs.	Avg.	AB	H	2B	3B	HR	RBI	BB	SO	OBP	Slg.
L	.202	163	33	4	0	4	14	14	36	.284	.301
R	.270	664	179	45	2	27	82	77	140	.350	.465

Year Team (League)	W	L	Pct.	ERA	WHIP	G	GS	CG	ShO	Hld.	Sv.-Opp.	IP	H	R	ER	HR	BB-IBB	SO	Avg.
2000— South Bend (Mid.)	10	4	.714	2.21	1.11	18	18	0	0		0-...	101.2	68	35	25	2	45-0	105	.193
2001— El Paso (Texas)	10	11	.476	5.31	1.63	28	28	2	2		0-...	159.1	184	109	94	13	75-0	167	.290
2002— Tucson (PCL)	4	1	.800	2.72	1.13	6	6	0	0		0-...	36.1	30	12	11	1	11-0	29	.227
2003— Tucson (PCL)	9	5	.643	3.34	1.23	23	23	0	0		0-...	142.2	133	66	53	9	43-2	108	.250
— Arizona (N.L.)	2	4	.333	4.64	1.15	9	5	0	0	1	0-0	33.0	27	19	17	3	11-1	23	.233
2004— Beloit (Midw.)	0	0		3.38	1.50	1	1	0	0		0-...	2.2	3	1	1	1	1-0	4	.300
— Indianapolis (Int'l)	0	1	.000	8.31	1.73	2	2	0	0		0-...	8.2	10	9	8	1	5-0	9	.294
— High Desert (Calif.)	0	1	.000	27.00	4.50	1	1	0	0		0-...	2.0	6	6	6	1	3-0	2	.600
— Milwaukee (N.L.)	6	8	.429	4.99	1.45	17	17	0	0		0-0	88.1	91	55	49	18	37-1	80	.269
2005— Milwaukee (N.L.)	18	12	.600	3.99	1.38	35	•35	0	0		0-0	219.0	212	105	97	31	91-6	176	.256
Major League totals (3 years)	26	24	.520	4.31	1.38	61	57	0	0	1	0-0	340.1	330	179	163	52	139-8	279	.258

CARLYLE, BUDDY — P

PERSONAL: Born December 21, 1977, in Omaha, Neb. ... 6-3/175. ... Throws right, bats left. ... Full name: Earl L. Carlyle. ... High school: Bellevue (Neb.) East.

TRANSACTIONS/CAREER NOTES: Selected by Cincinnati Reds organization in second round of free-agent draft (June 4, 1996). ... Traded by Reds to San Diego Padres for P Marc Kroon (April 8, 1998). ... Released by Padres (November 1, 2000). ... Contract sold by Padres to Hanshin of the Japan Central League (November 3, 2000). ... Signed as a free agent by Kansas City Royals organization (December 18, 2002). ... Signed as a free agent by New York Yankees organization (December 23, 2003). ... Signed as a free agent by Los Angeles Dodgers organization (November 26, 2004).

CAREER HITTING: 2-for-9 (.222), 1 R, 0 2B, 0 3B, 0 HR, 1 RBI.

BUDDY CARLYLE'S PITCHING ZONE

.000	.667	1.000
.167	.286	.143
.750	.500	.286

LEFTY-RIGHTY SPLITS

vs.	Avg.	AB	H	2B	3B	HR	RBI	BB	SO	OBP	Slg.
L	.296	27	8	2	0	2	9	2	7	.345	.593
R	.286	28	8	2	0	2	8	2	6	.355	.571

C

Year	Team (League)	W	L	Pct.	ERA	WHIP	G	GS	CG	ShO	Hld.	Sv.-Opp.	IP	H	R	ER	HR	BB-IBB	SO	Avg.
1996—	Princeton (Appal.)	2	4	.333	4.66	1.34	10	9	1	0	...	0-...	47.0	47	33	24	4	16-0	42	.255
1997—	Char., W.Va. (SAL)	14	5	.737	2.77	1.10	23	23	4	1	...	0-...	143.0	130	51	44	9	27-0	111	.240
1998—	Chattanooga (Sou.)	0	1	.000	5.40	1.20	1	1	0	0	...	0-...	5.0	6	3	3	0	0-0	3	.300
—	Mobile (Sou.)	14	6	.700	3.38	1.23	27	27	2	1	...	0-...	183.2	177	80	69	13	46-0	97	.256
1999—	Las Vegas (PCL)	11	8	.579	4.89	1.39	25	25	0	0	...	0-...	160.0	180	99	87	25	42-1	138	.286
—	San Diego (N.L.)	1	3	.250	5.97	1.41	7	7	0	0	0	0-...	37.2	36	28	25	7	17-...	29	.257
2000—	Las Vegas (PCL)	8	6	.571	4.29	1.38	27	27	1	0	...	0-...	151.0	165	93	72	25	44-0	127	.273
—	San Diego (N.L.)	0	0	...	21.00	3.00	4	0	0	0	0	0-...	3.0	6	7	7	0	3-...	2	.400
2001—	Hanshin (Jp. Cn.)	7	10	.412	3.87	1.40	28	26	0	0	...	0-...	154.0	151	73	66	22	64-0	111	...
2002—	Hanshin (Jp. Cn.)	0	2	.000	7.53	1.47	3	3	0	0	...	0-...	15.0	17	12	12	1	5-0	13	...
2003—	Omaha (PCL)	0	1	.000	5.40	1.20	2	0	0	0	...	0-...	5.0	5	3	3	2	1-0	4	.263
—	Wichita (Texas)	3	2	.600	1.98	0.93	15	0	0	0	...	3-...	28.0	19	6	6	0	7-0	41	.192
2004—	Trenton (East.)	4	0	1.000	0.72	0.71	8	5	0	0	...	0-...	38.0	23	4	3	0	4-0	48	.178
—	Columbus (Int'l)	8	5	.615	4.05	1.26	19	18	0	0	...	0-...	106.2	113	51	48	14	21-0	92	.274
2005—	Los Angeles (N.L.)	0	0	...	8.36	1.43	10	0	0	0	0	0-1	14.0	16	13	13	4	4-0	13	.291
—	GC Dodgers (GCL)	0	0	...	3.00	1.00	1	1	0	0	0	0-...	3.0	3	1	1	0	0-0	1	.273
—	Las Vegas (PCL)	1	2	.333	4.88	1.50	20	6	0	0	0	2-2	48.0	51	28	26	7	21-0	53	.280
Major League totals (3 years)		1	3	.250	7.41	1.50	21	7	0	0	0	0-1	54.2	58	48	45	11	24-0	44	.276

CARPENTER, CHRIS   P

PERSONAL: Born April 27, 1975, in Exeter, N.H. ... 6-6/230. ... Throws right, bats right. ... Full name: Christopher John Carpenter. ... High school: Trinity (Manchester, N.H.).
TRANSACTIONS/CAREER NOTES: Selected by Toronto Blue Jays organization in first round (15th pick overall) of 1993 free-agent draft. ... On disabled list (June 3-28, 1999); included rehabilitation assignment to St. Catharines. ... On disabled list (April 2-20, April 22-June 21 and August 14, 2002-remainder of season); included rehabilitation assignments to Tennessee and Syracuse. ... Released by Blue Jays (October 9, 2002). ... Signed by St. Louis Cardinals (December 13, 2002). ... On disabled list (March 27, 2003-entire season); included rehabilitation assignments to Palm Beach and Tennessee.
HONORS: Named N.L. Comeback Player of the Year by THE SPORTING NEWS (2004). ... Named N.L. Pitcher of the Year by the SPORTING NEWS (2005). ... Named N.L. Cy Young award winner by Baseball Writers' Association of America (2005).
CAREER HITTING: 12-for-150 (.080), 9 R, 2 2B, 0 3B, 0 HR, 3 RBI.

SCOUTING REPORT *Throws:* Carpenter throws a 91-95 mph fastball, a curveball at 74-79, and a changeup. *Tendencies:* He was dominant nearly all season, accenting his performance with a consistent, tight cut fastball. Can freeze hitters with a sharp curveball and occasional changeup. Has learned how to work hitters. Has a loose arm and a good delivery. *Outlook:* The cut fastball has made the biggest difference for Carpenter, who is healthy for the first time in three or four years. Will continue to be one of the game's best starters. *Grade 9.8*

CHRIS CARPENTER'S PITCHING ZONE

.207	.389	.130
.235	.407	.268
.181	.327	.263

LEFTY-RIGHTY SPLITS

vs.	Avg.	AB	H	2B	3B	HR	RBI	BB	SO	OBP	Slg.
L	.264	432	114	30	2	14	45	31	95	.313	.440
R	.199	452	90	16	1	4	31	20	118	.234	.265

Year	Team (League)	W	L	Pct.	ERA	WHIP	G	GS	CG	ShO	Hld.	Sv.-Opp.	IP	H	R	ER	HR	BB-IBB	SO	Avg.
1994—	Medicine Hat (Pio.)	6	3	.667	2.76	1.36	15	15	0	0	...	0-...	84.2	76	40	26	3	39-0	80	.243
1995—	Dunedin (Fla. St.)	3	5	.375	2.17	1.34	15	15	0	0	...	0-...	99.1	83	29	24	3	50-0	56	.229
—	Knoxville (Southern)	3	7	.300	5.18	1.59	12	12	0	0	...	0-...	64.1	71	47	37	3	31-1	53	.284
1996—	Knoxville (Southern)	7	9	.438	3.94	1.47	28	28	1	0	...	0-...	171.1	161	94	75	13	91-4	150	.250
1997—	Syracuse (Int'l)	4	9	.308	4.50	1.38	19	19	3	2	...	0-...	120.0	113	64	60	16	53-0	97	.257
—	Toronto (A.L.)	3	7	.300	5.09	1.78	14	13	1	1	0	0-0	81.1	108	51	46	7	37-0	55	.325
1998—	Toronto (A.L.)	12	7	.632	4.37	1.36	33	24	1	1	0	0-0	175.0	177	97	85	18	61-1	136	.265
1999—	Toronto (A.L.)	9	8	.529	4.38	1.50	24	24	4	1	0	0-0	150.0	177	81	73	16	48-1	106	.294
—	St. Catharines (NYP)	0	0	...	4.50	1.50	1	1	0	0	0	0-...	4.0	5	2	2	0	1-0	6	.294
2000—	Toronto (A.L.)	10	12	.455	6.26	1.64	34	27	2	0	0	0-...	175.1	204	*130	*122	30	83-1	113	.290
2001—	Toronto (A.L.)	11	11	.500	4.09	1.41	34	34	3	2	0	0-0	215.2	229	112	98	29	75-5	157	.274
2002—	Tennessee (Sou.)	0	1	.000	8.20	1.82	5	5	0	0	...	0-...	18.2	26	18	17	5	8-0	9	.338
—	Toronto (A.L.)	4	5	.444	5.28	1.58	13	13	1	0	0	0-0	73.1	89	45	43	11	27-0	45	.306
—	Syracuse (Int'l)	0	1	.000	4.50	1.67	1	1	0	0	...	0-...	6.0	8	3	3	1	2-0	6	.320
2003—	Palm Beach (FSL)	0	1	.000	1.29	1.00	4	4	0	0	...	0-...	7.0	6	3	1	1	1-0	6	.222
—	Memphis (PCL)	0	0	...	5.40	1.60	3	3	0	0	...	0-...	8.1	11	5	5	0	2-0	4	.333
—	Tennessee (Sou.)	0	1	.000	13.50	2.70	1	1	0	0	...	0-...	3.1	7	5	5	1	2-0	2	.438
2004—	St. Louis (N.L.)	15	5	.750	3.46	1.14	28	28	1	0	0	0-0	182.0	169	75	70	24	38-2	152	.245
2005—	St. Louis (N.L.)	21	5	.808	2.83	1.06	33	33	•7	4	0	0-0	241.2	204	82	76	18	51-0	213	.231
American League totals (6 years)		49	50	.495	4.83	1.51	152	135	12	5	0	0-0	870.2	984	520	467	111	331-8	612	.287
National League totals (2 years)		36	10	.783	3.10	1.09	61	61	8	4	0	0-0	423.2	373	157	146	42	89-2	365	.237
Major League totals (8 years)		85	60	.586	4.26	1.37	213	196	20	9	0	0-0	1294.1	1357	677	613	153	420-10	977	.271

DIVISION SERIES RECORD

Year	Team (League)	W	L	Pct.	ERA	WHIP	G	GS	CG	ShO	Hld.	Sv.-Opp.	IP	H	R	ER	HR	BB-IBB	SO	Avg.
2005—	St. Louis (N.L.)	1	0	1.000	0.00	1.00	1	1	0	0	0	0-0	6.0	3	0	0	0	3-0	3	.158

CHAMPIONSHIP SERIES RECORD

Year	Team (League)	W	L	Pct.	ERA	WHIP	G	GS	CG	ShO	Hld.	Sv.-Opp.	IP	H	R	ER	HR	BB-IBB	SO	Avg.
2005—	St. Louis (N.L.)	1	0	1.000	3.00	1.20	2	2	0	0	0	0-0	15.0	14	6	5	2	4-0	9	.255

ALL-STAR GAME RECORD

Year	Team (League)	W	L	Pct.	ERA	WHIP	G	GS	CG	ShO	Hld.	Sv.-Opp.	IP	H	R	ER	HR	BB-IBB	SO	Avg.
All-Star Game totals (1 year)		0	0	...	0.00	2.00	1	1	0	0	0	0-0	1.0	2	0	0	0	0-0	0	.500

CARRARA, GIOVANNI — P

PERSONAL: Born March 4, 1968, in Anzoategui, Venezuela. ... 6-2/230. ... Throws right, bats right. ... Full name: Giovanni Jimenez Carrara. ... Name pronounced: ka-RAH-rah.
TRANSACTIONS/CAREER NOTES: Signed as a non-drafted free agent by Toronto Blue Jays organization (January 23, 1990). ... Claimed on waivers by Cincinnati Reds (July 3, 1996). ... Signed as a free agent by Baltimore Orioles organization (November 12, 1996). ... Released by Orioles (May 14, 1997). ... Signed by Reds organization (May 17, 1997). ... Signed by Seibu of the Japan Pacific League (1998). ... Signed as a free agent by Reds organization (December 23, 1998). ... Signed as a free agent by Colorado Rockies organization (December 1, 1999). ... On disabled list (August 3-September 4, 2000); included rehabilitation assignment to Colorado Springs. ... Signed as a free agent by Los Angeles Dodgers organization (January 4, 2001). ... On disabled list (August 11-September 1, 2002). ... Released by Dodgers (March 26, 2003). ... Signed by Seattle Mariners (March 28, 2003). ... Signed as a free agent by Cleveland Indians organization (December 19, 2003). ... Released by Indians (March 27, 2004). ... Signed by Chicago Cubs organization (March 28, 2003). ... Released by Cubs (May 31, 2004). ... Signed by Dodgers organization (June 1, 2004).
CAREER HITTING: 3-for-31 (.097), 2 R, 0 2B, 0 3B, 0 HR, 0 RBI.

SCOUTING REPORT **Throws:** Carrara has three solid pitches: a fastball that ranges from 88-91 mph, a slider and a changeup. **Tendencies:** He likes to ride his four-seam fastball up in the zone. Slider acts more like a cutter. Change is very effective against lefthanders. Has learned to control his emotions better on the mound but still has a tendency to rush his motion. Can be effective when he gets his breaking ball over. **Outlook:** The durable Carrara can work in a variety of roles, from middle relief to setup work. ***Grade 6.5***

GIOVANNI CARRARA'S PITCHING ZONE

.167	.231	.188
.233	.436	.278
.059	.400	.333

LEFTY-RIGHTY SPLITS

vs.	Avg.	AB	H	2B	3B	HR	RBI	BB	SO	OBP	Slg.
L	.234	111	26	7	2	2	12	20	22	.351	.387
R	.248	157	39	9	1	4	24	18	34	.339	.395

C

Year	Team (League)	W	L	Pct.	ERA	WHIP	G	GS	CG	ShO	Hld.	Sv.-Opp.	IP	H	R	ER	HR	BB-IBB	SO	Avg.
1990—	Dom. B. Jays (DSL)	2	2	.500	2.62	1.35	15	14	4	0	...	0-...	86.0	88	31	25	...	28-...	55	...
1991—	St. Catharines (NYP)	5	2	.714	1.71	0.97	15	13	2	•2	...	0-...	89.2	66	26	17	5	21-0	83	.200
1992—	Dunedin (Fla. St.)	0	1	.000	4.63	1.41	5	4	0	0	...	0-...	23.1	22	13	12	1	11-0	16	.250
	— Myrtle Beach (SAL)	11	7	.611	3.14	1.22	22	16	1	1	...	0-...	100.1	86	40	35	12	36-0	100	.231
1993—	Dunedin (Fla. St.)	6	11	.353	3.45	1.39	27	24	1	0	...	0-...	140.2	136	69	54	11	59-0	108	.258
1994—	Knoxville (Southern)	13	7	.650	3.89	1.32	26	26	1	0	...	0-...	164.1	158	85	71	16	59-0	96	.251
1995—	Syracuse (Int'l)	7	7	.500	3.96	1.31	21	21	0	0	...	0-...	131.2	116	72	58	11	56-2	81	.232
	— Toronto (A.L.)	2	4	.333	7.21	1.83	12	7	1	0	0	0-0	48.2	64	46	39	10	25-1	27	.322
1996—	Toronto (A.L.)	0	1	.000	11.40	2.33	11	0	0	0	0	0-1	15.0	23	19	19	5	12-2	10	.359
	— Syracuse (Int'l)	4	4	.500	3.58	1.30	9	6	1	0	...	0-...	37.2	37	16	15	2	12-1	28	.253
	— Indianapolis (A.A.)	4	0	1.000	0.76	0.71	9	6	1	1	...	1-...	47.2	25	6	4	2	9-0	45	.152
	— Cincinnati (N.L.)	1	0	1.000	5.87	1.91	8	5	0	0	0	0-0	23.0	31	17	15	6	13-1	13	.323
1997—	Rochester (Int'l)	4	2	.667	4.44	1.31	8	8	1	0	...	0-...	46.2	45	23	23	4	16-0	48	.259
	— Indianapolis (A.A.)	12	5	.706	3.51	1.34	19	18	2	0	...	0-...	120.2	111	50	47	12	51-3	105	.247
	— Cincinnati (N.L.)	0	1	.000	7.84	1.94	2	2	0	0	0	0-0	10.1	14	9	9	4	6-1	5	.333
1998—	Seibu (Jp. East.)	2	0	1.000	4.50	1.13	4	0	0	0	...	0-...	8.0	8	4	4	...	1-...	8	...
	— Seibu (Jp. Pac.)	1	2	.333	4.91	1.47	33	0	0	0	...	1-...	73.1	68	44	40	...	40-...	50	...
1999—	Indianapolis (Int'l)	12	7	.632	3.47	1.28	39	21	2	1	...	0-...	158.0	144	68	61	20	58-3	114	.246
2000—	Colo. Springs (PCL)	7	2	.778	3.26	1.23	18	15	0	0	...	0-...	96.2	89	39	35	8	30-1	89	.245
	— Colorado (N.L.)	0	1	.000	12.83	2.40	8	0	0	0	0	0-1	13.1	21	19	19	5	11-2	15	.356
2001—	Las Vegas (PCL)	1	2	.333	3.10	1.24	6	6	0	0	...	0-...	29.0	27	10	10	5	9-0	35	.248
	— Los Angeles (N.L.)	6	1	.857	3.16	1.14	47	3	0	0	9	0-3	85.1	73	30	30	12	24-3	70	.231
2002—	Los Angeles (N.L.)	6	3	.667	3.28	1.27	63	1	0	0	14	1-6	90.2	83	34	33	14	32-4	56	.243
2003—	Seattle (A.L.)	2	0	1.000	6.83	1.86	23	0	0	0	4	0-0	29.0	40	22	22	6	14-0	13	.333
	— Tacoma (PCL)	1	1	.500	4.23	1.30	18	0	0	0	...	5-...	27.2	28	14	13	2	9-0	27	.264
2004—	Iowa (PCL)	1	2	.333	3.81	1.31	20	0	0	0	...	1-...	28.1	29	12	12	3	8-1	23	.279
	— Las Vegas (PCL)	0	1	.000	2.51	1.33	11	0	0	0	...	2-...	14.1	11	4	4	1	8-2	15	.208
	— Los Angeles (N.L.)	5	2	.714	2.18	1.23	42	0	0	0	6	2-3	53.2	46	15	13	1	20-3	48	.228
2005—	Los Angeles (N.L.)	7	4	.636	3.93	1.36	72	0	0	0	11	0-2	75.2	65	35	33	6	38-5	56	.243
	American League totals (3 years)	4	5	.444	7.77	1.92	46	7	1	0	4	0-1	92.2	127	87	80	21	51-3	50	.332
	National League totals (7 years)	25	12	.676	3.89	1.36	242	11	0	0	40	3-15	352.0	333	169	152	48	144-19	263	.252
	Major League totals (9 years)	29	17	.630	4.70	1.47	288	18	1	0	44	3-16	444.2	460	246	232	69	195-22	313	.269

DIVISION SERIES RECORD

Year	Team (League)	W	L	Pct.	ERA	WHIP	G	GS	CG	ShO	Hld.	Sv.-Opp.	IP	H	R	ER	HR	BB-IBB	SO	Avg.
2004—	Los Angeles (N.L.)	0	0	...	9.00	2.50	3	0	0	0	0	0-0	2.0	4	2	2	0	1-0	1	.444

CARRASCO, D.J. — P

PERSONAL: Born April 12, 1977, in Safford, Ariz. ... 6-1/215. ... Throws right, bats right. ... Full name: Daniel Carrasco. ... High school: Safford (Ariz.). ... Junior college: Pima (Ariz.) Community College.
TRANSACTIONS/CAREER NOTES: Selected by Baltimore Orioles organization in 20th round of 1997 free-agent draft. ... Released by Orioles (June 14, 1998). ... Signed by Cleveland Indians organization (June 18, 1998). ... Released by Indians (August 21, 1998). ... Signed by Pittsburgh Pirates organization (March 29, 1999). ... Selected by Kansas City Royals from Pirates organization in Rule 5 major league draft (December 16, 2002).
CAREER HITTING: 0-for-9 (.000), 0 R, 0 2B, 0 3B, 0 HR, 0 RBI.

SCOUTING REPORT **Throws:** He throws two- and four-seam fastballs that range from 88-92 mph. Also throws a slider, changeup and curveball. **Tendencies:** He is a contact pitcher who is very effective at keeping the ball down and getting ground balls. Has three-quarters to occasional sidearm action with very good tailing action on his two-seamer. Four-seamer runs up and in on righthanders. Slider has a big break without late bite and often is flat. Loses arm speed on his breaking ball. Change is hard with some sink. Rarely uses his curveball. **Outlook:** Carrasco's move into the rotation in May was smart; he is better suited to that role. Needs to tighten his breaking ball but throws strikes. ***Grade 6.1***

D.J. CARRASCO'S PITCHING ZONE

.333	.650	.292
.300	.362	.293
.348	.217	.222

LEFTY-RIGHTY SPLITS

vs.	Avg.	AB	H	2B	3B	HR	RBI	BB	SO	OBP	Slg.
L	.286	227	65	10	2	6	25	36	23	.387	.427
R	.292	219	64	12	0	5	31	15	26	.343	.416

Year	Team (League)	W	L	Pct.	ERA	WHIP	G	GS	CG	ShO	Hld.	Sv.-Opp.	IP	H	R	ER	HR	BB-IBB	SO	Avg.
1998—	Watertown (NYP)	1	1	.500	5.40	1.58	13	1	0	0	...	2-...	31.2	36	23	19	3	14-0	38	.281

Year Team (League)	W	L	Pct.	ERA	WHIP	G	GS	CG	ShO	Hld.	Sv.-Opp.	IP	H	R	ER	HR	BB-IBB	SO	Avg.
1999— Will. (NYP)	4	2	.667	2.96	1.28	18	4	0	0	...	0-...	51.2	43	20	17	2	23-0	49	.236
—Lynchburg (Caro.)	0	1	.000	6.35	2.12	2	0	0	0	...	0-...	5.2	9	8	4	0	3-0	4	.360
2000—Hickory (S. Atl.)	5	4	.556	1.34	1.36	27	0	0	0	...	6-...	40.1	35	10	6	0	20-1	40	.236
—Lynchburg (Caro.)	1	0	1.000	3.48	1.55	8	0	0	0	...	2-...	10.1	8	5	4	1	8-0	10	.222
—Altoona (East.)	1	1	.500	8.36	2.07	9	0	0	0	...	0-...	14.0	16	14	13	0	13-0	10	.296
2001—Lynchburg (Caro.)	4	0	1.000	1.50	0.89	22	0	0	0	...	7-...	36.0	18	7	6	0	14-1	40	.145
—Altoona (East.)	2	2	.500	4.14	1.59	27	1	0	0	...	1-...	37.0	34	22	17	2	25-2	35	.239
2002—Lynchburg (Caro.)	4	4	.500	1.61	0.96	55	0	0	0	...	29-...	72.2	52	18	13	1	18-1	83	.205
2003—Kansas City (A.L.)	6	5	.545	4.82	1.52	50	2	0	0	6	2-5	80.1	82	44	43	8	40-4	57	.271
2004—Omaha (PCL)	2	1	.667	3.20	1.38	32	1	0	0	...	3-...	56.1	60	22	20	2	18-0	50	.278
—Kansas City (A.L.)	2	2	.500	4.84	1.58	30	0	0	0	4	0-3	35.1	41	22	19	5	15-3	22	.287
2005—Kansas City (A.L.)	6	8	.429	4.79	1.57	21	20	1	0	0	0-0	114.2	129	67	61	11	51-2	49	.289
Major League totals (3 years)	14	15	.483	4.81	1.55	101	22	1	0	10	2-8	230.1	252	133	123	24	106-9	128	.283

CARRASCO, HECTOR   P

PERSONAL: Born October 22, 1969, in San Pedro de Macoris, Dominican Republic. ... 6-2/220. ... Throws right, bats right. ... Full name: Hector Pacheco Pipo Carrasco. ... Name pronounced: kuh-RASS-koh. ... High school: Liceo Mattias Mella (San Pedro de Macoris, D.R.).

TRANSACTIONS/CAREER NOTES: Signed as a non-drafted free agent by New York Mets organization (March 20, 1988). ... Released by Mets (January 6, 1992). ... Signed by Houston Astros organization (January 21, 1992). ... Traded by Astros with P Brian Griffiths to Florida Marlins for P Tom Edens (November 17, 1992). ... Traded by Marlins to Cincinnati Reds (September 10, 1993), completing deal in which Reds traded P Chris Hammond to Marlins for 3B Gary Scott and a player to be named (March 27, 1993). ... On disabled list (May 12-June 1, 1994). ... Traded by Reds with P Scott Service to Kansas City Royals for OF Jon Nunnally and IF/OF Chris Stynes (July 15, 1997). ... Selected by Arizona Diamondbacks in second round (49th pick overall) of expansion draft (November 18, 1997). ... Claimed on waivers by Minnesota Twins (April 3, 1998). ... On disabled list (April 3-June 25, 1999); included rehabilitation assignments to Fort Myers and Salt Lake. ... Traded by Twins to Boston Red Sox for OF Lew Ford (September 10, 2000). ... Signed as a free agent by Toronto Blue Jays organization (January 9, 2001). ... Released by Blue Jays (March 28, 2001). ... Signed by Twins organization (March 31, 2001). ... Signed as a free agent by Texas Rangers organization (January 18, 2002). ... Signed as a free agent by Baltimore Orioles organization (March 1, 2003). ... Signed as a free agent by Kintetsu of the Japan League (February 13, 2004). ... Signed as a free agent by Washington Nationals organization (December 23, 2004).

CAREER HITTING: 1-for-26 (.038), 1 R, 0 2B, 0 3B, 0 HR, 0 RBI.

SCOUTING REPORT **Throws:** Carrasco relies on an 89-94 mph fastball. Also has a curveball, slider and changeup. **Tendencies:** He is throwing better than in previous years after losing 20 pounds. Fastball velocity has increased; occasionally cuts the fastball to run it away from righthanders. Slider is quick and has good depth and velocity. Rarely throws his curve; pitch loops, making it a more effective change of speed. Releases his change at the same point as his fastball, making it sink like a splitter. **Outlook:** Carrasco has a very resilient arm and is best suited for middle relief. Can set up occasionally. **Grade 6.5**

HECTOR CARRASCO'S PITCHING ZONE

.111	.238	.188
.370	.143	.280
.111	.100	.158

LEFTY-RIGHTY SPLITS

vs.	Avg.	AB	H	2B	3B	HR	RBI	BB	SO	OBP	Slg.
L	.208	149	31	7	0	3	14	19	33	.306	.315
R	.178	157	28	5	0	3	18	19	42	.276	.268

Year Team (League)	W	L	Pct.	ERA	WHIP	G	GS	CG	ShO	Hld.	Sv.-Opp.	IP	H	R	ER	HR	BB-IBB	SO	Avg.
1988— GC Mets (GCL)	0	2	.000	4.17	1.36	14	2	0	0	...	0-...	36.2	37	29	17	0	13-0	21	.248
1989— Kingsport (Appalachian)	1	6	.143	5.74	1.93	12	10	0	0	...	0-...	53.1	69	49	34	6	34-1	55	.314
1990— Kingsport (Appalachian)	0	0	...	4.05	1.35	3	1	0	0	...	0-...	6.2	8	3	3	1	1-0	5	.308
1991— Pittsfield (NYP)	0	1	.000	5.40	1.97	12	1	0	0	...	1-...	23.1	25	17	14	1	21-0	20	.263
1992— Asheville (S. Atl.)	5	5	.500	2.99	1.44	49	0	0	0	...	8-...	78.1	66	30	26	5	47-6	67	.237
1993— Kane Co. (Midw.)	6	12	.333	4.11	1.54	28	28	0	0	...	0-...	149.0	153	90	68	11	76-6	127	.266
1994— Cincinnati (N.L.)	5	6	.455	2.24	1.28	45	0	0	0	3	6-8	56.1	42	17	14	3	30-1	41	.210
1995— Cincinnati (N.L.)	2	7	.222	4.12	1.51	64	0	0	0	11	5-9	87.1	86	45	40	1	46-5	64	.257
1996— Cincinnati (N.L.)	4	3	.571	3.75	1.39	56	0	0	0	15	0-2	74.1	58	37	31	6	45-5	59	.214
—Indianapolis (A.A.)	0	1	.000	2.14	1.48	13	2	0	0	...	1-...	21.0	18	7	5	1	13-1	17	.222
1997— Indianapolis (A.A.)	0	0	...	6.23	1.85	3	0	0	0	...	1-...	4.1	5	3	3	1	3-0	4	.294
—Cincinnati (N.L.)	1	2	.333	3.68	1.48	38	0	0	0	5	0-0	51.1	51	25	21	3	25-2	46	.250
—Kansas City (A.L.)	1	6	.143	5.45	1.30	28	0	0	0	3	0-2	34.2	29	21	21	4	16-3	30	.227
1998— Minnesota (A.L.)	4	2	.667	4.38	1.72	63	0	0	0	10	1-2	61.2	75	30	30	4	31-1	46	.304
1999— Fort Myers (FSL)	0	0	...	4.50	1.50	1	1	0	0	...	0-...	2.0	2	1	1	0	1-0	1	.286
—Salt Lake (PCL)	1	0	1.000	0.00	0.92	3	0	0	0	...	1-...	4.1	3	0	0	0	1-0	3	.188
—Minnesota (A.L.)	2	3	.400	4.96	1.35	39	0	0	0	7	1-2	49.0	48	29	27	3	18-0	35	.261
2000— Minnesota (A.L.)	4	3	.571	4.25	1.50	61	0	0	0	7	1-5	72.0	75	38	34	6	33-0	57	.271
—Boston (A.L.)	1	1	.500	9.45	3.00	8	1	0	0	1	0-1	6.2	15	8	7	2	5-1	7	.469
2001— Minnesota (A.L.)	4	3	.571	4.64	1.45	56	0	0	0	1	1-2	73.2	77	40	38	8	30-3	70	.277
2002—			Did not play.																
2003— Ottawa (Int'l)	4	2	.667	2.22	1.16	33	0	0	0	...	4-...	44.2	32	11	11	2	20-2	47	.208
—Baltimore (A.L.)	2	6	.250	4.93	1.57	40	0	0	0	8	1-3	38.1	40	22	21	5	20-3	27	.270
2004— Kintetsu (Jp. Pac.)	8	8	.500	5.57	1.46	53	5	0	0	...	5-...	76.0	74	52	47	12	37-...	70	...
2005— New Orleans (PCL)	1	0	1.000	0.00	0.75	6	0	0	0	...	4-4	8.0	4	1	0	0	2-0	10	.143
—Washington (N.L.)	5	4	.556	2.04	1.10	64	5	0	0	8	2-4	88.1	59	23	20	6	38-7	75	.193
American League totals (6 years)	18	24	.429	4.77	1.52	295	1	0	0	37	5-17	336.0	359	188	178	32	153-11	272	.277
National League totals (5 years)	17	22	.436	3.17	1.34	267	5	0	0	42	13-23	357.2	296	147	126	19	184-20	285	.225
Major League totals (10 years)	35	46	.432	3.94	1.43	562	6	0	0	79	18-40	693.2	655	335	304	51	337-31	557	.251

CHAMPIONSHIP SERIES RECORD

Year Team (League)	W	L	Pct.	ERA	WHIP	G	GS	CG	ShO	Hld.	Sv.-Opp.	IP	H	R	ER	HR	BB-IBB	SO	Avg.
1995— Cincinnati (N.L.)	0	0	...	0.00	0.75	1	0	0	0	...	0-...	1.1	1	0	0	...	0-...	3	...

CARROLL, JAMEY   2B/SS

PERSONAL: Born February 18, 1974, in Evansville, Ind. ... 5-9/170. ... Bats right, throws right. ... Full name: Jamey Blake Carroll. ... High school: Castle (Newburgh, Ind.). ... College: Evansville.

TRANSACTIONS/CAREER NOTES: Selected by Montreal Expos organization in 14th round of 1996 free-agent draft. ... Expos franchise transferred to Washington, D.C., and renamed Washington Nationals for 2005 season (December 3, 2004).
2005 GAMES PLAYED BY POSITION (MLB): 2B—63, SS—41, 3B—12.

SCOUTING REPORT Carroll is an overachiever with outstanding makeup. Has a short stroke. Is a gap hitter with limited power. Can run. Can play second or third base and has good hands. Has average range but makes quick pivots and has good instincts. *Grade 4.8*

JAMEY CARROLL'S HITTING ZONE

.240	.250	.320
.279	.237	.222
.308	.154	.214

LEFTY-RIGHTY SPLITS

vs.	Avg.	AB	H	2B	3B	HR	RBI	BB	SO	OBP	Slg.
L	.293	82	24	3	0	0	7	10	11	.362	.329
R	.235	221	52	5	1	0	15	24	44	.323	.267

Year Team (League)	Pos.	G	AB	R	H	2B	3B	HR	RBI	BB	SO	HBP	GDP	SB-CS	Avg.	OBP	SLG	OPS	E	Avg.
1996—Vermont (NYP) SS-2B-3B		54	203	40	56	6	1	0	17	29	25	0	1	16-11	.276	.363	.315	.679	9	.960
1997—W.P. Beach (FSL)	SS-2B	121	407	56	99	19	1	0	38	43	48	4	4	17-11	.243	.319	.295	.614	22	.951
1998—Jupiter (Fla. St.)	2B-SS	55	222	40	58	5	0	0	14	24	26	5	2	11-4	.261	.345	.284	.629	6	.977
—Harrisburg (East.)	2B-SS	75	261	43	66	11	3	0	20	41	29	5	4	11-5	.253	.365	.318	.683	17	.953
1999—Harrisburg (East.)	2B-SS	141	561	78	164	34	5	5	63	48	58	5	13	21-10	.292	.351	.398	.749	14	.979
2000—Ottawa (Int'l) 2B-3B-SS		91	349	53	97	17	2	2	23	33	32	2	9	6-3	.278	.342	.355	.697	13	.967
—Harrisburg (East.)	3B-SS	45	169	23	49	5	3	0	18	12	13	0	5	8-2	.290	.335	.355	.690	6	.960
2001—Ottawa (Int'l) 2B-SS-3B		83	267	26	64	8	2	0	16	18	41	2	5	5-5	.240	.292	.285	.576	9	.972
2002—Harrisburg (East.)	2B	3	9	1	4	0	0	0	1	3	0	0	0	0-0	.444	.583	.444	1.028	0	1.000
—Ottawa (Int'l) 2B-3B-SS		117	421	57	118	19	2	8	49	37	39	3	8	6-10	.280	.342	.392	.734	7	.983
—Montreal (N.L.)	3B-SS-2B	16	71	16	22	5	3	1	6	4	12	0	1	1-0	.310	.347	.507	.854	4	.925
2003—Montreal (N.L.) 3B-SS-2B																				
DH		105	227	31	59	10	1	1	10	19	39	3	10	5-2	.260	.323	.326	.649	5	.976
2004—Montreal (N.L.) 2B-SS-3B																				
OF		102	218	36	63	14	2	0	16	32	21	1	3	5-1	.289	.378	.372	.750	3	.988
2005—Washington (N.L.) 2B-SS-3B		113	303	44	76	8	1	0	22	34	55	5	2	3-4	.251	.333	.284	.617	5	.987
Major League totals (4 years)		336	819	127	220	37	7	2	54	89	127	9	16	14-7	.269	.344	.338	.682	17	.981

CARTER, LANCE   P

PERSONAL: Born December 18, 1974, in Bradenton, Fla. ... 6-1/190. ... Throws right, bats right. ... Full name: Lance David Carter. ... High school: Manatee (Bradenton, Fla.). ... Junior college: Manatee (Fla.) Community College.
TRANSACTIONS/CAREER NOTES: Selected by Minnesota Twins organization in 41st round of 1993 free-agent draft; did not sign. ... Selected by Kansas City Royals organization in 21st round of 1994 free-agent draft. ... Signed as a free agent by Tampa Bay Devil Rays organization (January 22, 2002). ... On suspended list (June 7-10, 2005).
CAREER HITTING: 0-for-0 (.000), 0 R, 0 2B, 0 3B, 0 HR, 0 RBI.

SCOUTING REPORT **Throws:** This former closer uses a sinking changeup as his out pitch. Also throws a fastball in the 85-89 mph range, a slider and a curveball. *Tendencies:* Carter will throw his change at any time. Has command of all his pitches to both sides of the plate. Fastball has good life down in the zone. Using his curve more than his slider; curve is a looping one to left-handers. Slider thrown to righthanders is more of a cut fastball. *Outlook:* The versatile Carter can pitch in most any role, but he's best suited for long and middle relief. Deception and ability to change speeds allow him to go through a batting order. *Grade 7*

LANCE CARTER'S PITCHING ZONE

.300	.429	.231
.268	.286	.364
.222	.308	.294

LEFTY-RIGHTY SPLITS

vs.	Avg.	AB	H	2B	3B	HR	RBI	BB	SO	OBP	Slg.
L	.309	110	34	8	2	3	27	2	12	.327	.500
R	.248	109	27	2	1	6	17	13	10	.320	.450

Year Team (League)	W	L	Pct.	ERA	WHIP	G	GS	CG	ShO	Hld.	Sv.-Opp.	IP	H	R	ER	HR	BB-IBB	SO	Avg.
1994—Eugene (Northwest)	1	0	1.000	5.47	1.56	8	7	0	0	...	0-...	26.1	26	17	16	2	15-0	23	.265
—GC Royals (GCL)	3	0	1.000	0.29	0.71	5	5	0	0	...	0-...	31.0	19	1	1	1	3-0	36	.179
1995—Springfield (Midw.)	9	5	.643	3.99	1.26	27	24	1	1	...	0-...	137.2	151	77	61	14	22-0	118	.276
1996—Wilmington (Caro.)	3	6	.333	6.34	1.50	16	12	0	0	...	0-...	65.1	81	50	46	8	17-2	49	.298
1997—			Did not play.																
1998—Lansing (Midw.)	3	1	.750	0.67	1.07	15	2	0	0	...	2-...	40.1	34	6	3	0	9-1	37	.231
—Wilmington (Caro.)	1	4	.200	3.29	1.23	28	1	0	0	...	5-...	52.0	50	21	19	5	14-1	61	.262
1999—Wichita (Texas)	5	2	.714	0.78	1.09	44	0	0	0	...	13-...	69.2	49	10	6	1	27-5	77	.195
—Kansas City (A.L.)	0	1	.000	5.06	1.13	6	0	0	0	0	0-0	5.1	3	3	3	2	3-0	3	.167
2000—Omaha (PCL)	2	8	.200	4.95	1.39	34	6	0	0	...	5-...	76.1	88	46	42	13	18-1	51	.295
2001—			Did not play.																
2002—Durham (Int'l)	12	2	.857	2.80	0.93	33	18	2	1	...	1-...	132.0	111	43	41	15	12-0	90	.230
—Tampa Bay (A.L.)	2	0	1.000	1.33	0.98	8	0	0	0	0	2-2	20.1	15	3	3	2	5-1	14	.203
2003—Tampa Bay (A.L.)	7	5	.583	4.33	1.15	62	0	0	0	2	26-33	79.0	72	39	38	12	19-6	47	.242
2004—Tampa Bay (A.L.)	3	3	.500	3.47	1.24	56	0	0	0	7	0-1	80.1	77	32	31	12	22-2	36	.252
2005—Durham (Int'l)	1	5	.167	5.14	1.49	8	7	0	0	...	0-0	35.0	40	24	20	8	12-0	30	.290
—Tampa Bay (A.L.)	1	2	.333	4.89	1.33	39	0	0	0	5	1-4	57.0	61	31	31	9	15-1	22	.279
Major League totals (5 years)	13	11	.542	3.94	1.21	171	0	0	0	14	29-40	242.0	228	108	106	37	65-10	122	.249

CARVAJAL, MARCOS　　　　　　　　　　P

PERSONAL: Born August 19, 1984, in Bolivar, Venezuela. ... 6-4/175. ... Throws right, bats right. ... Full name: Marcos Jose Carvajal.

TRANSACTIONS/CAREER NOTES: Signed as non-drafted free agent by Los Angeles Dodgers (September 26, 2000). ... Selected by Milwaukee Brewers from Dodgers organization in Rule 5 major league draft (December 13, 2004). ... Traded by Brewers to Colorado Rockies for cash (December 13, 2004).

CAREER HITTING: 1-for-4 (.250), 0 R, 0 2B, 0 3B, 0 HR, 2 RBI.

MARCOS CARVAJAL'S PITCHING ZONE

.192	.250	.214
.433	.250	.286
.125	.500	.000

LEFTY-RIGHTY SPLITS

vs.	Avg.	AB	H	2B	3B	HR	RBI	BB	SO	OBP	Slg.
L	.233	86	20	6	0	2	9	9	24	.305	.372
R	.278	115	32	7	0	6	25	12	23	.356	.496

Year Team (League)	W	L	Pct.	ERA	WHIP	G	GS	CG	ShO	Hld.	Sv.-Opp.	IP	H	R	ER	HR	BB-IBB	SO	Avg.
2001— La Pradera (VSL)	1	2	.333	2.12	1.18	9	6	0	0	...	1-...	29.2	24	11	7	0	11-0	26	...
2002— GC Dodgers (GCL)	3	2	.600	1.71	1.07	13	5	0	0	...	0-...	42.0	30	12	8	0	15-0	35	.201
2003— Ogden (Pion.)	2	1	.667	3.08	1.42	23	0	0	0	...	2-...	38.0	32	16	13	1	22-0	50	.224
2004— Columbus (S. Atl.)	4	2	.667	1.88	1.18	36	0	0	0	...	1-...	72.0	50	19	15	2	35-0	72	.198
—Jacksonville (Sou.)	0	0	...	0.00	1.33	1	0	0	0	...	0-...	3.0	2	0	0	0	2-0	2	.182
2005— Colorado (N.L.)	0	2	.000	5.09	1.38	39	0	0	0	0	0-1	53.0	52	30	30	8	21-0	47	.259
Major League totals (1 year)	0	2	.000	5.09	1.38	39	0	0	0	0	0-1	53.0	52	30	30	8	21-0	47	.259

C　　CASANOVA, RAUL　　　　　　　　　　C

PERSONAL: Born August 23, 1972, in Humacao, Puerto Rico. ... 6-0/216. ... Bats both, throws right. ... High school: Ponce (Puerto Rico).

TRANSACTIONS/CAREER NOTES: Selected by New York Mets organization in eighth round of 1990 free-agent draft. ... Traded by Mets to San Diego Padres (December 7, 1992), completing deal in which Padres traded SS Tony Fernandez to Mets for P Wally Whitehurst, OF D.J. Dozier and a player to be named (October 26, 1992). ... Traded by Padres with P Richie Lewis and OF Melvin Nieves to Detroit Tigers for Ps Sean Bergman and Cade Gaspar and OF Todd Steverson (March 22, 1996). ... On disabled list (June 19-August 13, 1996); included rehabilitation assignments to Jacksonville and Toledo. ... On disabled list (April 25-May 28 and July 21, 1998-remainder of season); included rehabilitation assignments to Toledo. ... On disabled list (March 31-July 12, 1999); included rehabilitation assignments to GCL Tigers, Lakeland and Toledo. ... Signed as a free agent by Colorado Rockies organization (December 15, 1999). ... Released by Rockies (March 24, 2000). ... Signed by Milwaukee Brewers organization (March 25, 2000). ... On disabled list (May 17-August 23, 2002); included rehabilitation assignment to Indianapolis. ... Released by Brewers (September 3, 2002). ... Signed by Baltimore Orioles (September 11, 2002). ... Released by Orioles (October 1, 2002). ... Signed by Rockies organization (December 27, 2002). ... Released by Rockies (July 29, 2003). ... Signed as a free agent by Boston Red Sox organization (May 14, 2004). ... Traded by Red Sox to Kansas City Royals for a player to be named (June 25, 2004). ... Signed as a free agent by Chicago White Sox organization (January 19, 2005).

2005 GAMES PLAYED BY POSITION (MLB): C—6.

LEFTY-RIGHTY SPLITS

vs.	Avg.	AB	H	2B	3B	HR	RBI	BB	SO	OBP	Slg.
L	.000	2	0	0	0	0	0	0	1	.000	.000
R	.333	3	1	0	0	0	0	0	0	.333	.333

								BATTING												FIELDING	
Year Team (League)	Pos.	G	AB	R	H	2B	3B	HR	RBI	BB	SO	HBP	GDP	SB-CS	Avg.	OBP	SLG	OPS		E	Avg.
1990— GC Mets (GCL)	C	23	65	4	5	0	0	0	1	4	16	0	2	0-1	.077	.130	.077	.207		8	.953
1991— GC Mets (GCL)	C	32	111	19	27	4	2	0	9	12	22	2	4	3-0	.243	.325	.315	.640		5	.979
—Kingsport (Appalachian)	C	5	18	0	1	0	0	0	0	1	10	0	1	0-0	.056	.105	.056	.161		1	.975
1992— Columbia (S. Atl.)	C	5	18	2	3	0	0	0	1	1	4	0	2	0-0	.167	.211	.167	.378		0	1.000
—Kingsport (Appalachian)	C	42	137	25	37	9	1	4	27	26	25	4	7	3-1	.270	.401	.438	.839		6	.982
1993— Waterloo (Midw.)	3B-C	76	227	32	58	12	0	6	30	21	46	1	5	0-1	.256	.321	.388	.709		10	.976
1994— Rancho Cuca. (Calif.)	C	123	471	83	160	27	2	23	120	43	97	9	16	1-4	.340	.403	.552	.955		14	.979
1995— Memphis (Sou.)	C-DH	89	306	42	83	18	0	12	44	25	51	4	7	4-1	.271	.330	.448	.778	*	12	.980
1996— Toledo (Int'l)	C-DH	49	161	23	44	11	0	8	28	20	24	2	11	0-1	.273	.353	.491	.844		2	.992
—Detroit (A.L.)	C-DH	25	85	6	16	1	0	4	9	6	18	0	...	0-0	.188	.242	.341	.583		3	.978
—Jacksonville (Sou.)	C-DH	8	30	5	10	2	0	4	9	2	7	0	0	0-0	.333	.375	.800	1.175		0	1.000
1997— Toledo (Int'l)	C	12	41	1	8	0	0	1	3	3	8	0	1	0-0	.195	.244	.268	.512		2	.977
—Detroit (A.L.)	C-DH	101	304	27	74	10	1	5	24	26	48	3	...	1-1	.243	.308	.332	.641		9	.985
1998— Detroit (A.L.)	C	16	42	4	6	2	0	1	3	5	10	1	...	0-0	.143	.250	.262	.512		3	.967
—Toledo (Int'l)	C-DH	50	171	17	44	8	0	7	26	22	28	1	6	0-0	.257	.350	.427	.777		9	.973
1999— GC Tigers (GCL)	C-C	2	5	1	4	0	0	1	1	0	0	0	0	0-0	.800	.800	1.400	2.200		1	1.000
—Lakeland (Fla. St.)	C-DH	4	12	3	6	2	0	1	6	0	1	1	0	0-0	.500	.538	.917	1.455		0	1.000
—Toledo (Int'l)	C-DH	44	160	21	33	9	0	6	23	7	28	1	9	0-0	.206	.243	.375	.618		3	.985
2000— Indianapolis (Int'l)	C	20	73	10	21	2	0	5	12	7	10	1	3	0-1	.288	.354	.521	.875		2	.985
—Milwaukee (N.L.)	C-DH	86	231	20	57	13	3	6	36	26	48	4	...	1-2	.247	.331	.407	.738		4	.990
2001— Milwaukee (N.L.)	C-DH	71	192	21	50	10	0	11	33	12	29	1	...	0-0	.260	.303	.484	.787		3	.991
2002— Milwaukee (N.L.)	C	31	87	3	16	1	0	1	8	10	18	1	...	0-0	.184	.273	.230	.503		1	.994
—Indianapolis (Int'l)	C	14	43	2	12	4	0	0	8	3	10	0	0	0-0	.279	.313	.372	.685		0	1.000
—Baltimore (A.L.)	C	2	1	0	0	0	0	0	0	0	1	0	0	0-0	.000	.000	.000	.000		0	1.000
2003— Colo. Springs (PCL)	C-1B	60	193	25	58	20	0	4	36	14	21	1	9	0-0	.301	.349	.466	.815		8	.978
—Ottawa (Int'l)	C-1B	26	91	12	26	5	0	3	14	10	15	2	4	0-0	.286	.365	.440	.805		2	.960
2004— Pawtucket (Int'l)	C-1B	23	74	4	20	2	1	1	9	10	15	0	1	0-0	.270	.353	.365	.718		2	.988
—Omaha (PCL)	C-1B	58	223	37	72	12	0	10	49	15	36	3	10	1-0	.323	.370	.511	.881		3	.993
2005— Charlotte (Int'l)	C-DH-1B	70	233	25	62	13	0	13	42	20	29	1	13	0-0	.266	.325	.489	.815		5	.990
—Chicago (A.L.)	C	6	5	0	1	0	0	0	0	0	1	0	0	0-0	.200	.200	.200	.400		0	1.000
American League totals (5 years)		150	437	37	97	13	1	10	36	37	78	4	...	1-1	.222	.288	.325	.613		15	.982
National League totals (3 years)		188	510	44	123	24	3	18	77	48	95	6	...	1-2	.241	.311	.406	.716		8	.991
Major League totals (7 years)		338	947	81	220	37	4	28	113	85	173	10	0	2-3	.232	.300	.369	.669		23	.987

PERSONAL: Born July 2, 1974, in Willingboro, N.J. ... 6-4/225. ... Bats left, throws right. ... Full name: Sean Thomas Casey. ... High school: Upper St. Clair (Pittsburgh). ... College: Richmond.

TRANSACTIONS/CAREER NOTES: Selected by Cleveland Indians organization in second round of 1995 free-agent draft. ... Traded by Indians to Cincinnati Reds for P Dave Burba (March 30, 1998). ... On disabled list (April 2-May 5, 1998); included rehabilitation assignment to Indianapolis. ... On disabled list (April 2-19, 2000). ... On disabled list (July 23-August 9 and September 10, 2002-remainder of season); included rehabilitation assignment to Louisville. ... On suspended list (July 2-4, 2003). ... On disabled list (June 28-July 14, 2004).

2005 GAMES PLAYED BY POSITION (MLB): 1B—134, DH—1.

SCOUTING REPORT *Offense:* Casey is an excellent contact hitter with a long stroke, but he has good plate coverage and the ability to adjust to off-speed and breaking pitches. Is good against lefthanders. More of a line-drive, gap hitter now. Likes to hit around the ball but goes with the pitch. Is quick enough to hook the ball on the inside part of the plate. *Defense:* Knee problems have affected his mobility, but Casey has good hands. Range to either side is limited. Doesn't have good lower-body flexibility now. *Outlook:* He is an outstanding individual in the clubhouse and one of the game's most popular players. Still a good offensive player but needs to show more power, especially in his home park. *Grade 8.4*

SEAN CASEY'S HITTING ZONE

.154	.632	.308
.370	.370	.286
.400	.286	.383

LEFTY-RIGHTY SPLITS

vs.	Avg.	AB	H	2B	3B	HR	RBI	BB	SO	OBP	Slg.
L	.335	197	66	13	0	2	21	16	20	.389	.431
R	.298	332	99	19	0	7	37	32	28	.361	.419

Year	Team (League)	Pos.	G	AB	R	H	2B	3B	HR	RBI	BB	SO	HBP	GDP	SB-CS	Avg.	OBP	SLG	OPS	E	Avg.
1995—Watertown (NYP)		1B	55	207	26	68	18	0	2	37	18	21	1	6	3-0	.329	.380	.444	.824	8	.985
1996—Kinston (Carol.)		1B-DH	92	344	62	114	31	3	12	57	36	47	6	5	1-1	.331	.402	.544	.946	6	.991
1997—Akron (East.)		1B-DH	62	241	38	93	19	1	10	66	23	34	5	5	0-1	.386	.448	.598	1.046	5	.988
—Buffalo (A.A.)		DH-1B	20	72	12	26	7	0	5	18	9	11	1	0	0-0	.361	.439	.667	1.106	0	1.000
—Cleveland (A.L.)		1B	6	10	1	2	0	0	0	1	1	2	1	0	0-0	.200	.333	.200	.533	0	1.000
1998—Cincinnati (N.L.)		1B	96	302	44	82	21	1	7	52	43	45	3	11	1-1	.272	.365	.417	.782	4	.994
—Indianapolis (Int'l)		1B-DH	27	95	14	31	8	1	1	13	14	10	1	0	0-0	.326	.418	.463	.881	2	.991
1999—Cincinnati (N.L.)		1B-DH	151	594	103	197	42	3	25	99	61	88	9	15	0-2	.332	.399	.539	.938	6	.995
2000—Cincinnati (N.L.)		1B	133	480	69	151	33	2	20	85	52	80	7	16	1-0	.315	.385	.517	.902	6	.995
2001—Cincinnati (N.L.)		1B-DH	145	533	69	165	40	4	13	89	43	63	9	16	3-1	.310	.369	.458	.827	7	.994
2002—Cincinnati (N.L.)		1B-DH	120	425	56	111	25	0	6	42	43	47	5	11	2-1	.261	.334	.362	.696	7	.993
—Louisville (Int'l)		DH	2	8	2	4	0	0	1	3	1	0	0	0	0-0	.500	.556	.875	1.431	...	...
2003—Cincinnati (N.L.)		1B	147	573	71	167	19	3	14	80	51	58	2	19	4-0	.291	.350	.408	.758	6	.996
2004—Cincinnati (N.L.)		1B-DH	146	571	101	185	44	2	24	99	46	36	10	16	2-0	.324	.381	.534	.915	8	.994
2005—Cincinnati (N.L.)		1B-DH	137	529	75	165	32	0	9	58	48	48	5	* 27	2-0	.312	.371	.423	.795	2	.998
American League totals (1 year)			6	10	1	2	0	0	0	1	1	2	1	0	0-0	.200	.333	.200	.533	0	1.000
National League totals (8 years)			1075	4007	588	1223	256	11	118	604	387	465	50	131	15-5	.305	.371	.463	.834	46	.995
Major League totals (9 years)			1081	4017	589	1225	256	11	118	605	388	467	51	131	15-5	.305	.371	.462	.833	46	.995

ALL-STAR GAME RECORD

	G	AB	R	H	2B	3B	HR	RBI	BB	SO	HBP	GDP	SB-CS	Avg.	OBP	SLG	OPS	E	Avg.
All-Star Game totals (2 years)	2	2	0	0	0	0	0	0	0	1	0	0	0-0	.000	.000	.000	.000	0	1.000

PERSONAL: Born December 6, 1977, in Tampa. ... 6-0/185. ... Bats right, throws right. ... Full name: Kevin Forrest Cash. ... High school: Gaither (Tampa). ... College: Florida State.

TRANSACTIONS/CAREER NOTES: Signed as a non-drafted free agent by Toronto Blue Jays organization (August 7, 1999). ... On disabled list (May 24-June 10, 2004). ... Traded by Blue Jays to Tampa Bay Devil Rays for P Chad Gaudin (December 12, 2004). ... On disabled list (March 26-May 7, 2005); included rehabilitation assignment to Durham.

2005 GAMES PLAYED BY POSITION (MLB): C—13.

SCOUTING REPORT *Offense:* He is a spray hitter who has not shown he can hit big-league pitching. Seems incapable of consistent strike zone judgment; either lays off everything or swings at everything. At one time showed an ability to use the gaps but began pulling too much, especially with a slow bat. *Defense:* He has a cannon arm, good footwork and soft hands and is adept at blocking pitches. Has a good mind for calling a game and has learned how to handle pitchers. *Outlook:* Plus arm makes him a defensive standout, but his below-average hitting skills will keep him in a reserve role. *Grade 5.8*

LEFTY-RIGHTY SPLITS

vs.	Avg.	AB	H	2B	3B	HR	RBI	BB	SO	OBP	Slg.
L	.250	8	2	0	0	1	1	1	4	.333	.625
R	.130	23	3	1	0	1	1	0	9	.167	.304

Year	Team (League)	Pos.	G	AB	R	H	2B	3B	HR	RBI	BB	SO	HBP	GDP	SB-CS	Avg.	OBP	SLG	OPS	E	Avg.
2000—Hagerstown (SAL)		C	59	196	28	48	10	1	10	27	22	54	1	7	5-3	.245	.323	.459	.782	10	.974
2001—Dunedin (Fla. St.)		C	105	371	55	105	27	0	12	66	43	80	8	11	4-3	.283	.369	.453	.822	12	.979
2002—Tennessee (Sou.)		C	55	213	38	59	15	1	8	44	36	44	1	4	5-2	.277	.381	.469	.850	4	.983
—Syracuse (Int'l)		C	67	236	27	52	18	0	10	26	25	72	2	3	0-1	.220	.299	.424	.723	4	.989
—Toronto (A.L.)		C	7	14	1	2	0	0	0	0	1	4	0	1	0-0	.143	.200	.143	.343	1	.968
2003—Syracuse (Int'l)		C-DH-3B	93	326	37	88	28	2	8	37	29	81	2	14	1-0	.270	.331	.442	.772	1	.998
—Toronto (A.L.)		C	34	106	10	15	3	0	1	8	4	22	1	6	0-0	.142	.179	.198	.377	1	.995
2004—Toronto (A.L.)		C	60	181	18	35	9	0	4	21	10	59	4	3	0-0	.193	.249	.309	.558	2	.994
2005—Tampa Bay (A.L.)		C	13	31	4	5	1	0	2	2	1	13	1	1	0-0	.161	.212	.387	.599	0	1.000
—Durham (Int'l)		C-DH-1B OF	42	147	25	43	10	0	9	27	12	42	3	3	0-0	.293	.354	.544	.898	3	.990
Major League totals (4 years)			114	332	33	57	13	0	7	31	16	98	6	13	0-0	.172	.221	.274	.495	4	.994

C

CASSIDY, SCOTT   P

PERSONAL: Born October 3, 1975, in Syracuse, N.Y. ... 6-2/175. ... Throws right, bats right. ... Full name: Scott Robert Cassidy. ... College: LeMoyne (N.Y.).
TRANSACTIONS/CAREER NOTES: Signed as non-drafted free agent by Toronto Blue Jays organization (May 21, 1998). ... Traded by Blue Jays to Boston Red Sox for cash (April 18, 2004). ... Traded by Red Sox to San Diego Padres for OF Adam Hyzdu (July 19, 2005).
CAREER HITTING: 0-for-1 (.000), 0 R, 0 2B, 0 3B, 0 HR, 0 RBI.

SCOTT CASSIDY'S PITCHING ZONE

.200	1.000	.250
.500	.667	.300
.000	.500	.333

LEFTY-RIGHTY SPLITS

vs.	Avg.	AB	H	2B	3B	HR	RBI	BB	SO	OBP	Slg.
L	.364	22	8	1	2	1	3	1	6	.391	.727
R	.333	33	11	3	0	2	10	2	6	.371	.606

Year Team (League)	W	L	Pct.	ERA	WHIP	G	GS	CG	ShO	Hld.	Sv.-Opp.	IP	H	R	ER	HR	BB-IBB	SO	Avg.
1998— Medicine Hat (Pio.)	8	1	.889	2.43	1.05	15	14	0	0	...	0-...	81.1	71	31	22	4	14-0	82	.236
1999— Hagerstown (SAL)	13	7	.650	3.27	1.06	27	27	1	0	...	0-...	170.2	151	78	62	13	30-0	178	.236
2000— Dunedin (Fla. St.)	9	3	.750	1.33	0.99	14	13	1	0	...	0-...	88.0	53	15	13	4	34-2	89	.177
— Tennessee (Sou.)	2	2	.500	5.91	1.48	8	7	0	0	...	0-...	42.2	48	30	28	7	15-0	39	.289
2001— Tennessee (Sou.)	6	6	.500	3.44	1.09	16	15	4	3	...	0-...	96.2	78	45	37	10	27-0	81	.218
— Syracuse (Int'l)	3	3	.500	2.71	1.37	11	11	0	0	...	0-...	63.0	60	24	19	6	26-0	48	.247
2002— Syracuse (Int'l)	1	0	1.000	4.00	0.89	3	2	0	0	...	0-...	9.0	8	4	4	2	0-0	4	.242
— Toronto (A.L.)	1	4	.200	5.73	1.47	58	0	0	0	7	0-7	66.0	52	42	42	12	32-3	48	.222
2003— Syracuse (Int'l)	3	4	.429	3.24	1.50	57	0	0	0	...	4-...	80.2	75	31	29	3	46-7	75	.253
2004— Pawtucket (Int'l)	5	3	.625	3.46	1.36	28	12	0	0	...	1-...	80.2	72	34	31	10	38-0	72	.242
2005— Boston (A.L.)	0	0	...	40.50	6.00	1	0	0	0	0	0-0	0.2	4	3	3	0	0-0	0	.667
— Pawtucket (Int'l)	6	3	.667	4.05	1.28	26	3	0	0	3	0-0	60.0	54	31	27	5	23-2	66	.243
— Portland (PCL)	0	1	.000	1.89	0.89	17	0	0	0	1	11-11	19.0	10	5	4	2	7-1	19	.156
— San Diego (N.L.)	1	1	.500	6.57	1.46	10	0	0	0	1	0-0	12.1	15	10	9	3	3-0	12	.306
American League totals (2 years)	1	4	.200	6.08	1.32	59	0	0	0	7	0-7	66.2	56	45	45	12	32-3	48	.233
National League totals (1 year)	1	1	.500	6.57	1.46	10	0	0	0	1	0-0	12.1	15	10	9	3	3-0	12	.306
Major League totals (2 years)	2	5	.286	6.15	1.34	69	0	0	0	8	0-7	79.0	71	55	54	15	35-3	60	.246

CASTILLA, VINNY   3B

PERSONAL: Born July 4, 1967, in Oaxaca, Mexico. ... 6-1/205. ... Bats right, throws right. ... Full name: Vinicio Soria Castilla. ... Name pronounced: cas-TEE-yah. ... High school: Instituto Carlos Gracida (Oaxaca, Mexico). ... College: Benito Suarez (Mexico).
TRANSACTIONS/CAREER NOTES: Contract sold by Saltillo to Atlanta Braves organization (March 19, 1990). ... Selected by Colorado Rockies in second round (40th pick overall) of expansion draft (November 17, 1992). ... On disabled list (May 20-June 4, 1993). ... Traded by Rockies to Tampa Bay Devil Rays for P Rolando Arrojo and IF Aaron Ledesma (December 13, 1999). ... On disabled list (March 25-April 11, June 14-July 3 and July 30-September 4, 2000); included rehabilitation assignment to Durham. ... Released by Devil Rays (May 10, 2001). ... Signed by Houston Astros (May 15, 2001). ... Signed as a free agent by Braves (December 11, 2001). ... Signed as a free agent by Rockies (December 11, 2003). ... Signed as a free agent by Montreal Expos (November 16, 2004). ... Expos franchise transferred to Washington, D.C., and renamed Washington Nationals for 2005 season (December 3, 2004). ... Traded by Nationals to San Diego Padres for P Brian Lawrence and cash (November 3, 2005).
2005 GAMES PLAYED BY POSITION (MLB): 3B—138.

SCOUTING REPORT *Offense:* Castilla still has a quick bat and is one of the best high fast-ball hitters in the majors. Has a long stroke and likes to hit early in the count. Will chase a lot of fastballs and still strikes out too much. Knee problems caused trouble hitting the ball the other way. Can't run or steal bases. *Defense:* He has very good hands and an extremely strong arm. Lost range and quickness because of his knee problems. Moves better to his left than his right. *Outlook:* Castilla is near the end of his career, so don't expect him to duplicate his 2004 season. But he still is an experienced hitter and could expand his numbers from 2005. *Grade 7.5*

VINNY CASTILLA'S HITTING ZONE

.278	.357	.207
.248	.378	.362
.315	.143	.368

LEFTY-RIGHTY SPLITS

vs.	Avg.	AB	H	2B	3B	HR	RBI	BB	SO	OBP	Slg.
L	.314	118	37	11	0	1	15	18	14	.401	.432
R	.234	376	88	25	1	11	51	25	68	.292	.394

Year Team (League)	Pos.	G	AB	R	H	2B	3B	HR	RBI	BB	SO	HBP	GDP	SB-CS	Avg.	OBP	SLG	OPS	E	Avg.
1987— Saltillo (Mex.)	3B	13	27	0	5	2	0	0	1	0	5	...	...	0-0	.185	...	.259	...	1	.976
1988— Salt.-Monc. (Mex.)	SS	50	124	22	30	2	2	5	18	8	29	...	...	1-4	.242	...	.411	...	13	.924
1989— Saltillo (Mex.)	3B-SS	128	462	70	142	25	13	10	58	33	70	...	...	11-12	.307	...	.483	...	34	.950
1990— Sumter (S. Atl.)	SS	93	339	47	91	15	2	9	53	28	54	8	8	2-5	.268	.334	.404	.738	23	.952
— Greenville (Sou.)	SS	46	170	20	40	5	1	4	16	13	23	2	7	4-4	.235	.296	.347	.643	7	.971
1991— Greenville (Sou.)	SS	66	259	34	70	17	3	7	44	9	35	2	4	0-1	.270	.296	.440	.736	11	.965
— Richmond (Int'l)	SS	67	240	25	54	7	4	7	36	14	32	3	4	1-1	.225	.271	.375	.646	12	.962
— Atlanta (N.L.)	SS	12	5	1	1	0	0	0	0	0	2	0	0	0-0	.200	.200	.200	.400	1	1.000
1992— Richmond (Int'l)	SS	127	449	49	113	29	1	7	44	21	68	4	19	1-2	.252	.288	.367	.655	31	.944
— Atlanta (N.L.)	3B-SS	9	16	1	4	1	0	0	1	1	4	1	0	0-0	.250	.333	.313	.646	1	.933
1993— Colorado (N.L.)	SS	105	337	36	86	9	7	9	30	13	45	2	10	2-5	.255	.283	.404	.686	11	.975
1994— Colorado (N.L.)	SS-2B-3B																			
	1B	52	130	16	43	11	1	3	18	7	23	0	7	2-1	.331	.357	.500	.857	2	.986
— Colo. Springs (PCL)	3B-2B-SS	22	78	13	19	6	1	1	11	7	11	1	6	0-0	.244	.303	.385	.688	3	.964
1995— Colorado (N.L.)	3B-SS	139	527	82	163	34	2	32	90	30	87	4	15	2-8	.309	.347	.564	.911	15	.959
1996— Colorado (N.L.)	3B	160	629	97	191	34	0	40	113	35	88	5	20	7-2	.304	.343	.548	.892	20	.960
1997— Colorado (N.L.)	3B	159	612	94	186	25	2	40	113	44	108	8	17	2-4	.304	.356	.547	.904	21	.954
1998— Colorado (N.L.)	3B-SS	•162	645	108	206	28	4	46	144	40	89	6	24	5-9	.319	.362	.589	.951	13	.954
1999— Colorado (N.L.)	3B	158	615	83	169	24	1	33	102	53	75	1	15	2-3	.275	.331	.478	.809	19	.954
2000— Tampa Bay (A.L.)	3B	85	331	22	73	19	1	6	42	14	41	3	9	1-2	.221	.254	.308	.562	8	.967
— Durham (Int'l)	3B	2	8	1	3	1	0	1	3	0	1	0	0	0-0	.375	.375	.875	1.250	0	1.000

Year Team (League)	Pos.	G	AB	R	H	2B	3B	HR	RBI	BB	SO	HBP	GDP	SB-CS	Avg.	OBP	SLG	OPS	E	Avg.
2001— Tampa Bay (A.L.)	3B	24	93	7	20	6	0	2	9	3	22	1	3	0-0	.215	.247	.344	.592	5	.934
— Houston (N.L.)	3B-SS	122	445	62	120	28	1	23	82	32	86	3	19	1-4	.270	.320	.492	.812	12	.963
2002— Atlanta (N.L.)	3B	143	543	56	126	23	2	12	61	22	69	7	22	4-1	.232	.268	.348	.616	6	.982
2003— Atlanta (N.L.)	3B	147	542	65	150	28	3	22	76	26	86	3	22	1-2	.277	.310	.461	.771	19	.955
2004— Colorado (N.L.)	3B	148	583	93	158	43	3	35	*131	51	113	6	22	0-0	.271	.332	.535	.867	6	.987
2005— Washington (N.L.)	3B	142	494	53	125	36	1	12	66	43	82	7	16	4-2	.253	.319	.403	.722	11	.970
American League totals (2 years)		109	424	29	93	15	1	8	51	17	63	4	12	1-2	.219	.253	.316	.569	13	.959
National League totals (14 years)		1658	6123	847	1728	324	27	307	1027	397	957	53	205	32-41	.282	.328	.494	.823	156	.967
Major League totals (15 years)		1767	6547	876	1821	339	28	315	1078	414	1020	57	217	33-43	.278	.324	.483	.806	169	.966

DIVISION SERIES RECORD

Year Team (League)	Pos.	G	AB	R	H	2B	3B	HR	RBI	BB	SO	HBP	GDP	SB-CS	Avg.	OBP	SLG	OPS	E	Avg.
1995— Colorado (N.L.)	3B	4	15	3	7	1	0	3	6	0	1	1	1	0-0	.467	.500	1.133	1.633	1	.941
2001— Houston (N.L.)	3B	3	11	1	3	0	0	1	1	0	3	0	1	0-0	.273	.273	.545	.818	0	1.000
2002— Atlanta (N.L.)	3B	5	18	5	7	0	0	1	4	2	2	0	0	0-0	.389	.450	.556	1.006	0	1.000
2003— Atlanta (N.L.)	3B	5	16	0	4	0	0	1	0	5	12	5	1	0-0	.250	.368	.250	.618	2	.895
Division series totals (4 years)		17	60	9	21	1	0	5	12	5	12	1	2	0-0	.350	.409	.617	1.026	3	.952

ALL-STAR GAME RECORD

	G	AB	R	H	2B	3B	HR	RBI	BB	SO	HBP	GDP	SB-CS	Avg.	OBP	SLG	OPS	E	Avg.
All-Star Game totals (2 years)	2	4	0	0	0	0	0	0	0	1	0	0	0-0	.000	.000	.000	.000	0	1.000

CASTILLO, ALBERTO — C

PERSONAL: Born February 10, 1970, in San Juan de la Maguana, Dominican Republic. ... 6-0/216. ... Bats right, throws right. ... Full name: Alberto Terrero Castillo. ... Name pronounced: cas-TEE-oh. ... High school: Mercedes Maria Mateo (Dominican Republic).

TRANSACTIONS/CAREER NOTES: Signed as a non-drafted free agent by New York Mets organization (April 15, 1987). ... Signed as a free agent by Philadelphia Phillies organization (November 5, 1998). ... Selected by St. Louis Cardinals from Phillies organization in Rule 5 major league draft (December 14, 1998). ... Traded by Cardinals with Ps Lance Painter and Matt DeWitt to Toronto Blue Jays for Ps Pat Hentgen and Paul Spoljaric (November 11, 1999). ... Released by Blue Jays (December 12, 2001). ... Signed by New York Yankees organization (December 21, 2001). ... Released by Yankees (October 10, 2002). ... Signed by San Francisco Giants organization (March 14, 2003). ... Loaned to Mexico City Red Devils and Laguna of the Mexican League (March 15, 2003). ... Returned to Giants (July 6, 2003). ... On disabled list (July 27-August 27, 2003); included rehabilitation assignment to Fresno. ... Released by Giants (March 17, 2004). ... Signed by Kansas City Royals organization (March 22, 2004). ... Released by Royals (August 5, 2005). ... Signed by Oakland Athletics organization (August 21, 2005).

2005 GAMES PLAYED BY POSITION (MLB): C—35.

SCOUTING REPORT His slow bat and long swing have doomed him to being a career backup, but he understands that is his role. Does not drive the ball, but will make contact and is fairly selective. Can be beaten with fastballs on the inner half. Is a much better hitter when he doesn't overswing. Has an above-average arm with a quick release. Receives the ball fine and has good mobility and energy behind the plate. ***Grade 4.6***

ALBERTO CASTILLO'S HITTING ZONE

.000	.000	.333
.353	.500	.100
.000	.167	.286

LEFTY-RIGHTY SPLITS

vs.	Avg.	AB	H	2B	3B	HR	RBI	BB	SO	OBP	Slg.
L	.139	36	5	0	1	1	4	2	9	.179	.278
R	.246	65	16	5	0	0	10	10	13	.347	.323

Year Team (League)	Pos.	G	AB	R	H	2B	3B	HR	RBI	BB	SO	HBP	GDP	SB-CS	Avg.	OBP	SLG	OPS	E	Avg.
1987— Kingsport (Appalachian)	C	7	9	1	1	0	0	0	0	5	3	0	0	1-0	.111	.429	.111	.540	1	1.000
1988— GC Mets (GCL)	C	22	68	7	18	4	0	0	10	4	4	2	3	2-0	.265	.312	.324	.635	1	.993
— Kingsport (Appalachian)	C	24	75	7	22	3	0	1	14	15	14	0	1	0-1	.293	.407	.373	.780	5	.973
1989— Kingsport (Appalachian)	1B-C	27	74	15	19	4	0	3	12	11	14	1	2	2-1	.257	.360	.432	.793	1	.994
— Pittsfield (NYP)	C	34	123	13	29	8	0	1	13	7	26	1	3	2-0	.236	.278	.325	.603	2	.991
1990— Columbia (S. Atl.)	C	30	103	8	24	4	3	1	14	10	21	0	1	1-1	.233	.296	.359	.655	5	.977
— Pittsfield (NYP)	1B-C-OF	58	187	19	41	8	1	4	24	26	35	5	7	3-3	.219	.327	.337	.664	9	.980
— St. Lucie (Fla. St.)	C	3	11	4	4	0	0	1	3	1	1	0	2	0-0	.364	.417	.636	1.053	0	1.000
1991— Columbia (S. Atl.)	C	90	267	35	74	20	3	3	47	43	44	5	6	6-6	.277	.382	.408	.791	15	.982
1992— St. Lucie (Fla. St.)	C	60	162	11	33	6	0	3	17	16	37	2	4	0-0	.204	.280	.296	.577	12	.967
1993— St. Lucie (Fla. St.)	C	105	333	37	86	21	0	5	42	28	46	3	5	0-2	.258	.315	.366	.682	12	.983
1994— Binghamton (East.)	1B-C	90	315	33	78	14	0	7	42	41	46	0	11	1-3	.248	.333	.359	.692	6	.991
1995— Norfolk (Int'l)	C-DH	69	217	23	58	13	1	4	31	26	32	1	6	2-3	.267	.346	.392	.737	7	.987
— New York (N.L.)	C	13	29	2	3	0	0	0	0	3	9	1	0	1-0	.103	.212	.103	.316	2	.974
1996— New York (N.L.)	C	6	11	1	4	0	0	0	2	1	3	0	1	0-0	.364	.364	.364	.727	0	1.000
— Norfolk (Int'l)	C	113	341	34	71	12	1	11	39	39	67	4	3	2-2	.208	.295	.346	.641	8	.990
1997— New York (N.L.)	C	35	59	3	12	1	0	0	7	9	16	0	3	0-1	.203	.304	.220	.525	2	.987
— Norfolk (Int'l)	C-OF	34	83	4	18	1	0	1	8	17	16	0	1	1-0	.217	.347	.265	.612	7	.968
1998— New York (N.L.)	C-DH	38	83	13	17	4	0	2	7	9	17	1	1	0-2	.205	.290	.325	.616	2	.990
— Norfolk (Int'l)	C-OF	21	49	4	9	2	0	1	6	11	12	0	0	0-0	.184	.333	.286	.619	1	.991
1999— St. Louis (N.L.)	C	93	255	21	67	8	0	4	31	24	48	2	6	1-0	.263	.326	.341	.667	5	.991
2000— Toronto (A.L.)	C	66	185	14	39	7	0	1	16	21	36	0	3	0-0	.211	.287	.265	.552	3	.993
2001— Toronto (A.L.)	C	66	131	9	26	4	0	1	4	7	30	3	2	1-1	.198	.255	.252	.507	4	.989
2002— New York (A.L.)	C	15	37	3	5	1	0	0	4	1	12	0	2	0-0	.135	.158	.216	.374	1	.990
— Columbus (Int'l)	C	30	91	7	25	7	0	0	8	9	8	2	3	1-0	.275	.340	.352	.701	4	.984
2003— M.C. R. Dev. (Mex.)	C	17	60	13	21	4	0	1	14	6	7	1	...	1-1	.350	.412	.467	.879	1	...
— Laguna (Mex.)	C	66	243	38	70	9	0	11	47	34	22	3	...	0-1	.288	.381	.461	.842	1	...
— Fresno (Int'l)	C	12	34	2	8	1	0	0	5	4	9	0	0	0-0	.235	.381	.265	.646	0	1.000
— San Francisco (N.L.)	C	11	15	3	3	1	0	1	4	0	5	0	0	0-0	.200	.200	.467	.667	1	.975
2004— Omaha (PCL)	C-DH-1B	48	161	15	41	9	0	1	15	20	20	3	3	0-0	.255	.348	.329	.677	5	.985
— Kansas City (A.L.)	C	29	89	12	24	6	0	1	11	14	10	0	0	0-2	.270	.365	.371	.736	1	.995
2005— Kansas City (A.L.)	C	34	100	13	21	5	1	1	14	12	21	0	1	1-0	.210	.292	.310	.602	2	.992

Year	Team (League)	Pos.	G	AB	R	H	2B	3B	HR	RBI	BB	SO	HBP	GDP	SB-CS	Avg.	OBP	SLG	OPS	E	Avg.
	— Sacramento (PCL)	C	4	13	2	1	0	0	0	0	0	4	0	0	0-0	.077	.143	.077	.220	1	.964
	— Oakland (A.L.)	C	1	1	0	0	0	0	0	0	0	1	0	0	0-0	.000	.000	.000	.000	0	1.000
	American League totals (5 years)		211	543	51	115	23	2	4	49	55	110	3	10	2-3	.212	.285	.284	.569	11	.992
	National League totals (6 years)		196	452	42	106	14	0	7	49	45	99	4	10	1-3	.235	.306	.312	.618	12	.989
	Major League totals (11 years)		407	995	93	221	37	2	11	98	100	209	7	20	3-6	.222	.295	.296	.591	23	.990

CASTILLO, FRANK — P

PERSONAL: Born April 1, 1969, in El Paso, Texas. ... 6-1/198. ... Throws right, bats right. ... Full name: Frank Anthony Castillo. ... Name pronounced: cas-TEE-oh. ... High school: Eastwood (El Paso, Texas).

TRANSACTIONS/CAREER NOTES: Selected by Chicago Cubs organization in sixth round of 1987 free-agent draft. ... On disabled list (August 11-27, 1991). ... On suspended list (September 20-24, 1993). ... On disabled list (March 20-May 12, 1994); included rehabilitation assignments to Daytona, Orlando and Iowa. ... Traded by Cubs to Colorado Rockies for P Matt Pool (July 15, 1997). ... Signed as a free agent by Detroit Tigers (December 11, 1997). ... On disabled list (March 24-April 28, 1998); included rehabilitation assignment to Lakeland. ... Signed as a free agent by Arizona Diamondbacks organization (January 12, 1999). ... Released by Diamondbacks (March 27, 1999). ... Signed by Pittsburgh Pirates organization (April 20, 1999). ... Signed as a free agent by Toronto Blue Jays organization (December 21, 1999). ... On disabled list (August 14-September 16, 2000). ... Signed as a free agent by Boston Red Sox (December 7, 2000). ... On disabled list (June 29-August 8, 2001); included rehabilitation assignment to Pawtucket. ... On suspended list (May 17-22 and July 1-5, 2002). ... Released by Red Sox (March 26, 2003). ... Signed by Oakland Athletics organization (April 9, 2003). ... Released by A's (June 9, 2003). ... Signed by Atlanta Braves organization (August 16, 2003). ... Released by Braves (September 2, 2003). ... Signed as a free agent by Red Sox organization (February 18, 2004). ... Signed as a free agent by Florida Marlins organization (November 11, 2004).

CAREER HITTING: 37-for-338 (.109), 7 R, 0 2B, 0 3B, 0 HR, 13 RBI.

Year	Team (League)	W	L	Pct.	ERA	WHIP	G	GS	CG	ShO	Hld.	Sv.-Opp.	IP	H	R	ER	HR	BB-IBB	SO	Avg.
1987	— Wytheville (App.)	10	1	.909	2.29	1.18	12	12	5	0	...	0-...	90.1	86	31	23	4	21-0	83	.252
	— Geneva (NY-Penn)	1	0	1.000	0.00	0.67	1	1	0	0	...	0-...	6.0	3	1	0	0	1-0	6	.136
1988	— Peoria (Midw.)	6	1	.857	0.71	0.69	9	8	2	2	...	0-...	51.0	25	5	4	1	10-0	58	.143
1989	— Win.-Salem (Car.)	9	6	.600	2.51	1.10	18	18	8	1	...	0-...	129.1	118	42	36	5	24-1	114	.240
	— Charlotte (Sou.)	3	4	.429	3.84	1.25	10	10	4	0	...	0-...	68.0	73	35	29	7	12-3	43	.277
1990	— Charlotte (Sou.)	6	6	.500	3.88	1.26	18	18	4	1	...	0-...	111.1	113	54	48	8	27-4	112	.265
1991	— Iowa (Am. Assoc.)	3	1	.750	2.52	1.08	4	4	1	1	...	0-...	25.0	20	7	7	0	7-0	20	.225
	— Chicago (N.L.)	6	7	.462	4.35	1.25	18	18	4	0	0	0-0	111.2	107	56	54	15	33-2	73	.252
1992	— Chicago (N.L.)	10	11	.476	3.46	1.18	33	33	0	0	0	0-0	205.1	179	91	79	19	63-6	135	.232
1993	— Chicago (N.L.)	5	8	.385	4.84	1.42	29	25	2	0	0	0-0	141.1	162	83	76	20	39-4	84	.293
1994	— Daytona (Fla. St.)	0	1	.000	4.50	1.75	1	1	0	0	...	0-...	4.0	7	3	2	0	0-0	1	.368
	— Orlando (South.)	1	0	1.000	1.29	0.71	1	1	0	0	...	0-...	7.0	4	2	1	0	1-0	2	.167
	— Iowa (Am. Assoc.)	4	2	.667	3.27	1.02	11	11	0	0	...	0-...	66.0	57	30	24	9	14-0	44	.228
	— Chicago (N.L.)	2	1	.667	4.30	1.30	4	4	1	0	0	0-0	23.0	25	13	11	3	5-0	19	.278
1995	— Chicago (N.L.)	11	10	.524	3.21	1.23	29	29	2	2	0	0-0	188.0	179	75	67	22	52-4	135	.248
1996	— Chicago (N.L.)	7	•16	.304	5.28	1.40	33	33	1	1	0	0-0	182.1	209	112	107	28	46-4	139	.288
1997	— Chicago (N.L.)	6	9	.400	5.42	1.60	20	19	0	0	0	0-0	98.0	113	64	59	9	44-1	67	.292
	— Colorado (N.L.)	6	3	.667	5.42	1.53	14	14	0	0	0	0-0	86.1	107	57	52	16	25-3	59	.308
1998	— Lakeland (Fla. St.)	1	0	1.000	0.00	0.40	1	1	0	0	...	0-...	5.0	2	0	0	0	4-0	4	.125
	— Detroit (A.L.)	3	9	.250	6.83	1.67	27	19	0	0	0	1-1	116.0	150	91	88	17	44-0	81	.316
1999	— Nashville (PCL)	7	5	.583	4.68	1.43	19	19	0	0	...	0-...	119.1	139	72	62	15	32-4	90	.290
2000	— Toronto (A.L.)	10	5	.667	3.59	1.22	25	24	0	0	0	0-0	138.0	112	58	55	18	56-0	104	.220
2001	— Boston (A.L.)	10	9	.526	4.21	1.27	26	26	0	0	0	0-0	136.2	138	72	64	14	35-2	89	.260
	— Pawtucket (Int'l)	0	0	...	0.00	0.91	2	2	0	0	0	0-0	7.2	7	1	0	0	0-0	3	.250
2002	— Boston (A.L.)	6	15	.286	5.07	1.42	36	23	0	0	0	1-2	163.1	174	101	92	19	58-6	112	.274
2003	— Sacramento (PCL)	5	4	.556	4.13	1.40	19	16	0	0	0	0-0	96.0	104	47	44	12	34-2	59	.280
	— Richmond (Int'l)	0	1	.000	1.50	1.50	4	3	0	0	0	0-0	18.0	23	5	3	1	4-0	14	.307
2004	— Boston (A.L.)	0	0	...	0.00	2.00	2	0	0	0	0	0-0	1.0	1	0	0	0	1-0	0	.333
	— Pawtucket (Int'l)	10	9	.526	4.38	1.21	27	25	0	0	0	0-0	168.1	169	87	82	28	34-0	123	.260
2005	— Florida (N.L.)	0	1	.000	10.38	2.08	1	1	0	0	0	0-0	4.1	4	5	5	0	5-0	4	.235
	— Albuquerque (PCL)	9	11	.450	5.53	1.53	27	24	0	0	0	0-0	143.1	161	102	88	20	58-3	80	.288
	American League totals (5 years)	29	38	.433	4.85	1.39	116	92	0	0	0	2-3	555.0	575	322	299	68	194-8	386	.267
	National League totals (8 years)	53	66	.445	4.41	1.34	181	176	10	3	0	0-0	1040.1	1085	556	510	122	312-24	715	.269
	Major League totals (13 years)	82	104	.441	4.56	1.36	297	268	10	3	0	2-3	1595.1	1660	878	809	190	506-32	1101	.268

CASTILLO, JOSE — 2B

PERSONAL: Born March 19, 1981, in Las Mercedes, Venezuela. ... 6-1/200. ... Bats right, throws right. ... Name pronounced: cas-TEE-oh.

TRANSACTIONS/CAREER NOTES: Signed as a non-drafted free agent by Pittsburgh Pirates organization (July 2, 1997). ... On disabled list (April 7-May 5; and August 23, 2005-remainder of season); included rehabilitation assignment to Indianapolis.

2005 GAMES PLAYED BY POSITION (MLB): 2B—100.

SCOUTING REPORT *Offense:* Castillo is extremely aggressive, with a long inside-out stroke. Is not selective and likes the ball out over the plate so he can hit to the opposite field. Is starting to develop power that will increase once he looks to pull the ball more. Has problems with breaking pitches and is not a good runner for a middle infielder. *Defense:* Castillo quickly is becoming one of the league's best second basemen. Reads the ball off the bat well and has improved his jumps to the right. Has the best throwing arm of any second basemen in the game, allowing him to go out deep on relays. Turns the double play exceptionally well and can turn it in a variety of ways. *Outlook:* Castillo showed much improvement before suffering a knee injury late in the season that required surgery. *Grade 7.3*

JOSE CASTILLO'S HITTING ZONE

.292	.278	.211
.267	.439	.297
.286	.444	.235

LEFTY-RIGHTY SPLITS

vs.	Avg.	AB	H	2B	3B	HR	RBI	BB	SO	OBP	Slg.
L	.258	97	25	3	2	2	16	7	19	.308	.392
R	.271	273	74	13	1	9	37	16	40	.307	.425

Year	Team (League)	Pos.	G	AB	R	H	2B	3B	HR	RBI	BB	SO	HBP	GDP	SB-CS	Avg.	OBP	SLG	OPS	E	Avg.
1999	— GC Pirates (GCL)	SS-2B	47	173	27	46	9	0	4	30	11	23	3	4	8-0	.266	.316	.387	.703	18	.923

Year	Team (League)	Pos.	G	AB	R	H	2B	3B	HR	RBI	BB	SO	HBP	GDP	SB-CS	Avg.	OBP	SLG	OPS	E	Avg.
																			BATTING	FIELDING	
2000—Hickory (S. Atl.)		SS	125	529	95	158	32	8	16	72	29	107	10	10	16-12	.299	.346	.480	.826	60	.908
2001—Lynchburg (Caro.)		SS	125	485	57	119	20	7	7	49	21	94	9	9	23-10	.245	.288	.359	.647	37	.939
2002—Lynchburg (Caro.)		SS	134	503	82	151	25	2	16	81	49	95	11	18	27-14	.300	.370	.453	.823	33	.951
2003—Altoona (East.)		2B-SS	126	498	68	143	24	6	5	66	40	81	3	18	19-10	.287	.339	.390	.728	23	.963
2004—Pittsburgh (N.L.)		2B-SS	129	383	44	98	15	2	8	39	23	92	1	12	3-2	.256	.298	.368	.666	11	.980
2005—Indianapolis (Int'l)		2B	4	13	2	5	1	0	2	2	2	1	0	0	0-0	.385	.467	.923	1.390	0	1.000
—Pittsburgh (N.L.)		2B	101	370	49	99	16	3	11	53	23	59	0	11	2-3	.268	.307	.416	.724	12	.977
Major League totals (2 years)			230	753	93	197	31	5	19	92	46	151	1	23	5-5	.262	.303	.392	.694	23	.979

CASTILLO, LUIS — 2B

PERSONAL: Born September 12, 1975, in San Pedro de Macoris, Dominican Republic. ... 5-11/190. ... Bats both, throws right. ... Full name: Luis Antonio Castillo. ... Name pronounced: cas-TEE-oh. ... High school: Colegio San Benito Abad (San Pedro de Macoris, D.R.).
TRANSACTIONS/CAREER NOTES: Signed as a non-drafted free agent by Florida Marlins organization (August 19, 1992). ... On disabled list (May 7-22, 1997). ... On disabled list (April 16-May 5, 2000); included rehabilitation assignment to Calgary.
HONORS: Won N.L. Gold Glove at second base (2003-05).
2005 GAMES PLAYED BY POSITION (MLB): 2B—120.

SCOUTING REPORT **Offense:** Castillo is a speedster with an unorthodox batting style. Has a lot of movement at the plate and is a slap-and-run hitter. Can bunt for hits, which forces infielders to move up and creates holes. Uses the whole field and is selective. Has no power and is not a run producer. Has better bat control than bat speed. Is an outstanding runner with good instincts. Is better from the right side. **Defense:** He has very good range to either side and extremely quick hands. Is as good as any player on the double play. **Outlook:** Castillo's intimidating speed is a real asset, but he is not running as much because of recurring leg problems. When healthy, he is a constant threat on the bases who can disrupt a pitcher. **Grade 7.8**

LUIS CASTILLO'S HITTING ZONE

.281	.154	.273
.419	.324	.278
.268	.385	.186

LEFTY-RIGHTY SPLITS

vs.	Avg.	AB	H	2B	3B	HR	RBI	BB	SO	OBP	Slg.
L	.423	111	47	9	2	4	14	8	8	.467	.649
R	.259	328	85	3	2	0	16	57	24	.368	.280

Year	Team (League)	Pos.	G	AB	R	H	2B	3B	HR	RBI	BB	SO	HBP	GDP	SB-CS	Avg.	OBP	SLG	OPS	E	Avg.
																			BATTING	FIELDING	
1993—Dom. Marlins (DSL)		IF	69	266	48	75	7	1	4	31	36	22	...		21-...	.282	...	.361		20	.943
1994—GC Marlins (GCL)		2B-SS	57	216	49	57	8	0	0	16	37	36	1	1	31-12	.264	.371	.301	.672	9	.972
1995—Kane Co. (Midw.)		2B	89	340	71	111	4	4	0	23	54	50	0	1	41-18	.326	.419	.362	.781	17	.962
1996—Portland (East.)		2B	109	420	83	133	15	7	1	35	66	68	2	2	51-28	.317	.411	.393	.804	14	.975
—Florida (N.L.)		2B	41	164	26	43	2	1	1	8	14	46	0	0	17-4	.262	.320	.305	.625	3	.986
1997—Florida (N.L.)		2B	75	263	27	63	8	0	0	8	27	53	0	6	16-10	.240	.310	.270	.580	9	.971
—Charlotte (Int'l)		2B	37	130	25	46	5	0	0	5	16	22	0	2	8-6	.354	.425	.392	.817	5	.970
1998—Charlotte (Int'l)		2B	100	381	74	109	11	2	0	15	75	68	0	6	41-15	.286	.403	.325	.728	16	.970
—Florida (N.L.)		2B	44	153	21	31	3	2	1	10	22	33	1	1	3-0	.203	.307	.268	.575	7	.970
1999—Florida (N.L.)		2B	128	487	76	147	23	4	0	28	67	85	0	3	50-17	.302	.384	.366	.750	15	.976
2000—Florida (N.L.)		2B	136	539	101	180	17	3	2	17	78	86	0	11	*62-22	.334	.418	.388	.806	11	.983
—Calgary (PCL)		2B	4	13	4	4	1	1	0	0	4	2	0	0	1-0	.308	.471	.538	1.009	1	.944
2001—Florida (N.L.)		2B	134	537	76	141	16	10	2	45	67	90	1	6	33-16	.263	.344	.341	.684	*13	.980
2002—Florida (N.L.)		2B	146	606	86	185	18	5	2	39	55	76	2	7	*48-15	.305	.364	.361	.726	13	.981
2003—Florida (N.L.)		2B	152	595	99	187	19	6	6	39	63	60	2	7	21-19	.314	.381	.397	.778	10	.986
2004—Florida (N.L.)		2B	150	564	91	164	12	7	2	47	75	68	1	15	21-4	.291	.373	.348	.720	6	.991
2005—Florida (N.L.)		2B	122	439	72	132	12	4	4	30	65	32	1	11	10-7	.301	.391	.374	.765	7	.988
Major League totals (10 years)			1128	4347	675	1273	130	42	20	271	533	629	8	67	281-114	.293	.370	.356	.726	94	.983

DIVISION SERIES RECORD

Year	Team (League)	Pos.	G	AB	R	H	2B	3B	HR	RBI	BB	SO	HBP	GDP	SB-CS	Avg.	OBP	SLG	OPS	E	Avg.
2003—Florida (N.L.)		2B	4	17	2	5	3	0	0	1	3	0	0	0	0-0	.294	.400	.471	.871	0	1.000

CHAMPIONSHIP SERIES RECORD

Year	Team (League)	Pos.	G	AB	R	H	2B	3B	HR	RBI	BB	SO	HBP	GDP	SB-CS	Avg.	OBP	SLG	OPS	E	Avg.
2003—Florida (N.L.)		2B	7	28	3	6	1	0	0	2	5	2	0	0	2-0	.214	.333	.250	.583	0	1.000

WORLD SERIES RECORD

Year	Team (League)	Pos.	G	AB	R	H	2B	3B	HR	RBI	BB	SO	HBP	GDP	SB-CS	Avg.	OBP	SLG	OPS	E	Avg.
2003—Florida (N.L.)		2B	6	26	1	4	0	0	0	1	0	1	0	0	1-1	.154	.154	.154	.308	0	1.000

ALL-STAR GAME RECORD

Year	Team (League)	Pos.	G	AB	R	H	2B	3B	HR	RBI	BB	SO	HBP	GDP	SB-CS	Avg.	OBP	SLG	OPS	E	Avg.
All-Star Game totals (3 years)			3	7	1	1	0	0	0	0	0	0	0	0	0-0	.143	.143	.143	.286	0	1.000

CASTRO, BERNIE — 2B

PERSONAL: Born July 14, 1979, in Santo Domingo, Dominican Republic. ... 5-10/160. ... Bats both, throws right. ... Full name: Bernabel Castro. ... College: None.
TRANSACTIONS/CAREER NOTES: Signed as a non-drafted free agent by New York Yankees organization (September 25, 1997). ... Traded by Yankees to San Diego Padres for OF Kevin Reese (December 18, 2001). ... Signed as a free agent by Washington Nationals (October 27, 2005).
2005 GAMES PLAYED BY POSITION (MLB): 2B—11, DH—9, OF—1.

BERNIE CASTRO'S HITTING ZONE

.143	.000	.400
.333	.364	.368
.200	.000	.250

LEFTY-RIGHTY SPLITS

vs.	Avg.	AB	H	2B	3B	HR	RBI	BB	SO	OBP	Slg.
L	.200	15	3	0	0	0	0	2	3	.294	.200
R	.308	65	20	3	1	0	7	7	7	.375	.385

Year	Team (League)	Pos.	G	AB	R	H	2B	3B	HR	RBI	BB	SO	HBP	GDP	SB-CS	Avg.	OBP	SLG	OPS	E	Avg.
																			BATTING	FIELDING	
1998—Dom. Yankees (DSL)			61	224	78	74	6	4	0	17	37	40	4	4	63-10	.330	.432	.393	.825	...	
1998—Dom. Yankees (DSL)		Did not play.																			

C

Year	Team (League)	Pos.	G	AB	R	H	2B	3B	HR	RBI	BB	SO	HBP	GDP	SB-CS	Avg.	OBP	SLG	OPS	E	Avg.
2000—Dom. Yankees (DSL)		2B	55	210	69	73	9	2	2	13	36	24	4	1	56-15	.348	.450	.438	.888	...	...
—GC Yankees (GCL)		2B	9	34	7	15	4	1	0	6	6	4	0	1	3-1	.441	.525	.618	1.143	2	.867
2001—Greensboro (S. Atl.)		2B	101	389	71	101	15	7	1	36	54	67	1	5	67-20	.260	.350	.342	.692	20	.956
—Staten Island (N.Y.-Penn.)		2B	15	57	6	20	1	0	0	7	11	12	1	0	8-3	.351	.464	.368	.832	1	.984
2002—Mobile (Sou.)		2B	109	419	61	109	13	3	0	32	52	67	3	1	53-20	.260	.345	.305	.650	11	.980
2003—Portland (PCL)		2B	105	425	57	132	17	5	2	24	25	43	1	5	49-13	.311	.349	.388	.737	14	.970
2004—Portland (PCL)		2B-OF	90	308	38	81	8	1	0	20	22	30	0	6	17-9	.263	.310	.295	.605	6	.920
2005—Ottawa (Int'l)		2B-DH	126	502	81	158	21	5	1	36	42	50	0	5	41-6	.315	.364	.382	.746	17	.972
—Baltimore (A.L.)		2B-DH-OF	24	80	14	23	3	1	0	7	9	10	0	0	6-2	.288	.360	.350	.710	4	.925
Major League totals (1 year)			24	80	14	23	3	1	0	7	9	10	0	0	6-2	.288	.360	.350	.710	4	.925

CASTRO, JUAN — 3B/SS

PERSONAL: Born June 20, 1972, in Los Mochis, Mexico. ... 5-11/195. ... Bats right, throws right. ... Full name: Juan Gabriel Castro. ... Name pronounced: KASS-tro. ... High school: CBTIS 43 (Los Mochis, Mexico).

TRANSACTIONS/CAREER NOTES: Signed as a non-drafted free agent by Los Angeles Dodgers organization (June 13, 1991). ... On disabled list (June 5-August 1, 1997). ... Traded by Dodgers to Cincinnati Reds for a player to be named and cash (April 1, 2000); Dodgers acquired P Kenny Lutz to complete deal (June 8, 2000). ... On disabled list (March 27-June 1, 2002); included rehabilitation assignment to Louisville. ... On disabled list (March 25-April 14, 2003); included rehabilitation assignment to Louisville. ... On disabled list (June 1-22, 2004); included rehabilitation assignment to Louisville. ... Signed as a free agent by Minnesota Twins (November 23, 2004). ... On disabled list (August 14-September 2, 2005).

2005 GAMES PLAYED BY POSITION (MLB): SS—73, 3B—22, 2B—5.

SCOUTING REPORT Castro is a dead pull hitter who cheats on the fastball because of a lack of bat speed. Has problems with breaking stuff. Defense is underrated. Is strictly a utility infielder. ***Grade 5.5***

JUAN CASTRO'S HITTING ZONE

.200	.500	.400
.170	.286	.265
.226	.417	.200

LEFTY-RIGHTY SPLITS

vs.	Avg.	AB	H	2B	3B	HR	RBI	BB	SO	OBP	Slg.
L	.247	89	22	5	0	2	14	3	10	.272	.371
R	.262	183	48	13	1	3	19	6	29	.283	.393

Year	Team (League)	Pos.	G	AB	R	H	2B	3B	HR	RBI	BB	SO	HBP	GDP	SB-CS	Avg.	OBP	SLG	OPS	E	Avg.
1991—Great Falls (Pio.)		2B-SS	60	217	36	60	4	2	1	27	33	31	0	2	7-6	.277	.369	.327	.696	21	.921
1992—Bakersfield (Calif.)		2B-SS	113	446	56	116	15	4	4	42	37	64	1	7	14-11	.260	.314	.339	.652	38	.928
1993—San Antonio (Texas)		2B-SS	118	424	55	117	23	8	7	41	30	40	2	14	12-11	.276	.325	.417	.742	28	.945
1994—San Antonio (Texas)		SS	123	445	55	128	25	4	4	44	31	66	1	9	4-7	.288	.334	.389	.723	29	.951
1995—Albuquerque (PCL)		SS-2B	104	341	51	91	18	4	3	43	20	42	1	11	4-4	.267	.307	.370	.677	14	.973
—Los Angeles (N.L.)		3B-SS	11	4	0	1	0	0	0	0	1	1	0	0	0-0	.250	.400	.250	.650	1	1.000
1996—Albuquerque (PCL)		3B-SS-2B	17	56	12	21	4	2	1	8	6	7	1	0	1-1	.375	.444	.571	1.016	2	.962
—Los Angeles (N.L.)		SS-3B-2B-OF	70	132	16	26	5	3	0	5	10	27	0	1	1-0	.197	.254	.280	.534	3	.979
1997—Los Angeles (N.L.)		SS-2B-3B	40	75	3	11	3	1	0	4	7	20	0	2	0-0	.147	.209	.213	.433	1	.990
—Albuquerque (PCL)		SS-2B	27	101	11	31	5	2	2	11	4	20	0	5	0-0	.307	.327	.455	.783	9	.928
1998—Los Angeles (N.L.)		SS-3B-2B	89	220	25	43	7	0	2	15	15	37	0	5	0-0	.195	.245	.255	.499	10	.965
1999—Albuquerque (PCL)		SS-3B-2B-DH	116	423	52	116	25	4	7	51	34	70	0	14	2-3	.274	.325	.402	.727	19	.956
—Los Angeles (N.L.)		2B-SS	2	1	0	0	0	0	0	0	0	1	0	0	0-0	.000	.000	.000	.000	0	1.000
2000—Louisville (Int'l)		SS-2B-3B	19	60	9	19	5	1	2	10	12	9	0	3	0-1	.317	.425	.533	.958	4	.956
—Cincinnati (N.L.)		SS-2B-3B-1B	82	224	20	54	12	2	4	23	14	33	0	9	0-1	.241	.283	.366	.649	2	.993
2001—Cincinnati (N.L.)		SS-2B-3B-1B	96	242	27	54	10	0	3	13	13	50	0	8	0-0	.223	.261	.302	.562	8	.970
2002—Louisville (Int'l)		SS-2B	5	17	2	3	0	0	0	3	1	3	0	0	0-0	.176	.222	.176	.399	1	.962
—Cincinnati (N.L.)		SS-2B-1B-3B	54	82	5	18	3	0	2	11	7	11	0	5	0-0	.220	.278	.329	.607	3	.971
2003—Louisville (Int'l)		SS-2B	9	32	3	7	0	0	0	2	1	3	0	1	0-0	.219	.257	.313	.570	2	.950
—Cincinnati (N.L.)		2B-3B-SS-1B	111	299	36	73	21	2	5	26	14	51	0	11	1-0	.244	.277	.378	.655	8	.973
2004—Louisville (Int'l)		3B-SS-2B	5	18	1	3	1	0	0	2	0	0	0	0	0-0	.167	.200	.222	.422	1	.955
—Cincinnati (N.L.)		SS-2B-3B	113	320	28	81	14	1	9	33	18	58	0	7	2-3	.253	.290	.388	.678	5	.987
2005—Minnesota (A.L.)		SS-3B-2B	97	272	27	70	18	1	5	33	9	39	0	8	0-1	.257	.279	.386	.665	9	.977
American League totals (1 year)			97	272	27	70	18	1	5	33	9	39	0	8	0-1	.257	.279	.386	.665	9	.977
National League totals (10 years)			668	1599	160	361	75	9	25	129	99	296	0	46	4-5	.226	.269	.331	.600	40	.979
Major League totals (11 years)			765	1871	187	431	93	10	30	162	108	335	0	54	4-6	.230	.271	.339	.609	49	.978

DIVISION SERIES RECORD

Year	Team (League)	Pos.	G	AB	R	H	2B	3B	HR	RBI	BB	SO	HBP	GDP	SB-CS	Avg.	OBP	SLG	OPS	E	Avg.
1996—Los Angeles (N.L.)		2B	2	5	0	1	1	0	0	1	1	0	0	0	0-0	.200	.333	.400	.733	0	1.000

CASTRO, RAMON — C

PERSONAL: Born March 1, 1976, in Vega Baja, Puerto Rico. ... 6-3/235. ... Bats right, throws right. ... Full name: Ramon Abraham Castro. ... High school: Lino P. Rivera (Vega Baja, Puerto Rico).

TRANSACTIONS/CAREER NOTES: Selected by Houston Astros organization in first round (17th pick overall) of 1994 free-agent draft. ... Traded by Astros to Florida Marlins for P Jay Powell and C Scott Makarewicz (July 6, 1998). ... On disabled list (May 17-June 8, 2002; and June 2, 2004-remainder of season). ... Signed as a free agent by New York Mets organization (December 22, 2004). ... On disabled list (May 16-June 2, 2005).

2005 GAMES PLAYED BY POSITION (MLB): C—99.

SCOUTING REPORT With the injury to Mike Piazza, Castro caught most of the games late last season. Has a big frame but moves well behind the plate. Has good arm strength and, even though he drops down slightly, his ball doesn't tail a lot. Is active blocking pitches in the dirt. Is a fastball hitter with a long stroke. Likes the ball out away from him so he can extend his arms. Has power from alley to alley. Isn't a good runner. ***Grade 5.3***

RAMON CASTRO'S HITTING ZONE

.273	.182	.222
.298	.323	.316
.160	.333	.000

LEFTY-RIGHTY SPLITS

vs.	Avg.	AB	H	2B	3B	HR	RBI	BB	SO	OBP	Slg.
L	.290	31	9	3	0	1	2	8	4	.436	.484
R	.236	178	42	13	0	7	39	17	54	.333	.427

Year	Team (League)	Pos.	G	AB	R	H	2B	3B	HR	RBI	BB	SO	HBP	GDP	SB-CS	Avg.	OBP	SLG	OPS	E	Avg.
1994—GC Astros (GCL)		C	37	123	17	34	7	0	3	14	17	14	2	4	5-5	.276	.373	.407	.780	4	.983

Year	Team (League)	Pos.	G	AB	R	H	2B	3B	HR	RBI	BB	SO	HBP	GDP	SB-CS	Avg.	OBP	SLG	OPS	E	Avg.
1995—Kissimmee (Fla. St.)		C	36	120	6	25	5	0	0	8	6	21	1	1	0-0	.208	.250	.250	.500	7	.967
—Auburn (NY-Penn)		C	63	224	40	67	17	0	9	49	24	27	0	6	0-1	.299	.358	.496	.854	2	.994
1996—Quad City (Midw.)		C	96	314	38	78	15	0	7	43	31	61	2	12	2-0	.248	.317	.363	.680	10	.987
1997—Kissimmee (Fla. St.)		C	115	410	53	115	22	1	8	65	53	73	2	17	1-0	.280	.357	.398	.755	6	.992
1998—Jackson (Texas)		C	48	168	27	43	6	0	8	25	13	31	4	3	0-1	.256	.324	.435	.759	10	.974
—Portland (East.)		C	31	88	9	22	3	0	3	11	8	21	0	3	0-0	.250	.306	.386	.692	5	.946
1999—Calgary (PCL)		C-DH	97	349	43	90	22	0	15	61	24	64	2	11	0-0	.258	.307	.450	.757	7	.989
—Florida (N.L.)		C	24	67	4	12	4	0	2	4	10	14	0	1	0-0	.179	.282	.328	.610	1	.992
2000—Calgary (PCL)		C	67	218	44	73	22	0	14	45	16	38	0	5	0-0	.335	.380	.628	1.009	4	.990
—Florida (N.L.)		C	50	138	10	33	4	0	2	14	16	36	1	1	0-0	.239	.318	.312	.630	6	.980
2001—Florida (N.L.)		C	7	11	0	2	0	0	0	1	1	1	0	0	0-0	.182	.250	.182	.432	0	1.000
—Calgary (PCL)		C	108	390	81	131	33	0	27	90	38	74	1	11	1-1	.336	.393	.628	1.021	7	.989
2002—Florida (N.L.)		C-DH	54	101	11	24	4	0	6	18	14	24	0	4	0-0	.238	.322	.455	.777	0	1.000
2003—Florida (N.L.)		C-DH	40	53	6	15	2	0	5	8	4	11	0	0	0-0	.283	.333	.604	.937	1	.982
2004—Florida (N.L.)		C	32	96	9	13	3	0	3	8	11	30	1	1	0-0	.135	.231	.260	.492	2	.990
2005—New York (N.L.)		C	99	209	26	51	16	0	8	41	25	58	0	7	1-0	.244	.321	.435	.756	3	.993
Major League totals (7 years)			306	675	66	150	33	0	26	94	81	174	2	14	1-0	.222	.304	.387	.690	13	.990

CATALANOTTO, FRANK — OF/IF

PERSONAL: Born April 27, 1974, in Smithtown, N.Y. ... 5-11/195. ... Bats left, throws right. ... Full name: Frank John Catalanotto. ... Name pronounced: ca-tal-a-NAH-tow. ... High school: Smithtown (N.Y.) East. ... College: C.W. Post (Brookville, N.Y.).

TRANSACTIONS/CAREER NOTES: Selected by Detroit Tigers organization in 10th round of 1992 free-agent draft. ... Selected by Oakland Athletics from Tigers organization in Rule 5 major league draft (December 9, 1996). ... Returned to Tigers organization (March 21, 1997). ... Traded by Tigers with Ps Justin Thompson, Francisco Cordero and Alan Webb, OF Gabe Kapler and C Bill Haselman to Texas Rangers for OF Juan Gonzalez, Danny Patterson and C Gregg Zaun (November 2, 1999). ... On disabled list (April 22-May 15, 2000); included rehabilitation assignment to Oklahoma. ... On disabled list (May 11-June 28 and August 17, 2002-remainder of season); included rehabilitation assignment to Tulsa. ... Signed as a free agent by Toronto Blue Jays (December 30, 2002). ... On disabled list (May 20-June 8, June 18-July 20 and August 21, 2004-remainder of season). ... On bereavement list (May 24-30, 2005).

2005 GAMES PLAYED BY POSITION (MLB): OF—111, DH—15.

SCOUTING REPORT **Offense:** Catalanotto has a long, looping swing with a slight uppercut. Has good bat control and speed and plate coverge. Can use the whole field. Has deceptive power and hits well with runners in scoring position. Is an above-average runner but does not steal bases. **Defense:** He was moved to left field from the infield to keep his bat in the lineup. Can't throw, doesn't get good jumps and has poor instincts. **Outlook:** Catalanotto is a platoon player limited to playing left feld against righthanded pitching. Must hit to continue playing. *Grade 7.3*

FRANK CATALANOTTO'S HITTING ZONE

.400	.286	.292
.333	.343	.307
.353	.346	.276

LEFTY-RIGHTY SPLITS

vs.	Avg.	AB	H	2B	3B	HR	RBI	BB	SO	OBP	Slg.
L	.290	31	9	3	0	1	4	2	2	.371	.484
R	.302	388	117	26	5	7	55	35	51	.367	.448

Year	Team (League)	Pos.	G	AB	R	H	2B	3B	HR	RBI	BB	SO	HBP	GDP	SB-CS	Avg.	OBP	SLG	OPS	E	Avg.
1992—Bristol (Appal.)		2B	21	50	6	10	2	0	0	4	8	8	0	0	0-1	.200	.310	.240	.550	2	.875
1993—Bristol (Appal.)		2B	55	199	37	61	9	5	3	22	15	19	3	3	3-6	.307	.364	.447	.811	10	.957
1994—Fayetteville (SAL)		2B	119	458	72	149	24	8	3	56	37	54	3	4	4-5	.325	.379	.432	.811	15	.973
1995—Jacksonville (Sou.)		2B	134	491	66	111	19	5	8	48	49	56	4	9	13-8	.226	.306	.334	.640	18	.974
1996—Jacksonville (Sou.)		2B	132	497	105	148	34	6	17	67	74	69	11	8	15-14	.298	.398	.493	.891	22	.968
1997—Toledo (Int'l)	2B-3B-OF DH		134	500	75	150	32	6	16	56	47	80	10	9	12-11	.300	.368	.472	.840	18	.966
—Detroit (A.L.)	2B-DH		13	26	2	8	2	0	0	3	3	7	0	0	0-0	.308	.379	.385	.764	0	1.000
1998—Detroit (A.L.)	2B-DH-1B 3B		89	213	23	60	13	2	6	25	12	39	4	4	3-2	.282	.325	.446	.771	3	.986
—Toledo (Int'l)	1B-2B-DH		28	105	20	35	6	3	4	28	14	21	7	2	0-0	.333	.438	.562	.999	2	.989
1999—Detroit (A.L.)	1B-2B-3B DH		100	286	41	79	19	0	11	35	15	49	9	5	3-4	.276	.327	.458	.785	5	.986
2000—Texas (A.L.)	2B-DH-1B OF		103	282	55	82	13	2	10	42	33	36	6	5	6-2	.291	.375	.457	.832	9	.969
—Oklahoma (PCL)	2B-OF		3	11	2	3	0	0	0	1	0	4	1	0	0-0	.273	.333	.273	.606	0	1.000
2001—Texas (A.L.)	OF-2B-3B 1B		133	463	77	153	31	6	11	54	39	55	8	5	15-5	.330	.391	.490	.882	4	.985
2002—Texas (A.L.)	OF-2B-1B DH		68	212	42	57	16	6	3	23	25	27	8	3	9-5	.269	.364	.443	.808	2	.990
—Tulsa (Texas)	1B-2B-OF		4	16	1	2	0	1	0	3	1	1	1	3	0-0	.125	.222	.250	.472	0	1.000
2003—Toronto (A.L.)	OF-DH-1B		133	489	83	146	34	6	13	59	35	62	6	9	2-2	.299	.351	.490	.823	3	.983
2004—Toronto (A.L.)	OF-DH		75	249	27	73	19	1	1	26	17	33	4	7	1-0	.293	.344	.390	.734	2	.971
2005—Toronto (A.L.)	OF-DH		130	419	56	126	29	5	8	59	37	53	10	9	0-2	.301	.367	.451	.818	0	1.000
Major League totals (9 years)			844	2639	406	784	176	27	63	326	216	361	55	47	39-22	.297	.359	.456	.815	28	.984

C

CEDENO, ROGER   OF

PERSONAL: Born August 16, 1974, in Valencia, Venezuela. ... 6-1/205. ... Bats both, throws right. ... Full name: Roger Leandro Cedeno. ... Name pronounced: sid-AIN-yo.

TRANSACTIONS/CAREER NOTES: Signed as a non-drafted free agent by Los Angeles Dodgers organization (March 28, 1991). ... On disabled list (March 25-April 17 and August 25, 1997-remainder of season); included rehabilitation assignment to Albuquerque. ... On disabled list (March 22-April 24, 1998); included rehabilitation assignment to Vero Beach. ... Traded by Dodgers with C Charles Johnson to New York Mets for C Todd Hundley and P Arnold Gooch (December 1, 1998). ... Traded by Mets with Ps Octavio Dotel and Kyle Kessel to Houston Astros for P Mike Hampton and OF Derek Bell (December 23, 1999). ... On disabled list (May 26-August 18, 2000); included rehabilitation assignment to New Orleans. ... Traded by Astros with C Mitch Meluskey and P Chris Holt to Detroit Tigers for C Brad Ausmus and Ps Doug Brocail and Nelson Cruz (December 11, 2000). ... Signed as a free agent by Mets (December 17, 2001). ... Traded by Mets to St. Louis Cardinals for IF Wilson Delgado and C Chris Widger (April 4, 2004). ... On disabled list (April 11-May 13, 2004); included rehabilitation assignment to Memphis. ... On suspended list (July 15-17, 2004). ... On disabled list (June 6-24, 2005); included rehabilitation assignment to Memphis. ... Released by Cardinals (June 29, 2005).

2005 GAMES PLAYED BY POSITION (MLB): OF—16.

ROGER CEDENO'S HITTING ZONE

.000	.500	.400
.182	.111	.250
.167	.000	.000

LEFTY-RIGHTY SPLITS

vs.	Avg.	AB	H	2B	3B	HR	RBI	BB	SO	OBP	Slg.
L	.333	12	4	1	0	0	3	0	3	.333	.333
R	.111	45	5	1	0	0	5	2	3	.163	.133

Year—Team (League)	Pos.	G	AB	R	H	2B	3B	HR	RBI	BB	SO	HBP	GDP	SB-CS	Avg.	OBP	SLG	OPS	E	Avg.
1991— Dom. Dodgers (DSL)	OF	58	209	25	50	1	1	0	7	0	0			26-13	.239	...	.254	...		...
1992— Great Falls (Pio.)	OF	69	256	60	81	6	5	2	27	51	53	2	4	40-9	.316	.431	.402	.833	8	.937
1993— San Antonio (Texas)	OF	122	465	70	134	12	8	4	30	45	90	1	5	28-20	.288	.352	.374	.726	9	.961
— Albuquerque (PCL)	OF	6	18	1	4	1	1	0	4	3	3	0	0	0-1	.222	.333	.389	.722	1	.923
1994— Albuquerque (PCL)	OF	104	383	84	123	18	5	4	49	51	57	0	4	30-13	.321	.395	.426	.820	8	.962
1995— Albuquerque (PCL)	OF-DH	99	367	67	112	19	9	2	44	53	56	2	5	23-18	.305	.393	.422	.815	3	.985
— Los Angeles (N.L.)	OF	40	42	4	10	2	0	0	3	3	10	0	1	1-0	.238	.283	.286	.568	1	.977
1996— Los Angeles (N.L.)	OF	86	211	26	52	11	1	2	18	24	47	1	0	5-1	.246	.326	.336	.663	2	.983
— Albuquerque (PCL)	OF	33	125	16	28	2	3	1	10	15	22	0	2	6-5	.224	.307	.312	.619	0	1.000
1997— Albuquerque (PCL)	OF	29	113	21	40	4	4	2	9	22	16	1	1	5-5	.354	.463	.513	.977	2	.964
— Los Angeles (N.L.)	OF	80	194	31	53	10	2	3	17	25	44	3	1	9-1	.273	.362	.392	.753	2	.987
1998— Vero Beach (FSL)	OF	6	21	5	9	0	1	1	6	5	5	0	2	1-0	.429	.538	.667	1.205	1	.933
— Los Angeles (N.L.)	OF	105	240	33	58	11	1	2	17	27	57	0	1	8-2	.242	.317	.321	.638	2	.978
1999— New York (N.L.)	OF-2B	155	453	90	142	23	4	4	36	60	100	3	5	66-17	.313	.396	.408	.804	3	.989
2000— Houston (N.L.)	OF	74	259	54	73	2	5	6	26	43	47	0	6	25-11	.282	.383	.398	.781	3	.978
— New Orleans (PCL)	OF	6	20	2	7	0	1	0	3	2	5	0	0	1-1	.350	.391	.450	.841	0	1.000
2001— Detroit (A.L.)	OF-DH	131	523	79	153	14	11	6	48	36	83	2	5	55-15	.293	.337	.396	.733	12	.953
2002— New York (N.L.)	OF	149	511	65	133	19	2	7	41	42	92	2	10	25-4	.260	.318	.346	.664	8	.966
2003— New York (N.L.)	OF	148	484	70	129	25	4	7	37	38	86	1	4	14-9	.267	.320	.378	.698	3	.987
2004— Memphis (PCL)	OF	7	23	3	5	0	0	0	1	2	6	0	0	0-0	.217	.280	.217	.497	0	1.000
— St. Louis (N.L.)	OF-DH	95	200	22	53	9	2	3	23	19	41	0	5	5-1	.265	.327	.375	.702	0	1.000
2005— New York (N.L.)	OF	37	57	4	9	1	0	0	8	2	6	1	2	0-2	.158	.197	.175	.372	2	.818
— Memphis (PCL)	OF	8	23	3	4	1	0	0	2	3	5	0	0	0-0	.174	.269	.217	.487	0	1.000
American League totals (1 year)		131	523	79	153	14	11	6	48	36	83	2	5	55-15	.293	.337	.396	.733	12	.953
National League totals (10 years)		969	2651	399	712	113	21	34	226	283	530	11	39	158-48	.269	.340	.366	.706	26	.981
Major League totals (11 years)		1100	3174	478	865	127	32	40	274	319	613	13	44	213-63	.273	.340	.371	.710	38	.976

DIVISION SERIES RECORD

Year Team (League)	Pos.	G	AB	R	H	2B	3B	HR	RBI	BB	SO	HBP	GDP	SB-CS	Avg.	OBP	SLG	OPS	E	Avg.
1999— New York (N.L.)	OF	4	7	1	2	0	0	0	2	1	1	0	1	1-0	.286	.333	.286	.619	0	1.000
2004— St. Louis (N.L.)		2	2	0	1	0	0	0	0	0	0	0	0	0-0	.500	.500	.500	1.000	0	...
Division series totals (2 years)		6	9	1	3	0	0	0	2	1	1	0	1	1-0	.333	.364	.333	.697	0	1.000

CHAMPIONSHIP SERIES RECORD

Year Team (League)	Pos.	G	AB	R	H	2B	3B	HR	RBI	BB	SO	HBP	GDP	SB-CS	Avg.	OBP	SLG	OPS	E	Avg.
1999— New York (N.L.)	OF	5	12	2	6	0	0	1	1	0	1	0	0	2-1	.500	.500	.583	1.083	0	1.000
2004— St. Louis (N.L.)	OF	6	6	1	1	0	0	0	1	0	2	0	0	0-0	.167	.167	.167	.333	0	...
Champ. series totals (2 years)		11	18	3	7	1	0	1	2	0	3	0	0	2-1	.389	.389	.444	.833	0	1.000

WORLD SERIES RECORD

Year Team (League)	Pos.	G	AB	R	H	2B	3B	HR	RBI	BB	SO	HBP	GDP	SB-CS	Avg.	OBP	SLG	OPS	E	Avg.
2004— St. Louis (N.L.)	OF	3	4	1	1	0	0	0	0	0	1	0	0	0-0	.250	.250	.250	.500	0	...

CEDENO, RONNY   SS

PERSONAL: Born February 2, 1983, in Carabobo, Venezuela. ... 6-0/180. ... Bats right, throws right. ... Full name: Ronny Alexander Cedeno. ... College: None.

TRANSACTIONS/CAREER NOTES: Signed as a non-drafted free agent by Chicago Cubs organization (August 27, 1999).

2005 GAMES PLAYED BY POSITION (MLB): SS—29, 2B—1.

SCOUTING REPORT Cedeno is a very live-bodied infielder with very quick feet and soft hands. Has excellent agility with plus range to either side and plays under control. Charges the ball well and has a very quick release. Is accurate on throws from the hole. Is an excellent runner. Is extremely aggressive at the plate and likes the ball up. Can be the Cubs' opening day shortstop with a good spring. ***Grade 5.9***

RONNY CEDENO'S HITTING ZONE

.333	...	.167
.348	.250	.400
.167	.667	.167

LEFTY-RIGHTY SPLITS

vs.	Avg.	AB	H	2B	3B	HR	RBI	BB	SO	OBP	Slg.
L	.256	39	10	3	0	0	2	1	4	.275	.333
R	.341	41	14	0	0	1	4	4	7	.426	.415

Year Team (League)	Pos.	G	AB	R	H	2B	3B	HR	RBI	BB	SO	HBP	GDP	SB-CS	Avg.	OBP	SLG	OPS	E	Avg.
2000— La Pradera (VSL)		51	167	35	48	8	3	3	14	19	37	3	1	13-10	.287	.370	.425	.795	...	...
2001— Lansing (Midw.)	SS-2B	17	56	9	11	4	1	1	2	2	18	1	1	0-2	.196	.237	.357	.594	5	.921

Year	Team (League)	Pos.	G	AB	R	H	2B	3B	HR	RBI	BB	SO	HBP	GDP	SB-CS	Avg.	OBP	SLG	OPS	E	Avg.
	— Ariz. Cubs (Ariz.)	SS-2B	52	206	36	72	13	4	1	17	13	32	5	3	17-10	.350	.398	.466	.864	22	.902
2002—	Lansing (Midw.)	SS-2B	98	376	44	80	17	4	2	31	22	74	8	6	14-10	.213	.269	.295	.564	26	.946
	— Boise (N'west)	SS-2B	29	110	17	24	5	2	0	6	9	25	0	1	8-2	.218	.275	.300	.575	8	.943
2003—	Daytona (Fla. St.)	SS-2B	107	380	43	80	18	1	4	36	21	82	4	5	19-6	.211	.257	.295	.552	29	.942
2004—	West Tenn (Sou.)	SS	116	384	39	107	19	5	6	48	24	74	8	10	10-10	.279	.328	.401	.729	18	.820
2005—	Iowa (PCL)	SS	65	245	42	87	14	1	8	36	20	31	1	9	11-3	.355	.403	.518	.921	12	.961
	— Chicago (N.L.)	SS-2B	41	80	13	24	3	0	1	6	5	11	2	4	1-0	.300	.356	.375	.731	1	.986
Major League totals (1 year)			41	80	13	24	3	0	1	6	5	11	2	4	1-0	.300	.356	.375	.731	1	.986

CEPICKY, MATT — OF

PERSONAL: Born November 10, 1977, in St. Louis. ... 6-2/215. ... Bats left, throws right. ... Full name: Matthew William Cepicky. ... Name pronounced: suh-PICK-ee. ... High school: Vianney (Kirkwood, Mo.). ... College: Southwest Missouri State.

TRANSACTIONS/CAREER NOTES: Selected by Montreal Expos organization in fourth round of 1999 free-agent draft. ... Expos franchise transferred to Washington, D.C., and renamed Washington Nationals for 2005 season (December 3, 2004).

2005 GAMES PLAYED BY POSITION (MLB): OF—6.

LEFTY-RIGHTY SPLITS

vs.	Avg.	AB	H	2B	3B	HR	RBI	BB	SO	OBP	Slg.
L	.000	2	0	0	0	0	0	0	2	.000	.000
R	.261	23	6	3	0	0	3	1	6	.292	.391

Year	Team (League)	Pos.	G	AB	R	H	2B	3B	HR	RBI	BB	SO	HBP	GDP	SB-CS	Avg.	OBP	SLG	OPS	E	Avg.
1999—	Vermont (NYP)	OF	74	323	50	99	15	5	12	53	20	49	1	6	10-9	.307	.349	.495	.844	1	.986
2000—	Jupiter (Fla. St.)	OF	131	536	61	160	32	7	5	88	24	64	2	9	32-13	.299	.328	.412	.740	4	.983
2001—	Harrisburg (East.)	OF	122	459	59	121	23	8	15	77	21	97	2	6	5-12	.264	.296	.447	.743	3	.986
2002—	Harrisburg (East.)	OF	109	419	54	116	25	2	16	76	33	94	2	14	7-1	.277	.327	.461	.787	2	.988
	— Montreal (N.L.)	OF	32	74	7	16	3	0	3	15	4	21	0	0	0-0	.216	.256	.378	.635	0	1.000
2003—	Montreal (N.L.)	OF	5	8	0	2	1	0	0	0	0	2	0	0	0-0	.250	.250	.375	.625	0	1.000
	— Edmonton (PCL)	OF-DH-1B	122	442	61	133	23	4	7	64	31	82	4	12	7-2	.301	.349	.419	.767	11	.948
2004—	Montreal (N.L.)	OF-DH-1B	32	60	4	13	4	0	1	3	1	18	0	1	1-0	.217	.230	.383	.563	0	1.000
	— Edmonton (PCL)	OF-DH-1B	82	312	51	84	15	3	15	67	18	75	0	4	2-1	.269	.305	.481	.786	4	.975
2005—	Washington (N.L.)	OF	11	25	1	6	0	0	0	3	1	8	0	1	0-1	.240	.269	.360	.629	0	1.000
	— New Orleans (PCL)	OF-1B-DH																			
		2B-3B	99	342	52	92	23	3	14	68	43	85	0	11	1-3	.269	.347	.477	.824	11	.975
Major League totals (4 years)			80	167	12	37	11	0	4	21	6	49	0	2	1-1	.222	.249	.359	.608	0	1.000

CERDA, JAIME — P

PERSONAL: Born October 26, 1978, in Fresno, Calif. ... 6-0/175. ... Throws left, bats left. ... Full name: Jaime Magana Cerda. ... Name pronounced: HY-may SER-da. ... High school: Selma (Calif.). ... Junior college: Fresno City (Calif.). ... College: Fresno City (CA) CC.

TRANSACTIONS/CAREER NOTES: Selected by New York Mets organization in 23rd round of 1998 free-agent draft. ... Traded by Mets to Kansas City Royals for P Shawn Sedlacek (January 26, 2004). ... Claimed on waivers by Colorado Rockies (October 4, 2005).

CAREER HITTING: 0-for-2 (.000), 0 R, 0 2B, 0 3B, 0 HR, 0 RBI.

SCOUTING REPORT *Throws:* Cerda's fastball ranges from 90-93 mph. Also has a slider and a changeup. *Tendencies:* Though his herky-jerky motion affects his command and makes him inconsistent, it also aids in his deception. Gets good tailing action on his fastball. Slider is very quick and runs away from lefthanded hitters. Has good arm speed and motion with his change but needs to be more consistent with it to set up his fastball on the inside half to righthanders. *Outlook:* The key for Cerda is to slow down his delivery and learn to pitch within himself so he can command his fastball. Long and middle relief for now. *Grade 5.7*

JAIME CERDA'S PITCHING ZONE

.000	.000	.250
.500	.200	.500
.500	.000	.286

LEFTY-RIGHTY SPLITS

vs.	Avg.	AB	H	2B	3B	HR	RBI	BB	SO	OBP	Slg.
L	.231	39	9	1	0	2	9	2	10	.262	.410
R	.343	35	12	4	0	1	5	9	8	.477	.543

Year	Team (League)	W	L	Pct.	ERA	WHIP	G	GS	CG	ShO	Hld.	Sv.-Opp.	IP	H	R	ER	HR	BB-IBB	SO	Avg.
1999—				Did not play.																
2000—	Pittsfield (NYP)	4	1	.800	0.57	0.83	20	1	0	0	...	5-...	47.0	33	6	3	0	6-1	51	.198
2001—	St. Lucie (Fla. St.)	2	1	.667	0.97	0.93	28	0	0	0	...	6-...	55.2	40	8	6	3	12-0	53	.204
	— Binghamton (East.)	1	0	1.000	3.10	1.13	12	0	0	0	...	3-...	20.1	17	7	7	1	6-0	22	.233
	— Norfolk (Int'l)	0	0	...	3.86	0.86	3	0	0	0	...	0-...	4.2	2	2	2	0	2-0	4	.125
2002—	Binghamton (East.)	5	1	.833	2.27	0.98	14	0	0	0	...	0-...	31.2	21	8	8	0	10-0	33	.193
	— Norfolk (Int'l)	0	0	...	0.43	0.81	12	0	0	0	...	1-...	21.0	10	2	1	0	7-1	17	.143
	— New York (N.L.)	0	0	...	2.45	1.40	32	0	0	0	4	0-0	25.2	22	7	7	0	14-0	21	.232
2003—	Norfolk (Int'l)	3	0	1.000	1.67	1.20	22	0	0	0	...	0-1	32.1	29	7	6	3	10-1	35	.246
	— New York (N.L.)	1	1	.500	5.85	1.61	27	0	0	0	2	0-1	32.1	32	21	21	4	20-1	19	.267
2004—	Omaha (PCL)	0	0	...	3.00	1.83	4	0	0	0	...	0-...	6.0	8	2	2	0	3-0	2	.348
	— Kansas City (A.L.)	1	4	.200	3.15	1.55	53	0	0	0	12	2-3	45.2	41	21	16	1	30-3	33	.244
2005—	Kansas City (A.L.)	1	4	.200	6.63	1.68	20	0	0	0	3	0-1	19.0	21	14	14	3	11-2	18	.284
	— Omaha (PCL)	4	1	.800	5.26	1.39	35	0	0	0	7	2-2	49.2	48	33	29	6	21-1	47	.249
American League totals (2 years)		2	8	.200	4.18	1.59	73	0	0	0	15	2-4	64.2	62	35	30	4	41-5	51	.256
National League totals (2 years)		1	1	.500	4.34	1.52	59	0	0	0	6	0-1	58.0	54	28	28	4	34-1	40	.251
Major League totals (4 years)		3	9	.250	4.26	1.56	132	0	0	0	21	2-5	122.2	116	63	58	8	75-6	91	.254

CHACIN, GUSTAVO — P

PERSONAL: Born December 4, 1980, in Maracaibo, Venezuela. ... 5-11/193. ... Throws left, bats left. ... Full name: Gustavo Adolfo Chacin. ... Name pronounced: Shah-SEEN.

TRANSACTIONS/CAREER NOTES: Signed as a non-drafted free agent by Toronto Blue Jays organization (July 3, 1998).

CAREER HITTING: 0-for-7 (.000), 1 R, 0 2B, 0 3B, 0 HR, 0 RBI.

SCOUTING REPORT *Throws:* Chacin has an 85-92 mph fastball, a curveball, a slider and a changeup. *Tendencies:* He has a complex, deceptive delivery with a lot of motion. Has good running action and command of fastball to both sides of the plate. Can cut the ball to either side. Has a big curveball, but it lacks tight spin; has a smaller break on his slider, but it is a better pitch. Gets good movement and has good arm speed on his changeup. *Outlook:* Chacin knows how to pitch and has good command, especially considering his violent delivery. *Grade 8*

GUSTAVO CHACIN'S PITCHING ZONE

.457	.273	.286
.250	.347	.318
.363	.184	.183

LEFTY-RIGHTY SPLITS

vs.	Avg.	AB	H	2B	3B	HR	RBI	BB	SO	OBP	Slg.
L	.225	169	38	10	0	2	18	15	33	.289	.320
R	.288	607	175	31	4	18	68	55	88	.350	.442

Year	Team (League)	W	L	Pct.	ERA	WHIP	G	GS	CG	ShO	Hld.	Sv.-Opp.	IP	H	R	ER	HR	BB-IBB	SO	Avg.
1998— Dom. B. Jays (DSL)		3	2	.600	2.70	1.17	9	6	2	2	...	0-...	36.2	28	12	11	...	15-...	56	...
1999— Medicine Hat (Pio.)		4	3	.571	3.09	1.42	15	9	0	0	...	1-...	64.0	68	33	22	6	23-0	50	.281
2000— Dunedin (Fla. St.)		9	5	.643	4.02	1.58	25	21	0	0	...	0-...	127.2	138	69	57	14	64-0	77	.269
— Tennessee (Sou.)		0	2	.000	12.60	3.20	2	2	0	0	...	0-...	5.0	10	7	7	1	6-0	5	.417
2001— Tennessee (Sou.)		11	8	.579	3.98	1.26	25	23	1	1	...	0-...	140.1	138	66	62	17	39-0	86	.257
2002— Tennessee (Sou.)		6	5	.545	4.66	1.59	35	13	1	0	...	1-...	119.2	131	73	62	12	59-0	68	.282
2003— New Haven (East.)		3	4	.429	4.15	1.54	46	2	0	0	...	2-...	69.1	78	39	32	1	29-1	55	.283
2004— Syracuse (Int'l)		2	0	1.000	2.31	1.63	2	2	0	0	...	0-...	11.2	16	4	3	0	3-0	14	.327
— New Hampshire (East.)		16	2	.889	2.92	1.14	25	25	0	0	...	0-...	141.2	113	53	46	15	49-0	109	.215
— Toronto (A.L.)		1	1	.500	2.57	0.79	2	2	0	0	0	0-0	14.0	8	4	4	0	3-0	6	.167
2005— Toronto (A.L.)		13	9	.591	3.72	1.39	34	34	0	0	0	0-0	203.0	213	93	84	20	70-3	121	.274
Major League totals (2 years)		14	10	.583	3.65	1.35	36	36	0	0	0	0-0	217.0	221	97	88	20	73-3	127	.268

C

CHACON, SHAWN   P

PERSONAL: Born December 23, 1977, in Anchorage, Alaska. ... 6-3/212. ... Throws right, bats right. ... Full name: Shawn Anthony Chacon. ... Name pronounced: chah-CONE. ... High school: Greeley (Colo.) Central.

TRANSACTIONS/CAREER NOTES: Selected by Colorado Rockies organization in third round of 1996 free-agent draft. ... On disabled list (May 10-June 6, 2002); included rehabilitation assignment to Colorado Springs. ... On disabled list (June 30-July 19 and August 18, 2003-remainder of season); included rehabilitation assignment to Colorado Springs. ... On disabled list (June 5-July 6, 2005); included rehabilitation assignment to Colorado Springs. ... Traded by Rockies to New York Yankees for Ps Ramon Ramirez and Eduardo Sierra (July 28, 2005).

CAREER HITTING: 23-for-148 (.155), 9 R, 3 2B, 0 3B, 1 HR, 9 RBI.

SCOUTING REPORT *Throws:* Chacon throws a fastball from 86-90 mph, a curveball, a slider and a changeup. *Tendencies:* He has excellent deception in his delivery and good action on his fastball down in the zone. Doesn't back off from hitters despite lack of velocity. Has a good curve that gives the appearance of breaking early out of his hand but breaks again late on top of the hitter. The ability to throw his curve for strikes makes his fastball better. Slider is also quick. Has good motion with his change. *Outlook:* Chacon is a better pitcher now than at any time in his career. *Grade 7.8*

SHAWN CHACON'S PITCHING ZONE

.150	.250	.212
.314	.281	.279
.209	.242	.191

LEFTY-RIGHTY SPLITS

vs.	Avg.	AB	H	2B	3B	HR	RBI	BB	SO	OBP	Slg.
L	.232	284	66	16	1	4	15	35	42	.326	.338
R	.252	274	69	19	1	10	38	31	37	.343	.438

Year	Team (League)	W	L	Pct.	ERA	WHIP	G	GS	CG	ShO	Hld.	Sv.-Opp.	IP	H	R	ER	HR	BB-IBB	SO	Avg.
1996— Ariz. Rockies (Ariz.)		1	2	.333	1.60	1.08	11	11	1	0		0-...	56.1	46	17	10	1	15-0	64	.209
— Portland (N'west)		0	2	.000	6.86	1.68	4	4	0	0		0-...	19.2	24	18	15	2	9-0	17	.293
1997— Asheville (S. Atl.)		11	7	.611	3.89	1.35	28	27	1	0		0-...	162.0	155	80	70	13	63-1	149	.252
1998— Salem (Carol.)		0	4	.000	5.30	1.50	12	12	0	0		0-...	56.0	53	35	33	5	31-0	54	.245
1999— Salem (Carol.)		5	5	.500	4.13	1.43	12	12	0	0		0-...	72.0	69	44	33	3	34-0	66	.250
2000— Carolina (Southern)		10	10	.500	3.16	1.36	27	27	4	3		0-...	173.2	151	71	61	10	85-1	172	.236
2001— Colo. Springs (PCL)		2	0	1.000	2.25	1.04	4	4	0	0		0-...	24.0	18	6	6	3	7-0	28	.207
— Colorado (N.L.)		6	10	.375	5.06	1.53	27	27	0	0	0	0-0	160.0	157	96	90	26	87-10	134	.260
2002— Colorado (N.L.)		5	11	.313	5.73	1.53	21	21	0	0	0	0-0	119.1	122	84	76	25	60-3	67	.264
— Colo. Springs (PCL)		2	0	1.000	4.79	1.60	4	4	0	0	0	0-...	20.2	23	12	11	3	10-0	15	.291
2003— Colo. Springs (PCL)		0	0	...	6.00	1.70	1	1	0	0	0	0-...	3.0	5	2	2	1	0-0	2	.385
— Colorado (N.L.)		11	8	.579	4.60	1.33	23	23	0	0	0	0-0	137.0	124	73	70	12	58-4	93	.243
2004— Colorado (N.L.)		1	9	.100	7.11	1.94	66	0	0	0	0	35-44	63.1	71	52	50	12	52-7	52	.282
2005— Colo. Springs (PCL)		0	2	.000	9.95	1.82	3	3	0	0	0	0-0	12.2	19	14	14	3	4-0	11	.345
— Colorado (N.L.)		1	7	.125	4.09	1.44	13	12	0	0	0	0-0	72.2	69	33	33	7	36-4	39	.260
— New York (A.L.)		7	3	.700	2.85	1.22	14	12	0	0	0	0-0	79.0	66	26	25	7	30-0	40	.225
American League totals (1 year)		7	3	.700	2.85	1.22	14	12	0	0	0	0-0	79.0	66	26	25	7	30-0	40	.225
National League totals (5 years)		24	45	.348	5.20	1.51	150	83	0	0	0	35-44	552.1	543	338	319	82	293-28	385	.259
Major League totals (5 years)		31	48	.392	4.90	1.48	164	95	0	0	0	35-44	631.1	609	364	344	89	323-28	425	.255

DIVISION SERIES RECORD

Year	Team (League)	W	L	Pct.	ERA	WHIP	G	GS	CG	ShO	Hld.	Sv.-Opp.	IP	H	R	ER	HR	BB-IBB	SO	Avg.
2005— New York (A.L.)		0	0	...	2.84	0.79	1	1	0	0	0	0-0	6.1	4	2	2	0	1-0	5	.190

CHAVEZ, ANGEL   SS

PERSONAL: Born July 22, 1981, in Panama City, Panama. ... 6-1/195. ... Bats right, throws right. ... Full name: Angel Aristedes Chavez. ... College: None.

TRANSACTIONS/CAREER NOTES: Signed as a non-drafted free agent by San Francisco Giants organization (October 30, 1998).

2005 GAMES PLAYED BY POSITION (MLB): 2B—5, SS—4, 3B—1.

LEFTY-RIGHTY SPLITS

vs.	Avg.	AB	H	2B	3B	HR	RBI	BB	SO	OBP	Slg.
L	.000	2	0	0	0	0	0	0	2	.000	.000
R	.294	17	5	1	0	0	1	0	1	.294	.353

Year	Team (League)	Pos.	G	AB	R	H	2B	3B	HR	RBI	BB	SO	HBP	GDP	SB-CS	Avg.	OBP	SLG	OPS	E	Avg.
1999— La Victoria (Pion.)			52	186	40	64	12	1	14	49	15	32	1	1	11-3	.344	.392	.645	1.037	...	...

Year	Team (League)	Pos.	G	AB	R	H	2B	3B	HR	RBI	BB	SO	HBP	GDP	SB-CS	Avg.	OBP	SLG	OPS	E	Avg.
2000—	Ariz. Giants (Ariz.)	SS	7	29	2	8	0	1	1	7	1	5	0	2	1-1	.276	.300	.448	.748	0	1.000
2001—	Hagerstown (SAL)	3B-SS	13	37	5	7	2	0	2	3	1	12	1	0	1-0	.189	.231	.405	.636	5	.865
	—San Jose (Calif.)	3B-SS-2B	84	316	37	77	22	2	3	28	16	60	1	9	10-4	.244	.280	.354	.634	16	.938
2002—	San Jose (Calif.)	3B-SS-2B	130	471	61	121	20	5	8	62	28	83	6	12	21-7	.257	.303	.372	.675	27	.941
2003—	San Jose (Calif.)	3B-SS-2B	120	478	69	134	23	6	10	58	22	60	4	13	20-11	.280	.314	.416	.730	25	.957
2004—	Norwich (East.)	SS-3B	89	308	22	61	8	2	0	21	24	53	3	10	6-4	.198	.261	.237	.498	15	.865
	—Ariz. Giants (Ariz.)	SS	4	16	2	6	0	0	1	5	1	3	0	1	2-0	.375	.389	.563	.952	1	.929
	—San Jose (Calif.)	3B-SS-2B	12	54	12	21	5	0	1	16	4	7	1	1	2-2	.389	.433	.537	.970	4	.000
2005—	San Jose (Calif.)	3B-SS-2B	30	120	22	34	2	1	5	19	5	21	0	7	4-0	.283	.310	.442	.751	4	.974
	—Fresno (PCL)	SS-2B-3B	89	334	46	94	17	3	11	64	17	59	3	6	5-1	.281	.320	.449	.769	11	.970
	—San Francisco (N.L.)	2B-SS-3B	10	19	1	5	1	0	0	1	0	3	0	0	0-0	.263	.263	.316	.579	1	.947
Major League totals (1 year)			10	19	1	5	1	0	0	1	0	3	0	0	0-0	.263	.263	.316	.579	1	.947

CHAVEZ, ENDY — OF

PERSONAL: Born February 7, 1978, in Valencia, Venezuela. ... 5-10/189. ... Bats left, throws left. ... Full name: Endy DeJesus Chavez. ... Name pronounced: SHAH-vez. ... High school: Liceo Bataila Carabobo (Venezuela).

TRANSACTIONS/CAREER NOTES: Signed as a non-drafted free agent by New York Mets organization (April 29, 1996). ... Selected by Kansas City Royals from Mets organization in Rule 5 major league draft (December 11, 2000). ... Returned to Mets organization (March 30, 2001). ... Traded by Mets to Royals for OF Michael Curry (March 30, 2001). ... Claimed on waivers by Detroit Tigers (December 20, 2001). ... Claimed on waivers by Mets (February 1, 2002). ... Claimed on waivers by Montreal Expos (February 22, 2002). ... Expos franchise transferred to Washington, D.C., and renamed Washington Nationals for 2005 season (December 3, 2004). ... Traded by Nationals to Philadelphia Phillies for OF Marlon Byrd (May 14, 2005).

2005 GAMES PLAYED BY POSITION (MLB): OF—57.

ENDY CHAVEZ'S HITTING ZONE

.000	.143	.273
.385	.000	.300
.000	.286	.167

LEFTY-RIGHTY SPLITS

vs.	Avg.	AB	H	2B	3B	HR	RBI	BB	SO	OBP	Slg.
L	.381	21	8	2	2	0	4	0	1	.381	.667
R	.179	95	17	2	1	0	7	7	13	.235	.221

Year	Team (League)	Pos.	G	AB	R	H	2B	3B	HR	RBI	BB	SO	HBP	GDP	SB-CS	Avg.	OBP	SLG	OPS	E	Avg.
1996—	Dom. Mets (DSL)	OF	48	164	42	58	11	1	7	29	22	16	...		3-...	.354	...	.561	...	3	.963
1997—	GC Mets (GCL)	OF	33	119	26	33	6	3	0	15	20	10	0	2	1-2	.277	.379	.378	.757	2	.967
	—Kingsport (Appalachian)	OF	19	73	16	22	4	0	0	4	13	10	0	2	5-2	.301	.407	.356	.763	2	.957
1998—	Kingsport (Appalachian)	OF	33	114	26	33	8	4	0	16	17	17	0	1	10-5	.289	.373	.430	.803	2	.941
1999—	Capital City (SAL)	OF	73	253	40	64	8	1	0	15	34	36	0	3	20-12	.253	.340	.292	.633	5	.967
	—St. Lucie (Fla. St.)	OF	45	183	33	57	8	3	2	18	22	22	0	5	9-3	.311	.383	.421	.804	2	.980
2000—	St. Lucie (Fla. St.)	OF	111	433	84	129	20	2	1	43	47	48	0	3	38-16	.298	.364	.360	.725	5	.980
2001—	Wichita (Texas)	OF	43	168	27	50	6	1	1	13	16	13	0	1	11-6	.298	.353	.363	.716	1	.980
	—Kansas City (A.L.)	OF	29	77	4	16	2	0	0	5	3	8	0	3	0-2	.208	.238	.234	.471	0	1.000
	—Omaha (PCL)	OF	23	104	18	35	6	0	0	4	0	13	0	1	4-3	.337	.333	.394	.728	0	1.000
2002—	Ottawa (Int'l)	OF	103	405	67	139	28	5	4	41	33	37	0	8	21-13	.343	.392	.467	.858	4	.985
	—Montreal (N.L.)	OF	36	125	20	37	8	5	1	9	5	16	0	0	3-5	.296	.321	.464	.785	1	.989
2003—	Montreal (N.L.)	OF	141	483	66	121	25	5	5	47	31	59	0	7	18-7	.251	.294	.354	.648	3	.990
2004—	Edmonton (PCL)	OF	14	61	9	21	3	2	0	7	7	7	0	0	5-2	.344	.406	.459	.865	0	1.000
	—Montreal (N.L.)	OF	132	502	65	139	20	6	5	34	30	40	1	6	32-7	.277	.318	.371	.688	5	.984
2005—	Washington (N.L.)	OF	7	9	2	2	1	0	0	1	3	1	0	1	0-1	.222	.417	.333	.750	0	1.000
	—New Orleans (PCL)	OF	23	87	11	22	6	0	1	4	10	7	0	2	6-1	.253	.330	.333	.663	2	.983
	—Philadelphia (N.L.)	OF	91	107	17	23	3	3	0	10	4	13	0	2	2-1	.215	.243	.299	.542	1	.980
American League totals (1 year)			29	77	4	16	2	0	0	5	3	8	0	3	0-2	.208	.238	.234	.471	0	1.000
National League totals (4 years)			407	1226	170	322	57	19	11	101	73	129	1	16	55-21	.263	.303	.367	.670	10	.987
Major League totals (5 years)			436	1303	174	338	59	19	11	106	76	137	1	19	55-23	.259	.299	.359	.659	10	.987

CHAVEZ, ERIC — 3B

PERSONAL: Born December 7, 1977, in Los Angeles. ... 6-1/206. ... Bats left, throws right. ... Full name: Eric Cesar Chavez. ... Name pronounced: shah-VEZ. ... High school: Mount Carmel (San Diego).

TRANSACTIONS/CAREER NOTES: Selected by Oakland Athletics organization in first round (10th pick overall) of 1996 free-agent draft. ... On disabled list (August 21-September 19, 1999); included rehabilitation assignment to Vancouver. ... On disabled list (June 2-July 9, 2004); included rehabilitation assignment to Sacramento.

HONORS: Won A.L. Gold Glove at third base (2001-05).

2005 GAMES PLAYED BY POSITION (MLB): 3B—153, DH—6.

***SCOUTING REPORT** Offense:* Chavez has an exceptionally quick bat despite a long swing. Uses his legs to drive the ball. Has good plate coverage. Tried to put more balls in play last season. Likes the ball up and has exceptional power to the alleys. Can drive the ball to all fields. Is slow out of the box because of his long swing. Tends to be streaky. *Defense:* Chavez has an unconventional approach to ground balls, with a bit of a stiff back and a preference for fielding the ball to the side. Has quick, soft hands. *Outlook:* Despite his off year at the plate in 2005, Chavez still is an outstanding third baseman. Still drove in 100 runs despite a lack of protection and a low average. *Grade 9.3*

ERIC CHAVEZ'S HITTING ZONE

.276	.357	.298
.313	.390	.295
.333	.417	.221

LEFTY-RIGHTY SPLITS

vs.	Avg.	AB	H	2B	3B	HR	RBI	BB	SO	OBP	Slg.
L	.264	216	57	16	0	6	41	20	61	.328	.421
R	.271	409	111	24	1	21	60	38	68	.329	.489

Year	Team (League)	Pos.	G	AB	R	H	2B	3B	HR	RBI	BB	SO	HBP	GDP	SB-CS	Avg.	OBP	SLG	OPS	E	Avg.
1997—	Visalia (Calif.)	3B-DH	134	520	67	141	30	3	18	100	37	91	2	20	13-7	.271	.321	.444	.765	32	.917
1998—	Huntsville (Sou.)	3B-DH	88	335	66	110	27	1	22	86	42	61	1	6	12-4	.328	.402	.612	1.014	14	.935
	—Edmonton (PCL)	3B-DH	47	194	38	63	18	0	11	40	12	32	1	4	2-3	.325	.364	.588	.951	7	.935
	—Oakland (A.L.)	3B	16	45	6	14	4	1	0	6	3	5	0	1	1-1	.311	.354	.444	.799	0	1.000
1999—	Oakland (A.L.)	3B-DH-SS	115	356	40	88	21	2	13	50	46	56	0	7	1-1	.247	.333	.427	.760	9	.961

Year	Team (League)	Pos.	G	AB	R	H	2B	3B	HR	RBI	BB	SO	HBP	GDP	SB-CS	Avg.	OBP	SLG	OPS	E	Avg.
2000— Oakland (A.L.)	3B-SS-DH		153	501	89	139	23	4	26	86	62	94	1	9	2-2	.277	.355	.495	.850	18	.951
2001— Oakland (A.L.)	3B-1B-DH																				
	SS		151	552	91	159	43	0	32	114	41	99	4	7	8-2	.288	.338	.540	.878	12	.972
2002— Oakland (A.L.)	3B-DH-OF		153	585	87	161	31	3	34	109	65	119	4	8	8-3	.275	.348	.513	.860	17	.961
2003— Oakland (A.L.)	3B		156	588	94	166	39	5	29	101	62	89	1	14	8-3	.282	.350	.514	.864	14	.971
2004— Sacramento (PCL)	DH-3B		3	13	2	4	1	0	0	0	1	2	0	0	0-0	.308	.357	.385	.742	0	...
— Oakland (A.L.)	3B-OF		125	475	87	131	20	0	29	77	* 95	99	3	21	6-3	.276	.397	.501	.898	13	.968
2005— Oakland (A.L.)	3B-DH		160	625	92	168	40	1	27	101	58	129	2	9	6-0	.269	.329	.466	.794	15	.966
Major League totals (8 years)			1029	3727	593	1026	221	16	190	644	432	690	12	76	40-15	.275	.350	.496	.846	98	.965

DIVISION SERIES RECORD

Year	Team (League)	Pos.	G	AB	R	H	2B	3B	HR	RBI	BB	SO	HBP	GDP	SB-CS	Avg.	OBP	SLG	OPS	E	Avg.
2000— Oakland (A.L.)	3B	5	21	4	7	3	0	0	4	0	5	0	1	0-0	.333	.333	.476	.810	0	1.000
2001— Oakland (A.L.)	3B	5	21	0	3	1	0	0	0	0	5	0	1	0-0	.143	.143	.190	.333	1	.938
2002— Oakland (A.L.)	3B	5	21	3	8	0	0	1	5	2	1	0	0	0-0	.381	.435	.524	.959	0	1.000
2003— Oakland (A.L.)	3B	5	22	1	1	1	0	0	0	1	3	0	0	1-0	.045	.087	.091	.178	2	.867
Division series totals (4 years)		20	85	8	19	5	0	1	9	3	14	0	2	1-0	.224	.250	.318	.568	3	.949

CHAVEZ, RAUL   C

PERSONAL: Born March 18, 1973, in Valencia, Venezuela. ... 5-11/215. ... Bats right, throws right. ... Full name: Raul Alexander Chavez.... Name pronounced: SHAH-vez.

TRANSACTIONS/CAREER NOTES: Signed as a non-drafted free agent by Houston Astros organization (January 10, 1990). ... Traded by Astros with P Dave Veres to Montreal Expos for 3B Sean Berry (December 20, 1995). ... Traded by Expos to Seattle Mariners for OF Robert Perez (May 8, 1998). ... Signed as a free agent by Astros organization (January 5, 2000).

2005 GAMES PLAYED BY POSITION (MLB): C—36.

SCOUTING REPORT Chavez is a good defensive catcher with exceptional arm strength and good accuracy. Controls the running game well. Must continually monitor his weight to retain his mobility in blocking and shifting behind the plate. Has a long swing and doesn't generate much bat speed but has some power when he extends his arms. Has never shown that he can hit enough to play more than once a week. *Grade 5.1*

RAUL CHAVEZ'S HITTING ZONE

.375	.000	.250
.182	.300	.222
.083	.333	.000

LEFTY-RIGHTY SPLITS

vs.	Avg.	AB	H	2B	3B	HR	RBI	BB	SO	OBP	Slg.
L	.133	30	4	0	0	0	0	4	5	.257	.133
R	.188	69	13	3	0	2	6	0	13	.186	.319

Year	Team (League)	Pos.	G	AB	R	H	2B	3B	HR	RBI	BB	SO	HBP	GDP	SB-CS	Avg.	OBP	SLG	OPS	E	Avg.
1990— GC Astros (GCL)	2B-3B-SS	48	155	23	50	8	1	0	23	7	12	2	7	5-3	.323	.358	.387	.745	9	.954
1991— Burlington (Midw.)	3B-SS	114	420	54	108	17	0	3	41	25	65	10	13	1-4	.257	.312	.319	.631	41	.914
1992— Asheville (S. Atl.)	C	95	348	37	99	22	1	2	40	16	39	4	11	1-0	.284	.320	.371	.691	13	.976
1993— Osceola (Fla. St.)	C	58	197	13	45	5	1	0	16	8	19	1	12	1-1	.228	.261	.264	.525	5	.986
1994— Jackson (Texas)	C	89	251	17	55	7	0	1	22	17	41	2	5	1-0	.219	.273	.259	.532	9	.986
1995— Jackson (Texas)	C	58	188	16	54	8	0	4	25	8	17	3	7	0-4	.287	.323	.394	.717	5	.987
— Tucson (PCL)	C	32	103	14	27	5	0	0	10	8	13	2	7	0-1	.262	.325	.311	.635	5	.980
1996— Ottawa (Int'l)	C	60	198	15	49	10	0	2	24	11	31	1	7	0-2	.247	.290	.328	.619	4	.990
— Montreal (N.L.)	C	3	5	1	1	0	0	0	0	0	1	1	0	1-0	.200	.333	.200	.533	0	1.000
1997— Ottawa (Int'l)	C-DH	92	310	31	76	17	0	4	46	18	42	4	9	1-3	.245	.293	.339	.631	15	.978
— Montreal (N.L.)	C	13	26	0	7	0	0	0	2	0	5	0	0	1-0	.269	.259	.269	.528	0	1.000
1998— Ottawa (Int'l)	C	11	31	2	7	0	0	0	1	1	5	0	0	1-0	.226	.333	.226	.559	0	1.000
— Tacoma (PCL)	C-DH	76	233	27	52	6	0	4	34	22	41	4	7	1-2	.223	.294	.300	.595	6	.992
— Seattle (A.L.)	C	1	1	0	0	0	0	0	0	0	0	0	0	0-0	.000	.000	.000	.000	0	1.000
1999— Tacoma (PCL)	C-DH-1B 2B-3B-SS	102	354	39	95	20	1	3	40	28	63	6	11	1-3	.268	.331	.356	.687	10	.987
2000— New Orleans (PCL)	C	99	303	31	74	13	0	2	36	34	44	4	12	3-0	.244	.325	.307	.632	8	.987
— Houston (N.L.)	C	14	43	3	11	2	0	1	5	3	6	0	5	0-0	.256	.298	.372	.670	1	.986
2001— New Orleans (PCL)	C-1B-3B	85	278	38	84	17	0	8	40	19	34	7	9	1-1	.302	.361	.450	.810	5	.992
2002— New Orleans (PCL)	C	111	373	24	85	10	0	3	36	21	50	7	11	3-4	.228	.278	.279	.557	7	.992
— Houston (N.L.)	C	2	4	1	1	1	0	0	0	0	1	0	0	0-0	.250	.500	.500	1.000	0	1.000
2003— New Orleans (PCL)	C-3B-DH	101	355	47	97	28	1	6	47	13	43	11	0	0-2	.273	.315	.408	.724	11	.977
— Houston (N.L.)	C	19	37	5	10	1	1	1	4	1	6	0	3	0-0	.270	.289	.432	.722	0	1.000
2004— Houston (N.L.)	C	64	162	9	34	8	0	0	23	10	38	0	9	0-1	.210	.256	.259	.515	4	.991
2005— Round Rock (PCL)	C	34	119	9	30	8	0	0	14	5	24	3	4	0-0	.252	.299	.319	.619	2	.992
— Houston (N.L.)	C	37	99	6	17	3	0	2	6	4	18	1	5	1-0	.172	.210	.263	.472	2	.991
American League totals (1 year)		1	1	0	0	0	0	0	0	0	0	0	0	0-0	.000	.000	.000	.000	0	1.000
National League totals (7 years)		152	376	25	81	15	1	4	40	20	74	2	23	3-1	.215	.257	.293	.549	7	.992
Major League totals (8 years)		153	377	25	81	15	1	4	40	20	74	2	23	3-1	.215	.256	.292	.548	7	.992

DIVISION SERIES RECORD

Year	Team (League)	Pos.	G	AB	R	H	2B	3B	HR	RBI	BB	SO	HBP	GDP	SB-CS	Avg.	OBP	SLG	OPS	E	Avg.
2004— Houston (N.L.)	C	2	5	1	3	0	0	0	1	0	0	0	0	0-0	.600	.600	1.200	1.800	1	.941
2005— Houston (N.L.)	C-1B	1	1	0	0	0	0	0	0	0	0	0	0	0-0	.000	.500	.000	.500	0	1.000
Division series totals (2 years)		3	6	1	3	0	0	0	1	0	0	0	0	0-0	.500	.571	1.000	1.571	1	.958

CHAMPIONSHIP SERIES RECORD

Year	Team (League)	Pos.	G	AB	R	H	2B	3B	HR	RBI	BB	SO	HBP	GDP	SB-CS	Avg.	OBP	SLG	OPS	E	Avg.
2004— Houston (N.L.)	C	2	4	0	1	0	0	0	1	0	1	0	0	0-0	.250	.250	.250	.500	0	1.000

CHEN, BRUCE — P

PERSONAL: Born June 19, 1977, in Panama City, Panama. ... 6-1/210. ... Throws left, bats left. ... Full name: Bruce Kastulo Chen. ... High school: Instituto Panamericano (Panama).
TRANSACTIONS/CAREER NOTES: Signed as a non-drafted free agent by Atlanta Braves organization (July 1, 1993). ... Traded by Braves with P Jimmy Osting to Philadelphia Phillies for P Andy Ashby (July 12, 2000). ... Traded by Phillies with P Adam Walker to New York Mets for Ps Turk Wendell and Dennis Cook (July 27, 2001). ... Traded by Mets with P Dicky Gonzalez, IF Luis Figueroa and a player to be named to Montreal Expos for Ps Scott Strickland and Phil Seibel and OF Matt Watson (April 5, 2002); Expos acquired P Saul Rivera to complete deal (July 14, 2002). ... Traded by Expos to Cincinnati Reds for P Jim Brower (June 14, 2002). ... Released by Reds (March 10, 2003). ... Signed by Houston Astros organization (March 14, 2003). ... Claimed on waivers by Boston Red Sox (May 7, 2003). ... Signed as a free agent by Toronto Blue Jays organization (November 26, 2003). ... Traded by Blue Jays to Baltimore Orioles for future considerations (May 1, 2004).
CAREER HITTING: 14-for-114 (.123), 4 R, 1 2B, 0 3B, 0 HR, 3 RBI.

SCOUTING REPORT

Throws: Chen has an 85-88 mph fastball, a curve and changeup. **Tendencies:** Chen creates some deception with hesitation in his delivery. Must maintain his arm speed to be successful. Fastball tails away on righthanders but can be cut inside. Velocity is down and he leaves the ball up too much, so he must locate his pitches well. Slider has a small break and he will throw it to both lefthanders and righthanders. Has a slow move to first base. Gives up a lot of fly balls. **Outlook:** He needs to pitch in a larger park to be effective, but he can still do well against righthanders. **Grade 6.7**

BRUCE CHEN'S PITCHING ZONE

.253	.286	.243
.198	.303	.322
.333	.278	.267

LEFTY-RIGHTY SPLITS

vs.	Avg.	AB	H	2B	3B	HR	RBI	BB	SO	OBP	Slg.
L	.324	182	59	8	1	8	24	25	22	.406	.511
R	.224	572	128	24	1	25	63	38	111	.280	.400

Year — Team (League)	W	L	Pct.	ERA	WHIP	G	GS	CG	ShO	Hld.	Sv.-Opp.	IP	H	R	ER	HR	BB-IBB	SO	Avg.
1994— GC Braves (GCL)	1	4	.200	3.80	1.05	9	7	0	0	...	1-...	42.2	42	21	18	2	3-0	26	.244
1995— Danville (Appal.)	4	4	.500	3.97	1.38	14	13	1	0	...	0-...	70.1	78	42	31	3	19-1	56	.276
1996— Eugene (Northwest)	4	1	.800	2.27	1.04	11	8	0	0	...	0-...	35.2	23	13	9	1	14-0	55	.173
1997— Macon (S. Atl.)	12	7	.632	3.51	1.12	28	28	1	1	...	0-...	146.1	120	67	57	19	44-0	182	.222
1998— Greenville (Sou.)	13	7	.650	3.29	1.11	24	23	1	0	...	0-...	139.1	106	57	51	12	48-0	164	.209
— Richmond (Int'l)	2	1	.667	1.88	1.50	4	4	0	0	...	0-...	24.0	17	5	5	1	19-0	29	.205
— Atlanta (N.L.)	2	0	1.000	3.98	1.57	4	4	0	0	0	0-0	20.1	23	9	9	3	9-1	17	.288
1999— Richmond (Int'l)	6	3	.667	3.81	1.27	14	14	0	0	0	0-0	78.0	73	36	33	10	26-0	90	.251
— Atlanta (N.L.)	2	2	.500	5.47	1.27	16	7	0	0	0	0-0	51.0	38	32	31	11	27-3	45	.208
2000— Atlanta (N.L.)	4	0	1.000	2.50	1.36	22	0	0	0	0	0-0	39.2	35	15	11	4	19-2	32	.232
— Richmond (Int'l)	1	0	1.000	0.00	1.00	1	1	0	0	0	0-0	6.0	5	0	0	0	1-0	6	.238
— Philadelphia (N.L.)	3	4	.429	3.63	1.14	15	15	0	0	0	0-0	94.1	81	39	38	14	27-2	80	.232
2001— Philadelphia (N.L.)	4	5	.444	5.00	1.40	16	16	0	0	0	0-0	86.1	90	53	48	19	31-4	79	.262
— Reading (East.)	1	0	1.000	0.00	0.50	1	1	0	0	...	0-...	6.0	3	0	0	0	0-0	7	.136
— Scran./W.B. (I.L.)	1	0	1.000	3.86	1.02	3	3	0	0	...	0-...	18.2	14	8	8	2	5-0	14	.212
— New York (N.L.)	3	2	.600	4.68	1.41	11	11	0	0	0	0-0	59.2	56	37	31	10	28-0	47	.255
2002— New York (N.L.)	0	0	...	0.00	1.50	1	0	0	0	0	0-0	2.0	1	0	0	0	0-0	0	.333
— Montreal (N.L.)	2	3	.400	6.99	1.88	15	5	0	0	0	0-0	37.1	47	29	29	9	23-3	43	.303
— Cincinnati (N.L.)	0	2	.000	4.31	1.44	39	0	0	0	4	0-0	39.2	37	24	19	7	20-2	37	.243
2003— Houston (N.L.)	0	0	...	6.00	1.83	11	0	0	0	1	0-0	12.0	14	8	8	2	8-1	8	.311
— Boston (A.L.)	0	1	.000	5.11	1.14	5	2	0	0	0	0-0	12.1	12	8	7	4	2-0	12	.255
— Pawtucket (Int'l)	5	5	.500	4.24	1.10	16	15	1	1	...	1-...	85.0	80	44	40	12	15-1	73	.244
2004— Syracuse (Int'l)	0	1	.000	8.71	2.13	3	3	0	0	...	0-...	10.1	17	12	10	4	5-1	8	.354
— Ottawa (Int'l)	4	3	.571	3.22	1.21	22	17	1	1	...	0-...	95.0	85	41	34	8	30-1	108	.235
— Baltimore (A.L.)	2	1	.667	3.02	1.15	8	7	1	0	0	0-0	47.2	39	19	16	7	16-0	32	.220
2005— Baltimore (A.L.)	13	10	.565	3.83	1.27	34	32	1	0	0	0-0	197.1	187	94	84	33	63-0	133	.248
American League totals (3 years)	15	12	.556	3.74	1.24	47	41	2	0	0	0-0	257.1	238	121	107	44	81-0	177	.243
National League totals (6 years)	20	18	.526	4.57	1.39	150	59	0	0	5	0-0	441.0	422	246	224	79	192-18	388	.251
Major League totals (8 years)	35	30	.538	4.27	1.34	197	100	2	0	5	0-0	698.1	660	367	331	123	273-18	565	.248

DIVISION SERIES RECORD

Year — Team (League)	W	L	Pct.	ERA	WHIP	G	GS	CG	ShO	Hld.	Sv.-Opp.	IP	H	R	ER	HR	BB-IBB	SO	Avg.
1999— Atlanta (N.L.)	Did not play.																		

CHAMPIONSHIP SERIES RECORD

Year — Team (League)	W	L	Pct.	ERA	WHIP	G	GS	CG	ShO	Hld.	Sv.-Opp.	IP	H	R	ER	HR	BB-IBB	SO	Avg.
1999— Atlanta (N.L.)	Did not play.																		

WORLD SERIES RECORD

Year — Team (League)	W	L	Pct.	ERA	WHIP	G	GS	CG	ShO	Hld.	Sv.-Opp.	IP	H	R	ER	HR	BB-IBB	SO	Avg.
1999— Atlanta (N.L.)	Did not play.																		

CHEN, CHIN-FENG — OF

PERSONAL: Born October 28, 1977, in Tainan City, Taiwan. ... 6-1/189. ... Bats right, throws right.
TRANSACTIONS/CAREER NOTES: Signed as a non-drafted free agent by Los Angeles Dodgers organization (January 5, 1999).
2005 GAMES PLAYED BY POSITION (MLB): OF—3.

LEFTY-RIGHTY SPLITS

vs.	Avg.	AB	H	2B	3B	HR	RBI	BB	SO	OBP	Slg.
L	.400	5	2	0	0	0	2	0	2	.400	.400
R	.000	3	0	0	0	0	0	0	2	.000	.000

Year — Team (League)	Pos.	G	AB	R	H	2B	3B	HR	RBI	BB	SO	HBP	GDP	SB-CS	Avg.	OBP	SLG	OPS	E	Avg.
1999— San Bern. (Calif.)	OF	131	510	98	161	22	6	31	123	75	129	5	7	31-7	.316	.404	.580	.984	6	.971
2000— San Antonio (Texas)	OF	133	516	66	143	27	3	6	67	61	131	3	7	23-15	.277	.355	.376	.731	3	.988
2001— Vero Beach (FSL)	OF	62	235	38	63	15	3	5	41	28	56	6	3	2-0	.268	.359	.421	.780	0	1.000
— Jacksonville (Sou.)	OF	64	224	47	70	16	2	17	50	41	65	2	7	5-4	.313	.422	.629	1.051	3	.966
2002— Las Vegas (PCL)	1B-OF	137	511	90	145	26	4	26	84	58	160	0	19	1-0	.284	.352	.503	.855	11	.988
— Los Angeles (N.L.)	OF	3	5	1	0	0	0	0	1	3	0	0	0	0-0	.000	.167	.000	.167	0	1.000

– 109 –

Year Team (League)	Pos.	G	AB	R	H	2B	3B	HR	RBI	BB	SO	HBP	GDP	SB-CS	BATTING Avg.	OBP	SLG	OPS	FIELDING E	Avg.
2003—Los Angeles (N.L.)		1	1	0	0	0	0	0	0	0	0	0	0	0-0	.000	.000	.000	.000	0	
—Las Vegas (PCL) OF-1B-DH		133	474	84	133	30	5	26	86	59	106	2	15	6-4	.281	.360	.530	.889	11	.963
2004—Las Vegas (PCL) OF-DH-1B		81	308	59	89	19	6	20	65	35	78	2	4	6-2	.289	.359	.584	.943	4	.971
—Los Angeles (N.L.) .... OF		8	8	1	0	0	0	0	0	2	3	0	1	0-0	.000	.200	.000	.200	0	1.000
2005—Los Angeles (N.L.) .... OF		7	8	1	2	0	0	0	2	0	4	0	0	0-0	.250	.250	.250	.500	0	1.000
Major League totals (4 years)		19	22	3	2	0	0	0		3	10	0	1	0-0	.091	.200	.091	.291	0	1.000

CHILDERS, MATT   P

PERSONAL: Born December 3, 1978, in Douglas, Ga. ... 6-5/195. ... Throws right, bats right. ... Full name: Matthew Wilkie Childers. ... Name pronounced: CHILL-ders. ... High school: Westside (Augusta, Ga.).

TRANSACTIONS/CAREER NOTES: Selected by Milwaukee Brewers organization in ninth round of free-agent draft (June 3, 1997). ... Signed as a free agent by Atlanta Braves organization (December 28, 2004).

CAREER HITTING: 0-for-1 (.000), 0 R, 0 2B, 0 3B, 0 HR, 0 RBI.

LEFTY-RIGHTY SPLITS

vs.	Avg.	AB	H	2B	3B	HR	RBI	BB	SO	OBP	Slg.
L	.125	8	1	1	0	0	0	3	1	.364	.250
R	.444	9	4	0	0	1	4	0	1	.500	.778

Year Team (League)	W	L	Pct.	ERA	WHIP	G	GS	CG	ShO	Hld.	Sv.-Opp.	IP	H	R	ER	HR	BB-IBB	SO	Avg.
1997—Helena (Pion.)	1	4	.200	6.20	1.72	14	10	0	0	...	1-...	61.0	81	49	42	5	24-0	19	.318
1998—Helena (Pion.)	1	0	1.000	0.64	0.93	2	2	1	1	...	0-...	14.0	9	1	1	0	4-1	4	.184
—Beloit (Midw.)	3	7	.300	5.10	1.63	14	12	3	0	...	0-...	67.0	89	55	38	5	20-0	49	.325
1999—Beloit (Midw.)	3	10	.231	5.94	1.59	20	19	0	0	...	0-...	100.0	129	72	66	9	30-1	52	.317
2000—Beloit (Midw.)	8	2	.800	2.71	1.11	12	12	1	1	...	0-...	73.0	64	33	22	4	17-0	47	.227
—Mudville (Calif.)	3	9	.250	4.75	1.57	15	15	0	0	...	0-...	86.0	103	59	45	10	32-0	43	.295
2001—High Desert (Calif.)	6	11	.353	6.44	1.56	20	20	0	0	...	0-...	118.0	155	95	84	19	29-0	76	.320
—Huntsville (Sou.)	2	2	.500	3.43	1.33	7	7	0	0	...	0-...	40.0	41	19	15	3	12-0	21	.268
2002—Huntsville (Sou.)	2	5	.286	4.50	1.59	35	10	0	0	...	12-...	82.0	103	47	41	6	27-0	57	.308
—Milwaukee (N.L.)	0	0	...	12.00	2.33	8	0	0	0	...	0-0	9.0	13	12	12	2	8-1	6	.342
—Indianapolis (Int'l)	0	0	...	0.00	0.60	3	0	0	0	...	0-0	5.0	1	0	0	0	2-0	4	.063
2003—Huntsville (Sou.)	1	0	1.000	2.93	1.24	36	1	0	0	...	8-...	73.2	67	32	24	3	24-0	44	.239
—Indianapolis (Int'l)	3	0	1.000	0.47	1.11	11	0	0	0	...	0-...	19.0	15	2	1	1	6-2	19	.224
2004—Indianapolis (Int'l)	5	5	.500	4.87	1.30	35	10	0	0	...	2-...	98.0	100	55	53	8	27-3	65	.265
2005—Atlanta (N.L.)	0	0	...	4.50	2.00	3	0	0	0	0	0-0	4.0	5	2	2	1	3-0	2	.294
—Richmond (Int'l)	4	2	.667	3.93	1.23	51	1	0	0	7	2-3	73.1	69	37	32	4	21-1	62	.247
Major League totals (2 years)	0	0	...	9.69	2.23	11	0	0	0	0	0-0	13.0	18	14	14	3	11-1	8	.327

CHOATE, RANDY   P

PERSONAL: Born September 5, 1975, in San Antonio. ... 6-2/195. ... Throws left, bats left. ... Full name: Randol Doyol Choate. ... Name pronounced: chote. ... High school: Winston Churchill (San Antonio). ... College: Florida State.

TRANSACTIONS/CAREER NOTES: Selected by New York Yankees organization in fifth round of 1997 free-agent draft. ... Traded by Yankees with 1B Nick Johnson and OF Juan Rivera to Montreal Expos for P Javier Vazquez (December 16, 2003). ... Traded by Expos to Arizona Diamondbacks for P John Patterson (March 27, 2004).

CAREER HITTING: 0-for-5 (.000), 0 R, 0 2B, 0 3B, 0 HR, 0 RBI.

LEFTY-RIGHTY SPLITS

vs.	Avg.	AB	H	2B	3B	HR	RBI	BB	SO	OBP	Slg.
L	.294	17	5	1	0	0	3	0	3	.333	.353
R	.250	12	3	2	0	0	5	5	1	.471	.417

Year Team (League)	W	L	Pct.	ERA	WHIP	G	GS	CG	ShO	Hld.	Sv.-Opp.	IP	H	R	ER	HR	BB-IBB	SO	Avg.
1997—Oneonta (NYP)	5	1	.833	1.73	0.98	10	10	0	0	...	0-...	62.1	49	12	12	1	12-1	61	.216
1998—Tampa (Fla. St.)	1	8	.111	5.27	1.50	13	13	0	0	...	0-...	70.0	83	57	41	6	22-2	55	.290
—Greensboro (S. Atl.)	1	5	.167	3.00	1.36	8	8	1	0	...	0-...	39.0	46	21	13	1	7-0	32	.293
1999—Tampa (Fla. St.)	2	2	.500	4.50	1.50	47	0	0	0	...	1-...	50.0	51	25	25	4	24-5	62	.263
2000—Columbus (Int'l)	2	0	1.000	2.04	1.36	33	0	0	0	...	1-...	35.1	34	8	8	2	14-3	37	.254
—New York (A.L.)	0	1	.000	4.76	1.29	22	0	0	0	2	0-0	17.0	14	10	9	3	8-0	12	.215
2001—New York (A.L.)	3	1	.750	3.35	1.26	37	0	0	0	3	0-0	48.1	34	21	18	0	27-2	35	.202
—Columbus (Int'l)	1	1	.500	2.08	2.31	4	0	0	0	...	0-...	4.1	7	1	1	0	3-0	4	.389
2002—Columbus (Int'l)	3	2	.600	1.72	1.09	31	0	0	0	...	1-...	36.2	25	8	7	0	15-1	32	.189
—New York (A.L.)	0	0	...	6.04	1.48	14	0	0	0	0	0-0	22.1	18	15	15	1	15-0	17	.217
2003—New York (A.L.)	0	0	...	7.36	2.18	5	0	0	0	0	0-0	3.2	7	3	3	0	1-0	0	.467
—Columbus (Int'l)	3	5	.375	3.91	1.40	54	3	0	0	...	1-...	71.1	75	35	31	4	24-3	56	.271
2004—Tucson (PCL)	0	0	...	5.68	1.42	15	0	0	0	...	1-...	12.2	10	8	8	1	8-1	7	.222
—Arizona (N.L.)	2	4	.333	4.62	1.38	74	0	0	0	11	0-2	50.2	52	26	26	1	28-11	49	.267
2005—Arizona (N.L.)	0	0	...	9.00	1.86	8	0	0	0	2	0-0	7.0	8	7	7	0	5-1	4	.276
—Tucson (PCL)	1	1	.500	3.38	1.65	47	0	0	0	5	3-4	40.0	44	22	15	4	22-1	20	.278
American League totals (4 years)	3	2	.600	4.43	1.36	82	0	0	0	5	0-0	91.1	73	52	45	4	51-2	64	.221
National League totals (2 years)	2	4	.333	5.15	1.61	82	0	0	0	13	0-2	57.2	60	33	33	1	33-12	53	.267
Major League totals (6 years)	5	6	.455	4.71	1.46	164	0	0	0	18	0-2	149.0	133	85	78	5	84-14	117	.240

DIVISION SERIES RECORD

Year Team (League)	W	L	Pct.	ERA	WHIP	G	GS	CG	ShO	Hld.	Sv.-Opp.	IP	H	R	ER	HR	BB-IBB	SO	Avg.
2000—New York (A.L.)	0	0	...	6.75	0.75	1	0	0	0	0	0-0	1.1	1	1	1	0	1-0	1	.000
2001—New York (A.L.)	Did not play.																		

CHAMPIONSHIP SERIES RECORD

Year Team (League)	W	L	Pct.	ERA	WHIP	G	GS	CG	ShO	Hld.	Sv.-Opp.	IP	H	R	ER	HR	BB-IBB	SO	Avg.
2000—New York (A.L.)	0	0	...	0.00	0.00	1	0	0	0	0	0-0	0.1	0	0	0	0	0-0	1	.000
2001—New York (A.L.)	Did not play.																		

WORLD SERIES RECORD

Year Team (League)	W	L	Pct.	ERA	WHIP	G	GS	CG	ShO	Hld.	Sv.-Opp.	IP	H	R	ER	HR	BB-IBB	SO	Avg.
2000—New York (A.L.)	Did not play.																		
2001—New York (A.L.)	0	0	...	2.45	2.18	2	0	0	0	0	0-0	3.2	7	4	1	0	1-1	2	.350

CHOI, HEE SEOP   1B

PERSONAL: Born March 16, 1979, in Chun-Nam, South Korea. ... 6-5/240. ... Bats left, throws left. ... Name pronounced: hee sop choy. ... High school: Kwang-Ju Jae (Kwang-Ju, Korea). ... College: Korea University.

TRANSACTIONS/CAREER NOTES: Signed as a non-drafted free agent by Chicago Cubs organization (March 8, 1999). ... On disabled list (June 8-30, 2003); included rehabilitation assignment to Iowa. ... Traded by Cubs with P Mike Nannini to Florida Marlins for 1B Derrek Lee (November 25, 2003). ... Traded by Marlins with Ps Brad Penny and Bill Murphy to Los Angeles Dodgers for C Paul Lo Duca, P Guillermo Mota and OF Juan Encarnacion (July 30, 2004).
2005 GAMES PLAYED BY POSITION (MLB): 1B—83.

SCOUTING REPORT

Offense: Choi is one of the streakiest hitters in the game. Has a long stroke and is extremely strong. Doesn't make a lot of adjustments. Has trouble handling the ball up but can hit it out of any part of the park when it's down. Doesn't hit off-speed pitches well and appears to be easily confused at the plate. Doesn't have real good bat speed and has problems with pitches on the inner half. *Defense:* He is a stiff player without quick feet and has a lot of trouble going to his right. Doesn't have a lot of agility and has heavy legs. *Outlook:* An all-or-nothing player prone to deep slumps and very hot streaks, Choi may never be a consistent hitter for average or power. *Grade 6*

HEE SEOP CHOI'S HITTING ZONE

.050	.500	.250
.194	.371	.324
.400	.412	.214

LEFTY-RIGHTY SPLITS

vs.	Avg.	AB	H	2B	3B	HR	RBI	BB	SO	OBP	Slg.
L	.207	29	6	2	0	1	2	3	12	.343	.379
R	.258	291	75	13	2	14	40	31	68	.335	.460

Year Team (League)	Pos.	G	AB	R	H	2B	3B	HR	RBI	BB	SO	HBP	GDP	SB-CS	Avg.	OBP	SLG	OPS	E	Avg.
1999— Lansing (Midw.)	1B	79	290	71	93	18	6	18	70	50	68	2	8	2-1	.321	.422	.610	1.032	18	.976
2000— Daytona (Fla. St.)	1B	96	345	60	102	25	6	15	70	37	78	6	7	4-1	.296	.369	.533	.902	4	.995
— West Tenn (Sou.)	1B	36	122	25	37	9	0	10	25	25	38	0	5	3-1	.303	.419	.623	1.042	1	.997
2001— Iowa (PCL)	1B	77	266	38	61	11	0	13	45	34	67	0	5	5-1	.229	.313	.417	.730	3	.995
2002— Iowa (PCL)	1B	135	478	94	137	24	3	26	97	95	119	6	6	3-2	.287	.406	.513	.919	12	.990
— Chicago (N.L.)	1B	24	50	6	9	1	0	2	4	7	15	0	2	0-0	.180	.281	.320	.601	2	.983
2003— Iowa (PCL)	1B	18	66	12	17	4	1	6	16	9	19	1	2	0-1	.258	.351	.621	.972	0	1.000
— Chicago (N.L.)	1B	80	202	31	44	17	0	8	28	37	71	4	2	1-1	.218	.350	.421	.771	5	.991
2004— Florida (N.L.)	1B	95	281	48	76	16	1	15	40	52	78	3	4	1-0	.270	.388	.495	.882	8	.990
— Los Angeles (N.L.)	1B	31	62	5	10	5	0	0	6	11	18	1	2	0-0	.161	.289	.242	.531	1	.994
2005— Los Angeles (N.L.)	1B	133	320	40	81	15	2	15	42	34	80	8	10	1-3	.253	.336	.453	.789	2	.997
Major League totals (4 years)		363	915	130	220	54	3	40	120	141	262	16	20	3-4	.240	.349	.437	.786	18	.992

DIVISION SERIES RECORD

Year Team (League)	Pos.	G	AB	R	H	2B	3B	HR	RBI	BB	SO	HBP	GDP	SB-CS	Avg.	OBP	SLG	OPS	E	Avg.
2004— Los Angeles (N.L.)		1	1	0	0	0	0	0	0	0	0	0	0	0-0	.000	.000	.000	.000	0	...

CHOO, SHIN-SOO — OF

PERSONAL: Born July 13, 1982, in Pusan, South Korea. ... 5-11/178. ... Bats left, throws left. ... Full name: Shin-Soo Choo.
TRANSACTIONS/CAREER NOTES: Signed as a non-drafted free agent by Seattle Mariners organization (August 14, 2000).
2005 GAMES PLAYED BY POSITION (MLB): OF—5.

LEFTY-RIGHTY SPLITS

vs.	Avg.	AB	H	2B	3B	HR	RBI	BB	SO	OBP	Slg.
L	.000	7	0	0	0	0	0	0	2	.000	.000
R	.091	11	1	0	0	0	1	3	2	.286	.091

Year Team (League)	Pos.	G	AB	R	H	2B	3B	HR	RBI	BB	SO	HBP	GDP	SB-CS	Avg.	OBP	SLG	OPS	E	Avg.
2001— Ariz. Mariners (Ariz.)	OF	51	199	51	60	10	10	4	35	34	49	9	1	12-4	.302	.420	.513	.933	1	.986
— Wisconsin (Midw.)	OF	3	13	1	6	0	0	0	3	1	3	1	0	2-0	.462	.533	.462	.995	1	.800
2002— Wisconsin (Midw.)	OF	119	420	69	127	24	8	6	48	70	98	13	2	34-21	.302	.417	.440	.857	4	.981
— San Bern. (Calif.)	OF	11	39	14	12	5	1	1	9	9	9	2	0	3-0	.308	.460	.564	1.024	0	1.000
2003— Inland Empire (Calif.)	OF	110	412	62	118	18	13	9	55	44	84	9	8	18-10	.286	.365	.459	.824	4	.980
2004— San Antonio (Texas)	OF	132	517	89	163	17	7	15	84	56	97	2	8	40-8	.315	.382	.462	.844	7	.781
2005— Tacoma (PCL)	OF-DH	115	429	73	121	21	5	11	54	69	97	1	8	20-10	.282	.382	.431	.813	4	.991
— Seattle (A.L.)	OF	10	18	1	1	0	0	0	1	3	4	0	0	0-0	.056	.190	.056	.246	0	1.000
Major League totals (1 year)		10	18	1	1	0	0	0	1	3	4	0	0	0-0	.056	.190	.056	.246	0	1.000

CHRISTIANSEN, JASON — P

PERSONAL: Born September 21, 1969, in Omaha, Neb. ... 6-5/241. ... Throws left, bats right. ... Full name: Jason Samuel Christiansen. ... High school: Elkhorn (Neb.). ... Junior college: Iowa Western Community College.
TRANSACTIONS/CAREER NOTES: Signed as a non-drafted free agent by Pittsburgh Pirates organization (July 5, 1991). ... On disabled list (March 31-June 19, 1997); included rehabilitation assignment to Carolina. ... On disabled list (May 7-28, July 29-August 21 and August 24-September 23, 1999); included rehabilitation assignments to Altoona and Nashville. ... Traded by Pirates to St. Louis Cardinals for SS Jack Wilson (July 30, 2000). ... On disabled list (March 23-May 7, 2001); included rehabilitation assignment to Memphis. ... Traded by Cardinals to San Francisco Giants for P Kevin Joseph and a player to be named (July 31, 2001); Cardinals acquired P Jason Farmer to complete the deal (October 22, 2001). ... On disabled list (April 16, 2002-remainder of season). ... On disabled list (March 25-June 3, 2003); included rehabilitation assignments to San Jose and Fresno. ... On disabled list (June 19-July 6, 2004). ... Traded by Giants to Los Angeles Angels of Anaheim for Ps Dustin Bergman and Ronald Ray (August 30, 2005).
CAREER HITTING: 1-for-10 (.100), 0 R, 0 2B, 0 3B, 0 HR, 1 RBI.

SCOUTING REPORT

Throws: He hits 88-91 mph with fastball and also throws a slider. *Tendencies:* Christiansen, who uses a three-quarters delivery, can run and sink his fastball, but he has problems hitting the inside part of the plate against righthanded hitters. Has a big-breaking slider with good depth. *Outlook:* Christiansen struggles with righthanded hitters, but he is effective enough against lefthanded hitters to be the second lefthanded pitcher in the bullpen. *Grade 6.2*

JASON CHRISTIANSEN'S PITCHING ZONE

.231	.750	.400
.319	.500	.217
.286	.545	.273

LEFTY-RIGHTY SPLITS

vs.	Avg.	AB	H	2B	3B	HR	RBI	BB	SO	OBP	Slg.
L	.280	93	26	5	1	0	18	10	12	.340	.355
R	.312	93	29	4	0	4	15	7	9	.356	.484

Year Team (League)	W	L	Pct.	ERA	WHIP	G	GS	CG	ShO	Hld.	Sv.-Opp.	IP	H	R	ER	HR	BB-IBB	SO	Avg.
1991— GC Pirates (GCL)	1	0	1.000	0.00	0.63	6	0	0	0	...	1-...	8.0	4	0	0	0	1-0	8	.143
— Welland (NYP)	0	1	.000	2.53	1.27	8	1	0	0	...	0-...	21.1	15	9	6	1	12-1	17	.208

Year	Team (League)	W	L	Pct.	ERA	WHIP	G	GS	CG	ShO	Hld.	Sv.-Opp.	IP	H	R	ER	HR	BB-IBB	SO	Avg.
1992—Augusta (S. Atl.)		1	0	1.000	1.80	1.00	10	0	0	0	...	2-...	20.0	12	4	4	0	8-0	21	.194
—Salem (Carol.)		3	1	.750	3.24	1.38	38	0	0	0	...	2-...	50.0	47	20	18	7	22-2	59	.254
1993—Salem (Carol.)		1	1	.500	3.15	1.01	57	0	0	0	...	4-...	71.1	48	30	25	5	24-2	70	.190
—Carolina (Southern)		0	0	...	0.00	1.50	2	0	0	0	...	0-...	2.2	3	0	0	0	1-0	2	.273
1994—Carolina (Southern)		2	1	.667	2.09	1.14	28	0	0	0	...	2-...	38.2	30	10	9	2	14-1	43	.216
—Buffalo (A.A.)		3	1	.750	2.41	1.04	33	0	0	0	...	0-...	33.2	19	9	9	3	16-0	39	.168
1995—Pittsburgh (N.L.)		1	3	.250	4.15	1.47	63	0	0	0	12	0-4	56.1	49	28	26	5	34-9	53	.234
1996—Pittsburgh (N.L.)		3	3	.500	6.70	1.69	33	0	0	0	2	0-2	44.1	56	34	33	7	19-2	38	.311
—Calgary (PCL)		1	0	1.000	3.27	0.91	6	2	2	0	...	0-...	11.0	9	4	4	1	1-0	10	.237
1997—Carolina (Southern)		0	1	.000	4.20	1.47	8	1	0	0	...	1-...	15.0	17	7	7	1	5-0	25	.293
—Pittsburgh (N.L.)		3	0	1.000	2.94	1.60	39	0	0	0	8	0-2	33.2	37	11	11	2	17-3	37	.274
1998—Pittsburgh (N.L.)		3	3	.500	2.51	1.21	60	0	0	0	15	6-10	64.2	51	22	18	2	27-7	71	.216
1999—Pittsburgh (N.L.)		2	3	.400	4.06	1.27	39	0	0	0	7	3-5	37.2	26	17	17	2	22-4	35	.197
—Altoona (East.)		0	0	...	0.00	0.67	2	1	0	0	...	0-...	3.0	1	0	0	0	1-0	2	.100
—Nashville (PCL)		0	0	...	0.00	1.50	2	0	0	0	...	0-...	2.0	0	0	0	0	0-0	1	.000
2000—Pittsburgh (N.L.)		2	8	.200	4.97	1.39	44	0	0	0	13	1-3	38.0	28	22	21	2	25-4	41	.207
—St. Louis (N.L.)		1	0	1.000	5.40	1.50	21	0	0	0	9	0-1	10.0	13	7	6	1	2-1	12	.317
2001—Memphis (PCL)		0	0	...	2.25	1.13	7	1	0	0	...	0-...	8.0	9	2	2	0	0-0	9	.281
—St. Louis (N.L.)		1	1	.500	4.66	1.29	30	0	0	0	4	3-3	19.1	15	10	10	4	10-1	19	.211
—San Francisco (N.L.)		1	0	1.000	1.59	1.12	25	0	0	0	7	0-1	17.0	14	3	3	1	5-0	12	.241
2002—San Francisco (N.L.)		0	1	.000	5.40	1.60	6	0	0	0	0	0-0	5.0	6	3	3	1	2-0	1	.316
2003—San Jose (Calif.)		0	0	...	1.93	1.70	5	1	0	0	...	0-...	4.2	5	1	1	0	3-0	2	.313
—Fresno (PCL)		0	0	...	5.40	1.20	4	1	0	0	...	0-...	5.0	5	3	3	0	1-0	2	.263
—San Francisco (N.L.)		0	0	...	5.19	1.38	40	0	0	0	7	0-1	26.0	25	15	15	3	11-0	22	.243
2004—San Francisco (N.L.)		4	3	.571	4.50	1.67	60	0	0	0	8	3-6	36.0	34	20	18	3	26-1	22	.250
2005—San Francisco (N.L.)		6	1	.857	5.36	1.50	56	0	0	0	10	0-2	42.0	48	27	25	4	15-2	17	.286
—Los Angeles (A.L.)		0	0	...	2.45	2.45	12	0	0	0	0	0-0	3.2	7	1	1	0	2-0	4	.389
American League totals (1 year)		0	0	...	2.45	2.45	12	0	0	0	0	0-0	3.2	7	1	1	0	2-0	4	.389
National League totals (11 years)		27	26	.509	4.31	1.43	516	0	0	0	102	16-40	430.0	402	219	206	37	215-34	380	.248
Major League totals (11 years)		27	26	.509	4.30	1.44	528	0	0	0	102	16-40	433.2	409	220	207	37	217-34	384	.249

DIVISION SERIES RECORD

Year	Team (League)	W	L	Pct.	ERA	WHIP	G	GS	CG	ShO	Hld.	Sv.-Opp.	IP	H	R	ER	HR	BB-IBB	SO	Avg.
2000—St. Louis (N.L.)		0	0	...	0.00	0.00	1	0	0	0	0	0-0	0.1	0	0	0	0	0-0	0	.000
2003—San Francisco (N.L.)		0	0	...	...	...	1	0	0	0	0	0-0	0	1	0	0	0	0-0	1	1.000
Division series totals (2 years)		0	0	...	0.00	3.00	2	0	0	0	0	0-0	0.1	1	0	0	0	0-0	1	.500

CHAMPIONSHIP SERIES RECORD

Year	Team (League)	W	L	Pct.	ERA	WHIP	G	GS	CG	ShO	Hld.	Sv.-Opp.	IP	H	R	ER	HR	BB-IBB	SO	Avg.
2000—St. Louis (N.L.)		0	0	...	0.00	0.00	2	0	0	0	0	0-0	2.0	0	0	0	0	0-0	1	.000

CHURCH, RYAN — OF

PERSONAL: Born October 14, 1978, in Santa Barbara, Calif. ... 6-1/190. ... Bats left, throws left. ... Full name: Ryan Matthew Church. ... High school: Lompoc (Calif.). ... College: Nevada.

TRANSACTIONS/CAREER NOTES: Selected by Cleveland Indians organization in 14th round of 2000 free-agent draft. ... Traded by Indians with SS Maicer Izturis to Montreal Expos for P Scott Stewart (January 5, 2004). ... Expos franchise transferred to Washington, D.C., and renamed Washington Nationals for 2005 season (December 3, 2004). ... On disabled list (June 23-July 13 and August 25-September 9, 2005); included rehabilitation assignment to Harrisburg.

2005 GAMES PLAYED BY POSITION (MLB): OF—85.

SCOUTING REPORT Church has a slight uppercut swing, but he generates good bat speed. Will expand his zone and chase high pitches. Is not patient and does not hit well with runners on. Is going to have power. Can play all three outfield spots but is best in left field. Plays shallow and has problems going back on balls. Has good lateral range and a strong arm. Needs to define his strike zone and cut down his strikeouts to reach his potential as a run producer. *Grade 5*

RYAN CHURCH'S HITTING ZONE

.267	.286	.273
.212	.520	.482
.214	.429	.152

LEFTY-RIGHTY SPLITS

vs.	Avg.	AB	H	2B	3B	HR	RBI	BB	SO	OBP	Slg.
L	.367	30	11	1	2	1	10	3	8	.441	.633
R	.277	238	66	14	1	8	32	21	62	.342	.445

Year	Team (League)	Pos.	G	AB	R	H	2B	3B	HR	RBI	BB	SO	HBP	GDP	SB-CS	Avg.	OBP	SLG	OPS	E	Avg.
2000—Mahoning Valley (N.Y.-Penn.)	OF	73	272	51	81	16	5	10	65	38	49	4	4	11-4	.298	.396	.504	.899	3	.973
2001—Columbus (S. Atl.)	OF	101	363	64	104	23	3	17	76	54	79	6	6	4-6	.287	.385	.507	.892	3	.987
—Kinston (Carol.)	OF	24	83	16	20	7	0	5	15	18	23	1	1	1-0	.241	.379	.506	.885	2	.947
2002—Kinston (Carol.)	OF	53	181	30	59	12	1	10	30	31	51	4	3	4-4	.326	.433	.569	1.002	3	.965
—Akron (East.)	OF	71	291	39	86	17	4	12	51	12	58	2	8	1-0	.296	.325	.505	.830	1	.993
2003—Akron (East.)	OF	99	371	47	97	17	3	13	52	32	64	4	17	4-3	.261	.325	.429	.754	6	.977
2004—Edmonton (PCL)	OF-DH	98	347	74	120	29	8	17	79	51	62	4	0	0-1	.346	.430	.622	1.041	2	.990
—Montreal (N.L.)	OF	30	63	6	11	1	0	1	6	7	16	0	3	0-0	.175	.257	.238	.495	0	1.000
2005—Harrisburg (East.)	OF	4	18	2	5	1	0	0	0	0	5	0	0	0-0	.278	.278	.333	.611	0	1.000
—Washington (N.L.)	OF	102	268	41	77	15	3	9	42	24	70	5	9	3-2	.287	.353	.466	.820	0	1.000
Major League totals (2 years)		132	331	47	88	16	3	10	48	31	86	5	9	3-2	.266	.335	.423	.758	0	1.000

CINTRON, ALEX — SS/2B

PERSONAL: Born December 17, 1978, in Humacao, Puerto Rico. ... 6-2/199. ... Bats both, throws right. ... Full name: Alexander Cintron. ... Name pronounced: SIN-tron. ... High school: Mech-Tech (Caguas, Puerto Rico).

TRANSACTIONS/CAREER NOTES: Selected by Arizona Diamondbacks organization in 36th round of 1997 free-agent draft.
2005 GAMES PLAYED BY POSITION (MLB): SS—39, 3B—32, 2B—23.

SCOUTING REPORT *Offense:* Cintron has better bat speed than his stroke would indicate. Has a big hitch in his swing. Is a much better fastball hitter than breaking-ball hitter. Has changes his stance to be more erect at the plate. Has surprising power. *Defense:* Cintron can play all four infield position but is best at second base, where he gets better jumps on the ball. Has good hands but can be erratic as he loses focus at times and lays back on the ball. Has very good range to his left. Has a strong arm making the pivot or coming across the bag on the double play. *Outlook:* Cintron is falling more into a utility role. Has the ability to be a good player but has been slow to mature and make adjustments. *Grade 5.9*

ALEX CINTRON'S HITTING ZONE

.125	.273	.313
.294	.297	.206
.278	.611	.167

LEFTY-RIGHTY SPLITS

vs.	Avg.	AB	H	2B	3B	HR	RBI	BB	SO	OBP	Slg.
L	.301	83	25	4	0	2	9	3	6	.326	.422
R	.263	247	65	15	2	6	39	9	27	.288	.413

Year	Team (League)	Pos.	G	AB	R	H	2B	3B	HR	RBI	BB	SO	HBP	GDP	SB-CS	Avg.	OBP	SLG	OPS	E	Avg.
																				FIELDING	
1997—	Ariz. D'backs (Ariz.)	SS	43	152	23	30	6	1	0	20	21	32	2	3	1-4	.197	.301	.250	.551	15	.931
	—Lethbridge (Pion.)	SS	1	3	0	1	0	0	0	0	0	1	0	0	0-0	.333	.333	.333	.667	1	.857
1998—	Lethbridge (Pion.)	SS	67	258	41	68	11	4	3	34	20	32	2	8	8-4	.264	.319	.372	.691	27	.921
1999—	High Desert (Calif.)	SS	128	499	78	153	25	4	3	64	19	65	3	14	15-8	.307	.333	.391	.724	28	.950
2000—	El Paso (Texas)	SS	125	522	83	157	30	6	4	59	29	56	2	22	9-9	.301	.336	.404	.740	32	.950
2001—	Tucson (PCL)	SS-2B	107	425	53	124	24	3	3	35	15	48	2	12	9-6	.292	.315	.384	.698	32	.936
	—Arizona (N.L.)	SS	8	7	0	2	0	1	0	0	0	0	0	0	0-0	.286	.286	.571	.857	0	1.000
2002—	Tucson (PCL)	SS-2B	85	351	53	113	22	3	4	26	11	33	2	8	9-5	.322	.345	.436	.781	14	.960
	—Arizona (N.L.)	2B-3B-SS	38	75	11	16	6	0	0	4	12	13	0	2	0-0	.213	.322	.293	.615	1	.989
2003—	Tucson (PCL)	SS-2B	26	107	21	42	11	2	2	21	8	6	0	0	1-0	.393	.435	.589	1.024	4	.970
	—Arizona (N.L.)	SS-3B-2B	117	448	70	142	26	6	13	51	29	33	2	7	2-3	.317	.359	.489	.848	11	.976
2004—	Arizona (N.L.)	SS-3B-2B	154	564	56	148	31	7	4	49	31	59	2	11	3-3	.262	.301	.363	.665	17	.973
2005—	Arizona (N.L.)	SS-3B-2B	122	330	36	90	19	2	8	48	12	33	1	8	1-2	.273	.298	.415	.713	8	.971
	Major League totals (5 years)		439	1424	173	398	82	16	25	152	84	138	5	28	6-8	.279	.320	.412	.732	37	.974

DIVISION SERIES RECORD

Year	Team (League)	Pos.	G	AB	R	H	2B	3B	HR	RBI	BB	SO	HBP	GDP	SB-CS	Avg.	OBP	SLG	OPS	E	Avg.
2002—	Arizona (N.L.)	3B	2	0	0	0	0	0	0	0	0	0	0	0	0-0	...	...	...	...	0	...

CIRILLO, JEFF — 3B/1B

PERSONAL: Born September 23, 1969, in Pasadena, Calif. ... 6-1/200. ... Bats right, throws right. ... Full name: Jeffrey Howard Cirillo. ... Name pronounced: suh-RILL-oh. ... High school: Providence (Burbank, Calif.). ... College: Southern California.
TRANSACTIONS/CAREER NOTES: Selected by Chicago Cubs organization in 37th round of 1987 free-agent draft; did not sign. ... Selected by Milwaukee Brewers organization in 11th round of 1991 free-agent draft. ... Traded by Brewers with P Scott Karl and cash to Colorado Rockies as part of three-team deal in which Brewers acquired P Jamey Wright and C Henry Blanco from Rockies and P Jimmy Haynes from Oakland Athletics, and A's acquired P Justin Miller and cash from Rockies (December 13, 1999). ... On disabled list (April 27-May 13, 2001); included rehabilitation assignment to Colorado Springs. ... Traded by Rockies to Seattle Mariners for Ps Jose Paniagua, Denny Stark and Brian Fuentes (December 15, 2001). ... On disabled list (July 24-August 19, 2003); included rehabilitation assignment to AZL Mariners. ... Traded by Mariners with P Brian Sweeney and cash to San Diego Padres for P Kevin Jarvis, IF Dave Hansen, C Wiki Gonzalez and OF Vince Faison (January 6, 2004). ... On disabled list (April 2-May 11, 2004); included rehabilitation assignment to Portland. ... Released by Padres (August 4, 2004). ... Signed by Milwaukee Brewers organization (February 4, 2005). ... On disabled list (June 25-September 1, 2005); included rehabilitation assignment to Nashville.
2005 GAMES PLAYED BY POSITION (MLB): 3B—53, 2B—3, 1B—1.

JEFF CIRILLO'S HITTING ZONE

.333	.111	.364
.265	.367	.364
.400	.200	.111

LEFTY-RIGHTY SPLITS

vs.	Avg.	AB	H	2B	3B	HR	RBI	BB	SO	OBP	Slg.
L	.400	55	22	7	0	2	10	8	5	.484	.636
R	.231	130	30	8	0	2	13	15	17	.324	.338

Year	Team (League)	Pos.	G	AB	R	H	2B	3B	HR	RBI	BB	SO	HBP	GDP	SB-CS	Avg.	OBP	SLG	OPS	E	Avg.
																				FIELDING	
1991—	Helena (Pion.)	3B-OF	70	286	60	100	16	2	10	51	31	28	4	11	3-1	.350	.418	.524	.942	15	.921
1992—	Stockton (Calif.)	3B	7	27	2	6	1	0	0	5	2	0	2	2	0-0	.222	.323	.259	.582	0	1.000
	—Beloit (Midw.)	2B-3B	126	444	65	135	27	3	9	71	84	85	6	7	21-12	.304	.417	.439	.856	26	.942
1993—	El Paso (Texas)	2B-3B	67	249	53	85	16	2	9	41	26	37	5	5	2-3	.341	.410	.530	.940	9	.962
	—New Orleans (A.A.)	3B-2B-SS	58	215	31	63	13	2	3	32	29	33	3	7	2-1	.293	.385	.414	.799	5	.974
1994—	New Orleans (A.A.)	3B-2B-DH																			
		SS	61	236	45	73	18	2	10	46	28	39	2	9	4-0	.309	.386	.530	.915	8	.963
	—Milwaukee (A.L.)	3B-2B	39	126	17	30	9	0	3	12	11	16	2	4	0-1	.238	.309	.381	.690	3	.965
1995—	Milwaukee (A.L.)	3B-2B-1B																			
		SS	125	328	57	91	19	4	9	39	47	42	4	9	7-2	.277	.371	.442	.813	15	.958
1996—	Milwaukee (A.L.)	3B-DH-1B																			
		2B	158	566	101	184	46	5	15	83	58	69	7	14	4-9	.325	.391	.504	.894	§ 18	.952
1997—	Milwaukee (A.L.)	3B-DH	154	580	74	167	46	2	10	82	60	74	14	13	4-3	.288	.367	.426	.793	17	.963
1998—	Milwaukee (N.L.)	3B-1B	156	604	97	194	31	1	14	68	79	88	4	* 26	10-4	.321	.402	.445	.847	11	.979
1999—	Milwaukee (N.L.)	3B	157	607	98	198	35	1	15	88	75	83	5	15	7-4	.326	.401	.461	.862	15	.967
2000—	Colorado (N.L.)	3B	157	598	111	195	53	2	11	115	67	72	6	19	3-4	.326	.392	.477	.869	15	.964
2001—	Colorado (N.L.)	3B	138	528	72	165	26	4	17	83	43	63	5	15	12-2	.313	.364	.473	.838	7	.982
	—Colo. Springs (PCL)	3B	1	4	2	3	1	0	0	3	1	0	0	0	0-0	.750	.800	1.000	1.800	0	1.000
2002—	Seattle (A.L.)	3B-1B	146	485	51	121	20	0	6	54	31	67	9	12	8-4	.249	.302	.328	.629	9	.976
2003—	Ariz. Mariners (Ariz.)	DH-3B	6	20	2	6	0	0	0	4	1	1	0	1	0-1	.300	.440	.300	.740	0	1.000
	—Inland Empire (Calif.)	3B-DH	5	15	1	3	1	0	0	1	3	1	0	1	0-0	.200	.333	.267	.600	1	.833
	—Tacoma (PCL)	3B	5	17	7	6	3	0	2	6	3	3	1	0	0-0	.353	.476	.882	1.359	0	1.000
	—Seattle (A.L.)	3B-1B-DH	87	258	24	53	11	0	2	23	24	32	5	6	1-1	.205	.284	.271	.555	4	.978
2004—	Portland (PCL)	3B-1B-2B																			
		DH-OF-SS	7	23	3	8	3	0	0	2	5	1	0	1	1-0	.348	.464	.478	.943	0	.960
	—San Diego (N.L.)	3B-1B-2B																			
		OF	33	75	12	16	3	0	1	7	5	14	0	0	0-0	.213	.259	.293	.553	2	.979

			BATTING																	FIELDING	
Year	Team (League)	Pos.	G	AB	R	H	2B	3B	HR	RBI	BB	SO	HBP	GDP	SB-CS	Avg.	OBP	SLG	OPS	E	Avg.
2005— Nashville (PCL)		3B-DH	9	29	2	7	1	0	0	6	0	5	1	1	0-1	.241	.250	.276	.526	1	.875
— Milwaukee (N.L.)		3B-2B-1B	77	185	29	52	15	0	4	23	23	22	4	3	4-2	.281	.373	.427	.800	5	.954
American League totals (6 years)			709	2343	324	646	151	11	45	293	231	300	41	57	24-20	.276	.348	.407	.755	66	.964
National League totals (6 years)			718	2597	419	820	163	8	62	384	292	342	24	78	36-16	.316	.386	.456	.842	55	.972
Major League totals (12 years)			1427	4940	743	1466	314	19	107	677	523	642	65	135	60-36	.297	.368	.433	.801	121	.968

ALL-STAR GAME RECORD

	G	AB	R	H	2B	3B	HR	RBI	BB	SO	HBP	GDP	SB-CS	Avg.	OBP	SLG	OPS	E	Avg.
All-Star Game totals (2 years)	2	2	0	0	0	0	0	0	0	1	0	0	0-0	.000	.000	.000	.000	0	1.000

CLARK, BRADY — OF

PERSONAL: Born April 18, 1973, in Portland, Ore. ... 6-2/202. ... Bats right, throws right. ... Full name: Brady William Clark. ... High school: Sunset (Beaverton, Ore.). ... College: San Diego.

TRANSACTIONS/CAREER NOTES: Signed as a non-drafted free agent by Cincinnati Reds organization (January 13, 1996). ... Released by Reds (April 10, 1996). ... Re-signed by Reds organization (February 15, 1997). ... Traded by Reds to New York Mets (September 9, 2002), completing deal in which Reds traded P Pedro Feliciano, OF Elvin Andujar and two players to be named to Mets for P Shawn Estes (August 15, 2002); Mets acquired OF Raul Gonzalez as part of deal (August 20, 2002). ... Claimed on waivers by Milwaukee Brewers (January 21, 2003). ... On disabled list (March 21-April 15, 2003); included rehabilitation assignment to Indianapolis. ... On disabled list (August 11-26, 2005).

2005 GAMES PLAYED BY POSITION (MLB): OF—145.

SCOUTING REPORT *Offense:* Clark hits from a wide stance with a deep crouch and little stride. Has an uppercut swing and showed improved bat speed last season. Can turn on inside pitches and has deceptive power. Hits well against all pitchers. Has improved with runners in scoring position. Is a good runner but will get picked off because he bites on first moves. *Defense:* Clark can play all three outfield positions but is most comfortable in center field. Gets good jumps and closes well on balls hit to the gaps. Plays deep and is better coming in than going back. Has good arm strength but a slow release. *Outlook:* Clark proved he could be an everyday player and has the ability to duplicate his 2005 numbers. *Grade 7.2*

BRADY CLARK'S HITTING ZONE

.310	.344	.229
.281	.382	.342
.333	.222	.344

LEFTY-RIGHTY SPLITS

vs.	Avg.	AB	H	2B	3B	HR	RBI	BB	SO	OBP	Slg.
L	.308	133	41	9	1	4	9	17	8	.403	.481
R	.305	466	142	22	0	9	44	30	47	.363	.410

			BATTING																	FIELDING	
Year	Team (League)	Pos.	G	AB	R	H	2B	3B	HR	RBI	BB	SO	HBP	GDP	SB-CS	Avg.	OBP	SLG	OPS	E	Avg.
1997— Burlington (Midw.)		OF	126	459	108	149	29	7	11	63	76	71	4	10	31-18	.325	.423	.490	.913	4	.986
1998— Chattanooga (Sou.)		OF	64	222	41	60	13	1	2	16	31	34	4	11	12-4	.270	.370	.365	.735	1	.993
1999— Chattanooga (Sou.)		OF-3B	138	506	103	165	37	4	17	75	89	58	2	6	25-17	.326	.425	.516	.941	5	.981
2000— Louisville (Int'l)		OF	132	487	90	148	41	6	16	79	72	51	9	14	12-8	.304	.397	.511	.908	6	.981
— Cincinnati (N.L.)		OF	11	11	1	3	1	0	0	2	0	2	0	0	0-0	.273	.273	.364	.636	0	1.000
2001— Louisville (Int'l)		OF	49	167	24	44	5	1	2	18	18	17	6	5	6-2	.263	.354	.341	.695	2	.981
— Cincinnati (N.L.)		OF-DH	89	129	22	34	3	0	6	18	22	16	1	6	4-1	.264	.373	.426	.799	1	.981
2002— Cincinnati (N.L.)		OF	51	66	6	10	3	0	0	9	6	9	1	1	1-2	.152	.233	.197	.430	1	.938
— Louisville (Int'l)		OF-3B	25	109	17	33	7	0	1	17	9	9	2	3	0-2	.303	.328	.395	.722	3	.955
— New York (N.L.)		OF	10	12	3	5	1	0	0	1	1	2	0	0	0-0	.417	.462	.500	.962	0	1.000
2003— Indianapolis (Int'l)		OF-DH	9	34	4	9	3	0	0	3	2	4	0	3	1-0	.265	.306	.353	.658	0	1.000
— Milwaukee (N.L.)		OF	128	315	33	86	21	1	3	32	40	40	9	12	13-2	.273	.330	.403	.733	5	.973
2004— Milwaukee (N.L.)		OF	138	353	41	99	18	1	7	46	53	48	9	15	15-8	.280	.385	.397	.782	4	.995
2005— Milwaukee (N.L.)		OF	145	599	94	183	31	1	13	53	47	55	18	13	10-13	.306	.372	.426	.798	2	.995
Major League totals (6 years)			572	1485	200	420	78	3	32	169	150	172	38	42	43-26	.283	.361	.404	.765	13	.986

CLARK, DOUG — OF

PERSONAL: Born March 5, 1976, in Springfield, Mass. ... 6-2/207. ... Bats left, throws right. ... Full name: Douglas Dwyer Clark. ... High school: Springfield (Mass.) Central. ... College: Massachusetts.

TRANSACTIONS/CAREER NOTES: Selected by San Francisco Giants organization in seventh round of 1998 free-agent draft.

LEFTY-RIGHTY SPLITS

vs.	Avg.	AB	H	2B	3B	HR	RBI	BB	SO	OBP	Slg.
L	.000	0	0	0	0	0	0	0	0	.000	.000
R	.000	5	0	0	0	0	0	1	2	.167	.000

			BATTING																	FIELDING	
Year	Team (League)	Pos.	G	AB	R	H	2B	3B	HR	RBI	BB	SO	HBP	GDP	SB-CS	Avg.	OBP	SLG	OPS	E	Avg.
1998— Salem-Keizer (N'west)		OF	59	227	49	76	8	6	3	41	32	31	3	1	12-8	.335	.422	.463	.885	5	.929
1999— Bakersfield (Calif.)		OF	118	420	67	137	17	2	11	58	59	89	5	5	17-11	.326	.415	.455	.870	9	.956
— Shreveport (Texas)		OF	15	50	6	11	3	0	1	6	4	9	0	2	0-0	.220	.278	.340	.618	0	1.000
2000— Shreveport (Texas)		OF	131	492	68	134	20	7	10	75	43	102	5	13	12-4	.272	.333	.402	.735	8	.982
2001— Shreveport (Texas)		OF	123	414	53	114	16	4	6	51	45	83	3	8	20-5	.275	.348	.377	.725	4	.982
2002— Shreveport (Texas)		OF	44	138	13	36	6	1	2	13	19	35	0	4	5-7	.261	.348	.362	.710	2	.974
— Fresno (PCL)		OF	70	212	24	57	9	1	5	19	15	52	5	3	3-3	.269	.330	.392	.722	2	.982
2003— Fresno (PCL)		OF	13	21	4	5	2	0	0	2	3	0	0	0	0-1	.238	.304	.238	.542	1	1.000
— Norwich (East.)		OF	113	396	47	119	23	4	4	49	45	67	2	9	8-5	.301	.371	.409	.780	1	1.000
2004— Norwich (East.)		OF	140	537	82	157	23	3	10	71	44	103	3	9	33-8	.292	.348	.439	.787	3	.906
2005— Fresno (PCL)		OF-DH	127	472	81	149	30	5	13	59	35	87	5	6	29-12	.316	.367	.483	.850	4	.992
— San Francisco (N.L.)		OF	8	5	2	0	0	0	0	0	1	2	0	0	0-0	.000	.167	.000	.167	0	...
Major League totals (1 year)			8	5	0	0	0	0	0	0	1	2	0	0	0-0	.000	.167	.000	.167	0	...

CLARK, JERMAINE   OF/2B

PERSONAL: Born September 29, 1976, in Berkeley, Calif. ... 5-10/170. ... Bats left, throws right. ... Full name: Jermaine Marcel Clark. ... High school: Will C. Wood (Vacaville, Calif.). ... College: San Francisco.

TRANSACTIONS/CAREER NOTES: Selected by Los Angeles Dodgers organization in 44th round of 1994 free-agent draft; did not sign. ... Selected by Seattle Mariners organzation in fifth round of 1997 free-agent draft. ... Selected by Detroit Tigers from Mariners organization in Rule 5 major league draft (December 11, 2000). ... Returned to Mariners (April 19, 2001). ... Traded by Mariners with P Derrick Van Dusen to Texas Rangers for P Ismael Valdes (August 18, 2002). ... Claimed on waivers by San Diego Padres (April 30, 2003). ... Traded by Padres to Rangers for cash (July 9, 2003). ... Signed as a free agent by Cincinnati Reds organization (January 9, 2004). ... Signed as a free agent by Oakland Athletics organization (November 19, 2004).

2005 GAMES PLAYED BY POSITION (MLB): 2B—2, OF—1.

LEFTY-RIGHTY SPLITS

vs.	Avg.	AB	H	2B	3B	HR	RBI	BB	SO	OBP	Slg.
L	.000	0	0	0	0	0	0	0	0	.000	.000
R	.000	0	0	0	0	0	0	1	0	1.000	.000

							BATTING										FIELDING	
Year — Team (League)	Pos.	G	AB	R	H	2B	3B	HR	RBI	BB	SO	HBP	GDP	SB-CS	Avg.	OBP	SLG	OPS	E	Avg.
1997— Everett (N'west)	2B-3B	59	199	42	67	13	2	3	29	34	31	3	1	22-3	.337	.437	.467	.904	9	.957
1998— Wisconsin (Midw.)	2B-OF	123	448	81	145	24	13	6	55	57	64	2	3	40-14	.324	.402	.475	.877	14	.970
1999— Lancaster (Calif.)	2B	126	502	112	158	27	8	6	61	58	80	2	10	33-15	.315	.386	.436	.822	10	.983
2000— New Haven (East.)	2B	133	447	80	131	23	9	2	44	87	69	14	7	38-8	.293	.421	.398	.819	13	.977
2001— Detroit (A.L.)	DH	3	0	1	0	0	0	0	0	0	0	0	0	0-0	...	...	...	...	0	...
— Tacoma (PCL)	2B	74	216	35	54	7	3	1	26	27	39	3	6	13-2	.250	.340	.324	.664	6	.980
2002— Tacoma (PCL)	2B-SS	108	368	47	98	14	4	6	36	62	59	2	...	29-14	.266	.370	.375	.745	8	.982
— Oklahoma (PCL)	2B-OF	13	57	13	17	2	1	1	4	7	11	0	...	6-2	.298	.375	.421	.796	1	.982
2003— San Diego (N.L.)	OF	1	2	0	0	0	0	0	1	0	1	0	0	0-1	.000	.000	.000	.000	0	1.000
— Portland (PCL)	OF-2B-SS 3B	50	160	27	40	2	2	4	10	22	24	1	1	14-3	.250	.342	.363	.705	4	.968
— Oklahoma (PCL)	OF-2B	49	171	24	38	6	4	6	24	16	26	1	3	11-1	.222	.291	.409	.700	2	.981
— Texas (A.L.)	OF-2B-DH	24	46	2	8	2	0	0	6	6	4	0	1	2-1	.174	.264	.217	.482	0	1.000
2004— Cincinnati (N.L.)	OF-2B	14	30	4	4	1	0	0	2	1	8	2	0	1-0	.133	.212	.167	.379	0	1.000
— Louisville (Int'l)	OF-2B-3B DH	115	398	77	113	15	5	10	52	63	54	7	4	24-9	.284	.386	.422	.808	2	.992
2005— Oakland (A.L.)	2B-OF	4	0	2	0	0	0	0	0	1	0	0	0	0-0	1.000	...	...	...	0	...
— Sacramento (PCL)	2B-3B-OF DH	70	256	32	64	13	4	5	28	41	33	2	5	14-8	.250	.353	.391	.744	2	.993
American League totals (3 years)		31	46	5	8	2	0	0	6	7	4	0	1	2-1	.174	.278	.217	.495	0	1.000
National League totals (2 years)		15	32	4	4	1	0	0	3	1	9	2	0	1-1	.125	.194	.156	.351	0	1.000
Major League totals (4 years)		46	78	9	12	3	0	0	9	8	13	2	1	3-2	.154	.244	.192	.437	0	1.000

CLARK, TONY   1B

PERSONAL: Born June 15, 1972, in Newton, Kan. ... 6-7/245. ... Bats both, throws right. ... Full name: Anthony Christopher Clark. ... High school: Valhalla (El Cajon, Calif.), then Christian (El Cajon, Calif.). ... College: San Diego State.

TRANSACTIONS/CAREER NOTES: Selected by Detroit Tigers organization in first round (second pick overall) of 1990 free-agent draft. ... On disabled list (May 26-June 10, 1999); included rehabilitation assignment to Toledo. ... On disabled list (May 13-June 12, July 15-September 1 and September 19, 2000-remainder of season); included rehabilitation assignments to Toledo. ... Claimed on waivers by Boston Red Sox (November 20, 2001). ... Signed as a free agent by New York Mets organization (February 20, 2003). ... Signed as a free agent by New York Yankees (January 12, 2004). ... Signed as a free agent by Arizona Diamondbacks (January 26, 2005).

2005 GAMES PLAYED BY POSITION (MLB): 1B—83, DH—7.

SCOUTING REPORT _Offense:_ Clark showed a dramatic increase in his bat speed in 2005. Has always been a better low-ball hitter but has shown the ability to catch up to the high fastball. Has a lot more power from the left side. Was a good hitter with runners in scoring position. _Defense:_ He has the strongest arm of any first baseman in baseball and is accurate. Has quick footwork around the bag and has good instincts to shift and field errant throws. Has good hands and range, especially with his long arms. _Outlook:_ After several subpar seasons, Clark once again showed he can be a good run producer. Appears to be rejuvenated in his work ethic. Look for him to have a similar season in 2006. _Grade 8.3_

TONY CLARK'S HITTING ZONE

.308	.400	.400
.422	.385	.448
.261	.429	.171

LEFTY-RIGHTY SPLITS

vs.	Avg.	AB	H	2B	3B	HR	RBI	BB	SO	OBP	Slg.
L	.313	115	36	8	0	6	27	16	15	.394	.539
R	.299	234	70	14	2	24	60	21	73	.352	.684

							BATTING										FIELDING	
Year — Team (League)	Pos.	G	AB	R	H	2B	3B	HR	RBI	BB	SO	HBP	GDP	SB-CS	Avg.	OBP	SLG	OPS	E	Avg.
1990— Bristol (Appal.)	OF	25	73	2	12	2	0	1	8	6	28	1	0	0-0	.164	.238	.233	.470	0	1.000
1991—	Did not play.
1992— Niagara Falls (NYP)	OF	27	85	12	26	9	0	5	17	9	34	0	0	1-0	.306	.372	.588	.961	0	1.000
1993— Lakeland (Fla. St.)	OF	36	117	14	31	4	1	1	22	18	32	0	1	0-1	.265	.358	.342	.700	2	.944
1994— Trenton (East.)	DH-1B	107	394	50	110	25	0	21	86	40	113	1	9	0-4	.279	.346	.503	.848	13	.977
— Toledo (Int'l)	1B-DH	25	92	10	24	4	0	2	13	12	25	0	1	2-0	.261	.340	.370	.709	0	1.000
1995— Toledo (Int'l)	1B-DH	110	405	50	98	17	2	14	63	52	129	3	8	0-2	.242	.330	.396	.728	13	.981
— Detroit (A.L.)	1B	27	101	10	24	5	1	3	11	8	30	0	2	0-0	.238	.294	.396	.690	4	.985
1996— Toledo (Int'l)	1B-DH	55	194	42	58	7	1	14	36	31	58	0	3	1-1	.299	.396	.562	.957	3	.993
— Detroit (A.L.)	1B-DH	100	376	56	94	14	0	27	72	29	127	0	7	0-1	.250	.299	.503	.802	6	.993
1997— Detroit (A.L.)	1B-DH	159	580	105	160	28	3	32	117	93	144	3	11	1-3	.276	.376	.500	.876	10	.993
1998— Detroit (A.L.)	1B-DH	157	602	84	175	37	4	34	103	63	128	3	16	3-3	.291	.358	.522	.880	13	.991
1999— Detroit (A.L.)	1B-DH	143	536	74	150	29	0	31	99	64	133	6	14	2-1	.280	.361	.507	.869	10	.992
— Toledo (Int'l)	1B	3	3	0	0	0	0	0	0	1	1	0	0	0-0	.000	.250	.000	.250	0	1.000
2000— Detroit (A.L.)	1B-DH	60	208	32	57	14	0	13	37	24	51	0	10	0-0	.274	.349	.529	.878	4	.993
— Toledo (Int'l)	1B	6	22	1	2	1	0	1	2	5	2	0	1	0-0	.091	.130	.273	.403	0	1.000
2001— Detroit (A.L.)	1B-DH	126	428	67	123	29	3	16	75	62	108	1	14	0-1	.287	.374	.481	.856	5	.996
2002— Boston (A.L.)	1B-DH	90	275	25	57	12	1	3	29	21	57	1	11	0-0	.207	.265	.291	.556	6	.992
2003— St. Lucie (Fla. St.)	1B	1	4	0	1	0	0	0	0	0	0	0	0	0-0	.250	.250	.250	.500	0	1.000
— New York (N.L.)	1B-OF	125	254	29	59	13	0	16	43	24	73	1	8	0-0	.232	.300	.472	.772	4	.992
2004— New York (A.L.)	1B-DH	106	253	37	56	12	0	16	49	26	92	2	6	0-0	.221	.297	.459	.755	4	.994

C

Year	Team (League)	Pos.	G	AB	R	H	2B	3B	HR	RBI	BB	SO	HBP	GDP	SB-CS	Avg.	OBP	SLG	OPS	E	Avg.
									BATTING											FIELDING	
2005— Arizona (N.L.)		1B-DH	130	349	47	106	22	2	30	87	37	88	1	10	0-0	.304	.366	.636	1.003	2	.997
American League totals (9 years)			968	3359	490	896	180	8	175	592	390	870	16	91	6-9	.267	.343	.481	.825	60	.992
National League totals (2 years)			255	603	76	165	35	2	46	130	61	161	2	18	0-0	.274	.339	.567	.906	6	.995
Major League totals (11 years)			1223	3962	566	1061	215	10	221	722	451	1031	18	109	6-9	.268	.343	.494	.837	66	.993

DIVISION SERIES RECORD

Year	Team (League)	Pos.	G	AB	R	H	2B	3B	HR	RBI	BB	SO	HBP	GDP	SB-CS	Avg.	OBP	SLG	OPS	E	Avg.
2004— New York (A.L.)		1B	1	1	0	0	0	0	0	0	1	0	0	0	0-0	.000	.000	.000	.000	0	1.000

CHAMPIONSHIP SERIES RECORD

Year	Team (League)	Pos.	G	AB	R	H	2B	3B	HR	RBI	BB	SO	HBP	GDP	SB-CS	Avg.	OBP	SLG	OPS	E	Avg.
2004— New York (A.L.)		1B	5	21	0	3	1	0	0	1	0	9	0	0	0-0	.143	.143	.190	.333	1	.976

ALL-STAR GAME RECORD

		G	AB	R	H	2B	3B	HR	RBI	BB	SO	HBP	GDP	SB-CS	Avg.	OBP	SLG	OPS	E	Avg.
All-Star Game totals (1 year)		1	1	0	0	0	0	0	0	1	0	0	0	0-0	.000	.000	.000		...	...

CLAUSSEN, BRANDON — P

PERSONAL: Born May 1, 1979, in Rapid City, S.D. ... 6-1/200. ... Throws left, bats right. ... Full name: Brandon Allen Falker Claussen. ... Name pronounced: CLAW-sin. ... High school: Goddard (Roswell, N.M.). ... Junior college: Howard (Texas). ... College: Howard (TX) JC.

TRANSACTIONS/CAREER NOTES: Selected by New York Yankees organization in 34th round of 1998 free-agent draft. ... Traded by Yankees with P Charlie Manning and cash to Cincinnati Reds for 3B Aaron Boone (July 31, 2003).

CAREER HITTING: 8-for-78 (.103), 4 R, 0 2B, 0 3B, 0 HR, 1 RBI.

SCOUTING REPORT *Throws:* His fastball is 86-92 mph, and he has a slider and changeup. *Tendencies:* His herky-jerky delivery causes him to be inconsistent with his command and velocity. Has good riding action to his four-seam fastball and a curveball that will be a good pitch for him when he doesn't rush it. Still is working on his straight changeup because he's inconsistent with his arm speed. Gets more life on his fastball up in the zone than down and is a fly-ball pitcher. *Outlook:* Claussen is projected to pitch at the back of the Reds' rotation. *Grade 6*

BRANDON CLAUSSEN'S PITCHING ZONE

.292	.261	.250
.246	.417	.333
.296	.550	.208

LEFTY-RIGHTY SPLITS

vs.	Avg.	AB	H	2B	3B	HR	RBI	BB	SO	OBP	Slg.
L	.242	132	32	6	0	8	19	9	31	.299	.470
R	.280	521	146	34	2	16	60	48	90	.344	.445

Year	Team (League)	W	L	Pct.	ERA	WHIP	G	GS	CG	ShO	Hld.	Sv.-Opp.	IP	H	R	ER	HR	BB-IBB	SO	Avg.
1999— GC Yankees (GCL)		0	1	.000	3.18	0.79	2	2	1	0	...	0-...	11.1	7	4	4	2	2-0	16	.175
— Staten Island (N.Y.-Penn.)		6	4	.600	3.38	1.14	12	12	1	0	...	0-...	72.0	70	30	27	4	12-2	89	.253
— Greensboro (S. Atl.)		0	1	.000	10.50	1.67	1	1	1	0	...	0-...	6.0	8	7	7	1	2-0	5	.296
2000— Greensboro (S. Atl.)		8	5	.615	4.05	1.38	17	17	1	0	...	0-...	97.2	91	49	44	9	44-0	98	.251
— Tampa (Fla. St.)		2	5	.286	3.10	1.26	9	9	1	1	...	0-...	52.1	49	24	18	1	17-0	44	.245
2001— Tampa (Fla. St.)		5	2	.714	2.73	1.07	8	8	0	0	...	0-...	56.0	47	21	17	2	13-0	69	.224
— Norwich (East.)		9	2	.818	2.13	1.19	21	21	1	1	...	0-...	131.0	101	42	31	6	55-0	151	.210
2002— Columbus (Int'l)		2	8	.200	3.28	1.40	15	15	0	0	...	0-...	93.1	85	47	34	4	46-3	73	.242
2003— Tampa (Fla. St.)		2	0	1.000	1.64	0.86	4	4	0	0	...	0-...	22.0	16	5	4	0	3-0	26	.198
— New York (A.L.)		1	0	1.000	1.42	1.42	1	1	0	0	0	0-0	6.1	8	2	1	1	1-0	5	.296
— Columbus (Int'l)		2	1	.667	2.75	1.03	11	11	1	0	0	0-0	68.2	53	28	21	4	18-0	39	.213
— Louisville (Int'l)		0	1	.000	7.47	1.47	3	3	0	0	0	0-0	15.2	17	13	13	3	6-0	16	.293
2004— Louisville (Int'l)		8	6	.571	4.66	1.45	18	18	0	0	0	0-...	100.1	98	56	52	10	47-0	111	.256
— Cincinnati (N.L.)		2	8	.200	6.14	1.74	14	14	0	0	0	0-0	66.0	80	50	45	9	35-2	45	.299
2005— Cincinnati (N.L.)		10	11	.476	4.21	1.41	29	29	0	0	0	0-0	166.2	178	89	78	24	57-5	121	.273
American League totals (1 year)		1	0	1.000	1.42	1.42	1	1	0	0	0	0-0	6.1	8	2	1	1	1-0	5	.296
National League totals (2 years)		12	19	.387	4.76	1.50	43	43	0	0	0	0-0	232.2	258	139	123	33	92-7	166	.280
Major League totals (3 years)		13	19	.406	4.67	1.50	44	44	0	0	0	0-0	239.0	266	141	124	34	93-7	171	.281

CLAYTON, ROYCE — SS

PERSONAL: Born January 2, 1970, in Burbank, Calif. ... 6-0/185. ... Bats right, throws right. ... Full name: Royce Spencer Clayton. ... High school: St. Bernard (Playa del Rey, Calif.).

TRANSACTIONS/CAREER NOTES: Selected by San Francisco Giants organization in first round (15th pick overall) of 1988 free-agent draft; pick received as compensation for Cincinnati Reds signing Type B free-agent OF Eddie Milner. ... Traded by Giants with a player to be named to St. Louis Cardinals for Ps Allen Watson, Rich DeLucia and Doug Creek (December 14, 1995); Cardinals acquired 2B Chris Wimmer to complete deal (January 16, 1996). ... On disabled list (June 24-July 9, 1998). ... Traded by Cardinals with P Todd Stottlemyre to Texas Rangers for P Darren Oliver, 3B Fernando Tatis and a player to be named (July 31, 1998); Cardinals acquired OF Mark Little to complete deal (August 9, 1998). ... On disabled list (May 1-21, 1999); included rehabilitation assignment to Oklahoma. ... Traded by Rangers to Chicago White Sox for Ps Aaron Myette and Brian Schmack (December 14, 2000). ... Released by White Sox (September 8, 2002). ... Signed by Milwaukee Brewers (December 11, 2002). ... Signed as a free agent by Colorado Rockies organization (January 5, 2004). ... Signed as a free agent by Arizona Diamondbacks (December 21, 2004).

2005 GAMES PLAYED BY POSITION (MLB): SS—141.

SCOUTING REPORT *Offense:* Clayton is a productive a No. 2 hitter despite high strikeout totals, because of his ability to bunt and move runners. Has a short stroke. Likes the ball up and out over the plate. Is a line-drive hitter whose power numbers continue to decline. Is not very selective and too often chases breaking pitches when behind in the count. *Defense:* An outstanding athlete, Clayton is very fluid with his actions and footwork. Has quick hands. Charges the ball well. Has good carry on throws from the hole and gets rid of the ball quickly. *Outlook:* Clayton is a very underrated shortstop. Offense has leveled off as his bat has begun to decline, but still can play every day. *Grade 6.5*

ROYCE CLAYTON'S HITTING ZONE

.286	.200	.214
.272	.406	.274
.261	.281	.387

LEFTY-RIGHTY SPLITS

vs.	Avg.	AB	H	2B	3B	HR	RBI	BB	SO	OBP	Slg.
L	.296	152	45	11	0	1	12	15	34	.361	.388
R	.259	370	96	17	4	1	32	23	71	.302	.335

Year Team (League)	Pos.	G	AB	R	H	2B	3B	HR	RBI	BB	SO	HBP	GDP	SB-CS	Avg.	OBP	SLG	OPS	E	Avg.
1988— Everett (N'west)	SS	60	212	35	55	4	0	3	29	27	54	3	8	10-4	.259	.348	.321	.669	35	.873
1989— Clinton (Midw.)	SS	104	385	39	91	13	3	0	24	39	101	4	6	28-16	.236	.309	.286	.595	31	.943
— San Jose (Calif.)	SS	28	92	5	11	2	0	0	4	13	27	1	5	10-1	.120	.236	.141	.377	8	.939
1990— San Jose (Calif.)	SS	123	460	80	123	15	10	7	71	68	98	4	13	33-15	.267	.364	.389	.753	37	.938
1991— Shreveport (Texas)	SS	126	485	84	136	28	8	5	68	61	104	3	7	36-10	.280	.361	.390	.751	29	.950
— San Francisco (N.L.)	SS	9	26	0	3	1	0	0	2	1	6	0	1	0-0	.115	.148	.154	.302	3	.880
1992— San Francisco (N.L.)	SS-3B	98	321	31	72	7	4	4	24	26	63	0	11	8-4	.224	.281	.308	.589	11	.973
— Phoenix (PCL)	SS	48	192	30	46	6	2	3	18	17	25	0	8	15-6	.240	.300	.339	.639	7	.971
1993— San Francisco (N.L.)	SS	153	549	54	155	21	5	6	70	38	91	5	16	11-10	.282	.331	.372	.702	27	.963
1994— San Francisco (N.L.)	SS	108	385	38	91	14	6	3	30	30	74	3	7	23-3	.236	.295	.327	.623	14	.973
1995— San Francisco (N.L.)	SS	138	509	56	124	29	3	5	58	38	109	3	7	24-9	.244	.298	.342	.640	20	.969
1996— St. Louis (N.L.)	SS	129	491	64	136	20	4	6	35	33	89	1	13	33-15	.277	.321	.371	.692	15	.973
1997— St. Louis (N.L.)	SS	154	576	75	153	39	5	9	61	33	109	3	19	30-10	.266	.306	.398	.704	19	.973
1998— St. Louis (N.L.)	SS	90	355	59	83	19	1	4	29	40	51	2	10	19-6	.234	.313	.327	.640	13	.970
— Texas (A.L.)	SS	52	186	30	53	12	1	5	24	13	32	1	6	5-5	.285	.330	.441	.771	7	.972
1999— Texas (A.L.)	SS	133	465	69	134	21	5	14	52	39	100	4	6	8-6	.288	.346	.445	.792	* 25	.961
— Oklahoma (PCL)	SS	2	7	1	1	0	0	0	1	3	0	0	0	0-0	.143	.400	.143	.543	0	1.000
2000— Texas (A.L.)	SS	148	513	70	124	21	5	14	54	42	92	3	21	11-7	.242	.301	.384	.685	16	.977
2001— Chicago (A.L.)	SS	135	433	62	114	21	4	9	60	33	72	3	16	10-7	.263	.315	.393	.708	7	.988
2002— Chicago (A.L.)	SS	112	342	51	86	14	2	7	35	20	67	3	7	5-1	.251	.295	.366	.661	5	.989
2003— Milwaukee (N.L.)	SS	146	483	49	110	16	1	11	39	49	92	3	25	5-2	.228	.301	.333	.634	14	.977
2004— Colorado (N.L.)	SS	146	574	95	160	36	4	8	54	48	125	4	13	10-5	.279	.338	.397	.735	9	.986
2005— Arizona (N.L.)	SS	143	522	59	141	28	4	2	44	38	105	1	19	13-3	.270	.320	.351	.670	11	.982
American League totals (5 years)		580	1939	282	511	89	17	49	225	147	363	14	56	39-26	.264	.317	.403	.720	60	.977
National League totals (11 years)		1314	4791	580	1228	230	37	58	446	374	914	25	141	176-67	.256	.312	.356	.668	156	.973
Major League totals (15 years)		1894	6730	862	1739	319	54	107	671	521	1277	39	197	215-93	.258	.313	.370	.683	216	.974

DIVISION SERIES RECORD

Year Team (League)	Pos.	G	AB	R	H	2B	3B	HR	RBI	BB	SO	HBP	GDP	SB-CS	Avg.	OBP	SLG	OPS	E	Avg.
1996— St. Louis (N.L.)	SS	2	6	1	2	0	0	0	0	3	1	0	0	0-1	.333	.556	.333	.889	0	1.000
1998— Texas (A.L.)	SS	3	9	0	2	0	0	0	0	0	4	0	1	0-0	.222	.222	.222	.444	1	.929
1999— Texas (A.L.)	SS	3	10	0	0	0	0	0	0	0	1	0	0	0-0	.000	.000	.000	.000	0	1.000
Division series totals (3 years)		8	25	1	4	0	0	0	0	3	6	0	1	0-1	.160	.250	.160	.410	1	.973

CHAMPIONSHIP SERIES RECORD

Year Team (League)	Pos.	G	AB	R	H	2B	3B	HR	RBI	BB	SO	HBP	GDP	SB-CS	Avg.	OBP	SLG	OPS	E	Avg.
1996— St. Louis (N.L.)	SS	5	20	4	7	0	0	0	0	0	0	0	0	1-1	.350	.381	.350	.731	2	.913

ALL-STAR GAME RECORD

		G	AB	R	H	2B	3B	HR	RBI	BB	SO	HBP	GDP	SB-CS	Avg.	OBP	SLG	OPS	E	Avg.
All-Star Game totals (1 year)		1	1	0	0	0	0	0	0	0	1	0	0	0-0	.000	.000	.000	.000	0	1.000

CLEMENS, ROGER — P

PERSONAL: Born August 4, 1962, in Dayton, Ohio. ... 6-4/235. ... Throws right, bats right. ... Full name: William Roger Clemens. ... High school: Spring Woods (Houston). ... College: Texas.

TRANSACTIONS/CAREER NOTES: Selected by New York Mets organization in 12th round of June 1981 free-agent draft; did not sign. ... Selected by Boston Red Sox organization in first round (19th pick overall) of June 1983 free-agent draft. ... On disabled list (July 8-August 3 and August 21, 1985-remainder of season). ... On suspended list (April 26-May 3, 1991). ... On disabled list (June 19-July 16, 1993); included rehabilitation assignment to Pawtucket. ... On disabled list (April 16-June 2, 1995); included rehabilitation assignments to Sarasota and Pawtucket. ... Signed as a free agent by Toronto Blue Jays (December 13, 1996). ... Traded by Blue Jays to New York Yankees for Ps David Wells and Graeme Lloyd and 2B Homer Bush (February 18, 1999). ... On disabled list (April 28-May 21, 1999; and June 15-July 2, 2000). ... On disabled list (July 13-August 7, 2002); included rehabilitation assignments to Tampa and Norwich. ... Signed as a free agent by Houston Astros (January 19, 2004).

RECORDS: Shares major league record for most strikeouts, 9-inning game—(20, April 29, 1986; and September 18, 1996).

HONORS: Named Major League Player of the Year by THE SPORTING NEWS (1986). ... Named A.L. Pitcher of the Year by THE SPORTING NEWS (1986, 1991, 1997, 1998 and 2001). ... Named A.L. Most Valuable Player by Baseball Writers' Association of America (1986). ... Named A.L. Cy Young Award winner by Baseball Writers' Association of America (1986, 1987, 1991, 1997, 1998 and 2001). ... Named N.L. Cy Young Award winner by Baseball Writers' Association of America (2004).

CAREER HITTING: 28-for-150 (.187), 5 R, 5 R, 2 2B, 0 3B, 0 HR, 12 RBI.

SCOUTING REPORT *Throws:* Clemens throws his fastball from 90-95 mph, a split-finger fastball from 85-89, a slider from 85-87 and a curveball from 73-76. *Tendencies:* The Rocket is using all his pitches now instead of relying on his fastball and splitter. Changes hitters' eye level by riding his four-seam fastball in and then using a diving splitter late in the count. Occasionally will throw a curve early in the count to a lefthanded hitter. Has late bite on his slider, which is a plus pitch. Is an intimidating presence. *Outlook:* In spite of his age, 2005 may have been Clemens' best year. Dominates with improved command down in the zone. *Grade 9.7*

ROGER CLEMENS'S PITCHING ZONE

.255	.111	.154
.279	.346	.182
.139	.188	.211

LEFTY-RIGHTY SPLITS

vs.	Avg.	AB	H	2B	3B	HR	RBI	BB	SO	OBP	Slg.
L	.195	364	71	12	1	3	14	28	83	.256	.258
R	.202	397	80	14	2	8	31	34	102	.265	.307

Year Team (League)	W	L	Pct.	ERA	WHIP	G	GS	CG	ShO	Hld.	Sv.-Opp.	IP	H	R	ER	HR	BB-IBB	SO	Avg.
1983— Winter Haven (FSL)	3	1	.750	1.24	0.76	4	4	3	1		0-...	29.0	22	4	4	0	0-0	36	.206
— New Britain (East.)	4	1	.800	1.38	0.83	7	7	1	1		0-...	52.0	31	8	8	1	12-0	59	.167
1984— Pawtucket (Int'l)	2	3	.400	1.93	1.14	7	6	3	1		0-...	46.2	39	12	10	3	14-0	50	.228
— Boston (A.L.)	9	4	.692	4.32	1.31	21	20	5	1	0	0-0	133.1	146	67	64	13	29-3	126	.271
1985— Boston (A.L.)	7	5	.583	3.29	1.22	15	15	3	1	0	0-0	98.1	83	38	36	5	37-0	74	.228
1986— Boston (A.L.)	* 24	4	* .857	* 2.48	0.97	33	33	10	1	0	0-0	254.0	179	77	70	21	67-0	238	* .195
1987— Boston (A.L.)	• 20	9	.690	2.97	1.18	36	36	* 18	• 7	0	0-0	281.2	248	100	93	19	83-4	256	.235
1988— Boston (A.L.)	18	12	.600	2.93	1.06	35	35	• 14	• 8	0	0-0	264.0	217	93	86	17	62-4	* 291	.231
1989— Boston (A.L.)	17	11	.607	3.13	1.22	35	35	8	3	0	0-0	253.1	215	101	88	20	93-5	230	.231
1990— Boston (A.L.)	21	6	.778	* 1.93	1.08	31	31	7	• 4	0	0-0	228.1	193	59	49	7	54-3	209	.228

Year	Team (League)	W	L	Pct.	ERA	WHIP	G	GS	CG	ShO	Hld.	Sv.-Opp.	IP	H	R	ER	HR	BB-IBB	SO	Avg.
1991— Boston (A.L.)		18	10	.643	*2.62	1.05	35	•35	13	*4	0	0-0	*271.1	219	93	79	15	65-12	*241	.221
1992— Boston (A.L.)		18	11	.621	*2.41	1.07	32	32	11	*5	0	0-0	246.2	203	80	66	11	62-5	208	.224
1993— Boston (A.L.)		11	14	.440	4.46	1.26	29	29	2	1	0	0-0	191.2	175	99	95	17	67-4	160	.244
—Pawtucket (Int'l)		0	0	...	0.00	1.36	1	1	0	0	0	0-...	3.2	1	0	0	0	4-0	8	.091
1994— Boston (A.L.)		9	7	.563	2.85	1.14	24	24	3	1	0	0-0	170.2	124	62	54	15	71-1	168	*.204
1995— Sarasota (Fla. St.)		0	0	...	0.00	0.50	1	1	0	0	0	0-...	4.0	0	0	0	0	2-0	7	.000
—Pawtucket (Int'l)		0	0	...	0.00	0.80	1	1	0	0	0	0-...	5.0	1	0	0	0	3-0	5	.063
—Boston (A.L.)		10	5	.667	4.18	1.44	23	23	0	0	0	0-0	140.0	141	70	65	15	60-0	132	.259
1996— Boston (A.L.)		10	13	.435	3.63	1.33	34	34	6	2	0	0-0	242.2	216	106	98	19	106-2	*257	.237
1997— Toronto (A.L.)		*21	7	.750	*2.05	1.03	34	34	•9	•3	0	0-0	•264.0	204	65	60	9	68-1	*292	.213
1998— Toronto (A.L.)		•20	6	.769	*2.65	1.10	33	33	5	3	0	0-0	234.2	169	78	69	11	88-0	*271	.198
1999— New York (A.L.)		14	10	.583	4.60	1.47	30	30	1	1	0	0-0	187.2	185	101	96	20	90-0	163	.261
2000— New York (A.L.)		13	8	.619	3.70	1.31	32	32	1	0	0	0-0	204.1	184	96	84	26	84-0	188	.236
2001— New York (A.L.)		20	3	*.870	3.51	1.26	33	33	0	0	0	0-0	220.1	205	94	86	19	72-1	213	.246
2002— New York (A.L.)		13	6	.684	4.35	1.31	29	29	0	0	0	0-0	180.0	172	94	87	18	63-6	192	.250
—Tampa (Fla. St.)		1	0	1.000	5.40	1.40	1	1	0	0	0	0-...	5.0	5	3	3	1	2-0	6	.263
—Norwich (East.)		0	1	.000	1.29	0.71	1	1	0	0	0	0-...	7.0	5	1	1	0	0-0	7	.200
2003— New York (A.L.)		17	9	.654	3.91	1.21	33	33	1	1	0	0-0	211.2	199	99	92	24	58-1	190	.247
2004— Houston (N.L.)		18	4	.818	2.98	1.16	33	33	0	0	0	0-0	214.1	169	76	71	15	79-5	218	.217
2005— Houston (N.L.)		13	8	.619	*1.87	1.01	32	32	1	0	0	0-0	211.1	151	51	44	11	62-5	185	*.198
American League totals (20 years)		310	160	.660	3.19	1.18	607	606	117	46	0	0-0	4278.2	3677	1672	1517	321	1379-52	4099	.231
National League totals (2 years)		31	12	.721	2.43	1.08	65	65	1	0	0	0-0	425.2	320	127	115	26	141-10	403	.208
Major League totals (22 years)		341	172	.665	3.12	1.17	672	671	118	46	0	0-0	4704.1	3997	1799	1632	347	1520-62	4502	.229

DIVISION SERIES RECORD

Year	Team (League)	W	L	Pct.	ERA	WHIP	G	GS	CG	ShO	Hld.	Sv.-Opp.	IP	H	R	ER	HR	BB-IBB	SO	Avg.
1995— Boston (A.L.)		0	0	...	3.86	0.86	1	1	0	0	0	0-0	7.0	5	3	3	0	1-0	5	.192
1999— New York (A.L.)		1	0	1.000	0.00	0.71	1	1	0	0	0	0-0	7.0	3	0	0	0	2-0	2	.125
2000— New York (A.L.)		0	2	.000	8.18	1.91	2	2	0	0	0	0-0	11.0	13	10	10	1	8-1	10	.302
2001— New York (A.L.)		0	1	.000	5.40	1.56	2	2	0	0	0	0-0	8.1	9	5	5	1	4-0	6	.265
2002— New York (A.L.)		0	0	...	6.35	1.94	1	1	0	0	0	0-0	5.2	8	4	4	1	3-0	5	.348
2003— New York (A.L.)		1	0	1.000	1.29	0.86	1	1	0	0	0	0-0	7.0	5	1	1	1	1-0	6	.192
2004— Houston (N.L.)		1	0	1.000	3.00	1.67	2	2	0	0	0	0-0	12.0	12	5	4	1	8-0	12	.267
2005— Houston (N.L.)		1	1	.500	5.63	1.25	2	1	0	0	0	0-0	8.0	7	5	5	1	3-0	6	.233
Division series totals (8 years)		4	4	.500	4.36	1.39	12	11	0	0	0	0-0	66.0	62	33	32	6	30-1	52	.247

CHAMPIONSHIP SERIES RECORD

Year	Team (League)	W	L	Pct.	ERA	WHIP	G	GS	CG	ShO	Hld.	Sv.-Opp.	IP	H	R	ER	HR	BB-IBB	SO	Avg.
1986— Boston (A.L.)		1	1	.500	4.37	1.28	3	3	0	0	0	0-0	22.2	22	12	11	1	7-0	17	.244
1988— Boston (A.L.)		0	0	...	3.86	0.86	1	1	0	0	0	0-0	7.0	6	3	3	1	0-0	8	.231
1990— Boston (A.L.)		0	1	.000	3.52	1.57	2	2	0	0	0	0-0	7.2	7	3	3	0	5-0	4	.259
1999— New York (A.L.)		0	1	.000	22.50	4.00	1	1	0	0	0	0-0	2.0	6	5	5	1	2-0	2	.462
2000— New York (A.L.)		1	0	1.000	0.00	0.33	1	1	1	0	0	0-0	9.0	1	0	0	0	2-0	15	.036
2001— New York (A.L.)		0	0	...	1.00	1.00	1	1	0	0	0	0-0	5.0	1	1	0	0	4-0	7	.063
2003— New York (A.L.)		1	0	1.000	5.00	1.44	2	2	0	0	0	0-0	9.0	11	6	5	2	2-0	8	.297
2004— Houston (N.L.)		1	1	.500	4.15	0.92	2	2	0	0	0	0-0	13.0	10	6	6	3	2-0	9	.217
2005— Houston (N.L.)		1	0	1.000	3.00	1.33	1	1	0	0	0	0-0	6.0	6	2	2	0	2-0	1	.286
Champ. series totals (9 years)		5	4	.556	3.87	1.18	14	14	1	1	0	0-0	81.1	70	37	35	8	26-0	71	.230

WORLD SERIES RECORD

Year	Team (League)	W	L	Pct.	ERA	WHIP	G	GS	CG	ShO	Hld.	Sv.-Opp.	IP	H	R	ER	HR	BB-IBB	SO	Avg.
1986— Boston (A.L.)		0	0	...	3.18	1.32	2	2	0	0	0	0-0	11.1	9	5	4	0	6-0	11	.225
1999— New York (A.L.)		1	0	1.000	1.17	0.78	1	1	0	0	0	0-0	7.2	4	1	1	0	2-0	4	.154
2000— New York (A.L.)		1	0	1.000	0.00	0.25	1	1	0	0	0	0-0	8.0	2	0	0	0	0-0	9	.074
2001— New York (A.L.)		1	0	1.000	1.35	1.05	2	2	0	0	0	0-0	13.1	10	2	2	0	4-0	19	.204
2003— New York (A.L.)		0	0	...	3.86	1.14	1	1	0	0	0	0-0	7.0	8	3	3	1	0-0	5	.286
2005— Houston (N.L.)		0	0	...	13.50	2.00	1	1	0	0	0	0-0	2.0	4	3	3	1	0-0	1	.400
World Series totals (6 years)		3	0	1.000	2.37	0.99	8	8	0	0	0	0-0	49.1	37	14	13	2	12-0	49	.206

ALL-STAR GAME RECORD

	Year	W	L	Pct.	ERA	WHIP	G	GS	CG	ShO	Hld.	Sv.-Opp.	IP	H	R	ER	HR	BB-IBB	SO	Avg.
All-Star Game totals (10 years)		1	1	.500	4.15	0.92	10	3	0	0	0	0-0	13.0	11	9	6	3	1-0	9	.224

CLEMENT, MATT   P

PERSONAL: Born August 12, 1974, in Butler, Pa. ... 6-3/210. ... Throws right, bats right. ... Full name: Matthew Paul Clement. ... Name pronounced: klah-MENT. ... High school: Butler (Pa.).

TRANSACTIONS/CAREER NOTES: Selected by San Diego Padres organization in third round of 1993 free-agent draft. ... Traded by Padres with OF Eric Owens and P Omar Ortiz to Florida Marlins for OFs Mark Kotsay and Cesar Crespo (March 28, 2001). ... Traded by Marlins with P Antonio Alfonseca to Chicago Cubs for Ps Julian Tavarez, Jose Cueto and Dontrelle Willis and C Ryan Jorgensen (March 27, 2002). ... Signed as a free agent by Boston Red Sox (December 21, 2004).

CAREER HITTING: 32-for-345 (.093), 21 R, 5 2B, 1 3B, 0 HR, 12 RBI.

SCOUTING REPORT **Throws:** His fastball ranges from 89-93 mph, his slider is in the mid-80s, and he also throws a split-finger fastball. **Tendencies:** Clement has exceptional stuff, but a lack of command and high pitch counts often result in five-inning outings. Hitters don't pick up the ball well off of him; they often swing and miss. Slider is sharp-breaking. Is starting to use a splitter late in the count to lefthanders. Can drive teammates playing behind him crazy with his lack of mound presence and 3-2 counts. Gets ahead and then nibbles. Inconsistent delivery also leads to being erratic. **Outlook:** He is an underachiever because he doesn't realize he has great stuff. Tries to be too fine and thread a needle when he should throw it down the middle and let his fastball run. *Grade 7*

MATT CLEMENT'S PITCHING ZONE

.293	.485	.263
.291	.318	.299
.307	.400	.237

LEFTY-RIGHTY SPLITS

vs.	Avg.	AB	H	2B	3B	HR	RBI	BB	SO	OBP	Slg.
L	.275	389	107	24	2	13	58	48	73	.354	.447
R	.244	349	85	20	0	5	29	20	73	.309	.344

Year	Team (League)	W	L	Pct.	ERA	WHIP	G	GS	CG	ShO	Hld.	Sv.-Opp.	IP	H	R	ER	HR	BB-IBB	SO	Avg.
1994—	Spokane (N'west)	1	1	.500	6.14	2.59	2	2	0	0	...	0-...	7.1	8	7	5	0	11-0	4	.296
—	Ariz. Padres (Ariz.)	8	5	.615	4.43	1.22	13	13	0	0	...	0-...	67.0	65	38	33	0	17-0	76	.248
1995—	Rancho Cuca. (Calif.)	3	4	.429	4.24	1.92	12	12	0	0	...	0-...	57.1	61	37	27	1	49-0	33	.295
—	Idaho Falls (Pio.)	6	3	.667	4.33	1.27	14	14	0	0	...	0-...	81.0	61	53	39	3	42-0	65	.214
1996—	Clinton (Midw.)	8	3	.727	2.80	1.22	16	16	1	1	...	0-...	96.1	66	31	30	3	52-0	109	.191
—	Rancho Cuca. (Calif.)	4	5	.444	5.59	1.54	11	11	0	0	...	0-...	56.1	61	40	35	8	26-0	75	.280
1997—	Rancho Cuca. (Calif.)	6	3	.667	1.60	1.04	14	14	2	1	...	0-...	101.0	74	30	18	3	31-1	109	.202
—	Mobile (Sou.)	6	5	.545	2.56	1.31	13	13	1	1	...	0-...	88.0	83	37	25	4	32-0	92	.249
1998—	Las Vegas (PCL)	10	9	.526	3.98	1.41	27	27	1	0	...	0-...	171.2	157	94	76	12	85-2	160	.245
—	San Diego (N.L.)	2	0	1.000	4.61	1.61	4	2	0	0	0	0-0	13.2	15	8	7	0	7-1	13	.283
1999—	San Diego (N.L.)	10	12	.455	4.48	1.53	31	31	0	0	0	0-0	180.2	190	106	90	18	86-2	135	.273
2000—	San Diego (N.L.)	13	17	.433	5.14	1.56	34	34	0	0	0	0-0	205.0	194	131	117	22	* 125-4	170	.248
2001—	Florida (N.L.)	9	10	.474	5.05	1.52	31	31	0	0	0	0-0	169.1	172	102	95	15	85-2	134	.268
2002—	Chicago (N.L.)	12	11	.522	3.60	1.20	32	32	3	2	0	0-0	205.0	162	84	82	18	85-7	215	.215
2003—	Chicago (N.L.)	14	12	.538	4.11	1.23	32	32	2	1	0	0-0	201.2	169	100	92	22	79-2	171	.227
2004—	Chicago (N.L.)	9	13	.409	3.68	1.28	30	30	0	0	0	0-0	181.0	155	79	74	23	77-4	190	.229
2005—	Boston (A.L.)	13	6	.684	4.57	1.36	32	32	1	0	0	0-0	191.0	192	102	97	18	68-1	146	.260
American League totals (1 year)		13	6	.684	4.57	1.36	32	32	1	0	0	0-0	191.0	192	102	97	18	68-1	146	.260
National League totals (7 years)		69	75	.479	4.34	1.38	194	192	5	3	0	0-0	1156.1	1057	610	557	118	544-22	1028	.243
Major League totals (8 years)		82	81	.503	4.37	1.38	226	224	6	3	0	0-0	1347.1	1249	712	654	136	612-23	1174	.246

DIVISION SERIES RECORD

Year	Team (League)	W	L	Pct.	ERA	WHIP	G	GS	CG	ShO	Hld.	Sv.-Opp.	IP	H	R	ER	HR	BB-IBB	SO	Avg.
2003—	Chicago (N.L.)	0	1	.000	7.71	2.57	1	1	0	0	0	0-0	4.2	8	4	4	1	4-0	3	.381
2005—	Boston (A.L.)	0	1	.000	21.60	2.10	1	1	0	0	0	0-0	3.1	7	8	8	3	0-0	0	.467
Division series totals (2 years)		0	2	.000	13.50	2.38	2	2	0	0	0	0-0	8.0	15	12	12	4	4-0	3	.417

CHAMPIONSHIP SERIES RECORD

Year	Team (League)	W	L	Pct.	ERA	WHIP	G	GS	CG	ShO	Hld.	Sv.-Opp.	IP	H	R	ER	HR	BB-IBB	SO	Avg.
2003—	Chicago (N.L.)	1	0	1.000	3.52	0.91	1	1	0	0	0	0-0	7.2	5	3	3	0	2-0	3	.192

ALL-STAR GAME RECORD

Year	Team (League)	W	L	Pct.	ERA	WHIP	G	GS	CG	ShO	Hld.	Sv.-Opp.	IP	H	R	ER	HR	BB-IBB	SO	Avg.
All-Star Game totals (1 year)		0	0	...	0.00	1.00	1	0	0	0	0	0-0	1.0	0	0	0	0	1-0	1	.000

CLOSSER, JD   C

PERSONAL: Born January 15, 1980, in Beech Grove, Ind. ... 5-10/176. ... Bats both, throws right. ... Full name: Jeffrey Darrin Closser. ... High school: Monroe Central (Parker City, Ind.).
TRANSACTIONS/CAREER NOTES: Selected by Arizona Diamondbacks organization in fifth round of 1998 free-agent draft. ... Traded by Diamondbacks with OF Jack Cust to Colorado Rockies for P Mike Myers (January 7, 2002).
2005 GAMES PLAYED BY POSITION (MLB): C—80.

SCOUTING REPORT Closser has a compact stroke but not good bat speed. Chases lots of bad pitches up out of the strike zone. Is a better lefthanded hitter, with power as his best asset. Likes the ball up and out over the plate. Doesn't throw well or have good footwork. Arm strength is below average and runners take liberties. Hands are a little stiff. Needs to have a good spring to make the club; may never be a really good catcher. ***Grade 4.3***

JD CLOSSER'S HITTING ZONE

.222	.333	.267
.241	.258	.293
.273	.222	.184

LEFTY-RIGHTY SPLITS

vs.	Avg.	AB	H	2B	3B	HR	RBI	BB	SO	OBP	Slg.
L	.270	37	10	2	0	2	8	5	7	.357	.486
R	.210	200	42	10	2	5	19	27	41	.306	.355

Year	Team (League)	Pos.	G	AB	R	H	2B	3B	HR	RBI	BB	SO	HBP	GDP	SB-CS	Avg.	OBP	SLG	OPS	FIELDING E	Avg.
1998—	Ariz. D'backs (Ariz.)	C-1B	45	150	26	47	13	2	4	21	37	36	2	3	3-2	.313	.453	.507	.959	13	.965
—	South Bend (Mid.)	C	4	14	3	3	1	0	0	2	2	7	0	0	0-0	.214	.313	.286	.598	0	1.000
1999—	South Bend (Mid.)	C	52	174	29	42	8	0	3	27	34	37	1	3	0-1	.241	.363	.339	.702	12	.951
—	Missoula (Pion.)	C	76	275	73	89	22	0	10	54	71	57	2	8	9-3	.324	.458	.513	.970	21	.964
2000—	South Bend (Mid.)	C-1B	101	331	54	74	19	1	8	37	60	61	3	7	6-2	.224	.347	.360	.706	12	.979
2001—	Lancaster (Calif.)	C-OF	128	468	85	136	26	6	21	87	65	106	2	9	6-7	.291	.377	.506	.883	16	.981
2002—	Carolina (Southern)	C	95	315	40	89	27	1	13	62	44	69	0	7	9-3	.283	.369	.498	.868	12	.977
2003—	Tulsa (Texas)	C-OF	118	410	62	116	28	5	13	54	47	79	3	10	3-2	.283	.359	.471	.829	18	.976
2004—	Colo. Springs (PCL)	C-DH	83	298	53	89	19	1	7	54	41	47	2	3	0-2	.299	.384	.440	.820	10	.983
—	Colorado (N.L.)	C	36	113	5	36	6	0	1	10	6	22	2	3	0-0	.319	.364	.398	.762	3	.986
2005—	Colorado (N.L.)	C	92	237	31	52	12	2	7	27	32	48	1	9	1-0	.219	.314	.376	.689	8	.982
Major League totals (2 years)			128	350	36	88	18	2	8	37	38	70	3	12	1-0	.251	.329	.383	.712	11	.983

COFFEY, TODD   P

PERSONAL: Born September 9, 1980, in Shelby, N.C. ... 6-5/230. ... Throws right, bats right. ... Full name: Justin Todd Coffey. ... High school: Chase (Forest City, N.C.).
TRANSACTIONS/CAREER NOTES: Selected by Cincinnati Reds organization in 41st round of 1998 free-agent draft. ... On disabled list (June 19-September 27, 2000).
CAREER HITTING: 0-for-3 (.000), 0 R, 0 2B, 0 3B, 0 HR, 0 RBI.

TODD COFFEY'S PITCHING ZONE

.538	.750	.313
.250	.472	.261
.412	.333	.308

LEFTY-RIGHTY SPLITS

vs.	Avg.	AB	H	2B	3B	HR	RBI	BB	SO	OBP	Slg.
L	.337	86	29	9	0	1	16	3	6	.363	.477
R	.348	158	55	9	2	4	22	8	20	.392	.506

Year	Team (League)	W	L	Pct.	ERA	WHIP	G	GS	CG	ShO	Hld.	Sv.-Opp.	IP	H	R	ER	HR	BB-IBB	SO	Avg.
1998—	Billings (Pion.)	0	0	...	3.00	1.17	3	2	0	0	...	0-...	12.0	13	4	4	1	1-0	8	.302
1999—	GC Reds (GCL)	1	1	.500	3.38	1.44	5	5	2	0	...	0-...	16.0	9	12	6	1	14-0	14	.145

Year Team (League)	W	L	Pct.	ERA	WHIP	G	GS	CG	ShO	Hld.	Sv.-Opp.	IP	H	R	ER	HR	BB-IBB	SO	Avg.
2000—	Did not play.																		
2001—GC Reds (GCL)	0	1	.000	4.26	1.26	3	2	0	0	...	0-...	12.2	11	11	6	1	5-0	15	.234
—Billings (Pion.)	2	2	.500	3.51	1.47	14	2	0	0	...	1-...	33.1	34	21	13	2	15-0	33	.258
2002—Dayton (Midw.)	6	4	.600	3.59	1.28	38	5	0	0	...	2-...	80.1	78	34	32	8	25-5	62	.260
2003—Dayton (Midw.)	3	3	.500	2.25	1.34	39	0	0	0	...	9-...	56.0	61	20	14	1	14-0	53	.289
—Potomac (Carol.)	0	2	.000	1.96	0.83	11	0	0	0	...	2-...	23.0	16	6	5	0	3-0	21	.208
2004—Chattanooga (Sou.)	4	1	.800	2.38	0.88	40	0	0	0	...	20-...	45.1	36	13	12	3	4-1	53	.209
—Louisville (Int'l)	1	0	1.000	5.27	1.24	15	0	0	0	...	4-...	13.2	15	8	8	1	2-0	11	.268
2005—Louisville (Int'l)	0	0	...	5.19	1.15	8	0	0	0	0	3-5	8.2	8	5	5	1	2-1	5	.242
—Cincinnati (N.L.)	4	1	.800	4.50	1.64	57	0	0	0	3	1-2	58.0	84	33	29	5	11-2	26	.344
Major League totals (1 year)	4	1	.800	4.50	1.64	57	0	0	0	3	1-2	58.0	84	33	29	5	11-2	26	.344

COLOME, JESUS — P

PERSONAL: Born December 23, 1977, in San Pedro de Macoris, Dominican Republic. ... 6-4/205. ... Throws right, bats right. ... Full name: Jesus Colome De La Cruz. ... Name pronounced: COL-um-ay.

TRANSACTIONS/CAREER NOTES: Signed as a non-drafted free agent by Oakland Athletics organization (September 29, 1996). ... Traded by A's with cash to Tampa Bay Devil Rays for Ps Jim Mecir and Todd Belitz (July 28, 2000). ... On disabled list (September 14, 2004-remainder of season). ... On disabled list (June 12-July 22, 2005); included rehabilitation assignment to Montgomery.

CAREER HITTING: 0-for-1 (.000), 0 R, 0 2B, 0 3B, 0 HR, 0 RBI.

SCOUTING REPORT *Throws:* Colome throws his fastball at 94-97 mph, and he also has a slider and a circle change. *Tendencies:* He's a long reliever with an outstanding arm but still is extremely inconsistent with his command. Has an extremely loose arm with a live, late finishing fastball that can overpower hitters up in the zone. Is staying on top of his slider and has tightened its break. Circle change is thrown hard and he lacks a feel for it. Three-quarters arm slot can flatten pitches, but showed improvement in his breaking ball in the second half of the season. *Outlook:* Colome, more of a long reliever now, is running out of time to harness his potential. *Grade 5.9*

JESUS COLOME'S PITCHING ZONE

.400	.333	.375
.385	.346	.182
.313	.500	.250

LEFTY-RIGHTY SPLITS

vs.	Avg.	AB	H	2B	3B	HR	RBI	BB	SO	OBP	Slg.
L	.291	86	25	5	0	4	17	10	12	.365	.488
R	.276	105	29	5	0	3	11	8	16	.339	.448

Year Team (League)	W	L	Pct.	ERA	WHIP	G	GS	CG	ShO	Hld.	Sv.-Opp.	IP	H	R	ER	HR	BB-IBB	SO	Avg.
1997—Dom. Athletics (DSL)	9	3	.750	2.70	1.06	18	7	3	0	...	0-...	90.0	73	33	27	...	22-...	55	
1998—Ariz. A's (Ariz.)	2	5	.286	3.18	1.11	12	11	0	0	...	0-...	56.2	47	27	20	1	16-0	62	.228
1999—Modesto (California)	8	4	.667	3.36	1.44	31	22	0	0	...	1-...	128.2	125	63	48	6	60-2	127	.256
2000—Midland (Texas)	9	4	.692	3.59	1.35	20	20	0	0	...	0-...	110.1	99	62	44	10	50-0	95	.239
—Orlando (South.)	1	2	.333	6.75	1.70	3	3	0	0	...	0-...	14.2	18	12	11	2	7-0	9	.290
2001—Durham (Int'l)	0	3	.000	6.23	1.62	13	0	0	0	...	0-...	17.1	22	13	12	1	6-0	18	.319
—Tampa Bay (A.L.)	2	3	.400	3.33	1.27	30	0	0	0	6	0-0	48.2	37	22	18	8	25-4	31	.208
2002—Tampa Bay (A.L.)	2	7	.222	8.27	2.15	32	0	0	0	3	0-5	41.1	56	44	38	6	33-5	33	.341
—Durham (Int'l)	2	2	.500	2.17	1.07	18	0	0	0	...	1-...	29.0	18	8	7	1	13-0	31	.176
2003—Tampa Bay (A.L.)	3	7	.300	4.50	1.55	54	0	0	0	11	2-8	74.0	69	37	37	9	46-5	69	.247
2004—Durham (Int'l)	2	1	.667	3.52	1.40	18	0	0	0	...	2-...	30.2	27	12	12	0	16-0	17	.243
—Tampa Bay (A.L.)	2	2	.500	3.27	1.11	33	0	0	0	8	3-4	41.1	28	16	15	4	18-1	40	.193
2005—Tampa Bay (A.L.)	2	3	.400	4.57	1.59	36	0	0	0	2	0-1	45.1	54	29	23	7	18-3	28	.283
Major League totals (5 years)	11	22	.333	4.70	1.53	185	0	0	0	30	5-18	250.2	244	145	131	34	140-18	201	.255

COLON, BARTOLO — P

PERSONAL: Born May 24, 1973, in Altamira, Dominican Republic. ... 5-11/250. ... Throws right, bats right. ... Name pronounced: bar-TOE-loh ko-LONE.

TRANSACTIONS/CAREER NOTES: Signed as a non-drafted free agent by Cleveland Indians organization (June 26, 1993). ... On disabled list (April 16-May 12, 2000); included rehabilitation assignment to Buffalo. ... On suspended list (July 28-August 2, 2001). ... Traded by Indians with future considerations to Montreal Expos for 1B Lee Stevens, SS Brandon Phillips, P Cliff Lee and OF Grady Sizemore (June 27, 2002); Expos acquired P Tim Drew to complete deal (June 28, 2002). ... Traded by Expos with 2B/SS Jorge Nunez to Chicago White Sox for P Orlando Hernandez, P Rocky Biddle, 3B/OF Jeff Liefer and cash (January 15, 2003). ... On suspended list (May 21-27, 2003). ... Signed as a free agent by Anaheim Angels (December 10, 2003). ... Angels franchise renamed Los Angeles Angels of Anaheim for 2005 season.

HONORS: Named A.L. Pitcher of the Year by the SPORTING NEWS (2005). ... Named A.L. Cy Young Award winner by Baseball Writers' Association of America (2005).

CAREER HITTING: 10-for-79 (.127), 1 R, 0 2B, 0 3B, 0 HR, 5 RBI.

SCOUTING REPORT *Throws:* Colon hits 93-98 mph with his two- and four-seam fastballs and 85-88 with his slider. Also has a changeup. *Tendencies:* He can pitch with his fastball and maintain his velocity for nine innings. Has good life up in the strike zone with the four-seam fastball and good tailing movement on the two-seam fastball. Has a quick, late-breaking slider. Doesn't throw many changeups. Has a short, extremely quick arm and powerful legs. *Outlook:* Colon put everything together in 2005, winning the A.L. Cy Young Award. Has learned to stay focused and not pitch to the level of the competition. *Grade 9.6*

BARTOLO COLON'S PITCHING ZONE

.281	.255	.273
.273	.286	.237
.310	.316	.282

LEFTY-RIGHTY SPLITS

vs.	Avg.	AB	H	2B	3B	HR	RBI	BB	SO	OBP	Slg.
L	.250	420	105	23	2	15	44	30	86	.300	.421
R	.258	427	110	19	3	11	42	13	71	.282	.393

Year Team (League)	W	L	Pct.	ERA	WHIP	G	GS	CG	ShO	Hld.	Sv.-Opp.	IP	H	R	ER	HR	BB-IBB	SO	Avg.
1993—Dom. Indians (DSL)	6	1	.857	2.59	1.17	11	10	2	1	...	1-...	66.0	44	24	19	...	33-...	48	
1994—Burlington (Appal.)	7	4	.636	3.14	1.36	12	12	0	0	...	0-...	66.0	46	32	23	3	44-0	84	.192
1995—Kinston (Carol.)	13	3	.813	1.96	1.11	21	21	0	0	...	0-...	128.2	91	31	28	8	39-0	152	.202
1996—Cant./Akr. (Eastern)	2	2	.500	1.74	1.11	13	12	0	0	...	0-...	62.0	44	17	12	2	25-0	56	.196
—Buffalo (A.A.)	0	0	...	6.00	1.60	8	0	0	0	...	0-...	15.0	16	10	10	2	8-0	19	.271
1997—Cleveland (A.L.)	4	7	.364	5.65	1.62	19	17	1	0	0	0-...	94.0	107	66	59	12	45-1	66	.286
—Buffalo (A.A.)	7	1	.875	2.22	1.20	10	10	1	1	...	0-...	56.2	45	15	14	4	23-0	54	.221

Year Team (League)	W	L	Pct.	ERA	WHIP	G	GS	CG	ShO	Hld.	Sv.-Opp.	IP	H	R	ER	HR	BB-IBB	SO	Avg.
1998— Cleveland (A.L.)	14	9	.609	3.71	1.39	31	31	6	2	0	0-0	204.0	205	91	84	15	79-5	158	.260
1999— Cleveland (A.L.)	18	5	.783	3.95	1.27	32	32	1	1	0	0-0	205.0	185	97	90	24	76-5	161	.242
2000— Cleveland (A.L.)	15	8	.652	3.88	1.39	30	30	2	1	0	0-0	188.0	163	86	81	21	98-4	212	.233
— Buffalo (Int'l)	1	0	1.000	1.80	1.20	1	1	0	0	0	0-...	5.0	6	1	1	0	0-0	4	.286
2001— Cleveland (A.L.)	14	12	.538	4.09	1.39	34	34	1	0	0	0-0	222.1	220	106	101	26	90-2	201	.261
2002— Cleveland (A.L.)	10	4	.714	2.55	1.16	16	16	4	2	0	0-0	116.1	104	37	33	11	31-1	75	.245
— Montreal (N.L.)	10	4	.714	3.31	1.32	17	17	4	1	0	0-0	117.0	115	48	43	9	39-4	74	.259
2003— Chicago (A.L.)	15	13	.536	3.87	1.20	34	34	•9	0	0	0-0	242.0	223	107	104	30	67-3	173	.248
2004— Anaheim (A.L.)	18	12	.600	5.01	1.37	34	34	0	0	0	0-0	208.1	215	122	116	38	71-1	158	.265
2005— Los Angeles (A.L.)	* 21	8	.724	3.48	1.16	33	33	2	0	0	0-0	222.2	215	93	86	26	43-0	157	.254
American League totals (9 years)	129	78	.623	3.99	1.31	263	261	26	6	0	0-0	1702.2	1637	805	754	203	600-22	1361	.254
National League totals (1 year)	10	4	.714	3.31	1.32	17	17	4	1	0	0-0	117.0	115	48	43	9	39-4	74	.259
Major League totals (9 years)	139	82	.629	3.94	1.31	280	278	30	7	0	0-0	1819.2	1752	853	797	212	639-26	1435	.254

DIVISION SERIES RECORD

Year Team (League)	W	L	Pct.	ERA	WHIP	G	GS	CG	ShO	Hld.	Sv.-Opp.	IP	H	R	ER	HR	BB-IBB	SO	Avg.
1997— Cleveland (A.L.)			Did not play.																
1998— Cleveland (A.L.)	0	0		1.59	1.41	1	1	0	0	0	0-0	5.2	5	1	1	1	3-1	3	.250
1999— Cleveland (A.L.)	0	1	.000	9.00	1.67	2	2	0	0	0	0-0	9.0	11	9	9	3	4-0	12	.306
2001— Cleveland (A.L.)	1	1	.500	1.84	1.23	2	2	0	0	0	0-0	14.2	12	3	3	0	6-0	13	.231
2004— Anaheim (A.L.)	0	0		4.50	1.67	1	1	0	0	0	0-0	6.0	7	3	3	1	3-0	3	.304
2005— Los Angeles (A.L.)	0	1	.000	4.50	1.50	2	2	0	0	0	0-0	8.0	10	4	4	0	2-0	7	.313
Division series totals (5 years)	1	3	.250	4.15	1.45	8	8	0	0	0	0-0	43.1	45	20	20	5	18-1	38	.276

CHAMPIONSHIP SERIES RECORD

Year Team (League)	W	L	Pct.	ERA	WHIP	G	GS	CG	ShO	Hld.	Sv.-Opp.	IP	H	R	ER	HR	BB-IBB	SO	Avg.
1997— Cleveland (A.L.)			Did not play.																
1998— Cleveland (A.L.)	1	0	1.000	1.00	0.89	1	1	1	0	0	0-0	9.0	4	1	1	0	4-0	3	.148

WORLD SERIES RECORD

Year Team (League)	W	L	Pct.	ERA	WHIP	G	GS	CG	ShO	Hld.	Sv.-Opp.	IP	H	R	ER	HR	BB-IBB	SO	Avg.
1997— Cleveland (A.L.)			Did not play.																

ALL-STAR GAME RECORD

	W	L	Pct.	ERA	WHIP	G	GS	CG	ShO	Hld.	Sv.-Opp.	IP	H	R	ER	HR	BB-IBB	SO	Avg.
All-Star Game totals (2 years)	1	0	1.000	13.50	2.00	2	0	0	0	0	0-0	2.0	3	3	3	1	1-0	1	.333

COLON, ROMAN — P

PERSONAL: Born August 13, 1979, in Montecristi, Dominican Republic. ... 6-6/225. ... Throws right, bats right. ... Full name: Roman Benedicto Colon. ...
TRANSACTIONS/CAREER NOTES: Signed as a non-drafted free agent by Atlanta Braves organization (August 14, 1995). ... Traded by Braves with P Zach Miner to Detroit Tigers for P Kyle Farnsworth (July 31, 2005).
CAREER HITTING: 0-for-7 (.000), 0 R, 0 2B, 0 3B, 0 HR, 0 RBI.

SCOUTING REPORT **Throws:** Colon's fastball tops out at 95 mph. Also throws a slider and a split-finger fastball. **Tendencies:** He has electric stuff but lacks control; as a result, he too often throws out over the plate. Rarely throws his splitter. Velocity starts to drop when his pitch count gets into the high 20s. **Outlook:** Unless his command improves, he will be an end-of-the-staff type guy versatile enough to start or work out of the bullpen. He could also turn into a Chris Reitsma type—a power arm who can set up. *Grade 6.5*

ROMAN COLON'S PITCHING ZONE

.267	.429	.421
.375	.385	.279
.273	.267	.320

LEFTY-RIGHTY SPLITS

vs.	Avg.	AB	H	2B	3B	HR	RBI	BB	SO	OBP	Slg.
L	.304	138	42	9	0	8	21	12	19	.355	.543
R	.282	142	40	5	1	9	23	9	28	.322	.521

Year Team (League)	W	L	Pct.	ERA	WHIP	G	GS	CG	ShO	Hld.	Sv.-Opp.	IP	H	R	ER	HR	BB-IBB	SO	Avg.
1996— Dominican Braves (DSL) ...	5	6	.455	3.52	1.52	14	14	0	0		0-0	64.0	59	45	25	0	38-...	39	.229
1997— GC Braves (GCL)	3	4	.429	4.29	1.52	14	12	0	0		0-...	63.0	68	47	30	2	28-0	44	.270
1998— Danville (Appal.)	1	7	.125	5.77	1.64	13	13	0	0		0-...	73.1	92	59	47	7	28-0	53	.302
1999— Jamestown (NYP)	7	5	.583	4.54	1.32	15	15	1	0		0-...	77.1	70	48	39	4	25-0	61	.258
2000—			Did not play.																
2001— Macon (S. Atl.)	7	7	.500	3.59	1.27	23	21	0	0		0-...	128.0	136	69	51	9	26-0	91	.271
2002— Myrtle Beach (Carol.)	9	8	.529	3.53	1.28	26	26	1	0		0-...	163.0	170	81	64	8	38-1	94	.269
2003— Greenville (Sou.)	11	3	.786	3.36	1.28	39	12	1	0		2-...	107.0	104	48	40	9	33-3	58	.261
2004— Richmond (Int'l)	4	1	.800	3.65	1.27	51	0	0	0		0-...	74.0	72	33	30	4	22-1	64	.258
— Greenville (Sou.)	1	0	1.000	0.00	0.33	3	0	0	0		0-...	3.0	1	0	0	0	0-0	5	.091
— Atlanta (N.L.)	2	1	.667	3.32	1.37	18	0	0	0	1	0-1	19.0	18	9	7	0	8-1	15	.254
2005— Mississippi (Sou.)	0	0		1.17	1.04	2	0	0	0		0-0	7.2	6	1	1	0	2-0	7	.222
— Atlanta (N.L.)	1	5	.167	5.28	1.38	23	4	0	0	2	0-0	44.1	47	28	26	10	14-1	30	.272
— Richmond (Int'l)	1	1	.500	1.93	1.21	3	3	0	0		0-0	14.0	12	3	3	0	5-0	9	.235
— Detroit (A.L.)	1	1	.500	6.12	1.68	12	3	0	0		0-1	25.0	35	17	17	7	7-0	17	.327
American League totals (1 year)	1	1	.500	6.12	1.68	12	3	0	0		0-1	25.0	35	17	17	7	7-0	17	.327
National League totals (2 years)	3	6	.333	4.69	1.37	41	4	0	0	3	0-1	63.1	65	37	33	10	22-2	45	.266
Major League totals (2 years)	4	7	.364	5.09	1.46	53	7	0	0	3	0-2	88.1	100	54	50	17	29-2	62	.285

CONINE, JEFF — OF/1B

PERSONAL: Born June 27, 1966, in Tacoma, Wash. ... 6-1/220. ... Bats right, throws right. ... Full name: Jeffrey Guy Conine. ... Name pronounced: COH-nine. ... High school: Eisenhower (Rialto, Calif.). ... College: UCLA.
TRANSACTIONS/CAREER NOTES: Selected by Kansas City Royals organization in 58th round of 1987 free-agent draft. ... Selected by Florida Marlins in first round (22nd pick overall) of expansion draft (November 17, 1992). ... Traded by Marlins to Royals for P Blaine Mull (November 20, 1997). ... On disabled list (March 25-May 5 and July 27-

August 19, 1998); included rehabilitation assignment to Omaha. ... Traded by Royals to Baltimore Orioles for P Chris Fussell (April 2, 1999). ... On disabled list (June 15-August 7, 2002). ... Traded by Orioles to Marlins for Ps Denny Bautista and Don Levinski (August 31, 2003).

2005 GAMES PLAYED BY POSITION (MLB): OF—61, 1B—45, DH—3.

SCOUTING REPORT

Offense: Conine still is a good fastball hitter. Attacks the ball with a short stroke and little movement. Has better bat control than bat speed and has problems handling the ball inside. Is a gap hitter who no longer is a real power threat. Is a below-average runner. **Defense:** He's better at first base than in the outfield. Has good agility around the bag. Range is limited and hands are a little rigid. **Outlook:** He is a professional hitter with a very good stroke, but his power and run production are starting to level off. Has a good approach and knows how to use the whole field. Better as a role player. **Grade 6.7**

JEFF CONINE'S HITTING ZONE

.300	.389	.077
.389	.368	.333
.273	.313	.333

LEFTY-RIGHTY SPLITS

vs.	Avg.	AB	H	2B	3B	HR	RBI	BB	SO	OBP	Slg.
L	.280	75	21	5	0	0	7	9	10	.353	.347
R	.312	260	81	15	2	3	26	29	48	.380	.419

Year Team (League)	Pos.	G	AB	R	H	2B	3B	HR	RBI	BB	SO	HBP	GDP	SB-CS	Avg.	OBP	SLG	OPS	FIELDING E	Avg.
1988— Baseball City (FSL)	1B-3B	118	415	63	113	23	9	10	59	46	77	0	6	26-12	.272	.342	.443	.785	22	.970
1989— Baseball City (FSL)	1B	113	425	68	116	12	7	14	60	40	91	3	14	32-13	.273	.338	.433	.771	18	.980
1990— Memphis (Sou.)	1B-3B	137	487	89	156	37	8	15	95	94	88	1	10	21-6	.320	.425	.522	.947	22	.983
— Kansas City (A.L.)	1B	9	20	3	5	2	0	0	2	2	5	0	1	0-0	.250	.318	.350	.668	1	.977
1991— Omaha (A.A.)	1B-OF	51	171	23	44	9	1	3	15	26	39	1	3	0-6	.257	.359	.374	.733	7	.984
1992— Omaha (A.A.)	1B-OF	110	397	64	120	24	5	20	72	54	67	2	6	4-5	.302	.383	.539	.922	6	.993
— Kansas City (A.L.)	OF-1B	28	91	10	23	5	2	0	9	8	23	0	1	0-0	.253	.313	.352	.665	0	1.000
1993— Florida (N.L.)	OF-1B	* 162	595	75	174	24	3	12	79	52	135	5	14	2-2	.292	.351	.403	.754	2	.995
1994— Florida (N.L.)	OF-1B	115	451	60	144	27	6	18	82	40	92	1	8	1-2	.319	.375	.526	.898	6	.986
1995— Florida (N.L.)	OF-1B	133	483	72	146	26	2	25	105	66	94	1	13	2-0	.302	.379	.520	.899	6	.981
1996— Florida (N.L.)	OF-1B	157	597	84	175	32	2	26	95	62	121	4	17	1-4	.293	.360	.484	.844	8	.985
1997— Florida (N.L.)	1B-OF	151	405	46	98	13	1	17	61	57	89	2	11	2-0	.242	.337	.405	.742	8	.992
1998— Kansas City (A.L.)	OF-1B-DH	93	309	30	79	26	0	8	43	26	68	2	8	3-0	.256	.312	.417	.729	1	.996
— Omaha (PCL)	DH-OF	2	9	0	0	0	0	0	0	0	3	0	0	0-0	.000	.000	.000	.000	0	1.000
1999— Baltimore (A.L.)	1B-DH-OF-3B	139	444	54	129	31	1	13	75	30	40	3	12	0-3	.291	.335	.453	.787	7	.992
2000— Baltimore (A.L.)	3B-1B-DH-OF	119	409	53	116	20	2	13	46	36	53	2	14	4-3	.284	.341	.438	.779	15	.969
2001— Baltimore (A.L.)	1B-OF-3B-DH	139	524	75	163	23	2	14	97	64	75	5	10	12-8	.311	.386	.443	.829	4	.995
2002— Baltimore (A.L.)	1B-DH-OF	116	451	44	123	26	4	15	63	25	66	2	10	8-0	.273	.307	.448	.755	10	.990
2003— Baltimore (A.L.)	1B-OF-3B	124	493	75	143	33	3	15	80	37	60	5	14	5-0	.290	.338	.460	.799	9	.992
— Florida (N.L.)	OF	25	84	13	20	7	0	5	13	13	10	0	2	0-0	.238	.337	.452	.789	0	1.000
2004— Florida (N.L.)	1B-OF	140	521	55	146	35	1	14	83	48	78	2	15	5-5	.280	.340	.432	.772	5	.993
2005— Florida (N.L.)	OF-1B-DH	131	335	42	102	20	2	3	33	38	58	3	12	2-0	.304	.374	.403	.777	7	.981
American League totals (8 years)		767	2741	344	781	166	14	78	415	228	390	19	72	32-14	.285	.339	.441	.780	47	.990
National League totals (8 years)		1014	3471	447	1005	180	17	120	553	376	677	18	92	15-13	.290	.358	.455	.813	42	.989
Major League totals (15 years)		1781	6212	791	1786	346	31	198	968	604	1067	37	164	47-27	.288	.350	.449	.798	89	.990

DIVISION SERIES RECORD

Year Team (League)	Pos.	G	AB	R	H	2B	3B	HR	RBI	BB	SO	HBP	GDP	SB-CS	Avg.	OBP	SLG	OPS	E	Avg.
1997— Florida (N.L.)	1B	3	11	3	4	1	0	0	1	0	1	0	0	0-0	.364	.417	.455	.871	1	.964
2003— Florida (N.L.)	OF	4	15	2	4	0	0	0	1	2	1	0	0	0-0	.267	.353	.267	.620	0	1.000
Division series totals (2 years)		7	26	5	8	1	0	0	2	2	1	0	0	0-0	.308	.379	.346	.725	1	.973

CHAMPIONSHIP SERIES RECORD

Year Team (League)	Pos.	G	AB	R	H	2B	3B	HR	RBI	BB	SO	HBP	GDP	SB-CS	Avg.	OBP	SLG	OPS	E	Avg.
1997— Florida (N.L.)	1B	6	18	1	2	0	0	0	1	1	4	0	1	0-0	.111	.158	.111	.269	0	1.000
2003— Florida (N.L.)	OF	7	24	4	11	1	1	1	4	4	2	0	0	0-0	.458	.500	.708	1.208	1	.875
Champ. series totals (2 years)		13	42	5	13	1	1	1	5	5	6	0	1	0-0	.310	.367	.452	.820	1	.979

WORLD SERIES RECORD

Year Team (League)	Pos.	G	AB	R	H	2B	3B	HR	RBI	BB	SO	HBP	GDP	SB-CS	Avg.	OBP	SLG	OPS	E	Avg.
1997— Florida (N.L.)	1B	6	13	1	3	0	0	0	2	0	1	0	1	0-0	.231	.231	.231	.462	0	1.000
2003— Florida (N.L.)	DH-OF	6	21	4	7	1	0	0	1	3	2	0	1	0-0	.333	.417	.381	.798	0	1.000
World Series totals (2 years)		12	34	5	10	1	0	0	3	3	2	0	1	0-0	.294	.351	.324	.675	0	1.000

ALL-STAR GAME RECORD

	G	AB	R	H	2B	3B	HR	RBI	BB	SO	HBP	GDP	SB-CS	Avg.	OBP	SLG	OPS	E	Avg.
All-Star Game totals (1 year)	1	1	1	1	0	0	1	1	0	0	0	0	0-0	1.000	1.000	4.000	5.000	...	...

CONTRERAS, JOSE — P

PERSONAL: Born December 6, 1971, in Havana, Cuba. ... 6-4/224. ... Throws right, bats right. ... Full name: Jose Ariel Contreras.
TRANSACTIONS/CAREER NOTES: Signed as a free agent by New York Yankees (February 6, 2003). ... On disabled list (June 7-August 24, 2003); included rehabilitation assignment to Tampa. ... Traded by Yankees with cash to Chicago White Sox for P Esteban Loaiza (July 31, 2003).
CAREER HITTING: 0-for-14 (.000), 0 R, 0 2B, 0 3B, 0 HR, 0 RBI.

SCOUTING REPORT

Throws: He throws a 91-95 mph fastball, a slider at 85-87 and a forkball in the upper 70s. **Tendencies:** Contreras was the White Sox's best pitcher down the stretch. Has renewed confidence in his fastball; it's very sneaky. Will occasionally cut it for a quick sliding effect. Slider is more of a cut fastball. Will throw the forkball more than 50 percent of the time on a given day. Will throw two different types, one that starts higher for a strike the other that starts in the middle and drops to the dirt for a strikeout. **Outlook:** He lived up to expectations with an outstanding playoff run. Has turned the corner in his career under Ozzie Guillen's tutelage and could win 20 games next year. **Grade 8.6**

JOSE CONTRERAS' PITCHING ZONE

.216	.133	.220
.229	.294	.352
.260	.268	.265

LEFTY-RIGHTY SPLITS

vs.	Avg.	AB	H	2B	3B	HR	RBI	BB	SO	OBP	Slg.
L	.231	386	89	10	3	12	40	48	74	.319	.365
R	.233	377	88	22	0	11	36	27	80	.295	.379

Year Team (League)	W	L	Pct.	ERA	WHIP	G	GS	CG	ShO	Hld.	Sv.-Opp.	IP	H	R	ER	HR	BB-IBB	SO	Avg.
2003— Columbus (Int'l)	2	0	1.000	1.20	0.80	3	3	0	0	0	0-...	15.0	10	2	2	1	2-0	18	.189

Year	Team (League)	W	L	Pct.	ERA	WHIP	G	GS	CG	ShO	Hld.	Sv.-Opp.	IP	H	R	ER	HR	BB-IBB	SO	Avg.
	— Trenton (East.)	0	0	...	0.00	1.80	1	1	0	0	...	0-...	1.2	1	0	0	0	2-0	3	.167
	— Tampa (Fla. St.)	0	0	...	4.50	1.75	1	1	0	0	...	0-...	4.0	4	2	2	0	3-0	5	.286
	— Staten Island (N.Y.-Penn.) .	0	0	...	0.00	0.29	1	1	0	0	...	0-...	7.0	2	0	0	0	0-0	15	.087
	— New York (A.L.)	7	2	.778	3.30	1.15	18	9	0	0	1	0-1	71.0	52	27	26	4	30-1	72	.202
2004	— Columbus (Int'l)	2	0	1.000	3.29	1.17	2	2	0	0	...	0-...	13.2	11	5	5	2	5-0	19	.216
	— New York (A.L.)	8	5	.615	5.64	1.41	18	18	0	0	0	0-0	95.2	93	66	60	22	42-1	82	.250
	— Chicago (A.L.)	5	4	.556	5.30	1.54	13	13	0	0	0	0-0	74.2	73	48	44	9	42-0	68	.256
2005	— Chicago (A.L.)	15	7	.682	3.61	1.23	32	32	1	0	0	0-0	204.2	177	91	82	23	75-2	154	.232
Major League totals (3 years)		**35**	**18**	**.660**	**4.28**	**1.31**	**81**	**72**	**1**	**0**	**1**	**0-1**	**446.0**	**395**	**232**	**212**	**58**	**189-4**	**376**	**.236**

DIVISION SERIES RECORD

Year	Team (League)	W	L	Pct.	ERA	WHIP	G	GS	CG	ShO	Hld.	Sv.-Opp.	IP	H	R	ER	HR	BB-IBB	SO	Avg.
2005	— Chicago (A.L.)	1	0	1.000	2.35	1.04	1	1	0	0	...	0-0	7.2	8	2	2	0	0-0	6	.258

CHAMPIONSHIP SERIES RECORD

Year	Team (League)	W	L	Pct.	ERA	WHIP	G	GS	CG	ShO	Hld.	Sv.-Opp.	IP	H	R	ER	HR	BB-IBB	SO	Avg.
2003	— New York (A.L.)	0	1	.000	5.79	1.71	4	0	0	0	2	0-1	4.2	6	3	3	0	2-0	7	.316
2005	— Chicago (A.L.)	1	1	.500	3.12	0.81	2	2	1	0	0	0-0	17.1	12	6	6	1	2-0	6	.197
Champ. series totals (2 years)		**1**	**2**	**.333**	**3.68**	**1.00**	**6**	**2**	**1**	**0**	**2**	**0-1**	**22.0**	**18**	**9**	**9**	**1**	**4-0**	**13**	**.225**

WORLD SERIES RECORD

Year	Team (League)	W	L	Pct.	ERA	WHIP	G	GS	CG	ShO	Hld.	Sv.-Opp.	IP	H	R	ER	HR	BB-IBB	SO	Avg.
2003	— New York (A.L.)	0	1	.000	5.68	1.58	4	0	0	0	0	0-0	6.1	5	4	4	0	5-0	10	.227
2005	— Chicago (A.L.)	1	0	1.000	3.86	0.86	1	1	0	0	0	0-0	7.0	6	3	3	1	0-0	2	.240
World Series totals (2 years)		**1**	**1**	**.500**	**4.73**	**1.20**	**5**	**1**	**0**	**0**	**0**	**0-0**	**13.1**	**11**	**7**	**7**	**1**	**5-0**	**12**	**.234**

COOK, AARON   P

PERSONAL: Born February 8, 1979, in Ft. Campbell, Ky. ... 6-3/205. ... Throws right, bats right. ... Full name: Aaron Lane Cook. ... High school: Hamilton (Ohio).
TRANSACTIONS/CAREER NOTES: Selected by Colorado Rockies organization in second round of 1997 free-agent draft. ... On disabled list (August 8, 2004-remainder of season). ... On disabled list (March 30-July 30, 2005); included rehabilitation assignments to Modesto, Tulsa and Colorado Springs.
CAREER HITTING: 15-for-104 (.144), 7 R, 0 2B, 1 3B, 0 HR, 5 RBI.

SCOUTING REPORT **Throws:** He has a heavy sinker that he throws at 87-93 mph. Also has a curveball, slider and changeup. **Tendencies:** His power sinkers is one of the best in the game; it bores in on righthanders. Has been slow to regain his velocity while coming back from surgery to remove blood clots from his lungs. Uses his curveball as a show pitch; does not have much rotation. Slider is much sharper. Working on his change. Has problems with lefthanders. Throws strikes. **Outlook:** Cook needs a pitch to combat lefthanders, but he still could be in line for a breakout year. **Grade 7**

AARON COOK'S PITCHING ZONE

.286	.250	.235
.394	.290	.323
.158	.313	.333

LEFTY-RIGHTY SPLITS

vs.	Avg.	AB	H	2B	3B	HR	RBI	BB	SO	OBP	Slg.
L	.317	189	60	16	0	4	17	8	13	.347	.466
R	.281	146	41	7	0	4	14	8	11	.318	.411

Year	Team (League)	W	L	Pct.	ERA	WHIP	G	GS	CG	ShO	Hld.	Sv.-Opp.	IP	H	R	ER	HR	BB-IBB	SO	Avg.
1997	— Ariz. Rockies (Ariz.)	1	3	.250	3.13	1.41	9	8	0	0	...	0-...	46.0	48	27	16	1	17-0	35	.261
1998	— Portland (N'west)	5	8	.385	4.88	1.59	15	15	1	0	...	0-...	79.1	87	50	43	8	39-0	38	.275
1999	— Asheville (S. Atl.)	4	12	.250	6.44	1.64	25	25	2	0	...	0-...	121.2	157	99	87	17	42-0	73	.310
2000	— Asheville (S. Atl.)	10	7	.588	2.96	1.07	21	21	4	2	...	0-...	142.2	130	54	47	10	23-0	118	.241
	— Salem (Carol.)	1	6	.143	5.44	1.49	7	7	1	0	...	0-...	43.0	52	33	26	4	12-0	37	.297
2001	— Salem (Carol.)	11	11	.500	3.08	1.26	27	27	0	0	...	0-...	155.0	157	73	53	4	38-0	122	.263
2002	— Carolina (Southern)	7	2	.778	1.42	0.97	14	14	2	2	...	0-...	95.0	73	24	15	4	19-0	58	.213
	— Colo. Springs (PCL)	4	4	.500	3.78	1.32	10	10	1	0	...	0-...	64.1	67	40	27	6	18-0	32	.264
	— Colorado (N.L.)	2	1	.667	4.54	1.51	9	5	0	0	1	0-0	35.2	41	18	18	4	13-0	14	.295
2003	— Colo. Springs (PCL)	1	1	.500	2.25	0.90	2	2	1	0	...	0-...	16.0	10	4	4	2	4-0	12	.175
	— Colorado (N.L.)	4	6	.400	6.02	1.75	43	16	1	0	1	0-0	124.0	160	89	83	8	57-7	43	.317
2004	— Colo. Springs (PCL)	3	1	.750	2.74	0.91	7	7	1	1	...	0-...	46.0	34	15	14	1	8-0	25	.206
	— Colorado (N.L.)	6	4	.600	4.28	1.56	16	16	1	0	0	0-0	96.2	112	47	46	7	39-5	40	.294
2005	— Modesto (California)	1	0	1.000	1.80	1.00	1	1	0	0	...	0-...	5.0	5	1	1	0	0-0	5	.263
	— Tulsa (Texas)	0	1	.000	17.18	3.00	1	0	0	0	...	0-...	3.2	10	9	7	2	1-0	1	.476
	— Colo. Springs (PCL)	0	1	.000	5.51	1.53	3	3	0	0	...	0-...	16.1	18	10	10	0	7-0	11	.295
	— Colorado (N.L.)	7	2	.778	3.67	1.40	13	13	0	0	0	0-0	83.1	101	38	34	8	16-2	24	.301
Major League totals (4 years)		**19**	**13**	**.594**	**4.80**	**1.59**	**81**	**50**	**4**	**0**	**2**	**0-0**	**339.2**	**414**	**192**	**181**	**27**	**125-14**	**121**	**.305**

COOPER, BRIAN   P

PERSONAL: Born August 19, 1974, in Hollywood, Calif. ... 6-1/185. ... Throws right, bats right. ... Full name: Brian John Cooper. ... High school: Glendora (Calif.). ... College: Southern California.
TRANSACTIONS/CAREER NOTES: Selected by Philadelphia Phillies organization in 39th round of 1994 free-agent draft; did not sign. ... Selected by California Angels organization in fourth round of 1995 free-agent draft. ... Angels franchise renamed Anaheim Angels for 1997 season. ... Traded by Angels to Toronto Blue Jays for DH/1B Brad Fullmer (January 17, 2002). ... Released by Blue Jays (September 30, 2002). ... Signed by Chicago White Sox organization (January 27, 2003). ... Signed as a free agent by San Francisco Giants organization (December 6, 2003).
CAREER HITTING: 1-for-9 (.111), 0 R, 0 2B, 0 3B, 0 HR, 0 RBI.

BRIAN COOPER'S PITCHING ZONE

.200	.250	.000
.316	.143	.333
.000	.333	.500

LEFTY-RIGHTY SPLITS

vs.	Avg.	AB	H	2B	3B	HR	RBI	BB	SO	OBP	Slg.
L	.190	21	4	1	0	0	2	5	1	.346	.238
R	.256	43	11	2	0	0	4	3	6	.304	.302

Year	Team (League)	W	L	Pct.	ERA	WHIP	G	GS	CG	ShO	Hld.	Sv.-Opp.	IP	H	R	ER	HR	BB-IBB	SO	Avg.
1995	— Boise (N'west)	3	2	.600	3.92	1.32	13	11	0	0	...	1-...	62.0	60	31	27	5	22-1	66	.260

Year	Team (League)	W	L	Pct.	ERA	WHIP	G	GS	CG	ShO	Hld.	Sv.-Opp.	IP	H	R	ER	HR	BB-IBB	SO	Avg.
1996— Lake Elsinore (Calif.)		7	9	.438	4.21	1.33	26	23	1	1	...	0-...	162.1	177	100	76	17	39-0	155	.277
1997— Lake Elsinore (Calif.)		7	3	.700	3.54	1.18	17	17	1	0	...	0-...	117.0	111	56	46	7	27-0	104	.246
1998— Midland (Texas)		8	10	.444	7.13	1.69	32	24	5	0	...	0-...	161.2	215	138	128	35	59-1	141	.320
1999— Erie (East.)		10	5	.667	3.30	1.11	22	22	*6	0	...	0-...	158.0	146	61	58	17	29-0	143	.246
— Edmonton (PCL)		2	1	.667	3.77	1.29	5	5	0	0	...	0-...	31.0	30	17	13	0	10-0	32	.256
— Anaheim (A.L.)		1	1	.500	4.88	1.48	5	5	0	0	0	0-0	27.2	23	15	15	3	18-0	15	.228
2000— Edmonton (PCL)		3	7	.300	7.23	1.72	11	11	1	0	...	0-...	61.0	87	51	49	12	18-0	37	.331
— Anaheim (A.L.)		4	8	.333	5.90	1.61	15	15	1	1	0	0-0	87.0	105	66	57	18	35-1	36	.300
— Lake Elsinore (Calif.)		0	0	...	0.00	0.86	1	1	0	0	...	0-...	7.0	4	1	0	0	2-0	3	.167
2001— Salt Lake (PCL)		12	8	.600	4.63	1.38	28	28	1	1	...	0-...	173.0	181	98	89	26	58-0	109	.273
— Anaheim (A.L.)		0	1	.000	2.63	1.02	7	1	0	0	0	0-0	13.2	10	5	4	2	4-0	7	.200
2002— Syracuse (Int'l)		9	9	.500	5.09	1.43	27	25	1	0	...	0-...	155.2	176	98	88	19	46-1	71	.289
— Toronto (A.L.)		0	1	.000	14.04	2.16	2	2	0	0	0	0-0	8.1	14	13	13	4	4-0	3	.400
2003— Charlotte (Int'l)		15	9	.625	3.98	1.30	28	28	2	0	...	0-...	174.1	195	91	77	18	35-2	106	.286
2004— San Francisco (N.L.)		0	2	.000	8.78	1.50	5	2	0	0	0	0-0	13.1	19	13	13	4	5-1	7	.288
— Fresno (PCL)		0	0	...	2.08	1.15	4	4	0	0	...	0-...	21.2	19	9	5	3	6-0	15	.247
2005— Fresno (PCL)		7	8	.467	4.53	1.41	29	21	0	0	1	0-...	137.0	139	72	69	23	54-1	82	.270
— San Francisco (N.L.)		0	1	.000	3.06	1.30	8	0	0	0	0	0-0	17.2	15	6	6	0	8-0	7	.234
American League totals (4 years)		5	11	.313	5.86	1.56	29	23	1	1	0	0-0	136.2	152	99	89	28	61-1	61	.284
National League totals (2 years)		0	3	.000	5.52	1.39	13	3	0	0	0	0-0	31.0	30	19	19	4	13-1	14	.259
Major League totals (6 years)		5	14	.263	5.80	1.53	42	26	1	1	0	0-0	167.2	182	118	108	32	74-2	75	.279

CORA, ALEX — 2B/SS

PERSONAL: Born October 18, 1975, in Caguas, Puerto Rico. ... 6-0/180. ... Bats left, throws right. ... Full name: Jose Alexander Cora. ... High school: Bautista (Caguas, Puerto Rico). ... College: Miami. ... Brother of Joey Cora, coach, Chicago White Sox, and second baseman with four major league teams (1987-98).

TRANSACTIONS/CAREER NOTES: Selected by Minnesota Twins organization in 12th round of 1993 free-agent draft; did not sign. ... Selected by Los Angeles Dodgers organization in third round of 1996 free-agent draft. ... On disabled list (March 25-June 27, 1999); included rehabilitation assignment to Albuquerque. ... Signed as a free agent by Cleveland Indians (January 18, 2005). ... Traded by Indians to Boston Red Sox for SS Ramon Vazquez (July 7, 2005).

2005 GAMES PLAYED BY POSITION (MLB): 2B—50, SS—35, 3B—5, OF—1.

SCOUTING REPORT **Offense:** Cora has a short stroke and will turn on inside pitches. Doesn't have a quick bat. Likes the ball down and has problems with hard throwers. Is a patient hitter but consistently is behind in the count. Is not a good runner and has below-average base-stealing instincts. **Defense:** Cora has quick, soft hands and good defensive instincts. Has good agility and plus range to either side. **Outlook:** Cora's struggles at the plate, particularly against left-handers, keep him from being a regular. *Grade 5.8*

ALEX CORA'S HITTING ZONE

.250	.167	.600
.125	.542	.224
.250	.000	.211

LEFTY-RIGHTY SPLITS

vs.	Avg.	AB	H	2B	3B	HR	RBI	BB	SO	OBP	Slg.
L	.273	33	9	1	1	0	5	3	8	.324	.364
R	.226	217	49	7	3	3	19	8	22	.267	.327

Year	Team (League)	Pos.	G	AB	R	H	2B	3B	HR	RBI	BB	SO	HBP	GDP	SB-CS	Avg.	OBP	SLG	OPS	E	Avg.
1996— Vero Beach (FSL)	OF-SS	61	214	26	55	4	4	0	26	12	36	3	1	5-5	.257	.306	.318	.623	16	.940
1997— San Antonio (Texas)	SS	127	448	52	105	20	4	3	48	25	60	3	17	12-9	.234	.279	.317	.596	20	.968
1998— Albuquerque (PCL)	2B-SS	81	299	42	79	17	5	5	45	15	38	3	1	10-7	.264	.303	.405	.708	18	.957
— Los Angeles (N.L.)	SS-2B	29	33	1	4	0	0	0	0	2	8	1	0	0-0	.121	.194	.182	.376	2	.965
1999— Albuquerque (PCL)	SS-2B-DH	80	302	51	93	11	7	4	37	12	37	8	8	9-5	.308	.348	.430	.778	12	.968
— Los Angeles (N.L.)	SS-2B	11	30	2	5	1	0	0	3	0	4	1	1	0-0	.167	.194	.200	.394	2	.943
2000— Albuquerque (PCL)	SS	30	110	18	41	8	3	0	20	7	10	2	1	5-3	.373	.417	.500	.917	7	.959
— Los Angeles (N.L.)	SS-2B	109	353	39	84	18	4	4	32	26	53	7	6	4-1	.238	.302	.357	.658	12	.973
2001— Los Angeles (N.L.)	SS-2B	134	405	38	88	18	4	4	29	31	58	8	16	0-2	.217	.285	.306	.591	6	.962
2002— Los Angeles (N.L.)	SS-2B	115	258	37	75	14	4	5	28	26	38	7	3	7-2	.291	.371	.434	.805	7	.977
2003— Los Angeles (N.L.)	2B-SS	148	477	39	119	24	3	4	34	16	59	10	4	4-2	.249	.287	.338	.625	15	.979
2004— Los Angeles (N.L.)	2B	138	455	47	107	9	4	10	47	47	41	18	9	3-4	.264	.364	.380	.745	8	.987
2005— Cleveland (A.L.)	SS-2B-OF	49	146	11	30	5	2	1	8	5	18	4	3	6-0	.205	.250	.288	.538	3	.984
— Boston (A.L.)	SS-2B-3B	47	104	14	28	3	2	2	16	6	12	1	3	1-2	.269	.310	.394	.704	5	.969
American League totals (1 year)		96	250	25	58	8	4	3	24	11	30	5	6	7-2	.232	.275	.332	.607	8	.977
National League totals (7 years)		684	1961	203	482	84	21	27	173	148	261	52	40	18-11	.246	.314	.351	.666	66	.975
Major League totals (8 years)		780	2211	228	540	92	25	30	197	159	291	57	46	25-13	.244	.310	.349	.659	74	.976

DIVISION SERIES RECORD

Year	Team (League)	Pos.	G	AB	R	H	2B	3B	HR	RBI	BB	SO	HBP	GDP	SB-CS	Avg.	OBP	SLG	OPS	E	Avg.
2004— Los Angeles (N.L.)	2B	4	15	1	2	0	1	0	1	0	2	0	2	0-0	.133	.188	.267	.454	0	1.000
2005— Boston (A.L.)	SS	1	0	0	0	0	0	0	0	0	0	0	0	...	...	...	...	...	0	...
Division series totals (2 years)		5	15	1	2	0	1	0	1	0	2	0	2	0-0	.133	.188	.267	.454	0	1.000

CORCORAN, TIM — P

PERSONAL: Born April 15, 1978, in Baton Rouge, La. ... 6-2/205. ... Throws right, bats right. ... Full name: Timothy Hugh Corcoran. ... College: Gulf Coast (FL) CC.

TRANSACTIONS/CAREER NOTES: Selected by New York Mets organization in 44th round of 1996 free-agent draft. ... Selected by Baltimore Orioles organization from Mets organization in Rule 5 minor league draft (December 11, 2000). ... Selected by Tampa Bay Devil Rays organization from Orioles orgainzation in Rule 5 minor league draft (December 15, 2003).

CAREER HITTING: 0-for-0 (.000), 0 R, 0 2B, 0 3B, 0 HR, 0 RBI.

TIM CORCORAN'S PITCHING ZONE

.000	.000	.286
.100	.300	.313
.500	.250	.250

LEFTY-RIGHTY SPLITS

vs.	Avg.	AB	H	2B	3B	HR	RBI	BB	SO	OBP	Slg.
L	.311	45	14	1	0	0	5	7	5	.404	.333
R	.128	39	5	0	0	1	4	5	8	.244	.205

Year	Team (League)	W	L	Pct.	ERA	WHIP	G	GS	CG	ShO	Hld.	Sv.-Opp.	IP	H	R	ER	HR	BB-IBB	SO	Avg.
1997— GC Mets (GCL)		3	0	1.000	3.00	1.48	10	0	0	0	...	3-...	21.0	16	8	7	0	15-0	20	.208
— Kingsport (Appalachian)		2	0	1.000	4.24	1.18	7	0	0	0	...	0-...	17.0	12	10	8	2	8-2	14	.194
1998— St. Lucie (Fla. St.)		0	0	...	8.22	1.57	4	0	0	0	...	0-...	7.2	10	7	7	1	2-0	8	.303
— Columbia (S. Atl.)		2	3	.400	2.61	1.20	20	1	0	0	...	4-...	48.1	43	21	14	4	15-0	38	.236

C

Year Team (League)	W	L	Pct.	ERA	WHIP	G	GS	CG	ShO	Hld.	Sv.-Opp.	IP	H	R	ER	HR	BB-IBB	SO	Avg.
1999— Columbia (S. Atl.)	0	3	.000	4.44	1.37	40	3	0	0	...	3-...	75.0	62	43	37	5	41-0	89	.225
2000— Columbia (S. Atl.)	3	5	.375	4.05	1.37	31	0	0	0	...	1-...	53.1	46	28	24	7	27-2	58	.231
2001— Frederick (Carolina)	6	5	.545	2.68	1.11	33	0	0	0	...	6-...	50.1	37	16	15	4	19-3	42	.208
— Bowie (East.)	1	0	1.000	0.77	0.60	7	0	0	0	...	0-...	11.2	4	1	1	0	3-0	13	.105
2002— Bowie (East.)	0	5	.000	3.67	1.84	35	0	0	0	...	1-...	49.0	61	31	20	5	29-3	48	.308
2003— Frederick (Carolina)	2	5	.286	5.74	1.79	22	3	0	0	...	0-...	47.0	57	38	30	3	27-2	41	.294
— Bowie (East.)	4	1	.800	4.09	1.27	26	2	0	0	...	3-...	44.0	37	22	20	1	19-2	33	.231
2004— Durham (Int'l)	3	3	.500	3.91	1.56	33	0	0	0	...	0-...	50.2	46	22	22	4	33-1	40	.242
— Montgom. (Sou.)	0	1	.000	2.76	1.04	6	2	0	0	...	0-...	16.1	14	5	5	2	3-0	12	.255
2005— Durham (Int'l)	5	1	.833	2.89	1.27	29	0	0	0	...	2	0-2	56.0	49	22	18	3	22-0	49	.230
— Tampa Bay (A.L.)	0	0	...	5.96	1.37	10	1	0	0	...	0-0	22.2	19	15	15	1	12-0	13	.226
Major League totals (1 year)	0	0	...	5.96	1.37	10	1	0	0	0	0-0	22.2	19	15	15	1	12-0	13	.226

CORDERO, CHAD   P

PERSONAL: Born March 18, 1982, in Upland, Calif. ... 6-0/198. ... Throws right, bats right. ... Full name: Chad Patrick Cordero. ... Name pronounced: cor-DAIR-oh. ... High school: Don Lugo (Chino, Calif.). ... College: Cal State Fullerton.
TRANSACTIONS/CAREER NOTES: Selected by San Diego Padres organization in 26th round of 2000 free-agent draft; did not sign. ... Selected by Montreal Expos organization in first round (20th pick overall) of 2003 free-agent draft. ... Expos franchise transferred to Washington, D.C., and renamed Washington Nationals for 2005 season (December 3, 2004).
CAREER HITTING: 0-for-2 (.000), 0 R, 0 2B, 0 3B, 0 HR, 0 RBI.

SCOUTING REPORT **Throws:** Cordero has two primary pitches—a fastball that ranges from 89-92 mph and a slider. **Tendencies:** He has plus stuff and is not afraid to challenge hitters. Fastball consistently bores in on righthanded hitters and has late life; hitters don't pick it up quickly. Slider is short and tight, with good bite and depth. Has really improved his command and often pitches only with his fastball. Is basically a one-speed pitcher. **Outlook:** Cordero is a closer in the Eddie Guardado mold: He essentially tells hitters, "Here it is try to hit it." **Grade 9**

CHAD CORDERO'S PITCHING ZONE

.154	.214	.000
.295	.261	.214
.207	.111	.259

LEFTY-RIGHTY SPLITS

vs.	Avg.	AB	H	2B	3B	HR	RBI	BB	SO	OBP	Slg.
L	.192	146	28	2	0	3	11	13	31	.265	.267
R	.205	132	27	1	0	6	12	4	30	.228	.348

Year Team (League)	W	L	Pct.	ERA	WHIP	G	GS	CG	ShO	Hld.	Sv.-Opp.	IP	H	R	ER	HR	BB-IBB	SO	Avg.
2003— Brevard County (FSL)	1	1	.500	2.05	1.03	19	0	0	0	...	6-...	26.1	17	8	6	1	10-0	17	.198
— Montreal (N.L.)	1	0	1.000	1.64	0.64	12	0	0	0	1	1-1	11.0	4	2	2	1	3-1	12	.111
2004— Montreal (N.L.)	7	3	.700	2.94	1.34	69	0	0	0	8	14-18	82.2	68	28	27	8	43-4	83	.222
2005— Washington (N.L.)	2	4	.333	1.82	0.97	74	0	0	0	*	47-54	74.1	55	24	15	9	17-2	61	.198
Major League totals (3 years)	10	7	.588	2.36	1.13	155	0	0	0	9	62-73	168.0	127	54	44	18	63-7	156	.205

ALL-STAR GAME RECORD

Year Team (League)	W	L	Pct.	ERA	WHIP	G	GS	CG	ShO	Hld.	Sv.-Opp.	IP	H	R	ER	HR	BB-IBB	SO	Avg.
All-Star Game totals (1 year)	0	0	...	0.00	0.00	1	0	0	0	0	0-0	0.1	0	0	0	0	0-0	1	.000

CORDERO, FRANCISCO   P

PERSONAL: Born May 11, 1975, in Santo Domingo, Dominican Republic. ... 6-2/235. ... Throws right, bats right. ... Full name: Francisco Javier Cordero. ... Name pronounced: cor-DAIR-oh. ... High school: Colegio Luz de Arroyo Hondo (Dominican Republic).
TRANSACTIONS/CAREER NOTES: Signed as a non-drafted free agent by Detroit Tigers organization (June 18, 1994). ... Traded by Tigers with Ps Justin Thompson and Alan Webb, OF Gabe Kapler, C Bill Haselman and 2B Frank Catalanotto to Texas Rangers for OF Juan Gonzalez, P Danny Patterson and C Gregg Zaun (November 2, 1999). ... On disabled list (March 23-June 19 and June 26, 2001-remainder of season); included rehabilitation assignment to Oklahoma. ... On disabled list (June 25-July 27, 2002); included rehabilitation assignment to Oklahoma.
CAREER HITTING: 0-for-1 (.000), 0 R, 0 2B, 0 3B, 0 HR, 0 RBI.

SCOUTING REPORT **Throws:** Cordero has a four-seam fastball that tops out at 98 mph and a hard slider that gets up to 87. **Tendencies:** His velocity picks up as he gets closer to putting away a hitter and closer to finishing a game. Fastball is overpowering enough that he can pitch up in the zone. Power slider moves late. Has good command of both pitches. **Outlook:** Cordero has gone from being one of the game's best setup relievers to being a top-notch closer. Can become even better if he continues to keep his emotions in check and doesn't overthrow. **Grade 8.7**

FRANCISCO CORDERO'S PITCHING ZONE

.333	.364	.077
.347	.241	.367
.280	.188	.313

LEFTY-RIGHTY SPLITS

vs.	Avg.	AB	H	2B	3B	HR	RBI	BB	SO	OBP	Slg.
L	.250	144	36	11	0	2	19	20	40	.347	.368
R	.214	117	25	4	1	3	18	10	39	.282	.342

Year Team (League)	W	L	Pct.	ERA	WHIP	G	GS	CG	ShO	Hld.	Sv.-Opp.	IP	H	R	ER	HR	BB-IBB	SO	Avg.
1994— Dom. Tigers (DSL)	4	3	.571	3.90	1.53	12	12	0	0	...	0-...	60.0	65	47	26	...	27-...	36	...
1995— Fayetteville (SAL)	0	3	.000	6.30	1.90	4	4	0	0	...	0-...	20.0	26	16	14	1	12-0	19	.342
— Jamestown (NYP)	4	7	.364	5.22	1.51	15	14	0	0	...	0-...	88.0	96	62	51	3	37-0	54	.282
1996— Fayetteville (SAL)	0	0	...	2.57	1.14	2	1	0	0	...	0-...	7.0	2	2	2	0	6-0	7	.095
— Jamestown (NYP)	0	0	...	0.82	0.64	2	2	0	0	...	0-...	11.0	5	1	1	0	2-0	10	.135
1997— W. Mich. (Mid.)	6	1	.857	0.99	0.94	50	0	0	0	...	35-...	54.1	36	13	6	2	15-2	67	.193
1998— Jacksonville (Sou.)	1	1	.500	4.86	1.68	17	0	0	0	...	8-...	16.2	19	12	9	1	6-0	18	.284
1999— Jacksonville (Sou.)	4	1	.800	1.38	1.09	47	0	0	0	...	27-...	52.1	35	9	8	3	22-0	58	.183
— Detroit (A.L.)	2	2	.500	3.32	1.95	20	0	0	0	...	0-0	19.0	19	7	7	2	18-2	19	.284
2000— Texas (A.L.)	1	2	.333	5.35	1.75	56	0	0	0	4	0-3	77.1	87	51	46	11	48-3	49	.285
— Oklahoma (PCL)	0	0	...	4.15	2.31	3	0	0	0	...	1-...	4.1	7	3	2	0	3-0	5	.350

Year Team (League)	W	L	Pct.	ERA	WHIP	G	GS	CG	ShO	Hld.	Sv.-Opp.	IP	H	R	ER	HR	BB-IBB	SO	Avg.
2001— Oklahoma (PCL)	0	1	.000	0.59	0.72	12	0	0	0	...	6-...	15.1	8	2	1	0	3-0	20	.148
— Texas (A.L.)	0	1	.000	3.86	2.14	3	0	0	0	...	0-0	2.1	3	1	1	0	2-1	1	.300
2002— Texas (A.L.)	2	0	1.000	1.79	1.01	39	0	0	0	1	10-12	45.1	33	12	9	2	13-1	41	.204
— Oklahoma (PCL)	0	2	.000	5.84	1.78	11	1	0	0	...	2-...	12.1	15	14	8	2	7-1	21	.278
2003— Texas (A.L.)	5	8	.385	2.94	1.31	73	0	0	0	18	15-25	82.2	70	33	27	4	38-6	90	.230
2004— Texas (A.L.)	3	4	.429	2.13	1.28	67	0	0	0	0	49-54	71.2	60	19	17	1	32-2	79	.226
2005— Texas (A.L.)	3	1	.750	3.39	1.32	69	0	0	0	0	37-45	69.0	61	28	26	5	30-2	79	.234
Major League totals (7 years)	16	18	.471	3.26	1.40	327	0	0	0	30	111-139	367.1	333	151	133	25	181-17	358	.242

CORDERO, WIL — 1B

PERSONAL: Born October 3, 1971, in Mayaguez, Puerto Rico. ... 6-2/232. ... Bats right, throws right. ... Full name: Wilfredo Nieva Cordero. ... Name pronounced: cor-DAIR-oh. ... High school: Centro de Servicios Education de Mayaguez (Puerto .

TRANSACTIONS/CAREER NOTES: Signed as a non-drafted free agent by Montreal Expos organization (May 24, 1988). ... Traded by Expos with P Bryan Eversgerd to Boston Red Sox for Ps Rheal Cormier and Shayne Bennett and 1B Ryan McGuire (January 10, 1996). ... On disabled list (May 21-August 12, 1996); included rehabilitation assignments to GCL Red Sox and Pawtucket. ... Released by Red Sox (September 28, 1997). ... Signed by Chicago White Sox (March 23, 1998). ... Signed as a free agent by Cleveland Indians (February 3, 1999). ... On disabled list (June 9-September 8, 1999); included rehabilitation assignment to Akron. ... Signed as a free agent by Pittsburgh Pirates (December 14, 1999). ... Traded by Pirates to Indians for OF Alex Ramirez and IF Enrique Wilson (July 28, 2000). ... On suspended list (September 19-23, 2000). ... On disabled list (June 11-26, 2001). ... Released by Indians (April 29, 2002). ... Signed by Expos (May 12, 2002). ... On disabled list (August 1-16, 2002). ... Signed as a free agent by Florida Marlins (February 6, 2004). ... On disabled list (May 17-September 7, 2004); included rehabilitation assignment to Jupiter. ... Signed as a free agent by Expos (December 13, 2004). ... Expos franchise transferred to Washington, D.C., and renamed Washington Nationals for 2005 season (December 3, 2004). ... On disabled list (April 8-May 30, 2005); included rehabilitation assignments to Potomac and Harrisburg. ... Released by Nationals (July 25, 2005). ... Signed by New York Mets organization (July 30, 2005). ... Released by Mets (August 14, 2005).

2005 GAMES PLAYED BY POSITION (MLB): 1B—12, DH—3.

SCOUTING REPORT Cordero's playing time continues to shrink, as does his bat speed. Has a compact stroke with a slight hitch, which he has trouble getting out of now. No longer drives the ball with authority. Doesn't run well and rarely plays in the field, where his lack of quickness can be a liability if forced to play a lot. Is nearing the end of his career. *Grade 4.5*

WIL CORDERO'S HITTING ZONE

.167	.000	1.000
.067	.000	1.000
.000	.333	.000

LEFTY-RIGHTY SPLITS

vs.	Avg.	AB	H	2B	3B	HR	RBI	BB	SO	OBP	Slg.
L	.105	19	2	0	0	0	0	1	7	.150	.105
R	.125	32	4	2	0	0	2	2	7	.167	.188

Year Team (League)	Pos.	G	AB	R	H	2B	3B	HR	RBI	BB	SO	HBP	GDP	SB-CS	Avg.	OBP	SLG	OPS	E	Avg.
1988— Jamestown (NYP)	SS	52	190	18	49	3	0	2	22	15	44	4	2	3-3	.258	.322	.305	.628	31	.886
1989— W.P. Beach (FSL)	SS	78	289	37	80	12	2	6	29	33	58	3	6	2-5	.277	.355	.394	.749	29	.922
— Jacksonville (Sou.)	SS	39	121	9	26	6	1	3	17	12	33	0	3	1-2	.215	.284	.355	.639	7	.957
1990— Jacksonville (Sou.)	SS	131	444	63	104	18	4	7	40	56	122	5	5	9-4	.234	.326	.340	.666	41	.928
1991— Indianapolis (A.A.)	SS	98	360	48	94	16	4	11	52	26	89	3	4	9-3	.261	.315	.419	.734	27	.943
1992— Indianapolis (A.A.)	SS	52	204	32	64	11	1	6	27	24	54	0	7	6-7	.314	.384	.466	.850	12	.949
— Montreal (N.L.)	SS-2B	45	126	17	38	4	1	2	8	9	31	1	3	0-0	.302	.353	.397	.750	8	.947
1993— Montreal (N.L.)	SS-3B	138	475	56	118	32	2	10	58	34	60	7	12	12-3	.248	.308	.387	.695	36	.937
1994— Montreal (N.L.)	SS	110	415	65	122	30	3	15	63	41	62	6	8	16-3	.294	.363	.489	.853	22	.952
1995— Montreal (N.L.)	SS-OF	131	514	64	147	35	2	10	49	36	88	9	11	9-5	.286	.341	.420	.761	22	.953
1996— Boston (A.L.)	2B-DH-1B	59	198	29	57	14	0	3	37	11	31	2	8	2-1	.288	.330	.404	.734	10	.951
— GC Red Sox (GCL)	DH-2B	3	10	1	3	0	0	1	3	0	2	0	1	0-0	.300	.273	.600	.873	0	1.000
— Pawtucket (Int'l)	2B-DH	4	10	2	3	1	0	1	2	2	3	0	1	0-0	.300	.417	.700	1.117	0	1.000
1997— Boston (A.L.)	OF-DH-2B	140	570	82	160	26	3	18	72	31	122	4	11	1-3	.281	.320	.432	.752	2	.992
1998— Birmingham (Sou.)	1B-DH	11	35	6	10	2	0	2	11	7	3	0	1	0-0	.286	.405	.514	.919	1	.989
— Chicago (A.L.)	1B-OF	96	341	58	91	18	2	13	49	22	66	3	7	2-1	.267	.314	.446	.759	7	.991
1999— Cleveland (A.L.)	OF-DH	54	194	35	58	15	0	8	32	15	37	6	7	2-0	.299	.364	.500	.864	1	.981
— Akron (East.)	OF-DH	3	11	2	4	2	0	0	0	0	3	1	1	0-0	.364	.417	.545	.962	0	...
2000— Pittsburgh (N.L.)	OF-DH	89	348	46	98	24	3	16	51	25	58	4	11	1-2	.282	.336	.506	.842	2	.983
— Cleveland (A.L.)	OF	38	148	18	39	11	2	0	17	7	18	3	7	0-0	.264	.310	.365	.675	0	1.000
2001— Cleveland (A.L.)	OF-1B-DH	89	268	30	67	11	1	4	21	22	50	4	8	0-0	.250	.313	.343	.656	2	.992
2002— Cleveland (A.L.)	OF-1B	6	18	1	4	1	0	0	1	0	3	0	1	0-0	.222	.222	.222	.444	0	1.000
— Montreal (N.L.)	OF-1B-DH	66	143	21	39	9	0	6	29	17	26	2	3	2-0	.273	.349	.462	.811	2	.983
2003— Montreal (N.L.)	1B-DH-OF	130	436	57	121	27	0	16	71	49	90	4	11	1-1	.278	.354	.450	.803	5	.996
2004— Jupiter (Fla. St.)	DH-1B	3	8	3	4	0	0	2	5	1	1	0	0	0-0	.500	.556	1.250	1.806	0	1.000
— Florida (N.L.)	1B-OF	27	66	6	13	3	0	1	6	3	19	2	2	1-0	.197	.250	.288	.538	1	.991
2005— Potomac (Carol.)	DH	2	7	2	3	1	0	0	2	1	0	0	0	0-0	.429	.500	1.429	1.929	0	...
— Harrisburg (East.)	DH	2	8	0	4	2	0	0	1	0	1	0	0	0-0	.500	.500	.750	1.250	0	...
— Washington (N.L.)	1B-DH	29	51	2	6	1	0	0	2	3	14	0	0	0-0	.118	.161	.157	.318	0	1.000
— Norfolk (Int'l)	1B-DH	8	31	3	4	2	0	0	2	1	5	1	0	0-0	.129	.150	.194	.444	0	1.000
American League totals (7 years)		482	1737	253	476	95	8	46	229	108	327	22	49	7-5	.274	.322	.417	.740	22	.987
National League totals (9 years)		765	2574	334	702	166	11	76	337	217	448	35	61	42-14	.273	.335	.434	.770	98	.969
Major League totals (14 years)		1247	4311	587	1178	261	19	122	566	325	775	57	110	49-19	.273	.330	.428	.758	120	.975

DIVISION SERIES RECORD

Year Team (League)	Pos.	G	AB	R	H	2B	3B	HR	RBI	BB	SO	HBP	GDP	SB-CS	Avg.	OBP	SLG	OPS	E	Avg.
1999— Cleveland (A.L.)	DH-OF	3	9	3	5	0	0	1	2	1	2	0	0	0-0	.556	.600	.889	1.489	0	1.000
2001— Cleveland (A.L.)	OF	1	1	0	0	0	0	0	0	0	0	0	0	0-0	.000	.000	.000	.000	0	1.000
Division series totals (2 years)		4	10	3	5	0	0	1	2	1	2	0	0	0-0	.500	.545	.800	1.345	0	1.000

ALL-STAR GAME RECORD

Year Team (League)	G	AB	R	H	2B	3B	HR	RBI	BB	SO	HBP	GDP	SB-CS	Avg.	OBP	SLG	OPS	E	Avg.
All-Star Game totals (1 year)	1	2	0	0	0	0	0	0	0	0	0	1	0-0	.000	.000	.000	.000	0	1.000

C

CORMIER, LANCE   P

PERSONAL: Born August 19, 1980, in Lafayette, La. ... 6-1/192. ... Throws right, bats right. ... Full name: Lance Robert Cormier. ... Name pronounced: COR-mee-ay. ... High school: Lafayette (La.). ... College: Alabama.

TRANSACTIONS/CAREER NOTES: Selected by Cincinnati Reds organization in 40th round of 1998 free-agent draft; did not sign. ... Selected by Houston Astros organization in 10th round of 2001 free-agent draft; did not sign. ... Selected by Arizona Diamondbacks organization in fourth round of 2002 free-agent draft.

CAREER HITTING: 4-for-14 (.286), 1 R, 1 2B, 0 3B, 0 HR, 2 RBI.

LANCE CORMIER'S PITCHING ZONE

.565	.333	.143
.259	.318	.302
.355	.400	.174

LEFTY-RIGHTY SPLITS

vs.	Avg.	AB	H	2B	3B	HR	RBI	BB	SO	OBP	Slg.
L	.300	130	39	7	1	3	19	22	29	.410	.438
R	.273	172	47	14	1	4	27	21	34	.359	.436

Year	Team (League)	W	L	Pct.	ERA	WHIP	G	GS	CG	ShO	Hld.	Sv.-Opp.	IP	H	R	ER	HR	BB-IBB	SO	Avg.
2002—	Yakima (N'west)	0	0	...	27.00	4.00	1	0	0	0	...	0-...	1.0	4	4	3	0	0-0	3	.500
—	South Bend (Mid.)	3	0	1.000	2.93	1.12	11	3	0	0	...	1-...	27.2	29	9	9	1	2-0	17	.259
2003—	Lancaster (Calif.)	6	5	.545	3.82	1.25	15	15	0	0	...	0-...	94.1	102	55	40	6	16-1	59	.280
—	Tucson (PCL)	1	1	.500	2.60	1.12	5	4	0	0	...	0-...	27.2	26	10	8	1	5-0	11	.260
—	El Paso (Texas)	2	3	.400	6.10	1.96	9	8	0	0	...	0-...	41.1	59	33	28	3	22-0	26	.337
2004—	El Paso (Texas)	2	3	.400	2.29	1.32	10	8	0	0	...	0-...	63.0	66	19	16	3	17-0	58	.277
—	Tucson (PCL)	3	3	.500	2.68	1.33	8	8	2	1	...	0-...	50.1	50	17	15	0	17-1	37	.260
—	Arizona (N.L.)	1	4	.200	8.14	1.92	17	5	0	0	2	0-0	45.1	62	42	41	13	25-2	24	.333
2005—	Tucson (PCL)	0	1	.000	14.73	3.00	1	1	0	0	...	0-...	3.2	6	6	6	1	5-0	5	.429
—	Arizona (N.L.)	7	3	.700	5.11	1.63	67	0	0	0	13	0-1	79.1	86	50	45	7	43-5	63	.285
Major League totals (2 years)		8	7	.533	6.21	1.73	84	5	0	0	15	0-1	124.2	148	92	86	20	68-7	87	.303

CORMIER, RHEAL   P

PERSONAL: Born April 23, 1967, in Moncton, New Brunswick. ... 5-10/195. ... Throws left, bats left. ... Full name: Rheal Paul Cormier. ... Name pronounced: ray-AL COR-mee-ay. ... High school: Polyvalente Louis J. Robichaud (New Brunswick, Canada). ... Junior college: Rhode Island Community College.

TRANSACTIONS/CAREER NOTES: Selected by St. Louis Cardinals organization in sixth round of 1988 free-agent draft. ... On disabled list (August 12-September 7, 1993). ... On disabled list (April 28-May 13 and May 21-August 3, 1994); included rehabilitation assignments to Arkansas and Louisville. ... Traded by Cardinals with OF Mark Whiten to Boston Red Sox for 3B Scott Cooper, P Cory Bailey and a player to be named (April 8, 1995). ... Traded by Red Sox with 1B Ryan McGuire and P Shayne Bennett to Montreal Expos for SS Wil Cordero and P Bryan Eversgerd (Jauary 10, 1996). ... On disabled list (August 26-September 10, 1996). ... Signed as a free agent by Cleveland Indians organization (December 18, 1997). ... Signed as a free agent by Red Sox organization (January 5, 1999). ... On suspended list (May 7-10, 1999). ... Signed as a free agent by Philadelphia Phillies (November 29, 2000). ... On disabled list (August 10-29, 2001); included rehabilitation assignment to Reading.

CAREER HITTING: 36-for-192 (.188), 15 R, 4 2B, 1 3B, 0 HR, 12 RBI.

SCOUTING REPORT

Throws: The aging Cormier's fastball has dipped into the upper 80s. Throws his slider at 83 and a split-finger fastball. ***Tendencies:*** Cormier has a good delivery and tailing action on a fastball that he runs away from righthanded hitters. Decline in velocity means he has trouble getting the ball inside to righties now. Slider no longer bites as sharply. Splitter has a big break yet still is quick. His 84 appearances in 2004 and advancing age have cut into his effectiveness. ***Outlook:*** No longer can he be considered for a setup role; is better pitching in the seventh inning or against better lefthanded hitters. Can no longer be stretched out or overexposed.

Grade 6.9

RHEAL CORMIER'S PITCHING ZONE

.583	.250	.300
.359	.353	.263
.444	.333	.100

LEFTY-RIGHTY SPLITS

vs.	Avg.	AB	H	2B	3B	HR	RBI	BB	SO	OBP	Slg.
L	.256	78	20	3	1	3	6	6	16	.326	.436
R	.324	111	36	11	0	6	22	10	18	.374	.586

Year	Team (League)	W	L	Pct.	ERA	WHIP	G	GS	CG	ShO	Hld.	Sv.-Opp.	IP	H	R	ER	HR	BB-IBB	SO	Avg.
1989—	St. Pete. (FSL)	12	7	.632	2.23	1.03	26	26	4	1	...	0-...	169.2	141	63	42	9	33-2	122	.225
1990—	Arkansas (Texas)	5	12	.294	5.04	1.34	22	21	3	1	...	0-...	121.1	133	81	68	9	30-2	102	.273
—	Louisville (A.A.)	1	1	.500	2.25	0.88	4	4	0	0	...	0-...	24.0	18	8	6	1	3-0	9	.202
1991—	Louisville (A.A.)	7	9	.438	4.23	1.34	21	21	3	3	...	0-...	127.2	140	64	60	5	31-1	74	.286
—	St. Louis (N.L.)	4	5	.444	4.12	1.21	11	10	2	0	0	0-0	67.2	74	35	31	5	8-1	38	.277
1992—	St. Louis (N.L.)	10	10	.500	3.68	1.22	31	30	3	0	0	0-0	186.0	194	83	76	15	33-2	117	.269
—	Louisville (A.A.)	0	1	.000	6.75	2.00	1	1	0	0	...	0-...	4.0	8	4	3	0	0-0	1	.400
1993—	St. Louis (N.L.)	7	6	.538	4.33	1.31	38	21	1	0	0	0-0	145.1	163	80	70	18	27-3	75	.284
1994—	St. Louis (N.L.)	3	2	.600	5.45	1.18	7	7	0	0	0	0-0	39.2	40	24	24	6	7-0	26	.256
—	Arkansas (Texas)	1	0	1.000	1.93	0.96	2	2	0	0	...	0-...	9.1	9	2	2	0	0-0	11	.257
—	Louisville (A.A.)	1	2	.333	4.50	1.32	3	3	1	0	...	0-...	22.0	21	11	11	3	8-1	13	.250
1995—	Boston (A.L.)	7	5	.583	4.07	1.41	48	12	0	0	9	0-2	115.0	131	60	52	12	31-2	69	.294
1996—	Montreal (N.L.)	7	10	.412	4.17	1.29	33	27	1	1	0	0-0	159.2	165	80	74	16	41-3	100	.270
1997—	Montreal (N.L.)	0	1	.000	33.75	3.75	1	1	0	0	0	0-0	1.1	4	5	5	1	1-0	0	.500
1998—	Akron (East.)	0	0	...	6.52	1.76	3	3	0	0	...	0-...	9.2	15	7	7	3	2-0	6	.366
1999—	Boston (A.L.)	2	0	1.000	3.69	1.25	60	0	0	0	15	0-3	63.1	61	34	26	4	18-2	39	.246
2000—	Boston (A.L.)	3	3	.500	4.61	1.33	64	0	0	0	9	0-2	68.1	74	40	35	7	17-2	43	.275
2001—	Philadelphia (N.L.)	5	6	.455	4.21	1.29	60	0	0	0	12	1-6	51.1	49	26	24	5	17-4	37	.247
—	Reading (East.)	0	0	...	0.00	0.50	1	1	0	0	...	0-...	2.0	0	0	0	0	1-0	2	.000
2002—	Philadelphia (N.L.)	5	6	.455	5.25	1.55	54	0	0	0	9	0-3	60.0	61	38	35	6	32-6	49	.266
2003—	Philadelphia (N.L.)	8	0	1.000	1.70	0.93	65	0	0	0	14	1-4	84.2	54	18	16	4	25-2	67	.182
2004—	Philadelphia (N.L.)	4	5	.444	3.56	1.19	84	0	0	0	28	0-7	81.0	70	32	32	7	26-1	46	.237
2005—	Philadelphia (N.L.)	4	2	.667	5.89	1.52	57	0	0	0	17	0-0	47.1	56	33	31	9	16-1	34	.296
American League totals (3 years)		12	8	.600	4.12	1.35	172	12	0	0	33	0-7	246.2	266	134	113	23	66-6	151	.276
National League totals (11 years)		57	53	.518	4.07	1.26	441	96	7	1	80	2-22	924.0	930	454	418	92	233-28	589	.262
Major League totals (14 years)		69	61	.531	4.08	1.28	613	108	7	1	113	2-29	1170.2	1196	588	531	115	299-34	740	.265

C

DIVISION SERIES RECORD

Year Team (League)	W	L	Pct.	ERA	WHIP	G	GS	CG	ShO	Hld.	Sv.-Opp.	IP	H	R	ER	HR	BB-IBB	SO	Avg.
1995— Boston (A.L.)	0	0	...	13.50	4.50	2	0	0	0	0	0-0	0.2	2	1	1	0	1-0	2	.500
1999— Boston (A.L.)	0	0	...	0.00	0.75	2	0	0	0	0	0-0	4.0	2	0	0	0	1-0	4	.154
Division series totals (2 years)	0	0	...	1.93	1.29	4	0	0	0	0	0-0	4.2	4	1	1	0	2-0	6	.235

CHAMPIONSHIP SERIES RECORD

Year Team (League)	W	L	Pct.	ERA	WHIP	G	GS	CG	ShO	Hld.	Sv.-Opp.	IP	H	R	ER	HR	BB-IBB	SO	Avg.
1999— Boston (A.L.)	0	0	...	0.00	1.64	4	0	0	0	0	0-0	3.2	3	0	0	0	3-1	4	.200

CORREIA, KEVIN — P

PERSONAL: Born August 24, 1980, in San Diego. ... 6-3/200. ... Throws right, bats right. ... Full name: Kevin John Correia. ... Name pronounced: cor-RAY-ah. ... High school: Grossmont (San Diego). ... College: Cal-Poly San Luis Obispo.

TRANSACTIONS/CAREER NOTES: Selected by St. Louis Cardinals organization in 23rd round of 2001 free-agent draft; did not sign. ... Selected by San Francisco Giants organization in fourth round of 2002 free-agent draft.

CAREER HITTING: 4-for-30 (.133), 2 R, 1 2B, 0 3B, 0 HR, 2 RBI.

SCOUTING REPORT *Throws:* His four-seam fastball hits 89-92 mph, and he has a curve and slider. *Tendencies:* Correia, who moved into the rotation late last season, throws mostly fastballs that have good late life. Slider is more of a slurve, and he wasn't consistent with it. Has the potential to have above-average stuff but won't make any difference until he develops command of his fastball. Gets into streaks of wildness and is slow to make adjustments. *Outlook:* Correia had shoulder problems in 2005 and likely wasn't healthy. *Grade 5*

KEVIN CORREIA'S PITCHING ZONE

.400	.364	.133
.314	.333	.368
.231	.176	.300

LEFTY-RIGHTY SPLITS

vs.	Avg.	AB	H	2B	3B	HR	RBI	BB	SO	OBP	Slg.
L	.311	103	32	8	2	4	8	23	16	.433	.544
R	.242	120	29	5	0	8	23	8	28	.311	.483

Year Team (League)	W	L	Pct.	ERA	WHIP	G	GS	CG	ShO	Hld.	Sv.-Opp.	IP	H	R	ER	HR	BB-IBB	SO	Avg.
2002— Salem-Keizer (N'west)	2	2	.500	4.54	1.35	10	8	0	0	...	0-...	37.2	37	20	19	1	14-0	31	.257
2003— Norwich (East.)	6	6	.500	3.65	1.27	16	14	0	0	...	0-...	86.1	80	38	35	3	30-0	73	.248
— Fresno (PCL)	1	0	1.000	2.84	0.95	3	3	0	0	...	0-...	19.0	16	8	6	3	2-0	23	.222
— San Francisco (N.L.)	3	1	.750	3.66	1.50	10	7	0	0	0	0-0	39.1	41	16	16	6	18-1	28	.275
2004— Fresno (PCL)	3	7	.300	4.53	1.45	29	16	0	0	...	0-...	105.1	118	61	53	12	35-3	70	.284
— San Francisco (N.L.)	0	1	.000	8.05	1.84	12	1	0	0	0	0-0	19.0	25	20	17	3	10-0	14	.333
2005— Fresno (PCL)	3	2	.600	6.07	1.59	31	3	0	0	...	7-7	46.0	50	38	31	6	23-0	35	.273
— San Jose (Calif.)	0	1	.000	2.57	1.43	1	1	0	0	0	0-0	7.0	5	2	2	0	5-0	7	.208
— San Francisco (N.L.)	2	5	.286	4.63	1.58	16	11	0	0	0	0-0	58.1	61	31	30	12	31-2	44	.274
Major League totals (3 years)	5	7	.417	4.86	1.59	38	19	0	0	0	0-0	116.2	127	67	63	21	59-3	86	.284

CORTES, DAVID — P

PERSONAL: Born October 15, 1973, in Mexicali, Mexico. ... 5-11/195. ... Throws right, bats right. ... Full name: David C. Cortes. ... Name pronounced: cor-tez. ... High school: Central Union (Calif.). ... Junior college: Imperial Valley College (Calif.).

TRANSACTIONS/CAREER NOTES: Signed as a non-drafted free agent by Atlanta Braves organization (July 13, 1996). ... On disabled list (June 4-July 5, 1998). ... Traded by Braves with P Mike Porzio to Colorado Rockies for 1B Greg Colbrunn (July 30, 1998). ... Traded by Rockies to Braves for a player to be named (August 19, 1998); Rockies acquired P Anthony Briggs to complete deal (September 8, 1998). ... On disabled list (April 2, 2000-entire season; and April 5-May 17, 2001). ... Signed as a free agent by Dos Laredos of the Mexican League (April 1, 2002). ... Contract purchased from Dos Laredos by Arizona Diamondbacks organization (August 24, 2002). ... Released by Diamondbacks (March 29, 2003). ... Signed by Dos Laredos (April 1, 2003). ... Contract purchased by Cleveland Indians organization (July 31, 2003). ... Signed as a free agent by Detroit Tigers organization (December 11, 2003). ... Loaned to Tijuana of the Mexican League (May 22, 2004). ... Released by Tigers (June 15, 2004). ... Signed by Colorado Rockies organization (December 22, 2004).

CAREER HITTING: 0-for-2 (.000), 0 R, 0 2B, 0 3B, 0 HR, 0 RBI.

DAVID CORTES' PITCHING ZONE

.200	.222	.125
.313	.188	.297
.143	.500	.333

LEFTY-RIGHTY SPLITS

vs.	Avg.	AB	H	2B	3B	HR	RBI	BB	SO	OBP	Slg.
L	.278	90	25	4	0	4	13	5	13	.313	.456
R	.229	109	25	3	1	5	14	5	23	.267	.413

Year Team (League)	W	L	Pct.	ERA	WHIP	G	GS	CG	ShO	Hld.	Sv.-Opp.	IP	H	R	ER	HR	BB-IBB	SO	Avg.
1996— Eugene (Northwest)	2	1	.667	0.73	0.77	15	0	0	0	...	4-...	24.2	13	2	2	0	6-0	33	.148
1997— Macon (S. Atl.)	3	0	1.000	0.57	0.64	27	0	0	0	...	15-...	31.1	16	3	2	0	4-0	32	.152
— Durham (Carol.)	2	0	1.000	2.33	1.03	19	0	0	0	...	8-...	19.1	15	5	5	1	5-0	16	.214
— Greenville (Sou.)	1	0	1.000	1.80	1.00	3	0	0	0	...	0-...	5.0	4	1	1	1	1-0	7	.211
1998— Richmond (Int'l)	3	3	.500	2.82	1.14	29	0	0	0	...	4-...	44.2	37	15	14	2	14-3	46	.227
— Colo. Springs (PCL)	1	0	1.000	7.71	2.29	6	0	0	0	...	0-...	7.0	14	6	6	0	2-0	5	.400
1999— Richmond (Int'l)	2	3	.400	3.35	1.40	47	0	0	0	...	22-...	45.2	50	19	17	2	14-5	42	.276
— Atlanta (N.L.)	0	0	...	4.91	1.91	4	0	0	0	0	0-0	3.2	3	3	2	0	4-0	2	.214
2000— Atlanta (N.L.)																Did not play.			
2001— Myrtle Beach (Carol.)	0	0	.000	5.91	1.50	9	0	0	0	...	2-...	10.2	11	7	7	2	5-0	9	.256
— Greenville (Sou.)	0	3	.000	8.15	1.70	14	0	0	0	...	0-...	17.2	19	18	16	2	11-2	10	.264
— Macon (S. Atl.)	1	0	1.000	7.11	1.50	10	0	0	0	...	0-...	12.2	14	11	10	1	5-0	8	.259
2002— Tucson (PCL)	0	0	...	0.00	0.75	3	0	0	0	...	0-...	4.0	1	0	0	0	0-0	1	.188
— Dos Laredos (Mex.)	3	1	.750	4.18	1.42	39	0	0	0	...	14-...	47.1	52	22	22	2	15-2	50	.278
2003— Dos Laredos (Mex.)	4	3	.571	2.70	1.43	48	0	0	0	...	18-...	53.1	58	17	16	3	18-1	39	.287
— Cleveland (A.L.)	0	0	...	12.00	2.67	2	0	0	0	0	0-0	3.0	8	5	4	1	0-0	1	.471
— Buffalo (Int'l)	1	0	1.000	2.70	0.60	5	0	0	0	...	1-...	6.2	4	3	2	1	0-0	6	.154
2004— Toledo (Int'l)	1	0	1.000	3.95	1.32	14	0	0	0	...	3-...	13.2	12	6	6	0	6-2	10	.235
— Tijuana (Mex.)	0	1	.000	5.17	1.40	14	0	0	0	...	3-...	15.2	16	10	9	3	6-1	18	.254
2005— Colo. Springs (PCL)	1	0	1.000	4.02	1.40	12	0	0	0	...	1-2	15.2	15	7	7	2	5-0	11	.250
— Colorado (N.L.)	2	0	1.000	4.10	1.14	50	0	0	0	4	2-3	52.2	50	24	24	9	10-2	36	.251
American League totals (1 year)	0	0	...	12.00	2.67	2	0	0	0	0	0-0	3.0	8	5	4	1	0-0	1	.471
National League totals (2 years)	2	0	1.000	4.15	1.19	54	0	0	0	4	2-3	56.1	53	27	26	9	14-2	38	.249
Major League totals (3 years)	2	0	1.000	4.55	1.26	56	0	0	0	4	2-3	59.1	61	32	30	10	14-2	39	.265

CORTEZ, FERNANDO — 2B

PERSONAL: Born August 10, 1981, in Stockton, Calif. ... 6-1/175. ... Bats left, throws right. ... Full name: Fernando Cortez. ... Name pronounced: cor-TEZ. ... College: Grossmont (Calif.).
TRANSACTIONS/CAREER NOTES: Selected by Tampa Bay Devil Rays organization in ninth round of 2001 free-agent draft.
2005 GAMES PLAYED BY POSITION (MLB): 2B—3, SS—2, 3B—1.

LEFTY-RIGHTY SPLITS

vs.	Avg.	AB	H	2B	3B	HR	RBI	BB	SO	OBP	Slg.
L	.000	0	0	0	0	0	0	0	0	.000	.000
R	.077	13	1	0	0	0	1	1	3	.143	.077

									BATTING									FIELDING	
Year Team (League)	Pos.	G	AB	R	H	2B	3B	HR	RBI	BB	SO	HBP	GDP	SB-CS	Avg.	OBP	SLG	OPS	E	Avg.
2001—Hudson Valley (NYP)	3B	55	234	36	65	14	3	1	25	15	26	3	5	6-3	.278	.327	.376	.703	22	.888
2002—Char., S.C. (SAL)	2B-SS-3B	127	475	60	127	14	5	2	49	41	59	4	9	37-16	.267	.327	.331	.658	19	.970
2003—Bakersfield (Calif.)		102	384	53	108	19	0	1	53	41	61	2	7	32-9	.281	.346	.339	.685	—	...
—Orlando (South.)	2B	30	114	15	36	3	1	1	6	3	22	0	2	1-2	.316	.333	.386	.719	4	.963
2004—Montgom. (Sou.)	2B-SS	94	359	51	103	20	5	3	30	32	60	1	3	7-7	.287	.345	.396	.741	10	.881
2005—Montgom. (Sou.)	2B-SS	55	219	39	73	11	4	0	23	15	42	2	3	12-3	.333	.377	.420	.797	7	.972
—Tampa Bay (A.L.)	2B-SS-3B	8	13	0	1	0	0	0	1	1	3	0	0	0-0	.077	.143	.077	.220	0	1.000
—Durham (Int'l)	2B	58	238	26	54	8	2	2	26	10	38	3	6	13-1	.227	.266	.303	.568	11	.963
Major League totals (1 year)		8	13	0	1	0	0	0	1	1	3	0	0	0-0	.077	.143	.077	.220	0	1.000

COSTA, SHANE — OF

PERSONAL: Born December 12, 1981, in Visalia, Calif. ... 6-0/220. ... Bats left, throws right. ... Full name: Shane Jeremy Costa. ... High school: Golden West (Visalia, Calif.). ... College: Cal State Fullerton.
TRANSACTIONS/CAREER NOTES: Selected by Kansas City Royals organization in second round of 2003 free-agent draft.
2005 GAMES PLAYED BY POSITION (MLB): OF—20, DH—4.

SHANE COSTA'S HITTING ZONE

.200	.000	.667
.000	.571	.261
.250	.000	.000

LEFTY-RIGHTY SPLITS

vs.	Avg.	AB	H	2B	3B	HR	RBI	BB	SO	OBP	Slg.
L	.000	10	0	0	0	0	1	2	2	.167	.000
R	.268	71	19	2	0	2	6	3	9	.307	.380

									BATTING									FIELDING	
Year Team (League)	Pos.	G	AB	R	H	2B	3B	HR	RBI	BB	SO	HBP	GDP	SB-CS	Avg.	OBP	SLG	OPS	E	Avg.
2003—Arizona Royals 2 (AZL)	OF	23	88	22	34	6	4	1	24	6	7	4	2	4-3	.386	.444	.580	1.024	4	.889
—Wilmington (Caro.)	OF	3	7	1	1	0	0	0	2	1	1	0	0	0-0	.143	.400	.286	.686	0	1.000
2004—Wilmington (Caro.)	OF	123	451	70	139	20	4	7	59	32	43	11	7	9-4	.308	.364	.417	.781	5	.500
2005—Kansas City (A.L.)	OF-DH	27	81	13	19	2	0	2	7	5	11	1	3	0-0	.235	.287	.333	.621	0	1.000
—Wichita (Texas)	OF-DH	75	277	37	78	18	2	8	43	24	23	8	10	5-1	.282	.349	.448	.797	6	.975
—Omaha (PCL)	OF	4	16	1	3	1	0	0	1	0	1	0	0	0-0	.188	.188	.250	.438	0	1.000
Major League totals (1 year)		27	81	13	19	2	0	2	7	5	11	1	3	0-0	.235	.287	.333	.621	0	1.000

COTA, HUMBERTO — C

PERSONAL: Born February 7, 1979, in San Luis Rio Colorado, Mexico. ... 6-0/210. ... Bats right, throws right. ... Full name: Humberto Figueroa Cota. ... Name pronounced: KOH-ta. ... High school: Preparatoria Abierta (Mexico).
TRANSACTIONS/CAREER NOTES: Signed as a non-drafted free agent by Atlanta Braves organization (December 22, 1995). ... Loaned by Braves organization to Mexico City Tigers of the Mexican League (June 23-September 23, 1996). ... Released by Braves (January 27, 1997). ... Signed by Tampa Bay Devil Rays organization (May 22, 1997). ... Traded by Devil Rays with C Joe Oliver to Pittsburgh Pirates for OF Jose Guillen and P Jeff Sparks (July 23, 1999). ... On disabled list (May 28-August 2, 2004); included rehabilitation assignment to Nashville.
2005 GAMES PLAYED BY POSITION (MLB): C—87.

SCOUTING REPORT Cota has a long stroke and likes to pull the ball. Will show a slider-speed bat but has some power on balls up and out over the plate. Swing has a lot of holes, especially against breaking stuff. Has some quickness behind the plate and likes to drop down to throw, but the ball has good carry. Sits up very wide early when preparing to catch breaking pitches, allowing hitters to pick up location. Doesn't have very soft hands and tends to push a lot of pitches out of the zone. Ideally is a backup. *Grade 5.2*

HUMBERTO COTA'S HITTING ZONE

.350	.100	.154
.317	.550	.333
.129	.455	.083

LEFTY-RIGHTY SPLITS

vs.	Avg.	AB	H	2B	3B	HR	RBI	BB	SO	OBP	Slg.
L	.294	85	25	5	1	3	20	3	21	.315	.482
R	.222	212	47	15	0	4	23	14	59	.274	.349

									BATTING									FIELDING	
Year Team (League)	Pos.	G	AB	R	H	2B	3B	HR	RBI	BB	SO	HBP	GDP	SB-CS	Avg.	OBP	SLG	OPS	E	Avg.
1996—M.C. Tigers (Mex.)			Did not play.																	
1997—GC Devil Rays (GCL)	C	44	133	14	32	6	1	2	20	17	27	3	1	3-1	.241	.333	.346	.679	5	.985
—Hudson Valley (NYP)	C	3	9	0	2	0	0	0	2	0	1	0	0	0-0	.222	.222	.222	.444	0	1.000
1998—Princeton (Appal.)	C	67	245	48	76	13	4	15	61	32	59	6	3	4-4	.310	.399	.580	.978	12	.973
1999—Char., S.C. (SAL)	C-1B	85	336	42	94	21	1	9	61	20	51	2	...	1-1	.280	.320	.429	.748	7	.986
—Hickory (S. Atl.)	C	37	133	28	36	11	2	2	20	21	20	0	...	3-1	.271	.365	.429	.794	2	.992
2000—Altoona (East.)	C-1B	112	429	49	112	20	1	8	44	21	80	3	8	6-4	.261	.297	.368	.665	17	.973
2001—Nashville (PCL)	C	111	377	61	112	22	2	14	72	25	74	8	8	7-2	.297	.351	.477	.829	8	.986
—Pittsburgh (N.L.)	C	7	9	0	2	0	0	0	1	0	5	0	0	0-0	.222	.222	.222	.444	0	1.000
2002—Nashville (PCL)	C-1B	118	404	51	108	27	1	9	54	31	106	5	11	5-8	.267	.321	.406	.727	4	.994
—Pittsburgh (N.L.)	C	7	17	2	5	1	0	0	0	0	4	0	0	0-0	.294	.333	.353	.686	0	1.000
2003—Pittsburgh (N.L.)	C	10	16	1	4	1	0	0	1	1	5	0	0	0-0	.250	.294	.313	.607	0	1.000

C

Year	Team (League)	Pos.	G	AB	R	H	2B	3B	HR	RBI	BB	SO	HBP	GDP	SB-CS	Avg.	OBP	SLG	OPS	E	Avg.
	— Nashville (PCL)	C-DH	62	200	23	41	9	0	8	27	20	59	2	4	2-0	.205	.284	.370	.654	0	1.000
2004—	Nashville (PCL)	C-DH	8	27	4	7	0	0	1	2	3	7	0	3	0-0	.259	.333	.370	.704	0	1.000
	— Pittsburgh (N.L.)	C	36	66	10	15	1	1	5	8	3	20	1	1	0-0	.227	.271	.500	.771	1	.991
2005—	Indianapolis (Int'l)	C	3	11	0	3	0	0	0	1	0	3	0	2	0-0	.273	.273	.273	.545	1	1.000
	— Pittsburgh (N.L.)	C	93	297	29	72	20	1	7	43	17	80	2	8	0-0	.242	.285	.387	.672	4	.992
	Major League totals (5 years)		153	405	42	98	23	2	12	53	22	114	3	9	0-0	.242	.284	.398	.682	5	.993

COTTS, NEAL — P

PERSONAL: Born March 25, 1980, in Belleville, Ill. ... 6-2/200. ... Throws left, bats left. ... Full name: Neal James Cotts. ... High school: Lebanon (Ill.). ... College: Illinois State.

TRANSACTIONS/CAREER NOTES: Selected by Oakland Athletics organization in second round of 2001 free-agent draft. ... Traded by Athletics with OF Dayton Holt to Chicago White Sox (December 16, 2002), completing deal in which White Sox traded Ps Keith Foulke and Joe Valentine and C Mark Johnson to Athletics for P Billy Koch and two players to be named (December 3, 2002).

CAREER HITTING: 1-for-1 (1.000), 0 R, 1 2B, 0 3B, 0 HR, 0 RBI.

SCOUTING REPORT *Throws:* His fastball is 88-93 mph, and he also has a slider and a changeup. *Tendencies:* He has a quick arm. Relies more on his late-moving fastball up in the zone. Slider is a quick breaking pitch that he throws more to lefthanders. Doesn't use his change in relief. *Outlook:* Cotts went from a starter to a successful setup reliever. Can rely totally on his fastball and has better command. Is effective pitching to lefthanded hitters in a specialty role. Probably will never start again. *Grade 8*

NEAL COTTS' PITCHING ZONE

.143	.375	.000
.269	.300	.163
.143	.333	.286

LEFTY-RIGHTY SPLITS

vs.	Avg.	AB	H	2B	3B	HR	RBI	BB	SO	OBP	Slg.
L	.206	102	21	7	0	0	14	9	33	.284	.275
R	.155	110	17	3	0	1	5	20	25	.288	.209

Year	Team (League)	W	L	Pct.	ERA	WHIP	G	GS	CG	ShO	Hld.	Sv.-Opp.	IP	H	R	ER	HR	BB-IBB	SO	Avg.
2001—	Vancouver (N'west)	1	0	1.000	3.09	1.17	9	7	0	0		0-...	35.0	28	14	12	2	13-0	44	.215
	— Visalia (Calif.)	3	2	.600	2.32	1.35	7	7	0	0		0-...	31.0	27	14	8	0	15-0	34	.225
2002—	Modesto (California)	12	6	.667	4.12	1.53	28	28	0	0		0-...	137.2	123	72	63	5	87-0	178	.239
2003—	Chicago (A.L.)	1	1	.500	8.10	2.40	4	4	0	0	0	0-0	13.1	15	12	12	1	17-0	10	.294
	— Birmingham (Sou.)	9	7	.563	2.16	1.14	21	21	0	0		0-...	108.1	67	32	26	2	56-1	133	.178
2004—	Chicago (A.L.)	4	4	.500	5.65	1.39	56	1	0	0	4	0-2	65.1	61	45	41	13	30-2	58	.247
2005—	Chicago (A.L.)	4	1	1.000	1.94	1.11	69	0	0	0	13	0-2	60.1	38	15	13	1	29-5	58	.179
	Major League totals (3 years)	9	5	.643	4.27	1.37	129	5	0	0	17	0-4	139.0	114	72	66	15	76-7	126	.224

DIVISION SERIES RECORD

Year	Team (League)	W	L	Pct.	ERA	WHIP	G	GS	CG	ShO	Hld.	Sv.-Opp.	IP	H	R	ER	HR	BB-IBB	SO	Avg.
2005—	Chicago (A.L.)	0	0		0.00	0.00	1	0	0	0	0	0-0	0.1	0	0	0	0	0-0	0	.000

CHAMPIONSHIP SERIES RECORD

Year	Team (League)	W	L	Pct.	ERA	WHIP	G	GS	CG	ShO	Hld.	Sv.-Opp.	IP	H	R	ER	HR	BB-IBB	SO	Avg.
2005—	Chicago (A.L.)	0	0		0.00	0.00	1	0	0	0	0	0-0	0.2	0	0	0	0	0-0	0	.000

WORLD SERIES RECORD

Year	Team (League)	W	L	Pct.	ERA	WHIP	G	GS	CG	ShO	Hld.	Sv.-Opp.	IP	H	R	ER	HR	BB-IBB	SO	Avg.
2005—	Chicago (A.L.)	1	0	1.000	0.00	1.50	4	0	0	0	2	0-0	1.1	1	0	0	0	1-0	2	.200

COUNSELL, CRAIG — 2B/SS

PERSONAL: Born August 21, 1970, in South Bend, Ind. ... 6-0/184. ... Bats left, throws right. ... Full name: Craig John Counsell. ... High school: Whitefish Bay (Milwaukee). ... College: Notre Dame.

TRANSACTIONS/CAREER NOTES: Selected by Colorado Rockies organization in 11th round of 1992 free-agent draft. ... On disabled list (May 1-July 15 and July 18-September 3, 1996). ... Traded by Rockies to Florida Marlins for P Mark Hutton (July 27, 1997). ... On disabled list (August 4, 1998-remainder of season). ... Traded by Marlins to Los Angeles Dodgers for a player to be named (June 15, 1999); Marlins acquired P Ryan Moskau to complete deal (July 15, 1999). ... Released by Dodgers (March 15, 2000). ... Signed by Arizona Diamondbacks organization (March 20, 2000). ... On disabled list (August 9, 2002-remainder of season). ... On disabled list (May 7-July 7, 2003); included rehabilitation assignment to Tucson. ... Traded by Diamondbacks with 2B Junior Spivey, 1B Lyle Overbay, C Chad Moeller and Ps Chris Capuano and Jorge de la Rosa to Milwaukee Brewers for 1B Richie Sexson, P Shane Nance and a player to be named (December 1, 2003); Diamondbacks acquired OF Noochie Varner to complete deal (December 15, 2003). ... Signed as a free agent by Arizona Diamondbacks (December 21, 2004).

2005 GAMES PLAYED BY POSITION (MLB): 2B—143, SS—1.

SCOUTING REPORT *Offense:* Counsell has an unorthodox stance and has problems catching up to good inside fastballs. Has a long swing and is losing bat speed. Handles the ball better down than up. Makes good contact and hangs in against lefthanded pitching. Has little power. Is a good runner who can steal bases. *Defense:* He was a shortstop when he broke in but now is strictly a second baseman. Has good agility and range to either side. Reads the ball well off the bat. Has good feet and soft, quick hands. Pivots well and is accurate on the double play. *Outlook:* Counsell's patience and ability to make contact make him a good table setter. *Grade 6.4*

CRAIG COUNSELL'S HITTING ZONE

.261	.333	.235
.184	.424	.282
.250	.222	.167

LEFTY-RIGHTY SPLITS

vs.	Avg.	AB	H	2B	3B	HR	RBI	BB	SO	OBP	Slg.
L	.269	119	32	6	1	2	13	18	20	.362	.387
R	.253	459	116	28	3	7	29	60	49	.347	.373

Year	Team (League)	Pos.	G	AB	R	H	2B	3B	HR	RBI	BB	SO	HBP	GDP	SB-CS	Avg.	OBP	SLG	OPS	E	Avg.
1992—	Bend (N'west)	2B-SS	18	61	11	15	6	1	0	8	9	10	1	2	1-2	.246	.352	.377	.729	2	.967
1993—	Central Valley (Cal.)	SS	131	471	79	132	26	3	5	59	95	68	3	8	14-8	.280	.401	.380	.781	35	.944
1994—	New Haven (East.)	2B-SS	83	300	47	84	20	1	5	37	37	32	5	6	4-1	.280	.366	.403	.770	27	.931

Year Team (League)	Pos.	G	AB	R	H	2B	3B	HR	RBI	BB	SO	HBP	GDP	SB-CS	Avg.	OBP	SLG	OPS	E	Avg.
1995— Colo. Springs (PCL)	SS	118	399	60	112	22	6	5	53	34	47	2	12	10-2	.281	.336	.404	.739	30	.950
— Colorado (N.L.)	SS	3	1	0	0	0	0	0	0	1	0	0	0	0-0	.000	.000	.000	.500	0	1.000
1996— Colo. Springs (PCL)	2B-3B-SS	25	75	17	18	3	0	2	10	24	7	0	2	4-3	.240	.424	.360	.784	4	.961
1997— Colo. Springs (PCL)	2B-SS	96	376	77	126	31	6	5	63	45	38	6	6	12-2	.335	.409	.489	.898	9	.981
— Colorado (N.L.)		1	0	0	0	0	0	0	0	0	0	0	0	0-0	...	...	...	...	0	...
— Florida (N.L.)	2B	51	164	20	49	9	2	1	16	18	17	3	5	1-1	.299	.376	.396	.773	3	.989
1998— Florida (N.L.)	2B	107	335	43	84	19	5	4	40	51	47	4	5	3-0	.251	.356	.373	.729	5	.991
1999— Florida (N.L.)	2B	37	66	4	10	1	0	0	5	5	10	0	1	0-0	.152	.211	.167	.378	1	.980
— Los Angeles (N.L.)	2B-SS	50	108	20	28	6	0	0	9	9	14	0	1	1-0	.259	.311	.315	.626	1	.993
2000— Tucson (PCL)	2B-3B-SS	50	198	45	69	14	3	3	27	22	20	1	1	4-1	.348	.413	.495	.908	4	.981
— Arizona (N.L.)	2B-3B-SS	67	152	23	48	8	1	2	11	20	18	2	4	3-3	.316	.400	.421	.821	6	.957
2001— Arizona (N.L.)	SS-2B-3B	141	458	76	126	22	3	4	38	61	76	2	9	6-8	.275	.359	.362	.721	8	.985
2002— Arizona (N.L.)	3B-SS-2B	112	436	63	123	22	1	2	51	45	52	1	10	7-5	.282	.348	.351	.699	8	.979
2003— Tucson (PCL)	2B-SS-3B	5	23	8	10	2	0	0	2	1	3	0	0	0-0	.435	.458	.522	.980	1	.963
— Arizona (N.L.)	3B-SS-2B-1B	89	303	40	71	6	3	3	21	41	32	2	4	11-4	.234	.328	.304	.631	3	.989
2004— Milwaukee (N.L.)	SS-3B	140	473	59	114	19	5	2	23	59	88	5	5	17-4	.241	.330	.315	.645	9	.983
2005— Arizona (N.L.)	2B-SS	150	578	85	148	34	4	9	42	78	69	8	8	26-7	.256	.350	.375	.726	8	.990
Major League totals (10 years)		948	3074	433	801	146	24	27	253	388	423	27	52	75-32	.261	.346	.350	.696	52	.986

DIVISION SERIES RECORD

Year Team (League)	Pos.	G	AB	R	H	2B	3B	HR	RBI	BB	SO	HBP	GDP	SB-CS	Avg.	OBP	SLG	OPS	E	Avg.
1997— Florida (N.L.)	2B	3	5	0	2	1	0	0	1	1	0	0	0	0-0	.400	.500	.600	1.100	1	.875
2001— Arizona (N.L.)	2B	5	16	2	3	0	0	1	3	2	2	0	1	0-0	.188	.278	.375	.653	0	1.000
Division series totals (2 years)		8	21	2	5	1	0	1	4	3	2	0	1	0-0	.238	.333	.429	.762	1	.963

CHAMPIONSHIP SERIES RECORD

Year Team (League)	Pos.	G	AB	R	H	2B	3B	HR	RBI	BB	SO	HBP	GDP	SB-CS	Avg.	OBP	SLG	OPS	E	Avg.
1997— Florida (N.L.)	2B	5	14	0	6	0	0	0	3	3	0	0	0	0-0	.429	.529	.429	.958	1	.941
2001— Arizona (N.L.)	2B-SS	5	21	5	8	3	0	0	4	3	6	0	0	1-0	.381	.381	.524	.905	0	1.000
Champ. series totals (2 years)		10	35	5	14	3	0	0	7	6	6	0	0	1-0	.400	.447	.486	.933	1	.972

WORLD SERIES RECORD

Year Team (League)	Pos.	G	AB	R	H	2B	3B	HR	RBI	BB	SO	HBP	GDP	SB-CS	Avg.	OBP	SLG	OPS	E	Avg.
1997— Florida (N.L.)	2B	7	22	4	4	1	0	0	2	6	5	0	0	1-0	.182	.345	.227	.572	1	.971
2001— Arizona (N.L.)	2B	6	24	1	2	0	0	1	1	0	7	1	0	0-0	.083	.120	.208	.328	0	1.000
World Series totals (2 years)		13	46	5	6	1	0	1	3	6	12	1	0	1-0	.130	.241	.217	.458	1	.984

CRAIN, JESSE — P

PERSONAL: Born July 5, 1981, in Toronto. ... 6-1/205. ... Throws right, bats right. ... Full name: Jesse Alan Crain. ... High school: Fairview (Colo.). ... College: Houston.
TRANSACTIONS/CAREER NOTES: Selected by Minnesota Twins organization in second round of 2002 free-agent draft.
CAREER HITTING: 0-for-0 (.000), 0 R, 0 2B, 0 3B, 0 HR, 0 RBI.

SCOUTING REPORT *Throws:* Crain throws two types of fastball—a two-seamer and a four-seamer ranging in velocity from 90-95 mph. Curve is thrown at 74, slider is in the upper 80s. *Tendencies:* Crain has outstanding arm speed even though he's a maximum-effort thrower. Is extremely aggressive and consistently challenges hitters. Has excellent deception. Fastball tends to jump when it's up in the zone but will tail if it's down. Hitters don't pick up the ball quickly from him. Curve is a big breaker but very quick. Slider is sharp with a small break. Throws strikes and is equally effective to lefthanders and righthanders. *Outlook:* One of the best setup/middle relievers in the league, Crain has Juan Rincon ahead of him in the pecking order; that leaves Crain as a sixth- or seventh-inning pitcher. *Grade 7.6*

JESSE CRAIN'S PITCHING ZONE

.158	.250	.138
.222	.217	.255
.211	.000	.375

LEFTY-RIGHTY SPLITS

vs.	Avg.	AB	H	2B	3B	HR	RBI	BB	SO	OBP	Slg.
L	.209	110	23	4	0	2	11	15	10	.307	.300
R	.225	169	38	2	0	4	18	14	15	.296	.308

Year Team (League)	W	L	Pct.	ERA	WHIP	G	GS	CG	ShO	Hld.	Sv.-Opp.	IP	H	R	ER	HR	BB-IBB	SO	Avg.
2002— Elizabethton (App.)	2	1	.667	0.57	0.70	9	0	0	0	...	2-...	15.2	4	2	1	0	7-3	18	.082
— Quad City (Midw.)	1	1	.500	1.50	0.83	9	0	0	0	...	1-...	12.0	6	3	2	0	4-0	11	.154
2003— Fort Myers (FSL)	2	1	.667	2.84	0.79	10	0	0	0	...	0-...	19.0	10	6	6	0	5-0	25	.154
— New Britain (East.)	1	1	.500	0.69	0.59	22	0	0	0	...	9-...	39.0	13	4	3	0	10-1	56	.099
— Rochester (Int'l)	3	1	.750	3.12	1.31	23	0	0	0	...	10-...	26.0	24	10	9	0	10-1	33	.245
2004— Rochester (Int'l)	3	2	.600	2.49	1.09	41	0	0	0	...	19-...	50.2	38	20	14	5	17-2	64	.208
— Minnesota (A.L.)	3	0	1.000	2.00	1.07	22	0	0	0	2	0-1	27.0	17	6	6	2	12-1	14	.179
2005— Minnesota (A.L.)	12	5	.706	2.71	1.13	75	0	0	0	11	1-4	79.2	61	28	24	6	29-7	25	.219
Major League totals (2 years)	15	5	.750	2.53	1.12	97	0	0	0	13	1-5	106.2	78	34	30	8	41-8	39	.209

DIVISION SERIES RECORD

Year Team (League)	W	L	Pct.	ERA	WHIP	G	GS	CG	ShO	Hld.	Sv.-Opp.	IP	H	R	ER	HR	BB-IBB	SO	Avg.
2004— Minnesota (A.L.)	0	0	...	0.00	3.00	1	0	0	0	0	0-0	0.1	1	0	0	0	0-0	0	.500

CRAWFORD, CARL — OF

PERSONAL: Born August 5, 1981, in Houston. ... 6-2/219. ... Bats left, throws left. ... Full name: Carl Demonte Crawford. ... High school: Jefferson Davis (Houston).
TRANSACTIONS/CAREER NOTES: Selected by Tampa Bay Devil Rays organization in second round of 1999 free-agent draft. ... On suspended list (July 19-22, 2003).
2005 GAMES PLAYED BY POSITION (MLB): OF—154, DH—1.

SCOUTING REPORT *Offense:* The game's best pure athlete is steadily improving his baseball skills. Hits with an open stance so he can stride into the ball and close his front hips. Made a change during the year by moving closer to the plate and began pulling and increasing his power. Has good bat speed and uses the whole field. Shows a good aptitude at the plate. His intimidating speed gives him the potential to steal 75 bases per year. *Defense:* He has outstanding body control and exceptional closing speed. Range eventually will make him a center fielder. Gets good jumps in all directions. Arm strength is short but improving. *Outlook:* He can be a dynamic offensive player with speed and power. Is a five-tool guy who could dominate the game soon. *Grade 8.9*

CARL CRAWFORD'S HITTING ZONE

.324	.111	.442
.339	.382	.329
.385	.308	.278

LEFTY-RIGHTY SPLITS

vs.	Avg.	AB	H	2B	3B	HR	RBI	BB	SO	OBP	Slg.
L	.244	193	47	4	3	2	17	12	41	.293	.326
R	.326	451	147	29	12	13	64	15	43	.348	.530

										BATTING								FIELDING	
Year	Team (League)	Pos.	G	AB	R	H	2B	3B	HR	RBI	BB	SO	HBP	GDP	SB-CS	Avg.	OBP	SLG	OPS	E	Avg.
1999— Princeton (Appal.)	OF	60	260	62	83	14	4	0	25	13	47	1	5	17-2	.319	.350	.404	.754	8	.934
2000— Char., S.C. (SAL)	OF	135	564	99	170	21	11	6	57	32	102	3	1	55-9	.301	.342	.410	.751	8	.968
2001— Orlando (South.)	OF	132	537	64	147	24	3	4	51	36	90	4	3	36-20	.274	.323	.352	.675	6	.981
2002— Durham (Int'l)	OF	85	353	59	105	17	9	7	52	20	69	2	5	26-8	.297	.335	.456	.791	1	.994
— Tampa Bay (A.L.)	OF	63	259	23	67	11	6	2	30	9	41	3	0	9-5	.259	.290	.371	.661	1	.994
2003— Tampa Bay (A.L.)	OF-DH	151	630	80	177	18	9	5	54	26	102	1	5	* 55-10	.281	.309	.362	.671	3	.992
2004— Tampa Bay (A.L.)	OF-DH	152	626	104	185	26	* 19	11	55	35	81	1	2	* 59-15	.296	.331	.450	.781	2	.994
2005— Tampa Bay (A.L.)	OF-DH	156	644	101	194	33	* 15	15	81	27	84	5	11	46-8	.301	.331	.469	.800	2	.995
Major League totals (4 years)		522	2159	308	623	88	49	33	220	97	308	10	18	169-38	.289	.320	.421	.740	8	.994

ALL-STAR GAME RECORD

	G	AB	R	H	2B	3B	HR	RBI	BB	SO	HBP	GDP	SB-CS	Avg.	OBP	SLG	OPS	E	Avg.
All-Star Game totals (1 year)	1	2	0	0	0	0	0	0	0	1	0	0	0-0	.000	.000	.000	.000	0	1.000

CREDE, JOE   3B

PERSONAL: Born April 26, 1978, in Jefferson City, Mo. ... 6-1/200. ... Bats right, throws right. ... Full name: Joseph Crede. ... Name pronounced: CREE-dee. ... High school: Fatima (Westphalia, Mo.).

TRANSACTIONS/CAREER NOTES: Selected by Chicago White Sox organization in fifth round of 1996 free-agent draft. ... On disabled list (August 26-September 10, 2005).

2005 GAMES PLAYED BY POSITION (MLB): 3B—130, SS—1, DH—1.

SCOUTING REPORT *Offense:* Crede is a streaky hitter with a long stroke. Likes the ball out over the plate. Has increased his bat speed and can handle inside pitches. Is a difficult out when he sees the ball well. Has power from right-center to the left-field line. Has poor depth perception, the reason for his struggles in certain parks. Is not fast but is a good baserunner. *Defense:* Crede is one of the most underrated defensive third basemen in baseball. Has good agility despite back problems and has a quick first step. Can dive to his right or range to his left. Has good hands. Arm is extremely strong and accurate. *Outlook:* His value increased during the playoffs, when he centered the ball better than he had all season. Defense continues to be a plus. *Grade 8.0*

JOE CREDE'S HITTING ZONE

.143	.400	.150
.247	.513	.314
.250	.348	.353

LEFTY-RIGHTY SPLITS

vs.	Avg.	AB	H	2B	3B	HR	RBI	BB	SO	OBP	Slg.
L	.277	83	23	4	0	4	13	8	9	.344	.470
R	.246	349	86	17	0	18	49	17	57	.292	.450

										BATTING								FIELDING	
Year	Team (League)	Pos.	G	AB	R	H	2B	3B	HR	RBI	BB	SO	HBP	GDP	SB-CS	Avg.	OBP	SLG	OPS	E	Avg.
1996— GC Whi. Sox (GCL)	3B	56	221	30	66	17	1	4	32	9	41	2	8	1-1	.299	.326	.439	.765	25	.857
1997— Hickory (S. Atl.)	3B	113	402	45	109	25	0	5	62	24	83	5	6	3-1	.271	.319	.371	.689	33	.905
1998— Win.-Salem (Car.)	3B	137	492	92	155	32	3	20	88	53	98	12	10	9-7	.315	.387	.514	.902	30	.929
1999— Birmingham (Sou.)	3B	74	291	37	73	14	1	4	42	22	47	1	15	2-6	.251	.303	.347	.650	20	.910
2000— Birmingham (Sou.)	3B	138	533	84	163	35	0	21	94	56	111	15	18	3-4	.306	.384	.490	.874	19	.942
— Chicago (A.L.)	3B-DH	7	14	2	5	1	0	0	3	0	3	0	0	0-0	.357	.333	.429	.762	1	.933
2001— Charlotte (Int'l)	3B	124	463	67	128	34	1	17	65	46	88	7	5	2-1	.276	.349	.464	.813	20	.946
— Chicago (A.L.)	3B	17	50	1	11	1	1	0	7	3	11	1	1	1-0	.220	.273	.280	.553	0	1.000
2002— Charlotte (Int'l)	3B	95	359	57	112	21	0	24	65	26	48	4	8	0-1	.312	.359	.571	.930	15	.938
— Chicago (A.L.)	3B	53	200	28	57	10	0	12	35	8	40	0	1	0-2	.285	.311	.515	.826	8	.938
2003— Chicago (A.L.)	3B	151	536	68	140	31	2	19	75	32	75	6	11	1-1	.261	.308	.433	.741	14	.964
2004— Chicago (A.L.)	3B	144	490	67	117	25	0	21	69	34	81	10	14	1-2	.239	.299	.418	.717	12	.965
2005— Chicago (A.L.)	3B-SS-DH	132	432	54	109	21	0	22	62	25	66	8	7	1-1	.252	.303	.454	.756	10	.972
Major League totals (6 years)		504	1722	220	439	89	3	74	251	102	276	25	34	4-6	.255	.303	.439	.743	45	.964

DIVISION SERIES RECORD

Year	Team (League)	Pos.	G	AB	R	H	2B	3B	HR	RBI	BB	SO	HBP	GDP	SB-CS	Avg.	OBP	SLG	OPS	E	Avg.
2005— Chicago (A.L.)	3B	3	9	2	1	0	0	0	1	1	1	0	0	0-0	.111	.200	.111	.311	1	.938

CHAMPIONSHIP SERIES RECORD

Year	Team (League)	Pos.	G	AB	R	H	2B	3B	HR	RBI	BB	SO	HBP	GDP	SB-CS	Avg.	OBP	SLG	OPS	E	Avg.
2005— Chicago (A.L.)	3B	5	19	2	7	2	0	2	7	0	3	0	0	0-1	.368	.350	.789	1.139	0	1.000

WORLD SERIES RECORD

Year	Team (League)	Pos.	G	AB	R	H	2B	3B	HR	RBI	BB	SO	HBP	GDP	SB-CS	Avg.	OBP	SLG	OPS	E	Avg.
2005— Chicago (A.L.)	3B	4	17	2	5	1	0	2	3	1	2	1	0	0-0	.294	.368	.706	1.074	0	1.000

CREEK, DOUG — P

PERSONAL: Born March 1, 1969, in Winchester, Va. ... 6-0/227. ... Throws left, bats left. ... Full name: Paul Douglas Creek. ... High school: Martinsburg (W.Va.). ... College: Georgia Tech.

TRANSACTIONS/CAREER NOTES: Selected by California Angels organization in fifth round of 1990 free-agent draft; did not sign. ... Selected by St. Louis Cardinals organization in seventh round of 1991 free-agent draft. ... Traded by Cardinals with Ps Allen Watson and Rich DeLucia to San Francisco Giants for SS Royce Clayton and a player to be named (December 14, 1995); Cardinals acquired 2B Chris Wimmer to complete deal (January 16, 1996). ... Traded by Giants to Chicago White Sox for cash (November 7, 1997). ... Contract sold by White Sox to Hanshin of the Japan Central League (December 4, 1997). ... Signed as a free agent by Chicago Cubs organization (January 29, 1999). ... Released by Cubs (September 13, 1999). ... Signed by Tampa Bay Devil Rays organization (February 1, 2000). ... Traded by Devil Rays to Seattle Mariners for cash (July 24, 2002). ... Released by Mariners (October 15, 2002). ... Signed by Toronto Blue Jays organization (October 29, 2002). ... On disabled list (May 17, 2003-remainder of season). ... Released by Blue Jays (October 8, 2003). ... Signed by Cardinals organization (February 14, 2004). ... Signed as a free agent by Detroit Tigers organization (January 8, 2005).

CAREER HITTING: 1-for-5 (.200), 1 R, 0 2B, 0 3B, 0 HR, 0 RBI.

DOUG CREEK'S PITCHING ZONE

.500	.200	.667
.286	.286	.313
.333	.364	.250

LEFTY-RIGHTY SPLITS

vs.	Avg.	AB	H	2B	3B	HR	RBI	BB	SO	OBP	Slg.
L	.282	39	11	1	1	3	8	2	5	.317	.590
R	.302	53	16	2	1	4	10	5	13	.356	.604

Year	Team (League)	W	L	Pct.	ERA	WHIP	G	GS	CG	ShO	Hld.	Sv.-Opp.	IP	H	R	ER	HR	BB-IBB	SO	Avg.
1991—Hamilton (NYP)		3	2	.600	5.12	1.47	9	5	0	0	...	1-...	38.2	39	22	22	2	18-0	45	.269
—Savannah (S. Atl.)		2	1	.667	4.45	1.41	5	5	0	0	...	0-...	29.0	24	14	14	2	17-0	32	.245
1992—Springfield (Midw.)		4	1	.800	2.58	1.15	6	6	0	0	...	0-...	39.0	32	11	11	4	13-1	43	.227
—St. Pete. (FSL)		5	4	.556	2.82	1.27	13	13	0	0	...	0-...	74.0	57	31	23	5	37-1	63	.221
1993—Arkansas (Texas)		11	10	.524	4.02	1.29	25	25	1	1	...	0-...	147.2	142	75	66	15	48-1	128	.254
—Louisville (A.A.)		0	0	...	3.21	1.36	2	2	0	0	...	0-...	14.0	10	5	5	0	9-0	9	.208
1994—Louisville (A.A.)		1	4	.200	8.54	2.22	7	7	0	0	...	0-...	27.0	37	26	25	2	23-0	16	.349
—Arkansas (Texas)		3	10	.231	4.40	1.43	17	17	1	0	...	0-...	92.0	96	54	45	4	36-0	65	.274
1995—Louisville (A.A.)		3	2	.600	3.23	1.34	26	0	0	0	...	0-...	30.2	20	12	11	1	21-0	29	.182
—Arkansas (Texas)		4	2	.667	2.88	1.14	26	0	0	0	...	1-...	35.0	24	12	11	4	16-2	50	.198
—St. Louis (N.L.)		0	0	...	0.00	0.75	6	0	0	0	0	0-0	6.2	2	0	0	0	3-0	10	.095
1996—San Francisco (N.L.)		0	2	.000	6.52	1.59	63	0	0	0	7	0-1	48.1	45	41	35	11	32-2	38	.243
1997—Phoenix (PCL)		8	6	.571	4.93	1.59	25	23	2	1	...	0-...	129.2	140	76	71	15	66-0	137	.276
—San Francisco (N.L.)		1	2	.333	6.75	1.95	3	3	0	0	0	0-0	13.1	12	12	10	1	14-0	14	.240
1998—Hanshin (Jp. West.)		9	1	.900	2.16	1.29	17	16	2		...	0-...	100.0	77	28	24		52-...	101	...
—Hanshin (Jp. Cn.)		0	4	.000	5.65	1.67	7	6	0	0	...	0-...	28.2	23	21	18	4	25-0	24	...
1999—Iowa (PCL)		7	3	.700	3.79	1.36	25	20	0	0	...	1-...	130.2	116	66	55	20	62-0	140	.241
—Chicago (N.L.)		0	0	...	10.50	2.33	3	0	0	0	0	0-0	6.0	6	7	7	1	8-1	6	.261
2000—Durham (Int'l)		0	0	...	1.96	1.26	10	1	0	0	...	0-...	19.0	10	5	4	1	14-0	22	.152
—Tampa Bay (A.L.)		1	3	.250	4.60	1.45	45	0	0	0	2	1-3	60.2	49	33	31	10	39-3	73	.224
2001—Tampa Bay (A.L.)		2	5	.286	4.31	1.60	66	0	0	0	15	0-3	62.2	51	34	30	7	49-5	66	.230
2002—Tampa Bay (A.L.)		2	1	.667	6.27	1.61	29	0	0	0	4	0-2	37.1	39	27	26	8	21-1	37	.264
—Seattle (A.L.)		1	1	.500	4.91	1.75	23	0	0	0	1	0-0	18.1	18	10	10	2	14-1	19	.257
2003—Toronto (A.L.)		0	0	...	3.29	1.90	21	0	0	0	2	0-1	13.2	14	6	5	0	12-3	11	.264
2004—Memphis (PCL)		2	1	.667	4.71	1.36	33	0	0	0	6	0-2	28.2	28	16	15	1	11-0	39	.246
2005—Toledo (Int'l)		2	2	.500	4.61	1.54	28	1	0	0	6	0-2	27.1	28	14	14	2	14-4	32	.267
—Detroit (A.L.)		0	0	...	6.85	1.52	20	0	0	0	1	0-...	22.1	27	18	17	1	7-0	18	.293
American League totals (5 years)		6	10	.375	4.98	1.58	204	0	0	0	25	1-9	215.0	198	128	119	36	142-13	224	.246
National League totals (4 years)		1	4	.200	6.30	1.64	75	3	0	0	7	0-1	74.1	65	60	52	13	57-3	68	.233
Major League totals (9 years)		7	14	.333	5.32	1.60	279	3	0	0	32	1-10	289.1	263	188	171	49	199-16	292	.243

CRISP, COCO — OF

PERSONAL: Born November 1, 1979, in Los Angeles. ... 6-0/185. ... Bats both, throws right. ... Full name: Covelli Loyce Crisp. ... High school: Inglewood (Los Angeles). ... Junior college: Los Angeles Pierce.

TRANSACTIONS/CAREER NOTES: Selected by St. Louis Cardinals organization in seventh round of 1999 free-agent draft. ... Traded by Cardinals to Cleveland Indians (August 6, 2002), completing deal in which Cardinals traded 1B Luis Garcia and a player to be named to Indians for P Chuck Finley (July 19, 2002). ... On disabled list (May 18-June 2, 2005).

2005 GAMES PLAYED BY POSITION (MLB): OF—145.

SCOUTING REPORT *Offense:* Crisp continues to improve in all phases of his game. Has really improved his swing from both sides of the plate and has good bat speed. Is a better left-handed hitter and hits more home runs from that side but has more raw power righthanded. Hitting third has allowed him to see more fastballs and his run production has increased. Is a good runner and has become more aggressive. *Defense:* Crisp is far more comfortable in left field than he was in center. Gets better jumps toward the line and has the speed to cover the gaps well. Arm is short but charges the ball and has a quick release. *Outlook:* Crisp has become a dependable offensive player for the Indians, with speed and developing power. *Grade 8.4*

COCO CRISP'S HITTING ZONE

.360	.324	.308
.337	.450	.322
.250	.222	.191

LEFTY-RIGHTY SPLITS

vs.	Avg.	AB	H	2B	3B	HR	RBI	BB	SO	OBP	Slg.
L	.252	202	51	13	0	5	20	16	34	.305	.391
R	.324	392	127	29	4	11	49	28	47	.366	.503

Year	Team (League)	Pos.	G	AB	R	H	2B	3B	HR	RBI	BB	SO	HBP	GDP	SB-CS	Avg.	OBP	SLG	OPS	E	Avg.
1999—Johnson City (App.)		2B	65	229	55	59	5	4	3	22	44	41	2	0	27-5	.258	.379	.354	.733	24	.912
2000—New Jersey (NYP)		OF-2B	36	134	18	32	5	0	0	14	11	22	1	1	25-3	.239	.301	.276	.577	2	.972
—Peoria (Midw.)		OF	27	98	14	27	9	0	0	7	16	15	0	1	7-3	.276	.377	.367	.745	0	1.000
2001—Potomac (Carol.)		OF	139	530	89	162	23	3	11	47	52	64	1	8	39-21	.306	.368	.423	.791	6	.975
2002—New Haven (East.)		OF	89	355	61	107	16	1	9	47	36	56	0		26-10	.301	.365	.428	.793	5	.985
—Akron (East.)		OF	7	32	9	13	1	0	1	4	3	3	0		4-0	.406	.457	.531	.988	0	1.000
—Cleveland (A.L.)		OF	32	127	16	33	9	2	1	9	11	19	0	0	4-1	.260	.316	.386	.700	1	.988
—Buffalo (Int'l)		OF	4	21	3	5	1	0	0	2	0	2	0	0	1-0	.238	.238	.286	.524	0	1.000
2003—Buffalo (Int'l)		OF	56	225	42	81	19	6	3	24	26	24	5	5	20-8	.360	.434	.511	.945	3	.982

Year Team (League)	Pos.	G	AB	R	H	2B	3B	HR	RBI	BB	SO	HBP	GDP	SB-CS	Avg.	OBP	SLG	OPS	E	Avg.
—Cleveland (A.L.)	OF-DH	99	414	55	110	15	6	3	27	23	51	0	4	15-9	.266	.302	.353	.655	1	.995
2004—Cleveland (A.L.)	OF-DH	139	491	78	146	24	2	15	71	36	69	0	8	20-13	.297	.344	.446	.790	4	.986
2005—Cleveland (A.L.)	OF	145	594	86	178	42	4	16	69	44	81	0	7	15-6	.300	.345	.465	.810	5	.985
Major League totals (4 years)		415	1626	235	467	90	14	35	176	114	220	0	19	54-29	.287	.332	.424	.756	11	.988

CROSBY, BOBBY — SS

PERSONAL: Born January 12, 1980, in Lakewood, Calif. ... 6-3/195. ... Bats right, throws right. ... Full name: Robert Edward Crosby. ... High school: La Quinta (Westminster, Calif.). ... College: Long Beach State. ... Son of Ed Crosby, infielder with three major league teams (1970-76).

TRANSACTIONS/CAREER NOTES: Selected by Anaheim Angels organization in 34th round of 1998 free-agent draft; did not sign. ... Selected by Oakland Athletics organization in first round (25th pick overall) of 2001 free-agent draft. ... On disabled list (April 7-May 30 and August 31-September 19, 2005); included rehabilitation assignments to Stockton and Sacramento.

HONORS: Named A.L. Rookie of the Year by THE SPORTING NEWS (2004). ... Named A.L. Rookie of the Year by Baseball Writers' Association of America (2004).

2005 GAMES PLAYED BY POSITION (MLB): SS—84.

SCOUTING REPORT *Offense:* His swing is a little long and has a slight uppercut motion, but Crosby still has good bat speed and should develop 25- to 30-home run power. Likes the ball away. Is aggressive but has become more patient. Doesn't hit well with runners in scoring position as he puts too much pressure on himself. Has improved against lefthanders. Is a very instinctive baserunner. *Defense:* Crosby is big for a middle infielder, yet has fluid actions. Has good hands. Range is very good to both sides, but is better to his left. Has good carry on his throws and is accurate despite using a slinging motion. *Outlook:* Crosby is a very athletic player who, despite his size, could become a good defensive shortstop. **Grade 7.7**

BOBBY CROSBY'S HITTING ZONE

.467	.333	.267
.321	.286	.171
.261	.286	.222

LEFTY-RIGHTY SPLITS

vs.	Avg.	AB	H	2B	3B	HR	RBI	BB	SO	OBP	Slg.
L	.314	102	32	8	2	4	11	13	15	.391	.549
R	.260	231	60	17	2	5	27	22	39	.325	.416

Year Team (League)	Pos.	G	AB	R	H	2B	3B	HR	RBI	BB	SO	HBP	GDP	SB-CS	Avg.	OBP	SLG	OPS	E	Avg.
2001—Modesto (California)	SS	11	38	7	15	5	0	1	3	3	8	0	1	0-0	.395	.439	.605	1.044	4	.889
2002—Modesto (California)	SS	73	280	47	86	17	2	2	38	33	43	7	5	5-0	.307	.393	.404	.796	19	.938
—Midland (Texas)	SS	59	228	31	64	16	0	7	31	19	41	0	9	9-2	.281	.335	.443	.778	13	.952
2003—Sacramento (PCL)	SS-DH	127	465	86	143	32	6	22	90	63	110	7	16	24-4	.308	.395	.544	.939	15	.973
—Oakland (A.L.)	SS-DH	11	12	1	0	0	0	0	0	1	5	1	0	0-0	.000	.143	.000	.143	2	.889
2004—Oakland (A.L.)	SS	151	545	70	130	34	1	22	64	58	141	9	20	7-3	.239	.319	.426	.744	19	.975
2005—Stockton (Calif.)	SS-DH	3	9	1	3	1	0	0	1	2	1	0	0	0-0	.333	.455	.444	.899	0	1.000
—Sacramento (PCL)	SS-DH	3	12	0	1	0	0	0	1	0	0	0	0	0-0	.083	.083	.167	0	1.000	
—Oakland (A.L.)	SS	84	333	66	92	25	4	9	38	35	54	1	10	0-0	.276	.346	.456	.802	7	.981
Major League totals (3 years)		246	890	137	222	59	5	31	102	94	200	11	30	7-3	.249	.326	.431	.758	28	.976

CROSBY, BUBBA — OF

PERSONAL: Born August 11, 1976, in Houston. ... 5-11/185. ... Bats left, throws left. ... Full name: Richard Stephen Crosby. ... High school: Bellaire (Texas). ... College: Rice.

TRANSACTIONS/CAREER NOTES: Selected by Los Angeles Dodgers organization in first round (23rd pick overall) in 1998 free-agent draft. ... Traded by Dodgers with P Scott Proctor to New York Yankees for IF Robin Ventura (July 31, 2003).

2005 GAMES PLAYED BY POSITION (MLB): OF—67, DH—4.

SCOUTING REPORT Crosby is a line-drive hitter with a short stroke and limited power. Slaps the ball to all fields and is a better fastball hitter. Has trouble with lefthanders. Is an outstanding runner and can play center field well. Gets good lateral jumps with range to either side. Arm is below average. Charges the ball well and makes accurate throws. **Grade 5**

BUBBA CROSBY'S HITTING ZONE

.333	.125	.182
.500	.125	.273
.000	.833	.300

LEFTY-RIGHTY SPLITS

vs.	Avg.	AB	H	2B	3B	HR	RBI	BB	SO	OBP	Slg.
L	.273	22	6	0	0	1	2	1	4	.304	.409
R	.276	76	21	0	1	0	4	3	10	.304	.303

Year Team (League)	Pos.	G	AB	R	H	2B	3B	HR	RBI	BB	SO	HBP	GDP	SB-CS	Avg.	OBP	SLG	OPS	E	Avg.
1998—San Bern. (Calif.)	OF	56	199	25	43	9	2	0	14	17	38	0	3	3-5	.216	.274	.281	.555	1	.990
1999—San Bern. (Calif.)	OF	96	371	53	110	21	3	1	37	42	71	6	6	19-8	.296	.376	.377	.754	5	.975
2000—Vero Beach (FSL)	OF	73	274	50	73	13	8	8	51	31	41	7	9	27-10	.266	.355	.460	.814	4	.969
—San Bern. (Calif.)		3	12	2	3	0	0	0	2	0	4	0	1	1-0	.250	.250	.250	.500	...	...
2001—Las Vegas (PCL)	OF	13	42	5	9	2	1	0	5	1	8	0	1	1-1	.214	.233	.310	.542	0	1.000
—Jacksonville (Sou.)	OF	107	384	68	116	22	5	6	47	37	60	8	7	22-6	.302	.369	.432	.802	3	.985
2002—Las Vegas (PCL)	OF	73	279	26	73	12	1	9	36	19	47	2	3	3-1	.262	.312	.409	.721	2	.989
—Jacksonville (Sou.)	OF	38	150	14	39	6	1	2	20	11	23	2	2	7-3	.260	.312	.367	.684	0	1.000
2003—Las Vegas (PCL)	OF-DH	76	277	57	100	24	8	12	57	25	47	3	6	8-0	.361	.410	.635	1.046	1	.991
—Los Angeles (N.L.)	OF	9	12	0	1	0	0	0	1	0	3	0	0	0-0	.083	.083	.167	1	.667	
—Columbus (Int'l)	OF	16	63	9	19	2	1	2	8	6	12	1	0	3-0	.302	.366	.460	.827	0	1.000
2004—Columbus (Int'l)	OF-DH	33	116	18	32	5	2	1	15	14	26	4	2	3-3	.276	.365	.379	.744	0	1.000
—New York (A.L.)	OF-DH	55	53	8	8	2	0	2	7	2	13	1	0	2-0	.151	.196	.302	.498	1	.973
2005—Columbus (Int'l)	OF-DH	42	160	18	37	7	1	4	22	12	28	6	2	2-1	.231	.306	.363	.668	2	1.000
—New York (A.L.)	OF-DH	76	98	15	27	0	1	1	6	4	14	0	1	4-1	.276	.304	.327	.630	1	1.000
American League totals (2 years)		131	151	23	35	2	1	3	13	6	27	1	1	6-1	.232	.266	.318	.584	1	.992
National League totals (1 year)		9	12	0	1	0	0	0	1	0	3	0	0	0-0	.083	.083	.167	0	.667
Major League totals (3 years)		140	163	23	36	2	1	3	14	6	30	1	1	6-1	.221	.253	.301	.554	2	.984

DIVISION SERIES RECORD

Year Team (League)	Pos.	G	AB	R	H	2B	3B	HR	RBI	BB	SO	HBP	GDP	SB-CS	Avg.	OBP	SLG	OPS	E	Avg.
2004— New York (A.L.)	OF	2	0	0	0	0	0	0	0	0	0	0	0	0-0	...	...	...	...	0	...
2005— New York (A.L.)	OF	3	8	0	2	0	0	0	1	0	1	0	0	1-0	.250	.250	.250	.500	0	1.000
Division series totals (2 years)		5	8	0	2	0	0	0	1	0	1	0	0	1-0	.250	.250	.250	.500	0	1.000

CHAMPIONSHIP SERIES RECORD

Year Team (League)	Pos.	G	AB	R	H	2B	3B	HR	RBI	BB	SO	HBP	GDP	SB-CS	Avg.	OBP	SLG	OPS	E	Avg.
2004— New York (A.L.)	OF	1	0	1	0	0	0	0	0	0	0	0	0	0-0	...	...	...	...	0	...

CROWELL, JIM — P

PERSONAL: Born May 14, 1974, in Minneapolis. ... 6-4/225. ... Throws left, bats right. ... Full name: James Everett Crowell. ... Name pronouncd: CROLL. ... High school: Valparaiso (Ind.). ... College: Indianapolis.
TRANSACTIONS/CAREER NOTES: Signed as a non-drafted free agent by Cleveland Indians organization (June 17, 1995). ... Traded by Indians with Ps Danny Graves and Scott Winchester and IF Damian Jackson to Cincinnati Reds for P John Smiley and IF Jeff Branson (July 31, 1997). ... Released by Reds (July 11, 2000). ... Signed by St. Louis Cardinals organization (July 22, 2000). ... Released by Cardinals (March 30, 2001). ... Signed by San Diego Padres organization (April 23, 2001). ... Released by Padres (July 2, 2001). ... Contract purchased by Philadelphia Phillies organization from Atlantic City of the independent Atlantic League (August 18, 2002). ... Signed as a free agent by Florida Marlins organization (November 19, 2004).
CAREER HITTING: 0-for-2 (.000), 0 R, 0 2B, 0 3B, 0 HR, 0 RBI.

LEFTY-RIGHTY SPLITS

vs.	Avg.	AB	H	2B	3B	HR	RBI	BB	SO	OBP	Slg.
L	.500	4	2	1	0	0	2	0	1	.500	.750
R	.533	15	8	4	0	1	8	0	1	.563	1.000

Year Team (League)	W	L	Pct.	ERA	WHIP	G	GS	CG	ShO	Hld.	Sv.-Opp.	IP	H	R	ER	HR	BB-IBB	SO	Avg.
1995—Watertown (NYP)	5	2	.714	2.86	1.36	12	9	0	0	...	0-...	56.2	50	22	18	1	27-1	48	.237
1996—Columbus (S. Atl.)	7	10	.412	4.14	1.40	28	28	3	0	...	0-...	165.1	163	89	76	16	69-0	104	.264
1997—Kinston (Carol.)	9	4	.692	2.37	1.07	17	17	0	0	...	0-...	114.0	96	41	30	4	26-0	94	.227
—Akron (East.)	1	0	1.000	4.50	1.33	3	3	0	0	...	0-...	18.0	13	12	9	2	11-0	7	.197
—Chattanooga (Sou.)	2	1	.667	2.84	1.26	3	3	0	0	...	0-...	19.0	19	6	6	2	5-0	14	.279
—Indianapolis (A.A.)	1	1	.500	2.75	1.37	3	3	1	1	...	0-...	19.2	19	7	6	0	8-0	6	.253
—Cincinnati (N.L.)	0	1	.000	9.95	2.68	2	1	0	0	...	0-...	6.1	12	7	7	2	5-0	3	.414
1998—Chattanooga (Sou.)	0	4	.000	8.51	2.26	5	5	0	0	...	0-...	24.1	38	27	23	2	17-0	10	.349
—Char., W.Va. (SAL)	0	4	.000	13.20	2.47	5	5	0	0	...	0-...	15.0	28	23	22	1	9-0	9	.400
—Indianapolis (Int'l)	0	0	...	6.75	1.75	1	1	0	0	...	0-...	4.0	7	3	3	0	0-0	2	.368
1999—Chattanooga (Sou.)	10	5	.667	5.10	1.74	27	27	0	0	...	0-...	148.1	173	98	84	12	85-0	80	.293
2000—Chattanooga (Sou.)	0	0	...	5.90	1.97	23	0	0	0	...	0-...	29.0	35	23	19	3	22-2	20	.289
—Arkansas (Texas)	1	1	.500	5.40	1.60	12	0	0	0	...	1-...	15.0	16	10	9	1	8-1	10	.276
2001—Portland (PCL)	0	0	...	5.49	1.88	11	2	0	0	...	0-...	19.2	22	15	12	3	15-0	7	.293
—Mobile (Sou.)	1	0	1.000	2.08	1.38	5	0	0	0	...	0-...	4.1	2	1	1	0	4-0	5	.154
2002—Atlantic City (Atl.)	8	4	.667	4.17	1.49	19	19	0	0	...	0-...	108.0	107	54	50	13	54-...	95	...
—Scran./W.B. (I.L.)	2	0	1.000	2.52	1.24	4	4	0	0	...	0-...	25.0	20	7	7	2	11-...	19	...
2003—Scran./W.B. (I.L.)	0	8	.000	4.12	1.60	54	0	0	0	...	9-...	54.2	63	31	25	5	23-5	42	.289
2004—Philadelphia (N.L.)	0	0	...	3.00	2.00	4	0	0	0	0	0-0	3.0	3	6	1	0	0-0	1	.333
—Scran./W.B. (I.L.)	7	3	.700	2.24	1.18	46	0	0	0	...	16-...	63.2	61	22	17	6	14-4	44	.250
2005—Florida (N.L.)	0	0	...	21.60	3.00	4	0	0	0	0	0-0	3.1	10	8	8	1	0-0	5	.526
—Albuquerque (PCL)	2	4	.333	2.67	1.12	55	0	0	0	13	12-15	60.2	54	19	18	6	14-2	44	.241
Major League totals (3 years)	0	1	.000	11.37	2.61	10	1	0	0	0	0-0	12.2	28	17	16	3	5-0	6	.424

CRUZ, DEIVI — SS

PERSONAL: Born November 6, 1972, in Nizao de Bani, Dominican Republic. ... 6-0/207. ... Bats right, throws right. ... Full name: Deivi Garcia Cruz. ... Name pronounced: DAY-vee. ... High school: Liceo Aliro Paulino Nizao (Dominican Republic).
TRANSACTIONS/CAREER NOTES: Signed as a non-drafted free agent by San Francisco Giants organization (April 23, 1993). ... Selected by Los Angeles Dodgers from Giants organization in Rule 5 major league draft (December 9, 1996). ... Traded by Dodgers with OF Juan Hernaiz to Detroit Tigers for 2B Jeff Berblinger (December 9, 1996). ... On disabled list (March 20-April 27, 1998); included rehabilitation assignments to Lakeland and Toledo. ... On disabled list (June 8-July 18, 2001); included rehabilitation assignment to Erie. ... Signed as a free agent by San Diego Padres (January 30, 2002). ... Signed as a free agent by Baltimore Orioles (December 15, 2002). ... Signed as a free agent by Tampa Bay Devil Rays organization (January 7, 2004). ... Released by Devil Rays (March 24, 2004). ... Signed by Giants organization (March 30, 2004). ... Traded by Giants to Washington Nationals for P Benjamin Cox (August 30, 2005).
2005 GAMES PLAYED BY POSITION (MLB): 2B—49, SS—24, 3B—5.

SCOUTING REPORT *Offense:* Cruz is a slashing-type hitter with a long stroke. Hits off his front foot but still makes very good contact. Doesn't have a very quick bat, yet covers the plate well. Will go with outside pitches and hit them to the opposite field. Is a better high-ball hitter. Rarely walks. Is much better against lefthanders than righthanders. Is not fast but is a solid baserunner. *Defense:* If Cruz can get to it, he'll catch it. Has very good hands. Gets into very good fielding position. Throws have good carry and are very accurate. *Outlook:* He isn't flashy, but this versatile veteran has value as a utility player. Can play both middle infield positions. Capable of hitting No. 2 in the batting order or in the lower third. *Grade 6.2*

DEIVI CRUZ'S HITTING ZONE

.379	.385	.091
.339	.464	.167
.167	.214	.250

LEFTY-RIGHTY SPLITS

vs.	Avg.	AB	H	2B	3B	HR	RBI	BB	SO	OBP	Slg.
L	.311	103	32	8	1	2	12	5	10	.343	.466
R	.236	157	37	3	0	3	8	6	24	.268	.312

Year Team (League)	Pos.	G	AB	R	H	2B	3B	HR	RBI	BB	SO	HBP	GDP	SB-CS	Avg.	OBP	SLG	OPS	E	Avg.
1993—Ariz. Giants (Ariz.)	1B-3B-SS	28	82	8	28	3	0	0	15	4	5	0	3	3-0	.341	.368	.378	.746	2	.972
1994—Ariz. Giants (Ariz.)	3B-SS	18	53	10	16	8	0	0	5	5	3	1	1	0-1	.302	.367	.453	.819	1	.980
1995—Burlington (Midw.)	2B-3B-SS	16	58	2	8	1	0	1	9	4	7	0	1	1-1	.138	.194	.207	.400	2	.969
—Bellingham (N'west)	2B-3B	64	223	32	66	17	0	3	28	19	21	0	5	6-3	.296	.348	.413	.761	10	.947
1996—Burlington (Midw.)	SS-3B	127	517	72	152	27	2	9	64	35	49	4	20	12-5	.294	.342	.406	.748	13	.979
1997—Detroit (A.L.)	SS	147	436	35	105	26	0	2	40	14	55	0	9	3-6	.241	.263	.314	.577	13	.979
1998—Lakeland (Fla. St.)	SS	2	9	0	0	0	0	0	0	0	0	0	0	0-0	.000	.000	.000	.000	0	1.000
—Toledo (Int'l)	SS	2	9	1	1	1	0	0	2	2	3	0	0	0-0	.111	.273	.222	.495	0	1.000
—Detroit (A.L.)	SS	135	454	52	118	22	3	5	45	13	55	3	11	3-4	.260	.288	.355	.639	11	.983

Year	Team (League)	Pos.	G	AB	R	H	2B	3B	HR	RBI	BB	SO	HBP	GDP	SB-CS	Avg.	OBP	SLG	OPS	E	Avg.
1999—	Detroit (A.L.)	SS	155	518	64	147	35	0	13	58	12	57	4	10	1-4	.284	.302	.427	.729	12	.983
2000—	Detroit (A.L.)	SS	156	583	68	176	46	5	10	82	13	43	4	25	1-4	.302	.318	.449	.767	13	.982
2001—	Detroit (A.L.)	SS-3B	110	414	39	106	28	1	7	52	17	46	4	13	4-1	.256	.291	.379	.670	17	.964
—	Erie (East.)	SS-3B	4	12	2	5	1	0	1	3	0	0	0	0	1-0	.417	.417	.750	1.167	1	.929
2002—	San Diego (N.L.)	SS-1B	151	514	49	135	28	2	7	47	22	58	3	20	2-3	.263	.294	.366	.660	15	.973
2003—	Baltimore (A.L.)	SS-DH	152	548	61	137	24	2	14	65	13	49	2	13	1-2	.250	.291	.378	.647	16	.975
2004—	Fresno (PCL)	SS-2B	12	42	5	13	3	0	1	6	3	2	0	1	0-0	.310	.348	.452	.800	1	.976
—	San Francisco (N.L.)	SS-2B-3B	127	397	46	116	30	2	7	55	17	32	3	11	1-3	.292	.322	.431	.752	8	.980
2005—	San Francisco (N.L.)	2B-3B-SS	81	209	26	56	10	1	5	19	10	31	0	5	0-1	.268	.347	.397	.698	3	.986
—	Washington (N.L.)	2B-SS	20	51	2	13	1	0	0	1	1	3	1	0	0-0	.255	.283	.275	.558	1	.986
American League totals (6 years)			855	2953	319	789	181	11	51	342	82	305	17	81	13-21	.267	.289	.388	.677	82	.979
National League totals (3 years)			379	1171	123	320	69	5	19	122	50	124	7	36	3-7	.273	.304	.389	.694	27	.978
Major League totals (9 years)			1234	4124	442	1109	250	16	70	464	132	429	24	117	16-28	.269	.293	.388	.682	109	.978

CRUZ, JACOB OF

PERSONAL: Born January 28, 1973, in Oxnard, Calif. ... 6-0/210. ... Bats left, throws left. ... High school: Channel Islands (Oxnard, Calif.). ... College: Arizona State.

TRANSACTIONS/CAREER NOTES: Selected by California Angels organization in 45th round of 1991 free-agent draft; did not sign. ... Selected by San Francisco Giants organization in supplemental round ("sandwich pick" between first and second round; 32nd pick overall) of free-agent draft (June 2, 1994); pick received as part of compensation for Texas Rangers signing Type A free-agent 1B Will Clark. ... Traded by Giants with P Steve Reed to Cleveland Indians for Ps Jose Mesa and Alvin Morman and IF Shawon Dunston (July 24, 1998). ... On disabled list (March 30-April 29 and August 3, 1999-remainder of season); included rehabilitation assignment to Buffalo. ... On disabled list (April 30, 2000-remainder of season). ... Traded by Indians to Colorado Rockies for C Josh Bard and OF Jody Gerut (June 2, 2001). ... On disabled list (July 17-August 17, 2001); included rehabilitation assignment to Colorado Springs. ... Released by Rockies (November 30, 2001). ... Signed by Detroit Tigers organization (December 21, 2001). ... On disabled list (June 1-18 and June 23, 2002-remainder of season); included rehabilitation assignment to Toledo. ... Released by Tigers (October 3, 2002). ... Signed by Cincinnati Reds organization (January 10, 2003).

2005 GAMES PLAYED BY POSITION (MLB): OF—20, 1B—5, DH—1.

SCOUTING REPORT Cruz shows good power in batting practice, but it doesn't transfer to games. Struggles to get good swings against lefthanders. Has a long swing and gets jammed by good fastballs. Lacks the speed and arm strength to play center field. Is best as a fifth outfielder.
Grade 5

JACOB CRUZ'S HITTING ZONE

.000	.000	.111
.083	.444	.185
.400	.250	.571

LEFTY-RIGHTY SPLITS

vs.	Avg.	AB	H	2B	3B	HR	RBI	BB	SO	OBP	Slg.
L	.400	10	4	2	0	0	4	1	5	.455	.600
R	.222	117	26	8	0	4	14	15	41	.313	.393

Year	Team (League)	Pos.	G	AB	R	H	2B	3B	HR	RBI	BB	SO	HBP	GDP	SB-CS	Avg.	OBP	SLG	OPS	E	Avg.
1994—	San Jose (Calif.)	OF	31	118	14	29	7	0	0	12	9	22	2	6	0-2	.246	.305	.305	.610	2	.957
1995—	Shreveport (Texas)	OF	127	458	88	136	33	1	13	77	57	72	8	15	9-8	.297	.383	.459	.841	1	.996
1996—	Phoenix (PCL)	OF-DH	121	435	60	124	26	4	7	75	62	77	10	16	5-9	.285	.378	.411	.790	3	.989
—	San Francisco (N.L.)	OF	33	77	10	18	3	0	3	10	12	24	2	2	0-1	.234	.352	.390	.741	1	.977
1997—	Phoenix (PCL)	OF-DH	127	493	97	178	45	3	12	95	64	64	3	11	18-3	.361	.434	.538	.971	8	.970
—	San Francisco (N.L.)	OF	16	25	3	4	1	0	0	3	3	4	0	3	0-0	.160	.241	.200	.441	1	.933
1998—	Fresno (PCL)	OF-DH	89	342	60	102	17	3	18	62	46	57	8	9	12-5	.298	.393	.523	.916	6	.963
—	San Francisco (N.L.)		3	3	0	0	0	0	0	0	0	2	0	0	0-0	.000	.000	.000	.000	0	...
—	Buffalo (Int'l)	OF	43	169	32	56	8	2	13	36	13	26	1	2	2-3	.331	.380	.633	1.014	4	.949
—	Cleveland (A.L.)		1	1	0	0	0	0	0	0	0	1	0	0	0-0	.000	.000	.000	.000	0	...
1999—	Buffalo (Int'l)	OF-DH	54	202	29	55	7	2	7	31	21	39	3	7	4-2	.272	.348	.431	.779	4	.953
—	Cleveland (A.L.)	OF-DH	32	88	14	29	5	1	3	17	5	13	1	4	0-2	.330	.368	.511	.880	0	1.000
2000—	Cleveland (A.L.)	OF	11	29	3	7	3	0	0	5	5	4	1	0	1-0	.241	.361	.345	.706	0	1.000
2001—	Cleveland (A.L.)	OF	28	68	12	15	4	0	3	11	5	23	3	4	1-0	.221	.303	.412	.714	1	.976
—	Colorado (N.L.)	OF	44	76	7	16	1	0	1	7	10	27	1	0	0-2	.211	.303	.263	.567	2	.931
—	Colo. Springs (PCL)	OF	20	86	18	28	5	2	6	25	1	23	1	2	1-0	.326	.337	.640	.977	0	1.000
2002—	Detroit (A.L.)	DH-OF-1B	35	88	12	24	3	1	2	6	13	20	3	3	3-1	.273	.377	.398	.775	1	.976
—	Toledo (Int'l)	OF	11	43	6	7	1	1	0	5	3	8	0	1	0-0	.163	.302	.233	.534	0	1.000
2003—	Louisville (Int'l)	OF-1B-DH	36	132	25	46	8	0	7	29	14	22	1	5	3-0	.348	.409	.568	.977	5	.953
2004—	Louisville (Int'l)	OF-1B-DH	17	54	12	17	4	0	3	7	10	10	0	2	0-0	.315	.415	.556	.971	0	1.000
—	Cincinnati (N.L.)	OF-1B-DH	96	147	22	33	8	0	3	28	16	43	4	0	0-0	.224	.317	.340	.658	0	1.000
2005—	Cincinnati (N.L.)	OF-1B-DH	110	127	12	30	10	0	4	18	16	46	1	0	0-0	.236	.324	.409	.734	0	1.000
American League totals (5 years)			107	274	41	75	15	2	8	39	28	61	8	9	4-5	.274	.354	.431	.784	2	.986
National League totals (6 years)			302	455	54	101	23	0	11	66	57	146	8	11	0-3	.222	.317	.345	.662	4	.976
Major League totals (9 years)			409	729	95	176	38	2	19	105	85	207	16	20	4-8	.241	.331	.377	.708	6	.981

CRUZ , JOSE OF

PERSONAL: Born April 19, 1974, in Arroyo, Puerto Rico. ... 6-0/210. ... Bats both, throws right. ... Full name: Jose Luis Cruz Jr.. ... High school: Bellaire (Houston). ... College: Rice. ... Son of Jose Cruz, coach, Houston Astros, and outfielder with three major league teams (1970-88); nephew of Hector Cruz, outfielder/third baseman with four major league teams (1973, 1975-82); nephew of Tommy Cruz, outfielder with two major league teams (1973-77).

TRANSACTIONS/CAREER NOTES: Selected by Atlanta Braves organization in 15th round of 1992 free-agent draft; did not sign. ... Selected by Seattle Mariners organization in first round (third pick overall) of 1995 free-agent draft. ... Traded by Mariners to Toronto Blue Jays for Ps Mike Timlin and Paul Spoljaric (July 31, 1997). ... On disabled list (June 24-July 9, 1999); included rehabilitation assignment to Syracuse. ... On disabled list (May 6-21, 2001; and August 10-September 15, 2002). ... Signed as a free agent by San Francisco Giants (January 28, 2003). ... Signed as a free agent by Tampa Bay Devil Rays (December 17, 2003). ... Traded by Devil Rays to Arizona Diamondbacks for P Casey Fossum (February 6, 2005). ... On disabled list (April 16-May 9, 2005); included rehabilitation assignment to Tucson. ... Traded by Diamondbacks to Boston Red Sox for P Kyle Bono and SS Kenny Perez (July 30, 2005). ... Claimed on waivers by Los Angeles Dodgers (August 9, 2005).

HONORS: Won N.L. Gold Glove as outfielder (2003).

2005 GAMES PLAYED BY POSITION (MLB): OF—107.

C

SCOUTING REPORT

Offense: Cruz has power but also a lot of holes in his swing. Is vulnerable to off-speed pitches. Hits around the ball more often than not. Has more power from the left side than the right. Chases high fastballs when behind in the count. Strikes out too much, especially with runners in scoring position. Is a good runner but no longer is a real basestealer. **Defense:** Cruz has good range and the speed to close on the ball in the gaps. Gets better jumps coming in than going back. Has arm strength but occasionally throws to the wrong base. **Outlook:** Cruz should be a much better player than he has showed. Has good tools but can be careless or inconsistent. **Grade 5.9**

JOSE CRUZ 'S HITTING ZONE

.111	.385	.314
.388	.357	.296
.160	.231	.184

LEFTY-RIGHTY SPLITS

vs.	Avg.	AB	H	2B	3B	HR	RBI	BB	SO	OBP	Slg.
L	.325	80	26	7	0	3	11	14	16	.426	.525
R	.231	290	67	17	2	15	39	52	85	.347	.459

Year	Team (League)	Pos.	G	AB	R	H	2B	3B	HR	RBI	BB	SO	HBP	GDP	SB-CS	Avg.	OBP	SLG	OPS	E	Avg.
1995—	Everett (N'west)	OF	3	11	6	5	0	0	0	2	3	3	0	0	1-0	.455	.571	.455	1.026	0	1.000
	— Riverside (Calif.)	OF	35	144	34	37	7	1	7	29	24	50	0	1	3-1	.257	.359	.465	.824	3	.961
1996—	Lancaster (Calif.)	OF-DH	53	203	38	66	17	1	6	43	39	33	0	4	7-1	.325	.423	.507	.931	1	.986
	— Port City (Sou.)	OF-DH	47	181	39	51	10	2	3	31	27	38	0	8	5-0	.282	.373	.409	.782	1	.990
	— Tacoma (PCL)	OF	22	76	15	18	1	2	6	15	18	12	0	1	1-1	.237	.383	.539	.922	0	1.000
1997—	Tacoma (PCL)	OF-DH	50	190	33	51	16	2	6	30	34	44	1	4	3-0	.268	.382	.468	.851	0	1.000
	— Seattle (A.L.)	OF	49	183	28	49	12	1	12	34	13	45	0	3	1-0	.268	.315	.541	.856	3	.966
	— Toronto (A.L.)	OF	55	212	31	49	7	0	14	34	28	72	0	2	6-2	.231	.316	.462	.778	2	.981
1998—	Toronto (A.L.)	OF	105	352	55	89	14	3	11	42	57	99	0	0	11-4	.253	.354	.403	.757	4	.985
	— Syracuse (Int'l)	OF	40	141	29	42	14	1	7	23	32	32	0	2	8-4	.298	.425	.560	.986	1	.991
1999—	Toronto (A.L.)	OF	106	349	63	84	19	3	14	45	64	91	0	6	14-4	.241	.358	.433	.791	3	.990
	— Syracuse (Int'l)	OF-DH	31	103	17	19	3	1	3	14	28	20	0	3	5-0	.184	.356	.320	.676	0	1.000
2000—	Toronto (A.L.)	OF	162	603	91	146	32	5	31	76	71	129	2	11	15-5	.242	.323	.466	.789	3	.993
2001—	Toronto (A.L.)	OF-DH	146	577	92	158	38	4	34	88	45	138	1	8	32-5	.274	.326	.530	.857	3	.990
2002—	Toronto (A.L.)	OF-DH	124	466	64	114	26	5	18	70	51	106	0	2	7-1	.245	.317	.438	.754	2	.992
2003—	San Francisco (N.L.)	OF	158	539	90	135	26	1	20	68	102	121	0	14	5-8	.250	.366	.414	.779	2	.994
2004—	Tampa Bay (A.L.)	OF	153	545	76	132	25	8	21	78	76	117	2	6	11-6	.242	.333	.433	.766	10	.970
2005—	Tucson (PCL)	OF	1	3	1	1	0	1	0	1	0	1	0	0	0-0	.333	.333	.667	1.000	0	1.000
	— Arizona (N.L.)	OF	64	202	23	43	9	0	12	28	42	54	0	6	0-1	.213	.347	.436	.783	2	1.000
	— Boston (A.L.)	OF	4	12	0	3	1	0	0	0	1	4	0	0	0-0	.250	.308	.333	.641	0	1.000
	— Los Angeles (N.L.)	OF	47	156	23	47	14	2	6	22	23	43	0	0	0-1	.301	.391	.532	.923	5	.954
American League totals (8 years)			904	3299	500	824	174	29	155	467	406	801	5	44	97-27	.250	.331	.460	.792	30	.985
National League totals (2 years)			269	897	136	225	49	3	38	118	167	218	0	24	5-10	.251	.366	.439	.805	9	.984
Major League totals (9 years)			1173	4196	636	1049	223	32	193	585	573	1019	5	68	102-37	.250	.338	.456	.795	39	.985

DIVISION SERIES RECORD

Year	Team (League)	Pos.	G	AB	R	H	2B	3B	HR	RBI	BB	SO	HBP	GDP	SB-CS	Avg.	OBP	SLG	OPS	E	Avg.
2003—	San Francisco (N.L.)	OF	4	11	0	0	0	0	0	1	2	4	0	0	0-0	.000	.154	.000	.154	1	.938

CRUZ, JUAN   P

PERSONAL: Born October 15, 1978, in Bonao, Dominican Republic. ... 6-2/165. ... Throws right, bats right. ... Full name: Juan Carlos Cruz. ... High school: Jallaco Bonao (Bonao, Dominican Republic).

TRANSACTIONS/CAREER NOTES: Signed as a non-drafted free agent by Chicago Cubs organization (July 4, 1997). ... On disabled list (August 10-25, 2002). ... Traded by Cubs with P Steve Smyth to Atlanta Braves for P Andy Pratt and IF Richard Lewis (March 25, 2004). ... Traded by Braves with P Dan Meyer and OF Charles Thomas to Oakland Athletics for P Tim Hudson (December 16, 2004).

CAREER HITTING: 8-for-47 (.170), 2 R, 1 2B, 1 3B, 0 HR, 2 RBI.

SCOUTING REPORT

Throws: Cruz's fastball range is 91-96. Throws his curveball at 80 and his slider from 86-88. **Tendencies:** There's nothing wrong with his stuff; his delivery is the problem. Has amazing arm strength and arm speed but consistently rushes and drops his hand under the ball, causing his pitches to flatten out. Slider is quick but flat. Doesn't have much command of the fastball. Needs to develop his curve for a change of speed. **Outlook:** The underachieving Cruz has the stuff to close but the poor mechanics and lack of command keep him back. Might not be able to handle heavy workload because of his slight build. **Grade 5.8**

JUAN CRUZ'S PITCHING ZONE

.333	.400	.286
.250	.462	.381
.444	.200	.000

LEFTY-RIGHTY SPLITS

vs.	Avg.	AB	H	2B	3B	HR	RBI	BB	SO	OBP	Slg.
L	.283	60	17	3	2	1	6	14	12	.423	.450
R	.296	71	21	2	1	4	15	8	22	.383	.521

Year	Team (League)	W	L	Pct.	ERA	WHIP	G	GS	CG	ShO	Hld.	Sv.-Opp.	IP	H	R	ER	HR	BB-IBB	SO	Avg.
1998—	Ariz. Cubs (Ariz.)	2	4	.333	6.10	1.81	12	6	0	0	...	0-...	41.1	61	48	28	2	14-0	36	.326
1999—	Eugene (Northwest)	5	6	.455	5.94	1.62	15	15	0	0	...	0-...	80.1	97	59	53	11	33-0	65	.297
2000—	Lansing (Midw.)	5	5	.500	3.28	1.41	17	17	2	1	...	0-...	96.0	75	50	35	6	60-0	106	.215
	— Daytona (Fla. St.)	3	0	1.000	3.25	1.08	8	7	1	0	...	0-...	44.1	30	22	16	5	18-0	54	.186
2001—	West Tenn (Sou.)	9	6	.600	4.01	1.38	23	23	0	0	...	0-...	121.1	107	56	54	6	60-0	137	.238
	— Chicago (N.L.)	3	1	.750	3.22	1.28	8	8	0	0	0	0-0	44.2	40	16	16	4	17-1	39	.244
2002—	Chicago (N.L.)	3	11	.214	3.98	1.47	45	9	0	0	3	1-4	97.1	84	56	43	11	59-4	81	.241
2003—	Iowa (PCL)	4	0	1.000	1.95	0.90	9	9	0	0	...	0-...	50.2	37	12	11	0	11-0	47	.207
	— Chicago (N.L.)	2	7	.222	6.05	1.54	25	6	0	0	1	0-1	61.0	66	44	41	7	28-0	65	.275
2004—	Atlanta (N.L.)	6	2	.750	2.75	1.24	50	0	0	0	2	0-0	72.0	59	24	22	7	30-1	70	.224
2005—	Oakland (A.L.)	0	3	.000	7.44	1.84	28	0	0	0	0	0-0	32.2	38	33	27	5	22-4	34	.290
	— Sacramento (PCL)	5	1	.833	1.05	1.84	13	13	0	0	...	0-0	75.0	51	23	20	4	28-0	90	.190
American League totals (1 year)		0	3	.000	7.44	1.84	28	0	0	0	0	0-0	32.2	38	33	27	5	22-4	34	.290
National League totals (4 years)		14	21	.400	3.99	1.39	128	23	0	0	6	1-5	275.0	249	140	122	29	134-6	255	.250
Major League totals (5 years)		14	24	.368	4.36	1.44	156	23	0	0	6	1-5	307.2	287	173	149	34	156-10	289	.250

Year Team (League)	W	L	Pct.	ERA	WHIP	G	GS	CG	ShO	Hld.	Sv.-Opp.	IP	H	R	ER	HR	BB-IBB	SO	Avg.
2003—Chicago (N.L.)	0	0	...	0.00	1.00	1	0	0	0	0	0-0	1.0	0	0	0	0	1-0	2	.000
2004—Atlanta (N.L.)	0	0	...	9.82	2.73	3	0	0	0	0	0-0	3.2	6	4	4	0	4-0	4	.353
Division series totals (2 years)	0	0	...	7.71	2.36	4	0	0	0	0	0-0	4.2	6	4	4	0	5-0	6	.300

CRUZ, NELSON — OF

PERSONAL: Born July 1, 1980, in Monte Cristi, Dominican Republic. ... 6-3/175. ... Bats right, throws right. ... Full name: Nelson Ramon Cruz.

TRANSACTIONS/CAREER NOTES: Signed as a non-drafted free agent by New York Mets organization (February 17, 1998). ... Traded by Mets to Oakland Athletics for SS Jorge Velandia (August 30, 2000). ... Traded by Athletics with P Justin Lehr to Milwaukee Brewers for IF Keith Ginter (December 15, 2004).

2005 GAMES PLAYED BY POSITION (MLB): OF—8.

LEFTY-RIGHTY SPLITS

vs.	Avg.	AB	H	2B	3B	HR	RBI	BB	SO	OBP	Slg.
L	.000	2	0	0	0	0	0	1	0	.333	.000
R	.333	3	1	1	0	0	0	1	0	.500	.667

								BATTING									FIELDING	
Year Team (League)	Pos.	G	AB	R	H	2B	3B	HR	RBI	BB	SO	HBP	GDP	SB-CS	Avg.	OBP	SLG	OPS	E	Avg.
1998—Dom. Mets (DSL)		30	70	10	19	0	0	1	13	7	21	3	1	6-0	.271	.363	.314	.677	...	...
1999—Dom. Mets (DSL)		35	90	7	18	4	1	0	11	6	21	1	1	6-1	.200	.255	.267	.522	...	...
— Dom. Mets 2 (DSL)		36	115	20	32	4	1	1	21	16	27	1	4	14-0	.278	.366	.357	.723	...	...
2000—Dom. Mets E (DSL)		69	259	60	91	14	4	15	80	33	56	8	5	17-4	.351	.434	.610	1.044	...	...
2001—Ariz. A's (Ariz.)	OF	23	88	11	22	3	1	3	16	4	29	0	1	6-3	.250	.283	.409	.692	0	1.000
2002—Vancouver (N'west)	OF	63	214	23	59	14	0	4	25	9	58	4	2	12-1	.276	.316	.397	.713	4	.961
2003—Kane Co. (Midw.)	OF	119	470	65	112	26	2	20	85	29	128	9	7	10-5	.238	.292	.430	.722	6	.979
2004—Modesto (California)	OF	66	261	54	90	27	1	11	52	24	73	4	2	8-4	.345	.407	.582	.989	3	.842
— Midland (Texas)	OF	67	262	51	82	14	2	14	45	26	69	1	4	8-3	.313	.377	.542	.919	4	.000
— Sacramento (PCL)	OF	4	13	4	3	1	0	1	2	1	7	0	0	0-0	.231	.286	.538	.824	0	...
2005—Huntsville (Sou.)	OF-DH	68	248	45	76	19	0	16	54	31	71	4	7	10-3	.306	.388	.577	.965	8	.967
— Nashville (PCL)	OF-DH	60	208	33	56	13	0	11	27	30	62	8	4	9-4	.269	.382	.490	.872	4	.933
— Milwaukee (N.L.)	OF	8	5	1	1	1	0	0	0	2	0	0	0	0-0	.200	.429	.400	.829	0	1.000
Major League totals (1 year)		8	5	1	1	1	0	0	0	2	0	0	0	0-0	.200	.429	.400	.829	0	1.000

CUDDYER, MICHAEL — 3B/2B

PERSONAL: Born March 27, 1979, in Norfolk, Va. ... 6-2/222. ... Bats right, throws right. ... Full name: Michael Brent Cuddyer. ... Name pronounced: cuh-DIE-er. ... High school: Great Bridge (Chesapeake, Va.).

TRANSACTIONS/CAREER NOTES: Selected by Minnesota Twins organization in first round (ninth pick overall) of 1997 free-agent draft. ... On disabled list (July 2-17, 2005); included rehabilitation assignment to Rochester.

2005 GAMES PLAYED BY POSITION (MLB): 3B—95, OF—20, 2B—11, 1B—8.

SCOUTING REPORT *Offense:* As one of the better athletes at this position, Cuddyer has a good stroke with decent bat speed. Has problems making contact. Likes the ball out over the plate, but is getting better at going to the opposite field with balls inside. Has problems recognizing breaking and off-speed pitches. Is an average runner with questionable instincts. Hasn't shown enough power to be a lock to start at third. *Defense:* Drafted as a shortstop, Cuddyer has successfully adjusted to third base. Has also played first and second base and outfield. Has good hands and has improved his reads and mobility. Occasionally is flat-footed but makes up for that with his strong arm. *Outlook:* His versatility is an asset, but he will have to improve his run production to play third regularly next season. *Grade 6.6*

MICHAEL CUDDYER'S HITTING ZONE

.269	.450	.258
.253	.341	.279
.238	.333	.333

LEFTY-RIGHTY SPLITS

vs.	Avg.	AB	H	2B	3B	HR	RBI	BB	SO	OBP	Slg.
L	.273	121	33	7	0	2	9	22	24	.382	.380
R	.259	301	78	18	3	10	33	19	69	.308	.439

								BATTING									FIELDING	
Year Team (League)	Pos.	G	AB	R	H	2B	3B	HR	RBI	BB	SO	HBP	GDP	SB-CS	Avg.	OBP	SLG	OPS	E	Avg.
1998—Fort Wayne (Midw.)	2B-SS	129	497	82	137	37	7	12	81	61	107	10	13	16-7	.276	.364	.451	.814	61	.907
1999—Fort Myers (FSL)	3B	130	466	87	139	24	4	16	82	76	91	10	20	14-4	.298	.403	.470	.873	28	.921
2000—New Britain (East.)	3B	138	490	72	129	30	8	6	61	55	93	12	16	5-4	.263	.351	.394	.745	34	.903
2001—New Britain (East.)	3B-1B-OF	141	509	95	153	36	3	30	87	75	106	6	6	5-9	.301	.395	.560	.955	28	.963
— Minnesota (A.L.)	1B-3B-DH	8	18	1	4	2	0	0	1	2	6	0	1	1-0	.222	.300	.333	.633	1	.975
2002—Edmonton (PCL)	OF-1B-3B	86	330	70	102	16	9	20	53	36	79	3	9	12-7	.309	.379	.594	.973	7	.970
— Minnesota (A.L.)	OF-3B-1B-DH	41	112	12	29	7	0	4	13	8	30	1	3	2-0	.259	.311	.429	.740	1	.990
2003—GC Twins (GCL)	DH-OF	2	5	1	4	0	0	1	3	1	0	1	0	0-1	.800	.857	1.400	2.257	0	1.000
— Rochester (Int'l)	OF-2B-DH																			
— Minnesota (A.L.)	3B-1B	53	186	25	57	17	0	3	34	25	49	1	4	5-4	.306	.381	.446	.827	1	.993
2004—Minnesota (A.L.)	OF-3B-1B DH-2B	35	102	14	25	1	3	4	8	12	19	0	6	1-1	.245	.325	.431	.756	1	.985
— Minnesota (A.L.)	2B-3B-OF 1B-DH	115	339	49	89	22	1	12	45	37	74	3	5	5-5	.263	.339	.440	.779	10	.968
2005—Rochester (Int'l)	3B-1B	3	9	1	1	0	0	0	0	3	1	0	0	2-0	.111	.333	.111	.444	0	1.000
— Minnesota (A.L.)	3B-OF-2B 1B	126	422	55	111	25	3	12	42	41	93	3	19	3-4	.263	.330	.422	.752	15	.959
Major League totals (5 years)		325	993	131	258	57	7	32	109	100	222	7	37	12-10	.260	.330	.428	.758	28	.968

Year Team (League)	Pos.	G	AB	R	H	2B	3B	HR	RBI	BB	SO	HBP	GDP	SB-CS	Avg.	OBP	SLG	OPS	E	Avg.
2002—Minnesota (A.L.)	OF	5	13	1	5	1	0	0	1	3	3	0	0	0-0	.385	.500	.462	.962	0	1.000
2003—Minnesota (A.L.)	DH	1	4	0	1	0	0	0	0	0	3	0	0	0-0	.250	.250	.250	.500	0	...
2004—Minnesota (A.L.)	2B-1B	4	15	1	7	0	0	0	2	0	3	0	0	0-2	.467	.467	.467	.933	0	1.000
Division series totals (3 years)		10	32	2	13	1	0	0	3	3	9	0	0	0-2	.406	.457	.438	.895	0	1.000

Year Team (League)	Pos.	G	AB	R	H	2B	3B	HR	RBI	BB	SO	HBP	GDP	SB-CS	Avg.	OBP	SLG	OPS	E	Avg.
2002—Minnesota (A.L.)	OF	3	5	0	1	0	0	0	0	1	1	0	0	0-0	.200	.333	.200	.533	0	1.000

C

CUMMINGS, MIDRE — OF

PERSONAL: Born October 14, 1971, in St. Croix, Virgin Islands. ... 6-0/195. ... Bats left, throws right. ... Full name: Midre Almeric Cummings. ... Name pronounced: MEE-dray. ... High school: Miami Edison Senior (Miami).

TRANSACTIONS/CAREER NOTES: Selected by Minnesota Twins organization in supplemental round ("sandwich pick" between first and second round, 29th pick overall) of 1990 free-agent draft; pick received as part of compensation for Boston Red Sox signing Type A free-agent P Jeff Reardon. ... Traded by Twins with P Denny Neagle to Pittsburgh Pirates for P John Smiley (March 17, 1992). ... Claimed on waivers by Philadelphia Phillies (July 8, 1997). ... Released by Phillies (February 24, 1998). ... Signed by Cincinnati Reds organization (February 27, 1998). ... Claimed on waivers by Boston Red Sox (March 19, 1998). ... On disabled list (July 29-September 7, 1998). ... Released by Red Sox (March 30, 1999). ... Signed by Twins organization (May 14, 1999). ... Traded by Twins to Red Sox for IF Hector De Los Santos (August 31, 2000). ... Signed as a free agent by Arizona Diamondbacks organization (December 15, 2000). ... Signed as a free agent by Milwaukee Brewers organization (February 8, 2002). ... Signed as a free agent by Chicago Cubs organization (January 13, 2003). ... Signed as a free agent by Tampa Bay Devil Rays organization (February 13, 2004). ... Released by Devil Rays (October 13, 2004). ... Signed as a free agent by Baltimore Orioles organization (January 18, 2005).

2005 GAMES PLAYED BY POSITION (MLB): OF—1.

LEFTY-RIGHTY SPLITS

vs.	Avg.	AB	H	2B	3B	HR	RBI	BB	SO	OBP	Slg.
L	.000	0	0	0	0	0	0	0	0	.000	.000
R	.000	2	0	0	0	0	0	0	1	.000	.000

									BATTING								FIELDING	
Year Team (League)	Pos.	G	AB	R	H	2B	3B	HR	RBI	BB	SO	HBP	GDP	SB-CS	Avg.	OBP	SLG	OPS	E	Avg.
1990—GC Twins (GCL)	OF	47	177	28	56	3	4	5	28	13	32	2	1	14-9	.316	.362	.463	.826	6	.926
1991—Kenosha (Midw.)	OF	106	382	59	123	20	4	4	54	22	66	6	7	28-10	.322	.367	.427	.793	• 13	.930
1992—Salem (Carol.)	OF	113	420	55	128	20	5	14	75	35	67	4	2	23-9	.305	.361	.476	.838	6	.964
1993—Carolina (Southern)	OF	63	237	33	70	17	2	6	24	14	23	1	3	5-3	.295	.337	.460	.797	4	.964
—Buffalo (A.A.)	OF	60	232	36	64	12	1	9	21	22	45	0	4	5-1	.276	.336	.453	.789	2	.978
—Pittsburgh (N.L.)	OF	13	36	5	4	1	0	0	3	4	9	0	1	0-0	.111	.200	.139	.339	0	1.000
1994—Buffalo (A.A.)	OF	49	183	23	57	12	4	2	22	13	26	2	11	5-0	.311	.360	.454	.814	0	1.000
—Pittsburgh (N.L.)	OF	24	86	11	21	4	0	1	12	4	18	1	0	0-0	.244	.278	.326	.603	2	.962
1995—Pittsburgh (N.L.)	OF	59	152	13	37	7	1	2	15	13	30	0	1	1-0	.243	.303	.342	.645	1	.988
—Calgary (PCL)	OF	45	159	19	44	9	1	1	16	6	27	2	1	1-1	.277	.302	.365	.667	6	.943
1996—Calgary (PCL)	OF-DH	97	368	60	112	24	3	8	55	21	60	1	6	6-4	.304	.341	.451	.792	5	.974
—Pittsburgh (N.L.)	OF	24	85	11	19	3	1	3	7	0	16	0	0	0-0	.224	.224	.388	.612	1	.980
1997—Pittsburgh (N.L.)	OF	52	106	11	20	6	2	3	8	8	26	1	1	0-0	.189	.246	.368	.614	0	1.000
—Philadelphia (N.L.)	OF	63	208	24	63	16	4	1	23	23	30	0	2	2-3	.303	.372	.433	.805	1	.991
1998—Boston (A.L.)	DH-OF	67	120	20	34	8	0	5	15	17	19	2	2	3-3	.283	.372	.475	.847	1	.941
1999—New Britain (East.)	OF	24	93	28	35	7	0	2	15	17	14	2	1	3-1	.376	.474	.516	.990	0	1.000
—Salt Lake (PCL)	OF	69	261	50	84	19	4	13	68	23	43	3	5	4-4	.322	.382	.575	.957	5	.954
—Minnesota (A.L.)	DH-OF	16	38	1	10	0	0	1	9	3	7	0	0	2-0	.263	.310	.342	.652	0	1.000
2000—Minnesota (A.L.)	OF-DH	77	181	28	50	10	0	4	22	11	25	3	4	0-0	.276	.328	.398	.726	0	1.000
—Boston (A.L.)	OF-DH	21	25	1	7	0	0	0	2	6	3	0	1	0-0	.280	.419	.280	.699	0	1.000
2001—Arizona (N.L.)	OF	20	20	1	6	1	0	0	1	0	4	0	2	0-0	.300	.286	.350	.636	0	1.000
—Tucson (PCL)	OF-1B	77	263	38	87	23	5	8	38	24	49	0	4	2-3	.331	.383	.544	.926	2	.985
2002—Indianapolis (Int'l)	OF	11	39	7	12	2	0	3	8	2	4	0	2	1-1	.308	.341	.590	.931	0	1.000
2003—Iowa (PCL)	OF-DH	114	385	53	98	22	2	19	54	40	86	4	10	1-3	.255	.328	.470	.798	2	.987
2004—Durham (Int'l)	DH-OF-1B	119	414	83	118	26	3	27	89	86	107	3	6	13-2	.285	.408	.558	.966	1	.983
—Tampa Bay (A.L.)	DH-OF	22	54	10	15	4	0	2	7	5	12	2	0	0-0	.278	.361	.463	.824	0	1.000
2005—Baltimore (A.L.)	OF	2	2	0	0	0	0	0	0	0	1	0	0	0-0	.000	.000	.000	.000	0	...
—Ottawa (Int'l)	OF-DH	74	264	39	75	14	0	12	40	36	69	4	3	0-1	.284	.372	.473	.846	4	.981
American League totals (5 years)		205	420	60	116	22	0	15	55	42	67	7	7	6-3	.276	.351	.414	.765	1	.989
National League totals (6 years)		255	693	76	170	38	8	10	69	52	133	2	7	3-3	.245	.297	.367	.664	5	.986
Major League totals (11 years)		460	1113	136	286	60	8	22	124	94	200	9	14	9-6	.257	.318	.385	.703	6	.987

DIVISION SERIES RECORD

									BATTING											
Year Team (League)	Pos.	G	AB	R	H	2B	3B	HR	RBI	BB	SO	HBP	GDP	SB-CS	Avg.	OBP	SLG	OPS	E	Avg.
1998—Boston (A.L.)		3	3	0	0	0	0	0	0	0	0	0	0	0-0	.000	.000	.000	.000	...	...
2001—Arizona (N.L.)		2	0	1	0	0	0	0	0	0	0	0	0	0-1	...	...	...	...	...	...
Division series totals (2 years)		5	3	1	0	0	0	0	0	0	0	0	0	0-1	.000	.000	.000	.000	...	...

CHAMPIONSHIP SERIES RECORD

									BATTING											
Year Team (League)	Pos.	G	AB	R	H	2B	3B	HR	RBI	BB	SO	HBP	GDP	SB-CS	Avg.	OBP	SLG	OPS	E	Avg.
2001—Arizona (N.L.)		1	1	0	0	0	0	0	0	0	0	0	0	0-0	.000	.000	.000	.000	...	...

WORLD SERIES RECORD

									BATTING											
Year Team (League)	Pos.	G	AB	R	H	2B	3B	HR	RBI	BB	SO	HBP	GDP	SB-CS	Avg.	OBP	SLG	OPS	E	Avg.
2001—Arizona (N.L.)	DH	2	0	2	0	0	0	0	0	0	0	0	0	0-0	...	...	...	...	...	...

DALLIMORE, BRIAN — 2B/3B

PERSONAL: Born November 15, 1973, in Las Vegas. ... 6-1/180. ... Bats right, throws right. ... Full name: Brian Scott Dallimore. ... High school: Clark (Las Vegas). ... College: Stanford.

TRANSACTIONS/CAREER NOTES: Selected by Florida Marlins organization in 37th round of 1995 free-agent draft; did not sign. ... Selected by Houston Astros organization in ninth round of 1996 free-agent draft. ... Traded by Astros to Arizona Diamondbacks for C Joshua McAfee (April 20, 2000). ... Signed as a free agent by San Francisco Giants organization (December 16, 2002).

2005 GAMES PLAYED BY POSITION (MLB): 2B—2, SS—1.

LEFTY-RIGHTY SPLITS

vs.	Avg.	AB	H	2B	3B	HR	RBI	BB	SO	OBP	Slg.
L	.167	6	1	1	0	0	0	0	0	.167	.333
R	.000	1	0	0	0	0	0	0	0	.000	.000

									BATTING								FIELDING	
Year Team (League)	Pos.	G	AB	R	H	2B	3B	HR	RBI	BB	SO	HBP	GDP	SB-CS	Avg.	OBP	SLG	OPS	E	Avg.
1996—Auburn (NY-Penn)	3B-2B-SS	74	290	50	77	17	3	5	30	18	38	10	5	7-5	.266	.326	.397	.723	24	.911
1997—Quad City (Midw.)	SS-3B-2B	130	492	80	128	23	3	6	48	38	76	20	19	24-8	.260	.335	.356	.691	46	.915
—Kissimmee (Fla. St.)	2B	1	3	0	0	0	0	0	0	0	0	0	0	0-0	.000	.000	.000	.000	0	1.000
1998—Kissimmee (Fla. St.)	3B-2B	62	240	34	61	11	1	0	19	19	42	5	6	7-5	.254	.321	.308	.629	9	.958
1999—Kissimmee (Fla. St.)	2B-3B-OF	19	74	12	20	2	0	0	3	4	10	3	1	2-1	.270	.329	.297	.627	6	.910
—Jackson (Texas)	2B-OF-3B																			
	SS	70	251	38	67	13	1	5	19	16	44	10	12	13-3	.267	.335	.386	.721	15	.943
2000—Round Rock (Texas)	SS	5	11	3	2	1	0	1	3	1	3	0	0	0-0	.182	.250	.545	.795	2	.667
—El Paso (Texas)	3B-2B-SS																			
	OF	107	356	50	99	16	1	4	53	25	55	6	13	17-3	.278	.332	.362	.694	22	.936

C

Year	Team (League)	Pos.	G	AB	R	H	2B	3B	HR	RBI	BB	SO	HBP	GDP	SB-CS	Avg.	OBP	SLG	OPS	E	Avg.
2001—El Paso (Texas)		3B-2B	127	517	74	169	38	6	8	67	30	56	13	9	11-13	.327	.378	.470	.848	25	.939
2002—Tucson (PCL)		3B-2B-OF-SS	122	419	62	123	26	2	6	50	28	72	9	10	13-4	.294	.346	.408	.754	13	.958
2003—Fresno (PCL)		2B-3B-OF	91	330	53	116	16	2	4	46	37	37	10	6	6-4	.352	.427	.448	.875	10	.975
2004—Fresno (PCL)		2B-3B-SS-OF-DH	111	432	72	140	21	4	8	67	40	53	15	13	9-2	.324	.396	.447	.842	15	.967
—San Francisco (N.L.)		2B-3B	20	43	8	12	2	0	1	7	4	7	1	0	0-1	.279	.347	.395	.742	2	.950
2005—San Francisco (N.L.)		2B-SS	7	7	1	1	0	0	0	0	0	0		1	0-0	.143	.143	.286	.429	0	1.000
—Fresno (PCL)		3B-2B-SS-1B	100	398	67	120	26	2	8	45	32	43	12	14	7-2	.302	.369	.437	.807	13	.966
Major League totals (2 years)			27	50	9	13	3	0	1	7	4	7	1	1	0-1	.260	.321	.380	.701	2	.957

DAMON, JOHNNY — OF

PERSONAL: Born November 5, 1973, in Fort Riley, Kan. ... 6-2/190. ... Bats left, throws left. ... Full name: Johnny David Damon. ... Name pronounced: DAY-mun. ... High school: Dr. Phillips (Orlando).

TRANSACTIONS/CAREER NOTES: Selected by Kansas City Royals organization in supplemental round ("sandwich pick" between first and second round, 35th pick overall) of 1992 free-agent draft; pick received as part of compensation for San Diego Padres signing Type A free-agent IF Kurt Stillwell. ... On suspended list (September 5-7, 1997). ... Traded by Royals with IF Mark Ellis and a player to be named to Oakland Athletics as part of three-team deal in which Royals acquired P Roberto Hernandez and A's acquired P Cory Lidle from Tampa Bay Devil Rays, Royals acquired C A.J. Hinch, IF Angel Berroa and cash from A's and Devil Rays acquired OF Ben Grieve and cash from A's (January 8, 2001). ... Signed as a free agent by Boston Red Sox (December 21, 2001).

RECORDS: Shares major league record for most doubles, game (4, July 18, 2000).

2005 GAMES PLAYED BY POSITION (MLB): OF—147, DH—1.

SCOUTING REPORT *Offense:* Damon is a catalyst at the top of the order. Has an unorthodox approach; hits with a sweeping swing and pulls off the ball, yet has good plate coverage and bat speed. Hits down on the ball to achieve the backspin that produces carry. Is deceptively strong with good pulling power. Will break more bats than any player; often gets out front and takes his top hand off the bat. Is a plus runner with good basestealing instincts. *Defense:* He is inconsistent with his jumps, but has good closing speed to balls in the gap. Occasionally will get beat directly over his head. Throwing mechanics are poor. *Outlook:* Damon brings speed, power and the ability to use the whole field to the leadoff spot. Had an injury to his throwing shoulder that slowed him in 2005. *Grade 8.9*

JOHNNY DAMON'S HITTING ZONE

.257	.304	.290
.309	.511	.274
.262	.387	.473

LEFTY-RIGHTY SPLITS

vs.	Avg.	AB	H	2B	3B	HR	RBI	BB	SO	OBP	Slg.
L	.327	208	68	13	2	2	30	19	32	.377	.438
R	.310	416	129	22	4	8	45	34	37	.361	.440

Year	Team (League)	Pos.	G	AB	R	H	2B	3B	HR	RBI	BB	SO	HBP	GDP	SB-CS	Avg.	OBP	SLG	OPS	E	Avg.
1992—GC Royals (GCL)		OF	50	192	58	67	12	9	4	24	31	21	4	1	33-6	.349	.449	.568	1.017	1	.988
—Baseball City (FSL)		OF	1	1	0	0	0	0	0	0	0	0	0	0	0-0	.000	.000	.000	.000	0	...
1993—Rockford (Midwest)		OF	127	511	82	148	25	13	5	50	52	83	6	4	59-18	.290	.360	.419	.779	6	.977
1994—Wilmington (Caro.)		OF	119	472	96	149	25	13	6	75	62	55	8	4	44-9	.316	.399	.462	.861	3	.989
1995—Wichita (Texas)		OF-DH	111	423	83	145	15	9	16	54	67	35	2	4	26-15	.343 *	.434	.534	.968	5	.984
—Kansas City (A.L.)		OF	47	188	32	53	11	5	3	23	12	22	1	2	7-0	.282	.324	.441	.765	1	.991
1996—Kansas City (A.L.)		OF-DH	145	517	61	140	22	5	6	50	31	64	3	4	25-5	.271	.313	.368	.680	6	.983
1997—Kansas City (A.L.)		OF-DH	146	472	70	130	12	8	8	48	42	70	3	3	16-10	.275	.338	.386	.723	4	.988
1998—Kansas City (A.L.)		OF	161	642	104	178	30	10	18	66	58	84	4	4	26-12	.277	.339	.439	.779	4	.990
1999—Kansas City (A.L.)		OF-DH	145	583	101	179	39	9	14	77	67	50	3	13	36-6	.307	.379	.477	.856	4	.987
2000—Kansas City (A.L.)		OF-DH	159	655	*136	214	42	10	16	88	65	60	1	7	*46-9	.327	.382	.495	.877	5	.986
2001—Oakland (A.L.)		OF-DH	155	644	108	165	34	4	9	49	61	70	5	7	27-12	.256	.324	.363	.687	3	.991
2002—Boston (A.L.)		OF-DH	154	623	118	178	34	*11	14	63	65	70	6	4	31-6	.286	.356	.443	.799	1	.997
2003—Boston (A.L.)		OF-DH	145	608	103	166	32	6	12	67	68	74	2	5	30-6	.273	.345	.405	.750	1	.997
2004—Boston (A.L.)		OF-DH	150	621	123	189	35	6	20	94	76	71	2	8	19-8	.304	.380	.477	.857	5	.986
2005—Boston (A.L.)		OF-DH	148	624	117	197	35	6	10	75	53	69	2	5	18-1	.316	.366	.439	.805	6	.985
Major League totals (11 years)			1555	6177	1073	1789	326	80	130	700	598	704	32	62	281-75	.290	.353	.431	.784	40	.989

DIVISION SERIES RECORD

Year	Team (League)	Pos.	G	AB	R	H	2B	3B	HR	RBI	BB	SO	HBP	GDP	SB-CS	Avg.	OBP	SLG	OPS	E	Avg.
2001—Oakland (A.L.)		OF	5	22	3	9	2	1	0	0	1	1	0	0	2-0	.409	.435	.591	1.026	0	1.000
2003—Boston (A.L.)		OF	5	19	2	6	2	0	1	3	2	1	1	1	2-0	.316	.409	.579	.988	0	1.000
2004—Boston (A.L.)		OF	3	15	4	7	1	0	0	0	1	2	0	0	3-0	.467	.500	.533	1.033	0	1.000
2005—Boston (A.L.)		OF	3	13	2	3	1	0	0	0	1	4	0	1	0-0	.231	.286	.308	.593	0	1.000
Division series totals (4 years)			16	69	11	25	6	1	1	3	5	8	1	2	7-0	.362	.413	.522	.935	0	1.000

CHAMPIONSHIP SERIES RECORD

Year	Team (League)	Pos.	G	AB	R	H	2B	3B	HR	RBI	BB	SO	HBP	GDP	SB-CS	Avg.	OBP	SLG	OPS	E	Avg.
2003—Boston (A.L.)		OF	5	20	1	4	1	0	0	1	3	3	0	1	1-0	.200	.304	.250	.554	0	1.000
2004—Boston (A.L.)		OF	7	35	5	6	0	0	2	7	2	8	0	1	2-1	.171	.216	.343	.559	0	1.000
Champ. series totals (2 years)			12	55	6	10	1	0	2	8	5	11	0	2	3-1	.182	.250	.309	.559	0	1.000

WORLD SERIES RECORD

Year	Team (League)	Pos.	G	AB	R	H	2B	3B	HR	RBI	BB	SO	HBP	GDP	SB-CS	Avg.	OBP	SLG	OPS	E	Avg.
2004—Boston (A.L.)		OF	4	21	4	6	2	1	1	2	0	1	0	1	0-0	.286	.286	.619	.905	0	1.000

ALL-STAR GAME RECORD

		G	AB	R	H	2B	3B	HR	RBI	BB	SO	HBP	GDP	SB-CS	Avg.	OBP	SLG	OPS	E	Avg.
All-Star Game totals (2 years)		2	5	2	2	0	0	0	0	0	1	0	0	1-0	.400	.400	.400	.800	0	1.000

DARENSBOURG, VIC — P

PERSONAL: Born November 13, 1970, in Los Angeles. ... 5-10/180. ... Throws left, bats left. ... Full name: Victor Anthony Darensbourg. ... Name pronounced: darens-berg. ... High school: Westchester (Los Angeles). ... College: Lewis-Clark State (Lewiston, Idaho).
TRANSACTIONS/CAREER NOTES: Signed as a non-drafted free agent by Florida Marlins organization (June 11, 1992). ... On disabled list (August 20-September 17, 2001). ... Traded by Marlins with C Charles Johnson, OF Preston Wilson and 2B Pablo Ozuna to Colorado Rockies for P Mike Hampton, OF Juan Pierre and cash (November 16, 2002). ... Released by Rockies (July 10, 2003). ... Signed by Montreal Expos organization (July 28, 2003). ... Signed as a free agent by Chicago White Sox organization (January 6, 2004). ... Released by White Sox (June 30, 2004). ... Signed by New York Mets organization (July 15, 2004). ... Signed as a free agent by Detroit Tigers organization (February 8, 2005).
CAREER HITTING: 2-for-18 (.111), 0 R, 0 2B, 0 3B, 0 HR, 0 RBI.

VIC DARENSBOURG'S PITCHING ZONE

.250	.000	.167
.381	.000	.500
.300	.250	.250

LEFTY-RIGHTY SPLITS

vs.	Avg.	AB	H	2B	3B	HR	RBI	BB	SO	OBP	Slg.
L	.231	39	9	1	0	1	5	2	6	.262	.333
R	.326	46	15	4	0	1	4	5	3	.385	.478

Year — Team (League)	W	L	Pct.	ERA	WHIP	G	GS	CG	ShO	Hld.	Sv.-Opp.	IP	H	R	ER	HR	BB-IBB	SO	Avg.
1992— GC Marlins (GCL)	2	1	.667	0.64	0.93	8	4	0	0	...	2-...	42.0	28	5	3	1	11-2	37	.190
1993— Kane Co. (Midw.)	9	1	.900	2.14	1.21	46	0	0	0	...	16-...	71.1	58	17	17	3	28-3	89	.221
— High Desert (Calif.)	0	0	...	0.00	0.00	1	0	0	0	...	0-...	1.0	0	0	0	0	0-0	1	.000
1994— Portland (East.)	10	7	.588	3.81	1.38	35	21	1	1	...	4-...	149.0	146	76	63	18	60-3	103	.264
1995— Florida (N.L.)		Did not play.																	
1996— Brevard County (FSL)	0	0	...	0.00	0.67	2	0	0	0	...	0-...	3.0	1	0	0	0	1-0	5	.111
— Charlotte (Int'l)	1	5	.167	3.69	1.47	47	0	0	0	...	7-...	63.1	61	30	26	7	32-3	66	.253
1997— Charlotte (Int'l)	4	2	.667	4.38	1.50	27	0	0	0	...	2-...	24.2	22	12	12	4	15-3	21	.242
1998— Florida (N.L.)	0	7	.000	3.68	1.15	59	0	0	0	13	1-2	71.0	52	29	29	5	30-6	74	.207
1999— Florida (N.L.)	0	1	.000	8.83	2.05	56	0	0	0	10	0-1	34.2	50	36	34	7	21-1	16	.340
— Calgary (PCL)	0	0	...	4.63	1.11	9	0	0	0	...	1-...	11.2	13	6	6	0	0-0	12	.289
2000— Florida (N.L.)	5	3	.625	4.06	1.44	56	0	0	0	3	0-1	62.0	61	32	28	7	28-1	59	.260
2001— Florida (N.L.)	1	2	.333	4.25	1.27	58	0	0	0	11	1-3	48.2	52	24	23	4	10-6	33	.277
2002— Florida (N.L.)	1	2	.333	6.14	1.80	42	0	0	0	3	0-0	48.1	61	34	33	10	26-4	33	.305
2003— Colorado (N.L.)	0	0	...	0.00	1.71	3	0	0	0	0	0-...	2.1	4	1	0	0	0-0	0	.333
— Colo. Springs (PCL)	2	2	.500	3.57	1.30	20	0	0	0	...	0-...	22.2	24	13	9	1	5-1	15	.273
— Edmonton (PCL)	1	1	.500	1.98	1.40	11	0	0	0	...	0-...	13.2	12	3	3	0	7-0	11	.235
— Montreal (N.L.)	0	0	...	10.80	2.10	6	0	0	0	0	0-...	6.2	13	8	8	2	1-0	4	.406
2004— Charlotte (Int'l)	3	3	.500	2.64	1.11	24	0	0	0	...	0-...	30.2	25	10	9	1	9-2	33	.229
— Chicago (A.L.)	0	0	...	0.00	1.50	2	0	0	0	0	0-...	1.1	1	0	0	0	1-0	0	.333
— Norfolk (Int'l)	1	1	.500	3.18	1.10	18	0	0	0	...	0-...	22.2	13	9	8	1	12-2	21	.169
— New York (N.L.)	0	1	.000	7.94	2.12	5	0	0	0	0	0-...	5.2	10	5	5	1	2-0	1	.435
2005— Toledo (Int'l)	2	0	1.000	0.29	0.91	44	0	0	0	12	7-8	30.2	17	3	1	0	11-1	30	.172
— Detroit (A.L.)	1	1	.500	2.82	1.39	22	0	0	0	1	0-0	22.1	24	7	7	2	7-2	9	.282
American League totals (2 years)	1	1	.500	2.66	1.39	24	0	0	0	1	0-0	23.2	25	7	7	2	8-2	9	.284
National League totals (7 years)	7	16	.304	5.16	1.51	285	0	0	0	40	2-7	279.1	303	169	160	32	118-18	220	.278
Major League totals (8 years)	8	17	.320	4.96	1.50	309	0	0	0	41	2-7	303.0	328	176	167	34	126-20	229	.279

DAUBACH, BRIAN — 1B/OF

PERSONAL: Born February 11, 1972, in Belleville, Ill. ... 6-1/230. ... Bats left, throws right. ... Full name: Brian Michael Daubach. ... Name pronounced: DAW-back. ... High school: Belleville (Ill.) West.
TRANSACTIONS/CAREER NOTES: Selected by New York Mets organization in 17th round of 1990 free-agent draft. ... Signed as a free agent by Florida Marlins organization (November 7, 1996). ... Released by Marlins (November 19, 1998). ... Signed by Boston Red Sox organization (December 18, 1998). ... On disabled list (August 15-September 2, 2001); included rehabilitation assignments to Pawtucket and Lowell. ... Signed as a free agent by Chicago White Sox organization (January 27, 2003). ... Released by White Sox (December 10, 2003). ... Signed by Red Sox organization (December 28, 2003). ... Signed as a free agent by Mets organization (March 8, 2005).
2005 GAMES PLAYED BY POSITION (MLB): 1B—6, DH—2.

LEFTY-RIGHTY SPLITS

vs.	Avg.	AB	H	2B	3B	HR	RBI	BB	SO	OBP	Slg.
L	.250	4	1	1	0	0	0	0	0	.250	.500
R	.095	21	2	1	0	1	3	7	5	.333	.286

Year — Team (League)	Pos.	G	AB	R	H	2B	3B	HR	RBI	BB	SO	HBP	GDP	SB-CS	Avg.	OBP	SLG	OPS	E	Avg.
1990— GC Mets (GCL)	1B	45	152	26	41	8	4	1	19	22	41	2	2	2-1	.270	.363	.395	.758	7	.976
1991— Kingsport (Appalachian)	1B	65	218	30	53	9	1	7	42	33	64	6	1	1-3	.243	.355	.390	.745	9	.986
1992— Pittsfield (NYP)	1B	72	260	26	63	15	2	2	40	30	61	3	5	4-0	.242	.323	.338	.662	12	.982
1993— Capital City (SAL)	1B-OF	102	379	50	106	19	3	7	72	52	84	5	14	6-1	.280	.368	.401	.769	5	.989
1994— St. Lucie (Fla. St.)	1B	129	450	52	123	30	2	6	74	58	120	4	3	14-9	.273	.360	.389	.749	12	.991
1995— Binghamton (East.)	1B-3B	135	469	61	115	25	2	10	72	51	104	7	5	6-2	.245	.324	.371	.695	10	.992
— Norfolk (Int'l)	1B	2	7	0	1	0	0	0	0	1	0	0	0	0-0	.125	.000	.125	.125	0	1.000
1996— Binghamton (East.)	1B-3B	122	436	80	129	24	1	22	76	74	103	7	8	7-9	.296	.403	.507	.910	11	.991
— Norfolk (Int'l)	1B	17	54	7	11	2	0	0	6	6	14	0	1	1-1	.204	.279	.241	.519	0	1.000
1997— Charlotte (Int'l)	1B	136	461	66	128	40	2	21	93	65	126	6	7	1-8	.278	.367	.510	.877	8	.991
1998— Charlotte (Int'l)	1B-OF	140	497	102	157	45	4	35	124	80	114	15	15	9-3	.316	.421	.634	1.055	3	.992
— Florida (N.L.)	1B	10	15	0	3	1	0	0	3	1	5	1	0	0-0	.200	.294	.267	.561	0	1.000
1999— Boston (A.L.)	1B-DH-OF 3B	110	381	61	112	33	3	21	73	36	92	5	5	0-1	.294	.360	.562	.921	8	.983
— Pawtucket (Int'l)	DH-1B-OF	9	31	4	9	2	0	1	6	6	8	2	0	0-0	.290	.436	.452	.888	1	.971
2000— Boston (A.L.)	1B-DH-OF 3B	142	495	55	123	32	2	21	76	44	130	6	6	1-1	.248	.315	.448	.764	3	.996
2001— Boston (A.L.)	1B-DH-OF	122	407	54	107	28	3	22	71	53	108	5	10	1-0	.263	.350	.509	.859	11	.988
— Pawtucket (Int'l)	DH	1	4	0	1	0	0	0	0	0	2	0	0	0-0	.250	.250	.250	.500	...	...
— Lowell (NY-Penn)	1B	2	2	0	0	0	0	0	0	1	1	0	0	0-0	.000	.333	.000	.333	0	1.000
2002— Boston (A.L.)	1B-OF-DH	137	444	62	118	24	2	20	78	51	126	7	10	2-1	.266	.348	.464	.812	5	.991
2003— Chicago (A.L.)	1B-DH-OF	95	183	26	42	11	0	6	21	34	54	1	3	1-0	.230	.352	.388	.740	2	.993
2004— Boston (A.L.)	1B-OF	30	75	9	17	8	0	0	10	8	21	1	0	0-0	.227	.326	.413	.739	2	.983
— Pawtucket (Int'l)	1B-DH-OF 3B	93	336	63	92	23	0	21	81	71	93	3	0	0-1	.274	.403	.530	.933	5	.992

Year Team (League)	Pos.	G	AB	R	H	2B	3B	HR	RBI	BB	SO	HBP	GDP	SB-CS	Avg.	OBP	SLG	OPS	E	Avg.
2005— New York (N.L.) 1B-DH		15	25	4	3	2	0	1	3	7	5	1	2	0-0	.120	.324	.320	.644	1	.977
— Norfolk (Int'l) 1B-DH-OF		99	345	63	112	29	1	16	62	62	68	1	6	1-2	.325	.426	.554	.979	4	.994
American League totals (6 years)		636	1985	267	519	136	10	92	327	228	531	23	35	5-3	.261	.342	.479	.821	31	.990
National League totals (2 years)		25	40	4	6	3	0	1	6	8	10	2	2	0-0	.150	.314	.300	.614	1	.985
Major League totals (8 years)		661	2025	271	525	139	10	93	333	236	541	25	37	5-3	.259	.341	.476	.817	32	.990

DIVISION SERIES RECORD

Year Team (League)	Pos.	G	AB	R	H	2B	3B	HR	RBI	BB	SO	HBP	GDP	SB-CS	Avg.	OBP	SLG	OPS	E	Avg.
1999— Boston (A.L.) 1B-DH		4	16	3	4	2	0	1	3	0	7	0	0	0-0	.250	.250	.563	.813	0	1.000

CHAMPIONSHIP SERIES RECORD

Year Team (League)	Pos.	G	AB	R	H	2B	3B	HR	RBI	BB	SO	HBP	GDP	SB-CS	Avg.	OBP	SLG	OPS	E	Avg.
1999— Boston (A.L.) 1B-DH		5	17	2	3	1	0	1	3	1	4	0	1	0-0	.176	.222	.412	.634	0	...

DAVANON, JEFF — OF

PERSONAL: Born December 8, 1973, in San Diego. ... 6-0/200. ... Bats both, throws right. ... Full name: Jeffrey Graham DaVanon. ... Name pronounced: duh-VAN-un. ... High school: Bellaire (Texas). ... College: San Diego State. ... Son of Jerry DaVanon, infielder with five major league teams (1969-77).

TRANSACTIONS/CAREER NOTES: Selected by Oakland Athletics organization in 26th round of 1995 free-agent draft. ... Traded by A's with P Elvin Nina and OF Nathan Haynes to Anaheim Angels for P Omar Olivares and 2B Randy Velarde (July 29, 1999). ... On disabled list (March 20, 2000-entire season). ... On disabled list (July 24-August 10, 2004); included rehabilitation assignment to Salt Lake. ... Angels franchise renamed Los Angeles Angels of Anaheim for 2005 season.

2005 GAMES PLAYED BY POSITION (MLB): OF—63, DH—30.

SCOUTING REPORT **Offense:** DaVanon is one of the league's better fourth outfielders. Has an unorthodox approach at the plate; tends to push the bat, and his swing has a short path to the ball. Takes no stride. Generates surprising power, especially from the left side. Is an above-average runner. **Defense:** DaVanon can play all three outfield positions. Has good lateral range but has problems tracking balls hit straight at him. Has more trouble going back than coming in. Has a strong arm and is accurate. **Outlook:** DaVanon, a very aggressive player, may never duplicate his 2004 numbers, but he has value with his versatility and as a switch hitter. *Grade 6*

JEFF DAVANON'S HITTING ZONE

.273	.100	.053
.222	.235	.296
.375	.167	.450

LEFTY-RIGHTY SPLITS

vs.	Avg.	AB	H	2B	3B	HR	RBI	BB	SO	OBP	Slg.
L	.393	28	11	1	0	1	3	6	7	.514	.536
R	.208	197	41	9	1	1	12	33	37	.322	.279

Year Team (League)	Pos.	G	AB	R	H	2B	3B	HR	RBI	BB	SO	HBP	GDP	SB-CS	Avg.	OBP	SLG	OPS	E	Avg.
1995— S. Oregon (N'west)	OF	57	167	29	42	6	2	1	17	34	49	0		6-5	.252	.376	.329	.706	8	.864
1996— W. Mich. (Mid.)	1B-2B-OF	89	289	43	70	13	4	2	33	49	66	1	6	5-7	.242	.353	.336	.689	2	.976
1997— Visalia (Calif.)	OF	119	408	70	104	17	3	6	38	81	101	0	7	23-14	.255	.377	.355	.732	10	.948
1998— Modesto (California)	OF	84	301	66	101	17	4	5	60	59	69	1	4	33-10	.336	.439	.468	.907	12	.902
1999— Midland (Texas)	OF-DH	100	374	87	128	29	11	11	60	53	68	4		18-10	.342	.424	.567	.991	13	.960
— Edmonton (PCL)	OF-DH	34	132	35	43	8	3	6	19	20	27	1	1	11-4	.326	.416	.568	.984	0	1.000
— Anaheim (A.L.)	OF-DH	4	20	4	4	0	1	1	4	2	7	0		0-1	.200	.273	.450	.723	0	1.000
2000—		Did not play.																		
2001— Salt Lake (PCL)	OF	69	256	46	80	19	8	10	48	32	57	3	4	8-3	.313	.390	.566	.956	1	.992
— Anaheim (A.L.)	OF-DH	40	88	7	17	2	1	1	9	11	29	0	1	1-3	.193	.280	.409	.689	1	.980
2002— Anaheim (A.L.)	OF	16	30	3	5	3	0	1	4	2	6	0	1	1-0	.167	.219	.367	.585	0	1.000
— Salt Lake (PCL)	OF	25	100	21	33	10	1	5	18	17	24	1	1	5-3	.330	.429	.600	1.029	2	.962
— Ariz. Angels (Ariz.)	OF	5	15	5	10	6	1	0	4	5	2	0		2-0	.667	.714	1.000	1.914	0	1.000
2003— Salt Lake (PCL)	OF-DH	16	60	11	18	4	1	2	14	9	9	1	1	4-1	.300	.400	.500	.900	2	.933
— Anaheim (A.L.)	OF-DH	123	330	56	93	16	1	12	43	42	59	1	6	17-5	.282	.360	.445	.805	4	.989
2004— Salt Lake (PCL)	OF	3	8	4	5	0	0	1	1	2	2	0		1-1	.625	.700	1.000	1.700	0	1.000
— Anaheim (A.L.)	OF-DH	108	285	41	79	11	4	7	34	46	54	0	2	18-3	.277	.372	.418	.790	1	.993
2005— Los Angeles (A.L.)	OF-DH	108	225	42	52	10	1	2	34	39	44	2	6	11-6	.231	.347	.311	.658	1	.991
Major League totals (6 years)		402	978	153	250	42	8	28	109	142	199	3	15	48-18	.256	.348	.401	.749	7	.987

DIVISION SERIES RECORD

Year Team (League)	Pos.	G	AB	R	H	2B	3B	HR	RBI	BB	SO	HBP	GDP	SB-CS	Avg.	OBP	SLG	OPS	E	Avg.
2004— Anaheim (A.L.)	OF	3	10	1	2	0	0	0	0	2	1	0		0-1	.200	.333	.200	.533	0	1.000
2005— Los Angeles (A.L.)	DH	1	0	1	0	0	0	0	0	0	0	0		0-0	...	...	...	...	0	...
Division series totals (2 years)		4	10	2	2	0	0	0	0	2	1	0		0-1	.200	.333	.200	.533	0	1.000

CHAMPIONSHIP SERIES RECORD

Year Team (League)	Pos.	G	AB	R	H	2B	3B	HR	RBI	BB	SO	HBP	GDP	SB-CS	Avg.	OBP	SLG	OPS	E	Avg.
2005— Los Angeles (A.L.)	DH	3	1	0	0	0	0	0	0	0	0	0	0	0-0	.000	.000	.000	.000	0	...

DAVIES, KYLE — P

PERSONAL: Born September 9, 1983, in Decatur, Ga. ... 6-2/205. ... Throws right, bats right. ... Full name: Hiram Kyle Davies. ... College: None.

TRANSACTIONS/CAREER NOTES: Selected by Atlanta Braves organization in fourth round of 2001 free-agent draft.

CAREER HITTING: 3-for-15 (.200), 0 R, 0 2B, 0 3B, 0 HR, 4 RBI.

KYLE DAVIES' PITCHING ZONE

.263	.292	.333
.283	.389	.302
.273	.250	.292

LEFTY-RIGHTY SPLITS

vs.	Avg.	AB	H	2B	3B	HR	RBI	BB	SO	OBP	Slg.
L	.264	174	46	11	0	4	15	27	32	.363	.397
R	.295	176	52	15	1	4	26	22	30	.377	.460

Year Team (League)	W	L	Pct.	ERA	WHIP	G	GS	CG	ShO	Hld.	Sv.-Opp.	IP	H	R	ER	HR	BB-IBB	SO	Avg.
2001— GC Braves (GCL)	4	2	.667	2.25	0.98	12	9	1	1	...	0-...	56.0	47	17	14	2	8-0	53	.224
— Macon (S. Atl.)	1	0	1.000	0.00	0.53	1	1	0	0	...	0-...	5.2	2	0	0	0	1-0	7	.105
2002— Macon (S. Atl.)	0	1	.000	6.00	1.67	2	1	0	0	...	0-...	6.0	6	4	4	1	4-0	4	.273
— Danville (Appal.)	5	3	.625	3.50	1.38	14	14	0	0	...	0-...	69.1	73	39	27	2	23-0	62	.263
2003— Rome (S. Atl.)	8	3	.727	2.89	1.24	27	27	1	0	...	0-...	146.1	128	52	47	9	53-0	148	.238

Year Team (League)	W	L	Pct.	ERA	WHIP	G	GS	CG	ShO	Hld.	Sv.-Opp.	IP	H	R	ER	HR	BB-IBB	SO	Avg.
2004— Myrtle Beach (Carol.)	9	2	.818	2.63	1.15	14	14	0	0	...	0-...	75.1	55	24	22	3	32-0	95	.208
— Greenville (Sou.)	4	0	1.000	2.32	1.00	11	10	0	0	...	0-...	62.0	40	18	16	9	22-0	73	.191
— Richmond (Int'l)	0	1	.000	9.00	1.60	1	1	0	0	...	0-...	5.0	5	5	5	0	3-0	5	.294
2005— Richmond (Int'l)	5	2	.714	3.44	1.36	13	13	0	0	0	0-0	73.1	66	28	28	6	34-2	62	.245
— Atlanta (N.L.)	7	6	.538	4.93	1.68	21	14	0	0	2	0-1	87.2	98	51	48	8	49-5	62	.280
Major League totals (1 year)	7	6	.538	4.93	1.68	21	14	0	0	2	0-1	87.2	98	51	48	8	49-5	62	.280

DAVIS, DOUG   P

PERSONAL: Born September 21, 1975, in Sacramento, Calif. ... 6-4/213. ... Throws left, bats right. ... Full name: Douglas P. Davis. ... High school: Northgate (Walnut Creek, Calif.). ... Junior college: San Francisco City College.
TRANSACTIONS/CAREER NOTES: Selected by Los Angeles Dodgers organization in 31st round of 1993 free-agent draft; did not sign. ... Selected by Texas Rangers organization in 10th round of 1996 free-agent draft. ... Claimed on waivers by Toronto Blue Jays (April 30, 2003). ... Signed as a free agent by Milwaukee Brewers organization (July 14, 2003).
CAREER HITTING: 13-for-161 (.081), 2 R, 3 2B, 1 3B, 0 HR, 3 RBI.

SCOUTING REPORT **Throws:** His fastball reaches 85-90 mph, and he also has a cut fastball, curveball and changeup. **Tendencies:** He has picked up his tempo and pitched aggressively while improving his command. Is not overpowering but has improved his ability to work both sides of the plate. Has a big-breaking curveball. Changes speeds well and has a good idea of how to pitch. Deceptive delivery makes him sneaky fast. **Outlook:** Davis struck out more than 200 batters with his stuff last season. Is a quality mid-rotation starter capable of winning 15 games a year. **Grade 7.7**

DOUG DAVIS' PITCHING ZONE

.250	.429	.138
.252	.384	.296
.200	.333	.159

LEFTY-RIGHTY SPLITS

vs.	Avg.	AB	H	2B	3B	HR	RBI	BB	SO	OBP	Slg.
L	.259	174	45	8	2	7	22	7	41	.299	.448
R	.228	661	151	41	2	19	71	86	167	.317	.383

Year Team (League)	W	L	Pct.	ERA	WHIP	G	GS	CG	ShO	Hld.	Sv.-Opp.	IP	H	R	ER	HR	BB-IBB	SO	Avg.
1996— GC Rangers (GCL)	3	1	.750	1.90	1.27	8	7	0	0	...	0-...	42.2	28	13	9	0	26-1	49	.193
1997— GC Rangers (GCL)	3	1	.750	1.71	1.38	4	4	0	0	...	0-...	21.0	14	5	4	0	15-0	27	.200
— Charlotte (Fla. St.)	5	3	.625	3.10	1.26	9	8	1	0	...	0-...	49.1	29	19	17	2	33-1	52	.175
1998— Charlotte (Fla. St.)	11	7	.611	3.24	1.31	27	27	1	1	...	0-...	155.1	129	69	56	8	74-0	* 173	.225
1999— Tulsa (Texas)	4	4	.500	2.42	1.21	12	12	1	0	...	0-...	74.1	65	26	20	9	25-0	79	.235
— Oklahoma (PCL)	7	0	1.000	3.00	1.38	13	11	0	0	...	0-...	78.0	77	27	26	4	31-0	74	.263
— Texas (A.L.)	0	0	...	33.75	4.50	2	0	0	0	0	0-0	2.2	12	10	10	3	0-0	3	.600
2000— Oklahoma (PCL)	8	3	.727	2.84	1.38	12	12	2	0	...	0-...	69.2	62	32	22	8	34-1	53	.248
— Texas (A.L.)	7	6	.538	5.38	1.69	30	13	1	0	2	0-3	98.2	109	61	59	14	58-3	66	.288
2001— Texas (A.L.)	11	10	.524	4.45	1.55	30	30	1	0	0	0-0	186.0	220	103	92	14	69-1	115	.295
— Oklahoma (PCL)	2	0	1.000	2.87	0.89	2	2	0	0	...	0-...	15.2	10	5	5	1	4-0	14	.189
2002— Texas (A.L.)	3	5	.375	4.98	1.49	10	10	1	1	0	0-0	59.2	67	36	33	7	22-0	28	.290
— Oklahoma (PCL)	4	3	.571	4.99	1.32	9	9	0	0	...	0-...	61.1	70	38	34	7	11-0	48	.290
2003— Oklahoma (PCL)	3	0	1.000	3.25	1.10	4	4	0	0	...	0-...	27.2	29	10	10	3	1-0	18	.271
— Texas (A.L.)	0	0	...	12.00	2.67	1	1	0	0	0	0-0	3.0	4	4	4	2	4-0	2	.308
— Toronto (A.L.)	4	6	.400	5.00	1.78	12	11	0	0	0	0-0	54.0	70	33	30	6	26-1	25	.318
— Huntsville (Sou.)	1	0	1.000	3.00	1.30	1	1	0	0	...	0-...	6.0	5	2	2	0	3-0	6	.227
— Indianapolis (Int'l)	1	2	.333	4.15	1.20	5	5	0	0	...	0-...	34.2	33	16	16	2	10-0	19	.250
— Milwaukee (N.L.)	3	2	.600	2.58	1.34	8	8	1	0	0	0-0	52.1	49	18	15	8	21-0	35	.247
2004— Milwaukee (N.L.)	12	12	.500	3.39	1.31	34	34	0	0	0	0-0	207.1	192	84	78	14	79-3	166	.247
2005— Milwaukee (N.L.)	11	11	.500	3.84	1.30	35	• 35	2	1	0	0-0	222.2	196	103	95	24	93-5	208	.235
American League totals (5 years)	25	27	.481	5.08	1.64	85	65	3	1	2	0-3	404.0	482	247	228	46	179-5	239	.300
National League totals (3 years)	26	25	.510	3.51	1.31	77	77	3	1	0	0-0	482.1	437	205	188	48	193-8	409	.241
Major League totals (7 years)	51	52	.495	4.22	1.46	162	142	6	2	2	0-3	886.1	919	452	416	94	372-13	648	.269

DAVIS, JASON   P

PERSONAL: Born May 8, 1980, in Chattanooga, Tenn. ... 6-6/210. ... Throws right, bats right. ... Full name: Jason Thomas Davis. ... High school: Charleston (Tenn.). ... College: Cleveland State.
TRANSACTIONS/CAREER NOTES: Selected by Cleveland Indians organization in 21st round of 1999 free-agent draft.
CAREER HITTING: 1-for-9 (.111), 1 R, 0 2B, 0 3B, 1 HR, 1 RBI.

JASON DAVIS' PITCHING ZONE

.333	.500	.400
.360	.500	.409
.000	.000	.250

LEFTY-RIGHTY SPLITS

vs.	Avg.	AB	H	2B	3B	HR	RBI	BB	SO	OBP	Slg.
L	.193	57	11	0	1	0	6	9	11	.319	.228
R	.333	99	33	7	0	4	19	11	21	.398	.525

Year Team (League)	W	L	Pct.	ERA	WHIP	G	GS	CG	ShO	Hld.	Sv.-Opp.	IP	H	R	ER	HR	BB-IBB	SO	Avg.
2000— Burlington (Appal.)	4	4	.500	4.40	1.42	10	10	0	0	...	0-...	45.0	48	27	22	5	16-0	35	.276
2001— Columbus (S. Atl.)	14	6	.700	2.70	1.24	27	27	1	1	...	0-...	160.0	147	72	48	9	51-1	115	.243
2002— Kinston (Carol.)	3	6	.333	4.15	1.38	17	17	1	1	...	0-...	99.2	107	64	46	7	31-2	68	.272
— Akron (East.)	6	2	.750	3.51	1.34	10	10	0	0	...	0-...	59.0	63	26	23	2	16-0	45	.278
— Cleveland (A.L.)	1	0	1.000	1.84	1.09	3	2	0	0	0	0-0	14.2	12	3	3	1	4-0	11	.218
2003— Cleveland (A.L.)	8	11	.421	4.68	1.32	27	27	1	0	0	0-0	165.1	172	101	86	25	47-4	85	.273
2004— Buffalo (Int'l)	3	2	.600	3.00	1.31	9	9	0	0	0	0-0	54.0	53	26	18	4	18-1	39	.261
— Cleveland (A.L.)	2	7	.222	5.51	1.74	26	19	0	0	1	0-0	114.1	148	81	70	13	51-1	72	.311
2005— Cleveland (A.L.)	4	2	.667	4.69	1.59	11	4	0	0	0	0-0	40.1	44	22	21	4	20-0	32	.282
— Buffalo (Int'l)	8	5	.615	4.61	1.39	16	16	1	0	0	0-0	95.2	106	65	49	9	27-0	77	.283
Major League totals (4 years)	15	20	.429	4.84	1.49	67	52	1	0	1	0-0	334.2	376	207	180	43	122-5	200	.285

D

DAVIS, J.J. — OF

PERSONAL: Born October 25, 1978, in Glendora, Calif. ... 6-5/250. ... Bats right, throws right. ... Full name: Jerry C. Davis. ... High school: Baldwin Park (Calif.).

TRANSACTIONS/CAREER NOTES: Selected by Pittsburgh Pirates organization in first round (eighth pick overall) of 1997 free-agent draft. ... On disabled list (May 19-June 25 and July 15, 2004-remainder of season); included rehabilitation assignment to Nashville. ... Traded by Pirates to Montreal Expos for OF Antonio Sucre (November 24, 2004). ... Expos franchise transferred to Washington, D.C., and renamed Washington Nationals for 2005 season (December 3, 2004). ... Traded by Nationals with P Zach Day to Colorado Rockies for OF Preston Wilson and cash (July 13, 2005).

2005 GAMES PLAYED BY POSITION (MLB): OF—10.

LEFTY-RIGHTY SPLITS

vs.	Avg.	AB	H	2B	3B	HR	RBI	BB	SO	OBP	Slg.
L	.158	19	3	0	0	0	1	1	5	.200	.158
R	.429	7	3	0	0	0	1	1	2	.500	.429

Year	Team (League)	Pos.	G	AB	R	H	2B	3B	HR	RBI	BB	SO	HBP	GDP	SB-CS	Avg.	OBP	SLG	OPS	E	Avg.
1997—	GC Pirates (GCL)	OF	45	165	19	42	10	2	1	18	14	44	2	4	0-0	.255	.315	.358	.673	0	1.000
—	Erie (N.Y.-Penn)	DH	4	13	1	1	0	0	0	0	0	4	0	0	0-0	.077	.077	.077	.154	—	—
1998—	Augusta (S. Atl.)	OF	30	106	11	21	6	0	4	11	3	24	0	4	1-1	.198	.220	.368	.588	3	.923
—	Erie (N.Y.-Penn)	OF	52	196	25	53	12	2	8	39	20	54	2	3	4-1	.270	.341	.474	.815	7	.932
1999—	Hickory (S. Atl.)	OF	86	317	58	84	26	1	19	65	44	99	4	3	2-5	.265	.360	.533	.893	4	.950
2000—	Lynchburg (Caro.)	OF	130	485	77	118	36	1	20	80	52	171	4	11	9-4	.243	.319	.445	.765	18	.925
2001—	Altoona (East.)	OF	67	228	21	57	13	3	4	26	21	79	2	1	2-5	.250	.317	.386	.703	0	1.000
—	GC Pirates (GCL)	OF	4	17	3	8	1	0	2	6	1	2	0	0	0-0	.471	.500	.882	1.382	1	.667
2002—	Altoona (East.)	OF	101	348	51	100	17	3	20	62	33	101	3	3	7-4	.287	.351	.526	.877	6	.971
—	Pittsburgh (N.L.)	OF	9	10	1	1	0	0	0	0	0	4	0	0	0-0	.100	.182	.100	.282	0	1.000
2003—	Nashville (PCL)	OF-DH	122	426	68	121	29	4	26	67	35	85	4	11	23-6	.284	.342	.554	.896	9	.964
—	Pittsburgh (N.L.)	OF	19	35	1	7	0	0	1	4	3	13	0	1	0-0	.200	.263	.286	.549	0	1.000
2004—	Pittsburgh (N.L.)	OF	25	35	4	5	1	0	0	3	4	10	0	0	2-0	.143	.225	.171	.396	2	.895
—	Nashville (PCL)	OF-DH	27	84	11	21	6	1	8	17	3	28	0	1	3-0	.250	.270	.631	.901	0	1.000
2005—	Washington (N.L.)	OF	14	26	0	6	0	0	0	2	7	0	2	1	1-1	.231	.286	.231	.516	0	1.000
—	New Orleans (PCL)	OF-DH-1B	51	174	34	49	10	0	12	31	18	53	3	4	3-4	.282	.359	.546	.905	7	.956
—	Colo. Springs (PCL)	OF-DH	21	67	12	15	3	0	3	15	7	20	1	2	1-1	.224	.295	.403	.698	0	1.000
Major League totals (4 years)			67	106	6	19	1	0	1	9	9	34	1	3	3-2	.179	.248	.217	.465	2	.962

DAVIS, KANE — P

D

PERSONAL: Born June 25, 1975, in Ripley, W.Va. ... 6-3/194. ... Throws right, bats right. ... Full name: Kane Thomas Davis. ... High school: Spencer (W.Va.).

TRANSACTIONS/CAREER NOTES: Selected by Pittsburgh Pirates organization in 13th round of 1993 free-agent draft. ... Signed by Cleveland Indians organization (December 22, 1999). ... Traded by Indians with P Paul Rigdon, 1B/OF Richie Sexson and a player to be named to Milwaukee Brewers for Ps Bob Wickman, Steve Woodard and Jason Bere (July 28, 2000); Brewers acquired 2B Marco Scutaro to complete deal (August 30, 2000). ... Traded by Brewers with P Juan Acevedo and IF Jose Flores to Colorado Rockies for Ps Mark Leiter and Mike DeJean and 2B/SS Elvis Pena (April 4, 2001). ... On disabled list (July 8-August 6, 2001); included rehabilitation assignment to Colorado Springs. ... Traded by Rockies to New York Mets for P Corey Brittan (February 21, 2002). ... On disabled list (May 13, 2002-remainder of season); included rehabilitation assignment to Norfolk. ... Signed as a free agent by Chicago Cubs organization (May 20, 2003). ... Signed as a free agent by Indians organization (May 16, 2004). ... Signed as a free agent by Brewers organization (December 8, 2004).

CAREER HITTING: 0-for-6 (.000), 0 R, 0 2B, 0 3B, 0 HR, 0 RBI.

KANE DAVIS' PITCHING ZONE

.500	.500	.000
.273	.000	.091
.000	.250	.000

LEFTY-RIGHTY SPLITS

vs.	Avg.	AB	H	2B	3B	HR	RBI	BB	SO	OBP	Slg.
L	.158	19	3	0	1	0	3	4	3	.304	.316
R	.171	41	7	1	0	1	3	6	8	.277	.268

Year	Team (League)	W	L	Pct.	ERA	WHIP	G	GS	CG	ShO	Hld.	Sv.-Opp.	IP	H	R	ER	HR	BB-IBB	SO	Avg.
1993—	GC Pirates (GCL)	0	4	.000	7.07	1.89	11	4	0	0		0-...	28.0	34	30	22	0	19-1	24	.293
1994—	Welland (NYP)	5	5	.500	2.65	1.24	15	15	2	0		0-...	98.1	90	36	29	4	32-1	74	.250
1995—	Augusta (S. Atl.)	12	6	.667	3.75	1.28	26	25	1	0		0-...	139.1	136	73	58	4	43-0	78	.251
1996—	Lynchburg (Caro.)	11	9	.550	4.29	1.37	26	26	3	1		0-...	157.1	160	84	75	12	56-0	116	.265
1997—	Carolina (Southern)	0	3	.000	3.77	1.33	6	6	0	0		0-...	28.2	22	17	12	2	16-1	23	.208
1998—	Augusta (S. Atl.)	0	0	—	6.00	1.22	2	2	0	0		0-...	9.0	8	6	6	0	3-0	6	.258
—	Carolina (Southern)	1	11	.083	9.24	1.89	18	16	0	0		0-...	74.0	102	84	76	12	38-2	39	.326
1999—	Altoona (East.)	4	6	.400	3.78	1.45	16	16	0	0		0-...	95.1	97	51	40	5	41-1	53	.261
—	Nashville (PCL)	3	2	.600	6.75	1.66	12	9	0	0		0-...	49.1	65	39	37	8	17-1	31	.323
2000—	Akron (East.)	0	1	.000	2.70	1.10	5	5	0	0		0-...	20.0	17	7	6	2	5-0	13	.233
—	Buffalo (Int'l)	2	0	1.000	4.20	1.40	6	4	0	0		0-...	30.0	30	16	14	2	5-0	19	.259
—	Cleveland (A.L.)	0	3	.000	14.73	2.55	5	2	0	0	0	0-0	11.0	20	21	18	3	8-0	2	.385
—	Milwaukee (N.L.)	0	0	—	6.75	3.00	3	0	0	0	0	0-...	4.0	7	3	3	1	6-0	2	.389
—	Indianapolis (Int'l)	1	1	.500	3.54	1.28	4	4	0	0		0-...	20.1	19	8	8	2	7-0	12	.250
2001—	Colorado (N.L.)	2	4	.333	4.35	1.43	57	0	0	0	9	0-5	68.1	66	36	33	11	32-4	47	.252
—	Colo. Springs (PCL)	0	0	—	3.60	1.60	4	0	0	0		0-...	5.0	5	2	2	0	3-1	7	.263
2002—	New York (N.L.)	1	1	.500	7.07	1.86	16	0	0	0	1	0-...	14.0	15	11	11	2	11-2	24	.273
—	Norfolk (Int'l)	0	0	—	0.00	1.00	1	0	0	0		0-...	1.0	1	0	0	0	0-0	2	.250
2003—	Camden (Atl.)	1	0	1.000	1.13	1.00	9	0	0	0		5-...	8.0	3	1	1	0	1-0	9	.107
—	Iowa (PCL)	2	1	.667	2.35	1.08	22	0	0	0		2-...	30.2	21	8	8	0	12-1	24	.198
2004—	Camden (Atl.)	2	0	1.000	0.00	0.92	5	0	0	0		3-...	4.1	2	0	0	0	2-0	7	.143
—	Buffalo (Int'l)	3	2	.600	6.15	1.85	32	0	0	0		2-...	45.1	59	35	31	2	25-1	45	.303
—	Akron (East.)	0	0	—	3.00	0.67	1	0	0	0		0-...	3.0	3	1	1	0	0-0	3	.182
2005—	Nashville (PCL)	4	2	.667	2.44	1.15	45	0	0	0	8	1-5	62.2	49	18	17	5	23-0	81	.216
—	Milwaukee (N.L.)	1	1	.500	2.70	1.20	15	0	0	0	0	0-2	16.2	10	6	5	2	10-0	11	.167
American League totals (1 year)		0	3	.000	14.73	2.55	5	2	0	0	0	0-0	11.0	20	21	18	3	8-0	2	.385
National League totals (4 years)		4	6	.400	4.54	1.51	91	0	0	0	10	0-7	103.0	98	56	52	16	58-6	84	.248
Major League totals (4 years)		4	9	.308	5.53	1.61	96	2	0	0	10	0-7	114.0	118	77	70	19	66-6	86	.264

DAY, ZACH — P

PERSONAL: Born June 15, 1978, in Cincinnati. ... 6-4/216. ... Throws right, bats right. ... Full name: Stephen Zachary Day. ... High school: La Salle (Cincinnati). ... College: Cincinnati.

TRANSACTIONS/CAREER NOTES: Selected by New York Yankees organization in fifth round of 1996 free-agent draft. ... Traded by Yankees to Cleveland Indians with P Jake Westbrook (July 24, 2000), completing deal in which Indians traded OF David Justice to Yankees for OF Ricky Ledee and two players to be named (June 29, 2000). ... Traded by Indians to Montreal Expos for OF Milton Bradley (July 31, 2001). ... On disabled list (May 29-July 26, 2003); included rehabilitation assignments to GCL Expos and Brevard

County. ... On disabled list (July 6-22 and August 2, 2004-remainder of season). ... Expos franchise transferred to Washington, D.C., and renamed Washington Nationals for 2005 season (December 3, 2004). ... On disabled list (May 31-July 13, 2005); included rehabilitation assignment to Harrisburg. ... Traded by Nationals with OF J.J. Davis to Colorado Rockies for OF Preston Wilson and cash (July 13, 2005). ... On disabled list (September 21, 2005-remainder of season).

CAREER HITTING: 6-for-93 (.065), 5 R, 0 2B, 0 3B, 1 HR, 3 RBI.

SCOUTING REPORT

Throws: He has a sinking fastball that tops out at 92 mph. Also has a curveball and slider. ***Tendencies:*** Day's sinker sets up everything. Likes to get ahead and get ground-ball outs. Is a quick worker. Can change the speed and look of his curve. Command of the low zone is inconsistent, most noticeably when his pitch counts elevate. Needs a consistent third pitch. ***Outlook:*** Shoulder problems make his health a question but he has the stuff to be a bottom-of-the-rotation starter. Might be even better in a setup role because his velocity likely would improve if he threw fewer pitches. ***Grade 6.4***

ZACH DAY'S PITCHING ZONE

.333	.500	.214
.389	.423	.171
.091	.538	.231

LEFTY-RIGHTY SPLITS

vs.	Avg.	AB	H	2B	3B	HR	RBI	BB	SO	OBP	Slg.
L	.330	94	31	6	2	2	15	22	8	.457	.500
R	.300	100	30	4	0	4	19	10	15	.366	.460

Year Team (League)	W	L	Pct.	ERA	WHIP	G	GS	CG	ShO	Hld.	Sv.-Opp.	IP	H	R	ER	HR	BB-IBB	SO	Avg.
1996— GC Yankees (GCL)	5	2	.714	5.61	1.31	7	5	0	0	...	0-...	33.2	41	26	21	3	3-0	23	.311
1997— Oneonta (NYP)	7	2	.778	2.15	1.14	14	14	0	0	...	0-...	92.0	82	26	22	2	23-0	92	.240
1998— Tampa (Fla. St.)	5	8	.385	5.49	1.74	18	17	0	0	...	0-...	100.0	142	89	61	5	32-4	69	.326
— Greensboro (S. Atl.)	1	2	.333	2.75	1.14	7	6	1	0	...	0-...	36.0	35	22	11	1	6-0	37	.245
1999— GC Yankees (GCL)	1	1	.500	3.78	1.44	5	4	0	0	...	0-...	16.2	20	10	7	1	4-0	17	.290
— Greensboro (S. Atl.)	0	1	.000	2.25	1.88	2	2	0	0	...	0-...	8.0	14	11	2	0	1-0	4	.359
2000— Greensboro (S. Atl.)	9	3	.750	1.90	1.21	13	13	1	1	...	0-...	85.1	72	29	18	6	31-0	101	.232
— Tampa (Fla. St.)	2	4	.333	4.19	1.40	7	7	0	0	...	0-...	34.1	33	22	16	2	15-1	36	.246
— Akron (East.)	4	2	.667	3.52	1.28	8	8	0	0	...	0-...	46.0	38	20	18	1	21-0	43	.232
2001— Akron (East.)	9	10	.474	3.10	1.23	22	22	2	0	...	0-...	136.2	123	54	47	8	45-1	94	.237
— Buffalo (Int'l)	1	0	1.000	1.50	0.67	1	1	0	0	...	0-...	6.0	3	1	1	0	1-0	4	.143
— Ottawa (Int'l)	2	2	.500	7.43	1.73	6	5	0	0	...	0-...	26.2	38	23	22	2	8-0	15	.349
2002— Ottawa (Int'l)	5	6	.455	3.50	1.21	17	16	1	0	...	0-...	90.0	77	38	35	5	32-0	68	.231
— Montreal (N.L.)	4	1	.800	3.62	1.15	19	2	0	0	...	1-2	37.1	28	18	15	3	15-2	25	.207
2003— GC Expos (GCL)	0	0	...	3.86	1.70	1	1	0	0	...	0-...	2.1	3	3	1	0	1-0	3	.300
— Brevard County (FSL)	0	0	...	1.69	0.80	1	1	0	0	...	0-...	5.1	3	1	1	0	1-0	3	.167
— Montreal (N.L.)	9	8	.529	4.18	1.45	23	23	1	0	0	0-0	131.1	132	64	61	8	59-3	61	.262
2004— Montreal (N.L.)	5	10	.333	3.93	1.39	19	19	1	1	0	0-0	116.2	117	53	51	13	45-7	61	.265
2005— Washington (N.L.)	2	2	.333	6.75	1.83	12	5	0	0	0	0-0	36.0	41	29	27	4	25-3	16	.289
— Harrisburg (East.)	1	0	1.000	2.77	1.15	3	3	0	0	...	0-...	13.0	14	4	4	1	1-0	10	.286
— Colo. Springs (PCL)	2	3	.400	5.89	1.66	7	7	0	0	...	0-...	36.2	46	29	24	4	15-0	17	.305
— Colorado (N.L.)	0	1	.000	7.15	2.38	5	3	0	0	0	0-1	11.1	20	11	9	2	7-1	7	.385
Major League totals (4 years)	19	22	.463	4.41	1.47	78	52	2	2	0	1-3	332.2	338	175	163	30	151-16	170	.265

DEJEAN, MIKE   P

PERSONAL: Born September 28, 1970, in Baton Rouge, La. ... 6-2/219. ... Throws right, bats right. ... Full name: Michel Dwain DeJean. ... Name pronounced: DAY-zhan. ... High school: Walker (La.). ... College: Livingston University (Ala.).

TRANSACTIONS/CAREER NOTES: Selected by New York Yankees organization in 24th round of 1992 free-agent draft. ... Traded by Yankees with a player to be named to Colorado Rockies for C Joe Girardi (November 20, 1995); Rockies acquired P Steve Shoemaker to complete deal (December 6, 1995). ... On disabled list (July 18-August 8, 1997); included rehabilitation assignment to New Haven. ... On disabled list (August 14-September 1, 1999); included rehabilitation assignment to Colorado Springs. ... On disabled list (March 29-April 28 and July 25-August 15, 2000); included rehabilitation assignment to Colorado Springs. ... Traded by Rockies with P Mark Leiter and 2B/SS Elvis Pena to Milwaukee Brewers for Ps Juan Acevedo and Kane Davis and IF Jose Flores (April 4, 2001). ... Traded by Milwaukee Brewers to St. Louis Cardinals for two players to be named (August 22, 2003); Brewers acquired Ps Mike Crudale (August 27, 2003) and John Novinsky (September 10, 2003) to complete deal. ... Signed as a free agent by Baltimore Orioles (January 8, 2004). ... Traded by Orioles to New York Mets for OF Karim Garcia (July 19, 2004). ... On disabled list (August 30, 2004-remainder of season). ... Released by Mets (June 20, 2005). ... Signed by Colorado Rockies (July 7, 2005).

CAREER HITTING: 1-for-17 (.059), 0 R, 1 2B, 0 3B, 0 HR, 0 RBI.

SCOUTING REPORT

Throws: He will deliver his fastball in the 88-94 mph range, his slider in the mid-80s and his split-finger pitch in the low 80s. ***Tendencies:*** DeJean has a herky-jerky delivery and gets the best sink on his fastball when he stays back over the rubber. Has a big, sweeping break on his slider and a splitter that he uses as his out pitch. Will struggle with his mechanics and control at times. Needs to establish command of his fastball to make the splitter effective. ***Outlook:*** He has good stuff, but is inconsistent. Should be a better setup reliever than he has shown. ***Grade 6.9***

MIKE DEJEAN'S PITCHING ZONE

.000	.286	.500
.256	.414	.289
.231	.400	.136

LEFTY-RIGHTY SPLITS

vs.	Avg.	AB	H	2B	3B	HR	RBI	BB	SO	OBP	Slg.
L	.252	107	27	5	0	1	13	14	15	.347	.327
R	.257	136	35	9	1	2	18	16	37	.335	.382

Year Team (League)	W	L	Pct.	ERA	WHIP	G	GS	CG	ShO	Hld.	Sv.-Opp.	IP	H	R	ER	HR	BB-IBB	SO	Avg.
1992— Oneonta (NYP)	0	0	...	0.44	0.73	20	0	0	0	...	16-...	20.2	12	3	1	1	3-0	20	.160
1993— Greensboro (S. Atl.)	2	3	.400	5.00	1.67	20	0	0	0	...	9-...	18.0	22	12	10	1	8-2	16	.286
1994— Tampa (Fla. St.)	0	2	.000	2.38	1.53	34	0	0	0	...	16-...	34.0	39	15	9	1	13-0	22	.283
— Albany (East.)	0	2	.000	4.38	1.50	16	0	0	0	...	4-...	24.2	14	12	12	1	15-3	13	.250
1995— Norwich (East.)	5	5	.500	2.99	1.17	59	0	0	0	...	20-...	78.1	58	29	26	5	34-2	57	.208
1996— Colo. Springs (PCL)	0	2	.000	5.13	1.81	30	0	0	0	...	1-...	40.1	52	24	23	3	21-3	31	.319
— New Haven (East.)	0	0	...	3.22	1.25	16	0	0	0	...	11-...	22.1	20	9	8	2	8-0	12	.247
1997— Colo. Springs (PCL)	0	1	.000	5.40	2.40	10	0	0	0	...	4-...	10.0	17	6	6	0	7-1	9	.405
— Colorado (N.L.)	5	0	1.000	3.99	1.45	55	0	0	0	13	2-4	67.2	74	34	30	4	24-2	38	.280
— New Haven (East.)	0	1	.000	6.00	1.67	2	0	0	0	...	0-...	3.0	3	2	2	0	2-0	2	.250
1998— Colorado (N.L.)	3	1	.750	3.03	1.37	59	1	0	0	11	2-3	74.1	78	29	25	4	24-1	27	.285
1999— Colorado (N.L.)	2	4	.333	8.41	1.89	56	0	0	0	...	0-4	61.0	83	61	57	13	32-8	31	.335

Year	Team (League)	W	L	Pct.	ERA	WHIP	G	GS	CG	ShO	Hld.	Sv.-Opp.	IP	H	R	ER	HR	BB-IBB	SO	Avg.
	—Colo. Springs (PCL)	0	0	—	0.00	1.00	1	0	0	0	...	0-...	1.0	1	0	0	0	0-0	...	.333
2000—	Colo. Springs (PCL)	1	1	.500	2.51	1.33	12	0	0	0	...	5-...	14.1	15	4	4	0	4-0	12	.273
	—Colorado (N.L.)	4	4	.500	4.89	1.58	54	0	0	0	7	0-4	53.1	54	31	29	9	30-6	34	.269
2001—	Milwaukee (N.L.)	4	2	.667	2.77	1.35	75	0	0	0	8	2-4	84.1	75	31	26	4	39-7	68	.236
2002—	Milwaukee (N.L.)	1	5	.167	3.12	1.40	68	0	0	0	8	27-30	75.0	66	28	26	7	39-8	65	.237
2003—	Milwaukee (N.L.)	4	7	.364	4.87	1.48	58	0	0	0	5	18-26	64.2	69	38	35	12	27-7	58	.271
	—St. Louis (N.L.)	1	1	.500	4.00	1.61	18	0	0	0	5	1-1	18.0	17	8	8	1	12-0	13	.262
2004—	Baltimore (A.L.)	0	5	.000	6.13	1.94	37	0	0	0	1	0-0	39.2	49	29	27	2	28-6	36	.308
	—New York (N.L.)	0	0	—	1.69	1.22	17	0	0	0	2	0-0	21.1	21	5	4	0	5-2	24	.256
2005—	New York (N.L.)	3	1	.750	6.31	2.10	28	0	0	0	2	0-0	25.2	36	19	18	3	18-2	17	.327
	—Colorado (N.L.)	2	3	.400	3.19	1.04	38	0	0	0	18	0-3	36.2	26	14	13	0	12-1	35	.195
American League totals (1 year)		0	5	.000	6.13	1.94	37	0	0	0	1	0-0	39.2	49	29	27	2	28-6	36	.308
National League totals (9 years)		29	28	.509	4.19	1.48	526	1	0	0	80	52-79	582.0	599	298	271	57	262-44	410	.269
Major League totals (9 years)		29	33	.468	4.31	1.51	563	1	0	0	81	52-79	621.2	648	327	298	59	290-50	446	.271

DEJESUS, DAVID — OF

PERSONAL: Born December 20, 1979, in Brooklyn, N.Y. ... 6-0/175. ... Bats left, throws left. ... Full name: David Christopher DeJesus. ... High school: Manalapan (N.J.). ... College: Rutgers.

TRANSACTIONS/CAREER NOTES: Selected by New York Mets organization in 43rd round of 1997 free-agent draft; did not sign. ... Selected by Kansas City Royals organization in fourth round of 2000 free-agent draft.

2005 GAMES PLAYED BY POSITION (MLB): OF—119.

SCOUTING REPORT** Offense:* DeJesus has a short stroke and can use the whole field, but he has a slider-speed bat. Will never have much power but is developing enough patience to be a lead-off hitter. Is an average runner who must improve his leads and ability to read moves. ***Defense: He doesn't have the speed most teams like in center field, but DeJesus compensates with good jumps. Will continue to improve his range. Tends to play shallow and has slightly below-average arm strength. ***Outlook:*** DeJesus still is a work in progress as a leadoff hitter and baserunner. Is not strong and has been injury-prone. ***Grade 5.7***

D

DAVID DEJESUS' HITTING ZONE

.375	.320	.394
.293	.429	.307
.263	.320	.176

LEFTY-RIGHTY SPLITS

vs.	Avg.	AB	H	2B	3B	HR	RBI	BB	SO	OBP	Slg.
L	.270	141	38	7	2	2	13	14	25	.350	.390
R	.303	320	97	24	4	7	43	28	51	.363	.469

									BATTING								FIELDING	
Year	Team (League)	Pos.	G	AB	R	H	2B	3B	HR	RBI	BB	SO	HBP	GDP	SB-CS	Avg.	OBP	SLG	OPS	E	Avg.
2001—	....					Did not play.														
2002—	Wilmington (Caro.)	OF	87	334	69	99	22	6	4	41	48	42	13	8	15-6	.296	.400	.434	.834	1	.994
	—Wichita (Texas)	OF	25	79	7	20	5	2	2	15	8	10	5	3	3-1	.253	.347	.443	.790	1	.976
2003—	Wichita (Texas)	OF	17	71	14	24	4	0	2	10	9	8	2	3	1-3	.338	.422	.479	.901	1	.980
	—Omaha (PCL)	OF-DH	59	215	49	64	16	3	5	23	34	30	9	9	8-4	.298	.412	.470	.881	0	1.000
	—Kansas City (A.L.)	OF	12	7	0	2	0	1	0	0	1	2	1	0	0-0	.286	.444	.571	1.016	0	1.000
2004—	Omaha (PCL)	OF	50	197	38	62	14	4	6	16	21	30	7	5	7-6	.315	.400	.518	.918	1	.991
	—Kansas City (A.L.)	OF	96	363	58	104	15	3	7	39	33	53	4	6	8-11	.287	.360	.402	.763	4	.984
2005—	Kansas City (A.L.)	OF	122	461	69	135	31	6	9	56	42	76	5	6	5-5	.293	.359	.445	.804	4	.987
Major League totals (3 years)			230	831	127	241	46	10	16	95	76	131	19	12	13-16	.290	.361	.427	.788	8	.986

DE LA ROSA, JORGE — P

PERSONAL: Born April 5, 1981, in Monterrey, Mexico. ... 6-1/190. ... Throws left, bats left. ... Full name: Jorge Alberto de la Rosa.

TRANSACTIONS/CAREER NOTES: Signed as a non-drafted free agent by Arizona Diamondbacks organization (March 20, 1998). ... Contract sold by Diamondbacks organization to Monterrey of the Mexican League (April 2, 2000). ... Contract purchased by Boston Red Sox organization from Monterrey (February 22, 2001). ... Traded with Ps Casey Fossum and Brandon Lyon and OF Mike Goss to Diamondbacks for P Curt Schilling (November 28, 2003). ... Traded with SS Craig Counsell, 2B Junior Spivey, 1B Lyle Overbay, C Chad Moeller and P Chris Capuano to Milwaukee Brewers for 1B Richie Sexson, P Shane Nance and a player to be named (December 1, 2003); Diamondbacks acquired OF Noochie Varner to complete deal (December 15, 2003).

CAREER HITTING: 0-for-6 (.000). 0 R, 0 2B, 0 3B, 0 HR, 0 RBI.

JORGE DE LA ROSA'S PITCHING ZONE

.333	.462	.000
.400	.333	.292
.333	.250	.286

LEFTY-RIGHTY SPLITS

vs.	Avg.	AB	H	2B	3B	HR	RBI	BB	SO	OBP	Slg.
L	.321	56	18	2	0	0	8	11	15	.426	.357
R	.273	110	30	12	1	1	16	27	27	.413	.427

Year	Team (League)	W	L	Pct.	ERA	WHIP	G	GS	CG	ShO	Hld.	Sv.-Opp.	IP	H	R	ER	HR	BB-IBB	SO	Avg.
1999—	High Desert (Calif.)	0	0	—	0.00	1.00	2	0	0	0	...	0-...	3.0	1	0	0	0	2-0	3	.100
	—Ariz. D'backs (Ariz.)	0	0	—	3.21	1.07	8	0	0	0	...	2-...	14.0	12	5	5	1	3-0	17	.226
	—Missoula (Pion.)	0	1	.000	7.98	2.11	13	0	0	0	...	2-...	14.2	22	17	13	2	9-0	14	.333
2000—	Monterrey (Mex.)	3	2	.600	6.28	1.81	37	0	0	0	...	1-...	38.2	38	27	27	2	32-...	50	
2001—	Sarasota (Fla. St.)	0	1	.000	1.21	0.84	12	0	0	0	...	2-...	29.2	13	7	4	0	12-0	27	.127
	—Trenton (East.)	1	3	.250	5.84	2.05	29	0	0	0	...	0-...	37.0	56	35	24	4	20-1	27	.348
2002—	Sarasota (Fla. St.)	7	7	.500	3.65	1.30	23	23	1	1	...	0-...	120.2	105	53	49	10	52-1	95	.231
	—Trenton (East.)	1	2	.333	5.50	1.44	4	4	0	0	...	0-...	18.0	12	11	11	0	9-0	15	.239
2003—	Portland (East.)	6	3	.667	2.80	1.23	22	20	0	0	...	1-...	99.2	87	39	31	6	36-0	102	.231
	—Pawtucket (Int'l)	1	3	.333	3.75	1.63	5	5	0	0	...	0-...	24.0	27	14	10	2	12-0	17	.278
2004—	Indianapolis (Int'l)	5	6	.455	4.52	1.35	20	20	0	0	...	0-...	85.2	80	45	43	9	36-1	86	.249
	—Milwaukee (N.L.)	0	3	.000	6.35	1.90	5	5	0	0	0	0-0	22.2	29	20	16	1	14-0	5	.289
2005—	Milwaukee (N.L.)	2	2	.500	4.46	2.03	38	5	0	0	...	5	0-2	42.1	48	23	21	1	38-4	42	.289
Major League totals (2 years)		2	5	.286	5.12	1.98	43	5	0	0	...	5	0-2	65.0	77	43	37	2	52-4	47	.296

DELCARMEN, MANNY P

PERSONAL: Born February 16, 1982, in Boston. ... 6-3/195. ... Throws right, bats right. ... Full name: Manuel Delcarmen.
TRANSACTIONS/CAREER NOTES: Selected by Boston Red Sox organization in second round of 2000 free-agent draft.
CAREER HITTING: 0-for-0 (.000), 0 R, 0 2B, 0 3B, 0 HR, 0 RBI.

SCOUTING REPORT *Throws:* His fastball tops out at 97 mph to go with a curve and a changeup. *Tendencies:* He can be overpowering with the fastball. Has one of the best curves in the Red Sox's system. Needs to learn how to take something off his fastball because it lacks movement. Was effective last year in outings up to 30 pitches. *Outlook:* Delcarmen is one of several youngsters the Red Sox hope will help shore up their bullpen. Should be at full strength this season, two full years after elbow surgery. *Grade 7.2*

LEFTY-RIGHTY SPLITS

vs.	Avg.	AB	H	2B	3B	HR	RBI	BB	SO	OBP	Slg.
L	.267	15	4	0	0	0	0	4	3	.421	.267
R	.222	18	4	1	0	0	2	3	6	.364	.278

Year Team (League)	W	L	Pct.	ERA	WHIP	G	GS	CG	ShO	Hld.	Sv.-Opp.	IP	H	R	ER	HR	BB-IBB	SO	Avg.
2001— GC Red Sox (GCL)	4	2	.667	2.54	1.17	11	8	0	0	...	1-...	46.0	35	16	13	0	19-0	62	.211
2002— Augusta (S. Atl.)	7	8	.467	4.10	1.32	26	24	0	0	...	0-...	136.0	124	77	62	15	56-0	136	.242
2003— Sarasota (Fla. St.)	1	1	.500	3.13	1.00	4	3	0	0	...	0-...	23.0	16	9	8	1	7-0	16	.200
2004— Sarasota (Fla. St.)	3	6	.333	4.68	1.42	19	18	0	0	...	0-...	73.0	84	43	38	10	20-1	76	.301
2005— Portland (East.)	4	4	.500	3.23	1.31	31	0	0	0	5	3-6	39.0	31	23	14	3	20-1	49	.212
— Pawtucket (Int'l)	3	1	.750	1.29	1.43	15	0	0	0	2	2-3	21.0	17	3	3	0	13-1	23	.218
— Boston (A.L.)	0	0	...	3.00	1.67	10	0	0	0	0	0-0	9.0	8	3	3	0	7-0	9	.242
Major League totals (1 year)	0	0	...	3.00	1.67	10	0	0	0	0	0-0	9.0	8	3	3	0	7-0	9	.242

DELGADO, CARLOS 1B

PERSONAL: Born June 25, 1972, in Aguadilla, Puerto Rico. ... 6-3/230. ... Bats left, throws right. ... Full name: Carlos Juan Delgado. ... Name pronounced: del-GAH-doh. ... High school: Jose de Diego (Aguadilla, Puerto Rico).
TRANSACTIONS/CAREER NOTES: Signed as a non-drafted free agent by Toronto Blue Jays organization (October 9, 1988). ... On disabled list (March 15-April 24, 1998); included rehabilitation assignments to Dunedin and Syracuse. ... On disabled list (August 9-25, 2002). ... On disabled list (May 30-July 6, 2004); included rehabilitation assignments to Dunedin and Syracuse. ... Signed as a free agent by Florida Marlins (January 27, 2005). ... On disabled list (July 28-August 13, 2005).
RECORDS: Shares major league record for home runs, game (4, September 25, 2003).
HONORS: Named Major League Player of the Year by THE SPORTING NEWS (2000).
2005 GAMES PLAYED BY POSITION (MLB): 1B—141, DH—1.

SCOUTING REPORT *Offense:* Delgado remains one of the best power hitters around. Has a pronounced inside-out swing with exceptionally strong hands and is more of a lift hitter. Has power to all fields. Most of his ground balls are to the right side, prompting defenses to employ a shift, but hits fly balls to all fields. Became less patient when he was pitched around. *Defense:* Indifferent to defense, Delgado has more problems moving to his right than his left. Hands are adequate. Has regressed as a fielder. *Outlook:* He's still an offensive force, but at this stage of his career, he'd be better as a DH. *Grade 8.6*

CARLOS DELGADO'S HITTING ZONE

.235	.444	.356
.280	.440	.321
.296	.214	.367

LEFTY-RIGHTY SPLITS

vs.	Avg.	AB	H	2B	3B	HR	RBI	BB	SO	OBP	Slg.
L	.234	141	33	9	1	7	27	9	37	.308	.461
R	.326	380	124	32	2	26	88	63	84	.431	.626

							BATTING											FIELDING	
Year Team (League)	Pos.	G	AB	R	H	2B	3B	HR	RBI	BB	SO	HBP	GDP	SB-CS	Avg.	OBP	SLG	OPS	E	Avg.
1989— St. Catharines (NYP)	C	31	89	9	16	5	0	0	11	23	39	0	4	0-0	.180	.345	.236	.581	2	.974
1990— St. Catharines (NYP)	C	67	228	30	64	13	0	6	39	35	65	5	2	2-7	.281	.382	.417	.799	7	.987
1991— Myrtle Beach (SAL)	C	132	441	72	126	18	2	18	70	75	97	8	7	9-10	.286	.396	.458	.854	19	.976
— Syracuse (Int'l)	C	1	3	0	0	0	0	0	0	0	2	0	0	0-0	.000	.000	.000	.000	0	1.000
1992— Dunedin (Fla. St.)	C	133	485	83	157	30	2	30	100	59	91	6	8	2-5	.324	.402	.579	.982	11	.986
1993— Knoxville (Southern)	C	140	468	91	142	28	0	25	102	102	98	6	11	10-3	.303	.430	.524	.954	14	.983
— Toronto (A.L.)	C-DH	2	1	0	0	0	0	0	0	1	0	0	0	0-0	.000	.500	.000	.500	0	1.000
1994— Toronto (A.L.)	OF-C	43	130	17	28	2	0	9	24	25	46	3	5	1-1	.215	.352	.438	.791	2	.967
— Syracuse (Int'l)	DH-C-1B	85	307	52	98	11	0	19	58	42	58	3	1	1-0	.319	.404	.541	.945	7	.974
1995— Toronto (A.L.)	OF-DH-1B	37	91	7	15	3	0	3	11	6	26	0	1	0-0	.165	.212	.297	.509	0	1.000
— Syracuse (Int'l)	1B-OF	91	333	59	106	23	4	22	74	45	78	5	8	0-4	.318	.403	.610	1.013	4	.995
1996— Toronto (A.L.)	DH-1B	138	488	68	132	28	2	25	92	58	139	6	9	0-0	.270	.353	.490	.843	4	.988
1997— Toronto (A.L.)	1B-DH	153	519	79	136	42	3	30	91	64	133	8	6	0-3	.262	.350	.528	.878	12	.988
1998— Dunedin (Fla. St.)	1B-DH	4	16	4	5	1	0	2	7	2	4	0	1	0-0	.313	.389	.750	1.139	0	1.000
— Syracuse (Int'l)	1B	2	7	4	4	2	0	1	6	2	0	0	0	0-0	.571	.667	1.286	1.952	0	1.000
— Toronto (A.L.)	1B-DH	142	530	94	155	43	1	38	115	73	139	11	8	3-0	.292	.385	.592	.978	10	.992
1999— Toronto (A.L.)	1B-DH	152	573	113	156	39	0	44	134	86	141	15	11	1-1	.272	.377	.571	.948	* 14	.990
2000— Toronto (A.L.)	1B	• 162	569	115	196	* 57	1	41	137	123	104	• 15	12	0-1	.344	.470	.664	1.134	13	.991
2001— Toronto (A.L.)	1B	• 162	574	102	160	31	1	39	102	111	136	16	9	3-0	.279	.408	.540	.948	9	.994
2002— Toronto (A.L.)	1B-DH	143	505	103	140	34	2	33	108	102	126	13	8	1-0	.277	.406	.549	.955	12	.991
2003— Toronto (A.L.)	1B-DH	161	570	117	172	38	1	42	* 145	109	137	19	9	0-0	.302	.426	.593	1.019	10	.993
2004— Dunedin (Fla. St.)	1B	2	8	1	2	0	0	1	2	0	0	0	0	0-0	.250	.250	.625	.875	0	1.000
— Syracuse (Int'l)	1B	2	9	2	5	2	0	1	4	0	0	0	1	0-0	.556	.556	1.111	1.667	0	1.000
— Toronto (A.L.)	1B-DH	128	458	74	123	26	0	32	99	69	115	13	11	0-1	.269	.372	.535	.907	5	.996
2005— Florida (N.L.)	1B-DH	144	521	81	157	41	3	33	115	72	121	17	16	0-0	.301	.399	.582	.981	14	.989
American League totals (12 years)		1423	5008	889	1413	343	11	336	1058	827	1242	122	93	9-7	.282	.392	.556	.949	91	.992
National League totals (1 year)		144	521	81	157	41	3	33	115	72	121	17	16	0-0	.301	.399	.582	.981	14	.989
Major League totals (13 years)		1567	5529	970	1570	384	14	369	1173	899	1363	139	109	9-7	.284	.393	.559	.952	105	.992

ALL-STAR GAME RECORD

	G	AB	R	H	2B	3B	HR	RBI	BB	SO	HBP	GDP	SB-CS	Avg.	OBP	SLG	OPS	E	Avg.
All-Star Game totals (2 years)	2	4	0	2	1	0	0	1	0	1	0	0	0-0	.500	.500	.750	1.250	0	1.000

DELLUCCI, DAVID   OF

PERSONAL: Born October 31, 1973, in Baton Rouge, La. ... 5-11/190. ... Bats left, throws left. ... Full name: David Michael Dellucci. ... Name pronounced: duh-LOO-chee. ... High school: Catholic (Baton Rouge, La.). ... College: Mississippi.

TRANSACTIONS/CAREER NOTES: Selected by Minnesota Twins in 11th round of 1994 free-agent draft; did not sign. ... Selected by Baltimore Orioles organization in 10th round of 1995 free-agent draft. ... Selected by Arizona Diamondbacks in second round (45th pick overall) of expansion draft (November 18, 1997). ... On disabled list (July 25, 1999-remainder of season). ... On disabled list (May 3-24, 2002); included rehabilitation assignment to Tucson. ... On disabled list (June 2-17, 2003). ... Traded by Diamondbacks with P Bret Prinz and C Jon-Mark Sprowl to New York Yankees for OF Raul Mondesi (July 29, 2003). ... On disabled list (August 28-September 27, 2003). ... Signed as a free agent by Texas Rangers (December 23, 2003).

2005 GAMES PLAYED BY POSITION (MLB): DH—67, OF—52.

SCOUTING REPORT **Offense:** Dellucci had a career year in 2005 after undergoing eye surgery. Is an extremely patient hitter with a compact stroke. Has improved his bat speed and has a slight lift to his swing. A good fastball hitter who likes the ball down. Can get on top of the fastball for power. Strikes out a lot when he starts to chase pitches above his zone. Is an average runner at best and is not a basestealer. **Defense:** He is an aggressive defender who is not afraid to leave his feet. Gets good jumps laterally and charges balls well. Arm is extremely short and runners frequently take an extra base on him. **Outlook:** He has become a productive offensive player, but he likely won't duplicate his home run totals. *Grade 7.8*

DAVID DELLUCCI'S HITTING ZONE

.286	.375	.433
.258	.471	.209
.429	.200	.188

LEFTY-RIGHTY SPLITS

vs.	Avg.	AB	H	2B	3B	HR	RBI	BB	SO	OBP	Slg.
L	.242	33	8	1	0	1	3	5	15	.342	.364
R	.251	402	101	16	5	28	62	71	106	.369	.525

Year	Team (League)	Pos.	G	AB	R	H	2B	3B	HR	RBI	BB	SO	HBP	GDP	SB-CS	Avg.	OBP	SLG	OPS	E	Avg.
1995—	Bluefield (Appal.)	OF	20	69	11	23	5	1	2	12	6	7	1	1	3-1	.333	.390	.522	.911	4	.846
—	Frederick (Carolina)	OF	28	96	16	27	3	0	1	10	12	10	3	3	1-2	.281	.378	.344	.722	1	.966
1996—	Frederick (Carolina)	OF	59	185	33	60	11	1	4	28	38	34	0	2	5-6	.324	.438	.459	.897	3	.972
—	Bowie (East.)	OF	66	251	27	73	14	1	2	33	28	56	1	4	2-7	.291	.363	.378	.741	3	.979
1997—	Bowie (East.)	OF-DH	107	385	71	126	29	3	20	55	58	69	5	6	11-4	.327	.421	.574	.995	1	.994
—	Baltimore (A.L.)	OF-DH	17	27	3	6	1	0	1	3	4	7	1	2	0-0	.222	.344	.370	.714	0	1.000
1998—	Tucson (PCL)	OF	17	72	17	22	4	1	1	11	5	8	0	2	4-0	.306	.346	.486	.832	0	1.000
—	Arizona (N.L.)	OF	124	416	43	108	19	* 12	5	51	33	103	3	6	3-5	.260	.318	.399	.717	3	.987
1999—	Arizona (N.L.)	OF-DH	63	109	27	43	7	1	1	15	11	24	3	1	0-0	.395	.463	.505	.968	0	1.000
2000—	Arizona (N.L.)	OF	34	50	2	15	3	0	0	2	4	9	0	0	0-2	.300	.352	.360	.712	0	1.000
—	Tucson (PCL)	OF	33	122	16	28	6	3	3	17	13	15	0	0	4-0	.230	.301	.402	.703	2	.966
—	Ariz. D'backs (Ariz.)	OF	2	6	0	2	1	0	0	1	0	0	0	0	0-0	.333	.333	.500	.833	0	
—	South Bend (Mid.)	OF	2	5	3	1	1	0	0	1	2	0	0	0	0-0	.200	.375	.400	.775	0	1.000
2001—	Arizona (N.L.)	OF	115	217	28	60	11	2	10	40	22	52	2	2	2-1	.277	.349	.479	.828	1	.989
2002—	Arizona (N.L.)	OF-DH	97	229	34	56	11	2	7	29	28	55	1	7	2-4	.245	.326	.402	.727	3	.967
—	Tucson (PCL)	OF	4	15	2	2	1	0	0	1	2	4	0	0	0-0	.133	.235	.200	.435	0	1.000
2003—	Arizona (N.L.)	OF	70	165	18	40	11	3	2	19	19	45	3	4	9-0	.242	.328	.382	.710	2	.976
—	New York (A.L.)	OF-DH	21	51	8	9	1	0	1	4	4	13	2	2	3-0	.176	.263	.255	.518	0	1.000
2004—	Texas (A.L.)	OF-DH	107	331	59	80	13	1	17	61	47	88	5	4	9-4	.242	.342	.441	.783	2	.989
2005—	Texas (A.L.)	DH-OF	128	435	97	109	17	5	29	65	76	121	5	4	5-3	.251	.367	.513	.879	3	.970
American League totals (4 years)			273	844	167	204	32	6	48	133	131	229	13	15	17-7	.242	.350	.464	.815	5	.985
National League totals (6 years)			503	1186	152	322	61	20	25	156	117	288	12	23	18-12	.272	.341	.420	.761	9	.984
Major League totals (9 years)			776	2030	319	526	93	26	73	289	248	517	25	38	35-19	.259	.345	.438	.784	14	.984

DIVISION SERIES RECORD

Year	Team (League)	Pos.	G	AB	R	H	2B	3B	HR	RBI	BB	SO	HBP	GDP	SB-CS	Avg.	OBP	SLG	OPS	E	Avg.
2001—	Arizona (N.L.)		2	0	0	0	0	0	0	0	0	0	0	0	0-0	...	...	...	...		...
2002—	Arizona (N.L.)	OF	3	7	1	2	0	0	0	2	0	1	0	0	0-0	.286	.286	.714	1.000	0	1.000
2003—	New York (A.L.)	DH	1	0	0	0	0	0	0	0	0	0	0	0	0-0	...	...	...	...		...
Division series totals (3 years)			6	7	1	2	0	0	0	2	0	1	0	0	0-0	.286	.286	.714	1.000	0	1.000

CHAMPIONSHIP SERIES RECORD

Year	Team (League)	Pos.	G	AB	R	H	2B	3B	HR	RBI	BB	SO	HBP	GDP	SB-CS	Avg.	OBP	SLG	OPS	E	Avg.
2001—	Arizona (N.L.)		2	2	1	1	0	0	0	0	0	0	0	0	0-0	.500	.500	.500	1.000	...	...
2003—	New York (A.L.)	DH-OF	3	3	2	1	0	0	0	0	0	1	0	0	1-0	.333	.500	.333	.833	0	...
Champ. series totals (2 years)			5	5	3	2	0	0	0	0	0	1	0	0	1-0	.400	.500	.400	.900	0	...

WORLD SERIES RECORD

Year	Team (League)	Pos.	G	AB	R	H	2B	3B	HR	RBI	BB	SO	HBP	GDP	SB-CS	Avg.	OBP	SLG	OPS	E	Avg.
2001—	Arizona (N.L.)	OF	2	2	0	1	0	0	0	0	0	0	0	0	0-0	.500	.500	.500	1.000	0	1.000
2003—	New York (A.L.)	OF-DH	4	2	1	0	0	0	0	0	0	0	0	0	0-0	.000	.000	.000	.000	0	1.000
World Series totals (2 years)			6	4	1	1	0	0	0	0	0	0	0	0	0-0	.250	.250	.250	.500	0	1.000

DE LOS SANTOS, VALERIO   P

PERSONAL: Born October 6, 1972, in Las Matas, Dominican Republic. ... 6-2/211. ... Throws left, bats left. ... Full name: Valerio Lorenzo de los Santos.

TRANSACTIONS/CAREER NOTES: Signed as a non-drafted free agent by Milwaukee Brewers organization (January 26, 1993). ... On disabled list (April 29-September 23, 1999; April 4, 2001-remainder of season; and April 27-May 27, 2003). ... Traded by Brewers to Philadelphia Phillies for cash (September 2, 2003). ... Signed as a free agent by Toronto Blue Jays (December 27, 2003). ... On disabled list (June 6, 2004-remainder of season). ... Signed as a free agent by Florida Marlins organization (May 13, 2005).

CAREER HITTING: 0-for-9 (.000), 0 R, 0 2B, 0 3B, 0 HR, 0 RBI.

VALERIO DE LOS SANTOS'S PITCHING ZONE

.200	.400	.250
.308	.250	.400
.125	.333	.200

LEFTY-RIGHTY SPLITS

vs.	Avg.	AB	H	2B	3B	HR	RBI	BB	SO	OBP	Slg.
L	.324	37	12	3	1	1	10	3	8	.405	.541
R	.250	52	13	3	0	3	10	9	8	.361	.481

Year	Team (League)	W	L	Pct.	ERA	WHIP	G	GS	CG	ShO	Hld.	Sv.-Opp.	IP	H	R	ER	HR	BB-IBB	SO	Avg.
1993—	Dom. Brewers (DSL)	1	7	.125	6.50	2.01	19	6	1	0		0-...	63.2	91	57	46		37-...	39	...
1994—	Dom. Brewers (DSL)	7	6	.538	3.69	1.38	17	16	1	1		0-...	90.1	90	52	37		35-...	50	...
1995—	Ariz. Brewers (Ariz.)	4	6	.400	2.20	1.13	14	12	0	0		0-...	82.0	81	34	20		12-2	57	.258

Year	Team (League)	W	L	Pct.	ERA	WHIP	G	GS	CG	ShO	Hld.	Sv.-Opp.	IP	H	R	ER	HR	BB-IBB	SO	Avg.
1996—	Beloit (Midw.)	10	8	.556	3.55	1.35	33	23	5	1	...	4-...	164.2	164	83	65	11	59-4	137	.257
1997—	El Paso (Texas)	6	10	.375	5.75	1.61	26	16	1	0	...	2-...	114.1	146	83	73	6	38-2	61	.314
1998—	El Paso (Texas)	6	2	.750	3.92	1.59	42	4	0	0	...	10-...	66.2	81	34	29	2	25-1	62	.299
	— Milwaukee (N.L.)	0	0	...	2.91	0.60	13	0	0	0	0	0-...	21.2	11	7	7	4	2-0	18	.151
	— Louisville (Int'l)	0	0	...	3.60	0.80	5	0	0	0	0	0-...	5.0	4	2	2	0	0-0	0	.211
1999—	Milwaukee (N.L.)	0	1	.000	6.48	2.28	7	0	0	0	0	0-0	8.1	12	6	6	1	7-0	5	.343
2000—	Milwaukee (N.L.)	2	3	.400	5.13	1.43	66	2	0	0	9	0-1	73.2	72	43	42	15	33-7	70	.254
2001—	Milwaukee (N.L.)	0	0	...	9.00	2.00	1	0	0	0	0	0-0	1.0	1	1	1	0	1-0	1	.250
2002—	Indianapolis (Int'l)	1	0	1.000	0.00	1.00	2	0	0	0	0	0-...	2.0	1	0	0	0	1-0	5	.143
	— Milwaukee (N.L.)	2	3	.400	3.12	1.18	51	0	0	0	7	0-0	57.2	42	21	20	4	26-3	38	.211
2003—	Milwaukee (N.L.)	3	3	.500	4.13	1.25	45	0	0	0	11	1-4	48.0	38	24	22	8	22-0	35	.225
	— Philadelphia (N.L.)	1	0	1.000	9.00	2.50	6	0	0	0	0	0-0	4.0	7	7	4	0	3-0	4	.389
2004—	Toronto (A.L.)	0	0	...	6.17	1.80	17	0	0	0	0	0-1	11.2	11	8	8	0	10-2	10	.250
2005—	Jupiter (Fla. St.)	0	0	...	0.00	1.50	3	0	0	0	0	0-0	4.0	4	0	0	0	2-0	4	.250
	— Florida (N.L.)	1	2	.333	6.14	1.68	27	0	0	0	1	0-1	22.0	25	15	15	4	12-3	16	.281
	— Albuquerque (PCL)	0	0	...	1.69	1.50	6	0	0	0	0	1-1	5.1	7	1	1	0	1-0	6	.304
	American League totals (1 year)	0	0	...	6.17	1.80	17	0	0	0	0	0-1	11.2	11	8	8	0	10-2	10	.250
	National League totals (7 years)	9	12	.429	4.46	1.33	216	2	0	0	28	1-6	236.1	208	124	117	36	106-13	187	.239
	Major League totals (8 years)	9	12	.429	4.54	1.35	233	2	0	0	28	1-7	248.0	219	132	125	36	116-15	197	.240

DEMARIA, CHRIS   P

PERSONAL: Born September 28, 1980, in Torrance, Calif. ... 6-3/210. ... Throws right, bats both. ... Full name: Christopher Neil Demaria. ... College: Long Beach State.
TRANSACTIONS/CAREER NOTES: Selected by Pittsburgh Pirates organization in 17th round of 2002 free-agent draft. ... Selected by Kansas City Royals organization from Pirates in Rule 5 minor league draft (December 13, 2004).
CAREER HITTING: 0-for-0 (.000), 0 R, 0 2B, 0 3B, 0 HR, 0 RBI.

LEFTY-RIGHTY SPLITS

vs.	Avg.	AB	H	2B	3B	HR	RBI	BB	SO	OBP	Slg.
L	.588	17	10	2	1	3	8	4	3	.667	1.353
R	.182	22	4	2	0	0	2	1	8	.217	.273

Year	Team (League)	W	L	Pct.	ERA	WHIP	G	GS	CG	ShO	Hld.	Sv.-Opp.	IP	H	R	ER	HR	BB-IBB	SO	Avg.
2002—	Will. (NYP)	1	1	.500	4.35	1.23	16	0	0	0	...	1-...	31.0	34	20	15	6	4-1	15	.272
2003—	Will. (NYP)	6	3	.667	2.68	0.98	25	1	0	0	...	3-...	47.0	36	15	14	3	10-1	48	.209
2004—	Hickory (S. Atl.)	8	3	.727	2.94	1.03	40	0	0	0	...	10-...	79.2	62	29	26	5	20-2	101	.209
2005—	High Desert (Calif.)	4	2	.667	2.23	1.10	48	0	0	0	1	19-24	60.2	57	19	15	8	10-1	73	.247
	— Wichita (Texas)	0	1	.000	1.76	0.91	10	0	0	0	0	1-2	15.1	12	3	3	3	2-0	19	.218
	— Kansas City (A.L.)	1	0	1.000	9.00	2.11	8	0	0	0	0	0-0	9.0	14	10	9	3	5-0	11	.359
	Major League totals (1 year)	1	0	1.000	9.00	2.11	8	0	0	0	0	0-0	9.0	14	10	9	3	5-0	11	.359

DEMPSTER, RYAN   P

PERSONAL: Born May 3, 1977, in Sechelt, British Columbia. ... 6-2/215. ... Throws right, bats right. ... Full name: Ryan Scott Dempster. ... High school: Elphinstone (Gibsons, B.C.).
TRANSACTIONS/CAREER NOTES: Selected by Texas Rangers organization in third round of 1995 free-agent draft. ... Traded by Rangers with a player to be named to Florida Marlins for P John Burkett (August 8, 1996); Marlins acquired P Rick Helling to complete deal (September 3, 1996). ... Traded by Marlins to Cincinnati Reds for OF Juan Encarnacion, OF/2B Wilton Guerrero and P Ryan Snare (July 11, 2002). ... On disabled list (May 23-June 7 and July 29, 2003-remainder of season); included rehabilitation assignment to Louisville. ... Released by Reds (November 4, 2003). ... Signed by Chicago Cubs (January 21, 2004). ... On disabled list (March 26-August 1, 2004); included rehabilitation assignments to Lansing and Iowa.
CAREER HITTING: 24-for-311 (.077), 12 R, 5 2B, 1 3B, 0 HR, 7 RBI.

SCOUTING REPORT **Throws:** Dempster has a fastball that ranges from 89-93 mph, a slider at 88 and a changeup. ***Tendencies:*** A former starter, Dempster is throwing harder two years removed from elbow surgery. Fastball has some sinking action. Slider is a power one with late life and is his most effective pitch. ***Outlook:*** With his two plus pitches, Dempster is poised to have a good year in 2006. ***Grade 7***

RYAN DEMPSTER'S PITCHING ZONE

.333	.211	.385
.354	.243	.289
.200	.500	.192

LEFTY-RIGHTY SPLITS

vs.	Avg.	AB	H	2B	3B	HR	RBI	BB	SO	OBP	Slg.
L	.278	144	40	7	0	2	19	29	39	.399	.368
R	.216	199	43	7	1	2	20	20	50	.300	.291

Year	Team (League)	W	L	Pct.	ERA	WHIP	G	GS	CG	ShO	Hld.	Sv.-Opp.	IP	H	R	ER	HR	BB-IBB	SO	Avg.
1995—	GC Rangers (GCL)	3	1	.750	2.36	1.49	8	6	1	0	...	0-...	34.1	34	21	9	1	17-0	37	.254
	— Hudson Valley (NYP)	1	0	1.000	3.18	1.41	1	1	0	0	...	0-...	5.2	7	2	2	0	1-0	6	.318
1996—	Char., S.C. (SAL)	7	11	.389	3.30	1.23	23	23	2	0	...	0-...	144.1	120	71	53	13	58-1	141	.229
	— Kane Co. (Midw.)	2	1	.667	2.73	1.37	4	4	1	1	...	0-...	26.1	18	10	8	0	18-0	16	.202
1997—	Brevard County (FSL)	10	9	.526	4.90	1.43	28	26	2	1	...	0-...	165.1	190	100	90	19	46-1	131	.290
1998—	Portland (East.)	4	3	.571	3.22	1.10	7	7	0	0	...	0-...	44.2	34	20	16	8	15-0	33	.214
	— Florida (N.L.)	1	5	.167	7.08	2.01	14	11	0	0	0	0-1	54.2	72	47	43	6	38-1	35	.336
	— Charlotte (Int'l)	3	1	.750	3.27	1.36	5	5	1	0	0	0-0	33.0	33	14	12	4	12-1	24	.270
1999—	Calgary (PCL)	1	1	.500	4.99	1.30	5	5	0	0	0	0-0	30.2	30	17	17	6	10-1	29	.252
	— Florida (N.L.)	7	8	.467	4.71	1.63	25	25	0	0	0	0-0	147.0	146	77	77	21	93-2	126	.262
2000—	Florida (N.L.)	14	10	.583	3.66	1.36	33	33	2	1	0	0-0	226.1	210	102	92	30	97-1	209	.243
2001—	Florida (N.L.)	15	12	.556	4.94	1.36	34	34	2	1	0	0-0	211.1	218	123	116	21	* 112-5	171	.269
2002—	Florida (N.L.)	5	8	.385	4.79	1.50	18	18	1	0	0	0-0	120.1	126	66	64	12	55-1	87	.281
	— Cincinnati (N.L.)	5	5	.500	6.19	1.58	15	15	1	0	0	0-0	88.2	102	61	‡ 61	16	38-1	66	.293
2003—	Louisville (Int'l)	1	1	.500	3.29	1.20	2	1	0	0	...	0-...	13.2	13	5	5	1	3-0	9	.255
	— Cincinnati (N.L.)	3	7	.300	6.54	1.76	22	20	0	0	0	0-0	115.2	134	89	84	14	70-4	84	.293
2004—	Lansing (Midw.)	0	0	...	1.96	1.20	5	5	0	0	...	0-...	18.1	20	5	4	3	2-0	21	.270
	— Iowa (PCL)	1	1	.500	3.86	1.38	6	4	0	0	...	0-...	21.0	19	9	9	1	10-0	20	.244
	— Chicago (N.L.)	1	1	.500	3.92	1.40	23	0	0	0	3	2-2	20.2	16	9	9	1	13-0	18	.208
2005—	Chicago (N.L.)	5	3	.625	3.13	1.43	63	6	0	0	3	33-35	92.0	83	35	32	4	49-7	89	.242
	Major League totals (8 years)	56	59	.487	4.83	1.55	247	162	8	2	3	35-38	1076.2	1107	609	578	125	565-28	885	.269

D

DENORFIA, CHRIS — OF

PERSONAL: Born July 15, 1980, in Bristol, Conn. ... 6-1/185. ... Bats right, throws right. ... Full name: Christopher Anthony Denorfia. ... College: Wheaton College.

TRANSACTIONS/CAREER NOTES: Selected by Cincinnati Reds organization in 19th round of 2002 free-agent draft.

2005 GAMES PLAYED BY POSITION (MLB): OF—12.

LEFTY-RIGHTY SPLITS

vs.	Avg.	AB	H	2B	3B	HR	RBI	BB	SO	OBP	Slg.
L	.273	11	3	1	0	1	1	3	3	.429	.636
R	.259	27	7	2	0	0	1	3	6	.333	.333

Year	Team (League)	Pos.	G	AB	R	H	2B	3B	HR	RBI	BB	SO	HBP	GDP	SB-CS	Avg.	OBP	SLG	OPS	E	Avg.
2002—	GC Reds (GCL)	OF	57	200	38	68	9	2	0	19	31	23	0	8	18-8	.340	.425	.405	.830	4	.966
	—Chattanooga (Sou.)	OF	3	7	0	3	2	1	0	0	2	1	0	0	0-0	.429	.556	1.000	1.556	0	1.000
	—Dayton (Midw.)	OF	3	10	2	0	0	0	0	0	0	3	0	1	0-0	.000	.000	.000	.000	1	1.000
2003—	Potomac (Carol.)	OF	128	470	60	111	10	5	4	39	54	106	1	10	20-7	.236	.317	.304	.621	5	.982
2004—	Potomac (Carol.)	OF	75	269	52	84	18	4	11	51	48	66	1	3	10-6	.312	.416	.532	.948	4	.846
	—Chattanooga (Sou.)	OF	61	221	30	55	10	2	6	27	30	42	1		5-2	.249	.340	.394	.734	2	.000
2005—	Chattanooga (Sou.)	OF	46	188	40	62	17	3	7	26	17	38	2	1	4-3	.330	.391	.564	.955	4	.979
	—Louisville (Int'l)	OF	91	323	50	100	12	6	13	61	41	54	4	7	8-3	.310	.391	.505	.895	0	1.000
	—Cincinnati (N.L.)	OF	18	38	8	10	3	0	1	2	6	9	0	1	1-0	.263	.364	.421	.785	1	.962
	Major League totals (1 year)		18	38	8	10	3	0	1	2	6	9	0	1	1-0	.263	.364	.421	.785	1	.962

DEPAULA, JORGE — P

PERSONAL: Born November 10, 1978, in Sabana Grande, Dominican Republic. ... 6-1/160. ... Throws right, bats right. ... Full name: Jorge DePaula.

TRANSACTIONS/CAREER NOTES: Signed as a non-drafted free agent by Colorado Rockies organization (January 13, 1997). ... Traded by Rockies to New York Yankees (April 20, 2001), completing deal in which Yankees traded P Craig Dingman to Rockies for a player to be named (April 20, 2001). ... On disabled list (April 17, 2004-remainder of season).

CAREER HITTING: 0-for-0 (.000), 0 R, 0 2B, 0 3B, 0 HR, 0 RBI.

LEFTY-RIGHTY SPLITS

vs.	Avg.	AB	H	2B	3B	HR	RBI	BB	SO	OBP	Slg.
L	.313	16	5	3	0	1	4	1	1	.353	.688
R	.273	11	3	0	0	1	2	2	2	.385	.545

Year	Team (League)	W	L	Pct.	ERA	WHIP	G	GS	CG	ShO	Hld.	Sv.-Opp.	IP	H	R	ER	HR	BB-IBB	SO	Avg.
1998—	Ariz. Rockies (Ariz.)	5	5	.500	3.81	1.33	17	9	0	0		2-..	54.1	54	30	23	1	18-1	62	.252
1999—	Portland (N'west)	6	6	.500	6.01	1.64	16	16	0	0		0-..	85.1	97	67	57	8	43-0	77	.290
2000—	Asheville (S. Atl.)	8	13	.381	4.70	1.37	28	27	1	1		0-..	155.0	151	90	81	16	62-0	187	.262
2001—	Asheville (S. Atl.)	1	1	.500	3.78	1.26	3	3	0	0		0-..	16.2	19	13	7	3	2-0	26	.268
	—Greensboro (S. Atl.)	6	1	.857	2.75	1.01	8	8	0	0		0-..	55.2	35	19	17	2	21-0	67	.179
	—Tampa (Fla. St.)	9	5	.643	3.58	1.42	16	13	0	0		0-..	83.0	65	43	33	3	53-2	77	.212
2002—	Norwich (East.)	14	6	.700	3.45	1.10	27	26	6	1		0-..	175.0	141	74	67	11	52-0	152	.221
2003—	Columbus (Int'l)	10	11	.476	4.35	1.34	27	27	3	2		0-..	167.2	168	90	81	22	57-2	125	.262
	—New York (A.L.)	0	0		0.79	0.35	4	1	0	0	0	0-0	11.1	3	1	1	1	1-0	7	.083
2004—	New York (A.L.)	0	1	.000	5.00	1.44	3	1	0	0	0	0-0	9.0	9	6	5	1	4-0	2	.257
2005—	New York (A.L.)	0	0		8.10	1.65	3	0	0	0	0	0-0	6.2	8	6	6	0	3-0	3	.296
	Major League totals (3 years)	0	1	.000	4.00	1.04	10	2	0	0	0	0-0	27.0	20	13	12	2	8-0	12	.211

DEROSA, MARK — IF/OF

PERSONAL: Born February 26, 1975, in Passaic, N.J. ... 6-1/205. ... Bats right, throws right. ... Full name: Mark Thomas DeRosa. ... High school: Bergen Catholic (Oradell, N.J.). ... College: Pennsylvania.

TRANSACTIONS/CAREER NOTES: Selected by Atlanta Braves organization in seventh round of 1996 free-agent draft. ... On disabled list (May 18-July 17, 2002); included rehabilitation assignments to Richmond and Myrtle Beach. ... Signed as a free agent by Texas Rangers organization (January 19, 2005).

2005 GAMES PLAYED BY POSITION (MLB): OF—25, 2B—17, SS—16, 3B—5, DH—4, 1B—1.

SCOUTING REPORT DeRosa basically is a utility player. Has a short stroke but poor bat speed. Will go with the pitch but isn't a good breaking-ball hitter. Is a much better hitter against lefthanded pitchers. Is a fluid infielder with good hands but isn't quick enough to play third base. Won't hit enough to be a regular. *Grade 5.3*

MARK DEROSA'S HITTING ZONE

.333	.200	.200
.227	.417	.412
.190	.267	.200

LEFTY-RIGHTY SPLITS

vs.	Avg.	AB	H	2B	3B	HR	RBI	BB	SO	OBP	Slg.
L	.322	59	19	3	0	5	12	9	12	.412	.627
R	.191	89	17	2	0	3	8	7	23	.265	.315

Year	Team (League)	Pos.	G	AB	R	H	2B	3B	HR	RBI	BB	SO	HBP	GDP	SB-CS	Avg.	OBP	SLG	OPS	E	Avg.
1996—	Eugene (Northwest)	SS	70	255	43	66	13	1	2	28	38	48	5	10	3-4	.259	.363	.341	.705	24	.921
1997—	Durham (Carol.)	SS	92	346	51	93	11	3	8	37	25	73	10	12	6-8	.269	.332	.387	.720	21	.948
1998—	Greenville (Sou.)	SS	125	461	67	123	26	2	8	49	60	57	5	18	7-13	.267	.356	.384	.740	20	.964
	—Atlanta (N.L.)	SS	5	3	2	1	0	0	0	0	0	1	0	0		.333	.333	.333	.667	0	1.000
1999—	Richmond (Int'l)	SS-DH	105	364	41	99	16	2	1	40	21	49	5	5	7-6	.272	.317	.335	.652	20	.951
	—Atlanta (N.L.)	SS	7	8	0	0	0	0	0	0	0	2	0	0	0-0	.000	.000	.000	.000	1	1.000
2000—	Richmond (Int'l)	SS-2B-3B	101	370	62	108	23	3	3	35	38	36	3	13	13-4	.292	.359	.392	.751	19	.958
	—Atlanta (N.L.)	SS	22	13	9	4	1	0	0	3	2	1	0	0	0-0	.308	.400	.385	.785	0	1.000
2001—	Richmond (Int'l)	SS-3B-2B	49	186	31	55	18	0	2	17	17	22	1	6	7-3	.296	.351	.425	.776	4	.978
	—Atlanta (N.L.)	SS-2B-DH 3B-OF	66	164	27	47	8	0	3	20	12	19	5	3	2-1	.287	.350	.390	.740	7	.966
2002—	Atlanta (N.L.)	2B-SS-OF 3B	72	212	24	63	9	2	5	23	12	24	3	5	2-3	.297	.339	.429	.768	6	.976
	—Richmond (Int'l)	2B-SS	16	55	9	14	3	0	0	6	5	2	2	4	2-0	.255	.339	.309	.648	3	.952
	—Myrtle Beach (Carol.)	2B	2	7	0	0	0	0	0	0	1	1	0	0	0-0	.000	.125	.000	.125	1	.889
2003—	Atlanta (N.L.)	2B-3B-SS DH-OF-1B	103	266	40	70	14	0	6	22	16	49	5	6	1-0	.263	.316	.383	.699	6	.976

Year Team (League)	Pos.	G	AB	R	H	2B	3B	HR	RBI	BB	SO	HBP	GDP	SB-CS	Avg.	OBP	SLG	OPS	E	Avg.
							BATTING												FIELDING	
2004— Atlanta (N.L.) ....3B-SS-2B OF		118	309	33	74	16	0	3	31	23	53	3	6	1-3	.239	.293	.320	.614	12	.942
2005— Texas (A.L.) OF-2B-SS 3B-DH-1B		66	148	26	36	5	0	8	20	16	35	2	5	1-0	.243	.325	.439	.764	3	.980
American League totals (1 year)		66	148	26	36	5	0	8	20	16	35	2	5	1-0	.243	.325	.439	.764	3	.980
National League totals (7 years)		393	975	135	259	48	2	17	99	65	149	16	20	6-7	.266	.318	.371	.690	31	.967
Major League totals (8 years)		459	1123	161	295	53	2	25	119	81	184	18	25	7-7	.263	.319	.380	.700	34	.968

DIVISION SERIES RECORD

Year Team (League)	Pos.	G	AB	R	H	2B	3B	HR	RBI	BB	SO	HBP	GDP	SB-CS	Avg.	OBP	SLG	OPS	E	Avg.
2001— Atlanta (N.L.)	SS	1	1	0	1	0	0	0	0	0	0	0	0	0-0	1.000	1.000	1.000	2.000	0	1.000
2002— Atlanta (N.L.)	2B	4	7	2	3	1	1	0	3	1	1	0	0	0-0	.429	.500	.857	1.357	0	1.000
2003— Atlanta (N.L.)	2B-3B	4	7	1	3	2	0	0	2	1	2	0	0	0-0	.429	.500	.714	1.214	0	1.000
Division series totals (3 years)		9	15	3	7	3	1	0	5	2	3	0	0	0-0	.467	.529	.800	1.329	0	1.000

CHAMPIONSHIP SERIES RECORD

Year Team (League)	Pos.	G	AB	R	H	2B	3B	HR	RBI	BB	SO	HBP	GDP	SB-CS	Avg.	OBP	SLG	OPS	E	Avg.
2001— Atlanta (N.L.)	SS	4	4	0	0	0	0	0	0	0	0	0	0	0-0	.000	.000	.000	.000	0	1.000

DESSENS, ELMER   P

PERSONAL: Born January 13, 1971, in Hermosillo, Mexico. ... 5-10/198. ... Throws right, bats right. ... Full name: Elmer Dessens Jusaino. ... Name pronounced: duh-SENZ. ... High school: Carrera Technica (Hermosillo, Mexico).

TRANSACTIONS/CAREER NOTES: Signed as a non-drafted free agent by Pittsburgh Pirates organization (January 27, 1993). ... Loaned by Pirates organization to Mexico City Red Devils of the Mexican League for 1993 and 1994 seasons; returned to Pirates organization for 1995 season. ... Loaned by Pirates organization to Red Devils (May 7, 1996). ... Returned to Pirates organization (June 21, 1996). ... On disabled list (July 31-September 10, 1996); included rehabilitation assignment to Carolina. ... Loaned by Pirates to Red Devils (March 27-September 5, 1997). ... On disabled list (April 8-24, 1998); included rehabilitation assignment to Nashville. ... Contract purchased by Yomiuri of the Japan League (March 31, 1999). ... Signed as a free agent by Cincinnati Reds organization (December 15, 1999). ... Traded by Reds with cash to Arizona Diamondbacks as part of four-team deal in which Reds acquired SS Felipe Lopez from Toronto Blue Jays, Blue Jays acquired a player to be named from Oakland Athletics and Athletics acquired 1B Erubiel Durazo from Diamondbacks (December 15, 2002); Blue Jays acquired P Jason Arnold to complete deal (December 16, 2002). ... Traded by Diamondbacks to Los Angeles Dodgers for OF Jereme Milons (August 19, 2004). ... On disabled list (April 24-June 15, 2005); included rehabilitation assignment to Las Vegas.

CAREER HITTING: 39-for-233 (.167), 12 R, 4 2B, 1 3B, 0 HR, 16 RBI.

SCOUTING REPORT **Throws:** Dessens has an 88-92 mph fastball, a curveball, a slider and a changeup. **Tendencies:** He is a control pitcher who must use all of his pitches and get groundballs to be effective. He is sneaky fast and has good life on his two-seam fastball, but it straightens out when it's up. Is most effective working inside. Has good rotation on his curveball and good depth on his slider. **Outlook:** Dessens has a history of arm problems, but he can be an effective No. 5 starter or long reliever if he can stay healthy and keep the ball down. ***Grade 6.2***

ELMER DESSENS'S PITCHING ZONE

.500	.167	.400
.216	.292	.280
.240	.385	.261

LEFTY-RIGHTY SPLITS

vs.	Avg.	AB	H	2B	3B	HR	RBI	BB	SO	OBP	Slg.
L	.243	111	27	6	0	4	14	11	17	.309	.405
R	.254	142	36	9	0	2	13	8	20	.294	.359

Year Team (League)	W	L	Pct.	ERA	WHIP	G	GS	CG	ShO	Hld.	Sv.-Opp.	IP	H	R	ER	HR	BB-IBB	SO	Avg.
1993— M.C. R. Dev. (Mex.)	3	1	.750	2.35	1.17	14	0	0	0	...	2-...	30.2	31	8	8	2	5-...	16	...
1994— M.C. R. Dev. (Mex.)	11	4	.733	2.04	1.20	37	15	4	1	...	3-...	127.2	121	37	29	5	32-...	51	...
1995— Carolina (Southern)	15	8	.652	2.49	1.26	27	27	1	0	...	0-...	152.0	170	62	42	10	21-3	68	.284
1996— Calgary (PCL)	2	2	.500	3.15	1.60	6	6	0	0	...	0-...	34.1	40	14	12	5	15-1	15	.305
— M.C. R. Dev. (Mex.)	7	0	1.000	1.26	1.08	7	7	1	0	...	0-...	50.0	44	12	7	1	10-...	17	...
— Pittsburgh (N.L.)	0	2	.000	8.28	1.76	15	3	0	0	3	0-0	25.0	40	23	23	2	4-0	13	.385
— Carolina (Southern)	0	1	.000	5.40	1.63	5	1	0	0	...	0-...	11.2	15	8	7	1	4-0	7	.300
1997— M.C. R. Dev. (Mex.)	16	5	.762	3.56	1.30	26	25	0	0	...	0-...	159.1	156	73	63	1	51-...	61	...
— Pittsburgh (N.L.)	0	0	.000	0.00	0.60	3	0	0	0	0	0-0	3.1	2	0	0	0	0-0	2	.167
1998— Pittsburgh (N.L.)	2	6	.250	5.67	1.54	43	5	0	0	6	0-1	74.2	90	50	47	10	25-2	43	.300
— Nashville (PCL)	3	1	.750	3.30	1.27	6	5	0	0	...	0-...	30.0	32	12	11	2	6-1	13	.274
1999— Yomiuri (Jp. East.)	4	3	.571	2.08	0.96	15	14	2	...	...	0-...	95.0	67	26	22	...	24-...	58	...
— Yomiuri (Jp. Cen.)	0	1	.000	3.86	1.71	8	0	0	0	...	0-...	16.1	24	7	7	...	4-...	6	...
2000— Louisville (Int'l)	2	1	.000	3.18	1.37	4	4	0	0	...	0-...	22.2	24	10	8	1	7-0	14	.270
— Cincinnati (N.L.)	11	5	.688	4.28	1.45	40	16	1	0	1	1-1	147.1	170	73	70	10	43-7	85	.296
2001— Cincinnati (N.L.)	10	14	.417	4.48	1.35	34	34	1	1	0	0-0	205.0	221	103	102	32	56-1	128	.279
2002— Cincinnati (N.L.)	7	8	.467	3.03	1.25	30	30	0	0	0	0-0	178.0	173	70	60	24	49-8	93	.257
2003— Arizona (N.L.)	8	8	.500	5.07	1.53	34	30	0	0	0	0-0	175.2	212	107	99	22	57-6	113	.299
2004— Arizona (N.L.)	1	6	.143	4.75	1.52	38	9	0	0	4	2-4	85.1	107	54	45	11	23-4	55	.301
— Los Angeles (N.L.)	1	0	1.000	3.20	1.22	12	1	0	0	0	0-1	19.2	16	7	7	4	8-0	18	.216
2005— Las Vegas (PCL)	0	0	...	3.38	1.00	3	3	0	0	0	0-0	8.0	6	3	3	1	2-0	6	.214
— Los Angeles (N.L.)	1	2	.333	3.56	1.25	28	7	0	0	0	0-0	65.2	63	30	26	6	19-2	37	.249
Major League totals (9 years)	41	51	.446	4.40	1.41	277	135	2	1	15	3-7	979.2	1094	517	479	121	284-30	587	.285

DIVISION SERIES RECORD

Year Team (League)	W	L	Pct.	ERA	WHIP	G	GS	CG	ShO	Hld.	Sv.-Opp.	IP	H	R	ER	HR	BB-IBB	SO	Avg.
2004— Los Angeles (N.L.)	0	0	...	6.75	0.75	1	0	0	0	0	0-0	1.1	1	1	1	1	0-0	1	.200

DEVINE, JOEY   P

PERSONAL: Born September 19, 1983, in Junction City, Kan. ... 5-11/195. ... Throws right, bats right. ... Full name: Joseph Devine. ... High school: Junction City (Kan.). ... College: North Carolina State.

TRANSACTIONS/CAREER NOTES: Selected by Atlanta Braves organization in first round (27th pick overall) of 2005 free-agent draft.

LEFTY-RIGHTY SPLITS

vs.	Avg.	AB	H	2B	3B	HR	RBI	BB	SO	OBP	Slg.
L	.429	7	3	0	0	1	4	1	0	.500	.857
R	.214	14	3	1	0	1	4	4	3	.389	.500

CAREER HITTING: 0-for-1 (.000), 0 R, 0 2B, 0 3B, 0 HR, 0 RBI.

Year Team (League)	W	L	Pct.	ERA	WHIP	G	GS	CG	ShO	Hld.	Sv.-Opp.	IP	H	R	ER	HR	BB-IBB	SO	Avg.
2005— Myrtle Beach (Carol.)	0	0		0.00	0.60	4	0	0	0	0	1-1	5.0	0	0	0	0	3-0	7	.000
— Mississippi (Sou.)	1	1	.500	2.70	1.55	18	0	0	0	0	5-6	20.0	19	13	6	2	12-1	28	.250
— Richmond (Int'l)	0	0		18.00	4.00	1	0	0	0	0	0-1	1.0	3	2	2	0	1-0	1	.600
— Atlanta (N.L.)	0	1	.000	12.60	2.20	5	0	0	0	1	0-0	5.0	6	7	7	2	5-1	3	.286
Major League totals (1 year)	0	1	.000	12.60	2.20	5	0	0	0	1	0-0	5.0	6	7	7	2	5-1	3	.286

DIVISION SERIES RECORD

Year Team (League)	W	L	Pct.	ERA	WHIP	G	GS	CG	ShO	Hld.	Sv.-Opp.	IP	H	R	ER	HR	BB-IBB	SO	Avg.
2005— Atlanta (N.L.)	0	1	.000	10.80	2.40	3	0	0	0	0	0-0	1.2	3	2	2	1	1-1	3	.375

DIAZ, EINAR — C

PERSONAL: Born December 28, 1972, in Chiriqui, Panama. ... 5-10/200. ... Bats right, throws right. ... Full name: Einar Antonio Diaz. ... Name pronounced: AY-een-ar.
TRANSACTIONS/CAREER NOTES: Signed as a non-drafted free agent by Cleveland Indians organization (October 5, 1990). ... On disabled list (August 23-September 30, 2002); included rehabilitation assignment to Mahoning Valley. ... Traded by Indians with P Ryan Drese to Texas Rangers for 1B Travis Hafner and P Aaron Myette (December 6, 2002). ... Traded by Rangers with P Justin Echols and cash to Montreal Expos for IF Josh McKinley and P Chris Young (April 3, 2004). ... Signed as a free agent by St. Louis Cardinals (December 14, 2004).
2005 GAMES PLAYED BY POSITION (MLB): C—50, 1B—3.

SCOUTING REPORT Diaz didn't catch much as Yadier Molina's backup; his skills regressed as a result. Has a very long swing and wraps the bat. Dives into the pitch, making him vulnerable inside. Hits down on the ball and doesn't have power. Is very impatient at the plate. Doesn't throw as well as he used to; consistently rushes to compensate and his mechanics cause the ball to really tail. Still very active in blocking and shifting to balls in the dirt. Works well with his pitching staff but can no longer be counted on to play a lot. Is nearing the end of his career. **Grade 4.4**

EINAR DIAZ'S HITTING ZONE

.167	.000	.500
.219	.273	.200
.182	.250	.143

LEFTY-RIGHTY SPLITS

vs.	Avg.	AB	H	2B	3B	HR	RBI	BB	SO	OBP	Slg.
L	.229	35	8	1	0	0	6	1	3	.270	.257
R	.200	95	19	5	0	1	11	4	9	.240	.284

Year Team (League)	Pos.	G	AB	R	H	2B	3B	HR	RBI	BB	SO	HBP	GDP	SB-CS	Avg.	OBP	SLG	OPS	E	Avg.
1991— Dom. Inds. (DSL)		62	239	35	67	6	3	1	29	14	5	...		10-...	.280		.343		9	
1992— Burlington (Appal.)	3B-SS	52	178	19	37	3	0	1	14	20	9	3	4	2-3	.208	.296	.242	.537	7	.959
1993— Burlington (Appal.)	3B-C	60	231	40	69	15	3	5	33	8	7	4	5	7-3	.299	.328	.455	.782	§ 10	.974
— Columbus (S. Atl.)	C	1	5	0	0	0	0	. 0	. 0	1	0	1	0	0-0	.000	.000	.000	.000	0	1.000
1994— Columbus (S. Atl.)	3B-C	120	491	67	137	23	2	16	71	17	34	21	18	4-4	.279	.330	.432	.762	9	.991
1995— Kinston (Carol.)	C-3B-DH	104	373	46	98	21	0	6	43	12	29	3	6	3-6	.263	.297	.367	.665	7	.991
1996— Cant./Akr. (Eastern)	C-3B	104	395	47	111	26	2	3	35	12	22	9	11	3-2	.281	.317	.380	.696	§ 15	.983
— Cleveland (A.L.)	C	4	1	0	0	0	0	0	0	0	0	0	0	0-0	.000	.000	.000	.000	0	1.000
1997— Buffalo (A.A.)	C-3B	109	336	40	86	18	2	3	31	18	34	4	12	0-0	.256	.302	.348	.650	§ 19	.974
— Cleveland (A.L.)	C	5	7	1	1	1	0	0	1	0	2	0	0	0-0	.143	.143	.286	.429	1	.955
1998— Buffalo (Int'l)	C	115	415	62	130	21	3	8	63	21	33	6	8	3-3	.313	.354	.436	.790	* 12	.986
— Cleveland (A.L.)	C	17	48	8	11	1	0	2	9	3	2	2	2	0-0	.229	.286	.375	.661	3	.973
1999— Cleveland (A.L.)	C	119	392	43	110	21	1	3	32	23	41	5	10	11-4	.281	.328	.362	.690	10	.988
2000— Cleveland (A.L.)	C-3B	75	250	29	68	14	2	4	25	11	29	8	4	4-2	.272	.323	.392	.715	4	.994
2001— Cleveland (A.L.)	C-2B	134	437	54	121	34	2	4	56	17	44	16	11	1-2	.277	.328	.387	.714	8	.992
2002— Mahoning Valley (NYP)	C	3	13	2	5	2	0	0	5	0	1	1	1	1-0	.385	.429	.538	.967	0	1.000
— Cleveland (A.L.)	C	102	320	34	66	19	0	2	16	17	27	6	13	0-1	.206	.258	.284	.542	8	.989
2003— Texas (A.L.)	C	101	334	30	86	14	1	9	34	9	32	10	12	3-1	.257	.294	.341	.635	8	.989
2004— Montreal (N.L.)	C-3B	55	139	9	31	6	1	1	11	11	10	4	6	2-0	.223	.293	.302	.595	3	.992
2005— St. Louis (N.L.)	C-1B	58	130	14	27	6	0	1	17	5	12	2	8	0-0	.208	.248	.277	.525	1	.995
American League totals (8 years)		557	1789	199	463	104	5	19	174	80	177	47	55	19-10	.259	.306	.354	.648	42	.990
National League totals (2 years)		113	269	23	58	12	1	2	28	16	22	6	14	2-0	.216	.272	.290	.562	4	.992
Major League totals (10 years)		670	2058	222	521	116	6	21	202	96	199	53	69	21-10	.253	.302	.346	.648	46	.990

DIVISION SERIES RECORD

Year Team (League)	Pos.	G	AB	R	H	2B	3B	HR	RBI	BB	SO	HBP	GDP	SB-CS	Avg.	OBP	SLG	OPS	E	Avg.
1998— Cleveland (A.L.)			Did not play.																	
1999— Cleveland (A.L.)	C	2	1	0	0	0	0	0	0	0	0	0	0	0-0	.000	.000	.000	.000	0	1.000
2001— Cleveland (A.L.)	C	5	16	3	5	0	0	0	2	2	1	0	0	0-0	.313	.389	.313	.701	1	.982
Division series totals (2 years)		7	17	3	5	0	0	0	2	2	1	0	0	0-0	.294	.368	.294	.663	1	.983

CHAMPIONSHIP SERIES RECORD

Year Team (League)	Pos.	G	AB	R	H	2B	3B	HR	RBI	BB	SO	HBP	GDP	SB-CS	Avg.	OBP	SLG	OPS	E	Avg.
1998— Cleveland (A.L.)	C	4	4	0	0	0	0	0	0	0	0	0	0	0-0	.000	.000	.000	.000	0	1.000

DIAZ, MATT — OF

PERSONAL: Born March 3, 1978, in Portland, Ore. ... 6-1/206. ... Bats right, throws right. ... Full name: Matthew Edward Diaz. ... High school: Sante Fe (Fla.). ... College: Florida State.
TRANSACTIONS/CAREER NOTES: Selected by Tampa Bay Devil Rays organization in 17th round of 1999 free-agent draft. ... On disabled list (June 11-July 18, 2005); included rehabilitation assignments to AZL Royals and Wichita. ... Claimed on waivers by Baltimore Orioles (February 18, 2005). ... Refused to report and became a free agent (February 22, 2005). ... Signed as a free agent by Kansas City Royals organization (February 24, 2005).
2005 GAMES PLAYED BY POSITION (MLB): OF—21, DH—7.

MATT DIAZ'S HITTING ZONE

.000	.600	.000
.300	.222	.200
.300	.600	.667

LEFTY-RIGHTY SPLITS

vs.	Avg.	AB	H	2B	3B	HR	RBI	BB	SO	OBP	Slg.
L	.370	54	20	2	0	1	8	3	4	.407	.463
R	.143	35	5	2	0	1	1	1	11	.189	.314

Year Team (League)	Pos.	G	AB	R	H	2B	3B	HR	RBI	BB	SO	HBP	GDP	SB-CS	Avg.	OBP	SLG	OPS	E	Avg.
1999— Hudson Valley (NYP)	OF	54	208	22	51	15	2	1	20	6	43	6	5	6-2	.245	.284	.351	.635	3	.972
2000— St. Pete. (FSL)	OF	106	392	37	106	21	3	6	53	11	54	11	21	2-3	.270	.305	.385	.691	10	.957
2001— Bakersfield (Calif.)	OF	131	524	79	172	40	2	16	81	24	73	14	11	11-5	.328	.370	.510	.880	10	.961
2002— Orlando (South.)	OF-1B	122	449	71	123	28	1	10	50	34	72	10	11	31-9	.274	.337	.408	.744	3	.987
2003— Orlando (South.)	OF	60	227	32	87	21	0	5	41	19	24	8	7	9-5	.383	.444	.542	.985	1	.994

Year Team (League)	Pos.	G	AB	R	H	2B	3B	HR	RBI	BB	SO	HBP	GDP	SB-CS	Avg.	OBP	SLG	OPS	E	Avg.
— Tampa Bay (A.L.)	DH-OF	4	9	2	1	0	0	0	0	1	3	0	0	0-0	.111	.200	.111	.311	1	.857
— Durham (Int'l)	OF-DH	67	253	35	83	18	3	8	45	16	45	8	8	6-2	.328	.382	.518	.900	1	.993
2004— Durham (Int'l)	OF-DH	134	503	81	167	47	5	21	93	26	96	13	9	15-4	.332	.377	.571	.947	7	.974
— Tampa Bay (A.L.)	DH-OF	10	21	3	4	1	1	1	3	1	6	2	0	0-0	.190	.292	.476	.768	0	1.000
2005— Arizona Royals (AZL)	OF-DH	3	13	2	6	2	0	0	2	0	2	0	1	0-1	.462	.462	.615	1.077	0	1.000
— Wichita (Texas)	OF-DH	7	26	6	7	0	0	1	6	3	5	0	1	1-0	.269	.333	.385	.718	0	1.000
— Omaha (PCL)	OF	65	259	48	96	22	4	14	56	12	49	5	14	10-3	.371	.408	.649	1.057	8	.969
— Kansas City (A.L.)	OF-DH	34	89	7	25	4	2	1	9	4	15	2	3	0-1	.281	.323	.404	.727	2	.950
Major League totals (3 years)		48	119	12	30	5	3	2	12	6	24	4	3	0-1	.252	.308	.395	.703	3	.948

DIAZ, VICTOR — OF

PERSONAL: Born December 10, 1981, in Santo Domingo, Dominican Republic. ... 6-0/200. ... Bats right, throws right. ... Full name: Victor Israel Diaz. ... High school: Roberto Clemente (Chicago). ... Junior college: Grayson County (Texas).
TRANSACTIONS/CAREER NOTES: Selected by Los Angeles Dodgers organization in 37th round of 2000 free-agent draft. ... Traded by Dodgers with Ps Kole Strayhorn and Jose Diaz to New York Mets for OF Jeromy Burnitz and cash (July 14, 2003).
2005 GAMES PLAYED BY POSITION (MLB): OF—81.

SCOUTING REPORT Diaz is an aggressive hitter with a long stroke. Has a big, uppercut swing with a lot of holes. Is susceptible to off-speed pitches. Will develop power. Is a converted infielder who needs a lot of work on tracking the ball in the outfield. Needs to improve arm strength. *Grade 5.3*

VICTOR DIAZ'S HITTING ZONE

.286	.417	.357
.297	.333	.147
.133	.417	.474

LEFTY-RIGHTY SPLITS

vs.	Avg.	AB	H	2B	3B	HR	RBI	BB	SO	OBP	Slg.
L	.259	54	14	2	0	1	4	7	12	.344	.352
R	.257	226	58	15	3	11	34	23	70	.325	.496

Year Team (League)	Pos.	G	AB	R	H	2B	3B	HR	RBI	BB	SO	HBP	GDP	SB-CS	Avg.	OBP	SLG	OPS	E	Avg.
2001— GC Dodgers (GCL)	2B-3B	53	195	36	69	22	2	3	31	16	23	6	3	6-3	.354	.414	.533	.947	12	.949
2002— South Georgia (S. Atl.)	3B-2B-1B	91	349	64	122	26	2	10	58	27	69	10	4	20-6	.350	.407	.521	.928	23	.903
— Jacksonville (Sou.)	1B-3B-2B	42	152	22	32	7	0	4	24	7	42	3	3	7-5	.211	.258	.336	.593	3	.989
2003— Jacksonville (Sou.)	2B	85	316	42	92	20	2	10	55	27	60	6	10	8-10	.291	.353	.462	.815	14	.962
— Binghamton (East.)	2B	45	175	29	62	11	0	6	23	8	32	1	3	7-5	.354	.382	.520	.902	6	.968
2004— Norfolk (Int'l)	OF-DH	141	528	81	154	31	1	24	94	31	133	5	12	6-8	.292	.332	.491	.816	9	.969
— New York (N.L.)	OF	15	51	8	15	3	0	3	8	1	15	1	3	0-0	.294	.321	.529	.850	2	.935
2005— Norfolk (Int'l)	1B-OF	42	170	30	51	11	0	10	34	14	47	0	6	6-2	.300	.353	.541	.894	2	.994
— New York (N.L.)	OF	89	280	41	72	17	3	12	38	30	82	1	13	6-2	.257	.329	.468	.797	3	.981
Major League totals (2 years)		104	331	49	87	20	3	15	46	31	97	2	16	6-2	.263	.328	.477	.805	5	.974

DICKEY, R.A. — P

PERSONAL: Born October 29, 1974, in Nashville. ... 6-3/220. ... Throws right, bats right. ... Full name: Robert Alan Dickey. ... High school: Montgomery Bell Academy (Nashville). ... College: Tennessee.
TRANSACTIONS/CAREER NOTES: Selected by Detroit Tigers organization in 10th round of 1993 free-agent draft; did not sign. ... Selected by Texas Rangers organization in first round (18th pick overall) of 1996 free-agent draft. ... On disabled list (June 25-July 19 and July 30-August 23, 2004); included rehabilitation assignment to Frisco. ... On disabled list (April 13-May 25, 2005); included rehabilitation assignment to Oklahoma.
CAREER HITTING: 1-for-1 (1.000), 0 R, 0 2B, 0 3B, 0 HR, 0 RBI.

SCOUTING REPORT *Throws:* He used to be a conventional pitcher but switched to the knuckleball because of arm problems. Dickey's fastball is in the 83-86 mph range. *Tendencies:* Dickey has an inconsistent release point and arm action. Starts games with good movement but loses it as the game goes along. Gets more downward movement than lateral movement. *Outlook:* Dickey still has work to do on his conversion to a knuckleball specialist, but he has outstanding makeup. *Grade 5.5*

R.A. DICKEY'S PITCHING ZONE

.286	.500	.100
.222	.462	.200
.300	.200	.273

LEFTY-RIGHTY SPLITS

vs.	Avg.	AB	H	2B	3B	HR	RBI	BB	SO	OBP	Slg.
L	.200	50	10	1	2	2	5	7	6	.293	.420
R	.297	64	19	5	0	2	15	10	9	.408	.469

Year Team (League)	W	L	Pct.	ERA	WHIP	G	GS	CG	ShO	Hld.	Sv.-Opp.	IP	H	R	ER	HR	BB-IBB	SO	Avg.
1997— Charlotte (Fla. St.)	1	4	.200	6.94	1.80	8	6	0	0	...	0-...	35.0	51	32	27	8	12-1	32	.340
1998— Charlotte (Fla. St.)	1	5	.167	3.30	1.33	57	0	0	0	...	38-...	60.0	58	31	22	9	22-3	53	.249
1999— Tulsa (Texas)	6	7	.462	4.55	1.53	35	11	0	0	...	10-...	95.0	105	60	48	13	40-1	59	.282
— Oklahoma (PCL)	2	2	.500	4.37	1.32	6	2	0	0	...	0-...	22.2	23	12	11	1	7-1	17	.261
2000— Oklahoma (PCL)	8	9	.471	4.49	1.47	30	23	2	0	...	1-...	158.1	167	83	79	13	65-1	85	.281
2001— Oklahoma (PCL)	11	7	.611	3.75	1.28	24	24	3	0	...	0-...	163.0	164	77	68	14	45-1	120	.262
— Texas (A.L.)	0	1	.000	6.75	1.67	4	0	0	0	...	0-0	12.0	13	9	9	3	7-1	4	.283
2002— Oklahoma (PCL)	8	7	.533	4.09	1.45	37	19	1	0	...	0-...	154.0	176	81	70	14	47-5	109	.295
2003— Oklahoma (PCL)	1	1	.500	1.20	1.10	3	2	0	0	...	0-...	15.0	14	3	2	1	3-0	4	.259
— Texas (A.L.)	9	8	.529	5.09	1.48	38	13	1	1	3	1-1	116.2	135	68	66	16	38-5	94	.292
2004— Frisco (Texas)	1	1	.500	1.98	1.24	4	4	0	0	...	0-...	13.2	16	5	3	0	1-0	9	.286
— Texas (A.L.)	6	7	.462	5.61	1.62	25	15	0	0	...	1-1	104.1	136	77	65	17	33-1	57	.311
2005— Oklahoma (PCL)	10	6	.625	5.99	1.57	19	17	1	1	...	0-...	121.2	152	88	81	12	39-0	81	.308
— Texas (A.L.)	1	2	.333	6.67	1.55	9	4	0	0	...	0-0	29.2	29	23	22	4	17-0	15	.254
Major League totals (4 years)	16	18	.471	5.55	1.55	76	32	1	1	3	2-2	262.2	313	177	162	40	95-7	170	.295

D

DIFELICE, MIKE C

PERSONAL: Born May 28, 1969, in Philadelphia. ... 6-2/205. ... Bats right, throws right. ... Full name: Michael William DiFelice. ... Name pronounced: DEE-fah-lease. ... High school: Bearden (Knoxville, Tenn.). ... College: Tennessee.

TRANSACTIONS/CAREER NOTES: Selected by St. Louis Cardinals organization in 11th round of 1991 free-agent draft. ... Selected by Tampa Bay Devil Rays in first round (20th pick overall) of expansion draft (November 18, 1997). ... Traded by Devil Rays with P Albie Lopez to Arizona Diamondbacks for OF Jason Conti and P Nick Bierbrodt (July 25, 2001). ... Released by Diamondbacks (September 4, 2001). ... Signed by Cardinals (November 20, 2001). ... Signed as a free agent by Kansas City Royals (January 9, 2003). ... On suspended list (September 4-6, 2003). ... Signed as a free agent by Detroit Tigers (December 18, 2003). ... Traded by Tigers to Chicago Cubs for a player to be named (August 31, 2004). ... Signed as a free agent by Florida Marlins organization (December 18, 2004). ... Released by Marlins (March 27, 2005). ... Signed by New York Mets organization (March 31, 2005).

LEFTY-RIGHTY SPLITS

vs.	Avg.	AB	H	2B	3B	HR	RBI	BB	SO	OBP	Slg.
L	.000	3	0	0	0	0	0	0	0	.000	.000
R	.143	14	2	0	0	0	0	2	5	.250	.143

2005 GAMES PLAYED BY POSITION (MLB): C—11.

Year Team (League)	Pos.	G	AB	R	H	2B	3B	HR	RBI	BB	SO	HBP	GDP	SB-CS	Avg.	OBP	SLG	OPS	E	Avg.
1991—Hamilton (NYP)	C	43	157	10	33	5	0	4	15	9	40	1	3	1-5	.210	.257	.318	.576	9	.974
1992—Hamilton (NYP)	1B-C	18	58	11	20	3	0	2	9	4	7	1	0	2-0	.345	.397	.500	.897	5	.969
—St. Pete. (FSL)	C	17	53	0	12	3	0	0	4	3	11	0	3	0-0	.226	.259	.283	.542	2	.977
1993—Springfield (Midw.)	C	8	20	5	7	1	0	0	3	2	3	1	0	0-1	.350	.435	.400	.835	0	1.000
—St. Pete. (FSL)	C	30	97	5	22	2	0	0	8	11	13	1	4	1-0	.227	.306	.247	.554	7	.964
1994—Arkansas (Texas)	C	71	200	19	50	11	2	2	15	12	48	2	9	0-1	.250	.296	.355	.651	6	.987
1995—Arkansas (Texas)	C	62	176	14	47	10	1	1	24	23	29	3	13	0-2	.267	.360	.352	.712	6	.984
—Louisville (A.A.)	C	21	63	8	17	4	0	0	3	5	11	0	4	1-0	.270	.324	.333	.657	2	.984
1996—Louisville (A.A.)	C	79	246	25	70	13	0	9	33	20	43	1	15	0-3	.285	.338	.447	.785	8	.984
—St. Louis (N.L.)	C	4	7	0	2	1	0	0	2	0	1	0	0	0-0	.286	.286	.429	.714	0	1.000
1997—Arkansas (Texas)	C	1	3	0	1	1	0	0	0	1	0	0	0	0-0	.333	.500	.667	1.167	0	1.000
—St. Louis (N.L.)	C-1B	93	260	16	62	10	1	4	30	19	61	3	11	1-1	.238	.297	.331	.628	6	.991
—Louisville (A.A.)	C	1	4	1	1	0	0	0	1	0	1	0	0	0-0	.250	.250	1.000	1.250	0	1.000
1998—Tampa Bay (A.L.)	C	84	248	17	57	12	3	3	23	15	56	1	12	0-0	.230	.274	.339	.613	4	.993
1999—Tampa Bay (A.L.)	C	51	179	21	55	11	0	6	27	8	23	3	1	0-0	.307	.346	.469	.815	5	.987
2000—Tampa Bay (A.L.)	C	60	204	23	49	13	1	6	19	12	40	0	8	0-0	.240	.280	.402	.682	8	.980
2001—Tampa Bay (A.L.)	C	48	149	13	31	5	1	2	9	8	39	3	3	1-1	.208	.259	.295	.555	6	.982
—Arizona (N.L.)	C	12	21	1	1	0	0	0	1	0	10	1	0	0-0	.048	.091	.048	.139	1	.982
—Tucson (PCL)	C-1B	7	26	6	9	0	0	1	2	3	6	0	2	0-0	.346	.414	.462	.875	3	.940
2002—St. Louis (N.L.)	C	70	174	17	40	11	0	4	19	17	42	1	4	0-0	.230	.297	.362	.660	3	.991
2003—Kansas City (A.L.)	C-DH	62	189	29	48	16	1	3	25	9	30	4	6	1-0	.254	.299	.397	.696	2	.994
2004—Detroit (A.L.)	C-DH	13	22	3	3	0	1	0	2	3	3	0	3	0-0	.136	.240	.227	.467	0	1.000
—Toledo (Int'l)	C-DH	64	237	20	64	14	0	5	36	14	37	1	7	1-0	.270	.311	.392	.703	4	.990
—Chicago (N.L.)	C	4	3	0	0	0	0	0	0	0	1	0	0	0-0	.000	.000	.000	.000	0	1.000
2005—Norfolk (Int'l)	C-DH	81	300	31	74	17	0	14	52	36	72	5	13	1-2	.247	.337	.443	.781	4	.993
—New York (N.L.)	C	11	17	0	2	0	0	0	2	2	5	0	1	0-0	.118	.211	.118	.328	1	.976
American League totals (6 years)		318	991	106	243	57	7	20	105	55	191	11	33	2-1	.245	.290	.377	.667	25	.988
National League totals (6 years)		194	482	34	107	22	1	8	52	38	120	5	16	1-1	.222	.284	.322	.605	11	.989
Major League totals (10 years)		512	1473	140	350	79	8	28	157	93	311	16	49	3-2	.238	.288	.359	.647	36	.989

CHAMPIONSHIP SERIES RECORD

Year Team (League)	Pos.	G	AB	R	H	2B	3B	HR	RBI	BB	SO	HBP	GDP	SB-CS	Avg.	OBP	SLG	OPS	E	Avg.
2002—St. Louis (N.L.)		1	1	0	0	0	0	0	0	0	0	0	0	0-0	.000	.000	.000	.000		

DILLON, JOE 3B

PERSONAL: Born August 2, 1975, in Modesto, Calif. ... 6-2/215. ... Bats right, throws right. ... Full name: Joseph William Dillon. ... College: Texas Tech.

TRANSACTIONS/CAREER NOTES: Selected by Kansas City Royals organization in seventh round of 1997 free-agent draft. ... Selected by Minnesota Twins from Royals in Rule 5 minor league draft (December 13, 2001). ... Released by Twins (March 24, 2003). ... Signed by Florida Marlins organization (March 17, 2004).

LEFTY-RIGHTY SPLITS

vs.	Avg.	AB	H	2B	3B	HR	RBI	BB	SO	OBP	Slg.
L	.222	9	2	0	0	0	0	0	1	.222	.222
R	.148	27	4	1	0	1	1	1	7	.207	.296

2005 GAMES PLAYED BY POSITION (MLB): 2B—4, OF—3, 3B—2, 1B—1.

Year Team (League)	Pos.	G	AB	R	H	2B	3B	HR	RBI	BB	SO	HBP	GDP	SB-CS	Avg.	OBP	SLG	OPS	E	Avg.
1997—Spokane (N'west)		19	70	6	15	3	0	2	6	5	13	1	2	1-0	.214	.276	.343	.619	...	...
1998—Lansing (Midw.)	1B-3B	73	268	37	70	17	2	15	43	36	57	0	6	9-2	.261	.349	.507	.856	7	.986
1999—Wilmington (Caro.)	3B-1B	134	503	73	133	31	2	16	90	59	124	7	12	9-6	.264	.347	.429	.776	28	.937
2000—Wichita (Texas)	3B	62	220	35	70	16	2	10	43	39	38	7	6	0-0	.318	.428	.545	.973	8	.950
—Omaha (PCL)	3B	45	149	19	42	11	2	1	11	17	26	2	6	1-0	.282	.363	.403	.766	4	.959
2001—Wichita (Texas)	3B	101	369	62	106	19	3	15	59	36	60	8	10	4-3	.287	.361	.477	.838	16	.974
2002—New Britain (East.)	3B-1B	103	344	47	90	20	2	9	50	54	62	6	10	3-1	.262	.368	.410	.778	19	.963
—Edmonton (PCL)	3B	6	18	5	3	1	0	0	2	2	2	0	1	1-0	.167	.250	.222	.472	0	1.000
2003— Did not play.																				
2004—Carolina (Southern)	3B	33	117	26	40	13	0	9	31	14	29	4	1	3-2	.342	.426	.684	1.110	3	.959
—Albuquerque (PCL)	3B-OF-2B	108	403	96	131	33	4	30	86	46	85	10	7	12-3	.325	.400	.665	1.065	17	.638
2005—Albuquerque (PCL)	3B-OF-2B	98	350	80	126	21	1	24	72	57	59	12	7	11-1	.360	.459	.631	1.090	14	.954
—Florida (N.L.)	2B-OF-3B-1B	27	36	6	6	1	0	1	1	1	8	1	3	0-0	.167	.211	.278	.488	1	.950
Major League totals (1 year)		27	36	6	6	1	0	1	1	1	8	1	3	0-0	.167	.211	.278	.488	1	.950

D

DINARDO, LENNY   P

PERSONAL: Born September 19, 1979, in Miami. ... 6-4/195. ... Throws left, bats left. ... Full name: Leonard Edward DiNardo. ... High school: Santa Fe (Alachua, Fla.). ... College: Stetson.
TRANSACTIONS/CAREER NOTES: Selected by Boston Red Sox organization in 10th round of 1998 free-agent draft; did not sign. ... Selected by New York Mets organization in third round of 2001 free-agent draft. ... Selected by Red Sox from Mets organization in Rule 5 major league draft (December 15, 2003). ... On disabled list (April 4-19 and July 5-September 16, 2004); included rehabilitation assignments to GCL Red Sox, Sarasota, Portland and Pawtucket.
CAREER HITTING: 0-for-0 (.000), 0 R, 0 2B, 0 3B, 0 HR, 0 RBI.

LENNY DINARDO'S PITCHING ZONE

.500	.000	.667
.125	.400	.400
.375	.000	.143

LEFTY-RIGHTY SPLITS

vs.	Avg.	AB	H	2B	3B	HR	RBI	BB	SO	OBP	Slg.
L	.263	19	5	1	0	0	3	1	4	.300	.316
R	.222	36	8	1	0	1	5	4	11	.293	.333

Year	Team (League)	W	L	Pct.	ERA	WHIP	G	GS	CG	ShO	Hld.	Sv.-Opp.	IP	H	R	ER	HR	BB-IBB	SO	Avg.
2001—	Brooklyn (N.Y.-Penn.)	1	2	.333	2.00	1.19	9	5	0	0	...	1-...	36.0	26	10	8	0	17-0	40	.200
2002—	Capital City (SAL)	5	5	.500	4.35	1.60	24	19	0	0	...	1-...	101.1	106	60	49	3	56-1	103	.274
2003—	Binghamton (East.)	1	3	.250	3.60	1.20	7	7	1	0	...	0-...	40.0	35	19	16	3	13-0	36	.236
—	St. Lucie (Fla. St.)	3	8	.273	2.01	0.92	19	13	1	0	...	1-...	85.0	64	27	19	1	14-0	93	.211
2004—	Sarasota (Fla. St.)	0	0	...	0.00	0.67	1	1	0	0	...	0-...	3.0	2	0	0	0	0-0	2	.182
—	Pawtucket (Int'l)	0	0	...	0.00	1.00	1	1	0	0	...	0-...	3.0	3	0	0	0	0-0	4	.250
—	Boston (A.L.)	0	0	...	4.23	1.66	22	0	0	0	0	0-0	27.2	34	17	13	1	12-1	21	.298
—	GC Red Sox (GCL)	0	0	...	0.00	1.00	2	1	0	0	...	0-...	3.0	3	0	0	0	0-0	5	.273
—	Portland (East.)	1	0	1.000	9.53	1.59	3	0	0	0	...	0-...	5.2	8	6	6	1	1-0	4	.333
2005—	Pawtucket (Int'l)	6	3	.667	3.15	1.33	23	22	0	0	0	0-0	108.2	109	51	38	7	35-0	93	.265
—	Boston (A.L.)	0	1	.000	1.84	1.23	8	1	0	0	0	0-0	14.2	13	6	3	1	5-1	15	.236
	Major League totals (2 years)	0	1	.000	3.40	1.51	30	1	0	0	0	0-0	42.1	47	23	16	2	17-2	36	.278

DINGMAN, CRAIG   P

PERSONAL: Born March 12, 1974, in Wichita, Kan. ... 6-4/215. ... Throws right, bats right. ... Full name: Craig Allen Dingman. ... High school: North (Wichita, Kan.). ... Junior college: Hutchinson (Kan.) Community College.
TRANSACTIONS/CAREER NOTES: Selected by New York Yankees organization in 36th round of 1993 free-agent draft. ... Traded by Yankees to Colorado Rockies for a player to be named (March 29, 2001); Yankees acquired P Jorge DePaula to complete deal (April 20, 2001). ... On disabled list (April 9-24, 2001; included rehabilitation assignment to Colorado Springs. ... Signed as a free agent by Cincinnati Reds organization (December 21, 2001). ... Traded by Reds to Yankees for cash (June 6, 2002). ... Signed as a free agent by Yucatan of the Mexican League (March 1, 2003). ... Signed by Cancun of the Mexican League (May 29, 2003). ... Contract purchased by Chicago Cubs organization from Cancun (July 22, 2003). ... Signed as a free agent by Detroit Tigers organization (December 19, 2003).
CAREER HITTING: 0-for-0 (.000), 0 R, 0 2B, 0 3B, 0 HR, 0 RBI.

CRAIG DINGMAN'S PITCHING ZONE

.273	.182	.000
.292	.385	.308
.000	.200	.400

LEFTY-RIGHTY SPLITS

vs.	Avg.	AB	H	2B	3B	HR	RBI	BB	SO	OBP	Slg.
L	.208	48	10	1	0	2	6	4	13	.269	.354
R	.294	68	20	4	0	3	8	5	11	.351	.485

Year	Team (League)	W	L	Pct.	ERA	WHIP	G	GS	CG	ShO	Hld.	Sv.-Opp.	IP	H	R	ER	HR	BB-IBB	SO	Avg.
1994—	GC Yankees (GCL)	0	5	.000	3.38	1.16	17	1	0	0	...	1-...	32.0	27	17	12	0	10-0	51	.239
1995—	Did not play - injured.																			
1996—	Oneonta (NYP)	0	2	.000	2.04	0.74	20	0	0	0	...	9-...	35.1	17	11	8	0	9-0	52	.136
1997—	Greensboro (S. Atl.)	2	0	1.000	1.91	0.94	30	0	0	0	...	19-...	33.0	19	7	7	0	12-0	41	.165
—	Tampa (Fla. St.)	0	4	.000	5.24	1.30	19	0	0	0	...	6-...	22.1	15	14	13	2	14-2	26	.195
1998—	Tampa (Fla. St.)	5	4	.556	2.93	1.23	50	0	0	0	...	7-...	70.2	48	29	23	8	39-9	95	.194
1999—	Norwich (East.)	8	6	.571	1.57	0.91	55	0	0	0	...	9-...	74.1	56	16	13	2	12-2	90	.206
2000—	Columbus (Int'l)	6	1	.857	3.05	1.09	47	2	0	0	...	1-...	73.2	60	31	25	9	20-2	65	.220
—	New York (A.L.)	0	0	...	6.55	1.91	10	0	0	0	0	0-...	11.0	18	8	8	1	3-0	8	.375
2001—	Colo. Springs (PCL)	3	5	.375	4.56	1.38	46	0	0	0	...	7-...	48.0	57	28	20	4	9-1	55	.294
—	Colorado (N.L.)	0	0	...	13.50	1.91	7	0	0	0	0	1-1	7.1	11	11	11	4	3-2	2	.355
2002—	Louisville (Int'l)	0	1	.000	4.15	1.27	22	0	0	0	...	0-...	26.0	20	12	12	3	13-0	26	.215
—	Columbus (Int'l)	0	0	...	13.50	5.25	2	0	0	0	...	0-...	1.1	6	6	2	0	1-1	2	.545
2003—	Yucatan (Mex.)	3	2	.600	3.08	1.29	27	0	0	0	...	14-...	26.1	25	10	9	3	9-...	22	.258
—	Cancun (Mex.)	1	5	.167	4.24	1.18	15	0	0	0	...	5-...	17.0	16	12	8	1	4-...	17	.254
—	West Tenn (Sou.)	0	1	.000	6.00	1.80	4	0	0	0	...	0-...	6.0	6	4	4	2	5-1	5	.257
—	Iowa (PCL)	1	0	1.000	2.00	1.20	11	0	0	0	...	0-...	18.0	14	4	4	0	7-0	12	.667
2004—	Toledo (Int'l)	1	2	.333	4.56	1.44	21	0	0	0	...	0-...	25.2	26	14	13	5	11-2	31	.260
—	Detroit (A.L.)	2	2	.500	6.75	1.88	24	0	0	0	0	0-2	29.1	33	22	22	3	22-3	16	.295
2005—	Toledo (Int'l)	2	1	.667	2.81	1.15	35	0	0	0	...	4-6	48.0	42	18	15	3	13-0	67	.230
—	Detroit (A.L.)	2	3	.400	3.66	1.22	34	0	0	0	0	4-5	32.0	30	14	13	5	9-0	24	.259
	American League totals (3 years)	4	5	.444	5.35	1.59	68	0	0	0	4	4-7	72.1	81	44	43	9	34-3	48	.293
	National League totals (1 year)	0	0	...	13.50	1.91	7	0	0	0	0	1-1	7.1	11	11	11	4	3-2	2	.355
	Major League totals (4 years)	4	5	.444	6.10	1.62	75	0	0	0	4	5-8	79.2	92	55	54	13	37-5	50	.300

DOBBS, GREG   3B

PERSONAL: Born July 2, 1978, in Los Angeles. ... 6-1/205. ... Bats left, throws right. ... Full name: Gregory Stuart Dobbs. ... High school: Canyon Springs (Calif.). ... Junior college: Riverside (Calif.) Community College. ... College: Oklahoma.
TRANSACTIONS/CAREER NOTES: Selected by Seattle Mariners organization in 52nd round of 1996 free-agent draft; did not sign. ... Selected by Houston Astros organiztion in 10th round of 1999 free-agent draft; did not sign. ... Signed as a non-drafted free agent by Seattle Mariners organization (May 28, 2001).
2005 GAMES PLAYED BY POSITION (MLB): DH—24, 1B—5, OF—4, 3B—2.

GREG DOBBS' HITTING ZONE

.200	.200	.250
.286	.333	.296
.333	.222	.357

LEFTY-RIGHTY SPLITS

vs.	Avg.	AB	H	2B	3B	HR	RBI	BB	SO	OBP	Slg.
L	.300	10	3	1	0	0	1	0	5	.300	.400
R	.242	132	32	6	1	1	19	9	20	.287	.326

									BATTING							FIELDING	
Year	Team (League)	Pos.	G	AB	R	H	2B	3B	HR	RBI	BB	SO	HBP	GDP	SB-CS	Avg.	OBP	SLG	OPS	E	Avg.
2001—	Everett (N'west)	1B-OF-3B	65	249	37	80	17	2	6	41	30	39	4	2	5-3	.321	.396	.478	.874	12	.972
—	San Bern. (Calif.)	OF	3	13	2	5	1	0	0	3	0	4	0	0	0-0	.385	.357	.692	1.049	0	1.000
2002—	Wisconsin (Midw.)	3B	86	320	43	88	16	2	10	48	31	50	1	3	13-3	.275	.338	.431	.769	23	.902
—	San Antonio (Texas)	OF-1B	27	96	13	35	2	0	5	15	9	17	1	2	1-3	.365	.425	.542	.966	4	.964
2003—	San Antonio (Texas)	3B	2	6	0	2	0	0	0	0	0	1	0	0	0-0	.333	.333	.667	1.000	0	1.000

Year	Team (League)	Pos.	G	AB	R	H	2B	3B	HR	RBI	BATTING BB	SO	HBP	GDP	SB-CS	Avg.	OBP	SLG	OPS	FIELDING E	Avg.
2004— San Antonio (Texas)		3B	51	203	25	66	14	4	5	34	11	23	5	5	5-4	.325	.373	.507	.866	10	.918
— Tacoma (PCL)		3B-DH	67	255	28	69	9	2	8	31	5	36	1	10	4-3	.271	.286	.416	.699	13	.931
— Seattle (A.L.)		3B-DH	18	53	4	12	1	0	1	9	1	14	1	0	0-0	.226	.250	.302	.552	2	.929
2005— Tacoma (PCL) 1B-3B-DH		OF	50	190	27	61	9	0	3	22	14	22	1	4	5-2	.321	.367	.416	.783	8	.977
— Seattle (A.L.) DH-1B-OF		3B	59	142	8	35	7	1	1	20	9	25	0	4	1-0	.246	.288	.331	.619	0	1.000
Major League totals (2 years)			77	195	12	47	8	1	2	29	10	39	1	4	1-0	.241	.278	.323	.601	2	.975

DOHMANN, SCOTT   P

PERSONAL: Born February 13, 1978, in New Orleans, La. ... 6-1/181. ... Throws right, bats right. ... Full name: Christopher Scott Dohmann. ... High school: St. Thomas More Catholic (Lafayette, La.). ... College: Louisiana-Lafayette.

TRANSACTIONS/CAREER NOTES: Selected by Colorado Rockies in sixth round of 2000 free-agent draft.

CAREER HITTING: 0-for-2 (.000), 0 R, 0 2B, 0 3B, 0 HR, 0 RBI.

SCOUTING REPORT **Throws:** His fastball is about 92 mph and his slider and changeup are in the 81-84 range. **Tendencies:** Dohman has a maximum-effort delivery; he throws over a stiff front leg. Fastball has some life down in the zone. Slider has some late break. Tends to overthrow all his pitches. Pitches behind in the count, resulting in a lot of home runs. Is effective against righthanders with his slider but doesn't have a pitch to get out lefthanders. Changeup acts like a splitter. **Outlook:** Dohmann has not shown a lot of progress and will continue to pitch in less critical roles until his command and ability to get out lefties improves. *Grade 5*

SCOTT DOHMANN'S PITCHING ZONE

.444	.833	.000
.348	.417	.000
.167	.500	.100

LEFTY-RIGHTY SPLITS

vs.	Avg.	AB	H	2B	3B	HR	RBI	BB	SO	OBP	Slg.
L	.328	58	19	1	3	2	13	11	10	.435	.552
R	.212	66	14	1	0	4	12	8	25	.297	.409

Year	Team (League)	W	L	Pct.	ERA	WHIP	G	GS	CG	ShO	Hld.	Sv.-Opp.	IP	H	R	ER	HR	BB-IBB	SO	Avg.
2000— Portland (N'west)		2	1	.667	0.78	0.83	5	4	0	0	...	0-...	23.0	14	3	2	0	5-0	23	.177
— Asheville (S. Atl.)		1	5	.167	6.06	1.56	7	7	0	0	...	0-...	32.2	43	24	22	3	8-0	36	.319
2001— Asheville (S. Atl.)		11	13	.458	4.32	1.14	28	28	3	1	...	0-...	173.0	165	88	83	27	33-5	154	.251
2002— Salem (Carol.)		13	5	.722	4.23	1.19	28	28	0	0	...	0-...	170.1	149	85	80	22	53-0	131	.233
2003— Tulsa (Texas)		9	4	.692	4.13	1.31	50	4	0	0	...	4-...	93.2	94	47	43	11	29-2	102	.259
2004— Colo. Springs (PCL)		1	0	1.000	1.64	1.32	18	0	0	0	...	2-...	22.0	22	5	4	1	7-1	31	.250
— Colorado (N.L.)		0	3	.000	4.11	1.30	41	0	0	0	4	0-4	46.0	41	22	21	8	19-0	49	.236
2005— Colo. Springs (PCL)		2	1	.667	4.38	1.46	34	0	0	0	5	1-3	39.0	41	19	19	5	16-1	53	.266
— Colorado (N.L.)		2	1	.667	6.10	1.68	32	0	0	0	7	0-3	31.0	33	21	21	6	19-1	35	.266
Major League totals (2 years)		2	4	.333	4.91	1.45	73	0	0	0	11	0-7	77.0	74	43	42	14	38-1	84	.248

DOMINGUEZ, JUAN   P

PERSONAL: Born May 18, 1980, in Ensanchez Ramirez, Dominican Republic. ... 6-2/195. ... Throws right, bats right. ... Full name: Juan Ramon Dominguez.

TRANSACTIONS/CAREER NOTES: Signed as a non-drafted free agent by Texas Rangers organization (December 26, 1999). ... On disabled list (June 12-September 13 and September 19, 2004-remainder of season); included rehabilitation assignments to Oklahoma and Frisco.

CAREER HITTING: 0-for-0 (.000), 0 R, 0 2B, 0 3B, 0 HR, 0 RBI.

JUAN DOMINGUEZ'S PITCHING ZONE

.300	.375	.200
.515	.391	.175
.235	.273	.208

LEFTY-RIGHTY SPLITS

vs.	Avg.	AB	H	2B	3B	HR	RBI	BB	SO	OBP	Slg.
L	.241	137	33	6	1	6	17	16	21	.318	.431
R	.310	145	45	5	0	5	15	9	24	.357	.448

Year	Team (League)	W	L	Pct.	ERA	WHIP	G	GS	CG	ShO	Hld.	Sv.-Opp.	IP	H	R	ER	HR	BB-IBB	SO	Avg.
2000— Dom. Rangers (DSL)		1	6	.143	4.52	1.58	14	14	0	0	...	0-...	67.2	69	49	34	2	38-...	56	...
2001— GC Rangers (GCL)		4	2	.667	4.01	1.17	11	9	1	1	...	0-...	58.1	56	29	26	4	12-0	55	.250
— Charlotte (Fla. St.)		1	0	1.000	3.60	1.00	2	0	0	0	...	0-...	5.0	4	2	2	1	1-0	5	.235
2002— Savannah (S. Atl.)		1	3	.250	2.16	1.07	16	9	0	0	...	1-...	66.2	50	23	16	4	21-1	70	.209
2003— Stockton (Calif.)		4	0	1.000	2.84	1.12	16	9	0	0	...	1-...	63.1	55	27	20	3	16-0	72	.233
— Oklahoma (PCL)		1	0	1.000	3.50	1.00	3	3	0	0	...	0-...	18.0	15	7	7	1	3-0	14	.227
— Frisco (Texas)		5	0	1.000	2.60	1.01	9	9	0	0	...	0-...	55.1	35	17	16	2	21-0	54	.178
— Texas (A.L.)		0	2	.000	7.16	1.71	6	3	0	0	...	0-...	16.1	16	14	13	6	12-0	13	.271
2004— Oklahoma (PCL)		5	1	.833	3.13	1.10	9	9	0	0	...	0-...	54.2	41	20	19	3	19-0	41	.205
— Frisco (Texas)		0	0	...	1.08	0.60	3	2	0	0	...	0-...	8.1	4	1	1	0	1-0	11	.143
— Texas (A.L.)		1	2	.333	3.91	1.30	4	4	0	0	...	0-0	23.0	25	11	10	2	5-0	14	.281
2005— Frisco (Texas)		2	0	1.000	2.63	1.04	15	2	0	0	1	2-2	37.2	30	14	11	4	9-1	31	.216
— Oklahoma (PCL)		2	1	.667	4.25	1.33	7	7	0	0	0	0-0	36.0	38	20	17	6	10-0	24	.266
— Texas (A.L.)		4	6	.400	4.22	1.46	22	10	0	0	...	0-1	70.1	78	37	33	11	25-0	45	.277
Major League totals (3 years)		5	10	.333	4.60	1.47	32	17	0	0	...	0-1	109.2	119	62	56	18	42-0	72	.277

D

DOMINIQUE, ANDY   C

PERSONAL: Born October 30, 1975, in Tarzana, Calif. ... 6-0/220. ... Bats right, throws right. ... Full name: Andrew John Dominique. ... High school: Alemany (Mission Hills, Calif.). ... College: Nevada-Reno.
TRANSACTIONS/CAREER NOTES: Selected by Philadelphia Phillies organization in 26th round of free-agent draft (June 4, 1997). ... Traded by Phillies to Boston Red Sox for future considerations (April 26, 2002). ... Signed as a free agent by New York Mets organization (December 23, 2004). ... Released by Mets (April 2, 2005). ... Signed by Toronto Blue Jays organization (April 5, 2005).
2005 GAMES PLAYED BY POSITION (MLB): C—1.

LEFTY-RIGHTY SPLITS

vs.	Avg.	AB	H	2B	3B	HR	RBI	BB	SO	OBP	Slg.
L	.000	0	0	0	0	0	0	0	0	.000	.000
R	.000	2	0	0	0	0	0	0	0	.333	.000

									BATTING										FIELDING	
Year	Team (League)	Pos.	G	AB	R	H	2B	3B	HR	RBI	BB	SO	HBP	GDP	SB-CS	Avg.	OBP	SLG	OPS	E	Avg.
1997—Batavia (NY-Penn)		1B	72	277	52	77	17	0	14	48	26	60	10	6	4-1	.278	.355	.491	.846	6	.990
1998—Piedmont (S. Atl.)		3B-1B	133	514	82	145	38	0	24	102	61	97	12	9	0-2	.282	.369	.496	.865	17	.961
1999—Clearwater (FSL)		C-1B	130	487	77	124	29	5	14	92	69	84	10	13	3-3	.255	.354	.421	.775	10	.984
2000—Reading (East.)		C-1B-3B	104	327	46	78	27	0	13	50	35	56	8	9	0-1	.239	.324	.440	.764	4	.994
2001—Reading (East.)		C-1B-3B	76	261	43	73	16	0	12	49	27	45	1	6	3-1	.280	.369	.479	.848	8	.985
—Scran./W.B. (I.L.)		1B-3B-C	40	135	16	23	6	0	3	18	12	34	1	4	0-0	.170	.243	.281	.525	5	.986
2002—Clearwater (FSL)		1B-OF	8	34	5	14	5	0	0	2	1	4	1	0	0-0	.412	.444	.559	1.003	0	1.000
—Trenton (East.)		1B-C	103	361	40	145	21	1	8	51	36	60	9	9	2-1	.271	.347	.402	.749	7	.991
2003—Portland (East.)		1B-C	32	97	18	35	7	0	3	21	16	15	3	1	0-0	.361	.454	.526	.980	3	.983
—Pawtucket (Int'l)		C-1B	79	289	42	88	18	0	13	57	22	45	7	10	2-1	.304	.364	.502	.866	3	.992
2004—Boston (A.L.)		1B-C	7	11	0	2	0	0	0	1	0	3	0	0	0-0	.182	.182	.182	.364	1	.964
—Pawtucket (Int'l)		DH-C-1B	111	419	54	112	28	0	15	69	55	87	8	11	0-2	.267	.360	.442	.791	6	.985
2005—Toronto (A.L.)		C	2	2	0	0	0	0	0	0	0	1	0	0	0-0	.000	.000	.000	.333	0	1.000
—Syracuse (Int'l)		C-DH	39	117	18	28	6	0	3	10	15	20	2	6	0-0	.239	.336	.368	.703	0	1.000
Major League totals (2 years)			9	13	0	2	0	0	0	1	0	3	1	0	0-0	.154	.214	.154	.368	1	.969

DONNELLY, BRENDAN   P

PERSONAL: Born July 4, 1971, in Washington, District of Columbia. ... 6-3/240. ... Throws right, bats right. ... Full name: Brendan Kevin Donnelly. ... High school: Sandia (Albuquerque, N.M.). ... Junior college: Mesa (Ari.) Community College.
TRANSACTIONS/CAREER NOTES: Selected by Chicago White Sox organization in 27th round of 1992 free-agent draft. ... Released by White Sox (April 16, 1993). ... Signed by Chicago Cubs organization (June 16, 1993). ... Released by Cubs (March 29, 1994). ... Signed by Ohio Valley of the independent Frontier League (July 1994). ... Signed by Cincinnati Reds organization (March 4, 1995). ... Released by Reds (April 3, 1999). ... Contract purchased by Tampa Bay Devil Rays organization from Nashua of the independent Atlantic League (May 15, 1999). ... Released by Devil Rays (August 12, 1999). ... Signed by Pittsburgh Pirates organization (August 18, 1999). ... Released by Pirates (August 25, 1999). ... Signed by Toronto Blue Jays organization (August 26, 1999). ... Released by Blue Jays (July 28, 2000). ... Signed by Cubs organization (August 10, 2000). ... Signed as a free agent by Anaheim Angels organization (January 9, 2001). ... On disabled list (March 26-June 17, 2004); included rehabilitation assignments to Rancho Cucamonga and Salt Lake. ... Angels franchise renamed Los Angeles Angels of Anaheim for 2005 season. ... On suspended list (July 1-9, 2005).
CAREER HITTING: 0-for-1 (.000), 0 R, 0 2B, 0 3B, 0 HR, 0 RBI.

SCOUTING REPORT **Throws:** The hard-nosed Donnelly has an 88-93 mph fastball, a slider and a split-finger fastball. ***Tendencies:*** Donnelly has a herky-jerky delivery and seems to throw himself at the hitter, making his ball difficult to pick up. Short, quick arm movement gives the hitter the appearance he throws harder than he does. Slider has a quick break. Uses splitter as an out pitch. Has lost a little off his fastball and the spread between his pitches has narrowed. ***Outlook:*** A heavy workload over the past several years is starting to show. ***Grade 7.9***

BRENDAN DONNELLY'S PITCHING ZONE

.125	.385	.200
.220	.542	.281
.250	.182	.091

LEFTY-RIGHTY SPLITS

vs.	Avg.	AB	H	2B	3B	HR	RBI	BB	SO	OBP	Slg.
L	.213	122	26	6	0	2	16	10	26	.278	.311
R	.274	124	34	4	0	7	12	9	27	.326	.476

Year	Team (League)	W	L	Pct.	ERA	WHIP	G	GS	CG	ShO	Hld.	Sv.-Opp.	IP	H	R	ER	HR	BB-IBB	SO	Avg.
1992—GC Whi. Sox (GCL)		0	3	.000	3.67	1.49	9	7	0	0	...	1-...	41.2	41	25	17	0	21-0	31	.256
1993—Geneva (NY-Penn)		4	0	1.000	6.28	1.58	21	3	0	0	...	1-...	43.0	39	34	30	4	29-0	29	.242
1994—Ohio Valley (Fron.)		1	1	.500	2.57	1.21	10	0	0	0	...	0-...	14.0	13	5	4	1	4-0	20	.250
1995—Char., W.Va. (SAL)		1	1	.500	1.19	0.69	24	0	0	0	...	12-...	30.1	14	4	4	0	7-1	33	.139
—Win.-Salem (Car.)		1	2	.333	1.02	0.96	23	0	0	0	...	2-...	35.1	20	6	4	1	14-2	32	.167
—Indianapolis (A.A.)		1	1	.500	23.63	3.38	3	0	0	0	...	0-...	2.2	7	8	7	2	2-0	1	.500
1996—Chattanooga (Sou.)		1	2	.333	5.52	1.50	22	0	0	0	...	0-...	29.1	27	21	18	4	17-2	22	.237
1997—Chattanooga (Sou.)		6	4	.600	3.27	1.31	62	0	0	0	...	6-...	82.2	71	43	30	6	37-4	64	.228
1998—Chattanooga (Sou.)		2	5	.286	2.98	1.48	38	0	0	0	...	13-...	45.1	43	16	15	4	24-5	47	.247
—Indianapolis (Int'l)		4	1	.800	2.65	1.21	19	1	0	0	...	0-...	37.1	29	16	11	3	16-3	39	.212
1999—Nashua (Atl.)		0	0	...	3.00	1.33	3	0	0	0	...	0-...	3.0	1	1	1	...	3-...	4	...
—Durham (Int'l)		5	5	.500	3.05	1.15	37	1	0	0	...	2-...	62.0	53	23	21	5	18-1	61	.240
—Altoona (East.)		0	0	...	7.71	2.57	2	0	0	0	...	1-...	2.1	4	2	2	0	2-0	5	.571
—Syracuse (Int'l)		0	1	.000	2.89	1.29	5	0	0	0	...	0-...	9.1	8	4	3	1	4-1	9	.242
2000—Syracuse (Int'l)		4	6	.400	5.48	1.73	37	0	0	0	...	0-...	42.2	47	34	26	5	27-2	34	.278
—Iowa (PCL)		0	3	.000	7.56	1.86	9	0	0	0	...	1-...	16.2	25	19	14	3	6-1	14	.338
2001—Arkansas (Texas)		4	1	.800	2.48	1.17	27	0	0	0	...	12-...	29.0	21	8	8	2	13-1	37	.200
—Salt Lake (PCL)		5	1	.833	2.40	1.11	29	0	0	0	...	1-...	41.1	38	11	11	4	8-0	50	.245
2002—Salt Lake (PCL)		4	0	1.000	3.48	1.13	25	0	0	0	...	6-...	33.2	27	13	13	5	11-0	42	.213
—Anaheim (A.L.)		1	1	.500	2.17	1.03	46	0	0	0	13	1-3	49.2	32	13	12	2	24-1	54	.184
2003—Anaheim (A.L.)		2	2	.500	1.58	1.07	63	0	0	0	* 29	3-5	74.0	55	14	13	2	24-1	79	.200
2004—Rancho Cuca. (Calif.)		0	0	...	0.00	1.33	2	0	0	0	...	0-...	3.0	3	0	0	0	1-0	5	.250
—Salt Lake (PCL)		0	0	...	7.71	1.71	3	0	0	0	...	0-...	2.1	2	2	2	0	2-0	6	.250
—Anaheim (A.L.)		5	2	.714	3.00	1.17	40	0	0	0	5	0-0	42.0	34	14	14	5	15-0	56	.224
2005—Los Angeles (A.L.)		9	3	.750	3.72	1.21	65	0	0	0	16	0-5	65.1	60	30	27	9	19-3	53	.244
Major League totals (4 years)		17	8	.680	2.57	1.12	214	0	0	0	63	4-13	231.0	181	71	66	18	77-7	242	.214

DIVISION SERIES RECORD

Year Team (League)	W	L	Pct.	ERA	WHIP	G	GS	CG	ShO	Hld.	Sv.-Opp.	IP	H	R	ER	HR	BB-IBB	SO	Avg.
2002— Anaheim (A.L.)	0	0	...	13.50	2.00	3	0	0	0	1	0-0	2.0	3	3	3	2	1-0	2	.333
2004— Anaheim (A.L.)	0	0	...	10.80	1.50	2	0	0	0	0	0-0	3.1	3	4	4	0	2-2	5	.231
2005— Los Angeles (A.L.)	0	0	...	27.00	9.00	1	0	0	0	0	0-0	0.1	2	2	1	0	1-0	0	.667
Division series totals (3 years)	0	0	...	12.71	2.12	6	0	0	0	1	0-0	5.2	8	9	8	2	4-2	7	.320

CHAMPIONSHIP SERIES RECORD

Year Team (League)	W	L	Pct.	ERA	WHIP	G	GS	CG	ShO	Hld.	Sv.-Opp.	IP	H	R	ER	HR	BB-IBB	SO	Avg.
2002— Anaheim (A.L.)	0	0	...	8.10	0.90	3	0	0	0	2	0-0	3.1	3	3	3	0	0-0	5	.231
2005— Los Angeles (A.L.)	0	0	...	0.00	0.90	3	0	0	0	0	0-0	3.1	2	0	0	0	1-0	5	.182
Champ. series totals (2 years)	0	0	...	4.05	0.90	6	0	0	0	2	0-0	6.2	5	3	3	0	1-0	10	.208

WORLD SERIES RECORD

Year Team (League)	W	L	Pct.	ERA	WHIP	G	GS	CG	ShO	Hld.	Sv.-Opp.	IP	H	R	ER	HR	BB-IBB	SO	Avg.
2002— Anaheim (A.L.)	1	0	1.000	0.00	0.65	5	0	0	0	0	0-0	7.2	1	0	0	0	4-0	6	.042

ALL-STAR GAME RECORD

	W	L	Pct.	ERA	WHIP	G	GS	CG	ShO	Hld.	Sv.-Opp.	IP	H	R	ER	HR	BB-IBB	SO	Avg.
All-Star Game totals (1 year)	1	0	1.000	0.00	0.00	1	0	0	0	0	0-0	1.0	0	0	0	0	0-0	1	.000

DOTEL, OCTAVIO   P

PERSONAL: Born November 25, 1973, in Santo Domingo, Dominican Republic. ... 6-0/210. ... Throws right, bats right. ... Full name: Octavio Eduardo Dotel. ... Name pronounced: Oc-TAH-vee-oh dough-TEL. ... High school: Liceo Eansino Afuera (Dominican Republic).

TRANSACTIONS/CAREER NOTES: Signed as a non-drafted free agent by New York Mets organization (March 20, 1993). ... Traded by Mets with OF Roger Cedeno and P Kyle Kessel to Houston Astros for P Mike Hampton and OF Derek Bell (December 23, 1999). ... Traded by Astros to Oakland Athletics as part of three-team deal in which Astros acquired OF Carlos Beltran and cash from Kansas City Royals and Royals acquired C John Buck and cash from Astros and P Mike Wood and 3B Mark Teahen from Athletics (June 24, 2004). ... On disabled list (May 20, 2005-remainder of season).

CAREER HITTING: 5-for-74 (.068), 3 R, 0 2B, 0 3B, 0 HR, 1 RBI.

SCOUTING REPORT *Throws:* Dotel's fastball is 94-98 mph, and his slider is 83-88. *Tendencies:* He essentially is a one-speed pitcher. Fastball can be overpowering, and slider runs sharply when mechanics are right. Erratic delivery and tendency to overthrow causes his stuff to flatten out at times. *Outlook:* His availability for 2006 is in question because of shoulder surgery, although he was ahead of schedule in his rehab. Is better as a setup man; doesn't have enough confidence to close. **Grade 7**

OCTAVIO DOTEL'S PITCHING ZONE

.000	.200	.000
.182	.750	.143
.000	.143	1.000

LEFTY-RIGHTY SPLITS

vs.	Avg.	AB	H	2B	3B	HR	RBI	BB	SO	OBP	Slg.
L	.269	26	7	3	0	1	4	9	6	.457	.500
R	.107	28	3	1	0	1	4	2	10	.167	.250

Year Team (League)	W	L	Pct.	ERA	WHIP	G	GS	CG	ShO	Hld.	Sv.-Opp.	IP	H	R	ER	HR	BB-IBB	SO	Avg.
1993— Dom. Mets (DSL)	6	2	.750	4.10	1.42	15	11	0	0	...	0-...	59.1	46	30	27	...	38-...	48	...
1994— Dom. Mets (DSL)	5	0	1.000	4.32	1.41	15	14	1	0	...	0-...	81.1	84	53	39	...	31-...	95	...
1995— GC Mets (GCL)	7	4	.636	2.18	0.87	13	12	2	0	...	0-...	74.1	48	23	18	0	17-1	86	.178
— St. Lucie (Fla. St.)	1	0	1.000	5.63	1.75	3	0	0	0	...	0-...	8.0	10	5	5	1	4-0	9	.323
1996— Capital City (SAL)	11	3	.786	3.59	1.20	22	19	0	0	...	0-...	115.1	89	49	46	7	49-0	142	.212
1997— St. Lucie (Fla. St.)	5	2	.714	2.52	1.34	9	8	1	1	...	0-...	50.0	44	18	14	2	23-0	39	.235
— Binghamton (East.)	3	4	.429	5.98	1.87	12	12	0	0	...	0-...	55.2	66	50	37	5	38-1	40	.293
— GC Mets (GCL)	0	0	...	0.96	1.18	3	2	0	0	...	1-...	9.1	9	1	1	0	2-0	7	.250
1998— Binghamton (East.)	4	2	.667	1.97	0.95	10	10	2	1	...	0-...	68.2	41	19	15	4	24-1	82	.175
— Norfolk (Int'l)	8	6	.571	3.45	1.26	17	16	1	0	...	0-...	99.0	82	47	38	9	43-1	118	.221
1999— St. Lucie (Fla. St.)	5	2	.714	3.84	1.22	13	13	1	0	...	0-...	70.1	52	33	30	9	34-1	90	.204
— New York (N.L.)	8	3	.727	5.38	1.38	19	14	0	0	0	0-0	85.1	69	52	51	12	49-1	85	.226
2000— Houston (N.L.)	3	7	.300	5.40	1.50	50	16	0	0	0	16-23	125.0	127	80	75	26	61-3	142	.265
2001— Houston (N.L.)	7	5	.583	2.66	1.20	61	4	0	0	14	2-4	105.0	79	35	31	5	47-2	145	.205
2002— Houston (N.L.)	6	4	.600	1.85	0.87	83	0	0	0	31	6-10	97.1	58	21	20	7	27-2	118	.173
2003— Houston (N.L.)	6	4	.600	2.48	0.97	76	0	0	0	* 33	4-6	87.0	53	25	24	9	31-2	97	.172
2004— Houston (N.L.)	0	4	.000	3.12	1.21	32	0	0	0	0	14-17	34.2	27	15	12	4	15-4	50	.213
— Oakland (A.L.)	6	2	.750	4.09	1.16	45	0	0	0	0	22-28	50.2	41	23	23	9	18-3	72	.220
2005— Oakland (A.L.)	1	2	.333	3.52	1.37	15	0	0	0	0	7-11	15.1	10	6	6	2	11-2	16	.185
American League totals (2 years)	7	4	.636	3.95	1.21	60	0	0	0	0	29-39	66.0	51	29	29	11	29-5	88	.213
National League totals (6 years)	30	27	.526	3.59	1.20	321	34	0	0	78	42-60	534.1	413	228	213	63	230-14	637	.213
Major League totals (7 years)	37	31	.544	3.63	1.20	381	34	0	0	78	71-99	600.1	464	257	242	74	259-19	725	.213

DIVISION SERIES RECORD

Year Team (League)	W	L	Pct.	ERA	WHIP	G	GS	CG	ShO	Hld.	Sv.-Opp.	IP	H	R	ER	HR	BB-IBB	SO	Avg.
1999— New York (N.L.)	0	0	...	54.00	9.00	1	0	0	0	0	0-0	0.1	1	2	2	0	2-0	0	.500
2001— Houston (N.L.)	0	0	...	5.40	1.50	2	0	0	0	0	0-0	3.1	5	2	2	1	0-0	5	.333
Division series totals (2 years)	0	0	...	9.82	2.18	3	0	0	0	0	0-0	3.2	6	4	4	1	2-0	5	.353

CHAMPIONSHIP SERIES RECORD

Year Team (League)	W	L	Pct.	ERA	WHIP	G	GS	CG	ShO	Hld.	Sv.-Opp.	IP	H	R	ER	HR	BB-IBB	SO	Avg.
1999— New York (N.L.)	1	0	1.000	3.00	2.00	1	0	0	0	0	0-0	3.0	4	1	1	0	2-1	5	.333

DOUGLASS, SEAN　　　　　　　　　　　P

PERSONAL: Born April 28, 1979, in Lancaster, Calif. ... 6-6/210. ... Throws right, bats right. ... Full name: Sean R. Douglass. ... High school: Antelope Valley (Lancaster, Calif.).
TRANSACTIONS/CAREER NOTES: Selected by Baltimore Orioles organization in second round of 1997 free-agent draft. ... Claimed on waivers by Minnesota Twins (October 14, 2003). ... Claimed on waivers by Toronto Blue Jays (March 31, 2004). ... Signed as a free agent by Detroit Tigers organization (November 12, 2004). ... Claimed on waivers by Cleveland Indians (October 10, 2005).
CAREER HITTING: 0-for-2 (.000), 0 R, 0 2B, 0 3B, 0 HR, 0 RBI.

SEAN DOUGLASS' PITCHING ZONE

.176	.182	.154
.440	.476	.341
.200	.308	.350

LEFTY-RIGHTY SPLITS

vs.	Avg.	AB	H	2B	3B	HR	RBI	BB	SO	OBP	Slg.
L	.315	178	56	10	3	9	35	18	24	.375	.556
R	.232	155	36	5	1	4	20	15	31	.301	.355

Year — Team (League)	W	L	Pct.	ERA	WHIP	G	GS	CG	ShO	Hld.	Sv.-Opp.	IP	H	R	ER	HR	BB—IBB	SO	Avg.
1997— GC Orioles (GCL)	1	3	.250	6.11	1.64	9	1	0	0	...	0-...	17.2	20	14	12	2	9-0	10	.308
1998— Bluefield (Appal.)	2	2	.500	3.23	1.11	10	0	0	0	...	0-...	53.0	45	20	19	6	14-0	62	.231
1999— Frederick (Carolina)	5	6	.455	3.32	1.63	16	16	1	0	...	0-...	97.2	101	48	36	9	58-0	161	.267
2000— Bowie (East.)	9	8	.529	4.02	1.31	27	27	2	0	...	0-...	159.0	174	88	71	17	34-1	105	.280
2001— Rochester (Int'l)	8	9	.471	3.49	1.36	27	27	0	0	...	0-...	162.1	160	79	63	13	61-0	156	.252
— Baltimore (A.L.)	2	1	.667	5.31	1.57	4	4	0	0	0	0-0	20.1	21	12	12	3	11-0	17	.259
2002— Rochester (Int'l)	4	6	.400	4.73	1.52	14	13	0	0	0	0-...	66.2	66	39	35	4	35-0	71	.256
— Baltimore (A.L.)	0	5	.000	6.08	1.74	15	8	0	0	0	0-0	53.1	58	41	36	10	35-2	44	.283
2003— Ottawa (Int'l)	10	8	.556	3.40	1.40	27	27	0	0	...	0-...	143.0	142	67	54	6	58-4	118	.256
— Baltimore (A.L.)	0	0	...	13.50	2.50	3	0	0	0	0	0-0	8.0	14	12	12	2	6-0	3	.378
2004— Syracuse (Int'l)	5	6	.455	4.75	1.45	18	18	1	0	...	0-...	89.0	92	53	47	7	37-0	74	.272
— Toronto (A.L.)	0	2	.000	6.28	1.68	14	3	0	0	0	0-0	38.2	37	27	27	6	28-4	36	.252
2005— Toledo (Int'l)	9	1	.900	2.87	1.08	14	14	0	0	0	0-0	81.2	61	26	26	5	27-1	76	.205
— Detroit (A.L.)	5	5	.500	5.56	1.43	18	16	0	0	0	0-0	87.1	92	57	54	13	33-2	55	.276
Major League totals (5 years)	**7**	**13**	**.350**	**6.11**	**1.61**	**54**	**31**	**0**	**0**	**0**	**0-0**	**207.2**	**222**	**149**	**141**	**34**	**113-8**	**155**	**.276**

DOUMIT, RYAN　　　　　　　　　　　C

PERSONAL: Born April 3, 1981, in Moses Lake, Wash. ... 6-0/200. ... Bats both, throws right. ... Full name: Ryan Matthew Doumit. ... High school: Moses Lake (Wash.).
TRANSACTIONS/CAREER NOTES: Selected by Pittsburgh Pirates organization in second round of 1999 free-agent draft.
2005 GAMES PLAYED BY POSITION (MLB): C—50, DH—6, OF—3.

SCOUTING REPORT *Offense:* He's a gap-to-gap hitter who could develop some serious power. Lack of experience causes him to miss mistakes he ought to hit, and he strikes out too much. Most of his power comes from the left side; he ought to give up trying to hit from the right side. Is in serious need of reps to gain any kind of consistent stroke. Is an average runner at best. *Defense:* Doumit has improved his footwork, throwing, framing and blocking to the point where he is adequate. Worked hard on his ability to handle pitchers. *Outlook:* If he can put together another injury-free season, he could hang around a while as a good backup catcher. *Grade 6.5*

RYAN DOUMIT'S HITTING ZONE

.308	.250	.250
.381	.389	.333
.214	.250	.269

LEFTY-RIGHTY SPLITS

vs.	Avg.	AB	H	2B	3B	HR	RBI	BB	SO	OBP	Slg.
L	.296	54	16	4	0	1	6	1	10	.361	.426
R	.243	177	43	9	1	5	29	10	38	.313	.390

							BATTING										FIELDING	
Year — Team (League)	Pos.	G	AB	R	H	2B	3B	HR	RBI	BB	SO	HBP	GDP	SB-CS	Avg.	OBP	SLG	OPS	E	Avg.
1999— GC Pirates (GCL)	C	29	85	17	24	5	0	1	7	15	14	4	0	4-2	.282	.410	.376	.786	2	.975
2000— Will. (NYP)	C	66	246	25	77	15	5	2	40	23	33	4	7	2-2	.313	.371	.439	.810	6	.985
2001— Hickory (S. Atl.)	C	39	148	14	40	6	0	2	14	10	32	4	2	2-1	.270	.333	.351	.684	3	.984
— GC Pirates (GCL)	C	7	17	2	4	2	0	0	3	2	0	0	0	0-0	.235	.316	.353	.669	1	.944
— Altoona (East.)	C	2	4	0	1	0	0	0	2	1	1	0	0	0-0	.250	.400	.250	.650	0	1.000
2002— Hickory (S. Atl.)	C	68	258	46	83	14	1	6	47	18	40	8	6	3-5	.322	.377	.453	.830	7	.968
2003— Lynchburg (Caro.)	C	127	458	75	126	38	1	11	77	45	79	13	4	4-0	.275	.351	.434	.785	9	.985
2004— Altoona (East.)	C	67	221	31	58	20	0	10	34	21	49	8	4	0-1	.262	.343	.489	.832	3	.983
2005— Indianapolis (Int'l)	C-DH-OF	51	165	41	57	11	0	12	35	16	36	5	3	1-3	.345	.415	.630	1.045	4	.984
— Pittsburgh (N.L.)	C-DH-OF	75	231	25	59	13	1	6	35	11	48	13	5	2-1	.255	.324	.398	.722	8	.975
Major League totals (1 year)		**75**	**231**	**25**	**59**	**13**	**1**	**6**	**35**	**11**	**48**	**13**	**5**	**2-1**	**.255**	**.324**	**.398**	**.722**	**8**	**.975**

DOWNS, SCOTT　　　　　　　　　　　P

PERSONAL: Born March 17, 1976, in Louisville, Ky. ... 6-2/190. ... Throws left, bats left. ... Full name: Scott Jeremy Downs. ... High school: Pleasure Ridge Park (Louisville, Ky.). ... College: Kentucky.
TRANSACTIONS/CAREER NOTES: Selected by Atlanta Braves organization in 12th round of 1994 free-agent draft; did not sign. ... Selected by Chicago Cubs organization in third round of 1997 free-agent draft. ... Traded by Cubs to Minnesota Twins (November 3, 1998), completing deal in which Twins traded P Mike Morgan to Cubs for cash and a player to be named (August 25, 1998). ... Traded by Twins with P Rick Aguilera to Cubs for Ps Kyle Lohse and Jason Ryan (May 21, 1999). ... Traded by Cubs to Montreal Expos for OF Rondell White (July 31, 2000). ... On disabled list (August 9, 2000-remainder of season; and March 23, 2001-entire season). ... On disabled list (March 27-June 10, 2002); included rehabilitation assignments to Brevard County and Ottawa. ... Released by Expos (November 23, 2004). ... Signed by Toronto Blue Jays organization (December 16, 2004).
CAREER HITTING: 3-for-44 (.068), 3 R, 0 2B, 0 3B, 0 HR, 1 RBI.

SCOUTING REPORT

Throws: Downs throws a two- and four-seam fastball in the upper 80s, a curveball and a straight changeup. **Tendencies:** He has good tailing action on his fastball and can run his two-seam fastball in on the hands of righthanded hitters. Throws a larger, looping curveball to righthanders and a harder, flatter curveball to lefthanders. Has good arm speed and motion on his changeup. Can use his off-speed pitches to set up his fastball. **Outlook:** Downs must have good control to win, but he is a good option at the back of the rotation. *Grade 6.6*

SCOTT DOWNS' PITCHING ZONE

.400	.125	.333
.371	.353	.229
.242	.346	.227

LEFTY-RIGHTY SPLITS

vs.	Avg.	AB	H	2B	3B	HR	RBI	BB	SO	OBP	Slg.
L	.234	107	25	1	0	3	10	9	28	.291	.327
R	.262	260	68	15	3	9	29	25	47	.338	.446

Year	Team (League)	W	L	Pct.	ERA	WHIP	G	GS	CG	ShO	Hld.	Sv.-Opp.	IP	H	R	ER	HR	BB-IBB	SO	Avg.
1997—	Will. (NYP)	0	2	.000	2.74	0.96	5	5	0	0	...	0-...	23.0	15	11	7	0	7-0	28	.181
—	Rockford (Midwest)	3	0	1.000	1.25	0.69	5	5	0	0	...	0-...	36.0	17	5	5	1	8-0	43	.144
1998—	Daytona (Fla. St.)	8	9	.471	3.90	1.45	27	27	2	0	...	0-...	161.2	179	83	70	12	55-0	117	.280
1999—	New Britain (East.)	0	0	...	8.69	2.19	6	3	0	0	...	0-...	19.2	33	21	19	5	10-1	22	.375
—	Fort Myers (FSL)	0	1	.000	0.00	1.34	2	2	0	0	...	0-...	9.2	7	3	0	0	6-0	9	.184
—	Daytona (Fla. St.)	5	0	1.000	1.88	1.08	7	7	1	1	...	0-...	48.0	41	12	10	2	11-0	41	.237
—	West Tenn (Sou.)	8	1	.889	1.35	1.05	13	12	1	0	...	0-...	80.0	56	13	12	2	28-0	101	.194
2000—	Chicago (N.L.)	4	3	.571	5.17	1.64	18	18	0	0	0	0-0	94.0	117	59	54	13	37-1	63	.310
—	Montreal (N.L.)	0	0	...	9.00	2.67	1	1	0	0	0	0-0	3.0	5	3	3	0	3-0	0	.385
2001—	Did not play.																			
2002—	Brevard County (FSL)	0	0	...	3.00	1.00	7	0	0	0	...	1-...	9.0	7	3	3	0	2-0	7	.206
—	Ottawa (Int'l)	2	1	.667	5.79	1.46	17	0	0	0	...	0-...	23.1	31	21	15	6	3-0	15	.320
2003—	Montreal (N.L.)	0	1	.000	15.00	2.67	1	1	0	0	0	0-0	3.0	5	5	5	2	3-2	4	.357
—	Edmonton (PCL)	8	9	.471	4.29	1.30	21	21	3	0	...	0-...	121.2	119	67	58	13	39-0	54	.263
2004—	Edmonton (PCL)	10	6	.625	3.53	1.25	22	22	2	2	...	0-...	135.1	143	57	53	16	26-0	67	.274
—	Montreal (N.L.)	3	6	.333	5.14	1.62	12	12	1	1	0	0-0	63.0	79	47	36	9	23-2	38	.310
2005—	Syracuse (Int'l)	2	3	.400	4.81	1.22	7	7	0	0	0	0-0	39.1	45	21	21	5	3-0	35	.285
—	Toronto (A.L.)	4	3	.571	4.31	1.35	26	13	0	0	0	0-0	94.0	93	49	45	12	34-0	75	.253
American League totals (1 year)		4	3	.571	4.31	1.35	26	13	0	0	0	0-0	94.0	93	49	45	12	34-0	75	.253
National League totals (3 years)		7	10	.412	5.41	1.67	32	32	1	1	0	0-0	163.0	206	114	98	24	66-5	105	.312
Major League totals (4 years)		11	13	.458	5.01	1.55	58	45	1	1	0	0-0	257.0	299	163	143	36	100-5	180	.291

D

DRESE, RYAN   P

PERSONAL: Born April 5, 1976, in San Francisco. ... 6-3/235. ... Throws right, bats right. ... Full name: Ryan Thomas Drese. ... Name pronounced: drees. ... High school: Bishop O'Dowd (Oakland). ... College: California.

TRANSACTIONS/CAREER NOTES: Selected by Oakland Athletics organization in fifth round of 1994 free-agent draft; did not sign. ... Selected by Athletics organization in 14th round of 1997 free-agent draft; did not sign. ... Selected by Cleveland Indians organization in fifth round of 1998 free-agent draft. ... Traded by Indians with C Einar Diaz to Texas Rangers for 1B Travis Hafner and P Aaron Myette (December 6, 2002). ... Claimed on waivers by Washington Nationals (June 10, 2005). ... On disabled list (August 24, 2005-remainder of season).

CAREER HITTING: 3-for-22 (.136), 1 R, 1 2B, 0 3B, 0 HR, 0 RBI.

SCOUTING REPORT

Throws: His sinking fastball ranges from 87-92 mph. Also throws a curveball, slider and changeup. **Tendencies:** Is effective when he's down. Makes too many mistakes in the middle of the plate and is not a strikeout pitcher. Shows a curve early in the count but doesn't have good rotation. Slider is a better breaking pitch. Has good movement on his straight change. **Outlook:** He is a question mark going into 2006 because he had a slight tear in his shoulder at the end of 2005. When healthy, is a better pitcher than his win-loss record. Is in an ideal park to increase his win total. *Grade 6.5*

RYAN DRESE'S PITCHING ZONE

.238	.300	.462
.330	.348	.354
.284	.400	.364

LEFTY-RIGHTY SPLITS

vs.	Avg.	AB	H	2B	3B	HR	RBI	BB	SO	OBP	Slg.
L	.303	238	72	17	1	3	29	30	15	.386	.420
R	.319	282	90	24	1	5	45	16	31	.361	.465

Year	Team (League)	W	L	Pct.	ERA	WHIP	G	GS	CG	ShO	Hld.	Sv.-Opp.	IP	H	R	ER	HR	BB-IBB	SO	Avg.
1998—	Watertown (NYP)	2	5	.286	4.07	1.29	9	9	0	0	...	0-...	42.0	40	21	19	1	14-0	40	.250
1999—	Kinston (Carol.)	5	4	.556	4.93	1.41	15	15	1	0	...	0-...	69.1	46	47	38	2	52-0	81	.189
—	Mahoning Valley (N.Y.-Penn.)	0	2	.000	2.65	0.88	5	5	0	0	...	0-...	17.0	8	6	5	1	7-0	26	.143
—	Columbus (S. Atl.)	0	2	.000	4.50	1.08	2	2	0	0	...	0-...	12.0	9	6	6	2	4-0	15	.200
2000—	Kinston (Carol.)	0	1	.000	3.86	1.29	1	1	0	0	...	0-...	2.1	2	1	1	0	1-0	4	.286
2001—	Akron (East.)	5	7	.417	3.35	1.08	14	13	1	1	...	0-...	86.0	64	34	32	4	29-0	73	.215
—	Buffalo (Int'l)	5	1	.833	4.01	1.27	11	10	0	0	...	0-...	60.2	60	28	27	7	17-0	52	.262
—	Cleveland (A.L.)	1	2	.333	3.44	1.28	9	4	0	0	0	0-0	36.2	32	15	14	2	15-2	24	.242
2002—	Cleveland (A.L.)	10	9	.526	6.55	1.73	26	26	1	0	0	0-0	137.1	176	104	100	15	62-1	102	.317
—	Buffalo (Int'l)	1	0	1.000	1.64	0.91	3	3	0	0	...	0-...	22.0	16	4	4	1	4-0	16	.200
2003—	Frisco (Texas)	1	1	.500	4.00	1.10	2	2	0	0	...	0-...	9.0	10	4	4	1	0-0	8	.278
—	Oklahoma (PCL)	8	6	.571	4.65	1.50	20	20	0	0	...	0-...	122.0	143	70	63	8	39-1	68	.300
—	Texas (A.L.)	2	4	.333	6.85	1.85	11	8	0	0	1	0-0	46.0	61	42	35	8	24-1	26	.314
2004—	Oklahoma (PCL)	1	0	1.000	1.80	1.20	1	1	0	0	...	0-...	5.0	6	1	1	1	0-0	4	.300
—	Texas (A.L.)	14	10	.583	4.20	1.40	34	33	4	0	0	0-0	207.2	233	104	97	16	58-6	98	.285
2005—	Texas (A.L.)	4	6	.400	6.46	1.72	12	12	1	0	0	0-0	69.2	96	52	50	5	24-1	20	.334
—	Washington (N.L.)	3	6	.333	4.98	1.47	11	11	0	0	0	0-0	59.2	66	38	33	3	22-1	26	.283
American League totals (5 years)		31	31	.500	5.36	1.57	92	83	4	0	1	0-0	497.1	598	317	296	46	183-11	270	.301
National League totals (1 year)		3	6	.333	4.98	1.47	11	11	0	0	0	0-0	59.2	66	38	33	3	22-1	26	.283
Major League totals (5 years)		34	37	.479	5.32	1.56	103	94	4	0	1	0-0	557.0	664	355	329	49	205-12	296	.299

PERSONAL: Born November 20, 1975, in Valdosta, Ga. ... 6-1/200. ... Bats left, throws right. ... Full name: David Jonathan Drew. ... High school: Lowndes County (Hahira, Ga.). ... College: Florida State. ... Brother of Tim Drew, pitcher with three major league teams (2000-04).

TRANSACTIONS/CAREER NOTES: Selected by San Francisco Giants organization in 20th round of 1994 free-agent draft; did not sign. ... Selected by Philadelphia Phillies organization in first round (second pick overall) of 1997 free-agent draft; did not sign. ... Signed by St. Paul of the independent Northern League (1997). ... Selected by St. Louis Cardinals organization in first round (fifth pick overall) of 1998 free-agent draft. ... On disabled list (May 16-June 17, 1999); included rehabilitation assignment to Memphis. ... On disabled list (July 8-27, 2000). ... On disabled list (June 18-July 31, 2001); included rehabilitation assignment to Peoria. ... On disabled list (June 28-July 13, 2002). ... On disabled list (March 21-April 20 and August 9-September 1, 2003); included rehabilitation assignment to Palm Beach. ... Traded by Cardinals with OF/C Eli Marrero to Atlanta Braves for Ps Jason Marquis, Ray King and Adam Wainwright (December 14, 2003). ... Signed as a free agent by Los Angeles Dodgers (January 11, 2005). ... On disabled list (July 4, 2005-remainder of season).

HONORS: Named College Player of the Year by THE SPORTING NEWS (1997).

2005 GAMES PLAYED BY POSITION (MLB): OF—72.

SCOUTING REPORT

Offense: Drew, an injury-plagued player, suffered a broken wrist and missed the last few months of 2005. Is a good tools player with a good approach at the plate. Hits with very little movement and has good bat speed. Can be too patient and frequently hits behind in the count, causing him to strike out a lot. Is a good fastball hitter, especially down in the zone, but looks lost at times with breaking stuff. Is a good runner with good basestealing instincts. **Defense:** Drew's arm is accurate, and he has a good over-the-top release to create good life and carry. Gets good reads and takes good routes. Doesn't make many mistakes. **Outlook:** Has the ability to be an All-Star but needs to stay on the field. Has not reached his potential. **Grade 7.8**

J.D. DREW'S HITTING ZONE

.300	.250	.600
.185	.393	.394
.143	.467	.163

LEFTY-RIGHTY SPLITS

vs.	Avg.	AB	H	2B	3B	HR	RBI	BB	SO	OBP	Slg.
L	.235	68	16	3	0	0	6	17	15	.416	.279
R	.304	184	56	9	1	15	30	34	35	.410	.609

Year Team (League)	Pos.	G	AB	R	H	2B	3B	HR	RBI	BB	SO	HBP	GDP	SB-CS	Avg.	OBP	SLG	OPS	FIELDING E	Avg.
1997—St. Paul (North.)	OF	44	170	51	58	6	1	18	50	30	40	2	1	5-3	.341	.443	.706	1.149	...	...
1998—St. Paul (North.)	OF	30	114	27	44	11	2	9	33	21	32	6	2	8-1	.386	.504	.754	1.258	...	...
—Arkansas (Texas)	OF	19	67	18	22	3	1	5	11	13	15	1	0	2-1	.328	.444	.627	1.071	1	.980
—Memphis (PCL)	OF	26	79	15	25	8	1	2	13	22	18	1	1	1-3	.316	.471	.519	.990	2	.966
—St. Louis (N.L.)	OF	14	36	9	15	3	1	5	13	4	10	0	4	0-0	.417	.463	.972	1.436	0	1.000
1999—St. Louis (N.L.)	OF	104	368	72	89	16	6	13	39	50	77	6	4	19-3	.242	.340	.424	.763	7	.972
—Memphis (PCL)	OF	25	87	11	26	5	1	2	15	8	20	2	0	6-1	.299	.371	.448	.819	0	1.000
2000—St. Louis (N.L.)	OF	135	407	73	120	17	2	18	57	67	99	6	3	17-9	.295	.401	.479	.880	9	.966
2001—St. Louis (N.L.)	OF	109	375	80	121	18	5	27	73	57	75	4	6	13-3	.323	.414	.613	1.027	6	.973
—Peoria (Midw.)	OF	3	11	3	6	2	0	0	0	1	0	0	1	0-0	.545	.583	.727	1.311	0	1.000
2002—St. Louis (N.L.)	OF	135	424	61	107	19	1	18	56	57	104	8	4	8-2	.252	.349	.429	.778	3	.987
2003—Palm Beach (FSL)	OF-DH	8	19	4	7	0	0	1	3	7	4	1	0	0-0	.368	.556	.526	1.082	0	1.000
—Atlanta (N.L.)	OF	100	287	60	83	13	3	15	42	36	48	3	6	2-2	.289	.374	.512	.886	1	.994
2004—Atlanta (N.L.)	OF-DH	145	518	118	158	28	8	31	93	118	116	5	7	12-3	.305	.436	.570	1.006	3	.990
2005—Los Angeles (N.L.)	OF	72	252	48	72	12	1	15	36	51	50	5	3	1-1	.286	.412	.520	.931	2	.987
Major League totals (8 years)		814	2667	521	765	126	27	142	409	440	579	37	37	72-23	.287	.393	.514	.907	31	.981

DIVISION SERIES RECORD

Year Team (League)	Pos.	G	AB	R	H	2B	3B	HR	RBI	BB	SO	HBP	GDP	SB-CS	Avg.	OBP	SLG	OPS	E	Avg.
2000—St. Louis (N.L.)	OF	2	6	1	1	0	0	0	0	2	1	0	0	2-0	.167	.375	.167	.542	0	1.000
2001—St. Louis (N.L.)	OF	5	13	1	2	0	0	1	2	3	1	0	0	0-0	.154	.313	.385	.697	0	1.000
2002—St. Louis (N.L.)	OF	2	9	1	2	0	0	1	1	1	2	0	0	0-0	.222	.300	.556	.856	0	1.000
2004—Atlanta (N.L.)	OF	5	20	1	4	0	0	0	2	4	7	0	0	1-1	.200	.333	.200	.533	1	.889
Division series totals (4 years)		14	48	4	9	0	0	2	4	10	11	0	0	3-1	.188	.328	.313	.640	1	.964

CHAMPIONSHIP SERIES RECORD

Year Team (League)	Pos.	G	AB	R	H	2B	3B	HR	RBI	BB	SO	HBP	GDP	SB-CS	Avg.	OBP	SLG	OPS	E	Avg.
2000—St. Louis (N.L.)	OF	5	12	2	4	1	0	1	0	3	0	0	0	0-0	.333	.333	.417	.750	0	1.000
2002—St. Louis (N.L.)	OF	5	13	1	5	0	0	1	1	2	0	1	0	0-0	.385	.429	.615	1.044	0	1.000
Champ. series totals (2 years)		10	25	3	9	1	0	1	2	5	0	1	0	0-0	.360	.385	.520	.905	0	1.000

PERSONAL: Born August 1, 1971, in Omaha, Neb. ... 6-0/215. ... Throws right, bats right. ... Full name: Travis Corey Driskill. ... High school: L.C. Anderson (Austin, Texas). ... College: Texas Tech.

TRANSACTIONS/CAREER NOTES: Selected by Houston Astros organization in 76th round of 1990 free-agent draft; did not sign. ... Selected by Cleveland Indians organization in fourth round of 1993 free-agent draft. ... Contract sold by Indians to Yakult of the Japan Central League (January 6, 1998). ... Signed as a free agent by Indians organization (August 3, 1998). ... Signed as a free agent by Astros organization (January 3, 2000). ... Signed as a free agent by Baltimore Orioles organization (November 16, 2001). ... Signed as a free agent by Colorado Rockies organization (December 17, 2003). ... Signed as a free agent by Astros organization (December 1, 2004).

LEFTY-RIGHTY SPLITS

vs.	Avg.	AB	H	2B	3B	HR	RBI	BB	SO	OBP	Slg.
L	.000	1	0	0	0	0	0	0	1	.000	.000
R	.333	3	1	0	0	0	0	0	1	.333	.333

CAREER HITTING: 0-for-5 (.000), 1 R, 0 2B, 0 3B, 0 HR, 0 RBI.

Year Team (League)	W	L	Pct.	ERA	WHIP	G	GS	CG	ShO	Hld.	Sv.-Opp.	IP	H	R	ER	HR	BB-IBB	SO	Avg.
1993—Watertown (NYP)	5	4	.556	4.14	1.32	21	8	0	0	...	3-...	63.0	62	38	29	4	21-0	53	.257
1994—Columbus (S. Atl.)	5	5	.500	2.52	1.26	62	0	0	0	...	35-...	64.1	51	25	18	2	30-4	88	.223
1995—Kinston (Carol.)	0	0	.000	2.74	0.96	15	0	0	0	...	0-...	23.0	17	7	7	2	5-1	24	.210
—Cant./Akr. (Eastern)	3	4	.429	4.66	1.40	33	0	0	0	...	4-...	46.1	46	24	24	3	19-1	39	.258
1996—Cant./Akr. (Eastern)	13	7	.650	3.61	1.35	29	24	4	2	...	0-...	172.0	169	89	69	8	63-0	148	.258
1997—Buffalo (A.A.)	8	7	.533	4.65	1.49	29	24	1	0	...	0-...	147.0	159	86	76	22	60-0	102	.277
1998—Yakult (Jp. Cen.)	1	6	.143	6.08	1.63	12	5	1	0	...	0-...	40.0	46	29	27	...	19-...	25	...
—Yakult (Jp. Cen.)	0	1	.000	4.80	1.80	7	3	0	0	...	0-...	15.0	21	9	8	...	6-...	7	...
—Akron (East.)	3	0	1.000	3.42	1.29	5	4	0	0	...	0-...	26.1	27	12	10	4	7-0	16	.270
—Buffalo (Int'l)	0	0	...	9.00	1.67	1	1	0	0	...	0-...	6.0	9	6	6	0	1-0	5	.333
1999—Buffalo (Int'l)	9	8	.529	4.83	1.35	31	18	0	0	...	0-...	132.1	146	78	71	21	32-2	90	.285

Year	Team (League)	W	L	Pct.	ERA	WHIP	G	GS	CG	ShO	Hld.	Sv.-Opp.	IP	H	R	ER	HR	BB-IBB	SO	Avg.
2000—New Orleans (PCL)		12	11	.522	4.01	1.37	28	28	2	1	...	0-...	* 179.1	201	101	80	15	45-0	113	.282
2001—New Orleans (PCL)		11	5	.688	3.78	1.16	28	28	1	0	...	0-...	* 178.2	175	83	75	21	33-2	145	.255
2002—Rochester (Int'l)		2	2	.500	1.64	0.82	4	4	1	1	...	0-...	22.0	17	8	4	1	1-0	15	.202
—Baltimore (A.L.)		8	8	.500	4.95	1.49	29	19	0	0	0	0-0	132.2	150	78	73	21	48-1	78	.284
2003—Baltimore (A.L.)		3	5	.375	6.00	1.48	20	0	0	0	0	1-1	48.0	62	35	32	8	9-2	33	.310
—Ottawa (Int'l)		4	0	1.000	2.84	1.00	9	9	0	0	0	0-...	50.2	46	17	16	8	6-0	36	.238
2004—Colorado (N.L.)		0	0	...	6.48	1.92	5	0	0	0	0	0-1	8.1	13	6	6	0	3-0	6	.361
—Colo. Springs (PCL)		5	5	.500	5.40	1.48	28	13	0	0	0	2-...	111.2	141	70	67	18	24-0	81	.311
2005—Round Rock (PCL)		9	5	.643	4.37	1.30	47	3	0	0	4	4-6	101.0	99	52	49	16	32-8	84	.261
—Houston (N.L.)		0	0	...	0.00	1.00	1	0	0	0	0	0-0	1.0	1	0	0	0	0-0	2	.250
American League totals (2 years)		11	13	.458	5.23	1.49	49	19	0	0	0	1-1	180.2	212	113	105	29	57-3	111	.291
National League totals (2 years)		0	0	...	5.79	1.82	6	0	0	0	0	0-1	9.1	14	6	6	0	3-0	8	.350
Major League totals (4 years)		11	13	.458	5.26	1.51	55	19	0	0	0	1-2	190.0	226	119	111	29	60-3	119	.294

DUBOIS, JASON — OF

PERSONAL: Born March 26, 1979, in Virginia Beach, Va. ... 6-5/220. ... Bats right, throws right. ... Full name: Jason Bradford Dubois. ... Name pronounced: DOO-boyce. ... High school: Frank W. Cox (Virginia Beach, Va.). ... College: Virginia Commonwealth.

TRANSACTIONS/CAREER NOTES: Selected by Chicago Cubs organization in 14th round of 2000 free-agent draft. ... Selected by Toronto Blue Jays from Cubs organization in Rule 5 major league draft (December 16, 2002). ... Returned to Cubs organization (March 15, 2003). ... Traded by Cubs to Cleveland Indians for OF Jody Gerut (July 19, 2005).

2005 GAMES PLAYED BY POSITION (MLB): OF—45, DH—10.

SCOUTING REPORT

Offense: He is a free swinger with good power potential. Chewed up minor league pitching but struggled in the majors after being traded to the Indians. Struck out in half of his 50 plate appearances. Still has a chance to develop improved plate discipline, which he will need if he wants to be an everyday player. Has below-average speed. **Defense:** His lack of speed seemed to hurt his ability to run routes well last season, though some say he's better than he first showed. Arm is considered above average. Can play first but not too well. **Outlook:** The Indians like Dubois, but he will need a strong spring to make the team as even a fourth outfielder. **Grade 6.3**

JASON DUBOIS'S HITTING ZONE

.111	.333	.000
.286	.500	.333
.276	.364	.267

LEFTY-RIGHTY SPLITS

vs.	Avg.	AB	H	2B	3B	HR	RBI	BB	SO	OBP	Slg.
L	.225	71	16	5	0	3	10	9	28	.321	.423
R	.241	116	28	7	0	6	14	3	46	.273	.457

Year	Team (League)	Pos.	G	AB	R	H	2B	3B	HR	RBI	BB	SO	HBP	GDP	SB-CS	Avg.	OBP	SLG	OPS	E	Avg.
2001—Lansing (Midw.)	OF-1B	118	443	76	131	28	9	24	92	46	120	14	8	1-2	.296	.377	.562	.940	7	.973
2002—Daytona (Fla. St.)	OF	99	361	64	116	25	1	20	85	57	95	9	7	6-2	.321	.422	.562	.985	4	.975
2003—West Tenn (Sou.)	OF-1B	130	443	57	119	31	4	15	73	57	118	15	12	2-4	.269	.367	.458	.825	9	.970
2004—Iowa (PCL)	OF-1B-DH	109	385	75	121	26	1	31	99	41	97	7	10	2-0	.314	.388	.629	1.009	4	.987
—Chicago (N.L.)	OF-1B	20	23	2	5	0	1	1	5	1	7	0	0	0-0	.217	.240	.435	.675	0	1.000
2005—Chicago (N.L.)	OF-DH	52	142	15	34	12	0	7	22	7	49	3	3	0-1	.239	.289	.472	.761	1	.980
—Iowa (PCL)	OF	4	17	4	9	1	0	1	6	1	3	0	0	0-0	.529	.556	.765	1.320	0	1.000
—Cleveland (A.L.)	OF-DH	14	45	6	10	0	0	2	2	5	25	0	0	0-0	.222	.300	.356	.656	0	1.000
—Buffalo (Int'l)	OF-DH	13	53	7	15	3	0	4	10	3	14	1	2	1-1	.283	.333	.566	.899	0	1.000
American League totals (1 year)		14	45	6	10	0	0	2	2	5	25	0	0	0-0	.222	.300	.356	.656	0	1.000
National League totals (2 years)		72	165	17	39	12	1	8	27	8	56	3	3	0-1	.236	.282	.467	.749	1	.986
Major League totals (2 years)		86	210	23	49	12	1	10	29	13	81	3	3	0-1	.233	.286	.443	.729	1	.986

DUBOSE, ERIC — P

PERSONAL: Born May 15, 1976, in Bradenton, Fla. ... 6-3/216. ... Throws left, bats left. ... Full name: Eric Ladell DuBose. ... Name pronounced: dew-BOWES. ... High school: Patrician Academy (Butler, Ala.). ... College: Mississippi State.

TRANSACTIONS/CAREER NOTES: Selected by Los Angeles Dodgers organization in sixth round of 1994 free-agent draft; did not sign. ... Selected by Oakland Athletics organization in first round (21st pick overall) of 1997 free-agent draft; pick received as compensation for Baltimore Orioles signing Type A free-agent SS Mike Bordick. ... Claimed on waivers by Cleveland Indians (September 8, 2000). ... Claimed on waivers by Detroit Tigers (September 22, 2000). ... Released by Tigers (March 31, 2001). ... Signed by Baltimore Orioles organization (February 4, 2002). ... On disabled list (June 20, 2004-remainder of season).

CAREER HITTING: 0-for-2 (.000), 0 R, 0 2B, 0 3B, 0 HR, 0 RBI.

ERIC DUBOSE'S PITCHING ZONE

.286	.200	.200
.444	.556	.091
.500	.333	.077

LEFTY-RIGHTY SPLITS

vs.	Avg.	AB	H	2B	3B	HR	RBI	BB	SO	OBP	Slg.
L	.146	48	7	1	0	2	2	6	9	.241	.292
R	.313	67	21	3	0	2	12	13	8	.432	.448

Year	Team (League)	W	L	Pct.	ERA	WHIP	G	GS	CG	ShO	Hld.	Sv.-Opp.	IP	H	R	ER	HR	BB-IBB	SO	Avg.
1997—S. Oregon (N'west)	1	0	1.000	0.00	1.10	3	1	0	0	...	0-...	10.0	5	0	0	0	6-0	15	.152
—Visalia (Calif.)	1	3	.250	7.04	1.85	10	1	0	0	...	0-...	38.1	43	37	30	4	28-0	39	.270
1998—Visalia (Calif.)	6	1	.857	3.38	1.13	17	10	0	0	...	1-...	72.0	56	34	27	5	25-0	85	.273
—Huntsville (Sou.)	7	6	.538	2.70	1.44	14	14	1	1	...	0-...	83.1	86	37	25	2	34-1	66	.273
1999—Midland (Texas)	4	2	.667	5.49	1.73	21	14	0	0	...	1-...	77.0	89	57	47	10	44-1	68	.293
2000—Midland (Texas)	5	1	.833	4.13	1.52	18	0	0	0	...	1-...	28.1	25	16	13	1	18-2	20	.227
—Visalia (Calif.)	0	1	.000	1.69	1.22	5	0	0	0	...	1-...	10.2	8	2	2	0	5-1	12	.200
2001—			Did not play.																
2002—Rochester (Int'l)	0	0	...	27.00	9.00	1	0	0	0	...	0-...	0.1	1	2	1	0	2-0	0	.333
—Bowie (East.)	5	3	.625	2.51	1.04	41	0	0	0	...	3-...	64.2	46	21	18	2	21-0	66	.198
—Baltimore (A.L.)	0	0	...	3.00	1.33	4	0	0	0	0	0-0	6.0	7	2	2	1	1-0	4	.304
2003—Ottawa (Int'l)	9	5	.643	3.39	1.30	19	19	0	0	...	0-...	114.0	112	49	43	7	34-2	107	.256
—Baltimore (A.L.)	3	6	.333	3.79	1.15	17	10	1	0	0	0-1	73.2	60	33	31	6	25-2	44	.222
2004—Baltimore (A.L.)	0	4	.000	6.39	1.61	14	14	0	0	0	0-0	74.2	76	55	53	12	44-0	48	.263
2005—Ottawa (Int'l)	0	1	.000	11.42	2.08	2	2	0	0	0	0-0	8.2	17	11	11	5	1-0	7	.395

D

Year	Team (League)	W	L	Pct.	ERA	WHIP	G	GS	CG	ShO	Hld.	Sv.-Opp.	IP	H	R	ER	HR	BB-IBB	SO	Avg.
	—Bowie (East.)	8	10	.444	3.25	1.16	21	20	0	0	0	0-0	122.0	113	52	44	10	29-0	114	.247
	—Baltimore (A.L.)	2	3	.400	5.52	1.60	15	3	0	0	3	0-0	29.1	28	21	18	4	19-0	17	.243
	Major League totals (4 years)	9	15	.375	5.10	1.42	50	27	1	0	4	0-1	183.2	171	111	104	23	89-2	113	.245

DUCHSCHERER, JUSTIN — P

PERSONAL: Born November 19, 1977, in Aberdeen, S.D. ... 6-3/190. ... Throws right, bats right. ... Full name: Justin Craig Duchscherer. ... Name pronounced: DUKE-sher. ... High school: Coronado (Lubbock, Texas).
TRANSACTIONS/CAREER NOTES: Selected by Boston Red Sox organization in eighth round of 1996 free-agent draft. ... Traded by Red Sox to Texas Rangers for C Doug Mirabelli (June 12, 2001). ... Traded by Rangers to Oakland Athletics for P Luis Vizcaino (March 18, 2002).
CAREER HITTING: 0-for-0 (.000), 0 R, 0 2B, 0 3B, 0 HR, 0 RBI.

SCOUTING REPORT **Throws:** He has a fastball that ranges from 83-89 mph, a cut fastball at 82-84, a curveball and a changeup. **Tendencies:** Duchscherer has a good feel for changing speeds and is not afraid to use any of his pitches, in any count. Will add and subtract speed off all his pitches. Goes to his curve when he needs to get an out; it has extremely tight rotation and breaks straight down. Has good tailing action on a changeup that he delivers with average deception. Throws lots of strikes but has little room for error. **Outlook:** One of the most versatile and durable pitchers in the league, he can pitch in any inning from the fifth to the eighth and can work multiple innings. **Grade 6.8**

JUSTIN DUCHSCHERER'S PITCHING ZONE

.263	.385	.188
.232	.333	.118
.222	.200	.308

LEFTY-RIGHTY SPLITS

vs.	Avg.	AB	H	2B	3B	HR	RBI	BB	SO	OBP	Slg.
L	.225	138	31	5	0	4	16	7	42	.260	.348
R	.208	173	36	4	1	3	21	12	43	.266	.295

Year	Team (League)	W	L	Pct.	ERA	WHIP	G	GS	CG	ShO	Hld.	Sv.-Opp.	IP	H	R	ER	HR	BB-IBB	SO	Avg.
1996	—GC Red Sox (GCL)	0	2	.000	3.13	1.21	13	8	0	0	...	1-...	54.2	52	26	19	0	14-0	45	.249
1997	—GC Red Sox (GCL)	2	3	.400	1.81	1.14	10	8	0	0	...	0-...	44.2	34	18	9	0	17-0	59	.204
	—Michigan (Midw.)	1	1	.500	5.63	1.50	4	4	0	0	...	0-...	24.0	26	17	15	1	10-0	19	.274
1998	—Michigan (Midw.)	7	12	.368	4.79	1.49	30	26	0	0	...	0-...	142.2	166	87	76	9	47-3	106	.298
1999	—Augusta (S. Atl.)	4	0	1.000	0.22	0.71	6	6	0	0	...	0-...	41.0	21	1	1	0	8-0	39	.148
	—Sarasota (Fla. St.)	7	7	.500	4.49	1.17	20	18	0	0	...	0-...	112.1	101	62	56	14	30-0	105	.237
2000	—Trenton (East.)	7	9	.438	3.39	1.18	24	24	2	2	...	0-...	143.1	134	59	54	7	35-1	126	.246
2001	—Trenton (East.)	6	3	.667	2.44	0.86	12	12	1	1	...	0-...	73.2	49	25	20	6	14-1	69	.179
	—Tulsa (Texas)	4	0	1.000	2.08	1.13	6	6	1	0	...	0-...	43.1	39	14	10	3	10-0	55	.242
	—Texas (A.L.)	1	1	.500	12.27	1.91	5	2	0	0	...	0-0	14.2	24	20	20	5	4-0	11	.353
	—Oklahoma (PCL)	3	3	.500	2.84	1.14	7	7	1	1	...	0-...	50.2	48	20	16	6	10-0	52	.255
2002	—Sacramento (PCL)	2	4	.333	5.57	1.43	14	11	0	0	...	0-...	63.0	73	45	39	7	17-0	52	.283
2003	—Sacramento (PCL)	14	2	.875	3.25	1.10	24	23	0	0	...	0-...	155.0	151	59	56	12	18-0	117	.254
	—Oakland (A.L.)	1	1	.500	3.31	1.22	4	3	0	0	...	0-0	16.1	17	7	6	1	3-0	15	.262
2004	—Oakland (A.L.)	7	6	.538	3.27	1.21	53	0	0	0	6	0-2	96.1	85	37	35	13	32-6	59	.241
2005	—Oakland (A.L.)	7	4	.636	2.21	1.00	65	0	0	0	10	5-7	85.2	67	25	21	4	19-3	85	.215
	Major League totals (4 years)	16	12	.571	3.46	1.18	127	5	0	0	16	5-9	213.0	193	89	82	26	58-9	170	.242

DUCKWORTH, BRANDON — P

PERSONAL: Born January 23, 1976, in Salt Lake City, Utah. ... 6-2/190. ... Throws right, bats right. ... Full name: Brandon J. Duckworth. ... High school: Kearns (Utah). ... College: Cal State Fullerton.
TRANSACTIONS/CAREER NOTES: Selected by Toronto Blue Jays organization in 30th round of 1995 free-agent draft; did not sign. ... Selected by Arizona Diamondbacks organization in 61st round of 1996 free-agent draft; did not sign. ... Signed as a non-drafted free agent by Philadelphia Phillies organization (August 13, 1997). ... On disabled list (March 21-April 20, 2003); included rehabilitation assignments to Clearwater and Reading. ... Traded by Phillies with Ps Taylor Buchholz and Ezequiel Astacio to Houston Astros for P Billy Wagner (November 3, 2003).
CAREER HITTING: 23-for-109 (.211), 7 R, 3 2B, 0 3B, 0 HR, 8 RBI.

BRANDON DUCKWORTH'S PITCHING ZONE

.000	1.000	.400
.200	.450	.455
.000	.200	.200

LEFTY-RIGHTY SPLITS

vs.	Avg.	AB	H	2B	3B	HR	RBI	BB	SO	OBP	Slg.
L	.258	31	8	1	0	1	3	2	6	.314	.387
R	.421	38	16	4	0	3	16	5	4	.532	.763

Year	Team (League)	W	L	Pct.	ERA	WHIP	G	GS	CG	ShO	Hld.	Sv.-Opp.	IP	H	R	ER	HR	BB-IBB	SO	Avg.
1998	—Piedmont (S. Atl.)	9	8	.529	2.80	0.95	21	21	5	3	...	0-...	147.2	116	58	46	10	24-0	119	.215
	—Clearwater (FSL)	6	2	.750	3.74	1.62	9	9	1	1	...	0-...	53.0	64	25	22	2	22-0	46	.306
1999	—Clearwater (FSL)	11	5	.688	4.84	1.55	27	17	0	0	...	1-...	132.0	164	84	71	13	40-0	101	.301
2000	—Reading (East.)	13	7	.650	3.16	1.19	27	27	1	0	...	0-...	165.0	145	70	58	17	52-0	178	.233
2001	—Scran./W.B. (I.L.)	13	2	.867	2.63	1.07	22	20	2	1	...	0-...	147.0	122	46	43	14	36-2	150	.228
	—Philadelphia (N.L.)	3	2	.600	3.52	1.25	11	11	0	0	...	0-0	69.0	57	29	27	2	29-5	40	.234
2002	—Philadelphia (N.L.)	8	9	.471	5.41	1.45	30	29	0	0	...	0-0	163.0	167	103	98	26	69-5	167	.261
2003	—Clearwater (FSL)	0	0	...	1.00	0.60	2	2	0	0	...	0-0	9.0	3	1	1	1	2-0	11	.100
	—Reading (East.)	0	0	...	4.50	0.50	1	1	0	0	...	0-0	2.0	1	1	1	1	0-0	2	.143
	—Scran./W.B. (I.L.)	2	1	.667	3.38	1.30	3	3	0	0	...	0-...	18.2	21	11	7	3	4-0	14	.280
	—Philadelphia (N.L.)	4	7	.364	4.94	1.53	24	18	0	0	...	0-0	93.0	98	58	51	12	44-3	68	.272
2004	—New Orleans (PCL)	5	5	.500	5.53	1.56	14	13	0	0	...	0-...	70.0	81	44	43	10	22-0	89	.286
	—Houston (N.L.)	1	2	.333	6.86	1.73	19	6	0	0	...	0-0	39.1	55	30	30	11	13-3	23	.337
2005	—Round Rock (PCL)	8	6	.571	4.62	1.52	20	19	0	0	...	0-...	115.0	138	68	59	17	37-2	89	.301
	—Houston (N.L.)	0	1	.000	11.02	1.90	7	2	0	0	...	0-0	16.1	24	20	20	4	7-1	10	.348
	Major League totals (5 years)	16	21	.432	5.34	1.48	91	66	0	0	...	0-0	380.2	401	240	226	55	162-17	308	.272

DUFFY, CHRIS — OF

PERSONAL: Born April 20, 1980, in Brattleboro, Vt. ... 5-10/180. ... Bats left, throws left. ... Full name: Christopher Ellis Duffy. ... High school: Mountain Ridge (Ariz.). ... College: Arizona State.
TRANSACTIONS/CAREER NOTES: Selected by Pittsburgh Pirates in eighth round of 2001 free-agent draft. ... On disabled list (August 28, 2005-remainder of season).
2005 GAMES PLAYED BY POSITION (MLB): OF—34.

D

SCOUTING REPORT

Offense: Duffy is a top-of-the-order hitter who makes consistent contact to all fields. Does not miss mistakes, though he hits too many balls into the air for a singles hitter. Has shown the ability to learn his strike zone but still strikes out too much. Is learning to take pitchers into deep counts. A legit switch hitter who squares the ball up on both sides of the plate, though he drives runs in better against righthanders. Has good speed and can steal. **Defense:** He has outstanding range in center and covers both gaps. Gets excellent reads and runs routes well. Has an above-average arm. **Outlook:** Duffy has an excellent chance to start the season as a regular in the Pirates' outfield. **Grade 7**

CHRIS DUFFY'S HITTING ZONE

.500	.000	.429
.353	.364	.438
.333	.333	.083

LEFTY-RIGHTY SPLITS

vs.	Avg.	AB	H	2B	3B	HR	RBI	BB	SO	OBP	Slg.
L	.355	31	11	0	0	0	2	1	4	.394	.355
R	.337	95	32	4	2	1	7	6	18	.382	.453

Year	Team (League)	Pos.	G	AB	R	H	2B	3B	HR	RBI	BB	SO	HBP	GDP	SB-CS	Avg.	OBP	SLG	OPS	E	Avg.
2001—Will. (NYP)		OF	64	221	50	70	12	4	1	24	33	33	17	0	30-5	.317	.440	.421	.861	1	.992
2002—Lynchburg (Caro.)		OF	132	539	85	162	27	5	10	52	33	101	12	1	22-7	.301	.353	.425	.778	3	.989
2003—Altoona (East.)		OF	137	494	84	135	23	6	1	42	44	78	20	7	34-12	.273	.355	.350	.705	4	.987
2004—Altoona (East.)		OF	113	453	84	140	23	6	8	41	33	77	17	4	30-8	.309	.378	.439	.817	2	.962
2005—Indianapolis (Int'l)		OF	78	308	55	95	13	7	7	31	16	57	10	4	17-9	.308	.358	.464	.822	4	.989
—Pittsburgh (N.L.)		OF	39	126	22	43	4	2	1	9	7	22	2	1	2-2	.341	.385	.429	.814	1	.988
Major League totals (1 year)			39	126	22	43	4	2	1	9	7	22	2	1	2-2	.341	.385	.429	.814	1	.988

DUKE, ZACH — P

PERSONAL: Born April 19, 1983, in Clifton, Texas. ... 6-2/212. ... Throws left, bats left. ... Full name: Zachary Thomas Duke. ... High school: Midway (Texas).
TRANSACTIONS/CAREER NOTES: Selected by Pittsburgh Pirates organization in 20th round of 2001 free-agent draft. ... On disabled list (August 27-September 16, 2005).
CAREER HITTING: 4-for-28 (.143), 1 R, 0 2B, 0 3B, 0 HR, 1 RBI.

SCOUTING REPORT

Throws: He uses a sneaky 88-92 mph fastball, a curveball and a circle changeup. **Tendencies:** Duke is extremely advanced for his age. Has a good delivery and deceptive arm speed. Can pitch inside to righthanded hitters or tail his fastball away from them. Has a tight, looping curveball and an effective, fading changeup that he can throw to both sides of the plate. **Outlook:** Duke probably will never be a No. 1 starter because he doesn't have a dominant pitch, but he should be an effective frontline starter. **Grade 7.9**

ZACH DUKE'S PITCHING ZONE

.455	.333	.250
.369	.435	.209
.163	.364	.000

LEFTY-RIGHTY SPLITS

vs.	Avg.	AB	H	2B	3B	HR	RBI	BB	SO	OBP	Slg.
L	.146	48	7	0	0	0	2	6	21	.241	.146
R	.273	264	72	17	1	3	17	17	37	.320	.379

Year	Team (League)	W	L	Pct.	ERA	WHIP	G	GS	CG	ShO	Hld.	Sv.-Opp.	IP	H	R	ER	HR	BB-IBB	SO	Avg.
2002—GC Pirates (GCL)		8	1	.889	1.95	0.93	11	11	1	1	...	0-...	60.0	38	15	13	2	18-0	48	.185
2003—Hickory (S. Atl.)		8	7	.533	3.11	1.20	26	26	1	1	...	0-...	141.2	124	66	49	7	46-0	113	.237
2004—Lynchburg (Caro.)		10	5	.667	1.39	0.96	17	17	1	0	...	0-...	97.0	73	24	15	3	20-1	106	.210
—Altoona (East.)		5	1	.833	1.58	0.99	9	9	0	0	...	0-...	51.1	41	11	9	2	10-0	36	.236
2005—Indianapolis (Int'l)		12	3	.800	2.92	1.21	16	16	1	0	0	0-0	108.0	108	39	35	2	23-1	66	.267
—Pittsburgh (N.L.)		8	2	.800	1.81	1.20	14	14	0	0	0	0-0	84.2	79	20	17	3	23-2	58	.253
Major League totals (1 year)		8	2	.800	1.81	1.20	14	14	0	0	0	0-0	84.2	79	20	17	3	23-2	58	.253

DUNCAN, CHRIS — 1B

PERSONAL: Born May 5, 1981, in Tucson, Ariz. ... 6-5/210. ... Bats left, throws right. ... Full name: Christopher E. Duncan. ... Son of Dave Duncan, coach with St. Louis Cardinals; and catcher with four major league teams (1964-76).
TRANSACTIONS/CAREER NOTES: Selected by St. Louis Cardinals organization in first round (46th pick overall) of 1999 free-agent draft.
2005 GAMES PLAYED BY POSITION (MLB): 1B—2, OF—1.

LEFTY-RIGHTY SPLITS

vs.	Avg.	AB	H	2B	3B	HR	RBI	BB	SO	OBP	Slg.
L	1.000	2	2	1	0	1	3	0	0	1.000	3.000
R	.000	8	0	0	0	0	0	0	5	.000	.000

Year	Team (League)	Pos.	G	AB	R	H	2B	3B	HR	RBI	BB	SO	HBP	GDP	SB-CS	Avg.	OBP	SLG	OPS	E	Avg.
1999—Johnson City (App.)		1B	55	201	23	43	8	1	6	34	25	62	1	4	3-1	.214	.300	.353	.653	12	.977
2000—Peoria (Midw.)		1B	122	450	52	115	34	0	8	57	36	111	6	11	1-2	.256	.318	.384	.702	35	.962
2001—Potomac (Carol.)		1B	49	168	12	30	6	0	3	16	10	47	1	5	4-4	.179	.229	.268	.497	9	.982
—Peoria (Midw.)		1B	80	297	44	91	23	2	13	59	36	55	3	10	13-3	.306	.386	.529	.915	21	.973
2002—Peoria (Midw.)		1B	129	487	58	132	25	4	16	75	44	118	7	8	5-5	.271	.337	.437	.774	19	.982
2003—Palm Beach (FSL)		1B	121	425	26	108	20	0	2	42	44	115	1	12	4-4	.254	.322	.315	.637	14	.987
—Tennessee (Sou.)		OF	10	25	1	5	1	0	1	3	0	6	0	0	0-0	.200	.200	.360	.560	1	.889
2004—Tennessee (Sou.)		OF	120	387	57	112	23	0	16	65	64	94	3	6	8-4	.289	.393	.473	.866	8	.994
2005—Memphis (PCL)		1B-OF-DH	128	431	57	114	21	2	21	73	63	104	2	14	1-3	.265	.358	.469	.827	21	.977
—St. Louis (N.L.)		1B-OF	9	10	2	2	1	0	1	3	0	5	0	1	0-0	.200	.200	.600	.800	0	1.000
Major League totals (1 year)			9	10	2	2	1	0	1	3	0	5	0	1	0-0	.200	.200	.600	.800	0	1.000

DUNN, ADAM — OF

PERSONAL: Born November 9, 1979, in Houston. ... 6-6/240. ... Bats left, throws right. ... Full name: Adam Troy Dunn. ... High school: New Caney (Texas).
TRANSACTIONS/CAREER NOTES: Selected by Cincinnati Reds organization in second round of 1998 free-agent draft. ... On suspended list (June 20-22, 2003). ... On disabled list (August 16, 2003-remainder of season).
RECORDS: Holds major league record for strikeouts, season (195, 2004). ... Shares major league record for strikeouts, nine-inning game (5, August 20, 2002).
2005 GAMES PLAYED BY POSITION (MLB): OF—133, 1B—33.

D

SCOUTING REPORT *Offense:* Dunn may have more power than any player in the game. Can hit the ball out of any park with his long, slightly uppercut swing. Has a quick bat. Doesn't take much of a stride but maintains good balance and leverage. Has a lot of holes and chases too many pitches out of the zone. Is a deceptive runner with good instincts. *Defense:* He is a good athlete who has improved his lateral jumps. Comes in well on the ball. His range could decline if he gets any bigger. Not throwing as well as in the past but has a quick release and accuracy on short throws. *Outlook:* Dunn is an all-or-nothing hitter with prodigious power; he's capable of becoming an outstanding run producer if he can cut down on his strikeouts. **Grade 7.7**

ADAM DUNN'S HITTING ZONE

.286	.400	.192
.393	.409	.288
.182	.167	.179

LEFTY-RIGHTY SPLITS

vs.	Avg.	AB	H	2B	3B	HR	RBI	BB	SO	OBP	Slg.
L	.197	188	37	9	1	13	35	31	62	.321	.463
R	.273	355	97	26	1	27	66	83	106	.421	.580

							BATTING								FIELDING	
Year	Team (League)	Pos.	G	AB	R	H	2B	3B	HR	RBI	BB	SO	HBP	GDP	SB-CS	Avg.	OBP	SLG	OPS	E	Avg.
1998— Billings (Pion.)		OF	34	125	26	36	3	1	4	13	22	33	3	3	4-2	.288	.404	.424	.828	6	.860
1999— Rockford (Midwest)		OF	93	313	62	96	16	2	11	44	46	64	10	6	21-9	.307	.409	.476	.885	8	.918
2000— Dayton (Midw.)		OF	122	420	101	118	29	1	16	79	100	101	12	10	24-5	.281	.428	.469	.897	9	.958
2001— Chattanooga (Sou.)		OF	39	140	30	48	9	0	12	31	24	31	3	1	6-3	.343	.449	.664	1.113	3	.961
— Louisville (Int'l)		OF	55	210	44	69	13	0	20	53	38	51	5	1	5-1	.329	.441	.676	1.117	5	.954
— Cincinnati (N.L.)		OF	66	244	54	64	18	1	19	43	38	74	4	4	4-2	.262	.371	.578	.949	2	.986
2002— Cincinnati (N.L.)		OF-1B-DH	158	535	84	133	28	2	26	71	128	170	9	8	19-9	.249	.400	.454	.854	15	.975
2003— Cincinnati (N.L.)		OF-1B-DH	116	381	70	82	12	1	27	57	74	126	10	4	8-2	.215	.354	.465	.819	11	.965
2004— Cincinnati (N.L.)		OF-1B-DH	161	568	105	151	34	0	46	102	108 * 195		5	8	6-1	.266	.388	.569	.956	8	.977
2005— Cincinnati (N.L.)		OF-1B	160	543	107	134	35	2	40	101	114 * 168		12	6	4-2	.247	.387	.540	.927	9	.983
Major League totals (5 years)			661	2271	420	564	127	6	158	374	462	733	40	30	41-16	.248	.383	.518	.901	45	.977

ALL-STAR GAME RECORD

		G	AB	R	H	2B	3B	HR	RBI	BB	SO	HBP	GDP	SB-CS	Avg.	OBP	SLG	OPS	E	Avg.
All-Star Game totals (1 year)		1	1	0	0	0	0	0	1	0	0	0	0	0-0	.000	.500	.000	.500	0	...

DURAZO, ERUBIEL   DH/1B

PERSONAL: Born January 23, 1975, in Hermosillo, Mexico. ... 6-3/240. ... Bats left, throws left. ... Full name: Erubiel Durazo Cardenas. ... Name pronounced: eh-ROO-bee-el du-RAH-zo. ... High school: Amphitheater (Tucson, Ariz.). ... Junior college: Pima (Ariz.) Community College.

TRANSACTIONS/CAREER NOTES: Signed by Monterrey, Mexican League (1997). ... Contract sold by Monterrey to Arizona Diamondbacks organization (December 16, 1998). ... On disabled list (May 30-June 24, June 27-July 13 and August 20, 2000-remainder of season); included rehabilitation assignments to Tuscon and AZL Diamondbacks. ... On disabled list (August 15-September 1, 2001); included rehabilitation assignment to Tucson. ... On disabled list (March 22-May 16 and June 30-July 27, 2002); included rehabilitation assignments to Tucson and El Paso. ... Traded by Diamondbacks to Oakland Athletics as part of four-team deal in which Diamondbacks acquired P Elmer Dessens from Cincinnati Reds, Reds acquired SS Felipe Lopez from Toronto Blue Jays and Blue Jays acquired a player to be named from A's (December 15, 2002); Blue Jays acquired P Jason Arnold to complete deal (December 16, 2002). ... On disabled list (May 27, 2005-remainder of season).

2005 GAMES PLAYED BY POSITION (MLB): DH—39, 1B—1.

SCOUTING REPORT *Offense:* Durazo missed most the season with elbow surgery. Had a lot of trouble handling the high fastball with his elbow problem. Bat speed and power have declined. Is patient going deep in the count. Prior to his injury was an extremely streaky hitter for power, but when he sees the ball well has good power to the big part of the park. Can't run and has poor instincts. *Defense:* He isn't good defensively and has stiff hands and almost no range. Doesn't have much lower body flexibility. Is basically a full-time DH. *Outlook:* He is difficult to evaluate because of his injury and decrease in power and bat speed. Limited to DH restricts his value to the A.L. **Grade 6.5**

ERUBIEL DURAZO'S HITTING ZONE

.286	.286	.154
.278	.409	.194
.167	.500	.313

LEFTY-RIGHTY SPLITS

vs.	Avg.	AB	H	2B	3B	HR	RBI	BB	SO	OBP	Slg.
L	.350	40	14	2	1	2	8	2	5	.381	.600
R	.196	112	22	4	0	2	8	12	19	.280	.286

							BATTING								FIELDING	
Year	Team (League)	Pos.	G	AB	R	H	2B	3B	HR	RBI	BB	SO	HBP	GDP	SB-CS	Avg.	OBP	SLG	OPS	E	Avg.
1997— Monterrey (Mex.)		1B-OF	110	358	47	101	21	10	8	61	52	43	...	...	3-7	.282	...	.464	...	3	.994
1998— Monterrey (Mex.)		1B-OF	119	420	84	147	32	2	19	98	99	71	...	...	4-3	.350	...	.571	...	0	1.000
1999— El Paso (Texas)		1B	64	226	53	91	18	3	14	55	44	37	2	5	2-1	.403	.498	.695	1.193	10	.982
— Tucson (PCL)		1B-DH	30	118	27	48	7	0	10	28	14	18	1	0	1-0	.407	.470	.720	1.190	1	.996
— Arizona (N.L.)		1B	52	155	31	51	4	2	11	30	26	43	1	1	1-1	.329	.427	.594	1.015	0	1.000
2000— Arizona (N.L.)		1B	67	196	35	52	11	0	8	33	34	43	1	3	1-0	.265	.373	.444	.817	5	.989
— Tucson (PCL)		1B	13	43	9	18	6	0	3	10	6	7	0	0	0-0	.419	.490	.767	1.257	3	.957
— AZL D'backs (Ariz.)		1B	2	5	2	3	0	0	1	2	1	0	0	0	0-0	.600	.667	1.200	1.867	0	1.000
2001— Arizona (N.L.)		1B-DH-OF	92	175	34	47	11	0	12	38	28	49	2	1	0-0	.269	.372	.537	.909	2	.993
— Tucson (PCL)		1B	3	11	3	3	0	0	1	1	1	3	0	0	0-0	.273	.333	.545	.879	0	1.000
2002— Tucson (PCL)		1B	7	22	5	7	2	1	1	3	0	2	1	1	0-0	.318	.348	.636	.984	1	.971
— Arizona (N.L.)		1B-DH-OF	76	222	46	58	12	2	16	48	49	60	2	1	0-1	.261	.395	.545	.944	7	.984
— El Paso (Texas)		1B	5	14	5	7	3	0	2	7	4	1	0	1	0-0	.500	.611	1.143	1.754	0	1.000
2003— Oakland (A.L.)		DH-1B	154	537	92	139	29	0	21	77	100	105	2	11	1-1	.259	.374	.430	.804	6	.981
2004— Oakland (A.L.)		DH-1B	142	511	80	164	35	1	22	88	56	104	9	7	3-2	.321	.396	.523	.919	2	.882
2005— Oakland (A.L.)		DH-1B	41	152	15	36	6	1	4	16	14	24	1	6	1-0	.237	.305	.368	.674	0	1.000
American League totals (3 years)			337	1200	187	339	70	2	47	181	170	233	12	24	5-3	.283	.375	.462	.836	8	.976
National League totals (4 years)			287	748	146	208	38	4	47	149	137	195	6	6	2-2	.278	.390	.528	.918	14	.991
Major League totals (7 years)			624	1948	333	547	108	6	94	330	307	428	18	30	7-5	.281	.381	.487	.868	22	.988

DIVISION SERIES RECORD

							BATTING								FIELDING	
Year	Team (League)	Pos.	G	AB	R	H	2B	3B	HR	RBI	BB	SO	HBP	GDP	SB-CS	Avg.	OBP	SLG	OPS	E	Avg.
1999— Arizona (N.L.)		1B	2	7	1	1	0	0	1	1	1	0	0	0	0-0	.143	.250	.571	.821	0	1.000
2001— Arizona (N.L.)			1	1	0	0	0	0	0	0	0	0	0	0	0-0	.000	.000	.000	.000	...	...
2002— Arizona (N.L.)		1B	2	4	0	0	0	0	0	1	1	0	0	0	0-0	.000	.200	.000	.200	0	1.000
2003— Oakland (A.L.)		DH	5	21	3	5	2	0	0	3	3	4	0	0	0-0	.238	.333	.333	.667	0	...
Division series totals (4 years)			10	33	4	6	2	0	1	4	5	5	0	0	0-0	.182	.289	.333	.623	0	1.000

CHAMPIONSHIP SERIES RECORD

Year Team (League)	Pos.	G	AB	R	H	2B	3B	HR	RBI	BB	SO	HBP	GDP	SB-CS	Avg.	OBP	SLG	OPS	E	Avg.
2001— Arizona (N.L.)	1B	2	3	1	1	0	0	1	2	0	1	0	0	0-0	.333	.333	1.333	1.667	0	1.000

WORLD SERIES RECORD

Year Team (League)	Pos.	G	AB	R	H	2B	3B	HR	RBI	BB	SO	HBP	GDP	SB-CS	Avg.	OBP	SLG	OPS	E	Avg.
2001— Arizona (N.L.)	DH	4	11	0	4	1	0	0	1	3	4	0	0	0-0	.364	.500	.455	.955	...	...

DURHAM, RAY — 2B

PERSONAL: Born November 30, 1971, in Charlotte, N.C. ... 5-8/196. ... Bats both, throws right. ... High school: Harding (Charlotte).

TRANSACTIONS/CAREER NOTES: Selected by Chicago White Sox organization in fifth round of 1990 free-agent draft. ... Traded by White Sox to Oakland Athletics for P Jon Adkins (July 25, 2002). ... Signed as a free agent by San Francisco Giants (December 7, 2002). ... On disabled list (May 11-26 and August 7-September 1, 2003). ... On disabled list (April 28-May 13 and May 23-June 15, 2004); included rehabilitation assignments to Fresno and San Jose.

2005 GAMES PLAYED BY POSITION (MLB): 2B—133, OF—1.

SCOUTING REPORT *Offense:* Durham is a catalyst at the top of the order with his speed and hitting ability. Is better overall from the right side but has more power lefthanded. Is a good high-ball hitter. Is a good baserunner but recurring hamstring problems have reduced his basestealing ability. *Defense:* He always has had stiff hands but appears to have regained some of his agility, especially to his backhand side. Doesn't make consistent reads and will occasionally break the wrong way. Doesn't have a real strong arm and relies on his footwork to turn the double play. *Outlook:* Durham played better at second base than he has in the past several years. Has retained his bat speed and is a catalyst at the top of the Giants' order. *Grade 7.5*

RAY DURHAM'S HITTING ZONE

.190	.211	.286
.444	.267	.357
.324	.222	.281

LEFTY-RIGHTY SPLITS

vs.	Avg.	AB	H	2B	3B	HR	RBI	BB	SO	OBP	Slg.
L	.290	93	27	7	0	3	12	9	10	.350	.462
R	.290	404	117	26	0	9	50	39	49	.357	.421

Year Team (League)	Pos.	G	AB	R	H	2B	3B	HR	RBI	BB	SO	HBP	GDP	SB-CS	Avg.	OBP	SLG	OPS	E	Avg.
1990— GC Whi. Sox (GCL)	2B-SS	35	116	18	32	3	3	0	13	15	36	4	0	23-9	.276	.375	.353	.728	15	.907
1991— Utica (N.Y.-Penn)	2B	39	142	29	36	2	7	0	17	25	44	2	0	12-1	.254	.371	.366	.737	12	.928
— GC Whi. Sox (GCL)	2B	6	23	3	7	1	0	0	4	3	5	0	0	5-1	.304	.385	.348	.732	0	1.000
1992— Sarasota (Fla. St.)	2B	57	202	37	55	6	3	0	7	32	36	10	2	28-8	.272	.398	.332	.729	10	.945
— GC Whi. Sox (GCL)	2B	5	13	3	7	2	0	0	2	3	1	0	0	1-0	.538	.625	.692	1.317	0	1.000
1993— Birmingham (Sou.)	2B	137	528	83	143	22	10	3	37	42	100	14	6	39-25	.271	.338	.367	.705	30	.945
1994— Nashville (A.A.)	2B	133	527	89	156	33	12	16	66	46	91	12	5	34-11	.296	.363	.495	.859	19	.973
1995— Chicago (A.L.)	2B-DH	125	471	68	121	27	6	7	51	31	83	6	8	18-5	.257	.309	.384	.693	15	.973
1996— Chicago (A.L.)	2B-DH	156	557	79	153	33	5	10	65	58	95	10	6	30-4	.275	.350	.406	.755	11	.984
1997— Chicago (A.L.)	2B-DH	155	634	106	172	27	5	11	53	61	96	6	14	33-16	.271	.337	.382	.719 *	18	.974
1998— Chicago (A.L.)	2B	158	635	126	181	35	8	19	67	73	105	6	5	36-9	.285	.363	.455	.808	19	.976
1999— Chicago (A.L.)	2B-DH	153	612	109	181	30	8	13	60	71	105	4	9	34-11	.296	.373	.435	.808	19	.974
2000— Chicago (A.L.)	2B	151	614	121	172	35	9	17	75	75	105	7	13	25-13	.280	.361	.450	.810	15	.980
2001— Chicago (A.L.)	2B-DH	152	611	104	163	42	10	20	65	64	110	4	10	23-10	.267	.337	.466	.804	10	.986
2002— Chicago (A.L.)	2B	96	345	71	103	20	2	9	48	49	59	5	13	20-5	.299	.390	.446	.836	15	.968
— Oakland (A.L.)	DH-2B	54	219	43	60	14	4	6	22	24	34	2	2	6-2	.274	.350	.457	.806	2	.967
2003— San Francisco (N.L.)	2B	110	410	61	117	30	5	8	33	50	82	3	4	7-7	.285	.366	.441	.807	5	.990
2004— San Jose (Calif.)	2B	1	3	0	1	0	0	0	0	0	0	0	0	0-0	.333	.333	.333	.667	0	1.000
— Fresno (PCL)	2B	5	14	4	8	0	1	1	5	2	2	1	0	0-1	.571	.647	.929	1.576	2	.944
— San Francisco (N.L.)	2B	120	471	95	133	28	8	17	65	57	60	6	6	10-4	.282	.364	.484	.848	16	.972
2005— San Francisco (N.L.)	2B-OF	142	497	67	144	33	0	12	62	48	59	7	19	6-3	.290	.356	.429	.785	11	.982
American League totals (8 years)			1200	4698	827	1306	263	57	112	506	508	792	50	80	225-75	.278	.352	.430	.782	123	.977
National League totals (3 years)			372	1378	223	394	91	13	37	160	155	201	16	29	23-14	.286	.362	.451	.813	32	.981
Major League totals (11 years)			1572	6076	1050	1700	354	70	149	666	663	993	66	109	248-89	.280	.354	.435	.789	155	.978

DIVISION SERIES RECORD

Year Team (League)	Pos.	G	AB	R	H	2B	3B	HR	RBI	BB	SO	HBP	GDP	SB-CS	Avg.	OBP	SLG	OPS	E	Avg.
2000— Chicago (A.L.)	2B	3	10	2	2	1	0	1	1	3	3	0	2	0-0	.200	.385	.600	.985	0	1.000
2002— Oakland (A.L.)	DH	5	21	7	7	3	0	2	2	2	4	1	0	1-0	.333	.417	.762	1.179	0	...
2003— San Francisco (N.L.)	2B	4	17	2	4	0	0	0	0	1	5	1	0	0-0	.235	.316	.235	.551	0	1.000
Division series totals (3 years)		12	48	11	13	4	0	3	3	6	12	2	2	1-0	.271	.375	.542	.917	0	1.000

ALL-STAR GAME RECORD

	G	AB	R	H	2B	3B	HR	RBI	BB	SO	HBP	GDP	SB-CS	Avg.	OBP	SLG	OPS	E	Avg.
All-Star Game totals (2 years)	2	3	2	2	0	0	0	0	1	0	0	0	0-0	.667	.667	.667	1.333	0	1.000

DURRINGTON, TRENT — 3B/2B

PERSONAL: Born August 27, 1975, in Sydney, Australia. ... 5-10/190. ... Bats right, throws right. ... Full name: Trent John Durrington. ... High school: The Southport School (Australia).

TRANSACTIONS/CAREER NOTES: Signed as a non-drafted free agent by California Angels organization (April 22, 1994). ... Angels franchise renamed Anaheim Angels for 1997 season. ... Released by Angels (August 29, 2000). ... Signed by Los Angeles Dodgers organization (December 27, 2000). ... Released by Dodgers (May 11, 2001). ... Signed by Angels organization (May 12, 2001). ... Signed as a free agent by Milwaukee Brewers organization (November 7, 2003).

CAREER PITCHING: 0-0, 0.00 ERA, 1 G, 0.1 IP, 0 H, 0 R, 0 ER, 0 BB, 0 SO.

2005 GAMES PLAYED BY POSITION (MLB): 3B—1.

LEFTY-RIGHTY SPLITS

vs.	Avg.	AB	H	2B	3B	HR	RBI	BB	SO	OBP	Slg.
L	.333	6	2	0	0	0	2	0	1	.333	.333
R	.125	8	1	1	0	0	1	2	2	.222	.250

Year Team (League)	Pos.	G	AB	R	H	2B	3B	HR	RBI	BB	SO	HBP	GDP	SB-CS	Avg.	OBP	SLG	OPS	E	Avg.
1994— Ariz. Angels (Ariz.)	2B-SS	16	52	13	14	3	0	1	2	11	16	1	1	5-1	.269	.406	.385	.791	5	.907
1995— Boise (N'west)	2B-SS	50	140	23	24	4	1	3	19	17	35	2	4	2-0	.171	.267	.279	.546	8	.959
1996— Cedar Rap. (Midw.)	2B	25	76	12	19	1	0	0	4	33	20	2	2	15-2	.250	.482	.263	.745	3	.969
— Boise (N'west)	2B-3B-SS	40	154	38	43	7	2	0	14	31	32	13	4	• 24-5	.279	.439	.351	.790	12	.969
1997— Lake Elsinore (Calif.)	2B-3B-OF	123	409	80	101	21	3	3	36	51	90	11	8	52-18	.247	.344	.335	.679	17	.969

Year Team (League)	Pos.	G	AB	R	H	2B	3B	HR	RBI	BB	SO	HBP	GDP	SB-CS	Avg.	OBP	SLG	OPS	E	Avg.
															BATTING				FIELDING	
1998— Midland (Texas)		112	351	62	79	10	1	1	30	50	74	17	5	24-12	.225	.346	.268	.614	13	.971
1999— Erie (East.)	2B	107	396	84	114	26	1	3	34	52	66	9	4	59-16	.288	.379	.381	.760	14	.974
—Anaheim (A.L.)	2B-DH	43	122	14	22	2	0	0	2	9	28	0	1	4-3	.180	.237	.197	.433	6	.966
2000— Edmonton (PCL)	2B-SS	28	105	19	23	4	1	3	14	16	25	1	3	8-6	.219	.325	.362	.687	2	.986
—Anaheim (A.L.)	2B	4	3	0	0	0	0	0	0	0	0	0	1	0-0	.000	.000	.000	.000	0	1.000
2001— Salt Lake (PCL)	2B-OF-3B-SS	39	122	20	40	11	4	3	21	11	24	...		7-4	.328		.557	...	4	.960
—Arkansas (Texas)	2B-SS-3B-OF	51	182	37	53	12	0	10	35	26	47	7	2	22-2	.291	.398	.522	.920	10	.949
—Las Vegas (PCL)	2B	22	55	10	12	4	1	-1	2	8	19	...		3-1	.218		.382	...	2	.973
2002— Arkansas (Texas)	C-2B-OF-3B-SS	107	382	59	94	18	4	9	47	39	71	11	3	25-14	.246	.328	.385	.713	14	.969
—Salt Lake (PCL)	OF-2B-3B-C	19	68	6	14	3	1	3	10	5	15	2	4	2-1	.206	.260	.412	.672	1	.984
2003— Salt Lake (PCL)	2B-3B-1B-DH-OF-C	117	447	81	136	27	5	7	54	61	75	6	6	35-8	.304	.390	.434	.824	10	.980
—Anaheim (A.L.)	2B-3B-DH-OF	12	14	5	2	0	0	0	3	0	0	0	0	1-1	.143	.294	.143	.437	0	1.000
2004— Indianapolis (Int'l)	2B-3B-OF-DH-1B	51	162	19	36	1	0	1	9	16	34	2	6	17-5	.222	.298	.247	.545	10	.945
—Milwaukee (N.L.)	3B-2B-DH-P	53	82	13	19	2	3	2	4	4	23	0	1	4-0	.232	.267	.402	.670	4	.907
2005— Nashville (PCL)	3B-OF-2B-1B-SS	92	313	61	94	15	2	5	31	41	63	5	5	30-12	.300	.389	.409	.798	14	.959
—Milwaukee (N.L.)	3B	28	14	3	3	1	0	0	2	1	3	0	0	5-2	.214	.267	.286	.552	3	.000
American League totals (3 years)		59	139	19	24	2	0	0	3	12	28	0	2	5-4	.173	.238	.187	.425	6	.968
National League totals (2 years)		81	96	16	22	3	3	2	6	5	26	0	1	9-2	.229	.267	.385	.653	7	.848
Major League totals (5 years)		140	235	35	46	5	3	2	9	17	54	0	3	14-6	.196	.250	.268	.518	13	.944

DYE, JERMAINE — OF

PERSONAL: Born January 28, 1974, in Vacaville, Calif. ... 6-5/220. ... Bats right, throws right. ... Full name: Jermaine Terrell Dye. ... Name pronounced: ger-MAIN. ... High school: Will C. Wood (Vacaville, Calif.). ... Junior college: Cosumnes River (Calif.).

TRANSACTIONS/CAREER NOTES: Selected by Atlanta Braves organization in 17th round of 1993 free-agent draft. ... Traded by Braves with P Jamie Walker to Kansas City Royals for OF Michael Tucker and IF Keith Lockhart (March 27, 1997). ... On disabled list (April 17-May 3, 1997); included rehabilitation assignment to Omaha. ... On disabled list (July 10-August 13, 1997); included rehabilitation assignment to Omaha. ... On disabled list (March 23-May 8 and September 1, 1998-remainder of season); included rehabilitation assignment to Omaha. ... Traded by Royals to Colorado Rockies for SS Neifi Perez (July 25, 2001). ... Traded by Rockies to Oakland Athletics for OF Mario Encarnacion, 2B/SS Jose Ortiz and P Todd Belitz (July 25, 2001). ... On disabled list (March 22-April 26, 2002); included rehabilitation assignments to Sacramento and Modesto. ... On disabled list (April 25-May 30 and July 7-September 1, 2003); included rehabilitation assignment to Sacramento. ... Signed as a free agent by Chicago White Sox (December 9, 2004).

HONORS: Won A.L. Gold Glove as outfielder (2000).

2005 GAMES PLAYED BY POSITION (MLB): OF—140, SS—1, DH—1, 1B—1.

SCOUTING REPORT

Offense: Dye has a good swing and has regained some bat speed. Has good plate coverage. Will use the whole field and has shown an ability to shorten his approach with two strikes. Is a good breaking-ball hitter. Has good alley-to-alley home run power. Doesn't steal a lot of bases but is a good runner from first to third. *Defense:* Dye's range into the gap has really improved. Is better at charging the ball than going back on it. Has a strong arm with excellent carry but has a slow release. Always plays under control and is much more mobile after recovering from a number of injuries. *Outlook:* A healthy Dye (he ended 2005 in his best shape since suffering a broken leg in 2002) is a good clutch hitter and regaining his outfield ability. *Grade 7.8*

JERMAINE DYE'S HITTING ZONE

.333	.391	.128
.301	.489	.300
.206	.320	.286

LEFTY-RIGHTY SPLITS

vs.	Avg.	AB	H	2B	3B	HR	RBI	BB	SO	OBP	Slg.
L	.252	131	33	7	1	8	20	18	34	.353	.504
R	.281	398	112	22	1	23	66	21	65	.326	.515

Year Team (League)	Pos.	G	AB	R	H	2B	3B	HR	RBI	BB	SO	HBP	GDP	SB-CS	Avg.	OBP	SLG	OPS	E	Avg.
															BATTING				FIELDING	
1993— GC Braves (GCL)	3B-OF	31	124	17	43	14	0	0	27	5	13	5	5	5-0	.347	.393	.460	.852	3	.948
—Danville (Appal.)	OF	25	94	6	26	6	1	2	12	8	10	0	2	19-1	.277	.327	.426	.752	2	.963
1994— Macon (S. Atl.)	OF	135	506	73	151	41	1	15	98	33	82	8	10	19-10	.298	.346	.472	.818	9	.969
1995— Greenville (Sou.)	OF	104	403	50	115	26	4	15	71	27	74	1	9	4-8	.285	.329	.481	.810	5	.981
1996— Richmond (Int'l)	OF	36	142	25	33	7	1	6	19	5	25	1	3	3-0	.232	.264	.423	.686	4	.955
—Atlanta (N.L.)	OF	98	292	32	82	16	0	12	37	8	67	3	11	1-4	.281	.304	.459	.763	6	.950
1997— Kansas City (A.L.)	OF	75	263	26	62	14	0	7	22	17	51	1	6	2-1	.236	.284	.369	.653	6	.966
—Omaha (A.A.)	OF-DH	39	144	21	44	6	0	10	25	9	25	1	3	0-2	.306	.348	.556	.904	0	1.000
1998— Omaha (PCL)	OF-1B-DH	41	157	29	47	6	0	12	35	19	29	1	8	7-0	.299	.374	.567	.941	1	.992
—Kansas City (A.L.)	OF	60	214	24	50	5	1	5	23	11	46	1	8	2-2	.234	.270	.336	.606	2	.987
1999— Kansas City (A.L.)	OF-DH	158	608	96	179	44	8	27	119	58	119	1	17	2-3	.294	.354	.526	.880	6	.984
2000— Kansas City (A.L.)	OF-DH	157	601	107	193	41	2	33	118	69	99	3	12	0-1	.321	.390	.561	.951	7	.976
2001— Kansas City (A.L.)	OF-DH	97	367	50	100	14	0	13	47	30	68	6	2	7-1	.272	.333	.417	.749	3	.984
—Oakland (A.L.)	OF	61	232	41	69	17	1	13	59	27	44	1	6	2-0	.297	.366	.547	.913	3	.971
2002— Sacramento (PCL)	DH	4	16	3	3	2	0	0	1	2	2	0	1	0-0	.188	.278	.313	.590	...	...
—Modesto (California)	OF	2	8	1	4	0	0	0	1	0	0	0	0	0-0	.500	.500	.875	1.375	0	1.000
—Oakland (A.L.)	OF-DH	131	488	74	123	27	1	24	86	52	108	10	15	2-0	.252	.333	.459	.792	5	.972
2003— Sacramento (PCL)	DH-OF	13	49	9	14	2	0	2	8	11	11	0	1	0-0	.286	.417	.444	.866	0	1.000
—Oakland (A.L.)	OF-DH	65	221	28	38	6	0	4	20	25	42	3	11	1-0	.172	.261	.253	.514	0	1.000
2004— Oakland (A.L.)	OF-DH	137	532	87	141	29	4	23	80	49	128	4	16	4-2	.265	.329	.464	.793	2	.992
2005— Chicago (A.L.)	OF-1B-SS-DH	145	529	74	145	29	2	31	86	39	99	9	15	11-4	.274	.333	.512	.846	8	.972
American League totals (9 years)		1086	4055	607	1100	226	19	180	660	377	804	39	108	33-14	.271	.336	.470	.805	42	.980
National League totals (1 year)		98	292	32	82	16	0	12	37	8	67	3	11	1-4	.281	.304	.459	.763	8	.950
Major League totals (10 years)		1184	4347	639	1182	242	19	192	697	385	871	42	119	34-18	.272	.334	.469	.803	50	.978

D

DIVISION SERIES RECORD

Year Team (League)	Pos.	G	AB	R	H	2B	3B	HR	RBI	BB	SO	HBP	GDP	SB-CS	Avg.	OBP	SLG	OPS	E	Avg.
1996—Atlanta (N.L.)	OF	3	11	1	2	0	0	1	1	0	6	0	0	1-0	.182	.182	.455	.636	0	1.000
2001—Oakland (A.L.)	OF	4	13	0	3	2	0	0	0	2	2	0	0	0-0	.231	.333	.385	.718	0	1.000
2002—Oakland (A.L.)	OF	5	20	3	8	2	0	1	1	1	5	0	0	0-0	.400	.429	.650	1.079	0	1.000
2003—Oakland (A.L.)	OF	4	13	2	3	0	0	1	3	0	2	1	0	0-0	.231	.286	.462	.747	0	1.000
2005—Chicago (A.L.)	OF	3	10	1	2	0	0	0	0	1	2	1	0	0-0	.200	.333	.200	.533	0	1.000
Division series totals (5 years)		19	67	7	18	4	0	3	5	4	17	2	0	1-0	.269	.329	.463	.791	0	1.000

CHAMPIONSHIP SERIES RECORD

Year Team (League)	Pos.	G	AB	R	H	2B	3B	HR	RBI	BB	SO	HBP	GDP	SB-CS	Avg.	OBP	SLG	OPS	E	Avg.
1996—Atlanta (N.L.)	OF	7	28	2	6	1	0	0	4	1	7	0	0	0-1	.214	.226	.250	.476	0	1.000
2005—Chicago (A.L.)	OF	5	19	3	5	2	0	0	3	3	3	0	0	0-0	.263	.364	.368	.732	0	1.000
Champ. series totals (2 years)		12	47	5	11	3	0	0	7	4	10	0	0	1-1	.234	.283	.298	.581	0	1.000

WORLD SERIES RECORD

Year Team (League)	Pos.	G	AB	R	H	2B	3B	HR	RBI	BB	SO	HBP	GDP	SB-CS	Avg.	OBP	SLG	OPS	E	Avg.
1996—Atlanta (N.L.)	OF	5	17	0	2	0	0	0	1	1	0	0	0	0-0	.118	.167	.118	.284	1	.938
2005—Chicago (A.L.)	OF	4	16	3	7	1	0	1	3	2	1	1	0	0-0	.438	.526	.688	1.214	0	1.000
World Series totals (2 years)		9	33	3	9	1	0	1	4	3	1	1	0	0-0	.273	.351	.394	.745	1	.955

ALL-STAR GAME RECORD

	G	AB	R	H	2B	3B	HR	RBI	BB	SO	HBP	GDP	SB-CS	Avg.	OBP	SLG	OPS	E	Avg.
All-Star Game totals (1 year)	1	2	1	0	0	0	0	0	0	0	0	0	0-0	.000	.333	.000	.333	0	1.000

EASLEY, DAMION — 2B/SS

PERSONAL: Born November 11, 1969, in New York. ... 5-11/190. ... Bats right, throws right. ... Full name: Jacinto Damion Easley. ... High school: Lakewood (Calif.). ... Junior college: Long Beach (Calif.) City College.

TRANSACTIONS/CAREER NOTES: Selected by California Angels organization in 30th round of 1988 free-agent draft. ... On disabled list (June 19-July 4 and July 28, 1993-remainder of season; and May 30-June 17, 1994). ... On disabled list (April 1-May 10, 1996); included rehabilitation assignment to Vancouver. ... Traded by Angels to Detroit Tigers for P Greg Gohr (July 31, 1996). ... On disabled list (April 10-25 and May 9-June 2, 2000); included rehabilitation assignments to Toledo. ... On disabled list (April 17-June 1, 2002) included rehabilitation assignment to Toledo. ... Released by Tigers (March 28, 2003). ... Signed by Tampa Bay Devil Rays (April 2, 2003). ... Released by Devil Rays (June 4, 2003). ... Signed by Florida Marlins organization (January 8, 2004).

RECORDS: Shares major league record for most times hit by pitch, game (3, May 31, 1999, and July 16, 2002).

2005 GAMES PLAYED BY POSITION (MLB): 2B—46, SS—30, 3B—10.

DAMION EASLEY'S HITTING ZONE

.519	.263	.071
.317	.219	.150
.267	.308	.000

LEFTY-RIGHTY SPLITS

vs.	Avg.	AB	H	2B	3B	HR	RBI	BB	SO	OBP	Slg.
L	.333	51	17	3	1	5	11	5	7	.390	.725
R	.218	216	47	16	0	4	19	21	40	.293	.347

									BATTING										FIELDING	
Year Team (League)	Pos.	G	AB	R	H	2B	3B	HR	RBI	BB	SO	HBP	GDP	SB-CS	Avg.	OBP	SLG	OPS	E	Avg.
1989—Bend (N'west)	2B	36	131	34	39	5	1	4	21	25	21	4	1	9-4	.298	.425	.443	.868	22	.863
1990—Quad City (Midw.)	SS	103	365	59	100	19	3	10	56	41	60	8	8	25-8	.274	.358	.425	.783	41	.893
1991—Midland (Texas)	SS	127	452	73	115	24	5	6	57	68	67	7	12	23-9	.254	.347	.369	.716	*47	.924
1992—Edmonton (PCL)	SS-3B	108	429	61	124	18	3	3	44	31	44	5	13	26-10	.289	.340	.366	.706	30	.943
— California (A.L.)	3B-SS	47	151	14	39	5	0	1	12	8	26	3	4	9-5	.258	.307	.311	.618	5	.964
1993—California (A.L.)	2B-3B-3B-SS	73	230	33	72	13	2	2	22	28	25	3	5	6-6	.313	.392	.413	.805	6	.978
1994—California (A.L.)	3B-2B	88	316	41	68	16	1	6	30	29	48	4	4	4-5	.215	.288	.329	.617	7	.977
1995—California (A.L.)	2B-SS	114	357	35	77	14	2	4	35	32	47	6	11	5-2	.216	.288	.300	.588	10	.979
1996—Vancouver (PCL)	SS-2B-3B	12	48	13	15	2	1	2	8	9	6	1	0	4-1	.313	.424	.521	.945	2	.958
— Midland (Texas)	3B-SS	4	14	1	6	2	0	2	0	0	0	0	0	1-0	.429	.429	.571	1.000	1	.944
— California (A.L.)	SS-2B-3B-DH-OF	28	45	4	7	1	0	2	7	6	12	0	0	0-0	.156	.255	.311	.566	3	.954
— Detroit (A.L.)	2B-SS-3B-DH	21	67	10	23	1	0	2	10	4	13	1	0	3-1	.343	.384	.448	.831	5	.958
1997—Detroit (A.L.)	2B-SS-DH	151	527	97	139	37	3	22	72	68	102	16	18	28-13	.264	.362	.471	.833	12	.982
1998—Detroit (A.L.)	2B-SS-DH	153	594	84	161	38	2	27	100	39	112	16	8	15-5	.271	.332	.478	.810	12	.985
1999—Detroit (A.L.)	2B-SS	151	549	83	146	30	1	20	65	51	124	19	15	11-3	.266	.346	.434	.779	8	.990
2000—Detroit (A.L.)	2B	126	464	76	120	27	2	14	59	55	79	11	11	13-4	.259	.350	.416	.766	6	.990
— Toledo (Int'l)	2B	4	13	3	3	1	0	1	4	4	2	2	0	0-0	.231	.474	.538	1.012	0	1.000
2001—Detroit (A.L.)	2B	154	585	77	146	27	7	11	65	52	90	13	10	10-5	.250	.321	.376	.699	14	.982
2002—Detroit (A.L.)	2B-DH	85	304	29	68	14	1	8	30	27	43	11	4	1-3	.224	.307	.355	.663	5	.980
— Toledo (Int'l)	2B	8	26	5	3	1	0	0	0	5	0	1	1	0-2	.115	.281	.154	.435	2	.949
2003—Tampa Bay (A.L.)	3B-DH-2B	36	107	8	20	3	1	1	7	2	18	0	3	0-0	.187	.202	.262	.464	4	.935
2004—Florida (N.L.)	2B-1B-SS-3B-OF-DH	98	223	26	53	20	1	9	43	24	36	8	6	4-1	.238	.331	.457	.788	7	.974
2005—Florida (N.L.)	2B-SS-3B	102	267	37	64	19	1	9	30	26	47	4	6	4-1	.240	.312	.419	.732	9	.973
American League totals (12 years)		1227	4296	591	1086	226	22	120	513	401	749	103	95	105-52	.253	.329	.399	.729	99	.982
National League totals (2 years)		200	490	63	117	39	2	18	73	50	83	12	12	8-2	.239	.321	.437	.758	16	.973
Major League totals (14 years)		1427	4786	654	1203	265	24	138	586	451	832	115	107	113-54	.251	.328	.403	.732	115	.981

ALL-STAR GAME RECORD

	G	AB	R	H	2B	3B	HR	RBI	BB	SO	HBP	GDP	SB-CS	Avg.	OBP	SLG	OPS	E	Avg.
All-Star Game totals (1 year)	1	1	1	1	0	0	0	0	0	0	0	0	0-0	1.000	1.000	1.000	2.000	0	...

EATON, ADAM — P

PERSONAL: Born November 23, 1977, in Seattle. ... 6-2/196. ... Throws right, bats right. ... Full name: Adam Thomas Eaton. ... High school: Snohomish (Wash.).

TRANSACTIONS/CAREER NOTES: Selected by Philadelphia Phillies organization in first round (11th pick overall) of 1996 free-agent draft. ... Traded by Phillies with Ps Carlton Loewer and Steve Montgomery to San Diego Padres for P Andy Ashby (November 10, 1999). ... On disabled list (July 6, 2001-remainder of season). ... On disabled list (March 27-September 1, 2002); included rehabilitation assignments to Lake Elsinore and Portland. ... On disabled list (May 5-20, 2003). ... On disabled list (June 22-August 1 and August 5-26, 2005); included rehabilitation assignments to Lake Elsinore and Portland.

CAREER HITTING: 48-for-251 (.191), 24 R, 13 2B, 1 3B, 2 HR, 19 RBI.

SCOUTING REPORT Throws: Eaton has a 90-93 mph fastball. Also throws a curveball, slider and changeup. **Tendencies:** Eaton has a tendency to throw across his body, which puts a lot of pressure on his arm, and consequently he has never pitched 200 innings in a season. Complements a live fastball with a hard curveball, but his other pitches lack consistency. Has a very quick curve but slider is a more consistent breaking ball. Has a feel for his changeup. **Outlook:** If he stays healthy, he could win 15 to 18 games for the Padres. **Grade 7.3**

ADAM EATON'S PITCHING ZONE

.222	.423	.313
.273	.293	.314
.294	.258	.333

LEFTY-RIGHTY SPLITS

vs.	Avg.	AB	H	2B	3B	HR	RBI	BB	SO	OBP	Slg.
L	.297	246	73	20	2	8	32	26	41	.366	.492
R	.255	263	67	18	0	6	29	18	59	.305	.392

Year	Team (League)	W	L	Pct.	ERA	WHIP	G	GS	CG	ShO	Hld.	Sv.-Opp.	IP	H	R	ER	HR	BB-IBB	SO	Avg.
1997—	Piedmont (S. Atl.)	5	6	.455	4.16	1.56	14	14	0	0	...	0-...	71.1	81	38	33	2	30-0	57	.287
1998—	Clearwater (FSL)	9	8	.529	4.44	1.51	24	23	1	0	...	0-...	131.2	152	68	65	9	47-1	89	.293
1999—	Clearwater (FSL)	5	5	.500	3.91	1.52	13	13	0	0	...	0-...	69.0	81	39	30	2	24-0	50	.293
	—Reading (East.)	5	4	.556	2.92	1.14	12	12	2	0	...	0-...	77.0	60	30	25	9	28-1	67	.214
	—Scran./W.B. (I.L.)	1	1	.500	3.00	1.10	3	3	0	0	...	0-...	21.0	17	10	7	1	6-0	10	.224
2000—	Mobile (Sou.)	4	1	.800	2.68	1.14	10	10	1	1	...	0-...	57.0	47	20	17	3	18-0	58	.219
	—San Diego (N.L.)	7	4	.636	4.13	1.44	22	22	0	0	0	0-0	135.0	134	63	62	14	61-3	90	.260
2001—	San Diego (N.L.)	8	5	.615	4.32	1.27	17	17	2	0	0	0-0	116.2	108	61	56	20	40-3	109	.241
2002—	Lake Elsinore (Calif.)	0	0	...	2.70	0.98	3	3	0	0	0	0-0	13.1	10	7	4	0	3-0	19	.196
	—Portland (PCL)	1	1	.500	2.92	0.97	2	2	0	0	0	0-0	12.1	9	9	4	3	3-0	6	.200
	—San Diego (N.L.)	1	1	.500	5.40	1.35	6	6	0	0	0	0-0	33.1	28	20	20	5	17-0	25	.235
2003—	San Diego (N.L.)	9	12	.429	4.08	1.32	31	31	1	0	0	0-0	183.0	173	91	83	20	68-6	146	.246
2004—	San Diego (N.L.)	11	14	.440	4.61	1.28	33	33	0	0	0	0-0	199.1	204	113	102	28	52-3	153	.266
2005—	Lake Elsinore (Calif.)	0	0	...	0.00	1.00	1	1	0	0	0	0-0	3.0	1	0	0	0	2-0	2	.111
	—Portland (PCL)	0	0	...	5.63	1.50	2	2	0	0	0	0-0	8.0	11	5	5	3	1-0	4	.344
	—San Diego (N.L.)	11	5	.688	4.27	1.43	24	22	0	0	0	0-0	128.2	140	70	61	14	44-6	100	.275
Major League totals (6 years)		47	41	.534	4.34	1.34	133	131	3	0	0	0-0	796.0	787	418	384	101	282-21	623	.257

ECKSTEIN, DAVID   SS

PERSONAL: Born January 20, 1975, in Sanford, Fla. ... 5-7/165. ... Bats right, throws right. ... Full name: David Mark Eckstein. ... Name pronounced: ECK-styne. ... High school: Seminole (Sanford, Fla.). ... College: Florida.
TRANSACTIONS/CAREER NOTES: Selected by Boston Red Sox organization in 19th round of 1997 free-agent draft. ... Claimed on waivers by Anaheim Angels (August 16, 2000). ... On disabled list (August 18-September 9, 2003). ... Signed as a free agent by St. Louis Cardinals (December 23, 2004).
2005 GAMES PLAYED BY POSITION (MLB): SS—156.

SCOUTING REPORT Offense: Eckstein is an outstanding contact hitter with exceptional bat control. Is one of the best two-strike hitters in the game. Handles the ball up or down, in or out. Has occasional power on pitches up. Is outstanding with the game on the line. Is an instinctive baserunner. **Defense:** His throwing dramatically improved after he went on a strength program and changed his mechanics. Arm is still short and he winds up to throw, but release is quicker. Has very good hands. Positioning makes up for average range. Adjusts his routes to grounders with short, choppy steps. **Outlook:** Eckstein gets the most from his ability of any player in the game, and he continues to get better. Has exceptional instincts and intangibles and an unmatched desire to succeed. **Grade 8**

DAVID ECKSTEIN'S HITTING ZONE

.393	.485	.243
.262	.397	.312
.209	.400	.393

LEFTY-RIGHTY SPLITS

vs.	Avg.	AB	H	2B	3B	HR	RBI	BB	SO	OBP	Slg.
L	.257	167	43	6	2	4	12	19	10	.346	.389
R	.307	463	142	20	5	4	49	39	34	.370	.397

E

Year	Team (League)	Pos.	G	AB	R	H	2B	3B	HR	RBI	BB	SO	HBP	GDP	SB-CS	Avg.	OBP	SLG	OPS	E	Avg.
1997—	Lowell (NY-Penn)	2B	68	249	43	75	11	4	4	39	33	29	12	2	21-5	.301	.407	.426	.832	9	.971
1998—	Sarasota (Fla. St.)	2B-SS	135	503	99	154	29	4	3	58	87	51	22	8	45-16	.306	.428	.398	.826	8	.986
1999—	Trenton (East.)	2B	131	483	109	151	22	5	6	52	89	48	25	8	32-13	.313	.440	.416	.856	8	.985
2000—	Pawtucket (Int'l)	2B-SS	119	422	77	104	20	0	1	31	60	45	20	8	11-8	.246	.364	.301	.665	4	.992
	—Edmonton (PCL)	2B	15	52	17	18	8	0	3	8	9	1	5	0	5-3	.346	.485	.673	1.158	0	1.000
2001—	Anaheim (A.L.)	SS-2B-DH	153	582	82	166	26	2	4	41	43	60	* 21	11	29-4	.285	.355	.357	.712	18	.969
2002—	Anaheim (A.L.)	SS-DH	152	608	107	178	22	6	8	63	45	44	* 27	7	21-13	.293	.363	.388	.752	14	.977
2003—	Anaheim (A.L.)	SS-DH	120	452	59	114	22	1	3	31	36	45	15	9	16-5	.252	.325	.325	.651	8	.984
2004—	Anaheim (A.L.)	SS-DH	142	566	92	156	24	1	2	35	42	49	13	11	16-5	.276	.339	.332	.671	6	.988
2005—	St. Louis (N.L.)	SS	158	630	90	185	26	7	8	61	58	44	13	13	11-8	.294	.363	.395	.758	15	.981
American League totals (4 years)			567	2208	340	614	94	10	17	170	166	198	76	38	82-27	.278	.347	.353	.700	46	.979
National League totals (1 year)			158	630	90	185	26	7	8	61	58	44	13	13	11-8	.294	.363	.395	.758	15	.981
Major League totals (5 years)			725	2838	430	799	120	17	25	231	224	242	89	51	93-35	.282	.351	.362	.713	61	.980

DIVISION SERIES RECORD

Year	Team (League)	Pos.	G	AB	R	H	2B	3B	HR	RBI	BB	SO	HBP	GDP	SB-CS	Avg.	OBP	SLG	OPS	E	Avg.
2002—	Anaheim (A.L.)	SS	4	18	2	5	0	0	0	1	0	0	1	0	1-0	.278	.316	.278	.594	0	1.000
2004—	Anaheim (A.L.)	SS	3	12	2	4	0	0	0	0	0	1	0	0	0-0	.333	.333	.333	.667	1	.917
2005—	St. Louis (N.L.)	SS	3	13	3	5	0	0	1	4	1	0	0	0	0-0	.385	.429	.615	1.044	2	.895
Division series totals (3 years)			10	43	7	14	0	0	1	5	1	1	1	0	1-0	.326	.356	.395	.751	3	.932

CHAMPIONSHIP SERIES RECORD

Year	Team (League)	Pos.	G	AB	R	H	2B	3B	HR	RBI	BB	SO	HBP	GDP	SB-CS	Avg.	OBP	SLG	OPS	E	Avg.
2002—	Anaheim (A.L.)	SS	5	21	1	6	0	0	0	2	0	2	1	0	0-0	.286	.318	.286	.604	1	.944
2005—	St. Louis (N.L.)	SS	6	20	5	4	0	0	0	3	2	2	2	0	1-1	.200	.346	.200	.546	1	.964
Champ. series totals (2 years)			11	41	6	10	0	0	0	5	2	4	3	0	1-1	.244	.333	.244	.577	2	.957

WORLD SERIES RECORD

Year	Team (League)	Pos.	G	AB	R	H	2B	3B	HR	RBI	BB	SO	HBP	GDP	SB-CS	Avg.	OBP	SLG	OPS	E	Avg.
2002—	Anaheim (A.L.)	SS	7	29	6	9	0	0	0	3	2	1	0	0	1-0	.310	.364	.310	.674	0	1.000

	G	AB	R	H	2B	3B	HR	RBI	BB	SO	HBP	GDP	SB-CS	Avg.	OBP	SLG	OPS	E	Avg.
All-Star Game totals (1 year)	1	2	0	0	0	0	0	0	0	0	0	0	0-0	.000	.000	.000	.000	0	1.000

EDMONDS, JIM — OF

PERSONAL: Born June 27, 1970, in Fullerton, Calif. ... 6-1/212. ... Bats left, throws left. ... Full name: James Patrick Edmonds. ... Name pronounced: ED-munds. ... High school: Diamond Bar (Calif.).

TRANSACTIONS/CAREER NOTES: Selected by California Angels organization in seventh round of 1988 free-agent draft. ... On disabled list (May 26-June 10 and June 12-July 18, 1996); included rehabilitation assignment to Lake Elsinore. ... Angels franchise renamed Anaheim Angels for 1997 season. ... On disabled list (August 1-16, 1997). ... On disabled list (March 30-August 2, 1999); included rehabilitation assignment to Lake Elsinore. ... Traded by Angels to St. Louis Cardinals for 2B Adam Kennedy and P Kent Bottenfield (March 23, 2000). ... On disabled list (June 1-16, 2002).

HONORS: Won A.L. Gold Glove as outfielder (1997-98). ... Won N.L. Gold Glove as outfielder (2000-05).

2005 GAMES PLAYED BY POSITION (MLB): OF—139.

SCOUTING REPORT

Offense: His stroke is one of the most fluid in the game, but his approach is unusual. Has an extremely quick bat and likes to uppercut the ball. Has power to all fields and is productive with runners in scoring position. Is a patient hitter who struggles when he chases high fastballs. Can be streaky, both with strikeouts and power. No longer runs well and has occasional hamstring problems. *Defense:* One of the best center fielders in the game (an eight-time Gold Glove winner), he gets outstanding jumps and takes excellent routes to the ball. Has a knack for making routine plays look spectacular. Arm is average, but has a quick release when he charges and is very accurate. *Outlook:* He seems to get better with age. Has become a better hitter who rises to the occasion. *Grade 9*

JIM EDMONDS' HITTING ZONE

.348	.344	.242
.351	.225	.279
.143	.393	.333

LEFTY-RIGHTY SPLITS

vs.	Avg.	AB	H	2B	3B	HR	RBI	BB	SO	OBP	Slg.
L	.296	125	37	10	1	8	29	15	38	.385	.584
R	.251	342	86	27	0	21	60	76	101	.385	.515

									BATTING										FIELDING	
Year Team (League)	Pos.	G	AB	R	H	2B	3B	HR	RBI	BB	SO	HBP	GDP	SB-CS	Avg.	OBP	SLG	OPS	E	Avg.
1988—Bend (N'west)	OF	35	122	23	27	4	0	0	13	20	44	0	2	4-0	.221	.329	.254	.583	1	.984
1989—Quad City (Midw.)	OF	31	92	11	24	4	0	1	4	7	34	0	3	1-0	.261	.313	.337	.650	3	.942
1990—Palm Springs (Calif.)	OF	91	314	36	92	18	6	3	56	27	75	2	10	5-2	.293	.351	.417	.768	10	.954
1991—Palm Springs (Calif.)	OF	60	187	28	55	15	1	2	27	40	57	0	2	2-2	.294	.417	.417	.834	1	1.000
1992—Midland (Texas)	OF	70	246	42	77	15	2	8	32	41	83	1	8	3-4	.313	.413	.488	.901	5	.967
—Edmonton (PCL)	OF	50	194	37	58	15	2	6	36	14	55	0	2	3-1	.299	.343	.490	.833	1	.988
1993—Vancouver (PCL)	OF	95	356	59	112	28	4	9	74	41	81	0	5	6-8	.315	.382	.492	.873	3	.983
—California (A.L.)	OF	18	61	5	15	4	1	0	4	2	16	0	1	0-2	.246	.270	.344	.614	1	.981
1994—California (A.L.)	OF-1B	94	289	35	79	13	1	5	37	30	72	1	3	4-2	.273	.343	.377	.720	3	.991
1995—California (A.L.)	OF	141	558	120	162	30	4	33	107	51	130	5	10	1-4	.290	.352	.536	.888	1	.998
1996—California (A.L.)	OF-DH	114	431	73	131	28	3	27	66	46	101	4	4	4-0	.304	.375	.571	.946	1	.997
—Lake Elsinore (Calif.)	OF-DH	5	15	4	6	2	0	1	4	1	1	0	0	0-0	.400	.471	.733	1.204	0	1.000
1997—Anaheim (A.L.)	OF-1B-DH	133	502	82	146	27	0	26	80	60	80	4	8	5-7	.291	.368	.500	.868	5	.988
1998—Anaheim (A.L.)	OF	154	599	115	184	42	1	25	91	57	114	1	16	7-5	.307	.368	.506	.874	5	.988
1999—Lake Elsinore (Calif.)	DH	5	19	4	8	2	0	0	3	4	2	0	0	2-0	.421	.522	.526	1.048	0	...
—Anaheim (A.L.)	OF-DH-1B	55	204	34	51	17	2	5	23	28	45	0	3	5-4	.250	.339	.426	.766	1	.993
2000—St. Louis (N.L.)	OF-1B	152	525	129	155	25	0	42	108	103	167	6	5	10-3	.295	.411	.583	.994	4	.990
2001—St. Louis (N.L.)	OF-1B	150	500	95	152	38	1	30	110	93	136	6	5	5-5	.304	.410	.564	.974	6	.983
2002—St. Louis (N.L.)	OF	144	476	96	148	31	2	28	83	86	134	8	9	4-3	.311	.420	.561	.981	5	.986
2003—St. Louis (N.L.)	OF-DH	137	447	89	123	32	2	39	89	77	127	4	11	1-3	.275	.385	.617	1.002	5	.986
2004—St. Louis (N.L.)	OF-1B-DH	153	498	102	150	38	3	42	111	101	150	5	4	8-3	.301	.418	.643	1.061	4	.988
2005—St. Louis (N.L.)	OF	142	467	88	123	37	1	29	89	91	139	4	6	5-5	.263	.385	.533	.918	2	.994
American League totals (7 years)		709	2644	464	768	161	12	121	408	274	558	15	49	26-24	.290	.359	.498	.856	17	.992
National League totals (6 years)		878	2913	599	851	201	9	210	590	551	853	31	43	33-22	.292	.406	.584	.989	26	.988
Major League totals (13 years)		1587	5557	1063	1619	362	21	331	998	825	1411	46	92	59-46	.291	.384	.543	.927	43	.990

DIVISION SERIES RECORD

Year Team (League)	Pos.	G	AB	R	H	2B	3B	HR	RBI	BB	SO	HBP	GDP	SB-CS	Avg.	OBP	SLG	OPS	E	Avg.
2000—St. Louis (N.L.)	OF	3	14	5	8	4	0	2	7	1	2	0	0	1-0	.571	.600	1.286	1.886	0	1.000
2001—St. Louis (N.L.)	OF	5	17	3	4	1	0	2	3	3	6	0	0	0-0	.235	.350	.647	.997	0	1.000
2002—St. Louis (N.L.)	OF	3	11	1	3	0	0	1	2	2	4	0	0	0-1	.273	.385	.545	.930	0	1.000
2004—St. Louis (N.L.)	OF	4	15	1	4	0	0	1	2	1	9	0	0	0-1	.267	.313	.467	.779	0	1.000
2005—St. Louis (N.L.)	OF	3	11	5	4	2	0	1	1	2	2	0	0	0-0	.364	.462	.818	1.280	0	1.000
Division series totals (5 years)		18	68	15	23	7	0	7	15	9	23	0	0	1-2	.338	.416	.750	1.166	0	1.000

CHAMPIONSHIP SERIES RECORD

Year Team (League)	Pos.	G	AB	R	H	2B	3B	HR	RBI	BB	SO	HBP	GDP	SB-CS	Avg.	OBP	SLG	OPS	E	Avg.
2000—St. Louis (N.L.)	OF	5	22	1	5	1	0	1	5	1	9	0	0	0-0	.227	.261	.409	.670	1	.933
2002—St. Louis (N.L.)	OF	5	20	2	8	2	0	1	4	2	5	0	0	0-0	.400	.455	.650	1.105	0	1.000
2004—St. Louis (N.L.)	OF	7	24	2	7	2	0	2	7	2	6	1	0	0-0	.292	.357	.625	.982	1	.952
2005—St. Louis (N.L.)	OF	6	19	2	4	1	0	0	0	5	5	0	1	1-0	.211	.375	.263	.638	1	.923
Champ. series totals (4 years)		23	85	7	24	6	0	4	16	10	25	1	1	1-0	.282	.361	.494	.855	3	.950

WORLD SERIES RECORD

Year Team (League)	Pos.	G	AB	R	H	2B	3B	HR	RBI	BB	SO	HBP	GDP	SB-CS	Avg.	OBP	SLG	OPS	E	Avg.
2004—St. Louis (N.L.)	OF	4	15	2	1	0	0	0	1	6	6	0	0	0-0	.067	.125	.067	.192	0	1.000

ALL-STAR GAME RECORD

	G	AB	R	H	2B	3B	HR	RBI	BB	SO	HBP	GDP	SB-CS	Avg.	OBP	SLG	OPS	E	Avg.
All-Star Game totals (4 years)	4	6	0	2	0	0	0	0	1	2	0	0	0-0	.333	.429	.333	.762	0	1.000

EDWARDS, MIKE — 3B/OF

PERSONAL: Born November 24, 1976, in Goshen, N.Y. ... 6-1/185. ... Bats right, throws right. ... Full name: Michael Donald Edwards. ... High school: Mechanicsburg (Pa.).

TRANSACTIONS/CAREER NOTES: Selected by Cleveland Indians organization in ninth round of 1995 free-agent draft. ... Signed as a free agent by Cincinnati Reds organization (November 8, 2001). ... Signed as a free agent by Oakland Athletics organization (November 8, 2002). ... Signed as a free agent by Los Angeles Dodgers organization (November 20, 2004).

2005 GAMES PLAYED BY POSITION (MLB): 3B—39, OF—34, DH—2, SS—1.

SCOUTING REPORT Edwards has too much movement at the plate, poor bat speed and little power. Stays inside the ball and is a good contact hitter. Is not a good breaking-ball hitter. Doesn't run well. Has good hands and an accurate arm but has limited range. Charges the ball well. Has to hit better to be a part of the Dodgers' plans for next season. ***Grade 5.0***

MIKE EDWARDS' HITTING ZONE

.231	.400	.118
.205	.333	.162
.444	.364	.167

LEFTY-RIGHTY SPLITS

vs.	Avg.	AB	H	2B	3B	HR	RBI	BB	SO	OBP	Slg.
L	.253	75	19	2	1	0	5	5	13	.309	.307
R	.244	164	40	7	1	3	10	11	21	.295	.354

Year	Team (League)	Pos.	G	AB	R	H	2B	3B	HR	RBI	BB	SO	HBP	GDP	SB-CS	Avg.	OBP	SLG	OPS	E	Avg.
1995— Burlington (Appal.)		SS	43	130	20	22	2	0	0	5	17	35	2	2	5-2	.169	.275	.185	.460	18	.897
1996— Burlington (Appal.)		3B-SS	58	206	31	58	13	1	1	17	37	26	3	4	5-4	.282	.394	.369	.763	13	.901
1997— Burlington (Appal.)	3B-SS-1B	OF	60	236	50	68	16	2	4	41	38	53	1	2	10-5	.288	.386	.424	.810	21	.903
1998— Columbus (S. Atl.)		3B-1B	124	497	82	146	34	4	8	81	66	95	3	13	16-6	.294	.379	.427	.806	31	.910
1999— Kinston (Carol.)		3B	133	456	76	132	25	4	16	89	93	117	9	12	8-3	.289	.413	.467	.880	28	.910
2000— Akron (East.)		1B-3B	136	481	72	142	25	2	11	63	68	86	5	9	7-3	.295	.386	.424	.810	20	.943
2001— Mahoning Valley (NYP)		3B	20	71	19	26	5	0	6	24	12	7	1	0	0-1	.366	.464	.690	1.154	1	.960
— Akron (East.)		1B-3B	29	111	21	37	7	3	6	24	13	26	0	3	0-0	.333	.403	.613	1.016	4	.978
— Buffalo (Int'l)		1B	3	9	1	2	0	0	1	1	1	3	0	1	0-0	.222	.300	.222	.522	0	1.000
2002— Chattanooga (Sou.)	OF-1B	3B	119	424	57	130	19	2	11	60	41	57	10	19	9-11	.307	.377	.439	.816	10	.981
— Louisville (Int'l)	OF	1B-P	15	57	7	23	5	1	2	8	6	9	0	1	0-0	.404	.460	.632	1.092	1	.976
2003— Sacramento (PCL)	OF-DH	3B-SS	125	436	78	130	23	4	14	95	60	78	6	17	5-2	.298	.387	.466	.853	3	.984
— Oakland (A.L.)	DH-OF		4	4	0	1	0	0	0	0	2	1	0	0	0-0	.250	.500	.250	.750	0	...
2004— Sacramento (PCL)	OF-1B-3B		140	551	91	158	41	4	13	81	76	100	13	14	11-2	.287	.384	.432	.816	24	.657
2005— Las Vegas (PCL)	OF-1B-3B	DH	32	118	18	33	6	0	4	21	11	21	3	4	3-1	.280	.353	.432	.786	1	.994
— Los Angeles (N.L.)	3B-OF-DH	SS	88	239	23	59	9	2	3	15	16	34	2	6	1-1	.247	.300	.339	.639	7	.950
American League totals (1 year)			4	4	0	1	0	0	0	0	2	1	0	0	0-0	.250	.500	.250	.750	0	...
National League totals (1 year)			88	239	23	59	9	2	3	15	16	34	2	6	1-1	.247	.300	.339	.639	7	.950
Major League totals (2 years)			92	243	23	60	9	2	3	15	18	35	2	6	1-1	.247	.304	.337	.642	7	.950

EISCHEN, JOEY — P

PERSONAL: Born May 25, 1970, in West Covina, Calif. ... 6-0/214. ... Throws left, bats left. ... Full name: Joseph Raymond Eischen. ... Name pronounced: EYE-shen. ... High school: West Covina (Calif.). ... Junior college: Pasadena (Calif.) City College.

TRANSACTIONS/CAREER NOTES: Selected by Chicago White Sox organization in fifth round of 1988 free-agent draft; did not sign. ... Selected by Texas Rangers in fourth round of 1989 free-agent draft. ... Traded by Rangers with P Jonathan Hurst and a player to be named to Montreal Expos for P Dennis Boyd (July 21, 1991); Expos acquired P Travis Buckley to complete deal (September 1, 1991). ... Traded by Expos with OF Roberto Kelly to Los Angeles Dodgers for OF Henry Rodriguez and IF Jeff Treadway (May 23, 1995). ... Traded by Dodgers with P John Cummings to Detroit Tigers for OF Chad Curtis (July 31, 1996). ... Traded by Tigers with P Cam Smith to San Diego Padres for C Brian Johnson and P Willie Blair (December 17, 1996). ... Traded by Padres to Cincinnati Reds for a player to be named (March 16, 1997); Padres acquired IF Ray Brown to complete deal (March 19, 1997). ... On disabled list (March 25-April 26 and April 29-July 18, 1997); included rehabilitation assignment to Indianapolis. ... Signed as a free agent by New York Yankees organization (February 3, 1998). ... Released by Yankees (March 11, 1998). ... Signed by Reds (March 19, 1998). ... Released by Reds (March 12, 1999). ... Signed by Arizona Diamondbacks organization (March 18, 1999). ... Released by Diamondbacks (July 1, 1999). ... Signed as a free agent by Cleveland Indians organization (December 23, 1999). ... Released by Indians (April 29, 2000). ... Signed as a free agent by Expos organization (July 12, 2000). ... On disabled list (March 26-August 2, 2004); included rehabilitation assignments to GCL Expos and Brevard County. ... Expos franchise transferred to Washington, D.C., and renamed Washington Nationals for 2005 season (December 3, 2004). ... On disabled list (May 2-July 1, 2005); included rehabilitation assignment to New Orleans.

JOEY EISCHEN'S PITCHING ZONE

.250	.333	.333
.565	.364	.133
.200	.000	.286

LEFTY-RIGHTY SPLITS

vs.	Avg.	AB	H	2B	3B	HR	RBI	BB	SO	OBP	Slg.
L	.250	72	18	2	1	1	8	6	20	.325	.375
R	.254	63	16	1	0	0	3	13	10	.405	.270

CAREER HITTING: 5-for-26 (.192), 4 R, 1 2B, 0 3B, 0 HR, 0 RBI.

Year	Team (League)	W	L	Pct.	ERA	WHIP	G	GS	CG	ShO	Hld.	Sv.-Opp.	IP	H	R	ER	HR	BB-IBB	SO	Avg.
1989— Butte (Pion.)		3	7	.300	5.30	1.67	12	12	0	0	...	0-...	52.2	50	45	31	4	38-0	57	.246
1990— Gastonia (S. Atl.)		3	7	.300	2.70	1.24	17	14	0	0	...	0-...	73.1	51	36	22	0	40-0	69	.195
1991— Charlotte (Fla. St.)		4	10	.286	3.41	1.42	18	18	1	0	...	0-...	108.1	99	59	41	5	55-1	80	.249
— W.P. Beach (FSL)		4	2	.667	5.17	1.54	8	8	1	0	...	0-...	38.1	35	27	22	3	24-0	26	.238
1992— W.P. Beach (FSL)		9	8	.529	3.08	1.24	27	26	3	2	...	0-...	169.2	128	68	58	5	83-2	167	.211
1993— Harrisburg (East.)		14	4	.778	3.62	1.53	20	20	1	0	...	0-...	119.1	122	62	48	11	60-0	110	.265
— Ottawa (Int'l)		2	2	.500	3.54	1.20	6	6	0	0	...	0-...	40.2	34	18	16	3	15-0	29	.238
1994— Ottawa (Int'l)		2	6	.250	4.94	1.52	48	2	0	0	...	2-...	62.0	54	38	34	7	40-4	57	.238
— Montreal (N.L.)		0	0	...	54.00	6.00	1	0	0	0	...	0-0	0.2	4	4	4	0	0-0	1	.667

Year	Team (League)	W	L	Pct.	ERA	WHIP	G	GS	CG	ShO	Hld.	Sv.-Opp.	IP	H	R	ER	HR	BB-IBB	SO	Avg.
1995—	Ottawa (Int'l)	2	1	.667	1.72	1.09	11	0	0	0	...	0-...	15.2	9	4	3	0	8-1	13	.173
	—Los Angeles (N.L.)	0	0	...	3.10	1.48	17	0	0	0	1	0-0	20.1	19	9	7	1	11-1	15	.232
	—Albuquerque (PCL)	3	0	1.000	0.00	0.67	13	0	0	0	...	2-...	16.1	8	0	0	0	3-0	14	.145
1996—	Los Angeles (N.L.)	0	1	.000	4.78	1.57	28	0	0	0	1	0-0	43.1	48	25	23	4	20-4	36	.282
	—Detroit (A.L.)	1	1	.500	3.24	1.64	24	0	0	0	1	0-2	25.0	27	11	9	3	14-3	15	.284
1997—	Indianapolis (A.A.)	1	0	1.000	1.27	1.27	26	5	0	0	...	2-...	42.2	41	7	6	1	13-1	26	.261
	—Cincinnati (N.L.)	0	0	...	6.75	2.25	1	0	0	0	0	0-0	1.1	2	2	1	0	1-0	2	.333
1998—	Indianapolis (Int'l)	2	5	.286	4.54	1.39	61	0	0	0	...	2-...	73.1	73	42	37	8	29-3	60	.258
1999—	Tucson (PCL)	1	3	.250	9.07	2.14	27	1	0	0	...	1-...	41.2	63	47	42	7	26-3	36	.350
	—Adirondack (North.)	4	2	.667	3.75	1.31	7	7	1	0	...	0-...	48.0	52	22	20	1	11-...	49	...
2000—	Buffalo (Int'l)	0	0	...	40.50	6.00	1	0	0	0	...	0-...	0.2	4	3	3	0	0-0	0	.667
	—Adirondack (North.)	7	1	.875	1.80	1.22	10	10	0	0	...	0-...	65.0	55	25	13	...	24-...	57	...
	—Ottawa (Int'l)	0	4	.000	3.64	1.30	10	9	0	0	...	0-...	59.1	55	31	24	8	22-0	34	.250
2001—	Ottawa (Int'l)	2	3	.400	2.24	1.01	34	1	0	0	...	7-...	52.1	42	16	13	6	11-0	54	.220
	—Montreal (N.L.)	0	1	.000	4.85	1.52	24	0	0	0	2	0-2	29.2	29	17	16	4	16-1	19	.257
2002—	Ottawa (Int'l)	1	0	1.000	0.00	0.79	11	0	0	0	...	4-...	14.0	8	4	0	0	3-0	15	.167
	—Montreal (N.L.)	6	1	.857	1.34	1.14	59	0	0	0	11	2-3	53.2	43	11	8	1	18-5	51	.224
2003—	Montreal (N.L.)	2	2	.500	3.06	1.32	70	0	0	0	15	1-4	53.0	57	27	18	7	13-1	40	.282
2004—	GC Expos (GCL)	0	0	...	0.00	0.00	2	1	0	0	...	0-...	1.0	0	0	0	0	0-0	2	.000
	—Brevard County (FSL)	0	0	...	0.00	1.00	4	4	0	0	...	0-...	6.0	5	4	0	0	1-0	7	.217
	—Montreal (N.L.)	0	1	.000	3.93	1.31	21	0	0	0	2	0-1	18.1	16	10	8	2	8-2	17	.232
2005—	New Orleans (PCL)	0	0	...	1.35	1.05	6	4	0	0	...	0-...	6.2	4	1	1	0	3-0	6	.167
	—Was. (N.L.)	2	1	.667	3.22	1.46	57	0	0	0	8	0-1	36.1	34	14	13	1	19-7	30	.252
	American League totals (1 year)	1	1	.500	3.24	1.64	24	0	0	0	1	0-2	25.0	27	11	9	3	14-3	15	.284
	National League totals (9 years)	10	7	.588	3.44	1.39	278	0	0	0	40	3-11	256.2	252	119	98	20	106-21	211	.258
	Major League totals (9 years)	11	8	.579	3.42	1.42	302	0	0	0	41	3-13	281.2	279	130	107	23	120-24	226	.261

ELARTON, SCOTT   P

PERSONAL: Born February 23, 1976, in Lamar, Colo. ... 6-8/240. ... Throws right, bats right. ... Full name: Vincent Scott Elarton. ... High school: Lamar (Colo.).

TRANSACTIONS/CAREER NOTES: Selected by Houston Astros organization in first round (25th pick overall) of 1994 free-agent draft. ... On disabled list (March 29-April 23, 2000); included rehabilitation assignments to New Orleans and Round Rock. ... On disabled list (July 17-September 4, 2001). ... Traded by Astros with a player to be named to Colorado Rockies for P Pedro Astacio and cash (July 31, 2001); Rockies acquired C Garrett Gentry to complete deal (September 27, 2001). ... On disabled list (July 31-September 4, 2001); included rehabilitation assignment to Colorado Springs. ... On disabled list (March 8, 2002-entire season). ... On disabled list (March 26-April 30, 2003); included rehabilitation assignment to Colorado Springs. ... Released by Rockies (May 20, 2004). ... Signed by Cleveland Indians organization (May 25, 2004).

CAREER HITTING: 22-for-162 (.136), 12 R, 2 2B, 0 3B, 0 HR, 3 RBI.

SCOUTING REPORT *Throws:* He uses a fastball that ranges from 87-91 mph, a curve in the low 70s, a slider at 81-83 and a changeup. *Tendencies:* Elarton has short arm action. Velocity has declined slightly. Is a fly-ball pitcher who has learned to pitch without his best fastball. Will cut his fastball and also throw a two-seamer at times. Curve has a big break but good rotation. Slider often is flat. Has good arm speed with his changeup. Holds runners on well. Has above-average command and a good idea of how to pitch. *Outlook:* He is a fifth starter who has increased his innings the past two seasons after dealing with arm problems. *Grade 7.3*

SCOTT ELARTON'S PITCHING ZONE

.257	.286	.196
.254	.394	.285
.274	.368	.286

LEFTY-RIGHTY SPLITS

vs.	Avg.	AB	H	2B	3B	HR	RBI	BB	SO	OBP	Slg.
L	.275	327	90	17	2	14	44	21	56	.315	.468
R	.261	380	99	16	1	18	47	27	47	.315	.450

Year	Team (League)	W	L	Pct.	ERA	WHIP	G	GS	CG	ShO	Hld.	Sv.-Opp.	IP	H	R	ER	HR	BB-IBB	SO	Avg.
1994—	GC Astros (GCL)	4	0	1.000	0.00	0.50	5	5	0	0	...	0-...	28.0	9	0	0	0	5-0	28	.103
	—Quad City (Midw.)	4	1	.800	3.29	1.10	9	9	0	0	...	0-...	54.2	42	23	20	4	18-0	42	.213
1995—	Quad City (Midw.)	13	7	.650	4.18	1.47	26	26	0	0	...	0-...	149.2	149	86	74	12	71-2	112	.259
1996—	Kissimmee (Fla. St.)	12	7	.632	2.92	1.21	27	27	3	1	...	0-...	172.1	154	67	56	13	54-0	130	.241
1997—	Jackson (Texas)	7	4	.636	3.24	1.13	20	20	2	0	...	0-...	133.1	103	57	48	6	47-3	141	.210
	—New Orleans (A.A.)	4	4	.500	5.33	1.26	9	9	0	0	...	0-...	54.0	51	36	32	5	17-1	50	.249
1998—	New Orleans (PCL)	9	4	.692	4.01	1.22	14	14	2	1	...	0-...	92.0	71	42	41	6	41-3	100	.212
	—Houston (N.L.)	2	1	.667	3.32	1.05	28	2	0	0	2	2-3	57.0	40	21	21	5	20-0	56	.196
1999—	Houston (N.L.)	9	5	.643	3.48	1.24	42	15	0	0	5	1-4	124.0	111	55	48	8	43-0	121	.238
2000—	New Orleans (PCL)	1	0	1.000	0.75	0.58	2	2	0	0	...	0-...	12.0	3	1	1	0	4-0	12	.081
	—Round Rock (Texas)	1	0	1.000	2.84	1.11	1	1	0	0	...	0-...	6.1	7	2	2	1	0-0	7	.280
	—Houston (N.L.)	17	7	.708	4.81	1.46	30	30	2	0	0	0-0	192.2	198	117	103	29	84-1	131	.263
2001—	Houston (N.L.)	4	8	.333	7.14	1.60	20	20	0	0	0	0-0	109.2	126	88	87	26	49-1	76	.290
	—Colo. Springs (PCL)	0	1	.000	7.04	1.83	2	2	0	0	...	0-...	7.2	14	6	6	2	0-0	8	.378
	—Colorado (N.L.)	0	2	.000	6.65	1.30	4	4	0	0	0	0-0	23.0	20	17	17	8	10-1	11	.233
2002—	Colorado (N.L.)			Did not play.																
2003—	Colo. Springs (PCL)	6	8	.429	5.31	1.60	20	20	0	0	...	0-...	118.2	146	81	70	15	39-1	92	.298
	—Colorado (N.L.)	4	4	.500	6.27	1.80	11	10	0	0	0	0-0	51.2	73	46	36	13	20-3	20	.329
2004—	Colorado (N.L.)	0	6	.000	9.80	1.86	8	8	0	0	0	0-0	41.1	57	45	45	8	20-1	23	.319
	—Buffalo (Int'l)	1	1	.500	3.15	1.20	3	3	1	1	...	0-...	20.0	19	7	7	1	5-0	10	.250
	—Cleveland (A.L.)	3	5	.375	4.53	1.27	21	21	1	1	0	0-0	117.1	107	62	59	25	42-2	80	.240
2005—	Cleveland (A.L.)	11	9	.550	4.61	1.30	31	31	1	0	0	0-0	181.2	189	100	93	32	48-1	103	.264
	American League totals (2 years)	14	14	.500	4.58	1.29	52	52	2	1	0	0-0	299.0	296	162	152	57	90-3	183	.257
	National League totals (6 years)	36	33	.522	5.36	1.45	143	89	2	0	7	3-7	599.1	625	389	357	97	246-7	438	.267
	Major League totals (7 years)	50	47	.515	5.10	1.40	195	141	4	1	7	3-7	898.1	921	551	509	154	336-10	621	.264

DIVISION SERIES RECORD

Year	Team (League)	W	L	Pct.	ERA	WHIP	G	GS	CG	ShO	Hld.	Sv.-Opp.	IP	H	R	ER	HR	BB-IBB	SO	Avg.
1998—	Houston (N.L.)	0	1	.000	4.50	1.00	1	0	0	0	0	0-0	2.0	1	1	1	0	1-0	3	.167
1999—	Houston (N.L.)	0	0	...	3.86	2.14	2	0	0	0	0	0-0	2.1	4	1	1	0	1-0	3	.400
	Division series totals (2 years)	0	1	.000	4.15	1.62	3	0	0	0	0	0-0	4.1	5	2	2	0	2-0	6	.313

ELDRED, BRAD — 1B

PERSONAL: Born July 12, 1980, in Fort Lauderdale, Fla. ... 6-5/245. ... Bats right, throws right. ... Full name: Bradley Ross Eldred. ... High school: Coconut Creek (Fla.). ... College: Florida International.
TRANSACTIONS/CAREER NOTES: Selected by Pittsburgh Pirates organization in sixth round of 2002 free-agent draft.
2005 GAMES PLAYED BY POSITION (MLB): 1B—50.

BRAD ELDRED'S HITTING ZONE

.364	.167	.000
.269	.300	.263
.500	.200	.000

SCOUTING REPORT *Offense:* He is a big, strong power hitter who feasts on mistakes, especially mistake fastballs. Strikes out too much, partly because he chases too many pitches. More big-league at-bats should help because he showed a more disciplined approach in the minors. Needs to use the rest of the field more. *Defense:* Eldred moves well for someone his size, and he has average skills around the base. *Outlook:* If the Pirates' top power-hitting prospect can improve his on-base percentage just a little, look for him to be in the middle of the order this season. *Grade 7.4*

LEFTY-RIGHTY SPLITS

vs.	Avg.	AB	H	2B	3B	HR	RBI	BB	SO	OBP	Slg.
L	.260	50	13	2	0	2	4	5	22	.321	.420
R	.207	140	29	7	0	10	23	8	55	.263	.471

Year Team (League)	Pos.	G	AB	R	H	2B	3B	HR	RBI	BB	SO	HBP	GDP	SB-CS	Avg.	OBP	SLG	OPS	E	Avg.
2002— Will. (NYP)	1B-OF	72	276	43	78	22	3	10	48	18	74	6	4	10-1	.283	.338	.493	.831	10	.982
2003— Hickory (S. Atl.)	1B	115	420	62	105	22	0	28	80	38	142	11	5	7-1	.250	.326	.502	.828	9	.990
2004— Lynchburg (Caro.)	1B	91	335	54	104	22	1	21	77	35	97	15	4	5-2	.310	.397	.570	.967	10	.994
— Altoona (East.)	1B	39	147	24	41	9	0	17	60	6	51	5	3	0-0	.279	.329	.687	1.016	2	.997
2005— Altoona (East.)	1B-DH	21	84	22	28	6	0	13	27	8	25	0	0	1-1	.333	.387	.869	1.256	2	.989
— Indianapolis (Int'l)	1B-DH	54	195	31	55	13	1	15	48	14	57	3	3	4-0	.282	.336	.590	.926	4	.989
— Pittsburgh (N.L.)	1B	55	190	23	42	9	0	12	27	13	77	3	5	1-1	.221	.279	.458	.737	7	.985
Major League totals (1 year)		55	190	23	42	9	0	12	27	13	77	3	5	1-1	.221	.279	.458	.737	7	.985

ELDRED, CAL — P

PERSONAL: Born November 24, 1967, in Cedar Rapids, Iowa. ... 6-4/240. ... Throws right, bats right. ... Full name: Calvin John Eldred. ... Name pronounced: EL-dred. ... Junior college: Urbana (Iowa) Community College. ... College: Iowa.
TRANSACTIONS/CAREER NOTES: Selected by Milwaukee Brewers organization in first round (17th pick overall) of 1989 free-agent draft. ... On disabled list (May 15, 1995-remainder of season). ... On disabled list (March 29-July 14, 1996); included rehabilitation assignment to New Orleans. ... On disabled list (July 26, 1998-remainder of season). ... On disabled list (March 29-April 20 and July 2-August 15, 1999); included rehabilitation assignments to Huntsville and Louisville. ... Traded by Brewers with SS Jose Valentin to Chicago White Sox for Ps Jaime Navarro and John Snyder (January 12, 2000). ... On disabled list (July 15-September 27, 2000); included rehabilitation assignment to Charlotte. ... On disabled list (April 12, 2001-remainder of season). ... Signed as a free agent by St. Louis Cardinals organization (December 18, 2002). ... On disabled list (April 15-June 12, 2005); included rehabilitation assignment to Springfield.
HONORS: Named A.L. Rookie Pitcher of the Year by THE SPORTING NEWS (1992).
CAREER HITTING: 8-for-72 (.111), 7 R, 2 2B, 0 3B, 0 HR, 4 RBI.

CAL ELDRED'S PITCHING ZONE

.250	.000	.222
.412	.500	.182
.214	.250	.385

SCOUTING REPORT *Throws:* Eldred features a fastball at 88-90 mph, a curveball at 75-77 and a changeup. *Tendencies:* Eldred's four-seam fastball has very good life. Pitches up in the zone but can change the hitter's focus with a tightly rotating curve that breaks straight down. Is more effective pitching to lefthanders than righthanders because of his curve and change. Is a fly-ball pitcher who will give up the long ball. *Outlook:* Eldred's stuff has declined and now is pitching less often and in less critical roles. Will provide innings when healthy, however. Is near the end of his career. *Grade 5.9*

LEFTY-RIGHTY SPLITS

vs.	Avg.	AB	H	2B	3B	HR	RBI	BB	SO	OBP	Slg.
L	.230	61	14	0	0	2	5	11	16	.347	.328
R	.284	74	21	4	0	1	7	7	13	.357	.378

Year Team (League)	W	L	Pct.	ERA	WHIP	G	GS	CG	ShO	Hld.	Sv.-Opp.	IP	H	R	ER	HR	BB-IBB	SO	Avg.
1989— Beloit (Midw.)	2	1	.667	2.30	1.09	5	5	0	0	...	0-...	31.1	23	10	8	0	11-1	32	.202
1990— Stockton (Calif.)	4	2	.667	1.62	1.00	7	7	3	1	...	0-...	50.0	31	12	9	2	19-0	75	.177
— El Paso (Texas)	5	4	.556	4.49	1.57	19	19	0	0	...	0-...	110.1	126	61	55	9	47-0	93	.293
1991— Denver (A.A.)	13	9	.591	3.75	1.32	29	29	3	1	...	0-...	185.0	161	82	77	13	84-2	168	.237
— Milwaukee (A.L.)	2	0	1.000	4.50	1.63	3	3	0	0	0	0-0	16.0	20	9	8	2	6-0	10	.299
1992— Denver (A.A.)	10	6	.625	3.00	1.16	19	19	4	1	0	0-...	141.0	122	49	47	9	42-0	99	.237
— Milwaukee (A.L.)	11	2	.846	1.79	0.99	14	14	2	1	0	0-0	100.1	76	21	20	4	23-0	62	.207
1993— Milwaukee (A.L.)	16	16	.500	4.01	1.25	36	•36	8	1	0	0-0	*258.0	232	120	115	32	91-5	180	.239
1994— Milwaukee (A.L.)	11	11	.500	4.68	1.35	25	•25	6	0	0	0-0	179.0	158	96	93	23	84-0	98	.236
1995— Milwaukee (A.L.)	1	1	.500	3.42	1.44	4	4	0	0	0	0-0	23.2	24	10	9	4	10-0	18	.261
1996— New Orleans (A.A.)	2	2	.500	3.34	1.27	6	6	0	0	0	0-...	32.1	24	12	12	2	17-0	30	.205
— Milwaukee (A.L.)	4	4	.500	4.46	1.42	15	15	0	0	0	0-0	84.2	82	43	42	8	38-0	50	.259
1997— Milwaukee (A.L.)	13	•15	.464	4.99	1.47	34	34	1	1	0	0-0	202.0	207	118	112	31	89-0	122	.266
1998— Milwaukee (A.L.)	4	8	.333	4.80	1.64	23	23	0	0	0	0-0	133.0	157	82	71	14	61-3	86	.297
1999— Huntsville (Sou.)	0	1	.000	7.50	1.33	2	2	1	0	0	0-...	12.0	13	10	10	2	3-0	10	.260
— Louisville (Int'l)	0	1	.000	5.30	1.55	4	4	0	0	0	0-0	18.2	19	12	11	4	10-0	21	.250
— Milwaukee (N.L.)	2	8	.200	7.79	1.79	20	15	0	0	0	0-0	82.0	101	75	71	19	46-0	60	.297
2000— Chicago (A.L.)	10	2	.833	4.58	1.45	20	20	0	0	0	0-0	112.0	103	61	57	12	59-0	97	.244
— Charlotte (Int'l)	0	1	.000	0.80	0.80	2	2	0	0	0	0-...	5.0	4	4	4	2	0-0	1	.211
2001— Chicago (A.L.)	0	1	.000	13.50	2.50	2	2	0	0	0	0-0	6.0	12	9	9	1	3-1	6	.429
2002—	Did not play.																		
2003— St. Louis (N.L.)	7	4	.636	3.74	1.38	62	0	0	0	11	8-14	67.1	62	32	28	9	31-4	67	.249
2004— St. Louis (N.L.)	4	2	.667	3.76	1.31	52	0	0	0	9	1-3	67.0	71	31	28	11	17-1	54	.276
2005— Springfield (Texas)	1	0	1.000	0.00	0.83	3	0	0	0	0	0-0	6.0	5	0	0	0	0-0	1	.238

Year Team (League)	W	L	Pct.	ERA	WHIP	G	GS	CG	ShO	Hld.	Sv.-Opp.	IP	H	R	ER	HR	BB-IBB	SO	Avg.
—St. Louis (N.L.)	1	0	1.000	2.19	1.43	31	1	0	0	2	0-1	37.0	35	9	9	3	18-3	29	.259
American League totals (9 years)	68	52	.567	4.26	1.34	153	153	19	4	0	0-0	981.2	914	487	465	117	403-6	643	.246
National League totals (5 years)	18	22	.450	4.82	1.55	188	39	0	0	22	9-18	386.1	426	229	207	56	173-11	296	.282
Major League totals (14 years)	86	74	.538	4.42	1.40	341	192	19	4	22	9-18	1368.0	1340	716	672	173	576-17	939	.257

DIVISION SERIES RECORD

Year Team (League)	W	L	Pct.	ERA	WHIP	G	GS	CG	ShO	Hld.	Sv.-Opp.	IP	H	R	ER	HR	BB-IBB	SO	Avg.
2004—St. Louis (N.L.)	0	0	...	0.00	4.50	2	0	0	0	0	0-0	0.2	1	0	0	0	2-0	0	.333
2005—St. Louis (N.L.)	0	0	...	27.00	4.50	1	0	0	0	0	0-0	0.2	2	2	2	0	1-0	0	.500
Division series totals (2 years)	0	0	...	13.50	4.50	3	0	0	0	0	0-0	1.1	3	2	2	0	3-0	0	.429

CHAMPIONSHIP SERIES RECORD

Year Team (League)	W	L	Pct.	ERA	WHIP	G	GS	CG	ShO	Hld.	Sv.-Opp.	IP	H	R	ER	HR	BB-IBB	SO	Avg.
2004—St. Louis (N.L.)	0	0	...	0.00	3.00	1	0	0	0	0	0-0	0.1	0	0	0	0	1-0	0	.000

WORLD SERIES RECORD

Year Team (League)	W	L	Pct.	ERA	WHIP	G	GS	CG	ShO	Hld.	Sv.-Opp.	IP	H	R	ER	HR	BB-IBB	SO	Avg.
2004—St. Louis (N.L.)	0	0	...	10.80	2.40	2	0	0	0	0	0-0	1.2	4	2	2	0	0-0	2	.444

ELLIS, MARK   2B/SS

PERSONAL: Born June 6, 1977, in Rapid City, S.D. ... 5-11/180. ... Bats right, throws right. ... Full name: Mark William Ellis. ... High school: Stevens (Rapid City, S.D.). ... College: Florida.

TRANSACTIONS/CAREER NOTES: Selected by Kansas City Royals organization in ninth round of 1999 free-agent draft. ... Traded by Royals with OF Johnny Damon and cash to Oakland Athletics as part of three-team deal in which Royals acquired P Roberto Hernandez from Tampa Bay Devil Rays, A's acquired P Cory Lidle from Devil Rays, Royals acquired C A.J. Hinch, IF Angel Berroa and cash from A's and Devil Rays received OF Ben Grieve and cash from A's (January 8, 2001). ... On disabled list (March 26, 2004-entire season).

2005 GAMES PLAYED BY POSITION (MLB): 2B—115, SS—7, 1B—2, DH—1.

SCOUTING REPORT Offense: Ellis is a steady player with a short stroke and good bat control. Regained his bat speed after missing 2004 because of shoulder surgery. Will go with the pitch to the opposite field. Is a contact hitter who likes the ball up but doesn't have much power. Is an average runner who doesn't steal a lot of bases. *Defense:* He does not throw as well as he did prior to the injury, but Ellis has a quick release and makes the pivot well on the double play. Gets hit a lot. Has good hands with good range to either side. Charges the ball well and has good instincts. *Outlook:* Ellis should continue to improve another year removed from surgery. Is an extremely professional player. *Grade 7.5*

MARK ELLIS' HITTING ZONE

.367	.357	.273
.284	.440	.243
.413	.233	.333

LEFTY-RIGHTY SPLITS

vs.	Avg.	AB	H	2B	3B	HR	RBI	BB	SO	OBP	Slg.
L	.313	112	35	7	3	3	15	15	10	.403	.509
R	.317	322	102	14	2	10	37	29	41	.377	.466

Year Team (League)	Pos.	G	AB	R	H	2B	3B	HR	RBI	BB	SO	HBP	GDP	SB-CS	Avg.	OBP	SLG	OPS	E	Avg.
1999—Spokane (N'west)	SS	71	281	67	92	14	0	7	47	47	40	3	1	21-7	.327	.424	.452	.876	16	.958
2000—Wilmington (Caro.)	2B-SS	132	484	83	146	27	4	6	62	78	72	7	11	25-7	.302	.404	.411	.815	31	.954
—Wichita (Texas)	2B	7	22	4	7	1	0	0	4	5	5	0	0	1-0	.318	.444	.364	.808	0	1.000
2001—Sacramento (PCL)	SS	132	472	71	129	38	0	10	53	54	78	5	13	21-7	.273	.351	.417	.768	19	.968
2002—Sacramento (PCL)	SS	21	84	14	25	10	1	0	5	6	13	4	1	4-0	.298	.372	.440	.813	3	.974
—Oakland (A.L.)	DH-SS-3B	98	345	58	94	16	4	6	35	44	54	4	3	4-2	.272	.359	.394	.753	11	.976
2003—Oakland (A.L.)	2B	154	553	78	137	31	5	9	52	48	94	7	7	6-2	.248	.313	.371	.684	14	.982
2004—Oakland (A.L.)							Did not play - injured.													
2005—Oakland (A.L.)	2B-SS-1B-DH	122	434	76	137	21	5	13	52	44	51	4	10	1-3	.316	.384	.477	.861	6	.989
Major League totals (3 years)		374	1332	212	368	68	14	28	139	136	199	15	20	11-7	.276	.348	.411	.759	31	.983

DIVISION SERIES RECORD

Year Team (League)	Pos.	G	AB	R	H	2B	3B	HR	RBI	BB	SO	HBP	GDP	SB-CS	Avg.	OBP	SLG	OPS	E	Avg.
2002—Oakland (A.L.)	2B	5	19	1	7	2	0	1	4	1	2	0	0	0-0	.368	.400	.632	1.032	1	.960
2003—Oakland (A.L.)	2B	5	17	2	2	0	0	0	0	4	7	1	0	0-0	.118	.318	.118	.436	1	.964
Division series totals (2 years)		10	36	3	9	2	0	1	4	5	9	1	0	0-0	.250	.357	.389	.746	2	.962

ELLISON, JASON   OF

PERSONAL: Born April 4, 1978, in Quincy, Calif. ... 5-10/180. ... Bats right, throws right. ... Full name: Jason Jerome Ellison. ... High school: South Kitsap High (Port Orchard, Wash.). ... College: Lewis-Clark State (Lewiston, Idaho).

TRANSACTIONS/CAREER NOTES: Selected by San Francisco Giants organization in 22nd round of 2000 free-agent draft.

2005 GAMES PLAYED BY POSITION (MLB): OF—122.

JASON ELLISON'S HITTING ZONE

.293	.500	.385
.207	.357	.370
.279	.400	.100

LEFTY-RIGHTY SPLITS

vs.	Avg.	AB	H	2B	3B	HR	RBI	BB	SO	OBP	Slg.
L	.328	119	39	7	1	2	8	9	16	.375	.454
R	.232	233	54	11	1	2	16	15	28	.286	.313

Year Team (League)	Pos.	G	AB	R	H	2B	3B	HR	RBI	BB	SO	HBP	GDP	SB-CS	Avg.	OBP	SLG	OPS	E	Avg.
2000—Salem-Keizer (N'west)	OF	74	300	67	90	15	2	0	28	29	45	7	1	13-7	.300	.374	.363	.737	4	.976
2001—Hagerstown (SAL)	OF	130	494	95	144	38	8	5	55	71	66	10	6	19-15	.291	.388	.429	.817	5	.984
2002—San Jose (Calif.)	OF	81	322	40	87	13	0	5	40	25	37	2	10	9-9	.270	.325	.357	.682	4	.980

E

Year Team (League)	Pos.	G	AB	R	H	2B	3B	HR	RBI	BB	SO	HBP	GDP	SB-CS	Avg.	OBP	SLG	OPS	E	Avg.
—Fresno (PCL)	OF	49	196	31	61	8	1	3	8	21	28	4	4	16-3	.311	.389	.408	.797	1	.992
2003—San Francisco (N.L.)	OF	7	10	1	1	0	0	0	0	0	1	0	0	0-0	.100	.100	.100	.200	0	1.000
—Fresno (PCL)	OF-DH	119	461	74	136	22	4	6	39	39	52	6	7	21-13	.295	.356	.399	.755	9	.974
2004—Fresno (PCL)	OF	125	505	90	159	32	7	9	40	40	66	3	8	27-12	.315	.368	.459	.827	6	.983
—San Francisco (N.L.)	OF	13	4	4	2	0	0	1	3	0	1	0	0	2-0	.500	.500	1.250	1.750	0	1.000
2005—Fresno (PCL)	OF	8	38	5	9	2	0	0	3	2	9	1	0	0-0	.237	.293	.289	.582	0	1.000
—San Francisco (N.L.)	OF	131	352	49	93	18	2	4	24	24	44	3	7	14-6	.264	.316	.361	.677	8	.968
Major League totals (3 years)		151	366	54	96	18	2	5	27	24	46	3	7	16-6	.262	.312	.363	.676	8	.969

EMBREE, ALAN   P

PERSONAL: Born January 23, 1970, in The Dalles, Ore. ... 6-2/190. ... Throws left, bats left. ... Full name: Alan Duane Embree. ... Name pronounced: EMM-bree. ... High school: Prairie (Vancouver, Wash.).

TRANSACTIONS/CAREER NOTES: Selected by Cleveland Indians organization in fifth round of 1989 free-agent draft. ... On disabled list (April 1-June 2 and June 2, 1993-remainder of season); included rehabilitation assignment to Canton/Akron. ... On disabled list (August 1-September 7, 1996); included rehabilitation assignment to Buffalo. ... Traded by Indians with OF Kenny Lofton to Atlanta Braves for OFs Marquis Grissom and David Justice (March 25, 1997). ... Traded by Braves to Arizona Diamondbacks for P Russ Springer (June 23, 1998). ... Traded by Diamondbacks to San Francisco Giants for OF Dante Powell (November 10, 1998). ... On disabled list (May 23-June 12, 2001); included rehabilitation assignment to Fresno. ... Traded by Giants to Chicago White Sox for P Derek Hasselhoff (June 29, 2001). ... Signed as a free agent by San Diego Padres (January 3, 2002). ... Traded by Padres with P Andy Shibilo to Boston Red Sox for Ps Brad Baker and Dan Giese (June 26, 2002). ... On disabled list (July 14-29, 2002). ... On disabled list (April 9-29, 2003); included rehabilitation assignment to Sarasota. ... Released by Red Sox (July 27, 2005). ... Signed by New York Yankees (July 30, 2005).

CAREER HITTING: 0-for-2 (.000), 0 R, 0 2B, 0 3B, 0 HR, 0 RBI.

SCOUTING REPORT **Throws:** Embree relies on a riding fastball that clocks from 90-94 mph. Also has a slider. **Tendencies:** Essentially, he is a one-speed pitcher who likes to work up in the zone. Tends to throw only fastballs. Has an easy motion and is easy for hitters to follow. Fastball lacks late movement and was not effective to lefthanders due to the lack of bite on his slider. **Outlook:** Embree has lost some off his fastball and rarely pitches at his upper velocity range. Lack of sharpness in his breaking ball is a bigger problem; that prevents him from doing his job, which is to get out lefthanders. *Grade 5.7*

ALAN EMBREE'S PITCHING ZONE

.294	.111	.176
.237	.619	.308
.412	.333	.292

LEFTY-RIGHTY SPLITS

vs.	Avg.	AB	H	2B	3B	HR	RBI	BB	SO	OBP	Slg.
L	.317	101	32	9	0	4	20	7	20	.360	.525
R	.278	108	30	12	1	6	23	7	18	.325	.574

Year Team (League)	W	L	Pct.	ERA	WHIP	G	GS	CG	ShO	Hld.	Sv.-Opp.	IP	H	R	ER	HR	BB-IBB	SO	Avg.
1990—Burlington (Appal.)	4	4	.500	2.64	1.43	15	15	0	0	...	0-...	81.2	87	36	24	3	30-0	58	.274
1991—Columbus (S. Atl.)	10	8	.556	3.59	1.31	27	26	3	1	...	0-...	155.1	126	80	62	4	77-1	137	.224
1992—Kinston (Carol.)	10	5	.667	3.30	1.20	15	15	1	0	...	0-...	101.0	89	48	37	10	32-0	115	.234
—Cant./Akr. (Eastern)	7	2	.778	2.28	1.13	12	12	0	0	...	0-...	79.0	61	24	20	2	28-1	56	.216
—Cleveland (A.L.)	0	2	.000	7.00	1.50	4	4	0	0	0	0-0	18.0	19	14	14	3	8-0	12	.271
1993—Cant./Akr. (Eastern)	0	0	...	3.38	1.13	1	1	0	0	0	...	5.1	3	2	2	0	3-0	4	.176
1994—Cant./Akr. (Eastern)	9	16	.360	5.50	1.57	30	27	2	1	...	0-...	157.0	183	106	96	15	64-3	81	.294
1995—Buffalo (A.A.)	3	4	.429	0.89	1.23	30	0	0	0	...	5-...	40.2	31	10	4	0	19-2	56	.211
—Cleveland (A.L.)	3	2	.600	5.11	1.58	23	0	0	0	6	1-1	24.2	23	16	14	2	16-0	23	.253
1996—Cleveland (A.L.)	1	1	.500	6.39	1.65	24	0	0	0	1	0-0	31.0	30	26	22	10	21-3	33	.259
—Buffalo (A.A.)	4	1	.800	3.93	1.17	20	0	0	0	...	5-...	34.1	26	16	15	1	14-0	46	.210
1997—Atlanta (N.L.)	3	1	.750	2.54	1.22	66	0	0	0	16	0-0	46.0	36	13	13	1	20-2	45	.221
1998—Atlanta (N.L.)	1	0	1.000	4.34	1.77	20	0	0	0	6	0-1	18.2	23	14	9	2	10-0	19	.307
—Arizona (N.L.)	3	2	.600	4.11	1.31	35	0	0	0	6	1-2	35.0	33	18	16	5	13-0	24	.248
1999—San Francisco (N.L.)	3	2	.600	3.38	1.16	68	0	0	0	22	0-3	58.2	42	22	22	6	26-2	53	.200
2000—San Francisco (N.L.)	3	5	.375	4.95	1.45	63	0	0	0	9	2-5	60.0	62	34	33	4	25-2	49	.274
2001—San Francisco (N.L.)	0	2	.000	11.25	2.20	22	0	0	0	0	0-1	20.0	34	26	25	7	10-2	25	.374
—Fresno (PCL)	1	0	1.000	1.13	0.75	7	0	0	0	...	1-...	8.0	5	3	1	0	1-0	6	.179
—Chicago (A.L.)	1	2	.333	5.03	1.12	39	0	0	0	9	0-2	34.0	31	21	19	7	7-0	34	.242
2002—San Diego (N.L.)	3	4	.429	1.26	1.12	36	0	0	0	10	0-2	28.2	23	7	4	2	9-2	38	.211
—Boston (A.L.)	1	2	.333	2.97	1.05	32	0	0	0	8	2-5	33.1	24	12	11	4	11-1	43	.203
2003—Sarasota (Fla. St.)	0	0	...	13.50	3.00	1	1	0	0	...	0-...	0.2	2	1	1	0	0-0	2	.500
—Boston (A.L.)	4	1	.800	4.25	1.18	65	0	0	0	14	1-2	55.0	49	26	26	5	16-3	45	.241
2004—Boston (A.L.)	2	2	.500	4.13	1.15	71	0	0	0	20	0-1	52.1	49	28	24	7	11-1	37	.244
2005—Boston (A.L.)	1	4	.200	7.65	1.41	43	0	0	0	4	1-3	37.2	42	33	32	8	11-2	30	.284
—New York (A.L.)	1	1	.500	7.53	1.60	24	0	0	0	6	0-0	14.1	20	14	12	2	3-1	8	.328
American League totals (8 years)	14	17	.452	5.21	1.30	325	4	0	0	68	5-14	300.1	287	190	174	48	104-11	265	.253
National League totals (6 years)	16	16	.500	4.11	1.37	310	0	0	0	69	3-14	267.0	253	134	122	27	113-10	253	.251
Major League totals (12 years)	30	33	.476	4.70	1.33	635	4	0	0	137	8-28	567.1	540	324	296	75	217-21	518	.252

DIVISION SERIES RECORD

Year Team (League)	W	L	Pct.	ERA	WHIP	G	GS	CG	ShO	Hld.	Sv.-Opp.	IP	H	R	ER	HR	BB-IBB	SO	Avg.
1996—Cleveland (A.L.)	0	0	...	9.00	0.00	3	0	0	0	1	0-0	1.0	0	1	1	0	0-0	1	.000
2000—San Francisco (N.L.)	0	0	...	0.00	0.00	2	0	0	0	1	0-0	1.2	0	0	0	0	0-0	0	.000
2003—Boston (A.L.)	0	0	...	0.00	0.50	3	0	0	0	1	0-1	2.0	1	0	0	0	0-0	3	.143
2004—Boston (A.L.)	0	0	...	0.00	1.00	2	0	0	0	0	0-0	1.0	1	0	0	0	0-0	1	.000
Division series totals (4 years)	0	0	...	1.59	0.35	10	0	0	0	3	0-1	5.2	2	1	1	0	0-0	5	.059

CHAMPIONSHIP SERIES RECORD

Year Team (League)	W	L	Pct.	ERA	WHIP	G	GS	CG	ShO	Hld.	Sv.-Opp.	IP	H	R	ER	HR	BB-IBB	SO	Avg.
1995—Cleveland (A.L.)	0	0	...	0.00	0.00	1	0	0	0	0	0-0	0.1	0	0	0	0	0-0	1	.000
1997—Atlanta (N.L.)	0	0	...	0.00	1.00	1	0	0	0	0	0-0	1.0	1	0	0	0	1-0	1	.000
2003—Boston (A.L.)	1	0	1.000	0.00	0.64	5	0	0	0	0	0-0	4.2	3	0	0	0	0-0	1	.214
2004—Boston (A.L.)	0	0	...	3.86	2.14	6	0	0	0	0	0-0	4.2	9	2	2	0	1-1	2	.409
Champ. series totals (4 years)	1	0	1.000	1.69	1.31	13	0	0	0	0	0-0	10.2	12	2	2	0	2-1	5	.308

E

Year Team (League)	W	L	Pct.	ERA	WHIP	G	GS	CG	ShO	Hld.	Sv.-Opp.	IP	H	R	ER	HR	BB-IBB	SO	Avg.
										WORLD SERIES RECORD									
1995—Cleveland (A.L.)	0	0	...	2.70	1.20	4	0	0	0	1	0-0	3.1	2	1	1	0	2-1	2	.182
2004—Boston (A.L.)	0	0	...	0.00	0.60	3	0	0	0	1	0-0	1.2	1	1	0	0	0-0	4	.167
World Series totals (2 years)	0	0	...	1.80	1.00	7	0	0	0	1	0-0	5.0	3	2	1	0	2-1	6	.176

ENCARNACION, EDWIN   3B

PERSONAL: Born January 7, 1983, in La Romana, Dominican Republic. ... 6-1/195. ... Bats right, throws right. ... Full name: Edwin Encarnacion. ... High school: Manuel Toro (Caguas, Puerto Rico).

TRANSACTIONS/CAREER NOTES: Selected by Texas Rangers organization in ninth round of 2000 free-agent draft. ... Traded by Rangers to with OF Ruben Mateo to Cincinnati Reds for P Rob Bell (June 15, 2001).

2005 GAMES PLAYED BY POSITION (MLB): 3B—56.

EDWIN ENCARNACION'S HITTING ZONE

.250	.333	.133
.400	.364	.095
.200	.714	.000

LEFTY-RIGHTY SPLITS

vs.	Avg.	AB	H	2B	3B	HR	RBI	BB	SO	OBP	Slg.
L	.246	65	16	6	0	3	8	9	12	.338	.477
R	.226	146	33	10	0	6	23	11	48	.294	.418

Year Team (League)	Pos.	G	AB	R	H	2B	3B	HR	RBI	BB	SO	HBP	GDP	SB-CS	Avg.	OBP	SLG	OPS	E	Avg.
									BATTING										**FIELDING**	
2000— GC Rangers (GCL)	3B	51	177	31	55	6	3	0	36	21	27	1	7	3-1	.311	.381	.379	.760	11	.927
2001— Savannah (S. Atl.)	3B	45	170	23	52	9	2	4	25	12	34	2	5	3-3	.306	.355	.453	.808	12	.891
— Dayton (Midw.)	3B-SS	9	37	2	6	2	0	1	6	1	5	0	1	0-1	.162	.184	.297	.481	1	.962
— Billings (Pion.)	3B	52	211	27	55	8	2	5	26	15	29	0	6	8-1	.261	.307	.389	.696	23	.863
2002— Dayton (Midw.)	3B-SS	136	518	80	146	32	4	17	73	40	108	7	15	25-7	.282	.338	.458	.796	40	.889
2003— Chattanooga (Sou.)	3B	67	254	40	69	13	1	5	36	22	44	3	3	8-3	.272	.331	.390	.721	23	.890
— Potomac (Carol.)	3B	58	215	40	69	15	1	6	29	24	32	1	2	7-1	.321	.387	.484	.871	17	.879
2004— Chattanooga (Sou.)	3B	120	469	73	132	35	1	13	76	53	79	5	9	17-3	.281	.352	.443	.795	25	.324
2005— Louisville (Int'l)	3B	78	290	44	91	23	0	15	54	33	53	4	8	7-2	.314	.388	.548	.936	19	.917
— Cincinnati (N.L.)	3B	69	211	25	49	16	0	9	31	20	60	3	8	3-0	.232	.308	.436	.744	10	.944
Major League totals (1 year)		69	211	25	49	16	0	9	31	20	60	3	8	3-0	.232	.308	.436	.744	10	.944

ENCARNACION, JUAN   OF

E

PERSONAL: Born March 8, 1976, in Las Matas de Farfan, Dominican Republic. ... 6-3/215. ... Bats right, throws right. ... Full name: Juan de Dios Encarnacion. ... Name pronounced: en-car-NAH-see-own. ... High school: Liceo Mercedes Maria Mateo (Las Matas de Farfan, Dominican Republic).

TRANSACTIONS/CAREER NOTES: Signed as a non-drafted free agent by Detroit Tigers organization (December 27, 1992). ... On disabled list (March 20-April 29, 1998); included rehabilitation assignment to Lakeland. ... On suspended list (May 27-29, 2000). ... Traded by Tigers with P Luis Pineda to Cincinnati Reds for OF Dmitri Young (December 11, 2001). ... Traded by Reds with OF/2B Wilton Guerrero and P Ryan Snare to Florida Marlins for P Ryan Dempster (July 11, 2002). ... Traded by Marlins to Los Angeles Dodgers for OF Travis Ezi (December 13, 2003). ... On disabled list (July 4-19, 2004). ... Traded by Dodgers with C Paul Lo Duca and P Guillermo Mota to Marlins for Ps Brad Penny and Bill Murphy and 1B Hee Seop Choi (July 30, 2004).

2005 GAMES PLAYED BY POSITION (MLB): OF—139.

SCOUTING REPORT *Offense:* Has a long swing with a slight uppercut but still has good bat speed. Regained his ability to get extension after being injured in 2004. Has become more of a pull hitter. Has a big loop in his swing and will strike out a lot. Has good power down in the zone. Can run but doesn't read pitchers well or get good jumps. *Defense:* Encarnacion is aggressive in charging the ball but inconsistent with his routes, especially when he has to go back. Has an above-average and accurate arm but release is slow. *Outlook:* Encarnacion has good tools for a run producer. Average and home runs will rise if he can lay off pitches up and out of the zone. *Grade 7*

JUAN ENCARNACION'S HITTING ZONE

.281	.263	.273
.337	.438	.357
.231	.304	.250

LEFTY-RIGHTY SPLITS

vs.	Avg.	AB	H	2B	3B	HR	RBI	BB	SO	OBP	Slg.
L	.309	94	29	6	0	3	14	14	18	.398	.468
R	.282	412	116	21	3	13	62	27	86	.337	.442

Year Team (League)	Pos.	G	AB	R	H	2B	3B	HR	RBI	BB	SO	HBP	GDP	SB-CS	Avg.	OBP	SLG	OPS	E	Avg.
									BATTING										**FIELDING**	
1993— Dom. Tigers (DSL)	OF	72	251	36	63	13	4	13	49	15	65			6-...	.251		.490		17	.879
1994— Bristol (Appal.)	OF	54	197	16	49	7	1	4	31	13	54	5	2	9-2	.249	.310	.355	.666	3	.968
— Fayetteville (SAL)	OF	24	83	6	16	1	1	1	4	8	36	1	2	1-1	.193	.272	.265	.537	2	.920
— Lakeland (Fla. St.)	OF	3	6	1	2	0	0	0	0	1	3	1	0	0-0	.333	.429	.333	.762	0	—
1995— Fayetteville (SAL)	OF	124	457	62	129	31	7	16	72	30	113	8	10	30-6	.282	.336	.486	.822	7	.956
1996— Lakeland (Fla. St.)	OF	131	499	54	120	31	2	15	58	24	104	12	10	11-5	.240	.290	.401	.691	6	.976
1997— Jacksonville (Sou.)	OF-DH	131	493	91	159	31	4	26	90	43	86	19	8	17-3	.323	.394	.560	.954	7	.987
— Detroit (A.L.)	OF	11	33	3	7	1	1	1	5	3	12	2	1	3-1	.212	.316	.394	.710	0	1.000
1998— Lakeland (Fla. St.)	OF	4	16	4	4	0	1	0	4	2	4	1	0	4-0	.250	.368	.375	.743	0	1.000
— Toledo (Int'l)	OF-DH	92	356	55	102	17	3	8	41	29	85	10	9	24-4	.287	.353	.419	.772	5	.973
— Detroit (A.L.)	OF-DH	40	164	30	54	9	4	7	21	7	31	1	2	4-0	.329	.354	.561	.915	1	.985
1999— Detroit (A.L.)	OF	132	509	62	130	30	6	19	74	14	113	9	12	33-12	.255	.287	.450	.736	9	.968
2000— Detroit (A.L.)	OF	141	547	75	158	25	6	14	72	29	90	7	15	16-4	.289	.330	.433	.764	5	.987
2001— Detroit (A.L.)	OF-DH	120	417	52	101	19	7	12	52	25	93	6	9	9-5	.242	.292	.408	.700	6	.977
2002— Cincinnati (N.L.)	OF	83	321	43	89	11	2	16	51	26	63	1	7	9-4	.277	.330	.474	.804	5	.977
— Florida (N.L.)	OF	69	263	34	69	11	3	8	34	20	50	3	6	8-0	.262	.317	.418	.735	1	.993
2003— Florida (N.L.)	OF	156	601	80	162	37	6	19	94	37	82	4	17	19-8	.270	.313	.446	.759	0	1.000
2004— Los Angeles (N.L.)	OF	86	324	42	76	18	1	13	43	21	53	4	9	3-3	.235	.289	.417	.705	4	.976
— Florida (N.L.)	OF	49	160	21	38	12	1	3	19	17	33	3	2	2-1	.238	.320	.381	.702	2	.980
2005— Florida (N.L.)	OF	141	506	59	145	27	3	16	76	41	104	9		6-5	.287	.349	.447	.795	4	.983
American League totals (5 years)		444	1670	222	450	84	24	53	224	78	339	25	39	68-26	.269	.310	.444	.753	21	.979
National League totals (4 years)		584	2175	279	579	116	16	75	317	162	385	24	55	51-26	.266	.322	.438	.759	16	.987
Major League totals (9 years)		1028	3845	501	1029	200	40	128	541	240	724	49	94	119-52	.268	.316	.440	.757	37	.983

DIVISION SERIES RECORD

Year Team (League)	Pos.	G	AB	R	H	2B	3B	HR	RBI	BB	SO	HBP	GDP	SB-CS	Avg.	OBP	SLG	OPS	E	Avg.
2003— Florida (N.L.)	OF	4	15	1	2	0	0	1	1	2	3	0	1	0-0	.133	.235	.333	.569	0	1.000

CHAMPIONSHIP SERIES RECORD

Year Team (League)	Pos.	G	AB	R	H	2B	3B	HR	RBI	BB	SO	HBP	GDP	SB-CS	Avg.	OBP	SLG	OPS	E	Avg.
2003— Florida (N.L.)	OF	5	12	1	3	1	0	1	1	0	4	0	1	0-0	.250	.250	.583	.833	0	1.000

WORLD SERIES RECORD

Year Team (League)	Pos.	G	AB	R	H	2B	3B	HR	RBI	BB	SO	HBP	GDP	SB-CS	Avg.	OBP	SLG	OPS	E	Avg.
2003— Florida (N.L.)	OF	6	11	1	2	0	0	0	1	1	5	0	0	0-0	.182	.231	.182	.413	0	1.000

ENSBERG, MORGAN — 3B

PERSONAL: Born August 26, 1975, in Hermosa Beach, Calif. ... 6-2/210. ... Bats right, throws right. ... Full name: Morgan Paul Ensberg. ... High school: Redondo Union (Redondo Beach, Calif.). ... College: Southern California.
TRANSACTIONS/CAREER NOTES: Selected by Seattle Mariners organization in 61st round of 1994 free-agent draft; did not sign. ... Selected by Houston Astros organization in ninth round of 1998 free-agent draft.
2005 GAMES PLAYED BY POSITION (MLB): 3B—148.

SCOUTING REPORT **Offense:** Ensberg continually makes adjustments at the plate. Likes the ball in and has good power when pulling the ball. Has good bat speed and above-average power from center field to left field. Has good hitting aptitude; can change his approach based on the way he feels at the plate. **Defense:** Though his range is limited, Ensberg has good hands and charges the ball well. Plays shallow. Has a strong arm and has improved his accuracy from different throwing angles. **Outlook:** Don't expect Ensberg to repeat his career-year numbers from 2005, but 25-30 home runs and 100 RBIs are reasonable targets because he plays at Minute Maid Park. Is not the best defender; as long as he is productive, that won't be a problem. *Grade 8.3*

MORGAN ENSBERG'S HITTING ZONE

.297	.391	.143
.295	.366	.299
.273	.444	.120

LEFTY-RIGHTY SPLITS

vs.	Avg.	AB	H	2B	3B	HR	RBI	BB	SO	OBP	Slg.
L	.299	134	40	10	0	9	20	24	25	.411	.575
R	.278	392	109	20	3	27	81	61	94	.380	.551

Year Team (League)	Pos.	G	AB	R	H	2B	3B	HR	RBI	BB	SO	HBP	GDP	SB-CS	Avg.	OBP	SLG	OPS	E	Avg.
1998— Auburn (NY-Penn)	3B-SS	59	196	39	45	10	1	5	31	46	51	6	5	15-3	.230	.388	.367	.755	11	.927
1999— Kissimmee (Fla. St.)	1B-3B-SS	123	427	72	102	25	2	15	69	68	90	9	9	17-6	.239	.353	.412	.765	35	.900
2000— Round Rock (Texas)	3B	137	483	95	145	34	0	28	90	92	107	8	15	9-12	.300	.416	.545	.960	24	.942
— Houston (N.L.)	3B	4	7	0	2	0	0	0	0	0	1	0	0	0-0	.286	.286	.286	.571	1	.667
2001— New Orleans (PCL)	3B-SS	87	316	65	98	20	0	23	61	45	60	3	12	6-3	.310	.397	.592	.989	17	.929
2002— Houston (N.L.)	3B	49	132	14	32	7	2	3	19	18	25	3	8	2-0	.242	.346	.394	.740	8	.929
— New Orleans (PCL)	3B-1B	83	292	50	84	12	3	7	37	50	56	7	9	9-5	.288	.401	.421	.822	19	.926
2003— Houston (N.L.)	3B-DH	127	385	69	112	15	1	25	60	48	60	6	10	7-2	.291	.377	.530	.907	9	.967
2004— Houston (N.L.)	3B-SS	131	411	51	113	20	3	10	66	36	46	0	17	6-4	.275	.330	.411	.742	13	.949
2005— Houston (N.L.)	3B	150	526	86	149	30	3	36	101	85	119	8	12	6-7	.283	.388	.557	.945	15	.964
Major League totals (5 years)		461	1461	220	408	72	9	74	246	187	251	17	47	21-13	.279	.365	.493	.858	46	.956

DIVISION SERIES RECORD

Year Team (League)	Pos.	G	AB	R	H	2B	3B	HR	RBI	BB	SO	HBP	GDP	SB-CS	Avg.	OBP	SLG	OPS	E	Avg.
2004— Houston (N.L.)	3B	5	19	1	7	2	0	0	5	3	1	0	1	0-1	.368	.455	.474	.928	0	1.000
2005— Houston (N.L.)	3B	4	18	2	5	2	0	0	7	2	3	0	1	0-0	.278	.350	.389	.739	1	.941
Division series totals (2 years)		9	37	3	12	4	0	0	12	5	4	0	2	0-1	.324	.405	.432	.837	1	.960

CHAMPIONSHIP SERIES RECORD

Year Team (League)	Pos.	G	AB	R	H	2B	3B	HR	RBI	BB	SO	HBP	GDP	SB-CS	Avg.	OBP	SLG	OPS	E	Avg.
2004— Houston (N.L.)	3B	7	22	2	3	0	0	1	2	1	3	2	1	0-1	.136	.240	.273	.513	0	1.000
2005— Houston (N.L.)	3B	6	21	1	5	1	0	0	2	2	2	0	1	0-0	.238	.292	.286	.577	1	.941
Champ. series totals (2 years)		13	43	3	8	1	0	1	4	3	5	2	2	0-1	.186	.265	.279	.544	1	.968

WORLD SERIES RECORD

Year Team (League)	Pos.	G	AB	R	H	2B	3B	HR	RBI	BB	SO	HBP	GDP	SB-CS	Avg.	OBP	SLG	OPS	E	Avg.
2005— Houston (N.L.)	3B	4	18	2	2	0	0	1	2	1	7	0	1	0-0	.111	.158	.278	.436	1	.938

ALL-STAR GAME RECORD

	G	AB	R	H	2B	3B	HR	RBI	BB	SO	HBP	GDP	SB-CS	Avg.	OBP	SLG	OPS	E	Avg.
All-Star Game totals (1 year)	1	2	0	0	0	0	0	0	0	1	0	0	0-0	.000	.000	.000	.000	0	1.000

ERICKSON, SCOTT — P

PERSONAL: Born February 2, 1968, in Long Beach, Calif. ... 6-4/230. ... Throws right, bats right. ... Full name: Scott Gavin Erickson. ... High school: Homestead (Cupertino, Calif.). ... Junior college: San Jose City College. ... College: Arizona.
TRANSACTIONS/CAREER NOTES: Selected by New York Mets organization in 36th round of June 1986 free-agent draft; did not sign. ... Selected by Houston Astros organization in 34th round of 1987 free-agent draft; did not sign. ... Selected by Toronto Blue Jays organization in 44th round of 1988 free-agent draft; did not sign. ... Selected by Minnesota Twins organization in fourth round of 1989 free-agent draft. ... On disabled list (June 30-July 15, 1991; April 3-18, 1993; and May 15-31, 1994). ... Traded by Twins to Baltimore Orioles for P Scott Klingenbeck and a player to be named (July 7, 1995); Twins acquired OF Kimera Bartee to complete deal (September 18, 1995). ... On disabled list (March 28-May 4 and July 28, 2000-remainder of season); included rehabilitation assignments to Frederick and Bowie. ... On disabled list (April 1, 2001-entire season; and March 28, 2003-entire season). ... Signed as a free agent by Mets organization (February 5, 2004). ... On disabled list (April 4-June 30, 2004); included rehabilitation assignments to St. Lucie and Norfolk. ... Traded by Mets to Texas Rangers for a player to be named (July 31, 2004); Mets acquired IF Josh Hoffpauir to complete deal (September 17, 2004). ... Signed as a free agent by Los Angeles Dodgers organization (January 25, 2005).
CAREER HITTING: 4-for-35 (.114), 4 R, 1 2B, 0 3B, 0 HR, 1 RBI.

SCOTT ERICKSON'S PITCHING ZONE

.143	.333	.353
.159	.469	.320
.214	.333	.304

LEFTY-RIGHTY SPLITS

vs.	Avg.	AB	H	2B	3B	HR	RBI	BB	SO	OBP	Slg.
L	.295	112	33	4	1	4	18	13	6	.375	.455
R	.282	103	29	2	0	8	18	12	9	.364	.534

Year	Team (League)	W	L	Pct.	ERA	WHIP	G	GS	CG	ShO	Hld.	Sv.-Opp.	IP	H	R	ER	HR	BB-IBB	SO	Avg.
1989—	Visalia (Calif.)	3	4	.429	2.97	1.28	12	12	2	0	...	0-...	78.2	79	29	26	3	22-0	59	.265
1990—	Orlando (South.)	8	3	.727	3.03	0.98	15	15	3	1	...	0-...	101.0	75	38	34	3	24-0	69	.205
—	Minnesota (A.L.)	8	4	.667	2.87	1.41	19	17	1	0	0	0-0	113.0	108	49	36	9	51-4	53	.256
1991—	Minnesota (A.L.)	• 20	8	.714	3.18	1.27	32	32	5	3	0	0-0	204.0	189	80	72	13	71-3	108	.248
1992—	Minnesota (A.L.)	13	12	.520	3.40	1.32	32	32	5	3	0	0-0	212.0	197	86	80	18	83-3	101	.252
1993—	Minnesota (A.L.)	8	* 19	.296	5.19	1.54	34	34	1	0	0	0-0	218.2	* 266	* 138	126	17	71-1	116	.305
1994—	Minnesota (A.L.)	8	11	.421	5.44	1.61	23	23	2	1	0	0-0	144.0	173	99	87	15	59-0	104	.299
1995—	Baltimore (A.L.)	4	6	.400	5.95	1.53	15	15	0	0	0	0-0	87.2	102	61	58	11	32-0	45	.291
—	Baltimore (A.L.)	9	4	.692	3.89	1.34	17	16	7	2	0	0-0	108.2	111	47	47	7	35-0	61	.273
1996—	Baltimore (A.L.)	13	12	.520	5.02	1.48	34	34	6	0	0	0-0	222.1	262	137	124	21	66-4	100	.297
1997—	Baltimore (A.L.)	16	7	.696	3.69	1.26	34	33	3	1	0	0-0	221.2	218	100	91	16	61-5	131	.257
1998—	Baltimore (A.L.)	16	13	.552	4.01	1.40	36	* 36	* 11	2	0	0-0	* 251.1	* 284	125	112	23	69-4	186	.281
1999—	Baltimore (A.L.)	15	12	.556	4.81	1.49	34	34	6	* 3	0	0-0	230.1	244	127	123	27	* 99-4	106	.280
2000—	Frederick (Carolina)	0	0	...	2.70	0.60	1	1	0	0	...	0-...	6.2	3	2	2	0	1-0	5	.130
—	Bowie (East.)	0	0	...	0.00	0.57	1	1	0	0	...	0-...	7.0	4	0	0	0	0-0	5	.160
—	Baltimore (A.L.)	5	8	.385	7.87	1.89	16	16	1	0	0	0-0	92.2	127	81	81	14	48-0	41	.331
2001—	Baltimore (A.L.)		Did not play.																	
2002—	Baltimore (A.L.)	5	12	.294	5.55	1.62	29	28	3	1	0	0-0	160.2	192	109	99	20	68-2	74	.303
2003—	Baltimore (A.L.)		Did not play.																	
2004—	St. Lucie (Fla. St.)	1	0	1.000	0.00	0.86	2	2	0	0	...	0-...	7.0	6	0	0	0	0-0	5	.222
—	Norfolk (Int'l)	3	3	.500	4.50	1.31	8	8	0	0	...	0-...	52.0	56	30	26	5	12-0	30	.279
—	New York (N.L.)	0	1	.000	7.88	2.38	2	2	0	0	0	0-0	8.0	15	9	7	1	4-0	3	.395
—	Texas (A.L.)	1	3	.250	6.16	2.05	4	4	0	0	0	0-0	19.0	23	13	13	2	16-0	6	.307
—	Oklahoma (PCL)	0	1	.000	9.82	2.36	2	2	0	0	...	0-...	11.0	17	13	12	1	9-0	11	.370
2005—	Los Angeles (N.L.)	1	4	.200	6.02	1.57	19	8	0	0	0	0-0	55.1	62	37	37	12	25-0	15	.289
—	Las Vegas (PCL)	2	4	.333	7.20	1.70	7	7	0	0	0	0-0	40.0	47	34	32	6	21-0	26	.294
American League totals (13 years)		141	131	.518	4.52	1.45	359	354	51	17	0	0-0	2286.0	2496	1248	1149	213	829-30	1232	.281
National League totals (2 years)		1	5	.167	6.25	1.67	21	10	0	0	0	0-0	63.1	77	46	44	13	29-0	18	.304
Major League totals (14 years)		142	136	.511	4.57	1.46	380	364	51	17	0	0-0	2349.1	2573	1294	1193	226	858-30	1250	.282

DIVISION SERIES RECORD

Year	Team (League)	W	L	Pct.	ERA	WHIP	G	GS	CG	ShO	Hld.	Sv.-Opp.	IP	H	R	ER	HR	BB-IBB	SO	Avg.
1996—	Baltimore (A.L.)	0	0	...	4.05	1.20	1	1	0	0	0	0-0	6.2	6	3	3	1	2-0	6	.240
1997—	Baltimore (A.L.)	1	0	1.000	4.05	1.35	1	1	0	0	0	0-0	6.2	7	3	3	0	2-0	6	.269
Division series totals (2 years)		1	0	1.000	4.05	1.28	2	2	0	0	0	0-0	13.1	13	6	6	1	4-0	12	.255

CHAMPIONSHIP SERIES RECORD

Year	Team (League)	W	L	Pct.	ERA	WHIP	G	GS	CG	ShO	Hld.	Sv.-Opp.	IP	H	R	ER	HR	BB-IBB	SO	Avg.
1991—	Minnesota (A.L.)	0	0	...	4.50	2.00	1	1	0	0	0	0-0	4.0	3	2	2	1	5-0	2	.214
1996—	Baltimore (A.L.)	0	1	.000	2.38	1.59	2	2	0	0	0	0-0	11.1	14	9	3	3	4-0	8	.286
1997—	Baltimore (A.L.)	1	0	1.000	4.26	1.26	2	2	0	0	0	0-0	12.2	15	7	6	2	1-0	6	.300
Champ. series totals (3 years)		1	1	.500	3.54	1.50	5	5	0	0	0	0-0	28.0	32	18	11	6	10-0	16	.283

WORLD SERIES RECORD

Year	Team (League)	W	L	Pct.	ERA	WHIP	G	GS	CG	ShO	Hld.	Sv.-Opp.	IP	H	R	ER	HR	BB-IBB	SO	Avg.
1991—	Minnesota (A.L.)	0	0	...	5.06	1.31	2	2	0	0	0	0-0	10.2	10	7	6	3	4-0	5	.233

E

ERSTAD, DARIN   1B

PERSONAL: Born June 4, 1974, in Jamestown, N.D. ... 6-2/210. ... Bats left, throws left. ... Full name: Darin Charles Erstad. ... Name pronounced: ER-stad. ... High school: Jamestown (N.D.). ... College: Nebraska.

TRANSACTIONS/CAREER NOTES: Selected by New York Mets organization in 13th round of 1992 free-agent draft; did not sign. ... Selected by California Angels organization in first round (first pick overall) of 1995 free-agent draft. ... Angels franchise renamed Anaheim Angels for 1997 season. ... On disabled list (August 4-19, 1998; and August 11-26, 1999). ... On disabled list (April 20-June 9 and August 7, 2003-remainder of season); included rehabilitation assignment to Salt Lake. ... On disabled list (May 9-June 14, 2004); included rehabilitation assignment to Salt Lake. ... Angels franchise renamed Los Angeles Angels of Anaheim for 2005 season.

HONORS: Won A.L. Gold Glove as outfielder (2000 and 2002). ... Won A.L. Gold Glove at first base (2004).

2005 GAMES PLAYED BY POSITION (MLB): 1B—147, DH—5.

SCOUTING REPORT **Offense:** Erstad's bat speed continues to slide, and he has health problems. A high-fastball hitter with a short stroke, is more of a line-drive gap hitter who hits down on the ball. No longer drives the ball for power and strikeout totals are increasing. Run production is dropping. Aggressive approach makes him susceptible to off-speed pitches. Is an aggressive runner who reads pitchers' moves. **Defense:** He is a Gold Glove winner with good hands and a quick first step to either side. Charges on bunts and has improved his accuracy throwing to bases. Is adept at fielding errant throws around the bag. Not afraid to leave his feet to knock down ground balls. **Outlook:** Concerns remain about his power and production. Plays all out, but injuries are starting to have an effect. *Grade 7.5*

DARIN ERSTAD'S HITTING ZONE

.308	.192	.385
.262	.250	.305
.448	.211	.304

LEFTY-RIGHTY SPLITS

vs.	Avg.	AB	H	2B	3B	HR	RBI	BB	SO	OBP	Slg.
L	.232	190	44	5	1	3	20	17	39	.298	.316
R	.291	419	122	28	2	4	46	30	70	.337	.396

Year	Team (League)	Pos.	G	AB	R	H	2B	3B	HR	RBI	BB	SO	HBP	GDP	SB-CS	Avg.	OBP	SLG	OPS	E	Avg.
									BATTING											FIELDING	
1995—	Ariz. Angels (Ariz.)	OF	4	18	2	10	1	0	0	1	1	1	0	0	1-0	.556	.579	.611	1.190	0	1.000
—	Lake Elsinore (Calif.)	OF	25	113	24	41	7	2	5	24	6	22	0	2	0-3	.363	.392	.593	.985	1	.985
1996—	Vancouver (PCL)	OF-1B-DH	85	351	63	107	22	5	6	41	44	53	3	5	11-6	.305	.385	.447	.832	1	.995
—	California (A.L.)	OF	57	208	34	59	5	1	4	20	17	29	0	3	3-3	.284	.333	.375	.708	3	.976
1997—	Anaheim (A.L.)	1B-DH-OF	139	539	99	161	34	4	16	77	51	86	4	5	23-8	.299	.360	.466	.839	11	.990
1998—	Anaheim (A.L.)	OF-1B-DH	133	537	84	159	39	3	19	82	43	77	6	2	20-6	.296	.353	.486	.839	1	.995
1999—	Anaheim (A.L.)	1B-OF-DH	142	585	84	148	22	5	13	53	47	101	1	16	13-7	.253	.308	.374	.683	1	.995
2000—	Anaheim (A.L.)	OF-DH-1B	157	* 676	121	* 240	39	6	25	100	64	82	1	18	28-8	.355	.409	.541	.951	3	.992
2001—	Anaheim (A.L.)	OF-1B-DH	157	631	89	163	35	1	9	63	62	113	10	8	24-10	.258	.331	.360	.691	1	.998
2002—	Anaheim (A.L.)	OF-1B-DH	150	625	99	177	28	4	10	73	27	67	2	9	23-3	.283	.313	.389	.702	1	.998

Year Team (League)	Pos.	G	AB	R	H	2B	3B	HR	RBI	BB	SO	HBP	GDP	SB-CS	Avg.	OBP	SLG	OPS	E	Avg.
2003—Salt Lake (PCL)	OF	7	27	6	11	0	0	0	4	2	1	0	0	1-0	.407	.448	.407	.856	0	1.000
—Anaheim (A.L.)	OF	67	258	35	65	7	1	4	17	18	40	4	8	9-1	.252	.309	.333	.642	0	1.000
2004—Salt Lake (PCL)	1B	4	16	2	2	0	0	0	3	1	1	0	0	0-0	.125	.176	.125	.301	1	.963
—Anaheim (A.L.)	1B	125	495	79	146	29	1	8	69	37	74	4	9	16-1	.295	.346	.400	.746	4	.996
2005—Los Angeles (A.L.)	1B-DH	153	609	86	166	33	3	7	66	47	109	1	8	10-3	.273	.325	.371	.696	4	.997
Major League totals (10 years)		1280	5163	810	1484	271	29	114	620	413	778	33	76	169-50	.287	.342	.417	.759	31	.995

DIVISION SERIES RECORD

Year Team (League)	Pos.	G	AB	R	H	2B	3B	HR	RBI	BB	SO	HBP	GDP	SB-CS	Avg.	OBP	SLG	OPS	E	Avg.
2002—Anaheim (A.L.)	OF	4	19	4	8	2	0	0	2	0	1	0	2	1-0	.421	.421	.526	.947	0	1.000
2004—Anaheim (A.L.)	1B	3	10	2	5	1	0	1	2	3	1	1	0	0-0	.500	.643	.900	1.543	0	1.000
2005—Los Angeles (A.L.)	1B	5	20	1	6	2	0	0	3	0	6	0	1	0-0	.300	.300	.400	.700	0	1.000
Division series totals (3 years)		12	49	7	19	5	0	1	7	3	8	1	3	1-0	.388	.434	.551	.985	0	1.000

CHAMPIONSHIP SERIES RECORD

Year Team (League)	Pos.	G	AB	R	H	2B	3B	HR	RBI	BB	SO	HBP	GDP	SB-CS	Avg.	OBP	SLG	OPS	E	Avg.
2002—Anaheim (A.L.)	OF	5	22	4	8	0	0	1	2	0	3	0	0	1-0	.364	.364	.500	.864	0	1.000
2005—Los Angeles (A.L.)	1B	5	17	1	4	1	0	0	1	1	2	0	0	1-0	.235	.278	.294	.572	0	1.000
Champ. series totals (2 years)		10	39	5	12	1	0	1	3	1	5	0	0	2-0	.308	.325	.410	.735	0	1.000

WORLD SERIES RECORD

Year Team (League)	Pos.	G	AB	R	H	2B	3B	HR	RBI	BB	SO	HBP	GDP	SB-CS	Avg.	OBP	SLG	OPS	E	Avg.
2002—Anaheim (A.L.)	OF	7	30	6	9	0	0	1	3	1	4	0	0	1-0	.300	.313	.500	.813	1	.955

ALL-STAR GAME RECORD

	G	AB	R	H	2B	3B	HR	RBI	BB	SO	HBP	GDP	SB-CS	Avg.	OBP	SLG	OPS	E	Avg.
All-Star Game totals (2 years)	2	4	1	0	0	0	0	1	0	0	0	0	0-0	.000	.000	.000	.000	0	1.000

ESCALONA, FELIX — SS

PERSONAL: Born March 12, 1979, in Puerto Cabello, Venezuela. ... 6-0/190. ... Bats right, throws right. ... Full name: Felix Eduardo Escalona.

TRANSACTIONS/CAREER NOTES: Signed as a non-drafted free agent by Houston Astros organization (October 2, 1995). ... Selected by San Francisco Giants from Astros organization in Rule 5 major league draft (December 13, 2001). ... Claimed on waivers by Tampa Bay Devil Rays (March 27, 2002). ... Claimed on waivers by Baltimore Orioles (May 19, 2003). ... Signed as a free agent by New York Yankees organization (February 4, 2004).

2005 GAMES PLAYED BY POSITION (MLB): SS—5, 3B—3, 2B—1, 1B—1.

LEFTY-RIGHTY SPLITS

vs.	Avg.	AB	H	2B	3B	HR	RBI	BB	SO	OBP	Slg.
L	.222	9	2	0	0	0	0	1	0	3	.300	.222
R	.400	5	2	1	0	0	1	1	1	1	.500	.600

Year Team (League)	Pos.	G	AB	R	H	2B	3B	HR	RBI	BB	SO	HBP	GDP	SB-CS	Avg.	OBP	SLG	OPS	E	Avg.
1996—GC Astros (GCL)	2B-3B	28	75	8	11	2	0	1	9	8	31	4	0	1-2	.147	.261	.213	.475	6	.924
1997—GC Astros (GCL)	2B	51	189	27	39	9	0	1	9	20	49	3	1	11-3	.206	.292	.270	.562	7	.969
—Kissimmee (Fla. St.)	2B	3	9	6	2	0	0	0	0	1	2	3	0	0-0	.222	.462	.222	.684	3	.833
1998—Kissimmee (Fla. St.)	3B	3	4	0	0	0	0	0	0	0	1	0	0	0-0	.000	.000	.000	.000	1	1.000
—Auburn (NY-Penn)	2B-3B-SS	51	149	22	31	5	0	1	17	11	33	6	4	4-2	.208	.282	.262	.544	14	.933
1999—Michigan (Midw.)	2B-3B-SS	116	396	78	114	29	4	6	49	29	60	17	4	7-7	.288	.360	.427	.786	21	.955
2000—Michigan (Midw.)	2B-SS	64	251	42	65	14	1	6	35	22	49	4	4	7-0	.259	.326	.394	.721	14	.953
—Kissimmee (Fla. St.)	2B-3B-SS	42	143	19	36	5	1	0	8	9	21	6	3	5-3	.252	.321	.301	.621	7	.955
2001—Lexington (S. Atl.)	2B-SS	130	536	92	155	42	2	16	64	30	85	16	8	46-12	.289	.342	.465	.807	23	.963
2002—Tampa Bay (A.L.)	SS-2B-3B DH	59	157	17	34	8	2	0	9	3	44	7	2	7-2	.217	.262	.293	.555	11	.949
2003—Orlando (South.)	SS-2B-3B DH	22	90	11	22	7	0	1	8	5	14	5	3	0-0	.244	.320	.356	.676	11	.896
—Tampa Bay (A.L.)	SS-2B-3B	10	27	2	5	2	0	0	2	2	6	0	0	1-0	.185	.241	.259	.501	0	1.000
—Bowie (East.)	2B	1	3	1	1	0	0	0	0	0	1	0	0	0-0	.333	.333	.333	.667	1	.950
—Ottawa (Int'l)	2B-SS	9	30	5	7	2	0	0	1	1	5	2	0	2-0	.233	.303	.300	.603	2	.950
2004—Columbus (Int'l)	SS-3B-2B	130	447	79	138	32	1	7	59	31	56	18	19	2-4	.309	.373	.432	.804	23	.958
—New York (A.L.)	SS-3B	5	8	1	0	0	0	0	0	1	2	0	0	0-0	.000	.111	.000	.111	0	1.000
2005—Columbus (Int'l)	SS-2B-3B	91	307	42	84	14	1	7	45	28	58	18	5	5-0	.274	.363	.394	.757	15	.963
—New York (A.L.)	SS-3B-1B 2B	10	14	0	4	1	0	0	2	1	1	0	1	0-0	.286	.375	.357	.732	0	1.000
Major League totals (4 years)		84	206	20	43	11	2	0	13	6	56	9	3	8-2	.209	.261	.282	.543	11	.962

ESCOBAR, KELVIM — P

PERSONAL: Born April 11, 1976, in La Guaira, Venezuela. ... 6-1/210. ... Throws right, bats right. ... Full name: Kelvim Jose Escobar. ... Name pronounced: kel-VEEM.

TRANSACTIONS/CAREER NOTES: Signed as a non-drafted free agent by Toronto Blue Jays organization (July 9, 1992). ... On disabled list (April 16-May 6, 1998); included rehabilitation assignment to Syracuse. ... Signed as a free agent by Anaheim Angels (November 24, 2003). ... Angels franchise renamed Los Angeles Angels of Anaheim for 2005 season. ... On disabled list (May 12-28 and June 9-September 6, 2005); included rehabilitation assignments to Salt Lake and Rancho Cucamonga.

CAREER HITTING: 1-for-17 (.059), 1 R, 0 2B, 0 3B, 0 HR, 1 RBI.

SCOUTING REPORT ***Throws:*** Throws a fastball between 92-97 mph, a curveball at 77-80, a slider at 85-88 and a split-finger fastball at 82-84. Also throws a changeup. ***Tendencies:*** Can overpower hitters up in the zone and cross them up with a tight, biting curveball. Has a power slider with late action and unusually large break on his split-finger fastball. Gives hitters fits trying to determine what pitch is coming, but needs to develop greater separation in the speed of his pitches ***Outlook:*** Escobar has the stuff to be a big winner, but he always has had something holding him back, whether it was a lack of command or concentration or an undefined role. Missed a couple of months last season with elbow problems and moved into a setup role when he returned. ***Grade 8.2***

KELVIM ESCOBAR'S PITCHING ZONE

.143	.375	.455
.163	.409	.267
.067	.222	.250

LEFTY-RIGHTY SPLITS

vs.	Avg.	AB	H	2B	3B	HR	RBI	BB	SO	OBP	Slg.
L	.278	108	30	7	4	3	16	12	31	.355	.500
R	.138	109	15	5	0	1	1	9	32	.210	.211

Year	Team (League)	W	L	Pct.	ERA	WHIP	G	GS	CG	ShO	Hld.	Sv.-Opp.	IP	H	R	ER	HR	BB-IBB	SO	Avg.
1993—	Dom. B. Jays (DSL)	2	1	.667	4.13	1.81	8	7	0	0	...	0-...	32.2	34	17	15	...	25-...	31	...
1994—	GC Jays (GCL)	4	4	.500	2.35	1.14	11	10	1	0	...	1-...	65.0	56	23	17	0	18-0	64	.237
1995—	Dom. B. Jays (DSL)	0	1	.000	1.72	1.21	3	2	0	0	...	0-...	15.2	14	3	3		5-...	20	...
	—Medicine Hat (Pio.)	3	3	.500	5.71	1.43	14	14	1	1	...	0-...	69.1	66	47	44	6	33-0	75	.253
1996—	Dunedin (Fla. St.)	9	5	.643	2.69	1.21	18	18	1	0	...	0-...	110.1	101	44	33	5	33-0	113	.240
	—Knoxville (Southern)	3	4	.429	5.33	1.57	10	10	0	0	...	0-...	54.0	61	36	32	7	24-0	44	.288
1997—	Dunedin (Fla. St.)	0	1	.000	3.75	1.58	3	2	0	0	...	0-...	12.0	16	9	5	0	3-0	16	.327
	—Knoxville (Southern)	2	1	.667	3.70	1.48	5	5	1	0	...	0-...	24.1	20	13	10	1	16-0	31	.222
	—Toronto (A.L.)	3	2	.600	2.90	1.52	27	0	0	0	1	14-17	31.0	28	12	10	1	19-2	36	.237
1998—	Toronto (A.L.)	7	3	.700	3.73	1.34	22	10	0	0	5	0-1	79.2	72	37	33	5	35-0	72	.238
	—Syracuse (Int'l)	2	2	.500	3.77	1.26	13	10	0	0	...	1-...	59.2	51	26	25	7	24-0	64	.229
1999—	Toronto (A.L.)	14	11	.560	5.69	1.63	33	30	1	0	...	0-0	174.0	203	118	110	19	81-2	129	.293
2000—	Toronto (A.L.)	10	15	.400	5.35	1.51	43	24	3	1	3	2-3	180.0	186	118	107	26	85-3	142	.267
2001—	Toronto (A.L.)	6	8	.429	3.50	1.15	59	11	1	1	13	0-0	126.0	93	51	49	8	52-5	121	.204
2002—	Toronto (A.L.)	5	7	.417	4.27	1.43	76	0	0	0		38-46	78.0	75	39	37	10	44-6	85	.246
2003—	Toronto (A.L.)	13	9	.591	4.29	1.48	41	26	1	1		4-5	180.1	189	94	86	15	78-3	159	.270
2004—	Anaheim (A.L.)	11	12	.478	3.93	1.29	33	33	0	0		0-0	208.1	192	91	91	21	76-2	191	.244
2005—	Rancho Cuca. (Calif.)	0	0	...	0.00	1.00	1	1	0	0		0-0	3.0	1	0	0	0	2-0	7	.100
	—Salt Lake (PCL)	1	0	1.000	2.51	1.53	4	4	0	0		0-0	14.1	14	4	4	2	8-0	22	.250
	—Los Angeles (A.L.)	3	2	.600	3.02	1.11	16	7	0	0	2	1-1	59.2	45	21	20	4	21-1	63	.207
Major League totals (9 years)		72	69	.511	4.38	1.41	350	141	6	3	24	59-73	1117.0	1083	581	543	109	491-24	998	.253

DIVISION SERIES RECORD

Year	Team (League)	W	L	Pct.	ERA	WHIP	G	GS	CG	ShO	Hld.	Sv.-Opp.	IP	H	R	ER	HR	BB-IBB	SO	Avg.
2004—	Anaheim (A.L.)	0	0	...	8.10	3.00	1	1	0	0		0-0	3.1	5	5	3	0	5-1	4	.333
2005—	Los Angeles (A.L.)	1	0	1.000	1.29	1.00	4	3	0	0	2	0-0	7.0	2	1	1	1	5-0	5	.091
Division series totals (2 years)		1	0	1.000	3.48	1.65	5	4	0	0	2	0-0	10.1	7	6	4	1	10-1	9	.189

CHAMPIONSHIP SERIES RECORD

Year	Team (League)	W	L	Pct.	ERA	WHIP	G	GS	CG	ShO	Hld.	Sv.-Opp.	IP	H	R	ER	HR	BB-IBB	SO	Avg.
2005—	Los Angeles (A.L.)	0	2	.000	2.08	1.38	2	0	0	0	0	0-1	4.1	4	3	1	1	2-0	10	.222

ESPOSITO, MIKE — P

PERSONAL: Born September 27, 1981, in Los Angeles, Calif. ... 6-0/190. ... Throws right, bats right. ... Full name: Michael Anthony Esposito. ... High school: Cimarron Memorial (Las Vegas). ... College: Arizona State.

TRANSACTIONS/CAREER NOTES: Selected by Colorado Rockies organization in 12th round of 2002 free-agent draft.

CAREER HITTING: 1-for-5 (.200) 0 R, 0 2B, 0 3B, 0 HR, 0 RBI.

MIKE ESPOSITO'S PITCHING ZONE

.333	1.000	.333
.167	.250	.409
.400	.333	.500

LEFTY-RIGHTY SPLITS

vs.	Avg.	AB	H	2B	3B	HR	RBI	BB	SO	OBP	Slg.
L	.432	37	16	2	2	1	8	6	4	.512	.676
R	.192	26	5	0	0	2	3	3	1	.276	.423

Year	Team (League)	W	L	Pct.	ERA	WHIP	G	GS	CG	ShO	Hld.	Sv.-Opp.	IP	H	R	ER	HR	BB-IBB	SO	Avg.
2003—	Visalia (Calif.)	12	6	.667	3.75	1.42	27	27	1	0	...	0-...	161.0	173	83	67	14	55-0	116	.277
2004—	Tulsa (Texas)	10	6	.625	3.33	1.21	24	24	1	0	...	0-...	143.1	138	57	53	12	35-1	90	.261
2005—	Colo. Springs (PCL)	8	9	.471	5.49	1.53	27	27	0	0	0	0-0	155.2	197	110	95	20	41-3	94	.308
	—Colorado (N.L.)	0	2	.000	6.75	2.05	3	3	0	0	0	0-0	14.2	21	11	11	3	9-1	5	.333
Major League totals (1 year)		0	2	.000	6.75	2.05	3	3	0	0	0	0-0	14.2	21	11	11	3	9-1	5	.333

ESTES, SHAWN — P

PERSONAL: Born February 18, 1973, in San Bernardino, Calif. ... 6-2/200. ... Throws left, bats right. ... Full name: Aaron Shawn Estes. ... Name pronounced: ES-tus. ... High school: Douglas (Minden, Nev.).

TRANSACTIONS/CAREER NOTES: Selected by Seattle Mariners organization in first round (11th pick overall) of 1991 free-agent draft. ... Traded by Mariners with IF Wilson Delgado to San Francisco Giants for P Salomon Torres (May 21, 1995). ... On disabled list (March 23-April 6, 1997). ... On disabled list (July 11-September 4, 1998); included rehabilitation assignments to Bakersfield and Fresno. ... On disabled list (March 29-April 17, 2000); included rehabilitation assignments to Fresno and San Jose. ... On disabled list (May 9-24 and August 23, 2001-remainder of season). ... Traded by Giants to New York Mets for OF Tsuyoshi Shinjo and SS Desi Relaford (December 16, 2001). ... Traded by Mets with cash to Cincinnati Reds for P Pedro Feliciano, OF Elvin Andujar and two players to be named (August 15, 2002); Mets acquired OF Raul Gonzalez (August 20, 2002) and OF Brady Clark (September 9, 2002) to complete deal. ... Signed as a free agent by Chicago Cubs (December 20, 2002). ... Signed as a free agent by Colorado Rockies organization (January 23, 2004). ... Signed as a free agent by Arizona Diamondbacks (January 12, 2005). ... On disabled list (July 7-September 9, 2005); included rehabilitation assignment to Tucson.

CAREER HITTING: 77-for-488 (.158), 49 R, 14 2B, 2 3B, 4 HR, 28 RBI.

SCOUTING REPORT *Throws:* Estes throws a fastball at 87-91 mph, a curve at 70-75 and a changeup in the low 80s. *Tendencies:* He throws over the top and pitches away from contact, keeping the ball away from righthanders. Often works behind in the count. Big-breaking curve is his best pitch; it starts high and hitters give up on it. Has good motion with his straight change, which turns over and runs from righthanders. *Outlook:* Estes is an underachiever. Nibbles off the plate, which creates high pitch counts and takes him out after five or six innings. Has to pitch in a big park because he's prone to the long ball. *Grade 5.8*

SHAWN ESTES' PITCHING ZONE

.319	.136	.227
.333	.375	.282
.273	.394	.100

LEFTY-RIGHTY SPLITS

vs.	Avg.	AB	H	2B	3B	HR	RBI	BB	SO	OBP	Slg.
L	.259	81	21	7	1	1	7	7	12	.333	.407
R	.284	391	111	23	2	14	51	38	51	.347	.460

Year Team (League)	W	L	Pct.	ERA	WHIP	G	GS	CG	ShO	Hld.	Sv.-Opp.	IP	H	R	ER	HR	BB-IBB	SO	Avg.
1991— Bellingham (N'west)	1	3	.250	6.88	2.41	9	9	0	0	...	0-...	34.0	27	33	26	2	55-0	35	.218
1992— Bellingham (N'west)	3	3	.500	4.32	1.68	15	15	0	0	...	0-...	77.0	84	55	37	6	45-0	77	.279
1993— Appleton (Midwest)	5	9	.357	7.24	1.92	19	18	0	0	...	0-...	83.1	108	85	67	3	52-1	65	.305
1994— Ariz. Mariners (Ariz.)	0	3	.000	3.15	1.10	5	5	0	0	...	0-...	20.0	16	9	7	0	6-0	31	.205
— Appleton (Midwest)	0	2	.000	4.58	1.83	5	4	0	0	...	0-...	19.2	19	13	10	1	17-0	28	.271
1995— Wisconsin (Midw.)	0	0	...	0.90	1.00	2	2	0	0	...	0-...	10.0	5	1	1	0	5-0	11	.156
— Burlington (Midw.)	0	0	...	4.11	1.63	4	4	0	0	...	0-...	15.1	13	8	7	2	12-0	22	.224
— San Jose (Calif.)	5	2	.714	2.17	0.99	9	8	0	0	...	0-...	49.2	32	13	12	1	17-0	61	.188
— Shreveport (Texas)	2	0	1.000	2.01	1.07	4	4	0	0	...	0-...	22.1	14	5	5	1	10-0	18	.184
— San Francisco (N.L.)	0	3	.000	6.75	1.21	3	3	0	0	0	0-0	17.1	16	14	13	2	5-0	14	.229
1996— Phoenix (PCL)	9	3	.750	3.43	1.18	18	18	0	0	0	0-0	110.1	92	43	42	7	38-1	95	.228
— San Francisco (N.L.)	3	5	.375	3.60	1.46	11	11	0	0	0	0-0	70.0	63	30	28	3	39-3	60	.243
1997— San Francisco (N.L.)	19	5	.792	3.18	1.30	32	32	3	2	0	0-0	201.0	162	80	71	12	* 100-2	181	.223
1998— San Francisco (N.L.)	7	12	.368	5.06	1.54	25	25	1	1	0	0-0	149.1	150	89	84	14	80-6	136	.269
— Bakersfield (Calif.)	0	0	...	0.00	0.92	1	1	0	0	0	0-...	4.1	3	0	0	0	1-0	5	.188
— Fresno (PCL)	1	0	1.000	1.80	1.20	1	1	0	0	0	0-...	5.0	3	1	1	0	3-0	6	.188
1999— San Francisco (N.L.)	11	11	.500	4.92	1.58	32	32	1	0	0	0-0	203.0	209	121	111	21	112-2	159	.268
2000— Fresno (PCL)	0	1	.000	9.00	2.33	1	1	0	0	...	0-0	3.0	5	9	3	2	2-0	2	.357
— San Jose (Calif.)	1	0	1.000	0.00	0.43	1	1	0	0	...	0-...	7.0	2	0	0	0	1-0	11	.095
— San Francisco (N.L.)	15	6	.714	4.26	1.59	30	30	4	2	0	0-0	190.1	194	99	90	11	108-1	136	.275
2001— San Francisco (N.L.)	9	8	.529	4.02	1.43	27	27	0	0	0	0-0	159.0	151	78	71	11	77-7	109	.253
2002— New York (N.L.)	4	9	.308	4.55	1.50	23	23	1	1	0	0-0	132.2	133	70	67	12	66-9	92	.267
— Cincinnati (N.L.)	1	3	.250	7.71	1.96	6	6	0	0	0	0-0	28.0	38	24	24	1	17-0	17	.345
2003— Chicago (N.L.)	8	11	.421	5.73	1.74	29	28	1	1	0	0-0	152.1	182	113	97	20	83-1	103	.305
2004— Atlanta (N.L.)	15	8	.652	5.84	1.62	34	34	1	0	0	0-0	202.0	223	* 133	* 131	30	105-5	117	.291
2005— Tucson (PCL)	0	0	...	1.64	0.82	2	2	0	0	0	0-0	11.0	5	2	2	1	4-0	9	.132
— Arizona (N.L.)	7	8	.467	4.80	1.43	21	21	2	0	0	0-0	123.2	132	70	66	15	45-0	63	.280
Major League totals (11 years)	99	89	.527	4.71	1.53	273	272	14	8	0	0-0	1628.2	1653	921	853	152	837-36	1187	.269

DIVISION SERIES RECORD

Year Team (League)	W	L	Pct.	ERA	WHIP	G	GS	CG	ShO	Hld.	Sv.-Opp.	IP	H	R	ER	HR	BB-IBB	SO	Avg.
1997— San Francisco (N.L.)	0	0	...	15.00	3.00	1	1	0	0	0	0-0	3.0	5	5	5	1	4-0	3	.357
2000— San Francisco (N.L.)	0	0	...	6.00	2.00	1	1	0	0	0	0-0	3.0	3	2	2	0	3-0	3	.250
Division series totals (2 years)	0	0	...	10.50	2.50	2	2	0	0	0	0-0	6.0	8	7	7	1	7-0	6	.308

ALL-STAR GAME RECORD

	W	L	Pct.	ERA	WHIP	G	GS	CG	ShO	Hld.	Sv.-Opp.	IP	H	R	ER	HR	BB-IBB	SO	Avg.
All-Star Game totals (1 year)	0	1	.000	18.00	2.00	1	0	0	0	...		1.0	1	2	2	1	1-0	1	.250

ESTRADA, JOHNNY   C

PERSONAL: Born June 27, 1976, in Hayward, Calif. ... 5-11/209. ... Bats both, throws right. ... Full name: Johnny P. Estrada. ... High school: Roosevelt (Fresno, Calif.). ... Junior college: College of the Sequoias (Calif.).

TRANSACTIONS/CAREER NOTES: Selected by Houston Astros organization in 71st round of 1994 free-agent draft; did not sign. ... Selected by Philadelphia Phillies organization in 17th round of 1997 free-agent draft. ... Traded by Phillies to Atlanta Braves for P Kevin Millwood (December 20, 2002). ... On suspended list (July 27-29, 2005). ... On disabled list (August 7-22, 2005).

2005 GAMES PLAYED BY POSITION (MLB): C—104.

E

SCOUTING REPORT *Offense:* Estrada, one of the Braves' most consistent hitters last year, will hit line drives to all fields with occasional power from the left side. Has a short, compact stroke, yet bat speed has declined. A good contact hitter who rarely overswings. Has learned to be patient. Can't run at all. *Defense:* Because his arm strength is below average, he relies on positioning and a quick release to throw out runners. Has only average hands and reflexes and has problems handling the ball down. Must watch his weight to retain his mobility. *Outlook:* Estrada didn't play a lot down the stretch due to back problems, but if he is healthy next spring he should continue to hit well. Throwing always will be his biggest problem. *Grade 7*

JOHNNY ESTRADA'S HITTING ZONE

.278	.182	.143
.297	.467	.358
.200	.091	.283

LEFTY-RIGHTY SPLITS

vs.	Avg.	AB	H	2B	3B	HR	RBI	BB	SO	OBP	Slg.
L	.214	103	22	5	0	1	5	4	10	.257	.291
R	.280	254	71	21	0	3	34	16	28	.321	.398

Year Team (League)	Pos.	G	AB	R	H	2B	3B	HR	RBI	BB	SO	HBP	GDP	SB-CS	Avg.	OBP	SLG	OPS	E	Avg.
1997— Batavia (NY-Penn)	1B-C	58	223	28	70	17	2	6	43	9	15	1	9	0-0	.314	.336	.489	.825	0	1.000
1998— Piedmont (S. Atl.)	C	77	303	33	94	14	2	7	44	6	19	5	11	0-1	.310	.331	.439	.770	6	.990
— Clearwater (FSL)	C	37	117	8	26	8	0	0	13	5	7	0	2	0-0	.222	.250	.291	.541	5	.979
1999— Clearwater (FSL)	C	98	346	35	96	15	0	9	52	14	26	2	12	1-0	.277	.303	.399	.702	5	.990
2000— Reading (East.)	C	95	356	42	105	18	0	12	42	10	20	4	8	1-0	.295	.322	.447	.768	7	.990
2001— Scran./W.B. (I.L.)	C	32	131	13	38	13	0	0	16	5	6	1	5	0-0	.290	.319	.389	.708	0	1.000
— Philadelphia (N.L.)	C	89	298	26	68	15	0	8	37	16	32	4	15	0-0	.228	.273	.359	.632	4	.993
2002— Scran./W.B. (I.L.)	C	118	434	49	121	27	0	11	67	26	53	5	19	1-0	.279	.322	.417	.739	4	.995
— Philadelphia (N.L.)	C	10	17	0	2	1	0	0	2	2	2	0	0	0-0	.118	.211	.176	.387	0	1.000
2003— Richmond (Int'l)	C-DH	106	354	40	116	29	0	10	66	30	30	12	11	0-0	.328	.393	.494	.887	4	.994
— Atlanta (N.L.)	C	16	36	2	11	0	0	2	6	3	3	1	0	0-0	.306	.359	.306	.665	0	1.000
2004— Atlanta (N.L.)	C	134	462	56	145	36	0	9	76	39	66	11	18	0-0	.314	.378	.450	.828	9	.989
2005— Atlanta (N.L.)	C	105	357	31	93	26	0	4	39	20	38	3	13	0-0	.261	.303	.367	.670	2	.997
Major League totals (5 years)		354	1170	115	319	78	0	21	156	77	141	21	47	0-0	.273	.326	.393	.719	15	.993

DIVISION SERIES RECORD

Year Team (League)	Pos.	G	AB	R	H	2B	3B	HR	RBI	BB	SO	HBP	GDP	SB-CS	Avg.	OBP	SLG	OPS	E	Avg.
2004— Atlanta (N.L.)	C	5	17	3	6	0	0	2	4	3	3	0	0	0-0	.353	.429	.706	1.134	0	1.000
2005— Atlanta (N.L.)	C	1	4	0	1	0	0	0	1	0	2	0	0	0-0	.250	.250	.250	.500	0	1.000
Division series totals (2 years)		6	21	3	7	0	0	2	5	3	5	0	0	0-0	.333	.400	.619	1.019	0	1.000

All-Star Game totals (1 year)	G	AB	R	H	2B	3B	HR	RBI	BB	SO	HBP	GDP	SB-CS	Avg.	OBP	SLG	OPS	E	Avg.
	1	2	0	0	0	0	0	0	0	1	0	0	0-0	.000	.000	.000	.000	0	1.000

ETHERTON, SETH — P

PERSONAL: Born October 17, 1976, in Laguna Beach, Calif. ... 6-1/200. ... Throws right, bats right. ... Full name: Seth Michael Etherton. ... High school: Dana Hills (Dana Point, Calif.). ... College: Southern California.
TRANSACTIONS/CAREER NOTES: Selected by Florida Marlins organization in 16th round of 1994 free-agent draft; did not sign. ... Selected by St. Louis Cardinals organization in ninth-round of 1997 free-agent draft; did not sign. ... Selected by Anaheim Angels organization in first round (18th pick overall) of 1998 free-agent draft. ... On disabled list (August 5, 2000-remainder of season) ... Traded by Angels to Cincinnati Reds for SS Wilmy Caceres (December 10, 2000). ... On disabled list (March 22, 2001-entire season). ... On disabled list (March 21-July 11 and July 23, 2002-remainder of season); included rehabilitation assignments to Dayton, Chattanooga and Louisville. ... Claimed on waivers by New York Yankees (July 11, 2002). ... Waiver claim voided by commissioner's office (July 23, 2002). ... Signed as a free agent by Oakland Athletics (November 1, 2004).
CAREER HITTING: 1-for-9 (.111), 1 R, 0 2B, 0 3B, 0 HR, 0 RBI.

SETH ETHERTON'S PITCHING ZONE

.333	.167	.000
.231	.364	.333
.167	.125	.200

LEFTY-RIGHTY SPLITS

vs.	Avg.	AB	H	2B	3B	HR	RBI	BB	SO	OBP	Slg.
L	.289	38	11	3	1	3	6	4	6	.357	.658
R	.167	30	5	1	0	1	5	1	4	.188	.300

Year	Team (League)	W	L	Pct.	ERA	WHIP	G	GS	CG	ShO	Hld.	Sv.-Opp.	IP	H	R	ER	HR	BB-IBB	SO	Avg.
1998—	Midland (Texas)	1	5	.167	6.14	1.43	9	7	1	0	...	0-...	48.1	57	36	33	9	12-0	35	.295
1999—	Erie (East.)	10	10	.500	3.27	1.17	24	24	4	1	...	0-...	167.2	153	72	61	14	43-0	153	.241
—	Edmonton (PCL)	0	2	.000	5.48	1.45	4	4	0	0	...	0-...	21.1	25	13	13	7	6-0	19	.291
2000—	Edmonton (PCL)	3	2	.600	4.01	1.35	9	9	0	0	...	0-...	58.1	60	30	26	6	19-0	50	.264
—	Anaheim (A.L.)	5	1	.833	5.52	1.49	11	11	0	0	...	0-0	60.1	68	38	37	16	22-0	32	.278
2001—	Cincinnati (N.L.)				Did not play.															
2002—	Dayton (Midw.)	0	0	...	0.00	1.00	1	1	0	0	...	0-...	1.0	1	0	0	0	0-0	2	.250
—	Chattanooga (Sou.)	0	1	.000	0.96	0.75	3	3	0	0	...	0-...	9.1	5	1	1	0	2-0	4	.161
—	Louisville (Int'l)	0	1	.000	8.22	1.76	5	5	0	0	...	0-...	15.1	21	16	14	4	6-0	10	.328
—	Norwich (East.)	0	0	...	0.00	1.00	1	1	0	0	...	0-...	2.0	1	1	0	0	1-0	2	.143
2003—	Louisville (Int'l)	7	7	.500	4.31	1.38	21	21	2	1	...	0-...	123.1	144	62	59	11	26-1	69	.297
—	Cincinnati (N.L.)	2	4	.333	6.90	1.80	7	7	0	0	0	0-0	30.0	39	23	23	4	15-1	17	.322
2004—	Chattanooga (Sou.)	4	1	.800	1.98	0.98	7	7	0	0	...	0-...	41.0	31	12	9	2	9-0	46	.204
—	Louisville (Int'l)	5	6	.455	3.47	1.24	19	19	3	1	...	0-...	111.2	107	45	43	13	32-1	110	.252
2005—	Oakland (A.L.)	1	1	.500	6.62	1.19	3	3	0	0	...	0-0	17.2	16	13	13	4	5-0	10	.235
—	Sacramento (PCL)	7	7	.500	2.72	1.09	20	19	0	0	...	0-...	112.1	93	44	34	11	30-1	99	.220
	American League totals (2 years)	6	2	.750	5.77	1.42	14	14	0	0	0	0-0	78.0	84	51	50	20	27-0	42	.268
	National League totals (1 year)	2	4	.333	6.90	1.80	7	7	0	0	0	0-0	30.0	39	23	23	4	15-1	17	.322
	Major League totals (3 years)	8	6	.571	6.08	1.53	21	21	0	0	0	0-0	108.0	123	74	73	24	42-1	59	.283

EVELAND, DANA — P

PERSONAL: Born October 29, 1983, in Olympia, Wash. ... 6-1/220. ... Throws left, bats left. ... Full name: Dana J. Eveland. ... College: College of the Canyons (Santa Clarita, Calif.).
TRANSACTIONS/CAREER NOTES: Selected by Milwaukee Brewers organization in 16th round of 2002 free-agent draft.
CAREER HITTING: 0-for-1 (.000), 0 R, 0 2B, 0 3B, 0 HR, 0 RBI.

DANA EVELAND'S PITCHING ZONE

.300	.500	.111
.500	.571	.200
.333	.286	.500

LEFTY-RIGHTY SPLITS

vs.	Avg.	AB	H	2B	3B	HR	RBI	BB	SO	OBP	Slg.
L	.324	34	11	2	1	0	5	5	9	.410	.441
R	.315	92	29	3	3	2	15	13	14	.402	.478

Year	Team (League)	W	L	Pct.	ERA	WHIP	G	GS	CG	ShO	Hld.	Sv.-Opp.	IP	H	R	ER	HR	BB-IBB	SO	Avg.
2003—	Helena (Pion.)	2	1	.667	2.08	1.46	19	0	0	0	...	14-...	26.0	30	9	6	1	8-1	41	.286
2004—	Beloit (Midw.)	9	6	.600	2.84	1.13	22	16	1	0	...	2-...	117.1	108	48	37	8	24-0	119	.244
—	Huntsville (Sou.)	0	2	.000	2.28	1.14	4	4	0	0	...	0-...	23.2	23	9	6	0	4-0	14	.261
2005—	Huntsville (Sou.)	10	4	.714	2.72	1.23	18	18	0	0	0	0-0	109.0	96	42	33	4	38-1	98	.237
—	Milwaukee (N.L.)	1	1	.500	5.97	1.83	27	0	0	0	7	1-2	31.2	40	21	21	2	18-3	23	.317
	Major League totals (1 year)	1	1	.500	5.97	1.83	27	0	0	0	7	1-2	31.2	40	21	21	2	18-3	23	.317

EVERETT, ADAM — SS

PERSONAL: Born February 5, 1977, in Austell, Ga. ... 6-0/170. ... Bats right, throws right. ... Full name: Jeffrey Adam Everett. ... High school: Harrison (Kennesaw, Ga.). ... College: South Carolina.
TRANSACTIONS/CAREER NOTES: Selected by Chicago Cubs organization in fourth round of 1995 free-agent draft; did not sign. ... Selected by Boston Red Sox organization in first round (12th pick overall) of 1998 free-agent draft. ... Traded by Red Sox with P Greg Miller to Houston Astros for OF Carl Everett (December 14, 1999). ... On disabled list (August 7-September 29, 2004).
2005 GAMES PLAYED BY POSITION (MLB): SS—150.

SCOUTING REPORT *Offense:* Everett isn't a very strong player physically. Has a slider-speed bat, yet handles fastballs better than breaking balls. Prefers the ball up. Likes to spread out at the plate to keep from lunging, but still has problems with the ball away. Strikes out too much. Is a very good runner who will improve as a basestealer. *Defense:* His agility is outstanding; he regains his feet very quickly after diving. Has well above-average range to his left. Has very soft hands and is under control when going to the hole. Has a plus arm with excellent carry but tends to guide the ball on routine plays. *Outlook:* Everett is a frontline defender and is beginning to show more power. Needs to make better contact to use his speed. *Grade 7.9*

ADAM EVERETT'S HITTING ZONE

.200	.250	.185
.328	.354	.200
.274	.176	.188

LEFTY-RIGHTY SPLITS

vs.	Avg.	AB	H	2B	3B	HR	RBI	BB	SO	OBP	Slg.
L	.227	154	35	5	1	0	9	8	24	.265	.273
R	.256	395	101	22	1	11	45	18	79	.299	.400

Year Team (League)	Pos.	G	AB	R	H	2B	3B	HR	RBI	BB	SO	HBP	GDP	SB-CS	Avg.	OBP	SLG	OPS	E	Avg.
																		BATTING	FIELDING	
1998— Lowell (NY-Penn)	SS	21	71	11	21	6	2	0	9	11	13	3	2	2-1	.296	.407	.437	.844	9	.918
1999— Trenton (East.)	SS	98	338	56	89	11	0	10	44	41	64	10	3	21-5	.263	.356	.385	.741	18	.959
2000— New Orleans (PCL)	SS	126	453	82	111	25	2	5	37	75	100	11	6	13-4	.245	.363	.342	.705	25	.959
2001— New Orleans (PCL)	SS	114	441	69	110	20	8	5	40	39	74	16	4	24-5	.249	.330	.365	.695	24	.956
— Houston (N.L.)	SS	9	3	1	0	0	0	0	0	0	1	0	1	1-0	.000	.000	.000	.000	2	.667
2002— Houston (N.L.)	SS	40	88	11	17	3	0	0	4	12	19	1	1	3-0	.193	.297	.227	.524	5	.962
— New Orleans (PCL)	SS	88	345	51	95	16	7	2	25	24	59	6	3	12-3	.275	.331	.380	.710	7	.984
2003— New Orleans (PCL)	SS-2B	25	100	23	25	1	1	9	7	16	1	1	3-1	.250	.306	.360	.666	2	.982
— Houston (N.L.)	SS	128	387	51	99	18	3	8	51	28	66	9	7	8-1	.256	.320	.380	.700	17	.970
2004— Houston (N.L.)	SS	104	384	66	105	15	2	8	31	17	56	9	4	13-2	.273	.317	.385	.703	10	.977
2005— Houston (N.L.)	SS	152	549	58	136	27	2	11	54	26	103	8	5	21-7	.248	.290	.364	.654	14	.978
Major League totals (5 years)		433	1411	187	357	63	7	27	140	83	245	27	17	46-10	.253	.305	.365	.670	48	.973

DIVISION SERIES RECORD

Year Team (League)	Pos.	G	AB	R	H	2B	3B	HR	RBI	BB	SO	HBP	GDP	SB-CS	Avg.	OBP	SLG	OPS	E	Avg.
2004— Houston (N.L.)	SS	2	0	0	0	0	0	0	0	0	0	0	0	0-0	...	...	...	...	0	...
2005— Houston (N.L.)	SS	4	14	1	3	0	0	0	1	1	1	0	1	0-0	.214	.250	.214	.464	1	.944
Division series totals (2 years)		6	14	1	3	0	0	0	1	1	1	0	1	0-0	.214	.250	.214	.464	1	.944

CHAMPIONSHIP SERIES RECORD

Year Team (League)	Pos.	G	AB	R	H	2B	3B	HR	RBI	BB	SO	HBP	GDP	SB-CS	Avg.	OBP	SLG	OPS	E	Avg.
2004— Houston (N.L.)	SS	3	1	0	0	0	0	0	0	0	0	0	0	0-0	.000	.000	.000	.000	1	1.000
2005— Houston (N.L.)	SS	6	23	2	7	1	1	0	2	0	4	0	0	0-0	.304	.304	.435	.739	1	.963
Champ. series totals (2 years)		9	24	2	7	1	1	0	2	0	4	0	0	0-0	.292	.292	.417	.708	1	.964

WORLD SERIES RECORD

Year Team (League)	Pos.	G	AB	R	H	2B	3B	HR	RBI	BB	SO	HBP	GDP	SB-CS	Avg.	OBP	SLG	OPS	E	Avg.
2005— Houston (N.L.)	SS	4	15	2	1	0	0	0	0	1	4	0	1	0-1	.067	.125	.067	.192	1	.962

EVERETT, CARL — OF

PERSONAL: Born June 3, 1971, in Tampa, Fla. ... 6-0/215. ... Bats both, throws right. ... Full name: Carl Edward Everett. ... High school: Hillsborough (Tampa).

TRANSACTIONS/CAREER NOTES: Selected by New York Yankees organization in first round (10th pick overall) of 1990 free-agent draft. ... Selected by Florida Marlins in second round (27th pick overall) of expansion draft (November 17, 1992). ... On disabled list (July 23-August 10, 1994). ... Traded by Marlins to New York Mets for 2B Quilvio Veras (November 29, 1994). ... On disabled list (April 12-27, 1996). ... Traded by Mets to Houston Astros for P John Hudek (December 22, 1997). ... On disabled list (July 16-August 6, 1999). ... Traded by Astros to Boston Red Sox for SS Adam Everett and P Greg Miller (December 14, 1999). ... On suspended list (July 24-August 5, 2000; and March 29-30, 2001). ... On disabled list (June 22-July 28, 2001); included rehabilitation assignments to Sarasota and GCL Red Sox. ... Traded by Red Sox to Texas Rangers for P Darren Oliver (December 13, 2001). ... On disabled list (May 5-21 and June 3-July 2, 2002); included rehabilitation assignment to Charlotte. ... Traded by Rangers to Chicago White Sox for three players to be named (July 1, 2003); Rangers acquired Ps Frank Francisco and Josh Rupe and OF Anthony Webster to complete deal (July 24, 2003). ... Signed as a free agent by Montreal Expos (December 19, 2003). ... On disabled list (April 15-May 17 and May 30-June 16, 2004); included rehabilitation assignment to Brevard County. ... Traded by Expos to White Sox for Ps Jon Rauch and Gary Majewski (July 18, 2004).

2005 GAMES PLAYED BY POSITION (MLB): DH—107, OF—22.

SCOUTING REPORT **Offense:** Everett has varying hitting styles. Stands on top of the plate batting lefthanded and is quick enough to get to the ball inside. Has a longer stroke righthanded and stands farther off the plate, but his bat speed is not as good. Is better from left side with more power, especially on low pitches. Has a big strike zone and is aggressive. Is a tough out with runners in scoring position. No longer runs as well because of persistent knee problems. **Defense:** His range has declined and he has trouble changing direction while going back on a ball. Has arm strength and is accurate. **Outlook:** Still a good offensive player, Everett is better suited to be a DH. Can be dangerous, especially if he doesn't have to play every day. **Grade 7**

CARL EVERETT'S HITTING ZONE

.286	.118	.192
.318	.342	.250
.357	.333	.205

LEFTY-RIGHTY SPLITS

vs.	Avg.	AB	H	2B	3B	HR	RBI	BB	SO	OBP	Slg.
L	.265	136	36	6	0	5	28	7	21	.295	.419
R	.246	354	87	11	2	18	59	35	78	.317	.441

Year Team (League)	Pos.	G	AB	R	H	2B	3B	HR	RBI	BB	SO	HBP	GDP	SB-CS	Avg.	OBP	SLG	OPS	E	Avg.
																		BATTING	FIELDING	
1990— GC Yankees (GCL)	OF	48	185	28	48	8	5	1	14	15	38	6	1	15-2	.259	.333	.373	.706	5	.932
1991— Greensboro (S. Atl.)	OF	123	468	96	127	18	0	4	40	57	122	23	1	28-19	.271	.376	.335	.711	7	.974
1992— Fort Laud. (FSL)	OF	46	183	30	42	8	2	2	9	12	40	4	1	11-3	.230	.291	.328	.619	3	.975
— Prince Will. (Car.)	OF	6	22	7	7	0	0	4	9	5	7	0	0	1-0	.318	.444	.864	1.308	0	1.000
1993— High Desert (Calif.)	OF	59	253	48	73	12	6	10	52	22	73	6	3	24-9	.289	.358	.502	.860	2	.985
— Florida (N.L.)	OF	11	19	0	2	0	0	0	0	1	9	0	0	1-0	.105	.150	.105	.255	1	.857
— Edmonton (PCL)	OF	35	136	28	42	13	4	6	16	19	45	2	1	12-1	.309	.401	.596	.997	2	.976
1994— Edmonton (PCL)	OF-DH	78	321	63	108	17	2	11	47	19	65	4	7	16-13	.336	.380	.505	.884	5	.989
— Florida (N.L.)	OF	16	51	7	11	1	0	2	6	3	15	0	0	4-0	.216	.259	.353	.612	0	1.000
1995— New York (N.L.)	OF	79	289	48	75	13	1	12	54	39	67	2	11	2-5	.260	.352	.436	.788	3	.981
— Norfolk (Int'l)	OF-DH-SS	67	260	52	78	16	4	6	35	20	47	4	2	12-6	.300	.358	.462	.820	3	1.000
1996— New York (N.L.)	OF	101	192	29	46	8	1	1	16	21	53	4	4	6-0	.240	.326	.307	.633	7	.935
1997— New York (N.L.)	OF	142	443	58	110	28	3	14	57	32	102	7	3	17-9	.248	.308	.420	.728	4	.971
1998— Houston (N.L.)	OF	133	467	72	138	34	4	15	76	44	102	3	11	14-12	.296	.359	.482	.840	4	.987
1999— Houston (N.L.)	OF-DH	123	464	86	151	33	3	25	108	50	94	11	5	27-7	.325	.398	.571	.969	6	.978
2000— Boston (A.L.)	OF-DH	137	496	82	149	32	4	34	108	52	113	8	4	11-4	.300	.373	.587	.959	6	.980
2001— Boston (A.L.)	OF-DH	102	409	61	105	24	4	14	58	27	104	13	3	9-2	.257	.323	.438	.761	5	.974
— Sarasota (Fla. St.)	DH	2	7	0	3	0	0	0	2	0	0	0	0	0-0	.429	.556	.429	.984	...	...
— GC Red Sox (GCL)	OF	3	10	2	2	0	0	0	2	1	3	0	0	0-0	.200	.273	.800	1.073	0	1.000
2002— Texas (A.L.)	OF-DH	105	374	47	100	16	0	16	62	33	77	6	7	2-3	.267	.333	.474	.772	5	.969
— Charlotte (Fla. St.)	OF	1	4	1	2	0	1	0	1	0	1	0	0	0-0	.500	.500	1.000	1.500	1	1.000
2003— Texas (A.L.)	OF-DH	74	270	53	74	13	3	18	51	31	48	5	2	4-1	.274	.356	.544	.900	2	.986
— Chicago (A.L.)	OF-DH	73	256	40	77	14	0	10	41	22	36	10	5	0-0	.301	.377	.473	.850	2	.987
2004— Brevard County (FSL)	OF-DH	5	15	2	6	1	0	0	3	2	3	0	0	0-0	.400	.444	.467	.911	0	1.000
— Montreal (N.L.)	OF-DH	39	127	8	32	10	0	2	14	8	19	5	8	0-0	.252	.319	.378	.697	3	.955

Year	Team (League)	Pos.	G	AB	R	H	2B	3B	HR	RBI	BB	SO	HBP	GDP	SB-CS	Avg.	OBP	SLG	OPS	E	Avg.
	—Chicago (A.L.)	DH-OF	43	154	21	41	7	1	5	21	8	26	5	3	1-0	.266	.320	.422	.742	0	1.000
2005—	Chicago (A.L.)	DH-OF	135	490	58	123	17	2	23	87	42	99	5	11	4-5	.251	.311	.435	.745	0	1.000
	American League totals (6 years)		669	2449	362	669	123	14	120	428	215	503	52	35	35-18	.273	.341	.482	.823	20	.980
	National League totals (8 years)		644	2052	308	565	127	12	71	331	198	461	32	42	71-33	.275	.346	.453	.799	31	.974
	Major League totals (13 years)		1313	4501	670	1234	250	26	191	759	413	964	84	77	106-51	.274	.344	.469	.812	51	.977

DIVISION SERIES RECORD

Year	Team (League)	Pos.	G	AB	R	H	2B	3B	HR	RBI	BB	SO	HBP	GDP	SB-CS	Avg.	OBP	SLG	OPS	E	Avg.
1998—	Houston (N.L.)	OF	4	13	1	2	0	0	0	0	0	4	0	1	0-0	.154	.154	.154	.308	0	1.000
1999—	Houston (N.L.)	OF	4	15	2	2	0	0	0	1	2	8	1	0	1-0	.133	.263	.133	.396	0	1.000
2005—	Chicago (A.L.)	DH	3	11	2	3	0	0	0	0	0	0	1	1	0-0	.273	.333	.273	.606	0	...
	Division series totals (3 years)		11	39	5	7	0	0	0	1	2	12	2	2	1-0	.179	.250	.179	.429	0	1.000

CHAMPIONSHIP SERIES RECORD

Year	Team (League)	Pos.	G	AB	R	H	2B	3B	HR	RBI	BB	SO	HBP	GDP	SB-CS	Avg.	OBP	SLG	OPS	E	Avg.
2005—	Chicago (A.L.)	DH	5	20	2	5	0	0	0	3	1	4	0	0	0-0	.250	.286	.250	.536	0	...

WORLD SERIES RECORD

Year	Team (League)	Pos.	G	AB	R	H	2B	3B	HR	RBI	BB	SO	HBP	GDP	SB-CS	Avg.	OBP	SLG	OPS	E	Avg.
2005—	Chicago (A.L.)	DH	4	9	1	4	0	0	0	0	0	2	0	0	0-1	.444	.444	.444	.889	0	...

ALL-STAR GAME RECORD

		G	AB	R	H	2B	3B	HR	RBI	BB	SO	HBP	GDP	SB-CS	Avg.	OBP	SLG	OPS	E	Avg.
	All-Star Game totals (2 years)	2	3	0	0	0	0	0	1	1	0	0	0	0-0	.000	.250	.000	.250	0	1.000

EYRE, SCOTT — P

PERSONAL: Born May 30, 1972, in Inglewood, Calif. ... 6-1/210. ... Throws left, bats left. ... Full name: Scott Alan Eyre. ... Name pronounced: AIR. ... High school: Cyprus (Magna, Utah). ... Junior college: Southern Idaho.

TRANSACTIONS/CAREER NOTES: Selected by Texas Rangers organization in ninth round of 1991 free-agent draft. ... Traded by Rangers to Chicago White Sox for SS Esteban Beltre (March 28, 1994). ... On disabled list (August 31-September 26, 1999); included rehabilitation assignment to Charlotte. ... Traded by White Sox to Toronto Blue Jays for P Gary Glover (November 7, 2000). ... Claimed on waivers by San Francisco Giants (August 8, 2002). ... On disabled list (March 27-April 22, 2004); included rehabilitation assignment to Fresno. ... Signed as a free agent by Chicago Cubs (Nov. 18, 2005).

CAREER HITTING: 2-for-11 (.182), 0 R, 0 2B, 0 3B, 0 HR, 0 RBI.

SCOUTING REPORT **Throws:** Eyre features a fastball that ranges from 89-94 mph, a slider and a changeup. ***Tendencies:*** He has very short, compact arm action, and his delivery makes it very difficult for hitters to pick up the ball. Fastball has gotten better, with very good running action. Has improved his command of the pitch. Slider is extremely quick with very late break. Has excellent arm speed on his change, making him effective against righthanders. ***Outlook:*** Eyre is one of the most improved setup relievers in the game. Is more aggressive and has a very resilient arm. Might be able to close now with improved velocity. ***Grade 9.2***

SCOTT EYRE'S PITCHING ZONE

.125	.545	.111
.297	.304	.242
.286	.286	.038

LEFTY-RIGHTY SPLITS

vs.	Avg.	AB	H	2B	3B	HR	RBI	BB	SO	OBP	Slg.
L	.182	99	18	6	0	0	4	11	30	.277	.242
R	.213	141	30	6	0	3	17	15	35	.292	.319

Year	Team (League)	W	L	Pct.	ERA	WHIP	G	GS	CG	ShO	Hld.	Sv.-Opp.	IP	H	R	ER	HR	BB-IBB	SO	Avg.
1992—	Butte (Pion.)	7	3	.700	2.90	1.36	15	14	2	1	...	0-...	80.2	71	30	26	6	39-0	94	.241
1993—	Char., S.C. (SAL)	11	7	.611	3.45	1.21	26	26	0	0	...	0-...	143.2	115	74	55	6	59-1	154	.220
1994—	South Bend (Mid.)	8	4	.667	3.47	1.30	19	18	2	0	...	0-...	111.2	108	56	43	7	37-0	111	.248
1995—	GC Whi. Sox (GCL)	0	2	.000	2.30	1.02	9	9	0	0	...	0-...	27.1	16	7	7	0	12-0	40	.174
1996—	Birmingham (Sou.)	12	7	.632	4.30	1.57	27	27	0	0	...	0-...	158.1	170	90	77	12	79-3	137	.277
1997—	Birmingham (Sou.)	13	5	.722	3.84	1.30	22	22	0	0	...	0-...	126.2	110	61	54	14	55-2	127	.231
	—Chicago (A.L.)	4	4	.500	5.04	1.53	11	11	0	0	0	0-0	60.2	62	36	34	11	31-1	36	.267
1998—	Chicago (A.L.)	3	8	.273	5.38	1.66	33	17	0	0	0	0-0	107.0	114	78	64	24	64-0	73	.271
1999—	Charlotte (Int'l)	6	4	.600	3.82	1.43	12	11	0	0	...	0-...	68.1	75	32	29	3	23-1	63	.284
	—Chicago (A.L.)	1	1	.500	7.56	2.12	21	0	0	0	1	0-0	25.0	38	22	21	6	15-2	17	.339
2000—	Chicago (A.L.)	1	1	.500	6.63	2.16	13	1	0	0	0	0-0	19.0	29	15	14	3	12-0	16	.372
	—Charlotte (Int'l)	3	2	.600	3.00	1.10	47	0	0	0	...	12-...	48.0	33	18	16	1	20-3	46	.200
2001—	Syracuse (Int'l)	4	6	.400	3.18	1.17	62	2	0	0	...	0-...	79.1	67	30	28	8	26-4	96	.224
	—Toronto (A.L.)	1	2	.333	3.45	1.40	17	0	0	0	3	2-3	15.2	15	6	6	1	7-2	16	.250
2002—	Toronto (A.L.)	2	4	.333	4.97	1.55	49	3	0	0	12	0-1	63.1	69	37	35	4	29-7	51	.278
	—San Francisco (N.L.)	0	0	...	1.59	1.59	21	0	0	0	6	0-...	11.1	11	4	2	0	7-1	7	.256
2003—	San Francisco (N.L.)	2	1	.667	3.32	1.51	74	0	0	0	20	1-3	57.0	60	23	21	4	26-0	35	.268
2004—	Fresno (PCL)	0	0	...	0.00	1.67	3	0	0	0	...	0-...	3.0	3	0	0	0	2-0	1	.250
	—San Francisco (N.L.)	2	2	.500	4.10	1.33	83	0	0	0	23	1-5	52.2	43	26	24	8	27-3	49	.221
2005—	San Francisco (N.L.)	2	2	.500	2.63	1.08	•86	0	0	0	•32	0-2	68.1	48	21	20	8	26-0	65	.200
	American League totals (6 years)	12	20	.375	5.39	1.67	144	32	0	0	16	2-4	290.2	327	194	174	49	158-12	209	.285
	National League totals (4 years)	6	5	.545	3.18	1.31	264	0	0	0	81	2-10	189.1	162	74	67	15	86-4	156	.230
	Major League totals (9 years)	18	25	.419	4.52	1.53	408	32	0	0	97	4-14	480.0	489	268	241	64	244-16	365	.264

DIVISION SERIES RECORD

Year	Team (League)	W	L	Pct.	ERA	WHIP	G	GS	CG	ShO	Hld.	Sv.-Opp.	IP	H	R	ER	HR	BB-IBB	SO	Avg.
2002—	San Francisco (N.L.)	0	0	...	0.00	0.75	3	0	0	0	1	0-0	1.1	1	0	0	0	0-0	0	.200
2003—	San Francisco (N.L.)	0	0	...	0.00	0.00	1	0	0	0	0	0-0	0.1	0	0	0	0	0-0	0	.000
	Division series totals (2 years)	0	0	...	0.00	0.60	4	0	0	0	1	0-0	1.2	1	0	0	0	0-0	0	.167

CHAMPIONSHIP SERIES RECORD

Year	Team (League)	W	L	Pct.	ERA	WHIP	G	GS	CG	ShO	Hld.	Sv.-Opp.	IP	H	R	ER	HR	BB-IBB	SO	Avg.
2002—	San Francisco (N.L.)	0	0	...	0.00	1.20	4	0	0	0	0	0-0	1.2	2	0	0	0	0-0	0	.286

WORLD SERIES RECORD

Year	Team (League)	W	L	Pct.	ERA	WHIP	G	GS	CG	ShO	Hld.	Sv.-Opp.	IP	H	R	ER	HR	BB-IBB	SO	Avg.
2002—	San Francisco (N.L.)	0	0	...	0.00	2.00	3	0	0	0	0	0-0	3.0	5	1	0	0	1-1	2	.385

FALKENBORG, BRIAN   P

PERSONAL: Born January 18, 1978, in Newport Beach, Calif. ... 6-6/190. ... Throws right, bats right. ... Full name: Brian Thomas Falkenborg. ... High school: Redmond (Wash.).
TRANSACTIONS/CAREER NOTES: Selected by Baltimore Orioles organization in second round of 1996 free-agent draft. ... On disabled list (March 23, 2000-entire season). ... Released by Orioles (December 19, 2000). ... Signed by Seattle Mariners organization (January 24, 2001). ... Signed as a free agent by Los Angeles Dodgers organization (November 10, 2003). ... On disabled list (April 5-24, 2004); included rehabilitation assignment to Las Vegas. ... Signed as a free agent by San Diego Padres organization (January 18, 2005). ... Signed as a free agent by St. Louis Cardinals organization (August 6, 2005).
CAREER HITTING: 0-for-2 (.000), 1 R, 0 2B, 0 3B, 0 HR, 0 RBI.

LEFTY-RIGHTY SPLITS

vs.	Avg.	AB	H	2B	3B	HR	RBI	BB	SO	OBP	Slg.
L	.316	19	6	2	1	1	2	3	2	.409	.684
R	.367	30	11	1	0	1	8	2	8	.406	.500

Year—Team (League)	W	L	Pct.	ERA	WHIP	G	GS	CG	ShO	Hld.	Sv.-Opp.	IP	H	R	ER	HR	BB-IBB	SO	Avg.
1996—GC Orioles (GCL)	0	3	.000	2.57	1.04	8	6	0	0	...	0-...	28.0	21	13	8	1	8-0	36	.196
—High Desert (Calif.)	0	0	...	0.00	1.00	1	0	0	0	...	0-...	1.0	1	0	0	0	0-0	1	.333
1997—Delmarva (S. Atl.)	7	9	.438	4.46	1.32	25	25	0	0	...	0-...	127.0	122	73	63	6	46-2	107	.253
—Bowie (East.)	0	1	.000	16.20	3.60	1	1	0	0	...	0-...	1.2	3	3	3	0	3-0	0	.375
1998—Frederick (Carolina)	5	5	.500	4.50	1.29	15	14	1	1	...	0-...	78.0	83	42	39	6	18-0	70	.267
1999—Bowie (East.)	3	6	.333	3.78	1.36	16	16	0	0	...	0-...	83.1	77	40	35	11	36-0	77	.242
—GC Orioles (GCL)	1	0	1.000	2.00	1.00	3	2	0	0	...	0-...	9.0	6	2	2	0	3-0	11	.176
—Baltimore (A.L.)	0	0	...	0.00	1.33	2	0	0	0	...	0-0	3.0	2	0	0	0	2-0	1	.200
2000—Baltimore (A.L.)			Did not play.																
2001—San Antonio (Texas)	5	6	.455	5.45	1.58	12	12	2	1	...	0-...	66.0	80	47	40	9	24-0	56	.305
—Tacoma (PCL)	2	4	.333	4.47	1.41	8	8	0	0	...	0-...	48.1	50	25	24	6	18-0	27	.273
2002—Tacoma (PCL)	4	4	.500	2.74	1.30	9	9	0	0	...	0-...	49.1	51	22	15	3	13-0	42	.267
2003—Tacoma (PCL)	4	2	.667	2.94	1.20	17	14	0	0	...	0-...	79.2	66	28	26	7	26-0	62	.221
2004—Los Angeles (N.L.)	1	0	1.000	7.53	1.95	6	0	0	0	...	0-0	14.1	19	14	12	2	9-0	11	.322
—Las Vegas (PCL)	4	6	.400	6.17	1.45	18	16	0	0	...	1-...	89.0	104	66	61	17	25-0	87	.286
2005—San Diego (N.L.)	0	0	...	8.18	2.00	10	0	0	0	...	0-0	11.0	17	11	10	2	5-1	10	.347
—Portland (PCL)	3	4	.429	5.25	1.56	28	0	0	0	3	1-2	36.0	35	25	21	2	21-1	26	.257
—Memphis (PCL)	1	0	1.000	1.69	0.94	13	0	0	0	5	5-5	16.0	10	3	3	1	5-0	14	.182
American League totals (1 year)	0	0	...	0.00	1.33	2	0	0	0	...	0-0	3.0	2	0	0	0	2-0	1	.200
National League totals (2 years)	1	0	1.000	7.82	1.97	16	0	0	0	...	0-0	25.1	36	25	22	4	14-1	21	.333
Major League totals (3 years)	1	0	1.000	6.99	1.91	18	0	0	0	...	0-0	28.1	38	25	22	4	16-1	22	.322

FARNSWORTH, KYLE   P

PERSONAL: Born April 14, 1976, in Wichita, Kan. ... 6-4/240. ... Throws right, bats right. ... Full name: Kyle Lynn Farnsworth. ... High school: Milton (Alpharetta, Ga.). ... Junior college: Abraham Baldwin (Tifton, Ga.).
TRANSACTIONS/CAREER NOTES: Selected by Chicago Cubs organization in 47th round of 1994 free-agent draft. ... On disabled list (April 10-June 4, 2002); included rehabilitation assignment to Iowa. ... On suspended list (June 26-28, 2003). ... On disabled list (August 28-September 12, 2004). ... Traded by Cubs to Detroit Tigers for P Roberto Novoa, OF Bo Flowers and SS Scott Moore (February 9, 2005). ... Traded by Tigers to Atlanta Braves for Ps Roman Colon and Zach Miner (July 31, 2005). ... On suspended list (August 9-14, 2005).
CAREER HITTING: 4-for-54 (.074), 3 R, 1 2B, 0 3B, 0 HR, 3 RBI.

SCOUTING REPORT **Throws:** Farnsworth's fastball ranges from 93-100 mph, and he also throws a slider. **Tendencies:** At times he's the hardest thrower in the game, but he can be hit hard. Is fairly easy to follow; hitters can time him as he goes deeper into the count, and he's predictable. Doesn't pitch inside enough. Has a power slider that has improved. **Outlook:** Farnsworth has a great arm and should be a dominant pitcher, but he is an underachiever. Was the Braves' closer down the stretch last season but Atlanta had a comfortable lead at the time. Playoffs proved that he belongs in a setup role. **Grade 7.9**

KYLE FARNSWORTH'S PITCHING ZONE

.211	.182	.176
.214	.333	.179
.280	.167	.111

LEFTY-RIGHTY SPLITS

vs.	Avg.	AB	H	2B	3B	HR	RBI	BB	SO	OBP	Slg.
L	.197	117	23	5	1	3	9	17	43	.301	.333
R	.165	127	21	1	0	2	14	10	44	.237	.220

Year—Team (League)	W	L	Pct.	ERA	WHIP	G	GS	CG	ShO	Hld.	Sv.-Opp.	IP	H	R	ER	HR	BB-IBB	SO	Avg.
1995—GC Cubs (GCL)	3	2	.600	0.87	1.06	16	0	0	0	...	1-...	31.0	22	8	3	0	11-0	18	.214
1996—Rockford (Midwest)	9	6	.600	3.70	1.40	20	20	1	0	...	0-...	112.0	122	62	46	7	35-0	82	.274
1997—Daytona (Fla. St.)	10	10	.500	4.09	1.44	27	27	2	0	...	0-...	156.1	178	91	71	13	47-1	105	.286
1998—West Tenn (Sou.)	8	2	.800	2.77	1.12	13	13	0	0	...	0-...	81.1	70	32	25	6	21-0	73	.231
—Iowa (PCL)	5	9	.357	6.93	1.61	18	18	0	0	...	0-...	102.2	129	88	79	18	36-0	79	.309
1999—Iowa (PCL)	2	2	.500	3.20	1.19	6	6	0	0	...	0-...	39.1	38	16	14	5	9-0	29	.262
—Chicago (N.L.)	5	9	.357	5.05	1.48	27	21	1	1	0	0-0	130.0	140	80	73	28	52-1	70	.271
2000—Chicago (N.L.)	2	9	.182	6.43	1.82	46	5	0	0	6	1-6	77.0	90	58	55	14	50-8	74	.291
—Iowa (PCL)	2	0	.000	3.20	1.66	22	0	0	0	...	9-...	25.1	24	10	9	1	18-2	22	.250
2001—Chicago (N.L.)	4	6	.400	2.74	1.15	76	0	0	0	24	2-3	82.0	65	26	25	8	29-2	107	.213
2002—Chicago (N.L.)	4	6	.400	7.33	1.65	45	0	0	0	6	1-7	46.2	53	47	38	9	24-7	46	.293
—Iowa (PCL)	0	1	.000	6.00	1.00	2	0	0	0	...	0-0	3.0	3	2	2	1	0-0	2	.273
2003—Chicago (N.L.)	3	2	.600	3.30	1.17	77	0	0	0	19	0-3	76.1	53	31	28	7	36-1	92	.196
2004—Chicago (N.L.)	4	5	.444	4.73	1.50	72	0	0	0	18	0-4	66.2	67	39	35	10	33-1	78	.260
2005—Detroit (A.L.)	1	1	.500	2.32	1.15	46	0	0	0	15	6-8	42.2	29	12	11	1	20-0	55	.192
—Atlanta (N.L.)	0	0	...	1.98	0.80	26	0	0	0	4	10-10	27.1	15	6	6	4	7-0	32	.161
American League totals (1 year)	1	1	.500	2.32	1.15	46	0	0	0	15	6-8	42.2	29	12	11	1	20-0	55	.192
National League totals (7 years)	22	37	.373	4.62	1.41	369	26	1	1	77	14-33	506.0	483	287	260	79	231-20	499	.250
Major League totals (7 years)	23	38	.377	4.45	1.39	415	26	1	1	92	20-41	548.2	512	299	271	80	251-20	554	.246

DIVISION SERIES RECORD

Year—Team (League)	W	L	Pct.	ERA	WHIP	G	GS	CG	ShO	Hld.	Sv.-Opp.	IP	H	R	ER	HR	BB-IBB	SO	Avg.
2003—Chicago (N.L.)	0	0	...	0.00	0.75	3	0	0	0	1	0-0	2.2	1	0	0	0	1-0	2	.111
2005—Atlanta (N.L.)	0	0	...	9.00	1.00	2	0	0	0	0	0-0	3.0	2	3	3	0	1-0	4	.182
Division series totals (2 years)	0	0	...	4.76	0.88	5	0	0	0	1	0-0	5.2	3	3	3	0	2-0	6	.150

F

Year	Team (League)	W	L	Pct.	ERA	WHIP	G	GS	CG	ShO	Hld.	Sv.-Opp.	IP	H	R	ER	HR	BB-IBB	SO	Avg.
2003—	Chicago (N.L.)	0	0	...	10.13	1.50	5	0	0	0	0	0-0	5.1	6	6	6	0	2-2	7	.300

FASANO, SAL   C

PERSONAL: Born August 10, 1971, in Chicago. ... 6-2/254. ... Bats right, throws right. ... Full name: Salvatore Frank Fasano. ... Name pronounced: fuh-SAH-noh. ... High school: Hoffman Estates (Ill.). ... College: Evansville.

TRANSACTIONS/CAREER NOTES: Selected by Kansas City Royals organization in 37th round of 1993 free-agent draft. ... On disabled list (April 20-May 9 and August 30, 1998-remainder of season); included rehabilitation assignment to Omaha. ... Traded by Royals to Oakland Athletics for cash (March 30, 2000). ... Contract purchased by Royals from A's (May 22, 2001). ... Traded by Royals with P Mac Suzuki to Colorado Rockies for C Brent Mayne (June 24, 2001). ... Signed as a free agent by Tampa Bay Devil Rays organization (January 28, 2002). ... Released by Devil Rays (June 1, 2002). ... Signed by Milwaukee Brewers organization (June 6, 2002). ... Traded by Brewers with OF Alex Ochoa to Anaheim Angels for C Jorge Fabregas and two players to be named (July 31, 2002); Brewers acquired IF Johnny Raburn (August 14, 2002) and P Pedro Liriano to complete deal (September 20, 2002). ... Released by Angels (November 5, 2002). ... Signed as a free agent by New York Yankees organization (January 14, 2004). ... Signed as a free agent by Baltimore Orioles organization (December 20, 2004).

2005 GAMES PLAYED BY POSITION (MLB): C—60, DH—3, 1B—1.

SCOUTING REPORT Fasano is strictly a backup; he won't hit enough to play much. Has a long stroke and not much bat speed. Does have very good power on pitches out over the plate. Doesn't adjust quickly to breaking balls. Has good hands as a receiver but sits down lower than most catchers and gets locked in where he can't move well or adjust quickly. Has arm strength but a slow release. *Grade 4.6*

SAL FASANO'S HITTING ZONE

.545	.125	.000
.417	.222	.167
.217	.400	.286

LEFTY-RIGHTY SPLITS

vs.	Avg.	AB	H	2B	3B	HR	RBI	BB	SO	OBP	Slg.
L	.310	42	13	1	0	6	6	4	7	.383	.762
R	.229	118	27	2	0	5	14	5	34	.283	.373

									BATTING										FIELDING	
Year	Team (League)	Pos.	G	AB	R	H	2B	3B	HR	RBI	BB	SO	HBP	GDP	SB-CS	Avg.	OBP	SLG	OPS	E	Avg.
1993—	Eugene (Northwest)	C	49	176	25	47	11	1	10	36	19	49	6	1	4-3	.267	.355	.511	.866	1	.997
1994—	Rockford (Midwest)	C-1B	97	345	61	97	16	1	25	81	33	66	16	10	8-3	.281	.366	.551	.917	12	.981
—	Wilmington (Caro.)	C-1B	23	90	15	29	7	0	7	32	13	24	0	3	0-0	.322	.408	.633	1.041	4	.957
1995—	Wilmington (Caro.)	C-1B	23	88	12	20	2	1	2	7	5	16	1	4	0-0	.227	.277	.341	.618	0	1.000
—	Wichita (Texas)	C-1B	87	317	60	92	19	2	20	66	27	61	16	8	3-6	.290	.373	.552	.925	14	.979
1996—	Kansas City (A.L.)	C	51	143	20	29	2	0	6	19	14	25	2	...	1-1	.203	.283	.343	.626	5	.984
—	Omaha (A.A.)	C-1B-3B	29	104	12	24	4	0	4	15	6	21	1	3	0-1	.231	.277	.385	.662	4	.982
1997—	Omaha (A.A.)	C-DH	49	152	17	25	7	0	4	14	12	53	5	1	0-0	.164	.247	.289	.536	4	.988
—	Kansas City (A.L.)	C-DH	13	38	4	8	2	0	1	1	1	12	0	...	0-0	.211	.231	.342	.573	1	.982
—	Wichita (Texas)	C-1B	40	131	27	31	5	0	13	27	20	35	7	2	0-2	.237	.360	.573	.933	4	.984
1998—	Kansas City (A.L.)	C-1B-3B	74	216	21	49	10	0	8	31	16	56	16	...	1-0	.227	.307	.384	.692	1	.996
—	Omaha (PCL)	C	4	14	1	3	1	0	1	2	1	4	0	1	0-1	.214	.267	.500	.767	0	1.000
1999—	Omaha (PCL)	C-DH-1B	88	280	63	77	15	0	21	49	42	69	26	7	4-2	.275	.415	.554	.969	† 12	.981
—	Kansas City (A.L.)	C	23	60	11	14	2	0	5	16	7	17	7	...	0-1	.233	.373	.517	.890	0	1.000
2000—	Oakland (A.L.)	C	52	126	21	27	6	0	7	19	14	47	3	...	0-0	.214	.306	.429	.734	5	.981
2001—	Oakland (A.L.)	C-DH	11	21	2	1	0	0	0	0	1	12	1	...	0-0	.048	.130	.048	.178	2	.952
—	Kansas City (A.L.)	C	3	1	0	0	0	0	0	0	0	0	0	...	0-0	.000	.000	.000	.000	0	1.000
—	Omaha (PCL)	C-1B	13	46	6	11	1	0	2	7	4	11	5	1	0-0	.239	.364	.391	.755	3	.966
—	Colo. Springs (PCL)	C	26	82	16	25	4	0	7	23	9	26	4	4	0-0	.305	.396	.610	1.006	4	.984
—	Colorado (N.L.)	C	25	63	10	16	5	0	3	9	4	19	3	...	0-0	.254	.329	.476	.805	3	.982
2002—	Durham (Int'l)	C	31	101	11	26	6	0	6	9	12	29	9	1	0-0	.257	.385	.495	.880	4	.984
—	Indianapolis (Int'l)	C-1B	34	97	5	20	9	0	1	11	3	24	6	2	0-0	.206	.271	.330	.601	3	.984
—	Salt Lake (PCL)	C	22	76	13	21	3	0	5	10	7	24	2	...	1-0	.276	.349	.513	.862	4	.978
—	Anaheim (A.L.)	C	2	1	0	0	0	0	0	0	0	1	0	...	0-0	.000	.000	.000	.000	1	1.000
2003—	....			Did not play.																	
2004—	Columbus (Int'l)	C	76	236	21	54	15	1	10	34	10	45	6	6	0-0	.229	.273	.428	.701	4	.993
2005—	Ottawa (Int'l)	C-1B-DH	14	45	6	12	3	0	4	12	2	15	2	1	0-0	.267	.327	.600	.927	1	.993
—	Baltimore (A.L.)	C-DH-1B	64	160	25	40	3	0	11	20	9	41	5	...	0-0	.250	.310	.475	.785	4	.987
American League totals (8 years)			293	766	104	168	25	0	38	106	56	211	34	5	2-2	.219	.300	.401	.701	19	.988
National League totals (1 year)			25	63	10	16	5	0	3	9	4	19	3	...	0-0	.254	.329	.476	.805	3	.982
Major League totals (8 years)			318	829	114	184	30	0	41	115	60	230	37	5	2-2	.222	.302	.407	.709	22	.988

DIVISION SERIES RECORD

Year	Team (League)	Pos.	G	AB	R	H	2B	3B	HR	RBI	BB	SO	HBP	GDP	SB-CS	Avg.	OBP	SLG	OPS	E	Avg.
2000—	Oakland (A.L.)	C	1	0	0	0	0	0	0	0	0	0	0	0	0-0	...	...	...	...	0	1.000

FASSERO, JEFF   P

PERSONAL: Born January 5, 1963, in Springfield, Ill. ... 6-1/200. ... Throws left, bats left. ... Full name: Jeffrey Joseph Fassero. ... Name pronounced: fuh-SAIR-oh. ... High school: Griffin (Springfield, Ill.). ... College: Mississippi.

TRANSACTIONS/CAREER NOTES: Selected by St. Louis Cardinals organization in 22nd round of June 1984 free-agent draft. ... Selected by Chicago White Sox organization from Cardinals organization in Rule 5 minor league draft (December 5, 1989). ... Released by White Sox (April 3, 1990). ... Signed by Cleveland Indians organization (April 9, 1990). ... Signed as a free agent by Montreal Expos organization (January 3, 1991). ... On disabled list (July 24-August 11, 1994). ... Traded by Expos with P Alex Pacheco to Seattle Mariners for C Chris Widger and Ps Trey Moore and Matt Wagner (October 29, 1996). ... On disabled list (March 22-April 12, 1998). ... Traded by Mariners to Texas Rangers for a player to be named (August 27, 1999); Mariners acquired OF Adrian Myers to complete deal (September 22, 1999). ... Signed as a free agent by Boston Red Sox (December 22, 1999). ... On disabled list (June 19-July 5, 2000). ... Signed as a free agent by Chicago Cubs (December 8, 2000). ... Traded by Cubs with cash to Cardinals for two players to be named (August 24, 2002); Cubs acquired Ps Jason Karnuth and Jared Blasdell to complete deal (September 24, 2002). ... On suspended list (May 2-4, 2003). ... Signed as a free agent by Colorado Rockies organization (January 13, 2004). ... Released by Rockies (September 24, 2004). ... Signed by Arizona Diamondbacks (September 29, 2004). ... Signed as a free agent by San Francisco Giants organization (December 14, 2004).

CAREER HITTING: 22-for-272 (.081), 19 R, 2 2B, 1 3B, 0 HR, 6 RBI.

JEFF FASSERO'S PITCHING ZONE

.364	.273	.222
.317	.269	.410
.350	.333	.207

LEFTY-RIGHTY SPLITS

vs.	Avg.	AB	H	2B	3B	HR	RBI	BB	SO	OBP	Slg.
L	.194	93	18	1	0	0	9	14	18	.294	.204
R	.296	250	74	16	2	7	43	17	42	.340	.460

Year	Team (League)	W	L	Pct.	ERA	WHIP	G	GS	CG	ShO	Hld.	Sv.-Opp.	IP	H	R	ER	HR	BB-IBB	SO	Avg.
1984—Johnson City (App.)	4	7	.364	4.59	1.56	13	11	2	0	...	1-...	66.2	65	42	34	2	39-0	59	.261
1985—Springfield (Midw.)	4	8	.333	4.01	1.43	29	15	1	0	...	1-...	119.0	125	78	53	11	45-3	65	.262
1986—St. Pete. (FSL)	13	7	.650	2.45	1.20	26	26	6	1	...	0-...	176.0	156	63	48	5	56-4	112	.239
1987—Arkansas (Texas)	10	7	.588	4.10	1.55	28	27	2	1	...	0-...	151.1	168	90	69	16	67-7	118	.283
1988—Arkansas (Texas)	5	5	.500	3.58	1.77	70	1	0	0	...	17-...	78.0	97	48	31	1	41-13	72	.301
1989—Louisville (A.A.)	3	10	.231	5.22	1.63	22	19	0	0	...	0-...	112.0	136	79	65	13	47-1	73	.302
—Arkansas (Texas)	4	1	.800	1.64	1.00	6	6	2	1	...	0-...	44.0	32	11	8	1	12-0	38	.200
1990—Cant./Akr. (Eastern)	5	4	.556	2.80	1.40	61	0	0	0	...	6-...	64.1	66	24	20	5	24-6	61	.263
1991—Indianapolis (A.A.)	3	0	1.000	1.47	0.98	18	0	0	0	...	4-...	18.1	11	3	3	1	7-3	12	.177
—Montreal (N.L.)	2	5	.286	2.44	1.01	51	0	0	0	7	8-11	55.1	39	17	15	1	17-1	42	.196
1992—Montreal (N.L.)	8	7	.533	2.84	1.34	70	0	0	0	12	1-7	85.2	81	35	27	1	34-6	63	.249
1993—Montreal (N.L.)	12	5	.706	2.29	1.16	56	15	1	0	6	1-3	149.2	119	50	38	7	54-0	140	.216
1994—Montreal (N.L.)	8	6	.571	2.99	1.15	21	21	1	0	0	0-0	138.2	119	54	46	13	40-4	119	.229
1995—Montreal (N.L.)	13	14	.481	4.33	1.49	30	30	1	0	0	0-0	189.0	207	102	91	15	74-3	164	.283
1996—Montreal (N.L.)	15	11	.577	3.30	1.17	34	34	5	1	0	0-0	231.2	217	95	85	20	55-3	222	.244
1997—Seattle (A.L.)	16	9	.640	3.61	1.32	35	•35	2	1	0	0-0	234.1	226	108	94	21	84-6	189	.249
1998—Seattle (A.L.)	13	12	.520	3.97	1.29	32	32	7	0	0	0-0	224.2	223	115	99	33	66-2	176	.259
1999—Seattle (A.L.)	4	14	.222	7.38	1.88	30	24	0	0	0	2	0-0	139.0	188	123	114	34	73-3	101	.321
—Texas (A.L.)	1	0	1.000	5.71	1.73	7	3	0	0	0	0-0	17.1	20	12	11	1	10-0	13	.286
2000—Boston (A.L.)	8	8	.500	4.78	1.56	38	23	0	0	0	5	0-0	130.0	153	72	69	16	50-2	97	.296
2001—Chicago (N.L.)	4	4	.500	3.42	1.21	82	0	0	0	25	12-17	73.2	66	31	28	6	23-5	79	.235
2002—Chicago (N.L.)	5	6	.455	6.18	1.71	57	0	0	0	6	0-1	51.0	65	37	35	5	22-5	44	.313
—St. Louis (N.L.)	3	0	1.000	3.00	1.17	16	0	0	0	8	0-2	18.0	16	6	6	4	5-0	12	.232
2003—St. Louis (N.L.)	1	7	.125	5.68	1.64	62	0	0	0	11	3-6	77.2	93	51	49	17	34-4	55	.296
2004—Colorado (N.L.)	3	8	.273	5.51	1.62	40	12	0	0	2	0-0	111.0	136	73	68	9	44-5	59	.306
—Arizona (N.L.)	0	0	...	0.00	0.00	1	0	0	0	0	0-0	1.0	0	0	0	0	0-0	1	.000
2005—San Francisco (N.L.)	4	7	.364	4.05	1.35	48	6	0	0	2	0-2	91.0	92	48	41	7	31-1	60	.268
American League totals (4 years)	42	43	.494	4.67	1.47	142	117	9	1		7	0-0	745.1	810	430	387	105	283-13	576	.276
National League totals (11 years)	78	80	.494	3.74	1.32	568	124	8	1		78	25-49	1273.1	1250	599	529	105	433-37	1060	.256
Major League totals (15 years)	120	123	.494	4.08	1.38	710	241	17	2		85	25-49	2018.2	2060	1029	916	210	716-50	1636	.264

DIVISION SERIES RECORD

Year	Team (League)	W	L	Pct.	ERA	WHIP	G	GS	CG	ShO	Hld.	Sv.-Opp.	IP	H	R	ER	HR	BB-IBB	SO	Avg.
1997—Seattle (A.L.)	1	0	1.000	1.13	0.88	1	1	0	0	0	0-0	8.0	3	1	1	0	4-0	3	.120
1999—Texas (A.L.)	0	0	...	9.00	3.00	1	0	0	0	0	0-0	1.0	1	1	1	0	1-0	1	.400
2002—St. Louis (N.L.)	2	0	1.000	0.00	1.13	3	0	0	0	0	0-0	2.2	3	0	0	0	0-0	2	.300
Division series totals (3 years)	3	0	1.000	1.54	1.11	5	1	0	0		0	0-0	11.2	8	2	2	0	5-0	6	.200

CHAMPIONSHIP SERIES RECORD

Year	Team (League)	W	L	Pct.	ERA	WHIP	G	GS	CG	ShO	Hld.	Sv.-Opp.	IP	H	R	ER	HR	BB-IBB	SO	Avg.
2002—St. Louis (N.L.)	0	0	...	0.00	0.00	1	0	0	0	0	0-0	0.2	0	0	0	0	0-0	1	.000

FELDMAN, SCOTT   P

PERSONAL: Born February 7, 1983, in Kailua, Hawaii. ... 6-5/210. ... Throws right, bats left. ... Full name: Scott Wayne Feldman. ... Junior college: San Mateo (Calif.).

TRANSACTIONS/CAREER NOTES: Selected by Texas Rangers organization in 30th round of 2003 free-agent draft.

CAREER HITTING: 0-for-0 (.000), 0 R, 0 2B, 0 3B, 0 HR, 0 RBI.

LEFTY-RIGHTY SPLITS

vs.	Avg.	AB	H	2B	3B	HR	RBI	BB	SO	OBP	Slg.
L	.308	13	4	0	0	0	0	1	0	.357	.308
R	.227	22	5	1	0	0	4	1	4	.261	.273

Year	Team (League)	W	L	Pct.	ERA	WHIP	G	GS	CG	ShO	Hld.	Sv.-Opp.	IP	H	R	ER	HR	BB-IBB	SO	Avg.
2003—Arizona Rangers (AZL)	1	1	.500	4.26	0.79	3	1	0	0	...	0-...	6.1	4	6	3	0	1-0	7	.138
2004—Arizona Rangers (AZL)	0	0	...	0.00	0.43	4	3	0	0	...	0-...	7.0	2	0	0	0	1-0	5	.091
2005—Bakersfield (Calif.)	0	0	...	0.00	0.78	6	0	0	0	0	3-3	9.0	5	2	0	0	2-0	11	.152
—Frisco (Texas)	1	2	.333	2.36	1.08	46	0	0	0	3	14-20	61.0	43	18	16	3	23-8	41	.202
—Texas (A.L.)	0	1	.000	0.96	1.18	8	0	0	0	1	0-0	9.1	9	1	1	0	2-1	4	.257
Major League totals (1 year)	0	1	.000	0.96	1.18	8	0	0	0		1	0-0	9.1	9	1	1	0	2-1	4	.257

FELIZ, PEDRO   3B/OF

PERSONAL: Born April 27, 1975, in Azua, Dominican Republic. ... 6-1/205. ... Bats right, throws right. ... Full name: Pedro Julio Feliz. ... High school: Los Toros (Azua, Dominican Republic).

TRANSACTIONS/CAREER NOTES: Signed as a non-drafted free agent by San Francisco Giants organization (February 7, 1994).

2005 GAMES PLAYED BY POSITION (MLB): 3B—79, OF—75, 1B—15.

SCOUTING REPORT *Offense:* Feliz is a run producer with power, but his high strikeout totals show a lack of discipline at the plate. Has an extremely long stroke and likes to extend his arms, yet has very good bat speed. Is not a patient hitter. Is a good high-fastball hitter who likes to pull the ball. Has not adjusted well to breaking pitches. *Defense:* He played nearly as many games in left field as he did at third base last year, and he spent time at first base. Arm strength is a plus for Feliz as an infielder, but he has a slow release and can be erratic when rushed. Has good hands but needs to work on getting better jumps, especially to his backhand side. *Outlook:* The slowly developing Feliz may never be a high-average hitter but he still has some offensive upside. *Grade 7.4*

PEDRO FELIZ'S HITTING ZONE

.368	.357	.192
.242	.403	.167
.260	.276	.154

LEFTY-RIGHTY SPLITS

vs.	Avg.	AB	H	2B	3B	HR	RBI	BB	SO	OBP	Slg.
L	.271	133	36	8	1	6	17	14	18	.340	.481
R	.243	436	106	22	3	14	64	24	84	.281	.404

Year	Team (League)	Pos.	G	AB	R	H	2B	3B	HR	RBI	BB	SO	HBP	GDP	SB-CS	Avg.	OBP	SLG	OPS	E	Avg.
1994—	Ariz. Giants (Ariz.)	3B	38	119	7	23	0	0	0	3	2	20	2	3	2-3	.193	.220	.193	.413	5	.953
1995—	Bellingham (N'west)	1B-3B	43	113	14	31	2	1	0	16	7	33	0	2	1-1	.274	.311	.310	.621	2	.971
1996—	Burlington (Midw.)	1B-3B	93	321	36	85	12	2	5	36	18	65	1	11	5-2	.265	.303	.361	.665	17	.937
1997—	Bakersfield (Calif.)	3B	135	515	59	140	25	4	14	56	23	90	7	15	5-7	.272	.310	.417	.728	23	.950
1998—	Shreveport (Texas)	3B	100	364	39	96	23	2	12	50	9	62	2	15	0-1	.264	.282	.437	.719	22	.926
	Fresno (PCL)	3B	7	7	1	3	1	0	1	3	1	0	0	1	0-0	.429	.500	1.000	1.500	0	1.000
1999—	Shreveport (Texas)	3B	131	491	52	124	24	6	13	77	19	90	3	18	4-2	.253	.282	.405	.687	27	.934
2000—	Fresno (PCL)	3B-SS	128	503	85	150	34	2	33	105	30	94	2	18	1-1	.298	.337	.571	.908	§ 24	.939
	San Francisco (N.L.)	3B	8	7	1	2	0	0	0	0	0	1	0	0	0-0	.286	.286	.286	.571	0	...
2001—	San Francisco (N.L.)	3B-DH	94	220	23	50	9	1	7	22	10	50	2	5	2-1	.227	.264	.373	.637	12	.908
2002—	San Francisco (N.L.)	3B-OF-SS	67	146	14	37	4	1	2	13	6	27	0	2	0-0	.253	.281	.336	.617	3	.982
2003—	San Francisco (N.L.)	3B-OF-1B	95	235	31	58	9	3	16	48	10	53	1	7	2-2	.247	.278	.515	.793	4	.982
2004—	San Francisco (N.L.)	1B-3B-SS OF	144	503	72	139	33	3	22	84	23	85	0	18	5-2	.276	.305	.485	.790	13	.983
2005—	San Francisco (N.L.)	3B-OF-1B	156	569	69	142	30	4	20	81	38	102	1	20	0-2	.250	.295	.422	.717	10	.976
	Major League totals (6 years)		564	1680	210	428	85	12	67	248	87	318	4	52	9-7	.255	.290	.439	.730	42	.974

DIVISION SERIES RECORD

Year	Team (League)	Pos.	G	AB	R	H	2B	3B	HR	RBI	BB	SO	HBP	GDP	SB-CS	Avg.	OBP	SLG	OPS	E	Avg.
2002—	San Francisco (N.L.)		1	1	0	0	0	0	0	0	0	1	0	0	0-0	.000	.000	.000	.000	...	...
2003—	San Francisco (N.L.)		3	3	1	2	0	1	0	1	0	1	0	0	0-0	.667	.667	1.333	2.000	0	...
	Division series totals (2 years)		4	4	1	2	0	1	0	1	0	2	0	0	0-0	.500	.500	1.000	1.500	0	...

CHAMPIONSHIP SERIES RECORD

Year	Team (League)	Pos.	G	AB	R	H	2B	3B	HR	RBI	BB	SO	HBP	GDP	SB-CS	Avg.	OBP	SLG	OPS	E	Avg.
2002—	San Francisco (N.L.)		1	1	0	0	0	0	0	0	0	0	0	0	0-0	.000	.000	.000	.000	...	...

WORLD SERIES RECORD

Year	Team (League)	Pos.	G	AB	R	H	2B	3B	HR	RBI	BB	SO	HBP	GDP	SB-CS	Avg.	OBP	SLG	OPS	E	Avg.
2002—	San Francisco (N.L.)	DH	3	5	0	0	0	0	0	0	0	2	0	0	0-0	.000	.000	.000	.000		

FICK, ROBERT   OF/1B

PERSONAL: Born March 15, 1974, in Torrance, Calif. ... 6-1/205. ... Bats left, throws right. ... Full name: Robert Charles Fick. ... High school: Newbury Park (Calif.). ... College: Cal State Northridge.

TRANSACTIONS/CAREER NOTES: Selected by Oakland Athletics organization in 45th round of 1992 free-agent draft; did not sign. ... Selected by Detroit Tigers organization in 43rd round of 1995 free-agent draft; did not sign. ... Selected by Tigers organization in fifth round of 1996 free-agent draft. ... On disabled list (March 31-September 7, 1999); included rehabilitation assignments to GCL Tigers, West Michigan and Toledo. ... On suspended list (May 23-26, 2000). ... On disabled list (July 6-September 1, 2000); included rehabilitation assignment to Toledo. ... On suspended list (September 22-27, 2001). ... Signed as a free agent by Atlanta Braves organization (January 6, 2003). ... On disabled list (April 13-29, 2003). ... Released by Braves (November 5, 2003). ... Signed by Tampa Bay Devil Rays (January 9, 2004). ... Released by Devil Rays (August 13, 2004). ... Signed by San Diego Padres organization (August 19, 2004).

2005 GAMES PLAYED BY POSITION (MLB): 1B—29, C—28, OF—13, DH—2, 3B—1.

SCOUTING REPORT *Offense:* Fick is a line-drive, gap hitter without much power. Has a sweeping type of swing and likes the ball better up than down. Handles righthanded pitching much better than lefthanders. *Defense:* In addition to playing first, he catches and can play third and the outfield, but defense is not his strong suit. Doesn't move well around the bag and has stiff hands. Can't run. *Outlook:* He's not an everyday player with his lack of a position and negligible power. More of a role player who can provide depth. *Grade 5.7*

ROBERT FICK'S HITTING ZONE

.125	.556	.250
.321	.414	.340
.214	.000	.227

LEFTY-RIGHTY SPLITS

vs.	Avg.	AB	H	2B	3B	HR	RBI	BB	SO	OBP	Slg.
L	.297	37	11	0	1	0	4	6	7	.409	.351
R	.259	193	50	10	1	3	26	20	26	.326	.368

Year	Team (League)	Pos.	G	AB	R	H	2B	3B	HR	RBI	BB	SO	HBP	GDP	SB-CS	Avg.	OBP	SLG	OPS	E	Avg.
1996—	Jamestown (NYP)	C	43	133	18	33	6	0	1	14	12	25	0	4	3-1	.248	.306	.316	.622	3	.982
1997—	W. Mich. (Mid.)	1B-3B-C	122	463	100	* 158	* 50	3	16	90	75	74	1	10	13-4	.341	.429	.566	.994	12	.989
1998—	Jacksonville (Sou.)	1B-C-OF	130	515	101	164	* 47	6	18	114	71	83	6	8	8-4	.318	.401	.538	.939	9	.985
	Detroit (A.L.)	C-DH-1B	7	22	6	8	1	0	3	7	2	7	0	1	1-0	.364	.417	.818	1.235	1	.966
1999—	GC Tigers (GCL)	1B-C-DH	3	9	2	3	1	0	0	2	2	0	0	0	1-0	.333	.455	.444	.899	0	1.000
	W. Mich. (Mid.)	1B-C-DH	3	11	2	3	0	0	0	0	2	0	0	0	1-0	.273	.385	.273	.657	2	.913
	Toledo (Int'l)	1B-C-DH 3B	14	48	11	15	0	1	2	8	8	5	1	0	1-0	.313	.414	.479	.893	5	.944
	Detroit (A.L.)	DH-C	15	41	6	9	0	0	3	10	7	6	0	1	1-0	.220	.327	.439	.766	0	1.000
2000—	Detroit (A.L.)	1B-C-DH	66	163	18	41	7	2	3	22	22	39	1	4	2-1	.252	.340	.374	.715	5	.983
	Toledo (Int'l)	1B	17	68	5	10	1	0	1	7	6	13	2	0	1-0	.147	.234	.265	.498	0	1.000

Year	Team (League)	Pos.	G	AB	R	H	2B	3B	HR	RBI	BB	SO	HBP	GDP	SB-CS	Avg.	OBP	SLG	OPS	E	Avg.
2001— Detroit (A.L.)	C-1B-DH																				
		OF	124	401	62	109	21	2	19	61	39	62	4	10	0-3	.272	.339	.476	.816	7	.989
2002— Detroit (A.L.)	OF-DH	148	556	66	150	36	2	17	63	46	90	7	17	0-1	.270	.331	.433	.764	*12	.963
2003— Atlanta (N.L.)	1B	126	409	52	110	26	1	11	80	42	47	2	9	1-0	.269	.335	.418	.753	14	.987
2004— Tampa Bay (A.L.)	DH-OF-1B																				
		C	76	214	12	43	5	2	6	26	20	32	2	2	0-0	.201	.273	.327	.600	3	.977
— Portland (PCL)	1B-C	12	50	8	19	4	0	2	6	2	11	0	0	1-0	.380	.404	.580	.984	1	.990
— San Diego (N.L.)	1B	13	12	2	2	0	0	0	0	2	4	1	0	0-0	.167	.333	.167	.500	0	1.000
2005— Portland (PCL)	1B-C	10	32	5	12	1	0	3	11	10	3	1	1	1-0	.375	.500	.688	1.210	1	.989
— San Diego (N.L.)	DH-3B	93	230	25	61	10	2	3	30	26	33	1	4	0-2	.265	.340	.365	.705	6	.986
American League totals (6 years)		436	1397	170	360	70	8	51	189	136	236	14	35	4-5	.258	.327	.429	.755	28	.981
National League totals (3 years)		232	651	79	173	36	3	14	110	70	84	4	13	1-2	.266	.337	.395	.731	20	.987
Major League totals (8 years)		668	2048	249	533	106	11	65	299	206	320	18	48	5-7	.260	.330	.418	.748	48	.984

DIVISION SERIES RECORD

Year	Team (League)	Pos.	G	AB	R	H	2B	3B	HR	RBI	BB	SO	HBP	GDP	SB-CS	Avg.	OBP	SLG	OPS	E	Avg.
2003— Atlanta (N.L.)	1B	4	11	0	0	0	0	0	0	1	2	0	1	0-0	.000	.083	.000	.083	0	1.000
2005— San Diego (N.L.)	1B	2	5	0	1	0	0	0	0	1	0	0	0	0-0	.200	.333	.200	.533	0	1.000
Division series totals (2 years)		6	16	0	1	0	0	0	0	2	2	0	1	0-0	.063	.167	.063	.229	0	1.000

ALL-STAR GAME RECORD

	G	AB	R	H	2B	3B	HR	RBI	BB	SO	HBP	GDP	SB-CS	Avg.	OBP	SLG	OPS	E	Avg.
All-Star Game totals (1 year)	1	2	1	1	0	0	0	0	0	0	0	0	1-0	.500	.500	.500	1.000	0	1.000

FIELD, NATE · P

PERSONAL: Born December 11, 1975, in Denver. ... 6-2/200. ... Throws right, bats right. ... Full name: Nathan Patrick Field. ... High school: Heritage (Littleton, Colo.). ... College: Fort Hays State (Kan.).

TRANSACTIONS/CAREER NOTES: Signed as a non-drafted free agent by Montreal Expos organization (June 11, 1998). ... Released by Expos (March 29, 2000). ... Contract purchased by Kansas City Royals organization from Sioux City of the independent Northern League (June 29, 2000). ... Claimed on waivers by New York Yankees (June 12, 2002). ... Signed as a free agent by Royals organization (January 6, 2003). ... On disabled list (August 11, 2004-remainder of season). ... Signed as a free agent by Colorado Rockies organization (November 8, 2005).

CAREER HITTING: 0-for-0 (.000), 0 R, 0 2B, 0 3B, 0 HR, 0 RBI.

LEFTY-RIGHTY SPLITS

vs.	Avg.	AB	H	2B	3B	HR	RBI	BB	SO	OBP	Slg.
L	.250	8	2	0	0	0	2	4	0	.500	.250
R	.500	22	11	1	1	1	9	1	4	.522	.773

Year	Team (League)	W	L	Pct.	ERA	WHIP	G	GS	CG	ShO	Hld.	Sv.-Opp.	IP	H	R	ER	HR	BB-IBB	SO	Avg.
1998— Vermont (NYP)	3	1	.750	3.09	1.23	25	0	0	0	...	2-...	35.0	32	16	12	1	11-0	39	.237
1999— Cape Fear (S. Atl.)	4	8	.333	5.40	1.49	42	0	0	0	...	2-...	65.0	75	49	39	8	22-2	55	.282
— Ottawa (Int'l)	0	0		3.00	2.67	2	0	0	0	...	0-...	3.0	4	1	1	0	4-0	4	.333
2000— Sioux City (Nor.)	3	0	1.000	1.93	1.37	11	0	0	0	...	0-...	23.1	17	10	5	0	15-...	19	...
— Char., W.Va. (SAL)	1	2	.333	2.23	1.18	17	0	0	0	...	0-...	36.1	28	10	9	2	15-0	31	.215
2001— Wichita (Texas)	4	2	.667	1.48	1.08	52	0	0	0	...	19-...	73.0	61	16	12	3	18-3	67	.222
2002— Omaha (PCL)	0	1	.000	3.31	1.84	18	0	0	0	...	7-...	16.1	22	10	6	0	8-0	13	.301
— Kansas City (A.L.)	0	0		9.00	2.20	5	0	0	0	0	0-0	5.0	8	5	5	2	3-1	3	.364
— Columbus (Int'l)	2	1	.667	6.75	1.73	21	2	0	0	...	3-...	38.2	46	30	29	6	21-1	25	.305
2003— Wichita (Texas)	1	0	1.000	3.60	1.40	15	0	0	0	...	3-...	20.0	20	9	8	2	8-1	20	.256
— Omaha (PCL)	2	2	.500	3.18	0.80	19	0	0	0	...	4-...	22.2	15	8	8	0	4-0	17	.188
— Kansas City (A.L.)	1	1	.500	4.15	1.52	19	0	0	0	2	0-0	21.2	19	10	10	3	14-1	19	.235
2004— Kansas City (A.L.)	2	3	.400	4.26	1.33	43	0	0	0	2	3-5	44.1	40	25	21	5	19-2	30	.241
2005— Kansas City (A.L.)	0	0		9.45	2.70	7	0	0	0	0	1	6.2	13	7	7	1	5-2	4	.433
— Omaha (PCL)	1	0	1.000	4.91	1.82	16	0	0	0	1	0-0	22.0	26	12	12	1	14-1	24	.295
Major League totals (4 years)	3	4	.429	4.98	1.56	74	0	0	0	5	3-5	77.2	80	47	43	11	41-6	56	.268

FIELDER, PRINCE · 1B

PERSONAL: Born May 18, 1984, in Ontario, Calif. ... 6-0/260. ... Bats left, throws right. ... Full name: Prince Semien Fielder. ... High school: Eau Gallie (Melbourne, Fla.). ... Son of Cecil Fielder, 1B/DH with five major league teams (1985-1998).

TRANSACTIONS/CAREER NOTES: Selected by Milwaukee Brewers organization in first round (seventh pick overall) of 2002 free-agent draft.

2005 GAMES PLAYED BY POSITION (MLB): 1B—7, DH—5.

SCOUTING REPORT

Offense: He is a power hitter who uses the whole field. Showed good pitch recognition in the minors. Rarely chases balls out of the zone and makes adjustments according to situations. Has quick hands to the inside of the hitting zone and generates tremendous bat speed over the outer third of the plate. Makes hard contact on high fastballs, especially for a lefthanded hitter. Has good instincts as a runner but is slow. **Defense:** He has soft hands but little range at first. Can handle the position well enough to play regularly and is helped by good hand-eye coordination and reflexes. Will never be an elite fielder. **Outlook:** The sky is the limit for Fielder power-wise. Must watch his weight and develop more plate discipline, but he will provide plenty of power if he does. **Grade 7.8**

PRINCE FIELDER'S HITTING ZONE

...	.500	.500
.200	.333	.400
.500	.000	.250

LEFTY-RIGHTY SPLITS

vs.	Avg.	AB	H	2B	3B	HR	RBI	BB	SO	OBP	Slg.
L	.500	2	1	0	0	0	1	0	1	.500	.500
R	.281	57	16	4	0	2	9	2	16	.300	.456

Year	Team (League)	Pos.	G	AB	R	H	2B	3B	HR	RBI	BB	SO	HBP	GDP	SB-CS	Avg.	OBP	SLG	OPS	E	Avg.
2002— Ogden (Pion.)		41	146	35	57	12	0	10	40	37	27	8	2	3-4	.390	.531	.678	1.209	6	.974
— Beloit (Midw.)		32	112	15	27	7	0	3	11	10	27	3	1	0-0	.241	.320	.384	.704	7	.973
2003— Beloit (Midw.)		137	502	81	157	22	2	27	112	71	80	15	14	2-1	.313	.409	.526	.935	18	.984
2004— Huntsville (Sou.)		135	497	70	135	29	1	23	78	65	93	11	11	11-7	.272	.366	.473	.839	15	.994
2005— Milwaukee (N.L.)	1B-DH	39	59	2	17	4	0	2	10	2	17	0	0	0-0	.288	.306	.458	.764	0	1.000
Major League totals (1 year)		39	59	2	17	4	0	2	10	2	17	0	0	0-0	.288	.306	.458	.764	0	1.000

F

PERSONAL: Born January 22, 1978, in Leary, Ga. ... 5-8/160. ... Bats both, throws right. ... Full name: Desmond DeChone Figgins. ... Name pronounced: shawn. ... High school: Brandon (Fla.).

TRANSACTIONS/CAREER NOTES: Selected by Colorado Rockies organization in fourth round of 1997 free-agent draft. ... Traded by Rockies to Anaheim Angels for OF Kimera Bartee (July 13, 2001). ... Angels franchise renamed Los Angeles Angels of Anaheim for 2005 season.

2005 GAMES PLAYED BY POSITION (MLB): OF—72, 3B—56, 2B—42, DH—7, SS—4.

SCOUTING REPORT

Offense: Figgins has an extremely short, compact stroke. Is a line-drive hitter with good bat speed and occasional power. Is a high-ball hitter who uses the whole field and makes quick adjustments. Is an outstanding baserunner with great acceleration. Has become a catalyst at the top of the order. *Defense:* He is versatile, playing all three outfield spots and three infield positions. Played mostly at third in 2005, showing improved reactions, good range and quick hand and feet. Has a plus arm but can be an erratic thrower. *Outlook:* Figgins is no longer considered a utility player because he has shown the ability to play every day. Doesn't have ideal power for third base but still figures to be a regular. *Grade 7.8*

CHONE FIGGINS'S HITTING ZONE

.229	.294	.121
.295	.440	.380
.268	.359	.200

LEFTY-RIGHTY SPLITS

vs.	Avg.	AB	H	2B	3B	HR	RBI	BB	SO	OBP	Slg.
L	.244	217	53	7	2	2	16	27	38	.328	.323
R	.313	425	133	18	8	6	41	37	63	.364	.435

									BATTING										FIELDING	
Year	Team (League)	Pos.	G	AB	R	H	2B	3B	HR	RBI	BB	SO	HBP	GDP	SB-CS	Avg.	OBP	SLG	OPS	E	Avg.
1997—Ariz. Rockies (Ariz.)		SS	54	214	41	60	5	6	1	23	35	51	3	2	30-12	.280	.386	.374	.760	40	.865
1998—Portland (N'west)		SS	69	269	41	76	9	3	1	26	24	56	2	3	25-4	.283	.345	.349	.694	16	.947
1999—Salem (Carol.)		SS	123	444	65	106	12	3	0	22	41	86	3	5	27-13	.239	.306	.279	.585	45	.925
2000—Salem (Carol.)		2B	134	522	92	145	26	14	3	48	42	107	1	7	37-19	.278	.338	.398	.756	28	.955
2001—Carolina (Southern)		2B-SS	86	332	41	73	14	5	2	25	40	73	2	0	27-8	.220	.306	.310	.616	16	.963
—Arkansas (Texas)		2B-SS-3B	39	138	21	37	12	2	0	12	14	26	0	0	7-2	.268	.329	.384	.713	10	.945
2002—Salt Lake (PCL)		2B-SS	125	511	100	156	25	18	7	62	53	83	0	0	39-8	.305	.345	.466	.830	23	.964
—Anaheim (A.L.)		2B	15	12	6	2	1	0	0	1	0	5	0	1	2-1	.167	.167	.250	.417	1	.941
2003—Salt Lake (PCL)		2B-SS-OF																			
		3B	68	285	55	89	14	15	4	30	29	36	3	4	16-6	.312	.379	.509	.888	17	.949
—Anaheim (A.L.)		OF-2B-SS																			
		DH	71	240	34	71	9	4	0	27	20	38	0	0	13-7	.296	.345	.367	.711	3	.985
2004—Anaheim (A.L.)		3B-OF-2B																			
		SS-DH	148	577	83	171	22	17	5	60	49	94	0	3	34-13	.296	.350	.419	.770	15	.964
2005—Los Angeles (A.L.)		OF-3B-2B																			
		DH-SS	158	642	113	186	25	10	8	57	64	101	0	9	* 62-17	.290	.352	.397	.749	10	.979
Major League totals (4 years)			392	1471	236	430	57	31	13	145	133	238	0	17	111-38	.292	.349	.400	.748	29	.974

DIVISION SERIES RECORD

Year	Team (League)	Pos.	G	AB	R	H	2B	3B	HR	RBI	BB	SO	HBP	GDP	SB-CS	Avg.	OBP	SLG	OPS	E	Avg.
2002—Anaheim (A.L.)		DH	1	0	1	0	0	0	0	0	0	0	0	0	1-0	...	...	...	...		
2004—Anaheim (A.L.)		2B-3B	3	14	0	2	0	0	0	0	5	1	0	1	1-0	.143	.200	.143	.343	2	.875
2005—Los Angeles (A.L.)		3B-OF	5	21	2	3	1	1	0	2	1	8	0	1	0-1	.143	.182	.286	.468	0	1.000
Division series totals (3 years)			9	35	3	5	1	1	0	2	1	13	1	1	2-1	.143	.189	.229	.418	2	.923

CHAMPIONSHIP SERIES RECORD

Year	Team (League)	Pos.	G	AB	R	H	2B	3B	HR	RBI	BB	SO	HBP	GDP	SB-CS	Avg.	OBP	SLG	OPS	E	Avg.
2002—Anaheim (A.L.)			3	1	2	1	0	0	0	0	0	0	0	0	0-0	1.000	1.000	1.000	2.000	...	...
2005—Los Angeles (A.L.)		3B-OF	5	17	1	2	1	0	0	1	3	0	0	0	1-0	.118	.167	.176	.343	1	.917
Champ. series totals (2 years)			8	18	3	3	1	0	0	1	3	0	0	0	1-0	.167	.211	.222	.433	1	.917

WORLD SERIES RECORD

Year	Team (League)	Pos.	G	AB	R	H	2B	3B	HR	RBI	BB	SO	HBP	GDP	SB-CS	Avg.	OBP	SLG	OPS	E	Avg.
2002—Anaheim (A.L.)			2	0	1	0	0	0	0	0	0	0	0	0	0-0	...	...	...	...		

FINLEY, STEVE   OF

F

PERSONAL: Born March 12, 1965, in Union City, Tenn. ... 6-2/194. ... Bats left, throws left. ... Full name: Steven Allen Finley. ... High school: Paducah (Ky.) Tilghman. ... College: Southern Illinois.

TRANSACTIONS/CAREER NOTES: Selected by Atlanta Braves organization in 11th round of June 1986 free-agent draft; did not sign. ... Selected by Baltimore Orioles organization in 13th round of 1987 free-agent draft. ... On disabled list (April 4-22 and July 29-September 1, 1989); included rehabilitation assignment to Hagerstown. ... Traded by Orioles with Ps Pete Harnisch and Curt Schilling to Houston Astros for 1B Glenn Davis (January 10, 1991). ... On disabled list (April 25-May 14, 1993). ... On disabled list (June 13-July 3, 1994); included rehabilitation assignment to Jackson. ... Traded by Astros with 3B Ken Caminiti, SS Andujar Cedeno, 1B Roberto Petagine, P Brian Williams and a player to be named to San Diego Padres for OFs Phil Plantier and Derek Bell, Ps Pedro Martinez and Doug Brocail, IF Craig Shipley and SS Ricky Gutierrez (December 28, 1994); Padres acquired P Sean Fesh to complete deal (May 1, 1995). ... On disabled list (April 20-May 6, 1997); included rehabilitation assignment to Rancho Cucamonga. ... Signed as a free agent by Arizona Diamondbacks (December 18, 1998). ... Traded by Diamondbacks with C Brent Mayne to Los Angeles Dodgers for C Koyie Hill, P Bill Murphy and OF Reggie Abercrombie (July 31, 2004). ... Signed as a free agent by Anaheim Angels (December 10, 2004). ... Angels franchise renamed Los Angeles Angels of Anaheim prior to 2005 season. ... On disabled list (June 20-July 14, 2005); included rehabilitation assignment to Rancho Cucamonga. ... Career major league pitching: 0-0, 0.00 ERA, 1 G, 1.0 IP, 0 H, 0 ER, 1 BB, 0 SO.

HONORS: Won N.L. Gold Glove as outfielder (1995, 1996, 1999, 2000 and 2004).

2005 GAMES PLAYED BY POSITION (MLB): OF—104, DH—5.

SCOUTING REPORT

Offense: Finley regressed offensively after changing leagues and suffering a shoulder injury early in 2005. Has a slight hitch and had trouble getting to the ball upstairs as his bat speed declined, which caused his strikeout total to rise. Was unable to drive the ball consistently. Is an instinctive runner and still moves well enough to snag the extra base. *Defense:* Finley still gets good jumps on the ball and takes consistent routes. Has good closing speed to the gaps and comes in on the ball well. Rarely makes a defensive mistake. Has a quick release and is accurate. *Outlook:* Still a good outfielder and, if his shoulder is healthy, should improve offensively in 2006. *Grade 7.5*

STEVE FINLEY'S HITTING ZONE

.105	.158	.310
.300	.214	.239
.211	.100	.283

LEFTY-RIGHTY SPLITS

vs.	Avg.	AB	H	2B	3B	HR	RBI	BB	SO	OBP	Slg.
L	.271	118	32	7	2	3	21	6	16	.317	.441
R	.201	288	58	13	1	9	33	20	55	.252	.347

									BATTING										FIELDING	
Year Team (League)	Pos.	G	AB	R	H	2B	3B	HR	RBI	BB	SO	HBP	GDP	SB-CS	Avg.	OBP	SLG	OPS	E	Avg.
1987— Newark (NY-Penn)	OF	54	222	40	65	13	2	3	33	22	24	2	4	26-5	.293	.359	.410	.769	4	.970
— Hagerstown (Car.)	OF	15	65	9	22	3	2	1	5	1	6	0	2	7-2	.338	.348	.492	.841	0	1.000
1988— Hagerstown (Car.)	OF	8	28	2	6	2	0	0	3	4	3	0	2	4-0	.214	.313	.286	.598	0	1.000
— Charlotte (Sou.)	OF	10	40	7	12	4	2	1	6	4	3	1	1	2-0	.300	.378	.575	.953	0	1.000
— Rochester (Int'l)	OF	120	456	61	143	19	7	5	54	28	55	0	4	20-11	.314	.352	.419	.771	12	.962
1989— Baltimore (A.L.)	DH-OF	81	217	35	54	5	2	2	25	15	30	1	3	17-3	.249	.298	.318	.616	2	.986
— Rochester (Int'l)	OF	7	25	2	4	0	0	0	2	1	5	0	0	3-0	.160	.192	.160	.352	0	1.000
— Hagerstown (East.)	OF	11	48	11	20	3	1	0	7	4	3	0	0	4-0	.417	.453	.521	.974	3	.925
1990— Baltimore (A.L.)	DH-OF	142	464	46	119	16	4	3	37	32	53	2	8	22-9	.256	.304	.328	.632	7	.977
1991— Houston (N.L.)	OF	159	596	84	170	28	10	8	54	42	65	2	8	34-18	.285	.331	.406	.737	5	.985
1992— Houston (N.L.)	OF	•162	607	84	177	29	13	5	55	58	63	3	10	44-9	.292	.355	.407	.762	3	.993
1993— Houston (N.L.)	OF	142	545	69	145	15	*13	8	44	28	65	3	8	19-6	.266	.304	.385	.689	4	.988
1994— Houston (N.L.)	OF	94	373	64	103	16	5	11	33	28	52	2	3	13-7	.276	.329	.434	.764	4	.982
— Jackson (Texas)	OF-DH	5	13	3	4	0	0	0	0	4	0	0	0	1-0	.308	.471	.308	.778	0	1.000
1995— San Diego (N.L.)	OF	139	562	104	167	23	8	10	44	59	62	3	8	36-12	.297	.366	.420	.786	7	.977
1996— San Diego (N.L.)	OF	161	655	126	195	45	9	30	95	56	87	4	20	22-8	.298	.354	.531	.885	7	.982
1997— San Diego (N.L.)	OF	143	560	101	146	26	5	28	92	43	92	3	10	15-3	.261	.313	.475	.788	4	.989
— Mobile (Sou.)	DH	1	4	1	2	0	0	1	2	1	2	0	0	0-0	.500	.600	1.250	1.850	...	...
— Rancho Cuca. (Calif.)	DH-OF	4	14	3	4	0	0	2	3	3	2	1	0	1-0	.286	.444	.714	1.159	0	...
1998— San Diego (N.L.)	OF	159	619	92	154	40	6	14	67	45	103	3	9	12-3	.249	.301	.401	.702	7	.981
1999— Arizona (N.L.)	OF-DH	156	590	100	156	32	10	34	103	63	94	3	4	8-4	.264	.336	.525	.861	2	.995
2000— Arizona (N.L.)	OF-DH	152	539	100	151	27	5	35	96	65	87	8	9	12-6	.280	.361	.544	.904	3	.992
2001— Arizona (N.L.)	OF-P	140	495	66	136	27	4	14	73	47	67	1	8	11-7	.275	.337	.430	.767	2	.994
2002— Arizona (N.L.)	OF	150	505	82	145	24	4	25	89	65	73	3	10	16-4	.287	.370	.499	.869	2	.994
2003— Arizona (N.L.)	OF	147	516	82	148	24	•10	22	70	57	94	6	6	15-8	.287	.363	.500	.863	5	.982
2004— Arizona (N.L.)	OF-DH	104	404	61	111	16	1	23	48	40	52	1	9	8-4	.275	.338	.490	.828	2	.991
— Los Angeles (N.L.)	OF	58	224	31	59	12	0	13	46	21	30	0	5	1-3	.263	.324	.491	.815	1	.993
2005— Rancho Cuca. (Calif.)	DH	1	4	2	2	1	0	0	0	1	0	0	0	0-0	.500	.600	.750	1.350	0	...
— Los Angeles (A.L.)	OF-DH	112	406	41	90	20	3	12	54	26	71	3	6	8-4	.222	.271	.374	.645	4	.985
American League totals (3 years)		335	1087	122	263	41	9	17	116	73	154	6	17	47-16	.242	.291	.343	.634	13	.982
National League totals (14 years)		2066	7790	1246	2163	384	103	280	1009	717	1086	45	127	266-102	.278	.340	.461	.801	58	.988
Major League totals (17 years)		2401	8877	1368	2426	425	112	297	1125	790	1240	51	144	313-118	.273	.334	.447	.781	71	.987

DIVISION SERIES RECORD

Year Team (League)	Pos.	G	AB	R	H	2B	3B	HR	RBI	BB	SO	HBP	GDP	SB-CS	Avg.	OBP	SLG	OPS	E	Avg.
1996— San Diego (N.L.)	OF	3	12	0	1	0	0	0	0	0	4	1	0	1-0	.083	.154	.083	.237	0	1.000
1998— San Diego (N.L.)	OF	4	10	2	1	1	0	0	1	1	4	0	0	0-0	.100	.182	.200	.382	0	1.000
1999— Arizona (N.L.)	OF	4	13	0	5	1	0	0	5	3	1	0	1	0-0	.385	.500	.462	.962	0	1.000
2001— Arizona (N.L.)	OF	5	19	1	8	1	0	0	2	0	2	0	0	0-0	.421	.421	.474	.895	0	1.000
2002— Arizona (N.L.)	OF	3	9	1	2	0	0	0	1	2	2	0	0	1-0	.222	.333	.222	.556	0	1.000
2004— Los Angeles (N.L.)	OF	4	16	0	2	1	0	0	2	1	0	0	0	0-0	.125	.176	.188	.364	0	1.000
2005— Los Angeles (A.L.)	OF	5	11	2	1	1	0	0	1	1	4	0	0	0-0	.091	.167	.182	.348	0	1.000
Division series totals (7 years)		28	90	6	20	5	0	0	13	8	17	1	1	2-0	.222	.290	.278	.568	0	1.000

CHAMPIONSHIP SERIES RECORD

Year Team (League)	Pos.	G	AB	R	H	2B	3B	HR	RBI	BB	SO	HBP	GDP	SB-CS	Avg.	OBP	SLG	OPS	E	Avg.
1998— San Diego (N.L.)	OF	6	21	3	7	1	0	0	2	6	2	0	0	1-0	.333	.481	.381	.862	0	1.000
2001— Arizona (N.L.)	OF	5	14	1	4	1	0	0	4	3	1	0	1	1-0	.286	.412	.357	.769	0	1.000
2005— Los Angeles (A.L.)	OF	3	9	1	2	0	0	0	0	0	2	0	1	0-0	.222	.222	.222	.444	0	1.000
Champ. series totals (3 years)		14	44	5	13	2	0	0	6	9	5	0	2	2-0	.295	.415	.341	.756	0	1.000

WORLD SERIES RECORD

Year Team (League)	Pos.	G	AB	R	H	2B	3B	HR	RBI	BB	SO	HBP	GDP	SB-CS	Avg.	OBP	SLG	OPS	E	Avg.
1998— San Diego (N.L.)	OF	3	12	0	1	1	0	0	0	0	2	0	0	1-0	.083	.083	.167	.250	0	1.000
2001— Arizona (N.L.)	OF	7	19	5	7	0	0	1	2	4	5	0	0	0-1	.368	.478	.526	1.005	0	1.000
World Series totals (2 years)		10	31	5	8	1	0	1	2	4	7	0	0	1-1	.258	.343	.387	.730	0	1.000

ALL-STAR GAME RECORD

		G	AB	R	H	2B	3B	HR	RBI	BB	SO	HBP	GDP	SB-CS	Avg.	OBP	SLG	OPS	E	Avg.
All-Star Game totals (2 years)		2	2	0	1	0	0	0	1	0	1	0	0	0-0	.500	.500	.500	1.000	0	1.000

FIORENTINO, JEFF   OF

PERSONAL: Born April 14, 1983, in Pembroke Pines, Fla. ... 6-1/188. ... Bats left, throws right. ... Full name: Jeffrey Philip Fiorentino. ... College: Florida Atlantic.

TRANSACTIONS/CAREER NOTES: Selected by Baltimore Orioles organization in third round of 2004 free-agent draft.

2005 GAMES PLAYED BY POSITION (MLB): OF—12.

LEFTY-RIGHTY SPLITS

vs.	Avg.	AB	H	2B	3B	HR	RBI	BB	SO	OBP	Slg.
L	.176	17	3	1	0	1	2	0	3	.176	.412
R	.296	27	8	1	0	0	3	2	7	.333	.333

									BATTING										FIELDING	
Year Team (League)	Pos.	G	AB	R	H	2B	3B	HR	RBI	BB	SO	HBP	GDP	SB-CS	Avg.	OBP	SLG	OPS	E	Avg.
2004— Aberdeen (N.Y.-Penn.)	OF-SS-C	14	46	9	16	7	1	2	12	9	4	2	0	3-1	.348	.474	.674	1.148	1	.909
— Delmarva (S. Atl.)	OF	49	179	40	54	15	2	10	36	20	50	3	1	2-2	.302	.379	.575	.954	5	.000
2005— Baltimore (A.L.)	OF	13	44	7	11	2	0	1	5	2	10	0	0	1-0	.250	.277	.364	.640	0	1.000
— Frederick (Carolina)	OF	103	413	70	118	18	4	22	66	34	90	4	5	12-6	.286	.346	.508	.854'	12	.968
Major League totals (1 year)		13	44	7	11	2	0	1	5	2	10	0	0	1-0	.250	.277	.364	.640	0	1.000

FLAHERTY, JOHN   C

PERSONAL: Born October 21, 1967, in New York. ... 6-1/200. ... Bats right, throws right. ... Full name: John Timothy Flaherty. ... High school: St. Joseph's Regional (Montvale, N.J.). ... College: George Washington.

TRANSACTIONS/CAREER NOTES: Selected by Boston Red Sox organization in 25th round of 1988 free-agent draft. ... Traded by Red Sox to Detroit Tigers for C Rich Rowland (April 1, 1994). ... Traded by Tigers with SS Chris Gomez to San Diego Padres for C Brad Ausmus, SS Andujar Cedeno and P Russ Spear (June 18, 1996). ... Traded by Padres

F

to Tampa Bay Devil Rays for P Brian Boehringer and IF Andy Sheets (November 18, 1997). ... On disabled list (May 26-June 20, 1998); included rehabilitation assignment to Durham. ... Signed as a free agent by New York Yankees organization (January 16, 2003).
2005 GAMES PLAYED BY POSITION (MLB): C—45, 1B—1.

SCOUTING REPORT
A solid professional with excellent instincts, Flaherty runs a pitching staff well. Has good hands and sets up well behind the plate. Arm strength has declined slightly but is quick to get rid of the ball and is accurate. Became the personal catcher for Randy Johnson. Offensively, he's a pull hitter who can handle pitches down and out over the plate with a little pop. Is not a good breaking-ball hitter and can be a very defensive swinger at times. Aptitude and experience are big pluses. If forced to play a lot, his offense will become a liability. **Grade 5.1**

JOHN FLAHERTY'S HITTING ZONE

.000	.200	.111
.216	.417	.375
.125	.000	.000

LEFTY-RIGHTY SPLITS

vs.	Avg.	AB	H	2B	3B	HR	RBI	BB	SO	OBP	Slg.
L	.161	31	5	0	0	0	0	4	6	.278	.161
R	.167	96	16	5	0	2	11	2	20	.180	.281

Year Team (League)	Pos.	G	AB	R	H	2B	3B	HR	RBI	BB	SO	HBP	GDP	SB-CS	Avg.	OBP	SLG	OPS	E	Avg.
1988— Elmira (N.Y.-Penn)	C	46	162	17	38	3	0	3	16	12	23	2	5	2-1	.235	.294	.309	.602	7	.975
1989— Winter Haven (FSL)	1B-C	95	334	31	87	14	2	4	28	20	44	3	19	1-0	.260	.306	.350	.657	9	.979
1990— Pawtucket (Int'l)	3B-C	99	317	35	72	18	0	4	32	24	43	2	11	1-1	.227	.284	.322	.606	10	.983
— Lynchburg (Caro.)	C	1	4	0	0	0	0	0	1	0	1	0	0	0-0	.000	.000	.000	.000	0	1.000
1991— New Britain (East.)	C	67	225	27	65	9	0	3	18	31	22	1	5	0-2	.289	.375	.369	.743	9	.977
— Pawtucket (Int'l)	C	45	156	18	29	7	0	3	13	15	14	0	1	0-1	.186	.257	.288	.546	9	.970
1992— Boston (A.L.)	C	35	66	3	13	2	0	0	2	3	7	0	0	0-0	.197	.229	.227	.456	2	.982
— Pawtucket (Int'l)	C	31	104	11	26	3	0	0	7	5	8	1	6	0-0	.250	.291	.279	.570	4	.978
1993— Pawtucket (Int'l)	C	105	365	29	99	22	0	6	35	26	41	5	9	0-2	.271	.327	.381	.707	10	.986
— Boston (A.L.)	C	13	25	3	3	2	0	0	2	2	6	1	0	0-0	.120	.214	.200	.414	0	1.000
1994— Toledo (Int'l)	C-DH	44	151	20	39	10	2	7	17	6	21	0	1	3-1	.258	.285	.490	.775	2	.994
— Detroit (A.L.)	C-DH	34	40	2	6	1	0	0	4	1	11	0	1	0-1	.150	.167	.175	.342	0	1.000
1995— Detroit (A.L.)	C	112	354	39	86	22	1	11	40	18	47	3	8	0-0	.243	.284	.404	.688	* 11	.982
1996— Detroit (A.L.)	C	47	152	18	38	12	0	4	23	8	25	1	5	1-0	.250	.290	.408	.698	5	.981
— San Diego (N.L.)	C	72	264	22	80	12	0	9	41	9	36	2	8	2-3	.303	.327	.451	.778	5	.990
1997— San Diego (N.L.)	C	129	439	38	120	21	1	9	46	33	62	0	11	4-4	.273	.323	.387	.710	11	.987
1998— Tampa Bay (A.L.)	C	91	304	21	63	11	0	3	24	22	46	1	9	0-5	.207	.261	.273	.534	4	.993
— Durham (Int'l)	C-DH	6	23	1	3	1	0	0	2	1	5	0	1	0-0	.130	.160	.174	.334	0	1.000
1999— Tampa Bay (A.L.)	C-DH	117	446	53	124	19	0	14	71	19	64	6	14	0-2	.278	.310	.415	.725	6	.993
2000— Tampa Bay (A.L.)	C	109	394	36	103	15	0	10	39	20	57	0	11	0-0	.261	.296	.376	.671	5	.993
2001— Tampa Bay (A.L.)	C	78	248	20	59	17	1	4	29	10	33	1	9	1-0	.238	.269	.363	.632	7	.986
2002— Tampa Bay (A.L.)	C	76	281	27	73	20	0	4	33	15	50	1	6	2-2	.260	.296	.374	.669	4	.992
2003— New York (A.L.)	C	40	105	16	28	8	0	4	14	4	19	1	6	0-0	.267	.297	.457	.754	2	.991
2004— New York (A.L.)	C	47	127	11	32	9	0	6	16	5	25	1	5	0-2	.252	.286	.465	.750	3	.989
2005— New York (A.L.)	C-1B	47	127	10	21	5	0	2	11	6	26	1	4	0-0	.165	.206	.252	.458	2	.994
American League totals (13 years)		846	2669	259	649	143	2	62	308	133	416	17	78	4-12	.243	.281	.368	.649	51	.990
National League totals (2 years)		201	703	60	200	33	1	18	87	42	98	2	19	6-7	.284	.324	.411	.736	16	.988
Major League totals (14 years)		1047	3372	319	849	176	3	80	395	175	514	19	97	10-19	.252	.290	.377	.667	67	.989

DIVISION SERIES RECORD

Year Team (League)	Pos.	G	AB	R	H	2B	3B	HR	RBI	BB	SO	HBP	GDP	SB-CS	Avg.	OBP	SLG	OPS	E	Avg.
1996— San Diego (N.L.)	C	2	4	0	0	0	0	0	0	0	1	0	0	0-0	.000	.000	.000	.000	0	1.000
2005— New York (A.L.)	C	1	0	0	0	0	0	0	0	1	0	0	0	0-0	...	1.000	...	...	0	1.000
Division series totals (2 years)		3	4	0	0	0	0	0	0	1	1	0	0	0-0	.000	.200	.000	.200	0	1.000

WORLD SERIES RECORD

Year Team (League)	Pos.	G	AB	R	H	2B	3B	HR	RBI	BB	SO	HBP	GDP	SB-CS	Avg.	OBP	SLG	OPS	E	Avg.
2003— New York (A.L.)	C	1	2	0	0	0	0	0	0	0	0	0	0	0-0	.000	.000	.000	.000	0	1.000

FLORES, RANDY   P

PERSONAL: Born July 31, 1975, in Bellflower, Calif. ... 6-0/180. ... Throws left, bats left. ... Full name: Randy Alan Flores. ... High school: El Rancho (Pico Rivera, Calif.). ... College: Southern California. ... Brother of Ron Flores, pitcher, Oakland Athletics.
TRANSACTIONS/CAREER NOTES: Selected by St. Louis Cardinals organization in 21st round of 1996 free-agent draft; did not sign. ... Selected by New York Yankees organization in ninth round of 1997 free-agent draft. ... Traded by Yankees with P Rosman Garcia to Texas Rangers (October 11, 2001), completing deal in which Rangers traded 2B Randy Velarde to Yankees for two players to be named (August 31, 2001). ... Claimed on waivers by Colorado Rockies (July 18, 2002). ... Signed as a free agent by Cardinals organization (November 21, 2003). ... On disabled list (June 24-July 9, 2005); included rehabilitation assignment to Memphis.
CAREER HITTING: 0-for-7 (.000), 0 R, 0 2B, 0 3B, 0 HR, 0 RBI.

RANDY FLORES' PITCHING ZONE

.500	.250	.429
.273	.263	.200
.333	.300	.250

LEFTY-RIGHTY SPLITS

vs.	Avg.	AB	H	2B	3B	HR	RBI	BB	SO	OBP	Slg.
L	.173	75	13	4	1	2	10	7	26	.250	.333
R	.304	79	24	2	0	3	13	6	17	.360	.443

Year Team (League)	W	L	Pct.	ERA	WHIP	G	GS	CG	ShO	Hld.	Sv.-Opp.	IP	H	R	ER	HR	BB-IBB	SO	Avg.
1997— Oneonta (NYP)	4	4	.500	3.25	1.17	13	13	2	1		0-...	74.2	64	32	27	3	23-1	70	.229
1998— Tampa (Fla. St.)	1	2	.333	6.46	1.86	5	5	0	0		0-...	23.2	28	23	17	2	16-2	15	.298
— Greensboro (S. Atl.)	12	7	.632	2.62	1.16	21	20	2	1		0-...	130.2	119	48	38	6	33-0	139	.243
1999— Norwich (East.)	0	1	.000	6.48	1.72	4	4	0	0		0-...	25.0	32	20	18	0	11-1	19	.302
— Tampa (Fla. St.)	11	4	.733	2.87	1.16	21	20	1	1		0-...	135.0	118	56	43	4	38-0	99	.235
2000— Norwich (East.)	10	9	.526	2.94	1.39	31	20	3	0		1-...	141.0	138	64	46	8	58-1	97	.259
— Columbus (Int'l)	1	2	.333	7.33	2.14	4	4	0	0		0-...	23.1	43	21	19	3	7-0	16	.391
2001— Columbus (Int'l)	0	1	.000	4.76	1.24	3	0	0	0		0-...	5.2	5	4	3	2	2-0	4	.238
— Norwich (East.)	14	6	.700	2.78	1.38	25	25	3	2		0-...	158.2	156	64	49	13	63-0	115	.258
2002— Oklahoma (PCL)	1	1	.500	5.75	1.33	15	0	0	0		1-...	20.1	22	13	13	4	5-1	16	.268

Year Team (League)	W	L	Pct.	ERA	WHIP	G	GS	CG	ShO	Hld.	Sv.-Opp.	IP	H	R	ER	HR	BB-IBB	SO	Avg.
—Texas (A.L.)	0	0	...	4.50	1.58	20	0	0	0	...	1-2	12.0	11	7	6	2	8-2	7	.268
—Colo. Springs (PCL)	2	2	.500	3.28	1.51	7	7	0	0	...	0-...	35.2	36	15	13	1	18-0	27	.269
—Colorado (N.L.)	0	2	.000	9.53	2.18	8	2	0	0	0	0-0	17.0	29	19	18	5	8-1	7	.382
2003—Colo. Springs (PCL)	10	8	.556	4.98	1.60	28	24	0	0	...	0-...	142.2	156	89	79	16	67-4	116	.279
2004—Memphis (PCL)	5	7	.417	3.82	1.31	36	15	1	1	...	2-...	122.2	115	60	52	10	46-1	99	.251
—St. Louis (N.L.)	1	0	1.000	1.93	1.14	9	1	0	0	0	0-0	14.0	13	3	3	0	3-1	7	.265
2005—Memphis (PCL)	1	0	1.000	6.43	1.14	6	0	0	0	1	0-1	7.0	8	6	5	1	0-0	6	.296
—St. Louis (N.L.)	3	1	.750	3.46	1.20	50	0	0	0	11	1-3	41.2	37	22	16	5	13-0	43	.240
American League totals (1 year)	0	0	...	4.50	1.58	20	0	0	0	2	1-2	12.0	11	7	6	2	8-2	7	.268
National League totals (3 years)	4	3	.571	4.58	1.42	67	3	0	0	11	1-3	72.2	79	44	37	10	24-2	57	.283
Major League totals (3 years)	4	3	.571	4.57	1.44	87	3	0	0	13	2-5	84.2	90	51	43	12	32-4	64	.281

DIVISION SERIES RECORD

Year Team (League)	W	L	Pct.	ERA	WHIP	G	GS	CG	ShO	Hld.	Sv.-Opp.	IP	H	R	ER	HR	BB-IBB	SO	Avg.
2005—St. Louis (N.L.)	0	0	...	4.50	1.00	3	0	0	0	1	0-0	2.0	2	1	1	1	0-0	3	.250

CHAMPIONSHIP SERIES RECORD

Year Team (League)	W	L	Pct.	ERA	WHIP	G	GS	CG	ShO	Hld.	Sv.-Opp.	IP	H	R	ER	HR	BB-IBB	SO	Avg.
2005—St. Louis (N.L.)	0	0	...	0.00	0.75	2	0	0	0	0	0-0	1.1	0	0	0	0	1-0	0	.000

FLORES, RON   P

PERSONAL: Born August 9, 1979, in Whittier, Calif. ... 5-11/190. ... Throws left, bats left. ... Full name: Ronald Joel Flores. ... College: Southern California. ... Brother of Randy Flores, pitcher, St. Louis Cardinals.
TRANSACTIONS/CAREER NOTES: Selected by Oakland Athletics organization in 29th round of 2000 free-agent draft.
CAREER HITTING: 0-for-0 (.000), 0 R, 0 2B, 0 3B, 0 HR, 0 RBI.

LEFTY-RIGHTY SPLITS

vs.	Avg.	AB	H	2B	3B	HR	RBI	BB	SO	OBP	Slg.
L	.154	13	2	0	0	0	1	0	4	.154	.154
R	.286	21	6	0	0	1	1	0	2	.286	.429

Year Team (League)	W	L	Pct.	ERA	WHIP	G	GS	CG	ShO	Hld.	Sv.-Opp.	IP	H	R	ER	HR	BB-IBB	SO	Avg.
2000—Vancouver (N'west)	1	1	.500	5.11	1.62	13	0	0	0	...	0-...	12.1	16	10	7	2	4-0	10	.296
2001—Modesto (California)	5	2	.714	2.86	1.24	47	0	0	0	...	6-...	66.0	53	24	21	4	29-7	71	.217
2002—Visalia (Calif.)	8	6	.571	3.25	1.32	53	0	0	0	...	11-...	80.1	90	41	29	7	16-2	92	.281
2003—Midland (Texas)	3	2	.600	2.88	0.99	39	0	0	0	...	6-...	59.1	44	19	19	6	15-3	66	.204
—Sacramento (PCL)	2	0	1.000	6.59	1.39	12	0	0	0	...	0-...	13.2	16	10	10	0	3-1	10	.302
2004—Sacramento (PCL)	4	3	.571	3.83	1.46	55	0	0	0	...	1-...	54.0	60	27	23	5	19-4	55	.271
2005—Sacramento (PCL)	5	3	.625	2.39	1.26	52	0	0	0	12	3-7	60.1	46	18	16	5	30-6	66	.213
—Oakland (A.L.)	0	0	...	1.04	0.92	11	0	0	0	1	0-0	8.2	8	1	1	1	0-0	6	.235
Major League totals (1 year)	0	0	...	1.04	0.92	11	0	0	0	1	0-0	8.2	8	1	1	1	0-0	6	.235

FLOYD, CLIFF   OF

PERSONAL: Born December 5, 1972, in Chicago. ... 6-4/230. ... Bats left, throws right. ... Full name: Cornelius Clifford Floyd. ... High school: Thornwood (South Holland, Ill.).
TRANSACTIONS/CAREER NOTES: Selected by Montreal Expos organization in first round (14th pick overall) of 1991 free-agent draft. ... On disabled list (May 16-September 11, 1995). ... Traded by Expos to Florida Marlins for OF Joe Orsulak and P Dustin Hermanson (March 26, 1997). ... On disabled list (May 9-24 and June 21-September 1, 1997); included rehabilitation assignment to Charlotte. ... On disabled list (March 30-April 27 and June 20-September 7, 1999); included rehabilitation assigment to Calgary. ... On disabled list (July 29-August 29, 2000). ... Traded by Marlins with P Claudio Vargas, OF/2B Wilton Guerrero, a player to be named and cash considerations to Expos for Ps Carl Pavano, Graeme Lloyd and Justin Wayne and IF Mike Mordecai (July 11, 2002); Expos acquired P Don Levinski to complete deal (August 5, 2002). ... Traded by Expos to Boston Red Sox for Ps Seung Song and Sun-Woo Kim (July 30, 2002). ... Signed as a free agent by New York Mets (December 20, 2002). ... On disabled list (August 19, 2003-remainder of season). ... On disabled list (April 12-May 13, 2004); included rehabilitation assignment to St. Lucie.
HONORS: Named Minor League Player of the Year by THE SPORTING NEWS (1993).
2005 GAMES PLAYED BY POSITION (MLB): OF—150.

SCOUTING REPORT **Offense:** Floyd was healthy for the first time in years and his offense really picked up. Has a long stroke with a slight lift to his swing. Has become more patient and with increased bat speed can cover the holes he had upstairs. Still has trouble with lefthanded pitching. Will shorten up and go the other way deep in the count. A good low-ball hitter with excellent power and is a clutch hitter. Running better than he has in years. **Defense:** He made considerable defensive improvements during the season. Gets better jumps and has increased range. Has improved his arm strength and is quick and accurate throwing to bases. Charges well when throwing home *Outlook:* An outstanding tool player whose offensive numbers should continue to rise as long as he has his legs. *Grade 8.1*

CLIFF FLOYD'S HITTING ZONE

.167	.296	.209
.167	.339	.358
.500	.290	.244

LEFTY-RIGHTY SPLITS

vs.	Avg.	AB	H	2B	3B	HR	RBI	BB	SO	OBP	Slg.
L	.224	143	32	2	0	9	25	10	37	.284	.427
R	.290	407	118	20	2	25	73	53	61	.382	.533

Year Team (League)	Pos.	G	AB	R	H	2B	3B	HR	RBI	BB	SO	HBP	GDP	SB-CS	Avg.	OBP	SLG	OPS	E	Avg.
1991—GC Expos (GCL)	1B	56	214	35	56	9	3	6	30	19	37	5	3	13-3	.262	.335	.416	.751	15	.970
1992—Albany (S. Atl.)	1B-OF	134	516	83	157	24	16	16	97	45	75	9	4	32-11	.304	.368	.506	.874	17	.964
—W.P. Beach (FSL)	OF	1	4	0	0	0	0	0	0	1	0	1	0	0-0	.000	.000	.000	.000	0	1.000
1993—Harrisburg (East.)	1B-OF	101	380	82	125	17	4	26	101	54	71	5	8	31-10	.329	.417	.600	1.017	19	.969
—Ottawa (Int'l)	1B	32	125	12	30	2	2	1	18	16	34	1	1	2-2	.240	.329	.336	.665	5	.983
—Montreal (N.L.)	1B	10	31	3	7	0	0	1	2	0	9	0	0	0-0	.226	.226	.323	.548	0	1.000
1994—Montreal (N.L.)	1B-OF	100	334	43	94	19	4	4	41	24	63	3	3	10-3	.281	.332	.398	.731	6	.990
1995—Montreal (N.L.)	1B-OF	29	69	6	9	1	0	1	8	7	22	1	1	3-0	.130	.221	.188	.409	3	.981
1996—Ottawa (Int'l)	OF-3B-DH	20	76	7	23	3	1	1	8	7	20	1	0	2-2	.303	.369	.408	.777	2	.951
—Montreal (N.L.)	OF-1B	117	227	29	55	15	4	6	26	30	52	5	3	7-1	.242	.340	.423	.763	5	.957
1997—Florida (N.L.)	OF-1B	61	137	23	32	9	1	6	19	24	33	2	3	6-2	.234	.354	.445	.799	3	.971
—Charlotte (Int'l)	OF-1B	39	131	27	48	10	0	9	33	10	29	1	2	7-2	.366	.415	.649	1.064	1	.988
1998—Florida (N.L.)	OF-DH	153	588	85	166	45	3	22	90	47	112	3	10	27-14	.282	.337	.481	.818	7	.974
1999—Florida (N.L.)	OF-DH	69	251	37	76	19	1	11	49	30	47	2	8	5-6	.303	.379	.486	.897	6	.952
—Calgary (PCL)	OF	9	31	6	12	1	0	3	8	2	8	0	0	0-1	.387	.424	.710	1.134	0	1.000
2000—Florida (N.L.)	OF-DH	121	420	75	126	30	6	22	91	50	82	8	4	24-3	.300	.378	.529	.906	9	.951
2001—Florida (N.L.)	OF-DH	149	555	123	176	44	4	31	103	59	101	10	8	18-3	.317	.390	.578	.968	8	.972

F

Year	Team (League)	Pos.	G	AB	R	H	2B	3B	HR	RBI	BB	SO	HBP	GDP	SB-CS	Avg.	OBP	SLG	OPS	E	Avg.
										BATTING										FIELDING	
2002— Florida (N.L.)		OF-DH	84	296	49	85	20	0	18	57	58	68	7	0	10-5	.287	.414	.537	.952	3	.983
— Montreal (N.L.)		OF	15	53	7	11	2	0	3	4	3	10	1	0	1-0	.208	.263	.415	.678	1	.941
— Boston (A.L.)		OF-DH	47	171	30	54	21	0	7	18	15	28	2	6	4-0	.316	.374	.561	.935	1	.977
2003— New York (N.L.)		OF-DH	108	365	57	106	25	2	18	68	51	66	3	10	3-0	.290	.376	.518	.894	5	.971
2004— St. Lucie (Fla. St.)		OF	1	4	2	2	0	0	0	1	0	2	0	0	0-0	.500	.500	.500	1.000	0	1.000
— New York (N.L.)		OF-DH	113	396	55	103	26	2	18	63	47	103	11	8	11-4	.260	.352	.462	.814	2	.988
2005— New York (N.L.)		OF	150	550	85	150	22	2	34	98	63	98	11	5	12-2	.273	.358	.505	.863	2	.993
American League totals (1 year)			47	171	30	54	21	0	7	18	15	28	2	6	4-0	.316	.374	.561	.935	1	.977
National League totals (13 years)			1279	4272	677	1196	277	21	195	719	493	866	67	64	137-43	.280	.361	.492	.852	60	.978
Major League totals (13 years)			1326	4443	707	1250	298	21	202	737	508	894	69	70	141-43	.281	.361	.494	.855	61	.978

DIVISION SERIES RECORD

Year	Team (League)	Pos.	G	AB	R	H	2B	3B	HR	RBI	BB	SO	HBP	GDP	SB-CS	Avg.	OBP	SLG	OPS	E	Avg.
1997— Florida (N.L.)		Did not play.																			

CHAMPIONSHIP SERIES RECORD

Year	Team (League)	Pos.	G	AB	R	H	2B	3B	HR	RBI	BB	SO	HBP	GDP	SB-CS	Avg.	OBP	SLG	OPS	E	Avg.
1997— Florida (N.L.)		Did not play.																			

WORLD SERIES RECORD

Year	Team (League)	Pos.	G	AB	R	H	2B	3B	HR	RBI	BB	SO	HBP	GDP	SB-CS	Avg.	OBP	SLG	OPS	E	Avg.
1997— Florida (N.L.)		DH	4	2	1	0	0	0	0	0	1	1	0	0	0-0	.000	.333	.000	.333	...	...

ALL-STAR GAME RECORD

			G	AB	R	H	2B	3B	HR	RBI	BB	SO	HBP	GDP	SB-CS	Avg.	OBP	SLG	OPS	E	Avg.
All-Star Game totals (1 year)			1	2	0	0	0	0	0	0	0	0	0	0	0-0	.000	.000	.000	.000	...	...

FLOYD, GAVIN — P

PERSONAL: Born January 27, 1983, in Annapolis, Md. ... 6-4/212. ... Throws right, bats right. ... Full name: Gavin Christopher Floyd. ... High school: Mount St. Joseph (Baltimore).

TRANSACTIONS/CAREER NOTES: Selected by Philadelphia Phillies organization in first round (fourth overall pick) of 2001 free-agent draft.

CAREER HITTING: 1-for-19 (.053), 0 R, 0 2B, 0 3B, 0 HR, 0 RBI.

SCOUTING REPORT **Throws:** His fastball reaches the mid-90s, and he has a curve and changeup. **Tendencies:** This highly regarded prospect struggled in April last year and was sent down to the minors. Tried to be too fine with his command and lacked endurance. Curve is his best pitch, but he has to be careful not to rely on it too much. **Outlook:** He will have an opportunity during spring training to make the rotation, but he will have to show a lot more than he did last year to break camp with the Phillies. **Grade 6.9**

GAVIN FLOYD'S PITCHING ZONE

.750	.333	.182
.231	.556	.167
.375	.667	.308

LEFTY-RIGHTY SPLITS

vs.	Avg.	AB	H	2B	3B	HR	RBI	BB	SO	OBP	Slg.
L	.283	46	13	3	1	3	10	9	5	.393	.587
R	.283	60	17	7	0	2	18	7	12	.386	.500

Year	Team (League)	W	L	Pct.	ERA	WHIP	G	GS	CG	ShO	Hld.	Sv.-Opp.	IP	H	R	ER	HR	BB-IBB	SO	Avg.
2002— Lakewood (S. Atl.)		11	10	.524	2.77	1.10	27	27	3	0	...	0-...	166.0	119	59	51	13	64-0	140	.200
2003— Clearwater (FSL)		7	8	.467	3.00	1.25	24	20	1	1	...	0-...	138.0	128	61	46	9	45-0	115	.247
2004— Reading (East.)		6	6	.500	2.57	1.17	20	20	2	1	...	0-...	119.0	93	39	34	5	46-1	94	.212
— Scran./W.B. (I.L.)		1	3	.250	4.99	1.57	5	5	0	0	...	0-...	30.2	39	20	17	4	9-0	18	.312
— Philadelphia (N.L.)		2	0	1.000	3.49	1.45	6	4	0	0	0	0-0	28.1	25	11	11	1	16-0	24	.240
2005— Scran./W.B. (I.L.)		6	9	.400	6.16	1.61	24	23	0	0	...	0-0	137.1	155	103	94	11	66-1	97	.290
— Philadelphia (N.L.)		1	2	.333	10.04	1.77	7	4	0	0	0	0-0	26.0	30	31	29	5	16-2	17	.283
Major League totals (2 years)		3	2	.600	6.63	1.60	13	8	0	0	0	0-0	54.1	55	55	40	6	32-2	41	.262

FOGG, JOSH — P

PERSONAL: Born December 13, 1976, in Lynn, Mass. ... 6-0/203. ... Throws right, bats right. ... Full name: Joshua Smith Fogg. ... High school: Cardinal Gibbons (Fort Lauderdale, Fla.). ... College: Florida.

TRANSACTIONS/CAREER NOTES: Selected by Chicago White Sox organization in third round of 1998 free-agent draft. ... Traded by White Sox with Ps Kip Wells and Sean Lowe to Pittsburgh Pirates for P Todd Ritchie and C Lee Evans (December 13, 2001). ... On disabled list (April 21-May 26, 2003); included rehabilitation assignment to Nashville.

CAREER HITTING: 24-for-200 (.120), 10 R, 2 2B, 0 3B, 0 HR, 8 RBI.

SCOUTING REPORT **Throws:** His fastball hits 86-91 mph, his curveball 74-78 and his slider 84-86. Also has a changeup. **Tendencies:** Fogg doesn't trust his stuff and tends to nibble. Fastball is short but has some sinking action when it is down. Throws strikes but is mistake-prone in the middle of the plate because his fastball upstairs doesn't do much. Curveball, which has tight spin but breaks early, is a better breaking pitch than his slider. Has good motion with his changeup. Success is determined by how well he gets his curve over. **Outlook:** Fogg was inconsistent throughout the year. Must spot his fastball and get his breaking ball over while behind in the count to win. **Grade 5.8**

JOSH FOGG'S PITCHING ZONE

.057	.167	.270
.358	.362	.363
.204	.350	.388

LEFTY-RIGHTY SPLITS

vs.	Avg.	AB	H	2B	3B	HR	RBI	BB	SO	OBP	Slg.
L	.340	315	107	18	3	15	45	30	34	.396	.559
R	.249	358	89	22	0	12	46	23	51	.301	.411

Year	Team (League)	W	L	Pct.	ERA	WHIP	G	GS	CG	ShO	Hld.	Sv.-Opp.	IP	H	R	ER	HR	BB-IBB	SO	Avg.
1998— Ariz. White Sox (Ariz.)		1	0	1.000	0.00	0.25	2	0	0	0	...	0-...	4.0	0	0	0	0	1-0	5	.000
— Hickory (S. Atl.)		1	3	.250	2.18	1.19	8	8	0	0	...	0-...	41.1	36	17	10	4	13-0	29	.228
— Win.-Salem (Car.)		0	1	.000	2.00	2.00	1	0	0	0	...	0-...	1.0	2	2	0	0	0-0	2	.333
1999— Win.-Salem (Car.)		10	5	.667	2.96	1.22	17	17	1	1	...	0-...	103.1	93	44	34	3	33-0	109	.235

Year — Team (League)	W	L	Pct.	ERA	WHIP	G	GS	CG	ShO	Hld.	Sv.-Opp.	IP	H	R	ER	HR	BB-IBB	SO	Avg.
— Birmingham (Sou.)	3	2	.600	5.89	1.53	10	10	0	0	...	0-...	55.0	66	37	36	8	18-0	40	.296
2000— Birmingham (Sou.)	11	7	.611	2.57	1.22	27	27	2	0	...	0-...	192.1	190	68	55	7	44-2	136	.261
2001— Charlotte (Int'l)	4	7	.364	4.79	1.39	40	16	0	0	...	4-...	114.2	129	68	61	19	30-1	89	.283
— Chicago (A.L.)	0	0	...	2.03	0.98	11	0	0	0	2	0-0	13.1	10	3	3	0	3-1	17	.208
2002— Pittsburgh (N.L.)	12	12	.500	4.35	1.38	33	33	0	0	0	0-0	194.1	199	102	94	28	69-12	113	.267
2003— Nashville (PCL)	0	1	.000	5.40	1.30	2	2	0	0	...	0-...	10.0	12	6	6	1	1-0	7	.324
— Pittsburgh (N.L.)	10	9	.526	5.26	1.45	26	26	1	0	0	0-0	142.0	166	90	83	22	40-0	71	.293
2004— Pittsburgh (N.L.)	11	10	.524	4.64	1.45	32	32	0	0	0	0-0	178.1	193	98	92	17	66-8	82	.283
2005— Pittsburgh (N.L.)	6	11	.353	5.05	1.47	34	28	0	0	0	0-0	169.1	196	106	95	27	53-11	85	.291
American League totals (1 year)	0	0	...	2.03	0.98	11	0	0	0	2	0-0	13.1	10	3	3	0	3-1	17	.208
National League totals (4 years)	39	42	.481	4.79	1.44	125	119	1	0	0	0-0	684.0	754	396	364	94	228-31	351	.283
Major League totals (5 years)	39	42	.481	4.74	1.43	136	119	1	0	2	0-0	697.1	764	399	367	94	231-32	368	.282

FONTENOT, MIKE — 2B

PERSONAL: Born June 9, 1980, in New Iberia, La. ... 5-8/160. ... Bats left, throws right. ... Full name: Michael Eugene Fontenot. ... College: Louisiana State.
TRANSACTIONS/CAREER NOTES: Selected by Baltimore Orioles organization in first round (19th pick overall) of 2001 free-agent draft. ... Traded by Orioles with 2B Jerry Hairston and P David Crouthers to Chicago Cubs for OF Sammy Sosa (January 30, 2005).

LEFTY-RIGHTY SPLITS

vs.	Avg.	AB	H	2B	3B	HR	RBI	BB	SO	OBP	Slg.
L	.000	0	0	0	0	0	0	1	0	1.000	.000
R	.000	2	0	0	0	0	0	1	0	.500	.000

							BATTING									FIELDING	
Year — Team (League)	Pos.	G	AB	R	H	2B	3B	HR	RBI	BB	SO	HBP	GDP	SB-CS	Avg.	OBP	SLG	OPS	E	Avg.
2002— Frederick (Carolina)	2B	122	481	61	127	16	4	8	53	42	117	10	3	13-9	.264	.333	.364	.697	25	.955
2003— Bowie (East.)	2B	126	449	63	146	24	5	12	66	50	89	8	6	16-5	.325	.399	.481	.880	18	.968
2004— Ottawa (Int'l)	2B	136	524	73	146	30	10	8	49	48	111	9	9	14-7	.279	.346	.420	.766	22	.829
2005— Chicago (N.L.)	PH-PR	7	2	4	0	0	0	0	0	2	0	1	0	0-0	.000	.600	.000	.600	0	...
— Iowa (PCL) ....2B-3B-DH SS-OF		111	379	60	103	22	10	6	39	59	77	6	4	3-2	.272	.377	.430	.807	13	.969
Major League totals (1 year)		7	2	4	0	0	0	0	0	2	0	1	0	0-0	.000	.600	.000	.600	0	...

FOPPERT, JESSE — P

PERSONAL: Born July 10, 1980, in Reading, Pa. ... 6-6/210. ... Throws right, bats right. ... Full name: Jesse W. Foppert. ... High school: San Raphael (Calif.). ... College: San Francisco.
TRANSACTIONS/CAREER NOTES: Selected by San Francisco Giants organization in second round of 2001 free-agent draft. ... On disabled list (August 21, 2003-remainder of season; and March 31-August 18, 2004); included rehabilitation assignments to AZL Giants, San Jose and Fresno. ... On disabled list (June 25-July 24, 2005). ... Traded by Giants with C Yorvit Torrealba to Seattle Mariners for OF Randy Winn (July 30, 2005).
CAREER HITTING: 3-for-37 (.081), 3 R, 1 2B, 1 3B, 0 HR, 1 RBI.

LEFTY-RIGHTY SPLITS

vs.	Avg.	AB	H	2B	3B	HR	RBI	BB	SO	OBP	Slg.
L	.200	15	3	0	0	1	4	2	.350	.200
R	.364	22	8	0	0	2	3	9	4	.545	.636

Year — Team (League)	W	L	Pct.	ERA	WHIP	G	GS	CG	ShO	Hld.	Sv.-Opp.	IP	H	R	ER	HR	BB-IBB	SO	Avg.
2001— Salem-Keizer (N'west)	8	1	.889	1.93	0.83	14	14	0	0	...	0-...	70.0	35	18	15	7	23-0	88	.150
2002— Shreveport (Texas)	3	3	.500	2.79	1.06	11	11	1	0	...	0-...	61.1	44	22	19	3	21-0	74	.199
— Fresno (PCL)	3	6	.333	3.99	1.34	14	14	0	0	...	0-...	79.0	71	37	35	12	35-0	109	.244
2003— Fresno (PCL)	0	0	...	1.80	0.60	1	1	0	0	...	0-...	5.0	3	1	1	0	0-0	9	.167
— San Jose (Calif.)	0	1	.000	9.00	1.67	1	1	0	0	...	0-...	3.0	5	3	3	0	0-0	3	.385
— San Francisco (N.L.)	8	9	.471	5.03	1.55	23	21	0	0	...	0-1	111.0	103	69	62	16	69-4	101	.249
2004— Ariz. Giants (Ariz.)	0	0	...	9.00	3.00	1	1	0	0	...	0-0	1.0	3	1	1	0	0-0	2	.500
— San Jose (Calif.)	0	0	...	1.93	0.86	4	4	0	0	...	0-0	9.1	4	2	2	1	4-0	11	.133
— Fresno (PCL)	0	2	.000	3.68	1.57	4	4	0	0	...	0-0	14.2	14	11	6	2	9-0	13	.241
— San Francisco (N.L.)	0	0	...	0.00	1.00	1	0	0	0	...	0-0	1.0	1	0	0	0	0-0	2	.250
2005— San Francisco (N.L.)	0	0	...	5.23	2.32	3	2	0	0	...	0-0	10.1	11	7	6	2	13-0	6	.297
— San Jose (Calif.)	1	0	1.000	2.08	1.27	3	3	0	0	...	0-0	8.2	5	2	2	0	6-0	9	.172
— Fresno (PCL)	3	1	.750	4.50	1.59	10	9	0	0	...	0-0	44.0	43	25	22	5	27-0	41	.250
— Tacoma (PCL)	0	1	.000	2.57	1.29	6	6	0	0	...	0-0	14.0	10	4	4	0	8-0	13	.200
Major League totals (3 years)	8	9	.471	5.00	1.61	27	23	0	0	...	0-0	122.1	115	76	68	18	82-4	109	.253

FORD, LEW — OF

PERSONAL: Born August 12, 1976, in Port Neches, Texas. ... 6-0/195. ... Bats right, throws right. ... Full name: Jon Lewis Ford. ... High school: Port Neches-Groves (Texarkana, Texas). ... College: Dallas Baptist.
TRANSACTIONS/CAREER NOTES: Selected by Boston Red Sox organization in 12th round of 1999 free-agent draft. ... Traded by Red Sox to Minnesota Twins for P Hector Carrasco (September 10, 2000). ... On disabled list (July 14-September 2, 2003); included rehabilitation assignment to Rochester.
2005 GAMES PLAYED BY POSITION (MLB): OF—95, DH—44.

SCOUTING REPORT *Offense:* Ford's numbers declined across the board as he started to see more off-speed pitches. Has a short, quick stroke and is more of a dead high-fastball hitter. Has gap power. Handles inside pitches well, especially when he becomes pull-conscious. Has trouble with lefthanded pitchers running the ball away. Is a plus runner and with good basestealing instincts. *Defense:* Ford gets good jumps laterally and shows solid range with closing speed. Had mental lapses on the field as he focused on his offensive woes. Throws well when he gets on top and ball has good life on throws that hit the ground. *Outlook:* Ford has played regularly the past two seasons but is better suited to be a fourth outfielder who can play all three positions. *Grade 6.6*

LEW FORD'S HITTING ZONE

.267	.269	.207
.337	.321	.302
.288	.375	.125

LEFTY-RIGHTY SPLITS

vs.	Avg.	AB	H	2B	3B	HR	RBI	BB	SO	OBP	Slg.
L	.233	150	35	10	0	1	9	13	24	.308	.320
R	.277	372	103	20	4	6	44	32	61	.351	.401

							BATTING									FIELDING	
Year — Team (League)	Pos.	G	AB	R	H	2B	3B	HR	RBI	BB	SO	HBP	GDP	SB-CS	Avg.	OBP	SLG	OPS	E	Avg.
1999— Lowell (NY-Penn)	OF	62	250	48	70	17	4	7	34	19	35	5	6	15-2	.280	.339	.464	.803	1	.993

F

Year	Team (League)	Pos.	G	AB	R	H	2B	3B	HR	RBI	BB	SO	HBP	GDP	SB-CS	Avg.	OBP	SLG	OPS	E	Avg.
																BATTING				**FIELDING**	
2000— Augusta (S. Atl.)		OF	126	514	122	162	35	11	9	74	52	83	12	12	52-4	.315	.390	.479	.868	2	.994
2001— Fort Myers (FSL)		OF	67	265	42	79	15	2	2	24	21	30	12	3	19-9	.298	.373	.392	.766	1	.993
— New Britain (East.)		OF	62	252	30	55	9	3	7	25	20	35	6	4	5-5	.218	.289	.361	.650	3	.974
2002— New Britain (East.)		OF	93	373	81	116	27	2	15	51	49	47	8	5	17-5	.311	.401	.515	.916	3	.986
— Edmonton (PCL)		OF	47	193	40	64	11	2	5	24	13	21	6	2	11-1	.332	.390	.487	.877	5	.964
2003— Rochester (Int'l)		OF-DH	53	211	33	64	18	2	3	31	10	28	8	1	4-5	.303	.357	.450	.807	1	.990
— Minnesota (A.L.)		OF-DH	34	73	16	24	7	1	3	15	8	9	1	1	2-0	.329	.402	.575	.978	3	.923
2004— Rochester (Int'l)		OF	1	5	0	1	0	0	0	0	0	1	0	0	0-0	.200	.200	.200	.400	0	1.000
— Minnesota (A.L.)		OF-DH	154	569	89	170	31	4	15	72	67	75	13	15	20-2	.299	.381	.446	.827	4	.986
2005— Minnesota (A.L.)		OF-DH	147	522	70	138	30	4	7	53	45	85	16	9	13-6	.264	.338	.377	.716	6	.972
Major League totals (3 years)			335	1164	175	332	68	9	25	140	120	169	30	25	35-8	.285	.363	.424	.787	13	.976

DIVISION SERIES RECORD

Year	Team (League)	Pos.	G	AB	R	H	2B	3B	HR	RBI	BB	SO	HBP	GDP	SB-CS	Avg.	OBP	SLG	OPS	E	Avg.
2003— Minnesota (A.L.)			1	1	0	0	0	0	0	0	0	0	0	0	0-0	.000	.000	.000	.000	0	...
2004— Minnesota (A.L.)		DH-OF	3	11	1	3	1	0	0	2	0	2	2	0	1-1	.273	.385	.364	.748	0	1.000
Division series totals (2 years)			4	12	1	3	1	0	0	2	0	3	2	0	1-1	.250	.357	.333	.690	0	1.000

FOSSUM, CASEY   P

PERSONAL: Born January 9, 1978, in Cherry Hill, N.J. ... 6-1/160. ... Throws left, bats left. ... Full name: Casey Paul Fossum. ... High school: Midway (Waco, Texas). ... College: Texas A&M.

TRANSACTIONS/CAREER NOTES: Selected by Arizona Diamondbacks organization in sixth round of 1996 free-agent draft; did not sign. ... Selected by Boston Red Sox organization in the supplemental round ("sandwich pick" between first and second round, 48th pick overall), of 1999 free-agent draft; pick received as part of compensation for Diamondbacks signing Type A free agent P Greg Swindell. ... On disabled list (June 8-July 17, 2003); included rehabilitation assignment to Portland. ... Traded by Red Sox with Ps Brandon Lyon and Jorge de la Rosa and a player to be named to Arizona Diamondbacks for P Curt Schilling (November 28, 2003); Diamondbacks acquired OF Michael Goss to complete deal (December 15, 2004). ... On disabled list (March 26-May 14, 2004); included rehabilitation assignments to El Paso and Tucson. ... Traded by Diamondbacks to Tampa Bay Devil Rays for OF Jose Cruz (February 6, 2005).

CAREER HITTING: 4-for-44 (.091), 3 R, 0 2B, 0 3B, 0 HR, 0 RBI.

SCOUTING REPORT ***Throws:*** Fossum has an 87-91 mph fastball, a big-breaking curveball, a quick slider and a changeup. ***Tendencies:*** He has a complex, long delivery, making it hard for him to stay on top of his pitches and keep them from flattening out. Has lost velocity on his fastball. Curveball rolls rather than breaking sharply. Makes too many mistakes over the middle of the plate with his slider. ***Outlook:*** Fossum has not improved and probably will never be a consistent starter. ***Grade 6.2***

CASEY FOSSUM'S PITCHING ZONE

.311	.235	.269
.352	.427	.313
.213	.375	.102

LEFTY-RIGHTY SPLITS

vs.	Avg.	AB	H	2B	3B	HR	RBI	BB	SO	OBP	Slg.
L	.234	167	39	5	0	5	22	12	31	.283	.353
R	.278	472	131	19	4	16	68	48	97	.363	.436

Year	Team (League)	W	L	Pct.	ERA	WHIP	G	GS	CG	ShO	Hld.	Sv.-Opp.	IP	H	R	ER	HR	BB-IBB	SO	Avg.
1999— Lowell (NY-Penn)		0	1	.000	1.26	0.77	5	5	0	0	...	0-...	14.1	6	2	2	1	5-0	16	.122
2000— Sarasota (Fla. St.)		9	10	.474	3.44	1.23	27	27	3	3	...	0-...	149.1	147	71	57	7	36-0	143	.257
2001— Trenton (East.)		3	7	.300	2.83	1.10	20	20	0	0	...	0-...	117.2	102	47	37	5	28-0	130	.231
— Boston (A.L.)		3	2	.600	4.87	1.44	13	7	0	0	0	0-0	44.1	44	26	24	4	20-1	26	.259
2002— Boston (A.L.)		5	4	.556	3.46	1.34	43	12	0	0	1	1-1	106.2	113	56	41	12	30-0	101	.270
— Pawtucket (Int'l)		0	3	.000	3.96	1.60	5	3	1	0	...	0-...	25.0	34	15	11	1	6-0	28	.337
2003— Portland (East.)		0	1	.000	6.75	2.00	3	2	0	0	...	0-...	4.0	5	3	3	1	3-0	7	.294
— Pawtucket (Int'l)		1	0	1.000	3.46	1.20	5	4	0	0	...	1-...	13.0	11	5	5	1	5-0	14	.234
— Boston (A.L.)		6	5	.545	5.47	1.47	19	14	0	0	0	1-1	79.0	82	55	48	9	34-0	63	.270
2004— El Paso (Texas)		0	0	...	2.08	1.38	2	2	0	0	...	0-...	4.1	3	1	1	0	3-0	5	.188
— Tucson (PCL)		2	0	1.000	0.00	0.93	3	3	0	0	...	0-...	15.0	11	2	0	0	3-0	16	.196
— Arizona (N.L.)		4	15	.211	6.65	1.65	27	27	0	0	0	0-0	142.0	171	111	105	31	63-5	117	.302
2005— Tampa Bay (A.L.)		8	12	.400	4.92	1.41	36	25	0	0	0	0-1	162.2	170	100	89	21	60-3	128	.266
American League totals (4 years)		22	23	.489	4.63	1.41	111	58	0	0	3	2-3	392.2	409	237	202	46	144-4	318	.267
National League totals (1 year)		4	15	.211	6.65	1.65	27	27	0	0	0	0-0	142.0	171	111	105	31	63-5	117	.302
Major League totals (5 years)		26	38	.406	5.17	1.47	138	85	0	0	3	2-3	534.2	580	348	307	77	207-9	435	.276

FOSTER, JOHN   P

PERSONAL: Born May 17, 1978, in Stockton, Calif. ... 6-0/200. ... Throws left, bats left. ... Full name: John Norman Foster. ... College: Lewis-Clark State (Lewiston, Idaho).

TRANSACTIONS/CAREER NOTES: Selected by Atlanta Braves organization in 25th round of 1999 free-agent draft. ... On disabled list (August 18, 2002-remainder of season); included rehabilitation assignment to Richmond. ... Traded by Braves with 3B Wes Helms to Milwaukee Brewers for P Ray King (December 16, 2002). ... Selected by Chicago Cubs organization from Brewers in Rule 5 minor league draft (December 15, 2003). ... Signed as a free agent by Atlanta Braves organization (March 10, 2005).

CAREER HITTING: 0-for-0 (.000), 0 R, 0 2B, 0 3B, 0 HR, 0 RBI.

JOHN FOSTER'S PITCHING ZONE

.000	.500	.125
.250	.182	.227
.222	.500	.182

LEFTY-RIGHTY SPLITS

vs.	Avg.	AB	H	2B	3B	HR	RBI	BB	SO	OBP	Slg.
L	.219	73	16	3	1	2	21	13	24	.345	.370
R	.204	54	11	1	0	1	4	6	8	.295	.278

Year	Team (League)	W	L	Pct.	ERA	WHIP	G	GS	CG	ShO	Hld.	Sv.-Opp.	IP	H	R	ER	HR	BB-IBB	SO	Avg.
1999— Danville (Appal.)		4	1	.800	1.38	0.87	18	0	0	0	...	1-...	39.0	28	10	6	0	6-0	36	.207
2000— Myrtle Beach (Carol.)		2	1	.667	1.85	1.27	38	0	0	0	...	3-...	48.2	48	13	10	2	14-4	46	.264
2001— Greenville (Sou.)		8	7	.533	3.01	1.51	50	0	0	0	...	7-...	68.2	71	30	23	6	33-7	63	.280
2002— Richmond (Int'l)		8	4	.667	4.21	1.53	55	0	0	0	...	8-...	62.0	67	34	29	5	28-8	48	.276

F

Year	Team (League)	W	L	Pct.	ERA	WHIP	G	GS	CG	ShO	Hld.	Sv.-Opp.	IP	H	R	ER	HR	BB-IBB	SO	Avg.
	— Atlanta (N.L.)	1	0	1.000	10.80	2.40	5	0	0	0	...	0-0	5.0	6	6	6	3	6-0	6	.286
2003	— Milwaukee (N.L.)	2	0	1.000	4.71	1.81	23	0	0	0	3	0-2	21.0	30	11	11	5	8-2	16	.341
	— Indianapolis (Int'l)	2	2	.500	3.70	1.38	27	0	0	0	...	0-...	41.1	44	21	17	4	13-1	37	.272
2004	Did not play (injured)																			
2005	— Richmond (Int'l)	0	0	...	1.59	0.53	3	0	0	0	0	1-1	5.2	2	1	1	0	1-0	5	.105
	— Atlanta (N.L.)	4	2	.667	4.15	1.33	62	0	0	0	12	1-2	34.2	27	17	16	3	19-0	32	.213
	Major League totals (3 years)	7	2	.778	4.90	1.58	90	0	0	0	15	1-4	60.2	63	34	33	11	33-2	54	.267

DIVISION SERIES RECORD

Year	Team (League)	W	L	Pct.	ERA	WHIP	G	GS	CG	ShO	Hld.	Sv.-Opp.	IP	H	R	ER	HR	BB-IBB	SO	Avg.
2005	Atlanta (N.L.)	0	0	...	54.00	12.00	2	0	0	0	0	0-0	0.1	2	2	2	0	2-1	1	.667

FOULKE, KEITH — P

PERSONAL: Born October 19, 1972, in Rapid City, S.D. ... 6-0/210. ... Throws right, bats right. ... Full name: Keith Charles Foulke. ... Name pronounced: FOLK. ... High school: Hargrove (Huffman, Texas). ... College: Lewis-Clark State (Lewiston, Idaho).
TRANSACTIONS/CAREER NOTES: Selected by Detroit Tigers organiztion in 14th round of 1993 free-agent draft; did not sign. ... Selected by San Francisco Giants organiza-tion in ninth round of 1994 free-agent draft. ... Traded by Giants with SS Mike Caruso, OF Brian Manning and Ps Lorenzo Barcelo, Bob Howry and Ken Vining to Chicago White Sox for Ps Wilson Alvarez, Danny Darwin and Roberto Hernandez (July 31, 1997). ... On disabled list (August 28, 1998-remainder of season). ... On suspended list (May 5-7, 2000). ... Traded by White Sox with C Mark Johnson, P Joe Valentine and cash to Oakland Athletics for P Billy Koch and two players to be named (December 3, 2002); White Sox acquired P Neal Cotts and OF Daylon Holt to complete deal (December 16, 2002). ... Signed as a free agent by Boston Red Sox (January 7, 2004). ... On disabled list (July 6-September 1, 2005); included rehabilitation assignment to Lowell.
HONORS: Named A.L. Reliever of the Year by THE SPORTING NEWS (2003).
CAREER HITTING: 2-for-16 (.125), 0 R, 0 2B, 0 3B, 0 HR, 0 RBI.

SCOUTING REPORT **Throws:** Foulke has a four-seam fastball that tops out at 91 mph, a two-seam fastball, a curveball and a changeup. *Tendencies:* Foulke uses deception to make up for his overall lack of stuff. Short arm motion makes it difficult for hitters to pick up the ball. Throws fast-ball and change with the same arm speed and from the same slot. Uses the four-seamer to set up his change. Occasionally will cut his fastball. Throws his change on any count. *Outlook:* If he does-n't regain the feel on his changeup, Foulke won't be effective as a closer. *Grade 7.5*

KEITH FOULKE'S PITCHING ZONE

.522	.429	.143
.229	.538	.333
.222	.000	.417

LEFTY-RIGHTY SPLITS

vs.	Avg.	AB	H	2B	3B	HR	RBI	BB	SO	OBP	Slg.
L	.255	106	27	6	0	3	17	12	25	.339	.396
R	.333	78	26	5	2	5	15	6	9	.402	.641

Year	Team (League)	W	L	Pct.	ERA	WHIP	G	GS	CG	ShO	Hld.	Sv.-Opp.	IP	H	R	ER	HR	BB-IBB	SO	Avg.
1994	— Everett (N'west)	2	0	1.000	0.93	1.03	4	4	0	0	...	0-...	19.1	17	4	2	0	3-0	22	.233
1995	— San Jose (Calif.)	13	6	.684	3.50	1.12	28	26	2	1	...	0-...	177.1	166	85	69	16	32-0	168	.247
1996	— Shreveport (Texas)	12	7	.632	2.76	1.01	27	27	4	2	...	0-...	182.2	149	61	56	16	35-0	129	.225
1997	— Phoenix (PCL)	5	4	.556	4.50	1.24	12	12	0	0	...	0-...	76.0	79	38	38	11	15-0	54	.270
	— San Francisco (N.L.)	1	5	.167	8.26	1.75	11	8	0	0	0	0-1	44.2	60	41	41	9	18-1	33	.324
	— Nashville (A.A.)	0	0	...	5.79	1.71	1	1	0	0	...	0-...	4.2	8	3	3	1	0-0	4	.400
	— Chicago (A.L.)	3	0	1.000	3.45	1.15	16	0	0	0	5	3-5	28.2	28	11	11	4	5-1	21	.255
1998	— Chicago (A.L.)	3	2	.600	4.13	1.09	54	0	0	0	13	1-2	65.1	51	31	30	9	20-3	57	.213
1999	— Chicago (A.L.)	3	3	.500	2.22	0.88	67	0	0	0	22	9-13	105.1	72	28	26	11	21-4	123	.188
2000	— Chicago (A.L.)	3	1	.750	2.97	1.00	72	0	0	0	3	34-39	88.0	66	31	29	9	22-2	91	.207
2001	— Chicago (A.L.)	4	9	.308	2.33	0.98	72	0	0	0		42-45	81.0	57	21	21	3	22-1	75	.199
2002	— Chicago (A.L.)	2	4	.333	2.90	1.00	65	0	0	0	8	11-14	77.2	65	26	25	7	13-2	58	.225
2003	— Oakland (A.L.)	9	1	.900	2.08	0.89	72	0	0	0		* 43-48	86.2	57	21	20	10	20-2	88	.184
2004	— Boston (A.L.)	5	3	.625	2.17	0.94	72	0	0	0		32-39	83.0	63	22	20	8	15-5	79	.206
2005	— Lowell (NY-Penn)	0	0	...	7.36	2.45	3	0	0	0	0	1-1	3.2	8	4	3	0	1-0	5	.421
	— Boston (A.L.)	5	5	.500	5.91	1.55	43	0	0	0	1	15-19	45.2	53	30	30	8	18-1	34	.288
	American League totals (9 years)	37	28	.569	2.89	1.01	533	0	0	0	52	190-224	661.1	512	221	212	69	156-21	626	.211
	National League totals (1 year)	1	5	.167	8.26	1.75	11	8	0	0	0	0-1	44.2	60	41	41	9	18-1	33	.324
	Major League totals (9 years)	38	33	.535	3.23	1.06	544	8	0	0	52	190-225	706.0	572	262	253	78	174-22	659	.219

DIVISION SERIES RECORD

Year	Team (League)	W	L	Pct.	ERA	WHIP	G	GS	CG	ShO	Hld.	Sv.-Opp.	IP	H	R	ER	HR	BB-IBB	SO	Avg.
2000	— Chicago (A.L.)	0	1	.000	11.57	2.57	2	0	0	0	0	0-0	2.1	4	3	3	2	2-0	2	.400
2003	— Oakland (A.L.)	0	1	.000	3.60	1.20	3	0	0	0	0	0-1	5.0	4	2	2	0	2-1	3	.211
2004	— Boston (A.L.)	0	0	...	0.00	1.00	2	0	0	0	0	1-1	3.0	2	0	0	0	1-1	5	.182
	Division series totals (3 years)	0	2	.000	4.35	1.45	7	0	0	0	0	1-2	10.1	10	5	5	2	5-2	10	.250

CHAMPIONSHIP SERIES RECORD

Year	Team (League)	W	L	Pct.	ERA	WHIP	G	GS	CG	ShO	Hld.	Sv.-Opp.	IP	H	R	ER	HR	BB-IBB	SO	Avg.
2004	— Boston (A.L.)	0	0	...	0.00	1.17	5	0	0	0	0	1-1	6.0	1	0	0	0	6-0	6	.053

WORLD SERIES RECORD

Year	Team (League)	W	L	Pct.	ERA	WHIP	G	GS	CG	ShO	Hld.	Sv.-Opp.	IP	H	R	ER	HR	BB-IBB	SO	Avg.
2004	— Boston (A.L.)	1	0	1.000	1.80	1.00	4	0	0	0	0	1-2	5.0	4	1	1	1	1-1	8	.200

ALL-STAR GAME RECORD

Year	Team (League)	W	L	Pct.	ERA	WHIP	G	GS	CG	ShO	Hld.	Sv.-Opp.	IP	H	R	ER	HR	BB-IBB	SO	Avg.
	All-Star Game totals (1 year)	0	0	...	0.00	0.00	1	0	0	0	0	1-1	1.0	0	0	0	0	0-0	0	.000

FOX, CHAD — P

PERSONAL: Born September 3, 1970, in Houston. ... 6-3/209. ... Throws right, bats right. ... Full name: Chad Douglas Fox. ... High school: Westfield (Houston). ... College: Tarleton State (Stephenville, Texas).
TRANSACTIONS/CAREER NOTES: Selected by Cincinnati Reds organization in 23rd round of 1992 free-agent draft. ... Traded by Reds with a player to be named to Atlanta Braves for OF Mike Kelly (January 9, 1996); Braves acquired P Ray King to complete deal (June 11, 1996). ... On disabled list (July 16-

LEFTY-RIGHTY SPLITS

vs.	Avg.	AB	H	2B	3B	HR	RBI	BB	SO	OBP	Slg.
L	.308	13	4	2	0	1	6	2	4	.400	.692
R	.250	16	4	1	0	1	4	6	7	.435	.500

F

September 3, 1996). ... Traded by Braves to Milwaukee Brewers for OF Gerald Williams (December 11, 1997). ... On disabled list (May 11-June 30, 1998); included rehabilitation assignment to Beloit. ... On disabled list (April 21, 1999-remainder of season; and March 28, 2000-entire season). ... On disabled list (March 30-May 31 and June 8, 2002-remainder of season); included rehabilitation assignment to Huntsville. ... Released by Brewers (October 15, 2002). ... Signed by Boston Red Sox (December 24, 2002). ... On disabled list (April 28-June 29, 2003); included rehabilitation assignments to Sarasota and Portland. ... Released by Red Sox (July 30, 2003). ... Signed by Florida Marlins organization (August 8, 2003). ... On disabled list (April 28, 2004-remainder of season). ... Signed as a free agent by Chicago Cubs organization (January 14, 2005) ... On disabled list (April 26, 2005-remainder of season).

CAREER HITTING: 0-for-7 (.000), 0 R, 0 2B, 0 3B, 0 HR, 0 RBI.

Year	Team (League)	W	L	Pct.	ERA	WHIP	G	GS	CG	ShO	Hld.	Sv.-Opp.	IP	H	R	ER	HR	BB-IBB	SO	Avg.
1992—	Princeton (Appal.)	4	2	.667	4.74	1.80	15	8	0	0	...	0-...	49.1	55	43	26	2	34-1	37	.275
1993—	Char., W.Va. (SAL)	9	12	.429	5.37	1.73	27	26	0	0	...	0-...	135.2	138	100	81	7	97-0	81	.268
1994—	Win.-Salem (Car.)	12	5	.706	3.86	1.38	25	25	1	0	...	0-...	156.1	121	77	67	18	94-0	137	.216
1995—	Chattanooga (Sou.)	4	5	.444	5.06	1.60	20	17	0	0	...	0-...	80.0	76	49	45	2	52-1	56	.250
1996—	Richmond (Int'l)	3	10	.231	4.73	1.50	18	18	1	0	...	0-...	93.1	91	57	49	9	49-1	87	.261
1997—	Richmond (Int'l)	1	0	1.000	3.70	1.56	13	0	0	0	...	0-...	24.1	24	10	10	1	14-0	25	.273
	— Atlanta (N.L.)	0	1	.000	3.29	1.46	30	0	0	0	7	0-1	27.1	24	12	10	4	16-0	28	.231
1998—	Milwaukee (N.L.)	1	4	.200	3.95	1.33	49	0	0	0	20	0-2	57.0	56	27	25	4	20-0	64	.260
	— Beloit (Midw.)	0	1	.000	4.50	0.50	2	1	0	0	...	0-...	2.0	1	1	1	0	0-0	3	.167
1999—	Milwaukee (N.L.)	0	0	...	10.80	2.25	6	0	0	0	1	0-0	6.2	11	8	8	1	4-0	12	.355
2000—	Milwaukee (N.L.)								Did not play.											
2001—	Indianapolis (Int'l)	3	0	1.000	1.50	1.17	4	0	0	0	...	0-...	6.0	4	1	1	0	3-0	8	.190
	— Milwaukee (N.L.)	5	2	.714	1.89	1.20	65	0	0	0	20	2-4	66.2	44	16	14	6	36-7	80	.181
2002—	Huntsville (Sou.)	0	1	.000	0.00	1.31	3	0	0	0	...	0-...	5.1	5	1	0	0	2-0	7	.263
	— Milwaukee (N.L.)	1	0	1.000	5.79	2.36	3	0	0	0	0	0-...	4.2	6	3	3	0	5-1	3	.316
2003—	Sarasota (Fla. St.)	0	0	...	4.50	1.50	2	1	0	0	...	0-...	2.0	2	1	1	0	1-0	1	.250
	— Pawtucket (Int'l)	0	0	...	13.50	3.00	1	0	0	0	...	0-...	1.1	3	3	2	1	1-0	2	.500
	— Portland (East.)	0	0	...	0.00	2.20	1	0	0	0	...	0-...	1.1	1	0	0	0	2-0	2	.200
	— Boston (A.L.)	1	2	.333	4.50	2.00	17	0	0	0	...	3-5	18.0	19	10	9	2	17-2	19	.264
	— Albuquerque (PCL)	0	0	...	3.86	2.10	3	0	0	0	...	0-...	2.1	4	1	1	0	1-0	5	.364
	— Florida (N.L.)	2	1	.667	2.13	1.18	21	0	0	0	7	0-0	25.1	16	6	6	1	14-2	27	.190
2004—	Florida (N.L.)	0	1	.000	6.75	1.59	12	0	0	0	5	0-2	10.2	9	8	8	1	8-0	17	.225
2005—	Chicago (N.L.)	0	0	...	6.75	2.00	11	0	0	0	3	1-1	8.0	8	6	6	2	8-0	11	.276
	American League totals (1 year)	1	2	.333	4.50	2.00	17	0	0	0	...	3-5	18.0	19	10	9	2	17-2	19	.264
	National League totals (8 years)	9	9	.500	3.49	1.38	197	0	0	0	63	3-10	206.1	174	86	80	19	111-10	242	.227
	Major League totals (8 years)	10	11	.476	3.57	1.43	214	0	0	0	63	6-15	224.1	193	96	89	21	128-12	261	.231

DIVISION SERIES RECORD

Year	Team (League)	W	L	Pct.	ERA	WHIP	G	GS	CG	ShO	Hld.	Sv.-Opp.	IP	H	R	ER	HR	BB-IBB	SO	Avg.
2003—	Florida (N.L.)	0	0	...	1.80	1.20	3	0	0	0	1	0-0	5.0	3	1	1	0	3-2	3	.188

CHAMPIONSHIP SERIES RECORD

Year	Team (League)	W	L	Pct.	ERA	WHIP	G	GS	CG	ShO	Hld.	Sv.-Opp.	IP	H	R	ER	HR	BB-IBB	SO	Avg.
2003—	Florida (N.L.)	1	0	1.000	5.40	2.10	3	0	0	0	0	0-0	3.1	5	2	2	1	2-0	2	.333

WORLD SERIES RECORD

Year	Team (League)	W	L	Pct.	ERA	WHIP	G	GS	CG	ShO	Hld.	Sv.-Opp.	IP	H	R	ER	HR	BB-IBB	SO	Avg.
2003—	Florida (N.L.)	0	0	...	6.00	2.67	3	0	0	0	0	0-0	3.0	4	2	2	1	4-1	4	.364

FRANCIS, JEFF   P

F

PERSONAL: Born January 8, 1981, in Vancouver. ... 6-5/200. ... Throws left, bats left. ... Full name: Jeffrey William Francis. ... High school: North Delta Senior (Delta, B.C.). ... College: British Columbia.

TRANSACTIONS/CAREER NOTES: Selected by Colorado Rockies organization in first round (ninth pick overall) of 2002 free-agent draft.

CAREER HITTING: 6-for-68 (.088), 8 R, 2 2B, 0 3B, 0 HR, 4 RBI.

SCOUTING REPORT *Throws:* He throws his fastball at 87-90 mph, a curve at 75, a slider at 80-81 and a changeup. *Tendencies:* Francis is a finesse pitcher who made a lot of improvements in his first full year in the major leagues. Has excellent mound presence with the ability to adjust quickly to hitters. Has very good life on his fastball down in the zone, running it away from righthanders. Curveball has a big, sweeping break. Slider occasionally is flat, but when he stays on top is quick and late. Good arm speed with his changeup. *Outlook:* Francis will be the Rockies' No. 1 starter. Is very advanced for his lack of experience. Is going to log a lot of innings. Will build on 14 wins from 2005 and is a candidate to win 20 eventually. *Grade 7.9*

JEFF FRANCIS' PITCHING ZONE

.360	.324	.154
.374	.395	.309
.346	.365	.138

LEFTY-RIGHTY SPLITS

vs.	Avg.	AB	H	2B	3B	HR	RBI	BB	SO	OBP	Slg.
L	.285	130	37	5	1	3	21	12	23	.342	.408
R	.317	603	191	45	4	23	92	58	105	.379	.519

Year	Team (League)	W	L	Pct.	ERA	WHIP	G	GS	CG	ShO	Hld.	Sv.-Opp.	IP	H	R	ER	HR	BB-IBB	SO	Avg.
2002—	Tri-Cities (NWL)	0	0	...	0.00	0.84	4	3	0	0	...	0-...	10.2	5	0	0	0	4-0	16	.143
	— Asheville (S. Atl.)	0	0	...	1.80	1.00	4	4	0	0	...	0-...	20.0	16	6	4	2	4-0	23	.232
2003—	Visalia (Calif.)	12	9	.571	3.47	1.12	27	27	2	2	...	0-...	160.2	135	66	62	8	45-1	153	.229
2004—	Tulsa (Texas)	13	1	.929	1.98	0.84	17	17	1	1	...	0-...	113.2	73	26	25	9	22-0	147	.180
	— Colo. Springs (PCL)	3	2	.600	2.85	1.02	7	7	0	0	...	0-...	41.0	35	16	13	3	7-0	49	.230
	— Colorado (N.L.)	3	2	.600	5.15	1.50	7	7	0	0	...	0-0	36.2	42	22	21	8	13-1	32	.286
2005—	Colorado (N.L.)	14	12	.538	5.68	1.62	33	33	0	0	...	0-0	183.2	228	119	116	26	70-5	128	.311
	Major League totals (2 years)	17	14	.548	5.60	1.60	40	40	0	0	...	0-0	220.1	270	141	137	34	83-6	160	.307

PERSONAL: Born September 17, 1960, in Brooklyn, N.Y. ... 5-10/185. ... Throws left, bats left. ... Full name: John Anthony Franco. ... High school: Lafayette (Brooklyn, N.Y.). ... College: St. John's.
TRANSACTIONS/CAREER NOTES: Selected by Los Angeles Dodgers organization in fifth round of June 1981 free-agent draft. ... Traded by Dodgers with P Brett Wise to Cincinnati Reds for IF Rafael Landestoy (May 9, 1983). ... Traded by Reds with OF Don Brown to New York Mets for Ps Randy Myers and Kip Gross (December 6, 1989). ... On disabled list (June 30-August 1 and August 26, 1992-remainder of season). ... On disabled list (April 17-May 7 and August 3-26, 1993). ... On disabled list (July 3-September 4, 1999); included rehabilitation assignment to Binghamton. ... On disabled list (March 21, 2002-entire season). ... On disabled list (March 28-May 30, 2003); included rehabilitation assignment to St. Lucie. ... Signed as a free agent by Houston Astros (February 9, 2005). ... Released by Astros (July 5, 2005).
HONORS: Named N.L. Fireman of the Year by THE SPORTING NEWS (1988, 1990 and 1994).
CAREER HITTING: 3-for-34 (.088), 2 R, 0 2B, 0 3B, 0 HR, 1 RBI.

JOHN FRANCO'S PITCHING ZONE

.000	.333	.500
.316	.750	.200
.625	.333	.333

LEFTY-RIGHTY SPLITS

vs.	Avg.	AB	H	2B	3B	HR	RBI	BB	SO	OBP	Slg.
L	.310	42	13	1	0	0	9	2	11	.356	.333
R	.400	25	10	3	0	0	4	7	5	.531	.520

Year Team (League)	W	L	Pct.	ERA	WHIP	G	GS	CG	ShO	Hld.	Sv.-Opp.	IP	H	R	ER	HR	BB-IBB	SO	Avg.
1981— Vero Beach (FSL)	7	4	.636	3.53	1.51	13	11	3	0		0-...	79.0	78	41	31	1	41-2	60	...
1982— Albuquerque (PCL)	1	2	.333	7.24	2.05	5	5	0	0		0-...	27.1	41	22	22	3	15-1	24	...
— San Antonio (Texas)	10	5	.667	4.96	1.74	17	17	3	0		0-...	105.1	137	70	58	11	46-1	76	...
1983— Albuquerque (PCL)	0	0		5.40	1.40	11	0	0	0		0-...	15.0	10	11	9	3	11-2	8	...
— Indianapolis (A.A.)	6	10	.375	4.85	1.65	23	18	2	0		2-...	115.0	148	69	62	10	42-3	54	...
1984— Wichita (A.A.)	1	0	1.000	5.79	1.29	6	0	0	0		0-...	9.1	8	6	6	1	4-0	11	.235
— Cincinnati (N.L.)	6	2	.750	2.61	1.39	54	0	0	0	1	4-9	79.1	74	28	23	3	36-4	55	.256
1985— Cincinnati (N.L.)	12	3	.800	2.18	1.24	67	0	0	0	11	12-15	99.0	83	27	24	5	40-8	61	.234
1986— Cincinnati (N.L.)	6	6	.500	2.94	1.33	74	0	0	0	1	29-38	101.0	90	40	33	7	44-12	84	.243
1987— Cincinnati (N.L.)	8	5	.615	2.52	1.26	68	0	0	0		32-41	82.0	76	26	23	4	27-6	61	.245
1988— Cincinnati (N.L.)	6	6	.500	1.57	1.01	70	0	0	0		* 39-42	86.0	60	18	15	3	27-3	46	.198
1989— Cincinnati (N.L.)	4	8	.333	3.12	1.40	60	0	0	0		32-39	80.2	77	35	28	3	36-8	60	.258
1990— New York (N.L.)	5	3	.625	2.53	1.29	55	0	0	0		* 33-39	67.2	66	22	19	4	21-2	56	.252
1991— New York (N.L.)	5	9	.357	2.93	1.43	52	0	0	0		30-35	55.1	61	27	18	2	18-4	45	.271
1992— New York (N.L.)	6	2	.750	1.64	1.06	31	0	0	0		15-17	33.0	24	6	6	1	11-2	20	.209
1993— New York (N.L.)	4	3	.571	5.20	1.79	35	0	0	0		10-17	36.1	46	24	21	6	19-3	29	.313
1994— New York (N.L.)	1	4	.200	2.70	1.32	47	0	0	0		* 30-36	50.0	47	20	15	2	19-0	42	.244
1995— New York (N.L.)	5	3	.625	2.44	1.26	48	0	0	0		29-36	51.2	48	17	14	4	17-2	41	.251
1996— New York (N.L.)	4	3	.571	1.83	1.39	51	0	0	0		28-36	54.0	54	15	11	2	21-0	48	.260
1997— New York (N.L.)	5	3	.625	2.55	1.15	59	0	0	0		36-42	60.0	49	18	17	3	20-2	53	.226
1998— New York (N.L.)	0	8	.000	3.62	1.47	61	0	0	0		38-46	64.2	66	28	26	4	29-7	59	.267
1999— New York (N.L.)	0	2	.000	2.88	1.45	46	0	0	0	1	19-21	40.2	40	14	13	1	19-0	41	.255
— Binghamton (East.)	0	0	...	0.00	0.00	1	1	0	0		0-...	1.1	0	0	0	0	0-0	1	.000
2000— New York (N.L.)	5	4	.556	3.40	1.29	62	0	0	0	20	4-4	55.2	46	24	21	4	26-6	56	.221
2001— New York (N.L.)	6	2	.750	4.05	1.39	58	0	0	0	17	2-7	53.1	55	25	24	8	19-2	50	.264
2002— New York (N.L.)			Did not play.																
2003— St. Lucie (Fla. St.)	0	1	.000	6.23	1.60	4	3	0	0		0-...	4.1	6	3	3	1	1-0	5	.316
— Norfolk (Int'l)	0	0	...	0.00	1.20	2	0	0	0		0-...	1.2	1	0	0	0	1-0	2	.167
— New York (N.L.)	0	3	.000	2.62	1.40	38	0	0	0	4	2-3	34.1	35	11	10	5	13-2	16	.265
2004— New York (N.L.)	2	7	.222	5.28	1.52	52	0	0	0	11	0-1	46.0	46	28	27	6	24-2	36	.258
2005— Houston (N.L.)	0	1	.000	7.20	2.13	31	0	0	0	6	0-1	15.0	23	13	12	0	9-2	16	.343
Major League totals (21 years)	**90**	**87**	**.508**	**2.89**	**1.33**	**1119**	**0**	**0**	**0**	**72**	**424-525**	**1245.2**	**1166**	**466**	**400**	**81**	**495-78**	**975**	**.249**

DIVISION SERIES RECORD

Year Team (League)	W	L	Pct.	ERA	WHIP	G	GS	CG	ShO	Hld.	Sv.-Opp.	IP	H	R	ER	HR	BB-IBB	SO	Avg.
1999— New York (N.L.)	1	0	1.000	0.00	0.27	3	0	0	0		0-0	3.2	1	0	0	0	0-0	2	.091
2000— New York (N.L.)	0	0	...	0.00	0.50	2	0	0	0		1-1	2.0	1	0	0	0	0-0	2	.167
Division series totals (2 years)	**1**	**0**	**1.000**	**0.00**	**0.35**	**5**	**0**	**0**	**0**		**1-1**	**5.2**	**2**	**0**	**0**	**0**	**0-0**	**4**	**.118**

CHAMPIONSHIP SERIES RECORD

Year Team (League)	W	L	Pct.	ERA	WHIP	G	GS	CG	ShO	Hld.	Sv.-Opp.	IP	H	R	ER	HR	BB-IBB	SO	Avg.
1999— New York (N.L.)	0	0	...	3.38	1.50	3	0	0	0		0-1	2.2	3	1	1	0	1-0	3	.333
2000— New York (N.L.)	0	0	...	6.75	1.88	3	0	0	0	2	0-0	2.2	3	2	2	0	2-0	2	.273
Champ. series totals (2 years)	**0**	**0**		**5.06**	**1.69**	**6**	**0**	**0**	**0**	**2**	**0-1**	**5.1**	**6**	**3**	**3**	**0**	**3-0**	**5**	**.300**

WORLD SERIES RECORD

Year Team (League)	W	L	Pct.	ERA	WHIP	G	GS	CG	ShO	Hld.	Sv.-Opp.	IP	H	R	ER	HR	BB-IBB	SO	Avg.
2000— New York (N.L.)	1	0	1.000	0.00	0.90	4	0	0	0	1	0-0	3.1	3	0	0	0	0-0	1	.273

ALL-STAR GAME RECORD

	W	L	Pct.	ERA	WHIP	G	GS	CG	ShO	Hld.	Sv.-Opp.	IP	H	R	ER	HR	BB-IBB	SO	Avg.
All-Star Game totals (2 years)	0	0		0.00	0.00	2	0	0	0		0-0	1.2	0	0	0	0	0-0	0	.000

FRANCO, JULIO   1B

PERSONAL: Born August 23, 1958, in San Pedro de Macoris, Dominican Republic. ... 6-1/188. ... Bats right, throws right. ... Full name: Julio Cesar Franco. ... High school: Divine Providence (San Pedro de Macoris, Dominican Republic).
TRANSACTIONS/CAREER NOTES: Signed as a non-drafted free agent by Philadelphia Phillies organization (June 23, 1978). ... Traded by Phillies with 2B Manny Trillo, OF George Vukovich, P Jay Baller and C Jerry Willard to Cleveland Indians for OF Von Hayes (December 9, 1982). ... On disabled list (July 13-August 8, 1987). ... Traded by Indians to Texas Rangers for 1B Pete O'Brien, OF Oddibe McDowell and 2B Jerry Browne (December 6, 1988). ... On disabled list (March 28-April 19, May 4-June 1 and July 9, 1992-remainder of season). ... Signed as a free agent by Chicago White Sox (December 15, 1993). ... Signed by Chiba Lotte Marines of Japan Pacific League (December 28, 1994). ... Signed as a free agent by Indians (December 7, 1995). ... On disabled list (July 7-25 and August 4-30, 1996). ... Released by Indians (August 13, 1997). ... Signed by Milwaukee Brewers (August 13, 1997). ... Signed by Chiba (1998). ... Signed as a free agent by Tampa Bay Devil Rays organization (February 19, 1999). ... Loaned by Devil Rays organization to Mexico City Tigers of the Mexican League (March 29-September 18, 1999). ... Contract purchased by Atlanta Braves organization from Mexico City (August 31, 2001). ... On disabled list (August 17-September 1, 2003).
2005 GAMES PLAYED BY POSITION (MLB): 1B—62, DH—4.

SCOUTING REPORT *Offense:* Franco can still hit despite being one of the oldest position players to play the game. Has a long stroke and wraps the bat around his head but knows how to hit and make adjustments. Bat speed has slowed but he can still cheat to the fastball. Likes the ball out over the plate and his power now is to the opposite field. *Defense:* His range is restricted, but his hands are still good enough to get him by. *Outlook:* Franco says he wants to play until he's 50, and he has the body to do it. Was an emotional leader on the Braves. Remains an offensive asset. **Grade 6.4**

JULIO FRANCO'S HITTING ZONE

.545	.091	.385
.323	.435	.286
.353	.429	.294

LEFTY-RIGHTY SPLITS

vs.	Avg.	AB	H	2B	3B	HR	RBI	BB	SO	OBP	Slg.
L	.271	107	29	4	0	5	21	16	27	.365	.449
R	.278	126	35	8	1	4	21	11	30	.333	.452

								BATTING											FIELDING	
Year	Team (League)	Pos.	G	AB	R	H	2B	3B	HR	RBI	BB	SO	HBP	GDP	SB-CS	Avg.	OBP	SLG	OPS	E	Avg.
1978—	Butte (Pion.)	SS	47	141	34	43	5	2	3	28	17	30	1	...	4-3	.305	.381	.433	.814	25	.781
1979—	Cen. Oregon (NWL)	SS	•71	299	57	•98	15	5	•10	45	24	59	3	...	22-9	.328	.381	.512	.893	31	.921
1980—	Peninsula (Caro.)	SS	•140	•555	105	178	25	6	11	•99	33	66	8	...	44-12	.321	.361	.447	.808	42	.934
1981—	Reading (East.)	SS	•139	•532	70	160	17	3	8	74	52	60	5	...	27-14	.301	.365	.389	.754	30	.958
1982—	Okla. City (A.A.)	3B-SS	120	463	80	139	19	5	21	66	39	56	3	...	33-11	.300	.357	.499	.856	§42	.930
—	Philadelphia (N.L.)	3B-SS	16	29	3	8	1	0	0	3	2	4	0	1	0-2	.276	.323	.310	.633	0	1.000
1983—	Cleveland (A.L.)	SS	149	560	68	153	24	8	8	80	27	50	2	21	32-12	.273	.306	.388	.693	28	.961
1984—	Cleveland (A.L.)	DH-SS	160	•658	82	188	22	5	3	79	43	68	6	23	19-10	.286	.331	.348	.679	*36	.955
1985—	Cleveland (A.L.)	2B-DH-SS	160	636	97	183	33	4	6	90	54	74	4	26	13-9	.288	.343	.381	.723	§36	.950
1986—	Cleveland (A.L.)		149	599	80	183	30	5	10	74	32	66	0	•28	10-7	.306	.338	.422	.760	19	.972
1987—	Cleveland (A.L.)	2B-DH-SS	128	495	86	158	24	3	8	52	57	56	3	23	32-9	.319	.389	.428	.818	18	.964
1988—	Cleveland (A.L.)	2B-DH	152	613	88	186	23	6	10	54	56	72	2	17	25-11	.303	.361	.409	.771	14	.982
1989—	Texas (A.L.)		150	548	80	173	31	5	13	92	66	69	1	•27	21-3	.316	.386	.462	.848	13	.980
1990—	Texas (A.L.)	2B-DH	157	582	96	172	27	1	11	69	82	83	2	12	31-10	.296	.383	.402	.785	•19	.975
1991—	Texas (A.L.)		146	589	108	201	27	3	15	78	65	78	3	13	36-9	•.341	.408	.474	.882	14	.979
1992—	Texas (A.L.)	DH-2B-OF	35	107	19	25	7	0	2	8	15	17	0	3	1-1	.234	.328	.355	.683	3	.927
1993—	Texas (A.L.)	DH	144	532	85	154	31	3	14	84	62	95	1	16	9-3	.289	.360	.438	.798	...	...
1994—	Chicago (A.L.)	DH-1B	112	433	72	138	19	2	20	98	62	75	5	14	8-1	.319	.406	.510	.916	3	.969
1995—	Chiba Lotte (Jap. Pac.)	1B	127	474	60	145	25	3	10	58					11-...	.306		.435			
1996—	Cleveland (A.L.)	1B	112	432	72	139	20	1	14	76	61	82	3	14	8-8	.322	.407	.470	.877	9	.990
1997—	Cleveland (A.L.)	DH-2B-1B	78	289	46	82	13	1	3	25	38	75	0	8	8-5	.284	.367	.367	.734	3	.983
—	Milwaukee (A.L.)	DH-1B	42	141	22	34	3	0	4	19	31	41	1	4	7-1	.241	.373	.348	.720	1	.992
1998—	Chiba Lotte (Jap. Pac.)		131	487	78	141	27	2	18	77					7-...	.290		.464			
1999—	Tigres (Mex.)	1B	93	326	90	138	22	6	14	77	80	44			9-1	.423		.656		2	.993
—	Tampa Bay (A.L.)	1B	1	1	0	0	0	0	0	0	0	1	0		0-0	.000	.000	.000	.000	0	1.000
2000—	Samsung (Kor.)		132	477		156			22	110					...-...	.327		.465			
2001—	Tigres (Mex.)	1B-DH-OF	110	407	90	•178	34	5	18	90	50	56			15-6	.437		.678		5	.991
—	Atlanta (N.L.)		25	90	13	27	4	0	3	11	10	20	1	3	0-0	.300	.378	.444	.821	1	.995
2002—	Atlanta (N.L.)	1B-DH	125	338	51	96	13	1	6	30	39	75	1	5	5-1	.284	.357	.382	.739	8	.990
2003—	Atlanta (N.L.)	1B	103	197	28	58	12	2	5	31	25	43	0	8	0-1	.294	.372	.452	.824	1	.998
2004—	Atlanta (N.L.)	1B-DH	125	320	37	99	18	3	6	57	36	68	1	10	4-2	.309	.378	.441	.818	2	.997
2005—	Atlanta (N.L.)	1B-DH	108	233	30	64	12	1	9	42	27	57	1	10	4-0	.275	.348	.451	.799	5	.990
	American League totals (15 years)			1875	7215	1101	2169	334	47	141	978	751	1002	33	254	260-99	.301	.366	.419	.785	216	.972
	National League totals (6 years)			502	1207	162	352	60	7	29	174	139	267	4	45	13-6	.292	.364	.425	.789	17	.994
	Major League totals (21 years)			2377	8422	1263	2521	394	54	170	1152	890	1269	37	299	273-105	.299	.366	.419	.785	233	.977

DIVISION SERIES RECORD

Year	Team (League)	Pos.	G	AB	R	H	2B	3B	HR	RBI	BB	SO	HBP	GDP	SB-CS	Avg.	OBP	SLG	OPS	E	Avg.
1996—	Cleveland (A.L.)	1B-DH	4	15	1	2	0	0	0	1	1	6	0	0	0-0	.133	.176	.133	.310	0	1.000
2001—	Atlanta (N.L.)	1B	3	13	3	4	0	0	1	1	0	1	0	0	0-1	.308	.308	.538	.846	0	1.000
2002—	Atlanta (N.L.)	1B	5	22	2	4	0	0	0	1	2	3	0	1	1-0	.182	.250	.182	.432	0	1.000
2003—	Atlanta (N.L.)	1B	4	8	1	4	1	0	0	0	2	2	0	0	0-0	.500	.600	.625	1.225	0	1.000
2004—	Atlanta (N.L.)	1B	3	4	0	0	0	0	0	0	0	1	0	0	0-0	.000	.000	.000	.000	0	1.000
2005—	Atlanta (N.L.)	1B	3	9	0	2	0	0	0	0	1	3	0	0	0-0	.222	.300	.222	.522	0	1.000
	Division series totals (6 years)		22	71	7	16	1	0	1	3	6	16	0	1	1-1	.225	.282	.282	.564	0	1.000

CHAMPIONSHIP SERIES RECORD

Year	Team (League)	Pos.	G	AB	R	H	2B	3B	HR	RBI	BB	SO	HBP	GDP	SB-CS	Avg.	OBP	SLG	OPS	E	Avg.
2001—	Atlanta (N.L.)	1B	5	23	2	6	0	1	0	2	0	2	0	0	0-0	.261	.261	.391	.652	0	1.000

ALL-STAR GAME RECORD

		G	AB	R	H	2B	3B	HR	RBI	BB	SO	HBP	GDP	SB-CS	Avg.	OBP	SLG	OPS	E	Avg.
All-Star Game totals (2 years)		2	6	0	2	1	0	0	2	0	0	0	0	0-0	.333	.333	.500	.833	0	1.000

FRANCOEUR, JEFF   OF

PERSONAL: Born January 8, 1984, in Atlanta, Ga. ... 6-4/220. ... Bats right, throws right. ... Full name: Jeffrey Braden Francoeur. ... High school: Parkview (Ga.).
TRANSACTIONS/CAREER NOTES: Selected by Atlanta Braves organization in first round (23rd pick overall) of 2002 free-agent draft.
2005 GAMES PLAYED BY POSITION (MLB): OF—67.

SCOUTING REPORT *Offense:* Francoeur is one of the best young players to enter the league in many years. Ball just explodes off his bat. Has outstanding bat speed and swings hard. Gets good extension and has the ability to use the whole field. Is a good fastball hitter. Is not a patient hitter. *Defense:* He is a natural right fielder who gets good jumps coming in on the ball and has good lateral range. Has an exceptional throwing arm, charges the ball well and has a quick, accurate release. *Outlook:* Francoeur's tools make him one of the most exciting players around; he has the potential to be a huge star, and he soon could be a Gold Glove and Silver Slugger winner. Will post elite power numbers in the near future. **Grade 7.8**

JEFF FRANCOEUR'S HITTING ZONE

.444	.600	.222
.326	.333	.233
.310	.313	.450

LEFTY-RIGHTY SPLITS

vs.	Avg.	AB	H	2B	3B	HR	RBI	BB	SO	OBP	Slg.
L	.379	66	25	8	1	6	17	2	15	.408	.803
R	.272	191	52	12	0	8	28	9	43	.310	.461

Year — Team (League)	Pos.	G	AB	R	H	2B	3B	HR	RBI	BB	SO	HBP	GDP	SB-CS	Avg.	OBP	SLG	OPS	FIELDING E	Avg.
2002— Danville (Appal.)	OF	38	147	31	48	12	1	8	31	15	34	3	2	8-5	.327	.395	.585	.980	1	.990
2003— Rome (S. Atl.)	OF	134	524	78	147	26	9	14	68	30	68	7	21	14-6	.281	.325	.445	.770	4	.986
2004— Myrtle Beach (Carol.)	OF	88	334	56	98	26	0	15	52	22	70	7	5	10-6	.293	.346	.506	.852	4	.765
— Greenville (Sou.)	OF	18	76	8	15	2	0	3	9	0	14	0	0	1-0	.197	.197	.342	.539	1	.000
2005— Mississippi (Sou.)	OF	84	335	40	92	28	2	13	62	21	76	5	7	13-4	.275	.322	.487	.808	6	.981
— Atlanta (N.L.)	OF	70	257	41	77	20	1	14	45	11	58	4	4	3-2	.300	.336	.549	.884	5	.966
Major League totals (1 year)		70	257	41	77	20	1	14	45	11	58	4	4	3-2	.300	.336	.549	.884	5	.966

DIVISION SERIES RECORD

Year — Team (League)	Pos.	G	AB	R	H	2B	3B	HR	RBI	BB	SO	HBP	GDP	SB-CS	Avg.	OBP	SLG	OPS	E	Avg.
2005— Atlanta (N.L.)	OF	4	17	2	4	1	1	0	1	2	4	1		0-0	.235	.350	.412	.762	0	1.000

FRANKLIN, RYAN — P

PERSONAL: Born March 5, 1973, in Fort Smith, Ark. ... 6-3/180. ... Throws right, bats right. ... Full name: Ryan Ray Franklin. ... High school: Spiro (Okla.). ... Junior college: Seminole (Okla.).

TRANSACTIONS/CAREER NOTES: Selected by Toronto Blue Jays organization in 25th round of 1991 free-agent draft; did not sign. ... Selected by Seattle Mariners organization in 23rd round of 1992 free-agent draft. ... On disabled list (June 28-July 15, 2002); included rehabilitation assignment to Everett. ... On restricted list (August 2-12, 2005).

CAREER HITTING: 1-for-11 (.091), 1 R, 0 2B, 0 3B, 0 HR, 0 RBI.

SCOUTING REPORT *Throws:* Franklin has an 87-91 mph fastball, an 83-86 slider, a 74-76 curve and a changeup. *Tendencies:* He throws a lot of different pitches, but the loss of velocity on his fastball has made them more similar and less effective. Appears to have lost confidence in his fastball and leaves it up too often. *Outlook:* He is starting to level off now with declining velocity and sharpness in his breaking ball. Could struggle to reach double-digit wins in 2006. *Grade 6.3*

RYAN FRANKLIN'S PITCHING ZONE

.325	.261	.292
.291	.299	.370
.310	.200	.156

LEFTY-RIGHTY SPLITS

vs.	Avg.	AB	H	2B	3B	HR	RBI	BB	SO	OBP	Slg.
L	.266	387	103	23	1	13	43	42	44	.338	.432
R	.295	370	109	14	3	15	53	20	49	.340	.470

Year — Team (League)	W	L	Pct.	ERA	WHIP	G	GS	CG	ShO	Hld.	Sv.-Opp.	IP	H	R	ER	HR	BB-IBB	SO	Avg.
1993— Bellingham (N'west)	5	3	.625	2.92	1.34	15	14	1	1	...	0-...	74.0	72	38	24	2	27-0	55	.250
1994— Appleton (Midwest)	9	6	.600	3.13	1.08	18	18	5	1	...	0-...	118.0	105	60	41	6	23-0	102	.234
— Riverside (Calif.)	4	2	.667	3.06	1.12	8	8	1	1	...	0-...	61.2	61	26	21	5	8-0	35	.249
— Calgary (PCL)	0	0	...	7.94	1.76	1	1	0	0	...	0-...	5.2	9	6	5	2	1-0	2	.333
1995— Port City (Sou.)	6	10	.375	4.32	1.34	31	20	1	1	...	0-...	146.0	153	84	70	13	43-4	102	.274
1996— Port City (Sou.)	6	12	.333	4.01	1.23	28	27	2	0	...	0-...	182.0	186	99	81	23	37-0	127	.265
1997— Memphis (Sou.)	4	2	.667	3.03	0.99	11	8	2	2	...	0-...	59.1	45	22	20	4	14-1	49	.208
— Tacoma (PCL)	5	5	.500	4.18	1.34	14	14	0	0	...	0-...	90.1	97	48	42	11	24-1	59	.281
1998— Tacoma (PCL)	5	6	.455	4.51	1.41	34	16	1	0	...	1-...	127.2	148	75	64	18	32-2	90	.292
1999— Tacoma (PCL)	6	9	.400	4.71	1.29	29	19	2	1	...	2-...	135.2	142	81	71	17	33-1	94	.270
— Seattle (A.L.)	0	0	...	4.76	1.59	6	0	0	0	1	0-0	11.1	10	6	6	2	8-1	6	.238
2000— Tacoma (PCL)	11	5	.688	3.90	1.11	31	22	4	0	...	0-0	164.0	147	85	71	28	35-1	142	.240
2001— Seattle (A.L.)	5	1	.833	3.56	1.28	38	0	0	0	5	0-1	78.1	76	32	31	13	24-4	60	.250
— Tacoma (PCL)	0	0	...	0.00	0.55	1	0	0	0	...	0-...	3.2	2	0	0	0	0-0	3	.167
2002— Seattle (A.L.)	7	5	.583	4.02	1.17	41	12	0	0	3	0-1	118.2	117	62	53	14	22-1	65	.255
— Everett (N'west)	0	0	...	0.00	0.75	1	1	0	0	...	0-...	2.2	2	1	0	0	0-0	1	.200
2003— Seattle (A.L.)	11	13	.458	3.57	1.23	32	32	2	1	0	0-0	212.0	199	93	84	• 34	61-3	99	.251
2004— Seattle (A.L.)	4	16	.200	4.90	1.42	32	32	2	1	0	0-0	200.1	224	116	109	33	61-1	104	.283
2005— Seattle (A.L.)	8	15	.348	5.10	1.44	32	30	2	1	0	0-0	190.2	212	110	108	28	62-4	93	.280
Major League totals (6 years)	35	50	.412	4.34	1.33	181	106	6	3	9	0-2	811.1	838	419	391	124	238-14	427	.267

FRANKLIN, WAYNE — P

PERSONAL: Born March 9, 1974, in Wilmington, Del. ... 6-2/204. ... Throws left, bats left. ... Full name: Gary Wayne Franklin. ... High school: Northeast (Md.). ... College: Maryland-Baltimore County.

TRANSACTIONS/CAREER NOTES: Selected by Los Angeles Dodgers organization in 36th round of 1996 free-agent draft. ... Selected by Houston Astros organization from Dodgers organization in Rule 5 minor league draft (December 14, 1998). ... Traded by Astros to Milwaukee Brewers (September 3, 2002), as part of deal in which Brewers traded IF Mark Loretta to Astros for two players to be named (August 31, 2002); Brewers acquired 2B Keith Ginter to complete deal (September 5, 2002). ... Traded by Brewers with P Leo Estrella to San Francisco Giants for Ps Carlos Villanueva and Glenn Woolard (March 30, 2004). ... On disabled list (July 29-August 18, 2004); included rehabilitation assignment to Fresno.

CAREER HITTING: 11-for-70 (.157), 3 R, 1 2B, 0 3B, 0 HR, 5 RBI.

LEFTY-RIGHTY SPLITS

vs.	Avg.	AB	H	2B	3B	HR	RBI	BB	SO	OBP	Slg.
L	.286	21	6	1	1	1	6	3	3	.385	.571
R	.200	25	5	1	0	0	2	5	7	.333	.240

Year — Team (League)	W	L	Pct.	ERA	WHIP	G	GS	CG	ShO	Hld.	Sv.-Opp.	IP	H	R	ER	HR	BB-IBB	SO	Avg.
1996— Yakima (N'west)	1	0	1.000	2.52	1.76	20	0	0	0	...	1-...	25.0	32	10	7	2	12-3	22	.311
1997— Savannah (S. Atl.)	5	3	.625	3.18	1.39	28	7	1	0	...	2-...	82.0	79	41	29	10	35-0	58	.246
— San Bern. (Calif.)	0	0	...	0.00	1.00	1	0	0	0	...	0-...	2.0	2	0	0	0	0-0	1	.286
1998— Vero Beach (FSL)	9	3	.750	3.53	1.23	48	0	0	0	...	10-...	86.2	81	43	34	7	26-0	78	.243
1999— Kissimmee (Fla. St.)	3	0	1.000	1.53	0.96	12	0	0	0	...	1-...	17.2	11	4	3	0	6-0	22	.180
— Jackson (Texas)	3	1	.750	1.61	0.93	46	0	0	0	...	20-...	50.1	31	11	9	4	16-3	40	.178
2000— New Orleans (PCL)	3	3	.500	3.63	1.57	48	0	0	0	...	4-...	44.2	51	29	18	4	19-3	37	.279
— Houston (N.L.)	0	0	...	5.48	1.69	25	0	0	0	8	0-0	21.1	24	14	13	2	12-1	21	.282
2001— Houston (N.L.)	0	0	...	6.75	2.17	11	0	0	0	1	0-0	12.0	17	9	9	4	9-0	9	.333
— New Orleans (PCL)	2	1	.667	3.81	1.31	41	0	0	0	...	0-...	49.2	47	28	21	6	18-2	51	.244
2002— New Orleans (PCL)	13	9	.591	3.12	1.18	29	27	1	0	...	0-...	179.0	153	68	62	14	59-2	* 141	.235
— Milwaukee (N.L.)	2	1	.667	2.63	1.38	4	4	0	0	...	0-...	24.0	16	8	7	1	17-1	17	.188
2003— Milwaukee (N.L.)	10	13	.435	5.50	1.52	36	34	1	0	...	0-...	194.2	201	* 129	• 119	* 36	94-2	116	.268
2004— Fresno (PCL)	0	2	.000	3.86	1.07	3	3	0	0	...	0-...	9.1	6	4	4	0	4-0	11	.182

F

Year	Team (League)	W	L	Pct.	ERA	WHIP	G	GS	CG	ShO	Hld.	Sv.-Opp.	IP	H	R	ER	HR	BB-IBB	SO	Avg.
— San Francisco (N.L.)		2	1	.667	6.39	1.52	43	2	0	0	5	0-1	50.2	55	37	36	11	22-2	40	.281
2005—Columbus (Int'l)		2	3	.400	3.61	1.11	42	0	0	0	11	1-1	42.1	36	18	17	4	11-1	50	.231
— New York (A.L.)		0	1	.000	6.39	1.50	13	0	0	0	3	0-3	12.2	11	12	9	1	8-0	10	.239
American League totals (1 year)		0	1	.000	6.39	1.50	13	0	0	0	3	0-3	12.2	11	12	9	1	8-0	10	.239
National League totals (5 years)		14	15	.483	5.47	1.54	119	40	1	1	14	0-1	302.2	313	197	184	54	154-6	203	.268
Major League totals (6 years)		14	16	.467	5.51	1.54	132	40	1	1	17	0-4	315.1	324	209	193	55	162-6	213	.267

FRASOR, JASON — P

PERSONAL: Born August 9, 1977, in Chicago. ... 5-10/170. ... Throws right, bats right. ... Full name: Jason Andrew Frasor. ... High school: Oak Forest (Ill.). ... College: Southern Illinois.

TRANSACTIONS/CAREER NOTES: Selected by Detroit Tigers organization in 33rd round of 1999 free-agent draft. ... Traded by Tigers to Los Angeles Dodgers (September 18, 2002), completing deal in which Tigers acquired OF Hiram Bocachica for P Tom Farmer and a player to be named (July 25, 2002). ... Traded by Dodgers to Toronto Blue Jays for OF Jayson Werth (March 29, 2004).

CAREER HITTING: 0-for-0 (.000), 0 R, 0 2B, 0 3B, 0 HR, 0 RBI.

SCOUTING REPORT *Throws:* Frasor's fastball ranges from 90-94 mph. Throws a hard curve at 78-80 and a straight change. *Tendencies:* He pitches with a high arm angle and has a very good delivery with a good downward plane, creating deception. Fastball is straight. Tends to pitch up in the zone too often, but his command has improved. Power curve breaks straight down and is more effective against lefthanded hitters. Change is improving; Frasor is using it more and being effective with it for a short-framed pitcher. *Outlook:* Frasor has been very good in a setup role for the Blue Jays. Is improving with the development of his changeup and improved control. **Grade 7.7**

JASON FRASOR'S PITCHING ZONE

.353	.000	.308
.104	.367	.459
.217	.368	.167

LEFTY-RIGHTY SPLITS

vs.	Avg.	AB	H	2B	3B	HR	RBI	BB	SO	OBP	Slg.
L	.236	123	29	3	0	1	10	9	32	.293	.285
R	.257	148	38	4	3	7	18	19	30	.347	.466

Year	Team (League)	W	L	Pct.	ERA	WHIP	G	GS	CG	ShO	Hld.	Sv.-Opp.	IP	H	R	ER	HR	BB-IBB	SO	Avg.
1999—Oneonta (NYP)		3	3	.500	1.69	0.99	12	11	0	0	...	0-...	58.2	36	16	11	3	22-0	69	.176
— W. Mich. (Midw.)		2	1	.667	2.63	1.08	4	4	1	1	...	0-...	24.0	17	10	7	2	9-0	33	.198
2000—W. Mich. (Midw.)		5	3	.625	3.28	1.18	14	14	0	0	...	0-...	71.1	55	32	26	2	29-0	65	.208
2001—	Did not play.																			
2002—Lakeland (Fla. St.)		5	6	.455	3.54	1.35	24	24	0	0	...	0-...	117.0	112	54	46	10	46-1	87	.257
2003—Vero Beach (Fla. St.) ...		1	0	1.000	1.85	0.82	15	0	0	0	...	6-...	24.1	16	7	5	0	4-0	36	.182
— Jacksonville (Sou.)		1	0	1.000	2.95	1.28	35	0	0	0	...	17-...	36.2	33	14	12	2	14-0	50	.241
2004— Syracuse (Int'l)		0	0	...	2.25	1.50	3	0	0	0	...	0-...	4.0	1	1	1	0	5-0	6	.077
— Toronto (A.L.)		4	6	.400	4.08	1.46	63	0	0	0	8	17-19	68.1	64	31	31	4	36-3	54	.251
2005— Toronto (A.L.)		3	5	.375	3.25	1.27	67	0	0	0	15	1-3	74.2	67	31	27	8	28-2	62	.247
Major League totals (2 years)		7	11	.389	3.65	1.36	130	0	0	0	23	18-22	143.0	131	62	58	12	64-5	116	.249

FREEL, RYAN — 2B/OF

PERSONAL: Born March 8, 1976, in Jacksonville. ... 5-10/180. ... Bats right, throws right. ... Full name: Ryan Paul Freel. ... High school: Englewood (Jacksonville). ... Junior college: Tallahassee (Fla.).

TRANSACTIONS/CAREER NOTES: Selected by St. Louis Cardinals organization in 14th round of 1994 free-agent draft; did not sign. ... Selected by Toronto Blue Jays organization in 10th round of 1995 free-agent draft. ... Signed as a free agent by Tampa Bay Devil Rays organization (November 8, 2001). ... Signed as a free agent by Cincinnati Reds organization (November 19, 2002). ... On disabled list (May 29-July 4, 2003). ... On disabled list (June 19-July 20 and August 16-September 5, 2005); included rehabilitation assignment to Chattanooga.

2005 GAMES PLAYED BY POSITION (MLB): OF—51, 2B—48, 3B—10.

SCOUTING REPORT *Offense:* One of the most versatile players in the game, Freel is a classic overachiever. Has a short, quick stroke and will make adjustments to use the whole field. Tries to work the count and keep his strikeout totals down. Doesn't have much power but is a good situational hitter. Is a plus runner who is extremely aggressive with excellent basestealing instincts. *Defense:* Freel is fearless, an outfielder who would run through a wall to make a play. Gets good lateral jumps and has good closing speed. Is stiff at third base, but is not afraid to get in front of the ball. Arm strength is average at third, slightly below average in the outfield. *Outlook:* Freel is a utility player who can play every day at a variety of positions. A self-made player any manager in baseball would love to have. **Grade 7**

RYAN FREEL'S HITTING ZONE

.364	.273	.056
.278	.333	.241
.296	.286	.167

LEFTY-RIGHTY SPLITS

vs.	Avg.	AB	H	2B	3B	HR	RBI	BB	SO	OBP	Slg.
L	.299	107	32	6	1	2	10	21	21	.419	.430
R	.260	262	68	13	2	2	11	30	38	.351	.347

										BATTING										FIELDING	
Year	Team (League)	Pos.	G	AB	R	H	2B	3B	HR	RBI	BB	SO	HBP	GDP	SB-CS	Avg.	OBP	SLG	OPS	E	Avg.
1995—St. Catharines (NYP)	2B	65	243	30	68	10	5	3	29	22	49	7	3	12-7	.280	.350	.399	.749	4	.940
1996—Dunedin (Fla. St.)	2B-3B	104	381	64	97	23	3	4	41	33	76	5	4	19-15	.255	.321	.362	.683	20	.959
1997—Knoxville (Sou.)	SS	33	94	18	19	1	1	0	4	19	13	2	1	5-3	.202	.348	.234	.582	13	.913
— Dunedin (Fla. St.)	2B-3B-OF-SS	61	181	42	51	8	2	3	17	46	28	9	3	24-5	.282	.447	.398	.845	18	.910
1998—Knoxville (Sou.)	2B-OF-SS	66	252	47	72	17	3	4	36	33	32	1	3	18-9	.286	.366	.425	.790	3	.982
— Syracuse (Int'l)	2B-OF	37	118	19	27	4	0	2	12	26	16	4	3	9-4	.229	.377	.314	.691	3	.962
1999—Knoxville (Sou.)	OF	11	46	9	13	5	1	1	9	8	4	1	0	4-2	.283	.382	.500	.882	0	1.000
— Syracuse (Int'l)	OF-SS	20	77	15	23	3	2	1	11	8	13	4	0	10-3	.299	.393	.429	.822	1	.976
2000—Dunedin (Fla. St.)	OF	4	18	7	9	1	0	1	6	9	5		0	0-0	.500	.500	1.056	1.556	0	1.000
— Tennessee (Sou.)	OF-2B	12	44	11	13	3	1	2	8	8	6	1	3	2-3	.295	.400	.409	.809	1	1.000
— Syracuse (Int'l)	OF-2B-3B-SS	80	283	62	81	14	5	10	30	35	44	7	3	30-7	.286	.380	.477	.857	9	.957
2001—Toronto (A.L.)	2B-3B	9	22	1	6	1	0	0	3	1	4	1	0	2-1	.273	.333	.318	.652	1	.969
— Syracuse (Int'l)	OF-2B-3B-SS	85	319	60	83	21	3	5	33	42	42	7	8	22-9	.260	.357	.392	.749	9	.959

Year Team (League)	Pos.	G	AB	R	H	2B	3B	HR	RBI	BB	SO	HBP	GDP	SB-CS	Avg.	OBP	SLG	OPS	E	Avg.
2002—Durham (Int'l)	2B-OF	119	448	65	117	27	4	8	48	38	51	14	10	37-10	.261	.337	.393	.730	7	.981
2003—Louisville (Int'l)	2B-OF-3B	54	215	38	59	11	1	3	12	21	32	0	2	25-6	.274	.336	.377	.713	2	.990
—Cincinnati (N.L.)	DH	43	137	23	39	6	1	4	12	9	13	4	2	9-4	.285	.344	.431	.775	1	.990
2004—Cincinnati (N.L.)	OF-2B-3B	143	505	74	140	21	8	3	28	67	88	12	7	37-10	.277	.375	.368	.743	15	.963
2005—Chattanooga (Sou.)	2B-OF-3B	5	17	3	3	0	0	0	1	3	5	0	1	0-1	.176	.286	.176	.462	0	1.000
—Cincinnati (N.L.)	OF-2B-3B	103	369	69	100	19	3	4	21	51	59	8	9	36-10	.271	.371	.371	.743	8	.978
American League totals (1 year)		9	22	1	6	1	0	0	3	1	4	1	0	2-1	.273	.333	.318	.652	1	.969
National League totals (3 years)		289	1011	166	279	46	12	11	61	127	160	24	18	82-24	.276	.370	.378	.748	24	.973
Major League totals (4 years)		298	1033	167	285	47	12	11	64	128	164	25	18	84-25	.276	.369	.377	.746	25	.972

FREEMAN, CHOO — OF

PERSONAL: Born October 20, 1979, in Pine Bluff, Ark. ... 6-2/200. ... Bats right, throws right. ... Full name: Raphael Freeman. ... High school: Dallas Christian.

TRANSACTIONS/CAREER NOTES: Selected by Colorado Rockies organization in supplemental round ("sandwich pick" between first and second rounds, 36th pick overall) of 1998 free-agent draft; pick received as part of compensation for Atlanta Braves signing Type A free-agent 1B Andres Galarraga.

2005 GAMES PLAYED BY POSITION (MLB): OF—6.

LEFTY-RIGHTY SPLITS

vs.	Avg.	AB	H	2B	3B	HR	RBI	BB	SO	OBP	Slg.
L	.231	13	3	0	1	0	0	0	2	.231	.385
R	.333	9	3	1	0	0	0	0	3	.333	.444

Year Team (League)	Pos.	G	AB	R	H	2B	3B	HR	RBI	BB	SO	HBP	GDP	SB-CS	Avg.	OBP	SLG	OPS	E	Avg.
1998—Ariz. Rockies (Ariz.)	OF	40	147	35	47	3	6	1	24	15	25	4	2	14-1	.320	.391	.442	.833	6	.880
1999—Asheville (S. Atl.)	OF	131	485	82	133	22	4	14	66	39	132	7	3	16-4	.274	.336	.423	.759	6	.975
2000—Salem (Carol.)	OF	127	429	73	114	18	7	5	54	37	104	4	7	16-8	.266	.326	.375	.702	8	.965
2001—Salem (Carol.)	OF	132	517	63	124	16	5	8	42	31	108	9	8	19-7	.240	.292	.337	.628	5	.979
2002—Carolina (Southern)	OF	124	430	81	125	16	4	12	64	64	101	15	15	15-13	.291	.400	.444	.844	6	.977
2003—Colo. Springs (PCL)	OF-DH	103	327	44	83	9	4	7	36	23	71	7	7	2-8	.254	.315	.370	.685	12	.936
2004—Colo. Springs (PCL)	OF	103	360	58	107	21	7	10	50	26	84	6	11	7-3	.297	.350	.478	.818	4	.983
—Colorado (N.L.)	OF	45	90	15	17	3	2	1	11	14	21	0	5	1-1	.189	.298	.300	.598	1	.986
2005—Colo. Springs (PCL)	OF	97	354	46	99	10	6	10	59	29	78	2	13	4-3	.280	.334	.427	.761	4	.989
—Colorado (N.L.)	OF	18	22	6	6	1	1	0	0	0	5	0	0	0-0	.273	.273	.409	.682	0	1.000
Major League totals (2 years)		63	112	21	23	4	3	1	11	14	26	0	5	1-1	.205	.294	.321	.615	1	.988

FREIRE, ALEJANDRO — 1B

PERSONAL: Born August 23, 1974, in Caracas, Venezuela. ... 6-2/185. ... Bats right, throws right. ... Full name: Alejandro Freire.

TRANSACTIONS/CAREER NOTES: Signed as a nondrafted free agent by Houston Astros organization (September 28, 1991). ... Selected by Detroit Tigers organization from Astros in Rule 5 minor league draft (December 9, 1996). ... Signed as a free agent by San Francisco Giants organization (February 2, 2002). ... Signed by Veracruz of the Mexican League (2004). ... Signed by Baltimore Orioles organization (April 1, 2005).

2005 GAMES PLAYED BY POSITION (MLB): 1B—16, DH—9, OF—1.

ALEJANDRO FREIRE'S HITTING ZONE

.500	.500	.200
.444	.286	.100
.167	.000	.000

LEFTY-RIGHTY SPLITS

vs.	Avg.	AB	H	2B	3B	HR	RBI	BB	SO	OBP	Slg.
L	.200	45	9	1	0	1	4	5	13	.294	.289
R	.350	20	7	2	0	0	0	1	4	.381	.450

Year Team (League)	Pos.	G	AB	R	H	2B	3B	HR	RBI	BB	SO	HBP	GDP	SB-CS	Avg.	OBP	SLG	OPS	E	Avg.
1993—Houston SP (DSL)		65	232	43	73	13	3	3	39	29	24	5	9	6-1	.315	.400	.435	.835	...	...
1994—GC Astros (GCL)	1B-3B	29	83	8	25	4	0	1	13	5	17	3	0	5-1	.301	.355	.386	.741	4	.981
1995—Quad City (Midw.)	1B-OF	125	417	71	127	23	1	15	65	50	83	6	9	9-5	.305	.381	.472	.853	7	.993
1996—Kissimmee (Fla. St.)	OF-1B	115	384	40	98	24	1	12	42	24	66	12	11	11-7	.255	.309	.417	.726	14	.972
1997—Lakeland (Fla. St.)	1B	130	477	85	154	30	2	24	92	50	84	12	10	13-4	.323	.396	.545	.941	17	.986
1998—Jacksonville (Sou.)	1B	130	494	79	136	30	0	16	78	33	83	17	16	3-1	.275	.336	.433	.769	15	.987
1999—Lakeland (Fla. St.)	1B	13	41	6	9	3	0	1	5	10	7	3	1	0-0	.220	.400	.366	.766	1	.986
—Jacksonville (Sou.)	1B-OF	66	243	45	72	20	0	10	43	23	44	6	8	2-0	.296	.366	.502	.868	6	.980
2000—Jacksonville (Sou.)	1B-OF	135	471	73	129	16	0	25	77	69	113	16	16	2-4	.274	.381	.467	.848	6	.989
2001—Erie (East.)	OF-1B	133	501	73	148	33	0	17	82	46	113	11	17	2-3	.295	.365	.463	.828	3	.978
2002—Shreveport (Texas)	1B	55	177	24	50	9	0	10	32	19	38	4	4	0-2	.282	.363	.503	.866	2	.973
—Fresno (PCL)	1B-OF-P	46	146	20	40	7	1	3	7	14	28	5	3	0-0	.274	.358	.397	.755	2	.988
2003—Norwich (East.)	1B-OF-P	137	498	71	155	31	1	18	80	48	87	13	21	1-0	.311	.383	.486	.869	7	.991
2004—Veracruz (Mex.)	1B	25	80	12	16	1	0	1	11	19	14	6	2	2-0	.200	.387	.250	.637	7	.996
2005—Ottawa (Int'l)	1B-DH	106	391	57	117	24	1	19	69	40	57	9	18	1-0	.299	.376	.512	.887	7	.988
—Bowie (East.)	DH-1B	3	13	0	5	0	0	0	2	0	1	0	2	0-0	.385	.357	.385	.742	0	1.000
—Baltimore (A.L.)	1B-DH-OF	25	65	7	16	3	0	1	4	6	17	1	4	0-0	.246	.319	.338	.658	1	.991
Major League totals (1 year)		25	65	7	16	3	0	1	4	6	17	1	4	0-0	.246	.319	.338	.658	1	.991

FUENTES, BRIAN — P

PERSONAL: Born August 9, 1975, in Merced, Calif. ... 6-4/220. ... Throws left, bats left. ... Full name: Brian Christopher Fuentes. ... Name pronounced: foo-WHEN-tayz. ... High school: Merced (Calif.). ... Junior college: Merced (Calif.).

TRANSACTIONS/CAREER NOTES: Selected by Seattle Mariners organization in 25th round of 1995 free-agent draft. ... Traded by Mariners with Ps Jose Paniagua and Denny Stark to Colorado Rockies for 3B Jeff Cirillo (December 15, 2001). ... On disabled list (June 7-August 15, 2004); included rehabilitation assignment to Colorado Springs.

CAREER HITTING: 0-for-1 (.000), 0 R, 0 2B, 0 3B, 0 HR, 0 RBI.

F

SCOUTING REPORT **Throws:** Fuentes has four pitches: an 88-91 mph fastball, a cut fastball, a slurve at 75 mph and a changeup. **Tendencies:** This sidearm slinger with the slight hesitation in his delivery makes life tough on hitters, especially lefthanders. Runs his fastball away from righthanders to set up his cut fastball on the inside. Is faster than he appears, and his fastball has very good late life. Uses the curve and changeup early in counts to righthanders. Has become more aggressive with renewed confidence in his fastball. **Outlook:** Fuentes had a career year for a bad team, but he wasn't a flash in the pan. Could save 40 in 2006. **Grade 8.5**

BRIAN FUENTES' PITCHING ZONE

.370	.250	.000
.325	.360	.179
.118	.176	.290

LEFTY-RIGHTY SPLITS

vs.	Avg.	AB	H	2B	3B	HR	RBI	BB	SO	OBP	Slg.
L	.167	72	12	3	0	0	4	8	35	.277	.208
R	.236	199	47	9	4	6	20	26	56	.343	.412

Year	Team (League)	W	L	Pct.	ERA	WHIP	G	GS	CG	ShO	Hld.	Sv.-Opp.	IP	H	R	ER	HR	BB-IBB	SO	Avg.
1996—	Everett (N'west)	0	1	.000	4.39	1.35	15	2	0	0	...	0-...	26.2	23	14	13	2	13-0	26	.230
1997—	Wisconsin (Midw.)	6	7	.462	3.56	1.21	22	22	0	0	...	0-...	118.2	84	52	47	6	59-0	153	.203
1998—	Lancaster (Calif.)	7	7	.500	4.17	1.70	24	22	0	0	...	0-...	118.2	121	73	55	8	81-0	137	.273
1999—	New Haven (East.)	3	3	.500	4.95	1.65	15	14	0	0	...	0-...	60.0	53	36	33	5	46-0	66	.255
2000—	New Haven (East.)	7	12	.368	4.51	1.41	26	26	1	0	...	0-...	139.2	127	80	70	7	70-0	152	.246
2001—	Tacoma (PCL)	3	2	.600	2.94	1.15	35	0	0	0	...	6-...	52.0	35	19	17	4	25-0	70	.206
—	Seattle (A.L.)	1	1	.500	4.63	1.20	10	0	0	0	1	0-1	11.2	6	6	6	2	8-0	10	.171
2002—	Colo. Springs (PCL)	3	3	.500	3.70	1.56	41	0	0	0	...	1-...	48.2	44	25	20	6	32-1	61	.246
—	Colorado (N.L.)	2	0	1.000	4.73	1.43	31	0	0	0	0	0-0	26.2	25	14	14	4	13-0	38	.250
2003—	Colorado (N.L.)	3	3	.500	2.75	1.30	75	0	0	0	19	4-6	75.1	64	24	23	7	34-2	82	.231
2004—	Colo. Springs (PCL)	0	0	...	0.00	0.80	5	5	0	0	...	0-...	5.0	1	0	0	0	3-0	6	.063
—	Colorado (N.L.)	2	4	.333	5.64	1.46	47	0	0	0	13	0-1	44.2	46	30	28	5	19-6	48	.269
2005—	Colorado (N.L.)	2	5	.286	2.91	1.25	78	0	0	0	6	31-34	74.1	59	25	24	6	34-4	91	.218
	American League totals (1 year)	1	1	.500	4.63	1.20	10	0	0	0	1	0-1	11.2	6	6	6	2	8-0	10	.171
	National League totals (4 years)	9	12	.429	3.62	1.33	231	0	0	0	38	35-41	221.0	194	93	89	22	100-12	259	.237
	Major League totals (5 years)	10	13	.435	3.67	1.32	241	0	0	0	39	35-42	232.2	200	99	95	24	108-12	269	.234

FULTZ, AARON   P

PERSONAL: Born September 4, 1973, in Memphis. ... 6-0/205. ... Throws left, bats left. ... Full name: Richard Aaron Fultz. ... High school: Munford (Tenn.). ... Junior college: North Florida.

TRANSACTIONS/CAREER NOTES: Selected by San Francisco Giants organization in sixth round of 1992 free-agent draft. ... Traded by Giants with SS Andres Duncan and P Greg Brummett to Minnesota Twins for P Jim Deshaies (August 28, 1993). ... Released by Twins (April 1, 1996). ... Signed by Giants organization (April 4, 1996). ... Signed as a free agent by Texas Rangers (December 31, 2002). ... On disabled list (June 23-July 11, 2003); included rehabilitation assignments to Oklahoma and Frisco. ... Signed as a free agent by Twins organization (January 11, 2004). ... Claimed on waivers by Philadelphia Phillies (October 14, 2004).
CAREER HITTING: 5-for-15 (.333), 2 R, 0 2B, 0 3B, 0 HR, 0 RBI.

SCOUTING REPORT **Throws:** Fultz is unique for a reliever because he throws a lot of different pitches, including a two-seam fastball, a curveball, a changeup and a slider. **Tendencies:** He throws from a three-quarters angle and has a very unorthodox arm action, making him deceptive. Has only marginal velocity but likes to cut the ball in on righthanders and expand the plate laterally with a running two-seamer. Has a big-sweeping, soft curve that he throws early in the count, but his slider is a more consistent, tighter breaking ball. Has good motion and movement with his straight change. **Outlook:** He is very effective in middle relief and can get both righthanders and lefthanders out. **Grade 6.5**

AARON FULTZ'S PITCHING ZONE

.250	.250	.200
.277	.474	.179
.179	.143	.050

LEFTY-RIGHTY SPLITS

vs.	Avg.	AB	H	2B	3B	HR	RBI	BB	SO	OBP	Slg.
L	.220	82	18	6	1	1	8	7	13	.312	.354
R	.170	171	29	4	0	5	16	16	41	.243	.281

Year	Team (League)	W	L	Pct.	ERA	WHIP	G	GS	CG	ShO	Hld.	Sv.-Opp.	IP	H	R	ER	HR	BB-IBB	SO	Avg.
1992—	Ariz. Giants (Ariz.)	3	2	.600	2.13	1.24	14	14	0	0	...	0-...	67.2	51	24	16	0	33-0	72	.213
1993—	Clinton (Midw.)	14	8	.636	3.41	1.32	26	25	2	1	...	0-...	148.0	132	63	56	8	64-2	144	.239
—	Fort Wayne (Midw.)	0	0	...	9.00	3.50	1	1	0	0	...	0-...	4.0	10	4	4	0	0-0	3	.476
1994—	Fort Myers (Fla. St.)	9	10	.474	4.33	1.50	28	28	3	0	...	0-...	168.1	193	95	81	9	60-5	132	.289
1995—	New Britain (East.)	0	2	.000	6.60	1.33	3	3	0	0	...	0-...	15.0	11	12	11	1	9-0	12	.208
—	Fort Myers (Fla. St.)	3	6	.333	3.25	1.28	21	21	2	2	...	0-...	122.0	115	52	44	10	41-1	127	.250
1996—	San Jose (Calif.)	9	5	.643	3.96	1.48	36	12	0	0	...	1-...	104.2	101	52	46	7	54-2	103	.262
1997—	Shreveport (Texas)	6	3	.667	2.83	1.20	49	0	0	0	...	0-...	70.0	65	30	22	6	19-0	60	.247
1998—	Shreveport (Texas)	5	7	.417	3.77	1.40	54	0	0	0	...	15-...	62.0	58	40	26	4	29-10	61	.252
—	Fresno (PCL)	0	0	...	5.06	1.50	16	0	0	0	...	0-...	16.0	22	10	9	2	2-1	13	.333
1999—	Fresno (PCL)	9	8	.529	4.98	1.40	37	20	1	0	...	0-...	137.1	141	87	76	32	51-1	151	.266
2000—	San Francisco (N.L.)	5	2	.714	4.67	1.37	58	0	0	0	7	1-3	69.1	67	38	36	8	28-0	62	.263
2001—	San Francisco (N.L.)	3	1	.750	4.56	1.28	66	0	0	0	12	1-2	71.0	70	40	36	9	21-3	67	.259
2002—	San Francisco (N.L.)	2	2	.500	4.79	1.40	60	0	0	0	4	0-1	41.1	47	22	22	4	19-3	31	.294
—	Fresno (PCL)	1	3	.250	3.18	1.28	17	0	0	0	...	4-...	22.2	18	8	8	1	11-2	22	.216
2003—	Oklahoma (PCL)	0	0	...	27.00	3.00	1	0	0	0	...	0-...	1.0	2	3	3	2	1-0	2	.400
—	Frisco (Texas)	0	0	...	9.00	2.00	1	0	0	0	...	0-...	1.0	2	1	1	0	0-0	0	.333
—	Texas (A.L.)	1	3	.250	5.21	1.51	64	0	0	0	19	0-0	67.1	75	43	39	9	27-7	53	.283
2004—	Rochester (Int'l)	0	0	...	1.08	1.32	7	0	0	0	...	0-...	8.1	6	1	1	0	5-0	5	.194
—	Minnesota (A.L.)	3	3	.500	5.04	1.46	55	0	0	0	5	1-4	50.0	50	28	28	5	23-2	37	.263
2005—	Philadelphia (N.L.)	1	0	1.000	2.24	0.97	62	0	0	0	2	0-1	72.1	47	21	18	6	23-2	54	.186
	American League totals (2 years)	4	6	.400	5.14	1.49	119	0	0	0	24	1-4	117.1	125	71	67	14	50-9	90	.279
	National League totals (4 years)	14	5	.737	3.97	1.27	229	0	0	0	25	2-7	254.0	231	121	112	27	91-8	214	.246
	Major League totals (6 years)	18	11	.621	4.34	1.34	348	0	0	0	49	3-11	371.1	356	192	179	41	141-17	304	.257

DIVISION SERIES RECORD

Year	Team (League)	W	L	Pct.	ERA	WHIP	G	GS	CG	ShO	Hld.	Sv.-Opp.	IP	H	R	ER	HR	BB-IBB	SO	Avg.
2000—	San Francisco (N.L.)	0	1	.000	6.75	2.25	1	0	0	0	...	0-0	1.1	3	1	1	1	0-0	0	.500
2002—	San Francisco (N.L.)	0	0	...	...	...	2	0	0	0	...	0-0	0.0	2	1	1	0	0-0	0	1.000
	Division series totals (2 years)	0	1	.000	13.50	3.75	3	0	0	0	...	0-0	1.1	5	2	2	1	0-0	0	.625

F

CHAMPIONSHIP SERIES RECORD

Year Team (League)	W	L	Pct.	ERA	WHIP	G	GS	CG	ShO	Hld.	Sv.-Opp.	IP	H	R	ER	HR	BB-IBB	SO	Avg.
2002— San Francisco (N.L.)	0	0	...	0.00	0.00	1	0	0	0	0	0-0	0.1	0	0	0	0	0-0	0	.000

WORLD SERIES RECORD

Year Team (League)	W	L	Pct.	ERA	WHIP	G	GS	CG	ShO	Hld.	Sv.-Opp.	IP	H	R	ER	HR	BB-IBB	SO	Avg.
2002— San Francisco (N.L.)	0	0	...	3.86	2.14	2	0	0	0	0	0-1	2.1	4	1	1	0	1-0	0	.400

FURCAL, RAFAEL   SS

PERSONAL: Born August 24, 1978, in Loma de Cabrera, Dominican Republic. ... 5-10/165. ... Bats both, throws right. ... Full name: Rafael Antoni Furcal. ... Name pronounced: fur-CALL. ... High school: Jose Cabrera (Loma De Cabrera, Dominican Republic).
TRANSACTIONS/CAREER NOTES: Signed as a non-drafted free agent by Atlanta Braves organization (November 9, 1996). ... On disabled list (June 13-29, 2000; and July 7, 2001-remainder of season).
RECORDS: Shares major league single-game record for most triples (3, April 21, 2002).
HONORS: Named N.L. Rookie Player of the Year by THE SPORTING NEWS (2000). ... Named N.L. Rookie of the Year by Baseball Writers' Association of America (2000).
2005 GAMES PLAYED BY POSITION (MLB): SS—152.

SCOUTING REPORT **Offense:** Furcal is an offensive catalyst with exceptional speed. Is a very aggressive hitter. Has a long, sweeping swing. Is a very good fastball hitter with deceptive power. Hits the ball as hard as any leadoff hitter in the league. Likes the ball up. Has very good basestealing instincts. Leads and jumps off bases are good as any player's. Knows how to maximize his speed. Will bunt. **Defense:** He gets excellent jumps on the ball to either side and has the game's strongest arm. Can win a game just with his arm strength. Has quick, agile feet and soft hands. Defensive instincts are very good. **Outlook:** Furcal continues to improve as a leadoff hitter and has become a much steadier defensive player. **Grade 8.7**

RAFAEL FURCAL'S HITTING ZONE

.139	.333	.271
.333	.444	.256
.387	.263	.232

LEFTY-RIGHTY SPLITS

vs.	Avg.	AB	H	2B	3B	HR	RBI	BB	SO	OBP	Slg.
L	.294	163	48	9	4	4	20	12	17	.339	.472
R	.280	453	127	22	7	8	38	50	61	.351	.413

									BATTING									FIELDING	
Year Team (League)	Pos.	G	AB	R	H	2B	3B	HR	RBI	BB	SO	HBP	GDP	SB-CS	Avg.	OBP	SLG	OPS	E	Avg.
1997— GC Braves (GCL)	2B-OF	50	190	31	49	5	4	1	9	20	21	2	1	15-2	.258	.335	.342	.677	10	.961
1998— Danville (Appal.)	2B	66	268	56	88	15	4	0	23	36	29	3	2	60-15	.328	.412	.414	.827	14	.965
1999— Macon (S. Atl.)	SS	83	335	73	113	15	1	1	29	41	36	5	4	73-22	.337	.417	.397	.814	30	.912
— Myrtle Beach (Carol.)	SS	43	184	32	54	9	3	0	12	14	42	0	3	23-8	.293	.343	.375	.718	4	.975
2000— Greenville (Sou.)	SS	3	10	1	2	0	0	1	3	1	0	0	0	0-0	.200	.273	.500	.773	1	.889
— Atlanta (N.L.)	SS-2B	131	455	87	134	20	4	4	37	73	80	3	2	40-14	.295	.394	.382	.776	24	.958
2001— Atlanta (N.L.)	SS	79	324	39	89	19	0	4	30	24	56	1	5	22-6	.275	.321	.370	.692	11	.970
2002— Atlanta (N.L.)	SS-2B	154	636	95	175	31	8	8	47	43	114	3	1	27-15	.275	.323	.387	.710	27	.964
2003— Atlanta (N.L.)	SS	156	664	130	194	35	* 10	15	61	60	76	3	1	25-2	.292	.352	.443	.794	31	.959
2004— Atlanta (N.L.)	SS-2B	143	563	103	157	24	5	14	59	58	71	1	9	29-6	.279	.345	.414	.758	24	.962
2005— Atlanta (N.L.)	SS	154	616	100	175	31	11	12	58	62	78	1	11	46-10	.284	.348	.429	.777	15	.981
Major League totals (6 years)		817	3258	554	924	180	38	57	292	320	475	12	36	189-53	.284	.348	.409	.756	132	.966

DIVISION SERIES RECORD

									BATTING									FIELDING	
Year Team (League)	Pos.	G	AB	R	H	2B	3B	HR	RBI	BB	SO	HBP	GDP	SB-CS	Avg.	OBP	SLG	OPS	E	Avg.
2000— Atlanta (N.L.)	2B-SS	3	11	2	1	0	0	0	0	3	0	0	0	1-1	.091	.286	.091	.377	1	.933
2002— Atlanta (N.L.)	SS	5	24	2	6	1	1	0	2	0	5	0	0	1-1	.250	.250	.375	.625	0	1.000
2003— Atlanta (N.L.)	SS	5	19	3	4	0	0	0	0	3	5	0	0	1-0	.211	.318	.211	.529	1	.968
2004— Atlanta (N.L.)	SS	5	21	5	8	0	1	2	4	3	3	1	0	3-0	.381	.480	.762	1.242	0	1.000
2005— Atlanta (N.L.)	SS	4	20	1	3	0	0	0	0	3	2	0	1	3-0	.150	.261	.150	.411	0	1.000
Division series totals (5 years)		22	95	13	22	1	2	2	6	12	15	1	1	9-2	.232	.324	.347	.671	2	.982

ALL-STAR GAME RECORD

	G	AB	R	H	2B	3B	HR	RBI	BB	SO	HBP	GDP	SB-CS	Avg.	OBP	SLG	OPS	E	Avg.
All-Star Game totals (1 year)	1	3	1	1	0	0	0	0	0	1	0		0-0	.333	.333	.333	.667	1	.500

FURMANIAK, J.J.   SS

PERSONAL: Born July 31, 1979, in Naperville, Ill. ... 6-3/190. ... Bats right, throws right. ... Full name: Jason Joseph Furmaniak. ... High school: Bolingbrook (Ill.). ... College: Lewis.
TRANSACTIONS/CAREER NOTES: Selected by San Diego Padres organization in 22nd round of 2000 free-agent draft. ... Traded by Padres to Pittsburgh Pirates for C David Ross (July 28, 2005).
2005 GAMES PLAYED BY POSITION (MLB): 2B—9, SS—2.

LEFTY-RIGHTY SPLITS

vs.	Avg.	AB	H	2B	3B	HR	RBI	BB	SO	OBP	Slg.
L	.000	0	0	0	0	0	0	1	0	1.000	.000
R	.192	26	5	1	1	0	1	3	4	.276	.308

									BATTING									FIELDING	
Year Team (League)	Pos.	G	AB	R	H	2B	3B	HR	RBI	BB	SO	HBP	GDP	SB-CS	Avg.	OBP	SLG	OPS	E	Avg.
2000— Idaho Falls (Pio.) SS-2B-3B		62	245	72	84	18	2	5	38	44	48	5	8	10-3	.343	.446	.494	.940	16	.950
2001— Fort Wayne (Midw.) SS-2B		123	436	57	96	24	3	5	35	55	117	4	10	11-6	.220	.309	.323	.632	28	.950
2002— Lake Elsinore (Calif.) 3B-SS-2B		106	381	50	98	16	6	7	43	26	100	6	8	11-9	.257	.311	.386	.697	22	.940
2003— Lake Elsinore (Calif.) 3B-SS-2B		78	309	65	97	22	8	9	54	36	55	8	5	10-4	.314	.397	.524	.921	22	.945
— Mobile (Sou.)	SS	31	103	10	27	4	1	3	11	8	27	1	0	0-0	.262	.336	.408	.744	9	.929
2004— Mobile (Sou.)	SS	14	51	10	10	4	0	1	8	7	15	1	0	1-0	.196	.305	.333	.638	2	.969
— Portland (PCL) 3B-SS-2B		120	425	71	125	24	4	17	73	33	86	6	10	8-5	.294	.348	.489	.837	27	.518
2005— Portland (PCL) 3B-SS-2B																				
	DH	99	387	54	103	16	4	14	47	28	86	6	8	9-5	.266	.324	.437	.761	15	.950
— Indianapolis (Int'l) SS-3B-2B																				
	OF	36	139	12	40	5	3	2	21	4	32	2	1	5-3	.288	.315	.410	.725	5	.968
— Pittsburgh (N.L.)	2B-SS	13	26	3	5	1	1	0	1	4	4	0	0	0-0	.192	.300	.308	.608	1	.967
Major League totals (1 year)		13	26	3	5	1	1	0	1	4	4	0	0	0-0	.192	.300	.308	.608	1	.967

F

GAGNE, ERIC   P

PERSONAL: Born January 7, 1976, in Montreal. ... 6-2/234. ... Throws right, bats right. ... Full name: Eric Serge Gagne. ... Name pronounced: gahn-yay. ... High school: Polyvalente Edouard Montpetit (Montreal). ... Junior college: Seminole (Okla.).
TRANSACTIONS/CAREER NOTES: Selected by Chicago White Sox organization in 30th round of 1994 free-agent draft; did not sign. ... Signed as a non-drafted free agent by Los Angeles Dodgers organization (July 26, 1995). ... On disabled list (April 2-May 14, 2005); included rehabilitation assignment to Las Vegas. ... On disabled list (June 15, 2005-remainder of season).
HONORS: Named N.L. Pitcher of the Year by THE SPORTING NEWS (2003). ... Named N.L. Reliever of the Year by THE SPORTING NEWS (2003 and 2004). ... Named N.L. Cy Young Award winner by Baseball Writers' Association of America (2003).
CAREER HITTING: 12-for-86 (.140), 5 R, 2 2B, 1 3B, 1 HR, 3 RBI.

SCOUTING REPORT *Throws:* Gagne, when healthy, has a fastball that tops out at 98 mph, a curveball and the hardest changeup in the game. *Tendencies:* He does not throw his curveball a lot, but it is effective against lefthanded hitters because of its speed change. Has outstanding motion on his circle change. Four-seam fastball has riding action. Curve has tight spin. Circle change moves like a split-finger fastball. Has absolutely no fear on the mound. *Outlook:* There is a great deal of uncertainty here because Gagne opted for rehab over surgery on his elbow. The injury most likely will limit him to one inning per game when he does return. *Grade 9*

ERIC GAGNE'S PITCHING ZONE

.000	1.000	.000
.429	.429	.143
.400	.000	.000

LEFTY-RIGHTY SPLITS

vs.	Avg.	AB	H	2B	3B	HR	RBI	BB	SO	OBP	Slg.
L	.217	23	5	2	0	1	3	1	11	.250	.435
R	.185	27	5	1	0	1	1	2	11	.241	.333

Year	Team (League)	W	L	Pct.	ERA	WHIP	G	GS	CG	ShO	Hld.	Sv.-Opp.	IP	H	R	ER	HR	BB-IBB	SO	Avg.
1996—	Savannah (S. Atl.)	7	6	.538	3.28	1.19	23	21	1	1	...	0-...	115.1	94	48	42	11	43-1	131	.221
1997—				Did not play.																
1998—	Vero Beach (Fla. St.)	9	7	.563	3.74	1.19	25	25	3	1	...	0-...	139.2	118	69	58	16	48-0	144	.225
1999—	San Antonio (Texas)	12	4	.750	2.63	1.11	26	26	0	0	...	0-...	167.2	122	55	49	17	64-0	185	.201
—	Los Angeles (N.L.)	1	1	.500	2.10	1.10	5	5	0	0	0	0-0	30.0	18	8	7	3	15-0	30	.175
2000—	Albuquerque (PCL)	5	1	.833	3.88	1.28	9	9	0	0	0	0-0	55.2	56	30	24	8	15-0	59	.260
—	Los Angeles (N.L.)	4	6	.400	5.15	1.64	20	19	0	0	0	0-0	101.1	106	62	58	20	60-1	79	.270
2001—	Los Angeles (N.L.)	6	7	.462	4.75	1.25	33	24	0	0	0	0-0	151.2	144	90	80	24	46-1	130	.251
—	Las Vegas (PCL)	3	0	1.000	1.52	0.97	4	4	0	0	0	0-...	23.2	15	4	4	2	8-0	31	.195
2002—	Los Angeles (N.L.)	4	1	.800	1.97	0.86	77	0	0	0	1	52-56	82.1	55	18	18	6	16-4	114	.189
2003—	Los Angeles (N.L.)	2	3	.400	1.20	0.69	77	0	0	0	*	55-55	82.1	37	12	11	2	20-2	137	.133
2004—	Los Angeles (N.L.)	7	3	.700	2.19	0.91	70	0	0	0	0	45-47	82.1	53	24	20	5	22-3	114	.181
2005—	Las Vegas (PCL)	0	0	...	0.00	0.00	3	0	0	0	1	0-0	4.0	0	0	0	0	0-0	7	.000
—	Los Angeles (N.L.)	1	0	1.000	2.70	0.98	14	0	0	0	1	8-8	13.1	10	4	4	2	3-0	22	.200
Major League totals (7 years)		**25**	**21**	**.543**	**3.28**	**1.11**	**296**	**48**	**0**	**0**	**1**	**160-166**	**543.1**	**423**	**218**	**198**	**62**	**182-11**	**626**	**.213**

DIVISION SERIES RECORD

Year	Team (League)	W	L	Pct.	ERA	WHIP	G	GS	CG	ShO	Hld.	Sv.-Opp.	IP	H	R	ER	HR	BB-IBB	SO	Avg.
2004—	Los Angeles (N.L.)	0	0		0.00	0.67	2	0	0	0	0	0-0	3.0	1	0	0	0	1-0	3	.111

ALL-STAR GAME RECORD

		W	L	Pct.	ERA	WHIP	G	GS	CG	ShO	Hld.	Sv.-Opp.	IP	H	R	ER	HR	BB-IBB	SO	Avg.
All-Star Game totals (3 years)		0	1	.000	12.00	2.00							3.0	5	4	4	2	1-0		.357

GALL, JOHN   OF

PERSONAL: Born April 2, 1978, in Stanford, Calif. ... 6-0/195. ... Bats right, throws right. ... Full name: John Christopher Gall. ... High school: St. Francis (Mountain View, Calif.). ... College: Stanford.
TRANSACTIONS/CAREER NOTES: Selected by St. Louis Cardinals organization in 11th round of 2000 free-agent draft.
2005 GAMES PLAYED BY POSITION (MLB): OF—10.

SCOUTING REPORT *Offense:* Gall is a power hitter who was tough on lefthanded pitchers but struggled against righthanders in limited time last season. Did a good job as a pinch hitter. Made consistent hard contact in the minors and knows how to use the whole field. Is not very athletic, and his speed is below average. *Defense:* A converted first baseman, Gall has adjusted to the outfield. Has a below-average arm, which makes him suitable only for left field. *Outlook:* He has too much difficulty against righthanders to have much of a chance of playing regularly or even being a fourth outfielder. Could stick in the majors as a pinch hitter and someone to hit against lefthanders. *Grade 6.6*

LEFTY-RIGHTY SPLITS

vs.	Avg.	AB	H	2B	3B	HR	RBI	BB	SO	OBP	Slg.
L	.313	16	5	1	0	2	8	1	4	.353	.750
R	.238	21	5	2	0	0	2	0	4	.227	.333

Year	Team (League)	Pos.	G	AB	R	H	2B	3B	HR	RBI	BB	SO	HBP	GDP	SB-CS	Avg.	OBP	SLG	OPS	E	Avg.
2000—	New Jersey (NYP)	1B-3B	71	259	28	62	10	0	2	27	25	37	1	7	16-5	.239	.304	.301	.605	10	.983
2001—	Peoria (Midw.)	1B	57	205	27	62	23	0	4	44	16	18	4	3	0-3	.302	.353	.473	.826	9	.993
—	Potomac (Carol.)	1B-3B	84	319	44	101	25	0	4	33	24	40	3	9	5-6	.317	.369	.433	.802	11	.978
2002—	New Haven (East.)	1B-3B-OF	135	526	82	166	45	3	20	81	38	75	2	26	4-1	.316	.362	.527	.889	16	.984
2003—	Memphis (PCL)	OF-1B-3B	123	461	62	144	24	1	16	73	39	56	2	13	5-2	.312	.368	.473	.841	7	.993
—	Tennessee (Sou.)	OF-1B	12	52	6	17	1	0	3	12	3	4	0	0	0-1	.327	.357	.519	.876	0	1.000
2004—	Memphis (PCL)	OF-1B-3B	135	506	77	148	34	0	22	84	48	68	1	19	1-1	.292	.350	.490	.840	5	.986
2005—	Memphis (PCL)	OF-1B-DH																			
		3B	114	374	61	101	22	0	13	64	45	42	1	12	9-2	.270	.345	.433	.778	9	.981
—	St. Louis (N.L.)	OF	22	37	5	10	3	0	2	10	1	8	0	0	0-0	.270	.282	.514	.796	0	1.000
Major League totals (1 year)			22	37	5	10	3	0	2	10	1	8	0	0	0-0	.270	.282	.514	.796	0	1.000

DIVISION SERIES RECORD

Year	Team (League)	Pos.	G	AB	R	H	2B	3B	HR	RBI	BB	SO	HBP	GDP	SB-CS	Avg.	OBP	SLG	OPS	E	Avg.
2005—	St. Louis (N.L.)		1	1	0	0	0	0	0	0	0	0	0	0	0-0	.000	.000	.000	.000	0	...

G

GALLO, MIKE   P

PERSONAL: Born April 2, 1977, in Long Beach, Calif. ... 6-0/175. ... Throws left, bats left. ... Full name: Michael Dwain Gallo. ... High school: Millikan (Calif.). ... College: Long Beach State.
TRANSACTIONS/CAREER NOTES: Selected by Houston Astros organization in fifth round of 1999 free-agent draft.
CAREER HITTING: 0-for-3 (.000), 0 R, 0 2B, 0 3B, 0 HR, 0 RBI.

MIKE GALLO'S PITCHING ZONE

.250	1.000	.333
.071	.556	.250
.000	1.000	.143

LEFTY-RIGHTY SPLITS

vs.	Avg.	AB	H	2B	3B	HR	RBI	BB	SO	OBP	Slg.
L	.268	41	11	2	1	1	5	4	5	.340	.439
R	.226	31	7	1	0	0	1	6	7	.368	.258

Year	Team (League)	W	L	Pct.	ERA	WHIP	G	GS	CG	ShO	Hld.	Sv.-Opp.	IP	H	R	ER	HR	BB-IBB	SO	Avg.
1999—	Auburn (NYP)	1	0	1.000	1.23	1.36	3	3	0	0	...	0-...	14.2	13	4	2	0	7-0	11	.232
—	Michigan (Midw.)	2	3	.400	5.85	1.65	12	12	0	0	...	0-...	60.0	76	47	39	6	23-0	32	.315
2000—	Michigan (Midw.)	8	3	.727	4.86	1.44	24	13	0	0	...	0-...	90.2	104	58	49	6	27-1	56	.285
2001—	Michigan (Midw.)	9	2	.818	3.84	1.21	44	0	0	0	...	4-...	84.1	83	38	36	4	19-1	67	.252
2002—	Lexington (S. Atl.)	4	4	.500	1.83	1.08	42	2	0	0	...	8-...	88.1	69	29	18	6	26-4	93	.211
—	Round Rock (Texas)	0	0	...	6.75	0.75	1	0	0	0	...	0-...	1.1	1	1	1	1	0-0	0	.200
2003—	Round Rock (Texas)	1	1	.500	1.37	1.17	17	0	0	0	...	2-...	19.2	17	3	3	1	6-2	22	.246
—	New Orleans (PCL)	3	0	1.000	2.08	0.92	16	0	0	0	...	0-...	17.1	13	4	4	0	3-0	11	.217
—	Houston (N.L.)	1	0	1.000	3.00	1.27	32	0	0	0	6	0-1	30.0	28	10	10	3	10-2	16	.267
2004—	New Orleans (PCL)	0	0	...	0.00	0.50	3	0	0	0	...	1-...	4.0	0	0	0	0	2-0	4	.000
—	Houston (N.L.)	2	0	1.000	4.74	1.52	69	0	0	0	4	0-1	49.1	55	27	26	12	20-7	34	.284
2005—	Round Rock (PCL)	4	2	.667	3.64	1.40	37	1	0	0	4	0-2	54.1	56	29	22	2	20-4	33	.271
—	Houston (N.L.)	0	1	.000	2.66	1.38	36	0	0	0	8	0-2	20.1	18	6	6	1	10-2	12	.250
Major League totals (3 years)		**3**	**1**	**.750**	**3.79**	**1.41**	**137**	**0**	**0**	**0**	**18**	**0-4**	**99.2**	**101**	**43**	**42**	**16**	**40-11**	**62**	**.272**

DIVISION SERIES RECORD

Year	Team (League)	W	L	Pct.	ERA	WHIP	G	GS	CG	ShO	Hld.	Sv.-Opp.	IP	H	R	ER	HR	BB-IBB	SO	Avg.
2004—	Houston (N.L.)	0	0	...	4.50	2.00	3	0	0	0	0	0-0	2.0	3	1	1	0	1-0	4	.333
2005—	Houston (N.L.)	0	0	...	0.00	1.20	3	0	0	0	1	0-0	1.2	1	0	0	0	1-1	0	.200
Division series totals (2 years)		**0**	**0**	**...**	**2.45**	**1.64**	**6**	**0**	**0**	**0**	**1**	**0-0**	**3.2**	**4**	**1**	**1**	**0**	**2-1**	**4**	**.286**

CHAMPIONSHIP SERIES RECORD

Year	Team (League)	W	L	Pct.	ERA	WHIP	G	GS	CG	ShO	Hld.	Sv.-Opp.	IP	H	R	ER	HR	BB-IBB	SO	Avg.
2005—	Houston (N.L.)	0	0	...	0.00	0.00	2	0	0	0	1	0-0	0.2	0	0	0	0	0-0	1	.000

WORLD SERIES RECORD

Year	Team (League)	W	L	Pct.	ERA	WHIP	G	GS	CG	ShO	Hld.	Sv.-Opp.	IP	H	R	ER	HR	BB-IBB	SO	Avg.
2005—	Houston (N.L.)	0	0	...	0.00	0.00	2	0	0	0	0	0-0	1.0	0	0	0	0	0-0	1	.000

GARABITO, EDDY   SS/2B

PERSONAL: Born December 2, 1976, in Manrreza, Dominican Republic. ... 5-8/188. ... Bats both, throws right. ... Full name: Eddy Jorge Garabito. ... College: None.
TRANSACTIONS/CAREER NOTES: Signed as a non-drafted free agent by Baltimore Orioles organization (March 30, 1996). ... Signed as a free agent by Colorado Rockies organization (November 18, 2004).
2005 GAMES PLAYED BY POSITION (MLB): 2B—18, SS—2.

EDDY GARABITO'S HITTING ZONE

.167	.000	.500
.231	.400	.350
.600	.600	.250

LEFTY-RIGHTY SPLITS

vs.	Avg.	AB	H	2B	3B	HR	RBI	BB	SO	OBP	Slg.
L	.192	26	5	2	0	0	0	0	9	.192	.269
R	.355	62	22	3	0	1	8	3	5	.452	.452

Year	Team (League)	Pos.	G	AB	R	H	2B	3B	HR	RBI	BB	SO	HBP	GDP	SB-CS	Avg.	OBP	SLG	OPS	E	Avg.
1996—	Dom. Orioles (DSL)		67	251	40	69	9	6	1	28	20	23	0		25-10	.275	.326	.371	.697	...	...
1997—	Delmarva (S. Atl.)		2	4	0	0	0	0	0	0	0	0	0		0-0	.000	.000	.000	.000	...	...
—	Bluefield (Appal.)	2B	61	231	47	70	12	3	5	44	21	30	3	5	26-9	.303	.359	.446	.805	11	.956
1998—	Delmarva (S. Atl.)	2B-3B	135	481	81	119	20	8	9	66	44	93	5	9	25-15	.247	.310	.378	.688	18	.973
—	Frederick (Carol.)	2B	4	19	4	4	1	1	0	2	1	5			0-1	.211	.250	.368	.618	1	.944
1999—	Frederick (Carol.)	2B	132	539	76	138	24	4	6	77	42	68	4	7	38-18	.256	.321	.349	.670	23	.960
2000—	Bowie (East.)	2B-SS	116	482	72	121	21	3	6	52	27	55	5	7	22-9	.251	.294	.344	.638	24	.953
—	Rochester (Int'l)	2B-3B	9	35	3	3	1	0	0	2	2	10	0	2	1-0	.086	.135	.114	.249	2	.931
2001—	Rochester (Int'l)	2B-SS	127	517	65	138	29	6	3	34	31	76	3	7	24-11	.267	.311	.364	.675	28	.951
2002—	Rochester (Int'l)	SS-2B-3B OF	110	434	52	112	20	4	4	32	24	48	4	11	11-8	.258	.300	.350	.650	19	.956
2003—	Ottawa (Int'l)	SS-2B	114	459	62	129	28	5	3	56	31	70	2	8	14-8	.281	.327	.383	.710	29	.941
2004—	Ottawa (Int'l)	SS-2B-OF	124	450	52	134	27	5	6	37	40	48	4	8	19-12	.298	.359	.420	.779	21	.750
2005—	Colorado (N.L.)	2B-SS	42	88	15	27	5	0	1	8	3	14	3	2	3-2	.307	.384	.398	.782	1	.987
—	Colo. Springs (PCL)	SS-2B	67	258	56	79	16	3	8	39	29	34	2	6	8-4	.306	.379	.484	.864	14	.959
Major League totals (1 year)			**42**	**88**	**15**	**27**	**5**	**0**	**1**	**8**	**3**	**14**	**3**	**2**	**3-2**	**.307**	**.384**	**.398**	**.782**	**1**	**.987**

GARCIA, FREDDY   P

PERSONAL: Born June 10, 1975, in Caracas, Venezuela. ... 6-4/240. ... Throws right, bats right. ... Full name: Freddy Antonio Garcia. ... **TRANSACTIONS/CAREER NOTES:** Signed as a non-drafted free agent by Houston Astros organization (October 21, 1993). ... Traded by Astros with SS Carlos Guillen and a player to be named to Seattle Mariners for P Randy Johnson (July 31, 1998); Mariners acquired P John Halama to complete deal (October 1, 1998). ... On disabled list (April

G

22-July 7, 2000); included rehabilitation assignments to Tacoma and Everett. ... Traded by Mariners with C Ben Davis to Chicago White Sox for C Miguel Olivo, OF Jeremy Reed and SS Michael Morse (June 27, 2004).
CAREER HITTING: 7-for-36 (.194), 0 R, 1 2B, 0 3B, 0 HR, 2 RBI.

SCOUTING REPORT *Throws:* Garcia's fastball hits 90-95 mph, and his curveball is in the mid-70s. Also throws a slider, a straight change and a split-finger fastball. *Tendencies:* He changed his approach and is using his fastball more. Has a better angle to the plate but will drop his arm slot at times; pays for it when it does. Has a late-breaking slider and has started to use more splitters against lefthanded hitters. *Outlook:* Garcia has restored his confidence and is going deeper in games. Should have a good year in 2006. *Grade 7.9*

FREDDY GARCIA'S PITCHING ZONE

.206	.237	.267
.289	.384	.312
.286	.255	.268

LEFTY-RIGHTY SPLITS

vs.	Avg.	AB	H	2B	3B	HR	RBI	BB	SO	OBP	Slg.
L	.268	440	118	17	2	17	42	41	54	.330	.432
R	.249	430	107	25	3	9	42	19	92	.283	.384

Year	Team (League)	W	L	Pct.	ERA	WHIP	G	GS	CG	ShO	Hld.	Sv.-Opp.	IP	H	R	ER	HR	BB-IBB	SO	Avg.
1994— Dom. Astros (DSL)		4	6	.400	5.29	1.39	16	15	0	0		0-...	85.0	80	61	50	...	38-...	68	
1995— GC Astros (GCL)		6	3	.667	4.47	1.27	11	11	0	0		0-...	58.1	60	32	29	2	14-0	58	.261
1996— Quad City (Midw.)		5	4	.556	3.12	1.38	13	13	0	0		0-...	60.2	57	27	21	3	27-0	50	.247
1997— Kissimmee (Fla. St.)		10	8	.556	2.56	1.20	27	27	5	2		0-...	179.0	165	63	51	6	49-3	131	.242
1998— Jackson (Texas)		6	7	.462	3.24	1.27	19	19	2	0		0-...	119.1	94	48	43	8	58-0	115	.215
— New Orleans (PCL)		1	0	1.000	3.14	1.05	2	2	0	0		0-...	14.1	14	5	5	2	1-0	13	.255
— Tacoma (PCL)		3	1	.750	3.86	1.32	5	5	0	0		0-...	32.2	30	14	14	6	13-0	30	.247
1999— Seattle (A.L.)		17	8	.680	4.07	1.47	33	33	2	1	0	0-0	201.1	205	96	91	18	90-4	170	.263
2000— Seattle (A.L.)		9	5	.643	3.91	1.42	21	20	0	0	0	0-0	124.1	112	62	54	16	64-4	79	.241
— Everett (N'west)		0	0		4.50	1.30	2	2	0	0		0-...	10.0	11	5	5	1	2-0	15	.262
— Tacoma (PCL)		1	0	1.000	2.57	1.00	1	1	0	0		0-...	7.0	5	2	2	2	2-0	11	.208
2001— Seattle (A.L.)		18	6	.750	* 3.05	1.12	34	34	4	3	0	0-0	* 238.2	199	88	81	16	69-6	163	* .225
2002— Seattle (A.L.)		16	10	.615	4.39	1.30	34	34	1	0	0	0-0	223.2	227	110	109	30	63-3	181	.260
2003— Seattle (A.L.)		12	14	.462	4.51	1.33	33	33	1	0	0	0-0	201.1	196	109	101	31	71-2	144	.255
2004— Seattle (A.L.)		4	7	.364	3.20	1.20	15	15	1	0	0	0-0	107.0	96	39	38	8	32-1	82	.236
— Chicago (A.L.)		9	4	.692	4.46	1.24	16	16	0	0	0	0-0	103.0	96	53	51	14	32-2	102	.247
2005— Chicago (A.L.)		14	8	.636	3.87	1.25	33	33	2	0	0	0-0	228.0	225	102	98	26	60-2	146	.259
Major League totals (7 years)		99	62	.615	3.93	1.29	219	218	11	4	0	0-0	1427.1	1356	659	623	159	481-24	1067	.249

DIVISION SERIES RECORD

Year	Team (League)	W	L	Pct.	ERA	WHIP	G	GS	CG	ShO	Hld.	Sv.-Opp.	IP	H	R	ER	HR	BB-IBB	SO	Avg.
2000— Seattle (A.L.)		0	0		10.80	2.70	1	1	0	0	0	0-0	3.1	6	4	4	1	3-0	2	.375
2001— Seattle (A.L.)		1	1	.500	3.86	1.37	2	2	0	0	0	0-0	11.2	13	6	5	1	3-0	13	.277
2005— Chicago (A.L.)		1	0	1.000	5.40	1.80	1	1	0	0	0	0-0	5.0	5	3	3	3	4-0	1	.278
Division series totals (3 years)		2	1	.667	5.40	1.70	4	4	0	0	0	0-0	20.0	24	13	12	5	10-0	16	.296

CHAMPIONSHIP SERIES RECORD

Year	Team (League)	W	L	Pct.	ERA	WHIP	G	GS	CG	ShO	Hld.	Sv.-Opp.	IP	H	R	ER	HR	BB-IBB	SO	Avg.
2000— Seattle (A.L.)		2	0	1.000	1.54	1.20	2	2	0	0	0	0-0	11.2	10	2	2	0	4-0	11	.227
2001— Seattle (A.L.)		0	1	.000	3.68	1.50	1	1	0	0	0	0-0	7.1	7	3	3	0	4-0	6	.292
2005— Chicago (A.L.)		1	0	1.000	2.00	0.78	1	1	1	0	0	0-0	9.0	6	2	2	0	1-0	5	.188
Champ. series totals (3 years)		3	1	.750	2.25	1.14	4	4	1	0	0	0-0	28.0	23	7	7	0	9-0	22	.230

WORLD SERIES RECORD

Year	Team (League)	W	L	Pct.	ERA	WHIP	G	GS	CG	ShO	Hld.	Sv.-Opp.	IP	H	R	ER	HR	BB-IBB	SO	Avg.
2005— Chicago (A.L.)		1	0	1.000	0.00	1.00	1	1	0	0	0	0-0	7.0	4	0	0	0	3-1	7	.174

ALL-STAR GAME RECORD

Year	Team (League)	W	L	Pct.	ERA	WHIP	G	GS	CG	ShO	Hld.	Sv.-Opp.	IP	H	R	ER	HR	BB-IBB	SO	Avg.
All-Star Game totals (2 years)		1	0	1.000	0.00	0.67	2	0	0	0	0	0-0	3.0	2	0	0	0	0-0	3	.182

GARCIA, JAIRO   P

PERSONAL: Born March 7, 1983, in Nizao, Dominican Republic. ... 6-0/164. ... Throws right, bats right. ... Full name: Jairo Paulino Garcia. ... Name pronounced: HY-ro.
TRANSACTIONS/CAREER NOTES: Signed as a non-drafted free agent by Oakland Athletics organization (January 31, 2000).
CAREER HITTING: 0-for-0 (.000), 0 R, 0 2B, 0 3B, 0 HR, 0 RBI.

LEFTY-RIGHTY SPLITS

vs.	Avg.	AB	H	2B	3B	HR	RBI	BB	SO	OBP	Slg.
L	.222	9	2	1	0	0	1	0	1	.222	.333
R	.000	2	0	0	0	0	0	1	0	.333	.000

Year	Team (League)	W	L	Pct.	ERA	WHIP	G	GS	CG	ShO	Hld.	Sv.-Opp.	IP	H	R	ER	HR	BB-IBB	SO	Avg.
2001— Ariz. A's (Ariz.)		4	2	.667	2.85	0.91	12	7	0	0	...	0-...	47.1	37	19	15	2	6-0	50	.214
2002— Ariz. A's (Ariz.)		2	1	.667	2.44	1.24	13	8	0	0	...	1-...	59.0	56	24	16	5	17-0	66	.258
— Vancouver (N'west)		0	3	.000	7.30	1.78	3	3	0	0	...	0-...	12.1	15	11	10	1	7-0	16	.300
2003— Kane Co. (Midw.)		0	1	.000	2.55	1.39	14	9	0	0	...	0-...	42.1	40	14	12	0	19-0	28	.250
2004— Kane Co. (Midw.)		1	0	1.000	0.30	0.73	25	0	0	0	...	16-...	30.0	16	2	1	0	6-2	49	.154
— Midland (Texas)		2	0	1.000	1.50	1.39	13	0	0	0	...	2-...	18.0	10	3	3	0	15-0	32	.161
— Sacramento (PCL)		1	2	.333	3.95	1.39	11	0	0	0	...	1-...	13.2	10	6	6	1	9-1	21	.208
— Oakland (A.L.)		0	0		12.71	2.47	4	0	0	0	0	0-0	5.2	5	8	8	1	4-0	5	.227
2005— Midland (Texas)		0	0		1.08	1.08	10	0	0	0	...	6-7	16.2	9	3	2	1	9-0	30	.153
— Sacramento (PCL)		3	6	.333	4.47	1.34	44	0	0	0	1	20-25	48.1	45	30	24	6	20-1	73	.239
— Oakland (A.L.)		0	0		3.00	1.00	3	0	0	0	0	0-0	3.0	2	1	1	0	1-0	1	.182
Major League totals (2 years)		0	0		9.35	1.96	7	0	0	0	0	0-0	8.2	7	9	9	3	10-0	6	.212

G

GARCIA, JESSE — SS/2B

PERSONAL: Born September 24, 1973, in Corpus Christi, Texas. ... 5-10/171. ... Bats right, throws right. ... Full name: Jesus Jesse Garcia. ... High school: Robstown (Texas). ... Junior college: Lee (Texas).

TRANSACTIONS/CAREER NOTES: Selected by Baltimore Orioles organization in 26th round of 1993 free-agent draft. ... Traded by Orioles to Atlanta Braves for IF Steve Sisco (December 18, 2000). ... Released by Braves (August 27, 2004). ... Signed by San Diego Padres organization (November 17, 2004).

2005 GAMES PLAYED BY POSITION (MLB): SS—13, 2B—2.

LEFTY-RIGHTY SPLITS

vs.	Avg.	AB	H	2B	3B	HR	RBI	BB	SO	OBP	Slg.
L	.357	14	5	0	0	1	3	3	2	.471	.571
R	.045	22	1	0	0	1	1	0	9	.045	.182

							BATTING												FIELDING	
Year Team (League)	Pos.	G	AB	R	H	2B	3B	HR	RBI	BB	SO	HBP	GDP	SB-CS	Avg.	OBP	SLG	OPS	E	Avg.
1993—GC Orioles (GCL)	2B-3B-SS	48	156	20	37	4	0	0	16	21	32	1	1	14-6	.237	.326	.263	.589	14	.934
1994—Bluefield (Appal.)								Did not play.												
1995—Frederick (Carol.)	2B	124	365	52	82	11	3	3	27	49	75	9	5	5-10	.225	.329	.296	.625	28	.952
1996—High Desert (Calif.)	2B-SS	137	459	94	122	21	5	10	66	57	81	8	7	25-7	.266	.354	.399	.753	22	.968
1997—Bowie (East.)	2B-3B-SS	141	437	52	103	18	1	5	42	38	71	6	9	7-7	.236	.304	.316	.620	13	.981
1998—Bowie (East.)	2B-OF-SS	86	258	46	73	13	1	2	20	34	37	1	9	12-3	.283	.369	.364	.733	9	.973
—Rochester (Int'l)	2B	44	160	20	47	6	4	0	18	7	22	3	3	7-5	.294	.329	.381	.711	8	.969
1999—Baltimore (A.L.)	SS-2B-3B DH	17	29	6	6	0	0	2	2	2	3	0	1	0-0	.207	.258	.414	.672	0	1.000
—Rochester (Int'l)	SS-2B	62	220	25	56	10	2	2	23	11	21	0	5	9-6	.255	.289	.345	.634	15	.944
2000—Baltimore (A.L.)	2B-SS	14	17	2	1	0	0	0	2	2	0	0	0	0-0	.059	.158	.059	.217	0	1.000
—Rochester (Int'l)	SS-2B-3B	106	372	44	90	12	2	1	23	27	60	4	8	9-4	.242	.300	.293	.593	18	.963
2001—Richmond (Int'l)	SS-2B-3B	105	375	50	100	23	3	2	22	22	54	4	4	18-6	.267	.313	.357	.671	20	.955
—Atlanta (N.L.)	2B-SS	22	5	3	1	0	0	0	0	1	0	0	0	6-2	.200	.200	.200	.400	0	1.000
2002—Richmond (Int'l)	2B-SS-3B OF	58	230	29	69	12	1	6	17	16	32	2	5	9-5	.300	.349	.439	.789	9	.966
—Atlanta (N.L.)	2B-SS-OF	39	61	6	12	1	0	0	5	0	14	0	1	2-2	.197	.197	.213	.410	1	.989
2003—Richmond (Int'l)	SS-2B-OF 3B-DH	110	425	45	130	17	3	2	30	12	50	4	4	29-9	.306	.329	.374	.703	18	.956
—Atlanta (N.L.)	2B-SS-3B	13	10	6	4	0	1	0	2	0	1	0	0	0-1	.400	.400	.600	1.000	0	1.000
2004—Atlanta (N.L.)	SS-2B-3B	50	115	14	29	4	1	1	10	1	16	1	1	1-2	.252	.265	.330	.595	7	.953
—Richmond (Int'l)	2B-SS	20	78	6	17	2	0	0	4	4	13	1	3	0-2	.218	.265	.244	.509	5	.943
2005—San Diego (N.L.)	SS-2B	16	36	4	6	0	0	2	4	3	11	0	0	0-0	.167	.231	.333	.564	0	1.000
—Mobile (Sou.)	SS-DH	7	31	4	6	2	0	1	3	0	4	1	0	1-1	.194	.212	.355	.567	3	.923
—Portland (PCL)	SS-3B	63	210	18	42	7	2	3	26	6	34	0	6	6-1	.200	.220	.295	.515	7	.964
American League totals (2 years)		31	46	8	7	0	0	2	4	4	5	0	1	0-0	.152	.220	.283	.503	0	1.000
National League totals (5 years)		140	227	33	52	5	2	3	21	4	43	1	3	7-6	.229	.246	.308	.554	8	.973
Major League totals (7 years)		171	273	41	59	5	2	5	23	8	48	1	4	7-6	.216	.241	.304	.545	8	.978

DIVISION SERIES RECORD

Year Team (League)	Pos.	G	AB	R	H	2B	3B	HR	RBI	BB	SO	HBP	GDP	SB-CS	Avg.	OBP	SLG	OPS	E	Avg.
2003—Atlanta (N.L.)	2B	2	0	1	0	0	0	0	0	0	0	0	0	0-0	...	...	...	...	0	1.000

GARCIAPARRA, NOMAR — SS

PERSONAL: Born July 23, 1973, in Whittier, Calif. ... 6-0/190. ... Bats right, throws right. ... Full name: Anthony Nomar Garciaparra. ... Name pronounced: no-mar GARCIA-par-uh. ... High school: St. John Bosco (Bellflower, Calif.). ... College: Georgia Tech.

TRANSACTIONS/CAREER NOTES: Selected by Milwaukee Brewers organization in fifth round of 1991 free-agent draft; did not sign. ... Selected by Boston Red Sox organization in first round (12th pick overall) of 1994 free-agent draft. ... On disabled list (May 9-28, 1998; and May 12-27, 2000). ... On disabled list (March 21-July 29 and August 27, 2001-remainder of season); included rehabilitation assignment to Pawtucket. ... On disabled list (March 26-June 9, 2004); included rehabilitation assignment to Pawtucket. ... Traded by Red Sox with OF Matt Murton to Chicago Cubs as part of four-team deal in which Red Sox acquired SS Orlando Cabrera from Expos and 1B Doug Mientkiewicz from Twins, Expos acquired SS Alex S. Gonzalez, P Francis Beltran and IF Brendan Harris from Cubs, and Twins acquired P Justin Jones from Cubs (July 31, 2004). ... On disabled list (April 21-August 5, 2005); included rehabilitation assignments to AZL Cubs, Peoria and West Tenn.

HONORS: Named A.L. Rookie Player of the Year by THE SPORTING NEWS (1997). ... Named A.L. Rookie of the Year by Baseball Writers' Association of America (1997).

2005 GAMES PLAYED BY POSITION (MLB): 3B—34, SS—26.

SCOUTING REPORT

Offense: Physical problems continue to plague Garciaparra, who finished last season at third base. Can drive the ball to all fields when healthy. Bat speed has declined due to inactivity. Is a very impatient hitter who attacks high fastballs, yet is very adept at taking breaking pitches the other way. ***Defense:*** The injuries have cut into his range. Has quick feet and is agile and athletic. Has very good hands. Will need to change his throwing mechanics at third base and come more from over the top. ***Outlook:*** Garciaparra probably will move to third full time to protect his legs and hope that his bat speed and offensive production will return with better health. ***Grade 7.5***

NOMAR GARCIAPARRA'S HITTING ZONE

.471	.667	.286
.308	.429	.300
.200	.182	.273

LEFTY-RIGHTY SPLITS

vs.	Avg.	AB	H	2B	3B	HR	RBI	BB	SO	OBP	Slg.
L	.281	89	25	4	0	2	11	3	9	.301	.393
R	.284	141	40	8	0	7	19	9	15	.331	.489

							BATTING												FIELDING	
Year Team (League)	Pos.	G	AB	R	H	2B	3B	HR	RBI	BB	SO	HBP	GDP	SB-CS	Avg.	OBP	SLG	OPS	E	Avg.
1994—Sarasota (Fla. St.)	SS	28	105	20	31	8	1	1	16	10	6	1	2	5-2	.295	.356	.419	.775	3	.974
1995—Trenton (East.)	SS	125	513	77	137	20	8	8	47	50	42	8	10	35-12	.267	.338	.384	.722	23	.963
1996—Pawtucket (Int'l)	SS	43	172	40	59	15	2	16	46	14	21	1	6	3-1	.343	.387	.733	1.120	5	.973
—GC Red Sox (GCL)	SS	5	14	4	4	2	1	0	4	1	0	1	1	0-0	.286	.375	.571	.946	1	.950
—Boston (A.L.)	SS-2B-DH	24	87	11	21	2	3	4	16	4	14	0	1	5-0	.241	.272	.471	.743	1	.989
1997—Boston (A.L.)	SS	153	*684	122	*209	44	*11	30	98	35	92	6	9	22-9	.306	.342	.534	.875	21	.971
1998—Boston (A.L.)	SS	143	604	111	195	37	8	35	122	33	62	8	20	12-6	.323	.362	.584	.946	25	.962
1999—Boston (A.L.)	SS	135	532	103	190	42	4	27	104	51	39	8	11	14-3	*.357	.418	.603	1.022	17	.972
2000—Boston (A.L.)	SS-DH	140	529	104	197	51	3	21	96	61	50	2	8	5-2	*.372	.434	.599	1.033	18	.971
2001—Pawtucket (Int'l)	SS	4	16	3	7	2	0	1	2	1	2	0	0	0-0	.438	.500	.750	1.250	1	.941
—Boston (A.L.)	SS	21	83	13	24	3	0	4	8	7	9	0	3	0-1	.289	.352	.470	.822	3	.968

G

Year Team (League)	Pos.	G	AB	R	H	2B	3B	HR	RBI	BB	SO	HBP	GDP	SB-CS	Avg.	OBP	SLG	OPS	E	Avg.
2002—Boston (A.L.)	SS	156	635	101	197	•56	5	24	120	41	63	6	17	5-2	.310	.352	.528	.880	*25	.965
2003—Boston (A.L.)	SS	156	658	120	198	37	13	28	105	39	61	11	10	19-5	.301	.345	.524	.870	20	.971
2004—Pawtucket (Int'l)	SS	6	21	1	5	1	0	1	3	1	3	0	0	0-0	.238	.273	.429	.701	0	1.000
—Boston (A.L.)	SS-DH	38	156	24	50	7	3	5	21	8	16	4	4	2-0	.321	.367	.500	.867	6	.957
—Chicago (N.L.)	SS	43	165	28	49	14	0	4	20	16	14	2	6	2-1	.297	.364	.455	.819	3	.982
2005—Ariz. Cubs (Ariz.)	SS	2	5	0	1	0	0	0	0	0	1	0	0	0-0	.200	.200	.200	.400	0	1.000
—Peoria (Midw.)	SS	2	5	1	1	0	0	0	2	2	0	0	0	0-0	.200	.429	.200	.629	0	1.000
—West Tenn (Sou.)	SS	4	13	2	3	0	0	0	0	1	1	1	0	0-0	.231	.333	.231	.564	1	.933
—Chicago (N.L.)	3B-SS	62	230	28	65	12	0	9	30	12	24	2	6	0-0	.283	.320	.452	.772	12	.937
American League totals (9 years)		966	3968	709	1281	279	50	178	690	279	406	46	80	84-28	.323	.370	.553	.923	136	.969
National League totals (2 years)		105	395	56	114	26	0	13	50	28	38	4	12	2-1	.289	.339	.453	.792	15	.958
Major League totals (10 years)		1071	4363	765	1395	305	50	191	740	307	444	50	92	86-29	.320	.367	.544	.911	151	.968

DIVISION SERIES RECORD

Year Team (League)	Pos.	G	AB	R	H	2B	3B	HR	RBI	BB	SO	HBP	GDP	SB-CS	Avg.	OBP	SLG	OPS	E	Avg.
1998—Boston (A.L.)	SS	4	15	4	5	1	0	3	11	1	0	0	1	0-0	.333	.333	1.000	1.333	0	1.000
1999—Boston (A.L.)	SS	4	12	6	5	2	0	2	4	3	3	1	0	0-0	.417	.563	1.083	1.646	0	1.000
2003—Boston (A.L.)	SS	5	20	2	6	1	0	0	0	3	2	0	1	1-0	.300	.391	.350	.741	1	.958
Division series totals (3 years)		13	47	12	16	4	0	5	15	7	5	1	2	1-0	.340	.421	.745	1.166	1	.980

CHAMPIONSHIP SERIES RECORD

Year Team (League)	Pos.	G	AB	R	H	2B	3B	HR	RBI	BB	SO	HBP	GDP	SB-CS	Avg.	OBP	SLG	OPS	E	Avg.
1999—Boston (A.L.)	SS	5	20	2	8	1	0	2	5	2	2	0	0	1-0	.400	.455	.800	1.255	4	.833
2003—Boston (A.L.)	SS	7	29	2	7	0	1	0	1	2	8	0	1	0-0	.241	.290	.310	.601	1	.966
Champ. series totals (2 years)		12	49	4	15	2	1	2	6	4	10	0	1	1-0	.306	.358	.510	.869	5	.906

ALL-STAR GAME RECORD

	G	AB	R	H	2B	3B	HR	RBI	BB	SO	HBP	GDP	SB-CS	Avg.	OBP	SLG	OPS	E	Avg.
All-Star Game totals (5 years)	5	7	1	1	0	0	0	0	0	0	0	0	0-0	.143	.143	.143	.286	2	.778

GARDNER, LEE — P

PERSONAL: Born January 16, 1975, in Hartland, Mich. ... 6-0/210. ... Throws right, bats right. ... Full name: Terrence Lee Gardner. ... High school: Hartland (Mich.). ... College: Central Michigan.

TRANSACTIONS/CAREER NOTES: Signed as a non-drafted free agent by Tampa Bay Devil Rays organization (May 19, 1998). ... Signed as a free agent by San Francisco Giants organization (December 22, 2003). ... Signed as a free agent by Tampa Bay Devil Rays organization (January 4, 2005).

CAREER HITTING: 0-for-0 (.000), 0 R, 0 2B, 0 3B, 0 HR, 0 RBI.

LEFTY-RIGHTY SPLITS

vs.	Avg.	AB	H	2B	3B	HR	RBI	BB	SO	OBP	Slg.
L	.500	16	8	2	1	2	8	1	1	.500	1.125
R	.222	18	4	0	0	0	1	1	3	.263	.222

Year Team (League)	W	L	Pct.	ERA	WHIP	G	GS	CG	ShO	Hld.	Sv.-Opp.	IP	H	R	ER	HR	BB-IBB	SO	Avg.
1998—St. Pete. (Fla. St.)	0	0	...	0.00	1.00	3	0	0	0	...	0-...	4.0	3	0	0	0	1-0	2	.214
—Char., S.C. (S. Atl.)	0	3	.000	4.04	1.18	28	0	0	0	...	3-...	35.2	38	18	16	3	4-0	55	.259
1999—St. Pete. (Fla. St.)	2	0	1.000	1.96	1.09	20	0	0	0	...	7-...	23.0	20	7	5	1	5-0	22	.233
—Orlando (Sou.)	0	0	...	9.00	2.00	1	0	0	0	...	0-...	2.0	3	2	2	0	1-0	1	.375
2000—Durham (Int'l)	1	0	1.000	3.38	1.13	21	0	0	0	...	5-...	18.2	12	7	7	1	9-1	8	.185
—Orlando (Sou.)	3	2	.600	3.40	1.07	36	0	0	0	...	12-...	45.0	34	19	17	0	14-1	48	.209
2001—Durham (Int'l)	5	2	.714	2.72	1.30	56	0	0	0	...	2-...	76.0	76	27	23	10	23-2	55	.259
—Orlando (Sou.)	0	0	...	0.00	0.00	1	0	0	0	...	0-...	1.2	0	0	0	0	0-0	0	.000
2002—Durham (Int'l)	2	1	.667	2.36	1.31	45	0	0	0	...	25-...	49.2	50	14	13	1	15-3	52	.262
—Tampa Bay (A.L.)	1	1	.500	4.05	1.50	12	0	0	0	1	0-2	13.1	12	11	6	3	8-0	8	.273
2003—Durham (Int'l)	3	7	.300	3.73	1.31	57	0	0	0	...	30-...	62.2	68	29	26	9	14-2	56	.273
2004—Fresno (PCL)	7	4	.636	4.46	1.43	57	0	0	0	...	1-...	70.2	79	40	35	8	22-3	42	.275
2005—Tampa Bay (A.L.)	0	0	...	4.91	1.91	5	0	0	0	0	0-0	7.1	12	9	4	2	2-0	4	.353
—Durham (Int'l)	4	3	.571	3.29	1.37	48	0	0	0	0	15-18	52.0	56	25	19	8	15-0	35	.277
Major League totals (2 years)	1	1	.500	4.35	1.65	17	0	0	0	1	0-2	20.2	24	20	10	5	10-0	12	.282

GARKO, RYAN — C

PERSONAL: Born January 2, 1981, in Pittsburgh. ... 6-2/225. ... Bats right, throws right. ... Full name: Ryan F. Garko. ... College: Stanford.

TRANSACTIONS/CAREER NOTES: Selected by Cleveland Indians organization in third round of 2003 free-agent draft.

2005 GAMES PLAYED BY POSITION (MLB): DH—1.

LEFTY-RIGHTY SPLITS

vs.	Avg.	AB	H	2B	3B	HR	RBI	BB	SO	OBP	Slg.
L	.000	0	0	0	0	0	0	0	0	.000	.000
R	.000	1	0	0	0	0	0	0	1	.000	.000

Year Team (League)	Pos.	G	AB	R	H	2B	3B	HR	RBI	BB	SO	HBP	GDP	SB-CS	Avg.	OBP	SLG	OPS	E	Avg.
2003—Mahoning Valley (NYP)	C	45	165	23	45	8	1	4	16	12	19	4	5	1-1	.273	.337	.406	.743	5	.982
2004—Kinston (Carol.)	1B-C	65	238	44	78	17	1	16	57	26	34	15	6	4-1	.328	.425	.609	1.034	3	.995
—Akron (East.)	C-1B	43	172	29	57	15	0	6	38	14	28	6	3	1-0	.331	.397	.523	.920	4	.991
—Buffalo (Int'l)	1B-C	5	20	2	7	1	0	0	4	2	3	0	0	0-0	.350	.391	.400	.791	0	1.000
2005—Buffalo (Int'l)	1B-C-DH	127	452	75	137	25	3	19	77	44	92	18	11	1-3	.303	.384	.498	.882	8	.992
—Cleveland (A.L.)	DH	1	1	0	0	0	0	0	0	0	0	1	0	0-0	.000	.000	.000	.000		...
Major League totals (1 year)		1	1	0	0	0	0	0	0	0	0	1	0	0-0	.000	.000	.000	.000		...

GARLAND, JON — P

PERSONAL: Born September 27, 1979, in Valencia, Calif. ... 6-6/210. ... Throws right, bats right. ... Full name: Jon Steven Garland. ... High school: John F. Kennedy (Granada Hills, Calif.).

TRANSACTIONS/CAREER NOTES: Selected by Chicago Cubs organization in first round (10th pick overall) of 1997 free-agent draft. ... Traded by Cubs to Chicago White Sox for P Matt Karchner (July 29, 1998). ... On disabled list (August 19-September 3, 2000); included rehabilitation assignment to Birmingham.

CAREER HITTING: 2-for-12 (.167), 0 R, 0 2B, 0 3B, 0 HR, 1 RBI.

SCOUTING REPORT

SCOUTING REPORT Throws: Garland mainly throws an 88-93 mph sinker, but he also has a curveball at 76-78, a slider at 81-85 and a changeup. **Tendencies:** He has a consistent sinker, especially for a pitcher who throws over the top. Has really improved the command of it to both sides of the plate and is pitching more off his fastball. Curve is extremely quick with good rotation. Has excellent arm speed with his change. Is starting to throw his slider more than the curve because of his ability to control it. **Outlook:** Garland is the most improved pitcher in the league and has renewed confidence to challenge hitters. Has lowered his pitch counts and worked deep into games. Could increase number of wins this season. Last year was not a fluke. **Grade 9**

JON GARLAND'S PITCHING ZONE

.167	.222	.373
.267	.308	.308
.141	.340	.280

LEFTY-RIGHTY SPLITS

vs.	Avg.	AB	H	2B	3B	HR	RBI	BB	SO	OBP	Slg.
L	.267	446	119	17	1	19	52	28	57	.308	.437
R	.242	384	93	20	1	7	37	19	58	.287	.354

Year Team (League)	W	L	Pct.	ERA	WHIP	G	GS	CG	ShO	Hld.	Sv.-Opp.	IP	H	R	ER	HR	BB-IBB	SO	Avg.
1997— Ariz. Cubs (Ariz.)	3	2	.600	2.70	1.18	10	7	0	0	...	0-...	40.0	37	14	12	3	10-0	39	.247
1998— Rockford (Midw.)	4	7	.364	5.03	1.57	19	19	1	0	...	0-...	107.1	124	69	60	11	45-0	70	.301
— Hickory (S. Atl.)	1	4	.200	5.40	1.84	5	5	0	0	...	0-...	26.2	36	20	16	2	13-0	19	.333
1999— Win.-Salem (Carol.)	5	7	.417	3.33	1.24	19	19	2	1	...	0-...	119.0	109	57	44	7	39-2	84	.244
— Birmingham (Sou.)	3	1	.750	4.38	1.46	7	7	0	0	...	0-...	39.0	39	22	19	4	18-0	27	.258
2000— Charlotte (Int'l)	9	2	.818	2.26	1.26	16	16	2	1	...	0-0	103.2	99	28	26	3	32-2	63	.251
— Chicago (A.L.)	4	8	.333	6.46	1.75	15	13	0	0	1	0-0	69.2	82	55	50	10	40-0	42	.292
— Birmingham (Sou.)	0	0	...	0.00	0.83	1	1	0	0	...	0-...	6.0	4	0	0	0	1-0	10	.200
2001— Charlotte (Int'l)	0	3	.000	2.73	1.27	5	5	1	0	...	0-...	33.0	31	10	10	1	11-1	26	.261
— Chicago (A.L.)	6	7	.462	3.69	1.52	35	16	0	0	2	1-1	117.0	123	59	48	16	55-2	61	.277
2002— Chicago (A.L.)	12	12	.500	4.58	1.41	33	33	1	1	0	0-0	192.2	188	109	98	23	83-1	112	.258
2003— Chicago (A.L.)	12	13	.480	4.51	1.37	32	32	0	0	0	0-0	191.2	188	103	96	28	74-1	108	.260
2004— Chicago (A.L.)	12	11	.522	4.89	1.38	34	33	1	0	0	0-0	217.0	223	125	118	34	76-2	113	.269
2005— Chicago (A.L.)	18	10	.643	3.50	1.17	32	32	3	* 3	0	0-0	221.0	212	93	86	26	47-3	115	.255
Major League totals (6 years)	64	61	.512	4.42	1.38	181	159	5	4	3	1-1	1009.0	1016	544	496	137	375-9	551	.265

CHAMPIONSHIP SERIES RECORD

Year Team (League)	W	L	Pct.	ERA	WHIP	G	GS	CG	ShO	Hld.	Sv.-Opp.	IP	H	R	ER	HR	BB-IBB	SO	Avg.
2005— Chicago (A.L.)	1	0	1.000	2.00	0.56	1	1	1	0	0	0-0	9.0	4	2	2	1	1-0	7	.138

WORLD SERIES RECORD

Year Team (League)	W	L	Pct.	ERA	WHIP	G	GS	CG	ShO	Hld.	Sv.-Opp.	IP	H	R	ER	HR	BB-IBB	SO	Avg.
2005— Chicago (A.L.)	0	0	...	2.57	1.29	1	1	0	0	0	0-0	7.0	7	4	2	1	2-0	4	.292

ALL-STAR GAME RECORD

	W	L	Pct.	ERA	WHIP	G	GS	CG	ShO	Hld.	Sv.-Opp.	IP	H	R	ER	HR	BB-IBB	SO	Avg.
All-Star Game totals (1 year)	0	0	...	0.00	2.00	1	1	0	0	0	0-0	1.0	0	0	0	0	2-0	0	.000

GASSNER, DAVE · P

PERSONAL: Born December 14, 1978, in Hortonville, Wis. ... 6-2/190. ... Throws left, bats right. ... Full name: David K. Gassner. ... High school: Hortonville (Wisc.). ... College: Purdue.
TRANSACTIONS/CAREER NOTES: Selected by Toronto Blue Jays organization in 24th round of 2001 free-agent draft. ... Traded by Blue Jays to Minnesota Twins (December 15, 2003); completed trade in which Twins traded OF Bobby Kielty to Blue Jays for OF Shannon Stewart and a player to be named (July 16, 2003).
CAREER HITTING: 0-for-0 (.000), 0 R, 0 2B, 0 3B, 0 HR, 0 RBI.

LEFTY-RIGHTY SPLITS

vs.	Avg.	AB	H	2B	3B	HR	RBI	BB	SO	OBP	Slg.
L	.250	8	2	0	1	0	0	0	2	.250	.500
R	.292	24	7	0	0	1	6	1	0	.308	.417

Year Team (League)	W	L	Pct.	ERA	WHIP	G	GS	CG	ShO	Hld.	Sv.-Opp.	IP	H	R	ER	HR	BB-IBB	SO	Avg.
2001— Char., W.Va. (S. Atl.)	4	4	.500	3.03	1.12	13	11	1	0	...	0-...	74.1	72	30	25	3	11-0	51	.247
2002— Dunedin (Fla. St.)	11	6	.647	3.44	1.15	23	21	2	1	...	0-...	146.2	143	64	56	17	26-1	104	.255
— Syracuse (Int'l)	0	1	.000	5.40	1.80	1	1	0	0	...	0-...	5.0	7	3	3	0	2-0	1	.333
— Tennessee (Sou.)	1	2	.333	2.49	1.14	4	4	0	0	...	0-...	25.1	22	8	7	1	7-1	14	.232
2003— New Haven (East.)	10	4	.714	2.79	1.15	35	19	1	0	...	1-...	145.1	139	54	45	10	28-1	92	.253
— Syracuse (Int'l)	1	0	1.000	1.80	1.20	1	1	0	0	...	0-...	5.0	5	1	1	0	1-0	4	.250
2004— Rochester (Int'l)	16	8	.667	3.41	1.18	28	28	0	0	...	0-...	174.1	175	72	66	16	30-1	93	.265
2005— Minnesota (A.L.)	1	0	1.000	5.87	1.30	2	2	0	0	0	0-0	7.2	9	7	5	1	1-0	2	.281
— Rochester (Int'l)	8	8	.500	4.95	1.47	22	20	2	0	0	0-0	116.1	138	65	64	18	33-0	64	.302
Major League totals (1 year)	1	0	1.000	5.87	1.30	2	2	0	0	0	0-0	7.2	9	7	5	1	1-0	2	.281

GATHRIGHT, JOEY · OF

PERSONAL: Born April 27, 1981, in Hattiesburg, Miss. ... 5-10/170. ... Bats left, throws right. ... Full name: Joey Renard Gathright. ... High school: Bonnabel (Kenner, La.).
TRANSACTIONS/CAREER NOTES: Selected by Tampa Bay Devil Rays organization in 32nd round of 2001 free-agent draft.
2005 GAMES PLAYED BY POSITION (MLB): OF-70, DH-1.

SCOUTING REPORT Offense: Gathright is one of the fastest players in the game. Needs to become more patient at the plate and keep the ball out of the air so he can use that speed. Still is learning to play. Doesn't have a quick bat and frequently is jammed. Is not going to have power. **Defense:** His arm is short, and he's going to have to charge the ball with a quick release because opponents will run on him. Doesn't get good jumps now in any direction, but speed allows him to make up the ground. **Outlook:** Gathright has game-changing speed, but unless he cuts down his swing and reduces his strikeouts, it's going to be useless. Won't have enough power to play a corner outfield spot. **Grade 5.3**

JOEY GATHRIGHT'S HITTING ZONE

.273	.300	.231
.192	.448	.326
.182	.000	.588

LEFTY-RIGHTY SPLITS

vs.	Avg.	AB	H	2B	3B	HR	RBI	BB	SO	OBP	Slg.
L	.353	17	6	1	0	0	0	1	4	.389	.412
R	.269	186	50	6	3	0	13	9	35	.310	.333

Year Team (League)	Pos.	G	AB	R	H	2B	3B	HR	RBI	BB	SO	HBP	GDP	SB-CS	Avg.	OBP	SLG	OPS	E	Avg.
2002— Char., S.C. (S. Atl.)	OF	59	208	30	55	1	0	0	14	21	36	10	1	22-7	.264	.360	.269	.629	1	.992
2003— Bakersfield (Calif.)	OF	89	340	65	110	6	3	0	23	41	54	6	3	57-13	.324	.406	.359	.765	3	.981
— Orlando (South.)	OF	22	85	12	32	1	0	0	5	5	15	2	0	12-3	.376	.419	.388	.808	1	.983

Year	Team (League)	Pos.	G	AB	R	H	2B	3B	HR	RBI	BB	SO	HBP	GDP	SB-CS	Avg.	OBP	SLG	OPS	E	Avg.
2004— Montgomery (Sou.)	OF-DH	32	126	23	43	5	1	0	8	11	30	1	1	10-6	.341	.399	.397	.795	1	.985
— Tampa Bay (A.L.)	OF-DH	19	52	11	13	0	0	0	1	2	14	3	2	6-1	.250	.316	.250	.566	0	1.000
— Durham (Int'l)	OF	60	236	34	77	9	1	0	8	19	46	3	5	33-13	.326	.384	.373	.749	4	.968
2005— Durham (Int'l)	OF-DH	58	226	46	69	10	5	1	18	29	47	2	0	31-8	.305	.384	.407	.795	14	.948
— Tampa Bay (A.L.)	OF-DH	76	203	29	56	7	3	0	13	10	39	2	5	20-5	.276	.316	.340	.656	5	.984
Major League totals (2 years)		95	255	40	69	7	3	0	14	12	53	5	7	26-6	.271	.316	.322	.638	3	.986

GAUDIN, CHAD — P

PERSONAL: Born March 24, 1983, in New Orleans. ... 5-11/165. ... Throws right, bats right. ... Full name: Chad Edward Gaudin. ... High school: Crescent City (Calif.).
TRANSACTIONS/CAREER NOTES: Selected by Tampa Bay Devil Rays organization in 34th round of 2001 free-agent draft. ... Traded by Devil Rays to Toronto Blue Jays for C Kevin Cash (December 12, 2004).
CAREER HITTING: 0-for-1 (.000), 0 R, 0 2B, 0 3B, 0 HR, 0 RBI.

CHAD GAUDIN'S PITCHING ZONE

.333	.500	.667
.800	.667	.545
.500	.250	.200

LEFTY-RIGHTY SPLITS

vs.	Avg.	AB	H	2B	3B	HR	RBI	BB	SO	OBP	Slg.
L	.481	27	13	1	0	3	8	3	4	.516	.852
R	.462	39	18	5	0	3	10	3	8	.512	.821

Year	Team (League)	W	L	Pct.	ERA	WHIP	G	GS	CG	ShO	Hld.	Sv.-Opp.	IP	H	R	ER	HR	BB-IBB	SO	Avg.
2002— Char., S.C. (S. Atl.)	4	6	.400	2.26	1.20	26	17	0	0	...	1-...	119.1	106	43	30	5	37-0	106	.244
2003— Bakersfield (Calif.)	5	3	.625	2.13	1.07	14	14	1	0	...	0-...	80.1	63	23	19	2	23-0	70	.214
— Orlando (Sou.)	2	0	1.000	0.47	0.58	3	3	1	1	...	0-...	19.0	8	1	1	0	3-0	23	.131
— Tampa Bay (A.L.)	2	0	1.000	3.60	1.33	15	3	0	0	0	0-0	40.0	37	18	16	4	16-0	23	.240
2004— Durham (Int'l)	1	3	.250	4.72	1.36	17	7	0	0	...	2-...	47.2	48	26	25	8	17-0	52	.264
— Tampa Bay (A.L.)	1	2	.333	4.85	1.76	26	4	0	0	5	0-1	42.2	59	27	23	4	16-4	30	.337
2005— Toronto (A.L.)	1	3	.250	13.15	2.85	5	3	0	0	0	0-0	13.0	31	19	19	6	6-0	12	.470
— Syracuse (Int'l)	9	8	.529	3.35	1.16	23	23	2	2	0	0-0	150.1	140	61	56	12	35-1	113	.251
Major League totals (3 years)	4	5	.444	5.46	1.72	46	10	0	0	5	0-1	95.2	127	64	58	14	38-4	65	.322

GEARY, GEOFF — P

PERSONAL: Born August 26, 1976, in Buffalo. ... 6-0/167. ... Throws right, bats right. ... Full name: Geoffrey Michael Geary. ... High school: Grossmont (El Cajon, Calif.). ... College: Oklahoma.
TRANSACTIONS/CAREER NOTES: Selected by Milwaukee Brewers organization in 41st round of 1997 free-agent draft; did not sign. ... Selected by Philadelphia Phillies organization in 15th round of 1998 free-agent draft. ... On disabled list (July 9-July 24, 2005); included rehabilitation assignment to Reading.
CAREER HITTING: 1-for-7 (.143), 0 R, 0 2B, 0 3B, 0 HR, 0 RBI.

GEOFF GEARY'S PITCHING ZONE

.304	.214	.294
.255	.313	.265
.071	.400	.333

LEFTY-RIGHTY SPLITS

vs.	Avg.	AB	H	2B	3B	HR	RBI	BB	SO	OBP	Slg.
L	.192	99	19	6	1	2	8	12	18	.279	.333
R	.294	119	35	5	1	3	25	9	24	.338	.429

Year	Team (League)	W	L	Pct.	ERA	WHIP	G	GS	CG	ShO	Hld.	Sv.-Opp.	IP	H	R	ER	HR	BB-IBB	SO	Avg.
1998— Batavia (NY-Penn)	9	1	.900	1.60	0.97	16	15	1	1	...	0-...	95.1	78	20	17	6	14-0	101	.222
1999— Clearwater (FSL)	10	5	.667	3.95	1.48	24	19	2	0	...	0-...	139.0	175	77	61	11	31-1	77	.310
2000— Reading (East.)	7	6	.538	4.11	1.26	22	22	1	0	...	0-...	129.1	141	66	59	15	22-0	112	.272
2001— Reading (East.)	9	7	.563	3.61	1.09	29	13	0	0	...	2-...	112.1	101	48	45	14	21-3	88	.245
— Scran./W.B. (I.L.)	0	3	.000	6.95	1.86	7	3	0	0	...	0-...	22.0	35	17	17	2	6-1	21	.376
2002— Scran./W.B. (I.L.)	4	2	.667	3.03	1.39	38	8	0	0	...	1-...	101.0	108	46	34	9	32-1	82	.277
2003— Scran./W.B. (I.L.)	9	4	.692	2.16	0.98	46	3	0	0	...	5-...	87.2	73	26	21	3	13-1	80	.229
— Philadelphia (N.L.)	0	0	...	4.50	1.83	5	0	0	0	0	0-0	6.0	8	3	3	0	3-0	3	.333
2004— Scran./W.B. (I.L.)	1	2	.333	2.31	1.41	21	0	0	0	0	10-...	23.1	20	7	6	1	13-4	23	.235
— Philadelphia (N.L.)	1	0	1.000	5.44	1.52	33	0	0	0	0	0-0	44.2	52	29	27	8	16-3	30	.292
2005— Reading (East.)	0	0	...	0.00	0.00	1	0	0	0	0	0-0	2.0	0	0	0	0	0-0	2	.000
— Scran./W.B. (I.L.)	1	2	.333	2.70	1.02	10	0	0	0	0	1-2	16.2	15	5	5	0	2-0	14	.238
— Philadelphia (N.L.)	2	1	.667	3.72	1.29	40	0	0	0	0	0-1	58.0	54	29	24	5	21-4	42	.248
Major League totals (3 years)	3	1	.750	4.47	1.42	78	0	0	0	3	0-1	108.2	114	61	54	13	40-7	75	.271

GERMAN, ESTEBAN — 3B/2B

PERSONAL: Born January 26, 1978, in Santo Domingo, Dominican Republic. ... 5-9/165. ... Bats right, throws right. ... Full name: Esteban German Guridi. ... Name pronounced: her-MAHN.
TRANSACTIONS/CAREER NOTES: Signed as a non-drafted free agent by Oakland Athletics organization (July 4, 1996). ... On disabled list (July 4-31, 2004); included rehabilitation assignment to Sacramento. ... Signed as a free agent by Texas Rangers organization (November 19, 2004).
2005 GAMES PLAYED BY POSITION (MLB): 2B—1, 3B—1, DH—1.

LEFTY-RIGHTY SPLITS

vs.	Avg.	AB	H	2B	3B	HR	RBI	BB	SO	OBP	Slg.
L	.000	0	0	0	0	0	0	0	0	.000	.000
R	.750	4	3	1	0	0	1	0	1	.750	1.000

Year	Team (League)	Pos.	G	AB	R	H	2B	3B	HR	RBI	BB	SO	HBP	GDP	SB-CS	Avg.	OBP	SLG	OPS	E	Avg.
1997— Dom. Athletics (DSL)		69	249	69	79	17	1	2	29	73	30	...	...	58-...	.317	...	.418	...	...	...
1998— Dom. Athletics (DSL)		10	32	9	10	1	1	0	4	7	2	...	...	1-...	.313	...	.406	...	...	...
— Ariz. A's (Ariz.)	2B	55	202	52	62	3	10	2	28	33	43	4	...	40-8	.307	.413	.451	.863	13	.940
1999— Modesto (Calif.)	2B	128	501	107	156	16	12	4	52	102	128	5	3	40-16	.311	.428	.415	.843	38	.932
2000— Midland (Texas)	2B	24	75	13	16	1	0	1	6	18	21	2	1	5-3	.213	.379	.267	.646	5	.951
— Visalia (Calif.)	2B-SS	109	428	82	113	14	10	2	35	61	86	5	4	78-8	.264	.361	.357	.718	25	.953
2001— Midland (Texas)	2B	92	335	79	95	20	3	6	30	63	66	12	4	31-11	.284	.415	.415	.830	16	.963

Year	Team (League)	Pos.	G	AB	R	H	2B	3B	HR	RBI	BB	SO	HBP	GDP	SB-CS	Avg.	OBP	SLG	OPS	E	Avg.
—Sacramento (PCL)	2B	38	150	40	56	8	0	4	14	18	20	6	4	17-2	.373	.457	.507	.964	7	.962
2002—Sacramento (PCL)	2B	121	458	72	126	16	4	4	43	78	66	8	7	26-14	.275	.390	.341	.730	8	.986
—Oakland (A.L.)	2B	9	35	4	7	0	0	0	0	4	11	1	0	1-0	.200	.300	.200	.500	1	.978
2003—Sacramento (PCL)	2B	115	467	86	143	20	8	3	51	56	64	2	17	32-8	.306	.379	.403	.781	13	.976
—Oakland (A.L.)	2B	5	4	0	1	0	0	0	1	0	1	0	1	0-0	.250	.250	.250	.500	0	1.000
2004—Sacramento (PCL) 2B-SS-DH		55	231	33	76	8	4	2	29	19	28	3	6	18-2	.329	.380	.424	.804	9	.961
—Oakland (A.L.) 3B-2B-DH		31	60	9	15	1	1	0	7	4	13	0	1	0-1	.250	.297	.300	.597	2	.967
2005—Texas (A.L.) 2B-3B-DH		5	4	3	3	1	0	0	1	0	1	0	0	2-0	.750	.750	1.000	1.750	1	.917
Major League totals (4 years)		50	103	16	26	2	1	0	9	8	26	1	2	3-1	.252	.313	.291	.604	4	.969

GERMAN, FRANKLYN   P

PERSONAL: Born January 20, 1980, in San Cristobal, Dominican Republic. ... 6-7/270. ... Throws right, bats right. ... Full name: Franklyn Miguel German. ... Name pronounced: her-MAHN.
TRANSACTIONS/CAREER NOTES: Signed as a non-drafted free agent by Oakland Athletics organization (July 2, 1996). ... Traded by A's with 1B Carlos Pena and a player to be named to Detroit Tigers as part of three-team deal in which New York Yankees acquired P Jeff Weaver from Tigers and A's acquired Ps Ted Lilly and Jason Arnold and OF John-Ford Griffin from Yankees (July 6, 2002); Tigers acquired P Jeremy Bonderman to complete deal (August 22, 2002).
CAREER HITTING: 0-for-1 (.000), 0 R, 0 2B, 0 3B, 0 HR, 0 RBI.

FRANKLYN GERMAN'S PITCHING ZONE

.294	.250	.400
.444	.304	.357
.211	.250	.158

LEFTY-RIGHTY SPLITS

vs.	Avg.	AB	H	2B	3B	HR	RBI	BB	SO	OBP	Slg.
L	.267	86	23	5	1	5	17	18	15	.413	.523
R	.294	136	40	3	1	2	12	16	23	.371	.375

Year	Team (League)	W	L	Pct.	ERA	WHIP	G	GS	CG	ShO	Hld.	Sv.-Opp.	IP	H	R	ER	HR	BB-IBB	SO	Avg.
1997—Dom. Athletics (DSL)		8	3	.727	2.33	1.09	13	13	5	...	...	0-...	89.0	66	33	23	...	31-...	80	...
1998—Ariz. A's (Ariz.)		2	1	.667	6.13	1.60	14	12	0	0	0	0-...	54.1	69	43	37	5	18-0	48	.317
1999—S. Oregon (N'west)		3	5	.375	5.99	1.82	15	15	0	0	0	0-...	73.2	89	52	49	10	45-1	58	.306
2000—Modesto (Calif.)		5	5	.500	5.50	1.74	17	14	0	0	0	0-...	72.0	88	55	44	4	37-0	52	.307
—Vancouver (N'west)		1	0	1.000	1.77	1.13	9	2	0	0	0	0-...	20.1	13	4	4	0	10-0	20	.173
2001—Visalia (Calif.)		2	4	.333	3.98	1.55	53	0	0	0	0	19-...	63.1	67	34	28	7	31-1	93	.262
2002—Midland (Texas)		1	1	.500	3.05	1.33	37	0	0	0	0	16-...	41.1	28	14	14	0	27-2	59	.194
—Toledo (Int'l)		1	1	.500	1.59	0.97	23	0	0	0	0	13-...	22.2	15	4	4	0	7-0	31	.188
—Detroit (A.L.)		1	0	1.000	0.00	0.75	7	0	0	0	1	1-1	6.2	3	0	0	0	2-1	6	.150
2003—Toledo (Int'l)		1	4	.200	2.45	1.00	24	0	0	0	0	4-...	29.1	21	9	8	2	9-1	32	.212
—Detroit (A.L.)		2	4	.333	6.04	2.06	45	0	0	0	4	5-7	44.2	47	32	30	5	45-3	41	.273
2004—Toledo (Int'l)		3	5	.375	4.59	1.45	49	0	0	0	0	27-...	49.0	46	25	25	6	25-2	60	.246
—Detroit (A.L.)		1	0	1.000	7.36	1.91	16	0	0	0	0	0-1	14.2	17	15	12	4	11-1	8	.279
2005—Detroit (A.L.)		4	0	1.000	3.66	1.64	58	0	0	0	4	1-3	59.0	63	26	24	7	34-4	38	.284
Major League totals (4 years)		8	4	.667	4.75	1.78	126	0	0	0	10	7-12	125.0	130	73	66	16	92-9	93	.274

GERUT, JODY   OF

PERSONAL: Born September 18, 1977, in Elmhurst, Ill. ... 6-0/190. ... Bats left, throws left. ... Full name: Joseph Diego Gerut. ... Name pronounced: GARE-et. ... High school: Willowbrook (Ill.). ... College: Stanford.
TRANSACTIONS/CAREER NOTES: Selected by Colorado Rockies organization in second round of 1998 free-agent draft. ... Traded by Rockies with C Josh Bard to Cleveland Indians for OF Jacob Cruz (June 1, 2001). ... On disabled list (September 19, 2004-remainder of season). ... On disabled list (March 20-May 13, 2005); included rehabilitation assignment to Buffalo. ... Traded by Indians to Chicago Cubs for OF Jason Dubois (July 19, 2005). ... Traded by Cubs to Pittsburgh Pirates for OF Matt Lawton (July 31, 2005). ... On disabled list (August 11, 2005-remainder of season).
HONORS: Named A.L. Rookie Player of the Year by THE SPORTING NEWS (2003).
2005 GAMES PLAYED BY POSITION (MLB): OF—47, DH—3.

SCOUTING REPORT **Offense:** Gerut doesn't have a fluid stroke. Hits down on the ball. Bat speed has declined slightly. Is a better high-ball hitter and will take the ball the other way. Is patient. Has a lot of problems with lefthanded pitching. Won't run a lot. ***Defense:*** He has the arm strength to play right field, but his accuracy is a question. Gets good jumps to the alley and is aggressive charging the ball but is unable to cover much ground because of his knee problems. ***Outlook:*** There are real concerns about his availability to start the season. ***Grade 5.6***

JODY GERUT'S HITTING ZONE

.273	.125	.308
.231	.308	.339
.000	.091	.238

LEFTY-RIGHTY SPLITS

vs.	Avg.	AB	H	2B	3B	HR	RBI	BB	SO	OBP	Slg.
L	.103	29	3	1	0	0	1	3	6	.188	.138
R	.284	141	40	10	1	1	13	17	14	.358	.390

Year	Team (League)	Pos.	G	AB	R	H	2B	3B	HR	RBI	BB	SO	HBP	GDP	SB-CS	Avg.	OBP	SLG	OPS	E	Avg.
1999—Salem (Carol.)	OF	133	499	80	144	33	11	11	63	61	65	3	10	25-12	.289	.367	.465	.832	7	.970
2000—Carolina (Sou.)	OF	109	362	48	103	32	3	3	57	76	54	2	9	18-11	.285	.405	.414	.819	4	.977
2001—				Did not play.																
2002—Akron (East.)	OF	65	256	44	72	15	2	9	39	34	30	1	7	17-8	.281	.368	.461	.829	3	.979
—Buffalo (Int'l)	OF	55	183	31	59	7	2	1	21	23	20	1	6	3-5	.322	.401	.399	.800	1	.993
2003—Buffalo (Int'l)	OF-DH	17	65	13	18	5	0	5	19	11	11	0	1	4-0	.277	.377	.585	.961	0	1.000
—Cleveland (A.L.)	OF-DH	127	480	66	134	33	2	22	75	35	70	7	13	4-5	.279	.336	.494	.830	4	.984
2004—Cleveland (A.L.)	OF-DH	134	481	72	121	31	5	11	51	54	59	7	9	13-6	.252	.334	.405	.739	4	.986
2005—Buffalo (Int'l)	OF-DH	12	48	12	21	5	0	3	8	6	7	2	2	0-0	.438	.518	.729	1.247	2	.947
—Cleveland (A.L.)	OF-DH	44	138	12	38	9	1	1	12	18	14	0	3	1-1	.275	.357	.377	.733	0	1.000
—Chicago (N.L.)	OF	11	14	1	1	0	0	0	0	2	3	0	1	0-0	.071	.188	.143	.330	0	1.000
—Pittsburgh (N.L.)	OF	4	18	2	4	1	0	0	2	0	2	0	0	0-0	.222	.222	.278	.500	0	1.000
American League totals (3 years)		305	1099	150	293	73	8	34	138	107	143	14	25	18-12	.267	.338	.440	.778	8	.986
National League totals (1 year)		15	32	3	5	2	0	0	2	2	5	0	1	0-0	.156	.206	.219	.425	0	1.000
Major League totals (3 years)		320	1131	153	298	75	8	34	140	109	149	14	26	18-12	.263	.334	.434	.768	8	.987

G

GIAMBI, JASON   1B/DH

PERSONAL: Born January 8, 1971, in West Covina, Calif. ... 6-3/230. ... Bats left, throws right. ... Full name: Jason Gilbert Giambi. ... Name pronounced: gee-OM-bee. ... High school: South Hills (West Covina, Calif.). ... College: Long Beach State. ... Brother of Jeremy Giambi, first baseman/outfielder with four major league teams (1998-2003).
TRANSACTIONS/CAREER NOTES: Selected by Milwaukee Brewers organization in 43rd round of 1989 free-agent draft; did not sign. ... Selected by Oakland Athletics organization in second round of 1992 free-agent draft. ... Signed as a free agent by New York Yankees (December 18, 2001). ... On disabled list (May 22-June 6 and July 26-September 14, 2004); included rehabilitation assignments to Tampa and Columbus.
HONORS: Named A.L. Most Valuable Player by Baseball Writers' Association of America (2000). ... Named A.L. Comeback Player of the Year by the SPORTING NEWS (2005).
2005 GAMES PLAYED BY POSITION (MLB): 1B—78, DH—60.

SCOUTING REPORT **Offense:** Giambi had a lot of trouble handling the ball inside and had some decline in bat speed early in the season. Handled low balls better, which is the pitch he can drive. Likes to pull the ball. An extremely patient hitter. Doesn't run well and can actually clog the bases. **Defense:** Never known for being a strong defensive player, he can catch what he gets to but doesn't have a lot of range. Has an accurate arm to start the double play. Doesn't have a really flexible lower body to shift well around the bag. **Outlook:** He is healthy now and is able to establish a firmer base at the plate, which increases his bat speed and power. Is more of a streak hitter now but still a quality run producer. **Grade 8.1**

JASON GIAMBI'S HITTING ZONE

.222	.304	.222
.294	.457	.292
.368	.417	.212

LEFTY-RIGHTY SPLITS

vs.	Avg.	AB	H	2B	3B	HR	RBI	BB	SO	OBP	Slg.
L	.261	138	36	4	0	8	28	25	42	.418	.464
R	.276	279	77	10	0	24	59	83	67	.451	.570

Year	Team (League)	Pos.	G	AB	R	H	2B	3B	HR	RBI	BB	SO	HBP	GDP	SB-CS	Avg.	OBP	SLG	OPS	E	Avg.
1992—	S. Oregon (N'west)	3B	13	41	9	13	3	0	3	13	9	6	0	0	1-1	.317	.440	.610	1.050	1	.962
1993—	Modesto (Calif.)	3B	89	313	72	91	16	2	12	60	73	47	10	12	2-3	.291	.436	.470	.906	19	.911
1994—	Huntsville (Sou.)	1B-3B	56	193	31	43	9	0	6	30	27	31	2	8	0-0	.223	.319	.363	.681	11	.945
—Tacoma (PCL)		3B-SS	52	176	28	56	20	0	4	38	25	32	0	1	1-0	.318	.388	.500	.888	8	.949
1995—	Edmonton (PCL)	3B-DH-1B	55	190	34	65	26	1	3	41	34	26	2	4	0-0	.342	.441	.537	.978	9	.938
—Oakland (A.L.)		3B-1B-DH	54	176	27	45	7	0	6	25	28	31	3	4	2-1	.256	.364	.398	.761	4	.984
1996—	Oakland (A.L.)	1B-OF-3B DH	140	536	84	156	40	1	20	79	51	95	5	15	0-1	.291	.355	.481	.836	11	.982
1997—	Oakland (A.L.)	OF-1B-DH	142	519	66	152	41	2	20	81	55	89	6	11	0-1	.293	.362	.495	.857	7	.987
1998—	Oakland (A.L.)	1B-DH	153	562	92	166	28	0	27	110	81	102	6	16	2-2	.295	.384	.489	.873	* 14	.990
1999—	Oakland (A.L.)	1B-DH-3B	158	575	115	181	36	1	33	123	105	106	9	11	1-1	.315	.422	.553	.975	7	.995
2000—	Oakland (A.L.)	1B-DH	152	510	108	170	29	1	43	137	* 137	96	9	2-0		.333	* .476	.647	1.123	6	.995
2001—	Oakland (A.L.)	1B-DH	154	520	109	178	* 47	2	38	120	* 129	83	13	17	2-0	.342	* .477	* .660	1.137	11	.992
2002—	New York (A.L.)	1B-DH	155	560	120	176	34	1	41	122	109	112	15	18	2-2	.314	.435	.598	1.034	4	.995
2003—	New York (A.L.)	1B-DH	156	535	97	134	25	0	41	* 107	* 129	140	* 21	9	2-1	.250	.412	.527	.939	4	.995
2004—	Tampa (Fla. St.)	1B	2	6	0	1	0	0	0	0	1	1	0	0	0-0	.167	.286	.167	.452	0	1.000
—New York (A.L.)		1B-DH	80	264	33	55	9	0	12	40	47	62	8	5	0-1	.208	.342	.379	.720	4	.990
2005—	New York (A.L.)	1B-DH	139	417	74	113	14	0	32	87	*108	109	19	7	0-0	.271	*.440	.535	.975	7	.988
Major League totals (11 years)			1483	5174	925	1526	310	8	313	1031	979	1025	111	122	13-10	.295	.413	.539	.953	79	.991

DIVISION SERIES RECORD

Year	Team (League)	Pos.	G	AB	R	H	2B	3B	HR	RBI	BB	SO	HBP	GDP	SB-CS	Avg.	OBP	SLG	OPS	E	Avg.
2000—	Oakland (A.L.)	1B	5	14	2	4	0	0	1	7	2	0	0	1-0		.286	.500	.286	.786	1	.976
2001—	Oakland (A.L.)	1B	5	17	2	6	0	0	1	4	2	0	1	0-0		.353	.455	.529	.984	1	.982
2002—	New York (A.L.)	1B-DH	4	14	5	5	0	0	1	3	4	1	1	0-0		.357	.526	.571	1.098	0	1.000
2003—	New York (A.L.)	DH	4	16	1	4	2	0	0	2	2	5	0	0-0		.250	.333	.375	.708	0	...
2005—	New York (A.L.)	1B-DH	5	19	1	8	3	0	0	3	4	1	0	0-0		.421	.500	.579	1.079	0	1.000
Division series totals (5 years)			23	80	11	27	5	0	2	12	20	14	1	2	1-0	.338	.466	.475	.941	2	.986

CHAMPIONSHIP SERIES RECORD

Year	Team (League)	Pos.	G	AB	R	H	2B	3B	HR	RBI	BB	SO	HBP	GDP	SB-CS	Avg.	OBP	SLG	OPS	E	Avg.
2003—	New York (A.L.)	DH	7	26	4	6	0	0	3	4	7	0	0	0-0		.231	.333	.577	.910	0	...

WORLD SERIES RECORD

Year	Team (League)	Pos.	G	AB	R	H	2B	3B	HR	RBI	BB	SO	HBP	GDP	SB-CS	Avg.	OBP	SLG	OPS	E	Avg.
2003—	New York (A.L.)	DH-1B	6	17	2	4	1	0	1	3	1	1	0	0-0		.235	.409	.471	.880	1	1.000

ALL-STAR GAME RECORD

			G	AB	R	H	2B	3B	HR	RBI	BB	SO	HBP	GDP	SB-CS	Avg.	OBP	SLG	OPS	E	Avg.
All-Star Game totals (5 years)			5	8	4	3	0	0	1	1	1	3	0	0-0		.375	.444	.750	1.194	0	1.000

G

GIARRATANO, TONY   SS

PERSONAL: Born November 29, 1982, in Queens, N.Y. ... 6-0/180. ... Bats both, throws right. ... Full name: Anthony J. Giarratano. ... College: Tulane.
TRANSACTIONS/CAREER NOTES: Selected by Detroit Tigers organization in third round of 2003 free-agent draft.
2005 GAMES PLAYED BY POSITION (MLB): SS—13.

LEFTY-RIGHTY SPLITS

vs.	Avg.	AB	H	2B	3B	HR	RBI	BB	SO	OBP	Slg.
L	.000	5	0	0	0	0	0	1	2	.167	.000
R	.162	37	6	0	0	1	4	4	5	.244	.243

Year	Team (League)	Pos.	G	AB	R	H	2B	3B	HR	RBI	BB	SO	HBP	GDP	SB-CS	Avg.	OBP	SLG	OPS	E	Avg.
2003—	Oneonta (NYP)	SS	47	189	31	62	11	4	3	27	12	22	2	3	9-4	.328	.369	.476	.845	8	.959
2004—	W. Mich. (Midw.)	SS	43	165	20	47	6	1	1	13	25	22	2	4	11-3	.285	.383	.352	.735	6	.824
—Lakeland (Fla. St.)		SS	53	202	30	76	11	0	5	25	16	38	1	4	14-8	.376	.421	.505	.926	8	.000
2005—	Detroit (A.L.)	SS	15	42	4	6	0	0	1	4	5	7	0	1	1-0	.143	.234	.214	.448	3	.949
—Erie (East.)		SS	89	346	40	92	22	3	3	32	32	75	5	9	12-5	.266	.334	.373	.707	18	.954
Major League totals (1 year)			15	42	4	6	0	0	1	4	5	7	0	1	1-0	.143	.234	.214	.448	3	.949

OF/1B

PERSONAL: Born March 2, 1977, in Rochester, Mich. ... 6-0/197. ... Bats left, throws left. ... Full name: Jay Jonathon Gibbons. ... High school: Mayfair (Lakewood, Calif.). ... College: Cal State Los Angeles.

TRANSACTIONS/CAREER NOTES: Selected by Toronto Blue Jays organization in 14th round of 1998 free-agent draft. ... Selected by Baltimore Orioles from Blue Jays organization in Rule 5 major league draft (December 11, 2000). ... On disabled list (August 5, 2001-remainder of season). ... On disabled list (May 26-June 14 and June 29-August 10, 2004); included rehabilitation assignments to Frederick and Bowie.

2005 GAMES PLAYED BY POSITION (MLB): OF—71, DH—42, 1B—22.

SCOUTING REPORT *Offense:* His production increased with a move up in the lineup, which provided more protection and better pitches to hit. Has a long, sweeping swing but good bat speed and is learning to hit the ball to the opposite field. Has problems with lefthanded pitching but has good power to all fields. Power numbers should continue to rise with more adjustments. Is not a good runner. *Defense:* His improvement in getting lateral jumps has made him a better right fielder. Still has more problems going back than coming in. Has surprising lateral range. Has arm strength but winds up to throw and has a slow release. *Outlook:* Gibbons is becoming a more compete offensive player. Doesn't strike out a lot because he rarely hits with two strikes. *Grade 7.4*

JAY GIBBONS'S HITTING ZONE

.100	.333	.244
.135	.395	.370
.400	.107	.343

LEFTY-RIGHTY SPLITS

vs.	Avg.	AB	H	2B	3B	HR	RBI	BB	SO	OBP	Slg.
L	.250	132	33	8	0	7	24	5	17	.277	.470
R	.287	356	102	25	3	19	55	23	39	.331	.534

Year Team (League)	Pos.	G	AB	R	H	2B	3B	HR	RBI	BB	SO	HBP	GDP	SB-CS	Avg.	OBP	SLG	OPS	E	Avg.
1998— Medicine Hat (Pio.)	1B	73	290	66	115	29	1	19	98	37	25	3	7	2-1	.397	.457	.700	1.157	6	.983
1999— Hagerstown (S. Atl.)	1B-OF	71	292	53	89	20	2	16	69	32	56	1	12	3-0	.305	.370	.551	.921	6	.975
— Dunedin (Fla. St.)	1B	60	212	34	66	14	0	9	39	25	38	0	4	2-1	.311	.382	.505	.887	5	.991
2000— Tennessee (Sou.)	1B-OF	132	474	85	152	38	1	19	75	61	67	10	10	3-1	.321	.404	.525	.929	8	.991
2001— Baltimore (A.L.)	DH-OF-1B	73	225	27	53	10	0	15	36	17	39	4	7	0-1	.236	.301	.480	.781	0	1.000
2002— Baltimore (A.L.)	OF-1B-DH	136	490	71	121	29	1	28	69	45	66	2	9	1-3	.247	.311	.482	.792	2	.995
2003— Baltimore (A.L.)	OF-1B-DH	160	625	80	173	39	2	23	100	49	89	3	12	0-0	.277	.330	.456	.786	6	.985
2004— Frederick (Carol.)	OF-DH	3	11	2	2	1	0	1	5	2	2	0	0	0-0	.182	.308	.545	.853	0	...
— Bowie (East.)	OF-DH	5	15	3	1	0	0	0	1	2	2	0	1	0-0	.067	.167	.067	.233	0	1.000
— Baltimore (A.L.)	OF-DH-1B	97	346	36	85	14	1	10	47	29	64	1	11	1-1	.246	.303	.379	.682	3	.988
2005— Baltimore (A.L.)	OF-DH-1B	139	488	72	135	33	3	26	79	28	56	1	15	0-0	.277	.317	.516	.833	3	.991
Major League totals (5 years)		605	2174	286	567	125	7	102	331	168	314	11	54	2-6	.261	.315	.466	.781	14	.991

C/IF

PERSONAL: Born August 7, 1975, in Oaxaca, Mexico. ... 6-2/234. ... Bats right, throws right. ... Name pronounced: heel.

TRANSACTIONS/CAREER NOTES: Contract purchased by Los Angeles Dodgers organization from Mexico City Red Devils of the Mexican League (February 15, 1996). ... Traded by Dodgers with P Kris Foster to Baltimore Orioles for P Mike Trombley (July 31, 2001). ... On disabled list (July 3-September 2, 2005); included rehabilitation assignment to Bowie.

2005 GAMES PLAYED BY POSITION (MLB): C—62.

SCOUTING REPORT Gil doesn't have a very quick bat and never has been able to shorten his swing. Likes the ball out over the plate; has a lot of trouble handling inside pitches. Doesn't adjust to breaking stuff, which he frequently chases in the dirt. Doesn't pull the ball a lot but has power. Has a strong arm but a slow release and is not very active behind the plate because of his weight. Range is limited. Has good hands. Calls a good game. Won't hit enough to play regularly. *Grade 4.6*

GERONIMO GIL'S HITTING ZONE

.000	.500	.000
.263	.364	.273
.125	.143	.143

LEFTY-RIGHTY SPLITS

vs.	Avg.	AB	H	2B	3B	HR	RBI	BB	SO	OBP	Slg.
L	.200	50	10	2	0	2	9	2	12	.231	.360
R	.187	75	14	1	0	2	8	3	11	.213	.280

Year Team (League)	Pos.	G	AB	R	H	2B	3B	HR	RBI	BB	SO	HBP	GDP	SB-CS	Avg.	OBP	SLG	OPS	E	Avg.
1993— M.C. R. Dev. (Mex.)	DH	1	1	0	0	0	0	0	0	0	1	...	...	0-0	.000	...	.000	...	...	...
1994—			Did not play.																	
1995— M.C. R. Dev. (Mex.)	OF	4	7	1	2	0	0	0	0	0	0	...	...	0-0	.286	...	.286	...	0	1.000
1996— Savannah (S. Atl.)	C	79	276	29	67	13	1	7	38	8	69	5	4	0-2	.243	.274	.373	.647	10	.983
1997— Vero Beach (Fla. St.)	C	66	213	30	53	13	1	6	24	15	41	4	5	3-0	.249	.310	.404	.714	13	.975
1998— San Antonio (Texas)	1B-C-OF	75	241	27	70	17	3	6	29	15	43	0	8	2-1	.290	.329	.461	.790	9	.972
1999— San Antonio (Texas)	1B-3B-C, OF	106	343	47	97	26	1	15	59	49	58	2	15	2-0	.283	.372	.496	.867	9	.986
2000— San Antonio (Texas)	1B-3B-C, OF	100	352	42	100	19	1	11	58	33	65	6	8	3-2	.284	.351	.438	.789	8	.988
— Albuquerque (PCL)	3B-C-OF	15	50	9	19	5	0	2	22	5	8	0	1	0-1	.380	.421	.600	1.021	3	.959
2001— Las Vegas (PCL)	C-1B-SS	82	281	40	83	15	0	9	40	16	56	2	9	0-1	.295	.334	.445	.779	3	.995
— Rochester (Int'l)	C	23	82	7	22	6	1	2	14	0	23	1	1	0-0	.268	.271	.439	.710	3	.986
— Baltimore (A.L.)	C	17	58	3	17	0	0	0	6	5	7	2	1	0-0	.293	.369	.328	.697	2	.985
2002— Baltimore (A.L.)	C	125	422	33	98	19	0	12	45	21	88	1	17	2-2	.232	.270	.363	.632	4	.995
2003— Ottawa (Int'l)	C-DH-1B	36	134	15	47	10	0	1	17	7	28	2	2	0-3	.351	.386	.448	.834	2	.992
— Baltimore (A.L.)	C	54	169	22	40	4	0	3	16	12	34	3	2	0-0	.237	.299	.314	.613	6	.984
2004— Ottawa (Int'l)	C-DH-1B	106	375	55	97	24	0	6	34	32	67	6	12	2-1	.259	.327	.371	.698	8	.990
— Baltimore (A.L.)	C	12	32	1	9	2	0	0	4	3	5	0	0	0-0	.281	.343	.344	.687	0	1.000
2005— Bowie (East.)	C	3	7	2	3	0	0	0	1	1	1	0	0	0-0	.429	.556	.429	.984	0	1.000
— Baltimore (A.L.)	C	64	125	7	24	3	0	2	17	1	10	0	0	0-0	.192	.220	.312	.532	2	.993
Major League totals (5 years)		272	806	66	188	30	0	19	88	46	157	6	30	2-2	.233	.279	.341	.620	14	.992

G

PERSONAL: Born January 20, 1971, in El Cajon, Calif. ... 5-10/205. ... Bats left, throws left. ... Full name: Brian Stephen Giles. ... Name pronounced: JYLES. ... High school: Granite Hills (El Cajon, Calif.). ... Brother of Marcus Giles, second baseman, Atlanta Braves.

TRANSACTIONS/CAREER NOTES: Selected by Cleveland Indians organization in 17th round of 1989 free-agent draft. ... On disabled list (June 1-July 7, 1998); included rehabilitation assignment to Buffalo. ... Traded by Indians to Pittsburgh Pirates for P Ricardo Rincon (November 18, 1998). ... On disabled list (April 11-May 7, 2003). ... Traded by Pirates to San Diego Padres for P Oliver Perez, OF Jason Bay and a player to be named (August 26, 2003); Padres acquired P Cory Stewart to complete deal (October 2, 2003).

2005 GAMES PLAYED BY POSITION (MLB): OF—155.

SCOUTING REPORT *Offense:* One of the game's most patient hitters, Giles led the league in walks in 2005. Hits for power and average with a sweeping type of swing. Likes to hook the ball and is a dominant pull hitter with good bat speed and a slight uppercut approach. Has a tendency to pull off the ball and can run into problems when he tries to pull outside pitches. Can be susceptible to off-speed stuff. *Defense:* Giles can play all three outfield positions. Has good throwing mechanics and gets on top of the ball. Charges the ball aggressively but is inconsistent breaking back on balls. Has surprising range going to the gaps. *Outlook:* His offensive numbers are down because he's getting used to a new ballpark with a big right field. Has an extremely aggressive makeup and is an effective run producer. *Grade 8.2*

BRIAN GILES' HITTING ZONE

.270	.414	.333
.319	.309	.287
.353	.326	.263

LEFTY-RIGHTY SPLITS

vs.	Avg.	AB	H	2B	3B	HR	RBI	BB	SO	OBP	Slg.
L	.289	166	48	11	4	2	23	32	25	.403	.440
R	.306	379	116	27	4	13	60	87	39	.431	.501

										BATTING								FIELDING	
Year	Team (League)	Pos.	G	AB	R	H	2B	3B	HR	RBI	BB	SO	HBP	GDP	SB-CS	Avg.	OBP	SLG	OPS	E	Avg.
1989— Burlington (Appal.)	OF	36	129	18	40	7	0	0	20	11	19	1	0	6-3	.310	.366	.364	.731	1	.982
1990— Watertown (NYP)	OF	70	246	44	71	15	2	1	23	48	23	0	3	11-8	.289	.403	.378	.781	1	.991
1991— Kinston (Carol.)	OF	125	394	71	122	14	0	4	47	68	70	2	5	19-7	.310	.411	.376	.787	5	.975
1992— Cant./Akr. (East.)	OF	23	74	6	16	4	0	0	3	10	10	0	4	3-1	.216	.310	.270	.580	0	1.000
— Kinston (Carol.)	OF	42	140	28	37	5	1	3	18	30	21	1	5	3-5	.264	.398	.379	.776	1	.987
1993— Cant./Akr. (East.)	OF	123	425	64	139	17	6	6	64	57	43	4	9	18-12	.327	.409	.438	.847	5	.974
1994— Charlotte (Int'l)	OF	128	434	74	136	18	3	16	58	55	61	2	5	8-5	.313	.390	.479	.869	4	.985
1995— Buffalo (A.A.)	OF-DH	123	413	67	128	18	8	15	67	54	40	8	9	7-3	.310	.395	.501	.896	5	.981
— Cleveland (A.L.)	OF-DH	6	9	6	5	0	0	1	3	0	1	0	0	0-0	.556	.556	.889	1.444	0	1.000
1996— Buffalo (A.A.)	OF	83	318	65	100	17	6	20	64	42	29	2	4	1-0	.314	.395	.594	.989	2	.986
— Cleveland (A.L.)	DH-OF	51	121	26	43	14	1	5	27	19	13	0	6	3-0	.355	.434	.612	1.045	0	1.000
1997— Cleveland (A.L.)	OF-DH	130	377	62	101	15	3	17	61	63	50	1	10	13-3	.268	.368	.459	.827	6	.972
1998— Cleveland (A.L.)	OF-DH	112	350	56	94	19	0	16	66	73	75	4	10	10-5	.269	.396	.460	.856	5	.978
— Buffalo (Int'l)	OF-DH	13	46	5	11	2	0	2	7	6	8	0	2	0-0	.239	.327	.413	.740	1	.947
1999— Pittsburgh (N.L.)	OF-DH	141	521	109	164	33	3	39	115	95	80	3	14	6-2	.315	.418	.614	1.032	3	.990
2000— Pittsburgh (N.L.)	OF	156	559	111	176	37	7	35	123	114	69	7	15	6-0	.315	.432	.594	1.026	6	.982
2001— Pittsburgh (N.L.)	OF	160	576	116	178	37	4	37	95	90	67	4	10	13-6	.309	.404	.590	.994	10	.969
2002— Pittsburgh (N.L.)	OF	153	497	95	148	37	5	38	103	135	74	7	10	15-6	.298	.450	.622	1.072	7	.973
2003— Pittsburgh (N.L.)	OF	105	388	70	116	30	4	16	70	85	48	6	8	0-3	.299	.430	.521	.951	2	.992
— San Diego (N.L.)	OF	29	104	23	31	4	2	4	18	20	10	2	4	4-0	.298	.414	.490	.904	2	.966
2004— San Diego (N.L.)	OF	159	609	97	173	33	7	23	94	89	80	4	12	10-3	.284	.374	.475	.849	7	.979
2005— San Diego (N.L.)	OF	158	545	92	164	38	6	15	83	* 119	64	2	14	13-5	.301	.423	.483	.905	4	.988
American League totals (4 years)		299	857	150	243	48	4	39	157	155	139	4	23	26-8	.284	.391	.485	.876	11	.976
National League totals (7 years)		1061	3799	713	1150	249	43	207	701	747	492	35	87	67-25	.303	.418	.554	.972	41	.981
Major League totals (11 years)		1360	4656	863	1393	297	47	246	858	902	631	39	110	93-33	.299	.413	.542	.954	52	.981

DIVISION SERIES RECORD

Year	Team (League)	Pos.	G	AB	R	H	2B	3B	HR	RBI	BB	SO	HBP	GDP	SB-CS	Avg.	OBP	SLG	OPS	E	Avg.
1996— Cleveland (A.L.)		1	1	0	0	0	0	0	0	0	0	0	0	0-0	.000	.000	.000	.000	...	...
1997— Cleveland (A.L.)	OF	3	7	0	1	0	0	0	0	0	1	0	0	0-0	.143	.143	.143	.286	0	1.000
1998— Cleveland (A.L.)	DH-OF	3	10	1	2	1	0	0	1	4	1	0	0	0-0	.200	.333	.300	.633	0	1.000
2005— San Diego (N.L.)	OF	3	13	0	3	0	0	0	1	1	2	0	1	1-0	.231	.286	.231	.516	0	1.000
Division series totals (4 years)		10	31	1	6	1	0	0	1	2	8	1	1	1-0	.194	.265	.226	.491	0	1.000

CHAMPIONSHIP SERIES RECORD

Year	Team (League)	Pos.	G	AB	R	H	2B	3B	HR	RBI	BB	SO	HBP	GDP	SB-CS	Avg.	OBP	SLG	OPS	E	Avg.
1997— Cleveland (A.L.)	OF	6	16	1	3	3	0	0	0	2	6	0	0	0-0	.188	.278	.375	.653	0	1.000
1998— Cleveland (A.L.)	OF	4	12	0	1	0	0	0	0	1	3	0	0	0-0	.083	.154	.083	.237	1	.875
Champ. series totals (2 years)		10	28	1	4	3	0	0	0	3	9	0	0	0-0	.143	.226	.250	.476	1	.941

WORLD SERIES RECORD

Year	Team (League)	Pos.	G	AB	R	H	2B	3B	HR	RBI	BB	SO	HBP	GDP	SB-CS	Avg.	OBP	SLG	OPS	E	Avg.
1997— Cleveland (A.L.)	OF	5	4	1	2	1	0	0	2	4	1	0	0	0-1	.500	.750	.750	1.500	0	1.000

ALL-STAR GAME RECORD

		G	AB	R	H	2B	3B	HR	RBI	BB	SO	HBP	GDP	SB-CS	Avg.	OBP	SLG	OPS	E	Avg.
All-Star Game totals (2 years)		2	3	0	0	0	0	0	0	0	0	0	0	0-0	.000	.000	.000	.000	...	...

G

PERSONAL: Born May 18, 1978, in San Diego. ... 5-8/180. ... Bats right, throws right. ... Full name: Marcus William Giles. ... Name pronounced: JYLES. ... High school: Granite Hills (Calif.). ... Junior college: Grossmont (Calif.). ... Brother of Brian Giles, outfielder, San Diego Padres.

TRANSACTIONS/CAREER NOTES: Selected by Atlanta Braves organization in 53rd round of 1996 free-agent draft. ... On disabled list (May 29-July 16, 2002); included rehabilitation assignment to Richmond. ... On disabled list (May 16-July 15, 2004); included rehabilitation assignments to Rome and Myrtle Beach.

RECORDS: Shares major league record for most doubles, game (4, July 27, 2003).

2005 GAMES PLAYED BY POSITION (MLB): 2B—149, 3B—1.

SCOUTING REPORT *Offense:* Giles has surprising power to the opposite field, but his aggressive approach leads to more strikeouts than walks. Likes to hit the ball up the middle. Is highly effective against lefthanded pitchers. Is an average runner but has good baserunning instincts. *Defense:* He isn't very fluid, and his hands are a little stiff, especially on balls hit right at him. Gets a good jump. Has improved his range to his right. Is aggressive coming across the bag to complete double plays. *Outlook:* Giles is a sparkplug on offense with his bat and aggressive makeup. Is an outstanding competitor and an overachiever who makes things happen both at the plate and in the field. *Grade 7.9*

MARCUS GILES' HITTING ZONE

.286	.280	.158
.339	.385	.342
.351	.298	.364

LEFTY-RIGHTY SPLITS

vs.	Avg.	AB	H	2B	3B	HR	RBI	BB	SO	OBP	Slg.
L	.298	141	42	10	0	4	12	13	13	.357	.454
R	.289	436	126	35	4	11	51	51	95	.367	.463

							BATTING										FIELDING	
Year Team (League)	Pos.	G	AB	R	H	2B	3B	HR	RBI	BB	SO	HBP	GDP	SB-CS	Avg.	OBP	SLG	OPS	E	Avg.
1997—Danville (Appal.)	2B	55	207	53	72	13	3	8	45	32	47	3	4	5-2	.348	.437	.556	.992	7	.962
1998—Macon (S. Atl.)	2B	135	505	111	166	38	3	37	108	85	103	10	15	12-5	.329	.433	.636	1.068	25	.954
1999—Myrtle Beach (Carol.)	2B	126	497	80	162	40	7	13	73	54	89	4	9	9-6	.326	.393	.513	.906	8	.985
2000—Greenville (Sou.)	2B	132	458	73	133	28	2	17	62	72	71	2	11	25-5	.290	.388	.472	.860	18	.973
2001—Richmond (Int'l)	2B-SS-3B																			
	OF	67	252	48	84	19	1	6	44	22	48	2	4	13-5	.333	.387	.488	.875	8	.975
—Atlanta (N.L.)	2B	68	244	36	64	10	2	9	31	28	37	0	8	2-5	.262	.338	.430	.769	6	.978
2002—Atlanta (N.L.)	2B-3B	68	213	27	49	10	1	8	23	25	41	2	5	1-1	.230	.311	.399	.714	8	.972
—Richmond (Int'l)	2B-3B	31	115	25	37	6	0	3	16	13	15	0	1	3-0	.322	.385	.452	.837	3	.970
2003—Atlanta (N.L.)	2B	145	551	101	174	49	2	21	69	59	80	11	7	14-4	.316	.390	.526	.917	14	.982
2004—Rome (S. Atl.)	DH	1	2	0	0	0	0	0	0	2	0	0	0	0-0	.000	.500	.000	.500	0	...
—Myrtle Beach (Carol.)	2B-DH	4	13	1	1	1	0	0	2	1	4	0	0	0-0	.077	.133	.154	.287	0	1.000
—Atlanta (N.L.)	2B	102	379	61	118	22	2	8	48	36	70	9	6	17-4	.311	.378	.443	.821	12	.975
2005—Atlanta (N.L.)	2B-3B	152	577	104	168	45	4	15	63	64	108	5	13	16-3	.291	.365	.461	.826	12	.984
Major League totals (5 years)		535	1964	329	573	136	11	61	234	212	336	27	39	50-17	.292	.366	.465	.831	52	.980

DIVISION SERIES RECORD

Year Team (League)	Pos.	G	AB	R	H	2B	3B	HR	RBI	BB	SO	HBP	GDP	SB-CS	Avg.	OBP	SLG	OPS	E	Avg.
2001—Atlanta (N.L.)	2B	3	12	2	3	1	0	0	1	0	3	0	0	0-0	.250	.250	.333	.583	0	1.000
2002—Atlanta (N.L.)	PH	3	2	0	1	0	0	0	0	0	0	0	0	0-0	.500	.500	.500	1.000	0	...
2003—Atlanta (N.L.)	2B	5	14	3	5	0	0	1	3	2	2	0	0	0-0	.357	.412	.571	.983	1	.955
2004—Atlanta (N.L.)	2B	5	24	1	3	0	0	0	1	0	6	0	0	1-0	.125	.125	.125	.250	0	1.000
2005—Atlanta (N.L.)	2B	4	20	5	4	1	0	0	0	2	5	1	0	0-0	.200	.304	.250	.554	0	1.000
Division series totals (5 years)		20	72	11	16	2	0	1	5	4	16	1	0	1-0	.222	.269	.292	.561	1	.990

CHAMPIONSHIP SERIES RECORD

Year Team (League)	Pos.	G	AB	R	H	2B	3B	HR	RBI	BB	SO	HBP	GDP	SB-CS	Avg.	OBP	SLG	OPS	E	Avg.
2001—Atlanta (N.L.)	2B	5	20	4	4	1	0	1	1	3	4	0	1	0-0	.200	.304	.400	.704	2	.917

GINTER, KEITH   3B/2B

PERSONAL: Born May 5, 1976, in Norwalk, Calif. ... 5-10/195. ... Bats right, throws right. ... Full name: Keith Michael Ginter. ... Name pronounced: GHIN-ter. ... High school: Fullerton (Calif.) Union. ... College: Texas Tech.

TRANSACTIONS/CAREER NOTES: Selected by Houston Astros organization in 10th round of 1998 free-agent draft. ... Traded by Astros to Milwaukee Brewers (September 5, 2002), completing deal in which Brewers traded IF Mark Loretta to Astros for two players to be named (August 31, 2002); Brewers acquired P Wayne Franklin as part of deal (September 3, 2002). ... On disabled list (July 25-August 28, 2004); included rehabilitation assignment to Indianapolis. ... Traded by Brewers to Oakland Athletics for OF Nelson Cruz and P Justin Lehr (December 15, 2004).

2005 GAMES PLAYED BY POSITION (MLB): 2B—25, 3B—12, DH—9, OF—2.

SCOUTING REPORT *Offense:* Ginter has a short, quick stroke and is a good fastball hitter. Likes to pull the ball and has some power. Will chase breaking pitches off the plate. *Defense:* He's a versatile player but isn't fluid in the field. Is better at third base than second because his range in the middle infield isn't good. Has a strong arm, slow release and only adequate hands. *Outlook:* Ginter must have a good spring to make the club. *Grade 4.7*

KEITH GINTER'S HITTING ZONE

.125	.000	.100
.208	.368	.091
.095	.429	.000

LEFTY-RIGHTY SPLITS

vs.	Avg.	AB	H	2B	3B	HR	RBI	BB	SO	OBP	Slg.
L	.164	61	10	3	0	0	14	4	11	.206	.213
R	.158	76	12	2	0	3	11	9	14	.256	.303

							BATTING										FIELDING	
Year Team (League)	Pos.	G	AB	R	H	2B	3B	HR	RBI	BB	SO	HBP	GDP	SB-CS	Avg.	OBP	SLG	OPS	E	Avg.
1998—Auburn (NYP)	2B	71	241	55	76	22	1	8	41	60	68	7	1	10-7	.315	.461	.515	.976	8	.971
1999—Kissimmee (Fla. St.)	2B	103	376	66	99	15	4	13	46	61	90	12	7	9-10	.263	.381	.428	.810	21	.959
—Jackson (Texas)	2B	9	34	9	13	1	0	1	6	4	6	2	0	0-0	.382	.463	.500	.963	2	.956
2000—Round Rock (Texas)	2B	125	462	108	154	30	3	26	92	82	127	24	9	24-11	.333	.457	.580	1.037	17	.972
—Houston (N.L.)	2B	5	8	3	2	0	0	1	3	1	3	0	0	0-0	.250	.300	.625	.925	0	1.000
2001—New Orleans (PCL)	2B-OF-3B	132	457	76	123	31	5	16	70	61	147	23	6	8-6	.269	.380	.464	.844	12	.975
—Houston (N.L.)		1	1	0	0	0	0	0	0	0	0	0	0	0-0	.000	.000	.000	.000	...	...
2002—New Orleans (PCL)	2B-3B-OF	121	435	70	115	28	1	12	54	56	97	12	7	3-4	.264	.362	.416	.778	22	.952
—Houston (N.L.)	3B-SS	5	5	1	1	0	0	0	0	2	1	1	0	0-0	.200	.500	.400	.900	1	.909
—Milwaukee (N.L.)	3B	21	76	6	18	8	0	1	8	15	14	0	0	0-0	.237	.363	.382	.744	2	.961
2003—Milwaukee (N.L.)	2B-3B-OF																			
	SS	127	358	51	92	15	2	14	44	37	87	17	8	1-1	.257	.352	.427	.779	8	.975
2004—Indianapolis (Int'l)	2B-3B-DH	4	14	3	3	2	0	1	3	1	4	0	0	0-0	.214	.267	.571	.838	0	1.000
—Milwaukee (N.L.)	2B-3B-DH																			
	OF	113	386	47	101	23	2	19	60	60	100	6	9	8-1	.262	.333	.479	.812	9	.974

G

Year	Team (League)	Pos.	G	AB	R	H	2B	3B	HR	RBI	BB	SO	HBP	GDP	SB-CS	BATTING Avg.	OBP	SLG	OPS	FIELDING E	Avg.
2005— Sacramento (PCL)	3B-2B-DH	14	57	9	19	8	0	3	12	4	11	1	0	0-0	.333	.387	.632	1.019	1	.974	
—Oakland (A.L.)	2B-3B-DH-OF	51	137	12	22	5	0	3	25	13	25	1	5	0-0	.161	.234	.263	.497	6	.959	
American League totals (1 year)		51	137	12	22	5	0	3	25	13	25	1	5	0-0	.161	.234	.263	.497	6	.959	
National League totals (5 years)		274	834	108	214	47	4	35	115	92	205	24	17	9-2	.257	.344	.448	.793	20	.973	
Major League totals (6 years)		325	971	120	236	52	4	38	140	105	230	25	22	9-2	.243	.329	.422	.751	26	.970	

GINTER, MATT   P

PERSONAL: Born December 24, 1977, in Winchester, Ky. ... 6-1/220. ... Throws right, bats right. ... Full name: Matthew Shane Ginter. ... Name pronounced: GHIN-ter. ... High school: George Rogers Clark (Winchester, Ky.). ... College: Mississippi State.

TRANSACTIONS/CAREER NOTES: Selected by New York Yankees organization in 17th round of 1996 free-agent draft; did not sign. ... Selected by Chicago White Sox organization in first round (22nd pick overall) of 1999 free-agent draft; pick received from New York Mets as compensation for signing Type A free-agent 3B Robin Ventura. ... Traded by White Sox to Mets for OF Timo Perez (March 27, 2004). ... On disabled list (September 11, 2004-remainder of season). ... Traded by Mets to Detroit Tigers for P Steve Colyer (April 2, 2005).

CAREER HITTING: 3-for-14 (.214), 1 R, 1 2B, 0 3B, 0 HR, 1 RBI.

MATT GINTER'S PITCHING ZONE

.600	.143	.200
.273	.579	.438
.333	.500	.333

LEFTY-RIGHTY SPLITS

vs.	Avg.	AB	H	2B	3B	HR	RBI	BB	SO	OBP	Slg.
L	.349	63	22	4	0	4	13	5	9	.391	.603
R	.333	81	27	4	1	2	12	4	6	.379	.481

Year	Team (League)	W	L	Pct.	ERA	WHIP	G	GS	CG	ShO	Hld.	Sv.-Opp.	IP	H	R	ER	HR	BB-IBB	SO	Avg.
1999— Ariz. White Sox (Ariz.)	1	0	1.000	3.24	0.96	3	3	0	0		1-...	8.1	5	4	3	0	3-0	10	.172
—Burlington (Midw.)	4	2	.667	4.05	1.43	9	9	0	0		0-...	40.0	38	20	18	3	19-0	29	.253
2000— Birmingham (Sou.)	11	8	.579	2.25	1.19	27	26	0	0		0-...	179.2	153	72	45	6	60-2	126	.233
—Chicago (A.L.)	1	0	1.000	13.50	2.68	7	0	0	0	0	0-1	9.1	18	14	14	5	7-0	6	.409
2001— Charlotte (Int'l)	2	3	.400	2.59	1.13	22	10	0	0	0	0-...	76.1	62	26	22	3	24-4	67	.219
—Chicago (A.L.)	1	0	1.000	5.22	1.21	20	0	0	0	0	0-0	39.2	34	23	23	2	14-2	24	.238
2002— Charlotte (Int'l)	1	0	1.000	3.94	1.88	13	0	0	0	0	0-0	16.0	20	8	7	3	10-1	9	.313
—Chicago (A.L.)	1	0	1.000	4.47	1.47	33	0	0	0	0	1-1	54.1	59	34	27	6	21-0	37	.278
2003— Chicago (A.L.)	0	0	...	13.50	0.90	3	0	0	0	0	0-0	3.1	2	5	5	1	1-0	0	.182
—Charlotte (Int'l)	3	5	.375	3.03	1.30	49	0	0	0	0	14-...	68.1	66	27	23	2	22-3	52	.249
2004— Norfolk (Int'l)	1	5	.167	2.95	0.98	11	11	0	0	0	0-...	64.0	55	26	21	4	8-1	49	.228
—New York (N.L.)	1	3	.250	4.54	1.47	15	14	0	0	0	0-0	69.1	82	41	35	8	20-5	38	.289
2005— Toledo (Int'l)	4	3	.571	4.33	1.19	17	10	0	0	3	0-0	68.2	72	35	33	9	10-0	49	.269
—Detroit (A.L.)	0	1	.000	6.17	1.66	14	1	0	0	0	0-0	35.0	49	25	24	6	9-1	15	.340
American League totals (5 years)	3	1	.750	5.91	1.51	77	1	0	0	0	1-2	141.2	162	101	93	20	52-3	82	.292
National League totals (1 year)	1	3	.250	4.54	1.47	15	14	0	0	0	0-0	69.1	82	41	35	8	20-5	38	.289
Major League totals (6 years)	4	4	.500	5.46	1.50	92	15	0	0	0	1-2	211.0	244	142	128	28	72-8	120	.291

GIPSON, CHARLES   OF/IF

PERSONAL: Born December 16, 1972, in Orange, Calif. ... 6-0/195. ... Bats right, throws right. ... Full name: Charles Wells Gipson. ... High school: Loara (Anaheim, Calif.). ... Junior college: Cypress (Calif.).

TRANSACTIONS/CAREER NOTES: Selected by Seattle Mariners organization in 63rd round of 1991 free-agent draft. ... On disabled list (July 11-September 1, 1999); included rehabilitation assignments to New Haven and Everett. ... Signed as a free agent by Chicago Cubs organization (January 21, 2003). ... Released by Cubs (March 29, 2003). ... Signed by New York Yankees organization (April 17, 2003). ... Signed as a free agent by Tampa Bay Devil Rays organization (February 13, 2004). ... Signed as a free agent by Houston Astros organization (January 6, 2005).

2005 GAMES PLAYED BY POSITION (MLB): OF—13.

LEFTY-RIGHTY SPLITS

vs.	Avg.	AB	H	2B	3B	HR	RBI	BB	SO	OBP	Slg.
L	.000	7	0	0	0	0	0	0	3	.000	.000
R	.500	4	2	1	0	0	1	1	0	.600	.750

Year	Team (League)	Pos.	G	AB	R	H	2B	3B	HR	RBI	BB	SO	HBP	GDP	SB-CS	BATTING Avg.	OBP	SLG	OPS	FIELDING E	Avg.
1992— Ariz. Mariners (Ariz.)		39	124	30	39	2	0	0	14	13	19	6	0	11-5	.315	.403	.331	.734	23	.876
1993— Appleton (Midw.)	2B-OF-SS	109	348	53	89	13	1	0	20	61	76	27	3	21-15	.256	.405	.299	.704	28	.933
1994— Riverside (Calif.)	OF	128	481	102	141	12	3	1	41	76	67	12	8	34-15	.293	.401	.337	.738	9	.972
1995— Port City (Sou.)	2B-OF	112	391	36	87	11	2	0	29	30	66	8	13	10-12	.223	.291	.261	.552	6	.977
1996— Port City (Sou.)	OF-SS	119	407	54	109	12	3	1	30	41	62	7	9	15-15	.268	.345	.319	.664	15	.961
1997— Memphis (Sou.)	2B-3B-OF-SS	88	320	56	79	9	4	1	28	34	71	13	4	31-6	.247	.342	.309	.652	23	.939
—Tacoma (PCL)	2B-3B-OF-SS	11	35	5	11	2	0	0	5	4	3	1	0	0-1	.314	.400	.371	.771	3	.912
1998— Seattle (A.L.)	OF-3B-DH	44	51	11	12	1	0	0	2	5	9	1	1	2-1	.235	.316	.255	.571	2	.957
—Tacoma (PCL)	2B-3B-OF-SS	75	278	39	67	16	2	0	11	27	50	6	17	14-11	.241	.322	.313	.634	11	.954
1999— Seattle (A.L.)	OF-3B-DH-SS-2B	55	80	16	18	5	2	0	6	6	13	1	4	3-4	.225	.287	.338	.625	1	.967
—Tacoma (PCL)	SS-OF-3B-2B-DH	47	174	26	52	6	3	0	21	14	24	0	5	18-4	.299	.361	.368	.729	9	.940
—New Haven (East.)	2B-3B-OF-OF-SS	5	18	2	0	0	0	0	3	0	0	0	0	1-0	.000	.143	.000	.143	1	.944
—Everett (N'west)	SS	1	2	0	1	0	1	0	1	2	0	0	0	1-0	.500	.750	1.500	2.250	0	1.000
2000— Seattle (A.L.)	OF-3B-SS-DH	59	29	7	9	1	0	0	3	4	0	0	0	2-3	.310	.394	.414	.808	1	1.000
—Tacoma (PCL)	OF-3B-SS-2B	67	214	27	53	6	0	1	22	31	38	3	7	16-7	.248	.347	.346	.692	6	.971
2001— Seattle (A.L.)	OF-DH-3B-SS-2B	94	64	16	14	2	0	0	5	4	20	2	1	1-1	.219	.282	.313	.594	2	.972
2002— Seattle (A.L.)	OF-3B-DH	79	72	22	17	5	2	0	8	9	14	1	3	4-0	.236	.329	.361	.690	2	.972
2003— New York (A.L.)	OF-DH	18	10	3	2	0	0	0	2	1	2	0	0	2-1	.200	.273	.200	.473	0	1.000
—Columbus (Int'l)	OF-3B-2B	31	120	17	33	6	1	0	5	18	5	1	0	5-6	.275	.351	.342	.692	3	.972

G

Year Team (League)	Pos.	G	AB	R	H	2B	3B	HR	RBI	BB	SO	HBP	GDP	SB-CS	Avg.	OBP	SLG	OPS	E	Avg.
2004—Tampa Bay (A.L.)	OF-SS-DH	5	4	1	2	0	0	0	0	0	1	0	0	1-0	.500	.500	.500	1.000	0	1.000
—Durham (Int'l)	OF-3B-2B DH-SS	96	297	50	88	14	3	2	27	35	57	7	5	8-8	.296	.381	.384	.765	8	.966
2005—Round Rock (PCL)	OF	110	393	58	119	24	3	2	25	25	75	8	3	19-9	.303	.356	.394	.750	10	.980
—Houston (N.L.)	OF	19	11	2	2	1	0	0	1	1	3	0	0	1-1	.182	.250	.273	.523	0	1.000
American League totals (7 years)		354	310	76	74	14	7	0	29	29	68	5	8	15-10	.239	.313	.329	.642	9	.972
National League totals (1 year)		19	11	2	2	1	0	0	1	1	3	0	0	1-1	.182	.250	.273	.523	0	1.000
Major League totals (8 years)		373	321	78	76	15	7	0	30	30	71	5	8	16-11	.237	.311	.327	.638	9	.973

DIVISION SERIES RECORD

Year Team (League)	Pos.	G	AB	R	H	2B	3B	HR	RBI	BB	SO	HBP	GDP	SB-CS	Avg.	OBP	SLG	OPS	E	Avg.
2000—Seattle (A.L.)		Did not play.																		
2001—Seattle (A.L.)		1	1	0	0	0	0	0	0	0	0	0	0	0-0	.000	.000	.000	.000	...	...

CHAMPIONSHIP SERIES RECORD

Year Team (League)	Pos.	G	AB	R	H	2B	3B	HR	RBI	BB	SO	HBP	GDP	SB-CS	Avg.	OBP	SLG	OPS	E	Avg.
2000—Seattle (A.L.)	OF	2	0	0	0	0	0	0	0	0	0	0	0	0-0	...	...	...	...	0	...
2001—Seattle (A.L.)	DH-OF	2	1	1	0	0	0	0	0	0	0	0	0	0-0	.000	.000	.000	.000	0	.000
Champ. series totals (2 years)		4	1	1	0	0	0	0	0	0	0	0	0	0-0	.000	.000	.000	.000	0	.000

GLAUS, TROY   3B

PERSONAL: Born August 3, 1976, in Tarzana, Calif. ... 6-5/240. ... Bats right, throws right. ... Full name: Troy Edward Glaus. ... Name pronounced: gloss. ... High school: Carlsbad (Calif.). ... College: UCLA.

TRANSACTIONS/CAREER NOTES: Selected by San Diego Padres organization in second round of 1994 free-agent draft; did not sign. ... Selected by Anaheim Angels organization in first round (third pick overall) of 1997 free-agent draft. ... On disabled list (July 22-August 11, 2003); included rehabilitation assignment to Rancho Cucamonga. ... On disabled list (May 12-August 29, 2004); included rehabilitation assignment to Rancho Cucamonga. ... Signed as a free agent by Arizona Diamondbacks (December 9, 2004).

2005 GAMES PLAYED BY POSITION (MLB): 3B—145, DH—1.

SCOUTING REPORT **Offense:** Glaus is one of the league's best pure power hitters. Swing is long and is vulnerable to off-speed stuff. Likes the ball over the plate. Has improved his bat speed and ability to extend his arms. Has exceptional power to all fields but is streaky and appears to guess at times. Isn't a good runner and has lost a step. **Defense:** Glaus has good hands and range, but he is a slightly below-average fielder. Charges the ball well. Has good arm strength and accuracy but has a slow release. Is agile for his size. **Outlook:** Glaus ended concerns about his surgically repaired shoulder with a solid 2005 season. *Grade 8.0*

TROY GLAUS' HITTING ZONE

.333	.316	.214
.301	.264	.270
.258	.296	.346

LEFTY-RIGHTY SPLITS

vs.	Avg.	AB	H	2B	3B	HR	RBI	BB	SO	OBP	Slg.
L	.244	131	32	6	0	10	27	32	30	.389	.519
R	.263	407	107	23	1	27	70	52	115	.353	.523

Year Team (League)	Pos.	G	AB	R	H	2B	3B	HR	RBI	BB	SO	HBP	GDP	SB-CS	Avg.	OBP	SLG	OPS	E	Avg.
1998—Midland (Texas)	3B	50	188	51	58	11	2	19	51	39	41	2	4	4-2	.309	.430	.691	1.122	11	.925
—Vancouver (PCL)	3B	59	219	33	67	16	0	16	42	21	55	3	1	3-2	.306	.374	.598	.973	13	.932
—Anaheim (A.L.)	3B	48	165	19	36	9	0	1	23	15	51	0	3	1-0	.218	.280	.291	.571	7	.941
1999—Anaheim (A.L.)	3B-DH	154	551	85	132	29	0	29	79	71	143	6	9	5-1	.240	.331	.450	.781	19	.954
2000—Anaheim (A.L.)	3B-SS-DH	159	563	120	160	37	1	*47	102	112	163	2	14	14-11	.284	.404	.604	1.008	§33	.934
2001—Anaheim (A.L.)	3B-DH-SS	161	588	100	147	38	2	41	108	107	158	6	16	10-3	.250	.367	.531	.898	19	.954
2002—Anaheim (A.L.)	3B-SS	156	569	99	142	24	1	30	111	88	144	6	12	10-3	.250	.352	.453	.805	20	.950
2003—Anaheim (A.L.)	3B-DH	91	319	53	79	17	2	16	50	46	73	1	8	7-2	.248	.343	.464	.807	16	.923
—Rancho Cuca. (Calif.)	DH	2	6	1	2	0	0	0	1	3	2	0	0	0-0	.333	.556	.333	.889	0	...
2004—Rancho Cuca. (Calif.)	DH	5	15	4	3	0	0	2	4	6	5	0	0	0-0	.200	.429	.600	1.029	0	...
—Anaheim (A.L.)	DH-3B	58	207	47	52	11	1	18	42	31	52	3	6	2-3	.251	.355	.575	.930	2	.950
2005—Arizona (N.L.)	3B-DH	149	538	78	139	29	1	37	97	84	145	7	7	4-2	.258	.363	.522	.885	24	.946
American League totals (7 years)		827	2962	523	748	165	7	182	515	470	784	24	68	49-23	.253	.357	.497	.854	116	.944
National League totals (1 year)		149	538	78	139	29	1	37	97	84	145	7	7	4-2	.258	.363	.522	.885	24	.946
Major League totals (8 years)		976	3500	601	887	194	8	219	612	554	929	31	75	53-25	.253	.358	.501	.859	140	.945

DIVISION SERIES RECORD

Year Team (League)	Pos.	G	AB	R	H	2B	3B	HR	RBI	BB	SO	HBP	GDP	SB-CS	Avg.	OBP	SLG	OPS	E	Avg.
2002—Anaheim (A.L.)	3B	4	16	4	5	0	0	3	3	1	3	1	0	0-0	.313	.389	.875	1.264	1	.929
2004—Anaheim (A.L.)	DH	3	11	3	4	2	0	2	3	2	4	0	0	0-0	.364	.462	1.091	1.552	0	...
Division series totals (2 years)		7	27	7	9	2	0	5	6	3	7	1	0	0-0	.333	.419	.963	1.382	1	.929

CHAMPIONSHIP SERIES RECORD

Year Team (League)	Pos.	G	AB	R	H	2B	3B	HR	RBI	BB	SO	HBP	GDP	SB-CS	Avg.	OBP	SLG	OPS	E	Avg.
2002—Anaheim (A.L.)	3B	5	19	4	6	0	1	1	2	5	0	0	0	0-0	.316	.381	.579	.960	0	1.000

WORLD SERIES RECORD

Year Team (League)	Pos.	G	AB	R	H	2B	3B	HR	RBI	BB	SO	HBP	GDP	SB-CS	Avg.	OBP	SLG	OPS	E	Avg.
2002—Anaheim (A.L.)	3B	7	26	7	10	3	0	3	8	4	6	0	1	0-0	.385	.467	.846	1.313	1	.938

ALL-STAR GAME RECORD

	G	AB	R	H	2B	3B	HR	RBI	BB	SO	HBP	GDP	SB-CS	Avg.	OBP	SLG	OPS	E	Avg.
All-Star Game totals (3 years)	3	5	0	0	0	0	0	0	0	2	0	0	0-0	.000	.000	.000	.000	0	1.000

GLAVINE, TOM   P

PERSONAL: Born March 25, 1966, in Concord, Mass. ... 6-0/185. ... Throws left, bats left. ... Full name: Thomas Michael Glavine. ... Name pronounced: GLA-vin. ... High school: Billerica (Mass.). ... Brother of Mike Glavine, first baseman with New York Mets (2003).

G

TRANSACTIONS/CAREER NOTES: Selected by Atlanta Braves organization in second round of June 1984 free-agent draft. ... Signed as a free agent by New York Mets (December 5, 2002).

HONORS: Named N.L. Pitcher of the Year by THE SPORTING NEWS (1991 and 2000). ... Named N.L. Cy Young Award winner by Baseball Writers' Association of America (1991 and 1998).

CAREER HITTING: 223-for-1195 (.187), 82 R, 23 2B, 2 3B, 1 HR, 83 RBI.

SCOUTING REPORT **Throws:** Glavine's fastball ranges from 84-88 mph, and he complements it with a curveball and changeup. **Tendencies:** He is the prototypical finesse pitcher with an exceptional feel for his craft. Doesn't throw hard but moves his fastball around the plate. Never throws the same pitch in the same spot to a hitter. Has total command of the strike zone and knows how to set up hitters. Varies his speeds and location, often expanding the plate laterally until the umpire forces him back in. Curve has good rotation, but the change might be his best pitch—he can throw it on any count and in any situation. **Outlook:** Preparation, instincts and experience allow Glavine to win despite declining stuff. *Grade 7.1*

TOM GLAVINE'S PITCHING ZONE

.379	.500	.217
.288	.365	.257
.305	.097	.302

LEFTY-RIGHTY SPLITS

vs.	Avg.	AB	H	2B	3B	HR	RBI	BB	SO	OBP	Slg.
L	.323	167	54	8	1	1	21	15	25	.383	.401
R	.267	648	173	35	4	11	65	46	80	.316	.384

Year Team (League)	W	L	Pct.	ERA	WHIP	G	GS	CG	ShO	Hld.	Sv.-Opp.	IP	H	R	ER	HR	BB-IBB	SO	Avg.
1984— GC Braves (GCL)	2	3	.400	3.34	1.30	8	7	0	0	...	0-...	32.1	29	17	12	0	13-0	34	.236
1985— Sumter (S. Atl.)	9	6	.600	2.35	1.11	26	26	2	1	...	0-...	168.2	114	58	44	6	73-0	174	.193
1986— Greenville (Sou.)	11	6	.647	3.41	1.37	22	22	2	1	...	0-...	145.1	129	62	55	14	70-3	114	.237
—Richmond (Int'l)	1	5	.167	5.63	1.68	7	7	1	1	...	0-...	40.0	40	29	25	4	27-0	12	.260
1987— Richmond (Int'l)	6	12	.333	3.35	1.32	22	22	4	1	...	0-...	150.1	142	70	56	15	56-3	91	.248
—Atlanta (N.L.)	2	4	.333	5.54	1.75	9	9	0	0	0	0-0	50.1	55	34	31	5	33-4	20	.279
1988— Atlanta (N.L.)	7	*17	.292	4.56	1.35	34	34	1	0	0	0-0	195.1	201	111	99	12	63-7	84	.270
1989— Atlanta (N.L.)	14	8	.636	3.68	1.14	29	29	6	4	0	0-0	186.0	172	88	76	20	40-3	90	.251
1990— Atlanta (N.L.)	10	12	.455	4.28	1.45	33	33	1	0	0	0-0	214.1	232	111	102	18	78-10	129	.281
1991— Atlanta (N.L.)	•20	11	.645	2.55	1.09	34	34	•9	1	0	0-0	246.2	201	83	70	17	69-6	192	.222
1992— Atlanta (N.L.)	•20	8	.714	2.76	1.19	33	33	7	•5	0	0-0	225.0	197	81	69	6	70-7	129	.235
1993— Atlanta (N.L.)	•22	6	.786	3.20	1.36	36	•36	4	2	0	0-0	239.1	236	91	85	16	90-7	120	.259
1994— Atlanta (N.L.)	13	9	.591	3.97	1.42	25	25	2	0	0	0-0	165.1	173	76	73	10	70-10	140	.268
1995— Atlanta (N.L.)	16	7	.696	3.08	1.25	29	29	3	1	0	0-0	198.2	182	76	68	9	66-0	127	.246
1996— Atlanta (N.L.)	15	10	.600	2.98	1.30	36	*36	1	0	0	0-0	235.1	222	91	78	14	85-7	181	.249
1997— Atlanta (N.L.)	14	7	.667	2.96	1.15	33	33	5	2	0	0-0	240.0	197	86	79	20	79-9	152	.226
1998— Atlanta (N.L.)	*20	6	.769	2.47	1.20	33	33	4	3	0	0-0	229.1	202	67	63	13	74-2	157	.238
1999— Atlanta (N.L.)	14	11	.560	4.12	1.46	35	*35	2	0	0	0-0	234.0	*259	115	107	18	83-14	138	.287
2000— Atlanta (N.L.)	*21	9	.700	3.40	1.19	35	*35	4	2	0	0-0	241.0	222	101	91	24	65-6	152	.244
2001— Atlanta (N.L.)	16	7	.696	3.57	1.41	35	*35	1	1	0	0-0	219.1	213	92	87	24	97-10	116	.261
2002— Atlanta (N.L.)	18	11	.621	2.96	1.28	36	*36	2	1	0	0-0	224.2	210	85	74	21	78-8	127	.252
2003— New York (N.L.)	9	14	.391	4.52	1.48	32	32	0	0	0	0-0	183.1	205	94	92	21	66-7	82	.288
2004— New York (N.L.)	11	14	.440	3.60	1.29	33	33	1	1	0	0-0	212.1	204	94	85	20	70-10	109	.252
2005— New York (N.L.)	13	13	.500	3.53	1.36	33	33	2	1	0	0-0	211.1	227	88	83	12	61-5	105	.279
Major League totals (19 years)	**275**	**184**	**.599**	**3.44**	**1.30**	**603**	**603**	**55**	**24**	**0**	**0-0**	**3951.2**	**3810**	**1664**	**1512**	**300**	**1337-132**	**2350**	**.255**

DIVISION SERIES RECORD

Year Team (League)	W	L	Pct.	ERA	WHIP	G	GS	CG	ShO	Hld.	Sv.-Opp.	IP	H	R	ER	HR	BB-IBB	SO	Avg.
1995— Atlanta (N.L.)	0	0	...	2.57	0.86	1	1	0	0	0	0-0	7.0	5	3	2	1	1-0	3	.185
1996— Atlanta (N.L.)	1	0	1.000	1.35	1.20	1	1	0	0	0	0-0	6.2	5	1	1	0	3-0	7	.217
1997— Atlanta (N.L.)	1	0	1.000	4.50	1.67	1	1	0	0	0	0-0	6.0	5	3	3	0	5-0	4	.217
1998— Atlanta (N.L.)	0	0	...	1.29	0.57	1	1	0	0	0	0-0	7.0	3	1	1	0	1-0	8	.136
1999— Atlanta (N.L.)	0	0	...	3.00	1.33	1	1	0	0	0	0-0	6.0	5	2	2	0	3-0	6	.238
2000— Atlanta (N.L.)	0	1	.000	27.00	3.00	1	1	0	0	0	0-0	2.1	6	7	7	2	1-0	2	.500
2001— Atlanta (N.L.)	1	0	1.000	0.00	0.25	1	1	0	0	0	0-0	8.0	6	0	0	0	2-0	3	.222
2002— Atlanta (N.L.)	0	2	.000	15.26	3.13	2	2	0	0	0	0-0	7.2	17	13	13	1	7-3	4	.459
Division series totals (8 years)	**3**	**3**	**.500**	**5.15**	**1.48**	**9**	**9**	**0**	**0**	**0**	**0-0**	**50.2**	**52**	**30**	**29**	**4**	**23-3**	**37**	**.271**

CHAMPIONSHIP SERIES RECORD

Year Team (League)	W	L	Pct.	ERA	WHIP	G	GS	CG	ShO	Hld.	Sv.-Opp.	IP	H	R	ER	HR	BB-IBB	SO	Avg.
1991— Atlanta (N.L.)	0	2	.000	3.21	1.29	2	2	0	0	0	0-0	14.0	12	5	5	1	6-2	11	.226
1992— Atlanta (N.L.)	0	2	.000	12.27	2.18	2	2	0	0	0	0-0	7.1	13	11	10	3	3-1	2	.382
1993— Atlanta (N.L.)	1	0	1.000	2.57	0.86	1	1	0	0	0	0-0	7.0	6	2	2	1	0-0	5	.222
1995— Atlanta (N.L.)	0	0	...	1.29	1.29	1	1	0	0	0	0-0	7.0	7	1	1	0	2-1	5	.292
1996— Atlanta (N.L.)	1	1	.500	2.08	0.77	2	2	0	0	0	0-0	13.0	10	3	3	2	0-0	9	.217
1997— Atlanta (N.L.)	1	1	.500	5.40	1.80	2	2	0	0	0	0-0	13.1	13	8	8	0	11-3	9	.271
1998— Atlanta (N.L.)	0	2	.000	2.31	1.89	2	2	0	0	0	0-0	11.2	13	6	3	0	9-0	8	.283
1999— Atlanta (N.L.)	1	0	1.000	0.00	1.14	1	1	0	0	0	0-0	7.0	7	0	0	0	1-0	5	.259
2001— Atlanta (N.L.)	1	1	.500	1.50	1.25	2	2	0	0	0	0-0	12.0	10	4	2	1	5-0	5	.217
Champ. series totals (9 years)	**5**	**9**	**.357**	**3.31**	**1.39**	**15**	**15**	**0**	**0**	**0**	**0-0**	**92.1**	**91**	**40**	**34**	**8**	**37-7**	**62**	**.259**

WORLD SERIES RECORD

Year Team (League)	W	L	Pct.	ERA	WHIP	G	GS	CG	ShO	Hld.	Sv.-Opp.	IP	H	R	ER	HR	BB-IBB	SO	Avg.
1991— Atlanta (N.L.)	1	1	.500	2.70	1.13	2	2	1	0	0	0-0	13.1	8	6	4	2	7-0	8	.174
1992— Atlanta (N.L.)	1	1	.500	1.59	0.82	2	2	0	0	0	0-0	17.0	10	3	3	2	4-0	8	.175
1995— Atlanta (N.L.)	2	0	1.000	1.29	0.71	2	2	0	0	0	0-0	14.0	4	2	2	1	6-0	11	.087
1996— Atlanta (N.L.)	0	1	.000	1.29	1.00	1	1	0	0	0	0-0	7.0	4	2	1	0	3-0	8	.174
1999— Atlanta (N.L.)	0	0	...	5.14	1.00	1	1	0	0	0	0-0	7.0	7	5	4	3	0-0	3	.250
World Series totals (5 years)	**4**	**3**	**.571**	**2.16**	**0.91**	**8**	**8**	**3**	**0**	**0**	**0-0**	**58.1**	**33**	**18**	**14**	**8**	**20-0**	**38**	**.165**

ALL-STAR GAME RECORD

	W	L	Pct.	ERA	WHIP	G	GS	CG	ShO	Hld.	Sv.-Opp.	IP	H	R	ER	HR	BB-IBB	SO	Avg.
All-Star Game totals (6 years)	**0**	**1**	**.000**	**10.13**	**2.50**	**6**	**2**	**0**	**0**	**0**	**0-0**	**8.0**	**16**	**9**	**9**	**0**	**4-0**	**7**	**.421**

G

GLOAD, ROSS — OF/1B

PERSONAL: Born April 5, 1976, in Brooklyn, N.Y. ... 6-0/185. ... Bats left, throws left. ... Full name: Ross Peter Gload. ... High school: East Hampton (N.Y.). ... College: South Florida.

TRANSACTIONS/CAREER NOTES: Selected by Florida Marlins organization in 13th round of 1997 free-agent draft. ... Traded by Marlins with P David Noyce to Chicago Cubs for OF Henry Rodriguez (July 31, 2000). ... Claimed on waivers by Colorado Rockies (September 12, 2001). ... Traded by Rockies with P Craig House to New York Mets as part of three-team deal in which Rockies acquired 1B/3B Todd Zeile, OF Benny Agbayani and cash from Mets, Mets acquired P Jeff D'Amico, OF Jeromy Burnitz, IF Lou Collier, OF/1B Mark Sweeney and cash from Milwaukee Brewers, and Brewers acquired P Glendon Rusch and IF Lenny Harris from Mets and OF Alex Ochoa from Rockies (January 21, 2002). ... Traded by Mets to Rockies for cash (January 27, 2002). ... Traded by Rockies to Chicago White Sox for P Wade Parrish (March 27, 2003). ... On disabled list (April 25-July 17, 2005); included rehabilitation assignment to Charlotte.
2005 GAMES PLAYED BY POSITION (MLB): 1B—24, OF—3.

SCOUTING REPORT** **Offense: Gload has a very fluid stroke and makes consistent contact. Is a line-drive hitter who uses the whole field but lacks power. Lost some bat speed after his shoulder injury last season. ***Defense:*** Gload is versatile and can play both the outfield and first base. Natural position is first, where he has excellent agility and soft, quick hands. Mobile moving to either side. ***Outlook:*** He's difficult to evaluate because of the shoulder injury, but he has a good stroke. Doesn't have enough power to play every day. ***Grade 5.8***

LEFTY-RIGHTY SPLITS

vs.	Avg.	AB	H	2B	3B	HR	RBI	BB	SO	OBP	Slg.
L	.000	5	0	0	0	0	0	0	2	.000	.000
R	.189	37	7	2	0	0	5	2	7	.231	.243

Year Team (League)	Pos.	G	AB	R	H	2B	3B	HR	RBI	BB	SO	HBP	GDP	SB-CS	Avg.	OBP	SLG	OPS	E	Avg.
1997—Utica (N.Y.-Penn)	1B	68	245	28	64	15	2	3	43	28	57	2	5	1-1	.261	.336	.376	.711	*16	.973
1998—Kane Co. (Midw.)	1B	132	501	77	157	*41	3	12	92	58	84	3	13	7-6	.313	.386	.479	.865	14	.989
1999—Brevard County (FSL)	1B	133	490	80	146	26	3	10	74	53	76	5	8	3-1	.298	.369	.424	.793	9	.993
2000—Portland (East.)	OF-1B	100	401	60	114	28	4	16	65	29	53	2	4	4-1	.284	.333	.494	.826	7	.986
—Iowa (PCL)	OF	28	104	24	42	10	2	14	39	9	13	1	2	1-1	.404	.452	.942	1.394	4	.917
—Chicago (N.L.)	OF-1B	18	31	4	6	0	1	1	3	3	10	1	1	0-0	.194	.257	.355	.612	0	1.000
2001—Iowa (PCL)	OF-1B	133	475	70	141	32	*10	15	93	35	88	3	8	9-7	.297	.344	.501	.845	3	.994
2002—Colo. Springs (PCL)	1B-OF	104	442	69	139	28	6	16	71	18	59	1	4	9-4	.314	.338	.514	.852	11	.987
—Colorado (N.L.)	1B-OF	26	31	4	8	1	0	1	4	3	7	0	0	0-0	.258	.324	.387	.711	0	1.000
2003—Charlotte (Int'l)	1B-OF	133	508	72	160	40	6	18	70	29	60	1	12	6-3	.315	.349	.524	.873	8	.991
2004—Chicago (A.L.)	1B-OF-DH	110	234	28	75	16	0	7	44	20	37	2	11	0-3	.321	.375	.479	.853	3	.990
2005—Charlotte (Int'l)	1B-DH-OF	60	236	45	86	22	1	15	45	22	37	1	2	0-1	.364	.416	.657	1.073	2	.995
—Chicago (A.L.)	1B-OF	28	42	2	7	2	0	0	5	2	9	0	1	0-0	.167	.205	.214	.419	1	.988
American League totals (2 years)		138	276	30	82	18	0	7	49	22	46	2	12	0-3	.297	.350	.438	.788	4	.989
National League totals (2 years)		44	62	8	14	1	1	2	7	6	17	1	1	0-0	.226	.290	.371	.661	0	1.000
Major League totals (4 years)		182	338	38	96	19	1	9	56	28	63	2	13	0-3	.284	.339	.426	.765	4	.990

GLOVER, GARY — P

PERSONAL: Born December 3, 1976, in Cleveland. ... 6-5/220. ... Throws right, bats right. ... Full name: John Gary Glover. ... High school: DeLand (Fla.).
TRANSACTIONS/CAREER NOTES: Selected by Toronto Blue Jays organization in 15th round of 1994 free-agent draft. ... Traded by Blue Jays to Chicago White Sox for P Scott Eyre (November 7, 2000). ... Traded by White Sox with Ps Scott Dunn and Tim Bittner to Anaheim Angels for Ps Scott Schoeneweis and Doug Nickle (July 30, 2003). ... Signed as a free agent by Chicago Cubs organization (December 18, 2003). ... Released by Cubs (June 5, 2004). ... Signed by Minnesota Twins organization (June 7, 2004). ... Released by Twins (July 2, 2004). ... Signed by Milwaukee Brewers organization (July 12, 2004).
CAREER HITTING: 2-for-28 (.071), 3 R, 0 2B, 0 3B, 0 HR, 1 RBI.

GARY GLOVER'S PITCHING ZONE

.333	.308	.286
.292	.409	.371
.500	.300	.400

LEFTY-RIGHTY SPLITS

vs.	Avg.	AB	H	2B	3B	HR	RBI	BB	SO	OBP	Slg.
L	.256	125	32	7	1	5	16	11	32	.321	.448
R	.318	132	42	11	2	5	20	9	26	.361	.545

Year Team (League)	W	L	Pct.	ERA	WHIP	G	GS	CG	ShO	Hld.	Sv.-Opp.	IP	H	R	ER	HR	BB-IBB	SO	Avg.
1994—GC Jays (GCL)	0	0	...	47.25	6.00	2	0	0	0	...	0-...	1.1	4	8	7	1	4-0	2	.500
1995—GC Jays (GCL)	3	7	.300	4.91	1.41	12	10	2	0	...	0-...	62.1	62	48	34	4	26-0	46	.264
1996—Medicine Hat (Pio.)	3	12	.200	7.75	1.77	15	15	2	0	...	0-...	83.2	119	94	72	14	29-1	54	.322
1997—Hagerstown (S. Atl.)	6	17	.261	3.73	1.28	28	28	3	0	...	0-...	173.2	165	94	72	2	58-1	155	.245
1998—Knoxville (Sou.)	0	5	.000	6.75	1.85	8	8	0	0	...	0-...	37.1	41	36	28	2	28-0	14	.277
—Dunedin (Fla. St.)	7	6	.538	4.28	1.40	19	18	0	0	...	0-...	109.1	117	66	52	8	36-0	88	.270
1999—Knoxville (Sou.)	8	2	.800	3.56	1.13	13	13	1	0	...	0-...	86.0	70	39	34	5	27-0	77	.224
—Syracuse (Int'l)	4	6	.400	5.19	1.68	14	14	0	0	...	0-...	76.1	93	50	44	10	35-0	57	.301
—Toronto (A.L.)	0	0	...	0.00	1.00	1	0	0	0	...	0-0	1.0	0	0	0	0	1-0	0	.000
2000—Syracuse (Int'l)	9	9	.500	5.02	1.46	27	27	1	0	...	0-...	166.2	181	104	93	21	62-0	119	.274
2001—Chicago (A.L.)	5	5	.500	4.93	1.30	46	11	0	0	7	0-1	100.1	98	61	55	16	32-3	63	.252
—Charlotte (Int'l)	2	1	.667	1.88	0.68	6	6	1	1	...	0-...	38.1	21	8	8	1	5-0	29	.158
2002—Chicago (A.L.)	7	8	.467	5.20	1.36	41	22	0	0	2	1-1	138.1	136	86	80	21	52-1	70	.253
2003—Chicago (A.L.)	1	0	1.000	4.54	1.60	24	0	0	0	1	0-0	35.2	43	18	18	3	14-2	23	.305
—Anaheim (A.L.)	1	0	1.000	1.00	1.56	18	0	0	0	0	0-0	27.0	34	15	15	3	8-1	14	.315
2004—Iowa (PCL)	3	2	.600	7.92	1.86	20	1	0	0	0	0-0	30.2	43	29	27	8	14-0	18	.328
—Rochester (Int'l)	0	1	.000	8.44	2.00	5	4	0	0	...	0-...	16.0	27	15	15	6	5-0	8	.386
—Indianapolis (Int'l)	3	3	.500	3.98	1.43	9	7	0	0	0	0-0	40.2	47	19	18	1	11-0	18	.307
—Milwaukee (N.L.)	2	1	.667	3.50	1.44	4	3	0	0	0	0-0	18.0	18	9	7	2	8-1	8	.265
2005—Nashville (PCL)	6	4	.600	3.03	1.30	17	16	1	0	0	1-1	92.0	91	39	31	9	25-1	75	.258
—Milwaukee (N.L.)	5	4	.556	5.57	1.45	15	11	0	0	0	0-0	64.2	74	41	40	10	20-0	58	.288
American League totals (4 years)	14	13	.519	5.00	1.38	130	33	0	0	10	1-2	302.1	311	180	168	43	107-7	170	.264
National League totals (2 years)	7	5	.583	5.12	1.45	19	14	0	0	0	0-0	82.2	92	50	47	12	28-1	66	.283
Major League totals (6 years)	21	18	.538	5.03	1.40	149	47	0	0	10	1-2	385.0	403	230	215	55	135-8	236	.268

G

GLYNN, RYAN   P

PERSONAL: Born November 1, 1974, in Portsmouth, Va. ... 6-3/200. ... Throws right, bats right. ... Full name: Ryan David Glynn. ... High school: Churchland (Portsmouth, Va.). ... College: Virginia Military.

TRANSACTIONS/CAREER NOTES: Selected by Texas Rangers organization in fourth round of 1995 free-agent draft. ... On disabled list (July 2-17 and August 12-29, 2000); included rehabilitation assignment to Oklahoma. ... On disabled list (June 1-July 1, 2001); included rehabilitation assignment to Oklahoma. ... Signed as a free agent by Milwaukee Brewers organization (January 11, 2002). ... Released by Brewers (June 6, 2002). ... Signed by Florida Marlins organization (June 14, 2002). ... Signed as a free agent by Atlanta Braves organization (January 14, 2003). ... Released by Braves (May 29, 2004). ... Signed by Toronto Blue Jays organization (June 1, 2004). ... Traded by Blue Jays to Oakland Athletics for cash (May 15, 2005).

CAREER HITTING: 0-for-4 (.000), 0 R, 0 2B, 0 3B, 0 HR, 0 RBI.

RYAN GLYNN'S PITCHING ZONE

.000	.500	.333
.455	.538	.308
.500	.000	.167

LEFTY-RIGHTY SPLITS

vs.	Avg.	AB	H	2B	3B	HR	RBI	BB	SO	OBP	Slg.
L	.385	39	15	2	0	4	11	5	5	.455	.744
R	.250	36	9	0	0	1	8	2	10	.289	.333

Year	Team (League)	W	L	Pct.	ERA	WHIP	G	GS	CG	ShO	Hld.	Sv.-Opp.	IP	H	R	ER	HR	BB-IBB	SO	Avg.
1995—Hudson Valley (NYP)		3	3	.500	4.70	1.64	9	8	0	0	...	0-...	44.0	56	27	23	0	16-1	21	.326
1996—Char., S.C. (S. Atl.)		8	7	.533	4.54	1.46	19	19	2	1	...	0-...	121.0	118	70	61	10	59-2	72	.264
1997—Charlotte (Fla. St.)		8	7	.533	4.97	1.43	23	22	5	1	...	1-...	134.0	148	81	74	13	44-0	96	.284
—Tulsa (Texas)		1	1	.500	3.38	1.45	3	3	0	0	...	0-...	21.1	21	9	8	1	10-0	18	.266
1998—Tulsa (Texas)		9	6	.600	3.44	1.30	26	24	4	1	...	0-...	157.0	140	66	60	12	64-0	111	.240
1999—Oklahoma (PCL)		6	2	.750	3.39	1.30	16	16	2	1	...	0-...	90.1	81	46	34	7	36-...	55	...
—Texas (A.L.)		2	4	.333	7.24	1.94	13	10	0	0	0	0-0	54.2	71	46	44	10	35-0	39	.316
2000—Oklahoma (PCL)		4	2	.667	3.55	1.25	15	14	2	2	...	0-...	83.2	72	36	33	5	33-1	66	.235
—Texas (A.L.)		5	7	.417	5.58	1.67	16	16	0	0	0	0-0	88.2	107	65	55	15	41-2	33	.293
2001—Texas (A.L.)		1	5	.167	7.04	1.85	12	9	0	0	0	0-0	46.0	59	38	36	7	26-1	15	.309
—Oklahoma (PCL)		2	6	.250	6.49	1.62	13	13	1	0	...	0-...	79.0	87	62	57	10	41-0	52	.282
2002—Indianapolis (Int'l)		3	6	.333	5.23	1.59	12	11	0	0	...	0-...	63.2	75	48	37	7	26-0	36	.286
—Calgary (PCL)		5	5	.500	6.00	1.65	14	14	0	0	...	0-...	78.0	102	58	52	7	27-0	48	.312
2003—Richmond (Int'l)		6	5	.545	2.91	1.20	16	16	0	0	...	0-...	92.2	84	31	30	4	31-3	75	.244
2004—Richmond (Int'l)		1	1	.500	5.60	2.26	11	0	0	0	...	0-...	17.2	26	11	11	0	14-0	19	.351
—Syracuse (Int'l)		7	2	.778	3.40	1.25	16	16	1	1	...	0-...	92.2	82	38	35	7	34-0	75	.236
—Toronto (A.L.)		1	0	1.000	4.05	1.35	6	2	0	0	0	0-0	20.0	19	9	9	4	8-1	14	.250
2005—Syracuse (Int'l)		2	4	.333	6.27	1.39	9	6	0	0	0	0-0	37.1	41	27	26	6	11-0	23	.283
—Oakland (A.L.)		0	4	.000	6.88	1.82	5	3	0	0	0	0-0	17.0	24	16	13	5	7-0	15	.320
—Sacramento (PCL)		3	1	.750	2.78	1.25	11	11	0	0	0	0-0	55.0	46	20	17	4	23-1	54	.225
Major League totals (5 years)		**9**	**20**	**.310**	**6.24**	**1.75**	**52**	**40**	**0**	**0**	**0**	**0-0**	**226.1**	**280**	**174**	**157**	**41**	**117-4**	**116**	**.300**

GOBBLE, JIMMY   P

PERSONAL: Born July 19, 1981, in Bristol, Tenn. ... 6-3/190. ... Throws left, bats left. ... Full name: Billy James Gobble. ... High school: John S. Battle (Bristol, Va.).

TRANSACTIONS/CAREER NOTES: Selected by Kansas City Royals organization in supplemental round ("sandwich" pick between first and second rounds, 43rd pick overall) of 1999 free-agent draft; Royals received pick as compensation for Detroit Tigers signing Type A free-agent 3B Dean Palmer.

CAREER HITTING: 0-for-2 (.000), 0 R, 0 2B, 0 3B, 0 HR, 0 RBI.

SCOUTING REPORT ***Throws:*** Gobble's fastball hits 88-92 mph, his curve 74-75 and he has a changeup. ***Tendencies:*** Gobble increased his velocity during the season and occasionally will show an above-average fastball with some tailing action. Can overthrow the pitch and leave it up, which causes problems. Curveball has been inconsistent both in break and command. Has a better changeup. ***Outlook:*** He needs to develop a more consistent breaking ball to get lefthanded hitters out, but he will compete for the fifth rotation spot next season. ***Grade 5.7***

JIMMY GOBBLE'S PITCHING ZONE

.462	.091	.200
.188	.464	.333
.400	.750	.167

LEFTY-RIGHTY SPLITS

vs.	Avg.	AB	H	2B	3B	HR	RBI	BB	SO	OBP	Slg.
L	.310	71	22	3	0	5	11	6	17	.364	.563
R	.294	143	42	9	1	4	24	24	21	.396	.455

Year	Team (League)	W	L	Pct.	ERA	WHIP	G	GS	CG	ShO	Hld.	Sv.-Opp.	IP	H	R	ER	HR	BB-IBB	SO	Avg.
1999—GC Royals (GCL)		0	0	...	2.70	1.65	4	1	0	0	...	0-...	6.2	6	3	2	0	5-0	8	.222
2000—Char., W.Va. (S. Atl.)		12	10	.545	3.66	1.23	25	25	3	2	...	0-...	145.0	144	75	59	10	34-0	115	.256
2001—Wilmington (Carol.)		10	6	.625	2.55	1.03	27	27	0	0	...	0-...	162.1	134	58	46	8	33-3	154	.226
2002—Wichita (Texas)		5	7	.417	3.38	1.30	13	13	0	0	...	0-...	69.1	71	29	26	3	19-2	52	.267
2003—Wichita (Texas)		12	8	.600	3.19	1.27	22	22	2	1	...	0-...	132.2	128	57	47	11	40-1	100	.254
—Kansas City (A.L.)		4	5	.444	4.61	1.35	9	9	0	0	0	0-0	52.2	56	32	27	8	15-0	31	.271
2004—Omaha (PCL)		3	1	.750	4.58	1.63	4	4	0	0	...	0-...	19.2	25	20	10	5	7-0	15	.298
—Kansas City (A.L.)		9	8	.529	5.35	1.35	25	24	1	0	0	0-0	148.0	157	94	88	24	43-0	49	.270
2005—Omaha (PCL)		2	7	.222	6.63	1.66	12	12	0	0	0	0-0	58.1	76	48	43	8	21-0	45	.314
—Kansas City (A.L.)		1	1	.500	5.70	1.75	28	4	0	0	4	0-0	53.2	64	34	34	9	30-4	38	.299
Major League totals (3 years)		**14**	**14**	**.500**	**5.27**	**1.44**	**62**	**37**	**1**	**0**	**4**	**0-0**	**254.1**	**277**	**160**	**149**	**41**	**88-4**	**118**	**.276**

GODWIN, TYRELL   OF

PERSONAL: Born July 10, 1979, in Wilmington, N.C. ... 6-0/200. ... Bats left, throws right. ... Full name: Carlton Tyrell Godwin. ... College: North Carolina.

TRANSACTIONS/CAREER NOTES: Selected by Toronto Blue Jays organization in third round of 2001 free-agent draft. ... Selected by Montreal Expos organization from Blue Jays in Rule 5 major league draft (December 13, 2004). ... Expos franchise moved to Washington, D.C., and was renamed Nationals for 2005 season (December 3, 2004). ... Returned by Nationals to Blue Jays organization (March 23, 2005). ... Traded by Blue Jays to Washington Nationals for P Aaron Wideman (March 23, 2005).

LEFTY-RIGHTY SPLITS

vs.	Avg.	AB	H	2B	3B	HR	RBI	BB	SO	OBP	Slg.
L	.000	0	0	0	0	0	0	0	0	.000	.000
R	.000	3	0	0	0	0	0	0	1	.000	.000

							BATTING											FIELDING	
Year	Team (League)	Pos.	G	AB	R	H	2B	3B	HR	RBI	BB	SO	HBP	GDP	SB-CS	Avg.	OBP	SLG	OPS	E	Avg.
2001—Auburn (NYP)		OF	33	117	26	43	8	2	2	15	19	27	2	1	9-5	.368	.464	.521	.985	0	1.000

Year Team (League)	Pos.	G	AB	R	H	2B	3B	HR	RBI	BB	SO	HBP	GDP	SB-CS	Avg.	OBP	SLG	OPS	E	Avg.
2002—Char., W.Va. (S. Atl.)	OF	48	185	31	52	8	5	0	16	20	23	4	2	10-2	.281	.364	.378	.742	2	.980
2003—Dunedin (Fla. St.)	OF	97	322	52	88	16	0	1	33	29	39	8	6	20-7	.273	.348	.332	.680	4	.982
— New Haven (East.)	OF	33	123	20	38	6	3	1	13	3	27	1	5	6-1	.309	.328	.431	.759	3	.940
2004—New Hampshire (East.)	OF	133	521	85	132	21	7	6	40	52	110	5	6	42-12	.253	.326	.355	.681	6	.925
2005—Was. (N.L.)		3	3	0	0	0	0	0	0	0	1	0	0	0-0	.000	.000	.000	.000	0	...
— New Orleans (PCL)	OF-DH	129	499	83	160	22	6	9	48	50	77	5	6	22-12	.321	.387	.443	.830	20	.959
Major League totals (1 year)		3	3	0	0	0	0	0	0	0	1	0	0	0-0	.000	.000	.000	.000	0	...

GOMES, JONNY — OF/DH

PERSONAL: Born November 22, 1980, in San Francisco. ... 6-1/205. ... Bats right, throws right. ... Full name: Jonny Johnson Gomes. ... High school: Casa Grande (Petaluma, Calif.). ... Junior college: Santa Rosa (Calif.).
TRANSACTIONS/CAREER NOTES: Selected by Tampa Bay Devil Rays organization in 18th round of 2001 free-agent draft.
RECORDS: Shares major league record for most times hit by pitch, game (3, August 15, 2005).
2005 GAMES PLAYED BY POSITION (MLB): OF—50, DH—49.

SCOUTING REPORT Gomes is one of the most aggressive young hitters in the game. Has exceptional bat speed and power to all fields. Is a good high-ball hitter but chases too many high pitches. Is not a good defensive left fielder; is better in right field. Needs to improve his jumps and routes but will get a chance to improve because his bat will keep him in the lineup. Has good arm strength. **Grade 6**

JONNY GOMES'S HITTING ZONE

.200	.389	.143
.369	.517	.289
.361	.471	.294

LEFTY-RIGHTY SPLITS

vs.	Avg.	AB	H	2B	3B	HR	RBI	BB	SO	OBP	Slg.
L	.288	104	30	4	0	6	11	12	37	.388	.500
R	.279	244	68	9	6	15	43	27	76	.365	.549

Year Team (League)	Pos.	G	AB	R	H	2B	3B	HR	RBI	BB	SO	HBP	GDP	SB-CS	Avg.	OBP	SLG	OPS	E	Avg.
2001—Princeton (Appal.)	OF	62	206	58	60	11	2	16	44	33	73	26	1	15-4	.291	.442	.597	1.039	7	.936
2002—Bakersfield (Calif.)	OF	134	446	102	124	24	9	30	72	91	173	31	4	15-3	.278	.432	.574	1.006	7	.961
2003—Orlando (Sou.)	OF-DH	120	442	68	110	28	3	17	56	53	148	16	5	23-2	.249	.348	.441	.789	4	.977
— Durham (Int'l)	OF-DH	5	19	2	6	2	1	0	1	2	5	2	0	0-0	.316	.435	.526	.961	0	1.000
— Tampa Bay (A.L.)	DH	8	15	1	2	1	0	0	0	0	6	1	0	0-0	.133	.188	.200	.388	0	...
2004—Tampa Bay (A.L.)	DH	14	14	0	1	0	0	0	1	1	6	0	0	0-0	.071	.133	.071	.205	0	...
— Durham (Int'l)	OF-DH	114	389	73	100	27	1	26	78	51	136	22	6	8-5	.257	.368	.532	.900	7	.962
2005—Durham (Int'l)	OF	45	162	34	52	13	0	14	46	30	44	8	2	7-1	.321	.446	.660	1.106	8	.948
— Tampa Bay (A.L.)	OF-DH	101	348	61	98	13	6	21	54	39	113	14	6	9-5	.282	.372	.534	.906	4	.963
Major League totals (3 years)		114	377	62	101	14	6	21	55	40	125	15	6	9-5	.268	.357	.504	.861	4	.963

GOMEZ, ALEXIS — OF

PERSONAL: Born August 6, 1978, in Loma de Cabrera, Dominican Republic. ... 6-2/180. ... Bats left, throws left. ... Full name: Alexis De Jesus Gomez. ... High school: Liceo General Jose Cabrera (Loma de Cabrera, D.R.).
TRANSACTIONS/CAREER NOTES: Signed as a non-drafted free agent by Kansas City Royals organization (February 21, 1997). ... Claimed on waivers by Detroit Tigers (October 1, 2004).
2005 GAMES PLAYED BY POSITION (MLB): OF—9.

LEFTY-RIGHTY SPLITS

vs.	Avg.	AB	H	2B	3B	HR	RBI	BB	SO	OBP	Slg.
L	.000	2	0	0	0	0	0	0	0	.000	.000
R	.214	14	3	0	0	0	1	2	2	.313	.214

Year Team (League)	Pos.	G	AB	R	H	2B	3B	HR	RBI	BB	SO	HBP	GDP	SB-CS	Avg.	OBP	SLG	OPS	E	Avg.
1997—Dom. Royals (DSL)		64	248	51	87	12	9	0	42	33	52	...	...	9-...	.351	...	.472	...	...	...
1998—Dom. Royals (DSL)		67	233	51	66	11	3	1	34	50	46	...	...	17-...	.283	...	.369	...	...	...
1999—GC Royals (GCL)	OF	56	214	44	59	12	1	5	31	32	48	1	1	13-5	.276	.371	.411	.782	2	.986
2000—Wilmington (Carol.)	OF	121	461	63	117	13	4	1	33	45	121	2	8	21-10	.254	.322	.306	.628	14	.950
2001—Wilmington (Carol.)	OF	48	169	29	51	8	2	1	9	11	43	1	4	7-3	.302	.348	.391	.739	5	.957
— Wichita (Texas)	OF	83	342	55	96	15	6	4	34	27	70	4	4	16-10	.281	.337	.395	.732	6	.971
2002—Wichita (Texas)	OF	114	461	72	136	21	8	14	75	45	84	3	9	36-24	.295	.359	.466	.825	•8	.967
— Kansas City (A.L.)	OF	5	10	0	2	0	0	0	0	0	2	0	0	0-0	.200	.200	.200	.400	0	1.000
2003—Omaha (PCL)	OF	121	457	49	123	23	8	8	58	26	92	1	12	4-5	.269	.307	.407	.714	9	.970
2004—Omaha (PCL)	OF	109	383	45	96	17	8	7	34	19	96	1	11	8-6	.251	.285	.392	.677	6	.971
— Kansas City (A.L.)	OF-DH	13	29	1	8	1	0	0	4	2	8	0	1	0-0	.276	.323	.310	.633	1	.955
2005—Detroit (A.L.)	OF	9	16	2	3	0	0	0	0	2	2	0	0	0-0	.188	.278	.188	.465	0	1.000
Major League totals (3 years)		27	55	3	13	1	0	0	5	4	12	0	1	0-0	.236	.288	.255	.543	1	.972

GOMEZ, CHRIS — SS/2B

PERSONAL: Born June 16, 1971, in Los Angeles. ... 6-1/188. ... Bats right, throws right. ... Full name: Christopher Cory Gomez. ... High school: Lakewood (Calif.). ... College: Long Beach State.
TRANSACTIONS/CAREER NOTES: Selected by California Angels organization in 37th round of 1989 free-agent draft; did not sign. ... Selected by Detroit Tigers organization in third round of 1992 free-agent draft. ... Traded by Tigers with C John Flaherty to San Diego Padres for C Brad Ausmus, SS Andujar Cedeno and P Russ Spear (June 18, 1996). ... On disabled list (June 2-July 31, 1999); included rehabilitation assignment to Las Vegas. ... On disabled list (June 22, 2000-remainder of season). ... Released by Padres (June 22, 2001). ... Signed by Tampa Bay Devil Rays organization (June 27, 2001). ... Released by Devil Rays (September 30, 2002). ... Signed by Minnesota Twins (January 2, 2003). ... On disabled list (June 7-July 5, 2003). ... Signed as a free agent by Toronto Blue Jays (January 7, 2004). ... Signed as a free agent by Baltimore Orioles organization (December 8, 2004). ... Selected by Philadelphia Phillies organization from Orioles organization in Rule 5 minor league draft (December 13, 2004). ... Traded by Phillies to Baltimore Orioles for cash (December 20, 2004).
2005 GAMES PLAYED BY POSITION (MLB): 1B—42, 2B—18, 3B—17, SS—10, DH—6.

G

SCOUTING REPORT Gomez doesn't have a lot of power, but he hits line drives to all fields. Has below-average speed but is a smart baserunner. Is a bottom-of-the-order hitter. No longer is quick enough to play in the middle infield for an extended period. Range is limited, forcing him to compensate through better positioning. Has very good hands. Arm is average. **Grade 5.4**

CHRIS GOMEZ'S HITTING ZONE

.429	.273	.100
.302	.292	.438
.269	.000	.250

LEFTY-RIGHTY SPLITS

vs.	Avg.	AB	H	2B	3B	HR	RBI	BB	SO	OBP	Slg.
L	.317	104	33	5	0	1	11	15	10	.400	.394
R	.243	115	28	6	0	0	7	12	7	.320	.296

Year — Team (League)	Pos.	G	AB	R	H	2B	3B	HR	RBI	BB	SO	HBP	GDP	SB-CS	Avg.	OBP	SLG	OPS	E	Avg.
1992— London (East.)	SS	64	220	20	59	13	2	1	19	20	34	3	11	1-3	.268	.337	.359	.697	14	.951
1993— Toledo (Int'l)	SS	87	277	29	68	12	2	0	20	23	37	3	4	6-2	.245	.308	.303	.611	16	.961
— Detroit (A.L.)	SS-2B-DH	46	128	11	32	7	1	0	11	9	17	1	2	2-2	.250	.304	.320	.625	5	.974
1994— Detroit (A.L.)	SS-2B	84	296	32	76	19	0	8	53	33	64	3	8	5-3	.257	.336	.402	.738	9	.978
1995— Detroit (A.L.)	SS-2B-DH	123	431	49	96	20	2	11	50	41	96	3	13	4-1	.223	.292	.355	.647	15	.974
1996— Detroit (A.L.)	SS	48	128	21	31	5	0	1	16	18	20	1	5	1-1	.242	.340	.305	.645	6	.970
— San Diego (N.L.)	SS	89	328	32	86	16	1	3	29	39	64	6	11	2-2	.262	.349	.345	.694	13	.967
1997— San Diego (N.L.)	SS	150	522	62	132	19	2	5	54	53	114	5	16	5-8	.253	.326	.326	.652	15	.978
1998— San Diego (N.L.)	SS	145	449	55	120	32	3	4	39	51	87	5	11	1-3	.267	.346	.379	.725	12	.980
1999— San Diego (N.L.)	SS	76	234	20	59	8	1	1	15	27	49	1	6	1-2	.252	.331	.308	.638	12	.961
— Las Vegas (PCL)	SS	10	27	3	9	1	0	0	4	2	6	1	1	0-0	.333	.400	.370	.770	2	.933
2000— San Diego (N.L.)	SS-2B	33	54	4	12	0	0	0	3	7	5	0	1	0-0	.222	.306	.222	.529	5	.933
2001— San Diego (N.L.)	SS-2B	40	112	6	21	3	0	0	7	9	14	0	5	1-0	.188	.244	.214	.458	6	.948
— Portland (PCL)	SS-2B	11	40	5	12	3	0	1	5	2	4	0	1	1-0	.300	.333	.450	.783	2	.959
— Durham (Int'l)	SS	23	93	16	28	5	1	4	17	11	5	0	5	1-1	.301	.375	.505	.880	2	.978
— Tampa Bay (A.L.)	SS	58	189	31	57	16	0	8	36	8	24	2	4	3-0	.302	.342	.513	.845	7	.968
2002— Tampa Bay (A.L.)	SS	130	461	51	122	31	3	10	46	21	58	7	8	1-3	.265	.305	.410	.715	12	.980
2003— Minnesota (A.L.)	2B-3B-SS DH	58	175	14	44	9	3	1	15	7	13	0	10	2-1	.251	.279	.354	.633	3	.982
2004— Toronto (A.L.)	SS-1B-3B DH-2B	109	341	41	96	11	1	3	37	28	41	2	4	3-2	.282	.337	.346	.683	12	.974
2005— Baltimore (A.L.)	1B-2B-3B SS-DH	89	219	27	61	11	0	1	18	27	17	1	14	2-1	.279	.359	.342	.701	5	.987
American League totals (9 years)		745	2368	277	615	129	10	43	282	192	350	20	68	23-14	.260	.319	.377	.696	73	.977
National League totals (6 years)		533	1699	179	430	78	7	13	147	186	333	17	50	10-15	.253	.331	.330	.661	63	.971
Major League totals (13 years)		1278	4067	456	1045	207	17	56	429	378	683	37	118	33-29	.257	.324	.358	.681	136	.974

DIVISION SERIES RECORD

Year — Team (League)	Pos.	G	AB	R	H	2B	3B	HR	RBI	BB	SO	HBP	GDP	SB-CS	Avg.	OBP	SLG	OPS	E	Avg.
1996— San Diego (N.L.)	SS	3	12	0	2	0	0	0	1	0	4	0	0	0-0	.167	.167	.167	.333	0	1.000
1998— San Diego (N.L.)	SS	4	11	1	3	0	0	0	0	4	1	0	0	0-0	.273	.467	.273	.739	1	.938
2003— Minnesota (A.L.)	2B	1	0	0	0	0	0	0	0	0	0	0	0	0-0	...	...	...	...	0	...
Division series totals (3 years)		8	23	1	5	0	0	0	1	4	5	0	0	0-0	.217	.333	.217	.551	1	.966

CHAMPIONSHIP SERIES RECORD

Year — Team (League)	Pos.	G	AB	R	H	2B	3B	HR	RBI	BB	SO	HBP	GDP	SB-CS	Avg.	OBP	SLG	OPS	E	Avg.
1998— San Diego (N.L.)	SS	6	20	2	3	1	0	0	0	2	5	0	3	0-0	.150	.227	.200	.427	1	.950

WORLD SERIES RECORD

Year — Team (League)	Pos.	G	AB	R	H	2B	3B	HR	RBI	BB	SO	HBP	GDP	SB-CS	Avg.	OBP	SLG	OPS	E	Avg.
1998— San Diego (N.L.)	SS	4	11	2	4	0	1	0	0	1	1	0	0	0-0	.364	.417	.545	.962	0	1.000

GONZALEZ, ADRIAN 1B

PERSONAL: Born May 8, 1982, in San Diego. ... 6-2/220. ... Bats left, throws left. ... High school: Eastlake High (Chula Vista, Calif.).

TRANSACTIONS/CAREER NOTES: Selected by Florida Marlins organization in first round (first pick overall) of 2000 draft. ... Traded by Marlins with P Ryan Snare and OF Will Smith to Texas Rangers for P Ugueth Urbina (July 11, 2003).

2005 GAMES PLAYED BY POSITION (MLB): DH—32, 1B—10, OF—1.

SCOUTING REPORT Gonzalez made an adjustment in his swing early in the season in an effort to develop more power. Not as fluid now with his stroke and tries to muscle the ball at times, which costs him bat speed. Is vulnerable to the ball inside and doesn't pull the ball much. Is an outstanding defensive first baseman and has some quickness and soft hands. Doesn't run well. Must show more power to play regularly. **Grade 5.7**

ADRIAN GONZALEZ'S HITTING ZONE

.200	.333	.400
.059	.375	.265
.250	.500	.188

LEFTY-RIGHTY SPLITS

vs.	Avg.	AB	H	2B	3B	HR	RBI	BB	SO	OBP	Slg.
L	.071	14	1	0	0	0	1	1	4	.133	.071
R	.243	136	33	7	1	6	16	9	33	.286	.441

Year — Team (League)	Pos.	G	AB	R	H	2B	3B	HR	RBI	BB	SO	HBP	GDP	SB-CS	Avg.	OBP	SLG	OPS	E	Avg.
2000— GC Marlins (GCL)	1B	53	193	24	57	10	1	0	30	32	35	2	6	0-0	.295	.397	.358	.755	7	.986
— Utica (NYP)	1B	8	29	7	9	3	0	0	3	7	6	0	0	0-0	.310	.444	.414	.858	2	.976
2001— Kane Co. (Midw.)	1B	127	516	86	161	37	1	17	103	57	83	5	17	5-5	.312	.382	.486	.868	14	.988
2002— Portland (East.)	1B	138	508	70	135	34	1	17	96	54	112	8	13	6-3	.266	.344	.437	.781	*16	.987
2003— Albuquerque (PCL)	1B	39	139	17	30	5	1	1	18	14	25	0	6	1-0	.216	.286	.288	.573	1	.997
— Carolina (Sou.)	1B	36	137	15	42	9	1	1	16	14	25	0	6	1-1	.307	.368	.409	.777	4	.987
— Frisco (Texas)	1B	45	173	16	49	6	2	3	17	11	27	1	6	0-0	.283	.326	.393	.719	7	.983

G

Year Team (League)	Pos.	G	AB	R	H	2B	3B	HR	RBI	BB	SO	HBP	GDP	SB-CS	Avg.	OBP	SLG	OPS	E	Avg.
2004—Oklahoma (PCL)	1B	123	457	61	139	28	3	12	88	39	73	6	17	1-1	.304	.364	.457	.813	6	.995
—Texas (A.L.)	1B-DH	16	42	7	10	3	0	1	7	2	6	0	0	0-0	.238	.273	.381	.654	1	.990
2005—Oklahoma (PCL)	1B-DH	84	328	61	111	17	1	18	65	32	44	4	13	0-0	.338	.399	.561	.960	5	.994
—Texas (A.L.) DH-1B-OF		43	150	17	34	7	1	6	17	10	37	0	3	0-0	.227	.272	.407	.678	3	.969
Major League totals (2 years)		59	192	24	44	10	1	7	24	12	43	0	3	0-0	.229	.272	.401	.673	4	.980

GONZALEZ, ALEX — SS

PERSONAL: Born February 15, 1977, in Cagua, Venezuela. ... 6-0/202. ... Bats right, throws right. ... Full name: Alexander Gonzalez. ... High school: Liceo Ramon Bastidas (Venezuela).

TRANSACTIONS/CAREER NOTES: Signed as a non-drafted free agent by Florida Marlins organization (April 18, 1994). ... On disabled list (July 28-September 1, 2000); included rehabilitation assignment to Brevard County. ... On disabled list (May 19, 2002-remainder of season); included rehabilitation assignment to GCL Marlins. ... On suspended list (June 3-5, 2004)

2005 GAMES PLAYED BY POSITION (MLB): SS—124.

SCOUTING REPORT **Offense:** Persistent elbow problems forced Gonzalez to change his swing and his approach at the plate last season. Shortened up and tried to hit to right field more. Cut down on his strikeouts. Inability to get full extension cost him power. Has very good bat speed when healthy and is one of the strongest middle infielders in the league. Is not a good runner and is not a basestealing threat. **Defense:** Gonzalez has good hands and agility and has exceptional range to his right. Had a lot of trouble throwing in the second half and became so erratic that he didn't play much down the stretch. **Outlook:** If he can maintain the changes in swing, he can become a better player. Has all the tools to be a very good defensive shortstop. **Grade 7**

ALEX GONZALEZ'S HITTING ZONE

.286	.188	.136
.324	.300	.278
.314	.333	.333

LEFTY-RIGHTY SPLITS

vs.	Avg.	AB	H	2B	3B	HR	RBI	BB	SO	OBP	Slg.
L	.216	88	19	5	0	1	3	8	20	.278	.307
R	.277	347	96	25	0	4	42	23	61	.329	.383

Year Team (League)	Pos.	G	AB	R	H	2B	3B	HR	RBI	BB	SO	HBP	GDP	SB-CS	Avg.	OBP	SLG	OPS	E	Avg.
1994—Dom. Marlins (DSL)	SS	54	239	30	54	7	3	3	31	15	36	...	...	4-...	.226	...	.318	...	34	.914
1995—Brevard County (Fla. St.) ...	SS	17	59	6	12	2	1	0	8	1	14	1	2	1-1	.203	.230	.271	.501	8	.906
—GC Marlins (GCL)	SS	53	187	30	55	7	4	2	30	19	27	2	2	11-2	.294	.358	.406	.765	17	.932
1996—GC Marlins (GCL)	SS	10	41	6	16	3	0	0	6	2	4	0	1	1-0	.390	.419	.463	.882	5	.898
—Kane Co. (Midw.)	SS	4	10	2	2	0	0	0	0	2	4	1	1	0-0	.200	.385	.200	.585	0	1.000
—Portland (East.)	SS	11	34	4	8	0	1	0	1	2	10	1	2	0-0	.235	.297	.294	.591	7	.887
1997—Portland (East.)	SS	133	449	69	114	16	4	19	65	27	83	7	1	4-7	.254	.305	.434	.739	37	.943
1998—Charlotte (Int'l)	SS	108	422	71	117	20	10	10	51	28	80	6	6	4-7	.277	.330	.443	.773	20	.960
—Florida (N.L.)	SS	25	86	11	13	2	0	3	7	9	30	1	2	0-0	.151	.240	.279	.519	2	.978
1999—Florida (N.L.)	SS	136	560	81	155	28	8	14	59	15	113	12	13	3-5	.277	.308	.430	.739	27	.955
2000—Florida (N.L.)	SS	109	385	35	77	17	4	7	42	13	77	2	7	7-1	.200	.229	.319	.548	19	.957
—Brevard County (Fla. St.) ...	SS	4	17	1	2	0	0	0	2	1	3	0	0	1-0	.118	.167	.118	.284	0	1.000
2001—Florida (N.L.)	SS-C	145	515	57	129	36	1	9	48	30	107	10	13	2-2	.250	.303	.377	.680	26	.960
2002—Florida (N.L.)	SS	42	151	15	34	7	1	2	18	12	32	4	2	3-1	.225	.296	.325	.620	3	.984
—GC Marlins (GCL)	SS	5	12	0	2	1	0	0	1	0	5	0	1	0-0	.167	.154	.250	.404	1	.923
2003—Florida (N.L.)	SS	150	528	52	135	33	6	18	77	33	106	13	8	0-4	.256	.313	.443	.756	16	.976
2004—Florida (N.L.)	SS	159	561	67	130	30	3	23	79	27	126	4	17	3-1	.232	.270	.419	.689	16	.976
2005—Florida (N.L.)	SS	130	435	45	115	30	0	5	45	31	81	5	11	5-3	.264	.319	.368	.686	16	.974
Major League totals (8 years)		896	3221	363	788	183	23	81	375	170	672	51	73	23-17	.245	.291	.391	.682	125	.968

DIVISION SERIES RECORD

Year Team (League)	Pos.	G	AB	R	H	2B	3B	HR	RBI	BB	SO	HBP	GDP	SB-CS	Avg.	OBP	SLG	OPS	E	Avg.
2003—Florida (N.L.)	SS	4	16	2	1	0	0	0	0	1	3	0	1	0-0	.063	.118	.063	.180	1	.929

CHAMPIONSHIP SERIES RECORD

Year Team (League)	Pos.	G	AB	R	H	2B	3B	HR	RBI	BB	SO	HBP	GDP	SB-CS	Avg.	OBP	SLG	OPS	E	Avg.
2003—Florida (N.L.)	SS	7	24	1	3	2	0	0	4	0	6	0	0	0-0	.125	.125	.208	.333	1	.970

WORLD SERIES RECORD

Year Team (League)	Pos.	G	AB	R	H	2B	3B	HR	RBI	BB	SO	HBP	GDP	SB-CS	Avg.	OBP	SLG	OPS	E	Avg.
2003—Florida (N.L.)	SS	6	22	3	6	2	0	1	2	0	7	0	1	0-1	.273	.273	.500	.773	0	1.000

ALL-STAR GAME RECORD

		G	AB	R	H	2B	3B	HR	RBI	BB	SO	HBP	GDP	SB-CS	Avg.	OBP	SLG	OPS	E	Avg.
All-Star Game totals (1 year)		1	1	0	0	0	0	0	0	0	0	0	0	0-0	.000	.000	.000	.000	0	1.000

GONZALEZ, ALEX S. — SS

PERSONAL: Born April 8, 1973, in Miami. ... 6-0/200. ... Bats right, throws right. ... Full name: Alexander Scott Gonzalez. ... High school: Miami Killian.

TRANSACTIONS/CAREER NOTES: Selected by Toronto Blue Jays organization in 14th round of 1991 free-agent draft. ... On disabled list (April 29-May 27, 1994); included rehabilitation assignment to Syracuse. ... On disabled list (August 13-September 14, 1997; and May 17, 1999-remainder of season). ... On disabled list (July 7-22, 2000); included rehabilitation assignment to Syracuse. ... Traded by Blue Jays to Chicago Cubs for P Felix Heredia and a player to be named (December 10, 2001); Blue Jays acquired IF James Deschaine to complete deal (December 13, 2001). ... On disabled list (May 10-25, 2002). ... On disabled list (May 6-July 19, 2004); included rehabilitation assignment to Iowa. ... Traded by Cubs with P Francis Beltran and IF Brendan Harris to Montreal Expos as part of four-team deal in which Cubs acquired SS Nomar Garciaparra and OF Matt Murton from Red Sox, Red Sox acquired SS Orlando Cabrera from Expos and 1B Doug Mientkiewicz from Twins, and Twins acquired P Justin Jones from Cubs (July 31, 2004). ... Traded by Expos to San Diego Padres for cash (September 16, 2004). ... Signed as a free agent by Tampa Bay Devil Rays (January 7, 2005). ... On disabled list (July 1-16, 2005).

RECORDS: Shares major league record for most strikeouts, game (6, September 9, 1998, 13 innings).

2005 GAMES PLAYED BY POSITION (MLB): 3B—98, SS—12.

G

SCOUTING REPORT *Offense:* Gonzalez generally tries to pull everything but he did begin to use the whole field more last season. Has a long stroke but can hit high fastballs. Will strike out too much; he's not selective and doesn't hit breaking balls well. Is more of a gap hitter but shows surprising power at times. *Defense:* He came up to the majors as a shortstop but has made the transition to third base without a lot of trouble. Has extremely good hands and a strong arm but is losing range. *Outlook:* Gonzalez is not an ideal run producer for the position, but his ability to play third base and shortstop makes him a good utility player. *Grade 6.5*

ALEX S. GONZALEZ'S HITTING ZONE

.306	.462	.222
.293	.378	.294
.255	.462	.200

LEFTY-RIGHTY SPLITS

vs.	Avg.	AB	H	2B	3B	HR	RBI	BB	SO	OBP	Slg.
L	.282	117	33	6	0	1	10	8	24	.331	.359
R	.263	232	61	14	1	8	28	18	50	.319	.435

Year	Team (League)	Pos.	G	AB	R	H	2B	3B	HR	RBI	BB	SO	HBP	GDP	SB-CS	Avg.	OBP	SLG	OPS	E	Avg.
1991—	GC Jays (GCL)	SS	53	191	29	40	5	4	0	10	12	41	3	1	7-2	.209	.267	.277	.544	21	.915
1992—	Myrtle Beach (S. Atl.)	SS	134	535	83	145	22	9	10	62	38	119	3	9	26-14	.271	.322	.402	.724	48	.932
1993—	Knoxville (Sou.)	SS	142	561	93	162	29	7	16	69	39	110	6	9	38-13	.289	.339	.451	.790	30	.956
1994—	Toronto (A.L.)	SS	15	53	7	8	3	1	0	1	4	17	1	2	3-0	.151	.224	.245	.469	6	.918
—	Syracuse (Int'l)	SS-DH	110	437	69	124	22	4	12	57	53	92	1	9	23-6	.284	.361	.435	.796	31	.943
1995—	Toronto (A.L.)	SS-3B-DH	111	367	51	89	19	4	10	42	44	114	1	7	4-4	.243	.322	.398	.720	19	.954
1996—	Toronto (A.L.)	SS	147	527	64	124	30	5	14	64	45	127	5	12	16-6	.235	.300	.391	.691	21	.973
1997—	Toronto (A.L.)	SS	126	426	46	102	23	2	12	35	34	94	5	15	15-6	.239	.302	.387	.689	8	.986
1998—	Toronto (A.L.)	SS	158	568	70	136	28	1	13	51	28	121	6	13	21-6	.239	.281	.361	.642	17	.976
1999—	Toronto (A.L.)	SS-DH	38	154	22	45	13	0	2	12	16	23	3	4	4-2	.292	.370	.416	.786	4	.980
2000—	Toronto (A.L.)	SS	141	527	68	133	31	2	15	69	43	113	4	14	4-4	.252	.313	.404	.717	16	.975
—	Syracuse (Int'l)	SS	1	5	0	0	0	0	0	0	0	2	0	0	0-0	.000	.000	.000	.000	0	1.000
2001—	Toronto (A.L.)	SS	154	636	79	161	25	5	17	76	43	149	7	16	18-11	.253	.303	.388	.692	10	.987
2002—	Chicago (N.L.)	SS	142	513	58	127	27	5	18	61	46	136	3	11	5-3	.248	.312	.425	.737	21	.965
2003—	Chicago (N.L.)	SS	152	536	71	122	37	0	20	59	47	123	6	17	3-3	.228	.295	.409	.704	10	.984
2004—	Iowa (PCL)	SS	8	24	7	8	0	0	0	4	4	7	0	1	1-0	.333	.429	.458	.887	0	1.000
—	Chicago (N.L.)	SS	37	129	15	28	10	0	3	8	4	26	0	4	1-1	.217	.241	.364	.605	5	.967
—	Montreal (N.L.)	SS	35	133	19	32	7	0	4	16	8	32	1	1	1-1	.241	.289	.383	.672	6	.960
—	San Diego (N.L.)	SS	11	23	2	4	1	1	0	3	2	6	0	0	0-0	.174	.240	.304	.544	0	1.000
2005—	Tampa Bay (A.L.)	3B-SS	109	349	47	94	20	1	9	38	26	74	3	13	2-1	.269	.323	.410	.733	16	.944
	American League totals (9 years)		999	3607	454	892	192	21	92	388	283	832	35	90	87-40	.247	.306	.389	.695	117	.973
	National League totals (3 years)		377	1334	165	313	82	6	45	147	107	323	10	35	10-8	.235	.295	.406	.701	42	.973
	Major League totals (12 years)		1376	4941	619	1205	274	27	137	535	390	1155	45	125	97-48	.244	.303	.393	.697	159	.973

DIVISION SERIES RECORD

Year	Team (League)	Pos.	G	AB	R	H	2B	3B	HR	RBI	BB	SO	HBP	GDP	SB-CS	Avg.	OBP	SLG	OPS	E	Avg.
2003—	Chicago (N.L.)	SS	5	12	1	3	0	0	1	1	2	3	0	0	0-1	.250	.357	.500	.857	0	1.000

CHAMPIONSHIP SERIES RECORD

Year	Team (League)	Pos.	G	AB	R	H	2B	3B	HR	RBI	BB	SO	HBP	GDP	SB-CS	Avg.	OBP	SLG	OPS	E	Avg.
2003—	Chicago (N.L.)	SS	7	28	5	8	2	0	3	7	2	7	0	0	0-0	.286	.333	.679	1.012	1	.968

GONZALEZ, EDGAR   P

PERSONAL: Born February 23, 1983, in Monterrey, Mexico. ... 6-0/215. ... Throws right, bats right. ... Full name: Edgar Gerardo Gonzalez Elizando.
TRANSACTIONS/CAREER NOTES: Signed as a non-drafted free agent by Arizona Diamondbacks organization (April 18, 2000). ... On suspended list for 2000 and 2001 seasons.
CAREER HITTING: 3-for-17 (.176), 1 R, 0 2B, 0 3B, 0 HR, 0 RBI.

LEFTY-RIGHTY SPLITS

vs.	Avg.	AB	H	2B	3B	HR	RBI	BB	SO	OBP	Slg.
L	.667	3	2	1	0	1	2	1	1	.750	2.000
R	.000	0	0	0	0	0	0	1	0	1.000	.000

Year	Team (League)	W	L	Pct.	ERA	WHIP	G	GS	CG	ShO	Hld.	Sv.-Opp.	IP	H	R	ER	HR	BB-IBB	SO	Avg.
2002—	South Bend (Midw.)	11	8	.579	2.91	1.16	23	23	4	2	...	0-...	151.1	141	66	49	4	34-0	110	.246
—	Lancaster (Calif.)	3	0	1.000	0.78	1.17	4	4	0	0	...	0-...	23.0	24	7	2	1	3-0	21	.264
2003—	El Paso (Texas)	2	2	.500	3.50	1.42	6	6	0	0	...	0-...	36.0	40	18	14	1	11-0	30	.282
—	Tucson (PCL)	8	7	.533	3.75	1.19	20	19	1	0	...	0-...	129.2	126	65	54	4	28-0	69	.255
—	Arizona (N.L.)	2	1	.667	4.91	1.91	9	2	0	0	0	0-1	18.1	28	10	10	3	7-2	14	.368
2004—	Tucson (PCL)	5	5	.500	4.88	1.32	15	15	1	1	...	0-...	94.0	99	52	51	15	25-0	66	.277
—	Arizona (N.L.)	0	9	.000	9.32	1.94	10	10	0	0	0	0-0	46.1	72	49	48	15	18-4	31	.362
2005—	Arizona (N.L.)	0	0		99.99	12.00	1	0	0	0	0	0-0	0.1	2	4	4	1	2-0	1	.667
—	Tucson (PCL)	11	6	.647	4.37	1.34	28	24	0	0	...	0-0	167.0	185	94	81	20	38-0	116	.283
	Major League totals (3 years)	2	10	.167	8.58	1.98	20	12	0	0	0	0-1	65.0	102	63	62	19	27-6	46	.367

GONZALEZ, JEREMI   P

PERSONAL: Born January 8, 1975, in Maracaibo, Venezuela. ... 6-0/220. ... Throws right, bats right. ... Full name: Geremis Segundo Gonzalez. ... High school: Colegio La Chinita (Maracaibo).
TRANSACTIONS/CAREER NOTES: Signed as a non-drafted free agent by Chicago Cubs organization (October 21, 1991). ... On disabled list (July 25, 1998-remainder of season). ... On disabled list (April 1, 1999-entire season); included rehabilitation assignments to Daytona, West Tenn and Iowa. ... On disabled list (March 28, 2000-entire season); included rehabilitation assignments to AZL Cubs and Lansing. ... Released by Cubs (March 13, 2001). ... Signed by Texas Rangers organization (December 18, 2001). ... Signed as a free agent by Tampa Bay Devil Rays organization (November 21, 2002). ... Released by Devil Rays (November 19, 2004). ... Signed by Boston Red Sox organization (February 1, 2005).
CAREER HITTING: 10-for-78 (.128), 1 R, 1 2B, 0 3B, 0 HR, 3 RBI.

JEREMI GONZALEZ'S PITCHING ZONE

.419	.273	.261
.286	.500	.308
.238	.286	.167

LEFTY-RIGHTY SPLITS

vs.	Avg.	AB	H	2B	3B	HR	RBI	BB	SO	OBP	Slg.
L	.340	100	34	5	1	3	15	6	13	.377	.500
R	.246	122	30	8	3	4	22	10	15	.304	.459

Year	Team (League)	W	L	Pct.	ERA	WHIP	G	GS	CG	ShO	Hld.	Sv.-Opp.	IP	H	R	ER	HR	BB-IBB	SO	Avg.
1992—	Ariz. Cubs (Ariz.)	0	5	.000	7.80	1.93	14	7	0	0	...	0-...	45.0	65	59	39	0	22-0	39	.325
1993—	Huntington (Appal.)	3	9	.250	6.25	1.77	12	12	1	0	...	0-...	67.2	82	59	47	6	38-0	42	.300

G

Year Team (League)	W	L	Pct.	ERA	WHIP	G	GS	CG	ShO	Hld.	Sv.-Opp.	IP	H	R	ER	HR	BB-IBB	SO	Avg.
1994— Peoria (Midw.)	1	7	.125	5.55	1.65	13	13	1	0		0-...	71.1	86	53	44	4	32-0	39	.306
— Will. (NYP)	4	6	.400	4.24	1.39	16	12	1	1		1-...	80.2	83	46	38	6	29-0	64	.266
1995— Rockford (Midw.)	4	4	.500	5.10	1.39	12	12	1	0		0-...	65.1	63	43	37	4	28-0	36	.247
— Daytona (Fla. St.)	5	1	.833	1.22	1.06	19	2	0	0		4-...	44.1	34	15	6	0	13-1	30	.211
1996— Orlando (Sou.)	6	3	.667	3.34	1.27	17	14	0	0		0-...	97.0	95	39	36	6	28-1	85	.250
1997— Iowa (A.A.)	2	2	.500	3.48	1.10	10	10	1	1		0-...	62.0	47	27	24	8	21-0	58	.209
— Chicago (N.L.)	11	9	.550	4.25	1.35	23	23	1	1	0	0-...	144.0	126	73	68	16	69-5	93	.236
1998— Chicago (N.L.)	7	7	.500	5.32	1.50	20	20	1	1	0	0-...	110.0	124	72	65	13	41-5	70	.281
1999— Daytona (Fla. St.)	0	0	...	0.00	0.43	2	2	0	0		0-...	4.2	2	0	0	0	0-0	4	.125
— West Tenn (Sou.)	0	0	...	1.74	1.55	3	3	0	0		0-...	10.1	7	2	2	0	9-0	12	.200
— Iowa (PCL)	0	1	.000	4.50	1.60	3	3	0	0		0-...	10.0	10	8	5	1	6-0	10	.270
2000— Ariz. Cubs (Ariz.)	0	1	.000	2.70	1.00	4	4	0	0		0-...	10.0	8	3	3	0	2-0	15	.211
— Lansing (Midw.)	0	0	...	0.00	0.00	1	1	0	0		0-...	0.2	0	0	0	0	0-0	2	.000
2001—			Did not play.																
2002— Oklahoma (PCL)	6	5	.545	3.33	1.36	46	5	0	0		14-...	92.0	86	40	34	8	39-5	93	.249
2003— Durham (Int'l)	1	0	1.000	2.53	0.90	7	6	0	0		0-...	32.0	24	11	9	2	6-0	33	.202
— Tampa Bay (A.L.)	6	11	.353	3.91	1.28	25	25	0	0	0	0-0	156.1	131	71	68	18	69-1	97	.228
2004— Tampa Bay (A.L.)	0	5	.000	6.97	1.83	11	8	0	0	0	0-0	50.1	72	42	39	9	20-0	22	.346
— Durham (Int'l)	4	2	.667	3.90	1.20	19	8	0	0		1-...	57.2	50	27	25	7	19-0	44	.233
2005— Pawtucket (Int'l)	5	2	.714	2.61	1.12	11	11	0	0		0-...	69.0	63	20	20	8	14-0	62	.245
— Boston (A.L.)	2	1	.667	6.11	1.43	28	3	0	0	1	0-0	56.0	64	39	38	7	16-2	28	.288
American League totals (3 years)	8	17	.320	4.97	1.42	64	36	2	0	1	0-0	262.2	267	152	145	34	105-3	147	.266
National League totals (2 years)	18	16	.529	4.71	1.42	43	43	2	2	0	0-...	254.0	250	145	133	29	110-10	163	.256
Major League totals (5 years)	26	33	.441	4.84	1.42	107	79	4	2	1	0-0	516.2	517	297	278	63	215-13	310	.261

DIVISION SERIES RECORD

Year Team (League)	W	L	Pct.	ERA	WHIP	G	GS	CG	ShO	Hld.	Sv.-Opp.	IP	H	R	ER	HR	BB-IBB	SO	Avg.
2005— Boston (A.L.)	0	0	...	15.43	1.29	1	0	0	0	0	0-...	2.1	2	4	4	1	1-0	0	.222

GONZALEZ, JUAN — OF

PERSONAL: Born October 16, 1969, in Vega Baja, Puerto Rico. ... 6-3/220. ... Bats right, throws right. ... Full name: Juan Alberto Gonzalez. ... High school: Vega Baja (Puerto Rico).

TRANSACTIONS/CAREER NOTES: Signed as a non-drafted free agent by Texas Rangers organization (May 30, 1986). ... On disabled list (March 30-April 26, 1991; April 16-June 1 and July 27-August 16, 1995; May 8-June 1, 1996; and March 24-May 2, 1997). ... Traded by Rangers with P Danny Patterson and C Gregg Zaun to Detroit Tigers for Ps Justin Thompson, Francisco Cordero and Alan Webb, OF Gabe Kapler, C Bill Haselman and 2B Frank Catalanotto (November 2, 1999). ... On disabled list (July 8-26, 2000). ... Signed as a free agent by Cleveland Indians (January 9, 2001). ... Signed as a free agent by Rangers (January 8, 2002). ... On disabled list (April 9-May 17, July 31, 2002-remainder of season and July 20, 2003-remainder of season). ... Signed as a free agent by Kansas City Royals (January 6, 2004). ... On disabled list (May 22, 2004-remainder of season); included rehabilitation assignment to AZL Royals. ... Signed as a free agent by Indians organization (January 1, 2005). ... On disabled list (March 31-May 31 and June 2, 2005-remainder of season); included rehabilitation assignment to Buffalo.

HONORS: Named A.L. Most Valuable Player by Baseball Writers' Association of America (1996 and 1998).

LEFTY-RIGHTY SPLITS

vs.	Avg.	AB	H	2B	3B	HR	RBI	BB	SO	OBP	Slg.
L	.000	0	0	0	0	0	0	0	0	.000	.000
R	.000	1	0	0	0	0	0	0	0	.000	.000

Year Team (League)	Pos.	G	AB	R	H	2B	3B	HR	RBI	BB	SO	HBP	GDP	SB-CS	Avg.	OBP	SLG	OPS	E	Avg.
1986— GC Rangers (GCL)	OF	60	233	24	56	4	1	0	36	21	57	1	9	7-5	.240	.302	.266	.568	6	.941
1987— Gastonia (S. Atl.)	OF	127	509	69	135	21	2	14	74	30	92	5	14	9-4	.265	.310	.397	.707	12	.953
1988— Charlotte (Fla. St.)	OF	77	277	25	71	14	3	8	43	25	64	4	7	5-2	.256	.325	.415	.740	4	.973
1989— Tulsa (Texas)	OF	133	502	73	147	30	7	21	85	31	98	9	8	1-8	.293	.342	.506	.848	9	.972
— Texas (A.L.)	OF	24	60	6	9	3	0	1	7	6	17	0	4	0-0	.150	.227	.250	.477	2	.964
1990— Okla. City (A.A.)	OF	128	496	78	128	29	4	29	101	32	109	1	11	2-2	.258	.300	.508	.808	8	.966
— Texas (A.L.)	DH-OF	25	90	11	26	7	1	4	12	2	18	2	2	0-1	.289	.316	.522	.838	0	1.000
1991— Texas (A.L.)	DH-OF	142	545	78	144	34	1	27	102	42	118	5	10	4-4	.264	.321	.479	.800	6	.981
1992— Texas (A.L.)	OF-DH	155	584	77	152	24	2	* 43	109	35	143	5	16	0-1	.260	.304	.529	.833	10	.975
1993— Texas (A.L.)	OF-DH	140	536	105	166	33	1	* 46	118	37	99	13	12	4-1	.310	.368	* .632	1.000	4	.985
1994— Texas (A.L.)	OF	107	422	57	116	18	4	19	85	30	66	7	18	6-4	.275	.330	.472	.802	2	.991
1995— Texas (A.L.)	DH-OF	90	352	57	104	20	2	27	82	17	66	0	15	0-0	.295	.324	.594	.917	1	1.000
1996— Texas (A.L.)	OF-DH	134	541	89	170	33	2	47	144	45	82	3	10	2-0	.314	.368	.643	1.012	4	.988
1997— Texas (A.L.)	DH-OF	133	533	87	158	24	3	42	131	33	107	3	12	0-0	.296	.335	.589	.924	4	.971
1998— Texas (A.L.)	OF-DH	154	606	110	193	* 50	2	45	* 157	46	126	6	20	2-1	.318	.366	.630	.997	4	.982
1999— Texas (A.L.)	OF-DH	144	562	114	183	36	1	39	128	51	105	4	10	3-3	.326	.378	.601	.980	4	.983
2000— Detroit (A.L.)	OF-DH	115	461	69	133	30	2	22	67	32	84	2	13	1-2	.289	.337	.505	.842	1	.992
2001— Cleveland (A.L.)	OF-DH	140	532	97	173	34	1	35	140	41	94	6	18	1-0	.325	.370	.590	.960	3	.987
2002— Texas (A.L.)	OF-DH	70	277	38	78	21	1	8	35	17	56	1	11	2-0	.282	.324	.451	.776	1	.992
2003— Texas (A.L.)	OF-DH	82	327	49	96	17	1	24	70	14	73	4	10	1-1	.294	.329	.572	.901	0	1.000
2004— Kansas City (A.L.)	OF-DH	33	127	17	35	4	1	5	17	9	19	1	3	0-1	.276	.326	.441	.767	3	.948
— AZL Royals (Ariz.)	DH	9	26	6	9	5	0	0	5	6	8	0	1	0-0	.346	.455	.538	.993	0	1.000
2005— Buffalo (Int'l)	OF-DH	5	21	1	6	0	0	0	1	3	0	0	1	0-0	.286	.286	.286	.571	0	1.000
— Cleveland (A.L.)		1	1	0	0	0	0	0	0	0	0	0	0	0-0	.000	.000	.000	.000	0	...
Major League totals (17 years)		1689	6556	1061	1936	388	25	434	1404	457	1273	62	184	26-19	.295	.343	.561	.904	46	.983

DIVISION SERIES RECORD

Year Team (League)	Pos.	G	AB	R	H	2B	3B	HR	RBI	BB	SO	HBP	GDP	SB-CS	Avg.	OBP	SLG	OPS	E	Avg.
1996— Texas (A.L.)	OF	4	16	5	7	0	0	5	9	3	2	0	0	0-0	.438	.526	1.375	1.901	0	1.000
1998— Texas (A.L.)	OF	3	12	1	1	1	0	0	0	0	3	0	0	0-0	.083	.083	.167	.250	0	1.000
1999— Texas (A.L.)	OF	3	11	1	2	0	0	1	1	1	3	0	1	0-0	.182	.250	.455	.705	0	1.000
2001— Cleveland (A.L.)	OF	5	23	4	8	3	0	2	5	0	7	0	1	0-0	.348	.348	.739	1.087	0	1.000
Division series totals (4 years)		15	62	11	18	4	0	8	15	4	15	0	2	0-0	.290	.333	.742	1.075	0	1.000

ALL-STAR GAME RECORD

		G	AB	R	H	2B	3B	HR	RBI	BB	SO	HBP	GDP	SB-CS	Avg.	OBP	SLG	OPS	E	Avg.
All-Star Game totals (3 years)		3	5	0	0	0	0	0	1	1	2	0	0	0-0	.000	.143	.000	.143	0	1.000

G

PERSONAL: Born September 3, 1967, in Tampa. ... 6-2/200. ... Bats left, throws right. ... Full name: Luis Emilio Gonzalez. ... High school: Jefferson (Tampa). ... College: South Alabama.

TRANSACTIONS/CAREER NOTES: Selected by Houston Astros organization in fourth round of 1988 free-agent draft. ... On disabled list (August 29-September 13, 1991; and July 21-August 5, 1992). ... Traded by Astros with C Scott Servais to Chicago Cubs for C Rick Wilkins (June 28, 1995). ... Signed as a free agent by Astros (December 19, 1996). ... Signed as a free agent by Detroit Tigers (December 9, 1997). ... Traded by Tigers to Arizona Diamondbacks for OF Karim Garcia (December 28, 1998). ... On disabled list (August 2, 2004-remainder of season). ... On bereavement list (June 25-29, 2005).

2005 GAMES PLAYED BY POSITION (MLB): OF—152.

SCOUTING REPORT

Offense: Gonzalez regained his power stroke after elbow surgery allowed him better extension with his arms. Has a fluid stroke and will use the whole field. Has good bat control and can handle the ball equally well inside or out. Is equally adept against left-handers and righthanders. Ball has good carry off his bat and he can drive the ball from left-center to right-center. Is an instinctive baserunner but not a basestealing threat. **Defense:** He's just an average left fielder now that his range has declined. Gets better jumps back than coming in. Arm is still short but is accurate. **Outlook:** His numbers have increased because of better health. Is a very steady offensive player with outstanding makeup. **Grade 7.7**

LUIS GONZALEZ'S HITTING ZONE

.136	.286	.423
.329	.328	.283
.273	.342	.346

LEFTY-RIGHTY SPLITS

vs.	Avg.	AB	H	2B	3B	HR	RBI	BB	SO	OBP	Slg.
L	.269	167	45	11	0	3	18	18	26	.359	.389
R	.272	412	112	26	0	21	61	60	64	.369	.488

Year	Team (League)	Pos.	G	AB	R	H	2B	3B	HR	RBI	BB	SO	HBP	GDP	SB-CS	Avg.	OBP	SLG	OPS	E	Avg.
1988—	Asheville (S. Atl.)	3B	31	115	13	29	7	1	2	14	12	17	2	4	2-2	.252	.333	.383	.716	6	.931
—	Auburn (NYP)	1B-3B-SS	39	157	32	49	10	3	5	27	12	19	1	1	2-0	.312	.354	.510	.864	13	.902
1989—	Osceola (Fla. St.)	DH	86	287	46	82	16	7	6	38	37	49	4	3	2-1	.286	.370	.453	.823	...	...
1990—	Columbus (Sou.)	1B-3B	138	495	86	131	30	6	• 24	89	54	100	6	6	27-9	.265	.337	.495	.832	23	.980
—	Houston (N.L.)	1B-3B	12	21	1	4	2	0	0	0	2	5	0	0	0-0	.190	.261	.286	.547	0	1.000
1991—	Houston (N.L.)	OF	137	473	51	120	28	9	13	69	40	101	8	9	10-7	.254	.320	.433	.753	5	.984
1992—	Houston (N.L.)	OF	122	387	40	94	19	3	10	55	24	52	2	6	7-7	.243	.289	.385	.674	2	.993
—	Tucson (PCL)	OF	13	44	11	19	4	2	1	9	5	7	1	0	4-1	.432	.490	.682	1.172	1	.963
1993—	Houston (N.L.)	OF	154	540	82	162	34	3	15	72	47	83	10	9	20-9	.300	.361	.457	.818	8	.978
1994—	Houston (N.L.)	OF	112	392	57	107	29	4	8	67	49	57	3	10	15-13	.273	.353	.429	.782	2	.991
1995—	Houston (N.L.)	OF	56	209	35	54	10	4	6	35	18	30	3	8	1-3	.258	.322	.431	.753	2	.980
—	Chicago (N.L.)	OF	77	262	34	76	19	4	7	34	39	33	3	4	5-5	.290	.384	.473	.858	4	.978
1996—	Chicago (N.L.)	OF-1B	146	483	70	131	30	4	15	79	61	49	4	13	9-6	.271	.354	.443	.797	3	.988
1997—	Houston (N.L.)	OF-1B	152	550	78	142	31	2	10	68	71	67	5	12	10-7	.258	.345	.376	.722	5	.982
1998—	Detroit (A.L.)	OF-DH	154	547	84	146	35	5	23	71	57	62	8	12	12-7	.267	.340	.475	.816	3	.988
1999—	Arizona (N.L.)	OF-DH	153	614	112	* 206	45	4	26	111	66	63	7	13	9-5	.336	.403	.549	.952	5	.983
2000—	Arizona (N.L.)	OF	• 162	618	106	192	47	2	31	114	78	85	12	12	2-4	.311	.392	.544	.935	3	.990
2001—	Arizona (N.L.)	OF	• 162	609	128	198	36	7	57	142	100	83	14	14	1-1	.325	.429	.688	1.117	0	1.000
2002—	Arizona (N.L.)	OF	148	524	90	151	19	3	28	103	97	76	5	12	9-2	.288	.400	.496	.896	4	.985
2003—	Arizona (N.L.)	OF	156	579	92	176	46	4	26	104	94	67	3	19	5-3	.304	.402	.532	.934	3	.989
2004—	Arizona (N.L.)	OF-DH	105	379	69	98	28	5	17	48	68	58	2	9	2-2	.259	.373	.493	.866	6	.965
2005—	Arizona (N.L.)	OF	155	579	90	157	37	0	24	79	78	90	11	14	4-1	.271	.366	.459	.825	3	.989
	American League totals (1 year)		154	547	84	146	35	5	23	71	57	62	8	9	12-7	.267	.340	.475	.816	3	.988
	National League totals (15 years)		2009	7219	1135	2068	460	58	293	1180	932	999	92	168	109-75	.286	.372	.488	.860	55	.986
	Major League totals (16 years)		2163	7766	1219	2214	495	63	316	1251	989	1061	100	177	121-82	.285	.369	.487	.857	58	.986

DIVISION SERIES RECORD

Year	Team (League)	Pos.	G	AB	R	H	2B	3B	HR	RBI	BB	SO	HBP	GDP	SB-CS	Avg.	OBP	SLG	OPS	E	Avg.
1997—	Houston (N.L.)	OF	3	12	0	4	0	0	0	0	0	1	0	0	0-0	.333	.333	.333	.667	1	.933
1999—	Arizona (N.L.)	OF	4	10	3	2	1	0	1	2	5	1	1	0	0-0	.200	.500	.600	1.100	0	1.000
2001—	Arizona (N.L.)	OF	5	19	1	5	0	0	1	1	2	4	0	0	0-0	.263	.333	.421	.754	0	1.000
	Division series totals (3 years)		12	41	4	11	1	0	2	3	7	6	1	0	0-0	.268	.388	.439	.827	1	.958

CHAMPIONSHIP SERIES RECORD

Year	Team (League)	Pos.	G	AB	R	H	2B	3B	HR	RBI	BB	SO	HBP	GDP	SB-CS	Avg.	OBP	SLG	OPS	E	Avg.
2001—	Arizona (N.L.)	OF	5	19	4	4	0	0	1	4	3	3	1	0	0-0	.211	.348	.368	.716	0	1.000

WORLD SERIES RECORD

Year	Team (League)	Pos.	G	AB	R	H	2B	3B	HR	RBI	BB	SO	HBP	GDP	SB-CS	Avg.	OBP	SLG	OPS	E	Avg.
2001—	Arizona (N.L.)	OF	7	27	4	7	2	0	1	5	1	11	2	1	0-0	.259	.333	.444	.778	0	1.000

ALL-STAR GAME RECORD

		G	AB	R	H	2B	3B	HR	RBI	BB	SO	HBP	GDP	SB-CS	Avg.	OBP	SLG	OPS	E	Avg.
	All-Star Game totals (5 years)	5	7	1	4	2	0	1	4	0	0	0	0	0-0	.571	.571	.857	1.429	0	...

PERSONAL: Born June 26, 1979, in Maracay, Venezuela. ... 5-11/170. ... Bats right, throws right. ... Full name: Luis Alberto Gonzalez.

TRANSACTIONS/CAREER NOTES: Signed as a non-drafted free agent by Cleveland Indians organization (July 5, 1996). ... Selected by Colorado Rockies from Indians organization in Rule 5 major league draft (December 15, 2003).

2005 GAMES PLAYED BY POSITION (MLB): 2B—83, SS—17, 3B—12, 1B—10, OF—8.

G

SCOUTING REPORT *Offense:* Gonzalez is an aggressive hitter with good bat speed. Has a long swing and lots of movement at the plate. Is a good fastball hitter with power to the opposite field. Has trouble with breaking pitches. Is an average runner but is slow out of the box. Doesn't steal bases. *Defense:* Gonzalez isn't quick enough to play the middle infield, but he has worked on his pivot at second base. Is accurate throwing on the move and off his back foot. *Outlook:* He could be a good hitter but needs to work on his agility. Could hit about 20 home runs a year if he learns to pull the ball. *Grade 6.1*

LUIS A. GONZALEZ'S HITTING ZONE

.409	.308	.105
.330	.361	.405
.286	.267	.368

LEFTY-RIGHTY SPLITS

vs.	Avg.	AB	H	2B	3B	HR	RBI	BB	SO	OBP	Slg.
L	.380	142	54	15	0	3	10	8	21	.413	.549
R	.244	262	64	10	0	6	34	12	42	.290	.351

									BATTING									FIELDING	
Year Team (League)	Pos.	G	AB	R	H	2B	3B	HR	RBI	BB	SO	HBP	GDP	SB-CS	Avg.	OBP	SLG	OPS	E	Avg.
1998—Columbus (S. Atl.)	SS	101	320	48	87	14	1	3	32	28	63	8	5	10-3	.272	.345	.350	.695	28	.940
1999—Kinston (Carol.)		1	1	0	0	0	0	0	0	0	0	0	0	0-0	.000	.000	.000	.000	...	...
—Columbus (S. Atl.)	SS-3B-2B	83	299	41	88	18	2	7	50	26	40	5	5	6-5	.294	.355	.438	.793	21	.931
2000—Kinston (Carol.)	2B-SS	79	284	32	70	11	0	2	33	21	54	6	6	6-6	.246	.310	.306	.616	12	.961
2001—Kinston (Carol.)	3B-2B-SS	52	183	31	59	14	0	5	19	14	36	8	1	3-5	.322	.391	.481	.872	9	.945
—Akron (East.)	2B-SS-3B	52	199	41	60	12	2	5	17	7	26	2	3	2-3	.302	.329	.457	.786	3	.987
2002—Buffalo (Int'l)	2B	6	19	0	2	0	0	0	1	1	4	1	1	0-0	.105	.190	.105	.296	1	.967
—Akron (East.)	2B-3B-SS OF-1B	73	263	42	70	10	3	6	24	12	37	5	6	4-0	.266	.304	.395	.700	8	.962
2003—Akron (East.)	1B-2B-OF 3B-SS	116	431	72	137	22	4	7	62	46	41	6	17	1-0	.318	.385	.436	.821	9	.985
2004—Colorado (N.L.)	2B-OF-3B SS-DH	102	322	42	94	17	3	12	40	15	67	4	5	1-5	.292	.330	.469	.799	2	.993
2005—Colorado (N.L.)	2B-SS-3B 1B-OF	128	404	51	118	25	0	9	44	20	63	6	7	3-4	.292	.333	.421	.753	4	.991
Major League totals (2 years)		230	726	93	212	42	2	21	84	35	130	10	12	4-9	.292	.332	.442	.774	6	.992

GONZALEZ, MIKE   P

PERSONAL: Born May 23, 1978, in Corpus Christi, Texas. ... 6-2/205. ... Throws left, bats right. ... Full name: Michael Vela Gonzalez. ... High school: Harvest Christian Academy (Pasadena, Texas). ... Junior college: San Jacinto (Texas).

TRANSACTIONS/CAREER NOTES: Selected by Pittsburgh Pirates organization in 17th round of 1996 free-agent draft; did not sign. ... Selected by Pittsburgh Pirates organization in 30th round of 1997 free-agent draft. ... Traded by Pirates with P Scott Sauerbeck to Boston Red Sox for Ps Brandon Lyon and Anastacio Martinez (July 22, 2003). ... Traded by Red Sox with IF Freddy Sanchez to Pirates for Ps Jeff Suppan, Brandon Lyon and Anastacio Martinez (July 31, 2003). ... On disabled list (June 23-August 16, 2005); included rehabilitation assignment to Indianapolis.

CAREER HITTING: 1-for-1 (1.000), 0 R, 1 2B, 0 3B, 0 HR, 2 RBI.

SCOUTING REPORT *Throws:* He throws a plus fastball that ranges from 91-94 mph. Also has a curve at 79-80, a slider at 84 and a changeup. *Tendencies:* Gonzalez has an outstanding arm with two plus pitches, his fastball and slider. Really labored with his control; delivery is very difficult to develop and keep in sync. Can overpower hitters up in the zone with his fastball. Breaking ball at times is more of a slurve. *Outlook:* If he can gain command of his fastball, he will be a candidate to close next season. Needs to stay healthy. *Grade 7.1*

MIKE GONZALEZ'S PITCHING ZONE

.600	.455	.077
.286	.000	.227
.375	.000	.167

LEFTY-RIGHTY SPLITS

vs.	Avg.	AB	H	2B	3B	HR	RBI	BB	SO	OBP	Slg.
L	.152	66	10	1	0	0	5	10	27	.260	.167
R	.223	112	25	9	0	2	13	21	31	.348	.357

Year Team (League)	W	L	Pct.	ERA	WHIP	G	GS	CG	ShO	Hld.	Sv.-Opp.	IP	H	R	ER	HR	BB-IBB	SO	Avg.
1997—GC Pirates (GCL)	2	0	1.000	2.48	1.00	7	3	0	0	...	0-...	29.0	21	9	8	0	8-0	33	.200
—Augusta (S. Atl.)	1	1	.500	1.86	0.98	4	3	0	0	...	0-...	19.1	11	5	4	1	8-0	22	.164
1998—Lynchburg (Carol.)	0	3	.000	6.67	1.87	7	7	0	0	...	0-...	28.1	40	21	21	5	13-0	22	.351
—Augusta (S. Atl.)	4	2	.667	2.84	1.36	11	9	0	0	...	0-...	50.2	43	24	16	2	26-0	72	.231
1999—Lynchburg (Carol.)	10	4	.714	4.02	1.44	20	20	0	0	...	0-...	112.0	98	55	50	10	63-0	119	.240
—Altoona (East.)	2	3	.400	8.10	1.99	7	5	0	0	...	0-...	26.2	34	25	24	4	19-0	31	.312
2000—GC Pirates (GCL)	1	0	1.000	4.50	2.00	2	1	0	0	...	0-...	6.0	8	6	3	1	4-0	7	.267
—Lynchburg (Carol.)	4	3	.571	4.66	1.63	12	10	0	0	...	0-...	56.0	57	34	29	6	34-0	53	.269
2001—Lynchburg (Carol.)	2	2	.500	2.93	1.14	14	2	0	0	...	0-...	30.2	28	14	10	3	7-1	32	.241
—Altoona (East.)	5	4	.556	3.71	1.34	14	14	1	0	...	0-...	87.1	81	38	36	4	36-0	66	.251
2002—GC Pirates (GCL)	2	0	1.000	0.00	0.60	2	2	0	0	...	0-...	13.1	5	1	0	0	3-0	14	.114
—Altoona (East.)	8	4	.667	3.80	1.45	16	16	0	0	...	0-...	85.1	77	38	36	4	47-2	82	.244
2003—Lynchburg (Carol.)	0	1	.000	5.14	1.71	5	0	0	0	...	0-...	7.0	7	9	4	0	5-0	9	.269
—Altoona (East.)	0	0	...	1.23	0.82	5	0	0	0	...	1-...	7.1	5	1	1	0	2-0	10	.154
—Pawtucket (Int'l)	0	0	...	0.00	1.80	2	0	0	0	...	0-...	1.2	2	0	0	0	1-0	2	.286
—Nashville (PCL)	0	0	...	4.50	1.30	7	0	0	0	...	2-...	10.0	9	5	5	0	4-1	10	.231
—Pittsburgh (N.L.)	0	1	.000	7.56	1.56	16	0	0	0	3	0-0	8.1	7	7	7	4	6-0	6	.233
2004—Nashville (PCL)	2	0	1.000	0.90	0.95	14	0	0	0	...	2-...	20.0	12	2	2	0	7-0	35	.185
—Pittsburgh (N.L.)	3	1	.750	1.25	0.88	47	0	0	0	13	1-4	43.1	32	7	6	2	6-0	55	.201
2005—Indianapolis (Int'l)	0	0	...	0.00	0.00	2	0	0	0	0	0-0	3.1	0	0	0	0	0-0	5	.000
—Pittsburgh (N.L.)	1	3	.250	2.70	1.32	51	0	0	0	15	3-3	50.0	35	15	15	2	31-2	58	.197
Major League totals (3 years)	4	5	.444	2.48	1.15	114	0	0	0	31	4-7	101.2	74	29	28	8	43-2	119	.202

G

GONZALEZ, WIKI   C

PERSONAL: Born May 17, 1974, in Aragua, Venezuela. ... 5-11/203. ... Bats right, throws right. ... Full name: Wiklenman Vicente Gonzalez. ... Name pronounced: WICK-ee.

TRANSACTIONS/CAREER NOTES: Signed as non-drafted free agent by Pittsburgh Pirates organization (February 12, 1992). ... Selected by San Diego Padres organization from Pirates organization in Rule 5 minor league draft (December 9, 1996). ... On disabled list (June 3-July 3, 2001); included rehabilitation assignment to Lake Elsinore. ... On disabled list (April 5-May 15 and July 18-August 24, 2002); included rehabilitation assignment to Lake Elsinore. ... Traded by Padres with P Kevin Jarvis, IF Dave Hansen and OF Vince Faison To Seattle Mariners for IF Jeff Cirillo, P Brian Sweeney and cash (January 6, 2004). ... On disabled list (May 15-July 1, 2005); included rehabilitation assignment to Tacoma.

2005 GAMES PLAYED BY POSITION (MLB): C—14.

LEFTY-RIGHTY SPLITS

vs.	Avg.	AB	H	2B	3B	HR	RBI	BB	SO	OBP	Slg.
L	.444	9	4	2	0	0	1	0	2	.444	.667
R	.222	36	8	3	0	0	1	2	1	.263	.306

Year Team (League)	Pos.	G	AB	R	H	2B	3B	HR	RBI	BB	SO	HBP	GDP	SB-CS	Avg.	OBP	SLG	OPS	E	Avg.
1992—Dom. Pirates (DSL)		63	190	20	48	6	1	3	33	22	12	4	6	4-1	.253	.338	.342	.680	...	...
1993—Dom. Pirates (DSL)		69	244	47	73	10	3	7	47	40	15	9	8	24-8	.299	.412	.451	.863	...	...
1994—GC Pirates (GCL)	C-1B-P	41	143	25	48	8	2	4	26	13	13	3	3	2-3	.336	.400	.503	.903	12	.962
1995—Augusta (S. Atl.)	C	84	278	41	67	17	0	3	36	26	32	2	7	5-4	.241	.305	.335	.640	6	.985
1996—Augusta (S. Atl.)	C	118	419	52	106	21	3	4	62	58	41	7	14	4-6	.253	.350	.346	.696	23	.976
1997—Rancho Cuca. (Calif.)	C	33	110	18	33	9	1	5	26	7	25	0	1	1-1	.300	.339	.536	.875	2	.985
—Mobile (Sou.)	C	47	143	15	39	7	1	4	25	10	12	2	5	1-1	.273	.327	.420	.747	3	.989
1998—Rancho Cuca. (Calif.)	C	75	292	51	84	24	2	10	59	26	54	2	6	0-0	.288	.346	.486	.832	3	.993
—Mobile (Sou.)	C	22	67	20	26	9	0	4	26	14	4	2	1	0-0	.388	.494	.701	1.195	0	1.000
1999—Mobile (Sou.)	C-DH	61	225	38	76	16	2	10	49	29	28	7	8	0-0	.338	.424	.560	.984	7	.982
—Las Vegas (PCL)	C-DH	24	92	13	25	6	0	6	12	5	10	3	4	0-0	.272	.330	.533	.863	3	.984
—San Diego (N.L.)	C	30	83	7	21	2	1	3	12	1	8	1	5	0-0	.253	.271	.410	.680	1	.991
2000—San Diego (N.L.)	C	95	284	25	66	15	1	5	30	30	31	3	5	1-2	.232	.311	.345	.656	5	.991
2001—San Diego (N.L.)	C-DH	64	160	16	44	6	0	8	27	11	28	4	3	2-0	.275	.335	.463	.798	3	.989
—Lake Elsinore (Calif.)	C	4	13	1	2	0	0	0	1	2	4	0	0		.154	.250	.154	.404	1	.973
2002—San Diego (N.L.)	C	56	164	16	36	8	1	1	20	27	24	1	10	0-0	.220	.330	.299	.629	6	.985
—Lake Elsinore (Calif.)	C	19	53	10	18	8	0	1	6	12	3	4	2	0-0	.340	.486	.547	1.033	2	.983
2003—San Diego (N.L.)	C-P	24	65	1	13	5	0	0	10	5	13	1	3	0-0	.200	.264	.277	.541	1	.993
—Portland (PCL)	C-DH	44	149	17	42	8	1	4	20	21	12	3	5	1-0	.282	.377	.430	.809	4	.987
2004—Tacoma (PCL)	C	13	52	9	16	5	0	5	14	2	3	0	0	0-0	.308	.333	.692	1.025	1	.991
2005—Seattle (A.L.)	C	14	45	7	12	5	0	0	2	2	3	0	1	0-0	.267	.298	.378	.676	0	1.000
—Tacoma (PCL)	C-DH	47	176	25	55	10	1	5	28	16	13	2	7	0-0	.313	.374	.466	.840	2	.993
American League totals (1 year)		14	45	7	12	5	0	0	2	2	3	0	1	0-0	.267	.298	.378	.676	0	1.000
National League totals (5 years)		269	756	65	180	36	3	17	99	74	104	10	26	3-2	.238	.312	.361	.674	16	.989
Major League totals (6 years)		283	801	72	192	41	3	17	101	76	107	10	27	3-2	.240	.312	.362	.674	16	.990

GOOD, ANDREW   P

PERSONAL: Born September 19, 1979, in San Diego. ... 6-1/209. ... Throws right, bats right. ... Full name: Andrew Richard Good. ... High school: Rochester (Rochester Hills, Mich.).

TRANSACTIONS/CAREER NOTES: Selected by Arizona Diamondbacks organization in eighth round of 1998 free-agent draft. ... On disabled list (July 9, 2004-remainder of season); included rehabilitation assignments to Tucson and El Paso. ... Released by Diamondbacks (December 13, 2004). ... Signed as a free agent by Detroit Tigers organization (December 20, 2004).

CAREER HITTING: 2-for-21 (.095), 0 R, 0 2B, 0 3B, 0 HR, 2 RBI.

LEFTY-RIGHTY SPLITS

vs.	Avg.	AB	H	2B	3B	HR	RBI	BB	SO	OBP	Slg.
L	.167	6	1	0	0	0	0	0	4	.167	.167
R	.231	13	3	0	0	1	3	1	3	.286	.462

Year Team (League)	W	L	Pct.	ERA	WHIP	G	GS	CG	ShO	Hld.	Sv.-Opp.	IP	H	R	ER	HR	BB-IBB	SO	Avg.
1998—Ariz. D'backs (Ariz.)	1	3	.250	4.28	1.57	9	9	0	0	...	0-...	33.2	46	25	16	1	7-0	25	.324
—South Bend (Midw.)	0	1	.000	3.00	1.33	2	0	0	0	...	0-...	6.0	7	4	2	0	1-0	6	.280
1999—South Bend (Midw.)	11	10	.524	4.10	1.31	27	27	0	0	...	0-...	153.2	160	80	70	9	42-0	146	.268
2000—Lancaster (Calif.)			Did not play.																
2001—Lancaster (Calif.)	8	6	.571	4.80	1.33	19	18	0	0	...	0-...	101.1	108	63	54	12	27-0	104	.267
—El Paso (Texas)	2	3	.400	5.88	1.75	10	9	0	0	...	0-...	56.2	79	44	37	2	20-0	46	.324
2002—El Paso (Texas)	13	6	.684	3.54	1.10	28	27	2	1	...	0-...	178.0	170	89	70	21	26-0	127	.248
2003—Arizona (N.L.)	4	2	.667	5.29	1.36	16	10	0	0	1	0-0	66.1	74	42	39	15	16-3	42	.281
—Tucson (PCL)	4	4	.500	5.00	1.44	11	11	0	0	...	0-0	63.0	78	36	35	12	13-0	45	.300
2004—Arizona (N.L.)	1	2	.333	5.31	1.38	17	2	0	0	0	0-0	40.2	43	25	24	8	13-0	26	.272
—El Paso (Texas)	0	0	...	0.93	1.03	4	4	0	0	...	0-0	9.2	7	2	1	0	3-0	9	.212
—Tucson (PCL)	3	2	.600	3.04	1.23	5	3	0	0	...	0-0	23.2	25	12	8	4	4-0	17	.266
2005—Detroit (A.L.)	0	0	...	5.40	1.00	2	0	0	0	...	0-0	5.0	4	3	3	1	1-0	7	.211
—Toledo (Int'l)	9	5	.643	3.68	1.27	23	23	0	0	...	0-0	134.1	129	61	55	18	42-3	89	.253
American League totals (1 year)	0	0	...	5.40	1.00	2	0	0	0	...	0-0	5.0	4	3	3	1	1-0	7	.211
National League totals (2 years)	5	4	.556	5.30	1.36	33	12	0	0	1	0-0	107.0	117	67	63	23	29-3	68	.278
Major League totals (3 years)	5	4	.556	5.30	1.35	35	12	0	0	1	0-0	112.0	121	70	66	24	30-3	75	.275

GORDON, TOM   P

PERSONAL: Born November 18, 1967, in Sebring, Fla. ... 5-10/190. ... Throws right, bats right. ... Full name: Thomas Gordon. ... High school: Avon Park (Fla.).

TRANSACTIONS/CAREER NOTES: Selected by Kansas City Royals organization in sixth round of June 1986 free-agent draft. ... On disabled list (August 12-September 1, 1992; and May 8-24, 1995). ... Signed as a free agent by Boston Red Sox (December 21, 1995). ... On disabled list (April 18-May 10 and June 12-September 27, 1999); included rehabilitation assignments to Trenton and Augusta. ... On disabled list (April 2, 2000-entire season). ... Signed as a free agent by Chicago Cubs (December 14, 2000). ... On disabled list (March 23-May 1, 2001); included rehabilitation assignments to Daytona and Iowa. ... On disabled list (March 28-July 2, 2002); included rehabilitation assignments to Daytona and Iowa. ... Traded by Cubs to Houston Astros for P Russ Rohlicek and two players to be named (August 22, 2002); Cubs acquired Ps Travis Anderson and Mike Nannini to complete deal (September 11, 2002). ... Signed as a free agent by Chicago White Sox (January 20, 2003). ... Signed as a free agent by New York Yankees (December 16, 2003).

HONORS: Named A.L. Rookie Pitcher of the Year by THE SPORTING NEWS (1989).

CAREER HITTING: 0-for-2 (.000), 0 R, 0 2B, 0 3B, 0 HR, 0 RBI.

SCOUTING REPORT Throws: Gordon has a riding four-seam fastball that he throws at 91-95 mph. His hard curveball is 77-82, and his slider is 85-88. All three are plus pitches. *Tendencies:* Gordon throws from directly over the top. Has used his slider more than his power curve, which used to be one of the best in the business. Still has a tight, biting curve but can command his slider better. Challenges hitters and is effective against righthanders and lefthanders. Has very good command overall and is deceptive. *Outlook:* He was one of the game's most dependable setup relievers; he'll close next season for some team. *Grade 9*

TOM GORDON'S PITCHING ZONE

.150	.143	.059
.255	.344	.214
.200	.263	.350

LEFTY-RIGHTY SPLITS

vs.	Avg.	AB	H	2B	3B	HR	RBI	BB	SO	OBP	Slg.
L	.187	134	25	4	1	2	14	18	39	.279	.276
R	.217	157	34	7	0	6	25	11	30	.266	.376

Year	Team (League)	W	L	Pct.	ERA	WHIP	G	GS	CG	ShO	Hld.	Sv.-Opp.	IP	H	R	ER	HR	BB-IBB	SO	Avg.
1986—	GC Royals (GCL)	3	1	.750	1.02	1.23	9	7	2	1	...	0-...	44.0	31	12	5	0	23-1	47	.194
—	Omaha (A.A.)	0	0	...	47.25	6.00	1	0	0	0	...	0-...	1.1	6	7	7	0	2-0	0	.600
1987—	Eugene (Northwest)	9	0	1.000	2.86	1.31	15	13	0	0	...	1-...	72.1	48	33	23	2	47-0	91	.183
—	Fort Myers (Fla. St.)	1	0	1.000	2.63	1.61	3	3	0	0	...	0-...	13.2	5	4	4	0	17-0	11	.122
1988—	Appleton (Midw.)	7	5	.583	2.06	0.95	17	17	5	1	...	0-...	118.0	69	30	27	3	43-1	172	.163
—	Memphis (Sou.)	6	0	1.000	0.38	0.70	6	6	2	2	...	0-...	47.1	16	3	2	1	17-0	62	.103
—	Omaha (A.A.)	3	0	1.000	1.33	1.28	3	3	0	0	...	0-...	20.1	11	3	3	0	15-0	29	.157
—	Kansas City (A.L.)	0	2	.000	5.17	1.47	5	2	0	0	...	0-0	15.2	16	9	9	1	7-0	18	.267
1989—	Kansas City (A.L.)	17	9	.654	3.64	1.28	49	16	1	1	3	1-7	163.0	122	67	66	10	86-4	153	.210
1990—	Kansas City (A.L.)	12	11	.522	3.73	1.49	32	32	6	1	0	0-0	195.1	192	99	81	17	99-1	175	.258
1991—	Kansas City (A.L.)	9	14	.391	3.87	1.37	45	14	1	0	4	1-4	158.0	129	76	68	16	87-6	167	.221
1992—	Kansas City (A.L.)	6	10	.375	4.59	1.45	40	11	0	0	0	0-2	117.2	116	67	60	9	55-4	98	.258
1993—	Kansas City (A.L.)	12	6	.667	3.58	1.30	48	14	2	0	2	1-6	155.2	125	65	62	11	77-5	143	.223
1994—	Kansas City (A.L.)	11	7	.611	4.35	1.44	24	24	0	0	0	0-0	155.1	136	79	75	15	87-3	126	.237
1995—	Kansas City (A.L.)	12	12	.500	4.43	1.55	31	31	2	0	0	0-0	189.0	204	110	93	12	89-4	119	.279
1996—	Boston (A.L.)	12	9	.571	5.59	1.64	34	34	4	1	0	0-0	215.2	249	143 *	134	28	105-5	171	.284
1997—	Boston (A.L.)	6	10	.375	3.74	1.28	42	25	2	1	0	11-13	182.2	155	85	76	10	78-1	159	.226
1998—	Boston (A.L.)	7	4	.636	2.72	1.01	73	0	0	0	0	* 46-47	79.1	55	24	24	2	25-1	78	.191
1999—	Boston (A.L.)	0	2	.000	5.60	1.64	21	0	0	0	1	11-13	17.2	17	11	11	2	12-2	24	.246
2000—	Boston (A.L.)				Did not play.															
2001—	Daytona (Fla. St.)	0	0	...	0.00	0.00	2	2	0	0	...	0-...	2.0	0	0	0	0	0-0	3	.000
—	Iowa (PCL)	0	0	...	0.00	1.00	2	0	0	0	...	0-...	2.0	1	0	0	0	1-0	2	.167
—	Chicago (N.L.)	1	2	.333	3.38	1.06	47	0	0	0	0	27-31	45.1	32	18	17	4	16-1	67	.188
2002—	Daytona (Fla. St.)	0	0	...	3.38	1.13	2	2	0	0	...	0-...	2.2	1	1	1	0	2-0	3	.100
—	Iowa (PCL)	0	0	...	16.20	2.40	2	0	0	0	...	1-...	1.2	1	4	3	0	3-0	0	.167
—	Chicago (N.L.)	1	1	.500	3.42	1.56	19	0	0	0	2	0-0	23.2	27	12	9	1	10-1	31	.293
—	Houston (N.L.)	0	2	.000	3.32	1.11	15	0	0	0	4	0-0	19.0	15	7	7	2	6-2	17	.217
2003—	Chicago (N.L.)	7	6	.538	3.16	1.19	66	0	0	0	7	12-17	74.0	57	29	26	4	31-3	91	.213
2004—	New York (A.L.)	9	4	.692	2.21	0.88	80	0	0	0	* 36	4-10	89.2	56	23	22	5	23-5	96	.180
2005—	New York (A.L.)	5	4	.556	2.57	1.09	79	0	0	0	• 33	2-9	80.2	59	25	23	8	29-4	69	.203
	American League totals (15 years)	125	110	.532	3.95	1.36	669	203	18	4	88	89-128	1889.1	1688	912	830	150	890-48	1687	.239
	National League totals (2 years)	2	5	.286	3.38	1.20	81	0	0	0	6	27-31	88.0	74	37	33	7	32-4	115	.224
	Major League totals (17 years)	127	115	.525	3.93	1.36	750	203	18	4	94	116-159	1977.1	1762	949	863	157	922-52	1802	.238

DIVISION SERIES RECORD

Year	Team (League)	W	L	Pct.	ERA	WHIP	G	GS	CG	ShO	Hld.	Sv.-Opp.	IP	H	R	ER	HR	BB-IBB	SO	Avg.
1998—	Boston (A.L.)	0	1	.000	9.00	2.67	2	0	0	0	0	0-1	3.0	4	3	3	0	4-0	1	.333
1999—	Boston (A.L.)	0	0	...	4.50	1.00	2	0	0	0	0	0-0	2.0	1	1	1	0	1-0	3	.143
2004—	New York (A.L.)	0	0	...	4.91	0.55	3	0	0	0	1	0-0	3.2	2	2	2	0	0-0	3	.143
2005—	New York (A.L.)	0	0	...	3.86	0.86	3	0	0	0	1	0-0	2.1	2	1	1	1	0-0	2	.200
	Division series totals (4 years)	0	1	.000	5.73	1.27	10	0	0	0	2	0-1	11.0	9	8	7	1	5-0	9	.209

CHAMPIONSHIP SERIES RECORD

Year	Team (League)	W	L	Pct.	ERA	WHIP	G	GS	CG	ShO	Hld.	Sv.-Opp.	IP	H	R	ER	HR	BB-IBB	SO	Avg.
1999—	Boston (A.L.)	0	0	...	13.50	2.00	3	0	0	0	0	0-0	2.0	3	3	3	2	1-0	3	.333
2004—	New York (A.L.)	0	0	...	8.10	1.80	6	0	0	0	3	0-0	6.2	10	6	6	2	2-0	3	.357
	Champ. series totals (2 years)	0	0	...	9.35	1.85	9	0	0	0	3	0-0	8.2	13	9	9	4	3-0	6	.351

ALL-STAR GAME RECORD

Year	Team (League)	W	L	Pct.	ERA	WHIP	G	GS	CG	ShO	Hld.	Sv.-Opp.	IP	H	R	ER	HR	BB-IBB	SO	Avg.
	All-Star Game totals (2 years)	0	0	...	13.50	3.00	2	0	0	0	0	0-0	1.1	3	2	2	0	1-0	0	.500

GORZELANNY, TOM   P   G

PERSONAL: Born July 12, 1982, in Evergreen Park, Ill. ... 6-2/207. ... Throws left, bats left. ... Full name: Thomas Stephen Gorzelanny. ... Name pronounced: gore-zah-LAWN-ee. ... High school: Marist (Ill.). ... Junior college: Triton (Ill.).

TRANSACTIONS/CAREER NOTES: Selected by Pittsburgh Pirates organization in second round of 2003 free-agent draft.

CAREER HITTING: 0-for-1 (.000), 0 R, 0 2B, 0 3B, 0 HR, 0 RBI.

LEFTY-RIGHTY SPLITS

vs.	Avg.	AB	H	2B	3B	HR	RBI	BB	SO	OBP	Slg.
L	.000	6	0	0	0	0	0	0	2	.000	.000
R	.455	22	10	3	0	1	5	3	1	.520	.727

Year	Team (League)	W	L	Pct.	ERA	WHIP	G	GS	CG	ShO	Hld.	Sv.-Opp.	IP	H	R	ER	HR	BB-IBB	SO	Avg.
2003—	Williamsport (NYP)	1	2	.333	1.78	1.09	8	8	0	0	...	0-...	30.1	23	6	6	1	10-0	22	.215
2004—	Hickory (S. Atl.)	7	2	.778	2.23	1.04	16	15	1	0	...	0-...	93.0	63	30	23	9	34-0	106	.194
—	Lynchburg (Carol.)	3	5	.375	4.85	1.31	10	10	0	0	...	0-...	55.2	54	31	30	6	19-0	61	.255
2005—	Altoona (East.)	8	5	.615	3.26	1.23	23	23	1	1	0	0-0	129.2	114	50	47	6	46-1	124	.236
—	Pittsburgh (N.L.)	0	1	.000	12.00	2.17	3	1	0	0	0	0-0	6.0	10	8	8	1	3-0	3	.357
	Major League totals (1 year)	0	1	.000	12.00	2.17	3	1	0	0	0	0-0	6.0	10	8	8	1	3-0	3	.357

GOSLING, MIKE — P

PERSONAL: Born September 23, 1980, in Madison, Wis. ... 6-0/210. ... Throws left, bats left. ... Full name: Michael Frederick Gosling. ... High school: East (Salt Lake City). ... College: Stanford.
TRANSACTIONS/CAREER NOTES: Selected by Minnesota Twins organization in 14th round of 1998 free-agent draft; did not sign. ... Selected by Arizona Diamondbacks organization in second round of 2001 free-agent draft.
CAREER HITTING: 0-for-12 (.000), 0 R, 0 2B, 0 3B, 0 HR, 0 RBI.

MIKE GOSLING'S PITCHING ZONE

.300	.250	.200
.423	.455	.273
.429	.500	.000

LEFTY-RIGHTY SPLITS

vs.	Avg.	AB	H	2B	3B	HR	RBI	BB	SO	OBP	Slg.
L	.231	39	9	5	0	0	1	4	5	.302	.359
R	.330	94	31	12	1	2	15	15	9	.422	.543

Year	Team (League)	W	L	Pct.	ERA	WHIP	G	GS	CG	ShO	Hld.	Sv.-Opp.	IP	H	R	ER	HR	BB-IBB	SO	Avg.
2002—	El Paso (Texas)	14	5	.737	3.13	1.27	27	27	2	2		0-...	166.2	149	66	58	7	62-4	115	.238
2003—	Tucson (PCL)	9	12	.429	5.61	1.80	26	26	0	0		0-...	136.1	190	106	85	13	56-0	89	.330
2004—	Tucson (PCL)	9	5	.643	5.82	1.66	24	21	0	0		0-...	128.1	160	101	83	16	53-0	67	.305
—	Arizona (N.L.)	1	1	.500	4.62	1.54	6	4	0	0	0	0-0	25.1	26	13	13	5	13-1	14	.274
2005—	Arizona (N.L.)	0	3	.000	4.45	1.82	13	5	0	0	0	0-0	32.1	40	20	16	2	19-2	14	.301
—	Tucson (PCL)	4	6	.400	5.95	1.72	18	17	0	0	0	0-0	92.1	129	70	61	11	30-0	76	.328
Major League totals (2 years)		1	4	.200	4.53	1.70	19	9	0	0	0	0-0	57.2	66	33	29	7	32-3	28	.289

GOTAY, RUBEN — 2B

PERSONAL: Born December 25, 1982, in Rio Piedras, Puerto Rico. ... 5-11/160. ... Bats both, throws right. ... Full name: Ruben A. Gotay. ... Name pronounced: GO-tie. ... High school: Dr. Santiago Veue Calzada (Fajardo, P.R.). ... Junior college: Indian Hills (Iowa) Community College.
TRANSACTIONS/CAREER NOTES: Selected by Kansas City Royals organization in 31st round of 2000 free-agent draft.
2005 GAMES PLAYED BY POSITION (MLB): 2B—81, DH—2.

SCOUTING REPORT Gotay is an inside-out hitter with little power from either side. Tries to pull the ball too much. Can run but does not trust his instincts. Is not fluid and has poor hands. Lacks arm strength and tends to play out of control. Has not progressed as rapidly as expected and will face an uphill battle to make the club next spring. *Grade 4.7*

RUBEN GOTAY'S HITTING ZONE

.364	.250	.111
.172	.333	.293
.429	.167	.226

LEFTY-RIGHTY SPLITS

vs.	Avg.	AB	H	2B	3B	HR	RBI	BB	SO	OBP	Slg.
L	.212	52	11	2	0	0	3	9	12	.323	.250
R	.230	230	53	12	2	5	26	13	39	.279	.365

Year	Team (League)	Pos.	G	AB	R	H	2B	3B	HR	RBI	BB	SO	HBP	GDP	SB-CS	Avg.	OBP	SLG	OPS	E	Avg.
2001—	GC Royals (GCL)	2B-3B	52	184	29	58	15	1	3	19	26	22	0	2	5-6	.315	.398	.457	.855	13	.937
2002—	Burlington (Midw.)	2B-3B	133	509	87	145	42	9	9	83	73	110	8	5	5-4	.285	.377	.456	.833	17	.974
2003—	Wilmington (Carol.)	2B	134	502	68	131	31	2	9	72	60	97	7	1	8-1	.261	.343	.384	.727	16	.973
2004—	Wichita (Texas)	2B-DH	106	405	71	117	22	6	9	68	51	60	6	9	9-10	.289	.373	.440	.806	15	.971
—	Kansas City (A.L.)	2B	44	152	17	41	7	3	1	16	9	36	2	4	0-1	.270	.315	.375	.690	3	.983
2005—	Kansas City (A.L.)	2B-DH	86	282	32	64	14	2	5	29	22	51	4	3	2-2	.227	.288	.344	.632	8	.980
—	Wichita (Texas)	2B-DH	28	110	22	27	8	0	3	15	12	13	0	2	0-2	.245	.320	.400	.720	0	1.000
Major League totals (2 years)			130	434	49	105	21	5	6	45	31	87	6	7	2-3	.242	.297	.355	.652	11	.981

GRABOW, JOHN — P

PERSONAL: Born November 4, 1978, in Arcadia, Calif. ... 6-2/210. ... Throws left, bats left. ... Full name: John William Grabow. ... Name pronounced: GRAY-bo. ... High school: San Gabriel (Calif.).
TRANSACTIONS/CAREER NOTES: Selected by Pittsburgh Pirates organization in third round of 1997 free-agent draft.
CAREER HITTING: 0-for-1 (.000), 0 R, 0 2B, 0 3B, 0 HR, 0 RBI.

SCOUTING REPORT *Throws:* Grabow throws a fastball at 88-92 mph as well as a slider and a changeup. *Tendencies:* He has good arm speed and a fastball that has good tailing action but tends to flatten out when he overthrows. Slider is quick but occasionally too big. Straight change is hard, but, with good arm speed, it has good sinking action as he turns it over. Is effective against lefthanders with his slider and against righthanders with his change. *Outlook:* He's proving he can be more than a situational lefthander out of the bullpen. *Grade 6.2*

JOHN GRABOW'S PITCHING ZONE

.375	.200	.125
.429	.313	.214
.133	.143	.133

LEFTY-RIGHTY SPLITS

vs.	Avg.	AB	H	2B	3B	HR	RBI	BB	SO	OBP	Slg.
L	.219	73	16	2	0	4	10	8	18	.313	.411
R	.250	120	30	7	0	2	11	17	24	.343	.358

Year	Team (League)	W	L	Pct.	ERA	WHIP	G	GS	CG	ShO	Hld.	Sv.-Opp.	IP	H	R	ER	HR	BB-IBB	SO	Avg.
1997—	GC Pirates (GCL)	2	7	.222	4.57	1.57	11	8	0	0		0-...	45.1	57	32	23	0	14-0	28	.305
1998—	Augusta (S. Atl.)	6	3	.667	5.78	1.65	17	16	0	0		0-...	71.2	84	59	46	7	34-0	67	.294
1999—	Hickory (S. Atl.)	9	10	.474	3.80	1.18	26	26	0	0		0-...	156.1	152	82	66	16	32-0	164	.259
2000—	Altoona (East.)	8	7	.533	4.33	1.44	24	24	1	0		0-...	145.1	145	81	70	10	65-0	109	.259
2001—	GC Pirates (GCL)	0	1	.000	3.75	1.25	6	6	0	0		0-...	12.0	11	6	5	3	4-0	9	.244
—	Lynchburg (Carol.)	1	3	.250	6.38	1.85	7	7	0	0		0-...	36.2	42	31	26	3	26-0	35	.294

G

Year	Team (League)	W	L	Pct.	ERA	WHIP	G	GS	CG	ShO	Hld.	Sv.-Opp.	IP	H	R	ER	HR	BB-IBB	SO	Avg.
—	Altoona (East.)	2	5	.286	3.38	1.36	10	10	0	0		0-...	50.2	30	23	19	1	39-0	42	.175
2002—	Altoona (East.)	8	13	.381	5.47	1.56	28	27	1	1		0-...	146.1	181	94	89	10	47-0	97	.308
2003—	Altoona (East.)	6	1	.857	3.36	1.28	24	9	0	0		1-...	83.0	87	34	31	9	19-2	73	.281
—	Nashville (PCL)	0	2	.000	4.74	1.54	17	0	0	0		0-...	24.2	31	17	13	0	7-2	26	.298
—	Pittsburgh (N.L.)	0	0	...	3.60	1.20	5	0	0	0	0	0-0	5.0	6	3	2	0	0-0	9	.273
2004—	Pittsburgh (N.L.)	2	5	.286	5.11	1.77	68	0	0	0	11	1-7	61.2	81	39	35	8	28-7	64	.323
2005—	Pittsburgh (N.L.)	2	3	.400	4.85	1.37	63	0	0	0	14	0-1	52.0	46	31	28	6	25-2	42	.238
Major League totals (3 years)		4	8	.333	4.93	1.57	136	0	0	0	25	1-8	118.2	133	73	65	14	53-9	115	.285

GRABOWSKI, JASON — OF

PERSONAL: Born May 24, 1976, in New Haven, Conn. ... 6-3/200. ... Bats left, throws right. ... Full name: Jason William Grabowski. ... High school: The Morgan School (Clinton, Conn.). ... College: Connecticut.

TRANSACTIONS/CAREER NOTES: Selected by New York Yankees organization in 17th round of 1994 free-agent draft; did not sign. ... Selected by Texas Rangers organization in second round of 1997 free-agent draft. ... Claimed on waivers by Seattle Mariners (December 18, 2000). ... Selected by Oakland Athletics from Mariners organization in Rule 5 major league draft (December 13, 2001). ... Traded by Athletics to Los Angeles Dodgers for cash (March 29, 2004). ... On disabled list (May 18-June 7, 2005).

2005 GAMES PLAYED BY POSITION (MLB): OF—32, 1B—3.

SCOUTING REPORT He has a slightly long uppercut stroke and only marginal bat speed, but he does have some power to the opposite field. Is selective but too often hits in a pitcher's count. Has limited defensive skills and poor range. Has problems reading balls off the bat, especially going back. **Grade 5**

JASON GRABOWSKI'S HITTING ZONE

.333	.167	.444
.200	.000	.250
.000	.000	.077

LEFTY-RIGHTY SPLITS

vs.	Avg.	AB	H	2B	3B	HR	RBI	BB	SO	OBP	Slg.
L	.111	9	1	0	0	0	0	1	2	1	.273	.111
R	.165	103	17	0	0	4	11	8	28	.223	.282

								BATTING											FIELDING	
Year	Team (League)	Pos.	G	AB	R	H	2B	3B	HR	RBI	BB	SO	HBP	GDP	SB-CS	Avg.	OBP	SLG	OPS	E	Avg.
1997—	Pulaski (Appal.)	C	50	174	36	51	14	0	4	24	40	32	0	2	6-1	.293	.423	.443	.866	8	.982
1998—	Savannah (S. Atl.)	1B-C	104	352	63	95	13	6	14	52	57	93	1	7	16-9	.270	.372	.460	.832	6	.990
1999—	Charlotte (Fla. St.)	3B-1B	123	434	68	136	31	6	12	87	65	66	5	8	13-10	.313	.407	.495	.903	27	.917
—	Tulsa (Texas)	DH	2	6	1	1	0	0	0	0	2	2	0	0	0-0	.167	.375	.167	.542	—	...
2000—	Tulsa (Texas)	3B	135	493	93	135	33	5	19	90	88	106	4	12	8-7	.274	.383	.477	.860	* 40	.898
2001—	Tacoma (PCL)	3B-OF-1B SS	114	394	60	117	32	3	9	58	61	94	2	8	7-4	.297	.390	.462	.852	21	.942
2002—	Sacramento (PCL)	OF-C-3B 1B	73	265	50	78	22	3	12	52	39	56	1	8	6-4	.294	.387	.536	.923	8	.962
—	Oakland (A.L.)	OF	4	8	3	3	1	1	0	1	3	1	0	0	0-0	.375	.545	.750	1.295	0	1.000
2003—	Ariz. A's (Ariz.)	DH	2	6	1	2	1	0	1	0	0	0			0-0	.333	.556	.500	1.056	0	...
—	Sacramento (PCL)	1B-3B	67	250	44	73	13	2	9	40	31	46	0	6	7-2	.292	.364	.468	.832	5	.969
—	Oakland (A.L.)	OF-3B-DH	8	8	0	0	0	0	0	0	1	5	0	4	0-0	.000	.111	.000	.111	0	1.000
2004—	Los Angeles (N.L.)	OF-1B-DH	113	173	18	38	7	0	7	20	19	50	0	4	0-0	.220	.297	.382	.678	1	.978
2005—	Las Vegas (PCL)	OF-DH-1B	52	181	37	56	16	1	6	33	30	26	0	5	0-0	.309	.408	.508	.916	6	.939
—	Los Angeles (N.L.)	OF-1B	65	112	14	18	0	0	4	12	10	29	0	4	1-0	.161	.228	.268	.495	1	.980
American League totals (2 years)			12	16	3	3	1	1	0	1	4	6	0	8	0-0	.188	.350	.375	.725	0	1.000
National League totals (2 years)			178	285	32	56	7	0	11	32	29	79	0	8	1-0	.196	.270	.337	.607	2	.979
Major League totals (4 years)			190	301	35	59	8	1	11	33	33	85	0	8	1-0	.196	.275	.339	.613	2	.981

DIVISION SERIES RECORD

Year	Team (League)	Pos.	G	AB	R	H	2B	3B	HR	RBI	BB	SO	HBP	GDP	SB-CS	Avg.	OBP	SLG	OPS	E	Avg.
2004—	Los Angeles (N.L.)		3	2	0	0	0	0	0	0	1	0	0	0		.000	.333	.000	.333		...

GRAFFANINO, TONY — 2B

PERSONAL: Born June 6, 1972, in Amityville, N.Y. ... 6-1/190. ... Bats right, throws right. ... Full name: Anthony Joseph Graffanino. ... Name pronounced: graf-a-NEEN-oh. ... High school: East Islip (Islip Terrace, N.Y.).

TRANSACTIONS/CAREER NOTES: Selected by Atlanta Braves organization in 10th round of 1990 free-agent draft. ... Released by Braves (April 2, 1999). ... Signed by Tampa Bay Devil Rays organization (April 9, 1999). ... Traded by Devil Rays to Chicago White Sox for P Tanyon Sturtze (May 31, 2000). ... On disabled list (August 26-September 30, 2002). ... Signed as a free agent by Kansas City Royals (December 16, 2003). ... On disabled list (May 1-28 and August 1, 2004-remainder of season; included rehabilitation assignment to Omaha. ... Traded by Royals to Boston Red Sox for P Juan Cedeno and OF Chip Ambres (July 19, 2005).

2005 GAMES PLAYED BY POSITION (MLB): 2B—73, 1B—22, 3B—17, SS—1, DH—1.

SCOUTING REPORT *Offense:* Graffanino has a long stroke and a slider-speed bat, making him vulnerable to inside pitches. Shows occasional power and can hit with runners in scoring position. Has become a better hitter as he has learned to look for pitches. Is a below-average runner. *Defense:* He has good hands and some quickness on the double-play pivot. Has a strong arm and a quick release. Has limited range. *Outlook:* Graffanino has become an ideal role player by improving at the plate. **Grade 6.1**

TONY GRAFFANINO'S HITTING ZONE

.273	.389	.348
.363	.429	.313
.317	.143	.286

LEFTY-RIGHTY SPLITS

vs.	Avg.	AB	H	2B	3B	HR	RBI	BB	SO	OBP	Slg.
L	.297	148	44	6	2	2	7	13	21	.358	.405
R	.316	231	73	11	1	5	31	18	30	.372	.437

								BATTING											FIELDING	
Year	Team (League)	Pos.	G	AB	R	H	2B	3B	HR	RBI	BB	SO	HBP	GDP	SB-CS	Avg.	OBP	SLG	OPS	E	Avg.
1990—	Pulaski (Appal.)	SS	42	131	23	27	5	1	0	11	26	17	2	3	6-3	.206	.344	.260	.603	24	.873

G

Year Team (League)	Pos.	G	AB	R	H	2B	3B	HR	RBI	BB	SO	HBP	GDP	SB-CS	Avg.	OBP	SLG	OPS	E	Avg.
																BATTING				FIELDING
1991—Idaho Falls (Pio.)	SS	66	274	53	95	16	4	4	56	27	37	3	2	19-4	.347	.408	.478	.887	*29	.912
1992—Macon (S. Atl.)	2B	112	400	50	96	15	5	10	31	50	84	8	6	9-6	.240	.333	.378	.711	17	.961
1993—Durham (Carol.)	2B	123	459	78	126	30	5	15	69	45	78	4	10	24-11	.275	.342	.460	.801	15	.968
1994—Greenville (Sou.)	2B-DH	124	440	66	132	28	3	7	52	50	53	2	8	29-7	.300	.372	.425	.797	14	.976
1995—Richmond (Int'l)	2B	50	179	20	34	6	0	4	17	15	49	1	4	2-2	.190	.254	.291	.544	4	.983
1996—Richmond (Int'l)	2B	96	353	57	100	29	2	7	33	34	72	3	3	11-7	.283	.350	.436	.787	10	.977
— Atlanta (N.L.)	2B	22	46	7	8	1	1	0	2	1	13	1	0	0-0	.174	.250	.239	.489	2	.969
1997—Atlanta (N.L.) 2B-3B-SS																				
	1B	104	186	33	48	9	1	8	20	26	46	1	3	6-4	.258	.344	.446	.790	5	.982
1998—Atlanta (N.L.) 2B-SS-3B		105	289	32	61	14	1	5	22	24	68	2	7	1-4	.211	.275	.318	.594	11	.971
1999—Durham (Int'l) 2B-DH-3B		87	345	66	108	25	6	9	58	37	46	3	9	16-9	.313	.379	.499	.878	1	.998
— Tampa Bay (A.L.) 2B-SS-3B																				
	DH	39	130	20	41	9	4	2	19	9	22	1	1	3-2	.315	.364	.492	.857	5	.973
2000—Tampa Bay (A.L.) 2B-3B-SS		13	20	8	6	1	0	0	1	1	2	1	1	0-0	.300	.364	.350	.714	0	1.000
— Durham (Int'l) SS-2B-1B																				
	3B	10	35	9	10	3	0	2	6	7	8	0	0	2-0	.286	.405	.543	.948	0	1.000
— Chicago (A.L.) SS-2B-3B																				
	DH	57	148	25	40	5	1	2	16	21	25	1	1	7-4	.270	.363	.358	.721	6	.968
2001— Chicago (A.L.) 3B-2B-SS																				
	DH-OF-1B	74	145	23	44	9	0	2	15	16	29	1	4	4-1	.303	.370	.407	.777	7	.957
2002—Chicago (A.L.) 3B-2B-SS		70	229	35	60	12	4	6	31	22	38	2	2	2-1	.262	.329	.428	.757	10	.953
2003—Chicago (A.L.) SS-2B-3B																				
	DH-1B	90	250	51	65	15	3	7	23	24	37	3	1	8-0	.260	.331	.428	.759	8	.972
2004—Omaha (PCL) 2B-DH		4	14	2	3	0	0	1	2	3	5	0	0	0-0	.214	.353	.429	.782	0	1.000
— Kansas City (A.L.) 2B		75	278	37	73	11	0	3	26	27	38	3	5	10-2	.263	.332	.335	.667	5	.988
2005—Kansas City (A.L.) 1B-2B-3B																				
	SS-DH	59	191	29	57	5	2	3	18	22	28	2	6	3-1	.298	.377	.393	.769	7	.974
— Boston (A.L.)	2B	51	188	39	60	12	1	4	20	9	23	2	4	4-1	.319	.355	.457	.812	3	.987
American League totals (7 years)		528	1579	267	446	79	15	29	169	151	242	16	29	41-12	.282	.349	.407	.756	51	.974
National League totals (3 years)		231	521	72	117	24	3	13	44	54	127	4	10	7-8	.225	.299	.357	.656	18	.975
Major League totals (10 years)		759	2100	339	563	103	18	42	213	205	369	20	39	48-20	.268	.336	.394	.731	69	.974

DIVISION SERIES RECORD

Year Team (League)	Pos.	G	AB	R	H	2B	3B	HR	RBI	BB	SO	HBP	GDP	SB-CS	Avg.	OBP	SLG	OPS	E	Avg.
1997—Atlanta (N.L.)	2B	3	3	0	0	0	0	0	0	2	1	0	0	0-0	.000	.400	.000	.400	0	1.000
1998—Atlanta (N.L.)		1	0	0	0	0	0	0	0	0	0	0	0	0-0	...	...	...	...		...
2000—Chicago (A.L.)	3B	1	0	0	0	0	0	0	0	0	0	0	0	0-0	...	...	...	...	0	1.000
2005—Boston (A.L.)	2B	3	12	0	3	2	0	0	0	0	0	0	0	0-0	.250	.250	.417	.667	1	.950
Division series totals (4 years)		8	15	0	3	2	0	0	0	2	1	0	0	0-0	.200	.294	.333	.627	1	.964

CHAMPIONSHIP SERIES RECORD

Year Team (League)	Pos.	G	AB	R	H	2B	3B	HR	RBI	BB	SO	HBP	GDP	SB-CS	Avg.	OBP	SLG	OPS	E	Avg.
1997—Atlanta (N.L.)	2B	3	8	1	2	1	0	0	0	0	3	0	1	0-0	.250	.250	.375	.625	0	1.000
1998—Atlanta (N.L.)	2B	4	3	2	1	1	0	0	1	2	1	0	0	0-0	.333	.600	.667	1.267	0	1.000
Champ. series totals (2 years)		7	11	3	3	2	0	0	1	2	4	0	1	0-0	.273	.385	.455	.839	0	1.000

GRAMAN, ALEX   P

PERSONAL: Born November 17, 1977, in Huntingburg, Ind. ... 6-4/210. ... Throws left, bats left. ... Full name: Alex Joseph Graman. ... Name pronounced: GRAY-mun. ... High school: Southridge (Huntingburg, Ind.). ... College: Indiana State.

TRANSACTIONS/CAREER NOTES: Selected by New York Yankees organization in third round of 1999 free-agent draft. ... Signed as a free agent by Cincinnati Reds organization (September 7, 2005).

CAREER HITTING: 0-for-0 (.000), 0 R, 0 2B, 0 3B, 0 HR, 0 RBI.

LEFTY-RIGHTY SPLITS

vs.	Avg.	AB	H	2B	3B	HR	RBI	BB	SO	OBP	Slg.
L	.750	4	3	1	0	1	4	0	0	.750	1.750
R	.000	3	0	0	0	0	0	0	2	.400	.000

Year Team (League)	W	L	Pct.	ERA	WHIP	G	GS	CG	ShO	Hld.	Sv.-Opp.	IP	H	R	ER	HR	BB-IBB	SO	Avg.
1999—Staten Island (NYP)	6	3	.667	2.99	1.11	14	14	0	0	...	0-...	81.1	74	30	27	7	16-0	85	.244
2000—Tampa (Fla. St.)	8	9	.471	3.65	1.24	28	•28	3	1	...	0-...	143.0	120	64	58	6	58-1	111	.226
— Norwich (East.)	0	1	.000	11.81	1.88	1	1	0	0	...	0-...	5.1	6	7	7	3	4-0	3	.300
2001— Norwich (East.)	12	9	.571	3.52	1.41	28	28	1	0	...	0-...	166.1	174	83	65	10	60-0	138	.267
2002— Norwich (East.)	5	2	.714	2.88	1.18	8	8	2	1	...	0-...	50.0	46	19	16	2	13-0	31	.242
— Columbus (Int'l)	6	9	.400	4.65	1.44	20	20	1	0	...	0-...	124.0	141	74	64	11	37-3	98	.291
2003— Columbus (Int'l)	9	10	.474	4.48	1.39	26	26	0	0	...	0-...	142.2	135	77	71	14	63-0	110	.250
2004— New York (A.L.)	0	0	...	19.80	3.20	3	2	0	0	0	0-0	5.0	14	11	11	1	2-0	4	.500
— Columbus (Int'l)	11	6	.647	3.37	1.28	24	22	1	1	...	0-...	131.0	115	56	49	12	53-0	129	.235
2005— Columbus (Int'l)	5	6	.455	3.18	1.36	23	16	0	0	1	1-1	96.1	95	40	34	12	36-2	96	.257
— New York (A.L.)	0	0	...	13.50	3.75	2	0	0	0	0	0-0	1.1	3	2	2	1	2-1	0	.429
— Louisville (Int'l)	2	1	.667	3.09	1.50	5	4	0	0	0	0-0	23.1	23	9	8	2	12-0	19	.258
Major League totals (2 years)	0	0	...	18.47	3.32	5	2	0	0	0	0-0	6.1	17	13	13	2	4-1	4	.486

G

PERSONAL: Born March 16, 1981, in Blue Island, Ill. ... 6-1/185. ... Bats left, throws right. ... High school: Thornton Fractional South (Lansing, Ill.). ... College: Illinois-Chicago.
TRANSACTIONS/CAREER NOTES: Selected by Detroit Tigers organization in third round of 2002 free-agent draft.
2005 GAMES PLAYED BY POSITION (MLB): OF—45.

SCOUTING REPORT Granderson is a good runner who has hitting potential. Has a quick, short stroke. Hits to all fields with surprising power and will become a good basestealer as he gains experience. Doesn't throw well and gets better jumps going back. Has above-average lateral range. Could win the regular job if he hits like he did during the last month of the season.
Grade 6.6

CURTIS GRANDERSON'S HITTING ZONE

.000	.500	.200
.375	.250	.281
.091	.429	.250

LEFTY-RIGHTY SPLITS

vs.	Avg.	AB	H	2B	3B	HR	RBI	BB	SO	OBP	Slg.
L	.320	25	8	1	1	2	5	3	8	.393	.680
R	.263	137	36	5	2	6	15	7	35	.299	.460

Year Team (League)	Pos.	G	AB	R	H	2B	3B	HR	RBI	BB	SO	HBP	GDP	SB-CS	Avg.	OBP	SLG	OPS	E	Avg.
2002—Oneonta (NYP)	OF	52	212	45	73	15	4	3	34	20	35	7	1	9-2	.344	.417	.495	.912	1	.989
2003—Lakeland (Fla. St.)	OF	127	476	71	136	29	10	11	51	49	91	12	5	10-7	.286	.365	.458	.823	5	.984
2004—Erie (East.)	OF	123	462	89	139	19	8	21	94	80	95	4	2	14-8	.301	.405	.513	.918	3	.991
—Detroit (A.L.)	OF	9	25	2	6	1	1	0	0	3	8	0	1	0-0	.240	.321	.360	.681	0	1.000
2005—Toledo (Int'l)	OF-DH	111	445	79	129	29	13	15	65	48	129	3	7	22-6	.290	.359	.515	.874	8	.985
—Detroit (A.L.)	OF	47	162	18	44	6	3	8	20	10	43	0	2	1-1	.272	.314	.494	.808	0	1.000
Major League totals (2 years)		56	187	20	50	7	4	8	20	13	51	0	3	1-1	.267	.315	.476	.791	0	1.000

PERSONAL: Born August 7, 1973, in Saigon, Vietnam. ... 6-0/185. ... Throws right, bats right. ... Full name: Daniel Peter Graves. ... High school: Brandon (Fla.). ... College: Miami.
TRANSACTIONS/CAREER NOTES: Selected by Cleveland Indians organization in fourth round of 1994 free-agent draft. ... Traded by Indians with Ps Jim Crowell and Scott Winchester and IF Damian Jackson to Cincinnati Reds for P John Smiley and IF Jeff Branson (July 31, 1997). ... On disabled list (August 19-September 3, 2004). ... Released by Reds (June 2, 2005). ... Signed by New York Mets (June 11, 2005).
CAREER HITTING: 8-for-76 (.105), 5 R, 0 2B, 0 3B, 2 HR, 3 RBI.

DANNY GRAVES' PITCHING ZONE

.400	.182	.400
.231	.375	.405
.214	.556	.389

LEFTY-RIGHTY SPLITS

vs.	Avg.	AB	H	2B	3B	HR	RBI	BB	SO	OBP	Slg.
L	.408	71	29	4	1	4	20	12	7	.500	.662
R	.303	99	30	8	0	5	24	8	13	.364	.535

Year Team (League)	W	L	Pct.	ERA	WHIP	G	GS	CG	ShO	Hld.	Sv.-Opp.	IP	H	R	ER	HR	BB-IBB	SO	Avg.
1995—Kinston (Carol.)	3	1	.750	0.82	0.95	38	0	0	0	...	21-...	44.0	30	11	4	0	12-2	46	.183
—Cant./Akr. (East.)	1	0	1.000	0.00	0.51	17	0	0	0	...	10-...	23.1	10	1	0	0	2-0	11	.133
—Buffalo (A.A.)	0	0	...	3.00	2.00	3	0	0	0	...	0-...	3.0	5	4	1	0	1-0	2	.333
1996—Buffalo (A.A.)	4	3	.571	1.48	1.03	43	0	0	0	...	19-...	79.0	57	14	13	1	24-2	46	.208
—Cleveland (A.L.)	2	0	1.000	4.55	1.31	15	0	0	0	0	0-1	29.2	29	18	15	2	10-0	22	.246
1997—Buffalo (A.A.)	2	3	.400	4.19	1.30	19	3	0	0	...	2-...	43.0	45	21	20	3	11-0	21	.276
—Cleveland (A.L.)	0	0	...	4.76	2.12	5	0	0	0	0	0-0	11.1	15	8	6	2	9-0	4	.326
—Indianapolis (A.A.)	1	0	1.000	3.09	1.03	11	0	0	0	...	5-...	11.2	7	4	4	1	5-0	5	.184
—Cincinnati (N.L.)	0	0	...	6.14	2.52	10	0	0	0	1	0-0	14.2	26	14	10	0	11-1	7	.413
1998—Indianapolis (Int'l)	1	0	1.000	1.93	1.29	13	0	0	0	...	0-...	14.0	15	3	3	0	3-0	11	.273
—Cincinnati (N.L.)	2	1	.667	3.32	1.28	62	0	0	0	6	8-8	81.1	76	31	30	6	28-4	44	.252
1999—Cincinnati (N.L.)	8	7	.533	3.08	1.25	75	0	0	0	7	27-36	111.0	90	42	38	10	49-4	69	.243
2000—Cincinnati (N.L.)	10	5	.667	2.56	1.35	66	0	0	0	0	30-35	91.1	81	31	26	8	42-7	53	.243
2001—Cincinnati (N.L.)	6	5	.545	4.15	1.26	66	0	0	0	0	32-39	80.1	83	41	37	7	18-6	49	.268
2002—Cincinnati (N.L.)	7	3	.700	3.19	1.26	68	4	0	0	0	32-39	98.2	99	37	35	7	25-9	58	.264
2003—Cincinnati (N.L.)	4	15	.211	5.33	1.45	30	26	2	1	0	2-2	169.0	204	108	100	30	41-6	60	.298
2004—Cincinnati (N.L.)	1	6	.143	3.95	1.32	68	0	0	0	0	41-50	68.1	77	39	30	12	13-6	40	.287
2005—Cincinnati (N.L.)	1	1	.500	7.36	2.29	20	0	0	0	0	10-12	18.1	30	18	15	4	12-3	8	.357
—Norfolk (Int'l)	0	1	.000	18.00	3.67	5	0	0	0	0	0-0	6.0	15	12	12	2	7-0	4	.484
—New York (N.L.)	0	0	...	5.75	1.82	20	0	0	0	1	0-0	20.1	29	17	13	5	8-1	12	.337
American League totals (2 years)	2	0	1.000	4.61	1.54	20	0	0	0	0	0-1	41.0	44	26	21	4	19-0	26	.268
National League totals (9 years)	39	43	.476	3.99	1.38	485	30	2	1	8	182-221	753.1	795	378	334	89	247-47	400	.274
Major League totals (10 years)	41	43	.488	4.02	1.39	505	30	2	1	8	182-222	794.1	839	404	355	93	266-47	426	.273

ALL-STAR GAME RECORD

	W	L	Pct.	ERA	WHIP	G	GS	CG	ShO	Hld.	Sv.-Opp.	IP	H	R	ER	HR	BB-IBB	SO	Avg.
All-Star Game totals (1 year)	0	0	...	0.00	1.00	1	0	0	0	...	0-0	1.0	1	0	0	0	0-0	1	.250

G

GREEN, ANDY — 3B/2B

PERSONAL: Born July 7, 1977, in Lexington, Ky. ... 5-9/180. ... Bats right, throws right. ... Full name: Andrew Mulligan Green. ... High school: Lexington (Ky.) Christian Academy. ... College: Kentucky.
TRANSACTIONS/CAREER NOTES: Selected by Arizona Diamondbacks organization in 24th round of 2000 free-agent draft.
2005 GAMES PLAYED BY POSITION (MLB): 2B—5, SS—2, OF—2.

LEFTY-RIGHTY SPLITS

vs.	Avg.	AB	H	2B	3B	HR	RBI	BB	SO	OBP	Slg.
L	.385	13	5	1	0	0	2	1	0	.400	.462
R	.111	18	2	0	0	0	0	6	3	.333	.111

Year	Team (League)	Pos.	G	AB	R	H	2B	3B	HR	RBI	BB	SO	HBP	GDP	SB-CS	Avg.	OBP	SLG	OPS	E	Avg.
2000—	South Bend (Midw.)	2B	3	9	1	0	0	0	0	0	0	1	2	0	0-0	.000	.182	.000	.182	0	1.000
—	Missoula (Pio.)	2B-3B	23	83	10	19	2	1	0	16	12	9	2	1	8-3	.229	.324	.277	.601	5	.949
2001—	South Bend (Midw.)	2B	128	477	76	143	18	6	5	59	59	50	7	7	51-15	.300	.379	.394	.773	16	.973
2002—	Tucson (PCL)	2B	27	99	13	22	8	0	1	13	9	17	1	2	2-1	.222	.294	.333	.627	2	.980
—	Lancaster (Calif.)	2B	102	401	74	124	36	4	6	50	60	59	5	7	15-10	.309	.401	.464	.865	10	.979
2003—	El Paso (Texas)	2B-SS-OF 3B	126	490	70	148	38	2	6	57	38	51	13	6	17-9	.302	.366	.400	.766	21	.962
2004—	Tucson (PCL)	3B-2B-SS OF-DH	77	309	56	101	31	3	9	45	34	45	3	3	10-4	.327	.394	.534	.923	11	.961
—	Arizona (N.L.)	3B-2B-OF	46	109	13	22	2	1	1	4	5	17	1	2	1-1	.202	.241	.266	.507	5	.946
2005—	Tucson (PCL)	2B-OF-3B DH-SS	135	530	125	182	46	13	19	80	68	82	6	9	9-6	.343	.422	.587	1.009	13	.976
—	Arizona (N.L.)	2B-SS-OF	17	31	5	7	1	0	0	2	7	3	0	1	0-0	.226	.359	.258	.617	0	1.000
Major League totals (2 years)			63	140	18	29	3	1	1	6	12	20	1	3	1-1	.207	.271	.264	.535	5	.959

GREEN, NICK — 2B/SS

PERSONAL: Born September 10, 1978, in Pensacola, Fla. ... 6-0/178. ... Bats right, throws right. ... Full name: Nicholas Anthony Green. ... High school: Duluth (Ga.). ... Junior college: Georgia Perimeter.
TRANSACTIONS/CAREER NOTES: Selected by Atlanta Braves organization in 32nd round of 1998 free-agent draft. ... On disabled list (March 22-April 24, 2002). ... Traded by Braves to Tampa Bay Devil Rays for P Jorge Sosa (March 31, 2005).
2005 GAMES PLAYED BY POSITION (MLB): 2B—91, 3B—13, DH—2, OF—1.

SCOUTING REPORT Green is quick, but he lacks strength at the plate. Has an inside-out approach and a slow bat. Hits the ball in the air too much for a guy with little power. Struggles against righthanders. Can hit the fastball but has problems with breaking stuff. Is a below-average runner. Has a strong arm on the double-play pivot and soft, quick hands. Is aggressive on pop flies.
Grade 5.0

NICK GREEN'S HITTING ZONE

.083	.182	.231
.297	.444	.267
.243	.381	.150

LEFTY-RIGHTY SPLITS

vs.	Avg.	AB	H	2B	3B	HR	RBI	BB	SO	OBP	Slg.
L	.292	96	28	7	0	2	7	12	26	.373	.427
R	.216	222	48	8	2	3	22	21	60	.310	.311

Year	Team (League)	Pos.	G	AB	R	H	2B	3B	HR	RBI	BB	SO	HBP	GDP	SB-CS	Avg.	OBP	SLG	OPS	E	Avg.
1999—	Jamestown (NYP)	2B	73	273	52	81	15	0	11	41	26	66	4	4	14-4	.297	.363	.473	.835	15	.955
—	Macon (S. Atl.)	2B	3	10	1	2	0	0	1	3	0	4	0	0	1-0	.200	.200	.500	.700	0	1.000
2000—	Macon (S. Atl.)	SS-2B	91	339	47	83	19	4	11	43	22	75	5	4	10-4	.245	.296	.422	.718	37	.911
—	Myrtle Beach (Carol.)	SS-2B	27	91	13	22	6	0	1	6	10	23	3	0	3-2	.242	.337	.341	.678	9	.890
2001—	Richmond (Int'l)	2B	2	5	0	1	0	0	0	1	0	3	0	0	0-0	.200	.200	.200	.400	1	.833
—	Myrtle Beach (Carol.)	2B-SS	80	297	49	79	18	1	10	42	32	70	7	2	9-2	.266	.348	.434	.782	13	.958
2002—	Greenville (Sou.)	2B-SS	94	355	49	85	16	2	15	50	36	92	8	9	2-5	.239	.321	.423	.743	14	.962
2003—	Richmond (Int'l)	2B-SS	124	399	40	99	26	1	11	51	26	79	7	5	7-5	.248	.303	.401	.704	20	.961
2004—	Richmond (Int'l)	2B-3B	22	77	8	29	4	1	0	11	6	9	4	2	0-3	.377	.443	.455	.871	3	.969
—	Atlanta (N.L.)	2B-3B-DH	95	264	40	72	15	3	3	26	12	63	4	0	1-2	.273	.312	.386	.698	8	.977
2005—	Tampa Bay (A.L.)	2B-3B-DH OF	111	318	53	76	15	2	5	29	33	86	11	5	3-1	.239	.329	.346	.675	7	.981
American League totals (1 year)			111	318	53	76	15	2	5	29	33	86	11	5	3-1	.239	.329	.346	.675	7	.981
National League totals (1 year)			95	264	40	72	15	3	3	26	12	63	4	0	1-2	.273	.312	.386	.698	8	.977
Major League totals (2 years)			206	582	93	148	30	5	8	55	45	149	15	5	4-3	.254	.321	.364	.686	15	.979

DIVISION SERIES RECORD

Year	Team (League)	Pos.	G	AB	R	H	2B	3B	HR	RBI	BB	SO	HBP	GDP	SB-CS	Avg.	OBP	SLG	OPS	E	Avg.
2004—	Atlanta (N.L.)		2	0	0	0	0	0	0	0	0	0	0	0	0-0	...	...	...	...	0	...

GREEN, SHAWN — 1B/OF

PERSONAL: Born November 10, 1972, in Des Plaines, Ill. ... 6-4/200. ... Bats left, throws left. ... Full name: Shawn David Green. ... High school: Tustin (Calif.).
TRANSACTIONS/CAREER NOTES: Selected by Toronto Blue Jays organization in first round (16th pick overall) of 1991 free-agent draft; pick received as compensation for San Francisco Giants signing Type A free-agent P Bud Black. ... Traded by Blue Jays with 2B Jorge Nunez to Los Angeles Dodgers for OF Raul Mondesi and P Pedro Borbon (November 8, 1999). ... Traded by Dodgers with cash to Arizona Diamondbacks for C Dioner Navarro and Ps William Juarez, Danny Muegge and Beltran Perez (January 11, 2005).
RECORDS: Shares major league single-game records for most home runs, game (4, May 23, 2002); and most runs scored, game (6, May 23, 2002).
HONORS: Won A.L. Gold Glove as outfielder (1999).
2005 GAMES PLAYED BY POSITION (MLB): OF—155.

G

SCOUTING REPORT *Offense:* Green's offensive numbers, especially his RBIs, really declined in 2005. Lost a bit of bat speed but has an extremely fluid and slightly long swing. Is a better hitter down than up and will use the whole field. Speeds up his bat when pitched away. Still capable of 30 home runs a year. Is not a good runner but has good instincts. *Defense:* He has lost a step defensively. Better in right field than center as his range is below average and has problems tracking the ball going back. Doesn't get good lateral jumps. Arm strength is an asset but has a slow release. *Outlook:* Green's numbers continue to slide as his bat speed slows. Has cut down his strikeouts by going the other way but may not have another 100-RBI year. Defense has slid even further. *Grade 7.2*

SHAWN GREEN'S HITTING ZONE

.207	.350	.267
.262	.426	.405
.267	.407	.254

LEFTY-RIGHTY SPLITS

vs.	Avg.	AB	H	2B	3B	HR	RBI	BB	SO	OBP	Slg.
L	.226	146	33	4	1	5	14	15	25	.299	.370
R	.306	435	133	33	3	17	59	47	70	.374	.513

										BATTING									FIELDING	
Year Team (League)	Pos.	G	AB	R	H	2B	3B	HR	RBI	BB	SO	HBP	GDP	SB-CS	Avg.	OBP	SLG	OPS	E	Avg.
1992— Dunedin (Fla. St.)	OF	114	417	44	114	21	3	1	49	28	66	4	9	22-9	.273	.319	.345	.665	5	.974
1993— Knoxville (Sou.)	OF	99	360	40	102	14	2	4	34	26	72	5	6	4-9	.283	.339	.367	.706	8	.956
— Toronto (A.L.)	OF-DH	3	6	0	0	0	0	0	0	0	1	0	0	0-0	.000	.000	.000	.000	0	1.000
1994— Syracuse (Int'l)	OF-DH	109	433	82	149	27	3	13	61	40	54	4	5	19-7	.344	.401	.510	.912	1	.996
— Toronto (A.L.)	OF	14	33	1	3	1	0	0	1	1	8	0	1	1-0	.091	.118	.121	.239	0	1.000
1995— Toronto (A.L.)	OF	121	379	52	109	31	4	15	54	20	68	3	4	1-2	.288	.326	.509	.835	6	.973
1996— Toronto (A.L.)	OF-DH	132	422	52	118	32	3	11	45	33	75	8	9	5-1	.280	.342	.448	.790	2	.992
1997— Toronto (A.L.)	OF-DH	135	429	57	123	22	4	16	53	36	99	1	4	14-3	.287	.340	.469	.809	3	.984
1998— Toronto (A.L.)	OF	158	630	106	175	33	4	35	100	50	142	5	6	35-12	.278	.334	.510	.844	7	.979
1999— Toronto (A.L.)	OF	153	614	134	190	*45	0	42	123	66	117	11	13	20-7	.309	.384	.588	.972	1	.997
2000— Los Angeles (N.L.)	OF	•162	610	98	164	44	4	24	99	90	121	8	18	24-5	.269	.367	.472	.839	6	.980
2001— Los Angeles (N.L.)	OF-1B	161	619	121	184	31	4	49	125	72	107	5	10	20-4	.297	.372	.598	.970	6	.982
2002— Los Angeles (N.L.)	OF-DH	158	582	110	166	31	1	42	114	93	112	5	26	8-5	.285	.385	.558	.944	2	.994
2003— Los Angeles (N.L.)	OF-DH	160	611	84	171	49	2	19	85	68	112	6	18	6-2	.280	.355	.460	.814	5	.982
2004— Los Angeles (N.L.)	1B-OF-DH	157	590	92	157	28	1	28	86	71	114	8	17	5-2	.266	.352	.459	.811	7	.993
2005— Arizona (N.L.)	OF	158	581	87	166	37	4	22	73	62	95	5	18	8-4	.286	.355	.477	.832	1	1.000
American League totals (7 years)		716	2513	402	718	164	15	119	376	206	510	28	37	76-25	.286	.344	.505	.849	19	.986
National League totals (6 years)		956	3593	592	1008	220	16	184	582	456	661	37	107	71-22	.281	.364	.504	.869	26	.990
Major League totals (13 years)		1672	6106	994	1726	384	31	303	958	662	1171	65	144	147-47	.283	.356	.505	.861	45	.989

DIVISION SERIES RECORD

Year Team (League)	Pos.	G	AB	R	H	2B	3B	HR	RBI	BB	SO	HBP	GDP	SB-CS	Avg.	OBP	SLG	OPS	E	Avg.
2004— Los Angeles (N.L.)	1B	4	16	3	4	0	0	0	3	0	3	0	0	0-0	.250	.250	.813	1.063	0	1.000

ALL-STAR GAME RECORD

	G	AB	R	H	2B	3B	HR	RBI	BB	SO	HBP	GDP	SB-CS	Avg.	OBP	SLG	OPS	E	Avg.
All-Star Game totals (2 years)	2	4	1	2	0	0	0	0	0	1	0	0	1-0	.500	.500	.500	1.000	0	1.000

GREENBERG, ADAM — OF

PERSONAL: Born February 21, 1981, in New Haven, Conn. ... 5-9/180. ... Bats left, throws left. ... Full name: Adam Daniel Greenberg. ... College: North Carolina.
TRANSACTIONS/CAREER NOTES: Selected by Chicago Cubs organization in ninth round of 2002 free-agent draft. ... On disabled list (July 10-28, 2005).

LEFTY-RIGHTY SPLITS

vs.	Avg.	AB	H	2B	3B	HR	RBI	BB	SO	OBP	Slg.
L	.000	0	0	0	0	0	0	0	0	1.000	.000
R	.000	0	0	0	0	0	0	0	0	.000	.000

										BATTING									FIELDING	
Year Team (League)	Pos.	G	AB	R	H	2B	3B	HR	RBI	BB	SO	HBP	GDP	SB-CS	Avg.	OBP	SLG	OPS	E	Avg.
2002— Lansing (Midw.)	OF	35	116	20	26	7	2	1	11	15	22	4	0	2-1	.224	.331	.345	.676	0	1.000
— Daytona (Fla. St.)	OF	21	73	20	28	5	3	1	9	14	18	3	0	15-2	.384	.500	.575	1.075	3	.943
2003— Daytona (Fla. St.)	OF	72	271	42	81	11	5	3	27	38	46	2	1	26-9	.299	.387	.410	.797	0	1.000
2004— Daytona (Fla. St.)	OF	91	323	52	94	10	12	3	28	42	65	7	4	16-8	.291	.381	.424	.805	0	1.000
— West Tenn (Sou.)	OF	32	112	22	31	7	2	3	10	14	30	3	1	3-0	.277	.366	.455	.821	2	.000
— Iowa (PCL)	OF	1	4	0	0	0	0	0	0	0	0	1	0	0-0	.000	.200	.000	.200	0	...
2005— Chicago (N.L.)		1	0	0	0	0	0	0	0	0	0	1	0	0-0	...	1.000	...	...	0	...
— West Tenn (Sou.)	OF	95	305	51	82	12	9	4	33	56	68	4	1	15-4	.269	.386	.407	.792	4	.988
Major League totals (1 year)		1	0	0	0	0	0	0	0	0	0	1	0	0-0	...	1.000	...	...	0	...

GREENE, KHALIL — SS

PERSONAL: Born October 21, 1979, in Butler, Pa. ... 5-11/210. ... Bats right, throws right. ... Full name: Khalil Thabit Greene. ... High school: Key West (Fla.). ... College: Clemson.
TRANSACTIONS/CAREER NOTES: Selected by Chicago Cubs organization in 14th round of 2001 free-agent draft; did not sign. ... Selected by San Diego Padres organization in first round (13th pick overall) of 2002 free-agent draft. ... On disabled list (April 18-May 9 and August 15-30, 2005); included rehabilitation assignment to Lake Elsinore.
2005 GAMES PLAYED BY POSITION (MLB): SS—121.

SCOUTING REPORT *Offense:* Greene is slightly rigid at the plate but he still has a very quick bat. Likes the ball on the inner half and is very quick to turn on it. Has problems when pitchers consistently run the ball away from him; needs to learn how to hit it the other way. Is a good runner but slow out of the box. Should steal more bases. *Defense:* Greene is exceptionally quick—in particular his first step—and has outstanding range to either side. Also has outstanding balance. Arm is strong from the hole. Excels at positioning and taking proper angles. *Outlook:* He could become one of the league's top fielding shortstops—if he can stay healthy. He averaged 130 games in his first two full big-league seasons. *Grade 7.8*

KHALIL GREENE'S HITTING ZONE

.353	.111	.308
.264	.327	.319
.341	.167	.429

LEFTY-RIGHTY SPLITS

vs.	Avg.	AB	H	2B	3B	HR	RBI	BB	SO	OBP	Slg.
L	.200	105	21	9	0	4	18	5	23	.234	.400
R	.266	331	88	21	2	11	52	20	70	.315	.441

										BATTING									FIELDING	
Year Team (League)	Pos.	G	AB	R	H	2B	3B	HR	RBI	BB	SO	HBP	GDP	SB-CS	Avg.	OBP	SLG	OPS	E	Avg.
2002— Eugene (N'west)	SS	10	37	5	10	1	0	0	6	5	6	3	1	0-0	.270	.400	.297	.697	3	.900
— Lake Elsinore (Calif.)	SS-2B-3B	46	183	33	58	9	1	9	32	12	33	4	7	0-0	.317	.368	.525	.893	9	.947

G

Year	Team (League)	Pos.	G	AB	R	H	2B	3B	HR	RBI	BB	SO	HBP	GDP	SB-CS	Avg.	OBP	SLG	OPS	E	Avg.
2003—Mobile (Sou.)	SS-DH	59	229	20	63	17	2	3	20	16	55	2	7	2-3	.275	.327	.406	.733	9	.949
—Portland (PCL)	SS	76	319	42	92	19	0	10	47	20	52	11	3	5-4	.288	.346	.442	.788	11	.967
—San Diego (N.L.)	SS	20	65	8	14	4	1	2	6	4	19	1	3	0-1	.215	.271	.400	.671	3	.963
2004—San Diego (N.L.)	SS	139	484	67	132	31	4	15	65	53	94	8	9	4-2	.273	.349	.446	.795	20	.965
2005—Lake Elsinore (Calif.)	SS	4	12	4	6	1	0	0	3	2	1	1	0	0-0	.500	.600	.583	1.183	0	1.000
—San Diego (N.L.)	SS	121	436	51	109	30	2	15	70	25	93	6	8	5-0	.250	.296	.431	.727	14	.971
Major League totals (3 years)		280	985	126	255	65	7	32	141	82	206	15	20	9-3	.259	.321	.437	.758	37	.968

DIVISION SERIES RECORD

Year	Team (League)	Pos.	G	AB	R	H	2B	3B	HR	RBI	BB	SO	HBP	GDP	SB-CS	Avg.	OBP	SLG	OPS	E	Avg.
2005—San Diego (N.L.)	SS	3	10	2	4	2	0	0	1	1	2	0	0	0-0	.400	.417	.600	1.017	2	.905

GREENE, TODD — C/DH

PERSONAL: Born May 8, 1971, in Augusta, Ga. ... 5-10/208. ... Bats right, throws right. ... Full name: Todd Anthony Greene. ... High school: Evans (Ga.). ... College: Georgia Southern.

TRANSACTIONS/CAREER NOTES: Selected by Atlanta Braves organization in 27th round of 1989 free-agent draft; did not sign. ... Selected by California Angels organization in 12th round of 1993 free-agent draft. ... Angels franchise renamed Anaheim Angels for 1997 season. ... On disabled list (August 20, 1997-remainder of season). ... On disabled list (March 19-August 5, 1998); included rehabilitation assignments to Lake Elsinore and Vancouver. ... On suspended list (May 13-16, 1999). ... Released by Angels (March 29, 2000). ... Signed by Toronto Blue Jays organization (April 10, 2000). ... On disabled list (June 7-23, 2000); included rehabilitation assignment to Dunedin. ... Released by Blue Jays (March 28, 2001). ... Signed by New York Yankees organization (April 5, 2001). ... Released by Yankees (March 26, 2002). ... Signed by Los Angeles Dodgers organization (April 2, 2002). ... Released by Dodgers (May 15, 2002). ... Signed by Texas Rangers (May 16, 2002). ... On disabled list (April 30-May 15, 2003); included rehabilitation assignment to Frisco. ... Signed as a free agent by Colorado Rockies organization (December 22, 2003). ... On disabled list (August 8-September 1, 2004); included rehabilitation assignment to Colorado Springs. ... On disabled list (June 6-August 17, 2005); included rehabilitation assignment to Colorado Springs.

2005 GAMES PLAYED BY POSITION (MLB): C—33.

SCOUTING REPORT Greene is physically strong, a dead-fastball pull hitter whose power is his best asset. Likes the ball out over the plate but does generate bat speed. Is a much better hitter in a platoon role against lefthanders than as an everyday player. Has benefited from playing in Coors Field. Has some value as a pinch hitter. Receiving skills are below average. Hands are stiff and lacks mobility and flexibility. Is in the big leagues strictly for his bat. *Grade 4.7*

TODD GREENE'S HITTING ZONE

.000	.500	.143
.296	.000	.077
.571	.375	.333

LEFTY-RIGHTY SPLITS

vs.	Avg.	AB	H	2B	3B	HR	RBI	BB	SO	OBP	Slg.
L	.294	51	15	2	0	3	8	5	5	.357	.510
R	.227	75	17	2	0	4	15	2	16	.256	.413

Year	Team (League)	Pos.	G	AB	R	H	2B	3B	HR	RBI	BB	SO	HBP	GDP	SB-CS	Avg.	OBP	SLG	OPS	E	Avg.
1993—Boise (N'west)	OF	76	305	55	82	15	3	15	71	34	44	9	3	4-3	.269	.356	.485	.841	3	.979
1994—Lake Elsinore (Calif.)	1B-C-OF	133	524	98	158	39	2	35	124	64	96	4	12	10-3	.302	.378	.584	.962	15	.979
1995—Midland (Texas)	C-DH	82	318	59	104	19	1	26	57	17	55	5	6	3-5	.327	.365	.638	1.004	3	.992
—Vancouver (PCL)	C-DH	43	168	28	42	3	1	14	35	11	36	4	3	1-0	.250	.308	.530	.838	1	.995
1996—Vancouver (PCL)	C-DH	60	223	27	68	18	0	5	33	16	36	1	6	0-2	.305	.347	.453	.800	3	.988
—California (A.L.)	C-DH	29	79	9	15	1	0	2	9	4	11	1	4	2-0	.190	.238	.278	.517	0	1.000
1997—Anaheim (A.L.)	C-DH-1B	34	124	24	36	6	0	9	24	7	25	0	1	2-0	.290	.328	.556	.885	0	1.000
—Vancouver (PCL)	OF	64	260	51	92	22	0	25	75	20	31	5	6	5-1	.354	.408	.727	1.135	3	.992
1998—Lake Elsinore (Calif.)	DH-1B	12	44	9	10	2	0	1	6	4	7	0	1	1-0	.227	.286	.341	.627	2	.833
—Vancouver (PCL)	DH-1B-C	30	108	16	30	12	0	7	20	12	17	3	2	1-0	.278	.360	.583	.943	1	1.000
—Anaheim (A.L.)	OF-DH-1B	29	71	3	18	4	0	1	7	2	20	0	0	0-0	.254	.274	.352	.626	0	1.000
1999—Anaheim (A.L.)	DH-OF-C	97	321	36	78	20	0	14	42	12	63	3	8	1-4	.243	.275	.436	.711	2	.980
—Edmonton (PCL)	OF-DH-C	19	74	10	18	8	0	5	14	0	12	1	4	0-0	.243	.253	.527	.780	0	1.000
2000—Syracuse (Int'l)	OF-C	24	91	14	27	3	0	7	14	6	16	0	3	1-0	.297	.337	.560	.897	1	.970
—Toronto (A.L.)	DH-C-OF	34	85	11	20	2	0	5	10	5	18	0	4	0-0	.235	.278	.435	.713	0	1.000
—Dunedin (Fla. St.)	OF	5	20	2	4	1	0	1	4	2	4	1	0	0-0	.200	.304	.400	.704	0	1.000
2001—Columbus (Int'l)	C-OF	34	131	16	33	8	0	6	17	4	19	1	3	3-2	.252	.279	.450	.730	4	.982
—New York (A.L.)	C-DH	35	96	9	20	4	0	1	11	3	21	1	3	0-0	.208	.240	.281	.521	0	1.000
2002—Las Vegas (PCL)	C-1B-OF	32	125	27	44	12	0	11	41	3	21	3	...		.352	.373	.712	1.085	2	.989
—Texas (A.L.)	1B-C-DH	42	112	15	30	5	0	6	19	2	23	1	4	0-0	.268	.282	.580	.862	3	.985
—Oklahoma (PCL)	C-OF-1B	39	152	21	46	9	0	6	29	9	27	1	...	2-0	.303	.339	.480	.820	2	.991
2003—Frisco (Texas)	C-1B	9	9	3	3	0	0	2	4	2	2	0	1	0-0	.333	.455	1.000	1.455	0	1.000
—Texas (A.L.)	C-DH-1B	62	205	25	47	10	1	10	20	2	47	2	2	0-0	.229	.243	.434	.677	4	.988
2004—Colo. Springs (PCL)	C-1B	4	12	2	4	1	0	1	4	3	0	0	0	0-0	.333	.385	.667	1.051	0	1.000
—Colorado (N.L.)	C	75	195	23	55	14	0	10	35	13	38	0	9	0-0	.282	.325	.508	.833	3	.989
2005—Colo. Springs (PCL)	C	11	33	4	13	0	0	3	8	1	3	0	2	0-0	.394	.412	.667	1.078	1	.980
—Colorado (N.L.)	C	38	126	10	32	4	0	7	23	7	21	1	5	0-0	.254	.299	.452	.751	4	.975
American League totals (8 years)		362	1093	132	264	52	1	52	142	37	228	8	26	5-4	.242	.270	.434	.704	9	.990
National League totals (2 years)		113	321	33	87	18	0	17	58	20	59	1	14	0-0	.271	.315	.486	.801	7	.984
Major League totals (10 years)		475	1414	165	351	70	1	69	200	57	287	9	40	5-4	.248	.281	.446	.726	16	.990

DIVISION SERIES RECORD

Year	Team (League)	Pos.	G	AB	R	H	2B	3B	HR	RBI	BB	SO	HBP	GDP	SB-CS	Avg.	OBP	SLG	OPS	E	Avg.
2001—New York (A.L.)		Did not play.																			

CHAMPIONSHIP SERIES RECORD

Year	Team (League)	Pos.	G	AB	R	H	2B	3B	HR	RBI	BB	SO	HBP	GDP	SB-CS	Avg.	OBP	SLG	OPS	E	Avg.
2001—New York (A.L.)	C	1	1	0	0	0	0	0	0	0	0	0	0	0-0	.000	.000	.000	.000	0	1.000

G

WORLD SERIES RECORD

Year Team (League)	Pos.	G	AB	R	H	2B	3B	HR	RBI	BB	SO	HBP	GDP	SB-CS	Avg.	OBP	SLG	OPS	E	Avg.
2001— New York (A.L.)	C	1	2	1	1	1	0	0	0	0	0	0	1	0-0	.500	.500	1.000	1.500	0	1.000

GREGG, KEVIN — P

PERSONAL: Born June 20, 1978, in Corvallis, Ore. ... 6-6/220. ... Throws right, bats right. ... Full name: Kevin Marschall Gregg. ... High school: Corvallis (Ore.).
TRANSACTIONS/CAREER NOTES: Selected by Oakland Athletics organization in 15th round of 1996 free-agent draft. ... Signed as a free agent by Anaheim Angels organization (November 19, 2002). ... Angels franchise renamed Los Angeles Angels of Anaheim for 2005 season.
CAREER HITTING: 0-for-0 (.000), 0 R, 0 2B, 0 3B, 0 HR, 0 RBI.

SCOUTING REPORT *Throws:* Gregg throws a sinking, 88-92 mph fastball, a slider and a split-finger fastball. *Tendencies:* He has a very deceptive windup and throws slighty across his body; hitters have a difficult time picking up the ball. Fastball has good sinking action but velocity has declined slightly. Can't afford to make mistakes up in the zone and is prone to the long ball. Break on the slider is quick but occasionally too big. Splitter breaks straight down and very late, making Gregg equally effective against righthanders and lefthanders. Needs better command of his fastball early in the count. *Outlook:* A middle reliever who can work often, Gregg provides valuable innings to save wear and tear on a pitching staff. *Grade 6.7*

KEVIN GREGG'S PITCHING ZONE

.133	.235	.313
.295	.318	.303
.250	.273	.368

LEFTY-RIGHTY SPLITS

vs.	Avg.	AB	H	2B	3B	HR	RBI	BB	SO	OBP	Slg.
L	.267	120	32	4	1	4	13	18	27	.362	.417
R	.279	136	38	6	0	4	21	11	25	.344	.412

Year Team (League)	W	L	Pct.	ERA	WHIP	G	GS	CG	ShO	Hld.	Sv.-Opp.	IP	H	R	ER	HR	BB-IBB	SO	Avg.
1996— Ariz. A's (Ariz.)	3	3	.500	3.10	1.25	11	9	0	0	...	0-...	40.2	30	14	14	1	21-0	48	.208
1997— Visalia (Calif.)	6	8	.429	5.70	1.65	25	24	0	0	...	0-...	115.1	116	81	73	8	74-0	136	.258
1998— Modesto (Calif.)	8	7	.533	3.81	1.49	30	24	0	0	...	1-...	144.0	139	72	61	7	76-2	141	.254
1999— Visalia (Calif.)	4	4	.500	3.80	1.30	13	11	1	1	...	0-...	64.0	60	34	27	3	23-0	48	.249
— Midland (Texas)	4	7	.364	3.74	1.16	16	16	2	0	...	0-...	91.1	75	45	38	7	31-1	66	.221
— Vancouver (PCL)	1	0	1.000	3.60	1.60	1	1	0	0	...	0-...	5.0	6	2	2	0	2-0	4	.316
2000— Midland (Texas)	5	14	.263	6.40	1.73	28	27	0	0	...	0-...	140.2	171	120	100	18	73-0	97	.304
2001— Midland (Texas)	5	5	.500	4.54	1.57	44	1	0	0	...	1-...	81.1	88	48	41	5	40-4	72	.274
2002— Midland (Texas)	3	3	.500	4.30	1.30	11	4	0	0	...	0-...	37.2	31	20	18	3	18-0	45	.221
— Visalia (Calif.)	2	1	.667	2.08	0.98	3	3	0	0	...	0-...	17.1	8	5	4	0	9-0	11	.140
— Sacramento (PCL)	2	5	.286	7.52	1.79	16	8	0	0	...	0-...	58.2	82	56	49	7	23-0	45	.332
2003— Arkansas (Texas)	4	3	.571	3.53	1.19	15	11	2	0	...	0-...	66.1	60	29	26	2	19-0	60	.241
— Salt Lake (PCL)	7	4	.636	4.03	1.18	15	15	0	0	...	0-...	91.2	90	47	41	10	18-0	75	.256
— Anaheim (A.L.)	2	0	1.000	3.28	1.05	5	3	0	0	0	0-0	24.2	18	9	9	3	8-0	14	.205
2004— Anaheim (A.L.)	5	2	.714	4.21	1.30	55	0	0	0	3	1-2	87.2	86	43	41	6	28-3	84	.255
2005— Salt Lake (PCL)	3	1	.750	3.89	1.33	7	6	0	0	0	0-0	34.2	36	15	15	2	10-0	36	.273
— Los Angeles (A.L.)	1	2	.333	5.04	1.54	33	2	0	0	1	0-1	64.1	70	37	36	8	29-2	52	.273
Major League totals (3 years)	**8**	**4**	**.667**	**4.38**	**1.35**	**93**	**5**	**0**	**0**	**4**	**1-3**	**176.2**	**174**	**89**	**86**	**17**	**65-5**	**150**	**.256**

DIVISION SERIES RECORD

Year Team (League)	W	L	Pct.	ERA	WHIP	G	GS	CG	ShO	Hld.	Sv.-Opp.	IP	H	R	ER	HR	BB-IBB	SO	Avg.
2004— Anaheim (A.L.)	0	0	...	0.00	2.00	1	0	0	0	0	0-0	2.0	3	0	0	0	1-0	1	.333

CHAMPIONSHIP SERIES RECORD

Year Team (League)	W	L	Pct.	ERA	WHIP	G	GS	CG	ShO	Hld.	Sv.-Opp.	IP	H	R	ER	HR	BB-IBB	SO	Avg.
2005— Los Angeles (A.L.)	0	0	...	0.00	1.00	1	0	0	0	0	0-0	2.0	1	0	0	0	1-0	3	.143

GREINKE, ZACK — P

PERSONAL: Born October 21, 1983, in Orlando. ... 6-2/200. ... Throws right, bats right. ... Full name: Donald Zackary Greinke. ... Name pronounced: GRAIN-key. ... High school: Apopka (Fla.).
TRANSACTIONS/CAREER NOTES: Selected by Kansas City Royals organization in first round (sixth pick overall) of 2002 free-agent draft.
HONORS: Named Minor League Player of the Year by THE SPORTING NEWS (2003).
CAREER HITTING: 1-for-4 (.250), 1 R, 0 2B, 0 3B, 1 HR, 1 RBI.

SCOUTING REPORT *Throws:* His two- and four-seam fastballs come in at 88-94 mph, but he pitches most often in the 89-91 range. Slider is 81-84 mph and has a late break. Curveball is 71-76. Also throws a changeup. *Tendencies:* Greinke pitches like a veteran; he has excellent feel and instincts. Has the ability to reach back and get a little extra. Has a simple delivery and is very efficient. Will have above-average control. Is not afraid to pitch inside and will back hitters off the plate. Curve is a big and looping with very good rotation and a downward break. Has excellent arm speed with his change. *Outlook:* He has all the intangibles to be a solid starter for years to come. Is unclear whether he is a power or finesse pitcher At times seems bored on the mound. *Grade 6.8*

ZACK GREINKE'S PITCHING ZONE

.268	.486	.338
.357	.361	.299
.208	.424	.327

LEFTY-RIGHTY SPLITS

vs.	Avg.	AB	H	2B	3B	HR	RBI	BB	SO	OBP	Slg.
L	.340	377	128	29	5	13	71	31	42	.395	.546
R	.279	377	105	19	2	10	41	22	72	.331	.419

Year Team (League)	W	L	Pct.	ERA	WHIP	G	GS	CG	ShO	Hld.	Sv.-Opp.	IP	H	R	ER	HR	BB-IBB	SO	Avg.
2002— GC Royals (GCL)	0	0	...	1.93	1.29	3	3	0	0	...	0-...	4.2	3	1	1	0	3-0	4	.200
— Spokane (N'west)	0	0	...	7.71	1.93	2	2	0	0	...	0-...	4.2	9	4	4	0	0-0	5	.391
— Wilmington (Carol.)	0	0	...	0.00	0.50	1	0	0	0	...	0-...	2.0	1	0	0	0	0-0	0	.167
2003— Wilmington (Carol.)	11	1	.917	1.14	0.79	14	14	3	1	...	0-...	87.0	56	16	11	5	13-0	78	.178
— Wichita (Texas)	4	3	.571	3.23	1.19	9	9	0	0	...	0-...	53.0	58	20	19	5	5-2	34	.286
2004— Omaha (PCL)	1	1	.500	2.51	1.08	6	6	0	0	...	0-...	28.2	25	8	8	2	6-0	23	.225
— Kansas City (A.L.)	8	11	.421	3.97	1.17	24	24	0	0	0	0-0	145.0	143	64	64	26	26-3	100	.256
2005— Kansas City (A.L.)	5	*17	.227	5.80	1.56	33	33	2	0	0	0-0	183.0	233	125	118	23	53-0	114	.309
Major League totals (2 years)	**13**	**28**	**.317**	**4.99**	**1.39**	**57**	**57**	**2**	**0**	**0**	**0-0**	**328.0**	**376**	**189**	**182**	**49**	**79-3**	**214**	**.286**

GREISINGER, SETH — P

PERSONAL: Born July 29, 1975, in Kansas City, Kan. ... 6-3/195. ... Throws right, bats right. ... Full name: Seth Adam Greisinger. ... Name pronounced: gry-sing-er. ... High school: McLean (Va.). ... College: Virginia.

TRANSACTIONS/CAREER NOTES: Selected by Cleveland Indians organization in seventh round of 1993 free-agent draft; did not sign. ... Selected by Detroit Tigers organization in first round (sixth pick overall) of 1996 free-agent draft. ... On disabled list (March 26, 1999-entire season); included rehabilitation assignments to Lakeland and Toledo. ... On disabled list (March 13, 2000-entire season; and March 30, 2001-entire sesaon). ... Signed as a free agent by Minnesota Twins organization (November 22, 2003). ... Released by Twins (November 10, 2004). ... Signed by Washington Nationals (December 23, 2004). ... Traded by Nationals to Atlanta Braves for a player to be named (March 26, 2005). ... Released by Braves (July 6, 2005).

CAREER HITTING: 1-for-6 (.167), 0 R, 0 2B, 0 3B, 0 HR, 1 RBI.

LEFTY-RIGHTY SPLITS

vs.	Avg.	AB	H	2B	3B	HR	RBI	BB	SO	OBP	Slg.
L	.556	9	5	1	0	1	1	0	1	.556	1.000
R	.182	11	2	1	0	0	1	1	1	.250	.273

Year	Team (League)	W	L	Pct.	ERA	WHIP	G	GS	CG	ShO	Hld.	Sv.-Opp.	IP	H	R	ER	HR	BB-IBB	SO	Avg.
1997—	Jacksonville (Sou.)	10	6	.625	5.20	1.55	28	28	1	0	...	0-...	159.1	194	103	92	29	53-0	105	.301
1998—	Toledo (Int'l)	3	4	.429	2.91	1.23	10	10	0	0	...	0-...	58.2	50	21	19	5	22-0	37	.229
—	Detroit (A.L.)	6	9	.400	5.12	1.46	21	21	0	0	0	0-0	130.0	142	79	74	17	48-2	66	.282
1999—	Lakeland (Fla. St.)	0	0	...	3.86	0.64	1	1	0	0	0	0-0	4.2	2	2	2	1	1-0	2	.125
—	Toledo (Int'l)	0	1	.000	5.87	1.57	2	2	0	0	...	0-...	7.2	9	5	5	0	3-0	4	.300
2000—	Detroit (A.L.)			Did not play.																
2001—	Detroit (A.L.)			Did not play.																
2002—	Erie (East.)	2	0	1.000	1.29	1.00	4	4	0	0	...	0-...	21.0	12	4	3	1	9-0	21	.160
—	Detroit (A.L.)	2	2	.500	6.21	1.57	8	8	0	0	0	0-0	37.2	46	26	26	4	13-2	14	.303
—	Toledo (Int'l)	1	1	.500	4.11	1.43	3	3	0	0	...	0-...	15.1	15	8	7	0	7-0	11	.278
2003—	Toledo (Int'l)	6	9	.400	3.97	1.30	25	21	2	1	...	0-...	136.0	154	77	60	16	23-3	80	.285
2004—	Minnesota (A.L.)	2	5	.286	6.18	1.63	12	9	0	0	0	0-0	51.0	68	40	35	12	15-1	36	.319
—	Rochester (Int'l)	5	5	.500	4.96	1.52	13	13	0	0	...	0-...	74.1	94	44	41	10	19-0	44	.319
2005—	Atlanta (N.L.)	0	0	...	3.60	1.60	1	1	0	0	0	0-0	5.0	7	2	2	1	1-0	2	.350
—	Richmond (Int'l)	4	7	.364	3.01	1.04	16	16	1	0	...	0-...	98.2	75	36	33	4	28-2	56	.212
American League totals (3 years)		**10**	**16**	**.385**	**5.56**	**1.52**	**41**	**38**	**0**	**0**	**0**	**0-0**	**218.2**	**256**	**145**	**135**	**33**	**76-5**	**116**	**.295**
National League totals (1 year)		**0**	**0**	**...**	**3.60**	**1.60**	**1**	**1**	**0**	**0**	**0**	**0-0**	**5.0**	**7**	**2**	**2**	**1**	**1-0**	**2**	**.350**
Major League totals (4 years)		**10**	**16**	**.385**	**5.51**	**1.52**	**42**	**39**	**0**	**0**	**0**	**0-0**	**223.2**	**263**	**147**	**137**	**34**	**77-5**	**118**	**.296**

GRIEVE, BEN — OF

PERSONAL: Born May 4, 1976, in Arlington, Texas. ... 6-4/216. ... Bats left, throws right. ... Full name: Benjamin Grieve. ... Name pronounced: greev. ... High school: James W. Martin (Arlington, Texas). ... Son of Tom Grieve, outfielder with four major league teams (1970-79).

TRANSACTIONS/CAREER NOTES: Selected by Oakland Athletics organization in first round (second pick overall) of 1994 free-agent draft. ... Traded by Athletics with cash to Tampa Bay Devil Rays as part of three-team deal in which Kansas City Royals acquired P Roberto Hernandez from Devil Rays, Athletics acquired P Cory Lidle from Devil Rays, Athletics acquired OF Johnny Damon, IF Mark Ellis and cash from Royals and Royals acquired C A.J. Hinch, IF Angel Berroa and cash from Athletics (January 8, 2001). ... On disabled list (April 18-May 22 and July 18, 2003-remainder of season). ... Signed as a free agent by Milwaukee Brewers (December 23, 2003). ... Traded by Brewers to Chicago Cubs for a player to be named and cash (August 31, 2004); Brewers acquired P Andy Pratt to complete deal (September 2, 2004). ... Signed as a free agent by Pittsburgh Pirates organization (January 24, 2005). ... Released by Pirates (April 1, 2005). ... Signed by Chicago Cubs organization (April 5, 2005).

HONORS: Named Minor League Player of the Year by THE SPORTING NEWS (1997). ... Named A.L. Rookie Player of the Year by THE SPORTING NEWS (1998). ... Named A.L. Rookie of the Year by Baseball Writers' Association of America (1998).

2005 GAMES PLAYED BY POSITION (MLB): OF—1.

LEFTY-RIGHTY SPLITS

vs.	Avg.	AB	H	2B	3B	HR	RBI	BB	SO	OBP	Slg.
L	.000	2	0	0	0	0	0	0	1	.000	.000
R	.278	18	5	0	0	0	1	5	6	.435	.278

Year	Team (League)	Pos.	G	AB	R	H	2B	3B	HR	RBI	BB	SO	HBP	GDP	SB-CS	Avg.	OBP	SLG	OPS	E	Avg.
1994—	S. Oregon (N'west)	OF	72	252	44	83	13	0	7	50	51	48	10	6	2-2	.329	.456	.464	.920	6	.959
1995—	W. Mich. (Mid.)	OF	102	371	53	97	16	1	4	62	60	75	8	10	11-3	.261	.371	.342	.713	8	.942
—	Modesto (California)	OF	28	107	17	28	5	0	2	14	14	15	0	3	2-0	.262	.341	.364	.706	2	.951
1996—	Modesto (California)	OF-DH	72	281	61	100	20	1	11	51	38	52	1	5	8-7	.356	.430	.552	.982	5	.956
—	Huntsville (Sou.)	OF-DH	63	232	34	55	8	1	8	32	35	53	2	3	0-3	.237	.338	.384	.722	4	.953
1997—	Huntsville (Sou.)	OF-DH	100	372	100	122	29	2	24	108	81	75	9	8	5-1	.328	.455	.610	1.065	•8	.961
—	Edmonton (PCL)	OF	27	108	27	46	11	1	7	28	12	16	1	4	0-1	.426	.484	.741	1.224	2	.964
—	Oakland (A.L.)	OF	24	93	12	29	6	0	3	24	13	25	1	1	0-0	.312	.402	.473	.875	0	1.000
1998—	Oakland (A.L.)	OF-DH	155	583	94	168	41	2	18	89	85	123	9	18	2-2	.288	.386	.458	.844	3	.993
1999—	Oakland (A.L.)	OF-DH	148	486	80	129	21	0	28	86	63	108	8	17	4-0	.265	.358	.481	.840	3	.988
2000—	Oakland (A.L.)	OF-DH	158	594	92	166	40	1	27	104	73	130	3	*32	3-0	.279	.359	.487	.845	4	.988
2001—	Tampa Bay (A.L.)	OF-DH	154	542	72	143	30	2	11	72	87	159	3	13	7-1	.264	.372	.387	.760	4	.984
2002—	Tampa Bay (A.L.)	OF-DH	136	482	62	121	30	0	19	64	69	121	8	15	8-2	.251	.353	.432	.784	3	.988
2003—	Tampa Bay (A.L.)	DH-OF	55	165	28	38	7	0	4	17	32	41	6	3	0-0	.230	.371	.345	.716	1	.947
2004—	Milwaukee (A.L.)	OF-DH	108	234	28	61	15	0	7	29	39	65	0	4	0-0	.261	.364	.415	.778	4	.964
—	Chicago (N.L.)	OF	15	16	2	4	2	0	0	6	0	5	2	0	0-0	.250	.316	.563	.878	0	1.000
2005—	Iowa (PCL)	OF-DH	86	293	44	78	16	1	14	51	48	59	1	9	0-3	.266	.371	.481	.853	4	.980
—	Chicago (N.L.)	OF	23	20	1	5	0	0	0	1	5	7	0	0	0-0	.250	.400	.250	.650	0	...
American League totals (7 years)			**830**	**2945**	**440**	**794**	**175**	**5**	**110**	**456**	**422**	**707**	**43**	**99**	**24-5**	**.270**	**.368**	**.444**	**.812**	**16**	**.988**
National League totals (2 years)			**146**	**270**	**31**	**70**	**17**	**0**	**8**	**36**	**44**	**77**	**2**	**4**	**0-0**	**.259**	**.364**	**.411**	**.775**	**4**	**.965**
Major League totals (9 years)			**976**	**3215**	**471**	**864**	**192**	**5**	**118**	**492**	**466**	**784**	**45**	**103**	**24-5**	**.269**	**.367**	**.442**	**.809**	**20**	**.986**

DIVISION SERIES RECORD

Year	Team (League)	Pos.	G	AB	R	H	2B	3B	HR	RBI	BB	SO	HBP	GDP	SB-CS	Avg.	OBP	SLG	OPS	E	Avg.
2000—	Oakland (A.L.)	OF	5	17	1	2	0	0	0	2	3	7	0	2	0-0	.118	.250	.118	.368	0	1.000

ALL-STAR GAME RECORD

			G	AB	R	H	2B	3B	HR	RBI	BB	SO	HBP	GDP	SB-CS	Avg.	OBP	SLG	OPS	E	Avg.
All-Star Game totals (1 year)			1	0	0	0	0	0	0	0	0	0	0	0	0-0	...	1.000	...	...	0	...

GRIFFEY, KEN — OF

PERSONAL: Born November 21, 1969, in Donora, Pa. ... 6-3/205. ... Bats left, throws left. ... Full name: George Kenneth Griffey Jr.. ... High school: Moeller (Cincinnati). ... Son of Ken Griffey, special consultant to general manager, Cincinnati Reds, and outfielder with four major league teams (1973-91).

TRANSACTIONS/CAREER NOTES: Selected by Seattle Mariners organization in first round (first pick overall) of 1987 free-agent draft. ... On disabled list (July 24-August 20, 1989; and June 9-25, 1992). ... On disabled list (May 27-August 15, 1995); included rehabilitation assignment to Tacoma. ... On disabled list (June 20-July 13, 1996). ...

G

Traded by Mariners to Cincinnati Reds for Ps Brett Tomko and Jake Meyer, OF Mike Cameron and IF Antonio Perez (February 10, 2000). ... On disabled list (April 29-June 15, 2001; and April 7-May 24 and June 24-July 22, 2002). ... On disabled list (April 6-May 13 and July 18, 2003-remainder of season). ... On disabled list (July 11-August 3 and August 12, 2004-remainder of season).

HONORS: Named Major League Player of the Year by THE SPORTING NEWS (1997). ... Named A.L. Most Valuable Player by Baseball Writers' Association of America (1997). ... Won A.L. Gold Glove as outfielder (1990-99). ... Named N.L. Comeback Player of the Year by the SPORTING NEWS (2005).

2005 GAMES PLAYED BY POSITION (MLB): OF—124, DH—2.

SCOUTING REPORT

Offense: Although his bat speed has declined, Griffey still has exceptional plate coverage. Has a slight lift to his swing. Is a smart hitter who will pick his spots. Still has good power to all fields. Was able to get his legs under him for the first time in several years and was able to drive the ball. No longer is a basestealing threat. ***Defense:*** His range has declined; he now relies on instincts, positioning and his ability to get good jumps. Rarely leaves his feet to dive. Doesn't throw as well now and makes little effort to build up his strength. ***Outlook:*** His renewed home run stroke should continue as long as he has his legs remain healthy. Is not the total package he was with the Mariners. ***Grade 7.7***

KEN GRIFFEY'S HITTING ZONE

.227	.478	.313
.364	.360	.336
.333	.367	.182

LEFTY-RIGHTY SPLITS

vs.	Avg.	AB	H	2B	3B	HR	RBI	BB	SO	OBP	Slg.
L	.278	169	47	11	0	11	31	20	35	.352	.538
R	.314	322	101	19	0	24	61	34	58	.378	.596

									BATTING								FIELDING	
Year Team (League)	Pos.	G	AB	R	H	2B	3B	HR	RBI	BB	SO	HBP	GDP	SB-CS	Avg.	OBP	SLG	OPS	E	Avg.
1987— Bellingham (N'west)	OF	54	182	43	57	9	1	14	40	44	42	0	2	13-6	.313	.445	.604	1.049	1	.992
1988— San Bern. (Calif.)	OF	58	219	50	74	13	3	11	42	34	39	2	3	32-9	.338	.431	.575	1.007	2	.987
— Vermont (East.)	OF	17	61	10	17	5	1	2	10	5	12	2	3	4-2	.279	.333	.492	.845	1	.977
1989— Seattle (A.L.)	DH-OF	127	455	61	120	23	0	16	61	44	83	2	4	16-7	.264	.329	.420	.748	• 10	.969
1990— Seattle (A.L.)	OF	155	597	91	179	28	7	22	80	63	81	2	12	16-11	.300	.366	.481	.847	7	.980
1991— Seattle (A.L.)	DH-OF	154	548	76	179	42	1	22	100	71	82	1	10	18-6	.327	.399	.527	.926	4	.989
1992— Seattle (A.L.)	OF-DH	142	565	83	174	39	4	27	103	44	67	5	15	10-5	.308	.361	.535	.896	1	.997
1993— Seattle (A.L.)	OF-DH-1B	156	582	113	180	38	3	45	109	96	91	6	14	17-9	.309	.408	.617	1.025	3	.991
1994— Seattle (A.L.)	OF-DH	111	433	94	140	24	4	* 40	90	56	73	2	9	11-3	.323	.402	.674	1.076	4	.983
1995— Seattle (A.L.)	OF-DH	72	260	52	67	7	0	17	42	52	53	0	4	4-2	.258	.379	.481	.860	2	.990
— Tacoma (PCL)	DH	1	3	0	0	0	0	0	0	1	0	0	0	0-0	.000	.000	.000	.000	...	...
1996— Seattle (A.L.)	OF-DH	140	545	125	165	26	2	49	140	78	104	7	7	16-1	.303	.392	.628	1.020	4	.990
1997— Seattle (A.L.)	OF-DH	157	608	* 125	185	34	3	* 56	* 147	76	121	8	12	15-4	.304	.382	* .646	1.028	6	.985
1998— Seattle (A.L.)	OF-DH-1B	161	633	120	180	33	3	* 56	146	76	121	7	14	20-5	.284	.365	.611	.977	5	.988
1999— Seattle (A.L.)	OF-DH	160	606	123	173	26	3	* 48	134	91	108	7	8	24-7	.285	.384	.576	.960	9	.978
2000— Cincinnati (N.L.)	OF	145	520	100	141	22	3	40	118	94	117	9	7	6-4	.271	.387	.556	.942	5	.987
2001— Cincinnati (N.L.)	OF-DH	111	364	57	104	20	2	22	65	44	72	4	8	2-0	.286	.365	.533	.898	3	.985
2002— Cincinnati (N.L.)	OF	70	197	17	52	8	0	8	23	28	39	3	6	1-2	.264	.358	.426	.784	3	.971
2003— Cincinnati (N.L.)	OF-DH	53	166	34	41	12	1	13	26	27	44	6	3	1-0	.247	.370	.566	.936	1	.989
2004— Cincinnati (N.L.)	OF-DH	83	300	49	76	18	0	20	60	44	67	2	8	1-0	.253	.351	.513	.864	1	.994
2005— Cincinnati (N.L.)	OF-DH	128	491	85	148	30	0	35	92	54	93	3	9	0-1	.301	.369	.576	.946	3	.990
American League totals (11 years)		1535	5832	1063	1742	320	30	398	1152	747	984	47	109	167-60	.299	.380	.569	.948	55	.986
National League totals (6 years)		590	2038	342	562	110	6	138	384	291	432	27	41	11-7	.276	.369	.539	.908	16	.987
Major League totals (17 years)		2125	7870	1405	2304	430	36	536	1536	1038	1416	74	150	178-67	.293	.377	.561	.938	71	.986

DIVISION SERIES RECORD

Year Team (League)	Pos.	G	AB	R	H	2B	3B	HR	RBI	BB	SO	HBP	GDP	SB-CS	Avg.	OBP	SLG	OPS	E	Avg.
1995— Seattle (A.L.)	OF	5	23	9	9	0	0	5	7	2	4	1	0	1-0	.391	.444	1.043	1.488	0	1.000
1997— Seattle (A.L.)	OF	4	15	0	2	0	0	0	2	1	3	0	0	2-0	.133	.188	.133	.321	0	1.000
Division series totals (2 years)		9	38	9	11	0	0	5	9	3	7	1	0	3-0	.289	.349	.684	1.033	0	1.000

CHAMPIONSHIP SERIES RECORD

Year Team (League)	Pos.	G	AB	R	H	2B	3B	HR	RBI	BB	SO	HBP	GDP	SB-CS	Avg.	OBP	SLG	OPS	E	Avg.
1995— Seattle (A.L.)	OF	6	21	2	7	2	0	1	4	4	0	0	0	2-1	.333	.440	.571	1.011	1	.929

ALL-STAR GAME RECORD

		G	AB	R	H	2B	3B	HR	RBI	BB	SO	HBP	GDP	SB-CS	Avg.	OBP	SLG	OPS	E	Avg.
All-Star Game totals (8 years)		8	23	4	10	2	0	1	5	2	4	0		1-0	.435	.480	.652	1.132	1	.900

GRIFFIN, JOHN-FORD   OF

PERSONAL: Born November 19, 1979, in Sarasota, Fla. ... 6-2/215. ... Bats left, throws left. ... Full name: John-Ford David Griffin. ... High school: Sarasota (Fla.). ... College: Florida State.

TRANSACTIONS/CAREER NOTES: Selected by New York Yankees organization in first round (23rd pick overall) of 2001 free-agent draft. ... Traded by Yankees with P Ted Lilly and P Jason Arnold to Oakland Athletics in three-team deal in which Yankees received P Jeff Weaver from Detroit Tigers and Tigers received IF Carlos Pena, P Franklyn German and a player to be named from Athletics (July 6, 2002); Tigers get P Jeremy Bonderman from Athletics to complete deal (August 22, 2002). ... Traded by Athletics to Toronto Blue Jays for player to be named (January 27, 2003); Athletics acquired OF Jason Perry to complete deal (June 23, 2003).

2005 GAMES PLAYED BY POSITION (MLB): DH—4.

LEFTY-RIGHTY SPLITS

vs.	Avg.	AB	H	2B	3B	HR	RBI	BB	SO	OBP	Slg.
L	1.000	1	1	0	0	1	1	0	0	1.000	4.000
R	.250	12	3	2	0	0	5	0	4	.250	.417

									BATTING								FIELDING	
Year Team (League)	Pos.	G	AB	R	H	2B	3B	HR	RBI	BB	SO	HBP	GDP	SB-CS	Avg.	OBP	SLG	OPS	E	Avg.
2001— Staten Island (NYP)	OF	66	238	46	74	17	1	5	43	40	41	3	5	10-4	.311	.413	.454	.867	5	.943
2002— Tampa (Fla. St.)	OF	65	255	32	68	16	1	3	31	29	45	3	9	1-0	.267	.344	.373	.717	3	.959
— Norwich (East.)	OF	18	67	17	22	3	0	5	10	8	13	0	5	0-1	.328	.400	.597	.997	2	.935
— Midland (Texas)	OF	2	7	0	1	0	0	0	0	0	3	1	0	0-0	.143	.250	.143	.393	0	1.000
2003— New Haven (East.)	OF	104	373	48	104	23	3	13	75	49	85	2	8	2-0	.279	.361	.461	.822	3	.977
2004— New Hampshire (East.)	OF-1B	129	467	66	116	28	1	22	81	56	128	4	15	1-1	.248	.330	.454	.784	4	.985
2005— Syracuse (Int'l)	OF-DH	135	512	80	130	21	1	30	103	62	140	3	10	1-2	.254	.335	.475	.810	6	.979
— Toronto (A.L.)	DH	7	13	3	4	2	0	1	6	0	4	0	0	0-0	.308	.308	.692	1.000	0	...
Major League totals (1 year)		7	13	3	4	2	0	1	6	0	4	0	0	0-0	.308	.308	.692	1.000	0	...

G

GRILLI, JASON   P

PERSONAL: Born November 11, 1976, in Royal Oak, Mich. ... 6-4/185. ... Throws right, bats right. ... Full name: Jason Michael Grilli. ... High school: C.W. Baker (Baldwinsville, N.Y.). ... College: Seton Hall. ... Son of Steve Grilli, pitcher with two major league teams (1975-79).
TRANSACTIONS/CAREER NOTES: Selected by New York Yankees organization in 24th round of 1994 free-agent draft; did not sign. ... Selected by San Francisco Giants organization in first round (fourth pick overall) of 1997 free-agent draft. ... Traded by Giants with P Nate Bump to Florida Marlins for P Livan Hernandez (July 24, 1999). ... Selected by Chicago White Sox from Marlins organization in Rule 5 major league draft (December 15, 2003). ... Released by White Sox (Feburary 3, 2005). ... Signed by Detroit Tigers organization (February 9, 2005).
CAREER HITTING: 3-for-9 (.333), 1 R, 0 2B, 0 3B, 1 HR, 3 RBI.

JASON GRILLI'S PITCHING ZONE

.000	.000	.667
.000	.333	.154
.333	.250	.400

LEFTY-RIGHTY SPLITS

vs.	Avg.	AB	H	2B	3B	HR	RBI	BB	SO	OBP	Slg.
L	.222	27	6	2	1	0	3	1	2	.241	.370
R	.286	28	8	1	0	1	3	5	3	.394	.429

Year	Team (League)	W	L	Pct.	ERA	WHIP	G	GS	CG	ShO	Hld.	Sv.-Opp.	IP	H	R	ER	HR	BB-IBB	SO	Avg.
1998	—Shreveport (Texas)	7	10	.412	3.79	1.22	21	21	3	0	...	0-...	123.1	113	60	52	11	37-0	100	.245
	—Fresno (PCL)	2	3	.400	5.14	1.60	8	8	0	0	...	0-...	42.0	49	30	24	7	18-0	37	.290
1999	—Fresno (PCL)	7	5	.583	5.54	1.62	19	19	1	0	...	0-...	100.2	124	69	62	22	39-0	76	.302
	—Calgary (PCL)	1	5	.167	7.68	1.93	8	8	0	0	...	0-...	41.0	56	48	35	7	23-0	27	.316
2000	—Calgary (PCL)	1	4	.200	7.19	1.96	8	8	0	0	...	0-...	41.1	58	37	33	4	23-0	21	.335
	—Florida (N.L.)	1	0	1.000	5.40	1.95	1	1	0	0	0	0-0	6.2	11	4	4	0	2-0	3	.379
2001	—Florida (N.L.)	2	2	.500	6.08	1.54	6	5	0	0	0	0-0	26.2	30	18	18	6	11-0	17	.297
	—Calgary (PCL)	1	2	.333	4.02	1.40	8	8	0	0	0	0-...	47.0	46	26	21	4	20-0	35	.256
	—GC Marlins (GCL)	0	0	...	0.00	0.50	2	2	0	0	0	0-...	4.0	2	0	0	0	0-0	6	.143
	—Brevard County (Fla. St.)	2	0	1.000	1.98	1.24	3	3	0	0	0	0-...	13.2	12	4	3	0	5-0	14	.231
	—Portland (East.)	0	1	.000	2.25	0.75	1	1	0	0	0	0-...	4.0	3	1	1	1	0-0	3	.200
2002	—Calgary (PCL)	0	1	.000	1.59	1.06	1	1	0	0	0	0-...	5.2	3	1	1	0	3-0	8	.158
2003	—Jupiter (Fla. St.)	4	2	.667	2.53	1.03	7	7	0	0	0	0-...	42.2	38	13	12	1	6-...	30	.236
	—Albuquerque (PCL)	6	2	.750	3.38	1.41	12	12	0	0	0	0-...	66.2	64	30	25	3	30-...	38	.260
2004	—Charlotte (Int'l)	9	9	.500	4.83	1.45	25	25	2	1	0	0-...	152.2	163	95	82	22	58-0	101	.276
	—Chicago (A.L.)	2	3	.400	7.40	1.60	8	8	1	0	0	0-0	45.0	52	38	37	11	20-0	26	.294
2005	—Toledo (Int'l)	12	9	.571	4.09	1.36	28	28	3	2	0	0-...	167.1	170	89	76	21	58-0	120	.263
	—Detroit (A.L.)	1	1	.500	3.38	1.25	3	2	0	0	0	0-0	16.0	14	6	6	1	6-0	5	.255
	American League totals (2 years)	3	4	.429	6.34	1.57	11	10	1	0	0	0-0	61.0	66	44	43	12	26-0	31	.284
	National League totals (2 years)	3	2	.600	5.94	1.62	7	6	0	0	0	0-0	33.1	41	22	22	6	13-0	20	.315
	Major League totals (4 years)	6	6	.500	6.20	1.55	18	16	1	0	0	0-0	94.1	107	66	65	18	39-0	51	.296

GRIMSLEY, JASON   P

PERSONAL: Born August 7, 1967, in Cleveland, Texas. ... 6-3/205. ... Throws right, bats right. ... Full name: Jason Alan Grimsley. ... High school: Tarkington (Cleveland, Texas).
TRANSACTIONS/CAREER NOTES: Selected by Philadelphia Phillies organization in 10th round of June 1985 free-agent draft. ... On disabled list (June 6-August 22, 1991); included rehabilitation assignments to Scranton/Wilkes-Barre. ... Traded by Phillies to Houston Astros for P Curt Schilling (April 2, 1992). ... On disabled list (May 14-June 14, 1992). ... Released by Astros (March 30, 1993). ... Signed by Cleveland Indians organization (April 7, 1993). ... Traded by Indians with P Pep Harris to California Angels for P Brian Anderson (February 15, 1996). ... Signed as a free agent by Detroit Tigers organization (January 17, 1997). ... Released by Tigers (March 20, 1997). ... Signed by Milwaukee Brewers (April 3, 1997). ... Traded by Brewers to Kansas City Royals for P Jamie Brewington (July 29, 1997). ... Signed as a free agent by Indians organization (January 8, 1998). ... Signed as a free agent by New York Yankees organization (January 26, 1999). ... On suspended list (August 11-15, 1999). ... Released by Yankees (November 20, 2000). ... Signed by Royals (January 19, 2001). ... On disabled list (June 4-22, 2002); included rehabilitation assignment to Wichita. ... Traded by Royals to Baltimore Orioles for P Denny Bautista (June 17, 2004). ... On disabled list (April 1-July 14 and August 19-September 2, 2005); included rehabilitation assignment to Bowie.
CAREER HITTING: 4-for-39 (.103), 3 R, 0 2B, 0 3B, 0 HR, 2 RBI.

SCOUTING REPORT *Throws:* Grimsley's fastball ranges from 91-95 mph, and his slider checks in at 85-86. *Tendencies:* Grimsley is a one-pitch pitcher; he relies on a very heavy sinker. Will throw it to both sides of the plate. Slider is very inconsistent and tends to flatten out. *Outlook:* Grimsley's ability to come back and pitch late last season after elbow surgery is a testimony to his makeup. Is entrenched as a setup man. *Grade 6*

JASON GRIMSLEY'S PITCHING ZONE

.000	.000	.429
.300	.250	.316
.333	.250	.600

LEFTY-RIGHTY SPLITS

vs.	Avg.	AB	H	2B	3B	HR	RBI	BB	SO	OBP	Slg.
L	.324	34	11	2	0	2	6	5	1	.400	.559
R	.265	49	13	2	1	3	11	4	9	.321	.531

Year	Team (League)	W	L	Pct.	ERA	WHIP	G	GS	CG	ShO	Hld.	Sv.-Opp.	IP	H	R	ER	HR	BB-IBB	SO	Avg.
1985	—Bend (N'west)	0	1	.000	13.50	3.26	6	1	0	0	...	0-...	11.1	12	21	17	0	25-0	10	...
1986	—Utica (NYP)	1	10	.091	6.40	2.16	14	14	3	0	...	0-...	64.2	63	61	46	3	* 77-0	46	.251
1987	—Spartanburg (S. Atl.)	7	4	.636	3.16	1.28	23	9	3	0	...	0-...	88.1	59	48	31	4	54-2	98	.190
1988	—Clearwater (Fla. St.)	4	7	.364	3.73	1.15	16	15	2	0	...	0-...	101.1	80	48	42	2	37-1	90	.217
	—Reading (East.)	1	3	.250	7.17	1.55	5	4	0	0	...	0-...	21.1	20	19	17	1	13-1	14	.247
1989	—Reading (East.)	11	8	.579	2.98	1.34	26	26	8	2	...	0-...	172.0	121	65	57	13	* 109-4	134	.202
	—Philadelphia (N.L.)	1	3	.250	5.89	2.07	4	4	0	0	0	0-0	18.1	19	13	12	2	19-1	7	.268
1990	—Scran./W.B. (Int'l)	8	5	.615	3.93	1.47	22	22	0	0	...	0-...	128.1	111	68	56	7	78-1	99	.236
	—Philadelphia (N.L.)	3	2	.600	3.30	1.57	11	11	0	0	0	0-0	57.1	47	21	21	1	43-0	41	.236
1991	—Philadelphia (N.L.)	1	7	.125	4.87	1.56	12	12	0	0	0	0-0	61.0	54	34	33	4	41-3	42	.242
	—Scran./W.B. (Int'l)	3	4	.400	4.35	1.65	9	9	1	0	...	0-...	51.2	48	28	25	3	37-2	43	.254
1992	—Tucson (PCL)	8	7	.533	5.05	1.66	26	20	0	0	...	0-...	124.2	152	79	70	4	55-0	90	.308
1993	—Charlotte (Int'l)	6	6	.500	3.39	1.38	28	19	3	1	0	0-...	135.1	138	64	51	10	49-1	90	.263
	—Cleveland (A.L.)	3	4	.429	5.31	1.70	10	6	0	0	1	0-0	42.1	52	26	25	8	20-1	27	.302
1994	—Charlotte (Int'l)	7	0	1.000	3.42	1.06	10	10	2	0	...	0-...	71.0	58	36	27	10	17-0	60	.218
	—Cleveland (A.L.)	5	2	.714	4.57	1.51	14	13	0	0	0	0-0	82.2	91	47	42	7	34-1	59	.283
1995	—Cleveland (A.L.)	0	0	...	6.09	2.03	15	2	0	0	0	1-1	34.0	37	24	23	4	32-1	25	.289
	—Buffalo (A.A.)	5	3	.625	2.91	1.18	10	10	2	0	...	0-...	68.0	61	26	22	4	19-0	40	.236

Year Team (League)	W	L	Pct.	ERA	WHIP	G	GS	CG	ShO	Hld.	Sv.-Opp.	IP	H	R	ER	HR	BB-IBB	SO	Avg.
1996— Vancouver (PCL)	2	0	1.000	1.20	0.73	2	2	1	0	...	0-...	15.0	8	2	2	0	3-0	11	.163
— California (A.L.)	5	7	.417	6.84	1.72	35	20	2	1	0	0-...	130.1	150	110	99	14	74-5	82	.286
1997— Tucson (PCL)	5	10	.333	5.70	1.63	36	10	0	0	...	4-...	85.1	96	70	54	6	43-2	65	.278
— Omaha (A.A.)	1	5	.167	6.68	2.10	7	6	0	0	...	0-...	31.0	36	26	23	3	29-0	22	.293
1998— Buffalo (Int'l)	6	3	.667	3.76	1.50	52	0	0	0	...	0-...	88.2	76	40	37	10	57-3	68	.234
1999— New York (A.L.)	7	2	.778	3.60	1.41	55	0	0	0	8	1-4	75.0	66	39	30	7	40-5	49	.231
2000— New York (A.L.)	3	2	.600	5.04	1.47	63	4	0	0	4	1-4	96.1	100	58	54	10	42-1	53	.268
2001— Kansas City (A.L.)	1	5	.167	3.02	1.23	73	0	0	0	26	0-7	80.1	71	32	27	8	28-5	61	.242
2002— Kansas City (A.L.)	4	7	.364	3.91	1.42	70	0	0	0	13	1-3	71.1	64	32	31	4	37-8	59	.236
— Wichita (Texas)	0	0	...	9.00	2.00	1	1	0	0	...	0-...	1.0	1	1	1	0	1-0	0	.250
2003— Kansas City (A.L.)	2	6	.250	5.16	1.65	76	0	0	0	28	0-7	75.0	88	47	43	6	36-5	58	.299
2004— Kansas City (A.L.)	3	3	.500	3.38	1.46	32	0	0	0	5	0-3	26.2	24	11	10	1	15-3	18	.238
— Baltimore (A.L.)	2	4	.333	4.21	1.57	41	0	0	0	12	0-6	36.1	37	25	17	3	20-3	21	.261
2005— Bowie (East.)	2	0	1.000	1.13	1.00	8	2	0	0	0	0-0	8.0	4	1	1	0	4-1	4	.143
— Baltimore (A.L.)	1	2	.333	5.73	1.50	22	0	0	0	3	0-3	22.0	24	15	14	5	9-2	10	.289
American League totals (11 years)	36	44	.450	4.84	1.54	506	45	3	1	100	4-38	772.1	804	466	415	72	387-40	522	.269
National League totals (3 years)	5	12	.294	4.35	1.63	27	27	0	0	0	0-0	136.2	120	68	66	7	103-4	90	.240
Major League totals (14 years)	41	56	.423	4.76	1.56	533	72	3	1	100	4-38	909.0	924	534	481	79	490-44	612	.265

DIVISION SERIES RECORD

Year Team (League)	W	L	Pct.	ERA	WHIP	G	GS	CG	ShO	Hld.	Sv.-Opp.	IP	H	R	ER	HR	BB-IBB	SO	Avg.
1999— New York (A.L.)									Did not play.										
2000— New York (A.L.)									Did not play.										

CHAMPIONSHIP SERIES RECORD

Year Team (League)	W	L	Pct.	ERA	WHIP	G	GS	CG	ShO	Hld.	Sv.-Opp.	IP	H	R	ER	HR	BB-IBB	SO	Avg.
1999— New York (A.L.)									Did not play.										
2000— New York (A.L.)	0	0	...	0.00	5.00	2	0	0	0	0	0-0	1.0	2	0	0	0	3-0	1	.400

WORLD SERIES RECORD

Year Team (League)	W	L	Pct.	ERA	WHIP	G	GS	CG	ShO	Hld.	Sv.-Opp.	IP	H	R	ER	HR	BB-IBB	SO	Avg.
1999— New York (A.L.)	0	0	...	0.00	1.71	1	0	0	0	0	0-0	2.1	2	0	0	0	2-0	0	.250
2000— New York (A.L.)									Did not play.										

GRISSOM, MARQUIS   OF

PERSONAL: Born April 17, 1967, in Atlanta. ... 5-11/208. ... Bats right, throws right. ... Full name: Marquis Deon Grissom. ... Name pronounced: mar-KEESE. ... High school: Lakeshore (College Park, Ga.). ... College: Florida A&M.

TRANSACTIONS/CAREER NOTES: Selected by Montreal Expos organization in third round of 1988 free-agent draft. ... On disabled list (May 29-June 30, 1990); included rehabilitation assignment to Indianapolis. ... Traded by Expos to Atlanta Braves for OFs Roberto Kelly and Tony Tarasco and P Esteban Yan (April 6, 1995). ... Traded by Braves with P Dave Justice to Cleveland Indians for OF Kenny Lofton and P Alan Embree (March 25, 1997). ... On disabled list (April 22-May 5, 1997). ... Traded by Indians with P Jeff Juden to Milwaukee Brewers for Ps Ben McDonald, Mike Fetters and Ron Villone (December 8, 1997). ... Traded by Brewers with a player to be named to Los Angeles Dodgers for OF Devon White (February 25, 2001); Dodgers acquired P Rudy Lugo to complete deal (June 1, 2001). ... On suspended list (July 18-24, 2001). ... Signed as a free agent by San Francisco Giants (December 7, 2002). ... On disabled list (May 20-June 4 and June 14-July 24, 2005); included rehabilitation assignment to Fresno. ... Released by Giants (August 4, 2005).

HONORS: Won N.L. Gold Glove as outfielder (1993-96).

2005 GAMES PLAYED BY POSITION (MLB): OF—36.

SCOUTING REPORT *Offense:* Grissom is a free swinger and a high-ball hitter. Has a short swing, but bat speed is down and has a lot of trouble handling good fastballs inside. Has gap-to-gap power. Is a better hitter down in the order, especially against lefthanded pitching. ***Defense:*** He has good instincts but his physical skills have declined and he no longer has good range, especially going back on the ball. Arm is very accurate and has quick release. ***Outlook:*** Grissom is nearing retirement and is only a fourth outfielder. Physically can no longer play every day. ***Grade 5.7***

MARQUIS GRISSOM'S HITTING ZONE

.071	.200	.500
.083	.583	.353
.158	.333	.143

LEFTY-RIGHTY SPLITS

vs.	Avg.	AB	H	2B	3B	HR	RBI	BB	SO	OBP	Slg.
L	.217	46	10	2	0	0	6	2	6	.245	.261
R	.209	91	19	2	0	2	9	5	12	.250	.297

Year Team (League)	Pos.	G	AB	R	H	2B	3B	HR	RBI	BB	SO	HBP	GDP	SB-CS	Avg.	OBP	SLG	OPS	E	Avg.
1988— Jamestown (NYP)	OF	74	291	69	94	14	7	8	39	35	39	2	2	23-7	.323	.393	.502	.895	3	.978
1989— Jacksonville (Sou.)	OF	78	278	43	83	15	4	3	31	24	31	7	1	24-6	.299	.365	.414	.779	3	.980
— Indianapolis (A.A.)	OF	49	187	28	52	10	4	2	21	14	23	0	2	16-4	.278	.327	.406	.733	0	1.000
— Montreal (N.L.)	OF	26	74	16	19	2	0	1	2	12	21	0	1	1-0	.257	.360	.324	.685	2	.943
1990— Montreal (N.L.)	OF	98	288	42	74	14	2	3	29	27	40	0	3	22-2	.257	.320	.351	.670	5	.988
— Indianapolis (A.A.)	OF	5	22	3	4	0	0	2	3	0	5	0	0	1-0	.182	.182	.455	.636	0	1.000
1991— Montreal (N.L.)	OF	148	558	73	149	23	9	6	39	34	89	1	8	* 76-17	.267	.310	.373	.683	6	.984
1992— Montreal (N.L.)	OF	159	* 653	99	180	39	6	14	66	42	81	5	12	* 78-13	.276	.322	.418	.741	7	.983
1993— Montreal (N.L.)	OF	157	630	104	188	27	2	19	95	52	76	3	9	53-10	.298	.351	.438	.789	7	.984
1994— Montreal (N.L.)	OF	110	475	96	137	25	4	11	45	41	66	1	10	36-6	.288	.344	.427	.771	5	.985
1995— Atlanta (N.L.)	OF	139	551	80	142	23	3	12	42	47	61	3	8	29-9	.258	.317	.376	.693	2	.994
1996— Atlanta (N.L.)	OF	158	671	106	207	32	10	23	74	41	73	3	12	28-11	.308	.349	.489	.838	1	.997
1997— Cleveland (A.L.)	OF	148	558	74	146	27	6	12	66	43	89	6	12	22-13	.262	.317	.396	.713	3	.992
1998— Milwaukee (N.L.)	OF	142	542	57	147	28	1	10	60	24	78	2	12	13-8	.271	.304	.382	.685	5	.991
1999— Milwaukee (N.L.)	OF	154	603	92	161	27	1	20	83	49	109	4	12	24-6	.267	.320	.415	.734	5	.987
2000— Milwaukee (N.L.)	OF	146	595	67	145	18	2	14	62	39	99	6	9	20-10	.244	.288	.351	.640	3	.992
2001— Los Angeles (N.L.)	OF-DH	135	448	56	99	17	4	21	60	16	107	2	12	7-5	.221	.250	.404	.654	0	1.000
2002— Los Angeles (N.L.)	OF	111	343	57	95	21	4	17	60	22	68	2	6	5-1	.277	.321	.510	.831	4	.978
2003— San Francisco (N.L.)	OF	149	587	82	176	33	3	20	79	20	82	1	14	11-3	.300	.322	.468	.790	8	.977
2004— San Francisco (N.L.)	OF	145	562	78	157	26	2	22	90	37	83	1	22	3-1	.279	.323	.450	.773	4	.994

Year Team (League)	Pos.	G	AB	R	H	2B	3B	HR	RBI	BB	SO	HBP	GDP	SB-CS	Avg.	OBP	SLG	OPS	E	Avg.
2005—Fresno (PCL)	OF-DH	4	15	4	3	0	0	1	2	0	3	0	0	0-0	.200	.200	.400	.600	0	1.000
—San Francisco (N.L.)	OF	44	137	8	29	4	0	2	15	7	18	0	9	1-1	.212	.248	.285	.533	1	.986
American League totals (1 year)		144	558	74	146	27	6	12	66	43	89	6	12	22-13	.262	.317	.396	.713	3	.992
National League totals (16 years)		2021	7717	1113	2105	359	50	215	901	510	1151	25	159	407-103	.273	.318	.416	.734	58	.988
Major League totals (17 years)		2165	8275	1187	2251	386	56	227	967	553	1240	31	171	429-116	.272	.318	.415	.732	61	.988

DIVISION SERIES RECORD

Year Team (League)	Pos.	G	AB	R	H	2B	3B	HR	RBI	BB	SO	HBP	GDP	SB-CS	Avg.	OBP	SLG	OPS	E	Avg.
1995—Atlanta (N.L.)	OF	4	21	5	11	2	0	3	4	0	3	0	0	2-1	.524	.524	1.048	1.571	0	1.000
1996—Atlanta (N.L.)	OF	3	12	2	1	0	0	0	0	1	2	0	0	1-0	.083	.154	.083	.237	1	.800
1997—Cleveland (A.L.)	OF	5	17	3	4	0	1	0	0	1	2	0	0	0-1	.235	.278	.353	.631	0	1.000
2003—San Francisco (N.L.)	OF	4	14	1	2	0	0	0	1	2	5	0	0	0-1	.143	.250	.143	.393	1	.889
Division series totals (4 years)		16	64	11	18	2	1	3	5	4	12	0	0	3-3	.281	.324	.484	.808	2	.946

CHAMPIONSHIP SERIES RECORD

Year Team (League)	Pos.	G	AB	R	H	2B	3B	HR	RBI	BB	SO	HBP	GDP	SB-CS	Avg.	OBP	SLG	OPS	E	Avg.
1995—Atlanta (N.L.)	OF	4	19	2	5	0	1	0	0	1	4	0	0	0-0	.263	.300	.368	.668	1	.889
1996—Atlanta (N.L.)	OF	7	35	7	10	1	0	1	3	0	8	0	0	2-0	.286	.286	.400	.686	1	.944
1997—Cleveland (A.L.)	OF	6	23	2	6	0	0	1	4	1	9	0	0	3-0	.261	.292	.391	.683	0	1.000
Champ. series totals (3 years)		17	77	11	21	1	1	2	7	2	21	0	0	5-0	.273	.291	.390	.681	2	.951

WORLD SERIES RECORD

Year Team (League)	Pos.	G	AB	R	H	2B	3B	HR	RBI	BB	SO	HBP	GDP	SB-CS	Avg.	OBP	SLG	OPS	E	Avg.
1995—Atlanta (N.L.)	OF	6	25	3	9	1	0	0	1	1	3	1	1	3-1	.360	.407	.400	.807	0	1.000
1996—Atlanta (N.L.)	OF	6	27	4	12	2	1	0	5	1	2	0	0	1-0	.444	.464	.593	1.057	1	.875
1997—Cleveland (A.L.)	OF	7	25	5	9	1	0	0	2	4	4	0	1	0-0	.360	.448	.400	.848	1	.950
World Series totals (3 years)		19	77	12	30	4	1	0	8	6	9	1	2	4-1	.390	.440	.468	.908	2	.951

ALL-STAR GAME RECORD

	G	AB	R	H	2B	3B	HR	RBI	BB	SO	HBP	GDP	SB-CS	Avg.	OBP	SLG	OPS	E	Avg.
All-Star Game totals (2 years)	2	4	1	1	0	0	1	1	1	0	0	0	0-0	.250	.400	1.000	1.400	0	1.000

GROOM, BUDDY   P

PERSONAL: Born July 10, 1965, in Dallas. ... 6-2/203. ... Throws left, bats left. ... Full name: Wedsel Gary Groom. ... High school: Red Oak (Texas). ... College: Mary Hardin-Baylor.

TRANSACTIONS/CAREER NOTES: Selected by Chicago White Sox organization in 12th round of 1987 free-agent draft. ... Selected by Detroit Tigers organization from White Sox organization in Rule 5 minor league draft (December 3, 1990). ... Traded by Tigers to Florida Marlins for a player to be named (August 7, 1995); Tigers acquired P Mike Myers to complete deal (August 9, 1995). ... Signed as a free agent by Oakland Athletics organization (November 27, 1995). ... Signed as a free agent by Baltimore Orioles (December 21, 1999). ... Signed as a free agent by New York Yankees (February 4, 2005). ... Traded by Yankees to Arizona Diamondbacks for player to be named (July 31, 2005).

CAREER HITTING: 0-for-0 (.000), 0 R, 0 2B, 0 3B, 0 HR, 0 RBI.

BUDDY GROOM'S PITCHING ZONE

.400	.000	.375
.379	.400	.226
.308	.545	.158

LEFTY-RIGHTY SPLITS

vs.	Avg.	AB	H	2B	3B	HR	RBI	BB	SO	OBP	Slg.
L	.244	78	19	2	1	2	10	4	9	.280	.372
R	.356	90	32	7	2	3	14	8	11	.417	.578

Year Team (League)	W	L	Pct.	ERA	WHIP	G	GS	CG	ShO	Hld.	Sv.-Opp.	IP	H	R	ER	HR	BB-IBB	SO	Avg.
1987—GC Whi. Sox (GCL)	1	0	1.000	0.75	1.17	4	1	0	0	...	1-...	12.0	12	1	1	0	2-0	8	.273
—Daytona Beach (Fla. St.)	7	2	.778	3.59	1.37	11	10	2	0	...	0-...	67.2	60	30	27	4	33-1	29	.236
1988—Tampa (Fla. St.)	13	10	.565	2.54	1.19	27	27	8	0	...	0-...	* 195.0	181	69	55	7	51-1	118	.247
1989—Birmingham (Sou.)	13	8	.619	4.52	1.49	26	26	3	1	...	0-...	167.1	172	101	84	13	78-1	94	.270
1990—Birmingham (Sou.)	6	8	.429	5.07	1.59	20	20	0	0	...	0-...	115.1	135	81	65	10	48-1	66	.290
1991—Toledo (Int'l)	2	5	.286	4.32	1.33	24	6	0	0	...	1-...	75.0	75	39	36	7	25-2	49	.264
—London (East.)	7	1	.875	3.48	1.22	11	7	0	0	...	1-...	51.2	51	20	20	7	12-1	39	.248
1992—Toledo (Int'l)	7	7	.500	2.80	1.14	16	16	1	0	...	0-...	109.1	102	41	34	8	23-1	71	.248
—Detroit (A.L.)	0	5	.000	5.82	1.81	12	7	0	0	0	1-2	38.2	48	28	25	4	22-4	15	.320
1993—Toledo (Int'l)	9	3	.750	2.74	1.25	16	15	0	0	...	0-...	102.0	98	34	31	5	30-1	78	.254
—Detroit (A.L.)	0	2	.000	6.14	1.66	19	3	0	0	1	0-...	36.2	48	25	25	4	13-5	15	.322
1994—Toledo (Int'l)	0	0		2.25	0.50	5	0	0	0	...	0-...	4.0	2	1	1	0	0-0	6	.154
—Detroit (A.L.)	0	0	.000	3.94	1.38	40	0	0	0	11	1-1	32.0	31	14	14	4	13-2	27	.256
1995—Detroit (A.L.)	1	3	.250	7.52	1.99	23	4	0	0	0	1-3	40.2	55	35	34	6	26-4	23	.322
—Toledo (Int'l)	2	3	.400	1.91	1.06	6	5	1	0	...	0-...	33.0	31	14	7	4	4-0	24	.247
—Florida (N.L.)	1	2	.333	7.20	2.13	14	0	0	0	0	0-0	15.0	26	12	12	2	6-0	12	.400
1996—Oakland (A.L.)	5	0	1.000	3.84	1.54	72	1	0	0	10	2-4	77.1	85	37	33	8	34-3	57	.281
1997—Oakland (A.L.)	2	2	.500	5.15	1.53	78	0	0	0	12	3-5	64.2	75	38	37	9	24-1	45	.292
1998—Oakland (A.L.)	3	1	.750	4.24	1.43	75	0	0	0	16	0-6	57.1	62	30	27	4	20-1	36	.274
1999—Oakland (A.L.)	3	2	.600	5.09	1.43	76	0	0	0	* 27	0-3	46.0	48	29	26	1	18-5	32	.274
2000—Baltimore (A.L.)	6	3	.667	4.85	1.42	70	0	0	0	27	4-11	59.1	63	37	32	5	21-2	44	.275
2001—Baltimore (A.L.)	1	4	.200	3.55	1.11	70	0	0	0	16	11-13	66.0	64	28	26	4	9-0	54	.252
2002—Baltimore (A.L.)	3	2	.600	1.60	0.90	70	0	0	0	19	2-4	62.0	44	11	11	4	12-3	48	.196
2003—Baltimore (A.L.)	1	3	.250	5.36	1.59	60	0	0	0	16	1-3	45.1	58	27	27	7	14-2	34	.309
2004—Baltimore (A.L.)	4	1	.800	4.78	1.58	60	0	0	0	8	0-2	52.2	67	30	28	8	16-1	32	.309
2005—Columbus (Int'l)	0	0		5.79	1.29	6	0	0	0	2	0-1	4.2	6	4	3	2	0-0	5	.333
—New York (A.L.)	1	0	1.000	4.91	1.52	24	0	0	0	3	0-0	25.2	32	14	14	3	7-2	13	.305
—Arizona (N.L.)	0	1	.000	4.70	1.57	23	0	0	0	4	1-1	15.1	19	8	8	2	5-1	7	.302
American League totals (14 years)	30	29	.508	4.59	1.46	749	15	0	0	166	26-57	704.1	780	383	359	69	249-35	475	.282
National League totals (2 years)	1	3	.250	5.93	1.85	37	0	0	0	4	1-1	30.1	45	20	20	4	11-1	19	.352
Major League totals (14 years)	31	32	.492	4.64	1.48	786	15	0	0	170	27-58	734.2	825	403	379	73	260-36	494	.285

GROSS, GABE   OF

PERSONAL: Born October 21, 1979, in Baltimore. ... 6-3/209. ... Bats left, throws right. ... Full name: Gabriel Jordan Gross. ... High school: Northview (Dothan, Ala.). ... College: Auburn.

G

TRANSACTIONS/CAREER NOTES: Selected by Toronto Blue Jays organization in first round (15th pick overall) of 2001 free-agent draft.
2005 GAMES PLAYED BY POSITION (MLB): OF—37, DH—2.

SCOUTING REPORT
Offense: He has good power potential which, to date, he has shown only in batting practice. Has good knowledge of the strike zone and good plate coverage. Hits too many weak fly balls because he can't get his timing down. Has yet to show he can aggressively attack mistake pitches. Is a below-average runner. *Defense:* Gross is an adequate corner outfielder with an average arm. Still is learning how to read the ball off the bat and get better jumps. *Outlook:* After bouncing back and forth between Class AAA and the Jays last season, Gross needs a strong spring to make the club. **Grade 5.9**

GABE GROSS'S HITTING ZONE

.000	.500	.286
.143	.333	.333
.250	.286	.267

LEFTY-RIGHTY SPLITS

vs.	Avg.	AB	H	2B	3B	HR	RBI	BB	SO	OBP	Slg.
L	.091	11	1	1	0	0	1	2	4	.231	.182
R	.272	81	22	3	1	1	6	8	17	.337	.370

Year— Team (League)	Pos.	G	AB	R	H	2B	3B	HR	RBI	BB	SO	HBP	GDP	SB-CS	Avg.	OBP	SLG	OPS	E	Fielding Avg.
2001— Dunedin (Fla. St.)	OF	35	126	23	38	9	2	4	15	26	29	2	2	4-2	.302	.426	.500	.926	5	.930
— Tennessee (Sou.)	OF	11	41	8	10	1	0	3	11	6	12	3	1	0-1	.244	.373	.488	.860	9	1.000
2002— Tennessee (Sou.)	OF	112	403	57	96	17	5	10	54	53	71	5	4	8-2	.238	.333	.380	.712	2	.991
2003— New Haven (East.)	OF	84	310	52	99	23	3	7	51	52	53	5	9	3-2	.319	.423	.481	.903	3	.980
— Syracuse (Int'l)	OF	53	182	22	48	16	2	5	23	31	56	3	2	1-1	.264	.380	.456	.836	2	.985
2004— Syracuse (Int'l)	DH-OF	103	377	52	111	29	2	9	54	53	81	1	8	4-5	.294	.381	.454	.833	3	.957
— Toronto (A.L.)	OF-DH	44	129	18	27	4	0	3	16	19	31	0	1	2-2	.209	.311	.310	.621	0	1.000
2005— Syracuse (Int'l)	OF-DH	102	390	64	116	29	4	6	46	52	83	2	5	14-2	.297	.380	.438	.819	8	.981
— Toronto (A.L.)	OF-DH	40	92	11	23	4	1	1	7	10	21	0	0	1-1	.250	.324	.348	.671	1	.981
Major League totals (2 years)		84	221	29	50	8	1	4	23	29	52	0	1	3-3	.226	.316	.326	.642	1	.992

GRUDZIELANEK, MARK — 2B

PERSONAL: Born June 30, 1970, in Milwaukee. ... 6-1/190. ... Bats right, throws right. ... Full name: Mark James Grudzielanek. ... Name pronounced: grud-zuh-LAN-nick. ... High school: J.M. Hanks (El Paso, Texas). ... Junior college: Trinidad State (Colo.).
TRANSACTIONS/CAREER NOTES: Selected by New York Mets organization in 17th round of 1989 free-agent draft; did not sign. ... Selected by Montreal Expos organization in 11th round of 1991 free-agent draft. ... Traded by Expos with P Carlos Perez and OF Hiram Bocachica to Los Angeles Dodgers for 2B Wilton Guerrero, P Ted Lilly, OF Peter Bergeron and 1B Jonathan Tucker (July 31, 1998). ... On disabled list (June 12-July 6, 1999); included rehabilitation assignment to San Bernardino. ... On disabled list (June 12-28, 2001). ... Traded by Dodgers with 1B Eric Karros and cash to Chicago Cubs for C Todd Hundley and OF Chad Hermansen (December 4, 2002). ... On disabled list (August 3-September 2, 2003); included rehabilitation assignment to Iowa. ... On disabled list (April 10-June 19, 2004); included rehabilitation assignment to Iowa. ... Signed as a free agent by St. Louis Cardinals (January 6, 2005).
2005 GAMES PLAYED BY POSITION (MLB): 2B—137.

SCOUTING REPORT
Offense: Grudzielanek has a short, compact stroke and uses the whole field. Has good bad control and doesn't strike out much. Is a gap hitter with little power. Can be effective in the No. 2 spot. Will attempt to steal some bases but still gets inconsistent jumps. *Defense:* Grudzielanek improved in the field while coming off an Achilles' injury in 2005. Got better jumps to each side. Has good hands and can charge the ball. Has a strong, very accurate arm. Goes out deeper than most second basemen on relays. Pivots well and teamed with David Eckstein to lead baseball in double plays. *Outlook:* Grudzielanek isn't flashy, but he is consistent. Is an asset on both sides of the field when healthy. **Grade 7.6**

MARK GRUDZIELANEK'S HITTING ZONE

.371	.414	.283
.207	.492	.333
.263	.357	.190

LEFTY-RIGHTY SPLITS

vs.	Avg.	AB	H	2B	3B	HR	RBI	BB	SO	OBP	Slg.
L	.303	155	47	7	2	2	17	13	20	.357	.413
R	.290	373	108	23	1	6	42	13	61	.324	.405

Year— Team (League)	Pos.	G	AB	R	H	2B	3B	HR	RBI	BB	SO	HBP	GDP	SB-CS	Avg.	OBP	SLG	OPS	E	Fielding Avg.
1991— Jamestown (NYP)	SS	72	275	44	72	9	3	2	32	18	43	3	6	14-4	.262	.311	.338	.649	23	.933
1992— Rockford (Midw.)	SS	128	496	64	122	12	5	5	54	22	59	5	10	25-4	.246	.285	.321	.605	41	.919
1993— W.P. Beach (Fla. St.)	2B-3B-OF	86	300	41	80	11	6	1	34	14	42	7	6	17-10	.267	.315	.353	.668	13	.949
1994— Harrisburg (East.)	3B-SS	122	488	92	157	37	3	11	66	43	66	8	15	32-10	.322	.382	.477	.860	23	.958
1995— Montreal (N.L.)	SS-3B-2B	78	269	27	66	12	2	1	20	14	47	7	7	8-3	.245	.300	.316	.616	10	.939
— Ottawa (Int'l)	SS	49	181	26	54	9	1	1	22	10	17	4	6	12-1	.298	.342	.376	.717	14	.939
1996— Montreal (N.L.)	SS	153	657	99	201	34	4	6	49	26	83	9	10	33-7	.306	.340	.397	.737	27	.959
1997— Montreal (N.L.)	SS	156	* 649	76	177	* 54	3	4	51	23	76	10	13	25-9	.273	.307	.384	.690	* 32	.955
1998— Montreal (N.L.)	SS	105	396	51	109	15	1	6	41	21	50	9	11	11-5	.275	.323	.379	.702	23	.950
— Los Angeles (N.L.)	SS	51	193	11	51	6	0	2	21	5	23	2	7	7-0	.264	.286	.326	.612	‡ 10	.962
1999— Los Angeles (N.L.)	SS	123	488	72	159	23	5	7	46	31	66	10	13	6-6	.326	.376	.418	.812	13	.973
— San Bern. (Calif.)	SS	4	16	2	4	0	0	0	0	0	1	0	1	0-2	.250	.250	.250	.500	0	1.000
2000— Los Angeles (N.L.)	2B-SS	148	617	101	172	35	6	7	49	45	91	9	16	12-3	.279	.335	.389	.724	17	.976
2001— Los Angeles (N.L.)	2B	133	539	83	146	21	3	13	55	28	83	11	9	4-4	.271	.317	.393	.711	10	.984
2002— Los Angeles (N.L.)	2B-DH	150	536	56	145	23	0	9	50	22	89	3	17	4-1	.271	.301	.364	.665	7	.989
2003— Iowa (PCL)	2B-DH	2	10	1	5	0	0	0	1	1	1	0	0	0-0	.500	.545	.500	1.045	0	1.000
— Chicago (N.L.)	2B	121	481	73	151	38	1	3	38	30	64	11	12	6-2	.314	.366	.416	.782	8	.986
2004— Iowa (PCL)	2B-DH	8	28	6	7	3	0	2	4	0	4	0	1	0-0	.250	.250	.571	.821	0	1.000
— Chicago (N.L.)	2B	81	257	32	79	12	1	6	23	15	32	1	1	1-1	.307	.347	.432	.779	5	.985
2005— St. Louis (N.L.)	2B	137	528	64	155	30	3	8	59	26	81	7	14	8-6	.294	.334	.407	.741	7	.990
Major League totals (11 years)		1436	5610	745	1611	303	29	74	502	286	774	89	136	125-47	.287	.330	.391	.721	169	.974

DIVISION SERIES RECORD

Year Team (League)	Pos.	G	AB	R	H	2B	3B	HR	RBI	BB	SO	HBP	GDP	SB-CS	Avg.	OBP	SLG	OPS	E	Avg.
2003— Chicago (N.L.)	2B	5	20	2	3	0	0	0	0	3	4	0	1	0-0	.150	.261	.150	.411	0	1.000
2005— St. Louis (N.L.)	2B	3	13	2	2	0	0	0	0	0	1	0	1	0-0	.154	.154	.154	.308	0	1.000
Division series totals (2 years)		8	33	4	5	0	0	0	0	3	5	0	2	0-0	.152	.222	.152	.374	0	1.000

G

CHAMPIONSHIP SERIES RECORD

Year Team (League)	Pos.	G	AB	R	H	2B	3B	HR	RBI	BB	SO	HBP	GDP	SB-CS	Avg.	OBP	SLG	OPS	E	Avg.
2003— Chicago (N.L.)	2B	7	30	2	6	1	1	0	3	0	5	0	0	0-0	.200	.200	.300	.500	2	.956
2005— St. Louis (N.L.)	2B	6	22	2	5	0	0	0	2	0	3	1	0	0-0	.227	.261	.227	.488	0	1.000
Champ. series totals (2 years)		13	52	4	11	1	1	0	5	0	8	1	0	0-0	.212	.226	.269	.496	2	.972

ALL-STAR GAME RECORD

	G	AB	R	H	2B	3B	HR	RBI	BB	SO	HBP	GDP	SB-CS	Avg.	OBP	SLG	OPS	E	Avg.
All-Star Game totals (1 year)	1	1	0	0	0	0	0	0	0	0	0	0	0-0	.000	.000	.000	.000	0	...

GRYBOSKI, KEVIN   P

PERSONAL: Born November 15, 1973, in Wilkes-Barre, Pa. ... 6-5/225. ... Throws right, bats right. ... Full name: Kevin John Gryboski. ... Name pronounced: gri-BOS-ski. ... High school: Bishop Hoban (Wilkes-Barre, Pa.). ... College: Wilkes University (Pa.).

TRANSACTIONS/CAREER NOTES: Selected by Cincinnati Reds organization in 16th round of 1994 free-agent draft; did not sign. ... Selected by Seattle Mariners organization in 16th round of 1995 free-agent draft. ... Traded by Mariners to Atlanta Braves for P Elvis Perez (January 18, 2002). ... On disabled list (July 24-August 20, 2002); included rehabilitation assignment to Macon. ... On disabled list (August 28-September 20, 2005). ... On disabled list (May 7-22, 2005); included rehabilitation assignment to Rome. ... Traded by Braves to Texas Rangers for P Matt Lorenzo (July 21, 2005).

CAREER HITTING: 0-for-1 (.000), 0 R, 0 2B, 0 3B, 0 HR, 0 RBI.

KEVIN GRYBOSKI'S PITCHING ZONE

.500	.000	.400
.467	.333	.208
.444	.333	.348

LEFTY-RIGHTY SPLITS

vs.	Avg.	AB	H	2B	3B	HR	RBI	BB	SO	OBP	Slg.
L	.227	44	10	0	1	0	7	10	6	.370	.273
R	.383	81	31	5	2	1	25	10	4	.458	.531

Year Team (League)	W	L	Pct.	ERA	WHIP	G	GS	CG	ShO	Hld.	Sv.-Opp.	IP	H	R	ER	HR	BB-IBB	SO	Avg.
1995— Everett (N'west)	1	5	.167	3.50	1.25	25	0	0	0	...	2-...	36.0	27	18	14	2	18-2	25	.206
1996— Wisconsin (Midw.)	10	5	.667	4.74	1.50	32	21	3	0	...	1-...	138.2	146	90	73	7	62-2	100	.270
1997— Lancaster (Calif.)	0	7	.000	9.89	2.06	21	15	0	0	...	0-...	67.1	113	82	74	13	26-0	41	.383
1998— Lancaster (Calif.)	5	5	.500	2.65	1.25	37	3	0	0	...	8-...	85.0	75	35	25	4	31-1	73	.240
— Orlando (Sou.)	0	0	...	9.00	1.80	2	0	0	0	...	0-...	5.0	8	5	5	1	1-0	4	.364
1999— New Haven (East.)	2	5	.286	2.89	1.40	47	0	0	0	...	10-...	62.1	67	27	20	5	20-4	41	.283
2000— New Haven (East.)	2	2	.500	2.50	1.28	16	0	0	0	...	9-...	18.0	15	5	5	0	8-1	20	.221
— Tacoma (PCL)	2	2	.500	4.83	1.66	31	0	0	0	...	2-...	41.0	45	23	22	3	23-4	35	.288
2001— Tacoma (PCL)	2	5	.286	3.90	1.38	58	0	0	0	...	22-...	60.0	64	29	26	8	19-2	50	.277
2002— Richmond (Int'l)	1	0	1.000	1.29	1.14	7	0	0	0	...	3-...	7.0	7	1	1	0	1-0	5	.280
— Atlanta (N.L.)	2	1	.667	3.48	1.68	57	0	0	0	11	0-2	51.2	50	20	20	6	37-5	33	.256
— Macon (S. Atl.)	0	0	...	0.00	1.00	2	1	0	0	...	0-...	2.0	1	0	0	0	1-0	2	.167
2003— Atlanta (N.L.)	6	4	.600	3.86	1.51	44.1	0	0	0	12	0-4	44.1	44	22	19	3	23-6	32	.272
2004— Atlanta (N.L.)	3	2	.600	2.84	1.52	69	0	0	0	16	2-4	50.2	54	22	16	2	23-4	24	.280
2005— Rome (S. Atl.)	0	0	...	0.00	1.00	1	1	0	0	...	0-...	1.0	1	0	0	0	0-0	0	.250
— Atlanta (N.L.)	0	0	...	2.95	1.69	31	0	0	0	2	0-2	21.1	24	10	7	0	12-3	8	.300
— Texas (A.L.)	1	1	.500	11.17	2.59	11	0	0	0	3	0-0	9.2	17	15	12	1	8-2	2	.378
— Oklahoma (PCL)	0	2	.000	5.23	1.94	9	0	0	0	2	0-1	10.1	14	7	6	2	6-1	5	.326
American League totals (1 year)	1	1	.500	11.17	2.59	11	0	0	0	3	0-0	9.2	17	15	12	1	8-2	2	.378
National League totals (4 years)	11	7	.611	3.32	1.59	221	0	0	0	41	2-12	168.0	172	74	62	11	95-18	97	.273
Major League totals (4 years)	12	8	.600	3.75	1.64	232	0	0	0	44	2-12	177.2	189	89	74	12	103-20	99	.280

DIVISION SERIES RECORD

Year Team (League)	W	L	Pct.	ERA	WHIP	G	GS	CG	ShO	Hld.	Sv.-Opp.	IP	H	R	ER	HR	BB-IBB	SO	Avg.
2002— Atlanta (N.L.)	0	0	...	0.00	1.09	3	0	0	0	0	0-0	3.2	2	0	0	0	2-1	3	.154
2003— Atlanta (N.L.)	0	0	...	3.00	1.33	5	0	0	0	2	0-0	3.0	2	1	1	0	2-1	4	.222
2004— Atlanta (N.L.)	0	0	...	2.08	0.92	5	0	0	0	0	0-0	4.1	3	1	1	0	1-0	3	.200
Division series totals (3 years)	0	0	...	1.64	1.09	13	0	0	0	2	0-0	11.0	7	2	2	0	5-2	10	.189

GUARDADO, EDDIE   P

PERSONAL: Born October 2, 1970, in Stockton, Calif. ... 6-0/205. ... Throws left, bats right. ... Full name: Edward Adrian Guardado. ... Name pronounced: gwar-DAH-doe. ... High school: Franklin (Stockton, Calif.). ... Junior college: San Joaquin Delta (Calif.).

TRANSACTIONS/CAREER NOTES: Selected by Minnesota Twins organization in 21st round of 1990 free-agent draft. ... On disabled list (May 22-June 28, 1999); included rehabilitation assignment to New Britain. ... On disabled list (June 5-20, 2001). ... Signed as a free agent by Seattle Mariners (December 16, 2003). ... On dsabled list (August 1, 2004-remainder of season).

CAREER HITTING: 0-for-1 (.000), 0 R, 0 2B, 0 3B, 0 HR, 0 RBI.

SCOUTING REPORT *Throws:* Guardado features a fastball at 89-90 mph, a slider at 80-82 and a split-finger fastball. *Tendencies:* His stuff is average, but Guardado is fearless. Challenges hitters and is confident he can get them out. Is tough on lefthanders. Neutralizes righthanders with his splitter. *Outlook:* There are lingering concerns about Guardado's heavy workload over the years and the wear on his shoulder and legs. *Grade 7.9*

EDDIE GUARDADO'S PITCHING ZONE

.393	.143	.143
.214	.217	.276
.200	.222	.250

LEFTY-RIGHTY SPLITS

vs.	Avg.	AB	H	2B	3B	HR	RBI	BB	SO	OBP	Slg.
L	.231	65	15	5	0	2	10	0	14	.231	.400
R	.242	153	37	8	0	5	15	15	34	.306	.392

Year Team (League)	W	L	Pct.	ERA	WHIP	G	GS	CG	ShO	Hld.	Sv.-Opp.	IP	H	R	ER	HR	BB-IBB	SO	Avg.
1991— Elizabethton (Appal.)	8	4	.667	1.86	1.07	14	13	3	1	...	0-...	92.0	67	30	19	5	31-0	106	.199
1992— Kenosha (Midw.)	5	10	.333	4.37	1.35	18	18	2	1	...	0-...	101.0	106	57	49	5	30-0	103	.274
— Visalia (Calif.)	7	0	1.000	1.64	1.16	7	7	1	1	...	0-...	49.1	47	13	9	1	10-0	39	.258
1993— Nashville (Sou.)	4	0	1.000	1.24	0.96	10	10	2	2	...	0-...	65.1	53	10	9	1	10-0	57	.219
— Minnesota (A.L.)	3	8	.273	6.18	1.68	19	16	0	0	...	0-0	94.2	123	68	65	13	36-2	46	.319
1994— Salt Lake (PCL)	12	7	.632	4.83	1.47	24	24	2	0	...	0-...	151.0	171	90	81	23	51-0	87	.290

Year Team (League)	W	L	Pct.	ERA	WHIP	G	GS	CG	ShO	Hld.	Sv.-Opp.	IP	H	R	ER	HR	BB-IBB	SO	Avg.
—Minnesota (A.L.)	0	2	.000	8.47	1.76	4	4	0	0	0	0-0	17.0	26	16	16	3	4-0	8	.351
1995—Minnesota (A.L.)	4	9	.308	5.12	1.58	51	5	0	0	5	2-5	91.1	99	54	52	13	45-2	71	.280
1996—Minnesota (A.L.)	6	5	.545	5.25	1.28	• 83	0	0	0	18	4-7	73.2	61	45	43	12	33-4	74	.228
1997—Minnesota (A.L.)	0	4	.000	3.91	1.35	69	0	0	0	13	1-1	46.0	45	23	20	7	17-2	54	.251
1998—Minnesota (A.L.)	3	1	.750	4.52	1.43	79	0	0	0	16	0-4	65.2	66	34	33	10	28-6	53	.265
1999—Minnesota (A.L.)	2	5	.286	4.50	1.29	63	0	0	0	15	2-4	48.0	37	24	24	6	25-4	50	.222
—New Britain (East.)	0	0	...	1.93	0.64	3	0	0	0	0	0-...	4.2	3	1	1	0	0-0	5	.176
2000—Minnesota (A.L.)	7	4	.636	3.94	1.30	70	0	0	0	8	9-11	61.2	55	27	27	14	25-3	52	.238
2001—Minnesota (A.L.)	7	1	.875	3.51	1.05	67	0	0	0	14	12-14	66.2	47	27	26	5	23-4	67	.197
2002—Minnesota (A.L.)	1	3	.250	2.93	1.05	68	0	0	0	0	* 45-51	67.2	53	22	22	9	18-2	70	.215
2003—Minnesota (A.L.)	3	5	.375	2.89	0.98	66	0	0	0	0	41-45	65.1	50	22	21	7	14-2	60	.207
2004—Seattle (A.L.)	2	2	.500	2.78	0.99	41	0	0	0	0	18-25	45.1	31	14	14	8	14-0	45	.194
2005—Seattle (A.L.)	2	3	.400	2.72	1.19	58	0	0	0	0	36-41	56.1	52	23	17	7	15-3	48	.239
Major League totals (13 years)	40	52	.435	4.28	1.30	738	25	0	0	89	170-208	799.1	745	399	380	114	297-34	698	.248

DIVISION SERIES RECORD

Year Team (League)	W	L	Pct.	ERA	WHIP	G	GS	CG	ShO	Hld.	Sv.-Opp.	IP	H	R	ER	HR	BB-IBB	SO	Avg.
2002—Minnesota (A.L.)	0	0	...	13.50	3.00	2	0	0	0	0	1-1	2.0	5	3	3	1	1-0	1	.455
2003—Minnesota (A.L.)	0	0	...	9.00	2.50	2	0	0	0	0	1-1	2.0	5	2	2	1	0-0	2	.455
Division series totals (2 years)	0	0	...	11.25	2.75	4	0	0	0	0	2-2	4.0	10	5	5	2	1-0	3	.455

CHAMPIONSHIP SERIES RECORD

Year Team (League)	W	L	Pct.	ERA	WHIP	G	GS	CG	ShO	Hld.	Sv.-Opp.	IP	H	R	ER	HR	BB-IBB	SO	Avg.
2002—Minnesota (A.L.)	0	0	...	0.00	1.00	1	0	0	0	0	1-1	1.0	0	0	0	0	1-0	2	.000

ALL-STAR GAME RECORD

	W	L	Pct.	ERA	WHIP	G	GS	CG	ShO	Hld.	Sv.-Opp.	IP	H	R	ER	HR	BB-IBB	SO	Avg.
All-Star Game totals (2 years)	0	0	...	9.00	2.00	2	0	0	0	0	0-0	1.0	2	1	1	0	0-0	2	.400

GUERRERO, VLADIMIR — OF

PERSONAL: Born February 9, 1976, in Nizao Bani, Dominican Republic. ... 6-3/220. ... Bats right, throws right. ... Full name: Vladimir Alvino Guerrero. ... Name pronounced: guh-RAR-oh. ... Brother of Wilton Guerrero, infielder/outfielder with four teams (1996-2004).

TRANSACTIONS/CAREER NOTES: Signed as a non-drafted free agent by Montreal Expos organization (March 1, 1993). ... On disabled list (March 30-May 2, June 5-21 and July 12-27, 1997); included rehabilitation assignment to West Palm Beach. ... On suspended list (March 30-April 3, 2003). ... On disabled list (June 5-July 21, 2003); included rehabilitation assignment to Brevard County. ... Signed as a free agent by Anaheim Angels (January 14, 2004). ... Angels franchise renamed Los Angeles Angels of Anaheim for 2005 season. ... On disabled list (May 22-June 10, 2005).

HONORS: Named Minor League Player of the Year by THE SPORTING NEWS (1996). ... Named A.L. Most Valuable Player by Baseball Writers' Association of America (2004).

2005 GAMES PLAYED BY POSITION (MLB): OF—120, DH—19.

SCOUTING REPORT *Offense:* Guerrero struggled in the playoffs as a result of a shoulder injury earlier in 2005. When healthy is the most aggressive hitter in the game, a first-ball hitter who swings at any pitch. Has tremendous bat speed with superior plate coverage. Has outstanding power to all fields and has become a very good situational hitter. Is an above-average runner with good instincts. *Defense:* His arm might be the game's best. Can be erratic because he rarely uses a cutoff man, but runners hesitate to take the extra base. Gets a better jump coming in than going back. Has above-average lateral range with closing speed in the gaps. *Outlook:* Guerrero has the best raw tools in the game and is one of its most dominant players with his arm, defense, speed, bat and power. *Grade 9.9*

VLADIMIR GUERRERO'S HITTING ZONE

.273	.316	.315
.306	.424	.301
.389	.714	.438

LEFTY-RIGHTY SPLITS

vs.	Avg.	AB	H	2B	3B	HR	RBI	BB	SO	OBP	Slg.
L	.313	150	47	12	0	9	27	16	9	.382	.573
R	.319	370	118	17	2	23	81	45	39	.399	.562

Year Team (League)	Pos.	G	AB	R	H	2B	3B	HR	RBI	BB	SO	HBP	GDP	SB-CS	Avg.	OBP	SLG	OPS	E	Avg.
1993—Dom. Expos (DSL)	OF	34	105	19	35	4	0	1	14	8	13	...	...	4-...	.333	...	.400	...	5	.943
1994—Dom. Expos (DSL)	OF	25	92	34	39	11	0	12	35	21	6	...	...	5-...	.424	...	.935	...	2	.957
—GC Expos (GCL)	OF	37	137	24	43	13	3	5	25	11	18	2	0	0-7	.314	.366	.562	.928	1	.986
1995—Albany (S. Atl.)	OF	110	421	77	140	21	10	16	63	30	45	7	8	12-7	.333	.383	.544	.927	11	.953
1996—W.P. Beach (Fla. St.)	OF	20	80	16	29	8	0	5	18	3	10	1	1	2-2	.363	.388	.650	1.038	3	.917
—Harrisburg (East.)	OF	118	417	84	150	32	8	19	78	51	42	9	8	17-10	.360	.438	.612	1.050	8	.961
—Montreal (N.L.)	OF	9	27	2	5	0	0	1	1	0	3	0	1	0-0	.185	.185	.296	.481	0	1.000
1997—W.P. Beach (Fla. St.)	OF	3	10	0	4	2	0	0	2	1	0	0	1	1-0	.400	.455	.600	1.055	0	1.000
—Montreal (N.L.)	OF	90	325	44	98	22	2	11	40	19	39	7	11	3-4	.302	.350	.483	.833	* 12	.929
1998—Montreal (N.L.)	OF	159	623	108	202	37	7	38	109	42	95	7	15	11-9	.324	.371	.589	.960	* 17	.951
1999—Montreal (N.L.)	OF	160	610	102	193	37	5	42	131	55	62	9	18	14-7	.316	.378	.600	.978	* 19	.948
2000—Montreal (N.L.)	OF-DH	154	571	101	197	28	11	44	123	58	74	8	15	9-10	.345	.410	.664	1.074	* 10	.969
2001—Montreal (N.L.)	OF	159	599	107	184	45	4	34	108	60	88	9	* 24	37-16	.307	.377	.566	.943	12	.965
2002—Montreal (N.L.)	OF	161	614	106	* 206	37	2	39	111	84	70	6	20	40-* 20	.336	.417	.593	1.010	* 10	.969
2003—Brevard County (Fla. St.) ...	OF-DH	3	6	2	3	0	0	1	1	0	1	0	0	0-0	.500	.571	1.000	1.571	0	1.000
—Montreal (N.L.)	OF	112	394	71	130	20	3	25	79	63	53	6	18	9-5	.330	.426	.586	1.012	* 7	.970
2004—Anaheim (A.L.)	OF-DH	156	612	* 124	206	39	2	39	126	52	74	6	19	15-3	.337	.391	.598	.989	9	.973
2005—Los Angeles (A.L.)	OF-DH	141	520	95	165	29	2	32	108	61	48	8	16	13-1	.317	.394	.565	.959	3	.988
American League totals (2 years)		297	1132	219	371	68	4	71	234	113	122	16	35	28-4	.328	.392	.583	.976	12	.979
National League totals (8 years)		1004	3763	641	1215	226	34	234	702	381	484	50	122	123-71	.323	.390	.588	.978	87	.959
Major League totals (10 years)		1301	4895	860	1586	294	38	305	936	494	606	66	157	151-75	.324	.391	.587	.977	99	.963

DIVISION SERIES RECORD

Year Team (League)	Pos.	G	AB	R	H	2B	3B	HR	RBI	BB	SO	HBP	GDP	SB-CS	Avg.	OBP	SLG	OPS	E	Avg.
2004—Anaheim (A.L.)	OF	3	12	1	2	0	0	1	6	2	4	0	0	0-0	.167	.286	.417	.702	0	1.000
2005—Los Angeles (A.L.)	OF	5	18	5	6	0	0	0	0	2	2	1	0	1-1	.333	.429	.333	.762	0	1.000
Division series totals (2 years)		8	30	6	8	0	0	1	6	4	6	1	0	1-1	.267	.371	.367	.738	0	1.000

CHAMPIONSHIP SERIES RECORD

Year—Team (League)	Pos.	G	AB	R	H	2B	3B	HR	RBI	BB	SO	HBP	GDP	SB-CS	Avg.	OBP	SLG	OPS	E	Avg.
2005— Los Angeles (A.L.)	OF-DH	5	20	0	1	0	0	1	0	1	0	2		0-0	.050	.050	.050	.100	1	.923

ALL-STAR GAME RECORD

		G	AB	R	H	2B	3B	HR	RBI	BB	SO	HBP	GDP	SB-CS	Avg.	OBP	SLG	OPS	E	Avg.
All-Star Game totals (6 years)		6	13	2	4	0	0	0	0	0	1	0	0	0-0	.308	.308	.308	.615	0	1.000

GUERRIER, MATT   P

PERSONAL: Born August 2, 1978, in Cleveland. ... 6-3/185. ... Throws right, bats right. ... Full name: Matthew Olson Guerrier. ... Name pronounced: GER-air. ... High school: Shaker Heights (Ohio). ... College: Kent State.

TRANSACTIONS/CAREER NOTES: Selected by Kansas City Royals organization in 33rd round of 1996 free-agent draft; did not sign. ... Selected by Chicago White Sox organization in 10th round of 1999 free-agent draft. ... Traded by White Sox to Pittsburgh Pirates for P Damaso Marte and IF Edwin Yan (March 27, 2002). ... Claimed on waivers by Minnesota Twins (November 20, 2003).

CAREER HITTING: 0-for-2 (.000), 0 R, 0 2B, 0 3B, 0 HR, 0 RBI.

MATT GUERRIER'S PITCHING ZONE

.350	.455	.400
.250	.444	.347
.111	.133	.200

LEFTY-RIGHTY SPLITS

vs.	Avg.	AB	H	2B	3B	HR	RBI	BB	SO	OBP	Slg.
L	.279	104	29	5	1	1	6	15	23	.375	.375
R	.247	170	42	8	1	5	22	9	23	.291	.394

Year	Team (League)	W	L	Pct.	ERA	WHIP	G	GS	CG	ShO	Hld.	Sv.-Opp.	IP	H	R	ER	HR	BB-IBB	SO	Avg.
1999—	Bristol (Appal.)	5	0	1.000	1.05	1.25	21	0	0	0	...	10-...	25.2	18	9	3	1	14-2	37	.196
—	Win.-Salem (Carol.)	0	0		5.40	0.90	4	0	0	0	...	2-...	3.1	3	2	2	0	0-0	5	.214
2000—	Win.-Salem (Carol.)	0	3	.000	1.30	1.07	30	0	0	0	...	19-...	34.2	25	13	5	0	12-0	35	.194
—	Birmingham (Sou.)	3	1	.750	2.70	1.24	23	0	0	0	...	7-...	23.1	17	9	7	1	12-1	19	.207
2001—	Birmingham (Sou.)	11	3	.786	3.10	1.19	15	15	1	1	...	0-...	98.2	85	42	34	8	32-1	75	.237
—	Charlotte (Int'l)	7	1	.875	3.54	1.14	12	12	3	0	...	0-...	81.1	75	33	32	7	18-0	43	.250
2002—	Nashville (PCL)	7	12	.368	4.59	1.28	27	26	2	1	...	0-...	157.0	154	88	80	20	47-3	130	.253
2003—	Nashville (PCL)	4	6	.400	4.53	1.20	20	19	0	0	...	0-...	105.1	108	56	53	15	18-1	78	.262
2004—	Rochester (Int'l)	5	10	.333	3.19	1.11	24	23	0	0	...	0-...	144.0	135	65	51	15	25-0	97	.248
—	Minnesota (A.L.)	0	1	.000	5.68	1.47	9	2	0	0	0	0-0	19.0	22	13	12	5	6-0	11	.293
2005—	Minnesota (A.L.)	0	3	.000	3.39	1.33	43	0	0	0	1	0-0	71.2	71	29	27	6	24-5	46	.259
Major League totals (2 years)		0	4	.000	3.87	1.36	52	2	0	0	1	0-0	90.2	93	42	39	11	30-5	57	.266

GUIEL, AARON   OF

PERSONAL: Born October 5, 1972, in Vancouver. ... 5-10/200. ... Bats left, throws right. ... Full name: Aaron Colin Guiel. ... Name pronounced: GUY-el. ... High school: Woodlands Senior (British Columbia). ... Junior college: Kwantlen (British Columbia).

TRANSACTIONS/CAREER NOTES: Selected by California Angels organization in 21st round of 1992 free-agent draft. ... Traded by Angels to San Diego Padres for C Angelo Encarnacion (August 25, 1997). ... Signed as a free agent by Oakland Athletics organization (March 18, 2000). ... Released by A's (March 30, 2000). ... Signed by Oaxaca of the Mexican League (April 2000). ... Signed by Kansas City Royals organization (June 13, 2000). ... On disabled list (May 13-July 17, 2004); included rehabilitation assignments to AZL Royals and Omaha.

2005 GAMES PLAYED BY POSITION (MLB): OF—30, DH—1.

SCOUTING REPORT Guiel has a short stroke with a slight uppercut. Has good balance at the plate. Bat speed has improved and is picking up the spin on pitches better after recovering from eye problems. Can drive the ball when he pulls it. Has a strong arm but only average range. Has problems tracking balls over his head. Could play regularly if he hits. *Grade 5.1*

AARON GUIEL'S HITTING ZONE

.167	.250	.000
.333	.357	.310
.000	.600	.500

LEFTY-RIGHTY SPLITS

vs.	Avg.	AB	H	2B	3B	HR	RBI	BB	SO	OBP	Slg.
L	.200	20	4	2	0	0	1	0	3	.292	.300
R	.315	89	28	3	0	4	6	6	18	.371	.483

Year	Team (League)	Pos.	G	AB	R	H	2B	3B	HR	RBI	BB	SO	HBP	GDP	SB-CS	Avg.	OBP	SLG	OPS	E	Avg.
1993—	Boise (N'west)	2B-OF	35	104	24	31	6	4	2	12	26	21	4	1	3-0	.298	.455	.490	.946	12	.874
1994—	Cedar Rap. (Midw.)	2B	127	454	84	122	30	1	18	82	64	93	6	7	21-7	.269	.364	.458	.822	32	.944
1995—	Lake Elsinore (Calif.)	2B	113	409	73	110	25	7	7	58	69	96	7	7	7-6	.269	.380	.416	.796	22	.944
1996—	Midland (Texas)	3B-2B-OF	129	439	72	118	29	7	10	48	56	71	10	6	11-7	.269	.364	.435	.799	28	.933
1997—	Midland (Texas)	OF-3B-2B	116	419	91	138	37	7	22	85	59	94	18	9	14-10	.329	.431	.609	1.039	8	.953
—	Mobile (Sou.)	OF	8	26	9	10	2	0	1	9	5	4	1	0	1-0	.385	.500	.577	1.077	0	1.000
1998—	Las Vegas (PCL)	OF-3B	60	183	33	57	15	4	5	31	28	51	4	4	5-1	.311	.410	.519	.929	4	.947
—	Ariz. Padres (Ariz.)	OF	8	16	8	8	3	1	1	6	5	5	0	0	1-1	.500	.667	1.000	1.667	0	1.000
1999—	Las Vegas (PCL)	OF	84	257	46	63	25	2	9	39	44	86	5	6	5-4	.245	.362	.498	.861	5	.944
2000—	Oaxaca (Mex.)		56	192	55	70	11	1	22	62	52	35		...	7-5	.365		.776		4	...
—	Omaha (PCL)	OF	73	258	47	74	15	2	13	40	35	54	8	3	6-0	.287	.389	.512	.900	4	.977
2001—	Omaha (PCL)	OF	121	442	78	118	27	3	21	73	51	92	13	12	6-4	.267	.355	.484	.840	6	.973
2002—	Omaha (PCL)	OF	61	215	44	76	11	1	9	50	29	34	8	4	8-1	.353	.443	.540	.983	3	.977
—	Kansas City (A.L.)	OF-DH	70	240	30	56	13	0	4	38	19	61	4	3	1-5	.233	.296	.338	.633	6	.962
2003—	Omaha (PCL)	OF	52	190	38	53	9	2	8	30	33	43	9	3	3-0	.279	.408	.474	.881	5	.962
—	Kansas City (A.L.)	OF-DH	99	354	63	98	30	0	15	52	27	63	13	3	3-5	.277	.346	.489	.835	3	.985
2004—	AZL Royals (Ariz.)	DH	4	17	3	8	1	0	2	5	0	2	1	0	0-0	.471	.500	.882	1.382	0	1.000
—	Wichita (Texas)	OF	6	20	7	5	0	0	0	2	5	5	0	0	0-0	.250	.516	.250	.766	1	.933
—	Omaha (PCL)	OF-DH	30	116	29	36	6	0	10	30	21	33	6	1	0-2	.310	.438	.621	1.058	1	.980
—	Kansas City (A.L.)	OF-DH	42	135	15	21	4	0	5	13	17	42	3	3	1-1	.156	.263	.296	.559	3	.966
2005—	Omaha (PCL)	OF-DH	128	496	94	137	32	4	30	95	64	103	15	14	6-3	.276	.371	.538	.909	4	.993
—	Kansas City (A.L.)	OF-DH	33	109	18	32	5	0	4	7	6	21	5	1	1-0	.294	.355	.450	.805	1	.985
Major League totals (4 years)			244	838	126	207	52	0	28	110	69	187	25	12	6-11	.247	.319	.409	.729	13	.973

G

GUILLEN, CARLOS   SS/3B

PERSONAL: Born September 30, 1975, in Maracay, Venezuela. ... 6-1/204. ... Bats both, throws right. ... Full name: Carlos Alfonso Guillen. ... Name pronounced: GHEE-yen.
TRANSACTIONS/CAREER NOTES: Signed as a non-drafted free agent by Houston Astros organization (September 19, 1992). ... Traded by Astros with P Freddy Garcia and a player to be named to Seattle Mariners for P Randy Johnson (July 31, 1998); Mariners acquired P John Halama to complete deal (October 1, 1998). ... On disabled list (April 7, 1999-remainder of season). ... On disabled list (April 13-28, 2000); included rehabilitation assignment to Tacoma. ... On disabled list (July 29-August 23, 2003); included rehabilitation assignment to Tacoma. ... Traded by Mariners to Detroit Tigers for IFs Ramon Santiago and Juan Gonzalez (January 8, 2004). ... On disabled list (June 11-26 and August 17-September 23, 2005).
2005 GAMES PLAYED BY POSITION (MLB): SS—75, DH—10.

SCOUTING REPORT **Offense:** Knee problems limited his ability to drive the ball last season. Has very good bat speed and plate coverage when healthy. Can use the whole field. Has power, especially on pitches out over the plate. Is a better hitter lefthanded. Bat control has really improved. Ability to adjust has led to more success with breaking pitches and with with runners in scoring position. Is a very good runner but doesn't steal because of his knees. **Defense:** Guillen has very good hands but his agility and mobility were limited because of his knee. Goes to the hole under control and has a very accurate arm with good carry. **Outlook:** Health was the concern entering the offseason, but if Guillen can come back strong and get some protection in the lineup, he could duplicate his 2004 numbers. *Grade 7.4*

CARLOS GUILLEN'S HITTING ZONE

.476	.273	.238
.412	.375	.241
.421	.250	.286

LEFTY-RIGHTY SPLITS

vs.	Avg.	AB	H	2B	3B	HR	RBI	BB	SO	OBP	Slg.
L	.368	76	28	3	2	1	7	2	7	.385	.500
R	.306	258	79	12	2	4	16	22	38	.364	.415

Year Team (League)	Pos.	G	AB	R	H	2B	3B	HR	RBI	BB	SO	HBP	GDP	SB-CS	Avg.	OBP	SLG	OPS	E	Avg.
1993—Dom. Astros (DSL)	IF	18	56	12	14	4	2	0	8	8	12	...	...	0-...	.250	...	.393	...	2	.956
1994—		Did not play.																		
1995—GC Astros (GCL)		30	105	17	31	4	2	2	15	9	17	1	0	17-1	.295	.350	.429	.779	...	...
1996—Quad City (Midw.)	SS	29	112	23	37	7	1	3	17	16	25	0	1	13-6	.330	.405	.491	.896	9	.929
1997—Jackson (Texas)	SS-DH	115	390	47	99	16	1	10	39	38	78	2	9	6-5	.254	.322	.377	.699	35	.932
—New Orleans (A.A.)	SS	3	13	3	4	1	0	0	0	0	4	0	0	0-0	.308	.308	.385	.692	0	1.000
1998—New Orleans (PCL)	SS	100	374	67	109	18	4	12	51	31	61	5	...	3-4	.291	.350	.457	.807	26	.943
—Tacoma (PCL)	2B	24	92	8	21	1	1	1	4	9	17	0	...	1-2	.228	.297	.293	.591	2	.982
—Seattle (A.L.)	2B	10	39	9	13	1	1	0	5	3	9	0	0	2-0	.333	.381	.410	.791	0	1.000
1999—Seattle (A.L.)	SS-2B	5	19	2	3	0	0	1	3	1	6	0	1	0-0	.158	.200	.316	.516	1	.964
2000—Seattle (A.L.)	3B-SS	90	288	45	74	15	2	7	42	28	53	2	6	1-3	.257	.324	.396	.720	21	.921
—Tacoma (PCL)	3B-SS	24	87	19	26	4	1	2	11	12	17	1	3	4-1	.299	.386	.437	.823	6	.926
2001—Seattle (A.L.)	SS-DH	140	456	72	118	21	4	5	53	53	89	1	9	4-1	.259	.333	.355	.689	10	.980
2002—Seattle (A.L.)	SS-DH	134	475	73	124	24	6	9	56	46	91	1	4	8-5	.261	.326	.394	.719	18	.966
2003—Tacoma (PCL)	3B-DH	4	14	2	5	1	0	2	4	0	1	1	2	0-0	.357	.400	.857	1.257	0	1.000
—Seattle (A.L.)	SS-3B-DH	109	388	63	107	19	3	7	52	52	64	1	12	4-4	.276	.359	.394	.753	14	.963
2004—Detroit (A.L.)	SS	136	522	97	166	37	10	20	97	52	87	2	12	12-5	.318	.379	.542	.921	17	.974
2005—Detroit (A.L.)	SS-DH	87	334	48	107	15	4	5	23	24	45	2	9	2-3	.320	.368	.434	.803	7	.978
Major League totals (8 years)		711	2521	409	712	132	30	54	331	259	444	9	57	29-21	.282	.349	.423	.771	88	.968

DIVISION SERIES RECORD

Year Team (League)	Pos.	G	AB	R	H	2B	3B	HR	RBI	BB	SO	HBP	GDP	SB-CS	Avg.	OBP	SLG	OPS	E	Avg.
2000—Seattle (A.L.)		1	1	0	1	0	0	0	1	0	0	0	0	0-0	1.000	1.000	1.000	2.000	...	...
2001—Seattle (A.L.)		Did not play.																		

CHAMPIONSHIP SERIES RECORD

Year Team (League)	Pos.	G	AB	R	H	2B	3B	HR	RBI	BB	SO	HBP	GDP	SB-CS	Avg.	OBP	SLG	OPS	E	Avg.
2000—Seattle (A.L.)	3B	2	5	1	1	0	0	1	2	2	2	0	0	0-1	.200	.429	.800	1.229	0	1.000
2001—Seattle (A.L.)	SS	3	8	1	2	0	0	0	0	1	1	0	0	0-0	.250	.250	.250	.500	0	1.000
Champ. series totals (2 years)		5	13	2	3	0	0	1	2	3	3	0	0	0-1	.231	.333	.462	.795	0	1.000

GUILLEN, JOSE   OF

PERSONAL: Born May 17, 1976, in San Cristobal, Dominican Republic. ... 5-11/190. ... Bats right, throws right. ... Full name: Jose Manuel Guillen. ... Name pronounced: GHEE-yen.
TRANSACTIONS/CAREER NOTES: Signed as a non-drafted free agent by Pittsburgh Pirates organization (August 19, 1992). ... Traded by Pirates with P Jeff Sparks to Tampa Bay Devil Rays for Cs Joe Oliver and Humberto Cota (July 23, 1999). ... On disabled list (March 28-April 12, 2000). ... On disabled list (May 17-June 24 and June 25-July 30, 2001); included rehabilitation assignments to Durham. ... Released by Devil Rays (November 27, 2001). ... Signed by Arizona Diamondbacks (December 18, 2001). ... Released by Diamondbacks (July 22, 2002). ... Signed by Colorado Rockies organization (July 29, 2002). ... Released by Rockies (August 1, 2002). ... Signed by Cincinnati Reds organization (August 20, 2002). .Traded by Reds to Oakland Athletics for Ps Aaron Harang, Joe Valentine and Jeff Bruksch (July 30, 2003). ... On suspended list (September 4-6, 2003). ... Signed as a free agent by Anaheim Angels (December 20, 2003). ... On Anaheim suspended list (September 26, 2004-remainder of season). ... Traded by Angels to Montreal Expos for OF Juan Rivera and SS Maicer Izturis (November 19, 2004). ... Expos franchise transferred to Washington, D.C., and renamed Washington Nationals for 2005 season (December 3, 2004). ... On suspended list (September 24-25, 2005).
2005 GAMES PLAYED BY POSITION (MLB): OF—142, DH—2.

SCOUTING REPORT **Offense:** He's an unusual hitter. Is very aggressive and loves to attack the first pitch. Will chase high fastballs late in the count and swing through pitches that are up. Has a slightly rigid swing and is more of an opposite-field hitter. Is vulnerable to the ball on the inside half. Can be a tough out with runners in scoring position but is much better against righthanders than left. Can run but doesn't steal bases. **Defense:** His arm is one of the game's finest. Teams alter their baserunning approach when he's in right field. Inconsistent with his routes when he doesn't get good reads but will run down balls in the gaps. **Outlook:** Guillen has an abundance of tools but is a high-maintenance player and can be a lightning rod for problems. *Grade 7.5*

JOSE GUILLEN'S HITTING ZONE

.290	.429	.257
.356	.268	.282
.313	.321	.214

LEFTY-RIGHTY SPLITS

vs.	Avg.	AB	H	2B	3B	HR	RBI	BB	SO	OBP	Slg.
L	.215	135	29	10	0	4	13	10	26	.282	.378
R	.305	416	127	22	2	20	63	21	76	.356	.512

Year Team (League)	Pos.	G	AB	R	H	2B	3B	HR	RBI	BB	SO	HBP	GDP	SB-CS	Avg.	OBP	SLG	OPS	E	Avg.
1993—Dom. Pirates (DSL)	OF	63	234	39	53	3	4	11	41	21	55			10-...	.227		.415		7	.947
1994—GC Pirates (GCL)	OF	30	110	17	29	4	1	4	11	7	15	6	0	2-1	.264	.341	.427	.769	2	.970
1995—Erie (NYP)	OF	66	258	41	81	17	1	12	46	10	44	12	5	1-5	.314	.367	.527	.894	13	.900
—Augusta (S. Atl.)	OF	10	34	6	8	1	1	2	6	2	9	2	0	0-0	.235	.316	.500	.816	0	1.000
1996—Lynchburg (Carol.)	OF-DH	136	528	78	170	30	0	21	94	20	73	13	16	24-13	.322	.357	.498	.855	13	.949
1997—Pittsburgh (N.L.)	OF	143	498	58	133	20	5	14	70	17	88	8	16	1-2	.267	.300	.412	.712	9	.963
1998—Pittsburgh (N.L.)	OF	153	573	60	153	38	2	14	84	21	100	6	7	3-5	.267	.298	.414	.712	10	.968
1999—Pittsburgh (N.L.)	OF	40	120	18	32	6	0	1	18	10	21	0	7	1-0	.267	.321	.342	.662	3	.952
—Nashville (PCL)	OF-DH	35	132	28	44	10	0	5	22	8	21	2	4	0-1	.333	.378	.523	.900	4	.939
—Durham (Int'l)	OF	9	34	8	13	1	0	3	12	7	7	0	2	0-1	.382	.476	.676	1.153	0	1.000
—Tampa Bay (A.L.)	OF	47	168	24	41	10	0	2	13	10	36	7	9	0-0	.244	.312	.339	.651	3	.966
2000—Durham (Int'l)	OF	19	78	20	33	8	2	9	31	8	11	1	2	0-1	.423	.477	.923	1.400	3	.912
—Tampa Bay (A.L.)	OF	105	316	40	80	16	5	10	41	18	65	13	6	3-1	.253	.320	.430	.750	4	.978
2001—Tampa Bay (A.L.)	OF-DH	41	135	14	37	8	0	3	11	6	26	3	2	2-3	.274	.317	.378	.695	3	.969
—Durham (Int'l)	OF	33	119	18	35	9	0	7	29	3	28	0	3	0-0	.294	.306	.546	.853	1	.982
2002—Arizona (N.L.)	OF-DH	54	131	13	30	4	0	4	15	7	25	2	7	3-4	.229	.277	.351	.628	0	1.000
—Colo. Springs (PCL)	OF	5	17	2	7	3	0	0	5	1	2	1	1	0-1	.412	.474	.588	1.062	0	1.000
—Louisville (Int'l)	OF	8	29	4	9	4	0	0	5	0	5	0	1	0-0	.310	.310	.655	.966	0	1.000
—Cincinnati (N.L.)	OF	31	109	12	27	3	0	4	16	7	18	1	6	1-1	.248	.299	.385	.684	1	.979
2003—Louisville (Int'l)	OF	4	15	4	5	1	0	0	3	1	3	0	1	1-0	.333	.353	.400	.753	0	1.000
—Cincinnati (N.L.)	OF	91	315	52	106	21	1	23	63	17	63	9	8	1-3	.337	.385	.629	1.013	8	.957
—Oakland (A.L.)	OF-DH	45	170	25	45	7	1	8	23	7	32	5	8	0-0	.265	.311	.459	.770	4	.942
2004—Anaheim (A.L.)	OF-DH	148	565	88	166	28	3	27	104	37	95	15	14	5-4	.294	.352	.497	.849	6	.979
2005—Washington (N.L.)	OF-DH	148	551	81	156	32	2	24	76	31	102	•19	14	1-1	.283	.338	.479	.817	7	.978
American League totals (5 years)		386	1354	191	369	66	9	50	192	78	251	43	39	10-8	.273	.331	.445	.776	20	.970
National League totals (6 years)		660	2297	294	637	124	10	84	342	110	417	45	65	11-16	.277	.320	.450	.770	38	.969
Major League totals (9 years)		1046	3651	485	1006	190	19	134	534	188	668	88	104	21-24	.276	.324	.448	.772	58	.970

DIVISION SERIES RECORD

Year Team (League)	Pos.	G	AB	R	H	2B	3B	HR	RBI	BB	SO	HBP	GDP	SB-CS	Avg.	OBP	SLG	OPS	E	Avg.
2003—Oakland (A.L.)	OF	4	11	1	5	1	0	0	1	3	2	0	0	0-0	.455	.571	.545	1.117	0	1.000

GUTHRIE, JEREMY — P

PERSONAL: Born April 8, 1979, in Roseburg, Ore. ... 6-1/200. ... Throws right, bats right. ... Full name: Jeremy Shane Guthrie. ... High school: Ashland (Ore.). ... College: Stanford.

TRANSACTIONS/CAREER NOTES: Selected by New York Mets organization in 15th round of 1997 free-agent draft; did not sign. ... Selected by Pittsburgh Pirates organization in third round of 2001 free-agent draft; did not sign. ... Selected by Cleveland Indians organization in first round (22nd pick overall) of 2002 free-agent draft.

CAREER HITTING: 0-for-0 (.000), 0 R, 0 2B, 0 3B, 0 HR, 0 RBI.

LEFTY-RIGHTY SPLITS

vs.	Avg.	AB	H	2B	3B	HR	RBI	BB	SO	OBP	Slg.
L	.375	16	6	1	0	0	1	0	2	.375	.438
R	.333	9	3	1	0	2	3	2	1	.417	1.111

Year Team (League)	W	L	Pct.	ERA	WHIP	G	GS	CG	ShO	Hld.	Sv.-Opp.	IP	H	R	ER	HR	BB-IBB	SO	Avg.
2003—Akron (East.)	6	2	.750	1.44	0.93	10	9	2	0		0-...	62.2	44	11	10	0	14-0	35	.196
—Buffalo (Int'l)	4	9	.308	6.52	1.64	18	18	1	0		0-...	96.2	129	75	70	15	30-1	62	.321
2004—Buffalo (Int'l)	1	2	.333	7.91	2.12	4	4	0	0		0-...	19.1	23	19	17	0	18-0	10	.303
—Akron (East.)	8	8	.500	4.21	1.43	23	21	0	0		0-...	130.1	145	76	61	16	42-0	94	.277
—Cleveland (A.L.)	0	0	...	4.63	1.29	6	0	0	0	0	0-0	11.2	9	6	6	1	6-0	7	.214
2005—Cleveland (A.L.)	0	0	...	6.00	1.83	1	0	0	0	0	0-0	6.0	9	4	4	2	2-0	3	.360
—Buffalo (Int'l)	12	10	.545	5.08	1.47	25	25	1	0		0-0	136.1	152	88	77	15	49-0	100	.286
Major League totals (2 years)	0	0	...	5.09	1.47	7	0	0	0	0	0-0	17.2	18	10	10	3	8-0	10	.269

GUTIERREZ, FRANKLIN — OF

PERSONAL: Born February 21, 1983, in Caricuao, Venezuela. ... 6-2/180. ... Bats right, throws right. ... Full name: Franklin Rafael Gutierrez.

TRANSACTIONS/CAREER NOTES: Signed as a non-drafted free agent by Los Angeles Dodgers organization (November 18, 2000). ... Traded by Dodgers with player to be named to Cleveland Indians for OF Milton Bradley (April 4, 2004); Indians acquired P Andrew Brown to complete deal (May 19, 2004).

2005 GAMES PLAYED BY POSITION (MLB): DH—3, OF—2.

LEFTY-RIGHTY SPLITS

vs.	Avg.	AB	H	2B	3B	HR	RBI	BB	SO	OBP	Slg.
L	.000	0	0	0	0	0	0	1	0	1.000	.000
R	.000	1	0	0	0	0	0	0	0	.000	.000

Year Team (League)	Pos.	G	AB	R	H	2B	3B	HR	RBI	BB	SO	HBP	GDP	SB-CS	Avg.	OBP	SLG	OPS	E	Avg.
2001—GC Dodgers (GCL)	OF	56	234	38	63	16	0	4	30	16	39	4	1	9-3	.269	.324	.389	.713	2	.980
2002—South Georgia (S. Atl.)	OF	92	361	61	102	18	4	12	45	31	88	6	5	13-4	.283	.344	.454	.798	3	.986
—Las Vegas (PCL)	OF	2	10	2	3	2	0	0	2	1	4	0	1	0-0	.300	.364	.500	.864	0	1.000
2003—Vero Beach (Fla. St.)	OF	110	425	65	120	28	5	20	68	39	111	3	9	17-5	.282	.345	.513	.858	4	.984
—Jacksonville (Sou.)	OF	18	67	12	21	3	2	4	12	7	20	1	1	3-3	.313	.387	.597	.984	0	1.000
2004—Akron (East.)	OF	70	262	38	79	24	2	5	35	23	77	9	4	6-3	.302	.372	.466	.838	3	.927
—Buffalo (Int'l)		7	27	4	4	1	0	1	3	1	11	0	0	0-0	.148	.179	.296	.475		...
2005—Akron (East.)	OF-DH	95	383	70	100	25	2	11	42	30	77	7	7	14-4	.261	.322	.423	.745	2	.995
—Buffalo (Int'l)	OF	19	67	10	17	6	0	0	7	6	13	1	1	2-2	.254	.320	.403	.723	0	1.000
—Cleveland (A.L.)	DH-OF	7	1	2	0	0	0	0	0	1	0	0	0	0-0	.000	.500	.000	.500	0	1.000
Major League totals (1 year)		7	1	2	0	0	0	0	0	1	0	0	0	0-0	.000	.500	.000	.500	0	1.000

GUZMAN, CRISTIAN — SS

PERSONAL: Born March 21, 1978, in Santo Domingo, Dominican Republic. ... 6-0/205. ... Bats both, throws right. ... Full name: Christian Antonio Guzman. ... Name pronounced: GOOZ-mahn.

TRANSACTIONS/CAREER NOTES: Signed as a non-drafted free agent by New York Yankees organization (August 24, 1994). ... Traded by Yankees with Ps Eric Milton and Danny Mota, OF Brian Buchanan and cash to Minnesota Twins for 2B Chuck Knoblauch (February 6, 1998). ... On disabled list (May 27-June 11, 1999). ... On suspended list (September 10-13, 1999). ... On disabled list (July 13-August 17, 2001); included rehabilitation assignment to GCL Twins. ... Signed as a free agent by Montreal Expos (November 16, 2004). ... Expos franchise transferred to Washington, D.C., and renamed Washington Nationals for 2005 season (December 3, 2004).

2005 GAMES PLAYED BY POSITION (MLB): SS—142.

G

SCOUTING REPORT Offense: Guzman had a very poor year after moving to the N.L. Was consistently late on balls, especially ones inside. Has a lot of movement at the plate. Is a slashing-type hitter who likes to hit off his front foot. Impatience often prevents him from having a chance at the plate. Doesn't have much power. Doesn't put his plus speed to use. **Defense:** His adjustment to grass after years of playing on the Metrodome carpet was difficult. No longer could play deep. Often fought the ball. Still has very good range to either side and a very strong arm. Can throw from any position. **Outlook:** Guzman can't be as bad as he was the first five months of last season. Was a prototypical turf player; needs to make the adjustment to grass. **Grade 7**

CRISTIAN GUZMAN'S HITTING ZONE

.313	.125	.147
.227	.304	.258
.200	.250	.220

LEFTY-RIGHTY SPLITS

vs.	Avg.	AB	H	2B	3B	HR	RBI	BB	SO	OBP	Slg.
L	.160	125	20	8	0	2	7	6	24	.198	.272
R	.242	331	80	11	6	2	24	19	52	.283	.329

							BATTING											FIELDING	
Year Team (League)	Pos.	G	AB	R	H	2B	3B	HR	RBI	BB	SO	HBP	GDP	SB-CS	Avg.	OBP	SLG	OPS	E	Avg.
1995— Dom. Yankees (DSL)	SS	46	160	24	43	6	5	3	20	12	23	...	...	11-...	.269	...	.425	...	13	.935
1996— GC Yankees (GCL)	SS	42	170	37	50	8	2	1	21	10	31	3	2	7-6	.294	.341	.382	.723	20	.890
1997— Greensboro (S. Atl.)	SS	124	495	68	135	21	4	4	52	17	105	10	3	23-12	.273	.309	.356	.665	37	.936
—Tampa (Fla. St.)	SS	4	14	4	4	0	0	0	1	1	1	0	0	0-1	.286	.333	.286	.619	2	.889
1998— New Britain (East.)	SS	140	566	68	157	29	5	1	40	21	111	1	13	23-14	.277	.304	.352	.655	* 32	.952
1999— Minnesota (A.L.)	SS	131	420	47	95	12	3	1	26	22	90	3	5	9-7	.226	.267	.276	.543	24	.959
2000— Minnesota (A.L.)	SS-DH	156	631	89	156	25	* 20	8	54	46	101	2	5	28-10	.247	.299	.388	.687	22	.967
2001— Minnesota (A.L.)	SS	118	493	80	149	28	* 14	10	51	21	78	5	6	25-8	.302	.337	.477	.814	* 21	.959
—GC Twins (GCL)	SS	5	16	4	4	0	1	0	0	2	4	1	1	0-1	.250	.368	.375	.743	0	1.000
2002— Minnesota (A.L.)	SS-DH	148	623	80	170	31	6	9	59	17	79	2	12	12-13	.273	.292	.385	.677	12	.981
2003— Minnesota (A.L.)	SS	143	534	78	143	15	* 14	3	53	30	79	5	4	18-9	.268	.311	.365	.676	11	.980
2004— Minnesota (A.L.)	SS	145	576	84	158	31	4	8	46	30	64	1	15	10-5	.274	.309	.384	.693	12	.983
2005— Washington (N.L.)	SS	142	456	39	100	19	6	4	31	25	76	1	12	7-4	.219	.260	.314	.574	15	.973
American League totals (6 years)		841	3277	458	871	142	61	39	289	166	491	18	47	102-52	.266	.303	.382	.685	102	.972
National League totals (1 year)		142	456	39	100	19	6	4	31	25	76	1	12	7-4	.219	.260	.314	.574	15	.973
Major League totals (7 years)		983	3733	497	971	161	67	43	320	191	567	19	59	109-56	.260	.298	.374	.671	117	.972

DIVISION SERIES RECORD

Year Team (League)	Pos.	G	AB	R	H	2B	3B	HR	RBI	BB	SO	HBP	GDP	SB-CS	Avg.	OBP	SLG	OPS	E	Avg.
2002— Minnesota (A.L.)	SS	5	21	5	6	2	0	1	2	2	4	0	0	2-0	.286	.348	.524	.872	1	.923
2003— Minnesota (A.L.)	SS	4	13	1	2	0	0	0	1	2	2	0	0	0-0	.154	.214	.154	.368	0	1.000
2004— Minnesota (A.L.)	SS	4	15	2	5	0	0	0	2	1	3	0	0	1-0	.333	.412	.333	.745	1	.964
Division series totals (3 years)		13	49	8	13	2	0	1	2	5	9	0	0	3-0	.265	.333	.367	.701	2	.966

CHAMPIONSHIP SERIES RECORD

Year Team (League)	Pos.	G	AB	R	H	2B	3B	HR	RBI	BB	SO	HBP	GDP	SB-CS	Avg.	OBP	SLG	OPS	E	Avg.
2002— Minnesota (A.L.)	SS	5	18	1	3	1	0	0	0	0	3	1	0	0-0	.167	.211	.222	.433	1	.962

ALL-STAR GAME RECORD

		G	AB	R	H	2B	3B	HR	RBI	BB	SO	HBP	GDP	SB-CS	Avg.	OBP	SLG	OPS	E	Avg.
All-Star Game totals (1 year)		1	1	0	0	0	0	0	0	0	1	0	0	0-0	.000	.000	.000	.000	0	...

HAAD, YAMID — C

PERSONAL: Born September 2, 1977, in Cartagena, Colombia. ... 6-2/204. ... Bats right, throws right. ... Full name: Yamid Salcedo Haad. ... Name pronounced: hawd.

TRANSACTIONS/CAREER NOTES: Signed as a non-drafted free agent by Pittsburgh Pirates organization (December 8, 1994). ... Signed as a free agent by Tampa Bay Devil Rays organization (December 23, 2001). ... Signed as a free agent by San Diego Padres organization (July 28, 2002). ... Signed as a free agent by San Francisco Giants organization (December 10, 2004).

2005 GAMES PLAYED BY POSITION (MLB): C—16.

LEFTY-RIGHTY SPLITS

vs.	Avg.	AB	H	2B	3B	HR	RBI	BB	SO	OBP	Slg.
L	.000	1	0	0	0	0	0	0	0	.000	.000
R	.074	27	2	1	0	0	1	3	7	.161	.111

							BATTING											FIELDING	
Year Team (League)	Pos.	G	AB	R	H	2B	3B	HR	RBI	BB	SO	HBP	GDP	SB-CS	Avg.	OBP	SLG	OPS	E	Avg.
1995— Dom. Pirates (DSL)		36	118	17	30	1	0	0	8	9	17	2	2	1-9	.254	.315	.263	.578	...	...
1996— Dom. Pirates (DSL)		56	205	29	66	9	0	5	28	10	38	1	0	8-7	.322	.353	.439	.792	...	...
1997— Erie (NYP)	C	43	155	27	45	7	3	1	19	7	27	0	5	3-3	.290	.310	.394	.704	3	.990
1998— Lynchburg (Carol.)	C	88	299	32	76	8	2	5	34	13	54	3	11	1-7	.254	.288	.344	.632	* 12	.982
1999— Lynchburg (Carol.)	C-DH																			
	1B-OF-3B	59	209	31	53	11	1	5	33	33	42	1	8	5-2	.254	.354	.388	.742	2	.994
—Altoona (East.)	C-1B-OF	43	137	20	25	3	0	6	10	19	32	0	4	7-3	.182	.280	.336	.616	10	.969
—Pittsburgh (N.L.)	PH	1	1	0	0	0	0	0	0	0	0	0	...	0-0	.000	.000	.000	.000	...	...
2000— Altoona (East.)	C-1B-OF	59	183	24	36	7	0	4	13	18	44	0	4	1-1	.197	.267	.301	.568	3	.991
—Lynchburg (Carol.)	C	25	91	14	23	8	0	3	9	11	16	0	4	2-0	.253	.330	.440	.770	5	.972
2001— Lynchburg (Carol.)	C	3	11	0	2	1	0	0	1	0	3	0	0	1-0	.182	.182	.273	.455	2	.943
—Altoona (East.)	1B-C-OF	1	3	0	0	0	0	0	0	0	0	0	0	0-0	.000	.000	.000	.000	0	1.000
—Nashville (PCL)	C-1B-P	51	144	14	37	5	0	2	10	7	27	0	2	0-3	.257	.291	.333	.624	3	.988
2002— Orlando (Sou.)	C	29	108	12	20	2	0	3	15	6	23	0	3	2-1	.185	.222	.287	.509	2	.991
—Durham (Int'l)	C	20	70	6	12	1	0	0	5	2	13	0	3	0-0	.171	.189	.186	.375	3	.982
—Mobile (Sou.)	C-1B	18	53	6	15	1	1	1	5	2	13	0	0	1-0	.283	.333	.358	.691	5	.957
2003— Portland (PCL)	C-1B	80	258	24	60	13	1	10	34	15	55	2	1	3-2	.233	.278	.407	.685	4	.984
—Mobile (Sou.)	1B-C	9	29	3	8	2	0	1	5	3	4	0	2	0-0	.276	.344	.448	.792	3	.950
2004— Portland (PCL)	C-1B	80	295	47	89	21	0	9	35	16	41	0	3	3-0	.302	.338	.464	.802	8	.988
2005— Fresno (PCL)	C-1B-DH	63	216	23	61	13	1	10	34	8	32	2	5	2-0	.282	.310	.491	.801	4	.991
—San Francisco (N.L.)	C	17	28	0	2	1	0	0	1	3	7	0	2	0-0	.071	.156	.107	.263	3	.957
Major League totals (2 years)		18	29	0	2	1	0	0	1	3	7	0	2	0-0	.069	.152	.103	.255	3	.957

G

HAFNER, TRAVIS — DH/1B

PERSONAL: Born June 3, 1977, in Jamestown, N.D. ... 6-3/240. ... Bats left, throws right. ... Full name: Travis Lee Hafner. ... Name pronounced: HAF-ner. ... High school: Sykeston (N.D.). ... Junior college: Cowley County (Kan.) Community College.

TRANSACTIONS/CAREER NOTES: Selected by Texas Rangers organization in 31st round of 1996 free-agent draft. ... Traded by Rangers with P Aaron Myette to Cleveland Indians for C Einar Diaz and P Ryan Drese (December 6, 2002). ... On disabled list (May 10-26, 2003); included rehabilitation assignment to Buffalo. ... On disabled list (July 26-August 4, 2005); included rehabilitation assignment to Akron.

2005 GAMES PLAYED BY POSITION (MLB): DH—130, 1B—1.

SCOUTING REPORT

Offense: Hafner, arguably one of the strongest players in baseball, simply can overpower the ball. Has exceptional power to all fields. Stays inside the ball well. Has improved his bat speed very much. Is an extremely patient hitter. Has become efficient with runners in scoring position. **Defense:** He was used primarily as a DH as he continues to have problems with his elbow. Is stiff with very limited range. **Outlook:** Hafner has become an outstanding offensive player with power and patience. Can only get better and may now be strictly a DH. **Grade 8.5**

TRAVIS HAFNER'S HITTING ZONE

.174	.500	.387
.403	.419	.376
.211	.435	.219

LEFTY-RIGHTY SPLITS

vs.	Avg.	AB	H	2B	3B	HR	RBI	BB	SO	OBP	Slg.
L	.269	156	42	15	0	7	36	23	52	.378	.500
R	.321	330	106	27	0	26	72	56	71	.423	.639

Year	Team (League)	Pos.	G	AB	R	H	2B	3B	HR	RBI	BB	SO	HBP	GDP	SB-CS	Avg.	OBP	SLG	OPS	E	Avg.
1997—	GC Rangers (GCL)	1B-OF	55	189	38	54	14	0	5	24	24	45	3	3	7-2	.286	.375	.439	.814	3	.991
1998—	Savannah (S. Atl.)	1B-3B-OF	123	405	62	96	15	4	16	84	68	139	6	8	7-3	.237	.351	.412	.764	12	.980
1999—	Savannah (S. Atl.)	1B-3B	134	480	94	140	30	4	28	111	67	151	11	11	5-4	.292	.387	.546	.933	15	.978
2000—	Charlotte (Fla. St.)	1B-3B	122	436	90	151	34	1	22	109	67	86	18	9	0-4	.346	.447	.580	1.027	13	.978
2001—	Tulsa (Texas)	1B	88	323	59	91	25	0	20	74	59	82	4	10	3-1	.282	.396	.545	.941	5	.993
2002—	Oklahoma (PCL)	1B	110	401	79	137	22	1	21	77	79	76	12	9	2-1	.342	.463	.559	1.022	4	.993
—	Texas (A.L.)	DH-1B	23	62	6	15	4	1	1	6	8	15	0	0	0-1	.242	.329	.387	.716	1	.909
2003—	Buffalo (Int'l)	1B-DH	29	100	15	27	4	0	2	10	25	26	1	2	2-1	.270	.421	.370	.791	3	.986
—	Cleveland (A.L.)	DH-1B	91	291	35	74	19	3	14	40	22	81	10	7	2-1	.254	.327	.485	.812	6	.985
2004—	Cleveland (A.L.)	DH-1B	140	482	96	150	41	3	28	109	68	111	•17	11	3-2	.311	.410	.583	.993	0	1.000
2005—	Akron (East.)		3	9	0	0	0	0	0	0	1	0	1	0	0-0	.000	.182	.000	.182	0	...
—	Cleveland (A.L.)	DH-1B	137	486	94	148	42	0	33	108	79	123	9	9	0-0	.305	.408	.595	1.003	0	1.000
Major League totals (4 years)			**391**	**1321**	**231**	**387**	**106**	**7**	**76**	**263**	**177**	**330**	**36**	**27**	**5-4**	**.293**	**.388**	**.556**	**.945**	**7**	**.986**

HAIRSTON, JERRY — OF

PERSONAL: Born May 29, 1976, in Naperville, Ill. ... 5-10/183. ... Bats right, throws right. ... Full name: Jerry Wayne Hairston Jr. ... High school: Naperville (Ill.) North. ... College: Southern Illinois. ... Son of Jerry Hairston, outfielder with two major league teams (1973-77 and 1981-89); brother of Scott Hairston, second baseman, Arizona Diamondbacks; nephew of John Hairston, catcher/outfielder with Chicago Cubs (1969); grandson of Sam Hairston, catcher with Chicago White Sox (1951).

TRANSACTIONS/CAREER NOTES: Selected by Baltimore Orioles organization in 42nd round of 1995 free-agent draft; did not sign. ... Selected by Orioles organization in 11th round of 1997 free-agent draft. ... On disabled list (May 21-September 4, 2003); included rehabilitation assignment to Bowie and Aberdeen. ... On disabled list (March 26-May 11 and August 18, 2004-remainder of season); included rehabilitation assignment to Bowie. ... Traded by Orioles with 2B Mike Fontenot and P David Crouthers to Chicago Cubs for OF Sammy Sosa and cash (February 2, 2005). ... On disabled list (August 4-19, 2005); included rehabilitation assignment to Iowa.

2005 GAMES PLAYED BY POSITION (MLB): OF—62, 2B—44, SS—1.

SCOUTING REPORT

Offense: Hairston is undisciplined and chases a lot of pitches. Has the bat speed to hit high fastballs but is more defensive when hitting breaking stuff. Has enough power to be home-run conscious but hits the ball in the air too much. Makes good contact and will use the whole field. Is a good runner but is not instinctive. **Defense:** He has quick hands and feet and good range to either side. Can be erratic and makes some dumb plays when he tries to do too much. Can play center field, adding to his value. **Outlook:** Hairston has a lot of natural ability but should have better instincts because he comes from a baseball family. Is too hyper at times and has an injury history. **Grade 5.8**

JERRY HAIRSTON'S HITTING ZONE

.211	.300	.350
.178	.326	.259
.421	.316	.125

LEFTY-RIGHTY SPLITS

vs.	Avg.	AB	H	2B	3B	HR	RBI	BB	SO	OBP	Slg.
L	.255	137	35	8	1	2	11	10	19	.306	.372
R	.263	243	64	17	1	2	19	21	27	.351	.366

Year	Team (League)	Pos.	G	AB	R	H	2B	3B	HR	RBI	BB	SO	HBP	GDP	SB-CS	Avg.	OBP	SLG	OPS	E	Avg.
1997—	Bluefield (Appal.)	SS	59	221	44	73	13	4	2	36	21	29	10	4	13-9	.330	.409	.452	.862	14	.949
1998—	Frederick (Carolina)	2B-SS	80	293	56	83	22	3	5	33	28	32	12	4	13-7	.283	.366	.430	.796	24	.943
—	Bowie (East.)	2B-SS	55	221	42	72	12	3	5	37	20	25	5	5	6-4	.326	.393	.475	.868	5	.980
—	Baltimore (A.L.)	2B	6	7	2	0	0	0	0	0	0	1	0	0	0-0	.000	.000	.000	.000	2	.750
1999—	Rochester (Int'l)	2B-SS	107	413	65	120	24	5	7	48	30	50	19	9	19-10	.291	.363	.424	.787	16	.968
—	Baltimore (A.L.)	2B	50	175	26	47	12	1	4	17	11	24	3	2	9-4	.269	.323	.417	.740	0	1.000
2000—	Baltimore (A.L.)	2B	49	180	27	46	5	0	5	19	21	22	6	8	8-5	.256	.353	.367	.719	5	.981
—	Rochester (Int'l)	2B-SS	58	201	43	59	15	1	4	21	29	32	5	2	6-4	.294	.392	.438	.830	11	.963
—	GC Orioles (GCL)	2B	4	10	3	3	2	0	0	3	3	2	0	1	4-0	.300	.500	.500	1.000	0	1.000
—	Frederick (Carolina)	2B	2	8	1	3	2	0	0	1	1	0	0	0	0-0	.375	.444	.625	1.069	0	1.000
2001—	Baltimore (A.L.)	2B	159	532	63	124	25	5	8	44	44	73	13	12	29-11	.233	.305	.344	.649	19	.976
2002—	Baltimore (A.L.)	2B	122	426	55	114	25	3	5	32	34	55	7	5	21-6	.268	.329	.376	.705	11	.979
2003—	Bowie (East.)	2B-DH	6	20	4	6	1	0	1	2	1	4	1	1	0-0	.300	.391	.500	.891	1	.941
—	Aberdeen (N.Y.-Penn.)	2B-DH	2	3	2	1	0	0	0	0	0	0	0	0	1-0	.333	.667	.333	1.000	0	1.000
—	Baltimore (A.L.)	2B-DH	58	218	25	59	12	2	2	21	23	25	6	8	14-5	.271	.353	.372	.725	5	.980
2004—	Bowie (East.)	2B	5	13	4	2	1	0	0	2	3	0	1	0	2-0	.154	.313	.231	.543	1	.929
—	Baltimore (A.L.)	OF-DH-2B 3B	86	287	43	87	19	1	2	24	29	29	8	3	13-8	.303	.378	.397	.775	2	.988

H

Year Team (League)	Pos.	G	AB	R	H	2B	3B	HR	RBI	BB	SO	HBP	GDP	SB-CS	Avg.	OBP	SLG	OPS	E	Avg.
2005— Iowa (PCL) 2B-OF-DH		5	22	3	7	0	1	0	2	0	3	2	0	3-0	.318	.360	.409	.769	0	1.000
—Chicago (N.L.) OF-2B-SS		114	380	51	99	25	2	4	30	31	46	12	5	8-9	.261	.336	.368	.704	7	.977
American League totals (7 years)		530	1825	241	477	98	12	26	160	162	229	43	38	94-39	.261	.334	.371	.705	44	.981
National League totals (1 year)		114	380	51	99	25	2	4	30	31	46	12	5	8-9	.261	.336	.368	.704	7	.977
Major League totals (8 years)		644	2205	292	576	123	14	30	190	193	275	55	43	102-48	.261	.334	.371	.705	51	.981

HAIRSTON, SCOTT   2B

PERSONAL: Born May 25, 1980, in Fort Worth, Texas. ... 6-0/188. ... Bats right, throws right. ... Full name: Scott Alexander Hairston. ... High school: Canyon del Oro (Tucson, Ariz.). ... Junior college: Central Arizona. ... Son of Jerry Hairston, outfielder with two major league teams (1973-77 and 1981-89); brother of Jerry Hairston, infielder/outfielder, Chicago Cubs; nephew of John Hairston, catcher/outfielder with Cubs (1969); grandson of Sam Hairston, catcher with Chicago White Sox (1951).

TRANSACTIONS/CAREER NOTES: Selected by Chicago White Sox organization in 18th round of 1999 free-agent draft; did not sign. ... Selected by Arizona Diamondbacks in third round of 2001 free-agent draft. ... On disabled list (September 2, 2005-remainder of season).

2005 GAMES PLAYED BY POSITION (MLB): OF—4, DH—2.

LEFTY-RIGHTY SPLITS

vs.	Avg.	AB	H	2B	3B	HR	RBI	BB	SO	OBP	Slg.
L	.182	11	2	1	0	0	0	0	2	.182	.273
R	.000	9	0	0	0	0	0	0	4	.000	.000

Year Team (League)	Pos.	G	AB	R	H	2B	3B	HR	RBI	BB	SO	HBP	GDP	SB-CS	Avg.	OBP	SLG	OPS	E	Avg.
2001—Missoula (Pion.)	2B	74	291	81	101	16	6	14	65	38	50	7	5	2-2	.347	.432	.588	1.020	21	.935
2002—South Bend (Mid.)	2B-3B	109	394	79	131	35	4	16	72	58	74	10	11	9-3	.332	.426	.563	.990	28	.944
—Lancaster (Calif.)	2B-3B	18	79	20	32	11	1	6	26	6	16	0	4	1-0	.405	.442	.797	1.239	2	.952
2003—El Paso (Texas)	2B	88	337	53	93	21	7	10	47	30	80	6	10	6-2	.276	.345	.469	.814	15	.960
—Tucson (PCL)		1	0	0	0	0	0	0	0	1	0	0	0	0-0	...	.000	...	...	0	.940
2004—Tucson (PCL)	2B-OF-DH	28	115	29	36	8	3	5	20	11	21	1	1	0-3	.313	.375	.565	.935	6	.940
—Arizona (N.L.)	2B-OF	101	339	39	84	15	6	13	29	21	88	1	4	3-3	.248	.293	.442	.735	11	.972
2005—Arizona (N.L.)	OF-DH	15	20	0	2	1	0	0	0	0	6	0	1	0-0	.100	.100	.150	.250	0	1.000
—Tucson (PCL)	OF-DH-2B	58	209	45	65	8	3	16	40	21	40	5	4	3-0	.311	.384	.608	.992	4	.979
Major League totals (2 years)		116	359	39	86	16	6	13	29	21	94	1	5	3-3	.240	.283	.426	.709	11	.972

HALAMA, JOHN   P

PERSONAL: Born February 22, 1972, in Brooklyn, N.Y. ... 6-5/215. ... Throws left, bats left. ... Full name: John Thadeuz Halama. ... Name pronounced: ha-LA-ma. ... High school: Bishop Ford (Brooklyn, N.Y.). ... College: St. Francis (N.Y.).

TRANSACTIONS/CAREER NOTES: Selected by Houston Astros organization in 23rd round of 1994 free-agent draft. ... Traded by Astros to Seattle Mariners (October 1, 1998), completing deal in which Mariners traded P Randy Johnson to Astros for SS Carlos Guillen, P Freddy Garcia and a player to be named (July 31, 1998). ... Signed as a free agent by Oakland Athletics (January 17, 2003). ... Signed as a free agent by Tampa Bay Devil Rays (November 14, 2003). ... Signed as a free agent by Boston Red Sox (December 17, 2004). ... Released by Red Sox (August 2, 2005). ... Signed by Washington Nationals organization (August 5, 2005). ... Released by Nationals (October 3, 2005).

CAREER HITTING: 3-for-26 (.115), 2 R, 1 2B, 0 3B, 0 HR, 0 RBI.

SCOUTING REPORT *Throws:* He features an 83-87 mph fastball, a curveball and a changeup. *Tendencies:* Halama relies on his ability to change speed with all his pitches and locate his fastball down in the zone. Command is essential to his success. Preys upon hitters' impatience by locating his fastball around, but not on, the plate. Will work both sides of the black. *Outlook:* Halama is versatile enough to work as a long reliever or a spot starter. *Grade 6.7*

JOHN HALAMA'S PITCHING ZONE

.389	.500	.600
.338	.286	.294
.283	.357	.353

LEFTY-RIGHTY SPLITS

vs.	Avg.	AB	H	2B	3B	HR	RBI	BB	SO	OBP	Slg.
L	.329	82	27	5	2	1	17	4	18	.404	.476
R	.277	188	52	14	3	5	28	13	19	.322	.463

Year Team (League)	W	L	Pct.	ERA	WHIP	G	GS	CG	ShO	Hld.	Sv.-Opp.	IP	H	R	ER	HR	BB-IBB	SO	Avg.
1994—Auburn (NY-Penn)	4	1	.800	1.29	0.82	6	3	0	0	...	1-...	28.0	18	5	4	1	5-0	27	.180
—Quad City (Midw.)	3	4	.429	4.56	1.58	9	9	1	1	...	0-...	51.1	63	31	26	2	18-1	37	.317
1995—Quad City (Midw.)	1	2	.333	2.02	1.12	55	0	0	0	...	2-...	62.1	48	16	14	7	22-1	56	.225
1996—Jackson (Texas)	9	10	.474	3.21	1.29	27	27	0	0	...	0-...	162.2	151	77	58	10	59-0	110	.248
1997—New Orleans (A.A.)	13	3	.813	2.58	1.06	26	24	1	0	...	0-...	171.0	150	57	49	8	32-1	126	.238
1998—Houston (N.L.)	1	1	.500	5.85	1.55	6	6	0	0	0	0-0	32.1	37	21	21	0	13-0	21	.297
—New Orleans (PCL)	12	8	.800	3.20	1.11	17	17	4	1	...	0-...	121.0	118	48	43	11	16-1	86	.255
1999—Seattle (A.L.)	11	10	.524	4.22	1.39	38	24	1	1	1	0-0	179.0	193	88	84	20	56-3	105	.282
2000—Seattle (A.L.)	14	9	.609	5.08	1.57	30	30	1	1	0	0-0	166.2	206	108	94	19	56-0	87	.308
2001—Seattle (A.L.)	10	7	.588	4.73	1.43	31	17	0	0	1	0-0	110.1	132	69	58	18	26-0	50	.296
—Tacoma (PCL)	2	0	1.000	0.47	0.47	3	3	1	0	...	0-...	19.0	9	2	1	1	0-0	22	.138
2002—Seattle (A.L.)	6	5	.545	3.56	1.44	31	0	0	0	0	0-...	101.0	112	45	40	9	33-5	70	.281
—Tacoma (PCL)	0	1	.000	6.14	1.36	2	2	0	0	...	0-...	14.2	19	11	10	0	1-1	9	.322
2003—Oakland (A.L.)	3	5	.375	4.22	1.41	35	13	0	0	3	0-0	108.2	117	68	51	18	36-2	51	.268
2004—Tampa Bay (A.L.)	7	6	.538	4.70	1.36	34	14	0	0	0	0-0	118.2	134	68	62	17	27-3	59	.284
2005—Boston (A.L.)	1	1	.500	6.18	1.49	30	1	0	0	0	0-0	43.2	56	33	30	5	9-3	26	.299
—New Orleans (PCL)	1	0	1.000	1.13	0.75	2	2	0	0	0	0-0	8.0	6	2	1	0	0-0	1	.194
—Washington (N.L.)	0	3	.000	4.64	1.45	10	3	0	0	0	0-0	21.1	23	11	11	1	8-0	11	.277
American League totals (7 years)	52	43	.547	4.55	1.44	229	109	2	2	5	0-0	828.0	950	479	419	106	243-16	448	.288
National League totals (2 years)	1	4	.200	5.37	1.51	16	9	0	0	0	0-0	53.2	60	32	32	1	21-0	32	.288
Major League totals (8 years)	53	47	.530	4.60	1.44	245	118	2	2	5	0-0	881.2	1010	511	451	107	264-16	480	.288

DIVISION SERIES RECORD

Year Team (League)	W	L	Pct.	ERA	WHIP	G	GS	CG	ShO	Hld.	Sv.-Opp.	IP	H	R	ER	HR	BB-IBB	SO	Avg.
2000—Seattle (A.L.)	Did not play.																		
2001—Seattle (A.L.)	0	0	...	0.00	1.00	2	0	0	0	0	0-0	3.0	3	0	0	0	0-0	3	.300

Year Team (League)	W	L	Pct.	ERA	WHIP	G	GS	CG	ShO	Hld.	Sv.-Opp.	IP	H	R	ER	HR	BB-IBB	SO	Avg.
2000— Seattle (A.L.)	0	0	...	2.89	1.61	2	0	0	0	0	0-0	9.1	10	3	3	0	5-0	3	.278
2001— Seattle (A.L.)	0	0	...	13.50	1.50	2	0	0	0	0	0-0	2.0	3	3	3	0	0-0	0	.333
Champ. series totals (2 years)	0	0	...	4.76	1.59	4	2	0	0	0	0-0	11.1	13	6	6	0	5-0	3	.289

HALL, BILL — 2B/SS

PERSONAL: Born December 28, 1979, in Nettleton, Miss. ... 6-0/195. ... Bats right, throws right. ... Full name: William Hall. ... High school: Nettleton (Miss.).
TRANSACTIONS/CAREER NOTES: Selected by Milwaukee Brewers organization in sixth round of 1998 free-agent draft.
2005 GAMES PLAYED BY POSITION (MLB): SS—66, 3B—59, 2B—23.

SCOUTING REPORT
Hall has gone from utility player to solid third-base candidate. Has defined his strike zone and is laying off bad breaking balls more often. Hits from a very wide stance. Has very good bat speed. Stroke is shorter and is beginning to show power especially on balls up. Defense has improved with better footwork and reads off the bat. Has good range to his left playing third. Tends to lay back on the ball playing short second. Has arm strength but can be very erratic. *Grade 6.8*

BILL HALL'S HITTING ZONE

.385	.429	.167
.380	.286	.302
.183	.261	.370

LEFTY-RIGHTY SPLITS

vs.	Avg.	AB	H	2B	3B	HR	RBI	BB	SO	OBP	Slg.
L	.336	125	42	17	1	3	13	14	25	.407	.560
R	.277	376	104	22	5	14	49	25	78	.319	.473

									BATTING									FIELDING	
Year Team (League)	Pos.	G	AB	R	H	2B	3B	HR	RBI	BB	SO	HBP	GDP	SB-CS	Avg.	OBP	SLG	OPS	E	Avg.
1998— Helena (Pion.)	SS	29	85	11	15	3	0	0	5	9	27	1	2	5-5	.176	.263	.212	.475	16	.876
1999— Ogden (Pion.)	SS	69	280	41	81	15	2	6	31	15	61	2	6	19-8	.289	.329	.421	.750	38	.894
2000— Beloit (Midw.)	SS	130	470	57	123	30	6	3	41	18	127	1	12	10-11	.262	.287	.370	.658	40	.939
2001— High Desert (Calif.)	SS	89	346	61	105	21	6	15	51	22	78	3	3	18-9	.303	.348	.529	.876	30	.929
— Huntsville (Sou.)	SS	41	160	14	41	8	1	3	14	5	46	0	5	5-3	.256	.279	.375	.654	15	.925
2002— Indianapolis (Int'l)	SS	134	465	35	106	20	1	4	31	25	105	4	12	17-10	.228	.272	.301	.573	41	.934
— Milwaukee (N.L.)	SS-3B	19	36	3	7	1	1	1	5	3	13	0	1	0-1	.194	.256	.361	.618	2	.951
2003— Indianapolis (Int'l)	2B-SS-OF	89	354	57	100	25	2	5	32	27	79	1	7	10-11	.282	.335	.407	.742	19	.957
— Milwaukee (N.L.)	2B-SS-3B	52	142	23	37	9	2	5	20	7	28	1	5	1-2	.261	.298	.458	.756	9	.948
2004— Milwaukee (N.L.)	SS-3B	126	390	43	93	20	3	9	53	20	119	1	4	12-6	.238	.276	.374	.650	19	.956
2005— Milwaukee (N.L.)	SS-3B-2B	146	501	69	146	39	6	17	62	39	103	1	11	18-6	.291	.342	.495	.837	16	.967
Major League totals (4 years)		343	1069	138	283	69	12	32	140	69	263	3	21	31-15	.265	.310	.442	.751	46	.959

HALL, TOBY — C

PERSONAL: Born October 21, 1975, in Tacoma, Wash. ... 6-3/240. ... Bats right, throws right. ... Full name: Toby Jason Hall. ... High school: El Dorado (Placentia, Calif.). ... College: UNLV.
TRANSACTIONS/CAREER NOTES: Selected by San Francisco Giants organization in 24th round of 1995 free-agent draft; did not sign. ... Selected by Tampa Bay Devil Rays organization in ninth round of 1997 free-agent draft.
2005 GAMES PLAYED BY POSITION (MLB): C—135, 1B—2.

SCOUTING REPORT
Offense: He has a long stroke and hits from a deep crouch. Doesn't pull the ball much, especially for a hitter with his strength. Is a very good contact hitter who doesn't strike out much because he rarely gets to two strikes. Has more power than numbers indicate. Gets defensive with his swing against breaking stuff. **Defense:** His arm strength is above average and his throws carry, but his footwork is inconsistent. Has good hands and has made improvements staying low and creating a good target for his pitches. Is beginning to frame pitches better. **Outlook:** Hall should be more productive offensively; he needs to improve his pitch selection to do so. Needs to stand more upright in the box to take advantage of his natural strength. *Grade 7.2*

TOBY HALL'S HITTING ZONE

.273	.222	.321
.265	.333	.260
.339	.360	.387

LEFTY-RIGHTY SPLITS

vs.	Avg.	AB	H	2B	3B	HR	RBI	BB	SO	OBP	Slg.
L	.302	129	39	4	0	3	15	6	10	.331	.403
R	.281	303	85	16	0	2	33	10	29	.308	.353

									BATTING									FIELDING	
Year Team (League)	Pos.	G	AB	R	H	2B	3B	HR	RBI	BB	SO	HBP	GDP	SB-CS	Avg.	OBP	SLG	OPS	E	Avg.
1997— Hudson Valley (NYP)	C	55	200	25	50	3	0	1	27	13	33	1	3	0-0	.250	.295	.280	.575	3	.989
1998— Char., S.C. (SAL)	C	105	377	59	121	25	1	6	50	39	32	5	15	3-7	.321	.386	.440	.827	18	.979
1999— Orlando (South.)	C	46	173	20	44	7	0	9	34	4	10	1	7	1-1	.254	.269	.451	.720	4	.986
— St. Pete. (FSL)	C	56	212	24	63	13	1	4	36	17	9	2	7	0-2	.297	.350	.425	.775	4	.986
2000— Orlando (South.)	C	68	271	37	93	14	0	9	50	17	24	1	6	3-2	.343	.378	.494	.872	7	.984
— Durham (Int'l)	C	47	184	21	56	15	0	7	35	3	19	2	9	0-0	.304	.314	.500	.814	2	.993
— Tampa Bay (A.L.)	C	4	12	1	2	0	0	1	1	1	0	0	0	0-0	.167	.231	.417	.647	6	1.000
2001— Durham (Int'l)	C	94	373	59	125	28	1	19	72	29	22	3	15	1-3	.335	.385	.568	.953	6	.987
— Tampa Bay (A.L.)	C	49	188	28	56	16	0	4	30	4	16	3	5	2-2	.298	.321	.447	.768	5	.986
2002— Tampa Bay (A.L.)	C	85	330	37	85	19	1	6	42	17	27	1	14	0-1	.258	.293	.376	.669	6	.993
— Durham (Int'l)	C	22	92	13	32	4	0	2	20	3	10	4	3	0-0	.348	.382	.457	.839	1	.993
2003— Tampa Bay (A.L.)	C	130	463	50	117	23	0	12	47	23	40	7	14	0-1	.253	.295	.380	.675	6	.988
2004— Tampa Bay (A.L.)	C	119	404	35	103	21	0	8	48	20	41	6	15	0-0	.255	.300	.366	.666	6	.992
2005— Tampa Bay (A.L.)	C-1B	135	432	28	124	20	0	5	48	16	39	5	15	0-0	.287	.315	.368	.683	9	.989
Major League totals (6 years)		522	1829	179	487	99	1	36	228	85	163	21	68	2-6	.266	.303	.381	.683	35	.989

H

HALLADAY, ROY — P

PERSONAL: Born May 14, 1977, in Denver. ... 6-6/230. ... Throws right, bats right. ... Full name: Harry Leroy Halladay. ... Name pronounced: HAL-luh-day. ... High school: Arvada (Colo.) West.
TRANSACTIONS/CAREER NOTES: Selected by Toronto Blue Jays organization in first round (17th pick overall) of 1995 free-agent draft. ... On disabled list (May 28-June 12 and July 17-September 21, 2004; and July 9, 2005-remainder of season).
HONORS: Named A.L. Pitcher of the Year by THE SPORTING NEWS (2003). ... Named A.L. Cy Young Award winner by Baseball Writers' Association of America (2003).
CAREER HITTING: 1-for-26 (.038), 2 R, 0 2B, 0 3B, 0 HR, 0 RBI.

SCOUTING REPORT *Throws:* Halladay's two- and four-seam fastballs hit 90-95 mph and his knuckle curve is around 78. Has a split-finger fastball. *Tendencies:* He has long arm action and a deceptive delivery. Can run the fastball in on hitters. Throws strikes, rarely pitching at top velocity. Likes to work low in the zone and is not afraid to challenge hitters inside. Has sweeping rotation on his knuckle curve. Uses his fastball as his out pitch and his knuckle-curve as a changeup. Rarely throws his splitter. *Outlook:* Halladay looked to be on the way to a second Cy Young award before a broken leg ended his 2005 season around the All-Star break. Has exceptional stuff and command of all his pitches. Will be a No. 1 starter for years. *Grade 9.3*

ROY HALLADAY'S PITCHING ZONE

.250	.545	.300
.250	.293	.174
.140	.286	.262

LEFTY-RIGHTY SPLITS

vs.	Avg.	AB	H	2B	3B	HR	RBI	BB	SO	OBP	Slg.
L	.217	277	60	8	0	4	16	13	50	.254	.289
R	.235	247	58	10	1	7	21	5	58	.266	.368

Year	Team (League)	W	L	Pct.	ERA	WHIP	G	GS	CG	ShO	Hld.	Sv.-Opp.	IP	H	R	ER	HR	BB-IBB	SO	Avg.
1995—	GC Jays (GCL)	3	5	.375	3.40	1.01	10	8	0	0		0-...	50.1	35	25	19	4	16-0	48	.190
1996—	Dunedin (Fla. St.)	15	7	.682	2.73	1.24	27	27	2	2		0-...	164.2	158	75	50	7	46-0	109	.251
1997—	Knoxville (Southern)	2	3	.400	5.40	1.55	7	7	0	0		0-...	36.2	46	26	22	4	11-0	30	.305
—Syracuse (Int'l)		7	10	.412	4.58	1.47	22	22	2	2		0-...	125.2	132	74	64	13	53-1	64	.276
1998—	Syracuse (Int'l)	9	5	.643	3.79	1.38	21	21	1	1		0-...	116.1	107	52	49	11	53-3	71	.246
—Toronto (A.L.)		1	0	1.000	1.93	0.79	2	2	1	0	0	0-0	14.0	9	4	3	2	2-0	13	.176
1999—	Toronto (A.L.)	8	7	.533	3.92	1.57	36	18	1	1	2	1-1	149.1	156	76	65	19	79-1	82	.270
2000—	Toronto (A.L.)	4	7	.364	10.64	2.20	19	13	0	0	0	0-0	67.2	107	87	80	14	42-0	44	.357
—Syracuse (Int'l)		2	3	.400	5.50	1.44	11	11	3	0		0-...	73.2	85	46	45	10	21-0	38	.290
2001—	Dunedin (Fla. St.)	0	1	.000	3.97	1.37	13	0	0	0		2-...	22.2	28	12	10	1	3-0	15	.304
—Tennessee (Sou.)		2	1	.667	2.12	0.91	5	5	3	0		0-...	34.0	25	9	8	2	6-0	29	.202
—Syracuse (Int'l)		1	0	1.000	3.21	0.86	2	2	0	0		0-...	14.0	12	5	5	2	0-0	13	.222
—Toronto (A.L.)		5	3	.625	3.16	1.16	17	16	1	1	0	0-0	105.1	97	41	37	3	25-0	96	.241
2002—	Toronto (A.L.)	19	7	.731	2.93	1.19	34	34	2	1	0	0-0	*239.1	223	93	78	10	62-6	168	.244
2003—	Toronto (A.L.)	*22	7	.759	3.25	1.07	36	*36	•9	•2	0	0-0	*266.0	*253	111	96	26	32-1	204	.247
2004—	Toronto (A.L.)	8	8	.500	4.20	1.35	21	21	1	1	0	0-0	133.0	140	66	62	13	39-1	95	.272
2005—	Toronto (A.L.)	12	4	.750	2.41	0.96	19	19	*5	2	0	0-0	141.2	118	39	38	11	18-2	108	.225
Major League totals (8 years)		**79**	**43**	**.648**	**3.70**	**1.26**	**184**	**159**	**20**	**8**	**2**	**1-1**	**1116.1**	**1103**	**517**	**459**	**98**	**299-11**	**810**	**.256**

ALL-STAR GAME RECORD

	W	L	Pct.	ERA	WHIP	G	GS	CG	ShO	Hld.	Sv.-Opp.	IP	H	R	ER	HR	BB-IBB	SO	Avg.
All-Star Game totals (1 year)	0	0	...	27.00	3.00	1	0	0	0	0	0-...	1.0	3	3	3	1	0-0	1	.500

HALSEY, BRAD — P

PERSONAL: Born February 14, 1981, in Houston. ... 6-1/180. ... Throws left, bats left. ... Full name: Bradford Alexander Halsey. ... High school: Westfield (Houston). ... Junior college: Hill College (Hillsboro, Texas). ... College: Texas.
TRANSACTIONS/CAREER NOTES: Selected by New York Yankees organization in 19th round of 2000 free-agent draft; did not sign. ... Selected by New York Yankees organization in eighth round of 2002 free-agent draft. ... Traded by Yankees with P Javier Vazquez, C Dioner Navarro and cash to Arizona Diamondbacks for P Randy Johnson (January 11, 2005). ... On suspended list (April 5-7, 2005).
CAREER HITTING: 4-for-50 (.080), 2 R, 0 2B, 0 3B, 0 HR, 2 RBI.

SCOUTING REPORT *Throws:* Halsey has a fastball that ranges from 87-90 mph, a slider and a circle change. *Tendencies:* Halsey has a good delivery but tends to pitch up in the zone. Has to have good command and spot his fastball. Is willing to pitch inside. Will change the speed and break of his slider. Struggles against righthanders because he is easy for them to follow. Must run his slider under their hands to negate this advantage. Change fades away from them. Is easy to run on. *Outlook:* Halsey has shown some improvement thanks to a tighter slider and his ability to pitch inside. Will begin the spring as the Diamondbacks' fifth starter. *Grade 6.3*

BRAD HALSEY'S PITCHING ZONE

.389	.333	.158
.429	.431	.283
.286	.206	.213

LEFTY-RIGHTY SPLITS

vs.	Avg.	AB	H	2B	3B	HR	RBI	BB	SO	OBP	Slg.
L	.267	135	36	8	0	3	18	6	22	.308	.393
R	.309	501	155	33	3	17	66	33	60	.357	.489

Year	Team (League)	W	L	Pct.	ERA	WHIP	G	GS	CG	ShO	Hld.	Sv.-Opp.	IP	H	R	ER	HR	BB-IBB	SO	Avg.
2002—	Staten Island (N.Y.-Penn.)	6	1	.857	1.93	1.00	11	10	0	0	...	0-...	56.0	39	15	12	0	17-0	53	.195
2003—	Tampa (Fla. St.)	10	4	.714	3.43	1.31	14	13	1	0	...	0-...	84.0	96	36	32	3	14-0	56	.287
—Trenton (East.)		7	5	.583	4.93	1.59	15	15	0	0	...	0-...	91.1	123	51	50	4	22-0	78	.325
2004—	Columbus (Int'l)	11	4	.733	2.63	1.15	24	23	3	2	...	0-...	144.0	128	46	42	8	37-0	109	.237
—New York (A.L.)		1	3	.250	6.47	1.72	8	7	0	0	0	0-0	32.0	41	26	23	4	14-0	25	.306
2005—	Arizona (N.L.)	8	12	.400	4.61	1.44	28	26	0	0	0	0-0	160.0	191	101	82	20	39-3	82	.300
American League totals (1 year)		**1**	**3**	**.250**	**6.47**	**1.72**	**8**	**7**	**0**	**0**	**0**	**0-0**	**32.0**	**41**	**26**	**23**	**4**	**14-0**	**25**	**.306**
National League totals (1 year)		**8**	**12**	**.400**	**4.61**	**1.44**	**28**	**26**	**0**	**0**	**0**	**0-0**	**160.0**	**191**	**101**	**82**	**20**	**39-3**	**82**	**.300**
Major League totals (2 years)		**9**	**15**	**.375**	**4.92**	**1.48**	**36**	**33**	**0**	**0**	**0**	**0-0**	**192.0**	**232**	**127**	**105**	**24**	**53-3**	**107**	**.301**

H

HAMMOND, CHRIS   P

PERSONAL: Born January 21, 1966, in Atlanta. ... 6-1/210. ... Throws left, bats left. ... Full name: Chris Andrew Hammond. ... High school: Vestavia Hills (Birmingham, Ala.). ... Junior college: Gulf Coast (Fla.) Community College. ... Brother of Steve Hammond, outfielder with Kansas City Royals (1982).

TRANSACTIONS/CAREER NOTES: Selected by Cincinnati Reds organization in sixth round of January 1986 free-agent draft. ... On disabled list (July 27-September 1, 1991). ... Traded by Reds to Florida Marlins for 3B Gary Scott and a player to be named (March 27, 1993); Reds acquired P Hector Carrasco to complete deal (September 10, 1993). ... On disabled list (June 11-August 3, 1994); included rehabilitation assignments to Portland and Brevard County. ... On disabled list (April 16-May 13 and August 3-19, 1995); included rehabilitation assignments to Brevard County and Charlotte. ... On disabled list (June 9-July 14, 1996); included rehabilitation assignments to Brevard County and Charlotte. ... Signed as a free agent by Boston Red Sox (December 17, 1996). ... On disabled list (June 30, 1997-remainder of season). ... Signed as a free agent by Kansas City Royals organization (January 12, 1998). ... Released by Royals (March 23, 1998). ... Signed by Marlins organization (March 27, 1998). ... Released by Marlins (June 2, 1998). ... Signed by Cleveland Indians organization (March 30, 2001). ... Released by Indians (July 3, 2001). ... Signed by Atlanta Braves organization (July 17, 2001). ... On suspended list (September 13-16, 2002). ... Signed as a free agent by New York Yankees (December 12, 2002). ... Traded by Yankees to Oakland Athletics for RHP Eduardo Sierra and SS J.T. Stotts (December 18, 2003). ... On disabled list (June 12-July 27, 2004); included rehabilitation assignment to Sacramento. ... Signed as a free agent by San Diego Padres (January 17, 2005). ... On disabled list (July 20-August 9, 2005).

CAREER HITTING: 48-for-238 (.202), 30 R, 7 2B, 1 3B, 4 HR, 14 RBI.

SCOUTING REPORT **Throws:** He delivers his fastball in the 79-82 mph range and also throws a curveball and changeup. **Tendencies:** Hammond is a soft-tosser with some deception in his delivery. Fastball is well below average, but ability to change speeds allows him to sneak it by hitters on the inside half. Likes to show his curveball to righthanders to set up his diving change away. Forces managers to turn over their lineup but can be very effective against righthanders with the change and curve. Is extremely effective against lefthanders, too. Never gives in to a hitter. **Outlook:** Hammond can fill a variety of roles, from a middle relief to situational lefthander. *Grade 7*

CHRIS HAMMOND'S PITCHING ZONE

.167	.200	.250
.244	.545	.306
.167	.143	.063

LEFTY-RIGHTY SPLITS

vs.	Avg.	AB	H	2B	3B	HR	RBI	BB	SO	OBP	Slg.
L	.164	73	12	3	0	2	13	4	15	.203	.288
R	.260	150	39	11	0	7	22	10	19	.315	.473

Year	Team (League)	W	L	Pct.	ERA	WHIP	G	GS	CG	ShO	Hld.	Sv.-Opp.	IP	H	R	ER	HR	BB-IBB	SO	Avg.
1986—	GC Reds (GCL)	3	2	.600	2.81	1.06	7	7	1	0	...	0-...	41.2	27	21	13	0	17-1	53	.172
—	Tampa (Fla. St.)	0	2	.000	3.32	1.75	5	5	0	0	...	0-...	21.2	25	8	8	0	13-1	21	.291
1987—	Tampa (Fla. St.)	11	11	.500	3.55	1.38	25	24	6	0	...	0-...	170.0	174	81	67	10	60-1	126	.258
1988—	Chattanooga (Sou.)	16	5	.762	1.72	1.12	26	26	4	2	...	0-...	182.2	127	48	35	2	77-3	127	.193
1989—	Nashville (A.A.)	11	7	.611	3.38	1.53	24	24	3	1	...	0-...	157.1	144	69	59	7	96-1	142	.245
1990—	Nashville (A.A.)	15	1	.938	2.17	1.21	24	24	5	3	...	0-...	149.0	118	43	36	7	63-1	149	.219
—	Cincinnati (N.L.)	0	2	.000	6.35	2.21	3	3	0	0	0	0-0	11.1	13	9	8	2	12-1	4	.302
1991—	Cincinnati (N.L.)	7	7	.500	4.06	1.40	20	18	0	0	0	0-0	99.2	92	51	45	4	48-3	50	.250
1992—	Cincinnati (N.L.)	7	10	.412	4.21	1.38	28	26	0	0	0	0-0	147.1	149	75	69	13	55-6	79	.266
1993—	Florida (N.L.)	11	12	.478	4.66	1.43	32	32	1	0	0	0-0	191.0	207	106	99	18	66-2	108	.277
1994—	Florida (N.L.)	4	4	.500	3.07	1.39	13	13	1	1	0	0-0	73.1	79	30	25	5	23-1	40	.281
—	Portland (East.)	0	0	...	0.00	0.00	1	1	0	0	...	0-...	2.0	0	0	0	0	0-0	2	.000
—	Brevard County (FSL)	0	0	...	1.23	0.95	2	2	0	0	...	0-...	7.1	4	3	1	0	3-0	5	.160
1995—	Brevard County (FSL)	0	0	...	0.00	0.75	1	1	0	0	...	0-...	4.0	3	1	0	0	0-0	4	.200
—	Charlotte (Int'l)	0	0	...	0.00	1.25	1	1	0	0	...	0-...	4.0	3	1	0	0	3-0	3	.176
—	Florida (N.L.)	9	6	.600	3.80	1.27	25	24	3	2	0	0-0	161.0	157	73	68	17	47-2	126	.256
1996—	Florida (N.L.)	5	8	.385	6.56	1.62	38	9	0	0	5	0-0	81.0	104	65	59	14	27-3	50	.315
—	Brevard County (FSL)	0	0	...	0.00	0.75	1	1	0	0	...	0-...	4.0	3	0	0	0	0-0	5	.214
—	Charlotte (Int'l)	1	0	1.000	7.20	1.00	1	1	0	0	...	0-...	5.0	5	4	4	0	0-0	3	.250
1997—	Boston (A.L.)	3	4	.429	5.92	1.65	29	8	0	0	4	1-2	65.1	81	45	43	5	27-4	48	.310
1998—	Charlotte (Int'l)	1	3	.250	4.82	1.75	5	5	0	0	...	0-...	28.0	35	17	15	2	14-2	22	.315
—	Florida (N.L.)	0	2	.000	6.59	2.05	3	3	0	0	0	0-0	13.2	20	11	10	3	8-0	8	.357
1999—				Did not play.																
2000—				Did not play.																
2001—	Buffalo (Int'l)	7	3	.700	3.31	1.41	28	4	0	0	...	0-...	51.2	53	22	19	5	20-1	54	.261
—	Richmond (Int'l)	3	1	.750	2.35	1.17	21	0	0	0	...	1-...	30.2	32	9	8	0	4-0	29	.281
2002—	Atlanta (N.L.)	7	2	.778	0.95	1.11	63	0	0	0	17	0-0	76.0	53	15	8	1	31-9	63	.195
2003—	New York (A.L.)	3	2	.600	2.86	1.21	62	0	0	0	17	1-4	63.0	65	23	20	5	11-0	45	.270
2004—	Sacramento (PCL)	0	0	...	0.00	1.50	3	3	0	0	...	0-...	4.0	6	0	0	0	0-0	5	.353
—	Oakland (A.L.)	4	1	.800	2.68	1.29	41	0	0	0	3	1-3	53.2	56	21	16	4	13-1	34	.277
2005—	San Diego (N.L.)	5	1	.833	3.84	1.11	55	0	0	0	6	0-3	58.2	51	25	25	9	14-0	34	.229
American League totals (3 years)		10	7	.588	3.91	1.39	132	8	0	0	24	3-9	182.0	202	89	79	14	51-5	127	.287
National League totals (10 years)		55	54	.505	4.10	1.38	280	128	5	3	28	0-5	913.0	925	460	416	86	331-27	562	.265
Major League totals (13 years)		65	61	.516	4.07	1.38	412	136	5	3	52	3-14	1095.0	1127	549	495	100	382-32	689	.268

DIVISION SERIES RECORD

Year	Team (League)	W	L	Pct.	ERA	WHIP	G	GS	CG	ShO	Hld.	Sv.-Opp.	IP	H	R	ER	HR	BB-IBB	SO	Avg.
2002—	Atlanta (N.L.)	0	0	...	6.75	1.88	3	0	0	0	0	0-0	2.2	2	2	2	0	3-1	2	.200

WORLD SERIES RECORD

Year	Team (League)	W	L	Pct.	ERA	WHIP	G	GS	CG	ShO	Hld.	Sv.-Opp.	IP	H	R	ER	HR	BB-IBB	SO	Avg.
2003—	New York (A.L.)	0	0	...	0.00	1.00	1	0	0	0	0	0-0	2.0	2	2	0	0	0-0	0	.250

HAMMONDS, JEFFREY   OF

PERSONAL: Born March 5, 1971, in Scotch Plains, N.J. ... 6-0/222. ... Bats right, throws right. ... Full name: Jeffrey Bryan Hammonds. ... High school: Scotch Plains (N.J.)-Fanwood. ... College: Stanford.

TRANSACTIONS/CAREER NOTES: Selected by Toronto Blue Jays organization in ninth round of 1989 free-agent draft; did not sign. ... Selected by Baltimore Orioles organization in first round (fourth pick overall) of 1992 free-agent draft. ... On disabled list (August 8-September 1 and September 28, 1993-remainder of season); included rehabilitation assignment to Bowie. ... On disabled list (May 4-June 16, 1994; July 18-September 3, 1995; and August 17-September 22, 1996). ... On disabled list (June 3-July 11, 1998); included rehabilitation assignment to Bowie. ... Traded by Orioles to Cincinnati Reds for 3B/OF Willie Greene (August 10, 1998). ... Traded by Reds with P Stan Belinda to Colorado Rockies for OF Dante Bichette and cash (October 30, 1999). ... On disabled list (April 4-22, 2000). ... Signed as a free agent by

LEFTY-RIGHTY SPLITS

vs.	Avg.	AB	H	2B	3B	HR	RBI	BB	SO	OBP	Slg.
L	.211	19	4	0	0	0	1	2	.286	.211
R	.231	13	3	1	0	0	1	1	2	.286	.308

Milwaukee Brewers (December 22, 2000). ... On disabled list (June 7, 2001-remainder of season); included rehabilitation assignment to AZL Brewers. ... On disabled list (April 15-June 4, 2003); included rehabilitation assignment to AZL and Fresno. ... Released by Brewers (June 4, 2003). ... Signed by San Francisco Giants organization (July 1, 2003). ... On disabled list (March 26-April 10, 2004). ... Released by Giants (June 3, 2004). ... Signed by Montreal Expos organization (December 13, 2004). ... Expos franchise transferred to Washington, D.C., and renamed Washington Nationals for 2005 season (December 3, 2004). ... On disabled list (May 23-June 9, 2005); included rehabilitation assignment to Harrisburg. ... On voluntarily retired list (June 10-November 9, 2005).

2005 GAMES PLAYED BY POSITION (MLB): OF—11, DH—1.

			BATTING																FIELDING	
Year	Team (League)	Pos.	G	AB	R	H	2B	3B	HR	RBI	BB	SO	HBP	GDP	SB-CS	Avg.	OBP	SLG	OPS	E	Avg.
1992	Hagerstown (East.)		Did not play.																		
1993	Bowie (East.)	OF	24	92	13	26	3	0	3	10	9	18	2	1	4-3	.283	.356	.413	.769	0	1.000
—	Rochester (Int'l)	OF	36	151	25	47	9	1	5	23	5	27	2	1	6-3	.311	.338	.483	.821	0	1.000
—	Baltimore (A.L.)	OF-DH	33	105	10	32	8	0	3	19	2	16	0	3	4-0	.305	.312	.467	.779	2	.961
1994	Baltimore (A.L.)	OF	68	250	45	74	18	2	8	31	17	39	2	3	5-0	.296	.339	.480	.819	6	.962
1995	Baltimore (A.L.)	OF-DH	57	178	18	43	9	1	4	23	9	30	1	3	4-2	.242	.279	.371	.650	1	.989
—	Bowie (East.)	OF-DH	9	31	7	12	3	1	1	11	10	7	0	0	3-0	.387	.524	.645	1.169	1	.923
1996	Baltimore (A.L.)	OF-DH	71	248	38	56	10	1	9	27	23	53	4	7	3-3	.226	.301	.383	.684	3	.980
—	Rochester (Int'l)	OF-DH	34	125	24	34	4	2	3	19	19	19	1	2	3-1	.272	.365	.408	.773	1	.987
1997	Baltimore (A.L.)	OF-DH	118	397	71	105	19	3	21	55	32	73	3	6	15-1	.264	.323	.486	.809	5	.980
1998	Baltimore (A.L.)	OF-DH	63	171	36	46	12	1	6	28	26	38	3	2	7-2	.269	.369	.456	.826	2	.980
—	Bowie (East.)	OF	3	6	4	2	0	0	0	0	2	2	1	0	3-1	.333	.556	.333	.889	0	1.000
—	Cincinnati (N.L.)	OF	26	86	14	26	4	1	0	11	13	18	0	0	1-1	.302	.390	.372	.762	1	.985
1999	Cincinnati (N.L.)	OF	123	262	43	73	13	0	17	41	27	64	1	4	3-6	.279	.347	.523	.870	0	1.000
2000	Colorado (N.L.)	OF	122	454	94	152	24	2	20	106	44	83	5	11	14-7	.335	.395	.529	.924	2	.991
2001	Milwaukee (N.L.)	OF	49	174	20	43	11	1	6	21	14	42	4	2	5-3	.247	.314	.425	.740	2	.982
—	Ariz. Brewers (Ariz.)	OF	1	3	0	1	0	0	0	0	0	0	0	0	0-0	.333	.333	.333	.667	0	...
2002	Milwaukee (N.L.)	OF	128	448	47	115	26	5	9	41	52	86	2	13	4-5	.257	.332	.397	.729	2	.992
2003	Milwaukee (N.L.)	OF	10	38	2	6	2	0	1	3	3	7	0	2	0-0	.158	.220	.289	.509	0	1.000
—	Ariz. Giants (Ariz.)	OF	4	10	4	5	1	1	3	6	1	1	0	2	0-0	.500	.545	1.700	2.245	0	1.000
—	Fresno (PCL)	OF-DH	11	36	7	12	1	0	2	2	3	3	0	1	1-0	.333	.385	.528	.912	0	1.000
—	San Francisco (N.L.)	OF	36	94	20	26	10	0	3	10	13	21	1	1	1-0	.277	.370	.479	.849	0	1.000
2004	San Francisco (N.L.)	OF	40	95	14	20	5	0	3	6	15	22	3	2	1-0	.211	.336	.358	.694	0	1.000
2005	New Orleans (PCL)	OF	19	60	10	15	5	1	2	9	7	5	2	2	1-0	.250	.343	.467	.810	0	1.000
—	Washington (N.L.)	OF-DH	13	32	3	7	1	0	0	1	2	4	1	0	0-0	.219	.286	.250	.536	0	1.000
—	Harrisburg (East.)	OF-DH	2	6	1	1	1	0	0	1	1	1	1	1	0-0	.167	.375	.333	.708	0	...
American League totals (6 years)			410	1349	218	356	76	8	51	183	109	249	13	24	38-8	.264	.322	.446	.767	19	.976
National League totals (8 years)			547	1683	257	468	96	9	59	240	183	347	17	35	29-22	.278	.352	.451	.803	7	.993
Major League totals (13 years)			957	3032	475	824	172	17	110	423	292	596	30	59	67-30	.272	.338	.449	.787	26	.985

DIVISION SERIES RECORD

Year	Team (League)	Pos.	G	AB	R	H	2B	3B	HR	RBI	BB	SO	HBP	GDP	SB-CS	Avg.	OBP	SLG	OPS	E	Avg.
1997	Baltimore (A.L.)	OF	4	10	3	1	1	0	0	2	2	2	0	0	1-0	.100	.250	.200	.450	0	1.000
2003	San Francisco (N.L.)	OF	3	5	1	2	0	0	0	0	1	0	1	0	0-0	.400	.571	.400	.971	0	1.000
Division series totals (2 years)			7	15	4	3	1	0	0	2	3	2	1	0	1-0	.200	.368	.267	.635	0	1.000

CHAMPIONSHIP SERIES RECORD

Year	Team (League)	Pos.	G	AB	R	H	2B	3B	HR	RBI	BB	SO	HBP	GDP	SB-CS	Avg.	OBP	SLG	OPS	E	Avg.
1997	Baltimore (A.L.)	OF	5	3	0	0	0	0	0	0	1	2	0	0	1-0	.000	.250	.000	.250	0	1.000

ALL-STAR GAME RECORD

	G	AB	R	H	2B	3B	HR	RBI	BB	SO	HBP	GDP	SB-CS	Avg.	OBP	SLG	OPS	E	Avg.
All-Star Game totals (1 year)	1	1	0	0	0	0	0	0	0	0	0	0	0-0	.000	.000	.000	.000	...	...

HAMPTON, MIKE — P

PERSONAL: Born September 9, 1972, in Brooksville, Fla. ... 5-10/195. ... Throws left, bats right. ... Full name: Michael William Hampton. ... High school: Crystal River (Fla.).

TRANSACTIONS/CAREER NOTES: Selected by Seattle Mariners organization in sixth round of 1990 free-agent draft. ... Traded by Mariners with OF Mike Felder to Houston Astros for OF Eric Anthony (December 10, 1993). ... On disabled list (May 15-June 13, 1995; June 16-July 4, 1998). ... Traded by Astros with OF Derek Bell to New York Mets for OF Roger Cedeno and Ps Octavio Dotel and Kyle Kessel (December 23, 1999). ... Signed as a free agent by Colorado Rockies (December 9, 2000). ... On suspended list (October 3-8, 2001). ... Traded by Rockies with OF Juan Pierre and cash to Florida Marlins for C Charles Johnson, P Vic Darensbourg, OF Preston Wilson and 2B Pablo Ozuna (November 16, 2002). ... Traded by Marlins with cash to Atlanta Braves for Ps Tim Spooneybarger and Ryan Baker (November 18, 2002). ... On disabled list (March 28-April 19, 2003). ... On disabled list (May 16-31, June 5-July 17, July 27-August 14 and August 24-September 11, 2005); included rehabilitation assignments to Richmond and GCL Braves.

HONORS: Named N.L. Pitcher of the Year by THE SPORTING NEWS (1999). ... Won N.L. Gold Glove at pitcher (2003).

MIKE HAMPTON'S PITCHING ZONE

.200	.200	.083
.397	.231	.417
.273	.267	.250

LEFTY-RIGHTY SPLITS

vs.	Avg.	AB	H	2B	3B	HR	RBI	BB	SO	OBP	Slg.
L	.338	65	22	4	0	3	10	5	9	.380	.538
R	.263	198	52	13	0	2	14	13	18	.308	.359

CAREER HITTING: 161-for-664 (.242), 88 R, 19 2B, 5 3B, 15 HR, 68 RBI.

Year	Team (League)	W	L	Pct.	ERA	WHIP	G	GS	CG	ShO	Hld.	Sv.-Opp.	IP	H	R	ER	HR	BB-IBB	SO	Avg.
1990	Ariz. Mariners (Ariz.)	7	2	.778	2.66	1.43	14	13	0	0	...	0-...	64.1	52	32	19	0	40-0	59	.213
1991	San Bern. (Calif.)	1	7	.125	5.25	1.60	18	15	1	1	...	0-...	73.2	71	58	43	3	47-1	57	.249
—	Bellingham (N'west)	5	2	.714	1.58	1.02	9	9	0	0	...	0-...	57.0	32	15	10	0	26-0	65	.162
1992	San Bern. (Calif.)	13	8	.619	3.12	1.35	25	25	6	2	...	0-...	170.0	163	75	59	8	66-1	132	.255
—	Jacksonville (Sou.)	0	1	.000	4.35	1.35	2	2	1	0	...	0-...	10.1	13	5	5	0	1-0	6	.317
1993	Seattle (A.L.)	1	3	.250	9.53	2.65	13	3	0	0	2	1-1	17.0	28	20	18	3	17-3	8	.368
—	Jacksonville (Sou.)	6	4	.600	3.71	1.19	15	14	1	0	...	0-...	87.1	71	43	36	3	33-1	84	.225
1994	Houston (N.L.)	2	1	.667	3.70	1.50	44	0	0	0	10	0-1	41.1	46	19	17	4	16-1	24	.282
1995	Houston (N.L.)	9	8	.529	3.35	1.26	24	24	0	0	0	0-0	150.2	141	73	56	13	49-3	115	.247
1996	Houston (N.L.)	10	10	.500	3.59	1.40	27	27	2	1	0	0-0	160.1	175	79	64	12	49-1	101	.280
1997	Houston (N.L.)	15	10	.600	3.83	1.32	34	34	7	2	0	0-0	223.0	217	105	95	16	77-2	139	.257
1998	Houston (N.L.)	11	7	.611	3.36	1.46	32	32	1	1	0	0-0	211.2	227	92	79	18	81-1	137	.278
1999	Houston (N.L.)	* 22	4	* .846	2.90	1.28	34	34	3	2	0	0-0	239.0	206	86	77	12	101-2	177	.241
2000	New York (N.L.)	15	10	.600	3.14	1.35	33	33	3	1	0	0-0	217.2	194	89	76	10	99-5	151	.241

Year Team (League)	W	L	Pct.	ERA	WHIP	G	GS	CG	ShO	Hld.	Sv.-Opp.	IP	H	R	ER	HR	BB-IBB	SO	Avg.
2001— Colorado (N.L.)	14	13	.519	5.41	1.58	32	32	2	1	0	0-0	203.0	236	138	122	31	85-7	122	.296
2002— Colorado (N.L.)	7	15	.318	6.15	1.79	30	30	1	0	0	0-0	178.2	228	* 135	122	24	91-4	74	.313
2003— Atlanta (N.L.)	14	8	.636	3.84	1.39	31	31	1	0	0	0-0	190.0	186	91	81	14	78-4	110	.255
2004— Atlanta (N.L.)	13	9	.591	4.28	1.53	29	29	1	0	0	0-0	172.1	198	86	82	15	65-3	87	.290
2005— Richmond (Int'l)	0	0	...	2.25	1.00	1	1	0	0	0	0-0	4.0	4	1	1	0	0-0	3	.250
— GC Braves (GCL)	0	0	...	0.00	1.20	1	1	0	0	0	0-0	5.0	6	0	0	0	0-0	4	.300
— Atlanta (N.L.)	5	3	.625	3.50	1.33	12	12	1	1	0	0-0	69.1	74	28	27	5	18-0	27	.281
American League totals (1 year)	1	3	.250	9.53	2.65	13	3	0	0	2	1-1	17.0	28	20	18	3	17-3	8	.368
National League totals (12 years)	137	98	.583	3.93	1.43	362	318	21	9	10	0-1	2057.0	2128	1021	898	174	809-33	1264	.270
Major League totals (13 years)	138	101	.577	3.97	1.44	375	321	21	9	12	1-2	2074.0	2156	1041	916	177	826-36	1272	.271

DIVISION SERIES RECORD

Year Team (League)	W	L	Pct.	ERA	WHIP	G	GS	CG	ShO	Hld.	Sv.-Opp.	IP	H	R	ER	HR	BB-IBB	SO	Avg.
1997— Houston (N.L.)	0	0	.000	11.57	2.14	1	1	0	0	0	0-0	4.2	2	6	6	1	8-0	2	.125
1998— Houston (N.L.)	0	0	...	1.50	0.50	1	1	0	0	0	0-0	6.0	2	1	1	0	1-0	2	.111
1999— Houston (N.L.)	0	0	...	3.86	1.00	1	1	0	0	0	0-0	7.0	6	3	3	1	1-0	9	.231
2000— New York (N.L.)	0	1	.000	8.44	1.69	1	1	0	0	0	0-0	5.1	6	5	5	1	3-1	2	.273
2003— Atlanta (N.L.)	0	1	.000	4.26	1.34	2	2	0	0	0	0-0	12.2	11	6	6	2	6-0	16	.224
2004— Atlanta (N.L.)	0	0	...	2.45	1.09	2	1	0	0	0	0-0	7.1	4	2	2	2	4-0	6	.174
Division series totals (6 years)	0	3	.000	4.81	1.26	8	7	0	0	0	0-0	43.0	31	23	23	7	23-1	37	.201

CHAMPIONSHIP SERIES RECORD

Year Team (League)	W	L	Pct.	ERA	WHIP	G	GS	CG	ShO	Hld.	Sv.-Opp.	IP	H	R	ER	HR	BB-IBB	SO	Avg.
2000— New York (N.L.)	2	0	1.000	0.00	0.81	2	2	1	1	0	0-0	16.0	9	0	0	0	4-0	12	.158

WORLD SERIES RECORD

Year Team (League)	W	L	Pct.	ERA	WHIP	G	GS	CG	ShO	Hld.	Sv.-Opp.	IP	H	R	ER	HR	BB-IBB	SO	Avg.
2000— New York (N.L.)	0	1	.000	6.00	2.17	1	1	0	0	0	0-0	6.0	8	4	4	1	5-1	4	.320

ALL-STAR GAME RECORD

Year Team (League)	W	L	Pct.	ERA	WHIP	G	GS	CG	ShO	Hld.	Sv.-Opp.	IP	H	R	ER	HR	BB-IBB	SO	Avg.
All-Star Game totals (2 years)	0	0	...	0.00	0.60	2	0	0	0	0	0-0	1.2	1	1	0	0	0-0	0	.143

HAMULACK, TIM — P

PERSONAL: Born November 14, 1976, in Ithaca, N.Y. ... 6-4/220. ... Throws left, bats left. ... Full name: Timothy William Alexander Hamulack. ... Junior college: Montgomery (Md.) CC.

TRANSACTIONS/CAREER NOTES: Selected by Houston Astros organization in 32nd round of 1995 free-agent draft. ... Selected by Kansas City Royals organization from Astros in Rule 5 minor league draft (December 11, 2000). ... Traded by Royals to Florida Marlins for cash (December 12, 2000). ... Signed as a free agent by Seattle Mariners organization (November 4, 2002). ... Signed as a free agent by Boston Red Sox (November 19, 2003). ... Signed as a free agent by New York Mets organization (February 1, 2005).

CAREER HITTING: 0-for-0 (.000), 0 R, 0 2B, 0 3B, 0 HR, 0 RBI.

LEFTY-RIGHTY SPLITS

vs.	Avg.	AB	H	2B	3B	HR	RBI	BB	SO	OBP	Slg.
L	.429	7	3	1	0	0	3	0	1	.429	.571
R	.800	5	4	0	0	3	6	1	1	.714	2.600

Year Team (League)	W	L	Pct.	ERA	WHIP	G	GS	CG	ShO	Hld.	Sv.-Opp.	IP	H	R	ER	HR	BB-IBB	SO	Avg.
1996— GC Astros (GCL)	4	1	.800	2.33	1.33	22	0	0	0	...	2-...	27.0	23	9	7	1	13-1	24	.230
1997— GC Astros (GCL)	1	1	.500	4.20	1.64	23	0	0	0	...	9-...	45.0	56	31	21	3	18-0	38	.311
1998— Quad City (Midw.)	0	2	.000	3.24	1.44	52	0	0	0	...	0-...	58.1	58	23	21	3	26-3	52	.265
1999— Michigan (Midw.)	3	0	1.000	3.04	1.28	25	0	0	0	...	0-...	26.2	23	9	9	0	11-0	32	.235
2000— Kissimmee (Fla. St.)	3	1	.750	4.98	1.57	41	0	0	0	...	1-...	56.0	67	37	31	3	21-1	54	.296
2001— Brevard County (FSL)	2	4	.333	3.15	1.46	40	0	0	0	...	1-...	71.1	83	42	25	3	21-1	39	.287
2002— Portland (East.)	8	4	.667	2.88	1.31	38	1	0	0	...	6-...	78.0	73	32	25	6	29-5	53	.252
2003— Tacoma (PCL)	1	0	1.000	3.86	1.71	10	0	0	0	...	1-...	14.0	16	6	6	1	8-0	12	.302
— San Antonio (Texas)	0	1	.000	2.09	0.99	40	0	0	0	...	1-...	47.1	32	13	11	0	15-2	54	.192
2004— Pawtucket (Int'l)	7	4	.636	6.98	2.12	35	0	0	0	...	2-...	29.2	44	26	23	4	19-2	25	.336
— Portland (East.)	2	0	1.000	3.52	1.50	7	0	0	0	...	0-...	15.1	16	6	6	0	7-0	16	.258
2005— Binghamton (East.)	2	2	.500	1.26	0.91	21	0	0	0	1	6-7	28.2	20	7	4	0	6-1	27	.187
— Norfolk (Int'l)	3	1	.750	1.02	0.82	28	0	0	0	4	6-8	35.1	20	5	4	1	9-1	34	.167
— New York (N.L.)	0	0	...	23.14	3.43	6	0	0	0	1	0-0	2.1	7	6	6	3	1-1	2	.583
Major League totals (1 year)	0	0	...	23.14	3.43	6	0	0	0	1	0-0	2.1	7	6	6	3	1-1	2	.583

HANCOCK, JOSH — P

PERSONAL: Born April 11, 1978, in Cleveland, Miss. ... 6-3/205. ... Throws right, bats right. ... Full name: Joshua Morgan Hancock. ... High school: Vestavia Hills (Ala.). ... College: Auburn.

TRANSACTIONS/CAREER NOTES: Selected by Milwaukee Brewers organization in fourth round of 1996 free-agent draft; did not sign. ... Selected by Boston Red Sox organization in fifth round of 1998 free-agent draft. ... Traded by Red Sox to Philadelphia Phillies for 1B/OF Jeremy Giambi (December 15, 2002). ... Traded by Phillies with SS Anderson Machado to Cincinnati Reds for P Todd Jones (July 30, 2004). ... On disabled list (April 2-September 1, 2005); included rehabilitation assignment to Louisville.

CAREER HITTING: 2-for-17 (.118), 1 R, 0 2B, 0 3B, 0 HR, 1 RBI.

JOSH HANCOCK'S PITCHING ZONE

.000	.000	...
.000	.143	.143
.000	.500	.500

LEFTY-RIGHTY SPLITS

vs.	Avg.	AB	H	2B	3B	HR	RBI	BB	SO	OBP	Slg.
L	.111	18	2	0	0	0	1	0	3	.111	.111
R	.257	35	9	3	0	1	4	1	2	.278	.429

Year Team (League)	W	L	Pct.	ERA	WHIP	G	GS	CG	ShO	Hld.	Sv.-Opp.	IP	H	R	ER	HR	BB-IBB	SO	Avg.
1998— GC Red Sox (GCL)	1	1	.500	3.38	0.90	5	1	0	0	...	0-...	13.1	9	5	5	1	3-0	21	.196
— Lowell (NY-Penn)	0	1	.000	2.25	2.25	1	1	0	0	...	0-...	4.0	5	2	1	0	4-0	4	.333
1999— Augusta (S. Atl.)	6	8	.429	3.80	1.43	25	25	0	0	...	0-...	139.2	154	79	59	12	46-0	106	.279
2000— Sarasota (Fla. St.)	5	10	.333	4.45	1.40	26	24	0	0	...	0-...	143.2	164	89	71	9	37-0	95	.284
2001— Trenton (East.)	8	6	.571	3.65	1.34	24	24	0	0	...	0-...	130.2	138	60	53	8	37-0	119	.273
2002— Trenton (East.)	3	4	.429	3.61	1.18	15	14	0	0	...	1-...	84.2	82	40	34	9	18-0	69	.250
— Pawtucket (Int'l)	4	2	.667	3.45	1.47	8	8	0	0	...	0-...	44.1	39	20	17	2	26-0	29	.235
— Boston (A.L.)	0	1	.000	3.68	0.95	3	1	0	0	0	0-0	7.1	5	3	3	1	2-0	6	.200

Year Team (League)	W	L	Pct.	ERA	WHIP	G	GS	CG	ShO	Hld.	Sv.-Opp.	IP	H	R	ER	HR	BB-IBB	SO	Avg.
2003— Scran./W.B. (I.L.)	10	9	.526	3.86	1.20	28	27	2	2	...	0-...	165.2	147	78	71	14	46-1	122	.238
— Philadelphia (N.L.)	0	0	...	3.00	0.67	2	0	0	0	0	0-0	3.0	2	1	1	0	0-0	4	.182
2004— Scran./W.B. (I.L.)	8	7	.533	4.01	1.19	18	18	1	0	...	0-...	107.2	107	52	48	10	21-1	65	.263
— Philadelphia (N.L.)	0	1	.000	9.00	1.78	4	2	0	0	0	0-0	9.0	13	9	9	3	3-0	5	.333
— Cincinnati (N.L.)	5	1	.833	4.45	1.55	12	9	0	0	0	0-0	54.2	60	34	27	14	25-2	31	.273
2005— Louisville (Int'l)	1	2	.333	5.93	1.73	11	8	0	0	1	0-0	44.0	59	33	29	5	17-0	38	.328
— Cincinnati (N.L.)	1	0	1.000	1.93	0.86	11	0	0	0	0	0-0	14.0	11	4	3	1	1-0	5	.208
American League totals (1 year)	0	1	.000	3.68	0.95	3	1	0	0	0	0-0	7.1	5	3	3	1	2-0	6	.200
National League totals (3 years)	6	2	.750	4.46	1.43	29	11	0	0	0	0-0	80.2	86	48	40	18	29-2	45	.266
Major League totals (4 years)	6	3	.667	4.40	1.39	32	12	0	0	0	0-0	88.0	91	51	43	19	31-2	51	.261

HANSEN, CRAIG   P

PERSONAL: Born November 15, 1983, in Glen Cove, N.Y. ... 6-6/210. ... Throws right, bats right. ... Full name: Craig R. Hansen. ... College: St. John's.

TRANSACTIONS/CAREER NOTES: Selected by Boston Red Sox organization in first round (26th pick overall) of 2005 free-agent draft.

CAREER HITTING: 0-for-0 (.000), 0 R, 0 2B, 0 3B, 0 HR, 0 RBI.

LEFTY-RIGHTY SPLITS

vs.	Avg.	AB	H	2B	3B	HR	RBI	BB	SO	OBP	Slg.
L	.600	5	3	0	0	1	0	0	0	.500	.600
R	.333	9	3	1	0	1	2	1	3	.400	.778

Year Team (League)	W	L	Pct.	ERA	WHIP	G	GS	CG	ShO	Hld.	Sv.-Opp.	IP	H	R	ER	HR	BB-IBB	SO	Avg.
2005— GC Red Sox (GCL)	1	0	1.000	0.00	0.67	2	1	0	0	0	0-0	3.0	2	0	0	0	0-0	4	.182
— Portland (East.)	0	0	...	0.00	1.03	8	0	0	0	2	1-1	9.2	9	0	0	0	1-0	10	.243
— Boston (A.L.)	0	0	...	6.00	2.33	4	0	0	0	0	0-1	3.0	6	2	2	1	1-0	3	.429
Major League totals (1 year)	0	0	...	6.00	2.33	4	0	0	0	0	0-1	3.0	6	2	2	1	1-0	3	.429

HANSEN, DAVE   3B/1B

PERSONAL: Born November 24, 1968, in Long Beach, Calif. ... 6-0/195. ... Bats left, throws right. ... Full name: David Andrew Hansen. ... High school: Rowland (Long Beach, Calif.).

TRANSACTIONS/CAREER NOTES: Selected by Los Angeles Dodgers organization in second round of June 1986 free-agent draft. ... On disabled list (May 9-28, 1994). ... Signed as a free agent by Chicago Cubs organization (January 22, 1997). ... Signed by Hanshin of the Japan Central League (November 7, 1997). ... Signed as a free agent by Dodgers (January 11, 1999). ... On disabled list (March 23-April 26, 2001); included rehabilitation assignment to Vero Beach. ... Signed as a free agent by San Diego Padres (December 10, 2002). ... Traded by Padres with P Kevin Jarvis, C Wiki Gonzalez and OF Vince Faison to Seattle Mariners for IF Jeff Cirillo and P Brian Sweeney (January 6, 2004). ... Traded by Mariners to Padres for P Jon Huber (July 30, 2004). ... Signed as a free agent by Chicago Cubs organization (February 4, 2005). ... Released by Cubs (March 31, 2005). ... Signed by Mariners organization (April 26, 2005). ... On disabled list (July 3-26, 2005).

2005 GAMES PLAYED BY POSITION (MLB): 1B—9, 3B—7, DH—5.

SCOUTING REPORT He's a role player whose best asset is his experience off the bench against righthanded pitching. Is a contact hitter with limited power. Is not a good defensive player, either at first base or third. Will have a job because he can hit in key situations. *Grade 4.9*

DAVE HANSEN'S HITTING ZONE

.000	1.000	.000
.273	.400	.222
.000	.167	.100

LEFTY-RIGHTY SPLITS

vs.	Avg.	AB	H	2B	3B	HR	RBI	BB	SO	OBP	Slg.
L	.000	2	0	0	0	0	0	0	2	.000	.000
R	.178	73	13	0	0	2	11	9	17	.262	.260

Year Team (League)	Pos.	G	AB	R	H	2B	3B	HR	RBI	BB	SO	HBP	GDP	SB-CS	Avg.	OBP	SLG	OPS	E	Avg.
1986— Great Falls (Pio.)	2B-3B-C																			
	OF	61	204	39	61	7	3	1	36	27	28	0	6	9-3	.299	.381	.377	.758	7	.901
1987— Bakersfield (Calif.)	3B-OF	132	432	68	113	22	1	3	38	65	61	4	11	4-2	.262	.363	.338	.701	45	.860
1988— Vero Beach (FSL)	3B	135	512	68	149	28	6	7	81	56	46	4	9	2-2	.291	.360	.410	.770	18	.953
1989— San Antonio (Texas)	3B	121	464	72	138	21	4	6	52	50	44	2	18	3-2	.297	.365	.399	.763	16	.949
— Albuquerque (PCL)	3B	6	30	6	8	1	0	2	10	2	3	0	1	0-0	.267	.313	.500	.813	3	.786
1990— Albuquerque (PCL)	3B-OF-SS	135	487	90	154	20	3	11	92	90	54	3	12	9-4	.316	.419	.437	.857	26	.926
— Los Angeles (N.L.)	3B	5	7	0	1	0	0	0	1	0	3	0	0	0-0	.143	.143	.143	.286	1	.500
1991— Albuquerque (PCL)	3B-SS	68	254	42	77	11	1	5	40	49	33	0	7	4-3	.303	.406	.413	.820	6	.966
— Los Angeles (N.L.)	3B-SS	53	56	3	15	4	0	1	5	2	12	0	2	1-0	.268	.293	.393	.686	0	1.000
1992— Los Angeles (N.L.)	3B	132	341	30	73	11	0	6	22	34	49	1	9	0-0	.214	.286	.299	.585	8	.968
1993— Los Angeles (N.L.)	3B	84	105	13	38	3	0	4	30	21	13	0	0	0-1	.362	.465	.505	.969	3	.927
1994— Los Angeles (N.L.)	3B	40	44	3	15	3	0	0	5	5	5	0	0	0-0	.341	.408	.409	.817	1	.857
1995— Los Angeles (N.L.)	3B	100	181	19	52	10	0	1	14	28	28	1	4	0-0	.287	.384	.359	.743	7	.933
1996— Los Angeles (N.L.)	3B-1B	80	104	7	23	1	0	0	6	11	22	0	0	0-0	.221	.293	.231	.524	1	.988
1997— Chicago (N.L.)	3B-1B-2B	90	151	19	47	8	2	3	21	31	32	1	0	1-2	.311	.429	.450	.880	7	.929
1998— Hanshin (Jp. Cn.)	3B	121	400	42	101	13	1	11	55	42	89	...	...	0-...	.253	...	.373	...	...	...
1999— Los Angeles (N.L.)	1B-3B-DH																			
	OF	100	107	14	27	8	1	2	17	26	20	2	2	0-0	.252	.404	.402	.806	3	.962
2000— Los Angeles (N.L.)	1B-3B-DH																			
	OF	102	121	18	35	6	2	8	26	26	32	0	3	0-1	.289	.415	.570	.985	2	.973
2001— Vero Beach (FSL)	3B	3	9	1	0	0	0	0	0	0	1	2	0	0-0	.000	.100	.000	.100	0	1.000
— Los Angeles (N.L.)	1B-3B-DH																			
	SS	92	140	13	33	10	0	2	20	32	29	0	3	0-1	.236	.371	.350	.721	6	.973
2002— Los Angeles (N.L.)	1B-3B-DH	96	120	15	35	6	0	2	17	14	22	0	1	1-0	.292	.363	.392	.755	2	.980
2003— San Diego (N.L.)	1B-3B-DH																			
	2B	110	135	13	33	4	1	2	15	23	25	1	4	1-0	.244	.358	.333	.692	1	.993
2004— Seattle (A.L.)	DH-1B-3B	57	78	14	22	5	0	2	12	18	16	0	3	0-0	.282	.412	.423	.835	0	1.000
— San Diego (N.L.)	3B	29	28	1	4	0	0	0	3	5	6	0	0	0-0	.143	.226	.143	.369	0	1.000
2005— Tacoma (PCL)	DH-1B-3B	6	20	2	6	0	0	0	3	1	4	0	0	0-0	.300	.348	.300	.648	1	.909
— Seattle (A.L.)	1B-3B-DH	60	75	5	13	0	0	2	11	9	19	0	1	1-0	.173	.256	.253	.509	0	1.000
American League totals (2 years)		117	153	19	35	5	0	4	23	27	35	0	4	1-0	.229	.339	.340	.679	0	1.000
National League totals (14 years)		1113	1640	168	431	74	6	31	199	256	297	6	36	4-7	.263	.362	.372	.734	42	.966
Major League totals (15 years)		1230	1793	187	466	79	6	35	222	283	332	6	40	5-7	.260	.360	.369	.729	42	.968

H

DIVISION SERIES RECORD

Year Team (League)	Pos.	G	AB	R	H	2B	3B	HR	RBI	BB	SO	HBP	GDP	SB-CS	Avg.	OBP	SLG	OPS	E	Avg.
1995— Los Angeles (N.L.)		3	3	0	2	0	0	0	0	0	0	0	0	0-0	.667	.667	.667	1.333	...	...
1996— Los Angeles (N.L.)	3B	2	2	0	0	0	0	0	0	0	0	0	0	0-0	.000	.000	.000	.000	0	1.000
Division series totals (2 years)		5	5	0	2	0	0	0	0	0	0	0	0	0-0	.400	.400	.400	.800	0	1.000

HARANG, AARON   P

PERSONAL: Born May 9, 1978, in San Diego. ... 6-7/240. ... Throws right, bats right. ... Full name: Aaron Michael Harang. ... Name pronounced: ha-RANG. ... High school: Patrick Henry (San Diego). ... College: San Diego State.
TRANSACTIONS/CAREER NOTES: Selected by Boston Red Sox organization in 22nd round of 1996 free-agent draft; did not sign. ... Selected by Texas Rangers organization in sixth round of 1999 free-agent draft. ... Traded by Rangers with P Ryan Cullen to Oakland Athletics for 2B Randy Velarde (December 12, 2000). ... Traded by Athletics with Ps Joe Valentine and Jeff Bruksch to Cincinnati Reds for OF Jose Guillen (July 30, 2003). ... On disabled list (June 2-26, 2004); included rehabilitation assignment to Louisville.
CAREER HITTING: 7-for-152 (.046), 2 R, 1 2B, 0 3B, 0 HR, 3 RBI.

SCOUTING REPORT *Throws:* His fastball ranges from 88-93 mph. Also throws a slider, changeup, curveball and split-finger fastball. *Tendencies:* He is an upright pitcher with a deceptive delivery who has improved his ability to throw downhill. Speeds vary widely because he will add and subtract from his fastball. Throws a big, slow looping curve to lefthanders and runs his slider away from righthanders. Is starting to use his splitter more as an out pitch. *Outlook:* Harang provided more quality innings and was the Reds' best overall pitcher last season. Is capable of winning 12 to 15 games per season while pitching in the middle of the rotation. *Grade 7.2*

AARON HARANG'S PITCHING ZONE

.291	.304	.291
.288	.395	.287
.250	.290	.192

LEFTY-RIGHTY SPLITS

vs.	Avg.	AB	H	2B	3B	HR	RBI	BB	SO	OBP	Slg.
L	.253	371	94	27	3	8	44	20	73	.291	.407
R	.279	441	123	25	5	14	46	31	90	.335	.454

Year Team (League)	W	L	Pct.	ERA	WHIP	G	GS	CG	ShO	Hld.	Sv.-Opp.	IP	H	R	ER	HR	BB-IBB	SO	Avg.
1999— Pulaski (Appalachian)	9	2	.818	2.30	1.03	16	10	1	1	...	1-...	78.1	64	22	20	5	17-1	87	.226
2000— Charlotte (Fla. St.)	13	5	.722	3.32	1.13	28	27	3	2	...	0-...	157.0	128	68	58	10	50-0	136	.220
2001— Midland (Texas)	10	8	.556	4.14	1.40	27	27	0	0	...	0-...	150.0	173	81	69	9	37-1	112	.285
2002— Midland (Texas)	2	0	1.000	1.08	1.14	3	3	0	0	...	0-...	16.2	12	3	2	0	7-0	21	.218
— Sacramento (PCL)	3	3	.500	3.26	1.29	8	8	0	0	...	0-...	38.2	41	17	14	0	9-0	39	.301
— Oakland (A.L.)	5	4	.556	4.83	1.57	16	15	0	0	0	0-0	78.1	78	44	42	7	45-2	64	.261
2003— Oakland (A.L.)	1	3	.250	5.34	1.65	7	6	0	0	0	0-0	30.1	41	19	18	5	9-0	16	.331
— Sacramento (PCL)	8	2	.800	2.71	1.10	12	12	0	0	0	0-0	69.2	62	24	21	5	17-0	60	.234
— Louisville (Int'l)	0	1	.000	15.00	2.30	1	1	0	0	0	0-0	3.0	5	5	5	1	2-0	4	.357
— Cincinnati (N.L.)	4	3	.571	5.28	1.26	9	9	0	0	0	0-0	46.0	48	28	27	6	10-0	26	.271
2004— Louisville (Int'l)	0	1	.000	12.00	4.00	1	1	0	0	...	0-...	3.0	9	8	4	1	3-0	3	.529
— Cincinnati (N.L.)	10	9	.526	4.86	1.43	28	28	1	1	0	0-0	161.0	177	90	87	26	53-5	125	.280
2005— Cincinnati (N.L.)	11	13	.458	3.83	1.27	32	32	1	0	0	0-0	211.2	217	93	90	22	51-3	163	.267
American League totals (2 years)	6	7	.462	4.97	1.59	23	21	0	0	0	0-0	108.2	119	63	60	12	54-2	80	.281
National League totals (3 years)	25	25	.500	4.39	1.33	69	69	2	1	0	0-0	418.2	442	211	204	54	114-8	314	.273
Major League totals (4 years)	31	32	.492	4.51	1.38	92	90	2	1	0	0-0	527.1	561	274	264	66	168-10	394	.274

HARDEN, RICH   P

PERSONAL: Born November 30, 1981, in Victoria, British Columbia. ... 6-1/180. ... Throws right, bats left. ... Full name: James Richard Harden. ... High school: Claremont Secondary (Victoria, B.C.). ... Junior college: Central Arizona.
TRANSACTIONS/CAREER NOTES: Selected by Seattle Mariners organization in 38th round of 1999 free-agent draft; did not sign. ... Selected by Oakland Athletics organization in 17th round of 2000 free-agent draft. ... On disabled list (May 15-June 21, 2005); included rehabilitation assignment to Sacramento.
CAREER HITTING: 0-for-5 (.000), 0 R, 0 2B, 0 3B, 0 HR, 0 RBI.

SCOUTING REPORT *Throws:* Harden has one of the game's best arms, throwing an overpowering fastball that can reach 97 mph. Also throws a hard slider and split-finger fastball. *Tendencies:* Harden's four-seam fastball may be the game's best, and it is almost impossible to catch up to it. Has exceptional arm speed, making his fastball appear even faster than it is. Has good command of his slider and late bite on his split-finger fastball. Has an improved delivery and takes outstanding angles to the plate. *Outlook:* The strained oblique muscle Harden suffered last season might continue to cause problems because of his size, but with three above-average pitches and solid command, he is on the verge of having an All-Star career. *Grade 8.7*

RICH HARDEN'S PITCHING ZONE

.267	.188	.294
.255	.347	.099
.323	.333	.103

LEFTY-RIGHTY SPLITS

vs.	Avg.	AB	H	2B	3B	HR	RBI	BB	SO	OBP	Slg.
L	.179	223	40	10	1	2	10	29	67	.276	.260
R	.221	240	53	10	0	5	22	14	54	.266	.325

Year Team (League)	W	L	Pct.	ERA	WHIP	G	GS	CG	ShO	Hld.	Sv.-Opp.	IP	H	R	ER	HR	BB-IBB	SO	Avg.
2001— Vancouver (N'west)	2	4	.333	3.39	1.14	18	14	0	0	...	0-...	74.1	47	29	28	3	38-0	100	.179
2002— Visalia (Calif.)	4	3	.571	2.93	1.08	12	12	1	0	...	0-...	67.2	49	27	22	4	24-0	85	.201
— Midland (Texas)	8	3	.727	2.95	1.39	16	16	1	0	...	0-...	85.1	67	33	28	2	52-1	102	.211
2003— Midland (Texas)	2	0	1.000	0.00	0.00	2	2	0	0	...	0-...	13.0	0	0	0	0	0-0	17	.000
— Sacramento (PCL)	9	4	.692	3.15	1.21	16	14	0	0	...	0-...	88.2	72	34	31	6	35-0	91	.226
— Oakland (A.L.)	5	4	.556	4.46	1.50	15	13	0	0	0	0-0	74.2	72	38	37	5	40-1	67	.259
2004— Sacramento (PCL)	0	0	...	5.40	1.80	1	1	0	0	...	0-...	5.0	6	3	3	0	3-0	6	.300
— Oakland (A.L.)	11	7	.611	3.99	1.33	31	31	0	0	0	0-0	189.2	171	90	84	16	81-6	167	.242
2005— Sacramento (PCL)	0	0	...	0.00	0.33	1	1	0	0	0	0-0	3.0	1	0	0	0	0-0	7	.100
— Oakland (A.L.)	10	5	.667	2.53	1.06	22	19	2	1	1	0-0	128.0	93	42	36	7	43-0	121	.201
Major League totals (3 years)	26	16	.619	3.60	1.27	68	63	2	1	1	0-0	392.1	336	170	157	28	164-7	355	.232

DIVISION SERIES RECORD

Year Team (League)	W	L	Pct.	ERA	WHIP	G	GS	CG	ShO	Hld.	Sv.-Opp.	IP	H	R	ER	HR	BB-IBB	SO	Avg.
2003— Oakland (A.L.)	1	1	.500	13.50	3.00	2	0	0	0	0	0-0	1.1	2	2	2	1	2-1	1	.333

H

HARDY, J.J.   SS

PERSONAL: Born August 19, 1982, in Tucson, Ariz. ... 6-2/181. ... Bats right, throws right. ... Full name: James Jerry Hardy. ... High school: Sabino (Ariz.).
TRANSACTIONS/CAREER NOTES: Selected by Milwaukee Brewers in second round of 2001 free-agent draft.
2005 GAMES PLAYED BY POSITION (MLB): SS—119.

J.J. HARDY'S HITTING ZONE

.450	.455	.294
.214	.378	.317
.079	.176	.235

SCOUTING REPORT **Offense:** After being overmatched early in the season, Hardy became more aggressive in the second half and improved his hitting. Began driving the ball to right-center. Stopped guessing at the plate. Has trouble with inside pitches. Needs to shorten his swing. Needs to get stronger. Is just an average runner at this point. **Defense:** Hardy is a very fluid infielder and has soft hands. Has a very angular frame with a long reach and range to either side. Will have an above-average and accurate arm. **Outlook:** There is no doubt about Hardy's defense, and his improved offense means that the Brewers' shortstop job is his to lose in spring training. Is just getting his feet on the ground at the major league level. *Grade 6*

LEFTY-RIGHTY SPLITS

vs.	Avg.	AB	H	2B	3B	HR	RBI	BB	SO	OBP	Slg.
L	.268	97	26	10	1	4	13	10	13	.336	.515
R	.240	275	66	12	0	5	37	34	35	.324	.338

									BATTING								FIELDING	
Year Team (League)	Pos.	G	AB	R	H	2B	3B	HR	RBI	BB	SO	HBP	GDP	SB-CS	Avg.	OBP	SLG	OPS	E	Avg.
2001— Ariz. Brewers (Ariz.)	SS	5	20	6	5	2	1	0	1	1	2	0	0	0-0	.250	.286	.450	.736	2	.931
— Ogden (Pion.)	SS	35	125	20	31	5	0	2	15	15	12	0	2	1-2	.248	.326	.336	.662	9	.948
2002— High Desert (Calif.)	SS	84	335	53	98	19	1	6	48	19	38	1	3	9-3	.293	.327	.409	.736	11	.973
— Huntsville (Sou.)	SS	38	145	14	33	7	0	1	13	9	19	0	4	1-2	.228	.269	.297	.566	10	.948
2003— Huntsville (Sou.)	SS	114	416	67	116	26	0	12	62	58	54	3	11	6-4	.279	.368	.428	.796	15	.970
2004— Indianapolis (Int'l)	SS	26	101	17	28	10	0	4	20	9	8	0	1	0-0	.277	.330	.495	.825	5	.925
2005— Milwaukee (N.L.)	SS	124	372	46	92	22	1	9	50	44	48	1	10	0-0	.247	.327	.384	.711	10	.975
Major League totals (1 year)		124	372	46	92	22	1	9	50	44	48	1	10	0-0	.247	.327	.384	.711	10	.975

HAREN, DANNY   P

PERSONAL: Born September 17, 1980, in Monterey Park, Calif. ... 6-5/220. ... Throws right, bats right. ... Full name: Daniel John Haren. ... High school: Bishop (La Puente, Calif.). ... College: Pepperdine.
TRANSACTIONS/CAREER NOTES: Selected by St. Louis Cardinals organization in second round of 2001 free-agent draft. ... Traded by Cardinals with P Kiko Calero and C Daric Barton to Oakland Athletics for P Mark Mulder (December 19, 2004).
CAREER HITTING: 4-for-42 (.095), 1 R, 3 2B, 0 3B, 0 HR, 3 RBI.

DANNY HAREN'S PITCHING ZONE

.318	.480	.315
.324	.313	.236
.288	.250	.185

SCOUTING REPORT **Throws:** Haren has a 90-94 mph fastball, a curve and a high-80s splitter. **Tendencies:** Haren has a deceptive delivery that can be tough for hitters to pick up. Has a live fastball both up and down in the zone and occasionally will throw a cutter. Has a big break to his curveball, but it has extremely tight spin. Splitter has excellent velocity with late sinking action and has become a quality out pitch for him. **Outlook:** Haren is turning the corner in his career. Should top 14 wins next season. With Rich Harden and Barry Zito, he gives the A's three excellent starters. *Grade 8*

LEFTY-RIGHTY SPLITS

vs.	Avg.	AB	H	2B	3B	HR	RBI	BB	SO	OBP	Slg.
L	.252	416	105	17	2	13	52	34	84	.305	.397
R	.258	414	107	23	2	13	38	19	79	.301	.418

Year Team (League)	W	L	Pct.	ERA	WHIP	G	GS	CG	ShO	Hld.	Sv.-Opp.	IP	H	R	ER	HR	BB-IBB	SO	Avg.
2001— New Jersey (NYP)	3	3	.500	3.10	1.05	12	8	0	0	...	1-...	52.1	47	22	18	6	8-0	57	.239
2002— Peoria (Midw.)	7	3	.700	1.95	0.99	14	14	1	0	...	0-...	101.2	89	32	22	6	12-0	89	.234
— Potomac (Carol.)	3	6	.333	3.62	1.18	14	14	1	0	...	0-...	92.0	90	43	37	8	19-2	82	.252
2003— Tennessee (Sou.)	6	0	1.000	0.82	0.76	8	8	0	0	...	0-...	55.0	36	8	5	2	6-0	49	.181
— Memphis (PCL)	2	1	.667	4.93	1.27	8	8	0	0	...	0-...	45.2	50	25	25	6	8-1	35	.272
— St. Louis (N.L.)	3	7	.300	5.08	1.46	14	14	0	0	0	0-0	72.2	84	44	41	9	22-0	43	.293
2004— Memphis (PCL)	11	4	.733	4.15	1.33	21	21	0	0	0	0-0	128.0	137	60	59	19	33-1	150	.276
— St. Louis (N.L.)	3	3	.500	4.50	1.35	14	5	0	0	0	0-0	46.0	45	23	23	4	17-2	32	.265
2005— Oakland (A.L.)	14	12	.538	3.73	1.22	34	34	3	0	0	0-0	217.0	212	101	90	26	53-5	163	.255
American League totals (1 year)	14	12	.538	3.73	1.22	34	34	3	0	0	0-0	217.0	212	101	90	26	53-5	163	.255
National League totals (2 years)	6	10	.375	4.85	1.42	28	19	0	0	0	0-0	118.2	129	67	64	13	39-2	75	.282
Major League totals (3 years)	20	22	.476	4.13	1.29	62	53	3	0	0	0-0	335.2	341	168	154	39	92-7	238	.265

DIVISION SERIES RECORD

Year Team (League)	W	L	Pct.	ERA	WHIP	G	GS	CG	ShO	Hld.	Sv.-Opp.	IP	H	R	ER	HR	BB-IBB	SO	Avg.
2004— St. Louis (N.L.)	1	0	1.000	0.00	1.00	1	0	0	0	0	0-0	2.0	1	0	0	0	1-0	3	.143

CHAMPIONSHIP SERIES RECORD

Year Team (League)	W	L	Pct.	ERA	WHIP	G	GS	CG	ShO	Hld.	Sv.-Opp.	IP	H	R	ER	HR	BB-IBB	SO	Avg.
2004— St. Louis (N.L.)	0	0	...	10.80	1.80	2	0	0	0	0	0-0	1.2	3	2	2	1	0-0	2	.375

WORLD SERIES RECORD

Year Team (League)	W	L	Pct.	ERA	WHIP	G	GS	CG	ShO	Hld.	Sv.-Opp.	IP	H	R	ER	HR	BB-IBB	SO	Avg.
2004— St. Louis (N.L.)	0	0	...	0.00	1.50	2	0	0	0	0	0-0	4.2	4	0	0	0	3-0	2	.222

H

HARIKKALA, TIM   P

PERSONAL: Born July 15, 1971, in West Palm Beach, Fla. ... 6-2/185. ... Throws right, bats right. ... Full name: Timothy Allan Harikkala. ... Name pronounced: ha-RICK-a-la. ... High school: Lake Worth Christian (Lantana, Fla.). ... College: Florida Atlantic.

TRANSACTIONS/CAREER NOTES: Selected by Seattle Mariners organization in 34th round of 1992 free-agent draft. ... Signed as a free agent by Boston Red Sox organization (December 14, 1998). ... Signed as a free agent by Milwaukee Brewers organization (April 17, 2000). ... Signed as a free agent by Oaxaca of the Mexican League (April 2003). ... Contract purchased from Oaxaca by Baltimore Orioles organization (July 21, 2003). ... Signed as a free agent by Colorado Rockies organization (November 11, 2003). ... Claimed on waivers by Oakland Athletics (October 6, 2004).

CAREER HITTING: 0-for-3 (.000), 0 R, 0 2B, 0 3B, 0 HR, 0 RBI.

TIM HARIKKALA'S PITCHING ZONE

.500	.000	.167
.273	.500	.333
.000	.000	.600

LEFTY-RIGHTY SPLITS

vs.	Avg.	AB	H	2B	3B	HR	RBI	BB	SO	OBP	Slg.
L	.370	27	10	3	0	2	7	2	4	.414	.704
R	.240	25	6	3	0	1	6	2	3	.296	.480

Year Team (League)	W	L	Pct.	ERA	WHIP	G	GS	CG	ShO	Hld.	Sv.-Opp.	IP	H	R	ER	HR	BB-IBB	SO	Avg.
1992— Bellingham (N'west)	2	0	1.000	2.70	1.59	15	2	0	0	...	1-...	33.1	37	15	10	2	16-0	18	.298
1993— Bellingham (N'west)	1	0	1.000	1.13	0.63	4	0	0	0	...	0-...	8.0	3	1	1	0	2-0	12	.111
— Appleton (Midwest)	3	3	.500	6.52	1.60	15	4	0	0	...	0-...	38.2	50	30	28	3	12-2	33	.316
1994— Appleton (Midwest)	8	3	.727	1.92	0.99	13	13	3	0	...	0-...	93.2	69	31	20	6	24-0	63	.204
— Riverside (Calif.)	4	0	1.000	0.62	0.90	4	4	0	0	...	0-...	29.0	16	6	2	1	10-0	30	.165
— Jacksonville (Sou.)	4	1	.800	3.98	1.64	9	9	0	0	...	0-...	54.1	70	30	24	4	19-0	22	.317
1995— Seattle (A.L.)	0	0	...	16.20	2.40	1	0	0	0	...	0-0	3.1	7	6	6	1	1-0	1	.412
— Tacoma (PCL)	5	12	.294	4.24	1.41	25	24	4	1	...	0-...	146.1	151	78	69	13	55-3	73	.263
1996— Tacoma (PCL)	8	12	.400	4.83	1.59	27	27	1	1	...	0-...	158.1	204	98	85	12	48-2	115	.312
— Seattle (A.L.)	0	1	.000	12.46	1.38	1	1	0	0	0	0-0	4.1	4	6	6	1	2-0	1	.250
1997— Tacoma (PCL)	6	8	.429	6.43	1.85	21	21	0	0	...	0-...	113.1	160	93	81	11	50-2	86	.336
— Memphis (Sou.)	3	1	.750	3.74	1.28	5	5	1	0	...	0-...	33.2	39	18	14	3	4-0	26	.283
1998— Orlando (South.)	5	7	.417	4.53	1.22	15	15	3	2	...	0-...	103.1	112	56	52	9	14-0	55	.279
— Tacoma (PCL)	2	3	.400	4.89	1.53	18	4	1	1	...	1-...	57.0	74	32	31	6	13-0	44	.307
1999— Pawtucket (Int'l)	1	2	.333	5.40	1.70	14	1	0	0	...	0-...	30.0	44	19	18	2	7-1	19	.336
— Boston (A.L.)	1	1	.500	6.23	1.62	7	0	0	0	0	0-0	13.0	15	9	9	0	6-1	7	.306
2000— Huntsville (Sou.)	5	3	.625	2.98	1.28	22	4	0	0	...	0-...	48.1	54	20	16	1	8-0	34	.281
— Indianapolis (Int'l)	4	2	.667	4.52	1.38	14	10	0	0	...	1-...	63.2	73	36	32	5	15-0	22	.285
2001— Indianapolis (Int'l)	11	10	.524	4.76	1.47	31	27	0	0	...	0-...	172.0	210	104	91	15	42-1	96	.304
2002— Indianapolis (Int'l)	8	10	.444	3.50	1.20	31	20	1	0	...	1-...	162.0	172	76	63	8	23-1	90	.271
2003— Oaxaca (Mex.)	3	7	.300	4.63	1.45	12	12	0	0	...	0-...	79.2	98	51	41	5	17-0	50	...
— Ottawa (Int'l)	5	0	1.000	0.81	0.80	20	0	0	0	...	2-...	44.1	27	4	4	0	7-1	29	.176
2004— Colo. Springs (PCL)	0	0	...	4.50	1.75	4	0	0	0	...	3-...	4.0	5	2	2	0	2-1	5	.263
— Colorado (N.L.)	6	6	.500	4.74	1.24	55	0	0	0	15	0-7	62.2	55	34	33	10	23-5	30	.235
2005— Sacramento (PCL)	1	2	.333	1.27	0.94	11	0	0	0	3	3-3	21.1	13	5	3	1	7-3	14	.181
— Oakland (A.L.)	0	0	...	6.39	1.58	8	0	0	0	...	0-...	12.2	16	9	9	3	4-0	7	.308
American League totals (4 years)	1	2	.333	8.10	1.65	17	1	0	0	0	0-0	33.1	42	30	30	5	13-1	16	.313
National League totals (1 year)	6	6	.500	4.74	1.24	55	0	0	0	15	0-7	62.2	55	34	33	10	23-5	30	.235
Major League totals (5 years)	7	8	.467	5.91	1.39	72	1	0	0	15	0-7	96.0	97	64	63	15	36-6	46	.264

HARPER, TRAVIS   P

PERSONAL: Born May 21, 1976, in Harrisonburg, Va. ... 6-4/192. ... Throws right, bats left. ... Full name: Travis Boyd Harper. ... High school: Circleville (W. Va.). ... College: James Madison.

TRANSACTIONS/CAREER NOTES: Selected by New York Mets organization in 14th round of 1994 free-agent draft; did not sign. ... Selected by Boston Red Sox organization in third round of 1997 free-agent draft. ... Contract with Red Sox voided due to pre-existing injury (October 29, 1997). ... Signed by Tampa Bay Devil Rays organization (June 29, 1998).

CAREER HITTING: 0-for-1 (.000), 0 R, 0 2B, 0 3B, 0 HR, 0 RBI.

SCOUTING REPORT **Throws:** His fastball ranges from 87-93 mph. Also has a curveball and a changeup. **Tendencies:** A very loose arm action creates deception with the fastball. Has good command of the pitch to both sides of the plate. Curve breaks early, but the break itself is very quick. Will sink his changeup away from lefthanders. Is very intelligent and has a very good idea of how to change speeds. Is a little more effective to lefthanders with his curve than to righthanders. **Outlook:** Harper basically is a middle reliever who can log innings and prevent his bullpen from being overused. *Grade 6.6*

TRAVIS HARPER'S PITCHING ZONE

.364	.105	.077
.429	.462	.338
.263	.308	.296

LEFTY-RIGHTY SPLITS

vs.	Avg.	AB	H	2B	3B	HR	RBI	BB	SO	OBP	Slg.
L	.292	113	33	5	2	8	27	14	16	.364	.584
R	.313	176	55	10	2	6	27	10	24	.353	.494

Year Team (League)	W	L	Pct.	ERA	WHIP	G	GS	CG	ShO	Hld.	Sv.-Opp.	IP	H	R	ER	HR	BB-IBB	SO	Avg.
1998— Hudson Valley (NYP)	6	2	.750	1.92	1.03	13	10	0	0	...	0-...	56.1	38	14	12	2	20-0	81	.192
1999— St. Pete. (FSL)	5	4	.556	3.43	1.29	14	14	0	0	...	0-...	81.1	82	36	31	4	23-0	79	.265
— Orlando (South.)	6	3	.667	5.38	1.38	14	14	1	1	...	0-...	72.0	73	45	43	10	26-0	68	.263
2000— Orlando (South.)	3	1	.750	2.63	1.17	9	9	0	0	...	0-...	51.1	49	19	15	1	11-0	33	.246
— Durham (Int'l)	7	4	.636	4.24	1.19	17	17	0	0	...	0-...	104.0	98	53	49	15	26-1	48	.246
— Tampa Bay (A.L.)	1	2	.333	4.78	1.41	6	5	1	1	0	0-0	32.0	30	17	17	5	15-0	14	.244
2001— Tampa Bay (A.L.)	0	2	.000	7.71	2.57	2	2	0	0	0	0-0	7.0	15	11	6	5	3-0	2	.455
— Durham (Int'l)	12	6	.667	3.70	1.14	25	25	1	1	...	0-...	155.1	140	70	64	25	38-0	115	.241
2002— Durham (Int'l)	1	2	.333	6.98	1.76	4	4	0	0	...	0-...	19.1	31	15	15	5	3-0	17	.383
— Tampa Bay (A.L.)	5	9	.357	5.46	1.49	37	7	0	0	...	3	1-2	85.2	101	54	52	14	27-3	60	.291
2003— Tampa Bay (A.L.)	4	8	.333	3.77	1.26	61	0	0	0	15	1-6	93.0	86	45	39	9	31-8	64	.252
2004— Durham (Int'l)	1	0	1.000	3.52	1.30	2	1	0	0	...	0-...	7.2	10	3	3	1	0-0	5	.294
— Tampa Bay (A.L.)	6	2	.750	3.89	1.17	52	0	0	0	9	0-1	78.2	69	37	34	8	23-3	59	.234
2005— Tampa Bay (A.L.)	4	6	.400	6.75	1.53	52	0	0	0	11	0-3	73.1	88	57	55	14	24-9	40	.304
Major League totals (6 years)	20	29	.408	4.94	1.39	210	14	1	1	38	2-12	369.2	389	221	203	55	123-23	239	.272

HARRIS, BRENDAN — 3B

PERSONAL: Born August 26, 1980, in Albany, N.Y. ... 6-1/200. ... Bats right, throws right. ... Full name: Brendan Michael Harris. ... High school: Queensbury (N.Y.). ... College: William & Mary.

TRANSACTIONS/CAREER NOTES: Selected by Chicago Cubs organization in fifth round of 2001 free-agent draft. ... Traded by Cubs with SS Alex S. Gonzalez and P Francis Beltran to Montreal Expos as part of four-team deal in which Cubs acquired SS Nomar Garciaparra and OF Matt Murton from Boston Red Sox, Red Sox acquired SS Orlando Cabrera from Expos and 1B Doug Mientkiewicz from Twins, and Twins acquired P Justin Jones from Cubs (July 31, 2004). ... Expos franchise transferred to Washington, D.C., and renamed Washington Nationals for 2005 season (December 3, 2004).

2005 GAMES PLAYED BY POSITION (MLB): 2B—2, 3B—1.

LEFTY-RIGHTY SPLITS

vs.	Avg.	AB	H	2B	3B	HR	RBI	BB	SO	OBP	Slg.
L	.500	2	1	0	0	1	2	0	0	.500	2.000
R	.286	7	2	1	0	0	1	0	0	.375	.429

Year — Team (League)	Pos.	G	AB	R	H	2B	3B	HR	RBI	BB	SO	HBP	GDP	SB-CS	Avg.	OBP	SLG	OPS	E	Avg.
2001—Lansing (Midw.)	2B-3B-SS	32	113	25	31	5	1	4	22	17	26	2	4	5-1	.274	.370	.442	.813	4	.966
2002—Daytona (Fla. St.)	3B-2B	110	425	82	140	35	6	13	54	43	57	4	7	16-4	.329	.395	.532	.926	16	.965
—West Tenn (Sou.)	3B-2B	13	53	8	17	4	1	2	11	2	5	0	1	1-1	.321	.345	.547	.893	0	1.000
2003—West Tenn (Sou.)	3B-2B-SS	120	435	56	122	34	7	5	52	51	72	8	10	6-7	.280	.364	.425	.789	17	.939
2004—Chicago (N.L.)	3B	3	9	0	2	1	0	0	1	1	1	0	0	0-0	.222	.300	.333	.633	1	.889
—Iowa (PCL)	2B-SS-3B																			
	DH	69	254	48	79	21	1	11	35	16	40	1	8	0-2	.311	.353	.531	.882	5	.983
—Edmonton (PCL)	3B	35	130	20	35	6	0	6	24	10	21	1	4	0-0	.269	.317	.454	.811	5	.943
—Montreal (N.L.)	2B-3B	20	50	4	8	2	0	1	2	2	11	1	0	0-0	.160	.208	.260	.468	2	.952
2005—Washington (N.L.)	2B-3B	4	9	1	3	1	0	1	3	0	0	1	2	0-0	.333	.400	.778	1.178	0	1.000
—New Orleans (PCL)	2B-3B-OF	127	470	67	127	22	4	13	81	40	77	3	12	9-5	.270	.329	.417	.746	15	.972
Major League totals (2 years)		27	68	5	13	4	0	2	6	3	12	2	2	0-0	.191	.247	.338	.585	3	.952

HARRIS, JEFF — P

PERSONAL: Born July 4, 1974, in Alameda, Calif. ... 6-1/190. ... Throws right, bats right. ... Full name: Jeffrey Austin Harris. ... College: San Francisco.

TRANSACTIONS/CAREER NOTES: Selected by Minnesota Twins organization in 28th round of 1995 free-agent draft. ... Released by Twins (January 11, 2001). ... Signed by Chico of the independent Western League (May 2002). ... Signed by Quebec of the independent Northeast league (May 2003). ... Signed by Aguascalientes of the Mexican league (April 2004). ... Signed by Quebec (May 2004). ... Signed as a free agent by Seattle Mariners organization (June 4, 2004).

CAREER HITTING: 0-for-0 (.000), 0 R, 0 2B, 0 3B, 0 HR, 0 RBI.

JEFF HARRIS' PITCHING ZONE

.286	.167	.071
.222	.417	.237
.333	.400	.167

LEFTY-RIGHTY SPLITS

vs.	Avg.	AB	H	2B	3B	HR	RBI	BB	SO	OBP	Slg.
L	.180	100	18	5	0	2	13	13	15	.276	.290
R	.294	102	30	2	0	7	16	7	10	.351	.520

Year — Team (League)	W	L	Pct.	ERA	WHIP	G	GS	CG	ShO	Hld.	Sv.-Opp.	IP	H	R	ER	HR	BB-IBB	SO	Avg.
1995—Elizabethton (App.)	1	3	.250	3.82	1.67	21	0	0	0	...	0-...	33.0	42	15	14	2	13-1	27	.309
1996—Fort Wayne (Midw.)	8	3	.727	3.11	1.37	42	0	0	0	...	3-...	89.2	90	35	31	4	33-1	85	.266
1997—Fort Myers (FSL)	2	4	.333	2.14	1.07	24	0	0	0	...	1-...	42.0	30	11	10	4	15-2	32	.207
—New Britain (East.)	2	1	.667	2.34	1.09	28	0	0	0	...	3-...	42.1	30	15	11	2	16-0	44	.199
1998—New Britain (East.)	1	0	1.000	1.66	0.68	26	0	0	0	...	5-...	38.0	21	7	7	3	5-0	40	.160
—Salt Lake (PCL)	8	0	1.000	5.91	1.78	25	0	0	0	...	0-...	32.0	38	24	21	4	19-4	24	.309
1999—Salt Lake (PCL)	4	3	.571	6.90	1.91	36	0	0	0	...	0-...	45.2	61	38	35	7	26-1	20	.332
—New Britain (East.)	3	1	.750	1.48	1.44	20	0	0	0	...	0-...	24.1	21	5	4	0	14-2	12	.239
2000—New Britain (East.)	2	0	1.000	4.82	1.61	24	0	0	0	...	0-...	28.0	35	17	15	5	10-0	28	.313
2001—Chico (West.)	11	7	.611	3.94	1.46	21	20	2	0	...	0-...	130.1	144	78	57	11	46-3	99	.277
2002—Chico (West.)	9	5	.643	2.85	1.11	20	19	3	1	...	0-...	135.2	120	64	43	11	31-2	109	.232
2003—Quebec (Northeast)	9	4	.692	2.51	1.00	18	18	3	2	...	0-...	129.1	107	42	36	6	22-0	119	.226
2004—Aguascal. (Mex.)	0	0	...	6.23	2.08	5	0	0	0	...	2-...	4.1	3	3	3	0	6-0	2	.200
—Tacoma (PCL)	5	3	.625	4.34	1.15	26	8	1	1	...	1-...	74.2	60	37	36	4	26-0	53	.223
—Quebec (Northeast)	0	0	...	0.75	1.08	2	2	0	0	...	0-...	12.0	9	1	1	0	4-1	12	.214
2005—San Antonio (Texas)	5	0	1.000	2.10	0.96	11	2	0	0	1	0-1	34.1	25	9	8	4	8-1	31	.200
—Tacoma (PCL)	5	2	.714	2.78	0.99	16	9	0	0	2	1-1	68.0	50	23	21	8	17-0	56	.207
—Seattle (A.L.)	2	5	.286	4.19	1.27	11	8	0	0	0	0-0	53.2	48	27	25	9	20-2	25	.238
Major League totals (1 year)	2	5	.286	4.19	1.27	11	8	0	0	0	0-0	53.2	48	27	25	9	20-2	25	.238

HARRIS, LENNY — OF

PERSONAL: Born October 28, 1964, in Miami. ... 5-10/234. ... Bats left, throws right. ... Full name: Leonard Anthony Harris. ... High school: Jackson (Miami). ... Junior college: Miami-Dade Community College North.

TRANSACTIONS/CAREER NOTES: Selected by Cincinnati Reds organization in fifth round of June 1983 free-agent draft. ... Loaned by Reds organization to Detroit Tigers organization (May 6-28, 1988). ... Traded by Reds with OF Kal Daniels to Los Angeles Dodgers for P Tim Leary and SS Mariano Duncan (July 18, 1989). ... Signed as a free agent by Reds (December 1, 1993). ... Traded by Reds to New York Mets for P John Hudek (July 3, 1998). ... Signed as a free agent by Colorado Rockies (November 9, 1998). ... Traded by Rockies to Arizona Diamondbacks for IF Belvani Martinez (August 31, 1999). ... Traded by Diamondbacks to Mets for P Bill Pulsipher (June 2, 2000). ... Traded by Mets with P Glendon Rusch to Milwaukee Brewers as part of three-team deal in which Brewers also acquired OF Alex Ochoa from Colorado Rockies, Mets acquired P Jeff D'Amico, OF Jeromy Burnitz, OF/1B Mark Sweeney and IF Lou Collier from Brewers and 1B/OF Ross Gload and P Craig House from Rockies, and Rockies acquired IF Todd Zeile, OF Benny Agbayani and cash from Mets (January 21, 2002). ... Signed as a free agent by Chicago Cubs organization (January 8, 2003). ... Released by Cubs (August 2, 2003). ... Signed by Florida Marlins organization (August 8, 2003). ... Career major league pitching: 0-0, 0.00 ERA, 1 G, 1.0 IP, 0 H, 0 R, 0 ER, 0 BB, 1 SO.

2005 GAMES PLAYED BY POSITION (MLB): 3B—2, DH—2, OF—2, 1B—1.

H

SCOUTING REPORT Harris, the career leader in pinch hits, is able to compensate for declining bat speed with a short stroke and knowledge of pitchers. Is a good fastball hitter who uses the whole field. Doesn't have much power. Has limited range and poor hands. *Grade 5.2*

LENNY HARRIS' HITTING ZONE

.556	.500	.000
.333	.429	.357
.250	.750	.250

LEFTY-RIGHTY SPLITS

vs.	Avg.	AB	H	2B	3B	HR	RBI	BB	SO	OBP	Slg.
L	.333	3	1	1	0	0	1	0	0	.333	.667
R	.313	67	21	3	0	1	12	7	11	.387	.403

Year — Team (League)	Pos.	G	AB	R	H	2B	3B	HR	RBI	BB	SO	HBP	GDP	SB-CS	Avg.	OBP	SLG	OPS	E	Avg.
1983— Billings (Pion.)	3B	56	224	37	63	8	1	1	26	13	35	1	...	7-1	.281	.322	.339	.661	22	.854
1984— Cedar Rap. (Midw.)	3B	132	468	52	115	15	3	6	53	42	59	3	14	31-10	.246	.308	.329	.637	34	.903
1985— Tampa (Fla. St.)	3B	132	499	66	129	11	8	3	51	37	57	1	9	15-8	.259	.307	.331	.638	35	.913
1986— Vermont (East.)	3B-SS	119	450	68	114	17	2	10	52	29	38	6	9	36-10	.253	.307	.367	.670	28	.924
1987— Nashville (A.A.)	3B-SS	120	403	45	100	12	3	2	31	27	43	5	10	30-12	.248	.302	.308	.610	34	.908
1988— Nashville (A.A.)	2B-3B-SS	107	422	46	117	20	2	0	35	22	36	0	13	45-22	.277	.313	.334	.647	25	.947
— Glens Falls (East.)	2B	17	65	9	22	5	1	1	7	9	6	0	1	6-2	.338	.419	.492	.911	5	.947
— Cincinnati (N.L.)	2B-3B	16	43	7	16	1	0	0	8	5	4	0	0	4-1	.372	.420	.395	.815	1	.979
1989— Nashville (A.A.)	2B	8	34	6	9	2	0	3	6	0	5	0	0	0-2	.265	.265	.588	.853	0	1.000
— Cincinnati (N.L.)	2B-3B-SS	61	188	17	42	4	0	2	11	9	20	1	5	10-6	.223	.263	.277	.539	13	.946
— Los Angeles (N.L.)	2B-3B-OF / SS	54	147	19	37	6	1	1	15	11	13	1	9	4-3	.252	.308	.327	.635	2	.978
1990— Los Angeles (N.L.)	2B-3B-OF / SS	137	431	61	131	16	4	2	29	29	31	1	8	15-10	.304	.348	.374	.722	11	.969
1991— Los Angeles (N.L.)	2B-3B-OF / SS	145	429	59	123	16	1	3	38	37	32	5	16	12-3	.287	.349	.350	.698	20	.949
1992— Los Angeles (N.L.)	2B-3B-OF / SS	135	347	28	94	11	0	0	30	24	24	1	10	19-7	.271	.318	.303	.621	27	.943
1993— Los Angeles (N.L.)	2B-3B-OF / OF	107	160	20	38	6	1	2	11	15	15	0	4	3-1	.238	.303	.325	.628	3	.982
1994— Cincinnati (N.L.)	3B-1B-OF / 2B	66	100	13	31	3	1	0	14	5	13	0	0	7-2	.310	.340	.360	.700	6	.903
1995— Cincinnati (N.L.)	3B-1B-OF / 2B	101	197	32	41	8	2	2	16	14	20	1	6	10-1	.208	.259	.310	.569	4	.982
1996— Cincinnati (N.L.)	OF-3B-1B / 2B	125	302	33	86	17	2	5	32	21	31	1	3	14-6	.285	.330	.404	.734	6	.978
1997— Cincinnati (N.L.)	OF-2B-3B / 1B	120	238	32	65	13	1	3	28	18	18	2	10	4-3	.273	.327	.374	.701	3	.983
1998— Cincinnati (N.L.)	OF-DH-P	57	122	12	36	8	0	0	10	8	9	1	8	1-3	.295	.338	.361	.699	3	.929
— New York (N.L.)	OF-3B-2B / 1B	75	168	18	39	7	0	6	17	9	12	1	5	5-2	.232	.272	.381	.653	2	.980
1999— Colorado (N.L.)	2B-OF-3B / DH	91	158	15	47	12	0	0	13	6	6	0	7	1-1	.297	.323	.373	.697	9	.926
— Arizona (N.L.)	3B-OF	19	29	2	11	1	0	1	7	0	1	0	0	1-0	.379	.367	.517	.884	0	1.000
2000— Arizona (N.L.)	3B-OF / 3B-OF-1B	36	85	9	16	1	1	1	13	3	5	0	3	5-0	.188	.209	.259	.468	4	.909
— New York (N.L.)	3B-OF-1B / 2B-DH	76	138	22	42	6	3	3	13	17	17	0	4	8-1	.304	.381	.457	.837	11	.904
2001— New York (N.L.)	3B-OF-1B / DH-2B	110	135	12	30	5	1	0	9	8	9	0	3	3-2	.222	.266	.274	.540	3	.943
2002— Milwaukee (N.L.)	OF-3B-2B / DH	122	197	23	60	8	2	3	17	14	17	2	4	4-1	.305	.355	.411	.766	0	1.000
2003— Chicago (N.L.)	3B-1B-OF	75	131	11	24	3	0	1	7	13	20	0	1	1-0	.183	.255	.229	.484	3	.953
— Albuquerque (PCL)	1B-3B-DH	8	24	3	4	1	0	0	1	4	3	0	1	0-0	.167	.286	.208	.494	1	.979
— Florida (N.L.)	OF	13	14	3	4	0	0	0	1	3	1	0	1	0-0	.286	.412	.286	.697	0	1.000
2004— Florida (N.L.)	OF-3B-DH	79	95	7	20	5	0	1	17	3	8	0	2	0-0	.211	.232	.295	.527	0	1.000
2005— Florida (N.L.)	3B-OF-DH / 1B	83	70	5	22	4	0	1	13	7	11	1	3	0-1	.314	.385	.414	.799	0	1.000
Major League totals (18 years)		1903	3924	460	1055	161	21	37	369	279	337	17	112	131-54	.269	.318	.349	.667	131	.959

DIVISION SERIES RECORD

Year — Team (League)	Pos.	G	AB	R	H	2B	3B	HR	RBI	BB	SO	HBP	GDP	SB-CS	Avg.	OBP	SLG	OPS	E	Avg.
1999— Arizona (N.L.)	3B	2	2	0	0	0	0	0	0	0	0	0	0	0-0	.000	.000	.000	.000	0	...
2000— New York (N.L.)	PH	2	2	1	0	0	0	0	0	0	0	0	0	1-0	.000	.000	.000	.000	0	...
2003— Florida (N.L.)	PH	2	2	0	1	0	0	0	0	0	0	0	0	0-0	.500	.500	.500	1.000	...	...
Division series totals (3 years)		6	6	1	1	0	0	0	0	0	0	0	0	1-0	.167	.167	.167	.333	0	...

CHAMPIONSHIP SERIES RECORD

Year — Team (League)	Pos.	G	AB	R	H	2B	3B	HR	RBI	BB	SO	HBP	GDP	SB-CS	Avg.	OBP	SLG	OPS	E	Avg.
1995— Cincinnati (N.L.)	PH	3	2	0	2	0	0	0	1	0	0	0	0	1-0	1.000	1.000	1.000	2.000	0	...
2000— New York (N.L.)	PH	2	1	0	0	0	0	0	0	0	1	0	0	0-0	.000	.000	.000	.000	0	...
2003— Florida (N.L.)	PH	3	2	0	0	0	0	0	0	1	0	0	0	0-0	.000	.333	.000	.333	0	...
Champ. series totals (3 years)		8	5	0	2	0	0	0	1	1	1	0	0	1-0	.400	.500	.400	.900	0	...

WORLD SERIES RECORD

Year — Team (League)	Pos.	G	AB	R	H	2B	3B	HR	RBI	BB	SO	HBP	GDP	SB-CS	Avg.	OBP	SLG	OPS	E	Avg.
2000— New York (N.L.)	DH	3	4	1	0	0	0	0	0	0	1	1	0	0-0	.000	.200	.000	.200		

H

HARRIS, WILLIE   2B/OF

PERSONAL: Born June 22, 1978, in Cairo, Ga. ... 5-9/170. ... Bats left, throws right. ... Full name: William Charles Harris. ... High school: Cairo (Ga.). ... College: Kennesaw State. ... Nephew of Ernest Riles, infielder with five major league teams (1985-1993).
TRANSACTIONS/CAREER NOTES: Selected by Pittsburgh Pirates organization in 28th round of 1996 free-agent draft; did not sign. ... Selected by Baltimore Orioles organization in 24th round of 1999 free-agent draft. ... Traded by Orioles to Chicago White Sox for OF Chris Singleton (January 29, 2002). ... On disabled list (May 22-June 16, 2003); included rehabilitation assignment to Charlotte.
2005 GAMES PLAYED BY POSITION (MLB): 2B—32, DH—9, SS—5.

SCOUTING REPORT *Offense:* Harris is a better hitter from the left side, but he has improved his bat control. Likes to hit up the middle. Has little power. Needs to keep the ball on the ground and use his speed; is a plus runner who can bunt. Has good basestealing instincts. *Defense:* He is more comfortable in center field than the infield. Doesn't have soft hands and gets inconsistent jumps. Has footwork problems and still has questionable instincts. *Outlook:* Harris has become a role player and he won't hit enough to play regularly. Can pinch hit and run, making him a valuable man off the bench. *Grade 5.8*

WILLIE HARRIS' HITTING ZONE

.000	.333	.143
.500	.643	.115
.000	.333	.286

LEFTY-RIGHTY SPLITS

vs.	Avg.	AB	H	2B	3B	HR	RBI	BB	SO	OBP	Slg.
L	.286	14	4	1	0	0	0	1	3	.333	.357
R	.252	107	27	1	1	1	8	12	22	.333	.308

										BATTING										FIELDING	
Year Team (League)	Pos.	G	AB	R	H	2B	3B	HR	RBI	BB	SO	HBP	GDP	SB-CS	Avg.	OBP	SLG	OPS		E	Avg.
1999— Bluefield (Appal.)	2B	5	22	3	6	1	0	0	3	4	2	0	1	1-0	.273	.370	.318	.689		1	.966
— Delmarva (S. Atl.)	2B-OF	66	272	42	72	13	3	2	32	20	41	1	4	11-11	.265	.313	.357	.670		11	.965
2000— Delmarva (S. Atl.)	2B-OF-SS	133	474	106	130	27	10	6	60	89	89	9	3	38-15	.274	.396	.411	.807		19	.968
2001— Bowie (East.)	2B-OF	133	525	83	160	27	4	9	49	46	71	5	6	54-16	.305	.364	.423	.787		14	.974
— Baltimore (A.L.)	OF	9	24	3	3	1	0	0	0	0	7	0	0	0-0	.125	.125	.167	.292		0	1.000
2002— Charlotte (Int'l)	2B-OF	89	360	54	102	16	5	5	33	33	61	2	4	32-14	.283	.345	.397	.742		6	.986
— Chicago (A.L.)	2B-OF	49	163	14	38	4	0	2	12	9	21	0	3	8-0	.233	.270	.294	.565		3	.986
2003— Charlotte (Int'l)	2B-OF	28	100	22	38	6	1	6	13	17	20	0	1	9-3	.380	.470	.640	1.110		0	1.000
— Chicago (A.L.)	OF-2B	79	137	19	28	3	1	0	5	10	28	0	1	12-2	.204	.259	.342	.499		2	.984
2004— Chicago (A.L.)	2B-OF-DH	129	409	68	107	15	2	2	27	51	79	1	4	19-7	.262	.343	.323	.665		5	.989
2005— Charlotte (Int'l)	2B	28	109	21	29	11	1	1	10	16	27	0	0	10-2	.266	.360	.413	.773		3	.977
— Chicago (A.L.)	2B-DH-SS	56	121	17	31	2	1	1	8	13	25	1	1	10-3	.256	.333	.314	.647		2	.986
Major League totals (5 years)		322	854	121	207	25	4	5	52	83	160	2	9	49-12	.242	.309	.299	.608		12	.987

DIVISION SERIES RECORD

										BATTING										FIELDING	
Year Team (League)	Pos.	G	AB	R	H	2B	3B	HR	RBI	BB	SO	HBP	GDP	SB-CS	Avg.	OBP	SLG	OPS		E	Avg.
2005— Chicago (A.L.)	2B	1	1	0	1	0	0	0	1	0	0	0	0	0-0	1.000	1.000	1.000	2.000		0	1.000

WORLD SERIES RECORD

										BATTING										FIELDING	
Year Team (League)	Pos.	G	AB	R	H	2B	3B	HR	RBI	BB	SO	HBP	GDP	SB-CS	Avg.	OBP	SLG	OPS		E	Avg.
2005— Chicago (A.L.)	2B	2	1	1	1	0	0	0	0	0	0	0	0	1-0	1.000	1.000	1.000	2.000		0	1.000

HART, COREY   3B

PERSONAL: Born March 24, 1982, in Bowling Green, Ky. ... 6-6/200. ... Bats right, throws right. ... Full name: Jon Corey Hart. ... High school: Greenwood (Bowling Green).
TRANSACTIONS/CAREER NOTES: Selected by Milwaukee Brewers organization in 11th round of 2000 free-agent draft.
2005 GAMES PLAYED BY POSITION (MLB): OF—16.

COREY HART'S HITTING ZONE

.000	.000	.000
.182	.333	.167
.167	1.000	.667

LEFTY-RIGHTY SPLITS

vs.	Avg.	AB	H	2B	3B	HR	RBI	BB	SO	OBP	Slg.
L	.211	19	4	0	0	1	4	2	2	.286	.368
R	.184	38	7	2	1	1	3	4	9	.262	.368

										BATTING										FIELDING	
Year Team (League)	Pos.	G	AB	R	H	2B	3B	HR	RBI	BB	SO	HBP	GDP	SB-CS	Avg.	OBP	SLG	OPS		E	Avg.
2000— Ogden (Pion.)	1B	57	216	32	62	9	1	2	30	13	27	2	6	6-0	.287	.332	.366	.698		11	.978
2001— Ogden (Pion.)	1B-OF	69	262	53	89	18	1	11	62	26	47	2	4	14-1	.340	.395	.542	.937		9	.985
2002— High Desert (Calif.)	3B-1B	100	393	76	113	26	10	22	84	37	101	5	3	24-11	.288	.356	.573	.928		22	.959
— Huntsville (Sou.)	3B-1B	28	94	16	25	3	0	2	15	7	16	4	1	3-2	.266	.340	.362	.701		10	.906
2003— Huntsville (Sou.)	3B-OF	130	493	70	149	40	1	13	94	28	101	5	7	25-8	.302	.340	.467	.807		32	.897
2004— Milwaukee (N.L.)	PH	1	0	0	0	0	0	0	0	0	1	0	0	0-0	.000	.000	.000	.000		0	...
— Indianapolis (Int'l)	OF-DH-1B	121	440	68	124	29	8	15	67	42	92	3	6	17-7	.282	.344	.486	.823		9	.954
2005— Nashville (PCL)	OF-DH-1B	113	429	85	132	29	9	17	69	48	88	3	11	31-7	.308	.377	.536	.913		6	.986
— Milwaukee (N.L.)	OF	21	57	9	11	2	1	2	7	6	11	0	6	2-0	.193	.270	.368	.638		1	.966
Major League totals (2 years)		22	58	9	11	2	1	2	7	6	12	0	6	2-0	.190	.266	.362	.628		1	.966

HARVEY, KEN — 1B/DH

PERSONAL: Born March 1, 1978, in Los Angeles. ... 6-2/240. ... Bats right, throws right. ... Full name: Kenneth Eugene Harvey. ... High school: Beverly Hills (Calif.). ... College: Nebraska.
TRANSACTIONS/CAREER NOTES: Selected by Kansas City Royals organization in fifth round of 1999 free-agent draft. ... On disabled list (August 21-September 5, 2004). ... On disabled list (May 19, 2005-remainder of season).
2005 GAMES PLAYED BY POSITION (MLB): DH—7, 1B—5.

LEFTY-RIGHTY SPLITS

vs.	Avg.	AB	H	2B	3B	HR	RBI	BB	SO	OBP	Slg.
L	.263	19	5	2	0	1	4	1	5	.300	.526
R	.192	26	5	1	0	0	1	2	8	.250	.231

Year	Team (League)	Pos.	G	AB	R	H	2B	3B	HR	RBI	BB	SO	HBP	GDP	SB-CS	Avg.	OBP	SLG	OPS	E	Avg.
1999—	Spokane (N'west)	1B	56	204	49	81	17	0	8	41	23	30	8	3	7-1	.397	.477	.598	1.075	5	.984
2000—	Wilmington (Caro.)	1B	46	164	20	55	10	0	4	25	14	29	7	4	0-2	.335	.411	.470	.880	3	.983
2001—	Wilmington (Caro.)	1B	35	137	22	52	9	1	6	27	13	21	6	5	3-1	.380	.455	.591	1.046	3	.984
—	Wichita (Texas)	1B-OF	79	314	54	106	20	3	9	63	18	60	4	12	3-0	.338	.372	.506	.878	5	.990
—	Kansas City (A.L.)	1B-DH	4	12	1	3	1	0	0	2	0	4	0	...	0-1	.250	.250	.333	.583	0	1.000
2002—	Omaha (PCL)	1B	128	488	75	135	30	1	20	75	42	87	8	22	8-3	.277	.342	.465	.807	* 15	.984
2003—	Kansas City (A.L.)	1B-DH	135	485	50	129	30	0	13	64	29	94	5	15	2-3	.266	.313	.408	.721	11	.988
2004—	Kansas City (A.L.)	1B-DH-OF	120	456	47	131	20	1	13	55	28	89	8	14	1-1	.287	.338	.421	.759	4	.994
2005—	Kansas City (A.L.)	DH-1B	12	45	4	10	3	0	1	5	3	13	0	0	0-0	.222	.271	.356	.626	0	1.000
—	Omaha (PCL)	1B-DH	25	104	10	36	4	1	3	18	5	18	0	2	0-0	.346	.373	.490	.863	2	.989
Major League totals (4 years)			271	998	102	273	54	1	27	126	60	200	13	29	3-5	.274	.322	.411	.733	15	.991

ALL-STAR GAME RECORD

	G	AB	R	H	2B	3B	HR	RBI	BB	SO	HBP	GDP	SB-CS	Avg.	OBP	SLG	OPS	E	Avg.
All-Star Game totals (1 year)	1	1	0	0	0	0	0	0	0	1	0	0	0-0	.000	.000	.000	.000	0	...

HARVILLE, CHAD — P

PERSONAL: Born September 16, 1976, in Selmer, Tenn. ... 5-9/185. ... Throws right, bats right. ... Full name: Chad Ashley Harville. ... High school: Hardin County (Savannah, Tenn.). ... College: Memphis.
TRANSACTIONS/CAREER NOTES: Selected by Oakland Athletics organization in second round of 1997 free-agent draft. ... On disabled list (March 31-June 9, 2001); included rehabilitation assignments to Visalia and Modesto. ... Traded by A's to Houston Astros for RHP Kirk Saarloos (April 17, 2004). ... On disabled list (May 6-31, 2004); included rehabilitation assignment to Round Rock. ... Claimed on waivers by Boston Red Sox (August 29, 2005).
CAREER HITTING: 0-for-2 (.000), 0 R, 0 2B, 0 3B, 0 HR, 0 RBI.

SCOUTING REPORT *Throws:* Harville has four pitches: a fastball that ranges from 90-95 mph, a hard curveball at 80, a slider at 85 and a changeup. *Tendencies:* He no longer is focused on power; he's using all his pitches and is developing a feel for pitching. Fastball is straight. More consistent curve allows him to change speeds more effectively. Slider is quick but inconsistent. Straight change is still thrown too hard. *Outlook:* Harville has not moved from middle relief. Makes too many mistakes out over the plate. *Grade 6*

CHAD HARVILLE'S PITCHING ZONE

.200	.333	.444
.296	.294	.172
.227	.667	.158

LEFTY-RIGHTY SPLITS

vs.	Avg.	AB	H	2B	3B	HR	RBI	BB	SO	OBP	Slg.
L	.244	82	20	4	0	4	17	13	18	.347	.439
R	.267	86	23	5	0	4	11	14	18	.394	.465

Year	Team (League)	W	L	Pct.	ERA	WHIP	G	GS	CG	ShO	Hld.	Sv.-Opp.	IP	H	R	ER	HR	BB-IBB	SO	Avg.
1997—	S. Oregon (N'west)	1	0	1.000	0.00	1.20	3	0	0	0	...	0-...	5.0	3	0	0	0	3-0	6	.176
—	Visalia (Calif.)	0	0	...	5.79	2.04	14	0	0	0	...	0-...	18.2	25	14	12	2	13-1	24	.325
1998—	Visalia (Calif.)	4	3	.571	3.00	1.30	24	7	0	0	...	4-...	69.0	59	25	23	0	31-0	76	.230
—	Huntsville (Sou.)	0	0	...	2.45	1.30	12	0	0	0	...	8-...	14.2	6	4	4	0	13-1	24	.122
1999—	Midland (Texas)	2	0	1.000	2.01	0.99	17	0	0	0	...	7-...	22.1	13	6	5	1	9-0	35	.165
—	Vancouver (PCL)	1	0	1.000	1.75	1.36	22	0	0	0	...	11-...	25.2	24	5	5	0	11-1	36	.240
—	Oakland (A.L.)	0	2	.000	6.91	1.95	15	0	0	0	0	0-0	14.1	18	11	11	2	10-1	15	.310
2000—	Sacramento (PCL)	5	3	.625	4.50	1.38	53	0	0	0	...	9-...	64.0	53	35	32	8	35-0	77	.222
2001—	Modesto (California)	0	0	...	3.00	0.67	2	1	0	0	...	0-...	3.0	2	1	1	0	0-0	3	.182
—	Visalia (Calif.)	0	0	...	0.00	1.00	1	1	0	0	...	0-...	3.0	3	0	0	0	0-0	3	.250
—	Sacramento (PCL)	5	2	.714	3.98	1.16	33	0	0	0	...	8-...	40.2	35	20	18	5	12-0	55	.230
—	Oakland (A.L.)	0	0	...	0.00	0.67	3	0	0	0	1	0-0	3.0	2	0	0	0	0-0	2	.182
2002—	Sacramento (PCL)	1	2	.333	5.40	1.50	24	0	0	0	...	5-...	30.0	32	19	18	5	13-1	26	.274
2003—	Sacramento (PCL)	3	5	.375	2.05	1.10	48	0	0	0	...	18-...	57.0	42	16	13	5	21-2	57	.202
—	Oakland (A.L.)	1	0	1.000	5.82	1.94	21	0	0	0	0	1-1	21.2	25	15	14	2	17-1	18	.294
2004—	Oakland (A.L.)	0	0	...	3.38	1.13	3	0	0	0	1	0-0	2.2	2	1	1	0	1-0	0	.200
—	Round Rock (Texas)	0	0	...	0.00	0.67	2	0	0	0	...	0-...	3.0	0	0	0	0	2-0	2	.000
—	Houston (N.L.)	3	2	.600	4.75	1.51	56	0	0	0	3	0-4	53.0	54	35	28	8	26-2	46	.260
2005—	Houston (N.L.)	0	2	.000	4.46	1.57	37	0	0	0	2	0-1	38.1	36	21	19	7	24-1	33	.254
—	Boston (A.L.)	0	1	.000	6.43	1.43	8	0	0	0	0	0-0	7.0	7	5	5	1	3-0	3	.269
American League totals (5 years)		1	3	.250	5.73	1.75	50	0	0	0	2	1-1	48.2	54	32	31	6	31-2	38	.284
National League totals (2 years)		3	4	.429	4.63	1.53	93	0	0	0	5	0-5	91.1	90	56	47	15	50-3	79	.257
Major League totals (5 years)		4	7	.364	5.01	1.61	143	0	0	0	7	1-6	140.0	144	88	78	21	81-5	117	.267

DIVISION SERIES RECORD

Year	Team (League)	W	L	Pct.	ERA	WHIP	G	GS	CG	ShO	Hld.	Sv.-Opp.	IP	H	R	ER	HR	BB-IBB	SO	Avg.
2004—	Houston (N.L.)	0	0	...	0.00	0.00	1	0	0	0	0	0-0	0.2	0	0	0	0	0-0	0	.000

CHAMPIONSHIP SERIES RECORD

Year	Team (League)	W	L	Pct.	ERA	WHIP	G	GS	CG	ShO	Hld.	Sv.-Opp.	IP	H	R	ER	HR	BB-IBB	SO	Avg.
2004—	Houston (N.L.)	0	0	...	13.50	3.00	3	0	0	0	0	0-0	1.1	3	2	2	1	1-0	3	.429

H

HASEGAWA, SHIGETOSHI   P

PERSONAL: Born August 1, 1968, in Kobe, Japan. ... 5-11/180. ... Throws right, bats right. ... Name pronounced: shig-eh-TOE-shi hoss-eh-GAWA. ... High school: Toyodai Himeji (Japan). ... College: Ritsumeikan University (Japan) .
TRANSACTIONS/CAREER NOTES: Signed as a free agent by Anaheim Angels (January 9, 1997). ... On disabled list (May 20-June 29, 2001); included rehabilitation assignment to Rancho Cucamonga. ... Signed as a free agent by Seattle Mariners (January 23, 2002).
CAREER HITTING: 0-for-1 (.000), 0 R, 0 2B, 0 3B, 0 HR, 0 RBI.

SCOUTING REPORT *Throws:* He has a sinker, a straight two-seam fastball that tops out at 90 mph, a slider and a forkball. *Tendencies:* Hasegawa, who has a herky-jerky delivery, seems to have lost some of the late action on his pitches; his frequent appearances the past several years have caught up to him. Fastball sinks when it's down in the zone and the slider breaks late. Splitter has more tumbling action than before. *Outlook:* Would pitch better if he wasn't overexposed. *Grade 6.9*

SHIGETOSHI HASEGAWA'S PITCHING ZONE

.250	.667	.375
.200	.263	.261
.100	.211	.200

LEFTY-RIGHTY SPLITS

vs.	Avg.	AB	H	2B	3B	HR	RBI	BB	SO	OBP	Slg.
L	.281	121	34	5	1	0	16	3	12	.302	.339
R	.239	134	32	5	0	4	15	13	18	.311	.366

Year Team (League)	W	L	Pct.	ERA	WHIP	G	GS	CG	ShO	Hld.	Sv.-Opp.	IP	H	R	ER	HR	BB-IBB	SO	Avg.
1991— Orix (Jap. Pacific)	12	9	.571	3.55	1.26	28	25	11	3	...	1-...	185.0	184	76	73	...	50-...	111	...
1992— Orix (Jap. Pacific)	6	8	.429	3.27	1.32	24	19	4	0	...	1-...	143.1	138	60	52	...	51-...	86	...
1993— Orix (Jap. Pacific)	12	6	.667	2.71	1.22	23	22	9	3	...	0-...	159.2	146	61	48	...	48-...	86	...
1994— Orix (Jap. Pacific)	11	9	.550	3.11	1.38	25	22	8	3	...	1-...	156.1	169	61	54	...	46-...	86	...
1995— Orix (Jap. Pacific)	12	7	.632	2.89	1.27	24	23	9	4	...	0-...	171.0	167	62	55	...	51-...	91	...
1996— Orix (Jap. Pacific)	4	6	.400	5.34	1.70	18	16	2	0	...	1-...	87.2	109	60	52	...	40-...	55	...
1997— Anaheim (A.L.)	3	7	.300	3.93	1.41	50	7	0	0	3	0-1	116.2	118	60	51	14	46-6	83	.269
1998— Anaheim (A.L.)	8	3	.727	3.14	1.21	61	0	0	0	10	5-7	97.1	86	37	34	14	32-2	73	.241
1999— Anaheim (A.L.)	4	6	.400	4.91	1.48	64	1	0	0	6	2-5	77.0	80	45	42	14	34-2	44	.276
2000— Anaheim (A.L.)	10	5	.667	3.48	1.44	66	0	0	0	19	9-18	95.2	100	42	37	11	38-6	59	.270
2001— Anaheim (A.L.)	5	6	.455	4.04	1.29	46	0	0	0	12	0-6	55.2	52	28	25	2	20-5	41	.248
— Rancho Cuca. (Calif.)	0	0	...	0.00	1.50	2	2	0	0	...	0-...	2.0	3	1	0	0	1-0	1	.375
2002— Seattle (A.L.)	8	3	.727	3.20	1.28	53	0	0	0	8	1-5	70.1	60	26	25	4	30-8	39	.238
2003— Seattle (A.L.)	2	4	.333	1.48	1.10	63	0	0	0	12	16-17	73.0	62	12	12	5	18-3	32	.235
2004— Seattle (A.L.)	4	6	.400	5.16	1.44	68	0	0	0	3	0-1	68.0	67	42	39	5	31-4	46	.260
2005— Seattle (A.L.)	1	3	.250	4.19	1.23	46	0	0	0	3	0-1	66.2	66	31	31	4	16-1	30	.259
Major League totals (9 years)	45	43	.511	3.70	1.33	517	8	0	0	85	33-65	720.1	691	323	296	76	265-37	447	.256

ALL-STAR GAME RECORD

	W	L	Pct.	ERA	WHIP	G	GS	CG	ShO	Hld.	Sv.-Opp.	IP	H	R	ER	HR	BB-IBB	SO	Avg.
All-Star Game totals (1 year)	0	0	...	54.00	6.00	1	0	0	0	0	0-0	0.2	3	4	4	1	1-0	1	.600

HATTEBERG, SCOTT   1B

PERSONAL: Born December 14, 1969, in Salem, Ore. ... 6-1/210. ... Bats left, throws right. ... Full name: Scott Allen Hatteberg. ... Name pronounced: HATT-eh-berg. ... High school: Eisenhower (Yakima, Wash.). ... College: Washington State.
TRANSACTIONS/CAREER NOTES: Selected by Philadelphia Phillies organization in 12th round of 1988 free-agent draft; did not sign. ... Selected by Boston Red Sox organization in supplemental round ("sandwich pick" between first and second round, 43rd pick overall) of 1991 free-agent draft; pick received as part of compensation for Kansas City Royals signing Type A free-agent P Mike Boddicker. ... On disabled list (April 15-May 7 and May 17-August 16, 1999); included rehabilitation assignments to Pawtucket, GCL Red Sox and Sarasota. ... Traded by Red Sox to Colorado Rockies for 2B Pokey Reese (December 19, 2001). ... Signed as a free agent by Oakland Athletics (January 2, 2002).
2005 GAMES PLAYED BY POSITION (MLB): DH—79, 1B—53.

SCOUTING REPORT *Offense:* Hatteberg, one of the most patient hitters in the A's lineup, has a compact stroke. Is a high-ball hitter but doesn't have a lot of power. Became more pull-conscious during the season and had problems with lefthanders. Still is a good situational hitter who makes contact. *Defense:* He catches what he can get to at first but doesn't have a lot of range. Has really learned to handle throws in the dirt well. *Outlook:* He's not the run-producing type of first baseman most clubs look for, but he has shown an ability to hit in the clutch. Better in a platoon role against righthanders. *Grade 6.5*

SCOTT HATTEBERG'S HITTING ZONE

.100	.233	.290
.311	.433	.289
.269	.182	.135

LEFTY-RIGHTY SPLITS

vs.	Avg.	AB	H	2B	3B	HR	RBI	BB	SO	OBP	Slg.
L	.214	117	25	4	0	2	17	15	23	.311	.299
R	.271	347	94	15	0	5	42	36	31	.342	.357

Year Team (League)	Pos.	G	AB	R	H	2B	3B	HR	RBI	BB	SO	HBP	GDP	SB-CS	Avg.	OBP	SLG	OPS	E	Avg.
1991— Winter Haven (FSL)	C	56	191	21	53	7	3	1	25	22	22	0	6	1-2	.277	.349	.361	.710	5	.983
— Lynchburg (Caro.)	C	8	25	4	5	1	0	0	2	7	6	0	0	0-0	.200	.375	.240	.615	0	1.000
1992— New Britain (East.)	C	103	297	28	69	13	2	1	30	41	49	2	6	1-3	.232	.327	.300	.626	11	.979
1993— New Britain (East.)	C	68	227	35	63	10	2	7	28	42	38	1	6	1-3	.278	.393	.432	.824	10	.978
— Pawtucket (Int'l)	C	18	53	6	10	0	0	1	3	6	12	1	0	0-0	.189	.283	.245	.529	5	.964
1994— New Britain (East.)	C	20	68	6	18	4	1	1	9	7	9	0	2	0-2	.265	.329	.397	.726	1	.993
— Pawtucket (Int'l)	C	78	238	26	56	14	0	7	19	32	49	3	14	2-1	.235	.332	.382	.714	7	.986
1995— Pawtucket (Int'l)	C-DH	85	251	36	68	15	1	7	27	40	39	4	8	2-0	.271	.376	.422	.798	• 8	.984
— Boston (A.L.)	C	2	2	1	1	0	0	0	0	0	1	0	0	0-0	.500	.500	.500	1.000	0	1.000
1996— Pawtucket (Int'l)	C-DH	90	287	52	77	16	0	12	49	58	66	2	6	1-1	.268	.391	.449	.841	6	.990
— Boston (A.L.)	C	10	11	3	2	1	0	0	3	2	0	0	0	0-0	.182	.357	.273	.630	0	1.000
1997— Boston (A.L.)	C-DH	114	350	46	97	23	4	10	44	40	70	2	11	0-1	.277	.354	.434	.788	11	.983

H

BATTING

Year Team (League)	Pos.	G	AB	R	H	2B	3B	HR	RBI	BB	SO	HBP	GDP	SB-CS	Avg.	OBP	SLG	OPS	FIELDING E	Avg.
1998— Boston (A.L.)	C	112	359	46	99	23	1	12	43	43	58	5	11	0-0	.276	.359	.446	.804	5	.993
1999— Boston (A.L.)	C-DH	30	80	12	22	5	0	1	11	18	14	1	2	0-0	.275	.410	.375	.785	1	.993
— Pawtucket (Int'l)	C-DH	10	34	3	6	2	0	0	4	4	6	0	2	0-0	.176	.263	.235	.498	0	1.000
— GC Red Sox (GCL)	C-DH	6	15	4	6	2	0	1	6	7	1	0	1	0-0	.400	.591	.733	1.324	0	1.000
— Sarasota (Fla. St.)	C	1	1	0	1	0	0	0	1	0	0	1	0	0-0	1.000	1.000	1.000	2.000	0	1.000
2000— Boston (A.L.)	C-DH-3B	92	230	21	61	15	0	8	36	38	39	0	8	0-0	.265	.367	.435	.801	6	.981
2001— Boston (A.L.)	C-DH	94	278	34	68	19	0	3	25	33	26	4	7	1-1	.245	.332	.345	.678	4	.992
2002— Oakland (A.L.)	1B-DH	136	492	58	138	22	4	15	61	68	56	6	8	0-1	.280	.374	.433	.807	5	.994
2003— Oakland (A.L.)	1B-DH	147	541	63	137	34	0	12	61	66	53	9	14	0-1	.253	.342	.383	.725	10	.992
2004— Oakland (A.L.)	1B-DH	152	550	87	156	30	0	15	82	72	48	5	10	0-0	.284	.367	.420	.787	10	.993
2005— Oakland (A.L.)	DH-1B	134	464	52	119	19	0	7	59	51	54	4	22	0-0	.256	.334	.343	.677	7	.985
Major League totals (11 years)		1023	3357	423	900	191	6	83	422	432	420	36	96	1-5	.268	.356	.403	.758	59	.991

DIVISION SERIES RECORD

Year Team (League)	Pos.	G	AB	R	H	2B	3B	HR	RBI	BB	SO	HBP	GDP	SB-CS	Avg.	OBP	SLG	OPS	E	Avg.
1998— Boston (A.L.)	C	3	9	0	1	0	0	0	0	3	1	0	0	0-0	.111	.333	.111	.444	0	1.000
1999— Boston (A.L.)	C	1	1	1	1	0	0	0	1	0	0	0	0	0-0	1.000	1.000	1.000	2.000	0	1.000
2002— Oakland (A.L.)	1B	5	14	5	7	2	0	1	3	3	0	0	0	0-0	.500	.588	.857	1.445	1	.973
2003— Oakland (A.L.)	1B	5	17	3	3	0	0	0	0	5	3	0	0	0-0	.176	.364	.176	.540	0	1.000
Division series totals (4 years)		14	41	9	12	2	0	1	4	11	4	0	0	0-0	.293	.442	.415	.857	1	.990

CHAMPIONSHIP SERIES RECORD

Year Team (League)	Pos.	G	AB	R	H	2B	3B	HR	RBI	BB	SO	HBP	GDP	SB-CS	Avg.	OBP	SLG	OPS	E	Avg.
1999— Boston (A.L.)	C	3	1	0	0	0	0	0	0	0	1	0	0	0-0	.000	.000	.000	.000	0	

HAWKINS, LATROY   P

PERSONAL: Born December 21, 1972, in Gary, Ind. ... 6-5/215. ... Throws right, bats right. ... Full name: LaTroy Hawkins. ... High school: West Side (Gary, Ind.).
TRANSACTIONS/CAREER NOTES: Selected by Minnesota Twins organization in seventh round of 1991 free-agent draft. ... Signed as a free agent by Chicago Cubs (December 3, 2003). ... On suspended list (August 13-17, 2004). ... Traded by Cubs to San Francisco Giants for Ps Jerome Williams and David Aardsma (May 28, 2005). ... On disabled list (June 17-July 4, 2005); included rehabilitation assignment to Fresno.
CAREER HITTING: 0-for-5 (.000), 0 R, 0 2B, 0 3B, 0 HR, 0 RBI.

SCOUTING REPORT Throws: His riding fastball clocks in at 92-97 mph. Also has a slider in the mid- to upper 80s and a changeup. *Tendencies:* The durable Hawkins has an extremely loose arm. Fastball is overpowering; it's light and lively with excellent riding action. Is able to keep the ball down better. No longer throws his curve. The one drawback to his stuff is that he's easy to follow and time. *Outlook:* Hawkins definitely can't close, as he has proven with several teams. Still can be one of the better setup relievers. *Grade 7.6*

LATROY HAWKINS' PITCHING ZONE

.438	.250	.269
.200	.462	.267
.238	.286	.154

LEFTY-RIGHTY SPLITS

vs.	Avg.	AB	H	2B	3B	HR	RBI	BB	SO	OBP	Slg.
L	.228	101	23	6	1	2	16	10	24	.295	.366
R	.297	118	35	5	0	5	14	14	19	.371	.466

Year Team (League)	W	L	Pct.	ERA	WHIP	G	GS	CG	ShO	Hld.	Sv.-Opp.	IP	H	R	ER	HR	BB-IBB	SO	Avg.
1991— GC Twins (GCL)	4	3	.571	4.75	1.60	11	11	0	0	...	0-...	55.0	62	34	29	2	26-0	47	.281
1992— GC Twins (GCL)	3	2	.600	3.22	1.27	6	6	1	0	...	0-...	36.1	36	19	13	1	10-0	35	.281
— Elizabethton (App.)	0	1	.000	3.38	1.20	5	5	1	0	...	0-...	26.2	21	12	10	2	11-0	36	.202
1993— Fort Wayne (Midw.)	15	5	.750	2.06	0.96	26	23	4	3	...	0-...	157.1	110	53	36	5	41-0	179	.195
1994— Fort Myers (FSL)	4	0	1.000	2.33	0.98	6	6	1	1	...	0-...	38.2	32	10	10	1	6-0	36	.224
— Nashville (Southern)	9	2	.818	2.33	1.06	11	11	1	0	...	0-...	73.1	50	23	19	2	28-0	53	.191
— Salt Lake (PCL)	5	4	.556	4.08	1.53	12	12	1	0	...	0-...	81.2	92	42	37	8	33-0	37	.296
1995— Minnesota (A.L.)	2	3	.400	8.67	1.89	6	6	1	0	0	0-0	27.0	39	29	26	3	12-0	9	.339
— Salt Lake (PCL)	9	7	.563	3.55	1.32	22	22	4	1	...	0-...	144.1	150	63	57	7	40-1	74	.271
1996— Minnesota (A.L.)	1	1	.500	8.20	1.94	7	6	0	0	0	0-0	26.1	42	24	24	8	9-0	24	.372
— Salt Lake (PCL)	9	8	.529	3.92	1.23	20	20	4	1	...	0-...	137.2	138	66	60	11	31-3	99	.263
1997— Minnesota (A.L.)	9	4	.692	5.45	1.53	14	13	2	1	0	0-0	76.0	100	53	46	4	16-1	53	.311
— Minnesota (A.L.)	6	12	.333	5.84	1.75	20	20	0	0	0	0-0	103.1	134	71	67	19	47-0	58	.317
1998— Minnesota (A.L.)	7	14	.333	5.25	1.51	33	33	0	0	0	0-0	190.1	227	126	111	27	61-1	105	.294
1999— Minnesota (A.L.)	10	14	.417	6.66	1.71	33	33	1	0	0	0-0	174.1	238	*136	*129	29	60-2	103	.323
2000— Minnesota (A.L.)	2	5	.286	3.39	1.33	66	0	0	0	7	14-14	87.2	85	34	33	7	32-1	59	.256
2001— Minnesota (A.L.)	1	5	.167	5.96	1.91	62	0	0	0	1	28-37	51.1	59	34	34	3	39-3	36	.291
2002— Minnesota (A.L.)	6	0	1.000	2.13	0.97	65	0	0	0	13	0-3	80.1	63	23	19	5	15-1	63	.217
2003— Minnesota (A.L.)	9	3	.750	1.86	1.09	74	0	0	0	28	2-8	77.1	69	20	16	4	15-1	75	.239
2004— Chicago (N.L.)	5	4	.556	2.63	1.05	77	0	0	0	4	25-34	82.0	72	27	24	10	14-5	69	.233
2005— Chicago (N.L.)	1	4	.200	3.32	1.32	21	0	0	0	4	4-8	19.0	18	9	7	4	7-0	13	.250
— Fresno (PCL)	0	0	...	0.00	1.00	2	0	0	0	1	0-0	2.0	2	0	0	0	0-0	1	.250
— San Francisco (N.L.)	1	4	.200	4.10	1.53	45	0	0	0	15	2-7	37.1	40	18	17	3	17-3	30	.272
American League totals (9 years)	44	57	.436	5.05	1.52	366	98	2	0	49	44-62	818.0	956	497	459	105	290-9	532	.293
National League totals (2 years)	7	12	.368	3.12	1.21	143	0	0	0	19	31-49	138.1	130	54	48	17	38-8	112	.246
Major League totals (11 years)	51	69	.425	4.77	1.48	509	98	2	0	68	75-111	956.1	1086	551	507	122	328-17	644	.287

DIVISION SERIES RECORD

Year Team (League)	W	L	Pct.	ERA	WHIP	G	GS	CG	ShO	Hld.	Sv.-Opp.	IP	H	R	ER	HR	BB-IBB	SO	Avg.
2002— Minnesota (A.L.)	0	0	...	0.00	0.00	3	0	0	0	1	0-0	2.1	0	0	0	0	0-0	5	.000
2003— Minnesota (A.L.)	1	0	1.000	6.00	1.67	3	0	0	0	1	0-0	3.0	5	3	2	0	0-0	5	.357
Division series totals (2 years)	1	0	1.000	3.38	0.94	6	0	0	0	2	0-0	5.1	5	3	2	0	0-0	10	.238

CHAMPIONSHIP SERIES RECORD

Year Team (League)	W	L	Pct.	ERA	WHIP	G	GS	CG	ShO	Hld.	Sv.-Opp.	IP	H	R	ER	HR	BB-IBB	SO	Avg.
2002— Minnesota (A.L.)	0	0	...	20.25	3.75	4	0	0	0	0	0-0	1.1	4	3	3	0	1-0	1	.571

H

HAWPE, BRAD — OF

PERSONAL: Born June 22, 1979, in Fort Worth, Texas. ... 6-3/200. ... Bats left, throws left. ... Full name: Bradley Bonte Hawpe. ... Name pronounced: HOP. ... High school: Boswell (Fort Worth). ... College: Louisiana State.
TRANSACTIONS/CAREER NOTES: Selected by Toronto Blue Jays organization in 46th round of 1997 free-agent draft; did not sign. ... Selected by Colorado Rockies organization in 11th round of 2000 free-agent draft. ... On disabled list (July 15-September 2, 2005); included rehabilitation assignment to Colorado Springs.
2005 GAMES PLAYED BY POSITION (MLB): OF—89.

SCOUTING REPORT Hawpe, a pitcher in college, has a strong arm even for a right fielder. Learning to get better jumps and take better routes but is a below-average runner who may not have much range. Has good bat speed and plate coverage. Will start to show more power as he learns to sit on pitches. **Grade 5.1**

BRAD HAWPE'S HITTING ZONE

.182	.455	.167
.333	.462	.302
.150	.500	.250

LEFTY-RIGHTY SPLITS

	Avg.	AB	H	2B	3B	HR	RBI	BB	SO	OBP	Slg.
L	.250	28	7	1	0	1	5	4	8	.344	.393
R	.264	277	73	9	3	8	42	39	62	.351	.404

| | | | | | | | | | BATTING | | | | | | | | | | | FIELDING | |
Year Team (League)	Pos.	G	AB	R	H	2B	3B	HR	RBI	BB	SO	HBP	GDP	SB-CS	Avg.	OBP	SLG	OPS	E	Avg.
2000— Portland (N'west)	OF-1B	62	205	38	59	19	2	7	29	40	51	2	1	2-0	.288	.398	.502	.900	5	.983
2001— Asheville (S. Atl.)	OF-1B	111	393	78	105	23	3	22	72	59	113	6	8	7-4	.267	.363	.506	.870	11	.981
2002— Salem (Carol.)	1B	122	450	87	156	38	2	22	97	81	84	2	7	1-1	.347	.447	.587	1.033	8	.994
2003— Tulsa (Texas)	OF-1B	93	346	52	96	27	0	17	68	31	84	1	5	1-3	.277	.338	.503	.841	6	.976
2004— Colo. Springs (PCL)	OF-DH	92	345	62	111	19	1	31	86	36	91	1	10	3-2	.322	.384	.652	1.035	3	.984
— Colorado (N.L.)	OF	42	105	12	26	3	2	3	9	11	34	1	4	1-1	.248	.322	.400	.722	1	.982
2005— Colo. Springs (PCL)	OF-DH	7	28	7	13	3	0	3	11	6	7	0	2	0-0	.464	.559	.893	1.452	0	1.000
— Colorado (N.L.)	OF	101	305	38	80	10	3	9	47	43	70	0	5	2-2	.262	.350	.403	.754	3	.981
Major League totals (2 years)		143	410	50	106	13	5	12	56	54	104	1	9	3-3	.259	.343	.402	.746	4	.982

HEILMAN, AARON — P

PERSONAL: Born November 12, 1978, in Logansport, Ind. ... 6-5/220. ... Throws right, bats right. ... Full name: Aaron Michael Heilman. ... Name pronounced: HILE-man. ... High school: Logansport (Ind.). ... College: Notre Dame.
TRANSACTIONS/CAREER NOTES: Selected by New York Yankees organization in 55th round of 1997 free-agent draft; did not sign. ... Selected by Minnesota Twins organization in supplemental round ("sandwich" pick between first and second rounds, 31st pick overall) of 2000 free-agent draft; did not sign; pick received as part of compensation for Baltimore Orioles signing Type A free-agent P Mike Trombley. ... Selected by New York Mets organization in first round (18th pick overall) of 2001 free-agent draft.
CAREER HITTING: 1-for-43 (.023), 1 R, 0 2B, 0 3B, 0 HR, 1 RBI.

SCOUTING REPORT Throws: He has a fastball that touches 94 mph, a slider, a changeup and a forkball. **Tendencies:** Heilman has dropped his arm angle to three-quarters, which creates more deception as he dives toward the hitter. Fastball has good late life as it dives from lefthanders with a sinking action; rides his four-seamer up and in on righthanders. Slider is more of a slurve, but often is flat. Forkball is similar in movement and velocity to his change. **Outlook:** One of the most improved N.L. pitchers in 2005, Heilman has a good idea of how to pitch and, as his confidence has risen, has become more aggressive in attacking the zone. Throws harder in relief appearances than in starts. **Grade 6.4**

AARON HEILMAN'S PITCHING ZONE

.214	.200	.217
.317	.294	.206
.161	.185	.340

LEFTY-RIGHTY SPLITS

	Avg.	AB	H	2B	3B	HR	RBI	BB	SO	OBP	Slg.
L	.208	183	38	6	0	3	17	25	47	.313	.290
R	.236	208	49	4	1	3	20	12	59	.286	.308

Year Team (League)	W	L	Pct.	ERA	WHIP	G	GS	CG	ShO	Hld.	Sv.-Opp.	IP	H	R	ER	HR	BB-IBB	SO	Avg.
2001— St. Lucie (Fla. St.)	0	1	.000	2.35	1.02	7	7	0	0	...	0-...	38.1	26	11	10	0	13-0	39	.190
2002— Binghamton (East.)	4	4	.500	3.82	1.17	17	17	0	0	...	0-...	96.2	85	43	41	7	28-2	97	.237
— Norfolk (Int'l)	2	3	.400	3.28	1.18	10	7	0	0	...	0-...	49.1	42	18	18	3	16-1	35	.240
2003— Norfolk (Int'l)	6	4	.600	3.24	1.39	16	16	0	0	...	0-...	94.1	99	37	34	5	32-0	71	.274
— New York (N.L.)	2	7	.222	6.75	1.84	14	13	0	0	0	0-0	65.1	79	53	49	13	41-2	51	.300
2004— Norfolk (Int'l)	7	10	.412	4.33	1.46	26	26	1	0	...	0-...	151.2	156	88	73	15	66-0	123	.264
— New York (N.L.)	1	3	.250	5.46	1.43	5	5	0	0	0	0-0	28.0	27	17	17	4	13-0	22	.257
2005— New York (N.L.)	5	3	.625	3.17	1.15	53	7	1	1	5	5-6	108.0	87	40	38	6	37-4	106	.223
Major League totals (3 years)	8	13	.381	4.65	1.41	72	25	1	1	5	5-6	201.1	193	110	104	23	91-6	179	.254

HEINTZ, CHRIS — C

PERSONAL: Born August 6, 1974, in Syosset, N.Y. ... 6-1/210. ... Bats right, throws right. ... Full name: Christopher John Heintz. ... College: South Florida.
TRANSACTIONS/CAREER NOTES: Selected by Chicago White Sox organization in 19th round of 1996 free-agent draft. ... Released by White Sox (January 8, 2002). ... Signed by St. Louis Cardinals organization (January 25, 2002). ... Signed as a free agent by Pittsburgh Pirates organization (December 2, 2002). ... Signed as a free agent by Minnesota Twins organization (November 21, 2003).
2005 GAMES PLAYED BY POSITION (MLB): C—8.

LEFTY-RIGHTY SPLITS

	Avg.	AB	H	2B	3B	HR	RBI	BB	SO	OBP	Slg.
L	.231	13	3	2	0	0	0	0	4	.231	.385
R	.167	12	2	1	0	0	2	1	2	.231	.250

| | | | | | | | | | BATTING | | | | | | | | | | | FIELDING | |
Year Team (League)	Pos.	G	AB	R	H	2B	3B	HR	RBI	BB	SO	HBP	GDP	SB-CS	Avg.	OBP	SLG	OPS	E	Avg.
1996— Bristol (Appal.)	1B	8	29	7	10	7	0	2	8	4	2	0	0	1-1	.345	.424	.793	1.217	4	.939
— South Bend (Mid.)	3B-1B	64	230	25	61	12	1	1	22	23	46	3	3	1-1	.265	.339	.339	.678	14	.943
1997— Hickory (S. Atl.)	1B-C	107	388	57	110	28	1	2	54	28	57	9	6	1-3	.284	.342	.376	.718	10	.990
1998— Win.-Salem (Car.)	1B-C-3B	130	508	66	147	21	4	8	79	31	87	5	17	10-8	.289	.331	.394	.725	18	.984
1999— Win.-Salem (Car.)	1B-C-3B	118	417	55	122	33	4	7	60	40	72	4	7	6-3	.293	.359	.432	.791	16	.982

H

Year	Team (League)	Pos.	G	AB	R	H	2B	3B	HR	RBI	BB	SO	HBP	GDP	SB-CS	Avg.	OBP	SLG	OPS	E	Avg.
																				FIELDING	
2000— Birmingham (Sou.)	C-3B	73	239	27	64	15	1	2	34	21	33	0	2	4-1	.268	.320	.364	.684	8	.984
2001— Birmingham (Sou.)	C-3B	37	119	14	28	8	0	2	8	10	23	2	2	0-2	.235	.303	.353	.656	4	.982
— Charlotte (Int'l)	C	5	10	1	1	1	0	0	1	0	3	0	0	0-0	.100	.091	.200	.291	0	1.000
2002— New Haven (East.)	C-1B-3B	105	373	40	117	29	1	7	45	19	61	2	13	1-0	.314	.349	.453	.802	8	.986
2003— Altoona (East.)	C	78	271	28	70	12	4	2	26	19	24	3	6	0-0	.258	.313	.354	.667	5	.991
2004— Rochester (Int'l)	C-3B	86	294	33	82	14	0	8	45	16	40	3	6	0-2	.279	.318	.408	.726	5	.991
2005— Rochester (Int'l)	DH-C-3B	89	329	38	100	18	2	8	58	22	61	0	16	0-0	.304	.343	.444	.786	5	.981
— Minnesota (A.L.)	C	8	25	1	5	3	0	0	2	1	6	0	1	0-0	.200	.231	.320	.551	0	1.000
Major League totals (1 year)		8	25	1	5	3	0	0	2	1	6	0	1	0-0	.200	.231	.320	.551	0	1.000

HELLING, RICK   P

PERSONAL: Born December 15, 1970, in Devils Lake, N.D. ... 6-3/241. ... Throws right, bats right. ... Full name: Ricky Allen Helling. ... High school: Lakota (Fargo, N.D.), then Shanley (Fargo, N.D.). ... College: Stanford.

TRANSACTIONS/CAREER NOTES: Selected by New York Mets organization in 50th round of 1990 free-agent draft; did not sign. ... Selected by Texas Rangers organization in first round (22nd pick overall) of 1992 free-agent draft. ... Traded by Rangers to Florida Marlins (September 3, 1996), completing deal in which Rangers acquired P John Burkett for P Ryan Dempster and a player to be named (August 8, 1996). ... Traded by Marlins to Rangers for P Ed Vosberg (August 12, 1997). ... Signed as a free agent by Arizona Diamondbacks (January 19, 2002). ... On Arizona disabled list (July 16-August 7, 2002); included rehabilitation assignment to Tucson. ... Signed as a free agent by Baltimore Orioles organization (February 11, 2003). ... Released by Orioles (August 18, 2003). ... Signed as a free agent by Marlins (August 22, 2003). ... Signed as a free agent by Minnesota Twins organization (January 13, 2004). ... Signed as a free agent by Rangers organization (June 8, 2004). ... Released by Rangers (July 16, 2004). ... Signed by Milwaukee Brewers organization (January 13, 2005).

CAREER HITTING: 6-for-101 (.059), 4 R, 1 2B, 0 3B, 0 HR, 1 RBI.

RICK HELLING'S PITCHING ZONE

.294	.000	.083
.250	.231	.214
.353	.111	.444

LEFTY-RIGHTY SPLITS

vs.	Avg.	AB	H	2B	3B	HR	RBI	BB	SO	OBP	Slg.
L	.219	73	16	2	0	1	9	10	12	.310	.288
R	.219	105	23	5	0	1	6	8	30	.287	.295

Year	Team (League)	W	L	Pct.	ERA	WHIP	G	GS	CG	ShO	Hld.	Sv.-Opp.	IP	H	R	ER	HR	BB-IBB	SO	Avg.
1992— Charlotte (Fla. St.)	1	1	.500	2.29	0.86	3	3	0	0	...	0-...	19.2	13	5	5	1	4-0	20	.181
1993— Tulsa (Texas)	12	8	.600	3.60	1.11	26	26	2	2	...	0-...	177.1	150	76	71	14	46-1	*188	.227
— Okla. City (A.A.)	1	1	.500	1.64	0.73	2	2	1	0	...	0-...	11.0	5	3	2	0	3-0	17	.135
1994— Texas (A.L.)	3	2	.600	5.88	1.54	9	9	1	1	0	0-0	52.0	62	34	34	14	18-0	25	.295
— Okla. City (A.A.)	4	12	.250	5.78	1.48	20	20	1	1	0	0-0	132.1	153	93	85	17	43-2	85	.295
1995— Texas (A.L.)	0	2	.000	6.57	2.03	3	3	0	0	0	0-0	12.1	17	11	9	2	8-0	5	.340
— Okla. City (A.A.)	4	8	.333	5.33	1.58	20	20	3	0	0	0-0	109.2	132	73	65	13	41-1	85	.304
1996— Okla. City (A.A.)	12	4	.750	2.96	1.16	23	22	0	1	...	0-...	140.0	124	54	46	10	38-1	157	.238
— Texas (A.L.)	1	2	.333	7.52	1.57	6	2	0	0	1	0-0	20.1	23	17	17	7	9-0	16	.280
— Florida (N.L.)	2	1	.667	1.95	0.76	5	4	0	0	0	0-0	27.2	14	6	6	2	7-0	26	.143
1997— Florida (N.L.)	2	6	.250	4.38	1.43	31	8	0	0	6	0-1	76.0	61	38	37	12	48-2	53	.232
— Texas (A.L.)	3	3	.500	4.58	1.24	10	8	0	0	0	0-0	55.0	47	29	28	5	21-0	46	.235
1998— Texas (A.L.)	*20	7	.741	4.41	1.33	33	33	4	2	0	0-0	216.1	209	109	106	27	78-6	164	.253
1999— Texas (A.L.)	13	11	.542	4.84	1.43	35	*35	3	0	0	0-0	219.1	228	127	118	*41	85-5	131	.272
2000— Texas (A.L.)	16	13	.552	4.48	1.43	35	•35	0	0	0	0-0	217.0	212	122	108	29	99-2	146	.252
2001— Texas (A.L.)	12	11	.522	5.17	1.48	34	34	2	1	0	0-0	215.2	*256	*134	*124	*38	63-2	154	.297
2002— Arizona (N.L.)	10	12	.455	4.51	1.30	30	30	0	0	0	0-0	175.2	180	94	88	31	48-6	120	.264
— Tucson (PCL)	1	0	1.000	1.29	0.71	1	1	0	0	...	0-...	7.0	4	1	1	0	1-0	7	.167
2003— Baltimore (A.L.)	7	8	.467	5.71	1.41	24	24	0	0	0	0-0	138.2	156	90	88	30	40-0	86	.286
— Florida (N.L.)	1	0	1.000	0.55	0.98	11	0	0	0	1	0-0	16.1	11	1	1	1	5-0	12	.193
2004— New Britain (East.)	1	2	.333	4.94	1.32	5	5	0	0	0	0-0	31.0	30	18	17	5	11-0	21	.261
— Rochester (Int'l)	1	0	1.000	0.00	0.71	1	1	1	1	0	0-0	7.0	4	0	0	0	1-0	2	.167
— Oklahoma (PCL)	1	4	.200	9.00	2.26	6	6	0	0	0	0-0	31.0	59	35	31	8	11-0	20	.440
2005— Nashville (PCL)	9	3	.750	4.13	1.36	21	21	0	0	0	0-0	130.2	128	74	60	12	50-1	105	.256
— Milwaukee (N.L.)	3	1	.750	2.39	1.16	15	7	0	0	2	0-0	49.0	39	13	13	2	18-1	42	.219
American League totals (9 years)	75	59	.560	4.96	1.42	189	183	10	4	1	0-0	1146.2	1210	673	632	193	421-15	773	.272
National League totals (5 years)	18	20	.474	3.79	1.25	92	49	0	0	9	0-1	344.2	305	152	145	48	126-9	253	.239
Major League totals (11 years)	93	79	.541	4.69	1.38	281	232	10	4	10	0-1	1491.1	1515	825	777	241	547-24	1026	.264

DIVISION SERIES RECORD

Year	Team (League)	W	L	Pct.	ERA	WHIP	G	GS	CG	ShO	Hld.	Sv.-Opp.	IP	H	R	ER	HR	BB-IBB	SO	Avg.
1998— Texas (A.L.)	0	1	.000	4.50	1.50	1	1	0	0	0	0-0	6.0	8	3	3	2	1-0	9	...
1999— Texas (A.L.)	0	1	.000	2.84	0.95	1	1	0	0	0	0-0	6.1	5	2	2	0	1-0	8	...
2002— Arizona (N.L.)	0	0	...	0.00	0.25	2	0	0	0	0	0-0	4.0	1	0	0	0	0-0	2	.077
2003— Florida (N.L.)	0	0	...	27.00	12.00	1	0	0	0	0	0-0	0.1	2	1	1	0	2-1	0	.667
Division series totals (4 years)	0	2	.000	3.24	1.20	5	2	0	0	0	0-0	16.2	16	6	6	2	4-1	19	1.000

CHAMPIONSHIP SERIES RECORD

Year	Team (League)	W	L	Pct.	ERA	WHIP	G	GS	CG	ShO	Hld.	Sv.-Opp.	IP	H	R	ER	HR	BB-IBB	SO	Avg.
2003— Florida (N.L.)	0	0	...	6.35	1.94	2	0	0	0	0	0-0	5.2	7	5	4	2	4-1	5	.304

WORLD SERIES RECORD

Year	Team (League)	W	L	Pct.	ERA	WHIP	G	GS	CG	ShO	Hld.	Sv.-Opp.	IP	H	R	ER	HR	BB-IBB	SO	Avg.
2003— Florida (N.L.)	0	0	...	6.75	0.75	1	0	0	0	0	0-0	2.2	2	2	2	1	0-0	2	.200

H

HELMS, WES   3B/1B

PERSONAL: Born May 12, 1976, in Gastonia, N.C. ... 6-4/231. ... Bats right, throws right. ... Full name: Wesley Ray Helms. ... High school: Ashbrook (Gastonia, N.C.).
TRANSACTIONS/CAREER NOTES: Selected by Atlanta Braves organization in 10th round of 1994 free-agent draft. ... On disabled list (April 3-July 15 and September 5, 1999-remainder of season); included rehabilitation assignment to GCL Braves. ... On disabled list (August 10-September 10, 2002). ... Traded by Braves with P John Foster to

Milwaukee Brewers for P Ray King (December 16, 2002). ... On disabled list (August 7-22, 2003); included rehabilitation assignment to Indianapolis. ... On disabled list (May 19-June 28, 2004); included rehabilitation assignment to Indianapolis.

2005 GAMES PLAYED BY POSITION (MLB): 3B—35, 1B—16, DH—3.

SCOUTING REPORT *Offense:* Helms is using his hands more after widening his stance and switching to a smaller stride. Is a good fastball hitter. Has good knowledge of the strike zone and is an effective pinch hitter. Is not a good runner or a threat to steal bases. *Defense:* Helms is a slightly rigid fielder who doesn't have much quickness or range. Has improved his throwing accuracy. Charges the ball well and has better agility to his left. *Outlook:* Helms is a good fit as a role player and has become a good pinch hitter, but he doesn't have enough power to play every day.
Grade 6.1

WES HELMS' HITTING ZONE

.455	.111	.300
.333	.600	.143
.333	.200	.273

LEFTY-RIGHTY SPLITS

vs.	Avg.	AB	H	2B	3B	HR	RBI	BB	SO	OBP	Slg.
L	.301	83	25	6	1	3	15	10	19	.375	.506
R	.294	85	25	7	0	1	9	4	11	.337	.412

											BATTING								FIELDING	
Year	Team (League)	Pos.	G	AB	R	H	2B	3B	HR	RBI	BB	SO	HBP	GDP	SB-CS	Avg.	OBP	SLG	OPS	E	Avg.
1994— GC Braves (GCL)	3B	56	184	22	49	15	1	4	29	22	36	4	3	6-1	.266	.355	.424	.779	20	.875
1995— Macon (S. Atl.)	3B	136	* 539	89	149	32	1	11	85	50	107	10	8	2-2	.276	.347	.401	.748	40	.900
1996— Durham (Carol.)	3B	67	258	40	83	19	2	13	54	12	51	7	7	1-1	.322	.367	.562	.929	15	.920
— Greenville (Sou.)	3B	64	231	24	59	13	2	4	22	13	48	4	6	2-1	.255	.306	.381	.687	12	.924
1997— Richmond (Int'l)	3B	32	110	11	21	4	0	3	15	10	34	5	4	1-1	.191	.286	.309	.595	9	.902
— Greenville (Sou.)	3B	86	314	50	93	14	1	11	44	33	50	6	14	3-4	.296	.371	.452	.823	11	.950
1998— Richmond (Int'l)	3B-DH	125	451	56	124	27	1	13	75	35	103	13	11	6-2	.275	.342	.426	.768	15	.952
— Atlanta (N.L.)	3B	7	13	2	4	1	0	1	2	0	4	0	0	0-0	.308	.308	.615	.923	1	.750
1999— GC Braves (GCL)	DH-1B	9	33	1	15	2	0	0	10	5	4	1	1	0-1	.455	.538	.515	1.054	0	1.000
— Greenville (Sou.)	1B	30	113	15	34	6	0	8	26	7	34	1	3	1-0	.301	.347	.566	.913	4	.984
2000— Richmond (Int'l)	3B	136	539	74	155	27	7	20	88	27	92	6	10	0-6	.288	.325	.475	.800	23	.933
— Atlanta (N.L.)	3B	6	5	0	1	0	0	0	0	0	2	0	0	0-0	.200	.200	.200	.400	1	.833
2001— Atlanta (N.L.)	1B-3B-OF	100	216	28	48	10	3	10	36	21	56	1	3	1-1	.222	.293	.435	.728	4	.992
2002— Atlanta (N.L.)	1B-3B-OF	85	210	20	51	16	0	6	22	11	57	3	5	1-1	.243	.283	.405	.687	5	.986
2003— Indianapolis (Int'l)	3B	2	5	0	2	0	0	0	0	1	1	0	0	0-0	.400	.500	.400	.900	0	1.000
— Milwaukee (N.L.)	3B	134	476	56	124	21	0	23	67	43	131	10	10	0-1	.261	.330	.450	.780	19	.945
2004— Indianapolis (Int'l)	3B-DH	6	19	4	6	1	0	0	1	3	4	0	0	0-0	.316	.409	.368	.778	2	.857
— Milwaukee (N.L.)	3B-1B	92	274	24	72	13	1	4	28	24	60	5	10	0-1	.263	.331	.361	.692	18	.925
2005— Milwaukee (N.L.)	3B-1B-DH	95	168	18	50	13	1	4	24	14	30	3	7	0-1	.298	.356	.458	.815	3	.982
Major League totals (7 years)		519	1362	148	350	74	5	48	179	113	340	22	35	2-5	.257	.320	.424	.744	51	.968

DIVISION SERIES RECORD

Year	Team (League)	Pos.	G	AB	R	H	2B	3B	HR	RBI	BB	SO	HBP	GDP	SB-CS	Avg.	OBP	SLG	OPS	E	Avg.
2002— Atlanta (N.L.)	1B	1	0	0	0	0	0	0	0	0	0	0	0	0-0	...	...	...	...	0	...

HELTON, TODD — 1B

PERSONAL: Born August 20, 1973, in Knoxville, Tenn. ... 6-2/204. ... Bats left, throws left. ... Full name: Todd Lynn Helton. ... High school: Knoxville (Tenn.) Central. ... College: Tennessee.

TRANSACTIONS/CAREER NOTES: Selected by San Diego Padres organization in second round of 1992 free-agent draft; did not sign. ... Selected by Colorado Rockies organization in first round (eighth pick overall) of 1995 free-agent draft. ... On disabled list (July 26-August 10, 2005); included rehabilitation assignment to Colorado Springs.

HONORS: Named N.L. Rookie Player of the Year by THE SPORTING NEWS (1998). ... Won N.L. Gold Glove at first base (2001, 2002 and 2004).

2005 GAMES PLAYED BY POSITION (MLB): 1B—144.

SCOUTING REPORT *Offense:* Helton is one of the game's best pure hitters. Has an outstanding swing and a consistent approach at the plate. Has exceptional balance and uses the whole field. Adjusts quickly to off-speed and breaking pitches. Keeps his bat in the hitting zone longer than most players. Is a good baserunner but has below-average speed. *Defense:* Helton, an excellent athlete for a first baseman, has good agility and soft hands. Is adept at handling throws in the dirt and starting double plays. Is aggressive in bunt situations. Has above-average arm strength and accuracy. *Outlook:* He's one of the game's steadiest players and is underrated because he plays at Coors Field; he would hit anywhere. Starting to show some frustration playing for a team that hasn't won. *Grade 9.4*

TODD HELTON'S HITTING ZONE

.385	.222	.357
.241	.400	.347
.256	.276	.322

LEFTY-RIGHTY SPLITS

vs.	Avg.	AB	H	2B	3B	HR	RBI	BB	SO	OBP	Slg.
L	.245	155	38	6	1	1	17	24	33	.361	.316
R	.353	354	125	39	1	19	62	82	47	.480	.630

											BATTING								FIELDING	
Year	Team (League)	Pos.	G	AB	R	H	2B	3B	HR	RBI	BB	SO	HBP	GDP	SB-CS	Avg.	OBP	SLG	OPS	E	Avg.
1995— Asheville (S. Atl.)	1B-DH	54	201	24	51	11	1	1	15	25	32	1	7	1-1	.254	.339	.333	.673	4	.990
1996— New Haven (East.)	1B-DH	93	319	46	106	24	2	7	51	51	37	1	8	2-5	.332	.425	.486	.911	5	.994
— Colo. Springs (PCL)	1B-OF	21	71	13	25	4	1	2	13	11	12	0	3	0-0	.352	.439	.521	.960	2	.988
1997— Colo. Springs (PCL)	1B-OF-DH	99	392	87	138	31	2	16	88	61	68	0	10	3-1	.352	.434	.564	.997	9	.987
— Colorado (N.L.)	OF-1B	35	93	13	26	2	1	5	11	8	11	0	1	0-1	.280	.337	.484	.821	0	1.000
1998— Colorado (N.L.)	1B	152	530	78	167	37	1	25	97	53	54	6	15	3-3	.315	.380	.530	.911	7	.995
1999— Colorado (N.L.)	1B	159	578	114	185	39	5	35	113	68	77	6	14	7-6	.320	.395	.587	.981	9	.993
2000— Colorado (N.L.)	1B	160	580	138	* 216	* 59	2	42	* 147	103	61	4	12	5-3	* .372	* .463	* .698	1.162	7	.995
2001— Colorado (N.L.)	1B	159	587	132	197	54	2	49	146	98	104	5	14	7-5	.336	.432	.685	1.116	2	.999
2002— Colorado (N.L.)	1B	156	553	107	182	39	4	30	109	99	91	5	10	5-1	.329	.429	.577	1.006	7	.995
2003— Colorado (N.L.)	1B	160	583	135	209	49	5	33	117	111	72	2	19	0-4	.358	.458	.630	1.088	11	.993
2004— Colorado (N.L.)	1B	154	547	115	190	49	2	32	96	127	72	3	12	3-0	.347	.469	.620	1.088	4	.997
2005— Colo. Springs (PCL)	1B	2	5	1	3	2	0	0	1	1	0	1	0	0-0	.600	.714	1.000	1.714	0	1.000
— Colorado (N.L.)	1B	144	509	92	163	45	2	20	79	106	80	9	14	3-0	.320	* .445	.534	.979	5	.996
Major League totals (9 years)		1279	4560	924	1535	373	24	271	915	773	622	40	111	33-23	.337	.433	.607	1.040	52	.996

H

All-Star Game totals (5 years)	G	AB	R	H	2B	3B	HR	RBI	BB	SO	HBP	GDP	SB-CS	Avg.	OBP	SLG	OPS	E	Avg.
	5	9	2	2	0	0	1	3	0	2	0	0	0-0	.222	.222	.556	.778	0	1.000

HENDRICKSON, MARK   P

PERSONAL: Born June 23, 1974, in Mount Vernon, Wash. ... 6-9/230. ... Throws left, bats left. ... Full name: Mark Allan Hendrickson. ... High school: Mount Vernon (Wash.). ... College: Washington State.

TRANSACTIONS/CAREER NOTES: Selected by Atlanta Braves organization in 12th round of 1992 free-agent draft; did not sign. ... Selected by San Diego Padres organization in 21st round of 1993 free-agent draft; did not sign. ... Selected by Braves organization in 32nd round of 1994 free-agent draft; did not sign. ... Selected by Detroit Tigers organization in 16th round of 1995 free-agent draft; did not sign. ... Selected by Texas Rangers organization in 19th round of 1996 free-agent draft; did not sign. ... Drafted by Philadelphia 76ers in second round (31st pick overall) of 1996 NBA draft. ... Played for four NBA teams (1997-2000). ... Selected by Toronto Blue Jays organization in 20th round of 1997 free-agent draft. ... Traded by Blue Jays to Tampa Bay Devil Rays as part of three-team deal in which Blue Jays acquired P Justin Speier from Colorado Rockies and Rockies acquired P Joe Kennedy from Devil Rays and a player to be named from Blue Jays (December 14, 2003); Rockies acquired P Sandy Nin to complete deal (December 15, 2003).

CAREER HITTING: 3-for-16 (.188), 2 R, 0 2B, 0 3B, 1 HR, 1 RBI.

SCOUTING REPORT *Throws:* His fastball hits 83-89 mph and his curve 73-75. Has a cut fastball. Also has a changeup. *Tendencies:* He is one of the league's tallest pitchers but isn't a hard thrower. Is deceptive because he has long lower-arm action, but does not have good arm speed. Fastball has a natural tailing action away from righthanders. Likes to pitch away and force hitters to chase balls until the umpire no longer calls strikes. Curveball is sweeping. Has good motion on his change, which he turns over. *Outlook:* He had his best year and could have been even better if he had better run support. Has a good idea of how to pitch around the plate. *Grade 7.3*

MARK HENDRICKSON'S PITCHING ZONE

.303	.500	.211
.330	.420	.288
.310	.347	.309

LEFTY-RIGHTY SPLITS

vs.	Avg.	AB	H	2B	3B	HR	RBI	BB	SO	OBP	Slg.
L	.258	178	46	11	1	3	22	10	28	.302	.382
R	.328	552	181	45	5	21	88	39	61	.369	.542

Year Team (League)	W	L	Pct.	ERA	WHIP	G	GS	CG	ShO	Hld.	Sv.-Opp.	IP	H	R	ER	HR	BB-IBB	SO	Avg.
1998—Dunedin (Fla. St.)	4	3	.571	2.37	1.42	16	5	0	0		1-...	49.1	44	16	13	2	26-1	38	.249
1999—Knoxville (Southern)	2	7	.222	6.63	1.69	12	11	0	0		0-...	55.2	73	46	41	4	21-0	39	.319
2000—Dunedin (Fla. St.)	2	2	.500	5.61	1.79	12	12	1	0		0-...	51.1	63	34	32	7	29-0	38	.315
—Tennessee (Sou.)	3	1	.750	3.63	1.11	6	6	0	0		0-...	39.2	32	17	16	5	12-0	29	.216
2001—Syracuse (Int'l)	2	9	.182	4.66	1.34	38	6	0	0		0-...	73.1	80	43	38	13	18-1	33	.274
2002—Syracuse (Int'l)	7	5	.583	3.52	1.22	19	14	0	0		0-...	92.0	90	38	36	12	22-0	68	.254
—Toronto (A.L.)	3	0	1.000	2.45	1.01	16	4	0	0		0-0	36.2	25	11	10	1	12-3	21	.202
2003—Syracuse (Int'l)	0	0		4.50	1.50	1	1	0	0	1	0-1	6.0	8	4	3	1	1-0	5	.333
—Dunedin (Fla. St.)	1	0	1.000	1.59	1.60	1	1	0	0		0-...	5.2	5	2	1	0	4-0	3	.227
—Toronto (A.L.)	9	9	.500	5.51	1.56	30	30	1	1		0-0	158.1	207	111	97	24	40-3	76	.317
2004—Tampa Bay (A.L.)	10	15	.400	4.81	1.40	32	30	2	0		0-0	183.1	211	113	98	21	46-5	87	.285
2005—Tampa Bay (A.L.)	11	8	.579	5.90	1.55	31	31	1	0		0-0	178.1	227	126	117	24	49-1	89	.311
Major League totals (4 years)	33	32	.508	5.21	1.47	109	95	4	1	1	0-1	556.2	670	361	322	70	147-12	273	.298

HENN, SEAN   P

PERSONAL: Born April 23, 1981, in Fort Worth, Texas. ... 6-4/215. ... Throws left, bats right. ... Full name: Sean Michael Henn. ... Junior college: McLennan (Texas) CC.

TRANSACTIONS/CAREER NOTES: Selected by New York Yankees organization in 26th round of 2000 free-agent draft.

CAREER HITTING: 0-for-0 (.000), 0 R, 0 2B, 0 3B, 0 HR, 0 RBI.

SEAN HENN'S PITCHING ZONE

.500	.500	1.000
.125	.000	.500
.857	.000	.000

LEFTY-RIGHTY SPLITS

vs.	Avg.	AB	H	2B	3B	HR	RBI	BB	SO	OBP	Slg.
L	.429	14	6	0	0	2	5	1	1	.467	.857
R	.333	36	12	5	0	1	7	10	2	.478	.556

Year Team (League)	W	L	Pct.	ERA	WHIP	G	GS	CG	ShO	Hld.	Sv.-Opp.	IP	H	R	ER	HR	BB-IBB	SO	Avg.
2001—Staten Island (N.Y.-Penn.)	3	1	.750	3.00	0.98	9	8	0	0		1-...	42.0	26	15	14	3	15-0	49	.178
2002—			Did not play.																
2003—Tampa (Fla. St.)	4	3	.571	3.61	1.47	16	16	0	0	...	0-...	72.1	69	31	29	3	37-0	52	.259
—GC Yankees (GCL)	1	1	.500	2.25	1.00	2	1	0	0	...	0-...	8.0	5	3	2	1	3-0	10	.167
2004—Trenton (East.)	6	8	.429	4.41	1.44	27	27	0	0	...	0-...	163.1	173	94	80	11	63-2	118	.280
2005—Trenton (East.)	2	1	.667	0.71	0.99	4	4	0	0	...	0-0	25.1	16	2	2	1	9-0	21	.188
—New York (A.L.)	0	3	.000	11.12	2.56	3	3	0	0	...	0-0	11.1	18	16	14	3	11-0	3	.360
—Columbus (Int'l)	5	5	.500	3.23	1.23	16	16	1	1	...	0-0	86.1	79	37	31	5	27-1	64	.254
Major League totals (1 year)	0	3	.000	11.12	2.56	3	3	0	0		0-0	11.1	18	16	14	3	11-0	3	.360

HENNESSEY, BRAD   P

PERSONAL: Born February 7, 1980, in Toledo, Ohio. ... 6-2/185. ... Throws right, bats right. ... Full name: Brad Martin Hennessey. ... High school: Whitmer (Toledo). ... College: Youngstown State.

TRANSACTIONS/CAREER NOTES: Selected by San Francisco Giants organization in first round (21st pick overall) of 2001 free-agent draft.

CAREER HITTING: 12-for-52 (.231), 4 R, 1 2B, 0 3B, 2 HR, 7 RBI.

BRAD HENNESSEY'S PITCHING ZONE

.316	.290	.263
.245	.327	.250
.410	.341	.280

LEFTY-RIGHTY SPLITS

vs.	Avg.	AB	H	2B	3B	HR	RBI	BB	SO	OBP	Slg.
L	.320	194	62	15	2	7	35	26	28	.395	.526
R	.244	266	65	12	1	8	22	26	36	.321	.387

Year Team (League)	W	L	Pct.	ERA	WHIP	G	GS	CG	ShO	Hld.	Sv.-Opp.	IP	H	R	ER	HR	BB-IBB	SO	Avg.
2001—Salem-Keizer (N'west)	1	0	1.000	2.38	1.15	9	9	0	0		0-...	34.0	28	9	9	1	11-0	22	.224
2002—			Did not play.																
2003—Hagerstown (SAL)	3	9	.250	4.20	1.36	15	15	1	0		0-...	79.1	81	49	37	6	27-0	44	.265

Year Team (League)	W	L	Pct.	ERA	WHIP	G	GS	CG	ShO	Hld.	Sv.-Opp.	IP	H	R	ER	HR	BB-IBB	SO	Avg.
2004— Norwich (East.)	5	5	.500	3.56	1.39	18	18	0	0	...	0-...	101.0	106	42	40	8	34-0	55	.272
— Fresno (PCL)	4	1	.800	2.02	1.15	5	5	0	0	...	0-...	35.2	26	8	8	2	15-0	16	.202
— San Francisco (N.L.)	2	2	.500	4.98	1.66	7	7	0	0	0	0-0	34.1	42	24	19	2	15-1	25	.294
2005— Fresno (PCL)	4	2	.667	5.19	1.43	11	11	0	0	0	0-0	67.2	75	40	39	7	22-1	46	.279
— San Francisco (N.L.)	5	8	.385	4.64	1.51	21	21	0	0	0	0-0	118.1	127	63	61	15	52-3	64	.276
Major League totals (2 years)	7	10	.412	4.72	1.55	28	28	0	0	0	0-0	152.2	169	87	80	17	67-4	89	.280

HENSLEY, CLAY   P

PERSONAL: Born August 31, 1979, in Tomball, Texas. ... 5-11/190. ... Throws right, bats right. ... Full name: Clayton Allen Hensley. ... College: Lamar.

TRANSACTIONS/CAREER NOTES: Selected by San Francisco Giants organization in eighth round of 2002 free-agent draft. ... Traded by Giants with a player to be named or cash to San Diego Padres for P Matt Herges (July 13, 2003); Padres acquired P R.D. Spiehs to complete deal (July 27, 2003).

CAREER HITTING: 1-for-6 (.167), 0 R, 1 2B, 0 3B, 0 HR, 0 RBI.

CLAY HENSLEY'S PITCHING ZONE

.250	.111	.333
.045	.200	.364
.100	.000	.500

LEFTY-RIGHTY SPLITS

vs.	Avg.	AB	H	2B	3B	HR	RBI	BB	SO	OBP	Slg.
L	.275	91	25	4	0	0	8	12	13	.359	.319
R	.103	78	8	1	1	0	6	5	15	.153	.141

Year Team (League)	W	L	Pct.	ERA	WHIP	G	GS	CG	ShO	Hld.	Sv.-Opp.	IP	H	R	ER	HR	BB-IBB	SO	Avg.
2002— Salem-Keizer (N'west)	7	0	1.000	2.53	1.19	15	15	1	0	...	0-...	81.2	72	31	23	3	25-0	84	.235
2003— Hagerstown (SAL)	4	3	.571	3.18	1.12	12	12	3	2	...	0-...	68.0	56	26	24	4	20-0	74	.223
— San Jose (Calif.)	2	3	.400	5.83	1.60	5	5	0	0	...	0-...	29.1	38	20	19	4	9-0	25	.336
— Lake Elsinore (Calif.)	3	4	.429	3.45	1.44	8	8	0	0	...	0-...	44.1	50	24	17	0	14-0	40	.286
2004— Mobile (Sou.)	11	10	.524	4.30	1.35	27	27	2	1	...	0-...	159.0	167	84	76	14	48-2	125	.271
2005— Portland (PCL)	2	2	.500	2.99	0.94	15	14	0	0	0	0-0	90.1	63	31	30	8	22-0	71	.197
— San Diego (N.L.)	1	1	.500	1.70	1.05	24	1	0	0	2	0-0	47.2	33	12	9	0	17-2	28	.195
Major League totals (1 year)	1	1	.500	1.70	1.05	24	1	0	0	2	0-0	47.2	33	12	9	0	17-2	28	.195

DIVISION SERIES RECORD

Year Team (League)	W	L	Pct.	ERA	WHIP	G	GS	CG	ShO	Hld.	Sv.-Opp.	IP	H	R	ER	HR	BB-IBB	SO	Avg.
2005— San Diego (N.L.)	0	0	...	3.86	1.50	3	0	0	0	0	0-...	4.2	4	2	2	0	3-0	1	.235

HEREDIA, FELIX   P

PERSONAL: Born June 20, 1975, in Barahona, Dominican Republic. ... 6-0/180. ... Throws left, bats left. ... Full name: Felix Perez Heredia. ... Name pronounced: heh-RAY-dee-ah. ... High school: Escuela Dominical (Barahona, Dominican Republic).

TRANSACTIONS/CAREER NOTES: Signed as a non-drafted free agent by Florida Marlins organization (November 22, 1992). ... Traded by Marlins with P Steve Hoff to Chicago Cubs for 3B Kevin Orie and Ps Todd Noel and Justin Speier (July 31, 1998). ... On disabled list (August 21-September 5 and September 18-October 3, 2001). ... Traded by Cubs with a player to be named to Toronto Blue Jays for SS Alex S. Gonzalez (December 10, 2001); Blue Jays acquired IF James Deschaine to complete deal (December 13, 2001). ... Signed as a free agent by Cincinnati Reds organization (January 7, 2003). ... Claimed on waivers by New York Yankees (August 25, 2003). ... On disabled list (April 10-May 17, 2004); included reha-bilitation assignment to Columbus. ... Traded by Yankees to New York Mets for P Mike Stanton and cash (December 3, 2004); included rehabilitation assignment to St. Lucie.

CAREER HITTING: 4-for-15 (.267), 0 R, 0 2B, 0 3B, 0 HR, 1 RBI.

LEFTY-RIGHTY SPLITS

vs.	Avg.	AB	H	2B	3B	HR	RBI	BB	SO	OBP	Slg.
L	.000	2	0	0	0	0	0	1	2	.500	.000
R	.167	6	1	0	0	0	0	0	0	.167	.167

Year Team (League)	W	L	Pct.	ERA	WHIP	G	GS	CG	ShO	Hld.	Sv.-Opp.	IP	H	R	ER	HR	BB-IBB	SO	Avg.
1993— GC Marlins (GCL)	5	1	.833	2.47	0.98	12	12	0	0	...	0-...	62.0	50	18	17	0	11-0	53	.238
1994— Kane Co. (Midw.)	4	5	.444	5.69	1.47	24	8	1	0	...	3-...	68.0	86	55	43	7	14-0	65	.305
1995— Brevard County (FSL)	6	4	.600	3.57	1.43	34	8	0	0	...	1-...	95.2	101	52	38	6	36-1	76	.271
1996— Portland (East.)	8	1	.889	1.50	1.05	55	0	0	0	...	5-...	60.0	48	11	10	3	15-2	42	.223
— Florida (N.L.)	1	1	.500	4.32	1.86	21	0	0	0	2	0-0	16.2	21	8	8	1	10-1	10	.313
1997— Florida (N.L.)	5	3	.625	4.29	1.46	56	0	0	0	7	0-1	56.2	53	30	27	3	30-1	54	.243
1998— Florida (N.L.)	0	3	.000	5.49	1.71	41	2	0	0	9	2-3	41.0	38	30	25	1	32-2	38	.241
— Chicago (N.L.)	3	0	1.000	4.08	1.42	30	0	0	0	8	0-2	17.2	19	9	8	1	6-1	16	.279
1999— Chicago (N.L.)	3	1	.750	4.85	1.56	69	0	0	0	12	1-7	52.0	56	35	28	6	25-2	50	.272
2000— Chicago (N.L.)	7	3	.700	4.76	1.35	74	0	0	0	12	2-5	58.2	46	31	31	6	33-4	52	.220
2001— Chicago (N.L.)	2	2	.500	6.17	1.74	48	0	0	0	8	0-3	35.0	45	27	24	6	16-1	28	.315
2002— Toronto (A.L.)	1	2	.333	3.61	1.47	53	0	0	0	7	0-2	52.1	51	29	21	5	26-3	31	.256
2003— Cincinnati (N.L.)	5	2	.714	3.00	1.24	57	0	0	0	7	1-4	72.0	61	27	24	9	28-5	41	.228
— New York (A.L.)	0	1	.000	1.20	1.20	12	0	0	0	1	0-1	15.0	13	5	2	1	5-2	4	.228
2004— Columbus (Int'l)	0	0	...	0.00	0.82	3	0	0	0	...	0-...	3.2	2	0	0	0	1-0	5	.154
— Tampa (Fla. St.)	0	0	...	1.80	1.40	2	2	0	0	...	0-...	5.0	4	1	1	0	3-0	3	.222
— Trenton (East.)	0	0	...	5.40	1.40	3	1	0	0	...	0-...	5.0	5	3	3	0	2-0	8	.350
— New York (A.L.)	1	1	.500	6.28	1.66	47	0	0	0	5	0-1	38.2	44	28	27	5	20-0	25	.278
2005— New York (N.L.)	0	0	...	0.00	0.75	3	0	0	0	0	0-0	2.2	1	0	0	0	1-0	2	.125
— St. Lucie (Fla. St.)	0	1	.000	13.50	2.00	5	0	0	0	0	0-1	4.0	6	6	6	0	2-0	1	.375
American League totals (3 years)	2	4	.333	4.25	1.50	112	0	0	0	13	0-4	106.0	108	62	50	11	51-5	60	.261
National League totals (8 years)	26	15	.634	4.47	1.48	399	2	0	0	65	6-25	352.1	340	197	175	34	181-17	291	.253
Major League totals (10 years)	28	19	.596	4.42	1.48	511	2	0	0	78	6-29	458.1	448	259	225	45	232-22	351	.255

DIVISION SERIES RECORD

Year Team (League)	W	L	Pct.	ERA	WHIP	G	GS	CG	ShO	Hld.	Sv.-Opp.	IP	H	R	ER	HR	BB-IBB	SO	Avg.
1997— Florida (N.L.)				Did not play.															
1998— Chicago (N.L.)	0	0	...	54.00	6.00	1	0	0	0	0	0-0	0.1	0	2	2	0	2-0	0	.000
2003— New York (A.L.)	0	0	...	0.00	1.00	1	0	0	0	0	0-0	2.0	1	0	0	0	1-1	1	.167
2004— New York (A.L.)	0	0	...	54.00	0.00	1	0	0	0	0	0-0	0.1	0	2	2	0	0-0	0	.000
Division series totals (3 years)	0	0	...	13.50	1.50	3	0	0	0	0	0-0	2.2	1	4	4	0	3-1	1	.125

H

Year Team (League)	W	L	Pct.	ERA	WHIP	G	GS	CG	ShO	Hld.	Sv.-Opp.	IP	H	R	ER	HR	BB-IBB	SO	Avg.
1997— Florida (N.L.)	0	0	...	5.40	1.50	2	0	0	0	0	0-0	3.1	3	2	2	0	2-0	4	.250
2003— New York (A.L.)	0	0	...	3.38	1.13	5	0	0	0	0	0-0	2.2	0	1	1	0	3-1	3	.000
2004— New York (A.L.)	0	0	...	0.00	0.75	3	0	0	0	0	0-0	1.1	1	0	0	0	0-0	1	.250
Champ. series totals (3 years)	0	0	...	3.68	1.23	10	0	0	0	0	0-0	7.1	4	3	3	0	5-1	8	.174

WORLD SERIES RECORD

Year Team (League)	W	L	Pct.	ERA	WHIP	G	GS	CG	ShO	Hld.	Sv.-Opp.	IP	H	R	ER	HR	BB-IBB	SO	Avg.
1997— Florida (N.L.)	0	0	...	0.00	0.56	4	0	0	0	0	0-0	5.1	2	0	0	0	1-0	5	.111

HERGES, MATT — P

PERSONAL: Born April 1, 1970, in Champaign, Ill. ... 6-0/200. ... Throws right, bats left. ... Full name: Matthew Tyler Herges. ... Name pronounced: hur-JISS. ... High school: Centennial (Champaign, Ill.). ... College: Illinois State.

TRANSACTIONS/CAREER NOTES: Signed as a non-drafted free agent by Los Angeles Dodgers organization (June 13, 1992). ... Traded by Dodgers with IF Jorge Nunez to Montreal Expos for P Guillermo Mota and OF Wilkin Ruan (March 24, 2002). ... Traded by Expos to Pittsburgh Pirates for Ps Chris Young and Jon Searles (December 20, 2002). ... Released by Pirates (March 26, 2003). ... Signed by San Diego Padres organization (April 11, 2003). ... Traded by Padres to San Francisco Giants for P Clay Hensley and a player to be named or cash (July 13, 2003); Padres acquired P R.D. Spiehs to complete the deal (July 27, 2003). ... Traded by Giants to Arizona Diamondbacks for OF Doug Devore (June 3, 2005).

CAREER HITTING: 6-for-27 (.222), 0 R, 0 2B, 0 3B, 0 HR, 1 RBI.

SCOUTING REPORT *Throws:* He will attack hitters with a sinking fastball that tops out at 92 mph. Also has a curveball and a changeup. *Tendencies:* Herges had problems with righthanders as his velocity dropped off and his ball stopped sinking. Was better against lefthanders with his tightly biting curve and change. *Outlook:* He must win a job in the spring. Likely will be in a middle-relief role if he does. *Grade 4.6*

MATT HERGES' PITCHING ZONE

.333	.333	.250
.290	.385	.375
.167	.500	.250

LEFTY-RIGHTY SPLITS

vs.	Avg.	AB	H	2B	3B	HR	RBI	BB	SO	OBP	Slg.
L	.256	43	11	5	2	1	10	6	5	.333	.535
R	.333	72	24	6	1	5	18	6	4	.392	.653

Year Team (League)	W	L	Pct.	ERA	WHIP	G	GS	CG	ShO	Hld.	Sv.-Opp.	IP	H	R	ER	HR	BB-IBB	SO	Avg.
1992— Yakima (N'west)	2	3	.400	3.22	1.28	27	0	0	0	...	9-...	44.2	33	21	16	2	24-1	57	.199
1993— Bakersfield (Calif.)	2	6	.250	3.69	1.39	51	0	0	0	...	2-...	90.1	70	49	37	6	56-6	84	.214
1994— Vero Beach (FSL)	8	9	.471	3.32	1.33	48	3	1	0	...	3-...	111.0	115	45	41	8	33-3	61	.268
1995— San Antonio (Texas)	0	3	.000	4.88	1.81	19	0	0	0	...	8-...	27.2	34	16	15	2	16-1	18	.306
— San Bern. (Calif.)	5	2	.714	3.66	1.41	22	2	0	0	...	1-...	51.2	58	29	21	3	15-0	35	.275
1996— San Antonio (Texas)	3	2	.600	2.71	1.34	30	6	0	0	...	3-...	83.0	83	38	25	3	28-0	45	.261
— Albuquerque (PCL)	4	1	.800	2.60	1.36	10	4	2	1	...	0-...	34.2	33	11	10	2	14-0	15	.270
1997— Albuquerque (PCL)	0	8	.000	8.89	1.95	31	12	0	0	...	0-...	85.0	120	92	84	13	46-1	61	.340
— San Antonio (Texas)	0	1	.000	8.80	2.09	4	3	0	0	...	0-...	15.1	22	15	15	2	10-0	12	.355
1998— Albuquerque (PCL)	3	5	.375	5.71	1.72	34	8	0	0	...	0-...	88.1	115	64	56	9	37-1	75	.325
— San Antonio (Texas)	0	0	...	0.00	0.83	3	0	0	0	...	0-...	6.0	3	0	0	0	2-0	3	.158
1999— Albuquerque (PCL)	8	3	.727	4.73	1.39	21	21	2	0	...	0-...	131.1	135	82	69	17	47-0	88	.272
— Los Angeles (N.L.)	0	0	.000	4.07	1.32	17	0	0	0	1	0-2	24.1	24	13	11	5	8-0	18	.255
2000— Los Angeles (N.L.)	11	3	.786	3.17	1.27	59	4	0	0	4	1-3	110.2	100	43	39	7	40-5	75	.249
2001— Los Angeles (N.L.)	9	8	.529	3.44	1.44	75	0	0	0	15	1-8	99.1	97	39	38	8	46-12	76	.259
2002— Montreal (N.L.)	2	5	.286	4.04	1.64	62	0	0	0	9	6-14	64.2	80	33	29	10	26-8	50	.305
2003— Portland (PCL)	0	0	...	1.80	0.60	4	0	0	0	...	0-...	5.0	1	1	1	0	2-0	5	.063
— San Diego (N.L.)	2	2	.500	2.86	1.36	40	0	0	0	4	3-5	44.0	40	16	14	2	20-2	40	.244
— San Francisco (N.L.)	1	0	1.000	2.31	1.06	27	0	0	0	5	0-1	35.0	28	11	9	1	9-0	28	.219
2004— San Francisco (N.L.)	4	5	.444	5.23	1.70	70	0	0	0	5	23-31	65.1	90	44	38	8	21-4	39	.338
2005— San Francisco (N.L.)	1	1	.500	4.71	1.43	21	0	0	0	3	0-0	21.0	23	11	11	2	7-1	6	.288
— Arizona (N.L.)	0	0	...	13.50	2.13	7	0	0	0	0	0-0	8.0	12	12	12	4	5-0	3	.343
— Tucson (PCL)	1	2	.333	3.14	1.64	26	0	0	0	5	0-0	28.2	39	13	10	3	8-0	29	.339
Major League totals (7 years)	30	26	.536	3.83	1.43	378	4	0	0	46	34-64	472.1	494	222	201	47	182-32	335	.274

DIVISION SERIES RECORD

Year Team (League)	W	L	Pct.	ERA	WHIP	G	GS	CG	ShO	Hld.	Sv.-Opp.	IP	H	R	ER	HR	BB-IBB	SO	Avg.
2003— San Francisco (N.L.)	0	0	...	0.00	0.69	3	0	0	0	...	0-0	4.1	1	0	0	0	2-0	5	.083

HERMANSON, DUSTIN — P

PERSONAL: Born December 21, 1972, in Springfield, Ohio. ... 6-2/200. ... Throws right, bats right. ... Full name: Dustin Michael Hermanson. ... Name pronounced: HERR-man-son. ... High school: Kenton Ridge (Springfield, Ohio). ... College: Kent State.

TRANSACTIONS/CAREER NOTES: Selected by Pittsburgh Pirates organization in 39th round of 1991 free-agent draft; did not sign. ... Selected by San Diego Padres organization in first round (third pick overall) of 1994 free-agent draft. ... Traded by Padres to Florida Marlins for 2B Quilvio Veras (November 21, 1996). ... Traded by Marlins with OF Joe Orsulak to Montreal Expos for OF/1B Cliff Floyd (March 26, 1997). ... On disabled list (May 15-30, 1998). ... Traded by Expos with P Steve Kline to St. Louis Cardinals for 3B Fernando Tatis and P Britt Reames (December 14, 2000). ... Traded by Cardinals to Boston Red Sox for OF Rick Asadoorian and 1B Luis Garcia and Dustin Brisson (December 15, 2001). ... On disabled list (April 4-July 20 and July 21-August 22, 2002); included rehabilitation assignments to Pawtucket and GCL Red Sox. ... Signed as a free agent by Cardinals (January 20, 2003). ... Released by Cardinals (June 26, 2003). ... Signed by San Francisco Giants organization (July 11, 2003). ... On disabled list (August 24-September 9, 2003). ... On disabled list (April 21-May 8, 2004). ... Signed as a free agent by Chicago White Sox (December 8, 2004). ... On suspended list (April 5-7, 2005).

CAREER HITTING: 30-for-322 (.093), 14 R, 5 2B, 0 3B, 2 HR, 10 RBI.

H

SCOUTING REPORT *Throws:* Hermanson's above-average fastball tops out at 91 mph. Also has a slider at 84 and a split-finger fastball in the mid-80s. *Tendencies:* He has a very loose arm. Gets some sinking action on his fastball when he keeps it down. Has a running slider that he uses on both sides of the plate, even though it sometimes goes flat. Has gotten away from his changeup in favor of a late-tumbling splitter that he's not afraid to throw to either lefthanded or righthanded hitters. Uses the splitter as an out pitch. *Outlook:* Back problems made it impossible for Hermanson to pitch back-to-back games, and ultimately he lost the closer's job to Bobby Jenks. Hermanson became an infrequent setup man. Doesn't have typical closer stuff; best role could be in middle relief. *Grade 7.2*

DUSTIN HERMANSON'S PITCHING ZONE

.333	.286	.059
.240	.296	.205
.313	.200	.286

LEFTY-RIGHTY SPLITS

vs.	Avg.	AB	H	2B	3B	HR	RBI	BB	SO	OBP	Slg.
L	.240	100	24	8	1	2	9	12	16	.321	.400
R	.206	107	22	3	1	2	10	5	17	.248	.308

Year Team (League)	W	L	Pct.	ERA	WHIP	G	GS	CG	ShO	Hld.	Sv.-Opp.	IP	H	R	ER	HR	BB-IBB	SO	Avg.
1994—Wichita (Texas)	1	0	1.000	0.43	0.90	16	0	0	0	0	8-...	21.0	13	1	1	0	6-2	30	.176
—Las Vegas (PCL)	0	0	...	6.14	1.50	7	0	0	0	0	3-...	7.1	6	5	5	1	5-0	6	.222
1995—Las Vegas (PCL)	0	1	.000	3.50	1.78	31	0	0	0	0	11-...	36.0	35	23	14	5	29-0	42	.245
—San Diego (N.L.)	3	1	.750	6.82	1.80	26	0	0	0	1	0-0	31.2	35	26	24	8	22-1	19	.280
1996—Las Vegas (PCL)	1	4	.200	3.13	1.48	42	0	0	0	0	21-...	46.0	41	20	16	3	27-7	54	.239
—San Diego (N.L.)	1	0	1.000	8.56	1.61	8	0	0	0	0	0-0	13.2	18	15	13	3	4-0	11	.340
1997—Montreal (N.L.)	8	8	.500	3.69	1.26	32	28	1	1	0	0-0	158.1	134	68	65	15	66-2	136	.234
1998—Montreal (N.L.)	14	11	.560	3.13	1.17	32	30	1	0	1	0-0	187.0	163	80	65	21	56-3	154	.234
1999—Montreal (N.L.)	9	14	.391	4.20	1.36	34	34	0	0	0	0-0	216.1	225	110	101	20	69-4	145	.271
2000—Montreal (N.L.)	12	14	.462	4.77	1.52	38	30	2	1	0	4-7	198.0	226	128	105	26	75-5	94	.290
2001—St. Louis (N.L.)	14	13	.519	4.45	1.39	33	33	0	0	0	0-0	192.1	195	106	95	34	73-3	123	.264
2002—Boston (A.L.)	1	1	.500	7.77	1.91	12	1	0	0	2	0-1	22.0	35	19	19	7	7-0	13	.354
—Pawtucket (Int'l)	0	1	.000	2.63	1.17	5	3	0	0	0	0-...	13.2	9	5	4	0	7-0	11	.191
—GC Red Sox (GCL)	0	0	...	9.00	2.50	1	1	0	0	0	0-...	2.0	5	3	2	0	0-0	1	.500
2003—St. Louis (N.L.)	1	2	.333	5.46	1.65	23	0	0	0	1	1-6	29.2	35	18	18	4	14-2	12	.315
—Fresno (PCL)	0	1	.000	4.85	1.20	4	4	0	0	0	0-...	26.0	29	16	14	2	3-1	17	.290
—San Francisco (N.L.)	2	1	.667	3.00	1.15	9	6	0	0	0	0-0	39.0	35	14	13	5	10-2	27	.238
2004—San Francisco (N.L.)	6	9	.400	4.53	1.36	47	18	0	0	1	17-20	131.0	132	71	66	15	46-5	102	.262
2005—Chicago (A.L.)	2	4	.333	2.04	1.10	57	0	0	0	5	34-39	57.1	46	17	13	4	17-4	33	.222
American League totals (2 years)	3	5	.375	3.63	1.32	69	1	0	0	7	34-40	79.1	81	36	32	7	24-4	46	.265
National League totals (9 years)	70	73	.490	4.25	1.36	282	179	4	2	5	22-33	1197.0	1198	636	565	151	435-27	823	.263
Major League totals (11 years)	73	78	.483	4.21	1.36	351	180	4	2	12	56-73	1276.1	1279	672	597	158	459-31	869	.263

DIVISION SERIES RECORD

Year Team (League)	W	L	Pct.	ERA	WHIP	G	GS	CG	ShO	Hld.	Sv.-Opp.	IP	H	R	ER	HR	BB-IBB	SO	Avg.
2001—St. Louis (N.L.)	0	0	...	0.00	0.00	1	0	0	0	1	0-0	3.0	0	0	0	0	0-0	0	.000
2003—San Francisco (N.L.)	0	0	...	0.00	2.00	1	0	0	0	0	0-0	1.0	1	0	0	0	1-0	0	.250
2005—Chicago (A.L.)			Did not play.																
Division series totals (3 years)	0	0	...	0.00	0.50	2	0	0	0	1	0-0	4.0	1	0	0	0	1-0	0	.077

CHAMPIONSHIP SERIES RECORD

Year Team (League)	W	L	Pct.	ERA	WHIP	G	GS	CG	ShO	Hld.	Sv.-Opp.	IP	H	R	ER	HR	BB-IBB	SO	Avg.
2005—Chicago (A.L.)			Did not play.																
Championship series total (1 year)			Did not play.																

WORLD SERIES RECORD

Year Team (League)	W	L	Pct.	ERA	WHIP	G	GS	CG	ShO	Hld.	Sv.-Opp.	IP	H	R	ER	HR	BB-IBB	SO	Avg.
2005—Chicago (A.L.)	0	0	...	0.00	3.00	1	0	0	0	0	0-1	0.1	1	0	0	0	0-0	1	.500

HERMIDA, JEREMY   OF

PERSONAL: Born January 30, 1984, in Marietta, Ga. ... 6-4/200. ... Bats left, throws right. ... Full name: Jeremy Ryan Hermida. ... Name pronounced: her-MEE-dah.
TRANSACTIONS/CAREER NOTES: Selected by Florida Marlins organization in first round (11th pick overall) of 2002 free-agent draft.
2005 GAMES PLAYED BY POSITION (MLB): OF—14.

SCOUTING REPORT *Offense:* Hermida is a gap hitter who has the potential to hit 25-30 home runs a year. Did not show the same kind of plate discipline he did in the minors. Looks for average fastballs up and out over the outer third of the plate. Has above-average speed and has shown he can steal bases. He could become a 30-30 man. *Defense:* He is a decent right fielder who could be better if he puts his mind to it. Has the makeup to become an accomplished defensive ballplayer but some scouts question if he has enough desire. *Outlook:* Hermida will be given the opportunity to be win the Marlins' right field job in spring training. *Grade 7.5*

LEFTY-RIGHTY SPLITS

vs.	Avg.	AB	H	2B	3B	HR	RBI	BB	SO	OBP	Slg.
L	.200	5	1	0	0	0	2	2	2	.429	.200
R	.306	36	11	2	0	4	11	4	10	.375	.694

Year Team (League)	Pos.	G	AB	R	H	2B	3B	HR	RBI	BB	SO	HBP	GDP	SB-CS	Avg.	OBP	SLG	OPS	E	Avg.
2002—GC Marlins (GCL)	OF	38	134	15	30	7	3	0	14	15	25	3	3	5-0	.224	.316	.321	.637	2	.950
—Jamestown (NYP)	OF	13	47	8	15	2	1	0	7	7	10	0	0	1-3	.319	.407	.404	.811	1	.947
2003—Greensboro (S. Atl.)	OF	133	468	73	133	23	5	6	49	80	100	2	3	28-2	.284	.387	.393	.780	8	.964
—Albuquerque (PCL)	OF	1	3	0	0	0	0	0	0	0	3	0	0	0-0	.000	.000	.000	.000	0	1.000
2004—Jupiter (Fla. St.)	OF	91	340	53	101	17	1	10	50	42	73	5	3	10-3	.297	.377	.441	.818	9	.500
2005—Carolina (Southern)	OF-DH	118	386	77	113	29	2	18	63	111	89	7	8	23-2	.293	.457	.518	.975	8	.982
—Florida (N.L.)	OF	23	41	9	12	2	0	4	11	6	12	0	1	2-0	.293	.383	.634	1.017	0	1.000
Major League totals (1 year)		23	41	9	12	2	0	4	11	6	12	0	1	2-0	.293	.383	.634	1.017	0	1.000

HERNANDEZ, ANDERSON   SS

PERSONAL: Born October 30, 1982, in Santo Domingo, Dominican Republic. ... 5-9/168. ... Bats both, throws right. ... Full name: Anderson Hernandez.
TRANSACTIONS/CAREER NOTES: Signed as a non-drafted free agent by Detroit Tigers organization (April 23, 2001). ... Traded by Tigers to New York Mets for C Vance Wilson (January 6, 2005).
2005 GAMES PLAYED BY POSITION (MLB): 2B—5, SS—2.

LEFTY-RIGHTY SPLITS

vs.	Avg.	AB	H	2B	3B	HR	RBI	BB	SO	OBP	Slg.
L	.000	0	0	0	0	0	0	1	0	.000	.000
R	.056	18	1	0	0	0	0	1	4	.105	.056

Year	Team (League)	Pos.	G	AB	R	H	2B	3B	HR	RBI	BB	SO	HBP	GDP	SB-CS	Avg.	OBP	SLG	OPS	E	Avg.
2001—GC Tigers (GCL)	SS-3B		55	216	37	57	5	11	0	18	13	38	0	0	34-8	.264	.303	.389	.692	21	.914
—Lakeland (Fla. St.)	SS		7	21	2	4	0	1	0	1	0	8	0	0	0-0	.190	.190	.286	.476	3	.917
2002—Lakeland (Fla. St.)	SS		123	410	52	106	13	7	2	42	33	102	0	2	16-14	.259	.310	.339	.649	27	.953
2003—Lakeland (Fla. St.)	SS		106	380	47	87	11	4	2	28	27	69	0	10	15-7	.229	.278	.295	.573	26	.947
2004—Lakeland (Fla. St.)	SS		32	122	20	36	4	3	0	11	6	26	0	0	7-0	.295	.326	.377	.703	3	.857
—Erie (East.)	SS		101	394	65	108	19	3	5	29	26	89	5	5	17-6	.274	.326	.376	.702	16	.000
2005—Binghamton (East.)	SS-2B-DH		66	273	46	89	14	1	7	24	14	58	1	0	11-9	.326	.360	.462	.821	14	.946
—Norfolk (Int'l)	2B-SS		66	261	34	79	6	4	2	30	22	46	1	2	24-9	.303	.354	.379	.733	9	.971
—New York (N.L.)	2B-SS		6	18	1	1	0	0	0	0	1	4	0	0	0-1	.056	.105	.056	.161	1	.964
Major League totals (1 year)			6	18	1	1	0	0	0	0	1	4	0	0	0-1	.056	.105	.056	.161	1	.964

HERNANDEZ, FELIX — P

PERSONAL: Born April 8, 1986, in Valencia, Venezuela. ... 6-3/225. ... Throws right, bats right. ... Full name: Felix Abraham Hernandez. ... College: None.
TRANSACTIONS/CAREER NOTES: Signed as a non-drafted free agent by Seattle Mariners organization (July 4, 2002).
CAREER HITTING: 0-for-0 (.000), 0 R, 0 2B, 0 3B, 0 HR, 0 RBI.

SCOUTING REPORT **Throws:** His fastball touches 98 mph and consistently is in the 95-mph range. Also throws an overhand curve and changeup. **Tendencies:** He is a power pitcher with excellent command and presence. Showed poise as a rookie. Complements his fastball with a plus curveball that he was confident enough in to throw on any count. Has an aggressive approach and uses all four edges of the strike zone. Is especially tough on lefthanded hitters. Is a good fielder. One negative is a stiff finish to his delivery, which can potentially create an arm injury. **Outlook:** If he avoids injury, he will be one of the best pitchers in the game for a long time, beginning this season. **Grade 8.7**

FELIX HERNANDEZ'S PITCHING ZONE

.273	.600	.375
.333	.231	.127
.250	.214	.185

LEFTY-RIGHTY SPLITS

vs.	Avg.	AB	H	2B	3B	HR	RBI	BB	SO	OBP	Slg.
L	.182	148	27	6	0	1	7	14	40	.255	.243
R	.224	152	34	3	0	4	17	9	37	.272	.322

Year	Team (League)	W	L	Pct.	ERA	WHIP	G	GS	CG	ShO	Hld.	Sv.-Opp.	IP	H	R	ER	HR	BB-IBB	SO	Avg.
2003—Everett (N'west)		7	2	.778	2.29	1.22	11	7	0	0	...	0-...	55.0	43	17	14	2	24-0	73	.218
—Wisconsin (Midw.)		0	0	...	1.93	0.86	2	2	0	0	...	0-...	14.0	9	4	3	1	3-0	18	.176
2004—Inland Empire (Calif.)		9	3	.750	2.74	1.21	16	15	0	0	...	0-...	92.0	85	31	28	5	26-0	114	.248
—San Antonio (Texas)		5	1	.833	3.30	1.19	10	10	1	1	...	0-...	57.1	47	23	21	8	21-0	58	.230
2005—Tacoma (PCL)		9	4	.692	2.25	1.25	19	14	1	0	...	2	0-0	88.0	62	24	22	3	48-0	100	.196
—Seattle (A.L.)		4	4	.500	2.67	1.00	12	12	0	0	0	0-0	84.1	61	24	25	5	23-0	77	.203
Major League totals (1 year)		4	4	.500	2.67	1.00	12	12	0	0	0	0-0	84.1	61	24	25	5	23-0	77	.203

HERNANDEZ, JOSE — 2B/SS

PERSONAL: Born July 14, 1969, in Vega Alta, Puerto Rico. ... 6-1/190. ... Bats right, throws right. ... Full name: Jose Antonio Hernandez. ... High school: Maestro Ladi (Vega Alta, Puerto Rico). ... College: Interamericana University (Puerto Rico).
TRANSACTIONS/CAREER NOTES: Signed as a non-drafted free agent by Texas Rangers organization (January 13, 1987). ... Claimed on waivers by Cleveland Indians (April 3, 1992). ... Traded by Indians to Chicago Cubs for P Heathcliff Slocumb (June 1, 1993). ... Traded by Cubs with P Terry Mulholland to Atlanta Braves for Ps Micah Bowie and Ruben Quevedo and a player to be named (July 31, 1999); Cubs acquired P Joey Nation to complete deal (August 24, 1999). ... Signed as a free agent by Milwaukee Brewers (December 16, 1999). ... On disabled list (August 10-September 1, 2000); included rehabilitation assignment to Indianapolis. ... Signed as a free agent by Colorado Rockies (January 24, 2003). ... Traded by Rockies to Chicago Cubs for IF Mark Bellhorn (June 20, 2003). ... Traded by Cubs with P Matt Bruback and a player to be named to Pittsburgh Pirates for 3B Aramis Ramirez, OF Kenny Lofton and cash (July 23, 2003); Pirates acquired IF Bobby Hill to complete deal (August 15, 2003). ... Released by Pirates (October 1, 2003). ... Signed by Los Angeles Dodgers organization (January 27, 2004). ... Signed as a free agent by Cleveland Indians (December 14, 2004).
2005 GAMES PLAYED BY POSITION (MLB): 1B—45, 3B—21, OF—6, 2B—4, SS—1, DH—1.

SCOUTING REPORT **Offense:** Hernandez, whose long stroke has a lot of holes, likes the ball out over the plate and has power against lefthanders. Is a platoon player because he struggles with breaking balls from righthanders. Power is to center and right-center, and the ball has good carry off his bat. **Defense:** He can play all four infield positions but is best suited at third because of his declining range. Has good hands and gets better jumps to his left than to his right. Can be erratic with his throwing and doesn't have very quick feet. **Outlook:** His greatest value is as a utility player. Has some power but strikeout total keeps him from playing every day. **Grade 6**

JOSE HERNANDEZ'S HITTING ZONE

.292	.167	.176
.383	.235	.273
.240	.000	.250

LEFTY-RIGHTY SPLITS

vs.	Avg.	AB	H	2B	3B	HR	RBI	BB	SO	OBP	Slg.
L	.269	145	39	6	0	6	23	5	30	.288	.434
R	.169	89	15	1	0	0	8	9	30	.260	.180

Year	Team (League)	Pos.	G	AB	R	H	2B	3B	HR	RBI	BB	SO	HBP	GDP	SB-CS	Avg.	OBP	SLG	OPS	E	Avg.
1987—GC Rangers (GCL)	SS		24	52	5	9	1	1	0	2	9	25	1	1	2-1	.173	.306	.231	.537	5	.932
1988—GC Rangers (GCL)	SS		55	162	19	26	7	1	1	13	12	36	0	5	4-1	.160	.217	.235	.452	8	.958
1989—Gastonia (S. Atl.)	2B-3B-OF SS		91	215	35	47	7	6	1	16	33	67	0	3	9-2	.219	.323	.321	.644	17	.941
1990—Charlotte (Fla. St.)	OF-SS		121	388	43	99	14	7	1	44	50	122	4	8	11-8	.255	.345	.335	.680	25	.958
1991—Tulsa (Texas)	SS		91	301	36	72	17	4	1	20	26	75	1	4	4-3	.239	.298	.332	.630	15	.968
—Okla. City (A.A.)	SS		14	46	6	14	1	1	1	3	4	10	1	0	0-0	.304	.353	.435	.788	5	.962
—Texas (A.L.)	3B-SS		45	98	8	18	2	1	0	4	3	31	0	2	0-1	.184	.208	.224	.432	4	.976
1992—Cant./Akr. (Eastern)			130	404	56	103	16	4	3	46	37	108	5	0	7-2	.255	.315	.337	.652	40	.932
—Cleveland (A.L.)	SS		3	4	0	0	0	0	0	0	0	0	2	0	0-0	.000	.000	.000	.000	1	.857
1993—Cant./Akr. (Eastern)	SS-3B		45	150	19	30	6	0	2	17	10	39	0	3	9-2	.200	.250	.280	.530	7	.968
—Orlando (South.)	SS		71	263	42	80	8	3	8	33	20	60	0	5	8-4	.304	.352	.449	.801	14	.961
—Iowa (Am. Assoc.)	SS		6	24	3	6	1	0	0	3	0	2	1	1	0-0	.250	.280	.292	.572	6	.976

H

Year	Team (League)	Pos.	G	AB	R	H	2B	3B	HR	RBI	BB	SO	HBP	GDP	SB-CS	Avg.	OBP	SLG	OPS	E	Avg.
									BATTING											**FIELDING**	
1994—Chicago (N.L.)	3B-SS-2B																				
		OF	56	132	18	32	2	3	1	9	8	29	1	4	2-2	.242	.291	.326	.617	4	.971
1995—Chicago (N.L.)	SS-2B-3B		93	245	37	60	11	4	13	40	13	69	0	8	1-0	.245	.281	.482	.762	9	.971
1996—Chicago (N.L.)	SS-3B-2B																				
		OF	131	331	52	80	14	1	10	41	24	97	1	10	4-0	.242	.293	.381	.674	20	.952
1997—Chicago (N.L.)	3B-SS-2B																				
		OF-1B-DH	121	183	33	50	8	5	7	26	14	42	0	5	2-5	.273	.323	.486	.810	8	.955
1998—Chicago (N.L.)	3B-OF-SS																				
		1B-2B	149	488	76	124	23	7	23	75	40	140	1	12	4-6	.254	.311	.471	.782	13	.970
1999—Chicago (N.L.)	SS-OF-1B		99	342	57	93	12	2	15	43	40	101	5	5	7-2	.272	.357	.450	.807	11	.973
—Atlanta (N.L.)	SS-1B-OF		48	166	22	42	8	0	4	19	12	44	0	5	4-1	.253	.302	.373	.675	6	.966
2000—Milwaukee (N.L.)	3B-SS-OF		124	446	51	109	22	1	11	59	41	125	6	12	3-7	.244	.315	.372	.687	19	.955
—Indianapolis (Int'l)	3B		2	9	2	3	0	0	2	3	1	3	0	0	0-0	.333	.400	1.000	1.400	0	1.000
2001—Milwaukee (N.L.)	SS-OF		152	542	67	135	26	2	25	73	39 *	185	2	9	5-4	.249	.300	.443	.743	18	.972
2002—Milwaukee (N.L.)	SS		152	525	72	151	24	2	24	73	52 *	188	4	19	3-5	.288	.356	.478	.834	19	.973
2003—Colorado (N.L.)	SS-1B		69	257	33	61	6	1	8	27	27	95	0	6	1-1	.237	.308	.362	.670	5	.984
—Chicago (N.L.)	3B-SS-OF																				
		2B	23	69	6	13	3	1	2	9	3	26	0	1	0-0	.188	.222	.348	.570	1	.977
—Pittsburgh (N.L.)	3B		58	193	19	43	9	1	3	21	16	56	1	9	1-0	.223	.282	.326	.608	8	.955
2004—Los Angeles (N.L.)	2B-SS-3B																				
		OF-1B	95	211	32	61	12	1	13	29	26	61	1	3	3-1	.289	.370	.540	.910	5	.981
2005—Cleveland (A.L.)	1B-3B-OF																				
		2B-DH	84	234	28	54	7	0	6	31	14	60	2	11	1-3	.231	.277	.338	.614	2	.995
American League totals (3 years)			132	336	36	72	9	1	6	35	17	93	2	13	1-4	.214	.254	.301	.555	7	.989
National League totals (11 years)			1370	4130	575	1054	180	31	159	549	355	1258	22	108	40-34	.255	.316	.429	.745	146	.968
Major League totals (14 years)			1502	4466	611	1126	189	32	165	584	372	1351	24	121	41-38	.252	.312	.420	.731	153	.971

DIVISION SERIES RECORD

Year	Team (League)	Pos.	G	AB	R	H	2B	3B	HR	RBI	BB	SO	HBP	GDP	SB-CS	Avg.	OBP	SLG	OPS	E	Avg.
1998—Chicago (N.L.)	SS		2	7	1	2	0	0	0	0	0	2	0	0	0-0	.286	.286	.286	.571	2	.750
1999—Atlanta (N.L.)	SS		4	11	1	1	0	0	0	0	1	3	0	1	1-0	.091	.167	.091	.258	1	.938
2004—Los Angeles (N.L.)			1	0	0	0	0	0	0	0	1	0	0	0	0-0	...	1.000	...	1.000	0	...
Division series totals (3 years)			7	18	2	3	0	0	0	0	2	5	0	1	1-0	.167	.250	.167	.417	3	.875

CHAMPIONSHIP SERIES RECORD

Year	Team (League)	Pos.	G	AB	R	H	2B	3B	HR	RBI	BB	SO	HBP	GDP	SB-CS	Avg.	OBP	SLG	OPS	E	Avg.
1999—Atlanta (N.L.)			2	2	0	1	0	0	0	1	0	1	0	0	0-0	.500	.500	.500	1.000	...	...

WORLD SERIES RECORD

Year	Team (League)	Pos.	G	AB	R	H	2B	3B	HR	RBI	BB	SO	HBP	GDP	SB-CS	Avg.	OBP	SLG	OPS	E	Avg.
1999—Atlanta (N.L.)	DH-SS		2	5	0	1	1	0	0	2	0	2	0	0	1-0	.200	.200	.400	.600	0	1.000

ALL-STAR GAME RECORD

	G	AB	R	H	2B	3B	HR	RBI	BB	SO	HBP	GDP	SB-CS	Avg.	OBP	SLG	OPS	E	Avg.
All-Star Game totals (1 year)	1	3	0	0	0	0	0	0	0	2	0	0	0-0	.000	.000	.000	.000	0	1.000

HERNANDEZ, LIVAN   P

PERSONAL: Born February 20, 1975, in Villa Clara, Cuba. ... 6-2/245. ... Throws right, bats right. ... Full name: Eisler Livan Hernandez. ... Name pronounced: lee-VAHN . ... Half-brother of Orlando Hernandez, pitcher, Chicago White Sox.

TRANSACTIONS/CAREER NOTES: Signed as a non-drafted free agent by Florida Marlins orgaization (January 13, 1996). ... Traded by Marlins to San Francisco Giants for Ps Jason Grilli and P Nate Bump (July 24, 1999). ... Traded by Giants with 3B/C Edwards Guzman and cash to Montreal Expos for P Jim Brower and a player to be named (March 24, 2003); Giants acquired P Matt Blank to complete deal (April 30, 2003). ... Expos franchise transferred to Washington, D.C., and renamed Washington Nationals for 2005 season (December 3, 2004).

CAREER HITTING: 153-for-646 (.237), 42 R, 28 2B, 2 3B, 7 HR, 62 RBI.

SCOUTING REPORT *Throws:* The crafty Hernandez attacks hitters with an 86-89 mph fastball, a slider, a changeup and a curveball. *Tendencies:* He is one of the game's true pitchers with an excellent idea of changing speeds and upsetting hitters timing. Doesn't throw hard but can spot his fastball to both sides of the plate. Throws a big, soft curve to lefthanders and a quick, short slider to righthanders. Changes speeds exceptionally well. Is not afraid to pitch to contact and is effective despite his below-average fastball. Is athletic despite his heavy frame. Is one of the better hitting pitchers in the game and a good fielder who knows how to control opponents' running games. *Outlook:* Hernandez is a solid starter but not a No. 1. Had knee surgery at the end of the season. *Grade 8.3*

LIVAN HERNANDEZ'S PITCHING ZONE

.268	.414	.220
.313	.347	.338
.293	.327	.240

LEFTY-RIGHTY SPLITS

vs.	Avg.	AB	H	2B	3B	HR	RBI	BB	SO	OBP	Slg.
L	.290	490	142	17	1	16	57	47	73	.358	.427
R	.278	454	126	31	5	9	54	37	74	.336	.427

Year	Team (League)	W	L	Pct.	ERA	WHIP	G	GS	CG	ShO	Hld.	Sv.-Opp.	IP	H	R	ER	HR	BB-IBB	SO	Avg.
1996—Charlotte (Int'l)		2	4	.333	5.14	1.94	10	10	0	0	...	0-...	49.0	61	32	28	3	34-1	45	.308
—Portland (East.)		9	2	.818	4.34	1.23	15	15	0	0	...	0-...	93.1	81	48	45	14	34-1	95	.233
—Florida (N.L.)		0	0	...	0.00	1.67	1	0	0	0	0	0-0	3.0	3	0	0	0	2-0	2	.273
1997—Charlotte (Int'l)		5	3	.625	3.98	1.40	14	14	0	0	...	0-...	81.1	76	39	36	5	38-2	58	.247
—Florida (N.L.)		9	3	.750	3.18	1.24	17	17	0	0	0	0-0	96.1	81	39	34	5	38-1	72	.229
—Portland (East.)		0	0	...	2.25	2.25	1	1	0	0	0	0-...	4.0	2	1	1	0	7-0	2	.154
1998—Florida (N.L.)		10	12	.455	4.72	1.57	33	33	9	0	0	0-0	234.1	* 265	133	123	37	104-8	162	.289
1999—Florida (N.L.)		5	9	.357	4.76	1.59	20	20	2	0	0	0-0	136.0	161	78	72	17	55-3	97	.294
—San Francisco (N.L.)		3	3	.500	4.38	1.37	10	10	0	0	0	0-0	63.2	66	32	31	6	21-2	47	.267
2000—San Francisco (N.L.)		17	11	.607	3.75	1.36	33	33	5	2	0	0-0	240.0	* 254	114	100	22	73-3	165	.273
2001—San Francisco (N.L.)		13	15	.464	5.24	1.55	34	34	2	0	0	0-0	226.2	* 266	* 143	* 132	24	85-7	138	.297
2002—San Francisco (N.L.)		12	• 16	.429	4.38	1.41	33	33	5	3	0	0-0	216.0	233	113	105	19	71-5	134	.283
2003—Montreal (N.L.)		15	10	.600	3.20	1.21	33	33	* 8	0	0	0-0	* 233.1	225	92	83	27	57-3	178	.253

– 277 –

H

Year Team (League)	W	L	Pct.	ERA	WHIP	G	GS	CG	ShO	Hld.	Sv.-Opp.	IP	H	R	ER	HR	BB-IBB	SO	Avg.
2004— Montreal (N.L.)	11	15	.423	3.60	1.24	35	•35	*9	2	0	0-0	*255.0	234	105	102	26	83-9	186	.248
2005— Washington (N.L.)	15	10	.600	3.98	1.43	35	•35	2	0	0	0-0	*246.1	*268	116	109	25	84-14	147	.284
Major League totals (10 years)	110	104	.514	4.11	1.40	284	283	42	7	0	0-0	1950.2	2056	965	891	208	673-55	1328	.274

DIVISION SERIES RECORD

Year Team (League)	W	L	Pct.	ERA	WHIP	G	GS	CG	ShO	Hld.	Sv.-Opp.	IP	H	R	ER	HR	BB-IBB	SO	Avg.
1997— Florida (N.L.)	0	0	...	2.25	0.75	1	0	0	0	0	0-0	4.0	3	1	1	0	0-0	3	.200
2000— San Francisco (N.L.)	1	0	1.000	1.17	1.30	1	1	0	0	0	0-0	7.2	5	1	1	0	5-0	5	.185
2002— San Francisco (N.L.)	1	0	1.000	3.24	1.20	1	1	0	0	0	0-0	8.1	8	3	3	0	2-0	6	.250
Division series totals (3 years)	2	0	1.000	2.25	1.15	3	2	0	0	0	0-0	20.0	16	5	5	0	7-0	14	.216

CHAMPIONSHIP SERIES RECORD

Year Team (League)	W	L	Pct.	ERA	WHIP	G	GS	CG	ShO	Hld.	Sv.-Opp.	IP	H	R	ER	HR	BB-IBB	SO	Avg.
1997— Florida (N.L.)	2	0	1.000	0.84	0.66	2	1	1	0	0	0-0	10.2	5	1	1	1	2-0	16	.143
2002— San Francisco (N.L.)	0	0	...	2.84	1.58	1	1	0	0	0	0-0	6.1	9	2	2	0	1-0	0	.360
Champ. series totals (2 years)	2	0	1.000	1.59	1.00	3	2	1	0	0	0-0	17.0	14	3	3	1	3-0	16	.233

WORLD SERIES RECORD

Year Team (League)	W	L	Pct.	ERA	WHIP	G	GS	CG	ShO	Hld.	Sv.-Opp.	IP	H	R	ER	HR	BB-IBB	SO	Avg.
1997— Florida (N.L.)	2	0	1.000	5.27	1.83	2	2	0	0	0	0-0	13.2	15	9	8	3	10-0	7	.283
2002— San Francisco (N.L.)	0	2	.000	14.29	3.18	2	2	0	0	0	0-0	5.2	9	10	9	0	9-3	4	.360
World Series totals (2 years)	2	2	.500	7.91	2.22	4	4	0	0	0	0-0	19.1	24	19	17	3	19-3	11	.308

ALL-STAR GAME RECORD

Year Team (League)	W	L	Pct.	ERA	WHIP	G	GS	CG	ShO	Hld.	Sv.-Opp.	IP	H	R	ER	HR	BB-IBB	SO	Avg.
All-Star Game totals (1 year)	0	0	...	18.00	3.00	1	0	0	0	0	0-0	1.0	2	2	2	0	1-0	0	.500

HERNANDEZ, ORLANDO — P

PERSONAL: Born October 11, 1969, in Havana, Cuba. ... 6-2/220. ... Throws right, bats right. ... Full name: Orlando P. Hernandez. ... Half-brother of Livan Hernandez, pitcher, Washington Nationals.

TRANSACTIONS/CAREER NOTES: Signed as a free agent by New York Yankees (March 23, 1998). ... On disabled list (July 18-August 6, 2000); included rehabilitation assignment to Tampa. ... On disabled list (June 1-August 21, 2001); included rehabilitation assignments to Tampa and Staten Island. ... On disabled list (May 16-June 27, 2002); included rehabilitation assignment to Columbus. ... On suspended list (July 21-28, 2002). ... Traded by Yankees to Chicago White Sox for Ps Antonio Osuna and Delvis Lantigua (January 15, 2003). ... Traded by White Sox with P Rocky Biddle, 3B/OF Jeff Liefer and cash to Montreal Expos for P Bartolo Colon and 2B/SS Jorge Nunez (January 15, 2003). ... On disabled list (March 21, 2003-entire season); included rehabilitation assignment to Brevard County. ... Signed as a free agent by Yankees (March 12, 2004). ... On disabled list (March 19-July 11, 2004); included rehabilitation assignments to Tampa and Columbus. ... Signed as a free agent by Chicago White Sox (January 3, 2005). ... On disabled list (May 22-June 3 and June 20-July 18, 2005).

CAREER HITTING: 2-for-22 (.091), 1 R, 0 2B, 0 3B, 0 HR, 0 RBI.

SCOUTING REPORT *Throws:* He has two- and four-seam fastballs that range from 86-90 mph, a curveball, slider and changeup. *Tendencies:* Hernandez will throw his riding four-seam fastball and running two-seam fastball late in the count. Likes to change speeds on his fastball but relies on his curve when runners are on. Varies the break and speed of his curveball and throws more of a slurve on occasion with a big, sweeping break. Stretches the pitch out of the zone as long as hitters chase it. Doesn't throw as hard now but has a real feel for pitching. *Outlook:* He has made an adjustment in his approach by throwing more breaking balls. Has increased his value with postseason relief performances but should start next season. *Grade 7.5*

ORLANDO HERNANDEZ'S PITCHING ZONE

.163	.387	.325
.316	.392	.279
.194	.467	.206

LEFTY-RIGHTY SPLITS

vs.	Avg.	AB	H	2B	3B	HR	RBI	BB	SO	OBP	Slg.
L	.291	268	78	18	4	9	39	28	33	.371	.489
R	.257	230	59	12	1	9	31	22	58	.329	.435

Year Team (League)	W	L	Pct.	ERA	WHIP	G	GS	CG	ShO	Hld.	Sv.-Opp.	IP	H	R	ER	HR	BB-IBB	SO	Avg.
1998— Tampa (Fla. St.)	1	1	.500	1.00	0.67	2	2	0	0	...	0-...	9.0	3	2	1	0	3-0	15	.100
— Columbus (Int'l)	6	0	1.000	3.83	1.37	7	7	0	0	...	0-...	42.1	41	19	18	2	17-0	59	.261
— New York (A.L.)	12	4	.750	3.13	1.17	21	21	3	1	0	0-0	141.0	113	53	49	11	52-1	131	.222
1999— New York (A.L.)	17	9	.654	4.12	1.28	33	33	2	1	0	0-0	214.1	187	108	98	24	87-2	157	.233
2000— New York (A.L.)	12	13	.480	4.51	1.21	29	29	3	0	0	0-0	195.2	186	104	98	34	51-2	141	.247
— Tampa (Fla. St.)	0	0	...	0.00	0.50	1	1	0	0	0	0-...	4.0	1	0	0	0	1-0	5	.077
2001— New York (A.L.)	4	7	.364	4.85	1.39	17	16	0	0	0	0-0	94.2	90	51	51	19	42-1	77	.248
— Tampa (Fla. St.)	0	0	...	0.00	1.00	2	2	0	0	0	0-...	7.0	6	2	0	0	1-0	8	.214
— Staten Island (N.Y.-Penn.) .	1	0	1.000	0.00	0.50	1	1	0	0	0	0-...	6.0	2	0	0	0	1-0	11	.100
2002— New York (A.L.)	8	5	.615	3.64	1.14	24	22	0	0	1	1-1	146.0	131	63	59	17	36-2	113	.236
— Columbus (Int'l)	1	0	1.000	1.59	1.41	1	1	0	0	0	0-...	5.2	7	2	1	0	1-0	5	.280
2003— Brevard County (FSL)	0	1	.000	10.80	1.80	2	2	0	0	0	0-...	5.0	5	6	6	0	4-0	7	.250
2004— Tampa (Fla. St.)	1	0	1.000	1.50	0.83	3	3	0	0	0	0-...	12.0	3	4	2	0	7-0	11	.079
— Columbus (Int'l)	2	1	.667	5.60	1.13	3	3	0	0	0	0-...	17.2	17	11	11	3	3-0	16	.243
— New York (A.L.)	8	2	.800	3.30	1.29	15	15	0	0	0	0-0	84.2	73	31	31	9	36-0	84	.230
2005— Charlotte (Int'l)	0	1	.000	2.25	1.00	1	1	0	0	0	0-...	4.0	4	1	1	0	0-0	2	.267
— Chicago (A.L.)	9	9	.500	5.12	1.46	24	22	0	0	0	1-1	128.1	137	77	73	18	50-1	91	.275
Major League totals (7 years)	70	49	.588	4.11	1.27	163	158	8	2	2	2-2	1004.2	917	487	459	132	354-9	794	.242

DIVISION SERIES RECORD

Year Team (League)	W	L	Pct.	ERA	WHIP	G	GS	CG	ShO	Hld.	Sv.-Opp.	IP	H	R	ER	HR	BB-IBB	SO	Avg.
1998— New York (A.L.)	Did not play.																		
1999— New York (A.L.)	1	0	1.000	0.00	1.00	1	1	0	0	0	0-0	8.0	2	0	0	0	6-0	4	.083
2000— New York (A.L.)	1	0	1.000	2.45	1.36	2	1	0	0	1	0-0	7.1	5	2	2	1	5-0	5	.200
2001— New York (A.L.)	1	0	1.000	3.18	1.76	1	1	0	0	0	0-0	5.2	8	2	2	0	2-0	5	.333
2002— New York (A.L.)	0	1	.000	2.84	0.79	2	1	0	0	0	0-0	6.1	5	2	2	0	0-0	7	.208
2004— New York (A.L.)	Did not play.																		
2005— Chicago (A.L.)	0	0	...	0.00	0.33	1	0	0	0	0	0-0	3.0	1	0	0	0	0-0	4	.100
Division series totals (5 years)	3	1	.750	1.78	1.12	7	4	0	0	1	0-0	30.1	21	6	6	1	13-0	25	.196

H

CHAMPIONSHIP SERIES RECORD

Year Team (League)	W	L	Pct.	ERA	WHIP	G	GS	CG	ShO	Hld.	Sv.-Opp.	IP	H	R	ER	HR	BB-IBB	SO	Avg.
1998— New York (A.L.)	1	0	1.000	0.00	0.71	1	1	0	0	0	0-0	7.0	3	0	0	0	2-0	6	.125
1999— New York (A.L.)	1	0	1.000	1.80	1.20	2	2	0	0	0	0-0	15.0	12	4	3	1	6-0	13	.207
2000— New York (A.L.)	2	0	1.000	4.20	1.40	2	2	0	0	0	0-0	15.0	13	7	7	2	8-2	14	.241
2001— New York (A.L.)	0	1	.000	7.20	2.00	1	1	0	0	0	0-0	5.0	5	5	4	1	5-0	7	.250
2004— New York (A.L.)	0	0	...	5.40	1.60	1	1	0	0	0	0-0	5.0	3	3	3	0	5-0	6	.167
2005— Chicago (A.L.)			Did not play.																
Champ. series totals (5 years)	4	1	.800	3.26	1.32	7	7	0	0	0	0-0	47.0	36	19	17	4	26-2	46	.207

WORLD SERIES RECORD

Year Team (League)	W	L	Pct.	ERA	WHIP	G	GS	CG	ShO	Hld.	Sv.-Opp.	IP	H	R	ER	HR	BB-IBB	SO	Avg.
1998— New York (A.L.)	1	0	1.000	1.29	1.29	1	1	0	0	0	0-0	7.0	6	1	1	0	3-0	7	.222
1999— New York (A.L.)	1	0	1.000	1.29	0.43	1	1	0	0	0	0-0	7.0	1	1	1	1	2-0	10	.048
2000— New York (A.L.)	0	1	.000	4.91	1.64	1	1	0	0	0	0-0	7.1	9	4	4	1	3-0	12	.300
2001— New York (A.L.)	0	0	...	1.42	1.26	1	1	0	0	0	0-0	6.1	4	1	1	1	4-0	5	.222
2005— Chicago (A.L.)	0	0	...	0.00	4.00	1	0	0	0	0	0-0	1.0	0	0	0	0	4-1	2	.000
World Series totals (5 years)	2	1	.667	2.20	1.26	5	4	0	0	0	0-0	28.2	20	7	7	3	16-1	36	.202

HERNANDEZ, RAMON — C

PERSONAL: Born May 20, 1976, in Caracas, Venezuela. ... 6-0/210. ... Bats right, throws right. ... Full name: Ramon Jose Hernandez.
TRANSACTIONS/CAREER NOTES: Signed as a non-drafted free agent by Oakland Athletics organization (February 18, 1994). ... On disabled list (July 26-August 27, 1999); included rehabilitation assignment to Vancouver. ... Traded by Athletics with OF Terrence Long to San Diego Padres for OF Mark Kotsay (November 26, 2003). ... On disabled list (June 21-July 26, 2004); included rehabilitation assignment to Portland. ... On disabled list (June 22-July 7 and July 29-September 2, 2005).
2005 GAMES PLAYED BY POSITION (MLB): C—97.

SCOUTING REPORT *Offense:* Likes the ball out over the plate, especially if it's up in the zone. Will go with the pitch and use the whole field. Has improved as a breaking-ball hitter. Has big-field power. Has some problems with lefthanded pitchers who change speeds. *Defense:* He is one of the league's best at handling a pitching staff. Has good hands and is mobile but must watch his weight. Tends to throw from a three-quarters arm angle but has arm strength and good carry. Has worked hard to improve his accuracy and footwork. *Outlook:* Hernandez has the ability to be a perennial All-Star. Continues to improve as a receiver and thrower. *Grade 8.3*

RAMON HERNANDEZ'S HITTING ZONE

.382	.353	.231
.359	.370	.264
.189	.360	.095

LEFTY-RIGHTY SPLITS

vs.	Avg.	AB	H	2B	3B	HR	RBI	BB	SO	OBP	Slg.
L	.238	80	19	2	1	3	18	6	10	.284	.400
R	.304	289	88	17	1	9	40	12	30	.333	.464

Year Team (League)	Pos.	G	AB	R	H	2B	3B	HR	RBI	BB	SO	HBP	GDP	SB-CS	Avg.	OBP	SLG	OPS	Fielding E	Avg.
1994— Dom. Athletics (DSL)	C	42	134	24	33	2	0	2	18	18	10			1-5	.246	...	.306	...	2	.991
1995— Ariz. A's (Ariz.)	1B-3B-C	48	143	37	52	9	6	4	37	39	16	8	3	6-2	.364	.510	.594	1.105	12	.972
1996— W. Mich. (Mid.)	C-DH-1B	123	447	62	114	26	2	12	68	69	62	4	22	2-3	.255	.355	.403	.758	20	.980
1997— Visalia (Calif.)	C-DH-1B	86	332	57	120	21	8	15	85	35	47	9	5	2-4	.361	.427	.572	.999	16	.976
— Huntsville (Sou.)	C-DH-1B																			
3B	44	161	27	31	3	0	4	24	18	23	3	8	0-0	.193	.281	.286	.567	1	.997
1998— Huntsville (Sou.)	DH-C-1B	127	479	83	142	24	1	15	98	57	61	19	15	4-5	.296	.389	.445	.833	11	.981
1999— Vancouver (PCL)	C-3B-1B	77	291	38	76	11	3	13	55	23	37	7	13	1-2	.261	.326	.454	.780	5	.980
— Oakland (A.L.)	C	40	136	13	38	7	0	3	21	18	11	1	5	1-0	.279	.363	.397	.760	6	.980
2000— Oakland (A.L.)	C	143	419	52	101	19	0	14	62	38	64	7	14	1-0	.241	.311	.387	.698	* 13	.984
2001— Oakland (A.L.)	C-1B	136	453	55	115	25	0	15	60	37	68	6	10	1-1	.254	.316	.408	.724	12	.988
2002— Oakland (A.L.)	C	136	403	51	94	20	0	7	42	43	64	5	11	0-0	.233	.313	.335	.648	7	.992
2003— Oakland (A.L.)	C	140	483	70	132	24	1	21	78	33	79	12	14	0-0	.273	.331	.458	.789	8	.991
2004— Portland (PCL)	C	7	19	2	6	1	0	0	6	2	3	0	1	0-0	.316	.381	.368	.749	2	.938
— San Diego (N.L.)	C	111	384	45	106	23	0	18	63	35	45	5	16	1-0	.276	.341	.477	.818	6	.992
2005— San Diego (N.L.)	C	99	369	36	107	19	2	12	58	18	40	1	14	1-0	.290	.322	.450	.772	8	.988
American League totals (5 years)		595	1894	241	480	95	1	60	263	169	286	31	54	3-1	.253	.322	.400	.721	46	.988
National League totals (2 years)		210	753	81	213	42	2	30	121	53	85	6	30	2-0	.283	.332	.463	.796	14	.991
Major League totals (7 years)		805	2647	322	693	137	3	90	384	222	371	37	84	5-1	.262	.325	.418	.742	60	.989

DIVISION SERIES RECORD

Year Team (League)	Pos.	G	AB	R	H	2B	3B	HR	RBI	BB	SO	HBP	GDP	SB-CS	Avg.	OBP	SLG	OPS	E	Avg.
2000— Oakland (A.L.)	C	5	16	3	6	2	0	0	3	0	3	1	0	0-0	.375	.412	.500	.912	1	.974
2001— Oakland (A.L.)	C	5	10	0	0	0	0	0	0	1	4	1	0	0-0	.000	.167	.000	.167	0	1.000
2002— Oakland (A.L.)	C	5	17	0	1	0	0	0	0	0	4	1	0	0-0	.059	.059	.059	.118	0	1.000
2003— Oakland (A.L.)	C	4	15	1	3	0	0	0	2	2	1	0	1	0-0	.200	.333	.200	.533	1	.974
2005— San Diego (N.L.)	C	3	11	2	5	0	0	1	1	2	1	0	1	0-0	.455	.538	.727	1.266	0	1.000
Division series totals (5 years)		22	69	6	15	2	0	1	6	5	13	3	2	0-0	.217	.299	.290	.589	2	.987

ALL-STAR GAME RECORD

	G	AB	R	H	2B	3B	HR	RBI	BB	SO	HBP	GDP	SB-CS	Avg.	OBP	SLG	OPS	E	Avg.
All-Star Game totals (1 year)	1	1	0	0	0	0	0	0	0	0	0	0	0-0	.000	.000	.000	.000	0	1.000

HERNANDEZ, ROBERTO — P

PERSONAL: Born November 11, 1964, in Santurce, Puerto Rico. ... 6-4/250. ... Throws right, bats right. ... Full name: Roberto Manuel Hernandez. ... High school: New Hampton (N.H.) Prep. ... College: South Carolina-Aiken.
TRANSACTIONS/CAREER NOTES: Selected by California Angels organization in first round (16th pick overall) of June 1986 free-agent draft; pick received as compensation for Baltimore Orioles signing Type A free-agent OF/IF Juan Beniquez. ... Traded by Angels with OF Mark Doran to Chicago White Sox for OF Mark Davis (August 2, 1989). ... Traded by White Sox with Ps Wilson Alvarez and Danny Darwin to San Francisco Giants for SS Mike Caruso, OF Brian Manning and Ps Lorenzo Barcelo, Keith Foulke, Bob Howry and Ken Vining (July 31, 1997). ... Signed as a free agent by Tampa Bay Devil Rays (November 18, 1997). ... Traded by Devil Rays to Kansas City Royals as part of three-team deal in which Devil Rays acquired OF Ben Grieve and cash from Oakland Athletics, A's acquired P Cory Lidle from Devil Rays and OF Johnny Damon, IF Mark Ellis and cash from Royals and Royals acquired C A.J. Hinch, IF Angel Berroa and cash from A's (January 8, 2001). ... On disabled list (March 22-May 2, 2002); included rehabil-

H

itation assignment to Omaha. ... Signed as a free agent by Atlanta Braves (January 22, 2003). ... On disabled list (June 12-27 and August 13-September 2, 2003); included rehabilitation assignment to Richmond. ... Signed as a free agent by Philadelphia Phillies (December 18, 2003). ... On disabled list (May 5-20, 2004). ... Signed as a free agent by New York Mets organization (January 18, 2005).

CAREER HITTING: 1-for-2 (.500), 0 R, 0 2B, 0 3B, 0 HR, 0 RBI.

SCOUTING REPORT Throws: Hernandez still hits the mid-90s with fastball, but his split-finger fastball still is his best pitch. Also throws a slider. *Tendencies:* He is using a slightly higher arm angle, which has given him better movement, especially on his slider. Has regained some velocity and late movement on his fastball. Can get hitters to chase the split-finger fastball out of the zone. *Outlook:* Hernandez still is a valuable middle reliever who can add good depth to a bullpen. *Grade 6.4*

ROBERTO HERNANDEZ'S PITCHING ZONE

.182	.143	.067
.237	.375	.273
.217	.368	.261

LEFTY-RIGHTY SPLITS

vs.	Avg.	AB	H	2B	3B	HR	RBI	BB	SO	OBP	Slg.
L	.244	123	30	6	0	4	16	15	32	.321	.390
R	.213	127	27	4	0	1	9	13	29	.296	.268

Year	Team (League)	W	L	Pct.	ERA	WHIP	G	GS	CG	ShO	Hld.	Sv.-Opp.	IP	H	R	ER	HR	BB-IBB	SO	Avg.
1986—	Salem (N'west)	2	2	.500	4.58	1.80	10	10	0	0	...	0-...	55.0	57	37	28	3	42-1	38	...
1987—	Quad City (Midw.)	2	3	.400	6.86	1.71	7	7	0	0	...	1-...	21.0	24	21	16	2	12-0	21	.273
1988—	Quad City (Midw.)	9	10	.474	3.17	1.24	24	24	6	1	...	0-...	164.2	157	70	58	8	48-0	114	.248
—	Midland (Texas)	0	2	.000	6.57	1.95	3	3	0	0	...	0-...	12.1	16	13	9	0	8-0	7	.320
1989—	Midland (Texas)	2	7	.222	6.89	1.94	12	12	0	0	...	0-...	64.0	94	57	49	4	30-0	42	.352
—	Palm Springs (Calif.)	1	4	.200	4.64	1.52	7	7	0	0	...	0-...	42.2	49	27	22	2	16-0	33	.295
—	South Bend (Mid.)	1	1	.500	3.33	1.07	4	4	0	0	...	0-...	24.1	19	9	9	1	7-0	17	.221
1990—	Birmingham (Sou.)	8	5	.615	3.67	1.35	17	17	1	0	...	0-...	108.0	103	53	44	6	43-2	62	.251
—	Vancouver (PCL)	3	5	.375	2.84	1.25	11	11	3	1	...	0-...	79.1	73	33	25	4	26-0	49	.247
1991—	Vancouver (PCL)	4	1	.800	3.22	1.43	7	7	0	0	...	0-...	44.2	41	17	16	2	23-0	40	.247
—	GC Whi. Sox (GCL)	0	0	...	0.00	0.33	1	1	0	0	...	0-...	6.0	2	0	0	0	0-0	7	.111
—	Birmingham (Sou.)	2	1	.667	1.99	0.75	4	4	0	0	...	0-...	22.2	11	5	5	2	6-0	25	.145
—	Chicago (A.L.)	1	0	1.000	7.80	1.67	9	3	0	0	0	0-0	15.0	18	15	13	1	7-0	6	.290
1992—	Chicago (A.L.)	7	3	.700	1.65	0.92	43	0	0	0	0	12-16	71.0	45	15	13	2	20-1	68	.180
—	Vancouver (PCL)	3	3	.500	2.61	1.16	9	0	0	0	0	2-...	20.2	13	9	6	0	11-1	23	.176
1993—	Chicago (A.L.)	3	4	.429	2.29	1.09	70	0	0	0	0	38-44	78.2	66	21	20	6	20-1	71	.228
1994—	Chicago (A.L.)	4	4	.500	4.91	1.32	45	0	0	0	0	14-20	47.2	44	29	26	9	19-1	50	.238
1995—	Chicago (A.L.)	3	7	.300	3.92	1.33	60	0	0	0	0	32-42	59.2	63	30	26	9	28-4	84	.266
1996—	Chicago (A.L.)	6	5	.545	1.91	1.22	72	0	0	0	0	38-46	84.2	65	21	18	2	38-5	85	.208
1997—	Chicago (A.L.)	5	1	.833	2.44	1.29	46	0	0	0	0	27-31	48.0	38	15	13	5	24-4	47	.216
—	San Francisco (N.L.)	5	2	.714	2.48	1.32	28	0	0	0	9	4-8	32.2	29	9	9	2	14-1	35	.238
1998—	Tampa Bay (A.L.)	2	6	.250	4.04	1.35	67	0	0	0	0	26-35	71.1	55	33	32	5	41-4	55	.212
1999—	Tampa Bay (A.L.)	2	3	.400	3.07	1.38	72	0	0	0	0	43-47	73.1	68	27	25	1	33-1	69	.245
2000—	Tampa Bay (A.L.)	4	7	.364	3.19	1.35	68	0	0	0	1	32-40	73.1	76	33	26	9	23-1	61	.272
2001—	Kansas City (A.L.)	5	6	.455	4.12	1.40	63	0	0	0	0	28-34	67.2	69	34	31	7	26-3	46	.266
2002—	Omaha (PCL)	0	0	...	0.00	1.50	2	0	0	0	0	0-...	2.0	0	1	0	0	3-0	3	.000
—	Kansas City (A.L.)	1	3	.250	4.33	1.42	53	0	0	0	0	26-33	52.0	62	29	25	6	12-2	39	.300
2003—	Richmond (Int'l)	1	1	.500	9.45	2.20	6	0	0	0	0	0-...	6.2	11	9	7	0	4-0	10	.333
—	Atlanta (N.L.)	5	3	.625	4.35	1.73	66	0	0	0	19	0-4	60.0	61	36	29	10	43-7	45	.263
2004—	Philadelphia (N.L.)	3	5	.375	4.76	1.68	63	0	0	0	9	0-4	56.2	66	39	30	9	29-3	44	.297
2005—	New York (N.L.)	8	6	.571	2.58	1.22	67	0	0	0	18	4-10	69.2	57	20	20	5	28-4	61	.228
American League totals (12 years)		43	49	.467	3.25	1.29	668	3	0	0	7	316-388	742.1	669	302	268	60	291-27	681	.239
National League totals (4 years)		21	16	.568	3.62	1.49	224	0	0	0	55	8-26	219.0	213	104	88	26	114-15	185	.258
Major League totals (15 years)		64	65	.496	3.33	1.34	892	3	0	0	62	324-414	961.1	882	406	356	86	405-42	866	.244

DIVISION SERIES RECORD

Year	Team (League)	W	L	Pct.	ERA	WHIP	G	GS	CG	ShO	Hld.	Sv.-Opp.	IP	H	R	ER	HR	BB-IBB	SO	Avg.
1997—	San Francisco (N.L.)	0	1	.000	20.25	6.00	3	0	0	0	0	0-0	1.1	5	3	3	0	3-1	1	.625
2003—	Atlanta (N.L.)	0	0	...	0.00	1.00	1	0	0	0	0	0-0	1.0	1	0	0	0	0-0	0	.333
Division series totals (2 years)		0	1	.000	11.57	3.86	4	0	0	0	0	0-0	2.1	6	3	3	0	3-1	1	.545

CHAMPIONSHIP SERIES RECORD

Year	Team (League)	W	L	Pct.	ERA	WHIP	G	GS	CG	ShO	Hld.	Sv.-Opp.	IP	H	R	ER	HR	BB-IBB	SO	Avg.
1993—	Chicago (A.L.)	0	0	...	0.00	1.00	4	0	0	0	0	1-1	4.0	4	0	0	0	0-0	1	.267

ALL-STAR GAME RECORD

	W	L	Pct.	ERA	WHIP	G	GS	CG	ShO	Hld.	Sv.-Opp.	IP	H	R	ER	HR	BB-IBB	SO	Avg.
All-Star Game totals (2 years)	0	0	...	0.00	0.50	2	0	0	0	0	0-0	2.0	1	0	0	0	0-0	0	.143

HERNANDEZ, RUNELVYS   P

PERSONAL: Born April 27, 1978, in Santo Domingo, Dominican Republic. ... 6-1/205. ... Throws right, bats right. ... Full name: Runelvys Antonio Hernandez. ... Name pronounced: roo-NEL-veez.

TRANSACTIONS/CAREER NOTES: Signed as a non-drafted free agent by Kansas City Royals organization (December 16, 1997). ... On disabled list (May 17-July 11 and August 17, 2003-remainder of season); included rehabilitation assignments to Omaha and Wichita. ... On disabled list (March 26, 2004-entire season; and August 22-September 6, 2005). ... On suspended list (September 6-17, 2005).

CAREER HITTING: 0-for-5 (.000), 0 R, 0 2B, 0 3B, 0 HR, 0 RBI.

SCOUTING REPORT Throws: Hernandez throws a four-seam fastball in the low-90 mph range, a slider and a circle change. *Tendencies:* Coming back from elbow problems, his velocity declined and his arm didn't appear to be loose. Fastball will run when it's down in the zone, but doesn't have much life up. Slider was not sharp, and was unable to maintain sufficient arm speed with his circle change. Gained a lot of weight. *Outlook:* He needs to focus on getting in better shape and regaining his velocity. Was a disappointment in 2005. *Grade 5.3*

RUNELVYS HERNANDEZ'S PITCHING ZONE

.226	.208	.263
.330	.424	.280
.171	.355	.204

LEFTY-RIGHTY SPLITS

vs.	Avg.	AB	H	2B	3B	HR	RBI	BB	SO	OBP	Slg.
L	.261	287	75	21	3	8	41	45	36	.362	.439
R	.290	335	97	19	3	10	53	25	52	.345	.454

H

Year	Team (League)	W	L	Pct.	ERA	WHIP	G	GS	CG	ShO	Hld.	Sv.-Opp.	IP	H	R	ER	HR	BB-IBB	SO	Avg.
1998—Dom. Royals (DSL)		0	2	.000	5.29	1.86	19	2	0	0	...	0-...	32.1	31	26	19	0	29-0	27	.263
1999—Dom. Royals (DSL)		2	2	.500	3.06	1.24	16	2	0	0	...	5-...	32.1	23	19	11	0	17-0	36	.192
2000—Dom. Royals (DSL)		7	3	.700	2.25	1.04	14	10	0	0	...	1-...	72.0	57	25	18	0	18-0	70	.210
2001—Burlington (Midw.)		7	5	.583	3.40	1.22	17	17	0	0	...	0-...	100.2	94	46	38	5	29-0	100	.241
2002—Wilmington (Caro.)		1	1	.500	3.75	1.08	2	2	0	0	...	0-...	12.0	12	6	5	0	1-0	9	.273
—Wichita (Texas)		8	3	.727	2.71	1.13	16	14	2	0	...	0-...	106.1	96	38	32	3	24-1	86	.249
—Kansas City (A.L.)		4	4	.500	4.36	1.36	12	12	0	0	0	0-0	74.1	79	36	36	8	22-0	45	.273
2003—Omaha (PCL)		1	0	1.000	1.80	1.00	1	1	0	0	0	0-...	5.0	3	1	1	0	2-0	5	.176
—Wichita (Texas)		0	2	.000	3.86	1.50	2	2	0	0	...	0-...	9.1	9	4	4	0	5-0	5	.257
—Kansas City (A.L.)		7	5	.583	4.61	1.35	16	16	0	0	0	0-...	91.2	87	51	47	9	37-0	48	.249
2004—Kansas City (A.L.)		Did not play.																		
2005—Kansas City (A.L.)		8	14	.364	5.52	1.52	29	29	0	0	0	0-0	159.2	172	101	98	18	70-0	88	.277
Major League totals (3 years)		19	23	.452	5.00	1.43	57	57	0	0	0	0-0	325.2	338	188	181	35	129-0	181	.268

HIDALGO, RICHARD   OF

PERSONAL: Born June 28, 1975, in Caracas, Venezuela. ... 6-3/220. ... Bats right, throws right. ... Full name: Richard Jose Hidalgo. ... Name pronounced: HUH-dahl-go.
TRANSACTIONS/CAREER NOTES: Signed as a non-drafted free agent by Houston Astros organization (July 2, 1991). ... On disabled list (May 30-July 21, 1998); included rehabilitation assignment to New Orleans. ... On disabled list (August 9, 1999-remainder of season; August 23-September 9, 2002; and May 23-June 8, 2003). ... Traded by Astros to New York Mets for Ps David Weathers and Jeremy Griffiths (June 17, 2004). ... Signed as a free agent by Texas Rangers (December 10, 2004). ... On disabled list (August 6, 2005-remainder of season).
RECORDS: Shares major league single-game record for most times hit by pitch (3, April 19, 2000).
2005 GAMES PLAYED BY POSITION (MLB): OF—85, DH—1.

SCOUTING REPORT **Offense:** Hidalgo has a long stroke but good bat speed. Has plus power to all fields. Can be vulnerable to off-speed stuff and pitches away. Can be streaky, both with strikeouts and homers. Has gained too much weight to be a good runner. **Defense:** He has a heavy lower body and no longer covers as much ground as he used to. Doesn't get good breaks, especially going back. Can be indecisive charging the ball. Has a strong arm but a slow release, yet is accurate. *Outlook:* A power threat, Hidalgo is streaky and continually must be reminded to stay on the ball and use the whole field. **Grade 7.5**

RICHARD HIDALGO'S HITTING ZONE

.148	.250	.167
.313	.333	.163
.250	.286	.083

LEFTY-RIGHTY SPLITS

vs.	Avg.	AB	H	2B	3B	HR	RBI	BB	SO	OBP	Slg.
L	.157	83	13	3	0	3	6	6	21	.231	.301
R	.244	225	55	9	0	13	37	20	53	.310	.458

								BATTING									FIELDING	
Year	Team (League)	Pos.	G	AB	R	H	2B	3B	HR	RBI	BB	SO	HBP	GDP	SB-CS	Avg.	OBP	SLG	OPS	E	Avg.
1992—GC Astros (GCL)	OF	51	184	20	57	7	3	1	27	13	27	3	1	14-5	.310	.360	.391	.756	0	1.000
1993—Asheville (S. Atl.)	OF	111	403	49	109	23	3	6	55	30	76	4	3	21-13	.270	.324	.417	.740	6	.974
1994—Quad City (Midw.)	OF	124	476	68	139	47	6	12	76	23	80	7	6	12-12	.292	.331	.492	.823	11	.953
1995—Jackson (Texas)	OF	133	489	59	130	28	6	14	59	32	76	2	11	8-9	.266	.309	.434	.743	5	.981
1996—Jackson (Texas)	OF-DH	130	513	66	151	34	2	14	78	29	55	11	24	11-7	.294	.341	.450	.791	6	.981
1997—New Orleans (A.A.)	OF-DH	134	526	74	147	37	5	11	78	35	57	8	16	6-10	.279	.330	.432	.761	9	.968
—Houston (N.L.)	OF	19	62	8	19	5	0	2	6	4	18	1	0	1-0	.306	.358	.484	.842	0	1.000
1998—Houston (N.L.)	OF	74	211	31	64	15	0	7	35	17	37	2	5	3-3	.303	.355	.474	.829	3	.978
—New Orleans (PCL)	OF	10	24	0	4	2	0	0	1	3	2	0	3	0-0	.167	.259	.250	.509	0	1.000
1999—Houston (N.L.)	OF	108	383	49	87	25	2	15	56	56	73	4	5	8-5	.227	.328	.420	.748	2	.991
2000—Houston (N.L.)	OF	153	558	118	175	42	3	44	122	56	110	21	4	13-6	.314	.391	.636	1.028	7	.984
2001—Houston (N.L.)	OF	146	512	70	141	29	3	19	80	54	107	16	15	3-5	.275	.356	.455	.811	3	.991
2002—Houston (N.L.)	OF	114	388	54	91	17	4	15	48	43	85	6	13	6-2	.235	.319	.415	.734	1	.995
2003—Houston (N.L.)	OF-DH	141	514	91	159	43	4	28	88	58	104	8	10	9-7	.309	.385	.572	.957	4	.987
2004—Houston (N.L.)	OF	58	199	21	51	15	2	4	30	17	53	0	7	1-2	.256	.309	.412	.721	2	.982
—New York (N.L.)	OF	86	324	46	74	11	1	21	52	27	76	5	12	3-2	.228	.296	.463	.759	4	.977
2005—Texas (A.L.)	OF-DH	88	308	43	68	12	0	16	43	26	74	4	8	1-2	.221	.289	.416	.705	2	.989
American League totals (1 year)		88	308	43	68	12	0	16	43	26	74	4	8	1-2	.221	.289	.416	.705	2	.989
National League totals (8 years)		899	3151	488	861	202	19	155	517	332	663	63	80	47-32	.273	.350	.497	.847	26	.987
Major League totals (9 years)		987	3459	531	929	214	19	171	560	358	737	67	88	48-34	.269	.345	.490	.835	28	.987

								DIVISION SERIES RECORD											
Year	Team (League)	Pos.	G	AB	R	H	2B	3B	HR	RBI	BB	SO	HBP	GDP	SB-CS	Avg.	OBP	SLG	OPS	E	Avg.
1997—Houston (N.L.)	OF	2	5	1	0	0	0	0	0	1	2	0	0	0-0	.000	.167	.000	.167	0	1.000
1998—Houston (N.L.)	OF	1	4	0	1	0	0	0	0	0	1	0	0	0-0	.250	.250	.250	.500	1	1.000
1999—Houston (N.L.)		Did not play.																	
2001—Houston (N.L.)	OF	3	8	1	1	0	0	0	0	3	2	0	0	0-0	.125	.364	.125	.489	0	1.000
Division series totals (3 years)		6	17	2	2	0	0	0	0	4	5	0	0	0-0	.118	.286	.118	.403	0	1.000

HIGGINSON, BOBBY   OF

PERSONAL: Born August 18, 1970, in Philadelphia. ... 5-11/195. ... Bats left, throws right. ... Full name: Robert Leigh Higginson. ... High school: Frankford (Philadelphia). ... College: Temple.
TRANSACTIONS/CAREER NOTES: Selected by Philadelphia Phillies organization in 18th round of 1991 free-agent draft; did not sign. ... Selected by Detroit Tigers organization in 12th round of 1992 free-agent draft. ... On disabled list (May 11-June 7, 1996); included rehabilitation assignment to Toledo. ... On disabled list (June 11-26, 1997). ... On suspended list (September 26, 1997). ... On disabled list (July 24-August 24, 1999). ... On suspended list (May 10-16, 1999). ... On disabled list (May 20-June 5, 2001; June 9-July 11, 2002; and June 29-July 25, 2003). ... On suspended list (September 2-4 and September 23-25, 2003). ... On disabled list (May 13, 2005-remainder of season).
2005 GAMES PLAYED BY POSITION (MLB): OF—7, DH—1.

LEFTY-RIGHTY SPLITS

vs.	Avg.	AB	H	2B	3B	HR	RBI	BB	SO	OBP	Slg.
L	.000	2	0	0	0	0	0	1	1	.333	.000
R	.083	24	2	0	0	0	1	0	4	.083	.083

Year	Team (League)	Pos.	G	AB	R	H	2B	3B	HR	RBI	BB	SO	HBP	GDP	SB-CS	Avg.	OBP	SLG	OPS	E	Avg.
1992—Niagara Falls (NYP)	OF	70	232	35	68	17	4	2	37	33	47	1	4	12-8	.293	.383	.427	.810	2	.983
1993—Lakeland (Fla. St.)	OF	61	223	42	67	11	7	3	25	40	31	1	6	8-3	.300	.406	.453	.859	2	.979
—London (East.)	OF	63	224	25	69	15	4	4	35	19	37	0	6	3-4	.308	.358	.464	.822	2	.982
1994—Toledo (Int'l)	OF	137	476	81	131	28	3	23	67	46	99	5	9	16-8	.275	.343	.492	.835	8	.973
1995—Detroit (A.L.)	OF-DH	131	410	61	92	17	5	14	43	62	107	5	5	6-4	.224	.329	.393	.721	4	.985
1996—Detroit (A.L.)	OF-DH	130	440	75	141	35	0	26	81	65	66	1	7	6-3	.320	.404	.577	.982	9	.963
—Toledo (Int'l)	OF	3	13	4	4	0	1	0	1	3	0	0	0	0-0	.308	.438	.462	.899	0	1.000
1997—Detroit (A.L.)	OF-DH	146	546	94	163	30	5	27	101	70	85	3	10	12-7	.299	.379	.520	.899	9	.972
1998—Detroit (A.L.)	OF-DH	157	612	92	174	37	4	25	85	63	101	6	16	3-3	.284	.355	.480	.835	8	.982
1999—Detroit (A.L.)	OF-DH	107	377	51	90	18	0	12	46	64	66	2	2	4-6	.239	.351	.382	.733	3	.983
2000—Detroit (A.L.)	OF-DH	154	597	104	179	44	4	30	102	74	99	2	5	15-3	.300	.377	.538	.915	7	.979
2001—Detroit (A.L.)	OF-DH	147	541	84	150	28	6	17	71	80	65	2	8	20-12	.277	.367	.445	.813	8	.976
2002—Detroit (A.L.)	OF-DH	119	444	50	125	24	3	10	63	41	45	6	8	12-5	.282	.345	.417	.762	7	.973
2003—Detroit (A.L.)	OF-DH	130	469	61	110	13	4	14	52	59	73	3	12	8-8	.235	.320	.369	.689	5	.981
2004—Detroit (A.L.)	OF-DH	131	448	63	110	24	2	12	64	70	84	1	10	5-2	.246	.354	.388	.742	6	.975
2005—Detroit (A.L.)	OF-DH	10	26	1	2	0	0	0	1	1	5	0	0	0-0	.077	.111	.077	.188	0	1.000
Major League totals (11 years)		1362	4910	736	1336	270	33	187	709	649	796	37	83	91-53	.272	.358	.455	.813	64	.977

HILL, AARON — 3B/SS

PERSONAL: Born March 21, 1982, in Visalia, Calif. ... 5-11/195. ... Bats right, throws right. ... Full name: Aaron Walter Hill. ... College: Louisiana State.
TRANSACTIONS/CAREER NOTES: Selected by Toronto Blue Jays organization in first round (13th pick overall) of 2003 free-agent draft.
2005 GAMES PLAYED BY POSITION (MLB): 3B—35, DH—34, 2B—22, SS—16.

SCOUTING REPORT Hill played second, shortstop and third in his first year and will at the least be a very good utility player. Has a compact, short swing. Likes the ball on the inside part of the plate. Should be a good breaking ball hitter. Doesn't have enough power to play third base regularly but is good enough defensively to play shortstop. Is a good runner but is not a threat to steal bases. Has a quick arm and can throw on the run. Has good hands and footwork but tends to lay back on the ball. ***Grade 5.4***

AARON HILL'S HITTING ZONE

.421	.286	.233
.257	.500	.265
.296	.130	.294

LEFTY-RIGHTY SPLITS

vs.	Avg.	AB	H	2B	3B	HR	RBI	BB	SO	OBP	Slg.
L	.298	104	31	9	1	1	10	15	13	.387	.433
R	.265	257	68	16	2	2	30	19	28	.323	.366

Year	Team (League)	Pos.	G	AB	R	H	2B	3B	HR	RBI	BB	SO	HBP	GDP	SB-CS	Avg.	OBP	SLG	OPS	E	Avg.
2003—Auburn (NY-Penn)	SS	33	122	22	44	4	0	4	34	16	20	6	2	1-1	.361	.446	.492	.938	8	.934
—Dunedin (Fla. St.)	SS	32	119	26	34	7	0	0	11	11	10	1	3	1-0	.286	.343	.345	.688	3	.930
2004—New Hampshire (East.)	SS	135	480	78	134	26	4	11	80	63	61	11	11	3-2	.279	.368	.410	.778	24	.724
2005—Syracuse (Int'l)	SS	38	156	22	47	11	0	5	18	4	17	6	6	2-0	.301	.339	.468	.807	10	.945
—Toronto (A.L.) 3B-DH-2B		105	361	49	99	25	3	3	40	34	41	5	5	2-1	.274	.342	.385	.727	6	.978
Major League totals (1 year)		105	361	49	99	25	3	3	40	34	41	5	5	2-1	.274	.342	.385	.727	6	.978

HILL, BOBBY — 2B/3B

PERSONAL: Born April 3, 1978, in San Jose, Calif. ... 5-9/180. ... Bats both, throws right. ... Full name: William Robert Hill. ... High school: Leland (Calif.). ... College: Miami.
TRANSACTIONS/CAREER NOTES: Selected by California Angels organization in fifth round of 1996 free-agent draft; did not sign. ... Selected by Chicago White Sox organization in second round of 1999 free-agent draft; did not sign. ... Signed by Newark of the independent Atlantic League (2000). ... Selected by Chicago Cubs organization in second round of 2000 free-agent draft. ... Traded by Cubs to Pittsburgh Pirates (August 15, 2003), completing deal in which Pirates acquired IF Jose Hernandez, P Matt Bruback and a player to be named for 3B Aramis Ramirez, OF Kenny Lofton and cash (July 23, 2003).
2005 GAMES PLAYED BY POSITION (MLB): 3B—24, 2B—1.

BOBBY HILL'S HITTING ZONE

.200	.667	.333
.250	.000	.346
.500	.333	.188

LEFTY-RIGHTY SPLITS

vs.	Avg.	AB	H	2B	3B	HR	RBI	BB	SO	OBP	Slg.
L	.357	14	5	0	0	0	2	4	4	.500	.357
R	.253	79	20	6	0	0	9	5	13	.310	.329

Year	Team (League)	Pos.	G	AB	R	H	2B	3B	HR	RBI	BB	SO	HBP	GDP	SB-CS	Avg.	OBP	SLG	OPS	E	Avg.
2000—Newark (Atl.)		132	481	109	157	22	9	13	82	101	57	4	...	81-15	.326	.442	.491	.933	38	...
2001—West Tenn (Sou.)	2B-SS	57	209	30	63	8	1	3	21	32	39	2	7	20-8	.301	.396	.392	.788	6	.973
—Ariz. Cubs (Ariz.)	2B	3	9	1	2	0	0	0	1	2	3	0	0	1-0	.222	.364	.222	.586	0	1.000
2002—Iowa (PCL)	2B	92	354	80	99	23	3	8	39	49	66	11	4	29-5	.280	.382	.429	.812	6	.980
—Chicago (N.L.)	2B-SS	59	190	26	48	7	2	4	20	17	42	4	0	6-1	.253	.327	.374	.701	3	.986
2003—Chicago (N.L.)	2B	5	4	0	1	0	0	0	1	2	0	1	0	0-0	.250	.400	.250	.650	0	1.000
—Iowa (PCL)	2B-3B	92	361	53	104	23	4	6	40	37	65	8	5	8-7	.288	.365	.424	.789	11	.973
—Nashville (PCL)	2B-DH	17	66	5	11	2	1	1	4	8	8	0	2	1-2	.167	.257	.273	.529	0	1.000
—Pittsburgh (N.L.)	2B	3	3	1	1	0	0	0	0	0	0	0	0	0-0	.333	.500	.333	.833	0	1.000
2004—Pittsburgh (N.L.)	2B-3B	126	233	28	62	7	2	2	27	20	39	12	12	0-3	.266	.353	.339	.692	2	.990
2005—Pittsburgh (N.L.)	3B-2B	58	93	12	25	6	0	0	11	9	17	2	3	0-0	.269	.343	.333	.676	2	.955
—Indianapolis (Int'l) 2B-3B-DH	SS	35	116	15	28	4	0	0	5	14	29	3	5	2-0	.241	.336	.276	.612	4	.929
Major League totals (4 years)		249	523	67	137	20	4	6	58	48	100	18	16	6-4	.262	.343	.350	.693	7	.985

H

HILL, KOYIE   C

PERSONAL: Born March 9, 1979, in Tulsa, Okla. ... 6-0/190. ... Bats both, throws right. ... Full name: Koyie Dolan Hill. ... Name pronounced: KOY-ee. ... High school: Eisenhower High (Lawton, Okla.). ... College: Wichita State.
TRANSACTIONS/CAREER NOTES: Selected by Los Angeles Dodgers organization in fourth round of 2000 free-agent draft. ... Traded with P Bill Murphy and OF Reggie Abercrombie to Arizona Diamondbacks for OF Steve Finley and C Brent Mayne (July 31, 2004). ... On disabled list (August 18, 2004-remainder of season).
2005 GAMES PLAYED BY POSITION (MLB): C—32.

SCOUTING REPORT** Offense:* Hill's swing is slow and long and he reaches for too many fast-balls up and away. Has trouble turning on inside heat and is fooled by average off-speed stuff. Does not get on top of the ball consistently, so he cannot use the gaps the way the Diamondbacks originally hoped. He needs to turn his hips into the ball in order to drive it. Is a slow runner. ***Defense: He knows how to handle pitchers and call a game. He has average to above-average footwork, hands, and blocking and framing skills. Has a plus arm but a slow release. ***Outlook:*** Until he can show more on offense—and he has a long way to go—he projects as a backup catcher. ***Grade 5.8***

KOYIE HILL'S HITTING ZONE

.667	.400	.000
.111	.667	.182
.667	.143	.125

LEFTY-RIGHTY SPLITS

vs.	Avg.	AB	H	2B	3B	HR	RBI	BB	SO	OBP	Slg.
L	.261	23	6	2	0	0	2	3	6	.333	.348
R	.200	55	11	3	0	0	4	8	21	.297	.255

Year	Team (League)	Pos.	G	AB	R	H	2B	3B	HR	RBI	BB	SO	HBP	GDP	SB-CS	Avg.	OBP	SLG	OPS	E	Avg.
2000—Yakima (N'west)		3B-C-2B	64	251	26	65	13	1	2	29	25	47	0	7	0-7	.259	.324	.343	.666	8	.941
2001—Wilmington (S. Atl.)		C	134	498	65	150	20	2	8	79	49	82	7	7	21-12	.301	.368	.398	.765	18	.977
2002—Jacksonville (Sou.)		C	130	468	67	127	25	1	11	64	76	88	0	14	5-3	.271	.368	.400	.768	17	.981
2003—Jacksonville (Sou.)		C-DH	25	101	9	23	7	0	0	7	6	19	0	3	2-1	.228	.271	.297	.568	2	.989
—Las Vegas (PCL)		C-DH-1B	85	312	48	98	18	0	3	36	15	39	1	7	5-0	.314	.345	.401	.746	9	.982
—Los Angeles (N.L.)			3	3	0	1	1	0	0	0	0	2	0	0	0-0	.333	.333	.667	1.000	0	...
2004—Las Vegas (PCL)		C-DH-1B																			
		3B	91	350	57	100	26	0	13	54	28	69	2	9	0-1	.286	.339	.471	.811	5	.992
—Arizona (N.L.)		C	13	36	3	9	1	0	1	6	2	6	0	1	1-0	.250	.289	.361	.651	1	.984
2005—Tucson (PCL)		C-DH	50	168	22	41	9	1	5	26	23	37	1	9	3-0	.244	.337	.399	.736	2	.993
—Arizona (N.L.)		C	34	78	6	17	5	0	0	6	11	27	0	0	0-1	.218	.308	.282	.590	0	1.000
Major League totals (3 years)			50	117	9	27	7	0	1	12	13	35	0	1	1-1	.231	.303	.316	.619	1	.995

HILL, RICH   P

PERSONAL: Born March 11, 1980, in Boston. ... 6-5/205. ... Throws left, bats left. ... Full name: Richard Joseph Hill. ... College: Michigan.
TRANSACTIONS/CAREER NOTES: Selected by Chicago Cubs organization in fourth round of 2002 free-agent draft.
CAREER HITTING: 2-for-6 (.333), 1 R, 0 2B, 0 3B, 0 HR, 0 RBI.

RICH HILL'S PITCHING ZONE

.636	.250	.333
.250	.250	.111
.125	.000	.400

LEFTY-RIGHTY SPLITS

vs.	Avg.	AB	H	2B	3B	HR	RBI	BB	SO	OBP	Slg.
L	.227	22	5	1	0	0	7	4	.414	.273
R	.270	74	20	5	0	3	12	10	17	.365	.459

Year	Team (League)	W	L	Pct.	ERA	WHIP	G	GS	CG	ShO	Hld.	Sv.-Opp.	IP	H	R	ER	HR	BB-IBB	SO	Avg.
2002—Boise (N'west)	0	2	.000	8.36	2.07	6	5	0	0	...	0-...	14.0	15	19	13	0	14-0	12	.268
2003—Lansing (Midw.)	0	1	.000	2.76	1.70	15	4	0	0	...	0-...	29.1	14	12	9	0	36-0	50	.141
—Boise (N'west)	1	6	.143	4.35	1.30	14	14	0	0	...	0-...	68.1	57	40	33	5	32-0	99	.233
2004—Daytona (Fla. St.)	7	6	.538	4.03	1.46	28	19	0	0	...	0-...	109.1	88	64	49	9	72-0	136	.221
2005—West Tenn (Sou.)	4	3	.571	3.28	1.09	10	10	0	0	0	0-0	57.2	42	22	21	9	21-0	90	.200
—Peoria (Midw.)	1	0	1.000	1.13	0.63	1	1	0	0	0	0-0	8.0	5	2	1	0	0-0	12	.179
—Iowa (PCL)	6	1	.857	3.60	1.03	11	10	0	0	0	0-0	65.0	53	28	26	11	14-0	92	.218
—Chicago (N.L.)	0	2	.000	9.13	1.77	10	4	0	0	0	0-0	23.2	25	24	24	3	17-1	21	.260
Major League totals (1 year)	0	2	.000	9.13	1.77	10	4	0	0	0	0-0	23.2	25	24	24	3	17-1	21	.260

HILLENBRAND, SHEA   1B/3B

PERSONAL: Born July 27, 1975, in Mesa, Ariz. ... 6-1/211. ... Bats right, throws right. ... Full name: Shea Matthew Hillenbrand. ... High school: Mountain View (Mesa, Ariz.). ... Junior college: Mesa (Ariz.) Community College.
TRANSACTIONS/CAREER NOTES: Selected by Boston Red Sox organization in 10th round of 1996 free-agent draft. ... On disabled list (August 31, 1999-remainder of season). ... Traded by Red Sox to Arizona Diamondbacks for P Byung-Hyun Kim (May 29, 2003). ... On disabled list (June 9-29, 2003); included rehabilitation assignment to Tucson. ... Traded by Diamondbacks to Toronto Blue Jays for P Adam Peterson (January 12, 2005).
2005 GAMES PLAYED BY POSITION (MLB): 1B—67, 3B—54, DH—33.

SCOUTING REPORT** Offense:* He showed renewed bat speed and was more aggressive in 2005. Has shortened his stroke and is using more of the whole field. Is quick enough to pull the ball inside and has power from right-center to the left-field line. Likes the ball up and has become better at hitting with runners in scoring position. ***Defense: He lost weight and was more mobile in the field. Still doesn't have really quick feet but catches what he gets to and handles errant throws well. Is better at first than third. ***Outlook:*** Hillenbrand has become a very dependable hitter over the past two seasons, but improved mobility around the bag has increased his value. ***Grade 8***

SHEA HILLENBRAND'S HITTING ZONE

.360	.207	.313
.321	.358	.304
.250	.351	.200

LEFTY-RIGHTY SPLITS

vs.	Avg.	AB	H	2B	3B	HR	RBI	BB	SO	OBP	Slg.
L	.325	160	52	11	0	7	22	6	18	.361	.525
R	.279	434	121	25	2	11	60	20	61	.336	.422

H

Year	Team (League)	Pos.	G	AB	R	H	2B	3B	HR	RBI	BB	SO	HBP	GDP	SB-CS	Avg.	OBP	SLG	OPS	E	Avg.
1996—	Lowell (NY-Penn)	1B-3B-SS	72	279	33	88	18	2	2	38	18	32	8	6	4-3	.315	.371	.416	.787	33	.938
1997—	Michigan (Midw.)	1B-3B	64	224	28	65	13	3	3	39	9	20	1	2	1-3	.290	.315	.415	.730	8	.950
—	Sarasota (Fla. St.)	1B-3B	57	220	25	65	12	0	2	28	7	29	2	4	9-8	.295	.320	.377	.698	20	.926
1998—	Michigan (Midw.)	1B-3B-C	129	498	80	174	33	4	19	93	19	49	10	11	13-7	.349	.383	.546	.929	14	.982
1999—	Trenton (East.)	C	69	282	41	73	15	0	7	36	14	27	3	6	6-5	.259	.298	.387	.685	5	.987
2000—	Trenton (East.)	1B-3B-DH	135	529	77	171	35	3	11	79	19	39	8	15	3-3	.323	.355	.463	.818	15	.979
2001—	Boston (A.L.)	3B-1B-DH	139	468	52	123	20	2	12	49	13	61	7	12	3-4	.263	.291	.391	.682	18	.950
2002—	Boston (A.L.)	3B	156	634	94	186	43	4	18	83	25	95	12	18	4-2	.293	.330	.459	.789 *	23	.943
2003—	Boston (A.L.)	3B-1B-DH	49	185	20	56	17	0	3	38	7	26	4	9	1-0	.303	.335	.443	.778	3	.989
—	Tucson (PCL)	1B-3B	3	10	0	3	1	0	0	1	0	1	0	0	0-0	.300	.300	.400	.700	0	1.000
—	Arizona (N.L.)	1B-3B	85	330	40	88	18	1	17	59	17	44	2	13	0-0	.267	.302	.482	.784	12	.978
2004—	Arizona (N.L.)	1B-3B	148	562	68	174	36	3	15	80	24	49	12	8	2-0	.310	.348	.464	.812	16	.987
2005—	Toronto (A.L.)	1B-3B-DH	152	594	91	173	36	2	18	82	26	79	* 22	21	5-1	.291	.343	.449	.792	12	.985
	American League totals (4 years)		496	1881	257	538	116	8	51	252	71	261	45	60	13-7	.286	.325	.438	.762	56	.970
	National League totals (2 years)		233	892	108	262	54	4	32	139	41	93	14	31	2-0	.294	.331	.471	.802	28	.984
	Major League totals (5 years)		729	2773	365	800	170	12	83	391	112	354	59	91	15-7	.288	.327	.448	.775	84	.977

ALL-STAR GAME RECORD

			G	AB	R	H	2B	3B	HR	RBI	BB	SO	HBP	GDP	SB-CS	Avg.	OBP	SLG	OPS	E	Avg.
All-Star Game totals (2 years)			2	2	0	0	0	0	0	0	0	1	0	0	0-0	.000	.000	.000	.000	0	1.000

HINSKE, ERIC — 3B

PERSONAL: Born August 5, 1977, in Menasha, Wis. ... 6-2/235. ... Bats left, throws right. ... Full name: Eric Scott Hinske. ... Name pronounced: HIN-skee. ... High school: Menasha (Wis.). ... College: Arkansas.

TRANSACTIONS/CAREER NOTES: Selected by Chicago Cubs organization in 17th round of 1998 free-agent draft. ... Traded by Cubs to Oakland Athletics for 2B Miguel Cairo (March 28, 2001). ... Traded by Athletics with P Justin Miller to Toronto Blue Jays for P Billy Koch (December 7, 2001). ... On disabled list (May 24-June 26, 2003); included rehabilitation assignment to Syracuse.

HONORS: Named A.L. Rookie Player of the Year by THE SPORTING NEWS (2002). ... Named A.L. Rookie of the Year by Baseball Writers' Association of America (2002).

2005 GAMES PLAYED BY POSITION (MLB): 1B—100, DH—43.

SCOUTING REPORT *Offense:* Hinske has lost bat speed and has to push the bat to get it started; he really keeps his hands inside the ball to hit. Will use the whole field and is patient but doesn't drive the ball consistently. Has better power on balls down. *Defense:* He's not an agile infielder and has a stiff lower body. Doesn't have much range around the bag and his hands are stiff. Doesn't throw well and can be a defensive liability with the ball in his hands. *Outlook:* Hinske still is searching for the run production and power most good first basemen possess. There are concerns if he will make the needed adjustments to play regularly at first. *Grade 6*

ERIC HINSKE'S HITTING ZONE

.269	.353	.286
.392	.390	.326
.125	.130	.295

LEFTY-RIGHTY SPLITS

vs.	Avg.	AB	H	2B	3B	HR	RBI	BB	SO	OBP	Slg.
L	.170	88	15	2	0	4	13	4	32	.215	.330
R	.283	389	110	29	2	11	55	42	89	.358	.452

Year	Team (League)	Pos.	G	AB	R	H	2B	3B	HR	RBI	BB	SO	HBP	GDP	SB-CS	Avg.	OBP	SLG	OPS	E	Avg.
1998—	Williamsport (N.Y.-Penn.)	1B	68	248	46	74	20	0	9	57	35	61	2	2	19-3	.298	.384	.488	.872	2	.997
—	Rockford (Midwest)	1B	6	20	8	9	4	0	1	4	5	6	0	0	1-0	.450	.538	.800	1.338	0	1.000
1999—	Daytona (Fla. St.)	1B-3B-OF	130	445	76	132	28	6	19	79	62	90	5	5	16-10	.297	.385	.515	.900	22	.965
—	Iowa (PCL)	1B-3B	4	15	3	4	0	1	1	2	1	4	0	0	0-0	.267	.313	.600	.913	1	.952
2000—	West Tenn (Sou.)	1B-3B-OF	131	436	76	113	21	9	20	73	78	133	3	7	14-5	.259	.373	.486	.859	28	.916
2001—	Sacramento (PCL)	3B-2B	121	436	71	123	27	1	25	79	54	113	10	6	20-7	.282	.373	.521	.893	17	.941
2002—	Toronto (A.L.)	3B	151	566	99	158	38	2	24	84	77	138	2	12	13-1	.279	.365	.481	.845	20	.946
2003—	Syracuse (Int'l)	3B	2	8	2	4	1	0	1	2	0	0	0	0	0-0	.500	.500	1.000	1.500	0	1.000
—	Toronto (A.L.)	3B	124	449	74	109	45	3	12	63	59	104	1	11	12-2	.243	.329	.437	.765	22	.930
2004—	Toronto (A.L.)	3B-DH	155	570	66	140	23	3	15	69	54	109	4	14	12-8	.246	.312	.375	.688	8	.978
2005—	Toronto (A.L.)	1B-DH	147	477	79	125	31	2	15	68	46	121	8	8	8-4	.262	.333	.430	.763	7	.993
	Major League totals (4 years)		577	2062	318	532	137	10	66	284	236	472	15	45	45-15	.258	.335	.430	.765	57	.971

HOCKING, DENNY — OF/SS

PERSONAL: Born April 2, 1970, in Torrance, Calif. ... 5-10/187. ... Bats both, throws right. ... Full name: Dennis Lee Hocking. ... Name pronounced: HAWK-ing. ... High school: West Torrance (Calif.). ... Junior college: El Camino (Calif.) Community College.

TRANSACTIONS/CAREER NOTES: Selected by Minnesota Twins organization in 52nd round of 1989 free-agent draft. ... On disabled list (March 22-April 30, May 30-June 29 and July 31-September 8, 1996); included rehabilitation assignments to Salt Lake. ... On disabled list (April 22-May 9, 2003). ... Signed as a free agent by Colorado Rockies organization (January 9, 2004). ... Released by Rockies (July 8, 2004). ... Signed by Chicago Cubs organization (July 23, 2004). ... Signed as a free agent by Kansas City Royals organization (January 18, 2005).

2005 GAMES PLAYED BY POSITION (MLB): 2B—13, 3B—1, SS—1.

DENNY HOCKING'S HITTING ZONE

.000	...	.000
.111	.286	.250
.200	.286	.400

LEFTY-RIGHTY SPLITS

vs.	Avg.	AB	H	2B	3B	HR	RBI	BB	SO	OBP	Slg.
L	.375	8	3	1	0	0	4	2	.583	.500
R	.250	52	13	0	0	0	7	6	8	.328	.250

Year	Team (League)	Pos.	G	AB	R	H	2B	3B	HR	RBI	BB	SO	HBP	GDP	SB-CS	Avg.	OBP	SLG	OPS	E	Avg.
1990—	Elizabethton (App.)	2B-3B-SS	54	201	45	59	6	2	6	30	40	26	6	6	14-4	.294	.422	.433	.855	20	.928
1991—	Kenosha (Midw.)	SS	125	432	72	110	17	8	2	36	77	69	6	6	22-10	.255	.372	.345	.717	42	.943
1992—	Visalia (Calif.)	SS	135	550	117	182	34	9	6	81	72	77	8	7	38-18	.331	.415	.464	.878	38	.947
1993—	Nashville (Southern)	SS	107	409	54	109	9	4	8	50	34	66	4	12	15-5	.267	.327	.367	.694	30	.937
—	Minnesota (A.L.)	SS-2B	15	36	7	5	1	0	0	0	6	8	0	0	1-0	.139	.262	.167	.429	1	.947
1994—	Salt Lake (PCL)	SS	112	394	61	110	14	6	5	57	28	57	2	6	13-7	.279	.327	.383	.710	26	.949

H

Year	Team (League)	Pos.	G	AB	R	H	2B	3B	HR	RBI	BB	SO	HBP	GDP	SB-CS	Avg.	OBP	SLG	OPS	E	Avg.
																		BATTING		**FIELDING**	
— Minnesota (A.L.)	SS	11	31	3	10	3	0	0	2	0	4	0	1	2-0	.323	.323	.419	.742	0	1.000
1995—Salt Lake (PCL)	SS-2B-DH	117	397	51	112	24	2	8	75	25	41	2	10	12-8	.282	.324	.413	.737	20	.966
— Minnesota (A.L.)	SS	9	25	4	5	0	2	0	3	2	2	0	1	1-0	.200	.259	.360	.619	1	.971
1996—Salt Lake (PCL)	SS-OF-DH 1B-2B-3B	37	130	18	36	6	2	3	22	10	17	2	4	2-2	.277	.333	.423	.756	3	.976
— Minnesota (A.L.)	OF-SS-2B 1B-DH	49	127	16	25	6	0	1	10	8	24	0	3	3-3	.197	.243	.268	.510	1	.987
1997—Minnesota (A.L.)	SS-3B-OF 2B-1B-DH	115	253	28	65	12	4	2	25	18	51	1	6	3-5	.257	.308	.360	.667	4	.985
1998—Minnesota (A.L.)	2B-SS-OF 3B-1B	110	198	32	40	6	1	3	15	16	44	0	2	2-1	.202	.259	.288	.547	4	.982
1999—Minnesota (A.L.)	SS-2B-OF 3B-1B	136	386	47	103	18	2	7	41	22	54	3	10	11-7	.267	.307	.378	.685	3	.992
2000—Minnesota (A.L.)	OF-2B-DH SS-1B-DH	134	373	52	111	24	4	4	47	48	77	0	2	7-5	.298	.373	.416	.789	5	.985
2001—Minnesota (A.L.)	SS-2B-OF 1B-DH-3B	112	327	34	82	16	2	3	25	29	67	2	7	6-1	.251	.315	.339	.654	5	.984
2002—Minnesota (A.L.)	2B-SS-3B 1B-DH	102	260	28	65	13	0	2	25	24	44	1	3	0-2	.250	.310	.323	.633	10	.968
2003—Minnesota (A.L.)	2B-3B-SS 1B-OF-DH	83	188	22	45	10	2	3	22	15	37	0	3	0-1	.239	.291	.362	.653	3	.988
2004—Colorado (N.L.)	OF-SS-2B 3B	55	94	7	19	2	0	0	4	7	20	0	0	0-1	.202	.257	.223	.481	4	.964
— Iowa (PCL)	3B-SS-2B OF	39	104	20	30	12	0	3	22	11	20	1	1	0-2	.288	.359	.490	.849	3	.975
2005—Omaha (PCL)	2B-SS-3B DH-1B-3B	68	230	37	66	14	2	0	24	25	44	0	5	1-0	.287	.353	.365	.718	6	.969
— Kansas City (A.L.)	2B-3B-SS	23	60	14	16	1	0	0	7	10	10	0	1	0-1	.267	.371	.283	.655	2	.977
American League totals (12 years)		899	2264	287	572	110	17	25	222	198	422	7	40	36-26	.253	.312	.349	.661	39	.984
National League totals (1 year)		55	94	7	19	2	0	0	4	7	20	0	3	0-1	.202	.257	.223	.481	4	.964
Major League totals (13 years)		954	2358	294	591	112	17	25	226	205	442	7	43	36-27	.251	.310	.344	.654	43	.983

DIVISION SERIES RECORD

Year	Team (League)	Pos.	G	AB	R	H	2B	3B	HR	RBI	BB	SO	HBP	GDP	SB-CS	Avg.	OBP	SLG	OPS	E	Avg.
2002—Minnesota (A.L.)	2B-OF	3	6	0	3	1	0	1	1	0	1	0	0	0-0	.500	.500	.667	1.167	0	1.000
2003—Minnesota (A.L.)	2B	1	0	0	0	0	0	0	0	0	0	0	0	0-0	...	...	...	...	0	...
Division series totals (2 years)		4	6	0	3	1	0	1	1	0	1	0	0	0-0	.500	.500	.667	1.167	0	1.000

HOFFMAN, TREVOR — P

PERSONAL: Born October 13, 1967, in Bellflower, Calif. ... 6-0/215. ... Throws right, bats right. ... Full name: Trevor William Hoffman. ... High school: Savanna (Anaheim). ... College: Arizona. ... Brother of Glenn Hoffman, coach, Los Angeles Dodgers and infielder with three major league teams (1980-87 and 1989).

TRANSACTIONS/CAREER NOTES: Selected by Cincinnati Reds organization in 11th round of 1989 free-agent draft. ... Played two seasons as a shortstop in Reds organization (1989-90). ... Selected by Florida Marlins in first round (eighth pick overall) of expansion draft (November 17, 1992). ... Traded by Marlins with Ps Jose Martinez and Andres Berumen to San Diego Padres for 3B Gary Sheffield and P Rich Rodriguez (June 24, 1993). ... On disabled list (March 25-September 2, 2003); included rehabilitation assignment to Lake Elsinore.

HONORS: Named N.L. Fireman of the Year by THE SPORTING NEWS (1996 and 1998).

CAREER HITTING: 4-for-33 (.121), 1 R, 2 2B, 0 3B, 0 HR, 5 RBI.

SCOUTING REPORT ***Throws:*** Hoffman has a four-seam fastball that tops out at 87 mph, but he also has one of the best changeups ever. ***Tendencies:*** He no longer relies on power but rather on his ability to speed up and slow down hitters' bats. Has outstanding deception and excellent command. Spots his fastball well but makes hitters hit his changeup. Throws the change with excellent arm speed and from the same release point as his fastball. Change almost stops at home plate. ***Outlook:*** Hoffman still is a reliable closer after he adjusted to a loss in velocity. ***Grade 8.5***

TREVOR HOFFMAN'S PITCHING ZONE

.182	.111	.500
.243	.294	.294
.217	.273	.238

LEFTY-RIGHTY SPLITS

vs.	Avg.	AB	H	2B	3B	HR	RBI	BB	SO	OBP	Slg.
L	.298	104	31	6	1	0	8	7	25	.342	.375
R	.179	117	21	5	1	3	14	5	29	.214	.316

Year	Team (League)	W	L	Pct.	ERA	WHIP	G	GS	CG	ShO	Hld.	Sv.-Opp.	IP	H	R	ER	HR	BB-IBB	SO	Avg.
1991—Cedar Rap. (Midw.)	1	1	.500	1.87	1.04	27	0	0	0	...	12-...	33.2	22	8	7	0	13-0	52	.188
—Chattanooga (Sou.)	1	0	1.000	1.93	1.21	14	0	0	0	...	8-...	14.0	10	4	3	0	7-0	23	.192
1992—Chattanooga (Sou.)	3	0	1.000	1.52	1.11	6	6	0	0	...	0-...	29.2	22	6	5	1	11-1	31	.212
—Nashville (A.A.)	4	6	.400	4.27	1.36	42	5	0	0	...	6-...	65.1	57	32	31	6	32-3	63	.234
1993—Florida (N.L.)	2	2	.500	3.28	1.21	28	0	0	0	8	2-3	35.2	24	13	13	6	19-7	26	.185
—San Diego (N.L.)	2	4	.333	4.31	1.40	39	0	0	0	7	3-5	54.1	56	30	26	5	20-6	53	.264
1994—San Diego (N.L.)	4	4	.500	2.57	1.05	47	0	0	0	1	20-23	56.0	39	16	16	4	20-6	68	.193
1995—San Diego (N.L.)	7	4	.636	3.88	1.16	55	0	0	0	0	31-38	53.1	48	25	23	10	14-3	52	.235
1996—San Diego (N.L.)	9	5	.643	2.25	0.92	70	0	0	0	0	42-49	88.0	50	23	22	6	31-5	111	.161
1997—San Diego (N.L.)	6	4	.600	2.66	1.02	70	0	0	0	0	37-44	81.1	59	25	24	9	24-4	111	.200
1998—San Diego (N.L.)	4	2	.667	1.48	0.85	66	0	0	0	0	* 53-54	73.0	41	12	12	2	21-2	86	.165
1999—San Diego (N.L.)	2	3	.400	2.14	0.94	64	0	0	0	0	40-43	67.1	48	23	16	5	15-2	73	.197
2000—San Diego (N.L.)	4	7	.364	2.99	1.00	70	0	0	0	0	43-50	72.1	61	29	24	7	11-4	85	.224
2001—San Diego (N.L.)	3	4	.429	3.43	1.14	62	0	0	0	0	43-46	60.1	48	25	23	10	21-2	63	.216
2002—San Diego (N.L.)	2	5	.286	2.73	1.18	61	0	0	0	0	38-41	59.1	52	20	18	2	18-2	69	.234
2003—Lake Elsinore (Calif.)	0	0	...	0.00	0.70	3	0	0	0	...	0-...	3.0	2	0	0	0	0-0	4	.182
—San Diego (N.L.)	0	0	...	2.00	1.11	9	0	0	0	...	0-...	9.0	7	2	2	1	3-0	11	.212
2004—San Diego (N.L.)	3	3	.500	2.30	0.91	55	0	0	0	0	41-45	54.2	42	14	14	5	8-1	53	.211
2005—San Diego (N.L.)	1	6	.143	2.97	1.11	60	0	0	0	0	43-46	57.2	52	23	19	3	12-1	54	.235
Major League totals (13 years)	49	53	.480	2.76	1.05	756	0	0	0	16	436-487	822.1	627	280	252	74	237-45	915	.208

H

DIVISION SERIES RECORD

Year	Team (League)	W	L	Pct.	ERA	WHIP	G	GS	CG	ShO	Hld.	Sv.-Opp.	IP	H	R	ER	HR	BB-IBB	SO	Avg.
1996— San Diego (N.L.)		0	1	.000	10.80	2.40	2	0	0	0	0	0-0	1.2	3	2	2	1	1-0	2	.375
1998— San Diego (N.L.)		0	0	...	0.00	1.33	4	0	0	0	0	2-2	3.0	3	1	0	0	1-1	4	.250
2005— San Diego (N.L.)		0	0	...	0.00	1.00	1	0	0	0	0	0-0	1.0	1	0	0	0	0-0	0	.250
Division series totals (3 years)		0	1	.000	3.18	1.59	7	0	0	0	0	2-2	5.2	7	3	2	1	2-1	6	.292

CHAMPIONSHIP SERIES RECORD

Year	Team (League)	W	L	Pct.	ERA	WHIP	G	GS	CG	ShO	Hld.	Sv.-Opp.	IP	H	R	ER	HR	BB-IBB	SO	Avg.
1998— San Diego (N.L.)		1	0	1.000	2.08	0.92	3	0	0	0	0	1-2	4.1	2	1	1	0	2-0	7	.143

WORLD SERIES RECORD

Year	Team (League)	W	L	Pct.	ERA	WHIP	G	GS	CG	ShO	Hld.	Sv.-Opp.	IP	H	R	ER	HR	BB-IBB	SO	Avg.
1998— San Diego (N.L.)		0	1	.000	9.00	1.50	1	0	0	0	0	0-1	2.0	2	2	2	1	1-0	0	.250

ALL-STAR GAME RECORD

	W	L	Pct.	ERA	WHIP	G	GS	CG	ShO	Hld.	Sv.-Opp.	IP	H	R	ER	HR	BB-IBB	SO	Avg.
All-Star Game totals (4 years)	0	0	...	10.80	1.50	4	0	0	0	1	0-0	3.1	5	4	4	1	0-0	5	.333

HOLBERT, AARON   SS/2B

PERSONAL: Born January 9, 1973, in Torrance, Calif. ... 6-0/160. ... Bats right, throws right. ... Full name: Aaron Keith Holbert. ... High school: David Starr Jordan (Long Beach, Calif.). ... Brother of Ray Holbert, infielder with four major league teams (1994-95, 1998-2000).

TRANSACTIONS/CAREER NOTES: Selected by St. Louis Cardinals organization in first round (18th pick overall) of 1990 free-agent draft; pick received as part of compensation for Boston Red Sox signing Type A free-agent C Tony Pena. ... Signed as a free agent by Seattle Mariners organization (April 7, 1998). ... Signed as a free agent by Tampa Bay Devil Rays organization (November 24, 1998). ... Signed as a free agent by Boston Red Sox organization (December 16, 1999). ... Traded by Red Sox to Florida Marlins for a player to be named (August 2, 2000); Red Sox acquired P Nelson Lara to complete deal (March 30, 2001). ... Signed as a free agent by Toronto Blue Jays organization (November 5, 2000). Signed as a free agent by Mariners organization (January 30, 2002). ... Signed as a free agent by Pittsburgh Pirates organization (November 7, 2002). ... Signed as a free agent by Cincinnati Reds (November 26, 2003).

LEFTY-RIGHTY SPLITS

vs.	Avg.	AB	H	2B	3B	HR	RBI	BB	SO	OBP	Slg.
L	.273	11	3	2	0	0	1	1	3	.333	.455
R	.188	16	3	1	0	0	2	2	5	.263	.250

2005 GAMES PLAYED BY POSITION (MLB): 2B—4, 3B—2, 1B—2.

							BATTING												FIELDING	
Year Team (League)	Pos.	G	AB	R	H	2B	3B	HR	RBI	BB	SO	HBP	GDP	SB-CS	Avg.	OBP	SLG	OPS	E	Avg.
1990— Johnson City (App.)	SS	54	174	27	30	4	1	1	18	24	31	3	2	4-5	.172	.282	.224	.506	* 30	.881
1991— Springfield (Midw.)	SS	59	215	22	48	5	1	1	24	15	28	6	3	5-8	.223	.290	.270	.560	15	.951
1992— Savannah (S. Atl.)	SS	119	438	53	117	17	4	1	34	40	57	8	4	62-25	.267	.337	.331	.668	47	.915
1993— St. Pete. (FSL)	SS-2B	121	457	60	121	18	3	2	31	28	61	4	6	45-* 22	.265	.312	.330	.642	32	.947
1994— Arkansas (Texas)	SS	59	233	41	69	10	6	2	19	14	25	2	5	9-7	.296	.340	.416	.756	17	.944
— Ariz. Cardinals (Ariz.)	SS	5	12	3	2	0	0	0	0	2	2	0	0	2-0	.167	.286	.167	.453	1	.950
1995— Louisville (A.A.)	SS	112	401	57	103	16	4	9	40	20	60	5	10	14-6	.257	.297	.384	.681	* 31	.936
1996— Louisville (A.A.) 2B-SS-DH	112	436	54	115	16	6	4	32	21	61	2	8	20-14	.264	.298	.356	.654	30	.946
— St. Louis (N.L.)	2B	1	3	0	0	0	0	0	0	0	0	...	...	0-0	.000	.000	.000	...	0	1.000
1997— Louisville (A.A.) SS-DH-2B	93	314	32	80	14	3	4	32	15	56	7	9	9-5	.255	.290	.357	.647	27	.935
1998— Orlando (South.)	SS-2B	68	251	46	72	13	5	3	34	22	41	5	3	10-14	.287	.355	.414	.769	10	.969
— Tacoma (PCL)	SS-2B																			
	2B-DH-P	56	229	38	72	12	0	9	31	12	40	1	3	6-6	.314	.355	.485	.840	14	.948
1999— Durham (Int'l) 2B-SS-DH																			
	OF-3B	100	347	77	108	18	4	12	56	25	56	5	4	14-5	.311	.361	.490	.851	11	.971
2000— Pawtucket (Int'l) SS-3B-2B	80	294	38	74	13	2	3	23	15	54	4	4	8-6	.252	.297	.340	.637	14	.941
— Calgary (PCL)	SS-2B	29	104	18	29	5	1	4	18	10	12	1	2	3-4	.279	.348	.462	.810	3	.979
2001— Syracuse (Int'l) 2B-3B-SS																			
	-OF	55	212	25	52	10	2	2	19	8	33	2	4	9-0	.245	.276	.340	.616	8	.961
2002— Tacoma (PCL) SS-2B-3B	120	399	62	124	24	3	7	42	19	50	12	12	17-13	.311	.358	.439	.797	19	.959
2003— Nashville (PCL) SS-2B-3B	116	397	57	107	20	7	3	37	19	78	8	6	29-13	.270	.314	.378	.692	20	.956
2004— Louisville (Int'l) 2B-1B-SS																			
	OF-P-3B	115	380	66	103	18	4	4	46	41	66	6	9	32-14	.271	.349	.361	.710	6	.991
2005— Louisville (Int'l) 2B-SS-3B																			
	1B-DH	68	230	33	70	14	2	6	23	11	31	6	5	12-5	.304	.351	.461	.812	11	.959
— Cincinnati (N.L.) 2B-1B-3B	22	27	3	6	3	0	0	2	3	8	0	1	1-0	.222	.290	.333	.624	1	.966
Major League totals (2 years)		23	30	3	6	3	0	0	2	3	8	0	1	1-0	.200	.265	.300	.565	1	.967

HOLLANDSWORTH, TODD   OF

PERSONAL: Born April 20, 1973, in Dayton, Ohio. ... 6-2/215. ... Bats left, throws left. ... Full name: Todd Mathew Hollandsworth. ... High school: Newport (Bellevue, Wash.).

TRANSACTIONS/CAREER NOTES: Selected by Los Angeles Dodgers organization in third round of 1991 free-agent draft; pick received as part of compensation for Kansas City Royals signing Type B free-agent OF/DH Kirk Gibson. ... On disabled list (May 3-July 7 and August 9-September 12, 1995); included rehabilitation assignments to San Bernardino and Albuquerque. ... On disabled list (August 1-16 and August 17-September 6, 1997); included rehabilitation assignment to San Bernardino. ... On disabled list (June 5, 1998-remainder of season). ... On disabled list (April 3-23 and June 4-19, 1999); included rehabilitation assignments to San Bernardino. ... Traded by Dodgers with OF Kevin Gibbs and P Randey Dorame to Colorado Rockies for OF Tom Goodwin and cash (July 31, 2000). ... On disabled list (May 12, 2001-remainder of season). ... Traded by Rockies with P Dennys Reyes to Texas Rangers for OF Gabe Kapler and 2B Jason Romano (July 31, 2002). ... On disabled list (August 4-20, 2002). ... Signed as a free agent by Florida Marlins (January 8, 2003). ... On disabled list (August 14-September 1, 2003). ... Signed as a free agent by Chicago Cubs (December 18, 2003). ... On disabled list (June 28, 2004-remainder of season). ... Traded by Cubs to Atlanta Braves for Ps Todd Blackford and Angelo Burrows (August 29, 2005).

HONORS: Named N.L. Rookie of the Year by Baseball Writers' Association of America (1996).

H

SCOUTING REPORT Hollandsworth is an experienced hitter with good power and the ability to deliver big hits off the bench. Likes the ball low and will look to pull. Combines patience with good bat speed and has become one of the league's best pinch hitters. Is a below-average runner. Can play a little in right field. Has a good arm but has poor range and gets inconsistent jumps. **Grade 5.4**

TODD HOLLANDSWORTH'S HITTING ZONE

.200	.273	.136
.250	.440	.275
.444	.286	.179

LEFTY-RIGHTY SPLITS

vs.	Avg.	AB	H	2B	3B	HR	RBI	BB	SO	OBP	Slg.
L	.293	41	12	5	0	0	6	4	7	.356	.415
R	.237	262	62	12	2	6	30	19	59	.289	.366

Year	Team (League)	Pos.	G	AB	R	H	2B	3B	HR	RBI	BB	SO	HBP	GDP	SB-CS	Avg.	OBP	SLG	OPS	E	Avg.
1991—	GC Dodgers (GCL)	OF	6	16	1	5	0	0	0	0	0	6	0	1	0-0	.313	.313	.313	.625	0	1.000
—	Yakima (N'west)	OF	56	203	34	48	5	1	8	33	27	57	4	2	11-1	.236	.338	.389	.727	4	.939
1992—	Bakersfield (Calif.)	OF	119	430	70	111	23	5	13	58	50	113	3	6	27-13	.258	.338	.426	.764	6	.975
1993—	San Antonio (Texas)	OF	126	474	57	119	24	9	17	63	29	101	5	7	24-12	.251	.298	.447	.746	12	.956
1994—	Albuquerque (PCL)	OF	132	505	80	144	31	5	19	91	46	96	0	15	15-9	.285	.343	.479	.822	13	.949
1995—	Los Angeles (N.L.)	OF	41	103	16	24	2	0	5	13	10	29	1	1	2-1	.233	.304	.398	.702	4	.938
—	San Bern. (Calif.)	OF	1	2	0	1	0	0	0	0	0	1	0	0	0-1	.500	.500	.500	1.000	0	...
—	Albuquerque (PCL)	OF	10	38	9	9	2	0	2	4	6	8	1	1	1-0	.237	.356	.447	.803	0	1.000
1996—	Los Angeles (N.L.)	OF	149	478	64	139	26	4	12	59	41	93	2	2	21-6	.291	.348	.437	.785	5	.978
1997—	Los Angeles (N.L.)	OF	106	296	39	73	20	2	4	31	17	60	0	8	5-5	.247	.286	.368	.654	3	.984
—	Albuquerque (PCL)	OF	13	56	13	24	4	3	1	14	4	4	0	2	2-3	.429	.467	.661	1.127	1	1.000
—	San Bern. (Calif.)	OF	2	8	1	2	0	1	0	2	1	2	0	0	0-0	.250	.333	.500	.833	0	1.000
1998—	Los Angeles (N.L.)	OF	55	175	23	47	6	4	3	20	9	42	1	2	4-3	.269	.308	.400	.708	4	.957
1999—	San Bern. (Calif.)	OF	4	13	3	5	2	0	0	3	2	4	1	1	0-1	.385	.500	.538	1.038	0	1.000
—	Los Angeles (N.L.)	OF-1B	92	261	39	74	12	2	9	32	24	61	1	2	5-2	.284	.345	.448	.793	3	.987
2000—	Los Angeles (N.L.)	OF	81	261	42	61	12	0	8	24	30	61	1	4	11-4	.234	.314	.372	.686	2	.987
—	Colorado (N.L.)	OF	56	167	39	54	8	0	11	23	11	38	0	4	7-3	.323	.365	.569	.934	1	.988
2001—	Colorado (N.L.)	OF	33	117	21	43	15	1	6	19	8	20	0	1	5-0	.368	.408	.667	1.075	1	.981
2002—	Colorado (N.L.)	OF	95	298	39	88	21	1	11	48	26	71	1	8	7-8	.295	.352	.483	.835	4	.973
—	Texas (A.L.)	OF	39	132	16	34	6	0	5	19	14	27	0	0	1-0	.258	.327	.417	.743	0	1.000
2003—	Florida (N.L.)	OF-DH	93	228	32	58	23	3	3	20	22	55	0	2	2-3	.254	.317	.421	.739	2	.983
2004—	Chicago (N.L.)	OF-1B-DH	57	148	28	47	6	2	8	22	17	26	1	2	1-1	.318	.382	.547	.939	1	.988
2005—	Chicago (N.L.)	OF-1B	107	268	23	68	17	2	5	35	18	53	1	4	4-4	.254	.301	.388	.689	2	.981
—	Atlanta (N.L.)	OF-1B	24	35	3	6	0	0	1	1	5	13	0	1	0-1	.171	.275	.257	.532	0	1.000
	American League totals (1 year)		39	132	16	34	6	0	5	19	14	27	0	0	1-0	.258	.327	.417	.743	0	1.000
	National League totals (11 years)		989	2835	408	782	168	21	86	347	238	622	9	41	74-41	.276	.332	.441	.773	32	.979
	Major League totals (11 years)		1028	2967	424	816	174	21	91	366	252	649	9	41	75-41	.275	.332	.440	.772	32	.980

DIVISION SERIES RECORD

Year	Team (League)	Pos.	G	AB	R	H	2B	3B	HR	RBI	BB	SO	HBP	GDP	SB-CS	Avg.	OBP	SLG	OPS	E	Avg.
1995—	Los Angeles (N.L.)	OF	2	2	0	0	0	0	0	0	0	0	0	0	0-0	.000	.000	.000	.000	0	...
1996—	Los Angeles (N.L.)	OF	3	12	1	4	3	0	0	1	0	3	0	0	0-0	.333	.333	.583	.917	0	1.000
2003—	Florida (N.L.)		3	3	1	1	0	0	0	0	0	2	0	0	0-0	.333	.333	.333	.667	0	...
	Division series totals (3 years)		8	17	2	5	3	0	0	1	0	5	0	0	0-0	.294	.294	.471	.765	0	1.000

CHAMPIONSHIP SERIES RECORD

Year	Team (League)	Pos.	G	AB	R	H	2B	3B	HR	RBI	BB	SO	HBP	GDP	SB-CS	Avg.	OBP	SLG	OPS	E	Avg.
2003—	Florida (N.L.)		4	3	2	3	1	0	0	2	1	0	0	0	0-0	1.000	1.000	1.333	2.333	0	...

WORLD SERIES RECORD

Year	Team (League)	Pos.	G	AB	R	H	2B	3B	HR	RBI	BB	SO	HBP	GDP	SB-CS	Avg.	OBP	SLG	OPS	E	Avg.
2003—	Florida (N.L.)		2	2	0	0	0	0	0	0	0	1	0	0	0-0	.000	.000	.000	.000	0	...

HOLLIDAY, MATT — OF

PERSONAL: Born January 15, 1980, in Stillwater, Okla. ... 6-4/235. ... Bats right, throws right. ... Full name: Matthew Thomas Holliday. ... High school: Stillwater (Okla.).
TRANSACTIONS/CAREER NOTES: Selected by Colorado Rockies organization in seventh round of 1998 free-agent draft. ... On disabled list (June 9-July 19, 2005); included rehabilitation assignment to Tulsa.
2005 GAMES PLAYED BY POSITION (MLB): OF—123.

SCOUTING REPORT Holliday has made a lot of progress as a hitter. Has good bat speed and has shortened his stroke. Is quick to inside pitches and can extend his arms to hit for power. Has the power to hit 30-40 home runs, especially playing in Coors Field. Has vastly improved his ability to get jumps in the outfield but still has problems tracking balls over his head. Is going to be a good run producer and will help protect Todd Helton. **Grade 6.3**

MATT HOLLIDAY'S HITTING ZONE

.391	.227	.125
.305	.409	.384
.196	.464	.429

LEFTY-RIGHTY SPLITS

vs.	Avg.	AB	H	2B	3B	HR	RBI	BB	SO	OBP	Slg.
L	.324	105	34	3	1	3	16	10	15	.393	.457
R	.302	374	113	21	6	16	71	26	64	.352	.519

Year	Team (League)	Pos.	G	AB	R	H	2B	3B	HR	RBI	BB	SO	HBP	GDP	SB-CS	Avg.	OBP	SLG	OPS	E	Avg.
1998—	Ariz. Rockies (Ariz.)	3B	32	117	20	40	4	1	5	23	15	21	2	0	2-1	.342	.413	.521	.934	10	.851
1999—	Asheville (S. Atl.)	3B	121	444	76	117	28	0	16	64	53	116	9	8	10-3	.264	.350	.435	.785	37	.871

H

Year	Team (League)	Pos.	G	AB	R	H	2B	3B	HR	RBI	BB	SO	HBP	GDP	SB-CS	Avg.	OBP	SLG	OPS	E	Avg.
2000—Salem (Carol.)		3B	123	460	64	126	28	2	7	72	43	74	2	12	11-5	.274	.335	.389	.724	32	.893
2001—Salem (Carol.)		OF	72	255	36	70	16	1	11	52	33	42	3	10	11-3	.275	.358	.475	.833	0	1.000
2002—Carolina (Southern)		OF	130	463	79	128	19	2	10	64	67	102	7	14	16-2	.276	.375	.391	.766	7	.961
2003—Tulsa (Texas)		OF	135	522	65	132	28	5	12	72	43	74	6	9	15-9	.253	.313	.395	.708	2	.991
2004—Colo. Springs (PCL)		OF	6	22	8	8	5	0	2	4	5	6	0	1	2-0	.364	.481	.864	1.345	0	1.000
—Colorado (N.L.)		OF	121	400	65	116	31	3	14	57	31	86	6	9	3-3	.290	.349	.488	.837	7	.963
2005—Tulsa (Texas)		OF	7	26	6	14	3	0	1	6	1	3	0	1	1-0	.538	.536	.769	1.305	0	1.000
—Colorado (N.L.)		OF	125	479	68	147	24	7	19	87	36	79	7	11	14-3	.307	.361	.505	.866	7	.972
Major League totals (2 years)			246	879	133	263	55	10	33	144	67	165	13	20	17-6	.299	.356	.497	.853	14	.968

HOLLINS, DAMON — OF

PERSONAL: Born June 12, 1974, in Fairfield, Calif. ... 5-11/180. ... Bats right, throws left. ... Full name: Damon Jamall Hollins. ... High school: Vallejo (Calif.).

TRANSACTIONS/CAREER NOTES: Selected by Atlanta Braves organization in fourth round of 1992 free-agent draft. ... Traded by Braves to Los Angeles Dodgers for 2B Jose Pimentel (September 9, 1998). ... Released by Dodgers (November 22, 1998). ... Signed by Cincinnati Reds organization (December 15, 1998). ... Signed as a free agent by Milwaukee Brewers organization (December 1, 1999). ... Signed as a free agent by Minnesota Twins organization (February 23, 2001). ... Traded by Twins to Braves for future considerations (July 22, 2001). ... On disabled list (August 31, 2003-remainder of season). ... Signed as a free agent by Tampa Bay Devil Rays organization (November 12, 2004).

2005 GAMES PLAYED BY POSITION (MLB): OF—116.

SCOUTING REPORT Hollins is an aggressive hitter who likes the ball up in the zone. Has gap power but needs to become a better breaking-ball hitter, though he can hit mistakes. Is not a prototypical center fielder because he is an average runner. Gets better jumps laterally and takes good routes. Lacks arm strength but is accurate. Has ideal makeup for a fourth outfielder. ***Grade 5***

DAMON HOLLINS' HITTING ZONE

.381	.375	.188
.210	.436	.261
.200	.294	.214

LEFTY-RIGHTY SPLITS

vs.	Avg.	AB	H	2B	3B	HR	RBI	BB	SO	OBP	Slg.
L	.250	112	28	4	0	6	19	8	19	.298	.446
R	.248	230	57	13	1	7	27	15	44	.296	.404

Year	Team (League)	Pos.	G	AB	R	H	2B	3B	HR	RBI	BB	SO	HBP	GDP	SB-CS	Avg.	OBP	SLG	OPS	E	Avg.
1992—GC Braves (GCL)		OF	49	179	35	41	12	1	1	15	30	22	2	3	15-2	.229	.346	.324	.670	1	.989
1993—Danville (Appal.)		OF	62	240	37	77	15	2	7	51	19	30	1	5	10-2	.321	.369	.488	.856	6	.946
1994—Durham (Carol.)		OF	131	485	76	131	28	0	23	88	45	115	4	9	12-7	.270	.335	.470	.805	13	.957
1995—Greenville (Sou.)		OF	129	466	64	115	26	2	18	77	44	120	4	7	6-6	.247	.313	.427	.741	8	.978
1996—Richmond (Int'l)		OF	42	146	16	29	9	0	0	8	16	37	0	2	2-3	.199	.278	.260	.538	3	.976
1997—Richmond (Int'l)		OF-DH	134	498	73	132	31	3	20	63	45	84	3	18	7-2	.265	.329	.460	.789	8	.977
1998—Richmond (Int'l)		OF-DH	119	436	61	115	26	3	13	48	45	85	0	16	10-2	.264	.330	.427	.757	5	.980
—Atlanta (N.L.)		OF	3	6	0	1	0	0	0	0	0	1	0	0	0-0	.167	.167	.167	.333	0	1.000
—Los Angeles (N.L.)		OF	9	9	1	2	0	0	0	2	0	2	0	0	0-1	.222	.222	.222	.444	0	1.000
1999—Indianapolis (Int'l)		OF	106	328	58	86	19	0	9	43	31	44	1	13	11-2	.262	.328	.402	.730	4	.983
2000—Indianapolis (Int'l)		OF	87	287	33	82	16	3	2	32	21	35	1	5	5-3	.286	.334	.383	.718	0	1.000
2001—Edmonton (PCL)		OF	69	232	29	64	8	2	6	30	22	44	2	8	3-3	.276	.342	.405	.748	5	.954
—Richmond (Int'l)		OF	43	160	27	42	10	2	5	24	14	34	0	7	2-2	.263	.318	.444	.762	2	.981
2002—Richmond (Int'l)		OF	128	498	66	139	34	1	12	59	35	77	1	13	10-2	.279	.326	.424	.750	4	.988
2003—Richmond (Int'l)		OF	91	307	39	84	23	4	11	45	22	62	2	10	7-2	.274	.324	.482	.806	4	.981
2004—Atlanta (N.L.)		OF	7	22	3	8	2	0	0	5	0	4	0	0	0-0	.364	.364	.455	.818	0	1.000
2005—Durham (Int'l)		OF-DH	109	356	50	107	26	2	20	67	24	57	0	9	5-3	.301	.341	.553	.895	7	.967
—Durham (Int'l)		OF-DH	22	81	11	24	5	0	2	17	15	17	2	3	3-2	.296	.414	.432	.846	0	1.000
—Tampa Bay (A.L.)		OF	120	342	44	85	17	1	13	46	23	63	1	8	8-1	.249	.296	.418	.714	6	.977
American League totals (1 year)			120	342	44	85	17	1	13	46	23	63	1	8	8-1	.249	.296	.418	.714	6	.977
National League totals (2 years)			15	37	4	11	2	0	0	7	0	7	0	0	0-1	.297	.297	.351	.649	0	1.000
Major League totals (3 years)			135	379	48	96	19	1	13	53	23	70	1	8	8-2	.253	.296	.412	.708	6	.979

HOOPER, KEVIN — 2B

PERSONAL: Born December 7, 1976, in Lawrence, Kan. ... 5-10/160. ... Bats right, throws right. ... Full name: Kevin J. Hooper. ... College: Wichita State.

TRANSACTIONS/CAREER NOTES: Selected by Florida Marlins organization in eighth round of free-agent draft (June 2, 1999). ... Called up by Florida from Albuquerque (September 26, 2003). ... Claimed on waivers by New York Yankees (May 26, 2004). ... Released by Yankees (August 6, 2004). ... Signed by Kansas City Royals organization (August 13, 2004). ... Signed as a free agent by Detroit Tigers organization (November 19, 2004).

2005 GAMES PLAYED BY POSITION (MLB): OF—3, SS—2, 2B—1.

LEFTY-RIGHTY SPLITS

vs.	Avg.	AB	H	2B	3B	HR	RBI	BB	SO	OBP	Slg.
L	.333	3	1	0	0	0	0	0	0	.333	.333
R	.000	2	0	0	0	0	0	0	1	.000	.000

Year	Team (League)	Pos.	G	AB	R	H	2B	3B	HR	RBI	BB	SO	HBP	GDP	SB-CS	Avg.	OBP	SLG	OPS	E	Avg.
1999—Utica (N.Y.-Penn)		2B	73	289	52	81	18	6	0	22	39	35	4	2	14-8	.280	.370	.384	.754	4	.989
2000—Kane Co. (Midw.)		2B	123	457	73	114	25	6	3	38	73	83	6	6	17-2	.249	.359	.350	.709	13	.978
2001—Kane Co. (Midw.)		2B	17	65	11	19	2	0	0	4	11	13	0	0	3-1	.292	.390	.323	.713	4	.957
—Portland (East.)		2B	117	468	70	144	19	6	2	39	59	78	1	8	24-12	.308	.392	.387	.779	7	.986
2002—Calgary (PCL)		2B-SS	117	452	70	130	21	3	2	38	34	51	4	7	17-10	.288	.341	.361	.702	12	.977
2003—Albuquerque (PCL)		2B-SS	130	493	77	131	9	4	1	54	35	62	10	5	25-9	.266	.325	.306	.631	11	.982
2004—Albuquerque (PCL)		2B-SS	39	155	21	43	3	2	0	17	14	24	0	1	6-5	.277	.335	.323	.658	3	.971
—Columbus (Int'l)		2B-SS-P	29	87	6	17	1	0	0	4	5	11	0	1	3-1	.195	.239	.207	.446	2	.000
—Omaha (PCL)		2B-SS	27	92	12	15	2	0	0	4	9	14	1	1	2-2	.163	.245	.185	.430	3	.000
2005—Detroit (A.L.)		OF-SS-2B	6	5	0	1	0	0	0	0	0	1	0	0	0-0	.200	.200	.200	.400	1	.900
Major League totals (1 year)			6	5	0	1	0	0	0	0	0	1	0	0	0-0	.200	.200	.200	.400	1	.900

H

HORGAN, JOE   P

PERSONAL: Born June 7, 1977, in Sacramento. ... 6-1/200. ... Throws left, bats left. ... Full name: Joseph Paul Horgan. ... High school: Cordova Senior (Rancho Cordova, Calif.). ... Junior college: Sacramento City College.

TRANSACTIONS/CAREER NOTES: Selected by New York Yankees organization in 42nd round of 1995 free-agent draft; did not sign. ... Selected by Cleveland Indians organization in 11th round of 1996 free-agent draft. ... Released by Indians (March 23, 1999). ... Signed by San Francisco Giants organization (April 11, 1999). ... Signed as a free agent by St. Louis Cardinals organization (November 6, 2003). ... Traded by Cardinals to Montreal Expos for P Benji DeQuin (May 7, 2004). ... Expos franchise transferred to Washington, D.C., and renamed Washington Nationals for 2005 season (December 3, 2004).

CAREER HITTING: 1-for-4 (.250), 0 R, 0 2B, 0 3B, 0 HR, 1 RBI.

LEFTY-RIGHTY SPLITS

vs.	Avg.	AB	H	2B	3B	HR	RBI	BB	SO	OBP	Slg.
L	.231	13	3	1	0	0	2	2	3	.375	.308
R	.667	24	16	7	0	0	12	2	2	.667	.958

Year—Team (League)	W	L	Pct.	ERA	WHIP	G	GS	CG	ShO	Hld.	Sv.-Opp.	IP	H	R	ER	HR	BB-IBB	SO	Avg.
1996—Burlington (Appal.)	1	2	.333	4.19	1.34	23	0	0	0	...	7-...	34.1	37	25	16	1	9-0	48	.257
1997—Watertown (NYP)	0	1	.000	6.10	1.72	15	4	0	0	...	0-...	38.1	48	31	26	4	18-1	31	.308
—Kinston (Carol.)	1	2	.333	7.27	1.85	4	2	0	0	...	0-...	17.1	23	15	14	1	9-0	9	.319
1998—Columbus (S. Atl.)	2	1	.667	2.38	1.18	22	1	0	0	...	0-...	34.0	19	9	9	3	21-0	27	.168
1999—Bakersfield (Calif.)	6	10	.375	5.22	1.47	25	19	1	0	...	0-...	117.1	129	76	68	18	43-0	101	.279
2000—San Jose (Calif.)	14	10	.583	4.60	1.54	27	27	1	0	...	0-...	166.1	190	104	85	15	66-0	92	.293
—Shreveport (Texas)	0	0		3.38	0.75	1	0	0	0	...	0-...	5.1	2	2	2	0	2-1	3	.111
2001—Shreveport (Texas)	3	5	.375	3.65	1.20	31	14	0	0	...	1-...	103.2	97	51	42	10	27-1	61	.246
—Fresno (PCL)	0	0		5.87	1.83	3	1	0	0	...	0-...	7.2	11	5	5	1	3-0	5	.333
2002—Fresno (PCL)	2	2	.500	5.93	1.49	27	4	0	0	...	0-...	57.2	65	38	38	8	21-0	37	.286
—Shreveport (Texas)	4	3	.571	4.34	1.59	10	10	1	0	...	0-...	56.0	69	35	27	5	20-1	35	.305
2003—Fresno (PCL)	7	7	.500	5.67	1.47	55	0	0	0	...	3-...	74.2	80	51	47	9	30-1	65	.276
2004—Memphis (PCL)	0	1	.000	6.52	1.76	10	0	0	0	...	0-...	9.2	14	7	7	3	3-0	8	.350
—Edmonton (PCL)	1	0	1.000	3.18	1.12	13	0	0	0	...	0-...	17.0	15	6	6	2	4-0	11	.234
—Montreal (N.L.)	4	1	.800	3.15	1.43	47	0	0	0	12	2-3	40.0	35	18	14	5	22-3	30	.230
2005—Washington (N.L.)	0	0		21.00	3.83	8	0	0	0	0	0-0	6.0	19	15	14	0	4-0	5	.543
—New Orleans (PCL)	4	3	.571	4.12	1.55	46	2	0	0	2	3-6	63.1	68	35	29	9	30-3	48	.278
Major League totals (2 years)	**4**	**1**	**.800**	**5.48**	**1.74**	**55**	**0**	**0**	**0**	**12**	**2-3**	**46.0**	**54**	**33**	**28**	**5**	**26-3**	**35**	**.286**

HOULTON, D.J.   P

PERSONAL: Born August 12, 1979, in Fullerton, Calif. ... 6-4/220. ... Throws right, bats right. ... Full name: Dennis Sean Houlton. ... High school: Servite (Anaheim, Calif.). ... College: Pacific.

TRANSACTIONS/CAREER NOTES: Selected by Houston Astros in 11th round of 2001 free-agent draft. ... Selected by Los Angeles Dodgers from Astros organization in Rule 5 major league draft (December 13, 2004).

CAREER HITTING: 3-for-30 (.100), 1 R, 1 2B, 0 3B, 0 HR, 1 RBI.

SCOUTING REPORT *Throws:* Houlton hits 87-91 mph with his fastball and also throws a curveball, slider and changeup. *Tendencies:* He has a great pitcher's body and a loose arm. Has deceptive arm speed but must keep his fastball down in the zone for it to have life. Varies the speed of his curveballs and gets better rotation as he takes more off of it. Tends to flatten his slider and does not use it much. Has a good changeup that he can sink. Sometimes tries to overthrow late in counts and has problems throwing strikes. Has problems keeping the ball down in early innings. *Outlook:* Houlton probably is better as a starter than as a reliever. *Grade 6*

D.J. HOULTON'S PITCHING ZONE

.171	.316	.381
.305	.500	.255
.217	.227	.292

LEFTY-RIGHTY SPLITS

vs.	Avg.	AB	H	2B	3B	HR	RBI	BB	SO	OBP	Slg.
L	.314	210	66	16	2	8	31	25	36	.387	.524
R	.271	292	79	20	1	13	43	27	54	.343	.479

Year—Team (League)	W	L	Pct.	ERA	WHIP	G	GS	CG	ShO	Hld.	Sv.-Opp.	IP	H	R	ER	HR	BB-IBB	SO	Avg.
2001—Martinsville (App.)	5	4	.556	2.50	1.03	13	13	1	0	...	0-...	72.0	67	24	20	7	7-0	71	.240
—Michigan (Midw.)	0	1	.000	5.40	1.60	1	1	0	0	...	0-...	5.0	7	5	3	0	1-0	4	.304
2002—Michigan (Midw.)	14	5	.737	3.14	1.07	35	16	0	0	...	2-...	140.2	120	57	49	12	30-0	138	.223
2003—Round Rock (Texas)	5	4	.556	3.47	1.11	18	18	1	1	...	0-...	109.0	93	45	42	11	28-1	101	.226
—New Orleans (PCL)	3	4	.429	5.40	1.44	11	11	0	0	...	0-...	61.2	70	39	37	12	19-0	48	.288
2004—Round Rock (Texas)	12	5	.706	2.94	1.18	28	28	3	1	...	0-...	159.0	141	59	52	14	47-2	159	.241
2005—Los Angeles (N.L.)	6	9	.400	5.16	1.53	35	19	0	0	0	0-0	129.0	145	79	74	21	52-3	90	.289
Major League totals (1 year)	**6**	**9**	**.400**	**5.16**	**1.53**	**35**	**19**	**0**	**0**	**0**	**0-0**	**129.0**	**145**	**79**	**74**	**21**	**52-3**	**90**	**.289**

HOWARD, RYAN   1B

PERSONAL: Born November 19, 1979, in St. Louis. ... 6-4/230. ... Bats left, throws left. ... Full name: Ryan James Howard. ... High school: Lafayette (St. Louis). ... College: Southwest Missouri State.

TRANSACTIONS/CAREER NOTES: Selected by Philadelphia Phillies in fifth round of 2001 free-agent draft.

HONORS: Named N.L. Rookie of the Year by Baseball Writers' Association of America (2005).

2005 GAMES PLAYED BY POSITION (MLB): 1B—84.

SCOUTING REPORT *Offense:* Howard is one of the best pure power hitters to come into the game in a long time. Hits from an open stance and dives toward the plate. Has very good bat speed but still has some holes to cover. Likes the ball down over the plate. Needs to improve hitting breaking stuff and lefthanded pitching. Has exceptional power to all fields. Is a better runner than his body would indicate. *Defense:* He was thought to be a liability, but in fact he was better at first last season than Jim Thome. Has good hands and has increased his mobility but will have to maintain his weight. Has a strong arm and starts the double play well. *Outlook:* He is farther along at this time in his career than either David Ortiz or Mo Vaughn, who had similar approaches and bat speed. Could hit 50 home runs, especially in homer-friendly Citizens Bank Park. *Grade 7.7*

RYAN HOWARD'S HITTING ZONE

.176	.313	.227
.364	.303	.455
.400	.273	.231

LEFTY-RIGHTY SPLITS

vs.	Avg.	AB	H	2B	3B	HR	RBI	BB	SO	OBP	Slg.
L	.148	61	9	1	1	1	6	2	26	.175	.246
R	.323	251	81	16	1	21	57	31	74	.396	.645

Year Team (League)	Pos.	G	AB	R	H	2B	3B	HR	RBI	BB	SO	HBP	GDP	SB-CS	Avg.	OBP	SLG	OPS	E	Avg.
2001— Batavia (NY-Penn)	1B	48	169	26	46	7	3	6	35	30	55	2	1	0-0	.272	.384	.456	.840	5	.987
2002— Lakewood (S. Atl.)	1B	135	493	56	138	20	6	19	87	66	145	5	9	5-4	.280	.367	.460	.828	17	.985
2003— Clearwater (FSL)	1B	130	490	67	149	32	1	23	82	50	151	8	12	0-0	.304	.374	.514	.889	10	.991
2004— Reading (East.)	1B-DH	102	374	73	111	18	1	37	102	46	129	10	2	1-2	.297	.386	.647	1.033	7	.992
— Scran./W.B. (I.L.)	1B	29	111	21	30	10	0	9	29	14	37	2	4	0-0	.270	.362	.604	.966	6	.977
— Philadelphia (N.L.)	1B	19	39	5	11	5	0	2	5	2	13	1	2	0-0	.282	.333	.564	.897	0	1.000
2005— Scran./W.B. (I.L.)	1B-DH	61	210	38	78	19	0	16	54	39	66	3	3	0-0	.371	.467	.690	1.157	8	.986
— Philadelphia (N.L.)	1B	88	312	52	90	17	2	22	63	33	100	1	6	0-1	.288	.356	.567	.924	5	.993
Major League totals (2 years)		107	351	57	101	22	2	24	68	35	113	2	8	0-1	.288	.354	.567	.921	5	.994

HOWELL, J.P.   P

PERSONAL: Born April 25, 1983, in Modesto, Calif. ... 6-0/175. ... Throws left, bats left. ... Full name: James Phillip Howell. ... High school: Jesuit (Carmichael, Calif.). ... College: Texas.
TRANSACTIONS/CAREER NOTES: Selected by Kansas City Royals organization in first round (31st pick overall) of 2004 free-agent draft
CAREER HITTING: 0-for-3 (.000), 0 R, 0 2B, 0 3B, 0 HR, 0 RBI.

SCOUTING REPORT *Throws:* He throws a fastball at 82-85 mph, a slider, a change and a split-finger fastball. *Tendencies:* Howell hooks his wrist and slings the ball to the plate, causing late tailing action away from righthanders. With mediocre velocity, he can't make mistakes over the plate. Slider isn't very sharp. Will occasionally throw a soft splitter that mimics his change. *Outlook:* Howell knows how to pitch, but he doesn't have a pitch that will consistently put hitters away. *Grade 5.7*

J.P. HOWELL'S PITCHING ZONE

.350	.250	.167
.196	.412	.316
.192	.353	.294

LEFTY-RIGHTY SPLITS

vs.	Avg.	AB	H	2B	3B	HR	RBI	BB	SO	OBP	Slg.
L	.229	48	11	2	0	1	7	7	10	.321	.333
R	.271	229	62	17	0	8	37	32	44	.372	.450

Year Team (League)	W	L	Pct.	ERA	WHIP	G	GS	CG	ShO	Hld.	Sv.-Opp.	IP	H	R	ER	HR	BB-IBB	SO	Avg.
2004— Idaho Falls (Pio.)	3	1	.750	2.77	1.08	6	4	0	0	...	0-...	26.0	16	9	8	1	12-0	38	.190
2005— High Desert (Calif.)	3	1	.750	1.96	1.24	8	8	0	0	0	0-0	46.0	33	16	10	2	24-0	48	.202
— Wichita (Texas)	2	0	1.000	2.50	0.94	3	3	0	0	0	0-0	18.0	12	5	5	2	5-0	23	.188
— Omaha (PCL)	3	1	.750	4.06	1.57	7	7	0	0	0	0-0	37.2	40	19	17	1	19-0	29	.286
— Kansas City (A.L.)	3	5	.375	6.19	1.54	15	15	0	0	0	0-0	72.2	73	55	50	9	39-0	54	.264
Major League totals (1 year)	3	5	.375	6.19	1.54	15	15	0	0	0	0-0	72.2	73	55	50	9	39-0	54	.264

HOWRY, BOB   P

PERSONAL: Born August 4, 1973, in Phoenix. ... 6-5/220. ... Throws right, bats left. ... Full name: Bobby Dean Howry. ... Name pronounced: HOW-ree. ... High school: Deer Valley (Phoenix). ... College: McNeese State.
TRANSACTIONS/CAREER NOTES: Selected by San Francisco Giants organization in fifth round of 1994 free-agent draft. ... Traded by Giants with SS Mike Caruso, OF Brian Manning and Ps Keith Foulke, Lorenzo Barcelo and Ken Vining to Chicago White Sox for Ps Wilson Alvarez, Danny Darwin and Roberto Hernandez (July 31, 1997). ... On suspended list (April 28-May 30, 2000). ... Traded by White Sox to Boston Red Sox for Ps Frank Francisco and Byeong An (July 31, 2002). ... On disabled list (August 22, 2003-remainder of season). ... Released by Red Sox (October 24, 2003). ... Signed by Cleveland Indians organization (December 17, 2003).
CAREER HITTING: 0-for-1 (.000), 0 R, 0 2B, 0 3B, 0 HR, 0 RBI.

SCOUTING REPORT *Throws:* Howry's fastball has improved to 92-95 mph, and his slider is in the mid- to high 80s. *Tendencies:* His elbow has really bounced back from surgery; he's throwing harder than ever and still has explosive sinking action. Comes right at hitters and is very effective to both righthanders and lefthanders. Is strictly a two-pitch reliever who has very good command. *Outlook:* He's one of the best setup relievers in the game, and he has the stuff to be a closer again. *Grade 8.1*

BOB HOWRY'S PITCHING ZONE

.056	.200	.278
.143	.393	.145
.182	.154	.333

LEFTY-RIGHTY SPLITS

vs.	Avg.	AB	H	2B	3B	HR	RBI	BB	SO	OBP	Slg.
L	.180	89	16	4	0	1	3	6	21	.232	.258
R	.198	167	33	4	1	3	14	10	27	.240	.287

Year Team (League)	W	L	Pct.	ERA	WHIP	G	GS	CG	ShO	Hld.	Sv.-Opp.	IP	H	R	ER	HR	BB-IBB	SO	Avg.
1994— Everett (N'west)	0	4	.000	4.74	2.05	5	5	0	0	0	0-...	19.0	29	15	10	3	10-2	16	.341
— Clinton (Midw.)	1	3	.250	4.20	1.56	9	8	0	0	0	0-...	49.1	61	29	23	1	16-0	22	.316
1995— San Jose (Calif.)	12	10	.545	3.54	1.36	27	25	0	0	0	0-...	165.1	171	79	65	6	54-0	107	.277
1996— Shreveport (Texas)	12	10	.545	4.65	1.40	27	27	1	0	0	0-...	156.2	163	90	81	17	56-3	57	.269
1997— Shreveport (Texas)	6	3	.667	4.91	1.44	48	0	0	0	0	22-...	55.0	58	35	30	6	21-0	43	.270
— Birmingham (Sou.)	0	0	...	2.84	1.50	12	0	0	0	0	0-...	12.2	16	4	4	1	3-0	3	.314
1998— Calgary (PCL)	1	2	.333	3.41	1.11	23	0	0	0	0	5-...	31.2	25	12	12	2	10-3	22	.216
— Chicago (A.L.)	0	3	.000	3.15	1.03	44	0	0	0	19	9-11	54.1	37	20	19	7	19-2	51	.194
1999— Chicago (A.L.)	5	3	.625	3.59	1.42	69	0	0	0	1	28-34	67.2	58	34	27	8	38-3	80	.226
2000— Chicago (A.L.)	2	4	.333	3.17	1.17	65	0	0	0	14	7-12	71.0	54	26	25	6	29-2	60	.216
2001— Chicago (A.L.)	4	5	.444	4.69	1.48	69	0	0	0	21	5-11	78.2	85	41	41	11	30-9	64	.279
2002— Chicago (A.L.)	2	2	.500	3.91	1.22	47	0	0	0	10	0-1	50.2	45	22	22	7	17-2	31	.245
— Boston (A.L.)	1	3	.250	5.00	1.44	20	0	0	0	5	0-1	18.0	22	15	10	2	4-2	14	.306
2003— Boston (A.L.)	0	0	...	12.46	3.23	4	0	0	0	0	0-1	4.1	11	6	6	1	3-1	4	.478
— Pawtucket (Int'l)	2	0	1.000	1.06	0.90	13	0	0	0	0	0-...	17.0	14	2	2	1	1-0	10	.215
2004— Buffalo (Int'l)	1	1	.500	5.19	1.08	26	0	0	0	0	0-...	26.0	22	16	15	3	6-0	24	.222
— Cleveland (A.L.)	4	2	.667	2.74	1.15	37	0	0	0	8	0-2	42.2	37	14	13	5	12-0	39	.228
2005— Cleveland (A.L.)	7	4	.636	2.47	0.89	79	0	0	0	29	3-5	73.0	49	23	20	4	16-1	48	.191
Major League totals (8 years)	25	26	.490	3.58	1.23	434	0	0	0	107	52-77	460.1	398	201	183	51	168-22	391	.235

H

DIVISION SERIES RECORD

Year Team (League)	W	L	Pct.	ERA	WHIP	G	GS	CG	ShO	Hld.	Sv.-Opp.	IP	H	R	ER	HR	BB-IBB	SO	Avg.
2000—Chicago (A.L.)	0	0	...	3.38	1.50	2	0	0	0	1	0-0	2.2	2	1	1	0	2-0	4	.222

HUBER, JUSTIN   1B

PERSONAL: Born July 1, 1982, in Melbourne, Australia. ... 6-2/200. ... Bats right, throws right. ... Full name: Justin Patrick Huber. ... Name pronounced: HYOO-ber. ... High school: Beacon Hill College (Victoria, Australia).

TRANSACTIONS/CAREER NOTES: Signed as a non-drafted free agent by New York Mets organization (July 26, 2000). ... Traded by Mets to Kansas City Royals for IF Jose Bautista to Pittsburgh Pirates (July 30, 2004).

2005 GAMES PLAYED BY POSITION (MLB): 1B—19, DH—4.

JUSTIN HUBER'S HITTING ZONE

.000	...	.333
.167	.364	.333
.250	.182	.167

LEFTY-RIGHTY SPLITS

vs.	Avg.	AB	H	2B	3B	HR	RBI	BB	SO	OBP	Slg.
L	.179	39	7	1	0	0	2	3	10	.256	.205
R	.256	39	10	2	0	0	4	2	10	.286	.308

									BATTING									FIELDING	
Year Team (League)	Pos.	G	AB	R	H	2B	3B	HR	RBI	BB	SO	HBP	GDP	SB-CS	Avg.	OBP	SLG	OPS	E	Avg.
2001—St. Lucie (Fla. St.)	C-OF	2	6	0	0	0	0	0	0	0	2	0	0	0-0	.000	.000	.000	.000	0	1.000
—Kingsport (Appalachian)	C	47	159	24	50	11	1	7	31	17	42	13	4	4-2	.314	.415	.528	.943	8	.981
—Brooklyn (N.Y.-Penn.)	C	3	9	0	0	0	0	0	0	0	4	0	1	0-0	.000	.000	.000	.000	0	1.000
2002—Capital City (S. Atl.)	C	95	330	49	96	22	2	11	78	45	81	23	5	1-2	.291	.408	.470	.878	8	.989
—St. Lucie (Fla. St.)	C-OF	28	100	15	27	2	1	3	15	11	18	6	3	0-0	.270	.370	.400	.770	3	.983
2003—St. Lucie (Fla. St.)	C-OF	50	183	26	52	15	0	9	36	17	30	9	9	1-1	.284	.370	.514	.884	5	.982
—Binghamton (East.)	C-1B	55	193	16	51	13	0	6	36	19	54	7	4	0-2	.264	.350	.425	.775	6	.979
2004—St. Lucie (Fla. St.)	C-OF	14	49	10	12	2	0	2	8	5	8	1	0	0-0	.245	.327	.408	.735	0	1.000
—Binghamton (East.)	C-1B	70	236	44	64	16	1	11	33	46	57	12	5	2-2	.271	.414	.487	.901	5	.991
—Norfolk (Int'l)	C	16	3	5	2	0	0	3	3	3	0	0	0	0-0	.313	.421	.313	.859	0	1.000
2005—Wichita (Texas)	1B-DH	88	335	68	115	22	3	16	74	51	70	5	11	7-3	.343	.432	.570	1.002	12	.981
—Omaha (PCL)	1B-DH	32	113	19	31	6	1	7	23	16	33	2	3	0-0	.274	.374	.531	.905	3	.990
—Kansas City (A.L.)	1B-DH	25	78	6	17	3	0	0	6	5	20	1	1	0-0	.218	.271	.256	.527	3	.978
Major League totals (1 year)		25	78	6	17	3	0	0	6	5	20	1	1	0-0	.218	.271	.256	.527	3	.978

HUCKABY, KEN   C

PERSONAL: Born January 27, 1971, in San Leandro, Calif. ... 6-1/210. ... Bats right, throws right. ... Full name: Kenneth Paul Huckaby. ... Name pronounced: HUCK-a-be. ... High school: Manteca (Calif.). ... Junior college: San Joaquin Delta (Calif.).

TRANSACTIONS/CAREER NOTES: Selected by Los Angeles Dodgers organization in 22nd round of 1991 free-agent draft. ... Signed as a free agent by Seattle Mariners organization (December 3, 1997). ... Released by Mariners (June 13, 1998). ... Signed by New York Yankees organization (June 28, 1998). ... Signed as a free agent by Arizona Diamondbacks organization (January 22, 1999). ... Released by Diamondbacks (October 29, 2001). ... Signed by Toronto Blue Jays organization (February 10, 2002). ... Signed as a free agent by Texas Rangers organization (November 13, 2003). ... Claimed on waivers by Baltimore Orioles (July 6, 2004). ... Signed as a free agent by Rangers organization (August 17, 2004). ... Signed as a free agent by Blue Jays organization (January 10, 2005).

2005 GAMES PLAYED BY POSITION (MLB): C—35.

KEN HUCKABY'S HITTING ZONE

.167	.000	.667
.286	.111	.300
.250	.000	.600

LEFTY-RIGHTY SPLITS

vs.	Avg.	AB	H	2B	3B	HR	RBI	BB	SO	OBP	Slg.
L	.267	30	8	2	0	0	1	4	9	.353	.333
R	.175	57	10	2	0	0	5	1	10	.190	.211

									BATTING									FIELDING	
Year Team (League)	Pos.	G	AB	R	H	2B	3B	HR	RBI	BB	SO	HBP	GDP	SB-CS	Avg.	OBP	SLG	OPS	E	Avg.
1991—Great Falls (Pio.)	C	57	213	39	55	16	0	3	37	17	38	4	4	3-2	.258	.321	.376	.696	12	.977
1992—Vero Beach (FSL)	C	73	261	14	63	9	0	0	21	7	42	1	5	1-1	.241	.262	.276	.538	9	.982
1993—Vero Beach (FSL)	C	79	281	22	75	14	1	4	41	11	35	2	3	2-1	.267	.297	.367	.664	12	.980
—San Antonio (Texas)	C	28	82	4	18	1	0	0	5	2	7	2	0	0-0	.220	.253	.232	.485	4	.978
1994—San Antonio (Texas)	C	11	41	3	11	1	0	1	9	1	1	0	1	1-0	.268	.286	.366	.652	6	.931
—Bakersfield (Calif.)	C	77	270	29	81	18	1	2	30	10	37	2	7	2-3	.300	.329	.396	.725	10	.986
1995—Albuquerque (PCL)	1B-C	89	278	30	90	16	2	1	40	12	26	4	16	3-1	.324	.359	.406	.766	16	.973
1996—Albuquerque (PCL)	C	103	287	37	79	16	2	3	41	17	35	2	10	0-0	.275	.319	.376	.696	6	.990
1997—Albuquerque (PCL)	C-DH	69	201	14	40	5	1	0	18	9	36	0	5	1-0	.199	.231	.234	.465	10	.975
1998—Tacoma (PCL)	C-1B	16	49	4	11	2	0	1	5	6	6	0	2	0-0	.224	.296	.265	.562	0	1.000
—Columbus (Int'l)	C	36	101	13	21	3	1	1	10	11	14	0	3	0-2	.208	.286	.287	.573	5	.978
1999—Tucson (PCL)	C-3B-1B DH	107	355	44	107	20	1	2	42	13	33	2	11	0-0	.301	.325	.380	.706	10	.987
2000—Tucson (PCL)	C-3B-OF 1B	76	243	31	67	11	1	4	33	10	30	2	10	2-2	.276	.306	.379	.685	8	.982
2001—El Paso (Texas)	1B-C	30	104	14	36	0	2	0	14	3	16	3	3	0-0	.346	.368	.442	.811	4	.983
—Tucson (PCL)	C-1B-3B 2B	78	262	31	76	15	1	2	34	7	62	2	3	1-3	.290	.313	.378	.690	14	.972
—Arizona (N.L.)	C	1	1	0	0	0	0	0	0	0	0	0	0	0-0	.000	.000	.000	.000	0	1.000
2002—Syracuse (Int'l)	C-1B	21	81	7	22	2	0	0	9	2	15	0	6	0-2	.272	.286	.296	.582	3	.981
—Toronto (A.L.)	C	88	273	29	67	6	1	3	22	9	44	0	10	0-0	.245	.270	.308	.577	6	.989
2003—Toronto (A.L.)	C	5	11	1	2	1	0	0	2	0	2	0	0	0-0	.182	.182	.273	.455	0	1.000
—Syracuse (Int'l)	C-1B-DH 3B	75	267	24	78	14	0	3	25	15	30	0	11	1-1	.292	.326	.378	.705	7	.987
2004—Baltimore (A.L.)	C	8	12	1	2	1	0	0	0	0	6	0	0	0-0	.167	.167	.250	.417	0	1.000
—Oklahoma (PCL)	C-1B	35	127	18	35	8	1	2	20	9	18	0	6	0-0	.276	.317	.402	.718	3	.988
—Texas (A.L.)	C	16	38	3	5	2	0	0	6	3	12	0	1	0-0	.132	.233	.184	.417	2	.978
2005—Syracuse (Int'l)	C-1B	15	56	3	15	1	0	3	11	1	13	0	1	0-0	.268	.281	.339	.620	1	.991
—Toronto (A.L.)	C	35	87	8	18	4	0	0	6	5	19	0	4	0-0	.207	.250	.253	.503	2	.987
American League totals (4 years)		152	421	42	94	14	1	3	30	19	77	0	15	0-0	.223	.257	.283	.539	10	.988
National League totals (1 year)		1	1	0	0	0	0	0	0	0	0	0	0	0-0	.000	.000	.000	.000	0	1.000
Major League totals (5 years)		153	422	42	94	14	1	3	30	19	78	0	15	0-0	.223	.256	.282	.538	10	.988

H

HUDSON, LUKE — P

PERSONAL: Born May 2, 1977, in Fountain Valley, Calif. ... 6-3/195. ... Throws right, bats right. ... Full name: Luke Stephen Hudson. ... High school: Fountain Valley (Calif.). ... College: Tennessee.

TRANSACTIONS/CAREER NOTES: Selected by Baltimore Orioles organization in fifth round of 1995 draft; did not sign. ... Selected by Colorado Rockies organization in fourth round of 1998 free-agent draft. ... Traded by Rockies with P Gabe White to Cincinnati Reds for 2B Pokey Reese and P Dennys Reyes (December 18, 2001). ... On disabled list (April 2-June 9, 2005); included rehabilitation assignment to Chattanooga.

CAREER HITTING: 10-for-41 (.244), 8 R, 2 2B, 0 3B, 0 HR, 5 RBI.

SCOUTING REPORT

Throws: Hudson has a fastball that ranges from 87-92 mph. Throws a curveball and a changeup, too. ***Tendencies:*** He was bothered by rotator cuff problems early in the season, which dropped his velocity a little. Fastball has good life when it's down but is straight when left up. Curveball break is big and difficult to control. Has good motion on his change. Pitched behind in the count too often. ***Outlook:*** There are concerns about Hudson's durability. In 2004 he showed promise to be a mid-rotation pitcher, but last season he lacked the crispness on his pitches that he had prior to his arm problems. ***Grade 5.8***

LUKE HUDSON'S PITCHING ZONE

.520	.286	.207
.212	.500	.310
.143	.273	.231

LEFTY-RIGHTY SPLITS

vs.	Avg.	AB	H	2B	3B	HR	RBI	BB	SO	OBP	Slg.
L	.255	141	36	7	1	5	21	24	27	.372	.426
R	.278	169	47	16	1	9	34	26	26	.394	.544

Year Team (League)	W	L	Pct.	ERA	WHIP	G	GS	CG	ShO	Hld.	Sv.-Opp.	IP	H	R	ER	HR	BB-IBB	SO	Avg.
1998— Portland (N'west)	3	6	.333	4.74	1.49	15	15	0	0	...	0-...	79.2	68	46	42	8	51-0	82	.226
1999— Asheville (S. Atl.)	6	5	.545	4.30	1.28	21	20	1	0	...	0-...	88.0	89	47	42	10	24-0	96	.265
2000— Salem (Carol.)	5	8	.385	3.27	1.23	19	19	2	2	...	0-...	110.0	101	47	40	9	34-0	80	.246
2001— Carolina (Southern)	7	12	.368	4.20	1.38	29	28	1	0	...	0-...	165.0	159	90	77	19	68-0	145	.250
2002— Louisville (Int'l)	5	9	.357	4.51	1.35	30	17	0	0	...	3-...	117.2	102	64	59	6	57-1	129	.233
— Cincinnati (N.L.)	0	0	...	4.50	1.83	3	0	0	0	1	0-0	6.0	5	5	3	1	6-0	7	.227
2003—			Did not play.																
2004— Chattanooga (Sou.)	7	7	.500	3.32	1.11	16	16	0	0	...	0-...	86.2	71	35	32	9	25-1	91	.225
— Louisville (Int'l)	2	1	.667	2.84	1.05	3	3	0	0	...	0-...	19.0	15	8	6	2	5-0	17	.214
— Cincinnati (N.L.)	4	2	.667	2.42	1.26	9	9	0	0	0	0-0	48.1	36	16	13	3	25-1	38	.208
2005— Chattanooga (Sou.)	0	1	.000	5.40	1.05	1	1	0	0	0	0-0	6.2	6	4	4	2	1-0	7	.231
— Cincinnati (N.L.)	6	9	.400	6.38	1.57	19	16	0	0	0	0-0	84.2	83	62	60	14	50-2	53	.268
Major League totals (3 years)	10	11	.476	4.92	1.47	31	25	0	0	1	0-0	139.0	124	83	76	18	81-3	98	.246

HUDSON, ORLANDO — 2B

PERSONAL: Born December 12, 1977, in Darlington, S.C. ... 6-0/185. ... Bats both, throws right. ... Full name: Orlando Thill Hudson. ... High school: Darlington (S.C.). ... College: Spartanburg Methodist (S.C.).

TRANSACTIONS/CAREER NOTES: Selected by Toronto Blue Jays organization in 33rd round of 1996 free-agent draft; did not sign. ... Selected by Blue Jays organization in 43rd round of 1997 free-agent draft. ... On disabled list (May 24-June 16, 2004).

HONORS: Won A.L. Gold Glove as second baseman (2005).

2005 GAMES PLAYED BY POSITION (MLB): 2B—130.

SCOUTING REPORT

Offense: Hudson doesn't get many pitches to hit at the bottom of the order. Has cut down on strikeouts, showing more patience. Has more bat speed and power from the left side. Is a gap hitter with occasional power. Has become a better high-ball hitter but still struggles to lay off off-speed pitches. Isn't as fast as he looks. Doesn't steal many bases but has good instincts. ***Defense:*** He has a live body. Shows good quickness and range on ground balls and popups. Has quick feet and is agile when making the pivot on the double play. ***Outlook:*** Hudson is an outstanding athlete who still is learning to play the game. Starting to level off at the .270 mark because of his inability to hit righthanded. ***Grade 7.2***

ORLANDO HUDSON'S HITTING ZONE

.190	.385	.222
.182	.298	.315
.275	.233	.377

LEFTY-RIGHTY SPLITS

vs.	Avg.	AB	H	2B	3B	HR	RBI	BB	SO	OBP	Slg.
L	.227	128	29	4	1	2	9	10	19	.286	.320
R	.288	333	96	21	4	8	54	20	46	.327	.447

Year Team (League)	Pos.	G	AB	R	H	2B	3B	HR	RBI	BB	SO	HBP	GDP	SB-CS	Avg.	OBP	SLG	OPS	E	Avg.
1998— Medicine Hat (Pio.)	2B	65	242	50	71	18	1	8	42	22	36	7	3	6-5	.293	.366	.475	.842	13	.959
1999— Hagerstown (SAL)	2B-3B-OF	132	513	66	137	36	6	7	74	42	85	2	10	8-6	.267	.322	.402	.724	21	.946
2000— Dunedin (Fla. St.)	2B-3B-SS	96	358	54	102	16	2	7	48	37	42	2	15	9-5	.285	.354	.399	.754	19	.941
— Tennessee (Sou.)	3B	39	134	17	32	4	3	2	15	15	18	2	3	3-2	.239	.320	.358	.678	11	.921
2001— Tennessee (Sou.)	2B-3B	84	306	51	94	22	8	4	52	37	42	3	12	8-3	.307	.385	.471	.856	8	.979
— Syracuse (Int'l)	2B-3B	55	194	31	59	14	3	4	27	23	34	2	1	11-3	.304	.378	.469	.847	4	.986
2002— Syracuse (Int'l)	2B	100	417	63	127	27	3	10	37	35	54	4	14	8-5	.305	.363	.456	.819	10	.982
— Toronto (A.L.)	2B	54	192	20	53	10	5	4	23	11	27	2	6	0-1	.276	.319	.443	.762	4	.986
2003— Toronto (A.L.)	2B	142	474	54	127	21	6	9	57	39	87	5	13	5-4	.268	.328	.395	.723	12	.984
2004— Toronto (A.L.)	2B	135	489	73	132	32	7	12	58	51	98	4	12	7-3	.270	.341	.438	.779	12	.984
2005— Toronto (A.L.)	2B	131	461	62	125	25	5	10	63	30	65	3	10	7-1	.271	.315	.412	.728	6	.991
Major League totals (4 years)		462	1616	209	437	88	23	35	201	131	277	14	41	19-9	.270	.328	.418	.746	34	.986

HUDSON, TIM — P

PERSONAL: Born July 14, 1975, in Columbus, Ga. ... 6-1/164. ... Throws right, bats right. ... Full name: Timothy Adam Hudson. ... High school: Glenwood (Phenix City, Ala.). ... College: Auburn.

TRANSACTIONS/CAREER NOTES: Selected by Oakland Athletics organization in 35th round of 1994 free-agent draft; did not sign. ... Selected by Athletics organization in sixth round of 1997 free-agent draft. ... On disabled list (June 23-August 7, 2004); included rehabilitation assignment to Sacramento. ... Traded by A's to Atlanta Braves for Ps Juan Cruz and Dan Meyer and OF Charles Thomas (December 16, 2004). ... On disabled list (June 16-July 16, 2005).

H

HONORS: Named A.L. Rookie Pitcher of the Year by THE SPORTING NEWS (1999).
CAREER HITTING: 12-for-91 (.132), 4 R, 3 2B, 1 3B, 0 HR, 7 RBI.

SCOUTING REPORT *Throws:* Hudson's bread-and-butter pitch is his heavy sinker, which runs from the low- to mid-90s. Throws a slider, changeup and split-finger fastball. *Tendencies:* He goes after hitters with the sinker, which bores in on righthanded hitters and away from left-handers. Has a tight, biting slider that has excellent depth. Regained the feel for his splitter, which has good late action, and used it more during the second half of the season. *Outlook:* Hudson bounced back from prolonged problems with an oblique muscle to throw well. Is still a top-notch starter. *Grade 9*

TIM HUDSON'S PITCHING ZONE

.278	.440	.275
.220	.420	.321
.254	.167	.290

LEFTY-RIGHTY SPLITS

vs.	Avg.	AB	H	2B	3B	HR	RBI	BB	SO	OBP	Slg.
L	.285	396	113	23	3	9	35	43	54	.365	.427
R	.240	337	81	14	1	11	40	22	61	.291	.386

Year Team (League)	W	L	Pct.	ERA	WHIP	G	GS	CG	ShO	Hld.	Sv.-Opp.	IP	H	R	ER	HR	BB-IBB	SO	Avg.
1997— S. Oregon (N'west)	3	1	.750	2.51	0.94	8	4	0	0	...	0-...	28.2	12	8	8	0	15-2	37	.128
1998— Modesto (California)	4	0	1.000	1.67	0.98	8	5	0	0	...	0-...	37.2	19	10	7	0	18-0	48	.148
— Huntsville (Sou.)	10	9	.526	4.54	1.54	22	22	2	0	...	0-...	134.2	136	84	68	13	71-2	104	.270
1999— Midland (Texas)	3	0	1.000	0.50	0.67	3	3	0	0	...	0-...	18.0	9	1	1	0	3-0	18	.153
— Vancouver (PCL)	4	0	1.000	2.20	1.20	8	8	0	0	...	0-...	49.0	38	16	12	2	21-0	61	.212
— Oakland (A.L.)	11	2	.846	3.23	1.34	21	21	1	0	0	0-0	136.1	121	56	49	8	62-2	132	.237
2000— Oakland (A.L.)	• 20	6	.769	4.14	1.24	32	32	2	2	0	0-0	202.1	169	100	93	24	82-5	169	.227
2001— Oakland (A.L.)	18	9	.667	3.37	1.22	35	• 35	3	0	0	0-0	235.0	216	100	88	20	71-5	181	.245
2002— Oakland (A.L.)	15	9	.625	2.98	1.25	34	34	4	2	0	0-0	238.1	237	87	79	19	62-9	152	.263
2003— Oakland (A.L.)	16	7	.696	2.70	1.08	34	34	3	• 2	0	0-0	240.0	197	84	72	15	61-9	162	.223
2004— Sacramento (PCL)	0	0	...	6.00	1.33	1	1	0	0	...	0-...	3.0	2	2	2	0	2-0	3	.167
— Oakland (A.L.)	12	6	.667	3.53	1.26	27	27	3	• 2	0	0-0	188.2	194	82	74	8	44-3	103	.267
2005— Atlanta (N.L.)	14	9	.609	3.52	1.35	29	29	2	0	0	0-0	192.0	194	79	75	20	65-5	115	.265
American League totals (6 years)	92	39	.702	3.30	1.22	183	183	16	8	0	0-0	1240.2	1134	509	455	94	382-33	899	.244
National League totals (1 year)	14	9	.609	3.52	1.35	29	29	2	0	0	0-0	192.0	194	79	75	20	65-5	115	.265
Major League totals (7 years)	106	48	.688	3.33	1.24	212	212	18	8	0	0-0	1432.2	1328	588	530	114	447-38	1014	.247

DIVISION SERIES RECORD

Year Team (League)	W	L	Pct.	ERA	WHIP	G	GS	CG	ShO	Hld.	Sv.-Opp.	IP	H	R	ER	HR	BB-IBB	SO	Avg.
2000— Oakland (A.L.)	0	1	.000	3.38	1.25	1	1	0	0	0	0-0	8.0	6	4	3	0	4-0	5	.194
2001— Oakland (A.L.)	1	0	1.000	0.93	0.93	2	1	0	0	0	0-0	9.2	8	1	1	1	1-0	5	.222
2002— Oakland (A.L.)	0	1	.000	6.23	1.96	2	2	0	0	0	0-0	8.2	13	11	6	2	4-0	8	.333
2003— Oakland (A.L.)	0	0	...	3.52	1.43	2	2	0	0	0	0-0	7.2	10	3	3	2	1-0	6	.323
2005— Atlanta (N.L.)	0	1	.000	5.27	1.39	2	2	0	0	0	0-0	13.2	13	8	8	0	6-1	8	.283
Division series totals (5 years)	1	3	.250	3.97	1.38	9	8	0	0	0	0-0	47.2	50	27	21	5	16-1	32	.273

ALL-STAR GAME RECORD

	W	L	Pct.	ERA	WHIP	G	GS	CG	ShO	Hld.	Sv.-Opp.	IP	H	R	ER	HR	BB-IBB	SO	Avg.
All-Star Game totals (1 year)	0	0	...	0.00	0.00	1	0	0	0	0	0-0	1.0	0	0	0	0	0-0	1	.000

HUFF, AUBREY   OF/1B

PERSONAL: Born December 20, 1976, in Marion, Ohio. ... 6-4/231. ... Bats left, throws right. ... Full name: Aubrey Lewis Huff. ... High school: Brewer (Fort Worth, Texas). ... College: Miami.
TRANSACTIONS/CAREER NOTES: Selected by Tampa Bay Devil Rays organization in fifth round of 1998 free-agent draft.
2005 GAMES PLAYED BY POSITION (MLB): OF—97, DH—33, 1B—25, 3B—4.

SCOUTING REPORT *Offense:* He has a fluid stroke that is slightly long, yet he generates good bat speed through the hitting zone. Has power to all fields but gets into streaks where he wants to pull the ball. Is a patient hitter, a necessary quality for him because he frequently is pitched around. Struggled against lefthanders this year as he saw a lot more breaking balls. Can't run and doesn't have baserunning instincts. *Defense:* He isn't too good at any position. Has a lot of trouble going back on the ball and doesn't track balls well to the gaps. Arm is short and runners can take extra bases on him. *Outlook:* Huff is a DH with home-run power. Was a steady run producer for a club that didn't give him much protection in the order. *Grade 7.8*

AUBREY HUFF'S HITTING ZONE

.308	.318	.308
.243	.367	.235
.286	.321	.288

LEFTY-RIGHTY SPLITS

vs.	Avg.	AB	H	2B	3B	HR	RBI	BB	SO	OBP	Slg.
L	.256	207	53	8	2	6	30	11	35	.300	.401
R	.264	368	97	18	0	16	62	38	53	.332	.443

Year Team (League)	Pos.	G	AB	R	H	2B	3B	HR	RBI	BB	SO	HBP	GDP	SB-CS	Avg.	OBP	SLG	OPS	E	Avg.
1998— Char., S.C. (SAL)	3B	69	265	38	85	19	1	13	54	24	40	0	5	3-1	.321	.371	.547	.918	8	.957
1999— Orlando (South.)	3B	133	491	85	148	40	3	22	78	64	77	4	14	2-3	.301	.385	.530	.915	29	.927
2000— Durham (Int'l)	3B-1B	108	408	73	129	36	3	20	76	51	72	2	15	2-3	.316	.394	.566	.960	21	.915
— Tampa Bay (A.L.)	3B	39	122	12	35	7	0	4	14	5	18	1	6	0-0	.287	.318	.443	.760	5	.939
2001— Durham (Int'l)	3B	17	66	14	19	6	0	3	10	5	7	0	3	0-0	.288	.338	.515	.853	4	.929
— Tampa Bay (A.L.)	3B-DH-1B	111	411	42	102	25	1	8	45	23	72	1	18	1-3	.248	.288	.372	.660	20	.940
2002— Durham (Int'l)	1B	32	126	18	41	9	0	3	20	12	13	1	4	0-0	.325	.386	.468	.854	0	1.000
— Tampa Bay (A.L.)	DH-1B-3B	113	454	67	142	25	0	23	59	37	55	1	17	4-1	.313	.364	.520	.884	8	.981
2003— Tampa Bay (A.L.)	OF-DH-1B	162	636	91	198	47	3	34	107	53	80	8	19	2-3	.311	.367	.555	.922	9	.977
2004— Tampa Bay (A.L.)	3B-1B-DH	157	600	92	178	27	2	29	104	56	74	6	5	5-1	.297	.360	.493	.853	13	.975
2005— Tampa Bay (A.L.)	OF-DH-1B	154	575	70	150	26	2	22	92	49	88	5	12	8-7	.261	.321	.428	.749	3	.992
Major League totals (6 years)	3B	736	2798	374	805	157	8	120	421	223	387	21	81	20-15	.288	.342	.478	.820	58	.972

H

HUGHES, TRAVIS   P

PERSONAL: Born May 25, 1978, in Newton, Kan. ... 6-5/240. ... Throws right, bats right. ... Full name: Travis Wade Hughes. ... High school: Elwood (Kan.). ... Junior college: Cowley County (Kan.) Community College.
TRANSACTIONS/CAREER NOTES: Selected by Texas Rangers organization in 19th round of 1997 free-agent draft. ... Claimed on waivers by Washington Nationals (April 7, 2005).
CAREER HITTING: 0-for-0 (.000), 0 R, 0 2B, 0 3B, 0 HR, 0 RBI.

TRAVIS HUGHES' PITCHING ZONE

.333	.200	.000
.143	.667	.375
.333	.667	.667

LEFTY-RIGHTY SPLITS

vs.	Avg.	AB	H	2B	3B	HR	RBI	BB	SO	OBP	Slg.
L	.313	16	5	0	0	2	3	3	3	.421	.688
R	.342	38	13	0	0	2	6	5	5	.432	.500

Year	Team (League)	W	L	Pct.	ERA	WHIP	G	GS	CG	ShO	Hld.	Sv.-Opp.	IP	H	R	ER	HR	BB-IBB	SO	Avg.
1998—	Pulaski (Appal.)	2	6	.250	3.89	1.32	22	3	0	0	...	2-...	41.2	30	25	18	2	25-1	48	.189
1999—	Savannah (S. Atl.)	11	7	.611	2.81	1.15	30	23	1	0	...	2-...	157.0	127	60	49	9	54-0	150	.221
2000—	Charlotte (Fla. St.)	9	9	.500	4.42	1.39	39	14	1	0	...	9-...	126.1	122	76	62	9	54-3	96	.254
2001—	Tulsa (Texas)	5	7	.417	4.64	1.56	47	5	0	0	...	8-...	87.1	91	52	45	8	45-2	86	.270
2002—	Tulsa (Texas)	9	7	.563	3.52	1.54	26	26	1	1	...	0-...	143.1	139	68	56	11	82-0	137	.255
2003—	Oklahoma (PCL)	1	3	.250	5.46	1.84	11	11	0	0	...	0-...	57.2	79	41	35	4	27-0	36	.329
—	Frisco (Texas)	4	8	.333	4.99	1.45	24	10	1	1	...	0-...	74.0	81	47	41	6	26-1	58	.277
2004—	Frisco (Texas)	3	6	.333	3.70	1.52	40	0	0	0	...	7-...	63.1	63	34	26	4	33-7	68	.256
—	Oklahoma (PCL)	1	2	.333	5.26	1.17	13	0	0	0	...	0-...	25.2	21	15	15	2	9-0	24	.221
—	Texas (A.L.)	0	0	...	13.50	4.50	2	0	0	0	0	0-0	1.1	4	2	2	0	2-0	4	.500
2005—	New Orleans (PCL)	2	5	.286	3.02	1.21	52	0	0	0	9	13-17	59.2	47	25	20	3	25-1	73	.214
—	Washington (N.L.)	1	1	.500	5.54	2.00	14	0	0	0	0	0-1	13.0	18	8	8	4	8-1	8	.333
American League totals (1 year)		0	0	...	13.50	4.50	2	0	0	0	0	0-0	1.1	4	2	2	0	2-0	4	.500
National League totals (1 year)		1	1	.500	5.54	2.00	14	0	0	0	0	0-1	13.0	18	8	8	4	8-1	8	.333
Major League totals (2 years)		1	1	.500	6.28	2.23	16	0	0	0	0	0-1	14.1	22	10	10	4	10-1	12	.355

HUNTER, TORII   OF

PERSONAL: Born July 18, 1975, in Pine Bluff, Ark. ... 6-2/211. ... Bats right, throws right. ... Full name: Torii Kedar Hunter. ... High school: Pine Bluff (Ark.).
TRANSACTIONS/CAREER NOTES: Selected by Minnesota Twins organization in first round (20th pick overall) of 1993 free-agent draft; pick recieved as part of compensation for Cincinnati Reds signing Type A free-agent P John Smiley. ... On disabled list (April 6-21, 2001; April 7-25, 2004; and July 30, 2005-remainder of season). ... On suspended list (July 20-23, 2002).
HONORS: Won A.L. Gold Glove as outfielder (2001-05).
2005 GAMES PLAYED BY POSITION (MLB): OF—93, DH—5.

SCOUTING REPORT Offense: He's a high-strikeout hitter because of his long swing and tendency to overswing. Has a very big zone. Had some decline in bat speed and gets into trouble when he becomes pull-conscious. Is a better high-ball hitter but consistently chases pitches up out of the zone. Has good power but needs to be conscious of taking the ball back through the middle. ***Defense:*** Hunter, a five-time Gold Glove winner, plays with reckless abandon and has no fear of the wall. Gets outstanding jumps with exceptional closing speed and agility. Has a plus arm with a quick release. Charges the ball well and is accurate. ***Outlook:*** Hunter is one of the game's best athletes, but must cut down his swing and strikeouts. Is coming back from a broken ankle suffered late last season. ***Grade 8.4***

TORII HUNTER'S HITTING ZONE

.409	.176	.273
.316	.450	.200
.333	.250	.067

LEFTY-RIGHTY SPLITS

vs.	Avg.	AB	H	2B	3B	HR	RBI	BB	SO	OBP	Slg.
L	.283	106	30	11	0	6	24	12	19	.355	.557
R	.263	266	70	13	1	8	32	22	46	.329	.410

Year	Team (League)	Pos.	G	AB	R	H	2B	3B	HR	RBI	BB	SO	HBP	GDP	SB-CS	Avg.	OBP	SLG	OPS	E	Avg.
1993—	GC Twins (GCL)	OF	28	100	6	19	3	0	0	8	4	23	9	1	4-2	.190	.283	.220	.503	6	.895
1994—	Fort Wayne (Midw.)	OF	91	335	57	98	17	1	10	50	25	80	10	5	8-10	.293	.358	.439	.796	7	.971
1995—	Fort Myers (FSL)	OF	113	391	64	96	15	2	7	36	38	77	12	8	7-4	.246	.330	.348	.678	7	.973
1996—	Fort Myers (FSL)	OF	4	16	1	3	0	0	0	1	2	5	0	0	1-1	.188	.278	.188	.465	0	1.000
—	New Britain (East.)	OF	99	342	49	90	20	3	7	33	28	60	7	7	7-7	.263	.331	.401	.731	4	.982
1997—	New Britain (East.)	OF-DH	127	471	57	109	22	2	8	56	47	94	3	6	8-8	.231	.305	.338	.642	7	.974
—	Minnesota (A.L.)		1	0	0	0	0	0	0	0	0	0	0	0	0-0	...	...	...	...	...	...
1998—	New Britain (East.)	OF	82	308	42	87	24	3	6	32	19	64	4	2	11-9	.282	.329	.438	.768	2	.989
—	Minnesota (A.L.)	OF	6	17	0	4	1	0	0	2	2	6	0	1	0-0	.235	.316	.294	.610	0	1.000
—	Salt Lake (PCL)	OF-DH	26	92	15	31	7	0	4	20	1	13	1	3	2-2	.337	.347	.543	.891	2	.966
1999—	Minnesota (A.L.)	OF	135	384	52	98	17	2	9	35	26	72	6	9	10-6	.255	.309	.380	.689	1	.997
2000—	Minnesota (A.L.)	OF	99	336	44	94	14	7	5	44	18	68	2	13	4-3	.280	.318	.408	.726	3	.989
—	Salt Lake (PCL)		55	209	58	77	17	2	18	61	11	54	3	4	11-3	.368	.403	.727	1.130	3	.973
2001—	Minnesota (A.L.)	OF	148	564	82	147	32	5	27	92	29	125	8	12	9-6	.261	.306	.479	.784	4	.992
2002—	Minnesota (A.L.)	OF-DH	148	561	89	162	37	4	29	94	35	118	5	17	23-8	.289	.334	.524	.859	3	.992
2003—	Minnesota (A.L.)	OF-DH	154	581	83	145	31	4	26	102	50	106	4	15	6-7	.250	.312	.451	.762	5	.991
2004—	Minnesota (A.L.)	OF	138	520	79	141	37	0	23	81	40	101	7	23	21-7	.271	.330	.475	.805	4	.988
2005—	Minnesota (A.L.)	OF-DH	98	372	63	100	24	1	14	56	34	65	6	8	23-7	.269	.337	.452	.788	3	.987
Major League totals (9 years)			927	3335	492	891	193	23	133	506	234	661	39	98	96-45	.267	.321	.458	.779	22	.991

DIVISION SERIES RECORD

Year	Team (League)	Pos.	G	AB	R	H	2B	3B	HR	RBI	BB	SO	HBP	GDP	SB-CS	Avg.	OBP	SLG	OPS	E	Avg.
2002—	Minnesota (A.L.)	OF	5	20	4	6	4	0	0	2	1	4	0	0	0-0	.300	.333	.500	.833	0	1.000
2003—	Minnesota (A.L.)	OF	4	14	3	6	0	1	1	2	2	2	0	0	0-0	.429	.500	.786	1.286	0	1.000
2004—	Minnesota (A.L.)	OF	4	17	5	6	1	0	1	2	1	1	0	0	2-0	.353	.368	.588	.957	0	1.000
Division series totals (3 years)			13	51	12	18	5	1	2	6	4	7	0	0	2-0	.353	.393	.608	1.001	0	1.000

H

Year Team (League)	Pos.	G	AB	R	H	2B	3B	HR	RBI	BB	SO	HBP	GDP	SB-CS	Avg.	OBP	SLG	OPS	E	Avg.
2002— Minnesota (A.L.)	OF	5	18	2	3	2	0	0	0	1	3	0	2	0-0	.167	.211	.278	.488	0	1.000

ALL-STAR GAME RECORD

		G	AB	R	H	2B	3B	HR	RBI	BB	SO	HBP	GDP	SB-CS	Avg.	OBP	SLG	OPS	E	Avg.
All-Star Game totals (1 year)		1	2	0	0	0	0	0	0	0	0	0	0	0-0	.000	.000	.000	.000	0	1.000

HYZDU, ADAM — OF

PERSONAL: Born December 6, 1971, in San Jose, Calif. ... 6-2/220. ... Bats right, throws right. ... Full name: Adam David Hyzdu. ... Name pronounced: HIGHS-doo. ... High school: Moeller (Cincinnati).

TRANSACTIONS/CAREER NOTES: Selected by San Francisco Giants organization in first round (15th pick overall) of 1990 free-agent draft; pick received as compensation for Houston Astros signing Type B free-agent IF Ken Oberkfell. ... Selected by Cincinnati Reds from Giants organization in Rule 5 major league draft (December 13, 1993). ... Released by Reds (March 23, 1996). ... Signed by Boston Red Sox organization (April 26, 1996). ... Signed as a free agent by Arizona Diamondbacks organization (January 2, 1998). ... Loaned by Diamondbacks organization to Monterrey of the Mexican League (April 7-May 17, 1998). ... On disabled list (June 30-August 23, 1998). ... Signed as a free agent by Red Sox organization (January 5, 1999). ... Released by Red Sox (May 5, 1999). ... Signed by Pittsburgh Pirates organization (May 10, 1999). ... Signed as a free agent by Red Sox organization (November 10, 2003). ... Traded by Red Sox to San Diego Padres for P Blaine Neal (March 22, 2005). ... Traded by Padres to Red Sox for P Scott Cassidy (July 19, 2005). ... Released by Red Sox (October 15, 2005). ... Signed by Texas Rangers organization (November 3, 2005).

2005 GAMES PLAYED BY POSITION (MLB): OF—24.

LEFTY-RIGHTY SPLITS

vs.	Avg.	AB	H	2B	3B	HR	RBI	BB	SO	OBP	Slg.
L	.167	18	3	1	0	0	3	5	5	.348	.222
R	.222	18	4	1	0	0	1	0	2	.211	.278

Year Team (League)	Pos.	G	AB	R	H	2B	3B	HR	RBI	BB	SO	HBP	GDP	SB-CS	Avg.	OBP	SLG	OPS	E	Avg.
1990—Everett (N'west)	OF	69	253	31	62	16	1	6	34	28	78	2	4	2-4	.245	.319	.387	.707	5	.963
1991—Clinton (Midw.)	OF	124	410	47	96	13	5	5	50	64	131	3	10	4-5	.234	.340	.327	.667	9	.955
1992—San Jose (Calif.)	OF	128	457	60	127	25	5	9	50	55	134	1	6	10-5	.278	.351	.414	.765	5	.976
1993—San Jose (Calif.)	OF	44	165	35	48	11	3	13	38	29	53	0	3	1-1	.291	.393	.630	1.023	3	.963
—Shreveport (Texas)	OF	86	302	30	61	17	0	6	25	20	82	1	5	0-5	.202	.253	.318	.571	4	.973
1994—Chattanooga (Sou.) OF-1B-DH	38	133	17	35	10	0	3	9	8	21	1	1	0-2	.263	.310	.406	.716	4	.949
—Win.-Salem (Car.)	OF-DH	55	210	30	58	11	1	15	39	18	33	2	3	1-5	.276	.336	.552	.889	4	.945
—Indianapolis (A.A.)	OF	12	25	3	3	2	0	0	3	1	5	0	0	0-0	.120	.143	.200	.343	1	.917
1995—Chattanooga (Sou.)	OF	102	312	55	82	14	1	13	48	45	56	4	4	3-2	.263	.362	.439	.801	1	.995
1996—Trenton (East.) ....OF-DH-C	109	374	71	126	24	3	25	80	56	75	2	7	1-8	.337	.424	.618	1.042	3	.980
1997—Pawtucket (Int'l)	OF	119	413	77	114	21	1	23	84	72	113	4	6	10-6	.276	.387	.499	.886	4	.978
1998—Monterrey (Mex.)	OF	29	110	20	36	3	0	5	22	14	17	...		7-1	.327	...	.491	...	0	1.000
—Tucson (PCL) ....OF-DH-P	34	100	21	34	7	1	4	14	15	23	0	2	0-1	.340	.419	.550	.969	1	.974
1999—Pawtucket (Int'l) ....OF-DH	12	35	4	8	0	1	0	6	4	13	0	1	0-0	.229	.308	.314	.622	0	1.000
—Altoona (East.) OF-1B-3B-DH	91	345	64	109	26	1	24	78	40	62	3	8	8-4	.316	.392	.612	1.003	11	.965
—Nashville (PCL)	OF	14	44	6	11	1	0	5	13	4	11	0	2	0-0	.250	.313	.614	.926	0	1.000
2000—Altoona (East.) OF-1B	142	514	96	149	39	2	31	106	94	102	8	6	3-7	.290	.405	.554	.960	1	.996
—Pittsburgh (N.L.)	OF	12	18	2	7	0	0	1	4	0	4	0	0	0-0	.389	.389	.667	1.056	0	1.000
2001—Nashville (PCL) OF-1B-3B	69	261	38	76	17	2	11	39	17	68	0	3	1-3	.291	.332	.498	.830	1	.994
—Pittsburgh (N.L.) OF-1B	51	72	7	15	1	0	5	9	4	18	1	1	0-1	.208	.253	.431	.690	0	1.000
2002—Nashville (PCL) OF-1B	65	243	33	59	17	0	10	50	29	59	0	4	1-2	.243	.318	.436	.754	3	.980
—Pittsburgh (N.L.) OF-1B	59	155	24	36	6	0	11	34	21	44	1	1	0-0	.232	.324	.484	.808	0	1.000
2003—Pittsburgh (N.L.)	OF	51	63	16	13	5	0	1	6	8	10	21	1	0-0	.206	.300	.333	.653	0	1.000
—Nashville (PCL) OF-1B	40	135	22	38	10	1	6	18	18	28	1	2	2-2	.281	.365	.504	.869	2	.981
2004—Pawtucket (Int'l) ....OF-DH	129	465	92	140	33	2	29	79	84	106	7	12	8-4	.301	.413	.568	.980	6	.976
—Boston (A.L.)	OF	17	10	3	3	2	0	1	2	1	5	0	0	0-0	.300	.364	.800	1.164	0	1.000
2005—San Diego (N.L.)	OF	17	20	1	3	1	0	0	4	3	4	0	1	0-0	.150	.250	.200	.450	0	1.000
—Portland (PCL)	OF	62	207	38	57	9	1	11	32	47	61	1	5	2-5	.275	.410	.488	.898	2	.993
—Pawtucket (Int'l) ....OF-DH	31	118	17	30	7	0	4	25	16	32	0	2	0-1	.254	.343	.415	.759	0	1.000
—Boston (A.L.)	OF	12	16	1	4	1	0	0	0	2	3	0	0	0-0	.250	.333	.313	.646	1	.909
American League totals (2 years)		29	26	4	7	3	0	1	2	3	5	0	0	0-0	.269	.345	.500	.845	1	.941
National League totals (5 years)		190	328	50	74	15	0	18	59	38	91	3	5	1-1	.226	.308	.436	.744	0	.995
Major League totals (6 years)		219	354	54	81	18	0	19	61	41	96	3	5	1-1	.229	.311	.441	.752	1	.995

DIVISION SERIES RECORD

Year Team (League)	Pos.	G	AB	R	H	2B	3B	HR	RBI	BB	SO	HBP	GDP	SB-CS	Avg.	OBP	SLG	OPS	E	Avg.
2005—Boston (A.L.)	OF	1	0	0	0	0	0	0	0	0	0	0	0	0-0	...	...	...	...	0	1.000

IBANEZ, RAUL — OF

PERSONAL: Born June 2, 1972, in New York. ... 6-2/200. ... Bats left, throws right. ... Full name: Raul Javier Ibanez. ... Name pronounced: ee-BON-yez. ... High school: Sunset (Miami). ... Junior college: Miami-Dade Community College South.

TRANSACTIONS/CAREER NOTES: Selected by Seattle Mariners organization in 36th round of 1992 free-agent draft. ... On disabled list (March 30-June 29, 1998); included rehabilitation assignment to Tacoma. ... On disabled list (May 18-June 3, 1999); included rehabilitation assignment to Tacoma. ... On disabled list (August 7-22, 2000); included rehabilitation assignment to Tacoma. ... Signed as a free agent by Kansas City Royals organization (January 22, 2001). ... Signed as a free agent by Mariners (November 19, 2003). ... On disabled list (June 3-July 10, 2004); included rehabilitation assignment to Tacoma.

2005 GAMES PLAYED BY POSITION (MLB): DH—101, OF—58, 1B—4.

SCOUTING REPORT *Offense:* He has a good stroke with good bat speed. His level swing keeps the bat in the zone. Will make adjustments and use the whole field. Has power when he pulls the ball. Is a good breaking-ball hitter with good bat control. Is an average runner but not a bases-stealer. *Defense:* He's a converted catcher who has played left field, right field and first base. His best position is right field, where he gets better jumps than in left. Has more problems going back than coming in. His arm strength is just below average, and he takes too long to get rid of the ball. *Outlook:* Ibanez is an underrated offensive player with a solid swing and deceptive power. Is a very good situational hitter. *Grade 7.4*

RAUL IBANEZ'S HITTING ZONE

.208	.300	.250
.222	.431	.338
.265	.250	.229

LEFTY-RIGHTY SPLITS

vs.	Avg.	AB	H	2B	3B	HR	RBI	BB	SO	OBP	Slg.
L	.275	189	52	7	0	7	38	19	39	.346	.423
R	.282	425	120	25	2	13	51	52	60	.359	.442

H

				BATTING																FIELDING	
Year	Team (League)	Pos.	G	AB	R	H	2B	3B	HR	RBI	BB	SO	HBP	GDP	SB-CS	Avg.	OBP	SLG	OPS	E	Avg.
1992— Ariz. Mariners (Ariz.)		1B-C-OF	33	120	25	37	8	2	1	16	9	18	2	3	1-2	.308	.366	.433	.800	4	.931
1993— Appleton (Midwest)		1B-C-OF	52	157	26	43	9	0	5	21	24	31	1	2	0-2	.274	.370	.427	.796	2	.980
— Bellingham (N'west)		C	43	134	16	38	5	2	0	15	21	23	0	0	0-3	.284	.378	.351	.729	1	.993
1994— Appleton (N'west)		1B-C-OF	91	327	55	102	30	3	7	59	32	37	2	3	10-5	.312	.375	.486	.861	10	.971
1995— Riverside (Calif.)		1B-C	95	361	59	120	23	9	20	108	41	49	2	7	4-3	.332	.395	.612	1.007	12	.977
1996— Tacoma (PCL)		OF-1B-DH	111	405	59	115	20	3	11	47	44	56	2	4	7-7	.284	.353	.430	.783	11	.951
— Port City (Sou.)		OF-DH-1B																			
		C	19	76	12	28	8	1	1	13	8	7	0	1	3-2	.368	.424	.539	.963	4	.905
		DH	4	5	0	0	0	0	0	0	0	1	1	0	0-0	.000	.167	.000	.167	0	...
1997— Tacoma (PCL)		OF	111	438	84	133	30	5	15	84	32	75	1	12	7-5	.304	.349	.498	.847	5	.976
— Seattle (A.L.)		OF-DH	11	26	3	4	0	1	1	4	0	6	0	0	0-0	.154	.154	.346	.500	0	1.000
1998— Tacoma (PCL)		OF-DH	52	190	24	41	8	1	6	25	24	47	0	3	1-1	.216	.301	.363	.664	1	.988
— Seattle (A.L.)		OF-1B-DH	37	98	12	25	7	1	2	12	5	22	0	4	0-0	.255	.291	.408	.699	1	.991
1999— Seattle (A.L.)		OF-1B-C																			
		DH	87	209	23	54	7	0	9	27	17	32	0	4	5-1	.258	.313	.421	.734	3	.988
— Tacoma (PCL)		OF-1B-DH	8	31	6	11	1	0	3	5	1	7	0	0	1-0	.355	.371	.677	1.052	0	1.000
2000— Seattle (A.L.)		OF-DH-1B	92	140	21	32	8	0	2	15	14	25	1	1	2-0	.229	.301	.329	.630	2	.980
— Tacoma (PCL)		OF	10	40	3	10	4	0	0	6	1	3	0	0	0-0	.250	.268	.350	.618	0	1.000
2001— Kansas City (A.L.)		OF-DH-1B																			
		3B	104	279	44	78	11	5	13	54	32	51	0	6	0-2	.280	.353	.495	.847	5	.962
— Omaha (PCL)		OF-SS	8	27	3	4	1	0	2	5	1	10	0	0	0-0	.148	.179	.407	.586	1	.857
2002— Kansas City (A.L.)		OF-1B-DH	137	497	70	146	37	6	24	103	40	76	2	11	5-3	.294	.346	.537	.883	3	.994
2003— Kansas City (A.L.)		OF-1B-DH	157	608	95	179	33	5	18	90	49	81	3	10	8-4	.294	.345	.454	.799	4	.991
2004— Tacoma (PCL)		DH-OF	4	17	2	4	1	0	0	1	0	6	0	0	0-0	.235	.235	.294	.529	0	1.000
— Seattle (A.L.)		OF-1B-DH	123	481	67	146	31	1	16	62	36	72	3	10	1-2	.304	.353	.472	.825	5	.984
2005— Seattle (A.L.)		DH-OF-1B	• 162	614	92	172	32	2	20	89	71	99	2	12	9-4	.280	.355	.436	.792	2	.986
Major League totals (10 years)			914	2957	427	836	166	21	105	456	264	465	12	58	30-16	.283	.341	.460	.801	25	.987

DIVISION SERIES RECORD

Year	Team (League)	Pos.	G	AB	R	H	2B	3B	HR	RBI	BB	SO	HBP	GDP	SB-CS	Avg.	OBP	SLG	OPS	E	Avg.
2000— Seattle (A.L.)		OF	3	8	2	3	0	0	0	0	0	0	0	0	0-0	.375	.375	.375	.750	0	1.000

CHAMPIONSHIP SERIES RECORD

Year	Team (League)	Pos.	G	AB	R	H	2B	3B	HR	RBI	BB	SO	HBP	GDP	SB-CS	Avg.	OBP	SLG	OPS	E	Avg.
2000— Seattle (A.L.)		OF	6	9	0	0	0	0	0	0	0	2	0	0	0-0	.000	.000	.000	.000	0	1.000

IGUCHI, TADAHITO — 2B

PERSONAL: Born December 4, 1974, in Tokyo. ... 5-10/185. ... Bats right, throws right. ... Full name: Tadahito Iguchi. ... Name pronounced: ta-da-HEAT-o ee-GOO-chee. ... College: Aoyama Gakuin.

TRANSACTIONS/CAREER NOTES: Played for Fukuoka of the Japan Pacific League (1997-2004). ... Signed as a free agent by Chicago White Sox (January 27, 2005).

2005 GAMES PLAYED BY POSITION (MLB): 2B—133.

SCOUTING REPORT *Offense:* Iguchi has an unorthodox long, sweeping swing and pulls off the ball, yet has good bat speed and control. Will use the whole field. Will move runners along. Has power from right-center to the left-field line. *Defense:* He has good instincts and soft hands. Plays deep but has good range to either side. Likes to keep the ball in front of him when moving to his right. Making quick pivots to turn the double play. *Outlook:* Iguchi, the second-best Japanese position player to play in the major leagues, made a huge difference in the White Sox's playoff drive. Should continue to improve as he learns the league *Grade 7.8*

TADAHITO IGUCHI'S HITTING ZONE

.294	.429	.219
.298	.392	.333
.293	.212	.250

LEFTY-RIGHTY SPLITS

vs.	Avg.	AB	H	2B	3B	HR	RBI	BB	SO	OBP	Slg.
L	.274	146	40	7	1	6	27	18	34	.353	.459
R	.279	365	102	18	5	9	44	29	80	.337	.430

				BATTING																FIELDING	
Year	Team (League)	Pos.	G	AB	R	H	2B	3B	HR	RBI	BB	SO	HBP	GDP	SB-CS	Avg.	OBP	SLG	OPS	E	Avg.
2005— Chicago (A.L.)		2B	135	511	74	142	25	6	15	71	47	114	6	16	15-5	.278	.342	.438	.780	14	.978
Major League totals (1 year)			135	511	74	142	25	6	15	71	47	114	6	16	15-5	.278	.342	.438	.780	14	.978

DIVISION SERIES RECORD

Year	Team (League)	Pos.	G	AB	R	H	2B	3B	HR	RBI	BB	SO	HBP	GDP	SB-CS	Avg.	OBP	SLG	OPS	E	Avg.
2005— Chicago (A.L.)		2B	3	12	1	3	0	0	1	4	0	3	0	0	0-0	.250	.250	.500	.750	0	1.000

CHAMPIONSHIP SERIES RECORD

Year	Team (League)	Pos.	G	AB	R	H	2B	3B	HR	RBI	BB	SO	HBP	GDP	SB-CS	Avg.	OBP	SLG	OPS	E	Avg.
2005— Chicago (A.L.)		2B	5	17	4	3	1	0	0	0	1	6	3	0	0-1	.176	.333	.235	.569	1	1.000

WORLD SERIES RECORD

Year	Team (League)	Pos.	G	AB	R	H	2B	3B	HR	RBI	BB	SO	HBP	GDP	SB-CS	Avg.	OBP	SLG	OPS	E	Avg.
2005— Chicago (A.L.)		2B	4	18	2	3	0	0	0	1	1	3	0	1	0-0	.167	.211	.167	.377	0	1.000

INFANTE, OMAR — 2B

PERSONAL: Born December 26, 1981, in Puerto la Cruz, Venezuela. ... 6-0/176. ... Bats right, throws right. ... Full name: Omar Rafael Infante. ... Name pronounced: in-FAHN-tay.

TRANSACTIONS/CAREER NOTES: Signed as a non-drafted free agent by Detroit Tigers organization (April 28, 1999).

2005 GAMES PLAYED BY POSITION (MLB): 2B—69, SS—50.

SCOUTING REPORT *Offense:* Infante's inability to adjust to breaking pitches has cost him an everyday position. Is a high-fastball hitter who struggles when he pulls the ball too much. Is not patient, has a long stroke and chases high pitches. Strikes out too much. *Defense:* He can play three infield positions and has good hands and feet. Has good agility and range to both sides. Makes quick pivots and gets good jumps on the ball. Throws well on the move but can airmail throws when he rushes. *Outlook:* Infante's bat always will be a question. Is ideally suited to be a utility infielder. *Grade 6.5*

OMAR INFANTE'S HITTING ZONE

.240	.258	.522
.152	.310	.286
.207	.381	.250

LEFTY-RIGHTY SPLITS

vs.	Avg.	AB	H	2B	3B	HR	RBI	BB	SO	OBP	Slg.
L	.174	92	16	4	0	2	9	3	16	.200	.283
R	.236	314	74	24	2	7	34	13	57	.269	.392

									BATTING									FIELDING	
Year	Team (League)	Pos.	G	AB	R	H	2B	3B	HR	RBI	BB	SO	HBP	GDP	SB-CS	Avg.	OBP	SLG	OPS	E	Avg.
1999— GC Tigers (GCL)	SS	25	97	11	26	4	0	0	7	4	11	0	1	4-0	.268	.294	.309	.603	8	.932
2000— Lakeland (Fla. St.)	SS	79	259	35	71	11	0	2	24	20	29	1	4	11-5	.274	.324	.340	.664	19	.951
— W. Mich. (Mid.)	SS	12	48	7	11	0	0	0	5	5	7	2	2	1-0	.229	.327	.229	.556	1	.983
2001— Erie (East.)	SS	132	540	86	163	21	4	2	62	46	87	2	9	27-12	.302	.355	.367	.721	27	.955
2002— Toledo (Int'l)	SS	120	436	49	117	16	8	4	51	28	49	0	5	19-15	.268	.309	.369	.678	26	.959
— Detroit (A.L.)	SS-2B	18	72	4	24	3	0	1	6	3	10	0	1	0-1	.333	.360	.417	.777	5	.945
2003— Toledo (Int'l)	SS	64	224	28	50	10	0	2	18	22	32	3	3	22-4	.223	.299	.295	.593	18	.942
— Detroit (A.L.)	SS-3B-2B	69	221	24	49	6	1	0	8	18	37	0	1	6-3	.222	.278	.258	.536	14	.961
2004— Detroit (A.L.)	2B-SS-3B OF	142	503	69	133	27	9	16	55	40	112	1	4	13-7	.264	.317	.449	.766	16	.974
2005— Detroit (A.L.)	2B-SS	121	406	36	90	28	2	9	43	16	73	2	5	8-0	.222	.254	.367	.621	10	.983
Major League totals (4 years)		350	1202	133	296	64	12	26	112	77	232	3	10	27-11	.246	.291	.384	.676	45	.973

INGE, BRANDON   3B/C

PERSONAL: Born May 19, 1977, in Lynchburg, Va. ... 5-11/195. ... Bats right, throws right. ... Full name: Charles Brandon Inge. ... Name pronounced: inj. ... High school: Brookville (Lynchburg, Lynchburg, Va.) ... College: Virginia Commonwealth.
TRANSACTIONS/CAREER NOTES: Selected by Detroit Tigers organization in second round of 1998 free-agent draft. ... On disabled list (June 25-August 6, 2001); included rehabilitation assignments to GCL Tigers, West Michigan and Toledo. ... On disabled list (May 12-May 27, 2002); included rehabilitation assignment to Toledo. ... On disabled list (June 26-July 15, 2004).
2005 GAMES PLAYED BY POSITION (MLB): 3B—160, OF—2.

SCOUTING REPORT *Offense:* The only time Inge isn't rigid at the plate is when the ball is inside; then he has good strength and quickness. Has problems with off-speed and breaking pitches. Needs to cut down his swing late in the count and use the whole field. May have problems making adjustments. *Defense:* Inge has made the most of his first opportunity to play every day. Doesn't have soft hands, but has agility. Needs a lot of help with his footwork. Range to his left is better than to his right. Has a strong arm but drops down to throw, leading to wildness. *Outlook:* His ability to play multiple positions makes Inge better suited as a utility player than an everyday third baseman. *Grade 6.8*

BRANDON INGE'S HITTING ZONE

.271	.375	.217
.228	.458	.254
.333	.302	.226

LEFTY-RIGHTY SPLITS

vs.	Avg.	AB	H	2B	3B	HR	RBI	BB	SO	OBP	Slg.
L	.281	128	36	8	0	5	18	22	27	.382	.461
R	.256	488	125	23	9	11	54	41	113	.315	.408

									BATTING									FIELDING	
Year	Team (League)	Pos.	G	AB	R	H	2B	3B	HR	RBI	BB	SO	HBP	GDP	SB-CS	Avg.	OBP	SLG	OPS	E	Avg.
1998— Jamestown (NYP)	C	51	191	24	44	10	1	8	29	17	53	6	4	8-8	.230	.312	.419	.730	6	.981
1999— W. Mich. (Mid.)	C	100	352	54	86	25	2	9	46	39	87	3	7	15-3	.244	.320	.403	.723	8	.990
2000— Jacksonville (Sou.)	C-OF	78	298	39	77	25	1	6	53	26	73	0	10	10-3	.258	.313	.409	.722	5	.990
— Toledo (Int'l)	C	55	190	24	42	9	3	5	20	15	51	1	5	2-1	.221	.280	.379	.659	3	.991
2001— Detroit (A.L.)	C	79	189	13	34	11	0	0	15	9	41	0	2	1-4	.180	.215	.238	.453	4	.989
— GC Tigers (GCL)	C	3	10	1	1	0	0	1	2	2	2	0	0	0-0	.100	.250	.400	.650	0	1.000
— W. Mich. (Mid.)	C	4	16	3	3	1	0	0	2	2	5	1	0	0-0	.188	.316	.250	.566	0	1.000
— Toledo (Int'l)	C	27	90	11	26	11	1	2	15	7	24	1	2	1-0	.289	.337	.500	.837	2	.989
2002— Toledo (Int'l)	C	21	65	10	17	2	4	3	13	11	16	2	2	1-3	.262	.380	.554	.934	4	.978
— Detroit (A.L.)	C-DH	95	321	27	65	15	3	7	24	24	101	4	7	1-3	.202	.266	.333	.599	1	.998
2003— Toledo (Int'l)	C-DH	39	142	15	39	9	0	5	15	11	23	0	6	3-1	.275	.327	.444	.770	0	1.000
— Detroit (A.L.)	C	104	330	32	67	15	3	8	30	24	79	5	8	4-4	.203	.265	.339	.605	2	.996
2004— Detroit (A.L.)	3B-C-OF	131	408	43	117	31	5	13	64	32	72	4	4	5-4	.287	.340	.453	.793	16	.966
2005— Detroit (A.L.)	3B-OF	160	616	75	161	31	9	16	72	63	140	3	14	7-6	.261	.330	.419	.749	23	.957
Major League totals (5 years)		569	1864	190	444	87	22	44	205	152	433	16	35	18-21	.238	.299	.379	.678	46	.981

ISHII, KAZUHISA   P

PERSONAL: Born September 9, 1973, in Chiba, Japan. ... 6-0/200. ... Throws left, bats left. ... Name pronounced: kaz-u-heesa ee-shee-ee.
TRANSACTIONS/CAREER NOTES: Signed as a free agent by Los Angeles Dodgers (February 8, 2002). ... On disabled list (September 9, 2002-remainder of season; and July 30-August 30, 2003). ... Traded by Dodgers to New York Mets for C Jason Phillips (March 20, 2005). ... On disabled list (April 22-May 17, 2005); included rehabilitation assignment to St. Lucie.
CAREER HITTING: 18-for-164 (.110), 10 R, 0 2B, 1 3B, 1 HR, 10 RBI.

SCOUTING REPORT

SCOUTING REPORT *Throws:* His fastball is 84-89 mph, and he throws a curveball and changeup. *Tendencies:* He lost a lot of velocity as last season progressed, but Ishii's pitching has leveled off largely because of command problems with his fastball. Doesn't have a compact delivery. Big, biting curveball is his best pitch, but he struggles locating it. Has good motion with his changeup. *Outlook:* Ishii ended in the bullpen because of his control problems. Rarely goes beyond five innings as a starter because of high pitch counts. Is always pitching in a hitter's count. *Grade 5.6*

KAZUHISA ISHII'S PITCHING ZONE

.333	.455	.182
.283	.282	.283
.300	.261	.182

LEFTY-RIGHTY SPLITS

vs.	Avg.	AB	H	2B	3B	HR	RBI	BB	SO	OBP	Slg.
L	.208	72	15	2	0	5	16	10	16	.305	.444
R	.271	266	72	21	1	8	39	39	37	.367	.447

Year Team (League)	W	L	Pct.	ERA	WHIP	G	GS	CG	ShO	Hld.	Sv.-Opp.	IP	H	R	ER	HR	BB-IBB	SO	Avg.
1992— Yakult (Jp. Cen.)	0	0	...	4.18	1.43	12	...	0	0	...	0-...	28.0	23	13	13	4	17-...	22	...
1993— Yakult (Jp. Cen.)	3	1	.750	4.70	1.45	19	...	1	0	...	0-...	59.1	48	32	31	8	38-...	66	...
1994— Yakult (Jp. Cen.)	7	5	.583	4.08	1.56	54	...	2	2	...	0-...	108.0	92	56	49	11	77-...	98	...
1995— Yakult (Jp. Cen.)	13	4	.765	2.76	1.24	26	...	3	0	...	1-...	153.0	112	49	47	14	77-...	159	...
1996— Yakult (Jp. Cen.)	1	5	.167	5.23	1.61	8	...	0	0	...	0-...	31.0	28	19	18	6	22-...	26	...
1997— Yakult (Jp. Cen.)	10	4	.714	1.91	1.05	18	...	2	2	...	0-...	117.2	73	28	25	5	50-...	120	...
1998— Yakult (Jp. Cen.)	14	6	.700	3.30	1.29	28	...	6	0	...	0-...	196.1	149	78	72	12	105-...	241	...
1999— Yakult (Jp. Cen.)	8	6	.571	4.80	1.46	23	...	2	1	...	0-...	133.0	123	75	71	16	71-...	162	...
2000— Yakult (Jp. Cen.)	10	9	.526	2.61	1.15	29	...	3	1	...	0-...	183.0	137	54	53	15	73-...	210	...
2001— Yakult (Jp. Cen.)	12	6	.667	3.39	1.19	27	...	0	0	...	0-...	175.0	135	74	66	18	73-...	173	...
2002— Los Angeles (N.L.)	14	10	.583	4.27	1.58	28	28	0	0		0-0	154.0	137	82	73	20	* 106-3	143	.240
2003— Los Angeles (N.L.)	9	7	.563	3.86	1.56	27	27	0	0		0-0	147.0	129	72	63	16	101-4	140	.238
2004— Los Angeles (N.L.)	13	8	.619	4.71	1.47	31	31	2	2		0-0	172.0	155	97	90	21	98-2	99	.246
2005— St. Lucie (Fla. St.)	0	0	...	0.00	0.25	1	1	0	0		0-...	4.0	0	0	0	0	1-0	3	.000
— Norfolk (Int'l)	2	2	.500	1.76	1.57	5	2	0	0		0-...	15.1	16	4	3	3	8-0	18	.267
— New York (N.L.)	3	9	.250	5.14	1.49	19	16	0	0		0-0	91.0	87	59	52	13	49-3	53	.257
Major League totals (4 years)	39	34	.534	4.44	1.53	105	102	2	2		0-0	564.0	508	310	278	70	354-12	435	.244

ISRINGHAUSEN, JASON P

PERSONAL: Born September 7, 1972, in Brighton, Ill. ... 6-3/230. ... Throws right, bats right. ... Full name: Jason Derek Isringhausen. ... Name pronounced: IS-ring-how-zin. ... High school: Southwestern (Brighton, Ill.). ... Junior college: Lewis & Clark (Ill.) Community College.
TRANSACTIONS/CAREER NOTES: Selected by New York Mets organization in 44th round of 1991 free-agent draft. ... On disabled list (August 13-September 1, 1996). ... On disabled list (March 24-August 27, 1997); included rehabilitation assignments to Norfolk, GCL Mets and St. Lucie. ... On disabled list (March 21, 1998-entire season). ... Traded by Mets with P Greg McMichael to Oakland Athletics for P Billy Taylor (July 31, 1999). ... Signed as a free agent by St. Louis Cardinals (December 11, 2001). ... On disabled list (March 21-June 10, 2003); included rehabilitation assignment to Tennessee. ... On disabled list (April 27-May 13, 2005).
CAREER HITTING: 21-for-102 (.206), 11 R, 4 2B, 1 3B, 2 HR, 16 RBI.

SCOUTING REPORT *Throws:* Isringhausen throws a fastball in the 93-97 mph range, a curve at 78-81 and a cutter at 86-89. *Tendencies:* He uses a riding fastball up in the zone to overpower hitters, especially late in the count. Using his cutter more with sharp and late slide, running it from righthanders and in on lefthanders. Curve is one of the best in the game; it has a big break but a tight spin and freezes hitters. Has good command. *Outlook:* He has proved to be steady and capable of closing big games, but he must be monitored and protected because of numerous physical problems over the years. *Grade 8.7*

JASON ISRINGHAUSEN'S PITCHING ZONE

.200	.300	.200
.243	.176	.222
.400	.250	.125

LEFTY-RIGHTY SPLITS

vs.	Avg.	AB	H	2B	3B	HR	RBI	BB	SO	OBP	Slg.
L	.168	95	16	1	0	1	7	14	27	.279	.211
R	.229	118	27	4	1	3	6	13	24	.305	.356

Year Team (League)	W	L	Pct.	ERA	WHIP	G	GS	CG	ShO	Hld.	Sv.-Opp.	IP	H	R	ER	HR	BB-IBB	SO	Avg.
1992— GC Mets (GCL)	2	4	.333	4.34	1.48	6	6	0	0	...	0-...	29.0	26	19	14	0	17-1	25	.230
— Kingsport (Appalachian)	4	1	.800	3.25	1.22	7	6	1	1	...	0-...	36.0	32	22	13	2	12-1	24	.222
1993— Pittsfield (NYP)	7	4	.636	3.29	1.06	15	15	2	0	...	0-...	90.1	68	45	33	7	28-0	104	.204
1994— St. Lucie (Fla. St.)	6	4	.600	2.23	1.02	14	14	6	3	...	0-...	101.0	76	31	25	2	27-2	59	.211
— Binghamton (East.)	5	4	.556	3.02	1.09	14	14	2	0	...	0-...	92.1	78	35	31	6	23-0	69	.234
1995— Binghamton (East.)	2	1	.667	2.85	0.93	6	6	1	0	...	0-...	41.0	26	15	13	1	12-0	59	.174
— Norfolk (Int'l)	9	1	.900	1.55	1.01	12	12	3	3	...	0-...	87.0	64	17	15	2	24-0	75	.203
— New York (N.L.)	9	2	.818	2.81	1.28	14	14	1	0	0	0-0	93.0	88	29	29	6	31-2	55	.254
1996— New York (N.L.)	6	14	.300	4.77	1.53	27	27	2	1	0	0-0	171.2	190	103	91	13	73-5	114	.284
1997— Norfolk (Int'l)	0	2	.000	4.05	1.40	3	3	0	0	...	0-0	20.0	20	10	9	4	8-0	17	.267
— GC Mets (GCL)	1	0	1.000	1.93	0.64	1	0	0	0	...	0-...	4.2	2	1	1	0	1-0	7	.125
— St. Lucie (Fla. St.)	1	0	1.000	0.00	1.08	2	2	0	0	...	0-...	12.0	8	1	0	0	5-0	15	.190
— New York (N.L.)	2	2	.500	7.58	2.09	6	6	0	0	0	0-0	29.2	40	27	25	3	22-0	25	.336
1998— New York (N.L.)					Did not play.														
1999— Norfolk (Int'l)	3	1	.750	2.29	1.04	12	8	0	0	...	0-...	51.0	33	18	13	4	20-0	51	.182
— New York (N.L.)	1	3	.250	6.41	1.65	13	5	0	0	0	1-1	39.1	43	29	28	7	22-2	31	.279
— Oakland (A.L.)	0	1	.000	2.13	1.30	20	0	0	0	0	8-8	25.1	20	6	6	2	12-2	20	.223
2000— Oakland (A.L.)	6	4	.600	3.78	1.43	66	0	0	0	0	33-40	69.0	67	34	29	6	32-5	57	.252
2001— Oakland (A.L.)	4	3	.571	2.65	1.08	65	0	0	0	0	34-43	71.1	54	24	21	5	23-5	74	.203
2002— St. Louis (N.L.)	3	2	.600	2.48	0.98	60	0	0	0	0	32-37	65.1	46	22	18	0	18-1	68	.199
2003— Tennessee (Sou.)	0	0	...	0.00	0.50	2	2	0	0	...	0-...	2.0	1	0	0	0	0-0	3	.143
— St. Louis (N.L.)	0	1	.000	3.04	1.17	40	0	0	0	1	22-25	42.0	31	14	11	2	18-1	41	.200
2004— St. Louis (N.L.)	4	2	.667	2.87	1.04	74	0	0	0	1	• 47-54	75.1	55	27	24	5	23-4	71	.194
2005— St. Louis (N.L.)	1	2	.333	2.14	1.19	63	0	0	0	1	39-43	59.0	43	14	14	4	27-5	51	.202
American League totals (3 years)	10	8	.556	3.04	1.26	151	0	0	0	0	75-91	165.2	142	64	56	13	67-12	151	.227
National League totals (8 years)	26	28	.481	3.75	1.34	297	52	3	1	2	141-160	575.1	536	265	240	40	234-20	456	.248
Major League totals (10 years)	36	36	.500	3.60	1.32	448	52	3	1	2	216-251	741.0	678	329	296	53	301-32	607	.243

DIVISION SERIES RECORD

Year Team (League)	W	L	Pct.	ERA	WHIP	G	GS	CG	ShO	Hld.	Sv.-Opp.	IP	H	R	ER	HR	BB-IBB	SO	Avg.
2000— Oakland (A.L.)	0	0	...	0.00	0.50	2	0	0	0	0	1-1	2.0	1	0	0	0	0-0	3	.143
2001— Oakland (A.L.)	0	0	...	0.00	1.00	2	0	0	0	0	2-2	2.0	1	0	0	0	1-0	3	.143
2002— St. Louis (N.L.)	0	0	...	0.00	0.00	2	0	0	0	0	2-2	2.0	0	0	0	0	0-0	1	.000
2004— St. Louis (N.L.)	0	0	...	4.50	1.50	2	0	0	0	0	0-0	2.0	1	1	1	1	2-0	2	.143
2005— St. Louis (N.L.)	0	0	...	3.00	2.00	3	0	0	0	0	1-1	3.0	5	1	1	0	1-0	4	.357
Division series totals (5 years)	0	0	...	1.64	1.09	11	0	0	0	0	6-6	11.0	8	2	2	1	4-0	13	.195

CHAMPIONSHIP SERIES RECORD

Year Team (League)	W	L	Pct.	ERA	WHIP	G	GS	CG	ShO	Hld.	Sv.-Opp.	IP	H	R	ER	HR	BB-IBB	SO	Avg.
2002— St. Louis (N.L.)	0	0	...	4.50	2.00	2	0	0	0	0	1-1	2.0	1	1	1	0	3-2	3	.167
2004— St. Louis (N.L.)	0	1	.000	4.70	1.04	6	0	0	0	0	3-4	7.2	4	4	4	1	4-2	3	.154
2005— St. Louis (N.L.)	1	0	1.000	0.00	0.75	3	0	0	0	0	1-1	4.0	3	1	0	0	0-0	2	.214
Champ. series totals (3 years)	1	1	.500	3.29	1.10	11	0	0	0	0	5-6	13.2	8	6	5	1	7-4	8	.174

WORLD SERIES RECORD

Year Team (League)	W	L	Pct.	ERA	WHIP	G	GS	CG	ShO	Hld.	Sv.-Opp.	IP	H	R	ER	HR	BB-IBB	SO	Avg.
2004— St. Louis (N.L.)	0	0	...	0.00	1.00	1	0	0	0	0	0-0	2.0	1	0	0	0	1-0	2	.143

ALL-STAR GAME RECORD

	W	L	Pct.	ERA	WHIP	G	GS	CG	ShO	Hld.	Sv.-Opp.	IP	H	R	ER	HR	BB-IBB	SO	Avg.
All-Star Game totals (1 year)	0	0	...	9.00	3.00	1	0	0	0	0	0-0	1.0	2	1	1	0	1-0	0	.400

IZTURIS, CESAR — SS

PERSONAL: Born February 10, 1980, in Barquisimeto, Venezuela. ... 5-9/175. ... Bats both, throws right. ... Full name: Cesar D. Izturis. ... Name pronounced: IS-tur-iss. ... Brother of Maicer Izturis, infielder, Los Angeles Angels of Anaheim.

TRANSACTIONS/CAREER NOTES: Signed as a non-drafted free agent by Toronto Blue Jays organization (July 11, 1996). ... Traded by Blue Jays with P Paul Quantrill to Los Angeles Dodgers for Ps Luke Prokopec and Chad Ricketts (December 13, 2001). ... On disabled list (July 1-15 and August 28, 2005-remainder of season).

HONORS: Won N.L. Gold Glove at shortstop (2004).

2005 GAMES PLAYED BY POSITION (MLB): SS—106.

SCOUTING REPORT **Offense:** Prior to his elbow injury, which required late-season surgery in 2005, Izturis had a quick bat and very good bat control, especially from the left side. Is a line drive hitter who uses the entire field. Handles high fastballs well batting lefthanded and low fastballs well batting righthanded. Doesn't have power from either side. Is an outstanding runner who has become an efficient basestealer. **Defense:** Izturis is one of the better defensive shortstops in the game. Has exceptionally soft and quick hands. Range to both sides is great. Charges the ball well and has a quick release. Has good overall instincts. **Outlook:** Izturis has the tools to be a very good player. Might not be available at the start of next season because of the surgery. **Grade 8.3**

CESAR IZTURIS' HITTING ZONE

.269	.350	.429
.267	.472	.207
.143	.333	.244

LEFTY-RIGHTY SPLITS

vs.	Avg.	AB	H	2B	3B	HR	RBI	BB	SO	OBP	Slg.
L	.303	109	33	7	1	1	11	5	8	.333	.413
R	.242	335	81	12	1	1	20	20	43	.292	.293

Year Team (League)	Pos.	G	AB	R	H	2B	3B	HR	RBI	BB	SO	HBP	GDP	SB-CS	Avg.	OBP	SLG	OPS	E	Avg.
1997— St. Catharines (NYP)	2B-3B-SS	70	231	32	44	3	0	1	11	15	27	1	3	6-3	.190	.241	.216	.457	16	.951
1998— Hagerstown (SAL)	2B-3B-SS	130	413	56	108	13	1	1	38	20	43	2	5	20-9	.262	.297	.305	.603	29	.952
1999— Dunedin (Fla. St.)	2B-3B-SS	131	536	77	165	28	12	3	77	22	58	6	9	32-16	.308	.337	.422	.758	21	.969
2000— Syracuse (Int'l)	SS	132	435	54	95	16	5	0	27	20	44	1	5	21-11	.218	.253	.278	.531	12	.981
2001— Syracuse (Int'l)	SS-2B	87	342	32	100	16	3	2	35	10	22	1	4	24-9	.292	.310	.374	.684	15	.962
— Toronto (A.L.)	2B-SS	46	134	19	36	6	2	2	9	2	15	0	0	8-1	.269	.279	.388	.667	3	.985
2002— Los Angeles (N.L.)	SS-2B-DH	135	439	43	102	24	2	1	31	14	39	0	12	7-7	.232	.253	.303	.556	10	.979
2003— Los Angeles (N.L.)	SS	158	558	47	140	21	6	1	40	25	70	0	8	10-5	.251	.282	.315	.597	16	.977
2004— Los Angeles (N.L.)	SS	159	670	90	193	32	9	4	62	43	70	0	6	25-9	.288	.330	.381	.710	10	.985
2005— Los Angeles (N.L.)	SS	106	444	48	114	19	2	2	31	25	51	4	11	8-8	.257	.302	.322	.624	11	.977
American League totals (1 year)		46	134	19	36	6	2	2	9	2	15	0	0	8-1	.269	.279	.388	.667	3	.985
National League totals (4 years)		558	2111	228	549	96	19	8	164	107	230	4	37	50-29	.260	.295	.335	.630	47	.980
Major League totals (5 years)		604	2245	247	585	102	21	10	173	109	245	4	37	58-30	.261	.295	.338	.633	50	.980

DIVISION SERIES RECORD

Year Team (League)	Pos.	G	AB	R	H	2B	3B	HR	RBI	BB	SO	HBP	GDP	SB-CS	Avg.	OBP	SLG	OPS	E	Avg.
2004— Los Angeles (N.L.)	SS	4	17	1	3	1	0	0	0	1	2	0	0	0-0	.176	.222	.235	.458	0	1.000

IZTURIS, MAICER — SS/2B

PERSONAL: Born September 12, 1980, in Barquisimeto, Venezuela. ... 5-8/155. ... Bats both, throws right. ... Full name: Maicer E. Izturis. ... Name pronounced: MY-seir IS-tur-iss. ... Brother of Cesar Izturis, shortstop, Los Angeles Dodgers

TRANSACTIONS/CAREER NOTES: Signed as a non-drafted free agent by Cleveland Indians organization (April 1, 1998). ... Traded by Indians with OF Ryan Church to Montreal Expos for P Scott Stewart (January 5, 2004). ... Traded by Expos with OF Juan Rivera to Anaheim Angels for OF Jose Guillen (November 23, 2004). ... Angels franchise renamed Los Angeles Angels of Anaheim for 2005 season. ... On disabled list (April 27-June 18, 2005); included rehabilitation assignment to Salt Lake.

2005 GAMES PLAYED BY POSITION (MLB): 3B—45, SS—29, 2B—1, OF—1.

MAICER IZTURIS' HITTING ZONE

.167	.231	.313
.333	.158	.267
.308	.200	.125

LEFTY-RIGHTY SPLITS

vs.	Avg.	AB	H	2B	3B	HR	RBI	BB	SO	OBP	Slg.
L	.191	47	9	1	0	1	5	6	6	.278	.277
R	.264	144	38	7	4	0	10	11	15	.316	.368

Year Team (League)	Pos.	G	AB	R	H	2B	3B	HR	RBI	BB	SO	HBP	GDP	SB-CS	Avg.	OBP	SLG	OPS	E	Avg.
1998— Burlington (Appal.)	SS	55	217	33	63	8	2	2	33	17	32	0	4	16-6	.290	.342	.373	.715	20	.929
1999— Columbus (S. Atl.)	SS	57	220	46	66	5	3	4	23	20	28	1	2	14-2	.300	.357	.405	.761	12	.939

Year	Team (League)	Pos.	G	AB	R	H	2B	3B	HR	RBI	BB	SO	HBP	GDP	SB-CS	Avg.	OBP	SLG	OPS	E	Avg.
2000—Columbus (S. Atl.)	SS	10	29	4	8	1	0	0	1	3	3	0	1	0-0	.276	.344	.310	.654	2	.846
2001—Kinston (Carol.)	2B	114	433	47	104	16	6	1	39	31	81	8	8	32-9	.240	.300	.312	.612	17	.959
2002—Kinston (Carol.)	2B	58	233	28	61	13	1	1	30	24	26	1	2	24-6	.262	.332	.339	.671	8	.967
—Akron (East.)	2B	67	253	34	70	12	7	0	32	17	28	3	10	8-4	.277	.326	.379	.706	11	.961
2003—Akron (East.)	2B-SS	53	218	31	61	11	5	1	20	24	23	1	4	14-6	.280	.351	.390	.741	12	.946
—Buffalo (Int'l.)	SS-2B	85	301	43	79	16	4	2	29	24	28	1	14	14-6	.262	.317	.362	.679	13	.967
2004—Edmonton (PCL)	SS-2B-DH	99	376	65	127	19	2	3	36	57	30	4	12	14-12	.338	.428	.423	.846	12	.969
—Montreal (N.L.)	SS-2B	32	107	10	22	5	2	1	4	10	20	2	1	4-0	.206	.286	.318	.603	8	.948
2005—Salt Lake (PCL)	SS-3B-DH-2B	10	31	10	14	4	0	0	2	7	4	0	2	4-2	.452	.553	.581	1.133	0	1.000
—Los Angeles (A.L.)	3B-SS-2B-OF	77	191	18	47	8	4	1	15	17	21	0	5	9-3	.246	.306	.346	.652	10	.950
American League totals (1 year)		77	191	18	47	8	4	1	15	17	21	0	5	9-3	.246	.306	.346	.652	10	.950
National League totals (1 year)		32	107	10	22	5	2	1	4	10	20	2	1	4-0	.206	.286	.318	.603	8	.948
Major League totals (2 years)		109	298	28	69	13	6	2	19	27	41	2	6	13-3	.232	.299	.336	.634	18	.949

CHAMPIONSHIP SERIES RECORD

Year	Team (League)	Pos.	G	AB	R	H	2B	3B	HR	RBI	BB	SO	HBP	GDP	SB-CS	Avg.	OBP	SLG	OPS	E	Avg.
2005—Los Angeles (A.L.)	SS	1	0	0	0	0	0	0	0	0	0	0	0	0-0	...	...	...	...	0	...

JACKSON, CONOR — 1B/OF

PERSONAL: Born May 7, 1982, in Austin, Texas. ... 6-2/225. ... Bats right, throws right. ... Full name: Conor S. Jackson. ... High school: El Camino Real (Woodland Hills, Calif.) ... College: California.

TRANSACTIONS/CAREER NOTES: Selected by Arizona Diamondbacks organization in first round (19th pick overall) of 2003 free-agent draft.

2005 GAMES PLAYED BY POSITION (MLB): 1B—20, OF—1.

SCOUTING REPORT Offense: Jackson has quick, disciplined hands through the hitting zone and unusually good recognition of pitches' spin for a young hitter. Is capable of using the whole field. Shows good power to right field and right-center. Has shown a consistent ability to draw walks. Is a below-average runner. *Defense:* He played mostly first base after being called up last season but also can play third base and left field. Is defensively challenged at them all, however. Has sub-par hands and not enough arm to play third base. *Outlook:* If the Diamondbacks will let Jackson settle into a position, he will hit. Is similar to the Padres' Xavier Nady, but with quicker hands and a better eye. *Grade 6.5*

CONOR JACKSON'S HITTING ZONE

.333	.125	.200
.158	.400	.100
.250	.500	.000

LEFTY-RIGHTY SPLITS

vs.	Avg.	AB	H	2B	3B	HR	RBI	BB	SO	OBP	Slg.
L	.258	31	8	2	0	2	4	4	3	.351	.516
R	.167	54	9	1	0	0	4	8	8	.274	.185

Year	Team (League)	Pos.	G	AB	R	H	2B	3B	HR	RBI	BB	SO	HBP	GDP	SB-CS	Avg.	OBP	SLG	OPS	E	Avg.
2003—Yakima (N'west)	OF	68	257	44	82	35	1	6	60	36	41	5	7	3-0	.319	.410	.533	.943	0	1.000
2004—Lancaster (Calif.)		67	258	64	89	19	2	11	54	45	36	3	3	4-3	.345	.438	.562	1.000	...	...
—El Paso (Texas)	OF-3B	60	226	33	68	13	2	6	37	24	36	2	4	3-3	.301	.367	.456	.823	3	.000
2005—Tucson (PCL)	1B-OF-DH	93	333	66	118	38	2	8	73	69	32	0	8	3-2	.354	.457	.553	1.010	11	.985
—Arizona (N.L.)	1B-OF	40	85	8	17	3	0	2	8	12	11	1	6	0-0	.200	.303	.306	.609	5	.973
Major League totals (1 year)		40	85	8	17	3	0	2	8	12	11	1	6	0-0	.200	.303	.306	.609	5	.973

JACKSON, DAMIAN — 2B/OF

PERSONAL: Born August 16, 1973, in Los Angeles. ... 5-11/185. ... Bats right, throws right. ... Full name: Damian Jacques Jackson. ... High school: Ygnacio Valley (Concord, Calif.). ... Junior college: Laney (Calif.).

TRANSACTIONS/CAREER NOTES: Selected by Cleveland Indians organization in 44th round of 1991 free-agent draft. ... Traded by Indians with Ps Danny Graves, Jim Crowell and Scott Winchester to Cincinnati Reds for P John Smiley and IF Jeff Branson (July 31, 1997). ... Traded by Reds with OF Reggie Sanders and P Josh Harris to San Diego Padres for OF Greg Vaughn and OF/1B Mark Sweeney (February 2, 1999). ... On disabled list (May 13-June 22, 2001); included rehabilitation assignment to Portland. ... Traded by Padres with C Matt Walbeck to Detroit Tigers for C Javier Cardona and OF Rich Gomez (March 24, 2002). ... On disabled list (April 7-22, 2002). ... Released by Tigers (November 20, 2002). ... Signed by Boston Red Sox (December 18, 2002). ... Signed as a free agent by Colorado Rockies organization (January 5, 2004). ... Released by Rockies (March 28, 2004). ... Signed by Chicago Cubs organization (April 1, 2004). ... Traded by Cubs to Kansas City Royals for IF Gookie Dawkins (May 31, 2004). ... Signed as a free agent by Padres organization (November 17, 2004). ... Signed as a free agent by Washington Nationals (October 27, 2005).

2005 GAMES PLAYED BY POSITION (MLB): OF—52, 2B—35, SS—26, 3B—8.

DAMIAN JACKSON'S HITTING ZONE

.364	.308	.077
.300	.357	.136
.407	.250	.000

LEFTY-RIGHTY SPLITS

vs.	Avg.	AB	H	2B	3B	HR	RBI	BB	SO	OBP	Slg.
L	.289	83	24	6	0	0	5	9	12	.366	.361
R	.240	192	46	3	0	5	18	21	33	.323	.333

Year	Team (League)	Pos.	G	AB	R	H	2B	3B	HR	RBI	BB	SO	HBP	GDP	SB-CS	Avg.	OBP	SLG	OPS	E	Avg.
1992—Burlington (Appal.)	SS	62	226	32	56	12	1	0	23	32	31	6	1	29-5	.248	.352	.310	.662	23	.933
1993—Columbus (S. Atl.)	SS	108	350	70	94	19	3	6	45	41	61	5	1	26-7	.269	.353	.391	.744	52	.908
1994—Cant./Akr. (Eastern)	OF-SS	138	531	85	143	29	5	5	60	48	97	5	6	37-16	.269	.346	.371	.717	54	.927
1995—Cant./Akr. (Eastern)	SS	131	484	67	120	20	2	8	34	65	103	9	6	40-22	.248	.348	.316	.664	36	.927
1996—Buffalo (A.A.)	SS	133	452	77	116	15	1	12	49	48	78	9	7	24-7	.257	.333	.374	.707	29	.954
—Cleveland (A.L.)	SS	5	10	2	3	2	0	0	1	1	4	0	0	0-0	.300	.364	.500	.864	0	1.000
1997—Buffalo (A.A.)	SS-2B-OF	73	266	51	78	12	0	4	13	37	45	3	...	20-8	.293	.383	.383	.767	23	.942
—Cleveland (A.L.)	SS-2B	8	9	2	1	0	0	0	0	0	1	1	0	1-0	.111	.200	.111	.311	0	1.000
—Indianapolis (A.A.)	2B-SS	19	71	12	19	6	1	0	7	10	17	1	...	4-1	.268	.361	.380	.742	5	.948
—Cincinnati (N.L.)	SS-2B	12	27	6	6	2	1	1	2	4	7	0	0	1-1	.222	.323	.481	.804	1	.971
1998—Cincinnati (N.L.)	SS-OF	13	38	4	12	5	0	0	7	6	4	0	1	2-0	.316	.400	.447	.847	1	.976
—Indianapolis (Int'l)	SS-2B-OF	131	517	102	135	36	10	6	49	62	125	10	2	25-10	.261	.349	.404	.753	44	.938
1999—San Diego (N.L.)	SS-2B-OF	133	388	56	87	20	2	6	37	39	105	3	2	34-10	.224	.320	.356	.676	26	.948
2000—San Diego (N.L.)	SS-2B-OF	138	470	68	120	27	6	6	37	53	108	3	7	28-6	.255	.345	.377	.721	25	.960

Year Team (League)	Pos.	G	AB	R	H	2B	3B	HR	RBI	BB	SO	HBP	GDP	SB-CS	Avg.	OBP	SLG	OPS	E	Avg.
2001—San Diego (N.L.)	2B-SS-OF	122	440	67	106	21	6	4	38	44	128	6	6	23-6	.241	.316	.343	.660	8	.986
—Portland (PCL)	SS	3	10	4	3	3	0	0	0	3	1	0	0	0-1	.300	.462	.600	1.062	0	1.000
2002—Detroit (A.L.)	2B-OF-SS DH-3B	81	245	31	63	20	1	1	25	21	36	3	3	12-3	.257	.320	.359	.679	8	.972
2003—Boston (A.L.)	2B-OF-SS DH-3B-1B	109	161	34	42	7	0	1	13	8	28	0	4	16-8	.261	.294	.323	.617	9	.951
2004—Iowa (PCL)	SS-OF-2B	28	97	18	27	6	5	3	13	11	20	0	0	3-1	.278	.352	.536	.888	1	.990
—Chicago (N.L.)	SS	7	15	1	1	0	0	1	1	3	6	0	0	0-0	.067	.222	.267	.489	1	.957
—Kansas City (A.L.)	OF-DH-2B SS	14	15	1	2	2	0	0	2	1	6	0	0	0-0	.133	.188	.267	.454	0	1.000
—Omaha (PCL)	SS-2B 2B-DH	48	169	46	52	13	1	8	27	30	36	6	3	12-2	.308	.425	.538	.964	9	.961
2005—Portland (PCL)	SS-3B-OF	14	51	14	18	4	1	3	10	13	9	0	0	1-1	.353	.477	.647	1.124	3	.939
—San Diego (N.L.)	OF-2B-SS 3B	118	275	44	70	9	0	5	23	30	45	4	4	15-2	.255	.335	.342	.677	9	.970
American League totals (5 years)		217	440	70	111	31	1	2	41	31	75	4	7	29-11	.252	.305	.341	.646	17	.966
National League totals (7 years)		543	1653	246	402	84	15	26	147	202	403	16	20	103-25	.243	.330	.359	.689	71	.966
Major League totals (10 years)		760	2093	316	513	115	16	28	188	233	478	20	27	132-36	.245	.325	.355	.680	88	.966

DIVISION SERIES RECORD

Year Team (League)	Pos.	G	AB	R	H	2B	3B	HR	RBI	BB	SO	HBP	GDP	SB-CS	Avg.	OBP	SLG	OPS	E	Avg.
2003—Boston (A.L.)	2B	4	5	0	0	0	0	0	0	0	2	0	0	0-0	.000	.000	.000	.000	0	1.000
2005—San Diego (N.L.)	OF	3	3	1	2	0	0	0	0	0	1	1	0	1-0	.667	.750	.667	1.417	0	1.000
Division series totals (2 years)		7	8	1	2	0	0	0	0	0	3	1	0	1-0	.250	.333	.250	.583	0	1.000

CHAMPIONSHIP SERIES RECORD

Year Team (League)	Pos.	G	AB	R	H	2B	3B	HR	RBI	BB	SO	HBP	GDP	SB-CS	Avg.	OBP	SLG	OPS	E	Avg.
2003—Boston (A.L.)	2B	5	3	0	1	0	0	0	0	0	1	0	0	0-1	.333	.333	.333	.667	1	.857

JACKSON, EDWIN P

PERSONAL: Born September 9, 1983, in Neu-Ulm, West Germany. ... 6-3/190. ... Throws right, bats right. ... High school: Shaw (Columbus, Ga.).
TRANSACTIONS/CAREER NOTES: Selected by Los Angeles Dodgers organization in sixth round of 2001 free-agent draft. ... On disabled list (July 9-September 7, 2004); included rehabilitation assignment to Las Vegas.
CAREER HITTING: 3-for-20 (.150), 0 R, 0 2B, 0 3B, 0 HR, 2 RBI.

SCOUTING REPORT *Throws:* His fastball hits 92-93 mph, and he has a slider and changeup. *Tendencies:* He relies more on his arm than his feel for pitching at this point. Pitch selection and knowledge of hitters need a lot of work. Has an easy delivery but his velocity has diminished, which is a major concern. Gets way too much plate in the big leagues, diminishing his natural aggressiveness. Given his loose arm action, should be able to go deep into games and get more sink on his fastball. *Outlook:* If he can gain control of his off-speed pitches, he could make the Dodgers' rotation. If he doesn't, a trip to the bullpen might be in order. **Grade 6.4**

EDWIN JACKSON'S PITCHING ZONE

.800	.000	.400
.389	.300	.333
.083	.333	.250

LEFTY-RIGHTY SPLITS

vs.	Avg.	AB	H	2B	3B	HR	RBI	BB	SO	OBP	Slg.
L	.333	42	14	4	1	0	10	6	3	.400	.476
R	.236	72	17	3	0	2	9	11	10	.345	.361

Year Team (League)	W	L	Pct.	ERA	WHIP	G	GS	CG	ShO	Hld.	Sv.-Opp.	IP	H	R	ER	HR	BB-IBB	SO	Avg.
2001—GC Dodgers (GCL)	2	1	.667	2.45	1.50	12	2	0	0	...	0-...	22.0	14	12	6	1	19-0	23	.173
2002—South Georgia (S. Atl.)	5	2	.714	1.98	1.07	19	19	0	0	...	0-...	104.2	79	34	23	2	33-0	85	.206
2003—Jacksonville (Sou.)	7	7	.500	3.70	1.17	27	27	0	0	...	0-...	148.1	121	68	61	9	53-0	157	.220
—Los Angeles (N.L.)	2	1	.667	2.45	1.27	4	3	0	0	0	0-0	22.0	17	6	6	2	11-1	19	.221
2004—Las Vegas (PCL)	6	4	.600	5.86	1.60	19	19	0	0	0	0-0	90.2	90	65	59	4	55-1	70	.265
—Los Angeles (N.L.)	2	1	.667	7.30	1.70	8	5	0	0	0	0-0	24.2	31	20	20	7	11-1	16	.307
2005—Las Vegas (PCL)	3	7	.300	8.62	2.04	12	11	1	0	0	0-0	55.1	76	61	53	13	37-2	33	.328
—Jacksonville (Sou.)	6	6	.600	3.48	1.13	11	11	0	0	0	0-0	62.0	52	31	24	7	18-0	44	.224
—Los Angeles (N.L.)	2	2	.500	6.28	1.67	7	6	0	0	0	0-0	28.2	31	22	20	2	17-0	13	.272
Major League totals (3 years)	6	4	.600	5.50	1.57	19	14	0	0	0	0-0	75.1	79	48	46	11	39-2	48	.271

JACOBS, MIKE 1B

PERSONAL: Born October 30, 1980, in Chula Vista, Calif. ... 6-2/180. ... Bats left, throws right. ... Full name: Michael James Jacobs. ... High school: Hilltop (Calif.). ... Junior college: Grossmont (Calif.).
TRANSACTIONS/CAREER NOTES: Selected by New York Mets organization in 38th round of 1999 free-agent draft.
2005 GAMES PLAYED BY POSITION (MLB): 1B—28.

SCOUTING REPORT Jacobs has an extremely fluid stroke. Hits with a high back elbow that indicates he'll be a dead low-ball hitter. Needs to adjust to the ball up. Likes to pull the ball, which carries well off his bat. Is going to have power but doesn't use the whole field. Is a converted catcher learning to play first and doesn't have really soft hands. Has more problems moving to his right than the left. **Grade 5.4**

MIKE JACOBS' HITTING ZONE

.250	.000	.200
.429	.286	.348
.600	.091	.438

LEFTY-RIGHTY SPLITS

vs.	Avg.	AB	H	2B	3B	HR	RBI	BB	SO	OBP	Slg.
L	.400	5	2	1	0	0	1	0	2	.400	.600
R	.305	95	29	6	0	11	22	10	20	.374	.716

Year Team (League)	Pos.	G	AB	R	H	2B	3B	HR	RBI	BB	SO	HBP	GDP	SB-CS	Avg.	OBP	SLG	OPS	E	Avg.
1999—GC Mets (GCL)	C-1B	44	147	18	49	12	0	4	30	14	30	1	3	2-0	.333	.383	.497	.880	7	.960
2000—Capital City (S. Atl.)	C	18	56	1	12	5	0	0	8	6	19	0	2	1-1	.214	.290	.304	.594	2	.989
—Kingsport (Appalachian)	C	59	204	28	55	15	4	7	40	33	62	1	3	6-3	.270	.371	.485	.856	8	.973
2001—Brooklyn (N.Y.-Penn.)	C	19	66	12	19	5	0	1	15	6	11	3	1	1-1	.288	.364	.409	.773	3	.977

Year	Team (League)	Pos.	G	AB	R	H	2B	3B	HR	RBI	BB	SO	HBP	GDP	SB-CS	Avg.	OBP	SLG	OPS	E	Avg.
								BATTING												FIELDING	
—Capital City (S. Atl.)	C	46	180	18	50	13	0	2	26	13	46	1	4	0-1	.278	.328	.383	.711	4	.988
2002—St. Lucie (Fla. St.)	C-1B	118	467	62	117	26	1	11	64	25	95	4	11	2-3	.251	.291	.381	.672	8	.984
2003—Binghamton (East.)	1B-C-OF	119	407	56	134	36	1	17	81	28	87	7	11	0-3	.329	.376	.548	.924	7	.987
2004—Norfolk (Int'l)	C-1B-SS	27	96	8	17	3	0	2	6	9	30	0	1	0-0	.177	.245	.271	.516	1	.992
2005—Binghamton (East.)	1B-C-DH-OF	117	433	66	139	37	2	25	93	35	94	7	11	1-2	.321	.376	.589	.965	14	.983
—New York (N.L.)	1B	30	100	19	31	7	0	11	23	10	22	1	5	0-0	.310	.375	.710	1.085	4	.984
Major League totals (1 year)		30	100	19	31	7	0	11	23	10	22	1	5	0-0	.310	.375	.710	1.085	4	.984

JAMES, CHUCK   P

PERSONAL: Born November 9, 1981, in Atlanta. ... 6-0/170. ... Throws left, bats left. ... Full name: Charles H. James. ... Junior college: Chattahoochie Valley (Ala.).

TRANSACTIONS/CAREER NOTES: Selected by Atlanta Braves organization in 20th round of 2002 free-agent draft.

CAREER HITTING: 1-for-1 (1.000), 0 R, 0 2B, 0 3B, 0 HR, 1 RBI.

LEFTY-RIGHTY SPLITS

vs.	Avg.	AB	H	2B	3B	HR	RBI	BB	SO	OBP	Slg.
L	.250	4	1	1	0	0	0	3	1	.571	.500
R	.188	16	3	0	0	0	1	0	4	.188	.188

Year	Team (League)	W	L	Pct.	ERA	WHIP	G	GS	CG	ShO	Hld.	Sv.-Opp.	IP	H	R	ER	HR	BB-IBB	SO	Avg.
2003—Danville (Appal.)	2	1	.667	1.25	0.89	11	11	0	0	...	0-...	50.1	26	9	7	1	19-0	68	.151
2004—Rome (S. Atl.)	10	5	.667	2.25	1.06	26	22	1	0	...	0-...	132.0	92	41	33	6	48-1	156	.203
2005—Myrtle Beach (Carol.)	3	3	.500	1.08	0.67	7	7	0	0	0	0-0	41.2	20	6	5	1	8-0	59	.139
—Mississippi (Sou.)	9	1	.900	2.09	0.93	16	16	0	0	0	0-0	86.0	62	25	20	4	18-0	104	.199
—Richmond (Int'l)	1	3	.250	3.48	0.92	6	6	0	0	0	0-0	33.2	21	13	13	4	10-0	30	.176
—Atlanta (N.L.)	0	0	...	1.59	1.24	2	0	0	0	0	0-0	5.2	4	1	1	0	3-0	5	.200
Major League totals (1 year)	0	0	...	1.59	1.24	2	0	0	0	0	0-0	5.2	4	1	1	0	3-0	5	.200

JARVIS, KEVIN   P

PERSONAL: Born August 1, 1969, in Lexington, Ky. ... 6-2/200. ... Throws right, bats left. ... Full name: Kevin Thomas Jarvis. ... High school: Tates Creek (Lexington, Ky.). ... College: Wake Forest.

TRANSACTIONS/CAREER NOTES: Selected by Cincinnati Reds organization in 21st round of 1991 free-agent draft. ... Claimed on waivers by Detroit Tigers (May 2, 1997). ... Claimed on waivers by Minnesota Twins (May 9, 1997). ... Claimed on waivers by Tigers (June 17, 1997). ... On disabled list (June 25-July 14, 1997); included rehabilitation assignment to Toledo. ... Released by Tigers (December 12, 1997). ... Signed by Chunichi of the Japan Central League (January 23, 1998). ... Signed as a free agent by Reds organization (August 27, 1998). ... Released by Reds (September 9, 1998). ... Signed by Oakland Athletics organization (January 4, 1999). ... On disabled list (April 19-June 4, 1999); included rehabilitation assignment to Modesto. ... Signed as a free agent by Colorado Rockies organization (December 1, 1999). ... On disabled list (July 28-September 1, 2000); included rehabilitation assignment to Colorado Springs. ... Signed as a free agent by San Diego Padres (January 5, 2001). ... On disabled list (April 18-May 5, May 10-June 27 and July 12, 2002-remainder of season); included rehabilitation assignments to Mobile and Lake Elsinore. ... On disabled list (March 26, 2003-June 13, 2003); included rehabilitation assignment to Lake Elsinore. ... Traded by Padres with IF Dave Hansen, C Wiki Gonzalez and OF Vince Faison to Seattle Mariners for IF Jeff Cirillo and RHP Brian Sweeney (January 6, 2004). ... Released by Mariners (May 4, 2004). ... Signed by Rockies organization (May 10, 2004). ... Released by Rockies (July 2, 2004). ... Signed as a free agent by St. Louis Cardinals organization (July 8, 2004). ... Signed as a free agent by Pittsburgh Pirates organization (February 16, 2005).

CAREER HITTING: 30-for-188 (.160), 19 R, 6 2B, 0 3B, 1 HR, 14 RBI.

LEFTY-RIGHTY SPLITS

vs.	Avg.	AB	H	2B	3B	HR	RBI	BB	SO	OBP	Slg.
L	.333	6	2	0	0	1	5	3	0	.600	.833
R	.167	6	1	0	0	0	0	0	2	.286	.167

Year	Team (League)	W	L	Pct.	ERA	WHIP	G	GS	CG	ShO	Hld.	Sv.-Opp.	IP	H	R	ER	HR	BB-IBB	SO	Avg.
1991—Princeton (Appal.)	5	6	.455	2.42	1.19	13	13	4	•1	...	0-...	85.2	73	34	23	6	29-3	79	.220
1992—Cedar Rap. (Midw.)	0	0	...	0.00	1.00	1	0	0	0	...	0-...	1.0	1	0	0	0	0-0	0	.333
—Char., W.Va. (SAL)	6	8	.429	3.11	1.20	28	18	2	1	...	0-...	133.0	123	59	46	3	37-1	131	.244
1993—Win.-Salem (Car.)	8	7	.533	3.41	1.25	21	20	2	1	...	0-...	145.0	133	68	55	13	48-2	101	.244
—Chattanooga (Sou.)	3	1	.750	1.69	0.99	7	3	2	0	...	0-...	37.1	26	7	7	0	11-0	18	.203
1994—Cincinnati (N.L.)	1	1	.500	7.13	1.53	6	3	0	0	0	0-0	17.2	22	14	14	4	5-0	10	.301
—Indianapolis (A.A.)	10	2	.833	3.54	1.28	21	20	2	0	0	0-0	132.1	136	55	52	13	34-2	90	.261
1995—Indianapolis (A.A.)	4	2	.667	4.45	1.32	10	10	2	1	0	0-0	60.2	62	33	30	2	18-1	37	.256
—Cincinnati (N.L.)	3	4	.429	5.70	1.56	19	11	1	0	0	0-0	79.0	91	56	50	13	32-2	33	.292
1996—Indianapolis (A.A.)	4	3	.571	5.06	1.34	8	8	0	0	0	0-0	42.2	45	27	24	3	12-0	32	.263
—Cincinnati (N.L.)	8	9	.471	5.98	1.62	24	20	2	1	0	0-0	120.1	152	93	80	17	43-5	63	.305
1997—Cincinnati (N.L.)	0	1	.000	10.13	2.10	9	0	0	0	0	1-1	13.1	21	16	15	4	7-0	12	.344
—Minnesota (A.L.)	0	0	...	12.46	2.38	6	2	0	0	0	0-0	13.0	23	18	18	4	8-0	9	.371
—Detroit (A.L.)	0	3	.000	5.40	1.66	17	3	0	0	0	0-0	41.2	55	28	25	9	14-0	27	.318
—Toledo (Int'l)	0	1	.000	6.75	1.38	2	2	0	0	0	0-0	8.0	7	6	6	0	4-0	5	.226
1998—Chunichi (Jp. Cn.)	1	2	.333	4.41	1.41	4	3	0	0	...	0-...	16.1	18	8	8	...	5-...	7	...
—Indianapolis (Int'l)	1	0	1.000	9.00	1.57	2	2	0	0	0	0-0	7.0	10	7	7	3	1-0	5	.323
1999—Oakland (A.L.)	0	1	.000	11.57	2.43	4	1	0	0	0	0-0	14.0	22	19	18	6	6-0	11	.418
—Modesto (California)	0	0	...	1.29	0.71	2	2	0	0	0	0-0	7.0	4	1	1	0	1-0	10	.138
—Vancouver (PCL)	10	2	.833	3.41	1.32	17	16	2	1	0	0-0	103.0	110	47	39	14	26-0	64	.270
2000—Colo. Springs (PCL)	3	2	.600	0.69	0.79	7	7	0	0	0	0-0	39.0	18	3	3	1	13-0	18	.138
—Colorado (N.L.)	3	4	.429	5.95	1.49	24	19	0	0	0	0-0	115.0	138	83	76	26	33-3	60	.300
2001—San Diego (N.L.)	12	11	.522	4.79	1.23	32	32	1	0	0	0-0	193.1	189	107	103	* 37	49-4	133	.254
2002—San Diego (N.L.)	2	4	.333	4.37	1.31	7	7	0	0	0	0-0	35.0	36	19	17	5	10-1	24	.269
—Mobile (Sou.)	0	0	...	0.00	0.67	1	1	0	0	0	0-0	3.0	2	0	0	0	1-0	3	.182
—Lake Elsinore (Calif.)	1	0	1.000	0.00	0.60	1	1	0	0	0	0-0	5.0	2	0	0	0	1-0	5	.133
2003—Lake Elsinore (Calif.)	2	1	.667	4.09	1.00	3	3	0	0	0	0-0	22.0	18	11	10	1	4-0	19	.222
—San Diego (N.L.)	4	8	.333	5.87	1.58	16	16	0	0	0	0-0	92.0	113	65	60	15	32-5	49	.304
2004—Seattle (A.L.)	1	0	1.000	8.31	1.92	8	2	0	0	0	0-0	13.0	20	12	12	4	5-0	7	.345
—Colo. Springs (PCL)	0	0	...	5.79	1.45	6	6	1	0	0	0-0	37.1	44	34	24	12	10-0	25	.293
—Colorado (N.L.)	0	0	...	27.00	5.00	2	0	0	0	0	0-0	2.0	6	6	6	1	4-2	0	.600
—Nashville (PCL)	2	5	.286	4.11	1.60	11	11	1	0	0	0-0	65.2	93	31	30	3	12-1	46	.322
2005—St. Louis (N.L.)	0	1	.000	13.50	1.80	4	0	0	0	0	0-1	3.1	5	5	5	1	3-0	2	.250
—Memphis (PCL)	11	6	.647	3.38	1.29	26	25	1	0	0	0-0	157.0	164	63	59	19	39-1	112	.272
American League totals (3 years)	1	4	.200	8.04	1.95	35	6	0	0	0	0-0	81.2	126	77	73	23	33-0	54	.355
National League totals (10 years)	33	43	.434	5.71	1.47	143	108	4	3	0	1-2	671.0	771	464	426	123	218-22	386	.288
Major League totals (11 years)	34	47	.420	5.97	1.53	178	114	4	3	0	1-2	752.2	897	541	499	146	251-22	440	.295

JENKINS, GEOFF   OF

PERSONAL: Born July 21, 1974, in Olympia, Wash. ... 6-1/212. ... Bats left, throws right. ... Full name: Geoff Scott Jenkins. ... High school: Cordova Senior (Rancho Cordova, Calif.). ... College: Southern California.
TRANSACTIONS/CAREER NOTES: Selected by Milwaukee Brewers organization in first round (ninth pick overall) of 1995 free-agent draft. ... On disabled list (May 7-29, 2000). ... On disabled list (May 2-19 and July 29-August 28, 2001); included rehabilitation assignment to Beloit. ... On disabled list (June 18, 2002-remainder of season). ... On disabled list (March 21-April 9 and August 29, 2003-remainder of season); included rehabilitation assignment to Huntsville.
RECORDS: Shares major league record for most strikeouts, extra-inning game (6, June 8, 2004, 17 innings).
2005 GAMES PLAYED BY POSITION (MLB): OF—144, DH—2.

SCOUTING REPORT Offense: Jenkins is a little rigid and has an uppercut. Stays inside the ball well. Will strike out a lot because he expands the zone up. Has improved against lefthanded pitching as he stays on the ball better. Is an aggressive baserunner who will slide hard into second base to break up the double play. ***Defense:*** He made the move from left to right and played very well after an adjustment period. Is technically sound with good hands. Range has declined slightly, but instincts help him compensate. One of the best, and most accurate, arms in the game. ***Outlook:*** Jenkins is a good run producer, and though he's not a fast runner, he is a solid outfielder. Needs more discipline at the plate and must cut down on strikeouts. ***Grade 7.8***

GEOFF JENKINS' HITTING ZONE

.440	.231	.259
.258	.381	.363
.333	.360	.362

LEFTY-RIGHTY SPLITS

vs.	Avg.	AB	H	2B	3B	HR	RBI	BB	SO	OBP	Slg.
L	.255	157	40	16	0	5	21	13	48	.354	.452
R	.307	381	117	26	1	20	65	43	90	.384	.538

									BATTING										FIELDING	
Year	Team (League)	Pos.	G	AB	R	H	2B	3B	HR	RBI	BB	SO	HBP	GDP	SB-CS	Avg.	OBP	SLG	OPS	E	Avg.
1995—	Helena (Pion.)	OF	7	28	2	9	0	1	0	9	3	11	0	0	0-2	.321	.375	.393	.768	0	1.000
	— Stockton (Calif.)	OF	13	47	13	12	2	0	3	12	10	12	0	0	2-0	.255	.373	.489	.862	2	.895
	— El Paso (Texas)	OF	22	79	12	22	4	1	1	13	8	23	0	1	3-1	.278	.341	.418	.759	7	.857
1996—	El Paso (Texas)	DH	22	77	17	22	5	4	1	11	12	21	2	2	1-2	.286	.391	.494	.885	—	—
	— Stockton (Calif.)	DH-OF	37	138	27	48	8	4	3	25	20	32	3	3	3-3	.348	.433	.529	.962	0	1.000
1997—	Tucson (PCL)	OF-SS	93	347	44	82	24	3	10	56	33	87	3	7	0-2	.236	.308	.409	.717	5	.961
1998—	Louisville (Int'l)	OF	55	215	38	71	10	4	7	52	14	39	5	6	1-1	.330	.381	.512	.893	2	.979
	— Milwaukee (N.L.)	OF	84	262	33	60	12	1	9	28	20	61	2	7	1-3	.229	.288	.386	.673	4	.968
1999—	Milwaukee (N.L.)	OF	135	447	70	140	43	3	21	82	35	87	7	10	5-1	.313	.371	.564	.935	7	.974
2000—	Milwaukee (N.L.)	OF	135	512	100	155	36	4	34	94	33	135	15	9	11-1	.303	.360	.588	.948	7	.975
2001—	Milwaukee (N.L.)	OF	105	397	60	105	21	1	20	63	36	120	8	11	4-2	.264	.334	.474	.808	3	.986
	— Beloit (Midw.)	OF	1	3	1	1	1	0	0	1	1	0	0	0	0-0	.333	.500	.667	1.167	0	...
2002—	Milwaukee (N.L.)	OF	67	243	35	59	17	1	10	29	22	60	6	8	1-2	.243	.320	.444	.764	1	.992
2003—	Huntsville (Sou.)	OF	6	20	6	5	0	0	2	3	1	7	0	0	1-0	.250	.286	.550	.836	0	1.000
	— Milwaukee (N.L.)	OF-DH	124	487	81	144	30	2	28	95	58	120	6	12	0-0	.296	.375	.538	.913	0	1.000
2004—	Milwaukee (N.L.)	OF	157	617	88	163	36	6	27	93	46	152	12	19	3-1	.264	.325	.473	.798	1	.996
2005—	Milwaukee (N.L.)	OF-DH	148	538	87	157	42	1	25	86	56	138	•19	13	0-0	.292	.375	.513	.888	5	.984
	Major League totals (8 years)		955	3503	554	983	237	19	174	570	306	873	75	89	25-10	.281	.349	.508	.857	28	.985

JENKS, BOBBY   P

PERSONAL: Born March 14, 1981, in Mission Hills, Calif. ... 6-3/270. ... Throws right, bats right. ... Full name: Robert Scott Jenks. ... High school: Inglemoor (Bothell, Wash.).
TRANSACTIONS/CAREER NOTES: Selected by Anaheim Angels organization in fifth round of 2000 free-agent draft. ... Claimed on waivers by Chicago White Sox (December 17, 2004).
CAREER HITTING: 0-for-0 (.000), 0 R, 0 2B, 0 3B, 0 HR, 0 RBI.

SCOUTING REPORT Throws: Jenks throws a fastball at 94-100 mph and a curveball in the low 80s. ***Tendencies:*** The hardest thrower in the game has two devastating pitches. Throws comfortably in the upper 90s. Cuts his fastball away from righthanders. Freezes hitters with a tightly biting curve. ***Outlook:*** Jenks has exceptional ability and showed an improved delivery and command as a rookie. Maturing quickly, he just needs to keep his feet on the ground to become a dominant closer. ***Grade 9***

BOBBY JENKS' PITCHING ZONE

.214	.333	.333
.500	.353	.235
.000	.273	.125

LEFTY-RIGHTY SPLITS

vs.	Avg.	AB	H	2B	3B	HR	RBI	BB	SO	OBP	Slg.
L	.105	57	6	3	0	1	6	7	21	.203	.211
R	.298	94	28	7	0	2	11	8	29	.359	.436

Year	Team (League)	W	L	Pct.	ERA	WHIP	G	GS	CG	ShO	Hld.	Sv.-Opp.	IP	H	R	ER	HR	BB-IBB	SO	Avg.
2000—	Butte (Pion.)	1	7	.125	7.86	1.99	14	12	0	0	...	0-...	52.2	61	57	46	2	44-0	42	.290
2001—	Cedar Rap. (Midw.)	3	7	.300	5.27	1.56	21	21	0	0	...	0-...	99.0	90	74	58	10	64-0	98	.245
	— Arkansas (Texas)	1	0	1.000	3.60	1.30	2	2	0	0	...	0-...	10.0	8	5	4	0	5-0	10	.200
2002—	Arkansas (Texas)	3	6	.333	4.66	1.60	10	10	1	0	...	0-...	58.0	49	34	30	2	44-0	58	.234
	— Rancho Cuca. (Calif.)	3	5	.375	4.82	1.47	11	10	1	1	...	0-...	65.1	50	42	35	4	46-0	64	.212
2003—	Arkansas (Texas)	7	2	.778	2.17	1.29	16	16	0	0	...	0-...	83.0	56	23	20	2	51-0	103	.191
	— Ariz. Angels (Ariz.)	0	0	...	0.00	0.50	1	1	0	0	...	0-...	4.0	2	0	0	0	0-0	5	.154
2004—	Salt Lake (PCL)	0	1	.000	8.76	2.03	3	3	0	0	...	0-...	12.1	19	15	12	1	6-0	13	.358
	— Ariz. Angels (Ariz.)	0	0	...	8.10	1.50	1	1	0	0	...	0-...	3.1	2	3	3	0	3-0	5	.182
	— Rancho Cuca. (Calif.)	0	1	.000	19.64	3.27	1	1	0	0	...	0-...	3.2	5	8	8	0	7-0	3	.385
2005—	Birmingham (Sou.)	1	2	.333	2.85	1.32	35	0	0	0	1	19-21	41.0	34	17	13	1	20-1	48	.224
	— Chicago (A.L.)	1	1	.500	2.75	1.25	32	0	0	0	3	6-8	39.1	34	15	12	3	15-3	50	.225
	Major League totals (1 year)	1	1	.500	2.75	1.25	32	0	0	0	3	6-8	39.1	34	15	12	3	15-3	50	.225

DIVISION SERIES RECORD

Year	Team (League)	W	L	Pct.	ERA	WHIP	G	GS	CG	ShO	Hld.	Sv.-Opp.	IP	H	R	ER	HR	BB-IBB	SO	Avg.
2005—	Chicago (A.L.)	0	0	...	0.00	0.67	2	0	0	0	...	2-2	3.0	1	0	0	0	1-0	1	.100

Year Team (League)	W	L	Pct.	ERA	WHIP	G	GS	CG	ShO	Hld.	Sv.-Opp.	IP	H	R	ER	HR	BB-IBB	SO	Avg.
2005— Chicago (A.L.)			Did not play.																

WORLD SERIES RECORD

Year Team (League)	W	L	Pct.	ERA	WHIP	G	GS	CG	ShO	Hld.	Sv.-Opp.	IP	H	R	ER	HR	BB-IBB	SO	Avg.
2005— Chicago (A.L.)	0	0	...	3.60	1.00	4	0	0	0	0	2-3	5.0	3	2	2	0	2-0	7	.176

JENNINGS, JASON — P

PERSONAL: Born July 17, 1978, in Dallas. ... 6-2/245. ... Throws right, bats left. ... Full name: Jason Ryan Jennings. ... High school: Dr. Ralph H. Poteet (Mesquite, Texas). ... College: Baylor.

TRANSACTIONS/CAREER NOTES: Selected by Arizona Diamondbacks organization in 54th round of 1996 free-agent draft; did not sign. ... Selected by Colorado Rockies organization in first round (16th pick overall) of 1999 free-agent draft. ... On disabled list (July 21, 2005-remainder of season).

HONORS: Named N.L. Rookie Pitcher of the Year by THE SPORTING NEWS (2002). ... Named N.L. Rookie of the Year by Baseball Writers' Association of America (2002).

CAREER HITTING: 58-for-240 (.242), 14 R, 13 2B, 0 3B, 2 HR, 23 RBI.

SCOUTING REPORT *Throws:* His fastball and sinker are in the 88-91-mph range. Also throws a slider and a circle changeup. *Tendencies:* Jennings' late-moving sinker is conducive to pitching in Coors Field. Needs to be more aggressive and get ahead in the count more often, then put hitters away quickly to keep pitch counts low. Nibbles too much. Slider occasionally is flat and at times is more of a slurve. Change has become more consistent. *Outlook:* Jennings will eat up innings. With his sinker, he should win more games. **Grade 7**

JASON JENNINGS' PITCHING ZONE

.242	.200	.294
.273	.368	.375
.345	.286	.211

LEFTY-RIGHTY SPLITS

vs.	Avg.	AB	H	2B	3B	HR	RBI	BB	SO	OBP	Slg.
L	.269	242	65	15	1	7	32	44	36	.380	.426
R	.279	233	65	17	0	4	34	18	39	.341	.403

Year Team (League)	W	L	Pct.	ERA	WHIP	G	GS	CG	ShO	Hld.	Sv.-Opp.	IP	H	R	ER	HR	BB-IBB	SO	Avg.
1999— Portland (N'west)	1	0	1.000	1.00	0.78	2	2	0	0	...	0-...	9.0	5	1	1	0	2-0	11	.161
—Asheville (S. Atl.)	2	2	.500	3.70	1.08	12	12	0	0	...	0-...	58.1	55	27	24	3	8-0	69	.247
2000— Salem (Carol.)	7	10	.412	3.47	1.18	22	22	3	1	...	0-...	150.1	136	66	58	6	42-0	133	.234
—Carolina (Southern)	1	3	.250	3.44	1.17	6	6	0	0	...	0-...	36.2	32	19	14	4	11-0	33	.234
2001— Carolina (Southern)	2	0	1.000	2.88	1.32	4	4	0	0	...	0-...	25.0	25	9	8	1	8-0	24	.258
—Colo. Springs (PCL)	7	8	.467	4.72	1.41	22	22	4	0	...	0-...	131.2	145	80	69	9	41-0	110	.281
—Colorado (N.L.)	4	1	.800	4.58	1.55	7	7	1	1	0	0-0	39.1	42	21	20	2	19-0	26	.276
2002— Colorado (N.L.)	16	8	.667	4.52	1.46	32	32	0	0	0	0-0	185.1	201	102	93	26	70-2	127	.280
2003— Colorado (N.L.)	12	13	.480	5.11	1.65	32	32	0	0	0	0-0	181.1	212	115	103	20	88-7	119	.299
2004— Colorado (N.L.)	11	12	.478	5.51	1.70	33	33	0	0	0	0-0	201.0	* 241	125	123	27	101-14	133	.299
2005— Colorado (N.L.)	6	9	.400	5.02	1.57	20	20	1	0	0	0-0	122.0	130	73	68	11	62-4	75	.274
Major League totals (5 years)	49	43	.533	5.02	1.60	124	124	3	1	0	0-0	729.0	826	436	407	86	340-27	480	.289

JENSEN, RYAN — P

PERSONAL: Born September 17, 1975, in Salt Lake City. ... 6-0/205. ... Throws right, bats right. ... Full name: Larry Ryan Jensen. ... High school: Cottonwood (Salt Lake City). ... College: Southern Utah.

TRANSACTIONS/CAREER NOTES: Selected by San Francisco Giants organization in eighth round of free-agent draft (June 4, 1996). ... On disabled list (April 10-May 9, 2003; included rehabilitation assignment to Fresno). ... Signed as a free agent by Kansas City Royals organization (November 19, 2004).

CAREER HITTING: 10-for-74 (.135), 5 R, 2 2B, 0 3B, 0 HR, 6 RBI.

RYAN JENSEN'S PITCHING ZONE

.300	.286	.200
.231	.316	.412
.400	1.000	.200

LEFTY-RIGHTY SPLITS

vs.	Avg.	AB	H	2B	3B	HR	RBI	BB	SO	OBP	Slg.
L	.269	52	14	3	1	3	1	5	12	.328	.538
R	.327	52	17	1	1	1	7	2	6	.368	.442

Year Team (League)	W	L	Pct.	ERA	WHIP	G	GS	CG	ShO	Hld.	Sv.-Opp.	IP	H	R	ER	HR	BB-IBB	SO	Avg.
1996— Bellingham (N'west)	2	4	.333	4.98	1.55	13	11	0	0	...	0-...	47.0	35	30	26	4	38-0	31	.208
1997— Bakersfield (Calif.)	0	0	...	13.50	2.25	1	1	0	0	...	0-...	1.1	3	2	2	1	0-0	2	.500
—Salem-Keizer (N'west)	7	3	.700	5.15	1.48	16	16	0	0	...	0-...	80.1	87	55	46	10	32-0	67	.278
1998— Bakersfield (Calif.)	11	12	.478	3.37	1.32	29	27	0	0	...	0-...	168.1	162	89	63	14	61-3	164	.249
—Fresno (PCL)	0	0	...	4.76	1.41	2	1	0	0	...	0-...	5.2	4	5	3	2	4-0	6	.200
1999— Fresno (PCL)	11	10	.524	5.12	1.46	27	27	0	0	...	0-...	156.1	160	96	89	17	68-1	150	.266
2000— Fresno (PCL)	5	8	.385	5.79	1.70	26	26	1	0	...	0-...	135.1	167	106	87	18	63-0	114	.305
2001— Fresno (PCL)	11	2	.846	3.48	1.24	20	17	1	1	...	0-...	106.0	97	43	41	11	34-0	95	.242
—San Francisco (N.L.)	1	2	.333	4.25	1.63	10	7	0	0	0	0-0	42.1	44	21	20	5	25-0	26	.268
2002— San Francisco (N.L.)	13	8	.619	4.51	1.45	32	30	1	0	0	0-0	171.2	183	93	86	21	66-4	105	.278
2003— San Francisco (N.L.)	0	0	...	10.80	1.95	6	2	0	0	0	0-0	13.1	21	16	16	6	5-0	3	.404
—Fresno (PCL)	1	10	.091	5.30	1.40	27	18	0	0	...	0-...	103.2	114	70	61	14	36-2	50	.285
2005— Kansas City (A.L.)	3	2	.600	7.11	1.50	9	3	0	0	0	0-1	25.1	31	20	20	4	7-1	18	.298
—Omaha (PCL)	2	11	.154	7.20	1.79	18	18	0	0	...	0-...	90.0	123	80	72	12	38-0	55	.325
American League totals (1 year)	3	2	.600	7.11	1.50	9	3	0	0	0	0-1	25.1	31	20	20	4	7-1	18	.298
National League totals (3 years)	14	10	.583	4.83	1.51	48	39	1	0	0	0-0	227.1	248	130	122	32	96-4	134	.284
Major League totals (4 years)	17	12	.586	5.06	1.51	57	42	1	0	0	0-1	252.2	279	150	142	36	103-5	152	.285

JETER, DEREK — SS

PERSONAL: Born June 26, 1974, in Pequannock, N.J. ... 6-3/195. ... Bats right, throws right. ... Full name: Derek Sanderson Jeter. ... Name pronounced: JEE-ter. ... High school: Central (Kalamazoo, Mich.).

TRANSACTIONS/CAREER NOTES: Selected by New York Yankees organization in first round (sixth pick overall) of 1992 free-agent draft. ... On disabled list (June 3-19, 1998; included rehabilitation assignment to Columbus. ... On disabled list (May 12-27, 2000; included rehabilitation assignment to Tampa. ... On disabled list (March 23-April 7, 2001). ... On disabled list (April 1-May 13, 2003; included rehabilitation assignment to Trenton).

HONORS: Named Minor League Player of the Year by THE SPORTING NEWS (1994). ... Named A.L. Rookie Player of the Year by THE SPORTING NEWS (1996). ... Named A.L. Rookie of the Year by Baseball Writers' Association of America (1996). ... Won A.L. Gold Glove at shortstop (2004-05).
2005 GAMES PLAYED BY POSITION (MLB): SS—157, DH—1.

SCOUTING REPORT *Offense:* Jeter slightly adjusted his natural inside-out swing a year ago; now he can handle pitches on the inner half and drive them to left field. Has extremely quick hands and very good bat control. Is a good two-strike hitter. Has above-average power. Is an outstanding, instinctive baserunner. *Defense:* His outstanding instincts are evident in the way he approaches grounders and avoids getting bad hops. Is very fluid. Has quick hands and is agile. Doesn't have really quick feet; his range is a product of positioning and very long arms. Charges the ball well and is quick on his transfer and release. Throws have good carry from the hole. *Outlook:* The Yankees' leader is one of the few "big-game" players around. No longer is a one-dimensional hitter. *Grade 9.5*

DEREK JETER'S HITTING ZONE

.381	.609	.170
.311	.476	.327
.260	.345	.205

LEFTY-RIGHTY SPLITS

vs.	Avg.	AB	H	2B	3B	HR	RBI	BB	SO	OBP	Slg.
L	.317	186	59	6	2	9	24	17	24	.382	.516
R	.306	468	143	19	3	10	46	60	93	.392	.423

J

										BATTING									FIELDING	
Year Team (League)	Pos.	G	AB	R	H	2B	3B	HR	RBI	BB	SO	HBP	GDP	SB-CS	Avg.	OBP	SLG	OPS	E	Avg.
1992— GC Yankees (GCL)	SS	47	173	19	35	10	6	3	25	19	36	5	4	2-2	.202	.296	.312	.609	12	.943
—Greensboro (S. Atl.)	SS	11	37	4	9	0	0	1	4	7	16	1	0	0-1	.243	.378	.324	.702	9	.813
1993—Greensboro (S. Atl.)	SS	128	515	85	152	14	11	5	71	56	95	11	9	18-9	.295	.374	.394	.768	56	.889
1994—Tampa (Fla. St.)	SS	69	292	61	96	13	8	0	39	23	30	3	4	28-2	.329	.380	.428	.808	12	.961
—Alb./Colon. (East.)	SS	34	122	17	46	7	2	2	13	15	16	1	3	12-2	.377	.446	.516	.962	6	.961
—Columbus (Int'l)	SS	35	126	25	44	7	1	3	16	20	15	1	6	10-4	.349	.439	.492	.931	7	.955
1995—Columbus (Int'l)	SS	123	486	96	154	27	9	2	45	61	56	4	9	20-12	.317	.394	.422	.816	29	.953
—New York (A.L.)	SS	15	48	5	12	4	1	0	7	3	11	0	0	0-0	.250	.294	.375	.669	2	.962
1996— New York (A.L.)	SS	157	582	104	183	25	6	10	78	48	102	9	13	14-7	.314	.370	.430	.800	22	.969
1997— New York (A.L.)	SS	159	654	116	190	31	7	10	70	74	125	10	14	23-12	.291	.370	.405	.775	18	.975
1998— New York (A.L.)	SS	149	626	*127	203	25	8	19	84	57	119	5	13	30-6	.324	.384	.481	.864	9	.986
—Columbus (Int'l)	SS	1	5	2	2	2	0	0	0	0	2	0	0	0-0	.400	.400	.800	1.200	1	.875
1999— New York (A.L.)	SS	158	627	134	*219	37	9	24	102	91	116	12	12	19-8	.349	.438	.552	.989	14	.978
2000— New York (A.L.)	SS	148	593	119	201	31	4	15	73	68	99	12	14	22-4	.339	.416	.481	.896	24	.961
—Tampa (Fla. St.)	SS	1	3	2	2	1	0	0	0	0	0	0	0	0-0	.667	.667	1.000	1.667	0	1.000
2001— New York (A.L.)	SS	150	614	110	191	35	3	21	74	56	99	10	13	27-3	.311	.377	.480	.858	15	.974
2002— New York (A.L.)	SS-DH	157	644	124	191	26	0	18	75	73	114	7	14	32-3	.297	.373	.421	.794	14	.977
2003— Trenton (East.)	SS	5	18	2	8	1	1	0	5	3	0	1	0	0-0	.444	.545	.611	1.157	1	.957
—New York (A.L.)	SS	119	482	87	156	25	3	10	52	43	88	13	10	11-5	.324	.393	.450	.844	14	.968
2004— New York (A.L.)	SS	154	643	111	188	44	1	23	78	46	99	14	19	23-4	.292	.352	.471	.823	13	.981
2005— New York (A.L.)	SS-DH	159	654	122	202	25	5	19	70	77	117	11	15	14-5	.309	.389	.450	.839	15	.979
Major League totals (11 years)		1525	6167	1159	1936	308	47	169	763	636	1089	103	137	215-57	.314	.386	.461	.847	160	.975

DIVISION SERIES RECORD

Year Team (League)	Pos.	G	AB	R	H	2B	3B	HR	RBI	BB	SO	HBP	GDP	SB-CS	Avg.	OBP	SLG	OPS	E	Avg.
1996— New York (A.L.)	SS	4	17	2	7	1	0	0	1	0	2	0	0	0-0	.412	.412	.471	.882	1	.947
1997— New York (A.L.)	SS	5	21	6	7	1	0	2	2	3	5	0	0	1-0	.333	.417	.667	1.083	0	1.000
1998— New York (A.L.)	SS	3	9	0	1	0	0	0	0	2	2	0	0	0-0	.111	.273	.111	.384	1	1.000
1999— New York (A.L.)	SS	3	11	3	5	1	1	0	0	2	3	0	0	0-0	.455	.538	.727	1.266	0	1.000
2000— New York (A.L.)	SS	5	19	1	4	0	0	0	2	3	1	0	0	0-1	.211	.318	.211	.529	0	1.000
2001— New York (A.L.)	SS	5	18	2	8	1	0	0	1	1	0	1	0	0-1	.444	.476	.500	.976	1	1.000
2002— New York (A.L.)	SS	4	16	6	8	0	0	2	3	2	3	0	0	0-0	.500	.526	.875	1.401	1	.944
2003— New York (A.L.)	SS	4	14	2	6	0	0	1	1	4	2	0	0	1-0	.429	.556	.643	1.198	1	.923
2004— New York (A.L.)	SS	4	19	3	6	1	0	1	4	1	4	0	1	1-0	.316	.350	.526	.876	1	.960
2005— New York (A.L.)	SS	5	21	4	7	0	0	2	5	1	5	0	0	1-0	.333	.348	.619	.967	0	1.000
Division series totals (10 years)		42	165	29	59	5	1	8	19	18	29	2	1	4-2	.358	.420	.545	.966	4	.978

CHAMPIONSHIP SERIES RECORD

Year Team (League)	Pos.	G	AB	R	H	2B	3B	HR	RBI	BB	SO	HBP	GDP	SB-CS	Avg.	OBP	SLG	OPS	E	Avg.
1996— New York (A.L.)	SS	5	24	5	10	2	0	1	1	0	5	0	0	2-0	.417	.417	.625	1.042	0	1.000
1998— New York (A.L.)	SS	6	25	3	5	1	1	0	2	2	5	0	1	3-0	.200	.259	.320	.579	0	1.000
1999— New York (A.L.)	SS	5	20	3	7	1	0	1	3	2	1	0	0	0-0	.350	.409	.550	.959	2	.909
2000— New York (A.L.)	SS	6	22	6	7	0	0	2	5	6	7	0	0	1-0	.318	.464	.591	1.055	0	1.000
2001— New York (A.L.)	SS	5	17	0	2	0	0	0	2	2	2	0	0	0-0	.118	.200	.118	.318	0	1.000
2003— New York (A.L.)	SS	7	30	3	7	2	0	1	2	2	4	0	0	1-0	.233	.281	.400	.681	0	1.000
2004— New York (A.L.)	SS	7	30	5	6	1	0	0	5	6	2	0	0	1-0	.200	.333	.233	.567	2	.956
Champ. series totals (7 years)		41	168	25	44	7	1	5	20	20	28	0	1	8-0	.262	.339	.405	.743	4	.979

WORLD SERIES RECORD

Year Team (League)	Pos.	G	AB	R	H	2B	3B	HR	RBI	BB	SO	HBP	GDP	SB-CS	Avg.	OBP	SLG	OPS	E	Avg.
1996— New York (A.L.)	SS	6	20	5	5	0	0	0	1	4	6	1	1	1-0	.250	.400	.250	.650	2	.949
1998— New York (A.L.)	SS	4	17	4	6	0	0	0	1	3	3	0	1	0-0	.353	.450	.353	.803	0	1.000
1999— New York (A.L.)	SS	4	17	4	6	1	0	1	1	3	3	0	0	3-1	.353	.389	.412	.801	0	1.000
2000— New York (A.L.)	SS	5	22	6	9	2	1	2	2	3	8	0	0	0-0	.409	.480	.864	1.344	0	1.000
2001— New York (A.L.)	SS	7	27	3	4	0	0	1	1	0	6	1	0	0-0	.148	.179	.259	.438	0	1.000
2003— New York (A.L.)	SS	6	26	5	9	3	0	0	3	1	7	1	2	0-0	.346	.393	.462	.854	1	.969
World Series totals (6 years)		32	129	27	39	6	1	3	8	12	33	3	4	4-1	.302	.375	.434	.809	3	.980

ALL-STAR GAME RECORD

		G	AB	R	H	2B	3B	HR	RBI	BB	SO	HBP	GDP	SB-CS	Avg.	OBP	SLG	OPS	E	Avg.
All-Star Game totals (6 years)		6	10	3	7	1	0	1	3	0	3	0	0	0-0	.700	.700	1.100	1.800	0	1.000

JIMENEZ, D'ANGELO — 2B

PERSONAL: Born December 21, 1977, in Santo Domingo, Dominican Republic. ... 6-0/195. ... Bats both, throws right. ... Name pronounced: he-MEN-ez.

TRANSACTIONS/CAREER NOTES: Signed as a non-drafted free agent by New York Yankees organization (August 1, 1994). ... On disabled list (March 23-August 24, 2000); included rehabilitation assignments to GCL Yankees, Tampa and Columbus. ... Traded by Yankees to San Diego Padres for P Jay Witasick (June 23, 2001). ... Traded by Padres to Chicago White Sox for OF Alex Fernandez and C Humberto Quintero (July 12, 2002). ... Traded by White Sox to Cincinnati Reds for P Scott Dunn (July 6, 2003). ... Career major league pitching: 0-0, 0.00 ERA, 1 G, 1.1 IP, 0 H, 0 R, 0 ER, 0 BB, 0 SO.

2005 GAMES PLAYED BY POSITION (MLB): 2B—27.

D'ANGELO JIMENEZ'S HITTING ZONE

.250	.125	.000
.250	.250	.200
.286	.429	.182

LEFTY-RIGHTY SPLITS

vs.	Avg.	AB	H	2B	3B	HR	RBI	BB	SO	OBP	Slg
L	.355	31	11	2	0	0	3	4	3	.429	.419
R	.176	74	13	5	0	0	2	10	20	.274	.243

Year	Team (League)	Pos.	G	AB	R	H	2B	3B	HR	RBI	BB	SO	HBP	GDP	SB-CS	Avg.	OBP	SLG	OPS	E	Avg.
1995—	GC Yankees (GCL)	SS	57	214	41	60	14	8	2	28	23	31	1	4	6-3	.280	.347	.449	.796	21	.927
1996—	Greensboro (S. Atl.)	SS	138	537	68	131	25	5	6	48	56	113	3	7	15-17	.244	.317	.343	.660	50	.922
1997—	Tampa (Fla. St.)	SS	94	352	52	99	14	6	6	48	50	50	2	3	8-14	.281	.368	.406	.775	21	.953
	— Columbus (Int'l)	SS	2	7	1	1	0	0	0	1	0	1	0	1	0-0	.143	.125	.143	.268	2	.833
1998—	Norwich (East.)	SS	40	152	21	41	6	2	2	21	25	26	2	3	5-5	.270	.378	.375	.753	12	.938
	— Columbus (Int'l)	2B-SS	91	344	55	88	19	4	8	51	46	67	1	7	6-6	.256	.341	.404	.745	26	.946
1999—	Columbus (Int'l)	SS-3B-2B	126	526	97	172	32	5	15	88	59	75	1	8	26-14	.327	.392	.492	.884	26	.957
	— New York (A.L.)	3B-2B	7	20	3	8	2	0	0	3	4	0	0	0	0-0	.400	.478	.500	.978	0	1.000
2000—	GC Yankees (GCL)	2B-SS	4	10	2	1	0	0	0	0	5	1	0	0	0-0	.100	.400	.100	.500	2	.900
	— Tampa (Fla. St.)	SS-2B	12	41	8	8	1	1	1	2	8	7	0	1	0-0	.195	.320	.341	.661	7	.875
	— Columbus (Int'l)	2B-3B-SS	21	73	11	17	3	1	1	9	7	12	1	2	2-0	.233	.309	.342	.651	4	.965
2001—	Columbus (Int'l)	2B-SS-3B	56	214	33	56	11	1	5	19	24	31	1	2	5-6	.262	.333	.393	.726	7	.965
	— San Diego (N.L.)	SS	86	308	45	85	19	0	3	33	39	68	0	9	2-3	.276	.355	.367	.722	21	.948
2002—	San Diego (N.L.)	2B-3B-P	87	321	39	77	11	4	3	33	34	63	0	10	4-2	.240	.311	.327	.638	12	.968
	— Charlotte (Int'l)	2B	42	157	24	44	11	1	6	18	24	14	0	2	6-2	.280	.372	.478	.849	6	.966
	— Chicago (A.L.)	2B-SS-3B	27	108	22	31	4	3	1	11	16	10	1	1	2-1	.287	.384	.407	.791	2	.985
2003—	Chicago (A.L.)	2B-3B	73	271	35	69	11	5	7	26	32	46	0	3	4-3	.255	.332	.410	.742	9	.970
	— Cincinnati (N.L.)	2B-3B	73	290	34	84	13	2	7	31	34	43	2	4	7-4	.290	.365	.421	.785	4	.990
2004—	Cincinnati (N.L.)	2B-SS	152	563	76	152	28	3	12	67	82	99	2	15	13-7	.270	.364	.394	.758	7	.990
2005—	Cincinnati (N.L.)	2B	35	105	14	24	7	0	0	5	14	23	0	1	2-1	.229	.319	.295	.615	2	.983
	— Chattanooga (Sou.)	SS-DH-2B	90	327	55	91	20	0	9	45	69	34	0	4	16-4	.278	.401	.422	.823	8	.978
American League totals (3 years)			107	399	60	108	17	8	8	41	51	60	1	4	6-4	.271	.354	.414	.768	11	.976
National League totals (5 years)			433	1587	208	422	78	9	25	169	203	296	4	39	28-17	.266	.349	.374	.723	46	.977
Major League totals (6 years)			540	1986	268	530	95	17	33	210	254	356	5	43	34-21	.267	.350	.382	.732	57	.977

JIMERSON, CHARLTON — OF

PERSONAL: Born September 22, 1979, in San Leandro, Calif. ... 6-3/210. ... Bats right, throws right. ... Full name: Charlton Maxwell Jimerson. ... High school: Mt. Eden (Calif.). ... College: Miami.

TRANSACTIONS/CAREER NOTES: Selected by Houston Astros organization in fifth round of 2001 free-agent draft.

2005 GAMES PLAYED BY POSITION (MLB): OF—1.

LEFTY-RIGHTY SPLITS

vs.	Avg.	AB	H	2B	3B	HR	RBI	BB	SO	OBP	Slg
L	.000	0	0	0	0	0	0	0	0	.000	.000
R	.000	0	0	0	0	0	0	0	0	.000	.000

Year	Team (League)	Pos.	G	AB	R	H	2B	3B	HR	RBI	BB	SO	HBP	GDP	SB-CS	Avg.	OBP	SLG	OPS	E	Avg.
2001—	Pittsfield (NYP)	OF	51	197	35	46	12	1	9	31	18	79	2	4	15-4	.234	.304	.442	.746	7	.903
2002—	Lexington (S. Atl.)	OF	125	439	65	100	22	4	14	57	36	168	7	7	34-9	.228	.295	.392	.687	8	.970
2003—	Salem (Carol.)	OF	97	336	53	89	19	3	12	55	25	109	2	4	27-4	.265	.317	.446	.763	3	.985
2004—	Round Rock (Texas)	OF	131	488	78	116	22	5	18	53	31	163	5	8	39-6	.238	.290	.414	.704	6	.857
2005—	Corpus Christi (Texas)	OF-DH	115	425	67	110	24	3	16	44	29	145	8	8	27-10	.259	.317	.442	.759	14	.971
	— Round Rock (PCL)	OF	7	23	1	7	1	0	0	1	0	7	0	0	3-0	.304	.292	.348	.639	2	.950
	— Houston (N.L.)	OF	1	0	0	0	0	0	0	0	0	0	0	0	0-0	...	...	...	...	0	...
Major League totals (1 year)			1	0	0	0	0	0	0	0	0	0	0	0	0-0	...	...	...	...	0	...

JOHNSON, BEN — OF

PERSONAL: Born June 18, 1981, in Memphis. ... 6-1/200. ... Bats right, throws right. ... Full name: Benjamin Joseph Johnson. ... High school: Germantown (Tenn.).

TRANSACTIONS/CAREER NOTES: Selected by St. Louis Cardinals organization in fourth round of 1999 free-agent draft. ... Traded by Cardinals with P Heathcliff Slocumb to San Diego Padres for C Carlos Hernandez and IF Nate Tebbs (July 31, 2000).

2005 GAMES PLAYED BY POSITION (MLB): OF—29.

BEN JOHNSON'S HITTING ZONE

.167	.500	.750
.368	.000	.111
.222	.000	.000

LEFTY-RIGHTY SPLITS

vs.	Avg.	AB	H	2B	3B	HR	RBI	BB	SO	OBP	Slg
L	.185	27	5	4	0	1	6	4	10	.281	.444
R	.229	48	11	4	1	2	7	7	13	.327	.479

Year	Team (League)	Pos.	G	AB	R	H	2B	3B	HR	RBI	BB	SO	HBP	GDP	SB-CS	Avg.	OBP	SLG	OPS	E	Avg.
1999—	Johnson City (App.)	OF	57	203	38	67	9	1	10	51	29	57	5	0	14-6	.330	.423	.532	.955	2	.978
2000—	Peoria (Midw.)	OF	93	330	58	80	22	1	13	46	53	78	5	8	17-6	.242	.353	.433	.786	6	.962
	— Fort Wayne (Midw.)	OF	29	109	11	21	6	2	3	13	7	25	3	0	0-3	.193	.261	.367	.628	0	1.000
2001—	Lake Elsinore (Calif.)	OF	136	503	79	139	35	6	12	63	54	141	11	15	22-7	.276	.358	.441	.799	12	.948
2002—	Mobile (Sou.)	OF	131	456	58	110	23	4	10	55	65	127	3	9	11-9	.241	.337	.375	.712	9	.965
2003—	Mobile (Sou.)	OF	44	127	8	23	5	0	1	10	10	36	2	0	0-1	.181	.252	.244	.496	1	.984

Year	Team (League)	Pos.	G	AB	R	H	2B	3B	HR	RBI	BB	SO	HBP	GDP	SB-CS	Avg.	OBP	SLG	OPS	E	Avg.
— Lake Elsinore (Calif.)	OF	52	184	30	49	9	0	8	29	20	49	5	5	6-1	.266	.354	.446	.800	4	.969
2004— Mobile (Sou.)	OF	136	475	80	119	28	6	23	85	55	136	7	0	5-6	.251	.334	.480	.814	9	.775
2005— Portland (PCL)	OF	107	414	79	129	27	0	25	83	51	88	6	7	6-1	.312	.394	.558	.952	8	.981
— San Diego (N.L.)	OF	31	75	10	16	8	1	3	13	11	23	0	4	0-2	.213	.310	.467	.777	2	.962
Major League totals (1 year)		31	75	10	16	8	1	3	13	11	23	0	4	0-2	.213	.310	.467	.777	2	.962

DIVISION SERIES RECORD

Year	Team (League)	Pos.	G	AB	R	H	2B	3B	HR	RBI	BB	SO	HBP	GDP	SB-CS	Avg.	OBP	SLG	OPS	E	Avg.
2005— San Diego (N.L.)	OF	2	2	0	0	0	0	0	0	0	2	0	0	0-0	.000	.000	.000	.000	0	...

JOHNSON, CHARLES   C

J

PERSONAL: Born July 20, 1971, in Fort Pierce, Fla. ... 6-3/225. ... Bats right, throws right. ... Full name: Charles Edward Johnson. ... High school: Westwood (Fort Pierce, Fla.). ... College: Miami. ... Nephew of Fred McGriff, first baseman with six major league teams (1986-2004).

TRANSACTIONS/CAREER NOTES: Selected by Montreal Expos organization in first round (10th pick overall) of 1989 free-agent draft; did not sign. ... Selected by Florida Marlins organization in first round (28th pick overall) of 1992 free-agent draft. ... On disabled list (August 9-September 1, 1995); included rehabilitation assignment to Portland. ... On disabled list (July 28-September 1, 1996). ... Traded by Marlins with OFs Gary Sheffield and Jim Eisenreich, 3B Bobby Bonilla and P Manuel Barrios to Los Angeles Dodgers for C Mike Piazza and 3B Todd Zeile (May 15, 1998). ... Traded by Dodgers with OF Roger Cedeno to New York Mets for C Todd Hundley and P Arnold Gooch (December 1, 1998). ... Traded by Mets to Baltimore Orioles for P Armando Benitez (December 1, 1998). ... Traded by Orioles with DH Harold Baines to Chicago White Sox for C Brook Fordyce and Ps Miguel Felix, Juan Figueroa and Jason Lakman (July 29, 2000). ... Signed as a free agent by Marlins (December 18, 2000). ... On disabled list (March 22-April 8 and July 28-August 16, 2002); included rehabilitation assignment to Jupiter. ... Traded by Marlins with P Vic Darensbourg, OF Preston Wilson and 2B Pablo Ozuna to Colorado Rockies for P Mike Hampton, OF Juan Pierre and cash (November 16, 2002). ... Traded by Rockies with P Christopher Narveson to Boston Red Sox for P Byung-Hyun Kim (March 30, 2005). ... Signed as a free agent by Tampa Bay Devil Rays (April 4, 2005). ... On restricted list (April 8-12, 2005). ... Released by Devil Rays (June 13, 2005).

HONORS: Won N.L. Gold Glove at catcher (1995-98).

2005 GAMES PLAYED BY POSITION (MLB): C—19.

Year	Team (League)	Pos.	G	AB	R	H	2B	3B	HR	RBI	BB	SO	HBP	GDP	SB-CS	Avg.	OBP	SLG	OPS	E	Avg.
1993— Kane Co. (Midw.)	C	135	488	74	134	29	5	19	94	62	111	2	12	9-1	.275	.356	.471	.827	12	.988
1994— Portland (East.)	C-DH	132	443	64	117	29	1	28	80	74	97	3	14	4-5	.264	.371	.524	.895	7	.991
— Florida (N.L.)	C	4	11	5	5	1	0	1	4	1	4	0	1	0-0	.455	.462	.818	1.280	0	1.000
1995— Florida (N.L.)	C	97	315	40	79	15	1	11	39	46	71	4	11	0-2	.251	.352	.410	.761	6	.992
— Portland (East.)	C	2	7	0	0	0	0	0	0	1	3	0	0	0-0	.000	.125	.000	.125	1	.958
1996— Florida (N.L.)	C	120	386	34	84	13	1	13	37	40	91	2	20	1-0	.218	.292	.358	.649	4	.995
1997— Florida (N.L.)	C	124	416	43	104	26	1	19	63	60	109	3	13	0-2	.250	.347	.454	.802	1	1.000
1998— Florida (N.L.)	C	31	113	13	25	5	0	7	23	16	30	0	3	0-1	.221	.315	.451	.766	2	.990
— Los Angeles (N.L.)	C	102	346	31	75	13	0	12	35	29	99	1	9	0-1	.217	.279	.358	.638	6	.992
1999— Baltimore (A.L.)	C	135	426	58	107	19	1	16	54	55	107	4	13	0-0	.251	.340	.413	.753	5	.994
2000— Baltimore (A.L.)	C-DH	84	286	52	84	16	0	21	55	32	69	0	8	2-0	.294	.364	.570	.934	3	.994
— Chicago (A.L.)	C	44	135	24	44	8	0	10	36	20	37	1	0	0-0	.326	.411	.607	1.019	3	.987
2001— Florida (N.L.)	C	128	451	51	117	32	0	18	75	38	133	4	8	0-0	.259	.321	.450	.771	4	.996
2002— Jupiter (Fla. St.)		5	16	5	7	0	0	3	9	2	4	0	0	0-0	.438	.500	1.000	1.500	0	1.000
— Florida (N.L.)	C	83	244	18	53	19	0	6	36	31	61	0	10	0-0	.217	.301	.369	.670	3	.994
2003— Colorado (N.L.)	C	108	356	49	82	20	0	20	61	49	84	1	3	1-3	.230	.320	.455	.775	4	.993
2004— Colorado (N.L.)	C	109	305	42	72	20	0	13	47	49	91	5	6	2-1	.236	.350	.430	.780	7	.988
2005— Tampa Bay	C	19	46	5	9	4	0	5	5	9	11	0	2	0-0	.196	.327	.283	.610	4	.959
American League totals (3 years)		282	893	139	244	47	1	47	150	116	224	5	23	2-0	.273	.358	.486	.844	15	.991
National League totals (9 years)		906	2943	326	696	164	3	120	420	359	773	20	89	4-10	.236	.321	.417	.738	36	.994
Major League totals (12 years)		1188	3836	465	940	211	4	167	570	475	997	25	112	6-10	.245	.330	.433	.762	51	.993

DIVISION SERIES RECORD

Year	Team (League)	Pos.	G	AB	R	H	2B	3B	HR	RBI	BB	SO	HBP	GDP	SB-CS	Avg.	OBP	SLG	OPS	E	Avg.
1997— Florida (N.L.)	C	3	8	5	2	1	0	1	2	3	2	1	0	0-0	.250	.500	.750	1.250	0	1.000
2000— Chicago (A.L.)	C	3	9	0	3	0	0	0	0	1	1	1	0	0-0	.333	.455	.333	.788	0	1.000
Division series totals (2 years)		6	17	5	5	1	0	1	2	4	3	2	0	0-0	.294	.478	.529	1.008	0	1.000

CHAMPIONSHIP SERIES RECORD

Year	Team (League)	Pos.	G	AB	R	H	2B	3B	HR	RBI	BB	SO	HBP	GDP	SB-CS	Avg.	OBP	SLG	OPS	E	Avg.
1997— Florida (N.L.)	C	6	17	1	2	2	0	0	5	3	8	1	0	0-1	.118	.286	.235	.521	2	.965

WORLD SERIES RECORD

Year	Team (League)	Pos.	G	AB	R	H	2B	3B	HR	RBI	BB	SO	HBP	GDP	SB-CS	Avg.	OBP	SLG	OPS	E	Avg.
1997— Florida (N.L.)	C	7	28	4	10	0	0	1	3	1	6	0	0	0-0	.357	.379	.464	.844	0	1.000

ALL-STAR GAME RECORD

	G	AB	R	H	2B	3B	HR	RBI	BB	SO	HBP	GDP	SB-CS	Avg.	OBP	SLG	OPS	E	Avg.
All-Star Game totals (2 years)	2	2	0	0	0	0	0	0	0	1	0	0	0-0	.000	.000	.000	.000	0	1.000

JOHNSON, DAN   1B

PERSONAL: Born August 10, 1979, in Coon Rapids, Minn. ... 6-2/220. ... Bats left, throws right. ... Full name: Daniel Ryan Johnson. ... College: Nebraska.

TRANSACTIONS/CAREER NOTES: Selected by Oakland Athletics organization in seventh round of 2001 free-agent draft.

2005 GAMES PLAYED BY POSITION (MLB): 1B—101, DH—5.

LEFTY-RIGHTY SPLITS

vs.	Avg.	AB	H	2B	3B	HR	RBI	BB	SO	OBP	Slg.
L	.222	9	2	1	0	0	1	1	3	.300	.333
R	.189	37	7	3	0	0	4	8	8	.333	.270

SCOUTING REPORT *Offense:* Johnson has showed that he can be a good hitter. Is extremely patient with almost as many walks as strikeouts. For his lack of experience doesn't mind hitting with two strikes. Stays inside the ball well and has good bat speed with the ability to use the whole field. Really stays in against lefthanders. Is going to develop more power when he begins to sit on pitches. *Defense:* He needs some work with his physical conditioning of his lower body to improve his agility and footwork around the bag. *Outlook:* Johnson is going to be a .300 hitter in the near future with the ability to hit 25-plus home runs a year. *Grade 7.1*

DAN JOHNSON'S HITTING ZONE

.188	.348	.174
.391	.262	.265
.500	.200	.286

LEFTY-RIGHTY SPLITS

vs.	Avg.	AB	H	2B	3B	HR	RBI	BB	SO	OBP	Slg.
L	.283	99	28	6	0	2	22	20	19	.395	.404
R	.272	276	75	15	0	13	36	30	33	.339	.467

J

Year Team (League)	Pos.	G	AB	R	H	2B	3B	HR	RBI	BB	SO	HBP	GDP	SB-CS	Avg.	OBP	SLG	OPS	E	Avg.
2001— Vancouver (N'west)	1B	69	247	36	70	15	2	11	41	27	63	2	6	0-0	.283	.354	.494	.848	12	.975
2002— Modesto (Calif.)	1B	126	426	56	125	23	1	21	85	57	87	0	8	4-1	.293	.371	.500	.871	7	.990
2003— Midland (Texas)	1B-OF	139	538	90	156	26	4	27	114	68	82	2	14	7-4	.290	.365	.504	.869	8	.992
— Sacramento (PCL)	1B-OF	1	4	0	1	0	0	0	0	0	0	0	0	0-0	.250	.250	.500	.750	0	1.000
2004— Sacramento (PCL)	1B-OF	142	536	95	160	29	5	29	111	89	93	9	15	0-1	.299	.403	.534	.937	12	.993
2005— Sacramento (PCL) 1B-OF-DH		47	182	36	59	17	0	8	41	32	24	1	1	0-1	.324	.424	.549	.973	4	.990
— Oakland (A.L.)	1B-DH	109	375	54	103	21	0	15	58	50	52	1	11	0-1	.275	.355	.451	.806	6	.994
Major League totals (1 year)		109	375	54	103	21	0	15	58	50	52	1	11	0-1	.275	.355	.451	.806	6	.994

JOHNSON, JASON   P

PERSONAL: Born October 27, 1973, in Santa Barbara, Calif. ... 6-6/217. ... Throws right, bats right. ... Full name: Jason Michael Johnson. ... High school: Conner (Hebron, Ky.).

TRANSACTIONS/CAREER NOTES: Signed as a non-drafted free agent by Pittsburgh Pirates organization (July 21, 1992). ... Selected by Tampa Bay Devil Rays in first round (14th pick overall) of expansion draft (November 18, 1997). ... On disabled list (July 4, 1998-remainder of season). ... Traded by Devil Rays to Baltimore Orioles for OF Danny Clyburn and a player to be named (March 29, 1999); Devil Rays acquired SS Bolivar Voquez to complete deal (April 22, 1999). ... On disabled list (April 25-June 7 and July 23-August 9, 2002); included rehabilitation assignment to Bowie. ... Signed as a free agent by Detroit Tigers (December 30, 2003).

CAREER HITTING: 3-for-24 (.125), 2 R, 0 2B, 0 3B, 1 HR, 1 RBI.

SCOUTING REPORT *Throws:* Johnson has a good fastball that ranges from 90-95 mph, a curveball at 74-78, and a changeup. *Tendencies:* Johnson is a fly-ball pitcher with a good arm and an erratic track record. Has a complicated delivery that makes it difficult for him to get into sync. When he does, his stuff can be dominating. Has a live fastball up and down in the strike zone, and his curve has a big break with a very tight spin. Never has developed a consistent feel for his changeup. Has good finishing action and varies the speed of his curveball; his harder curve is more of a sweeping slurve. *Outlook:* Johnson is an innings eater who still is considered an underachiever. *Grade 6.1*

JASON JOHNSON'S PITCHING ZONE

.216	.348	.291
.272	.385	.231
.345	.270	.450

LEFTY-RIGHTY SPLITS

vs.	Avg.	AB	H	2B	3B	HR	RBI	BB	SO	OBP	Slg.
L	.310	426	132	26	3	13	54	34	55	.362	.477
R	.258	391	101	11	1	10	47	15	38	.288	.368

Year Team (League)	W	L	Pct.	ERA	WHIP	G	GS	CG	ShO	Hld.	Sv.-Opp.	IP	H	R	ER	HR	BB-IBB	SO	Avg.
1992— GC Pirates (GCL)	2	0	1.000	3.68	1.64	5	0	0	0	...	0-...	7.1	6	3	3	0	6-0	3	.240
1993— GC Pirates (GCL)	1	4	.200	2.33	1.15	9	9	0	0	...	0-...	54.0	48	22	14	0	14-0	39	.239
— Welland (NYP)	1	5	.167	4.63	1.20	6	6	1	0	...	0-...	35.0	33	24	18	0	9-0	19	.243
1994— Augusta (S. Atl.)	2	12	.143	4.03	1.47	20	19	1	0	...	0-...	102.2	119	67	46	5	32-0	69	.285
1995— Augusta (S. Atl.)	3	5	.375	4.36	1.38	11	11	1	0	...	0-...	53.2	57	32	26	2	17-0	42	.271
— Lynchburg (Caro.)	1	4	.200	4.91	1.42	10	10	0	0	...	0-...	55.0	58	37	30	9	20-0	41	.275
1996— Lynchburg (Caro.)	1	4	.200	6.50	1.53	15	5	0	0	...	0-...	44.1	56	37	32	6	12-0	27	.303
— Augusta (S. Atl.)	4	4	.500	3.11	1.27	14	14	1	1	...	0-...	84.0	82	40	29	2	25-0	83	.256
1997— Lynchburg (Caro.)	8	4	.667	3.71	1.29	17	17	0	0	...	0-...	99.1	98	43	41	4	30-1	92	.266
— Carolina (Southern)	3	3	.500	4.08	1.26	9	9	1	0	...	0-...	57.1	56	31	26	6	16-0	63	.249
— Pittsburgh (N.L.)	0	0		6.00	1.83	3	0	0	0	0	0-0	6.0	10	4	4	2	1-0	3	.400
1998— Durham (Int'l)	1	0	1.000	2.92	0.65	2	2	0	0	0	0-0	12.1	6	4	4	2	2-0	14	.143
— Tampa Bay (A.L.)	2	5	.286	5.70	1.68	13	13	0	0	0	0-0	60.0	74	38	38	9	27-0	36	.306
1999— Rochester (Int'l)	4	2	.667	3.65	1.40	8	8	0	0	0	0-0	44.1	35	19	18	6	27-0	47	.212
— Baltimore (A.L.)	8	7	.533	5.46	1.52	22	21	0	0	0	0-0	115.1	120	74	70	16	55-0	71	.267
2000— Rochester (Int'l)	3	1	.750	1.47	0.96	8	8	1	1	0	0-0	55.0	32	12	9	2	21-0	56	.170
— Baltimore (A.L.)	1	10	.091	7.02	1.67	25	13	0	0	2	0-0	107.2	119	95	84	21	61-2	79	.278
2001— Baltimore (A.L.)	10	12	.455	4.09	1.38	32	32	2	0	0	0-0	196.0	194	109	89	28	77-3	114	.257
2002— Baltimore (A.L.)	5	14	.263	4.59	1.39	22	22	1	0	0	0-0	131.1	141	68	67	19	41-2	97	.276
— Bowie (East.)	1	0	1.000	0.00	1.00	1	1	0	0	0	0-...	5.0	4	0	0	0	1-0	6	.211
2003— Baltimore (A.L.)	10	10	.500	4.18	1.56	32	32	0	0	0	0-0	189.2	216	100	88	22	80-8	118	.283
2004— Detroit (A.L.)	8	15	.348	5.13	1.43	33	33	2	1	0	0-0	196.2	222	121	112	22	60-3	125	.284
2005— Detroit (A.L.)	8	13	.381	4.54	1.34	33	33	1	0	0	0-0	210.0	233	117	106	24	49-4	93	.285
American League totals (8 years)	52	86	.377	4.88	1.47	212	199	6	1	2	0-0	1206.2	1319	722	654	160	450-22	733	.278
National League totals (1 year)	0	0		6.00	1.83	3	0	0	0	0	0-0	6.0	10	4	4	2	1-0	3	.400
Major League totals (9 years)	52	86	.377	4.88	1.47	215	199	6	1	2	0-0	1212.2	1329	726	658	162	451-22	736	.278

JOHNSON, JOSH — P

PERSONAL: Born January 31, 1984, in Minneapolis. ... 6-7/240. ... Throws right, bats left. ... Full name: Joshua Michael Johnson.
TRANSACTIONS/CAREER NOTES: Selected by Florida Marlins organization in fourth round of 2002 free-agent draft.
CAREER HITTING: 1-for-4 (.250), 1 R, 0 2B, 0 3B, 0 HR, 0 RBI.

SCOUTING REPORT *Throws:* His fastball tops out at 96 mph, and he has a slider and changeup, which project as average pitches. *Tendencies:* He is an intimidating presence who throws easy heat. Fastball has late life. Has the ability to tweak his mechanics as circumstances dictate, which is unusual for a tall pitcher. Has superb mound presence and poise but is aggressive enough to throw inside to any hitter. *Outlook:* The Marlins see him as eventually being a No. 2 starter, but he'll likely spend next season in the minors gaining experience. *Grade 6.8*

LEFTY-RIGHTY SPLITS

vs.	Avg.	AB	H	2B	3B	HR	RBI	BB	SO	OBP	Slg.
L	.407	27	11	1	0	0	1	7	6	.529	.444
R	.000	16	0	0	0	0	0	3	4	.200	.000

Year Team (League)	W	L	Pct.	ERA	WHIP	G	GS	CG	ShO	Hld.	Sv.-Opp.	IP	H	R	ER	HR	BB-IBB	SO	Avg.
2002— GC Marlins (GCL)	2	0	1.000	0.60	0.73	4	3	0	0	...	0-...	15.0	8	3	1	0	3-0	11	.154
—Jamestown (N.Y.-Penn.)	0	2	.000	12.38	2.75	2	2	0	0	...	0-...	8.0	15	15	11	0	7-0	5	.385
2003— Greensboro (S. Atl.)	4	7	.364	3.61	1.19	17	17	0	0	...	0-...	82.1	69	44	33	5	29-0	59	.223
2004— Jupiter (Fla. St.)	5	12	.294	3.38	1.50	23	22	1	0	...	0-...	114.1	124	63	43	4	47-1	103	.285
2005— Carolina (Sou.)	12	4	.750	3.87	1.35	26	26	1	0	0	0-0	139.2	139	67	60	4	50-4	113	.261
—Florida (N.L.)	0	0	...	3.65	1.70	4	1	0	0	0	0-0	12.1	11	5	5	0	10-0	10	.256
Major League totals (1 year)	0	0	...	3.65	1.70	4	1	0	0	0	0-0	12.1	11	5	5	0	10-0	10	.256

JOHNSON, KELLY — OF

PERSONAL: Born February 22, 1982, in Austin, Texas. ... 6-1/205. ... Bats left, throws right. ... Full name: Kelly Andrew Johnson.
TRANSACTIONS/CAREER NOTES: Selected by Atlanta Braves organization in supplemental round ("sandwich" pick between first and second rounds, 38th pick overall) of 2000 free-agent draft; Braves received pick as compensation for Milwaukee Brewers signing Type A free-agent IF Jose Hernandez.
2005 GAMES PLAYED BY POSITION (MLB): OF—79, DH—1.

SCOUTING REPORT Johnson, a converted infielder with a short stroke, has a tendency to push the bat at times but has good bat speed and occasional power. Has some holes up in the zone and is a streaky hitter. Is still adjusting to playing the outfield and is not consistent with his jumps or routes. Is better coming in than going back. Needs to keep stretching out his arm and convert his mechanics. *Grade 5.7*

KELLY JOHNSON'S HITTING ZONE

.250	.214	.091
.256	.442	.239
.000	.353	.269

LEFTY-RIGHTY SPLITS

vs.	Avg.	AB	H	2B	3B	HR	RBI	BB	SO	OBP	Slg.
L	.257	74	19	3	1	2	12	8	23	.325	.405
R	.236	216	51	9	2	7	28	32	52	.337	.394

Year Team (League)	Pos.	G	AB	R	H	2B	3B	HR	RBI	BB	SO	HBP	GDP	SB-CS	Avg.	OBP	SLG	OPS	E	Avg.
								BATTING											FIELDING	
2000— GC Braves (GCL)	SS	53	193	27	52	12	3	4	29	24	45	0	4	6-1	.269	.349	.425	.774	17	.896
2001— Macon (S. Atl.)	SS	124	415	75	120	22	1	23	66	71	111	10	0	25-6	.289	.404	.513	.917	45	.905
2002— Myrtle Beach (Carol.)	SS-3B	126	482	62	123	21	5	12	49	51	105	1	5	12-15	.255	.325	.394	.719	24	.953
2003— Greenville (Sou.)	OF-3B-2B	98	334	46	92	22	5	6	45	35	81	0	4	10-3	.275	.340	.425	.765	16	.959
—GC Braves (GCL)	SS	6	26	10	10	1	1	1	3	3	4	1	2	1-1	.385	.467	.615	1.082	0	1.000
2004— Greenville (Sou.)	OF-3B-SS	135	479	70	135	35	3	16	50	49	102	3	5	9-9	.282	.350	.468	.818	11	.686
2005— Richmond (Int'l)	OF-3B-SS	44	155	35	48	12	3	8	22	34	22	2	3	7-1	.310	.438	.581	1.018	5	.974
—Atlanta (N.L.)	OF-DH	87	290	46	70	12	3	9	40	40	75	1	11	2-1	.241	.334	.397	.731	0	1.000
Major League totals (1 year)		87	290	46	70	12	3	9	40	40	75	1	11	2-1	.241	.334	.397	.731	0	1.000

DIVISION SERIES RECORD

Year Team (League)	Pos.	G	AB	R	H	2B	3B	HR	RBI	BB	SO	HBP	GDP	SB-CS	Avg.	OBP	SLG	OPS	E	Avg.
2005— Atlanta (N.L.)		4	2	0	0	0	0	0	0	1	0	0	0	0-0	.000	.333	.000	.333	0	...

JOHNSON, NICK — 1B

PERSONAL: Born September 19, 1978, in Sacramento. ... 6-3/224. ... Bats left, throws left. ... Full name: Nicholas Robert Johnson. ... High school: McClatchy (Sacramento). ... Nephew of Larry Bowa, shortstop with three major league teams (1970-85) and manager of San Diego Padres (1987-88) and Philadelphia Phillies (2001-04).
TRANSACTIONS/CAREER NOTES: Selected by New York Yankees organization in third round of 1996 free-agent draft. ... On disabled list (March 25, 2000-entire season). ... On disabled list (August 8-September 3, 2002); included rehabilitation assignment to Columbus. ... On disabled list (May 16-July 25, 2003); included rehabilitation assignment to Columbus. ... Traded by Yankees with OF Juan Rivera and P Randy Choate to Montreal Expos for P Javier Vazquez (December 16, 2003). ... On disabled list (March 31-May 28 and August 21, 2004-remainder of season); included rehabilitation assignments to Brevard County and Edmonton. ... Expos franchise transferred to Washington, D.C., and renamed Washington Nationals for 2005 season (December 3, 2004). ... On disabled list (July 4-26, 2005); included rehabilitation assignment to New Orleans.
2005 GAMES PLAYED BY POSITION (MLB): 1B—129.

SCOUTING REPORT *Offense:* Johnson has a long, fluid stroke and has made an adjustment in his stance that allows him to better handle the ball inside. Has good bat speed and is a better low-ball hitter but can catch up to the high fastball. Has good power and is driving the ball more frequently. Has become more aggressive early in the count. *Defense:* He has a fluid actions and good hands but doesn't have a real quick first step or range to either side. Shifts well on the bag to pick bad throws off the ground. Has a very strong, accurate arm to start the double play. *Outlook:* He is going to be a good run producer with plus power if he can stay healthy. Holes at the plate are starting to shrink. *Grade 8*

NICK JOHNSON'S HITTING ZONE

.323	.208	.107
.347	.440	.330
.250	.421	.206

LEFTY-RIGHTY SPLITS

vs.	Avg.	AB	H	2B	3B	HR	RBI	BB	SO	OBP	Slg.
L	.328	125	41	7	1	3	20	21	24	.444	.472
R	.274	328	90	28	2	12	54	59	63	.394	.482

Year	Team (League)	Pos.	G	AB	R	H	2B	3B	HR	RBI	BB	SO	HBP	GDP	SB-CS	Avg.	OBP	SLG	OPS	E	Avg.
													BATTING							FIELDING	
1996— GC Yankees (GCL)		1B	47	157	31	45	11	1	2	33	30	35	9	5	0-0	.287	.422	.408	.830	3	.991
1997— Greensboro (S. Atl.)		1B	127	433	77	118	23	1	16	75	76	99	18	5	16-3	.273	.398	.441	.839	16	.987
1998— Tampa (Fla. St.)		1B	92	303	69	96	14	1	17	58	68	76	19	5	1-4	.317	.466	.538	1.004	12	.986
1999— Norwich (East.)		1B	132	420	114	145	33	5	14	87	123	88	37	9	8-6	.345	.525	.548	1.073	20	.983
2000— New York (A.L.)			Did not play.																		
2001— Columbus (Int'l)		1B	110	359	68	92	20	0	18	49	81	105	14	6	9-2	.256	.407	.462	.870	10	.989
— New York (A.L.)		1B-DH	23	67	6	13	2	0	2	8	7	15	4	3	0-0	.194	.308	.313	.621	0	1.000
2002— Columbus (Int'l)		1B-DH-OF	129	378	56	92	15	0	15	58	48	98	12	11	1-3	.243	.347	.402	.749	7	.988
— Columbus (Int'l)		1B	3	11	1	1	0	0	0	0	1	4	0	*1	0-0	.091	.167	.091	.258	0	1.000
2003— Columbus (Int'l)		1B-DH	3	10	1	5	2	0	1	3	2	2	0	0	0-0	.500	.583	1.000	1.583	1	.952
— Trenton (East.)		1B	4	12	3	5	1	0	0	1	5	1	1	0	0-0	.417	.611	.500	1.111	0	1.000
— New York (A.L.)		1B-DH	96	324	60	92	19	0	14	47	70	57	8	9	5-2	.284	.422	.472	.894	5	.991
2004— Brevard County (Fla. St.)		1B	6	21	3	4	0	0	1	5	4	6	0	1	0-0	.190	.320	.333	.653	0	1.000
— Edmonton (PCL)		1B	3	9	2	2	1	0	0	0	4	3	0	1	0-0	.222	.462	.333	.795	0	1.000
— Montreal (N.L.)		1B	73	251	35	63	16	0	7	33	40	58	3	5	6-3	.251	.359	.398	.758	4	.994
2005— New Orleans (PCL)		1B	3	6	0	0	0	0	0	0	1	2	0	0	0-0	.000	.143	.000	.143	0	1.000
— Washington (N.L.)		1B	131	453	66	131	35	3	15	74	80	87	12	15	3-8	.289	.408	.479	.887	5	.996
American League totals (3 years)			248	769	122	197	36	0	31	113	125	170	24	23	6-5	.256	.376	.424	.800	12	.990
National League totals (2 years)			204	704	101	194	51	3	22	107	120	145	15	20	9-11	.276	.391	.450	.841	9	.995
Major League totals (5 years)			452	1473	223	391	87	3	53	220	245	315	39	43	15-16	.265	.383	.437	.820	21	.993

DIVISION SERIES RECORD

Year	Team (League)	Pos.	G	AB	R	H	2B	3B	HR	RBI	BB	SO	HBP	GDP	SB-CS	Avg.	OBP	SLG	OPS	E	Avg.
2002— New York (A.L.)		DH-1B	3	11	1	2	0	0	0	1	1	5	0	0	0-0	.182	.250	.182	.432	0	1.000
2003— New York (A.L.)		1B	4	13	2	1	1	0	0	2	3	2	1	0	0-0	.077	.294	.154	.448	0	1.000
Division series totals (2 years)			7	24	3	3	1	0	0	3	4	7	1	0	0-0	.125	.276	.167	.443	0	1.000

CHAMPIONSHIP SERIES RECORD

Year	Team (League)	Pos.	G	AB	R	H	2B	3B	HR	RBI	BB	SO	HBP	GDP	SB-CS	Avg.	OBP	SLG	OPS	E	Avg.
2003— New York (A.L.)		1B	7	26	4	6	1	0	1	3	2	4	0	1	0-0	.231	.286	.385	.670	0	1.000

WORLD SERIES RECORD

Year	Team (League)	Pos.	G	AB	R	H	2B	3B	HR	RBI	BB	SO	HBP	GDP	SB-CS	Avg.	OBP	SLG	OPS	E	Avg.
2003— New York (A.L.)		1B	6	17	3	5	1	0	0	0	2	3	0	1	0-0	.294	.368	.353	.721	0	1.000

JOHNSON, RANDY P

PERSONAL: Born September 10, 1963, in Walnut Creek, Calif. ... 6-10/231. ... Throws left, bats right. ... Full name: Randall David Johnson. ... High school: Livermore (Calif.). ... College: Southern California.

TRANSACTIONS/CAREER NOTES: Selected by Atlanta Braves organization in third round of June 1982 free-agent draft; did not sign. ... Selected by Montreal Expos organization in second round of June 1985 free-agent draft. ... Traded by Expos with Ps Brian Holman and Gene Harris to Seattle Mariners for P Mark Langston and a player to be named (May 25, 1989); Expos acquired P Mike Campbell to complete deal (July 31, 1989). ... On disabled list (June 11-27, 1992). ... On disabled list (May 15-August 6 and August 27, 1996-remainder of season); included rehabilitation assignment to Everett. ... On suspended list (April 24-27, 1998). ... Traded by Mariners to Houston Astros for SS Carlos Guillen, P Freddy Garcia and a player to be named (July 31, 1998); Mariners acquired P John Halama to complete deal (October 1, 1998). ... Signed as a free agent by Arizona Diamondbacks (December 10, 1998). ... On disabled list (April 12-27 and April 28-July 20, 2003); included rehabilitation assignment to Lancaster. ... Traded by Diamondbacks to New York Yankees for Ps Javier Vazquez and Brad Halsey, C Dioner Navarro and cash (January 11, 2005).

HONORS: Named A.L. Pitcher of the Year by THE SPORTING NEWS (1995). ... Named A.L. Cy Young Award winner by Baseball Writers' Association of America (1995). ... Named N.L. Cy Young Award winner by Baseball Writers' Association of America (1999, 2000, 2001 and 2002).

CAREER HITTING: 67-for-528 (.127), 17 R, 13 2B, 0 3B, 1 HR, 35 RBI.

SCOUTING REPORT

Throws: He throws a four-seam fastball that can hit 97 mph, a two-seam fastball in the low 90s, a slider around 90 and a split-finger fastball—which he uses as a changeup—at 88. **Tendencies:** Johnson is one of the premier power pitchers of all time. Still uses his fastball, which has late life because of his height, as his out pitch. Throws from a low release point without much effort and can overpower hitters high in the zone. Has to stay on top of his slider; when he does, it is difficult to hit. **Outlook:** The Big Unit didn't pitch up to expectations and he didn't appear healthy at times in 2005. Still is an intimidating frontline starter, though, and should improve in 2006. *Grade 9*

RANDY JOHNSON'S PITCHING ZONE

.367	.304	.255
.263	.390	.224
.299	.313	.132

LEFTY-RIGHTY SPLITS

vs.	Avg.	AB	H	2B	3B	HR	RBI	BB	SO	OBP	Slg.
L	.185	162	30	6	1	1	11	7	45	.244	.253
R	.257	689	177	32	2	31	82	40	166	.302	.444

Year	Team (League)	W	L	Pct.	ERA	WHIP	G	GS	CG	ShO	Hld.	Sv.-Opp.	IP	H	R	ER	HR	BB-IBB	SO	Avg.
1985— Jamestown (N.Y.-Penn.)		0	3	.000	5.93	1.94	8	8	0	0	...	0-...	27.1	29	22	18	2	24-0	21	.287
1986— W.P. Beach (Fla. St.)		8	7	.533	3.16	1.53	26	26	2	1	...	0-...	119.2	89	49	42	3	94-0	133	.211
1987— Jacksonville (Sou.)		11	8	.579	3.73	1.63	25	24	0	0	...	0-...	140.0	100	63	58	10	128-0	163	.204
1988— Indianapolis (A.A.)		8	7	.533	3.26	1.39	20	19	0	0	...	0-...	113.1	85	52	41	6	72-0	111	.209
— Montreal (N.L.)		3	0	1.000	2.42	1.15	4	4	1	0	0	0-0	26.0	23	8	7	3	7-0	25	.225
1989— Montreal (N.L.)		0	4	.000	6.67	1.85	7	6	0	0	0	0-0	29.2	29	25	22	2	26-1	26	.264
— Indianapolis (A.A.)		1	1	.500	2.00	1.22	3	3	0	0	0	0-0	18.0	13	5	4	0	9-0	17	.194
— Seattle (A.L.)		7	9	.438	4.40	1.44	22	22	2	0	0	0-0	131.0	118	75	64	11	70-1	104	.244
1990— Seattle (A.L.)		14	11	.560	3.65	1.34	33	33	5	2	0	0-0	219.2	174	103	89	26	*120-2	194	.216
1991— Seattle (A.L.)		13	10	.565	3.98	1.50	33	33	2	1	0	0-0	201.1	151	96	89	15	*152-0	228	.213
1992— Seattle (A.L.)		12	14	.462	3.77	1.42	31	31	6	2	0	0-0	210.1	154	104	88	13	*144-1	*241	.206
1993— Seattle (A.L.)		19	8	.704	3.24	1.11	35	34	10	*3		1-1	255.1	185	97	92	22	99-1	*308	.203
1994— Seattle (A.L.)		13	6	.684	3.19	1.19	23	23	*9	*4	0	0-0	172.0	132	65	61	14	72-2	*204	.216
1995— Seattle (A.L.)		18	2	*.900	*2.48	1.05	30	30	6	3	0	0-0	214.1	159	65	59	12	65-1	*294	.201
1996— Seattle (A.L.)		5	0	1.000	3.67	1.19	14	8	0	0		1-2	61.1	48	27	25	8	25-0	85	.211
— Everett (N'west)		0	0		0.00	0.00	1	1	0	0		0-...	2.0	0	0	0	0	0-0	5	.000
1997— Seattle (A.L.)		20	4	*.833	2.28	1.05	30	29	5	2	0	0-0	213.0	147	60	54	20	77-2	291	*.194
1998— Seattle (A.L.)		9	10	.474	4.33	1.29	23	23	6	2	0	0-0	160.0	146	90	77	19	60-0	213	.240
— Houston (N.L.)		10	1	.909	1.28	0.98	11	11	4	2	0	0-0	84.1	57	12	12	4	26-1	116	.191

Year Team (League)	W	L	Pct.	ERA	WHIP	G	GS	CG	ShO	Hld.	Sv.-Opp.	IP	H	R	ER	HR	BB-IBB	SO	Avg.
1999— Arizona (N.L.)	17	9	.654	* 2.48	1.02	35	• 35	* 12	2	0	0-0	* 271.2	207	86	75	30	70-3	* 364	.208
2000— Arizona (N.L.)	19	7	* .731	2.64	1.12	35	• 35	• 8	• 3	0	0-0	248.2	202	89	73	23	76-1	* 347	.224
2001— Arizona (N.L.)	21	6	.778	2.49	1.01	35	34	3	2	0	0-0	249.2	181	74	69	19	71-2	* 372	.203
2002— Arizona (N.L.)	* 24	5	* .828	* 2.32	1.03	35	35	* 8	4	0	0-0	* 260.0	197	78	67	26	71-1	* 334	* .208
2003— Tucson (PCL)	0	0	...	0.00	0.00	1	1	0	0	...	0-...	4.0	0	0	0	0	0-0	4	.000
— El Paso (Texas)	0	0	...	0.00	1.00	1	1	0	0	...	0-...	4.0	3	2	0	0	1-0	5	.231
— Lancaster (Calif.)	0	1	.000	6.00	1.80	1	1	0	0	...	0-...	6.0	11	5	4	1	0-0	6	.367
— Arizona (N.L.)	6	8	.429	4.26	1.33	18	18	1	1	0	0-0	114.0	125	61	54	16	27-3	125	.280
2004— Arizona (N.L.)	16	14	.533	2.60	0.90	• 35	35	4	2	0	0-0	245.2	177	88	71	18	44-1	* 290	* .197
2005— New York (A.L.)	17	8	.680	3.79	1.13	34	34	4	0	0	0-0	225.2	207	102	95	32	47-2	211	.243
American League totals (11 years)	147	82	.642	3.46	1.24	308	300	55	19	0	2-3	2064.0	1621	884	793	192	931-12	2373	.216
National League totals (9 years)	116	54	.682	2.65	1.06	215	213	41	18	0	0-0	1529.2	1198	521	450	141	418-13	1999	.215
Major League totals (18 years)	263	136	.659	3.11	1.16	523	513	96	37	0	2-3	3593.2	2819	1405	1243	333	1349-25	4372	.215

DIVISION SERIES RECORD

Year Team (League)	W	L	Pct.	ERA	WHIP	G	GS	CG	ShO	Hld.	Sv.-Opp.	IP	H	R	ER	HR	BB-IBB	SO	Avg.
1995— Seattle (A.L.)	2	0	1.000	2.70	1.10	2	1	0	0	0	0-0	10.0	5	3	3	1	6-1	16	.156
1997— Seattle (A.L.)	0	2	.000	5.54	1.54	2	2	1	0	0	0-0	13.0	14	8	8	3	6-0	16	.286
1998— Houston (N.L.)	0	2	.000	1.93	1.00	2	2	0	0	0	0-0	14.0	12	4	3	2	2-0	17	.226
1999— Arizona (N.L.)	0	1	.000	7.56	1.32	1	1	0	0	0	0-0	8.1	8	7	7	2	3-0	11	.250
2001— Arizona (N.L.)	0	1	.000	3.38	1.00	1	1	0	0	0	0-0	8.0	6	3	3	1	2-0	9	.222
2002— Arizona (N.L.)	0	1	.000	7.50	2.00	1	1	0	0	0	0-0	6.0	10	6	5	2	2-1	4	.370
2005— New York (A.L.)	0	0	...	6.14	1.77	2	1	0	0	0	0-0	7.1	12	5	5	2	1-0	4	.375
Division series totals (7 years)	2	7	.222	4.59	1.34	11	9	1	0	0	0-0	66.2	67	36	34	13	22-2	77	.266

CHAMPIONSHIP SERIES RECORD

Year Team (League)	W	L	Pct.	ERA	WHIP	G	GS	CG	ShO	Hld.	Sv.-Opp.	IP	H	R	ER	HR	BB-IBB	SO	Avg.
1995— Seattle (A.L.)	0	1	.000	2.35	0.91	2	2	0	0	0	0-0	15.1	12	6	4	1	2-0	13	.211
2001— Arizona (N.L.)	2	0	1.000	1.13	0.81	2	2	1	1	0	0-0	16.0	10	2	2	1	3-0	19	.169
Champ. series totals (2 years)	2	1	.667	1.72	0.86	4	4	1	1	0	0-0	31.1	22	8	6	2	5-0	32	.190

WORLD SERIES RECORD

Year Team (League)	W	L	Pct.	ERA	WHIP	G	GS	CG	ShO	Hld.	Sv.-Opp.	IP	H	R	ER	HR	BB-IBB	SO	Avg.
2001— Arizona (N.L.)	3	0	1.000	1.04	0.69	3	2	1	1	0	0-0	17.1	9	2	2	0	3-0	19	.150

ALL-STAR GAME RECORD

	W	L	Pct.	ERA	WHIP	G	GS	CG	ShO	Hld.	Sv.-Opp.	IP	H	R	ER	HR	BB-IBB	SO	Avg.
All-Star Game totals (8 years)	0	0	...	0.75	0.75	8	4	0	0	0			12.0	7	1	1	1	2-0	12	.171

JOHNSON, REED OF

PERSONAL: Born December 8, 1976, in Riverside, Calif. ... 5-10/180. ... Bats right, throws right. ... Full name: Reed Cameron Johnson. ... High school: Temecula Valley (Temecula, Calif.). ... College: Cal State Fullerton.
TRANSACTIONS/CAREER NOTES: Selected by Toronto Blue Jays organization in 17th round of 1999 free-agent draft.
RECORDS: Shares major league record for most times hit by pitch, game (3, April 16, 2005).
2005 GAMES PLAYED BY POSITION (MLB): OF—139.

SCOUTING REPORT Offense: He's short on natural ability but long on desire. Hits with a slight hand hitch and his swing is short. Is a high-ball hitter who likes the ball on the inner half. Has occasional power but is more of a line-drive gap hitter. Is not too disciplined. Can run but is not a basestealer. *Defense:* Johnson is capable of playing all three outfield positions. Arm strength is an asset, and he also has accuracy and a quick release. Gets good lateral jumps. Instincts have improved. Is learning to play under control more. *Outlook:* Ideally, Johnson would be a fourth outfielder. Can lead off and be a catalyst with his aggressive makeup. *Grade 6*

REED JOHNSON'S HITTING ZONE

.273	.250	.313
.345	.273	.294
.250	.348	.364

LEFTY-RIGHTY SPLITS

vs.	Avg.	AB	H	2B	3B	HR	RBI	BB	SO	OBP	Slg.
L	.279	165	46	10	2	3	22	7	31	.335	.418
R	.262	233	61	11	4	5	36	15	51	.329	.408

Year Team (League)	Pos.	G	AB	R	H	2B	3B	HR	RBI	BB	SO	HBP	GDP	SB-CS	Avg.	OBP	SLG	OPS	E	Avg.
1999— St. Catharines (NYP)	OF	60	191	24	46	8	2	2	23	24	31	2	4	5-5	.241	.326	.335	.661	3	.976
2000— Hagerstown (S. Atl.)	OF	95	324	66	94	24	5	8	70	62	49	14	9	14-2	.290	.422	.469	.891	1	.995
— Dunedin (Fla. St.)	OF	36	133	26	42	9	2	4	28	14	27	11	1	3-2	.316	.416	.504	.920	2	.975
2001— Tennessee (Sou.)	OF	136	554	104	174	29	4	13	74	45	79	18	11	42-12	.314	.383	.451	.834	4	.983
2002— Dunedin (Fla. St.)	OF	8	33	7	9	3	0	0	6	3	3	2	0	0-1	.273	.368	.364	.732	0	1.000
— Syracuse (Int'l)	OF	44	159	27	37	8	3	2	10	12	23	8	1	1-4	.233	.317	.358	.675	1	.991
2003— Syracuse (Int'l)	OF	26	101	14	33	4	1	2	16	3	13	5	2	3-1	.327	.369	.446	.815	0	1.000
— Toronto (A.L.)	OF-DH	114	412	79	121	21	2	10	52	20	67	20	10	5-3	.294	.353	.427	.780	4	.977
2004— Toronto (A.L.)	OF-DH	141	537	68	145	25	2	10	61	28	98	12	17	6-3	.270	.320	.380	.699	5	.989
2005— Toronto (A.L.)	OF	142	398	55	107	21	6	8	58	22	82	16	8	5-6	.269	.332	.412	.744	2	.990
Major League totals (3 years)		397	1347	202	373	67	10	28	171	70	247	48	35	16-12	.277	.334	.404	.737	9	.986

JOHNSON, RUSS IF

PERSONAL: Born February 22, 1973, in Baton Rouge, La. ... 5-10/198. ... Bats right, throws right. ... Full name: William Russell Johnson. ... High school: Denham Springs (La.). ... College: Louisiana State.
TRANSACTIONS/CAREER NOTES: Selected by Houston Astros organization in supplemental round ("sandwich pick" between first and second rounds, 30th pick overall) of 1994 free-agent draft; pick received as part of compensation for San Francisco Giants signing Type A free-agent P Mark Portugal. ... Traded by Astros to Tampa Bay Devil Rays for P Marc Valdes (May 27, 2000). ... On disabled list (May 16-31, 2001); included rehabilitation assignment to Orlando. ... On disabled list (March 28-April 15 and August 1-September 7, 2002); included rehabilitation assignments to Orlando and Durham. ... Traded by Devil Rays with 1B Josh Pressley to New York Mets (December 16, 2002), completing deal in which Rays acquired SS Rey Ordonez for two players to

LEFTY-RIGHTY SPLITS

vs.	Avg.	AB	H	2B	3B	HR	RBI	BB	SO	OBP	Slg.
L	.182	11	2	1	0	0	0	0	2	.250	.273
R	.286	7	2	1	0	0	0	1	2	.375	.429

be named (December 15, 2002). ... Released by Mets (November 13, 2003). ... Signed by Chicago Cubs organization (Feburary 19, 2004). ... Signed as a free agent by New York Yankees organization (November 15, 2004).

2005 GAMES PLAYED BY POSITION (MLB): 3B—8, 1B—7, DH—3, OF—3, 2B—1.

Year Team (League)	Pos.	G	AB	R	H	2B	3B	HR	RBI	BB	SO	HBP	GDP	SB-CS	Avg.	OBP	SLG	OPS	E	Avg.
																		BATTING → **FIELDING**		
1995— Jackson (Texas)	SS	132	475	65	118	16	2	9	53	50	60	8	11	10-5	.248	.327	.347	.674	13	.978
1996— Jackson (Texas)	SS	132	496	86	154	24	5	15	74	56	50	3	16	9-4	.310	.382	.470	.852	34	.949
1997— New Orleans (A.A.)	3B-SS-DH	122	445	72	123	16	6	4	49	66	78	1	10	7-4	.276	.370	.366	.736	21	.944
— Houston (N.L.)	3B-2B	21	60	7	18	1	0	2	9	6	14	0	...	1-1	.300	.364	.417	.780	1	.974
1998— New Orleans (PCL)	3B-2B-SS-DH	122	453	95	140	28	2	7	52	90	64	5	10	11-11	.309	.424	.426	.850	11	.966
— Houston (N.L.)	2B	8	13	2	3	1	0	0	0	1	5	1	...	1-0	.231	.333	.308	.641	0	1.000
1999— New Orleans (PCL)	2B-SS-OF	22	77	17	27	6	0	1	12	16	13	1	2	1-3	.351	.468	.468	.936	3	.968
— Houston (N.L.)	3B-2B-SS	83	156	24	44	10	0	5	23	20	31	0	...	2-3	.282	.358	.442	.800	7	.945
2000— Houston (N.L.)	SS-3B-2B	26	45	4	8	0	0	3	2	2	10	0	...	1-1	.178	.213	.178	.391	1	.962
— Tampa Bay (A.L.)	3B-2B-SS	74	185	28	47	8	0	2	17	25	30	1	...	4-1	.254	.344	.330	.674	5	.974
2001— Tampa Bay (A.L.)	3B-2B-SS-DH	85	248	32	73	19	2	4	33	34	57	1	...	2-2	.294	.380	.435	.816	7	.969
— Orlando (South.)	2B	1	3	0	2	0	0	0	0	1	0	0	1	0-0	.667	.750	.667	1.417	2	.818
2002— Orlando (South.)	3B-2B-OF	12	43	10	12	5	0	0	3	8	7	0	4	1-0	.279	.392	.395	.787	3	.885
— Durham (Int'l)	3B	10	33	9	9	0	1	2	5	4	5	0	...	1-0	.273	.351	.515	.866	3	.903
— Tampa Bay (A.L.)	3B-DH-SS-2B	45	111	15	24	5	0	1	12	16	22	1	...	5-2	.216	.320	.288	.609	1	.984
2003— Norfolk (Int'l)	3B-SS-1B-2B	100	349	37	99	16	0	3	39	44	45	3	8	6-5	.284	.362	.355	.717	12	.956
2004— Iowa (PCL)	2B-1B-3B P-OF-SS	129	415	71	122	38	2	14	78	70	63	2	8	7-3	.294	.396	.496	.892	13	.981
2005— New York (A.L.)	3B-1B-OF DH-2B	22	18	5	4	2	0	0	0	1	4	0	...	0-0	.222	.300	.333	.633	0	1.000
— Columbus (Int'l)	3B-OF-1B 2B-DH	73	281	43	82	26	0	9	40	39	50	1	8	5-5	.292	.377	.480	.857	3	.988
American League totals (4 years)		226	562	80	148	34	2	7	62	76	113	4	0	11-5	.263	.354	.368	.722	13	.975
National League totals (4 years)		138	274	37	73	12	0	7	35	29	60	1	...	5-5	.266	.336	.387	.722	9	.956
Major League totals (7 years)		364	836	117	221	46	2	14	97	105	173	5	0	16-10	.264	.348	.374	.722	22	.969

DIVISION SERIES RECORD

Year Team (League)	Pos.	G	AB	R	H	2B	3B	HR	RBI	BB	SO	HBP	GDP	SB-CS	Avg.	OBP	SLG	OPS	E	Avg.
1997— Houston (N.L.)		1	1	0	0	0	0	0	0	1	0	1	0	0-0	.000	.000	.000	.000	...	...
1999— Houston (N.L.)		2	1	0	1	1	0	0	0	0	0	0	0	0-0	1.000	1.000	2.000	3.000	...	...
Division series totals (2 years)		3	2	0	1	1	0	0	0	1	0	1	0	0-0	.500	.667	1.000	1.667		

JOHNSON, TYLER — P

PERSONAL: Born June 7, 1981, in Columbia, Mo. ... 6-2/180. ... Throws left, bats both. ... Full name: Tyler James Johnson. ... High school: Newbury Park (Calif.). ... Junior college: Moorpark (Calif.).

TRANSACTIONS/CAREER NOTES: Selected by St. Louis Cardinals organization in 34th round of 2000 free-agent draft. ... Selected by Oakland Athletics from Cardinals organization in Rule 5 major league draft (December 13, 2004). ... Returned to Cardinals (February 22, 2005).

CAREER HITTING: 0-for-0 (.000), 0 R, 0 2B, 0 3B, 0 RBI.

LEFTY-RIGHTY SPLITS

vs.	Avg.	AB	H	2B	3B	HR	RBI	BB	SO	OBP	Slg.
L	.400	5	2	0	0	0	0	2	2	.571	.400
R	.200	5	1	0	0	0	1	1	2	.333	.200

Year Team (League)	W	L	Pct.	ERA	WHIP	G	GS	CG	ShO	Hld.	Sv.-Opp.	IP	H	R	ER	HR	BB-IBB	SO	Avg.
2001— Johnson City (Appal.)	1	1	.500	2.66	1.16	9	9	0	0	...	0-...	40.2	26	17	12	1	21-0	58	...
— Peoria (Midw.)	0	3	.000	3.95	1.76	3	3	0	0	...	0-...	13.2	14	9	6	1	10-0	15	...
2002— Peoria (Midw.)	15	3	.833	2.00	1.14	22	18	0	0	...	0-...	121.1	96	35	27	7	42-1	132	...
2003— Palm Beach (PCL)	5	5	.500	3.08	1.48	22	10	0	0	...	0-...	79.0	79	29	27	2	38-2	81	...
— Tennessee (Sou.)	1	0	1.000	1.65	1.13	20	0	0	0	...	0-...	27.1	16	7	5	1	15-1	39	...
2004— Tennessee (Sou.)	2	2	.500	4.79	1.51	53	0	0	0	...	4-...	56.1	48	32	30	4	37-1	77	...
2005— Memphis (PCL)	2	1	.667	4.27	1.31	57	0	0	0	13	7-9	59.0	51	31	28	6	26-2	77	.232
— St. Louis (N.L.)	0	0	...	0.00	2.25	5	0	0	0	1	0-1	2.2	3	0	0	0	3-0	4	.300
Major League totals (1 year)	0	0	...	0.00	2.25	5	0	0	0	1	0-1	2.2	3	0	0	0	3-0	4	.300

JOHNSTON, MIKE — P

PERSONAL: Born March 30, 1979, in Philadelphia. ... 6-2/215. ... Throws left, bats left. ... Full name: Michael Charles Johnston. ... Junior college: Garrett Community College (McHenry, Md.).

TRANSACTIONS/CAREER NOTES: Selected by Pittsburgh Pirates organization in 20th round of 1998 free-agent draft. ... On disabled list (June 22-August 2, 2004); included rehabilitation assignments to GCL Pirates and Nashville.

CAREER HITTING: 0-for-0 (.000), 0 R, 0 2B, 0 3B, 0 HR, 0 RBI.

LEFTY-RIGHTY SPLITS

vs.	Avg.	AB	H	2B	3B	HR	RBI	BB	SO	OBP	Slg.
L	.500	2	1	0	1	0	2	0	1	.500	2.000
R	.600	5	3	0	0	1	2	0	1	.600	1.200

Year Team (League)	W	L	Pct.	ERA	WHIP	G	GS	CG	ShO	Hld.	Sv.-Opp.	IP	H	R	ER	HR	BB-IBB	SO	Avg.
1998— GC Pirates (GCL)	1	2	.333	3.34	1.28	13	3	0	0	...	0-...	29.2	28	17	11	1	10-0	17	.248
— Erie (N.Y.-Penn)	0	0	...	4.50	2.50	2	0	0	0	...	0-...	2.0	4	4	1	0	1-0	2	.364
1999— Williamsport (NYP)	3	2	.600	4.25	1.51	14	2	0	0	...	2-...	42.1	46	26	20	5	18-0	30	.267
2000— Hickory (S. Atl.)	4	2	.667	6.22	1.89	26	0	0	0	...	2-...	50.2	66	42	35	2	30-0	52	.320
2001— Hickory (S. Atl.)	4	5	.444	3.38	1.39	16	16	0	0	...	0-...	93.1	88	47	35	5	42-1	80	.249
— Lynchburg (Caro.)	4	4	.500	3.34	1.45	11	10	0	0	...	0-...	62.0	66	27	23	2	24-0	44	.272
2002— Lynchburg (Caro.)	4	2	.667	3.63	1.33	15	10	0	0	...	0-...	57.0	50	29	23	2	26-0	50	.230
2003— Altoona (East.)	4	2	.750	2.12	1.05	46	0	0	0	...	7-...	72.1	49	17	17	4	27-3	65	.199
2004— Pittsburgh (N.L.)	0	3	.000	4.37	1.94	24	0	0	0	4	0-1	22.2	29	16	11	2	15-1	18	.315
— Nashville (PCL)	0	0	...	8.40	2.13	19	0	0	0	...	0-...	15.0	19	14	14	3	13-1	6	.306
2005— Pittsburgh (N.L.)	0	0	...	36.00	4.00	1	0	0	0	0	0-0	1.0	4	4	4	2	0-0	1	.571
— Indianapolis (Int'l)	2	1	.667	2.97	1.27	52	0	0	0	14	0-4	57.2	43	21	19	5	30-2	52	.208
Major League totals (2 years)	0	3	.000	5.70	2.03	25	0	0	0	4	0-1	23.2	33	20	15	4	15-1	20	.333

JONES, ANDRUW — OF

PERSONAL: Born April 23, 1977, in Willemstad, Curacao. ... 6-1/210. ... Bats right, throws right. ... Full name: Andruw Rudolf Jones. ... High school: St. Paulus (Willemstad, Curacao).
TRANSACTIONS/CAREER NOTES: Signed as a non-drafted free agent by Atlanta Braves organization (July 1, 1993).
HONORS: Named Major League Player of the Year by the SPORTING NEWS (2005). ... Won N.L. Gold Glove as outfielder (1998-2005).
2005 GAMES PLAYED BY POSITION (MLB): OF—159.

SCOUTING REPORT

Offense: Jones spread his stance, stayed back behind the ball better in 2005 and led the majors in home runs. Has a long stroke but is extremely quick. Is a good high-ball hitter and an excellent mistake hitter. Is vulnerable to breaking pitches in the dirt when he falls behind in the count. Has plus power to all fields. Doesn't steal bases but is an instinctive baserunner. **Defense:** Aside from Torii Hunter, Jones probably is the best pure center fielder in the game. Has a fluid, gliding stride and exceptional range in all directions. Makes defense look easy by getting excellent breaks on balls. Has a plus arm and is accurate. **Outlook:** Jones is a five-tool player who is getting better. Can dominate a game with his defense, arm, speed and power.

Grade 9.6

ANDRUW JONES' HITTING ZONE

.407	.375	.250
.320	.429	.313
.231	.182	.250

LEFTY-RIGHTY SPLITS

vs.	Avg.	AB	H	2B	3B	HR	RBI	BB	SO	OBP	Slg.
L	.256	125	32	7	0	9	23	16	22	.349	.528
R	.265	461	122	17	3	42	105	48	90	.346	.588

								BATTING										FIELDING	
Year Team (League)	Pos.	G	AB	R	H	2B	3B	HR	RBI	BB	SO	HBP	GDP	SB-CS	Avg.	OBP	SLG	OPS	E	Avg.
1994— GC Braves (GCL)	OF	27	95	22	21	5	1	2	10	16	19	2	3	5-2	.221	.345	.358	.703	3	.968
— Danville (Appal.)	OF	36	143	20	48	9	2	1	16	9	25	3	0	16-9	.336	.385	.448	.832	2	.977
1995— Macon (S. Atl.)	OF	139	537	104	149	41	5	25	100	70	122	16	9	56-11	.277	.372	.512	.884	4	.988
1996— Durham (Carol.)	OF	66	243	65	76	14	3	17	43	42	54	3	5	16-4	.313	.419	.605	1.024	7	.963
— Greenville (Sou.)	OF	38	157	39	58	10	1	12	37	17	34	1	3	12-4	.369	.432	.675	1.107	1	.993
— Richmond (Int'l)	OF	12	45	11	17	3	1	5	12	1	9	0	0	2-2	.378	.391	.822	1.214	1	.972
— Atlanta (N.L.)	OF	31	106	11	23	7	1	5	13	7	29	0	1	3-0	.217	.265	.443	.709	2	.975
1997— Atlanta (N.L.)	OF	153	399	60	92	18	1	18	70	56	107	4	11	20-11	.231	.329	.474	.745	7	.977
1998— Atlanta (N.L.)	OF	159	582	89	158	33	8	31	90	40	129	4	10	27-4	.271	.321	.515	.836	2	.995
1999— Atlanta (N.L.)	OF •	162	592	97	163	35	5	26	84	76	103	9	12	24-12	.275	.365	.483	.848	10	.981
2000— Atlanta (N.L.)	OF	161	* 656	122	199	36	6	36	104	59	100	9	12	21-6	.303	.366	.461	.772	2	.996
2001— Atlanta (N.L.)	OF	161	625	104	157	25	2	34	104	56	142	3	10	11-4	.251	.312	.461	.772	6	.987
2002— Atlanta (N.L.)	OF-DH	154	560	91	148	34	0	35	94	83	135	10	14	8-3	.264	.366	.513	.878	3	.993
2003— Atlanta (N.L.)	OF	156	595	101	165	28	2	36	116	53	125	5	18	4-3	.277	.338	.513	.851	3	.993
2004— Atlanta (N.L.)	OF	154	570	85	149	34	4	29	91	71	147	3	24	6-6	.261	.345	.488	.833	3	.993
2005— Atlanta (N.L.)	OF	160	586	95	154	24	3	* 51	* 128	64	112	6	19	5-3	.263	.347	.575	.922	2	.995
Major League totals (10 years)		1451	5271	855	1408	274	32	301	894	565	1129	62	131	129-52	.267	.342	.503	.845	40	.990

DIVISION SERIES RECORD

																		FIELDING	
Year Team (League)	Pos.	G	AB	R	H	2B	3B	HR	RBI	BB	SO	HBP	GDP	SB-CS	Avg.	OBP	SLG	OPS	E	Avg.
1996— Atlanta (N.L.)	OF	3	0	0	0	0	0	0	1	0	0	0	0	0-0	...	1.000	...	1.000	0	1.000
1997— Atlanta (N.L.)	OF	3	5	1	0	0	0	0	1	1	1	0	0	0-0	.000	.167	.000	.167	0	1.000
1998— Atlanta (N.L.)	OF	3	9	2	0	0	0	0	1	3	2	0	0	2-0	.000	.231	.000	.231	0	1.000
1999— Atlanta (N.L.)	OF	4	18	1	4	1	0	0	2	1	3	0	0	0-0	.222	.263	.278	.541	0	1.000
2000— Atlanta (N.L.)	OF	3	9	3	1	0	0	1	1	4	1	0	1	0-1	.111	.385	.444	.829	0	1.000
2001— Atlanta (N.L.)	OF	3	12	2	6	0	0	1	1	0	3	0	0	0-0	.500	.500	.750	1.250	0	1.000
2002— Atlanta (N.L.)	OF	5	19	4	6	1	0	0	2	2	3	0	0	0-0	.316	.381	.368	.749	0	1.000
2003— Atlanta (N.L.)	OF	5	17	1	1	0	0	0	1	4	7	0	0	0-0	.059	.238	.059	.297	1	.900
2004— Atlanta (N.L.)	OF	5	19	4	10	2	0	2	5	2	3	0	1	1-0	.526	.571	.947	1.519	0	1.000
2005— Atlanta (N.L.)	OF	4	17	5	8	3	0	1	5	2	3	1	1	0-0	.471	.524	.824	1.347	0	1.000
Division series totals (10 years)		38	125	23	36	7	0	5	19	20	26	1	3	3-1	.288	.385	.464	.849	1	.990

CHAMPIONSHIP SERIES RECORD

																		FIELDING	
Year Team (League)	Pos.	G	AB	R	H	2B	3B	HR	RBI	BB	SO	HBP	GDP	SB-CS	Avg.	OBP	SLG	OPS	E	Avg.
1996— Atlanta (N.L.)	OF	5	9	3	2	0	0	1	3	3	2	0	0	0-0	.222	.417	.556	.972	0	1.000
1997— Atlanta (N.L.)	OF	5	9	0	4	0	0	0	1	1	1	0	0	0-0	.444	.500	.444	.944	0	1.000
1998— Atlanta (N.L.)	OF	6	22	3	6	0	0	1	2	1	4	0	0	1-1	.273	.292	.409	.701	0	1.000
1999— Atlanta (N.L.)	OF	6	23	5	5	0	0	0	1	4	3	0	1	0-1	.217	.333	.217	.551	0	1.000
2001— Atlanta (N.L.)	OF	5	17	4	3	0	0	1	1	1	5	0	0	0-0	.176	.222	.353	.575	0	1.000
Champ. series totals (5 years)		27	80	15	20	0	0	3	8	10	15	0	1	1-2	.250	.330	.363	.692	0	1.000

WORLD SERIES RECORD

																		FIELDING	
Year Team (League)	Pos.	G	AB	R	H	2B	3B	HR	RBI	BB	SO	HBP	GDP	SB-CS	Avg.	OBP	SLG	OPS	E	Avg.
1996— Atlanta (N.L.)	OF	6	20	4	8	1	0	2	6	3	6	1	0	1-2	.400	.500	.750	1.250	0	1.000
1999— Atlanta (N.L.)	OF	4	13	1	1	0	0	0	0	1	3	0	1	0-0	.077	.143	.077	.220	0	1.000
World Series totals (2 years)		10	33	5	9	1	0	2	6	4	9	1	1	1-2	.273	.368	.485	.853	0	1.000

ALL-STAR GAME RECORD

	G	AB	R	H	2B	3B	HR	RBI	BB	SO	HBP	GDP	SB-CS	Avg.	OBP	SLG	OPS	E	Avg.
All-Star Game totals (4 years)	4	8	4	4	1	0	2	6	1	3	0	0	0-0	.500	.556	1.375	1.931	0	1.000

JONES, CHIPPER — 3B

PERSONAL: Born April 24, 1972, in DeLand, Fla. ... 6-4/210. ... Bats both, throws right. ... Full name: Larry Wayne Jones. ... High school: The Bolles School (Jacksonville).
TRANSACTIONS/CAREER NOTES: Selected by Atlanta Braves organization in first round (first pick overall) of 1990 free-agent draft. ... On disabled list (March 20, 1994-entire season; and March 22-April 16, 1996). ... On disabled list (April 19-May 8, 2004); included rehabilitation assignment to Rome. ... On disabled list (June 6-July 18, 2005); included rehabilitation assignment to Rome.
HONORS: Named N.L. Rookie Player of the Year by THE SPORTING NEWS (1995). ... Named N.L. Most Valuable Player by Baseball Writers' Association of America (1999).
2005 GAMES PLAYED BY POSITION (MLB): 3B—101.

SCOUTING REPORT *Offense:* Jones can cover both sides of the plate and will hit to all fields. Is a better low-ball hitter lefthanded and a better high-ball hitter righthanded. Has more power and is more productive from the left side. Has to protect his hamstring, which limits his speed. *Defense:* Jones still has quick reflexes, but his range has declined because of his leg and hamstring problems. Has soft, quick hands and good arm strength and is an extremely accurate thrower. Moves better to his left and might be moved to first base next season to keep him on the field. *Outlook:* Jones' continued physical problems have caused a decline in his offensive output, but he still knows how to hit. But don't expect a dramatic drop-off from 2005 production. *Grade 8.2*

CHIPPER JONES' HITTING ZONE

.333	.500	.190
.345	.370	.269
.320	.207	.238

LEFTY-RIGHTY SPLITS

vs.	Avg.	AB	H	2B	3B	HR	RBI	BB	SO	OBP	Slg.
L	.270	74	20	6	0	3	13	12	12	.372	.473
R	.303	284	86	24	0	18	59	60	44	.422	.577

Year Team (League)	Pos.	G	AB	R	H	2B	3B	HR	RBI	BB	SO	HBP	GDP	SB-CS	Avg.	OBP	SLG	OPS	E	Avg.
1990— GC Braves (GCL)	SS	44	140	20	32	1	1	1	18	14	25	6	3	5-3	.229	.321	.271	.592	18	.919
1991— Macon (S. Atl.)	SS	136	473	104	154	24	11	15	98	69	70	3	6	40-11	.326	.407	.518	.925	56	.919
1992— Durham (Carol.)	SS	70	264	43	73	22	1	4	31	31	34	2	5	10-8	.277	.353	.413	.766	14	.956
— Greenville (Sou.)	SS	67	266	43	92	17	11	9	42	11	32	0	5	14-1	.346	.367	.594	.961	18	.945
1993— Richmond (Int'l)	SS	139	536	97	174	31	12	13	89	57	70	1	8	23-7	.325	.387	.500	.887	43	.931
— Atlanta (N.L.)	SS	8	3	2	2	1	0	0	0	1	1	0	0	0-0	.667	.750	1.000	1.750	0	1.000
1994— Atlanta (N.L.)					Did not play.															
1995— Atlanta (N.L.)	3B-OF	140	524	87	139	22	3	23	86	73	99	0	10	8-4	.265	.353	.450	.803	25	.935
1996— Atlanta (N.L.)	3B-SS-OF	157	598	114	185	32	5	30	110	87	88	0	14	14-1	.309	.393	.530	.923	17	.958
1997— Atlanta (N.L.)	3B-OF	157	597	100	176	41	3	21	111	76	88	0	19	20-5	.295	.371	.479	.850	15	.956
1998— Atlanta (N.L.)	3B	160	601	123	188	29	5	34	107	96	93	1	17	16-6	.313	.404	.547	.951	12	.971
1999— Atlanta (N.L.)	3B-SS	157	567	116	181	41	1	45	110	126	94	2	20	25-3	.319	.441	.633	1.074	17	.951
2000— Atlanta (N.L.)	3B-SS	156	579	118	180	38	1	36	111	95	64	2	14	14-7	.311	.404	.566	.970	25	.951
2001— Atlanta (N.L.)	3B-OF-DH	159	572	113	189	33	5	38	102	98	82	2	13	9-10	.330	.427	.605	1.032	18	.947
2002— Atlanta (N.L.)	OF	158	548	90	179	35	1	26	100	107	89	2	18	8-2	.327	.435	.537	.972	7	.975
2003— Atlanta (N.L.)	OF-DH	153	555	103	169	33	2	27	106	94	83	1	10	2-2	.305	.402	.517	.920	7	.968
2004— Rome (S. Atl.)	OF	1	4	0	0	0	0	0	0	0	0	0	0	0-0	.000	.000	.000	.000	0	1.000
— Atlanta (N.L.)	3B-OF-DH	137	472	69	117	20	1	30	96	84	96	0	14	2-0	.248	.362	.485	.847	6	.978
2005— Rome (S. Atl.)	3B-DH	3	6	1	3	0	0	0	2	3	1	0	1	0-0	.500	.667	.500	1.167	1	.833
— Atlanta (N.L.)	3B	109	358	66	106	30	0	21	72	72	56	0	9	5-1	.296	.412	.556	.968	5	.980
Major League totals (12 years)		1651	5974	1101	1811	355	27	331	1111	1009	933	14	158	123-41	.303	.401	.538	.939	154	.958

DIVISION SERIES RECORD

Year Team (League)	Pos.	G	AB	R	H	2B	3B	HR	RBI	BB	SO	HBP	GDP	SB-CS	Avg.	OBP	SLG	OPS	E	Avg.
1995— Atlanta (N.L.)	3B	4	18	4	7	2	0	2	4	2	2	0	2	0-0	.389	.450	.833	1.283	0	1.000
1996— Atlanta (N.L.)	3B	3	9	2	2	0	0	1	3	4	0	0	1	1-1	.222	.417	.556	.972	0	1.000
1997— Atlanta (N.L.)	3B	3	8	3	4	0	0	1	2	3	2	0	0	1-0	.500	.583	.875	1.458	1	.833
1998— Atlanta (N.L.)	3B	3	10	2	2	0	0	0	1	4	3	0	0	0-0	.200	.429	.200	.629	0	1.000
1999— Atlanta (N.L.)	3B	4	13	2	3	0	0	1	5	2	0	0	1	0-0	.231	.421	.231	.652	1	.875
2000— Atlanta (N.L.)	3B	3	12	3	4	1	0	0	1	1	5	0	0	0-0	.333	.385	.417	.801	2	.800
2001— Atlanta (N.L.)	3B	3	9	2	4	0	0	2	5	3	1	0	0	0-1	.444	.583	1.111	1.694	1	1.000
2002— Atlanta (N.L.)	OF	5	17	3	5	0	0	0	2	5	2	0	0	0-0	.294	.455	.294	.749	0	1.000
2003— Atlanta (N.L.)	OF	5	18	3	3	0	0	2	6	3	4	0	0	0-0	.167	.286	.500	.786	0	1.000
2004— Atlanta (N.L.)	3B	5	20	4	4	0	0	0	3	2	0	0	1	0-0	.200	.304	.200	.504	0	1.000
2005— Atlanta (N.L.)	3B	4	17	3	3	2	0	1	2	4	0	0	1	0-0	.176	.333	.471	.804	0	1.000
Division series totals (11 years)		42	151	30	41	5	0	9	26	36	30	0	7	2-2	.272	.407	.483	.891	4	.952

CHAMPIONSHIP SERIES RECORD

Year Team (League)	Pos.	G	AB	R	H	2B	3B	HR	RBI	BB	SO	HBP	GDP	SB-CS	Avg.	OBP	SLG	OPS	E	Avg.
1995— Atlanta (N.L.)	3B	4	16	3	7	0	0	1	3	3	1	0	0	1-0	.438	.526	.625	1.151	0	1.000
1996— Atlanta (N.L.)	3B	7	25	6	11	2	0	0	4	3	1	0	0	1-0	.440	.483	.520	1.003	1	.923
1997— Atlanta (N.L.)	3B	6	24	5	7	1	0	2	4	2	3	0	0	0-0	.292	.346	.583	.929	0	1.000
1998— Atlanta (N.L.)	3B	6	24	2	5	1	0	0	1	4	5	0	2	0-0	.208	.321	.250	.571	0	1.000
1999— Atlanta (N.L.)	3B	6	19	3	5	2	0	0	1	9	7	1	0	3-0	.263	.517	.368	.886	2	.867
2001— Atlanta (N.L.)	3B	5	19	1	5	1	0	0	2	3	6	0	0	0-0	.263	.364	.316	.679	1	.923
Champ. series totals (6 years)		34	127	20	40	7	0	3	15	24	23	1	2	5-0	.315	.425	.441	.866	4	.950

WORLD SERIES RECORD

Year Team (League)	Pos.	G	AB	R	H	2B	3B	HR	RBI	BB	SO	HBP	GDP	SB-CS	Avg.	OBP	SLG	OPS	E	Avg.
1995— Atlanta (N.L.)	3B	6	21	3	6	3	0	1	4	3	0	0	0	0-0	.286	.385	.429	.813	1	.947
1996— Atlanta (N.L.)	3B-SS	6	21	4	6	3	0	0	3	4	2	0	1	1-0	.286	.385	.429	.813	0	1.000
1999— Atlanta (N.L.)	3B	4	13	2	3	0	0	1	2	4	2	0	0	0-1	.231	.412	.462	.873	0	1.000
World Series totals (3 years)		16	55	8	15	6	0	1	6	12	7	0	1	1-1	.273	.391	.436	.828	1	.972

ALL-STAR GAME RECORD

Year Team (League)		G	AB	R	H	2B	3B	HR	RBI	BB	SO	HBP	GDP	SB-CS	Avg.	OBP	SLG	OPS	E	Avg.
All-Star Game totals (5 years)		5	10	3	4	0	0	1	1	1	0	0	1	0-0	.400	.455	.700	1.155	0	1.000

JONES, GREG   P

PERSONAL: Born November 15, 1976, in Clearwater, Fla. ... 6-2/195. ... Throws right, bats right. ... Full name: Greg Alan Jones. ... High school: Seminole, Fla. ... Junior college: Pasco Hernando (Fla.).

TRANSACTIONS/CAREER NOTES: Selected by Anaheim Angels organization in 42nd round of 1996 free-agent draft. ... On disabled list (March 26-June 7, 2004); included rehabilitation assignment to Salt Lake. ... Angels franchise renamed Los Angeles Angels of Anaheim for 2005 season.

CAREER HITTING: 0-for-0 (.000), 0 R, 0 2B, 0 3B, 0 HR, 0 RBI.

LEFTY-RIGHTY SPLITS

vs.	Avg.	AB	H	2B	3B	HR	RBI	BB	SO	OBP	Slg.
L	.444	9	4	1	0	1	3	1	2	.500	.889
R	.231	13	3	0	0	1	1	1	4	.286	.462

Year Team (League)	W	L	Pct.	ERA	WHIP	G	GS	CG	ShO	Hld.	Sv.-Opp.	IP	H	R	ER	HR	BB-IBB	SO	Avg.
1997— Boise (N'west)	2	2	.500	3.62	1.45	21	4	0	0	...	2-...	37.1	35	19	15	1	19-1	39	.243
1998— Boise (N'west)	0	2	.000	4.93	1.44	22	0	0	0	...	1-...	34.2	37	22	19	3	13-0	28	.278
1999— Cedar Rap. (Midw.)	2	4	.333	3.83	1.25	34	0	0	0	...	13-...	40.0	37	18	17	5	13-2	41	.247

Year Team (League)	W	L	Pct.	ERA	WHIP	G	GS	CG	ShO	Hld.	Sv.-Opp.	IP	H	R	ER	HR	BB-IBB	SO	Avg.
2000—Lake Elsinore (Calif.)	0	0	...	4.08	1.64	16	0	0	0		3-...	17.2	19	9	8	0	10-3	12	.284
—Erie (East.)	0	2	.000	5.40	1.53	11	0	0	0		2-...	15.0	19	9	9	1	4-0	7	.306
—Edmonton (PCL)	2	2	.500	7.65	2.13	25	0	0	0		1-...	42.1	57	42	36	5	33-1	21	.324
2001—Rancho Cuca. (Calif.)	1	3	.250	4.23	1.30	6	6	0	0		0-...	27.2	25	15	13	2	14-0	27	.238
—Ariz. Angels (Ariz.)	0	0	...	0.00	2.50	2	2	0	0		0-...	2.0	3	0	0	0	2-0	2	.375
2002—Salt Lake (PCL)	7	4	.636	4.31	1.44	39	0	0	0		2-...	62.2	68	35	30	5	22-0	55	.273
2003—Salt Lake (PCL)	2	3	.400	4.40	0.96	33	0	0	0		4-...	47.0	36	24	23	4	9-0	56	.207
—Anaheim (A.L.)	0	0	...	4.88	1.55	18	0	0	0	2	0-0	27.2	29	15	15	3	14-0	28	.261
2004—Salt Lake (PCL)	1	4	.200	5.74	1.54	36	0	0	0		3-...	53.1	63	38	34	11	19-0	43	.283
2005—Arkansas (Texas)	0	1	.000	2.70	0.90	3	0	0	0		0-...	3.1	2	1	1	0	1-0	2	.167
—Salt Lake (PCL)	2	4	.333	3.20	1.03	23	0	0	0		10-12	25.1	20	9	9	3	6-0	25	.215
—Los Angeles (A.L.)	0	0	...	6.75	1.69	6	0	0	0		0-0	5.1	7	4	4	2	2-0	6	.318
Major League totals (2 years)	0	0	...	5.18	1.58	24	0	0	0	2	0-0	33.0	36	19	19	5	16-0	34	.271

JONES, JACQUE — OF

J

PERSONAL: Born April 25, 1975, in San Diego. ... 5-10/195. ... Bats left, throws left. ... Full name: Jacque Dewayne Jones. ... High school: San Diego High. ... College: Southern California.

TRANSACTIONS/CAREER NOTES: Selected by Kansas City Royals organization in 31st round of 1993 free-agent draft; did not sign. ... Selected by Minnesota Twins organization in second round of 1996 free-agent draft. ... On disabled list (July 1-17, 2003).

2005 GAMES PLAYED BY POSITION (MLB): OF—132, DH—9.

SCOUTING REPORT **Offense:** A free swinger with power to the opposite field, Jones hits off his front foot. Likes to get on top of the high fastball with a quick bat. Has holes if pitchers continue to work him up in the zone. A streaky hitter who doesn't hit lefthanded pitching well. Is an above-average runner but could steal more. **Defense:** Jones' athleticism allows him to make plays even though his jumps aren't consistent. Has more trouble tracking the ball going back than coming in. Often airmails throws over the cutoff man, allowing runners to move up a base. **Outlook:** He is a catalyst type with speed and power. Average continues to drop even though his run production increases. Is not an outstanding hitter but certainly is a dangerous one. *Grade 7.3*

JACQUE JONES' HITTING ZONE

.310	.238	.275
.209	.488	.302
.176	.222	.294

LEFTY-RIGHTY SPLITS

vs.	Avg.	AB	H	2B	3B	HR	RBI	BB	SO	OBP	Slg.
L	.201	154	31	2	3	6	23	9	36	.247	.370
R	.268	369	99	20	1	17	50	42	84	.348	.466

Year Team (League)	Pos.	G	AB	R	H	2B	3B	HR	RBI	BB	SO	HBP	GDP	SB-CS	Avg.	OBP	SLG	OPS	E	Avg.
1996—Fort Myers (Fla. St.)	OF	1	3	0	2	1	0	0	1	0	0	0	0	0-1	.667	.667	1.000	1.667	0	...
1997—Fort Myers (Fla. St.)	OF	131	539	84	160	33	6	15	82	33	110	3	9	24-12	.297	.340	.464	.804	7	.979
1998—New Britain (East.)	OF-DH	134	518	78	155	39	3	21	85	37	134	4	4	18-11	.299	.349	.508	.856	10	.968
1999—Salt Lake (PCL)	OF	52	198	32	59	13	2	4	26	9	36	0	5	9-2	.298	.325	.444	.770	2	.987
—Minnesota (A.L.)	OF	95	322	54	93	24	2	9	44	17	63	4	7	3-4	.289	.329	.460	.789	2	.980
2000—Minnesota (A.L.)	OF	154	523	66	149	26	5	19	76	26	111	0	17	7-5	.285	.319	.463	.781	2	.994
2001—Minnesota (A.L.)	OF-DH	149	475	57	131	25	0	14	49	39	92	3	10	12-9	.276	.335	.417	.751	5	.983
2002—Minnesota (A.L.)	OF-DH	149	577	96	173	37	2	27	85	37	129	2	8	6-7	.300	.341	.511	.852	5	.986
2003—Minnesota (A.L.)	OF-DH	136	517	76	157	33	1	16	69	21	105	4	10	13-1	.304	.333	.464	.797	5	.977
2004—Minnesota (A.L.)	OF-DH	151	555	69	141	22	1	24	80	40	117	10	12	13-10	.254	.315	.427	.742	2	.994
2005—Minnesota (A.L.)	OF-DH	142	523	74	130	22	4	23	73	51	120	5	17	13-4	.249	.319	.438	.757	4	.986
Major League totals (7 years)		976	3492	492	974	189	15	132	476	231	737	28	81	67-40	.279	.327	.455	.782	28	.986

DIVISION SERIES RECORD

Year Team (League)	Pos.	G	AB	R	H	2B	3B	HR	RBI	BB	SO	HBP	GDP	SB-CS	Avg.	OBP	SLG	OPS	E	Avg.
2002—Minnesota (A.L.)	OF	5	20	3	5	3	0	0	1	1	8	1	1	0-0	.250	.318	.400	.718	1	.952
2003—Minnesota (A.L.)	OF	4	16	0	2	0	0	0	0	0	5	0	0	0-0	.125	.125	.125	.250	0	1.000
2004—Minnesota (A.L.)	OF	4	20	3	6	1	0	2	2	0	6	0	2	0-1	.300	.300	.650	.950	0	1.000
Division series totals (3 years)		13	56	6	13	4	0	2	3	1	19	1	3	0-1	.232	.259	.411	.669	1	.972

CHAMPIONSHIP SERIES RECORD

Year Team (League)	Pos.	G	AB	R	H	2B	3B	HR	RBI	BB	SO	HBP	GDP	SB-CS	Avg.	OBP	SLG	OPS	E	Avg.
2002—Minnesota (A.L.)	OF	5	20	0	2	1	0	0	2	0	4	0	0	0-0	.100	.095	.150	.245	0	1.000

JONES, TODD — P

PERSONAL: Born April 24, 1968, in Marietta, Ga. ... 6-3/230. ... Throws right, bats left. ... Full name: Todd Barton Jones. ... High school: Osborne (Ga.). ... College: Jacksonville (Ala.) State.

TRANSACTIONS/CAREER NOTES: Selected by New York Mets organization in 41st round of June 1986 free-agent draft; did not sign. ... Selected by Houston Astros organization in supplemental round ("sandwich pick" between first and second rounds, 27th pick overall) of 1989 free-agent draft; pick received as part of compensation for Texas Rangers signing Type A free-agent P Nolan Ryan. ... On suspended list (September 14-16, 1993). ... On disabled list (July 19-August 12 and August 18-September 12, 1996); included rehabilitation assignment to Tucson. ... Traded by Astros with OF Brian L. Hunter, IF Orlando Miller, P Doug Brocail and cash to Detroit Tigers for C Brad Ausmus, Ps Jose Lima, C.J. Nitkowski and Trever Miller and 1B Daryle Ward (December 10, 1996). ... Traded by Tigers to Minnesota Twins for P Mark Redman (July 28, 2001). ... Signed as a free agent by Colorado Rockies (January 15, 2002). ... Released by Rockies (June 30, 2003). ... Signed by Boston Red Sox (July 2, 2003). ... Signed as a free agent by Tampa Bay Devil Rays organization (January 11, 2004). ... Released by Devil Rays (March 24, 2004). ... Signed by Cincinnati Reds organization (March 25, 2004). ... Traded by Reds with OF Brad Correll to Philadelphia Phillies for P Josh Hancock and SS Anderson Machado (July 30, 2004). ... Signed as a free agent by Florida Marlins (December 13, 2004).

HONORS: Named A.L. Fireman of the Year by THE SPORTING NEWS (2000).

CAREER HITTING: 4-for-19 (.211), 1 R, 1 2B, 0 3B, 0 HR, 0 RBI.

SCOUTING REPORT

Throws: He has a fastball in the lower 90s and a cutter. **Tendencies:** Jones rediscovered his cut fastball and had good command to both sides of the plate. Has good deception. Threw a soft spinning off-speed curveball in the past but with the success of his cutter, rarely threw it in 2005. Overall has pinpoint control to the four corners with his fastball. Has outstanding makeup. **Outlook:** After going 40-for-45 in save opportunities for a team that went in the tank the last month of the season, Jones has re-established himself as a closer. **Grade 8.7**

TODD JONES'S PITCHING ZONE

.115	.304	.278
.209	.289	.273
.385	.182	.400

LEFTY-RIGHTY SPLITS

vs.	Avg.	AB	H	2B	3B	HR	RBI	BB	SO	OBP	Slg.
L	.231	134	31	3	1	1	10	7	30	.273	.291
R	.229	131	30	3	0	1	8	7	32	.279	.275

Year Team (League)	W	L	Pct.	ERA	WHIP	G	GS	CG	ShO	Hld.	Sv.-Opp.	IP	H	R	ER	HR	BB-IBB	SO	Avg.
1989— Auburn (NY-Penn)	2	3	.400	5.44	1.79	11	9	1	0	...	0-...	49.2	47	39	30	2	42-11	71	.240
1990— Osceola (Fla. St.)	12	10	.545	3.51	1.54	27	27	1	0	...	0-...	151.1	124	81	59	2	109-11	106	.223
1991— Osceola (Fla. St.)	4	4	.500	4.35	1.44	14	14	0	0	...	0-...	72.1	69	38	35	2	35-0	51	.256
— Jackson (Texas)	4	3	.571	4.88	1.63	10	10	0	0	...	0-...	55.1	51	37	30	2	39-1	37	.241
1992— Jackson (Texas)	3	7	.300	3.14	1.45	61	0	0	0	...	25-...	66.0	52	28	23	3	44-3	60	.213
— Tucson (PCL)	0	1	.000	4.50	2.75	3	0	0	0	...	0-...	4.0	1	2	2	0	10-1	4	.077
1993— Tucson (PCL)	4	2	.667	4.44	1.64	41	0	0	0	...	12-...	48.2	49	26	24	5	31-2	45	.265
— Houston (N.L.)	1	2	.333	3.13	1.15	27	0	0	0	6	2-3	37.1	28	14	13	4	15-2	25	.214
1994— Houston (N.L.)	5	2	.714	2.72	1.07	48	0	0	0	8	5-9	72.2	52	23	22	8	26-4	63	.202
1995— Houston (N.L.)	6	5	.545	3.07	1.41	68	0	0	0	8	15-20	99.2	89	38	34	8	52-17	96	.237
1996— Houston (N.L.)	6	3	.667	4.40	1.62	51	0	0	0	1	17-23	57.1	61	30	28	5	32-6	44	.277
— Tucson (PCL)	0	0	...	0.00	1.50	1	0	0	0	...	0-...	2.0	1	0	0	0	2-0	0	.200
1997— Detroit (A.L.)	5	4	.556	3.09	1.36	68	0	0	0	5	31-36	70.0	60	29	24	3	35-2	70	.231
1998— Detroit (A.L.)	1	4	.200	4.97	1.48	63	0	0	0	0	28-32	63.1	58	38	35	7	36-4	57	.243
1999— Detroit (A.L.)	4	4	.500	3.80	1.49	65	0	0	0	0	30-35	66.1	64	33	28	7	35-1	64	.259
2000— Detroit (A.L.)	2	4	.333	3.52	1.44	67	0	0	0	0	•42-46	64.0	67	28	25	6	25-1	67	.276
2001— Detroit (A.L.)	4	5	.444	4.62	1.68	45	0	0	0	3	11-17	48.2	60	31	25	6	22-1	39	.303
— Minnesota (A.L.)	1	0	1.000	3.26	1.76	24	0	0	0	7	2-4	19.1	27	8	7	3	7-0	15	.333
2002— Colorado (N.L.)	1	4	.200	4.70	1.36	79	0	0	0	30	1-3	82.1	84	43	43	10	28-3	73	.269
2003— Colorado (N.L.)	1	4	.200	8.24	2.01	33	1	0	0	3	0-5	39.1	61	39	36	8	18-0	28	.361
— Boston (A.L.)	2	1	.667	5.52	1.53	26	0	0	0	1	0-0	29.1	32	19	18	2	13-2	31	.269
2004— Cincinnati (N.L.)	8	2	.800	3.79	1.30	51	0	0	0	22	1-6	57.0	49	25	24	4	25-2	37	.243
— Philadelphia (N.L.)	3	3	.500	4.97	1.70	27	0	0	0	5	1-2	25.1	35	14	14	3	8-3	22	.330
2005— Florida (N.L.)	1	5	.167	2.10	1.03	68	0	0	0	7	40-45	73.0	61	19	17	2	14-2	62	.230
American League totals (6 years)	19	22	.463	4.04	1.50	360	0	0	0	16	144-170	361.0	368	183	162	34	173-11	343	.266
National League totals (8 years)	32	30	.516	3.82	1.36	452	1	0	0	84	82-116	544.0	520	245	231	47	218-39	450	.255
Major League totals (13 years)	51	52	.495	3.91	1.41	812	1	0	0	100	226-286	905.0	888	428	393	81	391-50	793	.260

CHAMPIONSHIP SERIES RECORD

Year Team (League)	W	L	Pct.	ERA	WHIP	G	GS	CG	ShO	Hld.	Sv.-Opp.	IP	H	R	ER	HR	BB-IBB	SO	Avg.
2003— Boston (A.L.)	0	0	...	0.00	6.00	1	0	0	0	0	0-0	0.1	1	0	0	0	1-0	1	.500

ALL-STAR GAME RECORD

Year Team (League)	W	L	Pct.	ERA	WHIP	G	GS	CG	ShO	Hld.	Sv.-Opp.	IP	H	R	ER	HR	BB-IBB	SO	Avg.
All-Star Game totals (1 year)	0	0	...	0.00	0.00	1	0	0	0	1	0-0	1.0	0	0	0	0	0-0	1	.000

JORDAN, BRIAN   OF

PERSONAL: Born March 29, 1967, in Baltimore. ... 6-1/225. ... Bats right, throws right. ... Full name: Brian O'Neal Jordan. ... High school: Milford (Baltimore). ... College: Richmond.

TRANSACTIONS/CAREER NOTES: Selected by Cleveland Indians organization in 20th round of June 1985 free-agent draft; did not sign. ... Selected by St. Louis Cardinals organization in supplemental round ("sandwich pick" between first and second rounds, 30th pick overall) of 1988 free-agent draft; pick received as part of compensation for New York Yankees signing Type A free-agent 1B/OF Jack Clark. ... Played defensive back for Atlanta Falcons of NFL (1989-91). ... On temporarily inactive list (July 3, 1991-remainder of season). ... On disabled list (May 23-June 22, 1992); included rehabilitation assignment to Louisville. ... On disabled list (July 10, 1994-remainder of season; and March 31-April 15, 1996). ... On disabled list (May 6-June 13, June 26-August 10 and August 25, 1997-remainder of season); included rehabilitation assignment to Louisville. ... Signed as a free agent by Atlanta Braves (November 23, 1998). ... On disabled list (April 4-19, 2000). ... Traded by Braves with Ps Odalis Perez and Andrew Brown to Los Angeles Dodgers for OF Gary Sheffield (January 15, 2002). ... On disabled list (August 17-September 1, 2002; and June 25, 2003-remainder of season). ... Signed as a free agent by Texas Rangers (January 8, 2004). ... On disabled list (March 27-April 27 and May 24-July 23, 2004); included rehabilitation assignments to Frisco and Oklahoma. ... Signed as a free agent by Braves (January 19, 2005). ... On disabled list (July 7-September 1, 2005); included rehabilitation assignment to Rome.

2005 GAMES PLAYED BY POSITION (MLB): OF—62.

SCOUTING REPORT

Offense: Jordan has not been sharp at the plate in recent years because he has had problems staying healthy. Is not a good breaking-ball hitter and continues to lose bat speed and power. Is still an average runner. **Defense:** Jordan's range and ability to get good jumps have decreased, but he is aggressive and charges the ball well. Has good instincts and arm strength. **Outlook:** Jordan's injuries have eroded his skills to the point he might be best suited coming off the bench against lefthanders. **Grade 5**

BRIAN JORDAN'S HITTING ZONE

.231	.333	.333
.220	.308	.237
.348	.462	.333

LEFTY-RIGHTY SPLITS

vs.	Avg.	AB	H	2B	3B	HR	RBI	BB	SO	OBP	Slg.
L	.263	76	20	3	1	2	8	6	11	.329	.408
R	.239	155	37	5	1	1	16	8	35	.277	.303

Year Team (League)	Pos.	G	AB	R	H	2B	3B	HR	RBI	BB	SO	HBP	GDP	SB-CS	Avg.	OBP	SLG	OPS	E	Avg.
1988— Hamilton (NYP)	OF	19	71	12	22	3	1	4	12	6	15	3	0	3-3	.310	.388	.549	.937	1	.971
1989— St. Pete. (FSL)	OF	11	43	7	15	4	1	2	11	8	2	1	1	0-2	.349	.378	.628	1.006	0	1.000
1990— Arkansas (Texas)	OF	16	50	4	8	1	0	0	0	0	11	1	1	0-0	.160	.176	.180	.356	2	.933

Year	Team (League)	Pos.	G	AB	R	H	2B	3B	HR	RBI	BB	SO	HBP	GDP	SB-CS	Avg.	OBP	SLG	OPS	E	Avg.
	—St. Pete. (Fla. St.)	OF	9	30	3	5	0	1	0	1	2	11	0	0	0-2	.167	.219	.233	.452	0	1.000
1991	—Louisville (A.A.)	OF	61	212	35	56	11	4	4	24	17	41	8	5	10-4	.264	.342	.410	.752	2	.987
1992	—St. Louis (N.L.)	OF	55	193	17	40	9	4	5	22	10	48	1	6	7-2	.207	.250	.373	.623	1	.991
	—Louisville (A.A.)	OF	43	155	23	45	3	1	4	16	8	21	4	1	13-2	.290	.337	.400	.737	1	.989
1993	—St. Louis (N.L.)	OF	67	223	33	69	10	6	10	44	12	35	4	6	6-6	.309	.351	.435	.894	4	.973
	—Louisville (A.A.)	OF	38	144	24	54	13	2	5	35	16	17	3	3	9-4	.375	.442	.597	1.040	1	1.000
1994	—St. Louis (N.L.)	OF-1B	53	178	14	46	8	2	5	15	16	40	1	6	4-3	.258	.320	.410	.730	1	.991
1995	—St. Louis (N.L.)	OF	131	490	83	145	20	4	22	81	22	79	11	5	24-9	.296	.339	.488	.827	1	.996
1996	—St. Louis (N.L.)	OF-1B	140	513	82	159	36	1	17	104	29	84	7	6	22-5	.310	.349	.483	.833	2	.994
1997	—St. Louis (N.L.)	OF	47	145	17	34	5	0	0	10	10	21	6	4	6-1	.234	.311	.269	.580	0	1.000
	—Louisville (A.A.)	OF-DH	6	20	1	3	0	0	0	2	1	2	1	0	1-0	.150	.227	.150	.377	0	1.000
1998	—St. Louis (N.L.)	OF-DH-3B	150	564	100	178	34	7	25	91	40	66	9	18	17-5	.316	.368	.534	.902	9	.970
1999	—Atlanta (N.L.)	OF	153	576	100	163	28	4	23	115	51	81	9	9	13-8	.283	.346	.465	.811	3	.990
2000	—Atlanta (N.L.)	OF	133	489	71	129	26	0	17	77	38	80	5	12	10-2	.264	.320	.421	.742	3	.990
2001	—Atlanta (N.L.)	OF-DH	148	560	82	165	32	3	25	97	31	88	6	18	3-2	.295	.334	.496	.830	3	.991
2002	—Los Angeles (N.L.)	OF-DH	128	471	65	134	27	3	18	80	34	86	6	10	2-2	.285	.338	.469	.807	4	.982
2003	—Los Angeles (N.L.)	OF-DH	66	224	28	67	9	0	6	28	23	30	4	3	1-1	.299	.372	.420	.791	1	.990
2004	—Frisco (Texas)	OF-DH	6	19	1	3	1	0	0	0	0	6	0	0	0-0	.158	.158	.211	.368	0	1.000
	—Oklahoma (PCL)	OF-DH	7	26	3	10	2	0	0	8	3	3	1	0	1-0	.385	.467	.462	.928	0	1.000
	—Texas (A.L.)	OF-DH	61	212	27	47	13	1	5	23	16	35	1	7	2-2	.222	.275	.363	.638	1	.990
2005	—Rome (S. Atl.)	DH-OF	5	16	5	8	1	0	1	7	2	2	0	0	1-0	.500	.500	.750	1.250	0	1.000
	—Atlanta (N.L.)	OF	76	231	25	57	8	2	3	24	14	46	3	5	2-0	.247	.295	.338	.632	0	1.000
American League totals (1 year)			61	212	27	47	13	1	5	23	16	35	1	7	2-2	.222	.275	.363	.638	1	.990
National League totals (13 years)			1347	4857	717	1386	252	36	176	788	330	784	72	108	117-46	.285	.337	.461	.798	32	.988
Major League totals (14 years)			1408	5069	744	1433	265	37	181	811	346	819	73	115	119-48	.283	.334	.457	.791	33	.988

DIVISION SERIES RECORD

Year	Team (League)	Pos.	G	AB	R	H	2B	3B	HR	RBI	BB	SO	HBP	GDP	SB-CS	Avg.	OBP	SLG	OPS	E	Avg.
1996	—St. Louis (N.L.)	OF	3	12	4	4	0	0	1	3	1	3	0	0	1-0	.333	.385	.583	.968	0	1.000
1999	—Atlanta (N.L.)	OF	4	17	2	8	1	0	1	7	1	2	0	0	0-1	.471	.474	.706	1.180	0	1.000
2000	—Atlanta (N.L.)	OF	3	11	1	4	1	0	0	4	1	1	0	0	0-0	.364	.417	.455	.871	0	1.000
2001	—Atlanta (N.L.)	OF	3	11	1	2	0	0	1	2	0	5	0	0	0-1	.182	.167	.455	.621	0	1.000
2005	—Atlanta (N.L.)	OF	3	5	0	1	1	0	0	0	0	0	0	0	0-0	.200	.200	.400	.600	0	1.000
Division series totals (5 years)			16	56	8	19	3	0	3	16	3	11	0	1	1-2	.339	.361	.554	.914	0	1.000

CHAMPIONSHIP SERIES RECORD

Year	Team (League)	Pos.	G	AB	R	H	2B	3B	HR	RBI	BB	SO	HBP	GDP	SB-CS	Avg.	OBP	SLG	OPS	E	Avg.
1996	—St. Louis (N.L.)	OF	7	25	3	6	1	1	1	2	1	3	0	1	0-0	.240	.269	.480	.749	0	1.000
1999	—Atlanta (N.L.)	OF	6	25	3	5	0	0	2	5	3	5	1	0	0-0	.200	.310	.440	.750	0	1.000
2001	—Atlanta (N.L.)	OF	5	21	1	4	2	0	0	3	0	6	0	1	0-0	.190	.190	.286	.476	0	1.000
Champ. series totals (3 years)			18	71	7	15	3	1	3	10	4	14	1	2	0-0	.211	.263	.408	.672	0	1.000

WORLD SERIES RECORD

Year	Team (League)	Pos.	G	AB	R	H	2B	3B	HR	RBI	BB	SO	HBP	GDP	SB-CS	Avg.	OBP	SLG	OPS	E	Avg.
1999	—Atlanta (N.L.)	OF	4	13	1	1	0	0	0	1	4	2	0	0	0-0	.077	.294	.077	.371	1	.889

ALL-STAR GAME RECORD

			G	AB	R	H	2B	3B	HR	RBI	BB	SO	HBP	GDP	SB-CS	Avg.	OBP	SLG	OPS	E	Avg.
All-Star Game totals (1 year)			1	1	0	1	0	0	0	0	1	0	0	0	0-1	1.000	1.000	1.000	2.000	0	...

JORGENSEN, RYAN   C

PERSONAL: Born May 4, 1979, in Jacksonville. ... 6-2/200. ... Bats right, throws right. ... Full name: Ryan Wayne Jorgensen. ... College: Louisiana State.

TRANSACTIONS/CAREER NOTES: Selected by Chicago Cubs organization in seventh round of 2000 free-agent draft. ... Traded by Cubs with RHPs Julian Tavarez, Jose Cueto and LHP Dontrelle Willis to Florida Marlins for RHPs Antonio Alfonseca and Matt Clement (March 27, 2002).

2005 GAMES PLAYED BY POSITION (MLB): C—3.

LEFTY-RIGHTY SPLITS

vs.	Avg.	AB	H	2B	3B	HR	RBI	BB	SO	OBP	Slg.
L	.000	0	0	0	0	0	0	0	0	.000	.000
R	.000	4	0	0	0	0	0	0	3	.000	.000

Year	Team (League)	Pos.	G	AB	R	H	2B	3B	HR	RBI	BB	SO	HBP	GDP	SB-CS	Avg.	OBP	SLG	OPS	E	Avg.
2000	—Eugene (N'west)	C	41	130	17	39	10	2	1	23	17	27	1	1	2-4	.300	.380	.431	.811	5	.986
2001	—Daytona (Fla. St.)	C	54	188	24	53	12	1	8	29	23	39	2	6	1-3	.282	.366	.484	.850	5	.986
	—West Tenn (Sou.)	C	32	109	8	13	4	0	2	7	11	38	0	5	0-0	.119	.195	.211	.406	5	.981
2002	—Jupiter (Fla. St.)	C	60	223	26	58	16	0	3	35	24	38	1	4	4-1	.260	.335	.372	.707	4	.990
	—Portland (East.)	C	41	144	15	32	4	0	2	14	12	33	1	3	3-1	.222	.287	.292	.579	5	.983
2003	—Carolina (Sou.)	C	67	211	28	51	16	0	6	34	30	53	2	2	1-0	.242	.337	.403	.740	6	.988
2004	—Albuquerque (PCL)	C	61	201	20	52	11	0	8	29	9	51	0	7	0-0	.259	.289	.433	.722	4	.988
2005	—Florida (N.L.)	C	4	4	0	0	0	0	0	0	0	3	0	0	0-0	.000	.000	.000	.000	0	1.000
	—Albuquerque (PCL)	C	53	137	20	27	5	0	2	11	21	46	1	1	1-0	.197	.308	.277	.586	3	.990
Major League totals (1 year)			4	4	0	0	0	0	0	0	0	3	0	0	0-0	.000	.000	.000	.000	0	1.000

JOURNELL, JIMMY   P

PERSONAL: Born December 29, 1977, in Springfield, Ohio. ... 6-4/205. ... Throws right, bats right. ... Full name: James Richard Journell. ... Name pronounced: JUR-nell. ... High school: Springfield North (Springfield, Ohio). ... College: Illinois.

TRANSACTIONS/CAREER NOTES: Selected by St. Louis Cardinals organization in fourth round of 1999 free-agent draft. ... On disabled list (August 18-September 6, 2003).

CAREER HITTING: 0-for-0 (.000), 0 R, 0 2B, 0 3B, 0 HR, 0 RBI.

LEFTY-RIGHTY SPLITS

vs.	Avg.	AB	H	2B	3B	HR	RBI	BB	SO	OBP	Slg.
L	1.000	3	3	0	0	0	2	2	0	1.000	1.000
R	.200	15	3	1	0	1	4	3	5	.333	.467

Year	Team (League)	W	L	Pct.	ERA	WHIP	G	GS	CG	ShO	Hld.	Sv.-Opp.	IP	H	R	ER	HR	BB-IBB	SO	Avg.
2000	—New Jersey (N.Y.-Penn.)	1	0	1.000	1.97	1.13	13	1	0	0	...	0-...	32.0	12	12	7	0	24-0	39	.111
2001	—Potomac (Carol.)	14	6	.700	2.50	1.08	26	26	0	0	...	0-...	151.0	121	54	42	8	42-0	156	.220

Year	Team (League)	W	L	Pct.	ERA	WHIP	G	GS	CG	ShO	Hld.	Sv.-Opp.	IP	H	R	ER	HR	BB-IBB	SO	Avg.
— New Haven (East.)		1	0	1.000	0.00	0.43	1	1	1	0	...	0-...	7.0	0	0	0	0	3-0	6	.000
2002— New Haven (East.)		3	3	.500	2.70	1.02	10	10	2	0	...	0-...	66.2	50	22	20	3	18-0	66	.206
— Memphis (PCL)		2	4	.333	3.68	1.53	7	7	0	0	...	0-...	36.2	38	16	15	3	18-0	32	.264
2003— Memphis (PCL)		6	6	.500	3.92	1.44	40	7	0	0	...	5-...	78.0	80	38	34	3	32-2	70	.268
— St. Louis (N.L.)		0	0	...	6.00	2.33	7	0	0	0	0	0-0	9.0	10	7	6	0	11-0	8	.278
2004— Memphis (PCL)		0	0	...	0.00	1.88	4	0	0	0	1	1-...	2.2	4	0	0	0	1-0	5	.333
2005— St. Louis (N.L.)		0	1	.000	10.38	2.54	5	0	0	0	0	0-0	4.1	6	6	5	1	5-0	5	.333
— Memphis (PCL)		1	4	.200	4.68	1.82	34	0	0	0	4	1-4	42.1	39	25	22	5	38-1	49	.245
Major League totals (2 years)		0	1	.000	7.43	2.40	12	0	0	0	0	0-0	13.1	16	13	11	1	16-0	13	.296

JULIO, JORGE   P

PERSONAL: Born March 3, 1979, in Caracas, Venezuela. ... 6-1/232. ... Throws right, bats right. ... Full name: Jorge Dandys Julio. ... Name pronounced: HOR-hay HOO-lee-oh. ... High school: Fundacion Bolivariana (Caracas, Venezuela).
TRANSACTIONS/CAREER NOTES: Signed as a non-drafted free agent by Montreal Expos organization (February 14, 1996). ... Traded by Expos to Baltimore Orioles for 3B Ryan Minor (December 22, 2000). ... On suspended list (September 24-28, 2004).
CAREER HITTING: 0-for-0 (.000), 0 R, 0 2B, 0 3B, 0 HR, 0 RBI.

SCOUTING REPORT *Throws:* Julio is a two-pitch pitcher, with a fastball at 90-95 mph and a slider at 85-87. *Tendencies:* He is overpowering but erratic and struggles with command. Overthrows all of his pitches. Doesn't have a good delivery. Rushes and really labors to throw. Is very hyper. Will resort to using only his fastball with the game on the line. *Outlook:* Julio has to prove he can become consistent enough to regain a closer's role. Is better in a setup role because of his lack of command. *Grade 6.5*

K

JORGE JULIO'S PITCHING ZONE

.143	.111	.350
.318	.333	.209
.385	.400	.350

LEFTY-RIGHTY SPLITS

vs.	Avg.	AB	H	2B	3B	HR	RBI	BB	SO	OBP	Slg.
L	.281	135	38	6	0	9	22	11	26	.331	.526
R	.257	148	38	4	0	5	17	13	32	.323	.385

Year	Team (League)	W	L	Pct.	ERA	WHIP	G	GS	CG	ShO	Hld.	Sv.-Opp.	IP	H	R	ER	HR	BB-IBB	SO	Avg.
1996— Dom. Expos (DSL)		1	1	.500	6.06	1.47	10	0	0	0	...	0-...	16.1	13	12	11		11-...	21	
1997— GC Expos (GCL)		5	6	.455	3.58	1.41	15	8	0	0	...	1-...	55.1	57	25	22	0	21-0	42	.256
— W.P. Beach (Fla. St.)		0	0	...	...	...	1	0	0	0	...	0-...	0.0	2	1	1	0	0-0	0	1.000
1998— Vermont (N.Y.-Penn.)		3	1	.750	2.57	1.07	7	7	0	0	...	0-...	42.0	30	12	12	1	15-0	52	.196
— Cape Fear (S. Atl.)		2	5	.500	5.68	1.42	6	6	0	0	...	0-...	31.2	33	24	20	4	12-0	20	.275
1999— Jupiter (Fla. St.)		4	8	.333	3.92	1.31	23	22	0	0	...	0-...	114.2	116	62	50	6	34-0	80	.260
2000— Jupiter (Fla. St.)		2	10	.167	5.90	1.61	21	15	0	0	...	1-...	79.1	93	60	52	4	35-0	67	.292
2001— Bowie (East.)		0	0	...	0.73	0.57	12	0	0	0	...	7-...	12.1	5	1	1	0	2-1	14	.125
— Baltimore (A.L.)		1	1	.500	3.80	1.59	18	0	0	0	3	0-1	21.1	25	13	9	2	9-0	22	.287
— Rochester (Int'l)		1	2	.333	3.74	1.34	34	0	0	0	...	12-...	43.1	39	27	18	4	19-3	48	.232
2002— Baltimore (A.L.)		5	6	.455	1.99	1.21	67	0	0	0	1	25-31	68.0	55	22	15	5	27-3	55	.213
2003— Baltimore (A.L.)		0	7	.000	4.38	1.52	64	0	0	0	2	36-44	61.2	60	36	30	10	34-4	52	.256
2004— Baltimore (A.L.)		2	5	.286	4.57	1.42	65	0	0	0	2	22-26	69.0	59	35	35	11	39-4	70	.228
2005— Baltimore (A.L.)		3	5	.375	5.90	1.40	67	0	0	0	12	0-2	71.2	76	50	47	14	24-4	58	.269
Major League totals (5 years)		11	24	.314	4.20	1.40	281	0	0	0	20	83-104	291.2	275	156	136	42	133-15	257	.245

KAPLER, GABE   OF

PERSONAL: Born August 31, 1975, in Hollywood, Calif. ... 6-2/200. ... Bats right, throws right. ... Full name: Gabriel Stefan Kapler. ... Name pronounced: CAP-ler. ... High school: Taft (Woodland Hills, Calif.). ... Junior college: Moorpark (Calif.).
TRANSACTIONS/CAREER NOTES: Selected by Detroit Tigers organization in 57th round of 1995 free-agent draft. ... Traded by Tigers with Ps Justin Thompson, Francisco Cordero and Alan Webb, C Bill Haselman and 2B Frank Catalanotto to Texas Rangers for OF Juan Gonzalez, P Danny Patterson and C Gregg Zaun (November 2, 1999). ... On disabled list (May 4-June 9, 2000); included rehabilitation assignments to Oklahoma and Tulsa. ... On disabled list (March 23-April 22, 2001); included rehabilitation assignment to Tulsa. ... On disabled list (June 24-July 16, 2002); included rehabilitation assignment to Oklahoma. ... Traded by Rangers with 2B Jason Romano to Colorado Rockies for OF Todd Hollandsworth and P Dennys Reyes (July 31, 2002). ... Released by Rockies (June 20, 2003). ... Signed by Boston Red Sox organization (June 26, 2003). ... Granted free agency (October 28, 2004). ... Signed with Yomiuri of the Japan league (November 22, 2004). ... Signed as free agent by Boston Red Sox (July 15, 2005). ... On disabled list (July 15-30, 2005); included rehabilitation assignments to Lowell and Pawtucket.
HONORS: Named Minor League Player of the Year by THE SPORTING NEWS (1998).
2005 GAMES PLAYED BY POSITION (MLB): OF-36.

GABE KAPLER'S HITTING ZONE

.077	.333	.200
.385	.200	.222
.250	.250	.400

LEFTY-RIGHTY SPLITS

vs.	Avg.	AB	H	2B	3B	HR	RBI	BB	SO	OBP	Slg.
L	.314	35	11	6	0	1	5	0	4	.306	.571
R	.210	62	13	1	0	4	3	11	.269	.226

Year	Team (League)	Pos.	G	AB	R	H	2B	3B	HR	RBI	BB	SO	HBP	GDP	SB-CS	Avg.	OBP	SLG	OPS	E	Avg.
																		BATTING		FIELDING	
1995— Jamestown (N.Y.-Penn.) ...	OF	63	236	38	68	19	4	4	34	23	37	2	4	1-2	.288	.351	.453	.804	9	.926
1996— Fayetteville (S. Atl.)	3B-OF	138	524	81	157	45	4	26	99	62	73	7	6	14-4	.300	.378	.534	.912	7	.968
1997— Lakeland (Fla. St.)	OF	137	519	87	153	40	6	19	87	54	68	5	8	8-6	.295	.361	.505	.865	6	.978
1998— Jacksonville (Sou.)	1B-OF	139	547	113	176	47	6	28	146	66	93	5	6	6-4	.322	.393	.583	.976	5	.984
— Detroit (A.L.)	OF-DH	7	25	3	5	0	1	0	1	0	5			2-0	.200	.231	.280	.511	0	1.000
1999— Detroit (A.L.)	OF-DH	130	416	60	102	22	4	18	49	42	74	2	7	11-5	.245	.315	.447	.762	5	.981
— Toledo (Int'l)	OF	14	54	11	17	6	2	3	14	9	10	0	0	0-1	.315	.400	.667	1.067	0	1.000
2000— Texas (A.L.)	OF	116	444	59	134	32	1	14	66	42	57	0	12	8-4	.302	.360	.473	.833	•10	.969
— Oklahoma (PCL)	OF	3	9	3	3	0	0	0	0	0	0			0-0	.333	.500	.333	.833	0	1.000
— Tulsa (Texas)	OF	3	12	3	7	0	0	1	4	1	2			0-0	.583	.615	.833	1.449	0	1.000
2001— Tulsa (Texas)	OF	5	15	2	5	0	0	0	2	0	0			0-0	.333	.524	.400	.924	0	1.000
— Texas (A.L.)	OF-DH	134	483	77	129	29	1	17	72	61	70	1	10	23-6	.267	.348	.437	.785	1	.997
2002— Texas (A.L.)	OF-1B-DH	72	196	25	51	12	1	0	17	8	30	0	3	5-2	.260	.285	.332	.617	3	.977

							BATTING													FIELDING	
Year	Team (League)	Pos.	G	AB	R	H	2B	3B	HR	RBI	BB	SO	HBP	GDP	SB-CS	Avg.	OBP	SLG	OPS	E	Avg.
	— Oklahoma (PCL)	OF	5	17	6	8	2	0	1	5	3	2	0	...	1-0	.471	.550	.765	1.315	0	1.000
	— Colorado (N.L.)	OF	40	119	12	37	4	3	2	17	8	23	1	2	6-2	.311	.359	.445	.805	0	1.000
2003—	Colorado (N.L.)	OF	39	67	10	15	2	0	0	4	8	18	0	3	2-0	.224	.307	.254	.560	1	.970
	— Colo. Springs (PCL)	OF	13	35	5	6	2	1	0	2	8	10	1	0	4-0	.171	.333	.286	.619	1	.955
	— Lowell (NY-Penn)	OF	1	3	2	2	0	0	0	0	1	0	0	1	1-0	.667	.750	.667	1.417	0	—
	— Portland (East.)	1B-OF	1	3	1	1	1	0	0	0	0	1	0	0	0-0	.333	.333	.667	1.000	0	1.000
	— Boston (A.L.) OF-1B-DH		68	158	29	46	11	1	4	23	14	23	0	5	4-2	.291	.349	.449	.798	6	.934
2004—	Boston (A.L.)	OF-DH	136	290	51	79	14	1	6	33	15	49	2	5	5-4	.272	.311	.390	.700	4	.978
2005—	Boston (A.L.)	OF	36	97	15	24	7	0	1	9	3	15	2	1	1-0	.247	.282	.351	.632	0	1.000
American League totals (8 years)			699	2109	319	570	127	10	60	269	186	322	9	43	59-23	.270	.329	.425	.754	30	.979
National League totals (2 years)			79	186	22	52	6	3	2	21	16	41	1	5	8-2	.280	.340	.376	.716	1	.990
Major League totals (8 years)			778	2295	341	622	133	13	62	290	202	363	10	48	67-25	.271	.330	.421	.751	31	.980

DIVISION SERIES RECORD

Year	Team (League)	Pos.	G	AB	R	H	2B	3B	HR	RBI	BB	SO	HBP	GDP	SB-CS	Avg.	OBP	SLG	OPS	E	Avg.
2003—	Boston (A.L.)	OF-DH	4	9	0	0	0	0	0	0	0	3	0	1	0-0	.000	.000	.000	.000	0	1.000
2004—	Boston (A.L.)	OF	2	5	2	1	0	0	0	0	0	0	0	0	0-0	.200	.200	.200	.400	0	1.000
Division series totals (2 years)			6	14	2	1	0	0	0	0	0	3	0	1	0-0	.071	.071	.071	.143	0	1.000

CHAMPIONSHIP SERIES RECORD

Year	Team (League)	Pos.	G	AB	R	H	2B	3B	HR	RBI	BB	SO	HBP	GDP	SB-CS	Avg.	OBP	SLG	OPS	E	Avg.
2003—	Boston (A.L.)	OF-DH	3	8	0	1	0	0	0	0	0	3	0	1	0-1	.125	.125	.125	.250	0	1.000
2004—	Boston (A.L.)	OF	2	3	0	1	0	0	0	0	0	0	0	0	0-0	.333	.333	.333	.667	0	1.000
Champ. series totals (2 years)			5	11	0	2	0	0	0	0	0	3	0	1	0-1	.182	.182	.182	.364	0	1.000

WORLD SERIES RECORD

Year	Team (League)	Pos.	G	AB	R	H	2B	3B	HR	RBI	BB	SO	HBP	GDP	SB-CS	Avg.	OBP	SLG	OPS	E	Avg.
2004—	Boston (A.L.)	OF	4	2	0	0	0	0	0	0	0	1	0	0	0-0	.000	.000	.000	.000	0	1.000

KARNUTH, JASON   P

PERSONAL: Born May 15, 1976, in LaGrange, Ill. ... 6-2/190. ... Throws right, bats right. ... Full name: Jason Andre Karnuth. ... Name pronounced: CAR-newth. ... High school: Glenbard South (Glen Ellyn, Ill.). ... College: Illinois State.
TRANSACTIONS/CAREER NOTES: Selected by St. Louis Cardinals organization in eighth round of 1997 free-agent draft. ... Traded by Cardinals with P Jared Blasdell to Chicago Cubs (September 24, 2002), completing deal in which Cardinals acquired P Jeff Fassero and cash for two players to be named (August 24, 2002).
CAREER HITTING: 0-for-0 (.000), 0 R, 0 2B, 0 3B, 0 HR, 0 RBI.

LEFTY-RIGHTY SPLITS

vs.	Avg.	AB	H	2B	3B	HR	BB	SO	OBP	Slg.
L	.000	4	0	0	0	0	0	0	.000	.000
R	.667	3	2	1	0	0	2	0	.667	1.000

Year	Team (League)	W	L	Pct.	ERA	WHIP	G	GS	CG	ShO	Hld.	Sv.-Opp.	IP	H	R	ER	HR	BB-IBB	SO	Avg.
1997—	New Jersey (NYP)	4	1	.800	1.86	1.09	7	7	0	0	...	0-...	38.2	33	8	8	0	9-0	23	.229
	— Peoria (Midw.)	0	3	.000	6.65	1.57	4	4	0	0	...	0-...	23.0	29	19	17	1	7-1	12	.315
1998—	Prince Will. (Car.)	8	1	.889	1.67	0.93	16	15	2	2	...	0-...	108.0	86	26	20	3	14-0	53	.224
1999—	Arkansas (Texas)	7	11	.389	5.22	1.43	26	26	2	0	...	0-...	161.0	175	105	93	16	55-0	71	.283
2000—	Arkansas (Texas)	2	3	.400	3.75	1.43	8	8	1	0	...	0-...	51.0	59	30	21	3	14-0	31	.292
	— Memphis (PCL)	5	4	.556	4.04	1.49	16	13	0	0	...	0-...	78.0	89	47	35	7	27-0	28	.294
2001—	Memphis (PCL)	4	4	.500	4.28	1.44	55	0	0	0	...	3-...	73.2	82	37	35	7	24-0	42	.284
	— St. Louis (N.L.)	0	0	...	1.80	2.00	4	0	0	0	...	0-...	5.0	6	1	1	1	4-...	1	.316
2002—	Memphis (PCL)	0	0	...	0.00	1.00	1	0	0	0	...	0-...	1.0	1	0	0	0	0-...	0	.250
	— New Haven (East.)	3	4	.429	3.60	1.39	58	0	0	0	...	4-...	70.0	74	34	28	7	23-2	46	.265
2003—	West Tenn (Sou.)	3	5	.375	3.35	1.31	45	0	0	0	...	13-...	49.0	53	21	18	3	11-2	36	.276
	— Iowa (PCL)	0	1	.000	4.74	1.84	13	0	0	0	...	1-...	19.0	23	12	10	4	12-0	7	.311
2004—	Erie (East.)	0	0	...	2.70	1.40	9	0	0	0	...	6-...	10.0	10	3	3	0	4-1	9	.256
	— Toledo (Int'l)	5	2	.714	3.74	1.09	46	0	0	0	...	2-...	56.0	45	26	23	4	16-2	34	.213
2005—	Toledo (Int'l)	7	2	.778	2.13	1.21	63	0	0	0	3	23-26	67.2	65	19	16	1	17-4	36	.261
	— Detroit (A.L.)	0	0	...	5.40	1.20	3	0	0	0	0	0-0	1.2	2	1	1	0	0-0	0	.286
American League totals (1 year)		0	0	...	5.40	1.20	3	0	0	0	0	0-0	1.2	2	1	1	0	0-0	0	.286
National League totals (1 year)		0	0	...	1.80	2.00	4	0	0	0	0	0-...	5.0	6	1	1	1	4-...	1	.316
Major League totals (2 years)		0	0	...	2.70	1.80	7	0	0	0	0	0-0	6.2	8	2	2	1	4-0	1	.308

KARSAY, STEVE   P

PERSONAL: Born March 24, 1972, in Flushing, N.Y. ... 6-3/210. ... Throws right, bats right. ... Full name: Stefan Andrew Karsay. ... Name pronounced: CAR-say. ... High school: Christ the King (Queens, N.Y.).
TRANSACTIONS/CAREER NOTES: Selected by Toronto Blue Jays organization in first round (22nd pick overall) of 1990 free-agent draft. ... Traded by Blue Jays with a player to be named to Oakland Athletics for OF Rickey Henderson (July 31, 1993); A's acquired OF Jose Herrera to complete deal (August 6, 1993). ... On disabled list (April 26, 1994-remainder of season; April 24, 1995-entire season; and August 6, 1997-remainder of season). ... Traded by A's to Cleveland Indians for P Mike Fetters (December 8, 1997). ... On disabled list (July 2-26 and August 25-September 22, 1999). ... Traded by Indians with P Steve Reed to Atlanta Braves for P John Rocker and 3B Troy Cameron (June 22, 2001). ... Signed as a free agent by New York Yankees (December 7, 2001). ... On disabled list (March 21, 2003-entire season). ... On disabled list (March 12-September 1, 2004); included rehabilitation assignments to Staten Island, Trenton and Columbus. ... Released by Yankees (May 12, 2005). ... Signed by Texas Rangers organization (May 15, 2005).
CAREER HITTING: 0-for-4 (.000), 1 R, 0 2B, 0 3B, 0 HR, 0 RBI.

SCOUTING REPORT **Throws:** His fastball is 90-92 mph, his curveball 77-79 and his splitfinger fastball 85. ***Tendencies:*** Karsay has shown a loose arm, which indicates he's on his way to recovery from a long series of shoulder problems, but he has yet to regain the late movement or sharpness to any pitch. Curveball rolls and splitter tumbles now. ***Outlook:*** It's difficult to define his role; he's not very durable, so when he warms ups must get in the game. Doubtful he can pitch on back-to-back days. Had an outstanding live arm at one time; now just trying to stay in the major leagues. Will be under the microscope in spring training. ***Grade 5.5***

STEVE KARSAY'S PITCHING ZONE

.500	.000	.429
.286	.625	.500
.333	.714	.167

LEFTY-RIGHTY SPLITS

vs.	Avg.	AB	H	2B	3B	HR	RBI	BB	SO	OBP	Slg.
L	.333	45	15	1	0	1	9	4	8	.380	.422
R	.404	52	21	2	1	1	11	3	6	.429	.538

K

Year	Team (League)	W	L	Pct.	ERA	WHIP	G	GS	CG	ShO	Hld.	Sv.-Opp.	IP	H	R	ER	HR	BB-IBB	SO	Avg.
1990—	St. Catharines (NYP)	1	1	.500	0.79	1.01	5	5	0	0	...	0-...	22.2	11	4	2	0	12-0	25	.141
1991—	Myrtle Beach (S. Atl)	4	9	.308	3.58	1.30	20	20	1	0	...	0-...	110.2	96	58	44	7	48-0	100	.240
1992—	Dunedin (Fla. St.)	6	3	.667	2.73	0.99	16	16	3	2	...	0-...	85.2	56	32	26	6	29-0	87	.187
1993—	Knoxville (Sou.)	8	4	.667	3.38	1.25	19	18	1	0	...	0-...	104.0	98	42	39	9	32-1	100	.251
	—Huntsville (Sou.)	0	0	...	5.14	1.14	2	2	0	0	...	0-...	14.0	13	8	8	2	3-0	22	.255
	—Oakland (A.L.)	3	3	.500	4.04	1.33	8	8	0	0	0	0-0	49.0	49	23	22	4	16-1	33	.258
1994—	Oakland (A.L.)	1	1	.500	2.57	1.21	4	4	1	0	0	0-0	28.0	26	8	8	1	8-0	15	.252
1995—	Oakland (A.L.)				Did not play.															
1996—	Modesto (Calif.)	0	1	.000	2.65	1.06	14	14	0	0	...	0-...	34.0	35	16	10	2	1-0	31	.255
1997—	Oakland (A.L.)	3	12	.200	5.77	1.61	24	24	0	0	0	0-0	132.2	166	92	85	20	47-3	92	.304
1998—	Buffalo (Int'l)	6	4	.600	3.76	1.32	16	14	0	0	...	0-...	79.0	89	39	33	5	15-0	63	.276
	—Cleveland (A.L.)	0	2	.000	5.92	1.52	11	1	0	0	2	0-0	24.1	31	16	16	3	6-1	13	.310
1999—	Cleveland (A.L.)	10	2	.833	2.97	1.28	50	3	0	0	9	1-3	78.2	71	29	26	6	30-3	68	.247
2000—	Cleveland (A.L.)	5	9	.357	3.76	1.36	72	0	0	0	11	20-29	76.2	79	33	32	5	25-4	66	.266
2001—	Cleveland (A.L.)	0	1	.000	1.25	0.85	31	0	0	0	8	1-1	43.1	29	6	6	1	8-2	44	.188
	—Atlanta (N.L.)	3	4	.429	3.43	1.37	43	0	0	0	4	7-11	44.2	44	21	17	4	17-8	39	.265
2002—	New York (A.L.)	6	4	.600	3.26	1.32	78	0	0	0	14	12-16	88.1	87	33	32	7	30-14	65	.258
2003—	New York (A.L.)				Did not play.															
2004—	Trenton (East.)	1	0	1.000	7.50	1.67	4	0	0	0	...	0-...	6.0	6	5	5	0	4-0	7	.273
	—Staten Island (N.Y.-Penn.)..	0	0	...	0.00	0.67	3	0	0	0	...	0-...	3.0	1	0	0	0	1-0	1	.100
	—Columbus (Int'l)	0	0	...	5.56	1.59	11	0	0	0	...	0-...	11.1	12	10	7	0	6-0	8	.255
	—New York (A.L.)	0	0	...	2.70	1.05	7	0	0	0	0	0-0	6.2	5	3	2	2	2-0	4	.217
2005—	New York (A.L.)	0	0	...	6.00	2.00	6	0	0	0	0	0-0	6.0	10	5	4	0	2-1	5	.385
	—Oklahoma (PCL)	0	1	.000	13.50	3.00	4	0	0	0	0	1	0-0	4.0	11	9	6	0	1-0	5	.458
	—Frisco (Texas)	1	2	.333	3.64	1.18	19	0	0	0	3	0-2	29.2	29	18	12	2	6-2	30	.248
	—Texas (A.L.)	0	1	.000	7.47	1.98	14	0	0	0	2	0-0	15.2	26	14	13	2	5-0	9	.366
American League totals (10 years)		**28**	**35**	**.444**	**4.03**	**1.38**	**305**	**40**	**1**	**0**	**46**	**34-49**	**549.1**	**579**	**262**	**246**	**51**	**179-29**	**414**	**.271**
National League totals (1 year)		**3**	**4**	**.429**	**3.43**	**1.37**	**43**	**0**	**0**	**0**	**4**	**7-11**	**44.2**	**44**	**21**	**17**	**4**	**17-8**	**39**	**.265**
Major League totals (10 years)		**31**	**39**	**.443**	**3.98**	**1.38**	**348**	**40**	**1**	**0**	**50**	**41-60**	**594.0**	**623**	**283**	**263**	**55**	**196-37**	**453**	**.271**

DIVISION SERIES RECORD

Year	Team (League)	W	L	Pct.	ERA	WHIP	G	GS	CG	ShO	Hld.	Sv.-Opp.	IP	H	R	ER	HR	BB-IBB	SO	Avg.
1999—	Cleveland (A.L.)	0	0	...	9.00	2.00	2	0	0	0	0	0-0	3.0	5	3	3	1	1-0	3	.357
2001—	Atlanta (N.L.)	0	0	...	0.00	0.00	1	0	0	0	1	0-0	1.0	0	0	0	0	0-0	1	.000
2002—	New York (A.L.)	1	0	1.000	6.75	1.13	4	0	0	0	1	0-0	2.2	3	2	2	1	0-0	1	.273
Division series totals (3 years)		**1**	**0**	**1.000**	**6.75**	**1.35**	**7**	**0**	**0**	**0**	**1**	**0-0**	**6.2**	**8**	**5**	**5**	**2**	**1-0**	**5**	**.286**

CHAMPIONSHIP SERIES RECORD

Year	Team (League)	W	L	Pct.	ERA	WHIP	G	GS	CG	ShO	Hld.	Sv.-Opp.	IP	H	R	ER	HR	BB-IBB	SO	Avg.
2001—	Atlanta (N.L.)	0	0	...	2.08	0.92	4	0	0	0	0	0-0	4.1	3	1	1	0	1-1	6	.176

KATA, MATT   2B

PERSONAL: Born March 14, 1978, in Fairview Park, Ohio. ... 6-1/185. ... Bats both, throws right. ... Full name: Matthew John Kata. ... Name pronounced: KATE-ah. ... High school: St. Ignatius (Cleveland). ... College: Vanderbilt.

TRANSACTIONS/CAREER NOTES: Selected by Minnesota Twins organization in 20th round of 1996 free-agent draft; did not sign. ... Selected by Arizona Diamondbacks organization in ninth round of 1999 free-agent draft. ... On disabled list (May 30, 2004-remainder of season). ... Traded by Diamondbacks to Philadelphia Phillies for P Tim Worrell (July 21, 2005).

2005 GAMES PLAYED BY POSITION (MLB): 2B—10, SS—1, DH—1, OF—1.

LEFTY-RIGHTY SPLITS

vs.	Avg.	AB	H	2B	3B	HR	RBI	BB	SO	OBP	Slg.
L	.214	14	3	1	0	0	0	2	2	.313	.286
R	.174	23	4	1	1	0	0	3	4	.269	.304

							BATTING												FIELDING	
Year	Team (League)	Pos.	G	AB	R	H	2B	3B	HR	RBI	BB	SO	HBP	GDP	SB-CS	Avg.	OBP	SLG	OPS		E	Avg.
1999—	South Bend (Mid.)	SS	78	318	40	83	14	5	3	33	28	46	4	5	5-6	.261	.328	.365	.692		22	.937
2000—	South Bend (Mid.) SS-2B-P																					
		P	133	521	82	133	22	9	6	59	52	58	6	10	38-12	.255	.327	.367	.694		39	.937
2001—	Lancaster (Calif.)	2B-SS	119	494	80	146	19	6	10	54	41	79	5	4	30-8	.296	.355	.419	.774		29	.952
	—El Paso (Texas)	2B	4	16	4	7	2	0	0	4	2	2	0	0	0-1	.438	.500	.563	1.063		0	1.000
2002—	El Paso (Texas)	2B-SS-3B	136	578	95	172	33	9	11	57	37	79	4	6	12-7	.298	.341	.443	.784		18	.972
2003—	Tucson (PCL)	2B-SS	48	201	31	58	13	5	3	25	9	29	3	1	2-3	.289	.327	.448	.775		10	.958
	—Arizona (N.L.)	2B-3B-SS	78	288	42	74	16	5	7	29	25	53	1	4	3-2	.257	.315	.420	.736		4	.987
2004—	Arizona (N.L.)	2B-3B-SS	42	162	17	40	9	2	2	13	13	29	0	1	4-1	.247	.301	.364	.665		2	.990
2005—	Arizona (N.L.)	2B-DH	30	31	6	6	2	1	0	6	5	4	0	0	0-1	.194	.306	.323	.628		0	1.000
	—Tucson (PCL)	2B-OF-SS																				
		3B-DH	46	200	25	62	10	3	3	28	6	25	1	4	5-1	.310	.329	.435	.764		9	.955
	—Scran./W.B. (I.L.)	2B-SS-OF																				
		3B	24	96	10	30	5	1	0	4	4	14	0	0	2-1	.313	.340	.385	.725		5	.955
	—Philadelphia (N.L.) 2B-SS-OF		10	6	1	1	0	0	0	0	2	0	0	0-0	.167	.167	.167	.333		0	...
Major League totals (3 years)			**160**	**487**	**66**	**121**	**27**	**8**	**9**	**42**	**43**	**88**	**1**	**5**	**7-4**	**.248**	**.308**	**.392**	**.701**		**6**	**.989**

KAZMIR, SCOTT   P

PERSONAL: Born January 24, 1984, in Houston. ... 6-0/170. ... Throws left, bats left. ... Full name: Scott Edward Kazmir. ... High school: Cypress Falls (Houston).
TRANSACTIONS/CAREER NOTES: Selected by New York Mets organization in first round (15th pick overall) of 2002 free-agent draft. ... Traded by Mets with P Jose Diaz to Tampa Bay Devil Rays for Ps Victor Zambrano and Bartolome Fortunato (July 30, 2004).
CAREER HITTING: 0-for-1 (.000), 0 R, 0 2B, 0 3B, 0 HR, 0 RBI.

SCOUTING REPORT *Throws:* Kazmir has an overpowering 93-97 mph fastball. Also has a slider and a changeup. *Tendencies:* He has as good stuff as any lefthander in the league. Fastball has a tendency to jump late and hitters can't get to it when it's up. Slider is very quick with a small break that he throws to both sides of the plate with improving command. Changeup shows good fade. Has good arm speed and throws without a lot of effort. Can be wild early in his starts until he settles in. Has worked on altering his warmup routine to have better command early. Might always be a high pitch-count pitcher. *Outlook:* He is going to be a 20-game winner and soon. Is one of the best arms to come into the league in years. *Grade 7.3*

SCOTT KAZMIR'S PITCHING ZONE

.277	.219	.188
.352	.379	.264
.265	.316	.182

LEFTY-RIGHTY SPLITS

vs.	Avg.	AB	H	2B	3B	HR	RBI	BB	SO	OBP	Slg.
L	.174	149	26	1	0	1	12	17	49	.256	.201
R	.268	544	146	40	5	11	67	83	125	.371	.421

Year — Team (League)	W	L	Pct.	ERA	WHIP	G	GS	CG	ShO	Hld.	Sv.-Opp.	IP	H	R	ER	HR	BB-IBB	SO	Avg.
2002— Brooklyn (N.Y.-Penn.)	0	1	.000	0.50	0.67	5	5	0	0		0-...	18.0	5	2	1	0	7-0	34	.089
2003— Capital City (S. Atl.)	4	4	.500	2.36	1.02	18	18	0	0		0-...	76.1	50	26	20	4	28-0	105	.185
— St. Lucie (Fla. St.)	1	2	.333	3.27	1.36	7	7	0	0		0-...	33.0	29	15	12	0	16-0	40	.240
2004— St. Lucie (Fla. St.)	1	2	.333	3.42	1.42	11	11	0	0		0-...	50.0	49	20	19	3	22-0	51	.257
— Binghamton (East.)	2	1	.667	1.73	0.96	4	4	0	0		0-...	26.0	16	6	5	0	9-0	29	.188
— Montgomery (Sou.)	1	2	.333	1.44	1.00	4	4	0	0		0-...	25.0	14	7	4	0	11-0	24	.171
— Tampa Bay (A.L.)	2	3	.400	5.67	1.62	8	7	0	0	0	0-0	33.1	33	22	21	4	21-0	41	.256
2005— Tampa Bay (A.L.)	10	9	.526	3.77	1.46	32	32	0	0	0	0-0	186.0	172	90	78	12	* 100-3	174	.248
Major League totals (2 years)	12	12	.500	4.06	1.49	40	39	0	0	0	0-0	219.1	205	112	99	16	121-3	215	.249

KEARNS, AUSTIN — OF

PERSONAL: Born May 20, 1980, in Lexington, Ky. ... 6-3/220. ... Bats right, throws right. ... Full name: Austin Ryan Kearns. ... High school: Lafayette (Lexington, Ky.).
TRANSACTIONS/CAREER NOTES: Selected by Cincinnati Reds organization in first round (seventh pick overall) of 1998 free-agent draft. ... On disabled list (August 27, 2002-remainder of season). ... On disabled list (July 9, 2003-remainder of season); included rehabilitation assignment to Chattanooga. ... On disabled list (April 27-May 19 and June 2-August 24, 2004); included rehabilitation assignments to Louisville.
2005 GAMES PLAYED BY POSITION (MLB): OF—107.

SCOUTING REPORT *Offense:* Kearns got off to such a poor start in 2005 that he was sent to Class AAA. Coming back from thumb problems, he was slow to regain his stroke but improved his bat speed and started to drive the ball more. Has 30-homer power. Has an erect stance and a short stride. Stands on top of the plate to inside-out the ball. Plate discipline is an issue. Puts too much pressure on himself. Is not a good hitter with runners on. *Defense:* A natural right fielder, Kearns has good instincts and takes excellent routes to the ball. Gets good jumps coming in. Excellent arm action creates good life on throws that hit the ground. *Outlook:* He has good physical tools but can't seem to stay healthy and retain his stroke; look for his numbers to increase next season, especially if he stays in Cincinnati. *Grade 7.3*

AUSTIN KEARNS' HITTING ZONE

.292	.250	.133
.321	.533	.262
.065	.120	.143

LEFTY-RIGHTY SPLITS

vs.	Avg.	AB	H	2B	3B	HR	RBI	BB	SO	OBP	Slg.
L	.233	103	24	4	0	4	13	22	28	.372	.388
R	.243	284	69	22	1	14	54	26	79	.317	.475

Year — Team (League)	Pos.	G	AB	R	H	2B	3B	HR	RBI	BB	SO	HBP	GDP	SB-CS	Avg.	OBP	SLG	OPS	E	Avg.
1998— Billings (Pion.)	OF	30	108	17	34	9	0	1	14	23	22	1	4	1-1	.315	.433	.426	.859	4	.905
1999— Rockford (Midwest)	OF	124	426	72	110	36	5	13	48	50	120	9	9	21-8	.258	.346	.458	.804	13	.939
2000— Dayton (Midw.)	OF	136	484	110	148	37	2	27	104	90	93	7	14	18-5	.306	.415	.558	.973	12	.955
2001— Chattanooga (Sou.)	OF	59	205	30	55	11	2	6	36	26	43	6	4	7-5	.268	.364	.429	.793	2	.979
— GC Reds (GCL)	OF	6	17	2	3	2	0	0	4	2	7	0	0	0-0	.176	.227	.294	.521	0	1.000
2002— Chattanooga (Sou.)	OF	12	41	10	11	2	0	5	13	9	9	3	0	1-0	.268	.434	.683	1.117	0	1.000
— Cincinnati (N.L.)	OF	107	372	66	117	24	3	13	56	54	81	6	11	6-3	.315	.407	.500	.907	4	.983
— Louisville (Int'l)	OF	1	4	3	3	2	0	0	2	1	0	0	0	0-0	.750	.800	1.250	2.050	0	1.000
2003— Cincinnati (N.L.)	OF	82	292	39	77	11	0	15	58	41	68	5	7	5-2	.264	.364	.455	.819	2	.990
— Chattanooga (Sou.)	OF	3	5	2	1	0	0	0	1	2	2	1	0	0-0	.200	.500	.200	.700	0	1.000
2004— Louisville (Int'l)	OF-DH	25	83	19	28	7	1	2	15	19	16	2	3	3-1	.337	.471	.518	.989	3	.949
— Cincinnati (N.L.)	OF	64	217	28	50	10	2	9	32	28	71	1	8	2-1	.230	.321	.419	.740	3	.975
2005— Louisville (Int'l)	OF-DH	28	111	24	38	15	1	7	21	11	30	1	9	0-0	.342	.407	.685	1.091	0	1.000
— Cincinnati (N.L.)	OF	112	387	62	93	26	1	18	67	48	107	8	8	0-0	.240	.333	.452	.785	3	.988
Major League totals (4 years)		365	1268	195	337	71	6	55	213	171	327	20	34	13-6	.266	.360	.461	.821	12	.985

KEISLER, RANDY — P

PERSONAL: Born February 24, 1976, in Richards, Texas. ... 6-3/190. ... Throws left, bats left. ... Full name: Randy Dean Keisler. ... Name pronounced: keyz-lur. ... High school: Navasota (Texas), then Palmer (Texas). ... College: Louisiana State.
TRANSACTIONS/CAREER NOTES: Selected by Cleveland Indians organization in 40th round of 1995 free-agent draft; did not sign. ... Selected by Indians organization in 57th round of 1996 free-agent draft; did not sign. ... Selected by New York Yankees organization in second round of 1998 free-agent draft. ... On disabled list (March 31, 2002-entire season). ... Released by Yankees (February 5, 2003). ... Signed by San Diego Padres organization (February 16, 2003). ... Signed as a free agent by Texas Rangers organization (June 16, 2003). ... Released by Rangers (July 14, 2003). ... Signed by Houston Astros organization (July 17, 2003). ... Signed as a free agent by New York Mets organization (March 5, 2004). ... Signed as a free agent by Cincinnati Reds organization (November 12, 2004). ... On disabled list (June 26-July 15, 2005); included rehabilitation assignment to Louisville.
CAREER HITTING: 4-for-19 (.211), 3 R, 2 2B, 0 3B, 1 HR, 2 RBI.

RANDY KEISLER'S PITCHING ZONE

.231	.333	.000
.259	.462	.318
.455	.375	.429

LEFTY-RIGHTY SPLITS

vs.	Avg.	AB	H	2B	3B	HR	RBI	BB	SO	OBP	Slg.
L	.304	69	21	2	0	5	20	8	10	.380	.551
R	.265	162	43	5	2	5	22	20	33	.346	.414

Year — Team (League)	W	L	Pct.	ERA	WHIP	G	GS	CG	ShO	Hld.	Sv.-Opp.	IP	H	R	ER	HR	BB-IBB	SO	Avg.
1998— Oneonta (N.Y.-Penn.)	1	1	.500	7.45	2.17	6	2	0	0		1-...	9.2	14	10	8	0	7-1	11	.341
1999— Greensboro (S. Atl.)	1	1	.500	2.38	0.97	4	4	0	0		0-...	22.2	12	6	6	1	10-0	42	.150
— Tampa (Fla. St.)	10	3	.769	3.30	1.19	15	15	1	0		0-...	90.0	67	43	33	2	40-0	77	.204

Year	Team (League)	W	L	Pct.	ERA	WHIP	G	GS	CG	ShO	Hld.	Sv.-Opp.	IP	H	R	ER	HR	BB-IBB	SO	Avg.
—	Norwich (East.)	3	4	.429	4.57	1.43	8	8	0	0	...	0-...	43.1	45	24	22	2	17-0	33	.273
2000—	Norwich (East.)	6	2	.750	2.60	1.33	11	11	1	0	...	0-...	72.2	63	29	21	4	34-1	70	.227
—	Columbus (Int'l)	8	3	.727	3.02	1.29	17	17	1	1	...	0-...	113.1	104	44	38	9	42-1	86	.244
—	New York (A.L.)	1	0	1.000	11.81	2.25	4	1	0	0	0	0-0	10.2	16	14	14	1	8-0	6	.364
2001—	Columbus (Int'l)	5	7	.417	5.18	1.54	18	18	3	1	...	0-...	97.1	111	67	56	10	39-0	88	.280
—	New York (A.L.)	1	2	.333	6.22	1.70	10	10	0	0	0	0-0	50.2	52	36	35	12	34-0	36	.259
2002—	New York (A.L.)			Did not play.																
2003—	Portland (PCL)	5	1	.833	2.61	1.09	8	6	0	0	...	0-...	41.1	33	12	12	6	12-0	24	.216
—	San Diego (N.L.)	0	1	.000	12.00	2.33	2	2	0	0	0	0-0	6.0	7	9	8	3	7-0	5	.292
—	Oklahoma (PCL)	0	2	.000	8.53	2.05	5	2	0	0	...	0-...	12.2	21	13	12	2	5-0	9	.389
—	New Orleans (PCL)	2	3	.400	4.28	1.53	9	9	0	0	...	0-...	48.1	53	24	23	3	21-2	27	.290
2004—	Norfolk (Int'l)	6	7	.462	3.81	1.46	22	21	1	0	...	0-...	130.0	145	72	55	13	45-1	110	.284
—	St. Lucie (Fla. St.)	1	0	1.000	0.00	0.82	1	0	0	0	...	0-...	3.2	3	0	0	0	0-0	1	.214
2005—	Louisville (Int'l)	5	2	.714	2.88	1.19	12	7	0	0	0	2-3	56.1	54	19	18	6	13-0	46	.250
—	Cincinnati (N.L.)	2	1	.667	6.27	1.64	24	4	0	0	0	0-0	56.0	64	45	39	10	28-2	43	.277
American League totals (2 years)		2	2	.500	7.19	1.79	14	11	0	0	0	0-0	61.1	68	50	49	13	42-0	42	.278
National League totals (2 years)		2	2	.500	6.82	1.71	26	6	0	0	0	0-0	62.0	71	54	47	13	35-2	48	.278
Major League totals (4 years)		4	4	.500	7.01	1.75	40	17	0	0	0	0-0	123.1	139	104	96	26	77-2	90	.278

KELLY, KENNY — OF

PERSONAL: Born January 26, 1979, in Plant City, Fla. ... 6-2/180. ... Bats right, throws right. ... Full name: Kenneth Alphonso Kelly. ... High school: Tampa Catholic. ... College: Miami.

TRANSACTIONS/CAREER NOTES: Selected by Tampa Bay Devil Rays organization in second round of 1997 free-agent draft. ... Traded by Devil Rays to Seattle Mariners for cash (April 4, 2001). ... Traded by Mariners for New York Mets for SS Rey Sanchez (July 29, 2003). ... Signed as a free agent by Cincinnati Reds organization (February 8, 2004). ... On disabled list (June 24-July 15, 2005); included rehabilitation assignments to Louisville and Sarasota. ... Claimed on waivers by Washington Nationals (July 20, 2005).

2005 GAMES PLAYED BY POSITION (MLB): OF—6, DH—1.

LEFTY-RIGHTY SPLITS

vs.	Avg.	AB	H	2B	3B	HR	RBI	BB	SO	OBP	Slg.
L	.333	9	3	1	0	0	0	0	3	.333	.444
R	.250	4	1	0	0	0	2	1	3	.400	.250

									BATTING								FIELDING	
Year	Team (League)	Pos.	G	AB	R	H	2B	3B	HR	RBI	BB	SO	HBP	GDP	SB-CS	Avg.	OBP	SLG	OPS	E	Avg.
1997—	GC Devil Rays (GCL)	OF-OF	27	99	21	21	2	1	2	7	11	24	2	1	6-3	.212	.304	.313	.617	2	.958
1998—	Char., S.C. (S. Atl.)	OF-OF	54	218	46	61	7	5	3	17	19	52	4	1	19-4	.280	.347	.399	.746	5	.964
1999—	St. Pete. (Fla. St.)	OF-OF	51	206	39	57	10	4	3	21	18	46	4	1	14-5	.277	.346	.408	.754	4	.970
2000—	Orlando (South.)	OF-OF	124	489	73	123	17	8	3	29	59	119	6	9	31-21	.252	.338	.337	.675	8	.974
—	Tampa Bay (A.L.)	DH	2	1	0	0	0	0	0	0	0	0	0	...	0-0	.000	.000	.000	.000	—	—
2001—	San Antonio (Texas)	OF-OF	121	478	72	125	20	5	11	46	45	111	3	9	18-12	.262	.326	.393	.719	5	.981
2002—	Tacoma (PCL)	OF-OF	122	391	51	97	13	10	11	53	26	93	2	11	11-3	.248	.296	.417	.713	8	.972
2003—	Tacoma (PCL)	OF	96	341	42	84	15	5	13	37	29	79	6	4	20-7	.246	.313	.434	.747	4	.981
—	Norfolk (Int'l)	OF	30	92	15	24	6	2	4	8	6	25	0	1	5-0	.261	.306	.500	.806	1	.981
2004—	Chattanooga (Sou.)	OF	51	191	33	68	15	3	5	28	26	46	4	2	13-7	.356	.441	.545	.986	0	1.000
—	Louisville (Int'l)	OF	78	268	44	68	15	4	9	43	24	71	3	3	7-4	.254	.318	.440	.758	0	1.000
2005—	Louisville (Int'l)	OF-DH	61	233	43	76	9	4	3	17	20	49	1	7	18-4	.326	.382	.438	.820	0	1.000
—	Sarasota (Fla. St.)	OF	3	12	1	2	1	0	0	1	2	0	0	0	0-0	.167	.231	.250	.481	0	1.000
—	Cincinnati (N.L.)	OF-DH	7	9	2	3	0	0	0	2	0	6	0	1	0-1	.333	.333	.333	.667	0	1.000
—	Harrisburg (East.)	OF	12	47	5	10	3	1	2	6	5	10	0	1	2-1	.213	.288	.447	.735	4	.939
—	New Orleans (PCL)	OF-DH	20	82	11	19	3	1	0	6	9	15	0	2	3-2	.232	.308	.293	.600	2	.974
—	Washington (N.L.)	OF	17	4	3	1	0	0	0	0	1	3	0	0	1-1	.250	.400	.500	.900	0	1.000
American League totals (1 year)			2	1	0	0	0	0	0	0	0	0	0	...	0-0	.000	.000	.000	.000	—	—
National League totals (1 year)			24	13	5	4	0	0	0	2	1	6	0	1	1-2	.308	.357	.385	.742	0	1.000
Major League totals (2 years)			26	14	5	4	1	0	0	2	1	6	0	0	1-2	.286	.333	.357	.690	0	1.000

KENDALL, JASON — C

PERSONAL: Born June 26, 1974, in San Diego. ... 6-0/195. ... Bats right, throws right. ... Full name: Jason Daniel Kendall. ... High school: Torrance (Calif.). ... Son of Fred Kendall, catcher/first baseman with three major league teams (1969-80).

TRANSACTIONS/CAREER NOTES: Selected by Pittsburgh Pirates organization in first round (23rd pick overall) of 1992 free-agent draft. ... On suspended list (July 21-23, 1998). ... On disabled list (July 5, 1999-remainder of season). ... On suspended list (September 19-20, 2001; July 29-August 1, 2003; and September 17-20, 2004). ... Traded by Pirates with cash to Oakland Athletics for Ps Mark Redman and Arthur Rhodes (November 29, 2004).

HONORS: Named N.L. Rookie Player of the Year by THE SPORTING NEWS (1996).

2005 GAMES PLAYED BY POSITION (MLB): C—147, DH—3.

SCOUTING REPORT *Offense:* Kendall is an outstanding contact hitter who uses an exaggerated open stance and a short, compact stroke. Is patient enough to hit at the top of the order and can hit line drives to the gaps but has no power. Has exceptional bat control but not bat speed. One of the better running catchers in the league and gives all-out effort on every ground ball. Has good instincts. *Defense:* A good defensive receiver, he has above-average range to both sides. Blocks and shifts well to balls in the dirt. Lacks natural arm strength; relies on footwork and agility to throw out runners. Doesn't generate a lot of velocity and throws tend to tail. *Outlook:* Kendall's running and hitting skills are unusual for a catcher. Is durable and should only improve. *Grade 8.2*

JASON KENDALL'S HITTING ZONE

.306	.105	.207
.272	.222	.310
.250	.400	.212

LEFTY-RIGHTY SPLITS

vs.	Avg.	AB	H	2B	3B	HR	RBI	BB	SO	OBP	Slg.
L	.293	164	48	7	0	0	13	18	10	.366	.335
R	.263	437	115	21	1	0	40	32	29	.337	.316

									BATTING								FIELDING	
Year	Team (League)	Pos.	G	AB	R	H	2B	3B	HR	RBI	BB	SO	HBP	GDP	SB-CS	Avg.	OBP	SLG	OPS	E	Avg.
1992—	GC Pirates (GCL)	C	33	111	7	29	2	0	0	10	8	9	2	3	2-2	.261	.317	.279	.596	5	.978
1993—	Augusta (S. Atl.)	C	102	366	43	101	17	4	1	40	22	30	7	17	8-5	.276	.325	.352	.677	20	.964
1994—	Salem (Carol.)	C	101	371	68	118	19	2	6	66	47	21	13	15	14-3	.318	.406	.437	.843	9	.980
—	Carolina (Southern)	C	13	47	6	11	2	0	0	6	2	3	2	0	0-0	.234	.294	.277	.571	2	.969

Year Team (League)	Pos.	G	AB	R	H	2B	3B	HR	RBI	BB	SO	HBP	GDP	SB-CS	Avg.	OBP	SLG	OPS	E	Avg.
1995—Carolina (Southern)	C	117	429	87	140	26	1	8	71	56	22	14	10	10-7	.326	.414	.448	.862	8	.989
1996—Pittsburgh (N.L.)	C	130	414	54	124	23	5	3	42	35	30	15	7	5-2	.300	.372	.401	.773	*18	.980
1997—Pittsburgh (N.L.)	C	144	486	71	143	36	4	8	49	49	53	31	11	18-6	.294	.391	.434	.825	11	.990
1998—Pittsburgh (N.L.)	C	149	535	95	175	36	3	12	75	51	51	*31	6	26-5	.327	.411	.484	.884	9	.992
1999—Pittsburgh (N.L.)	C	78	280	61	93	20	3	8	41	38	32	12	8	22-3	.332	.428	.511	.939	7	.988
2000—Pittsburgh (N.L.)	C	152	579	112	185	33	6	14	58	79	79	15	13	22-12	.320	.412	.470	.882	10	.991
2001—Pittsburgh (N.L.)	C-OF	157	606	84	161	22	2	10	53	44	48	20	18	13-14	.266	.335	.358	.693	17	.980
2002—Pittsburgh (N.L.)	C	145	545	59	154	25	3	3	44	49	29	9	11	15-8	.283	.350	.356	.706	9	.990
2003—Pittsburgh (N.L.)	C	150	587	84	191	29	3	6	58	49	40	25	9	8-7	.325	.399	.416	.815	10	.989
2004—Pittsburgh (N.L.)	C	147	574	86	183	32	0	3	51	60	41	19	12	11-8	.319	.399	.390	.789	10	.991
2005—Oakland (A.L.)	C-DH	150	601	70	163	28	1	0	53	50	39	20	*26	8-3	.271	.345	.321	.666	7	.993
American League totals (1 year)		150	601	70	163	28	1	0	53	50	39	20	26	8-3	.271	.345	.321	.666	7	.993
National League totals (9 years)		1252	4606	706	1409	256	29	67	471	454	403	177	95	140-65	.306	.387	.418	.805	101	.988
Major League totals (10 years)		1402	5207	776	1572	284	30	67	524	504	442	197	121	148-68	.302	.382	.407	.789	108	.989

ALL-STAR GAME RECORD

	G	AB	R	H	2B	3B	HR	RBI	BB	SO	HBP	GDP	SB-CS	Avg.	OBP	SLG	OPS	E	Avg.
All-Star Game totals (3 years)	3	3	0	1	0	0	0	0	0	1	0	0	0-0	.333	.333	.333	.667	0	1.000

KENNEDY, ADAM — 2B

PERSONAL: Born January 10, 1976, in Riverside, Calif. ... 6-1/185. ... Bats left, throws right. ... Full name: Adam Thomas Kennedy. ... High school: J.W. North (Riverside, Calif.). ... College: Cal State Northridge.

TRANSACTIONS/CAREER NOTES: Selected by St. Louis Cardinals organization in first round (20th pick overall) of 1997 free-agent draft. ... Traded by Cardinals with P Kent Bottenfield to Anaheim Angels for OF Jim Edmonds (March 23, 2000). ... On disabled list (March 23-April 13, 2001); included rehabilitation assignment to Rancho Cucamonga. ... On disabled list (April 7-22, 2003); included rehabilitation assignment to Rancho Cucamonga. ... Angels franchise renamed Los Angeles Angels of Anaheim for 2005 season. ... On disabled list (March 25-May 2, 2005); included rehabilitation assignments to Salt Lake and Rancho Cucamonga.

2005 GAMES PLAYED BY POSITION (MLB): 2B—127.

SCOUTING REPORT Offense: Kennedy has one of the most unusual strokes in baseball, swinging up and around the ball. Has become more efficient at using the whole field. Hit for more average last season after leveling his swing but also lost power. Is more consistent now. Can handle lefthanded pitching. **Defense:** He still is improving in the field, getting better reads and jumps. Has good hands and makes good pivots on double plays. **Outlook:** Kennedy has made a lot of improvements during the years, becoming a more complete player and a better hitter. **Grade 7.9**

ADAM KENNEDY'S HITTING ZONE

.263	.375	.409
.311	.293	.319
.259	.333	.375

LEFTY-RIGHTY SPLITS

vs.	Avg.	AB	H	2B	3B	HR	RBI	BB	SO	OBP	Slg.
L	.296	125	37	5	0	0	11	6	19	.348	.336
R	.302	291	88	18	0	2	26	23	45	.356	.385

Year Team (League)	Pos.	G	AB	R	H	2B	3B	HR	RBI	BB	SO	HBP	GDP	SB-CS	Avg.	OBP	SLG	OPS	E	Avg.
1997—New Jersey (N.Y.-Penn.)	SS	29	114	20	39	6	3	0	19	13	10	2	3	9-1	.342	.412	.447	.860	7	.951
—Prince Will. (Carol.)	SS	35	154	24	48	9	3	1	27	6	17	2	3	4-3	.312	.346	.429	.774	10	.939
1998—Prince Will. (Carol.)	2B-SS	17	69	9	18	6	0	0	7	5	12	0	1	5-2	.261	.307	.348	.654	5	.938
—Arkansas (Texas)	2B-SS	52	205	35	57	11	2	6	24	8	21	2	4	6-2	.278	.307	.439	.746	15	.940
—Memphis (PCL)	2B-SS	74	305	36	93	22	7	4	41	12	42	1	9	15-4	.305	.331	.462	.794	10	.972
1999—Memphis (PCL)	2B-SS-OF 3B-DH	91	367	69	120	22	4	10	63	29	36	4	7	20-6	.327	.378	.490	.868	18	.953
—St. Louis (N.L.)	2B	33	102	12	26	10	1	1	16	3	8	2	1	0-1	.255	.284	.402	.686	4	.971
2000—Anaheim (A.L.)	2B	156	598	82	159	33	11	9	72	28	73	3	10	22-8	.266	.300	.403	.703	*19	.976
2001—Rancho Cuca. (Calif.)	2B	3	8	3	3	2	0	0	1	2	1	1	0	3-0	.375	.545	.625	1.170	0	1.000
—Anaheim (A.L.)	2B	137	478	48	129	25	3	6	40	27	71	11	7	12-7	.270	.318	.372	.690	10	.984
2002—Anaheim (A.L.)	2B-DH-OF	144	474	65	148	32	6	7	52	19	80	7	5	17-4	.312	.345	.449	.795	11	.983
2003—Rancho Cuca. (Calif.)	2B	3	11	3	3	1	0	1	1	0	2	1	0	0-0	.273	.333	.636	.970	1	.923
—Anaheim (A.L.)	2B-DH	143	449	71	121	17	1	13	49	45	73	9	7	22-9	.269	.344	.394	.743	6	.990
2004—Anaheim (A.L.)	2B	144	468	70	130	20	5	10	48	41	92	13	10	15-5	.278	.351	.406	.757	12	.982
2005—Salt Lake (PCL)	2B-DH	4	17	4	7	1	0	0	4	2	2	0	0	2-0	.412	.450	.471	.921	0	1.000
—Rancho Cuca. (Calif.)	2B-DH	2	5	1	2	0	0	0	1	1	1	0	0	1-1	.400	.500	.400	.900	0	1.000
—Anaheim (A.L.)	2B	129	416	49	125	23	0	2	37	29	64	7	5	19-4	.300	.354	.370	.724	5	.991
American League totals (6 years)		853	2883	385	812	150	26	47	298	189	453	50	44	107-37	.282	.334	.401	.734	63	.984
National League totals (1 year)		33	102	12	26	10	1	1	16	3	8	2	1	0-1	.255	.284	.402	.686	4	.971
Major League totals (7 years)		886	2985	397	838	160	27	48	314	192	461	52	45	107-38	.281	.332	.401	.733	67	.983

DIVISION SERIES RECORD

Year Team (League)	Pos.	G	AB	R	H	2B	3B	HR	RBI	BB	SO	HBP	GDP	SB-CS	Avg.	OBP	SLG	OPS	E	Avg.
2002—Anaheim (A.L.)	2B	4	8	4	4	1	0	1	3	1	2	0	0	1-0	.500	.455	1.000	1.455	0	1.000
2005—Los Angeles (A.L.)	2B	5	17	0	4	0	1	0	2	0	3	0	0	0-2	.235	.235	.353	.588	0	1.000
Division series totals (2 years)		9	25	4	8	1	1	1	5	1	5	0	0	1-2	.320	.321	.560	.881	0	1.000

CHAMPIONSHIP SERIES RECORD

Year Team (League)	Pos.	G	AB	R	H	2B	3B	HR	RBI	BB	SO	HBP	GDP	SB-CS	Avg.	OBP	SLG	OPS	E	Avg.
2002—Anaheim (A.L.)	2B	4	14	5	5	0	0	3	5	0	2	0	0	1-0	.357	.357	1.000	1.357	0	1.000
2005—Los Angeles (A.L.)	2B	5	14	3	4	0	0	0	1	0	1	0	0	0-0	.286	.286	.286	.571	1	.952
Champ. series totals (2 years)		9	28	8	9	0	0	3	6	0	3	0	0	1-0	.321	.321	.643	.964	1	.977

WORLD SERIES RECORD

Year Team (League)	Pos.	G	AB	R	H	2B	3B	HR	RBI	BB	SO	HBP	GDP	SB-CS	Avg.	OBP	SLG	OPS	E	Avg.
2002—Anaheim (A.L.)	2B	7	25	1	7	2	0	0	2	0	7	1	0	0-0	.280	.308	.360	.668	0	1.000

KENNEDY, JOE   P

PERSONAL: Born May 24, 1979, in La Mesa, Calif. ... 6-4/237. ... Throws left, bats right. ... Full name: Joseph Darley Kennedy. ... High school: El Cajon Valley (El Cajon, Calif.). ... Junior college: Grossmont (Calif.).

TRANSACTIONS/CAREER NOTES: Selected by Tampa Bay Devil Rays organization in eighth round of 1998 free-agent draft. ... On suspended list (July 12-19, 2002). ... On disabled list (June 1-July 9, 2003); included rehabilitation assignments to Orlando and Durham. ... Traded by Devil Rays to Colorado Rockies as part of three-team deal in which Devil Rays acquired P Mark Hendrickson from Blue Jays, Blue Jays acquired P Justin Speier from Rockies and Rockies acquired a player to be named from Blue Jays (December 14, 2003); Rockies acquired P Sandy Nin to complete deal (December 15, 2003). ... On disabled list (July 3-August 10, 2004); included rehabilitation assignment to Colorado Springs. ... On suspended list (September 19-25, 2004). ... Traded by Rockies with P Jay Witasick to Oakland Athletics for OF Eric Byrnes and SS Omar Quintanilla (July 13, 2005).

CAREER HITTING: 15-for-88 (.170), 5 R, 1 2B, 1 3B, 0 HR, 6 RBI.

SCOUTING REPORT ***Throws:*** His fastball hits 87-91 mph, and his curveball is 71-76. Uses his straight changeup at 80-82. ***Tendencies:*** Kennedy is tough on lefthanded hitters. Is hard to hit in general when in command of his fastball because he will pitch to both sides of the plate. Is at his best when he is aggressive inside with his fastball, which sets up his changeup and breaking ball. Throws across his body, which gives him a lot of deception. Curve is big and rolling. ***Outlook:*** He is versatile enough to pitch in almost any role, and he moved into the Athletics' rotation after an injury to Rich Harden. Probably is better suited to relief work because he's not overpowering. Deceptive delivery makes him more effective when going through the order just once. ***Grade 6.5***

JOE KENNEDY'S PITCHING ZONE

.306	.417	.296
.336	.455	.242
.328	.326	.309

LEFTY-RIGHTY SPLITS

vs.	Avg.	AB	H	2B	3B	HR	RBI	BB	SO	OBP	Slg.
L	.265	132	35	6	0	4	24	11	27	.329	.402
R	.320	491	157	35	2	16	79	53	70	.388	.497

Year Team (League)	W	L	Pct.	ERA	WHIP	G	GS	CG	ShO	Hld.	Sv.-Opp.	IP	H	R	ER	HR	BB-IBB	SO	Avg.
1998— Princeton (Appal.)	6	4	.600	3.74	1.37	13	13	0	0	...	0-...	67.1	66	37	28	5	26-0	44	.264
1999— Hudson Valley (NYP)	6	5	.545	2.65	1.09	16	*16	1	1	...	0-...	*95.0	78	33	28	2	26-0	*101	.227
2000— Char., S.C. (S. Atl)	11	6	.647	3.30	1.11	22	22	3	2	...	0-...	136.1	122	59	50	6	29-1	142	.242
2001— Orlando (South.)	4	0	1.000	0.19	0.68	7	7	0	0	...	0-...	47.0	29	3	1	0	3-0	52	.178
— Durham (Int'l)	2	0	1.000	2.42	1.19	4	4	0	0	...	0-...	26.0	22	8	7	2	9-0	23	.227
— Tampa Bay (A.L.)	7	8	.467	4.44	1.33	20	20	0	0	0	0-0	117.2	122	63	58	16	34-0	78	.269
2002— Tampa Bay (A.L.)	8	11	.421	4.53	1.32	30	30	5	1	0	0-0	196.2	204	114	99	23	55-0	109	.269
2003— Orlando (South.)	0	0	...	8.10	2.10	1	1	0	0	...	0-...	3.1	6	3	3	0	1-0	3	.400
— Durham (Int'l)	1	0	1.000	1.42	0.90	1	1	0	0	...	0-...	6.1	6	1	1	0	0-0	4	.250
— Tampa Bay (A.L.)	3	12	.200	6.13	1.60	32	22	1	1	1	1-2	133.2	167	101	91	19	47-1	77	.303
2004— Colo. Springs (PCL)	1	1	.500	7.11	1.50	3	2	0	0	...	0-...	12.2	17	11	10	1	2-0	12	.321
— Colorado (N.L.)	9	7	.563	3.66	1.42	27	27	1	0	0	0-0	162.1	163	68	66	17	67-12	116	.265
2005— Colorado (N.L.)	4	8	.333	7.04	1.87	16	16	0	0	0	0-0	92.0	128	81	72	12	44-4	52	.334
— Oakland (A.L.)	4	5	.444	4.45	1.38	19	8	0	0	0	0-2	60.2	64	33	30	8	20-2	45	.267
American League totals (4 years)	22	36	.379	4.92	1.40	101	80	6	2	1	1-4	508.2	557	311	278	66	156-3	309	.278
National League totals (2 years)	13	15	.464	4.88	1.58	43	43	1	0	0	0-0	254.1	291	149	138	29	111-16	169	.292
Major League totals (5 years)	35	51	.407	4.91	1.46	144	123	7	2	1	1-4	763.0	848	460	416	95	267-19	478	.282

KENSING, LOGAN   P

PERSONAL: Born July 3, 1982, in San Antonio. ... 6-1/185. ... Throws right, bats right. ... Full name: Logan French Kensing. ... High school: Boerne (Texas). ... College: Texas A&M.

TRANSACTIONS/CAREER NOTES: Selected by Florida Marlins organization in second round of 2003 free-agent draft. ... On disabled list (June 17, 2005-remainder of season).

CAREER HITTING: 0-for-2 (.000), 0 R, 0 2B, 0 3B, 0 HR, 0 RBI.

LEFTY-RIGHTY SPLITS

vs.	Avg.	AB	H	2B	3B	HR	RBI	BB	SO	OBP	Slg.
L	.636	11	7	3	0	1	1	1	0	.667	1.182
R	.250	16	4	1	0	1	8	2	4	.316	.500

Year Team (League)	W	L	Pct.	ERA	WHIP	G	GS	CG	ShO	Hld.	Sv.-Opp.	IP	H	R	ER	HR	BB-IBB	SO	Avg.
2003— Jamestown (N.Y.-Penn.)	2	4	.333	5.73	1.64	8	6	0	0	...	0-...	33.0	48	23	21	1	6-0	20	.333
— Greensboro (S. Atl.)	0	2	.000	4.50	1.15	4	4	0	0	...	0-...	20.0	18	10	10	2	5-0	11	.243
2004— Jupiter (Fla. St.)	6	7	.462	2.96	1.21	23	23	1	0	...	0-...	127.2	120	53	42	5	35-1	100	.251
— Florida (N.L.)	0	3	.000	9.88	2.05	5	3	0	0	0	0-0	13.2	19	15	15	5	9-0	7	.345
2005— Carolina (Sou.)	4	1	.800	3.18	1.24	7	7	0	0	0	0-0	39.2	35	16	14	0	14-0	33	.229
— Florida (N.L.)	0	0	...	11.12	2.47	3	0	0	0	1	0-0	5.2	11	7	7	2	3-0	4	.407
Major League totals (2 years)	0	3	.000	10.24	2.17	8	3	0	0	1	0-0	19.1	30	22	22	7	12-0	11	.366

KENT, JEFF   2B

PERSONAL: Born March 7, 1968, in Bellflower, Calif. ... 6-1/210. ... Bats right, throws right. ... Full name: Jeffrey Frank Kent. ... High school: Edison (Huntington Beach, Calif.). ... College: California.

TRANSACTIONS/CAREER NOTES: Selected by Toronto Blue Jays organization in 20th round of 1989 free-agent draft. ... Traded by Blue Jays with a player to be named to New York Mets for P David Cone (August 27, 1992); Mets acquired OF Ryan Thompson to complete deal (September 1, 1992). ... On disabled list (July 6-21, 1995). ... Traded by New York Mets with IF Jose Vizcaino to Cleveland Indians for 2B Carlos Baerga and IF Alvaro Espinoza (July 29, 1996). ... Traded by Indians with IF Jose Vizcaino, P Julian Tavarez and a player to be named to San Francisco Giants for 3B Matt Williams and a player to be named (November 13, 1996); Indians traded P Joe Roa to Giants for OF Trenidad Hubbard to complete deal (December 16, 1996). ... On suspended list (August 22-25, 1997). ... On disabled list (June 10-July 10, 1998; August 3-21, 1999; and March 21-April 6, 2002). ... Signed as a free agent by Houston Astros (December 18, 2002). ... On disabled list (June 19-July 16, 2003); included rehabilitation assignment to Round Rock. ... On suspended list (August 6-9, 2003; and September 24-26, 2004). ... Signed as a free agent by Los Angeles Dodgers (December 9, 2004).

RECORDS: Holds major league record for home runs by a second baseman, career (306).

HONORS: Named N.L. Most Valuable Player by Baseball Writers' Association of America (2000).

2005 GAMES PLAYED BY POSITION (MLB): 2B—140, 1B—14.

SCOUTING REPORT *Offense:* Kent has a short, compact stroke and still has a quick bat. Likes the ball up and over the plate. Is adept at hitting the other way but is quick enough to pull the ball. Has good power to all fields. Gets in trouble when he tries to pull pitches away from him. Is a good mistake breaking-ball hitter. Remains one of the best with runners in scoring position. *Defense:* Kent is a slightly rigid fielder who doesn't have soft hands. Tends to play too upright and has restricted range. Has a plus arm and can shorten his throwing motion when making the pivot but doesn't have quick feet. *Outlook:* Kent has an unquestionable desire to win and demands it from his teammates, but he backs it up with his consistent, professional approach. *Grade 8.7*

JEFF KENT'S HITTING ZONE

.385	.267	.371
.290	.455	.233
.324	.423	.238

LEFTY-RIGHTY SPLITS

vs.	Avg.	AB	H	2B	3B	HR	RBI	BB	SO	OBP	Slg.
L	.306	121	37	7	0	4	23	16	12	.384	.463
R	.285	432	123	29	0	25	82	56	73	.375	.525

							BATTING										FIELDING	
Year — Team (League)	Pos.	G	AB	R	H	2B	3B	HR	RBI	BB	SO	HBP	GDP	SB-CS	Avg.	OBP	SLG	OPS	E	Avg.
1989— St. Catharines (NYP)	3B-SS	73	268	34	60	14	1	13	37	33	81	6	2	5-1	.224	.318	.429	.747	29	.906
1990— Dunedin (Fla. St.)	2B	132	447	72	124	32	2	16	60	53	98	6	4	17-7	.277	.360	.465	.825	15	.978
1991— Knoxville (Sou.)	2B	139	445	68	114	34	1	2	61	40	104	10	3	25-6	.256	.379	.351	.730	29	.957
1992— Toronto (A.L.)	3B-2B-1B	65	192	36	46	13	1	8	35	20	47	6	3	2-1	.240	.324	.443	.767	11	.941
— New York (N.L.)	2B-3B-SS	37	113	16	27	8	1	3	15	7	29	1	2	0-2	.239	.289	.407	.696	3	.981
1993— New York (N.L.)	2B-3B-SS	140	496	65	134	24	0	21	80	30	88	8	11	4-4	.270	.320	.446	.765	§ 22	.965
1994— New York (N.L.)	2B	107	415	53	121	24	5	14	68	23	84	10	7	1-4	.292	.341	.475	.816	• 14	.976
1995— New York (N.L.)	2B	125	472	65	131	22	3	20	65	29	89	8	9	3-3	.278	.327	.464	.791	10	.984
1996— New York (N.L.)	3B	89	335	45	97	20	1	9	39	21	56	1	7	4-3	.290	.331	.436	.766	21	.925
— Cleveland (A.L.)	1B-2B-3B DH	39	102	16	27	7	0	3	16	10	22	1	1	2-1	.265	.328	.422	.749	1	.994
1997— San Francisco (N.L.)	2B-1B	155	580	90	145	38	2	29	121	48	133	13	14	11-3	.250	.316	.472	.789	16	.981
1998— San Francisco (N.L.)	2B-1B	137	526	94	156	37	3	31	128	48	110	9	16	9-4	.297	.359	.555	.914	§ 20	.972
1999— San Francisco (N.L.)	2B-1B	138	511	86	148	40	2	23	101	61	112	5	12	13-6	.290	.366	.511	.877	10	.984
2000— San Francisco (N.L.)	2B-1B	159	587	114	196	41	7	33	125	90	107	9	17	12-9	.334	.424	.596	1.021	12	.985
2001— San Francisco (N.L.)	2B-1B	159	607	84	181	49	6	22	106	65	96	11	11	7-6	.298	.369	.507	.877	11	.987
2002— San Francisco (N.L.)	2B-1B	152	623	102	195	42	2	37	108	52	101	4	20	5-1	.313	.368	.565	.933	16	.979
2003— Round Rock (Texas)	2B-DH	3	10	1	3	0	0	1	6	1	1	0	1	0-1	.300	.333	.600	.933	1	.875
— Houston (N.L.)	2B	130	505	77	150	39	1	22	93	39	85	5	13	6-2	.297	.351	.509	.860	11	.983
2004— Houston (N.L.)	2B-DH	145	540	96	156	34	8	27	107	49	96	6	23	7-3	.289	.348	.531	.880	7	.989
2005— Los Angeles (N.L.)	2B-1B	149	553	100	160	36	0	29	105	72	85	8	19	6-2	.289	.377	.512	.889	18	.978
American League totals (2 years)		104	294	52	73	20	1	11	51	30	69	7	4	4-2	.248	.325	.435	.761	12	.966
National League totals (14 years)		1822	6863	1087	1997	454	41	320	1261	634	1271	98	181	88-52	.291	.355	.509	.864	191	.979
Major League totals (14 years)		1926	7157	1139	2070	474	42	331	1312	664	1340	105	185	92-54	.289	.354	.506	.860	203	.978

DIVISION SERIES RECORD

Year — Team (League)	Pos.	G	AB	R	H	2B	3B	HR	RBI	BB	SO	HBP	GDP	SB-CS	Avg.	OBP	SLG	OPS	E	Avg.
1996— Cleveland (A.L.)	1B-2B-3B	4	8	2	1	1	0	0	0	0	0	0	0	0-0	.125	.125	.250	.375	0	1.000
1997— San Francisco (N.L.)	1B-2B	3	10	2	3	0	0	2	2	1	0	0	0	0-0	.300	.417	.900	1.317	0	1.000
2000— San Francisco (N.L.)	1B-2B	4	16	3	6	1	0	0	1	1	3	0	0	1-0	.375	.412	.438	.849	0	1.000
2002— San Francisco (N.L.)	2B	5	19	1	5	2	0	0	1	2	7	1	0	0-0	.263	.364	.368	.732	1	.960
2004— Houston (N.L.)	2B	5	22	3	5	3	0	0	3	2	5	0	0	0-0	.227	.292	.364	.655	0	1.000
Division series totals (5 years)		21	75	11	20	7	0	2	7	7	16	1	2	1-0	.267	.337	.440	.777	1	.991

CHAMPIONSHIP SERIES RECORD

Year — Team (League)	Pos.	G	AB	R	H	2B	3B	HR	RBI	BB	SO	HBP	GDP	SB-CS	Avg.	OBP	SLG	OPS	E	Avg.
2002— San Francisco (N.L.)	2B	5	19	3	5	0	0	0	2	4	1	1	0	0-0	.263	.364	.263	.627	0	1.000
2004— Houston (N.L.)	2B	7	25	3	6	2	0	3	7	3	5	2	0	0-0	.240	.367	.680	1.047	0	1.000
Champ. series totals (2 years)		12	44	6	11	2	0	3	9	7	5	9	3	1	0-0	.250	.365	.500	.865	0	1.000

WORLD SERIES RECORD

Year — Team (League)	Pos.	G	AB	R	H	2B	3B	HR	RBI	BB	SO	HBP	GDP	SB-CS	Avg.	OBP	SLG	OPS	E	Avg.
2002— San Francisco (N.L.)	2B	7	29	6	8	1	0	3	7	1	7	0	0	0-0	.276	.290	.621	.911	0	1.000

ALL-STAR GAME RECORD

	G	AB	R	H	2B	3B	HR	RBI	BB	SO	HBP	GDP	SB-CS	Avg.	OBP	SLG	OPS	E	Avg.
All-Star Game totals (5 years)	5	8	2	2	1	0	0	1	1	0	1				.250	.333	.375	.708	2	.882

KIDA, MASAO   P

PERSONAL: Born September 12, 1968, in Tokyo, Japan. ... 6-3/210. ... Throws right, bats right. ... Name pronounced: muh-SOW KEY-duh.

TRANSACTIONS/CAREER NOTES: Signed as a free agent by Detroit Tigers (December 16, 1998). ... On disabled list (June 30-July 28, 1999); included rehabilitation assignment to Toledo. ... Released by Tigers (June 6, 2000). ... Signed by Orix of the Japan Pacific League (June 8, 2000). ... Signed as a free agent by Los Angeles Dodgers (February 5, 2003). ... Claimed on waivers by Seattle Mariners (September 1, 2004).

CAREER HITTING: 1-for-4 (.250), 0 R, 0 2B, 0 3B, 0 HR, 0 RBI.

LEFTY-RIGHTY SPLITS

vs.	Avg.	AB	H	2B	3B	HR	RBI	BB	SO	OBP	Slg.
L	.500	2	1	0	0	0	0	0	0	.500	.500
R	.167	6	1	0	0	1	1	0	0	.167	.667

Year — Team (League)	W	L	Pct.	ERA	WHIP	G	GS	CG	ShO	Hld.	Sv.-Opp.	IP	H	R	ER	HR	BB-IBB	SO	Avg.
1988— Miami (Fla. St.)	7	17	.292	3.99	1.30	27	27	9	1	...	0-...	162.1	149	88	72	9	62-3	100	
1989— Yomiuri (Jp. Cen.)	2	1	.667	4.62	1.49	8	4	1	0	...	0-...	37.0	41	19	19	...	14-...	26	
1990— Yomiuri (Jp. Cen.)	12	8	.600	2.71	0.99	32	17	13	1	...	0-...	182.2	130	56	55	...	51-...	182	
1991— Yomiuri (Jp. Cen.)	4	7	.364	6.44	1.63	19	5	2	0	...	1-...	50.1	51	41	36	...	31-...	44	
1992— Yomiuri (Jp. Cen.)	3	6	.333	4.53	1.48	29	11	2	1	...	0-...	93.1	103	48	47	...	35-...	87	
1993— Yomiuri (Jp. Cen.)	7	7	.500	3.35	1.28	35	17	1	1	...	2-...	131.2	129	50	49	...	40-...	97	
1994— Yomiuri (Jp. Cen.)	6	8	.429	4.93	1.40	28	12	1	0	...	1-...	87.2	86	52	48	...	37-...	61	
1995— Yomiuri (Jp. Cen.)	7	9	.438	3.40	1.22	40	12	2	1	...	0-...	121.2	117	49	46	...	31-...	97	
1996— Yomiuri (Jp. Cen.)	7	9	.438	3.78	1.25	33	16	3	2	...	0-...	123.2	121	53	52	...	34-...	99	
1997— Yomiuri (Jp. Cen.)	2	2	.500	1.99	1.39	39	0	0	0	...	7-...	49.2	47	13	11	...	22-...	53	
1998— Orix (Jp. Pacific)	4	7	.364	4.62	1.37	36	13	1	0	...	16-...	97.1	97	54	50	...	36-...	74	

Year Team (League)	W	L	Pct.	ERA	WHIP	G	GS	CG	ShO	Hld.	Sv.-Opp.	IP	H	R	ER	HR	BB-IBB	SO	Avg.
1999— Detroit (A.L.)	1	0	1.000	6.26	1.59	49	0	0	0	4	1-1	64.2	73	48	45	6	30-3	50	.289
— Toledo (Int'l)	0	0	...	3.18	1.24	3	0	0	0	...	0-...	5.2	6	2	2	2	1-0	4	.273
2000— Toledo (Int'l)	2	1	.667	2.16	1.00	21	0	0	0	...	7-...	25.0	21	6	6	3	4-1	26	.233
— Detroit (A.L.)	0	0	...	10.13	1.88	2	0	0	0	0	0-0	2.2	5	3	3	1	0-0	0	.385
— Orix (Jp. Pacific)	3	3	.500	5.66	1.77	24	0	0	0	...	3-...	41.1	55	29	26	7	18-...	31	...
2001— Orix (Jp. Pacific)	2	1	.667	3.72	1.24	13	0	0	0	...	1-...	19.1	15	9	8	4	9-...	18	...
2002— Orix (Jp. Pacific)	Did not play.																		
2003— Las Vegas (PCL)	2	4	.333	5.02	1.30	21	12	0	0	...	1-...	84.1	89	53	47	9	23-1	57	.271
— Los Angeles (N.L.)	0	1	.000	3.00	1.50	3	2	0	0	0	0-0	12.0	15	5	4	0	3-0	8	.300
2004— GC Dodgers (GCL)	0	0	...	0.00	0.50	2	2	0	0	...	0-...	4.0	2	0	0	0	0-0	6	.143
— Las Vegas (PCL)	3	1	.750	5.97	1.49	9	5	0	0	...	0-...	37.2	40	25	25	10	16-0	32	.274
— Los Angeles (N.L.)	0	0	...	0.00	1.07	3	0	0	0	0	0-0	4.2	4	0	0	0	1-0	5	.235
— Seattle (A.L.)	0	0	...	8.38	2.07	7	0	0	0	0	0-0	9.2	15	9	9	1	5-0	5	.366
2005— Seattle (A.L.)	0	0	...	4.50	1.00	1	0	0	0	0	0-0	2.0	2	1	1	1	0-0	0	.250
— Tacoma (PCL)	3	6	.333	4.08	1.25	53	0	0	0	4	22-27	79.1	72	37	36	6	27-1	66	.247
American League totals (4 years)	1	0	1.000	6.61	1.65	59	0	0	0	4	1-1	79.0	95	61	58	9	35-3	55	.302
National League totals (2 years)	0	1	.000	2.16	1.38	6	2	0	0	0	0-0	16.2	19	5	4	0	4-0	13	.284
Major League totals (5 years)	1	1	.500	5.83	1.60	65	2	0	0	4	1-1	95.2	114	66	62	9	39-3	68	.298

K KIELTY, BOBBY — OF

PERSONAL: Born August 5, 1976, in Fontana, Calif. ... 6-1/225. ... Bats both, throws right. ... Full name: Robert Michael Kielty. ... Name pronounced: kell-tee. ... High school: Canyon Springs (Moreno Valley, Calif.). ... College: Mississippi.

TRANSACTIONS/CAREER NOTES: Signed as a non-drafted free agent by Minnesota Twins organization (February 16, 1999). ... Traded by Twins to Toronto Blue Jays for OF Shannon Stewart and a player to be named (July 16, 2003); Twins acquired P Dave Gassner to complete deal (December 16, 2003). ... Traded by Blue Jays with cash to Oakland Athletics for P Ted Lilly (November 18, 2003).

2005 GAMES PLAYED BY POSITION (MLB): OF—96, DH—17.

SCOUTING REPORT **Offense:** Kielty hits so much better from the right side that he might want to consider hitting that way exclusively. Is patient and doesn't strike out much. Is not a good runner anymore and is not a threat on the bases. Has slightly more power hitting lefthanded. **Defense:** His arm strength and ability to play left or right are assets. Does not take consistent routes or get consistent jumps, especially going back. Has average range. **Outlook:** Kielty is an oft-injured fourth outfielder, but his versatility makes him valuable. *Grade 6.1*

BOBBY KIELTY'S HITTING ZONE

.278	.417	.125
.364	.364	.267
.231	.250	.207

LEFTY-RIGHTY SPLITS

vs.	Avg.	AB	H	2B	3B	HR	RBI	BB	SO	OBP	Slg.
L	.322	143	46	9	0	4	23	18	22	.398	.469
R	.226	234	53	11	0	6	34	32	45	.322	.350

Year Team (League)	Pos.	G	AB	R	H	2B	3B	HR	RBI	BB	SO	HBP	GDP	SB-CS	Avg.	OBP	SLG	OPS	E	Avg.
1999— Quad City (Midw.)	OF	69	245	52	72	13	1	13	43	43	56	3	7	12-3	.294	.401	.514	.916	3	.977
2000— New Britain (East.)	OF	129	451	79	118	30	3	14	65	98	109	5	16	6-4	.262	.396	.435	.831	3	.988
— Salt Lake (PCL)	OF	9	33	8	8	4	0	0	2	7	10	0	0	0-0	.242	.375	.364	.739	1	.957
2001— Edmonton (PCL)	OF	94	341	58	98	25	2	12	50	53	76	6	11	5-0	.287	.391	.478	.869	2	.991
— Minnesota (A.L.)	OF-DH	37	104	8	26	8	0	2	14	8	25	1	2	3-0	.250	.297	.385	.681	3	.956
2002— Edmonton (PCL)	OF	2	7	0	3	1	0	0	0	1	1	0	1	0-0	.429	.500	.571	1.071	0	1.000
— Minnesota (A.L.)	OF-DH-1B	112	289	49	84	14	3	12	46	52	66	5	4	4-1	.291	.405	.484	.890	0	1.000
2003— Minnesota (A.L.)	OF-DH	75	238	40	60	13	0	9	32	42	56	3	5	6-2	.252	.370	.420	.790	2	.972
— Toronto (A.L.)	OF-1B	62	189	31	44	13	1	4	25	29	36	4	6	2-1	.233	.342	.376	.718	1	.991
2004— Oakland (A.L.)	OF-DH	83	238	29	51	14	1	7	31	35	47	3	5	1-0	.214	.321	.370	.691	1	.990
2005— Oakland (A.L.)	OF-DH	116	377	55	99	20	0	10	57	50	67	2	14	3-2	.263	.350	.395	.746	3	.983
Major League totals (5 years)		485	1435	212	364	82	5	44	205	216	297	18	36	19-6	.254	.355	.410	.765	10	.986

DIVISION SERIES RECORD

Year Team (League)	Pos.	G	AB	R	H	2B	3B	HR	RBI	BB	SO	HBP	GDP	SB-CS	Avg.	OBP	SLG	OPS	E	Avg.
2002— Minnesota (A.L.)	OF-DH	3	4	0	0	0	0	0	0	0	1	0	0	0-0	.000	.000	.000	.000	1	1.000

CHAMPIONSHIP SERIES RECORD

Year Team (League)	Pos.	G	AB	R	H	2B	3B	HR	RBI	BB	SO	HBP	GDP	SB-CS	Avg.	OBP	SLG	OPS	E	Avg.
2002— Minnesota (A.L.)	DH-OF	4	3	0	0	0	0	0	1	1	2	0	0	0-0	.000	.250	.000	.250	0	...

KIM, BYUNG-HYUN — P

PERSONAL: Born January 19, 1979, in Gwangju, South Korea. ... 5-9/180. ... Throws right, bats right. ... Name pronounced: bee-yung hee-yun. ... High school: Kwang-ju (Korea). ... College: Sungkyunkwan (South Korea).

TRANSACTIONS/CAREER NOTES: Signed as a non-drafted free agent by Arizona Diamondbacks organization (February 19, 1999). ... On disabled list (July 28-September 7, 2000). ... On disabled list (April 30-May 27, 2003); included rehabilitation assignment to Tucson. ... Traded by Diamondbacks to Boston Red Sox for IF Shea Hillenbrand (May 30, 2003). ... On disabled list (March 26-April 29, 2004); included rehabilitation assignment to Sarasota. ... Traded by Red Sox to Colorado Rockies for P Christopher Narveson and C Charles Johnson (March 30, 2005).

CAREER HITTING: 9-for-70 (.129), 0 R, 1 2B, 0 3B, 0 HR, 5 RBI.

SCOUTING REPORT *Throws:* Kim is a submarine-style pitcher who has a 86-88 mph fastball, a sweeping slider and a changeup. *Tendencies:* His fastball has some sinking action, and Kim can bore it in on righthanded hitters or spot it to the outside corner against them. Has a wide, rising slider that is not sharp. Has good arm speed on his change. Loses focus quickly and becomes tentative in adverse situations. *Outlook:* Kim has closed and worked in a setup role, but he is better suited to starting, which he did for much of last season with the Rockies. *Grade 5.8*

BYUNG-HYUN KIM'S PITCHING ZONE

.150	.167	.185
.243	.500	.271
.382	.333	.233

LEFTY-RIGHTY SPLITS

vs.	Avg.	AB	H	2B	3B	HR	RBI	BB	SO	OBP	Slg.
L	.308	276	85	19	2	8	43	37	43	.406	.478
R	.244	291	71	21	2	9	38	34	72	.326	.423

Year	Team (League)	W	L	Pct.	ERA	WHIP	G	GS	CG	ShO	Hld.	Sv.-Opp.	IP	H	R	ER	HR	BB-IBB	SO	Avg.
1999—	El Paso (Texas)	2	0	1.000	2.11	0.70	10	0	0	0	...	0-...	21.1	6	5	5	0	9-0	32	.092
—	Tucson (PCL)	4	0	1.000	2.40	1.20	11	3	0	0	...	1-...	30.0	21	9	8	2	15-1	40	.196
—	Arizona (N.L.)	1	2	.333	4.61	1.46	25	0	0	0	3	1-4	27.1	20	15	14	2	20-2	31	.211
—	Ariz. D'backs (AZL)	0	0	...	0.00	1.00	1	1	0	0	...	0-...	2.0	1	0	0	0	1-0	2	.167
2000—	Arizona (N.L.)	6	6	.500	4.46	1.39	61	1	0	0	5	14-20	70.2	52	39	35	9	46-5	111	.200
—	Tucson (PCL)	0	0	...	0.00	0.60	2	2	0	0	...	0-...	8.1	1	0	0	0	4-0	13	.042
2001—	Arizona (N.L.)	5	6	.455	2.94	1.04	78	0	0	0	11	19-23	98.0	58	32	32	10	44-3	113	.173
2002—	Arizona (N.L.)	8	3	.727	2.04	1.07	72	0	0	0	0	36-42	84.0	64	20	19	5	26-2	92	.208
2003—	Tucson (PCL)	1	1	.500	2.55	1.00	3	3	0	0	...	0-...	17.2	17	5	5	2	1-0	8	.270
—	Arizona (N.L.)	1	5	.167	3.56	1.14	7	7	0	0	...	0-0	43.0	34	17	17	6	15-0	33	.214
—	Boston (A.L.)	8	5	.615	3.18	1.11	49	5	0	0	1	16-19	79.1	70	38	28	6	18-3	69	.230
2004—	Sarasota (Fla. St.)	0	0	...	0.00	0.00	1	1	0	0	...	0-...	2.0	0	0	0	0	0-0	2	.000
—	Pawtucket (Int'l)	2	6	.250	5.34	1.37	22	19	0	0	...	0-...	60.2	71	43	36	6	12-0	39	.289
—	Boston (A.L.)	2	1	.667	6.23	1.38	7	3	0	0	...	0-0	17.1	17	15	12	1	7-1	6	.258
2005—	Colorado (N.L.)	5	12	.294	4.86	1.53	40	22	0	0	1	0-2	148.0	156	82	80	17	71-8	115	.275
American League totals (2 years)		10	6	.625	3.72	1.16	56	8	0	0	1	16-19	96.2	87	53	40	7	25-4	75	.235
National League totals (6 years)		26	34	.433	3.76	1.29	283	30	0	0	20	70-91	471.0	384	205	197	49	222-20	495	.223
Major League totals (7 years)		36	40	.474	3.76	1.26	339	38	0	0	21	86-110	567.2	471	258	237	56	247-24	570	.225

DIVISION SERIES RECORD

Year	Team (League)	W	L	Pct.	ERA	WHIP	G	GS	CG	ShO	Hld.	Sv.-Opp.	IP	H	R	ER	HR	BB-IBB	SO	Avg.
2001—	Arizona (N.L.)	0	0	...	0.00	2.25	1	0	0	0	0	1-1	1.1	1	0	0	0	2-0	1	.250
2002—	Arizona (N.L.)	0	0	...	18.00	5.00	1	0	0	0	0	0-0	1.0	2	2	2	0	3-1	0	.400
2003—	Boston (A.L.)	0	0	...	13.50	1.50	1	0	0	0	0	0-0	0.2	1	1	1	0	1-0	1	.000
Division series totals (3 years)		0	0	...	9.00	3.00	3	0	0	0	0	1-1	3.0	3	3	3	0	6-1	2	.273

CHAMPIONSHIP SERIES RECORD

Year	Team (League)	W	L	Pct.	ERA	WHIP	G	GS	CG	ShO	Hld.	Sv.-Opp.	IP	H	R	ER	HR	BB-IBB	SO	Avg.
2001—	Arizona (N.L.)	0	0	...	0.00	0.20	3	0	0	0	0	2-2	5.0	0	0	0	0	1-0	3	.000

WORLD SERIES RECORD

Year	Team (League)	W	L	Pct.	ERA	WHIP	G	GS	CG	ShO	Hld.	Sv.-Opp.	IP	H	R	ER	HR	BB-IBB	SO	Avg.
2001—	Arizona (N.L.)	0	1	.000	13.50	2.10	2	0	0	0	0	0-2	3.1	8	5	5	3	1-0	6	.375

ALL-STAR GAME RECORD

		W	L	Pct.	ERA	WHIP	G	GS	CG	ShO	Hld.	Sv.-Opp.	IP	H	R	ER	HR	BB-IBB	SO	Avg.
All-Star Game totals (1 year)		0	0	...	54.00	9.00	1	0	0	0	0	0-0	0.1	3	2	2	0	0-0	0	.750

KIM, SUN-WOO   P

PERSONAL: Born September 4, 1977, in Inchon, South Korea. ... 6-1/185. ... Throws right, bats right. ... Full name: Sun-Woo Kim. ... College: Korea University.
TRANSACTIONS/CAREER NOTES: Signed as a non-drafted free agent by Boston Red Sox organization (November 21, 1997). ... Traded by Red Sox with P Seung Song and a player to be named to Montreal Expos for OF Cliff Floyd (July 30, 2002). ... Expos franchise transferred to Washington, D.C., and renamed Washington Nationals for 2005 season (December 3, 2004). ... Claimed on waivers by Colorado Rockies (August 5, 2005).
CAREER HITTING: 10-for-58 (.172), 5 R, 2 2B, 0 3B, 0 HR, 8 RBI.

SCOUTING REPORT *Throws:* He throws a fastball at 91-94 mph, a slider and a circle change. *Tendencies:* Kim has a herky-jerky motion with a short, three-quarters arm action that helps the ball jump at hitters. Is effective the first time through the order, but starts to rush and forces his motion to increase velocity, pushing his fastball up. Fastball down has good life. Tight slider has good velocity and late break. Circle change is hard but has good sinking action. *Outlook:* Kim is a versatile pitcher who is best used in a middle role so he's not overextended. Has shown improvement in both stuff and demeanor. *Grade 5.5*

SUN-WOO KIM'S PITCHING ZONE

.286	.400	.400
.304	.333	.333
.313	.304	.333

LEFTY-RIGHTY SPLITS

vs.	Avg.	AB	H	2B	3B	HR	RBI	BB	SO	OBP	Slg.
L	.279	147	41	4	1	2	18	6	21	.308	.361
R	.304	184	56	13	0	8	29	15	34	.361	.505

Year	Team (League)	W	L	Pct.	ERA	WHIP	G	GS	CG	ShO	Hld.	Sv.-Opp.	IP	H	R	ER	HR	BB-IBB	SO	Avg.
1998—	Sarasota (Fla. St.)	12	8	.600	4.82	1.30	26	24	5	0	...	0-...	153.0	159	88	82	18	40-1	132	.264
1999—	Trenton (East.)	9	8	.529	4.89	1.37	26	26	1	1	...	0-...	149.0	160	86	81	16	44-2	130	.275
2000—	Pawtucket (Int'l)	11	7	.611	6.03	1.58	26	25	0	0	...	0-...	134.1	170	98	90	17	42-1	116	.309
2001—	Pawtucket (Int'l)	6	7	.462	5.36	1.35	19	14	0	0	...	0-...	89.0	93	55	53	10	27-1	79	.272
—	Boston (A.L.)	0	2	.000	5.83	1.80	20	2	0	0	1	0-0	41.2	54	27	27	1	21-5	27	.312
2002—	Pawtucket (Int'l)	4	2	.667	3.18	1.10	8	8	1	0	...	0-...	45.1	34	18	16	4	16-0	37	.206
—	Boston (A.L.)	2	0	1.000	7.45	1.41	15	2	0	0	2	0-0	29.0	34	24	24	5	7-0	18	.288
—	Ottawa (Int'l)	3	0	1.000	1.24	1.03	7	7	1	1	...	0-...	43.2	29	11	6	2	16-0	28	.195
—	Montreal (N.L.)	1	0	1.000	0.89	1.23	4	3	0	0	0	0-0	20.1	18	2	2	0	7-2	11	.250
2003—	Montreal (N.L.)	0	1	.000	8.36	2.29	4	3	0	0	0	0-0	14.0	24	13	13	0	8-0	5	.407

K

Year	Team (League)	W	L	Pct.	ERA	WHIP	G	GS	CG	ShO	Hld.	Sv.-Opp.	IP	H	R	ER	HR	BB-IBB	SO	Avg.
	—Edmonton (PCL)	10	8	.556	5.03	1.50	22	22	3	2	...	0-...	132.1	147	83	74	18	53-1	83	.281
2004—	Montreal (N.L.)	4	6	.400	4.58	1.47	43	17	0	0	...	2	0-0	135.2	145	80	69	17	55-11	87	.275
2005—	New Orleans (PCL)	4	2	.667	2.76	1.24	9	9	0	0	0	0-0	49.0	46	23	15	4	15-0	38	.249
	—Washington (N.L.)	1	2	.333	6.14	1.67	12	2	0	0	0	0-0	29.1	41	20	20	3	8-2	17	.336
	—Colorado (N.L.)	5	1	.833	4.22	1.29	12	8	1	1	0	0-0	53.1	56	26	25	7	13-0	38	.268
American League totals (2 years)		2	2	.500	6.50	1.64	35	4	0	0	3	0-0	70.2	88	51	51	6	28-5	45	.302
National League totals (4 years)		11	10	.524	4.59	1.48	75	33	1	1	2	0-0	252.2	284	141	129	33	91-15	158	.287
Major League totals (5 years)		13	12	.520	5.01	1.52	110	37	1	1	5	0-0	323.1	372	192	180	39	119-20	203	.291

KING, RAY — P

PERSONAL: Born January 15, 1974, in Chicago. ... 6-1/242. ... Throws left, bats left. ... Full name: Raymond Keith King. ... High school: Ripley (Tenn.). ... College: Lambuth (Tenn.).

TRANSACTIONS/CAREER NOTES: Selected by Cincinnati Reds organization in eighth round of 1995 free-agent draft. ... Loaned by Reds organization to Atlanta Braves organization (March 22-June 11, 1996). ... Traded by Reds to Braves (June 11, 1996), completing deal in which Reds acquired OF Mike Kelly for P Chad Fox and a player to be named (January 9, 1996). ... Traded by Braves to Chicago Cubs for P Jon Ratliff (January 20, 1998). ... Traded by Cubs to Milwaukee Brewers for P Doug Johnston (April 14, 2000). ... On disabled list (April 4-19, 2002); included rehabilitation assignment to Indianapolis. ... Traded by Brewers to Braves for 3B Wes Helms and P John Foster (December 16, 2002). ... Traded by Braves with Ps Jason Marquis and Adam Wainwright to St. Louis Cardinals for OF J.D. Drew and C/OF Eli Marrero (December 14, 2003).

CAREER HITTING: 0-for-5 (.000), 0 R, 0 2B, 0 3B, 0 HR, 0 RBI.

SCOUTING REPORT

Throws: King has two pitches—a fastball that ranges from 89-92 mph, and a slider. *Tendencies:* His tight, running slider and running fastball work well against left-handed batters. Had problems with righthanders last season. Will struggle to command his fastball at times and will run up high pitch counts. Is a bulldog type with a resilient arm who loves to take the ball in key situations. *Outlook:* King can be effective if he isn't overextended. Lost his situational role late in the season because of his lack of command. Needs a change of scenery and to shed some pounds. *Grade 6.5*

RAY KING'S PITCHING ZONE

.267	.000	.222
.444	.435	.259
.333	.455	.188

LEFTY-RIGHTY SPLITS

vs.	Avg.	AB	H	2B	3B	HR	RBI	BB	SO	OBP	Slg.
L	.244	86	21	2	1	2	19	6	16	.313	.360
R	.352	71	25	4	2	2	9	10	7	.432	.549

Year	Team (League)	W	L	Pct.	ERA	WHIP	G	GS	CG	ShO	Hld.	Sv.-Opp.	IP	H	R	ER	HR	BB-IBB	SO	Avg.
1995—	Billings (Pion.)	3	0	1.000	1.67	1.07	28	0	0	0	...	5-...	43.0	31	11	8	1	15-3	43	.204
1996—	Macon (S. Atl.)	3	5	.375	2.80	1.17	18	10	1	0	...	0-...	70.2	63	34	22	4	20-0	63	.237
	—Durham (Carol.)	3	6	.333	4.46	1.44	14	14	2	0	...	0-...	82.2	104	54	41	3	15-2	52	.308
1997—	Greenville (Sou.)	5	5	.500	6.85	1.66	12	9	0	0	...	0-...	65.2	85	53	50	9	24-2	42	.304
	—Durham (Carol.)	6	9	.400	5.40	1.60	24	6	0	0	...	3-...	71.2	89	54	43	6	26-4	60	.300
1998—	West Tenn (Sou.)	1	2	.333	2.43	1.11	25	0	0	0	...	3-...	29.2	23	9	8	1	10-0	26	.213
	—Iowa (PCL)	1	3	.250	5.01	1.58	37	0	0	0	...	2-...	32.1	36	20	18	4	15-1	26	.283
1999—	Iowa (PCL)	4	4	.500	1.88	1.23	37	0	0	0	...	2-...	43.0	31	11	9	1	22-3	41	.200
	—Chicago (N.L.)	0	0	...	5.91	1.97	10	0	0	0	2	0-0	10.2	11	8	7	2	10-0	5	.289
2000—	Iowa (PCL)	1	0	1.000	0.00	0.75	1	0	0	0	...	0-...	1.1	1	0	0	0	0-0	1	.200
	—Indianapolis (Int'l)	0	3	.000	3.51	1.48	29	0	0	0	...	1-...	25.2	26	15	10	1	12-0	20	.271
	—Milwaukee (N.L.)	3	2	.600	1.26	0.98	36	0	0	0	5	0-1	28.2	18	7	4	0	10-1	19	.180
2001—	Milwaukee (N.L.)	0	4	.000	3.60	1.35	82	0	0	0	18	1-4	55.0	49	22	22	5	25-7	49	.241
2002—	Milwaukee (N.L.)	3	2	.600	3.05	1.31	76	0	0	0	15	0-1	65.0	61	24	22	5	24-6	50	.255
	—Indianapolis (Int'l)	0	0	...	0.00	1.00	1	0	0	0	...	0-...	1.0	1	0	0	0	1-0	1	.333
2003—	Atlanta (N.L.)	3	4	.429	3.51	1.24	80	0	0	0	18	0-1	59.0	46	30	23	3	27-2	43	.213
2004—	St. Louis (N.L.)	5	2	.714	2.61	1.08	86	0	0	0	31	0-1	62.0	43	19	18	1	24-0	40	.197
2005—	St. Louis (N.L.)	4	4	.500	3.38	1.55	77	0	0	0	16	0-6	40.0	46	17	15	4	16-0	23	.293
Major League totals (7 years)		18	18	.500	3.12	1.28	447	0	0	0	105	1-14	320.1	274	127	111	21	136-16	229	.234

DIVISION SERIES RECORD

Year	Team (League)	W	L	Pct.	ERA	WHIP	G	GS	CG	ShO	Hld.	Sv.-Opp.	IP	H	R	ER	HR	BB-IBB	SO	Avg.
2003—	Atlanta (N.L.)	0	0	...	0.00	2.00	4	0	0	0	1	0-0	1.0	1	0	0	0	1-0	0	.500
2004—	St. Louis (N.L.)	0	0	...	0.00	0.00	3	0	0	0	1	0-0	2.1	0	0	0	0	0-0	1	.000
Division series totals (2 years)		0	0	...	0.00	0.60	7	0	0	0	2	0-0	3.1	1	0	0	0	1-0	1	.111

CHAMPIONSHIP SERIES RECORD

Year	Team (League)	W	L	Pct.	ERA	WHIP	G	GS	CG	ShO	Hld.	Sv.-Opp.	IP	H	R	ER	HR	BB-IBB	SO	Avg.
2004—	St. Louis (N.L.)	0	0	...	10.80	2.40	4	0	0	0	1	0-0	1.2	4	2	2	0	0-0	1	.500

WORLD SERIES RECORD

Year	Team (League)	W	L	Pct.	ERA	WHIP	G	GS	CG	ShO	Hld.	Sv.-Opp.	IP	H	R	ER	HR	BB-IBB	SO	Avg.
2004—	St. Louis (N.L.)	0	0	...	0.00	0.75	3	0	0	0	0	0-0	2.2	1	0	0	0	1-0	1	.125

KINNEY, MATT — P

PERSONAL: Born December 16, 1976, in Bangor, Maine. ... 6-5/228. ... Throws right, bats right. ... Full name: Matthew John Kinney. ... High school: Bangor (Maine).

TRANSACTIONS/CAREER NOTES: Selected by Boston Red Sox organization in sixth round of 1995 free-agent draft. ... Traded by Red Sox with P Joe Thomas and OF John Barnes to Minnesota Twins for P Greg Swindell and 1B Orlando Merced (July 31, 1998). ... On disabled list (June 30-August 19, 2002); included rehabilitation assignments to GCL Twins, Fort Myers and New Britain. ... Traded by Twins with C Javier Valentin to Milwaukee Brewers for Ps Matt Yeatman and Gerard Oakes (November 15, 2002). ... Claimed on waivers by Kansas City Royals (August 13, 2004). ... Signed as a free agent by San Francisco Giants organization (December 10, 2004).

CAREER HITTING: 5-for-69 (.072), 3 R, 1 2B, 0 3B, 0 HR, 1 RBI.

LEFTY-RIGHTY SPLITS

vs.	Avg.	AB	H	2B	3B	HR	RBI	BB	SO	OBP	Slg.
L	.471	17	8	2	0	0	2	3	1	.550	.588
R	.333	30	10	1	0	2	6	3	2	.412	.567

Year	Team (League)	W	L	Pct.	ERA	WHIP	G	GS	CG	ShO	Hld.	Sv.-Opp.	IP	H	R	ER	HR	BB-IBB	SO	Avg.
1995—	GC Red Sox (GCL)	1	3	.250	2.93	1.41	8	2	0	0	...	2-...	27.2	29	13	9	0	10-0	11	.279
1996—	Lowell (NY-Penn)	3	9	.250	2.68	1.28	15	15	0	0	...	0-...	87.1	68	51	26	0	44-2	72	.207

K

Year Team (League)	W	L	Pct.	ERA	WHIP	G	GS	CG	ShO	Hld.	Sv.-Opp.	IP	H	R	ER	HR	BB-IBB	SO	Avg.
1997— Michigan (Midw.)	8	5	.615	3.53	1.46	22	22	2	1	...	0-...	117.1	93	59	46	4	78-2	123	.217
1998— Sarasota (Fla. St.)	9	6	.600	4.01	1.52	22	20	2	1	...	1-...	121.1	109	70	54	5	75-3	96	.241
— Fort Myers (FSL)	3	2	.600	3.13	1.31	7	7	0	0	...	0-...	37.1	31	18	13	0	18-0	39	.220
1999— New Britain (East.)	4	7	.364	7.12	1.73	14	13	0	0	...	0-...	60.2	69	54	48	8	36-0	50	.289
— GC Twins (GCL)	0	1	.000	4.76	1.59	3	3	0	0	...	0-...	5.2	6	4	3	0	3-0	8	.286
2000— New Britain (East.)	6	1	.857	2.71	1.26	15	15	0	0	...	0-...	86.1	74	31	26	7	35-0	93	.231
— Salt Lake (PCL)	5	2	.714	4.25	1.24	9	9	0	0	...	0-...	55.0	42	26	26	5	26-0	59	.211
— Minnesota (A.L.)	2	2	.500	5.10	1.56	8	8	0	0	0	0-0	42.1	41	26	24	7	25-1	24	.261
2001— Edmonton (PCL)	6	11	.353	5.07	1.56	29	29	2	0	...	0-...	161.2	178	101	91	25	74-0	146	.280
2002— Edmonton (PCL)	2	1	.667	8.89	1.68	5	5	0	0	...	0-...	27.1	42	27	27	9	4-0	21	.350
— Minnesota (A.L.)	2	7	.222	4.64	1.68	14	12	0	0	0	0-0	66.0	78	39	34	13	33-0	45	.295
— GC Twins (GCL)	0	0	...	3.00	1.00	2	2	0	0	...	0-...	6.0	2	2	2	1	4-0	7	.100
— Fort Myers (FSL)	0	0	...	0.00	1.40	1	1	0	0	...	0-...	5.0	4	2	0	0	3-0	5	.222
— New Britain (East.)	0	0	...	6.75	1.25	1	1	0	0	...	0-...	4.0	4	4	3	1	1-0	3	.250
2003— Milwaukee (N.L.)	10	13	.435	5.19	1.47	33	31	1	0	0	0-0	190.2	201	121	110	27	80-4	152	.272
2004— Milwaukee (N.L.)	3	4	.429	5.78	1.60	32	6	0	0	3	0-0	62.1	77	41	40	8	23-1	52	.301
— Kansas City (A.L.)	0	1	.000	7.16	2.08	11	0	0	0	0	0-0	16.1	27	14	13	3	7-1	21	.365
2005— San Jose (Calif.)	3	0	1.000	2.10	1.23	5	5	0	0	0	0-0	30.0	23	8	7	3	14-0	34	.215
— Fresno (PCL)	7	8	.467	5.21	1.42	19	19	1	0	0	0-0	114.0	117	68	66	18	45-0	110	.271
— San Francisco (N.L.)	2	0	1.000	6.00	2.00	5	1	0	0	0	0-1	12.0	18	8	8	2	6-0	3	.383
American League totals (3 years)	4	10	.286	5.13	1.69	33	20	0	0	0	0-0	124.2	146	79	71	23	65-2	90	.295
National League totals (3 years)	15	17	.469	5.37	1.53	70	38	1	0	3	0-1	265.0	296	170	158	37	109-5	207	.284
Major League totals (5 years)	19	27	.413	5.29	1.58	103	58	1	0	3	0-1	389.2	442	249	229	60	174-7	297	.287

KLESKO, RYAN — 1B

PERSONAL: Born June 12, 1971, in Westminster, Calif. ... 6-3/220. ... Bats left, throws left. ... Full name: Ryan Anthony Klesko. ... High school: Westminster (Calif.).

TRANSACTIONS/CAREER NOTES: Selected by Atlanta Braves organization in fifth round of 1989 free-agent draft. ... On disabled list (May 3-18, 1995); included rehabilitation assignment to Greenville. ... Traded by Braves with 2B Bret Boone and P Jason Shiell to San Diego Padres for 2B Quilvio Veras, 1B Wally Joyner and OF Reggie Sanders (December 22, 1999). ... On disabled list (September 1, 2003-remainder of season; and May 27-June 16, 2004).

2005 GAMES PLAYED BY POSITION (MLB): OF—121, DH—3, 1B—1.

SCOUTING REPORT *Offense:* His run production continued to drop off as a result of back problems in the second half of the season. Has a long uppercut stroke and bat speed has declined slightly. Still has above-average power. Has worked to use the whole field more. Has lot of holes up in the zone. Gets frustrated with off-speed stuff. Still is not comfortable hitting in his home park. *Defense:* He is not very mobile in the outfield and has problems going back. Doesn't have much range coming in. Arm is short, but he gets rid of the ball quickly. May move to first base where he lacks agility but his hands would be adequate. *Outlook:* Klesko needs to rededicate himself to his physical conditioning and work ethic. Finding a position for him has been a problem. *Grade 6.5*

RYAN KLESKO'S HITTING ZONE

.056	.308	.261
.196	.478	.263
.227	.286	.281

LEFTY-RIGHTY SPLITS

vs.	Avg.	AB	H	2B	3B	HR	RBI	BB	SO	OBP	Slg.
L	.200	100	20	4	1	0	8	15	27	.304	.260
R	.262	343	90	15	0	18	50	60	53	.373	.464

Year Team (League)	Pos.	G	AB	R	H	2B	3B	HR	RBI	BB	SO	HBP	GDP	SB-CS	Avg.	OBP	SLG	OPS	E	Avg.
1989— GC Braves (GCL)	DH	17	57	14	23	5	4	1	16	6	6	0	2	4-3	.404	.453	.684	1.137	...	...
— Sumter (S. Atl.)	1B	25	90	17	26	6	0	1	12	11	14	0	5	1-0	.289	.363	.389	.752	4	.979
1990— Sumter (S. Atl.)	1B	63	231	41	85	15	1	10	38	31	30	1	6	13-1	.368	.437	.571	1.008	14	.978
— Durham (Carol.)	1B	77	292	40	80	16	1	7	47	32	53	2	8	10-5	.274	.343	.408	.751	13	.976
1991— Greenville (Sou.)	1B	126	419	64	122	22	3	14	67	75	60	6	5	14-17	.291	.404	.458	.862	17	.985
1992— Richmond (Int'l)	1B	123	418	63	105	22	2	17	59	41	72	4	14	3-5	.251	.323	.435	.758	11	.989
— Atlanta (N.L.)	1B	13	14	0	0	0	0	0	1	0	5	1	0	0-0	.000	.067	.000	.067	0	1.000
1993— Richmond (Int'l)	1B-OF	98	343	59	94	14	2	22	74	47	69	2	8	4-3	.274	.361	.519	.880	12	.981
— Atlanta (N.L.)	1B-OF	22	17	3	6	1	0	2	5	3	4	0	0	0-0	.353	.450	.765	1.215	0	1.000
1994— Atlanta (N.L.)	OF-1B	92	245	42	68	13	3	17	47	26	48	1	8	1-0	.278	.344	.563	.907	7	.929
1995— Atlanta (N.L.)	OF-1B	107	329	48	102	25	2	23	70	47	72	2	8	5-4	.310	.396	.608	1.004	8	.944
— Greenville (Sou.)	DH-OF	4	13	1	3	0	0	1	4	2	1	0	1	0-0	.231	.333	.462	.795	0	1.000
1996— Atlanta (N.L.)	OF-1B	153	528	90	149	21	4	34	93	68	129	4	10	6-3	.282	.364	.530	.894	5	.977
1997— Atlanta (N.L.)	OF-1B	143	467	67	122	23	6	24	84	48	130	4	12	4-4	.261	.334	.490	.824	6	.977
1998— Atlanta (N.L.)	OF-1B	129	427	69	117	29	1	18	70	56	66	3	9	5-3	.274	.359	.473	.832	2	.990
1999— Atlanta (N.L.) 1B-OF-DH		133	404	55	120	28	2	21	80	53	69	6	5	5-2	.297	.376	.532	.908	6	.990
2000— San Diego (N.L.)	1B-OF	145	494	88	140	33	2	26	92	91	81	1	10	23-7	.283	.393	.516	.909	9	.992
2001— San Diego (N.L.)	1B	146	538	105	154	34	6	30	113	88	89	3	16	23-4	.286	.384	.539	.923	11	.991
2002— San Diego (N.L.) 1B-OF-DH		146	540	90	162	39	1	29	95	76	86	4	7	6-2	.300	.388	.537	.925	7	.993
2003— San Diego (N.L.)	1B-DH	121	397	47	100	18	0	21	67	65	83	3	11	2-5	.252	.354	.456	.810	6	.994
2004— San Diego (N.L.) OF-1B-DH		127	402	58	117	32	2	9	66	73	67	1	8	3-4	.291	.399	.448	.847	4	.986
2005— San Diego (N.L.) OF-DH-1B		137	443	61	110	19	1	18	58	75	80	1	6	3-4	.248	.358	.418	.775	4	.982
Major League totals (14 years)		1614	5245	823	1467	315	30	272	941	769	1009	28	111	86-40	.280	.371	.507	.878	75	.988

DIVISION SERIES RECORD

Year Team (League)	Pos.	G	AB	R	H	2B	3B	HR	RBI	BB	SO	HBP	GDP	SB-CS	Avg.	OBP	SLG	OPS	E	Avg.
1995— Atlanta (N.L.)	OF	4	15	5	7	1	0	1	1	0	3	0	1	0-0	.467	.467	.533	1.000	0	1.000
1996— Atlanta (N.L.)	OF	3	8	1	1	0	0	1	1	3	4	0	0	1-0	.125	.364	.500	.864	1	.667
1997— Atlanta (N.L.)	OF	3	8	2	2	1	0	1	1	0	2	0	1	0-0	.250	.250	.750	1.000	1	.750
1998— Atlanta (N.L.)	OF	3	11	3	3	0	0	1	4	0	3	0	0	0-0	.273	.273	.545	.818	0	1.000
1999— Atlanta (N.L.)	1B	4	12	3	4	0	0	0	0	1	4	0	0	0-0	.333	.385	.333	.718	0	1.000
2005— San Diego (N.L.)	OF	3	10	1	2	0	0	0	1	2	4	0	0	0-0	.200	.333	.200	.533	0	1.000
Division series totals (6 years)		20	64	13	19	2	0	3	8	6	20	0	2	1-0	.297	.357	.469	.826	2	.953

CHAMPIONSHIP SERIES RECORD

Year Team (League)	Pos.	G	AB	R	H	2B	3B	HR	RBI	BB	SO	HBP	GDP	SB-CS	Avg.	OBP	SLG	OPS	E	Avg.
1995— Atlanta (N.L.)	OF	4	7	0	0	0	0	0	0	3	4	0	0	0-1	.000	.300	.000	.300	0	1.000
1996— Atlanta (N.L.)	OF	6	16	1	4	0	0	1	3	2	6	0	1	0-0	.250	.333	.438	.771	0	1.000
1997— Atlanta (N.L.)	OF	5	17	2	4	0	0	2	4	2	3	0	0	0-0	.235	.316	.588	.904	0	1.000
1998— Atlanta (N.L.)	OF	5	12	1	1	0	0	0	1	6	3	0	0	0-0	.083	.389	.083	.472	1	.750
1999— Atlanta (N.L.)	1B	4	8	1	1	0	0	1	1	2	1	0	0	0-0	.125	.300	.500	.800	2	.935
Champ. series totals (5 years)		24	60	6	10	0	0	4	9	15	17	0	1	0-1	.167	.333	.367	.700	3	.944

WORLD SERIES RECORD

Year Team (League)	Pos.	G	AB	R	H	2B	3B	HR	RBI	BB	SO	HBP	GDP	SB-CS	Avg.	OBP	SLG	OPS	E	Avg.
1995— Atlanta (N.L.)	DH-OF	6	16	4	5	0	0	3	4	3	4	0	0	0-0	.313	.421	.875	1.296	0	1.000
1996— Atlanta (N.L.)	1B-DH-OF	5	10	2	1	0	0	0	1	2	4	0	0	0-0	.100	.250	.100	.350	1	.500
1999— Atlanta (N.L.)	1B	4	12	0	2	0	0	0	0	0	1	0	0	0-0	.167	.167	.167	.333	0	1.000
World Series totals (3 years)		15	38	6	8	0	0	3	5	5	9	0	0	0-0	.211	.302	.447	.750	1	.958

ALL-STAR GAME RECORD

	G	AB	R	H	2B	3B	HR	RBI	BB	SO	HBP	GDP	SB-CS	Avg.	OBP	SLG	OPS	E	Avg.
All-Star Game totals (1 year)	1	1	0	0	0	0	0	0	0	1	0	0	0-0	.000	.000	.000	.000	0	1.000

KLINE, STEVE — P

PERSONAL: Born August 22, 1972, in Sunbury, Pa. ... 6-1/215. ... Throws left, bats both. ... Full name: Steven James Kline. ... High school: Lewisburg (Pa.). ... College: West Virginia.

TRANSACTIONS/CAREER NOTES: Selected by Cleveland Indians organization in eighth round of 1993 free-agent draft. ... Traded by Indians to Montreal Expos for P Jeff Juden (July 31, 1997). ... On disabled list (April 11-27, 1999). ... Traded by Expos with P Dustin Hermanson to St. Louis Cardinals for 3B Fernando Tatis and P Britt Reames (December 14, 2000). ... On disabled list (April 29-May 31, 2002); included rehabilitation assignments to Peoria and New Haven. ... On disabled list (August 28-September 29, 2004). ... Signed as a free agent by Baltimore Orioles (December 20, 2004). ... On suspended list (July 22-26, 2005).

CAREER HITTING: 2-for-13 (.154), 1 R, 1 2B, 0 3B, 0 HR, 2 RBI.

SCOUTING REPORT **Throws:** Kline's fastball was in the 86-87 mph range, down from his 2004 numbers. His slider is in the low 80s. Has a changeup but rarely throws it. *Tendencies:* His slider wasn't as sharp as in the past and lefthanders gave him lots of trouble. Was far more effective against righthanders as he could use more of the plate in and away. *Outlook:* Kline never got over leaving St. Louis and had a down year in Baltimore. Needs to reestablish his slider to again be a reliable late-inning specialist. Will face a lot of righthanders as managers are forced to turn their lineups around when he's in the game. *Grade 6.4*

STEVE KLINE'S PITCHING ZONE

.231	.750	.125
.341	.385	.261
.286	.167	.211

LEFTY-RIGHTY SPLITS

vs.	Avg.	AB	H	2B	3B	HR	RBI	BB	SO	OBP	Slg.
L	.317	101	32	5	0	5	14	8	22	.364	.515
R	.209	129	27	3	0	6	19	22	14	.322	.372

Year Team (League)	W	L	Pct.	ERA	WHIP	G	GS	CG	ShO	Hld.	Sv.-Opp.	IP	H	R	ER	HR	BB-IBB	SO	Avg.
1993— Burlington (Appal.)	1	1	.500	4.91	1.77	2	1	0	0		0-...	7.1	11	4	4	0	2-1	4	.355
— Watertown (N.Y.-Penn.)	5	4	.556	3.19	1.13	13	13	2	1		0-...	79.0	77	36	28	3	12-0	45	.248
1994— Columbus (S. Atl.)	18	5	.783	3.01	1.14	28	28	2	1		0-...	185.2	175	67	62	14	36-0	174	.251
1995— Cant./Akr. (East.)	2	3	.400	2.42	1.30	14	14	0	0		0-...	89.1	86	34	24	6	30-3	45	.252
1996— Cant./Akr. (East.)	8	12	.400	5.46	1.52	25	24	0	0		0-...	146.2	168	98	89	16	55-2	107	.288
1997— Cleveland (A.L.)	3	1	.750	5.81	2.09	20	1	0	0	4	0-2	26.1	42	19	17	6	13-1	17	.365
— Buffalo (A.A.)	3	3	.500	4.03	1.29	20	4	0	0		1-...	51.1	53	26	23	4	13-1	41	.265
— Montreal (N.L.)	1	3	.250	6.15	1.56	26	0	0	0	1	0-1	26.1	31	18	18	4	10-3	20	.307
1998— Ottawa (Int'l)	0	0	...	0.00	0.38	2	0	0	0		0-...	2.2	1	0	0	0	0-0	1	.125
— Montreal (N.L.)	3	6	.333	2.76	1.44	78	0	0	0	18	1-2	71.2	62	25	22	4	41-7	76	.228
1999— Montreal (N.L.)	7	4	.636	3.75	1.28	82	0	0	0	16	0-2	69.2	56	32	29	8	33-6	69	.218
2000— Montreal (N.L.)	1	5	.167	3.50	1.40	83	0	0	0	12	14-18	82.1	88	36	32	8	27-2	64	.278
2001— St. Louis (N.L.)	3	3	.500	1.80	1.09	89	0	0	0	17	9-10	75.0	53	16	15	3	29-7	54	.203
2002— St. Louis (N.L.)	2	1	.667	3.39	1.29	66	0	0	0	21	6-8	58.1	54	23	22	3	21-2	41	.251
— Peoria (Midw.)	0	0	...	0.00	0.86	2	1	0	0		0-...	2.1	1	0	0	0	1-0	5	.111
— New Haven (East.)	0	0	...	0.00	0.50	1	1	0	0		0-...	2.0	0	0	0	0	1-0	2	.000
2003— St. Louis (N.L.)	5	5	.500	3.82	1.35	78	0	0	0	18	3-7	63.2	56	29	27	5	30-5	31	.237
2004— St. Louis (N.L.)	2	2	.500	1.79	1.07	67	0	0	0	15	3-4	50.1	37	12	10	3	17-4	35	.209
2005— Baltimore (A.L.)	2	4	.333	4.28	1.46	67	0	0	0	9	0-3	61.0	59	34	29	11	30-5	36	.257
American League totals (2 years)	5	5	.500	4.74	1.65	87	1	0	0	13	0-5	87.1	101	53	46	17	43-6	53	.293
National League totals (8 years)	24	29	.453	3.17	1.30	569	0	0	0	118	36-52	497.1	437	191	175	38	208-36	390	.238
Major League totals (9 years)	29	34	.460	3.40	1.35	656	1	0	0	131	36-57	584.2	538	244	221	55	251-42	443	.247

DIVISION SERIES RECORD

Year Team (League)	W	L	Pct.	ERA	WHIP	G	GS	CG	ShO	Hld.	Sv.-Opp.	IP	H	R	ER	HR	BB-IBB	SO	Avg.
2001— St. Louis (N.L.)	0	1	.000	2.08	1.38	4	0	0	0		2-2	4.1	4	1	1	0	2-1	0	.308
2002— St. Louis (N.L.)	0	0	...	0.00	1.50	2	0	0	0	2	0-0	1.1	1	0	0	0	1-0	0	.200
2004— St. Louis (N.L.)	0	0	...	0.00	0.00	2	0	0	0		0-0	1.1	0	0	0	0	0-0	0	.000
Division series totals (3 years)	0	1	.000	1.29	1.14	8	0	0	0	2	2-2	7.0	5	1	1	0	3-1	0	.192

CHAMPIONSHIP SERIES RECORD

Year Team (League)	W	L	Pct.	ERA	WHIP	G	GS	CG	ShO	Hld.	Sv.-Opp.	IP	H	R	ER	HR	BB-IBB	SO	Avg.
2002— St. Louis (N.L.)	0	0	...	0.00	0.86	4	0	0	0	1	0-0	2.1	2	0	0	0	0-0	1	.250
2004— St. Louis (N.L.)	0	0	...			1	0	0	0		0-0	0.0	2	0	0	0	0-0	0	1.000
Champ. series totals (2 years)	0	0	...	0.00	1.71	5	0	0	0	1	0-0	2.1	4	0	0	0	0-0	1	.400

KNOEDLER, JUSTIN   C

PERSONAL: Born July 17, 1980, in Springfield, Ill. ... 6-2/210. ... Bats right, throws right. ... Full name: Justin Joseph Knoedler. ... High school: Springfield (Ill.). ... Junior college: Lincoln Land CC (Springfield, Ill.). ... College: Miami (Ohio).
TRANSACTIONS/CAREER NOTES: Selected by St. Louis Cardinals organization in 41st round of 1998 free-agent draft; did not sign. ... Selected by San Francisco Giants organization in 13th round of 2000 free-agent draft; did not sign. ... Selected by Giants organization in fifth round of 2001 free-agent draft.
2005 GAMES PLAYED BY POSITION (MLB): C—4.

LEFTY-RIGHTY SPLITS

vs.	Avg.	AB	H	2B	3B	HR	RBI	BB	SO	OBP	Slg.
L	.000	1	0	0	0	0	0	0	0	.500	.000
R	.111	9	1	0	0	0	0	0	1	.111	.111

Year Team (League)	Pos.	G	AB	R	H	2B	3B	HR	RBI	BB	SO	HBP	GDP	SB-CS	Avg.	OBP	SLG	OPS	E	Avg.
2002—Hagerstown (S. Atl.)	C	86	280	32	72	16	2	5	33	37	56	4	8	6-5	.257	.349	.382	.731	15	.977
2003—San Jose (Calif.)	C	101	354	48	91	25	2	10	43	35	78	3	5	13-3	.257	.326	.424	.749	9	.989
2004—Norwich (East.)	C-DH-OF	115	409	64	112	28	3	9	47	32	98	8	7	5-3	.274	.335	.423	.758	7	.991
—San Francisco (N.L.)	C	1	1	0	0	0	0	0	0	0	0	0	0	0-0	.000	.000	.000	.000	0	1.000
2005—Norwich (East.)	C	4	10	2	3	0	0	0	0	2	0	0	1	2-1	.300	.417	.300	.717	0	1.000
—Lakeland (Fla. St.) OF-DH-1B		40	89	18	25	6	0	0	9	16	21	0	1	3-1	.281	.387	.348	.735	8	.915
—Fresno (PCL)	C-DH	85	287	35	78	19	1	4	32	26	61	7	2	5-5	.272	.345	.387	.731	4	.994
—Erie (East.)	OF-1B	32	79	10	18	6	0	1	8	10	26	1	1	1-0	.228	.322	.342	.664	0	1.000
—San Francisco (N.L.)	C	8	10	0	1	0	0	0	0	0	1	1	0	0-0	.100	.182	.100	.282	0	1.000
Major League totals (2 years)		9	11	0	1	0	0	0	0	0	1	1	0	0-0	.091	.167	.091	.258	0	1.000

KOLB, DAN   P

PERSONAL: Born March 29, 1975, in Sterling, Ill. ... 6-4/240. ... Throws right, bats right. ... Full name: Daniel Lee Kolb. ... High school: Walnut (Ill.). ... College: Illinois State.
TRANSACTIONS/CAREER NOTES: Selected by Minnesota Twins organization in 17th round of 1993 free-agent draft; did not sign. ... Selected by Texas Rangers organization in sixth round of 1995 free-agent draft. ... On disabled list (October 3, 1999-remainder of season; and May 29, 2000-remainder of season). ... On disabled list (March 23-July 11, 2001); included rehabilitation assignments to Charlotte and Tulsa. ... On disabled list (March 28-July 16, 2002); included rehabilitation assignments to Charlotte and Tulsa. ... Released by Rangers (March 26, 2003). ... Signed by Milwaukee Brewers organization (April 2, 2003). ... Traded by Brewers to Atlanta Braves for P Jose Capellan and a player to be named (December 11, 2004); Brewers acquired P Alec Zumwalt to complete deal (December 13, 2004).
CAREER HITTING: 0-for-1 (.000), 0 R, 0 2B, 0 3B, 0 HR, 0 RBI.

SCOUTING REPORT **Throws:** Kolb has a 92-95 mph fastball and a split-finger fastball at 80-83. ***Tendencies:*** He lost his confidence pitching for a contender and, though his fastball still was in the mid-90s, pitched at the lower range at times and didn't have command. Splitter was not as effective as his fastball. ***Outlook:*** He proved again that saves for second-division team don't necessarily translate to saves for a first-place team with the added pressure. ***Grade 6***

DAN KOLB'S PITCHING ZONE

.278	.222	.400
.422	.500	.250
.353	.154	.375

LEFTY-RIGHTY SPLITS

vs.	Avg.	AB	H	2B	3B	HR	RBI	BB	SO	OBP	Slg.
L	.336	110	37	8	1	2	17	18	22	.431	.482
R	.323	127	41	4	0	3	25	11	17	.377	.425

Year Team (League)	W	L	Pct.	ERA	WHIP	G	GS	CG	ShO	Hld.	Sv.-Opp.	IP	H	R	ER	HR	BB-IBB	SO	Avg.
1995—GC Rangers (GCL)	1	7	.125	2.21	1.25	12	11	0	0	...	0-...	53.0	38	22	13	0	28-0	46	.204
1996—Char., S.C. (S. Atl.)	8	6	.571	2.57	1.11	20	20	4	2	...	0-...	126.0	80	50	36	5	60-2	127	.181
—Charlotte (Fla. St.)	2	2	.500	4.26	1.37	6	6	0	0	...	0-...	38.0	38	18	18	1	14-0	28	.260
—Tulsa (Texas)	1	0	1.000	0.77	1.11	2	2	0	0	...	0-...	11.2	5	1	1	0	8-0	7	.139
1997—Charlotte (Fla. St.)	4	10	.286	4.87	1.56	24	23	3	0	...	0-...	133.0	146	91	72	10	62-1	83	.282
—Tulsa (Texas)	0	2	.000	4.76	1.59	2	2	0	0	...	0-...	11.1	7	7	6	1	11-0	6	.179
1998—Tulsa (Texas)	12	11	.522	4.82	1.62	28	28	2	0	...	0-...	162.1	187	104	87	11	76-1	83	.293
—Oklahoma (PCL)	0	0	...	0.00	2.00	1	0	0	0	...	0-...	1.0	1	0	0	0	0-0	0	.250
1999—Tulsa (Texas)	1	2	.333	2.79	1.45	7	7	1	1	...	0-...	38.2	38	16	12	0	18-0	32	.260
—Oklahoma (PCL)	5	3	.625	5.10	1.68	11	8	0	0	...	0-...	60.0	74	35	34	4	27-0	21	.320
—Texas (A.L.)	2	1	.667	4.65	1.55	16	0	0	0	0	0-0	31.0	33	18	16	2	15-0	15	.268
2000—Oklahoma (PCL)	4	1	.800	0.98	1.04	13	0	0	0	...	4-...	18.1	11	6	2	0	2-0	18	.175
—Texas (A.L.)	0	0	...	67.50	10.50	1	0	0	0	0	0-...	0.2	5	5	5	0	2-0	0	.833
2001—Charlotte (Fla. St.)	1	2	.333	3.86	1.23	7	7	0	0	...	0-...	18.2	21	8	8	1	0-0	16	.276
—Tulsa (Texas)	1	0	1.000	0.00	0.50	1	0	0	0	...	0-...	2.0	0	0	0	0	1-0	0	.000
—Oklahoma (PCL)	0	1	.000	1.42	0.89	12	0	0	0	...	3-...	19.0	13	3	3	1	4-0	21	.188
—Texas (A.L.)	0	0	...	4.70	1.63	17	0	0	0	7	0-0	15.1	15	8	8	2	10-1	15	.259
2002—Charlotte (Fla. St.)	1	0	1.000	1.50	1.50	4	0	0	0	...	0-...	6.0	5	1	1	0	4-0	2	.227
—Tulsa (Texas)	0	1	.000	2.16	1.44	5	1	0	0	...	0-...	8.1	9	2	2	0	3-0	4	.290
—Texas (A.L.)	3	6	.333	4.22	1.53	34	0	0	0	2	1-4	32.0	27	17	15	1	22-2	20	.227
2003—Indianapolis (Int'l)	0	1	.000	1.37	1.00	26	0	0	0	...	4-...	39.1	26	10	6	0	13-0	46	.183
—Milwaukee (N.L.)	1	2	.333	1.96	1.28	37	0	0	0	4	21-23	41.1	34	10	9	2	19-3	39	.221
2004—Milwaukee (N.L.)	0	4	.000	2.98	1.13	64	0	0	0	6	39-44	57.1	50	22	19	3	15-1	21	.234
2005—Atlanta (N.L.)	3	8	.273	5.93	1.86	65	0	0	0	6	11-18	57.2	78	39	38	5	29-5	39	.329
American League totals (4 years)	5	7	.417	5.01	1.63	68	0	0	0	9	1-4	79.0	80	48	44	5	49-3	50	.261
National League totals (3 years)	4	14	.222	3.80	1.44	166	0	0	0	11	71-85	156.1	162	71	66	10	63-9	99	.268
Major League totals (7 years)	9	21	.300	4.21	1.50	234	0	0	0	20	72-89	235.1	242	119	110	15	112-12	149	.266

ALL-STAR GAME RECORD

	W	L	Pct.	ERA	WHIP	G	GS	CG	ShO	Hld.	Sv.-Opp.	IP	H	R	ER	HR	BB-IBB	SO	Avg.
All-Star Game totals (1 year)	0	0	...	0.00	1.00	1	0	0	0	0	0-0	1.0	1	0	0	0	0-0	0	.250

KONERKO, PAUL — 1B

PERSONAL: Born March 5, 1976, in Providence, R.I. ... 6-2/215. ... Bats right, throws right. ... Full name: Paul Henry Konerko. ... Name pronounced: kone-err-coe. ... High school: Chaparral (Scottsdale, Ariz.).

TRANSACTIONS/CAREER NOTES: Selected by Los Angeles Dodgers organization in first round (13th pick overall) of 1994 free-agent draft. ... Traded by Dodgers with P Dennys Reyes to Cincinnati Reds for P Jeff Shaw (July 4, 1998). ... Traded by Reds to Chicago White Sox for OF Mike Cameron (November 11, 1998).

HONORS: Named A.L. Comeback Player of the Year by THE SPORTING NEWS (2004).

2005 GAMES PLAYED BY POSITION (MLB): 1B—146, DH—11.

SCOUTING REPORT

Offense: Konerko has one of the game's best strokes. Bat speed is exceptional. Ball really jumps off his bat. Has excellent power from right-center to the left-field line. Good breaking-ball hitter. Makes good contact and has showed he can make adjustments. Is increasingly better at handling inside pitches. Is one of the game's slowest runners. *Defense:* He improved defensively by playing every day at first base. Doesn't have a lot of range but hands have improved, as has his lower-body flexibility to receive throws. Has arm strength and has improved his accuracy to start double plays. *Outlook:* Konerko's stock rose during the playoffs with his power production. Was one of the more underrated offensive players prior to the postseason.

Grade 9.1

PAUL KONERKO'S HITTING ZONE

.324	.379	.222
.317	.400	.258
.404	.320	.105

LEFTY-RIGHTY SPLITS

vs.	Avg.	AB	H	2B	3B	HR	RBI	BB	SO	OBP	Slg.
L	.261	134	35	6	0	12	24	25	27	.381	.575
R	.290	441	128	18	0	28	76	56	82	.373	.522

Year	Team (League)	Pos.	G	AB	R	H	2B	3B	HR	RBI	BB	SO	HBP	GDP	SB-CS	Avg.	OBP	SLG	OPS	E	Avg.
1994—Yakima (N'west)		C-DH	67	257	25	74	15	2	6	58	36	52	6	6	1-0	.288	.379	.432	.811	5	.984
1995—San Bern. (Calif.)		C-DH	118	448	7	124	21	1	19	77	59	88	4	12	3-1	.277	.362	.455	.817	11	.985
1996—San Antonio (Texas)		1B-DH	133	470	78	141	23	2	29	86	72	85	8	7	1-3	.300	.397	.543	.939	14	.989
—Albuquerque (PCL)		1B	4	14	2	6	0	0	1	2	1	2	0	0	0-1	.429	.467	.643	1.110	0	1.000
1997—Albuquerque (PCL)		3B-1B-2B	130	483	97	156	31	1	37	127	64	61	8	16	2-3	.323	.407	.621	1.028	24	.952
—Los Angeles (N.L.)		1B-3B	6	7	0	1	0	0	0	0	1	2	0	1	0-0	.143	.250	.143	.393	0	1.000
1998—Los Angeles (N.L.)		1B-3B-OF-DH	49	144	14	31	1	0	4	16	10	30	2	5	0-1	.215	.272	.306	.578	2	.991
—Albuquerque (PCL)		OF-1B-3B	24	87	16	33	10	0	6	26	11	12	0	3	0-0	.379	.436	.701	1.137	3	.955
—Cincinnati (N.L.)		3B-1B-OF	26	73	7	16	3	0	3	13	6	10	1	5	0-0	.219	.284	.384	.668	0	1.000
—Indianapolis (Int'l)		3B	39	150	25	49	8	0	8	39	19	18	2	8	1-0	.327	.402	.540	.942	4	.957
1999—Chicago (A.L.)		1B-DH-3B	142	513	71	151	31	4	24	81	45	68	2	19	1-0	.294	.352	.511	.862	4	.995
2000—Chicago (A.L.)		1B-3B-DH	143	524	84	156	31	1	21	97	47	72	10	22	1-0	.298	.363	.481	.844	11	.990
2001—Chicago (A.L.)		1B-DH	156	582	92	164	35	0	32	99	54	89	9	17	1-0	.282	.349	.507	.856	8	.994
2002—Chicago (A.L.)		1B-DH	151	570	81	173	30	0	27	104	44	72	9	17	0-0	.304	.359	.498	.857	8	.993
2003—Chicago (A.L.)		1B-DH	137	444	49	104	19	0	18	65	43	50	4	*28	0-0	.234	.305	.399	.704	3	.998
2004—Chicago (A.L.)		1B-DH	155	563	84	156	22	0	41	117	69	107	6	23	1-0	.277	.359	.535	.894	6	.995
2005—Chicago (A.L.)		1B-DH	158	575	98	163	24	0	40	100	81	109	5	9	0-0	.283	.375	.534	.909	5	.996
American League totals (7 years)			1042	3771	559	1067	192	5	203	663	383	567	45	135	4-0	.283	.353	.498	.851	44	.995
National League totals (2 years)			81	224	21	48	4	0	7	29	17	42	3	11	0-1	.214	.275	.326	.601	2	.993
Major League totals (9 years)			1123	3995	580	1115	196	5	210	692	400	609	48	146	4-1	.279	.349	.488	.837	46	.995

DIVISION SERIES RECORD

Year	Team (League)	Pos.	G	AB	R	H	2B	3B	HR	RBI	BB	SO	HBP	GDP	SB-CS	Avg.	OBP	SLG	OPS	E	Avg.
2000—Chicago (A.L.)		1B	3	9	1	0	0	0	0	0	1	1	0	1	0-0	.000	.100	.000	.100	0	1.000
2005—Chicago (A.L.)		1B	3	12	3	3	0	0	2	4	0	1	0	0	0-0	.250	.250	.750	1.000	0	1.000
Division series totals (2 years)			6	21	4	3	0	0	2	4	1	2	0	1	0-0	.143	.182	.429	.610	0	1.000

CHAMPIONSHIP SERIES RECORD

Year	Team (League)	Pos.	G	AB	R	H	2B	3B	HR	RBI	BB	SO	HBP	GDP	SB-CS	Avg.	OBP	SLG	OPS	E	Avg.
2005—Chicago (A.L.)		1B	5	21	2	6	1	0	2	7	1	4	0	0	0-0	.286	.318	.619	.937	0	1.000

WORLD SERIES RECORD

Year	Team (League)	Pos.	G	AB	R	H	2B	3B	HR	RBI	BB	SO	HBP	GDP	SB-CS	Avg.	OBP	SLG	OPS	E	Avg.
2005—Chicago (A.L.)		1B	4	16	1	4	1	0	1	4	2	3	1	1	0-0	.250	.368	.500	.868	0	1.000

ALL-STAR GAME RECORD

			G	AB	R	H	2B	3B	HR	RBI	BB	SO	HBP	GDP	SB-CS	Avg.	OBP	SLG	OPS	E	Avg.
All-Star Game totals (2 years)			2	3	0	2	2	0	0	2	0	1	0	0	0-0	.667	.667	1.333	2.000	0	1.000

KOO, DAE-SUNG — P

PERSONAL: Born August 2, 1968, in Daejeon, South Korea. ... 6-1/187. ... Throws left, bats left. ... Full name: Dae-Sung Koo. ... College: Hanyang Univ. (South Korea).

TRANSACTIONS/CAREER NOTES: Played eight seasons in the Korea League (1993-2000). ... Played four seasons in the Japan League (2001-04). ... Signed as a free agent by New York Mets (January 12, 2005). ... On disabled list (June 2-21 and August 21-September 13, 2005).

CAREER HITTING: 1-for-2 (.500), 1 R, 1 2B, 0 3B, 0 HR, 0 RBI.

DAE-SUNG KOO'S PITCHING ZONE

.333	.200	.286
.100	.167	.471
.333	.333	.143

LEFTY-RIGHTY SPLITS

vs.	Avg.	AB	H	2B	3B	HR	RBI	BB	SO	OBP	Slg.
L	.239	46	11	2	0	1	12	9	14	.379	.348
R	.262	42	11	4	0	1	8	4	9	.313	.429

Year	Team (League)	W	L	Pct.	ERA	WHIP	G	GS	CG	ShO	Hld.	Sv.-Opp.	IP	H	R	ER	HR	BB-IBB	SO	Avg.
2005—New York (N.L.)		0	0	...	3.91	1.52	33	0	0	0	6	0-2	23.0	22	12	10	2	13-1	23	.250
Major League totals (1 year)		0	0	...	3.91	1.52	33	0	0	0	6	0-2	23.0	22	12	10	2	13-1	23	.250

KOPLOVE, MIKE   P

PERSONAL: Born August 30, 1976, in Philadelphia. ... 5-10/178. ... Throws right, bats right. ... Full name: Michael Paul Koplove. ... Name pronounced: COP-luv. ... High school: Chestnut Hill Academy (Philadelphia). ... College: Delaware.
TRANSACTIONS/CAREER NOTES: Selected by Arizona Diamondbacks organization in 29th round of 1998 free-agent draft. ... On disabled list (May 28-June 13 and June 19, 2003-remainder of season); included rehabilitation assignment to Tucson.
CAREER HITTING: 0-for-4 (.000), 0 R, 0 2B, 0 3B, 0 HR, 0 RBI.

MIKE KOPLOVE'S PITCHING ZONE

.000	.667	.167
.270	.174	.368
.300	.154	.200

LEFTY-RIGHTY SPLITS

vs.	Avg.	AB	H	2B	3B	HR	RBI	BB	SO	OBP	Slg.
L	.256	78	20	4	1	4	15	15	15	.385	.487
R	.257	109	28	4	1	2	28	5	13	.308	.367

Year — Team (League)	W	L	Pct.	ERA	WHIP	G	GS	CG	ShO	Hld.	Sv.-Opp.	IP	H	R	ER	HR	BB-IBB	SO	Avg.
1998— Ariz. D'backs (AZL)	0	0	...	9.00	1.50	2	0	0	0	...	0-...	4.0	4	4	4	0	2-0	5	.250
— Lethbridge (Pion.)	1	2	.333	3.54	0.93	12	1	0	0	...	2-...	28.0	23	12	11	2	3-0	22	.217
1999— South Bend (Mid.)	5	2	.714	2.04	1.18	45	45	0	0	...	7-...	84.0	70	23	19	5	29-0	98	.227
2000— High Desert (Calif.)	2	0	1.000	1.42	0.95	20	0	0	0	...	8-...	25.1	14	4	4	0	10-0	31	.163
— El Paso (Texas)	4	3	.571	4.46	1.41	35	0	0	0	...	6-...	40.1	38	28	20	2	19-1	47	.225
2001— El Paso (Texas)	3	2	.600	2.66	1.43	34	0	0	0	...	4-...	44.0	44	18	13	3	19-3	43	.263
— Tucson (PCL)	4	1	.800	2.82	1.21	17	0	0	0	...	9-...	22.1	17	7	7	1	10-1	22	.207
— Arizona (N.L.)	0	1	.000	3.60	1.70	9	0	0	0	1	0-0	10.0	8	7	4	1	9-1	14	.211
2002— Tucson (PCL)	1	2	.333	1.17	0.82	23	0	0	0	...	3-...	30.2	21	5	4	1	4-0	31	.196
— Arizona (N.L.)	6	1	.857	3.36	1.14	55	0	0	0	10	0-0	61.2	47	24	23	2	23-4	46	.213
2003— Arizona (N.L.)	3	0	1.000	2.15	1.09	31	0	0	0	5	0-1	37.2	31	11	9	3	10-1	27	.225
— Tucson (PCL)	0	1	.000	13.50	2.60	3	0	0	0	...	1-...	2.2	4	4	4	1	3-0	2	.333
2004— Arizona (N.L.)	4	4	.500	4.05	1.42	76	0	0	0	19	2-8	86.2	86	42	39	7	37-10	55	.269
2005— Arizona (N.L.)	2	1	.667	5.07	1.37	44	0	0	0	9	0-2	49.2	48	31	28	6	20-3	28	.257
— Tucson (PCL)	0	2	.000	13.00	2.11	9	0	0	0	1	0-1	9.0	12	13	13	1	7-0	6	.316
Major League totals (5 years)	**15**	**7**	**.682**	**3.77**	**1.30**	**215**	**0**	**0**	**0**	**44**	**2-11**	**245.2**	**220**	**115**	**103**	**19**	**99-19**	**170**	**.243**

DIVISION SERIES RECORD

Year — Team (League)	W	L	Pct.	ERA	WHIP	G	GS	CG	ShO	Hld.	Sv.-Opp.	IP	H	R	ER	HR	BB-IBB	SO	Avg.
2002— Arizona (N.L.)	0	1	.000	6.75	1.50	1	0	0	0	0	0-0	1.1	2	1	1	0	0-0	1	.400

KORONKA, JOHN   P

PERSONAL: Born July 3, 1980, in Clearwater, Fla. ... 6-1/180. ... Throws left, bats left. ... Full name: John Vincent Koronka. ... Name pronounced: CORE-on-kuh.
TRANSACTIONS/CAREER NOTES: Selected by Cincinnati Reds organization in 12th round of 1998 free-agent draft. ... Selected by Texas Rangers from Reds organization in Rule 5 major league draft (December 16, 2002). Returned to Reds (March 21, 2003). ... Traded by Reds to Chicago Cubs for P Phil Norton (August 25, 2003).
CAREER HITTING: 0-for-4 (.000), 0 R, 0 2B, 0 3B, 0 HR, 0 RBI.

JOHN KORONKA'S PITCHING ZONE

.333	...	.667
.300	.400	.222
.500	.000	.200

LEFTY-RIGHTY SPLITS

vs.	Avg.	AB	H	2B	3B	HR	RBI	BB	SO	OBP	Slg.
L	.385	13	5	1	0	0	2	0	3	.385	.462
R	.259	54	14	1	0	2	8	8	7	.355	.389

Year — Team (League)	W	L	Pct.	ERA	WHIP	G	GS	CG	ShO	Hld.	Sv.-Opp.	IP	H	R	ER	HR	BB-IBB	SO	Avg.
1998— Billings (Pion.)	0	3	.000	8.04	2.33	12	3	0	0	...	0-...	31.1	47	43	28	2	26-0	36	.326
1999— GC Reds (GCL)	3	3	.500	1.69	1.04	7	7	0	0	...	0-...	37.1	25	11	7	1	14-0	27	.194
— Billings (Pion.)	2	3	.400	5.58	1.44	7	7	0	0	...	0-...	40.1	41	26	25	1	17-0	34	.273
2000— Clinton (Midw.)	4	13	.235	4.33	1.55	20	18	4	0	...	0-...	104.0	123	65	50	7	38-2	74	.301
2001— Dayton (Midw.)	3	1	.750	0.75	1.29	5	5	0	0	...	0-...	24.0	23	12	2	0	8-0	25	.256
— Mudville (Calif.)	5	2	.714	4.94	1.65	12	12	0	0	...	0-...	71.0	78	44	39	10	39-0	66	.281
— Chattanooga (Sou.)	1	5	.167	5.73	1.64	9	9	0	0	...	0-...	55.0	62	37	35	7	28-0	44	.286
2002— Stockton (Calif.)	11	0	1.000	3.07	1.28	12	12	0	0	...	0-...	73.1	59	36	25	4	35-0	69	.214
— Chattanooga (Sou.)	2	8	.200	4.99	1.68	16	15	0	0	...	0-...	95.2	109	56	53	10	52-1	69	.298
2003— Chattanooga (Sou.)	7	13	.350	4.39	1.52	25	25	0	0	...	0-...	155.2	177	88	76	8	60-1	115	.298
— West Tenn (Sou.)	0	0	...	0.00	0.57	1	1	0	0	...	0-...	7.0	3	0	0	0	1-0	3	.136
2004— Iowa (PCL)	12	9	.571	4.34	1.49	29	23	2	2	...	0-...	153.1	164	86	74	19	65-3	116	.283
2005— Chicago (N.L.)	1	2	.333	7.47	1.72	4	3	0	0	...	0-0	15.2	19	13	13	2	8-0	10	.284
Major League totals (1 year)	**1**	**2**	**.333**	**7.47**	**1.72**	**4**	**3**	**0**	**0**	...	**0-0**	**15.2**	**19**	**13**	**13**	**2**	**8-0**	**10**	**.284**

KOSKIE, COREY   3B

PERSONAL: Born June 28, 1973, in Anola, Manitoba. ... 6-3/219. ... Bats left, throws right. ... Full name: Cordel Leonard Koskie. ... Name pronounced: KOSS-key. ... High school: Springfield Collegiate (Oakbank, Man.). ... College: University of Manitoba.
TRANSACTIONS/CAREER NOTES: Selected by Minnesota Twins organization in 26th round of 1994 free-agent draft. ... On disabled list (May 8-24, 2002; July 12-August 4, 2003; and May 12-27, 2004). ... Signed as a free agent by Toronto Blue Jays (December 14, 2004). ... On disabled list (May 20-July 26, 2005); included rehabilitation assignment to Syracuse.
RECORDS: Shares major league record for times hit by pitch, game (3, July 27, 2004).
2005 GAMES PLAYED BY POSITION (MLB): 3B—76, DH—19.

SCOUTING REPORT

Offense: Koskie never fully regained his stroke and bat speed last season after missing two months with injuries. Likes the ball out over the plate and down. Is most effective when he hits outside pitches to the opposite field. Has a lot of problem spots, especially up in the zone. Strikeout total is rising. Has problems with lefthanders. **Defense:** He always has had very good hands and footwork, but his range has declined in both directions. Spreads out his body to throw and has a slow, long release but throws have very good carry and accuracy. **Outlook:** Persistent physical problems have started to take a toll on his offense. Has great presence in the clubhouse but overall skills continue to slide. **Grade 7.2**

COREY KOSKIE'S HITTING ZONE

.222	.200	.355
.226	.368	.305
.143	.318	.176

LEFTY-RIGHTY SPLITS

vs.	Avg.	AB	H	2B	3B	HR	RBI	BB	SO	OBP	Sig.
L	.211	109	23	5	0	2	8	8	32	.269	.312
R	.265	245	65	15	0	9	28	36	58	.365	.437

Year	Team (League)	Pos.	G	AB	R	H	2B	3B	HR	RBI	BB	SO	HBP	GDP	SB-CS	Avg.	OBP	SLG	OPS	E	Avg.
1994	Elizabethton (App.)	3B	34	107	13	25	2	1	3	10	18	27	2	3	0-0	.234	.354	.355	.709	8	.930
1995	Fort Wayne (Midw.)	3B	123	462	64	143	37	5	16	78	38	79	9	10	2-4	.310	.370	.515	.885	36	.900
1996	Fort Myers (FSL)	3B	95	338	43	88	19	4	9	55	40	76	1	4	1-1	.260	.338	.420	.758	19	.926
1997	New Britain (East.)	3B-DH	131	437	88	125	26	6	23	79	90	106	7	13	9-5	.286	.414	.531	.945	22	.933
1998	Salt Lake (PCL)	3B-DH	135	505	91	152	32	5	26	105	51	104	8	17	15-7	.301	.368	.539	.906	23	.935
	—Minnesota (A.L.)	3B	11	29	2	4	0	0	1	2	2	10	0	0	0-0	.138	.194	.241	.435	1	.941
1999	—Minnesota (A.L.) 3B-OF-DH		117	342	42	106	21	0	11	58	40	72	5	6	4-4	.310	.387	.468	.855	8	.962
2000	—Minnesota (A.L.)	3B-DH	146	474	79	142	32	4	9	65	77	104	4	11	5-4	.300	.400	.441	.841	12	.966
2001	—Minnesota (A.L.)	3B-DH	153	562	100	155	37	2	26	103	68	118	12	16	27-6	.276	.362	.488	.850	15	.964
2002	—Minnesota (A.L.)	3B-DH	140	490	71	131	37	3	15	69	72	127	9	14	10-11	.267	.368	.447	.815	12	.969
2003	—Minnesota (A.L.)	3B	131	469	76	137	29	2	14	69	77	113	7	5	11-5	.292	.393	.452	.845	9	.973
2004	—Minnesota (A.L.)	3B-DH	118	422	68	106	24	2	25	71	49	103	12	6	9-3	.251	.342	.495	.837	11	.963
2005	—Syracuse (Int'l)	3B-DH	7	25	1	6	2	0	0	2	3	6	2	1	0-0	.240	.367	.320	.687	0	1.000
	—Toronto (A.L.)	3B-DH	97	354	49	88	20	0	11	36	44	90	4	10	4-1	.249	.337	.398	.735	7	.968
Major League totals (8 years)			913	3142	487	869	200	13	112	473	429	737	53	68	70-34	.277	.369	.455	.825	75	.966

DIVISION SERIES RECORD

Year	Team (League)	Pos.	G	AB	R	H	2B	3B	HR	RBI	BB	SO	HBP	GDP	SB-CS	Avg.	OBP	SLG	OPS	E	Avg.
2002	Minnesota (A.L.)	3B	5	21	3	3	0	1	1	5	2	6	1	0	0-0	.143	.250	.381	.631	1	.923
2003	Minnesota (A.L.)	3B	4	15	0	3	1	0	0	0	0	5	0	0	0-1	.200	.200	.267	.467	0	1.000
2004	Minnesota (A.L.)	3B	4	13	2	4	1	0	0	2	3	2	2	0	0-0	.308	.474	.385	.858	0	1.000
Division series totals (3 years)			13	49	5	10	2	1	1	7	5	13	3	0	0-1	.204	.310	.347	.657	1	.963

CHAMPIONSHIP SERIES RECORD

Year	Team (League)	Pos.	G	AB	R	H	2B	3B	HR	RBI	BB	SO	HBP	GDP	SB-CS	Avg.	OBP	SLG	OPS	E	Avg.
2002	Minnesota (A.L.)	3B	5	18	3	5	2	0	2	2	8	0	0	0-0		.278	.350	.389	.739	0	1.000

KOTCHMAN, CASEY — 1B

PERSONAL: Born February 22, 1983, in St. Petersburg, Fla. ... 6-3/210. ... Bats left, throws left. ... Full name: Casey John Kotchman. ... High school: Seminole (Fla.).
TRANSACTIONS/CAREER NOTES: Selected by Anaheim Angels organization in first round (13th pick overall) of 2001 free-agent draft. ... Angels franchise renamed Los Angeles Angels of Anaheim for 2005 season.
2005 GAMES PLAYED BY POSITION (MLB): DH—20, 1B—20.

SCOUTING REPORT

Offense: He has a short, compact swing and makes consistent contact. Tends to dive toward the plate and push the bat, which prevents him from keepins his weight on his backside. Can keep the ball fair when pitched in on his hands. Is starting to show power. Needs to adjust to lefthanders. **Defense:** He's a good defensive first baseman with soft hands, good agility and the ability to field bad throws. Has arm strength and is very accurate starting the double play. Is athletic and has good instincts. **Outlook:** Kotchman is going to continue to improve his power as he gains experience, but he already is fairly advanced for a young hitter. Twenty-five home runs a year will not be a stretch. **Grade 7**

CASEY KOTCHMAN'S HITTING ZONE

.500	.000	.250
.167	.556	.238
.286	.250	.000

LEFTY-RIGHTY SPLITS

vs.	Avg.	AB	H	2B	3B	HR	RBI	BB	SO	OBP	Sig.
L	.250	28	7	0	0	0	2	4	7	.344	.250
R	.286	98	28	5	0	7	20	11	11	.355	.551

Year	Team (League)	Pos.	G	AB	R	H	2B	3B	HR	RBI	BB	SO	HBP	GDP	SB-CS	Avg.	OBP	SLG	OPS	E	Avg.
2001	Ariz. Angels (AZL)	1B	4	15	5	9	1	0	1	5	3	2	0	0	0-0	.600	.632	.867	1.498	1	.974
	—Provo (Pion.)	1B	7	22	6	11	3	0	0	7	2	0	0	0	0-0	.500	.542	.636	1.178	0	1.000
2002	Cedar Rap. (Midw.)	1B	81	288	42	81	30	1	5	50	48	37	6	7	2-1	.281	.390	.444	.835	5	.992
2003	Ariz. Angels (Ariz.)	1B	7	27	5	9	1	0	2	6	3	1	0	0	0-0	.333	.379	.593	.972	0	1.000
	—Rancho Cuca. (Calif.)	1B	57	206	42	72	12	0	8	28	30	16	6	4	2-0	.350	.441	.524	.965	5	.988
2004	Arkansas (Texas)	1B-DH	28	114	19	42	11	0	3	18	10	7	5	6	0-0	.368	.438	.544	.960	1	1.000
	—Salt Lake (PCL)	1B-DH	49	199	32	74	22	0	5	38	14	25	5	9	0-0	.372	.423	.558	.967	3	.992
	—Anaheim (A.L.)	1B-DH	38	116	7	26	6	0	0	15	7	11	4	3	3-0	.224	.289	.276	.565	3	.988
2005	Salt Lake (PCL)		94	363	62	105	23	1	10	58	43	40	7	15	0-2	.289	.372	.441	.812	4	.995
	—Los Angeles (A.L.)	1B-DH	47	126	16	35	5	0	7	22	15	18	0	3	1-1	.278	.352	.484	.836	0	1.000
Major League totals (2 years)			85	242	23	61	11	0	7	37	22	29	4	6	4-1	.252	.322	.384	.707	3	.992

DIVISION SERIES RECORD

Year	Team (League)	Pos.	G	AB	R	H	2B	3B	HR	RBI	BB	SO	HBP	GDP	SB-CS	Avg.	OBP	SLG	OPS	E	Avg.
2004	Anaheim (A.L.)		2	1	0	0	0	0	0	0	0	0	0	0	0-0	.000	.000	.000	.000	0	...
2005	Los Angeles (A.L.)	DH	2	2	0	0	0	0	0	0	0	0	0	0	0-0	.000	.000	.000	.000	0	...
Division series totals (2 years)			4	3	0	0	0	0	0	0	0	0	0	0	0-0	.000	.000	.000	.000	0	...

CHAMPIONSHIP SERIES RECORD

Year	Team (League)	Pos.	G	AB	R	H	2B	3B	HR	RBI	BB	SO	HBP	GDP	SB-CS	Avg.	OBP	SLG	OPS	E	Avg.
2005	Los Angeles (A.L.)	DH	2	7	0	2	1	0	0	1	1	0	0	0	0-0	.286	.375	.429	.804	0	...

KOTSAY, MARK — OF

PERSONAL: Born December 2, 1975, in Whittier, Calif. ... 6-0/201. ... Bats left, throws left. ... Full name: Mark Steven Kotsay. ... Name pronounced: KAHT-say. ... High school: Santa Fe Springs (Calif.). ... College: Cal State Fullerton.
TRANSACTIONS/CAREER NOTES: Selected by Florida Marlins organization in first round (ninth pick overall) of 1996 free-agent draft. ... Traded by Marlins with OF Cesar Crespo to San Diego Padres for OF Eric Owens and Ps Matt Clement and Omar Ortiz (March 28, 2001). ... On disabled list (April 16-May 1, 2001; and May 19-June 5, 2003). ... Traded by Padres to Oakland Athletics for C Ramon Hernandez and OF Terrence Long (November 26, 2003).
2005 GAMES PLAYED BY POSITION (MLB): OF—137, DH—2.

SCOUTING REPORT** **Offense: He is an overly patient hitter who likes to take pitchers deep in the count. Is a high on-base percentage hitter with a short stroke. Is a line-drive hitter with increasing power and is starting to drive in runs. Good against lefthanded pitching. Is a very good runner with good baserunning instincts but doesn't steal a lot. ***Defense:*** He likes to play shallow but gets a good jump going back and has above-average lateral range. Takes precise routes and has good instincts. Has a slightly above-average arm, is accurate and gets rid of the ball quickly. ***Outlook:*** Kotsay is one of the more underrated players in the league and continues to improve. Is a complete player. Has the potential to raise his home run totals. ***Grade 8.4***

MARK KOTSAY'S HITTING ZONE

.500	.310	.167
.299	.321	.226
.450	.390	.293

LEFTY-RIGHTY SPLITS

vs.	Avg.	AB	H	2B	3B	HR	RBI	BB	SO	OBP	Slg.
L	.324	179	58	15	0	3	24	10	20	.359	.458
R	.261	403	105	20	1	12	58	30	31	.310	.404

									BATTING								FIELDING	
Year	Team (League)	Pos.	G	AB	R	H	2B	3B	HR	RBI	BB	SO	HBP	GDP	SB-CS	Avg.	OBP	SLG	OPS	E	Avg.
1996— Kane Co. (Midw.)	OF	17	60	16	17	5	0	2	8	16	8	1	3	3-0	.283	.436	.467	.903	0	1.000
1997— Portland (East.)	OF-DH	114	438	103	134	27	2	20	77	75	65	0	16	17-5	.306	.405	.514	.919	2	.992
— Florida (N.L.)	OF	14	52	5	10	1	1	0	4	4	7	0	1	3-0	.192	.250	.250	.500	0	1.000
1998— Florida (N.L.)	OF-1B	154	578	72	161	25	7	11	68	34	61	1	17	10-5	.279	.318	.403	.721	6	.984
1999— Florida (N.L.)	OF-1B	148	495	57	134	23	9	8	50	29	50	0	11	7-6	.271	.306	.402	.708	5	.987
2000— Florida (N.L.)	OF-1B	152	530	87	158	31	5	12	57	42	46	0	17	19-9	.298	.347	.443	.791	3	.990
2001— San Diego (N.L.)	OF	119	406	67	118	29	1	10	58	48	58	2	11	13-5	.291	.366	.441	.807	4	.986
2002— San Diego (N.L.)	OF	153	578	82	169	27	7	17	61	59	89	3	10	11-9	.292	.359	.452	.810	4	.989
2003— San Diego (N.L.)	OF	128	482	64	128	28	4	7	38	56	82	1	8	6-3	.266	.343	.384	.726	3	.991
2004— Oakland (A.L.)	OF-DH	148	606	78	190	37	3	15	63	55	70	2	6	8-5	.314	.370	.459	.829	6	.984
2005— Oakland (A.L.)	OF-DH	139	582	75	163	35	1	15	82	40	51	1	13	5-5	.280	.325	.421	.746	4	.987
American League totals (2 years)		287	1188	153	353	72	4	30	145	95	121	3	19	13-10	.297	.348	.440	.788	10	.985
National League totals (7 years)		868	3121	434	878	164	34	65	336	272	393	7	75	69-37	.281	.338	.418	.756	25	.988
Major League totals (9 years)		1155	4309	587	1231	236	38	95	481	367	514	10	94	82-47	.286	.341	.424	.765	35	.987

KRYNZEL, DAVE — OF

PERSONAL: Born November 7, 1981, in Dayton, Ohio. ... 6-1/180. ... Bats left, throws left. ... Full name: David Benjamin Krynzel. ... High school: Green Valley (Henderson, Nev.).
TRANSACTIONS/CAREER NOTES: Selected by Milwaukee Brewers organization in first round (11th pick overall) of 2000 free-agent draft.
2005 GAMES PLAYED BY POSITION (MLB): OF—1.

LEFTY-RIGHTY SPLITS

vs.	Avg.	AB	H	2B	3B	HR	RBI	BB	SO	OBP	Slg.
L	.000	0	0	0	0	0	0	0	0	.000	.000
R	.000	7	0	0	0	0	0	0	3	.000	.000

									BATTING								FIELDING	
Year	Team (League)	Pos.	G	AB	R	H	2B	3B	HR	RBI	BB	SO	HBP	GDP	SB-CS	Avg.	OBP	SLG	OPS	E	Avg.
2000— Ogden (Pion.)	OF	34	131	25	47	8	3	1	29	16	23	5	0	8-4	.359	.442	.489	.930	3	.955
2001— Beloit (Midw.)	OF	35	141	22	43	1	1	1	19	9	28	4	1	11-5	.305	.364	.348	.711	2	.970
— High Desert (Calif.)	OF	89	383	65	106	19	5	5	33	27	122	4	0	34-17	.277	.329	.392	.721	5	.977
2002— High Desert (Calif.)	OF	97	365	76	98	13	12	11	45	64	100	11	2	29-17	.268	.391	.460	.851	7	.971
— Huntsville (Sou.)	OF	31	129	13	31	2	3	2	13	4	30	1	0	13-5	.240	.269	.349	.617	2	.971
2003— Huntsville (Sou.)	OF	124	457	72	122	13	11	2	34	60	119	6	3	43-21	.267	.357	.357	.714	11	.963
2004— Ariz. Brewers (Ariz.)	OF	5	16	8	8	1	1	0	0	3	2	0	0	2-0	.500	.600	.688	1.266	0	1.000
— Indianapolis (Int'l)	OF-DH	69	258	36	70	10	4	6	26	20	63	3	0	10-8	.271	.327	.411	.741	1	.993
— Milwaukee (N.L.)	OF	16	41	6	9	1	0	0	3	3	15	3	0	0-0	.220	.319	.244	.563	1	.968
2005— Milwaukee (N.L.)	OF	5	7	0	0	0	0	0	0	0	3	0	0	0-0	.000	.000	.000	.000	0	1.000
— Nashville (PCL)	OF-DH	115	450	71	115	25	7	11	51	43	138	5	3	24-8	.256	.324	.416	.740	20	.959
Major League totals (2 years)		21	48	6	9	1	0	0	3	3	18	3	0	0-0	.188	.278	.208	.486	1	.970

KUO, HONG-CHIH — P

PERSONAL: Born July 23, 1981, in Tainan City, Taiwan. ... 6-0/200. ... Throws left, bats left. ... Full name: Hong-Chih Kuo.
TRANSACTIONS/CAREER NOTES: Signed as a non-drafted free agent by Los Angeles Dodgers organization (June 19, 1999).
CAREER HITTING: 0-for-0 (.000), 0 R, 0 2B, 0 3B, 0 HR, 0 RBI.

LEFTY-RIGHTY SPLITS

vs.	Avg.	AB	H	2B	3B	HR	RBI	BB	SO	OBP	Slg.
L	.385	13	5	3	0	1	2	3	5	.500	.846
R	.000	8	0	0	0	0	0	2	5	.200	.000

Year	Team (League)	W	L	Pct.	ERA	WHIP	G	GS	CG	ShO	Hld.	Sv.-Opp.	IP	H	R	ER	HR	BB-IBB	SO	Avg.
2000— San Bern. (Calif.)	0	0	...	0.00	0.00	1	1	0	0	...	0-...	3.0	0	0	0	0	0-0	7	.000
2001— GC Dodgers (GCL)	0	0	...	2.33	0.88	7	6	0	0	...	0-...	19.1	13	5	5	0	4-0	21	.186
2002— GC Dodgers (GCL)	0	0	...	4.50	0.83	3	3	0	0	...	0-...	6.0	4	3	3	0	1-0	9	.200
— Vero Beach (Fla. St.)	0	1	.000	6.75	1.63	4	4	0	0	...	0-...	8.0	11	6	6	0	2-0	8	.324
2004— Columbus (S. Atl.)	1	0	1.000	4.50	2.00	3	3	0	0	...	0-...	6.0	8	3	3	0	4-0	10	.308
2005— Vero Beach (Fla. St.)	1	1	.500	2.08	1.12	11	3	0	0	...	0-0	26.0	19	7	6	0	10-0	44	.202
— Jacksonville (Sou.)	1	1	.500	1.91	1.16	17	0	0	0	2	3-4	28.1	22	7	6	1	6-0	42	.210
— Los Angeles (N.L.)	0	1	.000	6.75	1.88	9	0	0	0	3	0-1	5.1	5	4	4	1	5-1	10	.238
Major League totals (1 year)	0	1	.000	6.75	1.88	9	0	0	0	3	0-1	5.1	5	4	4	1	5-1	10	.238

K

LACKEY, JOHN　　　　　　　　　　P

PERSONAL: Born October 23, 1978, in Abilene, Texas. ... 6-6/235. ... Throws right, bats right. ... Full name: John Derran Lackey. ... High school: Abilene (Texas). ... Junior college: Grayson County (Texas).
TRANSACTIONS/CAREER NOTES: Selected by Anaheim Angels organization in second round of 1999 free-agent draft. ... On suspended list (June 22-27, 2004). ... Angels franchise renamed Los Angeles Angels of Anaheim for 2005 season.
CAREER HITTING: 0-for-11 (.000), 0 R, 0 2B, 0 3B, 0 HR, 0 RBI.

SCOUTING REPORT **Throws:** Lackey has one of the game's better curveballs, a fastball in the 90-94 mph range and a changeup. **Tendencies:** He takes a good angle to the plate with his pitches and is keeping the ball down better. Has improved the command of his fastball and has been aggressive attacking hitters. Fastball down has good life. Is fast enough to pitch up with a four-seam fastball. Has a power curve that can look like a slider. Has improved his straight change both in arm speed and movement. **Outlook:** He has turned the corner in his career, controlling his emotions on the mound better. Has 20-win ability. *Grade 8.3*

JOHN LACKEY'S PITCHING ZONE

.234	.417	.313
.337	.342	.259
.263	.365	.270

LEFTY-RIGHTY SPLITS

vs.	Avg.	AB	H	2B	3B	HR	RBI	BB	SO	OBP	Slg.
L	.274	401	110	19	0	6	43	35	86	.338	.367
R	.241	406	98	24	1	7	38	36	113	.313	.357

Year Team (League)	W	L	Pct.	ERA	WHIP	G	GS	CG	ShO	Hld.	Sv.-Opp.	IP	H	R	ER	HR	BB-IBB	SO	Avg.
1999— Boise (N'west)	6	2	.750	4.98	1.61	15	15	1	0	...	0-...	81.1	81	59	45	7	50-1	77	.264
2000— Cedar Rap. (Midw.)	3	2	.600	2.08	0.82	5	5	0	0	...	0-...	30.1	20	7	7	1	5-0	21	.185
— Lake Elsinore (Calif.)	6	6	.500	3.40	1.35	15	15	2	1	...	0-...	100.2	94	56	38	9	42-0	74	.249
— Erie (East.)	6	1	.857	3.30	1.17	8	8	2	0	...	0-...	57.1	58	23	21	6	9-0	43	.260
2001— Arkansas (Texas)	9	7	.563	3.46	1.06	18	18	3	2	...	0-...	127.1	106	55	49	11	29-0	94	.227
— Salt Lake (PCL)	3	4	.429	6.71	1.58	10	10	1	0	...	0-...	57.2	75	44	43	5	16-0	42	.322
2002— Salt Lake (PCL)	8	2	.800	2.57	1.15	16	16	2	1	...	0-...	101.2	89	35	29	5	28-0	82	.235
— Anaheim (A.L.)	9	4	.692	3.66	1.35	18	18	1	0	0	0-0	108.1	113	52	44	10	33-0	69	.267
2003— Anaheim (A.L.)	10	16	.385	4.63	1.42	33	33	2	•2	0	0-0	204.0	223	117	105	31	66-4	151	.278
2004— Anaheim (A.L.)	14	13	.519	4.67	1.39	33	32	1	1	0	0-0	198.1	215	108	103	22	60-4	144	.278
2005— Los Angeles (A.L.)	14	5	.737	3.44	1.33	33	33	1	0	0	0-0	209.0	208	85	80	13	71-3	199	.258
Major League totals (4 years)	47	38	.553	4.15	1.37	117	116	5	3	0	0-0	719.2	759	362	332	76	230-11	563	.270

DIVISION SERIES RECORD

Year Team (League)	W	L	Pct.	ERA	WHIP	G	GS	CG	ShO	Hld.	Sv.-Opp.	IP	H	R	ER	HR	BB-IBB	SO	Avg.
2002— Anaheim (A.L.)	0	0	...	0.00	1.33	1	0	0	0	0	0-0	3.0	3	0	0	0	1-0	3	.250
2005— Los Angeles (A.L.)	0	0	...	2.38	1.41	2	2	0	0	0	0-0	11.1	7	3	3	0	9-0	9	.179
Division series totals (2 years)	0	0	...	1.88	1.40	3	2	0	0	0	0-0	14.1	10	3	3	0	10-0	12	.196

CHAMPIONSHIP SERIES RECORD

Year Team (League)	W	L	Pct.	ERA	WHIP	G	GS	CG	ShO	Hld.	Sv.-Opp.	IP	H	R	ER	HR	BB-IBB	SO	Avg.
2002— Anaheim (A.L.)	1	0	1.000	0.00	0.43	1	1	0	0	0	0-0	7.0	3	0	0	0	0-0	7	.130
2005— Los Angeles (A.L.)	0	1	.000	9.00	1.80	1	1	0	0	0	0-0	5.0	8	5	5	1	1-0	3	.381
Champ. series totals (2 years)	1	1	.500	3.75	1.00	2	2	0	0	0	0-0	12.0	11	5	5	1	1-0	10	.250

WORLD SERIES RECORD

Year Team (League)	W	L	Pct.	ERA	WHIP	G	GS	CG	ShO	Hld.	Sv.-Opp.	IP	H	R	ER	HR	BB-IBB	SO	Avg.
2002— Anaheim (A.L.)	1	0	1.000	4.38	1.62	3	2	0	0	0	0-0	12.1	15	6	6	0	5-4	7	.319

LAFOREST, PETE　　　　　　　　　　C

PERSONAL: Born January 17, 1978, in Hull, Quebec. ... 6-2/208. ... Bats left, throws right. ... Full name: Pierre-Luc LaForest. ... High school: Gatineau (Quebec).
TRANSACTIONS/CAREER NOTES: Selected by Montreal Expos organization in 16th round of 1995 free-agent draft. ... Contract voided by Commissioner's Office (August 15, 1995). ... Signed as a free agent by Tampa Bay Devil Rays (May 10, 1997).
2005 GAMES PLAYED BY POSITION (MLB): C—21, DH—2, 1B—1.

PETE LAFOREST'S HITTING ZONE

.000	.000	.333
.286	.500	.182
.000	.000	.333

LEFTY-RIGHTY SPLITS

vs.	Avg.	AB	H	2B	3B	HR	RBI	BB	SO	OBP	Slg.
L	.000	4	0	0	0	0	0	0	2	.000	.000
R	.183	60	11	3	0	1	4	6	21	.258	.283

Year Team (League)	Pos.	G	AB	R	H	2B	3B	HR	RBI	BB	SO	HBP	GDP	SB-CS	Avg.	OBP	SLG	OPS	E	Avg.
1995— GC Expos (GCL)	3B	2	6	1	0	0	0	0	0	2	4	0	0	0-0	.000	.250	.000	.250	0	...
1996—			Did not play.																	
1997— GC Devil Rays (GCL)	3B	34	107	21	28	7	2	3	21	10	18	1	1	4-3	.262	.328	.449	.777	7	.909
1998— Princeton (Appal.)	3B	25	91	18	25	7	1	2	14	12	18	1	0	4-1	.275	.365	.440	.805	7	.870
1999— Char., S.C. (S. Atl.)	3B-2B	125	445	64	114	21	3	13	53	55	97	5	11	9-3	.256	.343	.404	.747	37	.893
2000— St. Pete. (Fla. St.)	C	129	474	85	128	28	7	14	70	56	108	6	4	2-4	.270	.351	.447	.798	10	.974
2001— Orlando (South.)	C	7	21	3	2	0	0	1	1	5	9	0	0	0-0	.095	.269	.238	.507	2	.968
2002— Durham (Int'l)	C	17	66	7	17	3	0	3	15	3	28	0	1	0-1	.258	.290	.439	.729	5	.950
— Orlando (South.)	C-1B	106	359	57	97	18	1	20	64	60	94	2	4	9-6	.270	.374	.493	.867	13	.977
2003— Orlando (South.)	DH-C-3B	21	72	9	18	8	0	3	16	17	16	1	1	0-0	.250	.385	.486	.871	1	.981
— Durham (Int'l)	C-DH	61	201	40	54	14	2	14	38	36	56	2	2	2-1	.269	.382	.567	.949	3	.990
— Tampa Bay (A.L.)	DH-C	19	48	0	8	2	0	0	6	1	14	1	1	0-0	.167	.196	.208	.404	0	1.000
2004— Durham (Int'l)	C-1B	84	275	37	61	19	0	7	31	35	64	0	6	1-1	.222	.309	.367	.676	8	.984
2005— Tampa Bay (A.L.)	C-DH-1B	25	64	5	11	3	0	1	4	6	23	0	2	0-1	.172	.243	.266	.508	0	1.000
Major League totals (2 years)		44	112	5	19	5	0	1	10	7	37	1	3	0-1	.170	.223	.241	.464	0	1.000

LAIRD, GERALD   C

PERSONAL: Born November 13, 1979, in Westminster, Calif. ... 6-2/220. ... Bats right, throws right. ... Full name: Gerald Lee Laird. ... High school: La Quinta (Westminster,Calif.). ... Junior college: Cypress (Calif.).
TRANSACTIONS/CAREER NOTES: Selected by Oakland Athletics organization in second round of 1998 free-agent draft. ... Traded by A's with P Mario Ramos, 1B Jason Hart and OF Ryan Ludwick to Texas Rangers for P Mike Venafro and 1B Carlos Pena (January 14, 2002). ... On disabled list (May 21-July 23, 2004); included rehabilitation assignment to Oklahoma.
2005 GAMES PLAYED BY POSITION (MLB): C—13, OF—1.

LEFTY-RIGHTY SPLITS

vs.	Avg.	AB	H	2B	3B	HR	RBI	BB	SO	OBP	Slg.
L	.222	9	2	1	0	0	0	0	3	.222	.333
R	.226	31	7	1	0	1	4	2	4	.273	.355

									BATTING									FIELDING	
Year Team (League)	Pos.	G	AB	R	H	2B	3B	HR	RBI	BB	SO	HBP	GDP	SB-CS	Avg.	OBP	SLG	OPS	E	Avg.
1999— S. Oregon (N'west)	C	60	228	45	65	7	2	2	39	28	43	2	4	10-5	.285	.361	.360	.721	11	.972
2000— Ariz. A's (AZL)	C	14	50	10	15	2	1	0	9	6	7	1	3	2-0	.300	.379	.380	.759	0	1.000
—Visalia (Calif.)	C	33	103	14	25	3	0	0	13	14	27	1	3	7-2	.243	.333	.272	.605	8	.969
2001— Modesto (Calif.)	C-OF-1B																			
	2B-3B-SS	119	443	71	113	13	5	5	46	48	101	10	9	10-9	.255	.337	.341	.678	18	.976
2002— Tulsa (Texas)	C-OF	123	442	70	122	21	4	11	67	45	95	5	14	8-6	.276	.343	.416	.759	8	.988
2003— Oklahoma (PCL)	C-DH	99	338	50	88	20	5	9	42	37	61	7	7	9-3	.260	.344	.429	.773	11	.983
—Texas (A.L.)	C	19	44	9	12	2	1	1	4	5	11	1	2	0-0	.273	.360	.432	.792	1	.986
2004— Oklahoma (PCL)	C-DH	6	22	2	4	2	0	0	2	2	8	0	1	1-0	.182	.250	.273	.523	1	.955
—Texas (A.L.)	C	49	147	20	33	6	0	1	16	12	35	2	5	0-1	.224	.287	.286	.572	5	.983
2005— Texas (A.L.)	C-OF	13	40	7	9	2	0	1	4	2	7	0	1	0-0	.225	.262	.350	.612	3	.957
Major League totals (3 years)		81	231	36	54	10	1	3	24	19	53	3	8	0-1	.234	.297	.325	.622	9	.980

LAKER, TIM   C

PERSONAL: Born November 27, 1969, in Encino, Calif. ... 6-3/225. ... Bats right, throws right. ... Full name: Timothy John Laker. ... High school: Simi Valley (Calif.). ... Junior college: Oxnard (Calif.).
TRANSACTIONS/CAREER NOTES: Selected by Kansas City Royals organization in 49th round of 1987 free-agent draft; did not sign. ... Selected by Montreal Expos organization in sixth round of 1988 free-agent draft. ... On disabled list (March 29, 1996-entire season). ... Claimed on waivers by Baltimore Orioles (March 25, 1997). ... Signed as a free agent by Tampa Bay Devil Rays (December 19, 1997). ... Released by Devil Rays (June 26, 1998). ... Signed by Pittsburgh Pirates organization (July 9, 1998). ... Released by Pirates (December 18, 1998). ... Signed by Los Angeles Dodgers organization (January 11, 1999). ... Traded by Dodgers to Pirates for a player to be named (March 26, 1999); Dodgers acquired P Jay Ryan to complete the deal (June 1, 2001). ... Signed as a free agent by Cleveland Indians organization (December 20, 2000). ... Signed as a free agent by Devil Rays organization (December 16, 2005). ... Career major league pitching: 0-0, 0.00 ERA, 2 G, 2.0 IP, 2 H, 0 R, 0 ER, 2 BB, 1 SO.
2005 GAMES PLAYED BY POSITION (MLB): C—1.

LEFTY-RIGHTY SPLITS

vs.	Avg.	AB	H	2B	3B	HR	RBI	BB	SO	OBP	Slg.
L	.000	0	0	0	0	0	0	0	0	.000	.000
R	.000	1	0	0	0	0	0	0	1	.000	.000

L

									BATTING									FIELDING	
Year Team (League)	Pos.	G	AB	R	H	2B	3B	HR	RBI	BB	SO	HBP	GDP	SB-CS	Avg.	OBP	SLG	OPS	E	Avg.
1988— Jamestown (N.Y.-Penn.)	C-OF	47	152	14	34	9	0	0	17	8	30	0	4	2-1	.224	.261	.283	.544	2	.992
1989— Rockford (Midw.)	C	14	48	4	11	1	1	0	4	3	6	0	1	1-0	.229	.275	.292	.566	4	.960
—Jamestown (N.Y.-Penn.)	C	58	216	25	48	9	1	2	24	16	40	2	4	8-4	.222	.278	.301	.579	8	.984
1990— Rockford (Midw.)	C-OF	120	425	46	94	18	3	7	57	32	83	1	9	7-2	.221	.273	.327	.600	18	.981
—W.P. Beach (Fla. St.)	C	2	3	0	0	0	0	0	0	0	1	0	0	0-0	.000	.000	.000	.000	0	1.000
1991— W.P. Beach (Fla. St.)	C	100	333	35	77	15	2	5	33	22	51	2	9	10-1	.231	.280	.333	.613	14	.979
—Harrisburg (East.)	C	11	35	4	10	1	0	1	5	2	5	1	1	0-1	.286	.342	.400	.742	3	.959
1992— Harrisburg (East.)	C	117	409	55	99	19	3	15	68	39	89	5	10	3-1	.242	.312	.413	.725	14	.980
—Montreal (N.L.)	C	28	46	8	10	3	0	0	4	2	14	0	1	1-1	.217	.250	.283	.533	1	.991
1993— Montreal (N.L.)	C	43	86	3	17	2	1	0	7	2	16	1	2	2-0	.198	.222	.244	.466	2	.987
—Ottawa (Int'l)	C-1B	56	204	26	47	10	0	4	23	21	41	1	10	3-2	.230	.304	.338	.642	11	.972
1994— Ottawa (Int'l)	C-DH	118	424	68	131	32	2	12	71	47	96	3	10	11-6	.309	.381	.479	.860	11	.985
1995— Montreal (N.L.)	C	64	141	17	33	8	1	3	20	14	38	1	5	0-1	.234	.306	.369	.675	7	.977
1996— Montreal (N.L.)	C		Did not play.																	
1997— Rochester (Int'l)	DH-C	79	290	45	75	11	1	11	37	34	49	5	4	1-2	.259	.342	.417	.760	6	.980
—Baltimore (A.L.)	C	7	14	0	0	0	0	0	1	2	9	0	0	0-0	.000	.118	.000	.118	1	.966
1998— Durham (Int'l)	C-DH	40	134	36	32	7	0	11	26	28	32	1	4	1-1	.239	.372	.537	.909	2	.991
—Tampa Bay (A.L.)	C-DH	3	.5	1	0	0	0	0	0	1	1	0	0	0-0	.200	.333	.200	.533	0	1.000
—Nashville (PCL)	C-1B-DH	44	152	30	54	16	1	11	34	21	26	3	6	1-0	.355	.441	.691	1.131	4	.987
—Pittsburgh (N.L.)	1B-C	14	24	2	9	1	0	2	1	1	3	0	1	0-0	.375	.385	.542	.926	0	1.000
1999— Nashville (PCL)	C-1B-DH																			
	3B	112	405	48	109	29	3	12	65	29	68	4	10	3-0	.269	.322	.444	.766	15	.981
—Pittsburgh (N.L.)	C	6	9	0	3	0	0	0	0	0	2	0	0	0-0	.333	.333	.333	.667	0	1.000
2000— Nashville (PCL)	C-1B-3B	121	421	70	104	28	4	19	75	54	73	4	9	5-0	.247	.329	.468	.796	12	.984
2001— Buffalo (Int'l)	C-1B	86	320	45	79	13	0	20	57	28	53	4	10	2-1	.247	.314	.475	.789	6	.990
—Cleveland (A.L.)	C	16	33	5	6	0	0	1	5	6	8	0	1	0-0	.182	.308	.273	.580	1	.988
2002— Columbus (S. Atl.)	C	11	38	5	11	1	0	2	13	10	6	1	0	0-0	.289	.440	.474	.914	0	1.000
—Buffalo (Int'l)	C-1B	62	216	23	49	10	0	4	28	21	52	3	9	2-0	.227	.303	.329	.632	3	.992
2003— Cleveland (A.L.)	C-DH	52	162	17	39	11	0	3	21	9	38	0	4	2-2	.241	.281	.364	.645	5	.983
2004— Cleveland (A.L.)	C-P	44	117	12	25	2	0	3	17	7	28	1	5	0-0	.214	.262	.308	.570	4	.985
2005— Tampa Bay (A.L.)	C	1	1	0	0	0	0	0	0	0	1	0	0	0-0	.000	.000	.000	.000	0	1.000
—Durham (Int'l)	C-DH-P	89	327	48	74	19	0	11	44	37	80	2	12	0-0	.226	.305	.385	.691	6	.987
American League totals (6 years)		123	332	35	71	13	0	7	44	25	85	1	10	2-3	.214	.269	.316	.586	11	.983
National League totals (5 years)		155	306	30	72	14	2	4	33	19	73	2	9	3-2	.235	.282	.333	.615	10	.984
Major League totals (10 years)		278	638	65	143	27	2	11	77	44	158	3	19	5-5	.224	.275	.324	.600	21	.984

LAMB, MIKE — 1B/3B/OF

PERSONAL: Born August 9, 1975, in West Covina, Calif. ... 6-1/190. ... Bats left, throws right. ... Full name: Michael Robert Lamb. ... High school: Bishop Amat (La Puente, Calif.). ... College: Cal State Fullerton.

TRANSACTIONS/CAREER NOTES: Selected by Minnesota Twins organization in 31st round of 1996 free-agent draft; did not sign. ... Selected by Texas Rangers organization in seventh round of 1997 free-agent draft. ... Traded by Rangers to New York Yankees for P Jose Garcia (February 5, 2004). ... Traded by Yankees to Houston Astros for P Juan DeLeon (March 25, 2004).

2005 GAMES PLAYED BY POSITION (MLB): 1B—68, 3B—15, OF—13, DH—1.

SCOUTING REPORT *Offense:* He has an unusual approach at the plate that forces him to hit around the ball. Has some bat speed and deceptive power. Takes advantage of Minute Maid Park's short porch in left but also has the strength to hit it out in right. Plays mainly against righthanded pitchers. *Defense:* Lamb is versatile, but not very fluid. Is better at first than third. Has limited range to both sides. Arm, though not very strong, is adequate at starting the double play at first but can be erratic. Makes errors in bunches. *Outlook:* His bat will keep him in the big leagues, but his defensive limitations and shortcomings against lefthanders will keep him from being an everyday player. Is a power threat off the bench. *Grade 6.6*

MIKE LAMB'S HITTING ZONE

.333	.333	.200
.250	.308	.228
.105	.444	.260

LEFTY-RIGHTY SPLITS

vs.	Avg.	AB	H	2B	3B	HR	RBI	BB	SO	OBP	Slg.
L	.179	56	10	2	2	1	8	2	16	.217	.339
R	.248	266	66	11	3	11	45	20	49	.298	.436

									BATTING											FIELDING	
Year	Team (League)	Pos.	G	AB	R	H	2B	3B	HR	RBI	BB	SO	HBP	GDP	SB-CS	Avg.	OBP	SLG	OPS	E	Avg.
1997—	Pulaski (Appal.)	3B	60	233	59	78	19	3	9	47	31	18	4	5	7-2	.335	.412	.558	.970	25	.862
1998—	Charlotte (Fla. St.)	1B-3B	135	536	83	162	35	3	9	93	45	63	4	10	18-7	.302	.356	.429	.785	31	.933
1999—	Tulsa (Texas)	3B-C	137	544	98	176	51	5	21	100	53	65	7	11	4-3	.324	.386	.551	.937	28	.930
—	Oklahoma (PCL)	3B	2	2	0	1	0	0	0	0	1	0	1	0	0-1	.500	.750	.500	1.250	0	
2000—	Oklahoma (PCL)	3B	14	55	8	14	5	1	2	5	5	6	0	5	0-1	.255	.317	.491	.808	7	.806
—	Texas (A.L.)	3B-DH	138	493	65	137	25	2	6	47	34	60	4	10	0-2	.278	.328	.373	.702	• 33	.913
2001—	Oklahoma (PCL)	3B	69	273	35	81	19	3	8	40	13	31	3	8	0-2	.297	.331	.476	.807	15	.908
—	Texas (A.L.)	3B	76	284	42	87	18	0	4	35	14	27	5	6	2-1	.306	.348	.412	.760	18	.914
2002—	Oklahoma (PCL)	C-3B	6	28	3	11	1	0	0	4	1	4	0	1	0-0	.393	.414	.429	.842	3	.893
—	Texas (A.L.)	3B-C-2B / 1B-DH-OF	115	314	54	89	13	0	9	33	33	48	3	7	0-0	.283	.354	.411	.765	9	.980
2003—	Texas (A.L.)	DH-1B-OF / 3B	28	38	3	5	0	0	0	2	2	7	1	1	1-0	.132	.190	.132	.322	0	1.000
—	Oklahoma (PCL)	3B-1B-2B	73	274	45	79	19	4	9	46	42	45	2	4	1-1	.288	.383	.485	.869	11	.953
2004—	Houston (N.L.)	DH	112	278	38	80	14	3	14	58	31	63	0	4	1-1	.288	.356	.511	.867	14	.947
2005—	Houston (N.L.)	1B-3B-OF / DH	125	322	41	76	13	5	12	53	22	65	1	10	1-1	.236	.284	.419	.703	6	.989
	American League totals (4 years)		357	1129	164	318	56	2	19	117	83	142	13	24	3-3	.282	.336	.385	.721	60	.943
	National League totals (2 years)		237	600	79	156	27	8	26	111	53	128	1	14	2-2	.260	.318	.462	.779	20	.975
	Major League totals (6 years)		594	1729	243	474	83	10	45	228	136	270	14	38	5-5	.274	.329	.412	.741	80	.956

DIVISION SERIES RECORD

Year	Team (League)	Pos.	G	AB	R	H	2B	3B	HR	RBI	BB	SO	HBP	GDP	SB-CS	Avg.	OBP	SLG	OPS	E	Avg.
2004— Houston (N.L.)			4	3	0	0	0	0	0	0	0	0			0-0	.000	.000	.000	.000	0	...
2005— Houston (N.L.)		1B	2	6	1	3	0	0	1	1	2	0			0-0	.500	.625	1.000	1.625	0	1.000
Division series totals (2 years)			6	9	1	3	0	0	1	2	2	0			0-0	.333	.417	.667	1.083	0	1.000

CHAMPIONSHIP SERIES RECORD

Year	Team (League)	Pos.	G	AB	R	H	2B	3B	HR	RBI	BB	SO	HBP	GDP	SB-CS	Avg.	OBP	SLG	OPS	E	Avg.
2004— Houston (N.L.)		3B	2	5	2	2	0	0	2	2	1	1	0		0-0	.400	.500	1.600	2.100	0	1.000
2005— Houston (N.L.)		1B	4	16	3	3	1	0	1	2	0	3	0		0-0	.188	.188	.438	.625	1	.975
Champ. series totals (2 years)			6	21	5	5	1	0	3	4	1	4	0		0-0	.238	.273	.714	.987	1	.977

WORLD SERIES RECORD

Year	Team (League)	Pos.	G	AB	R	H	2B	3B	HR	RBI	BB	SO	HBP	GDP	SB-CS	Avg.	OBP	SLG	OPS	E	Avg.
2005— Houston (N.L.)		1B	4	10	1	2	1	0	1	1	2	3	0		0-0	.200	.333	.600	.933	0	1.000

LANE, JASON — OF

PERSONAL: Born December 22, 1976, in Santa Rosa, Calif. ... 6-2/220. ... Bats right, throws left. ... Full name: Jason Dean Lane. ... High school: Santa Rosa (Calif.). ... College: Southern California.

TRANSACTIONS/CAREER NOTES: Selected by Houston Astros organization in sixth round of 1999 free-agent draft.

2005 GAMES PLAYED BY POSITION (MLB): OF—141.

SCOUTING REPORT *Offense:* Lane looks ugly when he misses, but he has exceptional power. Has a sweeping swing and will pull off the ball. Looks for pitches inside and has good plate coverage against the fastball but struggles with breaking pitches. Will improve his average as he gains experience. Is an average runner. *Defense:* He has improved his arm strength through good mechanics. Has settled in right field, getting better jumps and showing average range to the gaps. *Outlook:* Lane is an underrated player who will continue to get better. He will average at least 30 home runs a year. *Grade 7.7*

JASON LANE'S HITTING ZONE

.250	.261	.250
.273	.393	.354
.233	.313	.412

LEFTY-RIGHTY SPLITS

vs.	Avg.	AB	H	2B	3B	HR	RBI	BB	SO	OBP	Slg.
L	.237	156	37	9	0	8	25	11	36	.300	.449
R	.280	361	101	25	4	18	53	21	69	.322	.521

									BATTING											FIELDING	
Year	Team (League)	Pos.	G	AB	R	H	2B	3B	HR	RBI	BB	SO	HBP	GDP	SB-CS	Avg.	OBP	SLG	OPS	E	Avg.
1999—	Auburn (N.Y.-Penn.)	1B-P	74	283	46	79	18	5	13	59	38	46	3	2	6-4	.279	.366	.516	.882	9	.986
2000—	Michigan (Midw.)	1B-OF	133	511	98	153	38	0	23	104	62	91	8	9	20-7	.299	.375	.509	.884	5	.986
2001—	Round Rock (Texas)	OF	137	526	103	166	36	4	38	124	61	86	21	6	14-2	.316	.407	.608	1.016	2	.992
2002—	New Orleans (PCL)	OF-1B	111	426	65	116	36	2	15	83	31	90	7	6	13-3	.272	.328	.472	.799	2	.993

Year Team (League)	Pos.	G	AB	R	H	2B	3B	HR	RBI	BB	SO	HBP	GDP	SB-CS	Avg.	OBP	SLG	OPS	E	Avg.
—Houston (N.L.)	OF	44	69	12	20	3	1	4	10	10	12	0	0	1-1	.290	.375	.536	.911	1	.980
2003—New Orleans (PCL)	OF-1B-DH	71	248	37	74	17	0	7	39	30	26	3	6	2-1	.298	.374	.452	.826	4	.976
—Houston (N.L.)	OF	18	27	5	8	2	0	4	10	0	2	0	0	0-0	.296	.296	.815	1.111	0	1.000
2004—Houston (N.L.)	OF-1B	107	136	21	37	10	2	4	19	16	33	1	2	1-0	.272	.348	.463	.812	2	.974
2005—Houston (N.L.)	OF	145	517	65	138	34	4	26	78	32	105	7	10	6-2	.267	.316	.499	.815	6	.976
Major League totals (4 years)		314	749	103	203	49	7	38	117	58	152	8	12	8-3	.271	.327	.507	.834	9	.977

DIVISION SERIES RECORD

Year Team (League)	Pos.	G	AB	R	H	2B	3B	HR	RBI	BB	SO	HBP	GDP	SB-CS	Avg.	OBP	SLG	OPS	E	Avg.
2004—Houston (N.L.)	OF	5	5	2	3	0	0	1	2	0	1	0	0	0-0	.600	.600	1.200	1.800	0	1.000
2005—Houston (N.L.)	OF	4	17	1	4	1	0	0	3	1	3	1	1	0-0	.235	.300	.294	.594	0	1.000
Division series totals (2 years)		9	22	3	7	1	0	1	5	1	4	1	1	0-0	.318	.360	.500	.860	0	1.000

CHAMPIONSHIP SERIES RECORD

Year Team (League)	Pos.	G	AB	R	H	2B	3B	HR	RBI	BB	SO	HBP	GDP	SB-CS	Avg.	OBP	SLG	OPS	E	Avg.
2004—Houston (N.L.)	OF	2	1	0	0	0	0	0	0	0	0	0	0	0-0	.000	.000	.000	.000	0	1.000
2005—Houston (N.L.)	OF	6	21	3	5	0	0	2	3	2	4	1	0	0-0	.238	.333	.524	.857	0	1.000
Champ. series totals (2 years)		8	22	3	5	0	0	2	3	2	4	1	0	0-0	.227	.320	.500	.820	0	1.000

WORLD SERIES RECORD

Year Team (League)	Pos.	G	AB	R	H	2B	3B	HR	RBI	BB	SO	HBP	GDP	SB-CS	Avg.	OBP	SLG	OPS	E	Avg.
2005—Houston (N.L.)	OF	4	18	1	4	1	0	1	2	1	5	0	1	1-0	.222	.263	.444	.708	0	1.000

LANGERHANS, RYAN — OF

PERSONAL: Born February 20, 1980, in San Antonio. ... 6-3/195. ... Bats left, throws left. ... Full name: Ryan David Langerhans. ... Name pronounced: lahn-ger-hahns. ... High school: Round Rock (Texas).

TRANSACTIONS/CAREER NOTES: Selected by Atlanta Braves organization in third round of 1998 free-agent draft.

2005 GAMES PLAYED BY POSITION (MLB): OF—114.

SCOUTING REPORT Langerhans is another young Braves outfielder with plenty of tools. Is an advanced hitter with good strength and bat speed. Will take the ball to all fields. Is going to have good power and has showed the ability to hit in the clutch. Is a good defensive outfielder, getting good jumps. Has good lateral closing speed and can go back on balls. Has an average arm but is accurate and has a quick release. Is going to be a good regular left fielder. *Grade 7*

RYAN LANGERHANS' HITTING ZONE

.231	.375	.182
.289	.348	.319
.316	.214	.286

LEFTY-RIGHTY SPLITS

vs.	Avg.	AB	H	2B	3B	HR	RBI	BB	SO	OBP	Slg.
L	.293	58	17	3	1	1	5	5	15	.369	.431
R	.261	268	70	19	2	7	37	32	60	.343	.425

Year Team (League)	Pos.	G	AB	R	H	2B	3B	HR	RBI	BB	SO	HBP	GDP	SB-CS	Avg.	OBP	SLG	OPS	E	Avg.
1998—GC Braves (GCL)	OF	43	148	15	41	10	4	2	19	19	38	0	0	2-5	.277	.357	.439	.796	2	.975
1999—Macon (S. Atl.)	OF	121	448	66	120	30	1	9	49	52	99	7	8	19-11	.268	.352	.400	.752	5	.976
2000—Myrtle Beach (Carol.)	OF	116	392	55	83	14	7	6	37	32	104	9	3	25-11	.212	.286	.329	.615	6	.961
2001—Myrtle Beach (Carol.)	OF	125	450	66	129	30	3	7	48	55	104	8	6	22-13	.287	.374	.413	.787	7	.972
2002—Greenville (Sou.)	OF	109	391	57	98	23	2	9	62	68	83	6	9	10-5	.251	.366	.389	.755	2	.992
—Atlanta (N.L.)	OF	1	1	0	0	0	0	0	0	0	0	0	0	0-0	.000	.000	.000	.000	0	...
2003—Greenville (Sou.)	OF	94	336	42	85	23	2	6	38	46	85	0	6	10-10	.253	.348	.387	.735	2	.991
—Richmond (Int'l)	OF	38	132	13	37	10	2	4	11	11	29	1	2	2-1	.280	.338	.477	.815	4	.949
—Atlanta (N.L.)	OF	16	15	2	4	0	0	0	0	6	6	1	0	0-0	.267	.267	.267	.533	0	1.000
2004—Richmond (Int'l)	OF	135	456	103	136	34	3	20	72	70	113	6	6	5-9	.298	.397	.518	.915	3	.933
2005—Atlanta (N.L.)	OF	128	326	48	87	22	3	8	42	37	75	5	2	0-2	.267	.348	.426	.774	1	.995
Major League totals (3 years)		145	342	50	91	22	3	8	42	37	81	5	3	0-2	.266	.344	.418	.762	1	.995

DIVISION SERIES RECORD

Year Team (League)	Pos.	G	AB	R	H	2B	3B	HR	RBI	BB	SO	HBP	GDP	SB-CS	Avg.	OBP	SLG	OPS	E	Avg.
2005—Atlanta (N.L.)	OF	4	12	1	4	1	0	0	0	3	3	1	0	1-0	.333	.500	.417	.917	0	1.000

LAROCHE, ADAM — 1B

PERSONAL: Born November 6, 1979, in Orange County, Calif. ... 6-3/180. ... Bats left, throws left. ... Full name: David Adam LaRoche. ... High school: Fort Scott (Kan.). ... Junior college: Fort Scott (Kan.), then Seminole (Okla.). ... Son of Dave LaRoche, pitcher for five major league clubs (1970-83).

TRANSACTIONS/CAREER NOTES: Selected by Florida Marlins organization in 18th round of 1998 free-agent draft; did not sign. ... Selected by Marlins organization in 42nd round of 1999 free-agent draft; did not sign. ... Selected by Atlanta Braves organization in 29th round of 2000 free-agent draft. ... On disabled list (May 29-July 2, 2004); included rehabilitation assignment to Richmond.

RECORDS: Shares major league record for most doubles, game (4, May 15, 2004).

2005 GAMES PLAYED BY POSITION (MLB): 1B—125.

SCOUTING REPORT **Offense:** His swing has a lot of moving parts. Has an inside-out approach, which creates a big loop that allows him to handle the ball downstairs. Is vulnerable above his hands, especially on the inner half. Has very deceptive power. Has been a very streaky hitter. **Defense:** LaRoche is a very fluid infielder, smooth around the bag, with soft hands and a strong arm. Has good range to his right and has good defensive instincts. **Outlook:** He's starting to show the type of power that was projected for him and his offensive production is on the rise. *Grade 7.8*

ADAM LAROCHE'S HITTING ZONE

.200	.600	.200
.305	.333	.269
.227	.419	.280

LEFTY-RIGHTY SPLITS

vs.	Avg.	AB	H	2B	3B	HR	RBI	BB	SO	OBP	Slg.
L	.188	48	9	2	0	1	5	1	9	.235	.292
R	.268	403	108	26	0	19	73	38	78	.330	.474

Year Team (League)	Pos.	G	AB	R	H	2B	3B	HR	RBI	BB	SO	HBP	GDP	SB-CS	Avg.	OBP	SLG	OPS	E	Avg.
2000—Danville (Appal.)	1B	56	201	38	62	13	3	7	45	24	46	2	2	4-1	.308	.381	.507	.888	2	.994

Year	Team (League)	Pos.	G	AB	R	H	2B	3B	HR	RBI	BB	SO	HBP	GDP	SB-CS	Avg.	OBP	SLG	OPS	E	Avg.
																BATTING				**FIELDING**	
2001— Myrtle Beach (Carol.)	1B-OF-P	126	471	49	118	31	0	7	47	30	108	9	13	10-8	.251	.305	.361	.666	4	.993
2002— Myrtle Beach (Carol.)		1B	69	250	30	84	17	0	9	53	27	37	4	3	0-2	.336	.406	.512	.918	5	.991
— Greenville (Sou.)		1B	45	173	17	50	9	0	4	19	19	38	1	6	1-1	.289	.363	.410	.773	1	.998
2003— Greenville (Sou.)	1B-P	61	219	42	62	12	1	12	37	34	53	3	6	1-2	.283	.381	.511	.892	2	.996
— Richmond (Int'l)		1B	72	264	33	78	21	0	8	35	27	58	3	6	1-2	.295	.360	.466	.826	4	.993
2004— Richmond (Int'l)		1B	4	11	1	2	0	0	1	2	1	0	0	2	0-0	.182	.250	.455	.705	0	1.000
— Atlanta (N.L.)		1B	110	324	45	90	27	1	13	45	27	78	1	10	0-0	.278	.333	.488	.821	5	.994
2005— Atlanta (N.L.)		1B	141	451	53	117	28	0	20	78	39	87	4	15	0-2	.259	.320	.455	.775	7	.994
Major League totals (2 years)			251	775	98	207	55	1	33	123	66	165	5	25	0-2	.267	.326	.468	.794	12	.994

DIVISION SERIES RECORD

Year	Team (League)	Pos.	G	AB	R	H	2B	3B	HR	RBI	BB	SO	HBP	GDP	SB-CS	Avg.	OBP	SLG	OPS	E	Avg.
2004— Atlanta (N.L.)	1B	5	17	1	4	1	0	1	4	2	5	0	1	0-0	.235	.316	.471	.786	0	1.000
2005— Atlanta (N.L.)	1B	3	8	2	4	1	0	1	6	3	1	0	0	0-0	.500	.636	1.000	1.636	0	1.000
Division series totals (2 years)		8	25	3	8	2	0	2	10	5	6	0	1	0-0	.320	.433	.640	1.073	0	1.000

LARUE, JASON — C

PERSONAL: Born March 19, 1974, in Houston. ... 5-11/200. ... Bats right, throws right. ... Full name: Michael Jason LaRue. ... Name pronounced: la-ROO. ... High school: Spring Valley (Spring Branch, Texas). ... College: Dallas Baptist .

TRANSACTIONS/CAREER NOTES: Selected by Cincinnati Reds organization in fifth round of 1995 free-agent draft. ... On disabled list (September 23, 2002-remainder of season). ... On disabled list (April 29-May 14, 2004); included rehabilitation assignment to Louisville. ... On bereavement list (June 12-15, 2005).

2005 GAMES PLAYED BY POSITION (MLB): C—109, OF—1.

SCOUTING REPORT

Offense: LaRue has a short, quick stroke and is very strong. Likes fastballs up out over the plate but also showed an ability to make adjustments with breaking balls. Still strikes out too often. Is impatient and doesn't like to hit late in the count. Power numbers are on the rise. **Defense:** He is an extremely aggressive receiver who shifts well on balls in the dirt and is adept at keeping them in front of him. Has a very quick release with above-average arm strength and is accurate. Can be stubborn; game-calling is not a strength. **Outlook:** LaRue has excellent makeup and his offensive output has improved. **Grade 6.2**

JASON LARUE'S HITTING ZONE

.333	.182	.000
.280	.326	.200
.333	.545	.200

LEFTY-RIGHTY SPLITS

vs.	Avg.	AB	H	2B	3B	HR	RBI	BB	SO	OBP	Slg.
L	.257	113	29	6	0	6	15	18	29	.368	.469
R	.262	248	65	21	0	8	45	23	72	.349	.444

Year	Team (League)	Pos.	G	AB	R	H	2B	3B	HR	RBI	BB	SO	HBP	GDP	SB-CS	Avg.	OBP	SLG	OPS	E	Avg.
																BATTING				**FIELDING**	
1995— Billings (Pion.)	C	58	183	35	50	8	1	5	31	16	28	12	2	3-5	.273	.366	.410	.776	8	.980
1996— Char., W.Va. (S. Atl.)	1B-C	37	123	17	26	8	0	2	14	11	28	2	2	3-0	.211	.287	.325	.612	6	.979
1997— Char., W.Va. (S. Atl.)	1B-3B-C OF	132	473	78	149	50	3	8	81	47	90	5	8	14-4	.315	.377	.484	.861	19	.977
1998— Chattanooga (Sou.)	1B-3B-C	105	386	71	141	39	8	14	82	40	60	10	13	4-3	.365	.429	.617	1.046	10	.985
— Indianapolis (Int'l)	C	15	51	5	12	4	0	0	5	4	8	0	2	0-1	.235	.286	.314	.599	0	1.000
1999— Indianapolis (Int'l)	C-DH	70	263	42	66	12	2	12	37	15	52	4	13	0-3	.251	.299	.449	.748	7	.984
— Cincinnati (N.L.)	C	36	90	12	19	7	0	3	10	11	32	2	4	4-1	.211	.311	.389	.700	2	.990
2000— Louisville (Int'l)	C	82	307	54	78	22	1	14	48	22	52	8	4	3-2	.254	.320	.469	.790	8	.984
— Cincinnati (N.L.)	C	31	98	12	23	3	0	5	12	5	19	4	1	0-0	.235	.299	.418	.717	2	.990
2001— Cincinnati (N.L.)	C-3B-OF 1B	121	364	39	86	21	2	12	43	27	106	9	11	3-3	.236	.303	.404	.707	7	.990
2002— Cincinnati (N.L.)	C	113	353	42	88	17	1	12	52	13	117	13	13	1-2	.249	.324	.405	.729	4	.994
2003— Cincinnati (N.L.)	C-1B-OF	118	379	52	87	23	1	16	50	33	111	20	9	3-3	.230	.321	.422	.743	11	.985
2004— Louisville (Int'l)	C	3	10	3	1	0	0	1	4	1	3	1	0	0-0	.100	.214	.400	.614	1	.917
— Cincinnati (N.L.)	C-DH-OF	114	390	46	98	24	2	14	55	26	108	24	7	0-2	.251	.334	.431	.765	8	.989
2005— Cincinnati (N.L.)	C-OF	110	361	38	94	27	0	14	60	41	101	13	8	0-0	.260	.355	.452	.806	5	.993
Major League totals (7 years)		643	2035	241	495	122	6	76	282	170	594	85	53	11-11	.243	.326	.421	.747	39	.990

LAWRENCE, BRIAN — P

PERSONAL: Born May 14, 1976, in Fort Collins, Colo. ... 6-0/197. ... Throws right, bats right. ... Full name: Brian Michael Lawrence. ... High school: Carthage (Texas). ... College: Northwestern State (La.).

TRANSACTIONS/CAREER NOTES: Selected by San Diego Padres organization in 17th round of 1998 free-agent draft. ... Traded by Padres with cash to Washington Nationals for 3B Vinny Castilla (November 3, 2005).

CAREER HITTING: 35-for-277 (.126), 15 R, 7 2B, 0 3B, 1 HR, 17 RBI.

SCOUTING REPORT

Throws: His sinker ranges from 81-84 mph, and he complements it with a slider and occasional changeup. **Tendencies:** Lawrence is a righthander who pitches more like a mediocre lefthander but has the know-how to win. Is a ground-ball pitcher who relies on his sinking fastball and pinpoint location. Has a quick-running slider and changes speeds with it, though the sinker is his money pitch. Has good deception in his delivery, a key factor for his success. Consistently moves his fastball around, always down in the zone, and stays away from big innings. **Outlook:** Lawrence gets a lot out of very little with his intelligent approach. Will provide innings at the back of the rotation. Should really benefit from moving to spacious RFK Stadium. **Grade 6.5**

BRIAN LAWRENCE'S PITCHING ZONE

.400	.333	.200
.290	.440	.355
.161	.326	.250

LEFTY-RIGHTY SPLITS

vs.	Avg.	AB	H	2B	3B	HR	RBI	BB	SO	OBP	Slg.
L	.300	360	108	29	2	10	37	31	36	.366	.475
R	.249	414	103	21	3	8	54	26	73	.295	.372

Year	Team (League)	W	L	Pct.	ERA	WHIP	G	GS	CG	ShO	Hld.	Sv.-Opp.	IP	H	R	ER	HR	BB-IBB	SO	Avg.
1998— Idaho Falls (Pion.)	3	0	1.000	2.45	1.23	4	4	2	1	...	0-...	22.0	22	7	6	1	5-0	21	.262
— Clinton (Midw.)	5	3	.625	2.80	1.00	12	12	2	0	...	0-...	80.1	67	34	25	5	13-0	79	.221
1999— Rancho Cuca. (Calif.)	12	8	.600	3.39	1.19	27	27	4	3	...	0-...	175.1	178	72	66	6	30-1	166	.265

Year Team (League)	W	L	Pct.	ERA	WHIP	G	GS	CG	ShO	Hld.	Sv.-Opp.	IP	H	R	ER	HR	BB-IBB	SO	Avg.
2000— Mobile (Sou.)	7	6	.538	2.42	1.00	21	21	0	0	...	0-...	126.2	99	40	34	6	28-0	119	.217
— Las Vegas (PCL)	4	0	1.000	1.93	1.18	8	8	0	0	...	0-...	46.2	48	13	10	6	7-0	46	.264
2001— Portland (PCL)	1	3	.250	3.80	1.31	9	8	0	0	...	1-...	45.0	42	22	19	3	17-2	42	.239
— San Diego (N.L.)	5	5	.500	3.45	1.23	27	15	1	0	0	0-0	114.2	107	53	44	10	34-5	84	.244
2002— San Diego (N.L.)	12	12	.500	3.69	1.34	35	31	2	2	1	0-0	210.0	230	97	86	16	52-6	149	.281
2003— San Diego (N.L.)	10	15	.400	4.19	1.25	33	33	1	0	0	0-0	210.2	206	106	98	27	57-8	116	.258
2004— San Diego (N.L.)	15	14	.517	4.12	1.38	34	34	2	1	0	0-0	203.0	226	101	93	26	55-7	121	.287
2005— San Diego (N.L.)	7	15	.318	4.83	1.37	33	33	1	0	0	0-0	195.2	211	106	105	18	57-7	109	.273
Major League totals (5 years)	49	61	.445	4.10	1.32	162	146	7	3	1	0-0	934.0	980	463	426	97	255-33	579	.271

DIVISION SERIES RECORD

Year Team (League)	W	L	Pct.	ERA	WHIP	G	GS	CG	ShO	Hld.	Sv.-Opp.	IP	H	R	ER	HR	BB-IBB	SO	Avg.
2005— San Diego (N.L.)	0	0	...	0.00	0.43	2	0	0	0	0	0-0	2.1	1	0	0	0	0-0	2	.125

LAWTON, MATT — OF

PERSONAL: Born November 3, 1971, in Gulfport, Miss. ... 5-10/195. ... Bats left, throws right. ... Full name: Matthew Lawton III. ... High school: Harrison Central (Gulfport, Miss.). ... Junior college: Mississippi Gulf Coast Community College. ... Brother of Marcus Lawton, outfielder with New York Yankees (1989).

TRANSACTIONS/CAREER NOTES: Selected by Minnesota Twins organization in 13th round of 1991 free-agent draft. ... On disabled list (June 9-July 18, 1999); included rehabilitation assignments to Fort Myers and GCL Twins. ... Traded by Twins to New York Mets for P Rick Reed (July 30, 2001). ... Traded by Mets with OF Alex Escobar, P Jerrod Riggan and two players to be named to Cleveland Indians for 2B Roberto Alomar, P Mike Bacsik and OF Danny Peoples (December 11, 2001); Indians acquired P Billy Traber and 1B Earl Snyder to complete deal (December 13, 2001). ... On disabled list (July 12-July 27 and September 4, 2002-remainder of season); included rehabilitation assignment to Akron. ... On disabled list (July 12-August 18 and September 6, 2003-remainder of season); included rehabilitation assignments to Akron. ... Traded by Indians with cash to Pittsburgh Pirates for P Arthur Rhodes and cash (December 11, 2004). ... Traded by Pirates to Chicago Cubs for OF Jody Gerut (July 31, 2005). ... Traded by Cubs to New York Yankees for P Justin Berg (August 27, 2005).

2005 GAMES PLAYED BY POSITION (MLB): OF—136.

SCOUTING REPORT **Offense:** Lawton was unable to get into a rhythm at the plate last season. Has a slightly long approach and likes to hit around the ball and hook it, but can take the ball the other way, too. Has average power when pulling the ball. Is patient enough to force pitchers deep into counts and can hit with two strikes. Has a lot of trouble with lefthanded pitchers who throw him breaking balls away. Still is a good runner with good basestealing instincts. **Defense:** He is a below-average fielder who has problems getting jumps and going back on the ball. Arm is below average and release is slow. Speed sometimes allows him to compensate for inadequate jumps. **Outlook:** Lawton in 2005 was suspended for the first 10 games of the 2006 season. Has value only in the A.L. because of his lack of defense. **Grade 6.4**

MATT LAWTON'S HITTING ZONE

.095	.333	.277
.239	.333	.260
.308	.500	.140

LEFTY-RIGHTY SPLITS

vs.	Avg.	AB	H	2B	3B	HR	RBI	BB	SO	OBP	Slg.
L	.207	145	30	4	0	4	14	18	23	.301	.317
R	.273	355	97	26	1	9	39	51	54	.377	.428

Year Team (League)	Pos.	G	AB	R	H	2B	3B	HR	RBI	BB	SO	HBP	GDP	SB-CS	Avg.	OBP	SLG	OPS	E	Avg.
1992— GC Twins (GCL)	2B	53	173	39	45	8	3	2	26	27	27	9	2	20-1	.260	.375	.376	.751	12	.958
1993— Fort Wayne (Midw.)	OF	111	340	50	97	21	3	9	38	65	42	8	8	23-15	.285	.410	.444	.854	3	.959
1994— Fort Myers (FSL)	OF	122	446	79	134	30	1	7	51	80	64	2	7	42-19	.300	.407	.419	.826	6	.971
1995— New Britain (East.)	OF-DH	114	412	75	111	19	5	13	54	56	70	12	8	26-9	.269	.371	.434	.805	2	.991
— Minnesota (A.L.)	OF-DH	21	60	11	19	4	1	1	12	7	11	3	1	1-1	.317	.414	.467	.881	1	.972
1996— Minnesota (A.L.)	OF-DH	79	252	34	65	7	1	6	42	28	28	4	6	4-4	.258	.339	.365	.704	3	.985
— Salt Lake (PCL)	OF-DH	53	212	40	63	16	1	7	33	26	34	3	2	2-4	.297	.379	.481	.860	6	.936
1997— Minnesota (A.L.)	OF	142	460	74	114	29	3	14	60	76	81	10	7	7-4	.248	.366	.415	.781	7	.976
1998— Minnesota (A.L.)	OF	152	557	91	155	36	6	21	77	86	64	15	10	16-8	.278	.387	.478	.864	4	.990
1999— Minnesota (A.L.)	OF-DH	118	406	58	105	18	0	7	54	57	42	6	11	26-4	.259	.353	.355	.708	4	.982
— Fort Myers (FSL)	OF	4	14	3	8	1	0	0	2	3	1	0	0	1-0	.571	.647	.643	1.290	0	1.000
— GC Twins (GCL)	OF	1	4	0	1	0	0	0	1	0	2	0	0	0-0	.250	.250	.250	.500	0	1.000
2000— Minnesota (A.L.)	OF-DH	156	561	84	171	44	2	13	88	91	63	7	10	23-7	.305	.405	.460	.865	5	.983
2001— Minnesota (A.L.)	OF-DH	103	376	71	110	25	0	10	51	63	46	3	14	19-6	.293	.396	.439	.835	4	.980
— New York (N.L.)	OF	48	183	24	45	11	1	3	13	22	34	8	2	10-2	.246	.352	.366	.718	0	1.000
2002— Cleveland (A.L.)	OF-DH	114	416	71	98	19	2	15	57	59	34	8	13	8-9	.236	.342	.399	.741	6	.975
— Akron (East.)	OF	3	10	1	0	0	0	0	0	3	1	0	0	0-0	.000	.231	.000	.231	1	1.000
2003— Akron (East.)	DH	5	19	1	1	0	0	0	1	2	6	0	1	0-0	.053	.143	.053	.195	0	...
— Cleveland (A.L.)	OF-DH	99	374	57	93	19	0	15	53	47	47	7	8	10-3	.249	.343	.420	.762	1	.993
2004— Cleveland (A.L.)	OF-DH	148	591	109	164	25	0	20	70	74	84	11	21	23-9	.278	.366	.421	.788	4	.986
2005— Pittsburgh (N.L.)	OF	101	374	53	102	28	1	10	44	58	61	9	7	16-9	.273	.380	.433	.813	1	.995
— Chicago (N.L.)	OF	19	78	8	19	2	0	1	5	4	8	1	3	1-0	.244	.289	.308	.597	1	.971
— New York (A.L.)	OF	21	48	6	6	0	0	2	4	7	8	2	0	1-0	.125	.263	.250	.513	1	.969
American League totals (11 years)		1155	4101	666	1100	226	15	124	568	595	508	76	101	138-55	.268	.369	.421	.790	40	.983
National League totals (2 years)		168	635	85	166	41	2	14	62	84	103	18	12	27-11	.261	.362	.398	.760	2	.994
Major League totals (11 years)		1323	4736	751	1266	267	17	138	630	679	611	94	113	165-66	.267	.368	.418	.786	42	.984

ALL-STAR GAME RECORD

	G	AB	R	H	2B	3B	HR	RBI	BB	SO	HBP	GDP	SB-CS	Avg.	OBP	SLG	OPS	E	Avg.
All-Star Game totals (2 years)	2	4	1	2	0	0	0	0	1	0	1	0	1-0	.500	.500	.500	1.000	0	...

LEAGUE, BRANDON P

PERSONAL: Born March 16, 1983, in Honolulu. ... 6-3/192. ... Throws right, bats right. ... Full name: Brandon Paul League. ... High school: Saint Louis (Honolulu).

TRANSACTIONS/CAREER NOTES: Selected by Toronto Blue Jays organization in second round of 2001 free-agent draft.

CAREER HITTING: 0-for-0 (.000), 0 R, 0 2B, 0 3B, 0 HR, 0 RBI.

BRANDON LEAGUE'S PITCHING ZONE

.000	.667	.600
.643	.316	.438
.000	.000	.261

LEFTY-RIGHTY SPLITS

vs.	Avg.	AB	H	2B	3B	HR	RBI	BB	SO	OBP	Slg.
L	.333	72	24	4	0	5	20	4	7	.377	.597
R	.269	67	18	3	0	3	10	16	10	.412	.448

Year	Team (League)	W	L	Pct.	ERA	WHIP	G	GS	CG	ShO	Hld.	Sv.-Opp.	IP	H	R	ER	HR	BB-IBB	SO	Avg.
2001— Medicine Hat (Pion.)		2	2	.500	4.66	1.22	9	9	0	0	...	0-...	38.2	36	23	20	3	11-1	38	.245
2002— Auburn (N.Y.-Penn.)		7	2	.778	3.15	1.20	16	16	0	0	...	0-...	85.2	80	42	30	2	23-0	72	.248
2003— Char., W.Va. (S. Atl.)		2	3	.400	1.91	1.08	12	12	0	0	...	0-...	70.2	58	15	15	1	18-0	61	.230
— Dunedin (Fla. St.)		4	3	.571	4.75	1.45	13	12	0	0	...	0-...	66.1	76	40	35	3	20-0	34	.288
2004— New Hampshire (East.)		6	4	.600	3.38	1.28	41	10	0	0	...	2-...	104.0	92	44	39	3	41-1	90	.240
— Toronto (A.L.)		1	0	1.000	0.00	0.86	3	0	0	0	1	0-0	4.2	3	0	0	0	1-0	2	.176
2005— Syracuse (Int'l)		4	4	.500	5.71	1.52	19	10	0	0	1	0-1	63.0	78	44	40	7	18-0	35	.306
— Toronto (A.L.)		1	0	1.000	6.56	1.74	20	0	0	0	1	0-0	35.2	42	27	26	8	20-1	17	.302
Major League totals (2 years)		2	0	1.000	5.80	1.64	23	0	0	0	2	0-0	40.1	45	27	26	8	21-1	19	.288

LECROY, MATTHEW C

PERSONAL: Born December 13, 1975, in Belton, S.C. ... 6-2/225. ... Bats right, throws right. ... Full name: Matthew Hanks LeCroy. ... Name pronounced: LEE-croy. ... High school: Belton-Honea Path (S.C.). ... College: Clemson.

TRANSACTIONS/CAREER NOTES: Selected by New York Mets organization in supplemental round ("sandwich" pick between second and third rounds, 63rd pick overall) of 1994 free-agent draft; did not sign; pick received as compensation for Atlanta Braves signing Type C free-agent C Charlie O'Brien. ... Selected by Minnesota Twins organization in supplemental round ("sandwich pick" between first and second rounds, 50th pick overall) of 1997 free-agent draft; pick received as compensation for failure to sign 1996 first-round pick Travis Lee. ... On disabled list (April 8-May 11, 2004).

2005 GAMES PLAYED BY POSITION (MLB): DH—63, 1B—23, C—1.

SCOUTING REPORT

He is basically a designated hitter and power is his best asset. Has a long, fluid stroke but his bat speed has declined. Likes the ball out over the plate and is a much better hitter against lefthanded pitching. Has become more of a pull hitter and with the decline in bat speed is having more problems catching up to high fastballs. Doesn't catch a lot as he can be a defensive liability. Doesn't throw well or stay on top; the ball really tails. Lacks mobility behind the plate and his hands are stiff. Better in the A.L. where he can DH, or as a No. 3 catcher instead of a No. 2. *Grade 5*

MATTHEW LECROY'S HITTING ZONE

.231	.200	.100
.321	.273	.348
.143	.353	.400

LEFTY-RIGHTY SPLITS

vs.	Avg.	AB	H	2B	3B	HR	RBI	BB	SO	OBP	Slg.
L	.306	124	38	0	0	13	24	20	32	.404	.621
R	.228	180	41	5	0	4	26	21	53	.319	.322

Year	Team (League)	Pos.	G	AB	R	H	2B	3B	HR	RBI	BB	SO	HBP	GDP	SB-CS	Avg.	OBP	SLG	OPS	E	Avg.
1998— Fort Wayne (Midw.)		C	64	225	33	62	17	1	9	40	34	45	8	9	0-0	.276	.387	.480	.867	1	.997
— Fort Myers (Fla. St.)		C	51	200	32	61	9	1	12	51	21	35	4	6	2-1	.305	.372	.540	.912	3	.991
— Salt Lake (PCL)		C	3	13	2	4	1	0	2	4	0	7	0	0	0-0	.308	.308	.846	1.154	0	1.000
1999— Fort Myers (Fla. St.)		C	89	333	54	93	20	1	20	69	42	51	3	10	0-0	.279	.364	.526	.890	8	.983
— Salt Lake (PCL)		C	29	119	23	36	4	1	10	30	5	22	1	8	0-1	.303	.331	.605	.936	0	1.000
2000— Minnesota (A.L.)		C-1B-DH	56	167	18	29	10	0	5	17	17	38	2	6	0-0	.174	.254	.323	.577	4	.989
— New Britain (East.)		C	54	195	33	55	12	1	10	38	29	34	6	8	0-0	.282	.391	.508	.899	10	.970
— Salt Lake (PCL)		C-1B	16	65	15	20	0	0	5	15	4	11	0	4	0-0	.308	.348	.615	.963	0	1.000
2001— Edmonton (PCL)		C-1B	101	396	53	130	17	0	20	80	36	95	6	8	0-2	.328	.390	.523	.913	5	.980
— Minnesota (A.L.)		DH-C-1B	15	40	6	17	5	0	3	12	0	8	1	0	0-1	.425	.429	.775	1.204	0	1.000
2002— Edmonton (PCL)		C-1B	46	174	36	61	7	1	12	50	17	34	4	1	2-0	.351	.412	.609	1.021	1	.993
— Minnesota (A.L.)		DH-1B-C	63	181	19	47	11	1	7	27	13	38	0	5	0-0	.260	.306	.448	.754	1	.984
2003— Minnesota (A.L.)		DH-C-1B	107	345	39	99	19	0	17	64	25	82	4	8	0-1	.287	.342	.490	.832	3	.985
2004— Minnesota (A.L.)		DH-C-1B	88	264	25	71	14	0	9	39	16	60	5	7	0-0	.269	.321	.424	.745	5	.983
2005— Minnesota (A.L.)		DH-1B-C	101	304	33	79	5	0	17	50	41	85	4	7	0-0	.260	.354	.444	.798	3	.986
Major League totals (6 years)			430	1301	140	342	64	1	58	209	112	311	16	33	0-4	.263	.327	.447	.774	16	.986

DIVISION SERIES RECORD

Year	Team (League)	Pos.	G	AB	R	H	2B	3B	HR	RBI	BB	SO	HBP	GDP	SB-CS	Avg.	OBP	SLG	OPS	E	Avg.
2002— Minnesota (A.L.)		DH	3	9	1	4	0	0	0	1	0	3	0	1	0-0	.444	.444	.444	.889	0	...
2003— Minnesota (A.L.)		DH	3	11	1	1	0	0	0	0	1	4	0	0	0-0	.091	.167	.091	.258	0	...
2004— Minnesota (A.L.)		1B-C	3	3	0	1	0	0	0	0	1	1	0	0	0-0	.333	.500	.333	.833	0	1.000
Division series totals (3 years)			9	23	2	6	0	0	0	1	2	8	0	1	0-0	.261	.320	.261	.581	0	1.000

CHAMPIONSHIP SERIES RECORD

Year	Team (League)	Pos.	G	AB	R	H	2B	3B	HR	RBI	BB	SO	HBP	GDP	SB-CS	Avg.	OBP	SLG	OPS	E	Avg.
2002— Minnesota (A.L.)		DH	1	3	0	1	0	0	0	0	0	1	0	0	0-0	.333	.333	.333	.667	0	...

LEDEE, RICKY OF

PERSONAL: Born November 22, 1973, in Ponce, Puerto Rico. ... 6-1/216. ... Bats left, throws left. ... Full name: Ricardo Alberto Ledee. ... Name pronounced: la-DAY. ... High school: Colonel Nuestra Sonora de Valvanera (Coano, Puerto.Rico).

TRANSACTIONS/CAREER NOTES: Selected by New York Yankees organization in 16th round of 1990 free-agent draft. ... Traded by Yankees with two players to be named to Cleveland Indians for OF David Justice (June 29, 2000); Indians acquired P Jake Westbrook and P Zach Day to complete deal (July 24, 2000). ... Traded by Indians to Texas Rangers for 1B/DH David Segui (July 28, 2000). ... On disabled list (March 23-June 13, 2001); included rehabilitation assignment to Oklahoma. ... Signed as a free agent by Philadelphia Phillies (January 29, 2002). ... On disabled list (June 23-July 8, 2004). ... Traded by Phillies with P Alfredo Simon to San Francisco Giants for P Felix Rodriguez (July 30, 2004). ... Signed as a free agent by Los Angeles Dodgers (December 7, 2004). ... On disabled list (June 7-July 8, 2005).
2005 GAMES PLAYED BY POSITION (MLB): OF—69.

SCOUTING REPORT **Offense:** Ledee is a low-ball hitter with a fluid stroke and good power. Has become a better breaking-ball hitter but still struggles against lefthanders. Is an average runner but not a basestealing threat. **Defense:** He can play all three outfield positions and has good lateral range, although he doesn't get consistent jumps and freezes on balls hit directly at him. Has a slightly below-average arm. **Outlook:** Ledee is a good role player but had a terrible time staying healthy during 2005 with prolonged hamstring problems. **Grade 5.7**

RICKY LEDEE'S HITTING ZONE

.125	.429	.400
.148	.636	.308
.267	.333	.294

LEFTY-RIGHTY SPLITS

vs.	Avg.	AB	H	2B	3B	HR	RBI	BB	SO	OBP	Slg.
L	.200	20	4	1	0	1	4	2	9	.273	.400
R	.286	217	62	15	1	6	35	18	46	.340	.447

Year	Team (League)	Pos.	G	AB	R	H	2B	3B	HR	RBI	BB	SO	HBP	GDP	SB-CS	Avg.	OBP	SLG	OPS	E	Avg.
																				FIELDING	
1990—	GC Yankees (GCL)	OF	19	37	5	4	2	0	0	1	6	18	0	1	2-0	.108	.233	.162	.395	1	1.000
1991—	GC Yankees (GCL)	OF	47	165	22	44	6	2	0	18	22	40	0	3	3-1	.267	.351	.327	.678	6	.934
1992—	GC Yankees (GCL)	OF	52	179	25	41	9	2	2	23	24	47	1	2	1-4	.229	.322	.335	.657	2	.971
1993—	Oneonta (N.Y.-Penn.)	OF	52	192	32	49	7	6	8	20	25	46	2	2	7-5	.255	.347	.479	.826	3	.970
1994—	Greensboro (S. Atl.)	OF	134	484	87	121	23	9	22	71	91	126	4	7	10-11	.250	.369	.471	.840	5	.973
1995—	Greensboro (S. Atl.)	OF	89	335	65	90	16	6	14	49	51	66	2	3	10-4	.269	.368	.478	.845	3	.982
1996—	Norwich (East.)	OF	39	137	27	50	11	1	8	37	16	25	1	4	2-2	.365	.421	.635	1.056	1	.980
—Columbus (Int'l)		OF	96	358	79	101	22	6	21	64	44	95	1	4	6-3	.282	.360	.553	.914	5	.952
1997—	Columbus (Int'l)	OF-DH	43	170	38	52	12	1	10	39	21	49	1	5	4-0	.306	.385	.565	.950	2	.966
—GC Yankees (GCL)		DH-OF	7	21	3	7	1	0	0	2	2	4	1	1	0-0	.333	.417	.381	.798	0	1.000
1998—	Columbus (Int'l)	OF-DH	96	360	70	102	21	1	19	41	54	108	4	7	7-2	.283	.378	.506	.884	4	.971
—New York (A.L.)		OF	42	79	13	19	5	2	1	12	7	29	0	1	3-1	.241	.299	.392	.691	1	.981
1999—	New York (A.L.)	OF-DH	88	250	45	69	13	5	9	40	28	73	0	2	4-3	.276	.346	.476	.822	9	.942
—Columbus (Int'l)		OF	30	115	18	29	7	1	4	15	17	29	0	1	4-2	.252	.346	.435	.781	3	.953
2000—	New York (A.L.)	OF-DH	62	191	23	46	11	1	7	31	26	39	1	7	7-3	.241	.332	.419	.751	2	.979
—Cleveland (A.L.)		OF	17	63	13	14	2	1	2	8	9	9	0	3	0-0	.222	.310	.381	.691	0	1.000
—Texas (A.L.)		OF	58	213	23	50	6	3	4	38	25	50	1	7	6-3	.235	.317	.347	.664	3	.977
2001—	Oklahoma (PCL)	OF	4	16	4	8	1	0	1	3	1	1	0	1	0-0	.500	.529	.750	1.279	0	1.000
—Texas (A.L.)		OF	78	242	33	56	21	1	2	36	23	58	3	3	3-3	.231	.303	.351	.654	3	.979
2002—	Philadelphia (N.L.)	OF	96	203	33	46	13	1	8	23	35	50	1	3	1-2	.227	.342	.419	.760	0	1.000
2003—	Philadelphia (N.L.)	OF-DH	121	255	37	63	15	2	13	46	34	59	0	4	0-0	.247	.334	.475	.809	0	1.000
2004—	Philadelphia (N.L.)	OF-DH	73	123	19	35	7	0	7	26	22	27	0	5	2-0	.285	.393	.512	.905	0	1.000
—San Francisco (N.L.)		OF	31	53	6	6	2	0	0	4	5	20	1	1	1-0	.113	.200	.151	.351	1	.960
2005—	Los Angeles (N.L.)	OF	102	237	31	66	16	1	7	39	20	55	3	5	0-0	.278	.335	.443	.778	2	.975
American League totals (4 years)			345	1038	150	254	58	13	25	165	117	258	5	23	23-13	.245	.322	.398	.720	18	.971
National League totals (4 years)			423	871	126	216	53	4	35	138	116	211	5	18	4-2	.248	.337	.439	.775	3	.992
Major League totals (8 years)			768	1909	276	470	111	17	60	303	233	469	10	41	27-15	.246	.329	.416	.745	21	.978

DIVISION SERIES RECORD

Year	Team (League)	Pos.	G	AB	R	H	2B	3B	HR	RBI	BB	SO	HBP	GDP	SB-CS	Avg.	OBP	SLG	OPS	E	Avg.
1998—	New York (A.L.)			Did not play.																	
1999—	New York (A.L.)	OF	3	11	1	3	2	0	0	2	1	5	0	0	0-0	.273	.333	.455	.788	0	1.000

CHAMPIONSHIP SERIES RECORD

Year	Team (League)	Pos.	G	AB	R	H	2B	3B	HR	RBI	BB	SO	HBP	GDP	SB-CS	Avg.	OBP	SLG	OPS	E	Avg.
1998—	New York (A.L.)	DH-OF	3	5	0	0	0	0	0	0	0	0	0	0	0-0	.000	.000	.000	.000	0	1.000
1999—	New York (A.L.)	DH-OF	3	8	2	2	0	0	1	4	1	4	0	0	0-1	.250	.333	.625	.958	1	.750
Champ. series totals (2 years)			6	13	2	2	0	0	1	4	1	4	0	0	0-1	.154	.214	.385	.599	1	.857

WORLD SERIES RECORD

Year	Team (League)	Pos.	G	AB	R	H	2B	3B	HR	RBI	BB	SO	HBP	GDP	SB-CS	Avg.	OBP	SLG	OPS	E	Avg.
1998—	New York (A.L.)	OF	4	10	1	6	3	0	0	4	2	1	0	0	0-1	.600	.615	.900	1.515	0	1.000
1999—	New York (A.L.)	OF	3	10	0	2	1	0	0	1	1	4	0	0	0-0	.200	.273	.300	.573	0	1.000
World Series totals (2 years)			7	20	1	8	4	0	0	5	3	5	0	0	0-1	.400	.458	.600	1.058	0	1.000

LEDEZMA, WILFREDO   P

PERSONAL: Born January 21, 1981, in Guarico, Venezuela. ... 6-4/212. ... Throws left, bats left. ... Full name: Wilfredo Jose Ledezma. ... Name pronounced: la-DEZ-ma. ... College: Cuidad Jardin University.
TRANSACTIONS/CAREER NOTES: Signed as a non-drafted free agent by Boston Red Sox organization (April 3, 1998). ... Selected by Detroit Tigers from Red Sox organization in Rule 5 major league draft (December 16, 2002).
CAREER HITTING: 0-for-0 (.000), 0 R, 0 2B, 0 3B, 0 HR, 0 RBI.

WILFREDO LEDEZMA'S PITCHING ZONE

.313	.300	.083
.485	.360	.391
.229	.545	.071

LEFTY-RIGHTY SPLITS

vs.	Avg.	AB	H	2B	3B	HR	RBI	BB	SO	OBP	Slg.
L	.352	54	19	1	2	2	17	3	6	.379	.556
R	.286	147	42	8	0	8	24	21	24	.376	.503

Year	Team (League)	W	L	Pct.	ERA	WHIP	G	GS	CG	ShO	Hld.	Sv.-Opp.	IP	H	R	ER	HR	BB-IBB	SO	Avg.
1999—	GC Red Sox (GCL)	5	1	.833	3.30	1.24	13	6	0	0	...	1-...	57.1	51	28	21	2	20-0	52	.233
2000—	Augusta (S. Atl.)	2	4	.333	5.13	1.65	14	14	0	0	...	0-...	52.2	51	33	30	3	36-0	60	.256
2001—				Did not play.																

Year	Team (League)	W	L	Pct.	ERA	WHIP	G	GS	CG	ShO	Hld.	Sv.-Opp.	IP	H	R	ER	HR	BB-IBB	SO	Avg.
2002—Augusta (S. Atl.)		2	2	.500	3.80	1.31	5	5	0	0	...	0-...	23.2	23	10	10	0	8-0	38	.250
—GC Red Sox (GCL)		0	0	...	6.00	1.33	1	0	0	0	...	0-...	3.0	4	2	2	0	0-0	3	.308
2003—Detroit (A.L.)		3	7	.300	5.79	1.60	34	8	0	0	1	0-1	84.0	99	55	54	12	35-3	49	.297
2004—Erie (East.)		10	3	.769	2.42	1.07	17	16	2	1	...	0-...	111.2	95	36	30	8	24-0	98	.228
—Detroit (A.L.)		4	3	.571	4.39	1.37	15	8	0	0	0	0-1	53.1	55	28	26	3	18-0	29	.272
2005—Detroit (A.L.)		2	4	.333	7.07	1.71	10	10	0	0	0	0-0	49.2	61	46	39	10	24-0	30	.303
—Toledo (Int'l)		5	3	.625	5.29	1.55	11	10	0	0	0	0-0	51.0	52	30	30	3	27-0	44	.260
Major League totals (3 years)		9	14	.391	5.73	1.56	59	26	0	0	1	0-2	187.0	215	129	119	25	77-3	108	.292

LEE, CARLOS — OF

PERSONAL: Born June 20, 1976, in Aguadulce, Panama. ... 6-2/240. ... Bats right, throws right. ... Full name: Carlos Noriel Lee. ... High school: Rodolfo Chiari (Panama).
TRANSACTIONS/CAREER NOTES: Signed as a non-drafted free agent by Chicago White Sox organization (February 8, 1994). ... On suspended list (April 28-May 1, 2000). ... Traded by White Sox to Milwaukee Brewers for OF Scott Podsednik, P Luis Vizcaino and a player to be named (December 13, 2004); White Sox acquired 1B Travis Hinton to complete the deal (January 10, 2005).
2005 GAMES PLAYED BY POSITION (MLB): OF—162.

SCOUTING REPORT *Offense:* He has a long stroke but displays excellent plate coverage and good bat speed. Has an inside-out swing and will use the whole field. Has become a good two-strike hitter and a dangerous run producer. Patience has improved. Slumped during the second half but still had solid run production numbers. Can run once he gets under way but is slow out of the box. *Defense:* He has made a lot of progress with his ability to read the ball off the bat and track it properly to the alley but has issues going directly back. Has deceptive arm strength with good accuracy. *Outlook:* Lee is a very good run producer and is becoming a very consistent offensive player. Has worked to improve his defense in left field. *Grade 8.1*

CARLOS LEE'S HITTING ZONE

.359	.269	.120
.297	.323	.281
.308	.214	.286

LEFTY-RIGHTY SPLITS

vs.	Avg.	AB	H	2B	3B	HR	RBI	BB	SO	OBP	Slg.
L	.261	157	41	10	0	7	30	21	20	.346	.459
R	.267	461	123	31	0	25	84	36	67	.316	.497

Year	Team (League)	Pos.	G	AB	R	H	2B	3B	HR	RBI	BB	SO	HBP	GDP	SB-CS	Avg.	OBP	SLG	OPS	E	Avg.
1994—GC Whi. Sox (GCL)		3B	29	56	6	7	1	0	0	1	4	8	0	1	0-1	.125	.183	.143	.326	2	.959
1995—Hickory (S. Atl.)		3B	63	218	18	54	9	1	4	30	8	34	1	7	1-5	.248	.278	.353	.631	19	.848
—Bristol (Appal.)		1B-3B	67	269	43	93	17	1	7	45	8	34	2	6	17-7	.346	.365	.494	.860	18	.914
1996—Hickory (S. Atl.)		1B-3B	119	480	65	150	23	6	8	70	23	50	0	15	18-13	.313	.337	.435	.772	32	.923
1997—Win.-Salem (Car.)		3B-DH	139	546	81	173	50	4	17	82	36	65	2	12	11-5	.317	.357	.516	.874	34	.906
1998—Birmingham (Sou.)		3B-DH	138	549	77	166	33	2	21	106	39	55	4	32	11-5	.302	.350	.485	.834	35	.902
1999—Charlotte (Int'l)		3B-OF-1B	25	94	16	33	5	0	4	20	8	14	1	3	2-1	.351	.396	.532	.928	4	.951
—Chicago (A.L.)		OF-DH-1B	127	492	66	144	32	2	16	84	13	72	4	11	4-2	.293	.312	.463	.775	5	.990
2000—Chicago (A.L.)		OF-DH	152	572	107	172	29	2	24	92	38	94	3	17	13-4	.301	.345	.484	.829	3	.990
2001—Chicago (A.L.)		OF-DH	150	558	75	150	33	3	24	84	38	85	6	15	17-7	.269	.321	.468	.789	8	.969
2002—Chicago (A.L.)		OF-DH	140	492	82	130	.26	2	26	80	75	73	2	5	1-4	.264	.359	.484	.843	1	.996
2003—Chicago (A.L.)		OF-DH	158	623	100	181	35	1	31	113	37	91	4	20	18-4	.291	.331	.499	.830	7	.978
2004—Chicago (A.L.)		OF-DH	153	591	103	180	37	0	31	99	54	86	7	10	11-5	.305	.366	.525	.891	6	1.000
2005—Milwaukee (N.L.)		OF	* 162	618	85	164	41	0	32	114	57	87	2	8	13-4	.265	.324	.487	.811	6	.981
American League totals (6 years)			880	3328	533	957	192	10	152	552	255	501	26	78	64-26	.288	.340	.488	.828	24	.985
National League totals (1 year)			162	618	85	164	41	0	32	114	57	87	2	8	13-4	.265	.324	.487	.811	6	.981
Major League totals (7 years)			1042	3946	618	1121	233	10	184	666	312	588	28	86	77-30	.284	.337	.488	.825	30	.985

DIVISION SERIES RECORD

Year	Team (League)	Pos.	G	AB	R	H	2B	3B	HR	RBI	BB	SO	HBP	GDP	SB-CS	Avg.	OBP	SLG	OPS	E	Avg.
2000—Chicago (A.L.)		OF	3	11	0	1	1	0	0	0	2	0	0	0	0-0	.091	.083	.182	.265	0	1.000

ALL-STAR GAME RECORD

			G	AB	R	H	2B	3B	HR	RBI	BB	SO	HBP	GDP	SB-CS	Avg.	OBP	SLG	OPS	E	Avg.
All-Star Game totals (1 year)			1	3	0	0	0	0	0	1	0	1	0	0	0-0	.000	.000	.000	.000	0	...

LEE, CLIFF — P

PERSONAL: Born August 30, 1978, in Benton, Ark. ... 6-3/190. ... Throws left, bats left. ... Full name: Clifton Phifer Lee. ... High school: Benton (Ark.). ... College: Arkansas.
TRANSACTIONS/CAREER NOTES: Selected by Montreal Expos organization in fourth round of 2000 free-agent draft. ... Traded by Expos with 1B Lee Stevens, SS Brandon Phillips and OF Grady Sizemore to Cleveland Indians for P Bartolo Colon and future considerations (June 27, 2002); Expos acquired P Tim Drew to complete deal (June 28, 2002). ... On disabled list (March 29-May 30, 2003); included rehabilitation assignment to Kinston. ... On suspended list (June 24-July 1, 2004).
CAREER HITTING: 1-for-11 (.091), 0 R, 0 2B, 0 3B, 0 HR, 0 RBI.

SCOUTING REPORT *Throws:* His fastball is 87-90 mph, his cutter is 85-87 and his curve is 74-77. Also throws a changeup. *Tendencies:* He has an unorthodox delivery in which he steps across his body yet throws over the top. Deceptive arm angle makes his fastball very sneaky and very difficult for hitters to pick up. Fastball naturally runs from righthanders, but he also cuts it to get inside, which allows him to pitch to both sides of the plate. Has improved the rotation of his curve and has excellent motion with his straight change which fades from righthanders. *Outlook:* Lee is one of the most improved pitchers in the league and is capable of repeating his 2005 performance. *Grade 9*

CLIFF LEE'S PITCHING ZONE

.212	.394	.278
.305	.341	.241
.265	.174	.236

LEFTY-RIGHTY SPLITS

vs.	Avg.	AB	H	2B	3B	HR	RBI	BB	SO	OBP	Slg.
L	.293	188	55	13	2	6	20	8	35	.321	.479
R	.237	586	139	33	1	16	64	44	108	.287	.379

Year	Team (League)	W	L	Pct.	ERA	WHIP	G	GS	CG	ShO	Hld.	Sv.-Opp.	IP	H	R	ER	HR	BB-IBB	SO	Avg.
2000—Cape Fear (S. Atl.)		1	4	.200	5.24	1.93	11	11	0	0	...	0-...	44.2	50	39	26	1	36-0	63	.281
2001—Jupiter (Fla. St.)		6	7	.462	2.79	1.13	21	20	0	0	...	0-...	109.2	78	43	34	13	46-0	129	.199

Year Team (League)	W	L	Pct.	ERA	WHIP	G	GS	CG	ShO	Hld.	Sv.-Opp.	IP	H	R	ER	HR	BB-IBB	SO	Avg.
2002— Harrisburg (East.)	7	2	.778	3.23	0.97	15	15	0	0	...	0-...	86.1	61	31	31	12	23-0	105	.197
—Akron (East.)	2	1	.667	5.40	1.26	3	3	0	0	...	0-...	16.2	11	11	10	1	10-0	18	.180
—Buffalo (Int'l)	3	2	.600	3.77	1.35	8	8	0	0	...	0-...	43.0	36	18	18	7	22-0	30	.229
—Cleveland (A.L.)	0	1	.000	1.74	1.35	2	2	0	0	0	0-0	10.1	6	2	2	0	8-1	6	.171
2003— Kinston (Carol.)	0	0	...	0.00	0.70	1	1	0	0	...	0-...	4.1	0	1	0	0	3-0	4	.000
—Akron (East.)	1	0	1.000	1.50	0.90	2	2	0	0	...	0-...	12.0	7	2	2	1	4-0	13	.167
—Buffalo (Int'l)	6	1	.857	3.27	1.50	11	11	0	0	...	0-...	63.1	62	24	23	4	31-0	61	.261
—Cleveland (A.L.)	3	3	.500	3.61	1.17	9	9	0	0	0	0-0	52.1	41	28	21	7	20-1	44	.220
2004— Cleveland (A.L.)	14	8	.636	5.43	1.50	33	33	0	0	0	0-0	179.0	188	113	108	30	81-1	161	.268
2005— Cleveland (A.L.)	18	5	* .783	3.79	1.22	32	32	1	0	0	0-0	202.0	194	91	85	22	52-1	143	.251
Major League totals (4 years)	35	17	.673	4.38	1.33	76	76	1	0	0	0-0	443.2	429	234	216	59	161-4	354	.253

LEE, DERREK — 1B

PERSONAL: Born September 6, 1975, in Sacramento. ... 6-5/245. ... Bats right, throws right. ... Full name: Derrek Leon Lee. ... High school: El Camino (Sacramento). ... Nephew of Leron Lee, outfielder with four major league teams (1969-76).

TRANSACTIONS/CAREER NOTES: Selected by San Diego Padres in first round (14th pick overall) of 1993 free-agent draft. ... Traded by Padres with Ps Rafael Medina and Steve Hoff to Florida Marlins for P Kevin Brown (December 15, 1997). ... Traded by Marlins to Chicago Cubs for 1B Hee Seop Choi and P Mike Nannini (November 25, 2003).

HONORS: Won N.L. Gold Glove at first base (2003 and 2005).

2005 GAMES PLAYED BY POSITION (MLB): 1B—158.

SCOUTING REPORT *Offense:* The league leader in hitting for 2005, Lee has become a much better all-around hitter. Likes to extend his arms and has outstanding leverage. Has shown the ability to make adjustments and can really handle inside pitch. Has a quick bat and good plate coverage and will use the whole field. Continues to cut down his strikeouts and has become more patient. Is one of the best baserunners in the game. *Defense:* He is extremely agile around the bag with outstanding hands, good range, quick feet and an above-average arm. Is adept at starting double plays and can handle balls in the dirt. *Outlook:* Lee is a complete player who was the first-half league MVP in 2005. Adjustments at the plate have allowed him to become one of the game's best. *Grade 9.8*

DERREK LEE'S HITTING ZONE

.172	.250	.357
.312	.518	.372
.392	.345	.257

LEFTY-RIGHTY SPLITS

vs.	Avg.	AB	H	2B	3B	HR	RBI	BB	SO	OBP	Slg.
L	.333	147	49	12	1	12	28	28	27	.439	.673
R	.336	447	150	38	2	34	79	57	82	.411	.658

Year Team (League)	Pos.	G	AB	R	H	2B	3B	HR	RBI	BB	SO	HBP	GDP	SB-CS	Avg.	OBP	SLG	OPS	E	Avg.
1993— Ariz. Padres (AZL)	1B	15	52	11	17	1	1	2	5	6	7	0	1	4-0	.327	.397	.500	.897	2	.985
—Rancho Cuca. (Calif.)	1B-DH	20	73	13	20	5	1	1	10	10	20	1	0	0-2	.274	.369	.411	.780	5	.960
1994— Rancho Cuca. (Calif.)	1B-DH	126	442	66	118	19	2	8	53	42	95	7	11	18-14	.267	.336	.373	.709	4	.988
1995— Rancho Cuca. (Calif.)	1B	128	502	82	151	25	2	23	95	49	130	7	8	14-7	.301	.366	.496	.862	18	.983
—Memphis (Sou.)	1B	2	9	0	1	0	0	0	1	2	0	0	0	0-0	.111	.111	.111	.222	0	1.000
1996— Memphis (Sou.)	1B-3B-DH	134	500	98	140	39	2	34	104	65	170	2	8	13-6	.280	.360	.570	.930	11	.991
1997— Las Vegas (PCL)	1B	125	472	86	153	29	2	13	64	60	116	0	9	17-3	.324	.399	.477	.876	9	.992
—San Diego (N.L.)	1B	22	54	9	14	3	0	1	4	9	24	0	1	0-0	.259	.365	.370	.735	0	1.000
1998— Florida (N.L.)	1B	141	454	62	106	29	1	17	74	47	120	10	12	5-2	.233	.318	.414	.732	8	.993
1999— Florida (N.L.)	1B	70	218	21	45	9	1	5	20	17	70	0	3	2-1	.206	.263	.326	.588	3	.994
—Calgary (PCL)	1B-DH	89	339	60	96	20	1	19	73	30	90	1	4	3-4	.283	.345	.516	.861	14	.983
2000— Florida (N.L.)	1B	158	477	70	134	18	3	28	70	63	123	4	14	0-3	.281	.368	.507	.875	8	.993
2001— Florida (N.L.)	1B	158	561	83	158	37	4	21	75	50	126	8	18	4-2	.282	.346	.474	.820	8	.994
2002— Florida (N.L.)	1B	• 162	581	95	157	35	7	27	86	98	164	5	14	19-9	.270	.378	.494	.872	12	.992
2003— Florida (N.L.)	1B	155	539	91	146	31	2	31	92	88	131	10	9	21-8	.271	.379	.508	.888	5	.996
2004— Chicago (N.L.)	1B	161	605	90	168	39	4	32	98	68	128	6	14	12-5	.278	.356	.504	.860	6	.996
2005— Chicago (N.L.)	1B	158	594	120	* 199	* 50	3	46	107	85	109	5	12	15-3	* .335	.418	* .662	*1.080	6	.996
Major League totals (9 years)		1185	4083	641	1127	251	22	208	626	525	995	50	97	78-33	.276	.363	.501	.864	56	.994

DIVISION SERIES RECORD

Year Team (League)	Pos.	G	AB	R	H	2B	3B	HR	RBI	BB	SO	HBP	GDP	SB-CS	Avg.	OBP	SLG	OPS	E	Avg.
2003— Florida (N.L.)	1B	4	16	2	4	1	0	0	2	1	2	2	0	1-0	.250	.368	.313	.681	0	1.000

CHAMPIONSHIP SERIES RECORD

Year Team (League)	Pos.	G	AB	R	H	2B	3B	HR	RBI	BB	SO	HBP	GDP	SB-CS	Avg.	OBP	SLG	OPS	E	Avg.
2003— Florida (N.L.)	1B	7	32	2	6	2	0	1	4	1	8	1	2	1-0	.188	.235	.344	.579	0	1.000

WORLD SERIES RECORD

Year Team (League)	Pos.	G	AB	R	H	2B	3B	HR	RBI	BB	SO	HBP	GDP	SB-CS	Avg.	OBP	SLG	OPS	E	Avg.
2003— Florida (N.L.)	1B	6	24	2	5	0	0	0	2	1	7	0	1	0-0	.208	.240	.208	.448	1	.977

ALL-STAR GAME RECORD

	G	AB	R	H	2B	3B	HR	RBI	BB	SO	HBP	GDP	SB-CS	Avg.	OBP	SLG	OPS	E	Avg.
All-Star Game totals (1 year)	1	3	0	1	1	0	0	0	0	1	0	0	0-0	.333	.333	.667	1.000	0	1.000

LEE, TRAVIS — 1B

PERSONAL: Born May 26, 1975, in San Diego. ... 6-3/225. ... Bats left, throws left. ... Full name: Travis Reynolds Lee. ... High school: Olympia (Wash.). ... College: San Diego State.

TRANSACTIONS/CAREER NOTES: Selected by Minnesota Twins organization in first round (second pick overall) of 1996 free-agent draft; did not sign. ... Signed by Arizona Diamondbacks organization (October 15, 1996). ... Loaned by Diamondbacks organization to Milwaukee Brewers organization (June 5, 1997-remainder of season). ... On disabled list (July 25-August 9, 1998; and August 16-September 9, 1999). ... On disabled list (May 25-June 9, 2000); included rehabilitation assignment to El Paso. ... Traded by Diamondbacks with Ps Vicente Padilla, Omar Daal and Nelson Figueroa to Philadelphia Phillies for P Curt Schilling (July 26, 2000). ... Signed as a free agent by Tampa Bay Devil Rays (February 6, 2003). ... On disabled list (April 14-29, 2003). ... Signed as a free agent by New York Yankees (March 2, 2004). ... On disabled list (March 29-April 17 and May 1, 2004-remainder of season); included rehabilitation assignment to Tampa. ... Signed as a free agent by Devil Rays (February 4, 2005). ... On disabled list (May 2-20, 2005).

2005 GAMES PLAYED BY POSITION (MLB): 1B—124.

SCOUTING REPORT

Offense: Lee has a fluid inside-out stroke with a slight uppercut but does not have good bat speed. Is a much better low-ball hitter than high-ball hitter. Has not regained his power stroke after shoulder surgery in 2004. Doesn't give in against lefthanders, but all his home runs are against righthanders. **Defense:** He has great hands and is one of the best when it comes to footwork and receiving throws. Is agile with good range to either side and has excellent instincts for the position. **Outlook:** He's not a middle-of-the-order power hitter, but he can work in the sixth or seventh spot and give a team 15 homers a year. Prevents runs with his defense. **Grade 5.9**

TRAVIS LEE'S HITTING ZONE

.231	.167	.321
.341	.447	.245
.500	.143	.305

LEFTY-RIGHTY SPLITS

vs.	Avg.	AB	H	2B	3B	HR	RBI	BB	SO	OBP	Slg.
L	.250	56	14	3	0	0	3	2	16	.276	.304
R	.276	348	96	19	2	12	46	33	50	.339	.445

Year	Team (League)	Pos.	G	AB	R	H	2B	3B	HR	RBI	BB	SO	HBP	GDP	SB-CS	Avg.	OBP	SLG	OPS	E	Avg.
1997—	High Desert (Calif.)	1B-DH	61	226	63	82	18	1	18	63	47	36	3	8	5-1	.363	.473	.690	1.163	1	.998
—	Tucson (PCL) 1B-DH-OF		59	227	42	68	16	2	14	46	31	46	2	10	2-0	.300	.387	.573	.960	3	.993
1998—	Arizona (N.L.)	1B	146	562	71	151	20	2	22	72	67	123	0	13	8-1	.269	.346	.429	.775	3	.998
1999—	Arizona (N.L.)	1B-OF	120	375	57	89	16	2	9	50	58	50	0	10	17-3	.237	.337	.363	.700	3	.997
2000—	Arizona (N.L.)	OF-1B	72	224	34	52	13	0	8	40	25	46	0	6	5-1	.232	.308	.397	.705	4	.983
—	El Paso (Texas)	1B-OF	3	10	0	2	0	0	0	0	2	1	0	1	0-0	.200	.333	.200	.533	0	1.000
—	Tucson (PCL)	1B-OF	7	30	4	11	4	0	0	3	1	6	0	1	1-0	.367	.387	.500	.887	0	1.000
—	Philadelphia (N.L.)	1B-OF	56	180	19	43	11	1	1	14	40	33	2	6	3-0	.239	.381	.328	.709	0	1.000
2001—	Philadelphia (N.L.)	1B	157	555	75	143	34	2	20	90	71	109	4	15	3-4	.258	.341	.434	.775	6	.996
2002—	Philadelphia (N.L.)	1B	153	536	55	142	26	2	13	70	54	104	0	12	5-3	.265	.331	.394	.725	6	.996
2003—	Tampa Bay (A.L.)	1B-DH	145	542	75	149	37	3	19	70	64	97	0	13	6-2	.275	.348	.459	.807	3	.996
2004—	Tampa (Fla. St.)	1B	3	12	-2	3	1	0	0	3	1	4	0	1	0-0	.250	.308	.333	.641	0	1.000
—	New York (A.L.)	1B	7	19	1	2	1	0	0	2	1	3	0	2	0-0	.105	.150	.158	.308	0	1.000
2005—	Tampa Bay (A.L.)	1B	129	404	54	110	22	2	12	49	35	66	1	7	7-4	.272	.331	.426	.757	4	.996
	American League totals (3 years)		281	965	130	261	60	5	31	121	100	166	1	22	13-6	.270	.337	.439	.777	7	.997
	National League totals (5 years)		704	2432	311	620	120	9	73	322	315	465	6	62	41-12	.255	.340	.402	.741	22	.996
	Major League totals (8 years)		985	3397	441	881	180	14	104	457	415	631	7	84	54-18	.259	.339	.412	.751	29	.996

LEHR, JUSTIN   P

PERSONAL: Born August 3, 1977, in Orange, Calif. ... 6-1/200. ... Throws right, bats right. ... Full name: Charles Larry Lehr. ... High school: West Covina (Calif.). ... College: Southern California.

TRANSACTIONS/CAREER NOTES: Selected by Detroit Tigers organization in 15th round of 1995 free-agent draft; did not sign. ... Selected by Anaheim Angels organization in 10th round of 1998 free-agent draft; did not sign. ... Selected by Oakland Athletics organization in eighth round of 1999 free-agent draft. ... Traded by A's with OF Nelson Cruz to Milwaukee Brewers for 3B Keith Ginter (December 15, 2004).

CAREER HITTING: 0-for-3 (.000), 0 R, 0 2B, 0 3B, 0 HR, 0 RBI.

SCOUTING REPORT

Throws: Lehr complements a fastball that tops out at around 92 mph with a curveball, slider and forkball. **Tendencies:** He is a converted catcher and doesn't have too much pitching experience, but he has a good arm. Is extremely deliberate. Fastball has some riding action. Curve breaks straight down but has a tendency to roll. Slider is more like a cut fastball but has good bite. Has improved his forkball with late sinking action; throws it to righthanded and lefthanders but is more effective against righties **Outlook:** He is a decent setup option, but he needs to cut down on his walks. **Grade 6**

JUSTIN LEHR'S PITCHING ZONE

.250	.500	.125
.348	.308	.273
.143	.333	.091

LEFTY-RIGHTY SPLITS

vs.	Avg.	AB	H	2B	3B	HR	RBI	BB	SO	OBP	Slg.
L	.207	58	12	2	0	0	1	10	9	.324	.241
R	.270	74	20	10	0	4	15	8	14	.345	.568

Year	Team (League)	W	L	Pct.	ERA	WHIP	G	GS	CG	ShO	Hld.	Sv.-Opp.	IP	H	R	ER	HR	BB-IBB	SO	Avg.
1999—	S. Oregon (N'west)	2	6	.250	5.95	1.87	14	4	0	0	...	0-...	42.1	62	36	28	3	17-3	40	.341
2000—	Sacramento (PCL)	0	0	...	11.25	2.50	1	1	0	0	...	0-...	4.0	7	5	5	1	3-0	3	.389
—	Modesto (Calif.)	13	6	.684	3.19	1.18	29	25	0	0	...	0-...	175.0	161	71	62	10	46-1	138	.249
2001—	Midland (Texas)	11	12	.478	5.45	1.60	29	27	0	0	...	0-...	155.1	206	107	94	20	43-1	103	.318
2002—	Midland (Texas)	8	3	.727	4.05	1.49	58	0	0	0	...	4-...	80.0	88	39	36	7	31-10	59	.290
2003—	Sacramento (PCL)	3	2	.600	3.72	1.35	53	0	0	0	...	0-...	75.0	74	34	31	3	27-3	64	.259
2004—	Sacramento (PCL)	4	2	.667	2.65	1.26	32	0	0	0	...	13-...	37.1	37	14	11	1	10-0	40	.250
—	Oakland (A.L.)	1	1	.500	5.23	1.50	27	0	0	0	5	0-1	32.2	35	19	19	3	14-2	16	.280
2005—	Nashville (PCL)	7	7	.500	3.99	1.52	27	11	0	0	1	1-1	88.0	102	49	39	8	32-2	68	.290
—	Milwaukee (N.L.)	1	1	.500	3.89	1.44	23	0	0	0	3	0-1	34.2	32	19	15	4	18-2	23	.242
	American League totals (1 year)	1	1	.500	5.23	1.50	27	0	0	0	5	0-1	32.2	35	19	19	3	14-2	16	.280
	National League totals (1 year)	1	1	.500	3.89	1.44	23	0	0	0	3	0-1	34.2	32	19	15	4	18-2	23	.242
	Major League totals (2 years)	2	2	.500	4.54	1.47	50	0	0	0	8	0-2	67.1	67	38	34	7	32-4	39	.261

LEICESTER, JON   P

PERSONAL: Born February 7, 1979, in Mariposa, Calif. ... 6-2/220. ... Throws right, bats right. ... Full name: Jonathan David Leicester. ... Name pronounced: lester. ... High school: Palisades Charter (Pacific Palisades, Calif.). ... College: Memphis.

TRANSACTIONS/CAREER NOTES: Selected by Chicago Cubs organization in 11th round of 2000 free-agent draft. ... Traded by Cubs to Texas Rangers for a player to be named (November 16, 2005).

CAREER HITTING: 0-for-1 (.000), 0 R, 0 2B, 0 3B, 0 HR, 0 RBI.

LEFTY-RIGHTY SPLITS

vs.	Avg.	AB	H	2B	3B	HR	RBI	BB	SO	OBP	Slg.
L	.462	13	6	1	0	1	1	5	3	.611	.769
R	.238	21	5	1	0	1	7	4	4	.407	.429

Year	Team (League)	W	L	Pct.	ERA	WHIP	G	GS	CG	ShO	Hld.	Sv.-Opp.	IP	H	R	ER	HR	BB-IBB	SO	Avg.
2000—	Eugene (Northwest)	1	5	.167	5.44	1.39	17	7	0	0	...	0-...	49.2	47	36	30	4	22-1	31	.247
2001—	Lansing (Midw.)	9	10	.474	5.29	1.57	28	27	1	0	...	0-...	153.0	182	117	90	16	58-0	109	.297
2002—	Daytona (Fla. St.)	2	3	.400	3.97	1.53	20	14	0	0	...	0-...	81.2	77	43	36	7	48-1	57	.248
—	West Tenn (Sou.)	2	2	.500	4.61	1.35	5	4	0	0	...	0-...	27.1	24	16	14	1	13-0	18	.231

Year	Team (League)	W	L	Pct.	ERA	WHIP	G	GS	CG	ShO	Hld.	Sv.-Opp.	IP	H	R	ER	HR	BB-IBB	SO	Avg.
2003— West Tenn. (Sou.)	6	7	.462	3.89	1.34	45	9	1	1	...	6-...	106.1	89	54	46	7	53-0	106	.227
— Iowa (PCL)	0	0	...	7.20	1.60	1	1	0	0	...	0-...	5.0	6	4	4	0	2-0	4	.316
2004— Iowa (PCL)	6	2	.750	3.70	1.48	12	12	0	0	...	0-...	65.2	61	31	27	3	36-0	60	.244
— Chicago (N.L.)	5	1	.833	3.89	1.32	32	0	0	0	5	0-2	41.2	40	20	18	7	15-0	35	.256
2005— Chicago (N.L.)	0	2	.000	9.00	2.22	6	1	0	0	0	0-0	9.0	11	10	9	2	9-0	7	.324
— Iowa (PCL)	3	8	.273	5.51	1.60	24	16	0	0	3	1-2	98.0	115	65	60	17	42-1	73	.294
Major League totals (2 years)	**5**	**3**	**.625**	**4.80**	**1.48**	**38**	**1**	**0**	**0**	**5**	**0-2**	**50.2**	**51**	**30**	**27**	**9**	**24-0**	**42**	**.268**

LEITER, AL   P

PERSONAL: Born October 23, 1965, in Toms River, N.J. ... 6-3/220. ... Throws left, bats left. ... Full name: Alois Terry Leiter. ... Name pronounced: LIGH-ter. ... High school: Central Regional (Bayville, N.J.). ... Brother of Mark Leiter, pitcher with eight major league teams (1990-99 and 2001).

TRANSACTIONS/CAREER NOTES: Selected by New York Yankees organization in second round of June 1984 free-agent draft. ... On disabled list (June 22-July 26, 1988); included rehabilitation assignment to Columbus. ... Traded by Yankees to Toronto Blue Jays for OF Jesse Barfield (April 30, 1989). ... On disabled list (May 11, 1989-remainder of season); included rehabilitation assignment to Dunedin. ... On disabled list (April 27, 1991-remainder of season); included rehabilitation assignments to Dunedin. ... On disabled list (April 24-May 9, 1993; and June 9-24, 1994). ... Signed as a free agent by Florida Marlins (December 14, 1995). ... On disabled list (May 1-20 and August 13-29, 1997). ... Traded by Marlins with 2B Ralph Milliard to New York Mets for Ps Jesus Sanchez and A.J. Burnett and OF Robert Stratton (February 6, 1998). ... On disabled list (June 27-July 18, 1998; April 21-May 18, 2001; June 30-July 20, 2003; and May 12-June 1, 2004). ... Signed as a free agent by Marlins (December 8, 2004). ... Traded by Marlins with cash to New York Yankees for a player to be named (July 16, 2005).

CAREER HITTING: 45-for-530 (.085), 15 R, 7 2B, 1 3B, 0 HR, 16 RBI.

SCOUTING REPORT **Throws:** Leiter throws a cut fastball in the upper to mid-80s, a four-seam fastball, a curveball and a changeup. **Tendencies:** He is no longer a power pitcher and has to be very fine to be effective. Has lost some bite on his cut fastball, which stays on the plate too much. Can't pitch up in the zone anymore and doesn't use his big curve or changeup much. **Outlook:** Leiter is nearing the end of his career and has lost the late sharpness on all his pitches. Has to finesse hitters now and has no margin for error. **Grade 6.5**

AL LEITER'S PITCHING ZONE

.238	.250	.200
.323	.333	.313
.429	.407	.389

LEFTY-RIGHTY SPLITS

vs.	Avg.	AB	H	2B	3B	HR	RBI	BB	SO	OBP	Slg.
L	.250	156	39	8	0	3	31	12	31	.312	.359
R	.294	391	115	25	3	10	61	86	66	.429	.450

Year	Team (League)	W	L	Pct.	ERA	WHIP	G	GS	CG	ShO	Hld.	Sv.-Opp.	IP	H	R	ER	HR	BB-IBB	SO	Avg.
1984— Oneonta (N.Y.-Penn.)	3	2	.600	3.63	1.37	10	10	0	0	...	0-...	57.0	52	32	23	1	26-0	48	.241
1985— Fort Laud. (Fla. St.)	1	6	.143	6.48	1.76	17	17	1	0	...	0-...	82.0	87	70	59	3	57-1	44	.270
— Oneonta (N.Y.-Penn.)	3	2	.600	2.37	1.37	6	6	2	0	...	0-...	38.0	27	14	10	0	25-0	34	.213
1986— Fort Laud. (Fla. St.)	4	8	.333	4.05	1.58	22	21	1	1	...	0-...	117.2	96	64	53	2	90-1	101	.226
1987— Columbus (Int'l)	1	4	.200	6.17	1.54	5	5	0	0	...	0-...	23.1	21	18	16	1	15-0	23	.250
— Alb./Colon. (East.)	3	3	.500	3.35	1.29	15	14	2	0	...	0-...	78.0	64	34	29	4	37-0	71	.227
— New York (A.L.)	2	2	.500	6.35	1.72	4	4	0	0	0	0-0	22.2	24	16	16	2	15-0	28	.273
1988— New York (A.L.)	4	4	.500	3.92	1.43	14	14	0	0	0	0-0	57.1	49	27	25	7	33-0	60	.231
— Columbus (Int'l)	0	2	.000	3.46	1.46	4	4	0	0	...	0-...	13.0	5	7	5	0	14-0	12	.122
1989— New York (A.L.)	1	2	.333	6.08	1.65	4	4	0	0	0	0-0	26.2	23	20	18	1	21-0	22	.235
— Toronto (A.L.)	0	0	...	4.05	1.65	1	1	0	0	0	0-0	6.2	9	3	3	1	2-0	4	.310
— Dunedin (Fla. St.)	0	2	.000	5.63	2.00	3	3	0	0	...	0-...	8.0	11	5	5	0	5-0	4	.324
1990— Dunedin (Fla. St.)	0	0	...	2.63	1.25	6	6	0	0	...	0-...	24.0	18	8	7	1	12-0	14	.209
— Syracuse (Int'l)	3	8	.273	4.62	1.63	15	14	1	1	...	0-...	78.0	59	43	40	4	68-0	69	.215
— Toronto (A.L.)	0	0	...	0.47	1.4	4	0	0	0	0	0-0	6.1	1	0	0	0	2-0	5	.050
1991— Toronto (A.L.)	0	0	...	27.00	4.80	3	0	0	0	0	0-0	1.2	3	5	5	0	5-0	1	.429
— Dunedin (Fla. St.)	0	0	...	1.86	1.24	4	3	0	0	...	0-...	9.2	5	2	2	0	7-0	5	.161
1992— Syracuse (Int'l)	8	9	.471	3.86	1.37	27	27	2	0	...	0-...	163.1	159	82	70	9	64-0	108	.256
— Toronto (A.L.)	0	0	...	9.00	3.00	1	0	0	0	0	0-0	1.0	1	1	1	0	2-0	0	.200
1993— Toronto (A.L.)	9	6	.600	4.11	1.42	34	12	1	1	3	2-3	105.0	93	52	48	9	56-2	66	.240
1994— Toronto (A.L.)	6	7	.462	5.08	1.70	20	20	1	0	0	0-0	111.2	125	68	63	6	65-3	100	.285
1995— Toronto (A.L.)	11	11	.500	3.64	1.48	28	28	2	1	0	0-0	183.0	162	80	74	15	* 108-1	153	.238
1996— Florida (N.L.)	16	12	.571	2.93	1.26	33	33	2	1	0	0-0	215.1	153	74	70	14	* 119-3	200	* .202
1997— Florida (N.L.)	11	9	.550	4.34	1.48	27	27	0	0	0	0-0	151.1	133	78	73	13	91-4	132	.241
1998— New York (N.L.)	17	6	.739	2.47	1.15	28	28	4	2	0	0-0	193.0	151	55	53	8	71-2	174	.216
1999— New York (N.L.)	13	12	.520	4.23	1.42	32	32	1	1	0	0-0	213.0	209	107	100	19	93-8	162	.252
2000— New York (N.L.)	16	8	.667	3.20	1.21	31	31	2	1	0	0-0	208.0	176	84	74	19	76-1	200	.228
2001— New York (N.L.)	11	11	.500	3.31	1.20	29	29	0	0	0	0-0	187.1	178	81	69	18	46-3	142	.252
2002— New York (N.L.)	13	13	.500	3.48	1.29	33	33	2	2	0	0-0	204.1	194	99	79	23	69-5	172	.250
2003— New York (N.L.)	15	9	.625	3.99	1.49	30	30	1	1	0	0-0	180.2	176	83	80	15	94-11	139	.260
2004— New York (N.L.)	10	8	.556	3.21	1.35	30	30	0	0	0	0-0	173.2	138	65	62	16	97-8	117	.218
2005— Florida (N.L.)	3	7	.300	6.64	1.85	17	16	0	0	0	0-0	80.0	88	61	59	9	60-2	52	.292
— New York (A.L.)	4	5	.444	5.49	1.67	16	10	0	0	0	0-0	62.1	66	42	38	4	38-0	45	.268
American League totals (10 years)	**37**	**37**	**.500**	**4.48**	**1.55**	**129**	**93**	**4**	**2**	**3**	**2-3**	**584.1**	**556**	**314**	**291**	**44**	**347-6**	**484**	**.251**
National League totals (10 years)	**125**	**95**	**.568**	**3.58**	**1.34**	**290**	**289**	**12**	**8**	**0**	**0-0**	**1806.2**	**1596**	**787**	**719**	**154**	**816-47**	**1490**	**.239**
Major League totals (19 years)	**162**	**132**	**.551**	**3.80**	**1.39**	**419**	**382**	**16**	**10**	**3**	**2-3**	**2391.0**	**2152**	**1101**	**1010**	**198**	**1163-53**	**1974**	**.242**

DIVISION SERIES RECORD

Year	Team (League)	W	L	Pct.	ERA	WHIP	G	GS	CG	ShO	Hld.	Sv.-Opp.	IP	H	R	ER	HR	BB-IBB	SO	Avg.
1997— Florida (N.L.)	0	0	...	9.00	2.50	1	1	0	0	0	0-0	4.0	7	4	4	1	3-0	3	.500
1999— New York (N.L.)	0	0	...	3.52	0.78	1	1	0	0	0	0-0	7.2	3	3	3	1	3-0	4	.125
2000— New York (N.L.)	0	0	...	2.25	1.00	1	1	0	0	0	0-0	8.0	5	2	2	0	3-0	6	.185
2005— New York (A.L.)	1	0	1.000	7.36	0.82	1	0	0	0	0	0-0	3.2	2	3	3	1	1-1	2	.200
Division series totals (4 years)	**1**	**0**	**1.000**	**4.63**	**1.16**	**7**	**3**	**0**	**0**	**0**	**0-0**	**23.1**	**17**	**12**	**12**	**3**	**10-1**	**15**	**.227**

CHAMPIONSHIP SERIES RECORD

Year	Team (League)	W	L	Pct.	ERA	WHIP	G	GS	CG	ShO	Hld.	Sv.-Opp.	IP	H	R	ER	HR	BB-IBB	SO	Avg.
1993— Toronto (A.L.)	0	0	...	3.38	2.25	2	0	0	0	0	1	0-0	2.2	4	1	1	0	2-1	2	.364

Year Team (League)	W	L	Pct.	ERA	WHIP	G	GS	CG	ShO	Hld.	Sv.-Opp.	IP	H	R	ER	HR	BB-IBB	SO	Avg.
1997— Florida (N.L.)	0	1	.000	4.32	1.80	2	1	0	0	0	0-0	8.1	13	4	4	1	2-0	6	.382
1999— New York (N.L.)	0	1	.000	6.43	1.29	2	2	0	0	0	0-0	7.0	5	6	5	0	4-0	5	.200
2000— New York (N.L.)	0	0	...	3.86	1.14	1	1	0	0	0	0-0	7.0	8	3	3	0	0-0	9	.286
Champ. series totals (4 years)	0	2	.000	4.68	1.52	7	4	0	0	1	0-0	25.0	30	14	13	1	8-1	22	.306

WORLD SERIES RECORD

Year Team (League)	W	L	Pct.	ERA	WHIP	G	GS	CG	ShO	Hld.	Sv.-Opp.	IP	H	R	ER	HR	BB-IBB	SO	Avg.
1993— Toronto (A.L.)	1	0	1.000	7.71	2.00	3	0	0	0	0	0-0	7.0	12	6	6	2	2-0	5	.375
1997— Florida (N.L.)	0	0	...	5.06	1.88	2	2	0	0	0	0-0	10.2	10	9	6	1	10-1	10	.244
2000— New York (N.L.)	0	1	.000	2.87	1.15	2	2	0	0	0	0-0	15.2	12	6	5	2	6-1	16	.207
World Series totals (3 years)	1	1	.500	4.59	1.56	7	4	0	0	0	0-0	33.1	34	21	17	5	18-2	31	.260

ALL-STAR GAME RECORD

Year Team (League)	W	L	Pct.	ERA	WHIP	G	GS	CG	ShO	Hld.	Sv.-Opp.	IP	H	R	ER	HR	BB-IBB	SO	Avg.
All-Star Game totals (2 years)	0	1	.000	6.75	2.25	1	0	0	0	0	0-0	1.1	2	2	1	0	1-0	1	.286

LEREW, ANTHONY   P

PERSONAL: Born October 28, 1982, in Carlisle, Pa. ... 6-3/220. ... Throws right, bats left. ... Full name: Anthony Allen Lerew.

TRANSACTIONS/CAREER NOTES: Selected by Atlanta Braves organization in 11th round of 2001 free-agent draft.

CAREER HITTING: 0-for-0 (.000), 0 R, 0 2B, 0 3B, 0 HR, 0 RBI.

LEFTY-RIGHTY SPLITS

vs.	Avg.	AB	H	2B	3B	HR	RBI	BB	SO	OBP	Slg.
L	.267	15	4	2	0	1	3	2	1	.353	.600
R	.313	16	5	2	0	0	4	3	4	.421	.438

Year Team (League)	W	L	Pct.	ERA	WHIP	G	GS	CG	ShO	Hld.	Sv.-Opp.	IP	H	R	ER	HR	BB-IBB	SO	Avg.
2001— GC Braves (GCL)	1	2	.333	2.92	1.16	12	7	0	0	...	0-...	49.1	43	25	16	3	14-0	40	.228
2002— Danville (Appal.)	8	3	.727	1.73	1.02	14	14	0	0	...	0-...	83.0	60	23	16	2	25-0	75	.205
2003— Rome (S. Atl.)	7	6	.538	2.38	1.08	25	25	0	0	...	0-...	143.2	112	45	38	7	43-2	127	.215
2004— Myrtle Beach (Carol.)	8	9	.471	3.75	1.33	27	27	0	0	...	0-...	144.0	145	75	60	12	46-0	125	.254
2005— Mississippi (Sou.)	6	2	.750	3.93	1.35	14	14	1	0	0	0-0	75.2	70	34	33	6	32-1	64	.246
— Richmond (Int'l)	4	4	.500	3.48	1.19	13	13	0	0	0	0-0	72.1	63	34	28	9	23-0	53	.232
— Atlanta (N.L.)	0	0	...	5.63	1.75	7	0	0	0	0	0-1	8.0	9	5	5	1	5-2	5	.290
Major League totals (1 year)	0	0	...	5.63	1.75	7	0	0	0	0	0-1	8.0	9	5	5	1	5-2	5	.290

LEVINE, AL   P

PERSONAL: Born May 22, 1968, in Park Ridge, Ill. ... 6-3/190. ... Throws right, bats left. ... Full name: Alan Brian Levine. ... Name pronounced: le-VINE. ... High school: Hoffman Estates (Ill.). ... College: Southern Illinois.

TRANSACTIONS/CAREER NOTES: Selected by Chicago White Sox in 11th round of 1991 free-agent draft. ... Traded by White Sox with P Larry Thomas to Texas Rangers for SS Benji Gil (December 19, 1997). ... Claimed on waivers by Anaheim Angels (April 2, 1999). ... On disabled list (July 31-August 19, 2000); included rehabilitation assignment to Erie. ... On disabled list (June 27-July 20, 2002); included rehabilitation assignment to Salt Lake. ... Signed as a free agent by St. Louis Cardinals (January 6, 2003). ... Released by Cardinals (March 26, 2003). ... Signed by Tampa Bay Devil Rays organization (April 2, 2003). ... Traded by Devil Rays to Kansas City Royals for cash (July, 31, 2003). ... Signed as a free agent by Detroit Tigers (December 18, 2003). ... Signed as a free agent by San Francisco Giants organization (March 1, 2005). ... On disabled list (May 11-June 3, 2005); included rehabilitation assignment to Fresno.

CAREER HITTING: 0-for-2 (.000), 0 R, 0 2B, 0 3B, 0 HR, 0 RBI.

LEFTY-RIGHTY SPLITS

vs.	Avg.	AB	H	2B	3B	HR	RBI	BB	SO	OBP	Slg.
L	.417	24	10	3	0	1	8	2	0	.462	.667
R	.261	23	6	0	0	1	4	2	4	.320	.391

Year Team (League)	W	L	Pct.	ERA	WHIP	G	GS	CG	ShO	Hld.	Sv.-Opp.	IP	H	R	ER	HR	BB-IBB	SO	Avg.
1991— Utica (N.Y.-Penn.)	6	4	.600	3.18	1.19	16	12	2	1	...	1-...	85.0	75	45	30	2	26-0	83	.231
1992— South Bend (Midw.)	9	5	.643	2.81	1.19	23	23	2	0	...	0-...	156.2	151	67	49	6	36-1	131	.253
— Sarasota (Fla. St.)	0	2	.000	4.02	1.40	3	2	0	0	...	0-...	15.2	17	11	7	1	5-1	11	.293
1993— Sarasota (Fla. St.)	11	8	.579	3.68	1.36	27	26	5	1	...	0-...	161.1	169	87	66	6	50-3	129	.271
1994— Birmingham (Sou.)	5	9	.357	3.31	1.41	18	18	1	0	...	0-...	114.1	117	50	42	7	44-1	94	.267
— Nashville (A.A.)	0	0	...	7.88	1.88	8	4	0	0	...	0-...	24.0	34	23	21	2	11-0	24	.343
1995— Nashville (A.A.)	0	2	.000	5.14	1.93	3	3	0	0	...	0-...	14.0	20	10	8	1	7-0	14	.323
— Birmingham (Sou.)	4	3	.571	2.34	1.18	43	1	0	0	...	7-...	73.0	61	22	19	2	25-5	68	.223
1996— Nashville (A.A.)	4	5	.444	3.65	1.33	43	0	0	0	...	12-...	61.2	58	27	25	4	24-6	45	.246
— Chicago (A.L.)	0	1	.000	5.40	1.58	16	0	0	0	0	0-1	18.1	22	14	11	1	7-1	12	.289
1997— Chicago (A.L.)	2	2	.500	6.91	1.87	25	0	0	0	3	0-1	27.1	35	22	21	4	16-1	22	.313
— Nashville (A.A.)	1	1	.500	7.13	1.95	26	0	0	0	...	2-...	35.1	58	32	28	3	11-1	29	.357
1998— Oklahoma (PCL)	1	3	.250	4.73	1.28	12	7	0	0	...	1-...	53.1	51	33	28	7	17-0	30	.252
— Texas (A.L.)	0	1	.000	4.50	1.45	30	0	0	0	0	0-0	58.0	68	30	29	6	16-1	19	.294
1999— Anaheim (A.L.)	1	1	.500	3.39	1.24	50	1	0	0	3	0-1	85.0	76	40	32	13	29-2	37	.266
2000— Anaheim (A.L.)	3	4	.429	3.87	1.54	51	0	0	0	5	2-2	95.1	98	44	41	10	49-5	42	.266
— Erie (East.)	0	0	...	0.00	1.50	1	1	0	0	...	0-...	2.0	3	2	0	0	0-0	0	.333
2001— Anaheim (A.L.)	8	10	.444	2.38	1.31	64	1	0	0	17	2-6	75.2	71	25	20	7	28-4	40	.257
2002— Anaheim (A.L.)	4	4	.500	4.24	1.49	52	0	0	0	10	5-7	63.2	61	35	30	8	34-3	40	.253
— Salt Lake (PCL)	0	0	...	3.00	1.67	2	0	0	0	...	0-...	3.0	5	1	1	0	0-0	0	.385
2003— Tampa Bay (A.L.)	3	5	.375	2.90	1.27	36	0	0	0	8	0-2	49.2	45	23	16	7	18-0	25	.243
— Kansas City (A.L.)	0	1	.000	2.53	1.55	18	0	0	0	2	1-2	21.1	22	6	6	2	11-1	5	.268
2004— Detroit (A.L.)	3	4	.429	4.58	1.51	65	0	0	0	16	0-1	70.2	83	37	36	10	24-1	32	.295
2005— Fresno (PCL)	0	0	...	2.84	1.50	9	0	0	0	1	1-1	12.2	12	5	4	0	7-1	6	.267
— San Francisco (N.L.)	0	0	...	9.58	1.94	9	0	0	0	0	0-0	10.1	16	11	11	2	4-1	4	.340
American League totals (9 years)	24	33	.421	3.85	1.44	407	7	0	0	64	10-23	565.0	581	276	242	68	232-19	274	.269
National League totals (1 year)	0	0	...	9.58	1.94	9	0	0	0	0	0-0	10.1	16	11	11	2	4-1	4	.340
Major League totals (10 years)	24	33	.421	3.96	1.45	416	7	0	0	64	10-23	575.1	597	287	253	70	236-20	278	.270

LIDGE, BRAD   P

PERSONAL: Born December 23, 1976, in Sacramento. ... 6-5/210. ... Throws right, bats right. ... Full name: Bradley Thomas Lidge. ... High school: Cherry Creek (Englewood, Colo.). ... College: Notre Dame.

TRANSACTIONS/CAREER NOTES: Selected by San Francisco Giants organization in 42nd round of 1995 free-agent draft; did not sign. ... Selected by Houston Astros organization in first round (17th pick overall) of 1998 free-agent draft; pick received as part of compensation for Colorado Rockies signing Type A free-agent P Darryl Kile.

L

CAREER HITTING: 2-for-7 (.286), 0 R, 1 2B, 0 3B, 0 HR, 2 RBI.

SCOUTING REPORT **Throws:** Lidge throws a 92-97 mph fastball and the best slider in the game, which is thrown at 87-89 mph. **Tendencies:** He comes right at hitters. Has a long arm action and puts a lot of strain on his shoulder, one reason he has had injury problems in his career. Almost impossible for hitters to lay off his slider; it's thrown with the same arm speed and from the same arm slot as his fastball, and it breaks just as it gets to the plate. Fastball has exceptional riding action. **Outlook:** Lidge is one of the most dominant relievers in either league. Appeared to have a tired arm in the playoffs but will bounce back. Astros should be cautious about using him for more than three outs. *Grade 9.7*

BRAD LIDGE'S PITCHING ZONE

.333	.556	.300
.273	.355	.382
.217	.250	.200

LEFTY-RIGHTY SPLITS

vs.	Avg.	AB	H	2B	3B	HR	RBI	BB	SO	OBP	Slg.
L	.244	131	32	7	0	1	13	11	38	.313	.321
R	.202	129	26	4	0	4	13	12	65	.273	.326

Year Team (League)	W	L	Pct.	ERA	WHIP	G	GS	CG	ShO	Hld.	Sv.-Opp.	IP	H	R	ER	HR	BB-IBB	SO	Avg.
1998—Quad City (Midw.)	0	1	.000	3.27	1.36	4	4	0	0		0-...	11.0	10	5	4	0	5-0	6	.227
1999—Kissimmee (Fla. St.)	0	2	.000	3.38	1.13	6	6	0	0		0-...	21.1	13	8	8	0	11-0	19	.183
2000—Kissimmee (Fla. St.)	2	1	.667	2.81	1.03	8	8	0	0		0-...	41.2	28	14	13	3	15-0	46	.190
2001—Round Rock (Texas)	2	0	1.000	1.73	1.08	5	5	0	0		0-...	26.0	21	5	5	1	7-0	42	.219
2002—Round Rock (Texas)	1	1	.500	2.45	1.09	5	0	0	0		0-...	11.0	9	4	3	0	3-0	18	.220
—Houston (N.L.)	1	0	1.000	6.23	2.42	6	1	0	0	0	0-0	8.2	12	6	6	0	9-1	12	.333
—New Orleans (PCL)	5	5	.500	3.39	1.16	24	19	0	0		0-...	111.2	83	47	42	9	47-0	110	.206
2003—Houston (N.L.)	6	3	.667	3.60	1.20	78	0	0	0	28	1-6	85.0	60	36	34	6	42-7	97	.202
2004—Houston (N.L.)	6	5	.545	1.90	0.92	80	0	0	0	17	29-33	94.2	57	21	20	8	30-5	157	.174
2005—Houston (N.L.)	4	4	.500	2.29	1.15	70	0	0	0	0	42-46	70.2	58	21	18	5	23-1	103	.223
Major League totals (4 years)	**17**	**12**	**.586**	**2.71**	**1.12**	**234**	**1**	**0**	**0**	**45**	**72-85**	**259.0**	**187**	**84**	**78**	**19**	**104-14**	**369**	**.203**

DIVISION SERIES RECORD

Year Team (League)	W	L	Pct.	ERA	WHIP	G	GS	CG	ShO	Hld.	Sv.-Opp.	IP	H	R	ER	HR	BB-IBB	SO	Avg.
2004—Houston (N.L.)	0	0	...	2.08	1.15	3	0	0	0	0	1-2	4.1	4	1	1	0	1-0	6	.286
2005—Houston (N.L.)	0	0	...	0.00	1.50	3	0	0	0	0	0-0	4.0	2	0	0	0	4-0	5	.143
Division series totals (2 years)	**0**	**0**	**...**	**1.08**	**1.32**	**6**	**0**	**0**	**0**	**0**	**1-2**	**8.1**	**6**	**1**	**1**	**0**	**5-0**	**11**	**.214**

CHAMPIONSHIP SERIES RECORD

Year Team (League)	W	L	Pct.	ERA	WHIP	G	GS	CG	ShO	Hld.	Sv.-Opp.	IP	H	R	ER	HR	BB-IBB	SO	Avg.
2004—Houston (N.L.)	1	0	1.000	0.00	0.38	4	0	0	0	0	2-2	8.0	1	0	0	0	2-0	14	.040
2005—Houston (N.L.)	0	1	.000	7.20	1.60	4	0	0	0	0	3-4	5.0	6	4	4	1	2-0	7	.300
Champ. series totals (2 years)	**1**	**1**	**.500**	**2.77**	**0.85**	**8**	**0**	**0**	**0**	**0**	**5-6**	**13.0**	**7**	**4**	**4**	**1**	**4-0**	**21**	**.156**

WORLD SERIES RECORD

Year Team (League)	W	L	Pct.	ERA	WHIP	G	GS	CG	ShO	Hld.	Sv.-Opp.	IP	H	R	ER	HR	BB-IBB	SO	Avg.
2005—Houston (N.L.)	0	2	.000	4.91	1.09	3	0	0	0	0	0-0	3.2	4	2	2	1	0-0	6	.286

ALL-STAR GAME RECORD

Year Team (League)	W	L	Pct.	ERA	WHIP	G	GS	CG	ShO	Hld.	Sv.-Opp.	IP	H	R	ER	HR	BB-IBB	SO	Avg.
All-Star Game totals (1 year)	**0**	**0**	**...**	**0.00**	**0.00**	**1**	**0**	**0**	**0**		**0-0**	**1.0**	**0**	**0**	**0**	**0**	**0-0**	**3**	**.000**

LIDLE, CORY   P

PERSONAL: Born March 22, 1972, in Hollywood, Calif. ... 5-11/192. ... Throws right, bats right. ... Full name: Cory Fulton Lidle. ... Name pronounced: LIE-dell. ... High school: South Hills (Covina, Calif.).

TRANSACTIONS/CAREER NOTES: Signed as a non-drafted free agent by Minnesota Twins organization (August 25, 1990). ... Released by Twins (April 1, 1993). ... Signed by Pocatello of the Pioneer League (May 28, 1993). ... Contract sold by Pocatello to Milwaukee Brewers organization (September 17, 1993). ... Traded by Brewers to New York Mets for C Kelly Stinnett (January 17, 1996). ... Selected by Arizona Diamondbacks in first round (13th pick overall) of expansion draft (November 18, 1997). ... On disabled list (March 31, 1998-entire season); included rehabilitation assignments to High Desert and Tucson. ... Claimed on waivers by Tampa Bay Devil Rays (October 7, 1998). ... On disabled list (March 23-September 18, 1999); included rehabilitation assignments to St. Petersburg and Durham. ... On suspended list (September 5-8, 2000). ... Traded by Devil Rays to Oakland Athletics as part of three-team deal in which Devil Rays acquired OF Ben Grieve and cash from A's, Kansas City Royals acquired P Roberto Hernandez from Devil Rays and C A.J. Hinch, IF Angel Berroa and cash from A's and A's received OF Johnny Damon, IF Mark Ellis and cash from Royals (January 8, 2001). ... On disabled list (May 13-30, 2002); included rehabilitation assignment to Sacramento. ... Traded by A's to Toronto Blue Jays for IF Michael Rouse and P Christopher Mowday (November 16, 2002). ... On disabled list (August 5-25, 2003); included rehabilitation assignment to Syracuse. ... Signed as a free agent by Cincinnati Reds (January 6, 2004). ... Traded by Reds to Philadelphia Phillies for OF Javon Moran, P Joe Wilson and a player to be named or cash (August 9, 2004); Reds acquired P Elizardo Ramirez to complete deal (August 11, 2004). ... On disabled list (August 25-September 9, 2005).

CAREER HITTING: 19-for-136 (.140), 7 R, 4 2B, 0 3B, 1 HR, 8 RBI.

SCOUTING REPORT **Throws:** Lidle throws his fastball is 87-92 mph; curveball is 71-75; changeup and split-finger fastball are 78-82. **Tendencies:** He basically is a sinkerball pitcher now that he he has abandoned his ineffective cutter. Has to use all his pitches and location is critical. Has very good sink to his fastball. Has a loose arm and good delivery and uses his curveball to lefthanders early in the count. Uses his splitter late in the count as an out pitch to both righthanders and lefthanders. **Outlook:** As a fifth starter he will eat innings but also will give up a lot of hits. Basically is a .500 pitcher. *Grade 7*

CORY LIDLE'S PITCHING ZONE

.400	.294	.235
.412	.391	.236
.291	.417	.254

LEFTY-RIGHTY SPLITS

vs.	Avg.	AB	H	2B	3B	HR	RBI	BB	SO	OBP	Slg.
L	.289	339	98	23	5	6	40	21	58	.329	.440
R	.289	388	112	24	2	12	52	19	63	.327	.454

Year Team (League)	W	L	Pct.	ERA	WHIP	G	GS	CG	ShO	Hld.	Sv.-Opp.	IP	H	R	ER	HR	BB-IBB	SO	Avg.
1991—GC Twins (GCL)	1	1	.500	5.79	1.07	4	0	0	0	0	0-...	4.2	5	3	3	0	0-0	5	.263
1992—Elizabethton (Appal.)	2	1	.667	3.71	1.40	19	2	0	0		6-...	43.2	40	29	18	2	21-0	32	.240
1993—Pocatello (Pion.)	8	4	.667	4.13	1.48	17	16	3	0		1-...	106.2	104	59	49	6	54-0	91	.261
1994—Stockton (Calif.)	1	2	.333	4.43	1.71	25	1	0	0		4-...	42.2	60	32	21	2	13-1	38	.323
—Beloit (Midw.)	3	4	.429	2.61	1.10	13	9	1	1		0-...	69.0	65	24	20	4	11-0	62	.245

L

Year Team (League)	W	L	Pct.	ERA	WHIP	G	GS	CG	ShO	Hld.	Sv.-Opp.	IP	H	R	ER	HR	BB-IBB	SO	Avg.
1995— El Paso (Texas)	5	4	.556	3.36	1.48	45	9	0	0		2-...	109.2	126	52	41	6	36-3	78	.292
1996— Binghamton (East.)	14	10	.583	3.31	1.23	27	27	6	1		0-...	190.1	186	78	70	13	49-4	141	.259
1997— Norfolk (Int'l)	4	2	.667	3.64	1.33	7	7	1	0		0-...	42.0	46	20	17	1	10-0	34	.279
— New York (N.L.)	7	2	.778	3.53	1.30	54	2	0	0	9	2-3	81.2	86	38	32	7	20-4	54	.274
1998— High Desert (Calif.)	0	0	...	0.00	1.50	1	1	0	0		0-...	2.2	2	1	0	0	2-0	6	.182
— Tucson (PCL)	0	0	...	0.00	0.86	1	1	0	0		0-...	4.2	2	0	0	0	2-0	2	.125
1999— St. Pete. (FSL)	0	0	...	0.00	0.80	2	2	0	0		0-...	5.0	2	0	0	0	2-0	1	.118
— Durham (Int'l)	0	0	...	4.76	1.76	3	2	0	0		0-...	5.2	9	3	3	0	1-0	6	.360
— Tampa Bay (A.L.)	1	0	1.000	7.20	2.00	5	1	0	0	0	0-0	5.0	8	4	4	0	2-0	4	.364
2000— Durham (Int'l)	6	2	.750	2.52	1.20	9	9	0	0		0-...	50.0	52	15	14	3	8-0	44	.267
— Tampa Bay (A.L.)	4	6	.400	5.03	1.48	31	11	0	0	2	0-...	96.2	114	61	54	13	29-3	62	.294
2001— Sacramento (PCL)	1	0	1.000	3.00	1.50	1	1	0	0		0-...	6.0	6	2	2	0	3-0	2	.261
— Oakland (A.L.)	13	6	.684	3.59	1.15	29	29	1	0	0	0-...	188.0	170	84	75	23	47-7	118	.242
2002— Oakland (A.L.)	8	10	.444	3.89	1.20	31	30	2	2	0	0-...	192.0	191	90	83	17	39-3	111	.258
— Sacramento (PCL)	0	0	...	2.25	1.25	1	1	0	0		0-...	4.0	2	1	1	0	3-0	3	.167
2003— Syracuse (Int'l)	0	0	...	0.00	1.20	1	1	0	0		0-...	4.0	5	0	0	0	3-0	3	.313
— Toronto (A.L.)	12	15	.444	5.75	1.43	31	31	2	0	0	0-0	192.2	216	* 133	• 123	24	60-3	112	.282
2004— Cincinnati (N.L.)	7	10	.412	5.32	1.44	24	24	3	1	0	0-0	149.0	170	95	88	24	44-4	93	.288
— Philadelphia (N.L.)	5	2	.714	3.90	1.14	10	10	2	§ 2	0	0-0	62.1	54	28	27	3	17-1	33	.236
2005— Philadelphia (N.L.)	13	11	.542	4.53	1.35	31	31	1	0	0	0-0	184.2	210	105	93	18	40-5	121	.289
American League totals (5 years)	38	37	.507	4.52	1.30	127	102	5	2	2	0-0	674.1	699	372	339	77	177-16	407	.267
National League totals (3 years)	32	25	.561	4.52	1.34	119	67	6	3	9	2-3	477.2	520	266	240	52	121-14	301	.279
Major League totals (8 years)	70	62	.530	4.52	1.32	246	169	11	5	11	2-3	1152.0	1219	638	579	129	298-30	708	.272

DIVISION SERIES RECORD

Year Team (League)	W	L	Pct.	ERA	WHIP	G	GS	CG	ShO	Hld.	Sv.-Opp.	IP	H	R	ER	HR	BB-IBB	SO	Avg.
2001— Oakland (A.L.)	0	1	.000	10.80	2.40	1	1	0	0	0	0-0	3.1	5	6	4	0	3-0	0	.357
2002— Oakland (A.L.)	0	0	...	9.00	2.00	1	0	0	0	0	0-0	1.0	2	1	1	0	0-0	0	.400
Division series totals (2 years)	0	1	.000	10.38	2.31	2	1	0	0	0	0-0	4.1	7	7	5	0	3-0	0	.368

LIEBER, JON   P

PERSONAL: Born April 2, 1970, in Council Bluffs, Iowa. ... 6-2/230. ... Throws right, bats left. ... Full name: Jonathan Ray Lieber. ... Name pronounced: LEE-ber. ... High school: Abraham Lincoln (Council Bluffs, Iowa.). ... Junior college: Iowa Western Community College-Council Bluffs. ... College: South Alabama.

TRANSACTIONS/CAREER NOTES: Selected by Chicago Cubs organization in ninth round of 1991 free-agent draft; did not sign. ... Selected by Kansas City Royals organization in second round of 1992 free-agent draft; pick received as part of compensation for New York Yankees signing Type A free-agent OF Danny Tartabull. ... Traded by Royals with P Dan Miceli to Pittsburgh Pirates for P Stan Belinda (July 31, 1993). ... On disabled list (August 21-September 15, 1998). ... Traded by Pirates to Chicago Cubs for OF Brant Brown (December 14, 1998). ... On disabled list (April 21-May 8, 1999; and August 2, 2002-remainder of season). ... Signed as a free agent by New York Yankees (February 4, 2003). ... On disabled list (March 21, 2003-entire season); included rehabilitation assignments to Tampa and GCL Yankees. ... On disabled list (March 19-May 1, 2004); included rehabilitation assignment to Tampa. ... Signed as a free agent by Philadelphia Phillies (December 8, 2004).

CAREER HITTING: 79-for-537 (.147), 34 R, 17 2B, 0 3B, 0 HR, 24 RBI.

SCOUTING REPORT **Throws:** Lieber relies on a sinking fastball at 88-91 mph, a slider at 80-84 and a changeup. **Tendencies:** Fielders have to stay on their toes when Lieber, one of the game's fastest workers, is on the mound. Is a control pitcher who has good sinking action on his fastball and really challenges hitters. Still has a plus slider with a quick lateral break. Has excellent arm speed on his changeup. **Outlook:** Lieber's sinker is a positive in Citizens Bank Park and he is a quality middle-rotation starter, but the Phillies counted on him to be their ace last season. **Grade 8.1**

JON LIEBER'S PITCHING ZONE

.253	.375	.203
.325	.338	.315
.235	.300	.240

LEFTY-RIGHTY SPLITS

vs.	Avg.	AB	H	2B	3B	HR	RBI	BB	SO	OBP	Slg.
L	.302	431	130	25	4	17	57	26	63	.342	.497
R	.223	417	93	14	1	16	45	15	86	.254	.376

Year Team (League)	W	L	Pct.	ERA	WHIP	G	GS	CG	ShO	Hld.	Sv.-Opp.	IP	H	R	ER	HR	BB-IBB	SO	Avg.
1992— Eugene (N'west)	3	0	1.000	1.16	0.90	5	5	0	0		0-...	31.0	26	6	4	1	2-0	23	.226
— Baseball City (Fla. St.)	3	3	.500	4.65	1.90	7	6	0	0		0-...	31.0	45	20	16	2	8-0	19	.344
1993— Wilmington (Carol.)	9	3	.750	2.67	1.17	17	16	1	0		0-...	114.2	125	47	34	4	9-1	89	.272
— Memphis (Sou.)	2	1	.667	6.86	1.81	4	4	0	0		0-...	21.0	32	16	16	4	6-0	17	.340
— Carolina (Sou.)	4	2	.667	3.97	1.44	6	6	0	0		0-...	34.0	39	15	15	3	10-0	28	.298
1994— Carolina (Sou.)	2	0	1.000	1.29	0.71	3	3	1	0		0-...	21.0	13	4	3	0	2-0	21	.171
— Buffalo (A.A.)	1	1	.500	1.69	0.80	3	3	0	0		0-...	21.1	16	4	4	1	1-0	21	.208
— Pittsburgh (N.L.)	6	7	.462	3.73	1.30	17	17	1	0	0	0-0	108.2	116	62	45	12	25-3	71	.279
1995— Pittsburgh (N.L.)	4	7	.364	6.32	1.61	21	12	0	0	3	0-1	72.2	103	56	51	7	14-0	45	.346
— Calgary (PCL)	1	5	.167	7.01	1.83	14	14	0	0		0-...	77.0	122	69	60	6	19-0	34	.354
1996— Pittsburgh (N.L.)	9	5	.643	3.99	1.30	51	15	0	0	9	1-4	142.0	156	70	63	19	28-2	94	.279
1997— Pittsburgh (N.L.)	11	14	.440	4.49	1.30	33	32	1	0	0	0-0	188.1	193	102	94	23	51-8	160	.263
1998— Pittsburgh (N.L.)	8	14	.364	4.11	1.30	29	28	2	0	0	1-1	171.0	182	93	78	23	40-4	138	.269
1999— Chicago (N.L.)	10	11	.476	4.07	1.34	31	31	3	1	0	0-0	203.1	226	107	92	28	46-6	186	.276
2000— Chicago (N.L.)	12	11	.522	4.41	1.20	35	• 35	6	1	0	0-0	* 251.0	248	130	123	36	54-3	192	.258
2001— Chicago (N.L.)	20	6	.769	3.80	1.15	34	34	5	1	0	0-0	232.1	226	104	98	25	41-4	148	.255
2002— Chicago (N.L.)	6	8	.429	3.70	1.17	21	21	3	0	0	0-0	141.0	153	64	58	15	12-2	87	.277
2003— GC Yankees (GCL)	0	0	...	4.50	1.30	2	2	0	0		0-...	6.0	8	3	3	0	0-0	6	.308
— Tampa (Fla. St.)	0	0	...	13.50	3.00	1	0	0	0		0-...	2.0	5	3	3	0	0-0	2	.455
2004— Tampa (Fla. St.)	1	0	1.000	0.00	0.29	1	1	0	0		0-...	7.0	2	0	0	0	0-0	4	.091
— New York (A.L.)	14	8	.636	4.33	1.32	27	27	0	0	0	0-0	176.2	216	95	85	20	18-2	102	.301
2005— Philadelphia (N.L.)	17	13	.567	4.20	1.21	35	• 35	1	0	0	0-0	218.1	223	107	102	33	41-6	149	.263
American League totals (1 year)	14	8	.636	4.33	1.32	27	27	0	0	0	0-0	176.2	216	95	85	20	18-2	102	.301
National League totals (10 years)	103	96	.518	4.19	1.26	307	260	22	3	12	2-6	1728.2	1826	895	804	221	352-38	1270	.270
Major League totals (11 years)	117	104	.529	4.20	1.27	334	287	22	3	12	2-6	1905.1	2042	990	889	241	370-40	1372	.273

Year	Team (League)	W	L	Pct.	ERA	WHIP	G	GS	CG	ShO	Hld.	Sv.-Opp.	IP	H	R	ER	HR	BB-IBB	SO	Avg.
											DIVISION SERIES RECORD									
2004— New York (A.L.)		0	0	...	4.05	1.20	1	1	0	0	0	0-0	6.2	7	3	3	0	1-0	4	.292

CHAMPIONSHIP SERIES RECORD

Year	Team (League)	W	L	Pct.	ERA	WHIP	G	GS	CG	ShO	Hld.	Sv.-Opp.	IP	H	R	ER	HR	BB-IBB	SO	Avg.
2004— New York (A.L.)		1	1	.500	3.14	0.91	2	2	0	0	0	0-0	14.1	12	5	5	1	1-0	5	.231

ALL-STAR GAME RECORD

	W	L	Pct.	ERA	WHIP	G	GS	CG	ShO	Hld.	Sv.-Opp.	IP	H	R	ER	HR	BB-IBB	SO	Avg.
All-Star Game totals (1 year)	0	0	...	18.00	3.00	1	0	0	0	0	0-0	1.0	3	2	2	2	0-0	1	.500

LIEBERTHAL, MIKE — C

PERSONAL: Born January 18, 1972, in Glendale, Calif. ... 6-0/190. ... Bats right, throws right. ... Full name: Michael Scott Lieberthal. ... Name pronounced: LEE-ber-thal. ... High school: Westlake (Westlake Village, Calif.).

TRANSACTIONS/CAREER NOTES: Selected by Philadelphia Phillies organization in first round (third pick overall) of 1990 free-agent draft. ... On disabled list (August 22, 1996-remainder of season; July 24-September 2, 1998; July 18-August 4 and September 11, 2000-remainder of season; and May 13, 2001-remainder of season).

HONORS: Won N.L. Gold Glove at catcher (1999). ... Named N.L. Comeback Player of the Year by THE SPORTING NEWS (2002).

2005 GAMES PLAYED BY POSITION (MLB): C—117.

SCOUTING REPORT **Offense:** His production is starting to plateau, but he had a better second half last season. Bat speed has declined. Is an extremely impatient hitter. Has a lot of trouble handling the ball on the inner half of the plate. Power has declined. Knee problems seem to have affected his ability to drive the ball. Is not a good runner. **Defense:** Arm strength is his best asset. Has a quick release and is accurate. Has good hands behind the plate but has a lot of trouble calling games. Mobility has declined some. **Outlook:** Lieberthal seems to be leveling off in all phases of the game. Should be a better player. Doesn't show much intensity. *Grade 7.5*

MIKE LIEBERTHAL'S HITTING ZONE

.152	.320	.241
.284	.310	.265
.333	.333	.353

LEFTY-RIGHTY SPLITS

vs.	Avg.	AB	H	2B	3B	HR	RBI	BB	SO	OBP	Slg.
L	.276	87	24	11	0	2	13	11	5	.354	.471
R	.259	305	79	14	0	10	34	24	30	.331	.403

Year	Team (League)	Pos.	G	AB	R	H	2B	3B	HR	RBI	BB	SO	HBP	GDP	SB-CS	Avg.	OBP	SLG	OPS	E	Avg.
1990— Martinsville (Appal.)	C	49	184	26	42	9	0	4	22	11	40	2	3	2-0	.228	.279	.342	.622	5	.990
1991— Spartanburg (S. Atl.)	C	72	243	34	74	17	0	0	31	23	25	5	4	1-2	.305	.372	.374	.747	10	.984
— Clearwater (Fla. St.)	C	16	52	7	15	2	0	0	7	3	12	1	2	0-0	.288	.333	.327	.660	1	.993
1992— Reading (East.)	C	86	309	30	88	16	1	2	37	19	26	10	15	4-1	.285	.342	.362	.705	7	.988
— Scran./W.B. (Int'l)	C	16	45	4	9	1	0	0	4	2	5	1	2	0-0	.200	.245	.222	.467	1	.989
1993— Scran./W.B. (Int'l)	C	112	382	35	100	17	0	7	40	24	32	6	15	2-0	.262	.313	.361	.674	11	.985
1994— Scran./W.B. (Int'l)	C-DH	84	296	23	69	16	0	1	32	21	29	2	7	1-1	.233	.286	.297	.583	9	.983
— Philadelphia (N.L.)	C	24	79	6	21	3	1	1	5	3	5	1	4	0-0	.266	.301	.367	.668	4	.969
1995— Philadelphia (N.L.)	C	16	47	1	12	2	0	0	4	5	5	0	1	0-0	.255	.327	.298	.625	1	.991
— Scran./W.B. (Int'l)	C-DH-3B	85	278	44	78	20	2	6	42	44	26	9	14	1-4	.281	.388	.432	.819	5	.991
1996— Philadelphia (N.L.)	C	50	166	21	42	8	0	7	23	10	30	2	4	0-0	.253	.297	.428	.724	3	.990
1997— Philadelphia (N.L.)	C-DH	134	455	59	112	27	1	20	77	44	76	4	10	3-4	.246	.314	.442	.755	12	.988
1998— Philadelphia (N.L.)	C	86	313	39	80	15	3	8	45	17	44	7	4	2-1	.256	.304	.399	.703	8	.988
1999— Philadelphia (N.L.)	C	145	510	84	153	33	1	31	96	44	86	11	15	0-0	.300	.363	.551	.914	3	.997
2000— Philadelphia (N.L.)	C	108	389	55	108	30	0	15	71	40	53	6	12	2-0	.278	.352	.470	.822	5	.994
2001— Philadelphia (N.L.)	C	34	121	21	28	8	0	2	11	12	21	3	2	0-0	.231	.316	.347	.663	2	.992
2002— Philadelphia (N.L.)	C	130	476	46	133	29	2	15	52	38	58	14	16	0-1	.279	.349	.443	.792	6	.993
2003— Philadelphia (N.L.)	C	131	508	68	159	30	1	13	81	38	59	12	14	0-0	.313	.373	.453	.825	9	.990
2004— Philadelphia (N.L.)	C	131	476	58	129	31	1	17	61	37	69	11	19	1-1	.271	.335	.447	.783	6	.993
2005— Philadelphia (N.L.)	C	118	392	48	103	25	0	12	47	35	35	11	6	0-0	.263	.336	.418	.755	6	.993
Major League totals (12 years)		1107	3932	506	1080	241	10	141	573	323	541	82	107	8-7	.275	.339	.449	.788	65	.992

ALL-STAR GAME RECORD

	G	AB	R	H	2B	3B	HR	RBI	BB	SO	HBP	GDP	SB-CS	Avg.	OBP	SLG	OPS	E	Avg.
All-Star Game totals (2 years)	2	3	1	1	0	0	0	0	0	0	0	1	0-0	.333	.333	.333	.667	0	1.000

LIEFER, JEFF — OF/3B

PERSONAL: Born August 17, 1974, in Fontana, Calif. ... 6-3/210. ... Bats left, throws right. ... Full name: Jeffrey David Liefer. ... Name pronounced: LEAF-er. ... High school: Upland (Calif.). ... College: Long Beach State.

TRANSACTIONS/CAREER NOTES: Selected by Cleveland Indians organization in sixth round of 1992 free-agent draft; did not sign. ... Selected by Chicago White Sox organization in first round (25th pick overall) of 1995 free-agent draft. ... On disabled list (March 25-April 17, 2000). ... Traded by White Sox with Ps Orlando Hernandez and Rocky Biddle and cash to Montreal Expos for P Bartolo Colon and 2B/SS Jorge Nunez (January 15, 2003). ... Claimed on waivers by Tampa Bay Devil Rays (June 6, 2003). ... Signed as a free agent by Milwaukee Brewers organization (January 5, 2004). ... Signed as a free agent by Indians organization (November 25, 2004).

2005 GAMES PLAYED BY POSITION (MLB): DH—9, 1B—5, OF—3.

JEFF LIEFER'S HITTING ZONE

.000	.000	.400
.000	.250	.533
.000	.000	.000

LEFTY-RIGHTY SPLITS

vs.	Avg.	AB	H	2B	3B	HR	RBI	BB	SO	OBP	Slg.
L	.000	6	0	0	0	0	0	0	3	.000	.000
R	.220	50	11	2	0	1	8	1	12	.235	.320

Year	Team (League)	Pos.	G	AB	R	H	2B	3B	HR	RBI	BB	SO	HBP	GDP	SB-CS	Avg.	OBP	SLG	OPS	E	Avg.
1996— South Bend (Mid.)	3B-DH	74	277	60	90	14	0	15	58	30	62	5	3	6-5	.325	.396	.538	.933	23	.802
— Prince Will. (Car.)	DH	37	147	17	33	6	0	1	13	11	27	1	6	0-0	.224	.277	.286	.562	0	—
1997— Birmingham (Sou.)	OF-DH	119	474	67	113	24	9	15	71	38	115	7	10	2-0	.238	.302	.422	.724	8	.955
1998— Birmingham (Sou.)	1B-DH-OF	127	471	84	137	33	6	21	89	60	125	9	9	1-2	.291	.381	.520	.901	11	.987
— Calgary (PCL)	OF-1B-DH	8	31	3	8	1	0	1	10	2	12	0	1	0-0	.258	.303	.452	.755	0	1.000
1999— Chicago (A.L.)	OF-1B-DH	45	113	8	28	7	1	0	14	8	28	0	3	2-0	.248	.295	.327	.623	0	1.000

Year	Team (League)	Pos.	G	AB	R	H	2B	3B	HR	RBI	BB	SO	HBP	GDP	SB-CS	Avg.	OBP	SLG	OPS	E	Avg.
	—Charlotte (Int'l)	1B-OF-3B	46	171	36	58	17	1	9	34	21	26	1	3	2-1	.339	.412	.608	1.021	3	.988
2000—	Charlotte (Int'l)	1B-OF-3B	120	445	75	125	29	1	32	91	53	107	2	17	2-3	.281	.356	.566	.923	9	.987
	—Chicago (A.L.)	OF-1B	5	11	0	2	0	0	0	0	0	4	0	0	0-0	.182	.182	.182	.364	1	.900
2001—	Charlotte (Int'l)	1B-3B	32	119	23	34	7	0	6	21	15	41	4	1	3-1	.286	.381	.496	.877	3	.989
	—Chicago (A.L.)	OF-1B-3B																			
		DH	83	254	36	65	13	0	18	39	20	69	2	6	0-1	.256	.313	.520	.833	7	.964
2002—	Chicago (A.L.)	OF-1B-DH	76	204	28	47	8	0	7	26	19	60	0	3	0-0	.230	.295	.373	.667	2	.992
2003—	Montreal (N.L.)	1B	35	88	6	17	3	0	3	18	3	26	0	2	0-1	.193	.247	.330	.547	3	.980
	—Tampa Bay (A.L.)	3B-DH-OF	9	25	4	3	1	0	1	3	3	13	0	0	0-0	.120	.214	.280	.494	1	.938
	—Durham (Int'l)	OF-DH-1B																			
		3B	44	157	20	41	10	3	7	24	14	49	1	2	0-0	.261	.326	.497	.822	1	.988
2004—	Milwaukee (N.L.)	DH-OF	16	28	2	6	2	0	1	5	2	8	0	2	0-0	.214	.258	.393	.651	0	1.000
	—Indianapolis (Int'l)	1B-OF-3B																			
		DH	107	370	60	104	25	1	20	83	47	63	4		1-0	.281	.364	.516	.880	4	.995
2005—	Buffalo (Int'l)	DH-1B-OF																			
		3B	89	321	59	103	27	2	19	68	35	62	2	8	2-1	.321	.388	.595	.983	2	.995
	—Cleveland (A.L.)	DH-1B-OF	19	56	5	11	2	0	1	8	1	15	0	1	0-0	.196	.211	.286	.496	1	.958
	American League totals (6 years)		237	663	81	156	31	1	27	90	51	189	2	13	2-1	.235	.290	.407	.698	12	.981
	National League totals (2 years)		51	116	8	23	5	0	4	23	5	34	0	4	0-1	.198	.228	.345	.572	3	.981
	Major League totals (7 years)		288	779	89	179	36	1	31	113	56	223	2	17	2-2	.230	.281	.398	.679	15	.981

LIGTENBERG, KERRY   P

PERSONAL: Born May 11, 1971, in Rapid City, S.D. ... 6-2/222. ... Throws right, bats right. ... Full name: Kerry Dale Ligtenberg. ... Name pronounced: lite-en-berg. ... High school: Park (Cottage Grove, Minn.). ... College: Minnesota.

TRANSACTIONS/CAREER NOTES: Contract sold by Minneapolis of the independent North Central League to Seattle Mariners organization (March 28, 1995). ... Released by Mariners (April 2, 1995). ... Contract sold by Minneapolis of the independent Prairie League to Atlanta Braves organization (January 27, 1996). ... On disabled list (April 3, 1999-entire season). ... Signed as a free agent by Baltimore Orioles (January 16, 2003). ... Signed as a free agent by Toronto Blue Jays (December 9, 2003). ... On disabled list (June 11-26, 2004). ... Released by Blue Jays (April 1, 2005). ... Signed by Arizona Diamondbacks organization (April 15, 2005).

CAREER HITTING: 0-for-1 (.000), 0 R, 0 2B, 0 3B, 0 HR, 0 RBI.

LEFTY-RIGHTY SPLITS

vs.	Avg.	AB	H	2B	3B	HR	RBI	BB	SO	OBP	Slg.
L	.250	16	4	2	0	1	7	1	1	.294	.563
R	.429	28	12	4	0	3	9	3	4	.484	.893

Year	Team (League)	W	L	Pct.	ERA	WHIP	G	GS	CG	ShO	Hld.	Sv.-Opp.	IP	H	R	ER	HR	BB-IBB	SO	Avg.
1994—	Minneapolis (N.Cen.Pra.) ..	5	5	.500	3.31	1.29	19	19	2	...	...	0-...	114.1	103	47	42	11	44-4	94	.239
1995—	Minneapolis (N.Cen.Pra.) ..	11	2	.846	2.73	1.17	17	15	4	...	...	0-...	108.2	101	41	33	...	26-...	100	...
1996—	Durham (Carol.)	7	4	.636	2.41	1.24	49	0	0	0	...	20-...	59.2	58	20	16	3	16-3	76	.251
1997—	Greenville (Sou.)	3	1	.750	2.04	0.96	31	0	0	0	...	16-...	35.1	20	8	8	3	14-1	43	.160
	—Richmond (Int'l)	0	3	.000	4.32	0.92	14	0	0	0	...	1-...	25.0	21	13	12	3	2-0	35	.236
	—Atlanta (N.L.)	1	0	1.000	3.00	1.07	15	0	0	0	0	1-1	15.0	12	5	5	4	4-2	19	.211
1998—	Atlanta (N.L.)	3	2	.600	2.71	1.03	75	0	0	0	11	30-34	73.0	51	24	22	6	24-1	79	.193
1999—	Atlanta (N.L.)			Did not play.																
2000—	Atlanta (N.L.)	2	3	.400	3.61	1.28	59	0	0	0	12	12-14	52.1	43	21	21	7	24-5	51	.226
	—Richmond (Int'l)	0	0	...	0.00	0.71	5	0	0	0	...	1-...	5.2	0	0	0	0	4-0	7	.000
2001—	Atlanta (N.L.)	3	3	.500	3.02	1.34	53	0	0	0	0	1-2	59.2	50	22	20	4	30-8	56	.226
	—Richmond (Int'l)	0	0	...	0.00	1.00	1	0	0	0	...	0-...	1.0	0	0	0	0	1-0	2	.000
2002—	Atlanta (N.L.)	3	4	.429	2.97	1.28	52	0	0	0	2	0-0	66.2	52	23	22	6	33-3	51	.213
2003—	Baltimore (A.L.)	4	2	.667	3.34	1.25	68	0	0	0	14	1-4	59.1	60	23	22	9	14-3	47	.263
2004—	Toronto (A.L.)	1	6	.143	6.38	1.78	57	0	0	0	4	3-5	55.0	73	40	39	6	25-7	49	.313
2005—	Arizona (N.L.)	0	0	...	13.97	2.07	7	0	0	0	0	0-0	9.2	16	15	15	4	4-0	15	.364
	—Tucson (PCL)	4	3	.571	3.24	1.16	38	0	0	0	5	1-4	50.0	51	18	18	4	7-1	50	.266
	American League totals (2 years)	5	8	.385	4.80	1.50	125	0	0	0	18	4-9	114.1	133	63	61	15	39-10	96	.289
	National League totals (6 years)	12	12	.500	3.42	1.24	261	0	0	0	25	44-51	276.1	224	110	105	31	119-19	261	.220
	Major League totals (8 years)	17	20	.459	3.82	1.32	386	0	0	0	43	48-60	390.2	357	173	166	46	158-29	357	.241

DIVISION SERIES RECORD

Year	Team (League)	W	L	Pct.	ERA	WHIP	G	GS	CG	ShO	Hld.	Sv.-Opp.	IP	H	R	ER	HR	BB-IBB	SO	Avg.
1998—	Atlanta (N.L.)	0	0	...	0.00	1.50	3	0	0	0	0	0-0	3.1	1	0	0	0	4-1	3	.111
2000—	Atlanta (N.L.)	0	0	...	5.40	0.60	3	0	0	0	0	0-0	1.2	0	1	1	0	1-1	3	.000
2001—	Atlanta (N.L.)			Did not play.																
2002—	Atlanta (N.L.)	0	0	...	0.00	0.00	1	0	0	0	0	0-0	2.0	0	0	0	0	0-0	1	.000
	Division series totals (3 years)	0	0	...	1.29	0.86	7	0	0	0	0	0-0	7.0	1	1	1	0	5-2	7	.048

CHAMPIONSHIP SERIES RECORD

Year	Team (League)	W	L	Pct.	ERA	WHIP	G	GS	CG	ShO	Hld.	Sv.-Opp.	IP	H	R	ER	HR	BB-IBB	SO	Avg.
1997—	Atlanta (N.L.)	0	0	...	0.00	0.33	2	0	0	0	0	0-0	3.0	1	0	0	0	0-0	4	.111
1998—	Atlanta (N.L.)	0	1	.000	7.36	1.36	4	0	0	0	0	0-0	3.2	3	3	3	2	2-0	5	.214
2001—	Atlanta (N.L.)	0	0	...	0.00	0.33	2	0	0	0	0	0-0	3.0	0	0	0	0	1-0	2	.000
	Champ. series totals (3 years)	0	1	.000	2.79	0.72	8	0	0	0	0	0-0	9.2	4	3	3	2	3-0	11	.129

LILLY, TED   P

PERSONAL: Born January 4, 1976, in Lomita, Calif. ... 6-1/190. ... Throws left, bats left. ... Full name: Theodore Roosevelt Lilly. ... Name pronounced: LILL-ee. ... High school: Yosemite (Oakhurst, Calif.). ... Junior college: Fresno City (Calif.).

TRANSACTIONS/CAREER NOTES: Selected by Los Angeles Dodgers organization in 23rd round of 1996 free-agent draft. ... Traded by Dodgers with 2B Wilton Guerrero, OF Peter Bergeron and 1B Jonathan Tucker to Montreal Expos for P Carlos Perez, SS Mark Grudzielanek and IF Hiram Bocachica (July 31, 1998). ... Traded by Expos to New York Yankees (March 17, 2000), as part of deal in which Yankees traded P Hideki Irabu to Expos for P Jake Westbrook and two players to be named (December 29, 1999); Yankees acquired P Christian Parker to complete deal (March 22, 2000). ... On disabled list (April 2-May 23, 2000); included rehabilitation assignments to Tampa and Columbus. ... On suspended list (August 11-17, 2001). ... Traded by Yankees with OF John-Ford Griffin and P Jason Arnold to Oakland Athletics as part of three-team deal in which Tigers acquired 1B Carlos Pena, P Franklyn German and a player to be named from A's and Yankees acquired P Jeff Weaver from Tigers (July 5, 2002); Tigers acquired P Jeremy Bonderman to complete deal (August 22, 2002). ... On disabled list (July 23-September 10, 2002). ... Traded by Athletics to Toronto Blue Jays for OF Bobby Kielty and cash (November 18, 2003). ... On disabled list (March 25-April 10 and July 30-September 6, 2005); included rehabilitation assignment to Syracuse.

CAREER HITTING: 1-for-20 (.050), 0 R, 0 2B, 0 3B, 0 HR, 0 RBI.

SCOUTING REPORT

Throws: He doesn't throw as hard as he once did, but he pitches in the 86-88 mph range. Throws a curveball and a changeup, too. **Tendencies:** His delivery and mechanics continue to be a problem. Is using his legs more but still recoils some, putting pressure on his shoulder; has had shoulder problems in the past. Velocity is down and fastball is up. Big looping curve has good rotation. Has good movement to change. Is a fly-ball pitcher. **Outlook:** Lilly may never be 100 percent, and with his delivery is always going to pitch up in the zone. **Grade 6.9**

TED LILLY'S PITCHING ZONE

.220	.333	.300
.321	.457	.300
.148	.200	.184

LEFTY-RIGHTY SPLITS

vs.	Avg.	AB	H	2B	3B	HR	RBI	BB	SO	OBP	Slg.
L	.336	134	45	8	2	4	18	10	26	.381	.515
R	.248	363	90	16	0	19	56	48	70	.337	.449

Year Team (League)	W	L	Pct.	ERA	WHIP	G	GS	CG	ShO	Hld.	Sv.-Opp.	IP	H	R	ER	HR	BB-IBB	SO	Avg.
1996—Yakima (N'west)	4	0	1.000	0.84	0.73	13	8	0	0	...	0-...	53.2	25	9	5	0	14-1	75	.135
1997—San Bern. (Calif.)	7	8	.467	2.81	1.10	23	21	2	1	...	0-...	134.2	116	52	42	9	32-0	158	.234
1998—San Antonio (Texas)	8	4	.667	3.30	1.35	17	17	0	0	...	0-...	111.2	114	50	41	8	37-0	96	.266
—Albuquerque (PCL)	1	3	.250	4.94	1.55	5	5	0	0	...	0-...	31.0	39	20	17	3	9-0	25	.310
—Ottawa (Int'l)	2	2	.500	4.85	1.64	7	7	0	0	...	0-...	39.0	45	28	21	8	19-0	49	.280
1999—Ottawa (Int'l)	8	5	.615	3.84	1.17	16	16	0	0	...	0-...	89.0	81	40	38	12	23-0	78	.241
—Montreal (N.L.)	0	1	.000	7.61	1.65	9	3	0	0	0	0-0	23.2	30	20	20	7	9-0	28	.309
2000—Tampa (Fla. St.)	0	0	...	1.35	0.90	1	1	0	0	0	0-0	6.2	5	3	1	0	1-0	6	.192
—Columbus (Int'l)	8	11	.421	4.19	1.49	22	22	3	1	...	0-...	137.1	157	77	64	14	48-0	127	.287
—New York (A.L.)	0	0	...	5.63	1.63	7	0	0	0	0	0-0	8.0	8	6	5	1	5-0	11	.235
2001—Columbus (Int'l)	0	0	...	2.84	0.95	5	5	0	0	...	0-...	25.1	16	10	8	2	8-0	30	.176
—New York (A.L.)	5	6	.455	5.37	1.47	26	21	0	0	0	0-0	120.2	126	81	72	20	51-1	112	.267
2002—New York (A.L.)	3	6	.333	3.40	1.06	16	11	2	1	0	0-0	76.2	57	31	29	10	24-3	59	.202
—Oakland (A.L.)	2	1	.667	4.63	1.29	5	5	0	0	0	0-0	23.1	23	12	12	5	7-0	18	.253
2003—Oakland (A.L.)	12	10	.545	4.34	1.33	32	31	0	0	0	0-0	178.1	179	92	86	24	58-3	147	.255
2004—Toronto (A.L.)	12	10	.545	4.06	1.32	32	32	2	1	0	0-0	197.1	171	92	89	26	89-2	168	.230
2005—Syracuse (Int'l)	0	1	.000	3.12	1.15	2	2	0	0	0	0-0	8.2	5	4	3	1	5-0	9	.172
—Toronto (A.L.)	10	11	.476	5.56	1.53	25	25	0	0	0	0-0	126.1	135	79	78	23	58-1	96	.272
American League totals (6 years)	44	44	.500	4.57	1.36	144	125	4	2	0	0-0	730.2	699	393	371	109	292-10	611	.248
National League totals (1 year)	0	1	.000	7.61	1.65	9	3	0	0	0	0-0	23.2	30	20	20	7	9-0	28	.309
Major League totals (7 years)	44	45	.494	4.67	1.37	153	128	4	2	0	0-0	754.1	729	413	391	116	301-10	639	.250

DIVISION SERIES RECORD

Year Team (League)	W	L	Pct.	ERA	WHIP	G	GS	CG	ShO	Hld.	Sv.-Opp.	IP	H	R	ER	HR	BB-IBB	SO	Avg.
2002—Oakland (A.L.)	0	1	.000	13.50	2.75	2	0	0	0	0	0-1	4.0	10	6	6	1	1-0	3	.476
2003—Oakland (A.L.)	0	0	...	0.00	0.44	2	1	0	0	0	0-0	9.0	2	1	0	0	2-0	7	.065
Division series totals (2 years)	0	1	.000	4.15	1.15	4	1	0	0	0	0-1	13.0	12	7	6	1	3-0	10	.231

ALL-STAR GAME RECORD

Year Team (League)	W	L	Pct.	ERA	WHIP	G	GS	CG	ShO	Hld.	Sv.-Opp.	IP	H	R	ER	HR	BB-IBB	SO	Avg.
All-Star Game totals (1 year)	0	0	...	0.00	2.00	1	0	0	0	0	0-0	1.0	2	0	0	0	0-0	1	.400

LIMA, JOSE   P

PERSONAL: Born September 30, 1972, in Santiago, Dominican Republic. ... 6-2/205. ... Throws right, bats right. ... Full name: Jose Desiderio Lima. ... Name pronounced: LEE-mah. ... High school: Escuela Primaria Las Charcas (Santiago, Dominican Republic).
TRANSACTIONS/CAREER NOTES: Signed as a non-drafted free agent by Detroit Tigers organization (July 5, 1989). ... Traded by Tigers with C Brad Ausmus, Ps C.J. Nitkowski and Trever Miller and 1B Daryle Ward to Houston Astros for OF Brian Hunter, IF Orlando Miller, Ps Doug Brocail and Todd Jones and cash (December 10, 1996). ... On suspended list (May 9-15, 2001). ... Traded by Astros to Detroit Tigers for P Dave Mlicki (June 23, 2001). ... Released by Tigers (September 7, 2002). ... Contract purchased by Kansas City Royals from Newark of the independent Atlantic League (June 4, 2003). ... On disabled list (August 2-18 and August 24-September 18, 2003). ... Signed as a free agent by Los Angeles Dodgers organization (January 27, 2004). ... Signed as a free agent by Royals (December 25, 2004).
CAREER HITTING: 38-for-287 (.132), 18 R, 4 2B, 0 3B, 0 HR, 10 RBI.

SCOUTING REPORT

Throws: He uses an 87-89 mph fastball, a curve, a slider and a changeup, but all his pitches are short. **Tendencies:** The most animated pitcher in the game, Lima is a slinger who has some tailing action to his fastball if he stays on top of the ball. Curve is big and sweeping to lefthanders while his slider has a tighter spin running from righthanders. Change is his best pitch because he can throw it on both sides of the plate to all batters. Makes too many mistakes in the middle of the plate. **Outlook:** He no longer has the arm speed to allow his pitches to bite late. Is near the end of his career. Will go into spring training looking for a job. **Grade 5.5**

JOSE LIMA'S PITCHING ZONE

.306	.306	.480
.470	.338	.342
.159	.286	.309

LEFTY-RIGHTY SPLITS

vs.	Avg.	AB	H	2B	3B	HR	RBI	BB	SO	OBP	Slg.
L	.302	324	98	28	3	17	65	37	29	.379	.565
R	.324	374	121	30	2	14	66	24	51	.367	.527

Year Team (League)	W	L	Pct.	ERA	WHIP	G	GS	CG	ShO	Hld.	Sv.-Opp.	IP	H	R	ER	HR	BB-IBB	SO	Avg.
1990—Bristol (Appal.)	3	8	.273	5.02	1.47	14	14	1	0	...	1-...	75.1	89	49	42	9	22-3	64	.299
1991—Lakeland (Fla. St.)	0	1	.000	10.38	2.08	4	1	0	0	...	0-...	8.2	16	10	10	1	2-0	5	.421
—Fayetteville (S. Atl.)	1	3	.250	4.97	1.34	18	7	0	0	...	0-...	58.0	53	38	32	4	25-0	60	.241
1992—Lakeland (Fla. St.)	5	11	.313	3.16	1.01	25	25	5	2	...	0-...	151.0	132	57	53	14	21-2	137	.237
1993—London (East.)	8	13	.381	4.07	1.24	27	27	2	0	...	0-...	177.0	160	96	80	19	59-4	138	.238
1994—Toledo (Int'l)	7	9	.438	3.60	1.21	23	22	3	2	...	0-...	142.1	124	70	57	16	48-1	117	.235
—Detroit (A.L.)	0	1	.000	13.50	2.10	3	1	0	0	0	0-0	6.2	11	10	10	2	3-1	7	.393
1995—Lakeland (Fla. St.)	3	1	.750	2.57	1.10	4	4	0	0	0	0-0	21.0	23	11	6	2	0-0	20	.271
—Toledo (Int'l)	5	3	.625	3.01	1.11	11	11	1	0	0	0-0	74.2	69	26	25	9	14-2	40	.247
—Detroit (A.L.)	3	9	.250	6.11	1.40	15	15	0	0	0	0-0	73.2	85	52	50	10	18-4	37	.288
1996—Toledo (Int'l)	5	4	.556	6.78	1.52	12	12	0	0	0	0-0	69.0	93	53	52	11	12-0	57	.322
—Detroit (A.L.)	5	6	.455	5.70	1.50	39	4	0	0	0	6	3-7	72.2	87	48	46	13	22-4	59	.296

Year	Team (League)	W	L	Pct.	ERA	WHIP	G	GS	CG	ShO	Hld.	Sv.-Opp.	IP	H	R	ER	HR	BB-IBB	SO	Avg.
1997—	Houston (N.L.)	1	6	.143	5.28	1.27	52	1	0	0	0	2-2	75.0	79	45	44	9	16-2	63	.271
1998—	Houston (N.L.)	16	8	.667	3.70	1.12	33	33	3	1	0	0-0	233.1	229	100	96	34	32-1	169	.256
1999—	Houston (N.L.)	21	10	.677	3.58	1.22	35	•35	3	0	0	0-0	246.1	256	108	98	30	44-2	187	.265
2000—	Houston (N.L.)	7	16	.304	6.65	1.62	33	33	0	0	0	0-0	196.1	251	*152	*145	*48	68-3	124	.313
2001—	Houston (N.L.)	1	2	.333	7.30	1.75	14	9	0	0	0	0-0	53.0	77	48	43	12	16-1	41	.350
—	Detroit (A.L.)	5	10	.333	4.71	1.26	18	18	2	0	0	0-0	112.2	120	66	59	23	22-2	43	.274
2002—	Detroit (A.L.)	4	6	.400	7.77	1.57	20	12	0	0	0	0-0	68.1	86	60	59	12	21-0	33	.314
2003—	Kansas City (A.L.)	8	3	.727	4.91	1.45	14	14	0	0	0	0-0	73.1	80	40	40	7	26-0	32	.280
2004—	Los Angeles (N.L.)	13	5	.722	4.07	1.24	36	24	0	0	1	0-0	170.1	178	81	77	33	34-6	93	.271
2005—	Kansas City (A.L.)	5	16	.238	6.99	1.66	32	32	1	0	0	0-0	168.2	219	*140	*131	31	61-1	80	.314
	American League totals (7 years)	30	51	.370	6.17	1.49	141	96	3	0	6	3-7	576.0	688	416	395	98	173-12	291	.297
	National League totals (6 years)	59	47	.557	4.65	1.31	203	135	6	1	4	2-2	974.1	1070	534	503	166	210-15	677	.279
	Major League totals (12 years)	89	98	.476	5.21	1.38	344	231	9	1	10	5-9	1550.1	1758	950	898	264	383-27	968	.286

DIVISION SERIES RECORD

Year	Team (League)	W	L	Pct.	ERA	WHIP	G	GS	CG	ShO	Hld.	Sv.-Opp.	IP	H	R	ER	HR	BB-IBB	SO	Avg.
1997—	Houston (N.L.)	0	0	...	0.00	1.00	1	0	0	0	0	0-0	1.0	0	0	0	0	1-0	1	.000
1998—	Houston (N.L.)			Did not play.																
1999—	Houston (N.L.)	0	1	.000	5.40	1.65	1	1	0	0	0	0-0	6.2	9	4	4	0	2-2	4	.333
2004—	Los Angeles (N.L.)	1	0	1.000	0.00	0.67	1	1	1	0	0	0-0	9.0	5	0	0	0	1-0	4	.161
	Division series totals (3 years)	1	1	.500	2.16	1.08	3	2	1	0	0	0-0	16.2	14	4	4	0	4-2	9	.233

ALL-STAR GAME RECORD

		W	L	Pct.	ERA	WHIP	G	GS	CG	ShO	Hld.	Sv.-Opp.	IP	H	R	ER	HR	BB-IBB	SO	Avg.
	All-Star Game totals (1 year)	0	0	...	0.00	1.00	1	0	0	0	0	0-0	1.0	1	0	0	0	0-0	0	.250

LINDEN, TODD — OF

PERSONAL: Born June 30, 1980, in Edmonds, Wash. ... 6-3/210. ... Bats both, throws right. ... Full name: Todd Anthony Linden. ... High school: Central Kitsap (Silverdale, Wash.). ... College: Louisiana State.

TRANSACTIONS/CAREER NOTES: Selected by San Francisco Giants in supplemental round ("sandwich pick" between first and second rounds, 41st pick overall) of 2001 free-agent draft; pick received as part of compensation for Cleveland Indians signing Type A free-agent OF Ellis Burks.

2005 GAMES PLAYED BY POSITION (MLB): OF—52.

TODD LINDEN'S HITTING ZONE

.222	.000	.211
.280	.250	.219
.400	.333	.154

LEFTY-RIGHTY SPLITS

vs.	Avg.	AB	H	2B	3B	HR	RBI	BB	SO	OBP	Slg.
L	.300	30	9	2	0	1	2	3	6	.364	.467
R	.199	141	28	6	0	3	11	7	48	.261	.305

Year	Team (League)	Pos.	G	AB	R	H	2B	3B	HR	RBI	BB	SO	HBP	GDP	SB-CS	Avg.	OBP	SLG	OPS	E	Avg.
2002—	Shreveport (Texas)	OF	111	392	64	123	26	2	12	52	61	101	4	12	9-5	.314	.419	.482	.901	3	.987
—	Fresno (PCL)	OF	29	100	18	25	2	1	3	10	20	35	1	2	2-0	.250	.380	.380	.760	0	1.000
2003—	Fresno (PCL)	OF-DH	125	471	75	131	24	3	11	56	40	105	17	9	14-4	.278	.356	.412	.768	4	.985
—	San Francisco (N.L.)	OF	18	38	2	8	1	0	1	6	1	8	0	2	0-0	.211	.231	.316	.547	1	.929
2004—	Fresno (PCL)	OF-DH	130	489	93	127	28	2	23	75	63	149	7	9	8-6	.260	.349	.466	.816	7	.976
—	San Francisco (N.L.)	OF	16	32	6	5	1	0	0	1	5	7	1	0	0-0	.156	.289	.188	.477	0	1.000
2005—	Fresno (PCL)	OF-DH	95	340	81	109	25	4	30	80	62	97	10	11	6-2	.321	.437	.682	1.120	8	.977
—	San Francisco (N.L.)	OF	60	171	20	37	8	0	4	13	10	54	5	5	3-0	.216	.280	.333	.613	2	.983
	Major League totals (3 years)		94	241	28	50	10	0	5	20	16	69	6	7	3-0	.207	.274	.311	.585	3	.978

LINEBRINK, SCOTT — P

PERSONAL: Born August 4, 1976, in Austin, Texas. ... 6-3/208. ... Throws right, bats right. ... Full name: Scott Cameron Linebrink. ... High school: McNeil (Austin, Texas). ... College: Texas State.

TRANSACTIONS/CAREER NOTES: Selected by San Francisco Giants organization in second round of 1997 free-agent draft. ... Traded by Giants to Houston Astros for P Doug Henry (July 30, 2000). ... On disabled list (May 20-June 17, 2002); included rehabilitation assignments to New Orleans and Round Rock. ... Claimed on waivers by San Diego Padres (May 29, 2003).

CAREER HITTING: 3-for-16 (.188), 0 R, 1 2B, 0 3B, 0 HR, 0 RBI.

SCOUTING REPORT ***Throws:*** Linebrink's fastball ranges from 91-94 mph. Throws both a changeup and a split-finger fastball in the mid-80s. Also has a slider. ***Tendencies:*** He comes right at hitters. Fastball occasionally will straighten out if it's up, but his delivery creates deception and hitters have a difficult time picking it up. Slider is very hard and tight. Uses his changeup early in the count and his splitter as an out pitch. Hitters have difficulty distinguishing between the change and splitter; both have very good life. ***Outlook:*** Linebrink is an underrated setup reliever who can be stretched out beyond one inning. ***Grade 7.8***

SCOTT LINEBRINK'S PITCHING ZONE

.063	.250	.188
.184	.219	.417
.056	.417	.250

LEFTY-RIGHTY SPLITS

vs.	Avg.	AB	H	2B	3B	HR	RBI	BB	SO	OBP	Slg.
L	.195	133	26	5	2	2	13	10	38	.252	.308
R	.223	130	29	4	1	2	11	13	32	.294	.315

Year	Team (League)	W	L	Pct.	ERA	WHIP	G	GS	CG	ShO	Hld.	Sv.-Opp.	IP	H	R	ER	HR	BB-IBB	SO	Avg.
1997—	Salem-Keizer (N'west)	0	0	...	4.50	1.30	3	3	0	0	...	0-...	10.0	7	5	5	1	6-0	6	.194
—	San Jose (Calif.)	2	1	.667	3.18	1.38	6	6	0	0	...	0-...	28.1	29	11	10	2	10-0	40	.243
1998—	Shreveport (Texas)	10	8	.556	5.02	1.41	21	21	0	0	...	0-...	113.0	101	66	63	12	58-1	128	.243
1999—	Shreveport (Texas)	3	8	.111	6.44	1.43	10	10	0	0	...	0-...	43.1	48	31	31	7	14-0	33	.279
2000—	Fresno (PCL)	1	4	.200	5.23	1.06	28	7	0	0	...	4-...	62.0	54	42	36	10	12-0	49	.225
—	San Francisco (N.L.)	0	0	...	11.57	3.86	2	0	0	0	0	0-0	2.1	7	3	3	1	2-0	0	.500

Year Team (League)	W	L	Pct.	ERA	WHIP	G	GS	CG	ShO	Hld.	Sv.-Opp.	IP	H	R	ER	HR	BB-IBB	SO	Avg.
—Houston (N.L.)	0	0	...	4.66	1.76	8	0	0	0	0	0-0	9.2	11	5	5	3	6-0	6	.289
—New Orleans (PCL)	2	0	1.000	1.80	1.47	11	0	0	0	0	1-...	15.0	15	4	3	0	7-0	22	.259
2001—Houston (N.L.)	0	0	...	2.61	1.16	9	0	0	0	0	0-0	10.1	6	4	3	0	6-0	9	.176
—New Orleans (PCL)	7	6	.538	3.50	1.06	50	0	0	0	0	8-...	72.0	52	28	28	4	24-6	72	.204
2002—Houston (N.L.)	0	0	...	7.03	1.81	22	0	0	0	1	0-0	24.1	31	21	19	2	13-4	24	.298
—New Orleans (PCL)	1	1	.500	6.00	1.87	13	0	0	0	0	0-...	15.0	17	11	10	1	11-3	16	.293
—Round Rock (Texas)	0	0	...	0.00	2.00	2	0	0	0	0	0-...	2.0	2	0	0	0	2-0	1	.286
2003—New Orleans (PCL)	0	2	.000	2.70	1.30	2	2	0	0	0	0-...	10.0	8	3	3	1	5-0	6	.222
—Houston (N.L.)	1	1	.500	4.26	1.64	9	6	0	0	0	0-0	31.2	38	15	15	4	14-1	17	.317
—San Diego (N.L.)	2	1	.667	2.82	1.27	43	0	0	0	0	6	0-0	60.2	55	22	19	5	22-3	51	.244
2004—San Diego (N.L.)	7	3	.700	2.14	1.04	73	0	0	0	28	0-5	84.0	61	22	20	8	26-2	83	.209
2005—San Diego (N.L.)	8	1	.889	1.83	1.06	73	0	0	0	26	1-6	73.2	55	17	15	4	23-4	70	.209
Major League totals (6 years)	18	6	.750	3.00	1.27	240	6	0	0	61	1-11	296.2	264	109	99	27	112-14	260	.242

DIVISION SERIES RECORD

Year Team (League)	W	L	Pct.	ERA	WHIP	G	GS	CG	ShO	Hld.	Sv.-Opp.	IP	H	R	ER	HR	BB-IBB	SO	Avg.
2005—San Diego (N.L.)	0	0	...	0.00	2.00	1	0	0	0	0	0-0	1.0	2	0	0	0	0-0	1	.400

LIRIANO, FRANCISCO   P

PERSONAL: Born October 26, 1983, in San Cristobal, Dominican Republic. ... 6-2/185. ... Throws left, bats left. ... Full name: Francisco Casillas Liriano. ... High school: Americo Pere (Dominican Republic).

TRANSACTIONS/CAREER NOTES: Signed as a nondrafted free agent by San Francisco Giants organization (September 9, 2000). ... Traded by Giants with Ps Boof Bonser and Joe Nathan to Minnesota Twins for C A.J. Pierzynski and cash (November 14, 2003).

CAREER HITTING: 0-for-0 (.000), 0 R, 0 2B, 0 3B, 0 HR, 0 RBI.

SCOUTING REPORT **Throws:** His fastball tops out at 97 mph, and he has a changeup, curve and slider. **Tendencies:** He is a hard-throwing lefthander who showed good stuff in a short call-up, but he must develop more command. Has the makeup and work ethic to gain the respect of any pitching coach. His body should fill out, giving him extra endurance and drive to the plate. **Outlook:** Barring a huge surprise in spring training, he will return to the minors for more development. Should be watched for a recurrence of shoulder problems. **Grade 7**

FRANCISCO LIRIANO'S PITCHING ZONE

.000	.250	.000
.263	.385	.333
.333	.333	.000

LEFTY-RIGHTY SPLITS

vs.	Avg.	AB	H	2B	3B	HR	RBI	BB	SO	OBP	Slg.
L	.222	18	4	1	0	1	3	2	10	.300	.444
R	.221	68	15	1	1	3	10	5	23	.274	.397

Year Team (League)	W	L	Pct.	ERA	WHIP	G	GS	CG	ShO	Hld.	Sv.-Opp.	IP	H	R	ER	HR	BB-IBB	SO	Avg.
2001—Ariz. Giants (Ariz.)	5	4	.556	3.63	1.21	13	12	0	0	...	0-...	62.0	51	26	25	3	24-0	67	.232
—Salem-Keizer (N'west)	0	0	...	5.00	0.89	2	2	0	0	...	0-...	9.0	7	5	5	2	1-0	12	.206
2002—Hagerstown (SAL)	3	6	.333	3.49	1.15	16	16	0	0	...	0-...	80.0	61	45	31	6	31-0	85	.210
2003—San Jose (Calif.)	0	1	.000	54.00	10.50	1	1	0	0	...	0-...	0.2	5	4	4	0	2-0	0	.714
—Ariz. Giants (Ariz.)	0	1	.000	4.32	1.32	4	4	0	0	...	0-...	8.1	5	4	4	1	6-0	9	.192
2004—Fort Myers (FSL)	6	7	.462	4.00	1.38	21	21	0	0	...	0-...	117.0	118	56	52	7	43-2	125	.269
—New Britain (East.)	3	2	.600	3.18	1.56	7	7	0	0	...	0-...	39.2	45	14	14	4	17-0	49	.287
2005—New Britain (East.)	3	5	.375	3.64	1.25	13	13	0	0	0	0-0	76.2	70	36	31	6	26-0	92	.242
—Rochester (Int'l)	9	2	.818	1.78	0.88	14	14	0	0	0	0-0	91.0	56	25	18	4	24-0	112	.177
—Minnesota (A.L.)	1	2	.333	5.70	1.10	6	4	0	0	0	0-0	23.2	19	15	15	4	7-0	33	.221
Major League totals (1 year)	1	2	.333	5.70	1.10	6	4	0	0	0	0-0	23.2	19	15	15	4	7-0	33	.221

LIRIANO, PEDRO   P

PERSONAL: Born October 23, 1980, in Fantino, Dominican Republic. ... 6-2/170. ... Throws right, bats right. ... Full name: Pedro Antonio Liriano. ... High school: Fourth Bachillerato (Dominican Republic). ... Cousin of Ramon Ortiz, pitcher, Cincinnati Reds.

TRANSACTIONS/CAREER NOTES: Signed as a non-drafted free agent by Anaheim Angels organization (November 10, 1998). ... Traded by Angels to Milwaukee Brewers (September 20, 2002), completing deal in which Angels acquired OF Alex Ochoa and C Sal Fasano from Brewers for C Jorge Fabregas and two players to be named (July 31, 2002); Brewers acquired 2B Johnny Raburn as part of deal (August 14, 2002). ... Claimed on waivers by Philadelphia Phillies (December 6, 2004).

CAREER HITTING: 0-for-1 (.000), 0 R, 0 2B, 0 3B, 0 HR, 0 RBI.

LEFTY-RIGHTY SPLITS

vs.	Avg.	AB	H	2B	3B	HR	RBI	BB	SO	OBP	Slg.
L	.400	15	6	3	1	1	6	0	0	.400	.933
R	.235	17	4	1	0	2	7	6	6	.458	.647

Year Team (League)	W	L	Pct.	ERA	WHIP	G	GS	CG	ShO	Hld.	Sv.-Opp.	IP	H	R	ER	HR	BB-IBB	SO	Avg.
1999—Dom. Angels (DSL)	7	2	.778	1.83	0.88	17	9	3	1	...	0-...	78.2	46	23	16	3	23-...	61	...
2000—Dom. Angels (DSL)	5	1	.833	1.25	0.82	12	11	1	1	...	0-...	79.0	36	19	11	3	29-...	78	...
2001—Provo (Pion.)	11	2	.846	2.78	1.43	15	14	0	0	...	0-...	77.2	80	39	24	3	31-0	76	.265
2002—Rancho Cuca. (Calif.)	10	14	.417	3.60	1.21	28	28	1	1	...	0-...	167.1	129	86	67	14	74-1	176	.212
2003—Huntsville (Sou.)	9	13	.409	3.79	1.40	27	26	0	0	...	0-...	142.2	138	77	60	12	62-2	116	.256
2004—Indianapolis (Int'l)	3	10	.231	5.20	1.58	29	21	1	0	...	1-...	126.1	149	81	73	21	50-1	97	.300
—Milwaukee (N.L.)	0	0	...	4.02	1.15	11	0	0	0	1	0-0	15.2	15	10	7	3	3-0	10	.238
2005—Scran./W.B. (I.L.)	4	9	.308	3.90	1.39	22	17	0	0	1	0-0	99.1	90	49	43	11	48-1	79	.245
—Philadelphia (N.L.)	0	0	...	10.57	2.09	5	0	0	0	0	0-0	7.2	10	11	9	3	6-0	6	.313
Major League totals (2 years)	0	0	...	6.17	1.46	16	0	0	0	1	0-0	23.1	25	21	16	6	9-0	16	.263

LOAIZA, ESTEBAN   P

PERSONAL: Born December 31, 1971, in Tijuana, Mexico. ... 6-3/215. ... Throws right, bats right. ... Full name: Esteban Antonio Veyna Loaiza. ... Name pronounced: ess-TAY-bahn low-EYE-zah. ... High school: Mar Vista (Imperial Beach, Calif.).

TRANSACTIONS/CAREER NOTES: Signed as a non-drafted free agent by Pittsburgh Pirates organization (March 21, 1991). ... Loaned by Pirates organization to Mexico City Red Devils of the Mexican League (May 7-28, 1993; and June 19-August 14, 1996). ... Traded by Pirates to Texas Rangers for P Todd Van Poppel and 2B Warren Morris (July 17, 1998). ... On disabled list (May 12-July 5, 1999); included rehabilitation assignment to Oklahoma City. ... Traded by Rangers to Toronto Blue Jays for P Darwin Cubillan and 2B/SS Michael Young (July 19, 2000). ... On disabled list (March 22-May 14, 2002); included rehabilitation assignments to Dunedin, Syracuse and Tennessee. ... Signed as a free agent by Chicago White Sox organization (January 27, 2003). ... Traded by White Sox to New York Yankees for P Jose Contreras and cash (July 31, 2004). ... Signed as a free agent by Washington Nationals (January 19, 2005).

CAREER HITTING: 43-for-253 (.170), 15 R, 4 2B, 1 3B, 0 HR, 15 RBI.

SCOUTING REPORT Throws: Loaiza, who used to throw every pitch in the book, now is a two-pitch guy who relies on a cutter that tops out at 91 mph and a straight changeup. ***Tendencies:*** He can be successful as long as he gets very late movement on his cut fastball, which has good depth. Uses the cutter on both sides of the plate and occasionally will ride it. Must have very good command to win. His change is a show pitch. Has a very good delivery. ***Outlook:*** Loaiza is an extremely durable starter, capable of logging more than 200 innings in a season. ***Grade 7.6***

ESTEBAN LOAIZA'S PITCHING ZONE

.340	.268	.275
.303	.337	.262
.217	.327	.167

LEFTY-RIGHTY SPLITS

vs.	Avg.	AB	H	2B	3B	HR	RBI	BB	SO	OBP	Slg.
L	.285	425	121	26	2	7	34	38	88	.346	.405
R	.255	415	106	16	0	11	48	17	85	.287	.373

Year	Team (League)	W	L	Pct.	ERA	WHIP	G	GS	CG	ShO	Hld.	Sv.-Opp.	IP	H	R	ER	HR	BB-IBB	SO	Avg.
1991—	GC Pirates (GCL)	5	1	.833	2.26	1.20	11	11	1	•1	...	0-...	51.2	48	17	13	0	14-0	41	.241
1992—	Augusta (S. Atl.)	10	8	.556	3.89	1.35	26	25	3	0	...	0-...	143.1	134	72	62	7	60-0	123	.249
1993—	Salem (Carol.)	6	7	.462	3.39	1.31	17	17	3	0	...	0-...	109.0	113	53	41	7	30-0	61	.268
—	M.C. R. Dev. (Mex.)	1	1	.500	5.18	1.48	4	3	0	0	...	0-...	24.1	32	18	14		4-...	15	...
—	Carolina (Southern)	2	1	.667	3.77	1.19	7	7	1	0	...	0-...	43.0	39	18	18	5	12-1	40	.241
1994—	Carolina (Southern)	10	5	.667	3.79	1.29	24	24	3	0	...	0-...	154.1	169	69	65	15	30-0	115	.280
1995—	Pittsburgh (N.L.)	8	9	.471	5.16	1.51	32	•31	1	0	0	0-0	172.2	205	*115	*99	21	55-3	85	.300
1996—	Calgary (PCL)	3	4	.429	4.02	1.24	12	11	1	0	...	0-...	69.1	61	34	31	5	25-2	38	.243
—	Pittsburgh (N.L.)	2	3	.400	4.96	1.59	10	10	1	1	0	0-0	52.2	65	34	29	11	19-2	32	.308
—	M.C. R. Dev. (Mex.)	2	0	1.000	2.43	1.26	5	5	0	0	...	0-...	33.1	28	12	9		14-...	16	...
1997—	Pittsburgh (N.L.)	11	11	.500	4.13	1.38	33	32	1	0	0	0-0	196.1	214	99	90	17	56-9	122	.279
1998—	Pittsburgh (N.L.)	6	5	.545	4.52	1.37	21	14	0	0	0	0-1	91.2	96	50	46	13	30-1	53	.275
—	Texas (A.L.)	3	6	.333	5.90	1.58	14	14	1	0	0	0-0	79.1	103	57	52	15	22-3	53	.316
1999—	Texas (A.L.)	9	5	.643	4.56	1.40	30	15	0	0	0	0-0	120.1	128	65	61	10	40-2	77	.275
—	Oklahoma (PCL)	0	0	...	0.00	1.38	2	2	0	0	...	0-...	4.1	3	0	0	0	3-0	6	.188
2000—	Texas (A.L.)	5	6	.455	5.37	1.53	20	17	0	0	0	1-1	107.1	133	67	64	21	31-1	75	.302
—	Toronto (A.L.)	5	7	.417	3.62	1.32	14	14	1	1	0	0-0	92.0	95	45	37	8	26-0	62	.270
2001—	Toronto (A.L.)	11	11	.500	5.02	1.47	36	30	1	0	0	0-0	190.0	239	113	106	27	40-1	110	.309
2002—	Toronto (A.L.)	9	10	.474	5.71	1.52	25	25	3	1	0	0-0	151.1	192	102	96	18	38-3	87	.309
—	Dunedin (Fla. St.)	0	0	...	0.00	0.80	2	2	0	0	...	0-...	5.0	2	0	0	0	2-0	2	.125
—	Syracuse (Int'l)	0	0	...	2.08	0.92	1	1	0	0	...	0-...	4.1	4	1	1	0	0-0	4	.250
—	Tennessee (Sou.)	2	0	1.000	1.88	0.77	2	2	0	0	...	0-...	14.1	10	3	3	0	1-0	13	.208
2003—	Chicago (A.L.)	21	9	.700	2.90	1.11	34	34	1	0	0	0-0	226.1	196	75	73	17	56-2	*207	.233
2004—	Chicago (A.L.)	9	5	.643	4.86	1.43	21	21	2	1	0	0-0	140.2	156	81	76	23	45-3	83	.283
—	New York (A.L.)	1	2	.333	8.50	2.06	10	6	0	0	0	0-0	42.1	61	43	40	9	26-2	34	.337
2005—	Was. (N.L.)	12	10	.545	3.77	1.30	34	34	0	0	0	0-0	217.0	227	93	91	18	55-3	173	.270
American League totals (7 years)		73	61	.545	4.74	1.42	204	176	9	4	0	1-1	1149.2	1303	648	605	148	324-17	790	.286
National League totals (5 years)		39	38	.506	4.37	1.40	130	121	3	1	0	0-1	730.1	807	389	355	80	215-18	465	.283
Major League totals (11 years)		112	99	.531	4.60	1.41	334	297	12	5	0	1-2	1880.0	2110	1037	960	228	539-35	1255	.285

DIVISION SERIES RECORD

Year	Team (League)	W	L	Pct.	ERA	WHIP	G	GS	CG	ShO	Hld.	Sv.-Opp.	IP	H	R	ER	HR	BB-IBB	SO	Avg.
1998—	Texas (A.L.)						Did not play.													
1999—	Texas (A.L.)	0	1	.000	3.86	0.86	1	1	0	0	0	0-0	7.0	5	3	3	1	1-0	4	.192
2004—	New York (A.L.)	0	0	...	0.00	2.00	1	0	0	0	0	0-0	2.0	4	0	0	0	0-0	0	.500
Division series totals (2 years)		0	1	.000	3.00	1.11	2	1	0	0	0	0-0	9.0	9	3	3	1	1-0	4	.265

CHAMPIONSHIP SERIES RECORD

Year	Team (League)	W	L	Pct.	ERA	WHIP	G	GS	CG	ShO	Hld.	Sv.-Opp.	IP	H	R	ER	HR	BB-IBB	SO	Avg.
2004—	New York (A.L.)	0	1	.000	1.42	1.26	2	0	0	0	0	0-0	6.1	5	1	1	0	3-0	5	.217

ALL-STAR GAME RECORD

		W	L	Pct.	ERA	WHIP	G	GS	CG	ShO	Hld.	Sv.-Opp.	IP	H	R	ER	HR	BB-IBB	SO	Avg.
All-Star Game totals (2 years)		0	0	...	0.00	1.00	2	1	0	0	0	0-0	3.0	2	0	0	0	1-0	1	.182

LO DUCA, PAUL   C

PERSONAL: Born April 12, 1972, in Brooklyn, N.Y. ... 5-10/185. ... Bats right, throws right. ... Full name: Paul Anthony Lo Duca. ... Name pronounced: low-duke-uh. ... High school: Apollo (Phoenix). ... College: Arizona State.

TRANSACTIONS/CAREER NOTES: Selected by Los Angeles Dodgers organization in 25th round of 1993 free-agent draft. ... On disabled list (April 29-May 21, 2001); included rehabilitation assignment to Las Vegas. ... Traded by Dodgers with P Guillermo Mota and OF Juan Encarnacion to Florida Marlins for Ps Brad Penny and Bill Murphy and 1B Hee Seop Choi (July 30, 2004).

2005 GAMES PLAYED BY POSITION (MLB): C—128.

SCOUTING REPORT *Offense:* A line-drive contact hitter, Lo Duca is difficult to defend because he hits the ball from line to line. Is a good high-ball and breaking-ball hitter and can make adjustments within the count. Has good bat speed and is quick on the inside part of the plate with occasional power. Is a below-average runner but has good instincts. *Defense:* A good defensive catcher, Lo Duca has quick footwork and is aggressive at blocking balls in the dirt. Has good hands and frames pitches well on both sides of the plate. Compensates for average arm strength with a quick release and accuracy. Calls a good game and is not afraid to challenge his pitching staff. *Outlook:* Lo Duca, who is a team leader, gets the most from his ability and makes everyone around him better. **Grade 7.9**

PAUL LO DUCA'S HITTING ZONE

.241	.400	.176
.348	.321	.293
.282	.350	.176

LEFTY-RIGHTY SPLITS

vs.	Avg.	AB	H	2B	3B	HR	RBI	BB	SO	OBP	Slg.
L	.314	86	27	8	1	1	9	5	2	.359	.465
R	.276	359	99	15	0	5	48	29	29	.328	.359

Year—Team (League)	Pos.	G	AB	R	H	2B	3B	HR	RBI	BB	SO	HBP	GDP	SB-CS	Avg.	OBP	SLG	OPS	E	Avg.
1993—Vero Beach (FSL)	C	39	134	17	42	6	0	0	13	13	22	2	2	0-0	.313	.380	.358	.738	2	.992
1994—Bakersfield (Calif.)	1B-C	123	455	65	144	32	1	6	68	52	49	3	5	16-9	.316	.387	.431	.818	5	.993
1995—San Antonio (Texas)	1B-3B-C	61	199	27	49	8	0	1	8	26	25	2	12	5-5	.246	.339	.302	.641	11	.973
1996—Vero Beach (FSL)	1B-3B-C	124	439	54	134	22	0	3	66	70	38	2	14	8-2	.305	.400	.376	.776	18	.980
1997—San Antonio (Texas)	1B-C	105	385	63	126	28	2	7	69	46	27	3	17	16-8	.327	.399	.465	.864	7	.990
1998—Albuquerque (PCL)	1B-3B-C	126	451	69	144	30	3	8	58	59	40	5	20	19-7	.319	.399	.452	.852	17	.980
—Los Angeles (N.L.)	C	6	14	2	4	1	0	0	1	0	1	0	0	0-0	.286	.286	.357	.643	0	1.000
1999—Los Angeles (N.L.)	C	36	95	11	22	1	0	3	11	10	9	2	3	1-2	.232	.312	.337	.649	2	.990
—Albuquerque (PCL)	C-1B-DH	26	76	17	28	9	0	1	8	10	1	6	0	1-1	.368	.478	.526	1.005	4	.978
2000—Albuquerque (PCL)	C-OF-1B																			
	3B-2B	78	279	47	98	27	3	4	54	33	14	2	13	8-5	.351	.421	.513	.933	9	.979
—Los Angeles (N.L.)	C-OF-3B	34	65	6	16	2	0	2	8	6	2	8	0	0-2	.246	.301	.369	.671	4	.993
2001—Los Angeles (N.L.)	C-1B-OF																			
	DH	125	460	71	147	28	0	25	90	39	30	6	10	1-4	.320	.374	.543	.917	9	.990
—Las Vegas (PCL)	C-1B	3	9	3	3	2	0	0	3	1	0	0	0	0-0	.333	.400	.556	.956	1	.950
2002—Los Angeles (N.L.)	C-1B-OF	149	580	74	163	38	1	10	64	34	31	10	20	3-1	.281	.330	.402	.731	9	.992
2003—Los Angeles (N.L.)	C-1B-OF	147	568	64	155	34	2	7	44	54	54	10	21	2-4	.273	.335	.444	.779	16	.988
2004—Los Angeles (N.L.)	C-OF-3B	91	349	41	105	18	1	10	49	22	27	6	15	2-4	.301	.351	.444	.795	3	.995
—Florida (N.L.)	C	52	186	27	48	11	1	3	31	14	22	3	7	2-1	.258	.314	.376	.690	1	.997
2005—Florida (N.L.)	C	132	445	45	126	23	1	6	57	34	31	4	16	4-3	.283	.334	.380	.714	8	.991
Major League totals (8 years)		**772**	**2762**	**341**	**786**	**156**	**6**	**66**	**363**	**203**	**213**	**41**	**95**	**14-19**	**.285**	**.339**	**.417**	**.756**	**49**	**.991**

ALL-STAR GAME RECORD

		G	AB	R	H	2B	3B	HR	RBI	BB	SO	HBP	GDP	SB-CS	Avg.	OBP	SLG	OPS	E	Avg.
All-Star Game totals (3 years)		3	4	0	1	0	0	0	0	0	0	0	1	0-0	.250	.250	.250	.500	0	1.000

LOE, KAMERON   P

PERSONAL: Born September 10, 1981, in Simi Valley, Calif. ... 6-8/225. ... Throws right, bats right. ... Full name: Kameron David Loe. ... High school: Granada Hills (Chatworth, Calif.). ... College: Cal State Northridge.
TRANSACTIONS/CAREER NOTES: Selected by Philadelphia Phillies organization in 39th round of 1999 free-agent draft; did not sign. ... Selected by Texas Rangers organization in 20th round of 2002 free-agent draft.
CAREER HITTING: 0-for-0 (.000), 0 R, 0 2B, 0 3B, 0 HR, 0 RBI.

KAMERON LOE'S PITCHING ZONE

.100	.333	.250
.233	.323	.302
.250	.192	.238

LEFTY-RIGHTY SPLITS

vs.	Avg.	AB	H	2B	3B	HR	RBI	BB	SO	OBP	Slg.
L	.284	169	48	9	1	5	21	18	12	.354	.438
R	.223	184	41	13	0	2	17	13	33	.278	.326

Year—Team (League)	W	L	Pct.	ERA	WHIP	G	GS	CG	ShO	Hld.	Sv.-Opp.	IP	H	R	ER	HR	BB-IBB	SO	Avg.
2002—Pulaski (Appalachian)	4	4	.500	4.47	1.39	14	11	0	0	...	1-...	58.1	64	34	29	3	17-0	55	.271
2003—Clinton (Midw.)	4	3	.571	1.95	1.00	23	11	0	0	...	2-...	97.0	78	34	21	3	19-0	94	.217
—Stockton (Calif.)	3	0	1.000	0.96	0.85	9	4	0	0	...	1-...	37.2	26	7	4	1	6-0	31	.183
2004—Frisco (Texas)	7	7	.500	3.10	1.33	19	19	0	0	...	0-...	113.1	122	42	39	6	29-3	97	.280
—Oklahoma (PCL)	5	2	.714	3.27	1.24	8	8	0	0	...	0-...	52.1	52	20	19	6	13-0	42	.265
—Texas (A.L.)	0	0	...	5.40	1.80	2	1	0	0	...	0-0	6.2	6	5	4	0	6-3	3	.273
2005—Oklahoma (PCL)	2	1	.667	5.08	1.48	5	5	0	0	...	0-0	28.1	32	17	16	5	10-1	23	.281
—Texas (A.L.)	9	6	.600	3.42	1.30	48	8	0	0	4	1-4	92.0	89	43	35	7	31-6	45	.252
Major League totals (2 years)	**9**	**6**	**.600**	**3.56**	**1.34**	**50**	**9**	**0**	**0**	**4**	**1-4**	**98.2**	**95**	**48**	**39**	**7**	**37-6**	**48**	**.253**

LOFTON, KENNY   OF

PERSONAL: Born May 31, 1967, in East Chicago, Ind. ... 6-0/180. ... Bats left, throws left. ... Full name: Kenneth Lofton. ... High school: Washington (East Chicago, Ind.). ... College: Arizona.
TRANSACTIONS/CAREER NOTES: Selected by Houston Astros organization in 17th round of 1988 free-agent draft. ... Traded by Astros with IF Dave Rohde to Cleveland Indians for P Willie Blair and C Eddie Taubensee (December 10, 1991). ... On disabled list (July 17-August 1, 1995). ... Traded by Indians with P Alan Embree to Atlanta Braves for OFs Marquis Grissom and David Justice (March 25, 1997). ... On disabled list (June 18-July 5 and July 6-28, 1997). ... Signed as a free agent by Indians (December 8, 1997). ... On disabled list (July 28-August 14 and August 17-September 1, 1999; April 30-May 12, 2000; and May 16-June 1, 2001). ... Signed as a free agent by Chicago White Sox (February 1, 2002). ... Traded by White Sox to San Francisco Giants for Ps Felix Diaz and Ryan Meaux (July 28, 2002). ... Signed as a free agent by Pittsburgh Pirates (March 14, 2003). ... Traded by Pirates with 3B Aramis Ramirez to Chicago Cubs for IF Jose Hernandez, P Matt Bruback and a player to be named (July 23, 2003); Pirates acquired IF Bobby Hill to complete deal (August 15, 2003). ... Signed as a free agent by New York Yankees (January 6, 2004). ... On disabled list (April 17-May 2 and May 28-June 12, 2004); included rehabilitation assignments to Tampa and Trenton. ... Traded by Yankees with cash to Philadelphia Phillies for P Felix Rodriguez (December 3, 2004). ... On disabled list (May 3-20, 2005).
HONORS: Won A.L. Gold Glove as outfielder (1993-96).
2005 GAMES PLAYED BY POSITION (MLB): OF—97, DH—1.

SCOUTING REPORT **Offense:** Lofton is a catalyst who still can run and knows how to use his speed. Will slash the ball to all fields. Has a sweeping swing and will pull off the ball. Makes good contact and is one of the game's best bunters. Still can steal but is not running as frequently because of recurring leg problems. **Defense:** He's not a pure center fielder; he doesn't get consistent jumps but has the speed to compensate. Has above-average lateral range predicated on that speed rather than on consistent routes. Will drift at times and makes plays more difficult than they should be. **Outlook:** Manager Charlie Manuel gets the most from Lofton, never allowing him to be overexposed. Can be a valuable addition to a team if he doesn't play more than 120 games. **Grade 7.2**

KENNY LOFTON'S HITTING ZONE

.368	.379	.217
.385	.375	.345
.231	.381	.375

LEFTY-RIGHTY SPLITS

vs.	Avg.	AB	H	2B	3B	HR	RBI	BB	SO	OBP	Slg.
L	.348	46	16	2	0	0	6	1	6	.375	.391
R	.333	321	107	13	5	2	30	31	35	.394	.424

									BATTING										FIELDING	
Year Team (League)	Pos.	G	AB	R	H	2B	3B	HR	RBI	BB	SO	HBP	GDP	SB-CS	Avg.	OBP	SLG	OPS		E	Avg.
1988— Auburn (NY-Penn)	OF	48	187	23	40	6	1	1	14	19	51	0	3	26-4	.214	.286	.273	.559		4	.961
1989— Auburn (NY-Penn)	OF	34	110	21	29	3	1	0	8	14	30	0	1	26-5	.264	.336	.309	.645		8	.837
— Asheville (S. Atl.)	OF	22	82	14	27	2	0	1	9	12	10	1	1	14-6	.329	.421	.390	.811		2	.951
1990— Osceola (Fla. St.)	OF	124	481	98	159	15	5	2	35	61	77	3	4	62-16	.331	.407	.395	.802		7	.974
1991— Tucson (PCL)	OF	130	545	93	168	19	17	2	50	52	95	0	4	40-23	.308	.367	.417	.784		9	.974
— Houston (N.L.)	OF	20	74	9	15	1	0	0	0	5	19	0	0	2-1	.203	.253	.216	.469		1	.977
1992— Cleveland (A.L.)	OF	148	576	96	164	15	8	5	42	68	54	2	7	* 66-12	.285	.362	.365	.726		8	.982
1993— Cleveland (A.L.)	OF	148	569	116	185	28	8	1	42	81	83	1	8	* 70-14	.325	.408	.408	.815		•9	.979
1994— Cleveland (A.L.)	OF	112	459	105	* 160	32	9	12	57	52	56	2	5	* 60-12	.349	.412	.536	.948		2	.993
1995— Cleveland (A.L.)	OF-DH	118	481	93	149	22	* 13	7	53	40	49	1	6	* 54-15	.310	.362	.453	.815		•8	.970
1996— Cleveland (A.L.)	OF	154	* 662	132	210	35	4	14	67	61	82	0	7	* 75-17	.317	.372	.446	.817		10	.975
1997— Atlanta (N.L.)	OF	122	493	90	164	20	6	5	48	64	83	2	10	27-20	.333	.409	.428	.837		5	.983
1998— Cleveland (A.L.)	OF	154	600	101	169	31	6	12	64	87	80	2	7	54-10	.282	.371	.413	.785		•8	.978
1999— Cleveland (A.L.)	OF-DH	120	465	110	140	28	6	7	39	79	84	6	6	25-6	.301	.405	.432	.838		3	.989
2000— Cleveland (A.L.)	OF-DH	137	543	107	151	23	5	15	73	79	72	4	11	30-7	.278	.369	.422	.791		4	.989
2001— Cleveland (A.L.)	OF	133	517	91	135	21	4	14	66	47	69	2	8	16-8	.261	.322	.398	.721		6	.981
2002— Chicago (A.L.)	OF	93	352	68	91	20	6	8	42	49	51	0	0	22-8	.259	.348	.418	.766		0	1.000
— San Francisco (N.L.)	OF	46	180	30	48	10	3	3	9	23	22	1	1	7-3	.267	.353	.406	.759		0	1.000
2003— Pittsburgh (N.L.)	OF	84	339	58	94	19	4	9	26	28	29	2	2	18-5	.277	.333	.437	.770		0	1.000
— Chicago (N.L.)	OF	56	208	39	68	13	4	3	20	18	22	2	4	12-4	.327	.381	.471	.852		3	.974
2004— Trenton (East.)	OF	4	14	0	3	1	0	0	2	1	3	0	0	0-0	.214	.267	.286	.552		0	1.000
— New York (A.L.)	OF-DH	83	276	51	76	10	7	3	18	31	27	1	4	7-3	.275	.346	.395	.741		2	.989
2005— Philadelphia (N.L.)	OF-DH	110	367	67	123	15	5	2	36	32	41	2	3	22-3	.335	.392	.420	.811		4	.981
American League totals (11 years)		1400	5500	1070	1630	265	76	98	563	674	707	21	69	479-112	.296	.372	.426	.798		60	.983
National League totals (5 years)		438	1661	293	512	78	22	22	139	170	216	9	20	88-36	.308	.374	.421	.795		13	.987
Major League totals (15 years)		1838	7161	1363	2142	343	98	120	702	844	923	30	89	567-148	.299	.373	.425	.797		73	.984

DIVISION SERIES RECORD

Year Team (League)	Pos.	G	AB	R	H	2B	3B	HR	RBI	BB	SO	HBP	GDP	SB-CS	Avg.	OBP	SLG	OPS	E	Avg.
1995— Cleveland (A.L.)	OF	3	13	1	2	0	0	0	0	1	3	1	0	0-0	.154	.267	.154	.421	2	.818
1996— Cleveland (A.L.)	OF	4	18	3	3	0	0	0	1	2	3	0	0	5-0	.167	.250	.167	.417	0	1.000
1997— Atlanta (N.L.)	OF	3	13	2	2	1	0	0	0	1	2	0	1	0-1	.154	.214	.231	.445	0	1.000
1998— Cleveland (A.L.)	OF	4	16	5	6	1	0	2	4	1	1	0	0	2-0	.375	.412	.813	1.224	0	1.000
1999— Cleveland (A.L.)	OF	5	16	5	2	1	0	0	1	5	4	0	0	2-0	.125	.333	.188	.521	1	.933
2001— Cleveland (A.L.)	OF	5	19	2	2	0	0	1	3	3	5	0	1	0-0	.105	.217	.263	.481	0	1.000
2002— San Francisco (N.L.)	OF	5	20	5	7	1	0	0	2	2	3	0	0	1-0	.350	.391	.400	.791	0	1.000
2003— Chicago (N.L.)	OF	5	21	3	6	1	0	0	1	2	2	0	1	3-1	.286	.348	.333	.681	0	1.000
2004— New York (A.L.)	DH	1	4	0	1	0	0	0	1	0	1	0	0	0-0	.250	.250	.250	.500	0	...
Division series totals (9 years)		35	140	26	31	5	0	3	13	17	26	1	3	13-2	.221	.306	.321	.628	3	.963

CHAMPIONSHIP SERIES RECORD

Year Team (League)	Pos.	G	AB	R	H	2B	3B	HR	RBI	BB	SO	HBP	GDP	SB-CS	Avg.	OBP	SLG	OPS	E	Avg.
1995— Cleveland (A.L.)	OF	6	24	4	11	0	2	0	3	4	6	0	0	5-0	.458	.517	.625	1.142	0	1.000
1997— Atlanta (N.L.)	OF	6	27	3	5	0	1	0	1	1	7	0	1	1-1	.185	.214	.259	.474	2	.833
1998— Cleveland (A.L.)	OF	6	27	2	5	1	0	1	3	1	7	0	0	1-0	.185	.214	.333	.548	1	.889
2002— San Francisco (N.L.)	OF	5	21	4	5	0	0	1	2	2	4	1	0	1-0	.238	.333	.381	.714	0	1.000
2003— Chicago (N.L.)	OF	7	31	8	10	1	0	0	2	3	4	0	0	1-0	.323	.382	.355	.737	0	1.000
2004— New York (A.L.)	DH	3	10	1	3	0	0	1	2	2	3	0	0	1-0	.300	.417	.600	1.017	0	...
Champ. series totals (6 years)		33	140	22	39	2	3	3	13	13	31	1	1	10-1	.279	.342	.400	.742	3	.962

WORLD SERIES RECORD

Year Team (League)	Pos.	G	AB	R	H	2B	3B	HR	RBI	BB	SO	HBP	GDP	SB-CS	Avg.	OBP	SLG	OPS	E	Avg.
1995— Cleveland (A.L.)	OF	6	25	6	5	1	0	0	0	3	1	0	0	6-1	.200	.286	.240	.526	0	1.000
2002— San Francisco (N.L.)	OF	7	31	7	9	1	1	0	2	2	2	0	0	3-0	.290	.333	.387	.720	1	.962
World Series totals (2 years)		13	56	13	14	2	1	0	2	5	3	0	0	9-1	.250	.311	.321	.633	1	.974

ALL-STAR GAME RECORD

		G	AB	R	H	2B	3B	HR	RBI	BB	SO	HBP	GDP	SB-CS	Avg.	OBP	SLG	OPS	E	Avg.
All-Star Game totals (5 years)		5	14	1	5	0	0	0	2	1	3	0	0	5-0	.357	.400	.357	.757	0	1.000

LOGAN, NOOK   OF

PERSONAL: Born November 28, 1979, in Natchez, Miss. ... 6-2/180. ... Bats both, throws right. ... Full name: Exavier Prente Logan. ... High school: Natchez (Miss.). ... Junior college: Copiah-Lincoln Community College.
TRANSACTIONS/CAREER NOTES: Selected by New York Yankees organization in 40th round of 1998 free-agent draft; did not sign. ... Selected by Detroit Tigers organization in third round of 2000 free-agent draft.
2005 GAMES PLAYED BY POSITION (MLB): OF—123, DH—3.

SCOUTING REPORT Logan is an outstanding athlete and may be the fastest player in the game. Doesn't have a good stroke or bat speed. Is stronger from the right side. Has no power and still is learning to use his speed to steal bases. Has an above-average arm. Doesn't get good jumps but makes up for it with his speed. Charges the ball better than he goes back. Will be a very good player as long as he hits. ***Grade 6.8***

NOOK LOGAN'S HITTING ZONE

.300	.083	.474
.260	.364	.318
.286	.208	.174

LEFTY-RIGHTY SPLITS

vs.	Avg.	AB	H	2B	3B	HR	RBI	BB	SO	OBP	Slg.
L	.281	89	25	5	2	1	3	6	15	.326	.416
R	.249	233	58	7	3	0	14	15	37	.297	.305

									BATTING								FIELDING	
Year — Team (League)	Pos.	G	AB	R	H	2B	3B	HR	RBI	BB	SO	HBP	GDP	SB-CS	Avg.	OBP	SLG	OPS	E	Avg.
2000— GC Tigers (GCL)	SS	43	136	29	38	2	2	0	14	31	36	1	1	20-3	.279	.412	.324	.735	21	.887
—Lakeland (Fla. St.)	SS	11	42	4	14	1	0	0	3	2	13	0	0	2-1	.333	.364	.357	.721	7	.860
2001— W. Mich. (Mid.)	OF	128	522	82	137	19	8	1	27	53	129	2	3	67-19	.262	.330	.335	.666	9	.968
2002— Lakeland (Fla. St.)	OF	124	506	75	136	14	7	2	26	40	111	0	2	55-16	.269	.321	.336	.657	10	.970
2003— Erie (East.)	OF	136	514	71	129	16	4	4	38	51	103	1	5	37-13	.251	.316	.333	.649	3	.991
2004— Toledo (Int'l)	OF	105	426	67	112	14	9	2	27	23	95	3	3	38-11	.263	.303	.352	.650	5	.979
—Detroit (A.L.)	OF	47	133	12	37	5	2	0	10	13	24	0	1	8-2	.278	.340	.346	.686	2	.984
2005— Detroit (A.L.)	OF-DH	129	322	47	83	12	5	1	17	21	52	1	5	23-6	.258	.305	.335	.641	6	.979
Major League totals (2 years)		176	455	59	120	17	7	1	27	34	76	1	6	31-8	.264	.316	.338	.654	8	.981

LOHSE, KYLE   P

PERSONAL: Born October 4, 1978, in Chico, Calif. ... 6-2/201. ... Throws right, bats right. ... Full name: Kyle Matthew Lohse. ... Name pronounced: lowshe. ... High school: Hamilton Union (Hamilton City, Calif.). ... Junior college: Butte (Calif.) Community College.
TRANSACTIONS/CAREER NOTES: Selected by Chicago Cubs organization in 29th round of 1996 free-agent draft. ... Traded by Cubs with P Jason Ryan to Minnesota Twins for Ps Rick Aguilera and Scott Downs (May 21, 1999).
CAREER HITTING: 4-for-20 (.200), 0 R, 1 2B, 0 3B, 0 HR, 1 RBI.

SCOUTING REPORT Throws: He has a fastball that ranges from 90-93 mph, an 84-86 slider and a straight changeup. ***Tendencies:*** Lohse has a good delivery and good stuff, but problems with command of his fastball have resulted in inconsistency. Fastball has good life up and down in the zone. Slider is a very quick late-biter. Has improved his straight change. Has a tendency to rely on his breaking ball with runners on and frequently will overthrow his fastball in those situations. Makes a lot of mistakes when ahead in the count. ***Outlook:*** He should be a better pitcher than he is because his stuff is at times above average. Should win 12 to 15 games per year. ***Grade 6.8***

KYLE LOHSE'S PITCHING ZONE

.304	.345	.255
.357	.421	.323
.175	.500	.286

LEFTY-RIGHTY SPLITS

vs.	Avg.	AB	H	2B	3B	HR	RBI	BB	SO	OBP	Slg.
L	.291	323	94	18	5	10	36	23	44	.343	.471
R	.305	383	117	14	1	12	45	21	42	.346	.441

Year — Team (League)	W	L	Pct.	ERA	WHIP	G	GS	CG	ShO	Hld.	Sv.-Opp.	IP	H	R	ER	HR	BB-IBB	SO	Avg.
1997— Ariz. Cubs (Ariz.)	2	2	.500	3.02	1.43	12	11	0	0	...	0-...	47.2	46	22	16	0	22-0	49	.249
1998— Rockford (Midwest)	13	8	.619	3.22	1.19	28	26	3	1	...	0-...	170.2	158	76	61	8	45-1	121	.246
1999— Daytona (Fla. St.)	5	3	.625	2.89	1.21	9	9	1	1	...	0-...	53.0	48	21	17	4	16-0	41	.242
—Fort Myers (FSL)	2	3	.400	5.18	1.34	7	7	0	0	...	0-...	41.2	47	28	24	5	9-0	33	.292
—New Britain (East.)	3	4	.429	5.89	1.56	11	11	1	0	...	0-...	70.1	87	49	46	9	23-0	41	.315
2000— New Britain (East.)	3	18	.143	6.04	1.50	28	28	0	0	...	0-...	167.0	196	123	112	23	55-0	124	.291
2001— New Britain (East.)	3	1	.750	2.37	0.95	6	6	0	0	...	0-...	38.0	32	10	10	5	4-0	32	.230
—Edmonton (PCL)	4	2	.667	3.12	1.29	8	8	1	1	...	0-...	49.0	50	21	17	3	13-0	48	.262
—Minnesota (A.L.)	4	7	.364	5.68	1.45	19	16	0	0	0	0-0	90.1	102	60	57	16	29-0	64	.284
2002— Minnesota (A.L.)	13	8	.619	4.23	1.39	32	31	1	1	0	0-1	180.2	181	92	85	26	70-2	124	.259
2003— Minnesota (A.L.)	14	11	.560	4.61	1.27	33	33	2	1	0	0-0	201.0	211	107	103	28	45-1	130	.268
2004— Minnesota (A.L.)	9	13	.409	5.34	1.63	35	34	1	1	0	0-0	194.0	240	128	115	28	76-5	111	.305
2005— Minnesota (A.L.)	9	13	.409	4.18	1.43	31	30	0	0	0	0-0	178.2	211	85	83	22	44-5	86	.299
Major League totals (5 years)	49	52	.485	4.72	1.43	150	144	4	3	0	0-1	844.2	945	472	443	120	264-13	515	.283

DIVISION SERIES RECORD

Year — Team (League)	W	L	Pct.	ERA	WHIP	G	GS	CG	ShO	Hld.	Sv.-Opp.	IP	H	R	ER	HR	BB-IBB	SO	Avg.
2002— Minnesota (A.L.)	0	0	...	0.00	0.50	2	0	0	0	0	0-0	4.0	2	0	0	0	0-0	5	.143
2003— Minnesota (A.L.)	0	1	.000	5.40	1.60	1	1	0	0	0	0-0	5.0	6	3	3	1	2-0	5	.286
2004— Minnesota (A.L.)	0	1	.000	4.50	0.50	1	1	0	0	0	0-0	2.0	1	1	1	0	0-0	3	.143
Division series totals (3 years)	0	2	.000	3.27	1.00	4	2	0	0	0	0-0	11.0	9	4	4	1	2-0	13	.214

CHAMPIONSHIP SERIES RECORD

Year — Team (League)	W	L	Pct.	ERA	WHIP	G	GS	CG	ShO	Hld.	Sv.-Opp.	IP	H	R	ER	HR	BB-IBB	SO	Avg.
2002— Minnesota (A.L.)	0	0	...	0.00	0.00	1	0	0	0	0	0-0	1.0	0	0	0	0	0-0	1	.000

LONG, TERRENCE   OF

PERSONAL: Born February 29, 1976, in Montgomery, Ala. ... 6-1/200. ... Bats left, throws left. ... Full name: Terrence Deon Long. ... High school: Stanhope Elmore (Millbrook, Ala.).
TRANSACTIONS/CAREER NOTES: Selected by New York Mets organization in first round (20th pick overall) of 1994 free-agent draft; pick received as compensation for Baltimore Orioles signing Type A free-agent P Sid Fernandez. ... Traded by Mets with P Leo Vasquez to Oakland Athletics for P Kenny Rogers (July 23, 1999). ... On suspended list (September 9-12, 2003). ... Traded by A's with C Ramon Hernandez to San Diego Padres for OF Mark Kotsay (November 26, 2003). ... Traded by Padres with P Dennis Tankersley and cash to Kansas City Royals for Ps Darrell May and Ryan Bukvich (November 8, 2004).
2005 GAMES PLAYED BY POSITION (MLB): OF—121, DH—4.

SCOUTING REPORT *Offense:* Long's offensive production continues to level off. Has a short stroke and declining bat speed. Has made some adjustments in his approach and is more willing to use the whole field. Doesn't hit with the power he did several years ago but also has reduced his strike outs. Is not a big run producer for a corner outfielder and is just an average runner with questionable instincts. *Defense:* He no longer has the range to play center field and has moved to left. Gets better jumps coming in. Charges the ball well but has average arm strength. *Outlook:* Long is beyond the point of getting at-bats based on past production. Doesn't have good natural instincts and could be destined for a fourth-outfielder role. **Grade 5.6**

TERRENCE LONG'S HITTING ZONE

.188	.286	.222
.310	.245	.362
.412	.292	.282

LEFTY-RIGHTY SPLITS

vs.	Avg.	AB	H	2B	3B	HR	RBI	BB	SO	OBP	Slg.
L	.291	103	30	1	1	0	14	3	19	.306	.320
R	.276	352	97	20	2	6	39	27	37	.325	.395

								BATTING										FIELDING	
Year	Team (League)	Pos.	G	AB	R	H	2B	3B	HR	RBI	BB	SO	HBP	GDP	SB-CS	Avg.	OBP	SLG	OPS	E	Avg.
1994— Kingsport (Appalachian)		1B-OF	60	215	39	50	9	2	12	39	32	52	4	2	9-3	.233	.340	.460	.800	5	.980
1995— Capital City (SAL)		OF	55	178	27	35	1	2	2	13	28	43	1	3	8-5	.197	.309	.258	.568	5	.937
— Pittsfield (NYP)		OF	51	187	24	48	9	4	4	31	18	36	1	2	11-4	.257	.324	.412	.735	1	.991
1996— Capital City (SAL)		DH-OF	123	473	66	136	26	9	12	78	36	120	5	9	32-7	.288	.342	.457	.798	5	.981
1997— St. Lucie (Fla. St.)		OF-DH	126	470	52	118	29	7	8	61	40	102	2	6	24-8	.251	.310	.394	.704	7	.972
1998— Binghamton (East.)		OF-DH	130	455	69	135	20	10	16	58	62	105	2	8	23-11	.297	.380	.490	.871	10	.958
1999— Norfolk (Int'l)		OF	78	304	41	99	20	4	7	47	23	41	1	6	14-6	.326	.374	.487	.861	4	.980
— New York (N.L.)			3	3	0	0	0	0	0	0	0	2	0	1	0-0	.000	.000	.000	.000	...	...
— Vancouver (PCL)		OF	40	154	16	38	6	2	2	21	10	29	1	4	7-5	.247	.297	.351	.648	4	.961
2000— Sacramento (PCL)		OF	15	60	11	24	6	0	3	15	4	4	0	2	0-3	.400	.431	.650	1.081	3	.903
— Oakland (A.L.)		OF	138	584	104	168	34	4	18	80	43	77	1	18	5-0	.288	.336	.452	.788	• 10	.971
2001— Oakland (A.L.)		OF	• 162	629	90	178	37	4	12	85	52	103	0	17	9-3	.283	.335	.412	.747	7	.980
2002— Oakland (A.L.)		OF	• 162	587	71	141	32	4	16	67	48	96	2	17	3-6	.240	.298	.390	.689	8	.980
2003— Oakland (A.L.)		OF-DH	140	486	64	119	22	2	14	61	31	67	3	9	4-1	.245	.293	.385	.678	4	.984
2004— San Diego (N.L.)		OF-DH	136	288	31	85	19	4	3	28	19	51	1	13	3-2	.295	.335	.420	.756	2	.986
2005— Kansas City (A.L.)		OF-DH	137	455	62	127	21	3	6	53	30	56	0	15	3-3	.279	.321	.378	.699	3	.986
American League totals (5 years)			739	2741	391	733	146	17	66	346	204	399	6	76	24-13	.267	.318	.405	.723	32	.979
National League totals (2 years)			139	291	31	85	19	4	3	28	19	53	1	14	3-2	.292	.332	.416	.748	2	.986
Major League totals (7 years)			878	3032	422	818	165	21	69	374	223	452	7	90	27-15	.270	.319	.406	.725	34	.980

DIVISION SERIES RECORD

Year	Team (League)	Pos.	G	AB	R	H	2B	3B	HR	RBI	BB	SO	HBP	GDP	SB-CS	Avg.	OBP	SLG	OPS	E	Avg.
2000— Oakland (A.L.)		OF	5	19	2	3	0	0	1	1	3	2	0	2	0-0	.158	.273	.316	.589	1	.923
2001— Oakland (A.L.)		OF	5	18	3	7	3	0	2	3	1	2	0	0	0-0	.389	.421	.889	1.310	0	1.000
2002— Oakland (A.L.)		OF	5	18	1	3	0	0	1	1	2	0	0	0	0-0	.167	.211	.333	.544	0	1.000
2003— Oakland (A.L.)		OF	4	8	0	2	0	0	0	0	1	3	0	0	0-0	.250	.333	.250	.583	0	1.000
Division series totals (4 years)			19	63	6	15	3	0	4	5	6	9	0	2	0-0	.238	.304	.476	.781	1	.974

L

LOOPER, BRADEN — P

PERSONAL: Born October 28, 1974, in Weatherford, Okla. ... 6-3/220. ... Throws right, bats right. ... Full name: Braden LaVern Looper. ... High school: Mangum (Okla.). ... College: Wichita State.

TRANSACTIONS/CAREER NOTES: Selected by St. Louis Cardinals organization in first round (third pick overall) of 1996 free-agent draft. ... Traded by Cardinals with P Armando Almanza and SS Pablo Ozuna to Florida Marlins for SS Edgar Renteria (December 14, 1998). ... Signed as a free agent by New York Mets (January 8, 2004).

CAREER HITTING: 1-for-8 (.125), 1 R, 0 2B, 0 3B, 0 HR, 0 RBI.

SCOUTING REPORT *Throws:* Looper's fastball ranges from 93-97 mph. Throws a slider at 85-88 and a split-finger fastball at 83-86. *Tendencies:* Command is an issue. Keeps his club on edge because of his inability to throw strikes. Has an overpowering fastball with good late life and a sharp, big-breaking slider. Splitter can be a good out pitch if he can set it up with his fastball. *Outlook:* Don't expect any easy saves from this streaky reliever. Has all the pitches to be successful but has yet to take the next step because of a fragile psyche. **Grade 7.2**

BRADEN LOOPER'S PITCHING ZONE

.083	.500	.280
.258	.389	.310
.167	.333	.192

LEFTY-RIGHTY SPLITS

vs.	Avg.	AB	H	2B	3B	HR	RBI	BB	SO	OBP	Slg.
L	.336	116	39	8	1	6	24	13	8	.408	.578
R	.210	124	26	4	0	1	5	9	19	.285	.266

Year	Team (League)	W	L	Pct.	ERA	WHIP	G	GS	CG	ShO	Hld.	Sv.-Opp.	IP	H	R	ER	HR	BB-IBB	SO	Avg.
1997— Prince Will. (Car.)		3	6	.333	4.48	1.49	12	12	0	0	...	0-...	64.1	71	38	32	6	25-0	58	.276
— Arkansas (Texas)		1	4	.200	5.91	1.45	19	0	0	0	...	5-...	21.1	24	14	14	2	7-2	20	.286
1998— St. Louis (N.L.)		0	1	.000	5.40	1.80	4	0	0	0	0	0-2	3.1	5	4	2	1	1-0	4	.357
— Memphis (PCL)		2	3	.400	3.10	1.38	40	0	0	0	...	20-...	40.2	43	16	14	3	13-1	43	.270
1999— Florida (N.L.)		3	3	.500	3.80	1.53	72	0	0	0	8	0-4	83.0	96	43	35	7	31-6	50	.293
2000— Florida (N.L.)		5	1	.833	4.41	1.59	73	0	0	0	18	2-5	67.1	71	41	33	3	36-6	29	.269
2001— Florida (N.L.)		3	3	.500	3.55	1.31	71	0	0	0	16	3-4	71.0	63	28	28	8	30-3	52	.242
2002— Florida (N.L.)		2	5	.286	3.14	1.17	78	0	0	0	16	13-16	86.0	73	31	30	8	28-3	55	.230
2003— Florida (N.L.)		6	4	.600	3.68	1.38	74	0	0	0	0	28-34	80.2	82	34	33	4	29-1	56	.266
2004— New York (N.L.)		2	5	.286	2.70	1.22	71	0	0	0	0	29-34	83.1	86	26	25	4	16-3	60	.266
2005— New York (N.L.)		4	7	.364	3.94	1.47	60	0	0	0	0	28-36	59.1	65	31	26	7	22-3	27	.271
Major League totals (8 years)		25	29	.463	3.57	1.37	503	0	0	0	58	103-137	534.0	541	240	212	43	193-25	333	.263

DIVISION SERIES RECORD

Year	Team (League)	W	L	Pct.	ERA	WHIP	G	GS	CG	ShO	Hld.	Sv.-Opp.	IP	H	R	ER	HR	BB-IBB	SO	Avg.
2003— Florida (N.L.)		1	0	1.000	0.00	1.80	2	0	0	0	1	0-0	1.2	1	1	0	0	2-1	0	.167

CHAMPIONSHIP SERIES RECORD

Year Team (League)	W	L	Pct.	ERA	WHIP	G	GS	CG	ShO	Hld.	Sv.-Opp.	IP	H	R	ER	HR	BB-IBB	SO	Avg.
2003— Florida (N.L.)	0	0	...	0.00	1.20	2	0	0	0	...	1-1	1.2	1	0	0	0	1-1	1	.167

WORLD SERIES RECORD

Year Team (League)	W	L	Pct.	ERA	WHIP	G	GS	CG	ShO	Hld.	Sv.-Opp.	IP	H	R	ER	HR	BB-IBB	SO	Avg.
2003— Florida (N.L.)	1	0	1.000	9.82	1.64	4	0	0	0	...	0-0	3.2	6	4	4	2	0-0	4	.353

LOPEZ, AQUILINO　　　　P

PERSONAL: Born April 21, 1975, in Villa Altagracia, Dominican Republic. ... 6-3/165. ... Throws right, bats right. ... Name pronounced: aquil-LEENO.

TRANSACTIONS/CAREER NOTES: Signed as a non-drafted free agent by Seattle Mariners organization (July 3, 1997). ... Selected by Toronto Blue Jays from Mariners organization in Rule 5 major league draft (December 16, 2002). ... Signed as a free agent by Los Angeles Dodgers organization (January 20, 2005). ... Signed as free agent by Colorado Rockies organization (July 29, 2005). ... Claimed on waivers by Philadelphia Phillies (August 2, 2005).

CAREER HITTING: 0-for-1 (.000), 1 R, 0 2B, 0 3B, 0 HR, 0 RBI.

AQUILINO LOPEZ'S PITCHING ZONE

.231	1.000	.000
.111	1.000	.364
.200	.000	.000

LEFTY-RIGHTY SPLITS

vs.	Avg.	AB	H	2B	3B	HR	RBI	BB	SO	OBP	Slg.
L	.346	26	9	3	0	1	3	4	7	.433	.577
R	.184	38	7	1	0	1	4	3	15	.244	.289

Year Team (League)	W	L	Pct.	ERA	WHIP	G	GS	CG	ShO	Hld.	Sv.-Opp.	IP	H	R	ER	HR	BB-IBB	SO	Avg.
1999— Everett (N'west)	7	6	.538	3.80	1.21	15	15	1	0	...	0-...	87.2	76	44	37	8	30-2	93	.230
2000— Wisconsin (Midw.)	6	1	.857	1.85	0.99	39	5	1	1	...	17-...	68.0	47	16	14	1	20-4	67	.193
2001— San Antonio (Texas)	4	3	.571	3.02	1.16	42	0	0	0	...	2-...	62.2	48	24	21	4	25-2	79	.209
2002— Tacoma (PCL)	4	4	.500	2.39	1.06	34	11	0	0	...	5-...	109.1	89	33	29	6	27-2	103	.221
2003— Toronto (A.L.)	1	3	.250	3.42	1.25	72	0	0	0	16	14-16	73.2	58	31	28	5	34-5	64	.212
2004— Toronto (A.L.)	1	1	.500	6.00	1.62	18	0	0	0	3	0-0	21.0	21	15	14	5	13-3	13	.266
— Syracuse (Int'l)	1	6	.143	7.17	1.59	32	0	0	0	...	5-...	42.2	58	36	34	8	10-0	32	.326
2005— Las Vegas (PCL)	3	4	.429	5.89	1.25	27	0	0	0	2	5-11	36.2	40	24	24	9	6-3	32	.276
— Colo. Springs (PCL)	2	0	1.000	2.75	0.92	14	0	0	0	3	0-1	19.2	14	10	6	2	4-0	25	.194
— Colorado (N.L.)	0	0	...	2.25	0.75	1	0	0	0	0	0-0	4.0	3	1	1	0	0-0	6	.200
— Scran./W.B. (I.L.)	0	0	...	1.00	0.67	4	0	0	0	2	0-0	9.0	5	1	1	0	1-0	11	.156
— Philadelphia (N.L.)	0	1	.000	2.13	1.58	10	0	0	0	0	0-0	12.2	13	4	3	2	7-1	16	.265
American League totals (2 years)	2	4	.333	3.99	1.33	90	0	0	0	19	14-16	94.2	79	46	42	10	47-8	77	.224
National League totals (1 year)	0	1	.000	2.16	1.38	11	0	0	0	0	0-0	16.2	16	5	4	2	7-1	22	.250
Major League totals (3 years)	2	5	.286	3.72	1.34	101	0	0	0	19	14-16	111.1	95	51	46	12	54-9	99	.228

LOPEZ, FELIPE　　　　SS

PERSONAL: Born May 12, 1980, in Bayamon, Puerto Rico. ... 6-1/185. ... Bats both, throws right. ... Full name: Felipe Lopez Jr.. ... High school: Lake Brantley (Altamonte Springs, Fla.).

TRANSACTIONS/CAREER NOTES: Selected by Toronto Blue Jays organization in first round (eighth pick overall) of 1998 free-agent draft. ... Traded by Blue Jays to Cincinnati Reds as part of four-team deal in which Blue Jays acquired a player to be named from Oakland Athletics, A's acquired 1B Erubiel Durazo from Arizona Diamondbacks and Diamondbacks acquired P Elmer Dessens and cash from Reds (December 15, 2002); Blue Jays acquired P Jason Arnold to complete deal (December 16, 2002).

2005 GAMES PLAYED BY POSITION (MLB): SS—140, 2B—7, 3B—1.

SCOUTING REPORT **Offense:** Lopez has learned to use the whole field. Has a short stroke and very good bat speed. Still strikes out too much but is becoming more patient. Beginning to really drive the ball when it's up and out over the plate. Is reading pitchers better and getting jumps on steal attempts. **Defense:** Lopez is extremely erratic in the field because he plays out of control and doesn't have very good instincts. Has a very strong arm from the hole but will rush throws on close plays and can be very erratic. Fields the ball too deep at times and lets the ball play him. Doesn't maintain concentration. **Outlook:** It's doubtful Lopez will hit for the kind of power he did in 2005, but he will hit for average. Will continue to frustrate on defense. ***Grade 8.2***

FELIPE LOPEZ'S HITTING ZONE

.300	.600	.162
.264	.423	.282
.343	.306	.393

LEFTY-RIGHTY SPLITS

vs.	Avg.	AB	H	2B	3B	HR	RBI	BB	SO	OBP	Slg.
L	.243	173	42	4	0	5	22	12	37	.291	.353
R	.312	407	127	30	5	18	63	45	74	.377	.543

									BATTING										FIELDING	
Year Team (League)	Pos.	G	AB	R	H	2B	3B	HR	RBI	BB	SO	HBP	GDP	SB-CS	Avg.	OBP	SLG	OPS	E	Avg.
1998— St. Catharines (NYP)	SS	19	83	14	31	5	2	1	11	3	14	0	1	4-2	.373	.395	.518	.913	9	.895
— Dunedin (Fla. St.)	SS	4	13	3	5	0	1	1	1	0	3	0	1	0-0	.385	.385	.769	1.154	4	.692
1999— Hagerstown (SAL)	SS	134	537	87	149	27	4	14	80	61	157	3	7	21-14	.277	.351	.421	.772	22	.960
2000— Tennessee (Sou.)	SS	127	463	52	119	18	4	9	41	31	110	1	6	12-11	.257	.303	.371	.675	44	.923
2001— Tennessee (Sou.)	SS-2B	19	72	12	16	2	1	2	4	9	23	0	1	4-4	.222	.309	.361	.670	8	.904
— Syracuse (Int'l)	SS-2B-3B	89	358	65	100	19	7	16	44	30	94	3	5	13-5	.279	.337	.506	.842	19	.950
— Toronto (A.L.)	3B-SS	49	177	21	46	5	4	5	23	12	39	0	2	4-3	.260	.304	.418	.722	9	.938
2002— Toronto (A.L.)	SS-3B-DH	85	282	35	64	15	3	8	34	23	90	1	4	5-4	.227	.287	.387	.673	8	.975
— Syracuse (Int'l)	SS	43	173	35	55	11	2	3	16	23	36	1	3	13-0	.318	.419	.457	.875	16	.934
2003— Cincinnati (N.L.)	SS-3B-2B	59	197	28	42	7	2	2	13	28	59	1	2	8-5	.213	.313	.299	.612	16	.928
— Louisville (Int'l)	SS-2B	35	143	22	40	11	0	2	18	12	38	0	0	2-5	.280	.333	.399	.732	9	.940
2004— Louisville (Int'l)	SS-3B-2B	75	293	50	80	11	3	9	43	25	71	2	2	2-2	.273	.329	.423	.752	13	.956
— Cincinnati (N.L.)	SS-3B-2B	79	264	35	64	18	2	7	31	25	81	3	1	1-1	.242	.314	.405	.719	15	.949
2005— Cincinnati (N.L.)	SS-2B-3B	148	580	97	169	34	5	23	85	57	111	6	8	15-7	.291	.352	.486	.838	17	.971
American League totals (2 years)		134	459	56	110	20	7	13	57	35	129	1	6	9-7	.240	.293	.399	.692	17	.964
National League totals (3 years)		286	1041	160	275	59	9	32	129	110	251	5	11	24-13	.264	.335	.430	.765	48	.956
Major League totals (5 years)		420	1500	216	385	79	16	45	186	145	380	6	17	33-20	.257	.322	.421	.743	65	.959

ALL-STAR GAME RECORD

	G	AB	R	H	2B	3B	HR	RBI	BB	SO	HBP	GDP	SB-CS	Avg.	OBP	SLG	OPS	E	Avg.
All-Star Game totals (1 year)	1	1	0	1	0	0	0	0	0	0	0	0	0-0	1.000	1.000	1.000	2.000	0	...

LOPEZ, JAVIER — P

PERSONAL: Born July 11, 1977, in San Juan, Puerto Rico. ... 6-4/200. ... Throws left, bats left. ... Full name: Javier Alfonso Lopez. ... High school: Robinson (Fairfax, Va.). ... College: Virginia.

TRANSACTIONS/CAREER NOTES: Selected by Arizona Diamondbacks organization in fourth round of 1998 free-agent draft. ... Selected by Boston Red Sox from Diamondbacks organization in Rule 5 major league draft (December 16, 2002). ... Traded by Red Sox to Colorado Rockies for future considerations (March 18, 2003); Red Sox acquired P Ryan Cameron to complete deal (March 29, 2003). ... Claimed on waivers by Diamondbacks (April 14, 2005).

CAREER HITTING: 1-for-7 (.143), 1 R, 0 2B, 0 3B, 0 HR, 1 RBI.

JAVIER LOPEZ'S PITCHING ZONE

.500	1.000	...
.375	.286	.500
.500	.500	.231

LEFTY-RIGHTY SPLITS

vs.	Avg.	AB	H	2B	3B	HR	RBI	BB	SO	OBP	Slg.
L	.286	35	10	3	0	1	10	5	6	.375	.457
R	.410	39	16	8	0	1	16	6	6	.500	.692

Year — Team (League)	W	L	Pct.	ERA	WHIP	G	GS	CG	ShO	Hld.	Sv.-Opp.	IP	H	R	ER	HR	BB-IBB	SO	Avg.
1998— South Bend (Mid.)	2	4	.333	6.55	2.05	16	9	0	0	...	0-...	44.0	60	36	32	2	30-0	31	.328
1999— South Bend (Mid.)	4	6	.400	6.00	1.67	20	20	0	0	...	0-...	99.0	122	74	66	9	43-0	70	.300
2000— High Desert (Calif.)	4	8	.333	5.22	1.53	30	21	0	0	...	2-...	136.1	152	87	79	14	57-0	98	.288
2001— Lancaster (Calif.)	1	3	.250	2.63	1.46	17	0	0	0	...	1-...	24.0	30	9	7	2	5-0	18	.313
— El Paso (Texas)	1	0	1.000	7.43	1.95	22	1	0	0	...	0-...	40.0	64	39	33	6	14-2	21	.370
2002— El Paso (Texas)	2	2	.500	2.72	1.08	61	0	0	0	...	6-...	46.1	34	16	14	3	16-1	47	.204
2003— Colorado (N.L.)	4	1	.800	3.70	1.20	75	0	0	0	15	1-2	58.1	58	25	24	5	12-2	40	.258
2004— Colo. Springs (PCL)	0	1	.000	4.00	1.33	8	0	0	0	...	0-...	9.0	10	4	4	2	2-0	9	.263
— Colorado (N.L.)	1	2	.333	7.52	1.75	64	0	0	0	12	0-1	40.2	45	34	34	1	26-4	20	.287
2005— Colorado (N.L.)	0	0	...	22.50	3.50	3	0	0	0	1	0-1	2.0	7	5	5	0	0-0	1	.538
— Arizona (N.L.)	1	1	.500	9.42	2.09	29	0	0	0	6	2-3	14.1	19	15	15	2	11-3	11	.311
— Tucson (PCL)	0	1	.000	2.22	1.19	27	0	0	0	2	2-2	24.1	17	7	6	0	12-1	16	.213
Major League totals (3 years)	**6**	**4**	**.600**	**6.09**	**1.54**	**171**	**0**	**0**	**0**	**33**	**3-7**	**115.1**	**129**	**79**	**78**	**8**	**49-9**	**72**	**.283**

LOPEZ, JAVY — C

PERSONAL: Born November 5, 1970, in Ponce, Puerto Rico. ... 6-3/224. ... Bats right, throws right. ... Full name: Javier Torres Lopez. ... Name pronounced: HAH-vee. ... High school: Academia Cristo Rey (Urb la Ramble Ponce, Puerto Rico).

TRANSACTIONS/CAREER NOTES: Signed as a non-drafted free agent by Atlanta Braves organization (November 6, 1987). ... On disabled list (July 6-22, 1997; June 21-July 15 and July 25, 1999-remainder of season; and August 1-16, 2002). ... Signed as a free agent by Baltimore Orioles (January 6, 2004). ... On disabled list (May 25-July 25, 2005); included rehabilitation assignment to Bowie.

HONORS: Named N.L. Comeback Player of the Year by THE SPORTING NEWS (2003).

2005 GAMES PLAYED BY POSITION (MLB): C—75, DH—28, 1B—1.

SCOUTING REPORT

Offense: Showed a dramatic dropoff in his numbers in 2005. Still generates bat speed despite a long stroke. Has an inside-out approach but likes to hook the ball for power and is becoming more pull-conscious. Is not a very patient hitter and doesn't like to hit behind in the count. Has not made an adjustment to seeing more off-speed pitches. *Defense:* He has natural arm strength, but his footwork is inconsistent. Accuracy improved accuracy as last season progressed. Has only adequate hands and doesn't like to be behind the plate every day. Team has considered him for first base and DH. *Outlook:* His offensive production has been declining as he approaches his mid-30s, and he never will be as good a run producer as he was years ago. *Grade 7.8*

JAVY LOPEZ'S HITTING ZONE

.435	.267	.333
.254	.375	.300
.178	.368	.263

LEFTY-RIGHTY SPLITS

vs.	Avg.	AB	H	2B	3B	HR	RBI	BB	SO	OBP	Slg.
L	.284	102	29	9	0	2	7	12	17	.362	.431
R	.276	293	81	15	1	13	42	7	51	.306	.468

Year — Team (League)	Pos.	G	AB	R	H	2B	3B	HR	RBI	BB	SO	HBP	GDP	SB-CS	Avg.	OBP	SLG	OPS	E	Avg.
1988— GC Braves (GCL)	C	31	94	8	18	4	0	1	9	3	19	0	0	1-0	.191	.214	.266	.480	7	.958
1989— Pulaski (Appalachian)	C	51	153	27	40	8	1	3	27	5	35	1	8	3-2	.261	.284	.386	.670	5	.983
1990— Burlington (Midw.)	C	116	422	48	112	17	3	11	55	14	84	5	10	0-2	.265	.297	.398	.695	11	.991
1991— Durham (Carol.)	C	113	384	43	94	14	2	11	51	25	88	3	10	10-3	.245	.294	.378	.672	6	.991
1992— Greenville (Sou.)	C	115	442	63	142	28	3	16	60	24	47	5	8	7-3	.321	.362	.507	.868	8	.990
— Atlanta (N.L.)	C	9	16	3	6	2	0	0	2	0	1	0	0	0-0	.375	.375	.500	.875	0	1.000
1993— Richmond (Int'l)	C	100	380	56	116	23	2	17	74	12	53	6	8	1-6	.305	.334	.511	.845	10	.987
— Atlanta (N.L.)	C	8	16	1	6	1	1	1	2	0	2	1	0	0-0	.375	.412	.750	1.162	1	.975
1994— Atlanta (N.L.)	C	80	277	27	68	9	0	13	35	17	61	5	12	0-2	.245	.299	.419	.718	3	.988
1995— Atlanta (N.L.)	C	100	333	37	105	11	4	14	51	14	57	2	13	0-1	.315	.344	.499	.842	8	.988
1996— Atlanta (N.L.)	C	138	489	56	138	19	1	23	69	28	84	3	17	1-6	.282	.322	.466	.788	6	.994
1997— Atlanta (N.L.)	C	123	414	52	122	28	1	23	68	40	82	5	9	1-1	.295	.361	.534	.895	6	.994
1998— Atlanta (N.L.)	C-DH	133	489	73	139	21	1	34	106	30	85	6	22	5-3	.284	.328	.540	.868	5	.995
1999— Atlanta (N.L.)	C	65	246	34	78	18	1	11	45	20	41	3	6	0-0	.317	.375	.533	.908	4	.991
2000— Atlanta (N.L.)	C	134	481	60	138	21	1	24	89	35	80	4	20	0-0	.287	.337	.484	.822	6	.993
2001— Atlanta (N.L.)	C	128	438	45	117	16	1	17	66	28	82	10	12	1-0	.267	.322	.425	.747	10	.989
2002— Atlanta (N.L.)	C	109	347	31	81	15	0	11	52	26	63	8	15	0-0	.233	.299	.372	.670	10	.986
2003— Atlanta (N.L.)	C-DH	129	457	89	150	29	3	43	109	33	90	4	10	0-1	.328	.378	.687	1.065	5	.994
2004— Baltimore (A.L.)	C-DH	150	579	83	183	33	3	23	86	47	97	6	16	0-0	.316	.370	.503	.873	5	.994
2005— Bowie (East.)	C-DH	4	15	1	6	1	0	2	3	0	0	0	0	0-0	.400	.375	.467	.842	0	1.000
— Baltimore (A.L.)	C-DH-1B	103	395	47	110	24	1	15	49	19	68	7	10	0-1	.278	.322	.458	.780	3	.994
American League totals (2 years)		**253**	**974**	**130**	**293**	**57**	**4**	**38**	**135**	**66**	**165**	**13**	**26**	**0-1**	**.301**	**.351**	**.485**	**.835**	**8**	**.994**
National League totals (12 years)		**1156**	**4003**	**508**	**1148**	**190**	**14**	**214**	**694**	**271**	**728**	**51**	**136**	**8-18**	**.287**	**.337**	**.502**	**.839**	**64**	**.992**
Major League totals (14 years)		**1409**	**4977**	**638**	**1441**	**247**	**18**	**252**	**829**	**337**	**893**	**64**	**162**	**8-19**	**.290**	**.340**	**.498**	**.838**	**72**	**.992**

DIVISION SERIES RECORD

Year Team (League)	Pos.	G	AB	R	H	2B	3B	HR	RBI	BB	SO	HBP	GDP	SB-CS	Avg.	OBP	SLG	OPS	E	Avg.
1995—Atlanta (N.L.)	C	3	9	0	4	0	0	0	3	0	3	0	0	0-1	.444	.400	.444	.844	0	1.000
1996—Atlanta (N.L.)	C	2	7	1	2	0	0	1	1	1	0	0	0	1-0	.286	.375	.714	1.089	1	.958
1997—Atlanta (N.L.)	C	2	7	3	2	2	0	0	1	2	1	0	0	0-0	.286	.444	.571	1.016	0	1.000
1998—Atlanta (N.L.)	C	2	7	1	2	0	0	1	1	1	1	0	0	0-0	.286	.375	.714	1.089	0	1.000
2000—Atlanta (N.L.)	C	3	11	0	1	0	0	0	0	0	1	0	0	0-1	.091	.091	.091	.182	0	1.000
2002—Atlanta (N.L.)	C	4	15	4	5	1	0	2	4	1	3	0	1	0-0	.333	.375	.800	1.175	0	1.000
2003—Atlanta (N.L.)	C	5	21	1	7	2	0	0	0	0	6	0	0	0-0	.333	.333	.429	.762	1	.977
Division series totals (7 years)		21	77	10	23	5	0	4	10	5	15	0	1	1-2	.299	.337	.519	.857	2	.989

CHAMPIONSHIP SERIES RECORD

Year Team (League)	Pos.	G	AB	R	H	2B	3B	HR	RBI	BB	SO	HBP	GDP	SB-CS	Avg.	OBP	SLG	OPS	E	Avg.
1992—Atlanta (N.L.)	C	1	1	0	0	0	0	0	0	0	0	0	0	0-0	.000	.000	.000	.000	0	1.000
1995—Atlanta (N.L.)	C	3	14	2	5	1	0	1	3	0	1	0	0	0-0	.357	.357	.643	1.000	0	1.000
1996—Atlanta (N.L.)	C	7	24	8	13	5	0	2	6	3	1	1	0	1-0	.542	.607	1.000	1.607	0	1.000
1997—Atlanta (N.L.)	C	5	17	0	1	0	0	0	2	1	7	0	0	0-0	.059	.100	.118	.218	0	1.000
1998—Atlanta (N.L.)	C	6	20	2	6	0	0	1	1	0	7	0	1	0-0	.300	.300	.450	.750	1	.978
2001—Atlanta (N.L.)	C	5	14	1	2	1	0	0	2	1	4	0	1	0-0	.143	.200	.357	.557	1	.957
Champ. series totals (6 years)		27	90	13	27	7	0	5	14	5	20	1	2	1-0	.300	.337	.544	.881	2	.990

WORLD SERIES RECORD

Year Team (League)	Pos.	G	AB	R	H	2B	3B	HR	RBI	BB	SO	HBP	GDP	SB-CS	Avg.	OBP	SLG	OPS	E	Avg.
1992—Atlanta (N.L.)		Did not play.																		
1995—Atlanta (N.L.)	C	6	17	1	3	2	0	1	3	1	1	1	1	0-0	.176	.263	.471	.734	0	1.000
1996—Atlanta (N.L.)	C	6	21	3	4	0	0	1	3	4	0	2		0-0	.190	.280	.190	.470	0	1.000
World Series totals (2 years)		12	38	4	7	2	0	1	4	5	1	3		0-0	.184	.273	.316	.589	0	1.000

ALL-STAR GAME RECORD

		G	AB	R	H	2B	3B	HR	RBI	BB	SO	HBP	GDP	SB-CS	Avg.	OBP	SLG	OPS	E	Avg.
All-Star Game totals (3 years)		3	4	1	1	0	0	1	0	1	0	0		0-0	.250	.250	1.000	1.250	0	1.000

LOPEZ, JOSE   SS

PERSONAL: Born November 24, 1983, in Anzoategui, Venezuela. ... 6-2/170. ... Bats right, throws right. ... Full name: Jose Celestino Lopez. ... High school: Unidad Educativa Cas Puerta Barcelona (Venezuela).

TRANSACTIONS/CAREER NOTES: Signed as a non-drafted free agent by Seattle Mariners organization (July 2, 2000).

2005 GAMES PLAYED BY POSITION (MLB): 2B—51, 3B—1.

SCOUTING REPORT *Offense:* Lopez is similar to the White Sox's Juan Uribe: He is a free swinger with above-average pop for a middle infielder. Has a tendency to chase high fastballs and off-speed pitches away. Tries to pull too much. Is an above-average runner who is a threat to steal. *Defense:* He has good raw tools that should translate to major league success. Is still growing physically. Still is making mental errors. Has soft hands, quick feet, good range and a strong arm. *Outlook:* He might still be a year or two away from being a productive major league player, but his defense last season should be enough to give him a shot to make the Mariners. *Grade 7.1*

JOSE LOPEZ'S HITTING ZONE

.250	.125	.429
.324	.278	.304
.250	.000	.429

LEFTY-RIGHTY SPLITS

vs.	Avg.	AB	H	2B	3B	HR	RBI	BB	SO	OBP	Slg.
L	.276	58	16	4	0	1	10	2	5	.306	.397
R	.235	132	31	15	0	1	15	4	20	.271	.371

Year Team (League)	Pos.	G	AB	R	H	2B	3B	HR	RBI	BB	SO	HBP	GDP	SB-CS	Avg.	OBP	SLG	OPS	E	Avg.
2001—Everett (N'west)	SS-2B	70	289	42	74	15	0	2	20	13	44	10	3	13-6	.256	.309	.638	.638	17	.950
2002—San Bern. (Calif.)	SS-2B	123	522	82	169	39	5	8	60	27	45	5	8	31-13	.324	.360	.464	.824	31	.939
2003—San Antonio (Texas)	SS-2B-3B	132	538	82	139	35	2	13	69	27	56	10	12	18-8	.258	.303	.403	.706	28	.954
2004—Ariz. Mariners (Ariz.)	3B-SS-2B	4	12	3	2	1	0	0	1	2	1	0	1	1-0	.167	.267	.250	.517	1	.933
—Tacoma (PCL)	SS-3B-2B DH	74	275	40	81	19	0	13	39	16	30	6	2	6-2	.295	.342	.505	.834	20	.934
—Seattle (A.L.)	SS-3B	57	207	28	48	13	0	5	22	8	31	1	1	0-1	.232	.263	.367	.630	10	.956
2005—Tacoma (PCL)	2B	44	182	29	58	19	0	5	31	8	25	2	6	2-3	.319	.354	.505	.860	6	.972
—Seattle (A.L.)	2B-3B	54	190	18	47	19	0	2	25	6	25	4	5	4-2	.247	.282	.379	.661	7	.976
Major League totals (2 years)		111	397	46	95	32	0	7	47	14	56	5	6	4-3	.239	.272	.373	.645	17	.967

LOPEZ, LUIS   3B/SS

PERSONAL: Born September 4, 1970, in Cirda, Puerto Rico. ... 5-11/175. ... Bats both, throws right. ... Full name: Luis Manuel Lopez. ... High school: San Jose (Caguas, Puerto Rico).

TRANSACTIONS/CAREER NOTES: Signed as a non-drafted free agent by San Diego Padres organization (September 9, 1987). ... On disabled list (April 24, 1995-entire season). ... On disabled list (March 29-April 18 and July 31-September 1, 1996); included rehabilitation assignments to Las Vegas. ... Traded by Padres to Houston Astros for P Sean Runyan (March 15, 1997). ... Traded by Astros to New York Mets for IF Tim Bogar (March 31, 1997). ... Traded by Mets to Milwaukee Brewers for P Bill Pulsipher (January 21, 2000). ... On disabled list (March 30-May 19, 2002); included rehabilitation assignment to Indianapolis. ... Released by Brewers (June 6, 2002). ... Signed by Baltimore Orioles organization (June 18, 2002). ... Released by Orioles (October 1, 2002). ... Signed by Colorado Rockies organization (December 27, 2002). ... Traded by Rockies to Orioles for cash considerations (July 1, 2003). ... Signed as a free agent by Cincinnati Reds organization (December 29, 2004). ... On disabled list (June 20, 2005-remainder of season).

2005 GAMES PLAYED BY POSITION (MLB): 3B—6, 2B—4.

LEFTY-RIGHTY SPLITS

vs.	Avg.	AB	H	2B	3B	HR	RBI	BB	SO	OBP	Slg.
L	.000	4	0	0	0	0	0	1	2	.200	.000
R	.261	23	6	3	0	0	2	0	4	.261	.391

Year Team (League)	Pos.	G	AB	R	H	2B	3B	HR	RBI	BB	SO	HBP	GDP	SB-CS	Avg.	OBP	SLG	OPS	E	Avg.
1988—Spokane (N'west)	SS	70	312	50	95	13	1	0	35	18	59	4	7	14-5	.304	.348	.353	.701	*47	.877
1989—Char., S.C. (SAL)	SS	127	460	50	102	15	1	1	29	17	85	2	9	12-9	.222	.251	.265	.516	*74	.895
1990—Riverside (Calif.)	SS	14	46	5	17	3	1	1	4	3	0	1	1	4-2	.370	.408	.543	.952	6	.903
1991—Wichita (Texas)	2B-SS	125	452	43	121	17	1	1	41	18	70	8	8	6-7	.268	.305	.316	.621	26	.959

Year — Team (League)	Pos.	G	AB	R	H	2B	3B	HR	RBI	BB	SO	HBP	GDP	SB-CS	Avg.	OBP	SLG	OPS	E	Avg.
1992—Las Vegas (PCL)	SS-OF	120	395	44	92	8	8	1	31	19	65	3	12	6-4	.233	.271	.301	.573	§30	.949
1993—Las Vegas (PCL)	SS-2B	131	491	52	150	36	6	6	58	27	62	5	7	8-0	.306	.346	.440	.786	29	.955
—San Diego (N.L.)	2B	17	43	1	5	1	0	0	1	0	8	0	0	0-0	.116	.114	.140	.253	1	.983
1994—Las Vegas (PCL)	2B	12	49	2	10	2	2	0	6	1	5	0	0	0-0	.204	.216	.327	.542	2	.973
—San Diego (N.L.)	SS-2B-3B	77	235	29	65	16	1	2	20	15	39	3	7	3-2	.277	.325	.379	.704	14	.952
1995—San Diego (N.L.)		Did not play.																		
1996—Las Vegas (PCL)	2B-SS	18	68	4	14	3	0	1	12	2	15	0	0	0-0	.206	.229	.294	.523	2	.976
—San Diego (N.L.)	SS-2B-3B	63	139	10	25	3	0	2	11	9	35	1	7	0-0	.180	.233	.245	.478	4	.975
1997—Norfolk (Int'l)	SS-2B-DH	48	203	32	67	12	1	4	19	9	29	1	1	2-6	.330	.358	.458	.816	14	.935
—New York (N.L.)	SS-2B-3B	78	178	19	48	12	1	1	19	12	42	4	2	2-4	.270	.330	.365	.695	9	.963
1998—New York (N.L.)	2B-SS-3B-OF	117	266	37	67	13	2	2	22	20	60	4	10	2-2	.252	.312	.338	.650	11	.960
1999—New York (N.L.)	SS-2B-3B	68	104	11	22	4	0	2	13	12	33	3	1	1-1	.212	.308	.308	.616	4	.962
2000—Milwaukee (N.L.)	SS-2B-3B	78	201	24	53	14	0	6	27	9	35	5	2	1-2	.264	.309	.423	.732	5	.969
2001—Milwaukee (N.L.)	3B-SS-2B	92	222	22	60	8	3	4	18	14	44	5	6	0-1	.270	.326	.387	.714	8	.959
2002—Indianapolis (Int'l)	SS-2B-3B	6	22	2	5	0	0	0	4	1	0			0-0	.227	.261	.227	.488	1	1.000
—Milwaukee (N.L.)	SS	6	8	1	0	0	0	0	0	2	1	0	0	0-0	.000	.200	.000	.200	0	1.000
—Rochester (Int'l)	2B-SS	17	68	12	22	6	0	3	8	3	11	1	1	0-0	.324	.361	.544	.905	1	.988
—Baltimore (A.L.)	SS-2B-1B-DH	52	109	10	23	6	0	2	9	3	20	0	3	1-0	.211	.232	.321	.553	3	.969
2003—Colo. Springs (PCL)	2B-SS-1B-3B	47	140	14	29	10	0	3	18	9	29	2	2	0-1	.207	.265	.343	.608	7	.961
—Ottawa (Int'l)	2B-SS-3B-3B	52	186	23	49	6	0	5	32	6	24	5	3	1-1	.263	.299	.376	.675	7	.969
2004—Baltimore (A.L.)	SS-3B-DH-1B-SS-1B	56	88	7	16	5	0	1	8	3	20	1	1	0-0	.182	.211	.273	.483	6	.923
2005—Louisville (Int'l)	SS-2B-DH	29	87	10	23	8	0	1	9	8	18	3	0	0-2	.264	.347	.391	.738	4	.958
—Cincinnati (N.L.)	3B-2B	17	27	0	6	3	0	0	2	1	6	0	1	0-0	.222	.250	.333	.583	1	.944
American League totals (2 years)		108	197	17	39	11	0	3	17	6	40	1	4	1-0	.198	.222	.299	.522	9	.949
National League totals (10 years)		613	1423	154	351	74	7	19	134	94	303	25	36	9-12	.247	.303	.349	.651	60	.963
Major League totals (11 years)		721	1620	171	390	85	7	22	151	100	343	26	40	10-12	.241	.293	.343	.636	69	.961

DIVISION SERIES RECORD

Year — Team (League)	Pos.	G	AB	R	H	2B	3B	HR	RBI	BB	SO	HBP	GDP	SB-CS	Avg.	OBP	SLG	OPS	E	Avg.
1996—San Diego (N.L.)		1	0	0	0	0	0	0	0	0	0	0	0	0-0	...	...	...	...	...	...
1999—New York (N.L.)		Did not play.																		

CHAMPIONSHIP SERIES RECORD

Year — Team (League)	Pos.	G	AB	R	H	2B	3B	HR	RBI	BB	SO	HBP	GDP	SB-CS	Avg.	OBP	SLG	OPS	E	Avg.
1999—New York (N.L.)		Did not play.																		

LOPEZ, PEDRO — SS/2B

PERSONAL: Born April 28, 1984, in Moca, Dominican Republic. ... 6-1/160. ... Bats right, throws right. ... Full name: Pedro Michel Lopez. ... College: None.

TRANSACTIONS/CAREER NOTES: Signed as a non-drafted free agent by Chicago White Sox (September 14, 2000).

2005 GAMES PLAYED BY POSITION (MLB): 2B—1, SS—1.

LEFTY-RIGHTY SPLITS

vs.	Avg.	AB	H	2B	3B	HR	RBI	BB	SO	OBP	Slg.
L	.333	6	2	0	0	0	2	0	1	.333	.333
R	.000	1	0	0	0	0	0	0	0	.000	.000

Year — Team (League)	Pos.	G	AB	R	H	2B	3B	HR	RBI	BB	SO	HBP	GDP	SB-CS	Avg.	OBP	SLG	OPS	E	Avg.
2001—Ariz. White Sox (Ariz.)	2B-SS-3B	50	199	26	62	11	3	1	19	16	24	0	4	12-6	.312	.359	.412	.771	19	.907
2002—Bristol (Appal.)	2B-SS	63	260	42	83	11	0	0	35	20	27	1	3	22-8	.319	.370	.362	.732	6	.980
2003—Kannapolis (S. Atl.)	2B-SS-3B	109	390	40	103	23	0	0	33	26	43	3	8	24-14	.264	.314	.323	.637	13	.972
—Win.-Salem (Car.)	SS-2B	4	13	1	3	0	0	0	0	1	0	0	0	0-0	.231	.286	.231	.517	2	.920
2004—Win.-Salem (Car.)	SS-2B	111	430	62	124	13	0	4	35	23	35	4	3	12-9	.288	.328	.347	.675	15	.667
—Birmingham (Sou.)	SS	7	23	3	5	0	1	0	0	5	2	1	0	2-0	.217	.379	.304	.683	1	.000
2005—Chicago (A.L.)	2B-SS	2	7	1	2	0	0	0	2	0	1	0	0	0-0	.286	.286	.286	.571	0	1.000
—Charlotte (Int'l)	SS-2B	55	188	14	38	6	0	3	17	7	24	2	4	1-1	.202	.236	.282	.518	13	.945
—Birmingham (Sou.)	SS	68	239	26	57	7	1	3	24	13	29	4	10	0-2	.238	.287	.314	.601	10	.970
Major League totals (1 year)		2	7	1	2	0	0	0	2	0	1	0	0	0-0	.286	.286	.286	.571	0	1.000

LOPEZ, RODRIGO — P

PERSONAL: Born December 14, 1975, in Tlalnepantla, Mexico. ... 6-1/190. ... Throws right, bats right. ... Full name: Rodrigo Munoz Lopez. ... Name pronounced: rod-REE-go.

TRANSACTIONS/CAREER NOTES: Contract sold by Aguila of the Mexican League to San Diego Padres organization (March 21, 1995). ... Loaned by Padres to Mexico City Red Devils of the Mexican League (March 13-August 19, 1998). ... Signed as a free agent by Baltimore Orioles organization (February 4, 2002). ... On disabled list (May 2-June 15, 2003); included rehabilitation assignment to Bowie.

HONORS: Named A.L. Rookie Pitcher of the Year by THE SPORTING NEWS (2002).

CAREER HITTING: 1-for-18 (.056), 1 R, 0 2B, 0 3B, 0 HR, 0 RBI.

SCOUTING REPORT *Throws:* Lopez attacks hitters with a 90-93 mph fastball, an 83-86 slider and a changeup. *Tendencies:* He has a good delivery with the ability to throw his fastball to both sides of the plate with command. Slider, his best pitch has only a small break, but it's a late one and he controls the pitch well, frequently starting it away from righthanders and forcing them to chase it off the plate. Shows good arm speed with his changeup. Is not overpowering and must keep the ball down. *Outlook:* He is an underrated starter who has three quality pitches and pitches deep into games. *Grade 7.9*

RODRIGO LOPEZ'S PITCHING ZONE

.298	.273	.298
.303	.446	.293
.261	.308	.254

LEFTY-RIGHTY SPLITS

vs.	Avg.	AB	H	2B	3B	HR	RBI	BB	SO	OBP	Slg.
L	.288	459	132	28	2	13	57	30	59	.335	.442
R	.262	381	100	24	4	15	58	33	59	.325	.465

Year	Team (League)	W	L	Pct.	ERA	WHIP	G	GS	CG	ShO	Hld.	Sv.-Opp.	IP	H	R	ER	HR	BB-IBB	SO	Avg.
1993— Aguila (Mex.)		0	0	...	36.00	6.00	2	0	0	0	...	0-...	1.0	3	4	4	0	3-...	0	...
1994— Aguila (Mex.)		0	0	...	4.97	1.42	10	0	0	0	...	0-...	12.2	15	7	7	2	3-...	5	...
1995— Ariz. Padres (Ariz.)		1	1	.500	5.45	1.59	11	7	0	0	...	1-...	34.2	41	29	21	0	14-0	33	.287
1996— Poza Rica (Mex.)		1	1	.500	3.54	1.52	7	3	0	0	...	1-...	20.1	15	8	8	2	16-...	22	...
— Idaho Falls (Pio.)		4	4	.500	5.70	1.55	15	14	0	0	...	1-...	71.0	76	52	45	3	34-0	72	.283
1997— Clinton (Midw.)		6	8	.429	3.18	1.19	37	14	2	0	...	9-...	121.2	103	49	43	6	42-1	123	.228
1998— M.C. R. Dev. (Mex.)		10	6	.625	3.35	1.49	26	26	1	0	...	0-...	163.2	165	73	61	9	79-...	95	...
— Mobile (Sou.)		3	0	1.000	1.40	0.97	4	4	2	1	...	0-...	25.2	21	11	4	1	4-0	20	.219
1999— Mobile (Sou.)		10	8	.556	4.41	1.45	28	28	2	1	...	0-...	169.1	187	91	83	14	58-3	138	.286
2000— Las Vegas (PCL)		8	7	.533	4.69	1.54	20	20	1	0	...	0-...	109.1	123	66	57	9	45-1	100	.289
— San Diego (N.L.)		0	3	.000	8.76	2.15	6	6	0	0	0	0-0	24.2	40	24	24	5	13-0	17	.377
2001— Lake Elsinore (Calif.)		0	1	.000	0.69	1.46	9	0	0	0	0	0-...	13.0	15	7	1	1	4-0	9	.278
— Portland (PCL)		2	2	.500	3.44	1.15	11	8	0	0	0	0-...	52.1	45	22	20	7	15-0	37	.230
2002— Baltimore (A.L.)		15	9	.625	3.57	1.19	33	28	1	0	0	0-0	196.2	172	83	78	23	62-4	136	.234
2003— Bowie (East.)		1	0	1.000	0.00	0.50	1	1	0	0	0	0-...	6.1	3	0	0	0	0-0	13	.143
— Baltimore (A.L.)		7	10	.412	5.82	1.57	26	26	3	1	0	0-0	147.0	188	101	95	24	43-6	103	.313
2004— Baltimore (A.L.)		14	9	.609	3.59	1.28	37	23	1	1	4	0-1	170.2	164	71	68	21	54-2	121	.252
2005— Baltimore (A.L.)		15	12	.556	4.90	1.41	35	35	0	0	0	0-0	209.1	232	126	114	28	63-1	118	.276
American League totals (4 years)		51	40	.560	4.42	1.35	131	112	5	2	4	0-1	723.2	756	381	355	96	222-13	478	.268
National League totals (1 year)		0	3	.000	8.76	2.15	6	6	0	0	0	0-0	24.2	40	24	24	5	13-0	17	.377
Major League totals (5 years)		51	43	.543	4.56	1.38	137	118	5	2	4	0-1	748.1	796	405	379	101	235-13	495	.271

LORETTA, MARK — 2B

PERSONAL: Born August 14, 1971, in Santa Monica, Calif. ... 6-0/186. ... Bats right, throws right. ... Full name: Mark David Loretta. ... High school: St. Francis (La Canada, Calif.). ... College: Northwestern.

TRANSACTIONS/CAREER NOTES: Selected by Milwaukee Brewers organization in seventh round of 1993 free-agent draft. ... On disabled list (June 3-August 16, 2000); included rehabilitation assignment to Indianapolis. ... On disabled list (March 27-May 19, 2001); included rehabilitation assignment to Indianapolis. ... Traded by Brewers to Houston Astros for two players to be named (August 31, 2002); Brewers acquired P Wayne Franklin (September 3, 2002) and 2B Keith Ginter (September 5, 2002) to complete deal. ... Signed as a free agent by San Diego Padres (December 16, 2002). ... On disabled list (May 24-July 18, 2005); included rehabilitation assignment to Portland. ... Career major league pitching: 0-0, 0.00 ERA, 1 G, 1.0 IP, 1 H, 0 R, 0 ER, 1 BB, 2 SO.

2005 GAMES PLAYED BY POSITION (MLB): 2B—105, 3B—1.

SCOUTING REPORT **Offense:** Loretta has a short, compact stroke and good bat control. Has lost bat speed because of a thumb injury but still makes good contact. Can adjust with the count and use the whole field. Could not drive the ball last season. Is a good hitter with runners on base and is deadly against lefthanded pitching. **Defense:** His technique is extremely sound, and his instincts are outstanding. Positions himself well and has good hands. Makes the pivot on the double play well and avoids contact. Has a accurate arm. Gets a good jump on balls to either side.

Outlook: Loretta is a steady, professional player with exceptional instincts and intelligence. Always plays under control and should have no complications coming back from the injury. **Grade 8.0**

MARK LORETTA'S HITTING ZONE

.375	.235	.185
.306	.261	.297
.286	.207	.381

LEFTY-RIGHTY SPLITS

vs.	Avg.	AB	H	2B	3B	HR	RBI	BB	SO	OBP	Slg.
L	.309	94	29	2	0	1	8	20	8	.426	.362
R	.271	310	84	14	1	2	30	25	26	.338	.342

Year	Team (League)	Pos.	G	AB	R	H	2B	3B	HR	RBI	BB	SO	HBP	GDP	SB-CS	Avg.	OBP	SLG	OPS	E	Avg.
1993— Helena (Pion.)		SS	6	28	5	9	1	0	1	8	1	4	1	1	0-0	.321	.367	.464	.831	0	1.000
— Stockton (Calif.)		3B-SS	53	201	36	73	4	1	4	31	22	17	2	6	8-2	.363	.427	.453	.880	15	.943
1994— El Paso (Texas)		P	77	302	50	95	13	6	0	38	27	33	2	12	8-5	.315	.369	.397	.766	11	.973
— New Orleans (A.A.)		2B-SS	43	138	16	29	7	0	1	14	12	13	3	2	2-1	.210	.282	.283	.565	11	.945
1995— New Orleans (A.A.)		SS-3B-2B																			
		DH	127	479	48	137	22	5	7	79	34	47	9	12	8-9	.286	.340	.397	.737	25	.959
— Milwaukee (A.L.)		SS-2B-DH	19	50	13	13	3	0	1	3	4	7	1	1	1-1	.260	.327	.380	.707	1	.984
1996— New Orleans (A.A.)		SS	19	71	10	18	5	1	0	11	9	8	2	1	1-1	.254	.345	.352	.697	5	.948
— Milwaukee (A.L.)		2B-3B-SS	73	154	20	43	3	0	1	13	14	15	0	7	2-1	.279	.339	.318	.657	2	.989
1997— Milwaukee (A.L.)		2B-SS-1B																			
		3B	132	418	56	120	17	5	5	47	47	60	2	15	5-5	.287	.354	.388	.742	15	.976
1998— Milwaukee (N.L.)		1B-SS-3B																			
		2B-OF	140	434	55	137	29	0	6	54	42	47	7	14	9-6	.316	.382	.424	.806	6	.991
1999— Milwaukee (N.L.)		SS-1B-2B																			
		3B	153	587	93	170	34	5	5	67	52	59	10	14	4-1	.290	.354	.390	.744	13	.986
2000— Milwaukee (N.L.)		SS-2B	91	352	49	99	21	1	7	40	37	38	1	9	0-3	.281	.350	.406	.757	2	.995
— Indianapolis (Int'l)		SS	10	25	6	6	1	0	0	5	2	4	1	1	0-0	.240	.310	.280	.590	0	1.000
2001— Indianapolis (Int'l)		SS-2B-3B	8	31	4	3	0	0	0	1	2	4	0	1	0-0	.097	.152	.097	.248	3	.850
— Milwaukee (N.L.)		2B-3B-SS																			
		DH-P	102	384	40	111	14	2	9	29	28	46	7	6	1-2	.289	.346	.352	.698	3	.978
2002— Milwaukee (N.L.)		3B-SS-1B																			
		2B-DH	86	217	23	58	14	0	2	19	23	32	5	6	0-0	.267	.350	.359	.709	3	.982
— Houston (N.L.)		3B-SS-2B	21	66	10	28	4	0	2	8	9	5	0	1	1-1	.424	.481	.576	1.056	2	.964
2003— San Diego (N.L.)		2B-SS	154	589	74	185	28	4	13	72	54	62	3	17	5-4	.314	.372	.441	.814	7	.990
2004— San Diego (N.L.)		2B	154	620	108	208	47	2	16	76	58	45	4	10	5-3	.335	.391	.495	.886	10	.987
2005— Portland (PCL)		2B-DH	3	10	0	1	0	0	0	0	2	1	0	1	0-0	.100	.250	.100	.350	0	1.000
— San Diego (N.L.)		2B-3B-DH	105	404	54	113	16	1	3	38	45	34	8	11	8-4	.280	.360	.347	.707	6	.987
American League totals (3 years)			224	622	89	176	23	5	7	63	65	82	3	23	8-7	.283	.349	.370	.718	18	.979
National League totals (8 years)			1006	3653	506	1109	207	15	56	403	348	368	50	88	33-24	.304	.368	.414	.783	57	.987
Major League totals (11 years)			1230	4275	595	1285	230	20	63	466	413	450	53	111	41-31	.301	.365	.408	.773	75	.986

DIVISION SERIES RECORD

Year	Team (League)	Pos.	G	AB	R	H	2B	3B	HR	RBI	BB	SO	HBP	GDP	SB-CS	Avg.	OBP	SLG	OPS	E	Avg.
2005— San Diego (N.L.)		2B	3	15	0	4	0	0	0	2	0	1	0	0	0-0	.267	.267	.267	.533	0	1.000

ALL-STAR GAME RECORD

			G	AB	R	H	2B	3B	HR	RBI	BB	SO	HBP	GDP	SB-CS	Avg.	OBP	SLG	OPS	E	Avg.
All-Star Game totals (1 year)			1	2	0	1	0	0	0	0	0	0	0	0	0-0	.500	.500	.500	1.000	0	1.000

LOWE, DEREK — P

PERSONAL: Born June 1, 1973, in Dearborn, Mich. ... 6-6/210. ... Throws right, bats right. ... Full name: Derek Christopher Lowe. ... High school: Edsel Ford (Dearborn, Mich.).

TRANSACTIONS/CAREER NOTES: Selected by Seattle Mariners organization in eighth round of 1991 free-agent draft. ... Traded by Mariners with C Jason Varitek to Boston Red Sox for P Heathcliff Slocumb (July 31, 1997). ... On suspended list (September 15-20, 2002). ... Signed as a free agent by Los Angeles Dodgers (January 12, 2005).

CAREER HITTING: 12-for-85 (.141), 3 R, 3 2B, 0 3B, 0 HR, 5 RBI.

SCOUTING REPORT *Throws:* Lowe primarily throws a sinking fastball at 89-93 mph, but he also has a curve at 78-80 and a slider at 84-87. *Tendencies:* He throws more fastballs than any pitcher in the league, continually pounding the zone with his sinker. Starts his sharp-biting slider away from righthanded hitters. Occasionally throws a curveball early in the count. Tends to nibble instead of starting his fastball down the middle and letting the movement take over. *Outlook:* Lowe has always had an outstanding sinker and good durability, but he needs to stay focused. Is still immature but has gotten better at handling adversity. **Grade 7.9**

DEREK LOWE'S PITCHING ZONE

.308	.273	.250
.261	.343	.340
.219	.344	.235

LEFTY-RIGHTY SPLITS

vs.	Avg.	AB	H	2B	3B	HR	RBI	BB	SO	OBP	Slg.
L	.296	460	136	25	1	17	64	36	68	.349	.465
R	.219	397	87	16	0	11	37	19	78	.257	.343

Year	Team (League)	W	L	Pct.	ERA	WHIP	G	GS	CG	ShO	Hld.	Sv.-Opp.	IP	H	R	ER	HR	BB-IBB	SO	Avg.
1991— Ariz. Mariners (Ariz.)		5	3	.625	2.41	1.11	12	12	0	0	...	0-...	71.0	58	26	19	2	21-0	60	.217
1992— Bellingham (N'west)		7	3	.700	2.42	1.06	14	13	0	•1	...	0-...	85.2	69	34	23	2	22-0	66	.216
1993— Riverside (Calif.)		12	9	.571	5.26	1.62	27	26	3	2	...	0-...	154.0	189	104	90	9	60-0	80	.304
1994— Jacksonville (Sou.)		7	10	.412	4.94	1.50	26	26	2	0	...	0-...	151.1	177	92	83	7	50-1	75	.291
1995— Ariz. Mariners (Ariz.)		1	0	1.000	0.93	0.72	2	2	0	0	...	0-...	9.2	5	1	1	0	2-0	11	.152
— Port City (Sou.)		1	6	.143	6.08	1.73	10	10	1	0	...	0-...	53.1	70	41	36	8	22-1	30	.327
1996— Port City (Sou.)		5	3	.625	3.05	1.12	10	10	0	0	...	0-...	65.0	56	27	22	7	17-0	33	.235
— Tacoma (PCL)		6	9	.400	4.54	1.48	17	16	1	1	...	0-...	105.0	118	64	53	7	37-1	54	.285
1997— Tacoma (PCL)		3	4	.429	3.45	1.27	10	9	1	0	...	0-...	57.1	53	26	22	3	20-0	49	.242
— Seattle (A.L.)		2	4	.333	6.96	1.49	12	9	0	0	0	0-0	53.0	59	43	41	11	20-2	39	.282
— Pawtucket (Int'l)		4	0	1.000	2.37	1.12	6	5	0	0	...	0-...	30.1	23	8	8	3	11-0	21	.213
— Boston (A.L.)		0	2	.000	3.38	1.13	8	0	0	0	1	0-2	16.0	15	6	6	0	3-1	13	.268
1998— Boston (A.L.)		3	9	.250	4.02	1.37	63	10	0	0	12	4-9	123.0	126	65	55	5	42-5	77	.267
1999— Boston (A.L.)		6	3	.667	2.63	1.00	74	0	0	0	22	15-20	109.1	84	35	32	7	25-1	80	.208
2000— Boston (A.L.)		4	4	.500	2.56	1.23	74	0	0	0	0	•42-47	91.1	90	27	26	6	22-5	79	.257
2001— Boston (A.L.)		5	10	.333	3.53	1.44	67	3	0	0	4	24-30	91.2	103	39	36	7	29-9	82	.285
2002— Boston (A.L.)		21	8	.724	2.58	0.97	32	32	1	1	0	0-0	219.2	166	65	63	12	48-0	127	.211
2003— Boston (A.L.)		17	7	.708	4.47	1.42	33	33	1	0	0	0-0	203.1	216	113	101	17	72-4	110	.272
2004— Boston (A.L.)		14	12	.538	5.42	1.61	33	33	0	0	0	0-0	182.2	224	*138	110	15	71-2	105	.299
2005— Los Angeles (N.L.)		12	15	.444	3.61	1.25	35	•35	2	2	0	0-0	222.0	223	113	89	28	55-1	146	.260
American League totals (8 years)		72	59	.550	3.88	1.30	396	120	2	1	39	85-108	1090.0	1083	531	470	80	332-29	712	.259
National League totals (1 year)		12	15	.444	3.61	1.25	35	35	2	2	0	0-0	222.0	223	113	89	28	55-1	146	.260
Major League totals (9 years)		84	74	.532	3.83	1.29	431	155	4	3	39	85-108	1312.0	1306	644	559	108	387-30	858	.259

DIVISION SERIES RECORD

Year	Team (League)	W	L	Pct.	ERA	WHIP	G	GS	CG	ShO	Hld.	Sv.-Opp.	IP	H	R	ER	HR	BB-IBB	SO	Avg.
1998— Boston (A.L.)		0	0	...	2.08	0.92	2	0	0	0	1	0-0	4.1	3	1	1	0	1-1	2	.200
1999— Boston (A.L.)		1	1	.500	4.32	0.84	3	0	0	0	0	0-0	8.1	6	7	4	2	1-0	7	.188
2003— Boston (A.L.)		0	1	.000	0.93	1.45	3	1	0	0	0	1-1	9.2	7	2	1	0	7-2	6	.200
2004— Boston (A.L.)		1	0	1.000	0.00	2.00	1	0	0	0	0	0-0	1.0	1	0	0	0	1-0	0	.333
Division series totals (4 years)		2	2	.500	2.31	1.16	9	1	0	0	1	1-1	23.1	17	10	6	2	10-3	15	.200

CHAMPIONSHIP SERIES RECORD

Year	Team (League)	W	L	Pct.	ERA	WHIP	G	GS	CG	ShO	Hld.	Sv.-Opp.	IP	H	R	ER	HR	BB-IBB	SO	Avg.
1999— Boston (A.L.)		0	0	...	1.42	1.26	3	0	0	0	0	0-1	6.1	6	3	1	0	2-0	7	.231
2003— Boston (A.L.)		0	2	.000	6.43	1.50	2	2	0	0	0	0-0	14.0	14	10	10	1	7-1	5	.255
2004— Boston (A.L.)		1	0	1.000	3.18	0.71	2	2	0	0	0	0-0	11.1	7	4	4	1	1-0	6	.175
Champ. series totals (3 years)		1	2	.333	4.26	1.17	7	4	0	0	0	0-1	31.2	27	17	15	2	10-1	18	.223

WORLD SERIES RECORD

Year	Team (League)	W	L	Pct.	ERA	WHIP	G	GS	CG	ShO	Hld.	Sv.-Opp.	IP	H	R	ER	HR	BB-IBB	SO	Avg.
2004— Boston (A.L.)		1	0	1.000	0.00	0.57	1	1	0	0	0	0-0	7.0	3	0	0	0	1-0	4	.130

ALL-STAR GAME RECORD

		W	L	Pct.	ERA	WHIP	G	GS	CG	ShO	Hld.	Sv.-Opp.	IP	H	R	ER	HR	BB-IBB	SO	Avg.
All-Star Game totals (2 years)		0	0	...	3.00	0.67	2	1	0	0	1	0-0	3.0	2	1	1	0	0-0	0	.182

LOWELL, MIKE — 3B

PERSONAL: Born February 24, 1974, in San Juan, Puerto Rico. ... 6-3/210. ... Bats right, throws right. ... Full name: Michael Averett Lowell. ... High school: Coral Gables (Fla.). ... College: Florida International.

TRANSACTIONS/CAREER NOTES: Selected by New York Yankees organization in 20th round of 1995 free-agent draft. ... Traded by Yankees to Florida Marlins for Ps Ed Yarnall, Mark Johnson and Todd Noel (February 1, 1999). ... On disabled list (March 26-May 29, 1999); included rehabilitation assignment to Calgary. ... On disabled list (May 13-29, 2000; and August 31-September 28, 2003).

HONORS: Won N.L. Gold Glove at third base (2005).

2005 GAMES PLAYED BY POSITION (MLB): 3B—135, 2B—9.

SCOUTING REPORT Offense: Lowell has lost some bat speed but poor plate discipline was his biggest problem in 2005. Is a better high-ball hitter and a good contact hitter. Loss of power was more worrisome than the loss of bat speed. Is vulnerable to off-speed stuff. Is not a good baserunner. **Defense:** Lowell is one of the better defensive third basemen around. Doesn't have great speed or range; compensates with good instincts and soft hands. Is better to his left. Has good agility and charges balls well. Has a quick release and good accuracy. **Outlook:** Lowell may never hit more than 25 home runs, but he still is a fine defensive player. **Grade 7.8**

MIKE LOWELL'S HITTING ZONE

.250	.091	.091
.325	.339	.100
.246	.350	.235

LEFTY-RIGHTY SPLITS

vs.	Avg.	AB	H	2B	3B	HR	RBI	BB	SO	OBP	Slg.
L	.304	92	28	10	0	2	22	10	8	.362	.478
R	.221	408	90	26	1	6	36	36	50	.283	.333

Year— Team (League)	Pos.	G	AB	R	H	2B	3B	HR	RBI	BB	SO	HBP	GDP	SB-CS	Avg.	OBP	SLG	OPS	E	Avg.
1995— Oneonta (NYP)	3B	72	281	36	73	18	0	1	27	23	34	3	5	3-1	.260	.316	.335	.651	24	.911
1996— Greensboro (S. Atl.)	3B-SS	113	433	58	122	33	0	8	64	46	43	4	7	10-3	.282	.355	.413	.768	32	.925
— Tampa (Fla. St.)	3B	24	78	8	22	5	0	0	11	3	13	0	2	1-1	.282	.298	.346	.644	3	.954
1997— Norwich (East.)	3B-SS	78	285	60	98	17	0	15	47	48	30	4	11	2-1	.344	.439	.561	1.000	15	.927
— Columbus (Int'l)	3B-SS	57	210	36	58	13	1	15	45	23	34	3	6	2-4	.276	.347	.562	.909	5	.954
1998— Columbus (Int'l)	1B-3B-SS	126	510	79	155	34	3	26	99	37	85	6	10	4-0	.304	.355	.535	.890	21	.950
— New York (A.L.)	3B-DH	8	15	1	4	0	0	0	0	0	1	0	0	0-0	.267	.267	.267	.533	0	1.000
1999— Calgary (PCL)	3B	24	83	11	26	3	0	2	9	8	19	0	0	0-0	.313	.374	.422	.795	4	.939
— Florida (N.L.)	3B	97	308	32	78	15	0	12	47	26	69	5	8	0-0	.253	.317	.419	.736	4	.981
2000— Florida (N.L.)	3B	140	508	73	137	38	0	22	91	54	75	9	4	4-0	.270	.344	.474	.818	12	.968
2001— Florida (N.L.)	3B	158	551	65	156	37	0	18	100	43	79	10	9	1-2	.283	.340	.448	.789	9	.976
2002— Florida (N.L.)	3B	160	597	88	165	44	0	24	92	65	92	4	16	4-3	.276	.346	.471	.816	14	.969
2003— Florida (N.L.)	3B-DH	130	492	76	136	27	1	32	105	56	78	3	14	3-1	.276	.350	.530	.881	9	.973
2004— Florida (N.L.)	3B-DH	158	598	87	175	44	1	27	85	64	77	6	17	5-1	.293	.365	.505	.870	7	.982
2005— Florida (N.L.)	3B-2B	150	500	56	118	36	1	8	58	46	58	2	14	4-0	.236	.298	.360	.658	7	.982
American League totals (1 year)		8	15	1	4	0	0	0	0	0	1	0	0	0-0	.267	.267	.267	.533	0	1.000
National League totals (7 years)		981	3554	477	965	241	3	143	578	354	528	39	82	21-7	.272	.339	.462	.801	62	.975
Major League totals (8 years)		989	3569	478	969	241	3	143	578	354	529	39	82	21-7	.272	.339	.461	.800	62	.976

DIVISION SERIES RECORD

Year— Team (League)	Pos.	G	AB	R	H	2B	3B	HR	RBI	BB	SO	HBP	GDP	SB-CS	Avg.	OBP	SLG	OPS	E	Avg.
2003— Florida (N.L.)	3B	2	3	0	0	0	0	0	0	0	1	0	0	0-0	.000	.000	.000	.000	0	1.000

CHAMPIONSHIP SERIES RECORD

Year— Team (League)	Pos.	G	AB	R	H	2B	3B	HR	RBI	BB	SO	HBP	GDP	SB-CS	Avg.	OBP	SLG	OPS	E	Avg.
2003— Florida (N.L.)	3B	7	20	5	4	0	0	2	3	3	4	0	0	0-0	.200	.304	.500	.804	1	1.000

WORLD SERIES RECORD

Year— Team (League)	Pos.	G	AB	R	H	2B	3B	HR	RBI	BB	SO	HBP	GDP	SB-CS	Avg.	OBP	SLG	OPS	E	Avg.
2003— Florida (N.L.)	3B	6	23	1	5	1	0	0	2	2	3	0	0	0-0	.217	.280	.261	.541	0	1.000

ALL-STAR GAME RECORD

		G	AB	R	H	2B	3B	HR	RBI	BB	SO	HBP	GDP	SB-CS	Avg.	OBP	SLG	OPS	E	Avg.
All-Star Game totals (3 years)		3	6	1	3	1	0	0	1	0	1	0	0	0-0	.500	.500	.667	1.167	0	1.000

L

LOWRY, NOAH   P

PERSONAL: Born October 10, 1980, in Ventura, Calif. ... 6-2/210. ... Throws left, bats right. ... Full name: Noah Ryan Lowry. ... High school: Nordhoff (Ojai, Calif.). ... College: Pepperdine.

TRANSACTIONS/CAREER NOTES: Selected by Texas Rangers organization in 19th round of 1999 free-agent draft; did not sign. ... Selected by San Francisco Giants organization in first round (30th pick overall) of 2001 free-agent draft.

CAREER HITTING: 23-for-94 (.245), 9 R, 8 2B, 0 3B, 0 HR, 7 RBI.

SCOUTING REPORT Throws: Lowry's 87-91 mph fastball has some sinking movement. Also throws a curve, slider and a good changeup. **Tendencies:** Lowry has a deceptive delivery that makes his fastball, which he throws to both sides of the plate, sneaky fast. Has good command, especially on his fastball. Doesn't use his curve much because it rolls, but his slider is a quicker, more consistent breaking ball that allows him to work the other side of the plate. Best pitch is an excellent changeup that will tail and fade. Will use his change on any count to any hitter and will throw it on back-to-back pitches. Sometimes uses it too much. **Outlook:** Lowry is advanced for a young pitcher and has the command to execute pitches. Will move up in the rotation next year and be a No. 2 or 3 starter. **Grade 7.5**

NOAH LOWRY'S PITCHING ZONE

.286	.226	.196
.297	.491	.205
.246	.364	.224

LEFTY-RIGHTY SPLITS

vs.	Avg.	AB	H	2B	3B	HR	RBI	BB	SO	OBP	Slg.
L	.213	178	38	8	0	3	14	22	43	.309	.309
R	.259	598	155	22	5	18	64	54	129	.324	.403

Year— Team (League)	W	L	Pct.	ERA	WHIP	G	GS	CG	ShO	Hld.	Sv.-Opp.	IP	H	R	ER	HR	BB-IBB	SO	Avg.
2001— Salem-Keizer (N'west)	1	1	.500	3.60	1.36	8	7	0	0	...	0-...	25.0	26	15	10	2	8-0	28	.265
2002— San Jose (Calif.)	6	5	.545	2.15	0.99	15	12	0	0	...	0-...	58.2	38	21	14	4	20-0	62	.186
2003— Norwich (East.)	9	6	.600	4.72	1.47	23	23	2	0	...	0-...	118.1	127	66	62	7	47-0	97	.285
— Fresno (PCL)	1	0	1.000	2.37	1.11	4	4	0	0	...	0-...	19.0	15	5	5	0	6-0	13	.227
— San Francisco (N.L.)	0	0	...	0.00	0.47	4	0	0	0	0	0-0	6.1	1	0	0	0	2-0	5	.048
2004— Fresno (PCL)	7	5	.583	4.13	1.41	17	17	1	1	...	0-...	89.1	98	53	41	9	28-0	73	.278
— San Francisco (N.L.)	6	0	1.000	3.82	1.29	16	14	2	1	0	0-0	92.0	91	41	39	10	28-1	72	.259
2005— San Francisco (N.L.)	13	13	.500	3.78	1.31	33	33	0	0	0	0-0	204.2	193	92	86	21	76-1	172	.249
Major League totals (3 years)	19	13	.594	3.71	1.29	53	47	2	1	0	0-0	303.0	285	133	125	31	106-2	249	.248

LUDWICK, RYAN — OF

PERSONAL: Born July 13, 1978, in Satellite Beach, Fla. ... 6-3/203. ... Bats right, throws left. ... Full name: Ryan Andrew Ludwick. ... High school: Durango (Las Vegas). ... College: UNLV. ... Brother of Eric Ludwick, pitcher for four major league teams (1996-99).

TRANSACTIONS/CAREER NOTES: Selected by Oakland Athletics organization in second round of 1999 free-agent draft. ... Traded by A's with 1B Jason Hart, P Mario Ramos and C Gerald Laird to Texas Rangers for 1B Carlos Pena and P Mike Venafro (January 14, 2002). ... Traded by Rangers to Cleveland Indians for P Ricardo Rodriguez (July 18, 2003). ... On disabled list (April 2-July 5, 2004); included rehabilitation assignment to Akron.

2005 GAMES PLAYED BY POSITION (MLB): OF—15, DH—3.

LEFTY-RIGHTY SPLITS

vs.	Avg.	AB	H	2B	3B	HR	RBI	BB	SO	OBP	Slg.
L	.200	25	5	0	0	3	4	6	10	.355	.560
R	.250	16	4	0	0	1	1	1	3	.294	.438

									BATTING										FIELDING	
Year	Team (League)	Pos.	G	AB	R	H	2B	3B	HR	RBI	BB	SO	HBP	GDP	SB-CS	Avg.	OBP	SLG	OPS	E	Avg.
1999—	Modesto (California)	OF	43	171	28	47	11	3	4	34	19	45	3	0	2-1	.275	.348	.444	.793	0	1.000
2000—	Modesto (California)	OF	129	493	86	130	26	3	29	102	68	128	9	6	10-6	.264	.359	.505	.864	5	.983
2001—	Midland (Texas)	OF	119	443	82	119	23	3	25	96	53	113	7	6	9-10	.269	.352	.503	.856	6	.977
	— Sacramento (PCL)	OF	17	57	10	13	3	0	1	7	2	16	0	0	2-0	.228	.246	.333	.579	1	.981
2002—	Oklahoma (PCL)	OF	78	305	62	87	27	4	15	52	38	76	5	6	2-2	.285	.370	.548	.918	5	.973
	— Texas (A.L.)	OF	23	81	10	19	6	0	1	9	7	24	0	4	2-1	.235	.295	.346	.641	0	1.000
2003—	Oklahoma (PCL)	OF-DH	81	317	51	96	24	3	17	63	33	71	5	9	1-1	.303	.372	.558	.931	3	.975
	— Texas (A.L.)	OF	8	26	3	4	1	0	0	0	4	9	0	0	0-0	.154	.267	.192	.459	0	1.000
	— Cleveland (A.L.)	OF-DH	39	136	14	36	7	1	7	26	8	39	0	1	2-0	.265	.306	.485	.791	0	1.000
2004—	Akron (East.)	OF-DH	8	26	4	7	2	0	1	5	1	5	0	0	0-0	.269	.286	.462	.747	0	1.000
	— Buffalo (Int'l)	OF-DH	44	166	25	45	15	0	8	30	16	52	4	4	0-0	.271	.346	.506	.852	1	.980
	— Cleveland (A.L.)	OF	15	50	3	11	2	0	2	4	2	14	2	0	0-0	.220	.278	.380	.658	1	.970
2005—	Cleveland (A.L.)	OF-DH	19	41	8	9	0	0	4	5	7	13	0	1	0-1	.220	.333	.512	.846	1	.957
	— Buffalo (Int'l)	OF	54	188	27	36	10	2	4	16	17	48	5	9	0-1	.191	.272	.330	.602	4	.983
Major League totals (4 years)			104	334	38	79	16	1	14	44	28	99	2	6	4-2	.237	.299	.416	.716	2	.989

LUGO, JULIO — SS

PERSONAL: Born November 16, 1975, in Barahona, Dominican Republic. ... 6-1/170. ... Bats right, throws right. ... Full name: Julio Cesar Lugo. ... Name pronounced: LOU-go. ... Junior college: Connors State (Okla.).

TRANSACTIONS/CAREER NOTES: Selected by Houston Astros organization in 43rd round of 1994 free-agent draft. ... On disabled list (August 13, 2002-remainder of season). ... Released by Astros (May 9, 2003). ... Signed by Tampa Bay Devil Rays (May 15, 2003).

2005 GAMES PLAYED BY POSITION (MLB): SS—156.

SCOUTING REPORT *Offense:* Lugo has become a very good offensive player. Has a very short stroke. Bat control makes him a good fit in the No. 2 spot. Can use the whole field. Is a very good situational hitter and can make adjustments according to the count. Has more gap power than home-run power yet is quick enough to turn on mistakes up and out over the plate. Is a very good runner. *Defense:* His throws have very good carry, but he can be erratic when he rushes the ball from the hole. Has very good hands. Is adept going to the hole and setting to throw. Range is better to his left. *Outlook:* This much-improved player has been showing signs of maturity. Will continue to be a productive player in the Rays' lineup. *Grade 8.1*

JULIO LUGO'S HITTING ZONE

.267	.379	.308
.290	.258	.375
.364	.423	.300

LEFTY-RIGHTY SPLITS

vs.	Avg.	AB	H	2B	3B	HR	RBI	BB	SO	OBP	Slg.
L	.306	183	56	13	1	1	15	17	13	.361	.404
R	.291	433	126	23	5	5	42	44	59	.363	.402

									BATTING										FIELDING	
Year	Team (League)	Pos.	G	AB	R	H	2B	3B	HR	RBI	BB	SO	HBP	GDP	SB-CS	Avg.	OBP	SLG	OPS	E	Avg.
1995—	Auburn (NY-Penn)	2B-OF-SS	59	230	36	67	6	3	1	16	26	31	2	7	17-7	.291	.368	.357	.725	12	.944
1996—	Quad City (Midw.)	2B-3B-SS	101	393	60	116	18	2	10	50	32	75	3	7	24-11	.295	.350	.427	.777	29	.934
1997—	Kissimmee (Fla. St.)	2B-3B-SS	125	505	89	135	22	14	7	61	46	99	2	8	35-8	.267	.329	.408	.736	41	.938
1998—	Kissimmee (Fla. St.)	SS	128	509	81	154	20	14	7	62	49	72	4	13	51-18	.303	.367	.418	.805	42	.921
1999—	Jackson (Texas)	SS-2B	116	445	77	142	24	5	10	42	44	53	3	6	25-11	.319	.381	.463	.844	29	.946
2000—	New Orleans (PCL)	2B-SS	24	101	22	33	4	1	3	12	11	20	0	2	12-7	.327	.393	.475	.868	4	.964
	— Houston (N.L.)	SS-OF-2B	116	420	73	119	22	5	10	40	37	93	4	9	22-9	.283	.346	.431	.777	17	.963
2001—	Houston (N.L.)	SS-OF-2B	140	513	93	135	20	3	10	37	46	116	5	7	12-11	.263	.326	.372	.698	22	.964
2002—	Houston (N.L.)	SS	88	322	45	84	15	1	8	35	28	74	2	6	9-3	.261	.322	.388	.710	8	.976
2003—	Houston (N.L.)	SS	22	65	6	16	3	0	0	2	9	12	0	2	2-1	.246	.338	.292	.630	3	.966
	— Tampa Bay (A.L.)	SS	117	433	58	119	19	4	15	53	35	88	4	5	10-3	.275	.333	.427	.760	17	.970
2004—	Tampa Bay (A.L.)	SS-2B-DH	157	581	83	160	41	4	7	75	54	106	5	8	21-5	.275	.338	.396	.734	26	.964
2005—	Tampa Bay (A.L.)	SS	158	616	89	182	36	6	6	57	61	72	6	5	39-11	.295	.362	.403	.765	24	.968
American League totals (3 years)			432	1630	230	461	90	14	28	185	150	266	15	18	70-19	.283	.346	.407	.753	67	.967
National League totals (4 years)			366	1320	222	354	60	9	28	114	120	295	11	24	45-24	.268	.332	.391	.723	50	.966
Major League totals (6 years)			798	2950	452	815	150	23	56	299	270	561	26	42	115-43	.276	.340	.400	.739	117	.967

DIVISION SERIES RECORD

									BATTING										FIELDING	
Year	Team (League)	Pos.	G	AB	R	H	2B	3B	HR	RBI	BB	SO	HBP	GDP	SB-CS	Avg.	OBP	SLG	OPS	E	Avg.
2001—	Houston (N.L.)	SS	3	8	1	0	0	0	0	0	0	2	0	1	0-0	.000	.000	.000	.000	3	.786

LUNA, HECTOR — SS/2B

PERSONAL: Born February 1, 1980, in Montecristi, Dominican Republic. ... 6-1/170. ... Bats right, throws right. ... Full name: Hector R. Luna.

TRANSACTIONS/CAREER NOTES: Signed as a non-drafted free agent by Cleveland Indians organization (February 2, 1999). ... Selected by Tampa Bay Devil Rays from Indians organization in Rule 5 major league draft (December 16, 2002); returned to Indians organization (April 2, 2003). ... Selected by St. Louis Cardinals from Indians organization in Rule 5 major league draft (December 15, 2003).

2005 GAMES PLAYED BY POSITION (MLB): OF—25, 2B—22, 3B—7, SS—6.

SCOUTING REPORT Luna is a line-drive hitter who has shortened his stroke and improved his bat speed. Is not patient. Will hit the ball where it is pitched. Is an average runner but has good instincts. Is not fluid but has improved his hands. Can play second or third base and shortstop. Has good arm strength and has improved going to his right. Will be a quality utility infielder because the Cardinals don't overexpose him. ***Grade 5.5***

HECTOR LUNA'S HITTING ZONE

.000	.333	.273
.375	.222	.235
.100	.375	.556

LEFTY-RIGHTY SPLITS

vs.	Avg.	AB	H	2B	3B	HR	RBI	BB	SO	OBP	Slg.
L	.310	58	18	5	1	1	8	3	10	.385	.483
R	.266	79	21	5	1	0	10	6	15	.314	.354

		BATTING																	FIELDING	
Year Team (League)	Pos.	G	AB	R	H	2B	3B	HR	RBI	BB	SO	HBP	GDP	SB-CS	Avg.	OBP	SLG	OPS	E	Avg.
1999—Dom. Indians (DSL)	SS	61	234	44	60	13	2	1	24	27	36	5	9	29-5	.256	.345	.342	.687	...	...
2000—Burlington (Appal.)	SS	55	201	25	41	5	0	1	15	27	35	3	4	19-4	.204	.306	.244	.550	26	.900
—Mahoning Valley (NYP)	SS	5	19	2	6	2	0	0	4	1	3	0	0	0-0	.316	.350	.421	.771	2	.875
2001—Columbus (S. Atl.)	SS	66	241	36	64	8	3	3	23	23	48	5	2	15-4	.266	.339	.361	.700	22	.933
2002—Kinston (Carol.)	SS	128	468	67	129	15	6	11	51	39	79	3	7	32-11	.276	.334	.404	.738	32	.947
2003—Akron (East.)	SS-2B	127	462	87	137	19	2	2	38	48	64	5	10	17-5	.297	.368	.359	.727	35	.936
2004—St. Louis (N.L.)	SS-2B-3B-OF	83	173	25	43	7	2	3	22	13	37	2	2	6-3	.249	.304	.364	.668	7	.962
2005—Memphis (PCL)	2B-SS	57	223	24	50	13	1	3	21	20	38	2	2	11-4	.224	.294	.332	.626	5	.980
—St. Louis (N.L.)	OF-2B-3B-SS	64	137	26	39	10	2	1	18	9	25	4	4	10-2	.285	.344	.409	.753	5	.967
Major League totals (2 years)		147	310	51	82	17	4	4	40	22	62	6	6	16-5	.265	.322	.384	.706	12	.964

CHAMPIONSHIP SERIES RECORD

Year Team (League)	Pos.	G	AB	R	H	2B	3B	HR	RBI	BB	SO	HBP	GDP	SB-CS	Avg.	OBP	SLG	OPS	E	Avg.
2004—St. Louis (N.L.)	2B-SS	2	4	0	0	0	0	0	0	0	2	0	0	0-0	.000	.000	.000	.000	0	1.000
2005—St. Louis (N.L.)	3B	2	4	0	0	0	0	0	0	0	2	0	0	0-0	.000	.000	.000	.000	2	.600
Champ. series totals (2 years)		4	8	0	0	0	0	0	0	0	4	0	0	0-0	.000	.000	.000	.000	2	.833

WORLD SERIES RECORD

Year Team (League)	Pos.	G	AB	R	H	2B	3B	HR	RBI	BB	SO	HBP	GDP	SB-CS	Avg.	OBP	SLG	OPS	E	Avg.
2004—St. Louis (N.L.)	2B	1	1	0	0	0	0	0	0	0	1	0	0	0-0	.000	.000	.000	.000	0	...

LYON, BRANDON — P

PERSONAL: Born August 10, 1979, in Salt Lake City. ... 6-1/185. ... Throws right, bats right. ... Full name: Brandon James Lyon. ... Name pronounced: lion. ... High school: Taylorsville (Salt Lake City). ... Junior college: Dixie College (Utah).

TRANSACTIONS/CAREER NOTES: Selected by New York Mets organization in 37th round of 1997 free-agent draft; did not sign. ... Selected by Toronto Blue Jays organization in 14th round of 1999 free-agent draft. ... Claimed on waivers by Boston Red Sox (October 9, 2002). ... On disabled list (July 24-September 1, 2003); included rehabilitation assignment to Pawtucket. ... Traded by Red Sox with P Anastacio Martinez to Pittsburgh Pirates for Ps Scott Sauerbeck and Mike Gonzalez (July 22, 2003). ... Traded by Pirates with Ps Jeff Suppan and Anastacio Martinez to Red Sox for IF Freddy Sanchez, P Mike Gonzalez and cash (July 31, 2003). ... Traded by Red Sox with Ps Casey Fossum and Jorge de la Rosa and OF Mike Goss to Arizona Diamondbacks for P Curt Schilling (November 28, 2003). ... On disabled list (April 3, 2004-entire season). ... On disabled list (April 13-August 13, 2005); included rehabilitation assignment to Tucson.

CAREER HITTING: 0-for-0 (.000), 0 R, 0 2B, 0 3B, 0 HR, 0 RBI.

BRANDON LYON'S PITCHING ZONE

.375	.000	.667
.308	.467	.190
.250	.333	.333

LEFTY-RIGHTY SPLITS

vs.	Avg.	AB	H	2B	3B	HR	RBI	BB	SO	OBP	Slg.
L	.317	63	20	4	0	3	10	4	7	.362	.524
R	.364	66	24	5	0	3	18	6	10	.425	.576

Year Team (League)	W	L	Pct.	ERA	WHIP	G	GS	CG	ShO	Hld.	Sv.-Opp.	IP	H	R	ER	HR	BB-IBB	SO	Avg.
2000—Queens (N.Y.-Penn.)	5	3	.625	2.39	0.81	15	13	0	0	...	0-...	60.1	43	20	16	1	6-0	55	.197
2001—Tennessee (Sou.)	5	0	1.000	3.68	1.13	9	9	0	0	...	0-...	58.2	57	25	24	7	9-0	45	.252
—Syracuse (Int'l)	5	3	.625	3.69	1.14	11	11	2	1	...	0-...	68.1	68	33	28	7	10-0	53	.257
—Toronto (A.L.)	5	4	.556	4.29	1.24	11	11	0	0	0	0-0	63.0	63	31	30	6	15-0	35	.266
2002—Toronto (A.L.)	1	4	.200	6.53	1.56	15	10	0	0	0	0-1	62.0	78	47	45	14	19-2	30	.308
—Syracuse (Int'l)	4	9	.308	5.11	1.56	14	14	0	0	...	0-...	75.2	99	54	43	4	19-0	35	.315
2003—Pawtucket (Int'l)	0	0	...	3.24	1.08	5	0	0	0	...	0-...	8.1	7	3	3	1	2-0	7	.219
—Boston (A.L.)	4	6	.400	4.12	1.56	49	0	0	0	2	9-12	59.0	73	33	27	6	19-5	50	.296
2004—Tucson (PCL)	2	3	.400	15.12	2.28	6	3	0	0	...	0-...	8.1	15	14	14	3	4-0	4	.366
2005—Tucson (PCL)	0	1	.000	5.40	1.00	5	4	0	0	0	0-0	5.0	5	3	3	0	0-0	4	.250
—Arizona (N.L.)	0	2	.000	6.44	1.84	32	0	0	0	1	14-15	29.1	44	25	21	6	10-2	17	.341
American League totals (3 years)	10	14	.417	4.99	1.45	75	21	0	0	2	9-13	184.0	214	111	102	26	53-7	115	.290
National League totals (1 year)	0	2	.000	6.44	1.84	32	0	0	0	1	14-15	29.1	44	25	21	6	10-2	17	.341
Major League totals (4 years)	10	16	.385	5.19	1.50	107	21	0	0	3	23-28	213.1	258	136	123	32	63-9	132	.298

MABRY, JOHN — OF/3B

PERSONAL: Born October 17, 1970, in Wilmington, Del. ... 6-4/210. ... Bats left, throws right. ... Full name: John Steven Mabry. ... Name pronounced: MAY-bree. ... High school: Bohemia Manor (Chesapeake City, Md.). ... College: West Chester (Pa.).

TRANSACTIONS/CAREER NOTES: Selected by St. Louis Cardinals organization in sixth round of 1991 free-agent draft. ... On disabled list (August 20-September 24, 1997). ... Signed as a free agent by Seattle Mariners (December 30, 1998). ... On disabled list (August 14, 1999-remainder of season). ... On disabled list (April 22-May 12, 2000); included rehabilitation assignment to Tacoma. ... Traded by Mariners with P Tom Davey to San Diego Padres for OF Al Martin (July 31, 2000). ... Signed as a free agent by Cardinals organization (January 5, 2001). ... Traded by Cardinals to Florida Marlins for cash (April 9, 2001). ... On disabled list (April 16-May 20, 2001); included rehabilitation assignment to Brevard County. ... Signed as a free agent by Philadelphia Phillies organization (January 28, 2002). ... Traded by Phillies to Oakland Athletics for 1B/OF Jeremy Giambi (May 22, 2002). ... Signed as a free agent by Mariners (January 15, 2003). ... On disabled list (May 28-June 20, 2003); included rehabilitation assignment to Tacoma. ... Signed as a free agent by Cardinals (December 7, 2004). ... Career major league pitching: 0-0, 63.00 ERA, 2 G, 1.0 IP, 6 H, 7 R, 7 ER, 4 BB, 0 SO.

2005 GAMES PLAYED BY POSITION (MLB): OF—70, 3B—18, 1B—14.

SCOUTING REPORT *Offense:* Mabry is a professional hitter with a good swing. Can power pitches that are out and over the plate. Has problems handling good stuff on his hands. Is patient. Hangs in against lefthanders. Has power on pitches down. Has below-average speed but good instincts. *Defense:* He can throw and will catch what he gets to, but his range is below average. Does not have the range to play center field. Can fill in at first and third. *Outlook:* Mabry is a productive role player who can be overexposed if he gets more than 300 at-bats. *Grade 5.8*

JOHN MABRY'S HITTING ZONE

.300	.400	.063
.235	.438	.322
.133	.200	.132

LEFTY-RIGHTY SPLITS

vs.	Avg.	AB	H	2B	3B	HR	RBI	BB	SO	OBP	Slg.
L	.226	31	7	1	0	0	0	1	12	.250	.258
R	.242	215	52	14	1	8	32	19	51	.301	.428

Year Team (League)	Pos.	G	AB	R	H	2B	3B	HR	RBI	BB	SO	HBP	GDP	SB-CS	Avg.	OBP	SLG	OPS	E	Avg.
1991—Hamilton (NYP)	OF	49	187	25	58	11	0	1	31	17	18	2	6	9-3	.310	.370	.385	.755	5	.943
—Savannah (S. Atl.)	OF	22	86	10	20	6	1	0	8	7	12	0	1	1-0	.233	.284	.326	.610	1	.974
1992—Springfield (Midw.)	OF	115	438	63	115	13	6	11	57	24	39	0	12	2-8	.263	.300	.395	.695	6	.969
1993—Arkansas (Texas)	OF	136	528	68	153	32	2	16	72	27	68	4	17	7-15	.290	.326	.449	.775	3	.989
—Louisville (A.A.)	OF	4	7	0	1	0	0	0	1	0	1	0	1	0-0	.143	.143	.143	.286	0	1.000
1994—Louisville (A.A.)	OF	122	477	76	125	30	1	15	68	32	67	3	14	2-6	.262	.311	.423	.735	2	.992
—St. Louis (N.L.)	OF	6	23	2	7	3	0	0	3	2	4	0	0	0-0	.304	.360	.435	.795	1	1.000
1995—St. Louis (N.L.)	1B-OF	129	388	35	119	21	1	5	41	24	45	2	6	0-3	.307	.347	.405	.752	4	.994
—Louisville (A.A.)	OF	4	12	0	1	0	0	0	0	0	0	0	0	0-0	.083	.083	.083	.167	1	.889
1996—St. Louis (N.L.)	1B-OF	151	543	63	161	30	2	13	74	37	84	3	21	3-2	.297	.342	.431	.773	8	.994
1997—St. Louis (N.L.)	OF-1B-3B	116	388	40	110	19	0	5	36	39	77	3	11	0-1	.284	.352	.371	.723	1	.998
1998—St. Louis (N.L.)	OF-3B-1B	142	377	41	94	22	0	9	46	30	76	1	6	0-2	.249	.305	.379	.684	9	.968
1999—Seattle (A.L.)	OF-3B-1B DH	87	262	34	64	14	0	9	33	20	60	0	6	2-1	.244	.297	.401	.698	10	.964
2000—Seattle (A.L.)	3B-OF-DH 1B-P	48	103	18	25	5	0	1	7	10	31	2	1	0-0	.243	.322	.320	.642	4	.934
—Tacoma (PCL)	1B-3B	4	14	1	3	1	0	0	1	0	4	0	0	0-0	.214	.214	.286	.500	1	.800
—San Diego (N.L.)	OF-1B	48	123	17	28	8	0	7	25	5	38	0	0	0-0	.228	.256	.463	.719	1	.983
2001—St. Louis (N.L.)	1B-OF	5	7	0	0	0	0	0	0	0	2	0	0	0-0	.000	.000	.000	.000	0	1.000
—Florida (N.L.)	OF-1B-DH	82	147	14	32	7	0	6	20	13	44	5	6	1-0	.218	.299	.388	.687	2	.964
—Brevard County (FSL)		4	13	0	2	0	0	0	4	2	1	0	0	0-0	.154	.250	.154	.404	0	1.000
2002—Philadelphia (N.L.)	1B-OF	21	21	1	6	0	0	0	3	1	5	0	0	0-0	.286	.304	.286	.590	0	1.000
—Oakland (A.L.)	OF-1B	89	193	27	53	13	1	11	40	14	37	1	7	1-1	.275	.322	.523	.846	2	.992
2003—Tacoma (PCL)	DH	3	11	1	4	0	0	0	0	2	1	0	0	0-0	.364	.462	.364	.825	0	...
—Seattle (A.L.)	OF-DH-1B	64	104	12	22	6	0	3	16	15	21	3	3	0-0	.212	.328	.356	.684	1	.987
2004—Memphis (PCL)	1B-OF-3B	39	136	27	46	7	0	12	35	17	29	2	3	0-0	.338	.406	.654	1.061	2	.991
—St. Louis (N.L.)	OF-3B-1B	87	240	32	71	11	0	13	40	26	63	1	6	0-1	.296	.363	.504	.867	6	.972
2005—St. Louis (N.L.)	OF-3B-1B	112	246	26	59	15	1	8	32	20	63	0	6	0-0	.240	.295	.407	.701	3	.980
American League totals (4 years)		288	662	91	164	38	1	24	96	59	149	6	17	3-3	.248	.313	.417	.730	17	.974
National League totals (10 years)		899	2503	271	687	136	4	66	320	197	501	15	65	4-9	.274	.328	.411	.740	34	.990
Major League totals (12 years)		1187	3165	362	851	174	5	90	416	256	650	21	82	7-12	.269	.325	.412	.738	51	.987

DIVISION SERIES RECORD

Year Team (League)	Pos.	G	AB	R	H	2B	3B	HR	RBI	BB	SO	HBP	GDP	SB-CS	Avg.	OBP	SLG	OPS	E	Avg.
1996—St. Louis (N.L.)	1B	3	10	1	3	0	1	0	1	1	1	0	0	0-0	.300	.364	.500	.864	0	1.000
2002—Oakland (A.L.)	1B-OF	2	2	0	0	0	0	0	0	0	1	0	0	0-0	.000	.000	.000	.000	0	1.000
2004—St. Louis (N.L.)		1	1	0	0	0	0	0	0	0	1	0	0	0-0	.000	.000	.000	.000	0	
2005—St. Louis (N.L.)	OF	2	2	0	1	0	0	0	0	0	0	0	0	0-0	.500	.500	.500	1.000	0	1.000
Division series totals (4 years)		8	15	1	4	0	1	0	1	1	3	0	0	0-0	.267	.313	.400	.713	0	1.000

CHAMPIONSHIP SERIES RECORD

Year Team (League)	Pos.	G	AB	R	H	2B	3B	HR	RBI	BB	SO	HBP	GDP	SB-CS	Avg.	OBP	SLG	OPS	E	Avg.
1996—St. Louis (N.L.)	1B-OF	7	23	1	6	0	0	0	0	0	6	1	0	0-0	.261	.292	.261	.553	0	1.000
2004—St. Louis (N.L.)		4	6	0	1	0	0	0	1	0	3	0	0	0-0	.167	.167	.167	.333	0	1.000
2005—St. Louis (N.L.)	OF-3B	5	8	0	1	1	0	0	1	0	3	0	1	0-0	.125	.125	.250	.375	0	1.000
Champ. series totals (3 years)		16	37	1	8	1	0	0	2	0	12	1	1	0-0	.216	.237	.243	.480	0	1.000

WORLD SERIES RECORD

Year Team (League)	Pos.	G	AB	R	H	2B	3B	HR	RBI	BB	SO	HBP	GDP	SB-CS	Avg.	OBP	SLG	OPS	E	Avg.
2004—St. Louis (N.L.)	OF	2	4	0	0	0	0	0	0	0	2	0	0		.000	.000	.000	.000	0	1.000

MACDOUGAL, MIKE   P

PERSONAL: Born March 5, 1977, in Las Vegas. ... 6-4/195. ... Throws right, bats both. ... Full name: Robert Meiklejohn MacDougal. ... High school: Mesa (Ariz.). ... College: Wake Forest.

TRANSACTIONS/CAREER NOTES: Selected by Baltimore Orioles organization in 22nd round of 1996 free-agent draft; did not sign. ... Selected by Orioles organization in 17th round of 1998 free-agent draft; did not sign. ... Selected by Kansas City Royals organization in first round (25th pick overall) of 1999 free-agent draft; pick received as part of compensation for Boston Red Sox signing Type A free-agent 2B Jose Offerman. ... On disabled list (March 26-April 24, 2004); included rehabilitation assignment to Wichita.

CAREER HITTING: 0-for-0 (.000), 0 R, 0 2B, 0 3B, 0 HR, 0 RBI.

SCOUTING REPORT *Throws:* His fastball ranges from 92-95 mph. Is developing a cut fastball. Also throws a slider, curveball and changeup. *Tendencies:* His recent change to a more over-the-top release has given him better command of his pitches. Has a tendency to rush and overthrow when he gets excited. Creates deception in his delivery. Fastball moves late and bores in on righthanders. Varies speed and break of breaking pitches. Curve has a big break, yet is very tight. *Outlook:* MacDougal regained his role as the Royals' closer after a trip to the minor leagues. Must work often to develop and stay consistent. Is better suited as a setup man. *Grade 5.5*

MIKE MACDOUGAL'S PITCHING ZONE

.222	.364	.250
.235	.324	.366
.176	.357	.214

LEFTY-RIGHTY SPLITS

vs.	Avg.	AB	H	2B	3B	HR	RBI	BB	SO	OBP	Slg.
L	.240	121	29	8	1	3	15	14	29	.328	.397
R	.270	148	40	8	0	3	17	10	43	.319	.385

Year Team (League)	W	L	Pct.	ERA	WHIP	G	GS	CG	ShO	Hld.	Sv.-Opp.	IP	H	R	ER	HR	BB-IBB	SO	Avg.
1999—Spokane (N'west)	2	2	.500	4.47	1.29	11	11	0	0	...	0-...	46.1	43	25	23	3	17-0	57	.251
2000—Wilmington (Caro.)	9	7	.563	3.92	1.32	26	25	0	0	...	1-...	144.2	115	79	63	5	76-0	129	.219
—Wichita (Texas)	0	1	.000	7.71	1.97	2	2	0	0	...	0-...	11.2	16	10	10	0	7-0	9	.356
2001—Omaha (PCL)	8	8	.500	4.68	1.52	28	27	1	0	...	0-...	144.1	144	90	75	13	76-0	110	.259
—Kansas City (A.L.)	1	1	.500	4.70	1.43	3	3	0	0	0	0-0	15.1	18	10	8	2	4-0	7	.290
2002—Omaha (PCL)	3	5	.375	5.60	2.02	12	10	0	0	...	0-...	53.0	52	42	33	4	55-0	30	.265
—Wichita (Texas)	1	1	.500	3.06	1.98	4	4	1	0	...	0-...	17.2	11	12	6	1	24-0	14	.193
—GC Royals (GCL)	0	0	...	3.00	1.00	1	1	0	0	...	0-...	3.0	3	1	1	0	0-0	3	.273
—Wilmington (Caro.)	0	1	.000	1.08	0.96	5	0	0	0	...	2-...	8.1	3	4	1	1	5-0	10	.107
—Kansas City (A.L.)	0	1	.000	5.00	1.33	6	0	0	0	...	0-...	9.0	5	5	5	0	7-1	10	.161
2003—Kansas City (A.L.)	3	5	.375	4.08	1.50	68	0	0	0	1	27-35	64.0	64	36	29	4	32-0	57	.267
2004—Omaha (PCL)	0	1	.000	5.65	1.60	14	0	0	0	...	2-...	14.1	12	9	9	1	11-0	8	.222
—Wichita (Texas)	1	0	1.000	1.47	1.53	17	2	0	0	...	1-...	18.1	14	7	3	0	14-0	13	.209
—Kansas City (A.L.)	1	1	.500	5.56	2.21	13	0	0	0	0	1-3	11.1	16	8	7	2	9-0	14	.314
2005—Kansas City (A.L.)	5	6	.455	3.33	1.32	68	0	0	0	1	21-25	70.1	69	32	26	6	24-2	72	.257
Major League totals (5 years)	10	14	.417	3.97	1.46	158	3	0	0	1	49-63	170.0	172	91	75	14	76-3	160	.263

MACHADO, ALEJANDRO — OF/2B

PERSONAL: Born April 26, 1982, in Caracas, Venezuela. ... 6-0/160. ... Bats right, throws right. ... Full name: Alejandro Jose Machado.

TRANSACTIONS/CAREER NOTES: Signed as non-drafted free agent by Atlanta Braves organization (July 2, 1998). ... Traded by Braves with P Brad Voyles to Kansas City Royals for SS Rey Sanchez (July 31, 2001). ... Traded by Kansas City Royals with P Wes Obermueller to Milwaukee Brewers for P Curtis Leskanic (July 2, 2003). ... Signed as a free agent by Montreal Expos organization (March 7, 2004). ... Expos franchise transferred to Washington, D.C., and renamed Washington Nationals for 2005 season (December 3, 2004). ... Traded by Nationals to Boston Red Sox for a player to be named (February 15, 2005); Nationals acquired 1B Carlos Torres to complete deal (March 28, 2005).

2005 GAMES PLAYED BY POSITION (MLB): OF—6, 2B—3, SS—1.

LEFTY-RIGHTY SPLITS

vs.	Avg.	AB	H	2B	3B	HR	RBI	BB	SO	OBP	Slg.
L	.000	0	0	0	0	0	0	0	0	.000	.000
R	.200	5	1	1	0	0	0	1	1	.333	.400

								BATTING									FIELDING	
Year Team (League)	Pos.	G	AB	R	H	2B	3B	HR	RBI	BB	SO	HBP	GDP	SB-CS	Avg.	OBP	SLG	OPS	E	Avg.
1999—GC Braves (GCL)	2B	56	223	45	62	11	0	0	14	20	22	5	3	19-6	.278	.348	.327	.675	5	.983
2000—Danville (Appal.)	2B-SS	61	217	45	74	6	2	0	16	53	29	6	3	30-12	.341	.477	.387	.864	8	.973
2001—Macon (S. Atl.)	2B-SS	82	306	43	83	6	3	1	24	34	56	13	1	20-13	.271	.368	.320	.688	5	.984
—Burlington (Midw.)	SS	28	109	17	26	5	0	0	11	10	16	2	2	5-2	.239	.311	.284	.595	3	.978
2002—Wilmington (Caro.)	SS-2B	101	325	53	102	9	1	2	29	27	43	12	2	20-6	.314	.381	.366	.747	18	.956
2003—Wichita (Texas)	2B-SS	78	289	59	83	13	5	1	31	34	45	4	4	19-9	.287	.368	.377	.745	4	.990
—Huntsville (Sou.)	2B	45	155	14	35	4	1	0	13	15	24	2	0	11-1	.226	.302	.265	.567	3	.985
2004—Brevard County (FSL)	SS-2B	46	186	34	66	10	2	1	19	22	27	1	2	11-6	.355	.424	.446	.870	8	.765
—Harrisburg (East.)	2B-SS	93	346	54	97	5	4	4	26	41	39	5	4	19-9	.280	.363	.353	.716	4	.000
2005—Pawtucket (Int'l) 2B-SS-OF																			
	DH	117	383	60	115	17	2	3	43	32	47	5	10	21-4	.300	.359	.379	.738	7	.986
—Boston (A.L.) OF-2B-SS		10	5	4	1	1	0	0	0	1	1	0	0	0-0	.200	.333	.400	.733	0	1.000
Major League totals (1 year)		10	5	4	1	1	0	0	0	1	1	0	0	0-0	.200	.333	.400	.733	0	1.000

DIVISION SERIES RECORD

									BATTING								FIELDING	
Year Team (League)	Pos.	G	AB	R	H	2B	3B	HR	RBI	BB	SO	HBP	GDP	SB-CS	Avg.	OBP	SLG	OPS	E	Avg.
2005—Boston (A.L.)		1	0	0	0	0	0	0	0	0	0	0	0	0-0	...	...	...	...	0	...

MACHADO, ANDERSON — SS

PERSONAL: Born January 25, 1981, in Caracas, Venezuela. ... 5-11/170. ... Bats both, throws right. ... Full name: Anderson Javier Machado. ... Name pronounced: ma-CHAH-do. ... High school: Liceo De Aplicacion (Caracas, Venezuela).

TRANSACTIONS/CAREER NOTES: Signed as non-drafted free agent by Philadelphia Phillies organization (January 14, 1998). ... On disabled list (March 26-April 29, 2004). ... Traded by Phillies with P Josh Hancock to Cincinnati Reds for P Todd Jones and OF Brad Correll (July 30, 2004). ... On disabled list (April 2-July 6, 2005); included rehabilitation assignment to Louisville. ... Claimed on waivers by Colorado Rockies (July 20, 2005).

2005 GAMES PLAYED BY POSITION (MLB): SS—4.

LEFTY-RIGHTY SPLITS

vs.	Avg.	AB	H	2B	3B	HR	RBI	BB	SO	OBP	Slg.
L	.000	7	0	0	0	0	2	2	3	.200	.000
R	.000	5	0	0	0	0	0	0	3	.000	.000

									BATTING								FIELDING	
Year Team (League)	Pos.	G	AB	R	H	2B	3B	HR	RBI	BB	SO	HBP	GDP	SB-CS	Avg.	OBP	SLG	OPS	E	Avg.
1998—Dom. Phillies (DSL)		68	219	26	44	7	0	0	17	30	44	...	...	4-...	.201	...	.233	...	...	...
1999—Clearwater (FSL)	SS	1	2	0	0	0	0	0	0	1	1	0	0	0-0	.000	.000	.000	.000	0	...
—GC Phillies (GCL) 2B-SS-3B		43	143	26	37	6	3	2	12	15	38	2	5	6-3	.259	.335	.385	.720	8	.958
—Piedmont (S. Atl.)	SS	20	60	7	14	4	2	0	7	7	20	1	0	2-1	.233	.324	.367	.690	8	.910
2000—Clearwater (FSL)	SS	117	417	55	102	19	7	1	35	54	103	0	7	32-18	.245	.330	.331	.661	43	.934
—Reading (East.)	SS	3	11	2	4	1	0	1	2	0	4	0	0	0-0	.364	.364	.727	1.091	1	.929
2001—Clearwater (FSL)	SS	82	272	49	71	8	5	8	36	31	66	4	3	23-9	.261	.342	.393	.735	16	.962
—Reading (East.)	SS	31	101	13	15	2	0	1	8	12	25	0	1	5-2	.149	.237	.198	.435	9	.941
2002—Reading (East.)	SS	126	450	71	113	24	3	12	77	72	118	2	5	40-11	.251	.353	.398	.751	28	.954
2003—Reading (East.)	SS	123	423	80	83	19	4	5	20	108	120	1	2	49-15	.196	.360	.296	.656	26	.951
—Philadelphia (N.L.)	SS	1	0	0	0	0	0	0	0	0	0	0	0	1-0	...	...	...	...	0	...
2004—Clearwater (FSL)	SS	7	22	0	5	0	0	0	4	2	0	0	0	0-0	.227	.346	.227	.573	4	.852
—Scran./W.B. (I.L.)	SS	78	295	51	67	12	5	6	26	50	73	1	1	11-6	.227	.337	.363	.700	20	.943
—Louisville (Int'l)	SS	31	109	14	25	5	2	0	12	10	26	1	1	3-2	.229	.295	.312	.607	9	.932
—Cincinnati (N.L.)	SS	17	56	6	15	5	1	0	4	10	26	0	0	3-1	.268	.379	.393	.772	4	.937
2005—Louisville (Int'l)	SS-2B	21	80	9	11	2	1	0	6	12	23	0	0	1-2	.138	.247	.188	.435	4	.949
—Cincinnati (N.L.)	SS	2	2	0	0	0	0	0	0	0	1	0	0	0-0	.000	.000	.000	.000	0	...
—Colorado (N.L.)	SS	4	10	1	0	0	0	0	2	0	5	0	0	0-0	.000	.154	.000	.154	1	.929
—Colo. Springs (PCL)	SS	25	63	6	10	3	1	0	6	16	17	0	1	0-1	.159	.325	.238	.563	6	.919
Major League totals (3 years)		24	68	7	15	5	1	0	6	12	32	0	0	4-1	.221	.333	.324	.657	5	.935

M

MACIAS, JOSE — 2B/OF

PERSONAL: Born January 25, 1972, in Panama City, Panama. ... 5-8/190. ... Bats both, throws right. ... Full name: Jose Prade Macias. ... Name pronounced: muh-SEE-us. ... High school: Instituto Technologico (Panama City, Panama).

TRANSACTIONS/CAREER NOTES: Signed as a non-drafted free agent by Montreal Expos organization (February 14, 1992). ... Selected by Detroit Tigers organization from Expos organization in Rule 5 minor league draft (December 9, 1996). ... Traded by Tigers to Expos for 3B Chris Truby (May 16, 2002). ... On disabled list (September 10, 2002-remainder of season). ... On suspended list (April 6-9, 2003). ... Traded by Expos to Chicago Cubs for P Wilton Chavez (December 19, 2003). ... On disabled list (March 26-April 14, 2004).

2005 GAMES PLAYED BY POSITION (MLB): 3B—23, 2B—20, OF—20.

SCOUTING REPORT

Offense: Macias is a slap hitter without power who will use the whole field but doesn't have much bat speed from either side of the plate. Is a better fastball hitter. Is a better lefthanded hitter. Not a threat with runners in scoring position. Is a good runner but not much of a basestealer. **Defense:** His best asset is his defensive versatility. Has good speed but hands are a little stiff. Gets good jumps in the outfield with average range and arm. **Outlook:** Macias never will hit enough to play every day. **Grade 5.7**

JOSE MACIAS' HITTING ZONE

.250	.250	.600
.364	.200	.353
.333	.250	.111

LEFTY-RIGHTY SPLITS

vs.	Avg.	AB	H	2B	3B	HR	RBI	BB	SO	OBP	Slg.
L	.277	47	13	3	0	1	3	4	5	.333	.404
R	.246	130	32	5	0	0	10	2	19	.252	.285

Year Team (League)	Pos.	G	AB	R	H	2B	3B	HR	RBI	BB	SO	HBP	GDP	SB-CS	Avg.	OBP	SLG	OPS	E	Avg.
1992—Dom. Expos (DSL)	OF	61	198	58	58	5	1	2	23	60	11	...	...	41-...	.293	...	.359		7	.942
1993—Dom. Expos (DSL)	OF	64	211	60	66	12	1	4	26	59	26	...	...	38-...	.313	...	.436		7	.954
1994—GC Expos (GCL)	2B-3B-OF	31	104	23	28	8	2	1	6	14	15	0	3	4-1	.269	.356	.413	.769	4	.937
1995—Vermont (NYP)	2B-3B-OF	53	176	24	42	4	2	0	9	19	19	2	3	11-7	.239	.320	.284	.604	9	.949
1996—Delmarva (S. Atl.)	2B-3B-OF	116	369	64	91	13	4	1	33	56	48	6	2	38-15	.247	.353	.312	.665	8	.970
1997—Lakeland (Fla. St.)	2B-OF	122	424	54	113	18	2	2	52	52	53	2	10	10-14	.267	.348	.333	.680	7	.989
1998—Jacksonville (Sou.)		128	511	82	156	28	10	12	71	52	46	4	4	6-9	.305	.372	.470	.842	14	.977
1999—Toledo (Int'l)	2B-OF-SS	112	438	44	107	18	8	2	36	36	60	4	8	10-5	.244	.306	.338	.642	18	.969
—Detroit (A.L.)	2B	5	4	2	1	0	0	1	2	0	1	0	0	0-0	.250	.250	1.000	1.250	0	1.000
2000—Toledo (Int'l)	OF-SS-2B	33	130	19	30	5	0	0	8	17	17	1	3	2-3	.231	.322	.269	.591	6	.940
—Detroit (A.L.)	DH-SS	73	173	25	44	3	5	2	24	18	24	1	3	2-0	.254	.328	.364	.692	4	.977
2001—Detroit (A.L.)	3B-OF-2B	137	488	62	131	24	6	8	51	32	54	3	7	21-6	.268	.316	.391	.707	12	.970
2002—Detroit (A.L.)	DH	33	107	10	25	4	0	0	6	8	13	1	4	3-2	.234	.291	.271	.562	5	.970
—Montreal (N.L.)	OF-3B-2B	90	231	33	59	17	1	7	33	13	44	1	2	5-6	.255	.294	.429	.723	6	.968
2003—Montreal (N.L.)	SS	111	272	31	65	15	2	4	22	11	45	2	4	4-3	.239	.273	.353	.626	5	.964
2004—Chicago (N.L.)	DH	98	194	23	52	6	3	3	22	5	38	2	2	4-1	.268	.292	.376	.668	1	.989
2005—Chicago (N.L.)	OF-3B-2B	112	177	15	45	8	0	1	13	6	24	0	6	4-3	.254	.274	.316	.591	4	.965
	3B-2B-OF																			
American League totals (4 years)		248	772	99	201	31	11	11	83	58	92	5	14	26-8	.260	.315	.372	.686	21	.970
National League totals (4 years)		411	874	102	221	46	6	15	90	35	151	5	15	17-13	.253	.283	.371	.654	16	.970
Major League totals (7 years)		659	1646	201	422	77	17	26	173	93	243	10	29	43-21	.256	.298	.371	.669	37	.970

MACKOWIAK, ROB — 3B/OF

PERSONAL: Born June 20, 1976, in Oak Lawn, Ill. ... 5-10/195. ... Bats left, throws right. ... Full name: Robert William Mackowiak. ... Name pronounced: mah-KOH-vee-ak. ... High school: Oak Lawn (Ill.), then Lake Central (Schererville) . ... Junior college: South Suburban (Ill.).

TRANSACTIONS/CAREER NOTES: Selected by Cincinnati Reds organization in 30th round of 1995 free-agent draft; did not sign. ... Selected by Pittsburgh Pirates organization in 53rd round of 1996 free-agent draft. ... On disabled list (July 20-August 18, 2001); included rehabilitation assignment to Nashville.

2005 GAMES PLAYED BY POSITION (MLB): 3B—65, OF—63, 2B—20, 1B—3.

SCOUTING REPORT

Offense: Mackowiak swings a live bat and has a short, compact stroke. Has good bat speed and can hit the high pitch. Slumps when he tries to pull too much. Is shorter and quicker to the ball when he goes to the opposite field. Has improved against lefthanded pitching. Strikes out too much because he's vulnerable to off-speed pitches. Is an extremely aggressive runner who runs out every ball. Has good speed. **Defense:** He has played all three outfield positions, as well as first and third base, but his feet aren't quick enough for the infield. Has good arm strength and has improved his outfield routes and jumps. **Outlook:** Mackowiak is an ideal N.L. player because of his versatility and power, but he needs to be more selective. Really wore down in the second half last season. **Grade 5.9**

ROB MACKOWIAK'S HITTING ZONE

.389	.278	.148
.365	.457	.221
.278	.375	.238

LEFTY-RIGHTY SPLITS

vs.	Avg.	AB	H	2B	3B	HR	RBI	BB	SO	OBP	Slg.
L	.275	69	19	3	1	0	10	6	18	.342	.348
R	.272	394	107	18	2	9	48	37	82	.336	.396

Year Team (League)	Pos.	G	AB	R	H	2B	3B	HR	RBI	BB	SO	HBP	GDP	SB-CS	Avg.	OBP	SLG	OPS	E	Avg.
1996—GC Pirates (GCL)	OF-SS	27	86	8	23	6	1	0	14	13	11	1	3	3-1	.267	.366	.360	.727	10	.796
1997—Erie (N.Y.-Penn)	1B-3B-C																			
	OF-P	61	203	26	58	14	2	1	25	21	47	7	5	1-7	.286	.371	.389	.760	6	.949
1998—Augusta (S. Atl.)	1B-OF	25	70	16	17	4	0	1	8	13	19	1	2	4-2	.243	.369	.343	.712	2	.941
—Lynchburg (Caro.)	2B-3B-OF	86	292	30	80	24	6	3	31	17	65	4	4	6-3	.274	.321	.428	.749	18	.916
1999—Lynchburg (Caro.)	2B-OF	74	263	51	80	7	4	9	30	18	57	6	5	9-3	.304	.362	.441	.803	1	.996
—Altoona (East.)	1B-OF	53	195	21	51	15	3	9	27	8	34	7	4	0-2	.262	.308	.415	.724	8	.971
2000—Altoona (East.)	2B-3B-OF																			
	SS	134	526	82	156	33	4	13	87	22	96	9	8	18-5	.297	.332	.449	.780	17	.965

M

Year Team (League)	Pos.	G	AB	R	H	2B	3B	HR	RBI	BB	SO	HBP	GDP	SB-CS	Avg.	OBP	SLG	OPS	E	Avg.
																		BATTING	**FIELDING**	
2001— Nashville (PCL)	OF-2B-3B	32	118	14	31	5	0	4	14	7	39	0	0	1-1	.263	.302	.407	.708	7	.940
— Pittsburgh (N.L.)	OF-2B-3B																			
	1B	83	214	30	57	15	2	4	21	15	52	3	3	4-3	.266	.319	.411	.730	6	.965
2002— Pittsburgh (N.L.)	OF-3B-2B	136	385	57	94	22	0	16	48	42	120	7	0	9-3	.244	.328	.426	.754	6	.974
2003— Nashville (PCL)	1B-3B-2B																			
	OF	59	217	21	50	11	1	2	23	18	51	0	3	7-3	.230	.286	.318	.604	9	.978
— Pittsburgh (N.L.)	OF-3B-2B	77	174	20	47	4	4	6	19	15	53	4	1	6-0	.270	.342	.443	.785	2	.983
2004— Pittsburgh (N.L.)	OF-3B-1B	155	491	65	121	22	6	17	75	50	114	6	3	13-4	.246	.319	.420	.739	9	.968
2005— Pittsburgh (N.L.)	3B-OF-2B																			
	1B	142	463	57	126	21	3	9	58	43	100	3		8-4	.272	.337	.389	.726	12	.968
Major League totals (5 years)		593	1727	229	445	84	15	52	221	165	439	23	14	40-14	.258	.328	.414	.742	35	.970

MADDUX, GREG   P

PERSONAL: Born April 14, 1966, in San Angelo, Texas. ... 6-0/185. ... Throws right, bats right. ... Full name: Gregory Alan Maddux. ... Name pronounced: MADD-ucks. ... High school: Valley (Las Vegas). ... Brother of Mike Maddux, coach, Milwaukee Brewers, and pitcher with nine major league teams (1986-2000).

TRANSACTIONS/CAREER NOTES: Selected by Chicago Cubs organization in second round of June 1984 free-agent draft. ... Signed as a free agent by Atlanta Braves (December 9, 1992). ... On disabled list (March 23-April 12, 2002). ... Signed as a free agent by Cubs (March 23, 2004).

HONORS: Named N.L. Pitcher of the Year by THE SPORTING NEWS (1992-95). ... Named N.L. Cy Young Award winner by Baseball Writers' Association of America (1992-95). ... Won N.L. Gold Glove at pitcher (1990-2002 and 2004-05).

CAREER HITTING: 248-for-1406 (.176), 97 R, 31 2B, 2 3B, 5 HR, 74 RBI.

SCOUTING REPORT **Throws:** Maddux's fastball ranges from 82-87 mph, his slider from 80-84 and his curve from 73-75. Also throws a circle change. **Tendencies:** Lack of velocity has no bearing on Maddux's success. Compensates with superior movement and location. Has late movement on his fastball and impeccable command to both sides of the plate. Has a tight curveball. Must have even better command than before. Is pitching in more hitters' counts now. Is a multiple Gold Glove winner. Might be the most intelligent pitcher of all time. **Outlook:** Maddux had his first losing season in many years, and his stuff has leveled off slightly. **Grade 7.5**

GREG MADDUX'S PITCHING ZONE

.326	.243	.205
.287	.417	.278
.250	.244	.290

LEFTY-RIGHTY SPLITS

vs.	Avg.	AB	H	2B	3B	HR	RBI	BB	SO	OBP	Slg.
L	.283	364	103	25	0	11	48	19	57	.324	.442
R	.270	504	136	25	2	18	56	17	79	.295	.435

Year Team (League)	W	L	Pct.	ERA	WHIP	G	GS	CG	ShO	Hld.	Sv.-Opp.	IP	H	R	ER	HR	BB-IBB	SO	Avg.
1984— Pikeville (Appal.)	6	2	.750	2.63	1.21	14	12	2	2	...	0-...	85.2	63	35	25	2	41-2	62	.205
1985— Peoria (Midw.)	13	9	.591	3.19	1.23	27	27	6	0	...	0-...	186.0	176	86	66	9	52-0	125	.245
1986— Pittsfield (East.)	4	3	.571	2.73	1.02	8	8	4	2	...	0-...	62.2	49	22	19	1	15-0	35	.214
— Iowa (Am. Assoc.)	10	1	.909	3.02	1.22	18	18	5	2	...	0-...	128.1	127	49	43	3	30-3	65	.259
— Chicago (N.L.)	2	4	.333	5.52	1.77	6	5	1	0	0	0-0	31.0	44	20	19	3	11-2	20	.336
1987— Chicago (N.L.)	6	14	.300	5.61	1.64	30	27	1	1	0	0-0	155.2	181	111	97	17	74-13	101	.294
— Iowa (Am. Assoc.)	3	0	1.000	0.98	1.05	4	4	2	2	...	0-...	27.2	17	3	3	1	12-0	22	.179
1988— Chicago (N.L.)	18	8	.692	3.18	1.25	34	34	9	3	0	0-0	249.0	230	97	88	13	81-16	140	.249
1989— Chicago (N.L.)	19	12	.613	2.95	1.28	35	35	7	1	0	0-0	238.1	222	90	78	13	82-13	135	.249
1990— Chicago (N.L.)	15	15	.500	3.46	1.32	35	•35	8	2	0	0-0	237.0	* 242	*116	91	11	71-10	144	.265
1991— Chicago (N.L.)	15	11	.577	3.35	1.13	37	*37	7	2	0	0-0	* 263.0	232	113	98	18	66-9	198	.232
1992— Chicago (N.L.)	• 20	11	.645	2.18	1.01	35	•35	9	4	0	0-0	* 268.0	201	68	65	7	70-7	199	.210
1993— Atlanta (N.L.)	20	10	.667	* 2.36	1.05	36	•36	• 8	1	0	0-0	* 267.0	228	85	70	14	52-7	197	.232
1994— Atlanta (N.L.)	• 16	6	.727	* 1.56	0.90	25	25	•10	•3	0	0-0	* 202.0	150	44	35	4	31-3	156	* .207
1995— Atlanta (N.L.)	* 19	2	.905	* 1.63	0.81	28	28	•10	•3	0	0-0	• 209.2	147	39	38	8	23-3	181	.197
1996— Atlanta (N.L.)	15	11	.577	2.72	1.03	35	35	5	1	0	0-0	245.0	225	85	74	11	28-11	172	.241
1997— Atlanta (N.L.)	19	4	* .826	2.20	0.95	33	33	5	2	0	0-0	232.2	200	58	57	9	20-6	177	.230
1998— Atlanta (N.L.)	18	9	.667	* 2.22	0.98	34	34	9	*5	0	0-0	251.0	201	75	62	13	45-10	204	.220
1999— Atlanta (N.L.)	19	9	.679	3.57	1.34	33	33	4	0	0	0-0	219.1	258	103	87	16	37-8	136	.294
2000— Atlanta (N.L.)	19	9	.679	3.00	1.07	35	•35	6	•3	0	0-0	249.1	225	91	83	19	42-12	190	.238
2001— Atlanta (N.L.)	17	11	.607	3.05	1.06	34	34	3	•3	0	0-0	233.0	220	86	79	20	27-10	173	.253
2002— Atlanta (N.L.)	16	6	.727	2.62	1.20	34	34	0	0	0	0-0	199.1	194	67	58	14	45-7	118	.257
2003— Atlanta (N.L.)	16	11	.593	3.96	1.18	36	*36	1	0	0	0-0	218.1	225	112	96	24	33-7	124	.268
2004— Chicago (N.L.)	16	11	.593	4.02	1.18	33	33	2	1	0	0-0	212.2	218	103	95	35	33-4	151	.269
2005— Chicago (N.L.)	13	15	.464	4.24	1.22	35	•35	3	0	0	0-0	225.0	239	112	106	29	36-4	136	.275
Major League totals (20 years)	318	189	.627	3.01	1.13	643	639	108	35	0	0-0	4406.1	4082	1675	1476	298	907-162	3052	.247

DIVISION SERIES RECORD

Year Team (League)	W	L	Pct.	ERA	WHIP	G	GS	CG	ShO	Hld.	Sv.-Opp.	IP	H	R	ER	HR	BB-IBB	SO	Avg.
1995— Atlanta (N.L.)	1	0	1.000	4.50	1.50	2	2	0	0	0	0-0	14.0	19	7	7	3	2-1	7	.365
1996— Atlanta (N.L.)	1	0	1.000	0.00	0.43	1	1	0	0	0	0-0	7.0	3	0	0	0	0-0	7	.125
1997— Atlanta (N.L.)	1	0	1.000	1.00	0.89	1	1	1	0	0	0-0	9.0	7	1	1	0	1-0	6	.219
1998— Atlanta (N.L.)	1	0	1.000	2.57	1.00	1	1	0	0	0	0-0	7.0	7	2	2	0	0-0	4	.250
1999— Atlanta (N.L.)	0	1	.000	2.57	2.14	2	1	0	0	0	0-0	7.0	10	5	2	1	5-2	5	.370
2000— Atlanta (N.L.)	0	1	.000	11.25	3.00	1	1	0	0	0	0-0	4.0	9	7	5	1	3-2	2	.429
2001— Atlanta (N.L.)	0	0	...	3.00	1.17	1	1	0	0	0	0-0	6.0	4	3	2	1	3-0	5	.190
2002— Atlanta (N.L.)	1	0	1.000	3.00	1.00	1	1	0	0	0	0-0	6.0	6	3	2	1	1-1	3	.238
2003— Atlanta (N.L.)	0	1	.000	3.00	1.17	1	1	0	0	0	0-0	6.0	6	2	2	0	1-0	1	.240
Division series totals (9 years)	5	3	.625	3.14	1.30	11	10	1	0	0	0-0	66.0	70	28	23	7	16-6	40	.279

CHAMPIONSHIP SERIES RECORD

Year Team (League)	W	L	Pct.	ERA	WHIP	G	GS	CG	ShO	Hld.	Sv.-Opp.	IP	H	R	ER	HR	BB-IBB	SO	Avg.
1989— Chicago (N.L.)	0	1	.000	13.50	2.32	2	2	0	0	0	0-0	7.1	13	12	11	2	4-2	5	.382
1993— Atlanta (N.L.)	1	1	.500	4.97	1.42	2	2	0	0	0	0-0	12.2	11	8	7	2	7-1	11	.224
1995— Atlanta (N.L.)	1	0	1.000	1.13	1.13	1	1	0	0	0	0-0	8.0	7	1	1	0	2-0	4	.226
1996— Atlanta (N.L.)	1	1	.500	2.51	1.19	2	2	0	0	0	0-0	14.1	15	9	4	1	2-1	10	.263

M

Year Team (League)	W	L	Pct.	ERA	WHIP	G	GS	CG	ShO	Hld.	Sv.-Opp.	IP	H	R	ER	HR	BB-IBB	SO	Avg.
1997— Atlanta (N.L.)	0	2	.000	1.38	1.00	2	2	0	0	0	0-0	13.0	9	7	2	0	4-1	16	.191
1998— Atlanta (N.L.)	0	1	.000	3.00	1.33	2	1	0	0	0	1-1	6.0	5	2	2	0	3-1	4	.217
1999— Atlanta (N.L.)	1	0	1.000	1.93	0.93	2	2	0	0	0	0-0	14.0	12	3	3	1	1-0	7	.222
2001— Atlanta (N.L.)	0	2	.000	5.40	1.60	2	2	0	0	0	0-0	10.0	14	8	6	0	2-1	7	.311
Champ. series totals (8 years)	4	8	.333	3.80	1.30	15	14	0	0	0	1-1	85.1	86	50	36	6	25-7	64	.253

WORLD SERIES RECORD

Year Team (League)	W	L	Pct.	ERA	WHIP	G	GS	CG	ShO	Hld.	Sv.-Opp.	IP	H	R	ER	HR	BB-IBB	SO	Avg.
1995— Atlanta (N.L.)	1	1	.500	2.25	0.75	2	1	1	0	0	0-0	16.0	9	6	4	1	3-1	8	.158
1996— Atlanta (N.L.)	1	1	.500	1.72	0.96	2	2	0	0	0	0-0	15.2	14	3	3	0	1-0	5	.246
1999— Atlanta (N.L.)	0	1	.000	2.57	1.14	1	1	0	0	0	0-0	7.0	5	4	2	0	3-0	5	.208
World Series totals (3 years)	2	3	.400	2.09	0.91	5	4	1	0	0	0-0	38.2	28	13	9	1	7-1	18	.203

ALL-STAR GAME RECORD

Year Team (League)	W	L	Pct.	ERA	WHIP	G	GS	CG	ShO	Hld.	Sv.-Opp.	IP	H	R	ER	HR	BB-IBB	SO	Avg.
All-Star Game totals (4 years)	0	0	...	3.24	1.20	4	3	0	0	0	0-0	8.1	9	3	3	2	1-0	3	.281

MADRITSCH, BOBBY — P

PERSONAL: Born February 28, 1976, in Oak Lawn, Ill. ... 6-2/190. ... Throws left, bats left. ... Full name: Robert A. Madritsch. ... High school: Reavis (Burbank, Ill.). ... Junior college: Point Park (Pa.).

TRANSACTIONS/CAREER NOTES: Selected by Cincinnati Reds organization in sixth round of 1998 free-agent draft. ... Released by Reds (March 24, 2001). ... Contract purchased by Seattle Mariners organization from Winnipeg of the independent Northern League (September 25, 2002). ... On disabled list (April 7, 2005-remainder of season). ... Claimed on waivers by Kansas City Royals (October 21, 2005).

CAREER HITTING: 0-for-0 (.000), 0 R, 0 2B, 0 3B, 0 HR, 0 RBI.

LEFTY-RIGHTY SPLITS

vs.	Avg.	AB	H	2B	3B	HR	RBI	BB	SO	OBP	Slg.
L	.250	4	1	0	0	0	0	0	1	.250	.250
R	.231	13	3	1	0	1	3	1	0	.286	.538

Year Team (League)	W	L	Pct.	ERA	WHIP	G	GS	CG	ShO	Hld.	Sv.-Opp.	IP	H	R	ER	HR	BB-IBB	SO	Avg.
1998— Billings (Pion.)	7	3	.700	2.80	1.33	14	13	0	0	...	0-...	80.1	72	30	25	3	35-1	87	.240
1999— Billings (Pion.)								Did not play.											
2000— GC Reds (GCL)	1	1	.500	2.01	1.07	6	4	0	0	...	0-...	22.1	15	5	5	0	9-0	27	.192
—Dayton (Midw.)	0	0	...	0.90	1.50	2	2	0	0	...	0-...	10.0	8	1	1	0	7-0	7	.222
2001— Rio Grande Valley (Tex.-La.) ..	3	4	.429	3.15	1.48	10	9	3	1	...	0-...	60.0	55	25	21	1	34-...	58	...
—San Angelo (Tex.-La.) ..	0	2	.000	1.73	0.77	3	3	1	0	...	0-...	26.0	14	8	5	2	6-...	27	...
—Chico (West.)	0	1	.000	11.74	2.61	5	0	0	0	...	0-...	7.2	14	12	10	2	6-...	12	...
2002— Winnipeg (North.)	11	4	.733	2.30	1.04	19	18	0	0	...	0-...	125.1	94	35	32	6	36-...	153	...
2003— San Antonio (Texas)	13	7	.650	3.63	1.26	27	27	2	1	...	0-...	158.2	133	75	64	11	67-0	154	.226
2004— Tacoma (PCL)	5	2	.714	3.75	1.40	12	12	0	0	...	0-...	62.1	61	33	26	3	26-0	53	.251
—Seattle (A.L.)	6	3	.667	3.27	1.22	15	11	1	0	0	0-0	88.0	74	33	32	3	33-2	60	.232
2005— Seattle (A.L.)	0	1	.000	6.23	1.15	1	1	0	0	0	0-0	4.1	4	3	3	1	1-0	1	.235
Major League totals (2 years)	6	4	.600	3.41	1.21	16	12	1	0	0	0-0	92.1	78	36	35	4	34-2	61	.232

MADSON, RYAN — P

PERSONAL: Born August 28, 1980, in Long Beach, Calif. ... 6-6/190. ... Throws right, bats left. ... Full name: Ryan Michael Madson. ... High school: Valley View High (Moreno County, Calif.).

TRANSACTIONS/CAREER NOTES: Selected by Philadelphia Phillies organization in ninth round of 1998 free-agent draft. ... On suspended list (April 16-19, 2004). ... On disabled list (July 26-September 3, 2004); included rehabilitation assignment to Reading.

CAREER HITTING: 0-for-9 (.000), 0 R, 0 2B, 0 3B, 0 HR, 0 RBI.

SCOUTING REPORT *Throws:* The tall, lanky Madson has a fastball at 89-93 mph, a curveball and a changeup. *Tendencies:* Madson has two quality pitches and—fastball and change—and is very durable. Has a very long, slinging arm action with deception. Fastball has some riding action. Curve wasn't as tight as in the past. Has excellent arm speed and movement on his straight change but relied on it too much with his curve absent. *Outlook:* His role going into 2006 is undefined. Could close or go back to starting (he was a starter in the minors). *Grade 7*

RYAN MADSON'S PITCHING ZONE

.400	.222	.310
.250	.356	.298
.118	.389	.250

LEFTY-RIGHTY SPLITS

vs.	Avg.	AB	H	2B	3B	HR	RBI	BB	SO	OBP	Slg.
L	.292	144	42	11	1	7	23	16	35	.364	.528
R	.233	180	42	8	0	4	25	9	44	.282	.344

Year Team (League)	W	L	Pct.	ERA	WHIP	G	GS	CG	ShO	Hld.	Sv.-Opp.	IP	H	R	ER	HR	BB-IBB	SO	Avg.
1998— Martinsville (App.)	3	3	.500	4.83	1.43	12	10	0	0	...	0-...	54.0	57	38	29	5	20-0	52	.265
1999— Batavia (NY-Penn)	5	5	.500	4.72	1.40	15	15	0	0	...	0-...	87.2	80	51	46	5	43-0	75	.247
2000— Piedmont (S. Atl.)	14	5	.737	2.59	1.16	21	21	2	1	...	0-...	135.2	113	50	39	5	45-0	123	.225
2001— Clearwater (FSL)	9	9	.500	3.90	1.58	22	21	1	0	...	0-...	117.2	137	68	51	4	49-1	101	.291
2002— Reading (East.)	16	4	.800	3.20	1.18	26	26	2	0	...	0-...	171.1	150	68	61	11	53-0	132	.242
2003— Clearwater (FSL)	0	0	...	5.63	1.63	2	2	0	0	...	0-...	8.0	11	5	5	0	2-0	9	.324
—Scran./W.B. (I.L.)	12	8	.600	3.50	1.27	26	26	0	0	...	0-...	157.0	157	70	61	9	42-2	138	.262
—Philadelphia (N.L.)	0	0	...	0.00	0.00	1	0	0	0	0	0-0	2.0	0	0	0	0	0-0	0	.000
2004— Reading (East.)	0	0	...	4.50	2.50	2	1	0	0	...	0-...	2.0	3	2	1	0	2-0	1	.375
—Philadelphia (N.L.)	9	3	.750	2.34	1.13	52	1	0	0	0	1-2	77.0	68	23	20	6	19-4	55	.238
2005— Philadelphia (N.L.)	6	5	.545	4.14	1.25	78	0	0	0	• 32	0-7	87.0	84	44	40	11	25-6	79	.259
Major League totals (3 years)	15	8	.652	3.25	1.18	131	1	0	0	39	1-9	166.0	152	67	60	17	44-10	134	.247

MAGRUDER, CHRIS   OF

PERSONAL: Born April 26, 1977, in Tacoma, Wash. ... 5-11/200. ... Bats both, throws right. ... Full name: Christopher James Magruder. ... High school: West Valley (Yakima, Wash.). ... College: Washington.
TRANSACTIONS/CAREER NOTES: Selected by San Francisco Giants in second round of 1998 free-agent draft; pick received as part of compensation for Tampa Bay Devil Rays signing Type A free-agent P Wilson Alvarez. ... Traded with Ps Todd Ozias and Erasmo Ramirez to Texas Rangers for 1B Andres Galarraga (July 24, 2001). ... Traded by Rangers to Cleveland Indians for OF Rashad Eldridge (April 4, 2002). ... Signed as a free agent by Milwaukee Brewers organization (November 11, 2003).
2005 GAMES PLAYED BY POSITION (MLB): OF—45.

CHRIS MAGRUDER'S HITTING ZONE

.167	.000	.200
.308	.357	.286
.000	.167	.176

LEFTY-RIGHTY SPLITS

vs.	Avg.	AB	H	2B	3B	HR	RBI	BB	SO	OBP	Slg.
L	.256	39	10	3	0	0	2	0	6	.293	.333
R	.182	99	18	6	0	2	11	7	27	.255	.303

Year	Team (League)	Pos.	G	AB	R	H	2B	3B	HR	RBI	BB	SO	HBP	GDP	SB-CS	Avg.	OBP	SLG	OPS	E	Avg.
1998—Salem-Keizer (N'west)		OF	47	177	43	59	8	5	3	18	37	21	8	2	14-7	.333	.464	.486	.950	2	.976
—Bakersfield (Calif.)		OF	22	92	21	28	7	0	1	4	13	16	0	2	3-0	.304	.390	.413	.804	0	1.000
1999—Shreveport (Texas)		OF	133	476	78	122	21	4	6	60	69	85	8	15	17-12	.256	.358	.355	.713	3	.988
2000—Shreveport (Texas)		OF	134	496	85	140	33	3	4	39	67	75	8	11	18-10	.282	.375	.385	.760	5	.983
2001—Fresno (PCL)		OF	54	214	37	60	7	1	10	30	18	45	7	...	3-1	.280	.354	.463	.817	1	.992
—Shreveport (Texas)		OF	40	149	22	38	6	3	2	11	15	27	3	2	5-3	.255	.335	.376	.711	2	.979
—Oklahoma (PCL)		OF	33	127	28	46	14	4	5	21	21	19	4	...	1-2	.362	.464	.654	1.118	1	.986
—Texas (A.L.)		OF	17	29	3	5	0	0	0	1	1	5	1	1	0-0	.172	.226	.172	.398	0	1.000
2002—Cleveland (A.L.)		OF	87	258	34	56	15	1	6	29	15	55	1	7	2-0	.217	.261	.353	.614	2	.987
—Buffalo (Int'l)		OF	54	191	28	51	10	2	5	16	26	34	3	2	3-2	.267	.364	.419	.782	1	.991
2003—Mahoning Valley (NYP)		OF-DH	3	11	5	2	2	0	0	0	2	1	1	0	0-0	.182	.357	.364	.721	0	1.000
—Akron (East.)		DH-OF	3	13	0	6	0	0	0	3	1	2	0	0	1-0	.462	.500	.462	.962	0	1.000
—Buffalo (Int'l)		OF	41	137	20	45	7	2	3	15	15	27	1	3	5-1	.328	.391	.474	.865	0	1.000
—Cleveland (A.L.)		OF	9	26	3	9	2	1	1	3	3	6	1	0	0-1	.346	.433	.615	1.049	0	1.000
2004—Indianapolis (Int'l)		OF-DH	79	305	37	83	17	4	6	39	21	55	10	4	7-4	.272	.337	.413	.750	0	1.000
—Milwaukee (N.L.)		OF	56	89	11	21	6	1	2	10	8	21	2	3	0-1	.236	.310	.393	.703	0	1.000
2005—Milwaukee (N.L.)		OF	101	138	16	28	9	0	2	13	7	33	5	3	3-0	.203	.265	.312	.576	2	.964
American League totals (3 years)			113	313	40	70	17	2	7	33	19	66	3	8	2-1	.224	.273	.358	.631	2	.989
National League totals (2 years)			157	227	27	49	15	1	4	23	15	54	7	6	3-1	.216	.283	.344	.626	2	.978
Major League totals (5 years)			270	540	67	119	32	3	11	56	34	120	10	14	5-2	.220	.277	.352	.629	4	.985

MAHAY, RON   P

PERSONAL: Born June 28, 1971, in Crestwood, Ill. ... 6-2/185. ... Throws left, bats left. ... Full name: Ronald Matthew Mahay. ... Name pronounced: MAY-hay. ... High school: Alan B. Shepard (Palos Heights, Ill.). ... Junior college: South Suburban (Ill.).
TRANSACTIONS/CAREER NOTES: Selected by Boston Red Sox organization in 18th round of 1991 free-agent draft. ... Played outfield in Red Sox organization (1991-95); played five games as an outfielder with Red Sox in 1995. ... Claimed on waivers by Oakland Athletics (March 30, 1999). ... Traded by A's to Florida Marlins for cash (May 11, 2000). ... Signed as a free agent by San Diego Padres organization (November 20, 2000). ... Released by Padres (May 15, 2001). ... Signed by Chicago Cubs organization (May 19, 2001). ... On disabled list (May 24-June 13, 2002); included rehabilitation assignment to Iowa. ... Released by Cubs (September 30, 2002). ... Signed by Texas Rangers (November 13, 2002). ... On disabled list (June 8-24, 2005); included rehabilitation assignment to Oklahoma.
CAREER HITTING: 6-for-27 (.222), 3 R, 3 2B, 0 3B, 1 HR, 3 RBI.

SCOUTING REPORT **Throws:** Mahay's fastball will range from 88-90 mph and his slider is at 80. Also throws a split-finger fastball at 82-83 mph. **Tendencies:** He has a good delivery and loose arm action. Fastball velocity was down last year; pitch tends to be straight if it's up. Became less effective as the difference in speeds narrowed. Slider wasn't as quick, causing problems against lefthanded hitters. Splitter was tumbling more than biting. **Outlook:** The quality of his three pitches dropped off dramatically from 2004. Will have to look for work this spring as a nonroster invitee. *Grade 5*

RON MAHAY'S PITCHING ZONE

.300	.500	.500
.235	.500	.389
.385	.364	.333

LEFTY-RIGHTY SPLITS

vs.	Avg.	AB	H	2B	3B	HR	RBI	BB	SO	OBP	Slg.
L	.302	63	19	2	0	5	14	4	13	.338	.571
R	.322	87	28	3	0	3	11	12	17	.404	.460

Year	Team (League)	W	L	Pct.	ERA	WHIP	G	GS	CG	ShO	Hld.	Sv.-Opp.	IP	H	R	ER	HR	BB-IBB	SO	Avg.
1996—Sarasota (Fla. St.)		2	2	.500	3.82	1.36	31	4	0	0	...	2-...	70.2	61	33	30	5	35-0	68	.236
—Trenton (East.)		0	1	.000	29.45	4.91	1	1	0	0	...	0-...	3.2	12	13	12	1	6-0	5	.522
1997—Trenton (East.)		3	5	.500	3.10	1.03	17	4	0	0	...	5-...	40.2	29	16	14	0	13-0	47	.193
—Pawtucket (Int'l)		1	0	1.000	0.00	0.86	1	1	0	0	...	0-...	4.2	3	0	0	0	1-0	6	.176
—Boston (A.L.)		3	0	1.000	2.52	1.20	28	0	0	0	6	0-2	25.0	19	7	7	3	11-0	22	.204
1998—Pawtucket (Int'l)		3	1	.750	4.17	1.37	23	1	0	0	...	3-...	41.0	37	20	19	8	19-2	41	.234
—Boston (A.L.)		1	1	.500	3.46	1.58	29	0	0	0	7	1-2	26.0	26	16	10	2	15-1	14	.263
1999—Vancouver (PCL)		7	2	.778	4.29	1.50	32	15	0	0	...	0-...	107.0	116	57	51	12	45-0	73	.280
—Oakland (A.L.)		2	0	1.000	1.86	0.57	6	1	0	0	0	1-1	19.1	8	4	4	2	3-0	15	.123
2000—Oakland (A.L.)		0	1	.000	9.00	2.19	5	2	0	0	0	0-0	16.0	26	18	16	4	9-0	5	.366
—Florida (N.L.)		1	0	1.000	6.04	1.86	18	0	0	0	2	0-0	25.1	31	17	17	6	16-1	27	.310
—Calgary (PCL)		0	1	.000	4.85	1.08	8	0	0	0	...	0-...	13.0	7	7	7	1	7-1	15	.175
2001—Portland (PCL)		1	2	.333	3.78	1.08	14	0	0	0	...	0-...	16.2	13	9	7	2	5-0	18	.210
—Iowa (PCL)		3	1	.750	2.31	0.84	36	0	0	0	...	14-...	46.2	29	12	12	5	10-1	52	.182
—Chicago (N.L.)		0	0	...	2.61	1.40	17	0	0	0	2	0-0	20.2	14	6	6	4	15-1	24	.197
2002—Iowa (PCL)		0	1	.000	1.93	1.01	39	1	0	0	...	2-...	46.2	32	11	10	3	15-1	50	.194
—Chicago (N.L.)		2	0	1.000	8.59	1.43	11	0	0	0	0	0-0	14.2	13	14	14	6	8-0	14	.228
2003—Oklahoma (PCL)		4	2	.667	4.22	1.10	26	0	0	0	...	3-...	42.2	36	21	20	5	10-0	51	.224

M

Year Team (League)	W	L	Pct.	ERA	WHIP	G	GS	CG	ShO	Hld.	Sv.-Opp.	IP	H	R	ER	HR	BB-IBB	SO	Avg.
—Texas (A.L.)	3	3	.500	3.18	1.17	35	0	0	0	9	0-3	45.1	33	19	16	3	20-7	38	.195
2004—Texas (A.L.)	3	0	1.000	2.55	1.33	60	0	0	0	14	0-2	67.0	60	23	19	5	29-5	54	.235
2005—Oklahoma (PCL)	0	0	...	0.00	0.82	3	0	0	0	1	0-0	3.2	2	0	0	0	1-0	5	.167
—Texas (A.L.)	0	2	.000	6.81	1.77	30	0	0	0	6	1-1	35.2	47	28	27	8	16-1	30	.313
—Frisco (Texas)	1	3	.250	7.78	1.68	5	5	0	0	0	0-0	19.2	24	19	17	3	9-0	20	.300
American League totals (7 years)	12	7	.632	3.80	1.37	193	3	0	0	42	3-11	234.1	219	115	99	27	103-14	178	.243
National League totals (3 years)	3	0	1.000	5.49	1.60	46	0	0	0	4	0-0	60.2	58	37	37	16	39-2	65	.254
Major League totals (9 years)	15	7	.682	4.15	1.42	239	3	0	0	46	3-11	295.0	277	152	136	43	142-16	243	.245

MAHOLM, PAUL   P

PERSONAL: Born June 25, 1982, in Greenwood, Miss. ... 6-2/225. ... Throws left, bats left. ... Full name: Paul G. Maholm. ... College: Mississippi State.
TRANSACTIONS/CAREER NOTES: Selected by Pittsburgh Pirates organization in first round (eighth pick overall) of 2003 free-agent draft.
CAREER HITTING: 2-for-15 (.133), 1 R, 0 2B, 0 3B, 0 HR, 0 RBI.

SCOUTING REPORT *Throws:* His fastball reaches 90 mph, and he has a curve, slider and changeup. *Tendencies:* He relies on movement and keeping his pitches low in the zone. Does a good job of establishing the strike zone with his breaking ball. Mixes his pitches intelligently. Is unflappable and shows good durability. From the windup he shows signs of using all four corners of the strike zone at will. Is solid against lefthanders. *Outlook:* He needs more experience before joining the rotation, but he was effective as a starter in his September call-up last year. If he doesn't make it as a starter, he could make an excellent situational reliever. *Grade 7.2*

PAUL MAHOLM'S PITCHING ZONE

.182	.400	.167
.222	.308	.250
.100	.200	.000

LEFTY-RIGHTY SPLITS

vs.	Avg.	AB	H	2B	3B	HR	RBI	BB	SO	OBP	Slg.
L	.087	23	2	0	0	0	0	0	5	.125	.087
R	.232	125	29	8	0	2	8	17	21	.333	.344

Year Team (League)	W	L	Pct.	ERA	WHIP	G	GS	CG	ShO	Hld.	Sv.-Opp.	IP	H	R	ER	HR	BB-IBB	SO	Avg.
2003—Will. (NYP)	2	1	.667	1.83	1.02	8	8	0	0	...	0-...	34.1	25	11	7	1	10-0	32	.197
2004—Lynchburg (Caro.)	1	3	.250	1.84	1.23	8	8	0	0	...	0-...	44.0	39	11	9	2	15-0	28	.245
—GC Pirates (GCL)	0	0	...	2.25	1.50	1	0	0	0	...	0-...	4.0	5	1	1	0	1-0	2	.294
—Hickory (S. Atl.)	0	2	.000	9.49	2.19	3	3	0	0	...	0-...	12.1	17	14	13	2	10-0	12	.354
2005—Altoona (East.)	6	2	.750	3.20	1.21	16	16	0	0	0	0-0	81.2	73	32	29	5	26-2	75	.243
—Indianapolis (Int'l)	1	1	.500	3.53	1.46	6	6	0	0	0	0-0	35.2	40	19	14	2	12-0	21	.286
—Pittsburgh (N.L.)	3	1	.750	2.18	1.16	6	6	0	0	0	0-0	41.1	31	10	10	2	17-0	26	.209
Major League totals (1 year)	3	1	.750	2.18	1.16	6	6	0	0	0	0-0	41.1	31	10	10	2	17-0	26	.209

MAHONEY, MIKE   C

PERSONAL: Born December 5, 1972, in Des Moines, Iowa. ... 6-1/200. ... Bats right, throws right. ... Full name: Michael John Mahoney. ... High school: Dowling (West Des Moines, Iowa). ... College: Creighton.
TRANSACTIONS/CAREER NOTES: Selected by Atlanta Braves organization in 39th round of 1995 free-agent draft. ... Released by Braves (October 7, 1999). ... Signed by Chicago Cubs organization (October 27, 1999). ... Signed as a free agent by St. Louis Cardinals organization (November 7, 2003).
2005 GAMES PLAYED BY POSITION (MLB): C—25.

MIKE MAHONEY'S HITTING ZONE

.250	.333	.111
.000	.200	.200
.375	.333	.000

LEFTY-RIGHTY SPLITS

vs.	Avg.	AB	H	2B	3B	HR	RBI	BB	SO	OBP	Slg.
L	.100	10	1	0	0	2	2	2	.308	.100
R	.167	54	9	1	0	1	4	2	8	.196	.241

Year Team (League)	Pos.	G	AB	R	H	2B	3B	HR	RBI	BB	SO	HBP	GDP	SB-CS	Avg.	OBP	SLG	OPS	E	Avg.
1995—Eugene (Northwest)	C	43	112	14	27	6	0	1	15	15	17	3	5	6-2	.241	.344	.321	.665	6	.981
1996—Durham (Carol.)	C	101	363	52	94	24	2	9	46	23	64	7	8	4-3	.259	.312	.410	.722	8	.990
1997—Greenville (Sou.)	C	87	298	46	68	17	0	8	46	28	75	3	10	1-0	.228	.299	.366	.665	10	.989
1998—Greenville (Sou.)	C	20	74	3	16	5	0	1	6	1	20	2	1	1-1	.216	.241	.324	.565	2	.987
—Richmond (Int'l)	C-P	71	208	26	44	10	0	5	28	24	49	5	10	1-1	.212	.302	.332	.634	7	.984
1999—Richmond (Int'l)	C-P	55	145	10	33	7	0	2	20	6	25	1	2	0-1	.228	.258	.317	.575	3	.989
2000—West Tenn. (Sou.)	C	24	76	12	23	7	0	0	7	7	16	2	0	0-0	.303	.372	.395	.767	1	.995
—Iowa (PCL)	1B-2B-C P	63	181	29	55	14	0	6	28	16	28	6	2	2-1	.304	.374	.481	.855	4	.988
—Chicago (N.L.)	C	4	7	1	2	1	0	0	1	1	0	1		0-0	.286	.444	.429	.873	0	...
2001—Iowa (PCL)	C-1B 3B-P-2B	95	289	22	65	14	1	3	27	16	63	4	8	1-3	.225	.287	.311	.598	3	.996
2002—Iowa (PCL)	C-1B P-2B	78	223	33	57	12	1	2	18	17	44	1	0	1-1	.256	.311	.345	.656	* 12	.978
—Chicago (N.L.)	C-1B-P	16	29	2	6	3	0	0	3	1	10	0		0-0	.207	.233	.310	.544	0	1.000
2003—Iowa (PCL)	2B	65	190	19	49	12	1	2	18	11	32	2	9	0-1	.258	.302	.363	.665	4	.989
2004—Memphis (PCL)	C	79	270	32	81	16	1	5	32	22	37	3	1	1-4	.300	.357	.422	.779	8	.986
2005—Memphis (PCL)	C	71	230	30	61	19	1	5	27	14	40	7	9	2-0	.265	.324	.422	.746	2	.996
—St. Louis (N.L.)	C	26	64	5	10	1	0	1	6	4	10	1	3	0-0	.156	.217	.219	.436	2	.984
Major League totals (3 years)		46	100	8	18	5	0	1	10	6	20	2	3	0-0	.180	.241	.260	.501	2	.990

MAINE, JOHN · P

PERSONAL: Born May 8, 1981, in Fredericksburg, Va. ... 6-4/193. ... Throws right, bats right. ... Full name: John K. Maine. ... High school: North Stafford (Va.). ... College: Charlotte.
TRANSACTIONS/CAREER NOTES: Selected by Baltimore Orioles organization in sixth round of 2002 free-agent draft.
CAREER HITTING: 0-for-0 (.000), 0 R, 0 2B, 0 3B, 0 HR, 0 RBI.

JOHN MAINE'S PITCHING ZONE

.222	.143	.500
.200	.357	.286
.286	.300	.174

LEFTY-RIGHTY SPLITS

vs.	Avg.	AB	H	2B	3B	HR	RBI	BB	SO	OBP	Slg.
L	.227	88	20	3	0	5	19	20	14	.364	.432
R	.275	69	19	3	0	3	8	4	10	.324	.449

Year	Team (League)	W	L	Pct.	ERA	WHIP	G	GS	CG	ShO	Hld.	Sv.-Opp.	IP	H	R	ER	HR	BB-IBB	SO	Avg.
2002—	Aberdeen (N.Y.-Penn.)	1	1	.500	1.74	0.87	4	2	0	0	...	0-...	10.1	6	2	2	0	3-0	21	.154
—	Delmarva (S. Atl.)	1	1	.500	1.36	0.76	6	5	0	0	...	0-...	33.0	21	8	5	0	4-0	39	.178
2003—	Delmarva (S. Atl.)	7	3	.700	1.53	0.80	14	14	1	0	...	0-...	76.1	43	16	13	1	18-0	108	.165
—	Frederick (Carolina)	6	1	.857	3.07	0.97	12	12	1	1	...	0-...	70.1	48	27	24	5	20-0	77	.190
2004—	Bowie (East.)	4	0	1.000	2.25	0.82	5	5	0	0	...	0-...	28.0	16	8	7	1	7-0	34	.160
—	Baltimore (A.L.)	0	1	.000	9.82	2.73	1	1	0	0	0	0-0	3.2	7	4	4	1	3-0	1	.438
—	Ottawa (Int'l)	5	7	.417	3.91	1.46	22	22	0	0	...	0-...	119.2	123	59	52	12	52-0	105	.266
2005—	Ottawa (Int'l)	6	11	.353	4.56	1.32	23	23	1	1	0	0-0	128.1	128	72	65	13	42-0	111	.257
—	Baltimore (A.L.)	2	3	.400	6.30	1.58	10	8	0	0	0	0-0	40.0	39	30	28	8	24-0	24	.248
Major League totals (2 years)		2	4	.333	6.60	1.67	11	9	0	0	0	0-0	43.2	46	34	32	9	27-0	25	.266

MAJEWSKI, GARY · P

PERSONAL: Born February 26, 1980, in Houston. ... 6-1/215. ... Throws right, bats right. ... Full name: Gary Wayne Majewski. ... Name pronounced: my-EV-ski. ... High school: St. Pius X (Houston).
TRANSACTIONS/CAREER NOTES: Selected by Chicago White Sox organization in second round of 1998 free-agent draft. ... Traded by White Sox with Ps Andre Simpson and Orlando Rodriguez to Los Angeles Dodgers for Ps Antonio Osuna and Carlos Ortega (March 22, 2001). ... Traded by Dodgers with P Onan Masaoka and OF Jeff Barry to White Sox for P James Baldwin (July 26, 2001). ... Selected by Toronto Blue Jays from White Sox organization in Rule 5 major league draft (December 16, 2002). ... Returned to White Sox (March 17, 2003). ... Traded by White Sox with P Jon Rauch to Montreal Expos for OF Carl Everett (July 18, 2004). ... Expos franchise transferred to Washington, D.C., and renamed Washington Nationals for 2005 season (December 3, 2004).
CAREER HITTING: 0-for-8 (.000), 0 R, 0 2B, 0 3B, 0 HR, 0 RBI.

GARY MAJEWSKI'S PITCHING ZONE

.300	.462	.167
.193	.400	.290
.269	.217	.242

LEFTY-RIGHTY SPLITS

vs.	Avg.	AB	H	2B	3B	HR	RBI	BB	SO	OBP	Slg.
L	.236	157	37	11	1	2	23	27	29	.353	.357
R	.259	166	43	6	1	0	13	10	21	.315	.307

Year	Team (League)	W	L	Pct.	ERA	WHIP	G	GS	CG	ShO	Hld.	Sv.-Opp.	IP	H	R	ER	HR	BB-IBB	SO	Avg.
1999—	Bristol (Appal.)	7	1	.875	3.05	1.36	13	13	1	1	...	0-...	76.2	67	34	26	4	37-0	91	.243
—	Burlington (Midw.)	0	0	...	37.80	4.50	2	0	0	0	...	0-...	3.1	11	14	14	3	4-0	1	.524
2000—	Burlington (Midw.)	6	7	.462	3.07	1.12	22	22	3	3	...	0-...	134.2	83	53	46	8	68-0	137	.182
—	Win.-Salem (Car.)	2	4	.333	5.11	1.32	6	6	0	0	...	0-...	37.0	32	21	21	1	17-0	24	.239
2001—	Vero Beach (FSL)	4	5	.444	6.24	1.85	23	13	0	0	...	1-...	75.0	103	57	52	9	36-0	41	.340
—	Win.-Salem (Car.)	4	2	.667	2.93	1.21	9	6	1	0	...	0-...	43.0	42	15	14	3	10-0	31	.266
2002—	Birmingham (Sou.)	5	3	.625	2.65	1.27	57	1	0	0	...	3-...	74.2	61	31	22	3	34-2	75	.221
2003—	Charlotte (Int'l)	6	4	.600	3.96	1.25	42	1	0	0	...	4-...	72.2	62	33	32	3	29-2	72	.231
2004—	Charlotte (Int'l)	3	3	.500	3.19	1.09	35	0	0	0	...	14-...	42.1	30	16	15	2	16-0	41	.208
—	Edmonton (PCL)	1	2	.333	3.86	1.59	15	0	0	0	...	0-...	16.1	18	8	7	0	8-1	17	.295
—	Montreal (N.L.)	0	1	.000	3.86	1.57	16	0	0	0	0	1-2	21.0	28	15	9	2	5-1	12	.326
2005—	New Orleans (PCL)	0	0	...	4.26	1.42	3	0	0	0	1	0-1	6.1	7	3	3	0	2-0	2	.292
—	Was. (N.L.)	4	4	.500	2.93	1.36	79	0	0	0	24	1-5	86.0	80	32	28	2	37-6	50	.248
Major League totals (2 years)		4	5	.444	3.11	1.40	95	0	0	0	24	2-7	107.0	108	47	37	4	42-7	62	.264

MANTEI, MATT · P

PERSONAL: Born July 7, 1973, in Tampa. ... 6-1/198. ... Throws right, bats right. ... Full name: Matthews Bruce Mantei. ... Name pronounced: MAN-tie. ... High school: River Valley (Three Oaks, Mich.).
TRANSACTIONS/CAREER NOTES: Selected by Seattle Mariners organization in 25th round of 1991 free-agent draft. ... Selected by Florida Marlins from Mariners organization in Rule 5 major league draft (December 5, 1994). ... On disabled list (April 20-June 18 and July 29-September 1, 1995); included rehabilitation assignments to Portland and Charlotte. ... On disabled list (June 19, 1996-remainder of season; March 31, 1997-entire season; and August 19-September 4, 1998). ... Traded by Marlins to Arizona Diamondbacks for Ps Vladimir Nunez and Brad Penny and a player to be named (July 9, 1999); Marlins acquired OF Abraham Nunez to complete deal (December 13, 1999). ... On disabled list (April 2-21 and May 5-21, 2000); included rehabilitation assignment to Tucson. ... On disabled list (April 25, 2001-remainder of season). ... On disabled list (March 22-June 27, 2002); included rehabilitation assignments to El Paso and Tucson. ... On disabled list (May 28-June 30, 2003); included rehabilitation assignment to Tucson. ... On disabled list (May 9, 2004-remainder of season). ... Signed as a free agent by Boston Red Sox (December 9, 2004). ... On disabled list (July 2, 2005-remainder of season).
CAREER HITTING: 1-for-5 (.200), 0 R, 0 2B, 0 3B, 0 HR, 0 RBI.

MATT MANTEI'S PITCHING ZONE

.214	.000	.111
.278	.417	.286
.444	.400	.167

LEFTY-RIGHTY SPLITS

vs.	Avg.	AB	H	2B	3B	HR	RBI	BB	SO	OBP	Slg.
L	.293	41	12	1	0	1	7	11	8	.473	.390
R	.200	55	11	6	0	0	5	13	14	.371	.309

Year	Team (League)	W	L	Pct.	ERA	WHIP	G	GS	CG	ShO	Hld.	Sv.-Opp.	IP	H	R	ER	HR	BB-IBB	SO	Avg.
1991—	Ariz. Mariners (Ariz.)	1	4	.200	6.69	2.03	17	5	0	0	...	0-...	40.1	54	40	30	0	28-2	29	.321
1992—	Ariz. Mariners (Ariz.)	1	1	.500	5.63	1.44	3	3	0	0	...	0-...	16.0	18	10	10	1	5-0	19	.286
1993—	Bellingham (N'west)	1	1	.500	5.96	1.60	26	0	0	0	...	12-...	25.2	26	19	17	2	15-0	34	.260
1994—	Appleton (Midwest)	5	1	.833	2.06	1.31	48	0	0	0	...	26-...	48.0	42	14	11	2	21-3	70	.240
1995—	Portland (East.)	1	0	1.000	2.38	1.32	8	0	0	0	...	1-...	11.1	10	3	3	0	5-0	15	.244
—	Charlotte (Int'l)	0	0	...	2.57	0.86	6	0	0	0	...	0-...	7.0	3	2	2	1	5-0	10	.050

M

Year	Team (League)	W	L	Pct.	ERA	WHIP	G	GS	CG	ShO	Hld.	Sv.-Opp.	IP	H	R	ER	HR	BB-IBB	SO	Avg.
	— Florida (N.L.)	0	1	.000	4.73	1.88	12	0	0	0	0	0-0	13.1	12	8	7	1	13-0	15	.245
1996—	Florida (N.L.)	1	0	1.000	6.38	1.85	14	0	0	0	0	0-1	18.1	13	13	13	2	21-1	25	.197
	— Charlotte (Int'l)	0	2	.000	4.70	1.70	7	0	0	0	...	2-...	7.2	6	4	4	1	7-0	8	.214
1997—	Brevard County (FSL)	0	0	...	6.00	1.67	4	0	0	0	...	0-...	6.0	4	4	4	1	6-0	11	.190
	— Portland (East.)	1	0	1.000	6.75	2.25	5	0	0	0	...	0-...	4.0	1	3	3	0	8-0	7	.083
1998—	Charlotte (Int'l)	1	2	.333	5.51	1.78	16	0	0	0	...	3-...	16.1	11	10	10	2	18-1	25	.196
	— Charlotte (Int'l)	3	4	.429	2.96	1.12	42	0	0	0	...	9-12	54.2	38	19	18	1	23-3	63	.203
1999—	Florida (N.L.)	1	2	.333	2.72	1.35	35	0	0	0	0	10-12	36.1	24	11	11	4	25-1	50	.186
	— Arizona (N.L.)	0	1	.000	2.79	1.34	30	0	0	0	0	22-25	29.0	20	10	9	1	19-0	49	.192
2000—	Tucson (PCL)	0	0	...	2.45	1.09	4	2	0	0	0	0-...	3.2	1	1	1	0	3-0	2	.100
	— Arizona (N.L.)	1	1	.500	4.57	1.46	47	0	0	0	0	17-20	45.1	31	24	23	4	35-1	53	.193
2001—	Arizona (N.L.)	0	0	...	2.57	1.43	8	0	0	0	1	2-2	7.0	6	2	2	2	4-0	12	.222
2002—	El Paso (Texas)	0	1	.000	2.25	1.00	4	3	0	0	...	0-...	4.0	3	3	1	0	4-0	5	.200
	— Tucson (PCL)	1	0	1.000	0.00	1.20	9	1	0	0	...	0-...	10.0	8	1	0	0	4-0	9	.211
	— Arizona (N.L.)	2	2	.500	4.73	1.50	31	0	0	0	2	0-1	26.2	28	15	14	3	12-0	26	.257
2003—	Tucson (PCL)	0	0	...	2.25	0.50	3	0	0	0	...	0-...	4.0	2	1	1	1	0-0	4	.154
	— Arizona (N.L.)	5	4	.556	2.62	1.00	50	0	0	0	0	29-32	55.0	37	17	16	6	18-1	68	.191
2004—	Arizona (N.L.)	0	3	.000	11.81	2.16	12	0	0	0	0	4-7	10.2	17	15	14	5	6-1	13	.354
2005—	Boston (A.L.)	1	0	1.000	6.49	1.78	34	0	0	0	8	0-0	26.1	23	20	19	1	24-1	22	.240
	American League totals (1 year)	1	0	1.000	6.49	1.78	34	0	0	0	8	0-0	26.1	23	20	19	1	24-1	22	.240
	National League totals (9 years)	13	18	.419	3.86	1.36	281	0	0	0	5	93-112	296.1	226	134	127	29	176-8	374	.210
	Major League totals (10 years)	14	18	.438	4.07	1.39	315	0	0	0	13	93-112	322.2	249	154	146	30	200-9	396	.213

DIVISION SERIES RECORD

Year	Team (League)	W	L	Pct.	ERA	WHIP	G	GS	CG	ShO	Hld.	Sv.-Opp.	IP	H	R	ER	HR	BB-IBB	SO	Avg.
1999—	Arizona (N.L.)	0	1	.000	4.50	2.00	1	0	0	0	0	0-0	2.0	1	1	1	1	3-1	1	.167
2002—	Arizona (N.L.)	0	0	...	54.00	6.00	1	0	0	0	0	0-0	0.1	1	2	2	0	1-0	0	.500
	Division series totals (2 years)	0	1	.000	11.57	2.57	2	0	0	0	0	0-0	2.1	2	3	3	1	4-1	1	.250

MARCUM, SHAUN   P

PERSONAL: Born December 14, 1981, in Kansas City, Mo. ... 6-0/180. ... Throws right, bats right. ... Full name: Shaun M. Marcum. ... College: SW Missouri State.

TRANSACTIONS/CAREER NOTES: Selected by Toronto Blue Jays organization in third round of 2003 free-agent draft.

CAREER HITTING: 0-for-0 (.000), 0 R, 0 2B, 0 3B, 0 HR, 0 RBI.

LEFTY-RIGHTY SPLITS

vs.	Avg.	AB	H	2B	3B	HR	RBI	BB	SO	OBP	Slg.
L	.176	17	3	1	0	0	0	0	2	.176	.235
R	.273	11	3	1	0	0	0	4	2	.467	.364

Year	Team (League)	W	L	Pct.	ERA	WHIP	G	GS	CG	ShO	Hld.	Sv.-Opp.	IP	H	R	ER	HR	BB-IBB	SO	Avg.
2003—	Auburn (NY-Penn)	1	0	1.000	1.32	0.65	21	0	0	0	...	8-...	34.0	15	6	5	1	7-0	47	.129
2004—	Char., W.Va. (SAL)	7	4	.636	3.19	1.01	13	13	1	1	...	0-...	79.0	64	32	28	7	16-0	83	.217
	— Dunedin (Fla. St.)	3	2	.600	3.12	1.13	12	12	0	0	...	0-...	69.1	74	30	24	6	4-0	72	.279
2005—	New Hampshire (East.)	7	1	.875	2.53	1.01	9	9	1	1	0	0-0	53.1	44	15	15	5	10-0	40	.229
	— Syracuse (Int'l)	6	4	.600	4.95	1.25	18	18	0	0	0	0-0	103.2	112	59	57	17	18-2	90	.271
	— Toronto (A.L.)	0	0	...	0.00	1.25	5	0	0	0	0	0-0	8.0	6	0	0	0	4-0	4	.214
	Major League totals (1 year)	0	0	...	0.00	1.25	5	0	0	0	0	0-0	8.0	6	0	0	0	4-0	4	.214

MAROTH, MIKE   P

PERSONAL: Born August 17, 1977, in Orlando. ... 6-0/190. ... Throws left, bats left. ... Full name: Michael Warren Maroth. ... Name pronounced: mah-ROTH. ... High school: William R. Boone (Orlando). ... College: Central Florida.

TRANSACTIONS/CAREER NOTES: Selected by Boston Red Sox organization in third round of 1998 free-agent draft. ... Traded by Red Sox to Detroit Tigers for P Bryce Florie (July 31, 1999).

CAREER HITTING: 4-for-16 (.250), 1 R, 0 2B, 0 3B, 0 HR, 2 RBI.

SCOUTING REPORT *Throws:* His fastball ranges from 86-88 mph, and he complements it with a curveball and changeup. *Tendencies:* Maroth has a very good delivery with good tailing action to his fastball. Will work both sides of the plate and is effective jamming righthanded hitters. Throws a big-looping curve to righthanders and turns over his changeup. Has a deceptive delivery and his fastball moves late. Has a good pickoff move to first base. Needs good location to be effective. *Outlook:* He is a durable starter who can be counted on to pitch 200 innings out of the middle of the rotation. *Grade 7.2*

MIKE MAROTH'S PITCHING ZONE

.327	.250	.273
.347	.370	.218
.261	.476	.203

LEFTY-RIGHTY SPLITS

vs.	Avg.	AB	H	2B	3B	HR	RBI	BB	SO	OBP	Slg.
L	.275	211	58	11	2	3	22	9	43	.304	.389
R	.293	604	177	22	2	27	92	42	72	.343	.470

Year	Team (League)	W	L	Pct.	ERA	WHIP	G	GS	CG	ShO	Hld.	Sv.-Opp.	IP	H	R	ER	HR	BB-IBB	SO	Avg.
1998—	GC Red Sox (GCL)	1	1	.500	0.00	0.87	4	2	0	0	...	0-...	12.2	9	3	0	0	2-0	14	.191
	— Lowell (NY-Penn)	2	3	.400	2.90	1.13	6	6	0	0	...	0-...	31.0	22	13	10	1	13-0	34	.200
1999—	Sarasota (Fla. St.)	11	6	.647	4.04	1.43	20	19	0	0	...	0-...	111.1	124	65	50	3	35-1	64	
	— Lakeland (Fla. St.)	2	1	.667	3.24	1.50	3	3	0	0	...	0-...	16.2	18	7	6	1	7-0	11	
	— Jacksonville (Sou.)	1	2	.333	4.79	1.65	4	4	0	0	...	0-...	20.2	27	15	11	2	7-0	10	.310
2000—	Jacksonville (Sou.)	9	14	.391	3.94	1.42	27	26	2	1	...	0-...	164.1	176	79	72	14	58-0	85	.289
2001—	Toledo (Int'l)	7	10	.412	4.65	1.58	24	23	0	0	...	0-...	131.2	158	80	68	11	50-1	63	.302
2002—	Toledo (Int'l)	8	1	.889	2.82	1.02	11	11	1	0	...	0-...	73.1	53	25	23	7	22-0	51	.201
	— Detroit (A.L.)	6	10	.375	4.48	1.34	21	21	0	0	0	0-0	128.2	136	68	64	7	36-1	58	.276
2003—	Detroit (A.L.)	9	* 21	.300	5.73	1.45	33	33	1	0	0	0-0	193.1	231	131 • 123	• 34	50-2	87	.299
2004—	Detroit (A.L.)	11	13	.458	4.31	1.40	33	33	0	0	0	0-0	217.0	244	112	104	25	59-1	108	.288
2005—	Detroit (A.L.)	14	14	.500	4.74	1.37	34	34	0	0	0	0-0	209.0	235	123	110	30	51-1	115	.288
	Major League totals (4 years)	40	58	.408	4.82	1.39	121	121	3	1	0	0-0	748.0	846	434	401	96	196-5	368	.289

MARQUIS, JASON   P

PERSONAL: Born August 21, 1978, in Manhasset, N.Y. ... 6-1/210. ... Throws right, bats left. ... Full name: Jason Scott Marquis. ... Name pronounced: mar-KEE. ... High school: Tottenville (Staten Island, N.Y.).
TRANSACTIONS/CAREER NOTES: Selected by Atlanta Braves organization in supplemental round ("sandwich" pick between first and second rounds, 35th pick overall) of 1996 free-agent draft; pick received as compensation for Braves' failure to sign 1995 first-round pick P Chad Hutchinson. ... On disabled list (April 22-May 12, 2002). ... Traded with Ps Ray King and Adam Wainwright to St. Louis Cardinals for OF J.D. Drew and C/OF Eli Marrero (December 14, 2003).
CAREER HITTING: 55-for-232 (.237), 25 R, 15 2B, 1 3B, 2 HR, 21 RBI.

SCOUTING REPORT **Throws:** He relies on an 88-93 mph fastball. Also has a curveball and changeup. **Tendencies:** He throws both a very good sinking fastball and a cutter, but too much of a reliance on the cutter could take away from his natural sinker. Doesn't throw as hard now and must keep the ball down. Is a contact pitcher. Curveball has a big break with good rotation. Shows good arm speed with movement and his change. Is one of the game's best hitting pitchers. **Outlook:** Marquis needs to use his sinker and stay out of the top part of the zone. Should improve from last year's 13-win season. **Grade 7.3**

JASON MARQUIS' PITCHING ZONE

.250	.452	.158
.300	.351	.273
.370	.208	.234

LEFTY-RIGHTY SPLITS

vs.	Avg.	AB	H	2B	3B	HR	RBI	BB	SO	OBP	Slg.
L	.238	340	81	9	0	11	36	41	43	.321	.362
R	.280	447	125	28	3	18	58	28	57	.326	.477

Year Team (League)	W	L	Pct.	ERA	WHIP	G	GS	CG	ShO	Hld.	Sv.-Opp.	IP	H	R	ER	HR	BB-IBB	SO	Avg.
1996—Danville (Appal.)	1	1	.500	4.63	1.59	7	4	0	0	...	0-...	23.1	30	18	12	0	7-0	24	.286
1997—Macon (S. Atl.)	14	10	.583	4.38	1.49	28	28	0	0	...	0-...	141.2	156	78	69	10	55-1	121	.278
1998—Danville (Carol.)	2	12	.143	4.87	1.40	22	22	1	0	...	0-...	114.2	120	65	62	3	41-0	135	.269
1999—Myrtle Beach (Carol.)	3	0	1.000	0.28	1.22	6	6	0	0	...	0-...	32.0	22	2	1	0	17-0	41	.191
—Greenville (Sou.)	3	4	.429	4.58	1.47	12	12	1	0	...	0-...	55.0	52	33	28	7	29-0	35	.241
2000—Greenville (Sou.)	4	2	.667	3.57	1.34	11	11	0	0	...	0-...	68.0	68	35	27	10	23-0	49	.262
—Atlanta (N.L.)	1	0	1.000	5.01	1.50	15	0	0	0	1	0-1	23.1	23	16	13	4	12-1	17	.261
—Richmond (Int'l)	0	3	.000	9.00	1.95	6	6	0	0	...	0-...	20.0	26	21	20	2	13-0	18	.321
2001—Atlanta (N.L.)	5	6	.455	3.48	1.33	38	16	0	0	2	0-2	129.1	113	62	50	14	59-4	98	.234
2002—Richmond (Int'l)	0	1	.000	3.60	1.20	1	1	0	0	...	0-...	5.0	5	2	2	0	1-0	6	.263
—Atlanta (N.L.)	8	9	.471	5.04	1.54	22	22	0	0	0	0-0	114.1	127	66	64	19	49-3	84	.283
2003—Atlanta (N.L.)	8	4	.667	3.35	1.40	15	15	3	1	0	0-0	94.0	93	40	35	4	34-0	75	.256
—Richmond (Int'l)	0	0	...	5.53	1.50	21	2	0	0	0	1-1	40.2	43	27	25	3	18-2	19	.270
2004—St. Louis (N.L.)	15	7	.682	3.71	1.42	32	32	0	0	0	0-0	201.1	215	90	83	26	70-1	138	.275
2005—St. Louis (N.L.)	13	14	.481	4.13	1.33	33	32	3	0	0	0-0	207.0	206	110	95	29	69-2	100	.262
Major League totals (6 years)	42	36	.538	4.15	1.40	161	104	3	1	3	1-4	716.0	727	371	330	95	277-13	456	.265

DIVISION SERIES RECORD

Year Team (League)	W	L	Pct.	ERA	WHIP	G	GS	CG	ShO	Hld.	Sv.-Opp.	IP	H	R	ER	HR	BB-IBB	SO	Avg.
2001—Atlanta (N.L.)	Did not play.																		
2004—St. Louis (N.L.)	0	0	...	8.10	2.40	1	1	0	0	0	0-0	3.1	4	3	3	3	4-0	0	.308

CHAMPIONSHIP SERIES RECORD

Year Team (League)	W	L	Pct.	ERA	WHIP	G	GS	CG	ShO	Hld.	Sv.-Opp.	IP	H	R	ER	HR	BB-IBB	SO	Avg.
2001—Atlanta (N.L.)	0	0	...	0.00	2.00	2	0	0	0	0	0-0	2.0	2	4	0	1	2-0	3	.222
2004—St. Louis (N.L.)	0	0	...	6.75	1.75	1	1	0	0	0	0-0	4.0	5	3	3	0	2-0	2	.294
2005—St. Louis (N.L.)	0	1	.000	3.38	1.69	3	0	0	0	0	0-0	5.1	6	3	2	0	3-0	4	.316
Champ. series totals (3 years)	0	1	.000	3.97	1.76	6	1	0	0	0	0-0	11.1	8	10	5	1	7-0	9	.289

WORLD SERIES RECORD

Year Team (League)	W	L	Pct.	ERA	WHIP	G	GS	CG	ShO	Hld.	Sv.-Opp.	IP	H	R	ER	HR	BB-IBB	SO	Avg.
2004—St. Louis (N.L.)	0	1	.000	3.86	1.86	2	1	0	0	0	0-0	7.0	6	3	3	1	7-1	5	.231

MARRERO, ELI   OF/C

PERSONAL: Born November 17, 1973, in Havana, Cuba. ... 6-1/180. ... Bats right, throws right. ... Full name: Elieser Marrero. ... Name pronounced: muh-RARE-ro. ... High school: Coral Gables (Fla.).
TRANSACTIONS/CAREER NOTES: Selected by St. Louis Cardinals organization in third round of 1993 free-agent draft. ... On disabled list (March 22-April 13, 1998). ... On disabled list (July 2-September 1, 2000); included rehabilitation assignment to Memphis. ... On disabled list (May 12-September 1, 2003); included rehabilitation assignment to Memphis. ... Traded with OF J.D. Drew to Atlanta Braves for Ps Jason Marquis, Ray King and Adam Wainwright (December 14, 2003). ... On disabled list (March 29-April 14 and April 25-May 29, 2004); included rehabilitation assignments to Greenville and Richmond. ... Traded by Braves to Kansas City Royals for P Luis Vasquez (December 16, 2004). ... Traded by Royals with cash to Baltimore Orioles for 2B Pete Maestrales (June 8, 2005). ... On disabled list (July 27, 2005-remainder of season).
2005 GAMES PLAYED BY POSITION (MLB): OF—36, 1B—9, DH—2.

SCOUTING REPORT Injuries continue to plague Marrero, who never has fulfilled expectations. Has a long stroke that's filled with holes. Doesn't make adjustments to the count. Has power but won't hit a lot of home runs because of his swing. Is adequate in left field; has better range laterally than going back. **Grade 5.5**

ELI MARRERO'S HITTING ZONE

.176	.000	.000
.154	.250	.200
.133	.385	1.000

LEFTY-RIGHTY SPLITS

vs.	Avg.	AB	H	2B	3B	HR	RBI	BB	SO	OBP	Slg.
L	.247	89	22	5	2	7	16	6	25	.293	.584
R	.061	49	3	2	0	0	3	5	13	.143	.102

Year Team (League)	Pos.	G	AB	R	H	2B	3B	HR	RBI	BB	SO	HBP	GDP	SB-CS	Avg.	OBP	SLG	OPS	E	Avg.
1993—Johnson City (App.)	C	18	61	10	22	8	0	2	14	12	9	1	0	2-2	.361	.467	.590	1.057	1	.994
1994—Savannah (S. Atl.)	C	116	421	71	110	16	3	21	79	39	92	5	6	5-4	.261	.328	.463	.791	15	.984

Year	Team (League)	Pos.	G	AB	R	H	2B	3B	HR	RBI	BB	SO	HBP	GDP	SB-CS	Avg.	OBP	SLG	OPS	E	Avg.
																BATTING				FIELDING	
1995—St. Pete. (FSL)	C	107	383	43	81	16	1	10	55	23	55	1	10	9-4	.211	.254	.337	.590	10	.984
1996—Arkansas (Texas)	C-DH	116	374	65	101	17	3	19	65	32	55	6	7	9-6	.270	.336	.484	.820	3	.996
1997—Louisville (A.A.)	C-DH	112	395	60	108	21	7	20	68	25	53	3	8	4-4	.273	.318	.514	.832	7	.991
—St. Louis (N.L.)	C	17	45	4	11	2	0	2	7	2	13	0	1	4-0	.244	.271	.422	.693	3	.969
1998—St. Louis (N.L.)	C-1B	83	254	28	62	18	1	4	20	28	42	0	5	6-2	.244	.318	.370	.688	4	.991
—Memphis (PCL)	C-DH	32	130	22	31	5	0	7	21	13	23	0	3	5-4	.238	.306	.438	.744	2	.991
1999—St. Louis (N.L.)	C-1B	114	317	32	61	13	1	6	34	18	56	1	14	11-2	.192	.236	.297	.533	7	.988
2000—St. Louis (N.L.)	C-1B	53	102	21	23	3	1	5	17	9	16	3	3	5-0	.225	.302	.422	.723	0	1.000
—Memphis (PCL)	C	6	15	1	1	0	0	0	0	0	2	0	1	0-0	.067	.067	.067	.133	0	1.000
2001—St. Louis (N.L.)	C-OF-1B	86	203	37	54	11	3	6	23	15	36	1	4	6-3	.266	.312	.438	.751	7	.983
2002—St. Louis (N.L.)	OF-C-1B	131	397	63	104	19	1	18	66	40	72	1	5	14-2	.262	.327	.451	.777	7	.981
2003—Memphis (PCL)	OF-DH	5	12	2	3	1	0	1	1	1	0	1	1	0-0	.250	.357	.583	.940	0	1.000
—St. Louis (N.L.)	OF-C-1B	41	107	10	24	4	2	2	20	7	14	0	0	0-1	.224	.267	.355	.622	1	.989
2004—Greenville (Sou.)	OF	3	12	3	5	1	0	2	5	2	6	1	0	0-0	.417	.500	1.000	1.500	0	1.000
—Richmond (Int'l)	OF	6	24	1	5	2	0	0	3	1	3	0	0	0-0	.208	.240	.292	.532	0	1.000
—Atlanta (N.L.)	OF	90	250	37	80	18	1	10	40	23	50	1	4	4-1	.320	.374	.520	.894	1	.992
2005—Kansas City (A.L.)	OF-1B-DH	32	88	11	14	4	0	4	9	7	18	1	2	1-0	.159	.222	.341	.563	2	.981
—Baltimore (A.L.)	OF	22	50	8	11	3	2	3	10	4	20	0	1	0-0	.220	.268	.540	.808	1	.966
American League totals (1 year)		54	138	19	25	7	2	7	19	11	38	1	3	1-0	.181	.239	.413	.652	3	.978
National League totals (8 years)		615	1675	232	419	88	10	53	227	142	303	5	36	50-11	.250	.307	.410	.717	30	.987
Major League totals (9 years)		669	1813	251	444	95	12	60	246	153	341	6	39	51-11	.245	.302	.410	.712	33	.987

DIVISION SERIES RECORD

Year	Team (League)	Pos.	G	AB	R	H	2B	3B	HR	RBI	BB	SO	HBP	GDP	SB-CS	Avg.	OBP	SLG	OPS	E	Avg.
2000—St. Louis (N.L.)			Did not play.																		
2001—St. Louis (N.L.)	C	3	7	0	0	0	0	0	0	0	0	0	0	0-0	.000	.000	.000	.000	0	1.000
2002—St. Louis (N.L.)	OF	2	6	0	0	0	0	0	1	0	1	0	0	0-0	.000	.000	.000	.000	0	1.000
2004—Atlanta (N.L.)	OF	3	5	0	1	0	0	0	0	0	2	0	0	0-0	.200	.200	.200	.400	0	...
Division series totals (3 years)		8	18	0	1	0	0	0	1	0	3	0	0	0-0	.056	.053	.056	.108	0	1.000

CHAMPIONSHIP SERIES RECORD

Year	Team (League)	Pos.	G	AB	R	H	2B	3B	HR	RBI	BB	SO	HBP	GDP	SB-CS	Avg.	OBP	SLG	OPS	E	Avg.
2000—St. Louis (N.L.)	C	4	4	0	0	0	0	0	0	1	0	0	0	0-0	.000	.000	.000	.000	0	1.000
2002—St. Louis (N.L.)	OF	4	16	1	3	1	0	1	1	1	1	0	0	0-0	.188	.235	.438	.673	0	1.000
Champ. series totals (2 years)		8	20	1	3	1	0	1	2	1	2	0	0	0-0	.150	.190	.350	.540	0	1.000

MARTE, ANDY — 3B

PERSONAL: Born October 21, 1983, in Villa Tapia, Dominican Republic. ... 6-1/185. ... Bats right, throws right. ... Full name: Andy M. Marte.
TRANSACTIONS/CAREER NOTES: Signed as a non-drafted free agent by Atlanta Braves organization (September 12, 2000).
2005 GAMES PLAYED BY POSITION (MLB): 3B—17.

ANDY MARTE'S HITTING ZONE

.125	.000	1.000
.222	.000	.111
.333	.333	.000

LEFTY-RIGHTY SPLITS

vs.	Avg.	AB	H	2B	3B	HR	RBI	BB	SO	OBP	Slg.
L	.174	23	4	2	1	0	2	4	6	.286	.348
R	.118	34	4	0	0	0	2	3	7	.184	.118

Year	Team (League)	Pos.	G	AB	R	H	2B	3B	HR	RBI	BB	SO	HBP	GDP	SB-CS	Avg.	OBP	SLG	OPS	E	Avg.
2001—Danville (Appal.)	3B-2B	37	125	12	25	6	0	1	12	20	45	0	3	3-0	.200	.306	.272	.578	6	.936
2002—Macon (S. Atl.)	3B	126	488	69	137	32	4	21	105	41	114	6	6	2-1	.281	.339	.492	.831	27	.917
2003—Myrtle Beach (Carol.)	3B	130	463	69	132	35	1	16	63	67	109	2	13	5-2	.285	.372	.469	.841	28	.911
2004—Greenville (Sou.)	3B	107	387	52	104	28	1	23	68	58	105	2	8	1-1	.269	.364	.525	.889	17	.717
—GC Braves (GCL)	2B-3B	4	15	4	7	4	0	1	6	2	2	0	0	0-0	.467	.529	.933	1.462	0	1.000
2005—Richmond (Int'l)	3B	109	389	51	107	26	2	20	74	64	83	0	8	0-3	.275	.372	.506	.878	15	.950
—Atlanta (N.L.)	3B	24	57	3	8	2	1	0	4	7	13	0	2	0-1	.140	.227	.211	.438	3	.857
Major League totals (1 year)		24	57	3	8	2	1	0	4	7	13	0	2	0-1	.140	.227	.211	.438	3	.857

MARTE, DAMASO — P

PERSONAL: Born February 14, 1975, in Santo Domingo, Dominican Republic. ... 6-2/200. ... Throws left, bats left. ... Full name: Damaso Savinon Marte. ... Name pronounced: da-muh-so mar-TAY.
TRANSACTIONS/CAREER NOTES: Signed as a non-drafted free agent by Seattle Mariners organization (October 28, 1992). ... Signed as a free agent by New York Yankees organization (November 16, 2000). ... Traded by Yankees to Pittsburgh Pirates for IF Enrique Wilson (June 13, 2001). ... Traded by Pirates with IF Edwin Yan to Chicago White Sox for P Matt Guerrier (March 27, 2002). ... On disabled list (June 30-July 14, 2005); included rehabilitation assignment to Charlotte.
CAREER HITTING: 0-for-5 (.000), 0 R, 0 2B, 0 3B, 0 HR, 0 RBI.

SCOUTING REPORT *Throws:* He has an 89-92 mph fastball, a slurve at 81-84 and a straight changeup. *Tendencies:* Marte has a low arm slot and good deception in his delivery. Occasionally lowers his angle to lefthanded hitters, making him tougher. The lower his arm slot gets, the less effective his ball moves late. Expands the plate with a sweeping slurve that he starts at lefthanders and backdoors to righthanders. Fastball has good life down in the zone and when going away from righthanders. Uses the change sparingly. *Outlook:* He's a setup reliever who's more effective against lefthanders. Can be extremely moody. *Grade 7.5*

DAMASO MARTE'S PITCHING ZONE

.333	.400	.273
.412	.154	.208
.100	.364	.267

LEFTY-RIGHTY SPLITS

vs.	Avg.	AB	H	2B	3B	HR	RBI	BB	SO	OBP	Slg.
L	.267	90	24	7	0	1	11	15	32	.389	.378
R	.244	86	21	5	0	4	8	18	22	.375	.442

M

Year	Team (League)	W	L	Pct.	ERA	WHIP	G	GS	CG	ShO	Hld.	Sv.-Opp.	IP	H	R	ER	HR	BB-IBB	SO	Avg.
1993— Dom. Mariners (DSL)	2	5	.286	6.55	1.99	17	15	2	0	...	0-...	56.1	62	48	41	...	50-...	29	...
1994— Dom. Mariners (DSL)	7	0	1.000	3.86	1.55	17	13	0	0	...	0-...	65.1	53	41	28	...	48-...	80	...
1995— Everett (N'west)	2	2	.500	2.21	0.95	11	11	5	0	...	0-...	36.2	25	11	9	2	10-0	39	.195
1996— Wisconsin (Midw.)	8	6	.571	4.49	1.47	26	26	2	1	...	0-...	142.1	134	82	71	8	75-5	115	.248
1997— Lancaster (Calif.)	8	8	.500	4.13	1.48	25	25	2	1	...	0-...	139.1	144	75	64	15	62-1	127	.272
1998— Orlando (South.)	7	6	.538	5.27	1.51	22	20	0	0	...	0-...	121.1	136	82	71	14	47-0	99	.281
1999— Tacoma (PCL)	3	3	.500	5.13	1.62	31	11	0	0	...	0-...	73.2	79	43	42	13	40-1	59	.271
— Seattle (A.L.)	0	1	.000	9.35	2.54	5	0	0	0	...	0-0	8.2	16	9	9	3	6-0	3	.390
2000— Ariz. Mariners (Ariz.) ...	0	0	...	0.00	0.20	2	2	0	0	...	0-...	5.0	1	0	0	0	0-0	6	.063
— New Haven (East.)	0	0	...	1.59	1.41	4	0	0	0	...	0-...	5.2	6	1	1	1	2-0	4	.286
2001— Norwich (East.)	3	1	.750	3.50	1.00	23	0	0	0	...	1-...	36.0	29	16	14	3	7-0	36	.215
— Nashville (PCL)	0	0	...	3.38	0.56	4	0	0	0	...	0-...	5.1	3	2	2	2	0-0	4	.167
— Pittsburgh (N.L.)	0	1	.000	4.71	1.27	23	0	0	0	0	0-0	36.1	34	21	19	5	12-3	39	.250
2002— Chicago (A.L.)	1	1	.500	2.83	1.03	68	0	0	0	14	10-12	60.1	44	19	19	5	18-2	72	.204
2003— Chicago (A.L.)	4	2	.667	1.58	1.05	71	0	0	0	14	11-18	79.2	50	16	14	3	34-6	87	.185
2004— Chicago (A.L.)	6	5	.545	3.42	1.22	74	0	0	0	21	6-12	73.2	56	28	28	10	34-4	68	.217
2005— Charlotte (Int'l)	0	0	...	5.40	3.00	1	0	0	0	0	0-0	1.2	4	1	1	0	1-0	2	.400
— Chicago (A.L.)	3	4	.429	3.77	1.72	66	0	0	0	22	4-8	45.1	45	21	19	5	33-4	54	.256
American League totals (5 years)	14	13	.519	2.99	1.26	284	0	0	0	71	31-50	267.2	211	93	89	26	125-16	284	.219
National League totals (1 year)	0	1	.000	4.71	1.27	23	0	0	0	0	0-0	36.1	34	21	19	5	12-3	39	.250
Major League totals (6 years)	14	14	.500	3.20	1.26	307	0	0	0	71	31-50	304.0	245	114	108	31	137-19	323	.223

DIVISION SERIES RECORD

Year	Team (League)	W	L	Pct.	ERA	WHIP	G	GS	CG	ShO	Hld.	Sv.-Opp.	IP	H	R	ER	HR	BB-IBB	SO	Avg.
2005— Chicago (A.L.)	0	0	...	...	...	1	0	0	0	0	0-0	0.0	1	0	0	0	2-0	0	1.000

WORLD SERIES RECORD

Year	Team (League)	W	L	Pct.	ERA	WHIP	G	GS	CG	ShO	Hld.	Sv.-Opp.	IP	H	R	ER	HR	BB-IBB	SO	Avg.
2005— Chicago (A.L.)	1	0	1.000	0.00	1.20	1	0	0	0	0	0-0	1.2	0	0	0	0	2-0	3	.000

MARTIN, TOM   P

PERSONAL: Born May 21, 1970, in Charleston, S.C. ... 6-1/206. ... Throws left, bats left. ... Full name: Thomas Edgar Martin. ... High school: Bay (Panama City, Fla.).

TRANSACTIONS/CAREER NOTES: Selected by Baltimore Orioles organization in sixth round of 1988 free-agent draft. ... Traded by Orioles with 3B Craig Worthington to San Diego Padres for P Jim Lewis and OF Steve Martin (February 17, 1992). ... Selected by Atlanta Braves organization from Padres organization in Rule 5 minor league draft (December 13, 1993). ... Loaned by Braves organization to Mexico City Tigers of the Mexican League (May 1-7, 1995). ... Released by Braves (January 25, 1996). ... Signed by Houston Astros organization (February 21, 1996). ... On disabled list (May 30-June 15, 1997). ... Selected by Arizona Diamondbacks in second round (29th pick overall) of expansion draft (November 18, 1997). ... Traded by Diamondbacks with 3B Travis Fryman and cash to Cleveland Indians for 3B Matt Williams (December 1, 1997). ... On disabled list (April 30-May 18 and August 31-September 19, 1998); included rehabilitation assignments to Buffalo. ... On disabled list (April 4-August 9, 1999); included rehabilitation assignment to Akron. ... On disabled list (June 13-August 4, 2000); included rehabilitation assignment to Buffalo. ... Traded by Indians to New York Mets for C Javier Ochoa (January 11, 2001). ... On disabled list (May 13-August 16, 2001); included rehabilitation assignments to Brooklyn and Norfolk. ... Released by Mets (October 11, 2001). ... Signed by Tampa Bay Devil Rays organization (January 28, 2002). ... On disabled list (April 23-September 30, 2002). ... Released by Devil Rays (September 30, 2002). ... Signed by Los Angeles Dodgers organization (February 26, 2003). ... Traded by Dodgers to Braves for P Matt Merricks (July 31, 2004). ... Released by Braves (April 15, 2005). ... Signed by Astros organization (April 22, 2005).

CAREER HITTING: 0-for-7 (.000), 0 R, 0 2B, 0 3B, 0 HR, 0 RBI.

LEFTY-RIGHTY SPLITS

vs.	Avg.	AB	H	2B	3B	HR	RBI	BB	SO	OBP	Slg.
L	.800	5	4	2	0	1	1	2	0	.857	1.800
R	.286	7	2	1	0	0	0	0	0	.286	.429

Year	Team (League)	W	L	Pct.	ERA	WHIP	G	GS	CG	ShO	Hld.	Sv.-Opp.	IP	H	R	ER	HR	BB-IBB	SO	Avg.
1989— Bluefield (Appal.)	3	3	.500	4.62	1.56	8	8	0	0	...	0-...	39.0	36	28	20	3	25-0	31	.242
— Erie (N.Y.-Penn)	0	5	.000	6.64	1.65	7	7	0	0	...	0-...	40.2	42	39	30	2	25-0	44	.259
1990— Wausau (Midw.)	2	3	.400	2.48	1.45	9	9	0	0	...	0-...	40.0	31	25	11	1	27-0	45	.209
1991— Kane Co. (Midw.)	4	10	.286	3.64	1.49	38	10	0	0	...	6-...	99.0	92	50	40	4	56-3	106	.247
1992— High Desert (Calif.)	0	2	.000	9.37	2.39	11	0	0	0	...	0-...	16.1	23	19	17	4	16-0	10	.333
— Waterloo (Midw.)	2	6	.250	4.25	1.53	39	2	0	0	...	3-...	55.0	62	38	26	3	22-4	57	.287
1993— Rancho Cuca. (Calif.)	1	4	.200	5.61	1.87	47	1	0	0	...	0-...	59.1	72	41	37	4	39-2	53	.305
1994— Greenville (Sou.)	5	6	.455	4.62	1.47	36	6	0	0	...	0-...	74.0	82	40	38	6	27-3	51	.288
1995— Richmond (Int'l)	0	0	...	9.00	2.22	7	0	0	0	...	0-...	9.0	10	9	9	4	10-2	3	.286
— M.C. Tigers (Mex.)	0	1	.000	27.00	4.50	1	1	0	0	...	0-...	1.1	5	5	4	0	1-...	0	...
1996— Tucson (PCL)	0	0	...	0.00	1.33	5	0	0	0	...	0-...	6.0	6	0	0	0	2-2	1	.261
— Jackson (Texas)	6	2	.750	3.24	1.51	57	0	0	0	...	3-...	75.0	71	35	27	8	42-4	58	.250
1997— Houston (N.L.)	5	3	.625	2.09	1.34	55	0	0	0	7	2-3	56.0	52	13	13	2	23-2	36	.254
1998— Cleveland (A.L.)	1	1	.500	12.89	2.80	14	0	0	0	3	0-0	14.2	29	21	21	3	12-0	9	.408
— Buffalo (Int'l)	3	1	.750	6.00	1.64	41	0	0	0	...	0-...	36.0	46	25	24	4	13-0	35	.309
1999— Akron (East.)	0	0	...	1.00	0.78	3	3	0	0	...	0-...	9.0	4	1	1	0	3-0	9	.138
— Cleveland (A.L.)	0	1	.000	8.68	1.71	6	0	0	0	2	0-...	9.1	13	9	9	2	3-1	8	.325
— Buffalo (Int'l)	1	0	1.000	3.00	1.00	5	0	0	0	...	0-...	6.0	5	2	2	1	1-0	6	.208
2000— Cleveland (A.L.)	1	0	1.000	4.05	1.41	31	0	0	0	9	0-...	33.1	32	16	15	3	15-2	21	.254
— Buffalo (Int'l)	0	1	.000	3.60	1.30	9	3	0	0	...	0-...	10.0	12	4	4	1	1-0	4	.300
2001— Norfolk (Int'l)	2	1	.667	6.26	1.78	23	0	0	0	...	1-...	23.0	31	17	16	4	10-0	24	.330
— New York (N.L.)	1	0	1.000	10.06	1.94	14	0	0	0	1	0-...	17.0	23	22	19	4	10-2	12	.319
— Brooklyn (N.Y.-Penn.)	0	0	...	0.00	2.00	1	1	0	0	...	0-...	1.0	2	0	0	0	1-0	0	.500
2002— Durham (Int'l)	0	0	...	0.00	1.20	4	0	0	0	...	2-...	3.1	3	0	0	0	1-0	6	.231
— Tampa Bay (A.L.)	0	0	...	16.20	3.60	2	0	0	0	0	0-...	1.2	5	3	3	0	1-0	1	.500
2003— Los Angeles (N.L.)	1	2	.333	3.53	1.18	80	0	0	0	28	0-1	51.0	36	21	20	6	24-4	51	.198
2004— Los Angeles (N.L.)	0	1	.000	4.13	1.62	47	0	0	0	5	1-1	28.1	32	13	13	3	14-1	18	.291
— Atlanta (N.L.)	0	0	...	3.71	1.29	29	0	0	0	7	0-3	17.0	17	7	7	4	5-2	12	.270
2005— Atlanta (N.L.)	0	0	...	19.29	3.43	4	0	0	0	0	0-0	2.1	6	5	5	1	2-0	0	.500
— Round Rock (PCL)	0	0	...	3.62	1.68	20	0	0	0	...	5-7	27.1	33	11	11	4	13-2	13	.308
American League totals (4 years)	2	2	.500	7.32	1.86	53	0	0	0	3	0-0	59.0	79	49	48	8	31-3	39	.320
National League totals (5 years)	7	7	.500	4.04	1.42	229	0	0	0	48	3-8	171.2	166	81	77	20	78-11	129	.258
Major League totals (9 years)	9	9	.500	4.88	1.53	282	0	0	0	51	3-8	230.2	245	130	125	28	109-14	168	.275

DIVISION SERIES RECORD

Year — Team (League)	W	L	Pct.	ERA	WHIP	G	GS	CG	ShO	Hld.	Sv.-Opp.	IP	H	R	ER	HR	BB-IBB	SO	Avg.
1997— Houston (N.L.)	0	0	...	0.00	3.00	2	0	0	0	0	0-0	0.2	1	1	0	0	1-0	1	.333
2004— Atlanta (N.L.)	0	0	...	54.00	15.00	2	0	0	0	0	0-0	0.1	4	2	2	0	1-0	0	1.000
Division series totals (2 years)	0	0	...	18.00	7.00	4	0	0	0	0	0-0	1.0	5	3	2	0	2-0	0	.714

MARTINEZ, PEDRO   P

PERSONAL: Born October 25, 1971, in Manoguayabo, Dominican Republic. ... 5-11/180. ... Throws right, bats right. ... Full name: Pedro Jaime Martinez. ... Brother of Ramon J. Martinez, pitcher with three major league teams (1988-2001).

TRANSACTIONS/CAREER NOTES: Signed as a non-drafted free agent by Los Angeles Dodgers organization (June 18, 1988). ... Traded by Dodgers to Montreal Expos for 2B Delino DeShields (November 19, 1993). ... On suspended list (April 1-9, 1997). ... Traded by Expos to Boston Red Sox for P Carl Pavano and a player to be named (November 18, 1997); Expos acquired P Tony Armas to complete deal (December 18, 1997). ... On disabled list (July 19-August 3, 1999; June 29-July 13, 2000; June 27-August 26 and September 8, 2001-remainder of season; and May 16-June 11, 2003). ... Signed as a free agent by New York Mets (December 17, 2004).

HONORS: Named Minor League Player of the Year by THE SPORTING NEWS (1991). ... Named N.L. Pitcher of the Year by THE SPORTING NEWS (1997). ... Named A.L. Pitcher of the Year by THE SPORTING NEWS (1999 and 2000). ... Named N.L. Cy Young Award winner by Baseball Writers' Association of America (1997). ... Named A.L. Cy Young Award winner by Baseball Writers' Association of America (1999 and 2000).

CAREER HITTING: 31-for-334 (.093), 16 R, 3 2B, 2 3B, 0 HR, 12 RBI.

SCOUTING REPORT

Throws: Martinez throws a low to mid-90s fastball and one of the best changeups in the game. Also has a slurve and a good cutter. **Tendencies:** Martinez now pitches at the lower range of his velocity, but he has such good command to both sides of the plate that he continues to be one of the game's best. Is not afraid to knock hitters off the plate. Has a quick-breaking, lateral breaking ball that he makes bigger as more hitters chase it. Will throw his circle changeup, which dives and fades, in any count. Can be dominant against righthanded hitters. Finishes pitches better than almost anyone. **Outlook:** He still is a top of the rotation starter despite a decline in pure stuff. Can adjust his approach faster than hitters can adjust theirs. **Grade 9**

PEDRO MARTINEZ'S PITCHING ZONE

.163	.256	.148
.248	.368	.204
.275	.143	.117

LEFTY-RIGHTY SPLITS

vs.	Avg.	AB	H	2B	3B	HR	RBI	BB	SO	OBP	Slg.
L	.215	391	84	23	1	9	33	35	93	.281	.348
R	.192	390	75	14	3	10	35	12	115	.221	.321

Year — Team (League)	W	L	Pct.	ERA	WHIP	G	GS	CG	ShO	Hld.	Sv.-Opp.	IP	H	R	ER	HR	BB-IBB	SO	Avg.
1988— Dom. Dodgers (DSL)	5	1	.833	3.10	1.24	8	7	1	0	...	0-...	49.1	45	25	17	...	16-...	28	...
1989— Dom. Dodgers (DSL)	7	2	.778	2.73	0.98	13	7	2	3	...	1-...	85.2	59	30	26	...	25-...	63	...
1990— Great Falls (Pio.)	8	3	.727	3.62	1.48	14	14	0	0	...	0-...	77.0	74	39	31	5	40-1	82	.253
1991— Bakersfield (Calif.)	8	0	1.000	2.05	0.98	10	10	0	0	...	0-...	61.1	41	17	14	3	19-0	83	.189
— San Antonio (Texas)	7	5	.583	1.76	1.15	12	12	4	3	...	0-...	76.2	57	21	15	1	31-1	74	.210
— Albuquerque (PCL)	3	3	.500	3.66	1.12	6	6	0	0	...	0-...	39.1	28	17	16	3	16-0	35	.201
1992— Albuquerque (PCL)	7	6	.538	3.81	1.28	20	20	3	1	...	0-...	125.1	104	57	53	10	57-0	124	.229
— Los Angeles (N.L.)	0	1	.000	2.25	0.88	2	1	0	0	0	0-0	8.0	6	2	2	0	1-0	8	.200
1993— Albuquerque (PCL)	0	0	...	3.00	0.67	1	1	0	0	...	0-...	3.0	1	1	1	0	1-0	4	.100
— Los Angeles (N.L.)	10	5	.667	2.61	1.24	65	2	0	0	14	2-3	107.0	76	34	31	5	57-4	119	.201
1994— Montreal (N.L.)	11	5	.688	3.42	1.11	24	23	1	1	0	1-1	144.2	115	58	55	11	45-3	142	.220
1995— Montreal (N.L.)	14	10	.583	3.51	1.15	30	30	2	2	0	0-0	194.2	158	79	76	21	66-1	174	.227
1996— Montreal (N.L.)	13	10	.565	3.70	1.20	33	33	4	1	0	0-0	216.2	189	100	89	19	70-3	222	.232
1997— Montreal (N.L.)	17	8	.680	* 1.90	0.93	31	31	* 13	4	0	0-0	241.1	158	65	51	16	67-5	305	* .184
1998— Boston (A.L.)	19	7	.731	2.89	1.09	33	33	3	2	0	0-0	233.2	188	82	75	26	67-3	251	.217
1999— Boston (A.L.)	* 23	4	* .852	* 2.07	0.92	31	29	5	1	0	0-0	213.1	160	56	49	9	37-1	* 313	.205
2000— Boston (A.L.)	18	6	.750	* 1.74	0.74	29	29	7	* 4	0	0-0	217.0	128	44	42	17	32-0	* 284	* .167
2001— Boston (A.L.)	7	3	.700	2.39	0.93	18	18	1	0	0	0-0	116.2	84	33	31	5	25-0	163	.199
2002— Boston (A.L.)	20	4	* .833	2.26	0.92	30	30	2	0	0	0-0	199.1	144	62	50	13	40-1	* 239	* .198
2003— Boston (A.L.)	14	4	.778	* 2.22	1.04	29	29	3	0	0	0-0	186.2	147	52	46	7	47-0	206	* .215
2004— Boston (A.L.)	16	9	.640	3.90	1.17	33	33	1	1	0	0-0	217.0	193	99	94	26	61-0	227	.238
2005— New York (N.L.)	15	8	.652	2.82	* 0.95	31	31	4	1	0	0-0	217.0	159	69	68	19	47-3	208	.204
American League totals (7 years)	117	37	.760	2.52	0.98	203	201	22	8	0	0-0	1383.2	1044	428	387	103	309-5	1683	.206
National League totals (7 years)	80	47	.630	2.96	1.07	216	151	24	9	14	3-4	1129.1	861	407	372	91	353-19	1178	.211
Major League totals (14 years)	197	84	.701	2.72	1.02	419	352	46	17	14	3-4	2513.0	1905	835	759	194	662-24	2861	.208

DIVISION SERIES RECORD

Year — Team (League)	W	L	Pct.	ERA	WHIP	G	GS	CG	ShO	Hld.	Sv.-Opp.	IP	H	R	ER	HR	BB-IBB	SO	Avg.
1998— Boston (A.L.)	1	0	1.000	3.86	0.86	1	1	0	0	0	0-0	7.0	6	3	3	2	0-0	8	.214
1999— Boston (A.L.)	1	0	1.000	0.00	0.70	2	1	0	0	0	0-0	10.0	3	0	0	0	4-0	11	.091
2003— Boston (A.L.)	1	0	1.000	3.86	1.29	2	2	0	0	0	0-0	14.0	13	6	6	0	5-0	9	.250
2004— Boston (A.L.)	1	0	1.000	3.86	1.14	1	1	0	0	0	0-0	7.0	6	3	3	0	2-0	6	.240
Division series totals (4 years)	4	0	1.000	2.84	1.03	6	5	0	0	0	0-0	38.0	28	12	12	2	11-0	34	.204

CHAMPIONSHIP SERIES RECORD

Year — Team (League)	W	L	Pct.	ERA	WHIP	G	GS	CG	ShO	Hld.	Sv.-Opp.	IP	H	R	ER	HR	BB-IBB	SO	Avg.
1999— Boston (A.L.)	1	0	1.000	0.00	0.57	1	1	0	0	0	0-0	7.0	2	0	0	0	2-0	12	.087
2003— Boston (A.L.)	0	1	.000	5.65	1.26	2	2	0	0	0	0-0	14.1	16	9	9	3	2-0	14	.276
2004— Boston (A.L.)	0	1	.000	6.23	1.77	3	2	0	0	0	0-0	13.0	14	9	9	2	9-0	14	.269
Champ. series totals (3 years)	1	2	.333	4.72	1.31	6	5	0	0	0	0-0	34.1	32	18	18	5	13-0	40	.241

WORLD SERIES RECORD

Year — Team (League)	W	L	Pct.	ERA	WHIP	G	GS	CG	ShO	Hld.	Sv.-Opp.	IP	H	R	ER	HR	BB-IBB	SO	Avg.
2004— Boston (A.L.)	1	0	1.000	0.00	0.71	1	1	0	0	0	0-0	7.0	3	0	0	0	2-0	6	.136

ALL-STAR GAME RECORD

Year — Team (League)	W	L	Pct.	ERA	WHIP	G	GS	CG	ShO	Hld.	Sv.-Opp.	IP	H	R	ER	HR	BB-IBB	SO	Avg.
All-Star Game totals (3 years)	1	0	1.000	0.00	0.50	3	1	0	0	0	0-0	4.0	2	0	0	0	0-0	8	.143

M

MARTINEZ, RAMON   IF

PERSONAL: Born October 10, 1972, in Philadelphia. ... 6-1/190. ... Bats right, throws right. ... Full name: Ramon E. Martinez. ... High school: Escuela Superior Catholica (Bayamon, Puerto Rico). ... Junior college: Vernon (Texas). ... Cousin of Geovany Soto, catcher, Chicago Cubs.
TRANSACTIONS/CAREER NOTES: Signed as a non-drafted free agent by Kansas City Royals organization (January 15, 1993). ... Traded by Royals to San Francisco Giants (December 11, 1996), completing deal in which Giants traded P Jamie Brewington to Royals for a player to be named (November 26, 1996). ... On disabled list (August 21-September 5, 1999; and June 1-16, 2002). ... Signed as a free agent by Chicago Cubs (January 2, 2003). ... On disabled list (September 16, 2004-remainder of season). ... Signed as a free agent by Detroit Tigers (January 4, 2005). ... On disabled list (April 9-29, 2005). ... Traded by Tigers with P Ugueth Urbina to Philadelphia Phillies for SS Placido Polanco (June 8, 2005).
2005 GAMES PLAYED BY POSITION (MLB): SS—15, 1B—12, 2B—5, 3B—4.

SCOUTING REPORT Martinez is an unselfish player who will play anywhere in the infield. Is a singles hitter who pulls the ball more than he hits it the other way. Can hit second or in the bottom half of the order. Makes all the routine plays at shortstop. Has limited range to his right. Probably isn't good enough to play every day on a good club, but is a good utilityman. Knows and understands his role and is always ready to play. ***Grade 5.4***

RAMON MARTINEZ'S HITTING ZONE

.250	.167	.125
.222	.438	.133
.385	.429	.286

LEFTY-RIGHTY SPLITS

vs.	Avg.	AB	H	2B	3B	HR	RBI	BB	SO	OBP	Slg.
L	.255	47	12	2	0	1	9	3	6	.296	.362
R	.292	65	19	1	0	0	5	3	5	.319	.308

									BATTING									FIELDING	
Year	Team (League)	Pos.	G	AB	R	H	2B	3B	HR	RBI	BB	SO	HBP	GDP	SB-CS	Avg.	OBP	SLG	OPS	E	Avg.
1993—GC Royals (GCL)		2B	37	97	16	23	5	0	0	9	8	6	2	5	3-0	.237	.303	.289	.591	5	.973
—Wilmington (Caro.)		2B-SS	24	75	8	19	4	0	0	6	11	9	1	2	1-4	.253	.352	.307	.659	6	.954
1994—Wilmington (Caro.)		2B	90	325	40	87	13	2	2	35	35	25	4	14	6-3	.268	.341	.338	.680	16	.964
—Rockford (Midwest)		2B	6	18	3	5	0	0	0	3	4	2	0	1	1-0	.278	.409	.278	.687	1	.955
1995—Wichita (Texas)		2B-SS	103	393	58	108	20	2	3	51	42	50	4	11	11-8	.275	.344	.359	.703	9	.982
1996—Omaha (A.A.)		2B	85	320	35	81	12	3	6	41	21	34	3	6	3-2	.253	.305	.366	.671	12	.969
—Wichita (Texas)		2B	26	93	16	32	4	1	1	8	7	8	0	4	4-1	.344	.390	.441	.831	6	.956
1997—Shreveport (Texas)		SS	105	404	72	129	32	4	5	54	40	48	3	6	4-5	.319	.382	.455	.838	18	.968
—Phoenix (PCL)		2B-SS	18	57	6	16	2	0	1	7	5	9	0	1	1-0	.281	.333	.368	.702	3	.959
1998—Fresno (PCL)		2B-SS	98	364	58	114	21	2	14	59	38	42	2	11	0-3	.313	.375	.497	.872	10	.980
—San Francisco (N.L.)		2B	19	19	4	6	1	0	0	0	4	2	0	0	0-0	.316	.435	.368	.803	0	1.000
1999—San Francisco (N.L.)	2B-SS-3B																			
		DH	61	144	21	38	6	0	5	19	14	17	0	2	1-2	.264	.327	.410	.737	6	.966
—Fresno (PCL)	SS-DH-3B		29	114	13	37	7	1	2	17	10	17	0	2	2-0	.325	.376	.456	.832	5	.951
2000—San Francisco (N.L.)	SS-2B-1B																			
		3B	88	189	30	57	13	2	6	25	15	22	1	6	3-2	.302	.354	.487	.841	1	.995
2001—San Francisco (N.L.)		3B-2B-SS	128	391	48	99	18	3	5	37	38	52	5	11	1-2	.253	.323	.353	.676	8	.980
2002—San Francisco (N.L.)	SS-2B-1B																			
		OF-3B	72	181	26	49	10	2	4	25	14	26	4	1	2-0	.271	.335	.414	.749	8	.965
2003—Chicago (N.L.)	2B-3B-SS																			
		1B	108	293	30	83	16	1	3	34	24	50	2	8	0-1	.283	.333	.375	.709	10	.966
2004—Chicago (N.L.)		SS-3B-2B	102	260	22	64	15	1	3	30	26	40	1	5	1-0	.246	.313	.346	.659	9	.970
2005—Toledo (Int'l)		SS-2B	3	15	4	11	0	0	0	1	1	1	0	0	0-0	.733	.750	.733	1.483	0	1.000
—Detroit (A.L.)	SS-2B-1B																			
		3B	19	56	4	15	1	0	0	5	3	4	0	1	0-0	.268	.300	.286	.586	4	.944
—Philadelphia (N.L.)	1B-3B-SS																			
		2B	33	56	7	16	2	0	1	9	3	7	1	1	0-0	.286	.317	.375	.692	1	.989
American League totals (1 year)			19	56	4	15	1	0	0	5	3	4	0	1	0-0	.268	.300	.286	.586	4	.944
National League totals (8 years)			611	1533	188	412	81	9	27	179	138	216	14	34	8-7	.269	.330	.386	.716	43	.975
Major League totals (8 years)			630	1589	192	427	82	9	27	184	141	220	14	35	8-7	.269	.329	.383	.712	47	.974

DIVISION SERIES RECORD

Year	Team (League)	Pos.	G	AB	R	H	2B	3B	HR	RBI	BB	SO	HBP	GDP	SB-CS	Avg.	OBP	SLG	OPS	E	Avg.
2000—San Francisco (N.L.)		2B-SS	2	6	0	2	0	0	0	0	0	2	0	0	0-0	.333	.333	.333	.667	0	1.000
2002—San Francisco (N.L.)			1	0	0	0	0	0	0	0	1	0	0	0	0-0	...	1.000	...	1.000	0	...
2003—Chicago (N.L.)		SS	2	4	0	0	0	0	0	0	0	2	0	0	0-0	.000	.000	.000	.000	0	1.000
Division series totals (3 years)			5	10	0	2	0	0	0	0	1	4	0	0	0-0	.200	.273	.200	.473	0	1.000

CHAMPIONSHIP SERIES RECORD

Year	Team (League)	Pos.	G	AB	R	H	2B	3B	HR	RBI	BB	SO	HBP	GDP	SB-CS	Avg.	OBP	SLG	OPS	E	Avg.
2002—San Francisco (N.L.)		SS	2	1	0	0	0	0	0	1	0	0	0	0	0-0	.000	.000	.000	.000	0	1.000
2003—Chicago (N.L.)		SS-2B	4	4	0	0	0	0	0	0	1	0	0	0	0-0	.000	.000	.000	.000	0	1.000
Champ. series totals (2 years)			6	5	0	0	0	0	0	1	1	0	0	0	0-0	.000	.000	.000	.000	0	1.000

WORLD SERIES RECORD

Year	Team (League)	Pos.	G	AB	R	H	2B	3B	HR	RBI	BB	SO	HBP	GDP	SB-CS	Avg.	OBP	SLG	OPS	E	Avg.
2002—San Francisco (N.L.)			2	2	0	0	0	0	0	0	0	2	0	0	0-0	.000	.000	.000	.000	0	...

MARTINEZ, TINO   1B

PERSONAL: Born December 7, 1967, in Tampa. ... 6-2/230. ... Bats left, throws right. ... Full name: Constantino Martinez. ... High school: Tampa Catholic. ... College: Tampa.
TRANSACTIONS/CAREER NOTES: Selected by Boston Red Sox organization in third round of June 1985 free-agent draft; did not sign. ... Selected by Seattle Mariners organization in first round (14th pick overall) of 1988 free-agent draft. ... On disabled list (August 10, 1993-remainder of season). ... Traded by Mariners with Ps Jeff Nelson and Jim Mecir to New York Yankees for P Sterling Hitchcock and 3B Russ Davis (December 7, 1995). ... Signed as a free agent by St. Louis Cardinals (December 19, 2001). ... Traded by Cardinals to Tampa Bay Devil Rays for P Evan Rust and 1B J.P. Davis (November 21, 2003). ... Signed as a free agent by Yankees (January 5, 2005).
2005 GAMES PLAYED BY POSITION (MLB): 1B—122, DH—1.

SCOUTING REPORT *Offense:* Martinez, who has a fluid stroke with a level swing, has lost some bat speed. Has become more of a streak hitter and no longer can be considered a dependable run producer for a whole season. Is a line-drive hitter who will go with the pitch. Likes the ball up and has become more vulnerable to pitches on his hands. He has to cheat on fastballs. *Defense:* He still has good hands and arm strength, but his range and mobility continue to decline. Has good instincts around the bag. *Outlook:* He had a home-run streak early last season that was impressive but is no longer capable of sustaining the type of offense he has shown in the past. Ideally a platoon player. *Grade 6.6*

TINO MARTINEZ'S HITTING ZONE

.333	.133	.476
.345	.314	.202
.154	.286	.227

LEFTY-RIGHTY SPLITS

vs.	Avg.	AB	H	2B	3B	HR	RBI	BB	SO	OBP	Slg.
L	.217	83	18	1	0	3	12	15	19	.340	.337
R	.250	220	55	8	0	14	37	23	35	.323	.477

Year Team (League)	Pos.	G	AB	R	H	2B	3B	HR	RBI	BB	SO	HBP	GDP	SB-CS	Avg.	OBP	SLG	OPS	E	Avg.
1989— Williamsport (East.)	1B	137	509	51	131	29	2	13	64	59	54	0	11	7-1	.257	.330	.399	.729	7	.995
1990— Calgary (PCL)	1B-3B	128	453	83	145	28	1	17	93	74	37	3	9	8-5	.320	.413	.499	.912	10	.991
— Seattle (A.L.)	1B	24	68	4	15	4	0	0	5	9	9	0	0	0-0	.221	.308	.279	.587	0	1.000
1991— Calgary (PCL)	1B-3B	122	442	94	144	34	5	18	86	82	44	3	5	3-3	.326	.428	.548	.976	9	.992
— Seattle (A.L.)	1B-DH	36	112	11	23	2	0	4	9	11	24	0	2	0-0	.205	.272	.330	.602	2	.993
1992— Seattle (A.L.)	1B-DH	136	460	53	118	19	2	16	66	42	77	2	24	2-1	.257	.316	.411	.727	4	.995
1993— Seattle (A.L.)	1B-DH	109	408	48	108	25	1	17	60	45	56	5	7	0-3	.265	.343	.456	.799	3	.997
1994— Seattle (A.L.)	1B-DH	97	329	42	86	21	0	20	61	29	52	1	9	1-2	.261	.320	.508	.828	2	.997
1995— Seattle (A.L.)	1B-DH	141	519	92	152	35	3	31	111	62	91	4	10	2-0	.293	.369	.551	.920	8	.993
1996— New York (A.L.)	1B-DH	155	595	82	174	28	0	25	117	68	85	2	18	2-1	.292	.364	.466	.830	5	.996
1997— New York (A.L.)	1B-DH	158	594	96	176	31	2	44	141	75	75	3	15	3-1	.296	.371	.577	.948	8	.994
1998— New York (A.L.)	1B	142	531	92	149	33	1	28	123	61	83	6	18	2-1	.281	.355	.505	.860	10	.995
1999— New York (A.L.)	1B	159	589	95	155	27	2	28	105	69	86	3	14	3-4	.263	.341	.458	.800	7	.995
2000— New York (A.L.)	1B	155	569	69	147	37	4	16	91	52	74	8	16	4-1	.258	.328	.422	.749	7	.994
2001— New York (A.L.)	1B-DH	154	589	89	165	24	2	34	113	42	89	2	12	1-2	.280	.329	.501	.830	5	.996
2002— St. Louis (N.L.)	1B	150	511	63	134	25	1	21	75	58	71	2	12	3-2	.262	.337	.438	.776	5	.996
2003— St. Louis (N.L.)	1B-DH	138	476	66	130	25	2	15	69	53	71	9	14	1-1	.273	.352	.429	.781	3	.997
2004— Tampa Bay (A.L.)	1B-DH	138	458	63	120	20	1	23	76	66	72	9	10	3-1	.262	.362	.461	.823	3	.997
2005— New York (A.L.)	1B-DH	131	303	43	73	9	0	17	49	38	54	3	10	2-0	.241	.328	.439	.767	8	.991
American League totals (14 years)		1735	6124	879	1661	315	18	303	1127	669	927	48	165	23-17	.271	.344	.477	.821	72	.995
National League totals (2 years)		288	987	129	264	50	3	36	144	111	142	11	26	4-3	.267	.345	.434	.778	8	.997
Major League totals (16 years)		2023	7111	1008	1925	365	21	339	1271	780	1069	59	191	27-20	.271	.344	.471	.815	80	.995

DIVISION SERIES RECORD

Year Team (League)	Pos.	G	AB	R	H	2B	3B	HR	RBI	BB	SO	HBP	GDP	SB-CS	Avg.	OBP	SLG	OPS	E	Avg.
1995— Seattle (A.L.)	1B	5	22	4	9	1	0	1	5	3	4	0	0	0-1	.409	.480	.591	1.071	0	1.000
1996— New York (A.L.)	1B	4	15	3	4	2	0	0	0	3	1	0	0	0-0	.267	.389	.400	.789	0	1.000
1997— New York (A.L.)	1B	5	18	1	4	1	0	1	4	2	4	1	0	0-0	.222	.333	.444	.778	0	1.000
1998— New York (A.L.)	1B	3	11	1	3	2	0	0	0	0	2	0	0	0-0	.273	.273	.455	.727	1	1.000
1999— New York (A.L.)	1B	3	11	2	2	0	0	0	0	2	3	0	0	0-0	.182	.308	.182	.490	1	.968
2000— New York (A.L.)	1B	5	19	2	8	2	0	0	4	1	3	0	0	0-0	.421	.429	.526	.955	1	.980
2001— New York (A.L.)	1B	5	18	1	2	0	0	1	2	1	6	2	0	0-0	.111	.238	.278	.516	0	1.000
2002— St. Louis (N.L.)	1B	3	11	2	0	0	0	0	0	2	1	0	0	0-0	.000	.154	.000	.154	0	1.000
2005— New York (A.L.)	1B	4	8	0	0	0	0	0	0	1	1	0	0	0-0	.000	.111	.000	.111	0	1.000
Division series totals (9 years)		37	133	16	32	8	0	3	15	15	25	3	0	0-1	.241	.329	.368	.697	2	.994

CHAMPIONSHIP SERIES RECORD

Year Team (League)	Pos.	G	AB	R	H	2B	3B	HR	RBI	BB	SO	HBP	GDP	SB-CS	Avg.	OBP	SLG	OPS	E	Avg.
1995— Seattle (A.L.)	1B	6	22	1	3	0	0	0	0	3	7	0	0	0-0	.136	.240	.136	.376	1	.980
1996— New York (A.L.)	1B	5	22	3	4	1	0	0	0	0	2	1	0	0-0	.182	.217	.227	.445	0	1.000
1998— New York (A.L.)	1B	6	19	1	2	1	0	0	1	6	8	1	0	2-0	.105	.333	.158	.491	1	.981
1999— New York (A.L.)	1B	5	19	3	5	1	0	1	3	2	4	1	0	0-0	.263	.364	.474	.837	0	1.000
2000— New York (A.L.)	1B	6	25	5	8	2	0	1	1	2	4	0	1	0-0	.320	.370	.520	.890	0	1.000
2001— New York (A.L.)	1B	5	20	3	5	1	0	1	3	0	4	0	0	0-1	.250	.250	.450	.700	0	1.000
2002— St. Louis (N.L.)	1B	4	14	1	2	0	0	0	1	2	1	0	0	1-0	.143	.250	.143	.393	0	1.000
Champ. series totals (7 years)		37	141	17	29	6	0	3	9	15	30	3	1	3-1	.206	.294	.312	.606	2	.994

WORLD SERIES RECORD

Year Team (League)	Pos.	G	AB	R	H	2B	3B	HR	RBI	BB	SO	HBP	GDP	SB-CS	Avg.	OBP	SLG	OPS	E	Avg.
1996— New York (A.L.)	1B	6	11	0	1	0	0	0	0	2	5	0	0	0-0	.091	.231	.091	.322	0	1.000
1998— New York (A.L.)	1B	4	13	4	5	0	0	1	4	4	2	0	0	0-0	.385	.529	.615	1.145	0	1.000
1999— New York (A.L.)	1B	4	15	3	4	0	0	1	5	2	4	0	0	0-0	.267	.353	.467	.820	0	1.000
2000— New York (A.L.)	1B	5	22	3	8	1	0	0	2	1	4	0	0	0-0	.364	.391	.409	.800	0	1.000
2001— New York (A.L.)	1B	6	21	1	4	0	0	1	3	2	2	0	0	0-0	.190	.261	.333	.594	0	1.000
World Series totals (5 years)		25	82	11	22	1	0	3	14	11	17	0	0	0-0	.268	.355	.390	.745	0	1.000

ALL-STAR GAME RECORD

		G	AB	R	H	2B	3B	HR	RBI	BB	SO	HBP	GDP	SB-CS	Avg.	OBP	SLG	OPS	E	Avg.
All-Star Game totals (2 years)		2	3	0	1	0	0	0	0	0	0	0	0	0-0	.333	.333	.333	.667	0	1.000

MARTINEZ, VICTOR   C

PERSONAL: Born December 23, 1978, in Ciudad Bolivar, Venezuela. ... 6-2/190. ... Bats both, throws right. ... Full name: Victor Jesus Martinez.

TRANSACTIONS/CAREER NOTES: Signed as a non-drafted free agent by Cleveland Indians organization (July 15, 1996). ... On disabled list (August 9-September 2, 2003); included rehabilitation assignment to Akron.

2005 GAMES PLAYED BY POSITION (MLB): C—142, DH—2.

SCOUTING REPORT *Offense:* One of the best hitting catchers in baseball, Martinez has a quick bat and is productive with runners on base. Likes the ball down when batting from the left side and up in the zone from the right side. Has power to all fields, and the ball jumps off his bat. Doesn't run well. *Defense:* He has made some progress in his receiving techniques. Arm strength has improved but release is unconventional. Has very good velocity and has become more accurate, though his ball will tail at times. Still needs some help with his footwork and setup. *Outlook:* Martinez has shown he can be a clutch hitter. Will continue to improve on defense and could be a front-line player for years to come. *Grade 8.6*

VICTOR MARTINEZ'S HITTING ZONE

.310	.394	.265
.406	.278	.372
.278	.440	.359

LEFTY-RIGHTY SPLITS

vs.	Avg.	AB	H	2B	3B	HR	RBI	BB	SO	OBP	Slg.
L	.274	168	46	9	0	3	19	22	31	.362	.381
R	.319	379	121	24	0	17	61	41	47	.385	.517

									BATTING									FIELDING	
Year Team (League)	Pos.	G	AB	R	H	2B	3B	HR	RBI	BB	SO	HBP	GDP	SB-CS	Avg.	OBP	SLG	OPS	E	Avg.
1997— Maracay 1 (VSL)		53	122	21	42	12	0	0	26	32	11	...	...	6-...	.344	...	.443	...	...	...
1998— Guacara 2 (VSL)		55	160	28	43	13	0	1	27	32	14	...	...	8-...	.269	...	.369	...	...	...
1999— Mahoning Valley (NYP)	C	64	235	37	65	9	0	4	36	27	31	1	4	0-1	.277	.346	.366	.712	6	.984
2000— Kinston (Carol.)	C	26	83	9	18	7	0	0	8	11	5	1	3	1-1	.217	.313	.301	.614	5	.980
— Columbus (S. Atl.)	C	21	70	11	26	9	1	2	12	11	6	1	1	0-0	.371	.452	.614	1.067	2	.988
2001— Kinston (Carol.)	C	114	420	59	138	33	2	10	57	39	60	8	12	3-3	.329	.394	.488	.882	16	.985
2002— Akron (East.)	C	121	443	84	149	40	0	22	85	58	62	8	10	3-3	.336	.417	.576	.993	10	.988
— Cleveland (A.L.)	C-DH	12	32	2	9	1	0	1	5	3	2	0	1	0-0	.281	.333	.406	.740	1	.983
2003— Buffalo (Int'l)	C-1B-DH	73	274	42	90	19	0	7	45	26	32	8	14	3-5	.328	.395	.474	.869	4	.993
— Akron (East.)	DH-C	3	12	1	4	0	0	0	2	0	1	0	1	0-0	.333	.333	.500	.833	0	1.000
— Cleveland (A.L.)	C-DH	49	159	15	46	4	0	1	16	13	21	1	8	1-1	.289	.345	.333	.678	1	.996
2004— Cleveland (A.L.)	C-DH	141	520	77	147	38	1	23	108	60	69	5	16	0-1	.283	.359	.492	.851	6	.994
2005— Cleveland (A.L.)	C-DH	147	547	73	167	33	0	20	80	63	78	5	16	0-1	.305	.378	.475	.853	5	.995
Major League totals (4 years)		349	1258	167	369	76	1	45	209	139	170	11	41	1-3	.293	.365	.463	.827	13	.994

ALL-STAR GAME RECORD

	G	AB	R	H	2B	3B	HR	RBI	BB	SO	HBP	GDP	SB-CS	Avg.	OBP	SLG	OPS	E	Avg.
All-Star Game totals (1 year)	1	1	0	0	0	0	0	0	0	0	0	0	0-0	.000	.000	.000	.000	0	1.000

MATEO, HENRY   2B

PERSONAL: Born October 14, 1976, in Santo Domingo, Dominican Republic. ... 6-0/176. ... Bats both, throws right. ... Full name: Henry Antonio Valera Mateo. ... Name pronounced: mah-TAY-oh. ... High school: Centro Estudios Libres (Santurce, Puerto Rico).

TRANSACTIONS/CAREER NOTES: Selected by Montreal Expos organization in second round of 1995 free-agent draft. ... Expos franchise transferred to Washington, D.C., and renamed Washington Nationals for 2005 season (December 3, 2004). ... On disabled list (March 16-May 9 and May 15-August 5, 2005); included rehabilitation assignments to Potomac, Harrisburg and New Orleans.

2005 GAMES PLAYED BY POSITION (MLB): 2B—1.

LEFTY-RIGHTY SPLITS

vs.	Avg.	AB	H	2B	3B	HR	RBI	BB	SO	OBP	Slg.
L	.000	1	0	0	0	0	0	1	0	.500	.000
R	.000	0	0	0	0	0	0	0	0	.000	.000

									BATTING									FIELDING	
Year Team (League)	Pos.	G	AB	R	H	2B	3B	HR	RBI	BB	SO	HBP	GDP	SB-CS	Avg.	OBP	SLG	OPS	E	Avg.
1995— GC Expos (GCL)	2B-SS	38	122	11	18	0	0	0	6	14	47	5	2	2-7	.148	.261	.148	.408	9	.951
1996— GC Expos (GCL)	2B	14	44	8	11	3	0	0	3	5	11	3	0	5-1	.250	.365	.318	.684	7	.901
1997— Vermont (NYP)	2B	67	228	32	56	9	3	1	31	30	44	7	4	21-11	.246	.348	.325	.673	14	.956
1998— Cape Fear (S. Atl.)	2B	114	416	72	115	20	5	4	41	40	111	13	4	22-16	.276	.355	.377	.733	15	.971
— Jupiter (Fla. St.)	2B	12	43	11	12	3	1	0	6	2	6	2	0	3-0	.279	.333	.395	.729	0	1.000
1999— Jupiter (Fla. St.)	2B	118	447	69	116	27	7	4	58	44	112	10	4	32-16	.260	.335	.378	.713	17	.962
2000— Harrisburg (East.)	2B	140	530	91	152	25	11	5	63	58	97	6	4	48-16	.287	.362	.404	.766	24	.962
2001— Ottawa (Int'l)	2B	118	500	71	134	14	12	5	43	33	89	7	2	47-14	.268	.322	.374	.696	22	.963
— Montreal (N.L.)	2B	9	9	1	3	1	0	0	0	0	1	0	0	0-0	.333	.333	.444	.778	2	.818
2002— Ottawa (Int'l)	2B-SS	74	285	35	73	10	6	5	25	18	53	3	6	15-6	.256	.306	.386	.692	12	.970
— Montreal (N.L.)	2B-SS	22	23	1	4	0	1	0	0	2	6	0	0	2-0	.174	.240	.261	.501	1	.950
2003— Montreal (N.L.)	2B-OF-DH																			
	SS	100	154	29	37	3	1	0	7	11	38	3	0	11-1	.240	.304	.273	.576	4	.973
2004— GC Expos (GCL)	2B	5	14	7	4	2	0	0	2	6	2	2	0	4-0	.286	.545	.429	.974	0	1.000
— Edmonton (PCL)	2B-DH	30	119	23	36	8	3	0	9	8	16	2	5	10-1	.303	.354	.420	.774	8	.937
— Montreal (N.L.)	2B-OF	40	44	3	12	2	0	0	0	1	9	0	1	2-3	.273	.289	.318	.607	4	.882
2005— Was. (N.L.)	2B	1	1	0	0	0	0	0	0	0	1	0	0	0-0	.000	.000	.000	.000	0	1.000
— Potomac (Carol.)	2B-DH	13	50	13	14	5	1	3	9	3	10	3	1	2-0	.280	.357	.600	.957	1	.974
— New Orleans (PCL)	2B	9	31	2	9	0	0	0	3	3	7	0	0	3-1	.290	.353	.290	.643	0	1.000
— Harrisburg (East.)	2B-DH	32	122	13	20	5	1	0	6	16	27	0	3	11-5	.164	.261	.221	.482	4	.972
Major League totals (5 years)		168	231	34	56	6	2	0	7	15	54	3	1	15-4	.242	.297	.286	.583	11	.949

MATEO, JULIO   P

PERSONAL: Born August 2, 1977, in Bani, Dominican Republic. ... 6-0/177. ... Throws right, bats right. ... Full name: Julio Cesar Mateo. ... Name pronounced: mah-TAY-oh.
TRANSACTIONS/CAREER NOTES: Signed as a non-drafted free agent by Seattle Mariners organization (May 15, 1996). ... On disabled list (July 29-September 16, 2004).
CAREER HITTING: 0-for-0 (.000), 0 R, 0 2B, 0 3B, 0 HR, 0 RBI.

SCOUTING REPORT *Throws:* Mateo's fastball tops out at 92 mph, he throws a slider in the low to mid-80s and has a changeup. *Tendencies:* Mateo has some deception in his delivery that makes his fastball sneaky. Will pitch inside, especially to righthanded hitters. Velocity on the slider has gotten better, and even though its break is big, it is very quick and runs down and away from righthanders. Has very good arm speed with his changeup, which he throws to lefthanders. *Outlook:* Mateo is coming off a good second half of last season. Is a durable middle reliever who can be stretched out. **Grade 7.2**

JULIO MATEO'S PITCHING ZONE

.190	.250	.158
.317	.278	.310
.156	.308	.208

LEFTY-RIGHTY SPLITS

vs.	Avg.	AB	H	2B	3B	HR	RBI	BB	SO	OBP	Slg.
L	.209	153	32	4	4	3	12	11	20	.261	.346
R	.261	180	47	10	0	9	20	6	32	.309	.467

Year Team (League)	W	L	Pct.	ERA	WHIP	G	GS	CG	ShO	Hld.	Sv.-Opp.	IP	H	R	ER	HR	BB-IBB	SO	Avg.
1996— Dom. Mariners (DSL)	4	2	.667	1.74	1.18	14	5	2	1	...	1-...	51.2	42	14	10	...	19-...	23	...
1997— Ariz. Mariners (Ariz.)	3	1	.750	3.30	1.13	13	6	0	0	...	1-...	60.0	45	32	22	1	23-0	54	.205
1998— Lancaster (Calif.)	0	0	...	6.75	1.50	1	0	0	0	...	0-...	1.1	1	1	1	0	1-0	1	.250
— Everett (N'west)	3	3	.500	4.70	1.49	28	0	0	0	...	4-...	38.1	40	25	20	6	17-1	37	.274
1999— Wisconsin (Midw.)	1	3	.250	4.34	1.34	20	0	0	0	...	4-...	29.0	31	18	14	2	8-2	27	.261
2000— Wisconsin (Midw.)	4	8	.333	4.19	1.25	36	1	0	0	...	4-...	68.2	63	38	32	12	23-1	73	.241
2001— San Bern. (Calif.)	5	4	.556	2.86	1.12	56	0	0	0	...	26-...	66.0	58	28	21	5	16-5	79	.230
2002— San Antonio (Texas)	1	0	1.000	0.52	0.58	12	0	0	0	...	0-...	17.1	7	3	1	2	3-0	18	.121
— Tacoma (PCL)	4	2	.667	4.06	1.48	20	0	0	0	...	6-...	31.0	39	15	14	2	7-1	23	.317
— Seattle (A.L.)	0	0	...	4.29	1.52	12	0	0	0	2	0-0	21.0	20	10	10	2	12-0	15	.247
2003— Seattle (A.L.)	4	0	1.000	3.15	0.96	50	0	0	0	2	1-1	85.2	69	32	30	14	13-1	71	.219
2004— Seattle (A.L.)	1	2	.333	4.68	1.25	45	0	0	0	6	1-4	57.2	56	30	30	11	16-3	43	.251
2005— Seattle (A.L.)	3	6	.333	3.06	1.09	55	1	0	0	8	0-2	88.1	79	32	30	12	17-6	52	.237
Major League totals (4 years)	**8**	**8**	**.500**	**3.56**	**1.12**	**162**	**1**	**0**	**0**	**18**	**2-7**	**252.2**	**224**	**104**	**100**	**39**	**58-10**	**181**	**.236**

MATHENY, MIKE — C

PERSONAL: Born September 22, 1970, in Reynoldsburg, Ohio. ... 6-3/220. ... Bats right, throws right. ... Full name: Michael Scott Matheny. ... Name pronounced: ma-THEE-nee. ... High school: Reynoldsburg (Ohio). ... College: Michigan.

TRANSACTIONS/CAREER NOTES: Selected by Toronto Blue Jays organization in 31st round of 1988 free-agent draft; did not sign. ... Selected by Milwaukee Brewers organization in eighth round of 1991 free-agent draft. ... On suspended list (June 20-23, 1996). ... On disabled list (June 15-July 12, 1998); included rehabilitation assignment to Beloit. ... Signed as a free agent by Blue Jays (December 23, 1998). ... Released by Blue Jays (November 16, 1999). ... Signed by St. Louis Cardinals (December 15, 1999). ... On suspended list (September 26-28, 2003). ... On disabled list (June 3-18, 2004). ... Signed as a free agent by San Francisco Giants (December 13, 2004). ... On bereavement list (August 1-4, 2005).

HONORS: Won N.L. Gold Glove at catcher (2000, 2003-05).

2005 GAMES PLAYED BY POSITION (MLB): C—132.

SCOUTING REPORT *Offense:* A contact-conscious hitter with a short stroke, he hits from a slight crouch and has good bat control. Is a line-drive hitter who uses the whole field and has limited power. Adjusts well with the count and is patient enough to stay on the breaking ball. Has excellent aptitude and is very productive with runners in scoring position. Can be overpowered by good fastballs. *Defense:* One of the best at blocking balls in the dirt, he has picture-perfect technique. Relies on a short, quick release to throw out runners. Has unmatched aptitude. *Outlook:* Matheny, the best defensive catcher in the game, hits well enough at the bottom of the order to be ranked among the best overall. **Grade 8.5**

MIKE MATHENY'S HITTING ZONE

.231	.368	.353
.288	.444	.341
.182	.120	.176

LEFTY-RIGHTY SPLITS

vs.	Avg.	AB	H	2B	3B	HR	RBI	BB	SO	OBP	Slg.
L	.269	104	28	9	0	3	14	6	18	.306	.442
R	.233	339	79	25	0	10	45	23	73	.291	.395

Year Team (League)	Pos.	G	AB	R	H	2B	3B	HR	RBI	BB	SO	HBP	GDP	SB-CS	Avg.	OBP	SLG	OPS	E	Avg.
1991— Helena (Pion.)	C	64	253	35	72	14	0	2	34	19	52	6	10	2-4	.285	.348	.364	.711	5	.991
1992— Stockton (Calif.)	C	106	333	42	73	13	2	6	46	35	81	3	11	2-2	.219	.297	.324	.621	8	.989
1993— El Paso (Texas)	C	107	339	39	86	21	2	2	28	17	73	2	6	1-4	.254	.292	.345	.638	9	.986
1994— Milwaukee (A.L.)	C	28	53	3	12	3	0	1	2	3	13	2	1	0-1	.226	.293	.340	.633	1	.989
— New Orleans (A.A.)	C-1B-DH	57	177	20	39	10	1	4	21	16	39	4	5	1-1	.220	.299	.356	.655	5	.987
1995— Milwaukee (A.L.)	C	80	166	13	41	9	1	0	21	12	28	2	3	2-1	.247	.306	.313	.619	4	.989
— New Orleans (A.A.)	C	6	17	3	6	2	0	3	4	0	5	3	0	0-0	.353	.450	1.000	1.450	0	1.000
1996— Milwaukee (A.L.)	C-DH	106	313	31	64	15	2	8	46	14	80	3	9	3-2	.204	.243	.342	.584	8	.989
— New Orleans (A.A.)	C-DH	20	66	3	15	4	0	1	6	2	17	0	1	1-0	.227	.246	.333	.580	0	1.000
1997— Milwaukee (A.L.)	C-1B	123	320	29	78	16	1	4	32	17	68	7	9	0-1	.244	.294	.338	.631	5	.993
1998— Milwaukee (A.L.)	C	108	320	24	76	13	0	6	37	11	63	7	6	1-0	.238	.278	.334	.612	8	.987
— Beloit (Midw.)	C-DH	2	8	1	2	1	0	0	2	1	3	0	0	0-0	.250	.333	.375	.708	1	1.000
1999— Toronto (A.L.)	C	57	163	16	35	6	0	3	17	12	37	1	3	0-0	.215	.271	.307	.578	2	.995
2000— St. Louis (N.L.)	C-1B	128	417	43	109	22	1	6	47	4	96	4	11	0-0	.261	.317	.362	.679	5	.994
2001— St. Louis (N.L.)	C-1B	121	381	40	83	12	0	7	42	28	76	4	11	0-1	.218	.276	.304	.581	4	.994
2002— St. Louis (N.L.)	C-1B	110	315	31	77	12	1	3	35	32	49	2	3	1-3	.244	.313	.317	.630	4	.994
2003— St. Louis (N.L.)	C-1B	141	441	43	111	18	2	8	47	44	81	2	11	1-1	.252	.320	.356	.676	0	.999
2004— St. Louis (N.L.)	C-1B	122	385	28	95	22	1	5	50	23	83	3	12	0-2	.247	.292	.348	.640	1	.999
2005— San Francisco (N.L.)	C	134	443	42	107	34	0	13	59	29	91	6	11	0-0	.242	.295	.406	.701	5	.999
American League totals (5 years)		394	1015	92	230	49	4	16	118	58	226	15	25	5-5	.227	.276	.330	.607	20	.994
National League totals (7 years)		864	2702	251	658	133	5	48	307	199	539	28	65	3-9	.244	.300	.350	.650	23	.996
Major League totals (12 years)		1258	3717	343	888	182	9	64	425	257	765	43	90	8-14	.239	.293	.344	.638	43	.994

DIVISION SERIES RECORD

Year Team (League)	Pos.	G	AB	R	H	2B	3B	HR	RBI	BB	SO	HBP	GDP	SB-CS	Avg.	OBP	SLG	OPS	E	Avg.
2000— St. Louis (N.L.)			Did not play.																	
2001— St. Louis (N.L.)	C	4	10	0	2	0	0	0	0	0	3	0	0	0-0	.200	.200	.200	.400	0	1.000

Year Team (League)	Pos.	G	AB	R	H	2B	3B	HR	RBI	BB	SO	HBP	GDP	SB-CS	Avg.	OBP	SLG	OPS	E	Avg.
2002—St. Louis (N.L.)	C	3	9	3	4	1	0	0	2	2	1	0	0	0-0	.444	.545	.556	1.101	0	1.000
2004—St. Louis (N.L.)	C	4	14	1	4	0	0	1	5	0	2	0	0	0-0	.286	.286	.500	.786	0	1.000
Division series totals (3 years)		11	33	4	10	1	0	1	7	2	6	0	0	0-0	.303	.343	.424	.767	0	1.000

CHAMPIONSHIP SERIES RECORD

Year Team (League)	Pos.	G	AB	R	H	2B	3B	HR	RBI	BB	SO	HBP	GDP	SB-CS	Avg.	OBP	SLG	OPS	E	Avg.
2000—St. Louis (N.L.)		Did not play.																		
2002—St. Louis (N.L.)	C	5	19	2	6	2	0	1	1	0	2	0	0	0-0	.316	.316	.579	.895	0	1.000
2004—St. Louis (N.L.)	C	7	19	0	2	0	0	0	0	1	8	0	0	0-0	.105	.150	.105	.255	0	1.000
Champ. series totals (2 years)		12	38	2	8	2	0	1	1	1	10	0	0	0-0	.211	.231	.342	.573	0	1.000

WORLD SERIES RECORD

Year Team (League)	Pos.	G	AB	R	H	2B	3B	HR	RBI	BB	SO	HBP	GDP	SB-CS	Avg.	OBP	SLG	OPS	E	Avg.
2004—St. Louis (N.L.)	C	4	8	0	2	0	0	0	0	0	3	0	0	0-0	.250	.200	.250	.450	0	1.000

MATHIS, JEFF — C

PERSONAL: Born March 31, 1983, in Marianna, Fla. ... 6-0/180. ... Bats right, throws right. ... Full name: Jeffery Stephen Mathis. ... High school: Marianna (Fla.).

TRANSACTIONS/CAREER NOTES: Selected by Anaheim Angels organization in first round of 2001 free-agent draft. ... Angels franchise renamed Los Angeles Angels of Anaheim for 2005 season.

2005 GAMES PLAYED BY POSITION (MLB): C—3, DH—2.

LEFTY-RIGHTY SPLITS

vs.	Avg.	AB	H	2B	3B	HR	RBI	BB	SO	OBP	Slg.
L	.000	0	0	0	0	0	0	0	0	.000	.000
R	.333	3	1	0	0	0	0	0	1	.333	.333

							BATTING												FIELDING	
Year Team (League)	Pos.	G	AB	R	H	2B	3B	HR	RBI	BB	SO	HBP	GDP	SB-CS	Avg.	OBP	SLG	OPS	E	Avg.
2001—Ariz. Angels (Ariz.)	C-OF	7	23	1	7	1	0	0	3	2	4	0	1	0-0	.304	.346	.348	.694	0	1.000
—Provo (Pion.)	C	22	77	14	23	6	3	0	18	11	13	2	1	1-0	.299	.387	.455	.842	2	.989
2002—Cedar Rap. (Midw.)	C	128	491	75	141	41	3	10	73	40	75	8	6	7-4	.287	.346	.444	.790	4	.994
2003—Rancho Cuca. (Pion.)		97	378	73	122	28	3	11	54	35	74	5	4	5-3	.323	.384	.500	.884	—	—
—Arkansas (Texas)	C	24	95	19	27	11	0	2	14	12	16	1	2	1-2	.284	.364	.463	.827	1	.995
2004—Arkansas (Texas)	C	117	432	57	98	24	3	14	55	49	102	5	5	2-1	.227	.310	.394	.704	14	.979
2005—Salt Lake (PCL)	C-DH	112	427	78	118	26	3	21	73	42	85	1	7	4-3	.276	.340	.499	.838	9	.986
—Los Angeles (A.L.)	C-DH	5	3	1	1	0	0	0	0	0	1	0	0	0-0	.333	.333	.333	.667	0	1.000
Major League totals (1 year)		5	3	1	1	0	0	0	0	0	1	0	0	0-0	.333	.333	.333	.667	0	1.000

MATOS, LUIS — OF

PERSONAL: Born October 30, 1978, in Bayamon, Puerto Rico. ... 6-0/208. ... Bats right, throws right. ... Full name: Luis David Matos. ... Name pronounced: MAH-tose. ... High school: Disciple of Christ Academy (Bayamon, Puerto Rico).

TRANSACTIONS/CAREER NOTES: Selected by Baltimore Orioles organization in 10th round of 1996 free-agent draft. ... On disabled list (March 30-August 24, 2001); included rehabilitation assignments to GCL Orioles, Frederick and Bowie. ... On disabled list (March 29-June 6, 2002); included rehabilitation assignment to Frederick. ... On disabled list (July 22, 2004-remainder of season). ... On disabled list (May 11-June 19, 2005); included rehabilitation assignment to Bowie.

2005 GAMES PLAYED BY POSITION (MLB): OF—120.

SCOUTING REPORT ***Offense:*** Matos improved a lot in 2005. Doesn't have a quick bat but still has reduced his strikeouts. Is a better fastball hitter but is learning to lay off breaking pitches. Has lost power as average and contact have increased. Gets jammed a lot. Is an aggressive baserunner but still questions his instincts and jumps. ***Defense:*** He has regressed on defense, struggling to go back on balls and taking some bad routes when moving laterally. Has a strong, accurate arm. ***Outlook:*** Matos gains on offense last season were canceled out by his setback on defense. ***Grade 5.7***

LUIS MATOS' HITTING ZONE

.375	.357	.316
.289	.313	.269
.239	.429	.273

LEFTY-RIGHTY SPLITS

vs.	Avg.	AB	H	2B	3B	HR	RBI	BB	SO	OBP	Slg.
L	.297	118	35	9	1	3	12	12	20	.368	.466
R	.273	271	74	11	1	1	20	15	38	.327	.332

							BATTING												FIELDING	
Year Team (League)	Pos.	G	AB	R	H	2B	3B	HR	RBI	BB	SO	HBP	GDP	SB-CS	Avg.	OBP	SLG	OPS	E	Avg.
1996—GC Orioles (GCL)	OF	43	130	21	38	2	0	0	13	15	18	2	3	12-7	.292	.374	.308	.682	1	.983
1997—Delmarva (S. Atl.)	OF	36	119	10	25	1	2	0	13	9	21	2	2	8-5	.210	.275	.252	.527	2	.972
—Bluefield (Appal.)	OF	61	240	37	66	7	3	2	35	20	36	4	5	26-4	.275	.340	.354	.694	3	.977
1998—Delmarva (S. Atl.)	OF	133	503	73	137	26	6	7	32	38	90	7	9	42-14	.272	.328	.390	.718	10	.964
—Bowie (East.)	OF	5	19	2	5	0	0	1	3	1	1	0	0	1-1	.263	.300	.421	.721	1	.833
1999—Frederick (Carolina)	OF	68	273	40	81	15	1	9	41	20	35	2	6	27-6	.297	.343	.436	.779	2	.987
—Bowie (East.)	OF	66	283	41	67	11	1	9	36	15	39	1	6	14-4	.237	.272	.378	.650	3	.982
2000—Rochester (Int'l)		11	35	2	6	1	0	0	3	3	8	1	0	2-0	.171	.256	.200	.456	0	1.000
—Bowie (East.)	OF	50	181	26	49	7	5	2	33	17	23	5	3	8-8	.271	.345	.398	.742	2	.984
—Baltimore (A.L.)	OF-DH	72	182	21	41	6	3	1	17	12	30	3	7	13-4	.225	.281	.308	.589	2	.988
2001—GC Orioles (GCL)	DH	3	14	1	4	2	0	0	2	0	3	0	0	0-0	.286	.286	.429	.714	...	...
—Frederick (Carolina)	DH	7	7	3	3	0	0	1	2	1	0	0	0	0-0	.429	.500	.857	1.357	...	...
—Bowie (East.)	OF	13	46	6	14	5	0	1	8	5	7	1	0	0-1	.304	.385	.478	.863	1	.955
—Baltimore (A.L.)	OF	31	98	16	21	7	0	4	12	11	30	1	1	7-0	.214	.300	.408	.708	1	.985
2002—Frederick (Carolina)	OF	3	12	2	4	1	0	0	2	3	0	0	0	1-0	.333	.429	.417	.845	0	1.000
—Bowie (East.)	OF	62	218	34	60	14	2	9	40	32	45	2	6	14-4	.275	.370	.482	.852	1	.992
—Baltimore (A.L.)	OF-DH	17	31	0	4	1	0	0	1	1	6	0	0	1-0	.129	.156	.161	.318	0	1.000
2003—Ottawa (Int'l)	OF	45	175	28	53	16	4	1	25	14	34	1	8	6-1	.303	.347	.457	.804	1	.990
—Baltimore (A.L.)	OF-DH	109	439	70	133	23	6	13	45	28	90	1	9	15-7	.303	.353	.458	.811	4	.987
2004—Baltimore (A.L.)	OF	89	330	36	74	18	0	6	28	19	60	5	7	12-4	.224	.275	.333	.609	1	.996
2005—Bowie (East.)	OF-DH	5	20	4	5	2	0	1	2	1	4	1	0	1-1	.250	.318	.400	.718	0	1.000
—Baltimore (A.L.)	OF	121	389	53	109	20	2	4	32	27	58	10	4	17-9	.280	.340	.373	.712	5	.984
Major League totals (6 years)		439	1469	196	382	75	8	28	135	98	274	26	29	65-24	.260	.316	.379	.695	13	.988

PERSONAL: Born January 8, 1977, in Orange, Calif. ... 6-0/170. ... Bats right, throws right. ... Full name: David Michael Matranga. ... High school: Aliso Viejo (Calif.). ... College: Pepperdine.
TRANSACTIONS/CAREER NOTES: Selected by Houston Astros organization in sixth round of 1998 free-agent draft. ... Signed as a free agent by Anaheim Angels organization (November 10, 2004). ... Franchise renamed Los Angeles Angels of Anaheim for 2005 season.
2005 GAMES PLAYED BY POSITION (MLB): 2B—1.

LEFTY-RIGHTY SPLITS

vs.	Avg.	AB	H	2B	3B	HR	RBI	BB	SO	OBP	Slg.
L	.000	0	0	0	0	0	0	0	0	.000	.000
R	.000	1	0	0	0	0	0	0	0	.000	.000

									BATTING										FIELDING	
Year	Team (League)	Pos.	G	AB	R	H	2B	3B	HR	RBI	BB	SO	HBP	GDP	SB-CS	Avg.	OBP	SLG	OPS	E	Avg.
1998—	Auburn (NY-Penn)	SS	40	144	34	44	13	1	4	24	25	38	5	0	16-3	.306	.423	.493	.916	10	.943
1999—	Kissimmee (Fla. St.)	SS	124	472	70	109	20	4	6	48	68	118	12	3	17-10	.231	.341	.328	.669	28	.954
2000—	Round Rock (Texas)	SS	120	373	50	87	14	3	6	44	48	99	17	1	5-5	.233	.346	.335	.681	27	.951
2001—	New Orleans (PCL)	2B-SS	4	16	3	5	1	0	1	3	0	5	1	0	1-0	.313	.333	.563	.896	0	1.000
—	Round Rock (Texas)	2B	103	387	78	117	34	2	10	60	45	91	14	2	17-7	.302	.391	.478	.869	6	.987
2002—	New Orleans (PCL)	2B-SS-3B	101	300	47	82	15	3	7	40	27	79	6	4	7-2	.273	.342	.413	.755	5	.982
2003—	Houston (N.L.)	2B	6	5	1	1	0	0	1	1	0	2	0	0	0-0	.200	.200	.800	1.000	0	1.000
—	New Orleans (PCL)	2B-SS-3B																			
		DH-OF	102	315	34	76	16	4	3	25	21	71	4	3	3-3	.241	.296	.346	.642	8	.980
2004—	Round Rock (Texas)	SS-3B-OF																			
		2B	112	392	61	95	20	2	7	48	34	81	17	7	14-4	.242	.327	.357	.684	9	.857
2005—	Los Angeles (A.L.)	2B	1	1	0	0	0	0	0	0	0	0	0	0	0-0	.000	.000	.000	.000	0	1.000
—	Salt Lake (PCL)	SS-3B-2B																			
		1B-DH	56	176	31	42	12	2	3	19	31	39	3	2	6-3	.239	.358	.381	.739	8	.966
—	Ariz. Angels (Ariz.)	2B-3B-SS																			
		DH	3	10	0	0	0	0	0	0	6	0	0	0	0-0	.000	.000	.000	.000	0	
—	Arkansas (Texas)	3B-2B-SS	9	26	4	5	2	0	1	2	1	6	0	0	0-1	.192	.214	.385	.599	2	.938
American League totals (1 year)			1	1	0	0	0	0	0	0	0	0	0	0	0-0	.000	.000	.000	.000	0	1.000
National League totals (1 year)			6	5	1	1	0	0	1	1	0	2	0	0	0-0	.200	.200	.800	1.000	0	1.000
Major League totals (2 years)			7	6	1	1	0	0	1	1	0	2	0	0	0-0	.167	.167	.667	.833	0	1.000

PERSONAL: Born June 12, 1974, in Kanazawa, Japan. ... 6-2/230. ... Bats left, throws right. ... Name pronounced: mat-SOO-ee. ... High school: Seiryo (Nagoya, Japan).
TRANSACTIONS/CAREER NOTES: Signed as a free agent by New York Yankees (December 19, 2002).
2005 GAMES PLAYED BY POSITION (MLB): OF—142, DH—19.

SCOUTING REPORT *Offense:* He's a professional hitter with an extremely quiet approach. Waits for the pitch with his bat in a perpendicular position, but has good bat speed. Is a line-drive hitter with deceptive power who has continued to improve as he gains experience in the major leagues. Has quality at bats with runners in scoring position. Is a slightly below-average runner but has good instincts. *Defense:* The only drawback to his game is lack of arm strength, but he gets rid of the ball quickly and charges well to compensate. Gets good lateral jumps but occasionally will freeze on balls hit over his head. Range is adequate. *Outlook:* This quiet front-line player is a very good run producer. The Yankees have considered possibly moving him to center field, the position he played in Japan. *Grade 8.8*

HIDEKI MATSUI'S HITTING ZONE

.355	.407	.306
.300	.452	.294
.353	.286	.250

LEFTY-RIGHTY SPLITS

vs.	Avg.	AB	H	2B	3B	HR	RBI	BB	SO	OBP	Slg.
L	.354	209	74	19	2	8	49	16	33	.393	.579
R	.281	420	118	26	1	15	67	47	45	.354	.455

									BATTING										FIELDING	
Year	Team (League)	Pos.	G	AB	R	H	2B	3B	HR	RBI	BB	SO	HBP	GDP	SB-CS	Avg.	OBP	SLG	OPS	E	Avg.
1993—	Yomiuri (Jp. Cen.)		57	184	27	41	9	0	11	27	...	...	...	...	1-0	.223	.296	.451	.747	1	...
1994—	Yomiuri (Jp. Cen.)		130	503	70	148	23	4	20	66	57	101	4	...	6-3	.294	.368	.475	.843	5	...
1995—	Yomiuri (Jp. Cen.)		131	501	76	142	31	1	22	80	62	93	2	...	9-7	.283	.363	.481	.844	3	...
1996—	Yomiuri (Jp. Cen.)		130	487	97	153	34	1	38	99	71	98	4	...	7-2	.314	.401	.622	1.023	6	...
1997—	Yomiuri (Jp. Cen.)		135	484	93	144	18	0	37	103	100	84	6	...	9-3	.298	.419	.564	.984	7	...
1998—	Yomiuri (Jp. Cen.)		135	487	103	142	24	3	34	100	104	101	8	...	3-5	.292	.421	.563	.984	4	...
1999—	Yomiuri (Jp. Cen.)		135	471	103	143	24	2	42	95	93	99	2	...	0-4	.304	.416	.631	1.047	1	...
2000—	Yomiuri (Jp. Cen.)		135	474	116	150	32	1	42	108	106	108	2	...	5-2	.316	.438	.654	1.092	2	...
2001—	Yomiuri (Jp. Cen.)		140	481	107	160	31	3	36	104	120	96	3	...	3-3	.333	.463	.617	1.081	6	...
2002—	Yomiuri (Jp. Cen.)		140	500	112	167	27	1	50	107	114	104	6	...	3-4	.334	.461	.692	1.153	2	...
2003—	New York (A.L.)	OF-DH	* 163	623	82	179	42	1	16	106	63	86	3	25	2-2	.287	.353	.435	.788	8	.977
2004—	New York (A.L.)	OF	* 162	584	109	174	34	2	31	108	88	103	3	11	3-0	.298	.390	.522	.912	7	.978
2005—	New York (A.L.)	OF-DH	* 162	629	108	192	45	3	23	116	63	78	3	16	2-2	.305	.367	.496	.863	3	.990
Major League totals (3 years)			487	1836	299	545	121	6	70	330	214	267	9	52	7-4	.297	.370	.484	.853	18	.981

DIVISION SERIES RECORD

									BATTING										FIELDING	
Year	Team (League)	Pos.	G	AB	R	H	2B	3B	HR	RBI	BB	SO	HBP	GDP	SB-CS	Avg.	OBP	SLG	OPS	E	Avg.
2003—	New York (A.L.)	OF	4	15	2	4	1	0	1	3	2	3	0	1	0-0	.267	.353	.533	.886	0	1.000
2004—	New York (A.L.)	OF	4	17	3	7	1	0	1	3	4	4	0	0	0-0	.412	.476	.647	1.123	0	1.000
2005—	New York (A.L.)	OF	5	20	4	4	1	0	1	1	2	3	0	2	0-0	.200	.273	.400	.673	1	.909
Division series totals (3 years)			13	52	9	15	3	0	3	7	7	10	0	3	0-0	.288	.367	.519	.886	1	.962

CHAMPIONSHIP SERIES RECORD

									BATTING										FIELDING	
Year	Team (League)	Pos.	G	AB	R	H	2B	3B	HR	RBI	BB	SO	HBP	GDP	SB-CS	Avg.	OBP	SLG	OPS	E	Avg.
2003—	New York (A.L.)	OF	7	26	3	8	3	0	0	4	1	3	0	1	0-0	.308	.321	.423	.745	1	.889
2004—	New York (A.L.)	OF	7	34	9	14	6	1	2	10	2	4	0	0	0-0	.412	.444	.824	1.268	0	1.000
Champ. series totals (2 years)			14	60	12	22	9	1	2	14	3	7	0	1	0-0	.367	.391	.650	1.041	1	.960

M

WORLD SERIES RECORD

Year	Team (League)	Pos.	G	AB	R	H	2B	3B	HR	RBI	BB	SO	HBP	GDP	SB-CS	Avg.	OBP	SLG	OPS	E	Avg.
2003—	New York (A.L.)	OF	6	23	1	6	0	0	1	4	3	2	1	0	0-0	.261	.370	.391	.762	0	1.000

ALL-STAR GAME RECORD

	G	AB	R	H	2B	3B	HR	RBI	BB	SO	HBP	GDP	SB-CS	Avg.	OBP	SLG	OPS	E	Avg.
All-Star Game totals (2 years)	2	3	0	1	0	0	0	0	0	1	0	0	0-0	.333	.333	.333	.667	0	1.000

MATSUI, KAZUO — 2B/SS

PERSONAL: Born October 23, 1975, in Osaka, Japan. ... 5-10/185. ... Bats both, throws right. ... Name pronounced: mat-SOO-ee. ... High school: PL Gakeun (Osaka, Japan).
TRANSACTIONS/CAREER NOTES: Signed as a free agent by New York Mets (December 10, 2003). ... On disabled list (August 9-September 24, 2004). ... On disabled list (June 21-August 9, 2005); included rehabilitation assignments to GCL Mets, Brooklyn and Binghamton.
2005 GAMES PLAYED BY POSITION (MLB): 2B—71.

SCOUTING REPORT
Offense: Matsui didn't fulfill expectations last season as he was bothered by knee problems. Has a long stroke and declining bat speed. Pulls off the ball. Likes the ball inside but is not patient and often gets himself out. Is a better hitter lefthanded but has little power. Runs well but doesn't steal bases. *Defense:* He did not appear comfortable with his move to second base. Had problems adjusting to the ball off the bat and appeared to lose confidence. Does not charge the ball well and still is learning to make the pivot. Has good range to both sides but is better to the left. *Outlook:* Matsui had a bad year on both sides of the ball and is rumored to be interested in a return to Japan. *Grade 6.0*

KAZUO MATSUI'S HITTING ZONE

.231	.143	.231
.364	.345	.265
.344	.389	.219

LEFTY-RIGHTY SPLITS

vs.	Avg.	AB	H	2B	3B	HR	RBI	BB	SO	OBP	Slg.
L	.279	68	19	1	1	0	7	3	9	.315	.324
R	.246	199	49	8	3	3	17	11	34	.295	.362

Year	Team (League)	Pos.	G	AB	R	H	2B	3B	HR	RBI	BB	SO	HBP	GDP	SB-CS	Avg.	OBP	SLG	OPS	E	Avg.
1995—Seibu (Jp. Pac.)			69	204	25	45	9	1	2	62	7	26	0	4	21-1	.221	.245	.304	.549	...	
1996—Seibu (Jp. Pac.)			130	473	54	134	22	5	1	29	14	93	3	2	50-9	.283	.307	.357	.664	...	
1997—Seibu (Jp. Pac.)			135	576	91	178	23	13	7	63	44	89	5	4	62-15	.309	.362	.431	.793	...	
1998—Seibu (Jp. Pac.)			135	575	92	179	38	5	9	58	55	89	1	10	43-14	.311	.370	.442	.812	...	
1999—Seibu (Jp. Pac.)			135	539	87	178	29	4	15	67	56	75	0	7	32-7	.330	.389	.482	.872	...	
2000—Seibu (Jp. Pac.)			135	550	99	177	40	11	23	90	46	60	2	8	26-3	.322	.372	.560	.932	...	
2001—Seibu (Jp. Pac.)			140	552	94	170	28	2	24	76	46	83	6	13	26-0	.308	.365	.496	.861	...	
2002—Seibu (Jp. Pac.)			140	582	119	193	46	6	36	87	53	112	4	4	33-11	.332	.389	.617	1.006	...	
2003—Seibu (Jp. Pac.)			140	587	104	179	36	4	33	84	55	124	4	4	13-0	.305	.365	.549	.914	...	
2004—New York (N.L.)	SS-2B		114	460	65	125	32	6	7	44	40	97	2	3	14-3	.272	.331	.396	.727	24	.955
2005—GC Mets (GCL)	2B-DH		3	9	3	4	0	0	1	3	1	3	1	0	0-0	.444	.545	.778	1.323	0	1.000
—Brooklyn (N.Y.-Penn.)	2B		1	3	0	0	0	0	0	1	2	0	0	0	0-0	.000	.400	.000	.400	1	.000
—Binghamton (East.)	2B		3	9	4	4	1	0	0	1	1	1	0	0	2-0	.444	.500	.556	1.056	0	1.000
—New York (N.L.)	2B		87	267	31	68	9	4	3	24	14	43	5	2	6-1	.255	.300	.352	.652	9	.970
Major League totals (2 years)			201	727	96	193	41	6	10	68	54	140	7	5	20-4	.265	.320	.380	.700	33	.961

MATTHEWS, GARY — OF

M

PERSONAL: Born August 25, 1974, in San Francisco. ... 6-3/225. ... Bats both, throws right. ... Full name: Gary Nathaniel Matthews Jr.. ... High school: Granada Hills (Calif.). ... Junior college: Mission (Calif.) Community College. ... Son of Gary Matthews, coach, Chicago Cubs, and outfielder with five major league teams (1972-87).
TRANSACTIONS/CAREER NOTES: Selected by San Diego Padres organization in 13th round of 1993 free-agent draft. ... Traded by Padres to Chicago Cubs for P Rodney Myers (March 23, 2000). ... Claimed on waivers by Pittsburgh Pirates (August 10, 2001). ... Traded by Pirates to New York Mets for cash (December 28, 2001). ... Traded by Mets to Baltimore Orioles for P John Bale (April 3, 2002). ... On disabled list (August 25-September 11, 2002). ... Claimed on waivers by Padres (May 23, 2003). ... Claimed on waivers by Atlanta Braves (November 24, 2003). ... Released by Braves (March 31, 2004). ... Signed by Texas Rangers organization (April 7, 2004). ... On disabled list (May 15-June 8, 2005); included rehabilitation assignment to Frisco.
2005 GAMES PLAYED BY POSITION (MLB): OF—123, DH—1.

SCOUTING REPORT
Offense: Though he has been with a lot of teams in a short span, Matthews has good overall tools. Shows good bat speed despite having a lot of movement at the plate. Has trouble with balls inside and swings through a lot of pitches. Has more raw power than the numbers show. Is extremely streaky. Has a long stroke and is better from the left side. Runs well and has good instincts. *Defense:* He basically is a corner outfielder, but Matthews played center field most of last year. Is very athletic and has above-average range. Has problems coming in on the ball. Has a strong, accurate arm. *Outlook:* Matthews should be a better player because of his speed and power but is so streaky he loses playing time. Needs to decide if he is a power or contact hitter to reach his potential. *Grade 6.3*

GARY MATTHEWS' HITTING ZONE

.310	.278	.350
.360	.278	.315
.219	.125	.192

LEFTY-RIGHTY SPLITS

vs.	Avg.	AB	H	2B	3B	HR	RBI	BB	SO	OBP	Slg.
L	.241	133	32	6	2	9	18	10	29	.294	.519
R	.260	342	89	19	3	8	37	37	61	.330	.404

Year	Team (League)	Pos.	G	AB	R	H	2B	3B	HR	RBI	BB	SO	HBP	GDP	SB-CS	Avg.	OBP	SLG	OPS	E	Avg.
1994—Spokane (N'west)	2B-OF		52	191	23	40	6	1	0	18	19	58	2	4	3-5	.209	.286	.251	.538	4	.961
1995—Clinton (Midw.)	OF		128	421	57	100	18	4	4	40	68	109	6	8	28-8	.238	.349	.314	.663	9	.966
1996—Rancho Cuca. (Calif.)	OF		123	435	65	118	21	11	6	54	60	102	6	11	7-8	.271	.366	.418	.784	16	.934
1997—Rancho Cuca. (Calif.)	OF		69	268	66	81	15	4	8	40	49	57	3	4	10-4	.302	.416	.478	.893	5	.959
—Mobile (Sou.)	OF		28	90	14	22	4	1	2	12	15	29	1	1	3-1	.244	.352	.378	.730	2	.960
1998—Mobile (Sou.)	OF		72	254	62	78	15	4	7	51	55	50	1	6	11-1	.307	.428	.480	.908	1	.995
1999—Las Vegas (PCL)	OF		121	422	57	108	19	6	9	52	58	104	7	13	17-6	.256	.352	.386	.739	7	.976
—San Diego (N.L.)	OF		23	36	4	8	0	0	0	7	9	9	0	1	2-0	.222	.378	.222	.600	0	1.000
2000—Iowa (PCL)	OF		60	211	27	51	11	3	5	22	18	41	0	4	6-1	.242	.300	.393	.693	4	.970
—Chicago (N.L.)	OF		80	158	24	30	1	2	4	14	15	28	1	4	3-0	.190	.264	.297	.562	2	.978
2001—Chicago (N.L.)	OF		106	258	41	56	9	3	9	30	38	55	1	4	5-3	.217	.320	.364	.684	4	.976

Year	Team (League)	Pos.	G	AB	R	H	2B	3B	HR	RBI	BB	SO	HBP	GDP	SB-CS	Avg.	OBP	SLG	OPS	E	Avg.
	—Pittsburgh (N.L.)	OF	46	147	22	36	6	1	5	14	22	45	0	4	3-2	.245	.341	.401	.743	3	.971
2002	—New York (N.L.)	PH	2	1	0	0	0	0	0	0	0	0	0	0	0-0	.000	.000	.000	.000	...	...
	—Baltimore (A.L.)	OF-DH	109	344	54	95	25	3	7	38	43	69	1	4	15-5	.276	.355	.427	.782	6	.969
2003	—Baltimore (A.L.)	OF-DH	41	162	21	33	12	1	2	20	9	29	1	4	0-3	.204	.250	.327	.577	0	1.000
	—San Diego (N.L.)	OF	103	306	50	83	19	1	4	22	34	66	1	4	12-5	.271	.346	.379	.725	1	.993
2004	—Oklahoma (PCL)	OF-DH	38	145	33	47	9	4	9	36	23	29	0	2	4-1	.324	.409	.628	1.037	2	.971
	—Texas (A.L.)	OF-DH	87	280	37	77	17	1	11	36	33	64	1	1	5-1	.275	.350	.461	.811	2	.990
2005	—Frisco (Texas)	OF	1	5	0	2	0	0	0	1	0	1	0	0	0-0	.400	.400	.400	.800	2	.500
	—Texas (A.L.)	OF-DH	131	475	72	121	25	5	17	55	47	90	0	11	9-2	.255	.320	.436	.756	6	.982
	American League totals (4 years)		368	1261	184	326	79	10	37	149	132	252	3	20	29-11	.259	.328	.425	.753	14	.983
	National League totals (5 years)		360	906	141	213	35	5	22	87	118	203	3	15	25-10	.235	.325	.358	.683	10	.981
	Major League totals (7 years)		728	2167	325	539	114	15	59	236	250	455	6	35	54-21	.249	.327	.397	.723	24	.982

MATTHEWS, MIKE   P

PERSONAL: Born October 24, 1973, in Fredericksburg, Va. ... 6-2/205. ... Throws left, bats left. ... Full name: Michael Scott Matthews. ... High school: Woodbridge Senior (Va.). ... Junior college: Montgomery (Md.) Community College.

TRANSACTIONS/CAREER NOTES: Selected by Cleveland Indians organization in second round of 1992 free-agent draft. ... Traded by Indians to Boston Red Sox for IF Jose Olmeda (August 4, 1999). ... Traded by Red Sox with C David Menham to St. Louis Cardinals for P Kent Mercker (August 24, 1999). ... On disabled list (July 16, 2000-remainder of season; and August 21-September 11, 2002). ... Traded by Cardinals to Milwaukee Brewers (September 11, 2002), completing deal in which Brewers traded P Jamey Wright and cash to Cardinals for OF Chris Morris and a player to be named (August 29, 2002). ... Claimed on waivers by San Diego Padres (March 26, 2003). ... Signed as a free agent by Cincinnati Reds organization (January 16, 2004). ... On disabled list (July 3-September 3, 2004); included rehabilitation assignment to Louisville. ... Signed as a free agent by New York Mets organization (January 28, 2005).

CAREER HITTING: 3-for-25 (.120), 2 R, 0 2B, 0 3B, 1 HR, 1 RBI.

LEFTY-RIGHTY SPLITS

vs.	Avg.	AB	H	2B	3B	HR	RBI	BB	SO	OBP	Slg.
L	.400	10	4	0	0	0	1	1	1	.417	.400
R	.455	11	5	3	0	0	4	3	1	.533	.727

Year	Team (League)	W	L	Pct.	ERA	WHIP	G	GS	CG	ShO	Hld.	Sv.-Opp.	IP	H	R	ER	HR	BB-IBB	SO	Avg.
1992	—Burlington (Appal.)	7	0	1.000	1.01	0.96	10	10	0	0	...	0-...	62.1	33	13	7	1	27-0	55	.156
	—Watertown (NYP)	1	0	1.000	3.27	1.64	2	2	2	0	...	0-...	11.0	10	4	4	0	8-0	5	.263
1993	—	Did not play.																		
1994	—Columbus (S. Atl.)	6	8	.429	3.08	1.37	23	23	0	0	...	0-...	119.2	120	53	41	8	44-1	99	.270
1995	—Cant./Akr. (Eastern)	5	8	.385	5.93	1.68	15	15	1	0	...	0-...	74.1	82	62	49	6	43-1	37	.283
1996	—Cant./Akr. (Eastern)	9	11	.450	4.66	1.55	27	27	3	0	...	0-...	162.1	178	96	84	13	74-3	112	.287
1997	—Buffalo (A.A.)	0	2	.000	7.71	2.00	5	5	0	0	...	0-...	21.0	32	19	18	7	10-0	17	.344
	—Akron (East.)	6	8	.429	3.82	1.53	19	19	3	1	...	0-...	113.0	116	62	48	13	57-0	69	.273
1998	—Buffalo (Int'l)	9	6	.600	4.63	1.57	24	23	0	0	...	0-...	130.1	137	79	67	19	68-1	86	.275
1999	—Buffalo (Int'l)	1	2	.333	7.59	1.92	25	0	0	0	...	0-...	21.1	23	18	18	3	18-0	16	.303
	—Akron (East.)	0	5	.000	8.77	1.99	6	6	0	0	...	0-...	25.2	36	30	25	7	15-0	10	.336
	—Trenton (East.)	0	0	...	4.63	1.71	3	3	0	0	...	0-...	11.2	11	7	6	1	9-0	8	.268
	—Arkansas (Texas)	2	0	1.000	0.00	0.33	2	2	1	1	...	0-...	12.0	3	0	0	0	1-0	10	.079
2000	—Memphis (PCL)	3	1	.750	3.12	1.25	9	9	0	0	...	0-...	52.0	33	19	18	4	32-1	50	.182
	—St. Louis (N.L.)	0	0	...	11.57	2.68	14	0	0	0	2	0-0	9.1	15	12	12	2	10-2	8	.349
2001	—St. Louis (N.L.)	3	4	.429	3.24	1.20	51	0	0	0	3	1-3	89.0	74	32	32	11	33-4	72	.227
2002	—St. Louis (N.L.)	2	1	.667	3.89	1.49	43	0	0	0	4	0-2	41.2	40	21	18	5	22-2	32	.260
	—Milwaukee (N.L.)	0	0	...	4.50	2.50	4	0	0	0	0	0-0	4.0	3	2	2	0	7-1	2	.214
2003	—San Diego (N.L.)	6	4	.600	4.45	1.45	77	0	0	0	16	0-3	64.2	65	34	32	4	29-5	44	.271
2004	—Louisville (Int'l)	1	0	1.000	1.53	0.96	13	3	0	0	...	1-...	17.2	12	3	3	1	5-0	16	.188
	—Cincinnati (N.L.)	2	1	.667	6.30	1.57	35	0	0	0	5	0-0	30.0	31	22	21	7	16-1	15	.265
2005	—New York (N.L.)	1	0	1.000	10.80	2.60	6	0	0	0	0	0-0	5.0	9	6	6	0	4-1	2	.429
	—Norfolk (Int'l)	0	1	.000	12.10	2.28	5	0	0	0	0	0-0	9.2	14	13	13	1	8-0	6	.341
	Major League totals (6 years)	14	10	.583	4.54	1.47	230	0	0	0	30	1-8	243.2	237	129	123	29	121-16	175	.259

DIVISION SERIES RECORD

Year	Team (League)	W	L	Pct.	ERA	WHIP	G	GS	CG	ShO	Hld.	Sv.-Opp.	IP	H	R	ER	HR	BB-IBB	SO	Avg.
2001	—St. Louis (N.L.)	0	1	.000	40.50	6.00	1	0	0	0	0	0-1	0.2	4	3	3	1	0-0	0	.667

MAUER, JOE   C

PERSONAL: Born April 19, 1983, in St. Paul, Minn. ... 6-4/220. ... Bats left, throws right. ... Full name: Joseph Patrick Mauer. ... High school: Cretin-Durham Hall (St. Paul).
TRANSACTIONS/CAREER NOTES: Selected by Minnesota Twins organization in first round (first pick overall) of 2001 free-agent draft ... On disabled list (April 7-June 2 and July 16, 2004-remainder of season); included rehabilitation assignments to Fort Myers and Rochester.
2005 GAMES PLAYED BY POSITION (MLB): C—116, DH—13.

SCOUTING REPORT *Offense:* Mauer, though only 22, already is one of the best all-around catchers in the game. Has a long stroke but knows the strike zone and can use the whole field. Stays inside on the ball and has the ability to drive it for power. Home run numbers should rise. Is a very good breaking-ball hitter and has shown the ability to make adjustments. Has questionable running skills. *Defense:* He is an excellent athlete and has quickness. Has an above-average arm with a good release. Has soft hands and good agility. Frames pitches well and is adept at working with his pitching staff. *Outlook:* Mauer projects as a consistent .300 hitter and has the potential to be a perennial All-Star; all he needs is to do is stay healthy. *Grade 7.9*

JOE MAUER'S HITTING ZONE

.417	.583	.381
.337	.242	.232
.286	.333	.178

LEFTY-RIGHTY SPLITS

vs.	Avg.	AB	H	2B	3B	HR	RBI	BB	SO	OBP	Slg.
L	.225	142	32	3	0	0	12	9	29	.268	.246
R	.323	347	112	23	2	9	43	52	35	.411	.478

Year	Team (League)	Pos.	G	AB	R	H	2B	3B	HR	RBI	BB	SO	HBP	GDP	SB-CS	Avg.	OBP	SLG	OPS	E	Avg.
2001	—Elizabethton (App.)	C	32	110	14	44	6	2	0	14	19	10	1	5	4-0	.400	.492	.491	.983	4	.980
2002	—Quad City (Midw.)	C-1B	110	411	58	124	23	1	4	62	61	42	2	16	0-0	.302	.393	.392	.785	6	.993
2003	—Fort Myers (FSL)	C-1B	62	233	25	78	13	1	1	44	24	24	1	11	3-0	.335	.395	.412	.807	0	1.000

Year Team (League)	Pos.	G	AB	R	H	2B	3B	HR	RBI	BB	SO	HBP	GDP	SB-CS	Avg.	OBP	SLG	OPS	E	Avg.
— New Britain (East.)	C	73	276	48	94	17	1	4	41	25	25	5	10	0-0	.341	.400	.453	.853	3	.992
2004— Fort Myers (FSL)	C-DH	2	6	0	4	0	0	0	2	2	2	0	0	0-0	.667	.750	.667	1.417	0	1.000
— Rochester (Int'l)	DH-C	5	19	1	6	3	0	0	2	1	4	0	1	0-0	.316	.333	.474	.807	0	1.000
— Minnesota (A.L.)	C-DH	35	107	18	33	8	1	6	17	11	14	1	1	1-0	.308	.369	.570	.939	2	.991
2005— Minnesota (A.L.)	C-DH	131	489	61	144	26	2	9	55	61	64	1	9	13-1	.294	.372	.411	.783	5	.993
Major League totals (2 years)		166	596	79	177	34	3	15	72	72	78	2	10	14-1	.297	.371	.440	.811	7	.993

MAY, DARRELL — P

PERSONAL: Born June 13, 1972, in San Bernardino, Calif. ... 6-2/185. ... Throws left, bats left. ... Full name: Darrell Kevin May. ... High school: Rogue River (Ore.). ... Junior college: Sacramento (Calif.) City College.

TRANSACTIONS/CAREER NOTES: Selected by Atlanta Braves organization in 46th round of 1992 free-agent draft. ... Claimed on waivers by Pittsburgh Pirates (April 4, 1996). ... Claimed on waivers by California Angels (September 6, 1996). ... Angels franchise renamed Anaheim Angels for 1997 season. ... Released by Angels (March 27, 1998). ... Signed by Hanshin of the Japan Central League (March 29, 1998). ... Signed by Yomiuri of the Japan Central League (December 18, 1999). ... Signed by Kansas City Royals organization (December 17, 2001). ... On disabled list (March 27-April 13 and April 14-May 18, 2002); included rehabilitation assignments to Omaha and Wichita. ... Traded by Royals with P Ryan Bukvich to San Diego Padres for OF Terrence Long, P Dennis Tankersley and cash (November 8, 2004). ... Traded by Padres with P Tim Redding to New York Yankees for P Paul Quantrill (July 2, 2005).

CAREER HITTING: 2-for-26 (.077), 1 R, 0 2B, 0 3B, 0 HR, 0 RBI.

DARRELL MAY'S PITCHING ZONE

.308	.400	.333
.431	.364	.213
.370	.500	.172

LEFTY-RIGHTY SPLITS

vs.	Avg.	AB	H	2B	3B	HR	RBI	BB	SO	OBP	Slg.
L	.226	62	14	5	1	1	11	3	11	.258	.387
R	.341	214	73	16	3	13	41	20	24	.396	.626

Year Team (League)	W	L	Pct.	ERA	WHIP	G	GS	CG	ShO	Hld.	Sv.-Opp.	IP	H	R	ER	HR	BB-IBB	SO	Avg.
1992— GC Braves (GCL)	4	3	.571	1.36	0.89	12	7	0	0	...	1-...	53.0	34	13	8	0	13-0	61	.182
1993— Macon (S. Atl.)	10	4	.714	2.24	0.99	17	17	0	0	...	0-...	104.1	81	29	26	6	22-1	111	.213
— Durham (Carol.)	5	2	.714	2.09	1.16	9	9	0	0	...	0-...	51.2	44	18	12	4	16-0	47	.232
1994— Durham (Carol.)	8	2	.800	3.01	1.22	12	12	1	0	...	0-...	74.2	74	29	25	6	17-1	73	.259
— Greenville (Sou.)	5	3	.625	3.11	1.23	11	11	1	0	...	0-...	63.2	61	25	22	4	17-0	42	.251
1995— Greenville (Sou.)	2	8	.200	3.55	1.11	15	15	0	0	...	0-...	91.1	81	44	36	18	20-0	79	.233
— Richmond (Int'l)	4	2	.667	3.71	1.35	9	9	0	0	...	0-...	51.0	53	21	21	1	16-1	42	.270
— Atlanta (N.L.)	0	0	...	11.25	2.50	2	0	0	0	0	0-0	4.0	10	5	5	0	0-0	1	.500
1996— Calgary (PCL)	7	6	.538	4.10	1.38	23	22	1	1	...	0-...	131.2	146	64	60	17	36-6	75	.284
— Pittsburgh (N.L.)	0	1	.000	9.35	2.19	5	2	0	0	1	0-0	8.2	15	10	9	5	4-0	5	.357
— California (A.L.)	0	0	...	10.13	1.88	5	0	0	0	0	0-0	2.2	3	3	3	1	2-0	1	.333
1997— Vancouver (PCL)	7	5	.583	3.26	1.20	13	12	2	2	...	0-...	80.0	65	31	29	10	31-0	62	.223
— Anaheim (A.L.)	2	1	.667	5.23	1.57	29	2	0	0	...	0-1	51.2	56	31	30	6	25-2	42	.277
1998— Hanshin (Jp. Cn.)	4	9	.308	3.47	1.37	21	21	1	1	...	0-...	129.2	122	55	50	...	55-...	94	...
— Hanshin (Jp. West.)	1	2	.333	5.82	1.24	5	3	0	0	...	0-...	17.0	19	11	11	...	2-...	11	...
1999— Hanshin (Jp. Cn.)	6	7	.462	4.25	1.24	18	18	0	0	...	0-...	112.1	101	56	53	...	38-...	113	...
— Hanshin (Jp. West.)	1	0	1.000	0.00	0.60	2	2	0	0	...	0-...	10.0	4	1	0	...	2-...	12	...
2000— Yomiuri (Jp. Cen.)	12	7	.632	2.95	1.05	24	24	3	3	...	0-...	155.1	123	52	51	...	40-...	165	...
— Yomiuri (Jp. East.)	0	0	...	0.00	0.75	1	0	0	0	...	0-...	4.0	2	0	0	...	1-...	4	...
2001— Yomiuri (Jp. Cen.)	10	8	.556	4.13	1.29	26	26	1	0	...	0-...	159.0	160	74	73	...	45-...	168	...
2002— Omaha (PCL)	1	0	1.000	0.75	0.67	2	2	0	0	...	0-...	12.0	8	1	1	0	0-0	9	.471
— Kansas City (A.L.)	4	10	.286	5.35	1.48	30	21	2	1	0	0-1	131.1	144	83	78	28	50-3	95	.277
— Wichita (Texas)	0	0	...	2.08	1.15	1	1	0	0	...	0-...	4.1	4	1	1	0	1-0	5	.235
2003— Kansas City (A.L.)	10	8	.556	3.77	1.19	35	32	2	1	0	0-1	210.0	197	98	88	31	53-1	115	.246
2004— Kansas City (A.L.)	9	*19	.321	5.61	1.55	31	31	3	1	0	0-0	186.0	234	130	116	38	55-4	120	.306
2005— San Diego (N.L.)	1	3	.250	5.61	1.57	22	8	0	0	0	0-0	59.1	73	38	37	10	20-1	32	.303
— New York (A.L.)	0	1	.000	16.71	2.43	2	1	0	0	0	0-0	7.0	14	13	13	4	3-0	3	.400
— Columbus (Int'l)	6	2	.750	4.17	1.23	10	7	0	0	0	0-0	58.1	67	29	27	6	5-0	39	.288
American League totals (6 years)	25	39	.391	5.01	1.42	132	87	7	3	0	0-3	588.2	648	358	328	108	188-10	376	.278
National League totals (3 years)	1	4	.200	6.38	1.69	29	10	0	0	1	0-0	72.0	98	53	51	15	24-1	38	.323
Major League totals (7 years)	26	43	.377	5.16	1.45	161	97	7	3	1	0-3	660.2	746	411	379	123	212-11	414	.283

MAYS, JOE — P

PERSONAL: Born December 10, 1975, in Flint, Mich. ... 6-1/192. ... Throws right, bats both. ... Full name: Joseph Emerson Mays. ... High school: Southeast (Bradenton, Fla.). ... Junior college: Manatee Community College (Bradenton, Fla.).

TRANSACTIONS/CAREER NOTES: Selected by Seattle Mariners organization in sixth round of 1994 free-agent draft. ... Traded by Mariners to Minnesota Twins (October 8, 1997), completing deal in which Twins traded OF Roberto Kelly to Mariners for P Jeromy Palki and a player to be named (August 20, 1997). ... On disabled list (April 15-July 20, 2002); included rehabilitation assignments to Fort Myers and New Britain. ... On disabled list (March 23, 2004-entire season).

CAREER HITTING: 4-for-15 (.267), 1 R, 1 2B, 0 3B, 0 HR, 0 RBI.

SCOUTING REPORT *Throws:* His fastball ranges from 88-91 mph, and he also has a curveball, slider and changeup. *Tendencies:* Coming off elbow surgery, Mays was slow to regain his velocity in 2005. Throws over the top but gets some sinking action. No longer is effective riding his fastball up in the zone. Tight rotation on a curve that breaks straight down; pitch is a better breaking ball than his slider. Has good arm speed with his changeup. *Outlook:* Mays could rebound but has to get better location with his fastball and stay consistently down in the zone to win. Projected as no better than a fifth starter going into the spring. *Grade 5.1*

JOE MAYS' PITCHING ZONE

.256	.310	.270
.447	.395	.327
.326	.267	.276

LEFTY-RIGHTY SPLITS

vs.	Avg.	AB	H	2B	3B	HR	RBI	BB	SO	OBP	Slg.
L	.273	319	87	18	3	12	48	20	29	.317	.461
R	.364	319	116	26	1	11	52	21	30	.404	.555

Year Team (League)	W	L	Pct.	ERA	WHIP	G	GS	CG	ShO	Hld.	Sv.-Opp.	IP	H	R	ER	HR	BB-IBB	SO	Avg.
1995— Ariz. Mariners (Ariz.)	2	3	.400	3.25	1.33	10	10	0	0	...	0-...	44.1	41	24	16	0	18-0	44	.247
1996— Everett (N'west)	4	4	.500	3.08	1.20	13	10	0	0	...	0-...	64.1	55	33	22	3	22-0	56	.227

M

Year Team (League)	W	L	Pct.	ERA	WHIP	G	GS	CG	ShO	Hld.	Sv.-Opp.	IP	H	R	ER	HR	BB-IBB	SO	Avg.
1997—Wisconsin (Midw.)	9	3	.750	2.09	1.04	13	13	1	0	...	0-...	81.2	62	20	19	3	23-1	79	.214
—Lancaster (Calif.)	7	4	.636	4.86	1.47	15	15	1	0	...	0-...	96.1	108	55	52	9	34-0	82	.290
1998—Fort Myers (FSL)	7	2	.778	3.04	1.31	16	15	0	0	...	0-...	94.2	101	45	32	7	23-0	83	.276
—New Britain (East.)	5	3	.625	4.99	1.46	11	10	0	0	...	0-...	57.2	63	40	32	4	21-0	45	.273
1999—Minnesota (A.L.)	6	11	.353	4.37	1.44	49	20	2	1	2	0-0	171.0	179	92	83	24	67-2	115	.270
2000—Minnesota (A.L.)	7	15	.318	5.56	1.62	31	28	2	1	0	0-0	160.1	193	105	99	20	67-1	102	.299
—Salt Lake (PCL)	2	0	1.000	1.72	1.15	3	3	0	0	...	0-...	15.2	16	4	3	0	2-0	18	.267
2001—Minnesota (A.L.)	17	13	.567	3.16	1.15	34	34	4	2	0	0-0	233.2	205	87	82	25	64-2	123	.235
2002—Minnesota (A.L.)	4	8	.333	5.38	1.45	17	17	1	1	0	0-0	95.1	113	60	57	14	25-0	38	.292
—Fort Myers (FSL)	0	1	.000	2.08	1.38	3	3	0	0	...	0-...	8.2	9	2	2	0	3-0	7	.273
—New Britain (East.)	1	0	1.000	1.29	0.43	1	1	0	0	...	0-...	7.0	2	1	1	1	1-0	5	.087
2003—Minnesota (A.L.)	8	8	.500	6.30	1.52	31	21	0	0	1	0-1	130.0	159	92	91	21	39-2	50	.302
2004—Minnesota (A.L.)	Did not play.																		
2005—Minnesota (A.L.)	6	10	.375	5.65	1.56	31	26	1	1	0	0-0	156.0	203	109	98	23	41-1	59	.318
Major League totals (6 years)	48	65	.425	4.85	1.43	193	146	10	6	3	0-1	946.1	1052	545	510	127	303-8	487	.282

DIVISION SERIES RECORD

Year Team (League)	W	L	Pct.	ERA	WHIP	G	GS	CG	ShO	Hld.	Sv.-Opp.	IP	H	R	ER	HR	BB-IBB	SO	Avg.
2002—Minnesota (A.L.)	0	1	.000	14.73	3.00	1	1	0	0	0	0-0	3.2	9	6	6	1	2-1	1	.474

CHAMPIONSHIP SERIES RECORD

Year Team (League)	W	L	Pct.	ERA	WHIP	G	GS	CG	ShO	Hld.	Sv.-Opp.	IP	H	R	ER	HR	BB-IBB	SO	Avg.
2002—Minnesota (A.L.)	1	0	1.000	2.03	0.90	2	2	0	0	0	0-0	13.1	12	4	3	3	0-0	3	.235

ALL-STAR GAME RECORD

Year Team (League)	W	L	Pct.	ERA	WHIP	G	GS	CG	ShO	Hld.	Sv.-Opp.	IP	H	R	ER	HR	BB-IBB	SO	Avg.
All-Star Game totals (1 year)	0	0	...	0.00	0.00	1	0	0	0	...	0-0	1.0	0	0	0	0	0-0	0	...

MCANULTY, PAUL — 1B

PERSONAL: Born February 24, 1981, in Oxnard, Calif. ... 5-10/220. ... Bats left, throws right. ... Full name: Paul Michael McAnulty. ... College: Long Beach State.

TRANSACTIONS/CAREER NOTES: Selected by San Diego Padres organization in 12th round of 2002 free-agent draft.

2005 GAMES PLAYED BY POSITION (MLB): OF—6, 1B—1.

LEFTY-RIGHTY SPLITS

vs.	Avg.	AB	H	2B	3B	HR	RBI	BB	SO	OBP	Slg.
L	.500	2	1	0	0	0	0	1	0	.667	.500
R	.182	22	4	0	0	0	0	2	7	.280	.182

Year Team (League)	Pos.	G	AB	R	H	2B	3B	HR	RBI	BB	SO	HBP	GDP	SB-CS	Avg.	OBP	SLG	OPS	E	Avg.
2002—Idaho Falls (Pio.)	1B	67	235	56	89	29	6	8	51	49	43	4	5	7-2	.379	.488	.604	1.092	11	.979
2003—Fort Wayne (Midw.)	1B-OF	133	455	48	124	27	0	7	73	67	82	9	7	5-3	.273	.370	.378	.748	16	.986
2004—Lake Elsinore (Calif.)	OF-1B	133	495	98	147	36	3	23	87	88	106	4	5	3-1	.297	.404	.521	.925	8	.984
2005—Mobile (Sou.)	OF-1B	79	298	39	84	17	2	10	42	34	66	6	3	5-2	.282	.364	.453	.817	10	.969
—Portland (PCL)	1B-OF-DH	38	151	27	52	15	0	6	27	16	29	0	4	0-0	.344	.405	.563	.968	2	.992
—San Diego (N.L.)	OF-1B	22	24	4	5	0	0	0	0	3	7	1	0	1-0	.208	.321	.208	.530	0	1.000
Major League totals (1 year)		22	24	4	5	0	0	0	0	3	7	1	0	1-0	.208	.321	.208	.530	0	1.000

MCBRIDE, MACAY — P

PERSONAL: Born October 24, 1982, in Augusta, Ga. ... 5-11/210. ... Throws left, bats left. ... Full name: Joseph Macay McBride.

TRANSACTIONS/CAREER NOTES: Selected by Atlanta Braves organization in first round (24th pick overall) of 2001 free-agent draft.

CAREER HITTING: 0-for-0 (.000), 0 R, 0 2B, 0 3B, 0 HR, 0 RBI.

MACAY MCBRIDE'S PITCHING ZONE

.333	.000	.000
.571	.286	.333
.400	.833	.200

LEFTY-RIGHTY SPLITS

vs.	Avg.	AB	H	2B	3B	HR	RBI	BB	SO	OBP	Slg.
L	.172	29	5	1	0	0	2	2	15	.226	.207
R	.433	30	13	1	0	0	5	5	7	.500	.467

Year Team (League)	W	L	Pct.	ERA	WHIP	G	GS	CG	ShO	Hld.	Sv.-Opp.	IP	H	R	ER	HR	BB-IBB	SO	Avg.
2001—GC Braves (GCL)	4	4	.500	3.76	1.35	13	11	0	0	...	0-...	55.0	51	30	23	0	23-1	67	.248
2002—Macon (S. Atl.)	12	8	.600	2.12	1.06	25	25	2	1	...	0-...	157.1	119	49	37	6	48-1	138	.209
2003—Myrtle Beach (Carol.)	9	8	.529	2.95	1.29	27	27	1	0	...	0-...	164.2	164	63	54	5	49-0	139	.262
2004—Greenville (Sou.)	1	7	.125	4.44	1.54	38	12	0	0	...	0-...	103.1	113	59	51	9	46-0	102	.277
2005—Mississippi (Sou.)	3	1	.750	3.65	1.34	6	3	0	0	0	0-2	24.2	21	11	10	2	12-1	16	.233
—Richmond (Int'l.)	1	5	.167	4.33	1.63	25	1	0	0	4	2-3	43.2	49	27	21	5	22-2	47	.290
—Atlanta (N.L.)	1	0	1.000	5.79	1.79	23	0	0	0	6	1-1	14.0	18	11	9	0	7-0	22	.305
Major League totals (1 year)	1	0	1.000	5.79	1.79	23	0	0	0	6	1-1	14.0	18	11	9	0	7-0	22	.305

DIVISION SERIES RECORD

Year Team (League)	W	L	Pct.	ERA	WHIP	G	GS	CG	ShO	Hld.	Sv.-Opp.	IP	H	R	ER	HR	BB-IBB	SO	Avg.
2005—Atlanta (N.L.)	0	0	...	0.00	0.00	1	0	0	0	0	0-0	1.0	0	0	0	0	0-0	1	.000

MCCANN, BRIAN — C

PERSONAL: Born February 20, 1984, in Athens, Ga. ... 6-3/210. ... Bats left, throws right. ... Full name: Brian Michael McCann.

TRANSACTIONS/CAREER NOTES: Selected by Atlanta Braves organization in second round of 2002 free-agent draft.

2005 GAMES PLAYED BY POSITION (MLB): C—57.

M

SCOUTING REPORT *Offense:* This lefthanded-hitting receiver has a very advanced approach at the plate for a young player. Has a quick bat and likes the ball down, but has enough bat speed to get on top of the ball upstairs. Will become a good breaking-ball hitter. Has power when he pulls the ball. Stays in against lefthanded pitching. Hits well with runners in scoring position. *Defense:* He has extremely soft hands and is quiet behind the plate. Is so far advanced that he catches John Smoltz. Frames pitches exceptionally well and has a strong, accurate arm to go with excellent footwork. *Outlook:* McCann is one of the most advanced catchers to come in to the league in many years. Will be a solid everyday catcher for years. Could force the Braves to move Johnny Estrada this winter. *Grade 7.8*

BRIAN McCANN'S HITTING ZONE

.000	.333	.444
.333	.381	.267
.500	.273	.182

LEFTY-RIGHTY SPLITS

vs.	Avg.	AB	H	2B	3B	HR	RBI	BB	SO	OBP	Slg.
L	.333	36	12	2	0	2	5	2	10	.385	.556
R	.264	144	38	5	0	3	18	16	16	.335	.361

										BATTING										FIELDING	
Year Team (League)	Pos.	G	AB	R	H	2B	3B	HR	RBI	BB	SO	HBP	GDP	SB-CS	Avg.	OBP	SLG	OPS		E	Avg.
2002— GC Braves (GCL)	C	29	100	9	22	5	0	2	11	10	22	1	0	0-0	.220	.295	.330	.625			.993
2003— Rome (S. Atl.)	C	115	424	40	123	31	3	12	71	24	73	2	5	7-4	.290	.329	.462	.791		3	.995
2004— Myrtle Beach (Carol.)	C	111	385	45	107	35	0	16	66	31	54	4	6	2-2	.278	.337	.494	.831		7	.988
2005— Mississippi (Sou.)	C-DH	48	166	27	44	13	2	6	26	25	26	2	2	2-3	.265	.359	.476	.834		1	.997
— Atlanta (N.L.)	C	59	180	20	50	7	0	5	23	18	26	1	5	1-1	.278	.345	.400	.745		3	.991
Major League totals (1 year)		59	180	20	50	7	0	5	23	18	26	1	5	1-1	.278	.345	.400	.745		3	.991

DIVISION SERIES RECORD

Year Team (League)	Pos.	G	AB	R	H	2B	3B	HR	RBI	BB	SO	HBP	GDP	SB-CS	Avg.	OBP	SLG	OPS	E	Avg.
2005— Atlanta (N.L.)	C	3	16	2	3	0	0	2	5	0	6	0	0	0-0	.188	.188	.563	.750	0	1.000

McCARTHY, BRANDON   P

PERSONAL: Born July 7, 1983, in Glendale, Calif. ... 6-7/190. ... Throws right, bats right. ... Full name: Brandon Patrick McCarthy. ... Junior college: Lamar (CO) Community College.
TRANSACTIONS/CAREER NOTES: Selected by Chicago White Sox organization in 17th round of 2002 free-agent draft.
CAREER HITTING: 0-for-2 (.000), 0 R, 0 2B, 0 3B, 0 HR, 0 RBI.

BRANDON McCARTHY'S PITCHING ZONE

.250	.429	.167
.360	.306	.359
.200	.091	.105

LEFTY-RIGHTY SPLITS

vs.	Avg.	AB	H	2B	3B	HR	RBI	BB	SO	OBP	Slg.
L	.205	122	25	8	0	3	13	9	28	.258	.344
R	.276	134	37	5	1	10	14	8	20	.326	.552

Year Team (League)	W	L	Pct.	ERA	WHIP	G	GS	CG	ShO	Hld.	Sv.-Opp.	IP	H	R	ER	HR	BB-IBB	SO	Avg.
2002— Ariz. White Sox (Ariz.)	4	4	.500	2.76	1.19	14	14	0	0	...	0-...	78.1	78	40	24	6	15-1	79	.255
2003— Great Falls (Pio.)	9	4	.692	3.65	1.19	16	15	1	0	...	0-...	101.0	105	49	41	7	15-0	125	.263
2004— Kannapolis (S. Atl.)	8	5	.615	3.64	1.07	15	15	3	1	...	0-...	94.0	80	41	38	10	21-0	113	.235
— Win.-Salem (Car.)	6	0	1.000	2.08	0.65	8	8	0	0	...	0-...	52.0	31	12	12	3	3-0	60	.171
— Birmingham (Sou.)	3	1	.750	3.46	1.12	4	4	0	0	...	0-...	26.0	23	10	10	2	6-1	29	.237
2005— Charlotte (Int'l)	7	7	.500	3.92	1.14	20	19	1	1	0	0-0	119.1	104	53	52	16	32-0	130	.233
— Chicago (A.L.)	3	2	.600	4.03	1.18	12	10	0	0	0	0-0	67.0	62	30	30	13	17-0	48	.242
Major League totals (1 year)	3	2	.600	4.03	1.18	12	10	0	0	0	0-0	67.0	62	30	30	13	17-0	48	.242

McCARTY, DAVE   1B/OF

PERSONAL: Born November 23, 1969, in Houston. ... 6-5/215. ... Bats right, throws left. ... Full name: David Andrew McCarty. ... High school: Sharpstown (Houston). ... College: Stanford.
TRANSACTIONS/CAREER NOTES: Selected by Minnesota Twins organization in first round (third pick overall) of 1991 free-agent draft. ... Traded by Twins to Cincinnati Reds for P John Courtright (June 8, 1995). ... Traded by Reds with OF Deion Sanders and Ps Ricky Pickett, Scott Service and John Roper to San Francisco Giants for OF Darren Lewis and Ps Mark Portugal and Dave Burba (July 21, 1995). ... On disabled list (June 6-27, 1996); included rehabilitation assignment to Phoenix. ... Traded by Giants to Seattle Mariners for OFs Jay Leach and Scott Smith (January 30, 1998). ... Signed as a free agent by Detroit Tigers organization (December 18, 1998). ... Signed as a free agent by Oakland Athletics organization (November 23, 1999). ... Traded by A's to Kansas City Royals for cash (March 24, 2000). ... Released by Royals (May 15, 2002). ... Signed by Tampa Bay Devil Rays organization (May 21, 2002). ... Released by Devil Rays (August 7, 2002). ... Signed by Athletics organization (November 18, 2002). ... Claimed on waivers by Boston Red Sox (August 4, 2003). ... On disabled list (August 13-September 14, 2004); included rehabilitation assignments to Lowell and Pawtucket. ... Career major league pitching: 0-0, 2.45 ERA, 3 G, 3.2 IP, 2 H, 1 R, 1 ER, 1 BB, 4 SO.
2005 GAMES PLAYED BY POSITION (MLB): 1B—12, OF—1.

LEFTY-RIGHTY SPLITS

vs.	Avg.	AB	H	2B	3B	HR	RBI	BB	SO	OBP	Slg.
L	.000	0	0	0	0	0	0	1	0	1.000	.000
R	.500	4	2	0	0	0	2	1	0	.600	.500

										BATTING									FIELDING	
Year Team (League)	Pos.	G	AB	R	H	2B	3B	HR	RBI	BB	SO	HBP	GDP	SB-CS	Avg.	OBP	SLG	OPS	E	Avg.
1991— Visalia (Calif.)	OF	15	50	16	19	3	0	3	8	13	7	3	0	3-1	.380	.530	.620	1.150	0	1.000
— Orlando (South.)	OF	28	88	18	23	4	0	3	11	10	20	2	1	0-1	.261	.350	.409	.759	1	.977
1992— Orlando (South.)	1B-OF	129	456	75	124	16	2	18	79	55	89	8	8	6-6	.272	.356	.434	.790	9	.977
— Portland (PCL)	1B-OF	7	26	7	13	2	0	1	8	5	3	1	1	1-0	.500	.594	.692	1.286	1	.977
1993— Portland (PCL)	OF-1B	40	143	42	55	11	0	8	31	27	25	1	3	5-2	.385	.477	.629	1.106	2	.990
— Minnesota (A.L.)	OF-1B-DH	98	350	36	75	15	2	2	21	19	80	1	13	2-6	.214	.257	.286	.542	8	.982
1994— Minnesota (A.L.)	1B-OF	44	131	21	34	8	2	1	12	7	32	5	2	2-1	.260	.322	.374	.696	5	.982
— Salt Lake (PCL)	OF-1B	55	186	32	47	9	3	3	19	35	34	4	9	1-3	.253	.379	.382	.761	5	.976
1995— Minnesota (A.L.)	1B-OF	25	55	10	12	3	1	0	4	4	16	1	5	0-0	.218	.279	.309	.588	1	.993
— Indianapolis (A.A.)	1B	37	140	31	47	10	1	8	32	15	30	1	0	0-0	.336	.401	.593	.994	2	.994
— Phoenix (PCL)	1B-OF-DH	37	151	31	53	19	2	4	19	17	27	6	6	1-1	.351	.434	.583	1.017	2	.995
— San Francisco (N.L.)	OF-1B	12	20	1	5	1	0	0	2	4	0	0	0	1-0	.250	.318	.300	.618	1	.990
1996— San Francisco (N.L.)	1B-OF	91	175	16	38	3	0	6	24	18	43	2	5	2-1	.217	.294	.337	.632	5	.990
— Phoenix (PCL)	OF-1B	6	25	4	10	1	1	1	7	2	4	0	0	0-0	.400	.429	.640	1.069	1	1.000
1997— Phoenix (PCL)	1B-DH-OF	121	434	85	153	27	5	22	92	49	75	2		9-4	.353	.419	.590	1.009	3	.995
1998— Tacoma (PCL)	OF-1B-DH	108	398	73	126	30	2	11	52	59	85	6	15	9-6	.317	.411	.485	.896	2	.996

Year	Team (League)	Pos.	G	AB	R	H	2B	3B	HR	RBI	BATTING BB	SO	HBP	GDP	SB-CS	Avg.	OBP	SLG	OPS	FIELDING E	Avg.
	—Seattle (A.L.)	OF-1B	8	18	1	5	0	0	1	2	5	4	0	0	1-0	.278	.435	.444	.879	0	1.000
1999	—Toledo (Int'l)	1B-OF-DH	132	466	85	125	24	3	31	77	70	110	4	9	6-6	.268	.366	.532	.899	2	.998
2000	—Kansas City (A.L.)	1B-OF-DH	103	270	34	75	14	2	12	53	22	68	0	6	0-0	.278	.329	.478	.807	5	.991
2001	—Kansas City (A.L.)	1B-OF-DH	98	200	26	50	10	0	7	26	24	45	1	8	0-0	.250	.328	.405	.733	8	.984
2002	—Kansas City (A.L.)	1B-DH	13	32	3	3	1	0	1	2	2	10	0	1	0-0	.094	.147	.219	.366	0	1.000
	—Durham (Int'l)	1B-OF	29	114	25	37	7	1	8	22	14	33	0	1	0-1	.325	.398	.614	1.012	2	.992
	—Tampa Bay (A.L.)	OF	12	34	2	6	0	0	1	2	4	9	2	0	0-0	.176	.300	.265	.565	0	1.000
2003	—Sacramento (PCL)	1B-DH-OF	91	352	69	95	23	2	15	72	44	71	3	12	4-1	.270	.351	.474	.826	4	.993
	—Oakland (A.L.)	1B-OF	8	26	2	7	2	0	0	2	1	7	0	0	0-0	.269	.286	.346	.632	1	.970
	—Boston (A.L.)	OF-1B-OF	16	27	4	11	3	0	1	6	2	7	0	0	0-0	.407	.448	.630	1.078	1	.970
2004	—Pawtucket (Int'l)	1B-DH	3	7	2	2	0	0	0	1	4	2	1	0	0-0	.286	.583	.286	.869	0	1.000
	—Lowell (NY-Penn)	1B	1	3	1	2	1	0	0	1	1	0	0	0	0-0	.667	.750	1.000	1.750	0	1.000
	—Boston (A.L.)	1B-OF-P	91	151	24	39	8	1	4	17	14	40	2	5	1-0	.258	.327	.404	.731	3	.991
2005	—Boston (A.L.)	1B-OF	13	4	2	2	0	0	0	2	2	0	0	0	0-0	.500	.667	.500	1.167	0	1.000
	American League totals (10 years)		529	1298	165	319	64	8	30	149	106	320	12	37	6-8	.246	.306	.377	.683	32	.987
	National League totals (2 years)		103	195	17	43	4	0	6	26	20	47	2	5	3-1	.221	.297	.333	.630	4	.988
	Major League totals (11 years)		632	1493	182	362	68	8	36	175	126	367	14	42	9-9	.242	.305	.371	.676	36	.987

DIVISION SERIES RECORD

Year	Team (League)	Pos.	G	AB	R	H	2B	3B	HR	RBI	BB	SO	HBP	GDP	SB-CS	Avg.	OBP	SLG	OPS	E	Avg.
2003	—Boston (A.L.)		1	0	0	0	0	0	0	0	0	0	0	0	0-0	...	...	...	...	0	...

CHAMPIONSHIP SERIES RECORD

Year	Team (League)	Pos.	G	AB	R	H	2B	3B	HR	RBI	BB	SO	HBP	GDP	SB-CS	Avg.	OBP	SLG	OPS	E	Avg.
2003	—Boston (A.L.)	PH	1	1	0	0	0	0	0	0	0	1	0	0	0-0	.000	.000	.000	.000	0	...

MCCLAIN, SCOTT — 3B

PERSONAL: Born May 19, 1972, in Simi Valley, Calif. ... 6-4/220. ... Bats right, throws right. ... Full name: Scott Michael McClain. ... High school: Atascadero (Calif.).

TRANSACTIONS/CAREER NOTES: Selected by Baltimore Orioles organization in 22nd round of 1990 free-agent draft. ... Traded by Orioles with IF Manny Alexander to New York Mets for P Hector Ramirez (March 22, 1997). ... Signed as a free agent by Tampa Bay Devil Rays organization (December 19, 1997). ... Released by Devil Rays (December 13, 1999). ... Signed by Colorado Rockies organization (February 15, 2000). ... Signed by Seibu of the Japan Pacific League (December 6, 2000). ... Signed by Chicago Cubs organization (December 15, 2003). ... Signed to play with Seibu of the Japan League (April 4, 2004). ... Signed by Cubs (August 27, 2005).

2005 GAMES PLAYED BY POSITION (MLB): 1B—4, 3B—3.

LEFTY-RIGHTY SPLITS

vs.	Avg.	AB	H	2B	3B	HR	RBI	BB	SO	OBP	Slg.
L	.000	3	0	0	0	0	0	1	0	.250	.000
R	.182	11	2	1	0	0	1	1	2	.250	.273

Year	Team (League)	Pos.	G	AB	R	H	2B	3B	HR	RBI	BATTING BB	SO	HBP	GDP	SB-CS	Avg.	OBP	SLG	OPS	FIELDING E	Avg.
1990	—Bluefield (Appal.)	3B-P-OF	40	107	20	21	2	0	4	15	22	35	2	1	2-3	.196	.333	.327	.660	8	.901
1991	—Kane Co. (Midw.)	3B	25	81	9	18	0	0	0	4	17	25	0	4	1-1	.222	.357	.222	.579	4	.942
	—Bluefield (Appal.)	3B-2B-SS	41	148	16	39	5	0	0	24	15	39	3	3	5-3	.264	.341	.297	.638	15	.882
1992	—Kane Co. (Midw.)	3B-SS-3B	96	316	43	84	12	2	3	30	48	62	6	5	7-4	.266	.372	.345	.717	26	.917
1993	—Frederick (Carolina)	1B-3B-SS	133	427	65	111	22	2	9	54	70	88	6	8	10-6	.260	.370	.384	.754	24	.936
1994	—Bowie (East.)	3B-SS	133	427	71	103	29	1	11	58	72	89	1	14	6-3	.241	.347	.391	.738	22	.933
1995	—Bowie (East.)	3B	70	259	41	72	14	1	13	61	25	44	3	13	2-1	.278	.344	.490	.834	16	.933
	—Rochester (Int'l)	3B	61	199	32	50	9	1	8	22	23	34	1	5	0-1	.251	.329	.427	.756	11	.940
1996	—Rochester (Int'l)	3B	131	463	76	130	23	4	17	69	61	109	1	8	8-6	.281	.361	.458	.819	17	.954
1997	—Norfolk (Int'l)	3B-SS-1B-DH	127	429	71	120	29	2	21	64	64	93	2	8	1-3	.280	.370	.503	.873	19	.958
1998	—Durham (Int'l)	3B-DH-SS	126	472	91	141	35	0	34	109	66	113	2	9	6-2	.299	.385	.589	.974	12	.964
	—Tampa Bay (A.L.)	1B-3B	9	20	2	2	0	0	0	0	2	6	...	...	0-0	.100	.182	.100	.282	1	.970
1999	—Durham (Int'l)	3B-DH-1B-C	137	533	106	134	33	1	28	104	73	156	3	11	4-2	.251	.341	.475	.816	18	.949
2000	—Colo. Springs (PCL)	3B	123	438	76	121	25	3	25	87	62	89	6	11	8-9	.276	.369	.518	.887	17	.948
2001	—Seibu (Jp. Pac.)		135	481	77	119	28	0	39	87	78	142	1	0	3-0	.247	.353	.549	.902	...	...
2002	—Seibu (Jp. Pac.)		19	63	6	15	0	0	2	5	8	20	1	0	0-0	.238	.381	.397	.778	...	...
2003	—Seibu (Jp. Pac.)		131	418	55	94	19	0	26	69	64	103	0	6	2-0	.225	.326	.457	.783	...	...
2004	—Seibu (Jp. Pac.)		35	76	10	14	0	0	4	10	8	19	1	...	0-0	.184	.271	.355	.626	0	1.000
2005	—Iowa (PCL)	3B-1B-DH-SS	121	423	75	123	27	2	30	93	45	84	4	17	1-1	.291	.358	.577	.934	12	.977
	—Chicago (N.L.)	1B-3B	13	14	1	2	1	0	0	1	2	2	0	1	0-0	.143	.250	.214	.464	0	1.000
	American League totals (1 year)		9	20	2	2	0	0	0	0	2	6	...	...	0-0	.100	...	.100	...	1	.970
	National League totals (1 year)		13	14	1	2	1	0	0	1	2	2	0	1	0-0	.143	.250	.214	.464	0	1.000
	Major League totals (2 years)		22	34	3	4	1	0	0	1	4	8	0	1	0-0	.118	.211	.147	.358	1	.980

MCCLUNG, SETH — P

PERSONAL: Born February 7, 1981, in Lewisburg, W.Va. ... 6-6/235. ... Throws right, bats left. ... Full name: Michael Seth McClung. ... High school: Greenbrier East (Lewisburg, W.Va.).

TRANSACTIONS/CAREER NOTES: Selected by Tampa Bay Devil Rays organization in fifth round of 1999 free-agent draft. ... On disabled list (May 23, 2003-remainder of season; and February 23-August 3, 2004); included rehabilitation assignments to Charleston, S.C., and Montgomery. ... On bereavement list (August 31-September 3, 2005).

CAREER HITTING: 0-for-0 (.000), 0 R, 0 2B, 0 3B, 0 HR, 0 RBI.

SCOUTING REPORT

Throws: His fastball reaches 90-96 mph and he complements it with a curve and change. **Tendencies:** Coming off surgery that cost him the 2004 season, McClung regained his good angle to the plate, keeping good life on his fastball. Has a tendency to drift and struggles with command. Will cut his fastball to give it a sliding effect. Can vary speeds on a tight curve to keep hitters from sitting on fastball. Has good arm speed with movement on his change that causes it to occasionally sink. **Outlook:** McClung has well above-average stuff that he just needs to command. Has no idea how good he could become. **Grade 6.1**

SETH McCLUNG'S PITCHING ZONE

.316	.250	.188
.218	.286	.380
.136	.233	.318

LEFTY-RIGHTY SPLITS

vs.	Avg.	AB	H	2B	3B	HR	RBI	BB	SO	OBP	Slg.
L	.294	228	67	15	3	15	51	31	49	.379	.583
R	.197	198	39	9	0	5	23	31	43	.318	.318

Year Team (League)	W	L	Pct.	ERA	WHIP	G	GS	CG	ShO	Hld.	Sv.-Opp.	IP	H	R	ER	HR	BB-IBB	SO	Avg.
1999—Princeton (Appal.)	2	4	.333	7.69	2.21	13	10	0	0	...	0-...	45.2	53	47	39	3	48-0	46	.285
2000—Char., S.C. (SAL)	2	1	.667	3.19	1.58	6	6	0	0	...	0-...	31.0	30	14	11	0	19-0	26	.246
—Hudson Valley (NYP)	2	2	.500	1.85	1.24	8	8	0	0	...	0-...	43.2	37	18	9	0	17-0	38	.227
2001—Char., S.C. (SAL)	10	11	.476	2.79	1.19	28	28	2	1	...	0-...	164.1	142	72	51	6	53-1	165	.231
2002—Bakersfield (Calif.)	3	2	.600	2.92	1.24	7	7	0	0	...	0-...	37.0	35	16	12	1	11-0	48	.243
—Orlando (South.)	5	7	.417	5.37	1.68	20	19	0	0	...	0-...	114.0	138	74	68	12	53-0	64	.299
2003—Tampa Bay (A.L.)	4	1	.800	5.35	1.50	12	5	0	0	1	0-0	38.2	33	23	23	6	25-1	25	.241
2004—Char., S.C. (SAL)	0	0	.000	0.00	0.96	3	3	0	0	...	0-...	9.1	5	0	0	0	4-0	10	.152
—Montgom. (Sou.)	1	1	.500	4.73	1.05	3	3	0	0	...	0-...	13.1	10	7	7	3	4-0	8	.208
—Durham (Int'l)	2	1	.667	3.29	1.24	11	0	0	0	...	0-...	13.2	10	5	5	0	7-0	12	.196
2005—Durham (Int'l)	2	0	1.000	3.93	1.58	6	3	0	0	0	0-0	18.1	23	12	8	1	6-1	19	.303
—Tampa Bay (A.L.)	7	11	.389	6.59	1.54	34	17	0	0	2	0-1	109.1	106	85	80	20	62-1	92	.249
Major League totals (2 years)	11	12	.478	6.26	1.53	46	22	0	0	3	0-1	148.0	139	108	103	26	87-2	117	.247

MCCRACKEN, QUINTON — OF

PERSONAL: Born August 16, 1970, in Wilmington, N.C. ... 5-7/188. ... Bats both, throws right. ... Full name: Quinton Antoine McCracken. ... High school: South Brunswick (Southport, N.C.). ... College: Duke.

TRANSACTIONS/CAREER NOTES: Selected by Colorado Rockies organization in 25th round of 1992 free-agent draft. ... Selected by Tampa Bay Devil Rays in first round (fourth pick overall) of expansion draft (November 18, 1997). ... On disabled list (May 25, 1999-remainder of season). ... Released by Devil Rays (November 27, 2000). ... Signed by St. Louis Cardinals (December 22, 2000). ... Released by Cardinals (March 28, 2001). ... Signed by Minnesota Twins organization (April 13, 2001). ... Signed as a free agent by Arizona Diamondbacks (January 9, 2002). ... Traded by Diamondbacks to Seattle Mariners for 1B Greg Colbrunn and cash (December 15, 2003). ... Released by Mariners (June 7, 2004). ... Signed by Diamondbacks organization (June 11, 2004).

2005 GAMES PLAYED BY POSITION (MLB): OF—59.

SCOUTING REPORT

He is a fourth outfielder/pinch hitter who is a good contact hitter but lacks power and doesn't have the patience to lead off. Is not a run producer. No longer runs well and has questionable instincts. Has below-average range, gets late jumps and has a weak arm. **Grade 4.7**

QUINTON McCRACKEN'S HITTING ZONE

.227	.250	.091
.267	.261	.371
.240	.000	.125

LEFTY-RIGHTY SPLITS

vs.	Avg.	AB	H	2B	3B	HR	RBI	BB	SO	OBP	Slg.
L	.261	46	12	1	0	1	5	6	8	.340	.348
R	.231	169	39	3	0	3	8	17	27	.305	.284

Year Team (League)	Pos.	G	AB	R	H	2B	3B	HR	RBI	BB	SO	HBP	GDP	SB-CS	Avg.	OBP	SLG	OPS	E	Avg.
1992—Bend (N'west)	2B-OF	67	232	37	65	13	2	0	27	25	39	0	6	18-6	.280	.347	.353	.701	†17	.930
1993—Central Valley (Cal.)	2B-OF	127	483	94	141	17	7	2	58	78	90	2	15	60-19	.292	.390	.369	.758	13	.946
1994—New Haven (East.)	OF	136	544	94	151	27	4	5	39	48	72	4	6	36-19	.278	.338	.369	.708	8	.972
1995—New Haven (East.)	OF-DH	55	221	33	79	11	4	1	26	21	32	3	2	26-8	.357	.419	.457	.876	3	.971
—Colo. Springs (PCL)	OF-DH	61	244	55	88	14	6	3	28	23	30	1	4	17-6	.361	.418	.504	.922	1	.991
—Colorado (N.L.)	OF	3	1	0	0	0	0	0	0	0	1	0	0	0-0	.000	.000	.000	.000	0	...
1996—Colorado (N.L.)	OF	124	283	50	82	13	6	3	40	32	62	1	5	17-6	.290	.363	.410	.773	6	.957
1997—Colorado (N.L.)	OF	147	325	69	95	11	1	3	36	42	62	1	6	28-11	.292	.374	.360	.734	4	.980
1998—Tampa Bay (A.L.)	OF	155	614	77	179	38	7	9	59	41	107	3	12	19-10	.292	.335	.410	.745	3	.992
1999—Tampa Bay (A.L.)	OF	40	148	20	37	6	1	1	18	14	23	1	7	6-5	.250	.317	.324	.641	1	.988
2000—Tampa Bay (A.L.)	OF	15	31	5	4	0	0	0	2	6	4	0	3	0-1	.129	.270	.129	.399	0	1.000
—Durham (Int'l)	OF	85	334	54	87	18	2	2	28	34	57	2	10	13-7	.260	.332	.344	.676	4	.971
2001—Edmonton (PCL)	OF-DH	81	361	53	122	27	4	4	45	21	54	1	5		.338	.374	.468	.842	5	.971
—Minnesota (A.L.)	OF-DH	24	64	7	14	2	2	0	3	5	13	0	2	0-1	.219	.275	.313	.588	1	1.000
2002—Arizona (N.L.)	OF	123	349	60	108	27	8	3	40	32	68	2	3	5-4	.309	.367	.458	.825	1	.995
2003—Arizona (N.L.)	OF-DH	115	203	17	46	5	2	0	18	15	34	0	4	5-1	.227	.276	.271	.547	1	.983
2004—Seattle (A.L.)	OF-DH	19	20	6	3	0	0	0	0	2	4	0	1	1-1	.150	.227	.150	.377	0	1.000
—Tucson (PCL)	OF	15	58	7	19	5	1	1	8	3	5	0	1	2-2	.328	.361	.500	.861	0	1.000
—Arizona (N.L.)	OF	55	156	20	45	11	4	2	13	13	23	0	2	1-2	.288	.341	.410	.751	1	.979
2005—Arizona (N.L.)	OF	134	215	23	51	4	3	1	13	23	35	1	4	4-0	.237	.313	.298	.610	2	.975
American League totals (5 years)		253	877	115	237	46	10	8	82	68	151	4	25	26-18	.270	.323	.373	.695	4	.992
National League totals (7 years)		701	1532	239	427	71	21	12	160	157	285	5	24	61-26	.279	.345	.376	.721	15	.979
Major League totals (11 years)		954	2409	354	664	117	31	20	242	225	436	9	49	87-44	.276	.337	.375	.712	19	.984

DIVISION SERIES RECORD

Year Team (League)	Pos.	G	AB	R	H	2B	3B	HR	RBI	BB	SO	HBP	GDP	SB-CS	Avg.	OBP	SLG	OPS	E	Avg.
2002—Arizona (N.L.)	OF	3	11	1	4	1	0	0	2	1	2	0	0	0-0	.364	.417	.455	.871	0	1.000

M

MCDONALD, JOHN — SS/2B

PERSONAL: Born September 24, 1974, in New London, Conn. ... 5-11/175. ... Bats right, throws right. ... Full name: John Joseph McDonald. ... High school: East Lyme (Conn.). ... College: Providence.

TRANSACTIONS/CAREER NOTES: Selected by Cleveland Indians organization in 12th round of 1996 free-agent draft. ... On disabled list (June 30-July 17 and August 27, 2003-remainder of season); included rehabilitation assignments to Mahoning Valley and Lake County. ... Traded by Indians to Toronto Blue Jays for a player to be named (December 2, 2004); Indians acquired P Thomas Mastny to complete deal (December 14, 2004). ... Traded by Blue Jays to Detroit Tigers for player to be named (July 22, 2005); Blue Jays received cash to complete deal (November 3, 2005). ... Traded by Tigers to Blue Jays for cash (November 10, 2005.)

2005 GAMES PLAYED BY POSITION (MLB): SS—54, 2B—13, 3B—1.

SCOUTING REPORT McDonald has a slow bat and is not patient. Hits the ball in the air too much for a hitter with no power. Is a spectacular fielder with exceptionally quick hands and feet. Has above-average range to both sides and amazing agility. Has one of the quickest pivots in the league and a strong, accurate arm. **Grade 4.4**

JOHN MCDONALD'S HITTING ZONE

.385	.125	.000
.324	.400	.278
.188	.091	.500

LEFTY-RIGHTY SPLITS

vs.	Avg.	AB	H	2B	3B	HR	RBI	BB	SO	OBP	Slg.
L	.291	86	25	3	0	0	11	6	16	.340	.326
R	.263	80	21	3	1	0	5	5	8	.310	.325

Year — Team (League)	Pos.	G	AB	R	H	2B	3B	HR	RBI	BB	SO	HBP	GDP	SB-CS	Avg.	OBP	SLG	OPS	FIELDING E	FIELDING Avg.
1996— Watertown (NYP)	SS	75	278	48	75	11	0	2	26	32	49	5	3	11-1	.270	.354	.331	.685	18	.946
1997— Kinston (Carol.)	SS	130	541	77	140	27	3	5	53	51	75	2	12	6-5	.259	.324	.348	.671	25	.961
1998— Akron (East.)	SS	132	514	68	118	18	2	2	43	43	61	6	7	17-6	.230	.293	.284	.578	23	.966
1999— Akron (East.)	SS-2B	55	226	31	67	12	0	1	26	19	26	2	5	7-3	.296	.351	.363	.713	8	.970
— Buffalo (Int'l)	SS-3B-2B	66	237	30	75	12	1	0	25	11	23	2	5	6-3	.316	.349	.376	.725	13	.956
— Cleveland (A.L.)	2B-SS	18	21	2	7	0	0	0	0	0	3	0	2	0-1	.333	.333	.333	.667	1	.967
2000— Buffalo (Int'l)	SS-2B	75	286	37	77	17	2	1	36	21	29	1	7	4-3	.269	.315	.353	.668	8	.975
— Mahoning Valley (NYP)	SS	5	17	0	2	1	0	0	1	2	3	0	0	0-0	.118	.211	.176	.387	0	1.000
— Cleveland (A.L.)	SS-2B	9	9	0	4	0	0	0	0	0	1	0	0	0-0	.444	.444	.444	.889	0	1.000
— Kinston (Carol.)	SS	1	3	0	1	0	0	0	0	0	0	0	0	0-0	.333	.333	.333	.667	0	1.000
2001— Cleveland (A.L.)	SS-2B-3B	17	22	1	2	1	0	0	0	1	7	1	0	0-0	.091	.167	.136	.303	1	.964
— Buffalo (Int'l)	SS-2B-3B	116	410	52	100	17	1	2	33	33	72	6	11	17-10	.244	.305	.305	.610	23	.955
2002— Cleveland (A.L.)	2B-SS-3B DH	93	264	35	66	11	3	1	12	10	50	5	4	3-0	.250	.288	.326	.614	8	.979
2003— Mahoning Valley (NYP)	SS	1	2	1	0	0	0	0	0	1	0	0	0	0-0	.000	.333	.000	.333	0	1.000
— Lake County (S.Atl.)	SS	1	3	0	0	0	0	0	0	0	0	0	0	0-0	.000	.000	.000	.000	0	1.000
— Cleveland (A.L.)	2B-SS-3B	82	214	21	46	9	1	1	14	11	31	2	4	3-3	.215	.258	.280	.538	10	.964
2004— Cleveland (A.L.)	SS-2B-3B DH	66	93	17	19	5	1	2	7	4	11	0	2	0-0	.204	.237	.344	.581	5	.965
2005— Toronto (A.L.)	SS-2B	37	93	8	27	3	0	0	12	6	12	2	3	5-0	.290	.340	.323	.662	3	.979
— Detroit (A.L.)	SS-2B-3B	31	73	10	19	3	1	0	4	5	12	0	1	1-1	.260	.308	.329	.636	5	.958
Major League totals (7 years)		353	789	94	190	32	6	4	49	37	127	10	18	12-5	.241	.281	.312	.593	33	.971

MCDOUGALL, MARSHALL — 3B

PERSONAL: Born December 19, 1978, in Jacksonville, Fla. ... 6-1/200. ... Bats right, throws right. ... Full name: Marshall James McDougall. ... College: Florida State.

TRANSACTIONS/CAREER NOTES: Selected by Oakland Athletics organization in ninth round of 2000 free-agent draft. ... Traded by Athletics to Cleveland Indians for P Ricky Rincon (July 30, 2002). ... Selected by Texas Rangers organization from Indians organization in Rule 5 major league draft (December 16, 2002). ... Returned to Indians (March 15, 2003). ... Traded by Indians to Rangers for P Derrick Van Dusen (March 15, 2003).

2005 GAMES PLAYED BY POSITION (MLB): 3B—5, OF—3, 2B—2, DH—2, SS—1.

LEFTY-RIGHTY SPLITS

vs.	Avg.	AB	H	2B	3B	HR	RBI	BB	SO	OBP	Slg.
L	.200	10	2	1	0	0	0	0	6	.200	.300
R	.125	8	1	0	0	0	0	0	4	.125	.125

Year — Team (League)	Pos.	G	AB	R	H	2B	3B	HR	RBI	BB	SO	HBP	GDP	SB-CS	Avg.	OBP	SLG	OPS	FIELDING E	FIELDING Avg.
2000— Vancouver (N'west)	2B-3B	27	102	17	28	4	2	0	11	18	19	0	1	5-3	.275	.380	.353	.733	7	.955
2001— Visalia (Calif.)	3B-2B-SS 1B-P	134	534	79	137	43	7	12	84	46	110	7	9	14-2	.257	.321	.431	.752	21	.951
2002— Midland (Texas)	1B-2B-3B SS-3B-SS -2B-1B	84	323	60	98	22	5	9	56	38	57	1	5	7-4	.303	.374	.486	.860	12	.959
— Mahoning Valley (N.Y.-Penn.)	3B-3B	2	5	0	1	0	0	0	0	1	1	0	0	0-0	.200	.333	.200	.533	0	1.000
— Akron (East.)	3B-3B	7	18	6	7	2	0	1	4	6	2	0	1	0-0	.389	.542	.667	1.209	1	.917
2003— Frisco (Texas)	SS-3B-2B	110	418	61	108	16	3	13	69	43	68	2	12	18-3	.258	.328	.404	.732	18	.962
— Oklahoma (PCL)	3B-SS	30	111	11	30	4	2	2	9	13	21	0	2	1-1	.270	.341	.396	.737	7	.933
2004— Frisco (Texas)	SS-3B-2B	18	73	17	23	7	0	2	14	8	12	0	3	0-0	.315	.383	.493	.876	1	.000
— Oklahoma (PCL)	3B-SS	94	354	48	100	23	0	19	69	35	80	1	8	2-1	.282	.349	.508	.857	17	.000
2005— Oklahoma (PCL)	3B-OF-DH SS-2B	57	223	40	76	16	2	11	64	30	45	0	4	5-0	.341	.416	.578	.994	6	.967
— Texas (A.L.)	3B-OF-2B DH-SS	18	18	3	3	1	0	0	0	0	10	0	1	0-0	.167	.167	.222	.389	0	1.000
Major League totals (1 year)		18	18	3	3	1	0	0	0	0	10	0	1	0-0	.167	.167	.222	.389	0	1.000

M

PERSONAL: Born October 19, 1972, in Bristol, Pa. ... 5-11/210. ... Bats right, throws right. ... Full name: Joseph Earl McEwing. ... High school: Bishop Egan (Fairless Hills, Pa.). ... Junior college: County College of Morris (Randolph, N.J.).
TRANSACTIONS/CAREER NOTES: Selected by St. Louis Cardinals organization in 28th round of 1992 free-agent draft. ... Traded by Cardinals to New York Mets for P Jesse Orosco (March 18, 2000). ... On disabled list (July 14-31, 2002); included rehabilitation assignments to Brooklyn and Binghamton. ... On disabled list (August 20, 2004-remainder of season). ... Released by Mets (March 17, 2005). ... Signed by Kansas City Royals organization (March 22, 2005).
2005 GAMES PLAYED BY POSITION (MLB): 3B—29, 1B—20, 2B—11, SS—6, DH—6, OF—5.

SCOUTING REPORT McEwing is not strong and has a long stroke with poor bat speed. Is not disciplined and strikes out too much. Is a good runner and can steal bases on occasion. Has a slow release. Is best suited for second base because he lacks arm strength and range. Is versatile enough to play every position except catcher. *Grade 4.5*

JOE MCEWING'S HITTING ZONE

.111	.200	.222
.190	.238	.143
.300	.500	.125

LEFTY-RIGHTY SPLITS

vs.	Avg.	AB	H	2B	3B	HR	RBI	BB	SO	OBP	Slg.
L	.237	97	23	3	0	1	4	3	18	.260	.299
R	.241	83	20	4	0	0	2	3	17	.267	.289

Year	Team (League)	Pos.	G	AB	R	H	2B	3B	HR	RBI	BB	SO	HBP	GDP	SB-CS	Avg.	OBP	SLG	OPS	E	Avg.
1992—	Ariz. Cardinals (Ariz.)	OF-SS	55	211	55	71	4	2	0	13	24	18	5	1	23-7	.336	.415	.374	.789	1	.991
1993—	Savannah (S. Atl.)	OF	138	511	94	127	35	4	0	43	89	73	4	7	22-9	.249	.362	.321	.683	5	.982
1994—	Madison (Midw.)	OF	90	346	58	112	24	2	4	47	32	53	1	5	18-15	.324	.380	.439	.819	5	.974
	— St. Pete. (FSL)	2B-OF	50	197	22	49	7	0	1	20	19	32	1	4	8-4	.249	.314	.299	.613	2	.985
1995—	St. Pete. (FSL)	2B-OF	75	281	33	64	13	0	1	23	25	49	1	5	2-3	.228	.289	.285	.574	15	.955
	— Arkansas (Texas)	2B-OF	42	121	16	30	4	0	2	12	9	13	1	4	3-2	.248	.305	.331	.636	0	1.000
1996—	Arkansas (Texas)	2B-OF	106	216	27	45	7	3	2	14	13	32	0	8	2-4	.208	.252	.296	.548	2	.987
1997—	Arkansas (Texas)	2B-OF	103	263	33	68	6	3	4	35	19	39	1	6	2-4	.259	.309	.350	.659	2	.988
1998—	Arkansas (Texas)	2B-OF	60	223	45	79	21	4	9	46	21	18	1	2	4-2	.354	.409	.605	1.014	1	.994
	— Memphis (PCL)	2B-3B-OF																			
		SS	78	329	52	110	30	7	6	46	21	39	3	4	11-10	.334	.379	.523	.901	3	.982
	— St. Louis (N.L.)	2B-OF	10	20	5	4	1	0	0	1	1	3	1	0	0-1	.200	.273	.250	.523	0	1.000
1999—	St. Louis (N.L.)	2B-OF-3B																			
		1B-SS	152	513	65	141	28	4	9	44	41	87	6	3	7-4	.275	.333	.398	.730	11	.981
2000—	Norfolk (Int'l)	OF-2B-3B																			
		SS	43	171	28	44	10	2	5	18	16	34	0	3	7-3	.257	.319	.427	.746	4	.973
	— New York (N.L.)	OF-3B-2B																			
		SS	87	153	20	34	14	1	2	19	5	29	1	2	3-1	.222	.248	.366	.614	5	.957
2001—	New York (N.L.)	OF-3B-SS																			
		2B-1B-DH	116	283	41	80	17	3	8	30	17	57	10	2	8-5	.283	.342	.449	.791	3	.981
2002—	New York (N.L.)	OF-SS-1B																			
		2B-3B	105	196	22	39	8	1	3	26	9	50	3	0	4-4	.199	.242	.296	.538	7	.967
	— Brooklyn (N.Y.-Penn.)	DH	1	4	0	1	0	0	0	1	0	0	0	0	0-0	.250	.250	.250	.500		...
	— Binghamton (East.)	2B-3B	1	5	0	0	0	0	0	0	0	1	0	0	0-0	.000	.000	.000	.000	0	1.000
2003—	Norfolk (Int'l)	OF-1B-2B																			
		3B	5	19	3	6	0	1	3	2	2	2	0	3-0	.316	.435	.474	.908	0	1.000
	— New York (N.L.)	2B-SS-OF																			
		1B-3B	119	278	31	67	11	0	1	16	25	57	3	6	3-0	.241	.309	.291	.601	3	.984
2004—	New York (N.L.)	2B-OF-SS																			
		1B-3B	75	138	17	35	3	1	1	16	9	32	0	4	4-1	.254	.297	.312	.609	3	.986
2005—	Omaha (PCL)	3B-2B	5	18	4	3	1	0	0	1	4	2	0	1	0-0	.167	.318	.222	.540	1	.938
	— Kansas City (A.L.)	3B-1B-2B																			
		SS-DH-OF	83	180	16	43	7	0	1	6	6	35	0	5	4-4	.239	.263	.294	.558	4	.984
	American League totals (1 year)		83	180	16	43	7	0	1	6	6	35	0	5	4-4	.239	.263	.294	.558	4	.984
	National League totals (7 years)		664	1581	201	400	82	10	24	152	107	315	24	13	29-16	.253	.307	.363	.671	35	.979
	Major League totals (8 years)		747	1761	217	443	89	10	25	158	113	350	24	18	33-20	.252	.303	.356	.659	39	.980

DIVISION SERIES RECORD

Year	Team (League)	Pos.	G	AB	R	H	2B	3B	HR	RBI	BB	SO	HBP	GDP	SB-CS	Avg.	OBP	SLG	OPS	E	Avg.
2000—	New York (N.L.)	3B-OF	4	1	0	1	0	0	0	0	0	0	0	0	0-0	1.000	1.000	1.000	2.000	0	...

CHAMPIONSHIP SERIES RECORD

Year	Team (League)	Pos.	G	AB	R	H	2B	3B	HR	RBI	BB	SO	HBP	GDP	SB-CS	Avg.	OBP	SLG	OPS	E	Avg.
2000—	New York (N.L.)	3B-OF	4	0	2	0	0	0	0	0	0	0	0	0	0-0	...	...	...	...	0	1.000

WORLD SERIES RECORD

Year	Team (League)	Pos.	G	AB	R	H	2B	3B	HR	RBI	BB	SO	HBP	GDP	SB-CS	Avg.	OBP	SLG	OPS	E	Avg.
2000—	New York (N.L.)	OF	3	1	1	0	0	0	0	0	0	0	0	0	0-0	.000	.000	.000	.000	0	1.000

MCGOWAN, DUSTIN   P

PERSONAL: Born March 24, 1982, in Savannah, Ga. ... 6-3/220. ... Throws right, bats right. ... Full name: Dustin Michael McGowan.
TRANSACTIONS/CAREER NOTES: Selected by Toronto Blue Jays organization in first round (33rd overall) of 2000 free-agent draft.
CAREER HITTING: 0-for-0 (.000), 0 R, 0 2B, 0 3B, 0 HR, 0 RBI.

SCOUTING REPORT *Throws:* His fastball tops out at 97 mph. Also has a slider, curve and changeup. *Tendencies:* He has the potential to be a legitimate four-pitch pitcher. Maintains consistent arm speed and slot on all his pitches. Touch and finish on all his pitches need work after an elbow injury interrupted his initial rapid progess. Fastball has late life. *Outlook:* Health is his biggest obstacle. Could be a fixture in the Blue Jays' rotation beginning this season. **Grade 7.1**

DUSTIN MCGOWAN'S PITCHING ZONE

.200	.571	.111
.310	.313	.278
.385	.167	.333

LEFTY-RIGHTY SPLITS

vs.	Avg.	AB	H	2B	3B	HR	RBI	BB	SO	OBP	Slg.
L	.243	74	18	4	1	5	10	10	12	.345	.527
R	.301	103	31	6	0	2	18	7	22	.364	.417

Year	Team (League)	W	L	Pct.	ERA	WHIP	G	GS	CG	ShO	Hld.	Sv.-Opp.	IP	H	R	ER	HR	BB-IBB	SO	Avg.
2000— Medicine Hat (Pio.)	0	3	.000	6.48	2.04	8	8	0	0	...	0-...	25.0	26	21	18	2	25-0	19	.274
2001— Auburn (NY-Penn)	3	6	.333	3.76	1.58	15	14	0	0	...	0-...	67.0	57	33	28	1	49-0	80	.234
2002— Char., W.Va. (SAL)	11	10	.524	4.19	1.36	28	28	1	0	...	0-...	148.1	143	77	69	10	59-0	163	.251
2003— Dunedin (Fla. St.)	5	6	.455	2.85	1.15	14	14	1	1	...	0-...	75.2	62	29	24	1	25-0	66	.223
— New Haven (East.)	7	0	1.000	3.17	1.27	14	14	1	0	...	0-...	76.2	78	28	27	1	19-0	72	.261
2004— New Hampshire (East.)	2	0	1.000	4.06	1.26	6	6	0	0	...	0-...	31.0	24	14	14	4	15-0	29	.209
2005— Dunedin (Fla. St.)	0	1	.000	4.29	1.24	5	5	0	0	0	0-0	21.0	21	12	10	2	5-0	20	.253
— New Hampshire (East.)	0	2	.000	3.34	1.29	6	6	0	0	0	0-0	35.0	35	16	13	6	10-0	33	.263
— Toronto (A.L.)	1	3	.250	6.35	1.46	13	7	0	0	0	1	0-0	45.1	49	34	32	7	17-0	34	.277
Major League totals (1 year)	1	3	.250	6.35	1.46	13	7	0	0	0	1	0-0	45.1	49	34	32	7	17-0	34	.277

MCLOUTH, NATE   OF

PERSONAL: Born October 28, 1981, in Muskegon, Mich. ... 5-11/185. ... Bats left, throws right. ... Full name: Nathan Richard McLouth.

TRANSACTIONS/CAREER NOTES: Selected by Pittsburgh Pirates organization in 25th round of 2000 free-agent draft.

2005 GAMES PLAYED BY POSITION (MLB): OF—29.

NATE MCLOUTH'S HITTING ZONE

.250	.333	.500
.333	.500	.231
.000	.667	.000

LEFTY-RIGHTY SPLITS

vs.	Avg.	AB	H	2B	3B	HR	RBI	BB	SO	OBP	Slg.
L	.100	20	2	0	0	1	2	1	4	.250	.250
R	.292	89	26	6	0	4	10	2	16	.319	.494

Year	Team (League)	Pos.	G	AB	R	H	2B	3B	HR	RBI	BB	SO	HBP	GDP	SB-CS	Avg.	OBP	SLG	OPS	E	Avg.
2001— Hickory (S. Atl.)	OF-2B	96	351	59	100	17	5	12	54	43	54	7	5	21-5	.285	.371	.464	.835	5	.972
2002— Lynchburg (Caro.)	OF	114	393	58	96	23	4	9	46	41	48	8	12	20-7	.244	.324	.392	.716	5	.968
2003— Lynchburg (Caro.)	OF	117	440	85	132	27	2	6	33	55	68	7	4	40-4	.300	.386	.411	.797	5	.979
2004— Altoona (East.)	OF	133	515	93	166	40	4	8	73	48	62	8	8	31-7	.322	.384	.462	.846	7	.781
2005— Indianapolis (Int'l)	OF-DH	110	397	64	118	20	3	5	39	39	58	7	10	34-8	.297	.364	.401	.765	6	.986
— Pittsburgh (N.L.)	OF	41	109	20	28	6	0	5	12	3	20	5	3	2-0	.257	.305	.450	.755	2	.958
Major League totals (1 year)		41	109	20	28	6	0	5	12	3	20	5	3	2-0	.257	.305	.450	.755	2	.958

MCPHERSON, DALLAS   3B

PERSONAL: Born July 23, 1980, in Greensboro, N.C. ... 6-4/230. ... Bats left, throws right. ... Full name: Dallas Lyle McPherson. ... High school: Randleman (N.C.). ... College: The Citadel.

TRANSACTIONS/CAREER NOTES: Selected by Atlanta Braves organization in 44th round of 1998 free-agent draft; did not sign. ... Selected by Anaheim Angels organization in second round of 2001 free-agent draft. ... Angels franchise renamed Los Angeles Angels of Anaheim for 2005 season. ... On disabled list (July 9, 2005-remainder of season); included rehabilitation assignments to AZL Angels, Rancho Cucamonga and Salt Lake.

2005 GAMES PLAYED BY POSITION (MLB): 3B—60.

SCOUTING REPORT *Offense:* McPherson never was healthy last season and missed the entire second half. Began the year slowly adjusting to off-speed and breaking pitches. Likes the ball down. Power numbers should increase so long as he's healthy, and as he pulls the ball more. Strikes out a lot. When healthy, has the natural bat speed to get a lot better. *Defense:* A hip injury limits his range and could spur a move to first base or designated hitter. Often looks stiff in the field. Will make the routine plays but agility is a concern. Needs help with his footwork and positioning. *Outlook:* The Angels never have seen him play for a whole season, but he has the ability to be a good hitter with power. **Grade 6.2**

DALLAS MCPHERSON'S HITTING ZONE

.250	.250	.067
.238	.462	.306
.286	.000	.280

LEFTY-RIGHTY SPLITS

vs.	Avg.	AB	H	2B	3B	HR	RBI	BB	SO	OBP	Slg.
L	.196	46	9	1	1	0	3	1	17	.213	.261
R	.258	159	41	13	1	8	23	13	47	.318	.503

Year	Team (League)	Pos.	G	AB	R	H	2B	3B	HR	RBI	BB	SO	HBP	GDP	SB-CS	Avg.	OBP	SLG	OPS	E	Avg.
2001— Provo (Pion.)	3B-1B	31	124	30	49	11	0	5	29	12	22	0	2	1-0	.395	.449	.605	1.053	11	.901
2002— Cedar Rap. (Midw.)	3B	132	499	71	138	24	3	15	88	78	128	7	9	30-6	.277	.381	.427	.807	31	.898
2003— Rancho Cuca. (Calif.)	3B	77	292	65	90	21	6	18	59	41	79	6	4	12-6	.308	.404	.606	1.010	14	.926
— Arkansas (Texas)	3B	28	102	22	32	9	1	5	27	19	25	1	4	4-0	.314	.426	.569	.995	2	.955
2004— Arkansas (Texas)	3B-DH	68	262	53	84	17	6	20	69	34	74	4	2	6-5	.321	.404	.660	1.056	12	.929
— Salt Lake (PCL)	3B-DH-OF	67	259	54	81	9	8	20	57	23	95	1	5	6-3	.313	.370	.680	1.047	17	.887
— Anaheim (A.L.)	3B	16	40	5	9	1	0	3	6	3	17	0	0	1-0	.225	.279	.475	.754	0	1.000
2005— Los Angeles (A.L.)	3B	61	205	29	50	14	8	26	14	64	1	5	3-3	.244	.295	.449	.744	7	.944

— 398 —

Year	Team (League)		Pos.	G	AB	R	H	2B	3B	HR	RBI	BB	SO	HBP	GDP	SB-CS	Avg.	OBP	SLG	OPS	E	Avg.
	— Ariz. Angels (Ariz.)		3B	3	9	1	2	1	1	0	2	0	5	0	0	0-0	.222	.222	.556	.778	0	1.000
	— Rancho Cuca. (Calif.)		3B-DH	5	16	3	7	2	0	2	5	3	4	1	0	1-1	.438	.550	.938	1.488	1	.857
	— Salt Lake (PCL)		3B-DH	14	54	8	15	1	2	6	19	7	20	0	1	1-2	.278	.349	.704	1.053	2	.931
	Major League totals (2 years)			77	245	34	59	15	2	11	32	17	81	1	5	4-3	.241	.293	.453	.746	7	.955

DIVISION SERIES RECORD

Year	Team (League)		Pos.	G	AB	R	H	2B	3B	HR	RBI	BB	SO	HBP	GDP	SB-CS	Avg.	OBP	SLG	OPS	E	Avg.
2004— Anaheim (A.L.)			3B	3	9	0	1	0	0	0	1	0	4	0	0	0-0	.111	.111	.111	.222	0	1.000

MEADOWS, BRIAN — P

PERSONAL: Born November 21, 1975, in Montgomery, Ala. ... 6-4/230. ... Throws right, bats right. ... Full name: Matthew Brian Meadows. ... High school: Charles Henderson (Troy, Ala.).

TRANSACTIONS/CAREER NOTES: Selected by Florida Marlins organization in third round of 1994 free-agent draft; pick received as compensation for Colorado Rockies signing Type B free-agent SS Walt Weiss. ... On disabled list (July 28-August 13, 1998). ... Traded by Marlins to San Diego Padres for P Dan Miceli (November 15, 1999). ... Traded by Padres to Kansas City Royals for P Jay Witasick (July 31, 2000). ... Signed as a free agent by Minnesota Twins organization (January 15, 2002). ... Released by Twins (March 30, 2002). ... Signed by Pittsburgh Pirates organization (April 5, 2002).

CAREER HITTING: 21-for-180 (.117), 12 R, 3 2B, 0 3B, 0 HR, 8 RBI.

SCOUTING REPORT *Throws:* He complements his 89-90 mph fastball with a curveball and?changeup. *Tendencies:* He has marginal velocity but his fastball has good sinking and tailing action when he keeps it down. Can't pitch up in the zone. Breaking ball has an in-between break like a curve, but it has the velocity of a slider; breaks short and down to lefthanders and bigger and wider to righthanders. *Outlook:* With an improving fastball, Meadows is a good middle-innings guy. *Grade 6*

BRIAN MEADOWS' PITCHING ZONE

.294	.300	.077
.294	.480	.390
.282	.300	.478

LEFTY-RIGHTY SPLITS

vs.	Avg.	AB	H	2B	3B	HR	RBI	BB	SO	OBP	Slg.
L	.301	103	31	9	0	2	16	7	14	.333	.447
R	.279	190	53	15	2	6	31	14	30	.321	.474

Year	Team (League)		W	L	Pct.	ERA	WHIP	G	GS	CG	ShO	Hld.	Sv.-Opp.	IP	H	R	ER	HR	BB-IBB	SO	Avg.
1994—	GC Marlins (GCL)		3	0	1.000	1.95	1.08	8	7	0	0	...	0-...	37.0	34	9	8	1	6-0	33	.236
1995—	Kane Co. (Midw.)		9	9	.500	4.22	1.39	26	26	1	1	...	0-...	147.0	163	90	69	11	41-0	103	.281
1996—	Brevard County (FSL)		8	7	.533	3.58	1.05	24	23	3	1	...	0-...	146.0	129	73	58	13	25-1	69	.231
	— Portland (East.)		0	1	.000	4.33	1.11	4	4	1	0	...	0-...	27.0	26	15	13	1	4-0	13	.263
1997—	Portland (East.)		9	7	.563	4.61	1.43	29	29	4	0	...	0-...	175.2	204	99	90	23	48-4	115	.292
1998—	Florida (N.L.)		11	13	.458	5.21	1.54	31	31	1	0	...	0-0	174.1	222	106	101	31	46-3	88	.315
1999—	Florida (N.L.)		11	15	.423	5.60	1.52	31	31	0	0	...	0-0	178.1	214	117	111	31	57-5	72	.302
2000—	San Diego (N.L.)		7	8	.467	5.34	1.60	22	22	0	0	...	0-0	124.2	150	80	74	24	50-6	53	.301
	— Kansas City (A.L.)		6	2	.750	4.77	1.37	11	10	2	0	...	0-0	71.2	84	39	38	8	14-0	26	.293
2001—	Kansas City (A.L.)		1	6	.143	6.97	1.69	10	10	0	0	...	0-0	50.1	73	41	39	12	12-2	21	.351
	— Omaha (PCL)		5	5	.545	6.17	1.55	18	18	0	0	...	0-...	105.0	143	73	72	21	20-1	74	.332
2002—	Nashville (PCL)		9	8	.529	4.27	1.25	23	22	1	1	...	0-...	126.1	132	69	60	15	26-1	98	.267
	— Pittsburgh (N.L.)		1	6	.143	3.88	1.21	11	11	0	0	...	0-0	62.2	62	29	27	7	14-8	31	.256
2003—	Nashville (PCL)		7	0	1.000	1.41	0.60	9	8	1	1	...	0-...	51.0	32	11	8	2	0-0	40	.178
	— Pittsburgh (N.L.)		2	1	.667	4.72	1.34	34	7	0	0	5	1-1	76.1	91	45	40	8	11-2	38	.290
2004—	Pittsburgh (N.L.)		2	4	.333	3.58	1.22	68	0	0	0	13	1-2	78.0	76	40	31	7	19-7	46	.259
2005—	Pittsburgh (N.L.)		3	1	.750	4.58	1.41	65	0	0	0	7	0-2	74.2	84	42	38	8	21-7	44	.287
	American League totals (2 years)		7	8	.467	5.68	1.50	21	20	2	0	0	0-0	122.0	157	80	77	20	26-2	47	.317
	National League totals (7 years)		37	48	.435	4.94	1.45	262	102	1	0	25	2-5	769.0	899	459	422	105	218-38	372	.294
	Major League totals (8 years)		44	56	.440	5.04	1.46	283	122	3	0	25	2-5	891.0	1056	539	499	125	244-40	419	.298

MECHE, GIL — P

PERSONAL: Born September 8, 1978, in Lafayette, La. ... 6-3/200. ... Throws right, bats right. ... Full name: Gilbert Allen Meche. ... Name pronounced: mesh. ... High school: Acadiana (Lafayette, La.).

TRANSACTIONS/CAREER NOTES: Selected by Seattle Mariners organization in first round (22nd pick overall) of 1996 free-agent draft. ... On disabled list (May 29-June 13 and July 31, 2000-remainder of season); included rehabilitation assignments to Tacoma, Wisconsin and Everett. ... On disabled list (March 31, 2001-entire season; and August 20-September 16, 2005).

HONORS: Named A.L. Comeback Player of the Year by THE SPORTING NEWS (2003).

CAREER HITTING: 2-for-9 (.222), 0 R, 0 2B, 0 3B, 0 HR, 1 RBI.

SCOUTING REPORT *Throws:* Meche is a power pitcher with a 90-94 mph fastball, a knuckle curve and a changeup. *Tendencies:* He has a very good delivery. Fastball has life up in the zone, but it is easy to follow. Isn't a strikeout pitcher despite his power; had almost as many walks as strikeouts. Must pitch inside and throw his fastball for strikes. Has tight spin and downward break on his curveball. Has good arm speed and movement on his straight change. *Outlook:* There is more in his arm than we have seen. Should consistently have 15-plus wins per season. Must trust his stuff. *Grade 7.7*

GIL MECHE'S PITCHING ZONE

.133	.300	.350
.284	.446	.213
.206	.278	.303

LEFTY-RIGHTY SPLITS

vs.	Avg.	AB	H	2B	3B	HR	RBI	BB	SO	OBP	Slg.
L	.266	308	82	12	0	12	42	36	56	.339	.422
R	.285	249	71	17	2	6	36	36	27	.378	.442

Year	Team (League)		W	L	Pct.	ERA	WHIP	G	GS	CG	ShO	Hld.	Sv.-Opp.	IP	H	R	ER	HR	BB-IBB	SO	Avg.
1996—	Ariz. Mariners (Ariz.)		0	1	.000	6.00	1.67	2	0	0	0	...	0-...	3.0	4	2	2	0	1-0	4	.333
1997—	Everett (N'west)		3	4	.429	3.98	1.33	12	12	1	0	...	0-...	74.2	75	40	33	7	24-0	62	.264

Year	Team (League)	W	L	Pct.	ERA	WHIP	G	GS	CG	ShO	Hld.	Sv.-Opp.	IP	H	R	ER	HR	BB-IBB	SO	Avg.
	—Wisconsin (Midw.)	0	2	.000	3.00	1.33	2	2	0	0	...	0-...	12.0	12	5	4	1	4-0	14	.261
1998—	Wisconsin (Midw.)	8	7	.533	3.44	1.34	26	0	0	0	...	0-...	149.0	136	77	57	9	63-0	168	.238
1999—	New Haven (East.)	3	4	.429	3.05	1.31	10	10	0	0	...	0-...	59.0	51	24	20	3	26-0	56	.231
	—Tacoma (PCL)	2	2	.500	3.19	1.42	6	6	0	0	...	0-...	31.0	31	12	11	3	13-0	24	.261
	—Seattle (A.L.)	8	4	.667	4.73	1.52	16	15	0	0	0	0-0	85.2	73	48	45	9	57-1	47	.237
2000—	Seattle (A.L.)	4	4	.500	3.78	1.34	15	15	1	1	0	0-0	85.2	75	37	36	7	40-0	60	.240
	—Tacoma (PCL)	1	1	.500	3.86	1.43	3	3	0	0	...	0-...	14.0	10	7	6	1	10-0	15	.200
	—Wisconsin (Midw.)	0	0	...	0.00	0.60	1	1	0	0	...	0-...	5.0	1	0	0	0	2-0	6	.067
	—Everett (N'west)	0	1	.000	9.00	3.00	1	1	0	0	...	0-...	1.0	1	1	1	0	0-0	0	.600
2001—	Seattle (A.L.)							Did not play.												
2002—	San Antonio (Texas)	4	6	.400	6.51	1.54	25	13	0	0	...	0-...	65.0	68	49	47	8	32-0	56	.271
2003—	Seattle (A.L.)	15	13	.536	4.59	1.34	32	32	1	0	0	0-0	186.1	187	97	95	30	63-2	130	.263
2004—	Tacoma (PCL)	1	3	.250	5.05	1.44	10	10	0	0	...	0-...	57.0	55	37	32	8	27-1	45	.249
	—Seattle (A.L.)	7	7	.500	5.01	1.46	23	23	0	0	0	0-0	127.2	139	73	71	21	47-0	99	.273
2005—	Seattle (A.L.)	10	8	.556	5.09	1.57	29	26	0	0	0	0-0	143.1	153	92	81	18	72-1	83	.275
Major League totals (5 years)		44	36	.550	4.70	1.44	115	111	3	2	0	0-0	628.2	627	347	328	85	279-4	419	.261

MECIR, JIM   P

PERSONAL: Born May 16, 1970, in Queens, N.Y. ... 6-1/230. ... Throws right, bats both. ... Full name: James Jason Mecir. ... Name pronounced: mah-SEAR. ... High school: Smithtown East (St. James, N.Y.). ... College: Eckerd (Fla.).

TRANSACTIONS/CAREER NOTES: Selected by Seattle Mariners organization in third round of 1991 free-agent draft. ... Traded by Mariners with 1B Tino Martinez and P Jeff Nelson to New York Yankees for P Sterling Hitchcock and 3B Russ Davis (December 7, 1995). ... Traded by Yankees to Boston Red Sox (September 29, 1997), completing deal in which Yankees traded P Tony Armas and a player to be named to Red Sox for C Mike Stanley and IF Randy Brown (August 13, 1997). ... Selected by Tampa Bay Devil Rays in second round (36th pick overall) of expansion draft (November 18, 1997). ... On disabled list (May 12, 1999-remainder of season; and April 27-May 23, 2000). ... Traded by Devil Rays with P Todd Belitz to Oakland Athletics for P Jesus Colome and a player to be named (July 28, 2000). ... On disabled list (August 2-September 5, 2001); included rehabilitation assignment to Sacramento. ... On suspended list (September 2-7, 2002). ... On disabled list (March 21-April 23 and July 24-August 13, 2003); included rehabilitation assignment to Sacramento. ... Signed as a free agent by Florida Marlins (February 2, 2005). ... On disabled list (August 8-September 4, 2005).

CAREER HITTING: 0-for-1 (.000), 0 R, 0 2B, 0 3B, 0 HR, 0 RBI.

SCOUTING REPORT *Throws:* Mecir throws an 89-90 mph fastball, but his screwball is his best pitch. *Tendencies:* Mecir has added some velocity to his fastball, which has good running action. Screwball dives down with good bite and is effective against lefthanders and righthanders because it has a good change in speed and direction. *Outlook:* Mecir's arm seems healthy, but his durability and use are concerns. Knee problems limit him, and he went on the D.L. with a sore shoulder. Can be an effective middle reliever as long as he's not overused. *Grade 6.3*

JIM MECIR'S PITCHING ZONE

.167	.000	.364
.188	.350	.243
.222	.286	.286

LEFTY-RIGHTY SPLITS

vs.	Avg.	AB	H	2B	3B	HR	RBI	BB	SO	OBP	Slg.
L	.226	62	14	2	0	1	12	10	19	.364	.306
R	.263	95	25	3	0	1	7	7	15	.317	.326

Year	Team (League)	W	L	Pct.	ERA	WHIP	G	GS	CG	ShO	Hld.	Sv.-Opp.	IP	H	R	ER	HR	BB-IBB	SO	Avg.
1991—	San Bern. (Calif.)	3	5	.375	4.22	1.55	14	12	0	0	...	1-...	70.1	72	40	33	3	37-0	48	.268
1992—	San Bern. (Calif.)	4	5	.444	4.67	1.59	14	11	0	0	...	0-...	61.2	72	40	32	8	26-0	53	.289
1993—	Riverside (Calif.)	9	11	.450	4.33	1.50	26	26	1	0	...	0-...	145.1	160	89	70	3	58-2	85	.281
1994—	Jacksonville (Sou.)	6	5	.545	2.69	1.34	46	0	0	0	...	13-...	80.1	73	28	24	5	35-3	53	.245
1995—	Tacoma (PCL)	1	4	.200	3.10	1.31	40	0	0	0	...	8-...	69.2	63	29	24	3	28-7	46	.238
	—Seattle (A.L.)	0	0	...	0.00	1.50	2	0	0	0	0	0-0	4.2	5	1	0	0	2-0	3	.263
1996—	Columbus (Int'l)	3	3	.500	2.27	1.09	33	0	0	0	...	7-...	47.2	37	14	12	2	15-2	52	.214
	—New York (A.L.)	1	1	.500	5.13	1.61	26	0	0	0	0	0-0	40.1	42	24	23	6	23-4	38	.275
1997—	Columbus (Int'l)	1	1	.500	1.00	0.74	24	0	0	0	...	11-...	27.0	14	4	3	0	6-0	34	.157
	—New York (A.L.)	0	4	.000	5.88	1.37	25	0	0	0	1	0-1	33.2	36	23	22	5	10-1	25	.279
1998—	Tampa Bay (A.L.)	7	2	.778	3.11	1.20	68	0	0	0	14	0-3	84.0	68	30	29	6	33-5	77	.225
1999—	Tampa Bay (A.L.)	0	1	.000	2.61	1.40	17	0	0	0	6	0-2	20.2	15	7	6	0	14-0	15	.205
2000—	Tampa Bay (A.L.)	7	2	.778	3.08	1.15	38	0	0	0	11	1-4	49.2	35	17	17	2	22-0	33	.201
	—Oakland (A.L.)	3	1	.750	2.80	1.39	25	0	0	0	10	4-9	35.1	35	14	11	2	14-2	37	.255
2001—	Oakland (A.L.)	2	8	.200	3.43	1.27	54	0	0	0	17	3-8	63.0	54	25	24	4	26-7	61	.231
	—Sacramento (PCL)	0	0	...	0.00	1.00	1	1	0	0	...	0-...	1.0	1	0	0	0	0-0	0	.250
2002—	Oakland (A.L.)	6	4	.600	4.26	1.43	61	0	0	0	20	1-6	67.2	68	36	32	5	29-4	53	.259
2003—	Sacramento (PCL)	0	0	...	5.40	2.10	3	2	0	0	...	0-...	3.1	5	4	2	0	2-0	3	.313
	—Oakland (A.L.)	2	3	.400	5.59	1.51	41	0	0	0	12	1-2	37.0	40	25	23	4	16-1	25	.280
2004—	Oakland (A.L.)	0	5	.000	3.59	1.34	65	0	0	0	21	2-7	47.2	45	21	19	5	19-2	49	.239
2005—	Florida (N.L.)	1	4	.200	3.12	1.29	52	0	0	0	13	0-4	43.1	39	17	15	2	17-2	34	.248
American League totals (10 years)		28	31	.475	3.83	1.35	422	0	0	0	112	12-42	483.2	443	223	206	39	208-26	416	.244
National League totals (1 year)		1	4	.200	3.12	1.29	52	0	0	0	13	0-4	43.1	39	17	15	2	17-2	34	.248
Major League totals (11 years)		29	35	.453	3.77	1.34	474	0	0	0	125	12-46	527.0	482	240	221	41	225-28	450	.244

DIVISION SERIES RECORD

Year	Team (League)	W	L	Pct.	ERA	WHIP	G	GS	CG	ShO	Hld.	Sv.-Opp.	IP	H	R	ER	HR	BB-IBB	SO	Avg.
2000—	Oakland (A.L.)	0	0	...	0.00	0.19	3	0	0	0	1	0-0	5.1	1	0	0	0	0-0	2	.059
2001—	Oakland (A.L.)	0	0	...	5.40	1.20	2	0	0	0	1	0-0	3.1	4	2	2	1	0-0	4	.286
2002—	Oakland (A.L.)	0	0	...	0.00	0.00	1	0	0	0	0	0-0	1.0	0	0	0	0	0-0	2	.000
2003—	Oakland (A.L.)	0	0	...	0.00	3.00	1	0	0	0	0	0-0	0.2	1	0	0	0	1-1	0	.333
Division series totals (4 years)		0	0	...	1.74	0.68	7	0	0	0	2	0-0	10.1	6	2	2	1	1-1	8	.162

MEDDERS, BRANDON — P

PERSONAL: Born January 26, 1980, in Tuscaloosa, Ala. ... 6-1/191. ... Throws right, bats right. ... Full name: Brandon Edward Medders. ... College: Mississippi State.
TRANSACTIONS/CAREER NOTES: Selected by Arizona Diamondbacks organization in eighth round of 2001 free-agent draft.
CAREER HITTING: 0-for-1 (.000), 0 R, 0 2B, 0 3B, 0 HR, 0 RBI.

BRANDON MEDDERS' PITCHING ZONE

.000	.500	.167
.300	.250	.333
.083	.200	.000

LEFTY-RIGHTY SPLITS

vs.	Avg.	AB	H	2B	3B	HR	RBI	BB	SO	OBP	Slg.
L	.239	46	11	0	0	0	0	5	14	.314	.239
R	.161	62	10	2	0	2	8	6	17	.239	.290

Year — Team (League)	W	L	Pct.	ERA	WHIP	G	GS	CG	ShO	Hld.	Sv.-Opp.	IP	H	R	ER	HR	BB-IBB	SO	Avg.
2001— Lancaster (Calif.)	1	2	.333	1.32	1.00	31	0	0	0	...	3-...	41.0	26	8	6	1	15-3	53	.182
2002— Lancaster (Calif.)	4	8	.333	5.38	1.49	43	12	0	0	...	15-...	98.2	111	73	59	9	36-1	104	.282
2003— El Paso (Texas)	5	3	.625	4.41	1.31	56	0	0	0	...	7-...	69.1	65	37	34	3	26-6	72	.244
2004— Tucson (PCL)	0	0	...	4.26	1.50	11	0	0	0	...	0-...	12.2	15	7	6	3	4-1	17	.273
2005— Tucson (PCL)	3	2	.600	2.48	1.35	36	0	0	0	1	8-10	36.1	31	11	10	3	18-3	44	.230
— Arizona (N.L.)	4	1	.800	1.78	1.05	27	0	0	0	2	0-0	30.1	21	6	6	2	11-0	31	.194
Major League totals (1 year)	4	1	.800	1.78	1.05	27	0	0	0	2	0-0	30.1	21	6	6	2	11-0	31	.194

MELHUSE, ADAM — C

PERSONAL: Born March 27, 1972, in Santa Clara, Calif. ... 6-2/200. ... Bats both, throws right. ... Full name: Adam Michael Melhuse. ... High school: Lincoln (Stockton, Calif.). ... College: UCLA.
TRANSACTIONS/CAREER NOTES: Selected by Toronto Blue Jays organization in 13th round of 1993 free-agent draft. ... Signed as a free agent by Los Angeles Dodgers organization (December 15, 1999). ... Traded by Dodgers to Colorado Rockies for cash (June 17, 2000). ... Signed as a free agent by Chicago Cubs organization (November 8, 2001). ... Released by Cubs (July 17, 2002). ... Signed by Rockies organization (July 18, 2002). ... Signed as a free agent by Oakland Athletics organization (November 6, 2002).
2005 GAMES PLAYED BY POSITION (MLB): C—24, DH—8.

SCOUTING REPORT Melhuse won't catch very much behind the extremely durable Jason Kendall. Can be very erratic with his throwing. Has arm strength but is inconsistent with his footwork. Blocks balls in the dirt well. Tends to sit back too much and reach for pitches that he should move in front to block. Has a long stroke but hits better and with more power from the left side. Didn't show good bat speed this season with his sporadic play. ***Grade 4.7***

ADAM MELHUSE'S HITTING ZONE

.286	.250	.222
.286	.300	.400
.250	.200	.000

LEFTY-RIGHTY SPLITS

vs.	Avg.	AB	H	2B	3B	HR	RBI	BB	SO	OBP	Slg.
L	.077	13	1	0	0	0	1	3	4	.250	.077
R	.274	84	23	7	0	2	11	2	24	.291	.429

											BATTING												FIELDING	
Year — Team (League)	Pos.	G	AB	R	H	2B	3B	HR	RBI	BB	SO	HBP	GDP	SB-CS	Avg.	OBP	SLG	OPS	E	Avg.
1993— St. Catharines (NYP)	3B	73	266	40	68	14	2	5	32	45	61	0	4	4-0	.256	.360	.380	.740	14	.927
1994— Hagerstown (SAL)	1B-C	118	422	61	109	16	3	11	58	53	77	1	13	6-8	.258	.338	.389	.727	13	.983
1995— Dunedin (Fla. St.)	1B-C-OF	123	428	43	92	20	0	4	41	61	87	1	7	6-1	.215	.312	.290	.601	13	.980
1996— Dunedin (Fla. St.)	1B-3B-C																			
—	OF	97	315	50	78	23	2	13	51	69	68	3	5	3-1	.248	.384	.457	.841	15	.978
— Knoxville (Southern)	C	32	94	13	20	3	0	1	6	14	29	0	3	0-1	.213	.312	.277	.589	2	.989
1997— Knoxville (Southern)	1B-C-OF	31	87	14	20	3	0	3	10	19	19	0	1	0-0	.230	.364	.368	.732	2	.990
— Syracuse (Int'l)	2B-C-OF	118	118	7	28	5	1	2	9	12	18	1	2	1-1	.237	.311	.347	.658	2	.992
1998— Knoxville (Southern)	1B-C-OF	76	240	56	72	22	0	15	43	70	39	0	6	4-4	.300	.458	.579	1.037	11	.977
— Syracuse (Int'l)	3B-C	12	38	4	11	3	0	1	7	7	6	0	0	0-0	.289	.391	.447	.839	2	.965
1999— Knoxville (Southern)	1B-3B-C	107	374	79	110	25	0	19	69	* 108	76	4	10	5-6	.294	.454	.513	.967	4	.986
— Syracuse (Int'l)	C	21	71	15	20	5	0	2	16	10	20	0	1	1-1	.282	.370	.437	.807	0	1.000
2000— San Antonio (Texas)	C-OF-1B																			
—	3B	16	58	17	23	7	0	2	9	11	9	2	2	3-0	.397	.500	.621	1.121	2	.973
— Albuquerque (PCL)	C-1B-3B																			
—	OF	36	108	21	37	9	0	1	19	22	21	...	0	4-2	.343	...	.454	...	0	1.000
— Los Angeles (N.L.)	C	1	1	0	0	0	0	0	0	0	1	0	0	0-0	.000	.000	.000	.000	...	...
— Colorado (N.L.)	1B-C-OF	23	23	3	4	0	1	0	4	3	5	0	1	0-0	.174	.269	.261	.530	0	1.000
— Colo. Springs (PCL)	OF-C-1B	42	140	23	39	5	1	3	18	21	35	...	...	2-3	.279	...	.393	...	2	.987
2001— Colo. Springs (PCL)	C-1B-OF	54	184	26	49	10	1	7	32	31	42	2	8	0-1	.266	.378	.446	.824	5	.986
— Colorado (N.L.)	C-1B	40	71	5	13	2	0	1	8	6	18	0	3	1-0	.183	.241	.254	.494	1	.991
2002— Iowa (PCL)	C-3B-1B																			
—	OF-SS	72	226	33	66	19	0	7	39	28	47	0	...	2-3	.292	.370	.469	.839	7	.983
— Colo. Springs (PCL)	C-1B	34	115	25	40	10	1	6	20	16	23	0	...	2-1	.348	.424	.609	1.033	4	.982
2003— Sacramento (PCL)	C-OF-3B																			
—	DH	45	147	26	42	9	0	3	17	26	32	1	5	0-1	.286	.394	.408	.802	2	.992
— Oakland (A.L.)	C-3B-1B	40	77	13	23	7	0	5	14	9	19	0	4	0-0	.299	.372	.584	.957	2	.986
2004— Oakland (A.L.)	C-3B-1B	64	214	23	55	11	0	11	31	16	47	0	4	0-1	.257	.309	.463	.771	3	.992
2005— Oakland (A.L.)	C-DH	39	97	11	24	7	0	2	12	5	28	0	0	0-0	.247	.284	.381	.666	0	1.000
American League totals (3 years)		148	388	47	102	25	0	18	57	30	94	0	6	0-1	.263	.316	.466	.782	5	.992
National League totals (2 years)		64	95	8	17	2	1	1	12	9	24	0	4	1-0	.179	.245	.253	.498	1	.992
Major League totals (5 years)		212	483	55	119	27	1	19	69	39	118	0	10	1-1	.246	.302	.424	.726	6	.992

M

Year	Team (League)	Pos.	G	AB	R	H	2B	3B	HR	RBI	BB	SO	HBP	GDP	SB-CS	Avg.	OBP	SLG	OPS	E	Avg.
2003—Oakland (A.L.)		C	2	5	1	3	0	1	0	1	0	1	0	0	0-0	.600	.600	1.000	1.600	0	1.000

MENCH, KEVIN — OF

PERSONAL: Born January 7, 1978, in Wilmington, Del. ... 6-0/225. ... Bats right, throws right. ... Full name: Kevin Ford Mench. ... High school: St. Mark's (Wilmington, Del.). ... College: Delaware.

TRANSACTIONS/CAREER NOTES: Selected by Texas Rangers organization in fourth round of 1999 free-agent draft; pick received as part of compensation for Arizona Diamondbacks signing Type A free-agent P Todd Stottlemyre. ... On disabled list (March 21-April 17 and July 9, 2003-remainder of season); included rehabilitation assignment to Frisco. ... On disabled list (May 24-June 12, 2004); included rehabilitation assignment to Frisco.

2005 GAMES PLAYED BY POSITION (MLB): OF—148, DH—1.

SCOUTING REPORT *Offense:* Mench is an aggressive high-ball hitter who has gotten better about using the whole field. Handles the breaking pitch well. Has good bat speed and above-average power to all fields. Is not a good runner, but he hustles. *Defense:* Mench has improved to the point the Rangers used him in center field for a few games last season. Continues to improve his reads. Comes in better than he goes back and has surprising range to the alley. Benefited from his exposure in center when he returned to right and left. *Outlook:* Mench can flat-out hit, and his power is increasing. Has outstanding makeup and gets the most from his ability. *Grade 7*

KEVIN MENCH'S HITTING ZONE

.333	.364	.314
.263	.339	.283
.185	.292	.316

LEFTY-RIGHTY SPLITS

vs.	Avg.	AB	H	2B	3B	HR	RBI	BB	SO	OBP	Slg.
L	.296	125	37	10	2	8	19	17	7	.380	.600
R	.255	432	110	23	1	17	54	33	61	.313	.431

Year	Team (League)	Pos.	G	AB	R	H	2B	3B	HR	RBI	BB	SO	HBP	GDP	SB-CS	Avg.	OBP	SLG	OPS	E	Avg.
1999—Pulaski (Appalachian)	OF	65	260	36	94	22	1	16	60	28	48	2	2	12-2	.362	.420	.638	1.059	4	.989
—Savannah (S. Atl.)	OF	6	23	4	7	1	1	2	8	2	4	0	1	0-0	.304	.360	.696	1.056	2	.900
2000—Charlotte (Fla. St.)	OF	132	491	118	164	39	9	27	121	78	72	7	9	19-7	.334	.427	.615	1.042	1	.996
2001—Tulsa (Texas)	OF	120	475	78	126	34	2	26	83	34	76	6	7	4-6	.265	.319	.509	.828	4	.983
2002—Oklahoma (PCL)	OF	26	98	17	21	8	0	6	15	17	33	2	7	0-0	.214	.342	.480	.821	2	.965
—Texas (A.L.)	OF-DH	110	366	52	95	20	2	15	60	31	83	8	4	1-1	.260	.327	.448	.775	2	.990
2003—Frisco (Texas)	OF	3	11	1	1	0	0	0	0	1	2	0	1	0-0	.091	.167	.091	.258	0	1.000
—Oklahoma (PCL)	OF	29	105	16	28	8	0	4	21	19	15	1	1	2-0	.267	.366	.457	.824	1	1.000
—Texas (A.L.)	OF	38	125	15	40	12	0	2	11	10	17	3	2	1-1	.320	.381	.464	.845	1	.984
2004—Frisco (Texas)	DH-OF	4	16	3	5	0	0	1	1	1	0	0	0	0-0	.313	.353	.500	.853	0	1.000
—Texas (A.L.)	OF-DH	125	438	69	122	30	3	26	71	33	63	6	0	0-0	.279	.335	.539	.874	1	.995
2005—Texas (A.L.)	OF-DH	150	557	71	147	33	3	25	73	50	68	5	6	4-3	.264	.328	.469	.797	4	.987
Major League totals (4 years)		423	1486	207	404	95	8	68	215	124	231	22	18	6-5	.272	.334	.484	.818	8	.990

MENDOZA, RAMIRO — P

PERSONAL: Born June 15, 1972, in Los Santos, Panama. ... 6-2/190. ... Throws right, bats right.

TRANSACTIONS/CAREER NOTES: Signed as a non-drafted free agent by New York Yankees organization (November 13, 1991). ... On disabled list (June 28-July 28 and August 4, 2000-remainder of season); included rehabilitation assignment to Tampa. ... On disabled list (March 26-April 10, 2001; and March 24-April 7, 2002). ... Signed as a free agent by Boston Red Sox (December 31, 2002). ... On disabled list (June 13-July 5 and August 3-September 3, 2003); included rehabilitation assignments to GCL Red Sox, Sarasota and Pawtucket. ... On disabled list (April 8-July 15, 2004); included rehabiltation assignments to Sarasota and Pawtucket. ... Signed as a free agent by Yankees organization (February 16, 2005).

CAREER HITTING: 0-for-3 (.000), 0 R, 0 2B, 0 3B, 0 HR, 0 RBI.

LEFTY-RIGHTY SPLITS

vs.	Avg.	AB	H	2B	3B	HR	RBI	BB	SO	OBP	Slg.
L	.000	1	0	0	0	0	0	0	0	.000	.000
R	.500	4	2	1	0	1	3	0	1	.500	1.500

Year	Team (League)	W	L	Pct.	ERA	WHIP	G	GS	CG	ShO	Hld.	Sv.-Opp.	IP	H	R	ER	HR	BB-IBB	SO	Avg.
1992—Dom. Yankees (DSL)	10	2	.833	2.13	1.10	15	15	5	0	...	0-...	109.2	93	37	26	...	28-...	79	...
1993—GC Yankees (GCL)	4	5	.444	2.79	0.98	15	9	0	0	...	1-...	67.2	59	26	21	3	7-0	61	.224
—Greensboro (S. Atl.)	0	1	.000	2.45	2.18	2	0	0	0	...	0-...	3.2	3	1	1	0	5-0	3	.231
1994—Tampa (Fla. St.)	12	6	.667	3.01	1.25	22	21	1	0	...	0-...	134.1	133	54	45	7	35-1	110	.258
1995—Norwich (East.)	5	6	.455	3.21	1.34	19	19	2	1	...	0-...	89.2	87	39	32	4	33-0	68	.254
—Columbus (Int'l)	1	0	1.000	2.57	0.86	2	2	0	0	...	0-...	14.0	10	4	4	0	2-0	13	.208
1996—Columbus (Int'l)	6	2	.750	2.51	1.19	15	15	0	0	...	0-0	97.0	96	30	27	2	19-0	61	.260
—New York (A.L.)	4	5	.444	6.79	1.70	12	11	0	0	0	0-0	53.0	80	43	40	5	10-1	34	.343
1997—Columbus (Int'l)	0	0	...	5.68	1.26	1	1	0	0	...	0-0	6.1	7	4	4	1	1-0	4	.233
—New York (A.L.)	8	6	.571	4.24	1.38	39	15	0	0	4	2-4	133.2	157	67	63	15	28-2	82	.292
1998—New York (A.L.)	10	2	.833	3.25	1.24	41	14	1	1	5	1-4	130.1	131	50	47	9	30-6	56	.264
1999—New York (A.L.)	9	9	.500	4.29	1.36	53	6	0	0	4	3-6	123.2	141	68	59	13	27-3	80	.284
2000—New York (A.L.)	7	4	.636	4.25	1.31	14	9	1	1	0	0-1	65.2	66	32	31	9	20-1	30	.260
—Tampa (Fla. St.)	0	2	.000	7.20	1.80	2	2	0	0	...	0-...	5.0	9	4	4	0	0-0	7	.409
2001—New York (A.L.)	8	4	.667	3.75	1.11	56	0	0	0	13	6-8	100.2	89	44	42	9	23-3	70	.241
2002—New York (A.L.)	8	4	.667	3.44	1.29	62	0	0	0	12	4-8	91.2	102	43	35	8	16-2	61	.275
2003—GC Red Sox (GCL)	0	0	...	0.00	0.40	2	2	0	0	...	0-0	7.0	3	0	0	0	0-0	4	.130
—Sarasota (Fla. St.)	1	0	1.000	0.00	0.60	1	1	0	0	...	0-0	5.0	2	0	0	0	1-0	4	.133
—Pawtucket (Int'l)	0	0	...	2.00	0.90	4	0	0	0	...	0-0	9.0	8	2	2	1	1-0	9	.235
—Boston (A.L.)	3	5	.375	6.75	1.77	37	0	0	0	3	0-1	66.2	98	51	50	10	20-4	36	.349
2004—Sarasota (Fla. St.)	0	1	.000	4.50	1.50	2	2	0	0	...	0-0	4.0	6	2	2	0	0-0	3	.353
—Pawtucket (Int'l)	0	0	...	4.15	1.50	6	0	0	0	...	0-0	8.2	13	5	4	2	0-0	3	.351
—Boston (A.L.)	2	1	.667	3.52	1.04	30	0	0	0	3	0-0	30.2	25	12	12	3	7-1	13	.225
2005—GC Yankees (GCL)	0	0	...	0.00	0.80	2	2	0	0	...	0-0	5.0	3	1	0	0	1-0	3	.167
—Columbus (Int'l)	1	0	1.000	0.75	0.42	8	0	0	0	...	1-1	12.0	7	1	1	0	4-1	15	.100
—New York (A.L.)	0	0	...	18.00	2.00	1	0	0	0	...	0-0	1.0	2	2	2	1	0-1	1	.400
Major League totals (10 years)	59	40	.596	4.30	1.35	342	62	2	2	44	16-32	797.0	891	412	381	82	181-23	463	.283

M

DIVISION SERIES RECORD

Year Team (League)	W	L	Pct.	ERA	WHIP	G	GS	CG	ShO	Hld.	Sv.-Opp.	IP	H	R	ER	HR	BB-IBB	SO	Avg.
1997— New York (A.L.)	1	1	.500	2.45	0.82	2	0	0	0	0	0-0	3.2	3	1	1	0	0-0	2	.250
1998— New York (A.L.)	Did not play.																		
1999— New York (A.L.)	Did not play.																		
2001— New York (A.L.)	0	0	...	0.00	0.69	3	0	0	0	1	0-0	4.1	2	0	0	0	1-1	5	.133
2002— New York (A.L.)	0	0	...	13.50	3.75	2	0	0	0	0	0-0	1.1	5	2	2	1	0-0	0	.625
Division series totals (3 years)	1	1	.500	2.89	1.18	7	0	0	0	1	0-0	9.1	10	3	3	1	1-1	7	.286

CHAMPIONSHIP SERIES RECORD

Year Team (League)	W	L	Pct.	ERA	WHIP	G	GS	CG	ShO	Hld.	Sv.-Opp.	IP	H	R	ER	HR	BB-IBB	SO	Avg.
1998— New York (A.L.)	0	0	...	0.00	0.92	2	0	0	0	1	0-0	4.1	4	0	0	0	0-0	1	.235
1999— New York (A.L.)	0	0	...	0.00	0.00	2	0	0	0	1	1-1	2.1	0	0	0	0	0-0	2	.000
2001— New York (A.L.)	0	0	...	1.69	0.94	3	0	0	0	1	0-0	5.1	3	1	1	1	2-1	4	.158
2004— Boston (A.L.)	0	1	.000	4.50	1.00	2	0	0	0	0	0-0	2.0	2	1	1	0	0-0	1	.250
Champ. series totals (4 years)	0	1	.000	1.29	0.79	9	0	0	0	3	1-1	14.0	9	2	2	1	2-1	8	.176

WORLD SERIES RECORD

Year Team (League)	W	L	Pct.	ERA	WHIP	G	GS	CG	ShO	Hld.	Sv.-Opp.	IP	H	R	ER	HR	BB-IBB	SO	Avg.
1998— New York (A.L.)	1	0	1.000	9.00	2.00	1	0	0	0	0	0-0	1.0	2	1	1	0	0-0	1	.500
1999— New York (A.L.)	0	0	...	10.80	2.40	1	0	0	0	0	0-0	1.2	3	2	2	0	1-0	0	.429
2001— New York (A.L.)	0	0	...	0.00	0.38	2	0	0	0	0	0-0	2.2	1	0	0	0	0-0	1	.111
World Series totals (3 years)	1	0	1.000	5.06	1.31	4	0	0	0	0	0-0	5.1	6	3	3	0	1-0	2	.300

MENECHINO, FRANK — 2B/SS

PERSONAL: Born January 7, 1971, in Staten Island, N.Y. ... 5-8/198. ... Bats right, throws right. ... Name pronounced: men-a-keen-o. ... High school: Susan E. Wagner (Staten Island, N.Y.). ... College: Alabama.

TRANSACTIONS/CAREER NOTES: Selected by Chicago White Sox organization in 45th round of 1993 free-agent draft. ... Selected by Oakland Athletics organization from White Sox organization in Rule 5 minor league draft (December 15, 1997). ... On disabled list (March 26-April 22, 2004); included rehabilitation assignment to Midland. ... Traded by Athletics to Toronto Blue Jays for future considerations (May 12, 2004). ... Career major league pitching: 0-0, 27.00 ERA, 2 G, 1.1 IP, 8 H, 4 R, 4 ER, 0 BB, 0 SO.

2005 GAMES PLAYED BY POSITION (MLB): 2B—26, DH—25, 3B—9, SS—1.

SCOUTING REPORT Menechino is a good hitter against mediocre pitching. Is a high-fastball hitter who looks for inside pitches to pull. Has some power but is not a good runner. Is not good defensively; has stiff hands, is not fluid and lacks range. *Grade 4.5*

FRANK MENECHINO'S HITTING ZONE

.222	.375	.000
.259	.438	.050
.200	.250	.000

LEFTY-RIGHTY SPLITS

vs.	Avg.	AB	H	2B	3B	HR	RBI	BB	SO	OBP	Slg.
L	.191	94	18	4	0	3	9	17	21	.339	.330
R	.259	54	14	3	0	1	4	8	12	.375	.370

Year Team (League)	Pos.	G	AB	R	H	2B	3B	HR	RBI	BB	SO	HBP	GDP	SB-CS	Avg.	OBP	SLG	OPS	E	Avg.
1993— GC Whi. Sox (GCL)	2B	17	45	10	11	4	1	1	9	12	4	4	1	3-1	.244	.443	.444	.887	1	.979
— Hickory (S. Atl.)	2B	50	178	35	50	6	3	4	19	33	28	4	4	11-2	.281	.403	.416	.819	6	.977
1994— South Bend (Mid.)	2B	106	379	77	113	21	5	5	48	78	70	9	8	15-8	.298	.427	.420	.847	10	.979
1995— Prince Will. (Car.)	2B	137	476	65	124	31	3	6	58	96	75	11	17	6-2	.261	.391	.767	.159	15	.975
1996— Birmingham (Sou.)	2B	125	415	77	121	25	3	12	62	64	84	8	5	7-9	.292	.391	.453	.844	13	.978
1997— Nashville (A.A.) 2B-3B-OF		37	113	20	26	4	0	4	11	26	31	6	2	3-2	.230	.397	.372	.769	9	.948
— Birmingham (Sou.)	2B-3B	90	318	78	95	28	4	12	60	79	77	11	7	7-3	.299	.447	.525	.972	11	.974
1998— Edmonton (PCL)	2B	106	378	72	105	11	7	10	40	70	75	10	11	9-10	.278	.403	.423	.826	7	.979
1999— Vancouver (PCL) 3B-SS-2B		130	501	103	155	31	6	15	88	73	97	9	12	4-5	.309	.403	.497	.900	10	.980
— Oakland (A.L.) ....SS-DH-3B DH		9	9	0	2	0	0	0	0	0	4	0	0	0-0	.222	.222	.222	.444	0	1.000
2000— Oakland (A.L.) ....2B-SS-3B DH-P		66	145	31	37	9	1	6	26	20	45	1	1	1-4	.255	.345	.455	.800	6	.974
— Sacramento (PCL)	SS-3B	9	38	8	12	2	0	2	2	5	4	0	0	1-0	.316	.395	.526	.922	0	1.000
2001— Oakland (A.L.) ....2B-SS-3B DH		139	471	82	114	22	2	12	60	79	97	19	13	2-3	.242	.369	.374	.742	16	.976
2002— Oakland (A.L.) ....2B-3B-SS DH		38	132	22	27	7	0	3	15	20	32	1	4	0-0	.205	.312	.326	.637	2	.986
— Sacramento (PCL) SS-2B-3B		84	314	50	78	12	0	6	50	46	58	8	10	10-3	.248	.356	.344	.700	22	.941
2003— Oakland (A.L.) ....2B-SS-3B DH		43	83	10	16	0	0	2	9	19	16	4	2	0-0	.193	.364	.265	.630	4	.962
2004— Midland (Texas)	2B-DH	4	13	1	4	0	0	0	0	2	1	0	0	0-0	.308	.400	.308	.708	1	.750
— Sacramento (PCL)	2B-DH	4	15	2	4	0	0	0	1	1	0	1	0	0-0	.267	.353	.267	.620	0	1.000
— Oakland (A.L.)	2B-DH	13	33	0	3	0	0	0	1	1	8	1	2	0-0	.091	.143	.091	.234	1	.978
— Toronto (A.L.) 2B-DH-SS 3B-P		72	236	40	71	13	4	9	25	36	44	3	3	0-2	.301	.400	.504	.904	1	.995
2005— Toronto (A.L.) ....2B-DH-3B SS		70	148	22	32	7	0	4	13	25	33	6	3	0-1	.216	.352	.345	.697	1	.992
Major League totals (7 years)		450	1257	207	302	58	7	36	149	200	279	35	28	3-10	.240	.358	.383	.741	31	.980

DIVISION SERIES RECORD

Year Team (League)	Pos.	G	AB	R	H	2B	3B	HR	RBI	BB	SO	HBP	GDP	SB-CS	Avg.	OBP	SLG	OPS	E	Avg.
2000— Oakland (A.L.)	P	1	0	0	0	0	0	0	0	0	0	0	0	0-0	...	...	...	...	0	1.000
2001— Oakland (A.L.)	2B	4	12	2	1	0	0	0	0	1	4	0	0	0-0	.083	.154	.083	.237	1	.957
2003— Oakland (A.L.)	2B	1	0	0	0	0	0	0	0	0	0	0	0	0-0	...	...	...	...	0	...
Division series totals (3 years)		6	12	2	1	0	0	0	0	1	4	0	0	0-0	.083	.154	.083	.237	1	.960

PERSONAL: Born February 1, 1968, in Indianapolis. ... 6-2/205. ... Throws left, bats left. ... Full name: Kent Franklin Mercker. ... High school: Dublin (Ohio).
TRANSACTIONS/CAREER NOTES: Selected by Atlanta Braves organization in first round (fifth pick overall) of June 1986 free-agent draft. ... On disabled list (August 9-24, 1991). ... Traded by Braves to Baltimore Orioles for Ps Joe Borowski and Rachaad Stewart (December 17, 1995). ... Traded by Orioles to Cleveland Indians for 1B Eddie Murray (July 21, 1996). ... Signed as a free agent by Cincinnati Reds (December 10, 1996). ... On disabled list (August 17-September 2, 1997). ... Signed as a free agent by St. Louis Cardinals (December 16, 1997). ... On disabled list (June 14-July 1, 1998). ... Traded by Cardinals to Boston Red Sox for P Mike Matthews and C David Benham (August 24, 1999). ... On disabled list (September 7-23, 1999). ... Signed as a free agent by Anaheim Angels organization (January 26, 2000). ... On disabled list (May 12-August 12, 2000); included rehabilitation assignment to Lake Elsinore. ... Signed as a free agent by Red Sox organization (January 5, 2001). ... Released by Red Sox (March 29, 2001). ... Signed by Colorado Rockies organization (January 31, 2002). ... On disabled list (June 6-July 30, 2002); included rehabilitation assignment to Colorado Springs. ... On suspended list (September 20-23, 2002). ... Signed as a free agent by Reds organization (January 7, 2003). ... On disabled list (June 25-July 10, 2003). ... Traded by Reds to Braves for a player to be named (August 12, 2003); Reds acquired P Matt Belisle to complete deal (August 14, 2003). ... Signed as a free agent by Chicago Cubs (December 19, 2003). ... On disabled list (May 16-June 4, 2004). ... On suspended list (September 13-15, 2004). ... Signed as a free agent by Reds (December 20, 2004).
CAREER HITTING: 28-for-248 (.113), 12 R, 5 2B, 2 3B, 1 HR, 18 RBI.

SCOUTING REPORT *Throws:* Mercker still can get his fastball to the plate at 93 mph and also throws a cut fastball and circle change. *Tendencies:* Mercker is throwing harder than he has in a while and with renewed aggressiveness, coming right after hitters. Is effective pitching inside to righthanders with his cut fastball and change. Prefers to attack lefties by lowering his arm angle and running his fastball away. Has a durable arm and some deception in his delivery. Has very good deception as his arm action makes it difficult to pick up the ball quickly. *Outlook:* More of a one- or two-inning reliever now, Mercker can maintain his fastball if not overworked. *Grade 7*

KENT MERCKER'S PITCHING ZONE

.333	.182	.111
.297	.440	.256
.308	.250	.500

LEFTY-RIGHTY SPLITS

vs.	Avg.	AB	H	2B	3B	HR	RBI	BB	SO	OBP	Slg.
L	.225	102	23	3	2	2	12	6	26	.286	.353
R	.304	135	41	13	1	6	24	13	19	.362	.548

Year	Team (League)	W	L	Pct.	ERA	WHIP	G	GS	CG	ShO	Hld.	Sv.-Opp.	IP	H	R	ER	HR	BB-IBB	SO	Avg.
1986—	GC Braves (GCL)	4	3	.571	2.47	1.12	9	8	0	0	...	0-...	47.1	37	21	13	1	16-1	42	.200
1987—	Durham (Carol.)	0	1	.000	5.40	1.46	3	3	0	0	...	0-...	11.2	11	8	7	1	6-0	14	.256
1988—	Durham (Carol.)	11	4	.733	2.75	1.17	19	19	5	0	...	0-...	127.2	102	44	39	5	47-0	159	.214
	Greenville (Sou.)	3	1	.750	3.35	1.28	9	9	0	0	...	0-...	48.1	36	20	18	2	26-1	60	.201
1989—	Richmond (Int'l)	9	12	.429	3.20	1.20	27	27	4	0	...	0-...	168.2	107	66	60	17	95-4	144	.183
	Atlanta (N.L.)	0	0	...	12.46	3.23	2	1	0	0	0	0-...	4.1	8	6	6	0	6-0	4	.400
1990—	Richmond (Int'l)	5	4	.556	3.55	1.49	12	10	0	0	0	1-...	58.1	60	30	23	1	27-1	69	.260
	Atlanta (N.L.)	4	7	.364	3.17	1.39	36	0	0	0	0	7-10	48.1	43	22	17	6	24-3	39	.236
1991—	Atlanta (N.L.)	5	3	.625	2.58	1.24	50	4	0	0	3	6-8	73.1	56	23	21	5	35-3	62	.211
1992—	Atlanta (N.L.)	3	2	.600	3.42	1.26	53	0	0	0	9	6-9	68.1	51	27	26	4	35-1	49	.207
1993—	Atlanta (N.L.)	3	1	.750	2.86	1.33	43	6	0	0	4	0-3	66.0	52	24	21	2	36-3	59	.214
1994—	Atlanta (N.L.)	9	4	.692	3.45	1.20	20	17	2	1	0	0-0	112.1	90	46	43	16	45-3	111	.220
1995—	Atlanta (N.L.)	7	8	.467	4.15	1.41	29	26	0	0	0	0-0	143.0	140	73	66	16	61-2	102	.258
1996—	Baltimore (A.L.)	3	6	.333	7.76	1.86	14	12	0	0	0	0-0	58.0	73	56	50	12	35-1	22	.307
	Buffalo (A.A.)	0	2	.000	3.94	1.25	3	3	0	0	...	0-...	16.0	11	7	7	3	9-0	11	.193
	Cleveland (A.L.)	1	0	1.000	3.09	1.11	10	0	0	0	2	0-0	11.2	10	4	4	1	3-1	7	.244
1997—	Cincinnati (N.L.)	8	11	.421	3.92	1.36	28	25	0	0	0	0-0	144.2	135	65	63	16	62-6	75	.250
1998—	St. Louis (N.L.)	11	11	.500	5.07	1.56	30	29	0	0	0	0-0	161.2	199	99	91	11	53-4	72	.310
1999—	St. Louis (N.L.)	6	5	.545	5.12	1.70	25	18	0	0	0	0-0	103.2	125	73	59	16	51-3	64	.303
	Boston (A.L.)	2	0	1.000	3.51	1.40	5	5	0	0	0	0-0	25.2	23	12	10	0	13-0	17	.235
2000—	Anaheim (A.L.)	1	3	.250	6.52	1.78	21	7	0	0	1	0-0	48.1	57	35	35	12	29-3	30	.300
	Lake Elsinore (Calif.)	0	0	...	0.00	0.00	1	1	0	0	...	0-...	4.0	0	0	0	0	0-0	3	.000
2001—	Did not play.																			
2002—	Colorado (N.L.)	3	1	.750	6.14	1.75	58	0	0	0	9	0-3	44.0	55	33	30	12	22-2	37	.299
	Colo. Springs (PCL)	0	0	...	21.60	3.00	2	0	0	0	...	0-...	1.2	3	4	4	2	2-0	0	.429
2003—	Cincinnati (N.L.)	0	2	.000	2.35	1.46	49	0	0	0	10	0-3	38.1	31	13	10	5	25-2	41	.225
	Atlanta (N.L.)	0	0	...	1.06	1.29	18	0	0	0	1	1-2	17.0	15	3	2	1	7-2	7	.231
2004—	Chicago (N.L.)	3	1	.750	2.55	1.25	71	0	0	0	16	0-3	53.0	39	15	15	4	27-2	51	.205
2005—	Cincinnati (N.L.)	3	1	.750	3.65	1.35	78	0	0	0	20	4-7	61.2	64	27	25	8	19-4	45	.270
	American League totals (3 years)	7	9	.438	6.20	1.69	50	24	0	0	3	0-0	143.2	163	107	99	25	80-5	76	.287
	National League totals (14 years)	65	57	.533	3.91	1.41	590	126	2	1	69	24-48	1139.2	1103	549	495	122	508-40	818	.256
	Major League totals (16 years)	72	66	.522	4.17	1.44	640	150	2	1	72	24-48	1283.1	1266	656	594	147	588-45	894	.259

DIVISION SERIES RECORD

Year	Team (League)	W	L	Pct.	ERA	WHIP	G	GS	CG	ShO	Hld.	Sv.-Opp.	IP	H	R	ER	HR	BB-IBB	SO	Avg.
1995—	Atlanta (N.L.)	0	0	...	0.00	0.00	1	0	0	0	0	0-0	0.1	0	0	0	0	0-0	0	.000
1999—	Boston (A.L.)	0	0	...	10.80	3.60	1	1	0	0	0	0-0	1.2	3	2	2	0	3-0	1	.500
2003—	Atlanta (N.L.)	0	0	...	0.00	1.00	1	0	0	0	0	0-0	1.0	0	0	0	0	1-0	1	.000
	Division series totals (3 years)	0	0	...	6.00	2.33	3	1	0	0	0	0-0	3.0	3	2	2	0	4-0	2	.333

CHAMPIONSHIP SERIES RECORD

Year	Team (League)	W	L	Pct.	ERA	WHIP	G	GS	CG	ShO	Hld.	Sv.-Opp.	IP	H	R	ER	HR	BB-IBB	SO	Avg.
1991—	Atlanta (N.L.)	0	1	.000	13.50	3.00	1	0	0	0	0	0-0	0.2	0	1	1	0	2-0	0	.000
1992—	Atlanta (N.L.)	0	0	...	0.00	0.67	2	0	0	0	0	0-0	3.0	1	0	0	0	1-0	1	.100
1993—	Atlanta (N.L.)	0	0	...	1.80	1.00	5	0	0	0	0	0-0	5.0	3	1	1	0	2-0	4	.176
1999—	Boston (A.L.)	0	1	.000	4.70	2.09	2	2	0	0	0	0-0	7.2	12	4	4	2	4-0	5	.353
	Champ. series totals (4 years)	0	2	.000	3.31	1.53	10	2	0	0	0	0-0	16.1	16	6	6	2	9-0	10	.254

WORLD SERIES RECORD

Year	Team (League)	W	L	Pct.	ERA	WHIP	G	GS	CG	ShO	Hld.	Sv.-Opp.	IP	H	R	ER	HR	BB-IBB	SO	Avg.
1991—	Atlanta (N.L.)	0	0	...	0.00	0.00	2	0	0	0	1	0-0	1.0	0	0	0	0	0-0	1	.000
1995—	Atlanta (N.L.)	0	0	...	4.50	1.50	1	0	0	0	0	0-0	2.0	1	1	1	0	2-0	2	.143
	World Series totals (2 years)	0	0	...	3.00	1.00	3	0	0	0	1	0-0	3.0	1	1	1	0	2-0	3	.100

M

MEREDITH, CLA — P

PERSONAL: Born June 4, 1983, in Richmond, Va. ... 6-0/180. ... Throws right, bats right. ... Full name: Olise C. Meredith. ... College: Virginia Commonwealth.

TRANSACTIONS/CAREER NOTES: Selected by Boston Red Sox organization in sixth round of 2004 free-agent draft.

CAREER HITTING: 0-for-0 (.000), 0 R, 0 2B, 0 3B, 0 HR, 0 RBI.

LEFTY-RIGHTY SPLITS

vs.	Avg.	AB	H	2B	3B	HR	RBI	BB	SO	OBP	Slg.
L	.500	8	4	1	1	0	3	2	0	.600	.875
R	.400	5	2	1	0	1	5	2	0	.625	1.200

Year — Team (League)	W	L	Pct.	ERA	WHIP	G	GS	CG	ShO	Hld.	Sv.-Opp.	IP	H	R	ER	HR	BB-IBB	SO	Avg.
2004— Augusta (S. Atl.)	1	0	1.000	0.00	0.72	13	0	0	0	...	6-...	15.1	8	0	0	0	3-0	18	.148
—Sarasota (Fla. St.)	0	2	.000	2.20	1.10	16	0	0	0	/	12-...	16.1	15	4	4	0	3-0	16	.234
2005— Portland (East.)	1	0	1.000	0.00	0.53	12	0	0	0	...	9-9	15.0	5	0	0	0	3-1	12	.106
— Boston (A.L.)	0	0		27.00	4.29	3	0	0	0	0	0-0	2.1	6	7	7	1	4-0	0	.462
— Wilmington (Caro.)	0	0		0.00	1.00	1	0	0	0	0	0-0	1.0	1	0	0	0	0-0	2	.250
— Pawtucket (Int'l)	2	5	.286	5.59	1.55	40	0	0	0	2	10-20	48.1	63	30	30	6	12-2	42	.312
Major League totals (1 year)	**0**	**0**		**27.00**	**4.29**	**3**	**0**	**0**	**0**	**0**	**0-0**	**2.1**	**6**	**7**	**7**	**1**	**4-0**	**0**	**.462**

MERLONI, LOU — 1B/3B

PERSONAL: Born April 6, 1971, in Framingham, Mass. ... 5-10/200. ... Bats right, throws right. ... Full name: Louis William Merloni. ... Name pronounced: mer-LONE-ee. ... High school: Framingham (Mass.) South. ... College: Providence.

TRANSACTIONS/CAREER NOTES: Selected by Boston Red Sox organization in 10th round of 1993 free-agent draft. ... On disabled list (June 29-September 12, 1998); included rehabilitation assignment to GCL Red Sox. ... Contract sold by Red Sox to Yokohama of the Japan Central League (November 22, 1999). ... Signed as a free agent by Red Sox organization (July 28, 2000). ... On disabled list (June 6-21, 2001); included rehabilitation assignment to Pawtucket. ... Claimed on waivers by San Diego Padres (March 25, 2003). ... On disabled list (June 9-July 4, 2003); included rehabilitation assignment to Lake Elsinore. ... Traded by Padres to Red Sox for P Rene Miniel (August 28, 2003). ... Signed as a free agent by Cleveland Indians organization (January 12, 2004). ... On disabled list (August 9-September 1, 2004); included rehabilitation assignment to Mahoning Valley. ... Signed as a free agent by Los Angeles Angels of Anaheim organization (January 21, 2005). ... On disabled list (May 2, 2005-remainder of season); included rehabilitation assignments to Salt Lake and AZL Angels.

2005 GAMES PLAYED BY POSITION (MLB): 3B—4, 1B—1.

LEFTY-RIGHTY SPLITS

vs.	Avg.	AB	H	2B	3B	HR	RBI	BB	SO	OBP	Slg.
L	.000	3	0	0	0	0	1	0	1	.000	.000
R	.000	2	0	0	0	0	0	1	1	.333	.000

						BATTING												FIELDING	
Year — Team (League)	Pos.	G	AB	R	H	2B	3B	HR	RBI	BB	SO	HBP	GDP	SB-CS	Avg.	OBP	SLG	OPS	E	Avg.
1993— GC Red Sox (GCL)	SS	4	14	4	5	1	0	0	1	1	1	1	0	1-1	.357	.438	.429	.866	1	.952
— Fort Laud. (FSL)	3B-SS	44	156	14	38	1	1	2	21	13	26	1	6	1-1	.244	.299	.301	.600	8	.951
1994— Sarasota (Fla. St.)	2B-3B-SS	113	419	59	120	16	2	1	63	36	57	7	11	5-2	.286	.345	.341	.687	18	.965
1995— Trenton (East.)	2B-3B-SS	93	318	42	88	16	1	1	30	39	50	11	1	7-7	.277	.373	.343	.716	20	.951
1996— Trenton (East.)	1B-2B-3B-SS	28	95	11	22	6	1	3	16	9	18	5	2	0-2	.232	.330	.411	.741	8	.930
— GC Red Sox (GCL)	2B	1	4	1	1	0	0	0	0	0	0	0	0	0-0	.250	.200	.250	.450	1	1.000
— Pawtucket (Int'l)	2B-3B-SS	38	115	19	29	6	0	1	12	10	20	3	1	0-1	.252	.328	.330	.659	8	.945
1997— Trenton (East.)	2B-3B-SS	69	255	49	79	17	4	5	37	30	43	12	2	3-2	.310	.402	.467	.869	9	.957
— Pawtucket (Int'l)	2B-3B-SS	49	165	24	49	10	0	5	24	15	20	4	4	0-2	.297	.368	.448	.816	4	.979
1998— Pawtucket (Int'l)	2B-3B-SS	27	88	17	34	3	1	8	22	16	13	8	2	2-2	.386	.518	.716	1.234	2	.976
— Boston (A.L.)	2B-3B-SS	39	96	10	27	6	0	1	15	7	20	2	1	1-0	.281	.343	.375	.718	5	.962
— GC Red Sox (GCL)	2B	1	1	0	0	0	0	0	0	0	0	0	0	0-0	.000	.000	.000	.000	0	...
1999— Boston (A.L.)	DH-1B-OF	43	126	18	32	7	0	1	13	8	16	2	6	0-0	.254	.307	.333	.640	10	.940
— Pawtucket (Int'l)	SS-3B-DH	66	229	45	64	14	1	7	36	30	38	9	4	1-1	.279	.383	.441	.824	12	.945
2000— Pawtucket (Int'l)	SS-1B-2B	11	39	6	16	2	0	1	5	3	3	0	2	0-1	.410	.452	.538	.991	4	.897
— Yo. Bay. (Jp. Cn.)	3B	42	94	10	20	4	0	1	3	7	15			0-...	.213	...	.287	...	...	...
— Boston (A.L.)	3B	40	128	10	41	11	2	0	18	4	22	1	0	1-0	.320	.341	.438	.778	7	.928
2001— Pawtucket (Int'l)	SS-2B-3B	52	195	30	51	12	0	4	20	15	37	5	6	2-0	.262	.330	.385	.715	10	.954
— Boston (A.L.)	SS-2B-3B	52	146	21	39	10	0	3	13	6	31	3	6	2-1	.267	.306	.397	.703	3	.983
2002— Boston (A.L.)	1B-OF	84	194	28	48	12	2	4	18	20	35	5	4	1-2	.247	.332	.392	.724	5	.982
— Pawtucket (Int'l)	3B-SS-OF	8	25	1	5	2	0	2	1	3	1	2	0	0-0	.200	.250	.280	.530	0	1.000
2003— Lake Elsinore (Calif.)	2B-3B-SS	5	19	3	9	3	0	1	7	1	0	0	0	0-0	.474	.476	.789	1.266	0	1.000
— San Diego (N.L.)	1B-OF	65	151	20	41	7	2	1	17	22	33	1	3	2-3	.272	.362	.364	.726	6	.962
— Boston (A.L.)	2B-3B-OF	15	30	4	7	1	0	1	4	4	8	0	0	0-0	.233	.324	.267	.590	0	1.000
2004— Mahoning Valley (N.Y.-Penn.)	DH	2	8	1	2	0	0	1	4	0	4	0	0	0-0	.250	.250	.625	.875	0	...
— Cleveland (A.L.)	OF-DH	71	190	25	55	12	1	4	28	14	41	3	9	1-2	.289	.343	.426	.769	4	.989
2005— Los Angeles (A.L.)	3B-1B	5	5	1	0	0	0	0	1	1	2	0	0	0-0	.000	.143	.000	.143	1	1.000
— Ariz. Angels (Ariz.)	3B-DH	6	15	3	5	1	0	2	2	2	0	0	0	0-0	.333	.412	.400	.812	0	1.000
— Salt Lake (PCL)	3B-DH-2B	6	25	6	8	3	0	1	2	2	5	1	1	0-0	.320	.393	.440	.833	0	1.000
American League totals (8 years)		**349**	**915**	**117**	**249**	**59**	**5**	**13**	**107**	**64**	**175**	**16**	**34**	**6-5**	**.272**	**.327**	**.390**	**.718**	**34**	**.973**
National League totals (1 year)		**65**	**151**	**20**	**41**	**7**	**2**	**1**	**17**	**22**	**33**	**1**	**3**	**2-3**	**.272**	**.362**	**.364**	**.726**	**6**	**.962**
Major League totals (8 years)		**414**	**1066**	**137**	**290**	**66**	**7**	**14**	**124**	**86**	**208**	**17**	**37**	**8-8**	**.272**	**.332**	**.386**	**.719**	**40**	**.971**

DIVISION SERIES RECORD

Year — Team (League)	Pos.	G	AB	R	H	2B	3B	HR	RBI	BB	SO	HBP	GDP	SB-CS	Avg.	OBP	SLG	OPS	E	Avg.
1999— Boston (A.L.)	SS	3	6	1	2	0	0	0	1	1	1	1	0	0-0	.333	.429	.333	.762	1	.833

CHAMPIONSHIP SERIES RECORD

Year — Team (League)	Pos.	G	AB	R	H	2B	3B	HR	RBI	BB	SO	HBP	GDP	SB-CS	Avg.	OBP	SLG	OPS	E	Avg.
1999— Boston (A.L.)		1	0	0	0	0	0	0	0	0	0	0	0	0-0	...	1.000	...	1.000	...	...

M

MESA, JOSE   P

PERSONAL: Born May 22, 1966, in Azua, Dominican Republic. ... 6-3/232. ... Throws right, bats right. ... Full name: Jose Ramon Mesa. ... Name pronounced: MAY-sa. ... High school: Santa School (Azua, Dominican Republic).

TRANSACTIONS/CAREER NOTES: Signed as a non-drafted free agent by Toronto Blue Jays organization (October 31, 1981). ... Traded by Blue Jays to Baltimore Orioles (September 4, 1987), completing deal in which Orioles traded P Mike Flanagan to Blue Jays for P Oswald Peraza and a player to be named (August 31, 1987). ... Traded by Orioles to Cleveland Indians for OF Kyle Washington (July 14, 1992). ... On suspended list (April 5-8, 1993). ... Traded by Indians with IF Shawon Dunston and P Alvin Morman to San Francisco Giants for P Steve Reed and OF Jacob Cruz (July 23, 1998). ... Signed as a free agent by Seattle Mariners (November 13, 1998). ... Signed as a free agent by Philadelphia Phillies (November 17, 2000). ... On suspended list (August 28-30, 2001). ... Signed as a free agent by Pittsburgh Pirates organization (January 29, 2004).

HONORS: Named A.L. Fireman of the Year by THE SPORTING NEWS (1995).

CAREER HITTING: 0-for-1 (.000), 1 R, 0 2B, 0 3B, 0 HR, 0 RBI.

SCOUTING REPORT

Throws: Mesa has a fastball at 91-95 mph, a slider at 85-88 and a curveball. **Tendencies:** Getting ahead and challenging hitters are keys for him. Uses his curve to catch up in the count against lefthanders. Fastball has good late life up in the zone. Slider is more like a quick cut fastball. Doesn't hold runners on well in crucial situations. Can usually tell with the first hitter whether he has it on a given day. **Outlook:** Mesa continues to be an effective closer but rarely has an easy save. Appears comfortable racking up saves for non-contenders. **Grade 7**

JOSE MESA'S PITCHING ZONE

.417	.300	.091
.370	.400	.364
.263	.300	.273

LEFTY-RIGHTY SPLITS

vs.	Avg.	AB	H	2B	3B	HR	RBI	BB	SO	OBP	Slg.
L	.309	97	30	5	0	4	18	15	13	.397	.485
R	.265	117	31	6	0	3	17	11	24	.331	.393

Year — Team (League)	W	L	Pct.	ERA	WHIP	G	GS	CG	ShO	Hld.	Sv.-Opp.	IP	H	R	ER	HR	BB-IBB	SO	Avg.
1982— GC Jays (GCL)	6	4	.600	2.70	0.94	13	12	6	3	...	1-...	83.1	58	34	25	1	20-0	40	...
1983— Florence (S. Atl.)	6	12	.333	5.48	1.74	28	27	1	0	...	0-...	141.1	153	116	86	14	93-0	91	...
1984— Florence (S. Atl.)	4	3	.571	3.76	1.64	7	7	0	0	...	0-...	38.1	38	24	16	3	25-0	35	.255
—Kinston (Carol.)	5	2	.714	3.91	1.56	10	9	0	0	...	0-...	50.2	51	23	22	2	28-0	24	.267
1985— Kinston (Carol.)	5	10	.333	6.16	1.77	30	20	0	0	...	1-...	106.2	110	89	73	11	79-2	71	.269
1986— Vent. Co. (Calif.)	10	6	.625	3.86	1.40	24	24	2	1	...	0-...	142.1	141	71	61	6	58-0	113	.256
—Knoxville (Southern)	2	2	.500	4.35	1.52	9	8	2	1	...	0-...	41.1	40	32	20	6	23-0	30	.242
1987— Knoxville (Southern)	10	13	.435	5.21	1.60	35	35	4	2	...	0-...	193.1	206	131	112	19	104-0	115	.273
—Baltimore (A.L.)	1	3	.250	6.03	1.69	6	5	0	0	1	0-0	31.1	38	23	21	7	15-0	17	.297
1988— Rochester (Int'l)	0	3	.000	8.62	2.23	11	2	0	0	...	0-...	15.2	21	20	15	2	14-0	15	.328
1989— Rochester (Int'l)	0	2	.000	5.40	1.60	7	1	0	0	...	0-...	10.0	10	6	6	2	6-0	3	.263
—Hagerstown (East.)	0	0	...	1.38	1.00	3	3	0	0	...	0-...	13.0	9	2	2	0	4-0	12	.191
1990— Hagerstown (East.)	5	5	.500	3.42	1.35	15	15	3	1	...	0-...	79.0	77	35	30	4	30-0	72	.258
—Rochester (Int'l)	1	2	.333	2.42	1.27	4	4	0	0	...	0-...	26.0	21	11	7	2	12-0	23	.223
—Baltimore (A.L.)	3	2	.600	3.86	1.37	7	7	0	0	0	0-0	46.2	37	20	20	2	27-2	24	.218
1991— Baltimore (A.L.)	6	11	.353	5.97	1.72	23	23	2	1	0	0-0	123.2	151	86	82	11	62-2	64	.307
—Rochester (Int'l)	3	3	.500	3.86	1.31	8	8	1	1	...	0-...	51.1	37	25	22	4	30-0	48	.203
1992— Baltimore (A.L.)	3	8	.273	5.19	1.54	13	12	0	0	0	0-0	67.2	77	41	39	9	27-1	22	.287
—Cleveland (A.L.)	4	4	.500	4.16	1.45	15	15	1	1	0	0-0	93.0	92	45	43	5	43-0	40	.262
1993— Cleveland (A.L.)	10	12	.455	4.92	1.41	34	33	3	0	0	0-0	208.2	232	122	114	21	62-2	118	.284
1994— Cleveland (A.L.)	7	5	.583	3.82	1.33	51	0	0	0	8	2-6	73.0	71	33	31	3	26-7	63	.254
1995— Cleveland (A.L.)	3	0	1.000	1.13	1.03	62	0	0	0	*	46-48	64.0	49	9	8	3	17-2	58	.216
1996— Cleveland (A.L.)	2	7	.222	3.73	1.34	69	0	0	0	0	39-44	72.1	69	32	30	6	28-4	64	.257
1997— Cleveland (A.L.)	4	4	.500	2.40	1.35	66	0	0	0	9	16-21	82.1	83	28	22	7	28-3	69	.259
1998— Cleveland (A.L.)	3	4	.429	5.17	1.50	44	0	0	0	7	1-3	54.0	61	36	31	7	20-3	35	.282
—San Francisco (N.L.)	5	3	.625	3.52	1.57	32	0	0	0	6	0-1	30.2	30	14	12	1	18-2	28	.256
1999— Seattle (A.L.)	3	6	.333	4.98	1.81	68	0	0	0	1	33-38	68.2	84	42	38	11	40-4	42	.305
2000— Seattle (A.L.)	4	6	.400	5.36	1.61	66	0	0	0	11	1-3	80.2	89	48	48	11	41-0	84	.280
2001— Philadelphia (N.L.)	3	3	.500	2.34	1.23	71	0	0	0	1	42-46	69.1	65	26	18	4	20-2	59	.246
2002— Philadelphia (N.L.)	4	6	.400	2.97	1.37	74	0	0	0	0	45-54	75.2	65	26	25	5	39-7	64	.231
2003— Philadelphia (N.L.)	5	7	.417	6.52	1.76	61	0	0	0	2	24-28	58.0	71	44	42	7	31-2	45	.296
2004— Pittsburgh (N.L.)	5	2	.714	3.25	1.41	70	0	0	0	0	43-48	69.1	78	26	25	6	20-3	37	.291
2005— Pittsburgh (N.L.)	2	8	.200	4.76	1.54	55	0	0	0	1	27-34	56.2	61	30	30	7	26-3	37	.285
American League totals (12 years)	53	72	.424	4.45	1.47	524	95	6	2	37	138-163	1066.0	1133	565	527	103	436-30	700	.275
National League totals (6 years)	24	29	.453	3.80	1.46	363	0	0	0	10	181-211	359.2	370	166	152	30	154-19	270	.267
Major League totals (17 years)	77	101	.433	4.29	1.47	887	95	6	2	47	319-374	1425.2	1503	731	679	133	590-49	970	.273

DIVISION SERIES RECORD

Year — Team (League)	W	L	Pct.	ERA	WHIP	G	GS	CG	ShO	Hld.	Sv.-Opp.	IP	H	R	ER	HR	BB-IBB	SO	Avg.
1995— Cleveland (A.L.)	0	0	...	0.00	1.00	2	0	0	0	0	0-0	2.0	0	0	0	0	2-0	0	.000
1996— Cleveland (A.L.)	0	1	.000	3.86	1.71	2	0	0	0	0	0-1	4.2	8	2	2	1	0-0	7	.381
1997— Cleveland (A.L.)	0	0	...	2.70	1.80	2	0	0	0	0	1-1	3.1	5	1	1	1	1-0	2	.333
2000— Seattle (A.L.)	1	0	1.000	0.00	0.50	2	0	0	0	0	0-0	2.0	0	0	0	0	1-1	2	.000
Division series totals (4 years)	1	1	.500	2.25	1.42	8	0	0	0	1	1-2	12.0	13	3	3	2	4-1	11	.277

CHAMPIONSHIP SERIES RECORD

Year — Team (League)	W	L	Pct.	ERA	WHIP	G	GS	CG	ShO	Hld.	Sv.-Opp.	IP	H	R	ER	HR	BB-IBB	SO	Avg.
1995— Cleveland (A.L.)	0	0	...	2.25	1.00	4	0	0	0	0	1-1	4.0	3	1	1	0	1-0	1	.214
1997— Cleveland (A.L.)	1	0	1.000	3.38	1.50	4	0	0	0	0	2-4	5.1	5	2	2	0	3-1	5	.238
2000— Seattle (A.L.)	0	0	...	12.46	1.85	3	0	0	0	0	0-0	4.1	5	6	6	2	3-0	3	.313
Champ. series totals (3 years)	1	0	1.000	5.93	1.46	11	0	0	0	0	3-5	13.2	13	9	9	3	7-1	9	.255

WORLD SERIES RECORD

Year — Team (League)	W	L	Pct.	ERA	WHIP	G	GS	CG	ShO	Hld.	Sv.-Opp.	IP	H	R	ER	HR	BB-IBB	SO	Avg.
1995— Cleveland (A.L.)	1	0	1.000	4.50	1.50	2	0	0	0	0	1-1	4.0	5	2	2	1	1-0	4	.333
1997— Cleveland (A.L.)	0	0	...	5.40	2.20	5	0	0	0	0	1-2	5.0	10	3	3	0	1-0	5	.417
World Series totals (2 years)	1	0	1.000	5.00	1.89	7	0	0	0	0	2-3	9.0	15	5	5	1	2-0	9	.385

							ALL-STAR GAME RECORD											
	W	L	Pct.	ERA	WHIP	G	GS	CG	ShO	Hld.	Sv.-Opp.	IP	H	R	ER	HR	BB-IBB	SO	Avg.
All-Star Game totals (1 year)	0	0	...	0.00	0.00	1	0	0	0	0	0-0	1.0	0	0	0	0	0-0	1	.000

MESSENGER, RANDY — P

PERSONAL: Born August 13, 1981, in Reno, Nev. ... 6-6/247. ... Throws right, bats right. ... Full name: Randall Jerome Messenger.
TRANSACTIONS/CAREER NOTES: Selected by Florida Marlins organization in 11th round of 1999 free-agent draft.
CAREER HITTING: 1-for-3 (.333), 0 R, 0 2B, 0 3B, 0 HR, 0 RBI.

RANDY MESSENGER'S PITCHING ZONE

.125	.471	.222
.333	.316	.375
.182	.143	.000

LEFTY-RIGHTY SPLITS

vs.	Avg.	AB	H	2B	3B	HR	RBI	BB	SO	OBP	Slg.
L	.271	59	16	2	1	1	9	16	11	.421	.390
R	.274	84	23	7	0	4	23	14	18	.370	.500

Year Team (League)	W	L	Pct.	ERA	WHIP	G	GS	CG	ShO	Hld.	Sv.-Opp.	IP	H	R	ER	HR	BB-IBB	SO	Avg.
1999— GC Marlins (GCL)	0	3	.000	7.52	1.78	13	2	0	0	...	2-...	26.1	28	25	22	1	19-0	23	.283
2000— GC Marlins (GCL)	2	2	.500	4.83	1.47	12	12	0	0	...	0-...	59.2	66	37	32	6	22-0	29	.280
2001— Kane Co. (Midw.)	2	1	.667	3.93	1.47	14	0	0	0	...	0-...	18.1	22	13	8	0	5-0	14	.301
— Brevard County (FSL)	7	4	.636	4.08	1.45	18	18	0	0	...	0-...	92.2	99	55	42	3	35-0	42	.277
2002— Jupiter (Fla. St.)	11	8	.579	4.37	1.51	28	27	1	0	...	0-...	156.2	178	94	76	4	58-0	96	.284
2003— Carolina (Southern)	5	7	.417	5.46	1.65	29	23	0	0	...	0-...	113.2	137	83	69	7	51-1	78	.296
2004— Carolina (Southern)	6	3	.667	2.58	1.38	58	0	0	0	...	21-...	69.2	67	21	20	4	29-3	71	.245
2005— Albuquerque (PCL)	4	2	.667	3.88	1.29	39	0	0	0	9	7-11	48.2	46	25	21	5	17-1	35	.251
— Florida (N.L.)	0	0	...	5.35	1.86	29	0	0	0	2	0-0	37.0	39	22	22	5	30-7	29	.273
Major League totals (1 year)	0	0	...	5.35	1.86	29	0	0	0	2	0-0	37.0	39	22	22	5	30-7	29	.273

MICELI, DAN — P

PERSONAL: Born September 9, 1970, in Newark, N.J. ... 6-0/215. ... Throws right, bats right. ... Full name: Daniel Miceli. ... Name pronounced: muh-SELL-ee. ... High school: Dr. Phillips (Orlando).
TRANSACTIONS/CAREER NOTES: Signed as a non-drafted free agent by Kansas City Royals organization (March 7, 1990). ... Traded by Royals with P Jon Lieber to Pittsburgh Pirates for P Stan Belinda (July 31, 1993). ... Traded by Pirates to Detroit Tigers for P Clint Sodowsky (November 1, 1996). ... Traded by Tigers with P Donne Wall and 3B Ryan Balfe to San Diego Padres for P Tim Worrell and OF Trey Beamon (November 19, 1997). ... Traded by Padres to Florida Marlins for P Brian Meadows (November 15, 1999). ... On disabled list (May 30-July 19, 2000); included rehabilitation assignments to GCL Marlins and Brevard County. ... Released by Marlins (June 25, 2001). ... Signed by Colorado Rockies organization (July 2, 2001). ... Signed as a free agent by Texas Rangers organization (January 29, 2002). ... Released by Rangers (May 6, 2002). ... Signed by Rockies organization (December 19, 2002). ... Signed as a free agent by Cleveland Indians organization (May 15, 2003). ... Traded by Indians with OF Karim Garcia to New York Yankees for cash (June 25, 2003). ... Traded by Yankees to Houston Astros for cash (July 29, 2003). ... On disabled list (August 22-September 9, 2004). ... On disabled list (August 7, 2005-remainder of season).
CAREER HITTING: 2-for-22 (.091), 0 R, 0 2B, 0 3B, 0 HR, 0 RBI.

DAN MICELI'S PITCHING ZONE

.000	.333	.250
.200	.500	.364
.286	.667	.333

LEFTY-RIGHTY SPLITS

vs.	Avg.	AB	H	2B	3B	HR	RBI	BB	SO	OBP	Slg.
L	.303	33	10	2	0	4	4	5	8	.395	.364
R	.243	37	9	2	0	1	7	8	11	.391	.378

Year Team (League)	W	L	Pct.	ERA	WHIP	G	GS	CG	ShO	Hld.	Sv.-Opp.	IP	H	R	ER	HR	BB-IBB	SO	Avg.
1990— GC Royals (GCL)	3	4	.429	3.91	1.40	27	0	0	0	...	4-...	53.0	45	27	23	0	29-5	48	.234
1991— Eugene (Northwest)	0	1	.000	2.14	1.07	25	0	0	0	...	10-...	33.2	18	8	8	1	18-0	43	.158
1992— Appleton (Midwest)	1	1	.500	1.93	0.69	23	0	0	0	...	9-...	23.1	12	6	5	0	4-1	44	.145
— Memphis (Sou.)	3	0	1.000	1.91	0.88	32	0	0	0	...	4-...	37.2	20	10	8	5	13-0	46	.160
1993— Memphis (Sou.)	6	4	.600	4.60	1.59	40	0	0	0	...	7-...	58.2	54	30	30	7	39-3	68	.242
— Carolina (Southern)	0	2	.000	5.11	1.22	13	0	0	0	...	10-...	12.1	11	8	7	2	4-1	19	.234
— Pittsburgh (N.L.)	0	0	...	5.06	1.69	9	0	0	0	0	0-0	5.1	6	3	3	0	3-0	4	.273
1994— Buffalo (A.A.)	1	1	.500	1.88	0.88	19	0	0	0	...	2-...	24.0	15	5	5	2	6-0	31	.185
— Pittsburgh (N.L.)	2	1	.667	5.93	1.43	28	0	0	0	4	2-3	27.1	28	19	18	5	11-2	27	.267
1995— Pittsburgh (N.L.)	4	4	.500	4.66	1.53	58	0	0	0	2	21-27	58.0	61	30	30	7	28-5	56	.270
1996— Pittsburgh (N.L.)	2	10	.167	5.78	1.68	44	0	0	0	4	1-1	85.2	99	65	55	15	45-5	66	.291
— Carolina (Southern)	1	0	1.000	1.00	0.56	3	0	0	0	...	1-...	9.0	4	1	1	0	1-0	17	.125
1997— Detroit (A.L.)	3	2	.600	5.01	1.39	71	0	0	0	11	3-8	82.2	77	49	46	13	38-4	79	.248
1998— San Diego (N.L.)	10	5	.667	3.22	1.25	67	0	0	0	20	2-8	72.2	64	28	26	6	27-4	70	.238
1999— San Diego (N.L.)	4	5	.444	4.46	1.50	66	0	0	0	9	2-4	68.2	67	39	34	7	36-5	59	.266
2000— Florida (N.L.)	6	4	.600	4.25	1.29	45	0	0	0	11	0-3	48.2	45	23	23	4	18-2	40	.242
— GC Marlins (GCL)	0	0	...	0.00	0.33	2	2	0	0	...	0-...	3.0	0	0	0	0	1-0	3	.000
— Brevard County (FSL)	1	0	1.000	3.00	0.50	5	4	0	0	...	0-...	6.0	3	2	2	0	0-0	7	.143
2001— Florida (N.L.)	0	5	.000	6.93	1.62	29	0	0	0	8	0-3	24.2	29	21	19	5	11-2	31	.287
— Colo. Springs (PCL)	0	0	...	6.00	1.00	4	0	0	0	...	1-1	3.0	2	2	2	0	1-1	4	.200
— Colorado (N.L.)	2	0	1.000	2.21	1.13	22	0	0	0	1	1-1	20.1	18	8	5	2	5-0	17	.231
2002— Texas (A.L.)	0	2	.000	8.64	1.92	9	0	0	0	1	0-1	8.1	13	8	8	1	3-0	5	.333
2003— Colorado (N.L.)	0	2	.000	5.66	1.60	14	0	0	0	1	0-0	20.2	24	13	13	7	9-1	18	.286
— Buffalo (Int'l)	0	1	.000	3.00	1.30	5	0	0	0	...	0-...	6.0	7	2	2	1	1-1	6	.280
— Cleveland (A.L.)	0	1	.500	1.20	1.00	13	0	0	0	4	0-...	15.0	9	4	2	1	6-1	19	.164
— New York (A.L.)	0	0	...	5.79	1.50	7	0	0	0	1	1-1	4.2	4	3	3	2	3-0	1	.211
— Houston (N.L.)	1	0	.500	2.10	0.97	23	0	0	0	3	0-0	30.0	22	7	7	3	7-1	20	.208
2004— Houston (N.L.)	6	6	.500	3.59	1.30	74	0	0	0	24	2-8	77.2	74	34	31	10	27-12	83	.247
2005— Colo. Springs (PCL)	0	0	...	5.40	1.20	5	0	0	0	...	0-0	5.0	4	3	3	1	2-0	8	.200
— Colorado (N.L.)	1	2	.333	5.89	1.75	19	0	0	0	5	0-2	18.1	19	12	12	1	13-0	19	.271
American League totals (3 years)	4	5	.444	4.80	1.38	100	0	0	0	12	4-11	110.2	103	64	59	17	50-5	104	.243
National League totals (11 years)	38	45	.458	4.45	1.43	498	0	0	0	91	31-60	558.0	556	302	276	72	240-39	510	.260
Major League totals (13 years)	42	50	.457	4.51	1.42	598	0	0	0	103	35-71	668.2	659	366	335	89	290-44	614	.257

DIVISION SERIES RECORD

Year Team (League)	W	L	Pct.	ERA	WHIP	G	GS	CG	ShO	Hld.	Sv.-Opp.	IP	H	R	ER	HR	BB-IBB	SO	Avg.
1998—San Diego (N.L.)	1	1	.500	2.70	0.60	3	0	0	0	1	0-0	3.1	2	1	1	0	0-0	4	.200
2004—Houston (N.L.)	0	1	.000	5.40	0.90	3	0	0	0	0	0-0	3.1	2	2	2	1	1-0	2	.167
Division series totals (2 years)	1	2	.333	4.05	0.75	6	0	0	0	1	0-0	6.2	4	3	3	1	1-0	6	.182

CHAMPIONSHIP SERIES RECORD

Year Team (League)	W	L	Pct.	ERA	WHIP	G	GS	CG	ShO	Hld.	Sv.-Opp.	IP	H	R	ER	HR	BB-IBB	SO	Avg.
1998—San Diego (N.L.)	0	0	...	13.50	6.00	3	0	0	0	1	0-0	0.2	4	1	1	0	0-0	1	.667
2004—Houston (N.L.)	0	2	.000	27.00	3.00	2	0	0	0	0	0-0	1.1	3	4	4	3	1-0	0	.429
Champ. series totals (2 years)	0	2	.000	22.50	4.00	5	0	0	0	1	0-0	2.0	7	5	5	4	1-0	1	.538

WORLD SERIES RECORD

Year Team (League)	W	L	Pct.	ERA	WHIP	G	GS	CG	ShO	Hld.	Sv.-Opp.	IP	H	R	ER	HR	BB-IBB	SO	Avg.
1998—San Diego (N.L.)	0	0	...	0.00	2.40	2	0	0	0	0	0-0	1.2	2	0	0	0	2-0	1	.286

MICHAELS, JASON — OF

PERSONAL: Born May 4, 1976, in Tampa. ... 6-0/204. ... Bats right, throws right. ... Full name: Jason Drew Michaels. ... High school: Jesuit (Tampa). ... College: Miami. ... Grandson of John Michaels, pitcher with Boston Red Sox (1932).

TRANSACTIONS/CAREER NOTES: Selected by San Diego Padres organization in 49th round of 1994 free-agent draft; did not sign. ... Selected by Tampa Bay Devil Rays organization in 44th round of 1996 free-agent draft; did not sign. ... Selected by St. Louis Cardinals organization in 15th round of 1997 free-agent draft; did not sign. ... Selected by Philadelphia Phillies organization in fourth round of 1998 free-agent draft. ... On disabled list (March 21-April 14, 2003); included rehabilitation assignment to Clearwater.

2005 GAMES PLAYED BY POSITION (MLB): OF—91.

SCOUTING REPORT Michaels can play all three outfield positions, but he is best in center field. Has improved his jumps as he has played more. Has problems going back on balls. Has average arm strength and a slow release. Hits with an inside-out approach and has improved his bat speed and power. Is covering holes in his swing and improving his discipline at the plate. Would be a regular for a lot of teams. *Grade 6.5*

JASON MICHAELS' HITTING ZONE

.250	.250	.278
.379	.417	.366
.295	.261	.231

LEFTY-RIGHTY SPLITS

vs.	Avg.	AB	H	2B	3B	HR	RBI	BB	SO	OBP	Slg.
L	.323	130	42	10	1	0	10	29	20	.438	.415
R	.289	159	46	6	1	4	21	15	25	.363	.415

Year Team (League)	Pos.	G	AB	R	H	2B	3B	HR	RBI	BB	SO	HBP	GDP	SB-CS	Avg.	OBP	SLG	OPS	E	Avg.
1998—Batavia (NY-Penn)	OF	67	235	45	63	14	3	11	49	40	69	4	5	4-2	.268	.381	.494	.874	5	.949
1999—Clearwater (FSL)	OF	122	451	91	138	31	6	14	65	68	103	3	7	10-7	.306	.396	.494	.890	1	.996
2000—Reading (East.)	OF	113	437	71	129	30	4	10	74	28	87	3	9	7-4	.295	.337	.451	.788	6	.977
2001—Scran./W.B. (I.L.)	OF	109	418	58	109	19	3	17	69	37	126	8	7	11-3	.261	.332	.443	.774	0	1.000
—Philadelphia (N.L.)	OF	6	6	0	1	0	0	0	1	0	2	0	0	0-0	.167	.167	.167	.333	0	...
2002—Scran./W.B. (I.L.)	OF	9	32	3	9	2	0	0	7	5	5	0	0	1-3	.281	.359	.344	.703	0	1.000
—Philadelphia (N.L.)	OF-DH-3B	81	105	16	28	10	3	2	11	13	33	1	1	1-1	.267	.347	.476	.823	2	.923
2003—Clearwater (FSL)	OF	4	14	1	0	0	0	0	0	2	4	0	0	0-0	.000	.125	.000	.125	0	1.000
—Philadelphia (N.L.)	OF	76	109	20	36	11	0	5	17	15	22	1	3	0-0	.330	.416	.569	.985	1	.976
2004—Philadelphia (N.L.)	OF-DH	115	299	44	82	12	0	10	40	42	80	2	3	2-2	.274	.364	.415	.779	3	.983
2005—Philadelphia (N.L.)	OF	105	289	54	88	16	2	4	31	44	45	4	3	3-3	.304	.399	.415	.814	2	.990
Major League totals (5 years)		383	808	134	235	49	5	21	100	114	182	8	10	6-6	.291	.380	.442	.822	8	.982

MIENTKIEWICZ, DOUG — 1B

PERSONAL: Born June 19, 1974, in Toledo, Ohio. ... 6-2/206. ... Bats left, throws right. ... Full name: Douglas Andrew Mientkiewicz. ... Name pronounced: mint-KAY-vich. ... High school: Westminster Christian (Miami). ... College: Florida State.

TRANSACTIONS/CAREER NOTES: Selected by Minnesota Twins organization in fifth round of 1995 free-agent draft. ... On disabled list (July 7-23, 2004). ... Traded by Twins to Boston Red Sox as part of four-team deal in which Twins acquired P Justin Jones from Cubs, Red Sox acquired SS Orlando Cabrera from Expos, Expos acquired SS Alex S. Gonzalez, P Francis Beltran and IF Brendan Harris from Cubs, and Cubs acquired SS Nomar Garciaparra and Matt Murton from Red Sox (July 31, 2004). ... Traded by Red Sox to New York Mets for 1B Ian Bladergroen (January 26, 2005). ... On disabled list (June 26-July 16 and August 9-September 2, 2005); included rehabilitation assignments to GCL Mets and St. Lucie.

HONORS: Won A.L. Gold Glove at first base (2001).

2005 GAMES PLAYED BY POSITION (MLB): 1B—83.

SCOUTING REPORT Offense: He's a singles hitter at a position that calls for power and run production. Is a nice complementary player who makes contact and goes deep in counts without striking out much. Pitchers can get inside on him because he doesn't have great bat speed. *Defense:* His exceptionally quick feet and agility to either side make him an outstanding defender. Will dive for balls and regains his feet quickly. Has excellent instincts with great lower-body flexibility, which helps when stretching for throws. *Outlook:* This is a player who always will be on the move because of his lack of power, but his defense is just great. *Grade 6.7*

DOUG MIENTKIEWICZ'S HITTING ZONE

.214	.364	.182
.256	.325	.206
.200	.188	.250

LEFTY-RIGHTY SPLITS

vs.	Avg.	AB	H	2B	3B	HR	RBI	BB	SO	OBP	Slg.
L	.214	42	9	2	0	3	8	6	7	.306	.476
R	.245	233	57	11	0	8	21	26	32	.324	.395

Year Team (League)	Pos.	G	AB	R	H	2B	3B	HR	RBI	BB	SO	HBP	GDP	SB-CS	Avg.	OBP	SLG	OPS	E	Avg.
1995—Fort Myers (FSL)	1B	38	110	9	27	6	1	1	15	18	19	1	1	2-2	.245	.357	.345	.702	1	.994
1996—Fort Myers (FSL)	1B	133	492	69	143	•36	4	5	79	66	47	3	10	12-2	.291	.374	.411	.784	3	.998

M

Year Team (League)	Pos.	G	AB	R	H	2B	3B	HR	RBI	BB	SO	HBP	GDP	SB-CS	Avg.	OBP	SLG	OPS	E	Avg.
1997— New Britain (East.)	1B-OF	132	467	87	119	28	2	15	61	98	67	7	8	21-8	.255	.390	.420	.810	5	.995
1998— New Britain (East.)	1B-OF	139	502	96	162	45	0	16	88	96	58	6	6	11-4	.323	.432	.508	.940	12	.991
— Minnesota (A.L.)	1B	8	25	1	5	1	0	0	2	4	3	0	0	1-1	.200	.310	.240	.550	0	1.000
1999— Minnesota (A.L.)	1B	118	327	34	75	21	3	2	32	43	51	4	13	1-1	.229	.324	.330	.655	3	.997
2000— Salt Lake (PCL)	1B-3B-2B-OF	130	485	96	162	32	3	18	96	61	68	3	17	9-5	.334	.406	.524	.929	10	.989
— Minnesota (A.L.)	1B	3	14	0	6	0	0	0	4	0	0	0	1	0-0	.429	.429	.429	.829	1	1.000
2001— Minnesota (A.L.)	1B-DH	151	543	77	166	39	1	15	74	67	92	9	10	2-6	.306	.387	.464	.851	4	.997
2002— Minnesota (A.L.)	1B	143	467	60	122	29	1	10	64	74	69	6	7	1-2	.261	.365	.392	.756	5	.996
2003— Minnesota (A.L.)	1B-OF-2B-3B-DH	142	487	67	146	38	1	11	65	74	55	5	9	4-1	.300	.393	.450	.843	4	.997
2004— Minnesota (A.L.)	1B	78	284	34	70	18	0	5	36	38	38	3	9	2-2	.246	.340	.363	.703	4	.994
— Boston (A.L.)	1B-2B	49	107	13	23	6	1	1	10	10	18	1	3	0-1	.215	.286	.318	.603	1	.997
2005— GC Mets (GCL)	1B-DH	4	10	2	5	1	0	1	5	4	1	0	0	0-0	.500	.643	.900	1.543	1	1.000
— St. Lucie (Fla. St.)	1B-DH	8	27	3	7	4	0	0	5	7	7	0	0	0-0	.259	.412	.407	.819	1	.985
— New York (N.L.)	1B	87	275	36	66	13	0	11	29	32	39	2	11	0-1	.240	.322	.407	.729	4	.995
American League totals (7 years)		692	2254	286	613	152	7	44	276	310	326	28	52	11-14	.272	.363	.404	.768	21	.996
National League totals (1 year)		87	275	36	66	13	0	11	29	32	39	2	11	0-1	.240	.322	.407	.729	4	.995
Major League totals (8 years)		779	2529	322	679	165	7	55	305	342	365	30	63	11-15	.268	.359	.405	.763	25	.996

DIVISION SERIES RECORD

Year Team (League)	Pos.	G	AB	R	H	2B	3B	HR	RBI	BB	SO	HBP	GDP	SB-CS	Avg.	OBP	SLG	OPS	E	Avg.
2002— Minnesota (A.L.)	1B	5	20	3	5	0	0	0	2	4	1	1	0	0-0	.250	.286	.550	.836	0	1.000
2003— Minnesota (A.L.)	1B	4	15	0	2	0	0	0	0	1	2	0	0	0-0	.133	.188	.133	.321	0	1.000
2004— Boston (A.L.)	1B	3	4	0	2	0	0	0	0	0	0	0	0	0-0	.500	.500	.500	1.000	0	1.000
Division series totals (3 years)		12	39	3	9	0	0	0	2	5	3	1	0	0-0	.231	.268	.385	.653	0	1.000

CHAMPIONSHIP SERIES RECORD

Year Team (League)	Pos.	G	AB	R	H	2B	3B	HR	RBI	BB	SO	HBP	GDP	SB-CS	Avg.	OBP	SLG	OPS	E	Avg.
2002— Minnesota (A.L.)	1B	5	18	1	5	1	0	0	2	1	2	0	0	0-0	.278	.316	.333	.649	0	1.000
2004— Boston (A.L.)	1B	4	4	0	2	1	0	0	0	1	0	0	0	0-0	.500	.500	.750	1.250	0	1.000
Champ. series totals (2 years)		9	22	1	7	2	0	0	2	1	3	0	0	0-0	.318	.348	.409	.757	0	1.000

WORLD SERIES RECORD

Year Team (League)	Pos.	G	AB	R	H	2B	3B	HR	RBI	BB	SO	HBP	GDP	SB-CS	Avg.	OBP	SLG	OPS	E	Avg.
2004— Boston (A.L.)	1B	4	1	0	0	0	0	0	0	0	0	0	0	0-0	.000	.000	.000	.000	0	1.000

MILES, AARON — 2B

PERSONAL: Born December 15, 1976, in Pittsburg, Calif. ... 5-7/180. ... Bats both, throws right. ... Full name: Aaron Wade Miles. ... High school: Antioch (Calif.).

TRANSACTIONS/CAREER NOTES: Selected by Houston Astros organization in 19th round of 1995 free-agent draft. ... Selected by Chicago White Sox organization from Astros organization in Rule 5 minor league draft (December 11, 2000). ... Traded by White Sox to Colorado Rockies for IF Juan Uribe (December 2, 2003). ... On disabled list (May 26-June 28, 2005); included rehabilitation assignment to Colorado Springs.

2005 GAMES PLAYED BY POSITION (MLB): 2B—79, SS—1.

SCOUTING REPORT *Offense:* Miles lost playing time in the second half of 2005 after Luis A. Gonzalez was moved to second base. Has a compact, short stroke, especially from the left side. Hits with an inside-out swing. Has better bat control than bat speed and makes good contact. Has no power and needs to use his speed more aggressively on the bases. *Defense:* Miles isn't fluid and his hands are stiff. Uses positioning and instincts to substitute for poor range. Is aggressive turning the double play. Can be a defensive liability if overextended. *Outlook:* Miles gets the most from his limited ability. Must have a good spring to get much playing time in 2006. *Grade 5.9*

AARON MILES' HITTING ZONE

.304	.294	.364
.341	.333	.365
.208	.188	.256

LEFTY-RIGHTY SPLITS

vs.	Avg.	AB	H	2B	3B	HR	RBI	BB	SO	OBP	Slg.
L	.234	64	15	2	0	1	8	2	11	.258	.313
R	.292	260	76	10	3	1	20	6	27	.317	.365

Year Team (League)	Pos.	G	AB	R	H	2B	3B	HR	RBI	BB	SO	HBP	GDP	SB-CS	Avg.	OBP	SLG	OPS	E	Avg.
1995— GC Astros (GCL)	SS-2B	47	171	32	44	9	3	0	18	14	14	0	3	9-6	.257	.312	.345	.657	14	.916
1996— GC Astros (GCL)	2B	55	214	48	63	3	2	0	15	20	18	1	3	14-7	.294	.357	.327	.685	10	.947
1997— Quad City (Midw.)	2B	97	370	55	97	13	2	1	35	30	45	2	8	18-11	.262	.318	.316	.634	14	.961
1998— Quad City (Midw.)	2B-3B-OF	108	369	42	90	22	6	2	37	25	52	1	7	28-13	.244	.293	.352	.645	28	.945
1999— Michigan (Midw.)	2B	112	470	72	149	28	8	10	71	28	33	2	8	17-12	.317	.353	.474	.828	11	.964
2000— Kissimmee (Fla. St.)	2B	75	295	40	86	20	1	2	36	28	29	0	7	11-6	.292	.352	.386	.738	17	.950
2001— Birmingham (Sou.)	3B-2B	84	343	53	89	16	3	8	42	26	35	2	10	3-5	.259	.313	.394	.706	6	.948
2002— Birmingham (Sou.)	2B-3B	138	531	67	171	39	1	9	68	40	45	2	4	25-16	.322	.369	.450	.819	26	.956
2003— Charlotte (Int'l)	2B-DH-3B	133	546	80	166	34	5	11	50	40	52	1	9	8-9	.304	.351	.445	.796	15	.973
— Chicago (A.L.)	2B-DH	8	12	3	4	3	0	0	2	0	0	0	0	0-0	.333	.333	.583	.917	0	1.000
2004— Colo. Springs (PCL)	2B	8	54	8	18	3	0	0	8	2	4	0	1	2-2	.333	.345	.389	.734	2	.968
— Colorado (N.L.)	2B	134	522	75	153	15	3	6	47	29	53	2	12	12-7	.293	.329	.368	.697	10	.984
2005— Colo. Springs (PCL)	2B	8	32	6	7	1	0	1	1	0	3	1	0	1-0	.219	.242	.281	.524	1	.978
— Colorado (N.L.)	2B-SS	99	324	37	91	12	3	2	28	8	38	4	6	4-2	.281	.306	.355	.661	7	.981
American League totals (1 year)		8	12	3	4	3	0	0	2	0	0	0	0	0-0	.333	.333	.583	.917	0	1.000
National League totals (2 years)		233	846	112	244	27	6	8	75	37	91	6	18	16-9	.288	.320	.363	.683	17	.983
Major League totals (3 years)		241	858	115	248	30	6	8	77	37	91	6	18	16-9	.289	.320	.366	.686	17	.983

MILLAR, KEVIN — OF/1B

PERSONAL: Born September 24, 1971, in Los Angeles. ... 6-0/210. ... Bats right, throws right. ... Full name: Kevin Charles Millar. ... Name pronounced: mi-LAR. ... High school: University (Los Angeles). ... College: Lamar. ... Nephew of Wayne Nordhagen, outfielder with four major league teams (1976-83).

TRANSACTIONS/CAREER NOTES: Contract purchased by Florida Marlins organization from Saint Paul of the independent Northern League (September 20, 1993). ... On disabled list (April 19, 1998-remainder of season); included rehabilitation assignment to Charlotte. ... On disabled list (May 4-28, 2002); included rehabilitation assignment to Portland. ... Claimed on waivers by Boston Red Sox (January 14, 2003); rejected claim. ... Traded by Marlins to Red Sox for cash considerations (February 15, 2003).
2005 GAMES PLAYED BY POSITION (MLB): 1B—110, OF—34.

SCOUTING REPORT *Offense:* Millar is an unorthodox hitter with a long approach. Will swing at anything on the inner half but has problems keeping the ball fair, sometimes because his top hand is dominant and he hooks the ball. Bat speed has declined and can no longer consistently pull the ball away from him. Is much more defensive on balls away. Will chase high pitches. *Defense:* Millar is stiff around the bag without good hands or range. Is not very accurate throwing to bases and doesn't have very quick feet. *Outlook:* He is showing signs of regression at the plate, and his holes are become more exploitable. Vocal presence in the clubhouse wears thin on some. **Grade 7.9**

KEVIN MILLAR'S HITTING ZONE

.260	.286	.150
.344	.280	.295
.348	.278	.211

LEFTY-RIGHTY SPLITS

vs.	Avg.	AB	H	2B	3B	HR	RBI	BB	SO	OBP	Slg.
L	.246	142	35	8	0	2	8	18	22	.341	.345
R	.283	307	87	20	1	7	42	36	52	.361	.423

Year Team (League)	Pos.	G	AB	R	H	2B	3B	HR	RBI	BB	SO	HBP	GDP	SB-CS	Avg.	OBP	SLG	OPS	E	FIELDING Avg.
1993— St. Paul (North.)	2B-3B	63	227	33	59	11	1	5	30	24	27	...	...	2-...	.260	...	.383	...	18	.911
1994— Kane Co. (Midw.)	1B	135	477	75	144	35	2	19	93	74	88	13	12	3-3	.302	.405	.503	.908	11	.990
1995— Brevard County (FSL)	1B	129	459	53	132	32	2	13	68	70	66	12	8	4-4	.288	.388	.451	.839	12	.991
1996— Portland (East.)	1B-3B	130	472	69	150	32	0	18	86	37	53	9	13	6-5	.318	.375	.500	.875	15	.983
1997— Portland (East.)	1B-3B	135	511	94	175	34	2	32	131	66	53	10	11	2-3	.342	.423	.605	1.027	17	.987
1998— Florida (N.L.)	3B	2	2	1	1	0	0	0	0	1	0	0	0	0-0	.500	.667	.500	1.167	1	.833
— Charlotte (Int'l)	1B-3B	14	46	14	15	3	0	4	15	9	7	2	3	1-0	.326	.448	.652	1.100	4	.930
1999— Calgary (PCL)	OF-3B-1B	36	143	24	43	11	1	7	26	11	19	0	5	2-0	.301	.348	.538	.887	2	.973
— Florida (N.L.)	1B-3B-OF	105	351	48	100	17	4	9	67	40	64	7	7	1-0	.285	.362	.433	.795	4	.995
2000— Florida (N.L.)	1B-OF-3B DH	123	259	36	67	14	3	14	42	36	47	8	5	0-0	.259	.364	.498	.862	5	.985
2001— Florida (N.L.)	OF-1B-DH DH	144	449	62	141	39	5	20	85	39	70	5	8	0-0	.314	.374	.557	.931	2	.993
2002— Portland (East.)		3	12	1	1	0	0	1	3	0	5	0	0	0-0	.083	.077	.333	.410	0	1.000
— Florida (N.L.)	OF-DH-1B 3B	126	438	58	134	41	0	16	57	40	74	5	15	0-2	.306	.366	.509	.875	4	.981
2003— Boston (A.L.)	1B-OF-DH	148	544	83	150	30	1	25	96	60	108	5	14	3-2	.276	.348	.472	.820	5	.995
2004— Boston (A.L.)	OF-1B-DH	150	508	74	151	36	0	18	74	57	91	•17	16	1-1	.297	.383	.474	.857	9	.986
2005— Boston (A.L.)	1B-OF	134	449	57	122	28	1	9	50	54	74	8	12	0-1	.272	.355	.399	.753	7	.992
American League totals (3 years)		432	1501	214	423	94	2	52	220	171	273	30	42	4-4	.282	.362	.451	.813	21	.992
National League totals (5 years)		500	1499	205	443	111	12	59	251	156	255	25	35	1-2	.296	.367	.504	.871	16	.990
Major League totals (8 years)		932	3000	419	866	205	14	111	471	327	528	55	77	5-6	.289	.365	.477	.842	37	.991

DIVISION SERIES RECORD

Year Team (League)	Pos.	G	AB	R	H	2B	3B	HR	RBI	BB	SO	HBP	GDP	SB-CS	Avg.	OBP	SLG	OPS	E	Avg.
2003— Boston (A.L.)	1B	5	21	0	5	0	0	0	0	2	4	0	0	0-0	.238	.304	.238	.542	0	1.000
2004— Boston (A.L.)	1B	3	10	2	3	0	0	1	4	1	1	0	0	0-0	.300	.364	.600	.964	0	1.000
2005— Boston (A.L.)	1B	2	3	0	1	1	0	0	1	0	1	0	0	0-0	.333	.333	.667	1.000	0	1.000
Division series totals (3 years)		10	34	2	9	1	0	1	5	3	6	0	0	0-0	.265	.324	.382	.707	0	1.000

CHAMPIONSHIP SERIES RECORD

Year Team (League)	Pos.	G	AB	R	H	2B	3B	HR	RBI	BB	SO	HBP	GDP	SB-CS	Avg.	OBP	SLG	OPS	E	Avg.
2003— Boston (A.L.)	1B	7	29	3	7	0	0	1	3	1	9	0	1	0-0	.241	.267	.345	.611	1	.986
2004— Boston (A.L.)	1B	7	24	4	6	3	0	0	2	5	4	0	1	0-0	.250	.379	.375	.754	0	1.000
Champ. series totals (2 years)		14	53	7	13	3	0	1	5	6	13	0	2	0-0	.245	.322	.358	.681	1	.992

WORLD SERIES RECORD

Year Team (League)	Pos.	G	AB	R	H	2B	3B	HR	RBI	BB	SO	HBP	GDP	SB-CS	Avg.	OBP	SLG	OPS	E	Avg.
2004— Boston (A.L.)	1B	4	8	2	1	1	0	0	0	2	2	1	0	0-0	.125	.364	.250	.614	1	.900

MILLER, CORKY   C

PERSONAL: Born March 18, 1976, in Yucaipa, Calif. ... 6-1/225. ... Bats right, throws right. ... Full name: Corky Abraham Philip Miller. ... High school: Yucaipa (Calif.). ... College: Nevada-Reno.
TRANSACTIONS/CAREER NOTES: Selected by California Angels organization in 23rd round of 1994 free-agent draft; did not sign. ... Signed as a non-drafted free agent by Cincinnati Reds organization (June 5, 1998). ... Claimed on waivers by Minnesota Twins (October 4, 2004).
2005 GAMES PLAYED BY POSITION (MLB): C—4, DH—1.

LEFTY-RIGHTY SPLITS

vs.	Avg.	AB	H	2B	3B	HR	RBI	BB	SO	OBP	Slg.
L	.000	6	0	0	0	0	0	0	2	.000	.000
R	.000	6	0	0	0	0	0	0	0	.000	.000

Year Team (League)	Pos.	G	AB	R	H	2B	3B	HR	RBI	BB	SO	HBP	GDP	SB-CS	Avg.	OBP	SLG	OPS	E	FIELDING Avg.
1998— Billings (Pion.)	C	45	129	28	35	8	0	5	24	24	24	21	2	1-4	.271	.455	.450	.904	14	.963
1999— Rockford (Midwest)	C	66	195	43	56	10	1	10	40	33	42	20	5	3-6	.287	.438	.503	.940	14	.975
— Chattanooga (Sou.)	C	33	104	20	23	10	0	4	16	11	30	11	3	0-0	.221	.354	.433	.787	3	.989
2000— Chattanooga (Sou.)	C	103	317	40	74	18	0	9	44	41	51	30	12	5-8	.233	.373	.375	.748	16	.983
2001— Chattanooga (Sou.)	C	59	170	25	47	12	0	9	42	25	32	19	1	1-2	.276	.425	.506	.931	7	.985
— Louisville (Int'l)	C	44	144	30	50	11	0	7	28	10	19	12	2	2-0	.347	.431	.569	1.001	3	.994
— Cincinnati (N.L.)	C	17	49	5	9	2	0	3	7	4	16	2	1	1-0	.184	.263	.408	.671	1	.991
2002— Louisville (Int'l)	C	43	134	14	31	5	0	6	21	16	21	6	4	1-2	.231	.340	.403	.743	2	.993
— Cincinnati (N.L.)	C	39	114	9	29	10	0	3	15	9	20	4	7	0-0	.254	.328	.421	.749	2	.992
2003— Louisville (Int'l)	C-DH	103	354	49	88	28	0	11	43	35	58	7	12	0-0	.249	.326	.421	.747	7	.985
— Cincinnati (N.L.)	C	14	30	3	8	0	0	0	1	5	7	2	1	0-0	.267	.395	.267	.661	0	1.000
2004— Louisville (Int'l)	C-DH	74	227	31	50	14	0	6	37	25	44	9	4	0-0	.220	.316	.361	.677	4	.990
— Cincinnati (N.L.)	C	13	39	2	1	0	0	0	3	6	12	3	2	0-0	.026	.204	.026	.230	1	.989
2005— Minnesota (A.L.)	C-DH	5	12	0	0	0	0	0	0	0	2	0	0	0-0	.000	.000	.000	.000	1	1.000

M

Year Team (League)	Pos.	G	AB	R	H	2B	3B	HR	RBI	BB	SO	HBP	GDP	SB-CS	Avg.	OBP	SLG	OPS	E	Avg.
— Rochester (Int'l)	C-DH-1B																			
	P	59	170	35	39	7	0	11	25	27	30	14	4	0-2	.229	.379	.465	.844	3	.994
American League totals (1 year)		5	12	0	0	0	0	0	0	0	2	0	0	0-0	.000	.000	.000	.000	0	1.000
National League totals (4 years)		83	232	20	47	12	0	6	26	24	55	11	12	1-0	.203	.301	.332	.633	4	.992
Major League totals (5 years)		88	244	20	47	12	0	6	26	24	57	11	12	1-0	.193	.289	.316	.604	4	.993

MILLER, DAMIAN   C

PERSONAL: Born October 13, 1969, in La Crosse, Wis. ... 6-3/220. ... Bats right, throws right. ... Full name: Damian Donald Miller. ... High school: West Salem (Wis.). ... College: Viterbo (Wis.).

TRANSACTIONS/CAREER NOTES: Selected by Minnesota Twins organization in 20th round of 1990 free-agent draft. ... Selected by Arizona Diamondbacks in second round (47th pick overall) of expansion draft (November 18, 1997). ... On disabled list (July 24-August 14, 2002); included rehabilitation assignment to Tucson. ... Traded by Diamondbacks to Chicago Cubs for P David Noyce and OF Gary Johnson (November 13, 2002). ... Traded by Cubs to Oakland Athletics for C Michael Barrett (December 21, 2003). ... Signed as a free agent by Milwaukee Brewers (November 24, 2004).

2005 GAMES PLAYED BY POSITION (MLB): C—111.

SCOUTING REPORT *Offense:* Miller is a steady .270 hitter with a short stroke but not too much patience. Strikes out too much. Has trouble with breaking stuff and has a slider-speed bat. Lack of patience is shown by his inability to hit with runners in scoring position. Has occasional power with the ball out over the plate. *Defense:* Miller has average arm strength and occasionally will drop his arm angle when he rushes. Has good hands but moves better to the right than left when blocking and shifting. *Outlook:* He isn't capable of playing more than 120 games a year, but he handles his pitching staff well. *Grade 6.2*

DAMIAN MILLER'S HITTING ZONE

.143	.421	.292
.328	.431	.245
.174	.273	.263

LEFTY-RIGHTY SPLITS

vs.	Avg.	AB	H	2B	3B	HR	RBI	BB	SO	OBP	Slg.
L	.231	91	21	5	0	0	6	10	25	.307	.286
R	.286	294	84	20	1	9	37	27	69	.351	.452

Year Team (League)	Pos.	G	AB	R	H	2B	3B	HR	RBI	BB	SO	HBP	GDP	SB-CS	Avg.	OBP	SLG	OPS	E	Avg.
1990— Elizabethton (App.)	C	14	45	7	10	1	0	1	6	9	3	0	2	1-0	.222	.352	.311	.663	2	.982
1991— Kenosha (Midw.)	1B-C-OF	80	267	28	62	11	1	3	34	24	53	2	4	3-2	.232	.297	.315	.612	4	.990
1992— Kenosha (Midw.)	C	115	377	53	110	27	2	5	56	53	66	7	13	6-1	.292	.385	.414	.799	9	.989
1993— Fort Myers (FSL)	C	87	325	31	69	12	1	1	26	31	44	0	5	6-3	.212	.281	.265	.546	8	.985
— Nashville (Southern)	C	4	13	0	3	0	0	0	0	2	4	0	0	0-0	.231	.333	.231	.564	0	1.000
1994— Nashville (Southern)	C	103	328	36	88	10	0	8	35	35	51	1	11	4-6	.268	.336	.372	.708	8	.989
1995— Salt Lake (PCL)	C-OF	83	295	39	84	23	1	3	41	15	39	3	11	2-4	.285	.324	.400	.724	1	.998
1996— Salt Lake (PCL)	1B-C	104	385	54	110	27	1	7	55	25	58	6	13	1-4	.286	.336	.416	.751	6	.992
1997— Salt Lake (PCL)	C-DH	85	314	48	106	19	3	11	82	29	62	3	7	6-1	.338	.395	.522	.918	6	.988
— Minnesota (A.L.)	C-DH	25	66	5	18	1	0	2	11	2	12	0	2	0-0	.273	.282	.379	.660	1	1.000
1998— Tucson (PCL)	C	18	63	14	22	7	1	0	11	9	9	2	2	0-0	.349	.434	.492	.926	3	.973
— Arizona (N.L.)	C-DH-OF / 1B	57	168	17	48	14	2	3	14	11	43	2	2	1-0	.286	.337	.446	.783	4	.986
1999— Arizona (N.L.)	C	86	296	35	80	19	0	11	47	19	78	2	6	0-0	.270	.316	.446	.762	6	.991
2000— Arizona (N.L.)	C-1B	100	324	43	89	24	0	10	44	36	74	1	6	2-2	.275	.347	.441	.788	7	.991
2001— Arizona (N.L.)	C	123	380	45	103	19	0	13	47	35	80	4	9	0-1	.271	.337	.424	.761	7	.993
2002— Arizona (N.L.)	C	101	297	40	74	22	0	11	42	38	88	3	14	0-0	.249	.340	.434	.775	2	.997
— Tucson (PCL)	C	3	9	1	3	1	0	0	0	0	1	0	1	0-0	.333	.333	.444	.778	0	1.000
2003— Chicago (N.L.)	C	114	352	34	82	19	1	9	36	39	91	1	15	1-0	.233	.310	.369	.680	3	.997
2004— Oakland (A.L.)	C	110	397	39	108	25	0	9	58	39	87	2	16	0-1	.272	.339	.403	.742	1	.999
2005— Milwaukee (N.L.)	C	114	385	50	105	25	1	9	43	37	94	4	16	0-1	.273	.340	.413	.753	3	.996
American League totals (2 years)		135	463	44	126	26	0	11	71	41	99	2	21	0-1	.272	.331	.400	.730	1	.999
National League totals (7 years)		695	2202	264	581	142	4	66	273	215	548	17	68	4-4	.264	.333	.422	.754	32	.994
Major League totals (9 years)		830	2665	308	707	168	4	77	344	256	647	19	89	4-5	.265	.332	.418	.750	33	.995

DIVISION SERIES RECORD

Year Team (League)	Pos.	G	AB	R	H	2B	3B	HR	RBI	BB	SO	HBP	GDP	SB-CS	Avg.	OBP	SLG	OPS	E	Avg.
2001— Arizona (N.L.)	C	5	15	1	4	0	0	0	0	1	3	1	0	0-0	.267	.353	.267	.620	0	1.000
2002— Arizona (N.L.)	C	1	2	0	1	1	0	0	0	2	0	0	0	0-0	.500	.750	1.000	1.750	0	1.000
2003— Chicago (N.L.)	C	4	11	0	1	1	0	0	1	2	5	0	0	0-0	.091	.231	.182	.413	0	1.000
Division series totals (3 years)		10	28	1	6	2	0	0	1	5	8	1	0	0-0	.214	.353	.286	.639	0	1.000

CHAMPIONSHIP SERIES RECORD

Year Team (League)	Pos.	G	AB	R	H	2B	3B	HR	RBI	BB	SO	HBP	GDP	SB-CS	Avg.	OBP	SLG	OPS	E	Avg.
2001— Arizona (N.L.)	C	5	17	0	3	0	0	0	0	2	5	0	2	0-0	.176	.263	.176	.440	0	1.000
2003— Chicago (N.L.)	C	4	10	0	2	1	0	0	1	2	2	0	0	0-0	.200	.333	.300	.633	0	1.000
Champ. series totals (2 years)		9	27	0	5	1	0	0	1	4	7	0	2	0-0	.185	.290	.222	.513	0	1.000

WORLD SERIES RECORD

Year Team (League)	Pos.	G	AB	R	H	2B	3B	HR	RBI	BB	SO	HBP	GDP	SB-CS	Avg.	OBP	SLG	OPS	E	Avg.
2001— Arizona (N.L.)	C	6	20	3	4	2	0	0	2	1	11	1	1	0-0	.200	.273	.300	.573	1	.982

ALL-STAR GAME RECORD

		G	AB	R	H	2B	3B	HR	RBI	BB	SO	HBP	GDP	SB-CS	Avg.	OBP	SLG	OPS	E	Avg.
All-Star Game totals (1 year)		1	3	1	2	2	0	0	1	0	0	0	0	0-0	.667	.667	1.333	2.000	0	1.000

MILLER, JUSTIN   P

PERSONAL: Born August 27, 1977, in Torrance, Calif. ... 6-2/209. ... Throws right, bats right. ... Full name: Justin Mark Miller. ... High school: Torrance (Calif.). ... Junior college: Los Angeles Harbor.

TRANSACTIONS/CAREER NOTES: Selected by San Francisco Giants organization in 34th round of 1995 free-agent draft; did not sign. ... Selected by Colorado Rockies organization in fifth round of 1997 free-agent draft. ... Traded by Rockies with cash to Oakland Athletics as part of three-team deal in which Brewers acquired P Jimmy Haynes from A's, Rockies acquired 3B Jeff Cirillo, P Scott Karl and cash from Brewers and Brewers acquired P Jamey Wright and C Henry Blanco from Rockies (December 13, 1999). ... Traded by A's with 3B Eric Hinske to Toronto Blue Jays for P Billy Koch (December 7, 2001). ... On disabled list (May 31-August 4, 2004).

CAREER HITTING: 0-for-2 (.000), 0 R, 0 2B, 0 3B, 0 HR, 0 RBI.

LEFTY-RIGHTY SPLITS

vs.	Avg.	AB	H	2B	3B	HR	RBI	BB	SO	OBP	Slg.
L	.333	3	1	0	0	1	2	0	2	.333	1.333
R	.444	9	4	0	0	2	4	0	.444	1.111

Year—Team (League)	W	L	Pct.	ERA	WHIP	G	GS	CG	ShO	Hld.	Sv.-Opp.	IP	H	R	ER	HR	BB-IBB	SO	Avg.
1997— Portland (N'west)	4	2	.667	2.14	1.31	14	11	0	0	...	0-...	67.1	68	26	16	3	20-0	54	.262
1998— Asheville (S. Atl.)	13	8	.619	3.69	1.33	27	27	3	1	...	0-...	163.1	177	89	67	14	40-0	142	.275
1999— Salem (Carol.)	1	2	.333	4.14	1.24	8	8	0	0	...	0-...	37.0	35	18	17	3	11-0	35	.245
2000— Midland (Texas)	5	4	.556	4.55	1.32	18	18	0	0	...	0-...	87.0	74	49	44	8	41-1	82	.230
—Sacramento (PCL)	4	1	.800	2.47	1.01	9	9	0	0	...	0-...	54.2	42	18	15	3	13-0	34	.210
2001— Sacramento (PCL)	7	10	.412	4.75	1.44	29	28	1	0	...	0-...	165.0	174	94	87	26	64-1	134	.276
2002— Syracuse (Int'l)	3	2	.600	1.61	1.12	8	8	0	0	...	0-...	44.2	34	11	8	0	16-0	29	.207
—Toronto (A.L.)	9	5	.643	5.54	1.65	25	18	0	0	1	0-0	102.1	103	70	63	12	66-2	68	.268
2003— Dunedin (Fla. St.)	0	1	.000	4.50	0.80	1	1	0	0	...	0-0	6.0	3	3	3	0	2-0	5	.167
2004— Syracuse (Int'l)	1	1	.500	2.16	1.20	3	3	0	0	...	0-0	16.2	16	6	4	2	4-0	21	.242
—Toronto (A.L.)	3	4	.429	6.06	1.75	19	15	0	0	0	0-0	81.2	101	58	55	14	42-3	47	.316
2005— Toronto (A.L.)	0	0	...	15.43	2.14	1	0	0	0	0	0-0	2.1	5	4	4	3	0-0	2	.417
—Syracuse (Int'l)	3	1	.750	2.32	1.05	28	4	0	0	8	2-4	50.1	39	15	13	3	14-0	56	.210
Major League totals (3 years)	**12**	**9**	**.571**	**5.89**	**1.70**	**45**	**33**	**0**	**0**	**1**	**0-0**	**186.1**	**209**	**132**	**122**	**29**	**108-5**	**117**	**.291**

MILLER, MATT   P

PERSONAL: Born November 23, 1971, in Greenwood, Miss. ... 6-3/215. ... Throws right, bats right. ... Full name: Matt Jacob Miller. ... High school: Monterey (Lubbock, Texas). ... College: Delta State.

TRANSACTIONS/CAREER NOTES: Signed as a free agent by Texas Rangers organization (December 1, 1997). ... Released by Rangers (March 29, 1998). ... Contract purchased by Rangers organization from Greenville of the independent Texas-Louisiana League (June 27, 1998). ... Signed as a free agent by San Diego Padres organization (November 5, 2000). ... Signed as a free agent by Oakland Athletics organization (November 19, 2001). ... Signed as a free agent by Colorado Rockies organization (November 20, 2002). ... Signed as a free agent by Cleveland Indians organization (January 5, 2004). ... On disabled list (July 16, 2005-remainder of season); included rehabilitation assignments to Mahoning Valley and Akron.

CAREER HITTING: 0-for-0 (.000), 0 R, 0 2B, 0 3B, 0 HR, 0 RBI.

SCOUTING REPORT **Throws:** Miller's fastball is in the 86-89 mph range, and he throws a slurve and a changeup. **Tendencies:** He throws with a sidearm action and the ball dives toward the hitter. Fastball down has good sinking action. The sweeping slurve starts away from righthanders, who will chase it if he continues to expand the zone with it. Starts it off the plate to lefthanders, forcing them to give up on it. Arm speed and motion with straight change is effective against lefthanders. **Outlook:** Miller has shown the past few years he's a solid bullpen arm. **Grade 5.9**

MATT MILLER'S PITCHING ZONE

.000	...	.200
.200	.444	.231
.111	.000	.375

LEFTY-RIGHTY SPLITS

vs.	Avg.	AB	H	2B	3B	HR	RBI	BB	SO	OBP	Slg.
L	.194	36	7	1	0	0	1	6	4	.326	.222
R	.221	68	15	3	0	1	7	4	19	.280	.309

Year—Team (League)	W	L	Pct.	ERA	WHIP	G	GS	CG	ShO	Hld.	Sv.-Opp.	IP	H	R	ER	HR	BB-IBB	SO	Avg.
1996— Greenville (BSL)	5	2	.714	6.07	1.82	19	6	0	0	...	1-...	69.2	77	51	47	2	50-0	54	.286
1997— Greenville (BSL)	12	3	.800	2.26	1.16	15	15	5	3	...	0-...	107.1	76	34	27	0	49-0	129	.203
1998— Greenville (BSL)	1	7	.125	2.85	1.21	8	8	4	0	...	0-...	53.2	46	26	17	1	19-1	49	.230
—Savannah (S. Atl.)	3	1	.750	2.29	0.99	17	0	0	0	...	3-...	35.1	25	9	9	0	10-0	46	.203
1999— Charlotte (Fla. St.)	1	2	.333	3.03	1.35	22	0	0	0	...	8-...	29.2	27	12	10	0	13-1	39	.231
—Tulsa (Texas)	6	4	.600	3.38	1.25	34	0	0	0	...	7-...	56.0	42	24	21	2	28-2	83	.213
2000— GC Rangers (GCL)	0	0	...	4.50	1.00	1	0	0	0	...	0-...	2.0	2	1	1	0	0-0	4	.250
—Tulsa (Texas)	0	0	...	14.73	3.00	3	0	0	0	...	0-...	3.2	7	7	6	0	4-0	4	.412
—Oklahoma (PCL)	3	3	.500	3.58	1.57	39	0	0	0	...	6-...	60.1	61	29	24	6	34-4	69	.264
2001— Portland (PCL)	1	7	.125	3.63	1.30	44	0	0	0	...	17-...	44.2	44	22	18	1	14-2	43	.254
2002— Sacramento (PCL)	3	7	.300	4.31	1.54	54	0	0	0	...	6-...	71.0	81	42	34	5	28-8	63	.286
2003— Colorado (N.L.)	0	0	...	2.08	1.62	4	0	0	0	0	0-0	4.1	5	1	1	0	2-0	5	.313
—Colo. Springs (PCL)	5	0	1.000	2.13	1.09	61	0	0	0	...	3-...	63.1	46	17	15	0	23-1	83	.200
2004— Buffalo (Int'l)	1	2	.333	1.93	1.14	13	0	0	0	...	2-...	14.0	10	4	3	0	6-1	17	.196
—Cleveland (A.L.)	4	1	.800	3.09	1.17	57	0	0	0	7	1-2	55.1	42	22	19	1	23-8	55	.216
2005— Buffalo (Int'l)	0	0	...	0.87	0.48	9	0	0	0	1	3-3	10.1	3	1	1	0	2-0	15	.088
—Cleveland (A.L.)	1	0	1.000	1.82	1.08	23	0	0	0	4	1-2	29.2	22	6	6	1	10-3	23	.212
—Mahoning Valley (N.Y.-Penn.)	0	0	...	54.00	7.50	1	0	0	0	0	0-0	0.2	5	4	4	0	0-0	1	.714
—Akron (East.)	0	0	...	0.00	0.00	1	0	0	0	0	0-0	1.0	0	0	0	0	0-0	0	.000
American League totals (2 years)	**5**	**1**	**.833**	**2.65**	**1.14**	**80**	**0**	**0**	**0**	**11**	**2-4**	**85.0**	**64**	**28**	**25**	**2**	**33-11**	**78**	**.215**
National League totals (1 year)	**0**	**0**	**...**	**2.08**	**1.62**	**4**	**0**	**0**	**0**	**0**	**0-0**	**4.1**	**5**	**1**	**1**	**0**	**2-0**	**5**	**.313**
Major League totals (3 years)	**5**	**1**	**.833**	**2.62**	**1.16**	**84**	**0**	**0**	**0**	**11**	**2-4**	**89.1**	**69**	**29**	**26**	**2**	**35-11**	**83**	**.220**

MILLER, TREVER   P

PERSONAL: Born May 29, 1973, in Louisville, Ky. ... 6-3/200. ... Throws left, bats right. ... Full name: Trever Douglas Miller. ... High school: Trinity (Louisville, Ky.).

TRANSACTIONS/CAREER NOTES: Selected by Detroit Tigers organization in supplemental round ("sandwich pick" between first and second rounds, 41st pick overall) of 1991 free-agent draft; pick received as part of compensation for Atlanta Braves signing Type A free-agent C Mike Heath. ... Traded by Tigers with C Brad Ausmus, Ps Jose Lima and C.J. Nitkowski and 1B Daryle Ward to Houston Astros for OF Brian Hunter, IF Orlando Miller, Ps Doug Brocail and Todd Jones and cash (December 10, 1996). ... On disabled list (August 23-September 7, 1998). ... Traded by Astros to Philadelphia Phillies for P Yorkis Perez (March 29, 2000). ... Claimed on waivers by Los Angeles

Dodgers (May 19, 2000). ... Signed as a free agent by Boston Red Sox organization (January 22, 2001). ... Signed as a free agent by Cincinnati Reds organization (December 21, 2001). ... Released by Reds (September 4, 2002). ... Signed by Toronto Blue Jays organization (October 30, 2002). ... Signed as a free agent by Tampa Bay Devil Rays (January 7, 2004). ... On disabled list (June 13-28, 2005).
CAREER HITTING: 1-for-6 (.167), 1 R, 1 2B, 0 3B, 0 HR, 0 RBI.

SCOUTING REPORT **Throws:** Miller has a fastball that hits 86-88 mph and a slider. **Tendencies:** He has changed his arm action, now dropping down to the side, especially against lefthanders. Stuff and velocity are marginal and pitches flatten out. Is successful if hitters chase his slurve out of the zone. **Outlook:** Miller primarily is a setup reliever. Must have good control to be effective. *Grade 6*

TREVER MILLER'S PITCHING ZONE

.167	.167	.125
.370	.429	.200
.167	.500	.278

LEFTY-RIGHTY SPLITS

vs.	Avg.	AB	H	2B	3B	HR	RBI	BB	SO	OBP	Slg.
L	.267	86	23	7	0	2	29	15	20	.393	.419
R	.289	76	22	2	0	2	9	14	15	.407	.395

Year	Team (League)	W	L	Pct.	ERA	WHIP	G	GS	CG	ShO	Hld.	Sv.-Opp.	IP	H	R	ER	HR	BB-IBB	SO	Avg.
1991—	Bristol (Appal.)	2	7	.222	5.67	1.65	13	13	0	0	...	0-...	54.0	60	44	34	7	29-0	46	.278
1992—	Bristol (Appal.)	3	• 8	.273	4.93	1.47	12	12	1	0	...	0-...	69.1	75	45	38	4	27-0	64	.271
1993—	Fayetteville (SAL)	8	13	.381	4.19	1.35	28	28	2	0	...	0-...	161.0	151	99	75	7	67-0	116	.245
1994—	Trenton (East.)	7	16	.304	4.39	1.43	26	26	6	0	...	0-...	174.1	198	95	85	9	51-0	73	.290
1995—	Jacksonville (Sou.)	8	2	.800	2.72	1.28	31	16	3	2	...	0-...	122.1	122	46	37	5	34-0	77	.261
1996—	Toledo (Int'l)	13	6	.684	4.90	1.40	27	27	0	0	...	0-...	165.1	167	98	90	19	65-1	115	.260
—Detroit (A.L.)		0	4	.000	9.18	2.22	5	4	0	0	0	0-0	16.2	28	17	17	3	9-0	8	.384
1997—	New Orleans (A.A.)	6	7	.462	3.30	1.41	29	27	2	0	...	0-...	163.2	177	71	60	15	54-1	99	.283
1998—	Houston (N.L.)	2	0	1.000	3.04	1.44	37	1	0	0	1	1-2	53.1	57	21	18	4	20-1	30	.266
1999—	Houston (N.L.)	3	2	.600	5.07	1.75	47	0	0	0	4	1-1	49.2	58	29	28	6	29-1	37	.299
2000—	Philadelphia (N.L.)	0	0	...	8.36	2.00	14	0	0	0	0	0-0	14.0	19	16	13	3	9-1	10	.317
—Los Angeles (N.L.)		0	0	...	23.14	4.71	2	0	0	0	0	0-0	2.1	8	6	6	0	3-0	1	.571
—Albuquerque (PCL)		4	2	.667	3.41	1.38	12	9	1	1	...	0-...	58.0	60	29	22	5	20-0	39	.268
2001—	Sarasota (Fla. St.)	0	0	...	2.25	0.50	3	2	0	0	...	0-...	8.0	3	2	2	0	1-0	6	.115
—Pawtucket (Int'l)		3	11	.214	5.20	1.52	33	15	0	0	...	0-...	116.0	142	79	67	16	34-2	93	.307
2002—	Louisville (Int'l)	9	5	.643	3.18	1.21	65	1	0	0	...	0-...	82.0	76	30	29	6	23-4	80	.242
2003—	Toronto (A.L.)	2	2	.500	4.61	1.41	* 79	0	0	0	16	3-4	52.2	46	30	27	7	28-3	44	.231
2004—	Tampa Bay (A.L.)	1	1	.500	3.12	1.29	60	0	0	0	9	1-3	49.0	48	21	17	3	15-4	43	.257
2005—	Tampa Bay (A.L.)	2	2	.500	4.06	1.67	61	0	0	0	11	0-3	44.1	45	23	20	4	29-6	35	.278
American League totals (4 years)		5	9	.357	4.48	1.52	205	4	0	0	36	4-10	162.2	167	91	81	17	81-13	130	.269
National League totals (3 years)		5	2	.714	4.90	1.70	100	1	0	0	5	2-3	119.1	142	72	65	13	61-3	78	.295
Major League totals (7 years)		10	11	.476	4.66	1.60	305	5	0	0	41	6-13	282.0	309	163	146	30	142-16	208	.280

DIVISION SERIES RECORD

Year	Team (League)	W	L	Pct.	ERA	WHIP	G	GS	CG	ShO	Hld.	Sv.-Opp.	IP	H	R	ER	HR	BB-IBB	SO	Avg.
1998—	Houston (N.L.)	0	0	...	...	...	1	0	0	0	0	0-0	0.0	0	0	0	0	1-0	0	...
1999—	Houston (N.L.)	0	0	...	0.00	0.75	2	0	0	0	1	0-0	1.1	1	0	0	0	0-0	2	.200
Division series totals (2 years)		0	0	...	0.00	1.50	3	0	0	0	1	0-0	1.1	1	0	0	0	1-0	2	.200

MILLER, WADE   P

PERSONAL: Born September 13, 1976, in Reading, Pa. ... 6-2/220. ... Throws right, bats right. ... Full name: Wade T. Miller. ... High school: Brandywine Heights (Pa.). ... College: Alvernia (Pa.).
TRANSACTIONS/CAREER NOTES: Selected by Houston Astros organization in 20th round of 1996 free-agent draft. ... On disabled list (April 15-May 29, 2002); included rehabilitation assignment to New Orleans. ... On disabled list (June 26, 2004-remainder of season). ... Signed as a free agent by Boston Red Sox (December 22, 2004). ... On disabled list (April 1-May 8 and August 8, 2005-remainder of season); incuded rehabilitation assignments to Pawtucket, Greenville and Wilmington.
CAREER HITTING: 45-for-262 (.172), 20 R, 9 2B, 0 3B, 0 HR, 17 RBI.

SCOUTING REPORT **Throws:** When healthy, Miller throws his fastball from 88-92 mph. Also throws a curve, slider and changeup. **Tendencies:** A poor delivery puts a lot of stress on his arm. Curveball still has good rotation. Slider was quick before last season's shoulder injury. Has developed a better change. Is an aggressive pitcher. **Outlook:** The big question with Miller is whether he can pitch a season without arm problems. Developed shoulder problems at midseason and missed the remainder of the season. Is a risk. *Grade 4.8*

WADE MILLER'S PITCHING ZONE

.275	.417	.324
.333	.286	.250
.152	.533	.300

LEFTY-RIGHTY SPLITS

vs.	Avg.	AB	H	2B	3B	HR	RBI	BB	SO	OBP	Slg.
L	.255	196	50	13	2	3	28	23	43	.336	.388
R	.282	163	46	10	3	5	21	24	21	.374	.472

Year	Team (League)	W	L	Pct.	ERA	WHIP	G	GS	CG	ShO	Hld.	Sv.-Opp.	IP	H	R	ER	HR	BB-IBB	SO	Avg.
1996—	GC Astros (GCL)	3	4	.429	3.79	1.07	11	10	0	0	...	0-...	57.0	49	26	24	1	12-0	53	.233
—Auburn (NY-Penn)		1	1	.500	5.00	1.33	2	2	0	0	...	0-...	9.0	8	9	5	0	4-0	11	.216
1997—	Quad City (Midw.)	5	3	.625	3.36	0.93	10	8	2	0	...	0-...	59.0	45	27	22	.7	10-0	50	.201
—Kissimmee (Fla. St.)		10	2	.833	1.80	0.93	14	14	4	1	...	0-...	100.0	79	28	20	3	14-1	76	.214
1998—	Jackson (Texas)	5	0	1.000	2.32	1.23	10	10	0	0	...	0-...	62.0	49	23	16	7	27-2	48	.213
1999—	New Orleans (PCL)	11	9	.550	4.38	1.36	26	26	2	0	...	0-...	162.1	156	85	79	16	64-0	135	.248
—Houston (N.L.)		0	1	.000	9.58	2.13	5	1	0	0	0	0-0	10.1	17	11	11	4	5-0	8	.362
2000—	New Orleans (PCL)	4	5	.444	3.67	1.26	16	15	0	0	...	0-...	105.1	95	46	43	6	38-1	81	.245
—Houston (N.L.)		6	6	.500	5.14	1.39	16	16	2	0	0	0-0	105.0	104	66	60	14	42-1	89	.257
2001—	Houston (N.L.)	16	8	.667	3.40	1.22	32	32	1	1	0	0-0	212.0	183	91	80	31	76-3	183	.234
2002—	Houston (N.L.)	15	4	.789	3.28	1.29	26	26	1	1	0	0-0	164.2	151	63	60	14	62-9	144	.249

M

Year	Team (League)	W	L	Pct.	ERA	WHIP	G	GS	CG	ShO	Hld.	Sv.-Opp.	IP	H	R	ER	HR	BB-IBB	SO	Avg.
—	New Orleans (PCL)	0	0	...	2.25	1.38	2	2	0	0	...	0-...	8.0	10	4	2	0	1-0	9	.323
2003—	Houston (N.L.)	14	13	.519	4.13	1.31	33	33	1	0	...	0-0	187.1	168	96	86	17	77-1	161	.242
2004—	Houston (N.L.)	7	7	.500	3.35	1.35	15	15	0	0	...	0-0	88.2	76	35	33	11	44-0	74	.228
2005—	Greenville (SAL)	0	0	...	3.86	1.07	1	1	0	0	0	0-0	4.2	4	2	2	1	1-0	4	.222
—	Wilmington (Caro.)	0	0	...	1.80	1.20	1	1	0	0	0	0-0	5.0	6	1	1	1	0-0	6	.316
—	Pawtucket (Int'l)	0	0	...	2.53	1.50	2	2	0	0	0	0-0	10.2	10	4	3	1	6-0	10	.250
—	Boston (A.L.)	4	4	.500	4.95	1.57	16	16	0	0	0	0-0	91.0	96	53	50	8	47-0	64	.267
American League totals (1 year)		4	4	.500	4.95	1.57	16	16	0	0	0	0-0	91.0	96	53	50	8	47-0	64	.267
National League totals (6 years)		58	39	.598	3.87	1.31	127	123	5	1	0	0-0	768.0	699	362	330	91	306-14	659	.244
Major League totals (7 years)		62	43	.590	3.98	1.34	143	139	5	1	0	0-0	859.0	795	415	380	99	353-14	723	.246

DIVISION SERIES RECORD

Year	Team (League)	W	L	Pct.	ERA	WHIP	G	GS	CG	ShO	Hld.	Sv.-Opp.	IP	H	R	ER	HR	BB-IBB	SO	Avg.
2001—	Houston (N.L.)	0	0	...	2.57	1.00	1	1	0	0	0	0-0	7.0	7	2	2	1	0-0	6	.292

MILLWOOD, KEVIN — P

PERSONAL: Born December 24, 1974, in Gastonia, N.C. ... 6-4/235. ... Throws right, bats right. ... Full name: Kevin Austin Millwood. ... High school: Bessemer City (N.C.).
TRANSACTIONS/CAREER NOTES: Selected by Atlanta Braves organization in 11th round of 1993 free-agent draft. ... On disabled list (May 7-July 20, 2001); included rehabilitation assignments to Macon and Greenville. ... Traded by Braves to Philadelphia Phillies for C Johnny Estrada (December 20, 2002). ... On disabled list (August 6-September 12, 2004). ... Signed as a free agent by Cleveland Indians (January 6, 2005). ... On disabled list (May 26-June 16, 2005). ... On suspended list (August 5-11, 2005).
CAREER HITTING: 53-for-428 (.124), 18 R, 14 2B, 0 3B, 2 HR, 24 RBI.

SCOUTING REPORT *Throws:* Millwood offers up a two- and a four-seam fastball, with an ability to maintain 90-94 mph velocity. Also has a mid-80s slider and a straight changeup. *Tendencies:* He is in his best physical shape in years and his velocity proves it. Has changed his delivery; is more straight up and driving more to the plate. Is working inside with good control. Has very good tilt to his slider, which breaks late. Has good arm speed and movement with his change. Challenges hitters. *Outlook:* Millwood was making a salary drive for 2006 with a much improved 2005. Is capable of posting 15-18 wins. *Grade 8.3*

KEVIN MILLWOOD'S PITCHING ZONE

.317	.275	.159
.205	.377	.348
.182	.227	.235

LEFTY-RIGHTY SPLITS

vs.	Avg.	AB	H	2B	3B	HR	RBI	BB	SO	OBP	Slg.
L	.269	368	99	21	1	10	36	32	83	.325	.413
R	.227	365	83	15	2	10	31	20	63	.274	.362

Year	Team (League)	W	L	Pct.	ERA	WHIP	G	GS	CG	ShO	Hld.	Sv.-Opp.	IP	H	R	ER	HR	BB-IBB	SO	Avg.
1993—	GC Braves (GCL)	3	3	.500	3.06	1.28	12	9	0	0	...	0-...	50.0	36	27	17	3	28-0	49	.196
1994—	Danville (Appal.)	3	3	.500	3.72	1.65	13	5	0	0	...	1-...	46.0	42	25	19	4	34-2	56	.247
—	Macon (S. Atl.)	0	5	.000	5.79	1.93	12	4	0	0	...	1-...	32.2	31	31	21	4	32-1	24	.242
1995—	Macon (S. Atl.)	5	6	.455	4.63	1.39	29	12	0	0	...	0-...	103.0	86	65	53	10	57-0	89	.219
1996—	Durham (Carol.)	6	9	.400	4.28	1.31	33	20	1	0	...	1-...	149.1	138	77	71	17	58-0	139	.248
1997—	Greenville (Sou.)	3	5	.375	4.11	1.35	11	11	0	0	...	0-...	61.1	59	37	28	8	24-0	61	.250
—	Richmond (Int'l)	7	0	1.000	1.93	0.89	9	9	1	0	...	0-...	60.2	38	13	13	2	16-0	46	.178
—	Atlanta (N.L.)	5	3	.625	4.03	1.48	12	8	0	0	0	0-0	51.1	55	26	23	1	21-1	42	.282
1998—	Atlanta (N.L.)	17	8	.680	4.08	1.33	31	29	3	1	1	0-0	174.1	175	86	79	18	56-3	163	.258
1999—	Atlanta (N.L.)	18	7	.720	2.68	1.00	33	33	2	0	0	0-0	228.0	168	80	68	24	59-2	205 *	.202
2000—	Atlanta (N.L.)	10	13	.435	4.66	1.29	36	•35	0	0	0	0-0	212.2	213	115	110	26	62-2	168	.258
2001—	Atlanta (N.L.)	7	7	.500	4.31	1.33	21	21	0	0	0	0-0	121.0	121	66	58	20	40-6	84	.260
—	Macon (S. Atl.)	0	0	...	0.00	0.00	1	1	0	0	0	0-0	3.0	0	0	0	0	1-0	5	.000
—	Greenville (Sou.)	0	1	.000	4.50	1.20	2	2	0	0	0	0-...	10.0	9	6	5	2	3-0	10	.243
2002—	Atlanta (N.L.)	18	8	.692	3.24	1.16	35	34	1	1	0	0-0	217.0	186	83	78	16	65-7	178	.230
2003—	Philadelphia (N.L.)	14	12	.538	4.01	1.25	35	35	5	•3	0	0-0	222.0	210	103	99	19	68-6	169	.250
2004—	Philadelphia (N.L.)	9	6	.600	4.85	1.46	25	25	0	0	0	0-0	141.0	155	81	76	14	51-5	125	.278
2005—	Cleveland (A.L.)	9	11	.450	* 2.86	1.22	30	30	1	0	0	0-0	192.0	182	72	61	20	52-0	146	.248
American League totals (1 year)		9	11	.450	2.86	1.22	30	30	1	0	0	0-0	192.0	182	72	61	20	52-0	146	.248
National League totals (8 years)		98	64	.605	3.89	1.25	228	220	11	5	1	0-0	1367.1	1283	640	591	138	422-32	1134	.247
Major League totals (9 years)		107	75	.588	3.76	1.24	258	250	12	5	1	0-0	1559.1	1465	712	652	158	474-32	1280	.247

DIVISION SERIES RECORD

Year	Team (League)	W	L	Pct.	ERA	WHIP	G	GS	CG	ShO	Hld.	Sv.-Opp.	IP	H	R	ER	HR	BB-IBB	SO	Avg.
1999—	Atlanta (N.L.)	1	0	1.000	0.90	0.10	2	1	1	0	0	1-1	10.0	1	1	1	1	0-0	9	.031
2000—	Atlanta (N.L.)	0	1	.000	7.71	1.50	1	1	0	0	0	0-0	4.2	4	4	4	2	3-0	3	.222
2001—	Atlanta (N.L.)		Did not play.																	
2002—	Atlanta (N.L.)	1	1	.500	3.27	0.64	2	2	0	0	0	0-0	11.0	7	4	4	3	0-0	14	.175
Division series totals (3 years)		2	2	.500	3.16	0.58	5	4	1	0	0	1-1	25.2	12	9	9	6	3-0	26	.133

CHAMPIONSHIP SERIES RECORD

Year	Team (League)	W	L	Pct.	ERA	WHIP	G	GS	CG	ShO	Hld.	Sv.-Opp.	IP	H	R	ER	HR	BB-IBB	SO	Avg.
1999—	Atlanta (N.L.)	1	0	1.000	3.55	1.11	2	2	0	0	0	0-0	12.2	13	6	5	1	1-0	9	.260
2001—	Atlanta (N.L.)	0	0	...	0.00	0.00	1	0	0	0	0	0-0	1.0	0	0	0	0	0-0	1	.000
Champ. series totals (2 years)		1	0	1.000	3.29	1.02	3	2	0	0	0	0-0	13.2	13	6	5	1	1-0	10	.245

WORLD SERIES RECORD

Year	Team (League)	W	L	Pct.	ERA	WHIP	G	GS	CG	ShO	Hld.	Sv.-Opp.	IP	H	R	ER	HR	BB-IBB	SO	Avg.
1999—	Atlanta (N.L.)	0	1	.000	18.00	5.00	1	1	0	0	0	0-0	2.0	8	5	4	0	2-0	2	.615

ALL-STAR GAME RECORD

Year	Team (League)	W	L	Pct.	ERA	WHIP	G	GS	CG	ShO	Hld.	Sv.-Opp.	IP	H	R	ER	HR	BB-IBB	SO	Avg.
All-Star Game totals (1 year)		0	0	...	0.00	1.00	1	0	0	0	0	0-0	1.0	1	0	0	0	0-0	1	.250

M

MILTON, ERIC   P

PERSONAL: Born August 4, 1975, in State College, Pa. ... 6-3/208. ... Throws left, bats left. ... Full name: Eric Robert Milton. ... High school: Bellefonte (Pa.). ... College: Maryland.

TRANSACTIONS/CAREER NOTES: Selected by New York Yankees organization in first round (20th pick overall) of 1996 free-agent draft. ... Traded by Yankees with P Danny Mota, OF Brian Buchanan, SS Cristian Guzman and cash to Minnesota Twins for 2B Chuck Knoblauch (February 6, 1998). ... On disabled list (August 7-September 2, 2002). ... On disabled list (March 13-September 14, 2003); included rehabilitation assignments to Fort Myers and New Britain. ... Traded by Twins to Philadelphia Phillies for P Carlos Silva, IF Nick Punto and a player to be named (December 3, 2003); Twins acquired P Bobby Korecky to complete deal (December 16, 2003). ... Signed as a free agent by Cincinnati Reds (December 27, 2004).

CAREER HITTING: 24-for-141 (.170), 12 R, 2 2B, 0 3B, 2 HR, 11 RBI.

SCOUTING REPORT *Throws:*
Milton throws four- and two-seam fastballs in the low 90s, a curveball, a slider and a changeup. *Tendencies:* He struggled in home run-friendly Great American Ballpark because he is a high-fastball pitcher. Trying to throw more two-seam fastballs to keep the ball out of the stands. Has good movement on his changeup. Has cutting movement on his slider, his best breaking pitch. Needs to have better command of his fastball. *Outlook:* Milton will continue to have problems with the home run. Has to work inside more with his fastball and be more consistent with his change, or rediscover the curve he had a few years ago. *Grade 7*

ERIC MILTON'S PITCHING ZONE

.403	.268	.194
.336	.430	.207
.377	.386	.186

LEFTY-RIGHTY SPLITS

vs.	Avg.	AB	H	2B	3B	HR	RBI	BB	SO	OBP	Slg.
L	.284	155	44	10	1	5	19	8	30	.329	.458
R	.307	629	193	45	6	35	111	44	93	.353	.564

Year Team (League)	W	L	Pct.	ERA	WHIP	G	GS	CG	ShO	Hld.	Sv.-Opp.	IP	H	R	ER	HR	BB-IBB	SO	Avg.
1997— Tampa (Fla. St.)	8	3	.727	3.09	0.99	14	14	1	0	...	0-...	93.1	78	35	32	8	14-0	95	.223
— Norwich (East.)	6	3	.667	3.13	1.22	14	14	1	0	...	0-...	77.2	59	29	27	2	36-0	67	.210
1998— Minnesota (A.L.)	8	14	.364	5.64	1.54	32	32	1	0	0	0-0	172.1	195	113	108	25	70-0	107	.282
1999— Minnesota (A.L.)	7	11	.389	4.49	1.23	34	34	5	2	0	0-0	206.1	190	111	103	43	63-2	163	.243
2000— Minnesota (A.L.)	13	10	.565	4.86	1.25	33	33	0	0	0	0-0	200.0	205	123	108	35	44-0	160	.260
2001— Minnesota (A.L.)	15	7	.682	4.32	1.28	35	34	2	1	0	0-0	220.2	222	109	106	35	61-0	157	.257
2002— Minnesota (A.L.)	13	9	.591	4.84	1.19	29	29	2	1	0	0-0	171.0	173	96	92	24	30-0	121	.258
2003— Fort Myers (FSL)	0	0	...	0.00	1.50	1	1	0	0	0	0-0	2.0	1	0	0	0	2-0	2	.143
— Minnesota (A.L.)	1	0	1.000	2.65	0.94	3	3	0	0	0	0-0	17.0	15	5	5	2	1-0	7	.234
2004— Philadelphia (N.L.)	14	6	.700	4.75	1.35	34	34	0	0	0	0-0	201.0	196	110	106	* 43	75-6	161	.255
2005— Cincinnati (N.L.)	8	15	.348	6.47	1.55	34	34	0	0	0	0-0	186.1	237	* 141	* 134	* 40	52-2	123	.302
American League totals (6 years)	57	51	.528	4.76	1.29	166	165	10	4	0	0-0	987.1	1000	557	522	149	269-2	715	.259
National League totals (2 years)	22	21	.512	5.58	1.45	68	68	0	0	0	0-0	387.1	433	251	240	83	127-8	284	.279
Major League totals (8 years)	79	72	.523	4.99	1.33	234	233	10	4	0	0-0	1374.2	1433	808	762	232	396-10	999	.265

DIVISION SERIES RECORD

Year Team (League)	W	L	Pct.	ERA	WHIP	G	GS	CG	ShO	Hld.	Sv.-Opp.	IP	H	R	ER	HR	BB-IBB	SO	Avg.
2002— Minnesota (A.L.)	1	0	1.000	2.57	1.00	1	1	0	0	0	0-0	7.0	6	2	2	1	1-0	3	.222
2003— Minnesota (A.L.)	0	0	...	0.00	0.60	1	0	0	0	0	0-0	3.1	2	0	0	0	0-0	2	.167
Division series totals (2 years)	1	0	1.000	1.74	0.87	2	1	0	0	0	0-0	10.1	8	2	2	1	1-0	5	.205

CHAMPIONSHIP SERIES RECORD

Year Team (League)	W	L	Pct.	ERA	WHIP	G	GS	CG	ShO	Hld.	Sv.-Opp.	IP	H	R	ER	HR	BB-IBB	SO	Avg.
2002— Minnesota (A.L.)	0	0	...	1.50	1.17	1	1	0	0	0	0-0	6.0	5	1	1	1	2-0	4	.217

MIRABELLI, DOUG   C

PERSONAL: Born October 18, 1970, in Kingman, Ariz. ... 6-1/220. ... Bats right, throws right. ... Full name: Douglas Anthony Mirabelli. ... Name pronounced: mirr-uh-BEL-ee. ... High school: Valley (Las Vegas). ... College: Wichita State.

TRANSACTIONS/CAREER NOTES: Selected by Detroit Tigers organization in sixth round of 1989 free-agent draft; did not sign. ... Selected by San Francisco Giants organization in fifth round of 1992 free-agent draft. ... Traded by Giants to Texas Rangers for cash (March 27, 2001). ... Traded by Rangers to Boston Red Sox for P Justin Duchscherer (June 12, 2001). ... On disabled list (May 20-June 12, 2005).

2005 GAMES PLAYED BY POSITION (MLB): C—43, DH—5.

SCOUTING REPORT *Offense:*
Mirabelli has good power, even though he doesn't have a quick bat. Likes fastballs away to take advantage of the Green Monster. Has become a good mistake hitter and is very streaky. *Defense:* He is a good defensive catcher who is especially valuable because of his ability to handle Tim Wakefield's knuckleball. Has good hands and is aggressive, whether blocking balls or blocking the plate. Has improved despite his advancing age. *Outlook:* Mirabelli is a tough, take-charge receiver with good makeup for the role he plays. Will always have a job as long as Wakefield keeps pitching. *Grade 6*

DOUG MIRABELLI'S HITTING ZONE

.000	.300	.375
.346	.375	.364
.192	.286	.000

LEFTY-RIGHTY SPLITS

vs.	Avg.	AB	H	2B	3B	HR	RBI	BB	SO	OBP	Slg.
L	.240	50	12	3	0	2	8	9	20	.356	.420
R	.221	86	19	4	0	4	10	5	28	.280	.407

Year Team (League)	Pos.	G	AB	R	H	2B	3B	HR	RBI	BB	SO	HBP	GDP	SB-CS	Avg.	OBP	SLG	OPS	E	Avg.
1992— San Jose (Calif.)	C	53	177	30	41	11	1	0	21	24	18	4	7	1-3	.232	.333	.305	.638	10	.973
1993— San Jose (Calif.)	C	113	371	58	100	19	2	1	48	72	55	4	7	0-4	.270	.390	.340	.730	9	.989
1994— Shreveport (Texas)	1B-C	85	255	23	56	8	0	4	24	36	48	0	6	3-1	.220	.316	.298	.614	3	.993
1995— Phoenix (PCL)	C	23	66	3	11	0	1	0	7	12	10	1	5	1-0	.167	.296	.197	.493	2	.985
— Shreveport (Texas)	1B-C	40	126	14	38	13	0	6	16	20	14	0	3	1-0	.302	.397	.405	.802	3	.986
1996— Shreveport (Texas)	C-DH-1B	115	380	60	112	23	0	21	70	76	49	6	9	0-1	.295	.419	.521	.940	7	.989
— Phoenix (PCL)	C	14	47	10	14	7	0	0	7	4	7	1	1	0-0	.298	.365	.447	.812	2	.982
— San Francisco (N.L.)	C	9	18	2	4	1	0	0	1	3	4	0	0	0-0	.222	.333	.278	.611	0	1.000

M

Year	Team (League)	Pos.	G	AB	R	H	2B	3B	HR	RBI	BB	SO	HBP	GDP	SB-CS	Avg.	OBP	SLG	OPS	E	Avg.
1997— Phoenix (PCL)		C-DH	100	332	49	88	23	2	8	48	58	69	7	9	1-2	.265	.384	.419	.803	4	.994
— San Francisco (N.L.)		C	6	7	0	1	0	0	0	0	1	3	0	0	0-0	.143	.250	.143	.393	0	1.000
1998— Fresno (PCL)		C-DH	85	265	45	69	12	2	13	53	52	55	3	9	2-0	.260	.386	.468	.854	3	.995
— San Francisco (N.L.)		C	10	17	2	4	2	0	1	4	2	6	0	0	0-0	.235	.316	.529	.845	1	.974
1999— Fresno (PCL)		C-1B-DH	86	320	63	100	24	1	14	51	48	56	1	6	8-2	.313	.398	.525	.923	5	.993
— San Francisco (N.L.)		C	33	87	10	22	6	0	1	10	9	25	1	1	0-0	.253	.327	.356	.683	0	1.000
2000— San Francisco (N.L.)		C	82	230	23	53	10	2	6	28	36	57	2	6	1-0	.230	.337	.370	.707	7	.985
2001— Texas (A.L.)		C-DH	23	49	4	5	2	0	2	3	10	21	0	1	0-0	.102	.254	.265	.520	1	.990
— Boston (A.L.)		C-DH	54	141	16	38	8	0	9	26	17	36	4	2	0-0	.270	.360	.518	.877	2	.995
2002— Boston (A.L.)		C-DH	57	151	17	34	7	0	7	25	17	33	3	6	0-0	.225	.312	.411	.723	0	1.000
2003— Boston (A.L.)		C-DH-1B	62	163	23	42	13	0	6	18	11	36	1	3	0-0	.258	.307	.448	.755	5	.986
2004— Boston (A.L.)		C-DH	59	160	27	45	12	0	9	32	19	46	3	5	0-0	.281	.368	.525	.893	2	.993
2005— Boston (A.L.)		C-DH	50	136	16	31	7	0	6	18	14	48	2	2	2-0	.228	.309	.412	.721	3	.988
American League totals (5 years)			305	800	103	195	49	0	39	122	88	220	13	19	2-0	.244	.327	.451	.778	13	.992
National League totals (5 years)			140	359	37	84	19	2	8	43	51	95	3	7	1-0	.234	.332	.365	.697	8	.989
Major League totals (10 years)			445	1159	140	279	68	2	47	165	139	315	16	26	3-0	.241	.328	.425	.753	21	.991

DIVISION SERIES RECORD

Year	Team (League)	Pos.	G	AB	R	H	2B	3B	HR	RBI	BB	SO	HBP	GDP	SB-CS	Avg.	OBP	SLG	OPS	E	Avg.
2000— San Francisco (N.L.)		C	2	2	0	0	0	0	0	0	1	1	0	0	0-0	.000	.333	.000	.333	0	1.000
2003— Boston (A.L.)		C	2	4	2	2	1	0	0	0	0	2	0	0	0-0	.500	.500	.750	1.250	0	1.000
2005— Boston (A.L.)		C	1	2	0	0	0	0	0	0	0	0	0	0	0-0	.000	.000	.000	.000	0	1.000
Division series totals (3 years)			5	8	2	2	1	0	0	0	1	3	0	0	0-0	.250	.333	.375	.708	0	1.000

CHAMPIONSHIP SERIES RECORD

Year	Team (League)	Pos.	G	AB	R	H	2B	3B	HR	RBI	BB	SO	HBP	GDP	SB-CS	Avg.	OBP	SLG	OPS	E	Avg.
2003— Boston (A.L.)		C	3	7	0	2	0	0	0	0	2	0	0	0	0-0	.286	.286	.286	.571	0	1.000
2004— Boston (A.L.)		C	1	1	0	0	0	0	0	0	0	0	0	0	0-0	.000	.000	.000	.000	0	1.000
Champ. series totals (2 years)			4	8	0	2	0	0	0	0	2	0	0	0	0-0	.250	.250	.250	.500	0	1.000

WORLD SERIES RECORD

Year	Team (League)	Pos.	G	AB	R	H	2B	3B	HR	RBI	BB	SO	HBP	GDP	SB-CS	Avg.	OBP	SLG	OPS	E	Avg.
2004— Boston (A.L.)		C	1	3	1	1	0	0	0	0	0	1	0	0	0-0	.333	.333	.333	.667	0	1.000

MITRE, SERGIO — P

PERSONAL: Born February 16, 1981, in Los Angeles. ... 6-4/210. ... Throws right, bats right. ... Full name: Sergio Armando Mitre. ... High school: Montgomery (Chula Vista, Calif.). ... Junior college: San Diego City College.

TRANSACTIONS/CAREER NOTES: Selected by Chicago Cubs organization in seventh round of 2001 free-agent draft.

CAREER HITTING: 6-for-28 (.214), 3 R, 2 2B, 0 3B, 0 HR, 1 RBI.

SERGIO MITRE'S PITCHING ZONE

.667	.143	.400
.211	.381	.349
.385	.200	.206

LEFTY-RIGHTY SPLITS

vs.	Avg.	AB	H	2B	3B	HR	RBI	BB	SO	OBP	Slg.
L	.294	102	30	2	1	5	12	13	8	.381	.480
R	.235	136	32	5	0	6	21	10	29	.289	.404

Year	Team (League)	W	L	Pct.	ERA	WHIP	G	GS	CG	ShO	Hld.	Sv.-Opp.	IP	H	R	ER	HR	BB-IBB	SO	Avg.
2001— Boise (N'west)		8	4	.667	3.07	1.13	15	15	1	1	...	0-...	91.0	85	37	31	2	18-1	71	.243
2002— Lansing (Midw.)		8	10	.444	2.83	1.14	27	27	2	0	...	0-...	168.2	166	72	53	7	27-1	96	.261
2003— West Tenn (Sou.)		7	9	.438	3.34	1.39	25	24	0	0	...	0-...	145.2	162	75	54	6	41-0	128	.282
— Chicago (N.L.)		0	1	.000	8.31	2.19	3	2	0	0	0	0-0	8.2	15	8	8	1	4-1	3	.395
2004— Iowa (PCL)		6	4	.600	2.98	1.32	18	15	1	1	...	1-...	102.2	97	38	34	9	39-1	95	.255
— Chicago (N.L.)		2	4	.333	6.62	1.76	12	9	0	0	0	0-0	51.2	71	38	38	6	20-1	37	.327
2005— Iowa (PCL)		5	6	.455	4.33	1.33	13	13	1	0	...	0-0	70.2	72	34	34	5	22-0	55	.263
— Chicago (N.L.)		2	5	.286	5.37	1.41	21	7	1	1	0	0-0	60.1	62	37	36	11	23-2	37	.261
Major League totals (3 years)		4	10	.286	6.12	1.62	36	18	1	1	0	0-0	120.2	148	83	82	18	47-4	77	.300

MOEHLER, BRIAN — P

PERSONAL: Born December 31, 1971, in Rockingham, N.C. ... 6-3/235. ... Throws right, bats right. ... Full name: Brian Merritt Moehler. ... Name pronounced: MOLE-er. ... High school: Richmond (N.C.) South. ... College: North Carolina-Greensboro.

TRANSACTIONS/CAREER NOTES: Selected by Detroit Tigers organization in sixth round of free-agent draft (June 3, 1993). ... On disabled list (August 7-22, 1997). ... On suspended list (May 3-13, 1999). ... On disabled list (April 17-May 19, 2000); included rehabilitation assignment to West Michigan. ... On disabled list (April 7, 2001-remainder of season); included rehabilitation assignment to Toledo. ... On disabled list (March 22-July 3, 2002); included rehabilitation assignment to Lakeland and Toledo. ... Traded by Tigers with IF Matt Boone to Cincinnati Reds for SS David Espinosa and two players to be named (July 23, 2002); Tigers acquired OF Gary Varner (August 30, 2002) and P Jorge Cordova (September 24, 2002) to complete deal. ... On disabled list (August 28-September 13, 2002). ... Signed as a free agent by Houston Astros (January 17, 2003). ... On disabled list (April 17, 2003-remainder of season); included rehabilitation assignment to New Orleans. ... Signed as a free agent by Atlanta Braves organization (February 17, 2004). ... Signed as a free agent by Florida Marlins organization (December 14, 2004).

CAREER HITTING: 3-for-70 (.043), 2 R, 1 2B, 0 3B, 0 HR, 3 RBI.

BRIAN MOEHLER'S PITCHING ZONE

.333	.212	.400
.374	.362	.248
.308	.429	.300

LEFTY-RIGHTY SPLITS

vs.	Avg.	AB	H	2B	3B	HR	RBI	BB	SO	OBP	Slg.
L	.320	334	107	19	2	9	44	22	53	.367	.470
R	.305	298	91	25	0	7	29	20	42	.350	.460

Year	Team (League)	W	L	Pct.	ERA	WHIP	G	GS	CG	ShO	Hld.	Sv.-Opp.	IP	H	R	ER	HR	BB-IBB	SO	Avg.
1993— Niagara Falls (NYP)		6	5	.545	3.22	1.33	12	11	0	0	...	0-...	58.2	51	33	21	3	27-0	38	.225
1994— Lakeland (Fla. St.)		12	12	.500	3.01	1.32	26	25	5	2	...	0-...	164.2	153	66	55	3	65-0	92	.254
1995— Jacksonville (Sou.)		8	10	.444	4.82	1.40	28	27	1	0	...	0-...	162.1	176	94	87	14	52-1	89	.279
1996— Jacksonville (Sou.)		15	6	.714	3.48	1.36	28	28	1	0	...	0-...	173.1	186	80	67	9	50-2	120	.263
— Detroit (A.L.)		0	1	.000	4.35	1.84	2	2	0	0	0	0-0	10.1	11	10	5	1	8-1	2	.262

M

Year Team (League)	W	L	Pct.	ERA	WHIP	G	GS	CG	ShO	Hld.	Sv.-Opp.	IP	H	R	ER	HR	BB-IBB	SO	Avg.
1997— Detroit (A.L.)	11	12	.478	4.67	1.48	31	31	2	1	0	0-0	175.1	198	97	91	22	61-1	97	.285
1998— Detroit (A.L.)	14	13	.519	3.90	1.25	33	33	4	3	0	0-0	221.1	220	103	96	30	56-1	123	.260
1999— Detroit (A.L.)	10	* 16	.385	5.04	1.47	32	32	2	2	0	0-0	196.1	229	116	110	22	59-5	106	.294
2000— Detroit (A.L.)	12	9	.571	4.50	1.47	29	29	2	0	0	0-0	178.0	222	99	89	20	40-0	103	.305
— W. Mich. (Mid.)	0	1	.000	4.26	0.95	1	1	0	0	...	0-...	6.1	5	3	3	1	1-0	4	.217
2001— Detroit (A.L.)	0	0	...	3.38	0.88	1	1	0	0	0	0-0	8.0	6	3	3	0	1-0	2	.207
— Toledo (Int'l)	0	2	.000	4.35	1.35	2	2	0	0	...	0-...	10.1	12	6	5	2	2-0	6	.279
2002— Lakeland (Fla. St.)	1	1	.500	2.92	0.89	2	2	0	0	...	0-...	12.1	10	9	4	2	1-0	7	.208
— Toledo (Int'l)	2	1	.667	4.88	1.29	4	4	0	0	...	0-...	24.0	28	15	13	3	3-0	7	.277
— Detroit (A.L.)	1	1	.500	2.29	0.97	3	3	0	0	0	0-0	19.2	17	5	5	3	2-0	13	.233
— Cincinnati (N.L.)	2	4	.333	6.02	1.66	10	9	0	0	0	0-0	43.1	61	34	29	8	11-0	18	.330
2003— Houston (N.L.)	0	0	...	7.90	2.05	3	3	0	0	0	0-0	13.2	22	12	12	4	6-0	5	.379
— New Orleans (PCL)	0	0	...	4.50	1.50	1	1	0	0	...	0-...	2.0	3	1	1	0	0-0	3	.375
2004— Greenville (Sou.)	3	9	.250	4.17	1.30	20	20	0	0	0	0-...	108.0	113	58	50	8	27-1	57	.276
2005— Florida (N.L.)	6	12	.333	4.55	1.52	37	25	0	0	1	0-0	158.1	198	82	80	16	42-9	95	.313
American League totals (7 years)	48	52	.480	4.44	1.40	131	131	10	6	0	0-0	809.0	903	433	399	98	227-8	446	.283
National League totals (3 years)	8	16	.333	5.06	1.58	50	37	0	0	1	0-0	215.1	281	128	121	28	59-9	118	.321
Major League totals (9 years)	56	68	.452	4.57	1.44	181	168	10	6	1	0-0	1024.1	1184	561	520	126	286-17	564	.291

MOELLER, CHAD   C

PERSONAL: Born February 18, 1975, in Upland, Calif. ... 6-3/210. ... Bats right, throws right. ... Full name: Chad Edward Moeller. ... Name pronounced: MOE-ler. ... High school: Upland (Calif.). ... College: Southern California.

TRANSACTIONS/CAREER NOTES: Selected by New York Yankees organization in 25th round of 1993 free-agent draft; did not sign. ... Selected by Minnesota Twins organization in seventh round of 1996 free-agent draft. ... On disabled list (August 12-30, 2000). ... Traded by Twins to Arizona Diamondbacks for SS Hanley Frias (March 28, 2001). ... Traded by Diamondbacks with SS Craig Counsell, 2B Junior Spivey, 1B Lyle Overbay and Ps Chris Capuano and Jorge de la Rosa to Milwaukee Brewers for 1B Richie Sexson, P Shane Nance and a player to be named (December 1, 2003); Diamondbacks acquired OF Noochie Varner to complete deal (December 15, 2003).
2005 GAMES PLAYED BY POSITION (MLB): C—65.

SCOUTING REPORT Moeller doesn't generate much bat speed with his short stroke and tends to push the bat. Hits with a slight hitch. Arm strength is below average, and his throws lose carry because he pushes the ball. Is in the majors purely for his defense, yet has trouble at times catching balls to his left and doesn't always show good reflexes. Is aggressive at blocking and shifting but moves better to his right. Calls a good game. Strictly a backup whose bat won't make up for lapses in defense. *Grade 4.8*

CHAD MOELLER'S HITTING ZONE

.182	.308	.000
.238	.381	.136
.240	.167	.000

LEFTY-RIGHTY SPLITS

vs.	Avg.	AB	H	2B	3B	HR	RBI	BB	SO	OBP	Slg.
L	.180	50	9	1	1	2	6	2	11	.212	.360
R	.215	149	32	8	0	5	17	11	37	.272	.369

								BATTING						FIELDING			
Year Team (League)	Pos.	G	AB	R	H	2B	3B	HR	RBI	BB	SO	HBP	GDP	SB-CS	Avg.	OBP	SLG	OPS	E	Avg.
1996— Elizabethton (App.)	C	17	59	17	21	4	0	4	13	18	9	2	3	1-2	.356	.519	.627	1.146	1	.991
1997— Fort Wayne (Midw.)	C	108	384	58	111	18	3	9	39	48	76	13	8	11-8	.289	.386	.422	.808	15	.984
1998— Fort Myers (FSL)	C	66	254	37	83	24	1	6	39	31	37	3	8	2-3	.327	.406	.500	.906	9	.980
— New Britain (East.)	C	58	187	21	44	10	0	6	23	24	41	3	4	2-1	.235	.332	.385	.717	6	.987
1999— New Britain (East.)	C	89	250	29	62	11	3	4	24	21	44	6	7	0-0	.248	.317	.364	.681	10	.984
2000— Salt Lake (PCL)	C	47	167	30	48	13	1	5	20	9	45	0	6	0-1	.287	.322	.467	.789	2	.993
— Minnesota (A.L.)	C	48	128	13	27	3	1	1	9	9	33	0	4	1-0	.211	.261	.273	.534	6	.979
2001— Tucson (PCL)	C	78	274	41	75	20	0	8	36	25	54	2	8	1-4	.274	.337	.434	.771	5	.989
— Arizona (N.L.)	C	25	56	8	13	0	1	1	2	6	12	0	2	0-0	.232	.306	.321	.628	0	1.000
2002— Tucson (PCL)	C	60	211	37	67	8	2	10	48	29	46	3	4	1-0	.318	.401	.517	.917	3	.994
— Arizona (N.L.)	C	37	105	10	30	11	1	2	16	17	23	0	6	0-1	.286	.385	.467	.852	1	.997
2003— Arizona (N.L.)	C	78	239	29	64	17	1	7	29	23	59	2	7	1-2	.268	.335	.435	.770	7	.987
2004— Milwaukee (N.L.)	C	101	317	25	66	13	1	5	27	21	74	4	12	0-1	.208	.265	.303	.568	1	.999
2005— Milwaukee (N.L.)	C	66	199	23	41	9	1	7	23	13	48	1	9	0-0	.206	.257	.367	.624	3	.994
American League totals (1 year)		48	128	13	27	3	1	1	9	9	33	0	4	1-0	.211	.261	.273	.534	6	.979
National League totals (5 years)		307	916	95	214	50	5	22	97	80	216	7	36	1-4	.234	.299	.371	.670	12	.995
Major League totals (6 years)		355	1044	108	241	53	6	23	106	89	249	7	40	2-4	.231	.294	.359	.654	18	.993

DIVISION SERIES RECORD

Year Team (League)	Pos.	G	AB	R	H	2B	3B	HR	RBI	BB	SO	HBP	GDP	SB-CS	Avg.	OBP	SLG	OPS	E	Avg.
2002— Arizona (N.L.)	C	3	5	0	2	0	0	0	0	0	1	0	0	0-0	.400	.400	.400	.800	0	1.000

MOHR, DUSTAN   OF

PERSONAL: Born June 19, 1976, in Hattiesburg, Miss. ... 6-1/214. ... Bats right, throws right. ... Full name: Dustan Kyle Mohr. ... High school: Oak Grove (Miss.). ... College: Alabama.

TRANSACTIONS/CAREER NOTES: Selected by California Angels organization in 20th round of 1994 free-agent draft; did not sign. ... Selected by Cleveland Indians organization in ninth round of 1997 free-agent draft. ... Released by Indians (March 31, 2000). ... Signed by Minnesota Twins organization (April 1, 2000). ... Traded by Twins to San Francisco Giants for P J.T. Thomas (December 15, 2003). ... Signed as free agent by Colorado Rockies (January 6, 2005). ... On disabled list (April 6-28, 2005); included rehabilitation assignment to Colorado Springs.
2005 GAMES PLAYED BY POSITION (MLB): OF—76.

SCOUTING REPORT *Offense:* Mohr lost bat speed after being injured on opening day; he was late on fastballs and struggled with breaking balls. Is a better high-ball hitter with power. Doesn't run well. *Defense:* He can play all three outfield positions and is a good fit in right field because of his arm strength. Has average range. *Outlook:* Mohr never got untracked last season, but he did provide some power. Is a platoon player who is better against lefthanded pitching. **Grade 5**

DUSTAN MOHR'S HITTING ZONE

.235	.455	.143
.339	.250	.258
.097	.273	.333

LEFTY-RIGHTY SPLITS

vs.	Avg.	AB	H	2B	3B	HR	RBI	BB	SO	OBP	Slg.
L	.274	113	31	7	2	7	15	12	36	.349	.558
R	.170	153	26	3	1	10	23	11	58	.228	.399

Year — Team (League)	Pos.	G	AB	R	H	2B	3B	HR	RBI	BB	SO	HBP	GDP	SB-CS	Avg.	OBP	SLG	OPS	E	Avg.
									BATTING										FIELDING	
1997— Watertown (NYP)	OF	74	275	52	80	20	2	7	53	31	76	4	1	3-6	.291	.366	.455	.821	1	.993
1998— Kinston (Carol.)	OF	134	491	60	119	23	9	19	65	39	146	9	7	8-4	.242	.309	.442	.751	7	.968
1999— Akron (East.)	OF	12	42	3	7	2	1	0	2	5	7	0	1	0-1	.167	.255	.262	.517	0	1.000
— Kinston (Carol.)	OF	112	429	46	120	29	3	8	60	26	104	1	13	6-6	.280	.322	.417	.739	6	.973
2000— Fort Myers (FSL)	OF	101	370	58	98	19	2	11	75	35	65	8	11	7-4	.265	.338	.416	.754	4	.978
2001— New Britain (East.)	OF	135	518	90	174	41	3	24	91	49	111	4	6	9-9	.336	.395	.566	.961	6	.978
— Minnesota (A.L.)	OF-DH	20	51	6	12	2	0	0	4	5	17	0	1	1-1	.235	.298	.275	.573	0	1.000
2002— Minnesota (A.L.)	OF-DH	120	383	55	103	23	2	12	45	31	86	1	5	6-3	.269	.325	.433	.759	2	.992
2003— Minnesota (A.L.)	OF-DH	121	348	50	87	22	0	10	36	33	106	1	10	5-2	.250	.314	.399	.714	6	.976
2004— San Francisco (N.L.)	OF-DH	117	263	52	72	20	1	7	28	46	64	8	5	0-3	.274	.394	.437	.831	3	.981
2005— Colo. Springs (PCL)	OF	3	12	2	3	2	0	1	4	0	4	0	1	0-0	.250	.250	.667	.917	0	1.000
— Colorado (N.L.)	OF	98	266	34	57	10	3	17	38	23	94	2	3	1-2	.214	.280	.466	.746	2	.987
American League totals (3 years)		261	782	111	202	47	2	22	85	69	209	2	15	12-6	.258	.319	.408	.726	8	.985
National League totals (2 years)		215	529	86	129	30	4	24	66	69	158	10	8	1-5	.244	.339	.452	.791	5	.984
Major League totals (5 years)		476	1311	197	331	77	6	46	151	138	367	12	23	13-11	.252	.327	.426	.753	13	.985

DIVISION SERIES RECORD

Year — Team (League)	Pos.	G	AB	R	H	2B	3B	HR	RBI	BB	SO	HBP	GDP	SB-CS	Avg.	OBP	SLG	OPS	E	Avg.
2002— Minnesota (A.L.)	OF	4	2	1	2	1	0	0	1	0	0	0	0	0-0	1.000	1.000	1.500	2.500	0	1.000

CHAMPIONSHIP SERIES RECORD

Year — Team (League)	Pos.	G	AB	R	H	2B	3B	HR	RBI	BB	SO	HBP	GDP	SB-CS	Avg.	OBP	SLG	OPS	E	Avg.
2002— Minnesota (A.L.)	OF	5	12	3	5	1	0	0	0	4	0	0	0	1-0	.417	.417	.500	.917	0	1.000

MOLINA, BENGIE   C

PERSONAL: Born July 20, 1974, in Rio Piedras, Puerto Rico. ... 5-11/220. ... Bats right, throws right. ... Full name: Benjamin Jose Molina. ... Name pronounced: mo-LEE-nah. ... High school: Maestro Ladi (Vega Alta, Puerto Rico). ... Junior college: Arizona Western Community College. ... Brother of Jose Molina, catcher, Los Angeles Angels of Anaheim; and of Yadier Molina, catcher, St. Louis Cardinals.

TRANSACTIONS/CAREER NOTES: Signed as a non-drafted free agent by California Angels organization (May 23, 1993). ... Angels franchise renamed Anaheim Angels for 1997 season. ... On disabled list (May 5-June 27, 2001); included rehabilitation assignments to Rancho Cucamonga and Salt Lake. ... On disabled list (July 17-August 1, 2002); included rehabilitation assignment to Rancho Cucamonga. ... On disabled list (September 5, 2003-remainder of season; and June 4-19 and August 1-17, 2004). ... Angels franchise renamed Los Angeles Angels of Anaheim for 2005 season. ... On disabled list (April 18-May 13, 2005).

HONORS: Won A.L. Gold Glove at catcher (2002 and 2003).

2005 GAMES PLAYED BY POSITION (MLB): C—105, DH—11.

SCOUTING REPORT *Offense:* An excellent contact hitter with a slightly long approach, Molina tends to swing up at the ball. Likes to hit early in the count and rarely walks. Has become a better low-ball hitter and has good bat speed with deceptive power to the left-center field alley. Likes pitches away that he can take to the opposite field. Has improved with runners in scoring position. Is incredibly slow running to first base. *Defense:* His receiving mechanics have regressed. Has a tendency to get very wide and reaches for too many pitches. Is lazy at times. Has a strong arm with a quick release and is accurate. Is instinctive at calling games and working with his pitching staff. *Outlook:* Molina has turned the corner offensively but needs to refresh his defense. **Grade 8.3**

BENGIE MOLINA'S HITTING ZONE

.158	.412	.300
.263	.419	.258
.269	.423	.391

LEFTY-RIGHTY SPLITS

vs.	Avg.	AB	H	2B	3B	HR	RBI	BB	SO	OBP	Slg.
L	.393	122	48	10	0	7	28	10	10	.430	.648
R	.253	288	73	7	0	8	41	17	31	.294	.361

Year — Team (League)	Pos.	G	AB	R	H	2B	3B	HR	RBI	BB	SO	HBP	GDP	SB-CS	Avg.	OBP	SLG	OPS	E	Avg.
									BATTING										FIELDING	
1993— Ariz. Angels (Ariz.)	C	27	80	9	21	6	2	0	10	10	4	1	1	0-2	.263	.348	.388	.735	0	1.000
1994— Cedar Rap. (Midw.)	C	48	171	14	48	6	0	3	16	8	12	3	3	1-2	.281	.324	.380	.704	10	.975
1995— Vancouver (PCL)		2	0	0	0	0	0	0	0	0	1	0	0	0-0	.000	.000	.000	.000	0	1.000
— Cedar Rap. (Midw.)	C	39	133	15	39	9	0	4	17	15	11	1	4	1-1	.293	.367	.451	.818	7	.978
— Lake Elsinore (Calif.)	C	27	96	21	37	7	2	2	12	8	7	4	2	0-0	.385	.450	.563	1.012	1	.995
1996— Midland (Texas)	C	108	365	45	100	21	2	8	54	25	25	6	16	0-1	.274	.327	.408	.735	7	.990
1997— Lake Elsinore (Calif.)	C	36	149	18	42	10	2	4	33	7	9	0	5	0-1	.282	.308	.456	.765	1	.996
— Midland (Texas)	C	29	106	18	35	8	0	6	30	10	7	0	6	0-0	.330	.381	.575	.957	2	.985
1998— Vancouver (PCL)	C	49	184	13	54	9	1	1	22	5	14	0	6	1-1	.293	.311	.370	.680	3	.986
— Midland (Texas)	C	41	154	28	55	8	0	9	39	14	7	3	7	0-1	.357	.419	.584	1.003	3	.981
— Anaheim (A.L.)	C	2	1	0	0	0	0	0	0	0	0	0	0	0-0	.000	.000	.000	.000	0	1.000
1999— Edmonton (PCL)	C-DH	65	241	28	69	16	0	7	41	15	17	6	7	1-2	.286	.338	.440	.778	5	.993
— Anaheim (A.L.)	C	31	101	8	26	5	0	1	6	6	2	5	0	0-1	.257	.312	.337	.649	2	.991
2000— Anaheim (A.L.)	C-DH	130	473	59	133	20	2	14	71	23	33	6	17	1-0	.281	.318	.421	.739	7	.991
2001— Anaheim (A.L.)	C-DH	96	325	31	85	11	0	6	40	16	51	8	8	0-1	.262	.309	.351	.660	5	.991
— Rancho Cuca. (Calif.)	C	3	11	1	6	1	0	0	2	0	1	0	0	0-0	.545	.545	.636	1.182	0	1.000
— Salt Lake (PCL)	C	5	18	2	5	1	0	0	3	2	3	0	2	0-0	.278	.350	.333	.683	0	1.000

Year	Team (League)	Pos.	G	AB	R	H	2B	3B	HR	RBI	BB	SO	HBP	GDP	SB-CS	Avg.	OBP	SLG	OPS	E	Avg.
			BATTING																	FIELDING	
2002—	Anaheim (A.L.)	C	122	428	34	105	18	0	5	47	15	34	4	15	0-0	.245	.274	.322	.596	1	.999
	— Rancho Cuca. (Calif.)	C	1	2	0	1	0	0	0	0	1	0	1	0	0-0	.500	.750	.500	1.250	0	1.000
2003—	Anaheim (A.L.)	C	119	409	37	115	24	0	14	71	13	31	2	17	1-1	.281	.304	.443	.746	5	.993
2004—	Anaheim (A.L.)	C-DH	97	337	36	93	13	0	10	54	18	35	2	18	0-1	.276	.313	.404	.717	3	.995
2005—	Los Angeles (A.L.)	C-DH	119	410	45	121	17	0	15	69	27	41	1	14	0-2	.295	.336	.446	.782	3	.996
Major League totals (8 years)			716	2484	250	678	108	2	65	362	118	231	25	94	2-6	.273	.309	.397	.705	26	.994

DIVISION SERIES RECORD

Year	Team (League)	Pos.	G	AB	R	H	2B	3B	HR	RBI	BB	SO	HBP	GDP	SB-CS	Avg.	OBP	SLG	OPS	E	Avg.
2002—	Anaheim (A.L.)	C	4	15	0	4	2	0	0	2	0	1	0	1	0-0	.267	.267	.400	.667	0	1.000
2004—	Anaheim (A.L.)	C	3	6	0	1	0	0	0	0	0	2	0	0	0-0	.167	.167	.167	.333	0	1.000
2005—	Los Angeles (A.L.)	C	5	18	5	8	0	0	3	5	0	0	1	0	0-0	.444	.474	.944	1.418	0	1.000
Division series totals (3 years)			12	39	5	13	2	0	3	7	0	3	1	1	0-0	.333	.350	.615	.965	0	1.000

CHAMPIONSHIP SERIES RECORD

Year	Team (League)	Pos.	G	AB	R	H	2B	3B	HR	RBI	BB	SO	HBP	GDP	SB-CS	Avg.	OBP	SLG	OPS	E	Avg.
2002—	Anaheim (A.L.)	C	5	14	0	3	0	1	0	2	1	2	1	0	0-0	.214	.313	.357	.670	0	1.000
2005—	Los Angeles (A.L.)	C-DH	5	17	0	2	0	0	0	1	0	2	1	0	0-0	.118	.167	.118	.284	0	1.000
Champ. series totals (2 years)			10	31	0	5	0	1	0	3	1	4	2	0	0-0	.161	.235	.226	.461	0	1.000

WORLD SERIES RECORD

Year	Team (League)	Pos.	G	AB	R	H	2B	3B	HR	RBI	BB	SO	HBP	GDP	SB-CS	Avg.	OBP	SLG	OPS	E	Avg.
2002—	Anaheim (A.L.)	C	7	21	2	6	2	0	0	2	3	1	0	2	0-0	.286	.375	.381	.756	1	.979

MOLINA, JOSE C

PERSONAL: Born June 3, 1975, in Bayamon, Puerto Rico. ... 6-2/220. ... Bats right, throws right. ... Full name: Jose Benjamin Molina. ... Name pronounced: mo-LEE-nah. ... High school: Maestro Ladi (Vega Alta, Puerto Rico). ... Brother of Bengie Molina, catcher, Los Angeles Angels of Anaheim; and of Yadier Molina, catcher, St. Louis Cardinals.
TRANSACTIONS/CAREER NOTES: Selected by Chicago Cubs organization in 14th round of 1993 free-agent draft. ... Released by Cubs (November 27, 2000). ... Signed by Anaheim Angels organization (May 17, 2001). ... On disabled list (May 21-July 1, 2001); included rehabilitation assignment to Salt Lake. ... Angels franchise renamed Los Angeles Angels of Anaheim for 2005 season.
2005 GAMES PLAYED BY POSITION (MLB): C—65, DH—5, 1B—4.

SCOUTING REPORT Molina has a long stroke and is a little rigid at the plate. Hits with a dead uppercut stroke and tries to pull the ball. Has problems handling pitches on the inner half of the plate, especially up. Has an above-average arm with quick feet and release. Has good hands and is mobile behind the plate with above-average range. Defense keeps him in the majors; won't ever hit enough to play regularly. ***Grade 4.8***

JOSE MOLINA'S HITTING ZONE

.167	.167	.200
.147	.364	.235
.391	.091	.091

LEFTY-RIGHTY SPLITS

vs.	Avg.	AB	H	2B	3B	HR	RBI	BB	SO	OBP	Slg.
L	.306	62	19	0	0	5	13	4	17	.368	.548
R	.189	122	23	4	0	1	12	9	24	.244	.246

Year	Team (League)	Pos.	G	AB	R	H	2B	3B	HR	RBI	BB	SO	HBP	GDP	SB-CS	Avg.	OBP	SLG	OPS	E	Avg.
			BATTING																	FIELDING	
1993—	GC Cubs (GCL)	1B-C	33	78	5	17	2	0	0	4	12	12	0	2	3-2	.218	.322	.244	.566	7	.960
	— Daytona (Fla. St.)	C	3	7	0	1	0	0	0	1	2	0	0	0	0-1	.143	.333	.143	.476	0	1.000
1994—	Peoria (Midw.)	C	78	253	31	58	13	1	1	33	24	61	4	5	4-3	.229	.302	.300	.602	13	.980
1995—	Daytona (Fla. St.)	C	82	233	27	55	9	1	1	19	29	53	7	7	1-0	.236	.336	.296	.632	8	.987
1996—	Rockford (Midwest)	C	96	305	35	69	10	1	2	27	36	71	3	8	2-4	.226	.310	.285	.596	11	.985
1997—	Daytona (Fla. St.)	C	55	179	17	45	9	1	0	23	14	25	1	5	4-0	.251	.306	.313	.619	8	.981
	— Iowa (Am. Assoc.)	C	1	3	0	1	0	0	0	0	1	1	0	1	0-0	.333	.500	.333	.833	0	1.000
	— Orlando (South.)	C	37	99	10	17	3	0	1	15	12	28	2	4	0-1	.172	.267	.232	.500	2	.993
1998—	West Tenn (Sou.)	1B-C	109	320	33	71	10	1	2	28	32	74	3	10	1-5	.222	.296	.278	.574	8	.991
1999—	West Tenn (Sou.)	C	14	35	2	6	3	0	0	5	2	14	0	1	0-0	.171	.211	.257	.468	2	.982
	— Iowa (PCL)	C	74	240	24	63	11	1	4	26	20	54	4	3	0-1	.263	.327	.367	.694	7	.987
	— Chicago (N.L.)	C	10	19	3	5	1	0	0	1	2	4	0	0	0-0	.263	.333	.316	.649	0	1.000
2000—	Iowa (PCL)	C-1B	76	248	22	58	9	0	1	17	23	61	0	6	1-4	.234	.296	.282	.578	11	.981
2001—	Salt Lake (PCL)	C	61	213	29	64	11	1	5	31	14	49	2	7	1-2	.300	.349	.432	.781	2	.996
	— Anaheim (A.L.)	C	15	37	8	10	3	0	2	4	3	8	0	2	0-0	.270	.325	.514	.839	0	1.000
2002—	Salt Lake (PCL)	C	79	290	30	89	14	2	4	43	12	60	4	4	0-3	.307	.341	.410	.751	4	.994
	— Anaheim (A.L.)	C	29	70	5	19	3	0	0	5	5	15	0	2	0-2	.271	.312	.314	.626	3	.983
2003—	Anaheim (A.L.)	C	53	114	12	21	4	0	0	6	1	26	3	1	0-0	.184	.210	.219	.429	1	.996
2004—	Anaheim (A.L.)	C-1B-DH	73	203	26	53	10	2	3	25	10	52	0	6	4-1	.261	.296	.374	.670	3	.994
2005—	Los Angeles (A.L.)	C-DH-1B	75	184	14	42	4	0	6	25	13	41	2	5	2-0	.228	.286	.348	.634	3	.994
American League totals (5 years)			245	608	65	145	24	2	11	65	32	142	5	16	6-3	.238	.281	.339	.620	10	.993
National League totals (1 year)			10	19	3	5	1	0	0	1	2	4	0	0	0-0	.263	.333	.316	.649	0	1.000
Major League totals (6 years)			255	627	68	150	25	2	11	66	34	146	5	16	6-3	.239	.283	.338	.621	10	.993

DIVISION SERIES RECORD

Year	Team (League)	Pos.	G	AB	R	H	2B	3B	HR	RBI	BB	SO	HBP	GDP	SB-CS	Avg.	OBP	SLG	OPS	E	Avg.
2004—	Anaheim (A.L.)	C	2	3	2	1	0	0	0	0	2	0	0	0	0-0	.333	.600	.333	.933	0	1.000
2005—	Los Angeles (A.L.)	C	1	1	1	1	0	0	0	1	0	0	0	0	0-0	1.000	1.000	1.000	2.000	0	1.000
Division series totals (2 years)			3	4	3	2	0	0	0	1	2	0	0	0	0-0	.500	.667	.500	1.167	0	1.000

CHAMPIONSHIP SERIES RECORD

Year	Team (League)	Pos.	G	AB	R	H	2B	3B	HR	RBI	BB	SO	HBP	GDP	SB-CS	Avg.	OBP	SLG	OPS	E	Avg.
2002—	Anaheim (A.L.)	C	3	1	0	0	0	0	0	0	0	0	0	0	0-0	.000	.000	.000	.000	0	1.000
2005—	Los Angeles (A.L.)	C	1	3	0	1	0	0	0	0	0	0	0	0	0-0	.333	.333	.333	.667	0	1.000
Champ. series totals (2 years)			4	4	0	1	0	0	0	0	0	0	0	0	0-0	.250	.250	.250	.500	0	1.000

Year	Team (League)	Pos.	G	AB	R	H	2B	3B	HR	RBI	BB	SO	HBP	GDP	SB-CS	Avg.	OBP	SLG	OPS	E	Avg.
2002— Anaheim (A.L.)		C	3	0	0	0	0	0	0	0	0	0	0	0	0-0	...	...	...	...	0	1.000

MOLINA, YADIER — C

PERSONAL: Born July 13, 1982, in Bayamon, Puerto Rico. ... 5-11/225. ... Bats right, throws right. ... Full name: Yadier B. Molina. ... Name pronounced: mo-LEE-nah. ... High school: Escuela Superior Maestro Ladi (Vega Alta, P.R.). ... Brother of Bengie Molina, catcher, Los Angeles Angels of Anaheim and Jose Molina, catcher, Angels.
TRANSACTIONS/CAREER NOTES: Selected by St. Louis Cardinals organization in fourth round of 2000 free-agent draft. ... On disabled list (July 17-August 18, 2005).
2005 GAMES PLAYED BY POSITION (MLB): C—114, 1B—1.

SCOUTING REPORT **Offense:** Molina's offense was well behind his defense in 2004, but he has shown a lot of improvement since. Is more selective but also has become more aggressive. Bat speed has improved as has his ability to take the ball the other way. Among the game's slowest baserunners. **Defense:** He is the best defensive catcher among the Molina brothers and is advancing quickly up the ladder among big-leaguers. Has extremely quick feet and an accurate, well-above-average arm that he loves to show off. Has very good defensive instincts and soft hands. Has made a lot of progress in calling games. **Outlook:** Molina has showed why the Cardinals could move Mike Matheny. Will be a frontline defensive catcher. Bat is coming around quicker than anticipated. Will be an All-Star. *Grade 7.6*

YADIER MOLINA'S HITTING ZONE

.308	.350	.259
.375	.263	.306
.071	.156	.269

LEFTY-RIGHTY SPLITS

vs.	Avg.	AB	H	2B	3B	HR	RBI	BB	SO	OBP	Slg.
L	.309	110	34	5	0	2	17	6	7	.339	.409
R	.229	275	63	10	1	6	32	17	23	.278	.338

Year	Team (League)	Pos.	G	AB	R	H	2B	3B	HR	RBI	BB	SO	HBP	GDP	SB-CS	Avg.	OBP	SLG	OPS	E	Avg.
2001— Johnson City (App.)		C	44	158	18	41	11	0	4	18	12	23	3	4	1-1	.259	.320	.405	.725	7	.986
2002— Peoria (Midw.)		C	112	393	39	110	20	0	7	50	21	36	10	14	2-7	.280	.331	.384	.715	14	.985
2003— Tennessee (Sou.)		C	104	364	32	100	13	1	2	51	25	45	5	11	0-1	.275	.327	.332	.660	8	.991
2004— Memphis (PCL)		C	37	129	19	39	6	0	1	14	17	14	2	2	0-0	.302	.387	.372	.750	0	1.000
— St. Louis (N.L.)		C	51	135	12	36	6	0	2	15	13	20	0	4	0-1	.267	.329	.356	.684	2	.993
2005— St. Louis (N.L.)		C-1B	114	385	36	97	15	1	8	49	23	30	2	10	2-3	.252	.295	.358	.654	7	.991
Major League totals (2 years)			165	520	48	133	21	1	10	64	36	50	2	14	2-4	.256	.304	.358	.662	9	.991

Year	Team (League)	Pos.	G	AB	R	H	2B	3B	HR	RBI	BB	SO	HBP	GDP	SB-CS	Avg.	OBP	SLG	OPS	E	Avg.
2005— St. Louis (N.L.)		C	3	13	1	3	0	0	0	3	0	1	0	0	0-0	.231	.231	.231	.462	0	1.000

Year	Team (League)	Pos.	G	AB	R	H	2B	3B	HR	RBI	BB	SO	HBP	GDP	SB-CS	Avg.	OBP	SLG	OPS	E	Avg.
2004— St. Louis (N.L.)		C	1	4	0	1	0	0	0	0	0	0	0	0	0-0	.250	.250	.250	.500	0	1.000
2005— St. Louis (N.L.)		C	6	22	1	7	3	0	0	0	0	2	0	1	0-0	.318	.318	.455	.773	0	1.000
Champ. series totals (2 years)			7	26	1	8	3	0	0	0	0	2	0	1	0-0	.308	.308	.423	.731	0	1.000

Year	Team (League)	Pos.	G	AB	R	H	2B	3B	HR	RBI	BB	SO	HBP	GDP	SB-CS	Avg.	OBP	SLG	OPS	E	Avg.
2004— St. Louis (N.L.)		C	3	3	0	0	0	0	0	0	0	0	1	0	0-0	.000	.000	.000	.000	0	1.000

M

MONDESI, RAUL — OF

PERSONAL: Born March 12, 1971, in San Cristoban, Dominican Republic. ... 5-11/230. ... Bats right, throws right. ... Full name: Raul Ramon Mondesi. ... Name pronounced: MON-de-see. ... High school: Liceo Manuel Maria Valencia (Dominican Republic).
TRANSACTIONS/CAREER NOTES: Signed as a non-drafted free agent by Los Angeles Dodgers organization (June 6, 1988). ... Traded by Dodgers with P Pedro Borbon to Toronto Blue Jays for OF Shawn Green and 2B Jorge Nunez (November 8, 1999). ... On disabled list (July 22-September 20, 2000). ... Traded by Blue Jays to New York Yankees for P Scott Wiggins (July 1, 2002). ... Traded by Yankees with cash to Arizona Diamondbacks for OF David Dellucci, P Bret Prinz and C Jon-Mark Sprowl (July 29, 2003). ... Signed as a free agent by Pittsburgh Pirates (February 24, 2004). ... On restricted list (May 11-19, 2004). ... Released by Pirates (May 19, 2004). ... Signed by Anaheim Angels (May 30, 2004). ... On disabled list (June 9-July 30, 2004); included rehabilitation assignment to Rancho Cucamonga. ... Released by Angels (July 30, 2004). ... Signed by Atlanta Braves (January 17, 2005). ... Released by Braves (June 6, 2005).
HONORS: Named N.L. Rookie Player of the Year by THE SPORTING NEWS (1994). ... Named N.L. Rookie of the Year by Baseball Writers' Association of America (1994). ... Won N.L. Gold Glove as outfielder (1995 and 1997).
2005 GAMES PLAYED BY POSITION (MLB): OF—40.

RAUL MONDESI'S HITTING ZONE

.182	.143	.143
.207	.200	.250
.167	.333	.333

LEFTY-RIGHTY SPLITS

vs.	Avg.	AB	H	2B	3B	HR	RBI	BB	SO	OBP	Slg.
L	.269	26	7	0	0	2	5	6	5	.406	.500
R	.198	116	23	7	1	2	12	6	30	.236	.328

Year	Team (League)	Pos.	G	AB	R	H	2B	3B	HR	RBI	BB	SO	HBP	GDP	SB-CS	Avg.	OBP	SLG	OPS	E	Avg.
1988— Dom. Dodgers (DSL)		OF	36	117	21	26	10	1	2	44	23	36	...	...	4-0	.222	...	.376	...	...	...
1989— Dom. Dodgers (DSL)		OF	46	156	32	43	15	3	2	27	16	26	...	...	8-0	.276	...	.449	...	...	...
1990— Great Falls (Pio.)		OF	44	175	35	53	10	4	8	31	11	30	2	0	30-6	.303	.349	.543	.892	1	.986
1991— Bakersfield (Calif.)		OF	28	106	23	30	7	2	3	13	3	1	9-4	.283	.330	.472	.802	3	.940		
— San Antonio (Texas)		OF	53	213	32	58	11	5	5	26	8	47	4	1	8-3	.272	.307	.441	.748	4	.964
— Albuquerque (PCL)		OF	2	9	3	3	1	0	0	0	1	0	1	0	1-0	.333	.333	.556	.889	1	1.000
1992— Albuquerque (PCL)		OF	35	138	23	43	4	7	4	15	9	35	1	0	2-3	.312	.358	.529	.887	7	.933
— San Antonio (Texas)		OF	18	68	8	18	2	2	2	14	1	24	0	1	3-2	.265	.264	.441	.705	1	.974
1993— Albuquerque (PCL)		OF	110	425	65	119	22	7	12	65	18	85	2	4	13-10	.280	.309	.449	.758	10	.957
— Los Angeles (N.L.)		OF	42	86	13	25	3	1	4	10	4	16	0	1	4-1	.291	.322	.488	.811	3	.951
1994— Los Angeles (N.L.)		OF	112	434	63	133	27	8	16	56	16	78	2	9	11-8	.306	.333	.516	.849	8	.965
1995— Los Angeles (N.L.)		OF	139	536	91	153	23	6	26	88	33	96	4	7	27-4	.285	.328	.496	.824	6	.980
1996— Los Angeles (N.L.)		OF	157	634	98	188	40	7	24	88	32	122	5	6	14-7	.297	.334	.495	.830	•12	.967
1997— Los Angeles (N.L.)		OF	159	616	95	191	42	5	30	87	44	105	6	11	32-15	.310	.360	.541	.901	4	.989
1998— Los Angeles (N.L.)		OF	148	580	85	162	26	5	30	90	30	112	3	6	16-10	.279	.316	.497	.813	6	.980
1999— Los Angeles (N.L.)		OF	159	601	98	152	29	5	33	99	71	134	3	3	36-9	.253	.332	.483	.815	6	.967
2000— Toronto (A.L.)		OF	96	388	78	105	22	2	24	67	32	73	3	8	22-6	.271	.329	.523	.852	7	.967

					BATTING														FIELDING	
Year	Team (League)	Pos.	G	AB	R	H	2B	3B	HR	RBI	BB	SO	HBP	GDP	SB-CS	Avg.	OBP	SLG	OPS	E	Avg.
2001—Toronto (A.L.)		OF	149	572	88	144	26	4	27	84	73	128	6	13	30-11	.252	.342	.453	.794	8	.972
2002—Toronto (A.L.)		OF-DH	75	299	51	67	16	1	15	45	31	57	3	8	9-2	.224	.301	.435	.736	2	.984
—New York (A.L.)		OF-DH	71	270	39	65	18	0	11	43	28	46	2	3	6-4	.241	.315	.430	.744	4	.969
2003—New York (A.L.)		OF-DH	98	361	56	93	23	3	16	49	38	66	2	6	17-7	.258	.330	.471	.801	3	.986
—Arizona (N.L.)		OF	45	162	27	49	8	1	8	22	18	31	1	3	5-4	.302	.372	.512	.884	3	.965
2004—Pittsburgh (N.L.)		OF	26	99	8	28	8	0	2	14	11	27	0	1	0-2	.283	.355	.424	.779	3	.939
—Anaheim (A.L.)		OF-DH	8	34	2	4	1	0	1	1	2	4	1	1	0-1	.118	.189	.235	.424	0	1.000
—Rancho Cuca. (Calif.)		DH-OF	2	8	2	1	0	0	0	0	1	2	0	1	0-0	.125	.222	.125	.347	0	1.000
—Salt Lake (PCL)		OF	2	6	1	2	0	0	1	2	1	2	0	0	0-0	.333	.429	.833	1.262	1	.800
2005—Atlanta (N.L.)		OF	41	142	17	30	7	1	4	17	12	35	0	5	0-1	.211	.271	.359	.630	1	.986
American League totals (5 years)			497	1924	314	478	106	10	94	289	204	374	17	39	84-31	.248	.324	.460	.785	24	.976
National League totals (10 years)			1028	3890	595	1111	213	39	177	571	271	756	24	54	145-61	.286	.334	.497	.831	52	.976
Major League totals (13 years)			1525	5814	909	1589	319	49	271	860	475	1130	41	93	229-92	.273	.331	.485	.815	76	.976

DIVISION SERIES RECORD

Year	Team (League)	Pos.	G	AB	R	H	2B	3B	HR	RBI	BB	SO	HBP	GDP	SB-CS	Avg.	OBP	SLG	OPS	E	Avg.
1995—Los Angeles (N.L.)		OF	3	9	0	2	0	0	0	1	0	2	1	0	0-0	.222	.300	.222	.522	0	1.000
1996—Los Angeles (N.L.)		OF	3	11	0	2	2	0	0	1	0	4	0	1	0-0	.182	.182	.364	.545	0	1.000
2002—New York (A.L.)		OF	4	12	1	3	0	0	0	1	3	1	2	0	0-0	.250	.471	.250	.721	0	1.000
Division series totals (3 years)			10	32	1	7	2	0	0	3	3	7	3	0	0-0	.219	.342	.281	.623	0	1.000

ALL-STAR GAME RECORD

			G	AB	R	H	2B	3B	HR	RBI	BB	SO	HBP	GDP	SB-CS	Avg.	OBP	SLG	OPS	E	Avg.
All-Star Game totals (1 year)			1	1	0	0	0	0	0	0	0	0	0	0	0-0	.000	.000	.000	.000	0	1.000

MONROE, CRAIG — OF

PERSONAL: Born February 27, 1977, in Texarkana, Texas. ... 6-1/220. ... Bats right, throws right. ... Full name: Craig Keystone Monroe. ... High school: Texas (Texarkana, Texas).

TRANSACTIONS/CAREER NOTES: Selected by Texas Rangers organization in eighth round of 1995 free-agent draft. ... Claimed on waivers by Detroit Tigers (February 1, 2002). ... On disabled list (July 21-August 7, 2004); included rehabilitation assignment to Toledo.

2005 GAMES PLAYED BY POSITION (MLB): OF—156, DH—1.

***SCOUTING REPORT* Offense:** Monroe is an athletic player who continues to improve each season. Has always been a better hitter against lefthanded pitchers but is improving against righthanders. Is a good fastball hitter who has learned to hit the breaking ball the other way. Still has some holes in his swing. Has power from gap to gap when he can extend his arms. **Defense:** Monroe doesn't have a lot of natural instincts, but he compensates with athleticism. Gets better reads playing a corner outfield spot. Has good closing speed when moving laterally. Has arm strength and accuracy. **Outlook:** He earned a regular spot in the Tigers' outfield in 2005 and responded with a good year. Can expand on those numbers next season if he can become more selective at the plate. **Grade 7.5**

CRAIG MONROE'S HITTING ZONE

.306	.421	.250
.383	.326	.246
.274	.250	.261

LEFTY-RIGHTY SPLITS

vs.	Avg.	AB	H	2B	3B	HR	RBI	BB	SO	OBP	Slg.
L	.303	122	37	7	1	7	23	12	25	.360	.549
R	.270	445	120	23	2	13	66	28	70	.311	.418

M

						BATTING														FIELDING	
Year	Team (League)	Pos.	G	AB	R	H	2B	3B	HR	RBI	BB	SO	HBP	GDP	SB-CS	Avg.	OBP	SLG	OPS	E	Avg.
1995—GC Rangers (GCL)		OF	54	193	22	48	6	2	0	33	18	25	2	1	13-2	.249	.316	.301	.617	4	.962
1996—Char., S.C. (SAL)		OF	49	153	11	23	11	1	0	9	18	48	3	3	2-2	.150	.253	.235	.488	4	.954
—Hudson Valley (NYP)		OF	67	268	53	74	16	6	5	29	23	63	2	4	21-7	.276	.336	.437	.772	6	.938
1997—Charlotte (Fla. St.)		OF	92	328	54	77	23	1	7	41	44	80	0	5	24-1	.235	.320	.375	.695	7	.959
1998—Charlotte (Fla. St.)		OF	132	472	73	114	26	7	17	76	66	102	3	15	50-13	.242	.334	.434	.768	11	.951
1999—Charlotte (Fla. St.)		OF	130	480	77	125	21	1	17	81	42	102	4	8	40-15	.260	.321	.415	.735	7	.980
—Oklahoma (PCL)		OF	6	16	2	4	1	0	0	1	1	4	4	0	0-0	.250	.429	.313	.741	0	1.000
2000—Tulsa (Texas)		OF	120	464	89	131	34	5	20	89	64	91	2	12	12-13	.282	.366	.506	.873	12	.948
2001—Oklahoma (PCL)		OF	114	410	60	115	25	5	20	75	46	85	5	11	10-8	.280	.358	.512	.870	5	.975
—Texas (A.L.)		OF-DH	27	52	8	11	1	0	2	5	6	18	0	1	2-0	.212	.293	.346	.639	1	1.000
2002—Toledo (Int'l)		OF	99	358	61	115	30	4	10	49	35	57	2	8	7-3	.321	.379	.511	.890	3	.983
—Detroit (A.L.)		OF-DH	13	25	3	3	1	0	1	1	0	5	1	1	0-2	.120	.154	.280	.434	1	.950
2003—Toledo (Int'l)		OF-DH	14	47	14	19	4	1	2	6	4	10	0	0	1-0	.404	.451	.660	1.111	0	1.000
—Detroit (A.L.)		OF-DH	128	425	51	102	18	1	23	70	27	89	2	10	4-2	.240	.287	.449	.736	7	.970
2004—Toledo (Int'l)		OF-DH	6	25	4	8	4	0	2	6	0	6	0	0	0-0	.320	.308	.720	1.028	0	1.000
—Detroit (A.L.)		OF-DH	128	447	65	131	27	3	18	72	29	79	2	8	3-4	.293	.337	.488	.824	11	.960
2005—Detroit (A.L.)		OF-DH	157	567	69	157	30	3	20	89	40	95	3	16	8-3	.277	.322	.446	.768	6	.981
Major League totals (5 years)			453	1516	196	404	77	7	64	237	102	286	8	36	17-11	.266	.313	.453	.766	25	.972

MORA, MELVIN — 3B

PERSONAL: Born February 2, 1972, in Agua Negra, Venezuela. ... 5-11/200. ... Bats right, throws right. ... Name pronounced: MORE-a. ... High school: Libertador (Valencia, Venezuela).

TRANSACTIONS/CAREER NOTES: Signed as a non-drafted free agent by Houston Astros organization (March 30, 1991). ... Signed as a free agent by New York Mets organization (July 24, 1998). ... On disabled list (May 13-30, 2000); included rehabilitation assignment to Norfolk. ... Traded by Mets with 3B Mike Kinkade and Ps Leslie Brea and Pat Gorman to Baltimore Orioles for SS Mike Bordick (July 28, 2000). ... On suspended list (September 13-16, 2002). ... On disabled list (August 1-September 2, 2003); included rehabilitation assignment to Bowie. ... On disabled list (July 3-18, 2004).

RECORDS: Shares major league record for times hit by pitch, game (3, July 18, 2002).

2005 GAMES PLAYED BY POSITION (MLB): 3B—148, DH—1.

SCOUTING REPORT *Offense:* Mora is a steady run producer with good power. Has a long swing and slightly uppercut stroke. Is a good breaking-ball hitter who likes the ball down. Has improved his bat speed and become more of a pull hitter. Still has a lot of holes and will chase balls up in the zone. Is a good baserunner with good instincts but does not steal many bases. *Defense:* Mora has improved at third base as he has become more comfortable. Has good hands and gets good jumps on the ball, especially to his left. Has soft hands and likes to field the ball to his side. Throws well and is accurate. *Outlook:* Mora is one of the league's steadiest players and has improved in all aspects of his game, particularly on defense. *Grade 8.9*

MELVIN MORA'S HITTING ZONE

.375	.194	.148
.257	.450	.333
.241	.429	.344

LEFTY-RIGHTY SPLITS

vs.	Avg.	AB	H	2B	3B	HR	RBI	BB	SO	OBP	Slg.
L	.232	168	39	8	0	10	22	14	35	.293	.458
R	.304	425	129	22	1	17	66	36	77	.369	.480

Year	Team (League)	Pos.	G	AB	R	H	2B	3B	HR	RBI	BB	SO	HBP	GDP	SB-CS	Avg.	OBP	SLG	OPS	E	Avg.
1991—	Dom. Astros (DSL)	....	58	211	38	63	18	1	0	20	19	22	...		21-...	.299		.393	...	...	...
1992—	GC Astros (GCL)	2B-3B-OF	49	144	28	32	3	0	0	8	18	16	5	2	16-3	.222	.327	.243	.570	4	.961
1993—	Asheville (S. Atl.)	....	108	365	66	104	22	2	2	31	36	46	9	7	20-13	.285	.356	.373	.729	17	.936
1994—	Osceola (Fla. St.)	3B-OF	118	425	57	120	29	4	8	46	37	60	10	8	24-16	.282	.352	.426	.777	15	.947
1995—	Jackson (Texas)	2B-3B-OF	123	467	63	139	32	0	3	45	32	57	9	11	22-11	.298	.350	.385	.735	6	.977
—	Tucson (PCL)	OF	2	5	3	3	0	1	0	1	2	0	0	0	1-0	.600	.714	1.000	1.714	0	1.000
1996—	Jackson (Texas)	2B-3B-OF																			
		SS	70	255	36	73	6	1	5	23	14	23	6	4	4-7	.286	.336	.376	.712	7	.959
—	Tucson (PCL)	2B-3B-OF	62	228	35	64	11	2	3	26	17	27	1	7	3-5	.281	.328	.386	.714	14	.912
1997—	New Orleans (A.A.)	....	119	370	55	95	15	3	2	38	47	52	11	7	7-7	.257	.356	.330	.686	11	.956
1998—	Mercury (Tai.)	....	...	164	34	55	11	2	3	11	...	...	...		-...	.335	...	.482	...	...	...
—	St. Lucie (Fla. St.)	2B-OF-SS	17	55	5	15	0	0	0	8	5	9	0	0	1-1	.273	.328	.273	.601	1	.985
—	Norfolk (Int'l)	2B-3B-OF	11	28	5	5	1	0	0	5	5	7	0	0	0-0	.179	.303	.214	.517	2	.875
1999—	Norfolk (Int'l)	SS-OF-2B																			
		3B	82	304	55	92	17	2	8	36	41	54	7	8	18-8	.303	.393	.451	.844	16	.942
—	New York (N.L.)	OF-2B-3B																			
		2B	66	31	6	5	0	0	0	1	4	7	1	0	2-1	.161	.278	.161	.439	0	1.000
2000—	New York (N.L.)	SS-OF-2B																			
		3B	79	215	35	56	13	2	6	30	18	48	2	3	7-3	.260	.317	.423	.740	8	.962
—	Norfolk (Int'l)	OF-2B-SS	8	27	7	9	2	0	0	7	7	3	0	0	2-0	.333	.471	.407	.878	0	1.000
—	Baltimore (A.L.)	SS-2B	53	199	25	58	3	2	7	17	17	32	4	2	5-8	.291	.359	.397	.756	12	.953
2001—	Baltimore (A.L.)	OF-SS-2B	128	436	49	109	28	0	7	48	41	91	14	6	11-4	.250	.329	.362	.692	11	.974
2002—	Baltimore (A.L.)	OF-SS-2B																			
		DH	149	557	86	130	30	4	19	64	70	108	20	7	16-10	.233	.338	.404	.742	12	.976
2003—	Bowie (East.)	OF	6	21	3	6	0	0	2	5	2	4	0	0	0-0	.286	.348	.571	.919	0	1.000
—	Baltimore (A.L.)	OF-SS-2B																			
		1B	96	344	68	109	17	1	15	48	49	71	12	3	6-3	.317	.418	.503	.921	2	.992
2004—	Baltimore (A.L.)	3B-DH-SS	140	550	111	187	41	0	27	104	66	95	11	10	11-6	.340 *	.419	.562	.981	21	.948
2005—	Baltimore (A.L.)	3B-DH	149	593	86	168	30	1	27	88	50	112	10	9	7-4	.283	.348	.474	.821	18	.957
American League totals (6 years)			715	2679	425	761	155	9	97	369	293	509	71	37	56-35	.284	.367	.457	.825	76	.966
National League totals (2 years)			145	246	41	61	13	2	6	31	22	55	3	3	9-4	.248	.312	.390	.702	8	.967
Major League totals (7 years)			860	2925	466	822	168	11	103	400	315	564	74	40	65-39	.281	.363	.452	.814	84	.966

DIVISION SERIES RECORD

Year	Team (League)	Pos.	G	AB	R	H	2B	3B	HR	RBI	BB	SO	HBP	GDP	SB-CS	Avg.	OBP	SLG	OPS	E	Avg.
1999—	New York (N.L.)	OF	3	1	1	0	0	0	0	0	1	0	0	0	0-0	.000	.500	.000	.500	0	1.000

CHAMPIONSHIP SERIES RECORD

Year	Team (League)	Pos.	G	AB	R	H	2B	3B	HR	RBI	BB	SO	HBP	GDP	SB-CS	Avg.	OBP	SLG	OPS	E	Avg.
1999—	New York (N.L.)	OF	6	14	3	6	0	0	1	2	2	2	0	0	2-0	.429	.500	.643	1.143	0	1.000

ALL-STAR GAME RECORD

			G	AB	R	H	2B	3B	HR	RBI	BB	SO	HBP	GDP	SB-CS	Avg.	OBP	SLG	OPS	E	Avg.
All-Star Game totals (2 years)			2	1	1	0	0	0	0	0	0	1	0	0	0-0	.000	.000	.000	.000	0	1.000

MORDECAI, MIKE — 3B/SS

PERSONAL: Born December 13, 1967, in Birmingham, Ala. ... 5-10/182. ... Bats right, throws right. ... Full name: Michael Howard Mordecai. ... Name pronounced: MORE-duh-kye. ... High school: Hewitt Trussville (Ala.). ... College: South Alabama.

TRANSACTIONS/CAREER NOTES: Selected by Pittsburgh Pirates organization in 33rd round of June 1986 free-agent draft; did not sign. ... Selected by Atlanta Braves organization in sixth round of 1989 free-agent draft. ... On disabled list (April 19-May 11, 1996); included rehabilitation assignment to Richmond. ... Signed as a free agent by Montreal Expos organization (March 27, 1998). ... On disabled list (June 24-July 24, 1998); included rehabilitation assignments to Jupiter and Ottawa. ... Traded by Expos with Ps Carl Pavano, Graeme Lloyd and Justin Wayne to Florida Marlins for OF Cliff Floyd, P Claudio Vargas, 2B/OF Wilton Guerrero, cash and a player to be named (July 11, 2002); Expos acquired P Don Levinski to complete deal (August 6, 2002).

2005 GAMES PLAYED BY POSITION (MLB): 2B—1, SS—1.

LEFTY-RIGHTY SPLITS

vs.	Avg.	AB	H	2B	3B	HR	RBI	BB	SO	OBP	Slg.
L	.000	0	0	0	0	0	0	0	0	.000	.000
R	.000	2	0	0	0	0	0	0	1	.000	.000

Year	Team (League)	Pos.	G	AB	R	H	2B	3B	HR	RBI	BB	SO	HBP	GDP	SB-CS	Avg.	OBP	SLG	OPS	E	Avg.
1989—	Burlington (Midw.)	3B-SS	65	241	39	61	11	1	1	22	33	43	5	2	12-5	.253	.352	.320	.672	21	.920
—	Greenville (Sou.)	2B-3B	4	8	0	3	0	0	1	1	1	1	0	0	0-0	.375	.444	.375	.819	0	1.000
1990—	Durham (Carol.)	SS	72	271	42	76	11	7	3	36	42	45	2	9	10-6	.280	.379	.406	.784	29	.920
1991—	Durham (Carol.)	SS	109	397	52	104	15	2	4	42	40	58	2	7	30-16	.262	.330	.340	.670	27	.945
1992—	Greenville (Sou.)	SS	65	222	31	58	13	1	4	31	29	31	0	6	9-6	.261	.344	.383	.727	11	.964
—	Richmond (Int'l)	2B-3B-SS	36	118	12	29	3	0	1	6	5	19	0	1	0-4	.246	.272	.297	.569	10	.943
1993—	Richmond (Int'l)	C	72	205	29	55	8	1	2	14	14	33	1	4	10-2	.268	.318	.346	.665	9	.967
1994—	Richmond (Int'l)	SS-1B-3B																			
		DH	99	382	67	107	25	1	14	57	35	50	2	5	14-7	.280	.340	.461	.800	22	.947
—	Atlanta (N.L.)	SS	4	4	1	1	0	0	1	3	1	0	0	0	0-0	.250	.400	1.000	1.400	0	1.000

Year Team (League)	Pos.	G	AB	R	H	2B	3B	HR	RBI	BB	SO	HBP	GDP	SB-CS	Avg.	OBP	SLG	OPS	E	Avg.
1995— Atlanta (N.L.) 2B-1B-3B																				
	SS-OF	69	75	10	21	6	0	3	11	9	16	0	0	0-0	.280	.353	.480	.833	0	1.000
1996— Atlanta (N.L.) 2B-3B-SS																				
	1B	66	108	12	26	5	0	2	8	9	24	0	1	1-0	.241	.297	.343	.639	2	.977
—Richmond (Int'l)	SS	3	11	2	2	0	0	1	2	0	3	0	0	0-0	.182	.167	.455	.621	0	1.000
1997— Atlanta (N.L.) 3B-2B-SS																				
	1B-DH-OF	61	81	8	14	2	1	0	3	6	16	0	4	0-1	.173	.227	.222	.449	0	1.000
—Richmond (Int'l)	2B-3B-DH																			
	SS	31	122	23	38	10	0	3	15	9	17	1	0	0-1	.311	.361	.467	.828	1	.989
1998— Montreal (N.L.) SS-2B-1B																				
	1B	73	119	12	24	4	2	3	10	9	20	0	2	1-0	.202	.258	.345	.602	5	.960
—Jupiter (Fla. St.)	2B-SS	2	8	0	0	0	0	0	0	1	3	0	1	0-0	.000	.111	.000	.111	0	1.000
—Ottawa (Int'l)	SS-2B	6	22	2	5	2	0	0	1	3	3	0	1	0-0	.227	.320	.318	.638	1	.969
1999— Montreal (N.L.) 2B-SS-3B																				
	1B	109	226	29	53	10	2	5	25	20	31	1	1	2-5	.235	.297	.363	.660	7	.970
2000— Montreal (N.L.) 3B-SS-2B																				
	1B	86	169	20	48	16	0	4	16	12	34	1	1	2-2	.284	.335	.450	.785	8	.942
2001— Montreal (N.L.) 3B-2B-SS																				
	1B-C-DH-OF	96	254	28	71	17	2	3	32	19	53	1	6	2-2	.280	.330	.398	.727	3	.985
2002— Montreal (N.L.) 3B-2B-1B																				
	SS-OF	55	74	9	15	4	0	0	4	8	14	1	2	1-1	.203	.289	.257	.546	4	.948
—Florida (N.L.)	SS-3B-1B	38	77	10	22	4	0	0	7	5	13	1	1	1-1	.286	.337	.338	.675	1	.989
2003— Florida (N.L.) SS-2B-3B																				
	1B	65	89	11	19	4	0	2	8	8	21	0	0	3-0	.213	.276	.326	.601	3	.961
2004— Florida (N.L.) 3B-2B-SS																				
	C	69	84	7	19	3	0	1	5	6	18	0	1	0-1	.226	.278	.298	.575	3	.945
2005— Florida (N.L.)	2B-SS	2	2	0	0	0	0	0	0	0	1	0	0	0-0	.000	.000	.000	.000	0	1.000
Major League totals (12 years)		793	1362	157	333	75	7	24	132	112	261	5	19	13-13	.244	.303	.363	.665	36	.970

DIVISION SERIES RECORD

Year Team (League)	Pos.	G	AB	R	H	2B	3B	HR	RBI	BB	SO	HBP	GDP	SB-CS	Avg.	OBP	SLG	OPS	E	Avg.
1995—Atlanta (N.L.)	SS	2	3	1	2	1	0	0	2	0	0	0	0	0-0	.667	.667	1.000	1.667	0	1.000
1996—Atlanta (N.L.)		Did not play.																		

CHAMPIONSHIP SERIES RECORD

Year Team (League)	Pos.	G	AB	R	H	2B	3B	HR	RBI	BB	SO	HBP	GDP	SB-CS	Avg.	OBP	SLG	OPS	E	Avg.
1995—Atlanta (N.L.)	SS	2	2	0	0	0	0	0	0	0	1	0	0	0-0	.000	.000	.000	.000	0	...
1996—Atlanta (N.L.)	2B-3B	4	4	1	1	0	0	0	0	0	1	0	0	0-0	.250	.250	.250	.500	1	1.000
2003—Florida (N.L.)	SS-2B	3	5	1	1	1	0	0	3	0	0	0	0	0-0	.200	.200	.400	.600	0	...
Champ. series totals (3 years)		9	11	2	2	1	0	0	3	0	2	0	0	0-0	.182	.182	.273	.455	1	1.000

WORLD SERIES RECORD

Year Team (League)	Pos.	G	AB	R	H	2B	3B	HR	RBI	BB	SO	HBP	GDP	SB-CS	Avg.	OBP	SLG	OPS	E	Avg.
1995—Atlanta (N.L.)	DH-SS	3	3	0	1	0	0	0	0	0	1	0	0	0-0	.333	.333	.333	.667	0	1.000
1996—Atlanta (N.L.)		1	1	0	0	0	0	0	0	0	0	0	0	0-0	.000	.000	.000	.000	...	...
World Series totals (2 years)		4	4	0	1	0	0	0	0	0	1	0	0	0-0	.250	.250	.250	.500	0	1.000

MORNEAU, JUSTIN   1B

M

PERSONAL: Born May 15, 1981, in New Westminster, British Columbia. ... 6-4/228. ... Bats left, throws right. ... Full name: Justin Ernest Morneau. ... Name pronounced: more-no. ... High school: New Westminster Academy (British Columbia).

TRANSACTIONS/CAREER NOTES: Selected by Minnesota Twins organization in third round of 1999 free-agent draft. ... On disabled list (April 7-22, 2005).

2005 GAMES PLAYED BY POSITION (MLB): 1B—138, DH—1.

SCOUTING REPORT **Offense:** The concussion he suffered early last season seemed to take away some of his aggressiveness at the plate. Has a fluid stroke but seemed to lose bat speed. Has some holes in the upper part of the zone. Is a low-ball hitter but isn't pulling the ball often enough. Stays inside the ball well. Appears to be more of a guess hitter. **Defense:** Morneau's hands are good, but his range is average. Is not very agile at first base and needs help with his footwork around the bag. Has arm strength and accuracy to start the double play. **Outlook:** At the end of 2004 there was no question he was going to hit and have power; with the injury in '05 and his decline in bat speed, he needs a big spring in 2006 to rebuild momentum. *Grade 7.8*

JUSTIN MORNEAU'S HITTING ZONE

.216	.091	.364
.333	.288	.297
.188	.238	.133

LEFTY-RIGHTY SPLITS

vs.	Avg.	AB	H	2B	3B	HR	RBI	BB	SO	OBP	Slg.
L	.201	154	31	8	0	4	24	8	32	.255	.331
R	.256	336	86	15	4	18	55	36	62	.325	.485

Year Team (League)	Pos.	G	AB	R	H	2B	3B	HR	RBI	BB	SO	HBP	GDP	SB-CS	Avg.	OBP	SLG	OPS	E	Avg.
1999—GC Twins (GCL)	DH	17	53	3	16	4	0	0	10	10	15	1	...	1-1	.302	.333	.377	.710	0	...
2000—GC Twins (GCL)	1B-C-OF	52	194	47	48	21	0	10	58	30	18	0	...	3-1	.402	.478	.510	.988	3	.992
—Elizabethton (App.)	C	6	23	4	5	0	0	1	3	1	6	0	0	0-0	.217	.250	.348	.598	0	1.000
2001—Quad City (Midw.)	1B	64	236	50	84	17	2	12	53	26	38	3	4	0-0	.356	.420	.597	1.018	8	.985
—Fort Myers (FSL)	1B	53	197	25	58	10	3	4	40	24	41	8	4	0-0	.294	.385	.437	.821	3	.994
—New Britain (East.)	1B	10	38	3	6	1	0	0	4	3	8	0	1	0-0	.158	.214	.184	.399	0	1.000
2002—New Britain (East.)	1B	126	494	72	147	31	4	16	80	42	88	6	8	7-0	.298	.356	.474	.830	13	.989
2003—New Britain (East.)	1B	20	79	14	26	3	1	6	13	7	14	0	0	0-0	.329	.384	.620	1.004	0	1.000
—Rochester (Int'l)	1B-DH	71	265	39	71	11	1	16	42	28	56	4	2	0-2	.268	.344	.498	.843	4	.993
—Minnesota (A.L.)	DH-1B	40	106	14	24	4	0	4	16	9	30	0	4	0-0	.226	.287	.377	.664	1	.971
2004—Rochester (Int'l)	1B-DH	72	288	51	88	23	0	22	63	32	47	3	7	1-1	.306	.377	.615	.992	4	.994
—Minnesota (A.L.)	1B-DH	74	280	39	76	17	0	19	58	28	54	2	4	0-0	.271	.340	.536	.875	3	.995
2005—Minnesota (A.L.)	1B-DH	141	490	62	117	23	4	22	79	44	94	4	12	0-2	.239	.304	.437	.741	8	.994
Major League totals (3 years)		255	876	115	217	44	4	45	153	81	178	6	20	0-2	.248	.313	.461	.775	12	.994

DIVISION SERIES RECORD

Year Team (League)	Pos.	G	AB	R	H	2B	3B	HR	RBI	BB	SO	HBP	GDP	SB-CS	Avg.	OBP	SLG	OPS	E	Avg.
2004— Minnesota (A.L.)	1B	4	17	1	4	2	0	0	2	0	3	0	0	0-0	.235	.235	.353	.588	0	1.000

MORRIS, MATT   P

PERSONAL: Born August 9, 1974, in Middletown, N.Y. ... 6-5/220. ... Throws right, bats right. ... Full name: Matthew Christian Morris. ... High school: Valley Central (Montgomery, N.Y.). ... College: Seton Hall.

TRANSACTIONS/CAREER NOTES: Selected by Milwaukee Brewers organization in 25th round of 1992 free-agent draft; did not sign. ... Selected by St. Louis Cardinals organization in first round (12th pick overall) of 1995 free-agent draft. ... On disabled list (March 24-April 11 and April 12-July 10, 1998); included rehabilitation assignments to Arkansas and Memphis. ... On disabled list (March 26, 1999-entire season). ... On disabled list (April 2-May 28, 2000); included rehabilitation assignments to Arkansas and Memphis. ... On disabled list (August 24-September 10, 2002; and July 22-August 23, 2003). ... On disabled list (April 3-19, 2005); included rehabilitation assignment to Palm Beach.

HONORS: Named N.L. Rookie Pitcher of the Year by THE SPORTING NEWS (1997). ... Named N.L. Comeback Player of the Year by THE SPORTING NEWS (2001).

CAREER HITTING: 65-for-419 (.155), 27 R, 11 2B, 0 3B, 1 HR, 28 RBI.

SCOUTING REPORT **Throws:** Morris' fastball hits 90-92 mph, and his curve goes 73-78. Straight changeup is improving. *Tendencies:* He's learning to pitch without a mid-90s fastball. Is most effective when he establishes the curveball, which has a big break and can freeze hitters. Is not afraid to challenge hitters despite his declining velocity. Is starting to rely more on a cut fastball and has improved his command. Is learning to spot his fastball on both sides of the plate and change speeds. *Outlook:* Morris should be a bigger winner in 2006. **Grade 7.9**

MATT MORRIS' PITCHING ZONE

.235	.214	.333
.245	.463	.359
.363	.262	.214

LEFTY-RIGHTY SPLITS

vs.	Avg.	AB	H	2B	3B	HR	RBI	BB	SO	OBP	Slg.
L	.279	351	98	20	3	11	49	20	58	.320	.447
R	.273	406	111	24	0	11	42	17	59	.310	.414

Year Team (League)	W	L	Pct.	ERA	WHIP	G	GS	CG	ShO	Hld.	Sv.-Opp.	IP	H	R	ER	HR	BB-IBB	SO	Avg.
1995— New Jersey (NYP)	2	0	1.000	1.64	1.36	2	2	0	0	...	0-...	11.0	12	3	2	1	3-0	13	.286
—St. Pete. (FSL)	3	2	.600	2.38	0.97	6	6	1	1	...	0-...	34.0	22	16	9	1	11-0	31	.182
1996— Arkansas (Texas)	12	12	.500	3.88	1.35	27	27	4	4	...	0-...	167.0	178	79	72	14	48-1	120	.274
—Louisville (A.A.)	0	1	.000	3.38	1.13	1	1	0	0	...	0-...	8.0	8	3	3	0	1-0	9	.258
1997— St. Louis (N.L.)	12	9	.571	3.19	1.28	33	33	3	0	0	0-0	217.0	208	88	77	12	69-2	149	.258
1998— Arkansas (Texas)	0	0	...	0.00	1.00	1	0	0	0	...	1-...	4.0	4	0	0	0	0-0	2	.235
—St. Louis (N.L.)	7	5	.583	2.53	1.26	17	17	2	1	0	0-0	113.2	101	37	32	8	42-6	79	.243
—Memphis (PCL)	1	0	1.000	4.50	1.43	4	4	0	0	...	0-...	14.0	16	8	7	1	4-0	21	.286
1999— St. Louis (N.L.)				Did not play.															
2000— Arkansas (Texas)	0	0	...	6.43	1.71	2	2	0	0	...	0-...	7.0	8	5	5	0	4-0	7	.296
—Memphis (PCL)	1	2	.333	7.98	1.77	3	3	0	0	...	0-...	14.2	20	13	13	2	6-1	8	.351
—St. Louis (N.L.)	3	3	.500	3.57	1.32	31	0	0	0	7	4-7	53.0	53	22	21	3	17-1	34	.261
2001— St. Louis (N.L.)	•22	8	.733	3.16	1.26	34	34	2	1	0	0-0	216.1	218	86	76	13	54-3	185	.265
2002— St. Louis (N.L.)	17	9	.654	3.42	1.30	32	32	1	1	0	0-0	210.1	210	86	80	16	64-3	171	.261
2003— St. Louis (N.L.)	11	8	.579	3.76	1.18	27	27	5	•3	0	0-0	172.1	164	76	72	20	39-1	120	.252
2004— St. Louis (N.L.)	15	10	.600	4.72	1.29	32	32	0	2	0	0-0	202.0	205	116	106	35	56-3	131	.266
2005— Palm Beach (FSL)	0	1	.000	6.52	1.45	2	2	0	0	0	0-0	9.2	12	7	7	0	2-0	15	.300
—St. Louis (N.L.)	14	10	.583	4.11	1.28	31	31	2	0	0	0-0	192.2	209	101	88	22	37-3	117	.276
Major League totals (8 years)	**101**	**62**	**.620**	**3.61**	**1.27**	**237**	**206**	**18**	**8**	**7**	**4-7**	**1377.1**	**1368**	**612**	**552**	**129**	**378-22**	**986**	**.261**

DIVISION SERIES RECORD

Year Team (League)	W	L	Pct.	ERA	WHIP	G	GS	CG	ShO	Hld.	Sv.-Opp.	IP	H	R	ER	HR	BB-IBB	SO	Avg.
2000— St. Louis (N.L.)	0	0	...	0.00	0.50	2	0	0	0	0	0-0	2.0	0	0	0	0	1-0	0	.000
2001— St. Louis (N.L.)	0	1	.000	1.20	1.20	2	2	0	0	0	0-0	15.0	13	2	2	1	5-0	12	.236
2002— St. Louis (N.L.)	1	0	1.000	1.29	1.29	1	1	0	0	0	0-0	7.0	7	2	1	0	2-0	3	.259
2004— St. Louis (N.L.)	0	1	.000	5.14	1.14	1	1	0	0	0	0-0	7.0	6	4	4	2	2-1	5	.231
2005— St. Louis (N.L.)	1	0	1.000	3.00	1.33	1	1	0	0	0	0-0	6.0	5	2	2	0	3-0	4	.217
Division series totals (5 years)	**2**	**2**	**.500**	**2.19**	**1.19**	**7**	**5**	**0**	**0**	**0**	**0-0**	**37.0**	**31**	**10**	**9**	**3**	**13-1**	**24**	**.226**

CHAMPIONSHIP SERIES RECORD

Year Team (League)	W	L	Pct.	ERA	WHIP	G	GS	CG	ShO	Hld.	Sv.-Opp.	IP	H	R	ER	HR	BB-IBB	SO	Avg.
2000— St. Louis (N.L.)	0	0	...	4.91	1.36	2	0	0	0	0	0-0	3.2	3	2	2	0	2-1	2	.214
2002— St. Louis (N.L.)	0	2	.000	6.23	1.69	2	2	0	0	0	0-0	13.0	16	9	9	2	6-1	6	.320
2004— St. Louis (N.L.)	0	0	...	5.40	1.90	2	2	0	0	0	0-0	10.0	11	6	6	3	8-1	6	.297
2005— St. Louis (N.L.)	0	1	.000	5.06	1.69	1	1	0	0	0	0-0	5.1	8	4	3	1	1-0	3	.333
Champ. series totals (4 years)	**0**	**3**	**.000**	**5.63**	**1.72**	**7**	**5**	**0**	**0**	**0**	**0-0**	**32.0**	**38**	**21**	**20**	**6**	**17-3**	**17**	**.304**

WORLD SERIES RECORD

Year Team (League)	W	L	Pct.	ERA	WHIP	G	GS	CG	ShO	Hld.	Sv.-Opp.	IP	H	R	ER	HR	BB-IBB	SO	Avg.
2004— St. Louis (N.L.)	0	1	.000	8.31	1.85	1	1	0	0	0	0-0	4.1	4	4	4	0	4-0	3	.250

ALL-STAR GAME RECORD

Year Team (League)	W	L	Pct.	ERA	WHIP	G	GS	CG	ShO	Hld.	Sv.-Opp.	IP	H	R	ER	HR	BB-IBB	SO	Avg.
All-Star Game totals (1 year)	0	0	...	0.00	1.00	1	1	0	0	0	0-0	1.0	1	0	0	0	0-0	1	.250

MORSE, MIKE   SS

PERSONAL: Born March 22, 1982, in Fort Lauderdale, Fla. ... 6-4/220. ... Bats right, throws right. ... Full name: Michael John Morse.

TRANSACTIONS/CAREER NOTES: Selected by Chicago White Sox organization in third round of 2000 free-agent draft. ... Traded by White Sox with OF Jeremy Reed and C Miguel Olivo to Mariners for P Freddy Garcia, C Ben Davis and cash (June 27, 2004). ... On suspended list (September 7-17, 2005).

2005 GAMES PLAYED BY POSITION (MLB): SS—55, DH—9, OF—8.

SCOUTING REPORT *Offense:* He's a good fastball hitter with the size and bat speed to develop some power. As a rookie, he tended to get pull-happy and chase high pitches, especially when behind in the count. Became a more disciplined hitter through the minors and showed signs of carrying that approach into the majors. *Defense:* Morse lacks quickness to the ball and has sub-par range, but his hands are soft and his arm is strong. Projects better at the corners. *Outlook:* After testing positive for steroids last September, his future has to be considered a bit uncertain. Considering he does not project to be an everyday shortstop in the majors and that the Mariners are set at the corners, he could be moved. *Grade 7*

MIKE MORSE'S HITTING ZONE

.375	.091	.273
.317	.522	.310
.286	.182	.286

LEFTY-RIGHTY SPLITS

vs.	Avg.	AB	H	2B	3B	HR	RBI	BB	SO	OBP	Slg.
L	.272	81	22	5	1	1	6	8	10	.352	.395
R	.282	149	42	5	0	2	17	10	40	.347	.356

Year Team (League)	Pos.	G	AB	R	H	2B	3B	HR	RBI	BB	SO	HBP	GDP	SB-CS	Avg.	OBP	SLG	OPS	E	Avg.
2000— Ariz. White Sox (Ariz.)	SS	45	180	32	46	6	1	2	24	15	29	1	6	5-2	.256	.308	.333	.641	18	.897
2001— Bristol (Appal.)	SS	57	181	23	41	7	3	4	27	17	57	9	4	6-2	.227	.324	.365	.689	14	.940
2002— Kannapolis (S. Atl.)	SS-3B	113	417	43	107	30	4	2	56	25	73	8	16	7-6	.257	.310	.362	.672	32	.934
2003— Win.-Salem (Car.)	SS	122	432	45	106	30	2	10	55	25	91	7	12	4-4	.245	.296	.394	.690	19	.959
2004— Birmingham (Sou.)	SS	54	209	30	60	9	5	11	38	15	46	1	4	0-3	.287	.336	.536	.872	11	.831
— San Antonio (Texas)	SS	41	157	18	43	10	1	6	33	9	27	4	8	0-2	.274	.326	.465	.791	9	.000
2005— Tacoma (PCL)	SS	49	182	20	46	12	2	4	23	16	36	2	6	1-0	.253	.317	.407	.723	4	.981
— Seattle (A.L.)	SS-DH-OF	72	230	27	64	10	1	3	23	18	50	8	9	3-1	.278	.349	.370	.718	12	.949
Major League totals (1 year)		72	230	27	64	10	1	3	23	18	50	8	9	3-1	.278	.349	.370	.718	12	.949

MOSQUERA, JULIO   C

PERSONAL: Born January 29, 1972, in Panama City, Panama. ... 6-0/204. ... Bats right, throws right. ... Full name: Julio Alberto Mosquera.

TRANSACTIONS/CAREER NOTES: Signed as non-drafted free agent by Toronto Blue Jays organization (May 16, 1991). ... Claimed on waivers by Tampa Bay Devil Rays (September 23, 1998). ... Signed as a free agent by New York Yankees organization (December 17, 1999). ... Signed as a free agent by Texas Rangers organization (January 29, 2002). ... Signed as a free agent by Seattle Mariners organization (November 6, 2002). ... Signed by Campeche of the Mexican League (April 2004). ... Signed as a free agent by Rangers (July 16, 2004). ... Signed as a free agent by Milwaukee Brewers organization (January 10, 2005).

LEFTY-RIGHTY SPLITS

vs.	Avg.	AB	H	2B	3B	HR	RBI	BB	SO	OBP	Slg.
L	.000	0	0	0	0	0	0	0	0	.000	.000
R	.000	1	0	0	0	0	0	0	0	.000	.000

Year Team (League)	Pos.	G	AB	R	H	2B	3B	HR	RBI	BB	SO	HBP	GDP	SB-CS	Avg.	OBP	SLG	OPS	E	Avg.
1991— Dom. B. Jays (DSL)	C	42	136	20	29	3	0	0	10	8	12	...		3-...	.213		.235			
— Toronto (DSL)	C	42	136	20	29	3	0	0	10	8	12	2	7	3-5	.213	.271	.235	.506	4	.975
1992— Dom. B. Jays (DSL)	C	67	235	47	85	12	1	3	39	17	20	...		17-...	.362		.460			
— Toronto W (DSL)	C	67	235	47	85	12	1	3	39	17	20	5	5	17-6	.362	.412	.460	.872	14	.956
1993— GC Jays (GCL)	C-SS	35	108	9	28	3	2	0	15	8	16	1	3	3-3	.259	.314	.324	.638	8	.965
1994— Medicine Hat (Pio.)	C	59	229	33	78	17	1	2	44	18	35	3	4	3-3	.341	.393	.450	.843	11	.971
1995— Hagerstown (SAL)	1B-C	108	406	64	118	22	5	3	46	29	53	13	13	5-5	.291	.353	.392	.745	7	.991
1996— Knoxville (Southern)	C	92	318	36	73	17	0	2	31	29	55	4	16	6-5	.230	.301	.302	.603	7	.991
— Syracuse (Int'l)	C	23	72	6	18	1	0	0	5	6	14	1		0-0	.250	.316	.264	.580	3	.983
— Toronto (A.L.)	C	8	22	2	5	2	0	0	2	0	3	...		0-1	.227	.227	.318	.545	0	1.000
1997— Knoxville (Southern)	C	87	309	47	90	23	1	5	50	22	56	5	10	3-4	.291	.345	.421	.766	7	.989
— Syracuse (Int'l)	C	10	35	5	8	1	0	0	1	2	5	1	2	0-0	.229	.289	.257	.546	1	.984
— Toronto (A.L.)	C	3	8	0	2	1	0	0	0	0	2	...		0-0	.250	.250	.375	.625	0	1.000
1998— Syracuse (Int'l)	C	28	94	10	20	6	0	2	4	5	12	4	2	1-0	.213	.279	.340	.619	0	1.000
— Knoxville (Southern)	C-DH-OF	12	43	4	12	1	0	0	8	4	7	0	0	1-0	.279	.333	.302	.635	1	.983
1999— Orlando (South.)	C-DH-OF	80	259	36	79	13	1	4	37	15	40	3	14	1-0	.305	.345	.464	.754	5	.988
2000— Norwich (East.)	C-1B	29	74	9	17	3	2	0	3	8	12	1	2	2-2	.230	.310	.324	.634	2	.988
— Columbus (Int'l)	C	35	101	17	24	6	2	1	14	8	20	6	3	6-0	.238	.328	.366	.694	3	.988
2001— Norwich (East.)	C-1B	88	268	31	72	18	0	9	33	14	64	7	3	2-1	.269	.317	.417	.754	6	.991
— Columbus (Int'l)	C	16	41	6	10	2	0	0	2	1	10	3	2	0-0	.244	.311	.293	.604	1	.989
2002— Savannah (S. Atl.)	C	5	15	1	4	0	0	0	1	3	4	1	0	2-1	.267	.421	.267	.688	0	1.000
— Tulsa (Texas)	C-OF	2	6	1	2	0	0	0	0	1	0	...		0-0	.333	.333	.333	.666	1	.833
— Oklahoma (PCL)	C-OF-3B	81	272	40	78	14	0	7	32	16	51	10	14	14-1	.287	.348	.415	.763	3	.992
2003— Tacoma (PCL)	C-3B	85	291	35	83	16	1	4	22	11	42	10	4	6-4	.285	.332	.388	.720	7	.986
2004— Campeche (Mex.)	C-1B	52	173	19	42	5	0	5	30	19	25	4	5	0-1	.243	.328	.347	.675	5	.983
— Newark (Atl.)	C	17	54	5	16	2	0	1	8	1	9	3	5	0-1	.296	.345	.389	.734	2	.982
— Frisco (Texas)	C-OF	31	116	23	36	4	0	8	36	9	17	3	5	0-0	.310	.375	.552	.927	2	.987
2005— Milwaukee (N.L.)	PH	1	1	0	0	0	0	0	0	0	0	0	0	0-0	.000	.000	.000	.000	0	...
— Nashville (PCL)	C	64	240	32	62	4	0	4	30	10	34	1	11	4-1	.258	.290	.383	.673	9	.983
American League totals (2 years)		11	30	2	7	3	0	0	2	0	5	...	...	0-1	.233	...	.333	...	0	1.000
National League totals (1 year)		1	1	0	0	0	0	0	0	0	0	0	0	0-0	.000	.000	.000	.000	0	...
Major League totals (3 years)		12	31	2	7	3	0	0	2	0	5	0	0	0-1	.226	.226	.323	.548	0	1.000

MOTA, GUILLERMO   P

PERSONAL: Born July 25, 1973, in San Pedro de Macoris, Dominican Republic. ... 6-4/205. ... Throws right, bats right. ... Full name: Guillermo Reynoso Mota. ... High school: Jose Joaquin Perez (San Pedro de Macoris, Dominican Republic).

TRANSACTIONS/CAREER NOTES: Signed as a non-drafted free agent by New York Mets organization (September 7, 1990). ... Played infield in Mets organization (1991-96). ... Selected by Montreal Expos organization from Mets organization in Rule 5 minor league draft (December 9, 1996). ... On disabled list (July 13-September 1, 2001); included rehabilitation assignment to Ottawa. ... Traded by Expos with OF Wilkin Ruan to Los Angeles Dodgers for P Matt Herges and IF Jorge Nunez (March 24, 2002). ... On sus-

pended list (March 30-April 4, 2003). ... Traded by Dodgers with C Paul Lo Duca and OF Juan Encarnacion to Florida Marlins for Ps Brad Penny and Bill Murphy and 1B Hee Seop Choi (July 30, 2004). ... On disabled list (May 1-27, 2005); included rehabilitation assignment to Jupiter.
CAREER HITTING: 7-for-33 (.212), 4 R, 1 2B, 0 3B, 2 HR, 6 RBI.

SCOUTING REPORT

Throws: Mota has a 93-97 mph fastball, a slider and a circle change. ***Tendencies:*** He has long and extremely loose arm action. Fastball has good life, especially down in the zone, and tends to move late. Arm action provides some deception. Slider is quick and has good tilt. Circle change is extremely effective and makes fastball look even faster. ***Outlook:*** Mota lost his closer's role after suffering elbow and shoulder problems. Needs to prove he is healthy next spring. ***Grade 7.5***

GUILLERMO MOTA'S PITCHING ZONE

.231	.250	.278
.171	.429	.353
.214	.421	.214

LEFTY-RIGHTY SPLITS

vs.	Avg.	AB	H	2B	3B	HR	RBI	BB	SO	OBP	Slg.
L	.243	111	27	7	3	4	26	20	23	.356	.468
R	.262	145	38	17	2	1	23	12	37	.318	.428

Year	Team (League)	W	L	Pct.	ERA	WHIP	G	GS	CG	ShO	Hld.	Sv.-Opp.	IP	H	R	ER	HR	BB-IBB	SO	Avg.
1997—	Cape Fear (S. Atl.)	5	10	.333	4.36	1.33	25	23	0	0	...	0-...	126.0	135	65	61	8	33-0	112	.278
1998—	Jupiter (Fla. St.)	3	2	.600	0.66	0.59	20	0	0	0	...	2-...	41.0	18	6	3	0	6-0	27	.130
—	Harrisburg (East.)	2	0	1.000	1.06	0.71	12	0	0	0	...	4-...	17.0	10	2	2	0	2-0	19	.172
1999—	Ottawa (Int'l)	2	0	1.000	1.89	1.11	14	0	0	0	...	5-...	19.0	16	6	4	0	5-0	17	.235
—	Montreal (N.L.)	2	4	.333	2.93	1.43	51	0	0	0	3	0-1	55.1	54	24	18	5	25-3	27	.257
2000—	Ottawa (Int'l)	4	5	.444	2.29	1.27	35	0	0	0	...	7-...	63.0	49	16	16	4	31-3	35	.220
—	Montreal (N.L.)	1	1	.500	6.00	1.30	29	0	0	0	5	0-0	30.0	21	20	20	3	12-0	24	.245
2001—	Montreal (N.L.)	1	3	.250	5.26	1.39	53	0	0	0	12	0-3	49.2	51	30	29	9	18-1	31	.264
—	Ottawa (Int'l)	0	0	...	2.25	0.25	4	0	0	0	...	0-...	4.0	1	1	1	0	0-0	4	.077
2002—	Las Vegas (PCL)	1	3	.250	2.95	1.15	20	0	0	0	...	1-...	36.2	34	13	12	1	8-1	38	.260
—	Los Angeles (N.L.)	1	3	.250	4.15	1.19	43	0	0	0	4	0-1	60.2	45	30	28	4	27-6	49	.202
2003—	Los Angeles (N.L.)	6	3	.667	1.97	0.99	76	0	0	0	13	1-3	105.0	78	23	23	7	26-4	99	.206
2004—	Los Angeles (N.L.)	8	4	.667	2.14	1.24	52	0	0	0	17	1-1	63.0	50	15	15	4	27-5	52	.228
—	Florida (N.L.)	1	4	.200	4.81	1.01	26	0	0	0	13	3-7	33.2	24	18	18	4	10-1	33	.200
2005—	Jupiter (Fla. St.)	0	0	...	0.00	1.13	2	2	0	0	...	0-0	2.2	3	1	0	0	4-0	3	.300
—	Florida (N.L.)	2	2	.500	4.70	1.45	56	0	0	0	14	2-4	67.0	65	38	35	5	32-7	60	.254
Major League totals (7 years)		22	24	.478	3.61	1.23	386	0	0	0	81	7-20	464.1	395	199	186	41	177-27	375	.231

MOYER, JAMIE   P

PERSONAL: Born November 18, 1962, in Sellersville, Pa. ... 6-0/175. ... Throws left, bats left. ... High school: Souderton (Pa.) Area. ... College: St. Joseph's (Pa.). ... Son-in-law of Digger Phelps, ESPN college basketball analyst and Notre Dame basketball coach (1971-72 through 1990-91).
TRANSACTIONS/CAREER NOTES: Selected by Chicago Cubs organization in sixth round of June 1984 free-agent draft. ... Traded by Cubs with OF Rafael Palmeiro and P Drew Hall to Texas Rangers for Ps Mitch Williams, Paul Kilgus and Steve Wilson, IFs Curtis Wilkerson and Luis Benitez and OF Pablo Delgado (December 5, 1988). ... On disabled list (May 31-September 1, 1989); included rehabilitation assignments to GCL Rangers and Tulsa. ... Released by Rangers (November 13, 1990). ... Signed by St. Louis Cardinals organization (January 9, 1991). ... Released by Cardinals (October 14, 1991). ... Signed by Cubs organization (January 8, 1992). ... Released by Cubs (March 30, 1992). ... Signed by Detroit Tigers organization (May 24, 1992). ... Signed as a free agent by Baltimore Orioles organization (December 14, 1992). ... Signed as a free agent by Boston Red Sox (January 2, 1996). ... Traded by Red Sox to Seattle Mariners for OF Darren Bragg (July 30, 1996). ... On disabled list (March 23-April 29, 1997); included rehabilitation assignment to Tacoma. ... On disabled list (April 15-June 2, 2000).
CAREER HITTING: 27-for-174 (.155), 11 R, 2 2B, 0 3B, 0 HR, 6 RBI.

SCOUTING REPORT

Throws: This crafty veteran is using more of a two-seam fastball in the low 80-mph range instead of a four-seamer. Cuts his fastball and throws a slider and a changeup. ***Tendencies:*** Moyer is a premier feel-and-touch pitcher who has command of all his pitches. Gets as much movement as he wants because he knows how to vary his grips. Will run a cutter in on righthanders; Slider is virtually the same pitch—with some tilt—for lefthanders. Will throw his changeup, one of the best in baseball, with a stiff or loose wrist, giving it dive-and-fade or dive-and-cut action. ***Outlook:*** Moyer can quickly adjust to hitters' approaches, but the decline in velocity is becoming dangerously large. ***Grade 7***

JAMIE MOYER'S PITCHING ZONE

.340	.125	.278
.324	.333	.293
.276	.361	.236

LEFTY-RIGHTY SPLITS

vs.	Avg.	AB	H	2B	3B	HR	RBI	BB	SO	OBP	Slg.
L	.294	221	65	18	0	4	27	8	34	.329	.430
R	.278	575	160	29	5	19	68	44	68	.331	.445

Year	Team (League)	W	L	Pct.	ERA	WHIP	G	GS	CG	ShO	Hld.	Sv.-Opp.	IP	H	R	ER	HR	BB-IBB	SO	Avg.
1984—	Geneva (NY-Penn)	9	3	.750	1.89	0.86	14	14	5	2	...	0-...	104.2	59	27	22	5	31-0	120	.160
1985—	Win.-Salem (Car.)	8	2	.800	2.30	1.11	12	12	6	2	...	0-...	94.0	82	36	24	1	22-3	94	.232
—	Pittsfield (East.)	7	6	.538	3.72	1.36	15	15	3	0	...	0-...	96.2	99	49	40	4	32-1	51	.265
1986—	Pittsfield (East.)	3	1	.750	0.88	1.05	6	6	0	0	...	0-...	41.0	27	10	4	2	16-0	42	.186
—	Iowa (Am. Assoc.)	3	2	.600	2.55	0.85	6	6	2	0	...	0-...	42.1	25	14	12	2	11-0	25	.162
—	Chicago (N.L.)	7	4	.636	5.05	1.71	16	16	1	1	0	0-0	87.1	107	52	49	10	42-1	45	.311
1987—	Chicago (N.L.)	12	15	.444	5.10	1.53	35	33	1	0	0	0-0	201.0	210	127	* 114	28	97-9	147	.271
1988—	Chicago (N.L.)	9	15	.375	3.48	1.32	34	30	3	1	0	0-2	202.0	212	84	78	20	55-7	121	.272
1989—	Texas (A.L.)	4	9	.308	4.86	1.54	15	15	1	0	0	0-0	76.0	84	51	41	10	33-0	44	.283
—	GC Rangers (GCL)	1	0	1.000	1.64	0.82	3	3	0	0	...	0-...	11.0	8	4	2	0	1-0	18	.195
—	Tulsa (Texas)	1	1	.500	5.11	1.54	2	2	1	1	...	0-...	12.1	15	8	7	1	3-0	9	.320
1990—	Texas (A.L.)	2	6	.250	4.66	1.50	33	10	1	0	1	0-0	102.1	115	59	53	6	39-4	58	.291
1991—	St. Louis (N.L.)	0	5	.000	5.74	1.72	8	7	0	0	0	0-0	31.1	38	21	20	5	16-0	20	.319
—	Louisville (A.A.)	5	10	.333	3.80	1.34	20	20	1	0	...	0-...	125.2	125	64	53	6	43-4	69	.260
1992—	Toledo (Int'l)	10	8	.556	2.86	1.19	21	20	5	0	...	0-...	138.2	128	48	44	8	37-3	80	.245
1993—	Rochester (Int'l)	6	0	1.000	1.67	1.02	8	8	1	1	...	0-...	54.0	42	13	10	2	13-0	41	.211
—	Baltimore (A.L.)	12	9	.571	3.43	1.26	25	25	3	1	0	0-0	152.0	154	63	58	11	38-2	90	.265
1994—	Baltimore (A.L.)	5	7	.417	4.77	1.32	23	23	0	0	0	0-0	149.0	158	81	79	23	38-3	87	.271
1995—	Baltimore (A.L.)	8	6	.571	5.21	1.27	27	18	0	0	0	0-0	115.2	117	70	67	18	30-0	65	.265

Year Team (League)	W	L	Pct.	ERA	WHIP	G	GS	CG	ShO	Hld.	Sv.-Opp.	IP	H	R	ER	HR	BB-IBB	SO	Avg.
1996— Boston (A.L.)	7	1	.875	4.50	1.53	23	10	0	0	1	0-0	90.0	111	50	45	14	27-2	50	.300
—Seattle (A.L.)	6	2	.750	3.31	1.20	11	11	0	0	0	0-0	70.2	66	36	26	9	19-3	29	.243
1997—Tacoma (PCL)	1	0	1.000	0.00	0.20	1	1	0	0	...	0-...	5.0	1	0	0	0	0-0	6	.063
—Seattle (A.L.)	17	5	.773	3.86	1.22	30	30	2	0	0	0-0	188.2	187	82	81	21	43-2	113	.256
1998—Seattle (A.L.)	15	9	.625	3.53	1.18	34	34	4	3	0	0-0	234.1	234	99	92	23	42-2	158	.256
1999—Seattle (A.L.)	14	8	.636	3.87	1.24	32	32	4	0	0	0-0	228.0	235	108	98	23	48-1	137	.267
2000—Seattle (A.L.)	13	10	.565	5.49	1.47	26	26	0	0	0	0-0	154.0	173	103	94	22	53-2	98	.281
2001—Seattle (A.L.)	20	6	.769	3.43	1.10	33	33	1	0	0	0-0	209.2	187	84	80	24	44-4	119	.239
2002—Seattle (A.L.)	13	8	.619	3.32	1.08	34	34	4	2	0	0-0	230.2	198	89	85	28	50-4	147	.233
2003—Seattle (A.L.)	21	7	.750	3.27	1.23	33	33	1	0	0	0-0	215.0	199	83	78	19	66-3	129	.246
2004—Seattle (A.L.)	7	13	.350	5.21	1.39	34	33	1	0	0	0-0	202.0	217	127	117	* 44	63-3	125	.272
2005—Seattle (A.L.)	13	7	.650	4.28	1.39	32	32	1	0	0	0-0	200.0	225	99	95	23	52-2	102	.283
American League totals (15 years)	177	113	.610	4.09	1.28	445	399	23	6	2	0-0	2618.0	2660	1284	1189	318	685-37	1551	.263
National League totals (4 years)	28	39	.418	4.50	1.49	93	86	5	2	0	0-2	521.2	567	284	261	63	210-17	333	.281
Major League totals (19 years)	205	152	.574	4.16	1.31	538	485	28	8	2	0-2	3139.2	3227	1568	1450	381	895-54	1884	.266

DIVISION SERIES RECORD

Year Team (League)	W	L	Pct.	ERA	WHIP	G	GS	CG	ShO	Hld.	Sv.-Opp.	IP	H	R	ER	HR	BB-IBB	SO	Avg.
1997—Seattle (A.L.)	0	1	.000	5.79	1.29	1	1	0	0	0	0-0	4.2	5	3	3	1	1-0	2	.278
2001—Seattle (A.L.)	2	0	1.000	1.50	0.83	2	2	0	0	0	0-0	12.0	8	2	2	0	2-0	10	.186
Division series totals (2 years)	2	1	.667	2.70	0.96	3	3	0	0	0	0-0	16.2	13	5	5	1	3-0	12	.213

CHAMPIONSHIP SERIES RECORD

Year Team (League)	W	L	Pct.	ERA	WHIP	G	GS	CG	ShO	Hld.	Sv.-Opp.	IP	H	R	ER	HR	BB-IBB	SO	Avg.
2001—Seattle (A.L.)	1	0	1.000	2.57	0.71	1	1	0	0	0	0-0	7.0	4	2	2	1	1-0	5	.167

ALL-STAR GAME RECORD

Year Team (League)	W	L	Pct.	ERA	WHIP	G	GS	CG	ShO	Hld.	Sv.-Opp.	IP	H	R	ER	HR	BB-IBB	SO	Avg.
All-Star Game totals (1 year)	0	0	...	0.00	0.00	1	0	0	0	0	0-0	1.0	0	0	0	0	0-0	1	.000

MUELLER, BILL   3B

PERSONAL: Born March 17, 1971, in Maryland Heights, Mo. ... 5-10/180. ... Bats both, throws right. ... Full name: William Richard Mueller. ... Name pronounced: MILL-er. ... High school: DeSmet (Creve Coeur, Mo.). ... College: Southwest Missouri State.

TRANSACTIONS/CAREER NOTES: Selected by San Francisco Giants organization in 15th round of 1993 free-agent draft. ... On disabled list (July 1-16, 1997). ... On disabled list (April 6-May 17, 1999); included rehabilitation assignment to Fresno. ... Traded by Giants to Chicago Cubs for P Tim Worrell (November 19, 2000). ... On disabled list (May 14-August 13, 2001); included rehabilitation assignment to Iowa. ... On disabled list (March 28-May 6, 2002); included rehabilitation assignment to Iowa. ... Traded by Cubs with cash to Giants for P Jeff Verplancke (September 3, 2002). ... Signed as a free agent by Boston Red Sox (January 14, 2003). ... On disabled list (May 20-July 2, 2004); included rehabilitation assignment to Pawtucket.

2005 GAMES PLAYED BY POSITION (MLB): 3B—142, 2B—5.

SCOUTING REPORT *Offense:* Mueller has a compact stroke and is basically a line-drive hitter. Makes excellent contact and can use the whole field. Is consistent and has extra-base power. Has more power from the left side. Is a good situational hitter, rarely swinging too hard or expanding his strike zone. Is selective and not afraid to hit with two strikes. *Defense:* He is not a particularly fluid fielder, but Mueller has excellent agility and quick feet. Regains his feet quickly after dives. Has good hands and has improved his range to both sides. Has average arm strength but compensates with a quick release and improved accuracy. *Outlook:* Mueller is a steady hitter who will be in the .290 range with double-digit home run power. Is good with runners in scoring position. Is underrated defensively. *Grade 8.0*

BILL MUELLER'S HITTING ZONE

.188	.294	.150
.400	.643	.275
.308	.300	.321

LEFTY-RIGHTY SPLITS

vs.	Avg.	AB	H	2B	3B	HR	RBI	BB	SO	OBP	Slg.
L	.275	142	39	8	0	2	20	14	21	.346	.373
R	.302	377	114	26	3	8	42	45	53	.378	.451

Year Team (League)	Pos.	G	AB	R	H	2B	3B	HR	RBI	BB	SO	HBP	GDP	SB-CS	Avg.	OBP	SLG	OPS	E	Avg.
1993— Everett (N'west)	2B	58	200	31	60	8	2	1	24	42	11	3	3	13-6	.300	.425	.425	.800	9	.966
1994— San Jose (Calif.) 2B-3B-SS		120	431	79	130	20	9	5	72	103	47	3	15	4-8	.302	.435	.425	.859	29	.925
1995— Shreveport (Texas) 2B-3B		88	330	56	102	16	2	1	39	53	36	4	9	6-5	.309	.406	.379	.784	5	.978
—Phoenix (PCL) 2B-3B		41	172	23	51	13	6	2	19	19	31	0	7	0-0	.297	.365	.477	.841	7	.941
1996— Phoenix (PCL) 3B-SS-2B-DH		106	440	73	133	14	6	4	36	44	40	1	11	2-5	.302	.365	.389	.753	11	.969
— San Francisco (N.L.)	3B-2B	55	200	31	66	15	1	0	19	24	26	1	1	0-0	.330	.401	.415	.816	6	.962
1997— San Francisco (N.L.)	3B	128	390	51	114	26	3	7	44	48	71	3	10	4-3	.292	.369	.428	.797	14	.956
1998— San Francisco (N.L.)	3B-2B	145	534	93	157	27	0	9	59	79	83	1	12	3-3	.294	.383	.395	.778	15	.953
1999— San Francisco (N.L.)	3B-2B	116	414	61	120	24	0	2	36	65	52	3	11	4-2	.290	.388	.362	.751	12	.959
—Fresno (PCL)	3B	3	12	3	5	0	1	0	6	4	0	0	0	0-0	.417	.385	.500	.885	3	.800
2000— San Francisco (N.L.)	3B-2B	153	560	97	150	29	4	10	55	52	62	6	16	4-2	.268	.333	.388	.721	9	.975
2001— Chicago (N.L.)	3B-2B	70	210	38	62	12	1	6	23	37	19	3	4	1-1	.295	.403	.448	.851	8	.942
—Iowa (PCL)	3B	8	26	3	11	3	0	4	1	2	0	0	0	0-0	.423	.444	.538	.983	0	1.000
2002— Chicago (N.L.)	3B	6	16	2	6	1	0	1	5	3	1	0	0	0-1	.375	.474	.625	1.099	1	.909
—Chicago (N.L.)	3B	103	353	51	94	19	4	7	37	51	41	0	8	0-0	.266	.355	.402	.757	6	.973
—San Francisco (N.L.)	3B	8	13	2	2	0	0	1	1	3	3	0	0	0-0	.154	.214	.154	.368	0	1.000
2003— Boston (A.L.) 3B-2B-DH	SS	146	524	85	171	45	5	19	85	59	77	7	11	1-4	* .326	.398	.540	.938	16	.956
2004— Pawtucket (Int'l)	3B	4	13	1	4	0	.0	2	2	2	0	0	0	0-0	.308	.400	.462	.862	1	.857
—Boston (A.L.)	3B-2B	110	399	75	113	27	1	12	57	51	56	4	8	2-2	.283	.365	.446	.811	17	.944
2005— Boston (A.L.)	3B-2B	150	519	69	153	34	3	10	62	59	74	6	22	0-0	.295	.369	.430	.799	11	.972
American League totals (3 years)		406	1442	229	437	106	9	41	204	169	207	17	41	3-6	.303	.378	.474	.853	44	.958
National League totals (7 years)		778	2674	422	765	152	13	41	274	357	355	17	63	16-11	.286	.370	.399	.769	74	.961
Major League totals (10 years)		1184	4116	651	1202	258	22	82	478	526	562	34	104	19-17	.292	.373	.425	.798	118	.960

DIVISION SERIES RECORD

Year Team (League)	Pos.	G	AB	R	H	2B	3B	HR	RBI	BB	SO	HBP	GDP	SB-CS	Avg.	OBP	SLG	OPS	E	Avg.
1997—San Francisco (N.L.)	3B	3	12	1	3	0	0	1	1	0	0	0	1	0-1	.250	.250	.500	.750	0	1.000
2000—San Francisco (N.L.)	3B	4	20	2	5	2	0	0	0	0	4	0	1	0-0	.250	.250	.350	.600	0	1.000
2003—Boston (A.L.)	3B	5	19	0	2	1	0	0	0	3	4	0	1	0-0	.105	.227	.158	.385	0	1.000
2004—Boston (A.L.)	3B	3	12	3	4	0	0	0	0	1	1	0	0	0-0	.333	.385	.333	.718	0	1.000
2005—Boston (A.L.)	3B	3	11	0	0	0	0	0	0	1	2	0	0	0-0	.000	.083	.000	.083	0	1.000
Division series totals (5 years)		18	74	6	14	3	0	1	1	5	11	0	3	0-1	.189	.241	.270	.511	0	1.000

CHAMPIONSHIP SERIES RECORD

Year Team (League)	Pos.	G	AB	R	H	2B	3B	HR	RBI	BB	SO	HBP	GDP	SB-CS	Avg.	OBP	SLG	OPS	E	Avg.
2003—Boston (A.L.)	3B	7	27	1	6	2	0	0	0	2	7	0	1	0-0	.222	.276	.296	.572	0	1.000
2004—Boston (A.L.)	3B	7	30	4	8	1	0	0	1	2	1	1	3	0-0	.267	.333	.300	.633	0	1.000
Champ. series totals (2 years)		14	57	5	14	3	0	0	1	4	8	1	4	0-0	.246	.306	.298	.605	0	1.000

WORLD SERIES RECORD

Year Team (League)	Pos.	G	AB	R	H	2B	3B	HR	RBI	BB	SO	HBP	GDP	SB-CS	Avg.	OBP	SLG	OPS	E	Avg.
2004—Boston (A.L.)	3B	4	14	3	6	2	0	0	2	4	0	0	1	0-0	.429	.556	.571	1.127	3	.850

MULDER, MARK   P

PERSONAL: Born August 5, 1977, in South Holland, Ill. ... 6-6/208. ... Throws left, bats left. ... Full name: Mark Alan Mulder. ... High school: Thornwood (South Holland, Ill.). ... College: Michigan State.

TRANSACTIONS/CAREER NOTES: Selected by Detroit Tigers organization in 55th round of 1995 free-agent draft; did not sign. ... Selected by Oakland Athletics organization in first round (second pick overall) of 1998 free-agent draft. ... On disabled list (April 12-May 10, 2002; and August 20, 2003-remainder of season). ... Traded by Athletics to St. Louis Cardinals for Ps Kiko Calero and Danny Haren and C Daric Barton (December 19, 2004).

CAREER HITTING: 10-for-84 (.119), 5 R, 0 2B, 0 3B, 0 HR, 4 RBI.

SCOUTING REPORT *Throws:* Mulder has a two-seam fastball that can hit 92 mph. Also has a four-seamer, a cut fastball, curve, changeup and a split-finger fastball. ***Tendencies:*** He has changed his pitching approach and now doesn't throw as hard. Is using his two-seamer more than his four-seamer. Tails his fastball away from righthanded hitters and cuts it away from lefthanded hitters. Has a good curve but doesn't throw it as often. Did not use his split-finger late in the season. ***Outlook:*** Mulder became more of a control pitcher last season and now knows how to move the ball around. Is a durable, top-of-the-rotation starter who can eat innings. ***Grade 8.7***

MARK MULDER'S PITCHING ZONE

.182	.227	.400
.360	.430	.271
.250	.250	.229

LEFTY-RIGHTY SPLITS

vs.	Avg.	AB	H	2B	3B	HR	RBI	BB	SO	OBP	Slg.
L	.201	139	28	7	0	3	8	15	30	.288	.317
R	.289	637	184	40	1	16	76	55	81	.350	.430

Year Team (League)	W	L	Pct.	ERA	WHIP	G	GS	CG	ShO	Hld.	Sv.-Opp.	IP	H	R	ER	HR	BB-IBB	SO	Avg.
1999—Vancouver (PCL)	6	7	.462	4.06	1.42	22	22	1	0	...	0-...	128.2	152	69	58	13	31-0	81	.300
2000—Sacramento (PCL)	1	1	.500	5.40	2.28	2	2	0	0	...	0-...	8.1	15	11	5	1	4-0	6	.375
—Oakland (A.L.)	9	10	.474	5.44	1.69	27	27	0	0		0-0	154.0	191	106	93	22	69-3	88	.308
2001—Oakland (A.L.)	* 21	8	.724	3.45	1.16	34	34	6	* 4	0	0-0	229.1	214	92	88	16	51-4	153	.249
2002—Oakland (A.L.)	19	7	.731	3.47	1.14	30	30	2	1	0	0-0	207.1	182	88	80	21	55-3	159	.232
2003—Oakland (A.L.)	15	9	.625	3.13	1.18	26	26	•9	•2	0	0-0	186.2	180	66	65	15	40-2	128	.259
2004—Oakland (A.L.)	17	8	.680	4.43	1.36	33	33	•5	1	0	0-0	225.2	223	119	111	25	83-1	140	.264
2005—St. Louis (N.L.)	16	8	.667	3.64	1.38	32	32	3	2	0	0-0	205.0	212	90	83	19	70-1	111	.273
American League totals (5 years)	81	42	.659	3.92	1.28	150	150	22	8	0	0-0	1003.0	990	471	437	99	298-13	668	.260
National League totals (1 year)	16	8	.667	3.64	1.38	32	32	3	2	0	0-0	205.0	212	90	83	19	70-1	111	.273
Major League totals (6 years)	97	50	.660	3.87	1.30	182	182	25	10	0	0-0	1208.0	1202	561	520	118	368-14	779	.262

DIVISION SERIES RECORD

Year Team (League)	W	L	Pct.	ERA	WHIP	G	GS	CG	ShO	Hld.	Sv.-Opp.	IP	H	R	ER	HR	BB-IBB	SO	Avg.
2000—Oakland (A.L.)		Did not play.																	
2001—Oakland (A.L.)	1	1	.500	2.45	1.45	2	2	0	0	0	0-0	11.0	14	5	3	0	2-0	7	.318
2002—Oakland (A.L.)	1	1	.500	2.08	1.31	2	2	0	0	0	0-0	13.0	14	3	3	1	3-1	12	.280
2005—St. Louis (N.L.)	1	0	1.000	1.35	1.35	1	1	0	0	0	0-0	6.2	8	1	1	0	1-0	2	.333
Division series totals (3 years)	3	2	.600	2.05	1.37	5	5	0	0	0	0-0	30.2	36	9	7	1	6-1	21	.305

CHAMPIONSHIP SERIES RECORD

Year Team (League)	W	L	Pct.	ERA	WHIP	G	GS	CG	ShO	Hld.	Sv.-Opp.	IP	H	R	ER	HR	BB-IBB	SO	Avg.
2005—St. Louis (N.L.)	0	2	.000	3.09	1.46	2	2	0	0	0	0-0	11.2	14	5	4	1	3-1	8	.311

ALL-STAR GAME RECORD

Year Team (League)	W	L	Pct.	ERA	WHIP	G	GS	CG	ShO	Hld.	Sv.-Opp.	IP	H	R	ER	HR	BB-IBB	SO	Avg.
All-Star Game totals (2 years)	1	0	1.000	4.50	1.75	2	1	0	0	0	0-0	4.0	7	2	2	1	0-0	2	.412

MULHOLLAND, TERRY   P

PERSONAL: Born March 9, 1963, in Uniontown, Pa. ... 6-3/220. ... Throws left, bats right. ... Full name: Terence John Mulholland. ... Name pronounced: mul-HOLLAND. ... High school: Laurel Highlands (Uniontown, Pa.). ... College: Marietta (Ohio).

TRANSACTIONS/CAREER NOTES: Selected by San Francisco Giants organization in first round (24th pick overall) of June 1984 free-agent draft; pick received as compensation for Detroit Tigers signing free-agent IF Darrell Evans. ... On disabled list (August 1, 1988-remainder of season). ... Traded by Giants with P Dennis Cook and 3B Charlie

Hayes to Philadelphia Phillies for P Steve Bedrosian and a player to be named (June 18, 1989); Giants acquired IF Rick Parker to complete deal (August 7, 1989). ... On disabled list (June 12-28, 1990); included rehabilitation assignment to Scranton/Wilkes-Barre. ... Traded by Phillies with a player to be named to New York Yankees for Ps Bobby Munoz and Ryan Karp and 2B Kevin Jordan (February 9, 1994); Yankees acquired P Jeff Patterson to complete deal (November 8, 1994). ... Signed as a free agent by Giants (April 8, 1995). ... On disabled list (June 6-July 4, 1995); included rehabilitation assignment to Phoenix. ... Signed as a free agent by Phillies organization (February 17, 1996). ... Traded by Phillies to Seattle Mariners for IF Desi Relaford (July 31, 1996). ... Signed as a free agent by Chicago Cubs (December 10, 1996). ... Claimed on waivers by Giants (August 8, 1997). ... Signed as a free agent by Cubs (February 2, 1998). ... Traded by Cubs with IF Jose Hernandez to Atlanta Braves for Ps Micah Bowie and Ruben Quevedo and a player to be named (July 31, 1999); Cubs acquired P Joey Nation to complete deal (August 24, 1999). ... Signed as a free agent by Pittsburgh Pirates (December 10, 2000). ... On disabled list (April 5-20 and June 12-August 1, 2001); included rehabilitation assignment to Altoona. ... Traded by Pirates to Los Angeles Dodgers for Ps Mike Fetters and Adrian Burnside (July 31, 2001). ... On disabled list (May 3-June 4, 2002). ... Traded by Dodgers with Ps Ricardo Rodriguez and Francisco Cruceta to Cleveland Indians for P Paul Shuey (July 28, 2002). ... Signed as a free agent by Mariners organization (February 10, 2004). ... Traded by Mariners to Minnesota Twins for cash (April 13, 2004).

CAREER HITTING: 69-for-619 (.111), 26 R, 13 2B, 1 3B, 2 HR, 23 RBI.

SCOUTING REPORT **Throws:** Mulholland's fastball is 81-86 mph. Also has a curveball, a cut fastball/slider and a changeup. **Tendencies:** This crafty veteran won't blow anyone away. Has a very short, quick arm motion. Spots his fastball well to both sides of the plate. Likes to start righthanded hitters off with a big, looping curve that he commands well. Runs his slider down and in on righthanders. Turns over his change and fades it; has some depth. Is the best in the game at holding runners. Has excellent makeup. **Outlook:** Mulholland is extremely versatile and can fill any role on a staff. **Grade 6.3**

TERRY MULHOLLAND'S PITCHING ZONE

.333	.583	.091
.325	.368	.243
.211	.364	.294

LEFTY-RIGHTY SPLITS

vs.	Avg.	AB	H	2B	3B	HR	RBI	BB	SO	OBP	Slg.
L	.202	84	17	3	1	1	8	4	12	.239	.298
R	.321	137	44	11	1	5	23	13	6	.386	.526

Year Team (League)	W	L	Pct.	ERA	WHIP	G	GS	CG	ShO	Hld.	Sv.-Opp.	IP	H	R	ER	HR	BB-IBB	SO	Avg.
1984— Everett (N'west)	1	0	1.000	0.00	0.74	3	3	0	0	...	0-...	19.0	10	2	0	0	4-0	15	...
— Fresno (Calif.)	5	2	.714	2.95	1.59	9	9	0	0	...	0-...	42.2	32	17	14	1	36-0	39	...
1985— Shreveport (Texas)	9	8	.529	2.90	1.43	26	26	8	3	...	0-...	176.2	166	79	57	9	87-2	122	.250
1986— Phoenix (PCL)	8	5	.615	4.46	1.51	17	17	3	0	...	0-...	111.0	112	60	55	6	56-4	77	.269
— San Francisco (N.L.)	1	7	.125	4.94	1.57	15	10	0	0	0	0-0	54.2	51	33	30	3	35-2	27	.251
1987— Phoenix (PCL)	7	12	.368	5.07	1.68	37	29	3	1	...	1-...	172.1	200	124	97	7	90-0	94	.291
1988— Phoenix (PCL)	7	3	.700	3.58	1.59	19	14	3	2	...	0-...	100.2	116	45	40	2	44-0	57	.291
— San Francisco (N.L.)	2	1	.667	3.72	1.24	9	6	2	1	1	0-0	46.0	50	20	19	3	7-0	18	.281
1989— Phoenix (PCL)	4	5	.444	2.99	1.19	13	10	3	0	...	0-0	78.1	67	30	26	3	26-2	61	.242
— San Francisco (N.L.)	0	0	...	4.09	1.73	5	1	0	0	1	0-0	11.0	15	5	5	0	4-0	6	.319
— Philadelphia (N.L.)	4	7	.364	5.00	1.48	20	17	2	1	0	0-0	104.1	122	61	58	8	32-3	60	.292
1990— Philadelphia (N.L.)	9	10	.474	3.34	1.18	33	26	6	1	0	0-1	180.2	172	78	67	15	42-7	75	.252
— Scran./W.B. (I.L.)	0	1	.000	3.00	1.83	1	1	0	0	...	0-...	6.0	9	4	2	0	2-0	2	.360
1991— Philadelphia (N.L.)	16	13	.552	3.61	1.21	34	34	8	3	0	0-0	232.0	231	100	93	15	49-2	142	.260
1992— Philadelphia (N.L.)	13	11	.542	3.81	1.19	32	32	* 12	2	0	0-0	229.0	227	101	97	14	46-3	125	.261
1993— Philadelphia (N.L.)	12	9	.571	3.25	1.14	29	28	7	2	0	0-0	191.0	177	80	69	20	40-2	116	.241
1994— New York (A.L.)	6	7	.462	6.49	1.55	24	19	2	0	0	0-0	120.2	150	94	87	24	37-1	72	.303
1995— San Francisco (N.L.)	5	13	.278	5.80	1.53	29	24	2	0	0	0-0	149.0	190	112	96	25	38-1	65	.313
— Phoenix (PCL)	0	0	...	2.25	1.25	1	1	0	0	...	0-...	4.0	4	3	1	0	1-0	4	.235
1996— Philadelphia (N.L.)	8	7	.533	4.66	1.34	21	21	3	0	0	0-0	133.1	157	74	69	17	21-1	52	.293
— Seattle (A.L.)	5	4	.556	4.67	1.49	12	12	0	0	0	0-0	69.1	75	38	36	5	28-3	34	.286
1997— Chicago (N.L.)	6	12	.333	4.07	1.32	25	25	1	0	0	0-0	157.0	162	79	71	20	45-2	74	.271
— San Francisco (N.L.)	0	1	.000	5.16	1.15	15	2	0	0	1	0-0	29.2	28	21	17	4	6-1	25	.248
1998— Chicago (N.L.)	6	5	.545	2.89	1.24	70	6	0	0	19	3-5	112.0	100	49	36	7	39-7	72	.235
1999— Chicago (N.L.)	6	6	.500	5.15	1.54	26	16	0	0	1	0-0	110.0	137	71	63	16	32-4	44	.309
— Atlanta (N.L.)	4	2	.667	2.98	1.28	16	8	0	0	3	1-1	60.1	64	24	20	5	13-2	39	.274
2000— Atlanta (N.L.)	9	9	.500	5.11	1.53	54	20	1	0	2	1-3	156.2	198	96	89	24	41-7	78	.308
2001— Pittsburgh (N.L.)	0	0	...	3.72	1.32	22	1	0	0	3	0-0	36.1	38	15	15	5	10-1	17	.277
— Altoona (East.)	0	2	.000	3.86	2.57	2	2	0	0	...	0-...	2.1	5	3	1	0	1-0	3	.417
— Los Angeles (N.L.)	1	1	.500	5.83	1.60	19	3	0	0	4	0-0	29.1	40	20	19	7	7-0	25	.315
2002— Los Angeles (N.L.)	0	0	...	7.31	1.63	21	0	0	0	0	0-0	32.0	45	29	26	10	7-0	17	.333
— Cleveland (A.L.)	3	2	.600	4.60	1.49	16	3	0	0	2	0-0	47.0	56	27	24	5	14-3	21	.301
2003— Cleveland (A.L.)	3	4	.429	4.91	1.56	45	3	0	0	2	0-2	99.0	117	60	54	17	37-6	42	.295
2004— Minnesota (A.L.)	5	9	.357	5.18	1.59	39	15	0	0	2	0-0	123.1	163	76	71	17	33-3	60	.327
2005— Minnesota (A.L.)	0	2	.000	4.27	1.32	49	0	0	0	6	0-1	59.0	61	30	28	6	17-4	18	.276
American League totals (6 years)	22	28	.440	5.21	1.52	185	52	2	0	9	0-3	518.1	622	325	300	74	166-20	247	.302
National League totals (15 years)	102	114	.472	4.20	1.32	495	280	44	10	35	5-10	2054.1	2204	1068	959	218	514-45	1077	.275
Major League totals (19 years)	124	142	.466	4.40	1.36	680	332	46	10	44	5-13	2572.2	2826	1393	1259	292	680-65	1324	.280

DIVISION SERIES RECORD

Year Team (League)	W	L	Pct.	ERA	WHIP	G	GS	CG	ShO	Hld.	Sv.-Opp.	IP	H	R	ER	HR	BB-IBB	SO	Avg.
1998— Chicago (N.L.)	0	1	.000	11.57	1.71	2	0	0	0	0	0-0	2.1	2	3	3	0	2-0	2	.222
1999— Atlanta (N.L.)	0	0	...	27.00	4.50	2	0	0	0	2	0-0	0.2	3	2	2	0	0-0	0	.600
2000— Atlanta (N.L.)	0	0	...	5.40	0.90	3	0	0	0	0	0-0	3.1	1	2	2	1	2-0	1	.100
2004— Minnesota (A.L.)	0	0	...	3.00	1.00	1	0	0	0	0	0-0	3.0	3	1	1	1	0-0	0	.250
Division series totals (4 years)	0	1	.000	7.71	1.39	8	0	0	0	2	0-0	9.1	9	8	8	1	4-0	3	.250

M

CHAMPIONSHIP SERIES RECORD

Year Team (League)	W	L	Pct.	ERA	WHIP	G	GS	CG	ShO	Hld.	Sv.-Opp.	IP	H	R	ER	HR	BB-IBB	SO	Avg.
1993— Philadelphia (N.L.)	0	1	.000	7.20	2.00	1	1	0	0	0	0-0	5.0	9	5	4	0	1-0	2	.391
1999— Atlanta (N.L.)	0	0	...	0.00	0.75	2	0	0	0	1	0-0	2.2	1	0	0	0	1-0	2	.143
Champ. series totals (2 years)	0	1	.000	4.70	1.57	3	1	0	0	1	0-0	7.2	10	5	4	0	2-0	4	.333

WORLD SERIES RECORD

Year Team (League)	W	L	Pct.	ERA	WHIP	G	GS	CG	ShO	Hld.	Sv.-Opp.	IP	H	R	ER	HR	BB-IBB	SO	Avg.
1993— Philadelphia (N.L.)	1	0	1.000	6.75	1.59	2	2	0	0	0	0-0	10.2	14	8	8	2	3-0	5	.326
1999— Atlanta (N.L.)	0	0	...	7.36	1.64	2	0	0	0	0	0-0	3.2	5	3	3	1	1-1	3	.313
World Series totals (2 years)	1	0	1.000	6.91	1.60	4	2	0	0	0	0-0	14.1	19	11	11	3	4-1	8	.322

ALL-STAR GAME RECORD

	W	L	Pct.	ERA	WHIP	G	GS	CG	ShO	Hld.	Sv.-Opp.	IP	H	R	ER	HR	BB-IBB	SO	Avg.
All-Star Game totals (1 year)	0	0	...	4.50	1.50	1	1	0	0	0	0-0	2.0	1	1	1	1	2-0	0	.143

MUNSON, ERIC — 3B

PERSONAL: Born October 3, 1977, in San Diego. ... 6-3/225. ... Bats left, throws right. ... Full name: Eric Walter Munson. ... High school: Mount Carmel (San Diego). ... College: Southern California.

TRANSACTIONS/CAREER NOTES: Selected by Atlanta Braves organization in second round of 1996 free-agent draft; did not sign. ... Selected by Detroit Tigers organization in first round (third pick overall) of 1999 free-agent draft. ... On disabled list (August 12, 2003-remainder of season). ... Signed as a free agent by Minnesota Twins organization (January 17, 2005). ... Released by Twins (March 27, 2005). ... Signed by Tampa Bay Devil Rays organization (April 3, 2005). ... On disabled list (July 2-August 3, 2005); included rehabilitation assignment to Durham. ... Released by Devil Rays (October 7, 2005).

2005 GAMES PLAYED BY POSITION (MLB): DH—3, 3B—2, 1B—1, OF—1.

LEFTY-RIGHTY SPLITS

vs.	Avg.	AB	H	2B	3B	HR	RBI	BB	SO	OBP	Slg.
L	.000	4	0	0	0	0	0	0	1	.000	.000
R	.214	14	3	1	0	0	2	4	2	.400	.286

								BATTING											FIELDING	
Year Team (League)	Pos.	G	AB	R	H	2B	3B	HR	RBI	BB	SO	HBP	GDP	SB-CS	Avg.	OBP	SLG	OPS	E	Avg.
1999— Lakeland (Fla. St.)	DH	2	6	0	2	0	0	0	1	1	1	0	0	0-0	.333	.429	.333	.762	...	...
— W. Mich. (Mid.)	1B-C	67	252	42	67	16	1	14	44	37	47	9	4	3-1	.266	.378	.504	.882	3	.991
2000— Jacksonville (Sou.)	1B	98	365	52	92	21	4	15	68	39	96	18	8	5-2	.252	.348	.455	.803	8	.989
—Detroit (A.L.)	1B	3	5	0	0	0	0	0	1	0	1	0	0	0-0	.000	.000	.000	.000	1	.941
2001— Erie (East.)	1B	142	519	88	135	35	1	26	102	84	141	11	4	0-3	.260	.371	.482	.853	17	.985
—Detroit (A.L.)	1B	17	66	4	10	3	1	1	6	3	21	0	2	0-1	.152	.188	.273	.461	1	.994
2002— Toledo (Int'l)	1B	136	477	77	125	30	4	24	84	77	114	7	9	1-3	.262	.367	.493	.860	12	.990
—Detroit (A.L.)	DH-1B	18	59	3	11	0	0	2	5	6	11	1	1	0-0	.186	.269	.288	.557	1	.970
2003—Detroit (A.L.)	3B-DH	99	313	28	75	9	0	18	50	35	61	1	4	3-0	.240	.312	.441	.753	19	.920
2004—Detroit (A.L.)	3B-DH-C	109	321	36	68	14	2	19	49	29	90	6	1	1-1	.212	.289	.445	.735	16	.934
2005— Durham (Int'l)	1B	100	382	67	109	22	0	25	71	38	81	2	11	1-1	.285	.351	.539	.891	16	.982
—Tampa Bay (A.L.) DH-3B-1B	OF	11	18	2	3	1	0	0	2	4	3	1	2	0-0	.167	.333	.222	.556	0	1.000
Major League totals (6 years)		257	782	73	167	27	3	40	113	77	187	9	10	4-2	.214	.288	.409	.698	38	.945

MUNTER, SCOTT — P

PERSONAL: Born March 7, 1980, in Norfolk, Neb. ... 6-6/240. ... Throws right, bats right. ... Full name: Scott Munter. ... Junior college: Butler County (Kan.) Community College.

TRANSACTIONS/CAREER NOTES: Selected by San Francisco Giants organization in 47th round of 2001 free-agent draft. ... On disabled list (August 12-September 2, 2005).

CAREER HITTING: 0-for-0 (.000), 0 R, 0 2B, 0 3B, 0 HR, 0 RBI.

SCOTT MUNTER'S PITCHING ZONE

.111	.625	.235
.278	.235	.333
.333	.273	.375

LEFTY-RIGHTY SPLITS

vs.	Avg.	AB	H	2B	3B	HR	RBI	BB	SO	OBP	Slg.
L	.353	51	18	2	1	0	3	6	5	.431	.431
R	.239	92	22	1	1	1	9	6	6	.283	.304

Year Team (League)	W	L	Pct.	ERA	WHIP	G	GS	CG	ShO	Hld.	Sv.-Opp.	IP	H	R	ER	HR	BB-IBB	SO	Avg.
2001— Salem-Keizer (N'west)	1	2	.333	5.91	1.54	15	0	0	0	...	0-...	35.0	42	26	23	3	12-0	28	.296
—Hagerstown (SAL)	1	0	1.000	3.38	1.13	1	1	0	0	...	0-...	5.1	5	3	2	0	1-0	2	.278
2002— Salem-Keizer (N'west)	1	1	.500	6.98	1.79	10	4	0	0	...	0-...	29.2	33	24	23	0	20-0	20	.287
—San Jose (Calif.)	0	0	...	10.38	3.69	3	0	0	0	...	0-...	4.1	12	5	5	0	4-0	2	.571
2003—Hagerstown (SAL)	3	5	.375	2.36	1.30	40	0	0	0	...	5-...	68.2	61	28	18	3	28-0	47	.243
2004— Norwich (East.)	2	4	.333	2.35	1.31	42	0	0	0	...	3-...	65.0	63	19	17	4	22-5	30	.246
—Fresno (PCL)	1	1	.500	3.45	1.53	13	0	0	0	...	1-...	15.2	20	8	6	1	4-0	5	.299
2005— Fresno (PCL)	1	3	.250	5.11	1.70	12	0	0	0	1	0-1	12.1	17	8	7	0	4-0	5	.362
—San Francisco (N.L.)	2	0	1.000	2.56	1.34	45	0	0	0	12	0-3	38.2	40	15	11	1	12-1	11	.280
Major League totals (1 year)	2	0	1.000	2.56	1.34	45	0	0	0	12	0-3	38.2	40	15	11	1	12-1	11	.280

MURPHY, DONNIE — 2B

PERSONAL: Born March 10, 1983, in Lakewood, Calif. ... 5-10/180. ... Bats right, throws right. ... Full name: Donald Rex Murphy. ... High school: Poly High (Riverside, Calif.). ... Junior college: Orange Coast Community College.

M

TRANSACTIONS/CAREER NOTES: Selected by Kansas City Royals organization in fifth round of 2002 free-agent draft. ... On disabled list (August 25-September 9, 2005).
2005 GAMES PLAYED BY POSITION (MLB): 2B—29, SS—2, DH—1.

DONNIE MURPHY'S HITTING ZONE

.200	.250	.000
.250	.111	.143
.250	.000	.000

SCOUTING REPORT Offense: Because of a lack of bat speed, he has not shown he can hit major league pitching. His wrists are not quick enough through the zone for his nervous hands, which make his swing too long for anything but mistakes. He wants to pull the ball, which makes him commit early. Is an easy target for pitchers who know what they're doing. *Defense:* He is a below-average fielder with limited range. Has good hands and a decent enough arm to make throws from the left side of the infield. *Outlook:* He will get a chance to make the roster, but he'll need a big spring. Could be tried at third base, depending on the Royals' needs going into camp. *Grade 5.9*

LEFTY-RIGHTY SPLITS

vs.	Avg.	AB	H	2B	3B	HR	RBI	BB	SO	OBP	Slg.
L	.146	41	6	2	0	1	5	5	13	.234	.268
R	.167	36	6	3	0	0	3	4	10	.250	.250

Year	Team (League)	Pos.	G	AB	R	H	2B	3B	HR	RBI	BB	SO	HBP	GDP	SB-CS	Avg.	OBP	SLG	OPS	E	Avg.
2002—Spokane (N'west)		SS	28	109	20	33	10	2	0	15	6	17	3	2	0-0	.303	.356	.431	.787	8	.931
—Burlington (Midw.)		SS	33	120	12	27	6	3	0	15	11	31	4	1	0-2	.225	.300	.325	.625	10	.934
2003—Burlington (Midw.)		2B-SS	132	504	77	158	29	6	5	98	65	78	9	8	15-6	.313	.397	.425	.821	14	.977
2004—Wilmington (Caro.)		2B-SS-DH	129	485	67	123	32	4	10	73	52	96	4	16	1-1	.254	.326	.398	.724	20	.969
—Kansas City (A.L.)		2B	7	27	1	5	3	0	0	3	0	7	0	1	1-0	.185	.185	.296	.481	0	1.000
2005—Wichita (Texas)		2B-SS-DH	50	214	33	67	13	1	10	32	13	32	4	6	1-1	.313	.362	.523	.885	6	.978
—Kansas City (A.L.)		2B-SS-DH	32	77	4	12	5	0	1	8	9	23	0	3	0-1	.156	.241	.260	.501	4	.963
Major League totals (2 years)			39	104	5	17	8	0	1	11	9	30	0	4	1-1	.163	.228	.269	.497	4	.971

MURTON, MATT   OF

PERSONAL: Born October 3, 1981, in Fort Lauderdale, Fla. ... 6-1/215. ... Bats right, throws right. ... Full name: Matthew Henry Murton. ... College: Georgia Tech.
TRANSACTIONS/CAREER NOTES: Selected by Boston Red Sox organization in first round (32nd pick overall) of 2003 free-agent draft. ... Traded by Red Sox with SS Nomar Garciaparra to Chicago Cubs in four-team deal in which Cubs sent 3B Brendan Harris, RHP Francis Beltran and SS Alex Gonzalez to Montreal Expos, Expos sent SS Orlando Cabrera to Red Sox, Twins sent 1B Doug Mientkiewicz to Red Sox and Cubs sent LHP Justin Jones to Minnesota Twins (July 31, 2004).
2005 GAMES PLAYED BY POSITION (MLB): OF—43.

SCOUTING REPORT Murton is an aggressive hitter who likes the fastball up. Has good bat speed and can turn on inside pitches. Is patient but often hits behind in the count and strikes out a lot. Is a good runner who will steal bases as he gains experience. Has good range and charges the ball well in the outfield. Needs to improve his routes breaking to the ball laterally and going back. Will have a chance to make the club, at least in a platoon role against lefthanded pitchers. *Grade 5.5*

MATT MURTON'S HITTING ZONE

.308	.571	.125
.353	.438	.167
.400	.500	.143

LEFTY-RIGHTY SPLITS

vs.	Avg.	AB	H	2B	3B	HR	RBI	BB	SO	OBP	Slg.
L	.380	71	27	2	1	3	8	8	8	.443	.563
R	.261	69	18	1	1	4	6	8	14	.329	.478

Year	Team (League)	Pos.	G	AB	R	H	2B	3B	HR	RBI	BB	SO	HBP	GDP	SB-CS	Avg.	OBP	SLG	OPS	E	Avg.
2003—Lowell (NY-Penn)		OF	53	189	30	54	11	2	2	29	27	39	4	5	9-3	.286	.374	.397	.771	2	.976
2004—Sarasota (Fla. St.)		OF	102	376	60	113	16	4	11	55	42	61	3	7	5-4	.301	.372	.452	.824	2	.857
—Daytona (Fla. St.)		OF	24	79	13	20	1	1	2	8	8	10	1	3	2-0	.253	.326	.367	.693	0	...
2005—West Tenn (Sou.)		OF	78	313	46	107	17	4	8	46	29	42	4	11	18-5	.342	.403	.498	.902	8	.971
—Iowa (PCL)		OF	9	34	4	12	2	0	1	3	4	8	0	2	0-0	.353	.421	.500	.921	2	.923
—Chicago (N.L.)		OF	51	140	19	45	3	2	7	14	16	22	0	4	2-1	.321	.386	.521	.908	2	.969
Major League totals (1 year)			51	140	19	45	3	2	7	14	16	22	0	4	2-1	.321	.386	.521	.908	2	.969

MUSSINA, MIKE   P

PERSONAL: Born December 8, 1968, in Williamsport, Pa. ... 6-2/185. ... Throws right, bats left. ... Full name: Michael Cole Mussina. ... Name pronounced: myoo-SEE-nuh. ... High school: Montoursville (Pa.). ... College: Stanford.
TRANSACTIONS/CAREER NOTES: Selected by Baltimore Orioles organization in 11th round of 1987 free-agent draft; did not sign. ... Selected by Orioles organization in first round (20th pick overall) of 1990 free-agent draft. ... On disabled list (July 22-August 20, 1993); included rehabilitation assignment to Bowie. ... On disabled list (April 17-May 3 and May 15-June 6, 1998). ... Signed as a free agent by New York Yankees (November 30, 2000). ... On disabled list (July 7-August 18, 2004); included rehabilitation assignment to Columbus.

HONORS: Won A.L. Gold Glove at pitcher (1996-99, 2001 and 2003).

CAREER HITTING: 8-for-41 (.195), 3 R, 1 2B, 0 3B, 0 HR, 5 RBI.

SCOUTING REPORT *Throws:* Mussina throws an 88-93 mph fastball, a 74-77 knuckle curve, an 82-84 slider, and a good changeup. *Tendencies:* He continually makes adjustments and often tailors his location and pitch selection to batters' swings. Has good command to both sides of the plate and constantly changes speeds. Is starting to throw his slider, which he has better command of, more than his knuckle curve, which remains a good pitch. Has lost some velocity. *Outlook:* Mussina had elbow problems during the year but didn't seem to lose much off his fastball. No longer is a dominant No. 1 starter but still is dependable. Is intelligent enough to continue adjusting and being effective as he loses his stuff. *Grade 8.1*

MIKE MUSSINA'S PITCHING ZONE

.167	.318	.180
.362	.468	.307
.286	.400	.246

LEFTY-RIGHTY SPLITS

vs.	Avg.	AB	H	2B	3B	HR	RBI	BB	SO	OBP	Slg.
L	.282	362	102	17	0	13	48	26	84	.334	.436
R	.286	339	97	19	1	10	41	21	58	.332	.437

Year	Team (League)	W	L	Pct.	ERA	WHIP	G	GS	CG	ShO	Hld.	Sv.-Opp.	IP	H	R	ER	HR	BB-IBB	SO	Avg.
1990—	Hagerstown (East.)	3	0	1.000	1.49	0.97	7	7	3	2	1	...	0-...	42.1	34	10	7	1	7-0	40	.214
	— Rochester (Int'l)	0	0	...	1.35	0.90	2	2	0	0	...	0-...	13.1	8	2	2	2	4-0	15	.174
1991—	Rochester (Int'l)	10	4	.714	2.87	1.14	19	19	3	1	...	0-...	122.1	108	42	39	9	31-0	107	.235
	— Baltimore (A.L.)	4	5	.444	2.87	1.12	12	12	2	0	0	0-0	87.2	77	31	28	7	21-0	52	.239
1992—	Baltimore (A.L.)	18	5	* .783	2.54	1.08	32	32	8	4	0	0-0	241.0	212	70	68	16	48-2	130	.239
1993—	Baltimore (A.L.)	14	6	.700	4.46	1.23	25	25	3	2	0	0-0	167.2	163	84	83	20	44-2	117	.256
	— Bowie (East.)	1	0	1.000	2.25	0.75	2	2	0	0	...	0-...	8.0	5	2	2	0	1-0	10	.172
1994—	Baltimore (A.L.)	16	5	.762	3.06	1.16	24	24	3	0	0	0-0	176.1	163	63	60	19	42-1	99	.248
1995—	Baltimore (A.L.)	* 19	9	.679	3.29	1.07	32	32	7	* 4	0	0-0	221.2	187	86	81	24	50-4	158	.226
1996—	Baltimore (A.L.)	19	11	.633	4.81	1.37	36	* 36	4	1	0	0-0	243.1	264	137	130	31	69-0	204	.275
1997—	Baltimore (A.L.)	15	8	.652	3.20	1.12	33	33	4	1	0	0-0	224.2	197	87	80	27	54-3	218	.234
1998—	Baltimore (A.L.)	13	10	.565	3.49	1.11	29	29	4	2	0	0-0	206.1	189	85	80	22	41-3	175	.242
1999—	Baltimore (A.L.)	18	7	.720	3.50	1.27	31	31	4	0	0	0-0	203.1	207	88	79	16	52-0	172	.268
2000—	Baltimore (A.L.)	11	15	.423	3.79	1.19	34	34	6	1	0	0-0	* 237.2	236	105	100	28	46-0	210	.255
2001—	New York (A.L.)	17	11	.607	3.15	1.07	34	34	4	3	0	0-0	228.2	202	87	80	20	42-2	214	.237
2002—	New York (A.L.)	18	10	.643	4.05	1.19	33	33	2	2	0	0-0	215.2	208	103	97	27	48-1	182	.253
2003—	New York (A.L.)	17	8	.680	3.40	1.08	31	31	2	1	0	0-0	214.2	192	86	81	21	40-4	195	.238
2004—	Columbus (Int'l)	0	0	...	0.00	0.67	1	1	0	0	...	0-...	3.0	2	0	0	0	0-0	5	.182
	— New York (A.L.)	12	9	.571	4.59	1.32	27	27	1	0	0	0-0	164.2	178	91	84	22	40-1	132	.276
2005—	New York (A.L.)	13	8	.619	4.41	1.37	30	30	2	2	0	0-0	179.2	199	93	88	23	47-0	142	.284
Major League totals (15 years)		224	127	.638	3.64	1.18	443	443	56	23	0	0-0	3013.0	2874	1296	1219	323	684-23	2400	.251

DIVISION SERIES RECORD

Year	Team (League)	W	L	Pct.	ERA	WHIP	G	GS	CG	ShO	Hld.	Sv.-Opp.	IP	H	R	ER	HR	BB-IBB	SO	Avg.
1996—	Baltimore (A.L.)	0	0	...	4.50	1.50	1	1	0	0	0	0-0	6.0	7	4	3	1	2-0	6	.280
1997—	Baltimore (A.L.)	2	0	1.000	1.93	0.71	2	2	0	0	0	0-0	14.0	7	3	3	3	3-0	16	.143
2001—	New York (A.L.)	1	0	1.000	0.00	0.71	1	1	0	0	0	0-0	7.0	4	0	0	0	1-0	4	.167
2002—	New York (A.L.)	0	0	...	9.00	1.50	1	1	0	0	0	0-0	4.0	6	4	4	1	0-0	2	.333
2003—	New York (A.L.)	0	1	.000	3.86	1.43	1	1	0	0	0	0-0	7.0	7	3	3	0	3-1	6	.280
2004—	New York (A.L.)	0	1	.000	2.57	1.14	1	1	0	0	0	0-0	7.0	7	2	2	1	1-0	7	.280
2005—	New York (A.L.)	1	1	.500	5.40	1.44	2	2	0	0	0	0-0	8.1	11	5	5	1	1-0	7	.306
Division series totals (7 years)		4	3	.571	3.38	1.13	9	9	0	0	0	0-0	53.1	49	21	20	7	11-1	48	.243

CHAMPIONSHIP SERIES RECORD

Year	Team (League)	W	L	Pct.	ERA	WHIP	G	GS	CG	ShO	Hld.	Sv.-Opp.	IP	H	R	ER	HR	BB-IBB	SO	Avg.
1996—	Baltimore (A.L.)	0	1	.000	5.87	1.30	1	1	0	0	0	0-0	7.2	8	5	5	1	2-0	6	.267
1997—	Baltimore (A.L.)	0	0	...	0.60	0.53	2	2	0	0	0	0-0	15.0	4	1	1	0	4-0	25	.082
2001—	New York (A.L.)	1	0	1.000	3.00	0.83	1	1	0	0	0	0-0	6.0	4	2	2	1	1-0	3	.182
2003—	New York (A.L.)	0	2	.000	4.11	1.30	3	2	0	0	0	0-0	15.1	16	7	7	5	4-1	17	.267
2004—	New York (A.L.)	1	0	1.000	4.26	0.95	2	2	0	0	0	0-0	12.2	10	6	6	0	2-0	15	.204
Champ. series totals (5 years)		2	3	.400	3.34	0.97	9	8	0	0	0	0-0	56.2	42	21	21	7	13-1	66	.200

WORLD SERIES RECORD

Year	Team (League)	W	L	Pct.	ERA	WHIP	G	GS	CG	ShO	Hld.	Sv.-Opp.	IP	H	R	ER	HR	BB-IBB	SO	Avg.
2001—	New York (A.L.)	0	1	.000	4.09	1.36	2	2	0	0	0	0-0	11.0	11	7	5	4	4-3	14	.256
2003—	New York (A.L.)	1	0	1.000	1.29	1.14	1	1	0	0	0	0-0	7.0	7	1	1	0	1-1	9	.259
World Series totals (2 years)		1	1	.500	3.00	1.28	3	3	0	0	0	0-0	18.0	18	8	6	4	5-4	23	.257

ALL-STAR GAME RECORD

		W	L	Pct.	ERA	WHIP	G	GS	CG	ShO	Hld.	Sv.-Opp.	IP	H	R	ER	HR	BB-IBB	SO	Avg.
All-Star Game totals (3 years)		0	0	...	0.00	1.00	3	0	0	0	0	0-0	3.0	2	0	0	0	1-0	3	.182

M

MYERS, BRETT   P

PERSONAL: Born August 17, 1980, in Jacksonville. ... 6-4/223. ... Throws right, bats right. ... Full name: Brett Allen Myers. ... High school: Englewood (Jacksonville).
TRANSACTIONS/CAREER NOTES: Selected by Philadelphia Phillies organization in first round (12th pick overall) of 1999 free-agent draft.
CAREER HITTING: 32-for-201 (.159), 10 R, 7 2B, 0 3B, 0 HR, 8 RBI.

SCOUTING REPORT **Throws:** Myers uses a four-seam fastball at 90-93 mph, a cut fastball, a power curve in the upper 70s and a changeup. *Tendencies:* He has two plus pitches—his fastball, which has very good life riding up in the zone, and a tightly biting hard curve that has a big downward break with very tight spin. Added a cutter that has very quick late slide; gives him a pitch he can run away from righthanders to complement the curve to lefthanders. *Outlook:* Myers has shown great improvement since coming up, and if he can control his emotions he can push the 20-win mark. Has the stuff to pitch at the top of the rotation. **Grade 7.5**

BRETT MYERS'S PITCHING ZONE

.273	.171	.147
.282	.329	.275
.220	.225	.222

LEFTY-RIGHTY SPLITS

vs.	Avg.	AB	H	2B	3B	HR	RBI	BB	SO	OBP	Slg.
L	.241	427	103	18	2	16	44	44	106	.317	.405
R	.233	387	90	26	0	15	46	24	102	.288	.416

Year Team (League)	W	L	Pct.	ERA	WHIP	G	GS	CG	ShO	Hld.	Sv.-Opp.	IP	H	R	ER	HR	BB-IBB	SO	Avg.
1999— GC Phillies (GCL)	2	1	.667	2.33	0.89	7	5	0	0	...	0-...	27.0	17	8	7	0	7-0	30	.177
2000— Piedmont (S. Atl.)	13	7	.650	3.18	1.33	27	27	2	1	...	0-...	175.1	165	78	62	7	69-0	140	.252
2001— Reading (East.)	13	4	.765	3.87	1.28	26	23	1	1	...	0-...	156.0	156	71	67	21	43-1	130	.258
2002— Scran./W.B. (I.L.)	9	6	.600	3.59	1.10	19	19	4	1	...	0-...	128.0	121	54	51	9	20-0	97	.252
—Philadelphia (N.L.)	4	5	.444	4.25	1.42	12	12	1	0	...	0-0	72.0	73	38	34	11	29-1	34	.277
2003— Philadelphia (N.L.)	14	9	.609	4.43	1.46	32	32	1	1	0	0-0	193.0	205	99	95	20	76-8	143	.272
2004— Philadelphia (N.L.)	11	11	.500	5.52	1.47	32	31	1	1	0	0-0	176.0	196	113	108	31	62-4	116	.281
2005— Philadelphia (N.L.)	13	8	.619	3.72	1.21	34	34	2	0	0	0-0	215.1	193	94	89	31	68-2	208	.237
Major League totals (4 years)	42	33	.560	4.47	1.37	110	109	5	2	0	0-0	656.1	667	344	326	93	235-15	501	.264

MYERS, GREG   C

PERSONAL: Born April 14, 1966, in Riverside, Calif. ... 6-2/225. ... Bats left, throws right. ... Full name: Gregory Richard Myers. ... High school: Riverside (Calif.) Polytechnical.
TRANSACTIONS/CAREER NOTES: Selected by Toronto Blue Jays organization in third round of June 1984 free-agent draft. ... On disabled list (March 26-June 5, 1989); included rehabilitation assignment to Knoxville. ... On disabled list (May 5-25, 1990); included rehabilitation assignment to Syracuse. ... Traded by Blue Jays with OF Rob Ducey to California Angels for P Mark Eichhorn (July 30, 1992). ... On disabled list (August 27, 1992-remainder of season). ... On disabled list (April 24-June 21, 1994); included rehabilitation assignments to Lake Elsinore. ... On disabled list (April 21-May 6, June 1-21 and September 30, 1995-remainder of season). ... Signed as a free agent by Minnesota Twins (December 8, 1995). ... On disabled list (July 14-August 2, 1996; and August 9-24, 1997). ... Traded by Twins to Atlanta Braves for a player to be named (September 5, 1997); Twins acquired 1B Steve Hacker to complete deal (December 18, 1997). ... Signed as a free agent by San Diego Padres (November 25, 1997). ... On disabled list (June 4-July 24, 1998); included rehabilitation assignments to Rancho Cucamonga and Las Vegas. ... On disabled list (June 29-July 26, 1999); included rehabilitation assignment to Rancho Cucamonga. ... Traded by Padres to Braves for P Doug Dent (July 26, 1999). ... Signed as a free agent by Baltimore Orioles (December 17, 1999). ... On disabled list (April 2-17, 2000). ... Released by Orioles (June 14, 2001). ... Signed by Oakland Athletics (June 23, 2001). ... Signed as a free agent by Blue Jays (December 11, 2002). ... On disabled list (April 27, 2004-remainder of season).
2005 GAMES PLAYED BY POSITION (MLB): C—4.

LEFTY-RIGHTY SPLITS

vs.	Avg.	AB	H	2B	3B	HR	RBI	BB	SO	OBP	Slg.
L	.000	0	0	0	0	0	0	0	0	.000	.000
R	.083	12	1	0	0	0	1	1	1	.154	.083

							BATTING										FIELDING	
Year Team (League)	Pos.	G	AB	R	H	2B	3B	HR	RBI	BB	SO	HBP	GDP	SB-CS	Avg.	OBP	SLG	OPS	E	Avg.
1984— Medicine Hat (Pio.)	C	38	133	20	42	9	0	2	20	16	6	0	4	0-0	.316	.387	.429	.815	4	.984
1985— Florence (S. Atl.)	C	134	489	52	109	19	2	5	62	39	54	2	12	0-0	.223	.279	.301	.580	7	.989
1986— Ventura (Calif.)	C	124	451	65	133	23	4	20	79	43	46	2	10	9-4	.295	.355	.497	.852	19	.980
1987— Syracuse (Int'l)	C	107	342	35	84	19	1	10	47	22	46	1	5	3-3	.246	.292	.395	.686	11	.984
—Toronto (A.L.)	C	7	9	1	1	0	0	0	0	0	3	0	2	0-0	.111	.111	.111	.222	0	1.000
1988— Syracuse (Int'l)	C	34	120	18	34	7	1	7	21	8	24	0	1	1-0	.283	.328	.533	.861	1	.986
1989— Knoxville (Southern)	C	29	90	11	30	10	0	5	19	3	16	0	2	1-0	.333	.351	.611	.962	1	.993
—Toronto (A.L.)	C-DH	17	44	0	5	2	0	0	1	2	9	0	2	0-1	.114	.152	.159	.311	0	1.000
—Syracuse (Int'l)	C	24	89	8	24	6	0	1	11	4	9	0	3	0-0	.270	.301	.371	.672	1	.985
1990— Toronto (A.L.)	C	87	250	33	59	7	1	5	22	22	33	0	12	0-1	.236	.293	.332	.625	3	.993
—Syracuse (Int'l)	C	3	11	0	2	1	0	0	2	1	1	0	0	0-0	.182	.231	.273	.503	0	1.000
1991— Toronto (A.L.)	C	107	309	25	81	22	0	8	36	21	45	0	13	0-0	.262	.306	.411	.717	11	.979
1992— Toronto (A.L.)	C	22	61	4	14	6	0	1	13	5	5	0	2	0-0	.230	.279	.377	.656	1	.991
—California (A.L.)	C-DH	8	17	4	4	1	0	0	0	0	6	0	0	0-0	.235	.235	.294	.529	0	1.000
1993— California (A.L.)	C-DH	108	290	27	74	10	0	7	40	17	47	2	8	3-3	.255	.298	.362	.660	6	.986
1994— California (A.L.)	C-DH	45	126	10	31	6	0	2	8	10	27	0	3	0-2	.246	.299	.341	.641	2	.991

Year	Team (League)	Pos.	G	AB	R	H	2B	3B	HR	RBI	BB	SO	HBP	GDP	SB-CS	Avg.	OBP	SLG	OPS	E	Avg.
	—Lake Elsinore (Calif.)	C-DH	10	32	4	8	2	0	0	5	2	6	0	2	0-0	.250	.286	.313	.598	0	1.000
1995—	California (A.L.)	C-DH	85	273	35	71	12	2	9	38	17	49	1	4	0-1	.260	.304	.418	.721	4	.989
1996—	Minnesota (A.L.)	C	97	329	37	94	22	3	6	47	19	52	0	11	0-0	.286	.320	.426	.746	8	.985
1997—	Minnesota (A.L.)	C-DH	62	165	24	44	11	1	5	28	16	29	0	4	0-0	.267	.328	.436	.764	3	.986
	—Atlanta (N.L.)	C	9	9	0	1	0	0	0	1	1	3	0	0	0-0	.111	.200	.111	.311	0	1.000
1998—	San Diego (N.L.)	C	69	171	19	42	10	0	4	20	17	36	0	6	0-1	.246	.312	.374	.686	4	.987
	—Rancho Cuca. (Calif.)	C-DH	3	9	1	0	0	0	0	0	2	1	0	1	0-0	.000	.182	.000	.182	0	1.000
	—Las Vegas (PCL)	C	3	9	0	5	0	0	1	0	0	0	0	0	0-0	.556	.556	.556	1.111	0	1.000
1999—	San Diego (N.L.)	C	50	128	9	37	4	0	3	15	13	14	0	5	0-0	.289	.355	.391	.745	3	.986
	—Rancho Cuca. (Calif.)	C-DH	3	3	0	0	0	0	0	0	1	1	0	0	0-0	.000	.250	.000	.250	0	1.000
	—Atlanta (N.L.)	C	34	72	10	16	2	0	2	9	13	16	0	1	0-0	.222	.337	.333	.671	1	.994
2000—	Baltimore (A.L.)	C-DH	43	125	9	28	6	0	3	12	8	29	0	7	0-0	.224	.271	.344	.615	0	1.000
2001—	Baltimore (A.L.)	DH-C	25	74	11	20	2	0	4	18	8	17	0	3	0-0	.270	.341	.459	.801	0	1.000
	—Sacramento (PCL)	C	2	5	0	0	0	0	0	1	3	2	0	1	0-0	.000	.375	.000	.375	0	1.000
	—Oakland (A.L.)	C-DH	33	87	13	16	1	0	7	13	13	21	0	2	0-0	.184	.290	.437	.727	0	1.000
2002—	Oakland (A.L.)	C-DH	65	144	15	32	5	0	6	21	26	36	0	4	0-0	.222	.341	.382	.723	1	.997
2003—	Toronto (A.L.)	C-DH	121	329	51	101	19	0	15	52	37	57	0	14	0-3	.307	.374	.502	.876	8	.982
2004—	Toronto (A.L.)	C-DH	8	18	0	4	2	0	0	1	2	4	0	1	0-0	.222	.300	.333	.633	0	1.000
2005—	Toronto (A.L.)	C	6	12	0	1	0	0	0	1	1	1	0	2	0-0	.083	.154	.083	.237	0	1.000
	American League totals (16 years)		946	2662	295	680	134	7	78	351	224	470	3	94	3-11	.255	.311	.399	.710	47	.989
	National League totals (3 years)		162	380	38	96	16	0	9	45	44	69	0	12	0-1	.253	.329	.366	.694	8	.989
	Major League totals (18 years)		1108	3042	333	776	150	7	87	396	268	539	3	106	3-12	.255	.313	.395	.708	55	.989

DIVISION SERIES RECORD

Year	Team (League)	Pos.	G	AB	R	H	2B	3B	HR	RBI	BB	SO	HBP	GDP	SB-CS	Avg.	OBP	SLG	OPS	E	Avg.
1998—	San Diego (N.L.)	C	1	0	0	0	0	0	0	0	0	0	0	0	0-0	...	...	...	...	0	...
1999—	Atlanta (N.L.)		Did not play.																		
2001—	Oakland (A.L.)	C	3	7	0	1	0	0	0	0	0	3	0	1	0-0	.143	.143	.143	.286	1	.929
2002—	Oakland (A.L.)	C	2	1	0	0	0	0	0	0	0	1	0	0	0-0	.000	.000	.000	.000	0	1.000
	Division series totals (3 years)		6	8	0	1	0	0	0	0	0	4	0	1	0-0	.125	.125	.125	.250	1	.944

CHAMPIONSHIP SERIES RECORD

Year	Team (League)	Pos.	G	AB	R	H	2B	3B	HR	RBI	BB	SO	HBP	GDP	SB-CS	Avg.	OBP	SLG	OPS	E	Avg.
1991—	Toronto (A.L.)		Did not play.																		
1998—	San Diego (N.L.)		2	1	1	1	0	0	1	2	1	0	0	0	0-0	1.000	1.000	4.000	5.000	...	...
1999—	Atlanta (N.L.)	C	2	2	0	0	0	0	0	0	1	1	0	0	0-0	.000	.333	.000	.333	0	1.000
	Champ. series totals (2 years)		4	3	1	1	0	0	1	2	2	1	0	0	0-0	.333	.600	1.333	1.933	0	1.000

WORLD SERIES RECORD

Year	Team (League)	Pos.	G	AB	R	H	2B	3B	HR	RBI	BB	SO	HBP	GDP	SB-CS	Avg.	OBP	SLG	OPS	E	Avg.
1998—	San Diego (N.L.)	C	2	4	0	0	0	0	0	0	0	2	0	0	0-0	.000	.000	.000	.000	0	1.000
1999—	Atlanta (N.L.)	C	4	6	0	2	0	0	0	1	1	0	0	0	0-0	.333	.429	.333	.762	0	1.000
	World Series totals (2 years)		6	10	0	2	0	0	0	1	1	2	0	0	0-0	.200	.273	.200	.473	0	1.000

M

MYERS, MIKE   P

PERSONAL: Born June 26, 1969, in Arlington Heights, Ill. ... 6-3/219. ... Throws left, bats left. ... Full name: Michael Stanley Myers. ... High school: Crystal Lake (Ill.) Central. ... College: Iowa State.

TRANSACTIONS/CAREER NOTES: Selected by San Francisco Giants organization in fourth round of 1990 free-agent draft. ... Selected by Florida Marlins from Giants organization in Rule 5 major league draft (December 7, 1992). ... On disabled list (June 7-August 5, 1994); included rehabilitation assignment to Brevard County. ... Traded by Marlins to Detroit Tigers (August 9, 1995), completing deal in which Tigers traded P Buddy Groom to Marlins for a player to be named (August 7, 1995). ... Traded by Tigers with P Rick Greene and SS Santiago Perez to Milwaukee Brewers for P Bryce Florie and a player to be named (November 20, 1997). ... Traded by Brewers to Colorado Rockies for P Curtis Leskanic (November 17, 1999). ... Traded by Rockies to Arizona Diamondbacks for OF Jack Cust and C J.D. Closser (January 7, 2002). ... Signed as a free agent by Seattle Mariners organization (January 16, 2004). ... Traded by Mariners to Boston Red Sox for a player to be named or cash (August 6, 2004). ... Signed as a free agent by St. Louis Cardinals (December 22, 2004). ... Traded by Cardinals to Red Sox for P Kevin Ool and OF Carlos De La Cruz (March 29, 2005).

CAREER HITTING: 0-for-1 (.000), 0 R, 0 2B, 0 3B, 0 HR, 0 RBI.

SCOUTING REPORT *Throws:* His fastball ranges from 84-89 mph, and he also throws a slurve. *Tendencies:* Myers will change his release point depending on whether he's facing a righthander or a lefthander. Will throw from three-quarters to sidearm to righties and submarine-style to lefties. Righthanders see him very well. Throws harder from the higher arm slot and has some running action to his fastball. Slurve actually rises and runs away from lefthanders. *Outlook:* Myers is a resilient situational reliever who can be expected to get in about 70 games a year. *Grade 6.3*

MIKE MYERS' PITCHING ZONE

.000	.286	.154
.250	.375	.350
.385	.500	.200

LEFTY-RIGHTY SPLITS

vs.	Avg.	AB	H	2B	3B	HR	RBI	BB	SO	OBP	Slg.
L	.158	95	15	2	0	1	9	5	18	.198	.211
R	.385	39	15	4	0	2	9	8	3	.510	.641

Year Team (League)	W	L	Pct.	ERA	WHIP	G	GS	CG	ShO	Hld.	Sv.-Opp.	IP	H	R	ER	HR	BB-IBB	SO	Avg.
1990— Everett (N'west)	4	5	.444	3.90	1.42	15	14	1	0	...	0-...	85.1	91	43	37	9	30-0	73	.269
1991— Clinton (Midw.)	5	3	.625	2.62	1.21	11	11	1	0	...	0-...	65.1	61	23	19	3	18-0	59	.253
— Ariz. Giants (Ariz.)	0	1	.000	12.00	2.33	1	0	0	0	...	0-...	3.0	5	5	4	0	2-0	2	.357
1992— San Jose (Calif.)	5	1	.833	2.30	1.10	8	8	0	0	...	0-...	54.2	43	20	14	1	17-0	40	.221
— Clinton (Midw.)	1	2	.333	1.19	0.96	7	7	0	0	...	0-...	37.2	28	11	5	0	8-0	32	.207
1993— Edmonton (PCL)	7	14	.333	5.18	1.53	27	27	3	0	...	0-...	161.2	195	109	93	20	52-1	112	.296
1994— Edmonton (PCL)	1	5	.167	5.55	1.65	12	11	0	0	...	0-...	60.0	78	42	37	9	21-0	55	.307
— Brevard County (FSL)	0	0	...	0.79	0.97	3	2	0	0	...	0-...	11.1	7	1	1	1	4-0	15	.184
1995— Florida (N.L.)	0	0	...	0.00	2.00	2	0	0	0	0	0-0	2.0	1	0	0	0	3-0	0	.167
— Charlotte (Int'l)	0	5	.000	5.65	1.53	37	0	0	0	...	0-...	36.2	41	25	23	6	15-1	24	.283
— Toledo (Int'l)	0	0	...	4.32	1.08	6	0	0	0	...	0-...	8.1	6	4	4	1	3-0	8	.194
— Detroit (A.L.)	1	0	1.000	9.95	2.21	11	0	0	0	1	0-1	6.1	10	7	7	1	4-0	4	.385
1996— Detroit (A.L.)	1	5	.167	5.01	1.61	83	0	0	0	17	6-8	64.2	70	41	36	6	34-8	69	.272
1997— Detroit (A.L.)	0	4	.000	5.70	1.55	88	0	0	0	18	2-5	53.2	58	36	34	12	25-2	50	.274
1998— Milwaukee (N.L.)	2	2	.500	2.70	1.32	70	0	0	0	* 23	1-3	50.0	44	19	15	5	22-1	40	.249
1999— Milwaukee (N.L.)	2	1	.667	5.23	1.43	71	0	0	0	14	0-3	41.1	46	24	24	7	13-1	35	.291
2000— Colorado (N.L.)	0	1	.000	1.99	1.06	78	0	0	0	15	1-2	45.1	24	10	10	2	24-3	41	.160
2001— Colorado (N.L.)	2	3	.400	3.60	1.40	73	0	0	0	10	0-2	40.0	32	17	16	2	24-7	36	.225
2002— Arizona (N.L.)	4	3	.571	4.38	1.51	69	0	0	0	17	4-9	37.0	39	18	18	2	17-0	31	.275
2003— Arizona (N.L.)	0	1	.000	5.70	1.62	64	0	0	0	6	0-3	36.1	38	23	23	4	21-1	21	.262
2004— Seattle (A.L.)	4	1	.800	4.88	1.66	50	0	0	0	8	0-0	27.2	29	15	15	3	17-4	23	.279
— Boston (A.L.)	1	0	1.000	4.20	1.47	25	0	0	0	2	0-0	15.0	16	7	7	2	6-1	9	.267
2005— Boston (A.L.)	3	1	.750	3.13	1.15	65	0	0	0	9	0-1	37.1	30	14	13	3	13-2	21	.224
American League totals (5 years)	10	11	.476	4.93	1.52	322	0	0	0	55	8-15	204.2	213	120	112	27	99-17	176	.269
National League totals (7 years)	10	11	.476	3.79	1.38	427	0	0	0	85	6-22	252.0	224	111	106	22	124-13	204	.243
Major League totals (11 years)	20	22	.476	4.30	1.45	749	0	0	0	140	14-37	456.2	437	231	218	49	223-30	380	.255

DIVISION SERIES RECORD

Year Team (League)	W	L	Pct.	ERA	WHIP	G	GS	CG	ShO	Hld.	Sv.-Opp.	IP	H	R	ER	HR	BB-IBB	SO	Avg.
2002— Arizona (N.L.)	0	0	...	0.00	1.20	2	0	0	0	0	0-0	1.2	2	0	0	0	0-0	1	.333
2004— Boston (A.L.)	0	0	...	27.00	3.00	2	0	0	0	1	0-0	0.1	0	1	1	0	1-0	1	.000
2005— Boston (A.L.)	0	0	...	...	...	1	0	0	0	0	0-0	0.0	0	0	0	0	1-0	0	...
Division series totals (3 years)	0	0	...	4.50	2.00	5	0	0	0	1	0-0	2.0	2	1	1	0	2-0	2	.286

CHAMPIONSHIP SERIES RECORD

Year Team (League)	W	L	Pct.	ERA	WHIP	G	GS	CG	ShO	Hld.	Sv.-Opp.	IP	H	R	ER	HR	BB-IBB	SO	Avg.
2004— Boston (A.L.)	0	0	...	7.71	2.57	3	0	0	0	0	0-0	2.1	5	2	2	1	1-0	4	.455

MYROW, BRIAN — 1B

PERSONAL: Born September 4, 1976, in Fort Worth, Texas. ... 5-11/190. ... Bats left, throws right. ... Full name: Brian Shawn Myrow. ... College: Louisiana Tech.

TRANSACTIONS/CAREER NOTES: Signed as a nondrafted free agent by New York Yankees (June 23, 2001). ... Traded by Yankees to Los Angeles Dodgers (May 15, 2004); completed May 10, 2004 deal in which Dodgers sent RHP Tanyon Sturtze to Yankees for a player to be named.

2005 GAMES PLAYED BY POSITION (MLB): 1B—5.

LEFTY-RIGHTY SPLITS

vs.	Avg.	AB	H	2B	3B	HR	RBI	BB	SO	OBP	Slg.
L	.000	0	0	0	0	0	0	0	0	.000	.000
R	.200	20	4	1	0	0	0	5	8	.360	.250

Year Team (League)	Pos.	G	AB	R	H	2B	3B	HR	RBI	BB	SO	HBP	GDP	SB-CS	Avg.	OBP	SLG	OPS	E	Avg.
1999— Winnipeg (N'west)	2B-3B	22	67	11	19	7	0	1	15	12	15	1	2	0-0	.284	.400	.433	.833	4	.932
2000— Winnipeg (N'west) 3B-OF-2B		60	190	26	58	14	2	4	29	42	37	5	2	1-0	.305	.439	.463	.902	14	.906
2001— Winnipeg (N'west)	2B	25	88	27	34	9	0	10	36	31	11	2	1	2-0	.386	.549	.830	1.379	8	.937
— Tampa (Fla. St.)	3B	48	149	30	38	11	1	3	28	32	29	5	4	5-1	.255	.399	.403	.802	12	.831
2002— Tampa (Fla. St.)	3B	61	225	29	63	12	1	5	40	42	45	9	4	0-0	.280	.409	.409	.818	2	.971
— Norwich (East.) 3B-2B-OF		61	188	37	57	16	0	3	30	41	42	6	4	5-0	.303	.441	.436	.877	10	.923
2003— Trenton (East.) 3B-2B-OF		137	461	99	141	31	8	18	78	107	113	16	3	6-3	.306	.447	.525	.972	28	.920
2004— Columbus (Int'l)	1B	47	164	28	44	12	3	3	15	23	37	4	0	3-4	.268	.365	.433	.798	9	.985
— Las Vegas (PCL) 1B-OF-3B		50	153	29	55	15	2	6	29	21	47	4	2	2-3	.359	.444	.601	1.045	3	.994
2005— Las Vegas (PCL) 1B-OF-DH																				
	3B	121	393	83	111	28	5	22	73	74	83	9	4	4-2	.282	.403	.547	.950	10	.989
— Los Angeles (N.L.)	1B	19	20	2	4	1	0	0	0	5	8	0	0	0-0	.200	.360	.250	.610	0	1.000
Major League totals (1 year)		19	20	2	4	1	0	0	0	5	8	0	0	0-0	.200	.360	.250	.610	0	1.000

NADY, XAVIER — OF/1B

PERSONAL: Born November 14, 1978, in Carmel, Calif. ... 6-2/205. ... Bats right, throws right. ... Full name: Xavier Clifford Nady. ... Name pronounced: ZAV-yer NAY-dee. ... High school: Salinas (Calif.). ... College: California.

TRANSACTIONS/CAREER NOTES: Selected by St. Louis Cardinals organization in fourth round of 1997 free-agent draft; did not sign. ... Selected by San Diego Padres organization in second round of 2000 free-agent draft.

2005 GAMES PLAYED BY POSITION (MLB): OF—68, 1B—44, 3B—3, DH—1.

SCOUTING REPORT Nady has an abundance of physical tools, but he has not become a regular because he is a streaky hitter and has not found a position he can adequately play. Has good bat speed but erratic timing. Can hit outside pitches with power to right field. Is not a good breaking-ball hitter and does not hit well with runners in scoring position. Has stiff hands and gets poor jumps as an infielder. Doesn't have the range or arm to play center field. *Grade 5.7*

XAVIER NADY'S HITTING ZONE

.250	.385	.105
.255	.447	.205
.286	.400	.238

LEFTY-RIGHTY SPLITS

vs.	Avg.	AB	H	2B	3B	HR	RBI	BB	SO	OBP	Slg.
L	.323	124	40	7	0	3	16	13	22	.400	.452
R	.223	202	45	8	2	10	27	9	45	.270	.431

| | | | | | | | | | BATTING | | | | | | | | | FIELDING | |
Year Team (League)	Pos.	G	AB	R	H	2B	3B	HR	RBI	BB	SO	HBP	GDP	SB-CS	Avg.	OBP	SLG	OPS	E	Avg.
2000—San Diego (N.L.)		1	1	1	1	0	0	0	0	0	0	0	0	0-0	1.000	1.000	1.000	2.000	...	...
2001—Lake Elsinore (Calif.)	1B	137	524	96	158	38	1	26	100	62	109	10	14	6-0	.302	.381	.527	.908	10	.989
2002—Lake Elsinore (Calif.)	OF	45	169	41	47	6	3	13	37	28	40	1	2	2-0	.278	.382	.580	.962	0	1.000
—Portland (PCL)	OF	85	315	46	89	12	1	10	43	20	60	3	11	0-1	.283	.329	.422	.752	2	.981
2003—Portland (PCL)	OF-DH	37	136	19	36	7	0	7	23	12	28	2	2	0-0	.265	.329	.471	.800	3	.954
—San Diego (N.L.)	OF	110	371	50	99	17	1	9	39	24	74	6	14	6-2	.267	.321	.391	.712	6	.968
2004—Portland (PCL)	OF-DH	74	291	52	97	19	1	22	70	22	42	7	7	3-0	.333	.394	.632	1.026	4	.981
—San Diego (N.L.)	OF-DH	34	77	7	19	4	0	3	9	5	13	1	4	0-0	.247	.301	.416	.717	2	.923
2005—San Diego (N.L.)	OF-1B-3B																			
	DH	124	326	40	85	15	2	13	43	22	67	7	5	2-1	.261	.321	.439	.760	6	.984
Major League totals (4 years)		269	775	98	204	36	3	25	91	51	154	14	23	8-3	.263	.320	.414	.734	14	.977

DIVISION SERIES RECORD

Year Team (League)	Pos.	G	AB	R	H	2B	3B	HR	RBI	BB	SO	HBP	GDP	SB-CS	Avg.	OBP	SLG	OPS	E	Avg.
2005—San Diego (N.L.)	1B	2	3	0	1	0	0	0	2	0	1	2	0	0-0	.333	.600	.333	.933	0	1.000

NAGEOTTE, CLINT — P

PERSONAL: Born October 25, 1980, in Parma, Ohio. ... 6-3/200. ... Throws right, bats right. ... Full name: Clinton Scott Nageotte. ... High school: Brooklyn (Ohio).

TRANSACTIONS/CAREER NOTES: Selected by Seattle Mariners organization in fifth round of 1999 free-agent draft. ... On disabled list (August 28, 2004-remainder of season).

CAREER HITTING: 0-for-2 (.000), 0 R, 0 2B, 0 3B, 0 HR, 0 RBI.

LEFTY-RIGHTY SPLITS

vs.	Avg.	AB	H	2B	3B	HR	RBI	BB	SO	OBP	Slg.
L	.500	6	3	1	0	0	1	1	0	.571	.667
R	.273	11	3	1	0	0	4	0	1	.333	.364

Year Team (League)	W	L	Pct.	ERA	WHIP	G	GS	CG	ShO	Hld.	Sv.-Opp.	IP	H	R	ER	HR	BB-IBB	SO	Avg.
2000—Ariz. Mariners (Ariz.)	4	1	.800	2.16	1.14	12	7	0	0	...	1-...	50.0	29	15	12	0	28-0	59	.167
2001—Wisconsin (Midw.)	11	8	.579	3.13	1.25	28	26	0	0	...	0-...	152.1	141	65	53	10	50-1	187	.246
2002—San Bern. (Calif.)	9	6	.600	4.54	1.34	29	29	1	0	...	0-...	164.2	153	101	83	10	68-0	214	.241
2003—San Antonio (Texas)	11	7	.611	3.10	1.26	27	27	2	1	...	0-...	154.0	127	60	53	6	67-1	157	.224
2004—Tacoma (PCL)	6	6	.500	4.46	1.40	14	14	0	0	...	0-...	80.2	78	42	40	7	35-0	63	.256
—Seattle (A.L.)	1	6	.143	7.36	2.05	12	5	0	0	0	0-0	36.2	48	31	30	3	27-1	24	.324
2005—Ariz. Mariners (Ariz.)	0	0	...	0.00	0.00	1	1	0	0	0	0-0	3.0	0	0	0	0	0-0	6	.000
—Seattle (A.L.)	0	0	...	6.75	1.75	3	0	0	0	0	0-0	4.0	6	3	3	0	1-0	1	.353
—Tacoma (PCL)	2	1	.667	2.65	1.26	19	0	0	0	4	2-4	34.0	21	16	10	2	22-0	35	.176
Major League totals (2 years)	1	6	.143	7.30	2.02	15	5	0	0	0	0-0	40.2	54	34	33	3	28-1	25	.327

NAKAMURA, NORIHIRO — 3B

PERSONAL: Born July 24, 1973, in Osaka, Japan. ... 5-10/203. ... Bats right, throws right. ... Full name: Norihiro Nakamura. ... High school: Shibuya (Japan).

TRANSACTIONS/CAREER NOTES: Played for Osaka of the Japan Pacific League (1992-2004). ... Signed as a free agent by Los Angeles Dodgers organization (February 3, 2005).

2005 GAMES PLAYED BY POSITION (MLB): 3B—10, 1B—4, SS—2, 2B—1.

LEFTY-RIGHTY SPLITS

vs.	Avg.	AB	H	2B	3B	HR	RBI	BB	SO	OBP	Slg.
L	.118	17	2	1	0	0	0	1	5	.167	.176
R	.136	22	3	1	0	0	3	1	2	.174	.182

| | | | | | | | | | BATTING | | | | | | | | | FIELDING | |
Year Team (League)	Pos.	G	AB	R	H	2B	3B	HR	RBI	BB	SO	HBP	GDP	SB-CS	Avg.	OBP	SLG	OPS	E	Avg.
2005—Los Angeles (N.L.)	3B-1B-SS																			
	2B	17	39	1	5	2	0	0	3	2	7	0	3	0-0	.128	.171	.179	.350	1	.975
—Las Vegas (PCL)	3B-1B-SS																			
	DH	101	357	54	89	17	1	22	67	45	70	1	19	0-0	.249	.331	.487	.818	20	.958
Major League totals (1 year)		17	39	1	5	2	0	0	3	2	7	0	3	0-0	.128	.171	.179	.350	1	.975

NATHAN, JOE — P

PERSONAL: Born November 22, 1974, in Houston. ... 6-4/205. ... Throws right, bats right. ... Full name: Joseph Michael Nathan. ... High school: Pine Bush (N.Y.). ... College: SUNY-Stony Brook.

TRANSACTIONS/CAREER NOTES: Selected by San Francisco Giants organization in sixth round of 1995 free-agent draft. ... Played shortstop in Giants' organization (1995). ... On disabled list (May 13-June 6 and July 14-August 19, 2000); included rehabilitation assignments to San Jose, Bakersfield and Fresno. ... Traded by Giants with Ps Boof Bonser and Francisco Liriano to Minnesota Twins for C A.J. Pierzynski and cash (November 14, 2003).
CAREER HITTING: 10-for-62 (.161), 4 R, 3 2B, 0 3B, 2 HR, 4 RBI.

SCOUTING REPORT *Throws:* Nathan has three plus pitches—a fastball at 92-97 mph, a curve at 77-78 and slider at 85-88. *Tendencies:* Nathan can attack hitters in a variety of ways. Rides his fastball and makes it difficult for hitters to lay off. Can drop a tight, biting curve in against lefthanders. Slider is one of the best in either league; it breaks very late, almost when it's on top of the plate. Has the second-best delivery among closers, behind Mariano Rivera. *Outlook:* With three out pitches and great command, Nathan is moving up the ladder as an elite closer. *Grade 9.6*

JOE NATHAN'S PITCHING ZONE

.188	.500	.208
.143	.281	.154
.364	.167	.308

LEFTY-RIGHTY SPLITS

vs.	Avg.	AB	H	2B	3B	HR	RBI	BB	SO	OBP	Slg.
L	.158	120	19	3	0	4	12	15	49	.248	.283
R	.206	131	27	8	0	1	7	7	45	.246	.290

Year Team (League)	W	L	Pct.	ERA	WHIP	G	GS	CG	ShO	Hld.	Sv.-Opp.	IP	H	R	ER	HR	BB-IBB	SO	Avg.
1996—			Did not play.																
1997—Salem-Keizer (N'west)	2	1	.667	2.47	1.27	18	5	0	0	...	2-...	62.0	53	22	17	7	26-0	44	.243
1998—San Jose (Calif.)	8	6	.571	3.32	1.21	22	22	0	0	...	0-...	122.0	100	51	45	13	48-0	118	.224
—Shreveport (Texas)	1	3	.250	8.80	1.89	4	4	0	0	...	0-...	15.1	20	15	15	4	9-0	10	.317
1999—Shreveport (Texas)	0	1	.000	3.12	1.38	2	2	0	0	...	0-...	8.2	5	4	3	0	7-0	7	.179
—San Francisco (N.L.)	7	4	.636	4.18	1.44	19	14	0	0	1-1	90.1	84	45	42	17	46-0	54	.243
—Fresno (PCL)	6	4	.600	4.46	1.39	13	13	1	0	...	0-...	74.2	68	44	37	11	36-0	82	.244
2000—San Francisco (N.L.)	5	2	.714	5.21	1.63	20	15	0	0	0-1	93.1	89	63	54	12	63-4	61	.255
—San Jose (Calif.)	0	1	.000	3.60	1.00	1	1	0	0	...	0-...	5.0	4	2	2	1	1-0	2	.235
—Bakersfield (Calif.)	1	0	1.000	5.06	1.69	1	1	0	0	...	0-...	5.1	2	3	3	0	7-0	6	.118
—Fresno (PCL)	0	2	.000	4.40	1.53	3	3	0	0	...	0-...	14.1	15	8	7	4	7-0	9	.268
2001—Fresno (PCL)	0	5	.000	7.77	2.07	10	10	0	0	...	0-...	46.1	63	47	40	13	33-0	21	.333
—Shreveport (Texas)	3	6	.333	6.93	1.76	21	7	0	0	...	0-...	62.1	73	49	48	11	37-5	33	.299
2002—Fresno (PCL)	6	12	.333	5.60	1.65	31	25	1	0	...	0-...	146.1	167	97	91	20	74-0	117	.283
—San Francisco (N.L.)	0	0	...	0.00	0.27	4	0	0	0	0-0	3.2	1	0	0	0	0-0	2	.083
2003—San Francisco (N.L.)	12	4	.750	2.96	1.06	78	0	0	0	20	0-3	79.0	51	26	26	7	33-3	83	.186
2004—Minnesota (A.L.)	1	2	.333	1.62	0.98	73	0	0	0	0	44-47	72.1	48	14	13	3	23-3	89	.187
2005—Minnesota (A.L.)	7	4	.636	2.70	0.97	69	0	0	0	0	43-48	70.0	46	22	21	5	22-1	94	.183
American League totals (2 years)	8	6	.571	2.15	0.98	142	0	0	0	0	87-95	142.1	94	36	34	8	45-4	183	.185
National League totals (4 years)	24	10	.706	4.12	1.38	121	29	0	0	20	1-5	266.1	225	134	122	36	142-7	200	.229
Major League totals (6 years)	32	16	.667	3.44	1.24	263	29	0	0	20	88-100	408.2	319	170	156	44	187-11	383	.214

DIVISION SERIES RECORD

Year Team (League)	W	L	Pct.	ERA	WHIP	G	GS	CG	ShO	Hld.	Sv.-Opp.	IP	H	R	ER	HR	BB-IBB	SO	Avg.
2003—San Francisco (N.L.)	0	1	.000	81.00	15.00	2	0	0	0	0	0-1	0.1	4	3	3	1	1-0	1	.800
2004—Minnesota (A.L.)	0	1	.000	3.60	1.40	3	0	0	0	0	1-1	5.0	2	2	2	0	5-2	6	.118
Division series totals (2 years)	0	2	.000	8.44	2.25	5	0	0	0	0	1-2	5.1	6	5	5	1	6-2	7	.273

ALL-STAR GAME RECORD

	W	L	Pct.	ERA	WHIP	G	GS	CG	ShO	Hld.	Sv.-Opp.	IP	H	R	ER	HR	BB-IBB	SO	Avg.
All-Star Game totals (2 years)	0	0	...	4.50	1.00	2	0	0	0	0	0-0	2.0	2	1	1	0	0-0	2	.250

NAVARRO, DIONER   C

PERSONAL: Born February 9, 1984, in Caracas, Venezuela. ... 5-10/190. ... Bats both, throws right. ... Full name: Dioner Faviau Navarro. ... Name pronounced: dee-o-nair.
TRANSACTIONS/CAREER NOTES: Signed as a non-drafted free agent by New York Yankees organization (August 21, 2000). ... Traded by Yankees with Ps Javier Vazquez and Brad Halsey and cash to Arizona Diamondbacks for P Randy Johnson (January 11, 2005). ... Traded by Diamondbacks with Ps William Juarez, Danny Muegge and Beltran Perez to Los Angeles Dodgers for OF Shawn Green and cash (January 11, 2005).
2005 GAMES PLAYED BY POSITION (MLB): C—50.

SCOUTING REPORT *Offense:* With a compact swing, he should be a productive hitter who hits 15-20 home runs. Has unusually good knowledge of the strike zone for a young hitter and consistently works pitchers into deep counts. Has an uncanny knack for picking up the release point, especially against lefthanders. Is not a fast runner. *Defense:* A converted infielder, Navarro has a strong, accurate arm. Also has quick footwork and lateral movement, and thus shows good framing and blocking skills. Hands are soft, and he is learning how to call a game and gain a pitcher's confidence. *Outlook:* He will enter spring training as the probable starter. *Grade 7.8*

DIONER NAVARRO'S HITTING ZONE

.167	.308	.400
.438	.471	.118
.222	.385	.308

LEFTY-RIGHTY SPLITS

vs.	Avg.	AB	H	2B	3B	HR	RBI	BB	SO	OBP	Slg.
L	.435	23	10	1	0	1	2	9	2	.594	.609
R	.248	153	38	8	0	2	12	11	19	.307	.340

Year Team (League)	Pos.	G	AB	R	H	2B	3B	HR	RBI	BB	SO	HBP	GDP	SB-CS	Avg.	OBP	SLG	OPS	E	Avg.
2001—GC Yankees (GCL)	C	43	143	27	40	10	1	2	22	17	23	0	4	6-0	.280	.345	.406	.751	3	.991
2002—Greensboro (S. Atl.)	C	92	328	41	78	12	2	8	36	39	61	5	9	1-2	.238	.326	.360	.686	8	.987
—Tampa (Fla. St.)	C	0	2	1	1	1	0	0	0	0	0	0	0	0-0	1.000	.500	2.000	3.000	0	1.000
2003—Tampa (Fla. St.)	C	52	197	28	59	16	4	3	28	17	27	4	4	1-0	.299	.364	.467	.831	3	.992
—Trenton (East.)	C	58	208	28	71	15	0	4	37	18	26	1	6	2-3	.341	.388	.471	.859	4	.986
2004—Trenton (East.)	C-DH	70	255	32	69	14	1	3	29	33	44	1	6	1-0	.271	.354	.369	.720	7	.984
—Columbus (Int'l)	C-DH	40	136	18	34	8	2	1	16	14	17	1	4	0-0	.250	.316	.360	.672	2	.994
—New York (A.L.)	C	5	7	2	3	0	0	0	1	0	0	1	0	0-0	.429	.429	.429	.857	0	1.000
2005—Las Vegas (PCL)	C-DH	75	241	31	64	12	0	6	29	38	24	2	9	2-2	.266	.366	.390	.756	1	.998

Year Team (League)	Pos.	G	AB	R	H	2B	3B	HR	RBI	BATTING BB	SO	HBP	GDP	SB-CS	Avg.	OBP	SLG	OPS	FIELDING E	Avg.
—Los Angeles (N.L.)	C	50	176	21	48	9	0	3	14	20	21	2	3	0-0	.273	.354	.375	.729	2	.995
American League totals (1 year)		5	7	2	3	0	0	0	1	0	0	0	1	0-0	.429	.429	.429	.857	0	1.000
National League totals (1 year)		50	176	21	48	9	0	3	14	20	21	2	3	0-0	.273	.354	.375	.729	2	.995
Major League totals (2 years)		55	183	23	51	9	0	3	15	20	21	2	4	0-0	.279	.356	.377	.733	2	.995

NEAL, BLAINE   P

PERSONAL: Born April 6, 1978, in Marlton, N.J. ... 6-5/248. ... Throws right, bats left. ... High school: Bishop Eustace Prep (Pennsauken, N.J.).

TRANSACTIONS/CAREER NOTES: Selected by Florida Marlins organization in fourth round of 1996 free-agent draft. ... Played one season as a first baseman in Marlins organization (1998). ... Traded by Marlins to San Diego Padres for P Ben Howard (April 3, 2004). ... Traded by Padres to Boston Red Sox for OF Adam Hyzdu (March 22, 2005). ... Claimed on waivers by Colorado Rockies (May 11, 2005). ... On disabled list (June 17-September 8, 2005); included rehabilitation assignment to Tulsa and Colorado Springs.

CAREER HITTING: 0-for-1 (.000), 0 R, 0 2B, 0 3B, 0 HR, 0 RBI.

BLAINE NEAL'S PITCHING ZONE

.250	.500	.143
.600	.438	.333
.286	.500	.667

LEFTY-RIGHTY SPLITS

vs.	Avg.	AB	H	2B	3B	HR	RBI	BB	SO	OBP	Slg.
L	.447	38	17	2	0	2	13	3	1	.465	.658
R	.321	56	18	1	0	2	9	9	10	.409	.446

Year Team (League)	W	L	Pct.	ERA	WHIP	G	GS	CG	ShO	Hld.	Sv.-Opp.	IP	H	R	ER	HR	BB-IBB	SO	Avg.
1996—GC Marlins (GCL)	1	1	.500	4.60	1.30	7	5	0	0	...	1-...	29.1	32	18	15	1	6-0	15	.274
1997—GC Marlins (GCL)	4	1	.800	3.63	1.57	10	0	0	0	...	1-...	22.1	24	11	9	1	11-0	19	.267
1999—Kane Co. (Midw.)	4	2	.667	2.32	1.00	26	0	0	0	...	6-...	31.0	21	8	8	2	10-0	31	.200
2000—Brevard County (FSL)	2	2	.500	2.15	1.18	41	0	0	0	...	11-...	54.1	40	27	13	1	24-3	65	.200
2001—Portland (East.)	2	3	.400	2.36	1.20	54	0	0	0	...	21-...	53.1	43	17	14	1	21-3	45	.218
—Florida (N.L.)	0	0	...	6.75	2.25	4	0	0	0	0	0-0	5.1	7	4	4	0	5-0	3	.304
2002—Calgary (PCL)	3	1	.750	2.90	1.35	29	0	0	0	...	11-...	31.0	27	11	10	2	15-1	26	.233
—Florida (N.L.)	3	0	1.000	2.73	1.39	32	0	0	0	2	0-0	33.0	32	12	10	1	14-2	33	.248
2003—Albuquerque (PCL)	3	2	.600	2.33	1.50	40	0	0	0	...	21-...	46.1	55	22	12	1	16-2	32	.304
—Florida (N.L.)	0	0	...	8.14	2.24	18	0	0	0	2	0-0	21.0	38	20	19	2	9-1	10	.413
2004—Portland (PCL)	4	2	.667	1.86	1.14	27	0	0	0	...	1-...	38.2	32	10	8	0	12-2	38	.225
—San Diego (N.L.)	1	1	.500	4.07	1.43	40	0	0	0	3	0-2	42.0	49	19	19	6	11-3	36	.295
2005—Boston (A.L.)	0	1	.000	9.00	2.25	8	0	0	0	0	0-0	8.0	15	9	8	2	3-0	3	.429
—Colorado (N.L.)	1	2	.333	6.14	1.98	11	0	0	0	0	0-2	14.2	20	10	10	2	9-2	8	.339
—Tulsa (Texas)	0	1	.000	9.00	1.67	4	1	0	0	0	0-0	3.0	4	4	3	1	1-0	2	.308
—Colo. Springs (PCL)	0	0	...	0.00	1.00	1	0	0	0	0	0-0	1.0	1	0	0	0	0-0	0	.250
American League totals (1 year)	0	1	.000	9.00	2.25	8	0	0	0	0	0-0	8.0	15	9	8	2	3-0	3	.429
National League totals (5 years)	5	3	.625	4.81	1.67	105	0	0	0	7	0-4	116.0	146	65	62	11	48-8	90	.311
Major League totals (5 years)	5	4	.556	5.08	1.71	113	0	0	0	7	0-4	124.0	161	74	70	13	51-8	93	.319

NELSON, JEFF   P

PERSONAL: Born November 17, 1966, in Baltimore. ... 6-8/225. ... Throws right, bats right. ... Full name: Jeffrey Allan Nelson. ... High school: Catonsville (Md.). ... Junior college: Catonsville (Md.) Community College. ... College: Catonsville (MD) CC.

TRANSACTIONS/CAREER NOTES: Selected by Los Angeles Dodgers organization in 22nd round of June 1984 free-agent draft. ... Selected by Seattle Mariners organization from Dodgers organization in Rule 5 minor league draft (December 9, 1986). ... On disabled list (July 16, 1989-remainder of season). ... Traded by Mariners with 1B Tino Martinez and P Jim Mecir to New York Yankees for P Sterling Hitchcock and 3B Russ Davis (December 7, 1995). ... On suspended list (September 3-5, 1996; and May 28-29, 1998). ... On disabled list (June 26-September 4, 1998); included rehabilitation assignment to Tampa. ... On disabled list (May 3-20 and June 3-August 11, 1999); included rehabilitation assignments to GCL Yankees and Tampa. ... Signed as a free agent by Mariners (December 4, 2000). ... On disabled list (May 8-June 27, 2002); included rehabilitation assignment to Everett. ... Traded by Mariners to Yankees for P Armando Benitez (August 6, 2003). ... Signed as a free agent by Texas Rangers (January 14, 2004). ... On disabled list (May 13-July 26 and August 1-September 1, 2004); included rehabilitation assignments to Frisco and Oklahoma. ... Signed as a free agent by Mariners organization (January 31, 2005). ... On bereavement list (August 2-5).

CAREER HITTING: 0-for-2 (.000), 0 R, 0 2B, 0 3B, 0 HR, 0 RBI.

SCOUTING REPORT **Throws:** Nelson throws a fastball at 87-89 mph and a slider. ***Tendencies:*** He has a slight pause in his delivery and creates some deception. Has lost a lot off his fastball and lives with his slider, which is more of a slurve. Throws slurve to both sides of the plate with a big break. Likes to start it away from lefthanders and will expand the zone with it if he forces hitters to chase it. Struggles with lefthanders. ***Outlook:*** Nelson is best as a situational reliever against righthanders at this point in his career. ***Grade 6***

JEFF NELSON'S PITCHING ZONE

.143	.571	.250
.250	.375	.125
.400	.167	.200

LEFTY-RIGHTY SPLITS

vs.	Avg.	AB	H	2B	3B	HR	RBI	BB	SO	OBP	Slg.
L	.342	38	13	3	0	2	8	6	7	.457	.579
R	.196	97	19	2	1		8	16	27	.319	.247

Year Team (League)	W	L	Pct.	ERA	WHIP	G	GS	CG	ShO	Hld.	Sv.-Opp.	IP	H	R	ER	HR	BB-IBB	SO	Avg.
1984—Great Falls (Pio.)	0	0	...	54.00	9.00	1	0	0	0	...	0-...	0.2	3	4	4	1	3-0	1	...
—GC Dodgers (GCL)	0	0	...	1.35	0.90	9	0	0	0	...	0-...	13.1	6	3	2	0	6-0	7	.122
1985—GC Dodgers (GCL)	0	5	.000	5.51	2.20	14	7	0	0	...	0-...	47.1	72	50	29	1	32-0	31	.344
1986—Bakersfield (Calif.)	0	7	.000	6.69	2.29	24	11	0	0	...	0-...	71.1	79	83	53	9	84-1	37	.252
—Great Falls (Pio.)	0	0	...	13.50	4.00	3	0	0	0	...	0-...	2.0	5	3	3	0	3-2	1	...
1987—Salinas (Calif.)	3	7	.300	5.74	1.89	17	16	1	0	...	0-...	80.0	80	61	51	2	71-0	43	.261
1988—San Bern. (Calif.)	8	9	.471	5.54	1.70	27	27	1	1	...	0-...	149.1	163	115	92	9	91-2	94	.287
1989—Williamsport (East.)	7	5	.583	3.31	1.35	15	15	2	0	...	0-...	92.1	72	41	34	2	53-1	61	.217
1990—Williamsport (East.)	1	4	.200	6.44	1.92	10	10	0	0	...	0-...	43.1	65	35	31	2	25-1	14	.359
—Peninsula (Caro.)	2	2	.500	3.15	1.20	18	7	1	0	...	6-...	60.0	47	21	21	2	25-1	49	.214

N

Year Team (League)	W	L	Pct.	ERA	WHIP	G	GS	CG	ShO	Hld.	Sv.-Opp.	IP	H	R	ER	HR	BB-IBB	SO	Avg.
1991—Jacksonville (Sou.)	4	0	1.000	1.27	1.13	21	0	0	0	...	12-...	28.1	23	5	4	0	9-0	34	.225
—Calgary (PCL)	3	4	.429	3.90	1.67	28	0	0	0	...	21-...	32.1	39	19	14	1	15-3	26	.310
1992—Calgary (PCL)	1	0	1.000	0.00	0.27	2	0	0	0	...	0-...	3.2	0	0	0	0	1-0	0	.000
—Seattle (A.L.)	1	7	.125	3.44	1.42	66	0	0	0	6	6-14	81.0	71	34	31	7	44-12	46	.245
1993—Calgary (PCL)	1	0	1.000	1.17	1.04	5	0	0	0	...	1-...	7.2	6	1	1	0	2-0	6	.222
—Seattle (A.L.)	5	3	.625	4.35	1.52	71	0	0	0	17	1-11	60.0	57	30	29	5	34-10	61	.258
1994—Seattle (A.L.)	0	0	...	2.76	1.30	28	0	0	0	2	0-0	42.1	35	18	13	3	20-4	44	.226
—Calgary (PCL)	1	4	.200	2.84	1.11	18	0	0	0	...	8-...	25.1	21	9	8	1	7-1	30	.236
1995—Seattle (A.L.)	7	3	.700	2.17	1.08	62	0	0	0	14	2-4	78.2	58	21	19	4	27-5	96	.209
1996—New York (A.L.)	4	4	.500	4.36	1.49	73	0	0	0	10	2-4	74.1	75	38	36	6	36-1	91	.262
1997—New York (A.L.)	3	7	.300	2.86	1.14	77	0	0	0	22	2-8	78.2	53	32	25	7	37-12	81	.191
1998—New York (A.L.)	5	3	.625	3.79	1.64	45	0	0	0	10	3-6	40.1	44	18	17	1	22-4	35	.278
—Tampa (Fla. St.)	0	0	...	0.00	1.00	2	1	0	0	...	0-...	2.0	1	1	0	0	1-0	4	.143
1999—New York (A.L.)	2	1	.667	4.15	1.62	39	0	0	0	10	1-2	30.1	27	14	14	2	22-2	35	.245
—GC Yankees (GCL)	0	0	...	0.00	1.00	2	2	0	0	...	0-...	2.0	1	0	0	0	1-0	3	.143
—Tampa (Fla. St.)	0	0	...	0.00	1.00	3	3	0	0	...	0-...	3.0	1	0	0	0	2-0	5	.100
2000—New York (A.L.)	8	4	.667	2.45	1.28	73	0	0	0	15	0-4	69.2	44	24	19	2	45-1	71	.183
2001—Seattle (A.L.)	4	3	.571	2.76	1.13	69	0	0	0	26	4-5	65.1	30	21	20	3	44-1	88	.136
2002—Seattle (A.L.)	3	2	.600	3.94	1.38	41	0	0	0	12	2-4	45.2	36	20	20	4	27-3	55	.221
—Everett (N'west)	0	1	.000	0.00	0.75	1	1	0	0	...	0-...	1.1	1	0	0	0	0-0	4	.200
2003—Seattle (A.L.)	3	2	.600	3.35	1.27	46	0	0	0	6	7-11	37.2	34	16	14	3	14-1	47	.246
—New York (A.L.)	1	0	1.000	4.58	1.53	24	0	0	0	8	1-3	17.2	17	9	9	1	10-2	21	.246
2004—Oklahoma (PCL)	0	1	.000	16.20	1.80	2	2	0	0	...	0-...	1.2	3	3	3	0	0-0	3	.375
—Frisco (Texas)	0	0	...	2.46	0.82	3	3	0	0	...	0-...	3.2	2	1	1	0	1-0	3	.154
—Texas (A.L.)	1	2	.333	5.32	1.52	29	0	0	0	9	1-1	23.2	17	16	14	3	19-0	22	.207
2005—Seattle (A.L.)	1	3	.250	3.93	1.47	49	0	0	0	9	1-4	36.2	32	17	16	3	22-0	34	.237
Major League totals (14 years)	48	44	.522	3.41	1.35	792	0	0	0	176	33-81	782.0	630	328	296	54	423-58	827	.223

DIVISION SERIES RECORD

Year Team (League)	W	L	Pct.	ERA	WHIP	G	GS	CG	ShO	Hld.	Sv.-Opp.	IP	H	R	ER	HR	BB-IBB	SO	Avg.
1995—Seattle (A.L.)	0	1	.000	3.18	1.76	3	0	0	0	0	0-0	5.2	7	2	2	0	3-0	7	.304
1996—New York (A.L.)	1	0	1.000	0.00	1.09	2	0	0	0	0	0-0	3.2	2	0	0	0	2-1	5	.154
1997—New York (A.L.)	0	0	...	0.00	1.50	4	0	0	0	2	0-0	4.0	4	0	0	0	2-0	0	.267
1998—New York (A.L.)	0	0	...	0.00	1.13	2	0	0	0	1	0-0	2.2	2	0	0	0	1-0	2	.222
1999—New York (A.L.)	0	0	...	0.00	1.20	3	0	0	0	1	0-0	1.2	1	0	0	0	1-0	3	.167
2000—New York (A.L.)	0	0	...	0.00	0.00	2	0	0	0	1	0-0	2.0	0	0	0	0	0-0	2	.000
2001—Seattle (A.L.)	0	0	...	0.00	0.67	3	0	0	0	1	0-0	3.0	1	0	0	0	1-0	5	.100
2003—Seattle (A.L.)	0	0	...	...	...	1	0	0	0	0	0-0	0.0	0	0	0	0	1-0	0	...
Division series totals (8 years)	1	1	.500	0.79	1.24	20	0	0	0	7	0-0	22.2	17	2	2	0	11-1	24	.207

CHAMPIONSHIP SERIES RECORD

Year Team (League)	W	L	Pct.	ERA	WHIP	G	GS	CG	ShO	Hld.	Sv.-Opp.	IP	H	R	ER	HR	BB-IBB	SO	Avg.
1995—Seattle (A.L.)	0	0	...	0.00	2.67	3	0	0	0	1	0-0	3.0	3	0	0	0	5-1	3	.333
1996—New York (A.L.)	0	1	.000	11.57	2.14	2	0	0	0	1	0-0	2.1	5	3	3	1	0-0	2	.385
1998—New York (A.L.)	0	1	.000	20.25	3.00	1	0	0	0	1	0-0	1.1	3	3	3	0	1-0	3	.429
1999—New York (A.L.)	0	0	...	0.00	0.00	2	0	0	0	1	0-0	0.2	0	0	0	0	0-0	0	.000
2000—New York (A.L.)	0	0	...	9.00	1.67	3	0	0	0	1	0-0	3.0	5	3	3	2	0-0	6	.357
2001—Seattle (A.L.)	0	0	...	0.00	0.86	2	0	0	0	1	0-0	2.1	1	0	0	0	1-0	3	.143
2003—New York (A.L.)	0	0	...	6.00	1.33	4	0	0	0	0	0-0	3.0	4	2	2	0	1-0	3	.364
Champ. series totals (7 years)	0	2	.000	6.32	1.79	19	0	0	0	4	0-0	15.2	21	11	11	3	7-1	20	.339

WORLD SERIES RECORD

Year Team (League)	W	L	Pct.	ERA	WHIP	G	GS	CG	ShO	Hld.	Sv.-Opp.	IP	H	R	ER	HR	BB-IBB	SO	Avg.
1996—New York (A.L.)	0	0	...	0.00	0.46	3	0	0	0	1	0-0	4.1	1	0	0	0	1-0	5	.071
1998—New York (A.L.)	0	0	...	0.00	1.29	3	0	0	0	1	0-0	2.1	2	1	0	0	1-0	4	.222
1999—New York (A.L.)	0	0	...	0.00	1.13	2	0	0	0	1	0-0	2.2	2	0	0	0	1-0	3	.200
2000—New York (A.L.)	1	0	1.000	10.13	2.25	3	0	0	0	1	0-0	2.2	5	3	3	1	1-0	1	.417
2003—New York (A.L.)	0	0	...	0.00	1.50	3	0	0	0	0	0-0	4.0	4	0	0	0	2-0	5	.267
World series totals (5 years)	1	0	1.000	1.69	1.25	16	0	0	0	3	0-0	16.0	14	4	3	1	6-0	18	.233

ALL-STAR GAME RECORD

	W	L	Pct.	ERA	WHIP	G	GS	CG	ShO	Hld.	Sv.-Opp.	IP	H	R	ER	HR	BB-IBB	SO	Avg.
All-Star Game totals (1 year)	0	0	...	0.00	1.00	1	0	0	0	1	0-0	1.0	0	0	0	0	1-0	1	.000

NEVIN, PHIL — 1B/DH

PERSONAL: Born January 19, 1971, in Fullerton, Calif. ... 6-2/231. ... Bats right, throws right. ... Full name: Phillip Joseph Nevin. ... High school: El Dorado (Placentia, Calif.). ... College: Cal State Fullerton.

TRANSACTIONS/CAREER NOTES: Selected by Los Angeles Dodgers organization in third round of 1989 free-agent draft; did not sign. ... Selected by Houston Astros organization in first round (first pick overall) of 1992 free-agent draft. ... Traded by Astros to Detroit Tigers (August 15, 1995), completing deal in which Tigers traded P Mike Henneman to Astros for a player to be named (August 10, 1995). ... On disabled list (March 21-April 16, 1997); included rehabilitation assignment to Lakeland. ... Traded by Tigers with C Matt Walbeck to Anaheim Angels for P Nick Skuse (November 20, 1997). ... On suspended list (June 12-15, 1998). ... Traded by Angels with P Keith Volkman to San Diego Padres for IF Andy Sheets and OF Gus Kennedy (March 29, 1999). ... On disabled list (April 1-16, 1999); included rehabilitaion assignment to Las Vegas. ... On disabled list (May 12-27 and May 30-July 12, 2002); included rehabilitation assignment to Lake Elsinore. ... On disabled list (March 25-July 23, 2003); included rehabilitation assignments to Lake Elsinore and Portland. ... On disabled list (July 5-21, 2004). ... On disabled list (June 26-July 18, 2005); included rehabilitation assignment to Portland. ... Traded by Padres to Texas Rangers for P Chan Ho Park (July 29, 2005).

2005 GAMES PLAYED BY POSITION (MLB): 1B—74, DH—25, C—2, 3B—1.

SCOUTING REPORT Offense: Nevin struggled to adjust after being traded. Is a dead fastball hitter with an uppercut. Has an inside-out approach. Bat speed has declined and has become vulnerable to the ball inside. Is impatient and frequently will chase balls up. Doesn't pull the ball

PHIL NEVIN'S HITTING ZONE

.143	.316	.214
.258	.364	.375
.154	.278	.059

LEFTY-RIGHTY SPLITS

vs.	Avg.	AB	H	2B	3B	HR	RBI	BB	SO	OBP	Slg.
L	.205	127	26	8	0	4	13	16	34	.292	.362
R	.253	253	64	8	1	8	42	11	63	.285	.387

but has power. Had a lot of trouble adjusting to more off-speed pitches. Struggled against lefthanders. **Defense:** He probably will be more of a DH in A.L. Doesn't have very quick feet and has stiff infield actions. Doesn't have good hands and has not been the same since coming back from shoulder surgery. Rarely leaves his feet for balls. **Outlook:** Nevin will have to make more adjustments to regain the stroke and bat speed he had years ago. Now is in a hitter's park (Ameriquest Field). *Grade 7.3*

Year	Team (League)	Pos.	G	AB	R	H	2B	3B	HR	RBI	BB	SO	HBP	GDP	SB-CS	Avg.	OBP	SLG	OPS	E	Avg.
1993—Tucson (PCL)		3B-OF	123	448	67	128	21	3	10	93	52	99	3	12	8-1	.286	.359	.413	.772	29	.898
1994—Tucson (PCL)		3B-OF	118	445	67	117	20	1	12	79	55	101	1	21	3-2	.263	.343	.393	.736	32	.907
1995—Tucson (PCL)		3B-DH	62	223	31	65	16	0	7	41	27	39	1	9	2-3	.291	.371	.457	.828	14	.923
—Houston (N.L.)		3B	18	60	4	7	1	0	0	1	7	13	1	2	1-0	.117	.221	.133	.354	3	.933
—Toledo (Int'l)		OF-DH	7	23	3	7	2	0	1	3	1	5	0	2	0-0	.304	.333	.522	.855	0	1.000
—Detroit (A.L.)		OF-DH	29	96	9	21	3	1	2	12	11	27	3	3	0-0	.219	.318	.333	.652	2	.963
1996—Jacksonville (Sou.)		C-DH-3B																			
		OF-1B	98	344	77	101	18	1	24	69	60	83	3	9	6-2	.294	.397	.561	.958	11	.977
—Detroit (A.L.)		3B-OF-C																			
		DH	38	120	15	35	5	0	8	19	8	39	1	1	1-0	.292	.338	.533	.872	5	.951
1997—Lakeland (Fla. St.)		1B-3B-DH	3	9	3	5	1	0	1	4	3	2	0	0	0-0	.556	.667	1.000	1.667	1	.929
—Toledo (Int'l)		1B-3B-DH	5	19	1	3	0	0	1	3	2	9	0	1	0-0	.158	.238	.316	.554	0	1.000
—Detroit (A.L.)		OF-DH-3B																			
		1B-C	93	251	32	59	16	1	9	35	25	68	1	5	0-1	.235	.306	.414	.720	2	.982
1998—Anaheim (A.L.)		C-DH-1B	75	237	27	54	8	1	8	27	17	67	5	6	0-0	.228	.291	.371	.663	5	.989
1999—Las Vegas (PCL)		C-1B-3B	3	10	2	2	0	0	2	2	0	2	0	1	0-0	.200	.200	.800	1.000	0	1.000
—San Diego (N.L.)		3B-C-OF																			
		1B-DH	128	383	52	103	27	0	24	85	51	82	1	7	1-0	.269	.352	.527	.880	5	.989
2000—San Diego (N.L.)		3B	143	538	87	163	34	1	31	107	59	121	4	17	2-0	.303	.374	.543	.916	* 26	.930
2001—San Diego (N.L.)		3B-DH	149	546	97	167	31	0	41	126	71	147	4	13	4-4	.306	.388	.588	.976	27	.930
2002—San Diego (N.L.)		3B-1B	107	407	53	116	16	0	12	57	38	87	1	12	4-0	.285	.344	.413	.757	18	.963
—Lake Elsinore (Calif.)		3B	2	6	2	2	1	0	1	6	1	2	0	0	0-0	.333	.375	1.000	1.375	2	.000
2003—Lake Elsinore (Calif.)		DH	5	15	1	4	1	0	0	5	2	2	0	1	0-0	.267	.300	.333	.633	0	...
—Portland (PCL)		1B-DH-OF	6	18	0	2	0	0	1	1	1	0	0	2	0-0	.111	.158	.111	.269	0	1.000
		1B-OF	59	226	30	63	8	0	13	46	21	44	0	9	2-0	.279	.339	.487	.825	2	.994
2004—San Diego (N.L.)		1B-DH-C	147	547	78	158	31	1	26	105	66	121	0	16	0-0	.289	.368	.492	.859	13	.990
2005—Portland (PCL)		1B	2	7	0	1	0	0	0	1	0	2	0	1	0-0	.143	.143	.143	.286	0	1.000
—San Diego (N.L.)		1B-C	73	281	31	72	11	1	9	47	19	67	1	2	1-0	.256	.301	.399	.699	4	.994
—Texas (A.L.)		DH-1B-3B	29	99	15	18	5	0	3	8	8	30	1	6	2-0	.182	.250	.323	.573	0	1.000
American League totals (5 years)			264	803	98	187	37	3	30	101	69	231	11	21	3-1	.233	.301	.399	.700	14	.981
National League totals (8 years)			824	2988	432	849	159	3	156	574	332	682	17	78	15-4	.284	.356	.496	.852	98	.975
Major League totals (11 years)			1088	3791	530	1036	196	6	186	675	401	913	28	99	18-5	.273	.345	.475	.820	112	.976

ALL-STAR GAME RECORD

	G	AB	R	H	2B	3B	HR	RBI	BB	SO	HBP	GDP	SB-CS	Avg.	OBP	SLG	OPS	E	Avg.
All-Star Game totals (1 year)	1	1	0	0	0	0	0	0	0	0	0	0	0-0	.000	.000	.000	.000	0	...

NEWHAN, DAVID   OF/3B

PERSONAL: Born September 7, 1973, in Fullerton, Calif. ... 5-10/180. ... Bats left, throws right. ... Full name: David Matthew Newhan. ... High school: Esperanza (Calif.). ... College: Pepperdine.

TRANSACTIONS/CAREER NOTES: Selected by Oakland Athletics organization in 17th round of 1995 free-agent draft. ... Traded by A's with P Don Wengert to San Diego Padres for P Doug Bochtler and SS Jorge Velandia (December 15, 1997). ... Traded by Padres to Philadelphia Phillies (August 7, 2000), completing deal in which Phillies traded SS Desi Relaford to Padres for a player to be named (August 4, 2000). ... On disabled list (April 15, 2001-remainder of season); included rehabilitation assignment to Scranton/Wilkes-Barre. ... Signed as a free agent by Los Angeles Dodgers organization (February 5, 2002). ... Signed as a free agent by Colorado Rockies organization (May 8, 2003). ... Signed as a free agent by Texas Rangers organization (November 10, 2003). ... Released by Rangers (June 17, 2004) ... Signed by Baltimore Orioles (June 18, 2004).

2005 GAMES PLAYED BY POSITION (MLB): OF—73, 3B—8, DH—7.

N

SCOUTING REPORT *Offense:* Newhan regressed in 2005. Bat speed declined and his swing became longer. Became more impatient and couldn't handle the ball upstairs. Did not display his power. Still is a good runner with first-step quickness and anticipation; can steal bases. *Defense:* Newhan can play just about anywhere in the infield or outfield. Has never shown really soft hands. Has good range to either side. Gets better jumps coming in than going back in the outfield. Arm is short but has a quick release. Not accurate from long distances. *Outlook:* His troubles last season prove he can't be overexposed; the rest of the league caught up to him. *Grade 5*

DAVID NEWHAN'S HITTING ZONE

.200	.125	.071
.240	.524	.220
.250	.133	.115

LEFTY-RIGHTY SPLITS

vs.	Avg.	AB	H	2B	3B	HR	RBI	BB	SO	OBP	Slg.
L	.250	28	7	1	0	1	6	2	8	.333	.393
R	.195	190	37	8	0	4	15	20	37	.270	.300

Year	Team (League)	Pos.	G	AB	R	H	2B	3B	HR	RBI	BB	SO	HBP	GDP	SB-CS	Avg.	OBP	SLG	OPS	E	Avg.
1995—S. Oregon (N'west)		OF	42	145	25	39	8	1	6	21	29	30	1	2	10-5	.269	.388	.462	.850	2	.964
—W. Mich. (Mid.)		OF	25	96	9	21	5	0	3	8	13	26	1	2	3-2	.219	.315	.365	.680	1	.976
1996—Modesto (California)		OF	117	455	96	137	27	3	25	75	62	106	4	8	17-8	.301	.386	.538	.924	5	.964
1997—Visalia (Calif.)		2B	67	241	52	67	15	2	7	48	44	58	3	5	9-3	.278	.389	.444	.833	10	.966
—Huntsville (Sou.)		2B	57	212	40	67	13	2	5	35	28	59	2	4	5-5	.316	.398	.467	.865	16	.934
1998—Mobile (Sou.)		2B-3B-SS	121	491	89	128	26	3	12	45	68	110	2	8	27-8	.261	.352	.399	.751	14	.975
1999—Las Vegas (PCL)		2B-SS	98	374	49	107	25	1	14	49	30	84	2	0	22-4	.286	.342	.471	.812	20	.952
—San Diego (N.L.)		2B-1B-3B	32	43	7	6	0	1	2	6	1	11	0	0	2-1	.140	.159	.302	.461	2	.970
2000—San Diego (N.L.)		OF-2B-3B	14	20	5	3	1	0	1	2	6	7	0	0	0-0	.150	.346	.350	.696	0	1.000
—Las Vegas (PCL)		2B-OF	66	244	41	62	5	2	5	35	37	61	0	9	9-3	.254	.352	.352	.704	7	.975
—Scran./W.B. (I.L.)		2B	25	83	10	21	3	0	3	8	11	15	0	0	3-1	.253	.337	.398	.734	1	.991

Year Team (League)	Pos.	BATTING																	FIELDING	
		G	AB	R	H	2B	3B	HR	RBI	BB	SO	HBP	GDP	SB-CS	Avg.	OBP	SLG	OPS	E	Avg.
— Philadelphia (N.L.)	2B	10	17	3	3	0	0	0	0	2	6	0	2	0-0	.176	.263	.176	.440	0	1.000
2001— Philadelphia (N.L.)	2B	7	6	2	2	1	0	0	1	1	0	0	0	0-0	.333	.375	.500	.875	0	1.000
— Scran./W.B. (I.L.)	2B	13	55	4	6	1	0	0	2	4	11	1	1	0-0	.109	.183	.127	.311	1	.969
2002— Los Angeles (N.L.)	Did not play.																			
2003— Colo. Springs (PCL) ....2B-1B-OF DH	DH	72	244	43	85	17	2	3	28	16	36	2	6	6-4	.348	.392	.471	.863	14	.959
2004— Oklahoma (PCL) 2B-DH-3B 1B	1B	61	262	57	86	21	6	9	38	26	55	1	3	10-0	.328	.387	.557	.944	10	.967
— Baltimore (A.L.) OF-DH-3B 1B	1B	95	373	66	116	15	7	8	54	27	72	4	4	11-1	.311	.361	.453	.814	5	.960
2005— Ottawa (Int'l)	OF	11	41	11	15	4	0	1	8	2	6	1	0	2-0	.366	.400	.537	.937	0	1.000
— Baltimore (A.L.) OF-3B-DH		96	218	31	44	9	0	5	21	22	45	2	2	9-2	.202	.279	.312	.591	1	.990
American League totals (2 years)		191	591	97	160	24	7	13	75	49	117	6	6	20-3	.271	.330	.401	.731	6	.974
National League totals (3 years)		63	86	17	14	3	0	3	9	10	24	0	2	2-1	.163	.247	.302	.550	2	.981
Major League totals (5 years)		254	677	114	174	27	7	16	84	59	141	6	8	22-4	.257	.320	.388	.708	8	.976

NIEKRO, LANCE   1B

PERSONAL: Born January 29, 1979, in Winter Haven, Fla. ... 6-3/210. ... Bats right, throws right. ... Full name: Lance Joseph Niekro. ... High school: George Jenkins (Lakeland, Florida). ... College: Florida Southern. ... Son of Joe Niekro, pitcher with seven major league teams (1967-88); nephew of Phil Niekro, pitcher with four major league teams (1964-87).

TRANSACTIONS/CAREER NOTES: Selected by Philadelphia Phillies organization in 13th round of 1997 free-agent draft; did not sign. ... Selected by San Francisco Giants organization in second round of 2000 free-agent draft. ... On disabled list (March 26-April 10, 2004).

2005 GAMES PLAYED BY POSITION (MLB): 1B—74, DH—1.

SCOUTING REPORT Showed good power in his first extended stay in the major leagues. Has a long swing and likes the ball out over the plate. Gets into trouble when he becomes pull conscious. Has some holes at the plate, particularly against righthanded pitching; struggles with breaking stuff. Needs to shorten his approach at the plate and hit to the opposite field better. Has good hands with a plus arm and has good footwork around the bag. Can be the heir apparent to J.T. Snow if he can hit righthanders. *Grade 5.9*

LANCE NIEKRO'S HITTING ZONE

.233	.500	.400
.306	.324	.192
.278	.500	.273

LEFTY-RIGHTY SPLITS

vs.	Avg.	AB	H	2B	3B	HR	RBI	BB	SO	OBP	Slg.
L	.324	108	35	7	1	9	26	7	17	.361	.657
R	.206	170	35	9	2	3	20	10	36	.251	.335

Year Team (League)	Pos.	BATTING																	FIELDING	
		G	AB	R	H	2B	3B	HR	RBI	BB	SO	HBP	GDP	SB-CS	Avg.	OBP	SLG	OPS	E	Avg.
2000— Salem-Keizer (N'west)	3B-3B	49	196	27	71	14	4	5	44	11	25	4	6	2-0	.362	.404	.551	.955	5	.939
2001— San Jose (Calif.)	3B-1B	42	163	18	47	11	0	3	34	4	14	0	4	4-2	.288	.298	.411	.709	8	.927
2002— Shreveport (Texas) 1B-1B-3B	3B	79	297	33	92	20	1	4	34	7	32	2	11	0-2	.310	.327	.424	.751	11	.979
2003— Fresno (PCL) 3B-1B-DH	1B-DH	98	381	43	115	15	2	4	41	19	39	1	12	3-3	.302	.334	.383	.717	15	.954
— San Francisco (N.L.)	1B	5	5	2	1	1	0	0	2	0	1	0	0	0-0	.200	.200	.400	.600	0	1.000
2004— San Jose (Calif.)	1B	15	61	13	19	7	1	1	14	2	5	0	5	0-0	.311	.328	.508	.836	1	.997
— Fresno (PCL)	1B-3B	67	241	42	72	21	4	12	47	14	32	1	5	1-1	.299	.339	.568	.907	6	.992
2005— Fresno (PCL)	1B	1	4	0	1	0	0	0	0	0	1	0	0	0-0	.250	.250	.250	.500	1	1.000
— San Francisco (N.L.)	1B-DH	113	278	32	70	16	3	12	46	17	53	2	11	0-2	.252	.295	.460	.755	5	.991
Major League totals (2 years)		118	283	34	71	17	3	12	48	17	54	2	11	0-2	.251	.293	.459	.753	5	.992

NIEVES, WIL   C

PERSONAL: Born September 25, 1977, in San Juan, Puerto Rico. ... 5-11/190. ... Bats right, throws right. ... Full name: Wilbert Nieves. ... Name pronounced: nee-AY-vas. ... Brother of Melvin Nieves, outfielder with four major league teams (1992-98).

TRANSACTIONS/CAREER NOTES: Selected by San Diego Padres organization in 47th round of 1995 free-agent draft. ... Claimed on waivers by Anaheim Angels (December 18, 2002). ... Angels franchise renamed Los Angeles Angels of Anaheim for 2005 season. ... Traded by Angels to New York Yankees for P Bret Prinz (March 29, 2005).

2005 GAMES PLAYED BY POSITION (MLB): C—3.

LEFTY-RIGHTY SPLITS

vs.	Avg.	AB	H	2B	3B	HR	RBI	BB	SO	OBP	Slg.
L	.000	1	0	0	0	0	0	0	1	.000	.000
R	.000	3	0	0	0	0	0	0	0	.000	.000

Year Team (League)	Pos.	BATTING																	FIELDING	
		G	AB	R	H	2B	3B	HR	RBI	BB	SO	HBP	GDP	SB-CS	Avg.	OBP	SLG	OPS	E	Avg.
1996— Ariz. Padres (Ariz.)	C-3B-OF	43	113	23	39	5	0	2	22	13	19	0	1	3-4	.345	.413	.442	.855	10	.960
1997— Ariz. Padres (Ariz.)	C-OF-3B	8	27	2	8	2	0	0	2	5	5	0	0	1-0	.296	.406	.370	.776	0	1.000
— Clinton (Midw.)	C	18	55	6	12	1	1	1	7	6	10	0	0	2-1	.218	.290	.327	.617	1	.952
1998— Clinton (Midw.)	C	115	380	47	97	22	0	3	55	47	69	7	16	7-9	.255	.343	.337	.680	14	.982
1999— Rancho Cuca. (Calif.)	C	120	427	58	140	26	2	7	61	40	54	5	12	2-7	.328	.389	.447	.836	5	.995
2000— Las Vegas (PCL)	PH	1	1	0	0	0	0	0	0	0	0	0	0	0-0	.000	.000	.000	.000	...	...
— Mobile (Sou.)	C-1B-2B	68	214	18	57	4	0	4	30	16	22	1	9	1-1	.266	.319	.341	.660	4	.991
— Rancho Cuca. (Calif.)	C	31	101	16	26	5	0	0	9	15	17	0	3	2-0	.257	.350	.307	.657	5	.984
2001— Mobile (Sou.)	C-1B-2B	95	330	28	99	24	0	3	41	18	40	2	8	1-0	.300	.336	.400	.736	3	.996
2002— Portland (PCL)	C-1B	70	237	24	73	20	2	7	29	5	40	0	7	0-0	.308	.321	.498	.819	3	.993

Year	Team (League)	Pos.	G	AB	R	H	2B	3B	HR	RBI	BB	SO	HBP	GDP	SB-CS	Avg.	OBP	SLG	OPS	E	Avg.
	— San Diego (N.L.)	C	28	72	2	13	3	1	0	3	4	15	0	...	1-0	.181	.224	.250	.474	5	.971
2003—	Salt Lake (PCL)	C-1B-3B	102	361	48	102	16	2	4	38	25	53	1	8	1-2	.283	.327	.371	.698	8	.988
2004—	Salt Lake (PCL)	C-1B-3B	108	421	60	125	22	8	10	53	12	64	0	11	3-6	.297	.316	.458	.774	7	.993
2005—	Columbus (Int'l)	C-DH	102	380	45	110	22	3	4	37	13	38	2	16	1-1	.289	.313	.395	.707	7	.991
	— New York (A.L.)	C	3	4	0	0	0	0	0	0	0	1	0	0	0-0	.000	.000	.000	.000	0	1.000
	American League totals (1 year)		3	4	0	0	0	0	0	0	0	1	0	0	0-0	.000	.000	.000	.000	0	1.000
	National League totals (1 year)		28	72	2	13	3	1	0	3	4	15	0	...	1-0	.181	.224	.250	.474	5	.971
	Major League totals (2 years)		31	76	2	13	3	1	0	3	4	16	0	...	1-0	.171	.213	.237	.449	5	.973

NIPPERT, DUSTIN   P

PERSONAL: Born May 6, 1981, in Wheeling, W.Va. ... 6-7/217. ... Throws right, bats right. ... Full name: Dustin David Nippert. ... High school: Beallsville (Ohio). ... College: West Virginia.

TRANSACTIONS/CAREER NOTES: Selected by Arizona Diamondbacks organization in 15th round of 2002 free-agent draft.

CAREER HITTING: 1-for-4 (.250), 0 R, 0 2B, 0 3B, 0 HR, 0 RBI.

DUSTIN NIPPERT'S PITCHING ZONE

.000	.000	.333
.125	.167	.231
.500	.200	.000

LEFTY-RIGHTY SPLITS

vs.	Avg.	AB	H	2B	3B	HR	RBI	BB	SO	OBP	Slg.
L	.182	22	4	2	0	0	1	9	6	.419	.273
R	.188	32	6	2	0	1	6	4	5	.297	.344

Year	Team (League)	W	L	Pct.	ERA	WHIP	G	GS	CG	ShO	Hld.	Sv.-Opp.	IP	H	R	ER	HR	BB-IBB	SO	Avg.
2002—	Missoula (Pion.)	4	2	.667	1.65	0.93	17	11	0	0	...	0-...	54.2	42	12	10	2	9-0	77	.208
2003—	South Bend (Mid.)	6	4	.600	2.82	1.02	17	17	0	0	...	0-...	95.2	66	32	30	4	32-3	96	.191
2004—	El Paso (Texas)	2	5	.286	3.64	1.63	14	14	0	0	...	0-...	71.2	77	45	29	0	40-1	73	.273
2005—	Tennessee (Sou.)	8	3	.727	2.38	1.17	18	18	3	2	0	0-0	117.1	95	33	31	4	42-1	97	.226
	— Missoula (Pion.)	1	1	.500	6.56	1.57	15	3	0	0	3	0-0	35.2	44	27	26	4	12-0	35	.291
	— Arizona (N.L.)	1	0	1.000	5.52	1.57	3	3	0	0	0	0-0	14.2	10	9	9	1	13-0	11	.185
	Major League totals (1 year)	1	0	1.000	5.52	1.57	3	3	0	0	0	0-0	14.2	10	9	9	1	13-0	11	.185

NITKOWSKI, C.J.   P

PERSONAL: Born March 9, 1973, in Suffern, N.Y. ... 6-3/200. ... Throws left, bats left. ... Full name: Christopher John Nitkowski. ... Name pronounced: nit-COW-ski. ... High school: Don Bosco Prep (N.J.). ... College: St. John's.

LEFTY-RIGHTY SPLITS

vs.	Avg.	AB	H	2B	3B	HR	RBI	BB	SO	OBP	Slg.
L	.571	7	4	1	0	0	1	2	2	.667	.714
R	.143	7	1	1	0	0	1	0	4	.143	.286

TRANSACTIONS/CAREER NOTES: Selected by Cincinnati Reds organization in first round (ninth pick overall) of 1994 free-agent draft. ... Traded by Reds with P David Tuttle and a player to be named to Detroit Tigers for P David Wells (July 31, 1995); Tigers acquired IF Mark Lewis to complete deal (November 16, 1995). ... On disabled list (August 11-29, 1996). ... Traded by Tigers with C Brad Ausmus, Ps Jose Lima and Trever Miller and 1B Daryle Ward to Houston Astros for OF Brian Hunter, IF Orlando Miller, Ps Doug Brocail and P Todd Jones and cash (December 10, 1996). ... Traded by Astros with C Brad Ausmus to Tigers for C Paul Bako, Ps Dean Crow, Mark Persails and Brian Powell and 3B Carlos Villalobos (January 14, 1999). ... On suspended list (May 28-30, 1999). ... Traded by Tigers with cash to New York Mets for a player to be named (September 1, 2001); Tigers acquired P Kyle Kessel to complete deal (December 13, 2001). ... Signed as a free agent by Astros organization (December 21, 2001). ... Released by Astros (June 6, 2002). ... Signed by St. Louis Cardinals organization (June 6, 2002). ... Released by Cardinals (July 21, 2002). ... Signed by Texas Rangers organization (July 29, 2002). ... Signed as a free agent by Atlanta Braves organization (December 6, 2003). ... Released by Braves (June 22, 2004). ... Signed by New York Yankees organization (June 29, 2004). ... Signed by Minnesota Twins organization (January 25, 2005). ... Released by Twins (May 27, 2005). ... Signed by Washington Nationals organization (May 27, 2005).

CAREER HITTING: 2-for-15 (.133), 1 R, 0 2B, 0 3B, 0 HR, 1 RBI.

Year	Team (League)	W	L	Pct.	ERA	WHIP	G	GS	CG	ShO	Hld.	Sv.-Opp.	IP	H	R	ER	HR	BB-IBB	SO	Avg.
1994—	Chattanooga (Sou.)	6	3	.667	3.50	1.35	14	14	0	0	...	0-...	74.2	61	30	29	4	40-0	60	.227
1995—	Chattanooga (Sou.)	4	2	.667	2.50	1.17	8	8	0	0	...	0-...	50.1	39	20	14	1	20-0	52	.217
	— Indianapolis (A.A.)	0	2	.000	5.20	1.37	6	6	0	0	...	0-...	27.2	28	16	16	3	10-0	21	.262
	— Cincinnati (N.L.)	1	3	.250	6.12	1.73	9	7	0	0	0	0-1	32.1	41	25	22	4	15-1	18	.306
	— Detroit (A.L.)	1	4	.200	7.09	1.86	11	11	0	0	0	0-0	39.1	53	32	31	7	20-2	13	.335
1996—	Toledo (Int'l)	4	6	.400	4.46	1.41	19	19	1	0	0	0-...	111.0	104	60	55	13	53-1	103	.254
	— Detroit (A.L.)	2	3	.400	8.08	2.19	11	8	0	0	0	0-0	45.2	62	44	41	7	38-1	36	.332
1997—	New Orleans (A.A.)	8	10	.444	3.98	1.37	28	28	1	0	...	0-...	174.1	183	82	77	10	56-2	* 141	.273
1998—	Houston (N.L.)	3	3	.500	3.77	1.21	43	0	0	0	8	3-5	59.2	49	27	25	4	23-2	44	.228
	— New Orleans (PCL)	0	1	.000	6.00	1.93	5	3	0	0	...	1-...	15.0	22	12	10	1	7-0	18	.338
1999—	Detroit (A.L.)	4	5	.444	4.30	1.32	68	7	0	0	11	0-0	81.2	63	44	39	11	45-3	66	.213
2000—	Detroit (A.L.)	4	9	.308	5.25	1.58	67	11	0	0	15	0-2	109.2	124	79	64	13	49-3	81	.286
2001—	Detroit (A.L.)	0	3	.000	5.56	1.81	56	0	0	0	6	0-6	45.1	51	30	28	7	31-7	38	.285
	— Toledo (Int'l)	0	0		0.00	1.00	1	0	0	0	0	0-...	1.0	1	0	0	0	0-0	1	.250
	— New York (N.L.)	1	0	1.000	0.00	1.06	5	0	0	0	0	0-0	5.2	3	0	0	0	3-1	4	.167
2002—	New Orleans (PCL)	1	2	.333	2.78	1.24	24	0	0	0	...	2-...	22.2	21	7	7	1	7-1	20	.244
	— Memphis (PCL)	1	2	.333	9.82	2.25	16	1	0	0	...	0-...	14.2	24	18	16	3	9-0	12	.348
	— Oklahoma (PCL)	1	1	.500	1.80	1.20	9	0	0	0	...	0-...	10.0	8	3	2	0	4-0	11	.211
	— Texas (A.L.)	0	1	.000	2.63	1.76	12	0	0	0	1	0-0	13.2	11	4	4	0	13-0	14	.224
2003—	Texas (A.L.)	0	0		7.45	2.59	6	0	0	0	1	0-0	9.2	17	8	8	0	8-1	5	.415
	— Oklahoma (PCL)	5	4	.556	4.09	1.50	33	6	0	0	...	2-...	81.1	88	40	37	6	31-2	53	.281
2004—	Atlanta (N.L.)	1	0	1.000	4.50	1.60	22	0	0	0	1	0-...	20.0	22	11	10	3	10-0	16	.275
	— Columbus (Int'l)	0	0		1.42	0.87	16	0	0	0	2	0-...	12.2	8	3	2	0	3-0	11	.182
	— New York (A.L.)	1	1	.500	7.62	1.85	19	0	0	0	0	0-0	13.0	18	11	11	4	6-0	15	.327
2005—	Indianapolis (Int'l)	2	0	1.000	0.83	0.69	18	0	0	0	8	2-2	21.2	6	5	2	0	9-0	18	.091
	— Was. (N.L.)	0	0		8.10	2.10	7	0	0	0	1	0-0	3.1	5	3	3	0	2-0	2	.357
	— New Orleans (PCL)	2	2	.500	3.62	1.33	27	0	0	0	6	4-4	32.1	36	15	13	3	7-0	24	.288
	American League totals (8 years)	12	26	.316	5.68	1.70	250	37	0	0	34	0-8	358.0	399	252	226	46	210-17	263	.285
	National League totals (5 years)	6	6	.500	4.46	1.43	86	7	0	0	9	3-6	121.0	120	66	60	11	53-4	84	.260
	Major League totals (10 years)	18	32	.360	5.37	1.63	336	44	0	0	43	3-14	479.0	519	318	286	57	263-21	347	.279

N

NIVAR, RAMON   OF

PERSONAL: Born February 22, 1980, in San Cristobal, Dominican Republic. ... 5-10/185. ... Bats right, throws right. ... Full name: Ramon A. Martinez Nivar. ... Name pronounced: nee-VAR.
TRANSACTIONS/CAREER NOTES: Signed as a non-drafted free agent by Texas Rangers organization (January 25, 1998). ... Traded by Rangers to Baltimore Orioles for P Matt Riley (March 30, 2005).
2005 GAMES PLAYED BY POSITION (MLB): OF—4.

LEFTY-RIGHTY SPLITS

vs.	Avg.	AB	H	2B	3B	HR	RBI	BB	SO	OBP	Slg.
L	.364	11	4	0	0	0	1	0	1	.364	.364
R	.000	2	0	0	0	0	0	0	1	.333	.000

Year Team (League)	Pos.	G	AB	R	H	2B	3B	HR	RBI	BB	SO	HBP	GDP	SB-CS	Avg.	OBP	SLG	OPS	E	Avg.
1998— Dom. Rangers (DSL)		54	179	23	51	13	0	3	21	8	7	4	8	2-7	.285	.328	.408	.736	...	...
1999— Dom. Rangers (DSL)		50	195	43	70	19	2	7	44	9	16	9	3	7-9	.359	.409	.585	.994	...	...
2000— Charlotte (Fla. St.)	SS-3B	42	152	12	44	7	1	1	20	5	28	0	2	8-3	.289	.310	.368	.679	11	.947
— Savannah (S. Atl.)	SS	39	164	19	51	9	0	1	17	2	29	3	3	6-5	.311	.331	.384	.716	15	.917
2001— Charlotte (Fla. St.)	2B-SS	128	515	69	124	20	1	2	32	28	65	5	7	28-18	.241	.286	.295	.581	29	.955
2002— Charlotte (Fla. St.)	2B-SS	114	472	98	144	21	8	3	41	32	44	6	15	39-15	.305	.353	.403	.755	10	.983
2003— Frisco (Texas)	2B-SS-OF	79	317	53	110	17	4	4	37	20	23	2	5	9-9	.347	.387	.464	.851	12	.970
— Oklahoma (PCL)	OF-2B	23	89	11	30	2	2	0	12	5	5	0	4	6-1	.337	.368	.472	.840	1	.987
— Texas (A.L.)	OF-DH	28	90	9	19	1	2	0	7	4	10	1	1	4-2	.211	.253	.267	.519	3	.961
2004— Texas (A.L.)	OF	7	18	3	4	0	0	0	4	0	7	0	0	1-1	.222	.211	.222	.433	0	1.000
— Oklahoma (PCL)	OF-2B-DH	113	462	62	122	21	0	10	52	14	43	4	10	15-15	.264	.290	.374	.665	5	.987
2005— Baltimore (A.L.)	OF	7	13	1	4	0	0	0	1	0	2	1	0	0-1	.308	.357	.308	.665	0	1.000
— Ottawa (Int'l)	OF-2B	33	111	13	22	4	0	1	5	3	10	2	4	9-4	.198	.231	.261	.492	7	.964
— Bowie (East.)	OF-DH	41	150	22	37	7	0	1	12	12	21	2	4	11-6	.247	.311	.313	.624	10	.941
Major League totals (3 years)		42	121	13	27	1	2	0	12	4	19	2	1	5-4	.223	.258	.264	.522	3	.970

NIX, LAYNCE   OF

PERSONAL: Born October 30, 1980, in Houston. ... 6-0/200. ... Bats left, throws left. ... Full name: Laynce Michael Nix. ... Name pronounced: nicks. ... High school: Midland (Texas).
TRANSACTIONS/CAREER NOTES: Selected by Texas Rangers organization in fourth round of 2000 free-agent draft. ... On disabled list (June 14-July 10, 2004); included rehabilitation assignment to Frisco. ... On disabled list (July 17, 2005-remainder of season).
2005 GAMES PLAYED BY POSITION (MLB): OF—61.

SCOUTING REPORT *Offense:* Nix has a short, inside-out stroke with a slight lift that makes him vulnerable to the ball upstairs. Has not defined his strike zone. Chases high fastballs and bad breaking balls. Has a chance for some power. Struggles with lefthanded pitching. Is a good runner but doesn't try to steal bases. *Defense:* Nix plays mostly in center, but he's not consistent with his jumps and doesn't always take good routes. Aggressive makeup can interfere with his instincts. Charges the ball well. Arm strength has improved but is not accurate with his throws. *Outlook:* Nix will hit 20 to 25 homers, but he needs to cut down his strikeouts. Is better suited to play a corner outfield spot but entered the offseason as the Rangers' center fielder. *Grade 6.2*

LAYNCE NIX'S HITTING ZONE

.286	.429	.273
.231	.400	.270
.000	.455	.167

LEFTY-RIGHTY SPLITS

vs.	Avg.	AB	H	2B	3B	HR	RBI	BB	SO	OBP	Slg.
L	.333	18	6	0	0	0	3	0	1	.333	.333
R	.232	211	49	12	3	6	29	9	44	.261	.403

Year Team (League)	Pos.	G	AB	R	H	2B	3B	HR	RBI	BB	SO	HBP	GDP	SB-CS	Avg.	OBP	SLG	OPS	E	Avg.
2000— GC Rangers (GCL)	OF	51	199	34	45	7	1	2	25	23	37	2	3	4-2	.226	.307	.302	.609	1	.991
2001— Savannah (S. Atl.)	OF	104	407	50	113	26	8	8	59	37	94	2	7	9-6	.278	.337	.440	.777	5	.976
— Charlotte (Fla. St.)	OF	9	37	4	11	3	1	0	2	1	13	0	2	0-0	.297	.316	.432	.748	0	1.000
2002— Charlotte (Fla. St.)	OF	137	512	86	146	27	3	21	110	72	105	6	9	17-11	.285	.374	.473	.847	3	.988
2003— Frisco (Texas)	OF-DH	87	335	52	95	23	0	15	63	34	68	0	4	9-2	.284	.344	.487	.831	3	.984
— Texas (A.L.)	OF-DH	53	184	25	47	10	0	8	30	9	53	0	1	3-0	.255	.289	.440	.729	5	.963
2004— Frisco (Texas)	OF	7	26	2	7	1	0	0	2	1	10	0	1	0-1	.269	.296	.308	.604	0	1.000
— Texas (A.L.)	OF	115	371	58	92	20	4	14	46	23	113	2	6	1-1	.248	.293	.437	.730	1	.996
2005— Oklahoma (PCL)	OF	10	36	8	12	1	1	3	6	9	6	0	0	0-1	.333	.467	.667	1.133	0	1.000
— Texas (A.L.)	OF	63	229	28	55	12	3	6	32	9	45	0	3	2-0	.240	.267	.397	.664	2	.988
Major League totals (3 years)		231	784	111	194	42	7	28	108	41	211	2	10	6-1	.247	.285	.426	.711	8	.985

NIXON, TROT   OF

PERSONAL: Born April 11, 1974, in Durham, N.C. ... 6-2/211. ... Bats left, throws left. ... Full name: Christopher Trotman Nixon. ... High school: New Hanover (Wilmington, N.C.).
TRANSACTIONS/CAREER NOTES: Selected by Boston Red Sox organization in first round (seventh pick overall) of 1993 free-agent draft. ... On disabled list (June 27-July 25, 2000); included rehabilitation assignment to GCL Red Sox. ... On disabled list (March 26-June 16 and July 25-September 7, 2004); included rehabilitation assignments to Pawtucket and Sarasota. ... On suspended list (May 3-5, 2005). ... On disabled list (July 27-August 23, 2005); included rehabilitation assignment to Pawtucket.
2005 GAMES PLAYED BY POSITION (MLB): OF—118, DH—2.

SCOUTING REPORT *Offense:* Nixon is an extremely aggressive hitter with a short stroke. Is a good high-ball hitter who can really get on top of the ball. Hits line drives and looks to pull the ball. Has become more disciplined at the plate. Stays on the breaking ball and goes the other way. Is good with runners in scoring position. Has problems with lefthanders. *Defense:* A natural right fielder with an average arm, Nixon is accurate when charging and throwing to bases. Has problems with balls hit directly at him. *Outlook:* Nixon is a hard-nosed and highly professional player. Has had injury issues, but when healthy is a very underrated player. Still is learning to channel his extreme competitiveness in a positive manner. *Grade 7*

TROT NIXON'S HITTING ZONE

.364	.357	.233
.220	.389	.354
.143	.278	.207

LEFTY-RIGHTY SPLITS

vs.	Avg.	AB	H	2B	3B	HR	RBI	BB	SO	OBP	Slg.
L	.224	85	19	2	1	1	9	12	18	.333	.306
R	.288	323	93	27	0	12	58	41	41	.364	.483

Year	Team (League)	Pos.	G	AB	R	H	2B	3B	HR	RBI	BB	SO	HBP	GDP	SB-CS	Avg.	OBP	SLG	OPS	E	Avg.
																			BATTING	FIELDING	
1994— Lynchburg (Caro.)	OF	71	264	33	65	12	0	12	43	44	53	3	5	10-3	.246	.357	.428	.785	4	.974
1995— Sarasota (Fla. St.)	OF	73	264	43	80	11	4	5	39	45	46	1	5	7-5	.303	.404	.432	.836	2	.986
— Trenton (East.)	OF	25	94	9	15	3	1	2	8	7	20	0	0	2-1	.160	.214	.277	.490	0	1.000
1996— Trenton (East.)	OF-DH	123	438	55	110	11	4	11	63	50	65	3	6	7-9	.251	.329	.370	.698	5	.979
— Boston (A.L.)	OF	2	4	2	2	1	0	0	0	0	1	0	0	1-0	.500	.500	.750	1.250	0	1.000
1997— Pawtucket (Int'l)	OF	130	475	80	116	18	3	20	61	63	86	1	11	11-4	.244	.331	.421	.753	4	.986
1998— Pawtucket (Int'l) OF-DH-1B	135	509	97	158	26	4	23	74	76	81	5	10	26-13	.310	.400	.513	.913	11	.957
— Boston (A.L.)	OF-DH	13	27	3	7	1	0	0	0	1	3	0	0	0-0	.259	.286	.296	.582	0	1.000
1999— Boston (A.L.)	OF	124	381	67	103	22	5	15	52	53	75	3	7	3-1	.270	.357	.472	.830	7	.968
2000— Boston (A.L.)	OF-DH	123	427	66	118	27	8	12	60	63	85	2	11	8-1	.276	.368	.461	.830	2	.991
— GC Red Sox (GCL)	OF	3	10	3	4	0	0	1	5	2	0	1	0	0-0	.400	.538	.700	1.238	0	1.000
2001— Boston (A.L.)	OF-DH	148	535	100	150	31	4	27	88	79	113	7	8	7-4	.280	.376	.505	.881	8	.973
2002— Boston (A.L.)	OF	152	532	81	136	36	3	24	94	65	109	5	7	4-2	.256	.338	.470	.808	5	.984
2003— Boston (A.L.)	OF-DH	134	441	81	135	24	6	28	87	65	96	3	4	4-2	.306	.396	.578	.975	4	.983
2004— Sarasota (Fla. St.)	OF	1	3	1	2	1	0	0	1	0	0	0	0	0-0	.667	.667	1.000	1.667	0	—
— Pawtucket (Int'l)	OF-DH	6	21	2	7	1	0	0	2	2	3	0	0	0-0	.333	.391	.381	.772	1	.750
— Boston (A.L.)	OF-DH	48	149	24	47	9	1	6	23	15	24	1	3	0-0	.315	.377	.510	.887	1	.985
2005— Pawtucket (Int'l)	OF-DH	2	6	3	3	0	0	1	2	2	2	0	0	0-0	.500	.556	1.000	1.556	0	1.000
— Boston (A.L.)	OF-DH	124	408	64	112	29	1	13	67	53	59	3	7	2-1	.275	.357	.446	.804	1	.996
Major League totals (9 years)		868	2904	488	810	180	28	125	471	394	565	24	46	29-11	.279	.366	.489	.855	28	.983

DIVISION SERIES RECORD

Year	Team (League)	Pos.	G	AB	R	H	2B	3B	HR	RBI	BB	SO	HBP	GDP	SB-CS	Avg.	OBP	SLG	OPS	E	Avg.
1998— Boston (A.L.)	OF	2	3	0	1	0	0	0	0	1	0	0	0	0-0	.333	.500	.333	.833	0	1.000
1999— Boston (A.L.)	OF	5	14	5	3	3	0	0	6	4	5	0	0	0-0	.214	.350	.429	.779	0	1.000
2003— Boston (A.L.)	OF	4	10	1	2	0	0	1	2	1	3	0	0	0-0	.200	.273	.500	.773	0	1.000
2004— Boston (A.L.)	OF	2	8	0	2	0	0	0	2	2	1	0	1	0-0	.250	.400	.250	.650	0	1.000
2005— Boston (A.L.)	OF	3	11	1	3	0	0	0	1	1	1	0	0	0-0	.273	.333	.273	.606	0	1.000
Division series totals (5 years)		16	46	7	11	3	0	1	11	9	10	0	1	0-0	.239	.351	.370	.720	0	1.000

CHAMPIONSHIP SERIES RECORD

Year	Team (League)	Pos.	G	AB	R	H	2B	3B	HR	RBI	BB	SO	HBP	GDP	SB-CS	Avg.	OBP	SLG	OPS	E	Avg.
1999— Boston (A.L.)	OF	4	14	2	4	2	0	0	1	5	0	0	0	0-0	.286	.333	.429	.762	0	1.000
2003— Boston (A.L.)	OF	7	24	3	8	1	0	3	5	3	7	1	1	1-2	.333	.429	.750	1.179	0	1.000
2004— Boston (A.L.)	OF	7	29	4	6	1	0	1	3	0	5	0	0	0-0	.207	.207	.345	.552	0	1.000
Champ. series totals (3 years)		18	67	9	18	4	0	4	8	4	17	1	1	1-2	.269	.319	.507	.827	0	1.000

WORLD SERIES RECORD

Year	Team (League)	Pos.	G	AB	R	H	2B	3B	HR	RBI	BB	SO	HBP	GDP	SB-CS	Avg.	OBP	SLG	OPS	E	Avg.
2004— Boston (A.L.)	OF	4	14	1	5	3	0	0	3	1	1	0	0	0-0	.357	.400	.571	.971	0	1.000

NOMO, HIDEO   P

PERSONAL: Born August 31, 1968, in Osaka, Japan. ... 6-2/210. ... Throws right, bats right. ... Name pronounced: hih-DAY-oh NO-mo. ... High school: Seijyo Kogyo (Japan).

TRANSACTIONS/CAREER NOTES: Signed as free agent by Los Angeles Dodgers organization (February 8, 1995). ... Loaned by Dodgers organization to Bakersfield of the California League (April 27-May 1, 1995). ... Traded by Dodgers with P Brad Clontz to New York Mets for Ps Dave Mlicki and Greg McMichael (June 4, 1998). ... Released by Mets (March 26, 1999). ... Signed by Chicago Cubs organization (April 2, 1999). ... Released by Cubs (April 23, 1999). ... Signed by Milwaukee Brewers organization (April 29, 1999). ... Claimed on waivers by Philadelphia Phillies (October 28, 1999). ... Signed as a free agent by Detroit Tigers organization (January 21, 2000). ... On disabled list (July 30-August 18, 2000). ... Released by Tigers (November 2, 2000). ... Signed by Boston Red Sox (December 15, 2000). ... Signed as a free agent by Dodgers (December 21, 2001). ... On disabled list (May 20-June 8 and July 1-September 1, 2004); included rehabilitation assignments to Las Vegas. ... Signed as a free agent by Tampa Bay Devil Rays organization (January 27, 2005). ... Released by Devil Rays (July 25, 2005). ... Signed by New York Yankees organization (July 27, 2005).

HONORS: Named N.L. Rookie Pitcher of the Year by THE SPORTING NEWS (1995). ... Named N.L. Rookie of the Year by Baseball Writers' Association of America (1995).

CAREER HITTING: 65-for-485 (.134), 22 R, 14 2B, 1 3B, 4 HR, 26 RBI.

HIDEO NOMO'S PITCHING ZONE

.273	.200	.250
.406	.438	.296
.300	.433	.308

LEFTY-RIGHTY SPLITS

vs.	Avg.	AB	H	2B	3B	HR	RBI	BB	SO	OBP	Slg.
L	.270	200	54	9	1	5	28	28	31	.362	.400
R	.356	205	73	16	2	11	47	23	28	.410	.615

Year	Team (League)	W	L	Pct.	ERA	WHIP	G	GS	CG	ShO	Hld.	Sv.-Opp.	IP	H	R	ER	HR	BB-IBB	SO	Avg.
1990— Kintetsu (Jp. Pac.)	18	8	.692	2.91	1.17	29	27	21	2	...	0-...	235.0	167	...	76	...	109-...	287	...
1991— Kintetsu (Jp. Pac.)	17	11	.607	3.05	1.28	31	29	22	4	...	1-...	242.1	183	...	82	...	128-...	287	...
1992— Kintetsu (Jp. Pac.)	18	8	.692	2.66	1.23	30	29	17	5	...	0-...	216.2	150	...	64	...	117-...	228	...
1993— Kintetsu (Jp. Pac.)	17	12	.586	3.70	1.43	32	32	14	2	...	0-...	243.1	201	...	100	...	148-...	276	...
1994— Kintetsu (Jp. Pac.)	8	7	.533	3.63	0.75	17	17	6	0	...	0-...	114.0	...	...	46	...	86-...	126	...
1995— Bakersfield (Calif.)	0	1	.000	3.38	1.31	1	1	0	0	...	0-...	5.1	6	2	2	0	1-0	6	.273
— Los Angeles (N.L.)	13	6	.684	2.54	1.06	28	28	4	•3	0	0-0	191.1	124	63	54	14	78-2	*236	*.182
1996— Los Angeles (N.L.)	16	11	.593	3.19	1.16	33	33	3	2	0	0-0	228.1	180	93	81	23	85-6	234	.218
1997— Los Angeles (N.L.)	14	12	.538	4.25	1.37	33	33	1	0	0	0-0	207.1	193	104	98	23	92-2	233	.243
1998— Los Angeles (N.L.)	2	7	.222	5.05	1.40	12	12	0	0	0	0-0	67.2	57	39	38	8	38-0	73	.228
— New York (N.L.)	4	5	.444	4.82	1.44	17	16	1	0	0	0-0	89.2	73	49	48	11	56-2	94	.224
1999— Iowa (PCL)	1	1	.500	3.71	1.41	3	3	0	0	...	0-...	17.0	12	7	7	1	12-0	18	.200
— Huntsville (Sou.)	1	0	1.000	0.00	0.86	1	1	0	0	...	0-...	7.0	5	0	0	0	1-0	7	.217
— Milwaukee (N.L.)	12	8	.600	4.54	1.42	28	28	1	0	0	0-0	176.1	173	96	89	27	78-2	161	.250
2000— Detroit (A.L.)	8	12	.400	4.74	1.47	32	31	1	0	0	0-0	190.0	191	102	100	31	89-1	181	.263
2001— Boston (A.L.)	13	10	.565	4.50	1.35	33	33	2	2	0	0-0	198.0	171	105	99	26	*96-2	*220	.231
2002— Los Angeles (N.L.)	16	6	.727	3.39	1.32	34	34	0	0	0	0-0	220.1	189	92	83	26	101-5	193	.236
2003— Los Angeles (N.L.)	16	13	.552	3.09	1.25	33	33	2	2	0	0-0	218.1	175	82	75	24	98-6	177	.223
2004— Las Vegas (PCL)	1	1	.500	5.71	1.73	4	4	0	0	...	0-...	17.1	22	11	11	4	8-0	25	.324
— Los Angeles (N.L.)	4	11	.267	8.25	1.75	18	18	0	0	0	0-0	84.0	105	77	77	19	42-1	54	.312
2005— Tampa Bay (A.L.)	5	8	.385	7.24	1.77	19	19	0	0	0	0-0	100.2	127	82	81	16	51-2	59	.314
— Columbus (Int'l)	2	3	.400	3.62	1.39	7	7	0	0	...	0-...	37.1	30	19	15	1	22-1	41	.221
American League totals (3 years)	26	30	.464	5.16	1.48	84	83	3	2	0	0-0	488.2	489	289	280	73	236-5	460	.261

Year Team (League)	W	L	Pct.	ERA	WHIP	G	GS	CG	ShO	Hld.	Sv.-Opp.	IP	H	R	ER	HR	BB-IBB	SO	Avg.
National League totals (8 years)	97	79	.551	3.90	1.31	236	235	13	7	0	0-0	1483.1	1269	695	643	175	668-26	1455	.232
Major League totals (11 years)	123	109	.530	4.21	1.35	320	318	16	9	0	0-0	1972.0	1758	984	923	248	904-31	1915	.239

DIVISION SERIES RECORD

Year Team (League)	W	L	Pct.	ERA	WHIP	G	GS	CG	ShO	Hld.	Sv.-Opp.	IP	H	R	ER	HR	BB-IBB	SO	Avg.
1995—Los Angeles (N.L.)	0	1	.000	9.00		1	1	0	0	0	0-0	5.0	7	5	5	2	2-1	6	.318
1996—Los Angeles (N.L.)	0	1	.000	12.27	2.73	1	1	0	0	0	0-0	3.2	5	5	5	1	5-0	3	.333
Division series totals (2 years)	0	2	.000	10.38	2.19	2	2	0	0	0	0-0	8.2	12	10	10	3	7-1	9	.324

ALL-STAR GAME RECORD

Year Team (League)	W	L	Pct.	ERA	WHIP	G	GS	CG	ShO	Hld.	Sv.-Opp.	IP	H	R	ER	HR	BB-IBB	SO	Avg.
All-Star Game totals (1 year)	0	0	...	0.00	0.50	1	1	0	0	0	0-0	2.0	1	0	0	0	0-0	3	.167

NOVOA, ROBERTO   P

PERSONAL: Born August 15, 1979, in Las Matas de Farfan, Dominican Republic. ... 6-5/200. ... Throws right, bats right.
TRANSACTIONS/CAREER NOTES: Signed as a non-drafted free agent by Pittsburgh Pirates organization (July 3, 1999). ... Traded by Pirates to Detroit Tigers (December 17, 2002), as part of deal in which Pirates acquired 1B Randall Simon for P Adrian Burnside and two players to be named (November 25, 2002); Tigers acquired 3B Kody Kirkland to complete deal (May 24, 2003). ... Traded by Tigers with SS Scott Moore and OF Bo Flowers to Chicago Cubs for P Kyle Farnsworth (February 9, 2005).
CAREER HITTING: 0-for-1 (.000), 0 R, 0 2B, 0 3B, 0 HR, 0 RBI.

SCOUTING REPORT *Throws:* His four-seam fastball gets up to 95 mph. Also has a slider, sinker and split-finger fastball. *Tendencies:* Novoa is a classic "grip-and-rip" pitcher. Mechanics surprisingly do not affect his command. Has a tendency to overly rely on his changeup and splitter. Has to be aggressive with his fastball. Has enough command to throw either his fastball or slider at any point in the count. Is a good athlete for his size. *Outlook:* Novoa pitched well enough with the Cubs to put himself in line for a seventh-inning role. Depends on how he pitches in spring training. *Grade 6.5*

ROBERTO NOVOA'S PITCHING ZONE

.250	.273	.333
.414	.364	.350
.143	.333	.300

LEFTY-RIGHTY SPLITS

vs.	Avg.	AB	H	2B	3B	HR	RBI	BB	SO	OBP	Slg.
L	.221	68	15	3	0	2	8	12	24	.338	.353
R	.291	110	32	7	3	2	15	13	23	.366	.464

Year Team (League)	W	L	Pct.	ERA	WHIP	G	GS	CG	ShO	Hld.	Sv.-Opp.	IP	H	R	ER	HR	BB-IBB	SO	Avg.
2000—Dom. Pirates (NYP)	4	6	.400	4.15	1.55	13	13	1	0	...	0-...	82.0	99	65	38	5	29-...	44	.289
2001—Williamsport (NYP)	5	5	.500	3.39	1.21	14	13	1	0	...	0-...	79.2	76	40	30	4	20-0	55	.255
2002—Hickory (S. Atl.)	1	5	.167	5.48	1.78	10	10	0	0	...	0-...	42.2	61	30	26	2	15-0	29	.335
—Williamsport (NYP)	8	3	.727	3.65	1.05	12	12	0	0	...	0-...	66.2	62	32	27	4	8-0	56	.240
2003—Lakeland (Fla. St.)	4	5	.444	3.73	1.19	19	15	2	0	...	0-...	99.0	93	45	41	8	25-0	71	.243
2004—Erie (East.)	7	0	1.000	2.96	1.03	41	0	0	0	...	4-...	79.0	63	32	26	7	18-1	59	.216
—Detroit (A.L.)	1	1	.500	5.57	1.48	16	0	0	0	3	0-1	21.0	25	15	13	4	6-0	15	.309
2005—Iowa (PCL)	2	2	.500	3.29	1.13	19	0	0	0	2	4-5	27.1	20	11	10	1	11-1	18	.217
—Chicago (N.L.)	4	5	.444	4.43	1.61	49	0	0	0	14	0-5	44.2	47	22	22	4	25-6	47	.264
American League totals (1 year)	1	1	.500	5.57	1.48	16	0	0	0	3	0-1	21.0	25	15	13	4	6-0	15	.309
National League totals (1 year)	4	5	.444	4.43	1.61	49	0	0	0	14	0-5	44.2	47	22	22	4	25-6	47	.264
Major League totals (2 years)	5	6	.455	4.80	1.57	65	0	0	0	17	0-6	65.2	72	37	35	8	31-6	62	.278

NUNEZ, ABRAHAM O.   3B/2B

PERSONAL: Born March 16, 1976, in Santo Domingo, Dominican Republic. ... 5-11/190. ... Bats both, throws right. ... Full name: Abraham Orlando Nunez. ... Name pronounced: NOON-yez. ... High school: Emmanuel (Santo Domingo, Dominican Republic).
TRANSACTIONS/CAREER NOTES: Signed as a non-drafted free agent by Toronto Blue Jays organization (May 5, 1994). ... Traded by Blue Jays with P Mike Halperin and C/OF Craig Wilson to Pittsburgh Pirates (December 11, 1996), completing deal in which Blue Jays traded Ps Jose Silva and Jose Pett, IF Brandon Cromer and three players to be named to Pirates for OF/1B Orlando Merced, IF Carlos Garcia and P Dan Plesac (November 14, 1996). ... Released by Pirates (November 29, 2004). ... Signed by St. Louis Cardinals' organization (December 25, 2004). ... Career major league pitching: 0-0, 0.00 ERA, 1 G, 0.1 IP, 0 H, 0 R, 0 ER, 0 BB, 0 SO
2005 GAMES PLAYED BY POSITION (MLB): 3B—98, 2B—22, SS—21.

SCOUTING REPORT Nunez gets on top of the ball and has some bat speed. Has limited power and is better hitting righthanded. Has quick feet, soft hands and very good reflexes. Has good first-step quickness to the line. Has a strong but sometimes erratic arm. Is an average runner but doesn't steal bases. *Grade 7.3*

N

ABRAHAM O. NUNEZ'S HITTING ZONE

.158	.381	.370
.298	.375	.240
.250	.136	.289

LEFTY-RIGHTY SPLITS

vs.	Avg.	AB	H	2B	3B	HR	RBI	BB	SO	OBP	Slg.
L	.324	74	24	2	0	1	8	9	9	.398	.392
R	.277	347	96	11	2	4	36	28	54	.331	.354

Year Team (League)	Pos.	G	AB	R	H	2B	3B	HR	RBI	BB	SO	HBP	GDP	SB-CS	Avg.	OBP	SLG	OPS	E	Avg.
1994—Dom. B. Jays (DSL)	2B	59	188	31	47	5	0	0	15	42	37			22-...	.250		.277	...	12	.938
1995—Dom. B. Jays (DSL)	2B	54	186	49	56	10	3	4	25	30	27			24-...	.301		.452	...	7	.962
1996—St. Catharines (NYP)	2B-SS	75	*297	43	83	6	4	3	26	31	43	4	2	37-14	.279	.353	.357	.710	15	.962
1997—Lynchburg (Caro.)	SS	78	304	45	79	9	4	3	32	23	47	1	5	29-14	.260	.313	.345	.658	15	.955
—Carolina (Southern)	SS	47	198	31	65	6	1	1	14	20	28	0	2	10-5	.328	.385	.384	.768	11	.949
—Pittsburgh (N.L.)	SS-2B	19	40	3	9	2	2	0	6	3	10	1	1	1-0	.225	.289	.375	.664	0	1.000
1998—Nashville (PCL)	SS	94	366	50	91	12	3	3	32	39	73	5	9	16-8	.249	.328	.322	.651	21	.953
—Lynchburg (Caro.)	SS-2B	5	18	2	4	1	0	0	2	3	1	0	2	1-0	.222	.333	.278	.611	1	.960
—Pittsburgh (N.L.)	SS	24	52	6	10	2	0	1	2	12	14	0	1	4-2	.192	.344	.288	.632	7	.930
1999—Pittsburgh (N.L.)	SS-2B	90	259	25	57	8	0	0	17	28	54	1	2	9-1	.220	.299	.251	.550	14	.959

Year	Team (League)	Pos.	G	AB	R	H	2B	3B	HR	RBI	BB	SO	HBP	GDP	SB-CS	Avg.	OBP	SLG	OPS	E	Avg.
— Nashville (PCL)	SS	15	58	12	18	0	0	0	3	5	8	0	2	1-0	.310	.365	.310	.675	2	.971
2000— Pittsburgh (N.L.)	SS-2B	40	91	10	20	1	0	1	8	8	14	0	3	0-0	.220	.283	.264	.547	2	.982
— Nashville (PCL)	SS-2B	90	351	49	97	11	1	3	29	36	46	1	7	20-6	.276	.344	.339	.683	13	.970
2001— Pittsburgh (N.L.)	2B-SS-3B																			
	OF	115	301	30	79	11	4	1	21	28	53	1	0	8-2	.262	.326	.336	.662	4	.990
2002— Pittsburgh (N.L.)	2B-SS-DH	112	253	28	59	14	1	2	15	27	44	2	2	3-4	.233	.311	.320	.631	7	.977
— Nashville (PCL)	SS-2B-OF	5	18	3	4	0	0	0	0	2	7	0	0	4-1	.222	.300	.222	.522	0	1.000
2003— Pittsburgh (N.L.)	2B-SS-3B	118	311	37	77	8	7	4	35	26	53	3	8	9-3	.248	.310	.357	.667	8	.980
2004— Pittsburgh (N.L.)	2B-SS-3B																			
	DH-P	112	182	17	43	9	0	2	13	10	36	0	8	1-3	.236	.275	.319	.593	3	.982
2005— St. Louis (N.L.)	3B-2B-SS	139	421	64	120	13	2	5	44	37	63	0	6	0-1	.285	.343	.361	.704	14	.963
Major League totals (9 years)		769	1910	220	474	68	16	16	161	179	341	8	31	35-16	.248	.314	.326	.640	59	.974

DIVISION SERIES RECORD

Year	Team (League)	Pos.	G	AB	R	H	2B	3B	HR	RBI	BB	SO	HBP	GDP	SB-CS	Avg.	OBP	SLG	OPS	E	Avg.
2005— St. Louis (N.L.)	3B	3	11	3	4	1	0	0	2	3	0	0	0	1-0	.364	.462	.455	.916	0	1.000

CHAMPIONSHIP SERIES RECORD

Year	Team (League)	Pos.	G	AB	R	H	2B	3B	HR	RBI	BB	SO	HBP	GDP	SB-CS	Avg.	OBP	SLG	OPS	E	Avg.
2005— St. Louis (N.L.)	3B	4	13	1	5	0	0	0	0	0	1	0	0	0-0	.385	.385	.385	.769	0	1.000

NUNEZ, FRANKLIN P

PERSONAL: Born January 18, 1977, in Nagua, Dominican Republic. ... 6-0/175. ... Throws right, bats right. ... Name pronounced: NOON-yez. ... High school: Escuela Cano Abajo (Dominican Republic).

TRANSACTIONS/CAREER NOTES: Signed as non-drafted free agent by Los Angeles Dodgers organization (September 1, 1994). ... Released by Dodgers (January 12, 1996). ... Signed by Philadelphia Phillies organization (June 20, 1998). ... On disabled list (July 13, 1999-remainder of season). ... Claimed on waivers by New York Mets (October 10, 2002). ... Signed as a free agent by Tampa Bay Devil Rays organization (February 13, 2004). ... On disabled list (March 25-May 28, 2005); included rehabilitation assignment to Durham.

CAREER HITTING: 0-for-0 (.000), 0 R, 0 2B, 0 3B, 0 HR, 0 RBI.

LEFTY-RIGHTY SPLITS

vs.	Avg.	AB	H	2B	3B	HR	RBI	BB	SO	OBP	Slg.
L	.333	6	2	0	0	0	2	2	0	.500	.333
R	.250	12	3	0	0	0	1	2	2	.357	.250

Year	Team (League)	W	L	Pct.	ERA	WHIP	G	GS	CG	ShO	Hld.	Sv.-Opp.	IP	H	R	ER	HR	BB-IBB	SO	Avg.
1995— Dom. Dodgers (DSL)	1	0	1.000	7.36	2.14	12	1	0	0	...	0-...	22.0	27	25	18	...	20-...	17	...
1996—	Did not play.																		
1997—	Did not play.																		
1998— Dom. Phillies (DSL)	0	2	.000	2.18	1.12	5	5	1	0	...	0-...	33.0	23	14	8	...	14-...	37	...
— Martinsville (App.)	2	2	.500	2.49	1.22	6	4	0	0	...	0-...	25.1	23	10	7	0	8-0	19	.232
1999— Piedmont (S. Atl.)	4	8	.333	3.39	1.22	13	13	1	0	...	0-...	77.0	69	39	29	4	25-0	88	.238
2000— Clearwater (FSL)	10	4	.714	3.62	1.51	23	14	1	0	...	2-...	112.0	112	54	45	4	57-0	81	.264
2001— Reading (East.)	8	7	.533	4.42	1.44	39	14	0	0	...	3-...	110.0	107	68	54	9	51-3	112	.252
2002— Scran./W.B. (I.L.)	2	1	.667	3.18	1.24	4	4	0	0	...	0-...	17.0	9	6	6	2	12-0	16	.158
— GC Phillies (GCL)	0	0	...	0.00	1.50	1	1	0	0	...	0-...	2.0	2	0	0	0	1-0	4	.250
2003— Brooklyn (N.Y.-Penn.)	0	0	...	5.06	1.69	7	0	0	0	...	0-...	5.1	5	4	3	0	4-0	8	.250
2004— Montgom. (Sou.)	0	1	.000	0.84	0.66	6	0	0	0	...	0-...	10.2	4	3	1	0	3-0	19	.114
— Durham (Int'l)	4	2	.667	2.81	1.36	40	0	0	0	...	9-...	51.1	36	21	16	1	34-0	70	.193
— Tampa Bay (A.L.)	0	3	.000	5.91	1.69	8	0	0	0	...	0-1	10.2	11	8	7	1	7-0	14	.268
2005— Tampa Bay (A.L.)	1	0	1.000	10.80	1.80	5	0	0	0	0	0-0	5.0	5	6	6	0	4-0	2	.250
— Durham (Int'l)	5	1	.833	6.34	1.62	27	0	0	0	4	3-5	32.2	32	27	23	1	21-0	34	.254
Major League totals (2 years)	1	3	.250	7.47	1.72	13	0	0	0	1	0-1	15.2	16	14	13	1	11-0	16	.271

NUNEZ, LEO P

PERSONAL: Born August 14, 1983, in Jamoa Norte, Dominican Republic. ... 6-1/160. ... Throws right, bats right. ... Full name: Leonel Nunez.

TRANSACTIONS/CAREER NOTES: Signed as a non-drafted free agent by Pittsburgh Pirates organization (February 16, 2000). ... Traded by Pirates to Kansas City Royals for C Benito Santiago (December 16, 2004).

CAREER HITTING: 0-for-0 (.000), 0 R, 0 2B, 0 3B, 0 HR, 0 RBI.

LEO NUNEZ'S PITCHING ZONE

.417	.308	.294
.372	.233	.368
.571	.333	.231

LEFTY-RIGHTY SPLITS

vs.	Avg.	AB	H	2B	3B	HR	RBI	BB	SO	OBP	Slg.
L	.374	91	34	7	2	4	29	10	9	.431	.626
R	.298	131	39	8	0	5	24	8	23	.350	.473

Year	Team (League)	W	L	Pct.	ERA	WHIP	G	GS	CG	ShO	Hld.	Sv.-Opp.	IP	H	R	ER	HR	BB-IBB	SO	Avg.
2000— Pittsburgh (DSL)	5	3	.625	2.19	1.12	14	14	1	0	...	0-...	86.0	69	26	21	0	27-0	82	...
2001— GC Pirates (GCL)	2	2	.500	4.39	1.33	10	7	1	1	...	0-...	53.1	62	28	26	4	9-0	34	.284
2002— GC Pirates (GCL)	4	2	.667	3.43	0.98	11	11	0	0	...	0-...	60.1	54	23	23	5	5-0	52	.238
— Hickory (S. Atl.)	0	0	...	0.00	2.00	1	1	0	0	...	0-...	4.0	5	0	0	0	3-0	1	.333
2003— Hickory (S. Atl.)	2	1	.667	5.59	1.51	13	7	0	0	...	0-...	48.1	59	34	30	6	14-0	37	.304
— Williamsport (NYP)	4	3	.571	3.05	1.12	8	8	0	0	...	0-...	38.1	31	14	13	0	12-0	41	.211
2004— Hickory (S. Atl.)	10	4	.714	3.06	1.16	27	20	3	0	...	1-...	144.0	121	53	49	16	46-0	140	.233
2005— High Desert (Calif.)	0	0	...	9.00	2.00	8	0	0	0	2	0-2	13.0	23	15	13	2	3-2	15	.377
— Wichita (Texas)	1	0	1.000	0.69	0.77	12	0	0	0	4	4-4	13.0	8	3	1	0	2-0	14	.170
— Kansas City (A.L.)	3	2	.600	7.55	1.70	41	0	0	0	2	0-1	53.2	73	45	45	9	18-2	32	.329
Major League totals (1 year)	3	2	.600	7.55	1.70	41	0	0	0	2	0-1	53.2	73	45	45	9	18-2	32	.329

OBERMUELLER, WES — P

PERSONAL: Born December 22, 1976, in Cedar Rapids, Iowa. ... 6-2/209. ... Throws right, bats right. ... Full name: Wesley Mitchell Obermueller. ... High school: Washington (Vinton, Iowa). ... College: Iowa.
TRANSACTIONS/CAREER NOTES: Selected by Kansas City Royals organization in second round of 1999 free-agent draft. ... Traded by Royals to Milwaukee Brewers for P Curtis Leskanic (July 2, 2003).
CAREER HITTING: 21-for-77 (.273), 4 R, 4 2B, 1 3B, 0 HR, 6 RBI.

WES OBERMUELLER'S PITCHING ZONE

.238	.538	.294
.304	.409	.250
.208	.474	.071

LEFTY-RIGHTY SPLITS

vs.	Avg.	AB	H	2B	3B	HR	RBI	BB	SO	OBP	Slg.
L	.262	103	27	1	0	3	15	19	11	.381	.359
R	.307	153	47	11	1	4	21	17	22	.383	.471

Year	Team (League)	W	L	Pct.	ERA	WHIP	G	GS	CG	ShO	Hld.	Sv.-Opp.	IP	H	R	ER	HR	BB-IBB	SO	Avg.
1999—	GC Royals (GCL)	2	1	.667	2.58	1.17	11	7	0	0	...	0-...	38.1	33	16	11	2	12-1	39	.228
2000—	Char., W.Va. (SAL)	3	0	1.000	1.14	0.76	8	7	0	0	...	0-...	31.2	19	6	4	0	5-0	29	.174
2001—	Wilmington (Caro.)	0	2	.000	3.08	1.42	20	6	0	0	...	0-...	38.0	38	15	13	3	16-1	28	.266
2002—	Wilmington (Caro.)	5	0	1.000	2.76	1.14	8	4	0	0	...	0-...	45.2	38	14	14	1	14-0	44	.228
—	Wichita (Texas)	9	5	.643	2.90	1.31	17	17	0	0	...	0-...	105.2	98	39	34	6	40-3	65	.250
—	Kansas City (A.L.)	0	2	.000	11.74	2.09	2	2	0	0	0	0-0	7.2	14	10	10	3	2-0	5	.378
2003—	Omaha (PCL)	10	5	.667	4.40	1.40	17	17	2	0	...	0-...	106.1	108	61	52	11	42-1	62	.262
—	Indianapolis (Int'l)	0	2	.000	4.70	1.60	3	3	0	0	...	0-...	15.1	19	9	8	1	6-0	11	.300
—	Milwaukee (N.L.)	2	5	.286	5.07	1.61	12	11	0	0	0	0-0	65.2	81	40	37	10	25-2	34	.301
2004—	Indianapolis (Int'l)	0	3	.000	5.19	1.42	4	4	1	0	...	0-...	26.0	30	16	15	3	7-0	17	.294
—	Milwaukee (N.L.)	6	8	.429	5.80	1.53	25	20	1	1	0	0-0	118.0	138	80	76	15	42-0	59	.291
2005—	Nashville (PCL)	3	1	.750	2.55	1.25	9	8	0	0	0	1-1	42.1	39	14	12	1	14-0	39	.255
—	Milwaukee (N.L.)	1	4	.200	5.26	1.69	23	8	0	0	0	0-0	65.0	74	41	38	7	36-2	33	.289
American League totals (1 year)		0	2	.000	11.74	2.09	2	2	0	0	0	0-0	7.2	14	10	10	3	2-0	5	.378
National League totals (3 years)		9	17	.346	5.47	1.59	60	39	1	1	0	0-0	248.2	293	161	151	32	103-4	126	.293
Major League totals (4 years)		9	19	.321	5.65	1.61	62	41	1	1	0	0-0	256.1	307	171	161	35	105-4	131	.296

OFFERMAN, JOSE — 1B

PERSONAL: Born November 11, 1968, in San Pedro de Macoris, Dominican Republic. ... 6-0/192. ... Bats both, throws right. ... Full name: Jose Antonio Offerman. ... High school: Colegio Biblico Cristiano (Dominican Republic).
TRANSACTIONS/CAREER NOTES: Signed as a non-drafted free agent by Los Angeles Dodgers organization (July 24, 1986). ... Traded by Dodgers to Kansas City Royals for P Billy Brewer (December 17, 1995). ... On disabled list (April 6-29, July 7-22 and August 14-September 6, 1997). ... Signed as a free agent by Boston Red Sox (November 16, 1998). ... On disabled list (May 27-June 10 and July 30-August 16, 2000). ... Traded by Red Sox to Seattle Mariners for cash considerations (August 8, 2002). ... Signed as a free agent by Montreal Expos organization (February 25, 2003). ... Released by Expos (March 28, 2003). ... Signed as a free agent by Minnesota Twins organization (February 10, 2004). ... Signed as a free agent by Philadelphia Phillies organization (January 19, 2005). ... Released by Phillies (May 25, 2005). ... Signed by New York Mets organization (June 8, 2005).
HONORS: Named Minor League Player of the Year by THE SPORTING NEWS (1990).
2005 GAMES PLAYED BY POSITION (MLB): 1B—15, 2B—1.

JOSE OFFERMAN'S HITTING ZONE

.000	.000	.333
.111	.467	.217
.333	.167	.250

LEFTY-RIGHTY SPLITS

vs.	Avg.	AB	H	2B	3B	HR	RBI	BB	SO	OBP	Slg.
L	.111	27	3	0	0	0	1	4	4	.226	.111
R	.269	78	21	3	1	2	12	7	13	.337	.410

Year	Team (League)	Pos.	G	AB	R	H	2B	3B	HR	RBI	BB	SO	HBP	GDP	SB-CS	Avg.	OBP	SLG	OPS	E	Avg.
1987—						Did not play.															
1988—	Vero Beach (FSL)	SS	4	14	4	4	2	0	0	2	2	0	0	0	0-0	.286	.375	.429	.804	5	.643
—	Great Falls (Pio.)	SS	60	251	75	83	11	5	2	28	38	42	2	3	57-10	.331	.421	.438	.859	18	.926
1989—	Bakersfield (Calif.)	SS	62	245	53	75	9	4	2	22	35	48	2	5	37-13	.306	.396	.400	.796	30	.901
—	San Antonio (Texas)	SS	68	278	47	80	6	3	2	22	40	39	1	1	32-13	.288	.379	.353	.732	20	.932
1990—	Albuquerque (PCL)	2B-SS	117	454	104	148	16	11	0	56	71	81	2	7	60-19	.326	.416	.410	.826	36	.937
—	Los Angeles (N.L.)	SS	29	58	7	9	0	0	1	7	4	14	0	0	1-0	.155	.210	.207	.417	4	.946
1991—	Albuquerque (PCL)	SS	79	289	58	86	8	4	0	29	47	58	0	5	32-15	.298	.396	.353	.749	17	.956
—	Los Angeles (N.L.)	SS	52	113	10	22	2	0	0	3	25	32	1	5	3-2	.195	.345	.212	.558	10	.945
1992—	Los Angeles (N.L.)	SS	149	534	67	139	20	8	1	30	57	98	0	5	23-16	.260	.331	.333	.664	* 42	.935
1993—	Los Angeles (N.L.)	SS	158	590	77	159	21	6	1	62	71	75	2	12	30-13	.269	.346	.331	.676	* 37	.950
1994—	Los Angeles (N.L.)	SS	72	243	27	51	8	4	1	25	38	38	0	6	2-1	.210	.314	.288	.603	11	.967
—	Albuquerque (PCL)	SS	56	224	43	74	7	5	1	31	37	48	0	4	9-4	.330	.419	.420	.839	13	.957
1995—	Los Angeles (N.L.)	SS	119	429	69	123	14	6	4	33	69	67	3	5	2-7	.287	.389	.375	.765	* 35	.932
1996—	Kansas City (A.L.)	1B-2B-SS OF	151	561	85	170	33	8	5	47	74	98	1	9	24-10	.303	.384	.417	.801	16	.986
1997—	Kansas City (A.L.)	2B-DH	106	424	59	126	23	6	2	39	41	64	0	5	9-10	.297	.359	.394	.753	9	.981
1998—	Kansas City (A.L.)	2B-DH	158	607	102	191	28	* 13	7	66	89	96	5	7	45-12	.315	.403	.438	.841	19	.974
1999—	Boston (A.L.)	2B-DH-1B	149	586	107	172	37	* 11	8	69	96	79	2	11	18-12	.294	.391	.435	.826	14	.977
2000—	Boston (A.L.)	2B-1B-DH	116	451	73	115	14	3	9	41	70	70	1	9	0-8	.255	.354	.359	.713	11	.983
2001—	Boston (A.L.)	2B-1B	128	524	76	140	23	3	9	49	61	97	1	9	5-2	.267	.342	.374	.716	14	.982
2002—	Boston (A.L.)	1B-DH-OF	72	237	39	55	10	0	4	27	33	29	1	9	8-5	.232	.325	.325	.650	3	.991
—	Seattle (A.L.)	1B-OF-DH 2B	29	47	9	11	2	1	1	4	4	9	0	3	1-1	.234	.294	.383	.677	0	1.000
2003—	Bridgeport (Atl.)		98	356	55	105	24	5	9	60	54	58	2	...	5-2	.295	.383	.466	.849	...	...
2004—	Minnesota (A.L.)	DH-1B-2B	77	172	22	44	14	2	2	22	29	31	0	1	1-1	.256	.363	.395	.759	3	.955
2005—	Philadelphia (N.L.)	1B	33	33	6	6	1	1	1	3	5	6	0	1	0-0	.182	.289	.364	.653	1	.938
—	New York (N.L.)	1B-2B	53	72	5	18	2	0	1	10	6	11	1	3	0-0	.250	.316	.319	.636	1	.988
American League totals (8 years)			986	3609	572	1024	184	47	47	364	497	573	11	63	111-61	.284	.370	.400	.770	89	.982
National League totals (7 years)			665	2072	268	527	68	25	10	173	275	341	7	37	61-39	.254	.342	.326	.668	141	.945
Major League totals (15 years)			1651	5681	840	1551	252	72	57	537	772	914	18	100	172-100	.273	.360	.373	.732	230	.969

Year Team (League)	Pos.	G	AB	R	H	2B	3B	HR	RBI	BB	SO	HBP	GDP	SB-CS	Avg.	OBP	SLG	OPS	E	Avg.
						DIVISION SERIES RECORD														
1995— Los Angeles (N.L.)		1	0	0	0	0	0	0	0	0	0	0	0	0-0	...	...	...	...		...
1999— Boston (A.L.)	2B	5	18	4	7	1	0	1	6	7	0	0	0	0-1	.389	.560	.611	1.171	0	1.000
2004— Minnesota (A.L.)		3	3	0	0	0	0	0	1	0	0	0	0	0-0	.000	.000	.000	.000	0	...
Division series totals (3 years)		9	21	4	7	1	0	1	7	7	0	0	0	0-1	.333	.500	.524	1.024	0	1.000
						CHAMPIONSHIP SERIES RECORD														
Year Team (League)	Pos.	G	AB	R	H	2B	3B	HR	RBI	BB	SO	HBP	GDP	SB-CS	Avg.	OBP	SLG	OPS	E	Avg.
1999— Boston (A.L.)	2B	5	24	4	11	0	1	0	2	1	3	0	1	1-0	.458	.480	.542	1.022	2	.917
						ALL-STAR GAME RECORD														
		G	AB	R	H	2B	3B	HR	RBI	BB	SO	HBP	GDP	SB-CS	Avg.	OBP	SLG	OPS	E	Avg.
All-Star Game totals (2 years)		2	1	0	0	0	0	0	0	0	0	0	0	0-0	.000	.000	.000	.000	1	.750

OHKA, TOMO   P

PERSONAL: Born March 18, 1976, in Kyoto, Japan. ... 6-1/200. ... Throws right, bats right. ... Full name: Tomokazu Ohka. ... Name pronounced: TOE-mo OH-kah. ... High school: Kyoto Siesio (Kyoto, Japan).

TRANSACTIONS/CAREER NOTES: Contract purchased by Boston Red Sox from Yokohama of the Japan Central League (November 20, 1998). ... Traded by Red Sox with P Rich Rundles to Montreal Expos for P Ugueth Urbina (July 31, 2001). ... On suspended list (September 24-30, 2002). ... On disabled list (June 11-September 14, 2004). ... Expos franchise transferred to Washington, D.C., and renamed Washington Nationals for 2005 season (December 3, 2004). ... Traded by Nationals to Milwaukee Brewers for 2B Junior Spivey (June 10, 2005).

CAREER HITTING: 28-for-207 (.135), 8 R, 1 2B, 0 3B, 0 HR, 9 RBI.

SCOUTING REPORT **Throws:** Ohka throws his fastball from 88-92 mph. Also throws a curve, a changeup and a split-finger fastball. **Tendencies:** Ohka relies on plus command and the ability to use all his pitches to be effective. Fastball down will occasionally sink but he can't make any mistakes with it. Curveball is not as effective as his slider, which has good bite and velocity. Uses a changeup early in the count and a splitter to put hitters away late. **Outlook:** Ohka is a fifth starter with good command. Will log innings and will give a club 30 plus starts a year and a .500 record. *Grade 6.1*

TOMO OHKA'S PITCHING ZONE

.229	.290	.136
.294	.434	.245
.327	.205	.188

LEFTY-RIGHTY SPLITS

vs.	Avg.	AB	H	2B	3B	HR	RBI	BB	SO	OBP	Slg.
L	.258	333	86	16	2	7	32	28	40	.314	.381
R	.277	372	103	26	3	15	42	27	58	.329	.484

Year Team (League)	W	L	Pct.	ERA	WHIP	G	GS	CG	ShO	Hld.	Sv.-Opp.	IP	H	R	ER	HR	BB-IBB	SO	Avg.
1994— Yo. Bay. (Jp. Cn.)	1	1	.500	4.18	1.68	15	2	0	0	...	0-...	28.0	29	13	13	...	18-...	18	...
1995— Yo. Bay. (Jp. Cn.)	0	0	...	1.93	1.71	3	1	0	0	...	0-...	9.1	3	2	2	...	13-...	6	...
1996— Yo. Bay. (Jp. Cn.)	0	1	.000	9.50	2.28	14	1	0	0	...	0-...	18.0	27	19	19	...	14-...	11	...
1997—			Did not play.																
1998— Yo. Bay. (Jp. Cn.)	0	0	...	9.00	2.00	2	0	0	0	...	0-...	2.0	2	2	2	...	2-...	1	...
1999— Trenton (East.)	8	0	1.000	3.00	1.22	12	12	0	0	...	0-...	72.0	63	26	24	9	25-0	53	.233
— Pawtucket (Int'l)	7	0	1.000	1.58	1.04	12	12	1	1	...	0-...	68.1	60	17	12	5	11-0	63	.230
— Boston (A.L.)	1	2	.333	6.23	2.08	8	2	0	0	0	0-0	13.0	21	12	9	2	6-0	8	.362
2000— Pawtucket (Int'l)	9	6	.600	2.96	1.03	19	19	3	2	...	0-...	130.2	111	52	43	15	23-1	78	.232
— Boston (A.L.)	3	6	.333	3.12	1.38	13	12	0	0	0	0-0	69.1	70	25	24	7	26-0	40	.263
2001— Boston (A.L.)	2	5	.286	6.19	1.68	12	11	0	0	0	0-0	52.1	69	40	36	7	19-0	37	.317
— Pawtucket (Int'l)	2	5	.286	5.57	1.52	8	8	1	0	...	0-...	42.0	55	35	26	5	9-0	33	.322
— Montreal (N.L.)	1	4	.200	4.77	1.37	10	10	0	0	0	0-0	54.2	65	30	29	8	10-0	31	.302
2002— Montreal (N.L.)	13	8	.619	3.18	1.24	32	31	2	0	0	0-0	192.2	194	83	68	19	45-7	118	.264
2003— Montreal (N.L.)	10	12	.455	4.16	1.40	34	34	2	0	0	0-0	199.0	233	106	92	24	45-11	118	.292
2004— Montreal (N.L.)	3	7	.300	3.40	1.39	15	15	0	0	0	0-0	84.2	98	40	32	11	20-1	38	.288
2005— Was. (N.L.)	4	3	.571	3.33	1.31	10	9	0	0	0	0-0	54.0	44	23	20	6	27-1	17	.224
— Milwaukee (N.L.)	7	6	.538	4.35	1.37	22	20	1	0	1	0-0	126.1	145	65	61	16	28-4	81	.285
American League totals (3 years)	6	13	.316	4.61	1.57	33	25	0	0	0	0-0	134.2	160	77	69	16	51-0	85	.295
National League totals (5 years)	38	40	.487	3.82	1.34	123	119	5	1	1	0-0	711.1	779	347	302	84	175-24	403	.279
Major League totals (7 years)	44	53	.454	3.95	1.38	156	144	5	1	1	0-0	846.0	939	424	371	100	226-24	488	.281

OHMAN, WILL   P

PERSONAL: Born August 13, 1977, in Frankfurt, West Germany. ... 6-2/195. ... Throws left, bats left. ... Full name: William McDaniel Ohman. ... Name pronounced: OH-min. ... High school: Ponderos (Parker, Colo.). ... College: Pepperdine.

TRANSACTIONS/CAREER NOTES: Selected by Chicago Cubs organization in eighth round of free-agent draft (June 2, 1998). ... On disabled list (March 15, 2002-entire season). ... On disabled list (March 28, 2003-entire season).

CAREER HITTING: 0-for-2 (.000), 0 R, 0 2B, 0 3B, 0 HR, 0 RBI.

WILL OHMAN'S PITCHING ZONE

.200	.286	.111
.346	.250	.176
.222	.333	.200

LEFTY-RIGHTY SPLITS

vs.	Avg.	AB	H	2B	3B	HR	RBI	BB	SO	OBP	Slg.
L	.173	81	14	0	0	4	8	10	26	.272	.321
R	.231	78	18	2	0	2	11	14	19	.362	.333

Year Team (League)	W	L	Pct.	ERA	WHIP	G	GS	CG	ShO	Hld.	Sv.-Opp.	IP	H	R	ER	HR	BB-IBB	SO	Avg.
1998— Williamsport (NYP)	4	4	.500	6.46	1.33	10	7	0	0	...	0-...	39.0	39	32	28	6	13-0	35	.260
— Rockford (Midwest)	1	1	.500	4.44	1.32	4	4	0	0	...	0-...	24.1	25	13	12	3	7-0	21	.269
1999— Daytona (Fla. St.)	4	7	.364	3.46	1.34	31	15	2	•2	...	5-...	106.2	102	59	41	11	41-1	97	.254
2000— West Tenn. (Sou.)	6	4	.600	1.89	1.25	59	0	0	0	...	3-...	71.1	53	20	15	3	36-5	85	.204
— Chicago (N.L.)	1	0	1.000	8.10	2.40	14	0	0	0	1	0-0	3.1	4	3	3	0	4-...	2	.308
2001— Iowa (PCL)	5	2	.714	4.06	1.35	40	1	0	0	...	4-...	51.0	51	24	23	9	18-3	66	.259
— Chicago (N.L.)	0	1	.000	7.71	1.71	11	0	0	0	1	0-0	11.2	14	10	10	2	6-...	12	.292

O

Year—Team (League)	W	L	Pct.	ERA	WHIP	G	GS	CG	ShO	Hld.	Sv.-Opp.	IP	H	R	ER	HR	BB-IBB	SO	Avg.
2002—Chicago (N.L.)	Did not play.																		
2003—Chicago (N.L.)	Did not play.																		
2004—Iowa (PCL)	3	3	.500	4.30	1.57	45	1	0	0	...	0-...	52.1	53	28	25	6	29-1	75	.249
2005—Iowa (PCL)	1	0	1.000	4.15	0.69	8	0	0	0	0	1-1	8.2	4	4	4	2	2-0	12	.138
—Chicago (N.L.)	2	2	.500	2.91	1.29	69	0	0	0	13	0-3	43.1	32	14	14	6	24-3	45	.201
Major League totals (3 years)	3	3	.500	4.17	1.44	86	0	0	0	15	0-3	58.1	50	27	27	8	34-3	59	.227

OJEDA, MIGUEL   C

PERSONAL: Born January 29, 1975, in Sonora, Mexico. ... 6-2/190. ... Bats right, throws right. ... Full name: Miguel Arturo Ojeda.
TRANSACTIONS/CAREER NOTES: Signed as a non-drafted free agent by Pittsburgh Pirates organization (May 28, 1993). ... Loaned by Pirates organization to Mexico City Reds of the Mexican League for the entire 1995, 1996 and 1997 seasons and part of the 1998 season. ... Traded by Pirates to Red Devils for future considerations (December 14, 1998). ... Signed as a free agent by San Diego Padres organization (January 12, 2003). ... Released by Padres (March 24, 2003). ... Contract purchased by Padres from Red Devils (May 17, 2003). ... On disabled list (August 16-September 1, 2004); included rehabilitation assignment to Portland. ... Traded by Padres with P Natanael Mateo to Seattle Mariners for C Miguel Olivo (July 30, 2005). ... Claimed on waivers by Colorado Rockies (October 11, 2005).
2005 GAMES PLAYED BY POSITION (MLB): C—41, OF—5, DH—1.

SCOUTING REPORT Ojeda is strictly a backup. Has a long stroke without good bat speed and hasn't shown the ability to make a lot of adjustments. Has problems catching up to good fastballs and doesn't pull the ball a lot. Is not a strong defensive catcher but does have some arm strength. Moves a lot behind the plate, which can cost his pitchers some calls. Has a tendency to drop pitches. *Grade 4.5*

MIGUEL OJEDA'S HITTING ZONE

.100	.000	.000
.100	.000	.167
.222	.200	.333

LEFTY-RIGHTY SPLITS

vs.	Avg.	AB	H	2B	3B	HR	RBI	BB	SO	OBP	Slg.
L	.108	37	4	2	0	0	2	4	8	.195	.162
R	.169	65	11	1	1	1	7	11	16	.289	.262

								BATTING								FIELDING	
Year—Team (League)	Pos.	G	AB	R	H	2B	3B	HR	RBI	BB	SO	HBP	GDP	SB-CS	Avg.	OBP	SLG	OPS	E	Avg.
1993—GC Pirates (GCL)	C	27	97	9	27	3	1	3	11	10	18	0	1	2-0	.278	.339	.423	.762	3	.983
1994—Welland (NYP)	C-1B-P	48	142	11	27	6	0	2	8	5	30	2	0	1-0	.190	.228	.275	.503	0	1.000
				Played for Mexico City (Mex.) — 1995-1997															
1998—Carolina (Southern)	C	18	58	4	9	2	0	1	4	3	12	1	0	0-0	.155	.210	.241	.451	1	.991
				Played for Mexico City (Mex.) — 1998-2003															
2003—San Diego (N.L.)	C-1B	61	141	13	33	6	0	4	22	18	26	3	2	1-1	.234	.331	.362	.693	6	.982
2004—Portland (PCL)	C	5	19	4	5	0	0	2	3	2	3	0	0	0-0	.263	.333	.579	.912	1	.974
—San Diego (N.L.)	C	62	156	23	40	3	0	8	26	15	34	1	0	0-0	.256	.322	.429	.751	1	.996
2005—San Diego (N.L.)	C-OF-DH	43	73	6	10	3	1	0	6	9	21	0	2	1-1	.137	.232	.205	.437	0	1.000
—Portland (PCL)	C-OF-DH	17	57	8	11	1	0	3	5	7	16	1	0	0-0	.193	.292	.368	.661	1	.991
—Tacoma (PCL)	C-DH-1B	9	33	7	11	1	0	3	11	1	5	0	0	0-0	.333	.371	.636	1.008	0	1.000
—Seattle (A.L.)	C	16	29	2	5	0	0	1	3	6	3	0	0	0-1	.172	.314	.276	.590	1	.986
American League totals (1 year)		16	29	2	5	0	0	1	3	6	3	0	0	0-1	.172	.314	.276	.590	1	.986
National League totals (3 years)		166	370	42	83	12	1	12	54	42	81	4	5	2-2	.224	.308	.359	.667	7	.990
Major League totals (3 years)		182	399	44	88	12	1	13	57	48	84	4	5	2-3	.221	.308	.353	.662	8	.990

OLERUD, JOHN   1B

PERSONAL: Born August 5, 1968, in Seattle. ... 6-5/225. ... Bats left, throws left. ... Full name: John Garrett Olerud. ... Name pronounced: OLE-le-RUDE. ... High school: Interlake (Bellevue, Wash.). ... College: Washington State. ... Cousin of Dale Sveum, coach, Milwaukee Brewers and infielder with seven major league teams (1986-99).
TRANSACTIONS/CAREER NOTES: Selected by New York Mets organization in 27th round of 1986 free-agent draft; did not sign. ... Selected by Toronto Blue Jays organization in third round of 1989 free-agent draft. ... Traded by Blue Jays with cash to Mets for P Robert Person (December 20, 1996). ... Signed as a free agent by Seattle Mariners (December 15, 1999). ... Released by Mariners (July 23, 2004). ... Signed by New York Yankees (August 3, 2004). ... Signed as a free agent by Boston Red Sox organization (May 1, 2005). ... On disabled list (August 1-17, 2005); included rehabilitation assignment to Pawtucket.
HONORS: Won A.L. Gold Glove at first base (2000, 2002 and 2003).
2005 GAMES PLAYED BY POSITION (MLB): 1B—80.

SCOUTING REPORT **Offense:** Olerud has a fluid swing and outstanding bat control. Is a very patient hitter. Approach at the plate is consistent. Has been able to compensate for a slight loss of bat speed. Is a line-drive hitter who occasionally will turn on pitches on the inner half of the plate for power. Has a great feel for hitting and an unflappable demeanor at the plate. **Defense:** Olerud still has soft hands and actually has shown more range than in the past few years. Not playing every day has kept him sharp in the field. Is proficient at scooping throws in the dirt. **Outlook:** Olerud is still a productive offensive player if he's not overextended. Has exceptional professional makeup. Is not a power hitter but rather a good complementary hitter. *Grade 7.3*

JOHN OLERUD'S HITTING ZONE

.462	.000	.300
.333	.357	.368
.200	.250	.286

LEFTY-RIGHTY SPLITS

vs.	Avg.	AB	H	2B	3B	HR	RBI	BB	SO	OBP	Slg.
L	.300	40	12	2	0	2	12	3	8	.341	.500
R	.286	133	38	5	0	5	25	13	12	.345	.436

								BATTING								FIELDING	
Year—Team (League)	Pos.	G	AB	R	H	2B	3B	HR	RBI	BB	SO	HBP	GDP	SB-CS	Avg.	OBP	SLG	OPS	E	Avg.
1989—Toronto (A.L.)	1B-DH	6	8	2	3	0	0	0	0	0	1	0	0	0-0	.375	.375	.375	.750	0	1.000
1990—Toronto (A.L.)	1B-DH	111	358	43	95	15	1	14	48	57	75	1	5	0-2	.265	.364	.430	.794	5	.986
1991—Toronto (A.L.)	1B-DH	139	454	64	116	30	1	17	68	68	84	6	12	0-2	.256	.353	.438	.791	5	.996
1992—Toronto (A.L.)	1B-DH	138	458	68	130	28	0	16	66	70	61	1	15	1-0	.284	.375	.450	.825	7	.994
1993—Toronto (A.L.)	1B-DH	158	551	109	200	* 54	2	24	107	114	65	7	12	0-2	* .363	* .473	.599	1.072	10	.992
1994—Toronto (A.L.)	1B-DH	108	384	47	114	29	2	12	67	61	53	3	11	1-2	.297	.393	.477	.870	6	.993
1995—Toronto (A.L.)	1B	135	492	72	143	32	0	8	54	84	54	4	17	0-0	.291	.398	.404	.802	4	.997
1996—Toronto (A.L.)	1B-DH	125	398	59	109	25	0	18	61	60	37	10	10	1-0	.274	.382	.472	.854	2	.998
1997—New York (N.L.)	1B	154	524	90	154	34	1	22	102	85	67	13	19	1-0	.294	.400	.489	.889	7	.995

Year Team (League)	Pos.	G	AB	R	H	2B	3B	HR	RBI	BB	SO	HBP	GDP	SB-CS	Avg.	OBP	SLG	OPS	E	Avg.
								BATTING											FIELDING	
1998— New York (N.L.)	1B	160	557	91	197	36	4	22	93	96	73	4	15	2-2	.354	.447	.551	.998	5	.996
1999— New York (N.L.)	1B	• 162	581	107	173	39	0	19	96	125	66	11	22	3-0	.298	.427	.463	.890	9	.994
2000— Seattle (A.L.)	1B	159	565	84	161	45	0	14	103	102	96	4	17	0-2	.285	.392	.439	.831	5	.996
2001— Seattle (A.L.)	1B	159	572	91	173	32	1	21	95	94	70	5	* 21	3-1	.302	.401	.472	.873	9	.993
2002— Seattle (A.L.)	1B-DH	154	553	85	166	39	0	22	102	98	66	5	19	0-0	.300	.403	.490	.893	5	.996
2003— Seattle (A.L.)	1B	152	539	64	145	35	0	10	83	84	67	6	20	0-1	.269	.372	.390	.761	3	.998
2004— Seattle (A.L.)	1B	78	261	29	64	13	1	5	22	40	41	6	6	0-0	.245	.354	.360	.714	1	.998
— New York (A.L.)	1B	49	164	16	46	7	0	4	26	21	20	2	5	0-0	.280	.367	.396	.763	1	.997
2005— Pawtucket (Int'l)	1B-DH	3	10	2	3	0	0	1	2	2	1	0	2	0-0	.300	.417	.600	1.017	0	1.000
— Boston (A.L.)	1B	87	173	18	50	7	0	7	37	16	20	1	6	0-0	.289	.344	.451	.795	1	.998
American League totals (14 years)		1758	5930	851	1715	391	8	192	939	969	810	60	176	6-12	.289	.390	.455	.845	61	.995
National League totals (3 years)		476	1662	288	524	109	5	63	291	306	206	28	56	5-2	.315	.425	.501	.926	21	.995
Major League totals (17 years)		2234	7592	1139	2239	500	13	255	1230	1275	1016	88	232	11-14	.295	.398	.465	.863	82	.995

DIVISION SERIES RECORD

Year Team (League)	Pos.	G	AB	R	H	2B	3B	HR	RBI	BB	SO	HBP	GDP	SB-CS	Avg.	OBP	SLG	OPS	E	Avg.
1999— New York (N.L.)	1B	4	16	3	7	0	0	1	6	3	2	0	0	0-0	.438	.526	.625	1.151	0	1.000
2000— Seattle (A.L.)	1B	3	10	2	3	0	0	1	2	2	1	1	1	0-0	.300	.462	.600	1.062	0	1.000
2001— Seattle (A.L.)	1B	5	17	1	3	0	0	0	1	3	5	0	1	0-0	.176	.300	.176	.476	0	1.000
2004— New York (A.L.)	1B	4	14	2	3	2	0	0	0	1	2	1	0	0-0	.214	.313	.357	.670	0	1.000
2005— Boston (A.L.)	1B	3	7	0	2	1	0	0	0	2	0	0	0	0-0	.286	.444	.429	.873	0	1.000
Division series totals (5 years)		19	64	8	18	3	0	2	9	11	10	2	2	0-0	.281	.403	.422	.824	0	1.000

CHAMPIONSHIP SERIES RECORD

Year Team (League)	Pos.	G	AB	R	H	2B	3B	HR	RBI	BB	SO	HBP	GDP	SB-CS	Avg.	OBP	SLG	OPS	E	Avg.
1991— Toronto (A.L.)	1B	5	19	1	3	0	0	0	3	3	1	0	0	0-0	.158	.273	.158	.431	0	1.000
1992— Toronto (A.L.)	1B	6	23	4	8	2	0	1	4	2	5	0	0	0-0	.348	.400	.565	.965	0	1.000
1993— Toronto (A.L.)	1B	6	23	5	8	1	0	0	3	4	1	1	1	0-0	.348	.464	.391	.856	1	.983
1999— New York (N.L.)	1B	6	27	4	8	0	0	2	6	2	3	0	1	0-0	.296	.345	.519	.863	2	.969
2000— Seattle (A.L.)	1B	6	20	3	7	2	0	2	2	2	2	0	1	1-0	.350	.391	.650	1.041	0	1.000
2001— Seattle (A.L.)	1B	5	19	2	4	0	0	1	3	2	4	0	1	0-0	.211	.286	.368	.654	0	1.000
2004— New York (A.L.)	1B	4	12	1	2	0	0	1	2	1	1	0	0	0-0	.167	.231	.417	.647	0	1.000
Champ. series totals (7 years)		38	143	20	40	6	0	6	23	16	17	1	4	1-0	.280	.354	.448	.802	3	.991

WORLD SERIES RECORD

Year Team (League)	Pos.	G	AB	R	H	2B	3B	HR	RBI	BB	SO	HBP	GDP	SB-CS	Avg.	OBP	SLG	OPS	E	Avg.
1992— Toronto (A.L.)	1B	4	13	2	4	0	0	0	0	4	0	0	0	0-0	.308	.308	.308	.615	0	1.000
1993— Toronto (A.L.)	1B	5	17	5	4	1	0	1	2	4	1	0	0	0-0	.235	.364	.471	.834	0	1.000
World series totals (2 years)		9	30	7	8	1	0	1	2	8	1	0	0	0-0	.267	.343	.400	.743	0	1.000

ALL-STAR GAME RECORD

		G	AB	R	H	2B	3B	HR	RBI	BB	SO	HBP	GDP	SB-CS	Avg.	OBP	SLG	OPS	E	Avg.
All-Star Game totals (2 years)		2	4	0	0	0	0	0	0	0	0	0	0	0-0	.000	.000	.000	.000	0	1.000

OLIVO, MIGUEL — C

PERSONAL: Born July 15, 1978, in Villa Vasquez, Dominican Republic. ... 6-0/215. ... Bats right, throws right. ... Full name: Miguel Eduardo Olivo.

TRANSACTIONS/CAREER NOTES: Signed as a non-drafted free agent by Oakland Athletics organization (September 30, 1996). ... Traded by A's to Chicago White Sox (December 12, 2000); completing deal in which White Sox traded P Chad Bradford to A's for player to be named (December 7, 2000). ... Traded by White Sox with OF Jeremy Reed and SS Michael Morse to Seattle Mariners for RHP Freddy Garcia and C Ben Davis (June 27, 2004). ... On disabled list (June 30-July 15, 2004); included rehabilitation assignment to Everett. ... On suspended list (October 2-3, 2004). ... Traded by Mariners to San Diego Padres for C Miguel Ojeda and P Natanael Mateo (July 30, 2005).

2005 GAMES PLAYED BY POSITION (MLB): C—91.

SCOUTING REPORT *Offense:* Olivo is a stiff hitter with a short stroke who hits from a wide stance. Will generate some bat speed and is a definite high-fastball hitter who gets in trouble when he tries to pull the ball too much. Isn't a disciplined hitter, but proved to be a better hitter with runners in scoring position. Has gap-to-gap power. *Defense:* His defense is not a strength. Doesn't have very soft, flexible hands and drops too many pitches. Has one of the stronger arms in the league and relies on velocity rather than footwork to throw out runners. Is not very efficient calling a game. *Outlook:* Olivo has unusual tools for a catcher in that he can really run and throw. Might hit, but not for power. Question if he can be a regular. *Grade 6.1*

MIGUEL OLIVO'S HITTING ZONE

.182	.250	.462
.204	.500	.160
.167	.333	.400

LEFTY-RIGHTY SPLITS

vs.	Avg.	AB	H	2B	3B	HR	RBI	BB	SO	OBP	Slg.
L	.284	74	21	3	1	6	9	1	17	.299	.595
R	.192	193	37	8	0	3	25	7	63	.227	.280

Year Team (League)	Pos.	G	AB	R	H	2B	3B	HR	RBI	BB	SO	HBP	GDP	SB-CS	Avg.	OBP	SLG	OPS	E	Avg.
								BATTING											FIELDING	
1997— Dom. Athletics (DSL)		63	221	37	60	11	4	6	57	34	36	...	...	6-...	.271	...	.439	...	...	...
1998— Ariz. A's (Ariz.)	C-OF	46	164	30	51	11	3	2	23	8	43	4	5	2-2	.311	.356	.451	.807	8	.977
1999— Modesto (California)	C	73	243	46	74	13	6	9	42	21	60	2	6	4-5	.305	.363	.519	.882	15	.977
2000— Modesto (California)	C	58	227	40	64	11	5	5	35	16	53	2	8	5-2	.282	.332	.441	.773	19	.959
— Midland (Texas)	C	19	59	8	14	2	0	1	9	5	15	0	3	0-0	.237	.297	.322	.619	2	.980
2001— Birmingham (Sou.)	C	93	316	45	82	23	1	14	55	37	62	7	4	6-3	.259	.347	.472	.819	9	.988
2002— Birmingham (Sou.)	C	106	359	51	110	24	10	6	49	40	66	5	11	29-13	.306	.381	.479	.860	13	.983
— Chicago (A.L.)	C	6	19	2	4	1	0	1	5	2	5	0	1	0-0	.211	.286	.421	.707	0	1.000
2003— Chicago (A.L.)	C	114	317	37	75	19	1	6	27	19	80	1	3	6-4	.237	.287	.360	.646	9	.988
2004— Chicago (A.L.)	C	46	141	21	38	7	2	7	26	10	29	0	4	5-4	.270	.316	.496	.812	4	.984
— Everett (N'west)	C	2	6	0	0	0	0	0	0	0	0	0	0	0-0	.000	.000	.000	.000	1	.909
— Seattle (A.L.)	C	50	160	25	32	8	2	6	14	10	55	3	2	2-2	.200	.260	.388	.648	1	.987
2005— Tacoma (PCL)	C-DH	24	90	13	21	4	1	3	21	7	19	1	1	8-1	.233	.293	.400	.693	0	1.000
— Seattle (A.L.)	C	54	152	14	23	4	0	5	18	4	49	1	3	1-1	.151	.172	.276	.448	4	.987
— San Diego (N.L.)	C	37	115	16	35	7	1	4	16	4	31	3	4	6-1	.304	.341	.487	.828	5	.979

O

Year Team (League)	Pos.	G	AB	R	H	2B	3B	HR	RBI	BB	SO	HBP	GDP	SB-CS	Avg.	OBP	SLG	OPS	E	Avg.
									BATTING										FIELDING	
American League totals (4 years)		270	789	99	172	39	5	25	90	45	218	7	11	14-11	.218	.265	.375	.640	18	.989
National League totals (1 year)		37	115	16	35	7	1	4	16	4	31	3	4	6-1	.304	.341	.487	.828	5	.979
Major League totals (4 years)		307	904	115	207	46	6	29	106	49	249	10	15	20-12	.229	.275	.389	.664	23	.988

DIVISION SERIES RECORD

Year Team (League)	Pos.	G	AB	R	H	2B	3B	HR	RBI	BB	SO	HBP	GDP	SB-CS	Avg.	OBP	SLG	OPS	E	Avg.
2005— San Diego (N.L.)		1	1	0	0	0	0	0	0	0	0	0	1	0-0	.000	.000	.000	.000	0	...

OLSEN, SCOTT   P

PERSONAL: Born January 12, 1984, in Kalamazoo, Mich. ... 6-4/198. ... Throws left, bats left. ... Full name: Scott M. Olsen. ... High school: Crystal Lake (Ill.) South.
TRANSACTIONS/CAREER NOTES: Selected by Florida Marlins organization in sixth round of 2002 free-agent draft.
CAREER HITTING: 0-for-3 (.000), 0 R, 0 2B, 0 3B, 0 HR, 0 RBI.

SCOTT OLSEN'S PITCHING ZONE

.250	.250	.500
.308	.455	.364
.000	.250	.200

LEFTY-RIGHTY SPLITS

vs.	Avg.	AB	H	2B	3B	HR	RBI	BB	SO	OBP	Slg.
L	.333	18	6	0	0	2	4	1	3	.368	.667
R	.238	63	15	2	0	3	5	9	18	.333	.413

Year Team (League)	W	L	Pct.	ERA	WHIP	G	GS	CG	ShO	Hld.	Sv.-Opp.	IP	H	R	ER	HR	BB-IBB	SO	Avg.
2002— GC Marlins (GCL)	2	3	.400	2.96	1.08	13	11	0	0	...	0-...	51.2	39	18	17	0	17-0	50	.204
2003— Greensboro (S. Atl.)	7	9	.438	2.81	1.25	25	24	0	0	...	0-...	128.1	101	51	40	4	59-0	129	.222
2004— Jupiter (Fla. St.)	7	6	.538	2.97	1.32	25	25	1	1	...	0-...	136.1	127	57	45	8	53-0	158	.252
2005— Carolina (Southern)	6	4	.600	3.92	1.27	14	14	1	1	0	0-0	80.1	75	38	35	7	27-0	94	.251
—Florida (N.L.)	1	1	.500	3.98	1.52	5	4	0	0	0	0-0	20.1	21	13	9	5	10-0	21	.259
Major League totals (1 year)	1	1	.500	3.98	1.52	5	4	0	0	0	0-0	20.1	21	13	9	5	10-0	21	.259

OLSON, TIM   3B/SS

PERSONAL: Born August 1, 1978, in Grand Forks, N.D. ... 6-2/200. ... Bats right, throws right. ... Full name: Timothy Lane Olson. ... High school: St. Mary's Central (Bismarck, N.D.). ... Junior college: Hutchinson (Kan.). ... College: Florida.
TRANSACTIONS/CAREER NOTES: Selected by Tampa Bay Devil Rays organization in 36th round of 1998 free-agent draft; did not sign. ... Selected by Arizona Diamondbacks organization in seventh round of 2000 free-agent draft. ... Signed as a free agent by Colorado Rockies organization (December 15, 2004).
2005 GAMES PLAYED BY POSITION (MLB): DH—1.

LEFTY-RIGHTY SPLITS

vs.	Avg.	AB	H	2B	3B	HR	RBI	BB	SO	OBP	Slg.
L	.000	1	0	0	0	0	0	1	1	.500	.000
R	.000	1	0	0	0	0	0	0	1	.000	.000

Year Team (League)	Pos.	G	AB	R	H	2B	3B	HR	RBI	BB	SO	HBP	GDP	SB-CS	Avg.	OBP	SLG	OPS	E	Avg.
										BATTING									FIELDING	
2000— South Bend (Mid.)	OF-3B	68	261	37	57	14	2	2	26	15	49	8	5	15-3	.218	.281	.310	.591	9	.947
2001— Lancaster (Calif.)	SS-3B-OF	61	239	36	69	12	4	6	32	14	49	3	4	13-9	.289	.336	.448	.784	24	.906
—El Paso (Texas)	SS	46	167	29	53	13	0	2	24	11	36	6	4	4-4	.317	.378	.431	.810	20	.914
2002— El Paso (Texas)	SS-OF-2B	126	433	61	118	24	2	10	64	27	91	19	13	9-11	.273	.337	.406	.744	31	.942
2003— El Paso (Texas)	SS-OF	14	56	5	11	2	0	2	8	5	19	0	1	0-2	.196	.258	.339	.597	4	.940
—Tucson (PCL)	SS-OF-2B	115	397	59	104	22	0	6	40	31	77	6	14	11-2	.262	.323	.363	.686	29	.943
2004— Arizona (N.L.)	3B-SS-2B	48	97	8	18	7	0	2	5	16	18	0	4	1-0	.186	.301	.320	.620	6	.946
—Tucson (PCL)	SS-OF-3B																			
	2B	37	147	32	44	11	0	7	25	16	28	2	2	5-1	.299	.373	.517	.883	5	.961
2005— Colorado (N.L.)	DH	3	2	0	0	0	0	0	0	1	2	0	0	0-0	.000	.333	.000	.333	0	...
—Colo. Springs (PCL)	3B-2B-OF																			
	SS-1B-DH	89	322	53	96	26	2	12	51	28	70	5	9	9-7	.298	.359	.503	.862	9	.971
Major League totals (2 years)		51	99	8	18	7	0	2	5	17	20	0	4	1-0	.182	.302	.313	.615	6	.946

ORDONEZ, MAGGLIO   OF

PERSONAL: Born January 28, 1974, in Caracas, Venezuela. ... 6-0/215. ... Bats right, throws right. ... Full name: Magglio Jose Ordonez. ... Name pronounced: or-DOAN-yez.
TRANSACTIONS/CAREER NOTES: Signed as a non-drafted free agent by Chicago White Sox organization (May 18, 1991). ... On suspended list (May 1-6, 2000). ... On disabled list (May 26-July 8 and July 22, 2004-remainder of season). ... Signed as a free agent by Detroit Tigers (February 7, 2005). ... On disabled list (April 15-July 1, 2005); included rehabilitation assignment to Toledo.
2005 GAMES PLAYED BY POSITION (MLB): OF—81, DH—1.

SCOUTING REPORT **Offense:** Ordonez missed the first half of the season with more injury problems. Has a long approach but quick hands helped his bat speed improve through the season. Is a better hitting going the other way but can turn on an inside pitch with power. Home-run production should to return to normal when he's back to full health. Is a very good baserunner but injuries have slowed him. **Defense:** He is a solid right fielder who gets a good jump on the ball, especially moving toward the line. Takes good lateral routes and has a strong, accurate arm. Range and ability to change direction quickly have declined as a result of his knee surgeries. **Outlook:** Showed flashes of his productive past and still is capable of putting up big numbers, but his home park is a disadvantage. Some concerns if he can stay healthy. **Grade 7.6**

MAGGLIO ORDONEZ'S HITTING ZONE

.450	.214	.400
.197	.423	.400
.235	.313	.462

LEFTY-RIGHTY SPLITS

vs.	Avg.	AB	H	2B	3B	HR	RBI	BB	SO	OBP	Slg.
L	.308	78	24	5	0	2	11	6	7	.357	.449
R	.300	227	68	12	0	6	35	24	28	.359	.432

Year Team (League)	Pos.	G	AB	R	H	2B	3B	HR	RBI	BB	SO	HBP	GDP	SB-CS	Avg.	OBP	SLG	OPS	E	Avg.
									BATTING										FIELDING	
1991— Dom. Orioles/W.S. (DSL) ..		25	94	17	28	3	1	0	8	6	12	...	...	4-...	.298		.351	...	...	...
1992— GC Whi. Sox (GCL)	OF	38	111	17	20	10	2	1	14	13	26	2	2	6-4	.180	.276	.333	.609	0	1.000

Year	Team (League)	Pos.	G	AB	R	H	2B	3B	HR	RBI	BB	SO	HBP	GDP	SB-CS	Avg.	OBP	SLG	OPS	E	Avg.
											BATTING									FIELDING	
1993—	Hickory (S. Atl.)	OF	84	273	32	59	14	4	3	20	26	66	0	6	5-5	.216	.284	.330	.614	6	.959
1994—	Hickory (S. Atl.)	OF	132	490	86	144	24	5	11	69	45	57	1	11	16-7	.294	.353	.431	.783	6	.980
1995—	Prince Will. (Car.)	OF	137	487	61	116	24	2	12	65	41	71	3	16	11-5	.238	.299	.370	.669	6	.978
1996—	Birmingham (Sou.)	OF	130	479	66	126	41	0	18	67	39	74	9	16	9-10	.263	.330	.461	.792	6	.976
1997—	Nashville (A.A.)	OF-DH	135	523	65	172	29	3	14	90	32	61	2	18	14-10	.329	.364	.476	.840	5	.983
—	Chicago (A.L.)	OF	21	69	12	22	6	0	4	11	2	8	0	1	1-2	.319	.338	.580	.918	0	1.000
1998—	Chicago (A.L.)	OF	145	535	70	151	25	2	14	65	28	53	9	19	9-7	.282	.326	.415	.741	5	.985
1999—	Chicago (A.L.)	OF-DH	157	624	100	188	34	3	30	117	47	64	1	24	13-6	.301	.349	.510	.858	3	.991
2000—	Chicago (A.L.)	OF	153	588	102	185	34	3	32	126	60	64	2	28	18-4	.315	.371	.546	.917	5	.983
2001—	Chicago (A.L.)	OF-DH	160	593	97	181	40	4	31	113	70	70	5	14	25-7	.305	.382	.533	.914	5	.983
2002—	Chicago (A.L.)	OF-DH	153	590	116	189	47	1	38	135	53	77	7	* 21	7-5	.320	.381	.597	.978	4	.986
2003—	Chicago (A.L.)	OF-DH	160	606	95	192	46	3	29	99	57	73	7	20	9-5	.317	.380	.546	.926	2	.994
2004—	Chicago (A.L.)	OF-DH	52	202	32	59	8	2	9	37	16	22	3	4	0-2	.292	.351	.485	.837	1	.990
2005—	Toledo (Int'l.)	OF-DH	4	14	3	3	1	0	1	2	2	0	0	0	0-0	.214	.313	.500	.813	0	1.000
—	Detroit (A.L.)	OF-DH	82	305	38	92	17	0	8	46	30	35	1	8	0-0	.302	.359	.436	.795	1	.993
Major League totals (9 years)			1083	4112	662	1259	257	15	195	749	363	466	35	139	82-38	.306	.364	.518	.882	26	.988

DIVISION SERIES RECORD

Year	Team (League)	Pos.	G	AB	R	H	2B	3B	HR	RBI	BB	SO	HBP	GDP	SB-CS	Avg.	OBP	SLG	OPS	E	Avg.
2000—	Chicago (A.L.)	OF	3	11	0	2	0	1	0	1	2	2	0	1	1-0	.182	.308	.364	.671	0	1.000

ALL-STAR GAME RECORD

			G	AB	R	H	2B	3B	HR	RBI	BB	SO	HBP	GDP	SB-CS	Avg.	OBP	SLG	OPS	E	Avg.
All-Star Game totals (4 years)			4	6	1	3	1	0	1	2	0	0	0	0	0-0	.500	.429	1.167	1.595	0	1.000

ORR, PETE   2B/3B

PERSONAL: Born June 8, 1979, in Richmond Hill, Ontario. ... 6-1/185. ... Bats left, throws right. ... Full name: Peterson Thomas Gordon Orr. ... College: Galveston (Texas) CC.

TRANSACTIONS/CAREER NOTES: Signed as a non-drafted free agent by Atlanta Braves (July 3, 1999).

2005 GAMES PLAYED BY POSITION (MLB): 2B—25, 3B—12, OF—3, SS—1, DH—1.

PETE ORR'S HITTING ZONE

.188	.750	.182
.389	.333	.333
.167	.400	.333

LEFTY-RIGHTY SPLITS

vs.	Avg.	AB	H	2B	3B	HR	RBI	BB	SO	OBP	Slg.
L	.391	23	9	2	0	0	1	1	5	.440	.478
R	.283	127	36	6	1	1	7	5	18	.311	.370

Year	Team (League)	Pos.	G	AB	R	H	2B	3B	HR	RBI	BB	SO	HBP	GDP	SB-CS	Avg.	OBP	SLG	OPS	E	Avg.
											BATTING									FIELDING	
2000—	Jamestown (NYP)	2B-3B-SS	69	265	40	64	8	1	2	15	24	51	6	4	9-5	.242	.314	.302	.616	18	.934
2001—	Myrtle Beach (Carol.)	SS-OF-2B																			
		3B	92	317	38	74	10	1	4	23	19	70	11	3	17-6	.233	.299	.309	.608	11	.965
2002—	Greenville (Sou.)	SS-2B-OF	89	305	36	76	10	2	4	36	21	47	3	8	23-4	.249	.302	.315	.617	9	.976
—	Myrtle Beach (Carol.)	SS-OF-2B																			
		3B	17	51	8	20	0	2	0	8	3	6	1	0	3-0	.392	.436	.471	.907	2	.960
2003—	Greenville (Sou.)	SS-2B-OF																			
		3B	98	257	22	58	10	2	4	31	25	48	3	3	14-5	.226	.299	.304	.603	13	.956
2004—	Richmond (Int'l.)	2B-3B-OF																			
		SS	115	460	69	147	16	10	1	35	20	59	2	7	24-11	.320	.349	.404	.753	4	.940
2005—	Atlanta (N.L.)	2B-3B-OF																			
		SS-DH	112	150	32	45	8	1	1	8	6	23	1	2	7-1	.300	.331	.387	.718	6	.950
Major League totals (1 year)			112	150	32	45	8	1	1	8	6	23	1	2	7-1	.300	.331	.387	.718	6	.950

DIVISION SERIES RECORD

Year	Team (League)	Pos.	G	AB	R	H	2B	3B	HR	RBI	BB	SO	HBP	GDP	SB-CS	Avg.	OBP	SLG	OPS	E	Avg.
2005—	Atlanta (N.L.)		3	2	0	0	0	0	0	0	0	0	0	0	0-0	.000	.000	.000	.000	0	...

ORTIZ, DAVID   1B/DH

PERSONAL: Born November 18, 1975, in Santo Domingo, Dominican Republic. ... 6-4/230. ... Bats left, throws left. ... Full name: David Americo Ortiz. ... Name pronounced: or-TEEZ. ... High school: Estudia Espallat (Dominican Republic). ... Formerly known as David Arias.

TRANSACTIONS/CAREER NOTES: Signed as a non-drafted free agent by Seattle Mariners organization (November 28, 1992). ... Traded by Mariners to Minnesota Twins (September 13, 1996), completing deal in which Twins traded 3B Dave Hollins to Mariners for a player to be named (August 29, 1996). ... On disabled list (May 10-July 9, 1998); included rehabilitation assignment to Salt Lake. ... On disabled list (May 5-July 21, 2001); included rehabilitation assignments to GCL Twins, Fort Myers and New Britain. ... On disabled list (April 19-May 12, 2002). ... Released by Twins (December 16, 2002). ... Signed by Boston Red Sox (January 22, 2003). ... On suspended list (August 1-7, 2004).

2005 GAMES PLAYED BY POSITION (MLB): DH—148, 1B—10.

SCOUTING REPORT **Offense:** Ortiz has become one of the game's best run producers. Made an adjustment in 2004 that allowed him to loosen up, and has learned to handle the ball inside. Has great ability to drive the ball to the opposite field. Has exceptional bat speed and extension and has become a good breaking-ball hitter. Can't run but will give the effort when it counts. **Defense:** A DH who doesn't play a lot in the field, Ortiz has some quickness but below-average range. Hands are adequate. **Outlook:** Ortiz has exceptional offensive tools and an outstanding clubhouse presence. Will be interesting to see how he hits if Manny Ramirez is gone and he's pitched around more. *Grade 9.5*

DAVID ORTIZ'S HITTING ZONE

.226	.100	.238
.438	.408	.402
.304	.211	.310

LEFTY-RIGHTY SPLITS

vs.	Avg.	AB	H	2B	3B	HR	RBI	BB	SO	OBP	Slg.
L	.302	205	62	14	0	11	46	20	38	.362	.532
R	.298	396	118	26	1	36	102	82	86	.413	.641

Year Team (League)	Pos.	G	AB	R	H	2B	3B	HR	RBI	BB	SO	HBP	GDP	SB-CS	Avg.	OBP	SLG	OPS	E	Avg.
1993— Dom. Mariners (DSL)		61	201	61	53	17	1	7	31	34	44	...	...	1-...	.264	...	.463	...	...	...
1994— Ariz. Mariners (Ariz.)	1B	53	167	14	41	10	1	2	20	14	46	2	2	1-4	.246	.305	.353	.658	6	.985
1995— Ariz. Mariners (Ariz.)	1B	48	184	30	61	18	4	4	37	23	52	1	2	2-0	.332	.403	.538	.941	5	.989
1996— Wisconsin (Midw.) ...1B-DH-3B		129	485	89	156	34	2	18	93	52	108	5	5	3-4	.322	.390	.511	.901	13	.989
1997— Fort Myers (FSL)	1B-DH	61	239	45	79	15	0	13	58	22	53	1	3	2-1	.331	.385	.556	.941	9	.984
— New Britain (East.)	DH-1B	69	258	40	83	22	2	14	56	21	78	4	6	2-6	.322	.379	.585	.964	3	.990
— Salt Lake (PCL)	1B-DH	10	42	5	9	1	0	4	10	2	11	0	4	0-1	.214	.250	.524	.774	1	1.000
— Minnesota (A.L.)	1B	15	49	10	16	3	0	1	6	2	19	0	1	0-0	.327	.353	.449	.802	1	.989
1998— Minnesota (A.L.)	1B-DH	86	278	47	77	20	0	9	46	39	72	5	8	1-0	.277	.371	.446	.817	6	.989
— Salt Lake (PCL)	1B-DH	11	37	5	9	3	0	2	6	3	9	0	0	0-0	.243	.300	.486	.786	3	.966
1999— Salt Lake (PCL)	1B-DH	130	476	85	150	35	3	30	110	79	105	3	8	2-2	.315	.412	.590	1.002	20	.980
— Minnesota (A.L.)	DH-1B-OF	10	20	1	0	0	0	0	0	5	12	0	2	0-0	.000	.200	.000	.200	1	1.000
2000— Minnesota (A.L.)	DH-1B	130	415	59	117	36	1	10	63	57	81	0	13	1-0	.282	.364	.446	.810	1	.996
2001— Minnesota (A.L.)	DH-1B	89	303	46	71	17	1	18	48	40	68	1	6	1-0	.234	.324	.475	.799	1	1.000
— GC Twins (GCL)	DH	4	10	3	4	0	0	0	1	3	1	0	0	1-0	.400	.538	.400	.938	...	...
— Fort Myers (FSL)	1B	1	3	0	0	0	0	0	0	1	0	0	0	0-0	.000	.250	.000	.250	0	1.000
— New Britain (East.)	1B	9	37	3	9	4	0	0	1	3	9	0	1	0-0	.243	.293	.351	.644	0	1.000
2002— Minnesota (A.L.)	DH-1B	125	412	52	112	32	1	20	75	43	87	3	5	1-2	.272	.339	.500	.839	1	.990
2003— Boston (A.L.)	DH-1B	128	448	79	129	39	2	31	101	58	83	1	9	0-0	.288	.369	.592	.961	3	.992
2004— Boston (A.L.)	DH-1B	150	582	94	175	47	3	41	139	75	133	4	12	0-0	.301	.380	.603	.983	4	.986
2005— Boston (A.L.)	DH-1B	159	601	119	180	40	1	47	* 148	102	124	1	13	1-0	.300	.397	.604	1.001	2	.976
Major League totals (9 years)		892	3108	507	877	234	9	177	626	421	679	15	69	5-2	.282	.366	.534	.901	18	.990

DIVISION SERIES RECORD

Year Team (League)	Pos.	G	AB	R	H	2B	3B	HR	RBI	BB	SO	HBP	GDP	SB-CS	Avg.	OBP	SLG	OPS	E	Avg.
2002— Minnesota (A.L.)	DH	4	13	0	3	2	0	0	2	0	5	0	0	0-0	.231	.231	.385	.615	...	...
2003— Boston (A.L.)	DH	5	21	0	2	1	0	0	2	2	7	0	0	0-0	.095	.174	.143	.317	0	...
2004— Boston (A.L.)	DH	3	11	4	6	2	0	1	4	5	2	0	0	0-0	.545	.688	1.000	1.688	0	...
2005— Boston (A.L.)	DH	3	12	2	4	2	0	1	1	0	3	0	0	0-0	.333	.333	.750	1.083	0	...
Division series totals (4 years)		15	57	6	15	7	0	2	9	7	17	0	0	0-0	.263	.344	.491	.835	0	...

CHAMPIONSHIP SERIES RECORD

Year Team (League)	Pos.	G	AB	R	H	2B	3B	HR	RBI	BB	SO	HBP	GDP	SB-CS	Avg.	OBP	SLG	OPS	E	Avg.
2002— Minnesota (A.L.)	DH	5	16	0	5	1	0	0	2	0	5	0	0	0-0	.313	.313	.375	.688	...	...
2003— Boston (A.L.)	DH	7	26	4	7	1	0	2	6	3	8	1	1	0-0	.269	.367	.538	.905	0	...
2004— Boston (A.L.)	DH	7	31	6	12	0	1	3	11	4	7	0	0	0-1	.387	.457	.742	1.199	0	...
Champ. series totals (3 years)		19	73	10	24	2	1	5	19	7	20	1	1	0-1	.329	.395	.589	.984	0	...

WORLD SERIES RECORD

Year Team (League)	Pos.	G	AB	R	H	2B	3B	HR	RBI	BB	SO	HBP	GDP	SB-CS	Avg.	OBP	SLG	OPS	E	Avg.
2004— Boston (A.L.)	1B-DH	4	13	3	4	1	0	1	4	4	1	0	0	0-0	.308	.471	.615	1.086	0	1.000

ALL-STAR GAME RECORD

		G	AB	R	H	2B	3B	HR	RBI	BB	SO	HBP	GDP	SB-CS	Avg.	OBP	SLG	OPS	E	Avg.
All-Star Game totals (2 years)		2	4	2	3	0	0	1	3	2	0	0	0	0-0	.750	.833	1.500	2.333	0	1.000

ORTIZ, RAMON — P

PERSONAL: Born May 23, 1973, in Cotui, Dominican Republic. ... 6-0/175. ... Throws right, bats right. ... Full name: Ramon Diogenes Ortiz. ... Name pronounced: or-TEEZ. ... High school: 8th Intermedian (Dominican Republic). ... Cousin of Pedro Liriano, pitcher, Milwaukee Brewers.

TRANSACTIONS/CAREER NOTES: Signed as a non-drafted free agent by California Angels organization (June 20, 1995). ... Angels franchise renamed Anaheim Angels for 1997 season. ... On disabled list (March 20-April 11, 2000); included rehabilitation assignment to Lake Elsinore. ... Traded by Angels to Cincinnati Reds for P Dustin Moseley (December 14, 2004). ... On disabled list (April 9-May 1, 2005).

CAREER HITTING: 4-for-76 (.053), 2 R, 2 2B, 0 3B, 0 HR, 0 RBI.

SCOUTING REPORT *Throws:* His fastball ranges from 90-93 mph, and he has a straight changeup. Also throws a slider. *Tendencies:* Ortiz throws from a low arm angle and when he flies open his stuff can get very flat. The higher his release point the better the velocity, movement and command. Slider is quick but flat. Not a strikeout pitcher and is prone to the home run. Has excellent arm speed with a change that fades away from lefthanders and that he will throw to righthanders. Goes through funks where he just throws instead of pitches. *Outlook:* He has a very good arm but needs to pitch in a bigger park. **Grade 6.1**

RAMON ORTIZ'S PITCHING ZONE

.513	.346	.280
.323	.439	.365
.258	.250	.224

LEFTY-RIGHTY SPLITS

vs.	Avg.	AB	H	2B	3B	HR	RBI	BB	SO	OBP	Slg.
L	.288	320	92	11	4	19	54	28	41	.346	.525
R	.315	362	114	30	2	15	52	55	59	.359	.533

Year Team (League)	W	L	Pct.	ERA	WHIP	G	GS	CG	ShO	Hld.	Sv.-Opp.	IP	H	R	ER	HR	BB-IBB	SO	Avg.
1995— Dom. Angels (DSL)	8	6	.571	2.23	1.37	16	.16	7	0	...	0-...	97.0	79	44	24	...	54-...	100	...
1996— Ariz. Angels (Ariz.)	5	4	.556	2.12	1.21	16	8	2	2	...	1-...	68.0	55	28	16	5	27-0	78	.216
— Boise (N'west)	1	1	.500	3.66	1.37	3	3	0	0	...	0-...	19.2	21	10	8	3	6-0	18	.263
1997— Cedar Rap. (Midw.)	11	10	.524	3.58	1.15	27	27	8	4	...	0-...	181.0	156	78	72	22	53-0	225	.230
1998— Midland (Texas)	2	1	.667	5.55	1.40	7	7	0	0	...	0-...	47.0	50	31	29	10	16-0	53	.275
1999— Erie (East.)	9	4	.692	2.82	1.25	15	15	2	2	...	0-...	102.0	88	38	32	12	40-0	86	.237
— Edmonton (PCL)	5	3	.625	4.05	1.22	9	9	0	0	...	0-...	53.1	46	26	24	7	19-0	64	.227
— Anaheim (A.L.)	2	3	.400	6.52	1.55	9	9	0	0	0	0-0	48.1	50	35	35	7	25-0	44	.265
2000— Lake Elsinore (Calif.)	1	0	1.000	3.00	1.67	1	1	0	0	0	0-...	6.0	8	2	2	0	2-0	7	.333
— Anaheim (A.L.)	8	6	.571	5.09	1.36	18	18	2	0	0	0-0	111.1	96	69	63	18	55-0	73	.236
— Edmonton (PCL)	6	6	.500	4.55	1.25	15	15	1	0	0	0-0	89.0	74	49	45	7	37-0	76	.223
2001— Anaheim (A.L.)	13	11	.542	4.36	1.43	32	32	2	0	0	0-0	208.2	223	114	101	26	76-6	135	.274
2002— Anaheim (A.L.)	15	9	.625	3.77	1.18	32	32	4	1	0	0-0	217.1	188	97	91	* 40	68-0	162	.230
2003— Anaheim (A.L.)	16	13	.552	5.20	1.51	32	32	1	0	0	0-0	180.0	209	121	104	28	63-0	94	.287

O

Year Team (League)	W	L	Pct.	ERA	WHIP	G	GS	CG	ShO	Hld.	Sv.-Opp.	IP	H	R	ER	HR	BB-IBB	SO	Avg.
2004— Anaheim (A.L.)	5	7	.417	4.43	1.38	34	14	0	0	0	0-0	128.0	139	64	63	18	38-4	82	.280
2005— Sarasota (Fla. St.)	0	1	.000	9.00	2.33	1	1	0	0	0	0-0	3.0	7	4	3	1	0-0	3	.412
— Cincinnati (N.L.)	9	11	.450	5.36	1.50	30	30	1	0	0	0-0	171.1	206	110	102	34	51-1	96	.302
American League totals (6 years)	59	49	.546	4.60	1.38	157	137	9	1	0	0-0	893.2	905	500	457	136	325-10	590	.262
National League totals (1 year)	9	11	.450	5.36	1.50	30	30	1	0	0	0-0	171.1	206	110	102	34	51-1	96	.302
Major League totals (7 years)	68	60	.531	4.72	1.40	187	167	10	1	0	0-0	1065.0	1111	610	559	170	376-11	686	.269

DIVISION SERIES RECORD

Year Team (League)	W	L	Pct.	ERA	WHIP	G	GS	CG	ShO	Hld.	Sv.-Opp.	IP	H	R	ER	HR	BB-IBB	SO	Avg.
2002— Anaheim (A.L.)	0	0	...	20.25	2.63	1	1	0	0	0	0-0	2.2	3	6	6	0	4-0	1	.333
2004— Anaheim (A.L.)	0	0	...	4.50	1.50	1	0	0	0	0	0-0	2.0	2	1	1	0	1-1	0	.250
Division series totals (2 years)	0	0	...	13.50	2.14	2	1	0	0	0	0-0	4.2	5	7	7	0	5-1	1	.294

CHAMPIONSHIP SERIES RECORD

Year Team (League)	W	L	Pct.	ERA	WHIP	G	GS	CG	ShO	Hld.	Sv.-Opp.	IP	H	R	ER	HR	BB-IBB	SO	Avg.
2002— Anaheim (A.L.)	1	0	1.000	5.06	2.06	1	1	0	0	0	0-0	5.1	10	3	3	0	1-0	3	.435

WORLD SERIES RECORD

Year Team (League)	W	L	Pct.	ERA	WHIP	G	GS	CG	ShO	Hld.	Sv.-Opp.	IP	H	R	ER	HR	BB-IBB	SO	Avg.
2002— Anaheim (A.L.)	1	0	1.000	7.20	1.80	1	1	0	0	0	0-0	5.0	5	4	4	2	4-1	3	.263

ORTIZ, RUSS — P

PERSONAL: Born June 5, 1974, in Encino, Calif. ... 6-1/208. ... Throws right, bats right. ... Full name: Russell Reid Ortiz. ... Name pronounced: or-TEEZ. ... High school: Montclair Prep (Van Nuys, Calif.). ... College: Oklahoma.

TRANSACTIONS/CAREER NOTES: Selected by San Francisco Giants organization in fourth round of 1995 free-agent draft. ... Traded by Giants to Atlanta Braves for Ps Damian Moss and Merkin Valdez (December 17, 2002). ... Signed as a free agent by Arizona Diamondbacks (December 10, 2004). ... On disabled list (June 18-August 13, 2005); included rehabilitation assignments to Lancaster and Tucson.

CAREER HITTING: 94-for-456 (.206), 42 R, 22 2B, 0 3B, 6 HR, 42 RBI.

SCOUTING REPORT

Throws: His best pitch is a 90-94 mph fastball. Also has a cut fastball that he throws at 82-85, a curveball at 77-80 and a changeup. **Tendencies:** Ortiz had an awful year as his command continued to be a major problem. Was hit hard because he couldn't be effective from behind in the count. Has good rotation on curveball, but it breaks early. Has a good changeup. **Outlook:** Ortiz needs to live up to the expectations of his big contract. Doesn't have the type of arm action that is going to allow him to throw a lot of strikes. Look for him to continue to struggle. **Grade 6.5**

RUSS ORTIZ'S PITCHING ZONE

.242	.316	.381
.361	.489	.375
.191	.517	.154

LEFTY-RIGHTY SPLITS

vs.	Avg.	AB	H	2B	3B	HR	RBI	BB	SO	OBP	Slg.
L	.329	246	81	12	8	6	30	31	17	.403	.516
R	.296	223	66	19	0	12	52	34	29	.388	.543

Year Team (League)	W	L	Pct.	ERA	WHIP	G	GS	CG	ShO	Hld.	Sv.-Opp.	IP	H	R	ER	HR	BB-IBB	SO	Avg.
1995— Bellingham (N'west)	2	0	1.000	0.52	0.93	25	0	0	0	...	11-...	34.1	19	4	2	1	13-0	55	.162
— San Jose (Calif.)	0	1	.000	1.50	1.00	5	0	0	0	...	0-...	6.0	4	1	1	0	2-0	7	.190
1996— San Jose (Calif.)	0	0	...	0.25	0.98	34	0	0	0	...	23-...	36.2	16	2	1	0	20-0	63	.131
— Shreveport (Texas)	1	2	.333	4.05	1.61	26	0	0	0	...	13-...	26.2	22	14	12	0	21-3	29	.220
1997— Shreveport (Texas)	2	3	.400	4.13	1.57	12	12	0	0	...	0-...	56.2	52	28	26	3	37-0	50	.252
— Phoenix (PCL)	4	3	.571	5.51	1.53	14	14	0	0	...	0-...	85.0	96	57	52	11	34-0	70	.287
1998— San Francisco (N.L.)	4	4	.500	4.99	1.54	22	13	0	0	1	0-0	88.1	90	51	49	11	46-1	75	.269
— Fresno (PCL)	3	1	.750	1.60	1.13	10	10	0	0	...	0-...	50.2	35	10	9	3	22-0	59	.198
1999— San Francisco (N.L.)	18	9	.667	3.81	1.51	33	33	3	0	0	0-0	207.2	189	109	88	24	* 125-5	164	.244
2000— San Francisco (N.L.)	14	12	.538	5.01	1.55	33	32	0	0	0	0-0	195.2	192	117	109	28	112-1	167	.261
2001— San Francisco (N.L.)	17	9	.654	3.29	1.27	33	33	1	1	0	0-0	218.2	187	90	80	13	91-3	169	.232
2002— San Francisco (N.L.)	14	10	.583	3.61	1.33	33	33	2	0	0	0-0	214.1	191	89	86	15	94-5	137	.241
2003— Atlanta (N.L.)	* 21	7	.750	3.81	1.31	34	34	1	1	0	0-0	212.1	177	101	90	17	* 102-7	149	.223
2004— Atlanta (N.L.)	15	9	.625	4.13	1.51	34	34	2	1	0	0-0	204.2	197	98	94	23	112-7	143	.258
2005— Lancaster (Calif.)	0	1	.000	42.43	5.57	1	1	0	0	0	0-0	2.1	12	11	11	2	1-0	1	.706
— Tucson (PCL)	0	1	.000	13.00	2.11	2	2	0	0	0	0-0	9.0	14	14	13	4	5-0	5	.341
— Arizona (N.L.)	5	11	.313	6.89	1.84	22	22	0	0	0	0-0	115.0	147	92	88	18	65-3	46	.313
Major League totals (8 years)	108	71	.603	4.23	1.45	244	234	9	3	1	0-0	1456.2	1370	747	684	149	747-32	1050	.251

DIVISION SERIES RECORD

Year Team (League)	W	L	Pct.	ERA	WHIP	G	GS	CG	ShO	Hld.	Sv.-Opp.	IP	H	R	ER	HR	BB-IBB	SO	Avg.
2000— San Francisco (N.L.)	0	0	...	1.69	1.13	1	1	0	0	0	0-0	5.1	2	1	1	0	4-1	4	.118
2002— San Francisco (N.L.)	2	0	1.000	2.19	1.38	2	2	0	0	0	0-0	12.1	9	3	3	0	8-1	8	.200
2003— Atlanta (N.L.)	1	1	.500	5.06	2.06	2	2	0	0	0	0-0	10.2	15	6	6	1	7-1	9	.333
2004— Atlanta (N.L.)	0	0	...	15.00	2.67	1	1	0	0	0	0-0	3.0	7	5	5	1	1-0	1	.467
Division series totals (4 years)	3	1	.750	4.31	1.69	6	6	0	0	0	0-0	31.1	33	15	15	2	20-3	22	.270

CHAMPIONSHIP SERIES RECORD

Year Team (League)	W	L	Pct.	ERA	WHIP	G	GS	CG	ShO	Hld.	Sv.-Opp.	IP	H	R	ER	HR	BB-IBB	SO	Avg.
2002— San Francisco (N.L.)	0	0	...	7.71	1.71	1	1	0	0	0	0-0	4.2	5	4	4	2	3-0	3	.263

WORLD SERIES RECORD

Year Team (League)	W	L	Pct.	ERA	WHIP	G	GS	CG	ShO	Hld.	Sv.-Opp.	IP	H	R	ER	HR	BB-IBB	SO	Avg.
2002— San Francisco (N.L.)	0	0	...	10.13	1.88	2	2	0	0	0	0-0	8.0	13	9	9	1	2-0	2	.361

ALL-STAR GAME RECORD

Year Team (League)	W	L	Pct.	ERA	WHIP	G	GS	CG	ShO	Hld.	Sv.-Opp.	IP	H	R	ER	HR	BB-IBB	SO	Avg.
All-Star Game totals (1 year)	0	0	...	0.00	1.00	1	0	0	0	0	0-0	1.0	0	0	0	0	1-0	2	.000

ORTMEIER, DAN — OF

PERSONAL: Born May 11, 1981, in Chattanooga, Tenn. ... 6-4/220. ... Bats both, throws left. ... Full name: Daniel D. Ortmeier. ... High school: Lewisville (Texas). ... College: Texas-Arlington.
TRANSACTIONS/CAREER NOTES: Selected by San Francisco Giants organization in third round of 2002 free-agent draft.
2005 GAMES PLAYED BY POSITION (MLB): OF—7.

LEFTY-RIGHTY SPLITS

vs.	Avg.	AB	H	2B	3B	HR	RBI	BB	SO	OBP	Slg.
L	.000	0	0	0	0	0	0	0	0	.000	.000
R	.136	22	3	0	0	0	1	3	5	.269	.136

									BATTING										FIELDING	
Year Team (League)	Pos.	G	AB	R	H	2B	3B	HR	RBI	BB	SO	HBP	GDP	SB-CS	Avg.	OBP	SLG	OPS	E	Avg.
2002— Salem-Keizer (N'west)	OF	49	195	32	57	9	1	5	31	18	37	1	5	3-0	.292	.352	.426	.778	1	.984
2003— San Jose (Calif.)	OF	115	408	62	124	32	6	8	56	39	89	11	13	13-6	.304	.378	.471	.849	3	.979
2004— Norwich (East.)	OF	106	377	55	95	23	6	10	48	47	110	12	5	18-2	.252	.352	.424	.776	2	.952
2005— Norwich (East.)	OF-DH	135	503	85	138	23	6	20	79	48	115	21	2	35-10	.274	.360	.463	.823	8	.983
— San Francisco (N.L.)	OF	15	22	1	3	0	0	0	1	3	5	1	2	1-0	.136	.269	.136	.406	0	1.000
Major League totals (1 year)		15	22	1	3	0	0	0	1	3	5	1	2	1-0	.136	.269	.136	.406	0	1.000

ORVELLA, CHAD — P

PERSONAL: Born October 1, 1980, in Renton, Wash. ... 5-11/190. ... Throws right, bats right. ... Full name: Chad Robert Orvella. ... High school: Eastlake (Wash.). ... Junior college: Columbia Basin (Wash.). ... College: North Carolina State.
TRANSACTIONS/CAREER NOTES: Selected by Tampa Bay Devil Rays organization in 13th round of 2003 free-agent draft.
CAREER HITTING: 0-for-0 (.000), 0 R, 0 2B, 0 3B, 0 HR, 0 RBI.

CHAD ORVELLA'S PITCHING ZONE

.400	.143	.250
.346	.286	.300
.350	.071	.176

LEFTY-RIGHTY SPLITS

vs.	Avg.	AB	H	2B	3B	HR	RBI	BB	SO	OBP	Slg.
L	.218	78	17	6	0	1	4	15	14	.344	.333
R	.265	113	30	9	0	3	23	8	29	.310	.425

Year Team (League)	W	L	Pct.	ERA	WHIP	G	GS	CG	ShO	Hld.	Sv.-Opp.	IP	H	R	ER	HR	BB-IBB	SO	Avg.
2003— Hudson Valley (NYP)	0	0	...	0.00	0.57	10	0	0	0	...	8-...	12.1	6	0	0	0	1-0	15	.140
2004— Char., S.C. (SAL)	1	0	1.000	1.33	0.70	22	0	0	0	...	4-...	47.1	28	9	7	4	5-0	76	.164
— Bakersfield (Calif.)	0	1	.000	3.06	0.96	15	0	0	0	...	4-...	17.2	13	7	6	2	4-1	24	.197
— Montgom. (Sou.)	0	0	...	0.00	0.00	6	0	0	0	...	4-...	7.0	0	0	0	0	0-0	14	.000
— Durham (Int'l)	0	0	...	5.40	1.20	2	0	0	0	...	0-...	1.2	1	1	1	1	1-0	2	.167
2005— Montgom. (Sou.)	0	0	...	0.36	0.84	16	0	0	0	0	9-10	25.0	15	1	1	0	6-0	29	.169
— Tampa Bay (A.L.)	3	3	.500	3.60	1.40	37	0	0	0	14	1-2	50.0	47	26	20	4	23-2	43	.246
Major League totals (1 year)	3	3	.500	3.60	1.40	37	0	0	0	14	1-2	50.0	47	26	20	4	23-2	43	.246

OSIK, KEITH — C

PERSONAL: Born October 22, 1968, in Port Jefferson, N.Y. ... 6-0/213. ... Bats right, throws right. ... Full name: Keith Richard Osik. ... Name pronounced: OH-sick. ... High school: Shoreham (N.Y.)-Wading River. ... College: Louisiana State.
TRANSACTIONS/CAREER NOTES: Selected by Texas Rangers organization in 47th round of 1987 free-agent draft; did not sign. ... Selected by Pittsburgh Pirates organization in 24th round of 1990 free-agent draft. ... On disabled list (July 16-August 13, 1996); included rehabilitation assignment to Erie. ... On disabled list (July 21-August 13, 1999); included rehabilitation assignment to Nashville. ... On disabled list (April 30-May 15, 2001). ... Signed as a free agent by Milwaukee Brewers organization (January 10, 2003). ... Signed as a free agent by Baltimore Orioles organization (January 14, 2004). ... Released by Orioles (June 1, 2004). ... Signed by Florida Marlins organization (June 10, 2004). ... Released by Marlins (July 15, 2004). ... Signed by Tampa Bay Devil Rays organization (July 28, 2004). ... Signed as free agent by Washington Nationals organization (December 23, 2004). ... Released by Nationals (March 24, 2005). ... Signed as free agent by Nationals (August 7, 2005). ... Released by Nationals (October 2, 2005). ... Career major league pitching: 0-0, 40.50 ERA, 2 G, 2.0 IP, 7 H, 9 R, 9 ER, 2 BB, 2 SO.
2005 GAMES PLAYED BY POSITION (MLB): C—5.

LEFTY-RIGHTY SPLITS

vs.	Avg.	AB	H	2B	3B	HR	RBI	BB	SO	OBP	Slg.
L	.000	2	0	0	0	0	0	0	1	.000	.000
R	.000	2	0	0	0	0	0	0	1	.000	.000

									BATTING										FIELDING	
Year Team (League)	Pos.	G	AB	R	H	2B	3B	HR	RBI	BB	SO	HBP	GDP	SB-CS	Avg.	OBP	SLG	OPS	E	Avg.
1990— Welland (NYP)	C	29	97	13	27	4	0	1	20	11	12	2	1	2-6	.278	.354	.351	.704	2	.978
1991— Salem (Carol.)	2B-3B-C	87	300	31	81	12	1	6	35	38	48	3	13	2-3	.270	.356	.377	.732	12	.970
— Carolina (Southern)	3B-C	17	43	9	13	3	1	0	5	5	5	0	1	0-0	.302	.375	.419	.794	2	.980
1992— Carolina (Southern)	P	129	425	41	110	17	1	5	45	52	69	15	12	2-9	.259	.357	.339	.696	19	.956
1993— Carolina (Southern)	C	103	371	47	104	21	2	10	47	30	46	9	13	0-2	.280	.348	.429	.777	6	.992
1994— Buffalo (A.A.)	C-OF-1B, DH-2B-P	83	260	27	55	16	0	5	33	28	41	3	5	0-1	.212	.294	.331	.624	8	.983
1995— Calgary (PCL)	C-1B-OF, P-3B	90	301	40	101	25	1	10	59	21	42	5	5	2-2	.336	.384	.525	.909	4	.992
1996— Pittsburgh (N.L.)	C-3B-OF	48	140	18	41	14	1	1	14	14	22	1	3	1-0	.293	.361	.429	.790	6	.978
— Erie (N.Y.-Penn)	C	3	10	1	3	1	0	0	2	1	2	1	0	0-0	.300	.417	.400	.817	0	1.000
1997— Pittsburgh (N.L.)	C-2B-1B, 3B	49	105	10	27	9	1	0	7	9	21	1	1	0-1	.257	.322	.362	.684	2	.989
1998— Pittsburgh (N.L.)	C-3B	39	98	8	21	4	0	0	7	13	16	2	4	1-2	.214	.316	.255	.571	1	.995
1999— Pittsburgh (N.L.)	C-P	66	167	12	31	3	1	2	13	11	30	1	8	0-0	.186	.239	.252	.490	1	.997
— Nashville (PCL)	C-OF	4	11	0	1	0	0	0	0	0	1	1	0	0-0	.091	.167	.091	.258	0	1.000
2000— Pittsburgh (N.L.)	C-3B-1B, DH-P	46	123	11	36	6	1	4	22	14	11	5	2	3-0	.293	.387	.455	.843	2	.989
2001— Pittsburgh (N.L.)	C-1B-3B, 2B-OF	56	120	9	25	4	0	2	13	13	24	3	1	1-0	.208	.299	.292	.591	1	.996
2002— Pittsburgh (N.L.)	C-3B-1B, 2B-OF	55	100	6	16	3	0	2	11	6	25	1	2	0-0	.160	.211	.250	.461	1	.994
2003— Milwaukee (N.L.)	C	80	241	22	60	12	0	2	21	31	44	3	7	0-1	.249	.342	.324	.665	5	.989
2004— Baltimore (A.L.)	C	11	25	0	2	0	0	0	0	0	7	0	1	0-0	.080	.080	.080	.160	1	1.000
— Albuquerque (PCL)	C	19	56	5	10	3	1	0	5	5	7	1	6	0-0	.179	.254	.321	.575	0	1.000

O

Year	Team (League)	Pos.	G	AB	R	H	2B	3B	HR	RBI	BB	SO	HBP	GDP	SB-CS	Avg.	OBP	SLG	OPS	E	Avg.
	—Durham (Int'l)	C	26	82	6	20	0	0	1	8	6	10	1	1	0-0	.244	.300	.280	.580	0	1.000
2005—	New Orleans (PCL)	C-1B	17	44	3	9	2	0	0	3	4	7	0	2	1-0	.205	.265	.250	.515	0	1.000
	—Was. (N.L.)	C	6	4	0	0	0	0	0	0	0	2	0	0	0-0	.000	.000	.000	.000	0	1.000
	American League totals (1 year)		11	25	0	2	0	0	0	0	0	7	0	1	0-0	.080	.080	.080	.160	0	1.000
	National League totals (9 years)		445	1098	96	257	55	4	13	108	111	195	17	28	6-4	.234	.313	.327	.640	19	.991
	Major League totals (10 years)		456	1123	96	259	55	4	13	108	111	202	17	29	6-4	.231	.308	.321	.630	19	.991

OSORIA, FRANQUELIS   P

PERSONAL: Born September 12, 1981, in Santiago, Dominican Republic. ... 6-0/165. ... Throws right, bats right. ... Full name: Franquelis Antonio Osoria..
TRANSACTIONS/CAREER NOTES: Signed as a non-drafted free agent by Los Angeles Dodgers organization (December 28, 1999).
CAREER HITTING: 0-for-3 (.000), 0 R, 0 2B, 0 3B, 0 HR, 0 RBI.

FRANQUELIS OSORIA'S PITCHING ZONE

.000	.333	.167
.133	.471	.321
.333	.000	.333

LEFTY-RIGHTY SPLITS

vs.	Avg.	AB	H	2B	3B	HR	RBI	BB	SO	OBP	Slg.
L	.392	51	20	1	1	2	15	3	4	.426	.569
R	.140	57	8	0	0	1	3	5	11	.246	.193

Year	Team (League)	W	L	Pct.	ERA	WHIP	G	GS	CG	ShO	Hld.	Sv.-Opp.	IP	H	R	ER	HR	BB-IBB	SO	Avg.
2000—	Dom. Dodgers (DSL)	3	4	.429	2.52	1.26	13	12	0	0	...	0-...	64.1	58	33	18	1	23-1	46	.230
2001—	Dom. Dodgers (DSL)	4	4	.500	3.16	1.10	15	11	0	0	...	0-...	77.0	69	38	27	5	16-0	67	.237
2002—	Vero Beach (FSL)	0	1	.000	2.45	0.82	3	0	0	0	...	0-...	7.1	4	2	2	0	2-0	10	.154
	—South Georgia (S. Atl.)	2	2	.500	3.32	1.22	21	1	0	0	...	1-...	43.1	40	22	16	1	13-1	30	.226
2003—	Vero Beach (FSL)	3	6	.333	3.00	1.17	33	3	0	0	...	6-...	75.0	69	34	25	4	19-5	53	.244
2004—	Jacksonville (Sou.)	8	5	.615	3.67	1.10	51	0	0	0	...	5-...	81.0	71	36	33	2	18-4	73	.229
	—Las Vegas (PCL)	0	0	...	6.48	1.68	4	0	0	0	...	0-...	8.1	13	6	6	0	1-0	3	.342
2005—	Las Vegas (PCL)	6	4	.600	2.62	1.38	40	0	0	0	8	9-13	55.0	63	18	16	3	13-6	35	.299
	—Los Angeles (N.L.)	0	2	.000	3.94	1.21	24	0	0	0	3	0-2	29.2	28	14	13	3	8-0	15	.259
	Major League totals (1 year)	0	2	.000	3.94	1.21	24	0	0	0	3	0-2	29.2	28	14	13	3	8-0	15	.259

OSUNA, ANTONIO   P

PERSONAL: Born April 12, 1973, in Sinaloa, Mexico. ... 5-11/227. ... Throws right, bats right. ... Full name: Antonio Pedro Osuna. ... Name pronounced: oh-SOON-a. ... High school: Secondaria Federal (Mexico).
TRANSACTIONS/CAREER NOTES: Signed as a non-drafted free agent by Los Angeles Dodgers organization (June 12, 1991). ... Loaned by Dodgers to Mexico City Tigres of the Mexican League (March 6-September 25, 1992). ... On disabled list (May 19-June 16, 1995); included rehabilitation assignment to San Bernardino. ... On disabled list (September 9, 1998-remainder of season). ... On disabled list (March 25-April 16, April 18-May 3 and May 19, 1999-remainder of season); included rehabilitation assignments to San Bernardino. ... On disabled list (March 31-May 5, 2000); included rehabilitation assignment to San Bernardino. ... Traded by Dodgers with P Carlos Ortega to Chicago White Sox for Ps Gary Majewski, Andre Simpson and Orlando Rodriguez (March 17, 2001). ... On disabled list (April 12, 2001-remainder of season). ... Traded by White Sox with P Delvis Lantigua to New York Yankees for P Orlando Hernandez and cash (January 15, 2003). ... On disabled list (April 23-May 14 and June 14-July 13, 2003); included rehabilitation assignments to Tampa and GCL Yankees. ... Signed as a free agent by San Diego Padres organization (February 5, 2004). ... On disabled list (May 12-31 and June 11-September 1, 2004); included rehabilitation assignment to Lake Elsinore. ... Signed as a free agent by Washington Nationals (January 19, 2005). ... On disabled list (April 18, 2005-remainder of season). ... Released by Nationals (October 3, 2005).
CAREER HITTING: 1-for-9 (.111), 0 R, 0 2B, 0 3B, 0 HR, 1 RBI.

LEFTY-RIGHTY SPLITS

vs.	Avg.	AB	H	2B	3B	HR	RBI	BB	SO	OBP	Slg.
L	.000	1	0	0	0	0	1	5	0	.714	.000
R	.643	14	9	1	0	2	9	2	0	.688	1.143

Year	Team (League)	W	L	Pct.	ERA	WHIP	G	GS	CG	ShO	Hld.	Sv.-Opp.	IP	H	R	ER	HR	BB-IBB	SO	Avg.
1991—	GC Dodgers (GCL)	0	0	...	0.82	0.73	8	0	0	0	...	4-...	11.0	8	5	1	0	0-0	13	.186
	—Yakima (N'west)	0	0	...	3.20	1.03	13	0	0	0	...	5-...	25.1	18	10	9	1	8-0	39	.205
1992—	M.C. Tigers (Mex.)	13	7	.650	4.05	1.53	28	26	3	1	...	0-...	166.2	181	80	75	16	74-...	129	...
1993—	Bakersfield (Calif.)	0	2	.000	4.91	1.31	14	2	0	0	...	2-...	18.1	19	10	10	2	5-0	20	.268
1994—	San Antonio (Texas)	1	2	.333	0.98	0.80	35	0	0	0	...	19-...	46.0	19	6	5	0	18-1	53	.127
	—Albuquerque (PCL)	0	0	...	0.00	1.00	6	0	0	0	...	4-...	6.0	5	1	0	0	1-0	8	.227
1995—	Los Angeles (N.L.)	2	4	.333	4.43	1.32	39	0	0	0	11	0-2	44.2	39	22	22	5	20-2	46	.241
	—San Bern. (Calif.)	0	0	...	1.29	1.14	5	0	0	0	...	0-...	7.0	3	1	1	1	5-0	11	.130
	—Albuquerque (PCL)	0	1	.000	4.42	1.31	19	0	0	0	...	11-...	18.1	15	9	9	2	9-0	19	.227
1996—	Los Angeles (N.L.)	0	0	...	0.00	2.00	1	0	0	0	...	0-...	1.0	2	0	0	0	0-0	1	.500
	—Los Angeles (N.L.)	9	6	.600	3.00	1.15	73	0	0	0	16	4-9	84.0	65	33	28	6	32-12	85	.229
1997—	Albuquerque (PCL)	1	1	.500	1.93	0.93	13	0	0	0	...	6-...	14.0	9	3	3	0	4-0	26	.176
	—Los Angeles (N.L.)	3	4	.429	2.19	1.45	48	0	0	0	10	0-0	61.2	46	15	15	6	19-2	68	.209
1998—	Los Angeles (N.L.)	7	1	.875	3.06	1.27	54	0	0	0	12	6-11	64.2	50	26	22	8	32-0	72	.213
1999—	San Bern. (Calif.)	0	0	...	2.33	1.29	13	4	0	0	...	0-...	19.1	19	6	5	0	6-0	27	.260
	—Los Angeles (N.L.)	0	0	...	7.71	1.50	5	0	0	0	2	0-0	4.2	4	5	4	0	3-0	5	.222
2000—	San Bern. (Calif.)	0	2	.000	4.91	0.95	3	3	0	0	...	0-...	7.1	4	4	4	2	3-0	11	.167
	—Albuquerque (PCL)	0	0	...	0.00	1.24	3	1	0	0	...	0-...	5.2	2	2	0	0	5-0	7	.095
	—Los Angeles (N.L.)	3	6	.333	3.74	1.37	46	0	0	0	4	0-3	67.1	57	30	28	7	35-2	70	.229
2001—	Chicago (A.L.)	0	0	...	20.77	2.31	4	0	0	0	...	0-1	4.1	8	10	10	3	2-1	6	.421
2002—	Chicago (A.L.)	8	2	.800	3.86	1.36	59	0	0	0	9	11-14	67.2	64	32	29	1	28-4	66	.250
2003—	GC Yankees (GCL)	0	0	...	0.00	1.00	1	1	0	0	...	0-...	1.0	1	0	0	0	0-0	2	.250
	—Tampa (Fla. St.)	0	0	...	0.00	0.50	2	2	0	0	...	0-...	4.0	1	0	0	0	1-0	5	.083
	—New York (A.L.)	2	5	.286	3.73	1.54	48	0	0	0	9	0-1	50.2	58	22	21	3	20-3	47	.282
2004—	Lake Elsinore (Calif.)	0	0	...	2.46	0.55	7	2	0	0	...	0-...	7.1	2	2	2	0	2-0	12	.083
	—San Diego (N.L.)	2	1	.667	2.45	1.17	31	0	0	0	2	0-2	36.2	32	11	10	3	11-0	36	.232
2005—	Was. (N.L.)	0	0	...	42.43	6.86	4	0	0	0	0	0-0	2.1	9	11	11	2	7-1	0	.600
	—New Orleans (PCL)	0	0	...	0.00	0.33	2	0	0	0	...	0-0	3.0	1	0	0	0	1-0	1	.111
	American League totals (3 years)	10	7	.588	4.40	1.47	111	0	0	0	18	11-16	122.2	130	64	60	7	50-8	119	.270
	National League totals (8 years)	26	22	.542	3.44	1.26	300	0	0	0	57	10-27	366.0	302	153	140	37	159-19	382	.227

0

Year Team (League)	W	L	Pct.	ERA	WHIP	G	GS	CG	ShO	Hld.	Sv.-Opp.	IP	H	R	ER	HR	BB-IBB	SO	Avg.
Major League totals (11 years)	36	29	.554	3.68	1.31	411	0	0	0	75	21-43	488.2	432	217	200	44	209-27	501	.238

DIVISION SERIES RECORD

Year Team (League)	W	L	Pct.	ERA	WHIP	G	GS	CG	ShO	Hld.	Sv.-Opp.	IP	H	R	ER	HR	BB-IBB	SO	Avg.
1995— Los Angeles (N.L.)	0	1	.000	2.70	1.20	3	0	0	0	0	0-0	3.1	3	1	1	0	1-1	3	.231
1996— Los Angeles (N.L.)	0	1	.000	4.50	2.00	2	0	0	0	0	0-0	2.0	3	1	1	1	1-0	4	.429
Division series totals (2 years)	0	2	.000	3.38	1.50	5	0	0	0	0	0-0	5.1	6	2	2	1	2-1	7	.300

OSWALT, ROY   P

PERSONAL: Born August 29, 1977, in Weir, Miss. ... 6-0/185. ... Throws right, bats right. ... Full name: Roy Edward Oswalt. ... Name pronounced: OWES-walt. ... High school: Weir (Miss.). ... Junior college: Holmes (Miss.).

TRANSACTIONS/CAREER NOTES: Selected by Houston Astros organization in 23rd round of 1996 free-agent draft. ... On suspended list (August 29-September 3, 2002). ... On disabled list (May 16-31, June 12-July 7 and July 30-September 8, 2003); included rehabilitation assignment to New Orleans.

HONORS: Named N.L. Rookie Pitcher of the Year by THE SPORTING NEWS (2001).

CAREER HITTING: 49-for-307 (.160), 14 R, 5 2B, 0 3B, 0 HR, 15 RBI.

SCOUTING REPORT *Throws:* Oswalt has a power arm, throwing a 92-96 mph fastball, a big curve from the low 60s to the high 70s, and a straight changeup. *Tendencies:* He has excellent command of his overpowering fastball to both sides of the plate, and it is almost impossible to center it high in the strike zone. Can pitch only with his fastball at times. Throws curve with tight downspin, forcing hitters to change their focus. Works quickly and continually challenges hitters. *Outlook:* Oswalt may have been baseball's best pitcher down the stretch, and he is the only pitcher with successive 20-win seasons the past two years. **Grade 9.6**

ROY OSWALT'S PITCHING ZONE

.156	.364	.207
.308	.365	.274
.361	.259	.259

LEFTY-RIGHTY SPLITS

vs.	Avg.	AB	H	2B	3B	HR	RBI	BB	SO	OBP	Slg.
L	.279	441	123	23	6	9	46	19	81	.312	.420
R	.247	486	120	25	2	9	33	29	103	.293	.362

Year Team (League)	W	L	Pct.	ERA	WHIP	G	GS	CG	ShO	Hld.	Sv.-Opp.	IP	H	R	ER	HR	BB-IBB	SO	Avg.
1997— GC Astros (GCL)	1	1	.500	0.64	1.13	5	5	0	0	...	0-...	28.1	25	7	2	2	7-0	28	.227
— Auburn (NY-Penn)	2	4	.333	4.53	1.26	9	9	1	1	...	0-...	51.2	50	29	26	1	15-1	44	.253
1998— GC Astros (GCL)	1	1	.500	2.25	0.69	4	4	0	0	...	0-...	16.0	10	6	4	2	1-0	27	.182
— Auburn (NY-Penn)	4	5	.444	2.18	1.14	11	11	0	0	...	0-...	70.1	49	24	17	3	31-0	67	.194
1999— Michigan (Midw.)	13	4	.765	4.46	1.31	22	22	2	0	...	0-...	151.1	144	78	75	8	54-0	143	.250
2000— Kissimmee (Fla. St.)	4	3	.571	2.98	1.39	8	8	0	0	...	0-...	45.1	52	15	15	1	11-0	47	.294
— Round Rock (Texas)	11	4	.733	1.94	0.99	19	18	2	2	...	0-...	129.2	106	37	28	5	22-1	141	.216
2001— New Orleans (PCL)	2	3	.400	4.35	1.23	5	5	0	0	...	0-...	31.0	32	16	15	4	6-0	34	.267
— Houston (N.L.)	14	3	.824	2.73	1.06	28	20	3	1	0	0-0	141.2	126	48	43	13	24-2	144	.235
2002— Houston (N.L.)	19	9	.679	3.01	1.19	35	34	0	0	0	0-0	233.0	215	86	78	17	62-4	208	.247
2003— New Orleans (PCL)	0	0	...	3.00	1.00	1	1	0	0	...	0-...	3.0	3	1	1	0	0-0	2	.250
— Houston (N.L.)	10	5	.667	2.97	1.14	21	21	0	0	0	0-0	127.1	116	48	42	15	29-0	108	.246
2004— Houston (N.L.)	* 20	10	.667	3.49	1.24	36	• 35	2	2	0	0-0	237.0	233	100	92	17	62-5	206	.260
2005— Houston (N.L.)	20	12	.625	2.94	1.20	35	• 35	4	1	0	0-0	241.2	243	85	79	18	48-3	184	.262
Major League totals (5 years)	83	39	.680	3.07	1.18	155	145	9	4	0	0-0	980.2	933	367	334	80	225-14	850	.252

DIVISION SERIES RECORD

Year Team (League)	W	L	Pct.	ERA	WHIP	G	GS	CG	ShO	Hld.	Sv.-Opp.	IP	H	R	ER	HR	BB-IBB	SO	Avg.
2004— Houston (N.L.)	1	0	1.000	2.38	1.68	2	2	0	0	0	0-0	11.1	15	3	3	2	4-0	8	.313
2005— Houston (N.L.)	1	0	1.000	3.68	1.09	1	1	0	0	0	0-0	7.1	6	3	3	0	2-0	7	.222
Division series totals (2 years)	2	0	1.000	2.89	1.45	3	3	0	0	0	0-0	18.2	21	6	6	2	6-0	15	.280

CHAMPIONSHIP SERIES RECORD

Year Team (League)	W	L	Pct.	ERA	WHIP	G	GS	CG	ShO	Hld.	Sv.-Opp.	IP	H	R	ER	HR	BB-IBB	SO	Avg.
2004— Houston (N.L.)	0	0	...	6.75	1.88	2	1	0	0	0	0-0	8.0	11	6	6	1	4-0	2	.367
2005— Houston (N.L.)	2	0	1.000	1.29	0.86	2	2	0	0	0	0-0	14.0	8	2	2	1	4-0	12	.163
Champ. series totals (2 years)	2	0	1.000	3.27	1.23	4	3	0	0	0	0-0	22.0	19	8	8	2	8-0	14	.241

WORLD SERIES RECORD

Year Team (League)	W	L	Pct.	ERA	WHIP	G	GS	CG	ShO	Hld.	Sv.-Opp.	IP	H	R	ER	HR	BB-IBB	SO	Avg.
2005— Houston (N.L.)	0	0	...	7.50	2.17	1	1	0	0	0	0-0	6.0	8	5	5	1	5-0	3	.320

ALL-STAR GAME RECORD

Year Team (League)	W	L	Pct.	ERA	WHIP	G	GS	CG	ShO	Hld.	Sv.-Opp.	IP	H	R	ER	HR	BB-IBB	SO	Avg.
All-Star Game totals (1 year)	0	0	...	18.00	3.00	1	0	0	0	0	0-0	1.0	2	2	2	0	1-0	1	.400

OTSUKA, AKINORI   P

PERSONAL: Born January 13, 1972, in Chiba, Japan. ... 6-0/200. ... Throws right, bats right. ... Name pronounced: oats-kah. ... High school: Yokoshiba (Japan). ... College: Tokai University.

TRANSACTIONS/CAREER NOTES: Signed as a free agent by San Diego Padres (December 9, 2003).

CAREER HITTING: 0-for-2 (.000), 0 R, 0 2B, 0 3B, 0 HR, 0 RBI.

SCOUTING REPORT *Throws:* His fastball ranges from 90-93 mph. Also has a curveball, slider and split-finger fastball. *Tendencies:* Otsuka has a very deliberate delivery that he slows down when nobody's on base, effectively keeping hitters off-balance. Has a good arm with good command. All of his breaking balls are average to above average. Fastball tends to be straight. *Outlook:* Otsuka, a veteran of the Japanese leagues, was reliable last year in a setup role. Could develop into a closer with more big-league experience. **Grade 7.7**

AKINORI OTSUKA'S PITCHING ZONE

.188	.333	.500
.342	.222	.448
.233	.111	.238

LEFTY-RIGHTY SPLITS

vs.	Avg.	AB	H	2B	3B	HR	RBI	BB	SO	OBP	Slg.
L	.207	121	25	4	0	2	10	20	35	.329	.289
R	.263	114	30	7	1	1	12	14	25	.344	.368

Year	Team (League)	W	L	Pct.	ERA	WHIP	G	GS	CG	ShO	Hld.	Sv.-Opp.	IP	H	R	ER	HR	BB-IBB	SO	Avg.
1997— Kintetsu (Jp. Pac.)		4	5	.444	2.07	1.09	52	0	0	0	...	7-...	82.2	44	22	19	2	46-0	127	...
1998— Kintetsu (Jp. Pac.)		.3	2	.600	2.11	1.23	49	0	0	0	...	35-...	55.1	43	19	13	5	25-0	74	...
1999— Kintetsu (Jp. Pac.)		1	4	.200	2.73	1.15	25	0	0	0	...	6-...	29.2	24	12	9	1	10-0	32	...
2000— Kintetsu (Jp. Pac.)		1	3	.250	2.38	1.06	39	0	0	0	...	24-...	41.2	31	11	11	3	13-0	49	...
2001— Kintetsu (Jp. Pac.)		2	5	.286	4.02	1.02	48	0	0	0	...	26-...	56.0	42	25	25	7	15-0	82	...
2002— Kintetsu (Jp. Pac.)		2	1	.667	1.28	0.59	41	0	0	0	...	22-...	42.1	22	7	6	4	3-0	54	...
2003— Chunichi (Jp. Cn.)		1	3	.250	2.09	0.84	51	0	0	0	...	17-...	43.0	31	10	10	4	5-0	56	.199
2004— San Diego (N.L.)		7	2	.778	1.75	1.06	73	0	0	0	* 34	2-7	77.1	56	16	15	6	26-6	87	.199
2005— San Diego (N.L.)		2	8	.200	3.59	1.42	66	0	0	0	22	1-7	62.2	55	28	25	3	34-8	60	.234
Major League totals (2 years)		**9**	**10**	**.474**	**2.57**	**1.22**	**139**	**0**	**0**	**0**	**56**	**3-14**	**140.0**	**111**	**44**	**40**	**9**	**60-14**	**147**	**.215**

DIVISION SERIES RECORD

Year	Team (League)	W	L	Pct.	ERA	WHIP	G	GS	CG	ShO	Hld.	Sv.-Opp.	IP	H	R	ER	HR	BB-IBB	SO	Avg.
2005— San Diego (N.L.)		0	0	...	0.00	0.67	3	0	0	0	0	0-0	3.0	1	0	0	0	1-1	0	.100

OVERBAY, LYLE — 1B

PERSONAL: Born January 28, 1977, in Centralia, Wash. ... 6-2/227. ... Bats left, throws left. ... Full name: Lyle Stefan Overbay. ... High school: Centralia (Wash.). ... College: Nevada.

TRANSACTIONS/CAREER NOTES: Selected by Arizona Diamondbacks organization in 18th round of 1999 free-agent draft. ... Traded by Diamondbacks with SS Craig Counsell, 2B Junior Spivey, C Chad Moeller and Ps Chris Capuano and Jorge de la Rosa to Milwaukee Brewers for 1B Richie Sexson, P Shane Nance and a player to be named (December 1, 2003); Diamondbacks acquired OF Noochie Varner to complete deal (December 15, 2003).

2005 GAMES PLAYED BY POSITION (MLB): 1B—154.

SCOUTING REPORT *Offense:* Although his average decreased in 2005, his power numbers increased. Is more of a gap-to-gap doubles hitter than a home-run and RBI producer. Is starting to pull the ball more but bat speed is just average. Has very good bat control and stays inside the ball well. Hits out of a very open stance. Doesn't run well. *Defense:* Overbay has good hands, but range to his right is limited. Has an accurate arm starting the double play and handles errant throws from a very erratic young infield well. *Outlook:* He has the stroke and the ability to make contact; now he's learning to sit on pitches better, which should increase his power. **Grade 7.9**

LYLE OVERBAY'S HITTING ZONE

.208	.333	.313
.306	.380	.306
.440	.433	.099

LEFTY-RIGHTY SPLITS

vs.	Avg.	AB	H	2B	3B	HR	RBI	BB	SO	OBP	Slg.
L	.269	145	39	6	1	6	25	5	36	.299	.448
R	.278	392	109	28	0	13	47	73	62	.390	.449

Year	Team (League)	Pos.	G	AB	R	H	2B	3B	HR	RBI	BB	SO	HBP	GDP	SB-CS	Avg.	OBP	SLG	OPS	E	FIELDING Avg.
1999— Missoula (Pion.)	1B-OF	75	306	66	105	25	7	12	101	40	53	2	14	10-3	.343	.418	.588	1.006	10	.986
2000— South Bend (Mid.)	1B	71	259	47	86	19	3	6	47	27	36	2	9	9-2	.332	.397	.498	.895	11	.974
— El Paso (Texas)	1B	62	244	43	86	16	2	8	49	28	39	2	6	3-2	.352	.420	.533	.953	12	.979
2001— El Paso (Texas)	1B-OF	138	532	82	187	49	3	13	100	67	92	5	6	5-4	.352	.423	.528	.951	13	.987
— Arizona (N.L.)		2	2	0	1	0	0	0	0	0	1	0	0	0-0	.500	.500	.500	1.000	...	...
2002— Tucson (PCL)	1B	134	525	83	180	* 40	0	19	109	42	86	1	12	0-0	.343	.396	.528	.923	10	.991
— Arizona (N.L.)		10	10	0	1	0	0	0	1	0	5	0	0	0-0	.100	.100	.100	.200	0	...
2003— Tucson (PCL)	1B-DH	35	119	24	34	11	0	4	16	28	19	0	2	0-0	.286	.419	.479	.898	5	.985
— Arizona (N.L.)	1B	86	254	23	70	20	0	4	28	35	67	2	8	1-0	.276	.365	.402	.767	2	.997
2004— Milwaukee (N.L.)	1B	159	579	83	174	* 53	1	16	87	81	128	2	11	2-1	.301	.385	.478	.863	11	.992
2005— Milwaukee (N.L.)	1B	158	537	80	148	34	1	19	72	78	98	2	17	1-0	.276	.367	.449	.816	10	.992
Major League totals (5 years)			415	1382	186	394	107	2	39	188	194	299	6	36	4-1	.285	.373	.450	.823	23	.993

OXSPRING, CHRIS — P

PERSONAL: Born May 13, 1977, in Ipswich, Australia. ... 6-0/185. ... Throws right, bats left. ... Full name: Chris Andrew Oxspring. ... High school: Ipswich State (Australia).

TRANSACTIONS/CAREER NOTES: Signed as a non-drafted free agent by San Diego Padres (October 31, 2000).

CAREER HITTING: 0-for-2 (.000), 0 R, 0 2B, 0 3B, 0 HR, 0 RBI.

LEFTY-RIGHTY SPLITS

vs.	Avg.	AB	H	2B	3B	HR	RBI	BB	SO	OBP	Slg.
L	.222	18	4	1	0	1	4	4	6	.364	.444
R	.227	22	5	0	0	1	5	2	5	.269	.364

Year	Team (League)	W	L	Pct.	ERA	WHIP	G	GS	CG	ShO	Hld.	Sv.-Opp.	IP	H	R	ER	HR	BB-IBB	SO	Avg.
2000— Cook County (Fron.)	1	0	1.000	3.10	1.52	13	2	0	0	...	1-...	29.0	29	18	10	1	15-0	29	.257
2001— Fort Wayne (Midw.)	4	1	.800	4.15	1.62	41	2	0	0	...	0-...	56.1	66	29	26	5	25-0	54	.297
— Lake Elsinore (Calif.)	0	0		0.64	1.14	7	0	0	0	...	0-...	14.0	10	2	1	1	6-0	17	.200
2002— Lake Elsinore (Calif.)	0	1	.000	4.78	1.22	15	1	0	0	...	0-...	26.1	24	16	14	2	8-0	30	.238
— Mobile (Sou.)	0	0		1.26	1.47	6	1	0	0	...	0-...	14.1	13	3	2	0	8-0	21	.245
2003— Mobile (Sou.)	10	6	.625	2.92	1.24	40	18	1	0	...	0-...	135.2	106	47	44	6	62-3	129	.211
2004— Portland (PCL)	6	4	.600	3.99	1.47	17	17	0	0	...	0-...	85.2	82	45	38	7	44-1	81	.255
2005— Portland (PCL)	12	6	.667	4.03	1.18	26	26	3	2	0	0-0	160.2	148	81	72	15	42-0	125	.243
— San Diego (N.L.)	0	0		3.75	1.25	5	0	0	0	0	0-0	12.0	9	8	5	2	6-0	11	.225
Major League totals (1 year)	**0**	**0**		**3.75**	**1.25**	**5**	**0**	**0**	**0**	**0**	**0-0**	**12.0**	**9**	**8**	**5**	**2**	**6-0**	**11**	**.225**

OZUNA, PABLO — 2B/SS

PERSONAL: Born August 25, 1974, in Santo Domingo, Dominican Republic. ... 5-10/186. ... Bats right, throws right. ... Full name: Pablo Jose Ozuna. ... Name pronounced: oh-ZU-na.

TRANSACTIONS/CAREER NOTES: Signed as non-drafted free agent by St. Louis Cardinals orgnaization (April 8, 1996). ... Traded by Cardinals with P Braden Looper and P Armando Almanza to Florida Marlins for SS Edgar Renteria (December 14, 1998). ... On disabled list (March 23, 2001-entire season). ... Traded by Marlins with C Charles Johnson, P Vic Darensbourg and OF Preston Wilson to Colorado Rockies for P Mike Hampton, OF Juan Pierre and cash (November 16, 2002). ... On disabled list (March 29-June 6, 2003); included rehabilitation assignment to Visalia. ... Released by Rockies (December 14, 2003). ... Signed by Detroit Tigers organization (January 14, 2004). ... Traded by Tigers to Philadelphia Phillies for cash (March 28, 2004). ... Signed as a free agent by Chicago White Sox organization (January 19, 2005).

HONORS: Named Midwest League Most Valuable Player (1998).

2005 GAMES PLAYED BY POSITION (MLB): 3B—32, SS—15, OF—10, 2B—6, DH—4, 1B—2.

O

SCOUTING REPORT

SCOUTING REPORT Ozuna is a valuable utility infielder. Is an aggressive hitter who likes the ball away and is vulnerable to inside pitches. Is better against lefthanders. Does not have much power. Doesn't hit breaking balls well. Is solid defensively at shortstop and second base but is less effective at third; doesn't react well there and often is fielding the ball off his chest. Has limited range. Has a strong arm but lacks accuracy. **Grade 4.6**

PABLO OZUNA'S HITTING ZONE

.421	.333	.385
.234	.286	.286
.231	.286	.250

LEFTY-RIGHTY SPLITS

vs.	Avg.	AB	H	2B	3B	HR	RBI	BB	SO	OBP	Slg.
L	.306	98	30	5	0	0	3	2	11	.340	.357
R	.248	105	26	2	2	0	8	5	15	.288	.305

									BATTING										FIELDING	
Year Team (League)	Pos.	G	AB	R	H	2B	3B	HR	RBI	BB	SO	HBP	GDP	SB-CS	Avg.	OBP	SLG	OPS	E	Avg.
1996— Dom. Cardinals (DSL)	SS	74	295	57	107	12	4	6	60	23	19	6	0	18-5.	.363	.415	.492	.907	32	.915
1997— Johnson City (App.)	SS	56	232	40	75	13	1	5	24	10	24	1	2	23-5	.323	.351	.453	.804	25	.898
1998— Peoria (Midw.)	SS	133	538	122	192	27	10	9	62	29	56	11	6	62-26	.357	.400	.494	.894	45	.929
1999— Portland (East.)	SS	117	502	62	141	25	7	7	46	13	50	13	8	31-16	.281	.315	.400	.715	28	.946
2000— Portland (East.)	SS-2B	118	464	74	143	25	6	7	59	40	55	7	9	35-24	.308	.368	.433	.801	25	.956
— Florida (N.L.)	2B	14	24	2	8	1	0	0	0	0	2	0	0	1-0	.333	.333	.375	.708	1	.967
2001— Florida (N.L.)					Did not play.															
2002— Calgary (PCL)	2B-OF	77	261	37	85	16	1	7	33	17	37	3	5	16-3	.326	.371	.475	.846	9	.961
— Florida (N.L.)	2B-OF	34	47	4	13	2	2	0	3	1	3	1	2	1-1	.277	.300	.404	.704	1	.967
2003— Visalia (Calif..)	2B-SS	2	8	1	5	0	0	0	1	1	1	0	0	1-1	.625	.667	.625	1.292	0	1.000
— Tulsa (Texas)	2B-SS-3B	12	59	4	15	3	0	0	4	2	5	0	0	4-2	.254	.279	.305	.584	3	.943
— Colo. Springs (PCL)	2B-OF-SS-3B	56	219	30	59	13	7	1	17	9	23	1	3	12-6	.269	.300	.406	.706	6	.970
— Colorado (N.L.)	2B-OF-SS	17	40	5	8	1	0	0	2	2	6	2	1	3-0	.200	.273	.225	.498	2	.969
2004— Scran./W.B. (I.L.)	2B-SS-OF	126	472	77	145	27	3	6	76	22	43	7	11	31-12	.307	.344	.415	.759	15	.786
2005— Chicago (A.L.)	3B-SS-OF																			
	2B-DH-1B	70	203	27	56	7	2	0	11	7	26	4	5	14-7	.276	.313	.330	.643	9	.951
American League totals (1 year)		70	203	27	56	7	2	0	11	7	26	4	5	14-7	.276	.313	.330	.643	9	.951
National League totals (3 years)		65	111	11	29	4	2	0	5	3	11	3	3	5-1	.261	.297	.333	.630	4	.968
Major League totals (4 years)		135	314	38	85	11	4	0	16	10	37	7	8	19-8	.271	.307	.331	.638	13	.958

CHAMPIONSHIP SERIES RECORD

Year Team (League)	Pos.	G	AB	R	H	2B	3B	HR	RBI	BB	SO	HBP	GDP	SB-CS	Avg.	OBP	SLG	OPS	E	Avg.
2005— Chicago (A.L.)	DH	2	0	1	0	0	0	0	0	0	0	0	0	1-0	...	...	...	...	0	...

PADILLA, JUAN P

PERSONAL: Born February 17, 1977, in Rio Piedras, Puerto Rico. ... 6-0/200. ... Throws right, bats right. ... Full name: Juan Miguel Padilla. ... Name pronounced: pa-DEE-ya. ... High school: Visual Arts (Santurce, Puerto Rico). ... Junior college: Tallahassee (Fla.) Community College. ... College: Jacksonville.

TRANSACTIONS/CAREER NOTES: Selected by Minnesota Twins in 24th round of 1998 free-agent draft. ... Traded by Twins to New York Yankees (September 2, 2003), completing deal in which Twins acquired P Jesse Orosco for a player to be named (August 31, 2003). ... Claimed on waivers by Cincinnati Reds (September 3, 2004). ... Signed as a free agent by New York Mets organization (December 2, 2004).

CAREER HITTING: 1-for-2 (.500), 0 R, 0 2B, 0 3B, 0 HR, 0 RBI.

SCOUTING REPORT *Throws:* Padilla's fastball tops out at 88 mph, but he throws his slider more. Also throws a split-finger fastball. *Tendencies:* He is a finesse pitcher with no true quality pitch, but he still did an excellent job of keeping hitters off-balance after his call-up last season. Stays on the corners and won't give in to hitters. Prefers to walk them rather than give them something too good when he's behind in the count. Has a fast delivery that borders on being a quick pitch. *Outlook:* After turning in a 1.49 ERA in 24 games, he is in line to handle a key spot in the Mets' bullpen this season, most likely as a seventh-inning setup man. Command will determine if he can be as successful as he was in 2005. **Grade 7.8**

JUAN PADILLA'S PITCHING ZONE

.000	.286	.182
.310	.167	.120
.000	.000	.250

LEFTY-RIGHTY SPLITS

vs.	Avg.	AB	H	2B	3B	HR	RBI	BB	SO	OBP	Slg.
L	.153	59	9	2	0	0	4	8	9	.254	.186
R	.203	74	15	2	1	0	3	5	8	.272	.257

Year Team (League)	W	L	Pct.	ERA	WHIP	G	GS	CG	ShO	Hld.	Sv.-Opp.	IP	H	R	ER	HR	BB-IBB	SO	Avg.
1998— GC Twins (GCL)	1	1	.500	1.40	0.78	17	0	0	0	...	10-...	25.2	19	4	4	1	1-0	27	.202
1999— Quad City (Midw.)	0	2	.000	2.40	1.60	12	0	0	0	...	0-...	15.0	18	8	4	0	6-2	16	.290
— New Britain (East.)	1	1	.500	6.63	2.00	11	0	0	0	...	2-...	19.0	31	15	14	3	7-0	12	.383
— Fort Myers (FSL)	2	2	.500	3.48	1.46	22	0	0	0	...	0-...	33.2	32	14	13	1	17-2	28	.260
2000— Quad City (Midw.)	2	2	.500	1.91	1.00	32	0	0	0	...	16-...	33.0	24	7	7	0	9-2	40	.200
— New Britain (East.)	0	1	.000	3.74	1.37	23	0	0	0	...	0-...	33.2	35	15	14	1	11-0	24	.269
2001— Fort Myers (FSL)	6	4	.600	2.99	1.40	56	0	0	0	...	23-...	69.1	72	35	23	2	25-6	77	.261
2002— New Britain (East.)	3	5	.375	3.31	1.33	54	0	0	0	...	29-...	65.1	69	30	24	2	18-6	52	.267
2003— Rochester (Int'l)	7	4	.636	3.36	1.22	57	0	0	0	...	6-...	91.0	94	40	34	7	17-3	68	.266
2004— Trenton (East.)	0	0	...	9.00	1.75	3	0	0	0	...	0-...	4.0	4	4	4	1	3-0	4	.267
— New York (A.L.)	0	0	...	3.97	1.76	6	0	0	0	0	0-0	11.1	16	5	5	1	4-0	5	.348
— Columbus (Int'l)	2	1	.667	2.03	0.95	44	0	0	0	...	2-...	57.2	49	20	13	1	6-2	52	.232
— Cincinnati (N.L.)	1	0	1.000	10.67	2.16	12	0	0	0	0	0-0	14.1	23	17	17	6	8-0	12	.359
2005— Norfolk (Int'l)	3	2	.600	1.42	0.85	37	2	0	0	3	11-14	63.1	45	13	10	4	9-0	59	.197

P

Year Team (League)	W	L	Pct.	ERA	WHIP	G	GS	CG	ShO	Hld.	Sv.-Opp.	IP	H	R	ER	HR	BB-IBB	SO	Avg.
— New York (N.L.)	3	1	.750	1.49	1.02	24	0	0	0	6	1-2	36.1	24	7	6	0	13-2	17	.180
American League totals (1 year)	0	0		3.97	1.76	6	0	0	0	0	0-0	11.1	16	5	5	1	4-0	5	.348
National League totals (2 years)	4	1	.800	4.09	1.34	36	0	0	0	6	1-2	50.2	47	24	23	6	21-2	29	.239
Major League totals (2 years)	4	1	.800	4.06	1.42	42	0	0	0	6	1-2	62.0	63	29	28	7	25-2	34	.259

PADILLA, VICENTE   P

PERSONAL: Born September 27, 1977, in Chinandega, Nicaragua. ... 6-2/219. ... Throws right, bats right. ... Full name: Vicente D. Padilla. ... Name pronounced: pa-DEE-ya. ... High school: Ruben Dario (Nicaragua).

TRANSACTIONS/CAREER NOTES: Signed as a non-drafted free agent by Arizona Diamondbacks organization (August 31, 1998). ... Traded by Diamondbacks with 1B/OF Travis Lee and Ps Omar Daal and Nelson Figueroa to Philadelphia Phillies for P Curt Schilling (July 26, 2000). ... On disabled list (May 4-30, 2001); included rehabilitation assignment to Scranton/Wilkes-Barre. ... On disabled list (May 30-August 10, 2004); included rehabilitation assignments to Scranton/Wilkes-Barre and Clearwater. ... On disabled list (March 30-April 19, 2005); included rehabilitation assignments to Scranton/Wilkes-Barre and Clearwater.

CAREER HITTING: 19-for-205 (.093), 7 R, 3 2B, 1 3B, 0 HR, 13 RBI.

SCOUTING REPORT *Throws:* He has a heavy fastball that tops out at 90-95 mph. Also has a curveball, slider and changeup. *Tendencies:* Padilla likes to experiment with his above-average stuff, but he makes too many mistakes because of it. Has very good life with fastballs down in the zone. Gets into trouble with a soft, looping curveball that hangs; slider is a much better breaking pitch because of its sharp, lateral break. Too often looks to pitch away from contact. *Outlook:* Padilla is a quality middle-rotation starter who has the stuff to be more. Needs to develop better focus and intensity on the mound. A high pitch count makes him unpredictable from one start to the next. *Grade 6.7*

VICENTE PADILLA'S PITCHING ZONE

.128	.387	.188
.258	.333	.343
.244	.226	.478

LEFTY-RIGHTY SPLITS

vs.	Avg.	AB	H	2B	3B	HR	RBI	BB	SO	OBP	Slg.
L	.297	283	84	25	0	18	51	43	37	.395	.576
R	.222	279	62	19	0	4	24	31	66	.308	.333

Year Team (League)	W	L	Pct.	ERA	WHIP	G	GS	CG	ShO	Hld.	Sv.-Opp.	IP	H	R	ER	HR	BB-IBB	SO	Avg.
1999— High Desert (Calif.)	4	1	.800	3.73	1.32	9	9	0	0	...	0-...	50.2	50	27	21	3	17-0	55	.253
— Tucson (PCL)	7	4	.636	3.75	1.40	18	14	0	0	...	0-...	93.2	107	47	39	6	24-7	58	.292
— Arizona (N.L.)	0	1	.000	16.88	3.75	5	0	0	0	1	0-1	2.2	7	5	5	1	3-0	0	.467
2000—Tucson (PCL)	0	1	.000	4.42	1.64	12	3	0	0	...	1-...	18.1	22	9	9	2	8-0	22	.306
— Arizona (N.L.)	2	1	.667	2.31	1.20	27	0	0	0	7	0-1	35.0	32	10	9	0	10-2	30	.242
— Philadelphia (N.L.)	2	6	.250	5.34	1.91	28	0	0	0	8	2-6	30.1	40	23	18	3	18-5	21	.328
2001— Philadelphia (N.L.)	3	1	.750	4.24	1.41	23	0	0	0	1	0-3	34.0	36	18	16	1	12-0	29	.273
— Scran./W.B. (I.L.)	7	0	1.000	2.42	0.92	16	16	0	0	...	0-...	81.2	64	24	22	8	11-0	75	.217
2002— Philadelphia (N.L.)	14	11	.560	3.28	1.22	32	32	1	1	...	0-...	206.0	198	83	75	16	53-5	128	.254
2003— Philadelphia (N.L.)	14	12	.538	3.62	1.24	32	32	1	1	...	0-...	208.2	196	94	84	22	62-4	133	.251
2004— Clearwater (FSL)	0	1	.000	9.00	2.00	1	1	0	0	...	0-...	2.0	3	2	2	0	1-0	1	.333
— Scran./W.B. (I.L.)	0	0	...	13.50	2.36	2	2	0	0	...	0-...	4.2	6	7	7	1	5-0	6	.286
— Philadelphia (N.L.)	7	7	.500	4.53	1.34	20	20	0	0	...	0-0	115.1	119	63	58	16	36-6	82	.267
2005— Clearwater (FSL)	0	1	.000	1.80	1.00	1	1	0	0	...	0-...	5.0	4	1	1	0	1-0	3	.200
— Scran./W.B. (I.L.)	1	0	1.000	3.60	1.60	1	1	0	0	...	0-...	5.0	6	2	2	0	2-0	4	.316
— Philadelphia (N.L.)	9	12	.429	4.71	1.50	27	27	0	0	...	0-0	147.0	146	79	77	22	74-9	103	.260
Major League totals (7 years)	51	51	.500	3.95	1.34	194	111	2	2	2	2-11	779.0	774	375	342	81	268-31	526	.261

ALL-STAR GAME RECORD

	W	L	Pct.	ERA	WHIP	G	GS	CG	ShO	Hld.	Sv.-Opp.	IP	H	R	ER	HR	BB-IBB	SO	Avg.
All-Star Game totals (1 year)	0	0	...	0.00	0.50	1	0	0	0	...	0-0	2.0	0	0	0	0	1-0	0	.000

PALMEIRO, ORLANDO   OF

PERSONAL: Born January 19, 1969, in Hoboken, N.J. ... 5-11/180. ... Bats left, throws left. ... Name pronounced: pahl-MARE-oh. ... High school: Southridge (Miami). ... College: Miami. ... Cousin of Rafael Palmeiro, first baseman, Baltimore Orioles.

TRANSACTIONS/CAREER NOTES: Selected by California Angels organization in 33rd round of 1991 free-agent draft. ... On disabled list (September 1-26, 1994). ... Angels franchise renamed Anaheim Angels for 1997 season. ... On disabled list (August 23-September 7, 1997). ... Signed as a free agent by St. Louis Cardinals (February 2, 2003). ... Signed as a free agent by Houston Astros (January 19, 2004).

2005 GAMES PLAYED BY POSITION (MLB): OF—71.

SCOUTING REPORT *Offense:* Palmeiro is a contact hitter with a short swing and good bat control, but he has poor bat speed. Is willing to take what the pitcher gives him and go to the opposite field. Is patient and prefers the ball up in the strike zone. Is a slightly below-average runner but has good instincts. *Defense:* He can play all three outfield positions, but Palmeiro rarely plays center field. Has good instincts and compensates for lost range with good jumps. Charges the ball well and has a quick release, compensating for below-average arm strength. *Outlook:* Palmeiro is a solid fourth outfielder who has become a better pinch hitter, but he doesn't hit enough to play regularly. *Grade 5.7*

ORLANDO PALMEIRO'S HITTING ZONE

.389	.000	.150
.231	.438	.462
.200	.417	.222

LEFTY-RIGHTY SPLITS

vs.	Avg.	AB	H	2B	3B	HR	RBI	BB	SO	OBP	Slg.
L	.136	22	3	0	0	0	2	3	5	.296	.136
R	.302	182	55	17	2	3	18	12	18	.347	.467

Year Team (League)	Pos.	G	AB	R	H	2B	3B	HR	RBI	BB	SO	HBP	GDP	SB-CS	Avg.	OBP	SLG	OPS	E	Avg.
1991—Boise (N'west)	OF	70	277	56	77	11	2	1	24	33	22	3	8	8-8	.278	.358	.343	.701	2	.986
1992—Quad City (Midw.)	OF	127	451	83	143	22	4	0	41	56	41	5	5	31-13	.317	.393	.384	.777	4	.973
1993—Midland (Texas)	OF	131	535	85	163	19	5	0	64	42	35	2	13	18-14	.305	.356	.359	.715	6	.973
1994—Vancouver (PCL)	OF	117	458	79	150	28	4	1	40	58	46	1	7	21-16	.328	.402	.413	.815	1	.996
1995—Vancouver (PCL)	OF-DH	107	398	66	122	21	4	0	47	41	34	3	11	16-7	.307	.371	.379	.751	1	.996
— California (A.L.)	OF-DH	15	20	3	7	0	0	0	1	1	1	0	0	0-0	.350	.381	.350	.731	0	1.000
1996—Vancouver (PCL)	OF	62	245	40	75	13	4	0	33	30	19	4	4	7-3	.306	.384	.392	.776	5	.959

P

Year Team (League)	Pos.	G	AB	R	H	2B	3B	HR	RBI	BB	SO	HBP	GDP	SB-CS	Avg.	OBP	SLG	OPS	E	Avg.
—California (A.L.)	OF-DH	50	87	6	25	6	1	0	6	8	13	2	1	0-1	.287	.361	.379	.740	0	1.000
1997—Anaheim (A.L.)	OF-DH	74	134	19	29	2	2	0	8	17	11	1	4	2-2	.216	.307	.261	.568	2	.975
1998—Vancouver (PCL)	OF	43	140	21	42	13	3	1	29	16	10	0	2	3-1	.300	.363	.457	.820	0	1.000
—Anaheim (A.L.)	OF-DH	75	165	28	53	7	2	0	21	20	11	0	2	5-4	.321	.395	.388	.782	0	1.000
1999—Anaheim (A.L.)	OF-DH	109	317	46	88	12	1	1	23	39	30	6	4	5-5	.278	.364	.331	.696	1	.994
2000—Anaheim (A.L.)	OF-DH	108	243	38	73	20	2	0	25	38	20	2	4	4-1	.300	.395	.399	.794	2	.984
2001—Anaheim (A.L.)	OF-DH	104	230	29	56	10	1	2	23	25	24	3	3	6-6	.243	.319	.322	.641	1	.989
2002—Anaheim (A.L.)	OF-DH	110	263	35	79	12	1	0	31	30	22	0	7	7-2	.300	.368	.354	.722	1	.993
2003—St. Louis (N.L.)	OF	141	317	37	86	13	1	3	33	32	31	2	1	3-3	.271	.336	.347	.683	0	1.000
2004—Houston (N.L.)	OF	102	133	19	32	5	0	3	12	18	19	3	1	2-1	.241	.344	.346	.690	0	1.000
2005—Houston (N.L.)	OF	114	204	22	58	17	2	3	20	15	23	4	4	3-1	.284	.341	.431	.772	1	.986
American League totals (8 years)		645	1459	204	410	69	10	3	138	178	132	14	25	29-21	.281	.361	.348	.710	7	.991
National League totals (3 years)		357	654	78	176	35	3	9	65	65	73	9	6	8-5	.269	.339	.373	.712	1	.996
Major League totals (11 years)		1002	2113	282	586	104	13	12	203	243	205	23	31	37-26	.277	.355	.356	.710	8	.992

DIVISION SERIES RECORD

Year Team (League)	Pos.	G	AB	R	H	2B	3B	HR	RBI	BB	SO	HBP	GDP	SB-CS	Avg.	OBP	SLG	OPS	E	Avg.
2004—Houston (N.L.)	OF	5	4	0	1	0	0	0	0	0	0	0	0	0-0	.250	.250	.250	.500	0	...
2005—Houston (N.L.)	OF	4	7	0	1	0	0	0	3	2	0	1	0	0-0	.143	.364	.143	.506	0	1.000
Division series totals (2 years)		9	11	0	2	0	0	0	3	2	0	1	0	0-0	.182	.333	.182	.515	0	1.000

CHAMPIONSHIP SERIES RECORD

Year Team (League)	Pos.	G	AB	R	H	2B	3B	HR	RBI	BB	SO	HBP	GDP	SB-CS	Avg.	OBP	SLG	OPS	E	Avg.
2002—Anaheim (A.L.)	OF	2	2	0	0	0	0	0	0	0	1	0	0	0-0	.000	.000	.000	.000	0	...
2004—Houston (N.L.)	OF	7	6	0	2	1	0	0	0	0	0	1	0	0-0	.333	.429	.500	.929	0	...
2005—Houston (N.L.)		4	3	0	1	0	0	0	0	1	0	0	0	0-0	.333	.500	.333	.833	0	...
Champ. series totals (3 years)		13	11	0	3	1	0	0	0	1	1	1	0	0-0	.273	.385	.364	.748	0	...

WORLD SERIES RECORD

Year Team (League)	Pos.	G	AB	R	H	2B	3B	HR	RBI	BB	SO	HBP	GDP	SB-CS	Avg.	OBP	SLG	OPS	E	Avg.
2002—Anaheim (A.L.)		4	4	1	1	1	0	0	0	0	2	0	0	0-0	.250	.250	.500	.750	0	...
2005—Houston (N.L.)	OF	2	2	0	0	0	0	0	0	2	0	0	0	0-0	.000	.500	.000	.500	0	...
World series totals (2 years)		6	6	1	1	1	0	0	0	2	2	0	0	0-0	.167	.375	.333	.708	0	...

PALMEIRO, RAFAEL — 1B/DH

PERSONAL: Born September 24, 1964, in Havana, Cuba. ... 6-0/214. ... Bats left, throws left. ... Full name: Rafael Corrales Palmeiro. ... Name pronounced: pahl-MARE-oh. ... High school: Jackson (Miami). ... College: Mississippi State. ... Cousin of Orlando Palmeiro, outfielder with Houston Astros.

TRANSACTIONS/CAREER NOTES: Selected by New York Mets organization in eighth round of June 1982 free-agent draft; did not sign. ... Selected by Chicago Cubs organization in first round (22nd pick overall) of June 1985 free-agent draft; pick received as compensation for San Diego Padres signing Type A free-agent P Tim Stoddard. ... Traded by Cubs with Ps Jamie Moyer and Drew Hall to Texas Rangers for Ps Mitch Williams, Paul Kilgus and Steve Wilson, IFs Curtis Wilkerson and Luis Benitez and OF Pablo Delgado (December 5, 1988). ... Signed as a free agent by Baltimore Orioles (December 12, 1993). ... Signed as a free agent by Rangers (December 4, 1998). ... Signed as a free agent by Orioles (January 14, 2004). ... On suspended list (August 1-11, 2005).

HONORS: Named Major League Player of the Year by THE SPORTING NEWS (1999). ... Won A.L. Gold Glove at first base (1997-99).

2005 GAMES PLAYED BY POSITION (MLB): 1B—93, DH—15.

SCOUTING REPORT **Offense:** Palmeiro has one of the most fluid strokes around, but his bat speed is on the decline. Strictly looks to pull the ball and has become home run conscious. Will go deep in the count but is vulnerable to off-speed pitches. **Defense:** He has very good hands, but his range is limited because of knee problems. Good at picking throws in the dirt. **Outlook:** There are more questions than answers concerning next year, but his skills are declining. **Grade 6.5**

RAFAEL PALMEIRO'S HITTING ZONE

.313	.333	.182
.459	.200	.265
.308	.176	.281

LEFTY-RIGHTY SPLITS

vs.	Avg.	AB	H	2B	3B	HR	RBI	BB	SO	OBP	Slg.
L	.221	95	21	1	0	3	20	5	12	.257	.326
R	.281	274	77	12	0	15	40	38	31	.366	.489

Year Team (League)	Pos.	G	AB	R	H	2B	3B	HR	RBI	BB	SO	HBP	GDP	SB-CS	Avg.	OBP	SLG	OPS	E	Avg.
1985—Peoria (Midw.)	OF	73	279	34	83	22	4	5	51	31	34	2	4	9-3	.297	.369	.459	.828	1	.992
1986—Pittsfield (East.)	OF	140	509	66	156	29	2	12	95	54	32	2	8	15-7	.306	.367	.442	.809	3	.988
—Chicago (N.L.)	OF	22	73	9	18	4	0	3	12	4	6	1	4	1-1	.247	.295	.425	.720	4	.900
1987—Iowa (A.A.)	1B-OF	57	214	36	64	14	3	11	41	22	22	3	2	4-3	.299	.366	.547	.913	2	.988
—Chicago (N.L.)	1B-OF	84	221	32	61	15	1	14	30	20	26	1	4	2-2	.276	.336	.543	.879	1	.995
1988—Chicago (N.L.)	1B-OF	152	580	75	178	41	5	8	53	38	34	6	11	12-2	.307	.349	.436	.785	5	.985
1989—Texas (A.L.)	1B-DH	156	559	76	154	23	4	8	64	63	48	6	18	4-3	.275	.354	.374	.728	12	.991
1990—Texas (A.L.)	1B-DH	154	598	72	* 191	35	6	14	89	40	59	3	24	3-3	.319	.361	.468	.829	7	.995
1991—Texas (A.L.)	1B-DH	159	631	115	203	* 49	3	26	88	68	72	6	17	4-3	.322	.389	.532	.922	* 12	.992
1992—Texas (A.L.)	1B-DH	159	608	84	163	27	4	22	85	72	83	10	10	2-3	.268	.352	.434	.786	7	.995
1993—Texas (A.L.)	1B	160	597	* 124	176	40	2	37	105	73	85	5	22	22-3	.295	.371	.554	.926	5	.997
1994—Baltimore (A.L.)	1B	111	436	82	139	32	0	23	76	54	63	4	11	7-3	.319	.392	.550	.942	4	.996
1995—Baltimore (A.L.)	1B	143	554	89	172	30	2	39	104	62	65	3	12	3-1	.310	.380	.583	.963	4	.997
1996—Baltimore (A.L.)	1B-DH	162	626	110	181	40	2	39	142	95	96	3	9	8-0	.289	.381	.546	.927	8	.995
1997—Baltimore (A.L.)	1B-DH	158	614	95	156	24	2	38	110	67	109	5	14	5-2	.254	.329	.485	.815	10	.993
1998—Baltimore (A.L.)	1B-DH	162	619	98	183	36	1	43	121	79	91	7	14	11-7	.296	.379	.565	.944	9	.994
1999—Texas (A.L.)	DH-1B	158	565	96	183	30	1	47	148	97	69	3	13	2-4	.324	.420	.630	1.050	1	.996
2000—Texas (A.L.)	1B-DH	158	565	102	163	29	3	39	120	103	77	3	14	2-1	.289	.397	.558	.954	4	.995
2001—Texas (A.L.)	1B-DH	160	600	98	164	33	0	47	123	101	90	7	8	1-1	.273	.381	.563	.944	8	.993
2002—Texas (A.L.)	1B-DH	155	546	99	149	34	0	43	105	104	94	6	10	2-0	.273	.391	.571	.962	5	.994
2003—Texas (A.L.)	DH-1B	154	561	92	146	21	2	38	112	84	77	5	7	2-0	.260	.359	.508	.867	2	.996
2004—Baltimore (A.L.)	1B-DH	154	550	68	142	29	0	23	88	86	61	6	15	2-1	.258	.359	.436	.796	5	.993

P

Year Team (League)	Pos.	G	AB	R	H	2B	3B	HR	RBI	BB	SO	HBP	GDP	SB-CS	Avg.	OBP	SLG	OPS	E	FIELDING Avg.
2005— Baltimore (A.L.)	1B-DH	110	369	47	98	13	0	18	60	43	43	2	9	2-0	.266	.339	.447	.786	4	.995
American League totals (17 years)		2573	9598	1547	2763	525	32	544	1740	1291	1282	82	213	82-35	.288	.373	.519	.892	110	.994
National League totals (3 years)		258	874	116	257	60	6	25	95	62	66	5	19	15-5	.294	.341	.462	.804	10	.982
Major League totals (20 years)		2831	10472	1663	3020	585	38	569	1835	1353	1348	87	232	97-40	.288	.371	.515	.885	120	.994

DIVISION SERIES RECORD

Year Team (League)	Pos.	G	AB	R	H	2B	3B	HR	RBI	BB	SO	HBP	GDP	SB-CS	Avg.	OBP	SLG	OPS	E	Avg.
1996— Baltimore (A.L.)	1B	4	17	4	3	1	0	1	2	1	6	1	0	0-0	.176	.263	.412	.675	1	.973
1997— Baltimore (A.L.)	1B	4	12	2	3	2	0	0	0	1	2	0	0	0-0	.250	.250	.417	.667	0	1.000
1999— Texas (A.L.)	DH	3	11	0	3	0	0	0	0	1	1	0	0	0-0	.273	.333	.273	.606	...	1.000
Division series totals (3 years)		11	40	6	9	3	0	1	2	3	9	1	0	0-0	.225	.279	.375	.654	1	.985

CHAMPIONSHIP SERIES RECORD

Year Team (League)	Pos.	G	AB	R	H	2B	3B	HR	RBI	BB	SO	HBP	GDP	SB-CS	Avg.	OBP	SLG	OPS	E	Avg.
1996— Baltimore (A.L.)	1B	5	17	4	4	0	0	2	4	4	4	0	0	0-0	.235	.364	.588	.952	0	1.000
1997— Baltimore (A.L.)	1B	6	25	3	7	2	0	1	2	0	10	1	1	0-0	.280	.308	.480	.788	0	1.000
Champ. series totals (2 years)		11	42	7	11	2	0	3	6	4	14	1	1	0-0	.262	.333	.524	.857	0	1.000

ALL-STAR GAME RECORD

		G	AB	R	H	2B	3B	HR	RBI	BB	SO	HBP	GDP	SB-CS	Avg.	OBP	SLG	OPS	E	Avg.
All-Star Game totals (4 years)		4	4	1	3	0	0	0	2	2	0	0	0	0-0	.750	.833	.750	1.583	0	1.000

PAPELBON, JONATHAN   P

PERSONAL: Born November 23, 1980, in Baton Rouge, La. ... 6-4/230. ... Throws right, bats right. ... Full name: Jonathan Robert Papelbon. ... High school: Bishop Kenny (Jacksonville). ... College: Mississippi State.

TRANSACTIONS/CAREER NOTES: Selected by Boston Red Sox organization in fourth round of 2003 free-agent draft.

CAREER HITTING: 0-for-0 (.000), 0 R, 0 2B, 0 3B, 0 HR, 0 RBI.

JONATHAN PAPELBON'S PITCHING ZONE

.143	.250	.214
.318	.857	.304
.333	.000	.125

LEFTY-RIGHTY SPLITS

vs.	Avg.	AB	H	2B	3B	HR	RBI	BB	SO	OBP	Slg.
L	.190	58	11	2	0	2	4	12	14	.338	.328
R	.319	69	22	6	0	2	7	5	20	.382	.493

Year Team (League)	W	L	Pct.	ERA	WHIP	G	GS	CG	ShO	Hld.	Sv.-Opp.	IP	H	R	ER	HR	BB-IBB	SO	Avg.
2003— Lowell (NY-Penn)	1	2	.333	6.34	1.59	13	6	0	0	...	0-...	32.2	43	23	23	2	9-0	36	.312
2004— Sarasota (Fla. St.)	12	7	.632	2.64	1.08	24	24	2	0	...	0-...	129.2	97	43	38	6	43-2	153	.210
2005— Portland (East.)	5	2	.714	2.48	0.94	14	14	0	0	0	0-0	87.0	59	28	24	9	23-3	83	.193
—Pawtucket (Int'l)	1	2	.333	2.93	0.87	7	4	0	0	0	1-1	27.2	21	9	9	2	3-0	27	.208
—Boston (A.L.)	3	1	.750	2.65	1.47	17	3	0	0	4	0-1	34.0	33	11	10	4	17-2	34	.260
Major League totals (1 year)	3	1	.750	2.65	1.47	17	3	0	0	4	0-1	34.0	33	11	10	4	17-2	34	.260

DIVISION SERIES RECORD

Year Team (League)	W	L	Pct.	ERA	WHIP	G	GS	CG	ShO	Hld.	Sv.-Opp.	IP	H	R	ER	HR	BB-IBB	SO	Avg.
2005— Boston (A.L.)	0	0	...	0.00	0.50	2	0	0	0	0	0-0	4.0	2	0	0	0	0-0	2	.143

PARK, CHAN HO   P

PERSONAL: Born June 30, 1973, in Kong Ju City, South Korea. ... 6-2/210. ... Throws right, bats right. ... Full name: Chan Ho Park. ... High school: Kong Ju (Kong Ju City, South Korea). ... College: Hanyang University (South Korea).

TRANSACTIONS/CAREER NOTES: Signed as a non-drafted free agent by Los Angeles Dodgers organization (January 14, 1994). ... On suspended list (June 8-17, 1999). ... Signed as a free agent by Texas Rangers (December 23, 2001). ... On disabled list (April 2-May 12 and August 7-23, 2002); included rehabilitation assignment to Oklahoma. ... On disabled list (April 28-June 7 and June 8, 2003-remainder of season); included rehabilitation assignments to Frisco and Oklahoma. ... On disabled list (May 20-August 26, 2004); included rehabilitation assignments to AZL Rangers, Frisco and Oklahoma. ... Traded by Rangers to San Diego Padres for IF Phil Nevin (July 29, 2005).

CAREER HITTING: 63-for-364 (.173), 26 R, 15 2B, 1 3B, 2 HR, 25 RBI.

SCOUTING REPORT *Throws:* He complements his 89-93 mph fastball with a curveball at 72-75, a slider at 80-85 and a changeup. *Tendencies:* Park showed flashes of the pitcher he was when be broke in with the Dodgers in the mid-1990s but still was extremely inconsistent. Worked on a two-seam fastball to keep the ball in the park, as he was very hittable up in the zone because of his declining velocity. Curve has a big, quick break and tight rotation. Slider is more like a cutter. Has good arm speed with his change. *Outlook:* He is an enigmatic starter who will pitch to the level of his competition. *Grade 5.2*

CHAN HO PARK'S PITCHING ZONE

.340	.353	.286
.265	.441	.345
.222	.194	.206

LEFTY-RIGHTY SPLITS

vs.	Avg.	AB	H	2B	3B	HR	RBI	BB	SO	OBP	Slg.
L	.305	328	100	23	1	9	51	45	61	.395	.463
R	.279	287	80	17	2	2	35	35	52	.366	.373

Year Team (League)	W	L	Pct.	ERA	WHIP	G	GS	CG	ShO	Hld.	Sv.-Opp.	IP	H	R	ER	HR	BB-IBB	SO	Avg.
1994— Los Angeles (N.L.)	0	0	...	11.25	2.50	2	0	0	0	0	0-0	4.0	5	5	5	1	5-0	6	.294
—San Antonio (Texas)	5	7	.417	3.55	1.46	20	20	0	0	...	0-...	101.1	91	52	40	4	57-0	100	.241
1995— Albuquerque (PCL)	6	7	.462	4.91	1.54	23	22	0	0	...	0-...	110.0	93	64	60	10	76-2	101	.233
—Los Angeles (N.L.)	0	0	...	4.50	1.00	2	1	0	0	0	0-0	4.0	2	2	2	1	2-0	7	.143
1996— Los Angeles (N.L.)	5	5	.500	3.64	1.41	48	10	0	0	4	0-0	108.2	82	48	44	7	71-3	119	.209
1997— Los Angeles (N.L.)	14	8	.636	3.38	1.14	32	29	2	0	0	0-0	192.0	149	80	72	24	70-1	166	.213
1998— Los Angeles (N.L.)	15	9	.625	3.71	1.34	34	34	2	0	0	0-0	220.2	199	101	91	16	97-1	191	.244
1999— Los Angeles (N.L.)	13	11	.542	5.23	1.58	33	33	0	0	0	0-0	194.1	208	120	113	31	100-4	174	.276
2000— Los Angeles (N.L.)	18	10	.643	3.27	1.31	34	34	3	1	0	0-0	226.0	173	92	82	21	124-4	217	.214

P

Year Team (League)	W	L	Pct.	ERA	WHIP	G	GS	CG	ShO	Hld.	Sv.-Opp.	IP	H	R	ER	HR	BB-IBB	SO	Avg.
2001— Los Angeles (N.L.)	15	11	.577	3.50	1.17	36	•35	2	1	0	0-0	234.0	183	98	91	23	91-1	218	.216
2002— Texas (A.L.)	9	8	.529	5.75	1.59	25	25	0	0	0	0-0	145.2	154	95	93	20	78-2	121	.273
— Oklahoma (PCL)	0	1	.000	27.00	4.00	1	1	0	0	...	0-...	3.0	9	9	9	0	3-0	3	.500
2003— Frisco (Texas)	1	0	1.000	2.45	1.30	2	2	0	0	0	0-...	11.0	10	5	3	0	4-0	6	.238
— Oklahoma (PCL)	1	0	1.000	5.89	1.90	3	3	0	0	0	0-...	18.1	27	12	12	4	8-0	12	.346
— Texas (A.L.)	1	3	.250	7.58	1.99	7	7	0	0	0	0-0	29.2	34	26	25	5	25-0	16	.306
2004— Rangers (Ariz.)	1	1	.500	1.71	1.00	4	4	0	0	0	0-0	21.0	15	6	4	0	6-0	20	.197
— Frisco (Texas)	0	2	.000	8.74	1.85	2	2	0	0	0	0-...	11.1	16	11	11	1	5-0	5	.356
— Oklahoma (PCL)	0	2	.000	3.72	1.24	4	4	0	0	0	0-0	19.1	21	8	8	4	3-0	19	.273
— Texas (A.L.)	4	7	.364	5.46	1.44	16	16	0	0	0	0-0	95.2	105	63	58	22	33-0	63	.281
2005— Texas (A.L.)	8	5	.615	5.66	1.68	20	20	0	0	0	0-0	109.2	130	70	69	8	54-1	80	.299
— San Diego (N.L.)	4	3	.571	5.91	1.66	10	9	0	0	0	0-0	45.2	50	33	30	3	26-0	33	.278
American League totals (4 years)	22	23	.489	5.79	1.61	68	68	0	0	0	0-0	380.2	423	254	245	55	190-3	280	.285
National League totals (9 years)	84	57	.596	3.88	1.33	231	185	9	2	4	0-0	1229.1	1051	579	530	127	586-14	1131	.232
Major League totals (12 years)	106	80	.570	4.33	1.40	299	253	9	2	4	0-0	1610.0	1474	833	775	182	776-17	1411	.245

ALL-STAR GAME RECORD

	W	L	Pct.	ERA	WHIP	G	GS	CG	ShO	Hld.	Sv.-Opp.	IP	H	R	ER	HR	BB-IBB	SO	Avg.
All-Star Game totals (1 year)	0	1	.000	9.00	1.00	1	1	0	0	0	0-0	1.0	1	1	1	1	0-0	1	.250

PARRISH, JOHN   P

PERSONAL: Born November 26, 1977, in Lancaster, Pa. ... 5-11/192. ... Throws left, bats left. ... Full name: John Henry Parrish Jr.. ... High school: J.P. McCaskey (Lancaster, Pa.).

TRANSACTIONS/CAREER NOTES: Selected by Baltimore Orioles organization in 25th round of 1996 free-agent draft. ... On disabled list (March 30, 2002-entire season; September 6, 2005-remainder of season).

CAREER HITTING: 0-for-1 (.000), 0 R, 0 2B, 0 3B, 0 HR, 0 RBI.

SCOUTING REPORT *Throws:* Parrish's fastball ranges from 90-92 mph and his slider from 81-84. Also has a changeup. *Tendencies:* He's an extremely aggressive pitcher with good life on his fastball, but he doesn't have good mechanics and throws across his body. Consistently works behind in the count. Overthrows all his pitches and lacks command. Slider can be very good with better command. Will turn over his change to righthanders, but he tends to speed up his arm when throwing it. *Outlook:* Parrish could develop quickly if he stops overthrowing and smooths out his mechanics. *Grade 6.2*

JOHN PARRISH'S PITCHING ZONE

.200	.000	.667
.500	.375	.500
.400	1.000	.143

LEFTY-RIGHTY SPLITS

vs.	Avg.	AB	H	2B	3B	HR	RBI	BB	SO	OBP	Slg.
L	.200	30	6	1	0	1	4	5	10	.314	.333
R	.342	38	13	3	0	0	6	12	15	.500	.421

Year Team (League)	W	L	Pct.	ERA	WHIP	G	GS	CG	ShO	Hld.	Sv.-Opp.	IP	H	R	ER	HR	BB-IBB	SO	Avg.
1996— GC Orioles (GCL)	2	0	1.000	1.86	1.24	11	0	0	0	...	2-...	19.1	13	5	4	0	11-0	33	.181
— Bluefield (Appal.)	2	1	.667	2.70	1.50	8	0	0	0	...	1-...	13.1	11	6	4	0	9-1	18	.229
1997— Delmarva (S. Atl.)	3	3	.500	3.84	1.39	23	10	0	0	...	1-...	72.2	69	39	31	7	32-3	76	.250
— Bowie (East.)	1	0	1.000	1.80	1.00	1	1	0	0	...	0-...	5.0	3	1	1	0	2-0	3	.167
— Frederick (Carolina)	1	3	.250	6.04	1.58	5	5	0	0	...	0-...	22.1	23	18	15	3	16-0	17	.274
1998— Frederick (Carolina)	4	4	.500	3.27	1.26	16	16	1	0	...	0-...	82.2	77	39	30	5	27-1	81	.246
1999— Delmarva (S. Atl.)	0	1	.000	7.20	1.50	4	0	0	0	...	0-...	10.0	9	8	8	1	6-1	10	.225
— Frederick (Carolina)	2	2	.500	4.17	1.25	6	6	0	0	...	0-...	36.2	34	17	17	4	12-0	44	.250
— Bowie (East.)	0	2	.000	4.04	1.65	12	10	0	0	...	0-...	55.2	49	28	25	4	43-1	42	.258
2000— Bowie (East.)	2	0	1.000	1.69	1.19	3	3	0	0	...	0-...	16.0	12	3	3	0	7-0	16	.214
— Rochester (Int'l)	6	7	.462	4.24	1.36	18	18	0	0	...	0-...	104.0	85	54	49	10	56-1	87	.235
— Baltimore (A.L.)	2	4	.333	7.18	2.06	8	8	0	0	0	0-...	36.1	40	32	29	6	35-0	28	.288
2001— Rochester (Int'l)	7	7	.500	3.52	1.25	26	19	1	0	...	0-...	133.0	115	68	52	11	51-4	126	.231
— Baltimore (A.L.)	1	2	.333	6.14	1.77	16	1	0	0	2	0-0	22.0	22	17	15	5	17-1	20	.256
2002— Baltimore (A.L.)	Did not play.																		
2003— Bowie (East.)	3	3	.500	2.00	1.20	49	0	0	0	...	6-...	76.1	58	22	17	5	33-0	85	.214
— Baltimore (A.L.)	0	1	.000	1.90	1.06	14	0	0	0	1	0-2	23.2	17	7	5	2	8-2	15	.205
2004— Baltimore (A.L.)	6	3	.667	3.46	1.58	56	1	0	0	2	1-1	78.0	68	39	30	6	55-6	71	.238
2005— Baltimore (A.L.)	1	0	1.000	3.12	2.08	14	0	0	0	1	0-0	17.1	19	6	6	1	17-1	25	.279
— Bowie (East.)	0	0	...	2.89	1.39	5	0	0	0	2	0-0	9.1	7	3	3	0	6-0	13	.212
Major League totals (5 years)	10	10	.500	4.31	1.68	108	10	0	0	6	1-3	177.1	166	101	85	18	132-10	159	.251

PATTERSON, COREY   OF

PERSONAL: Born August 13, 1979, in Atlanta. ... 5-9/180. ... Bats left, throws right. ... Full name: Donald Corey Patterson. ... High school: Harrison (Kennesaw, Ga.). ... Son of Don Patterson, defensive back with Detroit Lions (1979) and New York Giants (1980).

TRANSACTIONS/CAREER NOTES: Selected by Chicago Cubs organization in first round (third pick overall) of 1998 free-agent draft. ... On disabled list (July 7, 2003-remainder of season).

2005 GAMES PLAYED BY POSITION (MLB): OF—122.

SCOUTING REPORT *Offense:* Patterson has an abundance of tools but never has put them all together. Swing has gotten longer and has a lot of moving parts. Will continue to have problems at the plate until he can define the strike zone and lay off high pitches. Is slow to make adjustments. Is a very good baserunner with the instincts to steal. *Defense:* He should be a more complete center fielder. Has exceptional closing speed but is inconsistent with his routes. Will get late breaks coming in and doesn't appear to get consistent reads. Has a solid arm with good life and carry. Charges the ball well and is accurate. *Outlook:* Patterson has natural five-tool ability but may never reach his potential because of inability to make adjustments. At a crossroads in his career. *Grade 6.9*

COREY PATTERSON'S HITTING ZONE

.056	.143	.167
.302	.444	.184
.412	.231	.266

LEFTY-RIGHTY SPLITS

vs.	Avg.	AB	H	2B	3B	HR	RBI	BB	SO	OBP	Slg.
L	.169	118	20	5	1	3	6	5	36	.203	.305
R	.231	333	77	10	2	10	28	18	82	.272	.363

P

Year Team (League)	Pos.	G	AB	R	H	2B	3B	HR	RBI	BB	SO	HBP	GDP	SB-CS	Avg.	OBP	SLG	OPS	E	Avg.
1999—Lansing (Midw.)	OF	112	475	94	152	35	*17	20	79	25	85	5	5	33-9	.320	.358	.592	.949	9	.965
2000—West Tenn (Sou.)	OF	118	444	73	116	26	5	22	82	45	115	10	7	27-15	.261	.338	.491	.829	3	.990
—Chicago (N.L.)	OF	11	42	9	7	1	0	2	3	3	14	1	0	1-1	.167	.239	.333	.572	1	.963
2001—Iowa (PCL)	OF	89	367	63	93	22	3	7	32	29	65	1	2	19-8	.253	.308	.387	.694	6	.968
—Chicago (N.L.)	OF	59	131	26	29	3	0	4	14	6	33	3	1	4-0	.221	.266	.336	.602	2	.976
2002—Chicago (N.L.)	OF	153	592	71	150	30	5	14	54	19	142	8	8	18-3	.253	.284	.392	.676	3	.990
2003—Chicago (N.L.)	OF	83	329	49	98	17	7	13	55	15	77	1	5	16-5	.298	.329	.511	.839	4	.975
2004—Chicago (N.L.)	OF	157	631	91	168	33	6	24	72	45	168	5	7	32-9	.266	.320	.452	.771	1	.997
2005—Iowa (PCL)	OF	24	91	16	27	4	0	5	12	8	19	2	0	6-1	.297	.366	.505	.872	1	1.000
—Chicago (N.L.)	OF	126	451	47	97	15	3	13	34	23	118	1	0	15-5	.215	.254	.348	.602	5	.980
Major League totals (6 years)		589	2176	293	549	99	21	70	231	111	552	19	26	86-23	.252	.293	.414	.707	16	.986

PATTERSON, JOHN   P

PERSONAL: Born January 30, 1978, in Orange, Texas. ... 6-5/208. ... Throws right, bats right. ... Full name: John Hollis Patterson. ... High school: West Orange-Stark (Orange, Texas).

TRANSACTIONS/CAREER NOTES: Signed as a non-drafted free agent by Arizona Diamondbacks organization (November 7, 1996). ... On disabled list (April 6-24 and May 6-September 8, 2000). ... Traded by Diamondbacks to Montreal Expos for P Randy Choate (March 27, 2004). ... On disabled list (April 28-July 15, 2004); included rehabilitation assignments to Brevard County and Harrisburg. ... Expos franchise transferred to Washington, D.C., and renamed Washington Nationals for 2005 season (December 3, 2004). ... On disabled list (May 16-31, 2005).

CAREER HITTING: 12-for-115 (.104), 4 R, 3 2B, 0 3B, 0 HR, 2 RBI.

SCOUTING REPORT **Throws:** Patterson has a fastball at 89-93 mph, a curve at 74-76, a slider at 82-86 and a changeup. **Tendencies:** Patterson has developed good sink on his fastball. Curve has very tight spin. Doesn't throw his curve as much as he should; it can be a plus pitch for him and, when he has command of it, makes his fastball more effective. Slider is not as effective with a bigger, flatter break. Hitters have difficulty picking up the ball against him. **Outlook:** He has the type of stuff to be even better than last season. Could become the ace of the staff and would not be a stretch to win at least 15-18 games. *Grade 8.2*

JOHN PATTERSON'S PITCHING ZONE

.213	.138	.224
.293	.309	.219
.257	.282	.174

LEFTY-RIGHTY SPLITS

vs.	Avg.	AB	H	2B	3B	HR	RBI	BB	SO	OBP	Slg.
L	.229	375	86	15	0	9	29	34	88	.296	.341
R	.237	363	86	18	1	10	34	31	97	.300	.375

Year Team (League)	W	L	Pct.	ERA	WHIP	G	GS	CG	ShO	Hld.	Sv.-Opp.	IP	H	R	ER	HR	BB-IBB	SO	Avg.
1997—South Bend (Mid.)	1	9	.100	3.23	1.24	18	18	0	0	...	0-...	78.0	63	32	28	3	34-0	95	.221
1998—High Desert (Calif.)	8	7	.533	2.83	1.13	25	25	0	0	...	0-...	127.0	102	54	40	12	42-0	148	.217
1999—El Paso (Texas)	8	6	.571	4.77	1.40	18	18	2	0	...	0-...	100.0	98	61	53	16	42-0	117	.256
—Tucson (PCL)	1	5	.167	7.04	1.99	7	6	0	0	...	0-...	30.2	43	26	24	3	18-0	29	.331
2000—Tucson (PCL)	0	2	.000	7.80	2.00	3	2	0	0	...	0-...	15.0	21	14	13	1	9-0	10	.323
2001—Lancaster (Calif.)	0	0	...	5.79	1.29	2	2	0	0	...	0-...	9.1	9	6	6	3	3-0	9	.243
—El Paso (Texas)	1	2	.333	4.26	1.54	5	5	0	0	...	0-...	25.1	30	15	12	2	9-0	19	.297
—Tucson (PCL)	2	7	.222	5.85	1.67	13	12	0	0	...	0-...	67.2	82	50	44	9	31-3	40	.301
2002—Tucson (PCL)	10	5	.667	4.23	1.44	19	18	0	0	...	0-...	112.2	117	59	53	14	45-1	104	.265
—Arizona (N.L.)	2	0	1.000	3.23	1.11	7	5	0	0	0	0-0	30.2	27	11	11	7	7-0	31	.235
2003—Tucson (PCL)	10	5	.667	2.63	1.30	18	18	2	2	...	0-...	109.1	100	48	32	6	43-0	74	.244
—Arizona (N.L.)	1	4	.200	6.05	1.65	16	8	0	0	0	1-1	55.0	61	39	37	7	30-5	43	.281
2004—Harrisburg (East.)	0	0	...	0.00	0.50	1	1	0	0	...	0-...	4.0	0	0	0	0	2-0	9	.000
—Brevard County (FSL)	0	0	...	0.00	0.52	2	2	0	0	...	0-...	7.2	3	0	0	0	1-0	7	.111
—Montreal (N.L.)	4	7	.364	5.03	1.48	19	19	0	0	0	0-0	98.1	100	58	55	18	46-4	99	.260
2005—Was. (N.L.)	9	7	.563	3.13	1.19	31	31	2	1	0	0-0	198.1	172	71	69	19	65-11	185	.233
Major League totals (4 years)	16	18	.471	4.05	1.33	73	63	2	1	0	1-1	382.1	360	179	172	51	148-20	358	.247

PAUL, JOSH   C

PERSONAL: Born May 19, 1975, in Evanston, Ill. ... 6-1/200. ... Bats right, throws right. ... Full name: Joshua William Paul. ... High school: Buffalo Grove (Ill.). ... College: Vanderbilt.

TRANSACTIONS/CAREER NOTES: Selected by Chicago White Sox organization in second round of 1996 free-agent draft. ... Signed as a free agent by Chicago Cubs organization (July 4, 2003). ... Released by Cubs (October 31, 2003). ... Signed by Anaheim Angels organization (January 15, 2004). ... Angels franchise renamed Los Angeles Angels of Anaheim for 2005 season. ... On disabled list (August 12-September 1, 2005).

2005 GAMES PLAYED BY POSITION (MLB): C—29, OF—2, DH—1.

SCOUTING REPORT Paul is a good athlete who runs well for a catcher. Has below-average bat speed and lacks punch. Will spray balls to all fields and lay down bunts. Shows a knack for situational hitting. Can be used late in games as a pinch runner. Hands and receiving skills are only average. Versatility is his greatest asset. Has served well as the Angels' No. 3 catcher behind the Molina brothers. *Grade 4.4*

LEFTY-RIGHTY SPLITS

vs.	Avg.	AB	H	2B	3B	HR	RBI	BB	SO	OBP	Slg.
L	.143	7	1	0	0	1	2	0	0	.143	.571
R	.200	30	6	1	0	1	2	2	9	.250	.333

Year Team (League)	Pos.	G	AB	R	H	2B	3B	HR	RBI	BB	SO	HBP	GDP	SB-CS	Avg.	OBP	SLG	OPS	E	Avg.
1996—GC Whi. Sox (GCL)		1	0	0	0	0	0	0	0	1	0	0	0	0-0	...	1.000	...	1.000		
—Hickory (S. Atl.)	C	59	226	41	74	16	0	8	37	21	53	1	2	13-4	.327	.386	.504	.890	2	.991
1997—Birmingham (Sou.)	C	34	115	18	34	5	0	1	16	12	25	1	4	6-2	.296	.367	.365	.732	3	.988
—GC Whi. Sox (GCL)	C	5	14	3	6	0	1	0	0	1	5	0	1	1-0	.429	.467	.571	1.038	3	.900
1998—Win.-Salem (Car.)	C	123	444	66	113	20	7	11	63	38	91	5	11	20-8	.255	.319	.405	.724	3	.997
1999—Birmingham (Sou.)	C-DH	93	319	47	89	19	3	4	42	29	68	5	6	6-6	.279	.345	.395	.740	5	.992
—Chicago (A.L.)	C	6	18	2	4	1	0	0	1	0	6	0	0	0-0	.222	.222	.278	.500	1	1.000
2000—Chicago (A.L.)	C-OF	36	71	15	20	3	2	1	8	5	17	1	3	1-0	.282	.338	.423	.760	4	.974

P

Year Team (League)	Pos.	G	AB	R	H	2B	3B	HR	RBI	BB	SO	HBP	GDP	SB-CS	Avg.	OBP	SLG	OPS	E	Avg.
—Charlotte (Int'l)	C-OF	51	168	28	40	5	1	4	19	13	38	2	3	6-2	.238	.299	.351	.650	2	.994
2001—Chicago (A.L.)	C	57	139	20	37	11	0	3	18	13	25	0	3	6-2	.266	.327	.410	.737	6	.980
—Charlotte (Int'l)	C	22	75	11	21	4	0	4	14	7	18	0	0	0-0	.280	.337	.493	.831	0	1.000
2002—Charlotte (Int'l)	C-1B-OF	65	231	18	63	15	2	0	17	17	45	1	7	10-4	.273	.323	.355	.678	3	.993
—Chicago (A.L.)	C-OF	33	104	11	25	4	0	0	11	9	22	1	1	2-0	.240	.302	.279	.581	2	.991
2003—Charlotte (Int'l)	C-2B-DH	19	64	6	12	0	1	2	5	5	14	0	1	1-1	.188	.243	.313	.555	2	.982
—Chicago (A.L.)	C-DH	13	17	6	6	0	0	0	4	3	3	0	0	0-0	.353	.450	.353	.803	0	1.000
—Iowa (PCL)	C-OF-DH																			
	1B	47	146	12	37	4	0	2	15	8	30	1	5	0-2	.253	.297	.322	.619	1	.995
	C	3	6	0	0	0	0	0	0	0	3	0	0	0-0	.000	.000	.000	.000	1	1.000
2004—Anaheim (A.L.)	C-OF-DH	46	70	11	17	3	0	2	10	7	17	0	2	2-1	.243	.308	.371	.679	1	.993
2005—Salt Lake (PCL)	DH-C	9	33	6	9	4	0	0	6	6	7	0	0	1-0	.273	.385	.394	.779	0	1.000
—Los Angeles (A.L.)	C-OF-DH	34	37	4	7	1	0	2	9	2	9	0	1	0-0	.189	.231	.378	.609	1	.989
American League totals (7 years)		225	456	69	116	23	2	8	56	39	97	2	10	11-3	.254	.313	.366	.680	14	.986
National League totals (1 year)		3	6	0	0	0	0	0	0	0	3	0	0	0-0	.000	.000	.000	.000	0	1.000
Major League totals (7 years)		228	462	69	116	23	2	8	56	39	100	2	10	11-3	.251	.310	.361	.671	14	.986

DIVISION SERIES RECORD

Year Team (League)	Pos.	G	AB	R	H	2B	3B	HR	RBI	BB	SO	HBP	GDP	SB-CS	Avg.	OBP	SLG	OPS	E	Avg.
2000—Chicago (A.L.)	C	1	0	0	0	0	0	0	0	0	0	0	0	0-0	...	...	...	...	0	1.000
2005—Los Angeles (A.L.)		1	0	0	0	0	0	0	0	0	0	0	0	0-0	...	...	...	...	0	...
Division series totals (2 years)		2	0	0	0	0	0	0	0	0	0	0	0	0-0	...	...	...	...	0	1.000

CHAMPIONSHIP SERIES RECORD

Year Team (League)	Pos.	G	AB	R	H	2B	3B	HR	RBI	BB	SO	HBP	GDP	SB-CS	Avg.	OBP	SLG	OPS	E	Avg.
2005—Los Angeles (A.L.)	C	1	0	0	0	0	0	0	0	0	0	0	0	0-0	...	...	...	...	1	.800

PAULINO, RONNY — C/1B

PERSONAL: Born April 21, 1981, in Santo Domingo, Dominican Republic. ... 6-3/235. ... Bats right, throws right. ... Full name: Ronny Leonel Paulino. ... High school: Escuela (Santo Domingo, Dominican Republic).

TRANSACTIONS/CAREER NOTES: Signed as non-drafted free agent by Pittsburgh Pirates organization (December 29, 1997). ... Selected by Kansas City Royals from Pirates organization in Rule 5 major league draft (December 16, 2002). ... Returned to Pirates organization (March 13, 2003).

2005 GAMES PLAYED BY POSITION (MLB): C—2.

LEFTY-RIGHTY SPLITS

vs.	Avg.	AB	H	2B	3B	HR	RBI	BB	SO	OBP	Slg.
L	.500	2	1	0	0	0	0	1	0	.667	.500
R	.500	2	1	0	0	0	0	0	0	.500	.500

Year Team (League)	Pos.	G	AB	R	H	2B	3B	HR	RBI	BB	SO	HBP	GDP	SB-CS	Avg.	OBP	SLG	OPS	E	Avg.
1998—Pittsburgh (DSL)		53	170	18	40	5	0	4	26	17	27	4	2	6-4	.235	.318	.335	.653	...	...
1999—GC Pirates (GCL)	C	29	83	6	21	2	4	1	13	8	19	1	0	1-2	.253	.319	.410	.729	5	.974
2000—Hickory (S. Atl.)	C-1B-3B	88	301	38	87	16	2	6	39	27	71	4	9	3-2	.289	.354	.415	.769	9	.982
2001—Lynchburg (Caro.)	C	103	352	30	102	16	1	6	51	36	76	2	11	4-1	.290	.353	.394	.745	4	.994
2002—Lynchburg (Caro.)	1B-C-C	119	442	63	116	26	2	12	55	39	87	1	15	2-1	.262	.321	.412	.733	18	.982
2003—Altoona (East.)	C-1B	46	159	19	36	6	1	6	19	12	35	1	4	0-2	.226	.283	.390	.673	4	.988
—Lynchburg (Caro.)	C	23	81	8	19	3	0	1	12	8	16	1	6	1-0	.235	.308	.309	.617	2	.983
2004—Altoona (East.)	C-1B	99	369	54	105	23	2	15	60	32	62	3	7	3-2	.285	.344	.480	.824	10	.987
2005—Pittsburgh (N.L.)	C	2	4	1	2	0	0	0	0	1	0	0	0	0-0	.500	.600	.500	1.100	0	1.000
Major League totals (1 year)		2	4	1	2	0	0	0	0	1	0	0	0	0-0	.500	.600	.500	1.100	0	1.000

PAVANO, CARL — P

PERSONAL: Born January 8, 1976, in New Britain, Conn. ... 6-5/241. ... Throws right, bats right. ... Full name: Carl Anthony Pavano. ... Name pronounced: pa-VAH-no. ... High school: Southington (Conn.).

TRANSACTIONS/CAREER NOTES: Selected by Boston Red Sox organization in 13th round of 1994 free-agent draft. ... Traded by Red Sox with a player to be named to Montreal Expos for P Pedro Martinez (November 18, 1997); Expos acquired P Tony Armas to complete deal (December 18, 1997). ... On disabled list (July 12-September 11, 1999); included rehabilitation assignment to Ottawa. ... On disabled list (June 25, 2000-remainder of season). ... On disabled list (March 23-August 15, 2001); included rehabilitation assignments to Jupiter and Ottawa. ... Traded by Expos with Ps Graeme Lloyd and Justin Wayne and IF Mike Mordecai to Florida Marlins for OF Cliff Floyd, P Claudio Vargas, cash and a player to be named (July 11, 2002); Expos acquired P Don Levinski to complete deal (August 6, 2002). ... Signed as a free agent by New York Yankees (December 20, 2004). ... On disabled list (June 28, 2005-remainder of season); included rehabilitation assignment to GCL Yankees.

CAREER HITTING: 41-for-295 (.139), 14 R, 8 2B, 2 3B, 2 HR, 14 RBI.

SCOUTING REPORT Throws: Pavano lost some steam on his fastball, hitting the upper 80s and low 90s. Still has a very good slider. Also uses a split-finger fastball and a changeup. ***Tendencies:*** His fastball has good life down in the zone, and he is able to spot it on both sides of the plate. Has good command of sharp slider. Will show a changeup early in the count to a left-handed hitter but is starting to use the splitter late in counts. ***Outlook:*** Pavano missed a considerable amount of time during the season with rotator cuff problems and didn't pitch the second half. There are questions about his durability and ability to pitch in New York. ***Grade 7***

CARL PAVANO'S PITCHING ZONE

.286	.273	.353
.481	.531	.348
.250	.375	.262

LEFTY-RIGHTY SPLITS

vs.	Avg.	AB	H	2B	3B	HR	RBI	BB	SO	OBP	Slg.
L	.335	215	72	14	2	9	27	13	19	.380	.544
R	.294	194	57	6	3	8	29	5	37	.324	.479

Year Team (League)	W	L	Pct.	ERA	WHIP	G	GS	CG	ShO	Hld.	Sv.-Opp.	IP	H	R	ER	HR	BB-IBB	SO	Avg.
1994—GC Red Sox (GCL)	4	3	.571	1.84	0.86	9	7	0	0	...	0-...	44.0	31	14	9	1	7-0	47	.186
1995—Michigan (Midw.)	6	6	.500	3.45	1.21	22	22	1	0	...	0-...	141.0	118	63	54	7	52-0	138	.227
1996—Trenton (East.)	16	5	.762	2.63	1.09	27	26	6	2	...	0-...	185.0	154	66	54	16	47-2	146	.230
1997—Pawtucket (Int'l)	11	6	.647	3.12	1.13	23	23	3	0	...	0-...	161.2	148	62	56	13	34-2	147	.239
1998—Jupiter (Fla. St.)	0	0	...	6.60	1.53	4	4	0	0	...	0-...	15.0	20	11	11	1	3-0	14	.333
—Ottawa (Int'l)	1	0	1.000	2.41	1.02	3	3	0	0	...	0-...	18.2	12	5	5	1	7-0	14	.190

P

Year	Team (League)	W	L	Pct.	ERA	WHIP	G	GS	CG	ShO	Hld.	Sv.-Opp.	IP	H	R	ER	HR	BB-IBB	SO	Avg.
	—Montreal (N.L.)	6	9	.400	4.21	1.28	24	23	0	0	0	0-0	134.2	130	70	63	18	43-1	83	.251
1999—	Montreal (N.L.)	6	8	.429	5.63	1.46	19	18	1	1	0	0-0	104.0	117	66	65	8	35-1	70	.285
	—Ottawa (Int'l)	0	1	.000	9.00	1.40	2	2	0	0	...	0-...	5.0	7	5	5	1	0-0	3	.318
2000—	Montreal (N.L.)	8	4	.667	3.06	1.27	15	15	0	0	0	0-0	97.0	89	40	33	8	34-1	64	.248
2001—	Jupiter (Fla. St.)	1	1	.500	2.19	0.97	3	3	0	0	...	0-...	12.1	10	7	3	1	2-0	11	.213
	—Ottawa (Int'l)	2	1	.667	3.58	1.16	4	4	0	0	...	0-...	27.2	27	13	11	4	5-0	19	.248
	—Montreal (N.L.)	1	6	.143	6.33	1.76	8	8	0	0	0	0-0	42.2	59	33	30	7	16-1	36	.331
2002—	Montreal (N.L.)	3	8	.273	6.30	1.74	15	14	0	0	0	0-0	74.1	98	55	52	14	31-5	51	.318
	—Ottawa (Int'l)	3	0	1.000	3.10	1.23	3	3	0	0	...	0-...	20.1	23	8	7	2	2-0	9	.295
	—Florida (N.L.)	3	2	.600	3.79	1.46	22	8	0	0	3	0-0	61.2	76	33	26	5	14-3	41	.306
2003—	Florida (N.L.)	12	13	.480	4.30	1.26	33	32	2	0	0	0-0	201.0	204	99	96	19	49-10	133	.265
2004—	Florida (N.L.)	18	8	.692	3.00	1.17	31	31	2	2	0	0-0	222.1	212	80	74	16	49-13	139	.253
2005—	New York (A.L.)	4	6	.400	4.77	1.47	17	17	1	1	0	0-0	100.0	129	66	53	17	18-1	56	.315
	—GC Yankees (GCL)	0	0	...	1.80	0.40	1	1	0	0	0	0-0	5.0	2	2	1	1	0-0	5	.118
	—Tampa (Fla. St.)	0	1	.000	4.50	1.00	1	1	0	0	0	0-0	6.0	6	3	3	1	0-0	3	.250
	American League totals (1 year)	4	6	.400	4.77	1.47	17	17	1	1	0	0-0	100.0	129	66	53	17	18-1	56	.315
	National League totals (7 years)	57	58	.496	4.21	1.34	167	149	5	3	3	0-0	937.2	985	476	439	95	271-35	617	.271
	Major League totals (8 years)	61	64	.488	4.27	1.35	184	166	6	4	3	0-0	1037.2	1114	542	492	112	289-36	673	.276

DIVISION SERIES RECORD

Year	Team (League)	W	L	Pct.	ERA	WHIP	G	GS	CG	ShO	Hld.	Sv.-Opp.	IP	H	R	ER	HR	BB-IBB	SO	Avg.
2003—	Florida (N.L.)	2	0	1.000	0.00	0.75	3	0	0	0	0	0-0	2.2	1	0	0	0	1-1	1	.111

CHAMPIONSHIP SERIES RECORD

Year	Team (League)	W	L	Pct.	ERA	WHIP	G	GS	CG	ShO	Hld.	Sv.-Opp.	IP	H	R	ER	HR	BB-IBB	SO	Avg.
2003—	Florida (N.L.)	0	0	...	2.35	1.17	3	1	0	0	0	0-0	7.2	8	2	2	0	1-0	8	.286

WORLD SERIES RECORD

Year	Team (League)	W	L	Pct.	ERA	WHIP	G	GS	CG	ShO	Hld.	Sv.-Opp.	IP	H	R	ER	HR	BB-IBB	SO	Avg.
2003—	Florida (N.L.)	0	0	...	1.00	1.00	2	0	0	0	0	0-0	9.0	8	1	1	0	1-0	6	.250

ALL-STAR GAME RECORD

Year	Team (League)	W	L	Pct.	ERA	WHIP	G	GS	CG	ShO	Hld.	Sv.-Opp.	IP	H	R	ER	HR	BB-IBB	SO	Avg.
	All-Star Game totals (1 year)	0	0	...	9.00	1.50	1	0	0	0	0	0-0	2.0	3	2	2	1	0-0	1	.333

PAYTON, JAY   OF

PERSONAL: Born November 22, 1972, in Zanesville, Ohio. ... 5-10/185. ... Bats right, throws right. ... Full name: Jason Lee Payton. ... High school: Zanesville (Ohio). ... College: Georgia Tech.

TRANSACTIONS/CAREER NOTES: Selected by New York Mets organization in supplemental round ("sandwich pick" between first and second rounds, 29th pick overall) of 1994 free-agent draft; pick received as part of compensation for Baltimore Orioles signing Type A free-agent P Sid Fernandez. ... On disabled list (April 3, 1997-entire season). ... On disabled list (March 21-June 8, 1999); included rehabilitation assignment to St. Lucie. ... On disabled list (May 8-June 26, 2001); included rehabilitation assignment to St. Lucie. ... Traded by Mets with P Mark Corey and OF Robert Stratton to Colorado Rockies for P John Thomson and OF Mark Little (July 31, 2002). ... Signed as a free agent by San Diego Padres (January 13, 2004). ... Traded by Padres with SS Ramon Vazquez and P David Pauley to Boston Red Sox for OF Dave Roberts (December 20, 2004). ... Traded by Red Sox to Oakland Athletics for P Chad Bradford (July 13, 2005).

2005 GAMES PLAYED BY POSITION (MLB): OF—122.

SCOUTING REPORT **Offense:** Payton is an aggressive hitter who likes fastballs up out over the plate. Has good bat speed and the ball jumps off his bat. Improved his ability to hit with runners on because he became more selective. Is a line-drive hitter but is starting to show more power. Is a good runner but gets way from the plate slowly. Doesn't try to steal bases. **Defense:** Payton can play all outfield positions well. Doesn't always show good instincts, but his speed allows him to have slightly above-average range. Arm is just average. **Outlook:** Payton improved last season because he was given a chance to play every day in Oakland. Has always had good tools and is starting to show them. **Grade 7**

JAY PAYTON'S HITTING ZONE

.242	.417	.143
.288	.421	.327
.261	.444	.222

LEFTY-RIGHTY SPLITS

vs.	Avg.	AB	H	2B	3B	HR	RBI	BB	SO	OBP	Slg.
L	.283	152	43	7	0	5	22	11	13	.329	.428
R	.258	256	66	9	1	13	41	13	34	.292	.453

Year	Team (League)	Pos.	G	AB	R	H	2B	3B	HR	RBI	BB	SO	HBP	GDP	SB-CS	Avg.	OBP	SLG	OPS	E	Avg.
1994—	Pittsfield (NYP)	OF	58	219	47	80	16	2	3	37	23	18	9	1	10-2	.365	.439	.498	.937	5	.964
	—Binghamton (East.)	OF	8	25	3	7	1	0	0	1	2	3	1	1	1-1	.280	.357	.320	.677	1	.917
1995—	Binghamton (East.)	OF	85	357	59	123	20	3	14	54	29	32	2	11	16-7	.345	.395	.535	.930	3	.982
	—Norfolk (Int'l)	OF	50	196	33	47	11	4	4	30	11	22	2	5	11-3	.240	.284	.398	.682	2	.982
1996—	Norfolk (Int'l)	DH-OF	55	153	30	47	6	3	6	26	11	26	3	3	10-1	.307	.363	.503	.866	0	1.000
	—GC Mets (GCL)	DH	3	13	3	5	1	0	1	2	0	1	0	0	1-0	.385	.385	.692	1.077	...	...
	—St. Lucie (Fla. St.)	DH	9	26	4	8	2	0	0	1	4	5	0	1	2-1	.308	.400	.385	.785	...	...
	—Binghamton (East.)	DH	4	10	4	2	0	0	0	2	2	2	0	0	0-1	.200	.286	.200	.486	...	...
1997—							Did not play.														
1998—	Norfolk (Int'l)	OF-1B-DH	82	322	45	84	14	4	8	30	26	50	1	5	12-7	.261	.318	.404	.722	7	.980
	—St. Lucie (Fla. St.)	OF	3	7	0	1	0	0	0	0	3	1	0	0	0-0	.143	.400	.143	.543	0	1.000
	—New York (N.L.)	OF	15	22	2	7	1	0	0	0	1	4	0	0	0-0	.318	.348	.364	.711	0	1.000
1999—	St. Lucie (Fla. St.)	OF	7	26	3	9	1	1	0	3	4	5	0	0	0-1	.346	.433	.462	.895	1	.955
	—Norfolk (Int'l)	OF-DH	38	144	27	56	13	2	8	35	12	13	1	2	2-2	.389	.437	.674	1.110	1	.984
	—New York (N.L.)	OF	13	8	1	2	1	0	0	0	0	2	1	0	1-2	.250	.333	.375	.708	0	1.000
2000—	New York (N.L.)	OF	149	488	63	142	23	1	17	62	30	60	3	9	5-11	.291	.331	.447	.778	6	.981
2001—	New York (N.L.)	OF	104	361	44	92	16	1	8	34	18	52	5	11	4-3	.255	.298	.371	.669	4	.984
	—St. Lucie (Fla. St.)	OF	4	16	7	6	3	0	0	3	0	0	0	0	0-0	.375	.500	.563	1.063	0	1.000
2002—	New York (N.L.)	OF	87	275	33	78	6	3	8	21	9	34	1	8	4-1	.284	.336	.415	.750	1	.994
	—Colorado (N.L.)	OF	47	170	36	57	14	4	8	28	8	20	3	3	3-3	.335	.376	.606	.982	0	1.000
2003—	Colorado (N.L.)	OF	157	600	93	181	32	5	28	89	43	77	7	* 27	6-4	.302	.354	.512	.865	4	.987
2004—	San Diego (N.L.)	OF-DH	143	458	57	119	17	4	8	55	43	56	4	12	2-0	.260	.326	.367	.693	4	.989

P

Year Team (League)	Pos.	G	AB	R	H	2B	3B	HR	RBI	BB	SO	HBP	GDP	SB-CS	Avg.	OBP	SLG	OPS	E	Avg.
2005— Boston (A.L.)	OF	55	133	24	35	7	0	5	21	10	14	0	4	0-0	.263	.313	.429	.741	0	1.000
— Oakland (A.L.)	OF	69	275	38	74	9	1	13	42	14	33	0	4	0-1	.269	.302	.451	.753	0	1.000
American League totals (1 year)		124	408	62	109	16	1	18	63	24	47	0	8	0-1	.267	.306	.444	.749	0	1.000
National League totals (7 years)		715	2382	329	678	110	18	77	300	164	305	24	70	25-24	.285	.335	.443	.778	19	.987
Major League totals (8 years)		839	2790	391	787	126	19	95	363	188	352	24	78	25-25	.282	.330	.443	.773	19	.989

DIVISION SERIES RECORD

Year Team (League)	Pos.	G	AB	R	H	2B	3B	HR	RBI	BB	SO	HBP	GDP	SB-CS	Avg.	OBP	SLG	OPS	E	Avg.
2000— New York (N.L.)	OF	4	17	1	3	0	0	0	2	0	4	0	1	1-1	.176	.167	.176	.343	0	1.000

CHAMPIONSHIP SERIES RECORD

Year Team (League)	Pos.	G	AB	R	H	2B	3B	HR	RBI	BB	SO	HBP	GDP	SB-CS	Avg.	OBP	SLG	OPS	E	Avg.
2000— New York (N.L.)	OF	5	19	1	3	0	0	1	3	2	5	1	1	0-0	.158	.273	.316	.589	0	1.000

WORLD SERIES RECORD

Year Team (League)	Pos.	G	AB	R	H	2B	3B	HR	RBI	BB	SO	HBP	GDP	SB-CS	Avg.	OBP	SLG	OPS	E	Avg.
2000— New York (N.L.)	OF	5	21	3	7	0	0	1	3	0	5	0	0	0-0	.333	.333	.476	.810	2	.895

PEAVY, JAKE P

PERSONAL: Born May 31, 1981, in Mobile, Ala. ... 6-1/180. ... Throws right, bats right. ... Full name: Jacob Edward Peavy. ... Name pronounced: PEE-vee. ... High school: St. Paul (Mobile, Ala.).
TRANSACTIONS/CAREER NOTES: Selected by San Diego Padres organization in 15th round of 1999 free-agent draft. ... On disabled list (May 20-July 2, 2004); included rehabilitation assignment to Mobile.
CAREER HITTING: 31-for-200 (.155), 18 R, 5 2B, 0 3B, 0 HR, 8 RBI.

SCOUTING REPORT Throws: Peavy's best pitch is his changeup. Also throws a fastball that ranges from 89-94 mph, a curveball and a slider. **Tendencies:** His arm motion is loose, but he throws across his body and puts a lot of strain on his arm. Throws uphill with a high back elbow and a flat plane. Had some shoulder problems during the year. Runs fastball in against righthanded hitters. Can get lefthanded and righthanded hitters with his changeup but throws it too often. Throws a better slider than curveball. Is a great competitor and has excellent makeup.
Outlook: Peavy has above-average stuff, but his delivery is a concern. Can consistently win 15-17 games if he stays healthy. **Grade 8.3**

JAKE PEAVY'S PITCHING ZONE

.276	.154	.235
.160	.347	.275
.264	.378	.276

LEFTY-RIGHTY SPLITS

vs.	Avg.	AB	H	2B	3B	HR	RBI	BB	SO	OBP	Slg.
L	.223	359	80	23	5	9	28	28	100	.284	.390
R	.212	387	82	18	2	9	33	22	116	.258	.339

Year Team (League)	W	L	Pct.	ERA	WHIP	G	GS	CG	ShO	Hld.	Sv.-Opp.	IP	H	R	ER	HR	BB-IBB	SO	Avg.
1999— Ariz. Padres (Ariz.)	7	1	.875	1.34	1.02	13	11	1	0	...	0-...	73.2	52	16	11	4	23-0	90	.202
— Idaho Falls (Pio.)	2	0	1.000	0.00	0.55	2	2	0	0	...	0-...	11.0	5	0	0	0	1-0	13	.135
2000— Fort Wayne (Midw.)	13	8	.619	2.90	1.20	26	25	0	0	...	0-...	133.2	107	61	43	6	53-0	164	.216
2001— Mobile (Sou.)	2	1	.667	2.57	1.11	5	5	0	0	...	0-...	28.0	19	8	8	3	12-1	44	.192
— Lake Elsinore (Calif.)	7	5	.583	3.08	1.03	19	19	0	0	...	0-...	105.1	76	41	36	6	33-1	144	.200
2002— Mobile (Sou.)	4	5	.444	2.80	1.18	14	14	0	0	...	0-...	80.1	65	26	25	4	30-0	89	.220
— San Diego (N.L.)	6	7	.462	4.52	1.42	17	17	0	0	0	0-0	97.2	106	54	49	11	33-4	90	.274
2003— San Diego (N.L.)	12	11	.522	4.11	1.31	32	32	0	0	0	0-0	194.2	173	94	89	33	82-3	156	.238
2004— Mobile (Sou.)	0	1	.000	5.79	1.93	1	1	0	0	...	0-...	4.2	7	4	3	1	2-0	4	.318
— San Diego (N.L.)	15	6	.714	* 2.27	1.20	27	27	0	0	0	0-0	166.1	146	49	42	13	53-4	173	.236
2005— San Diego (N.L.)	13	7	.650	2.88	1.04	30	30	3	3	0	0-0	203.0	162	70	65	18	50-3	* 216	.217
Major League totals (4 years)	46	31	.597	3.33	1.22	106	106	3	3	0	0-0	661.2	587	267	245	75	218-14	635	.237

DIVISION SERIES RECORD

Year Team (League)	W	L	Pct.	ERA	WHIP	G	GS	CG	ShO	Hld.	Sv.-Opp.	IP	H	R	ER	HR	BB-IBB	SO	Avg.
2005— San Diego (N.L.)	0	1	.000	16.62	2.54	1	1	0	0	0	0-0	4.1	8	8	8	2	3-2	3	.400

ALL-STAR GAME RECORD

	W	L	Pct.	ERA	WHIP	G	GS	CG	ShO	Hld.	Sv.-Opp.	IP	H	R	ER	HR	BB-IBB	SO	Avg.
All-Star Game totals (1 year)	0	0	...	0.00	1.50	1	0	0	0	0	0-0	0.2	1	0	0	0	0-0	1	.333

PENA, BRAYAN C

PERSONAL: Born January 7, 1982, in Havana, Cuba. ... 5-11/220. ... Bats both, throws right. ... Full name: Brayan Eduardo Pena. ... Junior college: Espa Julio Trigo (Costa Rica).
TRANSACTIONS/CAREER NOTES: Signed as a non-drafted free agent by Atlanta Braves (November 2, 2000).
2005 GAMES PLAYED BY POSITION (MLB): C—15.

LEFTY-RIGHTY SPLITS

vs.	Avg.	AB	H	2B	3B	HR	RBI	BB	SO	OBP	Slg.
L	.273	11	3	1	0	0	0	0	1	.273	.364
R	.143	28	4	1	0	0	4	1	6	.172	.179

Year Team (League)	Pos.	G	AB	R	H	2B	3B	HR	RBI	BB	SO	HBP	GDP	SB-CS	Avg.	OBP	SLG	OPS	E	Avg.
2001— Danville (Appal.)	C	64	235	39	87	16	2	1	33	31	30	0	5	3-1	.370	.440	.468	.908	5	.984
2002— Macon (S. Atl.)	C	81	271	26	62	10	0	3	25	22	37	2	5	0-3	.229	.290	.299	.589	5	.990
— Myrtle Beach (Carol.)	C	6	19	3	4	1	0	0	1	3	4	0	0	0-0	.211	.318	.263	.581	0	1.000
2003— Myrtle Beach (Carol.)	C	82	286	24	84	14	1	2	27	11	28	1	8	2-5	.294	.320	.371	.691	2	.996
2004— Greenville (Sou.)	C	77	277	30	87	10	4	2	30	15	29	1	6	3-4	.314	.349	.401	.750	5	.986
2005— Richmond (Int'l)	C-DH-1B	81	282	27	92	21	2	0	25	28	19	0	15	3-1	.326	.383	.415	.798	4	.991
— Atlanta (N.L.)	C	18	39	2	7	2	0	0	4	1	7	0	1	0-0	.179	.200	.231	.431	0	1.000
Major League totals (1 year)		18	39	2	7	2	0	0	4	1	7	0	1	0-0	.179	.200	.231	.431	0	1.000

P

PERSONAL: Born May 17, 1978, in Santo Domingo, Dominican Republic. ... 6-2/215. ... Bats left, throws left. ... Full name: Carlos Felipe Pena. ... Name pronounced: PAIN-yuh. ... High school: Haverhill (Mass.). ... College: Northeastern.

TRANSACTIONS/CAREER NOTES: Selected by Texas Rangers organization in first round (10th pick overall) of 1998 free-agent draft. ... Traded by Rangers with P Mike Venafro to Oakland Athletics for 1B Jason Hart, P Mario Ramos, C Gerald Laird and OF Ryan Ludwick (January 14, 2002). ... Traded by A's to Detroit Tigers with P Franklyn German and a player to be named as part of three-team deal in which New York Yankees acquired P Jeff Weaver from Tigers and A's acquired P Ted Lilly, OF John-Ford Griffin and P Jason Arnold from Yankees (July 5, 2002); Tigers acquired P Jeremy Bonderman to complete deal (August 22, 2002). ... On disabled list (June 2-27, 2003); included rehabilitation assignment to Toledo.

2005 GAMES PLAYED BY POSITION (MLB): 1B—51, DH—24.

SCOUTING REPORT *Offense:* He has a good stroke, but it also has a lot of holes. Is a low-ball hitter who swings through a lot of pitches up in the zone. Doesn't make adjustments quickly. Power is a real asset but is not a good enough hitter to show the type of home-run production he should be capable of. Has problems with lefthanders. Doesn't run well. *Defense:* He's flashy and has quick hands and good footwork. Is one of the best at cheating off the bag on throws. Gets good jumps and has good range. Has become more consistent but will take offensive frustrations to the field. *Outlook:* Pena does have power, but he still has a lot of contact issues. Has been slow to develop and won't have a chance to reach his potential until he learns the zone. *Grade 7.1*

CARLOS PENA'S HITTING ZONE

.000	.286	.200
.250	.500	.354
.444	.235	.273

LEFTY-RIGHTY SPLITS

vs.	Avg.	AB	H	2B	3B	HR	RBI	BB	SO	OBP	Slg.
L	.157	51	8	1	0	4	8	1	26	.189	.412
R	.254	209	53	8	0	14	36	30	69	.355	.493

Year Team (League)	Pos.	G	AB	R	H	2B	3B	HR	RBI	BB	SO	HBP	GDP	SB-CS	Avg.	OBP	SLG	OPS	E	Avg.
1998—GC Rangers (GCL)	1B	2	5	1	2	0	0	0	0	3	1	0	0	1-1	.400	.625	.400	1.025	0	1.000
—Savannah (S. Atl.)	1B-OF	30	117	22	38	14	0	6	20	8	26	4	0	3-2	.325	.385	.598	.983	3	.986
—Charlotte (Fla. St.)	1B	7	22	1	6	1	0	0	3	2	8	1	0	0-1	.273	.360	.318	.678	1	.977
1999—Charlotte (Fla. St.)	1B	136	501	85	128	31	8	18	103	74	135	16	7	2-5	.255	.365	.457	.822	16	.986
2000—Tulsa (Texas)	1B	138	529	117	158	36	2	28	105	101	108	9	7	12-0	.299	.414	.533	.947	22	.982
2001—Oklahoma (PCL)	1B	119	431	71	124	38	3	23	74	80	127	8	6	11-3	.288	.408	.550	.958	11	.989
—Texas (A.L.)	1B-DH	22	62	6	16	4	1	3	12	10	17	0	1	0-0	.258	.361	.500	.861	2	.987
2002—Oakland (A.L.)	1B	40	124	12	27	4	0	7	16	15	38	1	2	0-0	.218	.305	.419	.724	1	.997
—Sacramento (PCL)	1B	44	175	30	42	10	1	10	33	24	49	4	3	3-0	.240	.340	.480	.820	3	.992
—Detroit (A.L.)	1B-DH	75	273	34	69	13	4	12	36	26	73	2	5	2-2	.253	.321	.462	.783	3	.996
2003—Toledo (Int'l)	1B-DH	8	30	4	10	4	1	0	5	4	7	1	0	0-0	.333	.429	.533	.962	1	.986
—Detroit (A.L.)	1B-DH	131	452	51	112	21	6	18	50	53	123	6	6	4-5	.248	.332	.440	.772	13	.990
2004—Detroit (A.L.)	1B-DH	142	481	89	116	22	4	27	82	70	146	6	11	7-1	.241	.338	.472	.810	6	.995
2005—Toledo (Int'l)	1B-DH	71	257	43	80	17	1	12	45	45	65	6	4	3-4	.311	.424	.525	.949	8	.986
—Detroit (A.L.)	1B-DH	79	260	37	61	9	0	18	44	31	95	4	3	0-1	.235	.325	.477	.802	3	.993
Major League totals (5 years)		489	1652	226	401	73	15	85	240	205	492	16	28	13-9	.243	.330	.459	.790	28	.993

PERSONAL: Born January 23, 1982, in Laguna Salada, Dominican Republic. ... 6-3/215. ... Bats right, throws right. ... Full name: Wily Modesto Pena. ... Name pronounced: willie.

TRANSACTIONS/CAREER NOTES: Signed as a non-drafted free agent by New York Mets organization (July 15, 1998); contract nullified by commissioner's office; was declared a free agent (February 26, 1999). ... Signed by New York Yankees organization (April 5, 1999). ... On disabled list (July 13, 2000-remainder of season). ... Traded by Yankees to Cincinnati Reds for 3B Drew Henson and OF Michael Coleman (March 21, 2001). ... On disabled list (July 5-30, 2003); included rehabilitation assignment to Louisville. ... On disabled list (May 9-June 7, 2005); included rehabilitation assignment to Louisville.

2005 GAMES PLAYED BY POSITION (MLB): OF—83.

SCOUTING REPORT *Offense:* Pena has good bat speed with exceptional power to all fields. Has almost as much power as teammate Adam Dunn, in fact. Can handle the fastball but has problems making adjustments to inside pitches and breaking balls. Chases breaking balls off the plate. If pitchers make a mistake, the river in right field at Great American Ball Park is in trouble. Is a plus runner but recurring leg problems prevent him from using his speed. *Defense:* His arm is above-average but his release is slow. Is inconsistent with his jumps and routes. *Outlook:* This tremendous physical specimen has never been consistent because of lack of patience and high strikeout totals. Is an all-or-nothing player clubs will always gamble on. *Grade 6.3*

WILY MO PENA'S HITTING ZONE

.067	.333	.080
.431	.464	.286
.167	.667	.357

LEFTY-RIGHTY SPLITS

vs.	Avg.	AB	H	2B	3B	HR	RBI	BB	SO	OBP	Slg.
L	.291	110	32	6	0	7	18	8	41	.345	.536
R	.234	201	47	11	0	12	33	12	75	.282	.468

Year Team (League)	Pos.	G	AB	R	H	2B	3B	HR	RBI	BB	SO	HBP	GDP	SB-CS	Avg.	OBP	SLG	OPS	E	Avg.
1999—GC Yankees (GCL)	OF	45	166	21	41	10	1	7	26	12	54	7	2	3-2	.247	.323	.446	.768	2	.947
2000—Greensboro (S. Atl.)	OF	67	249	41	51	7	1	10	28	18	91	5	9	6-5	.205	.268	.361	.630	4	.964
—Staten Island (N.Y.-Penn.)	OF	20	73	7	22	1	2	0	10	2	23	4	1	2-0	.301	.354	.370	.724	0	1.000
2001—Dayton (Midw.)	OF	135	511	87	135	25	5	26	113	33	177	17	6	26-10	.264	.327	.485	.813	9	.972
2002—Chattanooga (Sou.)	OF	105	388	47	99	23	1	11	47	36	126	9	8	8-0	.255	.330	.405	.735	4	.979
—Cincinnati (N.L.)	OF	13	18	1	4	0	0	1	1	0	11	0	0	0-0	.222	.222	.389	.611	0	1.000
2003—Louisville (Int'l)	OF-3B	14	51	16	19	3	0	4	14	5	13	3	0	0-0	.373	.450	.667	1.117	3	.933
—Cincinnati (N.L.)	OF	80	165	20	36	6	1	5	16	12	53	0	2	3-2	.218	.283	.358	.641	3	.978
2004—Cincinnati (N.L.)	OF	110	336	45	87	10	1	26	66	22	108	6	7	5-2	.259	.316	.527	.843	7	.969
2005—Louisville (Int'l)	OF-DH	7	24	1	7	1	0	1	4	1	10	0	0	0-0	.292	.320	.458	.778	2	.933
—Cincinnati (N.L.)	OF	99	311	42	79	17	0	19	51	20	116	3	7	2-1	.254	.304	.492	.796	4	.976
Major League totals (4 years)		302	830	108	206	33	2	51	134	54	288	12	16	10-5	.248	.303	.477	.780	13	.973

P

PERSONAL: Born October 13, 1984, in La Jolla, Calif. ... 6-3/185. ... Throws right, bats right. ... Full name: Hayden Andrew Penn. ... High school: Santana (Santee, Calif.).

TRANSACTIONS/CAREER NOTES: Selected by Baltimore Orioles organization in fifth round of 2002 free-agent draft.

CAREER HITTING: 0-for-1 (.000), 0 R, 0 2B, 0 3B, 0 HR, 0 RBI.

SCOUTING REPORT

Throws: His fastball tops out at 94 mph, and he has a changeup and a curveball. **Tendencies:** He has smarts and mound presence, especially for a young pitcher, but he must pitch better under adverse conditions. Has good pop on his fastball but has the sense to pitch to contact. Command improves when working the inside on righthanded hitters. Walked more than he struck out because of a lack of aggressiveness. **Outlook:** He will be given a chance to make the Orioles' rotation in spring training, but he also could be traded for someone with more experience. **Grade 7.4**

HAYDEN PENN'S PITCHING ZONE

.250	.500	.533
.316	.391	.316
.083	.091	.250

LEFTY-RIGHTY SPLITS

vs.	Avg.	AB	H	2B	3B	HR	RBI	BB	SO	OBP	Slg.
L	.289	83	24	6	2	0	14	11	9	.372	.410
R	.301	73	22	5	0	6	11	10	9	.386	.616

Year Team (League)	W	L	Pct.	ERA	WHIP	G	GS	CG	ShO	Hld.	Sv.-Opp.	IP	H	R	ER	HR	BB-IBB	SO	Avg.
2003— GC Orioles (GCL)	0	0	...	2.70	1.20	1	1	0	0		0-...	3.1	3	1	1	0	1-0	4	.273
— Bluefield (Appal.)	1	4	.200	4.30	1.47	12	11	0	0		0-...	52.1	58	27	25	4	19-0	38	.283
2004— Delmarva (S. Atl.)	4	1	.800	3.32	1.13	13	6	0	0		1-...	43.1	30	18	16	4	19-1	41	.201
— Frederick (Carolina)	6	5	.545	3.80	1.08	13	13	0	0		0-...	73.1	59	33	31	7	20-0	61	.224
— Bowie (East.)	3	0	1.000	4.87	1.52	4	4	0	0		0-0	20.1	22	12	11	0	9-0	20	.278
2005— Bowie (East.)	7	6	.538	3.83	1.25	20	19	1	0		0-0	110.1	101	51	47	11	37-0	120	.248
— Baltimore (A.L.)	3	2	.600	6.34	1.75	8	8	0	0		0-0	38.1	46	30	27	6	21-3	18	.295
Major League totals (1 year)	3	2	.600	6.34	1.75	8	8	0	0		0-0	38.1	46	30	27	6	21-3	18	.295

PERSONAL: Born May 24, 1978, in Broken Arrow, Okla. ... 6-4/250. ... Throws right, bats right. ... Full name: Bradley Wayne Penny. ... High school: Broken Arrow (Okla.).

TRANSACTIONS/CAREER NOTES: Selected by Arizona Diamondbacks organization in fifth round of 1996 free-agent draft. ... Traded by Diamondbacks with P Vladimir Nunez and a player to be named to Florida Marlins for P Matt Mantei (July 9, 1999); Marlins acquired OF Abraham Nunez to complete deal (December 13, 1999). ... On disabled list (July 20-September 2, 2000); included rehabilitation assignments to Brevard County and Calgary. ... On disabled list (May 19-July 2, 2002); included rehabilitation assignment to Jupiter. ... On suspended list (March 30-April 6, 2003). ... Traded with 1B Hee Seop Choi and P Bill Murphy to Los Angeles Dodgers for C Paul Lo Duca, P Guillermo Mota and OF Juan Encarnacion (July 30, 2004). ... On disabled list (August 9-September 22, 2004). ... On suspended list (August 31-September 6, 2005).

CAREER HITTING: 43-for-324 (.133), 13 R, 7 2B, 2 3B, 2 HR, 16 RBI.

SCOUTING REPORT

Throws: Penny's three main pitches are a fastball at 93-97 mph, a curveball at 79-81 and a changeup. **Tendencies:** He was healthy last season after biceps problems shut him down late in 2004. Four-seam fastball has a tendency to really jump late. Changes the hitter's focus with a tight curveball that bites straight down. Still working on his change as he's very inconsistent with its motion. Is slow to the plate and can be run on. **Outlook:** When he's healthy, he has dominant top-of-the-rotation stuff. Should be the Dodgers' No. 1 starter in 2006 and could have a breakout year. **Grade 7.8**

BRAD PENNY'S PITCHING ZONE

.207	.375	.306
.244	.386	.192
.280	.311	.315

LEFTY-RIGHTY SPLITS

vs.	Avg.	AB	H	2B	3B	HR	RBI	BB	SO	OBP	Slg.
L	.263	334	88	15	5	5	24	24	44	.315	.383
R	.276	352	97	21	2	12	46	17	78	.312	.449

Year Team (League)	W	L	Pct.	ERA	WHIP	G	GS	CG	ShO	Hld.	Sv.-Opp.	IP	H	R	ER	HR	BB-IBB	SO	Avg.
1996— Ariz. D'backs (Ariz.)	2	2	.500	4.80	1.01	11	8	0	0	...	0-...	49.2	36	18	13	1	14-0	52	.197
1997— South Bend (Mid.)	10	5	.667	2.73	1.13	25	25	0	0	...	0-...	118.2	91	44	36	4	43-2	116	.208
1998— High Desert (Calif.)	14	5	.737	2.96	1.05	28	28	1	0	...	0-...	164.0	138	65	54	15	35-0	207	.225
1999— El Paso (Texas)	2	7	.222	4.80	1.49	17	17	0	0	...	0-...	90.0	109	56	48	9	25-0	100	.303
— Portland (East.)	1	0	1.000	3.90	1.30	6	6	0	0	...	0-...	32.1	28	15	14	3	14-0	35	.231
2000— Florida (N.L.)	8	7	.533	4.81	1.50	23	22	0	0	0	0-0	119.2	120	70	64	13	60-4	80	.263
— Brevard County (FSL)	0	1	.000	1.13	1.13	2	2	0	0	...	0-...	8.0	5	2	1	0	4-0	11	.172
— Calgary (PCL)	2	0	1.000	1.80	1.20	3	3	0	0	...	0-...	15.0	8	8	3	1	10-0	16	.157
2001— Florida (N.L.)	10	10	.500	3.69	1.16	31	31	1	1	0	0-0	205.0	183	92	84	15	54-3	154	.240
2002— Florida (N.L.)	8	7	.533	4.66	1.53	24	24	1	1	0	0-0	129.1	148	76	67	18	50-7	93	.253
— Jupiter (Fla. St.)	0	0	...	0.00	0.65	2	2	0	0	...	0-...	7.2	5	0	0	0	0-0	9	.179
2003— Florida (N.L.)	14	10	.583	4.13	1.28	32	32	0	0	0	0-0	196.1	195	96	90	21	56-6	138	.264
2004— Florida (N.L.)	8	8	.500	3.15	1.24	21	21	0	0	0	0-0	131.1	124	50	46	10	39-6	105	.250
— Los Angeles (N.L.)	1	2	.333	3.09	1.03	3	3	0	0	0	0-0	11.2	6	5	4	2	6-0	6	.154
2005— Vero Beach (FSL)	1	0	1.000	1.80	0.60	1	1	0	0	0	0-0	5.0	2	1	1	1	1-0	3	.125
— Las Vegas (PCL)	1	0	1.000	3.00	1.17	1	1	0	0	0	0-0	6.0	5	2	2	0	2-0	9	.217
— Los Angeles (N.L.)	7	9	.438	3.90	1.29	29	29	1	0	0	0-0	175.1	185	78	76	17	41-2	122	.270
Major League totals (6 years)	56	53	.514	4.00	1.31	163	162	3	2	0	0-0	968.2	961	467	431	96	306-28	698	.260

DIVISION SERIES RECORD

Year Team (League)	W	L	Pct.	ERA	WHIP	G	GS	CG	ShO	Hld.	Sv.-Opp.	IP	H	R	ER	HR	BB-IBB	SO	Avg.
2003— Florida (N.L.)	0	0	...	6.35	1.06	2	1	0	0	0	0-1	5.2	5	4	4	0	1-0	6	.250

CHAMPIONSHIP SERIES RECORD

Year Team (League)	W	L	Pct.	ERA	WHIP	G	GS	CG	ShO	Hld.	Sv.-Opp.	IP	H	R	ER	HR	BB-IBB	SO	Avg.
2003— Florida (N.L.)	1	1	.500	15.75	3.00	3	1	0	0	0	0-0	4.0	9	7	7	2	3-1	0	.450

WORLD SERIES RECORD

Year Team (League)	W	L	Pct.	ERA	WHIP	G	GS	CG	ShO	Hld.	Sv.-Opp.	IP	H	R	ER	HR	BB-IBB	SO	Avg.
2003— Florida (N.L.)	2	0	1.000	2.19	1.62	2	2	0	0	0	0-0	12.1	15	4	3	1	5-0	7	.319

P

PERSONAL: Born May 28, 1982, in Santiago, Dominican Republic. ... 6-1/185. ... Bats right, throws right. ... Full name: Jhonny Antonio Peralta. ... Name pronounced: johnny pah-RALL-tah. ... High school: Collejo Pedagojico (Santiago, Dominican Republic).
TRANSACTIONS/CAREER NOTES: Signed as a non-drafted free agent by Cleveland Indians organization (April 14, 1999).
2005 GAMES PLAYED BY POSITION (MLB): SS—141.

SCOUTING REPORT **Offense:** His stroke is slightly long, but Peralta does have good bat speed. Hits to the opposite field well. Is a very good high-ball hitter. Can handle the ball inside but still likes it better away. Will make adjustments to cover up the holes in his swing. Power will improve once he pulls more pitches. **Defense:** He does not have a typical middle infielder's body and must watch his weight to maintain flexibility and range. Has better actions and range when moving to his left. Has a strong arm from the hole and is accurate. **Outlook:** Peralta has the ability to become a very good power-hitting shortstop. Could eventually move to third base if he outgrows his current position. Will be a very good run producer wherever he plays. **Grade 7.9**

JHONNY PERALTA'S HITTING ZONE

.276	.310	.240
.333	.516	.340
.289	.370	.125

LEFTY-RIGHTY SPLITS

vs.	Avg.	AB	H	2B	3B	HR	RBI	BB	SO	OBP	Slg.
L	.305	154	47	10	1	11	26	23	40	.394	.597
R	.286	350	100	25	3	13	52	35	88	.352	.486

Year	Team (League)	Pos.	G	AB	R	H	2B	3B	HR	RBI	BB	SO	HBP	GDP	SB-CS	Avg.	OBP	SLG	OPS	E	Avg.
2000—Columbus (S. Atl.)		SS-3B	106	349	52	84	13	1	3	34	59	102	2	13	7-6	.241	.352	.309	.661	26	.948
2001—Kinston (Carol.)		SS	125	441	57	106	24	2	7	47	58	148	1	9	4-8	.240	.328	.351	.680	27	.952
2002—Akron (East.)		SS	130	470	62	132	28	5	15	62	45	97	5	6	4-2	.281	.343	.457	.800	21	.965
2003—Buffalo (Int'l)		SS-3B	63	237	25	61	12	1	1	21	15	45	3	6	1-3	.257	.310	.329	.639	10	.969
—Cleveland (A.L.)		SS-3B	77	242	24	55	10	1	4	21	20	65	4	5	1-3	.227	.295	.326	.621	8	.977
2004—Buffalo (Int'l)		SS-3B-DH	138	556	109	181	44	2	15	86	54	126	4	16	8-4	.326	.384	.493	.876	27	.948
—Cleveland (A.L.)		SS-3B	8	25	2	6	1	0	0	2	3	6	0	0	0-1	.240	.321	.280	.601	3	.900
2005—Cleveland (A.L.)		SS	141	504	82	147	35	4	24	78	58	128	3	12	0-2	.292	.366	.520	.885	19	.970
Major League totals (3 years)			226	771	108	208	46	5	28	101	81	199	7	17	1-6	.270	.342	.451	.794	30	.970

PERSONAL: Born March 23, 1976, in Bonao, Dominican Republic. ... 5-11/170. ... Throws right, bats right. ... Full name: Joel Peralta. ... High school: 4th Bachillerato (Dominican Republic). ... Junior college: Ventura (Calif.) Community College.
TRANSACTIONS/CAREER NOTES: Signed as a non-drafted free agent by Oakland Athletics organization (July 4, 1996). ... Played one season as a fielder in Athletics organization. ... Released by A's (June 4, 1998). ... Signed by Anaheim Angels organization (February 25, 1999). ... Angels franchise renamed Los Angeles Angels of Anaheim for 2005 season. ... Claimed on waivers by Kansas City Royals (October 7, 2005).
CAREER HITTING: 0-for-0 (.000), 0 R, 0 2B, 0 3B, 0 HR, 0 RBI.

JOEL PERALTA'S PITCHING ZONE

.143	1.000	.333
.333	.167	.278
.214	.286	.083

LEFTY-RIGHTY SPLITS

vs.	Avg.	AB	H	2B	3B	HR	RBI	BB	SO	OBP	Slg.
L	.273	55	15	4	0	4	14	9	7	.369	.564
R	.178	73	13	3	0	2	4	5	23	.231	.301

Year	Team (League)	W	L	Pct.	ERA	WHIP	G	GS	CG	ShO	Hld.	Sv.-Opp.	IP	H	R	ER	HR	BB-IBB	SO	Avg.
1999—Anaheim SP (DSL)	2	3	.400	2.50	1.19	24	0	0	0	...	12-...	36.0	27	14	10	0	16-1	35	.201
2000—Butte (Pion.)	2	1	.667	6.63	1.79	10	1	0	0	...	1-...	19.0	24	15	14	2	10-1	17	.333
—Boise (N'west)	0	0		6.48	1.89	4	0	0	0	...	0-...	9.0	12	6	6	0	5-0	9	.353
2001—Cedar Rap. (Midw.)	0	0	...	2.13	0.74	41	0	0	0	...	23-...	43.0	27	13	10	3	5-0	53	.175
—Arkansas (Texas)	0	1	.000	6.30	2.00	9	0	0	0	...	2-...	10.0	15	10	7	2	5-0	14	.333
2002—Arkansas (Texas)	0	0		6.62	1.98	12	0	0	0	...	0-...	17.2	25	15	13	5	10-0	11	.338
—Cedar Rap. (Midw.)	5	0	1.000	0.95	0.81	41	0	0	0	...	21-...	48.0	28	7	5	2	11-3	53	.164
2003—Arkansas (Texas)	5	4	.556	2.24	0.96	47	0	0	0	...	20-...	53.0	39	13	13	3	12-2	48	.205
—Salt Lake (PCL)	0	0				1	0	0	0	...	0-...	0.0	0	0	0	0	1-0	0	
2004—Salt Lake (PCL)	4	2	.667	4.98	1.46	39	0	0	0	...	1-...	56.0	64	33	31	6	18-0	68	.276
—Ariz. Angels (Ariz.)	0	0		2.08	0.20	5	0	0	0	...	0-...	5.0	1	1	1	0	0-0	9	.077
—Rancho Cuca. (Calif.)	0	0		9.00	3.00	1	0	0	0	...	0-...	2.0	5	2	2	1	1-0	1	.455
2005—Los Angeles (A.L.)	1	0	1.000	3.89	1.21	28	0	0	0	0	0-0	34.2	28	15	15	6	14-2	30	.219
—Salt Lake (PCL)	4	1	.800	2.70	0.85	19	0	0	0	0	10-13	20.0	11	6	6	0	6-0	18	.159
Major League totals (1 year)	1	0	1.000	3.89	1.21	28	0	0	0	0	0-0	34.2	28	15	15	6	14-2	30	.219

P

PERSONAL: Born August 9, 1969, in Fontana, Calif. ... 6-3/235. ... Throws right, bats right. ... Full name: Troy Eugene Percival. ... High school: Moreno Valley (Calif.). ... College: UC-Riverside.
TRANSACTIONS/CAREER NOTES: Selected by California Angels organization in sixth round of 1990 free-agent draft. ... Played one season as a catcher in Angels organization (1990). ... Angels franchise renamed Anaheim Angels for 1997 season. ... On disabled list (April 7-May 16, 1997); included rehabilitation assignment to Lake Elsinore. ... On disabled list (August 5-26, 2000); included rehabilitation assignment to Lake Elsinore. ... On disabled list (April 3-18 and July 12-27, 2002; May 23-June 7, 2003; and June 2-27, 2004). ... Signed as a free agent by Detroit Tigers (November 17, 2004). ... On disabled list (May 9-June 5 and July 14, 2005-remainder of season).
CAREER HITTING: 0-for-1 (.000), 0 R, 0 2B, 0 3B, 0 HR, 0 RBI.

SCOUTING REPORT

Throws: Percival features a fastball that ranges from 91-95 mph, a hard curveball and a changeup. **Tendencies:** He is a maximum-effort pitcher but no longer can over-power hitters. Has exceptional arm speed. Can throw his curve for strikes. Will use his changeup but is prone to making mistakes with it up in the zone. **Outlook:** A biceps injury kept him out the second half of last season. Elected not to have surgery and will be a risk as a closer going into the spring. **Grade 7.2**

TROY PERCIVAL'S PITCHING ZONE

.300	.000	.222
.167	.375	.231
.000	1.000	1.000

LEFTY-RIGHTY SPLITS

vs.	Avg.	AB	H	2B	3B	HR	RBI	BB	SO	OBP	Slg.
L	.173	52	9	1	0	4	9	9	10	.306	.423
R	.250	40	10	2	0	3	7	2	10	.295	.525

Year Team (League)	W	L	Pct.	ERA	WHIP	G	GS	CG	ShO	Hld.	Sv.-Opp.	IP	H	R	ER	HR	BB-IBB	SO	Avg.
1991—Boise (N'west)	2	0	1.000	1.41	1.07	28	0	0	0	...	12-...	38.1	23	7	6	0	18-1	63	.172
1992—Palm Springs (Calif.)	1	1	.500	5.06	1.31	11	0	0	0	...	2-...	10.2	6	7	6	0	8-1	16	.188
—Midland (Texas)	3	0	1.000	2.37	1.53	20	0	0	0	...	5-...	19.0	18	5	5	1	11-1	21	.254
1993—Vancouver (PCL)	0	1	.000	6.27	1.98	18	0	0	0	...	4-...	18.2	24	14	13	0	13-1	19	.320
1994—Vancouver (PCL)	2	6	.250	4.13	1.51	49	0	0	0	...	15-...	61.0	63	31	28	4	29-5	73	.285
1995—California (A.L.)	3	2	.600	1.95	0.85	62	0	0	0	* 29	3-6	74.0	37	19	16	6	26-2	94	.147
1996—California (A.L.)	0	2	.000	2.31	0.93	62	0	0	0	2	36-39	74.0	38	20	19	8	31-4	100	.149
1997—Anaheim (A.L.)	5	5	.500	3.46	1.19	55	0	0	0	0	27-31	52.0	40	20	20	6	22-2	72	.205
—Lake Elsinore (Calif.)	0	0	...	0.00	0.50	2	1	0	0	...	0-...	2.0	1	0	0	0	0-0	3	.143
1998—Anaheim (A.L.)	2	7	.222	3.65	1.23	67	0	0	0	0	42-48	66.2	45	31	27	5	37-4	87	.186
1999—Anaheim (A.L.)	4	6	.400	3.79	1.05	60	0	0	0	0	31-39	57.0	38	24	24	9	22-0	58	.186
2000—Anaheim (A.L.)	5	5	.500	4.50	1.44	54	0	0	0	0	32-42	50.0	42	27	25	7	30-4	49	.228
—Lake Elsinore (Calif.)	0	0	...	4.50	1.00	2	2	0	0	0	0-...	2.0	1	1	1	0	1-0	1	.143
2001—Anaheim (A.L.)	4	2	.667	2.65	0.99	57	0	0	0	0	39-42	57.2	39	19	17	3	18-1	71	.187
2002—Anaheim (A.L.)	4	1	.800	1.92	1.12	58	0	0	0	0	40-44	56.1	38	12	12	5	25-1	68	.188
2003—Anaheim (A.L.)	0	5	.000	3.47	1.14	52	0	0	0	0	33-37	49.1	33	22	19	7	23-1	48	.184
2004—Anaheim (A.L.)	2	3	.400	2.90	1.25	52	0	0	0	0	33-38	49.2	43	19	16	7	19-3	33	.230
2005—Detroit (A.L.)	1	3	.250	5.76	1.20	26	0	0	0	0	8-11	25.0	19	16	16	7	11-3	20	.207
Major League totals (11 years)	30	41	.423	3.10	1.11	605	0	0	0	31	324-377	611.2	412	229	211	70	264-25	700	.187

DIVISION SERIES RECORD

Year Team (League)	W	L	Pct.	ERA	WHIP	G	GS	CG	ShO	Hld.	Sv.-Opp.	IP	H	R	ER	HR	BB-IBB	SO	Avg.
2002—Anaheim (A.L.)	0	0	...	5.40	1.80	3	0	0	0	0	2-2	3.1	6	2	2	0	0-0	4	.375

CHAMPIONSHIP SERIES RECORD

Year Team (League)	W	L	Pct.	ERA	WHIP	G	GS	CG	ShO	Hld.	Sv.-Opp.	IP	H	R	ER	HR	BB-IBB	SO	Avg.
2002—Anaheim (A.L.)	0	0	...	0.00	0.00	3	0	0	0	0	2-2	3.1	0	0	0	0	0-0	3	.000

WORLD SERIES RECORD

Year Team (League)	W	L	Pct.	ERA	WHIP	G	GS	CG	ShO	Hld.	Sv.-Opp.	IP	H	R	ER	HR	BB-IBB	SO	Avg.
2002—Anaheim (A.L.)	0	0	...	3.00	1.00	3	0	0	0	0	3-3	3.0	2	1	1	0	1-0	3	.182

ALL-STAR GAME RECORD

	W	L	Pct.	ERA	WHIP	G	GS	CG	ShO	Hld.	Sv.-Opp.	IP	H	R	ER	HR	BB-IBB	SO	Avg.
All-Star Game totals (3 years)	0	0	...	0.00	1.00	3	0	0	0	0	0-0	3.0	2	0	0	0	1-0	4	.182

PEREZ, ANTONIO — 2B/3B

PERSONAL: Born January 26, 1980, in Bani, Dominican Republic. ... 5-11/170. ... Bats right, throws right. ... Full name: Antonio Miguel Perez.

TRANSACTIONS/CAREER NOTES: Signed as a non-drafted free agent by Cincinnati Reds organization (March 21, 1998). ... Traded by Reds with OF Mike Cameron and Ps Brett Tomko and Jake Meyer to Seattle Mariners for OF Ken Griffey (February 10, 2000). ... Traded by Mariners to Tampa Bay Devil Rays for OF Randy Winn (October 28, 2002). ... Traded by Devil Rays to Los Angeles Dodgers for OF/IF Jason Romano (April 3, 2004). ... On disabled list (April 9-May 18, 2005); included rehabilitation assignment to Las Vegas.

2005 GAMES PLAYED BY POSITION (MLB): 3B—35, 2B—29, SS—9, DH—1, OF—1.

SCOUTING REPORT

Perez strictly is an offensive player who doesn't have a defensive position—his bat keeps him in the league. Has a short stroke but likes to hit off his front foot. Is aggressive but strikes out a lot. Has gap power and good bat speed. Can play second, shortstop or third but has stiff hands and is not fluid. Can be an erratic thrower. Is a good runner who can steal some bases. **Grade 5.9**

ANTONIO PEREZ'S HITTING ZONE

.250	.000	.273
.393	.387	.448
.267	.333	.375

LEFTY-RIGHTY SPLITS

vs.	Avg.	AB	H	2B	3B	HR	RBI	BB	SO	OBP	Slg.
L	.312	77	24	3	0	2	10	8	16	.386	.429
R	.291	182	53	10	2	1	13	13	45	.348	.385

									BATTING								FIELDING	
Year Team (League)	Pos.	G	AB	R	H	2B	3B	HR	RBI	BB	SO	HBP	GDP	SB-CS	Avg.	OBP	SLG	OPS	E	Avg.
1998—Dom. Reds (DSL)	SS	63	212	57	54	11	0	2	24	53	33	...		58-...	.255	.408	.335	.743	...	...
1999—Rockford (Midwest)	SS-2B	119	385	69	111	20	3	7	41	43	80	13	3	35-24	.288	.376	.410	.787	36	.929
2000—Lancaster (Calif.)	SS	98	395	90	109	36	6	17	63	58	99	8	3	28-16	.276	.376	.527	.903	27	.939
2001—San Antonio (Texas)	SS	5	21	3	3	0	0	0	0	0	7	0	0	0-0	.143	.143	.143	.286	6	.818
2002—Ariz. Mariners (Ariz.)	2B-SS	6	15	3	5	1	0	1	3	4	2	1	0	4-0	.333	.476	.600	1.076	1	1.000
—San Antonio (Texas)	2B-SS	72	240	30	62	8	2	2	24	11	64	10	3	15-9	.258	.312	.333	.645	13	.955
2003—Orlando (South.)	2B-DH	24	81	16	22	5	1	2	24	18	18	4	0	3-1	.272	.423	.432	.855	5	.967
—Durham (Int'l)	2B-DH	34	134	27	38	12	2	6	20	10	38	3	2	3-1	.284	.345	.537	.882	8	.958
—Tampa Bay (A.L.)	2B-3B-SS-DH	48	125	19	31	6	1	2	12	10	34		1	4-1	.248	.345	.360	.705	2	.985
2004—Las Vegas (PCL)	SS-2B-3B	125	476	92	141	24	6	22	88	61	87	7	1	23-12	.296	.379	.517	.890	20	.963
—Los Angeles (N.L.)	2B-SS	13	13	5	3	1	0	0	0	0	5	1	0	1-0	.231	.286	.308	.593	1	.857
2005—Las Vegas (PCL)	3B-SS	16	56	8	13	3	0	2	6	3	20	1	1	2-1	.232	.279	.393	.672	2	.941
—Los Angeles (N.L.)	3B-2B-SS-OF-DH	98	259	28	77	13	2	3	23	21	61	5	4	11-4	.297	.360	.398	.758	9	.961
American League totals (1 year)		48	125	19	31	6	1	2	12	18	34	1	1	4-1	.248	.345	.360	.705	2	.985
National League totals (2 years)		111	272	33	80	14	2	3	23	21	66	6	4	12-4	.294	.357	.393	.750	10	.958
Major League totals (3 years)		159	397	52	111	20	3	5	35	39	100	7	5	16-5	.280	.353	.383	.736	12	.968

P

PEREZ, EDDIE — C

PERSONAL: Born May 4, 1968, in Ciudad Ojeda, Venezuela. ... 6-1/220. ... Bats right, throws right. ... Full name: Eduardo Rafael Perez. ... High school: Doctor Raul Cuenca (Cuidad Ojeda, Venezuela).

TRANSACTIONS/CAREER NOTES: Signed as a non-drafted free agent by Atlanta Braves organization (September 27, 1986). ... On disabled list (August 30-September 14, 1996; and May 5, 2000-remainder of season). ... On disabled list (March 28-September 1, 2001); included rehabilitation assignment to Greenville. ... Traded by Braves to Cleveland Indians for a player to be named (March 21, 2002); Braves acquired OF Jason Fitzgerald to complete deal (September 18, 2002). ... Signed as a free agent by Milwaukee Brewers organization (January 24, 2003). ... Signed as a free agent by Braves organization (December 19, 2003). ... On disabled list (May 20-June 7 and June 8-September 9, 2005).

2005 GAMES PLAYED BY POSITION (MLB): C—13.

SCOUTING REPORT Perez, a career backup, is in the major leagues because of his defense. Is an instinctive receiver; his best assets are his ability to call a game and work with an experienced pitching staff. Had below-average arm strength because of a sore shoulder most of last season. Frames pitches well and has good hands but won't hit enough to play more than once or twice a week. ***Grade 4.5***

LEFTY-RIGHTY SPLITS

vs.	Avg.	AB	H	2B	3B	HR	RBI	BB	SO	OBP	Slg.
L	.333	12	4	0	0	1	3	1	1	.385	.583
R	.154	26	4	2	0	1	3	0	4	.154	.346

Year	Team (League)	Pos.	G	AB	R	H	2B	3B	HR	RBI	BB	SO	HBP	GDP	SB-CS	Avg.	OBP	SLG	OPS	E	Avg.
1987—	GC Braves (GCL)	C	31	89	8	18	1	0	1	5	8	14	1	4	0-0	.202	.273	.247	.520	4	.980
1988—	Burlington (Midw.)	1B-C	64	186	14	43	8	0	4	19	10	33	0	6	1-0	.231	.269	.339	.608	11	.963
1989—	Sumter (S. Atl.)	1B-C	114	401	39	93	21	0	5	44	44	68	5	10	2-6	.232	.312	.322	.634	§ 13	.985
1990—	Sumter (S. Atl.)	1B-C	41	123	11	22	7	1	3	17	14	18	2	7	0-0	.179	.271	.325	.597	3	.991
	—Durham (Carol.)	1B-C	31	93	9	22	1	0	3	10	1	12	1	3	0-0	.237	.250	.344	.594	3	.986
1991—	Durham (Carol.)	1B-C	92	277	38	75	10	1	9	41	17	33	3	7	0-3	.271	.317	.412	.728	8	.980
	—Greenville (Sou.)	1B	1	4	0	1	0	0	0	0	0	1	0	1	0-0	.250	.250	.250	.500	0	1.000
1992—	Greenville (Sou.)	1B-C	91	275	28	63	16	0	6	41	24	41	2	11	3-3	.229	.292	.353	.645	14	.980
1993—	Greenville (Sou.)	1B-C	28	84	15	28	6	0	6	17	2	8	0	4	1-0	.333	.341	.619	.960	3	.982
1994—	Richmond (Int'l)	1B-C	113	388	37	101	16	2	9	49	18	47	3	4	1-1	.260	.294	.381	.675	† 12	.985
1995—	Richmond (Int'l)	C-DH-1B	92	324	31	86	19	0	5	40	12	58	2	12	1-2	.265	.294	.370	.664	7	.989
	—Atlanta (N.L.)	C-1B	7	13	1	4	1	0	1	4	0	2	0	0	0-0	.308	.308	.615	.923	0	1.000
1996—	Atlanta (N.L.)	C-1B	68	156	19	40	9	1	4	17	8	19	1	6	0-0	.256	.293	.404	.697	3	.990
1997—	Atlanta (N.L.)	C-1B	73	191	20	41	5	0	6	18	10	35	2	8	0-1	.215	.259	.335	.594	5	.989
1998—	Atlanta (N.L.)	C-1B-DH	61	149	18	50	12	0	6	32	15	28	2	3	1-1	.336	.404	.537	.941	2	.994
1999—	Atlanta (N.L.)	C-1B	104	309	30	77	17	0	7	30	17	40	6	9	0-0	.249	.299	.372	.671	5	.993
2000—	Atlanta (N.L.)	C	7	22	0	4	1	0	0	3	0	2	0	0	0-0	.182	.182	.227	.409	1	.976
2001—	Greenville (Sou.)	C-1B	10	38	7	13	2	0	4	5	0	9	1	0	0-0	.342	.359	.711	1.070	1	.984
	—Atlanta (N.L.)	C	5	10	0	3	0	0	0	0	0	2	0	0	0-0	.300	.300	.300	.600	0	1.000
2002—	Cleveland (A.L.)	C	42	117	6	25	9	0	0	4	5	25	1	6	0-0	.214	.252	.291	.543	3	.988
2003—	Milwaukee (N.L.)	C	107	350	26	95	17	1	11	45	17	47	0	16	0-1	.271	.304	.420	.724	6	.991
2004—	Atlanta (N.L.)	C-1B	74	170	14	39	12	0	3	13	11	29	3	5	0-0	.229	.286	.353	.639	3	.991
2005—	Atlanta (N.L.)	C	16	38	3	8	2	0	2	6	1	5	0	1	0-0	.211	.231	.421	.652	0	1.000
American League totals (1 year)			42	117	6	25	9	0	0	4	5	25	1	6	0-0	.214	.252	.291	.543	3	.988
National League totals (10 years)			522	1408	131	361	76	2	40	168	79	209	14	48	1-4	.256	.300	.398	.699	25	.991
Major League totals (11 years)			564	1525	137	386	85	2	40	172	84	234	15	54	1-4	.253	.297	.390	.687	28	.991

DIVISION SERIES RECORD

Year	Team (League)	Pos.	G	AB	R	H	2B	3B	HR	RBI	BB	SO	HBP	GDP	SB-CS	Avg.	OBP	SLG	OPS	E	Avg.
1995—	Atlanta (N.L.)		Did not play.																	
1996—	Atlanta (N.L.)	C	1	3	0	1	0	0	0	0	0	0	0	0	0-0	.333	.333	.333	.667	0	1.000
1997—	Atlanta (N.L.)	C	1	3	0	0	0	0	0	0	0	1	0	0	0-0	.000	.000	.000	.000	0	1.000
1998—	Atlanta (N.L.)	C	1	5	1	1	0	0	0	4	0	2	0	0	0-0	.200	.200	.800	1.000	0	1.000
1999—	Atlanta (N.L.)	C	4	16	1	4	0	0	0	3	0	3	0	1	0-0	.250	.235	.250	.485	0	1.000
2001—	Atlanta (N.L.)		Did not play.																	
2004—	Atlanta (N.L.)	C	3	3	0	0	0	0	0	0	0	1	0	0	0-0	.000	.000	.000	.000	0	1.000
Division series totals (5 years)			10	30	2	6	0	0	0	7	0	7	0	1	0-0	.200	.194	.300	.494	0	1.000

CHAMPIONSHIP SERIES RECORD

Year	Team (League)	Pos.	G	AB	R	H	2B	3B	HR	RBI	BB	SO	HBP	GDP	SB-CS	Avg.	OBP	SLG	OPS	E	Avg.
1995—	Atlanta (N.L.)		Did not play.																	
1996—	Atlanta (N.L.)	1B-C	4	1	0	0	0	0	0	0	1	0	0	0	0-0	.000	.500	.000	.500	0	1.000
1997—	Atlanta (N.L.)	C	2	3	0	0	0	0	0	0	0	0	0	0	0-0	.000	.000	.000	.000	0	1.000
1998—	Atlanta (N.L.)	C	3	4	0	3	0	0	0	0	0	0	0	0	0-0	.750	.750	.750	1.500	0	1.000
1999—	Atlanta (N.L.)	C	6	20	2	10	2	0	2	5	1	3	0	0	0-0	.500	.524	.900	1.424	0	1.000
2001—	Atlanta (N.L.)		Did not play.																	
Champ. series totals (4 years)			15	28	2	13	2	0	2	5	2	3	0	0	0-0	.464	.500	.750	1.250	0	1.000

WORLD SERIES RECORD

Year	Team (League)	Pos.	G	AB	R	H	2B	3B	HR	RBI	BB	SO	HBP	GDP	SB-CS	Avg.	OBP	SLG	OPS	E	Avg.
1995—	Atlanta (N.L.)		Did not play.																	
1996—	Atlanta (N.L.)	C	2	1	0	0	0	0	0	0	0	0	0	0	0-0	.000	.000	.000	.000	0	1.000
1999—	Atlanta (N.L.)	C	3	8	0	1	0	0	0	0	1	3	0	1	0-0	.125	.222	.125	.347	0	1.000
World series totals (2 years)			5	9	0	1	0	0	0	0	1	3	0	1	0-0	.111	.200	.111	.311	0	1.000

PEREZ, EDUARDO — 1B/OF

PERSONAL: Born September 11, 1969, in Cincinnati. ... 6-4/240. ... Bats right, throws right. ... Full name: Eduardo Atanasio Perez. ... High school: Robinson (Santurce, Puerto Rico). ... College: Florida State. ... Son of Tony Perez, special assistant to general manager, Florida Marlins; infielder with four major league teams (1964-86) and manager of Cincinnati Reds (1993).

TRANSACTIONS/CAREER NOTES: Selected by California Angels organization in first round (17th pick overall) of 1991 free-agent draft. ... Traded by Angels to Cincinnati Reds for OF Will Pennyfeather (April 5, 1996). ... Released by Reds (December 14, 1998). ... Signed by St. Louis Cardinals organization (February 16, 1999). ... On disabled list (June 25-July 13 and August 13-September 1, 2000); included rehabilitation assignment to Memphis. ... Contract sold by Cardinals to Hanshin of the Japan Central League

(December 20, 2000). ... Signed as a free agent by Cardinals organization (February 8, 2002). ... Signed as a free agent by Tampa Bay Devil Rays (December 11, 2003). ... On disabled list (May 10, 2004-remainder of season).

2005 GAMES PLAYED BY POSITION (MLB): 1B—49, DH—7, OF—4, 3B—3.

SCOUTING REPORT

Perez has a slightly long stroke but is a productive hitter against left-handed pitching. Has good plate discipline and can take the ball to the opposite field. Has reduced his strikeouts and become a good situational hitter with power. Is strictly a platoon player whose bat will slow down if he gets overextended. Is not a good runner. Has good hands at first base but doesn't have much range to either side. Is a good role player whose power and professional approach make him a dangerous pinch hitter. *Grade 6.4*

EDUARDO PEREZ'S HITTING ZONE

.667	.000	.125
.323	.261	.238
.250	.222	.400

LEFTY-RIGHTY SPLITS

vs.	Avg.	AB	H	2B	3B	HR	RBI	BB	SO	OBP	Slg.
L	.259	135	35	6	0	10	24	21	25	.371	.526
R	.231	26	6	0	0	1	4	5	5	.355	.346

									BATTING								FIELDING	
Year Team (League)	Pos.	G	AB	R	H	2B	3B	HR	RBI	BB	SO	HBP	GDP	SB-CS	Avg.	OBP	SLG	OPS	E	Avg.
1991—Boise (N'west)	1B-OF	46	160	35	46	13	0	1	22	19	39	4	4	12-3	.288	.375	.388	.763	3	.969
1992—Palm Springs (Calif.)	3B-OF-SS	54	204	37	64	8	4	3	35	23	33	3	5	14-3	.314	.386	.436	.823	16	.882
—Midland (Texas)	1B-3B-OF	62	235	27	54	8	1	3	23	22	49	1	7	19-7	.230	.295	.311	.606	13	.920
1993—Vancouver (PCL)	3B-1B-OF	96	363	66	111	23	6	12	70	28	83	3	5	21-7	.306	.360	.501	.862	23	.922
—California (A.L.)	3B-DH	52	180	16	45	6	2	4	30	9	39	2	4	5-4	.250	.292	.372	.664	5	.962
1994—California (A.L.)	1B	38	129	10	27	7	0	5	16	12	29	0	5	3-0	.209	.275	.380	.654	1	.997
—Vancouver (PCL)	3B-DH	61	219	37	65	14	3	7	38	34	53	3	7	9-4	.297	.394	.484	.878	12	.926
—Ariz. Angels (Ariz.)	3B	1	3	0	0	0	0	0	0	1	1	0	0	0-0	.000	.250	.000	.250	0	1.000
1995—California (A.L.)	3B-DH	29	71	9	12	4	1	1	7	12	9	2	3	0-2	.169	.302	.296	.598	7	.883
—Vancouver (PCL)	3B-DH-1B	69	246	39	80	12	7	6	37	25	34	2	5	6-2	.325	.386	.504	.890	6	.968
1996—Indianapolis (A.A.)	3B-1B-DH	122	451	84	132	29	5	21	84	51	69	6	11	11-0	.293	.371	.519	.890	21	.939
—Cincinnati (N.L.)	1B-3B	18	36	8	8	0	0	3	5	5	9	0	2	0-0	.222	.317	.472	.789	0	1.000
1997—Cincinnati (N.L.)	1B-OF-3B																			
	DH	106	297	44	75	18	0	16	52	29	76	2	6	5-1	.253	.321	.475	.796	2	.996
1998—Cincinnati (N.L.)	1B-3B-OF	84	172	20	41	4	0	4	30	21	45	2	2	0-1	.238	.325	.331	.656	5	.985
1999—Memphis (PCL)	1B-3B-DH	119	416	67	133	31	0	18	82	45	92	6	11	7-8	.320	.393	.524	.917	9	.989
—St. Louis (N.L.)	OF-1B	21	32	6	11	2	0	1	9	7	6	0	0	0-0	.344	.462	.500	.962	1	.970
2000—St. Louis (N.L.)	1B-OF-3B	35	91	9	27	4	0	3	10	5	19	3	2	1-0	.297	.350	.440	.790	0	1.000
—Memphis (PCL)	3B-1B-OF	77	277	57	80	12	3	19	66	43	48	1	9	10-4	.289	.383	.560	.942	8	.980
2001—Hanshin (Jp. Cn.)		52	167	20	37	11	0	3	19	21	48	...		3-...	.222	...	.341		...	...
2002—St. Louis (N.L.)	OF-1B-3B																			
	DH	96	154	22	31	9	0	10	26	17	36	3	7	0-0	.201	.290	.455	.744	2	.982
2003—St. Louis (N.L.)	OF-3B-1B																			
	DH	105	253	47	72	16	0	11	41	29	53	4	7	5-2	.285	.365	.478	.843	7	.951
2004—Tampa Bay (A.L.)	1B-DH-OF																			
	3B	13	38	2	8	2	0	1	7	4	9	0	1	0-0	.211	.286	.342	.628	0	1.000
2005—Tampa Bay (A.L.)	1B-DH-OF																			
	3B	77	161	23	41	6	0	11	28	26	30	3	6	0-2	.255	.368	.497	.865	2	.993
American League totals (5 years)		209	579	60	133	25	3	22	88	63	116	7	19	8-8	.230	.311	.397	.709	15	.982
National League totals (7 years)		465	1035	156	265	53	0	48	173	113	244	14	26	11-4	.256	.335	.446	.781	17	.988
Major League totals (12 years)		674	1614	216	398	78	3	70	261	176	360	21	45	19-12	.247	.326	.429	.755	32	.986

DIVISION SERIES RECORD

Year Team (League)	Pos.	G	AB	R	H	2B	3B	HR	RBI	BB	SO	HBP	GDP	SB-CS	Avg.	OBP	SLG	OPS	E	Avg.
2002—St. Louis (N.L.)		1	1	0	0	0	0	0	0	0	0	0	0	0-0	.000	.000	.000	.000	0	...

CHAMPIONSHIP SERIES RECORD

Year Team (League)	Pos.	G	AB	R	H	2B	3B	HR	RBI	BB	SO	HBP	GDP	SB-CS	Avg.	OBP	SLG	OPS	E	Avg.
2002—St. Louis (N.L.)	OF	3	4	1	1	0	0	1	1	1	0	0	0	0-0	.250	.400	1.000	1.400	0	1.000

PEREZ, MIGUEL — C

PERSONAL: Born September 25, 1983, in Caracas, Venezuela. ... 6-3/190. ... Bats right, throws right. ... Full name: Miguel Angel Perez.

TRANSACTIONS/CAREER NOTES: Signed as a non-drafted free agent by Cincinnati Reds organization (November 15, 2000).

2005 GAMES PLAYED BY POSITION (MLB): C—1.

LEFTY-RIGHTY SPLITS

vs.	Avg.	AB	H	2B	3B	HR	RBI	BB	SO	OBP	Slg.
L	.000	1	0	0	0	0	0	0	0	.000	.000
R	.000	2	0	0	0	0	0	0	1	.000	.000

									BATTING								FIELDING	
Year Team (League)	Pos.	G	AB	R	H	2B	3B	HR	RBI	BB	SO	HBP	GDP	SB-CS	Avg.	OBP	SLG	OPS	E	Avg.
2001—Cagua (Pion.)		48	163	20	54	3	1	0	19	12	33	0	0	6-4	.331	.377	.362	.739	...	...
2002—Cagua (Pion.)		34	108	14	23	4	0	2	18	9	23	9	2	1-1	.213	.320	.306	.626	...	...
—GC Reds (GCL)	C-1B-3B-OF	26	86	12	31	1	0	0	11	2	9	3	2	3-0	.360	.396	.372	.768	5	.968
2003—Dayton (Midw.)	C	20	58	3	10	0	0	0	3	4	19	4	2	1-0	.172	.273	.172	.445	7	.950
—Billings (Pion.)	C	60	227	46	77	11	2	1	25	18	27	10	3	1-1	.339	.410	.419	.829	17	.967
2004—Dayton (Midw.)	C	74	249	22	59	7	0	1	22	16	62	11	5	2-2	.237	.309	.277	.586	16	.974
—Potomac (Carol.)	C	18	69	7	16	0	0	0	5	1	12	0	4	1-0	.232	.239	.261	.500	6	.950
2005—Sarasota (Fla. St.)	C-DH	80	291	36	78	11	0	4	33	16	63	1	3	7-1	.268	.305	.347	.653	9	.987
—Louisville (Int'l)	C	21	72	5	15	3	0	1	5	5	19	2	2	0-0	.208	.275	.292	.567	0	1.000
—Cincinnati (N.L.)	C	2	3	0	0	0	0	0	0	0	1	0	0	0-0	.000	.000	.000	.000	0	1.000
Major League totals (1 year)		2	3	0	0	0	0	0	0	0	1	0	0	0-0	.000	.000	.000	.000	0	1.000

P

PEREZ, NEIFI — SS/2B

PERSONAL: Born June 2, 1973, in Villa Mella, Dominican Republic. ... 6-0/197. ... Bats both, throws right. ... Full name: Neifi Neftali Perez. ... Name pronounced: NAY-fee PAIR-ez.

TRANSACTIONS/CAREER NOTES: Signed as a non-drafted free agent by Colorado Rockies organization (November 9, 1992). ... On disabled list (April 8-23, 2001). ... Traded by Rockies to Kansas City Royals for OF Jermaine Dye (July 25, 2001). ... Claimed on waivers by San Francisco Giants (November 20, 2002). ... Released by Giants (August 13, 2004). ... Signed by Chicago Cubs organization (August 19, 2004).

HONORS: Won N.L. Gold Glove as shortstop (2000).

2005 GAMES PLAYED BY POSITION (MLB): SS—130, 2B—26, 3B—4.

SCOUTING REPORT

Offense: Perez is a classic front-foot hitter. Has a slightly long stroke and a lot of movement at the plate from both sides. A line-drive hitter with gap power but can drive the ball down the line from the left side. Doesn't walk or strike out a lot as he likes to hit early in the count. Is an average runner but not a basestealer. **Defense:** He has very good hands with is agile. Has an extremely quick release making the pivot at second base. Has better range to his right than his left. Arm is above-average while moving to his right, but can be erratic when he charges and throws off the wrong foot. **Outlook:** Perez's versatility makes him a valuable player. Can play every day or off the bench. **Grade 6.3**

NEIFI PEREZ'S HITTING ZONE

.227	.421	.265
.346	.297	.234
.304	.313	.266

LEFTY-RIGHTY SPLITS

vs.	Avg.	AB	H	2B	3B	HR	RBI	BB	SO	OBP	Slg.
L	.267	150	40	12	0	5	16	4	21	.290	.447
R	.277	422	117	21	1	4	38	14	26	.301	.360

Year	Team (League)	Pos.	G	AB	R	H	2B	3B	HR	RBI	BB	SO	HBP	GDP	SB-CS	Avg.	OBP	SLG	OPS	E	Avg.
1993—	Bend (N'west)	2B-SS	75	296	35	77	11	4	3	32	19	43	2	3	19-14	.260	.306	.355	.661	25	.937
1994—	Central Valley (Cal.)	SS	134	506	64	121	16	7	1	35	32	79	2	6	9-7	.239	.284	.304	.589	39	.940
1995—	Colo. Springs (PCL)	SS	11	36	4	10	4	0	0	2	0	5	0	0	1-1	.278	.278	.389	.667	3	.936
—	New Haven (East.)	SS	116	427	59	108	28	3	5	43	24	52	2	6	5-2	.253	.295	.368	.663	18	.967
1996—	Colo. Springs (PCL)	SS	133	570	77	180	28	12	7	72	21	48	2	13	16-13	.316	.337	.444	.781	25	.963
—	Colorado (N.L.)	SS-2B	17	45	4	7	2	0	0	3	0	8	0	2	2-2	.156	.156	.200	.356	2	.961
1997—	Colo. Springs (PCL)	SS	68	303	68	110	24	3	8	46	17	27	0	3	8-2	.363	.393	.541	.934	8	.975
—	Colorado (N.L.)	SS-2B-3B	83	313	46	91	13	10	5	31	21	43	1	3	4-3	.291	.333	.444	.777	9	.981
1998—	Colorado (N.L.)	SS-C	•162	647	80	177	25	9	6	59	38	70	1	8	5-6	.274	.313	.382	.695	20	.975
1999—	Colorado (N.L.)	SS	157	•690	108	193	27	•11	12	70	28	54	1	4	13-5	.280	.307	.403	.710	14	.981
2000—	Colorado (N.L.)	SS	•162	651	92	187	39	11	10	71	30	63	0	9	3-6	.287	.314	.427	.741	18	.978
2001—	Colorado (N.L.)	SS	87	382	65	114	19	8	7	47	16	49	0	8	6-2	.298	.326	.445	.771	10	.976
—	Kansas City (A.L.)	SS-2B	49	199	18	48	7	1	1	12	10	19	1	2	3-4	.241	.277	.302	.579	5	.980
2002—	Kansas City (A.L.)	SS-2B	145	554	65	131	20	4	3	37	20	53	0	11	8-9	.236	.260	.303	.564	20	.971
2003—	San Francisco (N.L.)	2B-SS-3B	120	328	27	84	19	4	1	31	14	23	0	9	3-2	.256	.285	.348	.632	5	.989
2004—	San Francisco (N.L.)	SS-2B-3B	103	319	28	74	12	1	2	33	21	35	0	7	0-1	.232	.276	.295	.571	6	.986
—	Iowa (PCL)	SS	10	34	1	7	1	0	0	3	0	5	0	0	0-0	.206	.206	.235	.441	0	1.000
—	Chicago (N.L.)	SS-2B	23	62	12	23	5	0	2	6	3	6	0	1	1-0	.371	.400	.548	.948	2	.972
2005—	Chicago (N.L.)	SS-2B-3B	154	572	59	157	33	1	9	54	18	47	3	22	8-4	.274	.298	.383	.681	12	.982
	American League totals (2 years)		194	753	83	179	27	5	4	49	30	72	1	13	11-13	.238	.265	.303	.568	25	.974
	National League totals (9 years)		1068	4009	521	1107	194	55	57	405	189	398	6	73	45-31	.276	.307	.395	.702	98	.980
	Major League totals (10 years)		1262	4762	604	1286	221	60	61	454	219	470	7	86	56-44	.270	.301	.380	.681	123	.979

DIVISION SERIES RECORD

Year	Team (League)	Pos.	G	AB	R	H	2B	3B	HR	RBI	BB	SO	HBP	GDP	SB-CS	Avg.	OBP	SLG	OPS	E	Avg.
2003—	San Francisco (N.L.)	2B	3	3	1	1	0	0	0	0	1	0	0	0	0-0	.333	.500	.667	1.167	0	1.000

PEREZ, ODALIS — P

PERSONAL: Born June 7, 1977, in Las Matas de Farfan, Dominican Republic. ... 6-0/150. ... Throws left, bats left. ... Full name: Odalis Amadol Perez. ... Name pronounced: oh-DALL-iss. ... High school: Damian Davis Ortiz (Las Matas de Farfan, Dominican Republic).

TRANSACTIONS/CAREER NOTES: Signed as a non-drafted free agent by Atlanta Braves organization (July 2, 1994). ... On disabled list (July 23, 1999-remainder of season; and April 2, 2000-entire season). ... On disabled list (July 22-September 1, 2001); included rehabilitation assignment to Richmond. ... Traded by Braves with OF Brian Jordan and P Andrew Brown to Los Angeles Dodgers for OF Gary Sheffield (January 15, 2002). ... On disabled list (June 27-July 17, 2004). ... On disabled list (May 24-July 5 and August 22-September 24, 2005); included rehabilitation assignment to Las Vegas.

CAREER HITTING: 35-for-267 (.131), 17 R, 8 2B, 0 3B, 1 HR, 10 RBI.

SCOUTING REPORT

Throws: His fastball tops out at about 91 mph. Best pitch is a changeup. Also has a curveball. **Tendencies:** Perez's marginal-velocity fastball has natural tailing action and has good life when it's down, but he tends only to use it away to righthanders. Curve is more of a sweeping slurve that runs away from lefthanders. Throws an excellent circle change with good arm speed and movement. Has very good command of all his pitches. Becomes too one-dimensional and looks to pitch away from contact. **Outlook:** He needs to watch his weight and control his mood. Generally is considered an underachiever. **Grade 7.7**

ODALIS PEREZ'S PITCHING ZONE

.280	.421	.214
.322	.436	.205
.200	.310	.267

LEFTY-RIGHTY SPLITS

vs.	Avg.	AB	H	2B	3B	HR	RBI	BB	SO	OBP	Slg.
L	.256	86	22	0	1	2	12	6	23	.304	.349
R	.264	330	87	20	3	11	40	22	51	.309	.442

Year	Team (League)	W	L	Pct.	ERA	WHIP	G	GS	CG	ShO	Hld.	Sv.-Opp.	IP	H	R	ER	HR	BB-IBB	SO	Avg.
1995—	GC Braves (GCL)	3	5	.375	2.22	1.02	12	12	1	1	...	0-...	65.0	48	22	16	0	18-0	62	.200
1996—	Eugene (Northwest)	2	1	.667	3.80	1.56	10	6	0	0	...	0-...	23.2	26	16	10	2	11-0	38	.268
1997—	Macon (S. Atl.)	4	5	.444	1.65	1.08	36	0	0	0	...	5-...	87.1	67	31	16	4	27-1	100	.256
1998—	Greenville (Sou.)	6	5	.545	4.02	1.36	23	21	0	0	...	0-...	132.0	127	67	59	15	53-2	143	.256
—	Richmond (Int'l)	1	2	.333	2.96	1.36	13	0	0	0	...	3-...	24.1	26	10	8	4	7-1	22	.283
—	Atlanta (N.L.)	0	1	.000	4.22	1.31	10	0	0	0	5	0-1	10.2	10	5	5	1	4-0	5	.244

P

Year	Team (League)	W	L	Pct.	ERA	WHIP	G	GS	CG	ShO	Hld.	Sv.-Opp.	IP	H	R	ER	HR	BB-IBB	SO	Avg.
1999—	Atlanta (N.L.)	4	6	.400	6.00	1.65	18	17	0	0	0	0-0	93.0	100	65	62	12	53-2	82	.275
2000—	Atlanta (N.L.)			Did not play.																
2001—	Atlanta (N.L.)	7	8	.467	4.91	1.54	24	16	0	0	0	0-0	95.1	108	55	52	7	39-0	71	.290
—	Richmond (Int'l)	1	0	1.000	2.74	1.09	5	5	0	0	...	0-...	23.0	23	7	7	1	2-0	22	.256
2002—	Los Angeles (N.L.)	15	10	.600	3.00	0.99	32	32	4	2	0	0-0	222.1	182	76	74	21	38-5	155	.226
2003—	Los Angeles (N.L.)	12	12	.500	4.52	1.28	30	30	0	0	0	0-0	185.1	191	98	93	28	46-4	141	.267
2004—	Los Angeles (N.L.)	7	6	.538	3.25	1.14	31	31	0	0	0	0-0	196.1	180	76	71	26	44-4	128	.250
2005—	Las Vegas (PCL)	1	0	1.000	4.30	1.23	4	4	0	0	0	0-0	14.2	14	7	7	1	4-0	11	.255
—	Los Angeles (N.L.)	7	8	.467	4.56	1.26	19	19	0	0	0	0-0	108.2	109	59	55	13	28-2	74	.262
	Major League totals (7 years)	52	51	.505	4.07	1.24	164	145	4	2	5	0-1	911.2	880	434	412	108	252-17	656	.256

DIVISION SERIES RECORD

Year	Team (League)	W	L	Pct.	ERA	WHIP	G	GS	CG	ShO	Hld.	Sv.-Opp.	IP	H	R	ER	HR	BB-IBB	SO	Avg.
1998—	Atlanta (N.L.)	1	0	1.000	0.00	0.00	1	0	0	0	0	0-0	0.2	0	0	0	0	0-0	1	.000
2004—	Los Angeles (N.L.)	0	1	.000	14.40	3.00	2	2	0	0	0	0-0	5.0	8	8	8	4	7-0	3	.364
	Division series totals (2 years)	1	1	.500	12.71	2.65	3	2	0	0	0	0-0	5.2	8	8	8	4	7-0	4	.348

CHAMPIONSHIP SERIES RECORD

Year	Team (League)	W	L	Pct.	ERA	WHIP	G	GS	CG	ShO	Hld.	Sv.-Opp.	IP	H	R	ER	HR	BB-IBB	SO	Avg.
1998—	Atlanta (N.L.)	0	0	...	54.00	21.00	2	0	0	0	0	0-0	0.1	5	2	2	0	2-1	0	1.000

ALL-STAR GAME RECORD

		W	L	Pct.	ERA	WHIP	G	GS	CG	ShO	Hld.	Sv.-Opp.	IP	H	R	ER	HR	BB-IBB	SO	Avg.
	All-Star Game totals (1 year)	0	0	...	0.00	2.00	1	0	0	0	0	0-0	1.0	2	1	0	0	0-0	2	.400

PEREZ, OLIVER — P

PERSONAL: Born August 15, 1981, in Culiacan, Mexico. ... 6-0/190. ... Throws left, bats left. ... High school: Cobales (Culiacan, Mexico).
TRANSACTIONS/CAREER NOTES: Signed as a non-drafted free agent by San Diego Padres organization (March 4, 1999). ... Loaned by Padres organization to Yucatan of the Mexican League (June 2-22 and July 18, 2000-remainder of season). ... On disabled list (August 7-September 2, 2002). ... Traded by Padres with OF Jason Bay and a player to be named to Pittsburgh Pirates for OF Brian Giles (August 26, 2003); Pirates acquired P Cory Stewart to complete deal (October 2, 2003). ... On disabled list (June 28-September 3, 2005); included rehabilitation assignment to Indianapolis.
CAREER HITTING: 28-for-160 (.175), 4 R, 0 2B, 0 3B, 0 HR, 7 RBI.

SCOUTING REPORT *Throws:* Perez throws a power fastball that hits the mid-90s and has improved his curveball, slider and changeup *Tendencies:* Perez has a very deceptive delivery and hitters have a difficult time picking up the late movement on his fastball. Didn't throw as hard last season, pitching in the lower 90s. Needs to use both sides of the plate and falls into predictable patterns with his fastball. Has a tightly biting curve with good rotation. Has good arm speed with his changeup and is a quick worker. Is tough on lefthanders. *Outlook:* Perez has the ability to be a No. 1 starter, but he lacks the poise and maturity for it. Needs to learn to control his temper; one tantrum led to a broken toe late last season. *Grade 7.5*

OLIVER PEREZ'S PITCHING ZONE

.242	.381	.000
.340	.404	.261
.393	.400	.158

LEFTY-RIGHTY SPLITS

vs.	Avg.	AB	H	2B	3B	HR	RBI	BB	SO	OBP	Slg.
L	.313	64	20	3	1	6	11	12	18	.443	.672
R	.255	322	82	14	0	17	50	58	79	.370	.457

Year	Team (League)	W	L	Pct.	ERA	WHIP	G	GS	CG	ShO	Hld.	Sv.-Opp.	IP	H	R	ER	HR	BB-IBB	SO	Avg.
1999—	Ariz. Padres (Ariz.)	1	2	.333	5.08	1.55	15	2	0	0	...	3-...	28.1	28	20	16	1	16-0	37	.243
2000—	Yucatan (Mex.)	3	2	.600	4.40	1.30	11	6	0	0	...	1-...	43.0	39	24	21	...	17-...	37	
—	Idaho Falls (Pio.)	3	1	.750	4.07	1.36	5	5	0	0	...	0-...	24.1	24	14	11	1	9-0	27	.270
2001—	Fort Wayne (Midw.)	8	5	.615	3.46	1.25	19	19	0	0	...	0-...	101.1	84	46	39	9	43-0	98	.230
—	Lake Elsinore (Calif.)	2	4	.333	2.72	1.32	9	9	0	0	...	0-...	53.0	45	22	16	4	25-0	62	.225
2002—	Lake Elsinore (Calif.)	3	3	.500	1.85	1.23	9	8	0	0	...	0-...	48.2	36	13	10	0	24-0	66	.209
—	Mobile (Sou.)	1	0	1.000	1.17	1.17	4	4	0	0	...	0-...	23.0	11	3	3	1	16-0	34	.147
—	San Diego (N.L.)	4	5	.444	3.50	1.32	16	15	0	0	0	0-0	90.0	71	37	35	13	48-1	94	.218
2003—	Portland (PCL)	3	3	.500	3.02	1.20	8	8	0	0	...	0-...	47.2	44	20	16	6	12-0	48	.246
—	San Diego (N.L.)	4	7	.364	5.38	1.62	19	19	0	0	0	0-0	103.2	103	65	62	20	65-2	117	.258
—	Pittsburgh (N.L.)	0	3	.000	5.87	1.65	5	5	0	0	0	0-0	23.0	26	15	15	2	12-1	24	.283
2004—	Pittsburgh (N.L.)	12	10	.545	2.98	1.15	30	30	2	1	0	0-0	196.0	145	71	65	22	81-2	239	.207
2005—	Indianapolis (Int'l)	0	1	.000	9.90	2.60	3	3	0	0	...	0-...	10.0	14	11	11	3	12-1	4	.326
—	Pittsburgh (N.L.)	7	5	.583	5.85	1.67	20	20	0	0	0	0-0	103.0	102	68	67	23	70-1	97	.264
	Major League totals (4 years)	27	30	.474	4.26	1.40	90	89	2	1	0	0-0	515.2	447	256	244	80	276-7	571	.235

PEREZ, TIMO — OF

PERSONAL: Born April 8, 1975, in Bani, Dominican Republic. ... 5-9/167. ... Bats left, throws left. ... Full name: Timoniel Perez. ... High school: Juan Baron Palanque (Bani, Dominican Republic).
TRANSACTIONS/CAREER NOTES: Signed as a free agent by New York Mets organization (March 17, 2000). ... On disabled list (April 9-27, 2001); included rehabilitation assignment to Norfolk. ... On disabled list (May 26-June 10, 2003); included rehabilitation assignment to Norfolk. ... Traded by Mets to Chicago White Sox for P Matt Ginter (March 27, 2004).
2005 GAMES PLAYED BY POSITION (MLB): OF—50, DH—11, 1B—2.

SCOUTING REPORT Perez is a slashing type hitter who's not patient, but he still makes good contact and uses the whole field. Will chase hard stuff up in the zone and is not an instinctive baserunner. Has good arm strength but gets inconsistent jumps. Has excellent speed but average range. Can't play every day because he lacks power and struggles against lefthanders. *Grade 5.5*

TIMO PEREZ'S HITTING ZONE

.111	.000	.200
.200	.545	.231
.250	.300	.208

LEFTY-RIGHTY SPLITS

vs.	Avg.	AB	H	2B	3B	HR	RBI	BB	SO	OBP	Slg.
L	.105	19	2	1	0	0	3	1	6	.143	.158
R	.231	160	37	7	0	2	12	11	19	.281	.313

P

Year	Team (League)	Pos.	G	AB	R	H	2B	3B	HR	RBI	BB	SO	HBP	GDP	SB-CS	Avg.	OBP	SLG	OPS	E	Avg.
1994— Hiroshima (DSL)			51	206	40	70	9	8	0	21	31	7	...	...	8-...	.340	...	.461	...		
1995—			Did not play.																		
1996— Hiroshima (Jp. Cn.)			31	54	8	15	1	0	1	7	2	7	...	...	3-...	.278	...	.352	...		
1997— Hiroshima (Jp. West.)			19	69	9	21	3	1	2	12	10	3	...	...	9-...	.304	...	.464	...		
— Hiroshima (Jp. Cn.)			86	139	17	34	4	2	3	15	10	16	...	...	4-...	.245	...	.367	...		
1998— Hiroshima (Jp. West.)			2	7	0	2	0	0	0	0	0	0	...	...	0-...	.286	...	.286	...		
— Hiroshima (Jp. Cn.)			98	230	22	68	8	1	5	35	20	21	...	...	2-...	.296	...	.404	...		
1999— Hiroshima (Jp. West.)			60	160	19	58	13	4	1	24	34	13	...	...	6-...	.363	...	.513	...		
— Hiroshima (Jp. Cn.)			12	23	2	4	0	0	0	2	3	3	...	...	0-...	.174	...	.174	...		
2000— St. Lucie (Fla. St.)	OF		8	31	3	11	4	0	1	8	2	1	1	0	3-3	.355	.400	.581	.981	0	1.000
— Norfolk (Int'l)	OF		72	291	45	104	17	5	6	37	16	25	3	4	13-7	.357	.392	.512	.904	5	.976
— New York (N.L.)	OF		24	49	11	14	4	1	1	3	3	5	1	0	1-1	.286	.333	.469	.803	1	.970
2001— New York (N.L.)	OF		85	239	26	59	9	1	5	22	12	25	2	1	1-6	.247	.287	.356	.643	0	1.000
— Norfolk (Int'l)	OF		48	192	37	69	10	2	6	19	12	18	2	1	15-2	.359	.399	.526	.925	5	.951
2002— Norfolk (Int'l)	OF		5	21	5	12	2	1	1	5	2	2	0	1	3-1	.571	.609	.905	1.513	0	1.000
— New York (N.L.)	OF		136	444	52	131	27	6	8	47	23	36	2	10	10-6	.295	.331	.437	.768	6	.979
2003— Norfolk (Int'l)	OF		3	9	2	2	0	0	1	1	1	0	0	0	0-0	.222	.300	.556	.856	0	1.000
— New York (N.L.)	OF		127	346	32	93	21	0	4	42	18	29	2	5	5-6	.269	.301	.364	.666	2	.989
2004— Chicago (A.L.)	OF-DH		103	293	38	72	12	0	5	40	15	29	2	9	3-1	.246	.285	.338	.623	2	.986
2005— Chicago (A.L.) OF-DH-1B			76	179	13	39	8	0	2	15	12	25	0	3	2-2	.218	.266	.296	.562	4	.959
American League totals (2 years)			179	472	51	111	20	0	7	55	27	54	2	12	5-3	.235	.278	.322	.600	6	.975
National League totals (4 years)			372	1078	121	297	61	8	18	114	56	95	7	16	17-19	.276	.312	.397	.709	9	.986
Major League totals (6 years)			551	1550	172	408	81	8	25	169	83	149	9	28	22-22	.263	.302	.374	.676	15	.983

DIVISION SERIES RECORD

Year	Team (League)	Pos.	G	AB	R	H	2B	3B	HR	RBI	BB	SO	HBP	GDP	SB-CS	Avg.	OBP	SLG	OPS	E	Avg.
2000— New York (N.L.)			4	17	2	5	1	0	0	3	0	2	0	0	1-0	.294	.294	.353	.647	0	1.000
2005— Chicago (A.L.)	OF		1	1	0	0	0	0	0	0	0	0	0	0	0-0	.000	.000	.000	.000	0	1.000
Division series totals (2 years)			5	18	2	5	1	0	0	3	0	2	0	0	1-0	.278	.278	.333	.611	0	1.000

CHAMPIONSHIP SERIES RECORD

Year	Team (League)	Pos.	G	AB	R	H	2B	3B	HR	RBI	BB	SO	HBP	GDP	SB-CS	Avg.	OBP	SLG	OPS	E	Avg.
2000— New York (N.L.)	OF		5	23	8	7	2	0	0	0	1	3	0	1	2-1	.304	.333	.391	.725	1	.947

WORLD SERIES RECORD

Year	Team (League)	Pos.	G	AB	R	H	2B	3B	HR	RBI	BB	SO	HBP	GDP	SB-CS	Avg.	OBP	SLG	OPS	E	Avg.
2000— New York (N.L.)	OF		5	16	1	2	0	0	0	0	1	4	0	0	0-0	.125	.176	.125	.301	1	.900
2005— Chicago (A.L.)			1	1	0	0	0	0	0	0	0	0	0	0	0-0	.000	.000	.000	.000	0	...
World series totals (2 years)			6	17	1	2	0	0	0	0	1	4	0	0	0-0	.118	.167	.118	.284	1	.900

PEREZ, TOMAS — 1B/3B

PERSONAL: Born December 29, 1973, in Barquisimeto, Venezuela. ... 5-11/192. ... Bats both, throws right. ... Full name: Tomas Orlando Perez.

TRANSACTIONS/CAREER NOTES: Signed as a non-drafted free agent by Montreal Expos organization (July 11, 1991). ... Selected by California Angels from Expos organization in Rule 5 major league draft (December 5, 1994). ... Traded by Angels to Toronto Blue Jays for cash (December 5, 1994). ... On disabled list (June 25-July 25, 1997); included rehabilitation assignment to Syracuse. ... Traded by Blue Jays to Angels for IF Dave Hollins and cash (March 30, 1999). ... Signed as a free agent by Philadelphia Phillies organization (December 15, 1999). ... On disabled list (March 26-April 16, 2002); included rehabilitation assignment to Reading. ... Career major league pitching: 0-0, 0.00 ERA, 1 G, 0.1 IP, 0 H, 0 R, 0 ER, 0 BB, 0 SO.

2005 GAMES PLAYED BY POSITION (MLB): 1B—24, 3B—15, SS—14.

SCOUTING REPORT Perez has a long swing from both sides of the plate and often gets himself out. Is a dead fastball hitter who never has adjusted to off-speed pitches. Can run but isn't a threat to steal. Has extremely quick and soft hands and good agility. Has good range to both sides and can make throws from the hole. Tends to wear down and can't play for long stretches. ***Grade 5.1***

TOMAS PEREZ'S HITTING ZONE

.000	.200	.357
.235	.154	.242
.111	.308	.267

LEFTY-RIGHTY SPLITS

vs.	Avg.	AB	H	2B	3B	HR	RBI	BB	SO	OBP	Slg.
L	.283	46	13	3	0	0	6	3	4	.340	.348
R	.212	113	24	4	0	0	16	8	23	.268	.248

Year	Team (League)	Pos.	G	AB	R	H	2B	3B	HR	RBI	BB	SO	HBP	GDP	SB-CS	Avg.	OBP	SLG	OPS	E	Avg.
1992— Dom. Expos (DSL)	IF		44	151	35	46	7	0	1	19	27	20	...	...	12-...	.305	...	.371	...	12	.954
1993— GC Expos (GCL)	SS		52	189	27	46	3	1	2	21	23	25	0	5	8-3	.243	.322	.302	.624	12	.965
1994— Burlington (Midw.)	2B-SS		119	465	76	122	22	1	8	47	48	78	1	4	8-10	.262	.329	.366	.695	34	.944
1995— Toronto (A.L.)	SS-2B-3B		41	98	12	24	3	1	1	8	7	18	0	6	0-1	.245	.292	.327	.619	5	.962
1996— Syracuse (Int'l)	SS-2B		40	123	15	34	10	1	1	13	7	19	0	2	8-1	.276	.313	.398	.711	7	.962
— Toronto (A.L.)	2B-3B-SS		91	295	24	74	13	4	1	19	25	29	1	10	1-2	.251	.311	.332	.643	15	.964
1997— Syracuse (Int'l)	SS		89	303	32	68	13	1	0	20	37	67	0	9	3-4	.224	.308	.277	.585	12	.973
— Toronto (A.L.)	SS-2B		40	123	9	24	3	2	0	9	11	28	1	2	0-0	.195	.267	.252	.519	3	.984
1998— Syracuse (Int'l)	SS-2B		116	404	40	102	15	4	3	37	18	67	0	10	4-7	.252	.284	.332	.616	15	.977
— Toronto (A.L.)	SS-2B		6	9	1	1	0	0	0	1	3	1	0	1	0-0	.111	.200	.111	.311	0	1.000
1999— Edmonton (PCL)	SS-2B		83	296	31	77	17	1	4	40	19	43	2	1	2-2	.260	.306	.365	.671	11	.973
2000— Philadelphia (N.L.)	SS		45	140	17	31	7	1	1	13	11	30	0	3	1-1	.221	.278	.307	.585	4	.976
— Scran./W.B. (I.L.)	3B-SS-2B		77	279	44	82	16	2	10	56	16	48	2	2	4-1	.294	.334	.473	.808	9	.962
2001— Philadelphia (N.L.) 2B-3B-SS																					
	OF		62	135	11	41	7	1	3	19	7	22	2	2	0-1	.304	.347	.437	.784	1	.993
2002— Reading (East.)	2B-SS		2	9	2	4	0	0	1	0	1	1	0	0	0-0	.444	.444	.444	.889	0	1.000
— Philadelphia (N.L.) 2B-3B-SS																					
	1B-P		92	212	22	53	13	1	5	20	21	40	1	5	1-0	.250	.319	.392	.711	4	.985

P

Year Team (League)	Pos.	G	AB	R	H	2B	3B	HR	RBI	BB	SO	HBP	GDP	SB-CS	Avg.	OBP	SLG	OPS	E	Avg.
2003—Philadelphia (N.L.)	3B-2B-1B																			
	SS	125	298	39	79	18	1	5	33	23	54	0	7	0-1	.265	.316	.383	.698	9	.969
2004—Philadelphia (N.L.)	3B-2B-1B																			
	SS	86	176	22	38	13	2	6	21	9	44	1	2	0-0	.216	.257	.415	.671	6	.969
2005—Philadelphia (N.L.)	1B-3B-SS	94	159	17	37	7	0	0	22	11	27	2	6	1-0	.233	.289	.277	.566	0	1.000
American League totals (4 years)		178	525	46	123	19	7	2	36	44	78	2	19	2-4	.234	.295	.309	.604	23	.969
National League totals (6 years)		504	1120	128	279	65	6	20	128	82	217	6	25	3-3	.249	.303	.371	.674	24	.981
Major League totals (10 years)		682	1645	174	402	84	13	22	164	126	295	8	44	5-7	.244	.300	.351	.651	47	.977

PERISHO, MATT — P

PERSONAL: Born June 8, 1975, in Burlington, Iowa. ... 6-0/200. ... Throws left, bats left. ... Full name: Matthew Alan Perisho. ... Name pronounced: PAIR-ih-show. ... High school: McClintock (Tempe, Ariz.).

TRANSACTIONS/CAREER NOTES: Selected by California Angels organization in third round of 1993 free-agent draft. ... Angels franchise renamed Anaheim Angels for 1997 season. ... Traded by Angels to Texas Rangers for IF Mike Bell (October 31, 1997). ... Traded by Rangers to Detroit Tigers for Ps Kevin Mobley and Brandon Villafuerte (December 15, 2000). ... On disabled list (May 5-25, 2001); included rehabilitation assignment to Toledo. ... Released by Tigers (October 1, 2002). ... Signed by Tampa Bay Devil Rays organization (November 6, 2002). ... Released by Devil Rays (July 1, 2003). ... Signed by Arizona Diamondbacks organization (July 14, 2003). ... Released by Diamondbacks (July 27, 2003). ... Signed by Colorado Rockies organization (July 29, 2003). ... Signed as a free agent by Florida Marlins organization (December 19, 2003). ... Released by Marlins (August 3, 2005). ... Signed by Boston Red Sox organization (August 7, 2005). ... Released by Red Sox (September 15, 2005).

CAREER HITTING: 0-for-5 (.000), 0 R, 0 2B, 0 3B, 0 HR, 0 RBI.

MATT PERISHO'S PITCHING ZONE

1.000	.000	1.000
.400	.125	.222
.286	.000	.500

LEFTY-RIGHTY SPLITS

vs.	Avg.	AB	H	2B	3B	HR	RBI	BB	SO	OBP	Slg.
L	.346	26	9	4	0	1	8	9	4	.500	.615
R	.167	24	4	2	0	0	1	2	6	.259	.250

Year Team (League)	W	L	Pct.	ERA	WHIP	G	GS	CG	ShO	Hld.	Sv.-Opp.	IP	H	R	ER	HR	BB-IBB	SO	Avg.
1993—Ariz. Angels (Ariz.)	7	3	.700	3.66	1.27	11	11	1	1		0-...	64.0	58	32	26	1	23-0	65	.245
1994—Cedar Rap. (Midw.)	12	9	.571	4.33	1.71	27	27	0	0		0-...	147.2	165	90	71	11	88-0	107	.283
1995—Lake Elsinore (Calif.)	8	9	.471	6.32	1.71	24	22	0	0		0-...	115.1	137	91	81	10	60-0	68	.294
1996—Lake Elsinore (Calif.)	7	5	.583	4.20	1.47	21	18	1	1		0-...	128.2	131	72	60	9	58-0	97	.271
—Midland (Texas)	3	2	.600	3.21	1.28	8	8	0	0		0-...	53.1	48	22	19	4	20-0	50	.246
1997—Midland (Texas)	5	2	.714	2.96	1.18	10	10	3	1		0-...	73.0	60	26	24	5	26-1	62	.221
—Anaheim (A.L.)	0	2	.000	6.00	1.93	11	8	0	0	0	0-...	45.0	59	34	30	6	28-0	35	.324
—Vancouver (PCL)	4	4	.500	5.33	1.85	9	9	1	0		0-...	52.1	68	42	31	3	29-1	47	.313
1998—Tulsa (Texas)	0	0	...	6.00	2.00	1	1	0	0		0-...	3.0	3	2	2	0	3-0	1	.231
—Oklahoma (PCL)	8	5	.615	3.89	1.47	15	15	1	0		0-...	90.1	91	41	39	6	42-0	60	.267
—Texas (A.L.)	0	2	.000	27.00	4.60	2	2	0	0	0	0-...	5.0	15	17	15	2	8-0	2	.500
1999—Oklahoma (PCL)	15	7	.682	4.61	1.52	27	27	2	0		0-...	156.1	160	86	80	14	78-1	150	.270
—Texas (A.L.)	0	0	...	2.61	0.97	4	1	0	0	0	0-...	10.1	8	3	3	0	2-1	17	.211
2000—Texas (A.L.)	2	7	.222	7.37	1.93	34	13	0	0	0	0-1	105.0	136	99	86	20	67-3	74	.316
2001—Detroit (A.L.)	2	3	.400	5.72	1.73	30	4	0	0	0	0-2	39.1	54	29	25	5	14-1	19	.327
—Toledo (Int'l)	2	3	.400	1.71	1.26	25	2	0	0	0	9-...	42.0	42	10	8	3	11-0	28	.261
2002—Toledo (Int'l)	4	4	.500	2.45	1.23	51	0	0	0	0	1-...	66.0	62	20	18	4	19-4	44	.246
—Detroit (A.L.)	0	0	...	8.71	2.13	5	0	0	0	0	0-...	10.1	16	11	10	2	6-0	3	.372
2003—Durham (Int'l)	7	4	.636	6.52	1.40	34	0	0	0	0	1-...	38.2	43	29	28	5	12-2	41	.276
—Tucson (PCL)	0	0	...	9.82	1.60	4	0	0	0	0	0-...	3.2	4	4	1	0	2-2	5	.286
—Colo. Springs (PCL)	1	1	.500	3.42	1.60	8	4	0	0	0	0-...	23.2	25	16	9	1	14-2	15	.260
2004—Florida (N.L.)	5	3	.625	4.40	1.51	66	0	0	0	10	0-2	47.0	45	23	23	6	26-2	42	.247
2005—Florida (N.L.)	2	0	1.000	1.93	1.64	24	0	0	0	4	0-0	14.0	12	4	3	1	11-0	10	.245
—Albuquerque (PCL)	0	2	.000	11.93	2.23	17	1	0	0	0	1-2	14.1	25	20	19	4	7-0	10	.391
—Pawtucket (Int'l)	2	1	1.000	2.08	0.92	13	0	0	0	6	0-0	13.0	6	3	3	0	6-0	7	.140
—Boston (A.L.)	0	0	...	...	...	1	0	0	0	0	0-0	0.0	1	1	1	0	0-0	0	1.000
American League totals (7 years)	4	14	.222	7.12	1.93	87	28	0	0		0-3	215.0	289	194	170	35	125-5	150	.325
National League totals (2 years)	7	3	.700	3.84	1.54	90	0	0	0	14	0-2	61.0	57	27	26	7	37-2	52	.247
Major League totals (8 years)	11	17	.393	6.39	1.84	177	28	0	0	18	0-5	276.0	346	221	196	42	162-7	202	.309

PETAGINE, ROBERTO — 1B/OF

PERSONAL: Born June 2, 1971, in New York. ... 6-1/215. ... Bats left, throws left. ... Full name: Roberto Antonio Petagine. ... Name pronounced: PET-uh-GHEEN.

TRANSACTIONS/CAREER NOTES: Signed as non-drafted free agent by Houston Astros organization (February 13, 1990). ... Traded by Astros with 3B Ken Caminiti, OF Steve Finley, SS Andujar Cedeno, P Brian Williams and a player to be named to San Diego Padres for OFs Phil Plantier and Derek Bell, Ps Pedro A. Martinez and Doug Brocail, IF Craig Shipley and SS Ricky Gutierrez (December 28, 1994); Padres acquired P Sean Fesh to complete deal (May 1, 1995). ... Traded by Padres with P Scott Adair to New York Mets for Ps Luis Arroyo and Pete Walker (March 17, 1996). ... Traded by Mets to Cincinnati Reds for SS Yuri Sanchez (February 5, 1998). ... Contract sold by Reds to Yakult of Japan Central League (December 2, 1998). ... Signed as a free agent by Boston Red Sox organization (February 8, 2005).

2005 GAMES PLAYED BY POSITION (MLB): 1B—10, DH—3, OF—2.

LEFTY-RIGHTY SPLITS

vs.	Avg.	AB	H	2B	3B	HR	RBI	BB	SO	OBP	Slg.
L	.333	3	1	0	0	0	1	0	1	.333	.333
R	.276	29	8	2	0	1	8	4	4	.364	.448

Year Team (League)	Pos.	G	AB	R	H	2B	3B	HR	RBI	BB	SO	HBP	GDP	SB-CS	Avg.	OBP	SLG	OPS	E	Avg.
1990—GC Astros (GCL)	1B-OF	55	187	35	54	5	4	2	24	26	23	2	4	9-7	.289	.378	.390	.768	5	.990
1991—Burlington (Midw.)	1B	124	432	72	112	24	1	12	58	71	74	4	9	7-5	.259	.368	.403	.771	22	.978
1992—Osceola (Fla. St.)	1B	86	307	52	90	22	4	7	49	47	47	5	5	3-1	.293	.391	.459	.850	10	.987
—Jackson (Texas)	1B	21	70	8	21	4	0	4	12	6	15	2	4	1-0	.300	.363	.529	.892	0	1.000
1993—Jackson (Texas)	1B	128	437	73	146	36	2	15	90	84	89	4	6	6-5	.334	.442	.529	.971	14	.988
1994—Houston (N.L.)	1B	8	7	0	0	0	0	0	0	0	3	...	...	0-0	.000	.125	.000	.125	0	1.000
—Tucson (PCL)	1B	65	247	53	78	19	0	10	44	35	54	1	7	3-1	.316	.399	.514	.913	10	.984
1995—San Diego (N.L.)	1B-OF	89	124	15	29	8	0	3	17	26	41	...	...	0-0	.234	.367	.371	.738	1	.997
—Las Vegas (PCL)	1B-DH	19	56	8	12	2	1	1	5	13	17	0	0	1-0	.214	.362	.339	.701	3	.975
1996—Norfolk (Int'l)	1B-DH	95	314	49	100	24	1	12	65	51	75	4	4	4-1	.318	.421	.529	.950	15	.982
—New York (N.L.)	1B	50	99	10	23	3	0	4	17	9	27	...	...	0-2	.232	.296	.384	.680	1	.996
1997—Norfolk (Int'l)	1B-OF	129	441	90	140	32	3	31	100	85	92	8	6	0-1	.317	.430	.605	1.035	11	.990

P

		G	AB	R	H	2B	3B	HR	RBI	BB	SO			SB-CS	BA	OBP	SLG	OPS	E	Fld.
— New York (N.L.)	1B-OF	12	15	2	1	0	0	0	2	3	6	...	...	0-0	.067	.222	.067	.289	0	1.000
1998— Indianapolis (Int'l)	1B-OF-DH	102	363	79	120	30	1	24	109	70	71	3	14	3-1	.331	.436	.617	1.053	6	.992
— Cincinnati (N.L.)	1B-OF	34	62	14	16	2	1	3	7	16	11	...	...	1-0	.258	.410	.468	.878	0	1.000

					Played for Yakult (Jp. Cen.) — 1999-2002; Played for Yomiuri (Jp. Cen.) —2003-04															
2005— Boston (A.L.)	1B-DH-OF	18	32	4	9	2	0	1	9	4	5	0	3	0-0	.281	.361	.438	.799	1	.983
American League totals (1 year)		18	32	4	9	2	0	1	9	4	5	0	3	0-0	.281	.361	.438	.799	1	.983
National League totals (5 years)		193	307	41	69	13	1	10	43	55	88	...	...	1-2	.225	...	.371	...	2	.997
Major League totals (6 years)		211	339	45	78	15	1	11	52	59	93	0	3	1-2	.230	.344	.378	.722	3	.996

PETTITTE, ANDY   P

PERSONAL: Born June 15, 1972, in Baton Rouge, La. ... 6-5/225. ... Throws left, bats left. ... Full name: Andrew Eugene Pettitte. ... Name pronounced: pet-it. ... High school: Deer Park (Texas). ... Junior college: San Jacinto (Texas).

TRANSACTIONS/CAREER NOTES: Selected by New York Yankees organization in 22nd round of 1990 free-agent draft; did not sign. ... Signed as a non-drafted free agent by Yankees organization (May 25, 1991). ... On disabled list (March 26-April 17, 1999); included rehabilitation assignment to Tampa. ... On disabled list (April 8-26, 2000; and June 15-July 1, 2001). ... On disabled list (April 16-June 14, 2002); included rehabilitation assignments to Tampa and Norwich. ... Signed as a free agent by Houston Astros (December 16, 2003). ... On disabled list (April 7-29, May 27-June 29 and August 18, 2004-remainder of season); included rehabilitation assignment to Round Rock.

CAREER HITTING: 12-for-113 (.106), 1 R, 2 2B, 0 3B, 0 HR, 7 RBI.

SCOUTING REPORT **Throws:** Pettitte throws a four-seam fastball from 88-92 mph, a cut fastball, a two-seam fastball, a 12-6 curveball and a changeup. **Tendencies:** His delivery is outstanding, he has good command of all his pitches and has tremendous mound presence. Velocity has improved. Has good late tailing action on two-seam fastball. Can pound righthanded hitters with his cutter. Has an outstanding curve that breaks straight down and a good changeup that turns over. **Outlook:** Pettitte could have been a 20-game winner with more run support and a stronger early portion of the season. Is a complete pitcher with excellent command who will have a good year in 2006. *Grade 8.3*

ANDY PETTITTE'S PITCHING ZONE

.225	.381	.268
.258	.280	.196
.239	.265	.338

LEFTY-RIGHTY SPLITS

vs.	Avg.	AB	H	2B	3B	HR	RBI	BB	SO	OBP	Slg.
L	.200	180	36	7	1	2	11	6	38	.230	.283
R	.239	637	152	30	3	15	51	35	133	.279	.366

Year	Team (League)	W	L	Pct.	ERA	WHIP	G	GS	CG	ShO	Hld.	Sv.-Opp.	IP	H	R	ER	HR	BB-IBB	SO	Avg.
1991— GC Yankees (GCL)		4	1	.800	0.98	0.65	6	6	0	0		0-...	36.2	16	6	4	0	8-0	51	.127
— Oneonta (NYP)		2	2	.500	2.18	1.48	6	6	1	0		0-...	33.0	33	18	8	1	16-0	32	.252
1992— Greensboro (S. Atl.)		10	4	.714	2.20	1.17	27	27	2	1		0-...	168.0	141	53	41	4	55-0	130	.232
1993— Prince Will. (Car.)		11	9	.550	3.04	1.21	26	26	2	1		0-...	159.2	146	68	54	7	47-0	129	.248
— Albany (East.)		1	0	1.000	3.60	1.40	1	1	0	0		0-...	5.0	5	4	2	0	2-0	6	.250
1994— Alb./Colon. (East.)		7	2	.778	2.71	1.07	11	11	0	0		0-...	73.0	60	32	22	5	18-1	50	.220
— Columbus (Int'l)		7	2	.778	2.98	1.26	16	16	3	0		0-...	96.2	101	40	32	3	21-0	61	.272
1995— New York (A.L.)		12	9	.571	4.17	1.41	31	26	3	0	0	0-0	175.0	183	86	81	15	63-3	114	.272
— Columbus (Int'l)		0	0	...	0.00	0.60	2	2	0	0		0-...	11.2	7	0	0	0	0-0	8	.184
1996— New York (A.L.)		* 21	8	.724	3.87	1.36	35	34	0	0	0	0-0	221.0	229	105	95	23	72-2	162	.271
1997— New York (A.L.)		18	7	.720	2.88	1.24	35	• 35	4	1	0	0-0	240.1	233	86	77	7	65-0	166	.256
1998— New York (A.L.)		16	11	.593	4.24	1.45	33	32	5	0	0	0-0	216.1	226	110	102	20	87-1	146	.274
1999— Tampa (Fla. St.)		1	0	1.000	0.00	1.20	1	1	0	0		0-...	5.0	4	0	0	0	2-0	8	.222
— New York (A.L.)		14	11	.560	4.70	1.59	31	31	0	0	0	0-0	191.2	216	105	100	20	89-3	121	.289
2000— New York (A.L.)		19	9	.679	4.35	1.46	32	32	3	1	0	0-0	204.2	219	111	99	17	80-4	125	.271
2001— New York (A.L.)		15	10	.600	3.99	1.32	31	31	2	0	0	0-0	200.2	224	103	89	14	41-3	164	.281
2002— New York (A.L.)		13	5	.722	3.27	1.31	22	22	3	1	0	0-0	134.2	144	58	49	6	32-2	97	.272
— Tampa (Fla. St.)		0	0	...	0.00	0.60	2	2	0	0		0-...	5.0	3	0	0	0	0-0	4	.167
— Norwich (East.)		0	0	...	1.42	0.32	1	1	0	0		0-...	6.1	2	1	1	0	0-0	5	.095
2003— New York (A.L.)		21	8	.724	4.02	1.33	33	33	1	0	0	0-0	208.1	227	109	93	21	50-3	180	.272
2004— Round Rock (Texas)		0	0	...	2.25	0.75	2	2	0	0		0-...	8.0	4	2	2	1	2-0	9	.143
— Houston (N.L.)		6	4	.600	3.90	1.23	15	15	0	0	0	0-0	83.0	71	37	36	8	31-2	79	.226
2005— Houston (N.L.)		17	9	.654	2.39	1.03	33	33	0	0	0	0-0	222.1	188	66	59	17	41-0	171	.230
American League totals (9 years)		149	78	.656	3.94	1.38	283	276	23	3	0	0-0	1792.2	1901	873	785	143	579-21	1275	.273
National League totals (2 years)		23	13	.639	2.80	1.08	48	48	0	0	0	0-0	305.1	259	103	95	25	72-2	250	.229
Major League totals (11 years)		172	91	.654	3.78	1.34	331	324	23	3	0	0-0	2098.0	2160	976	880	168	651-23	1525	.267

DIVISION SERIES RECORD

Year	Team (League)	W	L	Pct.	ERA	WHIP	G	GS	CG	ShO	Hld.	Sv.-Opp.	IP	H	R	ER	HR	BB-IBB	SO	Avg.
1995— New York (A.L.)		0	0	...	5.14	1.71	1	1	0	0	0	0-0	7.0	9	4	4	1	3-0	0	.346
1996— New York (A.L.)		0	0	...	5.68	1.58	1	1	0	0	0	0-0	6.1	4	4	4	2	6-0	3	.190
1997— New York (A.L.)		0	2	.000	8.49	1.37	2	2	0	0	0	0-0	11.2	15	11	11	1	1-0	5	.333
1998— New York (A.L.)		1	0	1.000	1.29	0.43	1	1	0	0	0	0-0	7.0	3	1	1	0	0-0	8	.125
1999— New York (A.L.)		1	0	1.000	1.23	0.95	1	1	0	0	0	0-0	7.1	7	1	1	1	0-0	5	.241
2000— New York (A.L.)		1	0	1.000	3.97	1.59	2	2	0	0	0	0-0	11.1	15	5	5	0	3-0	7	.326
2001— New York (A.L.)		0	1	.000	1.42	1.42	1	1	0	0	0	0-0	6.1	7	1	1	0	2-0	4	.269
2002— New York (A.L.)		0	0	...	12.00	2.67	1	1	0	0	0	0-0	3.0	8	4	4	2	0-0	1	.471
2003— New York (A.L.)		1	0	1.000	1.29	1.00	1	1	0	0	0	0-0	7.0	3	1	1	0	3-0	10	.154
2005— Houston (N.L.)		1	0	1.000	3.86	0.86	1	1	0	0	0	0-0	7.0	4	3	3	2	2-0	6	.167
Division series totals (10 years)		5	3	.625	4.26	1.30	12	12	0	0	0	0-0	74.0	76	35	35	11	20-0	49	.268

CHAMPIONSHIP SERIES RECORD

Year	Team (League)	W	L	Pct.	ERA	WHIP	G	GS	CG	ShO	Hld.	Sv.-Opp.	IP	H	R	ER	HR	BB-IBB	SO	Avg.
1996— New York (A.L.)		1	0	1.000	3.60	1.00	2	2	0	0	0	0-0	15.0	10	6	6	4	5-0	7	.185
1998— New York (A.L.)		0	1	.000	11.57	2.36	1	1	0	0	0	0-0	4.2	8	6	6	4	3-0	1	.364
1999— New York (A.L.)		1	0	1.000	2.45	1.23	1	1	0	0	0	0-0	7.1	8	2	2	0	1-0	5	.296
2000— New York (A.L.)		1	0	1.000	2.70	1.50	1	1	0	0	0	0-0	6.2	9	2	2	0	1-0	4	.346
2001— New York (A.L.)		2	0	1.000	2.51	0.91	2	2	0	0	0	0-0	14.1	11	4	4	0	2-0	8	.224
2003— New York (A.L.)		1	0	1.000	4.63	1.80	2	2	0	0	0	0-0	11.2	17	6	6	2	4-0	10	.340
2005— Houston (N.L.)		0	1	.000	5.11	1.54	2	2	0	0	0	0-0	12.1	15	7	7	1	4-0	6	.313
Champ. series totals (7 years)		6	2	.750	4.13	1.36	11	11	0	0	0	0-0	72.0	78	33	33	11	20-0	39	.281

P

WORLD SERIES RECORD

Year Team (League)	W	L	Pct.	ERA	WHIP	G	GS	CG	ShO	Hld.	Sv.-Opp.	IP	H	R	ER	HR	BB-IBB	SO	Avg.
1996— New York (A.L.)	1	1	.500	5.91	1.41	2	2	0	0	0	0-0	10.2	11	7	7	1	4-0	5	.275
1998— New York (A.L.)	1	0	1.000	0.00	1.09	1	1	0	0	0	0-0	7.1	5	0	0	0	3-0	4	.192
1999— New York (A.L.)	0	0	...	12.27	3.00	1	1	0	0	0	0-0	3.2	10	5	5	0	1-0	1	.500
2000— New York (A.L.)	0	0	...	1.98	1.46	2	2	0	0	0	0-0	13.2	16	5	3	0	4-1	9	.302
2001— New York (A.L.)	0	2	.000	10.00	1.56	2	2	0	0	0	0-0	9.0	12	10	10	1	2-1	9	.324
2003— New York (A.L.)	1	1	.500	0.57	1.02	2	2	0	0	0	0-0	15.2	12	3	1	0	4-1	14	.207
2005— Houston (N.L.)	0	0	...	3.00	1.33	1	1	0	0	0	0-0	6.0	8	2	2	0	0-0	4	.320
World series totals (7 years)	3	4	.429	3.82	1.39	11	11	0	0	0	0-0	66.0	74	32	28	2	18-3	46	.286

ALL-STAR GAME RECORD

	W	L	Pct.	ERA	WHIP	G	GS	CG	ShO	Hld.	Sv.-Opp.	IP	H	R	ER	HR	BB-IBB	SO	Avg.
All-Star Game totals (1 year)	0	0	...	0.00	1.00	1	0	0	0	0	0-0	1.0	1	0	0	0	0-0	1	.250

PHELPS, JOSH   DH/1B

PERSONAL: Born May 12, 1978, in Anchorage, Alaska. ... 6-3/220. ... Bats right, throws right. ... Full name: Joshua Lee Phelps. ... High school: Lakeland (Rathdrum, Idaho).

TRANSACTIONS/CAREER NOTES: Selected by Toronto Blue Jays organization in 10th round of 1996 free-agent draft. ... On disabled list (July 7-25, 2003); included rehabilitation assignment to Syracuse. ... Traded by Blue Jays to Cleveland Indians for 1B Eric Crozier (August 6, 2004). ... Signed as a free agent by Tampa Bay Devil Rays (December 22, 2004).

2005 GAMES PLAYED BY POSITION (MLB): DH—42, 1B—1.

JOSH PHELPS' HITTING ZONE

.000	.200	.500
.387	.667	.250
.136	.333	.231

LEFTY-RIGHTY SPLITS

vs.	Avg.	AB	H	2B	3B	HR	RBI	BB	SO	OBP	Slg.
L	.217	46	10	2	0	1	4	3	13	.294	.326
R	.286	112	32	8	0	4	22	9	35	.341	.464

							BATTING											FIELDING	
Year Team (League)	Pos.	G	AB	R	H	2B	3B	HR	RBI	BB	SO	HBP	GDP	SB-CS	Avg.	OBP	SLG	OPS	E	Avg.
1996— Medicine Hat (Pio.)	C-OF	59	191	26	46	3	0	5	29	27	65	6	5	5-3	.241	.351	.335	.686	9	.964
1997— Hagerstown (SAL)	C	68	233	26	49	9	1	7	24	15	72	8	6	3-2	.210	.279	.348	.627	21	.965
1998— Hagerstown (SAL)	3B-C-OF	117	385	48	102	24	1	8	44	40	80	8	12	2-0	.265	.342	.395	.737	19	.975
1999— Dunedin (Fla. St.)	C	110	406	72	133	27	4	20	88	28	104	8	13	6-3	.328	.379	.562	.941	1	.994
2000— Tennessee (Sou.)	C	56	184	23	42	9	1	9	28	15	66	7	6	1-0	.228	.308	.435	.742	5	.983
— Toronto (A.L.)	C	1	1	0	0	0	0	0	0	0	1	0	0	0-0	.000	.000	.000	.000	0	1.000
— Dunedin (Fla. St.)	C	30	113	26	36	7	0	12	34	12	34	1	2	0-0	.319	.386	.699	1.085	1	.992
2001— Tennessee (Sou.)	C	136	486	95	142	36	1	31	97	80	127	17	5	3-3	.292	.406	.562	.968	2	.996
— Toronto (A.L.)	C	8	12	3	0	0	0	0	1	2	5	0	1	0-0	.000	.143	.000	.143	0	1.000
2002— Syracuse (Int'l)	C-1B	70	257	50	75	20	1	24	64	32	83	5	6	0-0	.292	.380	.658	1.037	4	.985
— Toronto (A.L.)	DH-1B	74	265	41	82	20	1	15	58	19	82	3	7	0-0	.309	.362	.562	.925	0	1.000
2003— Syracuse (Int'l)	DH	4	11	2	5	0	0	2	4	1	3	0	0	0-0	.455	.500	1.000	1.500	0	...
— Toronto (A.L.)	DH-1B	119	396	57	106	18	1	20	66	39	115	17	12	1-2	.268	.358	.470	.827	2	.967
2004— Toronto (A.L.)	DH-1B	79	295	38	70	13	2	12	51	18	73	7	9	0-0	.237	.296	.417	.713	2	.981
— Cleveland (A.L.)	DH-1B	24	76	13	23	6	0	5	10	4	20	0	4	0-0	.303	.338	.579	.916	1	.978
2005— Tampa Bay (A.L.)	DH-1B	47	158	21	42	10	0	5	26	12	48	4	3	0-0	.266	.328	.424	.752	0	1.000
— Durham (Int'l)	DH-1B	59	222	35	60	14	3	14	33	15	53	5	6	0-1	.270	.329	.550	.879	6	.971
Major League totals (6 years)		352	1203	173	323	67	4	57	212	94	344	31	36	2-2	.268	.336	.473	.809	5	.981

PHELPS, TOMMY   P

PERSONAL: Born March 4, 1974, in Seoul, South Korea. ... 6-3/215. ... Throws left, bats left. ... Full name: Thomas Allen Phelps. ... High school: Robinson (Tampa).

TRANSACTIONS/CAREER NOTES: Selected by Montreal Expos organization in eighth round of 1992 free-agent draft. ... Released by Expos (June 20, 1999). ... Signed by Detroit Tigers organization (November 23, 1999). ... Signed as a free agent by Florida Marlins organization (March 6, 2002). ... On disabled list (August 2-September 1, 2003); included rehabilitation assignment to Jupiter. ... Signed as a free agent by Milwaukee Brewers organization (December 15, 2004).

CAREER HITTING: 1-for-17 (.059), 1 R, 0 2B, 0 3B, 0 HR, 0 RBI.

TOMMY PHELPS' PITCHING ZONE

.333	.429	.000
.611	.313	.091
.000	.000	.200

LEFTY-RIGHTY SPLITS

vs.	Avg.	AB	H	2B	3B	HR	RBI	BB	SO	OBP	Slg.
L	.308	39	12	4	0	1	7	4	7	.372	.487
R	.245	53	13	4	0	1	6	8	7	.365	.377

Year Team (League)	W	L	Pct.	ERA	WHIP	G	GS	CG	ShO	Hld.	Sv.-Opp.	IP	H	R	ER	HR	BB-IBB	SO	Avg.
1993— Burlington (Midw.)	2	4	.333	3.73	1.20	8	8	0	0	...	0-...	41.0	36	18	17	4	13-0	33	.229
— Jamestown (NYP)	3	8	.273	4.58	1.51	16	15	1	0	...	0-...	92.1	102	62	47	4	37-1	74	.278
1994— Burlington (Midw.)	8	8	.500	5.55	1.61	23	23	1	1	...	0-...	118.1	143	91	73	9	48-1	82	.307
1995— W.P. Beach (FSL)	0	2	.000	16.20	4.20	2	2	0	0	...	0-...	5.0	10	10	9	0	11-0	5	.455
— Albany (S. Atl.)	10	9	.526	3.33	1.38	24	24	1	0	...	0-...	135.1	142	76	50	6	45-0	119	.262
1996— W.P. Beach (FSL)	10	2	.833	2.89	1.25	18	18	1	1	...	0-...	112.0	105	42	36	5	35-0	71	.246
— Harrisburg (East.)	2	2	.500	2.47	1.31	8	8	2	2	...	0-...	47.1	43	16	13	3	19-2	23	.249
1997— Harrisburg (East.)	10	6	.625	4.71	1.52	18	18	0	0	...	0-...	101.1	115	68	53	14	39-1	86	.285
1998— Jupiter (Fla. St.)	2	2	.500	4.39	1.39	7	7	0	0	...	0-...	41.0	42	21	20	3	15-0	21	.259
— Harrisburg (East.)	5	4	.556	3.62	1.39	12	10	0	0	...	0-...	59.2	57	29	24	5	26-0	26	.266
1999— Harrisburg (East.)	3	6	.333	5.71	1.58	13	13	1	0	...	0-...	64.2	76	53	41	13	26-0	36	.288
2000— Jacksonville (Sou.)	6	6	.500	4.94	1.34	38	11	0	0	...	0-...	102.0	111	59	56	17	26-2	62	.277
2001— Toledo (Int'l)	3	2	.600	3.62	1.56	29	0	0	0	...	1-...	59.2	74	30	24	4	19-3	53	.298
— Erie (East.)	1	1	.500	3.58	1.26	15	2	0	0	...	2-...	32.2	33	14	13	1	8-2	31	.268
2002— Calgary (PCL)	4	2	.667	3.15	1.30	51	0	0	0	...	2-...	74.1	76	27	26	8	21-3	62	.266
2003— Albuquerque (PCL)	0	0	...	1.17	1.04	5	0	0	0	...	0-...	7.2	5	1	1	1	3-0	13	.217
— Florida (N.L.)	3	2	.600	4.00	1.48	27	7	0	0	1	0-0	63.0	70	32	28	3	23-1	43	.282

P

Year	Team (League)	W	L	Pct.	ERA	WHIP	G	GS	CG	ShO	Hld.	Sv.-Opp.	IP	H	R	ER	HR	BB-IBB	SO	Avg.
—Jupiter (Fla. St.)		0	0	...	6.00	1.67	2	1	0	0	...	0-...	3.0	5	2	2	0	0-0	3	.357
2004—Florida (N.L.)		1	1	.500	4.76	1.35	19	4	0	0	4	0-0	34.0	34	20	18	6	12-0	28	.268
—GC Marlins (GCL)		0	0	...	0.00	0.00	1	1	0	0	...	0-...	1.0	0	0	0	0	0-0	1	.000
—Jupiter (Fla. St.)		0	0	...	0.00	1.50	1	0	0	0	...	0-...	1.1	2	3	0	0	0-0	1	.333
2005—Milwaukee (N.L.)		0	2	.000	4.63	1.59	29	0	0	0	4	1-2	23.1	25	12	12	2	12-4	14	.272
—Nashville (PCL)		1	0	1.000	1.13	0.94	5	4	0	0	...	0-0	16.0	13	3	2	0	2-0	14	.224
Major League totals (3 years)		4	5	.444	4.34	1.46	75	11	0	0	9	1-2	120.1	129	64	58	11	47-5	85	.276

PHILLIPS, ANDY — 1B

PERSONAL: Born April 6, 1977, in Tuscaloosa, Ala. ... 6-0/205. ... Bats right, throws right. ... Full name: George Andrew Phillips. ... High school: Demopolis Academy (Demopolis, Ala.). ... College: Alabama.

TRANSACTIONS/CAREER NOTES: Selected by New York Yankees in seventh round of 1999 free-agent draft.

RECORDS: Shares major league record for most strikeouts, game (5, May 2, 2005).

2005 GAMES PLAYED BY POSITION (MLB): 1B—19, DH—6, 3B—1, OF—1.

SCOUTING REPORT *Offense:* He can punish pitches over the plate when he extends his arms, but he can be pitched inside, where he'll hit popups. Commits early and pulls balls foul. Swings through high fastballs and breaking balls away. Waits for mistakes and works counts. Is a slow runner. *Defense:* He has limited range at first base, but he has learned the position well enough to not be a liability. Is adequate at handling throws. Has an average to below-average arm.

Outlook: He has proven himself at the minor league level but might not get much of an opportunity in the majors unless the Yankees trade him. Is best suited for a DH role. *Grade 6.3*

LEFTY-RIGHTY SPLITS

vs.	Avg.	AB	H	2B	3B	HR	RBI	BB	SO	OBP	Slg.
L	.150	20	3	1	0	1	3	1	7	.190	.350
R	.150	20	3	3	0	0	1	0	6	.150	.300

								BATTING											FIELDING	
Year	Team (League)	Pos.	G	AB	R	H	2B	3B	HR	RBI	BB	SO	HBP	GDP	SB-CS	Avg.	OBP	SLG	OPS	E	Avg.
1999—Staten Island (N.Y.-Penn.)	3B	64	233	35	75	11	7	7	48	37	40	3	4	3-3	.322	.417	.519	.936	16	.904
2000—Tampa (Fla. St.)	3B	127	478	66	137	33	2	13	58	46	98	2	9	2-0	.287	.346	.446	.792	30	.912
—Norwich (East.)	3B	7	28	5	7	2	1	0	3	3	11	0	1	1-0	.250	.323	.393	.715	2	.913
2001—Norwich (East.)	2B	51	183	23	49	9	2	6	25	21	54	0	6	1-0	.268	.340	.437	.777	17	.915
—Tampa (Fla. St.)	2B	75	288	43	87	17	4	11	50	25	55	3	6	3-3	.302	.353	.503	.856	10	.968
2002—Norwich (East.)	2B	73	272	58	83	24	2	19	51	30	56	3	6	4-3	.305	.381	.618	.999	7	.979
—Columbus (Int'l)	2B-1B	51	205	32	54	11	1	9	36	10	46	0	8	0-1	.263	.296	.459	.755	3	.985
2003—Columbus (Int'l)	3B	17	67	7	14	4	0	2	5	5	17	0	1	0-0	.209	.264	.358	.622	2	.955
2004—Trenton (East.)	3B-1B	10	42	8	15	2	1	4	16	3	1	0	0	3-0	.357	.383	.738	1.121	1	.982
—Columbus (Int'l)	1B-DH-2B-3B	115	434	82	137	19	6	25	84	51	61	2	19	2-1	.316	.386	.560	.955	13	.984
—New York (A.L.)	3B-DH	5	8	1	2	0	0	1	2	0	1	0	1	0-0	.250	.250	.625	.875	0	1.000
2005—Columbus (Int'l)	3B-1B-DH-2B	75	300	60	90	14	1	22	54	36	61	3	15	2-0	.300	.379	.573	.953	7	.979
—New York (A.L.)	1B-DH-3B-OF	27	40	7	6	4	0	1	4	1	13	0	1	0-0	.150	.171	.325	.496	1	.987
Major League totals (2 years)		32	48	8	8	4	0	2	6	1	14	0	2	0-0	.167	.184	.375	.559	1	.988

PHILLIPS, BRANDON — 2B

PERSONAL: Born June 28, 1981, in Raleigh, N.C. ... 5-11/185. ... Bats right, throws right. ... Full name: Brandon Emil Phillips. ... High school: Redan (Stone Mountain, Ga.).

TRANSACTIONS/CAREER NOTES: Selected by Montreal Expos organization in second round of 1999 free-agent draft. ... Traded by Expos with 1B Lee Stevens, P Cliff Lee and OF Grady Sizemore to Cleveland Indians for P Bartolo Colon and future considerations (June 27, 2002); Expos acquired P Tim Drew to complete deal (June 28, 2002).

2005 GAMES PLAYED BY POSITION (MLB): 2B—2, SS—1, DH—1.

SCOUTING REPORT *Offense:* He seems overmatched at the plate. Lacks the power to pull everything and can easily be set up for off-speed pitches. Has not shown the ability to make adjustments. Must find his stroke and define his own strike zone to have any major league success. Is fast when he reaches base. *Defense:* He is superb at second and shortstop with great footwork, lateral moves and an above-average arm. Turns double plays with ease. *Outlook:* By not calling him up in September, the Indians seemed to be saying they no longer see this once-touted prospect as an everyday player. A clean start might be best for Phillips and the Indians. *Grade 5.9*

LEFTY-RIGHTY SPLITS

vs.	Avg.	AB	H	2B	3B	HR	RBI	BB	SO	OBP	Slg.
L	.000	3	0	0	0	0	0	0	1	.000	.000
R	.000	6	0	0	0	0	0	0	3	.000	.000

								BATTING											FIELDING	
Year	Team (League)	Pos.	G	AB	R	H	2B	3B	HR	RBI	BB	SO	HBP	GDP	SB-CS	Avg.	OBP	SLG	OPS	E	Avg.
1999—GC Expos (GCL)	SS	47	169	23	49	11	3	1	21	15	35	3	6	12-3	.290	.358	.408	.767	17	.915
2000—Cape Fear (S. Atl.)	SS-2B	126	484	74	117	17	8	11	72	38	97	9	11	23-8	.242	.306	.378	.684	36	.941
2001—Jupiter (Fla. St.)	SS	55	194	36	55	12	2	4	23	38	45	6	3	17-3	.284	.414	.428	.842	18	.930
—Harrisburg (East.)	SS-2B-3B	67	265	35	79	19	0	7	36	12	42	4	9	13-6	.298	.337	.449	.786	12	.958
2002—Harrisburg (East.)	SS	60	245	40	80	13	2	9	35	16	33	5	7	6-3	.327	.380	.506	.886	14	.936
—Ottawa (Int'l)	SS	10	35	1	9	4	0	1	5	2	6	0	...	0-0	.257	.297	.457	.754	0	1.000
—Buffalo (Int'l)	SS-2B	55	223	30	63	14	0	8	27	14	39	1	...	8-2	.283	.321	.453	.774	15	.952
—Cleveland (A.L.)	2B	11	31	6	8	3	1	0	4	3	4	1	0	0-0	.258	.343	.419	.762	2	.957
2003—Buffalo (Int'l)	2B	43	154	14	27	7	0	3	13	12	24	3	3	7-3	.175	.247	.279	.526	3	.985
—Cleveland (A.L.)	2B	112	370	36	77	18	1	6	33	14	77	3	12	4-5	.208	.242	.311	.553	11	.981
2004—Buffalo (Int'l)	2B-SS	135	521	83	158	34	4	8	50	44	56	8	12	14-11	.303	.363	.430	.793	28	.955
—Cleveland (A.L.)	2B	6	22	1	4	2	0	0	1	2	5	0	1	0-2	.182	.250	.273	.523	1	.973
2005—Buffalo (Int'l)	2B-SS-DH	112	465	79	119	24	1	15	46	39	90	10	11	7-5	.256	.326	.409	.734	21	.958
—Cleveland (A.L.)	2B-SS-DH	6	9	1	0	0	0	0	0	1	0	0	0	0-0	.000	.000	.000	.000	1	.923
Major League totals (4 years)		135	432	43	89	23	2	6	38	19	92	4	13	4-7	.206	.246	.310	.556	15	.978

P

PHILLIPS, JASON   1B/C

PERSONAL: Born September 27, 1976, in La Mesa, Calif. ... 6-1/177. ... Bats right, throws right. ... Full name: Jason Lloyd Phillips. ... High school: El Capitan (Lakeside, Calif.). ... College: San Diego State.
TRANSACTIONS/CAREER NOTES: Selected by New York Mets organization in 24th round of 1997 free-agent draft. ... Traded by Mets to Los Angeles Dodgers for P Kazuhisa Ishii (March 20, 2005).
2005 GAMES PLAYED BY POSITION (MLB): C—93, 1B—21.

SCOUTING REPORT Phillips struggled most of the season and never hit for average. Has a very unusual swing; it's long with an inside-out approach, yet he likes to hook the ball. Has holes on the inside part of the plate. Has occasional power. Versatility is his best asset as he can catch and play first base. Is not a good defensive catcher; arm is short and doesn't have good enough carry to be accurate. Doesn't have a lot of quickness or range to block balls in the dirt, and has no range at first base. Is strictly a backup with attractive power off the bench. Can be overexposed quickly. **Grade 5.5**

JASON PHILLIPS' HITTING ZONE

.250	.467	.211
.229	.381	.425
.119	.353	.071

LEFTY-RIGHTY SPLITS

vs.	Avg.	AB	H	2B	3B	HR	RBI	BB	SO	OBP	Slg.
L	.270	89	24	6	0	4	16	12	7	.353	.472
R	.229	310	71	14	0	6	39	13	43	.267	.332

							BATTING											FIELDING	
Year	Team (League)	Pos.	G	AB	R	H	2B	3B	HR	RBI	BB	SO	HBP	GDP	SB-CS	Avg.	OBP	SLG	OPS	E	Avg.
1997—Pittsfield (NYP)		C	48	155	15	32	9	0	2	17	13	24	4	2	4-0	.206	.282	.303	.585	4	.990
1998—Capital City (SAL)		C	69	251	36	68	15	1	5	37	23	35	5	3	5-2	.271	.343	.398	.741	4	.994
—St. Lucie (Fla. St.)		C	8	28	4	13	2	0	0	2	2	1	0	1	0-0	.464	.500	.536	1.036	0	1.000
1999—St. Lucie (Fla. St.)		C	81	283	36	73	12	1	9	48	43	28	8	10	0-1	.258	.367	.403	.770	4	.992
—Binghamton (East.)		C	39	141	13	32	5	0	7	23	13	20	3	4	0-0	.227	.304	.411	.715	5	.984
2000—St. Lucie (Fla. St.)		C	80	297	53	82	21	0	6	41	23	19	8	12	1-1	.276	.343	.429	.751	6	.989
—Binghamton (East.)		C	27	98	16	38	4	0	0	13	7	9	2	3	0-0	.388	.435	.429	.864	3	.983
2001—Binghamton (East.)		C	93	317	42	93	21	0	11	55	31	25	5	9	0-1	.293	.362	.464	.826	3	.995
—New York (N.L.)		C	6	7	2	1	1	0	0	0	0	1	0	0	0-0	.143	.143	.286	.429	1	1.000
—Norfolk (Int'l)		C	19	66	8	20	2	0	2	14	7	8	0	2	0-0	.303	.365	.424	.789	0	1.000
2002—Norfolk (Int'l)		C	88	323	35	91	22	1	13	65	24	29	2	10	1-0	.282	.327	.477	.804	4	.993
—New York (N.L.)		C	11	19	4	7	0	0	1	3	1	1	1	0	0-0	.368	.409	.526	.935	0	1.000
2003—Norfolk (Int'l)		C-1B-DH	22	78	13	27	5	0	4	20	11	9	2	4	0-0	.346	.424	.564	.999	0	1.000
—New York (N.L.)		1B-C	119	403	45	120	25	0	11	58	39	50	10	21	0-1	.298	.373	.442	.815	8	.991
2004—New York (N.L.)		C-1B	128	362	34	79	18	0	7	34	35	42	8	11	0-1	.218	.298	.326	.624	1	.999
2005—Los Angeles (N.L.)		C-1B	121	399	38	95	20	0	10	55	25	50	4	16	0-0	.238	.287	.363	.650	5	.993
Major League totals (5 years)			385	1190	123	302	64	0	29	150	100	144	23	49	0-3	.254	.321	.381	.702	14	.994

PHILLIPS, PAUL   C

PERSONAL: Born April 15, 1977, in Demopolis, Ala. ... 5-11/185. ... Bats right, throws right. ... Full name: Paul Anthony Phillips. ... High school: West Lauderdale (Collinsville, Miss.). ... Junior college: Meridian. ... College: Alabama.
TRANSACTIONS/CAREER NOTES: Selected by Kansas City Royals organization in 59th round of 1995 free-agent draft; did not sign. ... Selected by Houston Astros organization in 25th round of 1996 free-agent draft; did not sign. ... Selected by Royals organization in ninth round of 1998 free-agent draft. ... On disabled list (April 5, 2001-entire season).
2005 GAMES PLAYED BY POSITION (MLB): C—20, DH—2.

SCOUTING REPORT Offense: Phillips showed after his call-up last season that he is a solid contact hitter; he had no walks in 67 at-bats but struck out only five times. With a long inside-out swing and slow bat speed, he does not project to hit with power. **Defense:** Phillips handles pitchers well and has decent receiving skills. Arm is average to below average with a quick release. **Outlook:** He's not likely to play much unless injuries open opportunities. **Grade 5.8**

PAUL PHILLIPS' HITTING ZONE

.143	.600	.333
.167	.000	1.000
.364	.333	.500

LEFTY-RIGHTY SPLITS

vs.	Avg.	AB	H	2B	3B	HR	RBI	BB	SO	OBP	Slg.
L	.227	22	5	2	1	1	4	0	2	.227	.545
R	.289	45	13	2	0	0	5	0	3	.289	.333

							BATTING											FIELDING	
Year	Team (League)	Pos.	G	AB	R	H	2B	3B	HR	RBI	BB	SO	HBP	GDP	SB-CS	Avg.	OBP	SLG	OPS	E	Avg.
1998—Spokane (N'west)		1B-C-OF	59	234	55	72	12	2	4	25	18	19	4	2	12-1	.308	.366	.427	.793	10	.978
—Wilmington (Caro.)		C	2	5	0	2	0	0	0	2	0	1	0	0	0-0	.400	.333	.400	.733	0	1.000
1999—Wichita (Texas)		C-OF-3B	108	393	58	105	20	2	3	56	26	38	2	8	8-9	.267	.314	.351	.665	10	.984
2000—Wichita (Texas)		C-OF	82	291	49	85	11	5	4	30	21	22	1	11	4-5	.292	.338	.405	.743	9	.983
2001—			Did not play.																		
2002—			Did not play.																		
2003—AZL Royals (Ariz.)		C	4	13	3	6	2	0	1	2	1	0	0	0	0-0	.462	.500	.846	1.346	1	.967
—Wilmington (Caro.)		C	13	46	1	11	1	0	0	6	1	6	1	3	0-1	.239	.271	.261	.532	1	.988
2004—Omaha (PCL)		C-DH-OF	86	311	40	97	17	1	6	41	20	36	3	10	4-3	.312	.358	.431	.783	3	.995
—Kansas City (A.L.)		C	4	5	2	1	0	0	0	0	0	1	1	0	0-0	.200	.333	.200	.533	0	1.000
2005—Omaha (PCL)		C-DH	87	332	45	89	21	1	7	42	21	44	4	7	1-4	.268	.317	.401	.717	6	.990
—Kansas City (A.L.)		C-DH	23	67	6	18	4	1	1	9	0	5	0	4	0-0	.269	.269	.403	.672	1	.990
Major League totals (2 years)			27	72	8	19	4	1	1	9	0	6	1	4	0-0	.264	.274	.389	.663	1	.991

P

PERSONAL: Born September 4, 1968, in Norristown, Pa. ... 6-3/215. ... Bats right, throws right. ... Full name: Michael Joseph Piazza. ... Name pronounced: pee-AH-zuh. ... High school: Phoenixville (Pa.) Area. ... Junior college: Miami-Dade CC North.

TRANSACTIONS/CAREER NOTES: Selected by Los Angeles Dodgers organization in 62nd round of 1988 free-agent draft. ... On disabled list (May 11-June 4, 1995). ... Traded by Dodgers with 3B Todd Zeile to Florida Marlins for OFs Gary Sheffield and Jim Eisenreich, 3B Bobby Bonilla, C Charles Johnson and P Manuel Barrios (May 15, 1998). ... Traded by Marlins to New York Mets for OF Preston Wilson and Ps Ed Yarnall and Geoff Goetz (May 22, 1998). ... On disabled list (April 10-25, 1999). ... On suspended list (April 2-6, 2003). ... On disabled list (May 17-August 13, 2003); included rehabilitation assignment to Norfolk. ... On disabled list (August 7-30, 2004); included rehabilitation assignment to St. Lucie. ... On disabled list (August 22-September 10, 2005).

RECORDS: Holds major league record for most home runs as a catcher, career (376).

HONORS: Named N.L. Rookie Player of the Year by THE SPORTING NEWS (1993). ... Named N.L. Rookie of the Year by Baseball Writers' Association of America (1993).

2005 GAMES PLAYED BY POSITION (MLB): C—101, DH—5.

SCOUTING REPORT

Offense: Piazza has been one of the best hitting catchers of all times but his bat speed has declined of late. Has a very long swing but generates exceptional leverage and lift with excellent opposite-field power. Can drive the ball to the biggest part of the park. Likes the ball out over the plate; has more difficulty handling the ball inside. Can't run at all. *Defense:* With his slow release, he must have a perfect ball to handle to throw out basestealers. Lack of mobility behind the plate and slowed reflexes have made him a liability. *Outlook:* Piazza needs to move to the A.L. and become a DH; he could regain some of his power and bat speed by doing so. Best years are past, however. *Grade 6.5*

MIKE PIAZZA'S HITTING ZONE

.400	.167	.280
.324	.317	.343
.067	.240	.182

LEFTY-RIGHTY SPLITS

vs.	Avg.	AB	H	2B	3B	HR	RBI	BB	SO	OBP	Slg.
L	.269	93	25	6	0	3	11	16	11	.376	.430
R	.246	305	75	17	0	16	51	25	56	.309	.459

Year	Team (League)	Pos.	G	AB	R	H	2B	3B	HR	RBI	BB	SO	HBP	GDP	SB-CS	Avg.	OBP	SLG	OPS	E	Avg.
1989—	Salem (N'west)	C	57	198	22	53	11	0	8	25	13	51	2	11	0-0	.268	.318	.444	.762	6	.977
1990—	Vero Beach (FSL)	1B-C	88	272	27	68	20	0	6	45	11	68	1	6	0-1	.250	.281	.390	.670	16	.967
1991—	Bakersfield (Calif.)	1B-C	117	448	71	124	27	2	29	80	47	83	3	19	0-3	.277	.344	.540	.884	15	.981
1992—	San Antonio (Texas)	C	31	114	18	43	11	0	7	21	13	18	0	2	0-0	.377	.441	.658	1.099	4	.981
—	Albuquerque (PCL)	C-1B	94	358	54	122	22	5	16	69	37	57	2	9	1-3	.341	.405	.564	.969	9	.985
—	Los Angeles (N.L.)	C	21	69	5	16	3	0	1	7	4	12	1	1	0-0	.232	.284	.319	.603	1	.990
1993—	Los Angeles (N.L.)	C-1B	149	547	81	174	24	2	35	112	46	86	3	10	3-4	.318	.370	.561	.932	† 11	.989
1994—	Los Angeles (N.L.)	C	107	405	64	129	18	0	24	92	33	65	1	11	1-3	.319	.370	.541	.910	* 10	.985
1995—	Los Angeles (N.L.)	C	112	434	82	150	17	0	32	93	39	80	1	10	1-0	.346	.400	.606	1.006	9	.990
1996—	Los Angeles (N.L.)	C	148	547	87	184	16	0	36	105	81	93	1	21	0-3	.336	.422	.563	.985	9	.992
1997—	Los Angeles (N.L.)	C-DH	152	556	104	201	32	1	40	124	69	77	3	19	5-1	.362	.431	.638	1.070	* 16	.986
1998—	Los Angeles (N.L.)	C	37	149	20	42	5	0	9	30	11	27	0	3	0-0	.282	.329	.497	.826	2	.993
—	Florida (N.L.)	C	5	18	1	5	0	1	0	5	0	0	0	0	0-0	.278	.263	.389	.652	1	.968
—	New York (N.L.)	C-DH	109	394	67	137	33	0	23	76	47	53	2	12	1-0	.348	.417	.607	1.024	8	.989
1999—	New York (N.L.)	C-DH	141	534	100	162	25	0	40	124	51	70	1	* 27	2-2	.303	.361	.575	.936	11	.989
2000—	New York (N.L.)	C-DH	136	482	90	156	26	0	38	113	58	69	3	15	4-2	.324	.398	.614	1.012	3	.997
2001—	New York (N.L.)	C-DH	141	503	81	151	29	0	36	94	67	87	2	20	0-2	.300	.384	.573	.957	3	.991
2002—	New York (N.L.)	C-DH	135	478	69	134	23	2	33	98	57	82	3	26	0-3	.280	.359	.544	.903	* 12	.986
2003—	Norfolk (Int'l)	C-1B-DH	5	17	2	3	0	0	1	2	1	0	0	0	0-0	.176	.222	.353	.575	0	1.000
—	New York (N.L.)	C-1B	68	234	37	67	13	0	11	34	35	40	1	11	0-0	.286	.377	.483	.860	7	.982
2004—	St. Lucie (Fla. St.)	1B-DH	2	6	0	3	1	0	0	2	1	0	0	0	0-0	.500	.500	.667	1.167	0	1.000
—	New York (N.L.)	1B-C-DH	129	455	47	121	21	0	20	54	68	78	2	14	0-0	.266	.362	.444	.806	13	.984
2005—	New York (N.L.)	C-DH	113	398	41	100	23	0	19	62	41	67	3	7	0-0	.251	.326	.452	.778	2	.997
Major League totals (14 years)			1703	6203	976	1929	308	6	397	1223	707	986	27	207	17-20	.311	.382	.555	.936	124	.989

DIVISION SERIES RECORD

Year	Team (League)	Pos.	G	AB	R	H	2B	3B	HR	RBI	BB	SO	HBP	GDP	SB-CS	Avg.	OBP	SLG	OPS	E	Avg.
1995—	Los Angeles (N.L.)	C	3	14	1	3	1	0	1	1	0	2	0	0	0-0	.214	.214	.500	.714	0	1.000
1996—	Los Angeles (N.L.)	C	3	10	1	3	0	0	0	2	1	2	0	0	0-0	.300	.333	.300	.633	0	1.000
1999—	New York (N.L.)	C	2	9	0	2	0	0	0	0	4	0	0	0	0-0	.222	.222	.222	.444	0	1.000
2000—	New York (N.L.)	C	4	14	1	3	1	0	0	0	0	7	0	0	0-0	.214	.389	.286	.675	0	1.000
Division series totals (4 years)			12	47	3	11	2	0	1	3	5	11	0	0	0-0	.234	.302	.340	.642	0	1.000

CHAMPIONSHIP SERIES RECORD

Year	Team (League)	Pos.	G	AB	R	H	2B	3B	HR	RBI	BB	SO	HBP	GDP	SB-CS	Avg.	OBP	SLG	OPS	E	Avg.
1999—	New York (N.L.)	C	6	24	1	4	0	0	1	4	1	6	0	0	0-0	.167	.192	.292	.484	3	.940
2000—	New York (N.L.)	C	5	17	7	7	3	0	2	4	5	0	0	1	0-0	.412	.545	.941	1.487	0	1.000
Champ. series totals (2 years)			11	41	8	11	3	0	3	8	6	6	0	1	0-0	.268	.354	.561	.915	3	.967

WORLD SERIES RECORD

Year	Team (League)	Pos.	G	AB	R	H	2B	3B	HR	RBI	BB	SO	HBP	GDP	SB-CS	Avg.	OBP	SLG	OPS	E	Avg.
2000—	New York (N.L.)	C-DH	5	22	3	6	2	0	2	4	0	4	0	0	0-1	.273	.273	.636	.909	0	1.000

ALL-STAR GAME RECORD

			G	AB	R	H	2B	3B	HR	RBI	BB	SO	HBP	GDP	SB-CS	Avg.	OBP	SLG	OPS	E	Avg.
All-Star Game totals (11 years)			11	25	2	6	1	0	2	5	1	5	0	0	0-0	.240	.269	.520	.789	0	1.000

P

PICKERING, CALVIN — 1B

PERSONAL: Born September 29, 1976, in St. Thomas, Virgin Islands. ... 6-5/267. ... Bats left, throws left. ... Full name: Calvin Elroy Pickering. ... High school: King (Tampa).

TRANSACTIONS/CAREER NOTES: Selected by Baltimore Orioles organization in 35th round of 1995 free-agent draft. ... On disabled list (June 20-August 6, 2000). ... Traded by Orioles to Cincinnati Reds for future considerations (August 30, 2001). ... Claimed on waivers by Boston Red Sox (September 6, 2001). ... On disabled list (March 22, 2002-entire season). ... Signed as a free agent by Seattle Mariners organization (January 16, 2003). ... Released by Mariners (March 18, 2003). ... Contract purchased by Cincinnati Reds organization from Vaqueros of the Mexican League (August 4, 2003). ... Signed as a free agent by Kansas City Royals organization (November 11, 2003).

2005 GAMES PLAYED BY POSITION (MLB): DH—7.

LEFTY-RIGHTY SPLITS

vs.	Avg.	AB	H	2B	3B	HR	RBI	BB	SO	OBP	Slg.
L	.000	7	0	0	0	0	0	0	3	.000	.000
R	.200	20	4	0	0	1	3	3	11	.292	.350

| | | | | | | | | BATTING | | | | | | | | | | FIELDING | |
Year Team (League)	Pos.	G	AB	R	H	2B	3B	HR	RBI	BB	SO	HBP	GDP	SB-CS	Avg.	OBP	SLG	OPS	E	Avg.
1995— GC Orioles (GCL)	1B-DH	15	60	8	30	10	0	1	22	2	6	0	3	0-0	.500	.508	.717	1.225	3	.968
1996— Bluefield (Appal.)	1B-DH	60	200	45	65	14	1	18	66	28	64	2	4	8-2	.325	.411	.675	1.086	9	.979
1997— Delmarva (S. Atl.)	1B-DH	122	444	88	138	31	1	25	79	53	139	9	14	6-3	.311	.394	.554	.949	27	.974
1998— Bowie (East.)	1B-OF-DH	139	488	93	151	28	2	31	114	98	119	11	20	4-6	.309	.434	.566	1.000	22	.981
— Baltimore (A.L.)	1B-DH	9	21	4	5	0	0	2	3	3	4	0	2	1-0	.238	.333	.524	.857	1	.969
1999— Rochester (Int'l)	1B-OF	103	372	63	106	20	0	16	63	60	99	11	10	1-3	.285	.396	.468	.864	13	.985
— Baltimore (A.L.)	1B-DH	23	40	4	5	1	0	1	5	11	16	0	1	0-0	.125	.314	.225	.539	2	.960
2000— Rochester (Int'l)	1B	60	197	20	43	10	0	6	30	36	70	1	4	2-2	.218	.339	.360	.699	12	.978
2001— Rochester (Int'l)	1B	131	461	62	130	25	0	21	98	64	149	10	16	0-1	.282	.379	.473	.852	8	.986
— Louisville (Int'l)	1B	1	4	1	1	0	0	1	1	1	2	0	0	0-0	.250	.400	1.000	1.400	0	1.000
— Cincinnati (N.L.)	DH	4	4	0	1	0	0	0	1	0	2	0	0	0-0	.250	.250	.250	.500	...	...
— Boston (A.L.)	1B-DH	17	50	4	14	1	0	3	7	8	13	0	4	0-0	.280	.379	.480	.859	0	1.000
2002— Boston (A.L.)			Did not play.																	
2003— Louisville (Int'l)	1B-DH	26	81	10	23	3	0	4	18	17	31	3	2	0-0	.284	.422	.469	.891	1	.991
2004— Omaha (PCL)	1B-DH	89	299	65	94	12	1	35	79	70	85	7	8	0-1	.314	.451	.712	1.164	12	.975
— Kansas City (A.L.)	DH-1B	35	122	21	30	8	1	7	26	18	42	0	6	0-0	.246	.338	.500	.838	0	1.000
2005— Kansas City (A.L.)	DH	7	27	4	4	0	0	1	3	3	14	0	0	0-0	.148	.226	.259	.485	0	...
— Omaha (PCL)	1B-DH	92	335	56	92	16	0	23	67	56	130	4	4	1-0	.275	.384	.528	.912	2	.975
American League totals (5 years)		91	260	37	58	10	1	14	44	43	89	0	13	1-0	.223	.330	.431	.761	3	.988
National League totals (1 year)		4	4	0	1	0	0	0	1	0	2	0	0	0-0	.250	.250	.250	.500	...	...
Major League totals (5 years)		95	264	37	59	10	1	14	45	43	91	0	13	1-0	.223	.329	.428	.757	3	.988

PIEDRA, JORGE — OF

PERSONAL: Born April 17, 1979, in Sun Valley, Calif. ... 6-0/190. ... Bats left, throws left. ... Full name: Jorge Moises Piedra. ... Name pronounced: pea-AY-dra. ... High school: Notre Dame (Van Nuys, Calif.).

TRANSACTIONS/CAREER NOTES: Signed as a non-drafted free agent by Los Angeles Dodgers organization (August 14, 1997). ... Traded by Dodgers with P Jamie Arnold to Chicago Cubs for P Ismael Valdez (July 26, 2000). ... Traded by Cubs to Colorado Rockies for cash (May 3, 2002).

2005 GAMES PLAYED BY POSITION (MLB): OF—26, DH—1.

JORGE PIEDRA'S HITTING ZONE

.571	.167	.250
.444	.364	.276
.000	.400	.286

LEFTY-RIGHTY SPLITS

vs.	Avg.	AB	H	2B	3B	HR	RBI	BB	SO	OBP	Slg.
L	.500	2	1	0	0	0	0	0	0	.500	.500
R	.309	110	34	8	1	6	16	10	15	.369	.564

| | | | | | | | | BATTING | | | | | | | | | | FIELDING | |
Year Team (League)	Pos.	G	AB	R	H	2B	3B	HR	RBI	BB	SO	HBP	GDP	SB-CS	Avg.	OBP	SLG	OPS	E	Avg.
1998— Great Falls (Pio.)	OF	72	282	72	108	22	7	2	33	39	29	1	4	16-7	.383	.460	.532	.992	7	.949
1999— San Bern. (Calif.)	OF	8	30	6	9	2	0	0	3	3	3	0	0	1-0	.300	.343	.367	.710	0	1.000
— Vero Beach (FSL)	OF	15	59	13	17	3	1	1	6	7	9	0	0	2-2	.288	.358	.424	.782	2	.933
2000— Vero Beach (FSL)	OF	92	360	59	102	11	6	6	52	29	57	5	6	21-5	.283	.339	.397	.736	6	.974
— Daytona (Fla. St.)	OF	34	139	24	48	11	1	1	17	6	15	0	0	8-4	.345	.367	.460	.828	0	1.000
2001— West Tenn (Sou.)	OF	124	441	55	108	26	6	8	54	37	80	8	8	12-5	.245	.310	.385	.696	5	.980
2002— West Tenn (Sou.)	OF	23	60	5	10	3	1	0	4	3	11	1	1	2-0	.167	.219	.250	.469	1	.971
— Salem (Carol.)	OF	104	392	64	118	37	12	13	64	37	55	8	4	10-2	.301	.366	.556	.922	5	.975
2003— Tulsa (Texas)	OF	96	357	56	98	17	7	18	53	31	50	8	6	5-2	.275	.342	.513	.854	5	.973
2004— Colo. Springs (PCL)	OF-DH	99	377	71	126	29	5	15	55	23	56	3	7	4-3	.334	.372	.557	.924	4	.978
— Colorado (N.L.)	OF	38	91	15	27	8	0	3	10	5	19	1	1	0-1	.297	.340	.484	.824	0	1.000
2005— Colo. Springs (PCL)	OF	47	186	35	58	20	1	6	45	18	23	1	4	4-2	.312	.372	.527	.899	6	.960
— Colorado (N.L.)	OF-DH	61	112	19	35	8	1	6	16	10	15	1	2	2-1	.313	.371	.563	.933	0	1.000
Major League totals (2 years)		99	203	34	62	16	1	9	26	15	34	2	3	2-2	.305	.357	.527	.885	0	1.000

PIERRE, JUAN — OF

PERSONAL: Born August 14, 1977, in Mobile, Ala. ... 6-0/180. ... Bats left, throws left. ... Full name: Juan D'Vaughn Pierre. ... High school: Alexandria (La.). ... College: South Alabama.

TRANSACTIONS/CAREER NOTES: Selected by Seattle Mariners organization in 30th round of 1995 free-agent draft; did not sign. ... Selected by Mariners organization in 48th round of 1996 free-agent draft; did not sign. ... Selected by Colorado Rockies organization in 13th round of 1998 free-agent draft. ... Traded by Rockies with P Mike Hampton and cash to Florida Marlins for C Charles Johnson, P Vic Darensbourg, OF Preston Wilson and 2B Pablo Ozuna (November 16, 2002).

2005 GAMES PLAYED BY POSITION (MLB): OF—160.

P

SCOUTING REPORT *Offense:* Pierre dropped 50 points off his average from 2004. Didn't take outside pitches the other way, instead rolled his wrists and hit weak ground balls to second base. Makes good contact but doesn't walk much. A slap line-drive hitter. Is the best directional bunter in the game, forcing infielders to play shallow and creating holes to drive the ball through. Is an aggressive baserunner who puts pressure on the defense. *Defense:* He charges the ball better than he goes back on it, but he can outrun his mistakes. Doesn't throw well, and runners consistently take the extra base. *Outlook:* An igniter, Pierre can control the game with his intimidating speed. Needs to return to the type of hitter who uses the whole field and puts pressure on the defense. **Grade 7.7**

JUAN PIERRE'S HITTING ZONE

.226	.382	.254
.324	.348	.310
.182	.393	.156

LEFTY-RIGHTY SPLITS

vs.	Avg.	AB	H	2B	3B	HR	RBI	BB	SO	OBP	Slg.
L	.299	144	43	3	0	0	4	7	11	.338	.319
R	.270	512	138	16	13	2	43	34	34	.323	.363

Year Team (League)	Pos.	G	AB	R	H	2B	3B	HR	RBI	BB	SO	HBP	GDP	SB-CS	Avg.	OBP	SLG	OPS	E	Avg.
1998— Portland (N'west)	OF	64	264	55	93	9	2	0	30	19	11	2	3	38-9	.352	.399	.402	.800	5	.955
1999— Asheville (S. Atl.)	OF	140	585	93	187	28	5	1	55	38	37	8	12	66-19	.320	.366	.390	.756	4	.981
2000— Carolina (Southern)	OF	107	439	63	143	16	4	0	32	33	26	5	4	46-12	.326	.376	.380	.757	2	.992
— Colo. Springs (PCL)	OF	4	17	3	8	0	1	0	1	0	0	0	0	1-1	.471	.471	.588	1.059	0	1.000
— Colorado (N.L.)	OF	51	200	26	62	2	0	0	20	13	15	1	2	7-6	.310	.353	.320	.673	3	.975
2001— Colorado (N.L.)	OF	156	617	108	202	26	11	2	55	41	29	10	6	•46-17	.327	.378	.415	.793	8	.979
2002— Colorado (N.L.)	OF	152	592	90	170	20	5	1	35	31	52	9	7	47-12	.287	.332	.343	.675	2	.995
2003— Florida (N.L.)	OF	162	*668	100	204	28	7	1	41	55	35	5	9	*65-20	.305	.361	.373	.734	3	.993
2004— Florida (N.L.)	OF	162	*678	100	*221	22	•12	3	49	45	35	8	9	45-24	.326	.374	.407	.781	2	.995
2005— Florida (N.L.)	OF	162	656	96	181	19	13	2	47	41	45	9	10	57-17	.276	.326	.354	.680	4	.988
Major League totals (6 years)		845	3411	520	1040	117	48	9	247	226	211	42	43	267-96	.305	.355	.375	.730	22	.989

DIVISION SERIES RECORD

Year Team (League)	Pos.	G	AB	R	H	2B	3B	HR	RBI	BB	SO	HBP	GDP	SB-CS	Avg.	OBP	SLG	OPS	E	Avg.
2003— Florida (N.L.)	OF	4	19	5	5	1	0	0	3	1	1	0	0	1-0	.263	.300	.316	.616	0	1.000

CHAMPIONSHIP SERIES RECORD

Year Team (League)	Pos.	G	AB	R	H	2B	3B	HR	RBI	BB	SO	HBP	GDP	SB-CS	Avg.	OBP	SLG	OPS	E	Avg.
2003— Florida (N.L.)	OF	7	33	5	10	1	2	0	1	2	1	0	0	1-3	.303	.343	.455	.797	0	1.000

WORLD SERIES RECORD

Year Team (League)	Pos.	G	AB	R	H	2B	3B	HR	RBI	BB	SO	HBP	GDP	SB-CS	Avg.	OBP	SLG	OPS	E	Avg.
2003— Florida (N.L.)	OF	6	21	2	7	2	0	0	3	5	2	1	0	1-1	.333	.481	.429	.910	0	1.000

PIERZYNSKI, A.J.   C

PERSONAL: Born December 30, 1976, in Bridgehampton, N.Y. ... 6-3/245. ... Bats left, throws right. ... Full name: Anthony John Pierzynski. ... Name pronounced: PEER-zin-skee. ... High school: Dr. Phillips (Orlando).

TRANSACTIONS/CAREER NOTES: Selected by Minnesota Twins organization in third round of 1994 free-agent draft. ... Traded by Twins with cash to San Francisco Giants for Ps Joe Nathan, Boof Bonser and Francisco Liriano (November 14, 2003). ... Released by Giants (December 16, 2004). ... Signed by Chicago White Sox (January 6, 2005).

2005 GAMES PLAYED BY POSITION (MLB): C—128.

SCOUTING REPORT *Offense:* He made a lot of improvements last season. Has a slightly long stroke but has shown better bat speed and is starting to drive the ball. Is a good contact hitter who likes the ball up. Has power from left-center field to the right-field line; home run production should continue to rise. Fights off tough pitches on the inside part of the plate and keep his at-bats alive. Can't run. *Defense:* He is throwing better and gets the ball up and out of his glove quickly. Is not afraid to block the plate. Game-calling has improved. *Outlook:* Pierzynski, who is a pest to opposing players, has made as much improvement as any catcher in the league. **Grade 8**

A.J. PIERZYNSKI'S HITTING ZONE

.286	.350	.238
.150	.375	.300
.400	.333	.269

LEFTY-RIGHTY SPLITS

vs.	Avg.	AB	H	2B	3B	HR	RBI	BB	SO	OBP	Slg.
L	.230	87	20	1	0	4	9	0	16	.247	.379
R	.263	373	98	20	0	14	47	23	52	.322	.429

Year Team (League)	Pos.	G	AB	R	H	2B	3B	HR	RBI	BB	SO	HBP	GDP	SB-CS	Avg.	OBP	SLG	OPS	E	Avg.
1994— GC Twins (GCL)	C-DH	43	152	21	44	8	1	1	19	12	19	0	3	0-2	.289	.337	.375	.712	8	.966
1995— Fort Wayne (Midw.)	C	22	84	10	26	5	1	2	14	2	10	0	1	0-0	.310	.322	.464	.786	10	.973
— Elizabethton (App.)	1B-C	56	205	29	68	13	1	7	45	14	23	0	6	0-2	.332	.373	.507	.880	† 12	.974
1996— Fort Wayne (Midw.)	C-DH-OF	114	431	48	118	30	3	7	70	22	53	2	10	0-4	.274	.308	.406	.714	§ 21	.972
1997— Fort Myers (FSL)	C-DH-1B	118	412	49	115	23	1	6	64	16	59	6	9	2-1	.279	.313	.405	.718	10	.987
1998— New Britain (East.)	C-DH	59	212	30	63	11	0	3	17	10	25	2	4	0-2	.297	.333	.392	.725	2	.996
— Salt Lake (PCL)	C	59	208	29	53	7	2	7	30	9	24	0	4	3-1	.255	.284	.409	.693	7	.983
— Minnesota (A.L.)	C	9	10	1	3	0	0	0	1	1	2	1	0	0-0	.300	.385	.300	.685	0	1.000
1999— Salt Lake (PCL)	C	67	228	29	59	10	1	1	25	16	29	0	11	0-0	.259	.307	.316	.623	7	.984
— Minnesota (A.L.)	C	9	22	3	6	2	0	0	3	1	4	1	0	0-0	.273	.333	.364	.697	0	1.000
2000— New Britain (East.)	C	62	228	36	68	17	2	4	34	8	22	9	13	0-0	.298	.341	.443	.784	6	.982
— Salt Lake (PCL)	C	41	155	22	52	14	1	4	25	5	22	1	3	1-1	.335	.354	.516	.870	3	.990
— Minnesota (A.L.)	C	33	88	12	27	5	1	2	11	5	14	2	1	0-0	.307	.354	.455	.809	0	1.000
2001— Minnesota (A.L.)	C-DH	114	381	51	110	33	2	7	55	16	57	4	7	1-7	.289	.322	.441	.763	10	.985
2002— Minnesota (A.L.)	C	130	440	54	132	31	6	6	49	13	61	11	14	1-2	.300	.334	.439	.773	5	.996
2003— Minnesota (A.L.)	C	137	487	63	152	35	3	11	74	24	55	15	13	3-1	.312	.360	.464	.824	6	.993
2004— San Francisco (N.L.)	C	131	471	45	128	28	2	11	77	19	27	15	* 27	0-1	.272	.319	.410	.729	1	.999
2005— Chicago (A.L.)	C	128	460	61	118	21	0	18	56	23	68	12	13	0-2	.257	.308	.420	.728	1	.999
American League totals (7 years)		558	1888	245	548	127	12	44	249	83	261	46	48	6-12	.290	.333	.440	.773	20	.994
National League totals (1 year)		131	471	45	128	28	2	11	77	19	27	15	27	0-1	.272	.319	.410	.729	1	.999
Major League totals (8 years)		689	2359	290	676	155	14	55	326	102	288	61	75	6-13	.287	.330	.434	.765	21	.995

P

DIVISION SERIES RECORD

Year Team (League)	Pos.	G	AB	R	H	2B	3B	HR	RBI	BB	SO	HBP	GDP	SB-CS	Avg.	OBP	SLG	OPS	E	Avg.
2002— Minnesota (A.L.)	C	5	16	4	7	0	1	1	4	2	2	0	0	0-0	.438	.500	.750	1.250	1	.969
2003— Minnesota (A.L.)	C	4	13	1	3	0	0	1	1	2	0	0	1	0-0	.231	.333	.462	.795	0	1.000
2005— Chicago (A.L.)	C	3	9	5	4	2	0	2	4	1	0	1	0	1-0	.444	.545	1.333	1.879	0	1.000
Division series totals (3 years)		12	38	10	14	2	1	4	9	5	2	1	1	1-0	.368	.455	.789	1.244	1	.987

CHAMPIONSHIP SERIES RECORD

Year Team (League)	Pos.	G	AB	R	H	2B	3B	HR	RBI	BB	SO	HBP	GDP	SB-CS	Avg.	OBP	SLG	OPS	E	Avg.
2002— Minnesota (A.L.)	C	5	16	1	4	0	0	0	2	0	2	0	0	0-1	.250	.235	.250	.485	2	.938
2005— Chicago (A.L.)	C	5	18	1	3	0	0	1	2	1	6	0	0	0-1	.167	.211	.333	.544	0	1.000
Champ. series totals (2 years)		10	34	2	7	0	0	1	4	1	8	0	0	0-2	.206	.222	.294	.516	2	.964

WORLD SERIES RECORD

Year Team (League)	Pos.	G	AB	R	H	2B	3B	HR	RBI	BB	SO	HBP	GDP	SB-CS	Avg.	OBP	SLG	OPS	E	Avg.
2005— Chicago (A.L.)	C	4	15	3	4	2	0	0	3	2	2	0	1	1-0	.267	.353	.400	.753	0	1.000

ALL-STAR GAME RECORD

	G	AB	R	H	2B	3B	HR	RBI	BB	SO	HBP	GDP	SB-CS	Avg.	OBP	SLG	OPS	E	Avg.
All-Star Game totals (1 year)	1	3	0	0	0	0	0	0	0	0	0	0	0-0	.000	.000	.000	.000		1.000

PINEIRO, JOEL — P

PERSONAL: Born September 25, 1978, in Rio Padres, Puerto Rico. ... 6-1/200. ... Throws right, bats right. ... Full name: Joel Alberto Pineiro. ... Name pronounced: pin-YER-oh. ... High school: Colonial (Orlando). ... Junior college: Edison (Fla.) Community College.

TRANSACTIONS/CAREER NOTES: Selected by Seattle Mariners organization in 12th round of 1997 free-agent draft. ... On suspended list (October 3-6, 2001). ... On disabled list (July 26, 2004-remainder of season).

CAREER HITTING: 2-for-20 (.100), 1 R, 1 2B, 0 3B, 0 HR, 2 RBI.

SCOUTING REPORT **Throws:** Pineiro's best pitch is a four-seam fastball that he throws at 90-94 mph. Also has an overhand curveball, a slider and a changeup. **Tendencies:** He changed his delivery to prevent him from arching his back so much, and that adjustment helps keep the ball down. Tends to pitch up in the zone. Has good rotation on his curveball but struggles to control it. Has a quick slider with improved command. Has good arm action and movement on his changeup. **Outlook:** Pineiro has a good arm, but he needs better command. Changing his arm slot would help his location and control. **Grade 7.4**

JOEL PINEIRO'S PITCHING ZONE

.372	.465	.269
.370	.365	.297
.217	.200	.286

LEFTY-RIGHTY SPLITS

vs.	Avg.	AB	H	2B	3B	HR	RBI	BB	SO	OBP	Slg.
L	.295	400	118	21	2	7	47	32	61	.344	.410
R	.305	347	106	22	1	16	65	24	46	.358	.513

Year Team (League)	W	L	Pct.	ERA	WHIP	G	GS	CG	ShO	Hld.	Sv.-Opp.	IP	H	R	ER	HR	BB-IBB	SO	Avg.
1997— Ariz. Mariners (Ariz.)	1	0	1.000	0.00	0.33	1	0	0	0	...	0-...	3.0	1	0	0	0	0-0	4	.100
— Everett (N'west)	4	2	.667	5.33	1.47	18	6	0	0	...	2-...	49.0	54	33	29	2	18-1	59	.267
1998— Wisconsin (Midw.)	8	4	.667	3.19	1.25	16	16	1	0	...	0-...	96.0	92	40	34	8	28-1	84	.252
— Lancaster (Calif.)	2	0	1.000	7.80	1.78	9	9	1	1	...	0-...	45.0	58	40	39	6	22-0	48	.307
— Orlando (South.)	1	0	1.000	5.40	1.80	1	1	0	0	...	0-...	5.0	7	4	3	0	2-0	2	.368
1999— New Haven (East.)	10	15	.400	4.72	1.46	28	25	4	0	...	0-...	166.0	190	105	87	18	52-0	116	.290
2000— New Haven (East.)	2	1	.667	4.13	1.03	9	9	0	0	...	0-...	52.1	42	25	24	6	12-0	43	.218
— Tacoma (PCL)	7	1	.875	2.80	1.23	10	9	2	2	...	0-...	61.0	53	20	19	3	22-1	41	.232
— Seattle (A.L.)	1	0	1.000	5.59	1.97	8	1	0	0	0	0-0	19.1	25	13	12	3	13-0	10	.316
2001— Tacoma (PCL)	6	3	.667	3.62	1.31	18	10	0	0	0	0-0	77.0	68	31	31	8	33-0	64	.242
— Seattle (A.L.)	6	2	.750	2.03	0.94	17	11	0	0	2	0-0	75.1	50	24	17	2	21-0	56	.191
2002— Seattle (A.L.)	14	7	.667	3.24	1.25	37	28	2	1	3	0-0	194.1	189	75	70	24	54-1	136	.256
2003— Seattle (A.L.)	16	11	.593	3.78	1.27	32	32	3	• 2	0	0-0	211.2	192	94	89	19	76-3	151	.241
2004— Seattle (A.L.)	6	11	.353	4.67	1.33	21	21	1	0	0	0-0	140.2	144	77	73	21	43-1	111	.265
2005— Tacoma (PCL)	0	0	...	1.29	0.71	1	1	0	0	0	0-0	7.0	5	1	1	1	0-0	6	.192
— Seattle (A.L.)	7	11	.389	5.62	1.48	30	30	2	0	0	0-0	189.0	224	118	118	23	56-4	107	.300
Major League totals (6 years)	50	42	.543	4.11	1.31	145	123	8	3	5	0-0	830.1	824	401	379	92	263-9	571	.260

DIVISION SERIES RECORD

Year Team (League)	W	L	Pct.	ERA	WHIP	G	GS	CG	ShO	Hld.	Sv.-Opp.	IP	H	R	ER	HR	BB-IBB	SO	Avg.
2001— Seattle (A.L.)	Did not play.																		

CHAMPIONSHIP SERIES RECORD

Year Team (League)	W	L	Pct.	ERA	WHIP	G	GS	CG	ShO	Hld.	Sv.-Opp.	IP	H	R	ER	HR	BB-IBB	SO	Avg.
2001— Seattle (A.L.)	0	0	...	4.50	3.00	1	0	0	0	0	0-0	2.0	4	1	1	0	2-0	5	.400

PODSEDNIK, SCOTT — OF

PERSONAL: Born March 18, 1976, in West, Texas. ... 6-0/188. ... Bats left, throws left. ... Full name: Scott Eric Podsednik. ... Name pronounced: pod-SED-nik. ... High school: West (Texas).

TRANSACTIONS/CAREER NOTES: Selected by Texas Rangers organization in third round of 1994 free-agent draft. ... Traded by Rangers to Florida Marlins (October 8, 1995), completing deal in which Marlins traded P Bobby Witt to Texas Rangers for two players to be named (August 8, 1995); Marlins acquired P Wilson Heredia as part of deal (August 11, 1995). ... Selected by Rangers organization from Marlins organization in Rule 5 minor league draft (December 15, 1997). ... Signed as a free agent by Seattle Mariners organization (November 1, 2000). ... Claimed on waivers by Milwaukee Brewers (October 13, 2002). ... Traded by Brewers with P Luis Vizcaino and a player to be named to Chicago White Sox for OF Carlos Lee (December 13, 2004). ... On disabled list (August 13-29, 2005); included rehabilitation assignment to Charlotte.

HONORS: Named N.L. Rookie Player of the Year by THE SPORTING NEWS (2003).

2005 GAMES PLAYED BY POSITION (MLB): OF—127.

P

SCOUTING REPORT

Offense: A catalyst in the leadoff position, Podsednik is a line-drive hitter with good bat speed and the ability to hit to all fields. Hits down on the ball to use his speed. A good low-ball hitter who has extra-base power. Creates holes with his intimidating speed and ability to bunt. Is an extremely aggressive basestealer with a basestealing mentality. **Defense:** Podsednik moved to left but plays the position as a center fielder. Will play deep but gets good lateral jumps and charges the ball well. Arm is short but compensates with his speed to cut the ball off and shorten his throws. **Outlook:** He gives the White Sox a dimension—speed—they lacked in the past, and he contributes to an improved defense. **Grade 7.8**

SCOTT PODSEDNIK'S HITTING ZONE

.412	.261	.425
.182	.397	.311
.192	.321	.246

LEFTY-RIGHTY SPLITS

vs.	Avg.	AB	H	2B	3B	HR	RBI	BB	SO	OBP	Slg.
L	.330	100	33	2	0	0	8	11	17	.404	.350
R	.280	407	114	26	1	0	17	36	58	.337	.349

Year Team (League)	Pos.	G	AB	R	H	2B	3B	HR	RBI	BB	SO	HBP	GDP	SB-CS	Avg.	OBP	SLG	OPS	E	FIELDING Avg.
1994— GC Rangers (GCL)	OF	60	211	34	48	7	1	1	17	41	34	3	1	18-5	.227	.357	.284	.641	0	1.000
1995— Hudson Valley (NYP)	OF	65	252	42	67	3	0	0	20	35	31	1	9	20-6	.266	.355	.278	.633	3	.978
1996— Brevard County (FSL)	OF	108	383	39	100	9	2	0	30	45	65	3	8	20-10	.261	.343	.295	.638	4	.984
1997— Kane Co. (Midw.)	OF	135	531	80	147	23	4	3	49	60	72	3	5	28-11	.277	.352	.352	.704	5	.977
1998— Charlotte (Fla. St.)	OF	81	302	55	86	12	4	4	39	44	32	0	2	26-8	.285	.369	.391	.760	2	.986
— Tulsa (Texas)	OF	17	75	9	18	4	1	0	4	6	11	0	3	5-2	.240	.296	.320	.616	0	1.000
1999— GC Rangers (GCL)	OF	5	17	6	7	2	0	0	5	2	3	0	1	1-0	.412	.474	.529	1.003	0	1.000
— Tulsa (Texas)	OF	37	116	10	18	4	0	0	1	5	13	0	3	4-2	.155	.190	.190	.380	1	.987
2000— Tulsa (Texas)	OF	49	169	20	42	7	2	2	13	30	33	1	4	19-4	.249	.361	.349	.710	3	.968
2001— Tacoma (PCL)	OF	66	269	46	78	15	4	3	30	13	46	2	0	12-5	.290	.327	.409	.736	5	.967
— Seattle (A.L.)	OF	5	6	1	1	0	1	0	3	0	1	0	1	0-0	.167	.167	.500	.667	0	1.000
2002— Tacoma (PCL)	OF	125	438	63	122	25	6	9	61	43	70	9	18	35-13	.279	.347	.425	.772	5	.985
— Seattle (A.L.)	OF-DH	14	20	2	4	0	0	1	5	4	6	0	1	0-0	.200	.320	.350	.670	4	.938
2003— Milwaukee (N.L.)	OF	154	558	100	175	29	8	9	58	56	91	4	11	43-10	.314	.379	.443	.822	3	.992
2004— Milwaukee (N.L.)	OF	154	640	85	156	27	7	12	39	58	105	7	7	* 70-13	.244	.313	.364	.677	4	.990
2005— Charlotte (Int'l)	OF	2	9	2	2	2	0	0	1	0	2	0	0	0-0	.222	.222	.444	.667	0	1.000
— Chicago (A.L.)	OF	129	507	80	147	28	1	0	25	47	75	3	7	59-* 23	.290	.351	.349	.700	3	.989
American League totals (3 years)		148	533	83	152	28	2	1	33	51	82	3	9	59-23	.285	.347	.351	.698	4	.987
National League totals (2 years)		308	1198	185	331	56	15	21	97	114	196	11	18	113-23	.276	.344	.401	.745	7	.991
Major League totals (5 years)		456	1731	268	483	84	17	22	130	165	278	14	27	172-46	.279	.345	.385	.730	11	.990

DIVISION SERIES RECORD

Year Team (League)	Pos.	G	AB	R	H	2B	3B	HR	RBI	BB	SO	HBP	GDP	SB-CS	Avg.	OBP	SLG	OPS	E	Avg.
2005— Chicago (A.L.)	OF	3	11	3	3	1	0	1	4	1	1	2	0	1-2	.273	.429	.636	1.065	0	1.000

CHAMPIONSHIP SERIES RECORD

Year Team (League)	Pos.	G	AB	R	H	2B	3B	HR	RBI	BB	SO	HBP	GDP	SB-CS	Avg.	OBP	SLG	OPS	E	Avg.
2005— Chicago (A.L.)	OF	5	17	4	5	0	1	0	0	6	5	0	0	3-1	.294	.478	.412	.890	0	1.000

WORLD SERIES RECORD

Year Team (League)	Pos.	G	AB	R	H	2B	3B	HR	RBI	BB	SO	HBP	GDP	SB-CS	Avg.	OBP	SLG	OPS	E	Avg.
2005— Chicago (A.L.)	OF	4	21	2	6	0	0	2	4	0	1	2	0	2-0	.286	.286	.619	.905	0	1.000

ALL-STAR GAME RECORD

		G	AB	R	H	2B	3B	HR	RBI	BB	SO	HBP	GDP	SB-CS	Avg.	OBP	SLG	OPS	E	Avg.
All-Star Game totals (1 year)		1	0	0	0	0	0	0	0	0	0	0	0	0-0	...	...	...	...	0	...

POLANCO, PLACIDO   2B/3B

PERSONAL: Born October 10, 1975, in Santo Domingo, Dominican Republic. ... 5-10/190. ... Bats right, throws right. ... Full name: Placido Enrique Polanco. ... Name pronounced: PLAH-si-doh poh-LAHN-co. ... High school: Santo Clara (Santo Domingo, Dominican Republic). ... Junior college: Miami-Dade CC Wolfson.

TRANSACTIONS/CAREER NOTES: Selected by St. Louis Cardinals in 19th round of 1994 free-agent draft. ... On disabled list (July 1-16, 2000). ... Traded by Cardinals with Ps Bud Smith and Mike Timlin to Philadelphia Phillies for 3B Scott Rolen and P Doug Nickle (July 29, 2002). ... On disabled list (April 16-May 1, 2003). ... On disabled list (May 8-June 7, 2004); included rehabilitation assignments to Reading and Scranton/Wilkes-Barre. ... Traded by Phillies to Detroit Tigers for 2B Ramon Martinez and P Ugueth Urbina (June 8, 2005). ... On disabled list (July 12-27, 2005).

2005 GAMES PLAYED BY POSITION (MLB): 2B—113, 3B—9, OF—5, SS—1.

SCOUTING REPORT

Offense: Polanco knows how to hit and makes quick adjustments. Has a short stroke and stays with breaking pitches. Is a line-drive hitter with occasional pop, especially on inside pitches. Is an ideal No. 2 hitter because he can work the count and control his bat. Is an average runner but has excellent instincts. **Defense:** He is much quicker than his body would indicate. Has extremely quick hands and gets good jumps on grounders, especially to his right. Makes the pivot on the double play well and has a strong enough arm to play third. **Outlook:** Polanco no longer is considered a utility player; he has become a steady, professional hitter. Is one of the best No. 2 hitters in the league. **Grade 7.9**

PLACIDO POLANCO'S HITTING ZONE

.444	.333	.321
.316	.473	.320
.266	.273	.261

LEFTY-RIGHTY SPLITS

vs.	Avg.	AB	H	2B	3B	HR	RBI	BB	SO	OBP	Slg.
L	.348	161	56	9	1	4	15	9	8	.387	.491
R	.324	340	110	18	1	5	41	24	17	.380	.426

Year Team (League)	Pos.	G	AB	R	H	2B	3B	HR	RBI	BB	SO	HBP	GDP	SB-CS	Avg.	OBP	SLG	OPS	E	FIELDING Avg.
1994— Ariz. Cardinals (Ariz.)	2B-SS	32	127	17	27	4	0	1	10	7	15	1	2	4-2	.213	.259	.268	.527	10	.932
1995— Peoria (Midw.)	2B-SS	103	361	43	96	7	4	2	41	18	30	2	8	7-6	.266	.303	.324	.627	21	.950
1996— St. Pete. (FSL)	2B	* 137	* 540	65	* 157	29	5	0	51	24	34	5	31	4-4	.291	.323	.363	.686	4	.993
1997— Arkansas (Texas)	2B	129	508	71	148	16	3	2	51	29	51	3	11	19-5	.291	.331	.346	.678	14	.977
1998— Memphis (PCL)	2B-SS	70	246	36	69	19	1	1	21	16	15	3	4	6-3	.280	.331	.378	.709	5	.984
— St. Louis (N.L.)	SS-2B	45	114	10	29	3	2	1	11	5	9	1	2	2-0	.254	.292	.342	.634	5	.961
1999— St. Louis (N.L.)	2B-3B-SS	88	220	24	61	9	3	1	19	15	24	0	7	1-3	.277	.321	.359	.680	8	.972

P

Year Team (League)	Pos.	G	AB	R	H	2B	3B	HR	RBI	BB	SO	HBP	GDP	SB-CS	Avg.	OBP	SLG	OPS	E	Avg.
—Memphis (PCL) 2B-SS-3B		29	120	18	33	4	1	0	10	3	11	1	7	2-0	.275	.296	.325	.621	2	.985
2000—St. Louis (N.L.) 2B-3B-SS	1B	118	323	50	102	12	3	5	39	16	26	1	8	4-4	.316	.347	.418	.765	3	.991
2001—St. Louis (N.L.) 3B-SS-2B	DH	144	564	87	173	26	4	3	38	25	43	6	22	12-3	.307	.342	.383	.725	4	.992
2002—St. Louis (N.L.) 3B-SS-2B		94	342	47	97	19	1	5	27	12	27	4	12	3-1	.284	.316	.389	.705	6	.978
—Philadelphia (N.L.) 3B		53	206	28	61	13	1	4	22	14	14	4	3	2-2	.296	.353	.427	.780	3	.983
2003—Philadelphia (N.L.) 2B-3B		122	492	87	142	30	3	14	63	42	38	8	16	14-2	.289	.352	.447	.799	6	.989
2004—Reading (East.) 2B		1	3	0	2	0	0	0	0	0	0	0	0	0-0	.667	.667	.667	1.333	0	1.000
—Scran./W.B. (I.L.) 2B		1	3	1	0	0	0	0	0	1	0	0	0	0-0	.000	.250	.000	.250	0	1.000
—Philadelphia (N.L.) 2B-3B		126	503	74	150	21	0	17	55	27	39	12	13	7-4	.298	.345	.441	.786	3	.995
2005—Philadelphia (N.L.) 2B-3B-OF	SS	43	158	26	50	7	0	3	20	9	3	3	3	0-0	.316	.376	.418	.793	0	1.000
—Detroit (A.L.) 2B-3B		86	343	58	116	20	2	6	36	21	16	8	9	4-3	.338	.386	.461	.846	3	.993
American League totals (1 year)		86	343	58	116	20	2	6	36	21	16	8	9	4-3	.338	.386	.461	.846	3	.993
National League totals (8 years)		833	2922	433	865	140	15	53	294	168	229	39	85	45-19	.296	.341	.410	.751	40	.987
Major League totals (8 years)		919	3265	491	981	160	19	59	330	189	245	47	94	49-22	.300	.346	.415	.761	43	.988

DIVISION SERIES RECORD

Year Team (League)	Pos.	G	AB	R	H	2B	3B	HR	RBI	BB	SO	HBP	GDP	SB-CS	Avg.	OBP	SLG	OPS	E	Avg.
2000—St. Louis (N.L.)	3B	3	10	1	3	0	0	0	3	1	0	0	0	1-0	.300	.364	.300	.664	0	1.000
2001—St. Louis (N.L.)	3B	5	15	1	4	0	0	0	1	1	1	0	1	1-0	.267	.294	.267	.561	1	.941
Division series totals (2 years)		8	25	2	7	0	0	0	4	2	1	0	1	2-0	.280	.321	.280	.601	1	.957

CHAMPIONSHIP SERIES RECORD

Year Team (League)	Pos.	G	AB	R	H	2B	3B	HR	RBI	BB	SO	HBP	GDP	SB-CS	Avg.	OBP	SLG	OPS	E	Avg.
2000—St. Louis (N.L.)	3B	4	5	0	1	0	0	0	0	2	1	0	0	0-0	.200	.429	.200	.629	0	1.000

POLITTE, CLIFF   P

PERSONAL: Born February 27, 1974, in St. Louis. ... 5-11/200. ... Throws right, bats right. ... Full name: Cliff Anthony Politte. ... Name pronounced: po-LEET. ... High school: Vianney (Kirkwood, Mo.). ... Junior college: Jefferson (Hillsboro, Mo.).

TRANSACTIONS/CAREER NOTES: Selected by St. Louis Cardinals organization in 54th round of 1995 free-agent draft. ... Traded by Cardinals with OF Ron Gant and P Jeff Brantley to Philadelphia Phillies for Ps Ricky Bottalico and Garrett Stephenson (November 19, 1998). ... On disabled list (March 31-July 6, 2001); included rehabilitation assignment to Clearwater. ... Traded by Phillies to Toronto Blue Jays for P Dan Plesac (May 26, 2002). ... On disabled list (June 29-July 25, 2003); included rehabilitation assignment to Syracuse. ... Signed as a free agent by Chicago White Sox (January 7, 2004).

CAREER HITTING: 4-for-33 (.121), 3 R, 1 2B, 0 3B, 0 HR, 3 RBI.

SCOUTING REPORT **Throws:** Politte can get his fastball up to 92-96 mph. Also has a slider. **Tendencies:** Basically, he's a one-speed pitcher who can overpower hitters up in the zone with his fastball. Has improved the command of it but it still tends to be straight. Has improved his breaking ball; it now has very late sharp movement. Has become more aggressive with his success and is throwing more strikes. **Outlook:** Politte turned the corner in his career with a solid postseason. The onetime closer fits well in a setup role. **Grade 7.5**

CLIFF POLITTE'S PITCHING ZONE

.067	.167	.190
.125	.286	.400
.056	.308	.167

LEFTY-RIGHTY SPLITS

vs.	Avg.	AB	H	2B	3B	HR	RBI	BB	SO	OBP	Slg.
L	.182	77	14	1	0	3	6	8	18	.267	.312
R	.181	155	28	9	1	4	17	13	39	.247	.329

Year Team (League)	W	L	Pct.	ERA	WHIP	G	GS	CG	ShO	Hld.	Sv.-Opp.	IP	H	R	ER	HR	BB-IBB	SO	Avg.
1996—Peoria (Midw.)	14	6	.700	2.59	1.04	25	25	0	0	...	0-...	149.2	108	50	43	8	47-0	151	.199
1997—Prince Will. (Car.)	11	1	.917	2.24	1.00	19	19	0	0	...	0-...	120.1	89	37	30	11	31-0	118	.203
—Arkansas (Texas)	4	1	.800	2.15	1.17	6	6	0	0	...	0-...	37.2	35	15	9	3	9-1	26	.257
1998—St. Louis (N.L.)	2	3	.400	6.32	1.70	8	8	0	0	0	0-0	37.0	45	32	26	6	18-0	22	.304
—Memphis (PCL)	1	4	.200	7.64	1.88	10	10	0	0	0	0-0	50.2	71	46	43	10	24-0	42	.332
—Arkansas (Texas)	5	3	.625	2.96	1.07	10	10	1	1	0	0-0	67.0	56	25	22	6	16-0	61	.230
1999—Reading (East.)	9	8	.529	3.63	1.33	37	13	1	0	...	5-...	109.0	112	45	44	12	33-3	97	.270
—Philadelphia (N.L.)	1	0	1.000	7.13	1.92	13	0	0	0	1	0-0	17.2	19	14	14	2	15-0	15	.275
2000—Scran./W.B. (I.L.)	8	4	.667	3.12	1.20	21	20	1	0	...	0-0	112.2	94	45	39	8	41-2	106	.227
—Philadelphia (N.L.)	4	3	.571	3.66	1.39	12	8	0	0	0	0-0	59.0	55	24	24	8	27-1	50	.248
2001—Clearwater (FSL)	0	1	.000	2.45	1.00	7	7	0	0	...	0-0	11.0	8	4	3	0	3-0	15	.200
—Philadelphia (N.L.)	2	3	.400	2.42	1.23	23	0	0	0	1	0-0	26.0	24	8	7	2	8-3	23	.250
2002—Philadelphia (N.L.)	2	0	1.000	3.86	1.71	13	0	0	0	0	0-1	16.1	19	10	7	0	9-1	15	.288
—Toronto (A.L.)	1	3	.250	3.61	0.99	55	0	0	0	25	1-3	57.1	38	23	23	5	19-1	57	.186
2003—Syracuse (Int'l)	0	0	...	0.00	0.00	1	0	0	0	...	0-...	1.0	0	0	0	0	0-0	1	.000
—Toronto (A.L.)	1	5	.167	5.66	1.40	54	0	0	0	8	12-18	49.1	52	32	31	11	17-4	40	.269
2004—Chicago (A.L.)	0	3	.000	4.38	1.44	54	0	0	0	19	1-1	51.1	52	26	25	6	22-5	48	.261
2005—Chicago (A.L.)	7	1	.875	2.00	0.94	68	0	0	0	23	1-2	67.1	42	15	15	7	21-4	57	.181
American League totals (4 years)	9	12	.429	3.75	1.17	231	0	0	0	75	15-24	225.1	184	96	94	29	79-14	202	.222
National League totals (5 years)	11	9	.550	4.50	1.53	69	16	0	0	2	0-1	156.0	162	88	78	18	77-5	125	.270
Major League totals (8 years)	20	21	.488	4.06	1.32	300	16	0	0	77	15-25	381.1	346	184	172	47	156-19	327	.242

DIVISION SERIES RECORD

Year Team (League)	W	L	Pct.	ERA	WHIP	G	GS	CG	ShO	Hld.	Sv.-Opp.	IP	H	R	ER	HR	BB-IBB	SO	Avg.
2005—Chicago (A.L.)	0	0	...	0.00	1.00	1	0	0	0		0-0	1.0	1	0	0	0	0-0	0	.250

CHAMPIONSHIP SERIES RECORD

Year Team (League)	W	L	Pct.	ERA	WHIP	G	GS	CG	ShO	Hld.	Sv.-Opp.	IP	H	R	ER	HR	BB-IBB	SO	Avg.
2005—Chicago (A.L.)	Did not play.																		

WORLD SERIES RECORD

Year Team (League)	W	L	Pct.	ERA	WHIP	G	GS	CG	ShO	Hld.	Sv.-Opp.	IP	H	R	ER	HR	BB-IBB	SO	Avg.
2005—Chicago (A.L.)	0	0	...	3.86	0.86	3	0	0	0	3	0-0	2.1	0	1	1	0	2-1	2	.000

P

PONSON, SIDNEY — P

PERSONAL: Born November 2, 1976, in Noord, Aruba. ... 6-1/266. ... Throws right, bats right. ... Full name: Sidney Alton Ponson. ... Name pronounced: pon-SONE. ... High school: Maria College (Aruba).

TRANSACTIONS/CAREER NOTES: Signed as a non-drafted free agent by Baltimore Orioles organization (August 17, 1993). ... On disabled list (April 16-May 9, 2001); included rehabilitation assignment to Bowie. ... On disabled list (August 7-September 1, 2002). ... Traded by Orioles to San Francisco Giants for Ps Kurt Ainsworth, Damian Moss and Ryan Hannaman (July 31, 2003). ... Signed as a free agent by Orioles (January 26, 2004). ... On disabled list (August 9-September 1, 2005). ... Released by Orioles (September 1, 2005).

CAREER HITTING: 6-for-50 (.120), 3 R, 3 2B, 0 3B, 0 HR, 0 RBI.

SCOUTING REPORT

Throws: Ponson features a 90-95 mph fastball, a curveball, a slider at 86-91 and a changeup. **Tendencies:** He is erratic from one start to the next. Doesn't maintain focus; is immature. Is working in the lower part of the zone better with his two-seam fastball yet is quick enough to ride his four-seamer. Doesn't throw his curve often. Slider is quick and bites late. Straight change has improved but often is thrown too hard. Throws strikes but is prone to making mistakes when ahead in the count. **Outlook:** Though he was released late in the season after off-the-field incidents, there's no question he will pitch for someone next year. With maturity, could make a difference in a club's rotation. **Grade 6**

SIDNEY PONSON'S PITCHING ZONE

.440	.214	.091
.373	.357	.346
.385	.323	.472

LEFTY-RIGHTY SPLITS

vs.	Avg.	AB	H	2B	3B	HR	RBI	BB	SO	OBP	Slg.
L	.360	283	102	19	0	8	43	33	33	.422	.512
R	.299	251	75	13	0	8	45	15	35	.339	.446

Year	Team (League)	W	L	Pct.	ERA	WHIP	G	GS	CG	ShO	Hld.	Sv.-Opp.	IP	H	R	ER	HR	BB-IBB	SO	Avg.
1994—	GC Orioles (GCL)	4	3	.571	2.96	1.16	12	10	1	0	...	0-...	73.0	68	30	24	5	17-0	53	.245
1995—	Bluefield (Appal.)	6	3	.667	4.17	1.22	13	13	0	0	...	0-...	77.2	79	44	36	7	16-0	56	.260
1996—	Frederick (Carolina)	7	6	.538	3.45	1.18	18	16	3	0	...	0-...	107.0	98	56	41	6	28-0	110	.244
1997—	Bowie (East.)	2	7	.222	5.42	1.46	13	13	1	1	...	0-...	74.2	77	51	45	11	32-2	56	.269
	— GC Orioles (GCL)	1	0	1.000	0.00	1.00	1	0	0	0	...	0-...	2.0	0	0	0	0	0-0	1	.000
1998—	Rochester (Int'l)	1	0	1.000	0.00	1.00	1	1	0	0	...	0-...	5.0	4	0	0	0	1-0	3	.211
	— Baltimore (A.L.)	8	9	.471	5.27	1.47	31	20	0	0	0	1-2	135.0	157	82	79	19	42-2	85	.293
1999—	Baltimore (A.L.)	12	12	.500	4.71	1.46	32	32	6	0	0	0-0	210.0	227	118	110	35	80-2	112	.282
2000—	Baltimore (A.L.)	9	13	.409	4.82	1.38	32	32	6	1	0	0-0	222.0	223	125	119	30	83-0	152	.258
2001—	Baltimore (A.L.)	5	10	.333	4.94	1.43	23	23	3	1	0	0-0	138.1	161	83	76	21	37-0	84	.289
	— Bowie (East.)	0	0	...	0.00	1.00	1	1	0	0	...	0-...	4.0	3	0	0	0	1-0	2	.231
2002—	Baltimore (A.L.)	7	9	.438	4.09	1.34	28	28	3	0	0	0-0	176.0	172	84	80	26	63-1	120	.258
2003—	Baltimore (A.L.)	14	6	.700	3.77	1.28	21	21	4	0	0	0-0	148.0	147	65	62	10	43-2	100	.258
	— San Francisco (N.L.)	3	6	.333	3.71	1.21	10	10	0	0	0	0-0	68.0	64	29	28	6	18-3	34	.255
2004—	Baltimore (A.L.)	11	15	.423	5.30	1.55	33	33	• 5	• 2	0	0-0	215.2	* 265	136	* 127	23	69-3	115	.305
2005—	Baltimore (A.L.)	7	11	.389	6.21	1.73	23	23	1	0	0	0-0	130.1	177	97	90	16	48-1	68	.331
American League totals (8 years)		73	85	.462	4.86	1.45	223	212	28	4	0	1-2	1375.1	1529	790	743	180	465-11	836	.283
National League totals (1 year)		3	6	.333	3.71	1.21	10	10	0	0	0	0-0	68.0	64	29	28	6	18-3	34	.255
Major League totals (8 years)		76	91	.455	4.81	1.44	233	222	28	4	0	1-2	1443.1	1593	819	771	186	483-14	870	.282

DIVISION SERIES RECORD

Year	Team (League)	W	L	Pct.	ERA	WHIP	G	GS	CG	ShO	Hld.	Sv.-Opp.	IP	H	R	ER	HR	BB-IBB	SO	Avg.
2003—	San Francisco (N.L.)	0	0	...	7.20	1.40	1	1	0	0	0	0-0	5.0	7	4	4	0	0-0	3	.318

POSADA, JORGE — C

PERSONAL: Born August 17, 1971, in Santurce, Puerto Rico. ... 6-2/205. ... Bats both, throws right. ... Full name: Jorge Rafael Posada. ... Name pronounced: hor-hay po-sa-da. ... High school: Colegio Alejandrino (Puerto Rico). ... Junior college: Calhoun (Ala.) Community College.

TRANSACTIONS/CAREER NOTES: Selected by New York Yankees organization in 24th round of 1990 free-agent draft. ... On suspended list (July 17-18, 2000; and September 26-October 2, 2001).

2005 GAMES PLAYED BY POSITION (MLB): C—133, DH—3.

SCOUTING REPORT

Offense: Posada is noted more for his offense than defense. Is an extremely patient hitter, but his bat speed has declined from both sides of the plate. Hits with more power and likes to pull the ball more from the left side. Is a tough out in key situations. Best offensive years are behind him. **Defense:** He has a quick release but his throws have a tendency to tail on him when he rushes. Still drops too many pitches and, at times, will reach for balls he could get in front of and block, especially to his right. Usually catches a veteran pitching staff and doesn't have to concern himself with calling the game. **Outlook:** Posada's slide continues and some in the organization have thought of moving him. Doubtful he can repeat his offensive production of several years ago. **Grade 8**

JORGE POSADA'S HITTING ZONE

.258	.259	.171
.375	.404	.278
.231	.286	.150

LEFTY-RIGHTY SPLITS

vs.	Avg.	AB	H	2B	3B	HR	RBI	BB	SO	OBP	Slg.
L	.281	171	48	9	0	7	25	21	34	.354	.456
R	.251	303	76	14	0	12	46	45	60	.350	.416

Year	Team (League)	Pos.	G	AB	R	H	2B	3B	HR	RBI	BB	SO	HBP	GDP	SB-CS	Avg.	OBP	SLG	OPS	E	FIELDING Avg.
1991—	Oneonta (NYP)	2B-C	71	217	34	51	5	5	4	33	51	51	4	3	6-4	.235	.388	.359	.748	21	.947
1992—	Greensboro (S. Atl.)	3B-C	101	339	60	94	22	4	12	58	58	87	6	8	11-6	.277	.389	.472	.861	11	.965
1993—	Prince Will. (Car.)	3B-C	118	410	71	106	27	2	17	61	67	90	6	7	17-5	.259	.366	.459	.825	15	.981
	— Albany (East.)	C	7	25	3	7	0	0	0	2	7	0	1	0	0-0	.280	.333	.280	.613	2	.958
1994—	Columbus (Int'l)	C-OF	92	313	46	75	13	3	11	48	32	81	1	5	5-5	.240	.308	.406	.713	11	.993
1995—	Columbus (Int'l)	C-DH	108	368	60	94	32	5	8	51	54	101	1	14	4-4	.255	.350	.435	.785	4	.993
	— New York (A.L.)	C	1	0	0	0	0	0	0	0	0	0	0	0	0-0	...	...	...	...	0	1.000
1996—	Columbus (Int'l)	C-DH-OF	106	354	76	96	22	6	11	62	79	86	3	13	3-3	.271	.405	.460	.866	10	.985
	— New York (A.L.)	C-DH	8	14	1	1	0	0	0	0	1	6	0	1	0-0	.071	.133	.071	.205	0	1.000
1997—	New York (A.L.)	C	60	188	29	47	12	0	6	25	30	33	3	2	1-2	.250	.359	.410	.768	3	.992
1998—	New York (A.L.)	C-DH-1B	111	358	56	96	23	0	17	63	47	92	0	14	0-1	.268	.350	.475	.824	4	.994

P

								BATTING												FIELDING	
Year Team (League)	Pos.	G	AB	R	H	2B	3B	HR	RBI	BB	SO	HBP	GDP	SB-CS	Avg.	OBP	SLG	OPS	E	Avg.
1999— New York (A.L.)	C-1B-DH	112	379	50	93	19	2	12	57	53	91	3	9	1-0	.245	.341	.401	.742	5	.993
2000— New York (A.L.)	C-1B-DH	151	505	92	145	35	1	28	86	107	151	8	11	2-2	.287	.417	.527	.943	8	.992
2001— New York (A.L.)	C-DH-1B	138	484	59	134	28	1	22	95	62	132	6	10	2-6	.277	.363	.475	.838	11	.990
2002— New York (A.L.)	C-DH	143	511	79	137	40	1	20	99	81	143	3	23	1-0	.268	.370	.468	.837	12	.988
2003— New York (A.L.)	C-DH	142	481	83	135	24	0	30	101	93	110	10	13	2-4	.281	.405	.518	.922	6	.994
2004— New York (A.L.)	C	137	449	72	122	31	0	21	81	88	92	9	• 24	1-3	.272	.400	.481	.881	9	.990
2005— New York (A.L.)	C-DH	142	474	67	124	23	0	19	71	66	94	2	8	1-0	.262	.352	.430	.782	3	.996
Major League totals (11 years)		1145	3843	588	1034	235	5	175	678	628	944	44	115	11-18	.269	.375	.469	.845	61	.992

DIVISION SERIES RECORD

Year Team (League)	Pos.	G	AB	R	H	2B	3B	HR	RBI	BB	SO	HBP	GDP	SB-CS	Avg.	OBP	SLG	OPS	E	Avg.
1995— New York (A.L.)		1	0	1	0	0	0	0	0	0	0	0	0	0-0	...	...	...	...	0	...
1997— New York (A.L.)	C	2	2	0	0	0	0	0	0	0	1	0	0	0-0	.000	.000	.000	.000	0	1.000
1998— New York (A.L.)	C	1	2	1	0	0	0	0	0	1	2	0	0	0-0	.000	.333	.000	.333	0	1.000
1999— New York (A.L.)	C	1	4	0	1	1	0	0	0	0	0	0	0	0-0	.250	.250	.500	.750	0	1.000
2000— New York (A.L.)	C	5	17	2	4	2	0	0	3	5	5	0	0	0-0	.235	.350	.353	.703	0	1.000
2001— New York (A.L.)	C	5	18	3	8	1	0	1	2	2	2	0	1	1-0	.444	.500	.667	1.167	0	1.000
2002— New York (A.L.)	C	4	17	2	4	0	0	1	3	0	3	0	1	0-0	.235	.222	.412	.634	1	.955
2003— New York (A.L.)	C	4	17	1	3	1	0	0	0	0	6	0	0	0-0	.176	.176	.235	.412	0	1.000
2004— New York (A.L.)	C	4	18	2	4	0	0	0	0	0	6	0	1	0-0	.222	.222	.222	.444	0	1.000
2005— New York (A.L.)	C	5	13	3	3	1	0	1	2	6	2	0	0	0-0	.231	.474	.538	1.012	0	1.000
Division series totals (10 years)		32	108	15	27	6	0	3	8	12	27	0	3	1-0	.250	.322	.389	.711	1	.995

CHAMPIONSHIP SERIES RECORD

Year Team (League)	Pos.	G	AB	R	H	2B	3B	HR	RBI	BB	SO	HBP	GDP	SB-CS	Avg.	OBP	SLG	OPS	E	Avg.
1998— New York (A.L.)	C	5	11	1	2	0	0	1	2	4	2	0	1	0-1	.182	.400	.455	.855	0	1.000
1999— New York (A.L.)	C	3	10	1	1	0	0	1	2	1	2	0	0	0-0	.100	.182	.400	.582	1	.955
2000— New York (A.L.)	C	6	19	2	3	1	0	0	3	5	5	1	0	0-1	.158	.360	.211	.571	0	1.000
2001— New York (A.L.)	C	5	14	4	3	1	0	0	6	7	0	0	0	0-0	.214	.450	.286	.736	0	1.000
2003— New York (A.L.)	C	7	27	5	8	4	0	1	6	3	4	0	1	0-0	.296	.367	.556	.922	0	1.000
2004— New York (A.L.)	C	7	27	4	7	1	0	0	2	7	1	1	1	0-0	.259	.417	.296	.713	0	1.000
Champ. series totals (6 years)		33	108	17	24	7	0	3	15	26	21	2	3	0-2	.222	.380	.370	.750	1	.996

WORLD SERIES RECORD

Year Team (League)	Pos.	G	AB	R	H	2B	3B	HR	RBI	BB	SO	HBP	GDP	SB-CS	Avg.	OBP	SLG	OPS	E	Avg.
1998— New York (A.L.)	C	3	9	2	3	0	0	1	2	2	2	0	0	0-0	.333	.455	.667	1.121	0	1.000
1999— New York (A.L.)	C	2	8	0	2	1	0	0	1	0	3	0	1	0-0	.250	.250	.375	.625	0	1.000
2000— New York (A.L.)	C	5	18	2	4	1	0	1	1	5	4	0	0	0-0	.222	.391	.278	.669	0	1.000
2001— New York (A.L.)	C	7	23	2	4	0	0	1	1	3	8	0	2	0-0	.174	.269	.348	.617	1	.986
2003— New York (A.L.)	C	6	19	0	3	1	0	0	1	5	7	0	0	1-1	.158	.333	.211	.544	0	1.000
World series totals (5 years)		23	77	6	16	4	0	2	6	15	24	0	5	1-1	.208	.337	.338	.675	1	.995

ALL-STAR GAME RECORD

	G	AB	R	H	2B	3B	HR	RBI	BB	SO	HBP	GDP	SB-CS	Avg.	OBP	SLG	OPS	E	Avg.
All-Star Game totals (4 years)	4	8	0	1	0	0	0	0	0	5	0	0	0-0	.125	.125	.250	.375	0	1.000

POWELL, JAY   P

PERSONAL: Born January 9, 1972, in Meridian, Miss. ... 6-4/230. ... Throws right, bats right. ... Full name: James Willard Powell. ... High school: West Lauderdale (Collinsville, Miss.). ... College: Mississippi State.

TRANSACTIONS/CAREER NOTES: Selected by San Diego Padres organization in 11th round of 1990 free-agent draft; did not sign. ... Selected by Baltimore Orioles organization in first round (19th pick overall) of 1993 free-agent draft. ... Traded by Orioles to Florida Marlins for IF Bret Barberie (December 6, 1994). ... On disabled list (April 20-May 10, 1996); included rehabilitation assignment to Brevard County. ... Traded by Marlins with C Scott Makarewicz to Houston Astros for C Ramon Castro (July 6, 1998). ... On disabled list (May 17-June 3, June 19-August 6 and August 18, 2000-remainder of season); included rehabilitation assignments to New Orleans and Round Rock. ... Traded by Astros to Colorado Rockies for P Ron Villone (June 27, 2001). ... Signed as a free agent by Texas Rangers (December 13, 2001). ... On disabled list (March 31-June 10, 2002); included rehabilitation assignment to Tulsa and Oklahoma. ... On disabled list (April 13-May 3, 2003); included rehabilitation assignment to Frisco. ... On disabled list (June 5, 2004-remainder of season). ... Signed as a free agent by Atlanta Braves organization (January 27, 2005). ... On disabled list (July 30, 2005-remainder of season).

LEFTY-RIGHTY SPLITS

vs.	Avg.	AB	H	2B	3B	HR	RBI	BB	SO	OBP	Slg.
L	.000	4	0	0	0	0	0	0	2	.333	.000
R	.143	7	1	0	0	0	1	2	1	.333	.143

CAREER HITTING: 2-for-12 (.167), 0 R, 0 2B, 0 3B, 0 HR, 1 RBI.

Year Team (League)	W	L	Pct.	ERA	WHIP	G	GS	CG	ShO	Hld.	Sv.-Opp.	IP	H	R	ER	HR	BB-IBB	SO	Avg.
1993— Albany (S. Atl.)	0	2	.000	4.55	1.52	6	6	0	0	...	0-...	27.2	29	19	14	0	13-0	29	.274
1994— Frederick (Carolina)	7	7	.500	4.96	1.51	26	20	0	0	...	1-...	123.1	132	79	68	13	54-0	87	.269
1995— Portland (East.)	5	4	.556	1.87	1.08	50	0	0	0	...	* 24-...	53.0	42	12	11	2	15-1	53	.219
— Florida (N.L.)	0	0	...	1.08	1.56	9	0	0	0	2	0-0	8.1	7	2	1	0	6-1	4	.241
1996— Florida (N.L.)	4	3	.571	4.54	1.50	67	0	0	0	10	2-5	71.1	71	41	36	5	36-1	52	.255
— Brevard County (FSL)	0	0	...	0.00	0.00	1	1	0	0	...	0-...	2.0	0	0	0	0	0-0	4	.000
1997— Florida (N.L.)	7	2	.778	3.28	1.27	74	0	0	0	24	2-4	79.2	71	35	29	3	30-3	65	.242
1998— Florida (N.L.)	4	4	.500	4.21	1.60	33	0	0	0	3	3-6	36.1	36	19	17	5	22-6	24	.263
— Houston (N.L.)	3	3	.500	2.38	1.09	29	0	0	0	3	4-5	34.0	22	9	9	1	15-3	38	.182
1999— Houston (N.L.)	5	4	.556	4.32	1.63	67	0	0	0	16	4-7	75.0	82	38	36	3	40-4	77	.282
2000— Houston (N.L.)	1	1	.500	5.67	1.78	29	0	0	0	5	0-0	27.0	29	18	17	1	19-1	16	.271
— New Orleans (PCL)	0	0	...	4.50	2.00	2	1	0	0	...	0-...	2.0	2	1	1	0	2-0	2	.286
— Round Rock (Texas)	0	0	...	0.00	0.50	1	1	0	0	...	0-...	2.0	0	0	0	0	1-0	1	.000
2001— Houston (N.L.)	2	2	.500	3.72	1.65	39	0	0	0	5	0-...	36.1	41	18	15	4	19-0	28	.275
— Colorado (N.L.)	3	1	.750	2.79	1.19	39	0	0	0	5	7-8	38.2	34	13	12	5	12-3	26	.245
2002— Tulsa (Texas)	0	0	...	0.00	0.50	2	0	0	0	...	0-...	2.0	0	0	0	0	1-0	0	.000
— Oklahoma (PCL)	2	0	1.000	12.38	2.13	8	0	0	0	...	0-0	8.0	14	11	11	2	3-1	8	.359
— Texas (A.L.)	3	2	.600	3.44	1.49	51	0	0	0	12	0-4	49.2	50	28	19	5	24-4	35	.253
2003— Frisco (Texas)	0	0	...	2.70	1.50	4	0	0	0	...	1-...	6.2	5	2	2	0	5-0	8	.208
— Texas (A.L.)	3	0	1.000	7.82	1.86	51	0	0	0	3	0-0	58.2	75	58	51	7	34-3	40	.319
2004— Texas (A.L.)	1	1	.500	3.38	1.46	23	0	0	0	6	0-0	24.0	24	11	9	3	11-1	17	.267
2005— GC Braves (GCL)	0	0	...	4.50	2.50	2	2	0	0	...	0-0	2.0	4	2	1	0	1-0	1	.444

Year Team (League)	W	L	Pct.	ERA	WHIP	G	GS	CG	ShO	Hld.	Sv.-Opp.	IP	H	R	ER	HR	BB-IBB	SO	Avg.
—Mississippi (Sou.)	2	0	1.000	0.64	0.64	11	0	0	0	3	0-0	14.0	6	1	1	0	3-1	8	.136
—Atlanta (N.L.)	0	0	...	0.00	1.50	5	0	0	0	1	0-0	3.1	1	0	0	0	4-0	1	.091
American League totals (3 years)	7	3	.700	5.37	1.65	125	0	0	0	18	0-4	132.1	149	97	79	15	69-8	92	.285
National League totals (8 years)	29	20	.592	3.78	1.46	387	0	0	0	69	22-40	410.0	394	198	172	27	203-22	331	.253
Major League totals (11 years)	36	23	.610	4.17	1.50	512	0	0	0	87	22-44	542.1	543	295	251	42	272-30	423	.261

DIVISION SERIES RECORD

Year Team (League)	W	L	Pct.	ERA	WHIP	G	GS	CG	ShO	Hld.	Sv.-Opp.	IP	H	R	ER	HR	BB-IBB	SO	Avg.
1997—Florida (N.L.)	Did not play.																		
1998—Houston (N.L.)	0	0		11.57	2.14	3	0	0	0	1	0-0	2.1	2	3	3	1	3-1	3	.222
1999—Houston (N.L.)	0	1	.000	6.00	1.33	3	0	0	0	0	0-0	3.0	3	2	2	0	1-1	3	.250
Division series totals (2 years)	0	1	.000	8.44	1.69	6	0	0	0	1	0-0	5.1	5	5	5	1	4-2	6	.238

CHAMPIONSHIP SERIES RECORD

Year Team (League)	W	L	Pct.	ERA	WHIP	G	GS	CG	ShO	Hld.	Sv.-Opp.	IP	H	R	ER	HR	BB-IBB	SO	Avg.
1997—Florida (N.L.)	0	0		0.00	0.00	1	0	0	0	1	0-0	0.2	0	0	0	0	0-0	1	.000

WORLD SERIES RECORD

Year Team (League)	W	L	Pct.	ERA	WHIP	G	GS	CG	ShO	Hld.	Sv.-Opp.	IP	H	R	ER	HR	BB-IBB	SO	Avg.
1997—Florida (N.L.)	1	0	1.000	7.36	2.45	4	0	0	0	0	0-0	3.2	5	3	3	1	4-0	2	.333

PRATT, TODD   C

PERSONAL: Born February 9, 1967, in Bellevue, Neb. ... 6-3/236. ... Bats right, throws right. ... Full name: Todd Alan Pratt. ... High school: Hilltop (Chula Vista, Calif.).

TRANSACTIONS/CAREER NOTES: Selected by Boston Red Sox organization in sixth round of June 1985 free-agent draft. ... Selected by Cleveland Indians organization from Red Sox organization in Rule 5 minor league draft (December 7, 1987). ... Returned to Red Sox organization (March 28, 1988). ... Signed as a free agent by Baltimore Orioles organization (November 13, 1991). ... Selected by Philadelphia Phillies from Orioles organization in Rule 5 major league draft (December 9, 1991). ... On disabled list (April 28-May 27, 1993); included rehabilitation assignment to Scranton/Wilkes-Barre. ... Signed as a free agent by Chicago Cubs organization (April 8, 1995). ... Signed as a free agent by Seattle Mariners organization (January 25, 1996). ... Released by Mariners (March 27, 1996). ... Signed by New York Mets organization (December 23, 1996). ... On disabled list (May 7-June 23, 1998); included rehabilitation assignments to St. Lucie, GCL Mets and Norfolk. ... Traded by Mets to Phillies for C Gary Bennett (July 23, 2001). ... On suspended list (May 17-20, 2004).

2005 GAMES PLAYED BY POSITION (MLB): C—57.

SCOUTING REPORT Pratt is the classic veteran backup who calls a good game and creates a good tempo for pitchers. Has good hands, is extremely aggressive and compensates for a lack of arm strength with a short, quick release. Is a stiff hitter with a long stroke but is extremely aggressive and overswings a lot. A dead-red hitter but has shown the ability to be patient and work the count. Likes to extend his arms and is strong enough to take mistake pitches out of the park. Has very good makeup for the role and works well with his pitching staff. *Grade 4.9*

TODD PRATT'S HITTING ZONE

.182	.375	.111
.311	.417	.250
.133	.200	.143

LEFTY-RIGHTY SPLITS

vs.	Avg.	AB	H	2B	3B	HR	RBI	BB	SO	OBP	Slg.
L	.300	40	12	1	0	5	13	6	9	.404	.700
R	.237	135	32	3	0	2	10	13	41	.309	.304

Year Team (League)	Pos.	G	AB	R	H	2B	3B	HR	RBI	BB	SO	HBP	GDP	SB-CS	Avg.	OBP	SLG	OPS	E	Avg.
1985—Elmira (N.Y.-Penn)	C	39	119	7	16	1	1	0	5	10	27	1	6	0-1	.134	.206	.160	.366	6	.979
1986—Greensboro (S. Atl.)	1B-C	107	348	63	84	16	0	12	56	75	114	5	10	0-1	.241	.380	.391	.770	† 15	.983
1987—Winter Haven (FSL)	1B-C-OF	118	407	57	105	22	0	12	65	70	94	1	10	0-1	.258	.364	.400	.764	15	.980
1988—New Britain (East.)	1B-C	124	395	41	89	15	2	8	49	41	110	3	7	1-4	.225	.299	.334	.633	15	.975
1989—New Britain (East.)	1B-C	109	338	30	77	17	1	2	35	44	66	7	10	1-2	.228	.325	.302	.627	§ 11	.977
1990—New Britain (East.)	1B-C	70	195	15	45	14	1	2	22	18	56	0	7	0-1	.231	.293	.344	.637	4	.978
1991—Pawtucket (Int'l)	1B-C	68	219	68	64	16	0	11	41	23	42	3	9	0-3	.292	.367	.516	.883	4	.985
1992—Reading (East.)	C	41	132	20	44	6	1	6	26	24	28	0	9	2-0	.333	.436	.530	.966	3	.970
—Scran./W.B. (I.L.)	C-1B	41	125	20	40	9	1	7	28	30	14	0	5	1-0	.320	.446	.576	1.022	4	.977
—Philadelphia (N.L.)	C	16	46	6	13	1	0	2	10	4	12	0	2	0-0	.283	.340	.435	.775	2	.972
1993—Philadelphia (N.L.)	C	33	87	8	25	6	0	5	13	5	19	1	2	0-0	.287	.330	.529	.859	2	.989
—Scran./W.B. (I.L.)	C	3	9	1	2	1	0	0	1	3	1	0	0	0-0	.222	.417	.333	.750	1	1.000
1994—Philadelphia (N.L.)	C	28	102	10	20	6	1	2	9	12	29	0	3	0-1	.196	.281	.333	.614	1	1.000
1995—Chicago (N.L.)	C	25	60	3	8	2	0	0	4	5	20	0	1	0-0	.133	.209	.167	.376	3	.981
—Iowa (Am. Assoc.)	C-1B-DH	23	58	3	19	1	0	0	5	4	17	0	0	0-0	.328	.371	.345	.716	2	.978
1996—	Did not play.																			
1997—Norfolk (Int'l)	C-DH	59	206	42	62	8	3	9	34	26	48	2	8	1-2	.301	.383	.500	.883	4	.988
—New York (N.L.)	C	39	106	12	30	6	0	2	19	13	32	2	1	0-0	.283	.372	.396	.768	2	.990
1998—Norfolk (Int'l)	DH-C-OF 1B	35	118	16	42	6	0	7	30	15	19	4	4	2-0	.356	.442	.585	1.027	2	.984
—New York (N.L.)	C-1B	41	69	9	19	9	1	2	18	2	20	0	0	0-0	.275	.296	.522	.818	2	.976
—St. Lucie (Fla. St.)	1B-C-OF	5	20	2	9	1	0	1	3	1	5	2	0	1-0	.450	.522	.650	1.172	0	1.000
—GC Mets (GCL)	C-OF	2	4	1	1	0	0	0	0	4	1	1	0	0-0	.250	.625	.250	.875	0	1.000
1999—New York (N.L.)	C-1B-OF	71	140	18	41	4	0	3	21	15	32	3	1	0-0	.293	.369	.386	.754	1	.996
2000—New York (N.L.)	C-DH	80	160	33	44	8	0	8	25	22	31	5	5	0-0	.275	.378	.463	.840	1	.997
2001—New York (N.L.)	C	45	80	6	13	5	0	2	4	15	36	2	4	0-0	.163	.306	.300	.606	1	.994
—Philadelphia (N.L.)	C-1B	35	93	12	19	3	0	2	7	19	25	1	2	0-0	.204	.345	.301	.646	3	.986
2002—Philadelphia (N.L.)	C-1B	39	106	14	33	11	0	3	16	24	28	4	3	2-0	.311	.449	.500	.949	1	1.000
2003—Philadelphia (N.L.)	C-1B	43	125	16	34	10	1	4	20	22	38	6	3	0-0	.272	.400	.464	.864	1	.997
2004—Philadelphia (N.L.)	C	45	128	16	33	5	0	4	14	8	15	5	6	1-0	.258	.351	.367	.719	0	1.000
2005—Philadelphia (N.L.)	C	60	175	17	44	4	0	7	23	19	50	2	3	0-0	.251	.332	.394	.726	1	.997
Major League totals (13 years)		600	1477	180	376	78	3	45	205	196	411	27	35	5-2	.255	.350	.403	.753	19	.994

P

DIVISION SERIES RECORD

Year — Team (League)	Pos.	G	AB	R	H	2B	3B	HR	RBI	BB	SO	HBP	GDP	SB-CS	Avg.	OBP	SLG	OPS	E	Avg.
1999—New York (N.L.)	C	3	8	2	1	0	0	1	1	2	1	0	0	0-0	.125	.300	.500	.800	0	1.000
2000—New York (N.L.)	C	1	1	0	0	0	0	0	0	0	0	0	0	0-0	.000	.000	.000	.000	0	1.000
Division series totals (2 years)		4	9	2	1	0	0	1	1	2	1	0	0	0-0	.111	.273	.444	.717	0	1.000

CHAMPIONSHIP SERIES RECORD

Year — Team (League)	Pos.	G	AB	R	H	2B	3B	HR	RBI	BB	SO	HBP	GDP	SB-CS	Avg.	OBP	SLG	OPS	E	Avg.
1993—Philadelphia (N.L.)	C	1	1	0	0	0	0	0	0	0	1	0	0	0-0	.000	.000	.000	.000	0	1.000
1999—New York (N.L.)	C	4	2	0	1	0	0	0	0	1	1	0	0	0-0	.500	.500	.500	1.000	0	1.000
2000—New York (N.L.)	Did not play.																			
Champ. series totals (2 years)		5	3	0	1	0	0	0	0	1	2	0	0	0-0	.333	.400	.333	.733	0	1.000

WORLD SERIES RECORD

Year — Team (League)	Pos.	G	AB	R	H	2B	3B	HR	RBI	BB	SO	HBP	GDP	SB-CS	Avg.	OBP	SLG	OPS	E	Avg.
1993—Philadelphia (N.L.)	Did not play.																			
2000—New York (N.L.)	C	1	2	1	0	0	0	0	0	1	2	2	0	0-0	.000	.600	.000	.600	0	1.000

PRIDE, CURTIS — OF

PERSONAL: Born December 17, 1968, in Washington, D.C. ... 6-0/210. ... Bats left, throws right. ... Full name: Curtis John Pride. ... High school: John F. Kennedy (Silver Spring, Md.). ... College: William & Mary (Va.).

LEFTY-RIGHTY SPLITS

vs.	Avg.	AB	H	2B	3B	HR	RBI	BB	SO	OBP	Slg.
L	.000	1	0	0	0	0	0	0	1	.000	.000
R	.100	10	1	1	0	0	0	0	3	.100	.200

TRANSACTIONS/CAREER NOTES: Selected by New York Mets organization in 10th round of June 1986 free-agent draft. ... Signed as a free agent by Montreal Expos organization (December 8, 1992). ... Signed as a free agent by Detroit Tigers (March 31, 1996). ... On disabled list (April 13-May 10, 1996); included rehabilitation assignment to Toledo. ... Signed as a free agent by Boston Red Sox organization (August 30, 1997). ... Signed as a free agent by Atlanta Braves organization (February 6, 1998). ... On suspended list (May 27-28, 1998). ... On disabled list (June 28-July 14, 1998); included rehabilitation assignment to Richmond. ... Released by Braves (December 1, 1998). ... Signed by Kansas City Royals organization (February 24, 1999). ... Released by Royals (March 4, 1999). ... Signed by Mets organization (January 20, 2000). ... Traded by Mets to Red Sox for a player to be named (April 26, 2000); Mets acquired SS Gavin Jackson to complete deal (July 9, 2000). ... Released by Red Sox (July 8, 2000). ... Signed by Los Angeles Dodgers organization (July 18, 2000). ... Signed as a free agent by Expos organization (December 21, 2000). ... On disabled list (June 18-August 21, 2001); included rehabilitation assignments to Jupiter and Ottawa. ... Signed as a free agent by Pittsburgh Pirates organization (March 5, 2002). ... Contract purchased by New York Yankees organization from Nashua of the independent Atlantic League (May 23, 2003). ... Signed as a free agent by Anaheim Angels organization (May 31, 2004). ... Angels franchise renamed Los Angeles Angels of Anaheim prior to 2005 season. ... On disabled list (May 30-June 22, 2005); included rehabilitation assignment to Salt Lake.

2005 GAMES PLAYED BY POSITION (MLB): OF—4, DH—3.

Year — Team (League)	Pos.	G	AB	R	H	2B	3B	HR	RBI	BB	SO	HBP	GDP	SB-CS	Avg.	OBP	SLG	OPS	E	Avg.
1986—Kingsport (Appalachian)	OF	27	46	5	5	0	0	1	4	6	24	1	0	5-0	.109	.226	.174	.400	0	1.000
1987—Kingsport (Appalachian)	OF	31	104	22	25	4	0	1	9	16	34	1	0	14-5	.240	.347	.308	.655	5	.894
1988—Kingsport (Appalachian)	OF	70	268	59	76	13	1	8	27	50	48	1	2	23-7	.284	.397	.429	.826	5	.961
1989—Pittsfield (NYP)	OF	55	212	35	55	7	3	6	23	25	47	2	1	9-2	.259	.342	.406	.747	4	.964
1990—Columbia (S. Atl.)	OF	53	191	38	51	4	4	6	25	21	45	0	3	11-8	.267	.338	.424	.762	11	.874
1991—St. Lucie (Fla. St.)	OF	116	392	57	102	21	7	9	37	43	94	2	4	24-5	.260	.336	.418	.755	8	.964
1992—Binghamton (East.)	OF	118	388	54	88	15	3	10	42	47	110	4	5	14-11	.227	.316	.358	.674	8	.964
1993—Harrisburg (East.)	OF	50	180	51	64	6	3	15	39	12	36	4	2	21-6	.356	.404	.672	1.076	2	.972
— Ottawa (Int'l)	OF	69	262	55	79	11	4	6	22	34	61	3	3	29-12	.302	.388	.443	.831	2	.986
— Montreal (N.L.)	OF	10	9	3	4	1	1	1	5	0	3	0	0	1-0	.444	.444	1.111	1.556	0	1.000
1994—W.P. Beach (FSL)	OF	3	8	5	6	1	0	1	3	4	2	0	0	2-2	.750	.833	1.250	2.083	0	1.000
— Ottawa (Int'l)	OF-DH	82	300	56	77	16	4	9	32	39	81	2	2	22-6	.257	.345	.427	.772	3	.982
1995—Ottawa (Int'l)	OF-DH	42	154	25	43	8	3	4	24	12	35	2	2	8-4	.279	.339	.448	.787	2	.974
— Montreal (N.L.)	OF	48	63	10	11	1	0	0	2	5	16	0	2	3-2	.175	.235	.190	.426	2	.920
1996—Detroit (A.L.)	OF-DH	95	267	52	80	17	5	10	31	31	63	0	2	11-6	.300	.372	.513	.886	3	.967
— Toledo (Int'l)	DH-OF	9	26	4	6	1	0	1	2	9	7	1	1	4-1	.231	.444	.385	.829	0	1.000
1997—Detroit (A.L.)	OF-DH	79	162	21	34	4	4	2	19	24	45	1	4	6-4	.210	.314	.321	.635	1	.980
— Pawtucket (Int'l)	OF	1	3	0	0	0	0	0	0	0	0	0	0	0-0	.000	.000	.000	.000	...	...
— Boston (A.L.)		2	2	1	1	0	0	0	1	0	1	0	0	0-0	.500	.500	.500	1.000	...	...
1998—Atlanta (N.L.)	OF-DH	70	107	19	27	6	1	3	9	9	29	3	2	4-0	.252	.325	.411	.736	0	1.000
— Richmond (Int'l)	OF-DH	21	78	11	19	2	1	2	6	15	17	0	3	8-0	.244	.366	.372	.737	1	.980
1999—Nashua (Atl.)	DH	14	32	0	2	0	0	0	2	7	11	...	...	0-0	.063	...	.063	...	...	...
2000—Norfolk (Int'l)	OF	15	31	9	9	2	2	1	4	11	7	2	2	3-2	.290	.500	.581	1.081	1	.929
— Pawtucket (Int'l)	OF	48	154	44	47	10	2	9	31	38	31	0	3	12-1	.305	.443	.571	1.014	1	.990
— Boston (A.L.)	OF-DH	9	20	4	5	1	0	0	1	1	7	0	0	2-0	.250	.286	.300	.586	0	1.000
— Albuquerque (PCL)	OF	38	133	30	39	7	3	6	17	20	37	0	2	7-5	.293	.383	.526	.909	3	.959
2001—Ottawa (Int'l)	OF	22	81	14	27	4	1	5	15	12	26	2	2	6-1	.333	.432	.593	1.024	1	.963
— Montreal (N.L.)	OF-DH	36	76	8	19	3	1	1	9	9	22	2	4	3-2	.250	.345	.355	.700	1	.968
— Jupiter (Fla. St.)	OF	6	21	3	4	1	0	0	0	1	6	0	0	0-1	.190	.292	.238	.530	0	1.000
2002—Nashville (PCL)	OF	110	385	71	114	22	1	10	46	33	75	7	7	22-8	.296	.362	.436	.798	6	.968
2003—New York (A.L.)	OF	4	12	1	1	0	0	1	1	0	2	0	1	0-0	.083	.083	.333	.417	0	1.000
— Columbus (Int'l)	OF-DH	55	225	44	65	11	4	7	34	20	48	4	7	7-7	.289	.357	.467	.824	1	.991
— Nashua (Atl.)	DH	16	61	10	21	1	5	5	25	4	12	0	0	5-...	.344	.391	.705	1.096	...	...
2004—Ariz. Angels (Ariz.)	DH	4	14	1	3	1	0	0	3	1	6	0	0	1-0	.214	.250	.286	.536	...	...
— Salt Lake (PCL)	OF-DH	19	65	13	28	8	1	2	10	4	12	1	1	2-0	.431	.465	.677	1.142	0	1.000
— Anaheim (A.L.)	DH	35	40	5	10	3	0	0	4	0	11	1	1	1-0	.250	.268	.325	.593	0	1.000
— Nashua (Atl.)	DH	17	65	12	29	3	0	1	12	10	10	0	0	4-...	.446	.513	.631	1.144	...	...
2005—Salt Lake (PCL)	OF-DH	82	280	44	81	16	7	6	56	49	65	1	6	10-5	.289	.397	.489	.886	4	.978
— Los Angeles (A.L.)	OF-DH	11	11	2	1	1	0	0	0	0	2	0	0	...	.091	.091	.182	.273	0	1.000
American League totals (6 years)		235	514	86	132	26	9	14	55	56	133	2	8	18-10	.257	.332	.424	.756	4	.979
National League totals (4 years)		164	255	40	61	11	3	5	25	23	70	5	8	11-4	.239	.313	.365	.678	2	.980
Major League totals (10 years)		399	769	126	193	37	12	19	80	79	203	7	16	29-14	.251	.326	.404	.730	6	.979

DIVISION SERIES RECORD

Year — Team (League)	Pos.	G	AB	R	H	2B	3B	HR	RBI	BB	SO	HBP	GDP	SB-CS	Avg.	OBP	SLG	OPS	E	Avg.
2004—Anaheim (A.L.)		2	2	0	0	0	0	0	0	0	1	0	0	0-0	.000	.000	.000	.000	0	...

PRIETO, CHRIS — OF

PERSONAL: Born August 24, 1972, in Carmel, Calif. ... 5-11/185. ... Bats left, throws left. ... Full name: Christian Michael Prieto. ... High school: Carmel (Calif.). ... College: Nevada.

TRANSACTIONS/CAREER NOTES: Selected by San Diego Padres organization in 24th round of 1993 free-agent draft. ... Signed as a free agent by Los Angeles Dodgers organization (January 20, 2000). ... Loaned by Dodgers to Mexico City Red Devils of Mexican League (July 18-September 6, 2000). ... Signed as a free agent by Houston Astros organization (December 17, 2001). ... Released by Astros (April 29, 2002). ... Signed by Oaxaca of Mexican League (May, 2002). ... Signed by Chico of the independent Western League (August, 2000). ... Signed by Oakland Athletics organization (November 8, 2002). ... Signed as a free agent by St. Louis Cardinals (January 7, 2004). ... Signed as a free agent by Anaheim Angels organization (December 14, 2004). ... Angels franchise renamed Los Angeles Angels of Anaheim for 2005 season.

2005 GAMES PLAYED BY POSITION (MLB): OF—2.

Year Team (League)	Pos.	G	AB	R	H	2B	3B	HR	RBI	BB	SO	HBP	GDP	SB-CS	Avg.	OBP	SLG	OPS	E	FIELDING Avg.
1993— Spokane (N'west)	OF	73	280	64	81	17	5	1	28	47	30	5	4	36-3	.289	.397	.396	.793	5	.962
1994— Rancho Cuca. (Calif.)	OF	102	353	64	87	10	3	1	29	52	49	5	3	29-11	.246	.348	.300	.648	3	.985
1995— Rancho Cuca. (Calif.)	OF	114	366	80	100	12	6	2	35	64	55	5	10	39-14	.273	.383	.355	.738	7	.957
1996— Rancho Cuca. (Calif.)	OF	55	216	36	52	11	2	2	23	39	36	0	4	23-8	.241	.357	.338	.695	1	.992
— Las Vegas (PCL)	OF	5	7	1	0	0	0	0	0	0	0	0	0	0-0	.000	.000	.000	.000	0	1.000
— Memphis (Sou.)	OF	7	12	1	4	0	1	0	0	1	2	0	0	2-0	.333	.385	.500	.885	0	1.000
1997— Rancho Cuca. (Calif.)	OF	22	82	21	23	4	0	4	12	19	16	0	0	4-3	.280	.416	.476	.892	0	1.000
— Mobile (Sou.)	OF	109	388	80	124	22	9	2	58	59	55	10	2	26-6	.320	.418	.438	.856	2	.991
1998— Las Vegas (PCL)	OF	92	352	65	107	18	6	2	35	40	48	1	4	20-11	.304	.377	.406	.783	6	.969
1999— Las Vegas (PCL)	OF	108	348	66	84	14	6	0	29	46	51	6	2	21-6	.241	.338	.368	.706	1	.994
2000— Albuquerque (PCL)	OF	85	248	53	69	13	3	8	31	50	42	4	3	25-5	.278	.406	.452	.858	3	.982
— Mex. R. Devils (Mex.)	OF	24	93	28	34	4	3	2	13	25	10	1	2	12-3	.366	.500	.538	1.038	0	1.000
2001— Las Vegas (PCL)	OF	118	446	98	130	27	4	19	58	67	79	13	6	25-7	.291	.398	.507	.905	3	.989
2002— New Orleans (PCL)	OF	21	86	10	17	2	0	0	1	8	11	1	0	0-1	.198	.274	.221	.495	2	.939
— Oaxaca (Mex.)	OF	63	252	58	73	18	7	7	51	30	32	9	5	18-0	.290	.384	.500	.884	2	.986
— Chico (West.)	OF	3	12	5	2	0	1	0	2	2	3	1	0	1-0	.167	.333	.417	.750	0	1.000
2003— Sacramento (PCL)	OF-P	111	390	70	110	12	7	4	54	48	40	7	7	5-3	.282	.366	.379	.745	0	1.000
2004— Memphis (PCL)	OF	130	451	73	128	17	6	3	41	51	56	9	4	28-8	.284	.366	.368	.734	4	.871
2005— Los Angeles (A.L.)	OF	2	2	0	0	0	0	0	0	0	0	0	0	0-0	.000	.000	.000	.000	0	1.000
— Salt Lake (PCL)	OF-DH	97	363	71	115	18	12	3	45	60	41	5	3	26-10	.317	.418	.457	.875	0	1.000
Major League totals (1 year)		2	2	0	0	0	0	0	0	0	0	0	0	0-0	.000	.000	.000	.000	0	1.000

LEFTY-RIGHTY SPLITS

vs.	Avg.	AB	H	2B	3B	HR	RBI	BB	SO	OBP	Slg.
L	.000	1	0	0	0	0	0	0	0	.000	.000
R	.000	1	0	0	0	0	0	0	0	.000	.000

PRINZ, BRET — P

PERSONAL: Born June 15, 1977, in Chicago Heights, Ill. ... 6-2/216. ... Throws right, bats right. ... Full name: Bret Randolph Prinz. ... High school: Centennial (Peoria, Ariz.). ... Junior college: Phoenix (Ariz.).

TRANSACTIONS/CAREER NOTES: Selected by Boston Red Sox organization in 30th round of 1997 free-agent draft; did not sign. ... Selected by Arizona Diamondbacks organization in 18th round of 1998 free-agent draft. ... On disabled list (April 1-July 24, 2003); included rehabilitation assignment to Tucson. ... Traded by Diamondbacks with OF David Dellucci and C Jon-Mark Sprowl to New York Yankees for OF Raul Mondesi and cash (July 29, 2003). ... Traded by Yankees to Los Angeles Angels of Anaheim for C Wilbert Nieves (March 29, 2005). ... On disabled list (April 11-September 1, 2005); included rehabilitation assignment to AZL Angels and Rancho Cucamonga. ... Released by Angels (September 1, 2005).

CAREER HITTING: 0-for-0 (.000), 0 R, 0 2B, 0 3B, 0 HR, 0 RBI.

Year Team (League)	W	L	Pct.	ERA	WHIP	G	GS	CG	ShO	Hld.	Sv.-Opp.	IP	H	R	ER	HR	BB-IBB	SO	Avg.
1998— Ariz. D'backs (Ariz.)	0	0	...	3.38	1.31	3	0	0	0	...	0-...	5.1	7	3	2	0	0-0	3	.304
— Lethbridge (Pion.)	4	2	.667	3.09	1.33	11	10	0	0	...	0-...	46.2	49	26	16	2	13-0	30	.262
1999— South Bend (Mid.)	6	10	.375	4.48	1.31	30	23	0	0	...	0-...	138.2	129	82	69	16	52-0	98	.247
2000— South Bend (Mid.)	1	0	1.000	0.00	0.41	6	0	0	0	...	1-...	7.1	2	2	0	0	1-0	10	.083
— El Paso (Texas)	9	1	.900	3.56	1.43	53	0	0	0	...	26-...	60.2	71	24	24	6	16-3	69	.293
2001— Tucson (PCL)	0	0	...	0.00	0.18	5	0	0	0	...	3-...	5.2	1	0	0	0	0-0	6	.056
— Arizona (N.L.)	4	1	.800	2.63	1.27	46	0	0	0	6	9-12	41.0	33	13	12	4	19-1	27	.220
2002— Arizona (N.L.)	0	2	.000	9.45	2.48	20	0	0	0	5	0-2	13.1	23	14	14	1	10-1	10	.404
— Tucson (PCL)	1	0	1.000	2.97	1.30	37	0	0	0	...	18-...	39.1	42	14	13	4	9-1	34	.269
— Lancaster (Calif.)	1	0	1.000	0.00	0.43	5	0	0	0	...	0-...	7.0	2	0	0	0	1-0	6	.083
2003— Arizona (N.L.)	0	0	...	0.00	2.00	1	0	0	0	0	0-0	1.0	1	0	0	0	1-1	1	.250
— Lancaster (Calif.)	0	0	...	0.00	0.00	1	1	0	0	...	0-...	1.0	0	0	0	0	0-0	2	.000
— El Paso (Texas)	0	0	...	4.50	2.00	2	0	0	0	...	0-...	2.0	3	1	1	0	1-0	2	.333
— Tucson (PCL)	0	0	.000	6.00	1.80	10	0	0	0	...	0-...	12.0	19	9	8	1	3-0	7	.345
— New York (A.L.)	0	0	...	18.00	4.50	2	0	0	0	0	0-0	2.0	6	4	4	1	3-1	2	.500
— Columbus (Int'l)	0	0	...	8.03	1.70	10	0	0	0	...	0-...	12.1	20	11	11	2	1-0	13	.364
2004— Columbus (Int'l)	3	1	.750	3.52	1.17	29	0	0	0	...	11-...	30.2	27	12	12	3	9-0	33	.259
— New York (A.L.)	1	0	1.000	5.08	1.48	26	0	0	0	1	0-0	28.1	28	17	16	5	14-0	22	.259
2005— Los Angeles (A.L.)	0	0	...	3.00	1.67	3	0	0	0	0	0-0	3.0	4	1	1	1	1-0	1	.308
— Ariz. Angels (Ariz.)	0	0	.000	12.00	2.33	2	2	0	0	0	0-0	3.0	5	5	4	1	2-0	6	.333
— Rancho Cuca. (Calif.)	0	0	...	1.80	1.00	2	0	0	0	0	0-0	5.0	3	1	1	0	3-0	6	.143
— Salt Lake (PCL)	0	0	...	5.59	1.86	5	0	0	0	0	1-1	9.2	12	7	6	1	6-0	8	.316
American League totals (3 years)	1	1	.500	5.67	1.68	31	0	0	0	1	0-0	33.1	38	22	21	7	18-1	25	.286
National League totals (3 years)	4	3	.571	4.23	1.57	67	0	0	0	11	9-14	55.1	57	27	26	5	30-3	38	.270
Major League totals (5 years)	5	4	.556	4.77	1.61	98	0	0	0	12	9-14	88.2	95	49	47	12	48-4	63	.276

LEFTY-RIGHTY SPLITS

vs.	Avg.	AB	H	2B	3B	HR	RBI	BB	SO	OBP	Slg.
L	.500	6	3	0	0	1	1	1	0	.571	.500
R	.143	7	1	0	0	1	0	1	0	.143	.571

PRIOR, MARK — P

PERSONAL: Born September 7, 1980, in San Diego. ... 6-5/230. ... Throws right, bats right. ... Full name: Mark William Prior. ... High school: University of San Diego High (Calif.). ... College: Southern California.

TRANSACTIONS/CAREER NOTES: Selected by New York Yankees organization in supplemental round ("sandwich" pick between first and second rounds, 43rd pick overall) of 1998 free-agent draft; did not sign; pick received as compensation for Yankees' failure to sign 1997 first-round pick of Tyrell Godwin. ... Selected by Chicago Cubs organization in first round (second pick overall) of 2001 free-agent draft. ... On disabled list (September 2-17, 2002; and July 12-August 4, 2003). ... On disabled list (March 26-June 4, 2004); included rehabilitation assignments to Lansing and Iowa. ... On disabled list (March 25-April 12 and May 28-June 26, 2005); included rehabilitation assignment to Iowa.

P

CAREER HITTING: 40-for-191 (.209), 19 R, 10 2B, 0 3B, 1 HR, 13 RBI.

SCOUTING REPORT **Throws:** Prior's fastball jumps out of his hand at 93-96 mph, and he also throws a big curve, a slurve and a changeup. **Tendencies:** The fastball is his best pitch because his easy delivery prevents batters from picking it up out of his hand, and it quickly gets on the hitter. Has excellent location on his fastball to both sides of the plate. Has a sharp, sweeping slurve. Can drop down against righthanded hitters when ahead in the count. Change shows some fade. **Outlook:** Prior's ceiling is unlimited, but injuries have prevented him from fulfilling his potential. Has an outstanding arm and the stuff to win a Cy Young Award. *Grade 8*

MARK PRIOR'S PITCHING ZONE

.216	.342	.246
.248	.387	.256
.234	.242	.171

LEFTY-RIGHTY SPLITS

vs.	Avg.	AB	H	2B	3B	HR	RBI	BB	SO	OBP	Slg.
L	.216	278	60	16	0	10	28	28	82	.291	.381
R	.236	352	83	14	0	15	41	31	106	.300	.403

Year Team (League)	W	L	Pct.	ERA	WHIP	G	GS	CG	ShO	Hld.	Sv.-Opp.	IP	H	R	ER	HR	BB-IBB	SO	Avg.
2002—West Tenn (Sou.)	4	1	.800	2.60	1.04	6	6	0	0	...	0-...	34.2	26	16	10	0	10-0	55	.198
—Iowa (PCL)	1	1	.500	1.65	1.29	3	3	0	0	...	0-...	16.1	13	10	3	1	8-0	24	.203
—Chicago (N.L.)	6	6	.500	3.32	1.17	19	19	1	0	0	0-0	116.2	98	45	43	14	38-0	147	.226
2003—Chicago (N.L.)	18	6	.750	2.43	1.10	30	30	3	1	0	0-0	211.1	183	67	57	15	50-4	245	.231
2004—Lansing (Midw.)	0	0	...	1.23	0.41	2	2	0	0	...	0-...	7.1	2	1	1	0	1-0	13	.087
—Iowa (PCL)	1	0	1.000	3.38	0.75	1	1	0	0	...	0-...	5.1	3	2	2	1	1-0	10	.158
—Chicago (N.L.)	6	4	.600	4.02	1.35	21	21	0	0	0	0-0	118.2	112	53	53	14	48-2	139	.251
2005—Iowa (PCL)	0	1	.000	10.50	1.67	1	1	0	0	0	0-0	6.0	9	7	7	0	1-0	7	.360
—Chicago (N.L.)	11	7	.611	3.67	1.21	27	27	1	0	0	0-0	166.2	143	73	68	25	59-2	188	.227
Major League totals (4 years)	**41**	**23**	**.641**	**3.24**	**1.19**	**97**	**97**	**5**	**1**	**0**	**0-0**	**613.1**	**536**	**238**	**221**	**68**	**195-8**	**719**	**.233**

DIVISION SERIES RECORD

Year Team (League)	W	L	Pct.	ERA	WHIP	G	GS	CG	ShO	Hld.	Sv.-Opp.	IP	H	R	ER	HR	BB-IBB	SO	Avg.
2003—Chicago (N.L.)	1	0	1.000	1.00	0.67	1	1	1	0	0	0-0	9.0	2	1	1	0	4-0	7	.071

CHAMPIONSHIP SERIES RECORD

Year Team (League)	W	L	Pct.	ERA	WHIP	G	GS	CG	ShO	Hld.	Sv.-Opp.	IP	H	R	ER	HR	BB-IBB	SO	Avg.
2003—Chicago (N.L.)	1	1	.500	3.14	1.33	2	2	0	0	0	0-0	14.1	14	8	5	2	5-0	11	.241

PROCTOR, SCOTT — P

PERSONAL: Born January 2, 1977, in Stuart, Fla. ... 6-1/198. ... Throws right, bats right. ... Full name: Scott Christopher Proctor. ... High school: Martin County (Stuart, Fla.). ... College: Florida State.
TRANSACTIONS/CAREER NOTES: Selected by New York Mets organization in 17th round of 1995 free-agent draft; did not sign. ... Selected by Los Angeles Dodgers organization in fifth round of 1998 free-agent draft. ... Traded by Dodgers with OF Bubba Crosby to New York Yankees for IF Robin Ventura (July 31, 2003).
CAREER HITTING: 0-for-0 (.000), 0 R, 0 2B, 0 3B, 0 HR, 0 RBI.

SCOTT PROCTOR'S PITCHING ZONE

.176	.250	.304
.241	.222	.370
.182	.600	.143

LEFTY-RIGHTY SPLITS

vs.	Avg.	AB	H	2B	3B	HR	RBI	BB	SO	OBP	Slg.
L	.315	73	23	3	1	6	15	10	9	.405	.630
R	.217	106	23	3	0	4	15	7	27	.270	.358

Year Team (League)	W	L	Pct.	ERA	WHIP	G	GS	CG	ShO	Hld.	Sv.-Opp.	IP	H	R	ER	HR	BB-IBB	SO	Avg.
1998—Yakima (N'west)	0	1	.000	10.80	2.00	3	1	0	0	...	2-...	5.0	9	8	6	1	1-0	4	.391
1999—Yakima (N'west)	4	2	.667	7.20	1.66	16	6	0	0	...	0-...	50.0	57	45	40	4	26-0	41	.286
2000—Vero Beach (FSL)	3	7	.300	5.16	1.65	35	5	0	0	...	1-...	89.0	93	65	51	13	54-1	70	.268
2001—Vero Beach (FSL)	6	4	.600	2.48	1.14	15	15	0	0	...	0-...	90.2	73	30	25	8	30-1	79	.226
—Jacksonville (Sou.)	4	3	.571	4.17	1.41	10	9	0	0	...	0-...	49.2	39	26	23	6	31-1	48	.220
2002—Jacksonville (Sou.)	7	9	.438	3.51	1.47	26	25	0	0	...	0-...	133.1	111	63	52	10	85-1	131	.227
2003—Jacksonville (Sou.)	1	2	.333	1.00	1.00	17	0	0	0	...	0-...	27.0	20	6	3	0	7-3	24	.208
—Las Vegas (PCL)	4	2	.667	3.66	1.22	24	0	0	0	...	1-...	39.1	35	17	16	2	13-3	35	.246
—Columbus (Int'l)	2	0	1.000	1.42	0.84	10	0	0	0	...	0-...	19.0	13	3	3	2	3-0	26	.197
2004—Columbus (Int'l)	2	3	.400	2.86	1.25	35	0	0	0	...	4-...	44.0	37	15	14	4	18-2	42	.233
—New York (A.L.)	2	1	.667	5.40	1.72	26	0	0	0	2	0-0	25.0	29	18	15	5	14-0	21	.284
2005—Columbus (Int'l)	6	1	.857	4.22	1.36	35	0	0	0	0	14-19	42.2	47	20	20	8	11-0	54	.280
—New York (A.L.)	1	0	1.000	6.04	1.41	29	1	0	0	0	0-0	44.2	46	32	30	10	17-4	36	.257
Major League totals (2 years)	**3**	**1**	**.750**	**5.81**	**1.52**	**55**	**1**	**0**	**0**	**2**	**0-0**	**69.2**	**75**	**50**	**45**	**15**	**31-4**	**57**	**.267**

DIVISION SERIES RECORD

Year Team (League)	W	L	Pct.	ERA	WHIP	G	GS	CG	ShO	Hld.	Sv.-Opp.	IP	H	R	ER	HR	BB-IBB	SO	Avg.
2005—New York (A.L.)	0	0	...	0.00	1.50	2	0	0	0	0	0-0	2.0	3	0	0	0	0-0	1	.375

PUFFER, BRANDON — P

PERSONAL: Born October 5, 1975, in Downey, Calif. ... 6-3/190. ... Throws right, bats right. ... Full name: Brandon Duane Puffer. ... High school: Capistrano Valley (Mission Viejo, Calif.).
TRANSACTIONS/CAREER NOTES: Selected by Minnesota Twins organization in 27th round of 1994 free-agent draft. ... Released by Twins (May 6, 1996). ... Signed by California Angels organization (May 28, 1996). ... Franchise renamed Anaheim Angels for 1997 season. ... Released by Angels (December 15, 1997). ... Signed as a free agent by Cincinnati Reds organization (January 14, 1998). ... Signed as a free agent by Colorado Rockies organization (November 18, 1999). ... Released by Rockies (May 18, 2000). ... Contract purchased by Houston Astros organization from Somerset of the independent Atlantic League (July 17, 2000). ... Released by Astros (November 19, 2003). ... Signed by San Diego Padres organization (January 7, 2004). ... Traded by Padres to Boston Red Sox for cash (July 2, 2004). ... Signed as a free agent by San Francisco Giants organization (December 14, 2004).
CAREER HITTING: 0-for-9 (.000), 0 R, 0 2B, 0 3B, 0 HR, 0 RBI.

LEFTY-RIGHTY SPLITS

vs.	Avg.	AB	H	2B	3B	HR	RBI	BB	SO	OBP	Slg.
L	.250	12	3	1	0	1	4	2	1	.357	.583
R	.353	17	6	3	0	1	5	0	0	.353	.706

Year Team (League)	W	L	Pct.	ERA	WHIP	G	GS	CG	ShO	Hld.	Sv.-Opp.	IP	H	R	ER	HR	BB-IBB	SO	Avg.
1994—GC Twins (GCL)	2	2	.500	3.06	1.47	18	0	0	0	...	2-...	35.1	33	18	12	1	19-0	40	.248

Year	Team (League)	W	L	Pct.	ERA	WHIP	G	GS	CG	ShO	Hld.	Sv.-Opp.	IP	H	R	ER	HR	BB-IBB	SO	Avg.
1995— GC Twins (GCL)		0	3	.000	2.88	1.23	14	5	0	0	...	1-...	40.2	29	21	13	0	21-0	35	.191
1996— Ariz. Angels (Ariz.)		0	1	.000	3.60	1.60	1	1	0	0	...	0-...	5.0	7	2	2	0	1-0	3	.318
— Boise (N'west)		2	0	1.000	4.45	1.25	16	0	0	0	...	1-...	30.1	27	19	15	3	11-0	22	.239
1997— Boise (N'west)		0	0	...	2.35	0.78	6	0	0	0	...	1-...	15.1	10	5	4	0	2-0	15	.169
— Cedar Rap. (Midw.)		0	0	...	2.60	1.04	10	0	0	0	...	0-...	17.1	8	6	5	0	10-0	11	.143
1998— Char., W.Va. (SAL)		2	7	.222	6.93	1.80	29	0	0	0	...	1-...	50.2	68	45	39	4	23-4	36	.325
— Chattanooga (Sou.)		0	0	...	3.12	0.58	7	0	0	0	...	0-...	8.2	2	3	3	2	3-0	6	.071
1999— Clinton (Midw.)		1	2	.333	1.99	1.22	59	0	0	0	...	34-...	63.1	53	20	14	2	24-3	60	.223
2000— Asheville (S. Atl.)		0	0	...	8.16	2.09	14	0	0	0	...	5-...	14.1	19	16	13	3	11-3	15	.322
— Somerset (Atl.)		2	2	.500	3.52	1.48	15	0	0	0	...	1-...	23.0	25	12	9	...	9-...	21	...
— Kissimmee (Fla. St.)		2	3	.400	1.27	1.36	18	0	0	0	...	9-...	21.1	18	6	3	0	11-4	26	.225
2001— Round Rock (Texas)		6	1	.857	2.07	1.05	56	0	0	0	...	8-...	82.2	52	19	19	4	35-2	91	.181
2002— New Orleans (PCL)		2	1	.667	1.80	0.80	11	0	0	0	...	0-...	15.0	8	3	3	1	4-0	13	.157
— Houston (N.L.)		3	3	.500	4.43	1.52	55	0	0	0	2	0-0	69.0	67	37	34	3	38-8	48	.258
2003— Houston (N.L.)		0	0	...	5.14	1.90	13	0	0	0	1	0-1	21.0	24	13	12	2	16-3	10	.300
— New Orleans (PCL)		7	3	.700	2.91	1.30	44	0	0	0	...	5-...	52.2	50	23	17	1	16-1	41	.253
2004— Portland (PCL)		1	1	.000	3.34	1.30	22	0	0	0	...	2-...	32.1	32	15	12	1	10-2	19	.254
— San Diego (N.L.)		0	1	.000	5.50	1.94	14	0	0	0	0	0-0	18.0	24	13	11	3	11-1	12	.320
— Pawtucket (Int'l)		3	2	.600	3.26	1.38	24	0	0	0	...	10-...	30.1	31	11	11	1	11-6	21	.263
2005— San Francisco (N.L.)		0	0	...	10.29	1.57	3	0	0	0	0	0-0	7.0	9	8	8	2	2-0	1	.310
— Fresno (PCL)		6	5	.545	5.52	1.47	54	0	0	0	5	0-5	73.1	85	54	45	9	23-3	48	.296
Major League totals (4 years)		3	4	.429	5.09	1.66	85	0	0	0	3	0-1	115.0	124	71	65	10	67-12	71	.279

PUJOLS, ALBERT   1B

PERSONAL: Born January 16, 1980, in Santo Domingo, Dominican Republic. ... 6-3/225. ... Bats right, throws right. ... Full name: Jose Albert Pujols. ... Name pronounced: POO-holes. ... High school: Fort Osage (Independence, Mo.). ... Junior college: Maple Woods (Mo.) Community College.

TRANSACTIONS/CAREER NOTES: Selected by St. Louis Cardinals organization in 13th round of 1999 free-agent draft. ... On suspended list (August 19-21, 2003).

HONORS: Named Most Valuable Player by Baseball Writers' Association of America (2005). ... Named N.L. Rookie Player of the Year by THE SPORTING NEWS (2001). ... Named N.L. Rookie of the Year by Baseball Writers' Association of America (2001). ... Named Major League Player of the Year by the SPORTING NEWS (2003).

2005 GAMES PLAYED BY POSITION (MLB): 1B—157.

SCOUTING REPORT *Offense:* Pujols simply is the best hitter in the game. Has an outstanding swing, hits without much of a stride and rarely is fooled. Has power to all fields and makes adjustments quickly. One of the few hitters who can keep the ball fair when pitched in off the plate. *Defense:* He is one of the league's best first basemen with good agility and increased mobility around the bag. Has good hands and footwork. Really improved his ability to field errant throws in the dirt and has very good instincts. Has a very strong arm and starts the double play well. Is very difficult to bunt on because he charges the ball well. *Outlook:* Pujols is one of the top three players in the game and continues to get better. Is on his way to Cooperstown. *Grade 10*

ALBERT PUJOLS'S HITTING ZONE

.389	.308	.320
.372	.574	.295
.333	.457	.242

LEFTY-RIGHTY SPLITS

vs.	Avg.	AB	H	2B	3B	HR	RBI	BB	SO	OBP	Slg.
L	.300	150	45	10	1	8	26	33	17	.424	.540
R	.340	441	150	28	1	33	91	64	48	.432	.633

								BATTING										FIELDING	
Year	Team (League)	Pos.	G	AB	R	H	2B	3B	HR	RBI	BB	SO	HBP	GDP	SB-CS	Avg.	OBP	SLG	OPS	E	Avg.
2000— Peoria (Midw.)		3B	109	395	62	128	32	6	17	84	38	37	5	10	2-4	.324	.389	.565	.953	19	.948
— Potomac (Carol.)		3B	21	81	11	23	8	1	2	10	7	8	0	3	1-1	.284	.341	.481	.822	3	.957
— Memphis (PCL)		3B-OF	3	14	1	3	1	0	0	2	1	2	0		1-0	.214	.267	.286	.552	0	1.000
2001— St. Louis (N.L.)		OF-3B-1B DH	161	590	112	194	47	4	37	130	69	93	9	21	1-3	.329	.403	.610	1.013	20	.967
2002— St. Louis (N.L.)		OF-1B-DH DH-SS	157	590	118	185	40	2	34	127	72	69	9	20	2-4	.314	.394	.561	.955	11	.975
2003— St. Louis (N.L.)		OF-1B-DH	157	591	*137	*212	*51	1	43	124	79	65	10	13	5-1	*.359	.439	.667	1.106	4	.993
2004— St. Louis (N.L.)		1B-DH	154	592	*133	196	51	2	46	123	84	52	7	21	5-5	.331	.415	.657	1.072	10	.994
2005— St. Louis (N.L.)		1B	161	591	*129	195	38	2	41	117	97	65	9	19	16-2	.330	.430	.609	1.039	14	.992
Major League totals (5 years)			790	2954	629	982	227	11	201	621	401	344	44	94	29-15	.332	.416	.621	1.037	59	.988

DIVISION SERIES RECORD

Year	Team (League)	Pos.	G	AB	R	H	2B	3B	HR	RBI	BB	SO	HBP	GDP	SB-CS	Avg.	OBP	SLG	OPS	E	Avg.
2001— St. Louis (N.L.)		1B-OF	5	18	1	2	0	0	1	2	2	2	0	1	0-0	.111	.200	.278	.478	1	.964
2002— St. Louis (N.L.)		OF-1B-3B	3	10	3	3	0	1	0	3	3	1	0	0	0-0	.300	.462	.500	.962	1	.833
2004— St. Louis (N.L.)		1B	4	15	4	5	0	0	2	5	3	0	0	1	0-0	.333	.444	.733	1.178	0	1.000
2005— St. Louis (N.L.)		1B	3	9	4	5	2	0	0	2	4	0	0		0-0	.556	.692	.778	1.470	0	1.000
Division series totals (4 years)			15	52	12	15	2	1	3	12	12	3	0	3	0-0	.288	.422	.538	.960	2	.982

CHAMPIONSHIP SERIES RECORD

Year	Team (League)	Pos.	G	AB	R	H	2B	3B	HR	RBI	BB	SO	HBP	GDP	SB-CS	Avg.	OBP	SLG	OPS	E	Avg.
2002— St. Louis (N.L.)		OF	5	19	2	5	1	0	1	2	2	5	1		0-0	.263	.364	.474	.837	1	1.000
2004— St. Louis (N.L.)		1B	7	28	10	14	0	0	4	9	4	3	0		0-0	.500	.563	1.000	1.563	0	1.000
2005— St. Louis (N.L.)		1B	6	23	3	7	2	0	2	6	1	3	0		0-0	.304	.320	.565	.885	0	1.000
Champ. series totals (3 years)			18	70	15	26	3	0	7	17	7	11	1		0-0	.371	.430	.714	1.145	0	1.000

WORLD SERIES RECORD

Year	Team (League)	Pos.	G	AB	R	H	2B	3B	HR	RBI	BB	SO	HBP	GDP	SB-CS	Avg.	OBP	SLG	OPS	E	Avg.
2004— St. Louis (N.L.)		1B	4	15	1	5	2	0	0	0	1	3	1		0-0	.333	.412	.467	.878	0	1.000

ALL-STAR GAME RECORD

	G	AB	R	H	2B	3B	HR	RBI	BB	SO	HBP	GDP	SB-CS	Avg.	OBP	SLG	OPS	E	Avg.
All-Star Game totals (4 years)	4	8	1	4	2	0	0	3	1	0	0		0-0	.500	.556	.750	1.306	0	1.000

P

PULSIPHER, BILL — P

PERSONAL: Born October 9, 1973, in Fort Benning, Ga. ... 6-3/200. ... Throws left, bats left. ... Full name: William Thomas Pulsipher. ... Name pronounced: PUL-sih-fir. ... High school: Fairfax (Va.).

TRANSACTIONS/CAREER NOTES: Selected by New York Mets organization in second round of free-agent draft (June 3, 1991). ... On disabled list (March 22, 1996-entire season). ... On disabled list (March 24-May 3, 1997); included rehabilitation assignment to Norfolk. ... Traded by Mets to Milwaukee Brewers for 3B Mike Kinkade (July 31, 1998). ... On disabled list (April 19-July 3, 1999); included rehabilitation assignment to Louisville. ... Traded by Brewers to Mets for IF Luis Lopez (January 21, 2000). ... Traded by Mets to Arizona Diamondbacks for IF/OF Lenny Harris (June 2, 2000). ... Signed by Tampa Bay Devil Rays organization (November 2, 2000). ... Released by Devil Rays (March 23, 2001). ... Signed by Boston Red Sox organization (April 18, 2001). ... Claimed on waivers by Chicago White Sox (August 23, 2001). ... Signed as a free agent by Texas Rangers organization (December 26, 2002). ... Signed by New York Yankees organization (April 17, 2002). ... Released by Yankees (May 23, 2002). ... Signed by Baltimore Orioles organization (December 2, 2002). ... Contract purchased by Seattle Mariners organization from Long Island of the independent Atlantic League (August 4, 2004). ... Released by Mariners (September 13, 2004). ... Signed by St. Louis Cardinals organization (February 15, 2005). ... On disabled list (April 12-May 5, 2005); included rehabilitation assignment to Memphis.

CAREER HITTING: 10-for-81 (.123), 7 R, 2 2B, 0 3B, 0 HR, 4 RBI.

LEFTY-RIGHTY SPLITS

vs.	Avg.	AB	H	2B	3B	HR	RBI	BB	SO	OBP	Slg.
L	.167	6	1	0	0	0	1	0	1	.167	.167
R	.500	8	4	0	0	0	2	2	0	.545	.500

Year — Team (League)	W	L	Pct.	ERA	WHIP	G	GS	CG	ShO	Hld.	Sv.-Opp.	IP	H	R	ER	HR	BB-IBB	SO	Avg.
1992— Pittsfield (NYP)	6	3	.667	2.84	1.52	14	14	0	0	...	0-...	95.0	88	40	30	3	56-0	83	.249
1993— Capital City (SAL)	2	3	.400	2.08	1.05	6	6	1	0	...	0-...	44.0	34	17	10	1	12-0	29	.213
— St. Lucie (Fla. St.)	7	3	.700	2.24	1.05	13	13	3	1	...	0-...	97.0	63	27	24	2	39-0	102	.190
1994— Binghamton (East.)	14	9	.609	3.22	1.33	28	28	5	1	...	0-...	201.0	179	90	72	18	89-2	171	.239
1995— Norfolk (Int'l)	6	4	.600	3.14	1.28	13	13	4	2	...	0-...	91.2	84	36	32	3	33-0	63	.251
— New York (N.L.)	5	7	.417	3.98	1.32	17	17	2	0	...	0-...	126.2	122	58	56	11	45-...	81	.255
1996— New York (N.L.)			Did not play.																
1997— Norfolk (Int'l)	0	5	.000	7.81	2.20	8	5	0	0	...	0-...	27.2	23	29	24	1	38-0	18	.230
— St. Lucie (Fla. St.)	1	4	.200	5.89	1.75	12	7	0	0	...	0-...	36.2	29	27	24	1	35-0	35	.213
— GC Mets (GCL)	0	0	...	1.80	0.80	2	2	0	0	...	0-...	5.0	3	1	1	0	1-0	4	.176
— Binghamton (East.)	0	0	...	1.42	1.42	10	0	0	0	...	0-...	12.2	11	3	2	0	7-1	12	.239
1998— Norfolk (Int'l)	7	5	.583	3.96	1.52	14	14	1	0	...	0-...	87.0	91	50	38	12	41-1	58	.273
— New York (N.L.)	0	0	...	6.91	1.95	15	1	0	0	...	0-...	14.1	23	11	11	2	5-...	13	.371
— Milwaukee (N.L.)	3	4	.429	4.66	1.53	11	10	0	0	...	0-...	58.0	63	30	30	6	26-...	38	.289
1999— Milwaukee (N.L.)	5	6	.455	5.98	1.56	19	16	0	0	0	0-0	87.1	100	65	58	19	36-...	42	.287
— Louisville (Int'l)	0	2	.000	4.28	1.46	6	6	0	0	...	0-...	28.0	22	14	13	1	19-0	21	.220
2000— Norfolk (Int'l)	2	3	.400	6.55	1.70	7	5	0	0	...	0-...	33.0	41	28	24	5	15-1	25	.308
— New York (N.L.)	0	2	.000	12.15	2.70	2	2	0	0	0	0-0	6.2	12	9	9	1	6-...	7	.387
— Tucson (PCL)	3	8	.273	3.95	1.56	13	13	0	0	...	0-...	70.2	73	39	31	7	37-0	51	.272
— Ariz. D'backs (Ariz.)	0	0	...	4.50	1.33	3	3	0	0	...	0-...	6.0	8	3	3	0	0-0	4	.348
2001— Pawtucket (Int'l)	1	1	.500	2.87	1.16	24	0	0	0	...	10-...	32.0	27	12	10	1	10-1	23	.229
— Boston (A.L.)	0	0	...	5.32	1.77	23	0	0	0	4	0-0	22.0	25	15	13	3	14-...	16	.294
— Chicago (A.L.)	0	0	...	7.88	2.25	14	0	0	0	2	0-0	8.0	11	8	7	2	7-...	4	.314
2002— Columbus (Int'l)	0	0	...	14.73	2.73	6	0	0	0	...	0-...	3.2	10	6	6	1	0-0	4	.500
2003— Ottawa (Int'l)	4	5	.444	5.63	1.60	51	0	0	0	...	3-...	55.0	59	43	34	3	29-5	43	.274
2004— Long Island (Atl.)	9	5	.643	3.67	1.34	18	17	0	4	...	0-...	116.0	121	58	47	9	34-0	85	.268
— Tacoma (PCL)	1	1	.500	2.92	1.31	2	2	0	0	...	0-...	13.0	13	5	4	1	4-0	5	.271
2005— St. Louis (N.L.)	0	0	...	6.75	1.75	5	0	0	0	0	0-0	4.0	5	3	3	0	2-1	1	.357
— Springfield (Texas)	1	0	1.000	2.70	1.35	1	1	0	0	0	0-0	6.2	8	2	2	2	1-0	7	.296
— Memphis (PCL)	6	7	.462	4.49	1.46	25	18	0	0	0	0-0	124.1	152	72	62	17	29-2	96	.301
American League totals (1 year)	0	0	...	6.00	1.90	37	0	0	0	6	0-0	30.0	36	23	20	5	21-...	20	.300
National League totals (5 years)	13	19	.406	5.06	1.50	69	46	2	0	0	0-0	297.0	325	176	167	39	120-1	182	.825
Major League totals (6 years)	13	19	.406	5.15	1.54	106	46	2	0	6	0-0	327.0	361	199	187	44	141-1	202	.702

PUNTO, NICK — 2B/SS

PERSONAL: Born November 8, 1977, in San Diego. ... 5-9/176. ... Bats both, throws right. ... Full name: Nicholas Paul Punto. ... Name pronounced: POON-toh. ... High school: Trabuco Hills (Mission Vieh Vijo, Calif.). ... Junior college: Saddleback (Calif.) Community College.

TRANSACTIONS/CAREER NOTES: Selected by Minnesota Twins organization in 33rd round of 1997 free-agent draft; did not sign. ... Selected by Philadelphia Phillies organization in 21st round of 1998 free-agent draft. ... Traded by Phillies with RHP Carlos Silva and a player to be named to Minnesota Twins for LHP Eric Milton (December 3, 2003); Twins acquired P Bobby Korecky to complete deal (December 16, 2003). ... On disabled list (May 9-June 30 and July 27, 2004-remainder of season); included rehabilitation assignment to Quad Cities. ... On disabled list (June 3-July 3, 2005); included rehabilitation assignment to Rochester.

2005 GAMES PLAYED BY POSITION (MLB): 2B—73, SS—34, 3B—12, DH—5, OF—3.

NICK PUNTO'S HITTING ZONE

.333	.533	.182
.179	.381	.299
.194	.222	.222

LEFTY-RIGHTY SPLITS

vs.	Avg.	AB	H	2B	3B	HR	RBI	BB	SO	OBP	Slg.
L	.210	81	17	5	0	0	2	8	17	.278	.272
R	.246	313	77	13	4	4	24	28	69	.307	.351

Year — Team (League)	Pos.	G	AB	R	H	2B	3B	HR	RBI	BB	SO	HBP	GDP	SB-CS	Avg.	OBP	SLG	OPS	E	Avg.
1998— Batavia (NY-Penn)	2B-SS	72	279	51	69	9	4	1	20	42	48	1	4	19-7	.247	.347	.319	.666	27	.924
1999— Clearwater (FSL)	SS	106	400	65	122	18	6	1	48	67	53	3	13	16-6	.305	.404	.388	.792	24	.958
2000— Reading (East.)	SS	121	456	77	116	15	4	5	47	69	71	2	5	33-10	.254	.351	.338	.689	20	.963
2001— Scran./W.B. (I.L.)	SS	123	463	57	106	19	5	1	39	68	114	0	15	33-9	.229	.327	.298	.625	21	.964
— Philadelphia (N.L.)	SS	4	5	0	2	0	0	0	0	0	0	0	0	0-0	.400	.400	.400	.800	1	1.000
2002— Philadelphia (N.L.)	2B-SS	9	6	0	1	0	0	0	0	0	3	0	0	0-0	.167	.167	.167	.333	1	.750
— Scran./W.B. (I.L.)	SS	115	443	74	120	12	5	1	29	76	84	2	5	42-8	.271	.378	.327	.705	19	.967
2003— Scran./W.B. (I.L.)	SS	25	111	19	35	7	1	0	9	7	13	0	0	7-1	.315	.353	.396	.749	4	.969
— Philadelphia (N.L.)	2B-3B-SS	64	92	14	20	2	0	1	5	7	22	0	0	2-1	.217	.273	.272	.544	2	.980
2004— Quad Cities (Mid.)	SS-2B-3B	4	16	4	7	3	0	1	6	2	2	0	0	1-0	.438	.500	.688	1.188	0	1.000
— Minnesota (A.L.)	2B-SS-DH	38	91	17	23	0	0	2	12	12	19	0	2	5-3	.253	.340	.319	.658	1	.991
2005— Rochester (Int'l)	2B	4	15	2	3	1	0	0	1	2	2	0	0	0-0	.200	.294	.267	.561	2	.900
— Minnesota (A.L.)	2B-SS-3B DH-OF	112	394	45	94	18	4	4	26	36	86	0	9	13-8	.239	.301	.335	.636	9	.981
American League totals (2 years)		150	485	62	117	18	4	6	38	48	105	0	11	19-8	.241	.308	.332	.640	10	.983
National League totals (3 years)		77	103	14	23	2	0	1	4	7	25	0	0	2-1	.223	.273	.272	.545	3	.972
Major League totals (5 years)		227	588	76	140	20	4	7	42	55	130	0	11	21-9	.238	.302	.321	.624	13	.981

PUTZ, J.J.   P

PERSONAL: Born February 22, 1977, in Trenton, Mich. ... 6-5/220. ... Throws right, bats right. ... Full name: Joseph Jason Putz. ... Name pronounced: pootz. ... High school: Trenton (Mich.). ... College: Michigan.

TRANSACTIONS/CAREER NOTES: Selected by Chicago White Sox organization in third round of 1995 free-agent draft; did not sign. ... Selected by Minnesota Twins organization in 17th round of 1998 free-agent draft; did not sign. ... Selected by Seattle Mariners organization in sixth round of 1999 free-agent draft.

CAREER HITTING: 0-for-0 (.000), 0 R, 0 2B, 0 3B, 0 HR, 0 RBI.

SCOUTING REPORT *Throws:* Putz has a fastball at 92-95 mph, a forkball and a slider. *Tendencies:* He throws from three-quarters from the stretch and has very good life on a plus fastball, which is heavy and bores in on righthanders. Is not afraid to pitch inside. Slider is quick with a sharp bite, but it occasionally gets too big. Will judiciously use his forkball as an out pitch, as it's more effective against righthanders. *Outlook:* A reliable part of the bullpen in 2005, Putz is the Mariners' closer of the future. ***Grade 7.2***

J.J. PUTZ'S PITCHING ZONE

.353	.154	.238
.515	.222	.342
.091	.214	.105

LEFTY-RIGHTY SPLITS

vs.	Avg.	AB	H	2B	3B	HR	RBI	BB	SO	OBP	Slg.
L	.321	106	34	4	0	6	22	9	26	.368	.528
R	.197	122	24	2	0	2	12	14	19	.288	.262

Year	Team (League)	W	L	Pct.	ERA	WHIP	G	GS	CG	ShO	Hld.	Sv.-Opp.	IP	H	R	ER	HR	BB-IBB	SO	Avg.
1999— Everett (N'west)		0	0	...	4.84	1.52	10	0	0	0	...	2-...	22.1	23	13	12	2	11-1	17	.288
2000— Wisconsin (Midw.)		12	6	.667	3.15	1.35	26	25	3	2	...	0-...	142.2	130	71	50	4	63-2	105	.247
2001— San Antonio (Texas)		7	9	.438	3.83	1.38	27	26	0	0	...	0-...	148.0	145	80	63	11	59-2	135	.259
2002— San Antonio (Texas)		3	10	.231	3.64	1.33	15	15	1	1	...	0-...	84.0	84	41	34	7	28-0	60	.264
— Tacoma (PCL)		2	4	.333	3.83	1.33	9	9	0	0	...	0-...	54.0	51	23	23	4	21-0	39	.258
2003— Tacoma (PCL)		0	3	.000	2.51	1.20	41	0	0	0	...	11-...	86.0	69	30	24	4	34-0	60	.225
— Seattle (A.L.)		0	0	...	4.91	1.91	3	0	0	0	...	0-0	3.2	4	2	2	0	3-0	3	.267
2004— Tacoma (PCL)		0	0	...	4.32	1.56	7	0	0	0	...	3-...	8.1	10	5	4	2	3-0	13	.294
— Seattle (A.L.)		0	3	.000	4.71	1.43	54	0	0	0	3	9-13	63.0	66	35	33	10	24-4	47	.274
2005— Seattle (A.L.)		6	5	.545	3.60	1.35	64	0	0	0	21	1-4	60.0	58	27	24	8	23-2	45	.254
Major League totals (3 years)		6	8	.429	4.19	1.41	121	0	0	0	24	10-17	126.2	128	64	59	18	50-6	95	.264

QUALLS, CHAD   P

PERSONAL: Born August 17, 1978, in Lomita, Calif. ... 6-5/220. ... Throws right, bats right. ... Full name: Chad Michael Qualls. ... High school: Narbonne (Harbor City, Calif.). ... Junior college: Los Angeles Harbor. ... College: Nevada.

TRANSACTIONS/CAREER NOTES: Selected by Toronto Blue Jays organization in 52nd round of 1997 free-agent draft; did not sign. ... Selected by Houston Astros organization in second round of 2000 free-agent draft.

CAREER HITTING: 0-for-2 (.000), 0 R, 0 2B, 0 3B, 0 HR, 0 RBI.

SCOUTING REPORT *Throws:* Qualls has a fastball that ranges from 91-94 mph, and a good slider. *Tendencies:* He basically is a two-pitch pitcher who is extremely aggressive attacking the zone. Throws an extremely heavy sinking fastball that bores in on righthanders. Slider is very sharp and has good tilt, giving him a pitch he can get on the other side of the plate. Command has improved as has his ability to maintain his release point. *Outlook:* Qualls is becoming one of the game's more dependable setup men, and he has the stuff to eventually be a closer. ***Grade 8.3***

CHAD QUALLS' PITCHING ZONE

.500	.375	.267
.315	.214	.308
.115	.429	.143

LEFTY-RIGHTY SPLITS

vs.	Avg.	AB	H	2B	3B	HR	RBI	BB	SO	OBP	Slg.
L	.218	133	29	2	1	2	10	12	21	.284	.293
R	.275	160	44	7	0	5	20	11	39	.339	.413

Year	Team (League)	W	L	Pct.	ERA	WHIP	G	GS	CG	ShO	Hld.	Sv.-Opp.	IP	H	R	ER	HR	BB-IBB	SO	Avg.
2001— Michigan (Midw.)		15	6	.714	3.72	1.11	26	26	3	2	...	0-...	162.0	149	77	67	8	31-0	125	.239
2002— Round Rock (Texas)		6	13	.316	4.36	1.48	29	29	0	0	...	0-...	163.0	174	92	79	9	67-3	142	.273
2003— Round Rock (Texas)		8	11	.421	3.85	1.34	28	28	3	2	...	0-...	175.1	174	85	75	12	61-0	132	.264
2004— New Orleans (PCL)		3	6	.333	5.57	1.54	32	14	1	0	...	1-...	106.2	134	69	66	8	30-3	72	.312
— Houston (N.L.)		4	0	1.000	3.55	1.27	25	0	0	0	9	1-2	33.0	34	13	13	3	8-1	24	.266
2005— Houston (N.L.)		6	4	.600	3.28	1.21	77	0	0	0	22	0-0	79.2	73	33	29	7	23-2	60	.249
Major League totals (2 years)		10	4	.714	3.36	1.22	102	0	0	0	31	1-2	112.2	107	46	42	10	31-3	84	.254

DIVISION SERIES RECORD

Year	Team (League)	W	L	Pct.	ERA	WHIP	G	GS	CG	ShO	Hld.	Sv.-Opp.	IP	H	R	ER	HR	BB-IBB	SO	Avg.
2004— Houston (N.L.)		0	0	...	6.75	1.25	4	0	0	0	1	0-1	4.0	4	3	3	1	1-0	3	.250
2005— Houston (N.L.)		0	0	...	6.00	2.33	2	0	0	0	0	0-0	3.0	5	2	2	0	2-1	1	.455
Division series totals (2 years)		0	0	...	6.43	1.71	6	0	0	0	1	0-1	7.0	9	5	5	1	3-1	4	.333

CHAMPIONSHIP SERIES RECORD

Year	Team (League)	W	L	Pct.	ERA	WHIP	G	GS	CG	ShO	Hld.	Sv.-Opp.	IP	H	R	ER	HR	BB-IBB	SO	Avg.
2004— Houston (N.L.)		0	1	.000	11.25	2.50	2	0	0	0	0	0-0	4.0	8	5	5	0	2-1	4	.444
2005— Houston (N.L.)		1	0	1.000	0.00	0.00	4	0	0	0	1	0-0	4.2	0	0	0	0	0-0	4	.000
Champ. series totals (2 years)		1	1	.500	5.19	1.15	6	0	0	0	1	0-0	8.2	8	5	5	0	2-1	8	.250

WORLD SERIES RECORD

Year	Team (League)	W	L	Pct.	ERA	WHIP	G	GS	CG	ShO	Hld.	Sv.-Opp.	IP	H	R	ER	HR	BB-IBB	SO	Avg.
2005— Houston (N.L.)		0	0	...	1.69	0.94	3	0	0	0	0	0-1	5.1	3	1	1	1	2-1	5	.167

QUANTRILL, PAUL — P

PERSONAL: Born November 3, 1968, in London, Ontario. ... 6-1/198. ... Throws right, bats left. ... Full name: Paul John Quantrill. ... Name pronounced: KWAN-trill. ... High school: Okemos (Mich.). ... College: Wisconsin.

TRANSACTIONS/CAREER NOTES: Selected by Los Angeles Dodgers organization in 26th round of June 1986 free-agent draft; did not sign. ... Selected by Boston Red Sox organization in sixth round of 1989 free-agent draft. ... Traded by Red Sox with OF Billy Hatcher to Philadelphia Phillies for OF Wes Chamberlain and P Mike Sullivan (May 31, 1994). ... Traded by Phillies to Toronto Blue Jays for 3B Howard Battle and P Ricardo Jordan (December 6, 1995). ... On disabled list (March 27-June 15, 1999); included rehabilitation assignments to Dunedin and Syracuse. ... Traded by Blue Jays with SS Cesar Izturis to Los Angeles Dodgers for Ps Luke Prokopec and Chad Ricketts (December 13, 2001). ... Signed as a free agent by New York Yankees (December 17, 2003). ... On suspended list (May 31-June 3, 2005). ... Traded by Yankees to San Diego Padres for Ps Darrell May and Tim Redding (July 2, 2005). ... Released by Padres (September 1, 2005). ... Signed as free agent by Florida Marlins (September 9, 2005).

CAREER HITTING: 7-for-67 (.104), 5 R, 0 2B, 0 3B, 0 HR, 0 RBI.

PAUL QUANTRILL'S PITCHING ZONE

.235	.125	.167
.339	.500	.353
.333	.176	.423

LEFTY-RIGHTY SPLITS

vs.	Avg.	AB	H	2B	3B	HR	RBI	BB	SO	OBP	Slg.
L	.336	125	42	5	1	4	27	9	19	.373	.488
R	.325	157	51	12	0	4	29	5	17	.341	.478

Year	Team (League)	W	L	Pct.	ERA	WHIP	G	GS	CG	ShO	Hld.	Sv.-Opp.	IP	H	R	ER	HR	BB-IBB	SO	Avg.
1989— GC Red Sox (GCL)		0	0	...	0.00	0.40	2	0	0	0	...	2-...	5.0	2	0	0	0	0-0	5	.111
—Elmira (N.Y.-Penn)		5	4	.556	3.43	1.34	20	7	5	0	...	2-...	76.0	90	37	29	5	12-2	55	.299
1990— Winter Haven (FSL)		2	5	.286	4.14	1.14	7	7	1	0	...	0-...	45.2	46	24	21	3	6-0	14	.264
—New Britain (East.)		7	11	.389	3.53	1.29	22	22	1	1	...	0-...	132.2	148	65	52	3	23-2	53	.290
1991— New Britain (East.)		2	1	.667	2.06	1.14	5	5	1	0	...	0-...	35.0	32	14	8	2	8-0	18	.248
—Pawtucket (Int'l)		10	7	.588	4.45	1.28	25	23	6	2	...	0-...	155.2	169	81	77	14	30-1	75	.282
1992— Pawtucket (Int'l)		6	8	.429	4.46	1.37	19	18	4	1	...	0-...	119.0	143	63	59	16	20-1	56	.300
—Boston (A.L.)		2	3	.400	2.19	1.42	27	0	0	0	3	1-5	49.1	55	18	12	1	15-5	24	.288
1993— Boston (A.L.)		6	12	.333	3.91	1.41	49	14	1	1	3	1-2	138.0	151	73	60	13	44-14	66	.279
1994— Boston (A.L.)		1	1	.500	3.52	1.30	17	0	0	0	2	0-2	23.0	25	10	9	4	5-1	15	.278
—Philadelphia (N.L.)		2	2	.500	6.00	1.63	18	1	0	0	1	1-2	30.0	39	21	20	3	10-3	13	.331
—Scran./W.B. (I.L.)		3	3	.500	3.47	1.07	8	8	1	1	...	0-...	57.0	55	25	22	5	6-0	36	.253
1995— Philadelphia (N.L.)		11	12	.478	4.67	1.43	33	29	0	0	0	0-0	179.1	212	102	93	20	44-3	103	.295
1996— Toronto (A.L.)		5	14	.263	5.43	1.66	38	20	0	0	1	0-2	134.1	172	90	81	27	51-3	86	.317
1997— Toronto (A.L.)		6	7	.462	1.94	1.36	77	0	0	0	16	5-10	88.0	103	25	19	5	17-3	56	.297
1998— Toronto (A.L.)		3	4	.429	2.59	1.38	82	0	0	0	* 27	7-14	80.0	88	26	23	1	1-0	2	.285
1999— Dunedin (Fla. St.)		0	1	.000	4.50	1.00	5	4	0	0	...	0-...	6.0	5	3	3	1	1-0	2	.238
—Syracuse (Int'l)		0	0	...	0.00	0.50	2	2	0	0	...	0-...	2.0	1	0	0	0	0-0	1	.167
—Toronto (A.L.)		3	2	.600	3.33	1.44	41	0	0	0	8	0-4	48.2	53	19	18	5	17-1	28	.282
2000— Toronto (A.L.)		2	5	.286	4.52	1.49	68	0	0	0	13	1-3	83.2	100	45	42	7	25-1	47	.298
2001— Toronto (A.L.)		11	2	.846	3.04	1.18	80	0	0	0	21	2-9	83.0	86	29	28	6	12-7	58	.274
2002— Los Angeles (N.L.)		5	4	.556	2.70	1.37	86	0	0	0	* 33	1-3	76.2	80	27	23	1	25-7	53	.267
2003— Los Angeles (N.L.)		2	5	.286	1.75	0.98	* 89	0	0	0	28	1-5	77.1	61	18	15	2	15-2	44	.227
2004— New York (A.L.)		7	3	.700	4.72	1.51	* 86	0	0	0	22	1-5	95.1	124	54	50	5	20-9	37	.316
2005— New York (A.L.)		1	0	1.000	6.75	1.72	22	0	0	0	0	0-1	32.0	48	24	24	5	7-2	11	.361
—San Diego (N.L.)		1	1	.500	3.41	1.23	22	0	0	0	1	0-0	31.2	37	13	12	2	2-1	24	.294
—Florida (N.L.)		0	0	...	8.44	2.44	6	0	0	0	0	0-0	5.1	8	7	5	1	5-0	1	.348
American League totals (11 years)		47	53	.470	3.85	1.45	587	34	1	1	116	18-57	855.1	1005	413	366	83	235-52	487	.297
National League totals (5 years)		21	25	.457	3.78	1.34	254	30	0	0	63	3-10	400.1	437	188	168	29	101-16	238	.281
Major League totals (14 years)		68	78	.466	3.83	1.42	841	64	1	1	179	21-67	1255.2	1442	601	534	112	336-68	725	.292

DIVISION SERIES RECORD

Year	Team (League)	W	L	Pct.	ERA	WHIP	G	GS	CG	ShO	Hld.	Sv.-Opp.	IP	H	R	ER	HR	BB-IBB	SO	Avg.
2004— New York (A.L.)		1	0	1.000	0.00	1.00	2	0	0	0	0	0-0	2.0	2	0	0	0	0-0	1	.250

CHAMPIONSHIP SERIES RECORD

Year	Team (League)	W	L	Pct.	ERA	WHIP	G	GS	CG	ShO	Hld.	Sv.-Opp.	IP	H	R	ER	HR	BB-IBB	SO	Avg.
2004— New York (A.L.)		0	1	.000	5.40	2.40	4	0	0	0	0	0-0	3.1	8	2	2	1	0-0	2	.444

ALL-STAR GAME RECORD

		W	L	Pct.	ERA	WHIP	G	GS	CG	ShO	Hld.	Sv.-Opp.	IP	H	R	ER	HR	BB-IBB	SO	Avg.
All-Star Game totals (1 year)		0	0	...	27.00	6.00						0-0	0.1	2	1	1	0	0-0	0	.667

QUINLAN, ROBB — 3B/1B

PERSONAL: Born March 17, 1977, in St. Paul, Minn. ... 6-1/200. ... Bats right, throws right. ... Full name: Robb William Quinlan. ... High school: Hill-Murray (Maplewood, Minn.). ... College: Minnesota. ... Brother of Tom Quinlan, infielder with three major league teams (1990, 1992, 1994 and 1996).

TRANSACTIONS/CAREER NOTES: Selected by California Angels organization in 33rd round of 1995 free-agent draft; did not sign. ... Selected by Anaheim Angels organization in 10th round of 1999 free-agent draft. ... On disabled list (August 16, 2004-remainder of season). ... Angels franchise renamed Los Angeles Angels of Anaheim for 2005 season. ... On disabled list (July 1-August 23, 2005); included rehabilitation assignments to AZL Angels and Salt Lake.

2005 GAMES PLAYED BY POSITION (MLB): 3B—33, 1B—9, OF—6.

SCOUTING REPORT Quinlan is a good contact hitter with a short stroke and occasional power. Hits line drives to all parts of the field but doesn't produce enough runs to be a regular. Can be jammed. Doesn't have the quickness to play third base and has limited range. Has an accurate arm. **Grade 5.5**

ROBB QUINLAN'S HITTING ZONE

.143	.600	.250
.286	.462	.238
.250	.167	.286

LEFTY-RIGHTY SPLITS

vs.	Avg.	AB	H	2B	3B	HR	RBI	BB	SO	OBP	Slg.
L	.289	83	24	6	0	5	13	3	10	.318	.542
R	.137	51	7	2	0	0	1	4	16	.200	.176

Year	Team (League)	Pos.	G	AB	R	H	2B	3B	HR	RBI	BB	SO	HBP	GDP	SB-CS	Avg.	OBP	SLG	OPS	E	Avg.
1999— Boise (N'west)		3B-2B-1B	73	295	51	95	20	1	9	77	35	52	4	5	5-3	.322	.400	.488	.888	27	.892
2000— Lake Elsinore (Calif.)		1B-OF	127	482	79	153	35	5	5	85	67	82	2	7	6-4	.317	.396	.442	.838	16	.986

Year	Team (League)	Pos.	G	AB	R	H	2B	3B	HR	RBI	BB	SO	HBP	GDP	SB-CS	Avg.	OBP	SLG	OPS	E	Avg.
2001— Arkansas (Texas)	1B-OF	129	492	82	145	33	7	14	79	53	84	6	12	0-4	.295	.366	.476	.841	8	.993
2002— Salt Lake (PCL)	OF-1B	136	528	95	176	31	13	20	112	41	93	4	16	8-2	.333	.376	.555	.931	3	.988
2003— Salt Lake (PCL)	1B-OF-DH	95	393	55	122	18	4	9	68	25	59	1	9	10-3	.310	.352	.445	.797	0	1.000
— Anaheim (A.L.)	1B-DH-OF	38	94	13	27	4	2	0	6	6	16	0	3	1-2	.287	.330	.372	.702	2	.988
2004— Salt Lake (PCL)	1B-3B-OF	27	108	15	32	9	1	2	17	14	14	0	2	1-1	.296	.377	.454	.831	3	.987
— Anaheim (A.L.) DH	3B-1B-OF	56	160	23	55	14	0	5	23	14	26	2	1	3-1	.344	.401	.525	.926	1	.994
2005— Ariz. Angels (Ariz.)	DH-1B-3B	4	12	3	3	2	0	0	3	2	3	0	0	1-0	.250	.333	.417	.750	0	1.000
— Salt Lake (PCL)	1B-3B-DH	15	60	13	23	6	0	1	4	2	8	0	4	0-0	.383	.403	.533	.937	1	.986
— Los Angeles (A.L.)	3B-1B-OF	54	134	17	31	8	0	5	14	7	26	1	4	0-1	.231	.273	.403	.676	7	.943
Major League totals (3 years)		148	388	53	113	26	2	10	41	27	68	3	8	4-4	.291	.340	.446	.786	10	.978

DIVISION SERIES RECORD

Year	Team (League)	Pos.	G	AB	R	H	2B	3B	HR	RBI	BB	SO	HBP	GDP	SB-CS	Avg.	OBP	SLG	OPS	E	Avg.
2005— Los Angeles (A.L.)	3B-DH	2	2	0	1	0	0	0	0	0	0	0	0	0-0	.500	.500	.500	1.000	0	1.000

CHAMPIONSHIP SERIES RECORD

Year	Team (League)	Pos.	G	AB	R	H	2B	3B	HR	RBI	BB	SO	HBP	GDP	SB-CS	Avg.	OBP	SLG	OPS	E	Avg.
2005— Los Angeles (A.L.)	3B	1	3	1	1	0	0	1	1	0	2	0	0	0-0	.333	.333	1.333	1.667	0	1.000

QUINTANILLA, OMAR   SS

PERSONAL: Born October 24, 1981, in El Paso, Texas. ... 5-9/190. ... Bats left, throws right. ... High school: Socorro (El Paso, Texas). ... College: Texas.
TRANSACTIONS/CAREER NOTES: Selected by Oakland Athletics organization in first round (33rd pick overall) of 2003 free-agent draft. ... Traded by Athletics with OF Eric Byrnes to Colorado Rockies for Ps Joe Kennedy and Jay Witasick (July 13, 2005).
2005 GAMES PLAYED BY POSITION (MLB): SS—31, 2B—6.

SCOUTING REPORT *Offense:* He is a light hitter who has quick hands through the hitting zone but little power and recognition of pitches' spin. Is fooled by almost any off-speed pitch. Needs to develop more patience. Has an inside-out approach that produces weak contact. Has average speed but is a smart baserunner who always is a threat to steal. *Defense:* He is above-average at shortstop and even better at second. He has a strong and accurate arm, good range and soft hands. *Outlook:* He needs more seasoning in the minors to see if his bat will come around; even if it does, his best role may be as a utilityman to back up both middle infield positions. *Grade 5.8*

OMAR QUINTANILLA'S HITTING ZONE

.250	.429	.125
.100	.500	.138
.125	.500	.235

LEFTY-RIGHTY SPLITS

vs.	Avg.	AB	H	2B	3B	HR	RBI	BB	SO	OBP	Slg.
L	.067	15	1	0	0	0	0	0	3	.067	.067
R	.239	113	27	1	1	0	7	9	12	.295	.265

Year	Team (League)	Pos.	G	AB	R	H	2B	3B	HR	RBI	BB	SO	HBP	GDP	SB-CS	Avg.	OBP	SLG	OPS	E	Avg.
2003— Vancouver (N'west)	SS	32	129	22	44	5	4	0	14	12	21	1	3	7-1	.341	.401	.442	.843	2	.983
— Modesto (Pion.)		8	36	9	15	3	0	2	6	3	6	0	1	0-0	.417	.462	.667	1.129	...	...
2004— Modesto (Pion.)		108	452	75	142	32	5	11	72	37	54	5	11	1-3	.314	.370	.480	.850	...	...
— Midland (Texas)	SS	23	94	20	33	10	0	2	20	10	9	1		2-0	.351	.419	.521	.940	4	.000
2005— Midland (Texas)	SS-2B	78	294	46	86	14	2	4	25	23	40	2	5	2-3	.293	.347	.395	.741	14	.960
— Colo. Springs (PCL)	SS	13	52	14	18	3	2	1	7	3	8	0	1	0-0	.346	.375	.538	.913	0	1.000
— Colorado (N.L.)	SS-2B	39	128	16	28	1	1	0	7	9	15	0	3	2-1	.219	.270	.242	.512	1	.993
Major League totals (1 year)		39	128	16	28	1	1	0	7	9	15	0	3	2-1	.219	.270	.242	.512	1	.993

QUINTERO, HUMBERTO   C

PERSONAL: Born August 8, 1979, in Maracaibo, Venezuela. ... 6-1/190. ... Bats right, throws right. ... High school: Andres Bello (Maracaibo, Venezuela).
TRANSACTIONS/CAREER NOTES: Signed as a non-drafted free agent by Chicago White Sox organization (January 16, 1997). ... Traded by White Sox with OF Alex Fernandez to San Diego Padres for IF D'Angelo Jimenez (July 12, 2002). ... Traded by Padres to Houston Astros for P Tim Redding (March 28, 2005). ... On disabled list (June 19-July 16, 2005); included rehabilitation assignments to Round Rock and Corpus Christi.
2005 GAMES PLAYED BY POSITION (MLB): C—16, 1B—1.

SCOUTING REPORT Quintero definitely will have to watch his weight in the future. Arm strength is his best tool but is not a good defensive receiver overall; lacks mobility and has stiff hands. Bat is slow. Doesn't drive the ball a lot. Hits with a hitch and has trouble handling pitches on the inner half of the plate. Question if he can even be a backup. *Grade 4.1*

HUMBERTO QUINTERO'S HITTING ZONE

.000	.000	.500
.444	.125	.125
.000	.500	.000

LEFTY-RIGHTY SPLITS

vs.	Avg.	AB	H	2B	3B	HR	RBI	BB	SO	OBP	Slg.
L	.200	15	3	1	0	0	4	0	2	.200	.267
R	.179	39	7	0	0	1	4	1	8	.200	.256

Year	Team (League)	Pos.	G	AB	R	H	2B	3B	HR	RBI	BB	SO	HBP	GDP	SB-CS	Avg.	OBP	SLG	OPS	E	Avg.
1997— Guacara 1 (VSL)	C	24	42	4	11	2	0	0	6	5	9			1-...	.262	.333	.310	.643	...	...
1998— Miranda (VSL)	C	30	73	6	15	1	0	0	1	3	12			0-...	.205	.266	.219	.475	...	...
1999— Bristol (Appal.)	C	48	155	30	43	5	2	0	15	9	19	6	8	11-1	.277	.341	.335	.677	6	.987
2000— Burlington (Midw.)	C	75	248	23	59	12	2	0	24	15	31	3	8	10-6	.238	.287	.302	.590	8	.986
— Ariz. White Sox (Ariz.)	C-OF	15	56	13	22	6	0	0	8	0	2	1		1-0	.393	.414	.500	.914	3	.976
2001— Kannapolis (S. Atl.)	C	60	197	32	53	7	1	1	20	8	20	2	5	7-3	.269	.321	.330	.651	3	.989
— Win.-Salem (Car.)	C	43	154	15	37	6	0	0	12	5	19	2	3	9-3	.240	.268	.279	.548	3	.992
— Birmingham (Sou.)	C	5	19	0	4	0	0	0	2	0	2	1	0	0-0	.211	.250	.211	.461	1	.971
2002— Birmingham (Sou.)	C	4	12	1	6	0	0	0	3	1	1	0	1	0-0	.500	.538	.500	1.038	0	1.000

Year	Team (League)	Pos.	G	AB	R	H	2B	3B	HR	RBI	BB	SO	HBP	GDP	SB-CS	Avg.	OBP	SLG	OPS	E	Avg.
— Charlotte (Int'l)	C	15	41	2	9	1	0	0	5	3			3	0-0	.220	.273	.244	.517	3	.964
— Win.-Salem (Car.)	C	52	160	15	31	1	1	0	12	8	23	4	4	2-3	.194	.247	.213	.460	4	.990
— Mobile (Sou.)	C	37	125	11	30	8	0	1	14	5	12	3	3	0-3	.240	.286	.328	.614	5	.983
2003— Mobile (Sou.)	C-DH	110	386	37	115	26	0	3	52	19	41	9	17	0-0	.298	.343	.389	.732	5	.995
— San Diego (N.L.)	C	12	23	1	5	0	0	0	2	1	6	0	0	0-0	.217	.250	.217	.467	1	.982
2004— Portland (PCL)	C-DH	68	259	36	82	25	0	5	30	8	18	5	7	0-0	.317	.348	.471	.819	6	.989
— San Diego (N.L.)	C	23	72	7	18	3	0	2	10	5	16	0	5	0-2	.250	.295	.375	.670	1	1.000
2005— Houston (N.L.)	C-1B	18	54	6	10	1	0	1	8	1	10	0	3	0-0	.185	.200	.259	.459	1	.989
Major League totals (3 years)		53	149	14	33	4	0	3	20	7	32	0	8	0-2	.221	.255	.309	.564	2	.993

QUIROZ, GUILLERMO   C

PERSONAL: Born November 29, 1981, in Maracaibo, Venezuela. ... 6-1/202. ... Bats right, throws right. ... Full name: Guillermo Antonio Quiroz.
TRANSACTIONS/CAREER NOTES: Signed as non-drafted free agent by Toronto Blue Jays organization (September 25, 1998).
2005 GAMES PLAYED BY POSITION (MLB): C—10, DH—2.

LEFTY-RIGHTY SPLITS

vs.	Avg.	AB	H	2B	3B	HR	RBI	BB	SO	OBP	Slg.
L	.095	21	2	1	0	0	2	1	7	.174	.143
R	.333	15	5	1	0	0	2	1	6	.375	.400

Year	Team (League)	Pos.	G	AB	R	H	2B	3B	HR	RBI	BB	SO	HBP	GDP	SB-CS	Avg.	OBP	SLG	OPS	E	Avg.
1999— Medicine Hat (Pio.)	C	63	208	25	46	7	0	6	28	18	55	4	4	0-2	.221	.296	.385	.680	10	.981
2000— Hagerstown (SAL)	C	43	136	14	22	4	0	1	12	16	44	4	3	0-1	.162	.269	.213	.482	2	.994
— Queens (N.Y.-Penn.)	C	55	196	27	44	9	0	5	29	27	48	4	4	1-2	.224	.329	.347	.676	7	.987
2001— Char., W.Va. (SAL)	C	82	261	25	52	12	0	5	25	29	67	6	5	5-1	.199	.294	.326	.620	9	.986
2002— Dunedin (Fla. St.)	C	111	411	50	107	28	1	12	68	35	91	9	18	1-0	.260	.330	.421	.751	11	.984
— Syracuse (Int'l)	C	13	45	7	10	4	0	1	6	3	14	0	1	0-0	.222	.271	.378	.649	2	.956
2003— New Haven (East.)	C	108	369	63	104	27	0	20	79	45	83	12	13	0-0	.282	.372	.518	.889	4	.994
2004— Syracuse (Int'l)	C-DH	76	255	32	58	19	1	8	32	28	54	3	8	1-0	.227	.309	.404	.706	3	.994
— Toronto (A.L.)	C-DH	17	52	2	11	2	0	0	6	2	8	2	1	1-0	.212	.263	.250	.513	2	.976
2005— Dunedin (Fla. St.)	DH-C	11	38	4	9	1	0	2	6	2	8	3	1	0-0	.237	.326	.421	.747	0	1.000
— Syracuse (Int'l)	C	25	83	11	19	3	0	6	18	9	19	1	5	0-0	.229	.309	.482	.790	2	.988
— Toronto (A.L.)	C-DH	12	36	3	7	2	0	0	4	2	13	1	0	0-0	.194	.256	.250	.506	0	1.000
Major League totals (2 years)		29	88	5	18	4	0	0	10	4	21	3	1	1-0	.205	.260	.250	.510	2	.986

RADKE, BRAD   P

PERSONAL: Born October 27, 1972, in Eau Claire, Wis. ... 6-2/184. ... Throws right, bats right. ... Full name: Brad William Radke. ... Name pronounced: RAD-key. ... High school: Jesuit (Tampa).
TRANSACTIONS/CAREER NOTES: Selected by Minnesota Twins organization in eighth round of 1991 free-agent draft. ... On disabled list (August 4-21, 2001). ... On disabled list (May 14-30 and May 31-August 3, 2002); included rehabilitation assignments to GCL Twins and Fort Myers. ... On suspended list (May 17-23, 2003).
CAREER HITTING: 3-for-28 (.107), 0 R, 0 2B, 0 3B, 0 HR, 0 RBI.

SCOUTING REPORT **Throws:** The consistent Radke has a fastball that ranges from 87-91 mph, a slider, a curveball and a changeup. **Tendencies:** Radke has been using his fastball more often than in previous seasons, and he complements it with a tight-biting, quick curve that he shows early in the count and a short, late-running slider that is more of cut fastball. Has an outstanding changeup that he throws on any count and in any situation with a consistent arm speed and release point. The changeup makes his average fastball more effective. Is one of the best control pitchers in the game. Goes after hitters. Has an excellent delivery and a great feel for pitching. **Outlook:** He is a dependable starter. Pitched through shoulder problems late in the year but has proven his durability. **Grade 8.6**

BRAD RADKE'S PITCHING ZONE

.197	.480	.281
.277	.491	.310
.236	.231	.340

LEFTY-RIGHTY SPLITS

vs.	Avg.	AB	H	2B	3B	HR	RBI	BB	SO	OBP	Slg.
L	.291	402	117	23	1	22	55	14	61	.315	.517
R	.252	385	97	15	4	11	37	9	56	.274	.397

Year	Team (League)	W	L	Pct.	ERA	WHIP	G	GS	CG	ShO	Hld.	Sv.-Opp.	IP	H	R	ER	HR	BB-IBB	SO	Avg.
1991— GC Twins (GCL)	3	4	.429	3.08	1.11	10	9	1	0	...	1-...	49.2	41	21	17	0	14-0	46	.220
1992— Kenosha (Midw.)	10	10	.500	2.93	1.18	26	25	4	1	...	0-...	165.2	149	70	54	8	47-1	127	.243
1993— Fort Myers (FSL)	3	5	.375	3.82	1.15	14	14	0	0	...	0-...	92.0	85	42	39	3	21-1	69	.243
— Nashville (Southern)	2	6	.250	4.62	1.28	13	13	1	0	...	0-...	76.0	81	42	39	6	16-0	76	.267
1994— Nashville (Southern)	12	9	.571	2.66	1.08	29	28	3	1	...	0-...	186.1	167	66	55	9	34-0	123	.240
1995— Minnesota (A.L.)	11	14	.440	5.32	1.34	29	28	2	1	0	0-0	181.0	195	112	107	*32	47-0	75	.275
1996— Minnesota (A.L.)	11	16	.407	4.46	1.24	35	35	3	0	0	0-0	232.0	231	125	115	*40	57-2	148	.256
1997— Minnesota (A.L.)	20	10	.667	3.87	1.19	35	•35	4	1	0	0-0	239.2	238	114	103	28	48-1	174	.257
1998— Minnesota (A.L.)	12	14	.462	4.30	1.32	32	32	5	1	0	0-0	213.2	238	109	102	23	43-1	146	.283
1999— Minnesota (A.L.)	12	14	.462	3.75	1.29	33	33	4	0	0	0-0	218.2	239	97	91	28	44-0	121	.287
2000— Minnesota (A.L.)	12	*16	.429	4.45	1.38	34	34	4	1	0	0-0	226.2	261	119	112	27	51-1	141	.287
2001— Minnesota (A.L.)	15	11	.577	3.94	1.15	33	33	3	0	0	0-0	226.0	235	105	99	24	26-0	137	.271
2002— Minnesota (A.L.)	9	5	.643	4.72	1.22	21	21	2	1	0	0-0	118.1	124	64	62	12	20-0	62	.272
— GC Twins (GCL)	0	0	...	0.67	1.00	1	1	0	0	0	0-...	3.0	2	0	0	0	0-0	4	.182
— Fort Myers (FSL)	0	1	.000	3.12	1.27	2	2	0	0	0	0-...	8.2	11	6	3	1	0-0	6	.289
2003— Minnesota (A.L.)	14	10	.583	4.49	1.27	33	33	1	0	0	0-0	212.1	242	111	106	32	28-2	120	.288
2004— Minnesota (A.L.)	11	8	.579	3.48	1.16	34	34	1	1	0	0-0	219.2	229	92	85	23	26-1	143	.267
2005— Minnesota (A.L.)	9	12	.429	4.04	1.18	31	31	3	1	0	0-0	200.2	214	98	90	33	23-1	117	.272
Major League totals (11 years)	136	130	.511	4.22	1.25	350	349	37	10	0	0-0	2288.2	2446	1146	1072	302	413-9	1384	.273

DIVISION SERIES RECORD

Year	Team (League)	W	L	Pct.	ERA	WHIP	G	GS	CG	ShO	Hld.	Sv.-Opp.	IP	H	R	ER	HR	BB-IBB	SO	Avg.
2002— Minnesota (A.L.)	2	0	1.000	1.54	1.29	2	2	0	0	0	0-0	11.2	14	6	2	1	1-0	7	.280
2003— Minnesota (A.L.)	0	1	.000	2.84	1.11	1	1	0	0	0	0-0	6.1	5	2	2	0	2-0	4	.227
2004— Minnesota (A.L.)	0	0	...	7.11	1.74	1	1	0	0	0	0-0	6.1	8	5	5	3	3-0	11	.320
Division series totals (3 years)	2	1	.667	3.33	1.36	4	4	0	0	0	0-0	24.1	27	13	9	4	6-0	11	.278

R

Year Team (League)	W	L	Pct.	ERA	WHIP	G	GS	CG	ShO	Hld.	Sv.-Opp.	IP	H	R	ER	HR	BB-IBB	SO	Avg.
2002— Minnesota (A.L.)	0	1	.000	2.70	0.90	1	1	0	0	...	0-0	6.2	5	2	2	0	1-0	4	.217

ALL-STAR GAME RECORD

	W	L	Pct.	ERA	WHIP	G	GS	CG	ShO	Hld.	Sv.-Opp.	IP	H	R	ER	HR	BB-IBB	SO	Avg.
All-Star Game totals (1 year)	0	0	...	9.00	3.00	1	0	0	0	0	0-0	1.0	2	1	1	0	1-0	1	.400

RAKERS, AARON   P

R

PERSONAL: Born January 22, 1977, in Highland, Ill. ... 6-3/205. ... Throws right, bats right. ... Full name: Aaron James Rakers. ... Name pronounced: Rockers. ... High school: Wesclin (Trenton, Ill.). ... College: Souther Illinois University-Edwardsville.
TRANSACTIONS/CAREER NOTES: Selected by Baltimore Orioles organzation in 23rd round of 1999 free-agent draft.
CAREER HITTING: 0-for-0 (.000), 0 R, 0 2B, 0 3B, 0 HR, 0 RBI.

AARON RAKERS'S PITCHING ZONE

.000	.000	.667
.250	.667	.200
.000	.333	.400

LEFTY-RIGHTY SPLITS

vs.	Avg.	AB	H	2B	3B	HR	RBI	BB	SO	OBP	Slg.
L	.227	22	5	1	1	0	1	3	2	.308	.364
R	.214	28	6	1	0	3	6	0	9	.207	.571

Year Team (League)	W	L	Pct.	ERA	WHIP	G	GS	CG	ShO	Hld.	Sv.-Opp.	IP	H	R	ER	HR	BB-IBB	SO	Avg.
1999— Bluefield (Appal.)	0	0	...	2.57	1.14	3	0	0	0	...	0-...	7.0	5	2	2	1	3-0	12	.200
— Delmarva (S. Atl.)	4	1	.800	1.42	0.87	18	0	0	0	...	8-...	25.1	9	6	4	0	13-0	38	.108
2000— Frederick (Carolina)	1	1	.500	1.55	0.86	26	0	0	0	...	8-...	40.2	23	8	7	2	12-1	57	.163
— Bowie (East.)	3	2	.600	2.79	1.03	24	0	0	0	...	8-...	29.0	20	11	9	5	10-0	21	.194
2001— Bowie (East.)	4	4	.500	2.39	1.21	51	0	0	0	...	14-...	60.1	53	21	16	8	20-1	74	.227
2002— Bowie (East.)	5	1	.833	2.06	1.06	36	0	0	0	...	10-...	48.0	39	12	11	3	12-2	45	.232
2003— Bowie (East.)	5	0	1.000	2.75	1.17	31	0	0	0	...	8-...	39.1	27	12	12	7	19-1	42	.196
— Ottawa (Int'l)	2	4	.333	5.13	1.14	21	0	0	0	...	1-...	26.1	19	18	15	1	11-2	26	.202
2004— Ottawa (Int'l)	4	5	.444	2.75	1.14	54	1	0	0	...	1-...	78.2	65	27	24	8	25-4	80	.229
— Baltimore (A.L.)	0	0	...	4.15	1.38	3	0	0	0	...	0-0	4.1	5	2	2	0	1-0	3	.278
2005— Ottawa (Int'l)	6	5	.545	2.57	1.17	57	0	0	0	7	7-11	77.0	69	26	22	9	21-4	92	.235
— Baltimore (A.L.)	1	0	1.000	3.29	1.02	10	0	0	0	1	0-0	13.2	11	5	5	3	3-0	11	.235
Major League totals (2 years)	1	0	1.000	3.50	1.11	13	0	0	0	1	0-0	18.0	16	7	7	3	4-0	14	.235

RAMIREZ, ARAMIS   3B

PERSONAL: Born June 25, 1978, in Santo Domingo, Dominican Republic. ... 6-1/215. ... Bats right, throws right. ... Full name: Aramis Nin Ramirez. ... Name pronounced: ah-RAH-mis. ... High school: Aida Cartagena Portalatin (Santo Domingo, Dominica.
TRANSACTIONS/CAREER NOTES: Signed as a non-drafted free agent by Pittsburgh Pirates organization (November 7, 1994). ... On suspended list (July 24-29, 1998). ... On disabled list (August 10-September 4, 1998); included rehabilitation assignment to Nashville. ... On disabled list (August 29, 2000-remainder of season). ... Traded by Pirates with OF Kenny Lofton to Chicago Cubs for IF Jose Hernandez, P Matt Bruback and a player to be named (July 23, 2003); Pirates acquired IF Bobby Hill to complete deal (August 15, 2003). ... On disabled list (August 26, 2005-remainder of season).
2005 GAMES PLAYED BY POSITION (MLB): 3B—119.

SCOUTING REPORT **Offense:** Ramirez has good bat speed and excellent plate coverage and has become a much better hitter as he has learned to hit to the opposite field. Continues to cut down on strikeouts. Stays on the breaking ball well. Likes the ball up. Has excellent power to all fields. **Defense:** He is an agile fielder, but he must watch his weight. Has good hands and has increased his mobility and range. Has improved his footwork and throwing accuracy. No longer lets offensive frustration affect his defense. Is getting better jumps, especially to his left. **Outlook:** Ramirez and Wrigley Field are an ideal match. Will be one of the premier third basemen for years to come as he puts up All-Star type offensive numbers. *Grade 9.4*

ARAMIS RAMIREZ'S HITTING ZONE

.333	.429	.100
.349	.366	.241
.333	.485	.294

LEFTY-RIGHTY SPLITS

vs.	Avg.	AB	H	2B	3B	HR	RBI	BB	SO	OBP	Slg.
L	.355	121	43	11	0	10	24	10	19	.418	.694
R	.284	342	97	19	0	21	68	25	41	.336	.523

Year Team (League)	Pos.	G	AB	R	H	2B	3B	HR	RBI	BB	SO	HBP	GDP	SB-CS	Avg.	OBP	SLG	OPS	E	FIELDING Avg.
1995— Dom. Pirates (DSL)	3B	64	214	41	63	13	0	11	54	42	26	...	...	2-...	.294	...	.509	...	19	.886
1996— Erie (N.Y.-Penn)	3B	61	223	37	68	14	4	9	42	31	41	7	7	0-0	.305	.403	.525	.928	11	.896
— Augusta (S. Atl.)	3B	6	20	3	4	1	0	1	2	1	7	2	0	0-2	.200	.304	.400	.704	2	.833
1997— Lynchburg (Caro.)	3B-DH	137	482	85	134	24	2	29	114	80	103	12	12	5-3	.278	.390	.517	.907	39	.897
1998— Nashville (PCL) 3B-DH-SS	47	168	19	46	10	0	5	18	24	28	4	3	0-2	.274	.374	.423	.796	4	.932
— Pittsburgh (N.L.)	3B	72	251	23	59	9	1	6	24	18	72	4	3	0-1	.235	.296	.351	.646	9	.941
1999— Nashville (PCL)	3B	131	460	92	151	35	1	21	74	73	56	9	11	5-3	.328	.425	.546	.971	42	.884
— Pittsburgh (N.L.)	3B	18	56	2	10	2	1	0	7	6	9	0	0	0-0	.179	.254	.250	.504	3	.930
2000— Pittsburgh (N.L.)	3B	73	254	19	65	15	2	6	35	10	36	5	9	0-0	.256	.293	.402	.695	14	.917
— Nashville (PCL)	3B	44	167	28	59	12	2	4	26	11	26	4	5	2-1	.353	.407	.521	.928	9	.930
2001— Pittsburgh (N.L.)	3B	158	603	83	181	40	0	34	112	40	100	8	9	5-4	.300	.350	.536	.885	25	.945
2002— Pittsburgh (N.L.)	3B-DH	142	522	51	122	26	0	18	71	29	95	8	17	2-0	.234	.279	.387	.666	19	.946
2003— Pittsburgh (N.L.)	3B	96	375	44	105	25	1	12	67	25	68	7	17	1-1	.280	.330	.448	.778	13	.924
— Chicago (N.L.)	3B	63	232	31	60	7	1	15	39	17	31	3	4	1-1	.259	.314	.491	.805	10	.939
2004— Chicago (N.L.)	3B	145	547	99	174	32	1	36	103	49	62	3	25	0-2	.318	.373	.578	.951	10	.969
2005— Chicago (N.L.)	3B	123	463	72	140	30	0	31	92	35	60	6	15	0-1	.302	.358	.568	.926	16	.947
Major League totals (8 years)		890	3303	424	916	186	7	158	550	229	533	44	99	9-10	.277	.329	.481	.810	129	.943

DIVISION SERIES RECORD

Year Team (League)	Pos.	G	AB	R	H	2B	3B	HR	RBI	BB	SO	HBP	GDP	SB-CS	Avg.	OBP	SLG	OPS	E	Avg.
2003— Chicago (N.L.)	3B	5	18	2	5	1	0	1	3	2	2	0	1	0-0	.278	.350	.500	.850	0	1.000

CHAMPIONSHIP SERIES RECORD

Year Team (League)	Pos.	G	AB	R	H	2B	3B	HR	RBI	BB	SO	HBP	GDP	SB-CS	Avg.	OBP	SLG	OPS	E	Avg.
2003— Chicago (N.L.)	3B	7	26	4	6	0	1	3	7	5	6	1	1	0-0	.231	.375	.654	1.029	0	1.000

ALL-STAR GAME RECORD

	G	AB	R	H	2B	3B	HR	RBI	BB	SO	HBP	GDP	SB-CS	Avg.	OBP	SLG	OPS	E	Avg.
All-Star Game totals (1 year)	1	2	0	1	0	0	0	0	1	0	0	1	0-0	.500	.667	.500	1.167	0	1.000

RAMIREZ, ELIZARDO — P

PERSONAL: Born January 28, 1983, in Villa Mella, Dominican Republic. ... 6-0/180. ... Throws right, bats both. ... High school: Liceo Pedregal (Dominican Republic).
TRANSACTIONS/CAREER NOTES: Signed as a non-drafted free agent by Philadelphia Phillies organization (July 2, 1999). ... Traded by Phillies to Cincinnati Reds (August 11, 2004) to complete deal in which Phillies acquired P Cory Lidle from Reds for OF Javon Moran, P Joe Wilson and a player to be named (August 9, 2004).
CAREER HITTING: 0-for-8 (.000), 0 R, 0 2B, 0 3B, 0 HR, 0 RBI.

ELIZARDO RAMIREZ'S PITCHING ZONE

.250	.250	.500
.143	.556	.250
.000	.143	.250

LEFTY-RIGHTY SPLITS

vs.	Avg.	AB	H	2B	3B	HR	RBI	BB	SO	OBP	Slg.
L	.386	57	22	6	0	5	14	4	4	.435	.754
R	.282	39	11	4	0	5	6	5	.391	.385

Year Team (League)	W	L	Pct.	ERA	WHIP	G	GS	CG	ShO	Hld.	Sv.-Opp.	IP	H	R	ER	HR	BB-IBB	SO	Avg.
2000— Dom. Phillies (DSL)	5	2	.714	1.88	0.91	11	9	0	0	...	1-...	57.1	47	19	12	1	5-...	67	...
2001— Dom. Phillies (DSL)	9	0	1.000	1.48	0.87	12	12	1	1	...	0-...	79.0	61	21	13	0	8-...	70	...
2002— GC Phillies (GCL)	7	1	.875	1.10	0.63	11	11	2	1	...	0-...	73.1	44	18	9	3	2-0	73	.165
2003— Clearwater (FSL)	13	9	.591	3.78	1.36	27	25	1	0	...	0-...	157.1	181	85	66	4	33-0	101	.290
2004— Clearwater (FSL)	5	1	.833	2.44	1.07	9	9	1	0	...	0-...	59.0	55	17	16	3	8-0	33	.249
— Philadelphia (N.L.)	0	0	...	4.80	1.47	7	0	0	0	0	0-0	15.0	17	8	8	3	5-1	9	.283
— Reading (East.)	2	5	.286	6.68	1.93	8	8	1	0	...	0-...	33.2	51	34	25	4	14-1	20	.345
— Chattanooga (Sou.)	1	0	1.000	3.19	1.26	5	5	1	1	...	0-...	31.0	35	11	11	6	4-1	23	.282
2005— Cincinnati (N.L.)	0	3	.000	8.46	1.93	6	4	0	0	0	0-0	22.1	33	22	21	5	10-2	9	.344
— Louisville (Int'l)	7	7	.500	3.77	1.28	21	21	0	0	...	0-...	131.1	150	63	55	14	18-1	82	.287
Major League totals (2 years)	0	3	.000	6.99	1.74	13	4	0	0	0	0-0	37.1	50	30	29	8	15-3	18	.321

RAMIREZ, ERASMO — P

PERSONAL: Born April 29, 1976, in Santa Ana, Calif. ... 6-0/190. ... Throws left, bats left. ... High school: Saddleback (Calif.). ... College: Cal State Fullerton.
TRANSACTIONS/CAREER NOTES: Selected by San Francisco Giants organization in 11th round of 1998 free-agent draft. ... Traded by Giants with P Todd Ozias and OF Chris Magruder to Texas Rangers for 1B Andres Galarraga (July 24, 2001). ... On disabled list (August 17-September 1, 2004). ... On disabled list (March 25-June 30, 2005); included rehabilitation assignment to Oklahoma.
CAREER HITTING: 0-for-0 (.000), 0 R, 0 2B, 0 3B, 0 HR, 0 RBI.

ERASMO RAMIREZ'S PITCHING ZONE

.429	.500	.000
.208	.250	.286
.167	.000	.600

LEFTY-RIGHTY SPLITS

vs.	Avg.	AB	H	2B	3B	HR	RBI	BB	SO	OBP	Slg.
L	.350	40	14	2	0	1	7	1	2	.381	.475
R	.208	48	10	1	0	2	7	2	4	.255	.354

Year Team (League)	W	L	Pct.	ERA	WHIP	G	GS	CG	ShO	Hld.	Sv.-Opp.	IP	H	R	ER	HR	BB-IBB	SO	Avg.
1998— Bakersfield (Calif.)	1	1	.500	3.38	0.75	14	0	0	0	...	3-...	21.1	10	8	8	0	6-0	17	.143
— Salem-Keizer (N'west)	0	1	.000	3.72	1.09	9	2	0	0	...	0-...	19.1	19	11	8	3	2-0	23	.247
1999— San Jose (Calif.)	2	0	1.000	2.67	0.87	31	0	0	0	...	5-...	57.1	42	18	17	2	8-0	52	.206
2000— Shreveport (Texas)	0	5	.000	6.44	1.72	39	2	0	0	...	1-...	58.2	80	45	42	7	21-5	46	.340
2001— San Jose (Calif.)	3	2	.600	3.41	0.88	17	0	0	0	...	1-...	31.2	23	14	12	2	5-0	33	.193
— Shreveport (Texas)	2	0	1.000	2.16	0.90	22	1	0	0	...	1-...	33.1	25	10	8	1	5-0	39	.205
— Tulsa (Texas)	2	1	.667	4.41	1.35	12	0	0	0	...	0-...	16.1	17	8	8	3	5-0	18	.270
2002— Tulsa (Texas)	4	2	.667	3.00	1.09	34	0	0	0	...	2-...	54.0	51	23	18	1	8-0	34	.254
— Oklahoma (PCL)	4	1	.800	1.29	0.90	25	0	0	0	...	1-...	21.0	15	5	3	0	4-1	17	.195
2003— Frisco (Texas)	1	0	1.000	6.00	1.67	3	0	0	0	...	0-...	3.0	4	2	2	1	1-0	4	.286
— Oklahoma (PCL)	2	1	.667	1.53	1.08	22	0	0	0	...	4-...	35.1	36	8	6	0	2-0	25	.257
— Texas (A.L.)	3	1	.750	3.86	1.12	34	0	0	0	2	0-1	49.0	46	21	21	4	9-0	28	.251
2004— Oklahoma (PCL)	1	0	1.000	6.16	1.42	14	0	0	0	...	0-...	19.0	23	15	13	2	4-1	9	.299
— Texas (A.L.)	5	3	.625	4.29	1.15	34	0	0	0	3	0-2	35.2	34	19	17	5	7-1	21	.252
2005— Oklahoma (PCL)	0	0	...	3.79	1.26	16	0	0	0	4	1-1	19.0	19	10	8	3	5-0	11	.253
— Texas (A.L.)	0	0	...	3.91	1.17	16	0	0	0	...	0-1	23.0	24	10	10	3	3-0	6	.273
Major League totals (3 years)	8	4	.667	4.01	1.14	84	0	0	0	5	0-4	107.2	104	50	48	12	19-1	55	.256

RAMIREZ, HANLEY — SS

PERSONAL: Born December 23, 1983, in Samana, Dominican Republic. ... 6-3/195. ... Bats right, throws right.
TRANSACTIONS/CAREER NOTES: Signed as a non-drafted free agent by Boston Red Sox organization (July 2, 2000).
2005 GAMES PLAYED BY POSITION (MLB): SS—2.

LEFTY-RIGHTY SPLITS

vs.	Avg.	AB	H	2B	3B	HR	RBI	BB	SO	OBP	Slg.
L	.000	0	0	0	0	0	0	0	0	.000	.000
R	.000	2	0	0	0	0	0	0	2	.000	.000

Year Team (League)	Pos.	G	AB	R	H	2B	3B	HR	RBI	BB	SO	HBP	GDP	SB-CS	Avg.	OBP	SLG	OPS	E	Avg.
2001— Dom. Red Sox (DSL)		54	197	32	68	18	2	5	34	15	22	4	9	13-4	.345	.397	.533	.930	...	...
2002— GC Red Sox (GCL)	SS-2B-3B	45	164	29	56	11	3	6	26	16	15	2	8-6	.341	.402	.555	.957	20	.915
— Lowell (NY-Penn)	SS	22	97	17	36	9	2	1	19	4	14	2	4-3	.371	.400	.536	.936	7	.935
2003— Augusta (S. Atl.)	SS	111	422	69	116	24	3	8	50	32	73	2	12	36-13	.275	.327	.403	.730	36	.926
2004— Sarasota (Fla. St.)	SS	62	239	33	74	8	4	1	24	17	39	4	2	12-7	.310	.364	.389	.753	17	.485

R

Year	Team (League)	Pos.	G	AB	R	H	2B	3B	HR	RBI	BB	SO	HBP	GDP	SB-CS	Avg.	OBP	SLG	OPS	E	Avg.
	—GC Red Sox (GCL)	SS-2B-3B	6	20	5	8	0	1	0	7	2	3	2	1	1-0	.400	.462	.500	.962	3	.885
	—Portland (East.)	SS	32	129	26	40	7	2	5	15	10	26	0	1	12-3	.310	.360	.512	.872	3	.000
2005—Portland (East.)		SS-2B-3B-DH	122	465	66	126	21	7	6	52	39	62	7	12	26-13	.271	.335	.385	.720	22	.957
	—Boston (A.L.)	SS	2	2	0	0	0	0	0	0	0	2	0	0	0-0	.000	.000	.000	.000	0	1.000
Major League totals (1 year)			2	2	0	0	0	0	0	0	0	2	0	0	0-0	.000	.000	.000	.000	0	1.000

RAMIREZ, HORACIO — P

PERSONAL: Born November 24, 1979, in Carson, Calif. ... 6-1/219. ... Throws left, bats left. ... High school: Inglewood (Calif.).
TRANSACTIONS/CAREER NOTES: Selected by Atlanta Braves organization in fifth round of 1997 free-agent draft. ... On disabled list (March 22-June 18, 2002); included rehabilitation assignment to Macon and Greenville. ... On disabled list (May 26-September 25, 2004); included rehabilitation assignment to Greenville.
CAREER HITTING: 24-for-155 (.155), 7 R, 3 2B, 1 3B, 0 HR, 5 RBI.

SCOUTING REPORT *Throws:* This prototypical crafty lefthander has a fastball that ranges from 88-91 mph, a slider/cutter and a screwball-like changeup. *Tendencies:* Ramirez has a very good delivery and is using his cutter more than ever, perhaps too much. Is throwing to one side of the plate (in on righthanders, away on lefthanders) too much and falls into predictable patterns. Keeps the ball down to induce grounders. Slider is very similar to his cutter. Has very good arm speed with his straight change. Needs to trust his stuff as he tries to spot the ball and loses his aggressiveness. *Outlook:* Ramirez figures to remain a bottom-of-the-rotation starter in Atlanta. **Grade 7.4**

HORACIO RAMIREZ'S PITCHING ZONE

.400	.258	.219
.315	.369	.356
.283	.366	.096

LEFTY-RIGHTY SPLITS

vs.	Avg.	AB	H	2B	3B	HR	RBI	BB	SO	OBP	Slg.
L	.267	180	48	5	1	4	21	12	27	.320	.372
R	.286	580	166	27	0	27	79	55	53	.345	.472

Year	Team (League)	W	L	Pct.	ERA	WHIP	G	GS	CG	ShO	Hld.	Sv.-Opp.	IP	H	R	ER	HR	BB-IBB	SO	Avg.
1997— GC Braves (GCL)		3	3	.500	2.25	1.09	11	8	0	0	...	0-...	44.0	30	13	11	1	18-0	61	.192
1998— Macon (S. Atl.)		1	7	.125	5.86	1.55	12	12	0	0	...	0-...	55.1	70	50	36	8	16-0	38	.310
— Eugene (Northwest)		2	7	.222	6.31	1.81	16	8	0	0	...	0-...	55.2	84	51	39	4	17-0	39	.346
1999— Macon (S. Atl.)		6	3	.667	2.67	1.22	17	14	1	1	...	0-...	77.2	70	30	23	6	25-0	43	.248
2000— Myrtle Beach (Carol.)		15	8	.652	3.22	1.20	27	26	3	2	...	0-...	148.1	136	57	53	14	42-0	125	.242
2001— Greenville (Sou.)		1	1	.500	4.91	1.70	3	3	0	0	...	0-...	14.2	17	8	8	4	8-0	17	.309
2002— Macon (S. Atl.)		0	2	.000	6.00	2.17	2	1	0	0	...	0-...	6.0	11	10	4	0	2-0	5	.355
— Greenville (Sou.)		9	5	.643	3.03	1.27	16	16	0	0	...	0-...	92.0	85	41	31	5	32-0	64	.253
2003— Atlanta (N.L.)		12	4	.750	4.00	1.39	29	29	1	0	0	0-0	182.1	181	91	81	21	72-10	100	.263
2004— Greenville (Sou.)		2	0	1.000	3.09	1.54	3	2	0	0	...	0-...	11.2	15	4	4	0	3-0	2	.349
— Richmond (Int'l)		0	0	...	8.00	1.78	2	2	0	0	...	0-...	9.0	15	8	8	1	1-0	3	.385
— Atlanta (N.L.)		2	4	.333	2.39	1.34	10	9	1	0	0	0-0	60.1	51	24	16	7	30-5	31	.226
2005— Atlanta (N.L.)		11	9	.550	4.63	1.39	33	32	1	1	0	0-0	202.1	214	108	104	31	67-4	80	.282
Major League totals (3 years)		25	17	.595	4.07	1.38	72	70	3	1	0	0-0	445.0	446	223	201	59	169-19	211	.266

RAMIREZ, JULIO — OF

PERSONAL: Born August 10, 1977, in San Juan de la Maguana, Dominican Republic. ... 5-11/170. ... Bats right, throws right. ... Full name: Julio Cesar Ramirez. ... High school: Escuela Otilia Pelaez (Santo Domingo, Dominican Re.
TRANSACTIONS/CAREER NOTES: Signed as non-drafted free agent by Florida Marlins organization (December 6, 1993). ... Traded by Marlins to Chicago White Sox for OF Jeff Abbott (December 10, 2000). ... Released by White Sox (March 13, 2002). ... Signed by Anaheim Angels organization (March 16, 2002). ... On disabled list (June 16-September 1, 2002); included rehabilitation assignment to Salt Lake. ... Signed as a free agent by San Francisco Giants organization (December 14, 2004).
2005 GAMES PLAYED BY POSITION (MLB): OF—6.

LEFTY-RIGHTY SPLITS

vs.	Avg.	AB	H	2B	3B	HR	RBI	BB	SO	OBP	Slg.
L	1.000	1	1	0	0	0	1	0	0	1.000	1.000
R	.000	3	0	0	0	0	0	0	1	.000	.000

Year	Team (League)	Pos.	G	AB	R	H	2B	3B	HR	RBI	BB	SO	HBP	GDP	SB-CS	Avg.	OBP	SLG	OPS	E	Avg.
1994— Dom. Marlins (DSL)	OF		67	274	54	75	18	0	7	32	28	41	0	0	29-8	.274	.337	.416	.753	10	.936
1995— GC Marlins (GCL)	OF-OF		48	204	35	58	9	4	2	13	13	42	1	2	17-6	.284	.330	.397	.727	2	.983
1996— GC Marlins (GCL)	OF-OF		43	174	35	50	5	4	0	16	15	34	3	0	26-7	.287	.354	.362	.716	2	.980
— Brevard County (FSL)	OF-OF		17	61	11	15	0	1	0	2	4	18	0	1	2-3	.246	.288	.279	.567	2	.950
1997— Kane Co. (Midw.)	OF-OF		99	376	70	96	18	7	14	53	37	122	5	1	41-6	.255	.329	.452	.781	4	.979
1998— Brevard County (FSL)	OF-OF		135	559	90	156	20	12	13	58	45	147	4	3	29-17	.279	.336	.428	.764	8	.979
1999— Portland (East.)	OF-OF		138	568	87	148	30	10	13	64	39	150	2	5	64-15	.261	.308	.417	.725	11	.969
— Florida (N.L.)			15	21	3	3	1	0	0	2	1	6	0	0	0-1	.143	.182	.190	.372	1	.950
2000— Calgary (PCL)	OF-OF		94	350	45	93	18	3	7	52	21	86	3	5	20-14	.266	.310	.394	.704	11	.954
2001— Chicago (A.L.)	OF		22	37	2	3	0	0	0	1	2	15	0	0	2-0	.081	.128	.081	.209	1	.978
— Charlotte (Int'l)	OF-OF		88	319	36	69	11	4	8	25	20	80	2	1	15-6	.216	.266	.332	.598	8	.962
2002— Salt Lake (PCL)	OF-OF		39	139	17	38	3	5	2	10	4	31	1	2	8-3	.273	.299	.410	.709	2	.976
— Anaheim (A.L.)	OF-DH		29	32	6	9	0	1	1	7	2	14	1	0	0-2	.281	.343	.438	.780	0	1.000
2003— Anaheim (A.L.)			6	2	1	0	0	0	0	0	0	0	0	0	0-0	.000	.000	.000	.000	1	.750
— Salt Lake (PCL)	OF-OF-DH		110	402	50	112	17	6	10	48	12	86	5	7	24-8	.279	.304	.425	.729	7	.975
2004— Tucson (PCL)	OF		125	441	67	120	26	9	7	64	22	118	4	5	21-11	.272	.310	.420	.730	7	.844
2005— Fresno (PCL)	OF-DH		113	386	57	93	13	1	23	60	22	113	3	10	22-8	.241	.286	.459	.744	6	.987
— San Francisco (N.L.)	OF		12	4	3	1	0	0	0	1	0	6	0	0	0-0	.250	.250	.250	.500	0	1.000
American League totals (3 years)			57	71	9	12	0	1	1	8	4	29	1	0	2-2	.169	.224	.239	.463	2	.974
National League totals (2 years)			27	25	6	4	1	0	0	3	1	7	0	0	0-1	.160	.192	.200	.392	1	.957
Major League totals (5 years)			84	96	15	16	1	1	1	11	5	36	1	0	2-3	.167	.216	.229	.445	3	.970

PERSONAL: Born May 30, 1972, in Santo Domingo, Dominican Republic. ... 6-0/213. ... Bats right, throws right. ... Full name: Manuel Aristides Ramirez. ... Name pronounced: ruh-MEER-ez. ... High school: George Washington (New York).

TRANSACTIONS/CAREER NOTES: Selected by Cleveland Indians organization in first round (13th pick overall) of 1991 free-agent draft. ... On suspended list (June 8-11, 1999). ... On disabled list (May 30-July 13, 2000); included rehabilitation assignments to Akron and Buffalo. ... Signed as a free agent by Boston Red Sox (December 13, 2000). ... On disabled list (May 14-June 25, 2002); included rehabilitation assignment to Pawtucket.

2005 GAMES PLAYED BY POSITION (MLB): OF—149, DH—2.

SCOUTING REPORT **Offense:** Outside of Albert Pujols, Ramirez is baseball's best righthand hitter and run producer. Has an exceptional approach at the plate with excellent balance and bat speed. Is a clutch hitter who will use the whole field. Can drive the best pitchers' best pitches. There is no single way to pitch to him, but he occasionally will chase high fastballs. Tends to give away at-bats. Is not an instinctive baserunner. **Defense:** He has some protection playing left field in Fenway Park, but he doesn't get very good jumps on the ball. Range is limited and hands are stiff. Is accurate with a quick release when he charges the ball. **Outlook:** Ramirez is a pure hitter and run producer with above-average power. Is one of the best in the league at making quick adjustments. **Grade 9.3**

MANNY RAMIREZ'S HITTING ZONE

.278	.333	.216
.364	.350	.347
.175	.412	.316

LEFTY-RIGHTY SPLITS

vs.	Avg.	AB	H	2B	3B	HR	RBI	BB	SO	OBP	Slg.
L	.236	165	39	9	0	13	36	30	29	.358	.527
R	.316	389	123	21	1	32	108	50	90	.401	.622

R

							BATTING											**FIELDING**	
Year Team (League)	Pos.	G	AB	R	H	2B	3B	HR	RBI	BB	SO	HBP	GDP	SB-CS	Avg.	OBP	SLG	OPS	E	Avg.
1991— Burlington (Appal.)	OF	59	215	44	70	11	4	19	63	34	41	6	4	7-8	.326	.426	.679	1.105	3	.966
1992— Kinston (Carol.)	OF	81	291	52	81	18	4	13	63	45	74	4	9	1-3	.278	.379	.502	.881	6	.956
1993— Cant./Akr. (Eastern)	OF	89	344	67	117	32	0	17	79	45	68	2	11	2-2	.340	.414	.581	.996	5	.967
—Charlotte (Int'l)	OF	40	145	38	46	12	0	14	36	27	35	2	1	1-1	.317	.424	.690	1.113	3	.961
—Cleveland (A.L.)	DH-OF	22	53	5	9	1	0	2	5	2	8	0	3	0-0	.170	.200	.302	.502	0	1.000
1994— Cleveland (A.L.)	OF-DH	91	290	51	78	22	0	17	60	42	72	0	6	4-2	.269	.357	.521	.878	1	.994
1995— Cleveland (A.L.)	OF-DH	137	484	85	149	26	1	31	107	75	112	5	13	6-6	.308	.402	.558	.960	9	.978
1996— Cleveland (A.L.)	OF-DH	152	550	94	170	45	3	33	112	85	104	3	18	8-5	.309	.399	.582	.981	7	.970
1997— Cleveland (A.L.)	OF-DH	150	561	99	184	40	0	26	88	79	115	7	19	2-3	.328	.415	.538	.953	7	.975
1998— Cleveland (A.L.)	OF-DH	150	571	108	168	35	2	45	145	76	121	6	18	5-3	.294	.377	.599	.976	7	.975
1999— Cleveland (A.L.)	OF-DH	147	522	131	174	34	3	44	* 165	96	131	13	12	2-4	.333	.442	* .663	1.105	7	.975
2000— Cleveland (A.L.)	OF-DH	118	439	92	154	34	2	38	122	86	117	3	9	1-1	.351	.457	* .697	1.154	2	.986
—Akron (East.)	DH	1	2	1	1	0	0	1	2	2	1	0	0	0-0	.500	.750	2.000	2.750	...	...
—Buffalo (Int'l)	DH	5	11	5	5	1	0	3	7	6	1	0	1	0-0	.455	.647	1.364	2.011	...	...
2001— Boston (A.L.)	DH-OF	142	529	93	162	33	2	41	125	81	147	8	9	0-1	.306	.405	.609	1.014	0	1.000
2002— Boston (A.L.)	OF-DH	120	436	84	152	31	0	33	107	73	85	8	13	0-0	* .349	* .450	.647	1.097	5	.959
—Pawtucket (Int'l)	OF	11	30	2	3	1	0	1	2	8	9	1	1	0-0	.100	.308	.233	.541	0	1.000
2003— Boston (A.L.)	OF-DH	154	569	117	185	36	1	37	104	97	94	8	22	3-1	.325	* .427	.587	1.014	4	.982
2004— Boston (A.L.)	OF-DH	152	568	108	175	44	0	* 43	130	82	124	6	17	2-4	.308	.397	* .613	1.009	7	.967
2005— Boston (A.L.)	OF-DH	152	554	112	162	30	1	45	144	80	119	10	20	1-0	.292	.388	.594	.982	7	.974
Major League totals (13 years)		1687	6126	1179	1922	411	15	435	1414	954	1349	77	179	34-30	.314	.409	.599	1.008	61	.977

DIVISION SERIES RECORD

Year Team (League)	Pos.	G	AB	R	H	2B	3B	HR	RBI	BB	SO	HBP	GDP	SB-CS	Avg.	OBP	SLG	OPS	E	Avg.
1995— Cleveland (A.L.)	OF	3	12	1	0	0	0	0	0	1	2	1	0	0-0	.000	.143	.000	.143	0	1.000
1996— Cleveland (A.L.)	OF	4	16	4	6	2	0	2	2	1	4	0	1	0-0	.375	.412	.875	1.287	0	1.000
1997— Cleveland (A.L.)	OF	5	21	2	3	1	0	0	3	0	3	0	2	0-0	.143	.143	.190	.333	1	.750
1998— Cleveland (A.L.)	OF	4	14	2	5	0	0	2	3	1	4	2	0	0-0	.357	.471	.929	1.399	0	1.000
1999— Cleveland (A.L.)	OF	5	18	5	1	1	0	0	1	4	8	1	0	0-0	.056	.261	.111	.372	0	1.000
2003— Boston (A.L.)	OF	5	20	2	4	0	0	1	3	3	7	0	0	0-0	.200	.304	.350	.654	0	1.000
2004— Boston (A.L.)	OF	3	13	3	5	2	0	1	7	1	4	0	0	0-0	.385	.375	.769	1.144	0	1.000
2005— Boston (A.L.)	OF	3	10	2	3	0	0	2	4	2	0	0	0	0-0	.300	.417	.900	1.317	0	1.000
Division series totals (8 years)		32	124	21	27	8	0	8	23	13	32	4	3		.218	.308	.476	.783	1	.978

CHAMPIONSHIP SERIES RECORD

Year Team (League)	Pos.	G	AB	R	H	2B	3B	HR	RBI	BB	SO	HBP	GDP	SB-CS	Avg.	OBP	SLG	OPS	E	Avg.
1995— Cleveland (A.L.)	OF	6	21	2	6	0	0	2	2	2	5	0	1	0-0	.286	.348	.571	.919	0	1.000
1997— Cleveland (A.L.)	OF	6	21	3	6	1	0	2	3	5	5	1	1	0-0	.286	.444	.619	1.063	1	.933
1998— Cleveland (A.L.)	OF	6	21	2	7	1	0	1	4	4	9	0	1	0-0	.333	.423	.667	1.090	0	1.000
2003— Boston (A.L.)	OF	7	29	6	9	1	0	2	4	1	4	0	2	0-1	.310	.333	.552	.885	0	1.000
2004— Boston (A.L.)	OF	7	30	3	9	1	0	0	0	5	4	0	1	0-0	.300	.400	.333	.733	1	.947
Champ. series totals (5 years)		32	122	16	37	4	0	8	13	17	27	1	6	0-1	.303	.390	.533	.923	2	.971

WORLD SERIES RECORD

Year Team (League)	Pos.	G	AB	R	H	2B	3B	HR	RBI	BB	SO	HBP	GDP	SB-CS	Avg.	OBP	SLG	OPS	E	Avg.
1995— Cleveland (A.L.)	OF	6	18	2	4	0	0	1	2	4	5	0	1	1-0	.222	.364	.389	.753	0	1.000
1997— Cleveland (A.L.)	OF	7	26	3	4	0	0	2	6	6	5	0	2	0-0	.154	.294	.385	.679	1	.944
2004— Boston (A.L.)	OF	4	17	2	7	0	0	1	4	3	3	0	0	0-0	.412	.500	.588	1.088	2	.750
World series totals (3 years)		17	61	7	15	0	0	4	12	13	13	0	3	1-0	.246	.368	.443	.811	3	.912

ALL-STAR GAME RECORD

		G	AB	R	H	2B	3B	HR	RBI	BB	SO	HBP	GDP	SB-CS	Avg.	OBP	SLG	OPS	E	Avg.
All-Star Game totals (7 years)		7	9	2	3	0	0	1	4	3	3	0	1	0-0	.333	.462	.667	1.128	0	1.000

RANDA, JOE 3B

PERSONAL: Born December 18, 1969, in Milwaukee. ... 5-11/190. ... Bats right, throws right. ... Full name: Joseph Gregory Randa. ... High school: Kettle-Moraine (Wales, Wis.). ... College: Tennessee.

TRANSACTIONS/CAREER NOTES: Selected by California Angels organization in 30th round of 1989 free-agent draft; did not sign. ... Selected by Kansas City Royals organization in 11th round of 1991 free-agent draft. ... On disabled list (May 5-27, 1996); included rehabilitation assignment to Omaha. ... Traded by Royals with Ps Jeff Granger, Jeff Martin and Jeff Wallace to Pittsburgh Pirates for SS Jay Bell and 1B Jeff King (December 13, 1996). ... On disabled list (June 28-July 27, 1997); included rehabilitation assignment to Calgary. ... Selected by Arizona Diamondbacks in third round (57th pick overall) of expansion draft (November 18, 1997). ... Traded by Diamondbacks with P Matt Drews and 3B Gabe Alvarez to Detroit Tigers for 3B Travis Fryman (November 18, 1997). ... Traded by Tigers to New York Mets for P Willie Blair (December 4, 1998). ... Traded by Mets to Royals for OF Juan LeBron (December 10, 1998). ... On disabled list (July 8-23, 2003; and June 28-July 24, 2004). ... Signed as a free agent by Cincinnati Reds (December 21, 2004). ... Traded by Reds to San Diego Padres for Ps Travis Chick and Justin Germano (July 23, 2005).

2005 GAMES PLAYED BY POSITION (MLB): 3B—142, DH—2.

R

SCOUTING REPORT *Offense:* He's a contact hitter whose power has declined with his bat speed. Has a long swing and is a better hitter when taking the ball the other way. Likes the ball up and over the plate. Is better against lefthanders. Is a good situational hitter who will shorten his stroke. Can't consistently handle good fastballs on the inner half of the plate. Doesn't run well. *Defense:* He has very good hands, but his range to both sides is limited. Has an unorthodox throwing motion with just average strength, yet is accurate. Will not be a defensive liability. *Outlook:* Randa is an average major league player whose lack of run production and power can be a problem at the corner position. Fits well on a club with power at other positions. *Grade 6.7*

JOE RANDA'S HITTING ZONE

.320	.000	.350
.342	.388	.226
.262	.317	.216

LEFTY-RIGHTY SPLITS

vs.	Avg.	AB	H	2B	3B	HR	RBI	BB	SO	OBP	Slg.
L	.306	157	48	14	0	3	22	15	18	.368	.452
R	.264	398	105	29	2	14	46	32	63	.322	.452

Year Team (League)	Pos.	G	AB	R	H	2B	3B	HR	RBI	BB	SO	HBP	GDP	SB-CS	Avg.	OBP	SLG	OPS	FIELDING E	Avg.
1991— Eugene (Northwest)	3B	72	275	53	93	20	2	11	59	46	29	6	8	6-1	.338	.438	.545	.984	14	.923
1992— Appleton (Midwest)	3B	72	266	55	80	13	0	5	43	34	37	6	6	6-2	.301	.385	.406	.791	12	.941
— Baseball City (FSL)	3B-SS	51	189	22	52	7	0	1	12	12	21	2	4	4-3	.275	.324	.328	.652	6	.961
1993— Memphis (Sou.)	3B	131	505	74	149	31	5	11	72	39	64	3	10	8-7	.295	.343	.442	.784	25	.942
1994— Omaha (A.A.)	3B	127	455	65	125	27	2	10	51	30	49	8	5	5-2	.275	.327	.409	.736	24	.945
1995— Kansas City (A.L.)	3B-2B-DH	34	70	6	12	2	0	1	5	6	17	0	2	0-1	.171	.237	.243	.480	3	.952
— Omaha (A.A.)	3B	64	233	33	64	10	2	8	33	22	33	2	9	2-2	.275	.341	.438	.779	4	.958
1996— Kansas City (A.L.)	DH	110	337	36	102	24	1	6	47	26	47	1	10	13-4	.303	.351	.433	.784	10	.960
— Omaha (A.A.)	3B	3	9	1	1	0	1	0	0	1	1	0	1	0-0	.111	.200	.333	.533	0	1.000
1997— Pittsburgh (N.L.)	3B-2B	126	443	58	134	27	9	7	60	41	64	6	10	4-2	.302	.366	.451	.817	21	.948
— Calgary (PCL)	3B	3	11	4	4	1	0	1	4	3	4	0	1	0-0	.364	.500	.727	1.227	1	.900
1998— Detroit (A.L.)	3B-2B-1B DH	138	460	56	117	21	2	9	50	41	70	7	9	8-7	.254	.323	.367	.690	7	.981
1999— Kansas City (A.L.)	3B	156	628	92	197	36	8	16	84	50	80	3	15	5-4	.314	.363	.473	.836	22	.952
2000— Kansas City (A.L.)	3B-DH	158	612	88	186	29	4	15	106	36	66	6	19	6-3	.304	.343	.438	.781	17	.957
2001— Kansas City (A.L.)	3B-DH-2B	151	581	59	147	34	2	13	83	42	80	6	15	3-2	.253	.307	.386	.693	13	.964
2002— Kansas City (A.L.)	3B-DH	151	549	63	155	36	5	11	80	46	69	9	13	2-1	.282	.341	.426	.768	10	.972
2003— Kansas City (A.L.)	3B-DH	131	502	80	146	31	1	16	72	41	61	7	12	1-0	.291	.348	.452	.800	5	.980
2004— Kansas City (A.L.)	3B-DH-1B	128	485	65	139	31	2	8	56	40	77	6	11	0-0	.287	.343	.408	.751	11	.969
2005— Cincinnati (N.L.)	3B-DH	92	332	44	96	26	1	13	48	33	52	2	6	0-0	.289	.356	.491	.847	6	.974
— San Diego (N.L.)	3B	58	223	27	57	17	1	4	20	14	29	2	5	0-1	.256	.303	.395	.698	6	.955
American League totals (9 years)		1157	4224	545	1201	244	25	95	583	328	567	45	106	38-23	.284	.338	.421	.760	102	.966
National League totals (2 years)		276	998	129	287	70	11	24	128	88	145	10	21	4-3	.288	.349	.452	.801	33	.957
Major League totals (11 years)		1433	5222	674	1488	314	36	119	711	416	712	55	127	42-26	.285	.340	.427	.768	135	.964

DIVISION SERIES RECORD

Year Team (League)	Pos.	G	AB	R	H	2B	3B	HR	RBI	BB	SO	HBP	GDP	SB-CS	Avg.	OBP	SLG	OPS	E	Avg.
2005— San Diego (N.L.)	3B	3	11	1	4	1	0	0	0	1	0	0	2	0-0	.364	.417	.455	.871	0	1.000

RASNER, DARRELL P

PERSONAL: Born January 13, 1981, in Carson City, Nev. ... 6-3/210. ... Throws right, bats right. ... Full name: Darrell Wayne Rasner. ... High school: Carson City (Nev.). ... College: Nevada.

TRANSACTIONS/CAREER NOTES: Selected by Montreal Expos organization in second round of 2002 free-agent draft. ... Expos franchise transferred to Washington, D.C., and renamed Washington Nationals for 2005 season (December 3, 2004).

CAREER HITTING: 0-for-0 (.000), 0 R, 0 2B, 0 3B, 0 HR, 0 RBI.

LEFTY-RIGHTY SPLITS

vs.	Avg.	AB	H	2B	3B	HR	RBI	BB	SO	OBP	Slg.
L	.143	14	2	1	0	0	2	2	2	.294	.214
R	.250	12	3	2	0	0	1	0	2	.308	.417

Year Team (League)	W	L	Pct.	ERA	WHIP	G	GS	CG	ShO	Hld.	Sv.-Opp.	IP	H	R	ER	HR	BB-IBB	SO	Avg.
2002— Vermont (NYP)	2	5	.286	4.33	1.42	10	10	0	0	...	0-...	43.2	44	27	21	1	18-0	49	.262
2003— Savannah (S. Atl.)	7	7	.500	4.19	1.35	22	22	2	0	...	0-...	105.1	106	53	49	8	36-0	90	.268
2004— Brevard County (FSL)	6	5	.545	3.17	1.37	22	21	0	0	...	0-...	119.1	133	55	42	6	31-0	88	.295
— Harrisburg (East.)	1	1	.500	1.21	1.01	5	5	0	0	...	0-...	29.2	21	4	4	1	9-1	15	.221
2005— Harrisburg (East.)	6	7	.462	3.59	1.19	27	26	1	0	1	0-0	150.1	150	66	60	10	29-2	96	.260
— Was. (N.L.)	0	1	.000	3.68	0.95	5	1	0	0	0	0-0	7.1	3	3	3	0	2-1	4	.192
Major League totals (1 year)	0	1	.000	3.68	0.95	5	1	0	0	0	0-0	7.1	3	3	3	0	2-1	4	.192

RAUCH, JON   P

PERSONAL: Born September 27, 1978, in Louisville, Ky. ... 6-11/260. ... Throws right, bats right. ... Full name: Jon Erich Rauch. ... Name pronounced: ROUSH. ... High school: Oldham County (Buckner, Ky.). ... College: Morehead State.
TRANSACTIONS/CAREER NOTES: Selected by Chicago White Sox organization in third round of 1999 free-agent draft. ... Traded by White Sox with P Gary Majewski to Montreal Expos for OF Carl Everett (July 18, 2004). ... On disabled list (August 14-September 14, 2004). ... On disabled list (May 26-September 6, 2005); included rehabilitation assignment to New Orleans.
HONORS: Named Minor League Player of the Year by THE SPORTING NEWS (2000).
CAREER HITTING: 2-for-13 (.154), 2 R, 0 2B, 0 3B, 1 HR, 3 RBI.

JON RAUCH'S PITCHING ZONE

.000	.273	.000
.250	.333	.067
.375	.250	.286

LEFTY-RIGHTY SPLITS

vs.	Avg.	AB	H	2B	3B	HR	RBI	BB	SO	OBP	Slg.
L	.255	51	13	3	1	1	4	8	9	.350	.412
R	.186	59	11	4	0	2	8	3	14	.238	.356

Year Team (League)	W	L	Pct.	ERA	WHIP	G	GS	CG	ShO	Hld.	Sv.-Opp.	IP	H	R	ER	HR	BB-IBB	SO	Avg.
1999— Bristol (Appal.)	4	4	.500	4.45	1.43	14	9	0	0	...	2-...	56.2	65	44	28	4	16-1	66	.269
— Win.-Salem (Car.)	0	0	...	3.00	1.17	1	1	0	0	...	0-...	6.0	4	3	2	1	3-0	7	.174
2000— Win.-Salem (Car.)	11	3	.786	2.86	1.23	18	18	1	0	...	0-...	110.0	102	49	35	10	33-0	124	.249
— Birmingham (Sou.)	5	1	.833	2.25	0.93	8	8	2	2	...	0-...	56.0	36	18	14	4	16-0	63	.179
2001— Charlotte (Int'l)	1	3	.250	5.79	1.25	6	6	0	0	...	0-...	28.0	28	20	18	4	7-0	27	.248
2002— Chicago (A.L.)	2	1	.667	6.59	1.47	8	6	0	0	0	0-0	28.2	28	26	21	7	14-2	19	.248
— Charlotte (Int'l)	7	8	.467	4.28	1.22	19	19	1	0	...	0-...	109.1	91	60	52	14	42-2	97	.226
2003— Charlotte (Int'l)	7	1	.875	4.11	1.30	24	23	1	0	...	0-...	124.2	121	60	57	16	35-1	94	.258
2004— Chicago (A.L.)	1	1	.500	6.23	2.31	2	2	0	0	0	0-0	8.2	16	6	6	0	4-0	4	.432
— Charlotte (Int'l)	6	3	.667	3.11	1.13	14	13	0	0	...	0-...	72.1	57	27	25	9	25-0	61	.218
— Edmonton (PCL)	1	1	.500	4.50	1.06	3	3	0	0	...	0-...	18.0	17	9	9	3	2-0	13	.246
— Montreal (N.L.)	3	0	1.000	1.54	0.90	9	2	0	0	0	0-0	23.1	14	4	4	1	7-2	18	.175
2005— New Orleans (PCL)	1	1	.500	2.53	0.98	7	5	0	0	...	0-...	21.1	19	7	6	3	2-0	25	.232
— Was. (N.L.)	2	4	.333	3.60	1.17	15	1	0	0	0	0-0	30.0	24	12	12	3	11-2	23	.218
American League totals (2 years)	3	2	.600	6.51	1.66	10	8	0	0	0	0-0	37.1	44	32	27	7	18-2	23	.293
National League totals (2 years)	5	4	.556	2.70	1.05	24	3	0	0	0	0-0	53.1	38	16	16	4	18-4	41	.200
Major League totals (3 years)	8	6	.571	4.27	1.30	34	11	0	0	0	0-0	90.2	82	48	43	11	36-6	64	.241

RAY, CHRIS   P

PERSONAL: Born January 12, 1982, in Tampa. ... 6-3/200. ... Throws right, bats right. ... Full name: Christopher T. Ray. ... College: William & Mary.
TRANSACTIONS/CAREER NOTES: Selected by Baltimore Orioles organization in third round of 2003 free-agent draft.
CAREER HITTING: 0-for-0 (.000), 0 R, 0 2B, 0 3B, 0 HR, 0 RBI.

CHRIS RAY'S PITCHING ZONE

.083	.200	.167
.192	.385	.400
.091	.500	.364

LEFTY-RIGHTY SPLITS

vs.	Avg.	AB	H	2B	3B	HR	RBI	BB	SO	OBP	Slg.
L	.284	67	19	2	1	3	10	7	16	.347	.478
R	.174	86	15	4	0	2	13	11	27	.276	.291

Year Team (League)	W	L	Pct.	ERA	WHIP	G	GS	CG	ShO	Hld.	Sv.-Opp.	IP	H	R	ER	HR	BB-IBB	SO	Avg.
2003— Aberdeen (N.Y.-Penn.)	2	0	1.000	2.82	1.10	9	8	0	0	...	0-...	38.1	32	15	12	0	10-0	44	.225
2004— Delmarva (S. Atl.)	2	3	.400	3.42	1.20	10	9	0	0	...	0-...	50.0	43	21	19	3	17-0	46	.240
— Frederick (Carolina)	6	3	.667	3.80	1.39	14	14	1	1	...	0-...	73.1	82	31	31	6	20-0	74	.296
2005— Bowie (East.)	1	2	.333	0.96	0.64	31	0	0	0	...	18-18	37.1	17	5	4	3	7-0	40	.140
— Baltimore (A.L.)	1	3	.250	2.66	1.28	41	0	0	0	8	0-4	40.2	34	15	12	5	18-3	43	.222
Major League totals (1 year)	1	3	.250	2.66	1.28	41	0	0	0	8	0-4	40.2	34	15	12	5	18-3	43	.222

REAMES, BRITT   P

PERSONAL: Born August 19, 1973, in Seneca, S.C. ... 5-10/180. ... Throws right, bats right. ... Full name: William Britt Reames. ... Name pronounced: REEMS. ... High school: Seneca (S.C.). ... College: The Citadel.
TRANSACTIONS/CAREER NOTES: Selected by St. Louis Cardinals organization in 17th round of 1995 free-agent draft. ... On disabled list (April 4, 1997-entire season; and April 10, 1998-entire season). ... Traded by Cardinals with 3B Fernando Tatis to Montreal Expos for Ps Dustin Hermanson and Steve Kline (December 14, 2000). ... Signed as a free agent by Oakland Athletics organization (January 8, 2004).
CAREER HITTING: 5-for-39 (.128), 3 R, 0 2B, 0 3B, 1 HR, 3 RBI.

LEFTY-RIGHTY SPLITS

vs.	Avg.	AB	H	2B	3B	HR	RBI	BB	SO	OBP	Slg.
L	.250	8	2	0	0	1	4	1	2	.300	.625
R	.471	17	8	2	0	1	4	1	2	.526	.765

Year Team (League)	W	L	Pct.	ERA	WHIP	G	GS	CG	ShO	Hld.	Sv.-Opp.	IP	H	R	ER	HR	BB-IBB	SO	Avg.
1995— New Jersey (NYP)	2	1	.667	1.52	1.04	5	5	0	0	...	0-...	29.2	19	7	5	1	12-0	42	.181
— Savannah (S. Atl.)	3	5	.375	3.46	1.02	10	10	1	0	...	0-...	54.2	41	23	21	7	15-0	63	.198
1996— Peoria (Midw.)	15	7	.682	1.90	0.86	25	25	2	•1	...	0-...	161.0	97	43	34	5	41-0	167	.170
1997—			Did not play.																
1998—			Did not play.																
1999— Potomac (Carol.)	3	2	.600	3.19	1.50	10	8	0	0	...	0-...	36.2	34	21	13	2	21-0	22	.250
2000— Arkansas (Texas)	2	3	.400	6.13	1.61	8	8	0	0	...	0-...	39.2	46	28	27	4	18-0	39	.291
— Memphis (PCL)	6	2	.750	2.28	1.00	13	13	2	1	...	0-...	75.0	55	20	19	2	20-0	77	.212
— St. Louis (N.L.)	2	1	.667	2.88	1.30	8	7	0	0	0	0-0	40.2	30	17	13	4	23-1	31	.207
2001— Montreal (N.L.)	4	8	.333	5.59	1.57	41	13	0	0	6	0-1	95.0	101	68	59	16	48-3	86	.273
— Ottawa (Int'l)	4	3	.571	3.50	1.11	8	8	1	0	...	0-...	54.0	47	24	21	4	13-0	38	.242
2002— Montreal (N.L.)	1	4	.200	5.03	1.59	42	6	0	0	6	0-1	68.0	70	42	38	8	38-6	76	.266
— Ottawa (Int'l)	3	2	.600	2.79	1.07	7	7	0	0	...	0-...	42.0	31	16	13	3	14-0	26	.207
2003— Montreal (N.L.)	0	0	...	27.00	4.50	2	0	0	0	0	0-0	1.1	4	4	4	0	2-0	1	.500
— Edmonton (PCL)	5	13	.278	5.42	1.63	25	20	0	0	...	0-...	118.0	146	80	71	8	46-1	86	.299
2004— Sacramento (PCL)	3	5	.375	4.67	1.60	34	3	0	0	...	8-...	52.0	55	27	27	5	28-5	57	.262

Year	Team (League)	W	L	Pct.	ERA	WHIP	G	GS	CG	ShO	Hld.	Sv.-Opp.	IP	H	R	ER	HR	BB-IBB	SO	Avg.
2005—	Oakland (A.L.)	0	0	...	9.53	2.12	2	0	0	0	0	0-0	5.2	10	6	6	2	2-0	4	.400
—	Sacramento (PCL)	6	6	.500	3.31	1.36	42	7	0	0	4	8-12	92.1	91	46	34	3	35-3	85	.253
American League totals (1 year)		0	0	...	9.53	2.12	2	0	0	0	0	0-0	5.2	10	6	6	2	2-0	4	.400
National League totals (4 years)		7	13	.350	5.00	1.54	93	26	0	0	12	0-2	205.0	205	131	114	28	111-10	194	.261
Major League totals (5 years)		7	13	.350	5.13	1.56	95	26	0	0	12	0-2	210.2	215	137	120	30	113-10	198	.265

DIVISION SERIES RECORD

Year	Team (League)	W	L	Pct.	ERA	WHIP	G	GS	CG	ShO	Hld.	Sv.-Opp.	IP	H	R	ER	HR	BB-IBB	SO	Avg.
2000—	St. Louis (N.L.)	1	0	1.000	0.00	0.90	2	0	0	0	...	0-0	3.1	0	0	0	0	3-0	2	...

CHAMPIONSHIP SERIES RECORD

Year	Team (League)	W	L	Pct.	ERA	WHIP	G	GS	CG	ShO	Hld.	Sv.-Opp.	IP	H	R	ER	HR	BB-IBB	SO	Avg.
2000—	St. Louis (N.L.)	0	0	...	1.42	1.42	2	0	0	0	...	0-0	6.1	5	1	1	1	4-1	6	...

R

REDDING, TIM — P

PERSONAL: Born February 12, 1978, in Rochester, N.Y. ... 6-0/200. ... Throws right, bats right. ... Full name: Timothy James Redding. ... High school: Churchville (N.Y.). ... Junior college: Monroe (N.Y.) Community College.

TRANSACTIONS/CAREER NOTES: Selected by Houston Astros organization in 20th round of 1997 free-agent draft. ... Traded by Astros to San Diego Padres for C Humberto Quintero (March 28, 2005). ... On disabled list (May 9-June 22, 2005); included rehabilitation assignment to Portland. ... Traded by Padres with P Darrell May to New York Yankees for P Paul Quantrill (July 2, 2005).

CAREER HITTING: 19-for-121 (.157), 5 R, 3 2B, 0 3B, 0 HR, 5 RBI.

TIM REDDING'S PITCHING ZONE

.143	.667	.400
.435	.391	.280
.167	.400	.556

LEFTY-RIGHTY SPLITS

vs.	Avg.	AB	H	2B	3B	HR	RBI	BB	SO	OBP	Slg.
L	.299	67	20	5	0	2	11	9	11	.385	.463
R	.387	62	24	4	1	5	20	8	8	.452	.726

Year	Team (League)	W	L	Pct.	ERA	WHIP	G	GS	CG	ShO	Hld.	Sv.-Opp.	IP	H	R	ER	HR	BB-IBB	SO	Avg.
1998—	Auburn (NY-Penn)	7	3	.700	4.52	1.34	16	15	0	0		1-...	73.2	49	44	37	2	50-0	98	.188
1999—	Michigan (Midw.)	8	6	.571	4.97	1.52	43	11	0	0		14-...	105.0	84	69	58	4	76-1	144	.221
2000—	Kissimmee (Fla. St.)	12	5	.706	2.68	1.18	24	24	0	0		0-...	154.2	125	62	46	5	57-1	170	.219
—	Round Rock (Texas)	2	0	1.000	3.46	1.38	5	5	0	0		0-...	26.0	14	12	10	4	22-0	22	.167
2001—	Round Rock (Texas)	10	2	.833	2.18	0.98	14	14	1	1		0-...	90.2	64	26	22	5	25-0	113	.192
—	New Orleans (PCL)	4	1	.800	4.54	1.09	6	6	0	0		0-...	37.2	22	21	19	4	19-0	42	.172
—	Houston (N.L.)	3	1	.750	5.50	1.54	13	9	0	0	0	0-0	55.2	62	38	34	11	24-0	55	.286
2002—	New Orleans (PCL)	3	3	.500	5.21	1.18	11	7	0	0	0	0-0	38.0	32	22	22	6	13-1	50	.232
—	Houston (N.L.)	3	6	.333	5.40	1.54	18	14	0	0	0	0-0	73.1	78	49	44	10	35-3	63	.276
2003—	Houston (N.L.)	10	14	.417	3.68	1.39	33	32	0	0	0	0-0	176.0	179	85	72	16	65-4	116	.261
2004—	New Orleans (PCL)	1	3	.250	6.04	1.48	5	5	0	0	0	0-0	28.1	30	21	19	2	12-0	26	.268
—	Houston (N.L.)	5	7	.417	5.72	1.67	27	17	0	0	0	0-0	100.2	125	73	64	15	43-3	56	.309
2005—	Portland (PCL)	0	0	...	0.90	0.90	2	2	0	0	0	0-0	10.0	7	1	1	0	2-0	5	.200
—	San Diego (N.L.)	0	5	.000	9.10	1.79	9	6	0	0	0	0-0	29.2	40	35	30	7	13-1	17	.328
—	New York (A.L.)	0	1	.000	54.00	8.00	1	1	0	0	0	0-0	1.0	6	6	6	0	4-0	2	.571
—	Columbus (Int'l)	3	4	.429	5.08	1.46	10	10	0	0	0	0-0	51.1	62	34	29	5	13-0	47	.295
American League totals (1 year)		0	1	.000	54.00	8.00	1	1	0	0	0	0-0	1.0	6	6	6	0	4-0	2	.571
National League totals (5 years)		21	33	.389	5.04	1.53	100	78	0	0	0	0-0	435.1	484	280	244	59	180-11	307	.283
Major League totals (5 years)		21	34	.382	5.16	1.54	101	79	0	0	0	0-0	436.1	488	286	250	59	184-11	309	.284

REDMAN, MARK — P

PERSONAL: Born January 5, 1974, in San Diego. ... 6-5/245. ... Throws left, bats left. ... Full name: Mark Allen Redman. ... High school: Escondido (Calif.). ... College: Oklahoma.

TRANSACTIONS/CAREER NOTES: Selected by Detroit Tigers organization in 41st round of 1992 free-agent draft; did not sign. ... Selected by Minnesota Twins organization in first round (13th pick overall) of 1995 free-agent draft. ... On disabled list (July 25-August 10, 1999). ... On disabled list (May 21-July 28, 2001); included rehabilitation assignment to Edmonton. ... Traded by Twins to Tigers for P Todd Jones (July 28, 2001). ... On disabled list (July 28-August 22, 2001); included rehabilitation assignment to Toledo. ... Traded by Tigers with P Jerrod Fuell to Florida Marlins for Ps Gary Knotts, Nate Robertson and Rob Henkel (January 11, 2003). ... On disabled list (April 30-May 30, 2003). ... Traded by Marlins to Oakland Athletics for Ps Mike Neu and Bill Murphy (December 16, 2003). ... Traded by A's with P Arthur Rhodes to Pittsburgh Pirates for C Jason Kendall and cash (November 29, 2004).

CAREER HITTING: 8-for-128 (.063), 2 R, 0 2B, 0 3B, 0 HR, 3 RBI.

SCOUTING REPORT *Throws:* He has an 82-85 mph fastball, a curveball and a changeup. *Tendencies:* Redman is a finesse pitcher, relying on location to be effective because his overall stuff is below average. Pushes the ball without velocity but is effective when he keeps his pitches down. Continually changes speeds and has a good idea what he wants to do. Likes to throw his curve to righthanders and has a good fading change. Changes his arm slot against lefthanders if ahead in the count. Hides the ball well and is deceptive but must stay away from the center of the plate. *Outlook:* He will go as far as his command takes him. **Grade 6.8**

MARK REDMAN'S PITCHING ZONE

.273	.375	.308
.252	.456	.234
.304	.318	.226

LEFTY-RIGHTY SPLITS

vs.	Avg.	AB	H	2B	3B	HR	RBI	BB	SO	OBP	Slg.
L	.256	133	34	9	2	4	17	14	30	.327	.444
R	.283	544	154	33	2	14	73	42	71	.334	.428

Year	Team (League)	W	L	Pct.	ERA	WHIP	G	GS	CG	ShO	Hld.	Sv.-Opp.	IP	H	R	ER	HR	BB-IBB	SO	Avg.
1995—	Fort Myers (FSL)	2	1	.667	2.76	1.26	8	5	0	0		0-...	32.2	28	13	10	4	13-0	26	.239
1996—	Fort Myers (FSL)	3	4	.429	1.85	1.17	13	13	0	0		0-...	82.2	63	24	17	1	34-0	75	.220
—	New Britain (East.)	7	7	.500	3.81	1.42	16	16	3	0		0-...	106.1	101	51	45	5	50-1	96	.251
—	Salt Lake (PCL)	0	0	...	9.00	2.25	1	1	0	0		0-...	4.0	7	4	4	1	2-0	4	.389
1997—	Salt Lake (PCL)	8	15	.348	5.81	1.79	29	28	0	0		1-...	158.1	204	123	111	19	80-3	125	.316
1998—	New Britain (East.)	4	2	.667	1.52	1.20	8	8	0	0		0-...	47.1	40	11	8	3	17-0	51	.237
—	Salt Lake (PCL)	6	7	.462	5.53	1.53	19	18	0	0		0-...	99.1	111	75	61	13	41-1	88	.282

Year	Team (League)	W	L	Pct.	ERA	WHIP	G	GS	CG	ShO	Hld.	Sv.-Opp.	IP	H	R	ER	HR	BB-IBB	SO	Avg.
1999— Salt Lake (PCL)		9	9	.500	5.05	1.44	24	24	1	0	…	0-…	133.2	141	87	75	12	51-1	114	.272
— Minnesota (A.L.)		1	0	1.000	8.53	1.89	5	1	0	0	0	0-0	12.2	17	13	12	3	7-0	11	.298
2000— Minnesota (A.L.)		12	9	.571	4.76	1.41	32	24	0	0	0	0-0	151.1	168	81	80	22	45-0	117	.286
2001— Minnesota (A.L.)		2	4	.333	4.22	1.55	9	9	0	0	0	0-0	49.0	57	26	23	6	19-0	29	.286
— Edmonton (PCL)		0	0	…	13.50	3.00	1	1	0	0	…	0-…	1.1	3	2	2	0	1-0	0	.500
— Toledo (Int'l)		0	1	.000	5.27	1.10	3	3	0	0	…	0-…	13.2	14	10	8	3	1-0	12	.259
— Detroit (A.L.)		0	2	.000	6.00	1.67	2	2	0	0	0	0-0	9.0	11	6	6	1	4-0	4	.306
2002— Detroit (A.L.)		8	15	.348	4.21	1.29	30	30	3	0	0	0-0	203.0	211	107	95	15	51-2	109	.268
2003— Florida (N.L.)		14	9	.609	3.59	1.22	29	29	3	0	0	0-0	190.2	172	82	76	16	61-3	151	.239
2004— Oakland (A.L.)		11	12	.478	4.71	1.50	32	32	2	0	0	0-0	191.0	218	110	100	28	68-6	102	.292
2005— Pittsburgh (N.L.)		5	15	.250	4.90	1.37	30	30	2	1	0	0-0	178.1	188	100	97	18	56-3	101	.278
American League totals (5 years)		34	42	.447	4.62	1.42	110	98	5	0	0		616.0	682	343	316	75	194-8	372	.281
National League totals (2 years)		19	24	.442	4.22	1.29	59	59	5	1	0		369.0	360	182	173	34	117-6	252	.258
Major League totals (7 years)		53	66	.445	4.47	1.37	169	157	10	1	0	0-0	985.0	1042	525	489	109	311-14	624	.273

DIVISION SERIES RECORD

Year	Team (League)	W	L	Pct.	ERA	WHIP	G	GS	CG	ShO	Hld.	Sv.-Opp.	IP	H	R	ER	HR	BB-IBB	SO	Avg.
2003— Florida (N.L.)		0	0	…	3.00	1.67	1	1	0	0	0	0-0	6.0	7	2	2	0	3-1	4	.280

CHAMPIONSHIP SERIES RECORD

Year	Team (League)	W	L	Pct.	ERA	WHIP	G	GS	CG	ShO	Hld.	Sv.-Opp.	IP	H	R	ER	HR	BB-IBB	SO	Avg.
2003— Florida (N.L.)		0	0	…	6.52	1.76	2	2	0	0	0	0-0	9.2	13	7	7	2	4-0	4	.342

WORLD SERIES RECORD

Year	Team (League)	W	L	Pct.	ERA	WHIP	G	GS	CG	ShO	Hld.	Sv.-Opp.	IP	H	R	ER	HR	BB-IBB	SO	Avg.
2003— Florida (N.L.)		0	1	.000	15.43	3.00	1	1	0	0	0	0-0	2.1	5	4	4	1	2-0	2	.500

REDMAN, TIKE   OF

PERSONAL: Born March 10, 1977, in Tuscaloosa, Ala. ... 5-11/172. ... Bats left, throws left. ... Full name: Julian Jawonn Redman. ... High school: Tuscaloosa (Ala.) Academy.
TRANSACTIONS/CAREER NOTES: Selected by Pittsburgh Pirates organization in fifth round of 1996 free-agent draft.
2005 GAMES PLAYED BY POSITION (MLB): OF—85.

SCOUTING REPORT **Offense:** Redman makes good contact for a leadoff man but needs to improve his patience to accentuate his speed. Is a sprinter with a short stroke but doesn't have good bat speed. Has bat control but no power. Is a streaky hitter and more of a line-drive gap hitter. Really bears down with runners on. **Defense:** With his speed, Redman is not a typical center fielder. Is inconsistent with his jumps and sometimes his effort. Doesn't have a lot of instincts and his arm is short. **Outlook:** Redman basically is a fourth outfielder. Will never be a big run producer. *Grade 4.8*

TIKE REDMAN'S HITTING ZONE

.143	.400	.280
.171	.160	.303
.273	.353	.212

LEFTY-RIGHTY SPLITS

vs.	Avg.	AB	H	2B	3B	HR	RBI	BB	SO	OBP	Slg.
L	.260	73	19	2	2	2	7	6	4	.316	.425
R	.248	246	61	10	2	0	19	13	23	.285	.305

Year	Team (League)	Pos.	G	AB	R	H	2B	3B	HR	RBI	BB	SO	HBP	GDP	SB-CS	Avg.	OBP	SLG	OPS	E	Avg.
1996— GC Pirates (GCL)		OF	26	104	20	31	4	1	1	16	12	12	0	0	15-3	.298	.368	.356	.752	1	.978
— Erie (N.Y.-Penn)		OF	43	170	31	50	4	6	2	21	17	30	0	1	7-3	.294	.353	.424	.776	7	.920
1997— Lynchburg (Caro.)		1B-OF	125	415	55	104	18	5	4	45	45	82	7	8	21-8	.251	.333	.347	.680	6	.975
1998— Lynchburg (Caro.)		OF	131	525	70	135	26	10	6	46	32	73	1	5	36-16	.257	.298	.379	.677	8	.971
1999— Altoona (East.)		OF	136	532	84	143	20	12	3	60	52	52	3	6	29-16	.269	.332	.368	.700	9	.972
2000— Nashville (PCL)		OF	121	506	62	132	24	11	4	51	32	73	3	4	24-18	.261	.306	.375	.682	5	.981
— Pittsburgh (N.L.)		OF	9	18	2	6	1	0	1	1	1	7	0	0	1-0	.333	.368	.556	.924	0	1.000
2001— Nashville (PCL)		OF	95	398	53	121	18	10	3	42	24	37	4	6	21-7	.304	.347	.422	.769	4	.970
— Pittsburgh (N.L.)		OF	37	125	8	28	4	1	1	4	4	25	0	2	3-5	.224	.246	.296	.542	2	.980
2002— Nashville (PCL)		OF	76	311	40	84	9	4	2	20	21	24	1	3	16-7	.270	.315	.344	.660	3	.982
— Pittsburgh (N.L.)		OF	56	230	36	76	16	5	3	19	14	18	2	1	7-3	.330	.374	.483	.857	2	.985
2003— Nashville (PCL)		OF-DH	100	360	60	106	12	7	4	29	36	32	0	5	42-9	.294	.357	.400	.757	3	.987
— Pittsburgh (N.L.)		OF	56	230	36	76	16	5	3	19	14	18	2	1	7-3	.330	.374	.483	.857	2	.985
2004— Pittsburgh (N.L.)		OF	155	546	65	153	19	4	8	51	23	52	3	6	18-6	.280	.310	.374	.684	5	.986
2005— Pittsburgh (N.L.)		OF	135	319	33	80	12	4	2	26	19	27	1	8	4-1	.251	.292	.332	.625	7	.962
Major League totals (5 years)			392	1238	144	343	52	14	15	101	61	129	6	17	33-15	.277	.312	.378	.690	16	.979

REDMOND, MIKE   C

PERSONAL: Born May 5, 1971, in Seattle. ... 5-11/200. ... Bats right, throws right. ... Full name: Michael Patrick Redmond. ... High school: Gonzaga Prep (Spokane, Wash.). ... College: Gonzaga.
TRANSACTIONS/CAREER NOTES: Signed as a non-drafted free agent by Florida Marlins organization (August 18, 1992). ... On disabled list (August 24-September 8, 1998). ... Signed as a free agent by Minnesota Twins (November 24, 2004).
2005 GAMES PLAYED BY POSITION (MLB): C—45.

SCOUTING REPORT **Offense:** Redmond makes good contact and has good bat control. Doesn't have good bat speed. Will make adjustments. Uses the whole field and has been dependable with runners in scoring position. **Defense:** He has enough arm strength to keep opposing runners in check. Works well with his pitchers and actively blocks and shifts behind the plate. Is a solid defensive replacement but can't be overexposed. **Outlook:** Redmond, one of the better backup catchers, gets the most from his ability. Could play every day because of his defense, but his bat would be a problem. *Grade 6.3*

MIKE REDMOND'S HITTING ZONE

.500	.600	.286
.190	.412	.278
.200	.250	.143

LEFTY-RIGHTY SPLITS

vs.	Avg.	AB	H	2B	3B	HR	RBI	BB	SO	OBP	Slg.
L	.345	58	20	4	0	0	9	3	2	.387	.414
R	.289	90	26	5	0	1	17	3	12	.326	.378

Year — Team (League)	Pos.	G	AB	R	H	2B	3B	HR	RBI	BB	SO	HBP	GDP	SB-CS	Avg.	OBP	SLG	OPS	E	Avg.
1993— Kane Co. (Midw.)	C	43	100	10	20	2	0	0	10	6	17	4	1	2-0	.200	.273	.220	.493	1	.996
1994— Kane Co. (Midw.)	C	92	306	39	83	10	0	1	24	26	31	9	10	3-4	.271	.344	.314	.658	6	.992
— Brevard County (FSL)	C	12	42	4	11	4	0	0	2	3	4	1	1	0-0	.262	.326	.357	.683	0	1.000
1995— Portland (East.)	3B-C	105	333	37	85	11	1	3	39	22	27	3	9	2-2	.255	.305	.321	.626	6	.992
1996— Portland (East.)	C	120	394	43	113	22	0	4	44	26	45	5	12	3-4	.287	.335	.373	.708	4	.996
1997— Charlotte (Int'l)	C	22	61	8	13	5	1	1	2	1	10	3	1	0-1	.213	.262	.377	.639	2	.985
— GC Marlins (GCL)	DH	16	55	7	19	3	0	0	5	9	5	3	1	2-0	.345	.463	.400	.863	...	...
— Brevard County (FSL)	1B	5	17	2	0	0	0	0	0	2	2	0	2	0-0	.000	.105	.000	.105	0	1.000
1998— Portland (East.)	C	8	28	7	9	4	0	1	7	2	2	2	2	0-0	.321	.406	.571	.978	1	.983
— Charlotte (Int'l)	C	18	58	4	14	2	0	2	7	0	3	1	3	0-0	.241	.246	.379	.625	0	1.000
— Florida (N.L.)	C	37	118	10	39	9	0	2	12	5	16	2	6	0-0	.331	.368	.458	.826	2	.992
1999— Florida (N.L.)	C	84	242	22	73	9	0	1	27	26	34	5	8	0-0	.302	.381	.351	.732	4	.992
2000— Florida (N.L.)	C	87	210	17	53	8	1	0	15	13	19	8	5	0-0	.252	.316	.300	.616	2	.996
2001— Florida (N.L.)	C	48	141	19	44	4	0	2	13	13	13	2	6	0-0	.312	.376	.426	.801	1	.994
2002— Florida (N.L.)	C-1B	89	256	19	78	15	0	2	28	21	34	4	4	0-2	.305	.372	.387	.758	4	.993
2003— Florida (N.L.)	C-1B-3B	59	125	12	30	7	1	0	11	7	16	5	2	0-0	.240	.302	.312	.614	1	.995
2004— Florida (N.L.)	C	81	246	19	63	15	0	2	25	14	28	8	10	1-0	.256	.315	.341	.656	2	.996
2005— Minnesota (A.L.)	C	45	148	17	46	9	0	1	26	6	14	3	9	0-0	.311	.350	.392	.742	0	1.000
American League totals (1 year)		45	148	17	46	9	0	1	26	6	14	3	9	0-0	.311	.350	.392	.742	0	1.000
National League totals (7 years)		485	1338	118	380	67	2	11	132	99	160	38	41	1-2	.284	.348	.362	.710	17	.994
Major League totals (8 years)		530	1486	135	426	76	2	12	158	105	174	41	50	1-2	.287	.348	.365	.713	17	.994

CHAMPIONSHIP SERIES RECORD

Year — Team (League)	Pos.	G	AB	R	H	2B	3B	HR	RBI	BB	SO	HBP	GDP	SB-CS	Avg.	OBP	SLG	OPS	E	Avg.
2003— Florida (N.L.)	C	1	0	1	0	0	0	0	0	1	0	0	0	0-0	...	1.000	...	1.000	0	1.000

WORLD SERIES RECORD

Year — Team (League)	Pos.	G	AB	R	H	2B	3B	HR	RBI	BB	SO	HBP	GDP	SB-CS	Avg.	OBP	SLG	OPS	E	Avg.
2003— Florida (N.L.)	C	1	1	0	0	0	0	0	0	0	0	0	0	0-0	.000	.000	.000	.000	1	1.000

REED, JEREMY · OF

PERSONAL: Born June 15, 1981, in San Dimas, Calif. ... 6-0/185. ... Bats left, throws left. ... Full name: Jeremy Thomas Reed. ... High school: Bonita (LaVerne, Calif.). ... College: Long Beach State.

TRANSACTIONS/CAREER NOTES: Selected by Chicago White Sox organization in second round of 2002 free-agent draft. ... Traded by White Sox with C Miguel Olivo and SS Michael Morse to Seattle Mariners for P Freddy Garcia and C Ben Davis (June 27, 2004).

2005 GAMES PLAYED BY POSITION (MLB): OF—137.

SCOUTING REPORT **Offense:** Reed hits from an open stance and moves toward the ball. Does not have much bat speed and pulls the ball too much. Is vulnerable inside. Doesn't exhibit good plate coverage. Has little power. Is an average runner but will steal bases. Is inconsistent in reading pitchers' moves and getting jumps. Will have a lot of trouble with lefthanders. **Defense:** Played too deep at times last season. Has improved his jumps, especially laterally, and has range with good body control. Still needs to work on his routes. Has an average arm, is accurate and has a quick release. Will be challenged to handle center in spacious Safeco Field but can handle other positions. **Outlook:** Reed will be a good defensive outfielder but must adjust his approach at the plate to be a solid hitter. **Grade 5.6**

JEREMY REED'S HITTING ZONE

.179	.429	.237
.263	.417	.243
.286	.160	.333

LEFTY-RIGHTY SPLITS

vs.	Avg.	AB	H	2B	3B	HR	RBI	BB	SO	OBP	Slg.
L	.200	105	21	3	2	0	12	10	16	.276	.267
R	.269	383	103	30	1	3	33	38	58	.335	.376

Year — Team (League)	Pos.	G	AB	R	H	2B	3B	HR	RBI	BB	SO	HBP	GDP	SB-CS	Avg.	OBP	SLG	OPS	E	Avg.
2002— Kannapolis (S. Atl.)	OF	57	210	37	67	15	0	4	32	11	24	11	7	17-5	.319	.377	.448	.825	0	1.000
2003— Win.-Salem (Car.)	OF	65	222	37	74	18	1	4	52	41	17	1	5	27-6	.333	.431	.477	.909	3	.979
— Birmingham (Sou.)	OF	66	242	51	99	17	3	7	43	29	19	2	7	18-13	.409	.474	.591	1.065	0	1.000
2004— Charlotte (Int'l)	OF-DH	73	276	44	76	14	1	8	37	36	34	3	7	12-7	.275	.357	.420	.771	1	.995
— Tacoma (PCL)	OF	61	233	40	71	10	5	5	36	23	22	0	6	14-2	.305	.366	.455	.821	3	.982
2005— Seattle (A.L.)	OF	18	58	11	23	4	0	0	5	7	4	1	2	3-1	.397	.470	.466	.935	1	.981
— Seattle (A.L.)	OF	141	488	61	124	33	3	3	45	48	74	2	10	12-11	.254	.322	.352	.675	3	.992
Major League totals (2 years)		159	546	72	147	37	3	3	50	55	78	3	12	15-12	.269	.338	.364	.703	4	.991

REED, KEITH · OF

PERSONAL: Born October 8, 1978, in Yarmouth Port, Mass. ... 6-4/205. ... Bats right, throws right. ... Full name: Keith A. Reed. ... College: Providence.

TRANSACTIONS/CAREER NOTES: Selected by Baltimore Orioles organization in first round (23rd pick overall) of 1999 free-agent draft.

2005 GAMES PLAYED BY POSITION (MLB): OF—6.

LEFTY-RIGHTY SPLITS

vs.	Avg.	AB	H	2B	3B	HR	RBI	BB	SO	OBP	Slg.
L	.000	3	0	0	0	0	0	1	1	.250	.000
R	.500	2	1	0	0	0	1	0	1	.500	.500

Year — Team (League)	Pos.	G	AB	R	H	2B	3B	HR	RBI	BB	SO	HBP	GDP	SB-CS	Avg.	OBP	SLG	OPS	E	Avg.
1999— Bluefield (Appal.)	OF	4	16	2	3	0	0	0	0	1	3	0	0	0-1	.188	.235	.188	.423	1	.667
— Delmarva (S. Atl.)	OF	61	240	36	62	14	3	4	25	22	53	3	4	3-2	.258	.326	.392	.718	7	.926
2000— Delmarva (S. Atl.)	OF	70	269	43	78	16	1	11	59	25	56	5	3	20-4	.290	.358	.480	.838	5	.962
— Frederick (Carolina)	OF	65	243	33	57	10	1	8	31	21	58	4	4	9-1	.235	.303	.383	.686	6	.953
2001— Frederick (Carolina)	OF	72	267	28	72	14	0	7	29	13	57	1	7	8-6	.270	.305	.401	.706	7	.948
— Bowie (East.)	OF	18	67	7	17	3	0	1	8	6	10	0	3	2-2	.254	.315	.343	.658	0	1.000
— Rochester (Int'l)	OF	20	74	11	23	7	1	2	11	5	14	0	1	1-1	.311	.354	.514	.868	2	.933
2002— Bowie (East.)	OF	137	488	57	120	20	1	15	64	40	107	10	13	3-10	.246	.314	.383	.697	5	.976
2003— Bowie (East.)	OF	114	419	63	108	11	1	10	39	31	94	5	7	16-9	.258	.314	.360	.674	5	.979
2004— Bowie (East.)	OF	121	464	62	137	32	0	16	65	31	101	6	12	3-6	.295	.345	.468	.813	9	.250

Year Team (League)	Pos.	G	AB	R	H	2B	3B	HR	RBI	BB	SO	HBP	GDP	SB-CS	Avg.	OBP	SLG	OPS	E	Avg.
2005—Baltimore (A.L.)	OF	6	5	1	1	0	0	0	1	1	2	0	0	0-0	.200	.333	.200	.533	0	1.000
—Aberdeen (N.Y.-Penn.)	DH-OF	16	62	10	16	2	0	4	11	7	18	0	0	2-0	.258	.333	.484	.817	0	1.000
—Ottawa (Int'l)	OF	80	271	39	79	19	1	8	37	10	55	1	5	1-3	.292	.316	.458	.773	6	.983
Major League totals (1 year)		6	5	1	1	0	0	0	1	1	2	0	0	0-0	.200	.333	.200	.533	0	1.000

REED, STEVE — P

PERSONAL: Born March 11, 1965, in Los Angeles. ... 6-2/212. ... Throws right, bats right. ... Full name: Steven Vincent Reed. ... High school: Chatsworth (Calif.). ... College: Lewis-Clark State (Lewiston, Idaho).

TRANSACTIONS/CAREER NOTES: Signed as a non-drafted free agent by San Francisco Giants organization (June 24, 1988). ... Selected by Colorado Rockies in third round (60th pick overall) of expansion draft (November 17, 1992). ... Signed as a free agent by Giants (December 24, 1997). ... Traded by Giants with OF Jacob Cruz to Cleveland Indians for Ps Jose Mesa and Alvin Morman and IF Shawon Dunston (July 23, 1998). ... Traded by Indians with P Steve Karsay to Atlanta Braves for P John Rocker and 3B Troy Cameron (June 22, 2001). ... Traded by Braves to San Diego Padres organization (January 23, 2002). ... Traded by Padres with P Jason Middlebrook to New York Mets for Ps Bobby M. Jones and Josh Reynolds and OF Jason Bay (July 31, 2002). ... Signed as a free agent by Rockies (January 24, 2003). ... On suspended list (September 25-27, 2004). ... Signed as a free agent by Baltimore Orioles (January 19, 2005). ... Released by Orioles (July 22, 2005).

CAREER HITTING: 4-for-25 (.160), 0 R, 0 2B, 0 3B, 0 HR, 1 RBI.

STEVE REED'S PITCHING ZONE

.200	.000	.000
.182	.600	.444
.333	.214	.385

LEFTY-RIGHTY SPLITS

vs.	Avg.	AB	H	2B	3B	HR	RBI	BB	SO	OBP	Slg.
L	.349	63	22	4	1	2	13	6	3	.400	.540
R	.271	70	19	4	0	3	13	5	12	.354	.457

Year Team (League)	W	L	Pct.	ERA	WHIP	G	GS	CG	ShO	Hld.	Sv.-Opp.	IP	H	R	ER	HR	BB-IBB	SO	Avg.
1988—Pocatello (Pion.)	4	1	.800	2.54	1.09	31	0	0	0	...	13-...	46.0	42	20	13	3	8-1	49	.237
1989—Clinton (Midw.)	5	3	.625	1.05	0.97	60	0	0	0	...	26-...	94.2	54	16	11	1	38-10	104	.171
—San Jose (Calif.)	0	0	...	0.00	0.50	2	0	0	0	...	0-...	2.0	0	0	0	0	1-0	3	.000
1990—Shreveport (Texas)	3	1	.750	1.64	1.21	45	1	0	0	...	8-...	60.1	53	20	11	2	20-6	59	.230
1991—Shreveport (Texas)	2	0	1.000	0.83	0.92	15	0	0	0	...	7-...	21.2	17	2	2	1	3-0	26	.218
—Phoenix (PCL)	2	3	.400	4.31	1.31	41	0	0	0	...	6-...	56.1	62	33	27	5	12-0	46	.279
1992—Shreveport (Texas)	1	0	1.000	0.62	0.62	27	0	0	0	...	23-...	29.0	18	3	2	1	0-0	33	.175
—Phoenix (PCL)	1	0	1.000	3.48	1.19	29	0	0	0	...	20-...	31.0	27	13	12	2	10-3	30	.237
—San Francisco (N.L.)	1	0	1.000	2.30	1.02	18	0	0	0	1	0-0	15.2	13	5	4	2	3-0	11	.220
1993—Colorado (N.L.)	9	5	.643	4.48	1.30	64	0	0	0	9	3-6	84.1	80	47	42	13	30-5	51	.259
—Colo. Springs (PCL)	0	0	...	0.00	0.89	11	0	0	0	...	7-...	12.1	8	1	0	0	3-1	10	.182
1994—Colorado (N.L.)	3	2	.600	3.94	1.64	61	0	0	0	14	3-10	64.0	79	33	28	8	26-3	51	.306
1995—Colorado (N.L.)	5	2	.714	2.14	0.98	71	0	0	0	11	3-3	84.0	61	24	20	8	21-3	79	.203
1996—Colorado (N.L.)	4	3	.571	3.96	1.13	70	0	0	0	* 22	0-6	75.0	66	38	33	11	19-0	51	.239
1997—Colorado (N.L.)	4	6	.400	4.04	1.22	63	0	0	0	10	6-13	62.1	49	28	28	10	27-1	43	.219
1998—San Francisco (N.L.)	2	1	.667	1.48	0.90	50	0	0	0	13	1-5	54.2	30	10	9	4	19-5	50	.160
—Cleveland (A.L.)	2	2	.500	6.66	1.32	20	0	0	0	8	0-1	25.2	26	19	19	4	8-0	23	.260
1999—Cleveland (A.L.)	3	2	.600	4.23	1.44	63	0	0	0	8	0-3	61.2	69	33	29	10	20-5	44	.285
2000—Cleveland (A.L.)	2	0	1.000	4.34	1.41	57	0	0	0	9	0-1	56.0	58	30	27	7	21-4	39	.269
2001—Cleveland (A.L.)	1	1	.500	3.62	1.17	31	0	0	0	6	0-1	27.1	22	11	11	3	10-2	21	.212
—Atlanta (N.L.)	2	2	.500	3.48	1.39	39	0	0	0	5	1-1	31.0	30	14	12	3	13-3	25	.259
2002—San Diego (N.L.)	2	4	.333	1.98	1.05	40	0	0	0	11	1-3	41.0	33	9	9	2	10-2	36	.228
—New York (N.L.)	0	1	.000	2.08	1.04	24	0	0	0	6	0-1	26.0	23	6	6	0	4-1	14	.240
2003—Colorado (N.L.)	5	3	.625	3.27	1.34	67	0	0	0	14	0-2	63.1	59	24	23	9	26-3	39	.254
2004—Colorado (N.L.)	3	8	.273	3.68	1.35	65	0	0	0	15	0-4	66.0	72	29	27	7	17-7	38	.281
2005—Baltimore (A.L.)	1	2	.333	6.61	1.59	30	0	0	0	4	0-0	32.2	41	24	24	5	11-2	15	.308
American League totals (5 years)	9	7	.563	4.87	1.41	201	0	0	0	35	0-6	203.1	216	117	110	29	70-13	142	.272
National League totals (11 years)	40	37	.519	3.25	1.21	632	0	0	0	131	18-57	667.1	595	267	241	78	215-33	488	.242
Major League totals (14 years)	49	44	.527	3.63	1.26	833	0	0	0	166	18-63	870.2	811	384	351	107	285-46	630	.249

DIVISION SERIES RECORD

Year Team (League)	W	L	Pct.	ERA	WHIP	G	GS	CG	ShO	Hld.	Sv.-Opp.	IP	H	R	ER	HR	BB-IBB	SO	Avg.
1995—Colorado (N.L.)	0	0	...	0.00	1.13	3	0	0	0	1	0-1	2.2	2	0	0	0	1-1	3	.200
1998—Cleveland (A.L.)	1	0	1.000	40.50	3.00	2	0	0	0	0	0-0	0.2	1	3	3	0	1-0	1	.333
1999—Cleveland (A.L.)	0	0	...	30.86	4.29	2	0	0	0	0	0-0	2.1	9	8	8	1	1-0	1	.600
2001—Atlanta (N.L.)	0	0	...	0.00	0.00	1	0	0	0	1	0-0	0.1	0	0	0	0	0-0	0	.000
Division series totals (4 years)	1	0	1.000	16.50	2.50	8	0	0	0	2	0-1	6.0	12	11	11	1	3-1	5	.414

CHAMPIONSHIP SERIES RECORD

Year Team (League)	W	L	Pct.	ERA	WHIP	G	GS	CG	ShO	Hld.	Sv.-Opp.	IP	H	R	ER	HR	BB-IBB	SO	Avg.
1998—Cleveland (A.L.)	0	0	...	0.00	0.60	3	0	0	0	0	0-0	1.2	0	0	0	0	1-0	0	.000
2001—Atlanta (N.L.)	0	0	...	...	...	1	0	0	0	...	0-...	0.0	0	0	0	0	0-0	0	...
Champ. series totals (2 years)	0	0	...	0.00	0.60	4	0	0	0	0	0-0	1.2	0	0	0	0	1-0	0	.000

REESE, KEVIN — OF

PERSONAL: Born March 11, 1978, in San Diego. ... 5-11/195. ... Bats left, throws left. ... Full name: Kevin Patrick Reese. ... College: San Diego.

TRANSACTIONS/CAREER NOTES: Selected by San Diego Padres organization in 27th round of 2000 free-agent draft. ... Traded by Padres to New York Yankees for 2B Bernie Castro (December 18, 2001).

2005 GAMES PLAYED BY POSITION (MLB): OF—2.

LEFTY-RIGHTY SPLITS

vs.	Avg.	AB	H	2B	3B	HR	RBI	BB	SO	OBP	Slg.
L	.000	0	0	0	0	0	0	0	0	.000	.000
R	.000	1	0	0	0	0	0	1	1	.500	.000

Year Team (League)	Pos.	G	AB	R	H	2B	3B	HR	RBI	BB	SO	HBP	GDP	SB-CS	Avg.	OBP	SLG	OPS	E	Avg.
2000—Idaho Falls (Pio.)	OF	53	201	51	72	14	4	2	36	43	30	3	5	12-3	.358	.474	.498	.972	5	.925
2001—Fort Wayne (Midw.)	OF	125	459	84	151	30	6	13	73	54	62	5	5	30-10	.329	.402	.505	.907	4	.984
2002—Norwich (East.)	OF	138	514	80	149	24	6	4	45	77	87	4	6	22-14	.290	.385	.383	.768	6	.980
2003—Columbus (Int'l)	OF	15	55	11	12	1	0	1	3	6	8	0	0	1-0	.218	.295	.291	.586	1	.963
—Trenton (East.)	OF	86	309	42	84	13	2	4	21	25	58	2	4	27-5	.272	.328	.366	.694	4	.980
2004—Trenton (East.)	OF	78	329	57	98	37	4	6	40	23	48	3	4	13-5	.298	.348	.489	.837	2	.966
—Columbus (Int'l)	OF	53	217	41	70	13	3	8	28	12	34	5	5	4-4	.323	.370	.521	.891	2	.000
2005—New York (A.L.)	OF	2	1	0	0	0	0	0	0	1	1	0	0	0-0	.000	.500	.000	.500	0	1.000
—Columbus (Int'l)	OF-DH	133	540	92	149	38	7	14	69	63	86	10	10	16-5	.276	.359	.450	.809	8	.984
Major League totals (1 year)		2	1	0	0	0	0	0	0	1	1	0	0	0-0	.000	.500	.000	.500	0	1.000

REGILIO, NICK P

PERSONAL: Born September 4, 1978, in Miami. ... 6-2/205. ... Throws right, bats right. ... Full name: Nicholas D. Regilio. ... High school: Father Lopez (Daytona, Fla.). ... College: Jacksonville.

TRANSACTIONS/CAREER NOTES: Selected by Texas Rangers organization in second round of 1999 free-agent draft. ... On disabled list (June 10, 2005-remainder of season); included rehabilitation assignment to AZL Rangers.

CAREER HITTING: 0-for-0 (.000), 0 R, 0 2B, 0 3B, 0 HR, 0 RBI.

NICK REGILIO'S PITCHING ZONE

.125	.000	.000
.400	.600	.333
.375	.167	.167

LEFTY-RIGHTY SPLITS

vs.	Avg.	AB	H	2B	3B	HR	RBI	BB	SO	OBP	Slg.
L	.214	28	6	1	0	1	6	3	5	.303	.357
R	.348	46	16	4	0	1	4	4	9	.400	.500

Year Team (League)	W	L	Pct.	ERA	WHIP	G	GS	CG	ShO	Hld.	Sv.-Opp.	IP	H	R	ER	HR	BB-IBB	SO	Avg.
1999— Pulaski (Appalachian)	4	2	.667	1.63	0.93	11	8	1	1	...	0-...	49.2	30	12	9	2	16-0	58	.172
2000— Charlotte (Fla. St.)	4	3	.571	4.52	1.44	20	20	0	0	...	0-...	85.2	94	54	43	8	29-0	63	.286
2001— Charlotte (Fla. St.)	6	2	.750	1.55	0.98	11	11	1	1	...	0-...	64.0	47	16	11	5	16-0	60	.200
— Tulsa (Texas)	1	3	.250	5.54	1.58	10	10	0	0	...	0-...	52.0	62	34	32	2	20-0	40	.297
2002— Oklahoma (PCL)	1	0	1.000	10.80	2.80	1	1	0	0	...	0-...	5.0	9	6	6	1	5-0	4	.391
— Tulsa (Texas)	6	8	.429	3.44	1.38	19	19	2	1	...	0-...	104.2	97	46	40	8	47-2	59	.245
2003— Rangers (Ariz.)	0	0	...	0.00	1.00	2	2	0	0	...	0-...	5.0	4	2	0	0	1-0	7	.235
— Frisco (Texas)	0	1	.000	21.60	3.60	1	0	0	0	...	0-...	1.2	5	4	4	0	1-0	2	.556
2004— Texas (A.L.)	0	4	.000	6.05	1.81	6	4	0	0	0	0-0	19.1	20	16	13	3	15-1	12	.277
— Oklahoma (PCL)	6	5	.545	4.71	1.57	17	17	0	0	...	0-...	91.2	98	49	48	6	46-0	72	.282
2005— Oklahoma (PCL)	0	0	...	0.00	1.00	1	0	0	0	0	0-0	2.0	1	0	0	0	1-0	2	.167
— Texas (A.L.)	1	2	.333	4.58	1.64	18	0	0	0	2	0-2	17.2	22	10	9	2	7-1	14	.297
— Arizona Rangers (AZL)	0	0	...	9.00	2.00	1	1	0	0	0	0-0	1.0	2	1	1	0	0-0	0	.400
Major League totals (2 years)	1	6	.143	5.35	1.73	24	4	0	0	2	0-2	37.0	42	26	22	5	22-2	26	.288

REITSMA, CHRIS P

PERSONAL: Born December 31, 1977, in Minneapolis. ... 6-5/235. ... Throws right, bats right. ... Full name: Christopher Michael Reitsma. ... Name pronounced: REETS-muh. ... High school: Calgary (Alberta) Christian.

TRANSACTIONS/CAREER NOTES: Selected by Boston Red Sox organization in supplemental round ("sandwich pick" between first and second rounds, 34th pick overall) of 1996 free-agent draft; pick received as compensation for Toronto Blue Jays signing free-agent P Erik Hanson. ... Selected by Tampa Bay Devil Rays from Red Sox organization in Rule 5 major league draft (December 13, 1999). ... Returned to Red Sox (March 28, 2000). ... Traded by Red Sox with P John Curtice to Cincinnati Reds for OF Dante Bichette (August 31, 2000). ... Traded by Reds to Atlanta Braves for Ps Jung Bong and Bubba Nelson (March 26, 2004).

CAREER HITTING: 9-for-87 (.103), 3 R, 1 2B, 0 3B, 0 HR, 5 RBI.

SCOUTING REPORT** **Throws: Reitsma's best pitches are a fastball that tops out at 95 mph and a changeup. Also throws a curveball. **Tendencies:** Reitsma has a herky-jerky delivery and doesn't have a loose arm. Can be erratic with his release point and command at times, but has some deception. Throws a heavy boring fastball that is sneaky. Has a very big but tightly spinning curve that he throws to lefthanders. Has outstanding motion and very good movement on his change, which occasionally sinks. Has the confidence to throw it on any count, in any situation. Change allows him to be more effective to lefthanders. Keeps the ball down and in the park. ***Outlook:*** He was overextended a little late in the season as the Braves' bullpen was out of sync. Is a quality setup reliever but not a closer. **Grade 7.8**

CHRIS REITSMA'S PITCHING ZONE

.400	.308	.150
.295	.333	.271
.129	.333	.321

LEFTY-RIGHTY SPLITS

vs.	Avg.	AB	H	2B	3B	HR	RBI	BB	SO	OBP	Slg.
L	.252	159	40	9	0	1	15	12	25	.301	.327
R	.298	131	39	4	0	2	19	2	17	.308	.374

Year Team (League)	W	L	Pct.	ERA	WHIP	G	GS	CG	ShO	Hld.	Sv.-Opp.	IP	H	R	ER	HR	BB-IBB	SO	Avg.
1996— GC Red Sox (GCL)	3	1	.750	1.35	0.94	7	6	0	0	...	0-...	26.2	24	7	4	0	1-0	32	.229
1997— Michigan (Midw.)	4	1	.800	2.90	1.41	9	9	0	0	...	0-...	49.2	57	23	16	4	13-0	41	.285
1998— Sarasota (Fla. St.)	0	0	...	2.84	1.34	8	8	0	0	...	0-...	12.2	12	6	4	0	5-0	9	.245
1999— Sarasota (Fla. St.)	4	10	.286	5.61	1.53	19	19	0	0	...	0-...	96.1	116	71	60	11	31-1	79	.294
2000— Sarasota (Fla. St.)	3	4	.429	3.66	1.16	11	11	0	0	...	0-...	64.0	57	29	26	3	17-0	47	.238
— Trenton (East.)	7	2	.778	2.58	1.09	14	14	1	0	...	0-...	90.2	78	28	26	7	21-1	58	.232
2001— Cincinnati (N.L.)	7	15	.318	5.29	1.42	36	29	0	0	...	1	0-0	182.0	209	121	107	23	49-6	96	.288
2002— Cincinnati (N.L.)	6	12	.333	3.64	1.37	32	21	1	1	0	0-0	138.1	144	73	56	17	45-5	84	.267
— Louisville (Int'l)	2	0	1.000	3.86	1.19	3	3	0	0	...	0-...	21.0	17	10	9	2	8-1	13	.224
2003— Louisville (Int'l)	1	2	.333	4.00	1.50	4	4	0	0	...	0-...	18.0	22	10	8	1	5-0	11	.293
— Cincinnati (N.L.)	9	5	.643	4.29	1.32	57	3	0	0	3	12-18	84.0	92	41	40	14	19-6	53	.281
2004— Atlanta (N.L.)	6	4	.600	4.07	1.37	84	0	0	0	31	2-9	79.2	89	38	36	9	20-3	60	.286
2005— Atlanta (N.L.)	3	6	.333	3.93	1.27	76	0	0	0	13	15-24	73.1	79	32	32	3	14-3	42	.272
Major League totals (5 years)	31	42	.425	4.38	1.36	285	53	1	1	48	29-51	557.1	613	305	271	66	147-23	335	.279

DIVISION SERIES RECORD

Year Team (League)	W	L	Pct.	ERA	WHIP	G	GS	CG	ShO	Hld.	Sv.-Opp.	IP	H	R	ER	HR	BB-IBB	SO	Avg.
2004— Atlanta (N.L.)	0	0	...	18.00	2.00	3	0	0	0	0	0-0	3.0	6	6	6	2	1-0	2	.417
2005— Atlanta (N.L.)	0	0	...	16.20	2.70	4	0	0	0	0	0-0	3.1	6	6	6	0	2-2	0	.438
Division series totals (2 years)	0	0	...	17.05	2.37	7	0	0	0	0	0-0	6.1	12	12	12	2	3-2	2	.429

RELAFORD, DESI — 2B/3B

PERSONAL: Born September 16, 1973, in Valdosta, Ga. ... 5-9/180. ... Bats both, throws right. ... Full name: Desmond Lamont Relaford. ... High school: Sandalwood (Jacksonville).

TRANSACTIONS/CAREER NOTES: Selected by Seattle Mariners organization in fourth round of 1991 free-agent draft. ... Traded by Mariners to Philadelphia Phillies for P Terry Mulholland (July 31, 1996). ... On disabled list (June 17-September 13, 1999); included rehabilitation assignment to Clearwater. ... Traded by Phillies to San Diego Padres for a player to be named (August 4, 2000); Phillies acquired IF David Newhan to complete deal (August 7, 2000). ... Claimed on waivers by New York Mets (October 12, 2000). ... Traded by Mets with OF Tsuyoshi Shinjo to San Francisco Giants for P Shawn Estes (December 16, 2001). ... Traded by Giants with cash to Mariners for 3B David Bell (January 25, 2002). ... Signed as a free agent by Kansas City Royals (January 10, 2003). ... On disabled list (April 6-29, 2004); included rehabilitation assignment to Omaha. ... Signed as a free agent by Colorado Rockies (January 7, 2005). ... On disabled list (March 25-April 12, 2005); included rehabilitation assignment to Colorado Springs. ... Released by Rockies (August 3, 2005). ... Signed by Toronto Blue Jays organization (August 11, 2005). ... Career major league pitching: 0-0, 0.00 ERA, 1G, 1.0 IP, 0 H, 0 R, 0 ER, 0 BB, 1 SO.

2005 GAMES PLAYED BY POSITION (MLB): SS—37, 3B—21, 2B—11, OF—4.

DESI RELAFORD'S HITTING ZONE

.250	.143	.222
.219	.269	.286
.200	.300	.152

LEFTY-RIGHTY SPLITS

vs.	Avg.	AB	H	2B	3B	HR	RBI	BB	SO	OBP	Slg.
L	.240	50	12	6	0	0	1	5	8	.309	.360
R	.219	160	35	7	2	1	15	17	34	.308	.306

Year	Team (League)	Pos.	G	AB	R	H	2B	3B	HR	RBI	BB	SO	HBP	GDP	SB-CS	Avg.	OBP	SLG	OPS	E	Avg.
1991—	Ariz. Mariners (Ariz.)	2B-SS	46	163	36	44	7	3	0	18	22	24	1	0	17-3	.270	.351	.350	.700	24	.885
1992—	Peninsula (Caro.)	SS	130	445	53	96	18	1	3	34	39	88	1	4	27-7	.216	.277	.281	.558	52	.913
1993—	Jacksonville (Sou.)	2B-3B-SS	133	472	49	115	16	4	8	47	50	103	7	4	16-12	.244	.323	.345	.668	38	.935
1994—	Jacksonville (Sou.)	SS	37	143	24	29	7	3	3	11	22	28	0	2	10-1	.203	.305	.357	.662	4	.979
—	Riverside (Calif.)	SS	99	374	95	116	27	5	5	59	78	78	4	7	27-6	.310	.429	.449	.878	36	.921
1995—	Port City (Sou.)	SS-2B-DH	90	352	51	101	11	2	7	27	41	58	2	4	25-9	.287	.365	.389	.754	31	.930
—	Tacoma (PCL)	2B-SS	30	113	20	27	5	1	2	7	13	24	0	2	6-0	.239	.313	.354	.666	6	.960
1996—	Tacoma (PCL)	2B-SS-SS-DH	93	317	27	65	12	0	4	32	23	58	1	7	10-6	.205	.259	.281	.539	20	.960
—	Philadelphia (N.L.)	SS-2B	15	40	2	7	2	0	0	1	3	9	0	1	1-0	.175	.233	.225	.458	2	.959
—	Scran./W.B. (I.L.)	SS	21	85	12	20	4	1	1	11	8	19	1	0	7-1	.235	.305	.341	.646	6	.938
1997—	Scran./W.B. (I.L.)	SS	131	517	82	138	34	4	9	53	43	77	7	12	29-8	.267	.329	.400	.729	34	.942
—	Philadelphia (N.L.)	SS	15	38	3	7	1	2	0	6	5	6	0	0	3-0	.184	.279	.316	.595	1	.977
1998—	Philadelphia (N.L.)	SS	142	494	45	121	25	3	5	41	33	87	3	9	9-5	.245	.293	.338	.631	24	.960
1999—	Philadelphia (N.L.)	SS	65	211	31	51	11	2	1	26	19	34	6	5	4-3	.242	.322	.327	.649	14	.952
—	Clearwater (FSL)	SS	2	7	1	2	0	0	0	1	1	1	0	0	0-0	.286	.375	.286	.661	1	.800
2000—	Philadelphia (N.L.)	SS	83	253	29	56	12	3	3	30	48	45	9	7	5-0	.221	.363	.328	.691	24	.930
—	San Diego (N.L.)	SS	45	157	26	32	2	0	2	16	27	26	3	3	8-0	.204	.330	.255	.585	‡7	.965
2001—	New York (N.L.)	2B-SS-3B P	120	301	43	91	27	0	8	36	27	65	5	4	13-5	.302	.364	.472	.836	11	.963
2002—	Seattle (A.L.)	SS-3B-OF 2B-DH	112	329	55	88	13	2	6	43	33	51	6	10	10-3	.267	.339	.374	.713	10	.965
2003—	Kansas City (A.L.)	2B-3B-OF SS-DH	141	500	70	127	27	5	8	59	40	70	6	10	20-4	.254	.315	.376	.691	16	.971
2004—	Omaha (PCL)	DH-2B-SS	4	15	1	4	1	0	0	3	2	1	0	0	0-0	.267	.353	.333	.686	0	1.000
—	Kansas City (A.L.)	SS	114	380	45	84	14	0	6	34	34	56	8	10	5-4	.221	.296	.305	.601	12	.968
2005—	Colo. Springs (PCL)	2B-3B-SS	3	12	4	4	1	0	0	3	3	1	0	0	1-0	.333	.500	.417	.917	1	.929
—	Colorado (N.L.)	SS-3B-2B OF	73	210	24	47	13	2	1	16	22	42	4	1	3-3	.224	.308	.319	.627	10	.956
—	Syracuse (Int'l)	2B-SS	22	76	15	16	2	0	2	6	13	12	4	1	5-0	.211	.355	.316	.671	2	.980
American League totals (3 years)			367	1209	170	299	54	7	20	136	107	177	20	26	35-11	.247	.316	.353	.669	38	.969
National League totals (7 years)			558	1704	203	412	93	12	20	172	184	314	30	30	46-16	.242	.324	.346	.670	93	.955
Major League totals (10 years)			925	2913	373	711	147	19	40	308	291	491	50	56	81-27	.244	.321	.349	.669	131	.960

REMLINGER, MIKE — P

PERSONAL: Born March 23, 1966, in Middletown, N.Y. ... 6-1/215. ... Throws left, bats left. ... Full name: Michael John Remlinger. ... Name pronounced: REM-lin-jurr. ... High school: Carver (Plymouth, Mass.). ... College: Dartmouth.

TRANSACTIONS/CAREER NOTES: Selected by San Francisco Giants organization in first round (16th pick overall) of 1987 free-agent draft. ... Traded by Giants with OF Kevin Mitchell to Seattle Mariners for Ps Bill Swift, Mike Jackson and Dave Burba (December 11, 1991). ... Signed as a free agent by New York Mets organization (November 22, 1993). ... Traded by Mets to Cincinnati Reds for OF Cobi Cradle (May 11, 1995). ... Traded by Reds to Kansas City Royals as part of three-team deal in which Reds acquired OF Andre King from St. Louis Cardinals and Cardinals acquired SS Luis Ordaz from Reds and OF Miguel Mejia from Royals (December 4, 1995). ... Claimed on waivers by Reds (April 4, 1996). ... Traded by Reds with 2B Bret Boone to Atlanta Braves for Ps Denny Neagle and Rob Bell and OF Michael Tucker (November 10, 1998). ... On disabled list (April 3-18, 1999; June 23-July 13, 2000; and August 8-24, 2002). ... Signed as a free agent by Chicago Cubs (December 3, 2002). ... On disabled list (March 26-May 22 and June 24-July 11, 2004); included rehabilitation assignment to Iowa. ... On disabled list (May 25-June 5, 2005). ... Traded by Cubs to Boston Red Sox for P Olivo Astacio (August 9, 2005). ... Released by Red Sox (August 29, 2005).

CAREER HITTING: 8-for-110 (.073), 5 R, 3 2B, 0 3B, 0 HR, 8 RBI.

MIKE REMLINGER'S PITCHING ZONE

.545	1.000	.182
.353	.444	.211
.188	.400	.273

LEFTY-RIGHTY SPLITS

vs.	Avg.	AB	H	2B	3B	HR	RBI	BB	SO	OBP	Slg.
L	.296	54	16	5	0	1	9	6	14	.367	.444
R	.283	106	30	7	1	6	22	11	21	.361	.538

Year	Team (League)	W	L	Pct.	ERA	WHIP	G	GS	CG	ShO	Hld.	Sv.-Opp.	IP	H	R	ER	HR	BB-IBB	SO	Avg.
1987—	Everett (N'west)	0	0	—	3.60	1.20	2	1	0	0		0-...	5.0	1	2	2	0	5-0	11	.071
—	Clinton (Midw.)	2	1	.667	3.30	1.17	6	5	0	0		0-...	30.0	21	12	11	2	14-0	43	.196
—	Shreveport (Texas)	4	2	.667	2.36	1.05	6	6	0	0		0-...	34.1	14	11	9	2	22-0	51	.120
1988—	Shreveport (Texas)	1	0	1.000	0.69	0.85	3	3	0	0		0-...	13.0	7	4	1	0	4-0	18	.163
1989—	Shreveport (Texas)	4	6	.400	2.98	1.56	16	16	0	0		0-...	90.2	68	43	30	4	73-0	92	.212
—	Phoenix (PCL)	1	6	.143	9.21	2.40	11	10	0	0		0-...	43.0	51	47	44	8	52-0	28	.290
1990—	Shreveport (Texas)	9	11	.450	3.90	1.50	25	25	2	1		0-...	147.2	149	82	64	7	72-1	75	.270
1991—	Phoenix (PCL)	5	5	.500	6.38	1.78	19	19	1	1		0-...	108.2	134	86	77	15	59-0	68	.305
—	San Francisco (N.L.)	2	1	.667	4.37	1.60	8	6	1	1	0	0-0	35.0	36	17	17	5	20-1	19	.271
1992—	Calgary (PCL)	1	7	.125	6.65	2.06	21	11	0	0		0-...	70.1	97	65	52	7	48-1	24	.342
—	Jacksonville (Sou.)	1	1	.500	3.46	1.38	5	5	0	0		0-...	26.0	25	15	10	1	11-0	21	.250
1993—	Calgary (PCL)	4	3	.571	5.53	1.80	19	18	0	0		0-...	84.2	100	57	52	8	52-0	51	.300

Year	Team (League)	W	L	Pct.	ERA	WHIP	G	GS	CG	ShO	Hld.	Sv.-Opp.	IP	H	R	ER	HR	BB-IBB	SO	Avg.
—	Jacksonville (Sou.)	1	3	.250	6.58	1.49	7	7	0	0	...	0-...	39.2	40	30	29	7	19-0	23	.261
1994—	Norfolk (Int'l)	2	4	.333	3.14	1.30	12	9	0	0	...	0-...	63.0	57	29	22	5	25-0	45	.242
—	New York (N.L.)	1	5	.167	4.61	1.65	10	9	0	0	1	0-0	54.2	55	30	28	9	35-4	33	.261
1995—	New York (N.L.)	0	1	.000	6.35	1.59	5	0	0	0	0	0-1	5.2	7	5	4	1	2-0	6	.292
—	Cincinnati (N.L.)	0	0	...	9.00	5.00	2	0	0	0	0	0-0	1.0	2	1	1	0	3-0	1	.500
—	Indianapolis (A.A.)	5	3	.625	4.05	1.54	41	1	0	0	...	0-...	46.2	40	24	21	4	32-4	58	.231
1996—	Indianapolis (A.A.)	4	3	.571	2.52	1.21	28	13	0	0	...	0-...	89.1	64	29	25	4	44-0	97	.203
—	Cincinnati (N.L.)	0	1	.000	5.60	1.57	19	4	0	0	1	0-0	27.1	24	17	17	4	19-2	19	.245
1997—	Cincinnati (N.L.)	8	8	.500	4.14	1.29	69	12	2	0	14	2-2	124.0	100	61	57	11	60-6	145	.223
1998—	Cincinnati (N.L.)	8	15	.348	4.82	1.53	35	28	1	1	0	0-0	164.1	164	96	88	23	87-1	144	.266
1999—	Atlanta (N.L.)	10	1	.909	2.37	1.21	73	0	0	0	21	1-3	83.2	66	24	22	9	35-5	81	.215
2000—	Atlanta (N.L.)	5	3	.625	3.47	1.27	71	0	0	0	23	12-16	72.2	55	29	28	6	37-1	72	.207
2001—	Atlanta (N.L.)	3	3	.500	2.76	1.20	74	0	0	0	31	1-5	75.0	67	25	23	9	23-4	93	.234
2002—	Atlanta (N.L.)	7	3	.700	1.99	1.12	73	0	0	0	30	0-5	68.0	48	17	15	3	28-3	69	.198
2003—	Chicago (N.L.)	6	5	.545	3.65	1.35	73	0	0	0	17	0-1	69.0	54	30	28	11	39-4	83	.211
2004—	Iowa (PCL)	0	0	...	16.20	1.80	2	0	0	0	...	0-...	1.2	3	3	3	1	0-0	1	.375
—	Chicago (N.L.)	1	2	.333	3.44	1.34	48	0	0	0	13	2-6	36.2	33	16	14	3	16-3	35	.246
2005—	Chicago (N.L.)	0	3	.000	4.91	1.30	35	0	0	0	5	0-1	33.0	31	19	18	5	12-2	30	.250
—	Boston (A.L.)	0	0	...	14.85	3.00	8	0	0	0	0	0-0	6.2	15	14	11	2	5-0	5	.417
American League totals (1 year)		0	0	...	14.85	3.00	8	0	0	0	0	0-0	6.2	15	14	11	2	5-0	5	.417
National League totals (13 years)		51	51	.500	3.81	1.36	595	59	4	2	156	18-40	850.0	742	387	360	99	416-36	830	.236
Major League totals (13 years)		51	51	.500	3.90	1.38	603	59	4	2	156	18-40	856.2	757	401	371	101	421-36	835	.238

DIVISION SERIES RECORD

Year	Team (League)	W	L	Pct.	ERA	WHIP	G	GS	CG	ShO	Hld.	Sv.-Opp.	IP	H	R	ER	HR	BB-IBB	SO	Avg.
1999—	Atlanta (N.L.)	0	0	...	9.82	1.91	2	0	0	0	0	0-1	3.2	4	4	4	1	3-2	4	.308
2000—	Atlanta (N.L.)	0	0	...	2.70	1.80	3	0	0	0	0	0-0	3.1	6	1	1	1	0-0	3	.375
2001—	Atlanta (N.L.)	0	0	...	0.00	0.00	1	0	0	0	1	0-0	0.1	0	0	0	0	0-0	0	.000
2002—	Atlanta (N.L.)	0	0	...	4.50	2.50	3	0	0	0	0	0-0	2.0	3	1	1	0	2-0	3	.333
2003—	Chicago (N.L.)	0	0	...	0.00	1.50	2	0	0	0	1	0-0	0.2	0	0	0	0	1-0	1	.000
Division series totals (5 years)		0	0	...	5.40	1.90	11	0	0	0	2	0-1	10.0	13	6	6	2	6-2	11	.317

CHAMPIONSHIP SERIES RECORD

Year	Team (League)	W	L	Pct.	ERA	WHIP	G	GS	CG	ShO	Hld.	Sv.-Opp.	IP	H	R	ER	HR	BB-IBB	SO	Avg.
1999—	Atlanta (N.L.)	0	1	.000	3.18	1.06	5	0	0	0	3	0-0	5.2	3	2	2	0	3-0	4	.158
2001—	Atlanta (N.L.)	0	0	...	0.00	2.14	3	0	0	0	0	0-0	2.1	3	0	0	0	2-0	2	.333
2003—	Chicago (N.L.)	0	0	...	2.70	1.20	5	0	0	0	0	1-1	3.1	3	1	1	1	1-0	2	.214
Champ. series totals (3 years)		0	1	.000	2.38	1.32	13	0	0	0	3	1-1	11.1	9	3	3	1	6-0	8	.214

WORLD SERIES RECORD

Year	Team (League)	W	L	Pct.	ERA	WHIP	G	GS	CG	ShO	Hld.	Sv.-Opp.	IP	H	R	ER	HR	BB-IBB	SO	Avg.
1999—	Atlanta (N.L.)	0	1	.000	9.00	2.00	2	0	0	0	0	0-0	1.0	1	1	1	1	1-0	0	.333

ALL-STAR GAME RECORD

	W	L	Pct.	ERA	WHIP	G	GS	CG	ShO	Hld.	Sv.-Opp.	IP	H	R	ER	HR	BB-IBB	SO	Avg.
All-Star Game totals (1 year)	0	0	...	27.00	3.00	1	0	0	0	1	0-0	0.2	1	2	2	0	1-0	1	.333

RENTERIA, EDGAR   SS

PERSONAL: Born August 7, 1975, in Barranquilla, Colombia. ... 6-1/200. ... Bats right, throws right. ... Full name: Edgar Enrique Renteria. ... Name pronounced: ren-ter-REE-ah. ... High school: Instituto Los Alpes (Barranquilla, Colombia).
TRANSACTIONS/CAREER NOTES: Signed as a non-drafted free agent by Florida Marlins organization (February 14, 1992). ... On disabled list (June 24-July 11, 1996); included rehabilitation assignment to Charlotte. ... On disabled list (August 25-September 9, 1998). ... Traded by Marlins to St. Louis Cardinals for Ps Braden Looper and Armando Almanza and SS Pablo Ozuna (December 14, 1998). ... Signed as a free agent by Boston Red Sox (December 17, 2004).
HONORS: Won N.L. Gold Glove at shortstop (2002 and 2003).
2005 GAMES PLAYED BY POSITION (MLB): SS—153.

SCOUTING REPORT Offense: His transition to a new league took longer than it should have. Bat speed decreased some, which isn't good with his long swing. Is a very good fastball hitter but saw more breaking pitches in the A.L. Will use the whole field but had more trouble handling the ball inside. Is much better against lefthanders. Is an excellent baserunner on a club that doesn't emphasize stolen bases. *Defense:* Renteria declined some in 2005. May have added some weight. Lower-body agility wasn't as good and had problems bending over for balls to his left. Has very good hands and a strong arm from the hole. Can get something on his throws from any angle. *Outlook:* Whether it was the change of league or the loss of quickness, Renteria simply didn't play as well in 2005. Should be better with another year of experience in the A.L. *Grade 8.2*

EDGAR RENTERIA'S HITTING ZONE

.350	.118	.353
.281	.386	.372
.253	.325	.233

LEFTY-RIGHTY SPLITS

vs.	Avg.	AB	H	2B	3B	HR	RBI	BB	SO	OBP	Slg.
L	.326	193	63	15	0	5	30	18	28	.384	.482
R	.253	430	109	21	4	3	40	37	72	.313	.342

Year	Team (League)	Pos.	G	AB	R	H	2B	3B	HR	RBI	BB	SO	HBP	GDP	SB-CS	Avg.	OBP	SLG	OPS	E	F. Avg.
1992—	GC Marlins (GCL)	SS	43	163	25	47	8	1	0	9	8	29	2	1	10-6	.288	.329	.350	.679	24	.897
1993—	Kane Co. (Midw.)	SS	116	384	40	78	8	0	1	35	35	94	0	3	7-8	.203	.268	.232	.500	34	.934
1994—	Brevard County (FSL)	SS	128	439	46	111	15	1	0	36	35	56	0	14	6-11	.253	.307	.292	.598	23	.959
1995—	Portland (East.)	SS	135	508	70	147	15	7	7	68	32	85	2	10	30-11	.289	.329	.388	.717	33	.944
1996—	Charlotte (Int'l)	SS	35	132	17	37	8	0	2	16	9	17	0	5	10-4	.280	.326	.386	.713	7	.959
—	Florida (N.L.)	SS	106	431	68	133	18	3	5	31	33	68	4	12	16-2	.309	.358	.399	.757	11	.975
1997—	Florida (N.L.)	SS	154	617	90	171	21	3	4	52	45	108	4	17	32-15	.277	.327	.340	.668	17	.975
1998—	Florida (N.L.)	SS	133	517	79	146	18	2	3	31	48	78	4	13	41-22	.282	.347	.342	.689	20	.966
1999—	St. Louis (N.L.)	SS	154	585	92	161	36	2	11	63	53	82	0	16	37-8	.275	.334	.400	.734	26	.969
2000—	St. Louis (N.L.)	SS	150	562	94	156	32	1	16	76	63	77	1	19	21-13	.278	.346	.423	.770	22	.958
2001—	St. Louis (N.L.) SS-1B-DH	141	493	54	128	19	3	10	57	39	73	3	15	17-4	.260	.314	.371	.685	24	.961
2002—	St. Louis (N.L.)	SS	152	544	77	166	36	2	11	83	49	57	4	17	22-7	.305	.364	.439	.803	19	.970

Year Team (League)	Pos.	G	AB	R	H	2B	3B	HR	RBI	BB	SO	HBP	GDP	SB-CS	Avg.	OBP	SLG	OPS	E	Avg.
2003—St. Louis (N.L.)	SS	157	587	96	194	47	1	13	100	65	54	1	21	34-7	.330	.394	.480	.874	16	.975
2004—St. Louis (N.L.)	SS	149	586	84	168	37	0	10	72	39	78	1	14	17-11	.287	.327	.401	.728	11	.983
2005—Boston (A.L.)	SS	153	623	100	172	36	4	8	70	55	100	3	15	9-4	.276	.335	.385	.721	30	.954
American League totals (1 year)		153	623	100	172	36	4	8	70	55	100	3	15	9-4	.276	.335	.385	.721	30	.954
National League totals (9 years)		1296	4922	734	1423	264	17	83	565	434	675	22	144	237-89	.289	.346	.400	.746	171	.969
Major League totals (10 years)		1449	5545	834	1595	300	21	91	635	489	775	25	159	246-93	.288	.345	.399	.743	201	.968

DIVISION SERIES RECORD

Year Team (League)	Pos.	G	AB	R	H	2B	3B	HR	RBI	BB	SO	HBP	GDP	SB-CS	Avg.	OBP	SLG	OPS	E	Avg.
1997—Florida (N.L.)	SS	3	13	1	2	0	0	0	1	2	4	0	1	0-0	.154	.267	.154	.421	2	.909
2000—St. Louis (N.L.)	SS	3	10	5	2	0	0	0	0	4	1	0	0	2-0	.200	.429	.200	.629	1	.909
2001—St. Louis (N.L.)	SS	5	17	2	4	1	0	1	1	2	4	0	1	0-0	.235	.316	.471	.786	1	.955
2002—St. Louis (N.L.)	SS	3	12	3	3	0	0	0	0	1	4	0	1	2-0	.250	.308	.250	.558	1	.909
2004—St. Louis (N.L.)	SS	4	11	4	5	2	0	0	4	3	1	1	0	1-1	.455	.600	.636	1.236	0	1.000
2005—Boston (A.L.)	SS	3	13	1	3	2	0	0	0	1	1	0	0	0-0	.231	.385	.385	.670	0	1.000
Division series totals (6 years)		21	76	16	19	5	0	1	6	13	12	1	3	5-1	.250	.367	.355	.722	5	.949

CHAMPIONSHIP SERIES RECORD

Year Team (League)	Pos.	G	AB	R	H	2B	3B	HR	RBI	BB	SO	HBP	GDP	SB-CS	Avg.	OBP	SLG	OPS	E	Avg.
1997—Florida (N.L.)	SS	6	22	4	5	1	0	0		3	6	1		1-0	.227	.346	.273	.619	0	1.000
2000—St. Louis (N.L.)	SS	5	20	4	6	1	0	0	4	0	2	0		3-0	.300	.286	.350	.636	1	1.000
2002—St. Louis (N.L.)	SS	5	19	0	3	0	0	0	1	0	2	1		0-0	.158	.190	.158	.348	1	.900
2004—St. Louis (N.L.)	SS	7	24	1	4	0	0	0	2	2	5	0		0-0	.167	.231	.167	.397	1	.989
Champ. series totals (4 years)		23	85	9	18	2	0	0	7	5	15	2		4-0	.212	.266	.235	.501	1	.989

WORLD SERIES RECORD

Year Team (League)	Pos.	G	AB	R	H	2B	3B	HR	RBI	BB	SO	HBP	GDP	SB-CS	Avg.	OBP	SLG	OPS	E	Avg.
1997—Florida (N.L.)	SS	7	31	3	9	2	0	0	3	3	5	0	0	0-0	.290	.353	.355	.708	1	.974
2004—St. Louis (N.L.)	SS	4	15	2	5	3	0	0	1	2	2	0	1	0-0	.333	.412	.533	.945	1	.941
World series totals (2 years)		11	46	5	14	5	0	0	4	5	7	0	1	0-0	.304	.373	.413	.786	2	.964

ALL-STAR GAME RECORD

	G	AB	R	H	2B	3B	HR	RBI	BB	SO	HBP	GDP	SB-CS	Avg.	OBP	SLG	OPS	E	Avg.
All-Star Game totals (4 years)	4	8	2	1	1	0	0			1			0-0	.125	.125	.250	.375	0	1.000

REPKO, JASON — OF

PERSONAL: Born December 27, 1980, in East Chicago, Ind. ... 5-11/175. ... Bats right, throws right. ... Full name: Jason Edward Repko. ... High school: Hanford (Wash.).

TRANSACTIONS/CAREER NOTES: Selected by Los Angeles Dodgers organization in first round (37th pick overall) of 1999 free-agent draft.

2005 GAMES PLAYED BY POSITION (MLB): OF—118, DH—1.

SCOUTING REPORT Repko is an aggressive player with the ability to run and throw. Can play all three outfield positions and appears to have good instincts. Gets good jumps and has the speed to close on the ball laterally. Charges the ball well and has good arm strength. Is a good runner but still is developing instincts. Is a dead fastball hitter who has problems with off-speed pitches. Is overaggressive and can be exploited. *Grade 5.1*

JASON REPKO'S HITTING ZONE

.385	.083	.154
.222	.158	.421
.196	.600	.111

LEFTY-RIGHTY SPLITS

vs.	Avg.	AB	H	2B	3B	HR	RBI	BB	SO	OBP	Slg.
L	.235	102	24	6	0	3	8	3	22	.278	.382
R	.213	174	37	9	3	5	13	13	58	.283	.385

Year Team (League)	Pos.	G	AB	R	H	2B	3B	HR	RBI	BB	SO	HBP	GDP	SB-CS	Avg.	OBP	SLG	OPS	E	Avg.
1999—Great Falls (Pio.)	SS	49	207	51	63	9	9	8	32	21	43	3	1	12-5	.304	.375	.551	.926	38	.859
2000—Yakima (N'west)	SS	8	17	3	5	2	0	0	1	1	7	0	0	0-0	.294	.333	.412	.745	3	.813
2001—Wilmington (S. Atl.)	SS	88	337	36	74	17	4	4	32	15	68	3	2	17-8	.220	.257	.329	.586	26	.921
2002—Vero Beach (FSL)	OF	120	470	73	128	29	5	9	53	25	92	8	3	29-13	.272	.319	.413	.732	7	.973
2003—Jacksonville (Sou.)	OF	119	416	62	100	14	5	10	23	42	89	6	1	21-8	.240	.317	.370	.687	5	.980
2004—Jacksonville (Sou.)	OF	46	189	26	55	11	2	6	19	13	43	2	1	10-5	.291	.341	.466	.807	3	.936
—Las Vegas (PCL)	OF	75	302	55	94	26	4	7	41	18	57	3	4	13-5	.311	.355	.493	.848	2	1.000
2005—Las Vegas (PCL)	OF	8	31	6	12	0	0	3	6	0	4	0	0	1-0	.387	.387	.677	1.065	0	1.000
—Los Angeles (N.L.)	OF-DH	129	276	43	61	15	3	8	30	16	80	7	7	5-0	.221	.281	.384	.665	6	.968
Major League totals (1 year)		129	276	43	61	15	3	8	30	16	80	7	7	5-0	.221	.281	.384	.665	6	.968

RESOP, CHRIS — P

PERSONAL: Born November 4, 1982, in Naples, Fla. ... 6-3/222. ... Throws right, bats right. ... Full name: Christopher Paul Resop. ... High school: Barron Collier (Naples, Fla.). ... College: None.

TRANSACTIONS/CAREER NOTES: Selected by Florida Marlins organization in fourth round of 2001 free-agent draft. ... Played two seasons as outfielder in Marlins organization (2001-02).

CAREER HITTING: 0-for-1 (.000), 0 R, 0 2B, 0 3B, 0 HR, 0 RBI.

CHRIS RESOP'S PITCHING ZONE

.333	.143	.333
.222	.600	.455
.000	.250	.333

LEFTY-RIGHTY SPLITS

vs.	Avg.	AB	H	2B	3B	HR	RBI	BB	SO	OBP	Slg.
L	.316	38	12	4	0	0	5	5	5	.395	.421
R	.333	30	10	3	1	1	11	4	10	.405	.600

Year Team (League)	W	L	Pct.	ERA	WHIP	G	GS	CG	ShO	Hld.	Sv.-Opp.	IP	H	R	ER	HR	BB-IBB	SO	Avg.
2003—Greensboro (S. Atl.)	0	1	.000	4.97	1.26	11	0	0	0	...	0-...	12.2	11	7	7	1	5-0	15	.224
2004—Greensboro (S. Atl.)	3	1	.750	1.94	0.79	41	0	0	0	...	13-...	41.2	26	11	9	1	7-0	68	.173
2005—Carolina (Southern)	3	2	.600	2.57	1.29	43	0	0	0	1	24-26	49.0	47	15	14	2	16-1	56	.242

Year Team (League)	W	L	Pct.	ERA	WHIP	G	GS	CG	ShO	Hld.	Sv.-Opp.	IP	H	R	ER	HR	BB-IBB	SO	Avg.
— Florida (N.L.)	2	0	1.000	8.47	1.82	15	0	0	0	0	0-0	17.0	22	16	16	1	9-0	15	.324
Major League totals (1 year)	2	0	1.000	8.47	1.82	15	0	0	0	0	0-0	17.0	22	16	16	1	9-0	15	.324

RESTOVICH, MICHAEL — OF

PERSONAL: Born January 3, 1979, in Rochester, Minn. ... 6-4/257. ... Bats right, throws right. ... Full name: Michael Jerome Restovich. ... Name pronounced: ress-TO-vich. ... High school: Mayo (Rochester, Minn.).

TRANSACTIONS/CAREER NOTES: Selected by Minnesota Twins organization in second round of 1997 free-agent draft. ... Claimed on waivers by Tampa Bay Devil Rays (March 30, 2005). ... Claimed on waivers by Colorado Rockies (April 6, 2005). ... Traded by Rockies to Pittsburgh Pirates for a player to be named later or cash considerations (May 11, 2005).

2005 GAMES PLAYED BY POSITION (MLB): OF—39.

MICHAEL RESTOVICH'S HITTING ZONE

.000	.667	.500
.269	.455	.133
.250	.667	.167

LEFTY-RIGHTY SPLITS

vs.	Avg.	AB	H	2B	3B	HR	RBI	BB	SO	OBP	Slg.
L	.250	88	22	5	1	3	6	8	20	.313	.432
R	.185	27	5	0	0	0	2	3	9	.267	.185

Year Team (League)	Pos.	G	AB	R	H	2B	3B	HR	RBI	BB	SO	HBP	GDP	SB-CS	Avg.	OBP	SLG	OPS	E	Avg.
1998—Elizabethton (App.)	OF	65	242	68	86	20	1	13	64	54	58	9	10	5-2	.355	.489	.607	1.096	9	.912
—Fort Wayne (Midw.)	OF	11	45	9	20	5	2	0	6	4	12	0	1	0-0	.444	.490	.644	1.134	0	1.000
1999—Quad City (Midw.)	3B-OF	131	493	91	154	30	6	19	107	74	100	13	9	7-9	.312	.412	.513	.925	9	.958
2000—Fort Myers (FSL)	OF	135	475	73	125	27	9	8	64	61	100	4	11	19-7	.263	.350	.408	.758	6	.975
2001—New Britain (East.)	1B-OF	140	501	69	135	33	4	23	84	54	125	6	8	15-7	.269	.345	.489	.834	3	.989
2002—Edmonton (PCL)	OF	138	518	95	148	32	7	29	98	53	151	4	10	11-7	.286	.353	.542	.896	6	.975
—Minnesota (A.L.)	OF-DH	8	13	3	4	0	0	1	1	1	4	0	2	1-0	.308	.357	.538	.896	1	1.000
2003—Rochester (Int'l)	OF-DH	119	454	75	125	34	2	16	72	47	117	4	10	10-3	.275	.346	.465	.811	3	.989
—Minnesota (A.L.)	OF-DH	24	53	10	15	3	2	0	4	10	12	1	3	0-0	.283	.406	.415	.821	0	1.000
2004—Rochester (Int'l)	OF-DH	106	425	65	105	20	3	20	63	25	104	2	13	4-3	.247	.291	.449	.740	5	.975
—Minnesota (A.L.)	OF-DH	29	47	9	12	3	0	2	6	4	10	0	0	0-0	.255	.314	.447	.761	0	1.000
2005—Colorado (N.L.)	OF	14	31	5	9	2	0	1	3	3	5	0	2	0-0	.290	.353	.452	.805		
—Pittsburgh (N.L.)	OF	52	84	10	18	3	1	2	5	8	24	1	0	0-0	.214	.283	.345	.628	1	.976
American League totals (3 years)		61	113	22	31	6	2	3	11	15	26	1	5	1-0	.274	.364	.442	.807	0	1.000
National League totals (1 year)		66	115	15	27	5	1	3	8	11	29	0	5	0-0	.235	.302	.374	.676	1	.983
Major League totals (4 years)		127	228	37	58	11	3	6	19	26	55	1	10	1-0	.254	.333	.408	.741	1	.991

REYES, AL — P

PERSONAL: Born April 10, 1970, in San Cristobal, Dominican Republic. ... 6-1/212. ... Throws right, bats right. ... Full name: Rafael Alberto Reyes. ... Name pronounced: RAY-ess. ... High school: Francisco del Rosario Sanche (Santo Domingo, Dominican Republic)..

TRANSACTIONS/CAREER NOTES: Signed as a non-drafted free agent by Montreal Expos organization (February 17, 1988). ... Selected by Milwaukee Brewers from Expos organization in Rule 5 major league draft (December 5, 1994). ... On disabled list (July 19, 1995-remainder of season). ... On disabled list (July 25-September 8, 1998); included rehabilitation assignment to Louisville. ... Traded by Brewers to Baltimore Orioles (July 21, 1999), completing deal in which Orioles traded P Rocky Coppinger to Brewers for a player to be named (July 16, 1999). ... Traded by Orioles to Los Angeles Dodgers for P Alan Mills and cash (June 13, 2000). ... Signed as a free agent by Pittsburgh Pirates organization (January 25, 2002). ... Released by Pirates (March 10, 2003). ... Signed by New York Yankees organization (March 19, 2003). ... Released by Yankees (July 25, 2003). ... Signed by Tampa Bay Devil Rays organization (January 12, 2004). ... Released by Devil Rays (June 1, 2004). ... Signed by St. Louis Cardinals organization (June 3, 2004).

CAREER HITTING: 3-for-12 (.250), 2 R, 0 2B, 0 3B, 0 HR, 0 RBI.

AL REYES' PITCHING ZONE

.286	.000	.111
.129	.261	.156
.231	.308	.176

LEFTY-RIGHTY SPLITS

vs.	Avg.	AB	H	2B	3B	HR	RBI	BB	SO	OBP	Slg.
L	.184	87	16	3	0	2	8	8	28	.276	.287
R	.172	128	22	6	0	3	13	12	39	.252	.289

Year Team (League)	W	L	Pct.	ERA	WHIP	G	GS	CG	ShO	Hld.	Sv.-Opp.	IP	H	R	ER	HR	BB-IBB	SO	Avg.
1989—Dom. Expos (DSL)	3	4	.429	2.79	1.42	12	10	1	0	...	0-...	71.0	68	36	22	...	33-...	49	...
1990—W.P. Beach (FSL)	5	4	.556	4.74	1.58	16	10	0	0	...	1-...	57.0	58	32	30	4	32-2	47	.272
1991—Rockford (Midwest)	0	1	.000	5.56	1.41	3	3	0	0	...	0-...	11.1	14	8	7	1	2-0	10	.304
1992—Albany (S. Atl.)	0	2	.000	3.95	1.35	27	0	0	0	...	4-...	27.1	24	14	12	0	13-0	29	.226
1993—Burlington (Midw.)	7	6	.538	2.68	1.05	53	0	0	0	...	11-...	74.0	52	33	22	7	26-3	80	.193
1994—Harrisburg (East.)	2	2	.500	3.25	1.17	60	0	0	0	...	35-...	69.1	68	26	25	4	13-0	60	.257
1995—Milwaukee (A.L.)	1	1	.500	2.43	1.11	27	0	0	0	4	1-1	33.1	19	9	9	3	18-2	29	.167
1996—Beloit (Midw.)	1	0	1.000	1.83	1.17	13	0	0	0	0	0-...	19.2	17	7	4	1	6-0	22	.227
—Milwaukee (A.L.)	1	0	1.000	7.94	1.76	5	0	0	0	0	0-0	5.2	8	5	5	1	2-0	2	.320
1997—Tucson (PCL)	2	4	.333	5.02	1.50	38	0	0	0	...	7-...	57.1	52	39	32	12	34-2	70	.243
—Milwaukee (A.L.)	1	2	.333	5.46	1.38	19	0	0	0	1	1-1	29.2	32	19	18	4	9-0	28	.274
1998—Milwaukee (N.L.)	5	1	.833	3.95	1.51	50	0	0	0	10	0-1	57.0	55	26	25	9	31-1	58	.255
—Louisville (Int'l)	0	1	.000	8.31	1.62	3	2	0	0	...	0-...	4.1	5	5	4	1	2-0	5	.294
1999—Louisville (Int'l)	0	0	...	8.38	1.97	6	0	0	0	...	0-...	9.2	12	9	9	2	7-2	8	.343
—Milwaukee (N.L.)	2	0	1.000	4.25	1.44	26	0	0	0	2	0-1	36.0	27	17	17	5	25-1	39	.204
—Baltimore (A.L.)	2	3	.400	4.85	1.31	27	0	0	0	4	0-3	29.2	23	16	16	4	14-2	28	.225
2000—Rochester (Int'l)	0	1	.000	7.71	1.89	9	0	0	0	...	2-...	11.2	13	11	10	2	9-1	17	.271
—Baltimore (A.L.)	1	0	1.000	6.92	1.85	13	0	0	0	2	0-1	13.0	13	10	10	2	11-1	10	.271
—Albuquerque (PCL)	3	2	.600	3.72	1.40	30	0	0	0	...	0-...	38.2	33	20	16	5	21-0	39	.226
—Los Angeles (N.L.)	0	0	...	0.00	0.45	6	0	0	0	1	0-0	6.2	2	0	0	0	1-0	8	.087
2001—Las Vegas (PCL)	0	1	.000	3.38	1.16	19	0	0	0	...	0-...	29.1	24	11	11	3	10-1	37	.218
—Los Angeles (N.L.)	2	1	.667	3.86	1.60	19	0	0	0	0	1-2	25.2	28	13	11	3	13-1	23	.271
2002—Nashville (PCL)	7	3	.700	2.70	0.93	43	0	0	0	...	1-...	66.2	40	23	20	5	22-2	90	.167
—Pittsburgh (N.L.)	0	0	...	2.65	0.94	15	0	0	0	3	0-1	17.0	16	5	5	1	7-0	21	.161
2003—Columbus (Int'l)	1	1	.500	3.71	1.20	15	0	0	0	...	0-...	17.0	16	7	7	1	5-0	15	.239
—New York (A.L.)	0	0	...	3.18	1.29	13	0	0	0	0	0-0	17.0	13	7	6	1	9-1	9	.203
2004—Durham (Int'l)	2	1	.667	2.46	1.23	20	0	0	0	...	10-...	22.0	22	6	6	0	5-1	22	.216
—Memphis (PCL)	2	2	.500	2.95	1.16	37	0	0	0	...	23-...	39.2	32	13	13	2	14-3	47	.219
—St. Louis (N.L.)	0	0	...	0.75	0.42	12	0	0	0	0	0-0	12.0	3	1	1	0	2-0	11	.067
2005—St. Louis (N.L.)	4	2	.667	2.15	0.93	65	0	0	0	16	3-3	62.2	38	15	15	5	20-2	67	.177
American League totals (6 years)	6	6	.500	4.49	1.35	104	0	0	0	11	2-7	128.1	108	66	64	15	65-6	106	.230
National League totals (7 years)	13	4	.765	3.07	1.20	193	2	0	0	32	4-8	217.0	162	77	74	20	99-5	227	.207
Major League totals (11 years)	19	10	.655	3.60	1.26	297	2	0	0	43	6-15	345.1	270	143	138	38	164-11	333	.216

Year Team (League)	W	L	Pct.	ERA	WHIP	G	GS	CG	ShO	Hld.	Sv.-Opp.	IP	H	R	ER	HR	BB-IBB	SO	Avg.
2004— St. Louis (N.L.)	0	0	...	0.00	0.00	2	0	0	0	...	0-0	1.1	0	0	0	0	0-0	0	.000

REYES, ANTHONY — P

PERSONAL: Born October 16, 1981, in Downey, Calif. ... 6-2/215. ... Throws right, bats right. ... Full name: Anthony Loza Reyes. ... High school: California (Whittier, Calif.). ... College: Southern California.

TRANSACTIONS/CAREER NOTES: Selected by St. Louis Cardinals organization in 15th round of 2003 free-agent draft.

CAREER HITTING: 0-for-4 (.000), 0 R, 0 2B, 0 3B, 0 HR, 0 RBI.

SCOUTING REPORT **Throws:** Reyes features a fastball that tops out around 96 mph and shows a curveball, slider and changeup. **Tendencies:** He primarily is a fastball-curveball pitcher who likes to work the high and low parts of the strike zone and is effective at changing speeds on his fastball. Has good feel for his four-seamer and a running two-seamer that reaches the low 90s. Mechanics are good, although he sometimes drops his arm slot on his breaking ball. Throws easy heat and despite some elbow problems, is able to maintain his velocity. **Outlook:** Reyes enters spring training with an excellent chance of making the Cardinals' rotation. **Grade 7.1**

LEFTY-RIGHTY SPLITS

vs.	Avg.	AB	H	2B	3B	HR	RBI	BB	SO	OBP	Slg.
L	.111	18	2	2	0	0	0	1	6	.158	.222
R	.148	27	4	0	0	2	4	3	6	.226	.370

R

Year Team (League)	W	L	Pct.	ERA	WHIP	G	GS	CG	ShO	Hld.	Sv.-Opp.	IP	H	R	ER	HR	BB-IBB	SO	Avg.
2004— Palm Beach (FSL)	3	0	1.000	4.66	1.31	7	7	0	0	...	0-...	36.2	41	21	19	5	7-0	38	.297
— Tennessee (Sou.)	6	2	.750	2.91	1.01	12	12	0	0	...	0-...	74.1	62	27	24	3	13-1	102	.230
2005— Memphis (PCL)	7	6	.538	3.64	1.08	23	23	2	1	0	0-0	128.2	105	55	52	13	34-1	136	.222
— St. Louis (N.L.)	1	1	.500	2.70	0.75	4	1	0	0	0	0-0	13.1	6	4	4	2	4-1	12	.133
Major League totals (1 year)	1	1	.500	2.70	0.75	4	1	0	0	0	0-0	13.1	6	4	4	2	4-1	12	.133

REYES, DENNYS — P

PERSONAL: Born April 19, 1977, in Higuera de Zaragoza, Mexico. ... 6-3/245. ... Throws left, bats right. ... Name pronounced: RAY-ess. ... High school: Ignacio Zaragoza (Higuera de Zaragoza, Mexico).

TRANSACTIONS/CAREER NOTES: Signed as a non-drafted free agent by Los Angeles Dodgers organization (July 5, 1993). ... Loaned by Dodgers organization to Mexico City Red Devils of the Mexican League (March 28-August 22, 1995). ... Traded by Dodgers with 1B/3B Paul Konerko to Cincinnati Reds for P Jeff Shaw (July 4, 1998). ... On disabled list (May 30-July 2, 2001). ... Traded by Reds with SS Pokey Reese to Colorado Rockies for Ps Gabe White and Luke Hudson (December 18, 2001). ... Traded by Rockies with OF Todd Hollandsworth to Texas Rangers for OF Gabe Kapler and 2B Jason Romano (July 31, 2002). ... Signed as a free agent by Pittsburgh Pirates organization (January 24, 2003). ... Signed as a free agent by Arizona Diamondbacks organization (June 11, 2003). ... Signed as a free agent by Kansas City Royals organization (October 30, 2003). ... Signed as a free agent by San Diego Padres (November 29, 2004). ... Released by Padres (July 17, 2005). ... Signed by New York Yankees organization (August 2, 2005).

CAREER HITTING: 4-for-54 (.074), 2 R, 1 2B, 0 3B, 0 HR, 0 RBI.

SCOUTING REPORT **Throws:** Reyes' fastball is in the 88-91 mph range. Also has a slider and a changeup. **Tendencies:** He has some deception in his delivery, and his marginal fastball can be sneaky with a natural tailing action when he keeps it down. Struggles with locating the fastball and doesn't pitch inside enough. Slider has a sweeping action and is without tight spin. Has good motion and movement on his change, which he turns over to righthanders. Doesn't hold runners on well. **Outlook:** Reyes can spot start or work in long relief, but he's prone to high pitch counts. **Grade 5.3**

DENNYS REYES'S PITCHING ZONE

.200	.500	.000
.468	.615	.261
.240	.143	.308

LEFTY-RIGHTY SPLITS

vs.	Avg.	AB	H	2B	3B	HR	RBI	BB	SO	OBP	Slg.
L	.208	53	11	3	0	0	6	8	11	.311	.264
R	.359	128	46	6	2	3	18	24	24	.464	.508

Year Team (League)	W	L	Pct.	ERA	WHIP	G	GS	CG	ShO	Hld.	Sv.-Opp.	IP	H	R	ER	HR	BB-IBB	SO	Avg.
1993— M.C. R. Dev. (Mex.)	0	1	.000	5.06	2.44	7	1	0	0	...	0-...	5.1	4	4	3	1	9-...	5	...
1994— Vero Beach (FSL)	2	4	.333	6.70	1.82	9	9	0	0	...	0-...	41.2	58	37	31	6	18-0	25	.324
— Great Falls (Pio.)	7	1	.875	3.78	1.44	14	9	0	0	...	0-...	66.2	71	37	28	0	25-0	70	.267
1995— M.C. R. Dev. (Mex.)	5	5	.500	6.60	1.99	17	15	1	0	...	0-...	58.2	76	49	43	4	41-...	44	...
— Vero Beach (FSL)	1	0	1.000	1.80	1.40	3	2	0	0	...	0-...	10.0	8	2	2	0	6-0	9	.222
1996— San Bern. (Calif.)	11	12	.478	4.17	1.46	29	28	0	0	...	0-...	166.0	166	106	77	11	77-0	176	.259
1997— San Antonio (Texas)	8	1	.889	3.02	1.33	12	12	1	0	...	0-...	80.1	79	33	27	6	28-1	66	.262
— Albuquerque (PCL)	6	3	.667	5.65	1.80	10	10	1	0	...	0-...	57.1	70	40	36	4	33-0	45	.303
— Los Angeles (N.L.)	2	3	.400	3.83	1.47	14	5	0	0	0	0-0	47.0	51	21	20	4	18-0	36	.280
1998— Albuquerque (PCL)	1	4	.200	1.44	1.12	7	7	1	1	...	0-...	43.2	31	13	7	0	18-0	58	.197
— Los Angeles (N.L.)	0	4	.000	4.71	1.64	11	4	0	0	0	0-0	28.2	27	17	15	1	20-4	33	.255
— Indianapolis (Int'l)	2	0	1.000	3.00	1.42	4	4	0	0	...	0-...	24.0	20	10	8	1	14-0	27	.233
— Cincinnati (N.L.)	3	1	.750	4.42	1.60	8	7	0	0	0	0-0	38.2	35	19	19	2	27-1	44	.255
1999— Cincinnati (N.L.)	2	2	.500	3.79	1.49	65	1	0	0	14	2-3	61.2	53	30	26	3	39-1	72	.232
2000— Cincinnati (N.L.)	2	1	.667	4.53	1.65	62	0	0	0	10	0-1	43.2	43	31	22	5	29-0	36	.262
2001— Cincinnati (N.L.)	2	6	.250	4.92	1.62	35	6	0	0	6	0-0	53.0	51	35	29	5	35-1	52	.248
— Louisville (Int'l)	4	2	.667	3.67	1.46	7	6	0	0	...	0-...	34.1	34	15	14	3	16-0	34	.260
2002— Colorado (N.L.)	0	1	.000	4.24	1.66	43	0	0	0	4	0-0	40.1	43	19	19	1	24-3	30	.279
— Texas (A.L.)	4	3	.571	6.38	1.80	15	5	0	0	0	0-0	42.1	55	33	30	9	21-1	29	.316
2003— Pittsburgh (N.L.)	0	0	...	10.45	1.84	12	0	0	0	2	0-0	10.1	10	13	12	1	9-1	11	.263
— Tucson (PCL)	2	1	.667	2.84	1.50	33	0	0	0	...	2-...	31.2	24	16	10	0	22-2	30	.207
— Arizona (N.L.)	0	0	...	11.57	2.57	3	0	0	0	0	0-0	2.1	5	3	3	1	1-0	5	.417
2004— Kansas City (A.L.)	4	8	.333	4.75	1.52	40	12	0	0	5	0-1	108.0	114	64	57	12	50-3	91	.273
2005— San Diego (N.L.)	3	2	.600	5.15	2.04	36	1	0	0	5	0-1	43.2	57	30	25	3	32-2	35	.315
American League totals (2 years)	8	11	.421	5.21	1.60	55	17	0	0	5	0-1	150.1	169	97	87	21	71-4	120	.286
National League totals (8 years)	14	20	.412	4.63	1.65	289	23	0	0	36	2-5	369.1	375	218	190	28	234-16	354	.266
Major League totals (9 years)	22	31	.415	4.80	1.63	344	40	0	0	41	2-6	519.2	544	315	277	49	305-20	474	.272

REYES, JOSE — SS

PERSONAL: Born June 11, 1983, in Villa Gonzalez, Dominican Republic. ... 6-0/160. ... Bats both, throws right. ... Full name: Jose Bernabe Reyes. ... Name pronounced: RAY-ess. ... High school: Attended Liceoi Delia Reyes, played for Felix de Leon, Dominican Republic).
TRANSACTIONS/CAREER NOTES: Signed as a non-drafted free agent by New York Mets organization (August 16, 1999). ... On disabled list (September 1, 2003-remainder of season). ... On disabled list (March 26-June 19 and August 13-September 24, 2004); included rehabilitation assignments to St. Lucie and Binghamton.
2005 GAMES PLAYED BY POSITION (MLB): SS—161.

SCOUTING REPORT

Offense: Reyes stands on top of the plate and hits off his front foot. Generates good bat speed despite having a sweeping stroke. Is a line-drive hitter to all fields with surprising power. Is better from his natural right side but has more power lefthanded. Speed Forces infielders to play shallow, creating holes. Is impatient and needs to cut down his strikeouts. Could lead the league in steals for many seasons. *Defense:* His footwork is exceptionally quick and he has outstanding range to either side. Has quick, soft hands and a plus arm from the hole with very good carry. *Outlook:* Intimidating speed makes him a catalyst at the top of the Mets' order. Can become one of the game's best shortstops if can play under control. **Grade 7.7**

JOSE REYES'S HITTING ZONE

.258	.357	.313
.349	.257	.266
.333	.396	.191

LEFTY-RIGHTY SPLITS

vs.	Avg.	AB	H	2B	3B	HR	RBI	BB	SO	OBP	Slg.
L	.288	153	44	6	2	1	18	6	16	.313	.373
R	.269	543	146	18	15	6	40	21	62	.297	.390

Year	Team (League)	Pos.	G	AB	R	H	2B	3B	HR	RBI	BB	SO	HBP	GDP	SB-CS	Avg.	OBP	SLG	OPS	E	Fielding Avg.
2000—	Kingsport (Appalachian)	SS-3B-2B-OF	49	132	22	33	3	3	0	8	20	37	3	1	10-4	.250	.359	.318	.677	11	.942
2001—	Capital City (SAL)	SS	108	407	71	125	22	15	5	48	18	71	2	4	30-10	.307	.337	.472	.809	18	.964
2002—	St. Lucie (Fla. St.)	SS	69	288	58	83	10	11	6	38	30	35	1	5	31-13	.288	.353	.462	.815	12	.967
—	Binghamton (East.)	SS	65	275	46	79	16	8	2	24	16	42	2	2	27-11	.287	.331	.425	.757	17	.940
2003—	Norfolk (Int'l)	SS-DH	42	160	28	43	6	4	0	13	15	25	1	2	26-5	.269	.333	.356	.690	5	.969
—	New York (N.L.)	SS	69	274	47	84	12	4	5	32	13	36	0	1	13-3	.307	.334	.434	.769	9	.973
2004—	St. Lucie (Fla. St.)	2B	6	23	3	6	2	0	0	1	0	3	0	1	2-0	.261	.261	.348	.609	2	.917
—	Binghamton (East.)	2B	4	18	2	2	0	0	0	3	2	4	0	0	3-1	.111	.190	.111	.302	0	1.000
—	New York (N.L.)	2B-SS	53	220	33	56	16	2	2	14	5	31	0	1	19-2	.255	.271	.373	.644	6	.975
2005—	New York (N.L.)	SS	161	696	99	190	24	17	7	58	27	78	2	7	*60-15	.273	.300	.386	.687	18	.974
Major League totals (3 years)			283	1190	179	330	52	23	14	104	45	145	2	9	92-20	.277	.303	.395	.698	33	.974

RHODES, ARTHUR — P

PERSONAL: Born October 24, 1969, in Waco, Texas. ... 6-2/212. ... Throws left, bats left. ... Full name: Arthur Lee Rhodes. ... High school: LaVega (Waco, Texas).
TRANSACTIONS/CAREER NOTES: Selected by Baltimore Orioles organization in second round of 1988 free-agent draft. ... On disabled list (May 16-August 2, 1993); included rehabilitation assignment to Rochester. ... On disabled list (May 2-20, 1994); included rehabilitation assignment to Frederick. ... On disabled list (August 25, 1995-remainder of season; and July 14-August 2 and August 6-September 27, 1996). ... On disabled list (July 5-August 17, 1998); included rehabilitation assignment to Rochester. ... Signed as a free agent by Seattle Mariners (December 21, 1999). ... Signed as a free agent by Oakland Athletics (December 23, 2003). ... On disabled list (June 28-August 18, 2004); included rehabilitation assignment to Sacramento. ... Traded by A's with P Mark Redman to Pittsburgh Pirates for C Jason Kendall and cash (November 29, 2004). ... Traded by Pirates with cash to Cleveland Indians for OF Matt Lawton and cash (December 11, 2004). ... On bereavement list (August 5-12, 2005). ... On disabled list (August 13-September 2, 2005); included rehabilitation assignment to Akron.
CAREER HITTING: 1-for-4 (.250), 0 R, 0 2B, 0 3B, 0 HR, 0 RBI.

SCOUTING REPORT

Throws: Rhodes' fastball ranges from 90-94 mph. Also has a slider. *Tendencies:* Rhodes uses a short-arm motion and has excellent arm speed and a good arm angle. Fastball naturally runs from righthanders but occasionally will cut it to move it in on them. Slider and cutter are basically the same pitch but the cutter isn't has hard and has some downward action. Is very effective keeping the ball in the park. *Outlook:* Rhodes was hampered by knee trouble last season; look for him to bounce back in 2006 and re-establish himself as a dependable setup/situational reliever. **Grade 7.2**

ARTHUR RHODES'S PITCHING ZONE

.333	.600	.273
.200	.286	.133
.200	.500	.313

LEFTY-RIGHTY SPLITS

vs.	Avg.	AB	H	2B	3B	HR	RBI	BB	SO	OBP	Slg.
L	.286	63	18	0	0	1	10	4	19	.328	.333
R	.155	97	15	4	0	1	6	8	24	.222	.227

Year	Team (League)	W	L	Pct.	ERA	WHIP	G	GS	CG	ShO	Hld.	Sv.-Opp.	IP	H	R	ER	HR	BB-IBB	SO	Avg.
1988—	Bluefield (Appal.)	3	4	.429	3.31	1.25	11	7	0	0	...	0-...	35.1	29	17	13	1	15-0	44	.210
1989—	Erie (N.Y.-Penn)	2	0	1.000	1.16	0.74	5	5	1	0	...	0-...	31.0	13	7	4	1	10-0	45	.114
—	Frederick (Carolina)	2	2	.500	5.18	1.56	7	6	0	0	...	0-...	24.1	19	16	14	2	19-0	28	.213
1990—	Frederick (Carolina)	4	6	.400	2.12	1.03	13	13	3	0	...	0-...	80.2	62	25	19	6	21-0	103	.207
—	Hagerstown (East.)	3	4	.429	3.73	1.40	12	12	0	0	...	0-...	72.1	62	32	30	3	39-0	60	.238
1991—	Hagerstown (East.)	7	4	.636	2.70	1.13	19	19	2	2	...	0-...	106.2	73	37	32	2	47-1	115	.194
—	Baltimore (A.L.)	0	3	.000	8.00	1.94	8	8	0	0	0	0-0	36.0	47	35	32	4	23-0	23	.320
1992—	Rochester (Int'l)	6	6	.500	3.72	1.28	17	17	1	0	...	0-...	101.2	84	48	42	7	46-0	115	.224
—	Baltimore (A.L.)	7	5	.583	3.63	1.33	15	15	2	1	0	0-0	94.1	87	39	38	6	38-2	77	.250
1993—	Baltimore (A.L.)	5	6	.455	6.51	1.63	17	17	0	0	0	0-0	85.2	91	62	62	16	49-1	49	.274
—	Rochester (Int'l)	1	1	.500	4.05	1.54	6	6	0	0	...	0-...	26.2	26	12	12	5	15-0	33	.263
1994—	Baltimore (A.L.)	3	5	.375	5.81	1.54	10	10	3	2	0	0-0	52.2	51	34	34	8	30-1	47	.254
—	Frederick (Carolina)	0	0	...	0.00	0.60	1	1	0	0	...	0-...	5.0	3	0	0	0	0-0	7	.176
—	Rochester (Int'l)	7	5	.583	2.79	1.15	15	15	3	0	...	0-...	90.1	70	41	28	7	34-1	86	.215
1995—	Baltimore (A.L.)	2	5	.286	6.21	1.54	19	9	0	0	0	0-1	75.1	68	53	52	13	48-1	77	.239
—	Rochester (Int'l)	2	1	.667	2.70	1.17	4	4	1	0	...	0-...	30.0	27	12	9	2	8-0	33	.239
1996—	Baltimore (A.L.)	9	1	.900	4.08	1.34	28	2	0	0	2	1-1	53.0	48	28	24	6	23-3	62	.239
1997—	Baltimore (A.L.)	10	3	.769	3.02	1.06	53	0	0	0	9	1-2	95.1	75	32	32	9	26-5	102	.218
1998—	Baltimore (A.L.)	4	4	.500	3.51	1.29	45	0	0	0	10	4-8	77.0	65	30	30	8	34-2	83	.233
—	Rochester (Int'l)	0	0	...	4.50	2.00	1	1	0	0	...	0-...	2.0	3	1	1	0	1-0	3	.333

Year Team (League)	W	L	Pct.	ERA	WHIP	G	GS	CG	ShO	Hld.	Sv.-Opp.	IP	H	R	ER	HR	BB-IBB	SO	Avg.
1999— Baltimore (A.L.)	3	4	.429	5.43	1.66	43	0	0	0	5	3-5	53.0	43	37	32	9	45-6	59	.221
2000— Seattle (A.L.)	5	8	.385	4.28	1.15	72	0	0	0	24	0-7	69.1	51	34	33	6	29-3	77	.205
2001— Seattle (A.L.)	8	0	1.000	1.72	0.85	71	0	0	0	* 32	3-7	68.0	46	14	13	5	12-0	83	.189
2002— Seattle (A.L.)	10	4	.714	2.33	0.83	66	0	0	0	27	2-7	69.2	45	18	18	4	13-1	81	.187
2003— Seattle (A.L.)	3	3	.500	4.17	1.31	67	0	0	0	18	3-6	54.0	53	25	25	4	18-2	48	.256
2004— Sacramento (PCL)	0	0	...	0.00	0.50	2	2	0	0	0	0-...	2.0	0	0	0	0	1-0	3	.000
— Oakland (A.L.)	3	3	.500	5.12	1.73	37	0	0	0	3	9-14	38.2	46	23	22	9	21-4	34	.293
2005— Akron (East.)	0	0	...	0.00	0.00	1	1	0	0	0	0-...	1.0	0	0	0	0	0-0	0	.000
— Cleveland (A.L.)	3	1	.750	2.08	1.04	47	0	0	0	16	0-3	43.1	33	13	10	2	12-2	43	.206
Major League totals (15 years)	75	55	.577	4.26	1.32	598	61	5	3	146	26-61	965.1	849	477	457	109	421-33	945	.237

DIVISION SERIES RECORD

Year Team (League)	W	L	Pct.	ERA	WHIP	G	GS	CG	ShO	Hld.	Sv.-Opp.	IP	H	R	ER	HR	BB-IBB	SO	Avg.
1996— Baltimore (A.L.)	0	0	...	9.00	2.00	2	0	0	0	0	0-0	1.0	1	1	1	0	1-0	1	.250
1997— Baltimore (A.L.)	0	0	...	0.00	0.00	1	0	0	0	0	0-0	2.1	0	0	0	0	0-0	4	.000
2000— Seattle (A.L.)	0	0	...	0.00	0.75	3	0	0	0	1	0-0	2.2	0	0	0	0	2-0	2	.000
2001— Seattle (A.L.)	0	0	...	0.00	0.38	3	0	0	0	2	0-0	2.2	1	0	0	0	0-0	1	.111
Division series totals (4 years)	0	0	...	1.04	0.58	9	0	0	0	3	0-0	8.2	2	1	1	0	3-0	8	.077

CHAMPIONSHIP SERIES RECORD

Year Team (League)	W	L	Pct.	ERA	WHIP	G	GS	CG	ShO	Hld.	Sv.-Opp.	IP	H	R	ER	HR	BB-IBB	SO	Avg.
1996— Baltimore (A.L.)	0	0	...	0.00	1.00	3	0	0	0	0	0-0	2.0	2	0	0	0	0-0	2	.286
1997— Baltimore (A.L.)	0	0	...	0.00	2.14	2	0	0	0	0	0-0	2.1	2	0	0	0	3-1	2	.250
2000— Seattle (A.L.)	0	1	.000	31.50	6.00	4	0	0	0	1	0-2	2.0	8	7	7	1	4-1	5	.615
2001— Seattle (A.L.)	0	0	...	4.50	1.00	2	0	0	0	0	0-1	2.0	2	1	1	1	0-0	2	.250
Champ. series totals (4 years)	0	1	.000	8.64	2.52	11	0	0	0	1	0-3	8.1	14	8	8	2	7-2	11	.389

RIEDLING, JOHN   P

PERSONAL: Born August 29, 1975, in Fort Lauderdale, Fla. ... 5-11/190. ... Throws right, bats right. ... Full name: John Richard Riedling. ... Name pronounced: READ-ling. ... High school: Ely (Pompano Beach, Fla.).
TRANSACTIONS/CAREER NOTES: Selected by Cincinnati Reds organization in 22nd round of 1994 free-agent draft. ... On disabled list (May 27-August 12 and August 31, 2001-remainder of season); included rehabilitation assignment to Louisville. ... On disabled list (March 26-May 1 and August 20-September 4, 2002; and June 12-27, 2003). ... Signed as a free agent by Florida Marlins (January 6, 2005). ... On disabled list (August 29, 2005-remainder of season). ... Released by Marlins (October 3, 2005).
CAREER HITTING: 4-for-27 (.148), 2 R, 0 2B, 0 3B, 0 HR, 2 RBI.

SCOUTING REPORT *Throws:* Riedling has a fastball that ranges from 88-92 mph. Also has a curveball and a slider. *Tendencies:* Riedling is a thrower whose lack of command prevents him from being consistent. Sinking fastball stays up when he overthrows it. Curve tends to roll rather than bite. Slider is better. Gives up too many walks and doesn't strike out enough batters. *Outlook:* Riedling is better suited for long and middle relief at this point. Can be effective as long as he keeps the ball down. *Grade 5.5*

JOHN RIEDLING'S PITCHING ZONE

.333	.200	.400
.375	.267	.458
.286	.125	.389

LEFTY-RIGHTY SPLITS

vs.	Avg.	AB	H	2B	3B	HR	RBI	BB	SO	OBP	Slg.
L	.306	62	19	2	1	2	8	6	5	.371	.468
R	.288	52	15	6	0	1	11	7	11	.373	.462

Year Team (League)	W	L	Pct.	ERA	WHIP	G	GS	CG	ShO	Hld.	Sv.-Opp.	IP	H	R	ER	HR	BB-IBB	SO	Avg.
1994— Billings (Pion.)	4	1	.800	5.48	2.03	15	15	0	0	...	0-...	44.1	62	36	27	0	28-0	27	.333
1995— Billings (Pion.)	2	2	.500	7.04	1.88	13	7	0	0	...	1-...	38.1	51	38	30	4	21-2	28	.305
1996— Char., W.Va. (SAL)	6	10	.375	3.99	1.44	26	26	0	0	...	0-...	140.0	135	85	62	2	66-6	90	.258
1997— Burlington (Midw.)	4	6	.400	5.26	1.44	35	16	0	0	...	0-...	102.2	101	70	60	8	47-0	104	.253
1998— Chattanooga (Sou.)	3	10	.231	5.00	1.68	24	20	0	0	...	0-...	102.2	112	70	57	10	60-5	86	.277
1999— Chattanooga (Sou.)	9	5	.643	3.43	1.45	40	0	0	0	...	5-...	42.0	41	23	16	2	20-3	38	.253
— Indianapolis (Int'l)	1	0	1.000	1.54	1.06	24	0	0	0	...	1-...	35.0	19	9	6	1	18-2	26	.160
2000— Louisville (Int'l)	6	3	.667	2.52	1.24	53	0	0	0	...	5-...	75.0	63	24	21	7	30-3	75	.226
— Cincinnati (N.L.)	3	1	.750	2.35	1.24	13	0	0	0	2	1-2	15.1	11	7	4	1	8-0	18	.208
2001— Cincinnati (N.L.)	1	1	.500	2.41	1.07	29	0	0	0	5	1-3	33.2	22	9	9	1	14-0	23	.186
— Louisville (Int'l)	0	0	...	0.00	1.00	1	0	0	0	...	0-...	1.0	0	0	0	0	1-0	1	.000
2002— Chattanooga (Sou.)	1	1	.500	11.05	2.45	6	0	0	0	...	0-...	7.1	13	11	9	0	5-2	5	.382
— Louisville (Int'l)	1	0	1.000	4.66	1.45	7	0	0	0	...	0-...	9.2	10	6	5	0	4-0	10	.256
— Cincinnati (N.L.)	2	4	.333	2.70	1.39	33	0	0	0	8	0-0	46.2	39	16	14	2	26-6	30	.234
2003— Cincinnati (N.L.)	2	3	.400	4.90	1.52	55	8	0	0	6	1-4	101.0	107	61	55	7	47-0	65	.270
2004— Cincinnati (N.L.)	5	3	.625	5.10	1.67	70	0	0	0	14	0-7	77.2	90	54	44	10	40-5	46	.286
2005— Albuquerque (PCL)	4	0	1.000	3.00	1.33	14	0	0	0	...	3-4	21.0	19	9	7	0	9-1	15	.250
— Florida (N.L.)	4	1	.800	7.16	1.70	29	0	0	0	2	0-0	27.2	34	23	22	3	13-2	16	.298
Major League totals (6 years)	17	13	.567	4.41	1.49	229	8	0	0	37	3-16	302.0	303	170	148	24	148-13	198	.260

RILEY, MATT   P

PERSONAL: Born August 2, 1979, in Antioch, Calif. ... 6-1/221. ... Throws left, bats left. ... Full name: Matthew Paul Riley. ... High school: Liberty Union (Oakley, Calif.). ... Junior college: Sacramento City College.
TRANSACTIONS/CAREER NOTES: Selected by Baltimore Orioles organization in third round of 1997 free-agent draft. ... On disabled list (September 29, 2000-remainder of season; April 1, 2001-entire season; and May 10-25, 2004). ... Traded by Orioles to Texas Rangers for 2B Ramon Nivar (March 30, 2005).
CAREER HITTING: 0-for-2 (.000), 0 R, 0 2B, 0 3B, 0 HR, 0 RBI.

MATT RILEY'S PITCHING ZONE

.800	.000	.000
.385	.400	.400
.500	.200	.333

LEFTY-RIGHTY SPLITS

vs.	Avg.	AB	H	2B	3B	HR	RBI	BB	SO	OBP	Slg.
L	.200	20	4	1	0	0	4	6	2	.407	.250
R	.400	30	12	2	0	2	8	4	2	.457	.667

Year Team (League)	W	L	Pct.	ERA	WHIP	G	GS	CG	ShO	Hld.	Sv.-Opp.	IP	H	R	ER	HR	BB-IBB	SO	Avg.
1998— Delmarva (S. Atl.)	5	4	.556	1.19	1.04	16	14	0	0	...	0-...	83.0	42	19	11	0	44-0	136	.152
1999— Frederick (Carolina)	3	2	.600	2.61	0.93	8	8	0	0	...	0-...	51.2	34	19	15	5	14-0	58	.188
— Bowie (East.)	10	6	.625	3.22	1.23	20	20	3	0	...	0-...	125.2	113	53	45	13	42-0	131	.241

Year	Team (League)	W	L	Pct.	ERA	WHIP	G	GS	CG	ShO	Hld.	Sv.-Opp.	IP	H	R	ER	HR	BB-IBB	SO	Avg.
	— Baltimore (A.L.)	0	0	...	7.36	2.73	3	3	0	0		0-...	11.0	17	9	9	4	13-0	6	.378
2000	— Rochester (Int'l)	0	2	.000	14.14	2.71	2	2	0	0	...	0-...	7.0	15	12	11	3	4-0	8	.417
	— Bowie (East.)	5	7	.417	6.08	1.66	19	14	2	0		1-...	74.0	74	56	50	9	49-0	66	.262
2001	— Baltimore (A.L.)								Did not play.											
2002	— Bowie (East.)	4	10	.286	6.34	1.68	22	22	0	0		0-...	109.1	136	84	77	12	48-1	105	.306
2003	— Bowie (East.)	5	2	.714	3.11	1.10	14	14	1	1		0-...	72.1	56	27	25	4	23-1	73	.210
	— Ottawa (Int'l)	4	2	.667	3.58	1.40	13	13	0	0		0-...	70.1	70	30	28	4	28-1	77	.261
	— Baltimore (A.L.)	1	0	1.000	1.80	1.20	2	2	0	0		0-0	10.0	7	2	2	1	5-0	8	.194
2004	— Ottawa (Int'l)	1	2	.333	1.71	1.17	10	10	0	0		0-...	42.0	26	9	8	3	23-0	51	.181
	— Baltimore (A.L.)	3	4	.429	5.63	1.63	14	13	0	0		0-0	64.0	60	43	40	11	44-0	60	.244
2005	— Texas (A.L.)	1	0	1.000	9.95	2.05	7	0	0	0		0-0	12.2	16	14	14	2	10-0	4	.320
	— Oklahoma (PCL)	0	1	.000	8.25	1.58	4	4	0	0		0-0	12.0	12	11	11	3	7-0	15	.245
	— Arizona Rangers (AZL)	0	0	...	0.00	0.00	1	0	0	0		0-0	0.2	0	0	0	0	0-0	2	.000
	Major League totals (4 years)	5	4	.556	5.99	1.76	26	18	0	0		0-0	97.2	100	68	65	18	72-0	78	.265

R

RINCON, JUAN — P

PERSONAL: Born January 23, 1979, in Maracaibo, Venezuela. ... 5-11/201. ... Throws right, bats right. ... Full name: Juan Manuel Rincon. ... Name pronounced: rin-CONE. ... High school: Instituto Cervantes (Maracaibo, Venezuela).
TRANSACTIONS/CAREER NOTES: Signed as a non-drafted free agent by Minnesota Twins organization (November 15, 1996). ... On restricted list (May 2-12, 2005).
CAREER HITTING: 1-for-2 (.500), 0 R, 0 2B, 0 3B, 0 HR, 0 RBI.

SCOUTING REPORT *Throws:* Rincon throws his fastball at 90-95 mph and his slider at 85-88. *Tendencies:* He has a very good delivery with excellent arm speed. Fastball has late riding action. Slider has very late bite and excellent tilt; it runs sharply away from righthanders. Throws strikes and is very resilient. *Outlook:* Rincon is one of the most valuable setup relievers in the majors. Forms, with closer Joe Nathan, probably the most effective late-inning relief combo in baseball. *Grade 8.9*

JUAN RINCON'S PITCHING ZONE

.417	.308	.235
.239	.273	.208
.192	.000	.167

LEFTY-RIGHTY SPLITS

vs.	Avg.	AB	H	2B	3B	HR	RBI	BB	SO	OBP	Slg.
L	.218	119	26	3	0	1	12	16	38	.311	.269
R	.228	162	37	3	1	1	11	14	46	.300	.278

Year	Team (League)	W	L	Pct.	ERA	WHIP	G	GS	CG	ShO	Hld.	Sv.-Opp.	IP	H	R	ER	HR	BB-IBB	SO	Avg.
1997	— GC Twins (GCL)	3	3	.500	2.95	1.36	11	10	1	0		0-...	58.0	55	21	19	0	24-0	46	.259
	— Elizabethton (App.)	0	1	.000	3.86	1.50	2	1	0	0		0-...	9.1	11	4	4	0	3-0	7	.289
1998	— Fort Wayne (Midw.)	6	4	.600	3.83	1.43	37	13	0	0		6-...	96.1	84	51	41	6	54-1	74	.232
1999	— Quad City (Midw.)	14	8	.636	2.92	1.30	28	28	0	0		0-...	163.1	146	67	53	8	66-3	153	.239
2000	— Fort Myers (FSL)	5	3	.625	2.13	1.18	13	13	0	0		0-...	76.0	67	26	18	3	23-2	55	.238
	— New Britain (East.)	3	9	.250	4.65	1.52	15	15	2	0		0-...	89.0	96	55	46	9	39-0	79	.267
2001	— New Britain (East.)	14	6	.700	2.88	1.22	29	23	2	1		0-...	153.1	130	60	49	9	57-5	133	.226
	— Minnesota (A.L.)	0	0		6.35	2.12	4	0	0	0	0	0-0	5.2	7	5	4	1	5-0	4	.318
2002	— Edmonton (PCL)	7	4	.636	4.78	1.44	19	16	3	0		0-...	101.2	111	56	54	12	35-0	75	.278
	— Minnesota (A.L.)	0	2	.000	6.28	1.85	10	3	0	0	0	0-1	28.2	44	23	20	5	9-0	21	.352
2003	— Rochester (Int'l)	0	2	.000	7.56	2.00	2	2	0	0		0-...	8.1	12	7	7	0	5-0	8	.364
	— Minnesota (A.L.)	5	6	.455	3.68	1.31	58	0	0	0	5	0-1	85.2	74	38	35	5	38-7	63	.231
2004	— Minnesota (A.L.)	11	6	.647	2.63	1.02	77	0	0	0	16	2-6	82.0	52	27	24	5	32-1	106	.181
2005	— Minnesota (A.L.)	6	6	.500	2.45	1.21	75	0	0	0	25	0-5	77.0	63	26	21	2	30-3	84	.224
	Major League totals (5 years)	22	20	.524	3.35	1.27	224	3	0	0	46	2-13	279.0	240	119	104	18	114-11	278	.232

DIVISION SERIES RECORD

Year	Team (League)	W	L	Pct.	ERA	WHIP	G	GS	CG	ShO	Hld.	Sv.-Opp.	IP	H	R	ER	HR	BB-IBB	SO	Avg.
2003	— Minnesota (A.L.)	0	0		0.00	2.14	3	0	0	0	0	0-0	2.1	1	0	0	0	4-0	1	.143
2004	— Minnesota (A.L.)	0	0		10.80	1.80	3	0	0	0	1	0-0	3.1	4	4	4	1	2-0	5	.308
	Division series totals (2 years)	0	0		6.35	1.94	6	0	0	0	1	0-0	5.2	5	4	4	1	6-0	6	.250

RINCON, RICARDO — P

PERSONAL: Born April 13, 1970, in Veracruz, Mexico. ... 5-9/190. ... Throws left, bats left. ... Full name: Ricardo Rincon (Espinoza). ... Name pronounced: rin-CONE.
TRANSACTIONS/CAREER NOTES: Contract purchased by Pittsburgh Pirates organization from Mexico City Red Devils of the Mexican League (March 30, 1997). ... On disabled list (March 22-April 18, 1998); included rehabilitation assignments to Carolina and Nashville. ... Traded by Pirates to Cleveland Indians for OF Brian Giles (November 18, 1998). ... On disabled list (April 12-May 14, 1999); included rehabilitation assignment to Akron. ... On disabled list (May 17-August 23, 2000); included rehabilitation assignment to Buffalo. ... Traded by Indians to Oakland Athletics for IF Marshall McDougall (July 30, 2002).
CAREER HITTING: 0-for-4 (.000), 0 R, 0 2B, 0 3B, 0 HR, 0 RBI.

SCOUTING REPORT *Throws:* Rincon's fastball has lost some velocity in the past year; it rarely reaches 90 mph now. Slider remains his best pitch. *Tendencies:* He has a nasty slider with a quick, late bite, and he tails it away from lefthanded hitters with good command. Will jam righthanders with the slider to set up a fastball that runs away from them. *Outlook:* This valuable veteran is at his best when he is called on to get out tough lefthanders, but he can get out righthanders, too. Logs a lot of appearances but faces few hitters in his role. *Grade 7.3*

RICARDO RINCON'S PITCHING ZONE

.200	.600	.000
.462	.222	.355
.333	.200	.071

LEFTY-RIGHTY SPLITS

vs.	Avg.	AB	H	2B	3B	HR	RBI	BB	SO	OBP	Slg.
L	.250	88	22	2	1	3	16	8	20	.316	.398
R	.240	50	12	2	0	4	6	12	7	.387	.520

Year	Team (League)	W	L	Pct.	ERA	WHIP	G	GS	CG	ShO	Hld.	Sv.-Opp.	IP	H	R	ER	HR	BB-IBB	SO	Avg.
1990	— Union Lag. (Mx.)	3	0	1.000	3.78	1.78	19	4	0	0	...	0-...	47.2	53	22	20	6	32-...	29	...
1991	— Union Lag. (Mx.)	2	8	.200	6.54	1.98	32	9	0	0	...	1-...	74.1	99	60	54	12	48-...	66	...
1992	— Union Lag. (Mx.)	6	5	.545	3.91	1.48	49	9	0	0	...	4-...	89.2	87	45	39	4	46-...	91	...

Year Team (League)	W	L	Pct.	ERA	WHIP	G	GS	CG	ShO	Hld.	Sv.-Opp.	IP	H	R	ER	HR	BB-IBB	SO	Avg.
1993— Torreon (Mex.)	7	3	.700	3.17	1.41	57	4	0	0	...	8-...	82.1	80	33	29	8	36-...	81	...
1994— M.C. R. Dev. (Mex.)	2	4	.333	3.21	1.44	20	9	0	0	...	1-...	53.1	57	23	19	4	20-...	38	...
1995— M.C. R. Dev. (Mex.)	6	6	.500	5.16	1.69	27	11	0	0	...	3-...	75.0	86	45	43	7	41-...	41	...
1996— M.C. R. Dev. (Mex.)	5	3	.625	2.97	1.08	50	0	0	0	...	10-...	78.2	58	28	26	2	27-...	60	...
1997— Pittsburgh (N.L.)	4	8	.333	3.45	1.25	62	0	0	0	18	4-6	60.0	51	26	23	5	24-6	71	.230
1998— Carolina (Southern)	0	0	...	6.00	2.33	2	0	0	0	...	0-...	3.0	5	2	2	1	2-0	1	.385
— Nashville (PCL)	0	0	...	0.00	0.00	1	0	0	0	...	0-...	1.0	0	0	0	0	0-0	1	.000
— Pittsburgh (N.L.)	0	2	.000	2.91	1.22	60	0	0	0	11	14-17	65.0	50	31	21	6	29-2	64	.208
1999— Cleveland (A.L.)	2	3	.400	4.43	1.46	59	0	0	0	11	0-2	44.2	41	22	22	6	24-5	30	.248
— Akron (East.)	0	0	...	5.40	1.20	2	2	0	0	...	0-...	1.2	2	1	1	1	0-0	2	.250
2000— Cleveland (A.L.)	2	0	1.000	2.70	1.50	35	0	0	0	10	0-0	20.0	17	7	6	1	13-1	20	.224
— Buffalo (Int'l)	0	0	...	0.00	0.50	2	0	0	0	...	0-...	2.0	1	1	0	0	0-0	2	.111
2001— Cleveland (A.L.)	2	1	.667	2.83	1.20	67	0	0	0	12	2-4	54.0	44	18	17	3	21-5	50	.223
2002— Cleveland (A.L.)	1	4	.200	4.79	1.23	46	0	0	0	11	0-3	35.2	36	21	19	3	8-1	30	.263
— Oakland (A.L.)	0	0	...	3.10	0.69	25	0	0	0	16	1-2	20.1	11	7	7	1	3-0	19	.164
2003— Oakland (A.L.)	8	4	.667	3.25	1.39	64	0	0	0	13	0-3	55.1	45	21	20	4	32-4	40	.230
2004— Oakland (A.L.)	1	1	.500	3.68	1.52	67	0	0	0	18	0-4	44.0	45	22	18	3	22-4	40	.256
2005— Oakland (A.L.)	1	1	.500	4.34	1.45	67	0	0	0	16	0-2	37.1	34	19	18	7	20-4	27	.246
American League totals (7 years)	17	14	.548	3.67	1.34	430	0	0	0	107	3-20	311.1	273	137	127	28	143-24	256	.237
National League totals (2 years)	4	10	.286	3.17	1.23	122	0	0	0	29	18-23	125.0	101	57	44	11	53-8	135	.219
Major League totals (9 years)	21	24	.467	3.53	1.31	552	0	0	0	136	21-43	436.1	374	194	171	39	196-32	391	.232

DIVISION SERIES RECORD

Year Team (League)	W	L	Pct.	ERA	WHIP	G	GS	CG	ShO	Hld.	Sv.-Opp.	IP	H	R	ER	HR	BB-IBB	SO	Avg.
1999— Cleveland (A.L.)	0	0	...	40.50	4.50	1	0	0	0	0	0-0	0.2	2	3	3	1	1-0	1	.500
2001— Cleveland (A.L.)	0	0	...	9.00	1.00	3	0	0	0	0	0-0	2.0	2	2	2	0	0-0	3	.286
2002— Oakland (A.L.)	0	0	...	0.00	0.67	2	0	0	0	1	0-0	3.0	2	0	0	0	0-0	2	.182
2003— Oakland (A.L.)	0	0	...	4.50	1.25	4	0	0	0	1	0-1	4.0	4	2	2	2	1-0	3	.267
Division series totals (4 years)	0	0	...	6.52	1.24	10	0	0	0	2	0-1	9.2	10	7	7	3	2-0	9	.270

RING, ROYCE — P

PERSONAL: Born December 21, 1980, in La Mesa, Calif. ... 6-0/220. ... Throws left, bats left. ... Full name: Roger Royce Ring. ... High school: Monte Vista (Spring Valley, Calif.). ... College: San Diego State.
TRANSACTIONS/CAREER NOTES: Selected by Chicago White Sox organization in first round (18th pick overall) of 2002 free-agent draft. ... Traded by White Sox with P Edwin Almonte and 2B Andrew Salvo to New York Mets for 2B Roberto Alomar (July 1, 2003).
CAREER HITTING: 0-for-0 (.000), 0 R, 0 2B, 0 3B, 0 HR, 0 RBI.

LEFTY-RIGHTY SPLITS

vs.	Avg.	AB	H	2B	3B	HR	RBI	BB	SO	OBP	Slg.
L	.250	24	6	0	0	0	3	7	6	.419	.250
R	.250	16	4	1	0	0	2	3	2	.368	.313

Year Team (League)	W	L	Pct.	ERA	WHIP	G	GS	CG	ShO	Hld.	Sv.-Opp.	IP	H	R	ER	HR	BB-IBB	SO	Avg.
2002— Ariz. White Sox (Ariz.)	0	0	...	0.00	0.40	3	0	0	0	...	0-...	5.0	2	0	0	0	0-0	9	.118
— Win.-Salem (Car.)	2	0	1.000	3.91	1.35	21	0	0	0	...	5-...	23.0	20	11	10	2	11-2	22	.247
2003— Birmingham (Sou.)	1	4	.200	2.52	1.32	36	0	0	0	...	19-...	35.2	33	11	10	1	14-1	44	.237
— Binghamton (East.)	3	0	1.000	1.66	1.11	18	0	0	0	...	7-...	21.2	13	4	4	2	11-0	18	.176
2004— Norfolk (Int'l)	3	1	.750	3.63	1.41	29	0	0	0	...	0-...	34.2	37	15	14	5	12-1	22	.266
— Binghamton (East.)	2	2	.500	3.77	1.26	19	0	0	0	...	2-...	28.2	25	13	12	5	11-1	23	.225
2005— New York (N.L.)	0	2	.000	5.06	1.88	15	0	0	0	3	0-0	10.2	10	6	6	0	10-1	8	.250
— Norfolk (Int'l)	3	0	1.000	3.26	1.22	33	0	0	0	9	2-2	38.2	34	16	14	2	13-1	26	.239
Major League totals (1 year)	0	2	.000	5.06	1.88	15	0	0	0	3	0-0	10.2	10	6	6	0	10-1	8	.250

RIOS, ALEX — OF

PERSONAL: Born February 18, 1981, in Coffee, Ala. ... 6-5/194. ... Bats right, throws right. ... Full name: Alexis Israel Rios. ... High school: San Pedro Martin (Guaynabo, Puerto Rico).
TRANSACTIONS/CAREER NOTES: Selected by Toronto Blue Jays organization in first round (19th pick overall) of 1999 free-agent draft.
2005 GAMES PLAYED BY POSITION (MLB): OF—142, DH—1.

SCOUTING REPORT **Offense:** Rios has a good stroke and has bat speed is improving. Likes to extend his arms. Is impatient and chases a lot of pitches up. Is better against righthanders than lefthanders. Has improved his ability to hit with runners in scoring position by taking the ball the other way. Will have plus power when he pulls the ball more. Is an above-average runner whose basestealing potential has been stymied by the organization. **Defense:** Rios has one of the best throwing arms of any young player, and he's accurate. Gets good jumps with above-average range and is fluid going to the ball. Can be an above-average defensive player. **Outlook:** Rios is a potential five-tool player who just needs to get stronger and develop better plate discipline. Will have enough power in time to be a quality run producer. **Grade 6.6**

ALEX RIOS'S HITTING ZONE

.333	.056	.320
.324	.320	.310
.275	.235	.308

LEFTY-RIGHTY SPLITS

vs.	Avg.	AB	H	2B	3B	HR	RBI	BB	SO	OBP	Slg.
L	.249	177	44	7	4	3	14	9	38	.291	.384
R	.270	304	82	16	2	7	45	19	63	.315	.405

Year Team (League)	Pos.	G	AB	R	H	2B	3B	HR	RBI	BB	SO	HBP	GDP	SB-CS	Avg.	OBP	SLG	OPS	E	Avg.
1999— Medicine Hat (Pio.)	OF	67	234	35	63	7	3	0	13	17	31	1	6	8-4	.269	.321	.325	.646	6	.955
2000— Hagerstown (SAL)		22	74	5	17	3	1	0	5	2	14	1	0	2-3	.230	.256	.297	.554	...	...
— Queens (N.Y.-Penn.)	OF	50	206	22	55	9	2	1	25	11	22	4	5	5-5	.267	.314	.345	.659	3	.957
2001— Char., W.Va. (SAL)	OF	130	480	40	126	20	9	2	58	25	59	4	16	22-14	.263	.296	.354	.651	13	.944
2002— Dunedin (Fla. St.)	OF	111	456	60	139	22	8	3	61	27	55	3	19	14-8	.305	.344	.408	.752	8	.967
2003— New Haven (East.)	OF	127	514	86	181	32	11	11	82	39	85	6	22	11-3	.352	.402	.521	.924	3	.990
2004— Syracuse (Int'l)	OF	46	185	14	48	10	1	3	23	9	30	0	10	2-1	.259	.292	.373	.665	4	.964
— Toronto (A.L.)	OF	111	426	55	122	24	7	1	28	31	84	2	14	15-3	.286	.338	.383	.720	2	.991
2005— Toronto (A.L.)	OF-DH	146	481	71	126	23	6	10	59	28	101	5	14	14-9	.262	.306	.397	.703	2	.992
Major League totals (2 years)		257	907	126	248	47	13	11	87	59	185	7	28	29-12	.273	.321	.390	.711	4	.992

R

RISKE, DAVID — P

PERSONAL: Born October 23, 1976, in Renton, Wash. ... 6-2/190. ... Throws right, bats right. ... Full name: David Richard Riske. ... Name pronounced: RISK-ee. ... High school: Lindbergh (Renton, Wash.). ... Junior college: Green River (Wash.) Community College.

TRANSACTIONS/CAREER NOTES: Selected by Cleveland Indians organization in 56th round of 1996 free-agent draft. ... On disabled list (March 25-April 28, May 29-September 4 and September 14, 2000-remainder of season); included rehabilitation assignment to Akron. ... On disabled list (June 19-July 17, 2002); included rehabilitation assignment to Akron. ... On suspended list (September 2-5, 2005).

CAREER HITTING: 0-for-0 (.000), 0 R, 0 2B, 0 3B, 0 HR, 0 RBI.

SCOUTING REPORT *Throws:* Riske's fastball ranges from 89-92 mph, his slider from 81-84. Also has a changeup that he holds like a split-finger fastball. *Tendencies:* He primarily was a middle reliever in the Indians' deep bullpen in 2005. Has a very live arm and deception in his delivery, but is prone to making mistakes up in the zone. His stuff can be similar to that of the Angels' Scot Shields. Fastball tends to jump late. Slider is big but quick; more a slurve on occasion. Change is thrown with good motion and is a effective pitch to lefthanders. *Outlook:* If he leaves Cleveland in the offseason, the versatile Riske could become a valuable setup man. Has closed before but was not as effective. *Grade 7.6*

DAVID RISKE'S PITCHING ZONE

.154	.250	.231
.267	.227	.259
.211	.267	.105

LEFTY-RIGHTY SPLITS

vs.	Avg.	AB	H	2B	3B	HR	RBI	BB	SO	OBP	Slg.
L	.213	108	23	5	0	6	11	8	23	.274	.426
R	.204	157	32	4	1	5	19	7	25	.250	.338

Year	Team (League)	W	L	Pct.	ERA	WHIP	G	GS	CG	ShO	Hld.	Sv.-Opp.	IP	H	R	ER	HR	BB-IBB	SO	Avg.
1997—	Kinston (Carol.)	4	4	.500	2.25	1.26	39	0	0	0	...	2-...	72.0	58	22	18	3	33-4	90	.227
1998—	Kinston (Carol.)	1	1	.500	2.33	1.17	53	0	0	0	...	33-...	54.0	48	15	14	4	15-0	67	.241
—	Akron (East.)	0	0		0.00	0.67	2	0	0	0	...	1-...	3.0	1	0	0	0	1-0	4	.100
1999—	Akron (East.)	0	0		1.90	0.76	23	0	0	0	...	12-...	23.2	5	6	5	1	13-0	33	.067
—	Buffalo (Int'l)	3	0	1.000	0.65	0.76	23	0	0	0	...	6-...	27.2	14	3	2	0	7-0	22	.151
—	Cleveland (A.L.)	1	1	.500	8.36	1.86	12	0	0	0	0	0-1	14.0	20	15	13	2	6-0	16	.333
2000—	Akron (East.)	0	0		0.00	0.50	3	1	0	0	...	1-...	4.0	2	0	0	0	0-0	4	.143
—	Buffalo (Int'l)	0	0		3.00	1.33	2	0	0	0	...	0-...	3.0	2	1	1	0	2-0	2	.182
2001—	Buffalo (Int'l)	1	2	.333	2.36	1.16	38	0	0	0	...	15-...	53.1	45	16	14	2	17-0	72	.232
—	Cleveland (A.L.)	2	0	1.000	1.98	1.39	26	0	0	0	3	1-1	27.1	20	7	6	3	18-3	29	.206
2002—	Cleveland (A.L.)	2	2	.500	5.26	1.64	51	0	0	0	5	1-1	51.1	49	32	30	8	35-4	65	.257
—	Akron (East.)	0	0		3.00	1.00	4	2	0	0	...	0-...	6.0	5	2	2	1	1-0	17	.217
—	Buffalo (Int'l)	0	1	.000	3.72	1.03	9	0	0	0	...	3-...	9.2	6	4	4	2	4-0	17	.182
2003—	Cleveland (A.L.)	2	2	.500	2.29	0.96	68	0	0	0	17	8-13	74.2	52	21	19	9	20-3	82	.196
2004—	Cleveland (A.L.)	7	3	.700	3.72	1.42	72	0	0	0	9	5-12	77.1	69	32	32	11	41-4	78	.240
2005—	Cleveland (A.L.)	3	4	.429	3.10	0.96	58	0	0	0	0	1-1	72.2	55	28	25	11	15-0	48	.208
Major League totals (6 years)		17	12	.586	3.55	1.26	287	0	0	0	34	16-29	317.1	265	135	125	44	135-14	318	.227

DIVISION SERIES RECORD

Year	Team (League)	W	L	Pct.	ERA	WHIP	G	GS	CG	ShO	Hld.	Sv.-Opp.	IP	H	R	ER	HR	BB-IBB	SO	Avg.
2001—	Cleveland (A.L.)	0	0		0.00	0.82	3	0	0	0	...	0-0	3.2	2	0	0	0	1-0	5	.154

RIVAS, LUIS — 2B

PERSONAL: Born August 30, 1979, in La Guaira, Venezuela. ... 5-11/186. ... Bats right, throws right. ... Full name: Luis Wilfredo Rivas. ... Name pronounced: REE-vas. ... High school: Riceniado Le Guaria (La Guaria, Venezuela).

TRANSACTIONS/CAREER NOTES: Signed as a non-drafted free agent by Minnesota Twins organization (October 9, 1995). ... On disabled list (April 7-June 4, 2002); included rehabilitation assignment to Fort Myers. ... On disabled list (May 19-June 8, 2004); included rehabilitation assignment to Rochester. ... On disabled list (June 1-17, 2005).

2005 GAMES PLAYED BY POSITION (MLB): 2B—53, SS—6, DH—1.

SCOUTING REPORT *Offense:* Rivas has a long swing and doesn't make quick adjustments. Is an impatient hitter who consistently gets himself out, particularly with runners on base. Likes the ball up. Tries to pull the ball too much and is not a good breaking-ball hitter. Is a plus runner with good basestealing instincts. *Defense:* He is very athletic, has good hands and is agile. Has plus range to either side. Likes to play deep and has a strong arm. Is excellent at turning double plays. Can be erratic when he lays back on the ball. *Outlook:* Rivas' skills have leveled off, in part because of his poor work ethic and the inability to make adjustments. He might wind up as a utility player. *Grade 5.8*

LUIS RIVAS'S HITTING ZONE

.111	.333	.333
.208	.400	.455
.167	.333	.167

LEFTY-RIGHTY SPLITS

vs.	Avg.	AB	H	2B	3B	HR	RBI	BB	SO	OBP	Slg.
L	.283	53	15	3	0	1	8	3	5	.316	.396
R	.241	83	20	0	1	0	4	6	12	.308	.367

Year	Team (League)	Pos.	G	AB	R	H	2B	3B	HR	RBI	BB	SO	HBP	GDP	SB-CS	Avg.	OBP	SLG	OPS	E	Avg.
1996—	GC Twins (GCL)	SS	53	201	29	52	12	1	1	13	18	37	0	2	35-10	.259	.320	.343	.663	21	.922
1997—	Fort Wayne (Midw.)	SS	121	419	61	100	20	6	1	30	33	90	5	1	28-18	.239	.301	.322	.623	58	.907
1998—	Fort Myers (FSL)	SS	126	463	58	130	21	5	4	51	14	75	3	11	34-8	.281	.302	.374	.676	55	.913
1999—	New Britain (East.)	SS-2B	132	527	78	134	30	7	7	49	41	92	2	16	31-14	.254	.309	.378	.687	39	.934
2000—	New Britain (East.)	2B-SS	82	328	56	82	23	6	3	40	36	41	4	3	11-4	.250	.329	.384	.713	11	.971
—	Salt Lake (PCL)	2B-SS	41	157	33	50	14	1	3	25	13	21	2	3	7-4	.318	.376	.478	.853	2	.971
—	Minnesota (A.L.)	2B-SS	16	58	8	18	4	1	0	6	2	4	0	2	2-0	.310	.323	.414	.736	1	.984
2001—	Minnesota (A.L.)	2B	153	563	70	150	21	6	7	47	40	99	6	15	31-11	.266	.319	.362	.682	15	.974
2002—	Minnesota (A.L.)	2B	93	316	46	81	23	4	4	35	19	51	3	12	9-4	.256	.305	.392	.697	5	.986
—	Fort Myers (FSL)	2B	6	22	1	2	0	1	0	3	2	4	0	1	0-0	.091	.167	.182	.348	2	.900
2003—	Minnesota (A.L.)	2B-DH	135	475	69	123	16	9	8	43	30	65	5	20	17-7	.259	.308	.381	.689	10	.982
2004—	Rochester (Int'l)	2B	3	14	2	3	0	0	0	1	0	2	1	0	1-0	.214	.267	.214	.481	0	1.000
—	Minnesota (A.L.)	2B	109	344	44	86	19	5	10	34	13	53	1	8	15-1	.256	.283	.432	.715	3	.994
2005—	Rochester (Int'l)	2B-SS	43	145	17	36	14	0	2	22	8	18	0	3	3-2	.248	.280	.386	.666	5	.971
—	Minnesota (A.L.)	2B-SS-DH	59	136	21	35	3	1	1	12	9	17	2	2	4-0	.257	.311	.316	.627	2	.984
Major League totals (6 years)			565	1884	258	493	86	26	30	177	113	289	17	59	78-23	.262	.307	.383	.690	36	.984

DIVISION SERIES RECORD

Year Team (League)	Pos.	G	AB	R	H	2B	3B	HR	RBI	BB	SO	HBP	GDP	SB-CS	Avg.	OBP	SLG	OPS	E	Avg.
2002—Minnesota (A.L.)	2B	4	12	2	3	1	0	0	1	2	0	2	0-0	.250	.308	.333	.641	0	1.000
2003—Minnesota (A.L.)	2B	4	13	0	0	0	0	0	1	0	4	0	1	0-0	.000	.000	.000	.000	0	1.000
2004—Minnesota (A.L.)	2B	3	1	0	0	0	0	0	0	0	0	0	0-0	.000	.000	.000	.000	0	1.000
Division series totals (3 years)		11	26	2	3	1	0	0	1	1	6	0	3	0-0	.115	.143	.154	.297	0	1.000

CHAMPIONSHIP SERIES RECORD

Year Team (League)	Pos.	G	AB	R	H	2B	3B	HR	RBI	BB	SO	HBP	GDP	SB-CS	Avg.	OBP	SLG	OPS	E	Avg.
2002—Minnesota (A.L.)	2B	5	12	1	3	0	0	0	0	1	3	0	2	0-0	.250	.308	.250	.558	0	1.000

RIVERA, JUAN   OF   R

PERSONAL: Born July 3, 1978, in Guarenas, Venezuela. ... 6-2/205. ... Bats right, throws right. ... Full name: Juan Luis Rivera.
TRANSACTIONS/CAREER NOTES: Signed as a non-drafted free agent by New York Yankees organization (April 12, 1996). ... On disabled list (June 9-August 19, 2002); included rehabilitation assignments to GCL Yankees and Columbus. ... Traded by Yankees with 1B Nick Johnson and P Randy Choate to Montreal Expos for Javier Vazquez (December 16, 2003). ... Traded by Expos with SS Maicer Izturis to Anaheim Angels for OF Jose Guillen (November 23, 2004). ... Angels franchise renamed Los Angeles Angels of Anaheim for 2005 season.
2005 GAMES PLAYED BY POSITION (MLB): OF—74, DH—28.

SCOUTING REPORT **Offense:** A good contact hitter, Rivera has shortened his stroke and is more willing to hit the ball to the opposite field. Has improved against breaking balls. Is a good high-ball hitter. Has power to all fields. Is very productive with runners in scoring position. Is a slightly below-average runner who will attempt to steal bases, but doesn't get good jumps. Handles righthanders better than lefthanders. **Defense:** Rivera, a natural right fielder, has an impressive, accurate arm. Gets good jumps on balls in the gaps and charges the ball well. Looks to have good instincts. **Outlook:** Rivera is starting to harness his impressive abilities and develop a better idea at the plate. **Grade 7.5**

JUAN RIVERA'S HITTING ZONE

.375	.350	.286
.292	.450	.291
.179	.143	.167

LEFTY-RIGHTY SPLITS

vs.	Avg.	AB	H	2B	3B	HR	RBI	BB	SO	OBP	Slg.
L	.252	139	35	7	0	4	21	10	12	.300	.388
R	.284	211	60	10	1	11	38	13	32	.326	.498

Year Team (League)	Pos.	G	AB	R	H	2B	3B	HR	RBI	BB	SO	HBP	GDP	SB-CS	Avg.	OBP	SLG	OPS	E	Avg.
1996—Dom. Yankees (DSL)	OF	10	18	0	3	0	0	0	2	0	1	...	...	0-...	.167	...	.167	...	0	1.000
1997—Maracay 1 (VSL)		52	142	25	40	9	0	0	14	12	16	...	...	12-...	.282	...	.345	...	...	...
1998—GC Yankees (GCL)	OF	57	210	43	70	9	1	12	45	26	27	1	10	8-5	.333	.408	.557	.965	2	.979
—Oneonta (NYP)	OF	6	18	2	5	0	0	1	3	1	4	0	1	1-1	.278	.316	.444	.760	0	1.000
1999—Tampa (Fla. St.)	OF	109	426	50	112	20	2	14	77	26	67	5	13	5-3	.263	.308	.418	.725	4	.979
—GC Yankees (GCL)	OF	5	18	7	6	0	0	1	4	4	1	0	1	0-0	.333	.455	.500	.955	0	1.000
2000—Norwich (East.)	OF	17	62	9	14	5	0	2	12	6	15	0	2	0-0	.226	.294	.403	.697	1	.955
—Tampa (Fla. St.)	1B-OF	115	409	62	113	26	1	14	69	33	56	6	9	11-7	.276	.336	.447	.783	5	.978
2001—Norwich (East.)	OF	77	316	50	101	18	3	14	58	15	50	3	10	5-7	.320	.353	.528	.882	6	.963
—Columbus (Int'l)	OF	55	199	39	65	11	1	14	40	15	31	1	7	4-5	.327	.372	.603	.975	4	.970
—New York (A.L.)	OF	3	4	0	0	0	0	0	0	0	0	0	0	0-0	.000	.000	.000	.000	0	1.000
2002—Columbus (Int'l)	OF	65	265	40	86	21	1	8	47	13	39	1	4	5-1	.325	.355	.502	.856	6	.955
—New York (A.L.)	OF	28	83	9	22	5	0	1	6	6	10	1	1	1-1	.265	.311	.361	.673	2	.966
—GC Yankees (GCL)	OF	4	13	1	4	2	0	0	4	2	3	1	1	0-0	.308	.438	.462	.899	0	1.000
2003—Columbus (Int'l)	OF	79	308	47	100	21	0	7	37	26	37	0	8	1-3	.325	.374	.461	.835	3	.982
—New York (A.L.)	OF	57	173	22	46	14	0	7	26	10	27	0	8	0-0	.266	.304	.468	.773	2	.979
2004—Montreal (N.L.)	OF-DH	134	391	48	120	24	1	12	49	34	45	1	11	6-2	.307	.364	.465	.829	3	.986
2005—Los Angeles (A.L.)	OF-DH	106	350	46	95	17	1	15	59	23	44	0	15	1-9	.271	.316	.454	.770	1	.992
American League totals (4 years)		194	610	77	163	36	1	23	91	39	81	0	27	2-10	.267	.310	.443	.752	5	.983
National League totals (1 year)		134	391	48	120	24	1	12	49	34	45	1	11	6-2	.307	.364	.465	.829	3	.986
Major League totals (5 years)		328	1001	125	283	60	2	35	140	73	126	1	38	8-12	.283	.331	.452	.783	8	.984

DIVISION SERIES RECORD

Year Team (League)	Pos.	G	AB	R	H	2B	3B	HR	RBI	BB	SO	HBP	GDP	SB-CS	Avg.	OBP	SLG	OPS	E	Avg.
2002—New York (A.L.)	OF	4	12	2	3	0	0	0	3	1	3	0	0	0-0	.250	.308	.250	.558	0	1.000
2003—New York (A.L.)	OF	4	12	2	4	0	0	0	0	1	0	0	1	0-0	.333	.385	.333	.718	0	1.000
2005—Los Angeles (A.L.)	DH	5	17	3	6	1	0	1	1	1	2	0	0	0-0	.353	.389	.588	.977	0	...
Division series totals (3 years)		13	41	7	13	1	0	1	4	3	5	0	1	0-0	.317	.364	.415	.778	0	1.000

CHAMPIONSHIP SERIES RECORD

Year Team (League)	Pos.	G	AB	R	H	2B	3B	HR	RBI	BB	SO	HBP	GDP	SB-CS	Avg.	OBP	SLG	OPS	E	Avg.
2003—New York (A.L.)	OF	2	2	0	0	0	0	0	0	0	1	0	0	0-0	.000	.000	.000	.000	0	1.000
2005—Los Angeles (A.L.)	OF-DH	3	9	1	1	1	0	0	0	0	1	0	0	0-0	.111	.111	.222	.333	0	1.000
Champ. series totals (2 years)		5	11	1	1	1	0	0	0	0	2	0	0	0-0	.091	.091	.182	.273	0	1.000

WORLD SERIES RECORD

Year Team (League)	Pos.	G	AB	R	H	2B	3B	HR	RBI	BB	SO	HBP	GDP	SB-CS	Avg.	OBP	SLG	OPS	E	Avg.
2003—New York (A.L.)	OF	4	6	0	1	1	0	1	1	1	1	0	0	0-0	.167	.286	.333	.619	0	1.000

RIVERA, MARIANO   P

PERSONAL: Born November 29, 1969, in Panama City, Panama. ... 6-2/170. ... Throws right, bats right. ... Cousin of Ruben Rivera, outfielder with five major league teams (1995-2003).
TRANSACTIONS/CAREER NOTES: Signed as a non-drafted free agent by New York Yankees organization (February 17, 1990). ... On disabled list (April 6-24, 1998). ... On disabled list (June 10-25, July 21-August 8 and August 18-September 21, 2002); included rehabilitation assignment to GCL Yankees. ... On disabled list (March 25-April 29, 2003).
HONORS: Named A.L. Fireman of the Year by THE SPORTING NEWS (1997 and 1999). ... Named A.L. Reliever of the Year by THE SPORTING NEWS (2001 and 2004).
CAREER HITTING: 0-for-0 (.000), 0 R, 0 2B, 0 3B, 0 HR, 0 RBI.

SCOUTING REPORT *Throws:* His main pitch is a four-seam cutter that he throws at 91-94 mph. *Tendencies:* Rivera has an outstanding, easy delivery that allows him to have impeccable command with his late-moving cutter, which he will use up and down in the zone. Hitters have a better chance to hit it when it's down. *Outlook:* This future Hall of Fame reliever arguably is the best closer of all time. Does the job year after year, and 2006 should be no different. *Grade 9.5*

MARIANO RIVERA'S PITCHING ZONE

.233	.067	.222
.125	.269	.190
.182	.500	.000

LEFTY-RIGHTY SPLITS

vs.	Avg.	AB	H	2B	3B	HR	RBI	BB	SO	OBP	Slg.
L	.177	141	25	2	1	1	5	5	36	.205	.227
R	.176	142	25	3	1	1	12	13	44	.263	.232

R

Year	Team (League)	W	L	Pct.	ERA	WHIP	G	GS	CG	ShO	Hld.	Sv.-Opp.	IP	H	R	ER	HR	BB-IBB	SO	Avg.
1990—	GC Yankees (GCL)	5	1	.833	0.17	0.46	22	1	1	1	...	1-...	52.0	17	3	1	0	7-0	58	.102
1991—	Greensboro (S. Atl.)	4	9	.308	2.75	1.21	29	15	1	0	...	0-...	114.2	103	48	35	2	36-0	123	.237
1992—	Fort Laud. (FSL)	5	3	.625	2.28	0.76	10	10	3	1	...	0-...	59.1	40	17	15	5	5-0	42	.191
1993—	Greensboro (S. Atl.)	1	0	1.000	2.06	1.17	10	10	0	0	...	0-...	39.1	31	12	9	0	15-0	32	.214
—	GC Yankees (GCL)	0	1	.000	2.25	0.75	2	2	0	0	...	0-...	4.0	2	1	1	0	1-0	6	.143
1994—	Tampa (Fla. St.)	3	0	1.000	2.21	1.25	7	7	0	0	...	0-...	36.2	34	12	9	2	12-0	27	.258
—	Alb./Colon. (East.)	3	0	1.000	2.27	1.04	9	9	0	0	...	0-...	63.1	58	20	16	5	8-0	39	.242
—	Columbus (Int'l)	4	2	.667	5.81	1.42	6	6	1	0	...	0-...	31.0	34	22	20	5	10-0	23	.268
1995—	Columbus (Int'l)	2	2	.500	2.10	0.93	7	7	1	1	...	0-...	30.0	25	10	7	2	3-0	30	.227
—	New York (A.L.)	5	3	.625	5.51	1.51	19	10	0	0	0	0-1	67.0	71	43	41	11	30-0	51	.266
1996—	New York (A.L.)	8	3	.727	2.09	0.99	61	0	0	0	* 27	5-8	107.2	73	25	25	1	34-3	130	.189
1997—	New York (A.L.)	6	4	.600	1.88	1.19	66	0	0	0	0	43-52	71.2	65	17	15	5	20-6	68	.237
1998—	New York (A.L.)	3	0	1.000	1.91	1.06	54	0	0	0	0	36-41	61.1	48	13	13	3	17-1	36	.213
1999—	New York (A.L.)	4	3	.571	1.83	0.88	66	0	0	0	0	* 45-49	69.0	43	15	14	2	18-3	52	.176
2000—	New York (A.L.)	7	4	.636	2.85	1.10	66	0	0	0	0	36-41	75.2	58	26	24	4	25-3	58	.208
2001—	New York (A.L.)	4	6	.400	2.34	0.90	71	0	0	0	0	* 50-57	80.2	61	24	21	5	12-2	83	.209
2002—	New York (A.L.)	1	4	.200	2.74	1.00	45	0	0	0	2	28-32	46.0	35	16	14	3	11-2	41	.203
—	GC Yankees (GCL)	0	0	...	0.00	1.50	1	1	0	0	0	0-...	2.0	2	0	0	0	1-0	3	.286
2003—	New York (A.L.)	5	2	.714	1.66	1.00	64	0	0	0	0	40-46	70.2	61	15	13	3	10-1	63	.235
2004—	New York (A.L.)	4	2	.667	1.94	1.08	74	0	0	0	0	* 53-57	78.2	65	17	17	3	20-3	66	.225
2005—	New York (A.L.)	7	4	.636	1.38	0.87	71	0	0	0	0	43-47	78.1	50	18	12	2	18-0	80	.177
Major League totals (11 years)		54	35	.607	2.33	1.05	657	10	0	0	29	379-431	806.2	630	229	209	42	215-24	728	.212

DIVISION SERIES RECORD

Year	Team (League)	W	L	Pct.	ERA	WHIP	G	GS	CG	ShO	Hld.	Sv.-Opp.	IP	H	R	ER	HR	BB-IBB	SO	Avg.
1995—	New York (A.L.)	1	0	1.000	0.00	0.75	3	0	0	0	0	0-0	5.1	3	0	0	0	1-1	8	.167
1996—	New York (A.L.)	0	0	...	0.00	0.21	2	0	0	0	1	0-0	4.2	0	0	0	0	1-0	1	.000
1997—	New York (A.L.)	0	0	...	4.50	1.00	2	0	0	0	0	1-2	2.0	2	1	1	1	0-0	1	.250
1998—	New York (A.L.)	0	0	...	0.00	0.60	3	0	0	0	0	2-2	3.1	1	0	0	0	1-0	2	.091
1999—	New York (A.L.)	0	0	...	0.00	0.33	2	0	0	0	0	2-2	3.0	1	0	0	0	0-0	3	.111
2000—	New York (A.L.)	0	0	...	0.00	0.40	3	0	0	0	0	3-3	5.0	2	0	0	0	0-0	2	.111
2001—	New York (A.L.)	0	0	...	0.00	0.80	3	0	0	0	0	2-2	4.0	3	0	0	0	0-0	4	.211
2002—	New York (A.L.)	0	0	...	0.00	1.00	1	0	0	0	0	1-1	1.0	1	0	0	0	0-0	0	.250
2003—	New York (A.L.)	0	0	...	0.00	0.00	2	0	0	0	0	2-2	4.0	0	0	0	0	0-0	4	.000
2004—	New York (A.L.)	1	0	1.000	0.00	0.35	4	0	0	0	0	0-1	5.2	2	0	0	0	0-0	2	.111
2005—	New York (A.L.)	0	0	...	3.00	0.67	2	0	0	0	0	2-2	3.0	1	1	1	0	1-0	2	.111
Division series totals (11 years)		2	0	1.000	0.43	0.50	27	0	0	0	1	15-17	42.0	17	3	2	1	4-1	29	.121

CHAMPIONSHIP SERIES RECORD

Year	Team (League)	W	L	Pct.	ERA	WHIP	G	GS	CG	ShO	Hld.	Sv.-Opp.	IP	H	R	ER	HR	BB-IBB	SO	Avg.
1996—	New York (A.L.)	1	0	1.000	0.00	1.75	2	0	0	0	0	0-0	4.0	6	0	0	0	1-0	5	.333
1998—	New York (A.L.)	0	0	...	0.00	0.18	4	0	0	0	0	1-1	5.2	0	0	0	0	1-0	5	.000
1999—	New York (A.L.)	1	0	1.000	0.00	1.07	3	0	0	0	0	2-2	4.2	5	0	0	0	0-0	3	.294
2000—	New York (A.L.)	0	0	...	1.93	0.86	3	0	0	0	0	1-1	4.2	4	1	1	0	0-0	1	.222
2001—	New York (A.L.)	1	0	1.000	1.93	0.64	4	0	0	0	0	2-2	4.2	2	1	1	0	1-0	3	.125
2003—	New York (A.L.)	1	0	1.000	1.13	0.63	4	0	0	0	0	2-2	8.0	5	1	1	0	0-0	6	.172
2004—	New York (A.L.)	0	0	...	1.29	1.14	5	0	0	0	0	2-4	7.0	6	1	1	0	2-0	6	.250
Champ. series totals (7 years)		4	0	1.000	0.93	0.85	25	0	0	0	1	10-12	38.2	28	4	4	0	5-0	29	.203

WORLD SERIES RECORD

Year	Team (League)	W	L	Pct.	ERA	WHIP	G	GS	CG	ShO	Hld.	Sv.-Opp.	IP	H	R	ER	HR	BB-IBB	SO	Avg.
1996—	New York (A.L.)	0	0	...	1.59	1.24	4	0	0	0	2	0-0	5.2	4	1	1	0	3-0	4	.214
1998—	New York (A.L.)	0	0	...	0.00	1.15	3	0	0	0	0	3-3	4.1	5	0	0	0	0-0	4	.294
1999—	New York (A.L.)	1	0	1.000	0.00	0.86	3	0	0	0	0	2-2	4.2	3	0	0	0	1-0	3	.188
2000—	New York (A.L.)	0	0	...	3.00	0.83	4	0	0	0	0	2-2	6.0	4	2	2	1	1-0	7	.182
2001—	New York (A.L.)	1	1	.500	1.42	1.11	4	0	0	0	0	1-2	6.1	6	2	1	0	1-1	7	.250
2003—	New York (A.L.)	0	0	...	0.00	0.50	2	0	0	0	0	1-1	4.0	2	0	0	0	0-0	4	.143
World series totals (6 years)		2	1	.667	1.16	0.97	20	0	0	0	2	9-10	31.0	24	5	4	1	6-1	29	.214

ALL-STAR GAME RECORD

		W	L	Pct.	ERA	WHIP	G	GS	CG	ShO	Hld.	Sv.-Opp.	IP	H	R	ER	HR	BB-IBB	SO	Avg.
All-Star Game totals (5 years)		0	0	...	0.00	0.69	5	0	0	0	0	2-2	4.1	3	1	0	0	0-0	2	.200

RIVERA, RENE   C

PERSONAL: Born July 31, 1983, in Bayamon, Puerto Rico. ... 5-10/190. ... Bats right, throws right. ... High school: Papa Juan XXIII (Bayamon, P.R.).
TRANSACTIONS/CAREER NOTES: Selected by Seattle Mariners organization in second round of 2001 free-agent draft.
2005 GAMES PLAYED BY POSITION (MLB): C—15.

LEFTY-RIGHTY SPLITS

vs.	Avg.	AB	H	2B	3B	HR	RBI	BB	SO	OBP	Slg.
L	.364	11	4	0	0	1	1	0	3	.364	.455
R	.405	37	15	2	0	1	5	1	8	.421	.541

Year	Team (League)	Pos.	G	AB	R	H	2B	3B	HR	RBI	BB	SO	HBP	GDP	SB-CS	Avg.	OBP	SLG	OPS	E	Avg.
2001—Everett (N'west)	C	15	45	3	4	1	0	2	3	1	19	0	1	0-0	.089	.106	.244	.351	1	.992
—Ariz. Mariners (Ariz.)	C	21	71	13	24	4	0	2	12	2	11	1	0	0-0	.338	.360	.479	.839	4	.977
2002—Everett (N'west)	C	62	227	29	55	18	1	1	26	16	38	9	3	5-2	.242	.314	.344	.657	7	.987
2003—Wisconsin (Midw.)	C	116	407	39	112	19	0	9	54	38	81	7	6	2-2	.275	.344	.388	.732	11	.987
2004—Tacoma (PCL)	C	4	15	3	6	1	0	1	1	0	3	0	0	0-0	.400	.400	.667	1.067	0	1.000
—Inland Empire (Calif.)	C-DH	107	379	41	89	22	1	6	53	28	70	9	17	0-1	.235	.300	.346	.646	7	.993
—Seattle (A.L.)	C	2	3	0	0	0	0	0	0	0	1	0	0	0-0	.000	.000	.000	.000	0	1.000
2005—San Antonio (Texas)	C	57	212	20	59	14	1	2	21	7	35	1	6	1-0	.278	.305	.382	.687	4	.990
—Tacoma (PCL)	C-DH	14	49	3	10	3	0	1	6	2	12	0	2	0-1	.204	.235	.327	.562	0	1.000
—Seattle (A.L.)	C	16	48	3	19	3	0	1	6	1	11	0	0	0-0	.396	.408	.521	.929	3	.961
Major League totals (2 years)		18	51	3	19	3	0	1	6	1	12	0	0	0-0	.373	.385	.490	.875	3	.963

ROBERTS, BRIAN — 2B

R

PERSONAL: Born October 9, 1977, in Durham, N.C. ... 5-9/176. ... Bats both, throws right. ... Full name: Brian Michael Roberts. ... High school: Chapel Hill (N.C.). ... College: North Carolina, then South Carolina.
TRANSACTIONS/CAREER NOTES: Selected by Baltimore Orioles organization in supplemental round ("sandwich pick" between first and second rounds, 50th pick overall) of 1999 free-agent draft; pick received as part of compensation for Texas Rangers signing Type A free-agent 1B Rafael Palmeiro.
2005 GAMES PLAYED BY POSITION (MLB): 2B—141.

SCOUTING REPORT **Offense:** Roberts showed improved bat speed last season. Is a better lefthanded hitter but has more power from the right side. Uses the whole field and can get on top of the high fastball. Flashed unexpected power. Is a good runner with good basestealing instincts. **Defense:** He has good hands and good mobility to either side. Has improved his footwork and gets better jumps to either side. Doesn't have great arm strength but is an accurate thrower. **Outlook:** It is difficult to predict how Roberts will return after a severe elbow injury ended his 2005 season. Will miss the first half of the 2006 season because of surgery on the elbow. *Grade 8.0*

BRIAN ROBERTS' HITTING ZONE

.194	.292	.286
.311	.424	.287
.267	.452	.421

LEFTY-RIGHTY SPLITS

vs.	Avg.	AB	H	2B	3B	HR	RBI	BB	SO	OBP	Slg.
L	.273	176	48	10	3	5	25	20	33	.352	.449
R	.332	385	128	35	4	13	48	47	50	.404	.545

Year	Team (League)	Pos.	G	AB	R	H	2B	3B	HR	RBI	BB	SO	HBP	GDP	SB-CS	Avg.	OBP	SLG	OPS	E	Avg.
1999—Delmarva (S. Atl.)	SS	47	167	22	40	12	1	0	21	27	42	1	0	17-5	.240	.347	.323	.670	8	.964
2000—Frederick (Carolina)	SS	48	163	27	49	6	3	0	16	27	24	1	4	13-10	.301	.403	.374	.777	8	.952
—GC Orioles (GCL)	SS	9	29	8	9	1	2	1	3	7	4	0	0	7-1	.310	.432	.586	1.019	2	.905
2001—Bowie (East.)	2B-SS	22	81	12	24	7	0	1	7	9	12	1	2	10-0	.296	.364	.420	.785	3	.968
—Rochester (Int'l)	SS	44	161	16	43	4	1	1	12	28	22	0	0	23-3	.267	.376	.323	.699	13	.927
—Baltimore (A.L.)	SS-2B-DH	75	273	42	69	12	3	2	17	13	36	0	3	12-3	.253	.284	.341	.624	16	.941
2002—Rochester (Int'l)	2B	78	313	49	86	9	7	3	30	40	46	3	3	22-4	.275	.361	.377	.738	7	.978
—Baltimore (A.L.)	2B-DH	38	128	18	29	6	0	1	11	15	21	1	3	9-2	.227	.308	.297	.605	3	.977
2003—Ottawa (Int'l)	2B-SS	44	178	36	56	13	1	0	15	27	12	0	3	19-6	.315	.401	.399	.800	4	.979
—Baltimore (A.L.)	2B-DH-SS	112	460	65	124	22	4	5	41	46	58	1	9	23-6	.270	.337	.367	.704	8	.983
2004—Baltimore (A.L.)	2B-DH	159	641	107	175	* 50	2	4	53	71	95	1	3	29-12	.273	.344	.376	.720	8	.988
2005—Baltimore (A.L.)	2B	143	561	92	176	45	7	18	73	67	83	3	6	27-10	.314	.387	.515	.903	8	.988
Major League totals (5 years)		527	2063	324	573	135	16	30	195	212	293	6	24	100-33	.278	.344	.402	.747	44	.981

ALL-STAR GAME RECORD

		G	AB	R	H	2B	3B	HR	RBI	BB	SO	HBP	GDP	SB-CS	Avg.	OBP	SLG	OPS	E	Avg.
All-Star Game totals (1 year)		1	2	1	1	1	0	0	0	0	0	0		0-0	.500	.500	1.000	1.500	0	1.000

ROBERTS, DAVE — OF

PERSONAL: Born May 31, 1972, in Okinawa, Japan. ... 5-10/180. ... Bats left, throws left. ... Full name: David Ray Roberts. ... High school: Rancho Buena Vista (Oceanside, Calif.). ... College: UCLA.
TRANSACTIONS/CAREER NOTES: Selected by Cleveland Indians organization in 47th round of 1993 free-agent draft; did not sign. ... Selected by Detroit Tigers organization in 28th round of 1994 free-agent draft. ... Loaned by Tigers organization to Oakland Athletics organization (March 30-August 30, 1996). ... Traded by Tigers with P Tim Worrell to Cleveland Indians for OF Geronimo Berroa (June 24, 1998). ... On disabled list (March 31-June 24, 2001); included rehabilitation assignment to Akron. ... Traded by Indians to Los Angeles Dodgers for Ps Christian Bridenbaugh and Nial Hughes (December 21, 2001). ... On disabled list (May 17-June 1 and July 2-26, 2003); included rehabilitation assignments to Las Vegas and Ogden. ... On disabled list (May 5-28, 2004); included rehabilitation assignment to Vero Beach. ... Traded by Dodgers to Boston Red Sox for OF Henri Stanley (July 31, 2004). ... Traded by Red Sox to San Diego Padres for OF Jay Payton, SS Ramon Vazquez and P David Pauley (December 20, 2004). ... On disabled list (March 30-April 18, 2005); included rehabilitation assignment to Lake Elsinore.
2005 GAMES PLAYED BY POSITION (MLB): OF—109.

SCOUTING REPORT **Offense:** Roberts is a singles hitter who feasts on average fastballs and thrives when he's patient and works the count. Has good bat control and uses the whole field. Is an excellent bunter and an outstanding runner who forces infielders to play up. Is an instinctive basestealer and aggressive but frequent leg problems are starting to take a toll. **Defense:** For a speed-oriented player, Roberts is just average defensively. Doesn't get consistent lateral jumps and has to make up for it with his speed. Doesn't have really good instincts and will take ill-advised dives. Has a below-average arm. **Outlook:** Roberts has a difficult time playing an entire season because of his leg injuries. *Grade 6.3*

DAVE ROBERTS' HITTING ZONE

.107	.500	.250
.314	.293	.306
.150	.313	.400

LEFTY-RIGHTY SPLITS

vs.	Avg.	AB	H	2B	3B	HR	RBI	BB	SO	OBP	Slg.
L	.258	66	17	1	1	1	3	10	13	.364	.348
R	.278	345	96	18	9	7	35	43	46	.355	.443

Year	Team (League)	Pos.	G	AB	R	H	2B	3B	HR	RBI	BB	SO	HBP	GDP	SB-CS	Avg.	OBP	SLG	OPS	E	Avg.
1994—Jamestown (NYP)	OF	54	178	33	52	7	2	0	12	29	27	1	0	12-8	.292	.392	.354	.746	1	1.000
1995—Lakeland (Fla. St.)	OF	92	357	67	108	10	5	3	30	39	43	1	7	30-8	.303	.371	.384	.755	1	.985

Year Team (League)	Pos.	G	AB	R	H	2B	3B	HR	RBI	BB	SO	HBP	GDP	SB-CS	Avg.	OBP	SLG	OPS	E	Avg.
1996—Visalia (Calif.)	OF	126	482	112	131	24	7	5	37	98	105	1	6	65-21	.272	.391	.382	.773	5	.977
—Jacksonville (Sou.)	OF	3	9	0	2	0	0	0	0	0	3	0	0	0-1	.222	.300	.222	.522	0	1.000
1997—Jacksonville (Sou.)	OF	105	415	76	123	24	2	4	41	45	62	2	5	23-5	.296	.366	.393	.759	4	.954
1998—Jacksonville (Sou.)	OF	69	279	71	91	14	5	5	42	53	59	3	4	21-9	.326	.434	.466	.900	0	1.000
—Akron (East.)	OF	56	227	49	82	10	5	7	33	35	30	1	3	28-6	.361	.447	.542	.989	1	.992
—Buffalo (Int'l)	OF	5	15	2	2	0	0	0	2	0	3	0	0	2-0	.133	.125	.133	.258	0	1.000
1999—Buffalo (Int'l)	OF-DH	89	350	65	95	17	10	0	38	43	52	2	1	39-3	.271	.351	.377	.728	1	.996
—Cleveland (A.L.)	OF	41	143	26	34	4	0	2	12	9	16	0	0	11-3	.238	.281	.308	.589	0	1.000
2000—Buffalo (Int'l)	OF	120	462	93	135	16	3	13	55	59	68	2	3	39-11	.292	.373	.424	.798	1	.997
—Cleveland (A.L.)	OF	19	10	1	2	0	0	0	0	2	2	0	0	1-1	.200	.333	.200	.533	0	1.000
2001—Akron (East.)	OF	17	64	9	13	5	0	0	2	9	8	1	1	4-0	.203	.307	.281	.588	1	.969
—Buffalo (Int'l)	OF	62	241	34	73	12	4	0	22	18	44	2	2	17-6	.303	.352	.386	.738	3	.978
—Cleveland (A.L.)	OF-DH	15	12	3	4	1	0	0	2	1	2	0	0	0-1	.333	.385	.417	.801	0	1.000
2002—Los Angeles (N.L.)	OF	127	422	63	117	14	7	3	34	48	51	2	1	45-10	.277	.353	.365	.718	0	1.000
2003—Las Vegas (PCL)	OF	2	5	2	0	0	0	0	0	1	0	0	0	0-0	.000	.167	.000	.167	0	...
—Ogden (Pion.)	OF	3	10	4	4	0	0	0	0	1	0	0	0	1-0	.400	.455	.400	.855	0	1.000
—Los Angeles (N.L.)	OF	107	388	56	97	6	5	2	16	43	39	4	0	40-14	.250	.331	.307	.638	5	.976
2004—Vero Beach (FSL)	OF	2	8	0	0	0	0	0	0	0	0	0	0	0-0	.000	.000	.000	.000	0	1.000
—Los Angeles (N.L.)	OF	68	233	45	59	4	7	2	21	28	31	4	2	33-1	.253	.340	.356	.696	3	.976
—Boston (A.L.)	OF-DH	45	86	19	22	10	0	2	14	10	17	1	2	5-2	.256	.330	.442	.772	1	.982
2005—Lake Elsinore (Calif.)	OF	3	10	2	2	1	0	0	3	0	1	0	0	0-1	.200	.385	.300	.685	0	1.000
—San Diego (N.L.)	OF	115	411	65	113	19	10	8	38	53	59	1	9	23-12	.275	.356	.428	.784	2	.992
American League totals (4 years)		120	251	49	62	15	0	4	28	22	37	1	2	17-7	.247	.306	.355	.660	1	.994
National League totals (4 years)		417	1454	229	386	43	29	15	109	172	180	11	12	141-37	.265	.346	.366	.712	10	.988
Major League totals (7 years)		537	1705	278	448	58	29	19	137	194	217	12	14	158-44	.263	.340	.364	.704	11	.989

DIVISION SERIES RECORD

Year Team (League)	Pos.	G	AB	R	H	2B	3B	HR	RBI	BB	SO	HBP	GDP	SB-CS	Avg.	OBP	SLG	OPS	E	Avg.
1999—Cleveland (A.L.)	OF	2	3	0	0	0	0	0	0	0	2	0	0	0-0	.000	.000	.000	.000	0	1.000
2004—Boston (A.L.)		1	0	0	0	0	0	0	0	0	0	0	0	0-0	...	...	...	...	0	...
2005—San Diego (N.L.)	OF	3	9	1	2	0	0	1	1	0	1	0	0	0-0	.222	.222	.556	.778	0	1.000
Division series totals (3 years)		6	12	1	2	0	0	1	1	0	3	0	0	0-0	.167	.167	.417	.583	0	1.000

CHAMPIONSHIP SERIES RECORD

Year Team (League)	Pos.	G	AB	R	H	2B	3B	HR	RBI	BB	SO	HBP	GDP	SB-CS	Avg.	OBP	SLG	OPS	E	Avg.
2004—Boston (A.L.)		2	0	2	0	0	0	0	0	0	0	0	0	1-0	...	...	...	...	0	...

WORLD SERIES RECORD

Year Team (League)	Pos.	G	AB	R	H	2B	3B	HR	RBI	BB	SO	HBP	GDP	SB-CS	Avg.	OBP	SLG	OPS	E	Avg.
2004—Boston (A.L.)		Did not play.																		

ROBERTSON, NATE   P

PERSONAL: Born September 3, 1977, in Wichita, Kan. ... 6-2/215. ... Throws left, bats right. ... Full name: Nathan Daniel Robertson. ... High school: Maize (Kan.). ... College: Wichita State.

TRANSACTIONS/CAREER NOTES: Selected by Chicago White Sox organization in 35th round of 1995 free-agent draft; did not sign. ... Selected by White Sox organization in 15th round of 1998 free-agent draft; did not sign. ... Selected by Florida Marlins organization in fifth round of 1999 free-agent draft. ... Traded by Marlins with Ps Gary Knotts and Rob Henkel to Detroit Tigers for Ps Mark Redman and Jerrod Fuell (January 11, 2003).

CAREER HITTING: 0-for-8 (.000). 0 R, 0 2B, 0 3B, 0 HR, 0 RBI.

SCOUTING REPORT **Throws:** His fastball is 89-92 mph, and he also throws a slider at 80-84 and a changeup. **Tendencies:** He lives on the outside part of the plate against righthanders with a naturally tailing fastball, but he doesn't pitch inside enough. Starting to throw more of a two-seam fastball. Slider is too flat. Has good motion with his changeup, which he turns over to righthanders. **Outlook:** He is a back-of-the-rotation starter but should pitch better in spacious Comerica Park. **Grade 6**

NATE ROBERTSON'S PITCHING ZONE

.348	.444	.120
.292	.417	.273
.293	.256	.212

LEFTY-RIGHTY SPLITS

vs.	Avg.	AB	H	2B	3B	HR	RBI	BB	SO	OBP	Slg.
L	.244	156	38	2	2	1	17	15	30	.316	.301
R	.272	604	164	32	5	27	82	50	92	.327	.475

Year Team (League)	W	L	Pct.	ERA	WHIP	G	GS	CG	ShO	Hld.	Sv.-Opp.	IP	H	R	ER	HR	BB-IBB	SO	Avg.
1999—Utica (N.Y.-Penn)	2	0	1.000	2.77	1.15	5	5	0	0	...	0-...	26.0	22	9	8	0	8-0	26	.244
—Kane Co. (Midw.)	6	1	.857	2.29	1.06	8	8	1	1	...	0-...	51.0	42	14	13	1	12-0	33	.230
2000—Kane Co. (Midw.)	0	2	.000	5.09	1.70	6	6	0	0	...	0-...	17.2	24	13	10	0	6-0	15	.324
2001—Brevard County (FSL)	11	4	.733	2.88	1.30	19	19	2	0	...	0-...	106.1	95	44	34	3	43-1	67	.244
2002—Portland (East.)	10	9	.526	3.42	1.26	27	27	3	0	...	0-...	163.0	156	77	62	12	50-2	109	.260
—Florida (N.L.)	0	1	.000	11.88	2.28	6	1	0	0	0	0-0	8.1	15	11	11	3	4-1	3	.375
2003—Toledo (Int'l)	9	7	.563	3.14	1.20	24	23	3	1	...	0-...	155.0	145	62	54	14	47-2	102	.250
—Detroit (A.L.)	1	2	.333	5.44	1.75	8	8	0	0	0	0-0	44.2	55	27	27	6	23-2	33	.306
2004—Detroit (A.L.)	12	10	.545	4.90	1.40	34	32	1	0	1	1-1	196.2	210	116	107	30	66-1	155	.274
2005—Detroit (A.L.)	7	16	.304	4.48	1.36	32	32	2	0	0	0-0	196.2	202	113	98	28	65-2	122	.266
American League totals (3 years)	20	28	.417	4.77	1.42	74	72	3	0	1	1-1	438.0	467	256	232	64	154-5	310	.274
National League totals (1 year)	0	1	.000	11.88	2.28	6	1	0	0	0	0-0	8.1	15	11	11	3	4-1	3	.375
Major League totals (4 years)	20	29	.408	4.90	1.43	80	73	3	0	1	1-1	446.1	482	267	243	67	158-6	313	.276

ROBLES, OSCAR — 3B/SS

PERSONAL: Born April 9, 1976, in Tijuana, Mexico. ... 5-11/155. ... Bats left, throws right. ... Full name: Oscar M. Robles. ... High school: Montgomery (San Diego).

TRANSACTIONS/CAREER NOTES: Selected by Houston Astros organization in third round of 1994 free-agent draft. ... Released by Astros (March 29, 1999). ... Signed as a free agent by Oakland Athletics organization (December 17, 2002). ... Returned to Oaxaca of the Mexican League (March 8, 2003). ... Rights acquired by San Diego Padres organization (March 15, 2003). ... Returned to Mexico City of the Mexican League (March 27, 2003). ... Contract purchased by Los Angeles Dodgers from Mexico City Red Devils (January 14, 2005).

2005 GAMES PLAYED BY POSITION (MLB): SS—54, 3B—40, 2B—1, DH—1.

OSCAR ROBLES'S HITTING ZONE

.316	.217	.250
.327	.263	.321
.143	.438	.262

LEFTY-RIGHTY SPLITS

vs.	Avg.	AB	H	2B	3B	HR	RBI	BB	SO	OBP	Slg.
L	.267	75	20	3	0	1	7	6	10	.329	.347
R	.273	289	79	15	1	4	27	25	23	.332	.374

									BATTING										FIELDING	
Year Team (League)	Pos.	G	AB	R	H	2B	3B	HR	RBI	BB	SO	HBP	GDP	SB-CS	Avg.	OBP	SLG	OPS	E	Avg.
1994—GC Astros (GCL)	SS-3B-2B	55	165	40	54	5	1	0	19	32	17	2	5	14-10	.327	.442	.370	.812	14	.930
1995—Auburn (NY-Penn)	SS	58	216	49	62	9	1	0	19	39	15	0	5	8-2	.287	.395	.338	.733	16	.949
1996—Kissimmee (Fla. St.)	2B	125	427	57	115	13	2	0	29	74	37	6	13	10-8	.269	.383	.309	.692	26	.957
1997—Kissimmee (Fla. St.)	2B	66	236	39	53	4	0	0	21	43	28	1	4	0-1	.225	.344	.242	.586	8	.973
— New Orleans (A.A.)	2B	2	3	0	1	0	0	0	0	1	1	0	0	0-0	.333	.500	.333	.833	0	1.000
1998—Kissimmee (Fla. St.)	2B	66	207	31	56	7	1	0	24	38	14	3	1	6-2	.271	.390	.314	.704	13	.954
— Jackson (Texas)	2B	4	5	0	1	0	0	0	0	1	1	0	0	0-0	.200	.333	.200	.533	0	1.000
1999—	Did not play.																			
2000—Mexico (Mex.)	2B-3B	1	0	1	0	0	0	0	0	1	0	0	0	...	1.000	...	1.000	0	1.000
— Oaxaca (Mex.)	3B-SS-OF																			
	OF	84	310	62	108	14	1	4	45	68	35	0	10	3-3	.348	.461	.439	.900	10	.970
2001—Oaxaca (Mex.)	3B-SS-2B																			
	OF	118	466	71	138	26	2	5	51	59	50	1	16	4-5	.296	.373	.393	.766	14	.971
2002—Oaxaca (Mex.)	3B-SS-2B																			
	OF	105	368	67	128	25	0	9	76	74	35	5	7	4-3	.348	.452	.489	.941	18	.960
2003—Mexico (Mex.)	2B-3B	99	398	81	123	13	9	8	53	69	29	0	10	6-3	.309	.404	.447	.851	10	.982
2004—Mexico (Mex.)	2B-3B	97	335	72	128	23	5	8	64	62	11	0	8	8-6	.382	.473	.552	1.025	11	.933
2005—Mexico (Mex.)	2B-OF	30	118	27	46	7	4	4	21	19	8	1	6	1-1	.390	.475	.551	1.026	2	.989
— Los Angeles (N.L.)	SS-3B-2B																			
	DH	110	364	44	99	18	1	5	34	31	33	2	8	0-8	.272	.332	.368	.700	7	.977
Major League totals (1 year)		110	364	44	99	18	1	5	34	31	33	2	8	0-8	.272	.332	.368	.700	7	.977

RODNEY, FERNANDO — P

PERSONAL: Born March 18, 1977, in Samana, Dominican Republic. ... 5-11/208. ... Throws right, bats right.

TRANSACTIONS/CAREER NOTES: Signed as a non-drafted free agent by Detroit Tigers organization (November 1, 1997). ... On disabled list (March 26, 2004-entire season). ... On disabled list (March 29-June 9, 2005); included rehabilitation assignment to Toledo.

CAREER HITTING: 0-for-0 (.000), 0 R, 0 2B, 0 3B, 0 HR, 0 RBI.

FERNANDO RODNEY'S PITCHING ZONE

.200	.500	.273
.238	.231	.259
.429	.333	.167

LEFTY-RIGHTY SPLITS

vs.	Avg.	AB	H	2B	3B	HR	RBI	BB	SO	OBP	Slg.
L	.265	68	18	7	0	3	10	8	16	.359	.500
R	.219	96	21	3	0	2	10	9	26	.286	.313

Year Team (League)	W	L	Pct.	ERA	WHIP	G	GS	CG	ShO	Hld.	Sv.-Opp.	IP	H	R	ER	HR	BB-IBB	SO	Avg.
1998— Dom. Tigers (DSL)	1	3	.250	3.38	1.38	11	5	0	0	...	1-...	32.0	25	16	12		19-...	37	...
— Detroit (DSL)	1	3	.250	3.38	1.38	11	5	0	0	...	1-...	32.0	25	16	12	4	19-2	37	.214
1999— GC Tigers (GCL)	3	3	.500	2.40	1.37	22	0	0	0	...	9-...	30.0	20	8	8	1	21-0	39	.200
— Lakeland (Fla. St.)	1	0	1.000	1.42	1.26	4	0	0	0	...	2-...	6.1	7	1	1	0	1-0	5	.304
2000— W. Mich. (Mid.)	6	4	.600	2.94	1.32	22	10	0	0	...	0-...	82.2	74	34	27	2	35-0	56	.238
2001— Lakeland (Fla. St.)	4	2	.667	3.42	1.30	16	9	0	0	...	0-...	55.1	53	26	21	2	19-1	44	.249
— GC Tigers (GCL)	0	0	...	0.00	1.00	1	1	0	0	...	0-...	1.0	0	0	0	0	1-0	1	.000
— Erie (East.)	0	0	...	4.26	1.58	4	0	0	0	...	1-...	6.1	7	3	3	1	3-0	8	.292
2002— Erie (East.)	1	0	1.000	1.33	0.93	21	0	0	0	...	11-...	20.1	14	4	3	0	5-0	18	.194
— Detroit (A.L.)	1	3	.250	6.00	1.94	20	0	0	0	0	0-4	18.0	25	15	12	2	10-2	10	.329
— Toledo (Int'l)	1	1	.500	0.81	0.99	20	0	0	0	...	4-...	22.1	13	4	2	1	9-0	25	.171
2003— Toledo (Int'l)	1	1	.500	1.33	0.86	38	0	0	0	...	23-...	40.2	22	6	6	0	13-0	58	.163
— Detroit (A.L.)	1	3	.250	6.07	1.75	27	0	0	0	3	3-6	29.2	35	20	20	2	17-1	33	.294
2004— Detroit (A.L.)	Did not play.																		
2005— Toledo (Int'l)	0	0	...	3.00	1.00	3	0	0	0	1	0-1	3.0	2	1	1	0	1-0	4	.182
— Detroit (A.L.)	2	3	.400	2.86	1.27	39	0	0	0	3	9-15	44.0	39	14	14	5	17-3	42	.238
Major League totals (3 years)	4	9	.308	4.52	1.56	86	0	0	0	6	12-25	91.2	99	49	46	9	44-6	85	.276

RODRIGUEZ, ALEX — 3B

PERSONAL: Born July 27, 1975, in New York. ... 6-3/210. ... Bats right, throws right. ... Full name: Alexander Emmanuel Rodriguez. ... High school: Westminster Christian (Miami).

TRANSACTIONS/CAREER NOTES: Selected by Seattle Mariners organization in first round (first pick overall) of 1993 free-agent draft. ... On disabled list (April 22-May 7, 1996); included rehabilitation assignment to Tacoma. ... On disabled list (June 12-27, 1997; April 7-May 14, 1999; and July 8-24, 2000). ... Signed as a free agent by Texas Rangers (December 11, 2000). ... Traded by Rangers to New York Yankees for 2B Alfonso Soriano and a player to be named (Feburary 16, 2004); Rangers acquired SS Joaquin Arias to complete deal (March 23, 2005). ... On suspended list (August 14-19, 2004).

HONORS: Named Major League Player of the Year by THE SPORTING NEWS (1996 and 2002). ... Named A.L. Most Valuable Player by Baseball Writers' Association of America (2003 and 2005). ... Won A.L. Gold Glove at shortstop (2002 and 2003).

2005 GAMES PLAYED BY POSITION (MLB): 3B—161, SS—3, DH—1.

SCOUTING REPORT *Offense:* A-Rod has an outstanding approach at the plate. Has exceptional extension and power to all fields. Is a good breaking-ball hitter. Civers the plate well. Tends to struggle with runners in scoring position because he puts too much pressure on himself and will chase high fastballs. Is an exceptional baserunner and has good instincts. *Defense:* After a slow start in the field last season, Rodriguez showed he was one of the best in the game. Is fluid and has a very quick first step and good range to either side. Has good hands and an outstanding, accurate arm. Is one of the best at charging balls and making off-balance throws. *Outlook:* Rodriguez arguably is the game's best player and has a Hall of Fame resume. Still needs to prove himself offensively in the playoffs, though. *Grade 10.0*

ALEX RODRIGUEZ'S HITTING ZONE

.382	.438	.263
.292	.441	.374
.292	.389	.350

LEFTY-RIGHTY SPLITS

vs.	Avg.	AB	H	2B	3B	HR	RBI	BB	SO	OBP	Slg.
L	.300	150	45	8	0	11	30	30	32	.414	.573
R	.327	455	149	21	1	37	100	61	107	.423	.622

Year Team (League)	Pos.	G	AB	R	H	2B	3B	HR	RBI	BB	SO	HBP	GDP	SB-CS	Avg.	OBP	SLG	OPS	E	Avg.
1994—Appleton (Midwest)	SS-DH	65	248	49	79	17	6	14	55	24	44	2	7	16-5	.319	.379	.605	.984	19	.934
—Jacksonville (Sou.)	SS	17	59	7	17	4	1	1	8	10	13	0	1	2-1	.288	.391	.441	.832	3	.964
—Seattle (A.L.)	SS	17	54	4	11	0	0	0	2	3	20	0	0	3-0	.204	.241	.204	.445	6	.915
—Calgary (PCL)	SS	32	119	22	37	7	4	6	21	8	25	1	1	2-4	.311	.359	.588	.948	3	.980
1995—Tacoma (PCL)	SS-DH	54	214	37	77	12	3	15	45	18	44	2	2	2-4	.360	.411	.654	1.065	10	.961
—Seattle (A.L.)	SS-DH	48	142	15	33	6	2	5	19	6	42	0	0	4-2	.232	.264	.408	.672	8	.953
1996—Seattle (A.L.)	SS	146	601	* 141	215	* 54	1	36	123	59	104	4	15	15-4	* .358	.414	.631	1.045	15	.977
—Tacoma (PCL)	SS	2	5	0	1	0	0	0	0	2	1	0	0	0-0	.200	.429	.200	.629	1	.833
1997—Seattle (A.L.)	SS-DH	141	587	100	176	40	3	23	84	41	99	5	14	29-6	.300	.350	.496	.846	* 24	.962
1998—Seattle (A.L.)	SS-DH	161	* 686	123	* 213	35	5	42	124	45	121	10	12	46-13	.311	.360	.560	.920	18	.977
1999—Seattle (A.L.)	SS	129	502	110	143	25	0	42	111	56	109	5	12	21-7	.285	.357	.586	.943	14	.977
2000—Seattle (A.L.)	SS	148	554	134	175	34	2	41	132	100	121	7	10	15-4	.316	.420	.607	1.026	10	.986
2001—Texas (A.L.)	SS-DH	•162	632	* 133	201	34	1	* 52	135	75	131	16	17	18-3	.318	.399	.622	1.021	18	.986
2002—Texas (A.L.)	SS	•162	624	125	187	27	2	* 57	* 142	87	122	10	14	9-4	.300	.392	.623	1.015	10	.987
2003—Texas (A.L.)	SS	•161	607	* 124	181	30	6	* 47	118	87	126	15	16	17-3	.298	.396	* .600	.995	8	.989
2004—New York (A.L.)	3B-SS	155	601	112	172	24	2	36	106	80	131	10	18	28-4	.286	.375	.512	.888	13	.966
2005—New York (A.L.)	3B-SS-DH	•162	605	* 124	194	29	1	* 48	130	91	139	16	8	21-6	.321	.421	* .610	*1.031	12	.971
Major League totals (12 years)		1592	6195	1245	1901	338	25	429	1226	730	1265	98	136	226-56	.307	.385	.577	.962	156	.976

DIVISION SERIES RECORD

Year Team (League)	Pos.	G	AB	R	H	2B	3B	HR	RBI	BB	SO	HBP	GDP	SB-CS	Avg.	OBP	SLG	OPS	E	Avg.
1995—Seattle (A.L.)	SS	1	1	1	0	0	0	0	0	0	0	0	0	0-0	.000	.000	.000	.000	0	...
1997—Seattle (A.L.)	SS	4	16	1	5	1	0	1	1	0	5	0	0	0-0	.313	.313	.563	.875	0	1.000
2000—Seattle (A.L.)	SS	3	13	0	4	1	0	0	2	0	2	0	1	0-1	.308	.308	.308	.615	0	1.000
2004—New York (A.L.)	3B	4	19	3	8	3	0	1	3	2	1	0	0	2-1	.421	.476	.737	1.213	0	1.000
2005—New York (A.L.)	3B	5	15	2	2	1	0	0	0	6	5	2	2	1-1	.133	.435	.200	.635	1	.933
Division series totals (5 years)		17	64	7	19	5	0	2	6	8	13	2	3	3-3	.297	.392	.469	.861	1	.984

CHAMPIONSHIP SERIES RECORD

Year Team (League)	Pos.	G	AB	R	H	2B	3B	HR	RBI	BB	SO	HBP	GDP	SB-CS	Avg.	OBP	SLG	OPS	E	Avg.
1995—Seattle (A.L.)		1	1	0	0	0	0	0	0	0	1	0	0	0-0	.000	.000	.000	...		...
2000—Seattle (A.L.)	SS	6	22	4	9	2	0	2	5	3	8	0	0	1-0	.409	.480	.773	1.253	0	1.000
2004—New York (A.L.)	3B	7	31	8	8	2	0	2	5	4	6	2	1	0-0	.258	.378	.516	.895	0	1.000
Champ. series totals (3 years)		14	54	12	17	4	0	4	10	7	15	2	1	1-0	.315	.413	.611	1.024	0	1.000

ALL-STAR GAME RECORD

		G	AB	R	H	2B	3B	HR	RBI	BB	SO	HBP	GDP	SB-CS	Avg.	OBP	SLG	OPS	E	Avg.
All-Star Game totals (8 years)		8	19	4	6	0	1	1	2	1	9	0	0	0-0	.316	.350	.579	.929	0	1.000

RODRIGUEZ, FELIX   P

PERSONAL: Born December 5, 1972, in Monte Cristi, Dominican Republic. ... 6-1/198. ... Throws right, bats right. ... Full name: Felix Antonio Rodriguez. ... High school: Liceo Bijiador (Monte Cristi, Dominican Republic).

TRANSACTIONS/CAREER NOTES: Signed as a non-drafted free agent by Los Angeles Dodgers organization (October 17, 1989). ... Played catcher in Dodgers organization (1990-92). ... Claimed on waivers by Cincinnati Reds (December 18, 1996). ... Traded by Reds to Arizona Diamondbacks for a player to be named (November 11, 1997); Reds acquired P Scott Winchester to complete deal (November 18, 1997). ... On disabled list (June 21-July 30, 1998); included rehabilitation assignments to AZL Diamondbacks and Tucson. ... Traded by Diamondbacks to San Francisco Giants for future considerations (December 8, 1998); Diamondbacks acquired P Troy Brohawn and OF Chris Van Rossum to complete deal (December 21, 1998). ... On disabled list (August 3-18, 2003). ... Traded by Giants to Philadelphia Phillies for OF Ricky Ledee and P Alfredo Simon (July 30, 2004). ... Traded by Phillies to New York Yankees for OF Kenny Lofton and cash (December 3, 2004). ... On disabled list (May 11-July 19, 2005); included rehabilitation assignments to Staten Island and Trenton.

CAREER HITTING: 4-for-16 (.250), 4 R, 1 2B, 0 3B, 1 HR, 3 RBI.

SCOUTING REPORT *Throws:* His fastball reaches into the upper 90s, and he also has a slider and a changeup. *Tendencies:* Rodriguez is a power pitcher with a loose arm but a predictable pitch pattern; he consistently works hitters away and rarely uses both sides of the plate. Is reluctant to throw his slider at times, and hitters can time his fastball the deeper he goes into the count. Has never developed an effective changeup. Is easy to follow and is reluctant to pitch inside even when he's being hit hard. *Outlook:* Rodriguez has a great arm but never has lived up to expectations. Used in longer-relief roles now as he's less dependable late in games. *Grade 6.7*

FELIX RODRIGUEZ'S PITCHING ZONE

.375	.444	.375
.421	.368	.118
.000	.143	.250

LEFTY-RIGHTY SPLITS

vs.	Avg.	AB	H	2B	3B	HR	RBI	BB	SO	OBP	Slg.
L	.239	46	11	2	0	1	5	10	11	.375	.348
R	.278	79	22	8	0	1	15	10	7	.374	.418

Year Team (League)	W	L	Pct.	ERA	WHIP	G	GS	CG	ShO	Hld.	Sv.-Opp.	IP	H	R	ER	HR	BB-IBB	SO	Avg.
1993—Vero Beach (FSL)	8	8	.500	3.75	1.36	32	20	2	1	...	0-...	132.0	109	71	55	15	71-1	80	.225
1994—San Antonio (Texas)	6	8	.429	4.03	1.42	26	26	0	0	...	0-...	136.1	106	70	61	8	* 88-3	126	.219
1995—Albuquerque (PCL)	3	2	.600	4.24	1.53	14	11	0	0	...	0-...	51.0	52	29	24	5	26-0	46	.269

Year Team (League)	W	L	Pct.	ERA	WHIP	G	GS	CG	ShO	Hld.	Sv.-Opp.	IP	H	R	ER	HR	BB-IBB	SO	Avg.
— Los Angeles (N.L.)	1	1	.500	2.53	1.50	11	0	0	0	0	0-1	10.2	11	3	3	2	5-0	5	.275
1996—Albuquerque (PCL)	3	9	.250	5.53	1.59	27	19	0	0	...	0-...	107.1	111	70	66	17	60-1	65	.280
1997—Indianapolis (A.A.)	3	3	.500	1.01	1.43	23	0	0	0	...	1-...	26.2	22	10	3	0	16-1	26	.212
— Cincinnati (N.L.)	0	0	...	4.30	1.65	26	1	0	0	0	0-0	46.0	48	23	22	2	28-2	34	.271
1998—Arizona (N.L.)	0	2	.000	6.14	1.66	43	0	0	0	0	5-8	44.0	44	31	30	5	29-1	36	.259
—Ariz. D'backs (Ariz.)	0	0	...	4.15	1.15	3	2	0	0	0	0-...	4.1	3	4	2	0	2-0	5	.200
—Tucson (PCL)	0	0	...	9.00	3.00	1	0	0	0	0	0-...	1.0	1	1	1	0	2-0	0	.250
1999—San Francisco (N.L.)	2	3	.400	3.80	1.45	47	0	0	0	3	0-1	66.1	67	32	28	6	29-2	55	.262
2000—San Francisco (N.L.)	4	2	.667	2.64	1.31	76	0	0	0	* 30	3-8	81.2	65	29	24	5	42-2	95	.220
2001—San Francisco (N.L.)	9	1	.900	1.68	1.00	80	0	0	0	* 32	0-3	80.1	53	16	15	5	27-2	91	.188
2002—San Francisco (N.L.)	8	6	.571	4.17	1.19	71	0	0	0	24	0-6	69.0	53	33	32	5	29-1	58	.259
2003—San Francisco (N.L.)	8	2	.800	3.10	1.44	68	0	0	0	19	2-3	61.0	59	21	21	5	29-2	46	.259
2004—San Francisco (N.L.)	3	5	.375	3.43	1.39	53	0	0	0	13	0-3	44.2	43	18	17	7	19-2	31	.250
—Philadelphia (N.L.)	2	3	.400	3.00	1.33	23	0	0	0	7	1-1	21.0	18	7	7	1	10-2	28	.231
2005—New York (A.L.)	0	0	...	5.01	1.64	34	0	0	0	3	0-0	32.1	33	18	18	2	20-0	18	.264
—Staten Island (N.Y.-Penn.)	0	0	...	3.00	1.33	2	2	0	0	0	0-0	3.0	4	1	1	1	0-0	5	...
—Trenton (East.)	0	0	...	0.00	1.33	2	2	0	0	0	0-0	3.0	1	0	0	0	3-...	3	...
American League totals (1 year)	0	0	...	5.01	1.64	34	0	0	0	3	0-0	32.1	33	18	18	2	20-0	18	.264
National League totals (9 years)	37	25	.597	3.41	1.35	498	1	0	0	128	11-34	524.2	461	213	199	43	247-16	479	.237
Major League totals (10 years)	37	25	.597	3.51	1.37	532	1	0	0	131	11-34	557.0	494	231	217	45	267-16	497	.238

DIVISION SERIES RECORD

Year Team (League)	W	L	Pct.	ERA	WHIP	G	GS	CG	ShO	Hld.	Sv.-Opp.	IP	H	R	ER	HR	BB-IBB	SO	Avg.
2000—San Francisco (N.L.)	0	1	.000	6.23	1.62	3	0	0	0	1	0-0	4.1	6	3	3	1	1-0	6	.316
2002—San Francisco (N.L.)	0	0	...	0.00	1.00	3	0	0	0	1	0-0	3.0	1	0	0	0	2-0	2	.111
2003—San Francisco (N.L.)	0	1	.000	2.25	1.25	3	0	0	0	0	0-0	4.0	4	3	1	0	1-1	5	.235
Division series totals (3 years)	0	2	.000	3.18	1.32	9	0	0	0	2	0-0	11.1	11	6	4	1	4-1	13	.244

CHAMPIONSHIP SERIES RECORD

Year Team (League)	W	L	Pct.	ERA	WHIP	G	GS	CG	ShO	Hld.	Sv.-Opp.	IP	H	R	ER	HR	BB-IBB	SO	Avg.
2002—San Francisco (N.L.)	0	0	...	1.93	1.07	4	0	0	0	0	0-0	4.2	3	1	1	0	2-0	2	.200

WORLD SERIES RECORD

Year Team (League)	W	L	Pct.	ERA	WHIP	G	GS	CG	ShO	Hld.	Sv.-Opp.	IP	H	R	ER	HR	BB-IBB	SO	Avg.
2002—San Francisco (N.L.)	0	1	.000	4.76	0.88	6	0	0	0	0	0-0	5.2	4	3	3	2	1-0	5	.190

RODRIGUEZ, FRANCISCO   P

PERSONAL: Born January 7, 1982, in Caracas, Venezuela. ... 6-0/185. ... Throws right, bats right. ... Full name: Francisco Jose Rodriguez. ... High school: Juan Lovera (Venezuela).

TRANSACTIONS/CAREER NOTES: Signed as a non-drafted free agent by Anaheim Angels organization (September 24, 1998). ... Angels franchise renamed Los Angeles Angels of Anaheim for 2005 season. ... On disabled list (May 15-June 1, 2005).

CAREER HITTING: 0-for-0 (.000), 0 R, 0 2B, 0 3B, 0 HR, 0 RBI.

SCOUTING REPORT *Throws:* Rodriguez has two dominant pitches, a fastball that tops out at 95 mph and a hard curve in the upper 70s. *Tendencies:* Rodriguez has exceptional arm speed and a deceptive delivery; he's as effective because of his motion as the quality of his pitches.. Can use a riding fastball to overpower hitters. Hard curve is almost impossible to hit; it has a big, sharp break. Hitters can't lay off it even though the pitch often breaks out of the strike zone. *Outlook:* Rodriguez can be dominant as a closer as long as he pitches within himself. Is very animated and the game moves too fast for him at times. *Grade 8.9*

FRANCISCO RODRIGUEZ'S PITCHING ZONE

.143	.571	.143
.219	.200	.194
.087	.417	.333

LEFTY-RIGHTY SPLITS

vs.	Avg.	AB	H	2B	3B	HR	RBI	BB	SO	OBP	Slg.
L	.213	127	27	4	2	4	14	15	48	.294	.370
R	.153	118	18	3	0	3	10	17	43	.259	.254

Year Team (League)	W	L	Pct.	ERA	WHIP	G	GS	CG	ShO	Hld.	Sv.-Opp.	IP	H	R	ER	HR	BB-IBB	SO	Avg.
1999—Butte (Pion.)	1	1	.500	3.31	1.05	12	9	1	0	...	0-...	51.2	33	21	19	1	21-1	69	.179
—Boise (N'west)	1	0	1.000	5.40	0.80	1	1	0	0	...	0-...	5.0	3	4	3	0	1-0	6	.150
2000—Lake Elsinore (Calif.)	4	4	.500	2.81	1.17	13	12	0	0	...	0-...	64.0	43	29	20	2	32-0	79	.189
2001—Rancho Cuca. (Calif.)	5	7	.417	5.38	1.60	20	20	1	1	...	0-...	113.2	127	72	68	13	55-1	147	.277
2002—Arkansas (Texas)	3	3	.500	1.96	1.14	23	0	0	0	...	9-...	41.1	32	13	9	2	15-0	61	.206
—Salt Lake (PCL)	2	3	.400	2.57	1.02	27	0	0	0	...	6-...	42.0	30	13	12	1	13-0	59	.204
—Anaheim (A.L.)	0	0	...	0.00	0.88	5	0	0	0	0	0-0	5.2	3	0	0	0	2-1	13	.167
2003—Anaheim (A.L.)	8	3	.727	3.03	0.99	59	0	0	0	7	2-6	86.0	50	30	29	12	35-5	95	.172
2004—Anaheim (A.L.)	4	1	.800	1.82	1.00	69	0	0	0	27	12-19	84.0	51	21	17	2	33-1	123	.174
2005—Los Angeles (A.L.)	2	5	.286	2.67	1.14	66	0	0	0	0	• 45-50	67.1	45	20	20	7	32-3	91	.184
Major League totals (4 years)	14	9	.609	2.44	1.03	199	0	0	0	34	59-75	243.0	149	71	66	21	102-10	322	.175

DIVISION SERIES RECORD

Year Team (League)	W	L	Pct.	ERA	WHIP	G	GS	CG	ShO	Hld.	Sv.-Opp.	IP	H	R	ER	HR	BB-IBB	SO	Avg.
2002—Anaheim (A.L.)	2	0	1.000	3.18	0.71	3	0	0	0	0	0-1	5.2	2	2	2	1	2-0	8	.105
2004—Anaheim (A.L.)	0	2	.000	3.86	1.50	2	0	0	0	0	0-0	4.2	4	2	2	0	3-1	5	.235
2005—Los Angeles (A.L.)	0	0	...	2.70	1.50	3	0	0	0	0	2-2	3.1	5	1	1	1	0-0	2	.357
Division series totals (3 years)	2	2	.500	3.29	1.17	8	0	0	0	0	2-3	13.2	11	5	5	2	5-1	15	.220

CHAMPIONSHIP SERIES RECORD

Year Team (League)	W	L	Pct.	ERA	WHIP	G	GS	CG	ShO	Hld.	Sv.-Opp.	IP	H	R	ER	HR	BB-IBB	SO	Avg.
2002—Anaheim (A.L.)	2	0	1.000	0.00	0.92	4	0	0	0	2	0-1	4.1	2	0	0	0	2-0	7	.143
2005—Los Angeles (A.L.)	0	0	...	0.00	2.14	2	0	0	0	0	1-1	2.1	2	2	0	0	3-0	3	.250
Champ. series totals (2 years)	2	0	1.000	0.00	1.35	6	0	0	0	2	1-2	6.2	4	2	0	0	5-0	10	.182

WORLD SERIES RECORD

Year Team (League)	W	L	Pct.	ERA	WHIP	G	GS	CG	ShO	Hld.	Sv.-Opp.	IP	H	R	ER	HR	BB-IBB	SO	Avg.
2002—Anaheim (A.L.)	1	1	.500	2.08	0.81	4	0	0	0	1	0-0	8.2	6	3	2	1	1-0	13	.194

	W	L	Pct.	ERA	WHIP	G	GS	CG	ShO	Hld.	Sv.-Opp.	IP	H	R	ER	HR	BB-IBB	SO	Avg.
All-Star Game totals (1 year)	0	0	...	0.00	0.00	1	0	0	0	0	0-0	0.2	0	0	0	0	0-0	0	.000

RODRIGUEZ, IVAN — C

PERSONAL: Born November 30, 1971, in Vega Baja, Puerto Rico. ... 5-9/218. ... Bats right, throws right. ... High school: Lina Padron Rivera (Vega Baja, Puerto Rico).
TRANSACTIONS/CAREER NOTES: Signed as a non-drafted free agent by Texas Rangers organization (July 27, 1988). ... On disabled list (June 6-27, 1992; July 25, 2000-remainder of season; May 2-17 and August 31, 2001-remainder of season). ... On disabled list (April 15-June 7, 2002; included rehabilitation assignment to Charlotte. ... On suspended list (September 28-29, 2002). ... Signed as a free agent by Florida Marlins (January 22, 2003). ... Signed as a free agent by Detroit Tigers (February 6, 2004). ... On suspended list (August 8-12, 2005).
HONORS: Named A.L. Most Valuable Player by Baseball Writers' Association of America (1999). ... Won A.L. Gold Glove at catcher (1992-2001 and 2004).
2005 GAMES PLAYED BY POSITION (MLB): C—123, DH—3.

R

SCOUTING REPORT **Offense:** Pudge is an outstanding player with an excellent approach at the plate. Has a short stroke with good bat control. Likes the ball out over the plate and adjusts quickly to breaking balls. Can hit for contact with good plate coverage. Power numbers have dropped dramatically. Has baserunning instincts but doesn't run as well as he used to. **Defense:** The 11-time Gold Glove winner has quick footwork and exceptional agility. Has quick, soft hands and frames pitches well. Sometimes reaches for pitches that he could get in front of and block. Can completely stop a running game with his arm. Doesn't call games well. **Outlook:** Rodriguez now is playing with more than just raw talent. Has improved his leadership and game-calling skills. Can nurture a young pitching staff. Is certain to make the Hall of Fame. *Grade 9.3*

IVAN RODRIGUEZ'S HITTING ZONE

.290	.667	.250
.304	.351	.326
.191	.344	.364

LEFTY-RIGHTY SPLITS

vs.	Avg.	AB	H	2B	3B	HR	RBI	BB	SO	OBP	Slg.
L	.294	109	32	7	2	4	15	5	18	.316	.505
R	.271	395	107	26	3	10	35	6	75	.283	.428

									BATTING									FIELDING	
Year Team (League)	Pos.	G	AB	R	H	2B	3B	HR	RBI	BB	SO	HBP	GDP	SB-CS	Avg.	OBP	SLG	OPS	E	Avg.
1989— Gastonia (S. Atl.)	C	112	386	38	92	22	1	7	42	21	58	2	6	2-5	.238	.278	.355	.633	11	.986
1990— Charlotte (Fla. St.)	C	109	408	48	117	17	7	2	55	12	50	1	6	1-0	.287	.316	.377	.693	14	.983
1991— Tulsa (Texas)	C	50	175	16	48	7	2	3	28	6	27	1	5	1-2	.274	.294	.389	.683	3	.988
— Texas (A.L.)	C	88	280	24	74	16	0	3	27	5	42	0	10	0-1	.264	.276	.354	.630	10	.983
1992— Texas (A.L.)	C-DH	123	420	39	109	16	1	8	37	24	73	1	15	0-0	.260	.300	.360	.659	* 15	.983
1993— Texas (A.L.)	C-DH	137	473	56	129	28	4	10	66	29	70	4	16	8-7	.273	.315	.412	.727	8	.991
1994— Texas (A.L.)	C	99	363	56	108	19	1	16	57	31	42	7	10	6-3	.298	.360	.488	.848	8	.992
1995— Texas (A.L.)	C-DH	130	492	56	149	32	2	12	67	16	48	4	11	0-2	.303	.327	.449	.776	8	.992
1996— Texas (A.L.)	C-DH	153	639	116	192	47	3	19	86	38	55	4	15	5-0	.300	.342	.473	.814	• 10	.989
1997— Texas (A.L.)	C-DH	150	597	98	187	34	4	20	77	38	89	8	18	7-3	.313	.360	.484	.844	7	.992
1998— Texas (A.L.)	C-DH	145	579	88	186	40	4	21	91	32	88	4	18	9-0	.321	.358	.513	.871	6	.994
1999— Texas (A.L.)	C-DH	144	600	116	199	29	1	35	113	24	64	1	* 31	25-12	.332	.356	.558	.914	7	.993
2000— Texas (A.L.)	C-DH	91	363	66	126	27	4	27	83	19	48	1	17	5-5	.347	.375	.667	1.042	2	.996
2001— Texas (A.L.)	C-DH	111	442	70	136	24	2	25	65	23	73	4	13	10-3	.308	.347	.541	.888	7	.990
2002— Texas (A.L.)	C-DH	108	408	67	128	32	2	19	60	25	71	2	13	5-4	.314	.353	.542	.895	7	.990
— Charlotte (Fla. St.)	C	3	9	1	3	0	0	0	0	0	3	0	0	0-0	.333	.333	.333	.667	1	1.000
2003— Florida (N.L.)	C-DH	144	511	90	152	36	3	16	85	55	92	6	18	10-6	.297	.369	.474	.843	8	.992
2004— Detroit (A.L.)	C-DH	135	527	72	176	32	2	19	86	41	91	3	15	7-4	.334	.383	.510	.893	11	.987
2005— Detroit (A.L.)	C-DH	129	504	71	139	33	5	14	50	11	93	2	19	7-3	.276	.290	.444	.735	4	.995
American League totals (14 years)		1743	6687	995	2038	409	35	248	965	356	947	44	221	94-47	.305	.341	.488	.829	107	.990
National League totals (1 year)		144	511	90	152	36	3	16	85	55	92	6	18	10-6	.297	.369	.474	.843	8	.992
Major League totals (15 years)		1887	7198	1085	2190	445	38	264	1050	411	1039	50	239	104-53	.304	.343	.487	.830	115	.990

DIVISION SERIES RECORD

Year Team (League)	Pos.	G	AB	R	H	2B	3B	HR	RBI	BB	SO	HBP	GDP	SB-CS	Avg.	OBP	SLG	OPS	E	Avg.
1996— Texas (A.L.)	C	4	16	1	6	1	0	0	2	2	3	0	0	0-0	.375	.444	.438	.882	0	1.000
1998— Texas (A.L.)	C	3	10	1	1	0	0	0	1	0	5	0	0	0-0	.100	.100	.100	.200	0	1.000
1999— Texas (A.L.)	C	3	12	1	3	1	0	0	0	0	2	0	1	1-0	.250	.250	.333	.583	0	1.000
2003— Florida (N.L.)	C	4	17	3	6	1	0	1	6	3	1	0	0	0-0	.353	.450	.588	1.038	0	1.000
Division series totals (4 years)		14	55	4	16	3	0	1	9	5	11	0	1	1-0	.291	.350	.400	.750	0	1.000

CHAMPIONSHIP SERIES RECORD

Year Team (League)	Pos.	G	AB	R	H	2B	3B	HR	RBI	BB	SO	HBP	GDP	SB-CS	Avg.	OBP	SLG	OPS	E	Avg.
2003— Florida (N.L.)	C	7	28	2	9	2	0	2	10	5	7	0	0	0-0	.321	.424	.607	1.031	1	.983

WORLD SERIES RECORD

Year Team (League)	Pos.	G	AB	R	H	2B	3B	HR	RBI	BB	SO	HBP	GDP	SB-CS	Avg.	OBP	SLG	OPS	E	Avg.
2003— Florida (N.L.)	C	6	22	2	6	2	0	1	1	1	4	0	1	0-0	.273	.292	.364	.655	0	1.000

ALL-STAR GAME RECORD

		G	AB	R	H	2B	3B	HR	RBI	BB	SO	HBP	GDP	SB-CS	Avg.	OBP	SLG	OPS	E	Avg.
All-Star Game totals (12 years)		12	32	4	10	1	1	0	3	1	6	0	1	1-0	.313	.333	.406	.740	0	1.000

RODRIGUEZ, JOHN — OF

PERSONAL: Born January 20, 1978, in New York. ... 6-0/205. ... Bats left, throws left. ... Full name: John Joseph Rodriguez. ... High school: Brandeis (New York).
TRANSACTIONS/CAREER NOTES: Signed as a non-drafted free agent by New York Yankees organization (November 17, 1996). ... Signed as a free agent by Cleveland Indians (November 16, 2004). ... Traded by Indians to St. Louis Cardinals for C Javier Cardona (June 11, 2005).
2005 GAMES PLAYED BY POSITION (MLB): OF—45.

JOHN RODRIGUEZ'S HITTING ZONE

.200	.667	.300
.500	.600	.389
.125	.375	.273

LEFTY-RIGHTY SPLITS

vs.	Avg.	AB	H	2B	3B	HR	RBI	BB	SO	OBP	Slg.
L	.296	27	8	0	0	0	3	6	12	.441	.296
R	.295	122	36	6	0	5	21	13	33	.367	.467

									BATTING									FIELDING	
Year Team (League)	Pos.	G	AB	R	H	2B	3B	HR	RBI	BB	SO	HBP	GDP	SB-CS	Avg.	OBP	SLG	OPS	E	Avg.
1997— GC Yankees (GCL)	OF	46	157	31	47	10	2	3	23	30	32	0	3	7-0	.299	.405	.446	.851	1	.985
1998— Greensboro (S. Atl.)	OF	119	408	64	103	18	4	10	49	64	93	4	7	14-3	.252	.357	.390	.747	6	.958

Year Team (League)	Pos.	G	AB	R	H	2B	3B	HR	RBI	BB	SO	HBP	GDP	SB-CS	Avg.	OBP	SLG	OPS	E	Avg.
1999—Tampa (Fla. St.)	OF	71	269	37	82	14	3	8	43	41	52	3	5	2-5	.305	.399	.468	.867	4	.966
—GC Yankees (GCL)	OF	3	7	1	2	0	1	0	1	3	0	0	0	0-0	.286	.500	.571	1.071	0	1.000
2000—Norwich (East.)	1B	17	56	4	11	4	0	1	10	8	22	1	1	0-0	.196	.308	.321	.629	2	.969
—Tampa (Fla. St.)	OF	105	362	59	97	14	2	16	44	40	81	8	6	3-2	.268	.354	.450	.804	2	.986
2001—Norwich (East.)	1B	103	393	64	112	31	1	22	66	26	117	11	7	2-3	.285	.345	.537	.882	4	.976
—GC Yankees (GCL)	OF	2	6	2	5	0	0	0	2	0	0	0	0	0-0	.833	.833	.833	1.666	0	...
2002—Norwich (East.)	1B	103	354	51	76	18	3	15	63	35	94	11	4	13-3	.215	.302	.410	.712	3	.985
2003—Columbus (Int'l)	OF	79	232	35	61	9	2	10	33	24	50	1	2	6-0	.263	.333	.448	.781	3	.981
2004—Columbus (Int'l)	OF	112	378	78	111	26	10	16	68	48	84	8	7	10-3	.294	.382	.542	.924	7	.865
2005—Buffalo (Int'l)	OF-DH	46	170	25	42	13	3	5	23	15	40	6	1	5-0	.247	.323	.447	.770	2	.989
—Memphis (PCL)	OF	34	120	24	41	5	0	17	47	13	28	3	2	1-1	.342	.419	.808	1.227	2	.983
—St. Louis (N.L.)	OF	56	149	15	44	6	0	5	24	19	45	3	0	2-0	.295	.382	.436	.818	2	.973
Major League totals (1 year)		56	149	15	44	6	0	5	24	19	45	3	0	2-0	.295	.382	.436	.818	2	.973

DIVISION SERIES RECORD

Year Team (League)	Pos.	G	AB	R	H	2B	3B	HR	RBI	BB	SO	HBP	GDP	SB-CS	Avg.	OBP	SLG	OPS	E	Avg.
2005—St. Louis (N.L.)		1	1	0	0	0	0	0	0	0	0	0	0	0-0	.000	.000	.000	.000	0	...

CHAMPIONSHIP SERIES RECORD

Year Team (League)	Pos.	G	AB	R	H	2B	3B	HR	RBI	BB	SO	HBP	GDP	SB-CS	Avg.	OBP	SLG	OPS	E	Avg.
2005—St. Louis (N.L.)		5	2	1	0	0	0	0	1	2	1	0	0	0-0	.000	.400	.000	.400	0	...

RODRIGUEZ, LUIS — 2B/3B

PERSONAL: Born June 27, 1980, in San Carlos, Venezuela. ... 5-9/180. ... Bats both, throws right. ... Full name: Luis Orlando Rodriguez. ... High school: Sixto Sosa (Cojedes, Venezuela). ... College: None.
TRANSACTIONS/CAREER NOTES: Signed as a non-drafted free agent by Minnesota Twins organization (June 1, 1997).
2005 GAMES PLAYED BY POSITION (MLB): 2B—40, 3B—27, SS—10, DH—3.

LUIS RODRIGUEZ'S HITTING ZONE

.500	.250	.222
.136	.563	.235
.000	.200	.222

LEFTY-RIGHTY SPLITS

vs.	Avg.	AB	H	2B	3B	HR	RBI	BB	SO	OBP	Slg.
L	.233	30	7	2	0	0	2	4	5	.324	.300
R	.276	145	40	8	2	2	18	14	18	.337	.400

Year Team (League)	Pos.	G	AB	R	H	2B	3B	HR	RBI	BB	SO	HBP	GDP	SB-CS	Avg.	OBP	SLG	OPS	E	Avg.
1997—Maracay-1 (Pion.)		51	107	21	33	6	1	0	12	12	6	0	2	5-0	.308	.357	.383	.740	...	...
1998—GC Twins (GCL)	2B-SS-3B	52	180	33	50	11	1	1	15	22	17	0	4	14-3	.278	.353	.367	.720	12	.949
1999—Quad City (Midw.)	2B-3B	119	434	63	117	20	0	3	50	53	49	4	10	8-4	.270	.348	.336	.684	11	.978
2000—Quad City (Midw.)	2B-3B	106	342	35	77	11	2	0	28	40	29	5	10	4-5	.225	.314	.269	.583	14	.971
2001—Fort Myers (FSL)	SS-2B-3B	125	463	71	127	21	3	4	64	82	42	6	14	11-8	.274	.387	.359	.746	21	.968
2002—New Britain (East.)	SS-2B	129	455	60	117	18	2	8	40	61	44	5	8	3-2	.257	.349	.358	.707	19	.970
2003—Rochester (Int'l)	2B-SS	131	518	65	153	35	2	1	44	46	46	3	15	6-8	.295	.354	.376	.730	13	.978
2004—Rochester (Int'l)	2B-SS	127	486	73	139	33	1	5	52	53	49	1	17	3-3	.286	.353	.389	.742	10	.878
2005—Rochester (Int'l)	2B-SS-3B	40	138	19	42	10	0	1	17	16	14	1	3	0-1	.304	.381	.399	.779	1	.994
—Minnesota (A.L.)	2B-3B-SS-DH	79	175	21	47	10	2	2	20	18	23	1	4	2-2	.269	.335	.383	.718	3	.986
Major League totals (1 year)		79	175	21	47	10	2	2	20	18	23	1	4	2-2	.269	.335	.383	.718	3	.986

RODRIGUEZ, RICARDO — P

PERSONAL: Born May 21, 1978, in Manga, Dominican Republic. ... 6-3/190. ... Throws right, bats right. ... Full name: Ricardo Antonio Rodriguez.
TRANSACTIONS/CAREER NOTES: Signed as a non-drafted free agent by Los Angeles Dodgers organization (September 2, 1996). ... Traded by Dodgers with Ps Terry Mulholland and Francisco Cruceta to Cleveland Indians for P Paul Shuey (July 28, 2002). ... On disabled list (June 9-26 and July 2, 2003-remainder of season); included rehabilitation assignment to Buffalo. ... Traded by Indians with OF Shane Spencer to Texas Rangers for OF Ryan Ludwick (July 18, 2003). ... On disabled list (July 23, 2004-remainder of season; and August 9, 2005-remainder of season).
CAREER HITTING: 1-for-8 (.125), 0 R, 0 2B, 0 3B, 0 HR, 1 RBI.

SCOUTING REPORT **Throws:** Rodriguez's fastball touches 95 mph when he's at full strength, which has been a while. Also throws a slider and a changeup. **Tendencies:** A sinker-slider pitcher who has spent at least two months on the disabled list in each of the past three seasons, Rodriguez does not hide his pitches well and lefthanded hitters particularly can pick up the baseball easily. Really starts to struggle the third time through a lineup. He has enough life on his pitches to get hitters out their first one or two at-bats. Could become a good ground-ball pitcher if he finds his touch. Must mix his pitches more intelligently and not overly rely on his sinker. **Outlook:** It is unsure whether his shattered elbow (suffered in 2004) has healed properly. Unless he gains fastball command in the low zone, Rodriguez could become a candidate for the bullpen, such that hitters would only see him for one at-bat. *Grade 7*

RICARDO RODRIGUEZ'S PITCHING ZONE

.182	.118	.063
.395	.393	.318
.455	.111	.200

LEFTY-RIGHTY SPLITS

vs.	Avg.	AB	H	2B	3B	HR	RBI	BB	SO	OBP	Slg.
L	.279	111	31	7	1	7	18	10	12	.339	.550
R	.298	121	36	6	0	4	16	7	12	.338	.446

Year Team (League)	W	L	Pct.	ERA	WHIP	G	GS	CG	ShO	Hld.	Sv.-Opp.	IP	H	R	ER	HR	BB-IBB	SO	Avg.
1997—San Dom. (In.-Am.)	1	2	.333	6.40	2.10	12	10	0	1	...	0-...	32.1	42	39	23	6	26-...	20	...
1998—Dom. Dodgers (DSL)	1	1	.500	3.55	1.88	13	9	1	1	...	0-...	33.0	28	19	13	1	34-...	36	...
1999—San Dom. (In.-Am.)	3	2	.600	3.43	1.24	9	9	0	0	...	0-...	42.0	34	22	16	2	18-...	51	...
2000—Great Falls (Pio.)	10	3	.769	1.88	0.93	15	15	2	0	...	0-...	95.2	66	32	20	2	23-0	129	.192
2001—Vero Beach (FSL)	14	6	.700	3.21	1.25	26	26	1	0	...	0-...	154.1	133	67	55	13	60-0	154	.232
2002—Jacksonville (Sou.)	5	4	.556	1.99	1.01	11	11	2	0	...	0-...	68.0	56	21	15	4	13-0	44	.224

R

Year	Team (League)	W	L	Pct.	ERA	WHIP	G	GS	CG	ShO	Hld.	Sv.-Opp.	IP	H	R	ER	HR	BB-IBB	SO	Avg.
	—Las Vegas (PCL)	1	0	1.000	3.86	1.54	2	2	0	0	...	0-...	11.2	13	5	5	1	5-0	7	.295
	—Buffalo (Int'l)	3	1	.750	3.60	1.32	4	4	0	0	...	0-...	25.0	26	10	10	1	7-0	14	.271
	—Cleveland (A.L.)	2	2	.500	5.66	1.40	7	7	0	0	0	0-0	41.1	40	27	26	5	18-3	24	.255
2003	—Cleveland (A.L.)	3	9	.250	5.73	1.43	15	15	0	0	0	0-0	81.2	89	57	52	16	28-1	41	.275
	—Buffalo (Int'l)	0	1	.000	4.32	1.10	2	2	0	0	...	0-...	8.1	6	4	4	2	3-0	7	.200
2004	—Oklahoma (PCL)	2	2	.500	5.11	1.46	6	6	1	0	...	0-...	37.0	42	23	21	5	12-0	18	.296
	—Texas (A.L.)	3	1	.750	2.03	1.50	5	4	1	1	0	0-0	26.2	28	10	6	1	12-0	15	.262
2005	—Texas (A.L.)	2	3	.400	5.53	1.47	12	10	0	0	0	0-0	57.0	67	39	35	11	17-0	24	.289
	—Oklahoma (PCL)	7	3	.700	2.91	1.08	13	12	3	2	0	0-0	80.1	64	30	26	8	23-0	48	.221
	Major League totals (4 years)	10	15	.400	5.18	1.45	39	36	1	1	0	0-0	206.2	224	133	119	33	75-4	104	.273

RODRIGUEZ, WANDY   P

PERSONAL: Born January 18, 1979, in Santiago, Dominican Republic. ... 5-11/160. ... Throws left, bats both. ... Full name: Wandy E. Rodriguez. ... College: None.
TRANSACTIONS/CAREER NOTES: Signed as a non-drafted free agent by Houston Astros organization (January 12, 1999).
CAREER HITTING: 6-for-40 (.150), 3 R, 0 2B, 0 3B, 0 HR, 1 RBI.

SCOUTING REPORT *Throws:* He throws two- and four-seam fastballs in the mid- to upper 80s, a big-breaking curveball and a straight changeup. *Tendencies:* Rodriguez must spot his fastball and keep it down to be effective. Has good tailing action on two-seam fastball, which is key to his success against righthanded hitters. Has tight spin on his curveball. Gets good arm speed and movement on his changeup. *Outlook:* Rodriguez needs to throw inside more, but he is an interesting option at the back of the rotation. *Grade 6.6*

WANDY RODRIGUEZ'S PITCHING ZONE

.567	.231	.333
.274	.429	.213
.311	.208	.257

LEFTY-RIGHTY SPLITS

vs.	Avg.	AB	H	2B	3B	HR	RBI	BB	SO	OBP	Slg.
L	.275	138	38	5	3	7	23	14	25	.359	.507
R	.273	355	97	22	0	12	44	39	55	.349	.437

Year	Team (League)	W	L	Pct.	ERA	WHIP	G	GS	CG	ShO	Hld.	Sv.-Opp.	IP	H	R	ER	HR	BB-IBB	SO	Avg.
1999	—Houston SP (DSL)	3	1	.750	3.61	1.59	19	7	0	0	...	2-...	52.1	61	27	21	1	22-0	51	.302
2000	—Houston (DSL)	3	3	.500	2.19	1.21	14	14	0	0	...	0-...	78.0	65	31	19	2	29-0	86	.226
2001	—Martinsville (App.)	4	3	.571	1.58	1.00	12	12	1	0	...	0-...	74.0	54	19	13	6	20-0	67	.208
2002	—Lexington (S. Atl.)	11	4	.733	3.78	1.32	28	28	0	0	...	0-...	159.1	167	74	67	12	44-0	137	.275
2003	—Salem (Carol.)	8	7	.533	3.49	1.29	20	20	1	1	...	0-...	111.0	102	51	43	9	41-1	72	.239
2004	—Round Rock (Texas)	11	6	.647	4.48	1.51	26	25	1	0	...	0-...	142.2	159	77	71	15	57-1	115	.286
2005	—Round Rock (PCL)	4	2	.667	3.69	1.27	8	8	0	0	0	0-0	46.1	43	20	19	7	16-0	48	.246
	—Corpus Christi (Texas)	0	0	...	2.70	1.50	1	1	0	0	0	0-0	3.1	3	1	1	0	2-1	3	.273
	—Houston (N.L.)	10	10	.500	5.53	1.46	25	22	0	0	0	0-0	128.2	135	82	79	19	53-2	80	.274
	Major League totals (1 year)	10	10	.500	5.53	1.46	25	22	0	0	0	0-0	128.2	135	82	79	19	53-2	80	.274

DIVISION SERIES RECORD

Year	Team (League)	W	L	Pct.	ERA	WHIP	G	GS	CG	ShO	Hld.	Sv.-Opp.	IP	H	R	ER	HR	BB-IBB	SO	Avg.
2005	—Houston (N.L.)	0	0	...	9.00	1.00	1	0	0	0	0	0-0	1.0	1	1	1	1	0-0	2	.250

WORLD SERIES RECORD

Year	Team (League)	W	L	Pct.	ERA	WHIP	G	GS	CG	ShO	Hld.	Sv.-Opp.	IP	H	R	ER	HR	BB-IBB	SO	Avg.
2005	—Houston (N.L.)	0	1	.000	2.45	2.45	2	0	0	0	0	0-0	3.2	4	1	1	1	5-1	2	.333

ROGERS, EDDIE   SS

PERSONAL: Born August 29, 1978, in San Pedro de Macoris, Dominican Republic. ... 6-1/172. ... Bats right, throws right. ... Full name: Edward Antonio Rogers.
TRANSACTIONS/CAREER NOTES: Signed as non-drafted free agent by Baltimore Orioles organization (November 1, 1997).
2005 GAMES PLAYED BY POSITION (MLB): DH—2, SS—1.

LEFTY-RIGHTY SPLITS

vs.	Avg.	AB	H	2B	3B	HR	RBI	BB	SO	OBP	Slg.
L	1.000	1	1	0	0	1	2	0	0	1.000	4.000
R	.000	0	0	0	0	0	0	0	0	.000	.000

Year	Team (League)	Pos.	G	AB	R	H	2B	3B	HR	RBI	BB	SO	HBP	GDP	SB-CS	Avg.	OBP	SLG	OPS	E	Avg.
1998	—Dom. Orioles/W.S. (DSL)	..	58	194	33	56	9	2	2	27	26	29	2	5	8-5	.289	.373	.387	.760	...	...
1999	—GC Orioles (GCL)	2B-3B-SS	53	177	34	51	5	1	1	19	23	22	4	2	20-3	.288	.379	.345	.724	10	.947
2000	—Delmarva (S. Atl.)	2B-SS	80	332	46	91	14	5	5	42	22	63	0	3	27-6	.274	.317	.392	.709	19	.947
	—Bowie (East.)	SS	13	49	4	14	3	0	1	8	3	15	0	1	1-1	.286	.321	.408	.729	0	1.000
2001	—Bowie (East.)	SS	53	191	11	38	10	1	0	13	6	40	2	4	10-2	.199	.231	.262	.493	10	.960
	—Frederick (Carolina)	SS	73	292	39	76	20	3	8	41	14	47	8	8	18-6	.260	.310	.432	.742	14	.956
2002	—Bowie (East.)	SS	112	422	59	110	26	2	11	57	16	70	10	9	14-4	.261	.300	.410	.710	20	.958
	—Baltimore (A.L.)	SS	5	3	0	0	0	0	0	0	0	0	0	0	0-0	.000	.000	.000	.000	0	1.000
2003	—Bowie (East.)	SS	97	340	48	72	13	1	6	35	12	64	6	7	27-8	.212	.249	.309	.558	17	.957
	—Aberdeen (N.Y.-Penn.)	SS	3	14	2	5	2	0	1	6	0	2	0	0	0-0	.357	.333	.714	1.047	1	.929
2004	—Bowie (East.)	3B-2B-SS / OF	124	482	71	137	32	1	4	37	37	78	4	4	20-7	.284	.340	.380	.720	14	.860
2005	—Ottawa (Int'l)	SS-3B-2B / OF	125	431	52	113	21	3	7	48	17	66	1	9	14-6	.262	.291	.374	.665	17	.967
	—Baltimore (A.L.)	DH-SS	8	1	4	1	0	0	1	2	0	0	0	0	0-2	1.000	1.000	4.000	5.000	0	...
	Major League totals (2 years)		13	4	4	1	0	0	1	2	0	0	0	0	0-2	.250	.250	1.000	1.250	0	1.000

ROGERS, KENNY — P

PERSONAL: Born November 10, 1964, in Savannah, Ga. ... 6-1/211. ... Throws left, bats left. ... Full name: Kenneth Scott Rogers. ... High school: Plant City (Fla.).

TRANSACTIONS/CAREER NOTES: Selected by Texas Rangers organization in 39th round of June 1982 free-agent draft. ... Signed as a free agent by New York Yankees (December 30, 1995). ... Traded by Yankees with IF Mariano Duncan and P Kevin Henthorne to San Diego Padres for OF Greg Vaughn and Ps Kerry Taylor and Chris Clark (July 4, 1997); trade voided because Vaughn failed physical (July 6, 1997). ... Traded by Yankees with cash to Oakland Athletics for a player to be named (November 7, 1997); Yankees acquired 3B Scott Brosius to complete deal (November 18, 1997). ... Traded by A's to New York Mets for OF Terrence Long and P Leo Vasquez (July 23, 1999). ... Signed as a free agent by Rangers (December 29, 1999). ... On disabled list (July 24, 2001-remainder of season). ... Signed as a free agent by Minnesota Twins (March 17, 2003). ... On suspended list (July 11-19, 2003). ... Signed as a free agent by Rangers (January 14, 2004). ... On suspended list (July 27-August 10, 2005).

HONORS: Won A.L. Gold Glove as pitcher (2000, 2002 and 2004-05).

CAREER HITTING: 8-for-56 (.143), 5 R, 0 2B, 1 3B, 0 HR, 4 RBI.

SCOUTING REPORT *Throws:* Rogers' fastball velocity improved into the low 90s, but his comfort level is 85-87. Has a cut fastball, a slow curveball and a changeup. *Tendencies:* He is using his four-seam fastball more and has abandoned his dead two-seam fastball. Has been more aggressive. Has good command and can pitch to both sides of the plate laterally and continually changes speeds. Likes to expand the plate. Will throw a big-breaking curve to lefthanded and righthanded hitters. Is an outstanding fielder with an excellent pickoff move. *Outlook:* Rogers rediscovered his fastball and showed a bigger separation in velocity between his pitches in 2005. Knows how to pitch and upset hitters' timing but needs to show up more in big games. *Grade 7.9*

KENNY ROGERS'S PITCHING ZONE

.353	.368	.120
.320	.288	.284
.284	.340	.214

LEFTY-RIGHTY SPLITS

vs.	Avg.	AB	H	2B	3B	HR	RBI	BB	SO	OBP	Slg.
L	.201	169	34	7	1	2	13	18	33	.292	.290
R	.291	587	171	35	4	13	68	35	54	.333	.431

Year Team (League)	W	L	Pct.	ERA	WHIP	G	GS	CG	ShO	Hld.	Sv.-Opp.	IP	H	R	ER	HR	BB-IBB	SO	Avg.
1982— GC Rangers (GCL)	0	0	...	0.00	0.00	2	0	0	0	...	0-...	3.0	0	0	0	0	0-0	4	...
1983— GC Rangers (GCL)	4	1	.800	2.36	1.13	15	6	0	0	...	1-...	53.1	40	21	14	0	20-0	36	...
1984— Burlington (Midw.)	4	7	.364	3.98	1.29	39	4	1	0	...	3-...	92.2	87	52	41	9	33-3	93	.246
1985— Daytona Beach (FSL)	0	1	.000	7.20	2.30	6	0	0	0	...	0-...	10.0	12	9	8	0	11-1	9	.300
— Burlington (Midw.)	2	5	.286	2.84	1.36	33	4	2	1	...	4-...	95.0	67	34	30	3	62-9	96	.202
1986— Tulsa (Texas)	0	3	.000	9.91	2.16	10	4	0	0	...	0-...	26.1	39	30	29	4	18-1	23	.333
— Salem (Carol.)	2	7	.222	6.27	1.53	12	12	0	0	...	0-...	66.0	75	54	46	9	26-0	46	.282
1987— Charlotte (Fla. St.)	0	3	.000	4.76	1.47	5	3	0	0	...	0-...	17.0	17	13	9	1	8-0	14	.258
— Tulsa (Texas)	1	5	.167	5.35	1.67	28	6	0	0	...	2-...	69.0	80	51	41	5	35-3	59	.291
1988— Charlotte (Fla. St.)	2	0	1.000	1.27	0.93	8	6	0	0	...	1-...	35.1	22	8	5	1	11-0	26	.179
— Tulsa (Texas)	4	6	.400	4.00	1.28	13	13	2	0	...	0-...	83.1	73	43	37	6	34-0	76	.233
1989— Texas (A.L.)	3	4	.429	2.93	1.38	73	0	0	0	15	2-5	73.2	60	28	24	2	42-9	63	.232
1990— Texas (A.L.)	10	6	.625	3.13	1.38	69	3	0	0	6	15-23	97.2	93	40	34	6	42-5	74	.249
1991— Texas (A.L.)	10	10	.500	5.42	1.66	63	9	0	0	11	5-6	109.2	121	80	66	14	61-7	73	.281
1992— Texas (A.L.)	3	6	.333	3.09	1.35	81	0	0	0	16	6-10	78.2	80	32	27	7	26-8	70	.261
1993— Texas (A.L.)	16	10	.615	4.10	1.35	35	33	5	0	1	0-0	208.1	210	108	95	18	71-2	140	.263
1994— Texas (A.L.)	11	8	.579	4.46	1.32	24	24	6	2	0	0-0	167.1	169	93	83	24	52-1	120	.260
1995— Texas (A.L.)	17	7	.708	3.38	1.29	31	31	3	1	0	0-0	208.0	192	87	78	26	76-1	140	.243
1996— New York (A.L.)	12	8	.600	4.68	1.46	30	30	2	1	0	0-0	179.0	179	97	93	16	83-2	92	.261
1997— New York (A.L.)	6	7	.462	5.65	1.54	31	22	0	0	1	0-0	145.0	161	100	91	18	62-1	78	.280
1998— Oakland (A.L.)	16	8	.667	3.17	1.18	34	34	7	1	0	0-0	238.2	215	96	84	19	67-0	138	.242
1999— Oakland (A.L.)	5	3	.625	4.30	1.47	19	19	3	0	0	0-0	119.1	135	66	57	8	41-0	68	.288
— New York (N.L.)	5	1	.833	4.03	1.30	12	12	0	0	0	0-0	76.0	71	35	34	8	28-1	58	.253
2000— Texas (A.L.)	13	13	.500	4.55	1.47	34	34	2	0	0	0-0	227.1	257	126	115	20	78-2	127	.285
2001— Texas (A.L.)	5	7	.417	6.19	1.65	20	20	0	0	0	0-0	120.2	150	88	83	18	49-2	74	.307
2002— Texas (A.L.)	13	8	.619	3.84	1.34	33	33	2	1	0	0-0	210.2	212	101	90	21	70-1	107	.261
2003— Minnesota (A.L.)	13	8	.619	4.57	1.42	33	31	0	0	0	0-0	195.0	227	108	99	22	50-5	116	.292
2004— Texas (A.L.)	18	9	.667	4.76	1.48	35	•35	2	1	0	0-0	211.2	248	117	112	24	66-0	126	.292
2005— Texas (A.L.)	14	8	.636	3.46	1.32	30	30	1	1	0	0-0	195.1	205	86	75	15	53-1	87	.271
American League totals (17 years)	**185**	**130**	**.587**	**4.22**	**1.40**	**675**	**388**	**34**	**8**	**50**	**28-44**	**2786.0**	**2914**	**1453**	**1306**	**278**	**989-47**	**1693**	**.270**
National League totals (1 year)	**5**	**1**	**.833**	**4.03**	**1.30**	**12**	**12**	**2**	**0**	**0**	**0-0**	**76.0**	**71**	**35**	**34**	**8**	**28-1**	**58**	**.253**
Major League totals (17 years)	**190**	**131**	**.592**	**4.21**	**1.40**	**687**	**400**	**36**	**9**	**50**	**28-44**	**2862.0**	**2985**	**1488**	**1340**	**286**	**1017-48**	**1751**	**.269**

DIVISION SERIES RECORD

Year Team (League)	W	L	Pct.	ERA	WHIP	G	GS	CG	ShO	Hld.	Sv.-Opp.	IP	H	R	ER	HR	BB-IBB	SO	Avg.
1996— New York (A.L.)	0	0	...	9.00	3.50	2	1	0	0	0	0-0	2.0	5	2	2	0	2-0	1	.455
1999— New York (A.L.)	0	1	.000	8.31	1.62	1	1	0	0	0	0-0	4.1	5	4	4	0	2-0	6	.278
2003— Minnesota (A.L.)	0	0	...	0.00	1.50	1	0	0	0	0	0-0	1.1	1	0	0	0	1-1	3	.200
Division series totals (3 years)	**0**	**1**	**.000**	**7.04**	**2.09**	**4**	**2**	**0**	**0**	**0**	**0-0**	**7.2**	**11**	**6**	**6**	**0**	**5-1**	**10**	**.324**

CHAMPIONSHIP SERIES RECORD

Year Team (League)	W	L	Pct.	ERA	WHIP	G	GS	CG	ShO	Hld.	Sv.-Opp.	IP	H	R	ER	HR	BB-IBB	SO	Avg.
1996— New York (A.L.)	0	0	...	12.00	2.33	1	1	0	0	0	0-0	3.0	5	4	4	1	2-0	3	.385
1999— New York (N.L.)	0	2	.000	5.87	2.35	3	1	0	0	0	0-0	7.2	11	5	5	2	7-2	2	.393
Champ. series totals (2 years)	**0**	**2**	**.000**	**7.59**	**2.34**	**4**	**2**	**0**	**0**	**0**	**0-0**	**10.2**	**16**	**9**	**9**	**3**	**9-2**	**5**	**.390**

WORLD SERIES RECORD

Year Team (League)	W	L	Pct.	ERA	WHIP	G	GS	CG	ShO	Hld.	Sv.-Opp.	IP	H	R	ER	HR	BB-IBB	SO	Avg.
1996— New York (A.L.)	0	0	...	22.50	3.50	1	1	0	0	0	0-0	2.0	5	5	5	1	2-0	0	.500

ALL-STAR GAME RECORD

	W	L	Pct.	ERA	WHIP	G	GS	CG	ShO	Hld.	Sv.-Opp.	IP	H	R	ER	HR	BB-IBB	SO	Avg.
All-Star Game totals (2 years)	0	0	...	13.50	2.00	2	0	0	0	0	0-1	2.0	4	3	3	2	0-0	3	.444

ROLEN, SCOTT — 3B

PERSONAL: Born April 4, 1975, in Jasper, Ind. ... 6-4/240. ... Bats right, throws right. ... Full name: Scott Bruce Rolen. ... Name pronounced: ROH-len. ... High school: Jasper (Ind.).

TRANSACTIONS/CAREER NOTES: Selected by Philadelphia Phillies organization in second round of 1993 free-agent draft. ... On disabled list (May 24-June 8, 2000). ... Traded by Phillies with P Doug Nickle to St. Louis Cardinals for IF/OF Placido Polanco and Ps Bud Smith and Mike Timlin (July 29, 2002). ... On disabled list (May 12-June 18 and July 22-remainder of season, 2005).

R

RECORDS: Shares major league record for most strikeouts, nine-inning game—5 (August 23, 1999).
HONORS: Named N.L. Rookie Player of the Year by THE SPORTING NEWS (1997). ... Named N.L. Rookie of the Year by Baseball Writers' Association of America (1997). ... Won N.L. Gold Glove at third base (1998 and 2000-04).
2005 GAMES PLAYED BY POSITION (MLB): 3B—56.

R

SCOUTING REPORT **Offense:** Rolen, when healthy, is one of he best run producers in the league. Has an unconventional approach for a hitter his size, hitting with a wide stance and from a deep crouch. Has extremely quick hands and generates good bat speed. Likes the ball out over the plate but is quick enough to turn on inside pitches. Has plus power and can drive the ball to all fields. Has become a better hitter with runners on and is a good breaking-ball hitter. Doesn't steal many bases but is the best baserunner in the game. **Defense:** Rolen may be the best defensive third baseman of all time. Is an exceptional athlete with great first-step quickness and outstanding footwork and agility. Can regain his feet after diving for a ball better than anyone. Has excellent range to either side and very soft hands. Has excellent accuracy even when charging and throwing off balance. Has the best arm of any third baseman in the majors. **Outlook:** The only question will be if he can regain his stroke after shoulder surgery. **Grade 9.6**

SCOTT ROLEN'S HITTING ZONE

.364	.000	.143
.343	.222	.222
.250	.125	.316

LEFTY-RIGHTY SPLITS

vs.	Avg.	AB	H	2B	3B	HR	RBI	BB	SO	OBP	Slg.
L	.237	59	14	4	0	2	11	9	10	.333	.407
R	.234	137	32	8	1	3	17	16	18	.318	.372

									BATTING									FIELDING	
Year	Team (League)	Pos.	G	AB	R	H	2B	3B	HR	RBI	BB	SO	HBP	GDP	SB-CS	Avg.	OBP	SLG	OPS	E	Avg.
1993— Martinsville (App.)		3B	25	80	8	25	5	0	0	12	10	15	7	3	3-4	.313	.429	.375	.804	10	.889
1994— Spartanburg (SAL)		3B	138	513	83	151	34	5	14	72	55	90	4	8	6-8	.294	.363	.462	.825	38	.917
1995— Clearwater (FSL)		3B	66	238	45	69	13	2	10	39	37	46	5	4	4-0	.290	.392	.487	.880	20	.899
—Reading (East.)		3B	20	76	16	22	3	0	3	15	7	14	1	2	1-0	.289	.353	.447	.800	4	.934
1996— Reading (East.)		3B	61	230	44	83	22	2	9	42	34	32	5	5	8-3	.361	.445	.591	1.037	9	.949
—Scran./W.B. (I.L.)		3B	45	168	23	46	17	0	2	19	28	28	0	9	4-5	.274	.376	.411	.786	6	.952
—Philadelphia (N.L.)		3B	37	130	10	33	7	0	4	18	13	27	1	4	0-2	.254	.322	.400	.722	4	.954
1997— Philadelphia (N.L.)		3B	156	561	93	159	35	3	21	92	76	138	13	6	16-6	.283	.377	.469	.846	24	.948
1998— Philadelphia (N.L.)		3B	160	601	120	174	45	4	31	110	93	141	11	10	14-7	.290	.391	.532	.923	14	.970
1999— Philadelphia (N.L.)		3B	112	421	74	113	28	1	26	77	67	114	3	8	12-2	.268	.368	.525	.893	14	.960
2000— Philadelphia (N.L.)		3B	128	483	88	144	32	6	26	89	51	99	5	4	8-1	.298	.370	.551	.920	10	.971
2001— Philadelphia (N.L.)		3B	151	554	96	160	39	1	25	107	74	127	13	6	16-5	.289	.378	.498	.876	12	.973
2002— Philadelphia (N.L.)		3B	100	375	52	97	21	4	17	66	52	68	8	12	5-2	.259	.358	.472	.830	8	.973
—St. Louis (N.L.)		3B	55	205	37	57	8	4	14	44	20	34	4	10	3-2	.278	.354	.561	.915	8	.958
2003— St. Louis (N.L.)		3B	154	559	98	160	49	1	28	104	82	104	9	19	13-3	.286	.382	.528	.910	13	.969
2004— St. Louis (N.L.)		3B	142	500	109	157	32	4	34	124	72	92	13	8	4-3	.314	.409	.598	1.007	10	.977
2005— St. Louis (N.L.)		3B	56	196	28	46	12	1	5	28	25	28	1	3	1-2	.235	.323	.383	.706	6	.966
Major League totals (10 years)			1251	4585	805	1300	308	29	231	859	625	972	81	90	92-35	.284	.375	.515	.890	123	.966

DIVISION SERIES RECORD

Year	Team (League)	Pos.	G	AB	R	H	2B	3B	HR	RBI	BB	SO	HBP	GDP	SB-CS	Avg.	OBP	SLG	OPS	E	Avg.
2002— St. Louis (N.L.)		3B	2	7	1	3	0	0	1	2	0	2	1	0	0-0	.429	.500	.857	1.357	0	1.000
2004— St. Louis (N.L.)		3B	4	12	1	0	0	0	0	0	6	3	0	0	0-0	.000	.333	.000	.333	0	1.000
Division series totals (2 years)			6	19	2	3	0	0	1	2	6	5	1	0	0-0	.158	.385	.316	.700	0	1.000

CHAMPIONSHIP SERIES RECORD

Year	Team (League)	Pos.	G	AB	R	H	2B	3B	HR	RBI	BB	SO	HBP	GDP	SB-CS	Avg.	OBP	SLG	OPS	E	Avg.
2004— St. Louis (N.L.)		3B	7	29	6	9	2	0	3	6	2	9	0	1	0-0	.310	.355	.690	1.044	0	1.000

WORLD SERIES RECORD

Year	Team (League)	Pos.	G	AB	R	H	2B	3B	HR	RBI	BB	SO	HBP	GDP	SB-CS	Avg.	OBP	SLG	OPS	E	Avg.
2004— St. Louis (N.L.)		3B	4	15	0	0	0	0	0	0	1	1	0	1	0-0	.000	.059	.000	.059	0	1.000

ALL-STAR GAME RECORD

			G	AB	R	H	2B	3B	HR	RBI	BB	SO	HBP	GDP	SB-CS	Avg.	OBP	SLG	OPS	E	Avg.
All-Star Game totals (3 years)			3	6	1	2	0	0	0	0	0	1	1	0	0-0	.333	.429	.333	.762	0	1.000

ROLLINS, JIMMY   SS

PERSONAL: Born November 27, 1978, in Oakland. ... 5-8/167. ... Bats both, throws right. ... Full name: James Calvin Rollins. ... High school: Encinal (Alameda, Calif.). ... Cousin of Tony Tarasco, outfielder with six major league teams (1988-99).
TRANSACTIONS/CAREER NOTES: Selected by Philadelphia Phillies organization in second round of 1996 free-agent draft.
2005 GAMES PLAYED BY POSITION (MLB): SS—157.

SCOUTING REPORT **Offense:** Rollins began concentrating on using the whole field and working the count late last season. Has a short, compact stroke and very good bat control. Has pop, especially from the left side. Is a better hitter righthanded. Needs to be more aggressive as a basestealer. Still tends to hit the ball in the air too much, which also neutralizes his speed. **Defense:** Rollins is a top-notch fielder who has become much steadier. Has very quick, soft hands. Excellent agility. Has really improved at getting a jump on the ball. Has exceptional range. Is very adept at going back on pop flies. Throws well. **Outlook:** One of the players who was instrumental in the Phillies' stretch drive last season, Rollins is putting things together and becoming more consistent in all facets. **Grade 9**

JIMMY ROLLINS'S HITTING ZONE

.433	.321	.259
.351	.407	.285
.265	.179	.200

LEFTY-RIGHTY SPLITS

vs.	Avg.	AB	H	2B	3B	HR	RBI	BB	SO	OBP	Slg.
L	.278	187	52	9	3	3	15	8	9	.311	.406
R	.294	490	144	29	8	9	39	39	62	.348	.441

									BATTING									FIELDING	
Year	Team (League)	Pos.	G	AB	R	H	2B	3B	HR	RBI	BB	SO	HBP	GDP	SB-CS	Avg.	OBP	SLG	OPS	E	Avg.
1996— Martinsville (App.)		SS	49	172	22	41	3	1	1	16	28	20	2	2	11-5	.238	.351	.285	.636	20	.906
1997— Piedmont (S. Atl.)		SS	139	560	94	151	22	8	6	59	52	80	0	4	46-6	.270	.330	.370	.700	26	.960
1998— Clearwater (FSL)		SS	119	495	72	121	18	9	6	35	41	62	4	9	23-9	.244	.306	.354	.659	29	.952

Year	Team (League)	Pos.	G	AB	R	H	2B	3B	HR	RBI	BB	SO	HBP	GDP	SB-CS	Avg.	OBP	SLG	OPS	E	Avg.
														BATTING						FIELDING	
1999—	Reading (East.)	SS	133	532	81	145	21	8	11	56	51	47	1	8	24-12	.273	.336	.404	.740	22	.965
	—Scran./W.B. (I.L.)	SS	4	13	0	1	1	0	0	0	1	1	0	0	1-0	.077	.143	.154	.297	1	.960
2000—	Scran./W.B. (I.L.)	SS	133	470	67	129	28	•11	12	69	49	55	2	4	24-7	.274	.341	.457	.798	26	.958
	—Philadelphia (N.L.)	SS	14	53	5	17	1	1	0	5	2	7	0	0	3-0	.321	.345	.377	.723	1	.978
2001—	Philadelphia (N.L.)	SS	158	656	97	180	29	*12	14	54	48	108	2	5	•46-8	.274	.323	.419	.743	14	.979
2002—	Philadelphia (N.L.)	SS-2B	154	*637	82	156	33	*10	11	60	54	103	4	14	31-13	.245	.306	.380	.686	14	.980
2003—	Philadelphia (N.L.)	SS	156	628	85	165	42	6	8	62	54	113	0	9	20-12	.263	.320	.387	.707	14	.979
2004—	Philadelphia (N.L.)	SS	154	657	119	190	43	•12	14	73	57	73	3	4	30-9	.289	.348	.455	.803	9	.986
2005—	Philadelphia (N.L.)	SS	158	677	115	196	38	11	12	54	47	71	4	9	41-6	.290	.338	.431	.770	12	.981
	Major League totals (6 years)		794	3308	503	904	186	52	59	308	262	475	13	41	171-48	.273	.328	.414	.742	64	.981

ALL-STAR GAME RECORD

		G	AB	R	H	2B	3B	HR	RBI	BB	SO	HBP	GDP	SB-CS	Avg.	OBP	SLG	OPS	E	Avg.
All-Star Game totals (3 years)		3	3	2	3	0	0	0	0	1	0	0	0	1-0	1.000	1.000	1.000	2.000	0	1.000

ROMANO, JASON — OF

PERSONAL: Born June 24, 1979, in Tampa. ... 6-0/185. ... Bats right, throws right. ... Full name: Jason Anthony Romano. ... High school: Hillsborough (Tampa).

TRANSACTIONS/CAREER NOTES: Selected by Texas Rangers organization in supplemental round ("sandwich pick" between first and second rounds, 39th pick overall) of 1997 free-agent draft; pick received as part of compensation for New York Yankees signing Type A free-agent P Mike Stanton. ... Traded by Rangers with OF Gabe Kapler to Colorado Rockies for OF Todd Hollandsworth and P Dennys Reyes (July 31, 2002). ... Traded by Rockies to Los Angeles Dodgers for OF Luke Allen (January 27, 2003). ... Traded by Dodgers to Tampa Bay Devil Rays for IF Antonio Perez (April 4, 2004). ... Claimed on waivers by Cincinnati Reds (April 22, 2004). ... On disabled list (July 26, 2004-remainder of season).

2005 GAMES PLAYED BY POSITION (MLB): OF—14.

LEFTY-RIGHTY SPLITS

vs.	Avg.	AB	H	2B	3B	HR	RBI	BB	SO	OBP	Slg.
L	.294	17	5	2	0	0	0	3	5	.429	.412
R	.231	13	3	0	0	1	3	0	4	.231	.462

Year	Team (League)	Pos.	G	AB	R	H	2B	3B	HR	RBI	BB	SO	HBP	GDP	SB-CS	Avg.	OBP	SLG	OPS	E	Avg.
														BATTING						FIELDING	
1997—	GC Rangers (GCL)	3B	34	109	27	28	5	3	2	11	13	19	3	1	13-4	.257	.349	.413	.762	15	.810
1998—	Savannah (S. Atl.)	2B	134	524	72	142	19	4	7	52	46	94	8	6	40-17	.271	.336	.363	.699	•32	.952
	—Charlotte (Fla. St.)	2B	7	24	3	5	1	0	0	1	2	2	0	0	1-2	.208	.259	.250	.509	1	.978
1999—	Charlotte (Fla. St.)	2B	120	459	84	143	27	14	13	71	39	72	13	4	34-15	.312	.376	.516	.893	23	.957
2000—	Tulsa (Texas)	2B	131	535	87	145	35	2	8	70	56	84	6	13	25-10	.271	.343	.389	.732	24	.963
2001—	Tulsa (Texas)	2B	46	186	19	45	9	1	1	19	16	31	1	8	8-3	.242	.304	.317	.621	8	.962
	—Oklahoma (PCL)	2B-OF	41	149	32	47	6	1	4	13	20	28	0	4	3-4	.315	.394	.450	.844	2	.981
	—GC Rangers (GCL)	2B-OF	5	21	2	3	0	0	0	1	0	8	0	0	1-0	.143	.182	.143	.325	5	.808
	—Charlotte (Fla. St.)	OF	3	10	3	4	2	0	0	1	4	1	0	0	1-0	.400	.571	.600	1.171	0	1.000
2002—	Oklahoma (PCL)	OF-2B-SS	48	196	28	53	8	1	4	28	19	41	0	...	10-3	.270	.329	.383	.711	5	.972
	—Texas (A.L.)	OF-2B-DH-3B	29	54	8	11	4	0	0	4	4	13	0	0	2-0	.204	.254	.278	.532	1	.981
	—Colo. Springs (PCL)	OF-2B-SS	31	129	20	40	7	2	0	9	6	27	0	...	8-3	.310	.338	.395	.734	3	.973
	—Colorado (N.L.)	2B-SS-SF-3B	18	37	9	12	0	0	1	3	3	11	0	0	4-1	.324	.375	.378	.753	4	.907
2003—	Las Vegas (PCL)	OF-2B-3B-SS	57	216	45	66	18	4	4	23	11	32	0	3	10-6	.306	.336	.481	.818	4	.977
	—Los Angeles (N.L.)	OF-2B-DH	37	36	3	3	0	0	0	0	1	8	0	2	2-0	.083	.108	.083	.191	0	1.000
2004—	Tampa Bay (A.L.)	2B-OF	4	8	0	1	0	0	0	1	0	2	0	0	0-0	.125	.125	.125	.250	1	.800
	—Louisville (Int'l)	OF	40	163	22	55	12	4	2	16	3	24	0	0	3-1	.337	.347	.497	.844	1	.989
	—Cincinnati (Int'l)	OF	22	26	3	4	0	0	1	3	2	10	0	0	0-0	.154	.214	.269	.484	0	1.000
2005—	Louisville (Int'l)	OF-DH	56	224	34	69	17	2	4	32	14	36	1	4	5-1	.308	.349	.455	.804	4	.985
	—Cincinnati (N.L.)	OF	19	30	3	8	2	0	1	3	3	9	1	0	0-0	.267	.353	.433	.786	1	.941
	—Albuquerque (PCL)	OF	1	1	0	0	0	0	0	0	1	0	0	0	0-0	.000	.500	.000	.500	0	1.000
	American League totals (2 years)		33	62	8	12	4	0	0	5	4	15	0	0	2-0	.194	.239	.258	.497	2	.965
	National League totals (4 years)		96	129	18	27	2	1	2	7	9	38	1	2	6-1	.209	.266	.287	.553	5	.943
	Major League totals (4 years)		129	191	26	39	6	1	2	12	13	53	1	2	8-1	.204	.257	.277	.535	7	.952

ROMERO, J.C. — P

PERSONAL: Born June 4, 1976, in Rio Piedras, Puerto Rico. ... 5-11/198. ...Throws left, bats both. ... Full name: Juan Carlos Romero. ... High school: Berwing (San Juan, Puerto Rico). ... College: Mobile (Ala.).

TRANSACTIONS/CAREER NOTES: Selected by Minnesota Twins organization in 21st round of 1997 free-agent draft. ... On disabled list (March 25-May 10, 2000); included rehabilitation assignment to Fort Myers.

CAREER HITTING: 1-for-3 (.333), 1 R, 1 2B, 0 3B, 0 HR, 0 RBI.

SCOUTING REPORT *Throws:* His fastball is 89-93 mph. Also throws a slider at 81-84 and a changeup. *Tendencies:* Romero has three quality pitches but still struggles with his control. Creates an excellent downward plane with his motion that makes his fastball ride up in the zone. Tends to fly open and has problems maintaining his arm slot. Slider is quick and has a big break; is very effective against lefthanders. Turns over his change to righthanders, doesn't throw it to lefthanders. Tends to work too fast at times, which hurts his control. *Outlook:* If he could harness his fastball, he'd be a more dependable setup man with the potential to close. *Grade 6.9*

J.C. ROMERO'S PITCHING ZONE

.350	.333	.429
.216	.313	.333
.360	.077	.250

LEFTY-RIGHTY SPLITS

vs.	Avg.	AB	H	2B	3B	HR	RBI	BB	SO	OBP	Slg.
L	.198	101	20	1	0	2	19	10	28	.308	.267
R	.268	112	30	6	1	4	13	29	20	.415	.446

Year	Team (League)	W	L	Pct.	ERA	WHIP	G	GS	CG	ShO	Hld.	Sv.-Opp.	IP	H	R	ER	HR	BB-IBB	SO	Avg.
1997—	Elizabethton (App.)	3	2	.600	4.88	1.42	18	0	0	0	...	3-...	24.0	27	16	13	4	7-0	29	.276
	—Fort Myers (FSL)	1	1	.500	4.38	1.22	7	1	0	0	...	0-...	12.1	11	6	6	1	4-0	9	.244
1998—	New Britain (East.)	6	3	.667	2.19	1.17	51	1	0	0	...	2-...	78.0	48	28	19	3	43-3	79	.178

Year Team (League)	W	L	Pct.	ERA	WHIP	G	GS	CG	ShO	Hld.	Sv.-Opp.	IP	H	R	ER	HR	BB-IBB	SO	Avg.
1999— New Britain (East.)	4	4	.500	3.40	1.60	36	1	0	0	...	7-...	53.0	51	25	20	6	34-0	53	.254
— Salt Lake (PCL)	4	1	.800	3.20	1.63	15	0	0	0	...	1-...	19.2	18	11	7	1	14-0	20	.250
— Minnesota (A.L.)	0	0	...	3.72	1.34	5	0	0	0	0	0-0	9.2	13	4	4	0	0-0	4	.333
2000— Fort Myers (FSL)	0	0	...	1.93	1.07	2	0	0	0	...	0-...	4.2	4	1	1	0	1-0	3	.222
— Salt Lake (PCL)	4	2	.667	3.44	1.30	17	11	1	0	...	4-...	65.1	60	40	25	6	25-0	38	.244
— Minnesota (A.L.)	2	7	.222	7.02	1.77	12	11	0	0	0	0-0	57.2	72	51	45	8	30-0	50	.312
2001— Minnesota (A.L.)	1	4	.200	6.23	1.46	14	11	0	0	0	0-0	65.0	71	48	45	10	24-1	39	.277
— Edmonton (PCL)	3	3	.500	3.68	1.43	12	10	0	0	...	0-...	63.2	67	33	26	4	24-0	55	.276
2002— Minnesota (A.L.)	9	2	.818	1.89	1.21	81	0	0	0	* 33	1-5	81.0	62	17	17	3	36-4	76	.213
2003— Minnesota (A.L.)	2	0	1.000	5.00	1.71	73	0	0	0	22	0-4	63.0	66	37	35	7	42-7	50	.272
2004— Rochester (Int'l)	0	0	...	2.25	1.13	3	3	0	0	...	0-...	8.0	4	2	2	1	5-0	11	.143
— Minnesota (A.L.)	7	4	.636	3.51	1.33	74	0	0	0	16	1-8	74.1	61	32	29	4	38-6	69	.224
2005— Minnesota (A.L.)	4	3	.571	3.47	1.56	68	0	0	0	11	0-1	57.0	50	26	22	6	39-8	48	.235
Major League totals (7 years)	25	20	.556	4.35	1.48	327	22	0	0	82	2-18	407.2	395	215	197	38	209-26	336	.256

DIVISION SERIES RECORD

Year Team (League)	W	L	Pct.	ERA	WHIP	G	GS	CG	ShO	Hld.	Sv.-Opp.	IP	H	R	ER	HR	BB-IBB	SO	Avg.
2002— Minnesota (A.L.)	0	0	...	0.00	1.20	3	0	0	0	2	0-0	3.1	3	0	0	0	1-0	2	.231
2003— Minnesota (A.L.)	0	0	...	0.00	1.50	3	0	0	0	0	0-0	3.1	3	0	0	0	2-1	1	.250
2004— Minnesota (A.L.)	0	0	...	9.00	1.00	2	0	0	0	0	0-0	1.0	1	1	1	0	1-0	1	.000
Division series totals (3 years)	0	0	...	1.17	1.30	8	0	0	0	2	0-0	7.2	6	1	1	0	4-1	4	.231

CHAMPIONSHIP SERIES RECORD

Year Team (League)	W	L	Pct.	ERA	WHIP	G	GS	CG	ShO	Hld.	Sv.-Opp.	IP	H	R	ER	HR	BB-IBB	SO	Avg.
2002— Minnesota (A.L.)	0	1	.000	22.50	3.00	4	0	0	0	0	0-0	2.0	4	5	5	1	2-0	3	.400

ROSE, MIKE — C

PERSONAL: Born August 25, 1976, in Sacramento. ... 6-1/185. ... Bats both, throws right. ... Full name: Michael John-Ferrero Rose. ... High school: Jesuit (Sacramento).

TRANSACTIONS/CAREER NOTES: Selected by Houston Astros organization in fifth round of 1995 free-agent draft. ... Released by Astros (March 16, 2000). ... Signed by Arizona Diamondbacks organization (March 21, 2000). ... Traded by Diamondbacks to Boston Red Sox for cash (August 18, 2001). ... Released by Red Sox (April 26, 2002). ... Signed by Kansas City Royals organization (May 1, 2002). ... Signed as a free agent by Oakland Athletics organization (November 6, 2002). ... Signed as a free agent by Los Angeles Dodgers organization (November 16, 2004). ... Claimed on waivers by Tampa Bay Devil Rays (October 14, 2005).

2005 GAMES PLAYED BY POSITION (MLB): C—13.

LEFTY-RIGHTY SPLITS

vs.	Avg.	AB	H	2B	3B	HR	RBI	BB	SO	OBP	Slg.
L	.125	16	2	0	0	0	0	0	1	.125	.125
R	.259	27	7	2	0	1	1	3	5	.333	.444

Year Team (League)	Pos.	G	AB	R	H	2B	3B	HR	RBI	BB	SO	HBP	GDP	SB-CS	Avg.	OBP	SLG	OPS	E	Avg.
1995— GC Astros (GCL)	C-1B	35	89	13	23	2	1	1	9	11	18	3	1	2-1	.258	.359	.337	.696	0	.996
1996— Kissimmee (Fla. St.)	C	2	1	0	0	0	0	0	0	0	1	0	0	0-0	.000	.000	.000	.000	0	1.000
— Auburn (NY-Penn)	C	61	180	20	45	5	1	2	11	30	41	1	5	9-3	.250	.360	.322	.682	7	.984
1997— Quad City (Midw.)	C	79	234	22	60	6	1	3	27	28	62	4	1	3-1	.256	.342	.329	.671	10	.983
1998— Kissimmee (Fla. St.)	C	18	62	9	14	4	0	3	9	8	14	0	2	1-0	.226	.314	.435	.750	3	.973
— Quad City (Midw.)	C-OF	88	267	48	81	13	2	7	40	52	56	1	5	10-8	.303	.417	.446	.863	8	.988
1999— Kissimmee (Fla. St.)	C	95	303	61	84	16	2	11	32	59	64	3	7	12-6	.277	.398	.452	.850	13	.981
— Jackson (Texas)	C	15	45	8	11	0	0	3	8	13	10	1	0	0-2	.244	.414	.444	.858	2	.983
2000— El Paso (Texas)	C-OF	117	352	58	100	22	1	10	62	68	70	1	16	8-11	.284	.398	.438	.835	16	.980
2001— Tucson (PCL)	C	20	55	9	10	1	2	0	8	12	16	0	3	0-0	.182	.324	.273	.596	0	1.000
— El Paso (Texas)	C-OF-3B	62	205	28	53	13	1	3	23	37	40	0	8	4-4	.259	.370	.376	.746	4	.984
— Trenton (East.)	C	9	24	3	4	0	0	1	2	6	10	0	0	0-0	.167	.333	.292	.625	0	1.000
2002— Trenton (East.)	C	10	29	1	3	1	1	0		5	7	0	2	0-0	.103	.235	.207	.442	0	1.000
— Omaha (PCL)	C	52	177	22	46	12	2	3	17	28	40	1	7	2-3	.260	.364	.401	.765	6	.981
— Wichita (Texas)	C-OF	14	59	13	18	5	0	2	14	7	11	0	3	0-1	.305	.379	.492	.870	1	.977
2003— Sacramento (PCL)	C-OF	70	221	44	58	10	1	8	30	44	50	4	6	2-1	.262	.390	.425	.815	8	.982
2004— Sacramento (PCL)	C-DH	107	349	56	98	20	2	6	49	76	80	3	14	0-0	.281	.407	.401	.808	8	.988
— Oakland (A.L.)	C	2	2	1	0	0	0	0	0	0	2	0	0	0-0	.000	.000	.000	.000	0	1.000
2005— Las Vegas (PCL)	C-OF-DH 1B	69	205	31	53	20	1	5	36	25	51	3	3	2-0	.259	.343	.439	.782	2	.995
— Los Angeles (N.L.)	C	15	43	2	9	2	0	1	1	3	6	0	0	0-0	.209	.261	.326	.586	2	.978
American League totals (1 year)		2	2	1	0	0	0	0	0	0	2	0	0	0-0	.000	.000	.000	.000	0	1.000
National League totals (1 year)		15	43	2	9	2	0	1	1	3	6	0	0	0-0	.209	.261	.326	.586	2	.978
Major League totals (2 years)		17	45	3	9	2	0	1	1	3	8	0	0	0-0	.200	.250	.311	.561	2	.978

ROSS, CODY — OF

PERSONAL: Born December 23, 1980, in Portales, N.M. ... 5-11/180. ... Bats right, throws left. ... Full name: Cody Joseph Ross. ... High school: Carlsbad (N.M.).

TRANSACTIONS/CAREER NOTES: Selected by Detroit Tigers organization in fourth round of 1999 free-agent draft. ... Traded by Tigers to Los Angeles Dodgers for P Steve Colyer and cash (April 1, 2004).

2005 GAMES PLAYED BY POSITION (MLB): OF—9.

LEFTY-RIGHTY SPLITS

vs.	Avg.	AB	H	2B	3B	HR	RBI	BB	SO	OBP	Slg.
L	.333	9	3	1	0	0	1	1	5	.400	.444
R	.063	16	1	0	0	0	0	0	5	.063	.063

Year Team (League)	Pos.	G	AB	R	H	2B	3B	HR	RBI	BB	SO	HBP	GDP	SB-CS	Avg.	OBP	SLG	OPS	E	Avg.
1999— GC Tigers (GCL)	OF	42	142	19	31	8	3	4	18	16	28	2	3	3-1	.218	.304	.401	.705	6	.980
2000— W. Mich. (Mid.)	OF	122	434	71	116	17	9	7	68	55	83	9	14	11-3	.267	.356	.396	.752	6	.978
2001— Lakeland (Fla. St.)	OF	127	482	84	133	34	5	15	80	44	96	5	9	28-5	.276	.337	.461	.798	4	.984
2002— Erie (East.)	OF	105	400	73	112	28	3	19	72	44	86	3	11	16-2	.280	.352	.508	.860	6	.975
2003— Toledo (Int'l)	OF-DH	124	470	74	135	35	6	20	61	32	86	5	12	15-6	.287	.333	.515	.848	6	.977
— Detroit (A.L.)	OF	6	19	1	4	1	0	1	5	1	3	1	0	0-0	.211	.286	.421	.707	2	.882
2004— Las Vegas (PCL)	OF	60	238	44	65	17	2	14	49	18	43	2	11	2-0	.273	.328	.538	.866	3	.500
2005— Los Angeles (N.L.)	OF	14	25	1	4	1	0	0	1	1	10	0	1	0-0	.160	.192	.200	.392	1	.933
— Las Vegas (PCL)	OF	115	393	79	105	21	4	22	63	49	103	2	8	4-2	.267	.348	.509	.857	2	.995
American League totals (1 year)		6	19	1	4	1	0	1	5	1	3	1	0	0-0	.211	.286	.421	.707	2	.882
National League totals (1 year)		14	25	1	4	1	0	0	1	1	10	0	1	0-0	.160	.192	.200	.392	1	.933
Major League totals (2 years)		20	44	2	8	2	0	1	6	2	13	1	1	0-0	.182	.234	.295	.529	3	.906

ROSS, DAVID   C

PERSONAL: Born March 19, 1977, in Bainbridge, Ga. ... 6-2/205. ... Bats right, throws right. ... Full name: David Wade Ross. ... High school: Florida (Tallahassee, Fla.). ... College: Florida.
TRANSACTIONS/CAREER NOTES: Selected by Los Angeles Dodgers organization in 19th round of 1995 free-agent draft; did not sign. ... Selected by Dodgers organization in seventh round of 1998 free-agent draft. ... Traded by Dodgers to Pittsburgh Pirates for cash (March 30, 2005). ... Traded by Pirates to San Diego Padres for IF J.J. Furmaniak (July 28, 2005).
2005 GAMES PLAYED BY POSITION (MLB): C—42.

SCOUTING REPORT Ross has not shown much ability to make adjustments to his long swing. Has a slider-speed bat and likes to extend his arms to hit. Has a lot of holes in his upper-cut stroke and his bat is not in the zone long. Has problems with breaking stuff. Is a better low-ball hitter who has occasional power. Is a good receiver with soft hands and a solid, average arm with good carry. Calls games aggressively and works with his staff. Bat will prevent him from being a regular. **Grade 5.2**

DAVID ROSS'S HITTING ZONE

.000	.167	.000
.391	.368	.263
.211	.500	.000

LEFTY-RIGHTY SPLITS

vs.	Avg.	AB	H	2B	3B	HR	RBI	BB	SO	OBP	Slg.
L	.200	30	6	1	1	0	2	1	2	.242	.300
R	.253	95	24	7	0	3	13	5	26	.291	.421

Year Team (League)	Pos.	G	AB	R	H	2B	3B	HR	RBI	BB	SO	HBP	GDP	SB-CS	Avg.	OBP	SLG	OPS	E	Avg.
1998— Yakima (N'west)	C	59	191	31	59	14	1	6	25	34	49	1	5	2-2	.309	.412	.487	.899	10	.979
1999— Vero Beach (FSL)	C-1B-OF	114	375	47	85	19	1	7	39	46	111	7	10	5-9	.227	.318	.339	.657	16	.979
2000— San Bern. (Calif.)	C	51	191	27	49	11	1	7	21	17	43	1	3	3-2	.257	.319	.435	.754	3	.992
— San Antonio (Texas)	C	24	67	11	14	2	1	3	12	9	17	1	0	1-0	.209	.308	.403	.711	1	.994
2001— Jacksonville (Sou.)	C	74	246	35	65	13	1	11	45	34	72	10	5	1-1	.264	.372	.459	.831	9	.985
2002— Las Vegas (PCL)	C	92	293	48	87	16	2	15	68	35	86	9	4	1-1	.297	.384	.519	.903	7	.989
— Los Angeles (N.L.)	C	8	10	2	2	1	0	1	2	2	1	0	0	0-0	.200	.385	.600	.985	0	1.000
2003— Las Vegas (PCL)	C	24	86	12	19	4	0	5	16	11	27	1	0	0-0	.221	.313	.442	.755	2	.989
— Los Angeles (N.L.)	C	40	124	19	32	7	0	10	18	13	42	2	4	0-0	.258	.336	.556	.892	4	.986
2004— Los Angeles (N.L.)	C	70	165	13	28	3	1	5	15	15	62	5	3	0-0	.170	.253	.291	.544	3	.992
2005— Pittsburgh (N.L.)	C	40	108	9	24	8	0	3	15	6	24	1	3	0-0	.222	.263	.380	.642	3	.986
— Indianapolis (Int'l)	C	6	19	1	4	1	0	0	1	3	7	0	0	0-0	.211	.304	.263	.568	1	.971
— Portland (PCL)	C	6	21	3	3	1	0	0	1	2	4	0	0	0-0	.143	.217	.190	.408	0	1.000
— San Diego (N.L.)	C	11	17	2	6	0	1	0	0	4	11	0	0	0-0	.353	.389	.471	.859	0	1.000
Major League totals (4 years)		169	424	45	92	19	2	19	50	36	136	8	10	0-0	.217	.288	.406	.694	10	.989

DIVISION SERIES RECORD

Year Team (League)	Pos.	G	AB	R	H	2B	3B	HR	RBI	BB	SO	HBP	GDP	SB-CS	Avg.	OBP	SLG	OPS	E	Avg.
2004— Los Angeles (N.L.)	C	2	3	0	0	0	0	0	0	1	0	0	0	0-0	.000	.250	.000	.250	0	.923

ROWAND, AARON   OF

PERSONAL: Born August 29, 1977, in Portland, Ore. ... 6-0/205. ... Bats right, throws right. ... Full name: Aaron Ryan Rowand. ... Name pronounced: ROE-und. ... High school: Glendora (Calif.). ... College: Cal State Fullerton.
TRANSACTIONS/CAREER NOTES: Selected by New York Mets organization in 40th round of 1995 free-agent draft; did not sign. ... Selected by Chicago White Sox organization in supplemental round ("sandwich pick" between first and second rounds, 35th pick overall) of 1998 free-agent draft; pick received as part of compensation for Tampa Bay Devil Rays signing Type A free-agent OF Dave Martinez.
2005 GAMES PLAYED BY POSITION (MLB): OF—157.

SCOUTING REPORT Offense: Rowand has a short, quick bat and is extremely short to the ball on the inside part of the plate. Has an erect stance and tends to hit around the ball. Is a good high-ball hitter on balls out over the plate with plus power. Is a very good runner and is aggressive on the bases. ***Defense:*** Rowand is one of the better defensive center fielders in the league. Has good range and takes precise routes to the ball in the gaps. Goes back well on the ball and has no fear. Has excellent throwing mechanics, gets on top and has very good carry. ***Outlook:*** Rowand, though not a household name, is a fine all-around player. Will continue to get better. **Grade 8**

AARON ROWAND'S HITTING ZONE

.235	.500	.185
.400	.308	.203
.259	.387	.237

LEFTY-RIGHTY SPLITS

vs.	Avg.	AB	H	2B	3B	HR	RBI	BB	SO	OBP	Slg.
L	.303	152	46	9	4	3	20	9	42	.354	.474
R	.258	426	110	21	1	10	49	23	74	.321	.383

Year Team (League)	Pos.	G	AB	R	H	2B	3B	HR	RBI	BB	SO	HBP	GDP	SB-CS	Avg.	OBP	SLG	OPS	E	Avg.
1998— Hickory (S. Atl.)	OF	61	222	42	76	13	3	5	32	21	36	6	5	7-3	.342	.410	.496	.906	3	.966
1999— Win.-Salem (Car.)	OF	133	512	96	143	37	3	24	88	33	94	13	13	15-9	.279	.336	.504	.840	5	.973
2000— Birmingham (Sou.)	OF	139	532	80	137	26	5	20	98	38	117	14	12	22-7	.258	.321	.438	.759	8	.975
2001— Charlotte (Int'l)	OF	82	329	54	97	28	0	16	48	21	47	9	9	8-2	.295	.353	.526	.879	6	.966
— Chicago (A.L.)	OF	63	123	21	36	5	0	4	20	15	28	4	2	5-1	.293	.385	.431	.816	1	.991
2002— Chicago (A.L.)	OF	126	302	41	78	16	2	7	29	12	54	6	8	0-1	.258	.298	.394	.692	4	.983
2003— Charlotte (Int'l)	OF	32	120	15	29	9	0	3	13	11	12	2	3	0-0	.242	.316	.392	.707	5	.950
— Chicago (A.L.)	OF-DH	93	157	22	45	8	0	6	24	7	21	3	1	0-0	.287	.327	.452	.780	1	1.000
2004— Chicago (A.L.)	OF	140	487	94	151	38	2	24	69	30	91	10	5	17-5	.310	.361	.544	.905	8	.975
2005— Chicago (A.L.)	OF	157	578	77	156	30	5	13	69	32	116	21	17	16-5	.270	.329	.407	.736	5	.992
Major League totals (5 years)		579	1647	255	466	97	9	54	211	96	310	44	33	38-12	.283	.337	.451	.788	16	.986

DIVISION SERIES RECORD

Year Team (League)	Pos.	G	AB	R	H	2B	3B	HR	RBI	BB	SO	HBP	GDP	SB-CS	Avg.	OBP	SLG	OPS	E	Avg.
2005— Chicago (A.L.)	OF	3	10	3	4	2	0	0	2	1	1	0	2	1-0	.400	.455	.600	1.055	0	1.000

CHAMPIONSHIP SERIES RECORD

Year Team (League)	Pos.	G	AB	R	H	2B	3B	HR	RBI	BB	SO	HBP	GDP	SB-CS	Avg.	OBP	SLG	OPS	E	Avg.
2005— Chicago (A.L.)	OF	5	18	3	3	0	0	1	1	2	1	1	1	0-0	.167	.238	.333	.571	0	1.000

WORLD SERIES RECORD

Year Team (League)	Pos.	G	AB	R	H	2B	3B	HR	RBI	BB	SO	HBP	GDP	SB-CS	Avg.	OBP	SLG	OPS	E	Avg.
2005— Chicago (A.L.)	OF	4	17	2	5	1	0	0	0	2	6	0	0	0-0	.294	.368	.353	.721	0	1.000

RUETER, KIRK P

PERSONAL: Born December 1, 1970, in Centralia, Ill. ... 6-2/212. ... Throws left, bats left. ... Full name: Kirk Wesley Rueter. ... Name pronounced: REE-ter. ... High school: Nashville (Ill.) Community. ... College: Murray State.

TRANSACTIONS/CAREER NOTES: Selected by Montreal Expos organization in 18th round of 1991 free-agent draft. ... On disabled list (May 10-26, 1996); included rehabilitation assignment to Ottawa. ... Traded by Expos with P Tim Scott to San Francisco Giants for P Mark Leiter (July 30, 1996). ... On disabled list (July 9-25 and July 26-August 24, 2003); included rehabilitation assignment to Fresno. ... On disabled list (July 30-August 14, 2005). ... Released by Giants (August 19, 2005).

HONORS: Named N.L. Rookie Pitcher of the Year by THE SPORTING NEWS (1993).

CAREER HITTING: 95-for-622 (.153), 44 R, 9 2B, 0 3B, 0 HR, 40 RBI.

SCOUTING REPORT *Throws:* He likes to cut his fastball, which is only 83-88 mph normally, so it moves in on righthanders and runs away from lefties. Also uses a curveball and changeup. *Tendencies:* He is unusually aggressive for a finesse pitcher. Uses a three-quarters arm slot, though he occasionally goes sidearm when cutting his fastball. Is very effective with his fastball to both sides of the plate. Sets up his fastball with effective changeups away from righthanders. *Outlook:* Rueter was released late last year, but because lefthanded starters are at a premium, he will go to spring training with an opportunity to win a job. Needs to reestablish the upper velocity range of his fastball. *Grade 6.5*

KIRK RUETER'S PITCHING ZONE

.261	.286	.200
.354	.480	.238
.313	.500	.333

LEFTY-RIGHTY SPLITS

vs.	Avg.	AB	H	2B	3B	HR	RBI	BB	SO	OBP	Slg.
L	.286	112	32	8	1	1	10	15	9	.367	.402
R	.311	318	99	21	3	11	58	32	16	.369	.500

Year Team (League)	W	L	Pct.	ERA	WHIP	G	GS	CG	ShO	Hld.	Sv.-Opp.	IP	H	R	ER	HR	BB-IBB	SO	Avg.
1991— GC Expos (GCL)	1	1	.500	0.95	1.05	5	4	0	0	...	0-...	19.0	16	5	2	0	4-0	19	.232
— Sumter (S. Atl.)	3	1	.750	1.33	1.03	8	5	0	0	...	0-...	40.2	32	8	6	3	10-0	27	.215
1992— Rockford (Midwest)	11	9	.550	2.58	1.07	26	26	6	2	...	0-...	174.1	150	68	50	5	36-2	153	.232
1993— Harrisburg (East.)	5	0	1.000	1.36	0.91	9	8	1	1	...	0-...	59.2	47	10	9	4	7-0	36	.218
— Ottawa (Int'l)	4	2	.667	2.70	1.13	7	7	1	0	...	0-...	43.1	46	20	13	7	3-0	27	.277
— Montreal (N.L.)	8	0	1.000	2.73	1.20	14	14	1	0	0	0-0	85.2	85	33	26	5	18-1	31	.264
1994— Montreal (N.L.)	7	3	.700	5.17	1.40	20	20	0	0	0	0-0	92.1	106	60	53	11	23-1	50	.294
— Ottawa (Int'l)	0	0	...	4.50	0.50	1	1	0	0	...	0-...	2.0	1	1	1	1	0-0	1	.143
1995— Montreal (N.L.)	5	3	.625	3.23	0.99	9	9	1	1	0	0-0	47.1	38	17	17	3	9-0	28	.224
— Ottawa (Int'l)	9	7	.563	3.06	1.20	20	20	3	1	...	0-...	120.2	120	50	41	7	25-0	67	.260
1996— Ottawa (Int'l)	1	2	.333	4.20	1.60	3	3	1	0	...	0-...	15.0	21	7	7	3	3-0	3	.333
— Montreal (N.L.)	5	6	.455	4.58	1.44	16	16	0	0	0	0-0	78.2	91	44	40	12	22-0	30	.295
— San Francisco (N.L.)	1	2	.333	1.93	0.99	4	3	0	0	0	0-0	23.1	18	6	5	0	5-0	16	.207
— Phoenix (PCL)	1	2	.333	3.51	1.44	5	5	0	0	...	0-...	25.2	25	12	10	2	12-0	15	.253
1997— San Francisco (N.L.)	13	6	.684	3.45	1.28	32	32	0	0	0	0-0	190.2	194	83	73	17	51-8	115	.264
1998— San Francisco (N.L.)	16	9	.640	4.36	1.33	33	33	1	0	0	0-0	187.2	193	100	91	27	57-3	102	.265
1999— San Francisco (N.L.)	15	10	.600	5.41	1.48	33	33	1	0	0	0-0	184.2	219	118	111	28	55-2	94	.297
2000— San Francisco (N.L.)	11	9	.550	3.96	1.45	32	31	0	0	0	0-0	184.0	205	92	81	23	62-5	71	.290
2001— San Francisco (N.L.)	14	12	.538	4.42	1.43	34	34	0	0	0	0-0	195.1	213	105	96	25	66-4	83	.283
2002— San Francisco (N.L.)	14	8	.636	3.23	1.27	33	33	0	0	0	0-0	203.2	204	83	73	22	54-7	76	.262
2003— Fresno (PCL)	0	0	...	0.00	0.60	1	1	0	0	0	0-...	4.2	1	0	0	0	2-0	6	.071
— San Francisco (N.L.)	10	5	.667	4.53	1.48	27	27	0	0	0	0-0	147.0	170	77	74	14	47-2	41	.297
2004— San Francisco (N.L.)	9	12	.429	4.73	1.53	33	33	0	0	0	0-0	190.1	225	108	100	21	66-5	56	.296
2005— San Francisco (N.L.)	2	7	.222	5.95	1.66	20	18	0	0	0	0-0	107.1	131	78	71	14	47-3	25	.305
Major League totals (13 years)	**130**	**92**	**.586**	**4.27**	**1.39**	**340**	**336**	**4**	**1**	**0**	**0-0**	**1918.0**	**2092**	**1004**	**911**	**220**	**582-41**	**818**	**.281**

DIVISION SERIES RECORD

Year Team (League)	W	L	Pct.	ERA	WHIP	G	GS	CG	ShO	Hld.	Sv.-Opp.	IP	H	R	ER	HR	BB-IBB	SO	Avg.
1997— San Francisco (N.L.)	0	0	...	1.29	1.00	1	1	0	0	0	0-0	7.0	4	1	1	1	3-0	5	.160
2000— San Francisco (N.L.)	0	0	...	0.00	0.92	1	0	0	0	0	0-0	4.1	3	0	0	0	1-0	1	.200
2002— San Francisco (N.L.)	0	1	.000	18.00	3.00	1	1	0	0	0	0-0	3.0	7	7	6	2	2-0	1	.500
2003— San Francisco (N.L.)	0	0	...	3.60	1.00	1	1	0	0	0	0-0	5.0	3	2	2	1	2-0	2	.167
Division series totals (4 years)	**0**	**1**	**.000**	**4.19**	**1.29**	**4**	**3**	**0**	**0**	**0**	**0-0**	**19.1**	**17**	**10**	**9**	**4**	**8-0**	**9**	**.236**

CHAMPIONSHIP SERIES RECORD

Year Team (League)	W	L	Pct.	ERA	WHIP	G	GS	CG	ShO	Hld.	Sv.-Opp.	IP	H	R	ER	HR	BB-IBB	SO	Avg.
2002— San Francisco (N.L.)	1	0	1.000	4.09	1.55	2	2	0	0	0	0-0	11.0	15	5	5	2	2-0	3	.326

WORLD SERIES RECORD

Year Team (League)	W	L	Pct.	ERA	WHIP	G	GS	CG	ShO	Hld.	Sv.-Opp.	IP	H	R	ER	HR	BB-IBB	SO	Avg.
2002— San Francisco (N.L.)	0	0	...	2.70	1.10	2	1	0	0	0	0-0	10.0	10	3	3	1	1-0	5	.263

RUPE, JOSH P

PERSONAL: Born August 18, 1982, in Portsmouth, Va. ... 6-2/200. ... Throws right, bats right. ... Full name: Joshua Matthew Rupe. ... Junior college: Louisburg (NC).

TRANSACTIONS/CAREER NOTES: Selected by Chicago White Sox organization in third round of 2002 free-agent draft. ... Traded by White Sox with OF Anthony Webster and P Frank Francisco to Texas Rangers (July 24, 2003); completed deal in which Rangers sent OF Carl Everett and cash to White Sox for three players to be named (July 1, 2003).

CAREER HITTING: 0-for-0 (.000), 0 R, 0 2B, 0 3B, 0 HR, 0 RBI.

LEFTY-RIGHTY SPLITS

vs.	Avg.	AB	H	2B	3B	HR	RBI	BB	SO	OBP	Slg.
L	.333	18	6	1	0	0	1	4	3	.478	.389
R	.071	14	1	0	0	0	0	2	3	.133	.071

Year Team (League)	W	L	Pct.	ERA	WHIP	G	GS	CG	ShO	Hld.	Sv.-Opp.	IP	H	R	ER	HR	BB-IBB	SO	Avg.
2002— Bristol (Appal.)	3	3	.500	5.26	1.59	17	2	0	0	0	0-...	37.2	38	23	22	4	22-1	40	.260

Year Team (League)	W	L	Pct.	ERA	WHIP	G	GS	CG	ShO	Hld.	Sv.-Opp.	IP	H	R	ER	HR	BB-IBB	SO	Avg.
2003— Kannapolis (S. Atl.)	5	5	.500	3.02	1.31	26	7	2	0	...	6-...	65.2	50	27	22	0	36-2	69	.212
— Clinton (Midw.)	4	1	.800	3.90	1.30	6	5	0	0	...	0-...	27.2	29	14	12	1	7-0	23	.266
2004— Stockton (Calif.)	2	0	1.000	0.98	0.87	4	3	0	0	...	0-...	18.1	12	4	2	0	4-0	14	.182
— Spokane (N'west)	2	0	1.000	1.50	0.94	4	3	0	0	...	0-...	18.0	14	3	3	1	3-0	19	.209
— Frisco (Texas)	2	2	.500	4.38	1.54	7	6	0	0	...	0-...	37.0	41	23	18	5	16-1	16	.281
2005— Frisco (Texas)	4	3	.571	3.74	1.38	11	10	0	0	0	0-0	65.0	64	29	27	7	26-0	55	.261
— Oklahoma (PCL)	6	7	.462	6.25	1.64	17	17	0	0	0	0-0	93.2	116	75	65	12	38-1	62	.306
— Texas (A.L.)	1	0	1.000	2.79	1.14	4	1	0	0	0	0-0	9.2	7	4	3	0	4-0	6	.219
Major League totals (1 year)	1	0	1.000	2.79	1.14	4	1	0	0	0	0-0	9.2	7	4	3	0	4-0	6	.219

RUSCH, GLENDON — P

PERSONAL: Born November 7, 1974, in Seattle. ... 6-1/220. ... Throws left, bats left. ... Full name: Glendon James Rusch. ... Name pronounced: RUSH. ... High school: Shorecrest (Seattle).

TRANSACTIONS/CAREER NOTES: Selected by Kansas City Royals organization in 17th round of 1993 free-agent draft. ... On disabled list (June 16-July 1, 1997); included rehabilitation assignment to Omaha. ... On disabled list (August 9-September 4, 1998); included rehabilitation assignment to Omaha. ... Traded by Royals to New York Mets for P Dan Murray (September 14, 1999). ... Traded by Mets with IF Lenny Harris to Milwaukee Brewers as part of three-team deal in which Brewers acquired OF Alex Ochoa from Colorado Rockies, Mets acquired P Jeff D'Amico, OF Jeromy Burnitz, IF Lou Collier, OF/1B Mark Sweeney from Brewers and 1B/OF Ross Gload and P Craig House from Rockies and Rockies acquired 1B/3B Todd Zeile, OF Benny Agbayani and cash from Mets (January 21, 2002). ... Signed as a free agent by Texas Rangers organization (January 21, 2004). ... Signed as a free agent by Chicago Cubs organization (April 1, 2004).

CAREER HITTING: 44-for-290 (.152), 15 R, 3 2B, 0 3B, 3 HR, 19 RBI.

SCOUTING REPORT **Throws:** He has an 86-91 mph fastball, a 71-74 curveball and a changeup. **Tendencies:** Rusch continually changes his release point, depending on the count, against lefthanded hitters. Has good life on his fastball, which he can tail away from righthanded hitters or cut so it runs inside. Likes to start hitters out with breaking stuff to set up his fastball. Has good motion and arm speed with a straight changeup. Is effective pitching to lefthanders. **Outlook:** He's a valuable spot starter and long reliever who has a good idea of how to pitch. **Grade 6.4**

GLENDON RUSCH'S PITCHING ZONE

.361	.480	.233
.317	.296	.281
.270	.529	.256

LEFTY-RIGHTY SPLITS

vs.	Avg.	AB	H	2B	3B	HR	RBI	BB	SO	OBP	Slg.
L	.333	117	39	12	1	5	20	3	20	.341	.581
R	.294	462	136	21	4	9	49	50	91	.360	.416

Year Team (League)	W	L	Pct.	ERA	WHIP	G	GS	CG	ShO	Hld.	Sv.-Opp.	IP	H	R	ER	HR	BB-IBB	SO	Avg.
1993— GC Royals (GCL)	4	2	.667	1.60	0.87	11	10	0	0	...	0-...	62.0	43	14	11	0	11-0	48	.197
— Rockford (Midwest)	0	1	.000	3.38	2.13	2	2	0	0	...	0-...	8.0	10	6	3	0	7-0	8	.313
1994— Rockford (Midwest)	8	5	.615	4.66	1.27	28	17	1	1	...	1-...	114.0	111	61	59	5	34-2	122	.256
1995— Wilmington (Caro.)	14	6	.700	1.74	0.87	26	26	1	1	...	0-...	165.2	110	41	32	5	34-3	147	.188
1996— Omaha (A.A.)	11	9	.550	3.98	1.28	28	28	1	0	...	0-...	169.2	177	88	75	15	40-3	117	.267
1997— Kansas City (A.L.)	6	9	.400	5.50	1.51	30	27	1	0	0	0-0	170.1	206	111	104	28	52-0	116	.301
— Omaha (A.A.)	0	1	.000	4.50	1.33	1	1	0	0	...	0-...	6.0	7	3	3	3	1-0	2	.292
1998— Kansas City (A.L.)	6	15	.286	5.88	1.56	29	24	1	1	0	1-1	154.2	191	104	101	22	50-0	94	.304
— Omaha (PCL)	1	1	.500	7.98	1.77	3	3	0	0	...	0-...	14.2	20	18	13	4	6-0	14	.317
1999— Omaha (PCL)	4	7	.364	4.42	1.54	20	20	1	0	...	0-...	114.0	143	68	56	10	33-0	102	.307
— GC Royals (GCL)	0	0	...	1.50	1.00	2	2	0	0	...	0-...	6.0	3	1	1	0	3-0	9	.136
— Kansas City (A.L.)	0	1	.000	15.75	2.50	3	0	0	0	0	0-0	4.0	7	7	7	1	3-0	4	.368
— New York (N.L.)	0	0	...	0.00	1.00	1	0	0	0	0	0-0	1.0	1	0	0	0	0-0	0	.333
2000— New York (N.L.)	11	11	.500	4.01	1.26	31	30	2	0	0	0-0	190.2	196	91	85	18	44-2	157	.267
2001— New York (N.L.)	8	12	.400	4.63	1.45	33	33	1	0	0	0-0	179.0	216	101	92	23	43-2	156	.301
2002— Milwaukee (N.L.)	10	• 16	.385	4.70	1.44	34	34	4	1	0	0-0	210.2	227	118	110	30	76-1	140	.279
2003— Indianapolis (Int'l)	1	1	.500	3.86	1.00	4	4	0	0	...	0-...	21.0	17	9	9	4	4-0	20	.218
— Milwaukee (N.L.)	1	12	.077	6.42	1.75	32	19	1	0	7	1-1	123.1	171	93	88	11	45-3	93	.331
2004— Iowa (PCL)	2	0	1.000	1.90	1.00	4	4	0	0	...	0-...	19.0	18	6	4	0	1-0	16	.257
— Chicago (N.L.)	6	2	.750	3.47	1.23	32	16	0	0	3	2-2	129.2	127	54	50	10	33-1	90	.256
2005— Chicago (N.L.)	9	8	.529	4.52	1.57	46	19	1	1	3	0-1	145.1	175	79	73	14	53-8	111	.302
American League totals (3 years)	12	25	.324	5.80	1.55	62	51	2	1	0	1-1	329.0	404	222	212	51	105-0	214	.303
National League totals (7 years)	45	61	.425	4.58	1.44	209	151	9	2	13	3-4	979.2	1113	536	498	106	294-17	747	.288
Major League totals (9 years)	57	86	.399	4.88	1.46	271	202	11	3	13	4-5	1308.2	1517	758	710	157	399-17	961	.292

DIVISION SERIES RECORD

Year Team (League)	W	L	Pct.	ERA	WHIP	G	GS	CG	ShO	Hld.	Sv.-Opp.	IP	H	R	ER	HR	BB-IBB	SO	Avg.
2000— New York (N.L.)	0	0	...	0.00	0.00	1	0	0	0	0	0-0	0.2	0	0	0	0	0-0	2	.000

CHAMPIONSHIP SERIES RECORD

Year Team (League)	W	L	Pct.	ERA	WHIP	G	GS	CG	ShO	Hld.	Sv.-Opp.	IP	H	R	ER	HR	BB-IBB	SO	Avg.
2000— New York (N.L.)	1	0	1.000	0.00	0.82	2	0	0	0	0	0-0	3.2	3	0	0	0	0-0	3	.250

WORLD SERIES RECORD

Year Team (League)	W	L	Pct.	ERA	WHIP	G	GS	CG	ShO	Hld.	Sv.-Opp.	IP	H	R	ER	HR	BB-IBB	SO	Avg.
2000— New York (N.L.)	0	0	...	2.25	2.00	3	0	0	0	0	0-0	4.0	6	1	1	0	2-1	2	.353

RYAN, B.J. — P

PERSONAL: Born December 28, 1975, in Bossier City, La. ... 6-6/249. ... Throws left, bats left. ... Full name: Robert Victor Ryan. ... High school: Airline (Bossier City, La.). ... College: Southwestern Louisiana.

TRANSACTIONS/CAREER NOTES: Selected by Cincinnati Reds organization in 17th round of 1998 free-agent draft. ... Traded by Reds with P Jacobo Sequea to Baltimore Orioles for P Juan Guzman (July 31, 1999). ...

CAREER HITTING: 0-for-2 (.000), 0 R, 0 2B, 0 3B, 0 HR, 0 RBI.

SCOUTING REPORT **Throws:** His fastball will range from 91-96 mph and his slider from 85-88. **Tendencies:** Ryan has an extreme herky-jerky delivery and is a slinger who is able to stay in sync with frequent work. Throws an extremely heavy running fastball, which has exceptional life up and down in the zone. Slider has excellent bite and runs away from lefthanders. Can be almost unhittable against lefties, who have trouble hanging tough when he occasionally drops down and gives the appearance he is starting the ball behind them. Has really improved his command. **Outlook:** Ryan moved into the closer's role at the beginning of last season and pitched exceptionally well. Has the stuff to save 40 games pitching for a better club. **Grade 9**

B.J. RYAN'S PITCHING ZONE

.222	.000	.154
.214	.367	.213
.333	.250	.286

LEFTY-RIGHTY SPLITS

vs.	Avg.	AB	H	2B	3B	HR	RBI	BB	SO	OBP	Slg.
L	.211	71	15	2	1	2	11	6	27	.288	.352
R	.206	189	39	5	0	2	11	20	73	.282	.265

Year	Team (League)	W	L	Pct.	ERA	WHIP	G	GS	CG	ShO	Hld.	Sv.-Opp.	IP	H	R	ER	HR	BB-IBB	SO	Avg.
1998—	Billings (Pion.)	2	1	.667	1.93	1.07	14	0	0	0	...	4-...	18.2	15	4	4	0	5-0	25	.211
—Char., W.Va. (SAL)		0	0	...	2.08	0.46	3	0	0	0	...	2-...	4.1	1	1	1	0	1-0	5	.077
—Chattanooga (Sou.)		1	0	1.000	2.20	1.16	16	0	0	0	...	4-...	16.1	13	4	4	0	6-0	21	.220
1999—	Chattanooga (Sou.)	2	1	.667	2.59	1.20	35	0	0	0	...	6-...	41.2	33	13	12	1	17-0	46	.217
—Indianapolis (Int'l)		1	0	1.000	4.00	1.33	11	0	0	0	...	0-...	9.0	9	4	4	0	3-1	12	.265
—Cincinnati (N.L.)		0	0	...	4.50	2.50	1	0	0	0	0	0-0	2.0	4	1	1	0	1-0	1	.500
—Rochester (Int'l)		0	0	...	2.51	0.84	11	0	0	0	0	1-...	14.1	8	4	4	2	4-1	20	.160
—Baltimore (A.L.)		1	0	1.000	2.95	1.15	13	0	0	0	0	0-0	18.1	9	6	6	0	12-1	28	.150
2000—	Baltimore (A.L.)	2	3	.400	5.91	1.57	42	0	0	0	7	0-3	42.2	36	29	28	7	31-1	41	.225
—Rochester (Int'l)		0	1	.000	4.74	1.30	14	4	0	0	...	0-...	24.2	23	13	13	4	9-0	28	.247
2001—	Baltimore (A.L.)	2	4	.333	4.25	1.45	61	0	0	0	14	2-4	53.0	47	31	25	6	30-4	54	.235
2002—	Baltimore (A.L.)	2	1	.667	4.68	1.46	67	0	0	0	12	1-2	57.2	51	31	30	7	33-4	56	.241
2003—	Baltimore (A.L.)	4	1	.800	3.40	1.37	76	0	0	0	19	0-2	50.1	42	19	19	1	27-0	63	.227
2004—	Baltimore (A.L.)	4	6	.400	2.28	1.14	76	0	0	0	21	3-7	87.0	64	24	22	4	35-9	122	.208
2005—	Baltimore (A.L.)	1	4	.200	2.43	1.14	69	0	0	0	0	36-41	70.1	54	20	19	4	26-2	100	.208
American League totals (7 years)		16	19	.457	3.54	1.31	404	0	0	0	73	42-59	379.1	303	160	149	29	194-21	464	.217
National League totals (1 year)		0	0	...	4.50	2.50	1	0	0	0	0	0-0	2.0	4	1	1	0	1-0	1	.500
Major League totals (7 years)		16	19	.457	3.54	1.32	405	0	0	0	73	42-59	381.1	307	161	150	29	195-21	465	.218

ALL-STAR GAME RECORD

	W	L	Pct.	ERA	WHIP	G	GS	CG	ShO	Hld.	Sv.-Opp.	IP	H	R	ER	HR	BB-IBB	SO	Avg.
All-Star Game totals (1 year)	0	0	...	13.50	1.50	1	0	0	0	...	0-0	0.2	1	1	1	0	0-0	0	.333

RYAN, MICHAEL — OF

PERSONAL: Born July 6, 1977, in Indiana, Pa. ... 6-0/193. ... Bats left, throws right. ... Full name: Michael Sean Ryan. ... High school: Indiana (Pa.).
TRANSACTIONS/CAREER NOTES: Selected by Minnesota Twins organization in fifth round of 1996 free-agent draft. ... On disabled list (June 14-July 20, 2004); included rehabilitation assignment to Rochester.
2005 GAMES PLAYED BY POSITION (MLB): OF—25, DH—13, 3B—1.

MICHAEL RYAN'S HITTING ZONE

.000	.333	.500
.000	.182	.393
.000	.667	.250

LEFTY-RIGHTY SPLITS

vs.	Avg.	AB	H	2B	3B	HR	RBI	BB	SO	OBP	Slg.
L	.167	6	1	0	0	0	0	1	3	.286	.167
R	.234	111	26	5	0	2	13	8	19	.283	.333

Year	Team (League)	Pos.	G	AB	R	H	2B	3B	HR	RBI	BB	SO	HBP	GDP	SB-CS	Avg.	OBP	SLG	OPS	E	Avg.
1996—	GC Twins (GCL)	3B	43	157	12	31	8	2	0	13	13	20	1	3	3-0	.197	.260	.274	.534	10	.910
1997—	Elizabethton (App.)	3B	62	220	44	66	10	4	3	29	38	39	3	8	2-2	.300	.404	.386	.790	28	.825
1998—	Fort Wayne (Midw.)	3B-1B	113	412	68	131	24	6	9	72	44	92	2	8	7-3	.318	.382	.471	.853	33	.906
1999—	Fort Myers (FSL)	2B	131	507	85	139	26	5	8	71	63	60	5	11	3-4	.274	.356	.393	.749	35	.949
2000—	New Britain (East.)	OF-2B	122	481	64	133	23	8	11	69	34	79	2	13	4-3	.277	.323	.428	.749	9	.965
—Salt Lake (PCL)		OF	3	9	1	2	0	0	0	2	3	2	0	1	0-0	.222	.417	.222	.639	1	1.000
2001—	Edmonton (PCL)	OF-2B	135	527	89	152	36	7	18	73	52	121	2	17	1-6	.288	.353	.486	.839	11	.966
2002—	Edmonton (PCL)	OF	131	540	92	141	36	6	31	101	55	124	2	9	4-5	.261	.330	.522	.852	3	.987
—Minnesota (A.L.)		OF-DH	7	11	3	1	0	0	0	0	0	2	0	0	0-0	.091	.091	.091	.182	0	1.000
2003—	Rochester (Int'l)	OF-DH	115	408	56	92	20	4	15	60	38	89	1	8	6-1	.225	.289	.404	.694	2	.988
—Minnesota (A.L.)		OF-DH	27	61	13	24	7	0	5	13	6	12	0	4	2-1	.393	.441	1.195	1.195	0	1.000
2004—	Minnesota (A.L.)	OF-DH	36	71	9	17	2	1	0	7	4	16	0	2	1-1	.239	.280	.296	.576	1	.947
—Rochester (Int'l)		OF-DH	50	175	29	37	7	1	6	16	16	38	1	3	3-4	.211	.281	.366	.647	1	.987
2005—	Rochester (Int'l)	OF-DH	46	152	16	43	7	1	6	26	15	34	0	4	0-3	.283	.343	.461	.804	0	1.000
—Minnesota (A.L.)		OF-DH-3B	57	117	7	27	5	0	2	13	9	22	0	5	1-2	.231	.283	.325	.608	1	1.000
Major League totals (4 years)			127	260	32	69	14	1	7	33	19	52	0	11	4-4	.265	.313	.408	.721	1	.989

DIVISION SERIES RECORD

Year	Team (League)	Pos.	G	AB	R	H	2B	3B	HR	RBI	BB	SO	HBP	GDP	SB-CS	Avg.	OBP	SLG	OPS	E	Avg.
2003—	Minnesota (A.L.)	PH	1	1	0	0	0	0	0	0	0	1	0	0	0-0	.000	.000	.000	.000		...

SAARLOOS, KIRK — P

PERSONAL: Born May 23, 1979, in Long Beach, Calif. ... 6-0/180. ... Throws right, bats right. ... Full name: Kirk Craig Saarloos. ... Name pronounced: SAR-lohs. ... High school: Valley Christian (Cerritos, Calif.). ... College: Cal State Fullerton.
TRANSACTIONS/CAREER NOTES: Selected by Houston Astros organization in third round of 2001 free-agent draft. ... Traded by Astros to Oakland Athletics for P Chad Harville (April 17, 2004). ... On disabled list (July 30, 2004-remainder of season).
CAREER HITTING: 2-for-36 (.056), 0 R, 1 2B, 0 3B, 0 HR, 3 RBI.

S

SCOUTING REPORT *Throws:* Saarloos' fastball is below average at 83-86 mph. Also has a slider and changeup. *Tendencies:* Changing speeds and deception are the keys to Saarloos' success. Has a very fast windup. Has a plus change that he will throw on any count; hitters, however, don't respect his fastball and they can sit on the change. Slider isn't very sharp. Improved his control and became more aggressive last season, which helped him get through the order more than once. *Outlook:* Saarloos worked his way into the fifth starter's role with the A's last season. Can work in relief, too. *Grade 6.3*

KIRK SAARLOOS'S PITCHING ZONE

.278	.333	.357
.375	.250	.323
.182	.235	.259

LEFTY-RIGHTY SPLITS

vs.	Avg.	AB	H	2B	3B	HR	RBI	BB	SO	OBP	Slg.
L	.304	322	98	14	2	4	25	34	27	.377	.398
R	.249	289	72	16	1	7	38	20	26	.311	.384

Year	Team (League)	W	L	Pct.	ERA	WHIP	G	GS	CG	ShO	Hld.	Sv.-Opp.	IP	H	R	ER	HR	BB-IBB	SO	Avg.
2001—	Lexington (S. Atl.)	1	1	.500	1.17	0.82	22	0	0	0	...	11-...	30.2	18	5	4	1	7-0	40	.165
2002—	Round Rock (Texas)	10	1	.909	1.40	0.83	13	13	1	1	...	0-...	83.1	48	17	13	1	21-0	82	.168
—	New Orleans (PCL)	2	0	1.000	2.25	0.88	4	2	0	0	...	0-...	16.0	12	4	4	1	2-0	19	.211
—	Houston (N.L.)	6	7	.462	6.01	1.49	17	17	1	1	0	0-0	85.1	100	59	57	12	27-5	54	.301
2003—	New Orleans (PCL)	5	0	1.000	3.08	1.10	13	7	2	1	0	0-0	61.1	54	22	21	4	11-1	34	.242
—	Houston (N.L.)	2	1	.667	4.93	1.46	36	4	0	0	4	0-0	49.1	55	31	27	4	17-3	43	.281
2004—	New Orleans (PCL)	0	2	.000	15.43	2.57	2	2	0	0	...	0-...	7.0	17	15	12	4	1-0	6	.447
—	Oakland (A.L.)	2	1	.667	4.44	1.60	6	5	0	0	0	0-0	24.1	27	13	12	4	12-0	10	.284
—	Sacramento (PCL)	2	0	1.000	3.54	1.38	5	5	0	0	0	0-0	20.1	19	8	8	1	9-0	17	.250
2005—	Oakland (A.L.)	10	9	.526	4.17	1.40	29	27	2	1	0	0-0	159.2	170	75	74	11	54-8	53	.278
	American League totals (2 years)	12	10	.545	4.21	1.43	35	32	2	1	0	0-0	184.0	197	88	86	15	66-8	63	.279
	National League totals (2 years)	8	8	.500	5.61	1.48	53	21	1	1	4	0-0	134.2	155	90	84	16	44-8	97	.294
	Major League totals (4 years)	20	18	.526	4.80	1.45	88	53	3	2	4	0-0	318.2	352	178	170	31	110-16	160	.285

SABATHIA, C.C.   P

PERSONAL: Born July 21, 1980, in Vallejo, Calif. ... 6-7/290. ... Throws left, bats left. ... Full name: Carsten Charles Sabathia. ... Name pronounced: sa-BATH-ee-a. ... High school: Vallejo (Calif.).

TRANSACTIONS/CAREER NOTES: Selected by Cleveland Indians organization in first round (20th pick overall) of 1998 free-agent draft. ... On disabled list (March 25-April 16, 2005).

HONORS: Named A.L. Rookie Pitcher of the Year by THE SPORTING NEWS (2001).

CAREER HITTING: 7-for-25 (.280), 2 R, 1 2B, 0 3B, 1 HR, 4 RBI.

SCOUTING REPORT *Throws:* He throws a 93-98 mph fastball, a 78-82 curve and a changeup. *Tendencies:* Sabathia has good command of his fastball and will run his four-seamer in and out to righthanded hitters. Has a sweeping curveball with good biting action and rotation. Has improved his changeup and will sink it to righthanders. Is an intimidating presence against lefthanders. Is athletic and a good fielder for his size. *Outlook:* Sabathia has overpowering stuff and is maturing into a dependable starter. Is able to control his weight and has become Cleveland's ace. *Grade 9*

C.C. SABATHIA'S PITCHING ZONE

.256	.294	.220
.262	.436	.315
.183	.203	.200

LEFTY-RIGHTY SPLITS

vs.	Avg.	AB	H	2B	3B	HR	RBI	BB	SO	OBP	Slg.
L	.248	109	27	5	0	4	16	13	34	.325	.404
R	.248	636	158	31	0	15	68	49	127	.308	.368

Year	Team (League)	W	L	Pct.	ERA	WHIP	G	GS	CG	ShO	Hld.	Sv.-Opp.	IP	H	R	ER	HR	BB-IBB	SO	Avg.
1998—	Burlington (Appal.)	1	0	1.000	4.50	1.56	5	5	0	0	...	0-...	18.0	20	14	9	1	8-0	35	.274
1999—	Mahoning Valley (N.Y.-Penn.)	0	0	...	1.83	1.07	6	6	0	0	...	0-...	19.2	9	5	4	0	12-0	27	.143
—	Columbus (S. Atl.)	2	0	1.000	1.08	0.78	3	3	0	0	...	0-...	16.2	8	2	2	1	5-0	20	.140
—	Kinston (Carol.)	3	3	.500	5.34	1.53	7	7	0	0	...	0-...	32.0	30	22	19	3	19-0	29	.256
2000—	Kinston (Carol.)	3	2	.600	3.54	1.29	10	10	2	2	...	0-...	56.0	48	23	22	4	24-0	69	.234
—	Akron (East.)	3	7	.300	3.59	1.36	17	17	0	0	...	0-...	90.1	75	41	36	6	48-0	90	.223
2001—	Cleveland (A.L.)	17	5	.773	4.39	1.35	33	33	0	0	0	0-0	180.1	149	93	88	19	95-1	171	.228
2002—	Cleveland (A.L.)	13	11	.542	4.37	1.36	33	33	2	0	0	0-0	210.0	198	109	102	17	88-2	149	.252
2003—	Cleveland (A.L.)	13	9	.591	3.60	1.30	30	30	2	1	0	0-0	197.2	190	85	79	19	66-3	141	.255
2004—	Cleveland (A.L.)	11	10	.524	4.12	1.32	30	30	1	1	0	0-0	188.0	176	90	86	20	72-3	139	.252
2005—	Akron (East.)	0	1	.000	1.00	0.67	2	2	0	0	0	0-0	9.0	4	3	1	0	2-0	9	.121
—	Cleveland (A.L.)	15	10	.600	4.03	1.26	31	31	1	0	0	0-0	196.2	185	92	88	19	62-1	161	.248
	Major League totals (5 years)	69	45	.605	4.10	1.32	157	157	6	2	0	0-0	972.2	898	469	443	94	383-10	761	.247

DIVISION SERIES RECORD

Year	Team (League)	W	L	Pct.	ERA	WHIP	G	GS	CG	ShO	Hld.	Sv.-Opp.	IP	H	R	ER	HR	BB-IBB	SO	Avg.
2001—	Cleveland (A.L.)	1	0	1.000	3.00	1.83	1	1	0	0	0	0-0	6.0	6	2	2	0	5-1	5	.261

ALL-STAR GAME RECORD

		W	L	Pct.	ERA	WHIP	G	GS	CG	ShO	Hld.	Sv.-Opp.	IP	H	R	ER	HR	BB-IBB	SO	Avg.
	All-Star Game totals (1 year)	0	0	...	27.00	4.00	1	0	0	0	0	0-0	1.0	4	3	3	0	0-0	0	.571

SADLER, RAY   OF

PERSONAL: Born September 19, 1980, in Clifton, Texas. ... 6-1/200. ... Bats right, throws right. ... Full name: Raymond Lee Sadler. ... Junior college: Hill (Texas).

TRANSACTIONS/CAREER NOTES: Selected by Chicago Cubs organization in 30th round of 1999 free-agent draft. ... Traded by Cubs to Pittsburgh Pirates for 1B Randall Simon (August 17, 2003).

2005 GAMES PLAYED BY POSITION (MLB): OF—3.

LEFTY-RIGHTY SPLITS

vs.	Avg.	AB	H	2B	3B	HR	RBI	BB	SO	OBP	Slg.
L	.167	6	1	0	0	1	1	0	0	.167	.667
R	.500	2	1	0	0	0	0	0	1	.500	.500

Year Team (League)	Pos.	G	AB	R	H	2B	3B	HR	RBI	BB	SO	HBP	GDP	SB-CS	Avg.	OBP	SLG	OPS	E	Avg.
2000— Ariz. Cubs (Ariz.)	OF	42	165	32	56	5	5	1	27	16	27	1	1	4-3	.339	.395	.448	.843	1	.988
2001— Lansing (Midw.)	OF	94	378	74	129	27	3	10	50	22	58	3	3	18-7	.341	.378	.508	.886	9	.942
2002— Daytona (Fla. St.)	OF	112	462	81	132	31	1	11	47	27	91	6	7	30-12	.286	.333	.429	.762	7	.971
— West Tenn (Sou.)	OF	10	30	4	2	1	0	0	1	5	5	3	3	2-0	.067	.263	.100	.363	0	1.000
2003— West Tenn (Sou.)	OF	110	412	56	120	31	5	6	42	33	81	7	8	17-7	.291	.352	.434	.786	3	.988
— Altoona (East.)	OF	14	53	8	14	5	0	1	7	3	16	1	0	0-0	.264	.310	.415	.725	0	1.000
2004— Altoona (East.)	OF	120	429	61	115	25	1	20	72	23	89	3	6	16-6	.268	.307	.471	.778	6	.769
2005— Pittsburgh (N.L.)	OF	3	8	1	2	0	0	1	1	0	1	0	0	0-0	.250	.250	.625	.875	0	1.000
— Altoona (East.)	OF-DH	62	209	23	51	17	2	5	23	17	54	0	4	4-4	.244	.301	.416	.717	6	.970
— Indianapolis (Int'l)	OF	69	251	28	65	9	1	10	30	15	57	5	5	8-6	.259	.310	.422	.733	6	.980
Major League totals (1 year)		3	8	1	2	0	0	1	1	0	1	0	0	0-0	.250	.250	.625	.875	0	1.000

SAENZ, OLMEDO   1B

PERSONAL: Born October 8, 1970, in Chitre Herrera, Panama. ... 5-11/221. ... Bats right, throws right. ... Full name: Olmedo Sanchez Saenz. ... Name pronounced: SIGNS.
TRANSACTIONS/CAREER NOTES: Signed as a non-drafted free agent by Chicago White Sox organization (May 11, 1990). ... Signed as a free agent by Oakland Athletics (November 13, 1998). ... On disabled list (July 26-August 16, 1999); included rehabilitation assignment to Vancouver. ... On disabled list (August 1-September 19, 2000); included rehabilitation assignment to Sacramento. ... Signed as a free agent by Los Angeles Dodgers organization (December 19, 2003).
2005 GAMES PLAYED BY POSITION (MLB): 1B—66, 3B—17, DH—8.

SCOUTING REPORT *Offense:* Saenz is a quality professional hitter with a good stroke. Can handle both the fastball and breaking ball and is effective using the whole field. Has power with the ball up and is a productive hitter with runners in scoring position. *Defense:* Leg problems restrict his lower-body quickness and agility, making him better suited to play first. Hands are average but range is not. *Outlook:* He is a good role player with a special tool: the ability to come off the bench and hit in clutch situations. Must be used wisely as he can be overextended. *Grade 6.6*

OLMEDO SAENZ'S HITTING ZONE

.476	.400	.286
.278	.370	.262
.143	.467	.133

LEFTY-RIGHTY SPLITS

vs.	Avg.	AB	H	2B	3B	HR	RBI	BB	SO	OBP	Slg.
L	.261	115	30	9	0	8	26	13	16	.338	.548
R	.265	204	54	15	0	7	37	14	47	.317	.441

Year Team (League)	Pos.	G	AB	R	H	2B	3B	HR	RBI	BB	SO	HBP	GDP	SB-CS	Avg.	OBP	SLG	OPS	E	Avg.
1991— South Bend (Mid.)	3B	56	192	23	47	10	1	2	22	21	48	5	3	5-3	.245	.332	.339	.670	12	.890
— Sarasota (Fla. St.)	3B	5	19	1	2	0	1	0	2	2	0	0	1	0-1	.105	.190	.211	.401	3	.842
1992— South Bend (Mid.)	1B-3B	132	493	66	121	26	4	7	59	36	52	11	16	16-13	.245	.309	.357	.666	48	.895
1993— Sarasota (Fla. St.)	3B	33	121	13	31	9	4	0	27	9	18	2	1	3-1	.256	.316	.397	.712	5	.933
— South Bend (Mid.)	3B	13	50	3	18	4	1	0	7	7	7	0	1	1-1	.360	.439	.480	.919	4	.913
— Birmingham (Sou.)	3B	49	173	30	60	17	2	6	29	20	21	5	7	2-1	.347	.427	.572	.999	14	.899
1994— Nashville (A.A.)	3B-DH	107	383	48	100	27	2	12	59	30	57	9	5	3-2	.261	.326	.436	.762	22	.917
— Chicago (A.L.)	3B	5	14	2	2	0	1	0	0	0	5	0	1	0-0	.143	.143	.286	.429	0	1.000
1995— Nashville (A.A.)	3B	111	415	60	126	26	1	13	74	45	60	12	11	0-2	.304	.385	.465	.850	24	.939
1996— Nashville (A.A.)	3B-DH	134	476	86	124	29	1	18	63	53	80	13	5	4-2	.261	.350	.439	.789	22	.939
1997— GC Whi. Sox (GCL)	DH	2	1	0	1	0	0	0	0	0	1	0	0	0-0	1.000	1.000	2.000	3.000	...	...
1998— Calgary (PCL)	3B-DH	124	466	89	146	29	0	29	102	45	49	22	16	3-3	.313	.394	.562	.957	21	.937
1999— Oakland (A.L.) 3B-1B-DH		97	255	41	70	18	0	11	41	22	47	15	6	1-1	.275	.363	.475	.837	8	.971
— Vancouver (PCL)	3B	2	5	1	3	1	0	0	2	0	1	0	0	0-0	.600	.571	.800	1.371	0	1.000
2000— Oakland (A.L.) DH-3B-1B		76	214	40	67	12	2	9	33	25	40	7	6	1-0	.313	.401	.514	.915	4	.977
— Sacramento (PCL)	DH	1	4	1	2	0	0	0	1	0	0	0	0	0-0	.500	.500	.500	1.000	...	...
2001— Oakland (A.L.) DH-1B-3B		106	305	33	67	21	1	9	32	19	64	13	9	0-1	.220	.291	.384	.675	5	.979
2002— Oakland (A.L.) 1B-3B-DH		68	156	15	43	10	1	6	18	13	31	7	2	1-1	.276	.354	.468	.822	5	.980
2003— Ariz. A's (Ariz.) 1B-3B-DH		13	45	13	15	2	0	2	8	8	6	2	1	1-0	.333	.455	.511	.966	1	.974
— Modesto (California)	DH	1	4	0	0	0	0	0	1	0	1	1	0	0-0	.000	.200	.000	.200	0	...
2004— Los Angeles (N.L.) 1B-DH-3B		77	111	17	31	1	0	8	22	10	33	2	4	0-0	.279	.352	.505	.856	2	.986
2005— Los Angeles (N.L.) 1B-3B-DH		109	319	39	84	24	0	15	63	27	63	3	12	0-1	.263	.325	.480	.804	3	.994
American League totals (5 years)		352	944	131	249	61	5	35	124	79	187	42	24	3-3	.264	.345	.450	.795	22	.977
National League totals (2 years)		186	430	56	115	25	0	23	85	39	96	5	16	0-1	.267	.332	.486	.818	5	.992
Major League totals (7 years)		538	1374	187	364	86	5	58	209	118	283	47	40	3-4	.265	.341	.461	.802	27	.983

DIVISION SERIES RECORD

Year Team (League)	Pos.	G	AB	R	H	2B	3B	HR	RBI	BB	SO	HBP	GDP	SB-CS	Avg.	OBP	SLG	OPS	E	Avg.
2000— Oakland (A.L.)	DH	4	13	1	3	0	0	1	4	0	2	1	1	0-0	.231	.267	.462	.728	...	...
2001— Oakland (A.L.)	DH	3	4	0	0	0	0	0	0	1	0	0	0	0-0	.000	.000	.000	.000	...	...
2002— Oakland (A.L.)	1B	1	0	0	0	0	0	0	0	1	0	0	0	0-0	...	1.000	...	1.000	0	1.000
Division series totals (3 years)		8	17	1	3	0	0	1	4	1	3	1	1	0-0	.176	.250	.353	.603	0	1.000

SANCHEZ, ALEX   OF

PERSONAL: Born August 26, 1976, in Havana, Cuba. ... 5-10/180. ... Bats left, throws left. ... Full name: Alexis Sanchez. ... Junior college: Miami-Dade Community College Wolfson.
TRANSACTIONS/CAREER NOTES: Selected by Tampa Bay Devil Rays organization in fifth round of 1996 free-agent draft. ... Claimed on waivers by Milwaukee Brewers (April 6, 2001). ... On disabled list (July 16-31, 2001; and September 2, 2002-remainder of season). ... Traded by Brewers to Detroit Tigers for P Chad Petty and OF Noochie Varner (May 27, 2003). ... On disabled list (July 8-29 and August 9, 2004-remainder of season); included rehabilitation assignment to Toledo. ... Signed as free agent by Devil Rays (March 19, 2005). ... On restricted list (April 4-14, 2005). ... Claimed on waivers by San Francisco Giants (June 23, 2005). ... On disabled list (July 24-August 9, 2005); included rehabilitation assignments to AZL Giants and Fresno.
2005 GAMES PLAYED BY POSITION (MLB): OF—41, DH—8.

ALEX SANCHEZ'S HITTING ZONE

.100	.500	.167
.414	.529	.486
.200	.571	.125

LEFTY-RIGHTY SPLITS

vs.	Avg.	AB	H	2B	3B	HR	RBI	BB	SO	OBP	Slg.
L	.304	23	7	2	0	1	6	0	6	.304	.522
R	.327	153	50	9	1	1	10	8	28	.360	.418

Year Team (League)	Pos.	G	AB	R	H	2B	3B	HR	RBI	BB	SO	HBP	GDP	SB-CS	Avg.	OBP	SLG	OPS	E	Avg.
1996—GC Devil Rays (GCL)	OF	56	227	36	64	7	6	1	22	10	35	6	2	20-12	.282	.328	.379	.707	3	.968
1997—Char., S.C. (SAL)	OF	131	537	73	155	15	6	0	34	37	72	3	7	92-40	.289	.336	.339	.675	11	.963
1998—St. Pete. (FSL)	OF	128	545	77	180	17	9	1	50	31	70	1	5	66-33	.330	.360	.400	.760	12	.965
1999—Orlando (South.)	OF	121	500	68	127	12	4	2	29	26	88	0	8	48-26	.254	.290	.306	.596	14	.958
—Durham (Int'l)	OF	3	10	2	2	1	0	0	0	1	0	0	0	0-0	.200	.273	.300	.573	0	1.000
2000—Durham (Int'l)	OF	107	446	76	130	18	3	2	33	30	66	5	6	52-20	.291	.342	.359	.700	6	.977
—Orlando (South.)	OF	20	86	12	25	2	1	0	4	1	13	1	1	2-6	.291	.307	.337	.644	1	.972
2001—Indianapolis (Int'l)	OF	83	335	52	105	14	5	1	26	22	44	2	2	27-8	.313	.359	.394	.753	6	.968
—Milwaukee (N.L.)	OF	30	68	7	14	3	2	0	4	5	13	0	0	6-2	.206	.260	.309	.569	1	.963
2002—Milwaukee (N.L.)	OF	112	394	55	114	10	7	1	33	31	62	2	4	37-14	.289	.343	.358	.701	5	.982
2003—Milwaukee (N.L.)	OF	43	163	15	46	10	3	0	10	7	28	2	1	8-6	.282	.316	.380	.696	1	.990
—Detroit (A.L.)	OF	101	394	43	114	13	5	1	22	18	46	1	4	44-18	.289	.320	.355	.675	6	.979
2004—Toledo (Int'l)	OF	2	10	0	0	0	0	0	0	0	6	0	0	0-0	.000	.000	.000	.000	0	1.000
—Detroit (A.L.)	OF-DH	79	332	41	107	9	3	2	26	7	50	0	5	19-13	.322	.335	.386	.721	9	.952
2005—Tampa Bay (A.L.)	OF-DH	43	133	28	46	8	1	2	13	7	25	0	3	6-3	.346	.373	.466	.839	3	.957
—San Francisco (N.L.)	OF-DH	19	43	4	11	3	0	0	3	1	9	1	0	2-2	.256	.289	.326	.614	3	.870
—Ariz. Giants (Ariz.)	OF	4	10	5	6	1	0	0	2	3	1	1	0	1-0	.600	.714	.700	1.414	2	.667
—Fresno (PCL)	OF	2	9	0	1	0	0	0	1	0	0	0	0	0-1	.111	.111	.111	.222	0	1.000
American League totals (3 years)		223	859	112	267	30	9	5	61	32	121	1	12	69-34	.311	.334	.384	.718	18	.967
National League totals (4 years)		204	668	81	185	26	12	1	50	44	112	5	5	53-24	.277	.325	.356	.681	10	.977
Major League totals (5 years)		427	1527	193	452	56	21	6	111	76	233	6	17	122-58	.296	.330	.372	.702	28	.971

S

SANCHEZ, DUANER   P

PERSONAL: Born October 14, 1979, in Cotui, Dominican Republic. ... 6-0/190. ... Throws right, bats right. ... High school: Francisco H. Carvajal (Cotui, Dominican Repblic).
TRANSACTIONS/CAREER NOTES: Signed as a non-drafted free agent by Arizona Diamondbacks organization (October 16, 1996). ... Traded by Diamondbacks to Pittsburgh Pirates for P Mike Fetters (July 6, 2002). ... Claimed on waivers by Los Angeles Dodgers (November 20, 2003).
CAREER HITTING: 1-for-8 (.125), 1 R, 1 2B, 0 3B, 0 HR, 2 RBI.

SCOUTING REPORT **Throws:** He has a 91-96 mph fastball, a curveball, a slider and a circle changeup. **Tendencies:** Sanchez tends to overthrow his fastball, but with his velocity he can ride it up in the strike zone, sink it or run it away from hitters. Has a tight curveball that can be difficult to command because of its big break. Has a big, sharp-breaking slider. Has excellent arm speed on his changeup and good sinking movement. **Outlook:** Sanchez probably is best as a setup man, but his four plus pitches make him a strong reliever. *Grade 7*

DUANER SANCHEZ'S PITCHING ZONE

.214	.368	.261
.216	.250	.283
.280	.273	.208

LEFTY-RIGHTY SPLITS

vs.	Avg.	AB	H	2B	3B	HR	RBI	BB	SO	OBP	Slg.
L	.310	155	48	10	1	5	28	18	29	.383	.484
R	.182	148	27	5	3	3	16	18	42	.280	.318

Year Team (League)	W	L	Pct.	ERA	WHIP	G	GS	CG	ShO	Hld.	Sv.-Opp.	IP	H	R	ER	HR	BB-IBB	SO	Avg.
1997—Dom. D-backs (DSL)	4	4	.500	5.13	1.76	21	6	0	0	...	1-...	59.2	57	50	34	...	48-...	44	...
1998—Dom. D-backs (DSL)	2	3	.400	1.79	1.19	14	8	1	0	...	1-...	50.1	36	19	10	...	24-...	44	...
1999—High Desert (Calif.)	0	0	...	7.53	1.67	3	3	0	0	...	0-...	14.1	15	13	12	2	9-0	9	.288
—Missoula (Pion.)	5	3	.625	3.13	1.22	13	11	0	0	...	0-...	63.1	54	34	22	3	23-0	51	.224
2000—South Bend (Mid.)	8	9	.471	3.65	1.25	28	28	4	0	...	0-...	165.1	152	80	67	6	54-1	121	.243
2001—El Paso (Texas)	3	7	.300	6.78	1.66	13	13	0	0	...	0-...	70.1	92	56	53	7	25-1	41	.324
—Lancaster (Calif.)	2	4	.333	4.58	1.41	10	10	1	0	...	0-...	59.0	65	44	30	7	18-0	49	.274
2002—El Paso (Texas)	4	3	.571	3.03	1.23	31	0	0	0	...	13-...	35.2	31	16	12	1	13-1	37	.223
—Arizona (N.L.)	0	0	...	4.91	2.18	6	0	0	0	1	0-1	3.2	3	2	2	1	5-0	4	.214
—Tucson (PCL)	1	1	.500	6.75	1.31	4	0	0	0	...	1-...	5.1	6	4	4	1	1-0	9	.261
—Nashville (PCL)	4	3	.000	4.76	1.50	20	0	0	0	...	6-...	22.2	23	12	12	2	11-2	20	.274
—Pittsburgh (N.L.)	0	0	...	15.43	2.14	3	0	0	0	0	0-0	2.1	3	4	4	1	2-0	2	.300
2003—Nashville (PCL)	4	4	.500	3.69	1.50	41	1	0	0	...	1-...	61.0	63	28	25	3	27-5	34	.265
—Pittsburgh (N.L.)	1	0	1.000	16.50	2.67	6	0	0	0	0	0-0	6.0	15	11	11	2	1-0	3	.500
2004—Los Angeles (N.L.)	3	1	.750	3.38	1.35	67	0	0	0	4	0-1	80.0	81	34	30	9	27-2	44	.266
2005—Los Angeles (N.L.)	4	7	.364	3.73	1.35	79	0	0	0	13	8-12	82.0	75	36	34	4	36-6	71	.248
Major League totals (4 years)	8	8	.500	4.19	1.43	161	0	0	0	18	8-14	174.0	177	87	81	21	71-8	124	.268

DIVISION SERIES RECORD

Year Team (League)	W	L	Pct.	ERA	WHIP	G	GS	CG	ShO	Hld.	Sv.-Opp.	IP	H	R	ER	HR	BB-IBB	SO	Avg.
2004—Los Angeles (N.L.)	0	0	...	0.00	1.00	2	0	0	0	0	0-0	2.0	1	0	0	0	1-0	3	.143

SANCHEZ, FREDDY   3B

PERSONAL: Born December 21, 1977, in Hollywood, Calif. ... 5-10/192. ... Bats right, throws right. ... Full name: Frederick Philip Sanchez. ... High school: Burbank (Calif.). ... Junior college: Oklahoma City Community College.
TRANSACTIONS/CAREER NOTES: Selected by Boston Red Sox organization in 11th round of 2000 free-agent draft. ... Traded by Red Sox with P Mike Gonzalez and cash to Pittsburgh Pirates for Ps Jeff Suppan, Brandon Lyon and Anastacio Martinez (July 31, 2003). ... On disabled list (March 26-July 9, 2004); included rehabilitation assignment to Nashville.
2005 GAMES PLAYED BY POSITION (MLB): 3B—65, 2B—58, SS—11.

FREDDY SANCHEZ'S HITTING ZONE

.320	.280	.192
.307	.321	.441
.310	.476	.214

LEFTY-RIGHTY SPLITS

vs.	Avg.	AB	H	2B	3B	HR	RBI	BB	SO	OBP	Slg.
L	.326	135	44	9	3	1	11	10	5	.369	.459
R	.277	318	88	17	1	4	24	17	31	.322	.374

Year	Team (League)	Pos.	G	AB	R	H	2B	3B	HR	RBI	BB	SO	HBP	GDP	SB-CS	Avg.	OBP	SLG	OPS	E	Avg.
2000—Lowell (NY-Penn)	SS	34	132	24	38	13	2	1	14	9	16	3	1	2-4	.288	.347	.439	.787	4	.974
—Augusta (S. Atl.)	SS	30	109	17	33	7	0	0	15	11	19	1	1	4-0	.303	.372	.367	.739	3	.976
2001—Sarasota (Fla. St.)	SS	69	280	40	95	19	4	1	24	22	30	2	3	5-3	.339	.388	.446	.834	17	.944
—Trenton (East.)	SS	44	178	25	58	20	0	2	19	9	21	2	6	3-1	.326	.363	.472	.835	9	.948
2002—Trenton (East.)	SS-2B	80	311	60	102	23	1	3	38	37	45	5	9	19-3	.328	.403	.437	.841	16	.955
—Pawtucket (Int'l)	SS-2B	45	183	25	55	10	1	4	28	12	21	3	3	5-3	.301	.350	.432	.782	13	.942
—Boston (A.L.)	2B-SS-DH	12	16	3	3	0	0	0	2	2	3	0	0	0-0	.188	.278	.188	.465	0	1.000
2003—Boston (A.L.)	3B-SS-2B	20	34	6	8	2	0	0	2	0	8	0	0	0-0	.235	.235	.294	.529	0	1.000
—Pawtucket (Int'l)	SS-2B-3B-DH	58	211	46	72	17	0	5	25	31	36	2	7	8-0	.341	.430	.493	.923	4	.983
—Nashville (PCL)	2B	1	5	1	2	1	0	0	0	0	1	0	0	0-0	.400	.400	.600	1.000	0	1.000
2004—Nashville (PCL)	2B-SS-DH	44	125	10	33	7	1	1	11	11	17	1	3	4-1	.264	.326	.360	.686	2	.983
—Pittsburgh (N.L.)	SS-2B-3B	9	19	2	3	0	0	0	2	0	3	0	0	0-0	.158	.158	.158	.316	1	.917
2005—Pittsburgh (N.L.)	3B-2B-SS	132	453	54	132	26	4	5	35	27	36	5	6	2-2	.291	.336	.400	.736	6	.986
American League totals (2 years)		32	50	9	11	2	0	0	4	2	11	0	0	0-0	.220	.250	.260	.510	0	1.000
National League totals (2 years)		141	472	56	135	26	4	5	37	27	39	5	6	2-2	.286	.329	.390	.719	7	.984
Major League totals (4 years)		173	522	65	146	28	4	5	41	29	50	5	6	2-2	.280	.322	.377	.699	7	.986

SANCHEZ, REY — 2B/SS

PERSONAL: Born October 5, 1967, in Rio Piedras, Puerto Rico. ... 5-9/170. ... Bats right, throws right. ... Full name: Rey Francisco Sanchez. ... Name pronounced: RAY SAN-chezz. ... High school: Live Oak (Morgan Hill, Calif.).

TRANSACTIONS/CAREER NOTES: Selected by Texas Rangers organization in 13th round of June 1986 free-agent draft. ... Traded by Rangers to Chicago Cubs for IF Bryan House (January 3, 1990). ... On disabled list (April 6, 1990-entire season). ... On disabled list (May 6-21, 1992); included rehabilitation assignment to Iowa. ... On disabled list (July 24-August 9, 1995). ... On disabled list (June 5-July 20 and August 11-September 1, 1996); included rehabilitation assignment to Iowa. ... Traded by Cubs to New York Yankees for P Frisco Parotte (August 16, 1997). ... Signed as a free agent by San Francisco Giants (January 22, 1998). ... Signed as a free agent by Kansas City Royals (December 11, 1998). ... Traded by Royals to Atlanta Braves for P Brad Voyles and 2B Alejandro Machado (July 31, 2001). ... Signed as a free agent by Boston Red Sox organization (February 27, 2002). ... On disabled list (June 13-July 11, 2002). ... On suspended list (September 15-16, 2002). ... Signed as a free agent by New York Mets (December 27, 2002). ... On disabled list (May 10-27 and June 6-July 1, 2003); included rehabilitation assignment to Binghamton. ... Traded by Mets with cash to Seattle Mariners for OF Kenny Kelly (July 29, 2003). ... Signed as a free agent by Tampa Bay Devil Rays (December 19, 2003). ... Signed as a free agent by New York Yankees (February 2, 2005). ... On disabled list (June 14, 2005-remainder of season).

2005 GAMES PLAYED BY POSITION (MLB): SS—10, 2B—9, DH—2, 3B—1.

SCOUTING REPORT Sanchez is a singles hitter with no power but makes good contact. Can take the ball to the opposite field. Has an inside-out swing and good bat control but is losing bat speed. Can play second or third base and shortstop. Has good hands and compensates for declining range with good instincts. Has lost arm strength and skill. **Grade 4.4**

LEFTY-RIGHTY SPLITS

vs.	Avg.	AB	H	2B	3B	HR	RBI	BB	SO	OBP	Slg.
L	.364	22	8	1	0	0	0	1	1	.417	.409
R	.190	21	4	0	0	0	2	1	2	.227	.190

Year	Team (League)	Pos.	G	AB	R	H	2B	3B	HR	RBI	BB	SO	HBP	GDP	SB-CS	Avg.	OBP	SLG	OPS	E	Avg.
1986—GC Rangers (GCL)	2B-SS	52	169	27	49	3	1	0	23	41	18	3	3	10-10	.290	.435	.320	.754	15	.938
1987—Gastonia (S. Atl.)	SS	50	160	19	35	1	2	1	10	22	17	2	9	6-3	.219	.321	.269	.589	18	.933
—Butte (Pion.)	SS	49	189	36	69	10	6	0	25	21	12	2	6	22-6	.365	.430	.481	.911	12	.953
1988—Charlotte (Fla. St.)	SS	128	418	60	128	6	5	0	38	35	24	5	14	29-11	.306	.364	.345	.709	35	.948
1989—Okla. City (A.A.)	SS	134	464	38	104	10	4	1	39	21	50	2	14	4-4	.224	.259	.269	.529	29	.958
1990—Iowa (Am. Assoc.)				Did not play.																	
1991—Iowa (Am. Assoc.)	SS	126	417	60	121	16	5	2	46	37	27	7	11	13-7	.290	.356	.367	.723	17	.971
—Chicago (N.L.)	2B-SS	13	23	1	6	0	0	0	2	4	3	0	0	0-0	.261	.370	.261	.631	0	1.000
1992—Chicago (N.L.)	SS-2B	20	76	12	26	3	0	0	3	4	1	0	0	6-3	.342	.375	.382	.757	5	.956
—Chicago (N.L.)	SS-2B	74	255	24	64	14	3	1	19	10	17	3	7	2-1	.251	.285	.341	.626	9	.975
1993—Chicago (N.L.)	SS	105	344	35	97	11	2	0	28	15	22	3	8	1-1	.282	.316	.326	.642	15	.969
1994—Chicago (N.L.)	2B-SS-3B	96	291	26	83	13	1	0	24	20	29	1	2	2-5	.285	.345	.337	.682	9	.980
1995—Chicago (N.L.)	2B-SS	114	428	57	119	22	2	3	27	14	48	1	9	6-4	.278	.301	.360	.661	7	.987
1996—Chicago (N.L.)	SS	95	289	28	61	9	0	1	12	22	42	3	6	7-1	.211	.272	.253	.525	11	.977
—Iowa (Am. Assoc.)	SS	3	12	2	2	0	0	0	1	1	2	0	0	2-0	.167	.231	.167	.397	1	.933
1997—Chicago (N.L.)	SS-2B-3B	97	205	14	51	9	0	1	12	11	26	0	7	4-2	.249	.287	.307	.594	6	.977
—New York (A.L.)	2B-SS	38	138	21	43	12	0	1	15	5	21	1	1	0-4	.312	.338	.420	.758	4	.978
1998—San Francisco (N.L.)	SS-2B	109	316	44	90	14	2	2	30	16	47	4	11	0-0	.285	.325	.361	.686	8	.981
1999—Kansas City (A.L.)	SS	134	479	66	141	18	6	2	56	22	48	4	14	11-5	.294	.329	.370	.698	13	.982
2000—Kansas City (A.L.)	SS	143	509	68	139	18	2	1	38	28	55	4	17	7-3	.273	.314	.322	.637	4	.994
2001—Kansas City (A.L.)	SS	100	390	40	118	14	5	0	28	11	34	2	11	9-1	.303	.322	.364	.686	4	.994
—Atlanta (N.L.)	SS	49	154	10	35	4	1	0	9	4	15	0	9	2-0	.227	.245	.266	.512	3	.986
2002—Boston (A.L.)	2B-SS	107	357	46	102	12	3	1	38	17	31	2	9	2-2	.286	.318	.345	.662	5	.988
2003—Binghamton (East.)	SS	3	9	1	1	0	0	0	0	1	1	0	3	0-0	.111	.200	.111	.311	1	.900
—New York (N.L.)	SS-2B	56	174	11	36	3	1	0	12	8	18	0	7	1-1	.207	.240	.236	.476	4	.981
—Seattle (A.L.)	SS	46	170	22	50	5	1	0	11	8	21	3	1	1-0	.294	.330	.335	.665	4	.979
2004—Tampa Bay (A.L.)	SS	91	285	23	70	14	3	2	26	12	28	3	6	0-1	.246	.281	.337	.617	5	.988
2005—New York (A.L.)	SS-2B-DH-3B	23	43	7	12	1	0	0	2	2	3	1	2	0-1	.279	.326	.302	.628	2	.969
American League totals (8 years)		682	2371	299	675	94	20	7	214	105	241	19	63	30-17	.285	.318	.350	.668	40	.987
National League totals (10 years)		808	2479	250	642	99	12	8	175	124	267	21	73	25-15	.259	.298	.318	.617	72	.979
Major League totals (15 years)		1490	4850	549	1317	193	32	15	389	229	508	40	136	55-32	.272	.308	.334	.642	112	.983

DIVISION SERIES RECORD

Year	Team (League)	Pos.	G	AB	R	H	2B	3B	HR	RBI	BB	SO	HBP	GDP	SB-CS	Avg.	OBP	SLG	OPS	E	Avg.
1997—New York (A.L.)	2B	5	15	1	3	1	0	0	1	1	2	0	0	0-0	.200	.250	.267	.517	0	1.000
2001—Atlanta (N.L.)	SS	3	9	1	2	1	0	0	0	1	2	0	1	0-0	.222	.222	.333	.556	1	.900
Division series totals (2 years)		8	24	2	5	2	0	0	1	2	4	0	1	0-0	.208	.240	.292	.532	1	.979

CHAMPIONSHIP SERIES RECORD

Year	Team (League)	Pos.	G	AB	R	H	2B	3B	HR	RBI	BB	SO	HBP	GDP	SB-CS	Avg.	OBP	SLG	OPS	E	Avg.
2001—Atlanta (N.L.)	SS	5	17	1	5	1	0	0	1	0	4	0	0	0-0	.294	.294	.353	.647	0	.900

SANDERS, DAVID — P

PERSONAL: Born August 29, 1979, in Oklahoma City. ... 6-0/200. ... Throws left, bats left. ... Full name: David Andrew Sanders. ... High school: Derby (Kan.). ... Junior college: Barton County Community College.
TRANSACTIONS/CAREER NOTES: Selected by Chicago White Sox organization in sixth round of 1999 free-agent draft.
CAREER HITTING: 0-for-0 (.000), 0 R, 0 2B, 0 3B, 0 HR, 0 RBI.

LEFTY-RIGHTY SPLITS

vs.	Avg.	AB	H	2B	3B	HR	RBI	BB	SO	OBP	Slg.
L	.500	4	2	2	0	0	1	0	1	.500	1.000
R	.250	4	1	0	0	1	2	1	0	.333	1.000

Year Team (League)	W	L	Pct.	ERA	WHIP	G	GS	CG	ShO	Hld.	Sv.-Opp.	IP	H	R	ER	HR	BB-IBB	SO	Avg.
1999— Ariz. White Sox (Ariz.)	1	0	1.000	1.10	1.10	7	1	0	0	...	1-...	16.1	12	3	2	0	6-3	26	.207
2000— Win.-Salem (Car.)	3	2	.600	5.21	1.61	51	0	0	0	...	6-...	48.1	39	35	28	4	39-1	50	.215
2001— Birmingham (Sou.)	3	0	1.000	2.65	1.53	36	0	0	0	...	0-...	34.0	27	12	10	1	25-1	25	.227
2002— Birmingham (Sou.)	3	1	.750	1.84	1.32	47	0	0	0	...	0-...	63.2	56	17	13	3	28-7	61	.234
2003— Chicago (A.L.)	0	0	...	6.14	1.64	20	0	0	0	...	0-0	22.0	25	16	15	5	11-0	14	.281
— Charlotte (Int'l)	1	1	.500	3.68	1.32	19	0	0	0	...	4-...	22.0	23	9	9	3	6-0	25	.264
2004— Charlotte (Int'l)	2	2	.500	6.06	1.63	40	0	0	0	...	0-...	52.0	61	38	35	7	24-0	45	.284
2005— Charlotte (Int'l)	4	2	.667	3.02	1.52	57	0	0	0	8	1-4	65.2	68	28	22	10	32-8	47	.268
— Chicago (A.L.)	0	0	...	13.50	2.00	2	0	0	0	0	0-0	2.0	3	3	3	1	1-0	1	.375
Major League totals (2 years)	0	0	...	6.75	1.67	22	0	0	0	0	0-0	24.0	28	19	18	6	12-0	15	.289

SANDERS, REGGIE — OF

PERSONAL: Born December 1, 1967, in Florence, S.C. ... 6-1/205. ... Bats right, throws right. ... Full name: Reginald Laverne Sanders. ... High school: Wilson (Florence, S.C.). ... Junior college: Spartanburg Methodist (S.C.).
TRANSACTIONS/CAREER NOTES: Selected by Cincinnati Reds organization in seventh round of 1987 free-agent draft. ... On disabled list (August 24-September 20, 1991; and May 13-29 and July 17-August 2, 1992). ... On suspended list (June 3-9, 1994). ... On disabled list (April 20-May 22, May 31-June 15 and September 17, 1996-remainder of season); included rehabilitation assignment to Indianapolis. ... On disabled list (April 19-May 6 and May 24-July 23, 1997); included rehabilitation assignments to Chattanooga and Indianapolis. ... Traded by Reds with SS Damian Jackson and P Josh Harris to San Diego Padres for OF Greg Vaughn and OF/1B Mark Sweeney (February 2, 1999). ... On disabled list (June 3-18, 1999). ... Traded by Padres with 2B Quilvio Veras and 1B Wally Joyner to Atlanta Braves for OF/1B Ryan Klesko, 2B Bret Boone and P Jason Shiell (December 22, 1999). ... On disabled list (April 30-May 23 and July 28-August 15, 2000). ... Signed as a free agent by Arizona Diamondbacks (January 5, 2001). ... On disabled list (March 23-April 8, 2001); included rehabilitation assignment to Tucson. ... Signed as a free agent by San Francisco Giants (January 8, 2002). ... Signed as a free agent by Pittsburgh Pirates (February 25, 2003). ... Signed as a free agent by St. Louis Cardinals (December 19, 2003). ... On disabled list (July 18-September 12, 2005).
2005 GAMES PLAYED BY POSITION (MLB): OF—81, DH—1.

SCOUTING REPORT *Offense:* Sanders rapidly regained his stroke and bat speed after returning from broken leg last season. Is one of the streakiest hitters in the game. Has a quick bat with a slight uppercut and a short follow-through. Is able to handle the ball up or down with excellent power. Extends the zone up when he slumps, and starts to strike out in bunches. Is a good baserunner. *Defense:* His arm is adequate for left field because he gets rid of the ball so quickly and is very accurate, especially to the bases. Doesn't get good jumps going back on the ball but closes well to the alley. *Outlook:* Sanders has a young body for a 37-year-old and has excellent makeup. Still is a dangerous run producer. *Grade 7.5*

REGGIE SANDERS'S HITTING ZONE

.450	.308	.200
.316	.269	.267
.233	.545	.231

LEFTY-RIGHTY SPLITS

vs.	Avg.	AB	H	2B	3B	HR	RBI	BB	SO	OBP	Slg.
L	.257	109	28	4	1	8	17	11	21	.328	.532
R	.280	186	52	10	1	13	37	17	54	.348	.554

Year Team (League)	Pos.	G	AB	R	H	2B	3B	HR	RBI	BB	SO	HBP	GDP	SB-CS	Avg.	OBP	SLG	OPS	E	Avg.
1988— Billings (Pion.)	SS	17	64	11	15	1	1	0	3	6	4	0	1	10-2	.234	.296	.281	.577	3	.944
1989— Greensboro (S. Atl.)	SS	81	315	53	91	18	5	9	53	29	63	3	3	21-7	.289	.353	.463	.817	42	.875
1990— Cedar Rap. (Midw.)	OF	127	466	89	133	21	4	17	63	59	97	4	8	40-15	.285	.370	.457	.827	10	.962
1991— Chattanooga (Sou.)	OF	86	302	50	95	15	8	8	49	41	67	1	5	15-2	.315	.394	.497	.890	3	.982
— Cincinnati (N.L.)	OF	9	40	6	8	0	0	1	3	0	9	0	1	1-1	.200	.200	.275	.475	0	1.000
1992— Cincinnati (N.L.)	OF	116	385	62	104	26	6	12	36	48	98	4	6	16-7	.270	.356	.462	.819	6	.978
1993— Cincinnati (N.L.)	OF	138	496	90	136	16	4	20	83	51	118	5	10	27-10	.274	.343	.444	.786	8	.975
1994— Cincinnati (N.L.)	OF	107	400	66	105	20	8	17	62	41 *	114	2	2	21-9	.263	.332	.480	.812	6	.975
1995— Cincinnati (N.L.)	OF	133	484	91	148	36	6	28	99	69	122	8	4	36-12	.306	.397	.579	.975	5	.982
1996— Cincinnati (N.L.)	OF	81	287	49	72	17	1	14	33	44	86	2	8	24-8	.251	.353	.463	.817	2	.988
— Indianapolis (A.A.)	OF-DH	4	12	3	5	2	0	0	1	1	4	1	0	0-1	.417	.500	.583	1.083	0	1.000
1997— Cincinnati (N.L.)	OF	86	312	52	79	19	2	19	56	42	93	3	9	13-7	.253	.347	.510	.857	5	.974
— Chattanooga (Sou.)	OF	3	11	3	6	1	1	1	3	1	2	1	0	0-0	.545	.615	1.091	1.706	0	1.000
— Indianapolis (A.A.)	OF	5	19	1	4	0	0	0	1	1	6	0	0	0-0	.211	.250	.211	.461	2	.750
1998— Cincinnati (N.L.)	OF	135	481	83	129	18	6	14	59	51	137	7	10	20-9	.268	.346	.418	.764	6	.978
1999— San Diego (N.L.)	OF-DH	133	478	92	136	24	7	26	72	65	108	6	10	36-13	.285	.376	.527	.904	6	.975
2000— Atlanta (N.L.)	OF	103	340	43	79	23	1	11	37	32	78	2	9	21-4	.232	.302	.403	.705	6	.964
2001— Tucson (PCL)	OF	2	6	0	2	1	0	0	1	2	0	0	2	0-0	.333	.500	.500	1.000	0	1.000
— Arizona (N.L.)	OF	126	441	84	116	21	3	33	90	46	126	5	2	14-10	.263	.337	.549	.886	1	.996
2002— San Francisco (N.L.)	OF	140	505	75	126	23	6	23	85	47	121	12	6	18-6	.250	.324	.455	.779	5	.984
2003— Pittsburgh (N.L.)	OF-DH	130	453	74	129	27	4	31	87	38	110	5	10	15-5	.285	.345	.567	.913	4	.983
2004— St. Louis (N.L.)	OF-DH	135	446	64	116	27	3	22	67	33	118	4	5	21-5	.260	.315	.482	.797	4	.981
2005— St. Louis (N.L.)	OF-DH	93	295	49	80	14	2	21	54	28	75	4	8	14-1	.271	.340	.546	.886	2	.983
Major League totals (15 years)		1665	5843	980	1563	311	59	292	923	635	1513	69	109	297-107	.267	.344	.491	.835	66	.980

DIVISION SERIES RECORD

Year Team (League)	Pos.	G	AB	R	H	2B	3B	HR	RBI	BB	SO	HBP	GDP	SB-CS	Avg.	OBP	SLG	OPS	E	Avg.
1995— Cincinnati (N.L.)	OF	3	13	3	2	1	0	1	2	1	9	0	0	2-0	.154	.214	.462	.676	1	.875
2000— Atlanta (N.L.)	OF	3	9	0	0	0	0	0	0	2	5	0	0	0-0	.000	.182	.000	.182	0	1.000
2001— Arizona (N.L.)	OF	5	14	2	5	1	0	1	3	3	3	0	0	1-0	.357	.471	.643	1.113	0	1.000
2002— San Francisco (N.L.)	OF	5	18	1	4	1	0	1	1	3	5	0	1	0-0	.222	.333	.278	.611	0	1.000
2004— St. Louis (N.L.)	OF	4	14	3	4	2	0	0	1	0	2	1	2	1-0	.286	.333	.500	.833	0	1.000
2005— St. Louis (N.L.)	OF	3	12	1	4	0	0	1	10	1	2	0	0	0-0	.333	.385	.750	1.135	0	1.000
Division series totals (6 years)		23	80	10	19	5	0	4	15	10	26	1	3	4-0	.238	.330	.450	.780	1	.981

S

CHAMPIONSHIP SERIES RECORD

Year Team (League)	Pos.	G	AB	R	H	2B	3B	HR	RBI	BB	SO	HBP	GDP	SB-CS	Avg.	OBP	SLG	OPS	E	Avg.
1995—Cincinnati (N.L.)	OF	4	16	0	2	0	0	0	2	10	0	2	0-1	.125	.222	.125	.347	1	.875
2001—Arizona (N.L.)	OF	5	17	2	2	0	0	0	1	5	5	0	1-0	.118	.318	.118	.436	0	1.000
2002—San Francisco (N.L.)	OF	4	16	0	1	0	0	0	0	4	0	0	0-0	.063	.063	.063	.125	0	1.000
2004—St. Louis (N.L.)	OF	6	21	1	4	2	0	0	0	1	5	0	1-0	.190	.227	.286	.513	0	1.000
2005—St. Louis (N.L.)	OF	5	18	1	3	0	0	1	2	1	8	0	1-0	.167	.211	.333	.544	0	1.000
Champ. series totals (5 years)		24	88	4	12	2	0	1	3	9	32	0	4	2-1	.136	.216	.193	.410	1	.983

WORLD SERIES RECORD

Year Team (League)	Pos.	G	AB	R	H	2B	3B	HR	RBI	BB	SO	HBP	GDP	SB-CS	Avg.	OBP	SLG	OPS	E	Avg.
2001—Arizona (N.L.)	OF	6	23	6	7	1	0	0	1	1	7	1	1	1-0	.304	.360	.348	.708	0	1.000
2002—San Francisco (N.L.)	OF	7	21	3	5	0	0	2	6	2	9	0	0	1-0	.238	.280	.524	.804	0	1.000
2004—St. Louis (N.L.)	OF-DH	4	9	1	0	0	0	0	0	4	5	0	0	1-0	.000	.308	.000	.308	0	1.000
World series totals (3 years)		17	53	10	12	1	0	2	7	7	21	1	1	3-0	.226	.317	.358	.676	0	1.000

ALL-STAR GAME RECORD

	G	AB	R	H	2B	3B	HR	RBI	BB	SO	HBP	GDP	SB-CS	Avg.	OBP	SLG	OPS	E	Avg.
All-Star Game totals (1 year)	1	1	0	0	0	0	0	0	0	1	0	0	0-0	.000	.000	.000	.000	0	...

SANDOVAL, DANNY   2B

PERSONAL: Born April 7, 1979, in Lara, Venezuela. ... 5-11/192. ... Bats both, throws right. ... Full name: Danny E. Sandoval. ... College: None.

TRANSACTIONS/CAREER NOTES: Signed as a non-drafted free agent by Chicago White Sox organization (December 8, 1996). ... Signed as a free agent by Philadelphia Phillies organization (November 14, 2003). ... Selected by Colorado Rockies from Phillies in Rule 5 minor league draft (December 15, 2003). ... Signed as a free agent by Phillies (October 29, 2004).

2005 GAMES PLAYED BY POSITION (MLB): SS—1.

LEFTY-RIGHTY SPLITS

vs.	Avg.	AB	H	2B	3B	HR	RBI	BB	SO	OBP	Slg.
L	.000	0	0	0	0	0	0	0	0	.000	.000
R	.000	2	0	0	0	0	0	0	1	.000	.000

									BATTING										FIELDING	
Year Team (League)	Pos.	G	AB	R	H	2B	3B	HR	RBI	BB	SO	HBP	GDP	SB-CS	Avg.	OBP	SLG	OPS	E	Avg.
1997—Guacara-1 (VSL)		31	82	16	28	0	1	0	9	11	7	0	2	8-0	.341	.398	.366	.764	...	...
1998—Hickory (S. Atl.)	SS	126	430	43	99	12	2	0	30	29	88	5	10	13-15	.230	.285	.267	.552	57	.912
1999—Burlington (Midw.)	SS	76	255	34	58	5	1	3	37	17	39	0	7	8-5	.227	.274	.290	.564	26	.929
2000—Burlington (Midw.)	SS	75	269	34	87	9	3	0	34	18	22	2	6	37-18	.323	.369	.379	.748	24	.927
—Win.-Salem (Car.)	2B-3B-SS	52	199	29	53	11	2	2	17	18	21	1	7	11-7	.266	.330	.372	.702	9	.956
—Charlotte (Int'l)	SS	2	8	0	1	0	0	0	1	1	1	0	0	0-0	.125	.222	.125	.347	1	.800
2001—Win.-Salem (Car.)	2B-3B-SS	48	176	25	48	11	0	3	14	11	31	3	3	11-2	.273	.323	.386	.709	16	.929
—Birmingham (Sou.)	SS-OF-3B	58	203	24	57	9	0	0	29	17	26	1	5	17-4	.281	.335	.325	.660	9	.948
2002—Birmingham (Sou.)	SS-OF-3B	135	504	86	133	30	2	5	45	45	56	5	12	39-24	.264	.329	.361	.690	23	.958
2003—Birmingham (Sou.)	SS-OF-3B	130	478	62	137	30	2	3	49	43	67	3	10	21-11	.287	.343	.377	.720	15	.972
2004—Tulsa (Texas)	SS	133	530	73	169	37	4	8	66	37	64	2	12	22-10	.319	.365	.449	.814	29	.726
2005—Philadelphia (N.L.)	SS	3	2	1	0	0	0	0	0	0	1	0	0	0-0	.000	.000	.000	.000	0	1.000
—Scran./W.B. (I.L.)	SS-2B	104	390	53	129	20	0	7	48	31	49	2	16	11-11	.331	.379	.436	.815	12	.976
Major League totals (1 year)		3	2	1	0	0	0	0	0	0	1	0	0	0-0	.000	.000	.000	.000	0	1.000

SANTANA, ERVIN   P

PERSONAL: Born January 10, 1983, in La Romana, Dominican Republic. ... 6-2/160. ... Throws right, bats right. ... Full name: Ervin Ramon Santana.

TRANSACTIONS/CAREER NOTES: Signed as a non-drafted free agent by Anaheim Angels organization (June 5, 2002). ... Angels franchise renamed Los Angeles Angels of Anaheim for 2005 season.

CAREER HITTING: 0-for-0 (.000), 0 R, 0 2B, 0 3B, 0 HR, 0 RBI.

SCOUTING REPORT ***Throws:*** Santana throws a fastball at 91-96 mph, a curveball, a slider and a change. ***Tendencies:*** Santana has excellent arm speed and a plus fastball that has good tailing action and can ride up in the zone. Fastball naturally runs away from lefthanders. Curve and slider are similar in breaks, but are thrown at different speeds. Change is very hard and he turns it over with good movement and arm speed. Should strike out more hitters with his velocity. ***Outlook:*** He was a big part of the Angels' division title run and proved mettle in playoffs. With improved command, should move rapidly up in rotation. ***Grade 7.6***

ERVIN SANTANA'S PITCHING ZONE

.220	.250	.333
.321	.320	.286
.313	.286	.300

LEFTY-RIGHTY SPLITS

vs.	Avg.	AB	H	2B	3B	HR	RBI	BB	SO	OBP	Slg.
L	.261	268	70	19	4	7	35	26	47	.331	.440
R	.271	255	69	15	1	10	31	21	52	.336	.455

Year Team (League)	W	L	Pct.	ERA	WHIP	G	GS	CG	ShO	Hld.	Sv.-Opp.	IP	H	R	ER	HR	BB-IBB	SO	Avg.
2001—Ariz. Angels (Ariz.)	3	2	.600	3.22	1.28	10	9	1	1	...	0-...	58.2	40	27	21	0	35-0	65	.184
—Provo (Pion.)	2	1	.667	7.71	1.66	4	4	0	0	...	0-...	18.2	19	17	16	1	12-1	22	.247
2002—Cedar Rap. (Midw.)	14	8	.636	4.16	1.23	27	27	0	0	...	0-...	147.0	133	75	68	10	48-3	146	.240
2003—Rancho Cuca. (Calif.)	10	2	.833	2.53	1.07	20	20	1	0	...	0-...	124.2	98	44	35	9	36-0	130	.212
—Arkansas (Texas)	1	1	.500	3.94	1.18	6	6	0	0	...	0-...	29.2	23	15	13	4	12-0	23	.211
2004—Arkansas (Texas)	2	1	.667	3.30	1.35	8	8	0	0	...	0-...	43.2	41	19	16	3	18-0	48	.247
2005—Arkansas (Texas)	5	1	.833	2.31	1.26	7	7	0	0	...	0-0	39.0	34	12	10	2	15-0	32	.234
—Salt Lake (PCL)	1	0	1.000	4.19	1.09	3	3	0	0	...	0-0	19.1	19	11	9	2	2-0	17	.260
—Los Angeles (A.L.)	12	8	.600	4.65	1.39	23	23	1	0	...	0-0	133.2	139	73	69	17	47-2	99	.266
Major League totals (1 year)	12	8	.600	4.65	1.39	23	23	1	0	...	0-0	133.2	139	73	69	17	47-2	99	.266

DIVISION SERIES RECORD

Year Team (League)	W	L	Pct.	ERA	WHIP	G	GS	CG	ShO	Hld.	Sv.-Opp.	IP	H	R	ER	HR	BB-IBB	SO	Avg.
2005—Los Angeles (A.L.)	1	0	1.000	5.06	1.31	1	1	0	0	0	0-0	5.1	5	3	3	1	2-0	2	.263

CHAMPIONSHIP SERIES RECORD

Year Team (League)	W	L	Pct.	ERA	WHIP	G	GS	CG	ShO	Hld.	Sv.-Opp.	IP	H	R	ER	HR	BB-IBB	SO	Avg.
2005—Los Angeles (A.L.)	0	1	.000	10.38	1.38	1	1	0	0	0	0-0	4.1	3	6	5	2	3-0	2	.188

S

SANTANA, JOHAN   P

PERSONAL: Born March 13, 1979, in Tovar Merida, Venezuela. ... 6-0/206. ... Throws left, bats left. ... Full name: Johan Alexander Santana. ... Name pronounced: YO-hahn. ... High school: Liceo Nucete Sardi (Venezuela).

TRANSACTIONS/CAREER NOTES: Signed as a non-drafted free agent by Houston Astros organization (July 2, 1995). ... Selected by Florida Marlins from Astros organization in Rule 5 major league draft (December 13, 1999). ... Traded by Marlins with cash to Minnesota Twins for P Jared Camp (December 13, 1999). ... On disabled list (July 7-September 21, 2001).

HONORS: Named A.L. Pitcher of the Year by THE SPORTING NEWS (2004). ... Named A.L. Cy Young Award winner by Baseball Writers' Association of America (2004).

CAREER HITTING: 6-for-22 (.273), 1 R, 0 2B, 0 3B, 0 HR, 2 RBI.

SCOUTING REPORT

Throws: Santana throws a four-seam fastball from 89-94 mph, a slider between 81-84 and an above-average changeup. ***Tendencies:*** He is a power pitcher with exceptional arm speed, a deceptive motion and good command to both sides of the plate. Has late life on his fastball and excellent depth on his tight, late-biting slider. Throws his changeup, which dives away from hitters, at the same arm speed as fastball. Has become more aggressive. ***Outlook:*** Santana is a solid No. 1 starter and should remain among the league's elite for years. Has become very dependable and goes deep into games. ***Grade 9.5***

JOHAN SANTANA'S PITCHING ZONE

.246	.239	.186
.230	.452	.200
.159	.286	.135

LEFTY-RIGHTY SPLITS

vs.	Avg.	AB	H	2B	3B	HR	RBI	BB	SO	OBP	Slg.
L	.256	156	40	8	2	6	15	7	43	.288	.449
R	.200	700	140	34	2	16	59	38	195	.242	.323

Year Team (League)	W	L	Pct.	ERA	WHIP	G	GS	CG	ShO	Hld.	Sv.-Opp.	IP	H	R	ER	HR	BB-IBB	SO	Avg.
1996—Dom. Astros (DSL).	4	3	.571	2.70	1.20	23	1	0	0	...	3-...	40.0	26	16	12		22-...	51	
1997—GC Astros (GCL)	0	4	.000	7.93	1.84	9	5	1	0	...	0-...	36.1	49	36	32	2	18-0	25	.322
—Auburn (NY-Penn)	0	0	...	2.25	1.75	1	1	0	0	...	0-...	4.0	1	1	1	0	6-0	5	.083
1998—Quad City (Midw.)	0	1	.000	9.45	2.55	2	1	0	0	...	0-...	6.2	14	7	7	1	3-0	6	.452
—Auburn (NY-Penn)	7	5	.583	4.36	1.18	15	15	1	1	...	0-...	86.2	81	52	42	9	21-0	88	.243
1999—Michigan (Midw.)	8	8	.500	4.66	1.35	27	26	1	0	...	0-...	160.1	162	94	83	14	55-0	150	.263
2000—Minnesota (A.L.)	2	3	.400	6.49	1.81	30	5	0	0	...	0-0	86.0	102	64	62	11	54-0	64	.302
2001—Minnesota (A.L.)	1	0	1.000	4.74	1.51	15	4	0	0	...	0-0	43.2	50	25	23	6	16-0	28	.292
2002—Edmonton (PCL)	5	2	.714	3.14	1.32	11	9	0	0	...	0-...	48.2	37	24	17	7	27-0	75	.202
—Minnesota (A.L.)	8	6	.571	2.99	1.23	27	14	0	0	3	1-1	108.1	84	41	36	7	49-0	137	.212
2003—Minnesota (A.L.)	12	3	.800	3.07	1.10	45	18	0	0	5	0-0	158.1	127	56	54	17	47-1	169	.216
2004—Minnesota (A.L.)	20	6	.769	* 2.61	0.92	34	34	1	1	0	0-0	228.0	156	70	66	24	54-0	* 265	* .192
2005—Minnesota (A.L.)	16	7	.696	2.87	* 0.97	33	33	3	2	0	0-0	231.2	180	77	74	22	45-1	* 238	* .210
Major League totals (6 years)	**59**	**25**	**.702**	**3.31**	**1.13**	**184**	**108**	**4**	**3**	**8**	**1-1**	**856.0**	**699**	**333**	**315**	**87**	**265-2**	**901**	**.221**

DIVISION SERIES RECORD

Year Team (League)	W	L	Pct.	ERA	WHIP	G	GS	CG	ShO	Hld.	Sv.-Opp.	IP	H	R	ER	HR	BB-IBB	SO	Avg.
2002—Minnesota (A.L.)	0	0	...	6.00	1.67	2	0	0	0	1	0-0	3.0	3	2	2	0	2-0	2	.250
2003—Minnesota (A.L.)	0	1	.000	7.04	1.57	2	2	0	0	0	0-0	7.2	9	6	6	0	3-1	6	.290
2004—Minnesota (A.L.)	1	0	1.000	0.75	1.50	2	2	0	0	0	0-0	12.0	14	1	1	0	4-0	12	.304
Division series totals (3 years)	**1**	**1**	**.500**	**3.57**	**1.54**	**6**	**4**	**0**	**0**	**1**	**0-0**	**22.2**	**26**	**9**	**9**	**0**	**9-1**	**20**	**.292**

CHAMPIONSHIP SERIES RECORD

Year Team (League)	W	L	Pct.	ERA	WHIP	G	GS	CG	ShO	Hld.	Sv.-Opp.	IP	H	R	ER	HR	BB-IBB	SO	Avg.
2002—Minnesota (A.L.)	0	1	.000	10.80	1.20	4	0	0	0	0	0-0	3.1	4	4	4	1	0-0	4	.286

ALL-STAR GAME RECORD

Year Team (League)	W	L	Pct.	ERA	WHIP	G	GS	CG	ShO	Hld.	Sv.-Opp.	IP	H	R	ER	HR	BB-IBB	SO	Avg.
All-Star Game totals (1 year)	**0**	**0**	**...**	**0.00**	**2.00**						**0-0**	**1.0**	**1**	**0**	**0**	**0**	**1-0**	**0**	**.333**

SANTANA, JULIO   P

PERSONAL: Born January 20, 1974, in San Pedro de Macoris, Dominican Republic. ... 6-0/225. ... Throws right, bats right. ... Full name: Julio Franklin Santana. ... High school: Divina Providence (Dominican Republic). ... Nephew of Rico Carty, outfielder with seven major league teams (1963-79).

TRANSACTIONS/CAREER NOTES: Signed as a non-drafted free agent by Texas Rangers organization (February 18, 1990). ... On disabled list (July 15-August 10, 1997). ... Claimed on waivers by Tampa Bay Devil Rays (April 27, 1998). ... On disabled list (May 3-24, 1999). ... Traded by Devil Rays to Boston Red Sox for a player to be named and cash (July 21, 1999); Devil Rays acquired P Will Silverthorn to complete deal (July 30, 1999). ... On disabled list (July 22, 1999-remainder of season). ... Released by Red Sox (June 15, 2000). ... Signed by Montreal Expos (June 18, 2000). ... Signed as a free agent by San Francisco Giants organization (November 11, 2000). ... Selected by New York Mets from Giants organization in Rule 5 major league draft (December 11, 2000). ... Returned to Giants organization (March 30, 2001). ... Signed as a free agent by Detroit Tigers organization (November 16, 2001). ... On disabled list (August 11, 2002-remainder of season). ... Released by Tigers (March 23, 2003). ... Signed by Philadelphia Phillies organization (March 30, 2003). ... Contract sold to Yomiuri of the Japan Central League by Phillies (June 9, 2003). ... Signed as free agent by Milwaukee Brewers organization (December 22, 2004). ... On disabled list (August 14-September 22, 2005).

CAREER HITTING: 2-for-15 (.133), 0 R, 0 2B, 0 3B, 0 HR, 1 RBI.

JULIO SANTANA'S PITCHING ZONE

.222	.333	.500
.188	.267	.444
.250	.250	.125

LEFTY-RIGHTY SPLITS

vs.	Avg.	AB	H	2B	3B	HR	RBI	BB	SO	OBP	Slg.
L	.247	73	18	4	0	3	12	8	20	.321	.425
R	.198	81	16	3	1	3	10	11	29	.284	.370

Year Team (League)	W	L	Pct.	ERA	WHIP	G	GS	CG	ShO	Hld.	Sv.-Opp.	IP	H	R	ER	HR	BB-IBB	SO	Avg.
1992—San Pedro (DSL)	0	1	.000	3.24	1.80	17	1	0	0	...	0-...	8.1	8	5	3	...	7-...	5	
—Texas (DSL)	0	1	.000	3.24	1.67	4	1	0	0	...	0-...	9.0	8	5	3	0	7-0	5	.222
1993—GC Rangers (GCL)	4	1	.800	1.38	0.97	26	0	0	0	...	7-...	39.0	31	9	6	0	7-0	50	.214
1994—Char., W.Va. (SAL)	6	7	.462	2.46	1.19	16	16	0	0	...	0-...	91.1	65	38	25	3	44-...	103	
—Tulsa (Texas)	7	2	.778	2.90	1.26	11	11	2	0	...	0-...	72.0	50	26	23	1	41-0	45	.205
—Char., S.C. (SAL)	6	7	.462	2.46	1.18	16	16	0	0	...	0-...	92.0	65	38	25	3	44-0	103	.198
1995—Okla. City (A.A.)	0	2	.000	39.00	5.33	2	2	0	0	...	0-...	3.0	9	14	13	3	7-0	6	.500
—Charlotte (Fla. St.)	0	3	.000	3.73	1.50	5	5	1	0	...	0-...	32.0	32	16	13	1	16-0	27	.271
—Tulsa (Texas)	6	4	.600	3.15	1.39	15	15	3	0	...	0-...	103.0	91	40	36	8	52-2	71	.239
1996—Okla. City (A.A.)	11	12	.478	4.02	1.28	29	* 29	4	1	...	0-...	185.2	171	102	83	12	66-1	113	.244

Year	Team (League)	W	L	Pct.	ERA	WHIP	G	GS	CG	ShO	Hld.	Sv.-Opp.	IP	H	R	ER	HR	BB-IBB	SO	Avg.
1997—	Texas (A.L.)	4	6	.400	6.75	1.83	30	14	0	0	...	0-1	104.0	141	86	78	16	49-2	64	.323
—	Okla. City (A.A.)	0	0	...	15.00	3.67	1	1	0	0	...	0-...	3.0	9	6	5	0	2-0	1	.500
1998—	Texas (A.L.)	0	0	...	8.44	2.06	3	0	0	0	...	0-0	5.1	7	5	5	0	4-1	1	.304
—	Tampa Bay (A.L.)	5	6	.455	4.23	1.44	32	19	1	0	...	0-0	140.1	144	72	66	18	58-2	60	.270
1999—	Tampa Bay (A.L.)	1	4	.200	7.32	1.77	22	5	0	0	0	0-0	55.1	66	49	45	10	32-0	34	.300
2000—	Pawtucket (Int'l)	5	3	.625	4.71	1.29	12	12	0	0	...	0-...	65.0	61	34	34	7	23-0	55	.249
—	Montreal (N.L.)	1	5	.167	5.67	1.53	36	4	0	0	1	0-2	66.2	69	45	42	11	33-2	58	.271
2001—	Fresno (PCL)	8	8	.500	5.83	1.58	25	25	0	0	...	0-...	132.2	160	94	86	28	50-0	125	.299
2002—	Toledo (Int'l)	0	1	.000	2.13	1.18	7	0	0	0	...	1-...	12.2	12	5	3	1	3-0	12	.250
—	Detroit (A.L.)	3	5	.375	2.84	1.35	38	0	0	0	7	0-1	57.0	49	19	18	8	28-2	38	.238
2003—	Scran./W.B. (Int'l)	1	1	.500	3.64	1.38	19	0	0	0	...	3-...	29.2	29	12	12	0	12-0	26	.261
—	Yomiuri (Jp. Cen.)	2	1	.667	4.94	1.46	25	0	0	0	...	5-...	28.0	35	15	15	3	6-0	21	...
2004—	Yomiuri (Jp. Cen.)	2	2	.500	1.89	0.96	29	0	0	0	...	4-...	33.1	30	7	7	2	2-0	33	...
2005—	Nashville (PCL)	2	0	1.000	1.50	1.00	8	0	0	0	0	1-1	12.0	8	2	2	0	4-0	15	.190
—	Milwaukee (N.L.)	3	5	.375	4.50	1.26	41	0	0	0	11	1-4	42.0	34	21	21	6	19-4	49	.221
	American League totals (4 years)	13	21	.382	5.27	1.60	125	38	1	0	7	0-2	362.0	407	231	212	52	171-7	197	.955
	National League totals (2 years)	4	10	.286	5.22	1.43	77	4	0	0	12	1-6	108.2	103	66	63	17	52-6	107	.252
	Major League totals (6 years)	17	31	.354	5.26	1.56	202	42	1	0	19	1-8	470.2	510	297	275	69	223-13	304	.611

SANTIAGO, BENITO — C

PERSONAL: Born March 9, 1965, in Ponce, Puerto Rico. ... 6-1/200. ... Bats right, throws right. ... Full name: Benito Rivera Santiago. ... Name pronounced: sahn-tee-AH-go. ... High school: John F. Kennedy (Ponce, Puerto Rico).

TRANSACTIONS/CAREER NOTES: Signed as a non-drafted free agent by San Diego Padres organization (September 1, 1982). ... On disabled list (June 15-August 10, 1990); included rehabilitation assignment to Las Vegas. ... On disabled list (May 31-July 11, 1992); included rehabilitation assignment to Las Vegas. ... Signed as a free agent by Florida Marlins (December 16, 1992). ... On suspended list (May 5-9, 1994). ... Signed as a free agent by Cincinnati Reds (April 17, 1995). ... On disabled list (May 8-July 4, 1995). ... Signed as a free agent by Philadelphia Phillies (January 30, 1996). ... Signed as a free agent by Toronto Blue Jays (December 9, 1996). ... On disabled list (April 14-29, 1997). ... On disabled list (March 18-September 3, 1998); included rehabilitation assignments to Dunedin and Syracuse. ... Signed as a free agent by Chicago Cubs (December 10, 1998). ... Signed as a free agent by Reds organization (February 24, 2000). ... Signed as a free agent by San Francisco Giants organization (March 17, 2001). ... On suspended list (September 20-22, 2002). ... On disabled list (July 14-29, 2003). ... Signed as a free agent by Kansas City Royals (December 11, 2003). ... On disabled list (June 19, 2004-remainder of season). ... Traded by Royals to Pittsburgh Pirates for P Leo Nunez (December 16, 2004). ... Released by Pirates (May 8, 2005). ... Signed by New York Mets organization (June 16, 2005).

HONORS: Named N.L. Rookie Player of the Year by THE SPORTING NEWS (1987). ... Named N.L. Rookie of the Year by Baseball Writers' Association of America (1987). ... Won N.L. Gold Glove at catcher (1988-90).

2005 GAMES PLAYED BY POSITION (MLB): C—6.

		LEFTY-RIGHTY SPLITS										
vs.	Avg.	AB	H	2B	3B	HR	RBI	BB	SO	OBP	Slg.
L	.125	8	1	0	0	0	0	0	0	.125	.125
R	.333	15	5	1	1	0	0	3	.333	.533	

Year	Team (League)	Pos.	G	AB	R	H	2B	3B	HR	RBI	BB	SO	HBP	GDP	SB-CS	Avg.	OBP	SLG	OPS	E	Avg.
1983—	Miami (Fla. St.)	C	122	429	34	106	25	3	5	56	11	79	7	...	3-7	.247	.276	.354	.630	21	.963
1984—	Reno (Calif.)	C	114	416	64	116	20	6	16	83	36	75	4	11	5-2	.279	.338	.471	.809	25	.969
1985—	Beaumont (Texas)	1B-3B-C	101	372	55	111	16	6	5	52	16	59	2	6	12-2	.298	.328	.414	.742	15	.976
1986—	Las Vegas (PCL)	C	117	437	55	125	26	3	17	71	17	81	1	12	19-7	.286	.312	.476	.788	21	.968
—	San Diego (N.L.)	C	17	62	10	18	2	0	3	6	2	12	0	0	0-1	.290	.308	.468	.775	5	.946
1987—	San Diego (N.L.)	C	146	546	64	164	33	2	18	79	16	112	5	12	21-12	.300	.324	.467	.791	* 22	.976
1988—	San Diego (N.L.)	C	139	492	49	122	22	2	10	46	24	82	1	18	15-7	.248	.282	.362	.643	* 12	.985
1989—	San Diego (N.L.)	C	129	462	50	109	16	3	16	62	26	89	1	9	11-6	.236	.277	.387	.664	* 20	.975
1990—	San Diego (N.L.)	C	100	344	42	93	8	5	11	53	27	55	3	4	5-5	.270	.323	.419	.741	12	.980
—	Las Vegas (PCL)	C	6	20	5	6	2	0	1	8	3	1	0	0	0-0	.300	.375	.550	.925	0	1.000
1991—	San Diego (N.L.)		152	580	60	155	22	3	17	87	23	114	4	* 21	8-10	.267	.296	.403	.700	§ 14	.987
1992—	San Diego (N.L.)	C	106	386	37	97	21	0	10	42	21	52	0	14	2-5	.251	.287	.383	.671	* 12	.982
—	Las Vegas (PCL)	C	4	13	3	4	0	0	1	2	1	1	0	0	0-0	.308	.357	.538	.896	0	1.000
1993—	Florida (N.L.)	C-OF	139	469	49	108	19	6	13	50	37	88	5	9	10-7	.230	.291	.380	.671	* 11	.987
1994—	Florida (N.L.)	C	101	337	35	92	14	2	11	41	25	57	1	11	1-2	.273	.322	.424	.746	5	.991
1995—	Cincinnati (N.L.)	C-1B	81	266	40	76	20	0	11	44	24	48	4	7	2-2	.286	.351	.485	.836	2	.996
1996—	Philadelphia (N.L.)	C-1B	136	481	71	127	21	2	30	85	49	104	1	8	2-0	.264	.332	.503	.835	11	.988
1997—	Toronto (A.L.)	C-DH	97	341	31	83	10	0	13	42	17	80	2	10	1-0	.243	.279	.387	.667	2	.997
1998—	Dunedin (Fla. St.)	DH-C	11	37	4	6	1	0	1	3	3	9	0	1	3-0	.162	.225	.270	.495	0	1.000
—	Syracuse (Int'l)	C	5	22	0	5	2	0	0	2	1	3	0	1	0-0	.227	.261	.318	.579	0	1.000
—	Toronto (A.L.)	C-DH	15	29	3	9	5	0	0	4	1	6	0	1	0-0	.310	.333	.483	.816	0	1.000
1999—	Chicago (N.L.)	C-1B	109	350	28	87	18	3	7	36	32	71	2	12	1-1	.249	.313	.377	.691	6	.990
2000—	Cincinnati (N.L.)	C	89	252	22	66	11	1	8	45	19	45	1	7	2-2	.262	.310	.409	.719	3	.994
2001—	San Francisco (N.L.)	C-1B	133	477	39	125	25	4	6	45	23	78	2	19	5-4	.262	.295	.369	.664	5	.994
2002—	San Francisco (N.L.)	C	126	478	56	133	24	5	16	74	27	73	2	19	4-2	.278	.315	.450	.765	4	.995
2003—	San Francisco (N.L.)	C	108	401	53	112	21	2	11	56	29	69	2	13	0-1	.279	.329	.424	.753	5	.993
2004—	Kansas City (A.L.)	C	49	175	15	48	10	0	6	23	8	32	2	9	1-2	.274	.312	.434	.746	1	.996
2005—	Pittsburgh (N.L.)	C	6	23	1	6	1	1	0	0	3	0	1	0	0-0	.261	.261	.391	.652	0	1.000
—	St. Lucie (Fla. St.)	C-DH	3	9	1	3	1	0	0	1	1	0	0	2	0-0	.333	.400	.444	.844	0	1.000
—	Norfolk (Int'l)	C-DH	9	33	5	8	1	0	0	4	4	8	1	1	0-0	.242	.333	.273	.606	0	1.000
	American League totals (3 years)		161	545	49	140	25	0	19	69	26	118	4	20	2-2	.257	.293	.407	.700	3	.997
	National League totals (17 years)		1817	6406	706	1690	298	41	198	851	404	1152	34	184	89-67	.264	.308	.416	.724	149	.987
	Major League totals (20 years)		1978	6951	755	1830	323	41	217	920	430	1270	38	204	91-69	.263	.307	.415	.722	152	.987

DIVISION SERIES RECORD

Year	Team (League)	Pos.	G	AB	R	H	2B	3B	HR	RBI	BB	SO	HBP	GDP	SB-CS	Avg.	OBP	SLG	OPS	E	Avg.
1995—	Cincinnati (N.L.)	C	3	9	2	3	0	0	1	3	3	3	0	0	0-0	.333	.462	.667	1.128	0	1.000
2002—	San Francisco (N.L.)	C	5	21	1	5	2	0	0	5	1	5	0	1	0-0	.238	.273	.333	.606	1	.971
2003—	San Francisco (N.L.)	C	4	11	0	2	0	0	0	0	1	2	0	0	0-0	.182	.250	.182	.432	0	1.000
	Division series totals (3 years)		12	41	3	10	2	0	1	8	5	10	0	1	0-0	.244	.319	.366	.685	1	.986

CHAMPIONSHIP SERIES RECORD

Year	Team (League)	Pos.	G	AB	R	H	2B	3B	HR	RBI	BB	SO	HBP	GDP	SB-CS	Avg.	OBP	SLG	OPS	E	Avg.
1995—	Cincinnati (N.L.)	C	4	13	0	3	0	0	0	0	3	2	0	1	0-0	.231	.333	.231	.564	0	1.000
2002—	San Francisco (N.L.)	C	5	20	2	6	0	0	2	6	2	4	0	1	0-0	.300	.364	.600	.964	0	1.000
	Champ. series totals (2 years)		9	33	2	9	0	0	2	6	4	7	0	2	0-0	.273	.351	.455	.806	0	1.000

SANTIAGO, JOSE — P

PERSONAL: Born November 5, 1974, in Fajardo, Puerto Rico. ... 6-3/225. ... Throws right, bats right. ... Full name: Jose Rafael Santiago. ... Name pronounced: SAWN-tea-ah-go. ... High school: Carlos Escobar Lopez (Loiza, Puerto Rico).

TRANSACTIONS/CAREER NOTES: Selected by Kansas City Royals organization in 70th round of 1994 free agent draft. ... On disabled list (June 18-July 9, 1997). ... On disabled list (June 20-September 13, 1999); included rehabilitation assignments to Gulf Coast Royals, Wichita and Omaha. ... Traded by Royals to Philadelphia Phillies for P Paul Byrd (June 5, 2001). ... Released by Phillies (October 11, 2002). ... Signed by Cleveland Indians organization (November 2, 2002). ... Signed as a free agent by Chicago White Sox organization (December 22, 2003). ... Signed as a free agent by New York Mets organization (March 1, 2005).

CAREER HITTING: 0-for-5 (.000), 0 R, 0 2B, 0 3B, 0 HR, 0 RBI.

LEFTY-RIGHTY SPLITS

vs.	Avg.	AB	H	2B	3B	HR	RBI	BB	SO	OBP	Slg.
L	.500	8	4	0	0	0	0	2	2	.600	.500
R	.375	16	6	4	0	0	2	0	1	.412	.625

Year Team (League)	W	L	Pct.	ERA	WHIP	G	GS	CG	ShO	Hld.	Sv.-Opp.	IP	H	R	ER	HR	BB-IBB	SO	Avg.
1994— GC Royals (GCL)	1	0	1.000	2.37	1.26	10	1	0	0	...	2-...	19.0	17	7	5	1	7-0	10	.224
1995— Spokane (N'west)	2	4	.333	3.14	1.64	22	0	0	0	...	1-...	48.2	60	26	17	1	20-4	32	.302
1996— Lansing (Midw.)	7	6	.538	3.74	1.29	54	0	0	0	...	19-...	77.0	78	34	32	4	21-3	55	.263
1997— Wilmington (Caro.)	1	1	.500	4.91	1.09	4	0	0	0	...	2-...	3.2	3	3	2	0	1-0	1	.200
— Lansing (Midw.)	1	0	1.000	2.08	1.23	9	0	0	0	...	1-...	13.0	10	6	3	0	6-1	8	.200
— Kansas City (A.L.)	0	0	...	1.93	1.93	4	0	0	0	0	0-0	4.2	7	2	1	0	2-1	1	.333
— Wichita (Texas)	2	1	.667	4.00	1.48	22	0	0	0	...	3-...	27.0	32	13	12	1	8-1	12	.299
1998— Wichita (Texas)	3	4	.429	3.61	1.47	52	0	0	0	...	22-...	72.1	79	36	29	9	27-7	31	.281
— Kansas City (A.L.)	0	0	...	9.00	2.00	2	0	0	0	0	0-0	2.0	4	2	2	0	0-0	2	.444
— Omaha (PCL)	0	0	...	7.04	1.96	4	0	0	0	...	1-...	7.2	10	9	6	0	2-0	4	.303
1999— Kansas City (A.L.)	3	4	.429	3.42	1.27	34	0	0	0	4	2-3	47.1	46	23	18	7	14-2	15	.251
— GC Royals (GCL)	0	0	...	1.80	0.20	3	3	0	0	...	0-...	5.0	1	1	1	0	0-0	4	.063
— Wichita (Texas)	0	1	.000	2.00	0.89	4	2	0	0	...	0-...	9.0	8	2	2	0	0-0	8	.258
— Omaha (PCL)	0	0	...	0.00	1.80	1	0	0	0	...	0-...	1.2	3	0	0	0	0-0	0	.429
2000— Kansas City (A.L.)	8	6	.571	3.91	1.39	45	0	0	0	5	2-8	69.0	70	33	30	7	26-3	44	.260
— Omaha (PCL)	0	1	.000	3.18	1.29	11	0	0	0	...	4-...	17.0	19	7	6	2	3-1	14	.279
2001— Kansas City (A.L.)	2	2	.500	6.75	1.67	20	0	0	0	0	0-1	29.1	40	22	22	2	9-1	15	.333
— Philadelphia (N.L.)	2	4	.333	3.61	1.27	53	0	0	0	9	0-1	62.1	66	25	25	3	13-1	28	.272
2002— Philadelphia (N.L.)	1	3	.250	6.70	1.51	42	0	0	0	9	0-1	47.0	56	35	35	7	15-1	30	.290
— Scran./W.B. (I.L.)	3	2	.600	1.29	1.25	22	0	0	0	...	7-...	28.0	28	6	4	0	7-1	21	.264
2003— Buffalo (Int'l)	3	3	.500	2.43	1.50	25	4	0	0	...	2-...	66.2	79	25	18	1	22-1	33	.298
— Cleveland (A.L.)	1	3	.250	2.84	1.61	25	0	0	0	4	0-2	31.2	37	11	10	2	14-3	15	.298
2004— Charlotte (Int'l)	9	9	.500	4.34	...	57	1	0	0	...	7-...	87.0	89	51	42	6	35-...	47	.255
2005— New York (N.L.)	0	0	...	3.18	2.12	4	0	0	0	0	0-0	5.2	10	2	2	0	2-0	3	.417
— Norfolk (Int'l)	7	6	.538	4.26	1.45	29	17	0	0	...	1	0-0	122.2	138	62	58	10	40-1	61	.288
American League totals (6 years)	14	15	.483	4.06	1.46	130	0	0	0	13	4-14	184.0	204	93	83	18	65-10	92	.281
National League totals (3 years)	3	7	.300	4.85	1.41	99	0	0	0	18	0-2	115.0	132	62	62	10	30-2	61	.287
Major League totals (8 years)	17	22	.436	4.36	1.44	229	0	0	0	31	4-16	299.0	336	155	145	28	95-12	153	.283

SANTIAGO, RAMON — SS/2B

PERSONAL: Born August 31, 1979, in Las Matas de Farfan, Dominican Republic. ... 5-11/167. ... Bats both, throws right. ... Full name: Ramon D. Santiago.

TRANSACTIONS/CAREER NOTES: Signed as a non-drafted free agent by Detroit Tigers organization (July 29, 1998). ... On disabled list (July 24-September 1, 2002). ... Traded by Tigers with SS Juan Gonzalez to Seattle Mariners for SS Carlos Guillen (January 8, 2004).

2005 GAMES PLAYED BY POSITION (MLB): 2B—2, SS—2.

LEFTY-RIGHTY SPLITS

vs.	Avg.	AB	H	2B	3B	HR	RBI	BB	SO	OBP	Slg.
L	.000	1	0	0	0	0	0	1	0	.667	.000
R	.143	7	1	0	0	0	0	0	2	.333	.143

Year Team (League)	Pos.	G	AB	R	H	2B	3B	HR	RBI	BB	SO	HBP	GDP	SB-CS	Avg.	OBP	SLG	OPS	E	Avg.
1999— GC Tigers (GCL)	SS	35	134	25	43	9	2	0	11	9	17	1	3	20-7	.321	.361	.418	.778	4	.974
— Oneonta (NYP)	SS	12	50	9	17	1	2	1	8	2	12	1	0	5-0	.340	.377	.500	.877	1	.979
2000— W. Mich. (Mid.)	SS	98	379	69	103	15	1	1	42	34	60	12	10	39-12	.272	.346	.325	.670	8	.976
2001— Lakeland (Fla. St.)	DH	120	429	64	115	15	3	2	46	54	60	11	7	34-8	.268	.361	.331	.692	...	...
2002— Erie (East.)	SS	22	75	9	21	1	0	2	6	3	12	3	2	6-0	.280	.329	.373	.703	5	.966
— Toledo (Int'l)	SS	9	28	8	12	1	0	2	6	3	4	2	0	0-2	.429	.515	.679	1.194	2	.956
— Detroit (A.L.)	SS-DH	65	222	33	54	5	5	2	20	13	48	8	2	8-5	.243	.306	.365	.671	7	.977
2003— Detroit (A.L.)	SS-2B	141	444	41	100	18	1	2	29	33	66	10	9	10-4	.225	.292	.284	.576	20	.970
2004— Tacoma (PCL)	SS-2B	71	243	35	47	7	2	1	24	24	31	10	3	9-6	.193	.288	.251	.539	6	.981
— Seattle (A.L.)	SS-DH	19	39	6	7	1	0	0	2	3	3	1	1	0-0	.179	.256	.205	.461	3	.946
2005— Tacoma (PCL)	2B-SS-3B-C	129	441	68	111	22	3	10	50	38	62	15	11	18-7	.252	.328	.383	.711	6	.990
— Seattle (A.L.)	2B-SS	8	8	2	1	0	0	0	0	1	2	3	0	0-0	.125	.417	.125	.542	1	.833
Major League totals (4 years)		233	713	84	162	24	6	6	51	50	119	22	12	18-9	.227	.297	.303	.600	31	.970

SANTOS, VICTOR — P

PERSONAL: Born October 2, 1976, in San Pedro de Macoris, Dominican Republic. ... 6-3/190. ... Throws right, bats right. ... Full name: Victor Irving Santos. ... High school: Passaic (N.J.).

TRANSACTIONS/CAREER NOTES: Signed as a non-drafted free agent by Detroit Tigers organization (June 11, 1995). ... Traded by Tigers with IF Ronnie Merrill to Colorado Rockies for P Jose Paniagua (March 25, 2002). ... Released by Rockies (October 9, 2002). ... Signed by Texas Rangers organization (November 13, 2002). ... Signed as a free agent by Milwaukee Brewers organization (December 3, 2003).

CAREER HITTING: 6-for-83 (.072), 1 R, 1 2B, 0 3B, 0 HR, 1 RBI.

SCOUTING REPORT *Throws:* Santos has a fastball at 88-91 mph, a curve at 71-75, a slider near 80 and a changeup. *Tendencies:* Santos has a herky-jerky delivery. As his velocity declines, he no longer can pitch upstairs, but has a lot of problems staying down. Deceptive curve is his best pitch. Slider lacks consistency and changeup will sink with occasional splitter action. *Outlook:* He is at best a fifth starter. Must have a good spring to break into someone's rotation or he will move into a middle-relief role. *Grade 5*

VICTOR SANTOS' PITCHING ZONE

.286	.353	.263
.232	.533	.293
.234	.125	.250

LEFTY-RIGHTY SPLITS

vs.	Avg.	AB	H	2B	3B	HR	RBI	BB	SO	OBP	Slg.
L	.259	259	67	14	2	9	31	29	41	.336	.432
R	.277	310	86	22	1	11	47	31	48	.350	.461

Year	Team (League)	W	L	Pct.	ERA	WHIP	G	GS	CG	ShO	Hld.	Sv.-Opp.	IP	H	R	ER	HR	BB-IBB	SO	Avg.
1995—	Dom. Tigers (DSL)	7	5	.583	3.72	1.37	15	12	3	2		0-...	77.1	88	46	32	...	18-...	75	...
1996—	Lakeland (Fla. St.)	2	2	.500	2.22	0.99	5	4	0	0		0-...	28.1	19	11	7	2	9-0	25	.194
	GC Tigers (GCL)	3	2	.600	1.98	1.14	9	9	0	0		0-...	50.0	44	12	11	1	13-0	39	.251
1997—	Lakeland (Fla. St.)	10	5	.667	3.23	1.34	26	26	4	2		0-...	145.0	136	74	52	10	59-1	108	.248
1998—	Lakeland (Fla. St.)	5	2	.714	2.51	1.12	16	15	0	0		1-...	100.1	88	38	28	9	24-1	74	.235
	Toledo (Int'l)	1	2	.333	11.05	2.32	5	3	0	0		0-...	14.2	24	22	18	5	10-0	12	.353
	Jacksonville (Sou.)	4	2	.667	4.17	1.50	6	6	0	0		0-...	36.2	40	20	17	2	15-1	37	.288
1999—	Jacksonville (Sou.)	12	6	.667	3.49	1.20	28	28	2	1		0-...	173.0	150	86	67	16	58-2	146	.230
2000—	GC Tigers (GCL)	0	0	...	0.00	1.33	1	1	0	0		0-...	3.0	2	1	0	0	2-0	5	.182
	Lakeland (Fla. St.)	1	0	1.000	0.00	1.20	1	1	0	0		0-...	5.0	5	0	0	0	1-0	4	.263
	Toledo (Int'l)	0	1	.000	11.37	2.05	2	2	0	0		0-...	6.1	7	8	8	4	6-0	2	.280
2001—	Detroit (A.L.)	2	2	.500	3.30	1.45	33	7	0	0	2	0-0	76.1	62	33	28	9	49-4	52	.222
	Toledo (Int'l)	2	1	.667	6.37	1.75	6	6	0	0		0-0	35.1	50	27	25	6	12-0	22	.340
2002—	Colo. Springs (PCL)	4	9	.308	5.72	1.61	21	21	1	1		0-...	118.0	147	81	75	17	43-0	134	.307
	Colorado (N.L.)	0	4	.000	10.38	2.42	24	2	0	0	1	0-0	26.0	41	30	30	3	22-3	25	.307
2003—	Texas (A.L.)	0	2	.000	7.01	1.75	8	4	0	0		0-0	25.2	29	21	20	5	16-1	15	.299
	Oklahoma (PCL)	5	4	.556	3.41	1.40	20	16	1	1		1-...	108.1	112	54	41	6	35-0	65	.264
2004—	Indianapolis (Int'l)	0	0	...	3.48	1.55	3	3	0	0		0-...	10.1	12	4	4	1	4-0	11	.308
	Milwaukee (N.L.)	11	12	.478	4.97	1.47	31	28	0	0		0-0	154.0	169	95	85	18	57-5	115	.278
2005—	Milwaukee (N.L.)	4	13	.235	4.57	1.50	29	24	1	0		0-0	141.2	153	87	72	20	60-8	89	.269
	American League totals (2 years)	2	4	.333	4.24	1.53	41	11	0	0	2	0-0	102.0	91	54	48	14	65-5	67	.242
	National League totals (3 years)	15	29	.341	5.23	1.56	84	54	1	0	1	0-0	321.2	363	212	187	41	139-16	229	.281
	Major League totals (5 years)	17	33	.340	4.99	1.55	125	65	1	0	3	0-0	423.2	454	266	235	55	204-21	296	.273

SARDINHA, DANE — C

PERSONAL: Born April 8, 1979, in Kahuku, Hawaii. ... 6-0/215. ... Bats right, throws right. ... Full name: Dane K.A.A. Sardinha. ... Name pronounced: sar-DEEN-uh. ... High school: Kamehameha High (Honolulu). ... College: Pepperdine.
TRANSACTIONS/CAREER NOTES: Selected by Cincinnati Reds organization in second round of 2000 free-agent draft.
2005 GAMES PLAYED BY POSITION (MLB): C—1.

LEFTY-RIGHTY SPLITS

vs.	Avg.	AB	H	2B	3B	HR	RBI	BB	SO	OBP	Slg.
L	.000	2	0	0	0	0	0	0	0	.000	.000
R	.000	1	0	0	0	0	0	0	1	.000	.000

Year	Team (League)	Pos.	G	AB	R	H	2B	3B	HR	RBI	BB	SO	HBP	GDP	SB-CS	Avg.	OBP	SLG	OPS	E	Avg.
2001—	Mudville (Calif.)	C	109	422	45	99	24	2	9	55	12	97	3	12	0-1	.235	.259	.365	.624	10	.991
2002—	Chattanooga (Sou.)	C	106	394	34	81	20	0	4	40	14	114	2	6	0-2	.206	.234	.287	.521	9	.990
2003—	Chattanooga (Sou.)	C	72	246	21	63	15	0	3	32	22	61	1	1	5-3	.256	.313	.354	.667	8	.985
	Cincinnati (N.L.)	C	1	2	0	0	0	0	0	0	0	0	0	0	0-0	.000	.000	.000	.000	0	1.000
2004—	Louisville (Int'l)	C	89	324	32	85	17	1	9	40	10	94	6	4	0-0	.262	.294	.404	.698	7	.987
2005—	Cincinnati (N.L.)	C	1	3	0	0	0	0	0	0	0	0	0	0	0-0	.000	.000	.000	.000	0	1.000
	Louisville (Int'l)	C	86	299	36	67	10	0	10	36	22	72	4	12	1-0	.224	.284	.358	.642	6	.991
	Major League totals (2 years)		2	5	0	0	0	0	0	0	0	0	0	0	0-0	.000	.000	.000	.000	0	1.000

SAUERBECK, SCOTT — P

PERSONAL: Born November 9, 1971, in Cincinnati. ... 6-3/200. ... Throws left, bats right. ... Full name: Scott William Sauerbeck. ... Name pronounced: SOW-er-beck. ... High school: Northwest (Cincinnati). ... College: Miami (Ohio).
TRANSACTIONS/CAREER NOTES: Selected by New York Mets organization in 23rd round of 1994 free-agent draft. ... Selected by Pittsburgh Pirates from Mets organization in Rule 5 major league draft (December 14, 1998). ... On disabled list (June 14-July 3, 2000); included rehabilitation assignment to Nashville. ... Traded by Pirates with P Jeff Suppan to Boston Red Sox for 2B Freddy Sanchez (July 31, 2003). ... Signed as a free agent by Cleveland Indians organization (March 20, 2004).
CAREER HITTING: 0-for-7 (.000), 0 R, 0 2B, 0 3B, 0 HR, 0 RBI.

SCOTT SAUERBECK'S PITCHING ZONE

.250	.400	.250
.300	.357	.320
.100	.286	.091

LEFTY-RIGHTY SPLITS

vs.	Avg.	AB	H	2B	3B	HR	RBI	BB	SO	OBP	Slg.
L	.162	74	12	3	0	3	10	10	25	.284	.324
R	.377	61	23	5	0	1	6	6	10	.441	.508

Year	Team (League)	W	L	Pct.	ERA	WHIP	G	GS	CG	ShO	Hld.	Sv.-Opp.	IP	H	R	ER	HR	BB-IBB	SO	Avg.
1994—	Pittsfield (NYP)	3	1	.750	2.05	1.20	21	0	0	0	...	1-...	48.1	39	16	11	0	19-2	39	.222
1995—	St. Lucie (Fla. St.)	0	1	.000	2.03	1.50	20	1	0	0	...	0-...	26.2	26	10	6	0	14-1	25	.231
	Capital City (SAL)	5	4	.556	3.27	1.27	19	0	0	0	...	2-...	33.0	28	14	12	2	14-1	33	.230
1996—	St. Lucie (Fla. St.)	6	6	.500	2.27	1.29	17	16	2	2	...	0-...	99.1	101	37	25	1	27-0	62	.269
	Binghamton (East.)	3	3	.500	3.47	1.29	8	8	2	0	...	0-...	46.2	48	24	18	4	12-0	30	.274
1997—	Binghamton (East.)	8	9	.471	4.93	1.48	27	20	2	0	...	0-...	131.1	144	89	72	15	50-0	88	.280
	Norfolk (Int'l)	1	0	1.000	3.60	1.40	1	1	0	0	...	0-...	5.0	3	2	2	0	4-0	4	.200
1998—	Norfolk (Int'l)	7	13	.350	3.93	1.54	27	27	0	0	...	0-...	160.1	178	82	70	8	69-1	119	.287
1999—	Pittsburgh (N.L.)	4	1	.800	2.00	1.34	65	0	0	0	10	2-5	67.2	53	19	15	6	38-5	55	.220
2000—	Pittsburgh (N.L.)	5	4	.556	4.04	1.81	75	0	0	0	13	1-4	75.2	76	36	34	4	61-8	83	.270
	Nashville (PCL)	0	0	...	0.00	0.50	2	0	0	0		0-...	2.0	1	0	0	0	0-0	0	.167
2001—	Pittsburgh (N.L.)	2	2	.500	5.60	1.61	70	0	0	0	19	2-4	62.2	61	41	39	4	40-6	79	.257
2002—	Pittsburgh (N.L.)	5	4	.556	3.21	1.23	70	0	0	0	28	0-0	62.2	50	18	16	4	27-4	70	.220

S

Year Team (League)	W	L	Pct.	ERA	WHIP	G	GS	CG	ShO	Hld.	Sv.-Opp.	IP	H	R	ER	HR	BB-IBB	SO	Avg.
2003— Pittsburgh (N.L.)	3	4	.429	4.05	1.38	53	0	0	0	16	0-4	40.0	30	20	18	5	25-2	32	.207
— Boston (A.L.)	0	1	.000	6.48	2.10	26	0	0	0	2	0-1	16.2	17	14	12	1	18-3	18	.266
2004— Cleveland (A.L.)	Did not play.																		
2005— Cleveland (A.L.)	1	0	1.000	4.04	1.43	58	0	0	0	14	0-2	35.2	35	18	16	4	16-2	35	.259
American League totals (2 years)	1	1	.500	4.82	1.64	84	0	0	0	16	0-3	52.1	52	32	28	5	34-5	53	.261
National League totals (5 years)	19	15	.559	3.56	1.49	341	0	0	0	86	5-17	308.2	270	134	122	23	191-25	319	.239
Major League totals (6 years)	20	16	.556	3.74	1.52	425	0	0	0	102	5-20	361.0	322	166	150	28	225-30	372	.242

CHAMPIONSHIP SERIES RECORD

Year Team (League)	W	L	Pct.	ERA	WHIP	G	GS	CG	ShO	Hld.	Sv.-Opp.	IP	H	R	ER	HR	BB-IBB	SO	Avg.
2003— Boston (A.L.)	0	0	...	0.00	6.00	1	0	0	0	0	0-0	0.1	1	0	0	0	1-0	0	.500

SAUNDERS, JOE   P

PERSONAL: Born June 16, 1981, in Falls Church, Va. ... 6-3/210. ... Throws left, bats left. ... Full name: Joseph Francis Saunders. ... High school: West Springfield (Va.). ... College: Virginia Tech.
TRANSACTIONS/CAREER NOTES: Selected by Anaheim Angels organization in first round (12th pick overall) of 2002 free-agent draft. ... Angels franchise renamed Los Angeles Angels of Anaheim for 2005 season.
CAREER HITTING: 0-for-0 (.000), 0 R, 0 2B, 0 3B, 0 HR, 0 RBI.

LEFTY-RIGHTY SPLITS

vs.	Avg.	AB	H	2B	3B	HR	RBI	BB	SO	OBP	Slg.
L	.417	12	5	1	0	1	5	2	1	.500	.750
R	.200	25	5	1	0	2	3	2	3	.259	.480

Year Team (League)	W	L	Pct.	ERA	WHIP	G	GS	CG	ShO	Hld.	Sv.-Opp.	IP	H	R	ER	HR	BB-IBB	SO	Avg.
2002— Provo (Pion.)	2	1	.667	3.62	1.58	8	8	0	0	...	0-...	32.1	40	19	13	1	11-0	21	.305
— Cedar Rap. (Midw.)	3	1	.750	1.88	0.87	5	5	0	0	...	0-...	28.2	16	7	6	2	9-0	27	.168
2003—	Did not play.																		
2004— Rancho Cuca. (Calif.)	9	7	.563	3.41	1.22	19	19	0	0	...	0-...	105.2	106	49	40	13	23-0	76	.265
— Arkansas (Texas)	4	3	.571	5.77	1.67	8	8	0	0	...	0-...	39.0	51	26	25	5	14-0	25	.327
2005— Arkansas (Texas)	7	4	.636	3.49	1.32	18	18	2	1	0	0-0	105.2	107	52	41	9	32-0	80	.263
— Salt Lake (PCL)	3	3	.500	4.58	1.56	9	9	1	1	0	0-0	55.0	65	38	28	3	21-0	29	.304
— Los Angeles (A.L.)	0	0	...	7.71	1.50	2	2	0	0	0	0-0	9.1	10	8	8	3	4-0	4	.270
Major League totals (1 year)	0	0	...	7.71	1.50	2	2	0	0	0	0-0	9.1	10	8	8	3	4-0	4	.270

SCHILLING, CURT   P

PERSONAL: Born November 14, 1966, in Anchorage, Alaska. ... 6-5/235. ... Throws right, bats right. ... Full name: Curtis Montague Schilling. ... Name pronounced: SHILL-ing. ... High school: Shadow Mountain (Phoenix). ... Junior college: Yavapai (Ariz.).
TRANSACTIONS/CAREER NOTES: Selected by Boston Red Sox organization in second round of January 1986 free-agent draft. ... Traded by Red Sox with OF Brady Anderson to Baltimore Orioles for P Mike Boddicker (July 29, 1988). ... Traded by Orioles with P Pete Harnisch and OF Steve Finley to Houston Astros for 1B Glenn Davis (January 10, 1991). ... Traded by Astros to Philadelphia Phillies for P Jason Grimsley (April 2, 1992). ... On disabled list (May 17-July 25, 1994); included rehabilitation assignments to Scranton/Wilkes-Barre and Reading. ... On disabled list (July 19, 1995-remainder of season). ... On disabled list (March 23-May 14, 1996); included rehabilitation assignments to Clearwater and Scranton/Wilkes-Barre. ... On disabled list (August 8-September 3, 1999). ... On disabled list (March 25-April 30, 2000); included rehabilitation assignments to Clearwater and Scranton/Wilkes-Barre. ... Traded by Phillies to Arizona Diamondbacks for 1B/OF Travis Lee and Ps Omar Daal, Vicente Padilla and Nelson Figueroa (July 26, 2000). ... On disabled list (April 18-May 3 and May 31-July 12, 2003); included rehabilitation assignment to Tucson. ... Traded by Diamondbacks to Boston Red Sox for Ps Casey Fossum, Brandon Lyon and Jorge de la Rosa and a player to be named (November 28, 2003); Diamondbacks acquired OF Michael Goss to complete deal (December 15, 2003). ... On disabled list (March 30-April 13 and April 24-July 13, 2005); included rehabilitation assignment to Pawtucket.
HONORS: Named N.L. Pitcher of the Year by THE SPORTING NEWS (2001 and 2002).
CAREER HITTING: 115-for-769 (.150), 39 R, 13 2B, 1 3B, 0 HR, 29 RBI.

SCOUTING REPORT *Throws:* His fastball ranges from 89-95 mph, his slider from 85-87, his split-finger fastball from 82-83 and his curve from 76-78. *Tendencies:* Schilling, who had recurring ankle problems that damaged his ability to push off the rubber and reduced the quality of his pitches, is one of the best control pitchers in the game when healthy. Has an above-average fastball, slider and split-finger. Has excellent life on his four-seam fastball up in the zone and on his two-seam fastball down. Uses curve, which is only average, as a change of pace. *Outlook:* Schilling is healthy and can regain his status as one of the most complete pitchers in the game, but he needs to have a good spring to shed some doubts. *Grade 8.5*

CURT SCHILLING'S PITCHING ZONE

.297	.313	.313
.311	.593	.469
.194	.600	.433

LEFTY-RIGHTY SPLITS

vs.	Avg.	AB	H	2B	3B	HR	RBI	BB	SO	OBP	Slg.
L	.290	207	60	16	2	4	29	15	51	.338	.444
R	.343	178	61	14	2	8	30	7	36	.368	.579

Year Team (League)	W	L	Pct.	ERA	WHIP	G	GS	CG	ShO	Hld.	Sv.-	IP	H	R	ER	HR	BB-IBB	SO	Avg.
1986— Elmira (N.Y.-Penn)	7	3	.700	2.59	1.30	16	15	2	1	...	0-...	93.2	92	34	27	3	30-1	75	.254
1987— Greensboro (S. Atl.)	8	15	.348	3.82	1.33	29	28	7	3	...	0-...	184.0	179	96	78	10	65-8	189	.255
1988— New Britain (East.)	8	5	.615	2.97	1.24	21	17	4	1	...	0-...	106.0	91	44	35	3	40-0	62	.232
— Charlotte (Sou.)	5	2	.714	3.18	1.30	7	7	2	1	...	0-...	45.1	36	19	16	3	23-0	32	.217
— Baltimore (A.L.)	0	3	.000	9.82	2.18	4	4	0	0	0	0-0	14.2	22	19	16	3	10-1	4	.355
1989— Rochester (Int'l)	13	11	.542	3.21	1.27	27	27	9	3	...	0-0	185.1	176	76	66	11	59-0	109	.254
— Baltimore (A.L.)	0	1	.000	6.23	1.50	5	1	0	0	0	0-0	8.2	10	6	6	2	3-0	6	.286
1990— Rochester (Int'l)	4	4	.500	3.92	1.37	15	14	1	0	...	0-0	87.1	95	46	38	0	25-1	83	.277
— Baltimore (A.L.)	1	2	.333	2.54	1.24	35	0	0	0	5	3-9	46.0	38	13	13	1	19-0	32	.229
1991— Houston (N.L.)	3	5	.375	3.81	1.56	56	0	0	0	5	8-11	75.2	79	35	32	2	39-7	71	.271
— Tucson (PCL)	0	1	.000	3.42	1.18	13	0	0	0	...	3-...	23.2	16	9	9	0	12-1	21	.186
1992— Philadelphia (N.L.)	14	11	.560	2.35	0.99	42	26	10	4	0	2-3	226.1	165	67	59	11	59-4	*147	.201
1993— Philadelphia (N.L.)	16	7	.696	4.02	1.24	34	34	7	2	0	0-0	235.1	234	114	105	23	57-6	186	.259
1994— Philadelphia (N.L.)	2	8	.200	4.48	1.40	13	13	1	0	0	0-0	82.1	87	42	41	10	28-3	58	.270
— Scran./W.B. (I.L.)	0	0	...	1.80	1.10	2	2	0	0	0	0-0	10.0	6	3	2	0	5-0	6	.171
— Reading (East.)	0	0	...	0.00	1.75	1	1	0	0	...	0-0	4.0	6	0	0	0	1-0	4	.375
1995— Philadelphia (N.L.)	7	5	.583	3.57	1.05	17	17	1	0	0	0-0	116.0	96	52	46	12	26-2	114	.220
1996— Clearwater (FSL)	2	0	1.000	1.29	0.71	2	2	0	0	0	0-0	14.0	5	2	2	0	1-0	17	.173
— Scran./W.B. (I.L.)	1	0	1.000	1.38	1.08	2	2	0	0	...	0-0	13.0	9	3	2	0	5-0	10	.200
— Philadelphia (N.L.)	9	10	.474	3.19	1.09	26	26	*8	2	0	0-0	183.1	149	69	65	12	50-5	182	.223
1997— Philadelphia (N.L.)	17	11	.607	2.97	1.05	35	*35	7	2	0	0-0	254.1	208	96	84	25	58-3	*319	.201
1998— Philadelphia (N.L.)	15	14	.517	3.25	1.11	35	*35	*15	2	0	0-0	*268.2	236	101	97	23	61-3	*300	.236
1999— Philadelphia (N.L.)	15	6	.714	3.54	1.13	24	24	8	1	0	0-0	180.1	159	74	71	25	44-0	152	.237

S

Year Team (League)	W	L	Pct.	ERA	WHIP	G	GS	CG	ShO	Hld.	Sv.-Opp.	IP	H	R	ER	HR	BB-IBB	SO	Avg.
2000—Clearwater (FSL)	1	0	1.000	1.31	0.58	4	4	0	0	...	0-...	20.2	10	3	3	0	2-0	23	.137
—Scran./W.B. (I.L.)	0	0	...	3.60	2.00	1	1	0	0	...	0-...	5.0	9	2	2	0	1-0	7	.375
—Philadelphia (N.L.)	6	6	.500	3.91	1.26	16	16	4	1	0	0-0	112.2	110	49	49	17	32-4	96	.253
—Arizona (N.L.)	5	6	.455	3.69	1.10	13	13	‡ 4	1	0	0-0	97.2	94	41	40	10	13-0	72	.257
2001—Arizona (N.L.)	• 22	6	.786	2.98	1.08	35	• 35	* 6	1	0	0-0	* 256.2	237	86	85	• 37	39-0	293	.245
2002—Arizona (N.L.)	23	7	.767	3.23	0.97	36	35	5	1	0	0-0	259.1	218	95	93	29	33-1	316	.224
2003—Tucson (PCL)	1	0	1.000	4.50	1.30	2	2	0	0	...	0-...	10.0	10	5	5	3	3-0	15	.256
—Arizona (N.L.)	8	-9	.471	2.95	1.05	24	24	3	2	0	0-0	168.0	144	58	55	17	32-2	194	.230
2004—Boston (A.L.)	* 21	6	.778	3.26	1.06	32	32	3	0	0	0-0	226.2	206	84	82	23	35-0	203	.239
2005—Pawtucket (Int'l)	0	2	.000	6.63	1.58	6	3	0	0	...	0-...	19.0	27	15	14	3	3-0	21	.321
—Boston (A.L.)	8	8	.500	5.69	1.53	32	11	0	0	0	9-11	93.1	121	59	59	12	22-0	87	.314
American League totals (5 years)	30	20	.600	4.07	1.25	108	48	3	0	5	12-20	389.1	397	181	176	41	89-1	332	.263
National League totals (13 years)	162	111	.593	3.30	1.11	406	333	79	19	5	10-14	2516.2	2216	979	922	257	571-40	2500	.235
Major League totals (18 years)	192	131	.594	3.40	1.13	514	381	82	19	10	22-34	2906.0	2613	1160	1098	298	660-41	2832	.239

DIVISION SERIES RECORD

Year Team (League)	W	L	Pct.	ERA	WHIP	G	GS	CG	ShO	Hld.	Sv.-Opp.	IP	H	R	ER	HR	BB-IBB	SO	Avg.
2001—Arizona (N.L.)	2	0	1.000	0.50	0.61	2	2	2	1	0	0-0	18.0	9	1	1	1	2-0	18	.143
2002—Arizona (N.L.)	0	0	...	1.29	1.14	1	1	0	0	0	0-0	7.0	7	1	1	1	1-0	7	.250
2004—Boston (A.L.)	1	0	1.000	2.70	1.65	1	1	0	0	0	0-0	6.2	9	3	2	2	2-0	4	.300
Division series totals (3 years)	3	0	1.000	1.14	0.95	4	4	2	1	0	0-0	31.2	25	5	4	4	5-0	29	.207

CHAMPIONSHIP SERIES RECORD

Year Team (League)	W	L	Pct.	ERA	WHIP	G	GS	CG	ShO	Hld.	Sv.-Opp.	IP	H	R	ER	HR	BB-IBB	SO	Avg.
1993—Philadelphia (N.L.)	0	0	...	1.69	1.00	2	2	0	0	0	0-0	16.0	11	4	3	0	5-0	19	.193
2001—Arizona (N.L.)	1	0	1.000	1.00	0.67	1	1	1	0	0	0-0	9.0	4	1	1	0	2-0	12	.133
2004—Boston (A.L.)	1	1	.500	6.30	1.20	2	2	0	0	0	0-0	10.0	10	7	7	1	2-0	5	.256
Champ. series totals (3 years)	2	1	.667	2.83	0.97	5	5	1	0	0	0-0	35.0	25	12	11	1	9-0	36	.195

WORLD SERIES RECORD

Year Team (League)	W	L	Pct.	ERA	WHIP	G	GS	CG	ShO	Hld.	Sv.-Opp.	IP	H	R	ER	HR	BB-IBB	SO	Avg.
1993—Philadelphia (N.L.)	1	1	.500	3.52	1.17	2	1	1	0	0	0-0	15.1	13	7	6	2	5-0	9	.236
2001—Arizona (N.L.)	1	0	1.000	1.69	0.66	3	3	0	0	0	0-0	21.1	12	4	4	2	2-0	26	.162
2004—Boston (A.L.)	1	0	1.000	0.00	0.83	1	1	0	0	0	0-0	6.0	4	1	0	0	1-0	4	.174
World series totals (3 years)	3	1	.750	2.11	0.99	6	6	1	0	0	0-0	42.2	29	12	10	4	8-0	39	.191

ALL-STAR GAME RECORD

Year Team (League)	W	L	Pct.	ERA	WHIP	G	GS	CG	ShO	Hld.	Sv.-Opp.	IP	H	R	ER	HR	BB-IBB	SO	Avg.
All-Star Game totals (3 years)	0	1	.000	3.00	1.17	3	2	0	0	0	0-0	6.0	6	2	2	0	1-0	9	.261

SCHMIDT, JASON   P

PERSONAL: Born January 29, 1973, in Lewiston, Idaho. ... 6-5/205. ... Throws right, bats right. ... Full name: Jason David Schmidt. ... High school: Kelso (Wash.).

TRANSACTIONS/CAREER NOTES: Selected by Atlanta Braves organization in eighth round of 1991 free-agent draft. ... On disabled list (July 15-August 30, 1996); included rehabilitation assignment to Greenville. ... Traded by Braves to Pittsburgh Pirates (August 30, 1996), completing deal in which Pirates traded P Denny Neagle to Braves for a player to be named (August 28, 1996). ... On disabled list (April 15-May 1 and June 10, 2000-remainder of season); included rehabilitation assignment to GCL Pirates. ... On disabled list (March 31-May 10, 2001); included rehabilitation assignments to Altoona and Nashville. ... Traded by Pirates with OF John Vander Wal to San Francisco Giants for OF Armando Rios and P Ryan Vogelsong (July 30, 2001). ... On disabled list (March 21-April 24, 2002); included rehabilitation assignment to Fresno. ... On disabled list (March 26-April 16, 2004); included rehabilitation assignment to San Jose. ... On disabled list (May 10-28, 2005).

HONORS: Named N.L. Pitcher of the Year by THE SPORTING NEWS (2004).

CAREER HITTING: 52-for-518 (.100), 23 R, 6 2B, 0 3B, 5 HR, 19 RBI.

SCOUTING REPORT **Throws:** Schmidt throws a four-seam fastball with late life, a slider and one of the best changeups in the game. Has lost some velocity on fastball because of arm problems, staying around 90-93. **Tendencies:** When healthy, he has good movement on his fastball down in the zone. Can pitch upstairs when hitting the mid-90s. Turns changeup over, running it away from lefthanded hitters. Has a quick slider but doesn't use it frequently. **Outlook:** Schmidt can again be a No. 1 starter, but there are a lot questions about his health. Needs a strong spring to reestablish his ability to anchor the Giants' rotation. **Grade 7.5**

JASON SCHMIDT'S PITCHING ZONE

.289	.276	.244
.339	.327	.200
.200	.317	.314

LEFTY-RIGHTY SPLITS

vs.	Avg.	AB	H	2B	3B	HR	RBI	BB	SO	OBP	Slg.
L	.264	364	96	24	2	7	48	46	93	.342	.398
R	.223	287	64	13	3	9	37	39	72	.323	.383

Year Team (League)	W	L	Pct.	ERA	WHIP	G	GS	CG	ShO	Hld.	Sv.-Opp.	IP	H	R	ER	HR	BB-IBB	SO	Avg.
1991—GC Braves (GCL)	3	4	.429	2.38	1.21	11	11	0	0	...	0-...	45.1	32	21	12	0	23-0	44	.189
1992—Pulaski (Appalachian)	3	4	.429	4.01	1.18	11	11	0	0	...	0-...	58.1	38	36	26	4	31-0	56	.170
—Macon (S. Atl.)	0	3	.000	4.01	2.03	7	7	0	0	...	0-...	24.2	31	18	11	2	19-0	33	.316
1993—Durham (Carol.)	7	11	.389	4.94	1.50	22	22	0	0	...	0-...	116.2	128	69	64	12	47-3	110	.286
1994—Greenville (Sou.)	8	7	.533	3.65	1.34	24	24	1	0	...	0-...	140.2	135	64	57	9	54-1	131	.255
1995—Atlanta (N.L.)	2	2	.500	5.76	1.80	9	2	0	0	0	0-1	25.0	27	17	16	2	18-3	19	.287
—Richmond (Int'l)	8	6	.571	2.25	1.25	19	19	0	0	...	0-...	116.0	97	40	29	2	48-3	95	.230
1996—Atlanta (N.L.)	3	4	.429	6.75	1.72	13	11	0	0	0	0-0	58.2	69	48	44	8	32-0	48	.296
—Richmond (Int'l)	3	0	1.000	2.56	1.20	7	7	0	0	...	0-...	45.2	36	17	13	2	19-1	41	.220
—Greenville (Sou.)	0	0	...	9.00	2.00	1	1	0	0	...	0-...	2.0	4	2	2	0	0-0	2	.444
—Pittsburgh (N.L.)	2	2	.500	4.06	1.59	6	6	1	0	0	0-0	37.2	39	19	17	2	21-0	26	.271
1997—Pittsburgh (N.L.)	10	9	.526	4.60	1.43	32	32	2	0	0	0-0	187.2	193	106	96	16	76-2	136	.265
1998—Pittsburgh (N.L.)	11	14	.440	4.07	1.40	33	33	0	0	0	0-0	214.1	228	106	97	24	71-3	158	.275
1999—Pittsburgh (N.L.)	13	11	.542	4.19	1.43	33	33	0	0	0	0-0	212.2	219	110	99	24	85-4	148	.262
2000—Pittsburgh (N.L.)	2	5	.286	5.40	1.77	11	11	0	0	0	0-0	63.1	71	43	38	6	41-2	51	.284
—GC Pirates (GCL)	0	0	...	2.25	1.25	1	1	0	0	...	0-...	4.0	4	2	1	0	1-0	7	.267
2001—Altoona (East.)	0	1	.000	0.96	0.86	3	3	0	0	...	0-...	9.1	7	1	1	0	1-0	17	.200

Year Team (League)	W	L	Pct.	ERA	WHIP	G	GS	CG	ShO	Hld.	Sv.-Opp.	IP	H	R	ER	HR	BB-IBB	SO	Avg.
—Nashville (PCL)	1	0	1.000	0.00	0.57	1	1	0	0	...	0-...	7.0	4	0	0	0	0-0	6	.160
—Pittsburgh (N.L.)	6	6	.500	4.61	1.30	14	14	1	0	0	0-0	84.0	81	46	43	11	28-2	77	.256
—San Francisco (N.L.)	7	1	.875	3.39	1.36	11	11	0	0	0	0-0	66.1	57	29	25	2	33-1	65	.230
2002—Fresno (PCL)	2	0	1.000	3.00	1.08	2	2	0	0	0	0-...	12.0	11	4	4	0	0	12	.262
—San Francisco (N.L.)	13	8	.619	3.45	1.19	29	29	2	2	0	0-0	185.1	148	78	71	15	73-1	196	.218
2003—San Francisco (N.L.)	17	5	.773	* 2.34	0.95	29	29	5	• 3	0	0-0	207.2	152	56	54	14	46-1	208 *	.200
2004—San Jose (Calif.)	1	0	1.000	0.00	0.60	1	1	0	0	...	0-...	5.0	2	0	0	0	1-0	7	.118
—San Francisco (N.L.)	18	7	.720	3.20	1.08	32	32	4	• 3	0	0-0	225.0	165	84	80	18	77-3	251	.202
2005—San Francisco (N.L.)	12	7	.632	4.40	1.42	29	29	0	0	0	0-0	172.0	160	90	84	16	85-4	165	.246
Major League totals (11 years)	116	81	.589	3.95	1.32	281	272	17	8	0	0-1	1739.2	1609	832	764	158	686-26	1548	.244

DIVISION SERIES RECORD

Year Team (League)	W	L	Pct.	ERA	WHIP	G	GS	CG	ShO	Hld.	Sv.-Opp.	IP	H	R	ER	HR	BB-IBB	SO	Avg.
2002—San Francisco (N.L.)	0	1	.000	6.75	1.31	1	1	0	0	0	0-0	5.1	3	4	4	0	4-1	5	.158
2003—San Francisco (N.L.)	1	0	1.000	0.00	0.33	1	1	1	1	0	0-0	9.0	3	0	0	0	0-0	5	.100
Division series totals (2 years)	1	1	.500	2.51	0.70	2	2	1	1	0	0-0	14.1	6	4	4	0	4-1	10	.122

CHAMPIONSHIP SERIES RECORD

Year Team (League)	W	L	Pct.	ERA	WHIP	G	GS	CG	ShO	Hld.	Sv.-Opp.	IP	H	R	ER	HR	BB-IBB	SO	Avg.
2002—San Francisco (N.L.)	1	0	1.000	1.17	0.65	1	1	0	0	0	0-0	7.2	4	1	1	1	1-0	8	.160

WORLD SERIES RECORD

Year Team (League)	W	L	Pct.	ERA	WHIP	G	GS	CG	ShO	Hld.	Sv.-Opp.	IP	H	R	ER	HR	BB-IBB	SO	Avg.
2002—San Francisco (N.L.)	1	0	1.000	5.23	1.94	2	2	0	0	0	0-0	10.1	16	6	6	2	4-0	14	.348

ALL-STAR GAME RECORD

	W	L	Pct.	ERA	WHIP	G	GS	CG	ShO	Hld.	Sv.-Opp.	IP	H	R	ER	HR	BB-IBB	SO	Avg.
All-Star Game totals (1 year)	0	0	...	0.00	0.50	1	1	0	0	0	0-0	2.0	1	0	0	0	0-0	3	.143

SCHMOLL, STEVE — P

PERSONAL: Born February 4, 1980, in Silver Spring, Md. ... 6-2/200. ... Throws right, bats right. ... Full name: Stephen John Schmoll. ... High school: Magruder (Md.). ... College: Maryland.
TRANSACTIONS/CAREER NOTES: Signed as a non-drafted free agent by Los Angeles Dodgers organization (May 25, 2003).
CAREER HITTING: 0-for-1 (.000), 0 R, 0 2B, 0 3B, 0 HR, 0 RBI.

STEVE SCHMOLL'S PITCHING ZONE

.375	.333	.300
.267	.476	.407
.294	.231	.000

LEFTY-RIGHTY SPLITS

vs.	Avg.	AB	H	2B	3B	HR	RBI	BB	SO	OBP	Slg.
L	.303	89	27	7	2	2	14	10	9	.376	.494
R	.244	82	20	4	0	2	15	12	20	.343	.366

Year Team (League)	W	L	Pct.	ERA	WHIP	G	GS	CG	ShO	Hld.	Sv.-Opp.	IP	H	R	ER	HR	BB-IBB	SO	Avg.
2003—Ogden (Pion.)	3	1	.750	3.68	1.15	24	1	0	0	...	7-...	36.2	27	23	15	2	15-0	53	.200
2004—Vero Beach (FSL)	3	3	.500	1.80	1.15	37	0	0	0	...	10-...	65.0	57	18	13	0	18-3	58	.226
—Jacksonville (Sou.)	0	2	.000	1.83	1.07	11	0	0	0	...	2-...	19.2	14	7	4	0	7-1	18	.197
2005—Las Vegas (PCL)	0	3	.000	4.78	1.41	22	0	0	0	4	5-7	26.1	24	15	14	1	13-1	31	.253
—Los Angeles (N.L.)	2	2	.500	5.01	1.48	48	0	0	0	9	3-4	46.2	47	29	26	4	22-2	29	.275
Major League totals (1 year)	2	2	.500	5.01	1.48	48	0	0	0	9	3-4	46.2	47	29	26	4	22-2	29	.275

SCHNEIDER, BRIAN — C

PERSONAL: Born November 26, 1976, in Jacksonville. ... 6-1/196. ... Bats left, throws right. ... Full name: Brian Duncan Schneider. ... High school: Northampton (Pa.).
TRANSACTIONS/CAREER NOTES: Selected by Montreal Expos organization in fifth round of 1995 free-agent draft. ... Expos franchise transferred to Washington, D.C., and renamed Washington Nationals for 2005 season (December 3, 2004).
2005 GAMES PLAYED BY POSITION (MLB): C—113.

SCOUTING REPORT *Offense:* A line-drive hitter, he swings with a shorter stroke and improved bat speed. Is quick to high pitches and has occasional power. Makes contact and doesn't strike out a lot. Stays in against lefthanders. Is not a threat on the basepaths. *Defense:* He is athletic and agile with quick footwork. Is an accurate thrower with a quick release and above-average arm strength. Aggressively blocks balls in the dirt and provides a good, low target. *Outlook:* The underrated Schneider should continue to improve at the plate. Could soon rank among the game's best defensive catchers. *Grade 7.5*

BRIAN SCHNEIDER'S HITTING ZONE

.261	.308	.300
.235	.471	.274
.333	.200	.279

LEFTY-RIGHTY SPLITS

vs.	Avg.	AB	H	2B	3B	HR	RBI	BB	SO	OBP	Slg.
L	.265	68	18	2	0	0	2	4	11	.324	.294
R	.269	301	81	18	1	10	42	25	37	.331	.435

Year Team (League)	Pos.	G	AB	R	H	2B	3B	HR	RBI	BB	SO	HBP	GDP	SB-CS	Avg.	OBP	SLG	OPS	E	Avg.
1995—GC Expos (GCL)	C	30	97	7	22	3	0	0	4	14	23	1	1	2-4	.227	.330	.258	.588	3	.982
1996—GC Expos (GCL)	C	52	144	26	44	5	2	0	23	24	15	3	3	2-3	.306	.415	.368	.783	3	.988
—Delmarva (S. Atl.)	C	5	9	0	3	0	0	1	1	1	1	1		0-0	.333	.455	.333	.788	0	1.000
1997—Cape Fear (S. Atl.)	C	113	381	46	96	20	1	4	49	53	45	4	9	3-6	.252	.345	.341	.687	10	.988
1998—Cape Fear (S. Atl.)	C	38	134	33	40	7	2	7	30	16	9	3	3	6-3	.299	.381	.537	.918	6	.980
—Jupiter (Fla. St.)	C	82	302	32	82	12	1	3	30	22	38	1	9	4-4	.272	.321	.348	.669	11	.981
1999—Harrisburg (East.)	C-1B	121	421	48	111	19	1	17	66	32	56	2	6	2-2	.264	.318	.435	.753	6	.982
2000—Ottawa (Int'l)	C-1B	67	238	22	59	22	3	4	31	16	42	0	5	1-0	.248	.285	.416	.701	8	.982
—Montreal (N.L.)	C	45	115	6	27	6	0	0	11	7	24	0	1	0-1	.235	.276	.287	.563	6	.974

Year Team (League)	Pos.	G	AB	R	H	2B	3B	HR	RBI	BB	SO	HBP	GDP	SB-CS	Avg.	OBP	SLG	OPS	E	Avg.
2001—Ottawa (Int'l)	C	97	338	33	93	27	1	6	43	27	55	4	5	2-0	.275	.336	.414	.750	4	.994
—Montreal (N.L.)	C	27	41	4	13	3	0	1	6	6	3	0	0	0-0	.317	.396	.463	.859	0	1.000
2002—Montreal (N.L.)	C-OF	73	207	21	57	19	2	5	29	21	41	0	7	1-2	.275	.339	.459	.798	3	.993
2003—Montreal (N.L.)	C-DH	108	335	34	77	26	1	9	46	37	75	2	12	0-2	.230	.309	.394	.703	3	.996
2004—Montreal (N.L.)	C	135	436	40	112	20	3	12	49	42	63	3	8	0-1	.257	.325	.399	.724	2	.998
2005—Was. (N.L.)	C	116	369	38	99	20	1	10	44	29	48	6	10	1-0	.268	.330	.409	.739	5	.993
Major League totals (6 years)		504	1503	143	385	94	7	37	185	142	254	11	38	2-6	.256	.323	.402	.725	19	.994

SCHOENEWEIS, SCOTT   P

PERSONAL: Born October 2, 1973, in Long Branch, N.J. ... 6-0/195. ... Throws left, bats left. ... Full name: Scott David Schoeneweis. ... Name pronounced: show-en-weiss. ... High school: Lenape (Medford, N.J.). ... College: Duke.

TRANSACTIONS/CAREER NOTES: Selected by California Angels organization in third round of 1996 free-agent draft. ... Angels franchise renamed Anaheim Angels for 1997 season. ... On disabled list (June 17-July 26, 2000); included rehabilitation assignments to Lake Elsinore and Edmonton. ... Traded by Anaheim Angels with P Doug Nickle to Chicago White Sox for Ps Gary Glover, Scott Dunn, and Tim Bittner (July 29, 2003). ... On disabled list (June 22-July 7 and August 5-September 30, 2004). ... Signed as a free agent by Toronto Blue Jays (January 10, 2005).

CAREER HITTING: 2-for-7 (.286), 0 R, 1 2B, 0 3B, 0 HR, 1 RBI.

SCOUTING REPORT **Throws:** His best pitch is a 90-93 mph sinker, and he also throws a slider. **Tendencies:** He only uses two pitches because he pitches in relief. Has a short, quick arm with consistent sinking action on his fastball. Tightly biting slider allows him to work both sides of the plate. **Outlook:** He is a former starter who now is on the verge of becoming a quality setup reliever. **Grade 7.5**

S

SCOTT SCHOENEWEIS'S PITCHING ZONE

.000	.200	.167
.343	.409	.280
.154	.294	.143

LEFTY-RIGHTY SPLITS

vs.	Avg.	AB	H	2B	3B	HR	RBI	BB	SO	OBP	Slg.
L	.188	112	21	1	1	1	13	10	24	.260	.241
R	.306	108	33	6	0	1	12	15	19	.405	.389

Year Team (League)	W	L	Pct.	ERA	WHIP	G	GS	CG	ShO	Hld.	Sv.-Opp.	IP	H	R	ER	HR	BB-IBB	SO	Avg.
1996—Lake Elsinore (Calif.)	8	3	.727	3.94	1.21	14	12	0	0		0-...	93.2	86	47	41	6	27-0	83	.244
1997—Midland (Texas)	7	5	.583	5.96	1.62	20	20	3	0		0-...	113.1	145	84	75	7	39-0	84	.313
1998—Vancouver (PCL)	11	8	.579	4.50	1.37	27	27	2	0		0-...	180.0	188	102	90	18	59-0	133	.266
1999—Anaheim (A.L.)	1	1	.500	5.49	1.55	31	0	0	0	3	0-0	39.1	47	27	24	4	14-1	22	.294
—Edmonton (PCL)	2	4	.333	7.64	1.98	9	7	0	0		0-...	35.1	58	35	30	6	12-0	29	.360
2000—Anaheim (A.L.)	7	10	.412	5.45	1.47	27	27	1	1	0	0-0	170.0	183	112	103	21	67-2	78	.276
—Lake Elsinore (Calif.)	0	0	...	1.93	1.29	1	1	0	0		0-...	4.2	3	1	1	0	3-0	3	.200
—Edmonton (PCL)	0	0	...	0.00	0.43	1	1	0	0		0-...	7.0	2	0	0	0	1-0	6	.083
2001—Anaheim (A.L.)	10	11	.476	5.08	1.48	32	32	1	0	0	0-0	205.1	227	122	116	21	77-2	104	.281
2002—Anaheim (A.L.)	9	8	.529	4.88	1.42	54	15	0	0	11	1-4	118.0	119	68	64	17	49-4	65	.264
2003—Anaheim (A.L.)	1	1	.500	3.96	1.22	39	0	0	0	4	0-1	38.2	37	19	17	2	10-3	29	.250
—Chicago (A.L.)	2	1	.667	4.50	1.35	20	0	0	0	0	0-1	26.0	26	16	13	1	9-2	27	.255
2004—Chicago (A.L.)	6	9	.400	5.59	1.58	20	19	0	0	0	0-0	112.2	129	74	70	17	49-0	69	.291
2005—Toronto (A.L.)	3	4	.429	3.32	1.39	80	0	0	0	21	1-4	57.0	54	23	21	2	25-5	43	.245
Major League totals (7 years)	39	45	.464	5.02	1.46	303	93	2	1	39	2-10	767.0	822	461	428	85	300-19	437	.275

DIVISION SERIES RECORD

Year Team (League)	W	L	Pct.	ERA	WHIP	G	GS	CG	ShO	Hld.	Sv.-Opp.	IP	H	R	ER	HR	BB-IBB	SO	Avg.
2002—Anaheim (A.L.)	0	0	...	27.00	6.00	3	0	0	0	0	0-1	0.1	2	1	1	0	0-0	0	.667

CHAMPIONSHIP SERIES RECORD

Year Team (League)	W	L	Pct.	ERA	WHIP	G	GS	CG	ShO	Hld.	Sv.-Opp.	IP	H	R	ER	HR	BB-IBB	SO	Avg.
2002—Anaheim (A.L.)	0	0	...	0.00	0.00	1	0	0	0	0	0-0	0.2	0	0	0	0	0-0	0	.000

WORLD SERIES RECORD

Year Team (League)	W	L	Pct.	ERA	WHIP	G	GS	CG	ShO	Hld.	Sv.-Opp.	IP	H	R	ER	HR	BB-IBB	SO	Avg.
2002—Anaheim (A.L.)	0	0	...	0.00	1.00	2	0	0	0	0	0-0	2.0	1	0	0	0	1-0	2	.167

SCHUMAKER, SKIP   OF

PERSONAL: Born February 3, 1980, in Torrance, Calif. ... 5-10/175. ... Bats left, throws right. ... Full name: Jared Michael Schumaker. ... High school: Aliso Niguel (Aliso Viejo, Calif.). ... College: California-Santa Barbara.

TRANSACTIONS/CAREER NOTES: Selected by St. Louis Cardinals organization in fifth round of 2001 free-agent draft.

2005 GAMES PLAYED BY POSITION (MLB): OF—21.

LEFTY-RIGHTY SPLITS

vs.	Avg.	AB	H	2B	3B	HR	RBI	BB	SO	OBP	Slg.
L	.500	2	1	0	0	0	0	0	1	.500	.500
R	.227	22	5	1	0	1	1	2	1	.292	.273

Year Team (League)	Pos.	G	AB	R	H	2B	3B	HR	RBI	BB	SO	HBP	GDP	SB-CS	Avg.	OBP	SLG	OPS	E	Avg.
2001—New Jersey (NYP)	OF	49	162	22	41	10	1	0	14	29	33	1	4	11-2	.253	.368	.327	.695	2	.971
2002—Potomac (Carol.)	OF	136	551	71	158	22	4	2	44	45	84	2	10	26-16	.287	.342	.352	.694	3	.988
2003—Tennessee (Sou.)	OF-3B	91	342	43	86	20	3	2	22	37	54	4	4	6-6	.251	.330	.345	.675	1	.994
2004—Tennessee (Sou.)	OF-3B	138	516	78	163	29	6	4	43	60	61	2	7	19-14	.316	.389	.419	.808	7	.821
2005—Memphis (PCL)	OF	115	443	66	127	24	3	7	34	29	54	2	14	14-3	.287	.330	.402	.732	2	.996
—St. Louis (N.L.)	OF	27	24	9	6	1	0	1	1	2	2	0	0	1-0	.250	.308	.292	.599	0	1.000
Major League totals (1 year)		27	24	9	6	1	0	1	1	2	2	0	0	1-0	.250	.308	.292	.599	0	1.000

SCOTT, LUKE   OF

PERSONAL: Born June 25, 1978, in Deleon Springs, Fla. ... 6-0/210. ... Bats left, throws right. ... Full name: Luke Brandon Scott. ... High school: DeLand (Fla.). ... Junior college: Indian River (Fla.). ... College: Oklahoma State.

TRANSACTIONS/CAREER NOTES: Selected by Cleveland Indians organization in ninth round of 2001 free-agent draft. ... Traded by Indians with OF Willy Taveras to Houston Astros for P Jeriome Robertson (March 31, 2004).
2005 GAMES PLAYED BY POSITION (MLB): OF—24.

SCOUTING REPORT Scott has a sweeping swing and a slider-speed bat. Is a better low-ball hitter. Doesn't turn on inside pitches but has good power to the opposite field. Is a below-average runner. Is better in left field than right. Doesn't go back on balls well. Has good arm strength. Will be a good fourth outfielder if he hits well. **Grade 5**

LUKE SCOTT'S HITTING ZONE

.000	.000	.000
.100	.333	.333
.000	.375	.300

LEFTY-RIGHTY SPLITS

vs.	Avg.	AB	H	2B	3B	HR	RBI	BB	SO	OBP	Slg.
L	.286	7	2	0	0	0	0	0	3	.286	.286
R	.178	73	13	4	2	0	4	9	20	.268	.288

									BATTING										FIELDING	
Year Team (League)	Pos.	G	AB	R	H	2B	3B	HR	RBI	BB	SO	HBP	GDP	SB-CS	Avg.	OBP	SLG	OPS	E	Avg.
2002—Columbus (S. Atl.)	OF	49	171	28	44	15	4	7	32	21	58	3	3	9-1	.257	.345	.515	.860	1	.971
—Kinston (Carol.)	OF-1B	48	163	22	39	7	1	8	30	16	47	5	2	2-1	.239	.326	.442	.768	2	.973
2003—Kinston (Carol.)	OF-1B	67	241	37	67	12	1	13	44	27	62	4	0	6-3	.278	.360	.498	.858	1	.989
—Akron (East.)	OF	50	183	21	50	13	1	7	37	11	37	2	2	0-1	.273	.317	.470	.787	2	.947
2004—Salem (Carol.)	OF	66	241	45	67	20	1	8	35	41	58	0	5	6-1	.278	.376	.469	.845	1	.500
—Round Rock (Texas)	OF	63	208	45	62	17	0	19	62	33	43	6	4	0-2	.298	.401	.654	1.055	1	.000
2005—Round Rock (PCL)	OF-DH	103	398	69	114	25	4	31	87	43	96	6	4	2-2	.286	.363	.603	.966	2	.996
—Houston (N.L.)	OF	34	80	6	15	4	2	0	4	9	23	0	0	1-1	.188	.270	.288	.557	1	.963
Major League totals (1 year)		34	80	6	15	4	2	0	4	9	23	0	0	1-1	.188	.270	.288	.557	1	.963

DIVISION SERIES RECORD

Year Team (League)	Pos.	G	AB	R	H	2B	3B	HR	RBI	BB	SO	HBP	GDP	SB-CS	Avg.	OBP	SLG	OPS	E	Avg.
2005—Houston (N.L.)	OF	2	2	1	0	0	0	0	1	0	0			0-0	.000	.333	.000	.333	0	...

SCUTARO, MARCO   2B/SS

S

PERSONAL: Born October 30, 1975, in San Felipe, Venezuela. ... 5-10/170. ... Bats right, throws right. ... Full name: Marcos Scutaro. ... Name pronounced: scoot-AH-roh. ... High school: Frederico Quiroz (Venezuela).
TRANSACTIONS/CAREER NOTES: Signed as a non-drafted free agent by Cleveland Indians organization (July 26, 1994). ... Traded by Indians to Milwaukee Brewers (August 30, 2000); completing deal in which Indians traded 1B Richie Sexson, Ps Paul Rigdon and Kane Davis and a player to be named to Brewers for Ps Bob Wickman, Jason Bere and Steve Woodard (July 28, 2000). ... Claimed on waivers by New York Mets (April 5, 2002). ... Claimed on waivers by Oakland Athletics (October 9, 2003).
2005 GAMES PLAYED BY POSITION (MLB): SS—81, 2B—30, 3B—5, OF—2.

SCOUTING REPORT **Offense:** Scutaro is an aggressive hitter with line-drive power, but he struggles against lefthanded pitchers. Uses the whole field. Has a long swing but still has good bat speed. Has cut down his strikeouts. Can drive pitches up in the zone and shows occasional power. **Defense:** He has good hands and quick feet. Gets himself into good position to field the ball. Has more than enough arm to play second or short and can make the double play. Can be too flashy, to the point of being careless. Has above-average range to his left. **Outlook:** The A's always try to get rid of Scutaro, but he has been a valuable piece the past two seasons because of injuries to regulars. Is a good infielder who has increased his value. **Grade 6.3**

MARCO SCUTARO'S HITTING ZONE

.381	.292	.091
.227	.319	.364
.205	.267	.059

LEFTY-RIGHTY SPLITS

vs.	Avg.	AB	H	2B	3B	HR	RBI	BB	SO	OBP	Slg.
L	.171	76	13	2	1	1	7	12	7	.284	.263
R	.266	305	81	20	2	8	30	24	41	.317	.423

									BATTING										FIELDING	
Year Team (League)	Pos.	G	AB	R	H	2B	3B	HR	RBI	BB	SO	HBP	GDP	SB-CS	Avg.	OBP	SLG	OPS	E	Avg.
1995—Dom. Inds. (DSL)	3B	66	262	71	103	18	6	0	38	20	11	...		32-...	.393	...	.508	...	17	.931
1996—Columbus (S. Atl.)	2B-3B-SS	85	315	66	79	12	3	10	45	38	86	4	6	6-3	.251	.334	.403	.737	17	.959
1997—Kinston (Carol.)	2B-3B	97	378	58	103	17	6	10	59	35	72	9	3	23-7	.263	.346	.429	.774	11	.972
—Buffalo (A.A.)	2B-3B-SS	21	57	8	15	3	0	1	6	6	8	0	4	0-1	.263	.328	.368	.697	3	.959
1998—Akron (East.)	2B-SS	124	462	68	146	27	6	11	62	47	71	10	8	33-16	.316	.387	.472	.859	15	.976
—Buffalo (Int'l)	2B-3B	8	26	3	6	3	0	0	4	0	2	0	0	0-0	.231	.231	.346	.577	2	.939
1999—Buffalo (Int'l)	2B-SS	129	462	76	126	24	2	8	51	61	69	6	5	21-6	.273	.362	.385	.747	16	.974
2000—Buffalo (Int'l)	2B-SS	124	425	67	117	20	5	5	54	61	53	9	...	9-6	.275	.373	.381	.754	15	.976
—Indianapolis (Int'l)	2B-SS	4	13	5	7	1	1	1	3	1	2	0	...	1-0	.538	.571	1.000	1.571	0	1.000
2001—Indianapolis (Int'l)	2B-3B-SS	132	495	87	146	29	3	11	50	62	83	10	9	11-11	.295	.382	.432	.815	19	.968
2002—Norfolk (Int'l)	2B-SS-OF 3B	97	354	48	113	22	6	7	28	30	61	2	7	7-8	.319	.375	.475	.849	10	.974
—New York (N.L.)	2B-SS-3B OF	27	36	2	8	0	1	1	6	0	11	0	1	0-1	.222	.216	.361	.577	1	.968
2003—Norfolk (Int'l)	3B-2B-SS OF-DH	70	244	42	76	18	3	9	32	33	34	0	6	11-6	.311	.401	.520	.921	7	.970
—New York (N.L.)	2B-SS	48	75	10	16	4	0	2	6	13	14	1	1	2-0	.213	.333	.347	.680	2	.981
2004—Oakland (A.L.)	2B-SS-3B	137	455	50	124	32	1	7	43	16	58	0	9	0-0	.273	.297	.393	.690	5	.992
2005—Oakland (A.L.)	SS-2B-3B OF	118	381	48	94	22	3	9	37	36	48	0	6	5-2	.247	.310	.391	.701	9	.982
American League totals (2 years)		255	836	98	218	54	4	16	80	52	106	0	15	5-2	.261	.303	.392	.695	14	.987
National League totals (2 years)		75	111	12	24	4	1	3	12	13	25	1	2	2-1	.216	.299	.351	.651	3	.978
Major League totals (4 years)		330	947	110	242	58	5	19	92	65	131	1	17	7-3	.256	.303	.388	.690	17	.986

SEABOL, SCOTT 3B/2B

PERSONAL: Born May 17, 1975, in McKeesport, Pa. ... 6-4/200. ... Bats right, throws right. ... Full name: Scott Anthony Seabol. ... Name pronounced: SEA-bowl. ... High school: South Allegheny (Pa.). ... College: West Virginia.

TRANSACTIONS/CAREER NOTES: Selected by New York Yankees organization in 88th round of 1996 free-agent draft. ... On disabled list (August 27, 2000-remainder of season). ... Signed as a free agent by Milwaukee Brewers organization (November 12, 2002). ... Released by Brewers (May 15, 2003). ... Signed by St. Louis Cardinals organization (May 27, 2003).

2005 GAMES PLAYED BY POSITION (MLB): 3B—20, 2B—8, 1B—5, OF—4, DH—3.

SCOTT SEABOL'S HITTING ZONE

.273	.167	.143
.267	.417	.167
.214	.400	.143

LEFTY-RIGHTY SPLITS

vs.	Avg.	AB	H	2B	3B	HR	RBI	BB	SO	OBP	Slg.
L	.224	49	11	4	0	0	5	5	9	.291	.306
R	.214	56	12	1	0	1	5	3	14	.254	.286

Year	Team (League)	Pos.	G	AB	R	H	2B	3B	HR	RBI	BB	SO	HBP	GDP	SB-CS	Avg.	OBP	SLG	OPS	E	Avg.
1996— Oneonta (NYP)	1B-3B-SS																				
	2B	43	142	16	30	9	1	3	10	15	30	6	1	2-3	.211	.313	.352	.665	11	.957
1997— Greensboro (S. Atl.)	OF-3B-SS	48	136	11	36	12	2	2	15	9	26	4	1	3-1	.265	.325	.426	.751	6	.887
1998— Greensboro (S. Atl.)	OF-3B-1B																			
	-SS	71	210	24	60	11	0	7	33	13	40	3	4	2-2	.286	.333	.438	.771	4	.960
1999— Greensboro (S. Atl.)	3B-OF-SS	138	543	86	171	55	6	15	89	45	91	9	9	6-5	.315	.370	.521	.891	24	.936
2000— Norwich (East.)	3B-OF-1B																			
	2B	132	493	82	146	45	2	20	78	42	108	4	11	2-4	.296	.355	.517	.872	22	.934
2001— New York (A.L.)	DH	1	1	0	0	0	0	0	0	0	0	0	0	0-0	.000	.000	.000	.000	...	...
— Columbus (Int'l)	1B-3B-SS																			
	OF-2B	78	282	32	75	19	1	10	42	14	56	4	6	3-4	.266	.308	.447	.755	13	.945
— Norwich (East.)	3B-OF-1B	31	128	16	32	7	0	4	19	5	30	3	4	1-1	.250	.290	.398	.688	11	.875
2002— Columbus (Int'l)	1B-SS-3B																			
	OF-2B	121	428	56	111	29	1	15	68	29	89	5	6	3-3	.259	.309	.437	.746	‡ 17	.980
2003— Indianapolis (Int'l)	1B-3B-OF	25	81	6	19	1	2	0	9	4	18	0	4	0-1	.235	.264	.296	.560	2	.985
— Memphis (PCL)	3B-2B-1B	88	307	40	92	22	1	16	58	32	64	8	5	2-0	.300	.376	.534	.910	14	.951
2004— Memphis (PCL)	3B-2B-1B	138	514	92	156	26	1	31	78	37	93	7	17	6-3	.304	.356	.539	.895	14	.853
2005— Memphis (PCL)	3B	54	203	34	54	18	2	9	33	20	40	0	5	0-0	.266	.330	.507	.838	7	.951
— St. Louis (N.L.)	3B-2B-1B																			
	OF-DH	59	105	11	23	5	0	1	10	8	23	0	1	0-0	.219	.272	.295	.567	3	.967
American League totals (1 year)		1	1	0	0	0	0	0	0	0	0	0	0	0-0	.000	.000	.000	.000	...	...
National League totals (1 year)		59	105	11	23	5	0	1	10	8	23	0	1	0-0	.219	.272	.295	.567	3	.967
Major League totals (2 years)		60	106	11	23	5	0	1	10	8	23	0	1	0-0	.217	.270	.292	.562	3	.967

SEANEZ, RUDY P

PERSONAL: Born October 20, 1968, in Brawley, Calif. ... 5-11/200. ... Throws right, bats right. ... Full name: Rudy Caballero Seanez. ... Name pronounced: SEE-ahn-ez. ... High school: Brawley (Calif.) Union.

TRANSACTIONS/CAREER NOTES: Selected by Cleveland Indians organization in fourth round of June 1986 free-agent draft. ... On disabled list (April 1-16 and July 30-September 2, 1991); included rehabilitation assignment to Colorado Springs. ... Traded by Indians to Los Angeles Dodgers for Ps Dennis Cook and Mike Christopher (December 10, 1991). ... On disabled list (March 29, 1992-entire season). ... Traded by Dodgers to Colorado Rockies for 2B Jody Reed (November 17, 1992). ... On disabled list (April 4-July 16, 1993); included rehabilitation assignments to Central Valley and Colorado Springs. ... Signed as a free agent by San Diego Padres organization (July 22, 1993). ... Released by Padres (November 18, 1993). ... Signed by Dodgers organization (January 12, 1994). ... On disabled list (May 28-June 16, 1995); included rehabilitation assignment to San Bernardino. ... Signed as a free agent by New York Mets organization (January 15, 1997). ... Traded by Mets to Kansas City Royals for future considerations (May 30, 1997). ... Signed as a free agent by Atlanta Braves organization (December 9, 1997). ... On disabled list (August 21, 1999-remainder of season). ... On disabled list (March 23-April 27, 2000 and June 14-remainder of season); included rehabilitation assignment to Greenville. ... Signed as a free agent by Padres organization (February 14, 2001). ... On disabled list (June 6-21, 2001). ... Traded by Padres to Braves for a player to be named (August 31, 2001); Padres acquired P Winston Abreu to complete deal (September 6, 2001). ... Signed as a free agent by Texas Rangers (January 28, 2002). ... On disabled list (May 30-September 2, 2002); included rehabilitation assignments to Oklahoma. ... Released by Rangers (May 3, 2003). ... Signed by Boston Red Sox organization (May 6, 2003). ... Released by Red Sox (July 30, 2003). ... Signed by Chicago Cubs organization (August 1, 2003). ... Signed by Kansas City Royals organization (February 12, 2004). ... Traded by Royals to Florida Marlins for OF Abraham Nunez (July 31, 2004). ... Signed as a free agent by Padres (November 24, 2004). ... On disabled list (July 18-August 12, 2005); included rehabilitation assignment to Lake Elsinore.

CAREER HITTING: 0-for-4 (.000), 1 R, 0 2B, 0 3B, 0 HR, 0 RBI.

SCOUTING REPORT *Throws:* His two-seam and four-seam fastballs top out in the low 90s. Has a hard slider that acts like a cutter, and a very hard circle change. *Tendencies:* Seanez likes to go right at hitters with his four-seamer. Has some boring action when the ball is waist-high and up, but it straightens out when the ball is down and over the center of the plate. Slider moves late and occasionally breaks straight down. Circle change is very hard and sinks, giving it the illusion of a splitter. Is equally effective against righthanded and lefthanded hitters. *Outlook:* Injury-prone with a history of back problems, Seanez still appeared in 57 games last season. Will prove to be a valuable free-agent acquisition. *Grade 7.8*

RUDY SEANEZ'S PITCHING ZONE

.133	.000	.300
.216	.346	.167
.280	.143	.571

LEFTY-RIGHTY SPLITS

vs.	Avg.	AB	H	2B	3B	HR	RBI	BB	SO	OBP	Slg.
L	.231	108	25	5	2	3	10	13	39	.320	.398
R	.212	113	24	4	0	1	11	9	45	.274	.274

Year	Team (League)	W	L	Pct.	ERA	WHIP	G	GS	CG	ShO	Hld.	Sv.-Opp.	IP	H	R	ER	HR	BB-IBB	SO	Avg.
1986— Burlington (Appal.)		5	2	.714	3.20	1.20	13	12	1	1	...	0-...	76.0	59	37	27	4	32-0	56	.212
1987— Waterloo (Midw.)		0	4	.000	6.75	1.67	10	10	0	0	...	0-...	34.2	35	29	26	6	23-0	23	.263
1988— Waterloo (Midw.)		6	6	.500	4.69	1.46	22	22	1	1	...	0-...	113.1	98	69	59	10	68-0	93	.230
1989— Kinston (Carol.)		8	10	.444	4.14	1.81	25	25	1	0	...	0-...	113.0	94	66	52	10	111-1	149	.223

S

Year	Team (League)	W	L	Pct.	ERA	WHIP	G	GS	CG	ShO	Hld.	Sv.-Opp.	IP	H	R	ER	HR	BB-IBB	SO	Avg.
—	Colo. Springs (PCL)	0	0	...	0.00	1.00	1	0	0	0	...	0-...	1.0	1	0	0	0	0-0	0	.250
—	Cleveland (A.L.)	0	0	...	3.60	1.00	5	0	0	0	0	0-0	5.0	1	2	2	0	4-1	7	.071
1990—	Cant./Akr. (Eastern)	1	0	1.000	2.16	1.26	15	0	0	0	...	5-...	16.2	9	4	4	0	12-0	27	.170
—	Cleveland (A.L.)	2	1	.667	5.60	1.72	24	0	0	0	3	0-0	27.1	22	17	17	2	25-1	24	.220
—	Colo. Springs (PCL)	1	4	.200	6.75	2.08	12	0	0	0	...	1-...	12.0	15	10	9	2	10-0	7	.313
1991—	Colo. Springs (PCL)	0	0	...	7.27	2.25	16	0	0	0	...	0-...	17.1	17	14	14	2	22-0	19	.274
—	Cant./Akr. (Eastern)	4	2	.667	2.58	1.23	25	0	0	0	...	7-...	38.1	17	12	11	2	30-1	73	.132
—	Cleveland (A.L.)	0	0	...	16.20	3.40	5	0	0	0	0	0-1	5.0	10	12	9	2	7-0	1	.385
1992—	Los Angeles (N.L.)				Did not play.															
1993—	Central Valley (Cal.)	0	2	.000	9.72	2.40	5	1	0	0	...	0-...	8.1	9	9	9	0	11-0	7	.265
—	Colo. Springs (PCL)	0	0	...	9.00	1.33	3	0	0	0	...	0-...	3.0	3	3	3	1	1-0	5	.250
—	Las Vegas (PCL)	0	1	.000	6.41	1.78	14	0	0	0	...	0-...	19.2	24	15	14	2	11-0	14	.308
—	San Diego (N.L.)	0	0	...	13.50	3.00	3	0	0	0	...	0-0	3.1	8	6	5	1	2-0	1	.471
1994—	Albuquerque (PCL)	2	1	.667	5.32	1.86	20	0	0	0	...	9-...	22.0	28	14	13	3	13-1	26	.308
—	Los Angeles (N.L.)	1	1	.500	2.66	1.39	17	0	0	0	1	0-1	23.2	24	7	7	2	9-1	18	.273
1995—	Los Angeles (N.L.)	1	3	.250	6.75	1.64	37	0	0	0	...	3-4	34.2	39	27	26	5	18-3	29	.285
—	San Bern. (Calif.)	2	0	1.000	0.00	0.83	4	0	0	0	...	1-...	6.0	2	0	0	0	3-0	5	.100
1996—	Albuquerque (PCL)	0	2	.000	6.52	1.97	21	0	0	0	...	6-...	19.1	27	18	14	0	11-1	20	.325
1997—	Norfolk (Int'l)	1	0	1.000	4.05	1.73	9	0	0	0	...	0-...	13.1	12	8	6	1	11-0	17	.231
—	Omaha (A.A.)	2	5	.286	6.51	1.66	28	3	0	0	...	0-...	47.0	53	42	34	13	25-0	46	.270
1998—	Richmond (Int'l)	2	0	1.000	1.29	0.95	16	0	0	0	...	7-...	21.0	13	9	3	1	7-1	33	.169
—	Atlanta (N.L.)	4	1	.800	2.75	1.14	34	0	0	0	8	2-4	36.0	25	13	11	2	16-0	50	.195
1999—	Atlanta (N.L.)	6	1	.857	3.35	1.27	56	0	0	0	18	3-8	53.2	47	21	20	3	21-1	41	.234
2000—	Greenville (Sou.)	0	0	...	0.00	1.00	2	1	0	0	...	0-...	2.0	2	0	0	0	0-0	3	.250
—	Atlanta (N.L.)	2	4	.333	4.29	1.14	23	0	0	0	6	2-3	21.0	15	11	10	3	9-1	20	.192
2001—	Lake Elsinore (Calif.)	2	0	1.000	2.08	1.04	7	0	0	0	...	0-...	8.2	7	3	2	1	2-0	8	.219
—	San Diego (N.L.)	0	2	.000	2.63	1.25	26	0	0	0	5	1-3	24.0	15	8	7	3	15-0	24	.176
—	Atlanta (N.L.)	0	0	...	3.00	1.00	12	0	0	0	4	0-0	12.0	8	4	4	1	4-0	17	.182
2002—	Texas (A.L.)	1	3	.250	5.73	1.58	33	0	0	0	10	0-4	33.0	28	25	21	5	24-1	40	.230
—	Oklahoma (PCL)	0	0	...	4.50	1.00	4	0	0	0	...	0-...	4.0	4	2	2	0	0-0	3	.267
2003—	Oklahoma (PCL)	0	1	.000	2.08	1.80	5	0	0	0	...	0-...	4.1	3	4	1	0	5-0	7	.176
—	Boston (A.L.)	0	1	.000	6.23	1.96	9	0	0	0	0	0-1	8.2	11	7	6	2	6-1	9	.297
—	Pawtucket (Int'l)	2	2	.500	6.10	1.50	17	0	0	0	...	3-...	20.2	20	14	14	5	10-1	24	.253
—	Iowa (PCL)	1	2	.333	3.46	1.60	13	0	0	0	...	2-...	13.0	12	10	5	1	9-2	13	.235
2004—	Omaha (PCL)	2	1	.667	1.57	0.90	24	0	0	0	...	3-...	34.1	19	8	6	3	12-0	41	.152
—	Kansas City (A.L.)	0	1	.000	3.91	1.39	16	0	0	0	1	0-1	23.0	21	10	10	0	11-2	21	.244
—	Florida (N.L.)	3	1	.750	2.74	1.13	23	0	0	0	3	0-1	23.0	18	7	7	0	8-1	25	.212
2005—	Lake Elsinore (Calif.)	0	1	.000	36.00	4.00	1	0	0	0	...	0-0	1.0	3	4	4	2	1-0	0	.500
—	San Diego (N.L.)	7	1	.875	2.69	1.18	57	0	0	0	11	0-2	60.1	49	19	18	4	22-4	84	.222
	American League totals (6 years)	3	6	.333	5.74	1.67	92	0	0	0	14	0-7	102.0	93	73	65	11	77-6	108	.242
	National League totals (9 years)	24	14	.632	3.55	1.28	288	0	0	0	62	11-26	291.2	248	123	115	27	124-11	309	.229
	Major League totals (14 years)	27	20	.574	4.12	1.38	380	0	0	0	76	11-33	393.2	341	196	180	38	201-17	417	.232

DIVISION SERIES RECORD

Year	Team (League)	W	L	Pct.	ERA	WHIP	G	GS	CG	ShO	Hld.	Sv.-Opp.	IP	H	R	ER	HR	BB-IBB	SO	Avg.
1998—	Atlanta (N.L.)	0	0	...	0.00	0.00	1	0	0	0	0	0-0	1.0	0	0	0	0	0-0	0	.000
2001—	Atlanta (N.L.)	1	0	1.000	0.00	1.00	1	0	0	0	0	0-0	1.0	0	0	0	0	1-0	0	.000
2005—	San Diego (N.L.)	0	0	...	6.00	1.33	2	0	0	0	0	0-0	3.0	3	2	2	0	1-0	4	.250
	Division series totals (3 years)	1	0	1.000	3.60	1.00	4	0	0	0	0	0-0	5.0	3	2	2	0	2-0	4	.167

CHAMPIONSHIP SERIES RECORD

Year	Team (League)	W	L	Pct.	ERA	WHIP	G	GS	CG	ShO	Hld.	Sv.-Opp.	IP	H	R	ER	HR	BB-IBB	SO	Avg.
1998—	Atlanta (N.L.)	0	0	...	6.00	1.00	4	0	0	0	1	0-0	3.0	2	2	2	0	1-0	4	.200
2001—	Atlanta (N.L.)	0	0	...	0.00	2.00	2	0	0	0	0	0-0	2.0	1	0	0	0	3-2	3	.143
	Champ. series totals (2 years)	0	0	...	3.60	1.40	6	0	0	0	1	0-0	5.0	3	2	2	0	4-2	7	.176

SEAY, BOBBY — P

PERSONAL: Born June 20, 1978, in Sarasota, Fla. ... 6-2/235. ... Throws left, bats left. ... Full name: Robert Michael Seay. ... Name pronounced: see. ... High school: Sarasota (Fla.).

TRANSACTIONS/CAREER NOTES: Selected by Chicago White Sox organization in first round (12th pick overall) of 1996 free-agent draft. ... Rights relinquished by White Sox (August 15, 1996). ... Signed by Tampa Bay Devil Rays organization (November 8, 1996). ... On disabled list (March 22-June 3, 2002); included rehabilitation assignment to Orlando. ... On disabled list (April 24-June 3, 2003). ... Traded by Devil Rays to Colorado Rockies for OF Reggie Taylor (April 8, 2005). ... On disabled list (April 18-June 5, 2005); inlcuded rehabilitation assignments to Tulsa and Colorado Springs.

CAREER HITTING: 0-for-0 (.000), 0 R, 0 2B, 0 3B, 0 HR, 0 RBI.

LEFTY-RIGHTY SPLITS

vs.	Avg.	AB	H	2B	3B	HR	RBI	BB	SO	OBP	Slg.
L	.421	19	8	1	0	1	3	4	4	.522	.632
R	.333	30	10	3	0	2	10	4	7	.412	.633

Year	Team (League)	W	L	Pct.	ERA	WHIP	G	GS	CG	ShO	Hld.	Sv.-Opp.	IP	H	R	ER	HR	BB-IBB	SO	Avg.
1997—	Char., S.C. (SAL)	3	4	.429	4.55	1.52	13	13	0	0	...	0-...	61.1	56	35	31	2	37-0	64	.249
1998—	Char., S.C. (SAL)	1	7	.125	4.30	1.28	15	15	0	0	...	0-...	69.0	59	40	33	10	29-0	74	.236
1999—	St. Pete. (FSL)	2	6	.250	3.00	1.39	12	11	0	0	...	0-...	57.0	56	25	19	0	23-0	45	.271
—	Orlando (South.)	1	2	.333	7.94	2.18	6	6	0	0	...	0-...	17.0	22	15	15	2	15-0	16	.319
2000—	Orlando (South.)	8	7	.533	3.88	1.40	24	24	0	0	...	0-...	132.1	132	64	57	13	53-1	106	.265
2001—	Orlando (South.)	2	5	.286	5.98	1.65	15	13	0	0	...	0-...	64.2	81	48	43	9	26-0	49	.310
—	Tampa Bay (A.L.)	1	1	.500	6.23	1.38	12	0	0	0	0	0-0	13.0	13	11	9	3	5-1	12	.260
2002—	Orlando (South.)	2	0	1.000	3.28	1.29	15	3	0	0	...	0-...	35.2	31	16	13	2	15-0	24	.237
—	Durham (Int'l)	0	0	...	6.00	1.13	10	0	0	0	...	0-...	15.0	15	10	10	1	2-0	14	.254
2003—	Tampa Bay (A.L.)	0	0	...	3.00	1.44	12	0	0	0	0	0-1	9.0	7	3	3	0	6-0	5	.226
—	Durham (Int'l)	3	0	1.000	2.10	1.30	25	0	0	0	...	0-...	30.0	23	10	7	1	15-0	29	.205
2004—	Durham (Int'l)	2	1	.667	1.72	0.95	29	0	0	0	...	1-...	36.2	26	9	7	1	9-0	35	.195
—	Tampa Bay (A.L.)	0	0	...	2.38	1.15	21	0	0	0	0	0-0	22.2	21	6	6	2	5-1	17	.239
2005—	Tulsa (Texas)	1	0	1.000	1.80	0.60	4	0	0	0	...	1-1	5.0	3	1	1	0	0-0	3	.188
—	Colorado (N.L.)	0	0	...	8.49	2.23	17	0	0	0	0	0-1	11.2	18	11	11	3	8-1	11	.367
—	Colo. Springs (PCL)	1	0	1.000	2.38	1.46	17	0	0	0	1	3-3	22.2	23	8	6	2	10-0	24	.271
	American League totals (3 years)	1	1	.500	3.63	1.28	45	0	0	0	0	0-1	44.2	41	20	18	5	16-2	34	.243
	National League totals (1 year)	0	0	...	8.49	2.23	17	0	0	0	0	0-1	11.2	18	11	11	3	8-1	11	.367
	Major League totals (4 years)	1	1	.500	4.63	1.47	62	0	0	0	0	0-2	56.1	59	31	29	8	24-3	45	.271

S

SELE, AARON   P

PERSONAL: Born June 25, 1970, in Golden Valley, Minn. ... 6-5/230. ... Throws right, bats right. ... Full name: Aaron Helmer Sele. ... Name pronounced: SEE-lee. ... High school: North Kitsap (Poulsbo, Wash.). ... College: Washington State.
TRANSACTIONS/CAREER NOTES: Selected by Minnesota Twins organization in 37th round of 1988 free-agent draft; did not sign. ... Selected by Boston Red Sox organization in first round (23rd pick overall) of 1991 free-agent draft. ... On disabled list (May 24, 1995-remainder of season); included rehabilitation assignments to Trenton, Sarasota and Pawtucket. ... On disabled list (August 14-September 1, 1996); included rehabilitation assignment to Pawtucket. ... Traded by Red Sox with P Mark Brandenburg and C Bill Haselman to Texas Rangers for C Jim Leyritz and OF Damon Buford (November 6, 1997). ... Signed as a free agent by Seattle Mariners (January 10, 2000). ... Signed as a free agent by Anaheim Angels (January 4, 2002). ... On disabled list (August 21-September 29, 2002). ... On disabled list (March 21-May 9, 2003); included rehabilitation assignments to Rancho Cucamonga and Salt Lake. ... On disabled list (June 11-26, 2004). ... Signed by Mariners organization (June 19, 2005). ... Released by Mariners (July 31, 2005).
HONORS: Named A.L. Rookie Pitcher of the Year by THE SPORTING NEWS (1993).
CAREER HITTING: 4-for-28 (.143), 3 R, 1 2B, 0 3B, 0 HR, 1 RBI.

SCOUTING REPORT **Throws:** Sele's fastball ranges from 83-87 mph, his curveball checks in at 71, and he also throws a backdoor slider and straight changeup. **Tendencies:** He's a finesse/control pitcher with marginal stuff. Tends to pitch up in the zone too often. Occasionally will throw a two-seam fastball away to righthanders so it can run back over the plate. Curveball is his best pitch; has tight spin and changes speeds with it. Fades his changeup from lefthanded hitters. Must have pinpoint control. **Outlook:** Because his velocity is decreasing, Sele must spot his pitches to both sides of the plate. Is a back-of-the-rotation starter. Is a fly-ball pitcher who needs a big park to be successful. *Grade 6*

AARON SELE'S PITCHING ZONE

.429	.250	.481
.347	.333	.330
.357	.217	.297

LEFTY-RIGHTY SPLITS

vs.	Avg.	AB	H	2B	3B	HR	RBI	BB	SO	OBP	Slg.
L	.325	252	82	15	2	12	42	23	22	.377	.544
R	.302	215	65	10	1	6	26	18	31	.361	.442

Year Team (League)	W	L	Pct.	ERA	WHIP	G	GS	CG	ShO	Hld.	Sv.-Opp.	IP	H	R	ER	HR	BB-IBB	SO	Avg.
1991— Winter Haven (FSL)	3	6	.333	4.96	1.41	13	11	4	0	...	1-...	69.0	65	42	38	2	32-2	51	.247
1992— Lynchburg (Caro.)	13	5	.722	2.91	1.18	20	19	2	1	...	0-...	127.0	104	51	41	5	46-0	112	.222
— New Britain (East.)	2	1	.667	6.27	1.76	7	6	1	0	...	0-...	33.0	43	29	23	2	15-0	29	.305
1993— Pawtucket (Int'l)	8	2	.800	2.19	1.03	14	14	2	1	...	0-...	94.1	74	30	23	8	23-0	87	.216
— Boston (A.L.)	7	2	.778	2.74	1.33	18	18	0	0	0	0-0	111.2	100	42	34	5	48-2	93	.237
1994— Boston (A.L.)	8	7	.533	3.83	1.40	22	22	0	0	0	0-0	143.1	140	68	61	13	60-2	105	.261
1995— Boston (A.L.)	3	1	.750	3.06	1.42	6	6	0	0	0	0-0	32.1	32	14	11	3	14-0	21	.252
— Trenton (East.)	0	1	.000	3.38	1.25	2	2	0	0	...	0-...	8.0	8	3	3	0	2-0	9	.286
— Sarasota (Fla. St.)	0	0	...	0.00	1.00	2	2	0	0	...	0-...	7.0	6	0	0	0	1-0	8	.231
— Pawtucket (Int'l)	0	0	...	9.00	2.20	1	1	0	0	...	0-...	5.0	9	5	5	3	2-0	1	.409
1996— Boston (A.L.)	7	11	.389	5.32	1.65	29	29	1	0	0	0-0	157.1	192	110	93	14	67-2	137	.303
— Pawtucket (Int'l)	0	0	...	6.00	1.33	1	1	0	0	...	0-...	3.0	3	2	2	0	1-0	4	.250
1997— Boston (A.L.)	13	12	.520	5.38	1.56	33	33	1	0	0	0-0	177.1	196	115	106	25	80-4	122	.279
1998— Texas (A.L.)	19	11	.633	4.23	1.52	33	33	3	2	0	0-0	212.2	239	116	100	14	84-6	167	.283
1999— Texas (A.L.)	18	9	.667	4.79	1.53	33	33	2	0	0	0-0	205.0	244	115	109	21	70-3	186	.293
2000— Seattle (A.L.)	17	10	.630	4.51	1.39	34	34	2	0	0	0-0	211.2	221	110	106	17	74-7	137	.271
2001— Seattle (A.L.)	15	5	.750	3.60	1.24	34	33	2	1	0	0-0	215.0	216	93	86	25	51-2	114	.261
2002— Anaheim (A.L.)	8	9	.471	4.89	1.49	26	26	1	1	0	0-0	160.0	190	92	87	21	49-2	82	.299
2003— Rancho Cuca. (Calif.)	0	0	...	4.50	1.90	3	2	0	0	...	0-...	8.0	12	4	4	0	3-0	7	.375
— Salt Lake (PCL)	1	2	.333	6.43	1.80	3	3	0	0	...	0-...	14.0	16	10	10	2	9-0	8	.296
— Anaheim (A.L.)	7	11	.389	5.77	1.59	25	25	0	0	0	0-0	121.2	135	82	78	17	58-1	53	.284
2004— Texas (A.L.)	9	4	.692	5.05	1.62	28	24	0	0	0	0-0	132.0	163	84	74	16	51-2	51	.310
2005— Seattle (A.L.)	6	12	.333	5.66	1.62	21	21	1	1	0	0-0	116.0	147	76	73	18	41-2	53	.315
— Oklahoma (PCL)	1	1	.500	8.03	1.95	2	2	0	0	...	0-...	12.1	22	12	11	2	2-0	6	.400
Major League totals (13 years)	**137**	**104**	**.568**	**4.59**	**1.48**	**342**	**337**	**15**	**9**	**0**	**0-0**	**1996.0**	**2215**	**1117**	**1018**	**209**	**747-35**	**1321**	**.282**

DIVISION SERIES RECORD

Year Team (League)	W	L	Pct.	ERA	WHIP	G	GS	CG	ShO	Hld.	Sv.-Opp.	IP	H	R	ER	HR	BB-IBB	SO	Avg.
1998— Texas (A.L.)	0	1	.000	6.00	1.50	1	1	0	0	0	0-0	6.0	8	4	4	2	1-0	4	.320
1999— Texas (A.L.)	0	1	.000	5.40	2.20	1	1	0	0	0	0-0	5.0	6	4	3	0	5-2	3	.286
2000— Seattle (A.L.)	0	0	...	1.23	0.82	1	1	0	0	0	0-0	7.1	3	1	1	0	3-0	1	.143
2001— Seattle (A.L.)	0	1	.000	9.00	2.50	1	1	0	0	0	0-0	2.0	5	4	2	0	0-0	0	.417
Division series totals (4 years)	**0**	**3**	**.000**	**4.43**	**1.52**	**4**	**4**	**0**	**0**	**0**	**0-0**	**20.1**	**22**	**13**	**10**	**2**	**9-2**	**8**	**.278**

CHAMPIONSHIP SERIES RECORD

Year Team (League)	W	L	Pct.	ERA	WHIP	G	GS	CG	ShO	Hld.	Sv.-Opp.	IP	H	R	ER	HR	BB-IBB	SO	Avg.
2000— Seattle (A.L.)	0	1	.000	6.00	1.50	1	1	0	0	0	0-0	6.0	9	4	4	2	0-0	4	.333
2001— Seattle (A.L.)	0	2	.000	3.60	1.50	2	2	0	0	0	0-0	10.0	11	8	4	3	4-0	5	.282
Champ. series totals (2 years)	**0**	**3**	**.000**	**4.50**	**1.50**	**3**	**3**	**0**	**0**	**0**	**0-0**	**16.0**	**20**	**12**	**8**	**5**	**4-0**	**9**	**.303**

ALL-STAR GAME RECORD

Year Team (League)	W	L	Pct.	ERA	WHIP	G	GS	CG	ShO	Hld.	Sv.-Opp.	IP	H	R	ER	HR	BB-IBB	SO	Avg.
All-Star Game totals (1 year)	0	0	...	0.00	1.00	1	0	0	0	0	0-0	1.0	1	0	0	0	0-0	0	.250

SELF, TODD   OF

PERSONAL: Born November 9, 1978, in Shreveport, La. ... 6-5/215. ... Bats left, throws right. ... Full name: Todd Douglas Self. ... High school: Southwood (Shreveport, La.). ... College: Louisiana-Monroe.
TRANSACTIONS/CAREER NOTES: Selected by Houston Astros organization in 15th round of 2000 free-agent draft. ... Claimed on waivers by New York Mets (September 9, 2005).
2005 GAMES PLAYED BY POSITION (MLB): OF—15, DH—1.

LEFTY-RIGHTY SPLITS

vs.	Avg.	AB	H	2B	3B	HR	RBI	BB	SO	OBP	Slg.
L	.167	6	1	1	0	0	0	0	1	.167	.333
R	.205	39	8	1	0	1	4	3	8	.262	.308

| | | | | | | BATTING | | | | | | | | | | | | FIELDING | |
Year Team (League)	Pos.	G	AB	R	H	2B	3B	HR	RBI	BB	SO	HBP	GDP	SB-CS	Avg.	OBP	SLG	OPS	E	Avg.
2000— Auburn (NY-Penn)	OF	52	160	13	31	3	1	1	19	28	42	4	1	10-4	.194	.326	.244	.570	6	.930
2001— Pittsfield (NYP)	OF	73	261	52	79	13	4	3	49	46	61	2	2	10-6	.303	.403	.418	.821	2	.979
2002— Michigan (Midw.)	OF-1B	136	491	81	152	36	5	12	94	65	104	9	1	10-1	.310	.394	.477	.871	5	.992

Year	Team (League)	Pos.	G	AB	R	H	2B	3B	HR	RBI	BB	SO	HBP	GDP	SB-CS	Avg.	OBP	SLG	OPS	E	Avg.
2003—Salem (Carol.)	1B-OF	126	431	84	137	27	2	6	57	87	93	5	9	2-1	.318	.433	.432	.865	6	.994
2004—Round Rock (Texas)	1B-OF	131	476	86	150	34	1	11	81	89	95	1	8	8-0	.315	.420	.460	.880	7	.997
2005—Houston (N.L.)	OF-DH	21	45	7	9	2	0	1	4	3	9	0	2	0-0	.200	.250	.311	.561	0	1.000
—Round Rock (PCL)	OF-1B-DH	100	326	42	97	25	2	8	47	58	91	4	5	4-1	.298	.407	.460	.867	8	.977
Major League totals (1 year)		21	45	7	9	2	0	1	4	3	9	0	2	0-0	.200	.250	.311	.561	0	1.000

SEO, JAE WEONG   P

PERSONAL: Born May 24, 1977, in Kwanju, South Korea. ... 6-1/215. ... Throws right, bats right. ... Full name: Jae Weong Seo. ... Name pronounced: jay wong sew. ... High school: First (Kwanju, South Korea). ... College: Inha (South Korea).
TRANSACTIONS/CAREER NOTES: Signed as a non-drafted free agent by New York Mets organization (December 17, 1997). ... On disabled list (April 6, 2000-entire season).
CAREER HITTING: 13-for-112 (.116), 7 R, 3 2B, 0 3B, 0 HR, 5 RBI.

SCOUTING REPORT *Throws:* Seo's fastball ranges from 88-91 mph. Curve is 71-74, slider is at 82. Also throws a changeup and a split-finger fastball. *Tendencies:* He pitched very well after being put in the Mets' rotation in midseason. Has a slow, very deceptive windup. Spots his fastball well to both sides of the plate. Curve has very good rotation and he changes speeds with it. Slider is more like a quick cutter. Uses his change early in the count to lefthanders and his splitter late to both lefthanders and righthanders. Splitter has good diving action. Has very good command of all his pitches. *Outlook:* Seo is versatile enough to be a fifth starter or long reliever. Pitched well enough down the stretch to earn a shot at starting full time. *Grade 6.6*

JAE WEONG SEO'S PITCHING ZONE

.400	.250	.207
.333	.281	.214
.120	.333	.353

LEFTY-RIGHTY SPLITS

vs.	Avg.	AB	H	2B	3B	HR	RBI	BB	SO	OBP	Slg.
L	.233	176	41	6	0	5	11	11	35	.275	.352
R	.272	158	43	11	0	4	14	5	24	.297	.418

Year	Team (League)	W	L	Pct.	ERA	WHIP	G	GS	CG	ShO	Hld.	Sv.-Opp.	IP	H	R	ER	HR	BB-IBB	SO	Avg.
1998—St. Lucie (Fla. St.)	3	1	.750	2.27	1.01	8	7	0	0	...	0-...	35.2	26	13	9	2	10-0	37	.206
—GC Mets (GCL)	0	0	...	0.00	0.80	2	0	0	0	...	0-...	5.0	4	0	0	0	0-0	0	.235
1999—St. Lucie (Fla. St.)	2	0	1.000	1.84	0.68	3	3	0	0	...	0-...	14.2	8	3	3	0	2-0	14	.154
2000—St. Lucie (Fla. St.)	Did not play.																		
2001—St. Lucie (Fla. St.)	2	3	.400	3.55	1.07	6	5	0	0	...	0-...	25.1	21	11	10	2	6-0	19	.221
—Binghamton (East.)	5	1	.833	1.94	0.91	12	10	0	0	...	0-...	60.1	44	14	13	3	11-1	47	.206
—Norfolk (Int'l)	2	2	.500	3.42	1.25	9	9	0	0	...	0-...	47.1	53	18	18	4	6-1	25	.296
2002—Binghamton (East.)	0	0	...	5.40	1.20	1	0	0	0	...	0-...	5.0	5	3	3	1	1-0	6	.250
—Norfolk (Int'l)	6	9	.400	3.99	1.30	26	24	1	0	...	0-...	128.2	145	66	57	14	22-1	87	.284
—New York (N.L.)	0	0	...	0.00	0.00	1	0	0	0	...	0-0	1.0	0	0	0	0	0-0	1	.000
2003—New York (N.L.)	9	12	.429	3.82	1.27	32	31	0	0	...	0-0	188.1	193	94	80	18	46-11	110	.260
2004—Norfolk (Int'l)	0	2	.000	2.82	1.34	4	4	0	0	...	0-...	22.1	22	7	7	1	8-0	20	.272
—New York (N.L.)	5	10	.333	4.90	1.56	24	21	0	0	...	0-0	117.2	133	67	64	17	50-7	54	.299
2005—Norfolk (Int'l)	7	4	.636	4.29	1.28	19	19	0	0	...	0-0	121.2	126	64	58	13	30-0	111	.268
—New York (N.L.)	8	2	.800	2.59	1.11	14	14	1	0	...	0-0	90.1	84	26	26	9	16-0	59	.251
Major League totals (4 years)	22	24	.478	3.85	1.31	71	66	1	0		0-0	397.1	410	187	170	44	112-18	224	.269

SEXSON, RICHIE   1B

PERSONAL: Born December 29, 1974, in Portland. ... 6-8/237. ... Bats right, throws right. ... Full name: Richmond Lockwood Sexson. ... Name pronounced: SECKS-un. ... High school: Prairie (Brush Prairie, Wash.).
TRANSACTIONS/CAREER NOTES: Selected by Cleveland Indians organization in 24th round of 1993 free-agent draft. ... Traded by Indians with Ps Paul Rigdon and Kane Davis and a player to be named to Milwaukee Brewers for Ps Bob Wickman, Steve Woodard and Jason Bere (July 28, 2000); Brewers acquired 2B Marco Scutaro to complete deal (August 30). ... Traded by Brewers with P Shane Nance and a player to be named to Arizona Diamondbacks for SS Craig Counsell, 2B Junior Spivey, 1B Lyle Overbay, C Chad Moeller and Ps Chris Capuano and Jorge de la Rosa (December 1, 2003); Diamondbacks acquired OF Noochie Varner to complete deal (December 15, 2003). ... On disabled list (April 29-May 21 and May 23, 2004-remainder of season). ... On suspended list (September 23-24, 2005). ... Signed as a free agent by Seattle Mariners (December 15, 2004).
RECORDS: Shares major league record for most strikeouts, nine-inning game (5, May 29, 2001).
2005 GAMES PLAYED BY POSITION (MLB): 1B—151, DH—5.

SCOUTING REPORT *Offense:* Sexson, coming back from a shoulder injury, quickly regained his power stroke last season. Has a long swing yet generates good bat speed. Likes to extend his arms at the plate but can adjust to the ball inside. Still has a lot of holes and swings through a lot of pitches. Has exceptional power to all fields. *Defense:* He's agile for his size and is very mobile around the bag. Has always had good hands and a strong, accurate arm. Is not a defensive liability and is athletic enough to play left field. *Outlook:* Sexson is a high risk/high reward offensive player who now is healthy. Will produce even higher numbers with more protection in the lineup. *Grade 8.8*

RICHIE SEXSON'S HITTING ZONE

.152	.474	.100
.391	.413	.286
.167	.364	.308

LEFTY-RIGHTY SPLITS

vs.	Avg.	AB	H	2B	3B	HR	RBI	BB	SO	OBP	Slg.
L	.333	123	41	11	1	9	31	28	34	.458	.659
R	.244	435	106	25	0	30	90	61	133	.342	.508

Year	Team (League)	Pos.	G	AB	R	H	2B	3B	HR	RBI	BB	SO	HBP	GDP	SB-CS	Avg.	OBP	SLG	OPS	E	Avg.
1993—Burlington (Appal.)	1B	40	97	11	18	3	0	1	5	18	21	1	1	1-1	.186	.316	.247	.564	4	.988
1994—Columbus (S. Atl.)	1B	130	488	88	133	25	2	14	77	37	87	14	5	7-3	.273	.338	.418	.756	10	.990
1995—Kinston (Carol.)	1B	131	494	80	151	34	0	22	85	43	115	10	8	4-6	.306	.368	.508	.876	12	.990
1996—Cant./Akr. (Eastern)	1B	133	518	85	143	33	3	16	76	39	118	6	13	2-1	.276	.331	.444	.775	11	.989
1997—Buffalo (A.A.)	1B-DH	115	434	57	113	20	2	31	88	27	87	4	11	5-1	.260	.307	.530	.837	4	.996
—Cleveland (A.L.)	1B	5	11	1	3	0	0	0	0	0	2	0	2	0-0	.273	.273	.273	.545	0	1.000
1998—Buffalo (Int'l)	OF-1B-DH	89	344	58	102	20	1	21	74	50	68	3	11	1-2	.297	.386	.544	.929	5	.990
—Cleveland (A.L.)	1B-OF-DH	49	174	28	54	14	1	11	35	6	42	3	3	1-1	.310	.344	.592	.936	6	.984

Year Team (League)	Pos.	G	AB	R	H	2B	3B	HR	RBI	BB	SO	HBP	GDP	SB-CS	Avg.	OBP	SLG	OPS	E	Avg.
														BATTING					**FIELDING**	
1999—Cleveland (A.L.) 1B-OF-DH		134	479	72	122	17	7	31	116	34	117	4	19	3-3	.255	.305	.514	.818	7	.989
2000—Cleveland (A.L.) OF-1B-DH		91	324	45	83	16	1	16	44	25	96	4	8	1-0	.256	.315	.460	.774	1	.997
—Milwaukee (N.L.)	1B	57	213	44	63	14	0	14	47	34	63	3	3	1-0	.296	.398	.559	.957	5	.991
2001—Milwaukee (N.L.)	1B	158	598	94	162	24	3	45	125	60	178	6	20	2-4	.271	.342	.547	.889	8	.995
2002—Milwaukee (N.L.) 1B-DH		157	570	86	159	37	2	29	102	70	136	8	17	0-0	.279	.364	.504	.867	7	.995
2003—Milwaukee (N.L.)	1B	162	606	97	165	28	2	45	124	98	151	9	18	2-3	.272	.379	.548	.927	11	.993
2004—Arizona (N.L.)	1B	23	90	20	21	4	0	9	23	14	21	0	2	0-0	.233	.337	.578	.914	1	.996
2005—Seattle (A.L.) 1B-DH		156	558	99	147	36	1	39	121	89 *	167	6	14	1-1	.263	.369	.541	.910	7	.995
American League totals (5 years)		435	1546	245	409	83	10	97	316	154	424	17	46	6-5	.265	.335	.519	.854	21	.992
National League totals (5 years)		557	2077	341	570	107	7	142	421	276	549	26	60	5-7	.274	.365	.538	.902	32	.994
Major League totals (9 years)		992	3623	586	979	190	17	239	737	430	973	43	106	11-12	.270	.352	.530	.882	53	.993

DIVISION SERIES RECORD

Year Team (League)	Pos.	G	AB	R	H	2B	3B	HR	RBI	BB	SO	HBP	GDP	SB-CS	Avg.	OBP	SLG	OPS	E	Avg.
1998—Cleveland (A.L.)	1B	3	2	0	0	0	0	0	0	2	1	0	0	0-0	.000	.500	.000	.500	0	1.000
1999—Cleveland (A.L.)	1B-OF	3	6	1	1	0	0	0	1	1	3	0	0	0-0	.167	.286	.167	.452	0	1.000
Division series totals (2 years)		6	8	1	1	0	0	0	1	3	4	0	0	0-0	.125	.364	.125	.489	0	1.000

CHAMPIONSHIP SERIES RECORD

Year Team (League)	Pos.	G	AB	R	H	2B	3B	HR	RBI	BB	SO	HBP	GDP	SB-CS	Avg.	OBP	SLG	OPS	E	Avg.
1998—Cleveland (A.L.)	1B	3	6	0	0	0	0	0	0	0	3	0	1	0-0	.000	.000	.000	.000	0	1.000

ALL-STAR GAME RECORD

		G	AB	R	H	2B	3B	HR	RBI	BB	SO	HBP	GDP	SB-CS	Avg.	OBP	SLG	OPS	E	Avg.
All-Star Game totals (2 years)		2	3	0	0	0	0	0	0	0	0	0	1	0-0	.000	.000	.000	.000	0	1.000

SHABALA, ADAM — OF

PERSONAL: Born February 6, 1978, in Streator, Ill. ... 6-1/190. ... Bats left, throws right. ... Full name: Adam Jason Shabala. ... High school: Streator (Ill.). ... Junior college: Kishwaukee (Ill.). ... College: Nebraska.

TRANSACTIONS/CAREER NOTES: Selected by San Francisco Giants organization in 10th round of 2000 free-agent draft.

2005 GAMES PLAYED BY POSITION (MLB): OF—5.

LEFTY-RIGHTY SPLITS

vs.	Avg.	AB	H	2B	3B	HR	RBI	BB	SO	OBP	Slg.
L	.333	3	1	0	0	0	2	0	0	.333	.333
R	.167	12	2	0	0	0	2	1	5	.214	.167

Year Team (League)	Pos.	G	AB	R	H	2B	3B	HR	RBI	BB	SO	HBP	GDP	SB-CS	Avg.	OBP	SLG	OPS	E	Avg.
														BATTING					**FIELDING**	
2000—Salem-Keizer (N'west)	OF	59	176	27	38	6	3	4	19	30	60	2	4	2-1	.216	.335	.352	.687	2	.971
2001—San Jose (Calif.)	OF	3	7	1	1	0	0	0	0	2	4	0	0	0-0	.143	.333	.143	.476	0	...
—Shreveport (Texas)	OF	12	35	9	12	0	0	1	4	7	10	0	0	2-0	.343	.452	.429	.881	0	1.000
—Hagerstown (SAL)	OF	70	256	37	80	16	2	1	29	37	37	6	9	11-4	.313	.411	.402	.813	2	.982
2002—San Jose (Calif.)	OF	73	244	42	80	18	2	7	45	36	64	1	2	11-7	.328	.412	.504	.916	1	.991
—Shreveport (Texas)	OF	40	148	14	32	8	0	1	16	4	35	1	3	3-1	.216	.250	.291	.541	0	1.000
2003—Norwich (East.)	OF	132	513	71	137	22	6	9	54	46	99	2	11	10-7	.267	.328	.386	.714	3	.990
2004—Fresno (PCL)	OF	118	401	63	126	17	5	9	48	32	81	1	5	21-3	.314	.365	.449	.814	3	.842
2005—San Francisco (N.L.)	OF	6	15	1	3	0	0	0	4	1	5	0	1	0-0	.200	.235	.200	.435	1	.875
—Fresno (PCL)	OF-DH	95	373	58	102	24	1	14	42	35	73	4	4	10-2	.273	.341	.456	.797	4	.989
Major League totals (1 year)		6	15	1	3	0	0	0	4	1	5	0	1	0-0	.200	.235	.200	.435	1	.875

SHACKELFORD, BRIAN — P

PERSONAL: Born August 30, 1976, in McAlester, Okla. ... 6-1/195. ... Throws left, bats left. ... Full name: Brian Wesley Shackelford. ... High school: McAlester (Okla.). ... College: Oklahoma.

TRANSACTIONS/CAREER NOTES: Selected by Kansas City Royals organization in 13th round of 1998 free-agent draft. ... Played in the outfield and first base in Royals organization(1998-2002); Traded by Royals with P Jeff Austin to Cincinnati Reds for 3B Damaso Espino and OF Alan Moye (March 6, 2003).

CAREER HITTING: 0-for-1 (.000), 0 R, 0 2B, 0 3B, 0 HR, 0 RBI.

BRIAN SHACKELFORD'S PITCHING ZONE

.286	.400	.000
.125	.385	.267
.250	.333	.000

LEFTY-RIGHTY SPLITS

vs.	Avg.	AB	H	2B	3B	HR	RBI	BB	SO	OBP	Slg.
L	.205	39	8	0	1	1	1	2	11	.295	.333
R	.203	64	13	3	0	1	5	7	6	.307	.297

Year Team (League)	W	L	Pct.	ERA	WHIP	G	GS	CG	ShO	Hld.	Sv.-Opp.	IP	H	R	ER	HR	BB-IBB	SO	Avg.
2001—Wichita (Texas)	0	0	...	18.00	4.00	1	0	0	0	...	0-...	1.0	3	2	2	0	1-0	0	.500
2002—Wichita (Texas)	3	1	.750	3.51	1.91	22	0	0	0	...	0-...	25.2	23	12	10	1	26-2	15	.258
2003—Chattanooga (Sou.)	3	2	.600	6.30	2.00	13	0	0	0	...	1-...	20.0	26	18	14	3	14-2	19	.313
—Potomac (Carol.)	0	1	.000	1.98	0.91	18	0	0	0	...	1-...	27.1	17	6	6	1	8-0	20	.181
—Louisville (Int'l)	1	0	1.000	2.30	1.40	12	0	0	0	...	0-...	15.2	15	4	4	0	7-0	10	.259
2004—Louisville (Int'l)	8	1	.889	3.58	1.37	59	0	0	0	9	1-2	73.0	58	31	29	6	42-1	63	.213
2005—Louisville (Int'l)	1	6	.143	5.23	1.38	31	0	0	0	9	1-2	32.2	35	19	19	1	10-0	21	.282
—Cincinnati (N.L.)	1	0	1.000	2.43	1.01	37	0	0	0	3	0-0	29.2	21	9	8	2	9-1	17	.204
Major League totals (1 year)	1	0	1.000	2.43	1.01	37	0	0	0	3	0-0	29.2	21	9	8	2	9-1	17	.204

SHEALY, RYAN   1B

PERSONAL: Born August 29, 1979, in Fort Lauderdale, Fla. ... 6-5/240. ... Bats right, throws right. ... Full name: Ryan Nelson Shealy. ... High school: Cardinal Gibbons (Fort Lauderdale, Fla.). ... College: Florida.
TRANSACTIONS/CAREER NOTES: Selected by Colorado Rockies organization in 11th round of 2002 free-agent draft.
2005 GAMES PLAYED BY POSITION (MLB): 1B—19, DH—5.

RYAN SHEALY'S HITTING ZONE

.667	.500	.500
.421	.167	.154
.417	.400	.250

LEFTY-RIGHTY SPLITS

vs.	Avg.	AB	H	2B	3B	HR	RBI	BB	SO	OBP	Slg.
L	.125	16	2	1	0	0	3	3	5	.263	.188
R	.373	75	28	6	0	2	13	10	17	.447	.533

								BATTING												FIELDING	
Year Team (League)	Pos.	G	AB	R	H	2B	3B	HR	RBI	BB	SO	HBP	GDP	SB-CS	Avg.	OBP	SLG	OPS		E	Avg.
2002—Casper (Pion.)	1B	69	231	55	85	21	1	19	70	50	52	18	7	0-0	.368	.497	.714	1.211		6	.991
2003—Visalia (Pion.)		93	341	70	102	31	1	14	73	42	72	14	5	0-0	.299	.391	.519	.910		...	...
2004—Tulsa (Texas)	1B	132	469	88	149	32	3	29	99	61	123	16	10	1-1	.318	.411	.584	.995		4	.998
2005—Colo. Springs (PCL)	1B-DH-OF	108	411	85	135	30	2	26	88	41	81	7	13	4-0	.328	.393	.601	.994		13	.987
—Colorado (N.L.)	1B-DH	36	91	14	30	7	0	2	16	13	22	0	6	1-0	.330	.413	.473	.886		0	1.000
Major League totals (1 year)		36	91	14	30	7	0	2	16	13	22	0	6	1-0	.330	.413	.473	.886		0	1.000

SHEETS, BEN   P

PERSONAL: Born July 18, 1978, in Baton Rouge, La. ... 6-1/218. ... Throws right, bats right. ... Full name: Ben M. Sheets. ... High school: St. Amant (La.). ... College: Northeast Louisiana.
TRANSACTIONS/CAREER NOTES: Selected by Milwaukee Brewers organization in first round (10th pick overall) of 1999 free-agent draft. ... On disabled list (August 6-September 21, 2001; April 21-May 28 and August 27, 2005-remainder of season).
CAREER HITTING: 24-for-288 (.083), 8 R, 1 2B, 0 3B, 0 HR, 7 RBI.

SCOUTING REPORT **Throws:** Sheets has a superior fastball that tops out at 96 mph. Curveball ranges from 73-80. Also has a changeup. **Tendencies:** Sheets can blow away hitters with his live fastball and also can dominate with a tight-biting curveball. Changes speeds better off his curve than with his straight changeup. Has good movement on the change but lacks consistency with it because he varies his arm speed too much. **Outlook:** Sheets continues to have injury issues, losing most of the second half to shoulder problems in 2005. Is an aggressive No. 1 starter and perennial All-Star who is underrated because he can't stay healthy. When right, he's one of the game's true finishers. **Grade 8.2**

BEN SHEETS' PITCHING ZONE

.395	.235	.281
.247	.286	.315
.212	.333	.143

LEFTY-RIGHTY SPLITS

vs.	Avg.	AB	H	2B	3B	HR	RBI	BB	SO	OBP	Slg.
L	.234	303	71	17	2	10	28	15	84	.269	.403
R	.241	295	71	8	1	9	34	10	57	.270	.366

Year Team (League)	W	L	Pct.	ERA	WHIP	G	GS	CG	ShO	Hld.	Sv.-Opp.	IP	H	R	ER	HR	BB-IBB	SO	Avg.
1999—Ogden (Pion.)	0	1	.000	5.63	1.25	2	2	0	0	...	0-...	8.0	8	5	5	2	2-0	12	.267
—Stockton (Calif.)	1	0	1.000	3.58	1.34	5	5	0	0	...	0-...	27.2	23	11	11	1	14-0	28	.232
2000—Huntsville (Sou.)	5	3	.625	1.88	1.11	13	13	0	0	...	0-...	72.0	55	17	15	4	25-0	60	.215
—Indianapolis (Int'l)	3	5	.375	2.87	1.32	14	13	1	0	...	0-...	81.2	77	31	26	4	31-0	59	.251
2001—Milwaukee (N.L.)	11	10	.524	4.76	1.41	25	25	1	1	0	0-0	151.1	166	89	80	23	48-6	94	.283
—Indianapolis (Int'l)	1	1	.500	3.38	1.59	2	2	0	0	0	0-0	10.2	14	5	4	0	3-0	6	.318
2002—Milwaukee (N.L.)	11	•16	.407	4.15	1.42	34	34	1	0	0	0-0	216.2	237	105	100	21	70-10	170	.281
2003—Milwaukee (N.L.)	11	13	.458	4.45	1.25	34	34	1	0	0	0-0	220.2	232	122	109	29	43-2	157	.268
2004—Milwaukee (N.L.)	12	14	.462	2.70	0.98	34	34	5	0	0	0-0	237.0	201	85	71	25	32-1	264	.226
2005—Milwaukee (N.L.)	10	9	.526	3.33	1.07	22	22	3	0	0	0-0	156.2	142	66	58	19	25-1	141	.237
Major League totals (5 years)	55	62	.470	3.83	1.22	149	149	11	1	0	0-0	982.1	978	467	418	117	218-20	826	.258

ALL-STAR GAME RECORD

	W	L	Pct.	ERA	WHIP	G	GS	CG	ShO	Hld.	Sv.-Opp.	IP	H	R	ER	HR	BB-IBB	SO	Avg.
All-Star Game totals (2 years)	0	0	...	0.00	0.00	2	0	0	0	0	0-0	1.1	0	0	0	0	0-0	1	.000

SHEFFIELD, GARY   OF

PERSONAL: Born November 18, 1968, in Tampa. ... 6-0/205. ... Bats right, throws right. ... Full name: Gary Antonian Sheffield. ... High school: Hillsborough (Tampa). ... Nephew of Dwight Gooden, pitcher with five major league teams (1984-2000).
TRANSACTIONS/CAREER NOTES: Selected by Milwaukee Brewers organization in first round (sixth pick overall) of June 1986 free-agent draft. ... On disabled list (July 14-September 9, 1989). ... On suspended list (August 31-September 3, 1990). ... On disabled list (June 15-July 3 and July 25, 1991-remainder of season). ... Traded by Brewers with P Geoff Kellogg to San Diego Padres for P Ricky Bones, SS Jose Valentin and OF Matt Mieske (March 27, 1992). ... Traded by Padres with P Rich Rodriguez to Florida Marlins for Ps Trevor Hoffman, Jose Martinez and Andres Berumen (June 24, 1993). ... On suspended list (July 9-12, 1993). ... On disabled list (May 10-25 and May 28-June 12, 1994); included rehabilitation assignment to Portland. ... On disabled list (June 11-September 1, 1995; and May 14-29, 1997). ... Traded by Marlins with 3B Bobby Bonilla, C Charles Johnson, OF Jim Eisenreich and P Manuel Barrios to Los Angeles Dodgers for C Mike Piazza and 3B Todd Zeile (May 15, 1998). ... On suspended list (August 4-6, 1998; and August 23-27, 2000). ... On disabled list (May 24-June 8, 2001). ... Traded by Dodgers to Atlanta Braves for OF Brian Jordan and Ps Odalis Perez and Andrew Brown (January 15, 2002). ... Signed as a free agent by New York Yankees (December 19, 2003). ... On suspended list (August 30-31, 2005).
HONORS: Named Minor League co-Player of the Year by THE SPORTING NEWS (1988). ... Named Major League Player of the Year by THE SPORTING NEWS (1992). ... Named N.L. Comeback Player of the Year by THE SPORTING NEWS (1992).
2005 GAMES PLAYED BY POSITION (MLB): OF—131, DH—23.

SCOUTING REPORT

Offense: Despite having a lot of movement at the plate, Sheffield sports the best pure bat speed in the game. Hits with a very big hitch but has exceptional timing and never seems to be late. Is a line-drive hitter who uses the entire field, and is one of the best high-ball hitters ever. Good breaking-ball hitter with exceptional power. Has outstanding plate coverage. Is an above-average runner with good instincts. **Defense:** Sheffield is underrated defensively. Has improved his jumps, especially in going back on the ball, and his range is deceptively good to the alleys. Has an above-average arm and is extremely accurate with a quick release. **Outlook:** Sheffield is a five-tool player and is one of the game's best offensive players. Suffered through shoulder problems late in 2005. **Grade 9.8**

GARY SHEFFIELD'S HITTING ZONE

.273	.270	.321
.376	.524	.236
.183	.321	.304

LEFTY-RIGHTY SPLITS

vs.	Avg.	AB	H	2B	3B	HR	RBI	BB	SO	OBP	Slg.
L	.359	156	56	7	0	14	50	20	23	.436	.673
R	.266	428	114	20	0	20	73	58	53	.359	.453

Year	Team (League)	Pos.	G	AB	R	H	2B	3B	HR	RBI	BB	SO	HBP	GDP	SB-CS	Avg.	OBP	SLG	OPS	E	FIELDING Avg.
1986—	Helena (Pion.)	SS	57	222	53	81	12	2	15	71	20	14	3	3	14-4	.365	.413	.640	1.052	24	.911
1987—	Stockton (Calif.)	SS	129	469	84	130	23	3	17	103	81	49	8	7	25-15	.277	.388	.448	.836	39	.937
1988—	El Paso (Texas)	3B-OF-SS	77	296	70	93	19	3	19	65	35	41	3	9	5-4	.314	.386	.591	.978	23	.936
	—Denver (A.A.)	3B-SS	57	212	42	73	9	5	9	54	21	22	5	5	8-4	.344	.407	.561	.969	8	.950
	—Milwaukee (A.L.)	SS	24	80	12	19	1	0	4	12	7	7	0	5	3-1	.238	.295	.400	.695	3	.967
1989—	Milwaukee (A.L.)	3B-DH-SS	95	368	34	91	18	0	5	32	27	33	4	4	10-6	.247	.303	.337	.640	16	.955
	—Denver (A.A.)	SS	7	29	3	4	1	0	0	0	2	0	0	1	0-0	.138	.194	.241	.435	0	1.000
1990—	Milwaukee (A.L.)	3B	125	487	67	143	30	1	10	67	44	41	3	11	25-10	.294	.350	.421	.771	25	.934
1991—	Milwaukee (A.L.)	3B-DH	50	175	25	34	12	2	2	22	19	15	3	3	5-5	.194	.277	.320	.597	8	.922
1992—	San Diego (N.L.)	3B	146	557	87	184	34	3	33	100	48	40	6	19	5-6	*.330	.385	.580	.965	16	.961
1993—	San Diego (N.L.)	3B	68	258	34	76	12	2	10	36	18	30	3	5	5-1	.295	.344	.473	.817	15	.905
	—Florida (N.L.)	3B	72	236	33	69	8	3	10	37	29	34	6	2	12-4	.292	.378	.479	.857	19	.894
1994—	Florida (N.L.)	OF	87	322	61	89	16	1	27	78	51	50	6	10	12-6	.276	.380	.584	.964	5	.970
	—Portland (East.)	OF	2	7	1	2	1	0	0	1	3	0	0	0	0-0	.286	.375	.429	.804	0	1.000
1995—	Florida (N.L.)	OF	63	213	46	69	8	0	16	46	55	45	4	3	19-4	.324	.467	.587	1.054	7	.942
1996—	Florida (N.L.)	OF	161	519	118	163	33	1	42	120	142	66	10	16	16-9	.314	*.465	.624	1.090	6	.976
1997—	Florida (N.L.)	OF-DH	135	444	86	111	22	1	21	71	121	79	15	7	11-7	.250	.424	.446	.870	5	.980
1998—	Florida (N.L.)	OF	40	136	21	37	11	1	6	28	26	16	2	3	4-2	.272	.392	.500	.892	1	.986
	—Los Angeles (N.L.)	OF	90	301	52	95	16	1	16	57	69	30	6	4	18-5	.316	.444	.535	.979	1	.994
1999—	Los Angeles (N.L.)	OF-DH	152	549	103	165	20	0	34	101	101	64	4	10	11-5	.301	.407	.523	.930	7	.972
2000—	Los Angeles (N.L.)	OF-DH	141	501	105	163	24	3	43	109	101	71	4	13	4-6	.325	.438	.643	1.081	•10	.954
2001—	Los Angeles (N.L.)	OF-DH	143	515	98	160	28	2	36	100	94	67	4	12	10-4	.311	.417	.583	1.000	6	.972
2002—	Atlanta (N.L.)	OF-DH	135	492	82	151	26	0	25	84	72	53	11	16	12-2	.307	.404	.512	.916	4	.984
2003—	Atlanta (N.L.)	OF	155	576	126	190	37	2	39	132	86	55	8	16	18-4	.330	.419	.604	1.023	4	.986
2004—	New York (A.L.)	OF-DH-3B	154	573	117	166	30	1	36	121	92	83	11	16	5-6	.290	.393	.534	.927	6	.979
2005—	New York (A.L.)	OF-DH	154	584	104	170	27	0	34	123	78	76	8	11	10-2	.291	.379	.512	.891	3	.968
	American League totals (6 years)		602	2267	359	623	118	4	91	377	267	255	29	50	58-30	.275	.354	.451	.805	61	.958
	National League totals (12 years)		1588	5619	1052	1722	295	20	358	1099	1013	700	89	140	157-65	.306	.416	.557	.973	106	.965
	Major League totals (18 years)		2190	7886	1411	2345	413	24	449	1476	1280	955	118	190	215-95	.297	.399	.527	.925	167	.962

DIVISION SERIES RECORD

Year	Team (League)	Pos.	G	AB	R	H	2B	3B	HR	RBI	BB	SO	HBP	GDP	SB-CS	Avg.	OBP	SLG	OPS	E	Avg.
1997—	Florida (N.L.)	OF	3	9	3	5	1	0	1	1	5	0	0	1	1-0	.556	.714	1.000	1.714	0	1.000
2002—	Atlanta (N.L.)	OF	5	16	3	1	0	0	1	1	7	3	0	1	0-0	.063	.348	.250	.598	0	1.000
2003—	Atlanta (N.L.)	OF	4	14	0	2	0	0	0	1	2	5	0	1	0-0	.143	.294	.143	.437	0	1.000
2004—	New York (A.L.)	OF	4	18	2	4	1	0	1	2	3	1	0	1	0-1	.222	.333	.444	.778	0	1.000
2005—	New York (A.L.)	OF	5	21	1	6	0	0	0	2	1	2	0	0	0-0	.286	.318	.286	.604	1	.900
	Division series totals (5 years)		21	78	9	18	2	0	3	7	18	6	1	2	1-1	.231	.381	.372	.753	1	.971

CHAMPIONSHIP SERIES RECORD

Year	Team (League)	Pos.	G	AB	R	H	2B	3B	HR	RBI	BB	SO	HBP	GDP	SB-CS	Avg.	OBP	SLG	OPS	E	Avg.
1997—	Florida (N.L.)	OF	6	17	6	4	0	0	1	1	7	3	0	0	0-0	.235	.458	.412	.870	1	1.000
2004—	New York (A.L.)	OF	7	30	7	10	3	0	1	5	6	8	0	1	0-0	.333	.444	.533	.978	0	1.000
	Champ. series totals (2 years)		13	47	13	14	3	0	2	6	13	11	0	1	0-0	.298	.450	.489	.939	0	1.000

WORLD SERIES RECORD

Year	Team (League)	Pos.	G	AB	R	H	2B	3B	HR	RBI	BB	SO	HBP	GDP	SB-CS	Avg.	OBP	SLG	OPS	E	Avg.
1997—	Florida (N.L.)	OF	7	24	4	7	1	0	1	5	8	5	1	2	0-0	.292	.485	.458	.943	1	.941

ALL-STAR GAME RECORD

		G	AB	R	H	2B	3B	HR	RBI	BB	SO	HBP	GDP	SB-CS	Avg.	OBP	SLG	OPS	E	Avg.
All-Star Game totals (9 years)		9	12	3	2	0	0	1	2	2	0	0	2	0-0	.167	.286	.417	.702	0	1.000

SHELTON, CHRIS — 1B

PERSONAL: Born June 26, 1980, in Salt Lake City. ... 6-0/220. ... Bats right, throws right. ... Full name: Christopher Bob Shelton. ... High school: Cottonwood (Salt Lake City). ... Junior college: Salt Lake Community College (Salt Lake City). ... College: Utah.
TRANSACTIONS/CAREER NOTES: Selected by Pittsburgh Pirates organization in 33rd round of 2001 free-agent draft. ... Selected by Detroit Tigers from Pirates organization in Rule 5 major league draft (December 15, 2003). ... On disabled list (May 31-July 10, 2004); included rehabilitation assignment to Toledo.
2005 GAMES PLAYED BY POSITION (MLB): 1B—84, DH—15, OF—1.

SCOUTING REPORT

Offense: Shelton is extremely strong with great power when he pulls the ball. Has a chance to be a great all-around hitter. Has shown the ability to handle the ball inside and stays on the breaking ball. Has a good knowledge of the strike zone and has proven to be a good hitter with runners in scoring position. Is advanced for a hitter who has less than one year of major league experience. **Defense:** Defensively, he is still looking for a position he can play regularly. Made 6 errors in only 84 games in 2005 and is a stiff player with limited range and doesn't have very quick hands. Has a lot to learn about playing first because he came up as a catcher. **Outlook:** There's no doubt he's going to hit and have power, but finding a position he's comfortable with could be a problem. Can always be a DH in his league. **Grade 6.8**

CHRIS SHELTON'S HITTING ZONE

.125	.286	.333
.328	.406	.321
.286	.294	.438

LEFTY-RIGHTY SPLITS

vs.	Avg.	AB	H	2B	3B	HR	RBI	BB	SO	OBP	Slg.
L	.278	97	27	3	0	4	14	10	20	.345	.433
R	.306	291	89	19	3	14	45	24	67	.364	.536

Year Team (League)	Pos.	G	AB	R	H	2B	3B	HR	RBI	BB	SO	HBP	GDP	SB-CS	Avg.	OBP	SLG	OPS	E	Avg.
2001— Will. (NYP)	C-1B	50	174	22	53	11	0	2	33	33	31	2	1	4-1	.305	.415	.402	.817	7	.985
2002— Hickory (S. Atl.)	1B-C-OF	93	332	72	113	27	2	17	65	47	74	5	1	0-0	.340	.425	.587	1.013	1	.998
2003— Lynchburg (Caro.)	1B-C	95	315	71	113	24	1	21	69	68	67	5	6	1-4	.359	.478	.641	1.119	4	.993
— Altoona (East.)	1B-C	35	122	17	34	10	1	0	14	8	23	2	1	0-1	.279	.331	.377	.708	2	.993
2004— Toledo (Int'l)	1B-DH	18	62	5	21	2	0	0	7	10	13	0	0	0-0	.339	.425	.371	.796	2	.973
— Detroit (A.L.)	DH-1B-C																			
	OF	27	46	6	9	1	0	1	3	9	14	0	2	0-0	.196	.321	.283	.604	0	1.000
2005— Toledo (Int'l)	1B-DH-C	48	181	34	60	19	0	8	39	25	33	3	3	0-2	.331	.417	.569	.986	4	.987
— Detroit (A.L.)	1B-DH-OF	107	388	61	116	22	3	18	59	34	87	5	11	0-0	.299	.360	.510	.870	6	.993
Major League totals (2 years)		134	434	67	125	23	3	19	62	43	101	5	13	0-0	.288	.355	.486	.841	6	.993

SHERRILL, GEORGE   P

PERSONAL: Born April 19, 1977, in Memphis. ... 6-0/210. ... Throws left, bats left. ... Full name: George Friederich Sherrill. ... High school: Evangelical Christian (Memphis). ... Junior college: Jackson State Community College. ... College: Austin Peay.
TRANSACTIONS/CAREER NOTES: Signed as a free agent by Seattle Mariners organization (July 2, 2003). ... On disabled list (September 17, 2004-remainder of season).
CAREER HITTING: 0-for-0 (.000), 0 R, 0 2B, 0 3B, 0 HR, 0 RBI.

SCOUTING REPORT *Throws:* His fastball tops out at 90 mph. Also throws a slider, a curveball and a changeup. *Tendencies:* His sneaky fastball will naturally run away from righthanders, but he has problems moving it to the other side of the plate. Relies on his breaking ball early in the count; rides his four-seam fastball up and in on lefthanders late in the count. Curve has a big, early break. Best pitch is his slider, which runs from lefthanders with a big, sweeping break. Is very effective against lefthanders. *Outlook:* Sherrill is best as a situational reliever **Grade 5.5**

GEORGE SHERRILL'S PITCHING ZONE

.000	1.000	.667
.000	.286	.300
.200	.500	.200

LEFTY-RIGHTY SPLITS

vs.	Avg.	AB	H	2B	3B	HR	RBI	BB	SO	OBP	Slg.
L	.156	45	7	2	0	2	8	0	18	.170	.333
R	.273	22	6	0	0	1	3	7	6	.448	.409

Year Team (League)	W	L	Pct.	ERA	WHIP	G	GS	CG	ShO	Hld.	Sv.-Opp.	IP	H	R	ER	HR	BB-IBB	SO	Avg.
1999— Evansville (Fron.)	2	4	.333	3.15	1.45	22	4	1	1	...	2-...	40.0	40	20	14	3	18-...	33	...
2000— Evansville (Fron.)	3	5	.375	4.66	1.41	13	13	1	0	...	0-...	75.1	71	45	39	5	35-...	61	...
2001— Sioux Falls (Nor.)	4	4	.500	2.45	1.14	48	2	0	0	...	0-...	58.2	53	20	16	3	14-...	45	...
2002— Winnipeg (North.)	3	5	.375	3.07	1.17	38	0	0	0	...	2-...	41.0	35	15	14	6	13-...	61	...
2003— Winnipeg (North.)	1	0	1.000	1.13	0.75	16	0	0	0	...	1-...	16.0	8	2	2	0	4-...	30	...
— San Antonio (Texas)	3	0	1.000	0.33	1.13	16	0	0	0	...	0-...	27.1	19	2	1	1	12-1	31	.198
2004— Tacoma (PCL)	4	2	.667	2.33	1.01	36	0	0	0	...	13-...	50.1	42	13	13	4	9-1	62	.223
— Seattle (A.L.)	2	1	.667	3.80	1.39	21	0	0	0	3	0-0	23.2	24	12	10	3	9-1	16	.258
2005— Ariz. Mariners (Ariz.)	0	0	...	0.00	0.00	3	2	0	0	0	0-0	4.0	0	0	0	0	0-0	5	.000
— Tacoma (PCL)	1	3	.250	2.28	1.06	22	0	0	0	1	7-9	23.2	19	7	6	0	6-0	38	.209
— Seattle (A.L.)	4	3	.571	5.21	1.05	29	0	0	0	9	0-0	19.0	13	12	11	3	7-2	24	.194
Major League totals (2 years)	6	4	.600	4.43	1.24	50	0	0	0	12	0-0	42.2	37	24	21	6	16-3	40	.231

SHIELDS, SCOT   P

PERSONAL: Born July 22, 1975, in Fort Lauderdale, Fla. ... 6-1/170. ... Throws right, bats right. ... Full name: Robert Scot Shields. ... High school: Fort Lauderdale (Fla.). ... College: Lincoln Memorial (Tenn.).
TRANSACTIONS/CAREER NOTES: Selected by Anaheim Angels organization in 38th round of 1997 free-agent draft. ... Angels franchise renamed Los Angeles Angels of Anaheim for 2005 season.
CAREER HITTING: 0-for-2 (.000), 0 R, 0 2B, 0 3B, 0 HR, 0 RBI.

SCOUTING REPORT *Throws:* Shields ranges his fastball from 88-94 mph, Also throws a curve and slider. *Tendencies:* Shields has an outstanding motion. Throws slightly across his body, but his fastball really moves late. Has a very big but quick, sweeping curve. Slider is a hard slurve. Creates outstanding deception and is equally effective against lefthanded and righthanded hitters. *Outlook:* Shields is the Angels' most valuable pitcher because of his versatility and his above-average stuff. Possibly the most valuable setup man and most versatile pitcher in the game. **Grade 9.5**

SCOT SHIELDS'S PITCHING ZONE

.133	.462	.243
.214	.417	.167
.241	.294	.048

LEFTY-RIGHTY SPLITS

vs.	Avg.	AB	H	2B	3B	HR	RBI	BB	SO	OBP	Slg.
L	.199	171	34	10	0	2	19	21	60	.289	.292
R	.203	158	32	0	1	3	15	16	38	.276	.272

Year Team (League)	W	L	Pct.	ERA	WHIP	G	GS	CG	ShO	Hld.	Sv.-Opp.	IP	H	R	ER	HR	BB-IBB	SO	Avg.
1997— Boise (N'west)	7	2	.778	2.94	1.33	30	0	0	0	...	2-...	52.0	45	20	17	1	24-4	61	.233
1998— Cedar Rap. (Midw.)	6	5	.545	3.65	1.23	58	0	0	0	...	7-...	74.0	62	33	30	5	29-0	81	.232
1999— Lake Elsinore (Calif.)	10	3	.769	2.52	1.21	24	9	2	1	...	1-...	107.1	91	37	30	1	39-4	113	.233
— Erie (East.)	4	4	.500	2.89	1.11	10	10	1	1	...	0-...	74.2	57	26	24	10	26-0	81	.216
2000— Edmonton (PCL)	7	13	.350	5.41	1.47	27	27	4	1	...	0-...	163.0	158	114	98	16	82-0	156	.250
2001— Salt Lake (PCL)	6	11	.353	4.97	1.25	21	21	4	0	...	0-...	137.2	141	84	76	24	31-0	104	.267
— Anaheim (A.L.)	0	0	...	0.00	1.36	8	0	0	0	0	0-0	11.0	8	1	0	0	7-0	7	.200
2002— Salt Lake (PCL)	2	2	.500	3.06	0.96	28	1	0	0	...	1-...	47.0	39	18	16	5	6-0	50	.223
— Anaheim (A.L.)	5	3	.625	2.20	1.06	29	1	0	0	3	0-0	49.0	31	13	12	4	21-1	30	.188
2003— Anaheim (A.L.)	5	6	.455	2.85	1.19	44	13	0	0	3	1-1	148.1	138	56	47	12	38-6	111	.247
2004— Anaheim (A.L.)	8	2	.800	3.33	1.30	60	0	0	0	17	4-7	105.1	97	42	39	6	40-5	109	.238
2005— Los Angeles (A.L.)	10	11	.476	2.75	1.12	78	0	0	0	•33	7-13	91.2	66	33	28	5	37-2	98	.201
Major League totals (5 years)	28	22	.560	2.80	1.19	219	14	0	0	56	12-21	405.1	340	145	126	27	143-14	355	.227

DIVISION SERIES RECORD

Year — Team (League)	W	L	Pct.	ERA	WHIP	G	GS	CG	ShO	Hld.	Sv.-Opp.	IP	H	R	ER	HR	BB-IBB	SO	Avg.
2004— Anaheim (A.L.)	0	0	...	6.00	2.33	2	0	0	0	0	0-0	3.0	5	2	2	1	2-1	3	.357
2005— Los Angeles (A.L.)	1	1	.500	3.60	1.40	4	0	0	0	0	0-1	5.0	4	2	2	0	3-0	5	.211
Division series totals (2 years)	1	1	.500	4.50	1.75	6	0	0	0	0	0-1	8.0	9	4	4	1	5-1	8	.273

CHAMPIONSHIP SERIES RECORD

Year — Team (League)	W	L	Pct.	ERA	WHIP	G	GS	CG	ShO	Hld.	Sv.-Opp.	IP	H	R	ER	HR	BB-IBB	SO	Avg.
2005— Los Angeles (A.L.)	0	0	...	0.00	0.83	4	0	0	0	0	0-0	6.0	4	0	0	0	1-1	5	.200

WORLD SERIES RECORD

Year — Team (League)	W	L	Pct.	ERA	WHIP	G	GS	CG	ShO	Hld.	Sv.-Opp.	IP	H	R	ER	HR	BB-IBB	SO	Avg.
2002— Anaheim (A.L.)	0	0	...	5.40	3.00	1	0	0	0	0	0-0	1.2	5	5	1	2	0-0	1	.455

SHOPPACH, KELLY — C

PERSONAL: Born April 29, 1980, in Fort Worth, Texas. ... 6-1/210. ... Bats right, throws right. ... Full name: Kelly Brian Shoppach. ... High school: Brewer (Fort Worth, Texas). ... College: Baylor.

TRANSACTIONS/CAREER NOTES: Selected by Boston Red Sox organization in second round of 2001 free-agent draft.

2005 GAMES PLAYED BY POSITION (MLB): C—7, DH—2.

LEFTY-RIGHTY SPLITS

vs.	Avg.	AB	H	2B	3B	HR	RBI	BB	SO	OBP	Slg.
L	.000	3	0	0	0	0	0	0	1	.250	.000
R	.000	12	0	0	0	0	0	0	6	.000	.000

							BATTING								FIELDING	
Year — Team (League)	Pos.	G	AB	R	H	2B	3B	HR	RBI	BB	SO	HBP	GDP	SB-CS	Avg.	OBP	SLG	OPS	E	Avg.
2002— Sarasota (Fla. St.)	C	116	414	54	112	35	1	10	66	59	112	6	11	2-1	.271	.369	.432	.801	9	.986
2003— Portland (East.)	C	92	340	45	96	30	2	12	60	35	83	5	10	0-0	.282	.353	.488	.841	11	.982
2004— Pawtucket (Int'l)	C	113	399	62	93	25	0	22	64	46	138	6	7	0-0	.233	.320	.461	.781	8	.988
2005— Pawtucket (Int'l)	C-DH	102	371	60	94	16	0	26	75	46	116	12	9	0-0	.253	.352	.507	.859	5	.993
— Boston (A.L.)	C-DH	9	15	1	0	0	0	0	0	0	7	1	0	0-0	.000	.063	.000	.063	0	1.000
Major League totals (1 year)		9	15	1	0	0	0	0	0	0	7	1	0	0-0	.000	.063	.000	.063	0	1.000

SHORT, RICK — 2B

PERSONAL: Born December 6, 1972, in Elgin, Ill. ... 6-0/200. ... Bats right, throws right. ... Full name: Richard Ryan Short. ... College: Western Illinois.

TRANSACTIONS/CAREER NOTES: Selected by Baltimore Orioles organization in 33rd round of 1994 free-agent draft. ... Signed as a free agent by Chicago Cubs (November 26, 2000). ... Signed as a free agent by Anaheim Angels (December 7, 2001). ... Signed by Chiba of Japanese league (2003). ... Signed as a free agent by Kansas City Royals (December 15, 2003). ... Traded by Royals to Montreal Expos for RHP Scott Randall (July 23, 2004). ... Expos franchise transferred to Washington, D.C., and was renamed Nationals for 2005 season (December 3, 2005). ... On disabled list (September 24, 2005-remainder of season).

2005 GAMES PLAYED BY POSITION (MLB): 2B—6, 1B—1.

LEFTY-RIGHTY SPLITS

vs.	Avg.	AB	H	2B	3B	HR	RBI	BB	SO	OBP	Slg.
L	1.000	2	2	0	0	1	1	0	0	1.000	2.500
R	.308	13	4	2	0	1	3	1	1	.357	.692

							BATTING								FIELDING	
Year — Team (League)	Pos.	G	AB	R	H	2B	3B	HR	RBI	BB	SO	HBP	GDP	SB-CS	Avg.	OBP	SLG	OPS	E	Avg.
1994— Bluefield (Appal.)	3B	64	229	39	69	8	0	4	35	22	23	2	3	4-6	.301	.365	.389	.754	14	.918
1995— Frederick (Carolina)	3B	5	13	1	1	0	0	0	2	1	2	0	0	1-0	.077	.143	.077	.220	1	.800
— Bluefield (Appal.)	3B	11	39	9	11	2	0	2	12	2	1	1	2	2-1	.282	.326	.487	.813	2	.953
— High Desert (Calif.)	2B-3B-SS	29	98	14	41	3	0	4	12	10	5	2	2	1-2	.418	.482	.571	1.053	7	.944
1996— Frederick (Carolina)	3B	126	474	68	148	33	0	3	54	29	44	5	14	12-7	.312	.355	.401	.756	33	.914
1997— Frederick (Carolina)	3B	126	480	73	153	29	1	10	72	38	44	12	20	10-7	.319	.382	.446	.828	22	.947
1998— Bowie (East.)	3B-2B-OF																			
	1B	34	87	12	20	4	0	2	18	13	18	0	0	0-0	.230	.317	.345	.662	2	.946
— Frederick (Carolina)	3B	59	221	36	68	14	0	6	28	18	29	8	12	3-2	.308	.376	.452	.828	3	.982
— Rochester (Int'l)	3B-OF-1B	13	34	3	6	0	1	0	4	4	1	0	0	0-0	.176	.275	.294	.569	0	1.000
1999— Bowie (East.)	3B-2B-OF																			
	1B	112	392	60	123	19	1	6	62	43	48	9	9	6-1	.314	.390	.485	.875	7	.982
2000— Bowie (East.)	3B-2B-OF																			
	1B	116	447	63	148	39	1	9	82	44	54	8	14	3-3	.331	.394	.483	.877	7	.975
— Rochester (Int'l)	3B-OF-1B	13	37	3	9	1	0	1	3	4	4	2	0	0-0	.243	.349	.351	.700	2	.933
2001— West Tenn (Sou.)	1B-3B-OF																			
	2B	8	19	5	5	0	0	0	0	5	1	1	0	0-1	.263	.440	.263	.703	0	1.000
— Iowa (PCL)	3B-2B-1B																			
	OF	105	313	38	86	19	1	5	34	22	42	3	13	2-1	.275	.327	.390	.717	6	.965
2002— Salt Lake (PCL)	1B-2B-OF																			
	3B	105	410	71	146	29	2	7	68	23	43	9	4	3-2	.356	.399	.488	.887	5	.976
2003— Chiba Lotte (Jp.)		127	472	61	143	32	0	12	58	39	60	6	18	3-3	.303	.362	.447	.809	9	...
2004— Omaha (PCL)	3B-2B-OF	89	316	30	89	16	0	7	48	15	39	4	15	1-1	.282	.320	.399	.719	10	.981
— Edmonton (PCL)	1B-3B-2B	40	152	13	51	13	0	2	19	10	7	1	5	1-1	.336	.378	.461	.839	1	.996
2005— New Orleans (PCL)	1B-2B-3B																			
	DH-OF-C	108	376	72	144	35	1	11	70	46	27	7	8	5-4	.383	.456	.569	1.025	11	.979
— Washington (N.L.)	2B-1B	11	15	4	6	2	0	1	4	1	1	0	0	0-0	.400	.471	.933	1.404	1	.952
Major League totals (1 year)		11	15	4	6	2	0	1	4	1	1	0	0	0-0	.400	.471	.933	1.404	1	.952

SHOUSE, BRIAN — P

PERSONAL: Born September 26, 1968, in Effingham, Ill. ... 5-11/190. ... Throws left, bats left. ... Full name: Brian Douglas Shouse. ... High school: Effingham (Ill.). ... College: Bradley.

TRANSACTIONS/CAREER NOTES: Selected by Pittsburgh Pirates organization in 13th round of 1990 free-agent draft. ... Released by Pirates (May 16, 1996). ... Signed by Baltimore Orioles organization (May 22, 1996). ... Signed as a free agent by Boston Red Sox organization (October 28, 1997). ... Contract sold by Red Sox to Kintetsu of the Japan Pacific League (June 25, 1998). ... Signed as a free agent by Arizona Diamondbacks organization (November 19, 1998). ... On disabled list (September 18, 1999-remainder of season). ... Signed as a free agent by New York Mets organization (December 2, 1999). ... Released by Mets (April 14, 2000). ... Signed by Orioles organization (May 13, 2000). ... Signed as a free agent by Houston Astros organization (December 22, 2000). ... Signed as a free agent by Kansas City Royals organization (December 7, 2001). ... On disabled list (April 28-May 13, 2002). ... Released by Royals (June 27, 2002). ... Signed by Astros organization (July 22, 2002). ... Signed as a free agent by Texas Rangers organization (November 13, 2002). ... On disabled list (March 27-May 13, 2004); included rehabilitation assignment to Oklahoma.

CAREER HITTING: 0-for-0 (.000), 0 R, 0 2B, 0 3B, 0 HR, 0 RBI.

SCOUTING REPORT

Throws: The sidearming Shouse throws his fastball at 83-86 mph, and he also has a slurve. **Tendencies:** Shouse relies on his deceptive low-sidearm action to baffle left-handers, who get the impression he is starting the ball behind them. Relies on command to be effective and needs to keep his fastball down. Breaking ball has a wide sweeping action. Worked behind in the count too much last season. Righthanders give him a lot of trouble. **Outlook:** Shouse is a situational reliever who can't be overexposed. **Grade 6.4**

BRIAN SHOUSE'S PITCHING ZONE

.143	.333	.500
.368	.273	.360
.324	.300	.286

LEFTY-RIGHTY SPLITS

vs.	Avg.	AB	H	2B	3B	HR	RBI	BB	SO	OBP	Slg.
L	.209	115	24	5	0	4	23	8	27	.271	.357
R	.337	92	31	8	0	3	19	10	8	.402	.522

Year — Team (League)	W	L	Pct.	ERA	WHIP	G	GS	CG	ShO	Hld.	Sv.-Opp.	IP	H	R	ER	HR	BB-IBB	SO	Avg.
1990— Welland (NYP)	4	3	.571	5.22	1.44	17	1	0	0	...	2-...	39.2	50	27	23	2	7-0	39	.309
1991— Augusta (S. Atl.)	2	3	.400	3.19	1.00	26	0	0	0	...	8-...	31.0	22	13	11	1	9-1	32	.200
— Salem (Carol.)	2	1	.667	2.94	1.49	17	0	0	0	...	3-...	33.2	35	12	11	2	15-2	25	.269
1992— Carolina (Southern)	5	6	.455	2.44	1.28	59	0	0	0	...	4-...	77.1	71	31	21	3	28-4	79	.252
1993— Buffalo (A.A.)	1	0	1.000	3.83	1.37	48	0	0	0	...	2-...	51.2	54	24	22	7	17-2	25	.276
— Pittsburgh (N.L.)	0	0	...	9.00	2.25	6	0	0	0	0	0-0	4.0	7	4	4	1	2-0	3	.368
1994— Buffalo (A.A.)	3	4	.429	3.63	1.13	43	0	0	0	...	0-...	52.0	44	22	21	6	15-4	31	.232
1995— Carolina (Southern)	7	6	.538	4.47	1.26	21	20	0	0	...	0-...	114.2	126	64	57	14	19-2	76	.281
— Calgary (PCL)	4	4	.500	6.18	1.75	8	8	1	0	...	0-...	39.1	62	35	27	2	7-0	17	.354
1996— Calgary (PCL)	1	0	1.000	10.66	2.05	12	1	0	0	...	0-...	12.2	22	15	15	4	4-1	12	.367
— Rochester (Int'l)	1	2	.333	4.50	1.38	32	0	0	0	...	2-...	50.0	53	27	25	6	16-1	45	.270
1997— Rochester (Int'l)	6	2	.750	2.27	0.97	54	0	0	0	...	9-...	71.1	48	21	18	6	21-4	81	.191
1998— Pawtucket (Int'l)	2	0	1.000	2.90	0.90	22	1	0	0	...	6-...	31.0	21	11	10	7	7-0	25	.188
— Boston (A.L.)	0	1	.000	5.63	1.63	7	0	0	0	1	0-0	8.0	9	5	5	2	4-0	5	.281
— Kintetsu (Jp. Pac.)	0	2	.000	6.58	2.04	13	3	0	0	...	0-...	26.0	40	20	19	...	13-...	20	...
— Kintetsu (Jp. West.)	1	0	1.000	1.38	1.23	5	2	0	0	...	0-...	13.0	9	2	2	2	7-...	9	...
1999— Tucson (PCL)	3	4	.429	6.25	1.81	30	0	0	0	...	0-...	44.2	63	35	31	4	18-3	32	.339
2000— Norfolk (Int'l)	0	1	.000	15.00	2.67	4	0	0	0	...	0-...	3.0	6	5	5	2	2-0	1	.429
— Rochester (Int'l)	4	4	.500	2.79	1.33	43	0	0	0	...	0-...	58.0	63	20	18	4	14-1	52	.279
2001— New Orleans (PCL)	2	2	.500	2.89	1.25	56	1	0	0	...	1-...	53.0	51	21	17	4	15-0	56	.249
2002— Kansas City (A.L.)	0	0	...	6.14	1.64	23	0	0	0	2	0-0	14.2	15	10	10	3	9-1	11	.259
— Omaha (PCL)	0	0	...	11.57	3.43	5	0	0	0	...	0-...	2.1	7	3	3	0	1-0	2	.538
— New Orleans (PCL)	1	0	1.000	3.43	0.95	19	0	0	0	...	0-...	21.0	17	10	8	2	3-0	20	.215
2003— Oklahoma (PCL)	0	1	.000	3.68	1.50	6	0	0	0	...	1-...	7.1	8	3	3	0	3-0	2	.286
— Texas (A.L.)	0	1	.000	3.10	1.25	62	0	0	0	10	1-1	61.0	62	24	21	1	14-6	40	.267
2004— Oklahoma (PCL)	0	0	...	6.14	2.18	9	0	0	0	...	0-...	7.1	12	5	5	1	4-1	3	.375
— Texas (A.L.)	2	0	1.000	2.23	1.22	53	0	0	0	12	0-0	44.1	36	12	11	3	18-3	34	.224
2005— Texas (A.L.)	3	2	.600	5.23	1.37	64	0	0	0	11	0-2	53.1	55	37	31	7	18-4	35	.266
American League totals (5 years)	5	4	.556	3.87	1.32	209	0	0	0	36	1-3	181.1	177	88	78	16	63-14	125	.257
National League totals (1 year)	0	0	...	9.00	2.25	6	0	0	0	0	0-0	4.0	7	4	4	1	2-0	3	.368
Major League totals (6 years)	5	4	.556	3.98	1.34	215	0	0	0	36	1-3	185.1	184	92	82	17	65-14	128	.260

SIERRA, RUBEN — DH/OF

PERSONAL: Born October 6, 1965, in Rio Piedras, Puerto Rico. ... 6-1/215. ... Bats both, throws right. ... Full name: Ruben Angel Sierra. ... High school: Dr. Secario Rosario (Rio Piedras, Puerto Rico).

TRANSACTIONS/CAREER NOTES: Signed as a non-drafted free agent by Texas Rangers organization (November 21, 1982). ... Traded by Rangers with Ps Jeff Russell and Bobby Witt and cash to Oakland Athletics for OF Jose Canseco (August 31, 1992). ... On disabled list (July 7-22, 1995). ... Traded by A's with P Jason Beverlin to New York Yankees for OF/DH Danny Tartabull (July 28, 1995). ... Traded by Yankees with P Matt Drews to Detroit Tigers for 1B/DH Cecil Fielder (July 31, 1996). ... Traded by Tigers to Cincinnati Reds for OF Decomba Conner and P Ben Bailey (October 28, 1996). ... Released by Reds (May 9, 1997). ... Signed by Toronto Blue Jays organization (May 11, 1997). ... Released by Blue Jays (June 16, 1997). ... Signed by Chicago White Sox organization (January 9, 1998). ... Released by White Sox (May 29, 1998). ... Signed by New York Mets organization (June 20, 1998). ... Signed as a free agent by Cleveland Indians organization (December 23, 1999). ... Released by Indians (March 20, 2000). ... Signed by Rangers organization (May 1, 2000). ... On disabled list (July 27-August 11, 2001). ... Signed as a free agent by Seattle Mariners (January 3, 2002). ... Signed as a free agent by Rangers organization (January 27, 2003). ... Traded by Rangers to Yankees for OF Marcus Thames (June 6, 2003). ... On disabled list (April 21-May 20 and July 19-September 1, 2005).

HONORS: Named A.L. Player of the Year by THE SPORTING NEWS (1989). ... Named A.L. Comeback Player of the Year by THE SPORTING NEWS (2001).

2005 GAMES PLAYED BY POSITION (MLB): DH—30, OF—18.

SCOUTING REPORT

Offense: His plate approach is long and includes a high front-leg lift, but he still generates good bat speed. Is a classic switch hitter: a high-ball hitter from the right side, a low-ball hitter from the left. Has above-average power batting lefthanded. Likes the ball away and pulls almost everything. **Defense:** He's not a good defensive outfielder. Doesn't get good jumps but charges the ball well. Has arm strength but is an erratic thrower. **Outlook:** Sierra basically is a DH and a potential liability when he is in the field. Still is a dangerous hitter with power. **Grade 5.9**

RUBEN SIERRA'S HITTING ZONE

.100	.167	.071
.400	.200	.304
.222	.308	.455

LEFTY-RIGHTY SPLITS

vs.	Avg.	AB	H	2B	3B	HR	RBI	BB	SO	OBP	Slg.
L	.221	77	17	7	0	2	11	6	13	.277	.390
R	.237	93	22	5	0	2	18	3	28	.255	.355

Year — Team (League)	Pos.	G	AB	R	H	2B	3B	HR	RBI	BB	SO	HBP	GDP	SB-CS	Avg.	OBP	SLG	OPS	E	Avg.
1983— GC Rangers (GCL)	OF	48	182	26	44	7	3	1	26	16	38	1	...	3-4	.242	.300	.330	.630	4	.948
1984— Burlington (Midw.)	OF	138	482	55	127	33	5	6	75	49	97	1	9	13-9	.263	.331	.390	.721	20	.928
1985— Tulsa (Texas)	OF	137	545	63	138	34	8	13	74	35	111	1	8	22-7	.253	.297	.417	.713	15	.943
1986— Okla. City (A.A.)	OF	46	189	31	56	11	2	9	41	15	27	0	5	8-2	.296	.341	.519	.860	2	.983
— Texas (A.L.)	DH-OF	113	382	50	101	13	10	16	55	22	65	1	8	7-8	.264	.302	.476	.779	6	.972

Year	Team (League)	Pos.	G	AB	R	H	2B	3B	HR	RBI	BB	SO	HBP	GDP	SB-CS	Avg.	OBP	SLG	OPS	E	Avg.
1987— Texas (A.L.)		OF	158	* 643	97	169	35	4	30	109	39	114	2	18	16-11	.263	.302	.470	.771	11	.963
1988— Texas (A.L.)		DH-OF	156	615	77	156	32	2	23	91	44	91	1	15	18-4	.254	.301	.424	.725	7	.979
1989— Texas (A.L.)			• 162	634	101	194	35	* 14	29	* 119	43	82	2	7	8-2	.306	.347	* .543	.889	9	.973
1990— Texas (A.L.)		DH-OF	159	608	70	170	37	2	16	96	49	86	1	15	9-0	.280	.330	.426	.756	10	.967
1991— Texas (A.L.)		OF	161	661	110	203	44	5	25	116	56	91	0	17	16-4	.307	.357	.502	.859	7	.979
1992— Texas (A.L.)		OF-DH	124	500	66	139	30	6	14	70	31	59	0	9	12-4	.278	.315	.446	.761	7	.970
— Oakland (A.L.)		OF-DH	27	101	17	28	4	1	3	17	14	9	0	2	2-0	.277	.359	.426	.785	0	1.000
1993— Oakland (A.L.)		OF-DH	158	630	77	147	23	5	22	101	52	97	0	17	25-5	.233	.288	.390	.678	7	.977
1994— Oakland (A.L.)		OF-DH	110	426	71	114	21	1	23	92	23	64	0	15	8-5	.268	.298	.484	.781	* 9	.948
1995— Oakland (A.L.)		OF-DH	70	264	40	70	17	0	12	42	24	42	0	2	4-4	.265	.323	.466	.789	4	.957
— New York (A.L.)		DH-OF	56	215	33	56	15	0	7	44	22	34	0	6	1-0	.260	.322	.428	.750	1	.950
1996— Campeche (Mex.)		DH	1	1	0	0	0	0	0	0	0	0	...	...	0-0	.000	...	.000	...	...	...
— New York (A.L.)		DH-OF	96	360	39	93	17	1	11	52	40	58	0	10	1-3	.258	.327	.403	.730	1	.984
— Detroit (A.L.)		OF-DH	46	158	22	35	9	1	1	20	20	25	0	2	3-1	.222	.306	.310	.616	5	.914
1997— Cincinnati (N.L.)		OF	25	90	6	22	5	1	2	7	6	21	0	1	0-0	.244	.292	.389	.681	0	1.000
— Syracuse (Int'l)		OF	8	32	5	7	2	0	1	5	2	6	0	0	0-0	.219	.265	.375	.640	1	.923
— Toronto (A.L.)		OF-DH	14	48	4	10	0	2	1	5	3	13	0	0	0-0	.208	.250	.354	.604	1	.929
1998— Chicago (A.L.)		OF-DH	27	74	7	16	4	1	4	11	3	11	0	1	2-0	.216	.247	.459	.706	0	1.000
— Norfolk (Int'l)		OF-DH	28	108	16	28	5	0	3	19	13	18	0	4	3-0	.259	.331	.389	.720	1	1.000
1999— Atlantic City (Atl.)		DH-OF	112	422	76	124	22	2	28	82	59	63	...	...	3-2	.294	...	.555	...	3	.960
2000— Cancun (Mex.)		OF	16	62	8	22	2	1	3	12	10	10	...	...	0-1	.355	...	.565	...	0	1.000
— Oklahoma (PCL)		OF	112	439	70	143	26	3	18	82	55	63	0	24	5-2	.326	.398	.522	.919	6	.962
— Texas (A.L.)		DH	20	60	5	14	0	0	1	7	4	9	0	1	1-0	.233	.281	.283	.565	...	...
2001— Oklahoma (PCL)		OF	24	94	14	25	2	1	3	12	10	14	0	5	2-0	.266	.337	.404	.741	0	1.000
— Texas (A.L.)		DH-OF	94	344	55	100	22	1	23	67	19	52	0	13	2-0	.291	.322	.561	.884	4	.937
2002— Seattle (A.L.)		OF-DH	122	419	47	113	23	0	13	60	31	66	0	17	4-0	.270	.319	.418	.736	2	.979
2003— Oakland (A.L.)		OF-DH	43	133	14	35	9	0	3	12	14	27	0	2	1-1	.263	.333	.399	.732	1	.962
— New York (A.L.)		DH-OF	63	174	19	48	8	1	6	31	13	20	0	7	1-0	.276	.323	.437	.760	0	1.000
2004— New York (A.L.)		DH-OF	107	307	40	75	12	1	17	55	25	55	0	5	1-0	.244	.296	.456	.752	1	.977
2005— Columbus (Int'l)			3	11	2	2	0	0	1	1	2	3	0	0	0-0	.182	.308	.455	.762	0	...
— New York (A.L.)		DH-OF	61	170	14	39	12	0	4	29	9	41	0	2	0-0	.229	.265	.371	.636	1	.958
American League totals (19 years)			2147	7926	1075	2125	422	58	304	1311	600	1211	7	192	142-52	.268	.316	.451	.767	94	.970
National League totals (1 year)			25	90	6	22	5	1	2	7	6	21	0	1	0-0	.244	.292	.389	.681	0	1.000
Major League totals (19 years)			2172	8016	1081	2147	427	59	306	1318	606	1232	7	193	142-52	.268	.316	.450	.766	94	.970

DIVISION SERIES RECORD

Year	Team (League)	Pos.	G	AB	R	H	2B	3B	HR	RBI	BB	SO	HBP	GDP	SB-CS	Avg.	OBP	SLG	OPS	E	Avg.
1995— New York (A.L.)		DH	5	23	2	4	2	0	2	5	2	7	0	0	0-0	.174	.231	.522	.753	0	...
2003— New York (A.L.)		OF	1	2	0	0	0	0	0	0	0	0	0	0	0-0	.000	.000	.000	.000	0	...
2004— New York (A.L.)		DH	3	12	1	2	0	0	1	3	2	3	0	0	1-0	.167	.286	.417	.702	0	...
2005— New York (A.L.)		OF	3	3	0	1	0	0	0	1	0	1	0	0	0-0	.333	.333	.333	.667	0	...
Division series totals (4 years)			12	40	3	7	2	0	3	9	4	11	0	0	1-0	.175	.244	.450	.694	0	...

CHAMPIONSHIP SERIES RECORD

Year	Team (League)	Pos.	G	AB	R	H	2B	3B	HR	RBI	BB	SO	HBP	GDP	SB-CS	Avg.	OBP	SLG	OPS	E	Avg.
1992— Oakland (A.L.)		OF	6	24	4	8	2	1	1	7	2	1	0	1	1-2	.333	.357	.625	.982	0	1.000
2003— New York (A.L.)		OF	3	2	1	1	0	0	1	1	1	0	0	0	0-0	.500	.667	2.000	2.667	0	...
2004— New York (A.L.)		DH	5	21	1	7	1	1	0	2	3	8	0	0	0-0	.333	.417	.476	.893	0	...
Champ. series totals (3 years)			14	47	6	16	3	2	2	10	6	9	0	1	1-2	.340	.400	.617	1.017	0	1.000

WORLD SERIES RECORD

Year	Team (League)	Pos.	G	AB	R	H	2B	3B	HR	RBI	BB	SO	HBP	GDP	SB-CS	Avg.	OBP	SLG	OPS	E	Avg.
2003— New York (A.L.)		OF	5	4	0	1	0	1	0	2	1	3	0	0	0-0	.250	.400	.750	1.150	0	...

ALL-STAR GAME RECORD

			G	AB	R	H	2B	3B	HR	RBI	BB	SO	HBP	GDP	SB-CS	Avg.	OBP	SLG	OPS	E	Avg.
All-Star Game totals (4 years)			4	9	3	4	0	0	1	3	2	2	0	0	0-0	.444	.444	.778	1.222	0	1.000

SILVA, CARLOS   P

PERSONAL: Born April 23, 1979, in Bolivar, Venezuela. ... 6-4/240. ... Throws right, bats right. ... High school: U.E. General Ezequiel Zamora Bolivar.

TRANSACTIONS/CAREER NOTES: Signed as a non-drafted free agent by Philadelphia Phillies organization (March 22, 1996). ... On disabled list (May 27-June 14, 2002); included rehabilitation assignment to Reading. ... On suspended list (July 17-22, 2003). ... Traded by Phillies with IF Nick Punto and a player to be named to Minnesota Twins for P Eric Milton (December 3, 2003); Twins acquired P Bobby Korecky to complete deal (December 16, 2003). ... On disabled list (April 7-22, 2005); included rehabilitation assignment to Beloit.

CAREER HITTING: 2-for-16 (.125), 0 R, 1 2B, 0 3B, 0 HR, 1 RBI.

SCOUTING REPORT *Throws:* His best pitch is his excellent sinker. Also throws an 87-93 mph fastball, a 79-81 mph slurve and a changeup. *Tendencies:* He doesn't throw as hard as he did as a reliever. Has consistent sinking action on his fastball and has a compact delivery. Has the best command of any pitcher in baseball with an unheard-of total of nine walks last season. Breaking ball is a sweeping slurve and is starting to throw a more consistent change. Can be wild within the strike zone, giving up a lot more hits than innings pitched. *Outlook:* Knee surgery at the end of the season might affect his sinker. Barring complications, can win more than 15 games next year. *Grade 7.8*

CARLOS SILVA'S PITCHING ZONE

.212	.263	.340
.263	.333	.345
.341	.300	.292

LEFTY-RIGHTY SPLITS

vs.	Avg.	AB	H	2B	3B	HR	RBI	BB	SO	OBP	Slg.
L	.302	394	119	21	1	14	40	8	42	.315	.467
R	.277	336	93	12	0	11	33	1	29	.282	.411

Year	Team (League)	W	L	Pct.	ERA	WHIP	G	GS	CG	ShO	Hld.	Sv.-Opp.	IP	H	R	ER	HR	BB-IBB	SO	Avg.
1996— Martinsville (App.)		0	0	...	4.00	1.39	7	1	0	0	...	0-...	18.0	20	11	8	1	5-0	16	.299
1997— Martinsville (App.)		2	2	.500	5.15	1.39	11	11	0	0	...	0-...	57.2	66	46	33	9	14-0	31	.284
1998— Martinsville (App.)		1	4	.200	5.05	1.27	7	7	1	0	...	0-...	41.0	48	24	23	2	4-0	21	.284

Year	Team (League)	W	L	Pct.	ERA	WHIP	G	GS	CG	ShO	Hld.	Sv.-Opp.	IP	H	R	ER	HR	BB-IBB	SO	Avg.
— Batavia (NY-Penn)		2	3	.400	6.35	1.54	9	7	0	0	...	0-...	45.1	61	37	32	4	9-0	27	.314
1999— Piedmont (S. Atl.)		11	8	.579	3.12	1.32	26	26	3	1	...	0-...	164.1	176	79	57	6	41-2	99	.273
2000— Clearwater (FSL)		8	13	.381	3.57	1.45	26	24	4	0	...	0-...	176.1	229	99	70	7	26-1	82	.314
2001— Reading (East.)		15	8	.652	3.90	1.24	28	28	4	1	...	0-...	180.0	197	85	78	20	27-0	100	.284
2002— Philadelphia (N.L.)		5	0	1.000	3.21	1.31	68	0	0	0	8	1-5	84.0	88	34	30	4	22-6	41	.282
— Reading (East.)		0	0	...	0.00	0.00	2	0	0	0	...	1-...	3.0	0	0	0	0	0-0	1	.000
2003— Philadelphia (N.L.)		3	1	.750	4.43	1.48	62	1	0	0	4	1-3	87.1	92	43	43	7	37-5	48	.280
2004— Minnesota (A.L.)		14	8	.636	4.21	1.43	33	33	1	1	0	0-0	203.0	255	100	95	23	35-2	76	.310
2005— Beloit (Midw.)		0	0	...	1.80	1.00	1	1	0	0	0	0-0	5.0	5	1	1	1	0-0	3	.263
— Minnesota (A.L.)		9	8	.529	3.44	1.17	27	27	2	0	0	0-0	188.1	212	83	72	25	9-2	71	.290
American League totals (2 years)		23	16	.590	3.84	1.31	60	60	3	1	0	0-0	391.1	467	183	167	48	44-4	147	.301
National League totals (2 years)		8	1	.889	3.83	1.39	130	1	0	0	12	2-8	171.1	180	77	73	11	59-11	89	.281
Major League totals (4 years)		31	17	.646	3.84	1.33	190	61	3	1	12	2-8	562.2	647	260	240	59	103-15	236	.295

DIVISION SERIES RECORD

Year	Team (League)	W	L	Pct.	ERA	WHIP	G	GS	CG	ShO	Hld.	Sv.-Opp.	IP	H	R	ER	HR	BB-IBB	SO	Avg.
2004— Minnesota (A.L.)		0	1	.000	10.80	2.00	1	1	0	0	...	0-0	5.0	10	6	6	1	0-0	1	.417

SIMPSON, ALLAN — P

PERSONAL: Born August 26, 1977, in Springfield, Ill. ... 6-4/185. ... Throws right, bats right. ... Full name: Larry Allan Simpson. ... High school: Cheyenne (North Las Vegas, Nev.). ... Junior college: Taft (Calif.). ... College: Long Beach State.

TRANSACTIONS/CAREER NOTES: Selected by Seattle Mariners organization in eighth round of 1997 free-agent draft. ... Traded by Mariners to Colorado Rockies for P Chris Buglovsky (December 15, 2003). ... Traded by Rockies to Cincinnati Reds for P Jose Acevedo (April 9, 2005).

CAREER HITTING: 0-for-1 (.000), 0 R, 0 2B, 0 3B, 0 HR, 0 RBI.

LEFTY-RIGHTY SPLITS

vs.	Avg.	AB	H	2B	3B	HR	RBI	BB	SO	OBP	Slg.
L	.143	7	1	0	0	1	2	3	2	.364	.571
R	.263	19	5	0	0	3	5	4	.440	.368

Year	Team (League)	W	L	Pct.	ERA	WHIP	G	GS	CG	ShO	Hld.	Sv.-Opp.	IP	H	R	ER	HR	BB-IBB	SO	Avg.
1997— Everett (N'west)		0	3	.000	6.84	1.90	16	0	0	0	...	0-...	26.1	26	23	20	1	24-1	26	.263
1998— Wisconsin (Midw.)		3	5	.375	4.44	1.61	19	19	0	0	...	0-...	93.1	89	52	46	5	61-0	86	.257
— Ariz. Mariners (Ariz.)		1	0	1.000	0.96	1.18	3	0	0	0	...	1-...	9.1	8	2	1	1	3-0	12	.235
1999— Wisconsin (Midw.)		2	9	.182	4.38	1.45	24	13	1	0	...	0-...	90.1	83	56	44	4	48-0	88	.245
— Lancaster (Calif.)		0	0	...	6.33	1.45	4	0	0	0	...	0-...	21.1	17	16	15	4	14-0	25	.218
2000— Lancaster (Calif.)		3	2	.600	2.08	1.17	46	0	0	0	...	6-...	52.0	34	17	12	1	27-1	67	.184
2001— San Bern. (Calif.)		1	0	1.000	1.80	1.03	16	0	0	0	...	9-...	30.0	19	7	6	1	12-1	40	.178
— San Antonio (Texas)		2	1	.667	1.86	1.03	22	0	0	0	...	9-...	38.2	25	8	8	1	15-1	37	.184
2002— San Antonio (Texas)		10	5	.667	3.06	1.25	56	0	0	0	...	7-...	82.1	53	33	28	4	50-5	99	.189
2003— Tacoma (PCL)		2	5	.286	4.16	1.63	43	0	0	0	...	1-...	62.2	60	30	29	7	42-1	69	.251
2004— Colo. Springs (PCL)		2	1	.667	2.80	1.13	27	0	0	0	...	4-...	35.1	30	14	11	1	10-0	43	.236
— Colorado (N.L.)		2	1	.667	5.08	1.64	32	0	0	0	1	0-1	39.0	44	26	22	4	20-0	46	.289
2005— Colorado (N.L.)		0	0	...	67.50	9.00	2	0	0	0	0	0-0	0.2	3	5	5	0	3-0	1	.750
— Louisville (Int'l)		4	4	.500	4.06	1.38	50	0	0	0	9	1-5	64.1	51	30	29	5	38-1	89	.213
— Cincinnati (N.L.)		0	1	.000	6.75	1.20	9	0	0	0	0	0-1	6.2	3	5	5	1	5-0	6	.136
Major League totals (2 years)		2	2	.500	6.22	1.68	43	0	0	0	1	0-2	46.1	50	36	32	5	28-0	52	.281

SINGLETON, CHRIS — OF

PERSONAL: Born August 15, 1972, in Martinez, Calif. ... 6-2/217. ... Bats left, throws left. ... Full name: Christopher Verdell Singleton. ... High school: Pinole (Calif.) Valley. ... College: Nevada.

TRANSACTIONS/CAREER NOTES: Selected by San Francisco Giants organization in second round of 1993 free-agent draft. ... Traded by Giants with P Alberto Castillo to New York Yankees for 3B Charlie Hayes and cash (November 11, 1997). ... Traded by Yankees to Chicago White Sox for a player to be named (December 8, 1998). ... Yankees acquired P Rich Pratt to complete deal (January 10, 1999). ... Traded by White Sox to Baltimore Orioles for 2B/OF Willie Harris (January 29, 2002). ... Signed as a free agent by Oakland Athletics (December 23, 2002). ... Signed as a free agent by Pittsburgh Pirates organization (January 3, 2004). ... Failed physical; contract voided by Pirates (March 4, 2004). ... Signed as a free agent by Tampa Bay Devil Rays organization (January 24, 2005). ... Released by Devil Rays (July 4, 2005).

2005 GAMES PLAYED BY POSITION (MLB): OF—19, DH—4.

CHRIS SINGLETON'S HITTING ZONE

.000	.000	.000
.286	.333	.250
1.000	.250	.375

LEFTY-RIGHTY SPLITS

vs.	Avg.	AB	H	2B	3B	HR	RBI	BB	SO	OBP	Slg.
L	.000	3	0	0	0	0	0	0	2	.000	.000
R	.286	56	16	5	0	0	11	6	12	.365	.375

Year	Team (League)	Pos.	G	AB	R	H	2B	3B	HR	RBI	BB	SO	HBP	GDP	SB-CS	Avg.	OBP	SLG	OPS	E	Avg.
1993— Everett (N'west)		OF-OF	58	219	39	58	14	4	3	18	18	46	1	3	14-3	.265	.322	.406	.728	3	.974
1994— San Jose (Calif.)		OF-OF	113	425	51	106	17	5	2	49	27	62	3	9	19-6	.249	.297	.327	.624	13	.952
1995— San Jose (Calif.)		OF-OF	94	405	55	112	13	5	2	31	17	49	5	5	33-13	.277	.313	.348	.661	7	.955
1996— Shreveport (Texas)		OF-OF	129	500	68	149	31	9	5	72	24	58	6	12	27-12	.298	.333	.426	.759	4	.986
— Phoenix (PCL)		OF	9	32	3	4	0	0	0	0	1	2	0	0	0-0	.125	.152	.125	.277	0	1.000
1997— Shreveport (Texas)		OF-OF	126	464	85	147	26	10	9	61	22	50	1	7	27-11	.317	.343	.474	.817	7	.974
1998— Columbus (Int'l)		OF-OF	121	413	55	105	17	10	6	45	27	78	4	7	9-3	.254	.304	.387	.691	7	.974
1999— Chicago (A.L.)		OF-DH	133	496	72	149	31	6	17	72	22	45	1	10	20-5	.300	.328	.490	.818	4	.990
2000— Chicago (A.L.)		OF-DH	147	511	83	130	22	5	11	62	35	85	4	9	22-7	.254	.301	.382	.683	3	.992
2001— Chicago (A.L.)		OF-DH	140	392	57	117	21	5	7	45	20	61	1	5	12-11	.298	.331	.426	.762	3	.991
2002— Baltimore (A.L.)		OF-DH	136	466	67	122	30	6	9	50	21	83	4	8	20-2	.262	.296	.410	.706	4	.986
2003— Oakland (A.L.)		OF	120	306	38	75	24	1	1	36	26	55	1	2	7-2	.245	.301	.340	.641	6	.969
2004—	Did not play.																				
2005— Tampa Bay (A.L.)		OF-DH	28	59	9	16	5	0	0	11	6	14	1	0	0-0	.271	.348	.356	.704	1	.973
— Durham (Int'l)		OF	1	3	0	1	0	0	0	0	0	1	0	0	0-0	.333	.333	.333	.667	0	1.000
Major League totals (6 years)			704	2230	326	609	133	23	45	276	130	343	9	32	81-27	.273	.312	.414	.726	21	.987

DIVISION SERIES RECORD

Year	Team (League)	Pos.	G	AB	R	H	2B	3B	HR	RBI	BB	SO	HBP	GDP	SB-CS	Avg.	OBP	SLG	OPS	E	Avg.
2000— Chicago (A.L.)		OF	3	9	1	1	0	1	0	1	0	2	0	...	0-0	.111	.111	.333	.444	0	1.000
2003— Oakland (A.L.)		OF	2	7	2	2	0	0	0	0	1	1	0	1	1-0	.286	.444	.571	1.016	0	1.000
Division series totals (2 years)			5	16	3	3	0	1	0	1	1	3	0	1	1-0	.188	.278	.438	.715	0	1.000

SISCO, ANDREW   P

PERSONAL: Born January 13, 1983, in Steamboat Springs, Colo. ... 6-10/270. ... Throws left, bats left. ... Full name: Andrew Frank Sisco.
TRANSACTIONS/CAREER NOTES: Selected by Chicago Cubs organization in second round of 2001 free-agent draft. ... Selected by Kansas City Royals from Cubs in Rule 5 major league draft (December 13, 2004).
CAREER HITTING: 0-for-1 (.000), 0 R, 0 2B, 0 3B, 0 HR, 0 RBI.

ANDREW SISCO'S PITCHING ZONE

.308	.143	.111
.387	.222	.188
.286	.412	.259

LEFTY-RIGHTY SPLITS

vs.	Avg.	AB	H	2B	3B	HR	RBI	BB	SO	OBP	Slg.
L	.216	88	19	1	1	2	9	10	22	.297	.318
R	.255	192	49	7	1	4	29	32	54	.363	.365

Year	Team (League)	W	L	Pct.	ERA	WHIP	G	GS	CG	ShO	Hld.	Sv.-Opp.	IP	H	R	ER	HR	BB-IBB	SO	Avg.
2001—	Ariz. Cubs (Ariz.)	1	0	1.000	5.24	1.34	10	7	0	0	...	0-...	34.1	36	28	20	1	10-0	31	.267
2002—	Boise (N'west)	7	2	.778	2.43	1.16	14	14	0	0	...	0-...	77.2	51	23	21	3	39-0	101	.188
2003—	Lansing (Midw.)	6	8	.429	3.54	1.14	19	19	3	0	...	0-...	94.0	76	44	37	3	31-0	99	.220
2004—	Daytona (Fla. St.)	4	10	.286	4.21	1.45	26	25	0	0	...	0-...	126.0	118	64	59	11	65-1	134	.262
2005—	Kansas City (A.L.)	2	5	.286	3.11	1.46	67	0	0	0	14	0-5	75.1	68	27	26	6	42-4	76	.243
	Major League totals (1 year)	2	5	.286	3.11	1.46	67	0	0	0	14	0-5	75.1	68	27	26	6	42-4	76	.243

S

SIZEMORE, GRADY   OF

PERSONAL: Born August 2, 1982, in Seattle, Wash. ... 6-2/200. ... Bats left, throws left. ... Full name: Grady Sizemore III. ... High school: Cascade (Everett, Wash.).
TRANSACTIONS/CAREER NOTES: Selected by Montreal Expos organization in third round of 2000 free-agent draft. ... Traded by Expos with 1B Lee Stevens, IF Brandon Phillips and P Cliff Lee to Cleveland Indians for P Bartolo Colon and future considerations (June 27, 2002); Expos acquired P Tim Drew to complete deal (June 28, 2002).
2005 GAMES PLAYED BY POSITION (MLB): OF—155.

SCOUTING REPORT *Offense:* Sizemore has an outstanding stroke and good bat speed. Has advanced mechanics and bat control and quick hands. Strikes out a lot, especially on high fastballs and breaking stuff away. Hits well with runners in scoring position. Uses the whole field and will develop 30-home run power. Is an outstanding runner and basestealer. Doesn't pull the ball consistently, limiting his power production. *Defense:* He moves well laterally and coming in on the ball but still needs to improve going back. Has exceptional body control and instincts. Charges the ball well and has a quick, accurate release. *Outlook:* Sizemore is one of the most gifted players to come along in years; look for him to take his play to an All-Star level in 2006. *Grade 8.2*

GRADY SIZEMORE'S HITTING ZONE

.231	.346	.128
.303	.421	.377
.241	.356	.297

LEFTY-RIGHTY SPLITS

vs.	Avg.	AB	H	2B	3B	HR	RBI	BB	SO	OBP	Slg.
L	.245	184	45	9	2	3	17	12	49	.296	.364
R	.307	456	140	28	9	19	64	40	83	.369	.533

Year	Team (League)	Pos.	G	AB	R	H	2B	3B	HR	RBI	BB	SO	HBP	GDP	SB-CS	Avg.	OBP	SLG	OPS	E	Avg.
2000—	GC Expos (GCL)	OF-1B	55	205	31	60	8	3	1	14	23	24	6	1	16-2	.293	.380	.376	.756	3	.975
2001—	Clinton (Midw.)	OF	123	451	64	121	16	4	2	61	81	92	4	7	32-11	.268	.381	.335	.716	7	.972
2002—	Brevard County (FSL)	OF	75	256	37	66	15	4	0	26	36	41	2	6	9-9	.258	.351	.348	.699	3	.977
—	Kinston (Carol.)	OF	47	172	31	59	9	3	3	20	33	30	1	1	14-7	.343	.451	.483	.934	4	.949
2003—	Akron (East.)	OF	128	496	96	151	26	11	13	78	46	73	11	5	10-9	.304	.373	.480	.853	4	.986
2004—	Buffalo (Int'l)	OF-DH	101	418	73	120	23	8	8	51	42	72	8	6	15-10	.287	.360	.438	.787	1	.996
—	Cleveland (A.L.)	OF	43	138	15	34	6	2	4	24	14	34	5	0	2-0	.246	.333	.406	.739	1	.991
2005—	Cleveland (A.L.)	OF	158	640	111	185	37	11	22	81	52	132	7	17	22-10	.289	.348	.484	.832	3	.992
	Major League totals (2 years)		201	778	126	219	43	13	26	105	66	166	12	17	24-10	.281	.345	.470	.816	4	.992

SLEDGE, TERRMEL   OF

PERSONAL: Born March 18, 1977, in Fayetteville, N.C. ... 6-0/185. ... Bats left, throws left. ... Full name: Terrmel Sledge. ... Name pronounced: tur-MEL. ... High school: John F. Kennedy (Granada Hills, Calif.). ... College: Long Beach State.
TRANSACTIONS/CAREER NOTES: Selected by Cincinnati Reds organization in 45th round of 1998 free-agent draft; did not sign. ... Selected by Seattle Mariners organization in eighth round of 1999 free-agent draft. ... Traded by Mariners to Montreal Expos (September 27, 2000), completing deal in which Mariners acquired C Chris Widger for two players to be named (August 8, 2000); Expos acquired P Sean Spencer as part of deal (August 10, 2000). ... Expos franchise transferred to Washington, D.C., and renamed Washington Nationals for 2005 season (December 3, 2004). ... On disabled list (May 3, 2005-remainder of season).
2005 GAMES PLAYED BY POSITION (MLB): OF—13.

LEFTY-RIGHTY SPLITS

vs.	Avg.	AB	H	2B	3B	HR	RBI	BB	SO	OBP	Slg.
L	.000	1	0	0	0	0	1	0	0	.000	.000
R	.250	36	9	0	1	1	7	7	8	.364	.389

Year	Team (League)	Pos.	G	AB	R	H	2B	3B	HR	RBI	BB	SO	HBP	GDP	SB-CS	Avg.	OBP	SLG	OPS	E	Avg.
1999—	Everett (N'west)	OF	62	233	43	74	8	3	5	32	27	35	9	2	9-8	.318	.406	.442	.848	4	.958
2000—	Wisconsin (Midw.)	OF	7	23	5	5	2	2	0	3	3	3	1	2	1-0	.217	.333	.478	.812	0	1.000
—	Lancaster (Calif.)	OF	103	384	90	130	22	7	11	75	72	49	17	4	35-11	.339	.458	.518	.976	3	.981
2001—	Harrisburg (East.)	1B-OF	129	448	66	124	22	6	9	48	51	72	4	5	30-8	.277	.359	.413	.772	15	.985
2002—	Harrisburg (East.)	OF-1B	102	396	74	119	18	6	8	43	55	70	12	4	11-8	.301	.401	.437	.838	4	.996
—	Ottawa (Int'l)	OF-1B	24	80	12	21	5	2	1	11	11	15	1	2	1-1	.263	.359	.413	.771	2	.972
2003—	Edmonton (PCL)	OF-1B	131	497	95	161	26	9	22	92	61	93	5	10	13-5	.324	.397	.545	.942	8	.972
2004—	Montreal (N.L.)	OF-1B	133	398	45	107	20	6	15	62	40	66	1	2	3-3	.269	.336	.462	.799	3	.990
2005—	Was. (N.L.)	OF	20	37	7	9	0	1	1	8	7	8	0	0	2-1	.243	.348	.378	.726	0	1.000
	Major League totals (2 years)		153	435	52	116	20	7	16	70	47	74	1	2	5-4	.267	.337	.455	.793	3	.990

SMALL, AARON   P

PERSONAL: Born November 23, 1971, in Oxnard, Calif. ... 6-5/225. ... Throws right, bats right. ... Full name: Aaron James Small. ... High school: South Hills (Covina, Calif.).
TRANSACTIONS/CAREER NOTES: Selected by Toronto Blue Jays organization in 22nd round of 1989 free-agent draft. ... Traded by Blue Jays to Florida Marlins for a player to be named (April 26, 1995); Blue Jays acquired P Ernie Delgado to complete deal (September 19, 1995). ... Claimed on waivers by Seattle Mariners (January 23, 1996). ... Claimed on waivers by Oakland Athletics (January 29, 1996). ... Claimed on waivers by Arizona Diamondbacks (June 26, 1998). ... Released by Diamondbacks (March 30, 1999). ... Signed by Milwaukee Brewers organization (April 12, 1999). ... Released by Brewers (May 23, 1999). ... Signed by Tampa Bay Devil Rays organization (May 27, 1999). ... Signed as a free agent by Colorado Rockies organization (January 5, 2000). ... Signed as a free agent by Anaheim Angels organization (December 21, 2000). ... Released by Angels (May 4, 2001). ... Signed by Atlanta Braves organization (May 10, 2001). ... Released by Braves (September 30, 2002). ... Signed by Chicago Cubs organization (January 13, 2003). ... Released by Cubs (March 29, 2003). ... Signed by Marlins organization (April 30, 2003). ... Signed as a free agent by New York Yankees organization (January 28, 2005).
CAREER HITTING: 0-for-3 (.000), 0 R, 0 2B, 0 3B, 0 HR, 0 RBI.

SCOUTING REPORT **Throws:** Small throws a fastball at 88-91 mph, a curve and a change. **Tendencies:** He came out of nowhere to turn in a career year for Yankees. Has a slight hesitation in his delivery that creates deception. Has marginal velocity but good sinking action down in the zone. Will cut his fastball but it is very flat. Curve has good rotation, but more of an in-between break at higher speeds. Will use change to set up fastball. Is a contact pitcher who doesn't like to pitch inside. **Outlook:** Small turned a corner in his career in terms of command, confidence and consistency with his pitches. ***Grade 6.7***

AARON SMALL'S PITCHING ZONE

.250	.375	.333
.283	.292	.250
.200	.143	.310

LEFTY-RIGHTY SPLITS

vs.	Avg.	AB	H	2B	3B	HR	RBI	BB	SO	OBP	Slg.
L	.252	135	34	7	2	0	13	16	17	.331	.333
R	.248	149	37	9	1	4	16	8	20	.304	.403

Year Team (League)	W	L	Pct.	ERA	WHIP	G	GS	CG	ShO	Hld.	Sv.-Opp.	IP	H	R	ER	HR	BB-IBB	SO	Avg.
1989— Medicine Hat (Pio.)	1	7	.125	5.86	1.57	15	14	0	0	...	0-...	70.2	80	55	46	2	31-1	40	.279
1990— Myrtle Beach (SAL)	9	9	.500	2.80	1.40	27	27	1	0	...	0-...	147.2	150	72	46	6	56-2	96	.262
1991— Dunedin (Fla. St.)	8	7	.533	2.73	1.15	24	23	1	0	...	0-...	148.1	129	51	45	5	42-1	92	.240
1992— Knoxville (Southern)	5	12	.294	5.27	1.58	27	24	2	1	...	0-...	135.0	152	94	79	13	61-0	79	.283
1993— Knoxville (Southern)	4	4	.500	3.39	1.49	48	9	0	0	...	16-...	93.0	99	44	35	5	40-4	44	.273
1994— Knoxville (Southern)	5	5	.500	2.99	1.35	29	11	1	1	...	5-...	96.1	92	37	32	4	38-0	75	.258
— Syracuse (Int'l)	3	2	.600	2.22	1.15	13	0	0	0	...	0-...	24.1	19	8	6	2	9-2	15	.218
— Toronto (A.L.)	0	0	...	9.00	3.50	1	0	0	0	...	0-0	2.0	5	2	2	1	2-0	0	.500
1995— Syracuse (Int'l)	0	0	...	5.40	2.40	1	0	0	0	...	0-0	1.2	3	1	1	1	1-0	2	.375
— Charlotte (Int'l)	2	1	.667	2.88	1.13	33	0	0	0	...	10-...	40.2	36	15	13	2	10-1	31	.229
— Florida (N.L.)	1	0	1.000	1.42	2.05	7	0	0	0	...	0-0	6.1	7	2	1	1	6-0	5	.269
1996— Oakland (A.L.)	1	3	.250	8.16	2.06	12	3	0	0	0	0-0	28.2	37	28	26	3	22-1	17	.308
— Edmonton (PCL)	8	6	.571	4.29	1.16	25	19	1	1	...	1-...	119.2	111	65	57	9	28-0	83	.244
1997— Edmonton (PCL)	1	0	1.000	0.00	0.20	1	1	0	0	...	0-0	5.0	1	0	0	0	4-0	4	.063
— Oakland (A.L.)	9	5	.643	4.28	1.54	71	0	0	0	...	4-6	96.2	109	50	46	6	40-6	57	.294
1998— Oakland (A.L.)	1	1	.500	7.25	1.81	24	0	0	0	3	0-0	36.0	51	34	29	3	14-3	19	.333
— Arizona (N.L.)	3	1	.750	3.69	1.26	23	0	0	0	1	0-2	31.2	32	14	13	5	8-1	14	.269
1999— Louisville (Int'l)	1	1	.500	9.43	2.52	11	0	0	0	...	0-...	21.0	38	23	22	3	15-1	11	.400
— Durham (Int'l)	4	6	.400	6.34	1.51	21	18	0	0	...	0-...	99.1	118	81	70	16	32-2	52	.295
2000— Colo. Springs (PCL)	11	6	.647	5.61	1.48	36	18	0	0	...	0-...	131.2	152	87	82	14	43-0	85	.285
2001— Salt Lake (PCL)	0	1	.000	1.69	1.69	3	0	0	0	...	0-...	5.1	8	1	1	1	1-0	5	.364
— Richmond (Int'l)	10	7	.588	3.83	1.33	41	11	0	0	...	0-...	96.1	97	50	41	14	31-5	61	.257
2002— Richmond (Int'l)	0	3	.000	6.39	2.00	14	4	0	0	...	0-...	31.0	48	27	22	7	14-1	19	.364
— Atlanta (N.L.)	0	0	...	27.00	12.00	1	0	0	0	...	0-0	0.1	2	1	1	0	2-0	1	.667
— GC Braves (GCL)	0	0	...	6.00	1.50	5	5	0	0	...	0-0	6.0	9	4	4	0	0-0	3	.360
2003— Carolina (Southern)	3	4	.429	4.83	1.50	8	7	0	0	...	0-...	41.0	47	23	22	5	14-0	24	.290
— Albuquerque (PCL)	6	4	.600	4.63	1.30	14	14	0	0	...	0-...	89.1	95	50	46	12	18-0	56	.270
2004— Albuquerque (PCL)	9	9	.500	5.06	1.47	27	24	2	0	...	0-...	154.2	199	95	87	18	29-2	109	.315
— Florida (N.L.)	0	0	...	8.27	1.90	7	0	0	0	1	0-0	16.1	24	15	15	5	7-0	8	.343
2005— Trenton (East.)	1	0	1.000	3.60	1.60	1	1	0	0	0	0-0	5.0	7	3	2	1	1-0	3	.333
— Columbus (Int'l)	1	4	.200	4.96	1.43	11	10	0	0	0	0-0	49.0	62	30	27	5	8-0	21	.310
— New York (A.L.)	10	0	1.000	3.20	1.25	15	9	1	1	0	0-1	76.0	71	27	27	4	24-0	37	.250
American League totals (5 years)	**21**	**9**	**.700**	**4.89**	**1.57**	**123**	**12**	**1**	**1**	**11**	**4-7**	**239.1**	**273**	**141**	**130**	**17**	**102-10**	**130**	**.291**
National League totals (4 years)	**4**	**1**	**.800**	**4.94**	**1.61**	**38**	**0**	**0**	**0**	**2**	**0-2**	**54.2**	**65**	**32**	**30**	**11**	**23-1**	**28**	**.298**
Major League totals (8 years)	**25**	**10**	**.714**	**4.90**	**1.57**	**161**	**12**	**1**	**1**	**13**	**4-9**	**294.0**	**338**	**173**	**160**	**28**	**125-11**	**158**	**.292**

DIVISION SERIES RECORD

Year Team (League)	W	L	Pct.	ERA	WHIP	G	GS	CG	ShO	Hld.	Sv.-Opp.	IP	H	R	ER	HR	BB-IBB	SO	Avg.
2005— New York (A.L.)	0	1	.000	6.75	1.50	1	0	0	0	0	0-0	2.2	4	2	2	0	0-0	2	.364

SMITH, JASON   2B/SS

PERSONAL: Born July 24, 1977, in Meridian, Miss. ... 6-3/199. ... Bats left, throws right. ... Full name: Jason William Smith. ... High school: Demopolis (Ala.). ... Junior college: Meridian (Miss.) Community College.
TRANSACTIONS/CAREER NOTES: Selected by Los Angeles Dodgers organization in 42nd round of 1995 free-agent draft; did not sign. ... Selected by Chicago Cubs organization in 23rd round of 1996 free-agent draft. ... Traded by Cubs to Tampa Bay Devil Rays (August 5, 2001), completing deal in which Devil Rays traded 1B Fred McGriff to Cubs for P Manny Aybar and a player to be named (July 27, 2001). ... Signed as a free agent by Detroit Tigers organization (December 8, 2003). ... Signed as a free agent by Colorado Rockies organization (November 8, 2005).
2005 GAMES PLAYED BY POSITION (MLB): SS—15, 2B—6, 3B—3, DH—1, 1B—1.

JASON SMITH'S HITTING ZONE

.000	.000	.000
.143	.333	.250
.000	.500	.500

LEFTY-RIGHTY SPLITS

vs.	Avg.	AB	H	2B	3B	HR	RBI	BB	SO	OBP	Slg.
L	.143	7	1	0	0	0	0	0	3	.143	.143
R	.196	51	10	1	2	0	2	0	13	.212	.294

Year — Team (League)	Pos.	G	AB	R	H	2B	3B	HR	RBI	BB	SO	HBP	GDP	SB-CS	Avg.	OBP	SLG	OPS	E	Avg.
1997— Will. (NYP)	SS	51	205	25	59	5	2	0	11	10	44	0	0	9-2	.288	.321	.332	.653	19	.930
— Rockford (Midwest)	SS	9	33	4	6	0	1	0	3	2	11	0	1	1-0	.182	.229	.242	.471	5	.884
1998— Rockford (Midwest)	SS	126	464	67	111	15	9	7	60	31	122	1	2	23-6	.239	.286	.356	.642	38	.939
1999— Daytona (Fla. St.)	SS	39	142	22	37	5	2	5	26	12	29	3	2	9-3	.261	.329	.430	.759	7	.953
2000— West Tenn (Sou.)	SS	119	481	55	114	22	7	12	61	22	130	2	7	16-10	.237	.273	.387	.659	37	.927
2001— Iowa (PCL)	SS	70	240	31	56	8	6	4	15	12	71	1	4	6-3	.233	.271	.367	.637	19	.942
— Chicago (N.L.)	SS	2	1	0	0	0	0	0	0	0	1	0	0	0-0	.000	.000	.000	.000	0	1.000
— Durham (Int'l)	SS	8	31	2	6	1	0	0	3	0	11	0	0	0-0	.194	.194	.226	.419	3	.917
2002— Tampa Bay (A.L.)	3B-SS-2B																			
	DH	26	65	9	13	1	2	1	6	2	24	0	0	3-0	.200	.224	.323	.547	6	.905
— Durham (Int'l)	SS-3B	54	206	29	57	11	2	4	28	10	44	1	2	5-1	.277	.312	.408	.720	16	.936
2003— Tampa Bay (A.L.)	SS-2B-3B	1	4	0	1	0	0	0	0	0	0	0	0	0-0	.250	.250	.250	.500	2	.500
— Durham (Int'l)	SS-3B																			
	DH	130	515	76	147	20	14	15	71	11	128	5	1	14-9	.285	.304	.466	.770	23	.959
2004— Toledo (Int'l)	3B	33	122	18	33	8	2	3	13	6	26	0	1	5-1	.270	.300	.443	.743	6	.938
— Detroit (A.L.)	2B-SS-3B																			
	DH	61	155	20	37	7	4	5	19	8	37	1	0	1-2	.239	.280	.432	.713	5	.977
2005— Detroit (A.L.)	1B-DH	27	58	4	11	1	2	0	16	1	0	0	0	2-1	.190	.203	.276	.479	1	.989
— Toledo (Int'l)	1B-2B-3B																			
	SS-OF-DH	55	187	24	43	11	2	6	25	11	53	0	1	8-4	.230	.269	.406	.675	6	.977
American League totals (4 years)		115	282	33	62	9	8	6	27	10	77	2	0	6-3	.220	.252	.372	.624	14	.963
National League totals (1 year)		2	1	0	0	0	0	0	0	0	1	0	0	0-0	.000	.000	.000	.000	0	1.000
Major League totals (5 years)		117	283	33	62	9	8	6	27	10	78	2	0	6-3	.219	.251	.371	.622	14	.963

SMITH, TRAVIS   P

PERSONAL: Born November 7, 1972, in Springfield, Ore. ... 5-10/165. ... Throws right, bats right. ... Full name: Travis William Smith. ... High school: Bend (Ore.). ... College: Texas Tech.

TRANSACTIONS/CAREER NOTES: Selected by Milwaukee Brewers organization in 19th round of 1995 free-agent draft. ... On disabled list (June 23, 1998-remainder of season). ... Signed as a free agent by Houston Astros organization (November 1, 2000). ... Signed as a free agent by St. Louis Cardinals organization (November 21, 2001). ... Signed as a free agent by Atlanta Braves organization (November 10, 2003). ... Signed as a free agent by Florida Marlins organization (November 11, 2004).

CAREER HITTING: 4-for-27 (.148), 0 R, 0 2B, 0 3B, 0 HR, 2 RBI.

LEFTY-RIGHTY SPLITS

vs.	Avg.	AB	H	2B	3B	HR	RBI	BB	SO	OBP	Slg.
L	.500	24	12	5	1	0	3	3	3	.556	.792
R	.227	22	5	0	0	1	6	2	6	.280	.364

Year — Team (League)	W	L	Pct.	ERA	WHIP	G	GS	CG	ShO	Hld.	Sv.-Opp.	IP	H	R	ER	HR	BB-IBB	SO	Avg.
1995— Helena (Pion.)	4	2	.667	2.41	1.07	20	7	0	0		5-...	56.0	41	16	15	4	19-0	63	.207
1996— Stockton (Calif.)	6	1	.857	1.84	1.31	14	6	0	0		1-...	58.2	56	17	12	4	21-0	48	.260
— El Paso (Texas)	7	4	.636	4.18	1.47	17	17	3	1		0-...	107.2	119	56	50	6	39-0	68	.281
1997— El Paso (Texas)	16	3	.842	4.15	1.45	28	28	5	1		0-...	184.1	210	106	85	12	58-2	107	.288
1998— Louisville (Int'l)	4	6	.400	5.32	1.51	12	11	0	0		0-...	67.2	77	44	40	9	25-1	36	.294
— Milwaukee (N.L.)	0	0	...	0.00	0.50	1	0	0	0	0	0-0	2.0	1	0	0	0	0-0	1	.143
1999— Ogden (Pion.)	0	0	...	0.00	0.00	1	1	0	0		0-...	1.0	0	0	0	0	0-0	3	.000
— Stockton (Calif.)	0	2	.000	6.14	1.64	3	3	0	0		0-...	7.1	9	6	5	1	3-0	8	.300
— Huntsville (Sou.)	3	2	.600	5.87	1.51	7	7	0	0		0-...	38.1	40	27	25	3	18-0	23	.268
2000— Huntsville (Sou.)	12	7	.632	3.73	1.15	27	24	1	1		0-...	154.1	141	77	64	13	37-0	113	.242
— Indianapolis (Int'l)	1	1	.500	12.66	2.63	3	3	0	0		0-...	10.2	18	15	15	6	9-1	6	.413
2001— Round Rock (Texas)	15	8	.652	3.09	1.12	29	22	1	0		1-...	160.1	154	66	55	7	26-0	85	.251
— New Orleans (PCL)	0	0	...	0.00	2.00	1	0	0	0		0-...	2.0	3	0	0	0	1-0	0	.333
2002— Memphis (PCL)	4	7	.364	2.31	1.05	16	13	1	0		0-...	85.2	76	24	22	7	14-1	62	.238
— St. Louis (N.L.)	4	2	.667	7.17	1.63	12	10	0	0	0	0-0	54.0	69	44	43	10	20-0	32	.322
2003—			Did not play.																
2004— Richmond (Int'l)	10	2	.833	2.59	1.15	20	19	1	0		0-...	107.2	98	31	31	6	26-0	93	.246
— Atlanta (N.L.)	2	3	.400	6.20	1.48	16	4	0	0	1	0-0	40.2	48	28	28	12	12-2	26	.293
2005— Florida (N.L.)	0	0	...	6.75	2.06	12	0	0	0	0	0-0	10.2	17	8	8	1	5-1	9	.370
— Albuquerque (PCL)	7	8	.467	4.08	1.33	18	17	0	0		0-...	103.2	107	54	47	12	31-1	73	.268
Major League totals (4 years)	6	5	.545	6.62	1.60	41	14	0	0	1	0-0	107.1	135	80	79	23	37-3	68	.313

SMOLTZ, JOHN   P

PERSONAL: Born May 15, 1967, in Warren, Mich. ... 6-3/220. ... Throws right, bats right. ... Full name: John Andrew Smoltz. ... High school: Waverly (Lansing, Mich.).

TRANSACTIONS/CAREER NOTES: Selected by Detroit Tigers organization in 22nd round of June 1985 free-agent draft. ... Traded by Tigers to Atlanta Braves for P Doyle Alexander (August 12, 1987). ... On suspended list (June 20-29, 1994). ... On disabled list (March 29-April 15 and May 24-June 20, 1998); included rehabilitation assignments to Greenville and Macon. ... On disabled list (May 17-June 1 and July 5-24, 1999); included rehabilitation assignment to Greenville. ... On disabled list (April 2, 2000-entire season). ... On disabled list (March 23-May 17 and June 10-July 22, 2001); included rehabilitation assignments to Macon and Greenville. ... On disabled list (August 27-September 20, 2003).

HONORS: Named N.L. Pitcher of the Year by THE SPORTING NEWS (1996). ... Named N.L. Cy Young Award winner by Baseball Writers' Association of America (1996).

CAREER HITTING: 137-for-807 (.170), 70 R, 22 2B, 2 3B, 5 HR, 54 RBI.

SCOUTING REPORT *Throws:* Smoltz's fastball still hits 93-98 mph, his split-finger fastball can reach 91, and his hard slider is one of the game's best. *Tendencies:* Smoltz didn't appear to lose much when he moved back into the rotation last season. Has one of the best deliveries in baseball with a loose arm and command of all his pitches. Has an overpowering fastball that he can ride up in the zone and will occasionally cut. Throws a power slider with late break that is hard for righthanders to take. Didn't use his splitter as much, but it still is an out pitch. *Outlook:* Smoltz was sorely missed in the Braves' bullpen but once again was one of the league's best starters. Is a true professional pitcher. *Grade 9.1*

JOHN SMOLTZ'S PITCHING ZONE

.250	.184	.241
.242	.378	.308
.250	.350	.268

LEFTY-RIGHTY SPLITS

vs.	Avg.	AB	H	2B	3B	HR	RBI	BB	SO	OBP	Slg.
L	.252	473	119	29	2	10	48	34	82	.301	.385
R	.233	391	91	15	1	8	31	19	87	.268	.338

Year Team (League)	W	L	Pct.	ERA	WHIP	G	GS	CG	ShO	Hld.	Sv.-Opp.	IP	H	R	ER	HR	BB-IBB	SO	Avg.
1986— Lakeland (Fla. St.)	7	8	.467	3.56	1.22	17	14	2	1	...	0-...	96.0	86	44	38	7	31-0	47	.242
1987— Glens Falls (East.)	4	10	.286	5.68	1.63	21	21	0	0	...	0-...	130.0	131	89	82	17	81-2	86	.268
— Richmond (Int'l)	0	1	.000	6.19	1.75	3	3	0	0	...	0-...	16.0	17	11	11	2	11-0	5	.266
1988— Richmond (Int'l)	10	5	.667	2.79	1.15	20	20	3	0	...	0-...	135.1	118	49	42	5	37-1	115	.233
— Atlanta (N.L.)	2	7	.222	5.48	1.67	12	12	0	0	0	0-0	64.0	74	40	39	10	33-4	37	.285
1989— Atlanta (N.L.)	12	11	.522	2.94	1.12	29	29	5	0	0	0-0	208.0	160	79	68	15	72-2	168	.212
1990— Atlanta (N.L.)	14	11	.560	3.85	1.28	34	34	6	2	0	0-0	231.1	206	109	99	20	* 90-3	170	.240
1991— Atlanta (N.L.)	14	13	.519	3.80	1.23	36	36	5	0	0	0-0	229.2	206	101	97	16	77-1	148	.243
1992— Atlanta (N.L.)	15	12	.556	2.85	1.16	35	* 35	9	3	0	0-0	246.2	206	90	78	17	80-5	* 215	.224
1993— Atlanta (N.L.)	15	11	.577	3.62	1.26	35	35	3	1	0	0-0	243.2	208	104	98	23	100-12	208	.230
1994— Atlanta (N.L.)	6	10	.375	4.14	1.25	21	21	1	0	0	0-0	134.2	120	69	62	15	48-4	113	.239
1995— Atlanta (N.L.)	12	7	.632	3.18	1.24	29	29	2	1	0	0-0	192.2	166	76	68	15	72-8	193	.232
1996— Atlanta (N.L.)	* 24	8	* .750	2.94	1.00	35	35	6	2	0	0-0	* 253.2	199	93	83	19	55-3	* 276	.216
1997— Atlanta (N.L.)	15	12	.556	3.02	1.16	35	* 35	7	2	0	0-0	* 256.0	* 234	97	86	21	63-9	241	.242
1998— Greenville (Sou.)	0	1	.000	2.57	1.00	3	3	0	0	...	0-...	14.0	11	4	4	2	3-0	16	.216
— Macon (S. Atl.)	0	0	...	3.60	0.80	2	2	0	0	...	0-...	10.0	7	4	4	1	1-0	14	.179
— Atlanta (N.L.)	17	3	* .850	2.90	1.13	26	26	2	2	0	0-0	167.2	145	58	54	10	44-2	173	.231
1999— Atlanta (N.L.)	11	8	.579	3.19	1.12	29	29	1	1	0	0-0	186.1	168	70	66	14	40-2	156	.245
— Greenville (Sou.)	0	0	...	4.50	1.50	2	1	0	0	...	0-...	4.0	5	2	2	0	1-0	7	.294
2000— Atlanta (N.L.)			Did not play.																
2001— Greenville (Sou.)	0	0	...	0.00	0.50	3	1	0	0	...	0-0	6.0	3	0	0	0	0-0	6	.150
— Macon (S. Atl.)	0	0	...	1.80	0.80	1	1	0	0	...	0-...	5.0	4	1	1	0	0-0	5	.235
— Atlanta (N.L.)	3	3	.500	3.36	1.07	36	5	0	0	5	10-11	59.0	53	24	22	7	10-2	57	.238
2002— Atlanta (N.L.)	3	2	.600	3.25	1.03	75	0	0	0	0	* 55-59	80.1	59	30	29	4	24-1	85	.206
2003— Atlanta (N.L.)	0	2	.000	1.12	0.87	62	0	0	0	0	45-49	64.1	48	9	8	2	8-1	73	.204
2004— Atlanta (N.L.)	0	1	.000	2.76	1.08	73	0	0	0	0	44-49	81.2	75	25	25	8	13-2	85	.245
2005— Atlanta (N.L.)	14	7	.667	3.06	1.15	33	33	3	1	0	0-0	229.2	210	83	78	18	53-7	169	.243
Major League totals (17 years)	177	128	.580	3.26	1.17	635	394	50	15	5	154-168	2929.1	2537	1157	1060	234	882-68	2567	.233

DIVISION SERIES RECORD

Year Team (League)	W	L	Pct.	ERA	WHIP	G	GS	CG	ShO	Hld.	Sv.-Opp.	IP	H	R	ER	HR	BB-IBB	SO	Avg.
1995— Atlanta (N.L.)	0	0	...	7.94	1.06	1	1	0	0	0	0-0	5.2	5	5	5	2	1-0	6	.238
1996— Atlanta (N.L.)	1	0	1.000	1.00	0.67	1	1	0	0	0	0-0	9.0	4	1	1	0	2-0	7	.129
1997— Atlanta (N.L.)	1	0	1.000	1.00	0.44	1	1	0	0	0	0-0	9.0	3	1	1	1	1-0	11	.097
1998— Atlanta (N.L.)	1	0	1.000	1.17	0.65	1	1	0	0	0	0-0	7.2	5	1	1	1	0-0	6	.185
1999— Atlanta (N.L.)	1	0	1.000	5.14	1.29	1	1	0	0	0	0-0	7.0	6	4	4	2	3-0	3	.222
2001— Atlanta (N.L.)	0	0	...	2.25	0.75	3	0	0	0	0	2-2	4.0	3	1	1	1	0-0	3	.214
2002— Atlanta (N.L.)	0	0	...	2.70	1.20	2	0	0	0	0	0-0	3.1	2	1	1	1	2-0	7	.182
2003— Atlanta (N.L.)	1	0	1.000	6.00	1.33	2	0	0	0	0	1-2	3.0	4	2	2	0	0-0	1	.364
2004— Atlanta (N.L.)	1	0	1.000	0.00	1.20	2	0	0	0	0	0-0	5.0	4	0	0	0	2-0	4	.235
2005— Atlanta (N.L.)	1	0	1.000	1.29	1.14	1	1	0	0	0	0-0	7.0	7	1	1	0	1-1	5	.259
Division series totals (10 years)	7	0	1.000	2.52	0.91	15	6	1	0	0	3-4	60.2	43	17	17	8	12-1	53	.198

CHAMPIONSHIP SERIES RECORD

Year Team (League)	W	L	Pct.	ERA	WHIP	G	GS	CG	ShO	Hld.	Sv.-Opp.	IP	H	R	ER	·HR	BB-IBB	SO	Avg.
1991— Atlanta (N.L.)	2	0	1.000	1.76	1.11	2	2	1	1	0	0-0	15.1	14	3	3	2	3-0	15	.230
1992— Atlanta (N.L.)	2	0	1.000	2.66	1.18	3	3	0	0	0	0-0	20.1	14	7	6	1	10-2	19	.194
1993— Atlanta (N.L.)	0	1	.000	0.00	2.05	1	1	0	0	0	0-0	6.1	8	2	0	0	5-0	10	.296
1995— Atlanta (N.L.)	0	0	...	2.57	1.29	1	1	0	0	0	0-0	7.0	7	2	2	0	2-0	2	.269
1996— Atlanta (N.L.)	2	0	1.000	1.20	1.00	2	2	0	0	0	0-0	15.0	12	2	2	0	3-0	12	.214
1997— Atlanta (N.L.)	0	1	.000	7.50	1.67	1	1	0	0	0	0-0	6.0	5	5	5	1	5-2	9	.227
1998— Atlanta (N.L.)	0	0	...	3.95	1.39	2	2	0	0	0	0-0	13.2	13	6	6	2	6-0	13	.250
1999— Atlanta (N.L.)	0	0	...	6.23	0.92	3	1	0	0	0	1-1	8.2	8	6	6	2	0-0	8	.235
2001— Atlanta (N.L.)	0	0	...	0.00	0.00	2	0	0	0	0	0-0	3.0	0	0	0	0	0-0	1	.000
Champ. series totals (9 years)	6	2	.750	2.83	1.21	17	13	1	1	0	1-1	95.1	81	33	30	8	34-4	89	.226

WORLD SERIES RECORD

Year Team (League)	W	L	Pct.	ERA	WHIP	G	GS	CG	ShO	Hld.	Sv.-Opp.	IP	H	R	ER	HR	BB-IBB	SO	Avg.
1991— Atlanta (N.L.)	0	0	...	1.26	0.98	2	2	0	0	0	0-0	14.1	13	2	2	1	1-0	11	.241
1992— Atlanta (N.L.)	1	0	1.000	2.70	1.50	2	2	0	0	0	0-0	13.1	13	5	4	0	7-0	12	.255
1995— Atlanta (N.L.)	0	0	...	15.43	3.43	1	1	0	0	0	0-0	2.1	6	4	4	0	2-0	4	.462
1996— Atlanta (N.L.)	1	0	.500	0.64	1.00	2	2	0	0	0	0-0	14.0	6	2	1	0	8-0	14	.125
1999— Atlanta (N.L.)	0	1	.000	3.86	1.29	1	1	0	0	0	0-0	7.0	6	3	3	0	3-1	11	.222
World series totals (5 years)	2	2	.500	2.47	1.27	8	8	0	0	0	0-0	51.0	44	16	14	1	21-1	52	.228

ALL-STAR GAME RECORD

	W	L	Pct.	ERA	WHIP	G	GS	CG	ShO	Hld.	Sv.-Opp.	IP	H	R	ER	HR	BB-IBB	SO	Avg.
All-Star Game totals (6 years)	1	2	.333	3.18	1.41	6	1	0	0	0	0-0	5.2	7	2	2	1	1-0	2	.304

SNELL, IAN — P

PERSONAL: Born October 30, 1981, in Dover, Del. ... 5-11/170. ... Throws right, bats right. ... Full name: Ian Dante Snell, formerly Ian Oquendo. ... High school: Caesar Rodney (Camden, Del.).

TRANSACTIONS/CAREER NOTES: Selected by Pittsburgh Pirates organization in 26th round of 2000 free-agent draft.

CAREER HITTING: 0-for-10 (.000), 0 R, 0 2B, 0 3B, 0 HR, 0 RBI.

SCOUTING REPORT *Throws:* His fastball touches the low to mid-90s. Has a slider, curve and changeup. *Tendencies:* He is a power pitcher who struggled with his control in his limited big-league starts last season. Must keep his fastball down to be successful because it's not hard enough to be successful up high. Will work inside and shows mental toughness. His slider is projected as a plus pitch, but his curve was more effective last season. *Outlook:* The Pirates hope he will be a key member of their rotation, but he has not shown he's ready for that kind of role yet. Would be better off getting more starts in the minors. *Grade 6.9*

IAN SNELL'S PITCHING ZONE

.000	.308	.333
.370	.263	.346
.222	.250	.250

LEFTY-RIGHTY SPLITS

vs.	Avg.	AB	H	2B	3B	HR	RBI	BB	SO	OBP	Slg.
L	.304	69	21	6	0	3	12	15	14	.429	.522
R	.239	92	22	6	1	2	12	9	20	.311	.391

Year Team (League)	W	L	Pct.	ERA	WHIP	G	GS	CG	ShO	Hld.	Sv.-Opp.	IP	H	R	ER	HR	BB-IBB	SO	Avg.
2000—GC Pirates (GCL)	1	0	1.000	2.35	0.78	4	0	0	0	...	0-...	7.2	5	2	2	1	1-0	8	.200
2001—GC Pirates (GCL)	3	0	1.000	0.47	0.89	3	3	0	0	...	0-...	19.0	12	2	1	0	5-0	13	.185
—Will. (NYP)	7	0	1.000	1.39	1.01	10	9	1	0	...	0-...	64.2	55	16	10	2	10-0	56	.230
2002—Hickory (S. Atl.)	11	6	.647	2.71	1.23	24	22	0	0	...	0-...	139.2	127	49	42	8	45-0	149	.243
2003—Lynchburg (Caro.)	10	3	.769	3.33	1.19	20	20	1	1	...	0-...	116.1	105	46	43	3	33-1	122	.244
—Altoona (East.)	4	0	1.000	1.96	1.25	6	6	0	0	...	0-...	36.2	36	13	8	2	10-0	23	.252
2004—Altoona (East.)	11	7	.611	3.16	1.24	26	26	3	2	...	0-...	151.0	147	54	53	16	40-2	142	.259
—Pittsburgh (N.L.)	0	1	.000	7.50	1.92	3	1	0	0	...	0-0	12.0	14	10	10	2	9-0	9	.298
2005—Indianapolis (Int'l)	11	3	.786	3.70	1.01	18	18	2	1	0	0-0	112.0	90	49	46	14	23-0	104	.216
—Pittsburgh (N.L.)	1	2	.333	5.14	1.60	15	5	0	0	1	0-0	42.0	43	25	24	5	24-3	34	.267
Major League totals (2 years)	1	3	.250	5.67	1.67	18	6	0	0	1	0-0	54.0	57	35	34	7	33-3	43	.274

SNELLING, CHRIS — OF

PERSONAL: Born December 3, 1981, in North Miami, Fla. ... 5-10/165. ... Bats left, throws left. ... Full name: Christopher Doyle Snelling. ... High school: Corpus Christi College Tuggerah (Australia).

TRANSACTIONS/CAREER NOTES: Signed as a non-drafted free agent by Seattle Mariners organization (March 2, 1999). ... On disabled list (June 5, 2002-remainder of season; and March 21-April 29, 2003). ... On disabled list (March 26, 2004-entire season); included rehabilitation assignment to AZL Mariners. ... On disabled list (April 1-14 and August 12, 2005-remainder of season); included rehabilitation assignment to Tacoma.

2005 GAMES PLAYED BY POSITION (MLB): OF—10.

LEFTY-RIGHTY SPLITS

vs.	Avg.	AB	H	2B	3B	HR	RBI	BB	SO	OBP	Slg.
L	.333	3	1	0	0	0	0	0	0	.333	.333
R	.269	26	7	2	0	1	5	2	.387	.462

Year Team (League)	Pos.	G	AB	R	H	2B	3B	HR	RBI	BB	SO	HBP	GDP	SB-CS	Avg.	OBP	SLG	OPS	E	Avg.
1999—Everett (N'west)	OF-OF	69	265	46	81	15	3	10	50	33	24	6	4	8-9	.306	.388	.498	.886	1	.993
2000—Wisconsin (Midw.)	OF-OF	72	259	44	79	9	5	9	56	34	34	6	2	7-4	.305	.386	.483	.869	2	.983
2001—San Bern. (Calif.)	OF-OF	114	450	90	151	29	10	7	73	45	63	21	7	12-5	.336	.418	.491	.909	4	.978
2002—San Antonio (Texas)	OF-OF	23	89	10	29	9	2	1	12	12	11	4	1	5-1	.326	.429	.506	.935	0	1.000
—Seattle (A.L.)	OF	8	27	2	4	0	0	1	3	2	4	0	2	0-0	.148	.207	.259	.466	0	1.000
2003—San Antonio (Texas)	OF	47	186	24	62	12	2	3	25	8	30	5	0	1-7	.333	.371	.468	.839	0	1.000
—Tacoma (PCL)	OF	18	67	11	18	2	0	3	10	5	12	2	0	1-0	.269	.333	.433	.766	0	1.000
2004—Ariz. Mariners (Ariz.)	OF	10	32	8	10	4	1	0	9	7	3	3	2	1-0	.313	.476	.500	.976	2	.846
2005—Tacoma (PCL)	OF-DH	65	246	50	91	17	2	8	46	36	43	4	1	2-3	.370	.452	.553	1.005	4	.976
—Seattle (A.L.)	OF	15	29	4	8	2	0	1	1	5	2	0	0	0-2	.276	.382	.448	.831	0	1.000
Major League totals (2 years)		23	56	6	12	2	0	2	4	7	6	0	2	0-2	.214	.302	.357	.659	0	1.000

SNOW, J.T. — 1B

PERSONAL: Born February 26, 1968, in Long Beach, Calif. ... 6-2/209. ... Bats left, throws left. ... Full name: Jack Thomas Snow. ... High school: Los Alamitos (Calif.). ... College: Arizona. ... Son of Jack Snow, wide receiver with Los Angeles Rams (1965-75).

TRANSACTIONS/CAREER NOTES: Selected by New York Yankees organization in fifth round of 1989 free-agent draft. ... Traded by Yankees with Ps Jerry Nielsen and Russ Springer to California Angels for P Jim Abbott (December 6, 1992). ... Traded by Angels to San Francisco Giants for Ps Allen Watson and Fausto Macey (November 27, 1996). ... On disabled list (May 27-June 14, June 24-July 15 and July 27-August 7, 2001); included rehabilitation assignments to Fresno. ... On disabled list (June 18-July 3 and August 17-September 1, 2003). ... On disabled list (May 22-June 25, 2004); included rehabilitation assignment to Fresno.

HONORS: Won A.L. Gold Glove at first base (1995-96). ... Won N.L. Gold Glove at first base (1997-2000).

2005 GAMES PLAYED BY POSITION (MLB): 1B—108.

SCOUTING REPORT *Offense:* Snow has a very fluid stroke but has had a slight decline in bat speed and a decline in power. Is a gap-to-gap hitter with line-drive power. Is more of a high-ball hitter. Has trouble with lefthanded pitching. Will be selective at the plate. Does not have the run production typical of the position. *Defense:* Snow is an outstanding, athletic first baseman with soft, quick hands and excellent agility. Gets good jumps on balls to either side and also is good on short hops. *Outlook:* His offensive numbers should continue to decline as he begins his 15th big-league season. Is more valuable on a club that has a lot of power at other positions. *Grade 7.9*

J.T. SNOW'S HITTING ZONE

.231	.435	.364
.319	.259	.302
.235	.304	.210

LEFTY-RIGHTY SPLITS

vs.	Avg.	AB	H	2B	3B	HR	RBI	BB	SO	OBP	Slg.
L	.243	37	9	1	0	0	4	1	8	.282	.270
R	.279	330	92	16	2	4	36	31	53	.350	.376

Year Team (League)	Pos.	G	AB	R	H	2B	3B	HR	RBI	BB	SO	HBP	GDP	SB-CS	Avg.	OBP	SLG	OPS	E	Avg.
1989—Oneonta (NYP)	1B	73	274	41	80	18	2	8	51	29	35	2	9	4-1	.292	.359	.460	.819	6	.991
1990—Prince Will. (Car.)	1B	138	520	57	133	25	1	8	72	46	65	5	20	2-0	.256	.318	.354	.672	12	.991
1991—Alb./Colon. (East.)	1B	132	477	78	133	33	1	13	76	67	78	3	10	5-1	.279	.364	.442	.807	8	.993
1992—Columbus (Int'l)	1B-OF	135	492	81	154	26	4	15	78	70	65	1	9	3-3	.313	.395	.474	.869	8	.993
—New York (A.L.)	1B-DH	7	14	1	2	1	0	0	2	5	5	0	0	0-0	.143	.368	.214	.583	0	1.000
1993—California (A.L.)	1B	129	419	60	101	18	2	16	57	55	88	2	10	3-0	.241	.328	.408	.736	6	.995
—Vancouver (PCL)	1B	23	94	19	32	9	1	5	24	10	13	1	2	0-0	.340	.410	.617	1.027	2	.991
1994—Vancouver (PCL)	1B-DH	53	189	35	56	13	2	8	43	22	32	0	5	1-2	.296	.364	.513	.877	1	.998
—California (A.L.)	1B	61	223	22	49	4	0	8	30	19	48	3	2	0-1	.220	.289	.345	.634	2	.996
1995—California (A.L.)	1B	143	544	80	157	22	1	24	102	52	91	3	16	2-1	.289	.353	.465	.818	4	.997
1996—California (A.L.)	1B	155	575	69	148	20	1	17	67	56	96	5	19	1-6	.257	.324	.384	.711	10	.993
1997—San Francisco (N.L.)	1B	157	531	81	149	36	2	28	104	96	124	1	8	6-4	.281	.387	.510	.898	1	.995
1998—San Francisco (N.L.)	1B	138	435	65	108	29	1	15	79	58	84	0	12	1-2	.248	.332	.423	.755	1	.999
1999—San Francisco (N.L.)	1B	161	570	93	156	25	2	24	98	86	121	5	16	0-4	.274	.370	.451	.821	6	.996
2000—San Francisco (N.L.)	1B	155	536	82	152	33	2	19	96	66	129	11	20	1-3	.284	.365	.459	.824	6	.995
2001—San Francisco (N.L.)	1B	101	285	43	70	12	1	8	34	55	81	4	2	0-0	.246	.371	.379	.750	1	.999
—Fresno (PCL)	1B	4	12	0	0	0	0	0	2	7	0	0	0	0-0	.000	.143	.000	.143	0	1.000
2002—San Francisco (N.L.)	1B	143	422	47	104	26	2	6	53	59	90	7	11	0-0	.246	.344	.360	.704	7	.995
2003—San Francisco (N.L.)	1B	103	330	48	90	18	3	8	51	55	55	8	7	1-2	.273	.387	.418	.806	5	.994

Year Team (League)	Pos.	G	AB	R	H	2B	3B	HR	RBI	BB	SO	HBP	GDP	SB-CS	Avg.	OBP	SLG	OPS	E	Avg.
2004— Fresno (PCL)	1B	2	7	1	2	0	0	1	2	0	1	0	0	0-0	.286	.286	.714	1.000	0	1.000
— San Francisco (N.L.)	1B	107	346	62	113	32	1	12	60	58	61	7	5	4-0	.327	.429	.529	.958	4	.995
2005— San Francisco (N.L.)	1B	117	367	40	101	17	2	4	40	32	61	7	6	1-0	.275	.343	.365	.708	3	.997
American League totals (5 years)		495	1775	232	457	65	4	65	258	187	328	13	47	6-8	.257	.331	.408	.739	22	.995
National League totals (9 years)		1182	3822	561	1043	228	15	124	615	565	806	50	87	14-15	.273	.369	.438	.807	40	.996
Major League totals (14 years)		1677	5597	793	1500	293	19	189	873	752	1134	63	134	20-23	.268	.357	.428	.786	62	.996

DIVISION SERIES RECORD

Year Team (League)	Pos.	G	AB	R	H	2B	3B	HR	RBI	BB	SO	HBP	GDP	SB-CS	Avg.	OBP	SLG	OPS	E	Avg.
1997— San Francisco (N.L.)	1B	3	6	0	1	0	0	0	0	1	1	0	0	0-0	.167	.286	.167	.452	0	1.000
2000— San Francisco (N.L.)	1B	4	10	1	4	0	0	1	3	4	1	0	0	0-0	.400	.571	.700	1.271	0	1.000
2002— San Francisco (N.L.)	1B	5	19	3	6	2	0	1	3	1	5	0	0	0-0	.316	.350	.579	.929	0	1.000
2003— San Francisco (N.L.)	1B	4	16	0	5	0	0	0	3	0	3	0	0	0-0	.313	.313	.313	.625	2	.929
Division series totals (4 years)		16	51	4	16	2	0	2	9	6	10	0	0	0-0	.314	.386	.471	.857	2	.982

CHAMPIONSHIP SERIES RECORD

Year Team (League)	Pos.	G	AB	R	H	2B	3B	HR	RBI	BB	SO	HBP	GDP	SB-CS	Avg.	OBP	SLG	OPS	E	Avg.
2002— San Francisco (N.L.)	1B	5	20	1	5	1	1	0	2	1	4	0	1	0-0	.250	.286	.400	.686	0	1.000

WORLD SERIES RECORD

Year Team (League)	Pos.	G	AB	R	H	2B	3B	HR	RBI	BB	SO	HBP	GDP	SB-CS	Avg.	OBP	SLG	OPS	E	Avg.
2002— San Francisco (N.L.)	1B	7	27	6	11	1	0	1	4	2	1	0	0	0-0	.407	.448	.556	1.004	0	1.000

SNYDER, CHRIS — C

PERSONAL: Born February 12, 1981, in Houston. ... 6-3/220. ... Bats right, throws right. ... Full name: Christopher Ryan Snyder. ... High school: Spring Woods (Houston). ... College: Houston.

TRANSACTIONS/CAREER NOTES: Selected by Arizona Diamondbacks organization in second round of 2002 free-agent draft.

2005 GAMES PLAYED BY POSITION (MLB): C—113.

SCOUTING REPORT *Offense:* Snyder hasn't shown a great deal of bat speed but does have some power. Has a lot of holes and doesn't recognize breaking pitches well. Swing is too long and has problems handling inside pitches. *Defense:* Snyder eventually will be a good defensive catcher. Has soft hands. Blocks and shifts well to either side on balls in the dirt. Is very efficient calling games for a young pitching staff. *Outlook:* Snyder needs to make some offensive adjustments if he is to become a regular. *Grade 5.9*

CHRIS SNYDER'S HITTING ZONE

.211	.267	.182
.221	.472	.259
.109	.176	.000

LEFTY-RIGHTY SPLITS

vs.	Avg.	AB	H	2B	3B	HR	RBI	BB	SO	OBP	Slg.
L	.260	77	20	3	0	2	11	15	17	.380	.377
R	.185	249	46	11	0	4	17	25	70	.270	.277

Year Team (League)	Pos.	G	AB	R	H	2B	3B	HR	RBI	BB	SO	HBP	GDP	SB-CS	Avg.	OBP	SLG	OPS	E	Avg.
2002— Lancaster (Calif.)	C-DH	60	217	31	56	16	0	9	44	25	54	3	7	0-0	.258	.337	.456	.794	3	.992
2003— Lancaster (Calif.)	C-DH	69	245	53	77	16	2	10	53	35	43	8	4	0-1	.314	.414	.518	.932	7	.984
— El Paso (Texas)	C-DH	53	188	21	38	14	0	4	26	19	29	4	9	0-0	.202	.286	.340	.627	3	.991
2004— El Paso (Texas)	C-DH-1B	99	346	66	104	31	0	15	57	46	57	6	7	3-1	.301	.389	.520	.909	9	.987
— Arizona (N.L.)	C	29	96	10	23	6	0	5	15	13	25	0	0	0-0	.240	.327	.458	.786	0	1.000
2005— Arizona (N.L.)	C	115	326	24	66	14	0	6	28	40	87	4	6	0-1	.202	.297	.301	.598	2	.997
Major League totals (2 years)		144	422	34	89	20	0	11	43	53	112	4	6	0-1	.211	.304	.336	.641	2	.998

SNYDER, KYLE — P

PERSONAL: Born September 9, 1977, in Houston. ... 6-8/220. ... Throws right, bats both. ... Full name: Kyle Ehren Snyder. ... High school: Riverview (Sarasota, Fla.). ... College: North Carolina.

TRANSACTIONS/CAREER NOTES: Selected by Tampa Bay Devil Rays organization in 27th round of 1996 free-agent draft; did not sign. ... Selected by Kansas City Royals organization in first round (seventh pick overall) of 1999 free-agent draft. ... On disabled list (July 1-21 and August 6, 2003-remainder of season); included rehabilitation assignments to AZL Royals and Wichita. ... On disabled list (March 26, 2004-entire season). ... On disabled list (May 12-July 13, 2005); included rehabilitation assignments to Omaha and Wichita.

CAREER HITTING: 0-for-2 (.000), 0 R, 0 2B, 0 3B, 0 HR, 0 RBI.

SCOUTING REPORT *Throws:* Has a fastball at 88-91 mph, a curveball, a slider and a changeup. *Tendencies:* Snyder has a long history of arm problems. Has lost some off his fastball and doesn't have a loose arm. Will cut his fastball to run from righthanders. Starting to rely more on his slider, especially with runners on, because it has a sharp, late biting break. Good motion with sinking action on his change. *Outlook:* Snyder is destined for middle relief. Much-improved slider that could prove to be his salvation in this role. *Grade 4.9*

KYLE SNYDER'S PITCHING ZONE

.750	.500	.143
.316	.571	.682
.313	.333	.250

LEFTY-RIGHTY SPLITS

vs.	Avg.	AB	H	2B	3B	HR	RBI	BB	SO	OBP	Slg.
L	.333	63	21	4	2	1	9	6	8	.400	.508
R	.366	93	34	12	0	2	14	4	11	.384	.559

Year Team (League)	W	L	Pct.	ERA	WHIP	G	GS	CG	ShO	Hld.	Sv.-Opp.	IP	H	R	ER	HR	BB-IBB	SO	Avg.
1999— Spokane (N'west)	1	0	1.000	4.13	1.13	7	7	0	0	...	0-...	24.0	20	13	11	1	7-0	25	.220
2000— GC Royals (GCL)	0	0	...	0.00	0.50	1	1	0	0	...	0-...	2.0	1	0	0	0	0-0	4	.143
— Wilmington (Caro.)	0	0	...	...	...	1	1	0	0	...	0-...	0.0	0	0	0	0	1-0	1	...
2001	Did not play.																		

Year Team (League)	W	L	Pct.	ERA	WHIP	G	GS	CG	ShO	Hld.	Sv.-Opp.	IP	H	R	ER	HR	BB-IBB	SO	Avg.
2002— Wilmington (Caro.)	0	2	.000	2.98	1.24	15	15	0	0	...	0-...	48.1	49	19	16	1	11-0	48	.261
— Wichita (Texas)	2	2	.500	4.21	1.09	6	6	0	0	...	0-...	25.2	21	12	12	4	7-1	18	.226
2003— Omaha (PCL)	3	0	1.000	2.79	1.17	5	5	0	0	...	0-...	29.0	28	9	9	3	6-0	15	.259
— Royals-1 (Ariz.)	0	0	...	4.50	1.50	1	1	0	0	...	0-...	2.0	3	1	1	0	0-0	1	.375
— Arizona Royals 1 (AZL)	0	0	...	4.50	1.50	1	1	0	0	...	0-...	2.0	3	1	1	0	0-0	1	.375
— Wichita (Texas)	0	0	...	0.00	0.40	1	1	0	0	...	0-...	5.0	2	0	0	0	0-0	2	.125
— Kansas City (A.L.)	1	6	.143	5.17	1.35	15	15	0	0	0	0-0	85.1	94	52	49	11	21-3	39	.283
2004— Kansas City (A.L.)				Did not play.															
2005— Wichita (Texas)	1	0	1.000	5.40	1.20	1	1	0	0	0	0-0	5.0	5	3	3	1	1-0	1	.263
— Omaha (PCL)	2	3	.400	3.55	1.26	15	12	0	0	1	0-0	66.0	61	32	26	3	22-0	48	.244
— Kansas City (A.L.)	1	3	.250	6.75	1.81	13	3	0	0	0	0-0	36.0	55	29	27	3	10-1	19	.353
Major League totals (2 years)	**2**	**9**	**.182**	**5.64**	**1.48**	**28**	**18**	**0**	**0**	**0**	**0-0**	**121.1**	**149**	**81**	**76**	**14**	**31-4**	**58**	**.305**

SORENSEN, ZACH   2B

PERSONAL: Born January 3, 1977, in Salt Lake City. ... 6-0/190. ... Bats both, throws right. ... Full name: Zach Hart Sorensen. ... High school: Highland (Salt Lake City). ... College: Wichita State.

TRANSACTIONS/CAREER NOTES: Selected by Cleveland Indians organization in second round of 1998 free-agent draft. ... Signed as free agent by Anaheim Angels organization (May 22, 2004). ... Angels franchise renamed Los Angeles Angels of Anaheim for 2005 season. ... Waived by Angels (November 16, 2005).

2005 GAMES PLAYED BY POSITION (MLB): 2B—5, 3B—1, DH—1.

LEFTY-RIGHTY SPLITS

vs.	Avg.	AB	H	2B	3B	HR	RBI	BB	SO	OBP	Slg.
L	.167	6	1	1	0	0	0	0	1	.167	.333
R	.167	6	1	0	0	0	0	0	1	.167	.167

								BATTING											FIELDING	
Year Team (League)	Pos.	G	AB	R	H	2B	3B	HR	RBI	BB	SO	HBP	GDP	SB-CS	Avg.	OBP	SLG	OPS	E	Avg.
1998— Watertown (NYP)	SS	53	200	38	60	7	8	4	26	35	35	0	2	14-4	.300	.404	.475	.879	12	.951
1999— Kinston (Carol.)	SS	130	508	79	121	16	7	7	59	62	126	2	6	24-12	.238	.322	.339	.661	22	.963
2000— Akron (East.)	SS	96	382	62	99	17	4	6	38	42	62	2	8	16-6	.259	.333	.372	.705	18	.961
— Buffalo (Int'l)	SS	12	38	5	10	1	1	0	2	3	9	0	2	1-0	.263	.310	.342	.652	2	.972
2001— Mahoning Valley (NYP)	SS	14	53	10	13	0	1	1	11	2	8	0	2	2-0	.245	.263	.340	.603	1	.970
— Akron (East.)	SS	46	194	24	45	6	1	5	16	11	30	1	3	10-8	.232	.273	.351	.624	10	.956
— Buffalo (Int'l)	SS-2B	2	7	2	2	0	0	0	1	0	0	0	0	0-0	.286	.286	.286	.572	0	1.000
2002— Buffalo (Int'l)	2B-SS	120	455	55	120	12	12	7	54	24	72	1	9	13-6	.264	.300	.389	.689	13	.978
2003— Buffalo (Int'l)	2B-OF-SS																			
	3B	61	238	39	57	12	3	6	29	22	42	0	3	12-5	.239	.299	.353	.652	10	.957
— Cleveland (A.L.)	2B-SS-3B																			
	DH-OF	36	37	2	5	1	0	1	2	7	13	0	0	0-3	.135	.273	.243	.516	2	.955
2004— Buffalo (Int'l)	SS	4	8	0	0	0	0	0	0	1	3	0	0	0-0	.000	.111	.000	.111	0	1.000
— Akron (East.)	SS	26	93	12	24	2	1	1	9	17	19	0	0	9-1	.258	.366	.333	.699	2	.975
— Salt Lake (PCL)	SS-1B-2B																			
	OF-3B	95	359	73	111	16	4	3	37	45	58	0	6	22-5	.309	.380	.401	.781	11	.000
2005— Salt Lake (PCL)	SS-1B-2B																			
	OF-3B-DH	78	287	47	87	11	3	2	41	34	55	1	5	21-9	.303	.372	.383	.755	3	.993
— Los Angeles (A.L.)	2B-3B-DH	12	12	3	2	1	0	0	2	0	2	0	0	0-0	.167	.167	.250	.417	1	.929
Major League totals (2 years)		**48**	**49**	**5**	**7**	**2**	**0**	**1**	**2**	**7**	**15**	**0**	**0**	**0-3**	**.143**	**.250**	**.245**	**.495**	**3**	**.948**

SORIANO, ALFONSO   2B

PERSONAL: Born January 7, 1976, in San Pedro de Macoris, Dominican Republic. ... 6-1/180. ... Bats right, throws right. ... Full name: Alfonso Guilleard Soriano. ... Name pronounced: soar-ee-AH-no. ... High school: Eugenio Maria de Osto (Dominican Republic).

TRANSACTIONS/CAREER NOTES: Signed by Hiroshima of the Japan Central League (November 1994). ... Retired from Japan Central League and declared a free agent by Major League Baseball (1998). ... Signed by New York Yankees (September 29, 1998). ... Traded by Yankees with a player to be named to Texas Rangers for SS Alex Rodriguez (February 16, 2004); Rangers acquired SS Joaquin Arias to complete deal (March 13, 2005).

2005 GAMES PLAYED BY POSITION (MLB): 2B—153, DH—2.

SCOUTING REPORT **Offense:** Soriano is an outstanding hitter with an extremely live bat. Has a long swing but has excellent plate coverage and bat speed. Is not patient but is a good bad-ball hitter. Has deceptive strength and power to all fields. Can steal bases and is a consistent 30-30 guy. **Defense:** Soriano is athletic but not fundamentally sound, and his struggles at second base might force a move to center field. Often fields balls off balance and tends to lay back. Likes to play deep and has good range to either side. Has improved fielding balls to his back hand. Has a plus arm which makes up for poor footwork on double plays. Is an erratic thrower when he rushes. **Outlook:** Soriano has speed and power and is one of the game's best offensive players, but he's not steady in the field and has showed no improvement in that area. ***Grade 9.0***

ALFONSO SORIANO'S HITTING ZONE

.348	.400	.326
.304	.421	.253
.247	.375	.259

LEFTY-RIGHTY SPLITS

vs.	Avg.	AB	H	2B	3B	HR	RBI	BB	SO	OBP	Slg.
L	.257	140	36	7	1	4	10	14	29	.327	.407
R	.272	497	135	36	1	32	94	19	96	.304	.541

								BATTING											FIELDING	
Year Team (League)	Pos.	G	AB	R	H	2B	3B	HR	RBI	BB	SO	HBP	GDP	SB-CS	Avg.	OBP	SLG	OPS	E	Avg.
1995— Hiroshima (Jp. West.)		63	227	52	83	12	3	4	55	30	19	...	...	8-...	.366	...	.498	...	...	...
1996— Hiroshima (Jp. West.)		57	131	11	28	...	...	0	13	...	...	...	...	...-...	.214	...	.214	...	...	...
1997— Hiroshima (Jp. West.)		68	242	28	61	13	2	8	34	13	35	...	...	14-...	.252	...	.421	...	...	...
— Hiroshima (Jp. Cn.)	OF	9	17	2	2	0	0	0	2	4	4	...	...	0-...	.118	...	.118	...	...	...
1998—					Did not play.															
1999— Norwich (East.)	SS-DH	89	361	57	110	20	3	15	68	32	67	4	9	24-16	.305	.363	.501	.865	27	.937
— GC Yankees (GCL)	SS-DH	5	19	7	5	2	0	1	5	1	3	1	1	0-0	.263	.318	.526	.844	1	.929
— Columbus (Int'l)	SS-3B-2B	20	82	8	15	5	1	2	11	5	18	0	1	1-1	.183	.225	.341	.566	3	.955
— New York (A.L.)	DH-SS	9	8	2	1	0	0	1	1	0	3	0	0	0-1	.125	.125	.500	.625	1	.500
2000— Columbus (Int'l)	SS-2B	111	459	90	133	32	6	12	66	25	85	3	8	14-7	.290	.327	.464	.791	21	.952
— New York (A.L.)	3B-SS-2B																			
	DH	22	50	5	9	3	0	2	3	1	15	0	0	2-0	.180	.196	.360	.556	7	.837
2001— New York (A.L.)	2B-DH	158	574	77	154	34	3	18	73	29	125	3	7	43-14	.268	.304	.432	.736	19	.973
2002— New York (A.L.)	2B-DH	156	* 696	* 128	* 209	51	2	39	102	23	157	14	8	* 41-13	.300	.332	.547	.880	* 23	.968

S

Year Team (League)	Pos.	G	AB	R	H	2B	3B	HR	RBI	BB	SO	HBP	GDP	SB-CS	Avg.	OBP	SLG	OPS	E	Avg.
									BATTING										**FIELDING**	
2003— New York (A.L.)	2B	156	* 682	114	198	36	5	38	91	38	130	12	8	35-8	.290	.338	.525	.863	19	.975
2004— Texas (A.L.)	2B-DH	145	608	77	170	32	4	28	91	33	121	10	7	18-5	.280	.324	.484	.807	23	.969
2005— Texas (A.L.)	2B-DH	156	637	102	171	43	2	36	104	33	125	7	6	30-2	.268	.309	.512	.821	21	.972
Major League totals (7 years)		802	3255	505	912	199	16	162	465	157	676	46	36	169-43	.280	.320	.500	.820	113	.970

DIVISION SERIES RECORD

Year Team (League)	Pos.	G	AB	R	H	2B	3B	HR	RBI	BB	SO	HBP	GDP	SB-CS	Avg.	OBP	SLG	OPS	E	Avg.
2001— New York (A.L.)	2B	5	18	2	4	0	0	0	3	1	5	0	0	2-1	.222	.263	.222	.485	0	1.000
2002— New York (A.L.)	2B	4	17	2	2	1	0	1	2	1	4	1	0	1-0	.118	.211	.353	.563	1	.958
2003— New York (A.L.)	2B	4	19	2	7	1	0	0	4	0	6	0	0	2-0	.368	.368	.421	.789	1	.938
Division series totals (3 years)		13	54	6	13	2	0	1	9	2	15	1	1	5-1	.241	.281	.333	.614	2	.964

CHAMPIONSHIP SERIES RECORD

Year Team (League)	Pos.	G	AB	R	H	2B	3B	HR	RBI	BB	SO	HBP	GDP	SB-CS	Avg.	OBP	SLG	OPS	E	Avg.
2001— New York (A.L.)	2B	5	15	5	6	0	0	1	2	3	3	1	0	2-0	.400	.526	.600	1.126	1	.955
2003— New York (A.L.)	2B	7	30	0	4	1	0	0	3	1	11	1	1	2-0	.133	.188	.167	.354	1	.973
Champ. series totals (2 years)		12	45	5	10	1	0	1	5	4	14	2	1	4-0	.222	.314	.311	.625	2	.966

WORLD SERIES RECORD

Year Team (League)	Pos.	G	AB	R	H	2B	3B	HR	RBI	BB	SO	HBP	GDP	SB-CS	Avg.	OBP	SLG	OPS	E	Avg.
2001— New York (A.L.)	2B	7	25	1	6	0	0	1	2	0	7	0	0	0-1	.240	.240	.360	.600	3	.927
2003— New York (A.L.)	2B-OF	6	22	2	5	0	0	1	2	2	9	0	1	1-1	.227	.292	.364	.655	0	1.000
World series totals (2 years)		13	47	3	11	0	0	2	4	2	16	0	1	1-2	.234	.265	.362	.627	3	.955

ALL-STAR GAME RECORD

	G	AB	R	H	2B	3B	HR	RBI	BB	SO	HBP	GDP	SB-CS	Avg.	OBP	SLG	OPS	E	Avg.
All-Star Game totals (4 years)	4	9	3	3	0	0	2	4	0	3	0	0	0-0	.333	.333	1.000	1.333	0	1.000

SORIANO, RAFAEL   P

PERSONAL: Born December 19, 1979, in San Jose, Dominican Republic. ... 6-1/175. ... Throws right, bats right. ... Full name: Rafael Soriano. ... Name pronounced: soar-ee-AH-no.

TRANSACTIONS/CAREER NOTES: Signed as a non-drafted free agent by Seattle Mariners organization (August 30, 1996). ... Played first base and outfield in Mariners organization (1997-98). ... On disabled list (July 3-August 2, 2002). ... On disabled list (May 10, 2004-remainder of season); included rehabilitation assignment to Tacoma. ... On disabled list (April 1-September 5, 2005); included rehabilitation assignments to Everett, Inland Empire, San Antonio and Tacoma.

HONORS: Named A.L. Rookie Pitcher of the Year by THE SPORTING NEWS (2003).

CAREER HITTING: 0-for-4 (.000), 0 R, 0 2B, 0 3B, 0 HR, 0 RBI.

SCOUTING REPORT *Throws:* His fastball reaches the plate in the low to mid-90s. Also has a slider in the low 80s and a changeup. *Tendencies:* Soriano, who had arm problems last season, has a loose arm with some deception. Fastball tends to jump on the hitter. Slider will gain a few miles once he builds up arm strength. *Outlook:* Soriano needs to come to spring training and prove he's 100 percent. Can be a very valuable part of the Mariners' bullpen. *Grade 6.7*

LEFTY-RIGHTY SPLITS

vs.	Avg.	AB	H	2B	3B	HR	RBI	BB	SO	OBP	Slg.
L	.571	7	4	1	0	0	0	1	2	.625	.714
R	.100	20	2	1	0	0	2	0	7	.136	.150

Year Team (League)	W	L	Pct.	ERA	WHIP	G	GS	CG	ShO	Hld.	Sv.-Opp.	IP	H	R	ER	HR	BB-IBB	SO	Avg.
1999— Everett (N'west)	5	4	.556	3.11	1.39	14	14	0	0	...	0-...	75.1	56	34	26	8	49-0	83	.208
2000— Wisconsin (Midw.)	8	4	.667	2.87	1.20	21	21	1	0	...	0-...	122.1	97	41	39	3	50-0	90	.225
2001— San Bern. (Calif.)	6	3	.667	2.53	0.99	15	15	* 2	1	...	0-...	89.0	49	28	25	4	39-0	98	.164
— San Antonio (Texas)	2	2	.500	3.35	0.99	8	8	0	0	...	0-...	48.1	34	18	18	5	14-0	53	.192
2002— San Antonio (Texas)	2	3	.400	2.31	1.01	10	8	0	0	...	0-...	46.2	32	13	12	6	15-0	52	.190
— Seattle (A.L.)	0	3	.000	4.56	1.29	10	8	0	0	...	1-1	47.1	45	25	24	8	16-1	32	.243
2003— Tacoma (PCL)	4	3	.571	3.19	0.90	11	10	0	0	...	0-...	62.0	43	24	22	2	12-0	63	.192
— Seattle (A.L.)	3	0	1.000	1.53	0.79	40	0	0	0	5	1-2	53.0	30	9	9	2	12-1	68	.162
2004— Inland Empire (Calif.)	0	0	...	2.25	1.00	2	2	0	0	...	0-...	8.0	7	3	2	1	1-0	9	.241
— San Antonio (Texas)	1	0	1.000	1.13	0.50	2	2	0	0	...	0-...	8.0	4	1	1	0	0-0	10	.154
— Seattle (A.L.)	0	3	.000	13.50	3.60	6	0	0	0	0	0-1	3.1	9	6	5	0	3-0	3	.450
— Tacoma (PCL)	0	0	...	2.46	1.09	3	3	0	0	...	0-...	3.2	2	1	1	1	2-0	5	.154
2005— Inland Empire (Calif.)	0	0	...	0.00	0.50	3	3	0	0	0	0-0	4.0	2	0	0	0	0-0	5	.154
— San Antonio (Texas)	0	0	...	0.00	0.00	1	1	0	0	0	0-0	1.0	0	0	0	0	0-0	0	.000
— Everett (N'west)	0	0	...	3.00	1.33	4	4	0	0	0	0-0	6.0	6	3	2	0	2-0	8	.250
— Tacoma (PCL)	1	0	1.000	0.00	0.75	5	0	0	0	1	0-0	5.1	3	0	0	0	1-0	11	.158
— Seattle (A.L.)	0	0	...	2.45	0.95	7	0	0	0	1	0-0	7.1	6	2	2	0	1-0	9	.222
Major League totals (4 years)	3	6	.333	3.24	1.10	63	8	0	0	6	2-4	111.0	90	42	40	10	32-2	112	.216

SOSA, JORGE   P

PERSONAL: Born April 28, 1977, in Santo Domingo, Dominican Republic. ... 6-2/170. ... Throws right, bats both. ... Full name: Jorge Bolivar Sosa. ... Name pronounced: hor-hey.

TRANSACTIONS/CAREER NOTES: Signed as a non-drafted free agent by Colorado Rockies organization (June 23, 1995). ... Played outfield in Rockies organization (1995-2000). ... Selected by Seattle Mariners organization from Rockies organization in Rule 5 minor league draft (December 11, 2000). ... Selected by Milwaukee Brewers from Mariners organization in Rule 5 major league draft (December 13, 2001). ... Claimed on waivers by Tampa Bay Devil Rays (March 18, 2002). ... On disabled list (May 26-June 25, 2002); included rehabilitation assignment to Orlando. ... Traded by Devil Rays to Atlanta Braves for 2B Nick Green (March 31, 2005).

CAREER HITTING: 3-for-31 (.097), 1 R, 0 2B, 0 3B, 0 HR, 0 RBI.

JORGE SOSA'S PITCHING ZONE

.105	.292	.324
.222	.357	.241
.276	.457	.167

LEFTY-RIGHTY SPLITS

vs.	Avg.	AB	H	2B	3B	HR	RBI	BB	SO	OBP	Slg.
L	.247	251	62	16	3	8	25	40	33	.351	.430
R	.235	255	60	9	0	4	14	24	52	.299	.318

Year Team (League)	W	L	Pct.	ERA	WHIP	G	GS	CG	ShO	Hld.	Sv.-Opp.	IP	H	R	ER	HR	BB-IBB	SO	Avg.
2001— Everett (N'west)	3	1	.750	1.69	1.09	21	7	0	0	...	7-...	58.2	45	22	11	2	19-0	57	.204
— Wisconsin (Midw.)	0	0	...	9.00	1.50	2	0	0	0	...	0-...	2.0	3	2	2	1	0-0	4	.333
2002— Tampa Bay (A.L.)	2	7	.222	5.53	1.43	31	14	0	0	1	0-0	99.1	88	63	61	16	54-0	48	.236
— Orlando (South.)	0	0	...	0.00	0.71	2	2	0	0	...	0-...	7.0	4	2	0	1	1-0	3	.167
2003— Durham (Int'l)	1	1	.500	5.47	1.70	4	4	0	0	...	0-...	24.2	32	15	15	3	9-0	17	.314
— Tampa Bay (A.L.)	5	12	.294	4.62	1.53	29	19	1	1	0	0-0	128.2	137	71	66	14	60-4	72	.278

Year Team (League)	W	L	Pct.	ERA	WHIP	G	GS	CG	ShO	Hld.	Sv.-Opp.	IP	H	R	ER	HR	BB-IBB	SO	Avg.
2004—Durham (Int'l)	1	2	.333	2.77	0.85	3	3	0	0	...	0-...	13.0	11	5	4	0	0-0	23	.224
—Tampa Bay (A.L.)	4	7	.364	5.53	1.55	43	8	0	0	6	1-1	99.1	100	67	61	17	54-3	94	.259
2005—Atlanta (N.L.)	13	3	* .813	2.55	1.39	44	20	0	0	4	0-0	134.0	122	42	38	12	64-8	85	.241
American League totals (3 years)	11	26	.297	5.17	1.51	103	41	1	1	7	1-1	327.1	325	201	188	47	168-7	214	.260
National League totals (1 year)	13	3	.813	2.55	1.39	44	20	0	0	4	0-0	134.0	122	42	38	12	64-8	85	.241
Major League totals (4 years)	24	29	.453	4.41	1.47	147	61	1	1	11	1-1	461.1	447	243	226	59	232-15	299	.254

DIVISION SERIES RECORD

Year Team (League)	W	L	Pct.	ERA	WHIP	G	GS	CG	ShO	Hld.	Sv.-Opp.	IP	H	R	ER	HR	BB-IBB	SO	Avg.
2005—Atlanta (N.L.)	0	1	.000	4.50	1.50	1	1	0	0	...	0-0	6.0	7	3	3	1	2-2	3	.304

SOSA, SAMMY   OF

PERSONAL: Born November 12, 1968, in San Pedro de Macoris, Dominican Republic. ... 6-0/220. ... Bats right, throws right. ... Full name: Samuel Peralta Sosa.

TRANSACTIONS/CAREER NOTES: Signed as a non-drafted free agent by Texas Rangers organization (July 30, 1985). ... Traded by Rangers with SS Scott Fletcher and P Wilson Alvarez to Chicago White Sox for OF Harold Baines and IF Fred Manrique (July 29, 1989). ... Traded by White Sox with P Ken Patterson to Chicago Cubs for OF George Bell (March 30, 1992). ... On disabled list (June 13-July 27, and August 7-September 16, 1992); included rehabilitation assignment to Iowa. ... On disabled list (August 21, 1996-remainder of season). ... On suspended list (June 11-18, 2003). ... On disabled list (May 16-June 18, 2004); included rehabilitation assignment to West Tenn. ... Traded by Cubs with cash to Baltimore Orioles for 2B/OF Jerry Hairston, 2B Mike Fontenot and P David Crouthers (February 2, 2005). ... On disabled list (May 5-24 and August 28, 2005-remainder of season).

HONORS: Named Major League Player of the Year by THE SPORTING NEWS (1998). ... Named N.L. Most Valuable Player by Baseball Writers' Association of America (1998).

2005 GAMES PLAYED BY POSITION (MLB): OF—66, DH—35.

S

SCOUTING REPORT
Offense: Sosa really regressed during the 2005 season. Bat speed showed a dramatic decline but he didn't change his swing, which is still very long. Had a lot of trouble handling the fastball up or inside. Swings through a lot of pitches. Ball no longer sounds the same off his bat and is not exploding as in the past. Is not a good runner. ***Defense:*** Sosa doesn't get a good jump on the ball coming in or going back, and as his speed has declined, so has his range. Doesn't take good lateral routes, with his first step usually in. Arm has good life but is erratic. Often misses the cutoff man. ***Outlook:*** Sosa is at a crossroads with rapidly declining skills. Could be a late-winter pickup for a club that will take him to spring training. ***Grade 7***

SAMMY SOSA'S HITTING ZONE

.182	.273	.346
.175	.406	.214
.255	.316	.154

LEFTY-RIGHTY SPLITS

vs.	Avg.	AB	H	2B	3B	HR	RBI	BB	SO	OBP	Slg.
L	.288	104	30	5	1	4	10	14	22	.370	.471
R	.196	276	54	10	0	10	35	25	62	.266	.341

Year Team (League)	Pos.	G	AB	R	H	2B	3B	HR	RBI	BB	SO	HBP	GDP	SB-CS	Avg.	OBP	SLG	OPS	E	Avg.
1986—GC Rangers (GCL)	OF	61	229	38	63	19	1	4	28	22	51	0	4	11-3	.275	.336	.419	.755	6	.944
1987—Gastonia (S. Atl.)	OF	129	519	73	145	27	4	11	59	21	123	5	7	22-8	.279	.312	.410	.722	17	.920
1988—Charlotte (Fla. St.)	OF	131	507	70	116	13	12	9	51	35	106	4	14	42-24	.229	.282	.355	.637	7	.971
1989—Tulsa (Texas)	OF	66	273	45	81	15	4	7	31	15	52	3	4	16-11	.297	.338	.458	.796	4	.967
—Texas (A.L.)	DH-OF	25	84	8	20	3	0	1	3	0	20	0	3	0-2	.238	.238	.310	.548	2	.944
—Okla. City (A.A.)	OF	10	39	2	4	2	0	0	2	0	6	0	1	4-2	.103	.146	.154	.300	2	.917
—Vancouver (PCL)	OF	13	49	7	18	3	0	1	5	0	20	0	1	0-1	.367	.367	.490	.857	0	1.000
—Chicago (A.L.)	OF	33	99	19	27	5	0	3	10	11	27	2	3	7-3	.273	.351	.414	.765	2	.969
1990—Chicago (A.L.)	OF	153	532	72	124	26	10	15	70	33	150	6	10	32-16	.233	.283	.404	.687	* 13	.962
1991—Chicago (A.L.)	DH-OF	116	316	39	64	10	1	10	33	14	98	2	5	13-6	.203	.240	.335	.576	6	.973
—Vancouver (PCL)	OF	32	116	19	31	7	2	3	19	17	32	1	2	9-2	.267	.358	.440	.797	3	.970
1992—Chicago (N.L.)	OF	67	262	41	68	7	2	8	25	19	63	4	4	15-7	.260	.317	.393	.710	6	.961
—Iowa (Am. Assoc.)	OF	5	19	3	6	2	0	0	1	1	2	0	0	5-0	.316	.350	.421	.771	0	1.000
1993—Chicago (N.L.)	OF	159	598	92	156	25	5	33	93	38	135	4	14	36-11	.261	.309	.485	.794	9	.976
1994—Chicago (N.L.)	OF	105	426	59	128	17	6	25	70	25	92	2	7	22-13	.300	.339	.545	.884	7	.973
1995—Chicago (N.L.)	OF	* 144	564	89	151	17	3	36	119	58	134	5	8	34-7	.268	.340	.500	.840	* 13	.962
1996—Chicago (N.L.)	OF	124	498	84	136	21	2	40	100	34	134	5	14	18-5	.273	.323	.564	.888	10	.964
1997—Chicago (N.L.)	OF	* 162	642	90	161	31	4	36	119	45	* 174	2	16	22-12	.251	.300	.480	.779	8	.977
1998—Chicago (N.L.)	OF	159	643	* 134	198	20	0	66	* 158	73	* 171	1	20	18-9	.308	.377	.647	1.024	9	.975
1999—Chicago (N.L.)	OF	* 162	625	114	180	24	2	63	141	78	* 171	3	17	7-8	.288	.367	.635	1.002	6	.978
2000—Chicago (N.L.)	OF	156	604	106	193	38	1	* 50	138	91	168	2	12	7-4	.320	.406	.634	1.040	* 10	.970
2001—Chicago (N.L.)	OF	160	577	* 146	189	34	5	64	* 160	116	153	6	6	0-2	.328	.437	.737	1.174	6	.982
2002—Chicago (N.L.)	OF	150	556	* 122	160	19	2	* 49	108	103	144	3	14	2-0	.288	.399	.594	.993	6	.980
2003—Chicago (N.L.)	OF	137	517	99	144	22	0	40	103	62	143	5	14	0-1	.279	.358	.553	.911	5	.977
2004—West Tenn (Sou.)	DH	2	6	0	2	1	0	0	1	1	2	0	0	0-0	.333	.429	.500	.929		...
—Chicago (N.L.)	OF-DH	126	478	69	121	21	0	35	80	56	133	2	9	0-0	.253	.332	.517	.849	4	.984
2005—Baltimore (A.L.)	OF-DH	102	380	39	84	15	1	14	45	39	84	2	15	1-1	.221	.295	.376	.671	3	.976
American League totals (4 years)		429	1411	177	319	59	12	43	161	97	379	12	36	53-28	.226	.279	.376	.656	26	.967
National League totals (13 years)		1811	6990	1245	1985	296	32	545	1414	798	1815	44	155	181-79	.284	.358	.569	.928	102	.974
Major League totals (17 years)		2240	8401	1422	2304	355	44	588	1575	895	2194	56	191	234-107	.274	.345	.537	.882	128	.973

DIVISION SERIES RECORD

Year Team (League)	Pos.	G	AB	R	H	2B	3B	HR	RBI	BB	SO	HBP	GDP	SB-CS	Avg.	OBP	SLG	OPS	E	Avg.
1998—Chicago (N.L.)	OF	3	11	0	2	1	0	0	0	1	4	0	0	0-2	.182	.250	.273	.523	0	1.000
2003—Chicago (N.L.)	OF	5	16	1	3	1	0	0	1	6	4	0	1	1-0	.188	.409	.250	.659	0	1.000
Division series totals (2 years)		8	27	1	5	2	0	0	1	7	8	0	1	1-2	.185	.353	.259		0	1.000

CHAMPIONSHIP SERIES RECORD

Year Team (League)	Pos.	G	AB	R	H	2B	3B	HR	RBI	BB	SO	HBP	GDP	SB-CS	Avg.	OBP	SLG	OPS	E	Avg.
2003—Chicago (N.L.)	OF	7	26	7	8	1	0	2	2	6	9	1	0	0-0	.308	.455	.577	1.031	0	1.000

ALL-STAR GAME RECORD

		G	AB	R	H	2B	3B	HR	RBI	BB	SO	HBP	GDP	SB-CS	Avg.	OBP	SLG	OPS	E	Avg.
All-Star Game totals (6 years)		6	13	0	2	0	0	0	0	1	4	0	0	0-0	.154	.154	.154	.308	0	1.000

SOTO, GEOVANY   C

PERSONAL: Born January 20, 1983, in San Juan, Puerto Rico. ... 6-1/195. ... Bats right, throws right. ... Full name: Geovany Soto. ... Cousin of Ramon Martinez, infielder, Philadelphia Phillies.

TRANSACTIONS/CAREER NOTES: Selected by Chicago Cubs organization in 11th round of 2001 free-agent draft.

LEFTY-RIGHTY SPLITS

vs.	Avg.	AB	H	2B	3B	HR	RBI	BB	SO	OBP	Slg.
L	.000	0	0	0	0	0	0	0	0	.000	.000
R	.000	1	0	0	0	0	0	0	0	.000	.000

Year	Team (League)	Pos.	G	AB	R	H	2B	3B	HR	RBI	BB	SO	HBP	GDP	SB-CS	Avg.	OBP	SLG	OPS	E	Avg.
2001—Ariz. Cubs (Ariz.)		C-1B-3B-																			
		OF	41	150	18	39	16	0	1	20	15	33	3	3	1-0	.260	.339	.387	.726	7	.975
2002—Ariz. Cubs (Ariz.)		C-1B-3B-																			
		OF	44	156	24	42	10	2	3	24	13	35	3	2	0-2	.269	.333	.417	.750	1	.992
—Boise (N'west)		C	1	5	1	2	0	0	0	0	0	1	0	0	0-0	.400	.400	.400	.800	0	1.000
2003—Daytona (Fla. St.)		C-3B	89	297	26	72	12	2	2	38	31	58	2	10	0-0	.242	.313	.316	.629	9	.987
2004—West Tenn (Sou.)		C-1B	104	332	47	90	16	0	9	48	40	71	5	10	1-2	.271	.355	.401	.756	6	.993
2005—Iowa (PCL)		C-DH	91	292	30	74	14	0	4	39	48	77	0	15	0-1	.253	.357	.342	.699	4	.995
—Chicago (N.L.)			1	1	0	0	0	0	0	0	0	0	0	0	0-0	.000	.000	.000	.000	0	...
Major League totals (1 year)			1	1	0	0	0	0	0	0	0	0	0	0	0-0	.000	.000	.000	.000	0	...

SPEIER, JUSTIN   P

PERSONAL: Born November 6, 1973, in Walnut Creek, Calif. ... 6-4/205. ... Throws right, bats right. ... Full name: Justin James Speier. ... Name pronounced: SPY-er. ... High school: Brophy College Prep (Phoenix). ... College: Nicholls State. ... Son of Chris Speier, coach, Chicago Cubs, and infielder with five major league teams (1971-89).

TRANSACTIONS/CAREER NOTES: Selected by Chicago Cubs organization in 55th round of 1995 free-agent draft. ... Traded by Cubs with 3B Kevin Orie and P Todd Noel to Florida Marlins for Ps Felix Heredia and Steve Hoff (July 31, 1998). ... Traded by Marlins to Atlanta Braves for a player to be named (April 1, 1999); Marlins acquired P Matthew Targac to complete deal (June 11, 1999). ... Claimed on waivers by Cleveland Indians (November 23, 1999). ... Traded by Indians to New York Mets for OF Brian Jenkins (May 19, 2001). ... Claimed on waivers by Colorado Rockies (May 29, 2001). ... On disabled list (March 31-May 6, 2002); included rehabilitation assignment to Colorado Springs. ... Traded by Rockies to Toronto Blue Jays as part of three-team deal in which Rockies acquired P Joe Kennedy from Devil Rays and a player to be named from Blue Jays, and Devil Rays acquired P Mark Hendrickson from Blue Jays (December 14, 2003); Rockies acquired P Sandy Nin to complete deal (December 15, 2003). ... On disabled list (May 11-June 8, 2004); included rehabilitation assignment to Dunedin.

CAREER HITTING: 3-for-17 (.176), 0 R, 0 2B, 0 3B, 0 HR, 0 RBI.

SCOUTING REPORT **Throws:** Speier uses a 90-92 mph sinker, a slider and a split-finger fastball. **Tendencies:** When he stays on top of the ball, his sinker is good. Slider is more like a slurve. Splitter has a big break and is effective against lefthanders. Struggles with mechanics; pitches tend to flatten out. **Outlook:** He should be a better pitcher than he is but he makes too many mistakes over the plate. With his durability, is better suited to set up. **Grade 6.4**

JUSTIN SPEIER'S PITCHING ZONE

.444	.182	.429
.245	.000	.235
.194	.091	.188

LEFTY-RIGHTY SPLITS

vs.	Avg.	AB	H	2B	3B	HR	RBI	BB	SO	OBP	Slg.
L	.167	96	16	2	0	4	8	6	22	.216	.313
R	.219	146	32	7	0	6	17	9	34	.278	.390

Year	Team (League)	W	L	Pct.	ERA	WHIP	G	GS	CG	ShO	Hld.	Sv.-Opp.	IP	H	R	ER	HR	BB-IBB	SO	Avg.
1995—Will. (NYP)		2	1	.667	1.49	0.85	30	0	0	0	...	12-...	36.1	27	6	6	1	4-0	39	.203
1996—Daytona (Fla. St.)		2	4	.333	3.76	1.33	33	0	0	0	...	13-...	38.1	32	19	16	3	19-3	34	.225
—Orlando (South.)		4	1	.800	2.05	1.06	24	0	0	0	...	6-...	26.1	23	7	6	2	5-1	14	.228
1997—Orlando (South.)		6	5	.545	4.48	1.28	50	0	0	0	...	6-...	78.1	77	46	39	8	23-0	63	.260
—Iowa (Am. Assoc.)		2	0	1.000	0.00	0.49	8	0	0	0	...	1-...	12.1	5	0	0	0	1-0	9	.128
1998—Iowa (PCL)		3	3	.500	5.05	1.37	45	0	0	0	...	12-...	51.2	52	31	29	10	19-1	49	.261
—Chicago (N.L.)		0	0	...	13.50	2.25	1	0	0	0	0	0-0	1.1	2	2	2	0	1-0	2	.333
—Florida (N.L.)		0	3	.000	8.38	1.91	18	0	0	0	1	0-1	19.1	25	18	18	7	12-1	15	.325
1999—Richmond (Int'l)		2	4	.333	5.62	1.75	27	0	0	0	...	3-...	41.2	51	28	26	4	22-4	39	.293
—Atlanta (N.L.)		0	0	...	5.65	1.43	19	0	0	0	0	0-0	28.2	28	18	18	8	13-1	22	.248
2000—Buffalo (Int'l)		0	0	...	4.15	1.23	13	0	0	0	...	9-...	13.0	13	6	6	0	3-0	12	.255
—Cleveland (A.L.)		5	2	.714	3.29	1.24	47	0	0	0	6	0-1	68.1	57	27	25	9	28-3	69	.226
2001—Cleveland (A.L.)		2	0	1.000	6.97	1.55	12	0	0	0	0	0-0	20.2	24	16	16	5	8-0	15	.293
—Colorado (N.L.)		4	3	.571	3.70	1.05	42	0	0	0	4	0-1	56.0	47	24	23	8	12-3	47	.229
—Colo. Springs (PCL)		1	0	1.000	1.46	1.38	11	0	0	0	...	2-...	12.1	10	2	2	0	7-0	16	.227
2002—Colo. Springs (PCL)		2	0	1.000	3.86	1.64	12	0	0	0	...	2-...	14.0	20	7	6	2	3-1	14	.333
—Colorado (N.L.)		5	1	.833	4.33	1.12	63	0	0	0	18	1-4	62.1	51	31	30	9	19-4	47	.216
2003—Colorado (N.L.)		3	1	.750	4.05	1.31	72	0	0	0	12	9-12	73.1	73	37	33	11	23-6	66	.257
2004—Dunedin (Fla. St.)		0	0	...	4.50	1.50	2	0	0	0	...	0-...	2.0	3	1	1	1	0-0	2	.333
—Toronto (A.L.)		3	8	.273	3.91	1.25	62	0	0	0	7	7-11	69.0	61	32	30	8	25-6	52	.239
2005—Toronto (A.L.)		3	2	.600	2.57	0.95	65	0	0	0	11	0-4	66.2	48	20	19	10	15-2	56	.198
American League totals (4 years)		13	12	.520	3.61	1.18	186	0	0	0	24	7-16	224.2	190	95	90	32	76-11	192	.229
National League totals (5 years)		12	8	.600	4.63	1.27	215	0	0	0	35	10-18	241.0	226	130	124	43	80-15	199	.245
Major League totals (8 years)		25	20	.556	4.14	1.23	401	0	0	0	59	17-34	465.2	416	225	214	75	156-26	391	.237

S

SPEIER, RYAN — P

PERSONAL: Born July 24, 1979, in Frankfort, Ky. ... 6-7/200. ... Throws right, bats right. ... Full name: Ryan Andrew Speier. ... College: Radford.
TRANSACTIONS/CAREER NOTES: Signed as a non-drafted free agent by Colorado Rockies organization (July 23, 2001).
CAREER HITTING: 0-for-2 (.000), 0 R, 0 2B, 0 3B, 0 HR, 0 RBI.

RYAN SPEIER'S PITCHING ZONE

.000	...	.500
.429	.286	.313
.333	.500	.182

LEFTY-RIGHTY SPLITS

vs.	Avg.	AB	H	2B	3B	HR	RBI	BB	SO	OBP	Slg.
L	.289	38	11	4	0	0	5	9	5	.426	.395
R	.268	56	15	1	0	0	10	4	5	.323	.286

Year	Team (League)	W	L	Pct.	ERA	WHIP	G	GS	CG	ShO	Hld.	Sv.-Opp.	IP	H	R	ER	HR	BB-IBB	SO	Avg.
2001—Casper (Pion.)		1	2	.333	3.16	1.09	17	0	0	0	...	1-...	25.2	19	12	9	2	9-4	24	.196
2002—Asheville (S. Atl.)		3	1	.750	3.93	1.23	28	0	0	0	...	1-...	36.2	32	21	16	3	13-1	39	.235
—Salem (Carol.)		2	2	.500	3.94	1.44	24	0	0	0	...	4-...	32.0	35	21	14	0	11-2	33	.285
2003—Visalia (Calif.)		4	2	.667	1.53	1.14	56	0	0	0	...	18-...	58.2	50	14	10	2	17-2	73	.226
2004—Tulsa (Texas)		3	1	.750	2.04	0.94	61	0	0	0	...	37-...	61.2	33	14	14	3	25-1	70	.151
2005—Colo. Springs (PCL)		2	2	.500	4.99	1.68	45	0	0	0	4	6-7	52.1	70	30	29	2	18-0	45	.327
—Colorado (N.L.)		2	1	.667	3.65	1.58	22	0	0	0	2	0-1	24.2	26	12	10	0	13-0	10	.277
Major League totals (1 year)		2	1	.667	3.65	1.58	22	0	0	0	2	0-1	24.2	26	12	10	0	13-0	10	.277

SPIEZIO, SCOTT — 3B/1B

PERSONAL: Born September 21, 1972, in Joliet, Ill. ... 6-2/220. ... Bats both, throws right. ... Full name: Scott Edward Spiezio. ... Name pronounced: SPEE-zee-oh. ... High school: Morris (Ill.). ... College: Illinois. ... Son of Ed Spiezio, third baseman with three major league teams (1964-72).
TRANSACTIONS/CAREER NOTES: Selected by Oakland Athletics organization in sixth round of 1993 free-agent draft. ... On disabled list (June 8-25, 1997); included rehabilitation assignment to Southern Oregon. ... On disabled list (June 15-July 31, 1998); included rehabilitation assignment to Edmonton. ... Signed as a free agent by Anaheim Angels (January 11, 2000). ... Signed as a free agent by Seattle Mariners (December 19, 2003). ... On disabled list (March 28-April 17, 2004); included rehabilitation assignment to Inland Empire. ... On disabled list (April 19-July 1, 2005); included rehabilitation assignment to Tacoma. ... Released by Mariners (August 19, 2005).
2005 GAMES PLAYED BY POSITION (MLB): 3B—6, DH—5, 1B—4, 2B—1.

LEFTY-RIGHTY SPLITS

vs.	Avg.	AB	H	2B	3B	HR	RBI	BB	SO	OBP	Slg.
L	.000	17	0	0	0	0	0	1	8	.056	.000
R	.100	30	3	1	0	1	1	3	10	.182	.233

Year	Team (League)	Pos.	G	AB	R	H	2B	3B	HR	RBI	BB	SO	HBP	GDP	SB-CS	Avg.	OBP	SLG	OPS	E	Avg.
1993—S. Oregon (N'west)		1B-3B	31	125	32	41	10	2	3	19	16	18	0	1	0-1	.328	.404	.512	.916	9	.928
—Modesto (California)		1B-3B	32	110	12	28	9	1	1	13	23	19	1	4	1-5	.255	.388	.382	.770	5	.949
1994—Modesto (California)		1B-3B-SS	127	453	84	127	32	5	14	68	88	72	7	15	5-0	.280	.399	.466	.864	18	.951
1995—Huntsville (Sou.)		1B-2B-3B	141	528	78	149	33	8	13	86	67	78	4	10	10-3	.282	.359	.449	.808	29	.935
1996—Edmonton (PCL)		3B-1B-DH	140	523	87	137	30	4	20	91	56	66	4	7	6-5	.262	.335	.449	.784	15	.970
—Oakland (A.L.)		3B-DH	9	29	6	9	2	0	2	8	4	4	0	0	0-0	.310	.394	.586	.980	2	.846
1997—Oakland (A.L.)		2B-3B	147	538	58	131	28	4	14	65	44	75	1	13	9-3	.243	.300	.388	.688	7	.990
—S. Oregon (N'west)		2B-DH	2	9	1	5	0	0	0	2	2	1	0	0	0-0	.556	.583	.556	1.139	1	.875
1998—Oakland (A.L.)		2B-DH	114	406	54	105	19	1	9	50	44	56	2	10	1-3	.259	.333	.377	.709	13	.975
—Edmonton (PCL)		2B-DH	5	13	3	3	1	0	1	4	3	2	0	0	0-0	.231	.375	.538	.913	1	.889
1999—Oakland (A.L.)		2B-3B-1B-DH	89	247	31	60	24	0	8	33	29	36	2	5	0-0	.243	.324	.437	.761	7	.976
—Vancouver (PCL)		2B-3B-1B	28	105	27	41	7	1	6	27	15	16	2	0	0-0	.390	.475	.648	1.123	4	.969
2000—Anaheim (A.L.)		DH-1B-3B-OF-2B	123	297	47	72	11	2	17	49	40	41	3	5	1-2	.242	.334	.465	.799	3	.984
2001—Anaheim (A.L.)		1B-DH-OF-3B-2B	139	457	57	124	29	4	13	54	34	65	5	6	5-2	.271	.326	.438	.764	2	.998
2002—Anaheim (A.L.)		1B-3B-OF-2B	153	491	80	140	34	2	12	82	67	52	4	12	6-7	.285	.371	.436	.807	5	.996
2003—Anaheim (A.L.)		1B-3B-OF	158	521	69	138	36	2	16	83	46	66	5	12	6-3	.265	.326	.453	.779	11	.988
2004—Inland Empire (Calif.)			2	5	0	0	0	0	0	1	0	1	0	0	0-0	.000	.000	.000	.000	0	1.000
—Seattle (A.L.)		3B-1B-DH	112	367	38	79	12	3	10	41	36	60	4	7	4-1	.215	.288	.346	.634	11	.977
2005—Tacoma (PCL)		1B-DH-3B-2B	14	58	11	19	3	1	2	9	1	9	1	2	0-0	.328	.333	.517	.851	1	1.000
—Seattle (A.L.)		3B-DH-1B-2B	29	47	2	3	1	0	1	4	4	18	0	1	0-0	.064	.137	.149	.286	0	1.000
Major League totals (10 years)			1073	3400	442	861	196	23	102	466	348	488	26	71	32-22	.253	.324	.414	.739	61	.988

DIVISION SERIES RECORD

Year	Team (League)	Pos.	G	AB	R	H	2B	3B	HR	RBI	BB	SO	HBP	GDP	SB-CS	Avg.	OBP	SLG	OPS	E	Avg.
2002—Anaheim (A.L.)		1B	4	15	2	6	1	0	1	6	2	1	0	0	0-0	.400	.471	.667	1.137	0	1.000

CHAMPIONSHIP SERIES RECORD

Year	Team (League)	Pos.	G	AB	R	H	2B	3B	HR	RBI	BB	SO	HBP	GDP	SB-CS	Avg.	OBP	SLG	OPS	E	Avg.
2002—Anaheim (A.L.)		1B	5	17	5	6	2	0	1	5	2	1	0	0	1-0	.353	.421	.647	1.068	0	1.000

WORLD SERIES RECORD

Year	Team (League)	Pos.	G	AB	R	H	2B	3B	HR	RBI	BB	SO	HBP	GDP	SB-CS	Avg.	OBP	SLG	OPS	E	Avg.
2002—Anaheim (A.L.)		1B	7	23	3	6	1	1	1	8	6	1	0	1	1-0	.261	.400	.522	.922	0	1.000

SPILBORGHS, RYAN — OF

PERSONAL: Born September 5, 1979, in Santa Barbara, Calif. ... 6-1/190. ... Bats right, throws right. ... Full name: Ryan A. Spilborghs. ... College: Cal-Santa Barbara.
TRANSACTIONS/CAREER NOTES: Selected by Colorado Rockies organization in seventh round of 2002 free-agent draft.
2005 GAMES PLAYED BY POSITION (MLB): OF—1.

LEFTY-RIGHTY SPLITS

vs.	Avg.	AB	H	2B	3B	HR	RBI	BB	SO	OBP	Slg.
L	.000	2	0	0	0	0	0	0	1	.000	.000
R	1.000	2	2	0	0	0	1	0	0	1.000	1.000

S

Year Team (League)	Pos.	G	AB	R	H	2B	3B	HR	RBI	BB	SO	HBP	GDP	SB-CS	Avg.	OBP	SLG	OPS	E	Avg.
2002—Tri-Cities (NWL)		71	261	34	60	11	1	4	34	29	61	3	5	11-7	.230	.313	.326	.639	3	.977
2003—Asheville (S. Atl.)	OF	119	434	78	122	22	2	15	61	63	96	8	4	10-11	.281	.379	.445	.824	4	.982
2004—Visalia (Pion.)		125	444	59	115	26	3	8	57	64	98	6	13	8-6	.259	.357	.385	.742		...
2005—Tulsa (Texas)	OF-DH	71	255	52	87	23	3	6	54	42	49	2	8	10-3	.341	.435	.525	.961	2	.991
—Colorado (N.L.)	OF	1	4	0	2	0	0	0	1	0	1	0	0	0-0	.500	.500	.500	1.000	0	1.000
—Colo. Springs (PCL)	OF	60	227	49	77	23	5	5	30	22	53	3	5	7-3	.339	.405	.551	.955	4	.979
Major League totals (1 year)		1	4	0	2	0	0	0	1	0	1	0	0	0-0	.500	.500	.500	1.000	0	1.000

SPIVEY, JUNIOR — 2B

PERSONAL: Born January 28, 1975, in Oklahoma City. ... 6-0/201. ... Bats right, throws right. ... Full name: Ernest Lee Spivey. ... Name pronounced: SPY-vee. ... High school: Douglass (Oklahoma City). ... Junior college: Cowley County (Kan.) Community College.

TRANSACTIONS/CAREER NOTES: Selected by St. Louis Cardinals organization in 28th round of 1995 free-agent draft; did not sign. ... Selected by Arizona Diamondbacks organization in 36th round of 1996 free-agent draft. ... Loaned by Diamondbacks organization to Texas Rangers organization (July 18-August 29, 1998). ... On disabled list (June 11-26, 2002). ... On disabled list (June 15-July 21, 2003); included rehabilitation assignments to El Paso and Tucson. ... Traded by Diamondbacks with SS Craig Counsell, 1B Lyle Overbay, C Chad Moeller and Ps Chris Capuano and Jorge de la Rosa to Milwaukee Brewers for 1B Richie Sexson, P Shane Nance and a player to be named (December 1, 2003); Diamondbacks acquired OF Noochie Varner to complete deal (December 15, 2003). ... On disabled list (July 3, 2004-remainder of season). ... Traded by Brewers to Washington Nationals for P Tomo Ohka (June 10, 2005). ... On disabled list (July 13-September 17, 2005).

2005 GAMES PLAYED BY POSITION (MLB): 2B—70.

SCOUTING REPORT **Offense:** Spivey is a better fastball hitter than breaking-ball hitter. Has problems with righthanded pitching. Is better at going with the pitch but still tries to pull outside pitches. Will drive balls up in the zone for power. Needs to be more selective. Can run but still is learning to read moves. **Defense:** He isn't a fluid infielder, but his athleticism and quickness allow him to compensate. Has good range to either side. Is aggressive going back on popups and turns the double play quickly. Has a strong arm but has poor accuracy. **Outlook:** Spivey can't seem to play an entire season without an injury, but his versatility makes him valuable when he's healthy. **Grade 6.6**

JUNIOR SPIVEY'S HITTING ZONE

.214	.167	.000
.246	.350	.217
.333	.368	.231

LEFTY-RIGHTY SPLITS

vs.	Avg.	AB	H	2B	3B	HR	RBI	BB	SO	OBP	Slg.
L	.306	72	22	8	1	4	9	10	20	.390	.611
R	.203	187	38	7	0	3	15	19	63	.286	.289

Year Team (League)	Pos.	G	AB	R	H	2B	3B	HR	RBI	BB	SO	HBP	GDP	SB-CS	Avg.	OBP	SLG	OPS	E	Avg.
1996—Ariz. D'backs (Ariz.)	2B-3B-SS	20	69	13	23	0	0	0	3	12	16	4	0	11-2	.333	.453	.333	.787	3	.970
—Lethbridge (Pion.)	2B-SS	31	107	30	36	3	4	2	25	23	24	3	2	8-3	.336	.459	.495	.955	10	.930
1997—High Desert (Calif.)	2B	136	491	88	134	24	6	6	53	69	115	11	9	14-9	.273	.373	.383	.756	33	.949
1998—High Desert (Calif.)	2B-3B-SS	79	285	64	80	14	5	5	35	64	61	3	4	34-12	.281	.416	.418	.834	20	.949
—Tulsa (Texas)	2B	34	119	26	37	10	1	3	16	28	25	3	1	8-4	.311	.450	.487	.938	3	.980
1999—El Paso (Texas)	2B-SS	44	164	40	48	10	4	3	19	36	27	2	5	14-10	.293	.424	.457	.881	9	.963
2000—Tucson (PCL)	2B-SS-3B	28	117	21	33	8	4	3	16	11	17	0	4	3-1	.282	.341	.496	.837	6	.958
—El Paso (Texas)	2B	6	19	5	8	5	0	1	2	0	5	0	1	0-0	.421	.421	.842	1.263	0	1.000
2001—Tucson (PCL)	2B-SS	54	194	25	45	7	0	6	27	27	32	0	4	9-6	.232	.326	.356	.681	3	.990
—Arizona (N.L.)	2B-SS	72	163	33	42	6	3	5	21	23	47	2	2	3-0	.258	.355	.423	.778	3	.985
2002—Arizona (N.L.)	2B	143	538	103	162	34	6	16	78	65	100	16	10	11-6	.301	.389	.476	.865	15	.977
2003—El Paso (Texas)	2B	4	11	2	5	1	0	1	2	2	1	1	1	2-0	.455	.533	.545	1.079	1	.909
—Tucson (PCL)	2B	4	15	3	4	2	0	0	1	1	1	0	0	0-0	.267	.313	.400	.713	0	1.000
—Arizona (N.L.)	2B-OF	106	365	52	93	22	2	13	50	33	95	7	7	4-3	.255	.326	.433	.759	8	.982
2004—Milwaukee (N.L.)	2B-SS	59	228	33	62	13	0	7	28	25	48	7	5	5-3	.272	.359	.421	.780	11	.963
2005—Milwaukee (N.L.)	2B	49	182	22	43	8	1	5	17	18	57	1	3	7-3	.236	.308	.374	.682	7	.968
—Was. (N.L.)	2B	28	77	15	17	7	0	2	8	11	26	2	0	2-0	.221	.330	.390	.719	0	1.000
Major League totals (5 years)		457	1553	258	419	90	12	48	201	175	373	35	30	32-15	.270	.354	.436	.790	44	.977

DIVISION SERIES RECORD

Year Team (League)	Pos.	G	AB	R	H	2B	3B	HR	RBI	BB	SO	HBP	GDP	SB-CS	Avg.	OBP	SLG	OPS	E	Avg.
2002—Arizona (N.L.)	2B	3	13	0	2	0	0	0	0	1	3	0	0	0-0	.154	.214	.154	.368	0	1.000

ALL-STAR GAME RECORD

	G	AB	R	H	2B	3B	HR	RBI	BB	SO	HBP	GDP	SB-CS	Avg.	OBP	SLG	OPS		Avg.
All-Star Game totals (1 year)	1	2	0	0	0	0	0	0	0	1	0	0	0-0	.000	.000	.000	.000		1.000

SPRINGER, RUSS — P

PERSONAL: Born November 7, 1968, in Alexandria, La. ... 6-4/211. ... Throws right, bats right. ... Full name: Russell Paul Springer. ... High school: Grant (Dry Prong, La.). ... College: Louisiana State.

TRANSACTIONS/CAREER NOTES: Selected by New York Yankees organization in seventh round of 1989 free-agent draft. ... Traded by Yankees with 1B J.T. Snow and P Jerry Nielsen to California Angels for P Jim Abbott (December 6, 1992). ... On disabled list (August 2, 1993-remainder of season). ... Traded by Angels to Philadelphia Phillies (August 15, 1995), completing deal in which Phillies traded OF Dave Gallagher to Angels for 2B Kevin Flora and a player to be named (August 9, 1995). ... Released by Phillies (December 20, 1996). ... Signed by Houston Astros organization (December 30, 1996). ... On disabled list (June 17-July 10, 1997); included rehabilitation assignment to Jackson. ... Selected by Arizona Diamondbacks in third round (61st pick overall) of expansion draft (November 18, 1997). ... Traded by Diamondbacks to Atlanta Braves for P Alan Embree (June 23, 1998). ... On disabled list (August 6-21, 1998). ... On disabled list (April 3-May 17, 1999); included rehabilitation assignment to Richmond. ... Signed as a free agent by Diamondbacks (December 3, 1999). ... On disabled list (May 23, 2001-remainder of season); included rehabilitation assignment to Tucson. ... Signed as a free agent by St. Louis Cardinals organization (December 19, 2002). ... On disabled list (May 1-August 30, 2003); included rehabilitation assignment to Memphis. ... Signed as a free agent by Astros organization (June 19, 2004).

CAREER HITTING: 2-for-26 (.077), 1 R, 0 2B, 0 3B, 0 HR, 0 RBI.

SCOUTING REPORT

Throws: He throws a fastball at 90-92 mph, a curve and a slider. **Tendencies:** Springer has a three-quarters delivery with good velocity, but tends to pitch most hitters away. Light fastball tends to flatten out when tries to cut it. Curve has tight spin and quick, but early, break. Slider is more of a quick running fastball. **Outlook:** Springer tends to nibble too much; he has never really trusted his stuff. Good at filling up the middle innings as long as they're not meaningful. **Grade 5.2**

RUSS SPRINGER'S PITCHING ZONE

.412	.214	.154
.209	.240	.240
.313	.091	.286

LEFTY-RIGHTY SPLITS

vs.	Avg.	AB	H	2B	3B	HR	RBI	BB	SO	OBP	Slg.
L	.209	91	19	4	1	4	10	10	23	.287	.407
R	.231	130	30	4	0	5	22	11	31	.306	.377

Year	Team (League)	W	L	Pct.	ERA	WHIP	G	GS	CG	ShO	Hld.	Sv.-Opp.	IP	H	R	ER	HR	BB-IBB	SO	Avg.
1989—	GC Yankees (GCL)	3	0	1.000	1.50	1.00	6	6	0	0	...	0-...	24.0	14	8	4	0	10-0	34	.167
1990—	GC Yankees (GCL)	0	2	.000	1.20	0.93	4	4	0	0	...	0-...	15.0	10	6	2	0	4-0	17	.172
—	Greensboro (S. Atl.)	2	3	.400	3.67	1.46	10	10	0	0	...	0-...	56.1	51	33	23	3	31-0	51	.236
1991—	Fort Laud. (FSL)	5	9	.357	3.49	1.18	25	25	2	0	...	0-...	152.1	118	68	59	9	62-1	139	.213
—	Alb./Colon. (East.)	1	0	1.000	1.80	1.00	2	2	0	0	...	0-...	15.0	9	4	3	0	6-1	16	.167
1992—	Columbus (Int'l)	8	5	.615	2.69	1.16	20	20	1	0	...	0-...	123.2	89	46	37	11	54-0	95	.204
—	New York (A.L.)	0	0	...	6.19	1.75	14	0	0	0	2	0-0	16.0	18	11	11	0	10-0	12	.281
1993—	Vancouver (PCL)	5	4	.556	4.27	1.54	11	9	1	0	...	0-...	59.0	58	37	28	5	33-1	40	.256
—	California (A.L.)	1	6	.143	7.20	1.75	14	9	1	0	0	0-0	60.0	73	48	48	11	32-1	31	.303
1994—	Vancouver (PCL)	7	4	.636	3.04	1.16	12	12	4	0	...	0-...	83.0	77	35	28	7	19-0	58	.242
—	California (A.L.)	2	2	.500	5.52	1.47	18	5	0	0	1	2-3	45.2	53	28	28	9	14-0	28	.291
1995—	California (A.L.)	1	2	.333	6.10	1.65	19	6	0	0	0	1-2	51.2	60	37	35	11	25-1	38	.290
—	Vancouver (PCL)	2	0	1.000	3.44	1.38	6	6	0	0	...	0-...	34.0	24	16	13	3	23-0	23	.207
—	Philadelphia (N.L.)	0	0	...	3.71	1.20	14	0	0	0	0	0-0	26.2	22	11	11	5	10-3	32	.227
1996—	Philadelphia (N.L.)	3	10	.231	4.66	1.49	51	7	0	0	6	0-3	96.2	106	60	50	12	38-6	94	.272
1997—	Houston (N.L.)	3	3	.500	4.23	1.36	54	0	0	0	9	3-7	55.1	48	28	26	4	27-2	74	.232
—	Jackson (Texas)	0	0	...	9.00	2.00	1	0	0	0	...	0-...	1.0	2	1	1	0	0-0	2	.400
1998—	Arizona (N.L.)	4	3	.571	4.13	1.32	26	0	0	0	1	0-3	32.2	26	16	15	4	14-1	37	.232
—	Atlanta (N.L.)	1	1	.500	4.05	1.90	22	0	0	0	6	0-1	20.0	22	10	9	0	16-3	19	.301
1999—	Richmond (Int'l)	1	0	1.000	1.17	0.65	11	0	0	0	...	2-...	15.1	9	2	2	0	1-0	13	.170
—	Atlanta (N.L.)	2	1	.667	3.42	1.12	49	0	0	0	8	1-1	47.1	31	20	18	5	22-2	49	.185
2000—	Arizona (N.L.)	2	4	.333	5.08	1.56	52	0	0	0	3	0-2	62.0	63	36	35	11	34-6	59	.261
2001—	Arizona (N.L.)	0	0	...	7.13	1.36	18	0	0	0	2	1-1	17.2	20	16	14	5	4-0	12	.274
—	Tucson (PCL)	0	0	...	4.91	1.36	7	3	0	0	...	0-...	7.1	7	4	4	0	3-0	6	.250
2002—	Did not play.																			
2003—	Memphis (PCL)	0	0	...	1.42	0.90	7	0	0	0	...	0-...	6.1	2	1	1	0	4-0	5	.105
—	St. Louis (N.L.)	1	1	.500	8.31	1.44	17	0	0	0	5	0-1	17.1	19	16	16	4	6-0	11	.271
2004—	New Orleans (PCL)	1	2	.333	3.48	1.45	26	0	0	0	...	6-...	31.0	31	13	12	3	14-3	33	.263
—	Houston (N.L.)	1	0	1.000	2.63	1.54	16	0	0	0	5	0-0	13.2	15	4	4	1	6-0	9	.278
2005—	Houston (N.L.)	4	4	.500	4.73	1.19	62	0	0	0	10	0-3	59.0	49	34	31	9	21-3	54	.222
	American League totals (4 years)	4	10	.286	6.33	1.64	65	20	1	0	3	3-5	173.1	204	124	122	31	81-2	109	.294
	National League totals (10 years)	20	28	.417	4.60	1.39	381	7	0	0	55	5-22	448.1	424	251	229	64	198-26	450	.247
	Major League totals (13 years)	24	38	.387	5.08	1.46	446	27	1	0	58	8-27	621.2	628	375	351	95	279-28	559	.260

DIVISION SERIES RECORD

Year	Team (League)	W	L	Pct.	ERA	WHIP	G	GS	CG	ShO	Hld.	Sv.-Opp.	IP	H	R	ER	HR	BB-IBB	SO	Avg.
1997—	Houston (N.L.)	0	0	...	5.40	1.80	2	0	0	0	0	0-0	1.2	2	1	1	0	1-0	3	.286
1998—	Atlanta (N.L.)			Did not play.																
1999—	Atlanta (N.L.)	0	0	...	0.00	3.00	1	0	0	0	0	0-0	1.0	2	0	0	0	1-0	1	.400
2004—	Houston (N.L.)	0	1	.000	18.00	2.00	2	0	0	0	0	0-0	2.0	3	4	4	1	1-0	5	.333
2005—	Houston (N.L.)	0	0	...	3.86	2.57	2	0	0	0	0	0-0	2.1	5	1	1	0	1-0	1	.556
	Division series totals (4 years)	0	1	.000	7.71	2.29	7	0	0	0	0	0-0	7.0	12	6	6	1	4-0	10	.400

CHAMPIONSHIP SERIES RECORD

Year	Team (League)	W	L	Pct.	ERA	WHIP	G	GS	CG	ShO	Hld.	Sv.-Opp.	IP	H	R	ER	HR	BB-IBB	SO	Avg.
1998—	Atlanta (N.L.)			Did not play.																
1999—	Atlanta (N.L.)	1	0	1.000	0.00	0.50	2	0	0	0	0	0-0	2.0	0	0	0	0	1-0	1	.000
2005—	Houston (N.L.)	0	0	...	0.00	1.00	1	0	0	0	0	0-0	1.0	0	0	0	0	1-0	1	.000
	Champ. series totals (2 years)	1	0	1.000	0.00	0.67	3	0	0	0	0	0-0	3.0	0	0	0	0	2-0	2	.000

WORLD SERIES RECORD

Year	Team (League)	W	L	Pct.	ERA	WHIP	G	GS	CG	ShO	Hld.	Sv.-Opp.	IP	H	R	ER	HR	BB-IBB	SO	Avg.
1999—	Atlanta (N.L.)	0	0	...	0.00	0.43	2	0	0	0	0	0-0	2.1	1	0	0	0	0-0	1	.125
2005—	Houston (N.L.)	0	0	...	4.50	1.00	2	0	0	0	0	0-0	2.0	2	1	1	0	0-0	1	.250
	World series totals (2 years)	0	0	...	2.08	0.69	4	0	0	0	0	0-0	4.1	3	1	1	0	0-0	2	.188

SPURLING, CHRIS   P

PERSONAL: Born June 28, 1977, in Dayton, Ohio. ... 6-5/228. ... Throws right, bats right. ... Full name: Christopher Michael Spurling. ... High school: Northridge (Johnstown, Ohio). ... Junior college: Sinclair (Ohio) Community College.

TRANSACTIONS/CAREER NOTES: Selected by New York Yankees organization in 41st round of 1997 free-agent draft. ... Traded by Yankees to Pittsburgh Pirates for IF Luis Sojo (August 7, 2000). ... Selected by Atlanta Braves from Pirates organization in Rule 5 major league draft (December 16, 2002). ... Traded by Braves to Detroit Tigers for P Matt Coenen (March 25, 2003). ... On disabled list (April 2, 2004-entire season).

CAREER HITTING: 0-for-0 (.000), 0 R, 0 2B, 0 3B, 0 HR, 0 RBI.

CHRIS SPURLING'S PITCHING ZONE

.250	.333	.154
.256	.333	.214
.409	.125	.313

LEFTY-RIGHTY SPLITS

vs.	Avg.	AB	H	2B	3B	HR	RBI	BB	SO	OBP	Slg.
L	.223	94	21	3	0	4	10	13	10	.312	.383
R	.234	158	37	8	0	4	20	9	16	.279	.361

Year Team (League)	W	L	Pct.	ERA	WHIP	G	GS	CG	ShO	Hld.	Sv.-Opp.	IP	H	R	ER	HR	BB-IBB	SO	Avg.
1998— GC Yankees (GCL)	2	1	.667	2.28	1.32	13	6	0	0	...	1-...	51.1	57	21	13	3	11-0	44	.279
— Greensboro (S. Atl.)	1	0	1.000	3.00	1.33	1	1	0	0	...	0-...	6.0	7	2	2	1	1-0	5	.292
1999— Greensboro (S. Atl.)	4	6	.400	3.66	1.32	49	0	0	0	...	4-...	76.1	78	34	31	8	23-3	68	.265
2000— Lynchburg (Caro.)	1	0	1.000	0.98	0.60	9	0	0	0	...	5-...	18.1	8	2	2	1	3-0	17	.129
— Tampa (Fla. St.)	4	6	.400	3.79	1.26	34	0	0	0	...	1-...	57.0	50	27	24	1	22-5	55	.237
2001— Altoona (East.)	5	7	.417	3.11	1.32	34	15	0	0	...	1-...	121.2	133	48	42	9	28-1	63	.279
2002— Altoona (East.)	4	3	.571	2.19	0.94	51	0	0	0	...	20-...	70.0	54	18	17	8	12-1	60	.210
2003— Detroit (A.L.)	1	3	.250	4.68	1.30	66	0	0	0	5	3-6	77.0	78	42	40	9	22-1	38	.266
2004— Detroit (A.L.)	Did not play.																		
2005— Toledo (Int'l)	2	1	.667	4.12	1.07	12	0	0	0	2	1-2	19.2	18	10	9	2	3-0	15	.243
— Detroit (A.L.)	3	4	.429	3.44	1.13	56	0	0	0	11	0-1	70.2	58	30	27	8	22-6	26	.230
Major League totals (2 years)	4	7	.364	4.08	1.22	122	0	0	0	16	3-7	147.2	136	72	67	17	44-7	64	.250

STAIRS, MATT — OF/1B

PERSONAL: Born February 27, 1968, in Saint John, New Brunswick. ... 5-9/210. ... Bats left, throws right. ... Full name: Matthew Wade Stairs. ... High school: Fredericton (New Brunswick).

TRANSACTIONS/CAREER NOTES: Signed as a non-drafted free agent by Montreal Expos organization (January 17, 1989). ... Contract sold by Expos to Chunichi of the Japan Central League (June 8, 1993). ... Signed as a free agent by Expos organization (December 15, 1993). ... Traded by Expos to Boston Red Sox for cash (February 18, 1994). ... Signed as a free agent by Oakland Athletics organization (December 1, 1995). ... Traded by A's to Chicago Cubs for P Eric Ireland (November 20, 2000). ... Signed as a free agent by Milwaukee Brewers (January 25, 2002). ... On disabled list (May 16-June 3, 2002). ... Signed as a free agent by Pittsburgh Pirates organization (December 18, 2002). ... On disabled list (May 19-June 10, 2003); included rehabilitation assignment to Nashville. ... Signed as a free agent by Kansas City Royals (December 9, 2003). ... On disabled list (August 7-22, 2004).

2005 GAMES PLAYED BY POSITION (MLB): 1B—64, DH—40, OF—15.

SCOUTING REPORT *Offense:* Stairs is an aggressive hitter who loves high fastballs. Has a long stroke and good bat speed but still has to start his swing early. Is vulnerable to off-speed stuff. Likes to pull the ball and has average power. Is a below-average runner but is aggressive and will break up the double play. *Defense:* Stairs' best position is right field, but he played mostly at first base last season. Has arm strength but a slow release. Doesn't have a lot of range to either side. Is inconsistent with reads on balls hit directly at him. Has stiff hands and limited range at first. Becomes a defensive liability if overexposed. *Outlook:* Stairs is a bulldog type who has excellent makeup and is a good role player. *Grade 5.9*

MATT STAIRS' HITTING ZONE

.063	.300	.344
.250	.273	.282
.222	.250	.422

LEFTY-RIGHTY SPLITS

vs.	Avg.	AB	H	2B	3B	HR	RBI	BB	SO	OBP	Slg.
L	.259	54	14	4	0	1	15	12	11	.400	.389
R	.278	342	95	22	1	12	51	48	58	.369	.453

									BATTING									FIELDING	
Year Team (League)	Pos.	G	AB	R	H	2B	3B	HR	RBI	BB	SO	HBP	GDP	SB-CS	Avg.	OBP	SLG	OPS	E	Avg.
1989— W.P. Beach (FSL)	2B-3B-SS	36	111	12	21	3	1	1	9	9	18	0	3	0-0	.189	.248	.261	.509	4	.956
— Jamestown (NYP)	2B-3B	14	43	8	11	1	0	1	5	3	5	0	0	1-2	.256	.304	.349	.653	6	.893
— Rockford (Midwest)	3B	44	141	20	40	9	2	2	14	15	29	2	4	5-4	.284	.358	.418	.777	7	.929
1990— W.P. Beach (FSL)	2B-3B	55	183	30	62	9	3	3	30	41	19	5	5	15-2	.339	.468	.470	.937	17	.899
— Jacksonville (Sou.)	2B-3B-OF																			
	SS	79	280	26	71	17	0	3	34	22	43	3	6	5-3	.254	.310	.346	.656	22	.893
1991— Harrisburg (East.)	2B-3B-OF	129	505	87	168	30	10	13	78	66	47	3	14	23-11	.333	.411	.509	.920	22	.958
1992— Indianapolis (A.A.)	OF	110	401	57	107	23	4	11	56	49	61	4	10	11-11	.267	.351	.426	.777	3	.985
— Montreal (N.L.)	OF	13	30	2	5	2	0	0	5	7	7	0	0	0-0	.167	.316	.233	.549	1	.933
1993— Ottawa (Int'l)	OF	34	125	18	35	4	2	3	20	11	15	2	3	4-1	.280	.348	.416	.764	0	1.000
— Montreal (N.L.)	OF	6	8	1	3	1	0	0	2	0	1	0	1	0-0	.375	.375	.500	.875	0	1.000
— Chunichi (Jp. Cn.)		60	132	10	33	6	0	6	23	...	34	...	...	1-...	.250	...	.432	...	...	...
1994— New Britain (East.) OF-DH-1B		93	317	44	98	25	2	9	61	53	38	3	10	10-7	.309	.407	.486	.893	3	.975
1995— Pawtucket (Int'l)	OF-DH	75	271	40	77	17	0	13	56	29	41	1	10	3-3	.284	.352	.491	.843	0	1.000
— Boston (A.L.)	OF-DH	39	88	8	23	7	1	1	17	4	14	1	4	0-1	.261	.298	.398	.696	2	.913
1996— Oakland (A.L.) OF-DH-1B		61	137	21	38	5	1	10	23	19	23	1	2	1-1	.277	.367	.547	.915	1	.987
— Edmonton (PCL)	DH-OF-1B	51	180	35	62	16	1	8	41	21	34	0	4	0-0	.344	.401	.578	.979	3	.944
1997— Oakland (A.L.) OF-DH-1B		133	352	62	105	19	0	27	73	50	60	3	6	3-2	.298	.386	.582	.969	4	.974
1998— Oakland (A.L.) DH-OF-1B		149	523	88	154	33	4	26	106	59	93	6	13	8-3	.294	.370	.511	.880	1	1.000
1999— Oakland (A.L.) OF-DH-1B		146	531	94	137	26	3	38	102	89	124	2	8	2-7	.258	.366	.533	.899	5	.989
2000— Oakland (A.L.) OF-DH-1B		143	476	74	108	26	0	21	81	78	122	1	5	5-2	.227	.333	.414	.747	4	.980
2001— Chicago (N.L.) 1B-OF-DH																				
	2B	128	340	48	85	21	0	17	61	52	76	7	4	2-3	.250	.358	.462	.820	4	.993
2002— Milwaukee (N.L.)	OF	107	270	41	66	15	0	16	41	36	50	8	7	2-0	.244	.349	.478	.827	1	.993
2003— Nashville (PCL) OF-1B-DH		7	18	4	3	0	0	2	3	7	2	2	1	0-0	.167	.444	.500	.944	0	1.000
— Pittsburgh (N.L.) OF-1B-DH		121	305	49	89	20	1	20	57	45	64	5	7	0-1	.292	.389	.561	.950	3	.990
2004— Kansas City (A.L.) OF-1B-DH		126	439	48	117	21	3	18	66	49	92	5	15	1-0	.267	.345	.451	.796	5	.986
2005— Kansas City (A.L.) 1B-DH-OF		127	396	55	109	26	1	13	66	60	69	5	7	1-2	.275	.373	.444	.818	4	.993
American League totals (8 years)		924	2942	450	791	163	10	154	534	408	597	24	64	21-18	.269	.360	.488	.848	25	.985
National League totals (5 years)		375	953	141	248	59	1	53	166	140	198	20	19	4-4	.260	.364	.491	.855	9	.991
Major League totals (13 years)		1299	3895	591	1039	222	11	207	700	548	795	44	83	25-22	.267	.361	.489	.850	34	.988

DIVISION SERIES RECORD

Year Team (League)	Pos.	G	AB	R	H	2B	3B	HR	RBI	BB	SO	HBP	GDP	SB-CS	Avg.	OBP	SLG	OPS	E	Avg.
1995— Boston (A.L.)		1	1	0	0	0	0	0	0	0	1	0	0	0-0	.000	.000	.000	.000	...	...
2000— Oakland (A.L.)	OF	3	9	0	1	1	0	0	0	0	1	0	0	0-0	.111	.111	.222	.333	0	1.000
Division series totals (2 years)		4	10	0	1	1	0	0	0	0	2	0	0	0-0	.100	.100	.200	.300	0	1.000

S

STANDRIDGE, JASON — P

PERSONAL: Born November 9, 1978, in Birmingham, Ala. ... 6-4/230. ... Throws right, bats right. ... Full name: Jason Wayne Standridge. ... High school: Hewitt-Trussville (Ala.).
TRANSACTIONS/CAREER NOTES: Selected by Tampa Bay Devil Rays organization in first round (31st pick overall) of 1997 free-agent draft. ... On disabled list (March 24-May 19, 2004); included rehabilitation assignments to Montgomery and Durham. ... Signed as a free agent by Texas Rangers organization (November 19, 2004). ... Signed as a free agent by Cincinnati Reds organization (July 1, 2005).
CAREER HITTING: 0-for-0 (.000), 0 R, 0 2B, 0 3B, 0 HR, 0 RBI.

JASON STANDRIDGE'S PITCHING ZONE

.333	.750	.000
.348	.222	.450
.273	.667	.625

LEFTY-RIGHTY SPLITS

vs.	Avg.	AB	H	2B	3B	HR	RBI	BB	SO	OBP	Slg.
L	.356	45	16	4	0	1	8	4	7	.420	.511
R	.319	91	29	5	1	2	13	13	12	.404	.462

Year	Team (League)	W	L	Pct.	ERA	WHIP	G	GS	CG	ShO	Hld.	Sv.-Opp.	IP	H	R	ER	HR	BB-IBB	SO	Avg.
1997—GC Devil Rays (GCL)		0	6	.000	3.59	1.20	13	13	0	0	...	0-...	57.2	56	30	23	3	13-1	55	.250
1998—Princeton (Appal.)		4	4	.500	7.00	1.75	12	12	0	0	...	0-...	63.0	82	61	49	4	28-0	47	.314
1999—Char., S.C. (SAL)		9	1	.900	2.02	0.96	18	18	3	3	...	0-...	116.0	80	35	26	3	31-1	84	.197
—St. Pete. (FSL)		4	4	.500	3.91	1.43	8	8	0	0	...	0-...	48.1	49	21	21	0	20-0	26	.268
2000—St. Pete. (FSL)		2	4	.333	3.38	1.36	10	10	1	0	...	0-...	56.0	45	28	21	4	31-0	41	.214
—Orlando (South.)		6	8	.429	3.62	1.32	17	17	2	0	...	0-...	97.0	85	46	39	4	43-0	55	.237
2001—Durham (Int'l)		5	10	.333	5.28	1.76	20	20	0	0	...	0-...	102.1	130	73	60	13	50-0	48	.315
—Tampa Bay (A.L.)		0	0		4.66	1.71	9	1	0	0	0	0-0	19.1	19	10	10	5	14-1	9	.260
—Orlando (South.)		0	2	.000	5.59	1.66	2	2	0	0	0	0-0	9.2	12	6	6	0	4-0	7	.300
2002—Durham (Int'l)		10	9	.526	3.12	1.34	29	29	0	0	...	0-...	173.0	168	71	60	12	64-1	111	.259
—Tampa Bay (A.L.)		0	0		9.00	3.67	1	0	0	0	0	0-0	3.0	7	3	3	1	4-0	1	.500
2003—Tampa Bay (A.L.)		0	5	.000	6.37	1.53	8	7	1	0	0	0-0	35.1	38	25	25	7	16-0	20	.270
—Durham (Int'l)		2	4	.333	4.50	1.50	12	10	0	0	...	1-...	60.0	62	32	30	5	28-0	37	.270
2004—Montgom. (Sou.)		1	0	1.000	3.60	1.70	2	2	0	0	0	0-0	10.0	13	4	4	1	4-0	8	.361
—Tampa Bay (A.L.)		0	0		9.00	1.80	3	1	0	0	0	0-0	10.0	14	10	10	5	4-0	7	.326
—Durham (Int'l)		8	4	.667	3.85	1.37	20	20	2	0	...	0-...	119.1	120	56	51	7	44-0	76	.265
2005—Oklahoma (PCL)		5	3	.625	4.50	1.57	15	10	0	0	...	0-...	76.0	83	41	38	3	36-0	47	.288
—Texas (A.L.)		0	0		11.57	3.43	2	0	0	0	0	0-0	2.1	7	3	3	0	1-1	2	.467
—Louisville (Int'l)		0	0		16.20	2.40	2	0	0	0	0	0-0	1.2	3	3	3	0	1-0	4	.375
—Cincinnati (N.L.)		2	2	.500	4.06	1.74	32	0	0	0	5	0-0	31.0	38	14	14	3	16-7	17	.314
American League totals (5 years)		0	5	.000	6.56	1.77	23	9	1	0	0	0-0	70.0	85	51	51	18	39-2	39	.300
National League totals (1 year)		2	2	.500	4.06	1.74	32	0	0	0	5	0-0	31.0	38	14	14	3	16-7	17	.314
Major League totals (5 years)		2	7	.222	5.79	1.76	55	9	1	0	5	0-0	101.0	123	65	65	21	55-9	56	.304

STANTON, MIKE — P

PERSONAL: Born June 2, 1967, in Houston. ... 6-1/215. ... Throws left, bats left. ... Full name: William Michael Stanton. ... High school: Midland (Texas). ... Junior college: Alvin (Texas) Community College.
TRANSACTIONS/CAREER NOTES: Selected by Atlanta Braves organization in 13th round of 1987 free-agent draft. ... On disabled list (April 27, 1990-remainder of season); included rehabilitation assignments to Greenville. ... Traded by Braves with a player to be named to Boston Red Sox for two players to be named (July 31, 1995); Red Sox acquired P Matt Murray and Braves acquired OF Marc Lewis and P Mike Jacobs to complete deal (August 31, 1995). ... Traded by Red Sox to Texas Rangers for Ps Mark Brandenburg and Kerry Lacy (July 31, 1996). ... Signed as a free agent by New York Yankees (December 11, 1996). ... On suspended list (July 3-10, 1998). ... Signed as a free agent by New York Mets (December 16, 2002). ... On disabled list (May 22-June 6 and June 11-July 13, 2003); included rehabilitation assignments to Binghamton and Brooklyn. ... Traded by Mets with cash to Yankees for P Felix Heredia (December 3, 2004). ... Released by Yankees (July 11, 2005). ... Signed as free agent by Washington Nationals (July 13, 2005). ... Traded by Nationals to Boston Red Sox for Ps Rhys Taylor and Yader Peralta (September 29, 2005).
CAREER HITTING: 8-for-20 (.400), 3 R, 1 2B, 0 3B, 0 HR, 3 RBI.

SCOUTING REPORT **Throws:** His fastball will reach 91 mph, and he complements it with a curveball, slider, changeup and split-finger fastball. ***Tendencies:*** Stanton has lost a little off his fastball and pitched up in the zone more last year. Consistently challenges hitters on the inside half. Will throw a big-breaking curve early in the count to righthanders and a slider to lefties. Has been more effective against righthanded hitters with his splitter than against lefthanders, who lay off the pitch. Needs to pitch inside more to lefthanders. ***Outlook:*** Stanton has exceptional makeup and always will take the ball. Is more of a situational reliever. ***Grade 5.8***

MIKE STANTON'S PITCHING ZONE

.200	.571	.071
.435	.381	.333
.438	.429	.176

LEFTY-RIGHTY SPLITS

vs.	Avg.	AB	H	2B	3B	HR	RBI	BB	SO	OBP	Slg.
L	.235	85	20	2	0	0	8	4	15	.270	.259
R	.358	81	29	9	1	3	14	11	12	.430	.605

Year	Team (League)	W	L	Pct.	ERA	WHIP	G	GS	CG	ShO	Hld.	Sv.-Opp.	IP	H	R	ER	HR	BB-IBB	SO	Avg.
1987—Pulaski (Appalachian)		4	8	.333	3.24	1.27	15	13	3	2	...	0-...	83.1	64	37	30	7	42-0	82	.212
1988—Burlington (Midw.)		11	5	.688	3.62	1.45	30	23	1	1	...	0-...	154.0	154	86	62	7	69-2	160	.258
—Durham (Carol.)		1	0	1.000	1.46	1.54	2	2	1	1	...	0-...	12.1	14	3	2	0	5-0	14	.280
1989—Greenville (Sou.)		4	1	.800	1.58	1.23	47	0	0	0	...	19-...	51.1	32	10	9	1	31-3	58	.189
—Richmond (Int'l)		2	0	1.000	0.00	0.95	13	0	0	0	...	8-...	20.0	6	0	0	0	13-2	20	.097
—Atlanta (N.L.)		0	1	.000	1.50	1.04	20	0	0	0	2	7-8	24.0	17	4	4	0	8-1	27	.207
1990—Atlanta (N.L.)		0	3	.000	18.00	2.86	7	0	0	0	0	2-3	7.0	16	16	14	1	4-2	7	.444
—Greenville (Sou.)		0	1	.000	1.59	1.76	4	4	0	0	...	0-...	5.2	7	1	1	1	3-0	4	.292
1991—Atlanta (N.L.)		5	5	.500	2.88	1.06	74	0	0	0	15	7-10	78.0	62	27	25	6	21-6	54	.217
1992—Atlanta (N.L.)		5	4	.556	4.10	1.24	65	0	0	0	15	8-11	63.2	59	32	29	6	20-2	44	.247
1993—Atlanta (N.L.)		4	6	.400	4.67	1.54	63	0	0	0	5	27-33	52.0	51	35	27	4	29-7	43	.255
1994—Atlanta (N.L.)		3	1	.750	3.55	1.47	49	0	0	0	10	3-4	45.2	41	18	18	2	26-3	35	.248
1995—Atlanta (N.L.)		1	1	.500	5.59	1.91	26	0	0	0	4	1-2	19.1	31	14	12	3	6-2	13	.369
—Boston (A.L.)		1	0	1.000	3.00	1.19	22	0	0	0	4	0-1	21.0	17	9	7	3	8-0	10	.224
1996—Boston (A.L.)		4	3	.571	3.83	1.44	59	0	0	0	15	1-5	56.1	58	24	24	9	23-4	46	.275
—Texas (A.L.)		0	1	.000	3.22	1.07	22	0	0	0	7	0-1	22.1	20	8	8	2	4-1	14	.241

Year Team (League)	W	L	Pct.	ERA	WHIP	G	GS	CG	ShO	Hld.	Sv.-Opp.	IP	H	R	ER	HR	BB-IBB	SO	Avg.
1997— New York (A.L.)	6	1	.857	2.57	1.26	64	0	0	0	26	3-5	66.2	50	19	19	3	34-2	70	.205
1998— New York (A.L.)	4	1	.800	5.47	1.23	67	0	0	0	18	6-10	79.0	71	51	48	13	26-1	69	.239
1999— New York (A.L.)	2	2	.500	4.33	1.43	73	1	0	0	21	0-5	62.1	71	30	30	5	18-4	59	.289
2000— New York (A.L.)	2	3	.400	4.10	1.35	69	0	0	0	15	0-4	68.0	68	32	31	5	24-2	75	.263
2001— New York (A.L.)	9	4	.692	2.58	1.36	76	0	0	0	23	0-1	80.1	80	25	23	4	29-9	78	.263
2002— New York (A.L.)	7	1	.875	3.00	1.29	79	0	0	0	17	6-9	78.0	73	29	26	4	28-3	44	.256
2003— Binghamton (East.)	0	1	.000	9.00	6.00	1	1	0	0	...	0-...	1.0	6	3	1	0	0-0	1	.750
— Brooklyn (N.Y.-Penn.)	0	0	...	0.00	0.50	1	1	0	0	...	0-...	2.0	1	0	0	0	0-0	1	.167
— New York (N.L.)	2	7	.222	4.57	1.24	50	0	0	0	10	5-7	45.1	37	25	23	6	19-4	34	.219
2004— New York (N.L.)	2	6	.250	3.16	1.34	83	0	0	0	25	0-6	77.0	70	32	27	6	33-6	58	.237
2005— New York (N.L.)	1	2	.333	7.07	1.64	28	0	0	0	4	0-0	14.0	17	11	11	1	6-0	12	.298
— Was. (N.L.)	2	1	.667	3.58	1.45	30	0	0	0	5	0-1	27.2	31	13	11	2	9-4	14	.292
— Boston (A.L.)	0	0	...	0.00	1.00	1	0	0	0	0	0-0	1.0	1	0	0	0	0-0	1	.333
American League totals (9 years)	36	18	.667	3.72	1.32	560	1	0	0	150	16-41	549.0	526	238	227	49	200-26	478	.255
National League totals (10 years)	24	35	.407	3.89	1.34	467	0	0	0	91	60-85	439.2	415	216	190	36	175-37	329	.250
Major League totals (17 years)	60	53	.531	3.80	1.33	1027	1	0	0	241	76-126	988.2	941	454	417	85	375-63	807	.252

DIVISION SERIES RECORD

Year Team (League)	W	L	Pct.	ERA	WHIP	G	GS	CG	ShO	Hld.	Sv.-Opp.	IP	H	R	ER	HR	BB-IBB	SO	Avg.
1995— Boston (A.L.)	0	0	...	0.00	0.43	3	0	0	0	0	0-0	2.1	1	0	0	0	0-0	4	.125
1996— Texas (A.L.)	0	1	.000	2.70	1.50	3	0	0	0	1	0-0	3.1	2	2	1	1	3-0	3	.200
1997— New York (A.L.)	0	0	...	0.00	2.00	3	0	0	0	0	0-0	1.0	1	0	0	0	1-0	3	.250
1998— New York (A.L.)			Did not play.																
1999— New York (A.L.)			Did not play.																
2000— New York (A.L.)	1	0	1.000	2.08	1.38	3	0	0	0	0	0-0	4.1	5	1	1	0	1-0	3	.294
2001— New York (A.L.)	1	0	1.000	0.00	0.64	3	0	0	0	1	0-0	4.2	3	0	0	0	0-0	1	.176
2002— New York (A.L.)	0	1	.000	10.13	2.63	3	0	0	0	0	0-1	2.2	6	3	3	0	1-1	1	.500
Division series totals (6 years)	2	2	.500	2.45	1.31	16	0	0	0	1	0-1	18.1	18	6	5	1	6-1	15	.265

CHAMPIONSHIP SERIES RECORD

Year Team (League)	W	L	Pct.	ERA	WHIP	G	GS	CG	ShO	Hld.	Sv.-Opp.	IP	H	R	ER	HR	BB-IBB	SO	Avg.
1991— Atlanta (N.L.)	0	0	...	2.45	1.91	3	0	0	0	1	0-0	3.2	4	1	1	0	3-1	3	.333
1992— Atlanta (N.L.)	0	0	...	0.00	0.92	5	0	0	0	2	0-0	4.1	2	1	0	0	2-1	5	.154
1993— Atlanta (N.L.)	0	0	...	0.00	2.00	1	0	0	0	0	0-0	1.0	1	0	0	0	1-0	0	.250
1998— New York (A.L.)	0	0	...	0.00	0.82	3	0	0	0	1	0-0	3.2	2	0	0	0	1-1	4	.167
1999— New York (A.L.)	0	0	...	0.00	6.00	3	0	0	0	0	0-0	0.1	1	0	0	0	1-0	0	.500
2000— New York (A.L.)			Did not play.																
2001— New York (A.L.)	0	0	...	27.00	3.00	2	0	0	0	0	0-0	1.0	1	3	3	0	2-1	0	.200
Champ. series totals (6 years)	0	0	...	2.57	1.50	17	0	0	0	4	0-0	14.0	11	5	4	0	10-4	12	.229

WORLD SERIES RECORD

Year Team (League)	W	L	Pct.	ERA	WHIP	G	GS	CG	ShO	Hld.	Sv.-Opp.	IP	H	R	ER	HR	BB-IBB	SO	Avg.
1991— Atlanta (N.L.)	1	0	1.000	0.00	0.95	5	0	0	0	0	0-0	7.1	5	0	0	0	2-2	7	.200
1992— Atlanta (N.L.)	0	0	...	0.00	1.00	4	0	0	0	1	1-1	5.0	3	0	0	0	2-2	4	.188
1998— New York (A.L.)	0	0	...	27.00	4.50	1	0	0	0	0	0-0	0.2	3	2	2	0	0-0	1	.600
1999— New York (A.L.)	0	0	...	0.00	0.00	1	0	0	0	1	0-0	0.1	0	0	0	0	0-0	1	.000
2000— New York (A.L.)	2	0	1.000	0.00	0.00	4	0	0	0	0	0-0	4.1	0	0	0	0	0-0	7	.000
2001— New York (A.L.)	0	0	...	3.18	0.71	5	0	0	0	1	0-0	5.2	3	2	2	0	1-0	3	.167
World series totals (6 years)	3	0	1.000	1.54	0.81	20	0	0	0	3	1-1	23.1	14	4	4	0	5-4	20	.182

ALL-STAR GAME RECORD

	W	L	Pct.	ERA	WHIP	G	GS	CG	ShO	Hld.	Sv.-Opp.	IP	H	R	ER	HR	BB-IBB	SO	Avg.
All-Star Game totals (1 year)	0	0	...	0.00	0.00	1	0	0	0	1	0-0	0.2	1	0	0	0	0-0	0	.000

STAUFFER, TIM   P

PERSONAL: Born June 2, 1982, in Portland, Maine. ... 6-1/214. ... Throws right, bats right. ... Full name: Timothy James Stauffer. ... College: Richmond.
TRANSACTIONS/CAREER NOTES: Selected by San Diego Padres organization in first round (fourth pick overall) of 2003 free-agent draft.
CAREER HITTING: 3-for-24 (.125), 1 R, 1 2B, 0 3B, 0 HR, 1 RBI.

SCOUTING REPORT *Throws:* Stauffer's fastball tops out in the high 80. Also has a slurve and a changeup. *Tendencies:* He is a soft-tosser who has an uncanny ability to throw to all four quadrants of the strike zone. Tends to keep the ball up in the zone too much for someone who doesn't throw hard, however. Seems to tire at around the 80-pitch mark. Seemed to have lost confidence in his changeup, which was a plus pitch in Class AAA. Hitters will sit on his breaking pitches. Needs to use his sinker more. *Outlook:* Stauffer should get a chance to be a fifth starter in spring training. **Grade 6.3**

TIM STAUFFER'S PITCHING ZONE

.154	.600	.176
.310	.435	.344
.231	.300	.217

LEFTY-RIGHTY SPLITS

vs.	Avg.	AB	H	2B	3B	HR	RBI	BB	SO	OBP	Slg.
L	.289	149	43	14	1	5	21	15	18	.358	.497
R	.283	173	49	13	0	5	23	14	31	.340	.445

Year Team (League)	W	L	Pct.	ERA	WHIP	G	GS	CG	ShO	Hld.	Sv.-Opp.	IP	H	R	ER	HR	BB-IBB	SO	Avg.
2004— Lake Elsinore (Calif.)	2	0	1.000	1.78	1.05	6	6	0	0	...	0-...	35.1	28	10	7	0	9-0	30	.222
— Mobile (Sou.)	3	2	.600	2.63	1.34	8	8	1	0	...	0-...	51.1	56	17	15	3	13-1	33	.290
— Portland (PCL)	6	3	.667	3.54	1.34	14	14	0	0	...	0-...	81.1	83	46	32	15	26-1	50	.286
2005— San Diego (N.L.)	3	6	.333	5.33	1.49	15	14	0	0	0	0-0	81.0	92	50	48	10	29-0	49	.286
— Portland (PCL)	3	5	.375	5.14	1.42	13	13	1	0	...	0-0	75.1	90	48	43	5	17-0	64	.296
Major League totals (1 year)	3	6	.333	5.33	1.49	15	14	0	0	0	0-0	81.0	92	50	48	10	29-0	49	.286

STEMLE, STEVE   P

PERSONAL: Born May 20, 1977, in Louisville, Ky. ... 6-4/200. ... Throws right, bats right. ... Full name: Stephen J. Stemle. ...High school: New Albany (Ind.). ... College: Western Kentucky.
TRANSACTIONS/CAREER NOTES: Selected by St. Louis Cardinals organization in fifth round of 1998 free-agent draft. ... Signed as a free agent by Kansas City Royals organization (November 15, 2004). ... On disabled list (June 11, 2005-remainder of season).
CAREER HITTING: 0-for-0 (.000), 0 R, 0 2B, 0 3B, 0 HR, 0 RBI.

LEFTY-RIGHTY SPLITS

vs.	Avg.	AB	H	2B	3B	HR	RBI	BB	SO	OBP	Slg.
L	.211	19	4	1	0	0	1	1	6	.250	.263
R	.300	20	6	0	0	0	3	3	3	.391	.300

Year	Team (League)	W	L	Pct.	ERA	WHIP	G	GS	CG	ShO	Hld.	Sv.-Opp.	IP	H	R	ER	HR	BB-IBB	SO	Avg.
1998—	New Jersey (NYP)	3	3	.500	1.83	1.15	9	9	0	0	...	0-...	44.1	37	17	9	1	14-0	47	.219
1999—	Peoria (Midw.)	7	10	.412	5.47	1.65	28	28	0	0	...	0-...	148.0	177	104	90	11	67-0	113	.292
2000—	Potomac (Carol.)	9	10	.474	4.80	1.52	26	26	1	0	...	0-...	150.0	169	89	80	15	59-1	84	.286
2001—	New Haven (East.)	7	10	.412	4.77	1.51	26	25	0	0	...	0-...	134.0	159	76	71	12	43-2	75	.293
2002—	New Haven (East.)	5	2	.714	4.36	1.38	8	7	0	0	...	0-...	43.1	45	24	21	3	15-1	26	.280
—	Memphis (PCL)	7	4	.636	3.65	1.28	20	11	0	0	...	0-...	93.2	97	41	38	8	23-1	55	.266
2003—	Memphis (PCL)	6	11	.353	3.46	1.22	26	26	1	0	...	0-...	156.0	155	71	60	12	36-4	89	.260
2004—	Palm Beach (FSL)	2	0	1.000	1.50	0.83	3	1	0	0	...	0-...	6.0	5	1	1	0	0-0	2	.217
—	Memphis (PCL)	6	3	.667	3.30	1.27	54	0	0	0	...	3-...	76.1	85	28	28	7	12-2	42	.269
2005—	Omaha (PCL)	1	1	.500	0.45	0.80	14	0	0	0	...	3	3-3	20.0	13	3	1	0	3-0	12	.191
—	Kansas City (A.L.)	0	0	...	5.06	1.31	6	0	0	0	...	1	0-0	10.2	10	6	6	0	4-0	9	.256
Major League totals (1 year)		0	0	...	5.06	1.31	6	0	0	0	...	1	0-0	10.2	10	6	6	0	4-0	9	.256

STERN, ADAM   OF

PERSONAL: Born February 12, 1980, in London, Ontario. ... 5-11/180. ... Bats left, throws right. ... Full name: Adam Jeremy Stern. ... College: Nebraska.
TRANSACTIONS/CAREER NOTES: Selected by Atlanta Braves organization in third round of 2001 free-agent draft. ... Selected by Boston Red Sox organization from Braves in Rule 5 major league draft (December 13, 2004). ... On disabled list (April 1-July 7 and August 20-September 4, 2005); included rehabilitation assignment to Pawtucket.
2005 GAMES PLAYED BY POSITION (MLB): OF—21.

LEFTY-RIGHTY SPLITS

vs.	Avg.	AB	H	2B	3B	HR	RBI	BB	SO	OBP	Slg.
L	.000	6	0	0	0	0	0	0	1	.000	.000
R	.222	9	2	0	0	1	2	0	3	.300	.556

Year	Team (League)	Pos.	G	AB	R	H	2B	3B	HR	RBI	BB	SO	HBP	GDP	SB-CS	Avg.	OBP	SLG	OPS	E	Avg.
2001—	Jamestown (NYP)	OF	21	75	20	23	4	2	0	11	5	11	0	0	9-4	.307	.413	.413	.826	0	1.000
2002—	Myrtle Beach (Carol.)	OF	119	462	65	117	22	10	3	47	27	89	3	3	40-8	.253	.298	.364	.662	3	.990
2003—	GC Braves (GCL)	OF	7	29	6	10	1	0	1	6	6	3	0	1	2-2	.345	.457	.483	.940	0	1.000
—	Myrtle Beach (Carol.)	OF	28	103	11	20	2	0	0	6	13	21	0	1	7-3	.194	.282	.214	.496	0	1.000
2004—	Greenville (Sou.)		102	394	64	127	26	6	8	47	35	58	2	2	27-10	.322	.378	.480	.858	...	...
2005—	Pawtucket (Int'l)	OF	20	81	16	26	8	0	2	14	8	10	1	0	3-1	.321	.385	.494	.878	2	.980
—	Boston (A.L.)	OF	36	15	4	2	0	0	1	2	0	4	1	0	1-1	.133	.188	.333	.521	0	1.000
Major League totals (1 year)			36	15	4	2	0	0	1	2	0	4	1	0	1-1	.133	.188	.333	.521	0	1.000

STEWART, SHANNON   OF

PERSONAL: Born February 25, 1974, in Cincinnati. ... 5-11/200. ... Bats right, throws right. ... Full name: Shannon Harold Stewart. ... High school: Southridge Senior (Miami).
TRANSACTIONS/CAREER NOTES: Selected by Toronto Blue Jays organization in first round (19th pick overall) of 1992 free-agent draft; pick received as part of compensation for Los Angeles Dodgers signing Type A free-agent P Tom Candiotti. ... On disabled list (April 29-May 14, 2000); included rehabilitation assignment to Dunedin. ... On disabled list (May 1-16, 2002). ... On disabled list (May 29-June 23, 2003); included rehabilitation assignment to Syracuse. ... Traded by Blue Jays to Minnesota Twins for OF Bobby Kielty (July 16, 2003). ... On disabled list (May 18-July 15, 2004); included rehabilitation assignment to Rochester.
RECORDS: Shares major league record for most doubles, game (4, July 18, 2000).
2005 GAMES PLAYED BY POSITION (MLB): OF—125, DH—5.

SCOUTING REPORT *Offense:* Stewart has a short stroke and stays inside the ball well but has had some decline in bat speed. Is a line-drive gap hitter with speed who really benefits from playing on turf. Has good plate coverage but has become more impatient and strikeout totals have risen. Is a good runner but does not steal much because of his tight lower body, which is prone to muscle pulls. *Defense:* He never has been able to throw, but compensates with speed and a quick release. Still, runners consistently take the extra base. Gets good lateral jumps but can get turned around going back at times. *Outlook:* Stewart is one of the league's better leadoff hitters when healthy. A fragile player from the waist down and no longer runs much. Starting to show signs of offensive decline. *Grade 7.6*

SHANNON STEWART'S HITTING ZONE

.167	.400	.318
.434	.298	.211
.236	.263	.200

LEFTY-RIGHTY SPLITS

vs.	Avg.	AB	H	2B	3B	HR	RBI	BB	SO	OBP	Slg.
L	.244	131	32	3	2	1	7	9	24	.310	.344
R	.283	420	119	24	1	8	49	25	49	.327	.402

Year	Team (League)	Pos.	G	AB	R	H	2B	3B	HR	RBI	BB	SO	HBP	GDP	SB-CS	Avg.	OBP	SLG	OPS	E	Avg.
1992—	GC Jays (GCL)	OF	50	172	44	40	1	0	1	11	24	27	3	3	32-5	.233	.333	.256	.589	1	.988
1993—	St. Catharines (NYP)	OF	75	301	53	84	15	2	3	29	33	43	2	7	25-10	.279	.351	.372	.723	0	1.000
1994—	Hagerstown (SAL)	OF	56	225	39	73	10	5	4	25	23	39	1	3	15-11	.324	.386	.467	.853	1	.990
1995—	Knoxville (Southern)	OF-DH	138	498	89	143	24	6	5	55	89	61	6	13	42-16	.287	.398	.390	.788	6	.980
—	Toronto (A.L.)	OF	12	38	2	8	0	0	1	5	5	1	0	2	2-0	.211	.318	.211	.529	1	.955
1996—	Syracuse (Int'l)	OF	112	420	77	125	26	8	6	42	54	61	2	6	35-8	.298	.377	.440	.818	5	.983
—	Toronto (A.L.)	OF	7	17	2	3	1	0	0	2	1	4	0	1	1-0	.176	.222	.235	.458	1	.800
1997—	Toronto (A.L.)	OF-DH	44	168	25	48	13	7	0	22	19	24	4	1	10-3	.286	.368	.446	.814	2	.980
—	Syracuse (Int'l)	OF	58	208	41	72	13	1	5	24	36	26	4	1	9-6	.346	.452	.490	.942	5	.980
1998—	Toronto (A.L.)	OF	144	516	90	144	29	3	12	55	67	77	15	5	51-18	.279	.377	.417	.794	6	.980
1999—	Toronto (A.L.)	OF-DH	145	608	102	185	28	2	11	67	59	83	6	12	37-14	.304	.371	.411	.782	5	.981
2000—	Toronto (A.L.)	OF	136	583	107	186	43	5	21	69	37	79	6	12	20-5	.319	.363	.518	.882	2	.993
—	Dunedin (Fla. St.)	OF	3	13	2	3	1	0	1	2	0	0	0	0	0-1	1.000	1.000	1.333	2.333	0	...
2001—	Toronto (A.L.)	OF-DH	155	640	103	202	44	7	12	60	46	72	11	9	27-10	.316	.371	.463	.834	1	.981
2002—	Toronto (A.L.)	OF-DH	141	577	103	175	38	6	10	45	54	60	8	17	14-2	.303	.371	.442	.813	2	.990

Year Team (League)	Pos.	G	AB	R	H	2B	3B	HR	RBI	BB	SO	HBP	GDP	SB-CS	Avg.	OBP	SLG	OPS	E	Avg.
												BATTING							FIELDING	
2003— Syracuse (Int'l)	OF	1	3	0	0	0	0	0	0	1	0	0	0	0-0	.000	.250	.000	.250	0	1.000
— Toronto (A.L.)	OF-DH	71	303	47	89	22	2	7	35	27	30	2	6	1-2	.294	.347	.449	.796	4	.974
— Minnesota (A.L.)	OF-DH	65	270	43	87	22	0	6	38	25	36	4	4	3-4	.322	.384	.470	.854	1	.993
2004— Rochester (Int'l)	DH-OF	3	9	3	3	1	0	0	0	1	2	0	0	0-0	.333	.400	.444	.844	0	...
— Minnesota (A.L.)	OF-DH	92	378	46	115	17	2	11	47	47	44	1	5	6-3	.304	.380	.447	.827	3	.972
2005— Minnesota (A.L.)	OF-DH	132	551	69	151	27	3	10	56	34	73	8	11	7-5	.274	.323	.388	.711	4	.985
Major League totals (11 years)		1144	4649	739	1393	284	37	100	497	421	587	69	85	179-66	.300	.364	.441	.805	36	.983

DIVISION SERIES RECORD

Year Team (League)	Pos.	G	AB	R	H	2B	3B	HR	RBI	BB	SO	HBP	GDP	SB-CS	Avg.	OBP	SLG	OPS	E	Avg.
2003— Minnesota (A.L.)	OF	4	15	0	6	2	0	0	0	2	4	0	0	1-0	.400	.471	.533	1.004	0	1.000
2004— Minnesota (A.L.)	OF-DH	4	20	1	4	0	0	0	2	0	2	0	0	0-0	.200	.190	.200	.390	0	1.000
Division series totals (2 years)		8	35	1	10	2	0	0	2	2	6	0	0	1-0	.286	.316	.343	.659	0	1.000

STINNETT, KELLY   C

PERSONAL: Born February 4, 1970, in Lawton, Okla. ... 5-11/225. ... Bats right, throws right. ... Full name: Kelly Lee Stinnett. ... Name pronounced: sti-NETT. ... High school: Lawton (Okla.). ... Junior college: Seminole (Okla.).

TRANSACTIONS/CAREER NOTES: Selected by Cleveland Indians organization in 11th round of 1989 free-agent draft. ... Selected by New York Mets from Indians organization in Rule 5 major league draft (December 13, 1993). ... Traded by Mets to Milwaukee Brewers for P Cory Lidle (January 17, 1996). ... On disabled list (July 27-September 2, 1997). ... Selected by Arizona Diamondbacks in third round (65th pick overall) of expansion draft (November 18, 1997). ... Signed as a free agent by Cincinnati Reds (January 9, 2001). ... On disabled list (September 4, 2001-remainder of season). ... On disabled list (April 6-July 15, 2002); included rehabilitation assignments to Louisville. ... Traded by Reds to Philadelphia Phillies for OF Eric Valent (August 31, 2003). ... Signed as a free agent by Kansas City Royals (December 19, 2003). ... On disabled list (June 20, 2004-remainder of season). ... Signed as a free agent by Diamondbacks organization (December 13, 2004). ... Signed as a free agent by Mets organization (March 29, 2005). ... Released by Mets (April 1, 2005). ... Signed by Diamondbacks organization (May 10, 2005). ... On disabled list (July 19-August 9, 2005); included rehabilitation assignment to Lancaster.

2005 GAMES PLAYED BY POSITION (MLB): C—56.

SCOUTING REPORT Stinnett's defense has kept him in the big leagues; he throws well and has good hands. Works well with a young pitching staff but has never hit enough to play regularly. Has a slow bat but does have some power. A righthanded hitter who has trouble with lefthanders who consistently run the ball away. Doesn't make quick adjustments. **Grade 4.2**

KELLY STINNETT'S HITTING ZONE

.500	.750	.167
.214	.300	.273
.190	.571	.167

LEFTY-RIGHTY SPLITS

vs.	Avg.	AB	H	2B	3B	HR	RBI	BB	SO	OBP	Slg.
L	.214	28	6	1	0	1	2	5	7	.333	.357
R	.257	101	26	3	0	5	10	7	25	.312	.436

Year Team (League)	Pos.	G	AB	R	H	2B	3B	HR	RBI	BB	SO	HBP	GDP	SB-CS	Avg.	OBP	SLG	OPS	E	Avg.
												BATTING							FIELDING	
1990— Watertown (NYP)	1B-C	60	192	29	46	10	2	2	21	40	43	4	8	3-7	.240	.378	.344	.722	18	.957
1991— Columbus (S. Atl.)	1B-C	102	384	49	101	15	1	14	74	26	70	9	17	4-1	.263	.321	.417	.737	28	.966
1992— Cant./Akr. (Eastern)	C	91	296	37	84	10	0	6	32	16	43	4	8	7-6	.284	.326	.378	.704	13	.979
1993— Charlotte (Int'l)	C	98	288	42	79	10	3	6	33	17	52	2	4	0-0	.274	.318	.392	.711	8	.985
1994— New York (N.L.)	C	47	150	20	38	6	2	2	14	11	28	5	3	2-0	.253	.323	.360	.683	5	.979
1995— New York (N.L.)	C	77	196	23	43	8	1	4	18	29	65	6	3	2-0	.219	.338	.332	.669	7	.983
1996— Milwaukee (A.L.)	C-DH	14	26	1	2	0	0	0	0	2	11	1	0	0-0	.077	.172	.077	.249	2	.960
— New Orleans (A.A.)	C-DH-3B	95	334	63	96	21	1	27	70	31	83	13	6	3-3	.287	.366	.599	.966	11	.980
1997— Tucson (PCL)	C-DH-1B	64	209	50	67	15	3	10	43	42	46	6	2	1-1	.321	.444	.565	1.009	2	.989
— Milwaukee (A.L.)	C-DH	30	36	2	9	4	0	0	3	3	9	0	0	0-0	.250	.308	.361	.669	1	.989
1998— Arizona (N.L.)	C-DH	92	274	35	71	14	1	11	34	35	74	6	9	0-1	.259	.353	.438	.791	8	.984
1999— Arizona (N.L.)	C	88	284	36	66	13	0	14	38	24	83	5	4	2-1	.232	.302	.426	.728	6	.990
2000— Arizona (N.L.)	C	76	240	22	52	7	0	8	33	19	56	6	5	0-1	.217	.291	.346	.636	6	.990
2001— Cincinnati (N.L.)	C-DH	63	187	27	48	11	0	9	25	17	61	5	5	2-2	.257	.333	.460	.793	12	.966
2002— Cincinnati (N.L.)	C	34	93	10	21	5	0	3	13	15	25	0	1	2-0	.226	.333	.376	.710	2	.990
— Louisville (Int'l)	C	30	86	6	17	6	0	0	5	3	24	0	1	0-0	.198	.225	.267	.492	2	.988
2003— Cincinnati (N.L.)	C	60	179	14	41	13	0	3	19	13	51	4	3	0-0	.229	.294	.352	.646	2	.990
— Philadelphia (N.L.)	C	7	7	0	3	0	0	0	0	1	1	0	0	0-0	.429	.500	.429	.929	0	1.000
2004— Kansas City (A.L.)	C	20	59	10	18	0	0	3	7	5	16	2	0	0-0	.305	.379	.458	.836	3	.971
2005— Tucson (PCL)	C	11	35	4	8	2	0	1	5	2	12	2	0	0-0	.229	.325	.371	.696	2	.973
— Lancaster (Calif.)	C-DH	3	11	4	3	1	0	1	5	2	1	0	0	0-0	.273	.385	.636	1.021	0	1.000
— Arizona (N.L.)	C	59	129	15	32	4	0	6	12	12	32	1	4	0-0	.248	.317	.419	.736	6	.977
American League totals (3 years)		64	121	13	29	4	0	3	10	10	36	3	0	0-0	.240	.313	.347	.661	6	.975
National League totals (9 years)		603	1739	202	415	81	4	60	206	176	476	38	37	10-5	.239	.321	.393	.714	54	.984
Major League totals (12 years)		667	1860	215	444	85	4	63	216	186	512	41	37	10-5	.239	.320	.390	.711	60	.984

DIVISION SERIES RECORD

Year Team (League)	Pos.	G	AB	R	H	2B	3B	HR	RBI	BB	SO	HBP	GDP	SB-CS	Avg.	OBP	SLG	OPS	E	Avg.
1999— Arizona (N.L.)	C	4	14	1	2	1	0	0	0	0	4	0	0	0-0	.143	.200	.214	.414	0	1.000

S

STONE, RICKY P

PERSONAL: Born February 28, 1975, in Hamilton, Ohio. ... 6-1/195. ... Throws right, bats right. ... Full name: Ricky L. Stone. ... High school: Hamilton (Ohio).

TRANSACTIONS/CAREER NOTES: Selected by Los Angeles Dodgers organization in fourth round of 1994 free-agent draft. ... Signed as a free agent by Houston Astros organization (January 8, 2001). ... Claimed on waivers by San Diego Padres (June 18, 2004). ... Signed as a free agent by Cincinnati Reds organization (November 1, 2004).

CAREER HITTING: 0-for-10 (.000), 0 R, 0 2B, 0 3B, 0 HR, 0 RBI.

RICKY STONE'S PITCHING ZONE

.667	.200	.500
.278	.333	.667
.333	.167	.308

LEFTY-RIGHTY SPLITS

vs.	Avg.	AB	H	2B	3B	HR	RBI	BB	SO	OBP	Slg.
L	.333	57	19	4	0	3	15	4	7	.387	.561
R	.387	75	29	7	0	5	16	3	8	.407	.680

Year	Team (League)	W	L	Pct.	ERA	WHIP	G	GS	CG	ShO	Hld.	Sv.-Opp.	IP	H	R	ER	HR	BB-IBB	SO	Avg.
1994—	Great Falls (Pio.)	2	2	.500	4.44	1.56	13	7	0	0	...	2-...	50.2	55	40	25	5	24-0	48	.268
1995—	San Bern. (Calif.)	3	5	.375	6.52	1.79	12	12	0	0	...	0-...	58.0	79	50	42	7	25-0	31	.333
	—Yakima (N'west)	4	4	.500	5.25	1.54	16	6	0	0	...	2-...	48.0	54	31	28	5	20-0	28	.289
1996—	Savannah (S. Atl.)	2	1	.667	3.98	1.36	5	5	0	0	...	0-...	31.2	34	15	14	2	9-0	31	.288
	—Vero Beach (FSL)	8	6	.571	3.83	1.43	21	21	1	0	...	0-...	112.2	115	58	48	9	46-0	74	.267
1997—	San Antonio (Texas)	0	3	.000	5.47	1.77	25	5	0	0	...	3-...	52.2	63	33	32	4	30-0	46	.304
	—San Bern. (Calif.)	3	3	.500	3.35	0.93	8	8	0	0	...	0-...	53.2	40	22	20	4	10-0	40	.209
1998—	San Antonio (Texas)	7	2	.778	3.84	1.24	13	13	1	1	...	0-...	82.0	76	40	35	4	26-0	69	.251
	—Albuquerque (PCL)	5	5	.500	5.38	1.53	18	16	0	0	...	0-...	105.1	120	69	63	13	41-0	85	.287
1999—	Albuquerque (PCL)	6	10	.375	5.50	1.65	27	27	2	0	...	0-...	167.0	205	123	102	23	71-4	132	.306
2000—	Albuquerque (PCL)	9	5	.643	4.94	1.56	48	7	0	0	...	5-...	120.1	146	79	66	9	42-3	75	.309
2001—	New Orleans (PCL)	6	3	.667	3.59	1.31	51	8	0	0	...	2-...	95.1	98	42	38	8	27-4	78	.269
	—Houston (N.L.)	0	0	...	2.35	1.30	6	0	0	0	0	0-0	7.2	8	3	2	1	2-1	4	.258
2002—	Houston (N.L.)	3	3	.500	3.61	1.45	78	0	0	0	12	1-2	77.1	78	36	31	9	34-3	63	.266
2003—	Houston (N.L.)	6	4	.600	3.69	1.29	65	0	0	0	7	1-1	83.0	76	36	34	11	31-4	47	.250
2004—	New Orleans (PCL)	1	0	1.000	4.50	1.00	2	0	0	0	...	0-...	2.0	2	1	1	0	0-0	0	.250
	—Houston (N.L.)	1	1	.500	5.68	1.74	16	0	0	0	1	0-0	19.0	26	12	12	5	7-3	16	.317
	—Portland (PCL)	0	0	...	3.38	2.06	3	0	0	0	...	0-...	5.1	9	5	2	2	2-0	2	.409
	—San Diego (N.L.)	1	1	.500	6.89	1.50	27	0	0	0	0	0-0	32.2	40	27	25	6	9-0	22	.301
2005—	Louisville (Int'l)	2	1	.667	2.57	0.93	9	0	0	0	1	3-4	14.0	10	4	4	0	3-0	15	.192
	—Cincinnati (N.L.)	0	0	...	6.75	1.79	23	0	0	0	2	0-0	30.2	48	24	23	8	7-2	15	.364
	—Memphis (PCL)	1	1	.500	1.65	0.86	14	0	0	0	0	6-7	16.1	12	5	3	0	2-0	16	.203
Major League totals (5 years)		11	9	.550	4.57	1.46	215	0	0	0	22	2-3	250.1	276	138	127	40	90-13	167	.282

STREET, HUSTON P

PERSONAL: Born August 2, 1983, in Austin, Texas. ... 6-0/185. ... Throws right, bats right. ... Full name: Huston Lowell Street. ... High school: Westlake, (Austin, Texas). ... College: Texas.

TRANSACTIONS/CAREER NOTES: Selected by Oakland Athletics organization in first round (40th pick overall) of 2004 free-agent draft.

HONORS: Named A.L. Rookie of the Year by THE SPORTING NEWS (2005). ... Named A.L. Rookie of the Year by Baseball Writers' Association of America (2005).

CAREER HITTING: 0-for-0 (.000), 0 R, 0 2B, 0 3B, 0 HR, 0 RBI.

HUSTON STREET'S PITCHING ZONE

.250	.250	.250
.167	.297	.225
.208	.100	.105

LEFTY-RIGHTY SPLITS

vs.	Avg.	AB	H	2B	3B	HR	RBI	BB	SO	OBP	Slg.
L	.224	116	26	8	0	2	14	17	29	.321	.345
R	.172	157	27	3	0	1	9	9	43	.225	.210

Year	Team (League)	W	L	Pct.	ERA	WHIP	G	GS	CG	ShO	Hld.	Sv.-Opp.	IP	H	R	ER	HR	BB-IBB	SO	Avg.
2004—	Kane Co. (Midw.)	0	1	.000	1.69	1.31	9	0	0	0	...	4-...	10.2	9	2	2	0	5-1	14	.220
	—Midland (Texas)	1	0	1.000	1.35	0.98	10	0	0	0	...	3-...	13.1	10	2	2	0	3-0	14	.200
	—Sacramento (PCL)	0	0	...	0.00	1.00	2	0	0	0	...	1-...	2.0	2	0	0	0	0-0	2	.250
2005—	Oakland (A.L.)	5	1	.833	1.72	1.01	67	0	0	0	...	23-27	78.1	53	17	15	3	26-4	72	.194
Major League totals (1 year)		5	1	.833	1.72	1.01	67	0	0	0	0	23-27	78.1	53	17	15	3	26-4	72	.194

STRICKLAND, SCOTT P

PERSONAL: Born April 26, 1976, in Houston. ... 5-11/180. ... Throws right, bats right. ... Full name: Scott Michael Strickland. ... High school: Klein Oak (Spring, Texas). ... College: New Mexico.

TRANSACTIONS/CAREER NOTES: Selected by Montreal Expos organization in 10th round of 1997 free-agent draft. ... On disabled list (May 3-July 3, 2000); included rehabilitation assignment to Ottawa. ... Traded by Expos with OF Matt Watson and P Phil Seibel to New York Mets for Ps Bruce Chen and Dicky Gonzalez, SS/2B Luis Figueroa and a player to be named (April 5, 2002); Expos acquired P Saul Rivera to complete deal (July 14, 2002). ... On disabled list (May 11, 2003-remainder of season). ... On disabled list (March 31, 2004-remainder of season); included rehabilitation assignment to GCL Mets and St. Lucie. ... Signed as a free agent by Houston Astros organization (May 25, 2005).

CAREER HITTING: 0-for-6 (.000), 0 R, 0 2B, 0 3B, 0 HR, 0 RBI.

LEFTY-RIGHTY SPLITS

vs.	Avg.	AB	H	2B	3B	HR	RBI	BB	SO	OBP	Slg.
L	.400	5	2	0	0	1	2	0	0	.400	1.000
R	.182	11	2	0	0	1	2	0	2	.182	.455

Year	Team (League)	W	L	Pct.	ERA	WHIP	G	GS	CG	ShO	Hld.	Sv.-Opp.	IP	H	R	ER	HR	BB-IBB	SO	Avg.
1997—	Vermont (NYP)	5	2	.714	3.82	1.23	15	9	1	0	...	0-...	62.0	56	27	26	5	20-0	69	.250

Year	Team (League)	W	L	Pct.	ERA	WHIP	G	GS	CG	ShO	Hld.	Sv.-Opp.	IP	H	R	ER	HR	BB-IBB	SO	Avg.
	—Cape Fear (S. Atl.)	0	1	.000	6.35	1.59	3	1	0	0	...	1-...	5.2	8	7	4	0	1-0	8	.320
1998—	Cape Fear (S. Atl.)	0	3	.000	4.46	1.30	15	2	0	0	...	4-...	37.0	36	19	18	3	12-0	53	.254
	—Jupiter (Fla. St.)	4	3	.571	3.39	1.22	22	11	0	0	...	2-...	69.0	64	28	26	5	20-0	51	.251
1999—	Jupiter (Fla. St.)	1	1	.500	3.51	0.97	12	1	0	0	...	2-...	25.2	21	11	10	1	4-1	33	.221
	—Harrisburg (East.)	1	1	.500	2.48	1.21	14	1	0	0	...	3-...	29.0	25	8	8	1	10-0	36	.238
	—Ottawa (Int'l)	3	0	1.000	1.63	1.23	19	0	0	0	...	5-...	27.2	23	5	5	0	11-2	34	.223
	—Ottawa (Int'l)	0	1	.000	4.50	1.44	17	0	0	0	2	0-0	18.0	15	10	9	3	11-0	23	.231
2000—	Montreal (N.L.)	4	3	.571	3.00	1.13	49	0	0	0	6	9-13	48.0	38	18	16	3	16-2	48	.215
	—Ottawa (Int'l)	0	0	...	0.00	0.25	3	0	0	0	0	0-...	4.0	1	0	0	0	0-0	4	.077
2001—	Montreal (N.L.)	2	6	.250	3.21	1.33	77	0	0	0	12	9-12	81.1	67	36	29	9	41-5	85	.222
2002—	Montreal (N.L.)	0	0	...	0.00	0.00	1	0	0	0	0	0-0	1.0	0	0	0	0	0-0	2	.000
	—New York (N.L.)	6	9	.400	3.59	1.39	68	0	0	0	15	2-6	67.2	61	29	27	7	33-9	67	.236
2003—	New York (N.L.)	0	2	.000	2.25	1.30	19	0	0	0	4	0-1	20.0	16	6	5	1	10-1	16	.219
2004—	GC Mets (GCL)	0	0	...	0.00	0.00	2	1	0	0	0	0-...	2.0	0	0	0	0	0-0	2	.000
	—St. Lucie (Fla. St.)	0	1	.000	9.45	1.95	6	1	0	0	0	0-...	6.2	11	8	7	0	2-0	5	.355
2005—	St. Lucie (Fla. St.)	0	0	...	10.80	2.40	1	0	0	0	0	0-0	1.2	4	2	2	1	0-0	2	.444
	—Norfolk (Int'l)	0	3	.000	5.40	1.63	13	0	0	0	0	5-6	11.2	14	9	7	1	5-1	9	.298
	—Round Rock (PCL)	2	0	1.000	2.37	0.79	15	0	0	0	3	5-7	19.0	11	5	5	2	4-0	20	.167
	—Houston (N.L.)	0	0	...	6.75	1.00	5	0	0	0	0	0-0	4.0	4	3	3	0	0-0	2	.250
Major League totals (6 years)		12	21	.364	3.34	1.30	236	0	0	0	39	20-32	240.0	201	102	89	25	111-17	243	.225

STRONG, JAMAL — OF

PERSONAL: Born August 5, 1978, in Pasadena, Calif. ... 5-10/180. ... Bats right, throws right. ... Full name: Jamal Najar Strong. ... High school: Pasadena High (Calif.). ... College: Nebraska.

TRANSACTIONS/CAREER NOTES: Selected by Pittsburgh Pirates organization in 38th round of 1996 free-agent draft; did not sign. ... Selected by Pirates organization in 35th round of 1997 free-agent draft; did not sign. ... Selected by Seattle Mariners organization in sixth round of 2000 free-agent draft. ... On restricted list (April 26-May 5,2005). ... On disabled list (September 13, 2005-remainder of season).

2005 GAMES PLAYED BY POSITION (MLB): OF—11, DH—3.

LEFTY-RIGHTY SPLITS

vs.	Avg.	AB	H	2B	3B	HR	RBI	BB	SO	OBP	Slg.
L	.273	11	3	0	0	0	2	1	4	.357	.273
R	.222	9	2	0	1	0	0	1	2	.300	.444

Year	Team (League)	Pos.	G	AB	R	H	2B	3B	HR	RBI	BB	SO	HBP	GDP	SB-CS	Avg.	OBP	SLG	OPS	E	Avg.
2000—	Everett (N'west)	OF	75	296	63	93	7	3	1	28	52	29	4	0	60-14	.314	.422	.368	.790	2	.988
2001—	Wisconsin (Midw.)	OF	51	184	41	65	12	1	0	19	40	27	5	2	35-4	.353	.478	.429	.907	1	.988
	—San Bern. (Calif.)	OF	81	331	74	103	11	2	0	32	51	60	5	4	47-8	.311	.411	.356	.767	4	.977
2002—	San Antonio (Texas)	OF	127	503	63	140	16	5	1	31	62	87	10	7	46-16	.278	.366	.336	.702	6	.980
2003—	Ariz. Mariners (Ariz.)	OF	2	7	5	5	0	1	0	4	3	1	1	0	3-0	.714	.692	1.000	1.692	1	.889
	—Tacoma (PCL)	OF	56	210	38	64	6	1	2	19	25	38	5	3	26-11	.305	.390	.371	.761	6	.958
	—Seattle (A.L.)	DH-OF	12	2	2	0	0	0	0	0	0	0	0	0	0-0	.000	.000	.000	.000	0	...
2004—	Tacoma (PCL)	OF	64	238	46	77	11	2	3	24	38	28	3	3	19-6	.324	.421	.424	.845	2	.833
2005—	Tacoma (PCL)	OF-DH	93	382	57	112	16	5	4	36	43	67	5	4	25-6	.293	.371	.393	.764	10	.976
	—Seattle (A.L.)	OF-DH	16	20	6	5	0	1	0	2	2	6	0	0	0-0	.250	.333	.350	.683	0	1.000
Major League totals (2 years)			28	22	8	5	0	1	0	2	2	6	0	0	0-0	.227	.308	.318	.626	0	1.000

STURTZE, TANYON — P

PERSONAL: Born October 12, 1970, in Worcester, Mass. ... 6-5/200. ... Throws right, bats right. ... Full name: Tanyon James Sturtze. ... Name pronounced: sturts. ... High school: St. Peter-Marian (Worcester, Mass.). ... Junior college: Quinsigamond (Mass.) Community College.

TRANSACTIONS/CAREER NOTES: Selected by Oakland Athletics organization in 23rd round of 1990 free-agent draft. ... Selected by Chicago Cubs from A's organization in Rule 5 major league draft (December 5, 1994). ... Signed as a free agent by Texas Rangers (November 20, 1996). ... Signed as a free agent by Chicago White Sox organization (November 23, 1998). ... On suspended list (May 1-3, 2000). ... Traded by White Sox to Tampa Bay Devil Rays for IF Tony Graffanino (May 31, 2000). ... On disabled list (August 27, 2000-remainder of season). ... Signed as a free agent by Toronto Blue Jays (December 22, 2002). ... On suspended list (September 26-28, 2003). ... Signed as a free agent by Los Angeles Dodgers organization (December 19, 2003). ... Released by Dodgers (March 29, 2004). ... Signed by Florida Marlins organization (March 30, 2004). ... Released by Marlins (April 2, 2004). ... Signed by Dodgers organization (April 14, 2004). ... Traded by Dodgers to New York Yankees for 1B Bryan Myrow (May 15, 2004). ... On suspended list (August 12-15, 2004). ... On disabled list (April 18-May 5, 2005); included rehabilitation assignment to Tampa.

CAREER HITTING: 1-for-16 (.063), 0 R, 0 2B, 0 3B, 0 HR, 0 RBI.

TANYON STURTZE'S PITCHING ZONE

.400	.100	.235
.294	.419	.297
.211	.400	.217

LEFTY-RIGHTY SPLITS

vs.	Avg.	AB	H	2B	3B	HR	RBI	BB	SO	OBP	Slg.
L	.233	120	28	7	0	3	13	12	15	.308	.367
R	.273	176	48	10	4	7	32	15	30	.343	.449

Year	Team (League)	W	L	Pct.	ERA	WHIP	G	GS	CG	ShO	Hld.	Sv.-Opp.	IP	H	R	ER	HR	BB-IBB	SO	Avg.
1990—	Ariz. A's (Ariz.)	2	5	.286	5.44	1.71	12	10	0	0		0-...	48.0	55	41	29	3	27-0	30	.276
1991—	Madison (Midw.)	10	5	.667	3.09	1.19	27	27	0	0		0-...	163.0	136	77	56	5	58-5	88	.223
1992—	Modesto (California)	7	11	.389	3.75	1.46	25	25	1	0		0-...	151.0	143	72	63	6	78-1	126	.254
1993—	Huntsville (Sou.)	5	12	.294	4.78	1.53	28	28	1	0		0-...	165.2	169	102	88	16	85-2	112	.269
1994—	Huntsville (Sou.)	6	3	.667	3.22	1.35	17	17	1	0		0-...	103.1	100	40	37	5	39-1	63	.259
	—Tacoma (PCL)	4	5	.444	4.04	1.65	11	9	0	0		0-...	64.2	73	36	29	5	34-2	28	.290
1995—	Chicago (N.L.)	0	0	...	9.00	1.50	2	0	0	0	0	0-0	2.0	2	2	2	1	1-0	1	.250
	—Iowa (Am. Assoc.)	4	7	.364	6.80	1.74	23	17	1	1		0-...	86.0	108	66	65	18	42-1	48	.314
1996—	Iowa (Am. Assoc.)	6	4	.600	4.85	1.56	51	1	0	0		4-...	72.1	80	42	39	7	33-2	51	.290

Year	Team (League)	W	L	Pct.	ERA	WHIP	G	GS	CG	ShO	Hld.	Sv.-Opp.	IP	H	R	ER	HR	BB-IBB	SO	Avg.
	—Chicago (N.L.)	1	0	1.000	9.00	1.91	6	0	0	0	0	0-0	11.0	16	11	11	3	5-0	7	.348
1997	—Okla. City (A.A.)	8	6	.571	5.10	1.57	25	19	1	0	...	0-...	114.2	133	76	65	10	47-1	79	.295
	—Texas (A.L.)	1	1	.500	8.27	1.93	9	5	0	0	0	0-0	32.2	45	30	30	6	18-0	18	.338
1998	—GC Rangers (GCL)	0	1	.000	7.71	2.29	3	3	0	0	0	0-...	7.0	12	7	6	1	4-0	10	.364
	—Charlotte (Fla. St.)	0	1	.000	6.00	1.00	1	0	0	0	0	0-...	3.0	2	3	2	0	1-0	3	.200
	—Tulsa (Texas)	1	0	1.000	5.40	2.40	1	0	0	0	0	0-...	1.2	2	1	1	1	2-0	3	.400
	—Oklahoma (PCL)	3	1	.750	3.34	1.46	13	3	0	0	...	0-...	35.0	33	13	13	3	18-0	31	.252
1999	—Charlotte (Int'l)	9	4	.692	4.05	1.19	33	14	2	1	...	3-...	104.1	83	53	47	7	41-1	107	.214
	—Chicago (A.L.)	0	0	...	0.00	1.00	1	1	0	0	0	0-0	6.0	4	0	0	0	2-0	2	.200
2000	—Chicago (A.L.)	1	2	.333	12.06	2.55	10	1	0	0	0	0-0	15.2	25	23	21	4	15-0	6	.379
	—Tampa Bay (A.L.)	4	0	1.000	2.56	1.16	19	5	0	0	0	0-0	52.2	47	16	15	4	14-1	38	.236
2001	—Tampa Bay (A.L.)	11	12	.478	4.42	1.43	39	27	0	0	3	1-3	195.1	200	98	96	23	79-0	110	.271
2002	—Tampa Bay (A.L.)	4	* 18	.182	5.18	1.61	33	33	4	0	0	0-0	224.0	* 271	* 141	* 129	33	* 89-2	137	.302
2003	—Toronto (A.L.)	7	6	.538	5.94	1.68	40	8	0	0	1	0-0	89.1	107	67	59	14	43-3	54	.296
2004	—Las Vegas (PCL)	3	0	1.000	2.50	1.06	6	6	0	0	...	0-...	36.0	26	11	10	2	12-0	32	.203
	—New York (A.L.)	6	2	.750	5.47	1.40	28	3	0	0	1	1-1	77.1	75	49	47	9	33-2	56	.254
2005	—Tampa (Fla. St.)	0	1	.000	6.00	1.33	2	2	0	0	0	0-0	3.0	4	2	2	0	0-0	4	.286
	—New York (A.L.)	5	3	.625	4.73	1.32	64	1	0	0	16	1-6	78.0	76	43	41	10	27-1	45	.257
	American League totals (8 years)	39	44	.470	5.11	1.52	243	84	4	0	21	3-10	771.0	850	467	438	103	320-9	466	.283
	National League totals (2 years)	1	0	1.000	9.00	1.85	8	0	0	0	0	0-0	13.0	18	13	13	4	6-0	7	.333
	Major League totals (10 years)	40	44	.476	5.18	1.52	251	84	4	0	21	3-10	784.0	868	480	451	107	326-9	473	.284

DIVISION SERIES RECORD

Year	Team (League)	W	L	Pct.	ERA	WHIP	G	GS	CG	ShO	Hld.	Sv.-Opp.	IP	H	R	ER	HR	BB-IBB	SO	Avg.
2004	—New York (A.L.)	0	0	...	6.75	2.63	2	0	0	0	0	0-0	2.2	4	2	2	1	3-0	4	.333
2005	—New York (A.L.)	0	0	...	13.50	1.50	2	0	0	0	0	0-0	0.2	1	1	1	1	0-0	0	.333
	Division series totals (2 years)	0	0	...	8.10	2.40	4	0	0	0	0	0-0	3.1	5	3	3	2	3-0	4	.333

CHAMPIONSHIP SERIES RECORD

Year	Team (League)	W	L	Pct.	ERA	WHIP	G	GS	CG	ShO	Hld.	Sv.-Opp.	IP	H	R	ER	HR	BB-IBB	SO	Avg.
2004	—New York (A.L.)	0	0	...	2.70	1.20	4	0	0	0	2	0-0	3.1	2	1	1	1	2-0	2	.182

SULLIVAN, CORY — OF

PERSONAL: Born August 20, 1979, in Tulsa, Okla. ... 6-0/180. ... Bats left, throws left. ... Full name: Cory Sullivan. ... High school: North Alleghney (Pa.). ... Junior college: Cypress (Calif.). ... College: Wake Forest.

TRANSACTIONS/CAREER NOTES: Selected by Colorado Rockies organization in seventh round of 2001 free-agent draft.

2005 GAMES PLAYED BY POSITION (MLB): OF—114.

SCOUTING REPORT Sullivan doesn't have much strength, but he can run. Has an inside-out swing but a slider-speed bat. Is not patient for a leadoff hitter and hits the ball in the air too much. Is a good defensive center fielder, getting good jumps and showing good range with instincts. Has a solid arm, a quick release and good accuracy. Must improve his patience to be a leadoff candidate in 2006. *Grade 5.3*

CORY SULLIVAN'S HITTING ZONE

.200	.286	.296
.413	.290	.394
.316	.158	.300

LEFTY-RIGHTY SPLITS

vs.	Avg.	AB	H	2B	3B	HR	RBI	BB	SO	OBP	Slg.
L	.250	44	11	1	1	0	2	3	11	.292	.318
R	.299	334	100	14	3	4	28	25	72	.350	.395

Year	Team (League)	Pos.	G	AB	R	H	2B	3B	HR	RBI	BB	SO	HBP	GDP	SB-CS	Avg.	OBP	SLG	OPS	E	Avg.
2001	—Asheville (S. Atl.)	OF	67	258	36	71	12	1	5	22	25	56	2	2	13-9	.275	.344	.388	.732	2	.985
2002	—Salem (Carol.)	OF	138	560	90	161	42	6	12	67	36	70	12	8	26-5	.288	.340	.448	.788	4	.987
2003	—Tulsa (Texas)	OF	135	557	81	167	34	8	5	61	39	83	4	4	17-13	.300	.347	.417	.764	2	.994
2004	—Tulsa (Texas)	Did not play.																			
2005	—Colorado (N.L.)	OF	139	378	64	111	15	4	4	30	28	83	3	6	12-3	.294	.343	.386	.729	3	.986
	Major League totals (1 year)		139	378	64	111	15	4	4	30	28	83	3	6	12-3	.294	.343	.386	.729	3	.986

SUPPAN, JEFF — P

PERSONAL: Born January 2, 1975, in Oklahoma City. ... 6-2/220. ... Throws right, bats right. ... Full name: Jeffrey Scot Suppan. ... Name pronounced: SOO-pahn. ... High school: Crespi (Encino, Calif.).

TRANSACTIONS/CAREER NOTES: Selected by Boston Red Sox organization in second round of 1993 free-agent draft. ... On disabled list (August 25, 1996-remainder of season). ... Selected by Arizona Diamondbacks in first round (third pick overall) of expansion draft (November 18, 1997). ... Traded by Diamondbacks to Kansas City Royals for cash (September 3, 1998). ... Signed as a free agent by Pittsburgh Pirates (January 31, 2003). ... Traded by Pirates with Ps Brandon Lyon and Anastacio Martinez to Boston Red Sox for 2B Freddy Sanchez, P Mike Gonzalez and cash (July 31, 2003). ... Signed as a free agent by St. Louis Cardinals (December 18, 2003).

CAREER HITTING: 37-for-196 (.189), 12 R, 3 2B, 0 3B, 1 HR, 9 RBI.

SCOUTING REPORT *Throws:* Suppan's two-seam fastball ranges from 87-92 mph. Also throws a curveball, a changeup and a slider. *Tendencies:* He does not have an overpowering fastball, but he does have good command to both sides of the plate and is effective at keeping the ball down. Curve has a tight, downward biting action and good rotation. Likes to use his slider to get in on lefthanders. Changes speeds off all his pitches and continually moves the ball around to stay away from the middle of the plate. Uses the change against lefthanders and righthanders. Has good command and a solid game plan; really knows how to set up hitters. *Outlook:* Suppan has moved from back-end starter to solid mid-rotation starter. *Grade 7.4*

JEFF SUPPAN'S PITCHING ZONE

.200	.474	.361
.320	.329	.319
.224	.300	.202

LEFTY-RIGHTY SPLITS

vs.	Avg.	AB	H	2B	3B	HR	RBI	BB	SO	OBP	Slg.
L	.271	350	95	15	1	10	40	27	43	.325	.406
R	.279	398	111	19	3	14	42	36	71	.344	.447

Year Team (League)	W	L	Pct.	ERA	WHIP	G	GS	CG	ShO	Hld.	Sv.-Opp.	IP	H	R	ER	HR	BB-IBB	SO	Avg.
1993— GC Red Sox (GCL)	4	3	.571	2.18	1.18	10	9	2	1	...	0-...	57.2	52	20	14	0	16-0	64	.237
1994— Sarasota (Fla. St.)	13	7	.650	3.26	1.17	27	27	4	2	...	0-...	174.0	153	74	63	10	50-0	173	.236
1995— Trenton (East.)	6	2	.750	2.36	1.13	15	15	1	1	...	0-...	99.0	86	35	26	5	26-1	88	.232
— Boston (A.L.)	1	2	.333	5.96	1.50	8	3	0	0	1	0-0	22.2	29	15	15	4	5-1	19	.312
— Pawtucket (Int'l)	2	3	.400	5.32	1.29	7	7	0	0	...	0-...	45.2	50	29	27	9	9-0	32	.278
1996— Boston (A.L.)	1	1	.500	7.54	1.85	8	4	0	0	0	0-0	22.2	29	19	19	3	13-0	13	.330
— Pawtucket (Int'l)	10	6	.625	3.22	1.07	22	22	7	1	0	0-...	145.1	130	66	52	16	25-1	142	.233
1997— Pawtucket (Int'l)	5	1	.833	3.71	1.09	9	9	2	1	0	0-...	60.2	51	26	25	7	15-0	40	.233
— Boston (A.L.)	7	3	.700	5.69	1.57	23	22	0	0	0	0-0	112.1	140	75	71	12	36-1	67	.305
1998— Arizona (N.L.)	1	7	.125	6.68	1.56	13	13	1	0	0	0-0	66.0	82	55	49	12	21-1	39	.301
— Tucson (PCL)	4	3	.571	3.63	1.37	13	12	0	0	...	0-...	67.0	75	29	27	4	17-1	62	.277
— Kansas City (A.L.)	0	0	...	0.71	0.79	4	1	0	0	0	0-0	12.2	9	1	1	1	1-0	12	.200
1999— Kansas City (A.L.)	10	12	.455	4.53	1.36	32	32	4	1	0	0-0	208.2	222	113	105	28	62-4	103	.274
2000— Kansas City (A.L.)	10	9	.526	4.94	1.49	35	33	3	1	0	0-0	217.0	240	121	119	* 36	84-3	128	.284
2001— Kansas City (A.L.)	10	14	.417	4.37	1.38	34	34	1	0	0	0-0	218.1	227	120	106	31	74-3	120	.267
2002— Kansas City (A.L.)	9	16	.360	5.32	1.43	33	33	3	1	0	0-0	208.0	229	134	123	32	68-3	109	.279
2003— Pittsburgh (N.L.)	10	7	.588	3.57	1.26	21	21	3	2	0	0-0	141.0	147	57	56	11	31-5	78	.268
— Boston (A.L.)	3	4	.429	5.57	1.43	11	10	0	0	0	0-0	63.0	70	41	39	12	20-0	32	.281
2004— St. Louis (N.L.)	16	9	.640	4.16	1.37	31	31	0	0	0	0-0	188.0	192	98	87	25	65-1	110	.265
2005— St. Louis (N.L.)	16	10	.615	3.57	1.38	32	32	0	0	0	0-0	194.1	206	93	77	24	63-1	114	.275
American League totals (9 years)	51	61	.455	4.96	1.44	188	172	11	3	1	0-0	1085.1	1195	639	598	154	363-15	603	.280
National League totals (4 years)	43	33	.566	4.11	1.37	97	97	4	2	0	0-0	589.1	627	303	269	72	180-8	341	.273
Major League totals (11 years)	94	94	.500	4.66	1.41	285	269	15	5	1	0-0	1674.2	1822	942	867	226	543-23	944	.278

DIVISION SERIES RECORD

Year Team (League)	W	L	Pct.	ERA	WHIP	G	GS	CG	ShO	Hld.	Sv.-Opp.	IP	H	R	ER	HR	BB-IBB	SO	Avg.
2004— St. Louis (N.L.)	1	0	1.000	2.57	0.71	1	1	0	0	0	0-0	7.0	2	2	2	1	3-0	2	.091

CHAMPIONSHIP SERIES RECORD

Year Team (League)	W	L	Pct.	ERA	WHIP	G	GS	CG	ShO	Hld.	Sv.-Opp.	IP	H	R	ER	HR	BB-IBB	SO	Avg.
2004— St. Louis (N.L.)	1	1	.500	3.00	1.00	2	2	0	0	0	0-0	12.0	8	5	4	2	4-0	9	.186
2005— St. Louis (N.L.)	0	0	...	1.80	1.20	1	1	0	0	0	0-0	5.0	3	1	1	1	3-0	5	.167
Champ. series totals (2 years)	1	1	.500	2.65	1.06	3	3	0	0	0	0-0	17.0	11	6	5	3	7-0	14	.180

WORLD SERIES RECORD

Year Team (League)	W	L	Pct.	ERA	WHIP	G	GS	CG	ShO	Hld.	Sv.-Opp.	IP	H	R	ER	HR	BB-IBB	SO	Avg.
2004— St. Louis (N.L.)	0	1	.000	7.71	1.93	1	1	0	0	0	0-0	4.2	8	4	4	1	1-0	4	.364

SURHOFF, B.J.   OF/DH

PERSONAL: Born August 4, 1964, in Bronx, N.Y. ... 6-1/210. ... Bats left, throws right. ... Full name: William James Surhoff. ... High school: Rye (N.Y.). ... College: North Carolina. ... Son of Dick Surhoff, forward with two NBA teams (1952-53 and 1953-54); brother of Rich Surhoff, pitcher with Philadelphia Phillies and Texas Rangers (1985).
TRANSACTIONS/CAREER NOTES: Selected by New York Yankees organization in fifth round of June 1982 free-agent draft; did not sign. ... Selected by Milwaukee Brewers organization in first round (first pick overall) of June 1985 free-agent draft. ... On suspended list (August 23-25, 1990). ... On disabled list (March 25-April 16, April 20-May 23 and July 7, 1994-remainder of season); included rehabilitation assignments to El Paso and New Orleans. ... Signed as a free agent by Baltimore Orioles (December 20, 1995). ... On disabled list (May 18-June 2, 1996). ... Traded by Orioles with P Gabe Molina to Atlanta Braves for OF Trenidad Hubbard, C Fernando Lunar and P Luis Rivera (July 31, 2000). ... On disabled list (April 28, 2002-remainder of season). ... Signed as a free agent by Orioles organization (February 12, 2002). ... On disabled list (May 4-28 and July 25-August 12, 2003; and June 19-July 27, 2004). ... On disabled list (June 22-July 7 and August 9-24, 2005).
HONORS: Named College Player of the Year by THE SPORTING NEWS (1985).
2005 GAMES PLAYED BY POSITION (MLB): OF—60, 1B—18, DH—7.

SCOUTING REPORT *Offense:* Surhoff is a professional hitter who has lost some bat speed. Has a good approach and will adjust. Is a line-drive hitter who likes the ball up and out over the plate. Is a good contact hitter who can shorten his stroke. *Defense:* Surhoff's lack of speed restricts him to left field, where his arm is weak but accurate. Has below-average range and relies on positioning to compensate. *Outlook:* Surhoff still is a good complementary player who can help a club with his offense and his clubhouse presence. *Grade 5.7*

B.J. SURHOFF'S HITTING ZONE

.412	.300	.364
.314	.286	.232
.357	.222	.209

LEFTY-RIGHTY SPLITS

vs.	Avg.	AB	H	2B	3B	HR	RBI	BB	SO	OBP	Slg.
L	.255	98	25	3	1	2	17	1	12	.260	.367
R	.259	205	53	8	1	3	17	10	20	.293	.351

Year Team (League)	Pos.	G	AB	R	H	2B	3B	HR	RBI	BB	SO	HBP	GDP	SB-CS	Avg.	OBP	SLG	OPS	E	Avg.
1985—Beloit (Midw.)	C	76	289	39	96	13	4	7	58	22	35	0	3	10-9	.332	.373	.478	.851	3	.994
1986—Vancouver (PCL)	C	116	458	71	141	19	3	5	59	29	30	8	16	21-8	.308	.356	.395	.751	7	* .989
1987—Milwaukee (A.L.)	C-DH	115	395	50	118	22	3	7	68	36	30	0	13	11-10	.299	.350	.423	.773	11	.985
1988—Milwaukee (A.L.)	C	139	493	47	121	21	0	5	38	31	49	3	12	21-6	.245	.292	.318	.611	8	.988
1989—Milwaukee (A.L.)	3B-C-DH	126	436	42	108	17	4	5	55	25	29	3	8	14-12	.248	.287	.339	.626	10	.983
1990—Milwaukee (A.L.)	3B-C	135	474	55	131	21	4	6	59	41	37	1	8	18-7	.276	.331	.376	.706	12	.983
1991—Milwaukee (A.L.)		143	505	57	146	19	4	5	68	26	33	0	* 21	5-8	.289	.319	.372	.691	4	.995
1992—Milwaukee (A.L.)	C-1B-DH OF-3B	139	480	63	121	19	1	4	62	46	41	2	9	14-8	.252	.314	.321	.635	6	.992
1993—Milwaukee (A.L.)	3B-OF-1B C-DH	148	552	66	151	38	3	7	79	36	47	2	9	12-9	.274	.318	.391	.709	18	.956
1994—El Paso (Texas)	OF	3	12	2	3	1	0	0	0	0	2	0	0	0-0	.250	.250	.333	.583	0	1.000
—Milwaukee (A.L.)	3B-C-1B OF-1B	40	134	20	35	11	2	5	22	16	14	0	5	0-1	.261	.336	.485	.821	4	.974
—New Orleans (A.A.)	3B-OF-1B C	5	19	3	6	2	0	0	1	1	2	0	0	0-0	.316	.350	.421	.771	0	1.000
1995—Milwaukee (A.L.)	OF-1B-DH DH	117	415	72	133	26	3	13	73	37	43	4	7	7-3	.320	.378	.492	.870	5	.991
1996—Baltimore (A.L.)	3B-OF-DH 1B	143	537	74	157	27	6	21	82	47	79	3	7	0-1	.292	.352	.482	.834	15	.955
1997—Baltimore (A.L.)	OF-DH-1B 3B	147	528	80	150	30	4	18	88	49	60	5	7	1-1	.284	.345	.458	.803	2	.993
1998—Baltimore (A.L.)	OF-1B	162	573	79	160	34	1	22	92	49	81	1	13	9-7	.279	.332	.457	.789	3	.986
1999—Baltimore (A.L.)	OF-DH-3B	* 162	* 673	104	207	38	1	28	107	43	78	2	15	5-1	.308	.347	.492	.839	0	1.000
2000—Baltimore (A.L.)	OF-DH	103	411	56	120	27	0	13	57	29	46	2	5	7-2	.292	.341	.453	.793	3	.987
—Atlanta (N.L.)	OF	44	128	13	37	9	2	1	11	12	12	1	5	3-0	.289	.352	.414	.766	0	1.000
2001—Atlanta (N.L.)	OF-DH	141	484	68	131	33	1	10	58	38	48	1	5	9-3	.271	.321	.405	.726	3	.986
2002—Atlanta (N.L.)		25	75	5	22	5	0	0	9	9	5	0	1	1-3	.293	.369	.360	.729	0	1.000
2003—Baltimore (A.L.)	DH-OF-1B	93	319	32	94	20	0	5	41	29	29	1	4	2-2	.295	.353	.404	.758	2	.991
2004—Baltimore (A.L.)	OF-DH-1B	100	343	49	106	12	1	8	50	30	46	1	9	2-0	.309	.365	.420	.785	2	.989
2005—Baltimore (A.L.)	OF-1B-DH	91	303	30	78	11	2	5	34	11	32	1	6	0-0	.257	.282	.356	.639	2	.992
American League totals (17 years)		2103	7571	976	2136	393	39	177	1075	581	774	31	158	128-78	.282	.332	.414	.746	107	.986
National League totals (3 years)		210	687	86	190	47	3	11	78	59	65	2	11	13-6	.277	.332	.402	.734	3	.992
Major League totals (19 years)		2313	8258	1062	2326	440	42	188	1153	640	839	33	169	141-84	.282	.332	.413	.745	110	.986

DIVISION SERIES RECORD

Year Team (League)	Pos.	G	AB	R	H	2B	3B	HR	RBI	BB	SO	HBP	GDP	SB-CS	Avg.	OBP	SLG	OPS	E	Avg.
1996—Baltimore (A.L.)	OF	4	13	3	5	0	0	3	5	0	1	0	0	0-0	.385	.385	1.077	1.462	0	1.000
1997—Baltimore (A.L.)	OF	3	11	0	3	1	0	0	2	0	2	0	0	0-0	.273	.273	.364	.636	0	1.000
2000—Atlanta (N.L.)		2	2	0	1	0	0	0	0	0	0	0	0	0-0	.500	.500	.500	1.000	...	...
2001—Atlanta (N.L.)	OF	3	11	1	3	1	0	0	0	0	1	0	1	1-0	.273	.333	.455	.697	0	1.000
Division series totals (4 years)		12	37	4	12	2	0	3	7	0	3	1	1	1-0	.324	.342	.622	.964	0	1.000

CHAMPIONSHIP SERIES RECORD

Year Team (League)	Pos.	G	AB	R	H	2B	3B	HR	RBI	BB	SO	HBP	GDP	SB-CS	Avg.	OBP	SLG	OPS	E	Avg.
1996—Baltimore (A.L.)	OF	5	15	0	4	0	0	0	2	1	2	0	1	0-0	.267	.294	.267	.561	0	1.000
1997—Baltimore (A.L.)	1B-OF	6	25	1	5	2	0	0	1	2	2	0	1	0-0	.200	.259	.280	.539	0	1.000
2001—Atlanta (N.L.)	OF	4	13	1	3	0	0	1	2	0	1	0	0	0-1	.231	.231	.462	.692	0	1.000
Champ. series totals (3 years)		15	53	2	12	2	0	1	5	3	5	0	2	0-1	.226	.263	.321	.584	0	1.000

ALL-STAR GAME RECORD

		G	AB	R	H	2B	3B	HR	RBI	BB	SO	HBP	GDP	SB-CS	Avg.	OBP	SLG	OPS	E	Avg.
All-Star Game totals (1 year)		1	2	0	0	0	0	0	0	0	0	0	0	0-0	.000	.000	.000	.000	0	...

SUZUKI, ICHIRO — OF

PERSONAL: Born October 22, 1973, in Kasugai, Japan. ... 5-9/172. ... Bats left, throws right. ... Name pronounced: ee-chee-row. ... High school: Aikoudai Meiden (Kasugai, Japan).

TRANSACTIONS/CAREER NOTES: Signed as a free agent by Seattle Mariners (November 18, 2000).

RECORDS: Holds major league record for most hits, season (262, 2004).

HONORS: Named A.L. Rookie Player of the Year by THE SPORTING NEWS (2001). ... Named A.L. Rookie of the Year by Baseball Writers' Association of America (2001). ... Named A.L. Most Valuable Player by Baseball Writers' Association of America (2001). ... Won A.L. Gold Glove as outfielder (2001-05).

2005 GAMES PLAYED BY POSITION (MLB): OF—158, DH—3.

SCOUTING REPORT *Offense:* He is one of the game's best pure hitters and has the best hand-eye coordination of any player in history. Is a line-drive hitter with deceptive power who sprays the ball to all fields. Has outstanding bat control and keeps at-bats alive by fouling off good pitches. Is an outstanding runner with good instincts. *Defense:* A natural right fielder, Suzuki has an exceptionally strong, accurate arm and a quick release. Gets excellent lateral jumps on the ball coming in. Has issues going directly back on balls, but his speed allows him to compensate. *Outlook:* One of the game's premier five-tool players can dominate a game. Started last season with aspirations of hitting .400 but fell well short as he appeared to tire and struggled in the second half. *Grade 9.5*

ICHIRO SUZUKI'S HITTING ZONE

.197	.440	.257
.329	.348	.279
.300	.311	.333

LEFTY-RIGHTY SPLITS

vs.	Avg.	AB	H	2B	3B	HR	RBI	BB	SO	OBP	Slg.
L	.352	196	69	5	5	5	17	14	19	.394	.505
R	.284	483	137	16	7	10	51	34	47	.332	.408

Year Team (League)	Pos.	G	AB	R	H	2B	3B	HR	RBI	BB	SO	HBP	GDP	SB-CS	Avg.	OBP	SLG	OPS	E	Avg.
									BATTING										FIELDING	
1992— Orix (Jp. Pacific)		40	95	9	24	5	0	0	5	3	11	...	...	3-2	.253	...	.305	...	...	...
1993— Orix (Jp. Pacific)		43	64	4	12	2	0	1	3	2	7	...	...	0-2	.188	...	.266	...	...	...
1994— Orix (Jp. Pacific)		130	546	111	210	41	5	13	54	51	53	...	...	29-7	.385	...	.549	...	...	...
1995— Orix (Jp. Pacific)		130	524	104	179	23	4	25	80	68	52	...	...	49-9	.342	...	.544	...	...	...
1996— Orix (Jp. Pacific)		130	542	104	193	24	4	16	84	56	52	...	...	35-3	.356	...	.504	...	...	...
1997— Orix (Jp. Pacific)		135	536	94	185	31	4	17	91	62	36	...	...	39-4	.345	...	.513	...	...	...
1998— Orix (Jp. Pacific)		135	506	79	181	36	3	13	71	43	35	...	...	11-4	.358	...	.518	...	...	...
1999— Orix (Jp. Pacific)		103	411	80	141	27	2	21	68	45	46	...	...	12-1	.343	...	.572	...	...	...
2000— Orix (Jp. Pacific)		105	395	73	153	22	1	12	74	54	36	...	...	21-...	.387	...	.539	...	...	...
2001— Seattle (A.L.)	OF-DH	157	*692	127	*242	34	8	8	69	30	53	8	3	*56-14	*.350	.381	.457	.838	1	.997
2002— Seattle (A.L.)	OF-DH	157	647	111	208	27	8	8	51	68	62	5	8	31-15	.321	.388	.425	.813	3	.991
2003— Seattle (A.L.)	OF	159	679	111	212	29	8	13	62	36	69	6	3	34-8	.312	.352	.436	.788	2	.994
2004— Seattle (A.L.)	OF-DH	161	*704	101	*262	24	5	8	60	49	63	4	6	36-11	*.372	.414	.455	.869	3	.992
2005— Seattle (A.L.)	OF-DH	•162	*679	111	206	21	12	15	68	48	66	4	5	33-8	.303	.350	.436	.786	2	.995
Major League totals (5 years)		796	3401	561	1130	135	41	52	310	231	313	27	25	190-56	.332	.377	.442	.819	11	.994

DIVISION SERIES RECORD

Year Team (League)	Pos.	G	AB	R	H	2B	3B	HR	RBI	BB	SO	HBP	GDP	SB-CS	Avg.	OBP	SLG	OPS	E	Avg.
2001— Seattle (A.L.)	OF	5	20	4	12	1	0	0	2	1	0	0	0	1-2	.600	.619	.650	1.269	1	.900

CHAMPIONSHIP SERIES RECORD

Year Team (League)	Pos.	G	AB	R	H	2B	3B	HR	RBI	BB	SO	HBP	GDP	SB-CS	Avg.	OBP	SLG	OPS	E	Avg.
2001— Seattle (A.L.)	OF	5	18	3	4	1	0	0	1	4	4	0	0	2-0	.222	.364	.278	.641	0	1.000

ALL-STAR GAME RECORD

	G	AB	R	H	2B	3B	HR	RBI	BB	SO	HBP	GDP	SB-CS	Avg.	OBP	SLG	OPS	E	Avg.
All-Star Game totals (5 years)	5	12	2	3	1	0	0	2	2	0	0	0	1-0	.250	.357	.333	.690	0	1.000

SWEENEY, MARK — OF/1B

PERSONAL: Born October 26, 1969, in Framingham, Mass. ... 6-1/215. ... Bats left, throws left. ... Full name: Mark Patrick Sweeney. ... High school: Holliston (Mass.). ... College: Maine.

TRANSACTIONS/CAREER NOTES: Selected by Los Angeles Dodgers organization in 39th round of 1990 free-agent draft; did not sign. ... Selected by California Angels organization in ninth round of 1991 free-agent draft. ... Traded by Angels with a player to be named to St. Louis Cardinals for P John Habyan (July 8, 1995); Cardinals acquired IF Rod Correia to complete deal (January 31, 1996). ... Traded by Cardinals with Ps Danny Jackson and Rich Batchelor to San Diego Padres for P Fernando Valenzuela, 3B Scott Livingstone and OF Phil Plantier (June 13, 1997). ... Traded by Padres with OF Greg Vaughn to Cincinnati Reds for OF Reggie Sanders, SS Damian Jackson and P Josh Harris (February 2, 1999). ... Traded by Reds with a player to be named to Milwaukee Brewers for OF Alex Ochoa (January 14, 2000); Brewers acquired P Gene Altman to complete deal (May 15, 2000). ... On disabled list (March 31-May 7 and July 18-August 14, 2000); included rehabilitation assignments to Indianapolis. ... Traded by Brewers with P Jeff D'Amico, OF Jeromy Burnitz, IF Lou Collier and cash to New York Mets as part of three-team deal in which Mets also acquired 1B/OF Ross Gload and P Craig House from Colorado Rockies, Rockies acquired IF Todd Zeile, OF Benny Agbayani and cash from Mets and Brewers acquired P Glendon Rusch and IF/OF Lenny Harris from Mets and OF Alex Ochoa from Rockies (January 21, 2002). ... Released by Mets (March 13, 2002). ... Signed by Padres organization (March 16, 2002). ... On disabled list (June 6-26, 2002). ... Released by Padres (July 15, 2002). ... Signed by Rockies organization (January 21, 2003). ... Signed as a free agent by Padres (December 22, 2004).

2005 GAMES PLAYED BY POSITION (MLB): 1B—53, OF—6, DH—5.

SCOUTING REPORT Sweeney has always been a role player whose best asset is pinch hitting. Has a good stroke and the ability to hit in the clutch. Doesn't have a real quick bat and has problems with good fastballs up. Doesn't hit lefthanders well and has never been a big home-run or RBI player. Not a good defensive first baseman; has stiff hands and doesn't have a lot of range. Will always have a job because of his professional approach at the plate and occasional power but can't be counted on to play regularly. *Grade 5*

MARK SWEENEY'S HITTING ZONE

.429	.500	.176
.440	.471	.313
.455	.250	.250

LEFTY-RIGHTY SPLITS

vs.	Avg.	AB	H	2B	3B	HR	RBI	BB	SO	OBP	Slg.
L	.200	20	4	0	0	0	3	4	6	.320	.200
R	.303	201	61	12	1	8	37	36	52	.402	.493

Year Team (League)	Pos.	G	AB	R	H	2B	3B	HR	RBI	BB	SO	HBP	GDP	SB-CS	Avg.	OBP	SLG	OPS	E	Avg.
1991— Boise (N'west)	OF	70	234	45	66	10	3	4	34	51	42	5	7	9-5	.282	.416	.402	.818	4	.954
1992— Quad City (Midw.)	OF	120	424	65	115	20	5	14	76	47	85	4	6	15-11	.271	.346	.441	.787	4	.981
1993— Palm Springs (Calif.)	OF-1B	66	245	41	87	18	3	3	47	42	29	2	4	9-6	.355	.449	.490	.938	7	.955
— Midland (Texas)	OF	51	188	41	67	13	2	9	32	27	22	6	5	1-1	.356	.444	.590	1.035	1	.989
1994— Vancouver (PCL)	DH-1B-OF	103	344	59	98	12	3	8	49	59	50	5	5	3-3	.285	.394	.407	.801	2	.994

Year	Team (League)	Pos.	G	AB	R	H	2B	3B	HR	RBI	BB	SO	HBP	GDP	SB-CS	Avg.	OBP	SLG	OPS	E	Avg.
	—Midland (Texas)	OF-1B-DH	14	50	13	15	3	0	3	18	10	10	0	3	1-1	.300	.403	.540	.943	2	.973
1995—	Vancouver (PCL)	OF-DH-1B	69	226	48	78	14	2	7	59	43	33	2	6	3-1	.345	.452	.518	.970	2	.981
	—Louisville (A.A.)	1B	22	76	15	28	8	0	2	22	14	8	2	0	2-0	.368	.468	.553	1.021	2	.990
	—St. Louis (N.L.)	1B-OF	37	77	5	21	2	0	2	13	10	15	0	3	1-1	.273	.348	.377	.725	2	.988
1996—	St. Louis (N.L.)	OF-1B	98	170	32	45	9	0	3	22	33	29	1	4	3-0	.265	.387	.371	.758	3	.977
1997—	St. Louis (N.L.)	OF-1B	44	61	5	13	3	0	0	4	9	14	1	2	0-1	.213	.319	.262	.582	0	1.000
	—San Diego (N.L.)	OF-1B	71	103	11	33	4	0	2	19	11	18	0	1	2-2	.320	.383	.417	.800	2	.957
1998—	San Diego (N.L.)	OF-1B-DH	122	192	17	45	8	3	2	15	26	37	1	5	1-2	.234	.324	.339	.663	1	.994
1999—	Cincinnati (N.L.)	1B-OF	37	31	6	11	3	0	2	7	4	9	0	2	0-0	.355	.429	.645	1.074	0	1.000
	—Indianapolis (Int'l)	OF-DH-1B	86	311	66	100	17	1	12	51	59	40	4	7	3-2	.322	.432	.498	.931	5	.982
2000—	Milwaukee (N.L.)	DH-1B-OF	71	73	9	16	6	0	1	6	12	18	1	1	0-0	.219	.337	.342	.680	1	1.000
	—Indianapolis (Int'l)	1B-OF	18	55	13	28	8	0	2	14	10	8	0	3	0-0	.509	.585	.764	1.348	0	1.000
2001—	Indianapolis (Int'l)	OF-1B	109	404	65	116	34	1	6	69	56	71	2	6	3-1	.287	.373	.421	.793	1	.993
	—Milwaukee (N.L.)	OF-1B	48	89	9	23	3	1	3	11	12	23	0	0	2-1	.258	.347	.416	.762	1	.971
2002—	San Diego (N.L.)	1B-OF-DH	48	65	3	11	3	0	1	4	4	19	0	1	0-0	.169	.217	.262	.479	2	.956
	—Portland (PCL)	1B	1	1	0	1	0	0	0	0	0	0	0	0	0-0	1.000	1.000	1.000	2.000	0	...
2003—	Colo. Springs (PCL)	OF-1B-DH	51	165	24	49	10	1	5	35	34	32	0	5	1-4	.297	.407	.461	.867	2	.985
	—Colorado (N.L.)	OF-1B-DH	67	97	13	25	9	0	2	14	9	27	0	2	0-1	.258	.321	.412	.733	0	1.000
2004—	Colorado (N.L.)	OF-1B-DH	122	177	25	47	12	2	9	40	32	51	2	2	1-0	.266	.377	.508	.885	0	1.000
2005—	San Diego (N.L.)	1B-OF-DH	135	221	31	65	12	1	8	40	40	58	0	6	4-0	.294	.395	.466	.861	5	.986
Major League totals (11 years)			900	1356	166	355	74	7	35	195	202	318	6	29	14-8	.262	.356	.404	.760	16	.986

DIVISION SERIES RECORD

Year	Team (League)	Pos.	G	AB	R	H	2B	3B	HR	RBI	BB	SO	HBP	GDP	SB-CS	Avg.	OBP	SLG	OPS	E	Avg.
1996—	St. Louis (N.L.)		1	1	0	1	0	0	0	0	0	0	0	0	0-0	1.000	1.000	1.000	2.000	...	...
1998—	San Diego (N.L.)		2	1	0	0	0	0	0	0	1	0	0	0	0-1	.000	.500	.000	.500	...	...
2005—	San Diego (N.L.)	1B	3	3	1	2	1	0	0	0	2	1	0	0	0-0	.667	.800	1.000	1.800	0	1.000
Division series totals (3 years)			6	5	1	3	1	0	0	0	3	1	0	0	0-1	.600	.750	.800	1.550	0	1.000

CHAMPIONSHIP SERIES RECORD

Year	Team (League)	Pos.	G	AB	R	H	2B	3B	HR	RBI	BB	SO	HBP	GDP	SB-CS	Avg.	OBP	SLG	OPS	E	Avg.
1996—	St. Louis (N.L.)	OF	5	4	1	0	0	0	0	0	2	0	0	0	0-0	.000	.000	.000	.000	0	1.000
1998—	San Diego (N.L.)		3	2	1	0	0	0	0	0	1	1	0	0	0-0	.000	.333	.000	.333	...	...
Champ. series totals (2 years)			8	6	2	0	0	0	0	0	1	3	0	0	0-0	.000	.143	.000	.143	0	1.000

WORLD SERIES RECORD

Year	Team (League)	Pos.	G	AB	R	H	2B	3B	HR	RBI	BB	SO	HBP	GDP	SB-CS	Avg.	OBP	SLG	OPS	E	Avg.
1998—	San Diego (N.L.)		3	3	0	2	0	0	0	1	0	0	0	0	0-0	.667	.667	.667	1.333	...	...

SWEENEY, MIKE   1B

PERSONAL: Born July 22, 1973, in Orange, Calif. ... 6-3/225. ... Bats right, throws right. ... Full name: Michael John Sweeney. ... High school: Ontario (Calif.).

TRANSACTIONS/CAREER NOTES: Selected by Kansas City Royals organization in 10th round of 1991 free-agent draft. ... On suspended list (August 17-27, 2001). ... On disabled list (July 14-August 13, 2002); included rehabilitation assignment to Omaha. ... On disabled list (June 21-August 8, 2003); included rehabilitation assignment to Omaha. ... On disabled list (August 22, 2004-remainder of season). ... On disabled list (June 20-July 1, 2005).

2005 GAMES PLAYED BY POSITION (MLB): DH—73, 1B—49.

SCOUTING REPORT *Offense:* When healthy, Sweeney has an excellent approach. Hits without a stride and can really wait on the ball. Has good balance, making him a good breaking-ball hitter. Is strong and stays inside the ball and hits to the opposite field with plus power. Still quick enough to handle the ball inside. Is not a good runner. ***Defense:*** He is used mostly as a DH to protect his back and keep him in the lineup. Doesn't have a lot of range or mobility but is very aggressive. ***Outlook:*** Sweeney is becoming a fragile player whose availability is almost a day-to-day issue. Is still an effective run producer in a weak lineup. ***Grade 7.3***

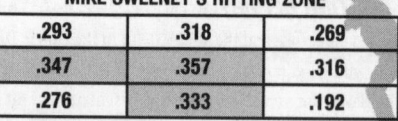

MIKE SWEENEY'S HITTING ZONE

.293	.318	.269
.347	.357	.316
.276	.333	.192

LEFTY-RIGHTY SPLITS

vs.	Avg.	AB	H	2B	3B	HR	RBI	BB	SO	OBP	Slg.
L	.279	129	36	13	0	6	29	17	14	.358	.519
R	.308	341	105	26	0	15	54	16	47	.342	.516

Year	Team (League)	Pos.	G	AB	R	H	2B	3B	HR	RBI	BB	SO	HBP	GDP	SB-CS	Avg.	OBP	SLG	OPS	E	Avg.
1991—	GC Royals (GCL)	1B-C	38	102	8	22	3	0	1	11	11	9	0	2	1-0	.216	.287	.275	.561	4	.972
1992—	Eugene (Northwest)	C	59	199	17	44	12	1	4	28	13	54	4	0	3-3	.221	.280	.352	.632	14	.967
1993—	Eugene (Northwest)	C	53	175	32	42	10	2	6	29	30	41	3	2	1-0	.240	.359	.423	.782	5	.983
1994—	Rockford (Midwest)	C	86	276	47	83	20	3	10	52	55	43	9	8	0-1	.301	.427	.504	.931	6	.988
1995—	Wilmington (Caro.)	C-DH-3B	99	332	61	103	23	1	18	53	60	39	9	4	6-1	.310	.424	.548	.972	7	.989
	—Kansas City (A.L.)	C	4	4	1	1	0	0	0	0	0	0	0	0	0-0	.250	.250	.250	.500	1	.875

S

Year Team (League)	Pos.	G	AB	R	H	2B	3B	HR	RBI	BB	SO	HBP	GDP	SB-CS	Avg.	OBP	SLG	OPS	E	Avg.
1996— Wichita (Texas)	DH-C	66	235	45	75	18	1	14	51	32	29	2	5	3-2	.319	.399	.583	.982	1	.995
— Omaha (A.A.)	C-DH	25	101	14	26	9	0	3	16	6	13	3	0	0-0	.257	.318	.436	.754	0	1.000
— Kansas City (A.L.)	C-DH	50	165	23	46	10	0	4	24	18	21	4	7	1-2	.279	.358	.412	.770	1	.994
1997— Kansas City (A.L.)	C-DH	84	240	30	58	8	0	7	31	17	33	6	8	3-2	.242	.306	.363	.668	3	.993
— Omaha (A.A.)	C-DH	40	144	22	34	8	1	10	29	18	20	2	3	0-2	.236	.323	.514	.837	1	.996
1998— Kansas City (A.L.)	C	92	282	32	73	18	0	8	35	24	38	2	7	2-3	.259	.320	.408	.728	• 9	.984
1999— Kansas City (A.L.)	1B-DH-C	150	575	101	185	44	2	22	102	54	48	10	21	6-1	.322	.387	.520	.907	12	.981
2000— Kansas City (A.L.)	1B-DH	159	618	105	206	30	0	29	144	71	67	• 15	15	8-3	.333	.407	.542	.916	9	.991
2001— Kansas City (A.L.)	1B-DH	147	559	97	170	46	0	29	99	64	64	2	13	10-3	.304	.374	.542	.916	12	.989
2002— Kansas City (A.L.)	1B-DH	126	471	81	160	31	1	24	86	61	46	6	9	9-7	.340	.417	.563	.979	9	.991
— Omaha (PCL)	1B	3	12	2	3	1	0	1	4	1	2	0	1	0-0	.250	.286	.583	.869	0	1.000
2003— Omaha (PCL)	DH	2	8	3	2	1	0	1	1	1	1	0	0	0-0	.250	.333	.750	1.083	0	...
— Kansas City (A.L.)	DH-1B	108	392	62	115	18	1	16	83	64	56	2	13	3-2	.293	.391	.467	.858	4	.990
2004— Kansas City (A.L.)	1B-DH	106	411	56	118	23	0	22	79	33	44	6	7	3-2	.287	.347	.504	.851	4	.992
2005— Kansas City (A.L.)	DH-1B	122	470	63	141	39	0	21	83	33	61	4	16	3-0	.300	.347	.517	.864	1	.998
Major League totals (11 years)		1148	4187	651	1273	267	4	182	766	439	478	57	116	48-25	.304	.374	.500	.874	65	.990

ALL-STAR GAME RECORD

	G	AB	R	H	2B	3B	HR	RBI	BB	SO	HBP	GDP	SB-CS	Avg.	OBP	SLG	OPS	E	Avg.
All-Star Game totals (4 years)	4	4	0	0	0	0	0	0	1	0	0		0-0	.000	.000	.000	.000	0	1.000

SWISHER, NICK   OF

PERSONAL: Born November 25, 1980, in Parkersburg, W.Va. ... 6-0/194. ... Bats both, throws left. ... Full name: Nicolas Thompson Swisher. ... High school: Parkersburg (W. Va.). ... College: Ohio State. ... Son of Steve Swisher, catcher with three major league teams (1974-82).

TRANSACTIONS/CAREER NOTES: Selected by Oakland Athletics organization in first round (16th pick overall) of 2002 free-agent draft. ... On disabled list (May 2-25, 2005); included rehabilitation assignment to Sacramento. ... On bereavement list (August 14-19, 2005).

2005 GAMES PLAYED BY POSITION (MLB): OF—121, 1B—21.

SCOUTING REPORT **Offense:** He has a strong, compact body. Has some power and can drive the ball to all parts of the park. Patience early in the season took away his aggressiveness, which is his strength. Has a quick bat and is a good fastball hitter down in the zone, especially from the left side. Is much better hitting lefthanded and has far more power from there. Is not going to steal many bases. **Defense:** Swisher has the arm strength to play right field but is inconsistent with his jumps and routes. Also can play first base, where he showed some agility and good hands. **Outlook:** He is going to hit and have power but needs to cut down on his strikeouts. Is a high-maintenance player at this stage of his career but will be a good one. **Grade 6.3**

NICK SWISHER'S HITTING ZONE

.389	.500	.233
.231	.388	.297
.167	.313	.103

LEFTY-RIGHTY SPLITS

vs.	Avg.	AB	H	2B	3B	HR	RBI	BB	SO	OBP	Slg.
L	.203	123	25	6	0	3	18	16	21	.310	.325
R	.248	339	84	26	1	18	56	39	89	.326	.490

Year Team (League)	Pos.	G	AB	R	H	2B	3B	HR	RBI	BB	SO	HBP	GDP	SB-CS	Avg.	OBP	SLG	OPS	E	Avg.
2002— Vancouver (N'west)	OF	13	44	10	11	3	0	2	12	13	11	2	0	3-0	.250	.433	.455	.888	0	1.000
— Visalia (Calif.)	OF	49	183	22	44	13	2	4	23	26	48	2	3	3-1	.240	.340	.399	.739	4	.953
2003— Modesto (California)	OF-1B	51	189	38	56	14	2	10	43	41	49	2	4	0-2	.296	.418	.550	.968	4	.969
— Midland (Texas)	OF-1B	76	287	36	66	24	2	5	43	37	76	6	8	0-1	.230	.324	.380	.704	5	.971
2004— Sacramento (PCL) OF-DH-1B		125	443	109	119	28	2	29	92	103	109	3	16	3-3	.269	.406	.537	.940	7	.977
— Oakland (A.L.) OF-1B-DH		20	60	11	15	4	0	2	8	8	11	2	2	0-0	.250	.352	.417	.769	3	.935
2005— Oakland (A.L.)	OF-1B	131	462	66	109	32	1	21	74	55	110	4	9	0-1	.236	.322	.446	.768	2	.994
— Sacramento (PCL)	OF-DH	6	23	4	9	3	0	0	1	2	7	...		0-1	.391	.462	.522	.984	...	...
Major League totals (2 years)		151	522	77	124	36	1	23	82	63	121	6	11	0-1	.238	.325	.443	.768	5	.986

SWITZER, JON   P

PERSONAL: Born August 13, 1979, in Houston. ... 6-3/191. ... Throws left, bats left. ... Full name: Jon Michael Switzer. ... High school: Clear Lake (Texas). ... College: Arizona State.

TRANSACTIONS/CAREER NOTES: Selected by Pittsburgh Pirates organization in 26th round of 1998 free-agent draft; did not sign. ... Selected by Tampa Bay Devil Rays organization in second round of 2001 free-agent draft. ... On disabled list (April 8, 2004-entire season).

CAREER HITTING: 0-for-0 (.000), 0 R, 0 2B, 0 3B, 0 HR, 0 RBI.

LEFTY-RIGHTY SPLITS

vs.	Avg.	AB	H	2B	3B	HR	RBI	BB	SO	OBP	Slg.
L	.167	6	1	0	0	0	0	1	3	.286	.167
R	.333	12	4	1	0	0	5	6	2	.556	.417

Year Team (League)	W	L	Pct.	ERA	WHIP	G	GS	CG	ShO	Hld.	Sv.-Opp.	IP	H	R	ER	HR	BB-IBB	SO	Avg.
2001— Hudson Valley (NYP)	2	0	1.000	0.63	0.77	5	0	0	0	...	0-...	14.1	9	3	1	0	2-0	20	.173
2002— Bakersfield (Calif.)	7	5	.583	4.27	1.30	20	20	0	0	...	0-...	103.1	108	55	49	8	26-0	129	.269
2003— Orlando (South.)	8	8	.500	3.43	1.18	22	22	2	0	...	0-...	126.0	117	63	48	10	32-1	100	.246
— Durham (Int'l)	1	0	1.000	1.80	1.20	1	1	0	0	...	0-...	5.0	6	1	1	1	0-0	3	.316
— Tampa Bay (A.L.)	0	0	...	7.45	1.66	5	0	0	0	0	0-0	9.2	13	8	8	2	3-0	7	.342
2004— Tampa Bay (A.L.)					Did not play.														
2005— Montgom. (Sou.)	3	1	.750	3.45	1.21	6	6	0	0	0	0-0	31.1	33	14	12	2	5-0	20	.268
— Tampa Bay (A.L.)	0	0	...	6.75	3.00	2	0	0	0	0	0-0	4.0	5	4	3	0	7-0	5	.278
— Durham (Int'l)	0	5	.000	7.11	1.94	17	8	0	0	2	0-0	44.1	64	38	35	6	22-1	28	.342
Major League totals (2 years)	0	0	...	7.24	2.05	7	0	0	0	0	0-0	13.2	18	12	11	2	10-0	12	.321

TADANO, KAZUHITO   P

PERSONAL: Born April 25, 1980, in Tokyo. ... 6-0/180. ... Throws right, bats right. ... Name pronounced: kaz-oo-hee-toh tuh-DAHN-oh. ... College: Rikkyo (Japan).

TRANSACTIONS/CAREER NOTES: Signed as a non-drafted free agent by Cleveland Indians organization (March 8, 2003). ... On disabled list (September 16, 2004-remainder of season).

CAREER HITTING: 1-for-3 (.333), 1 R, 0 2B, 0 3B, 0 HR, 0 RBI.

LEFTY-RIGHTY SPLITS

vs.	Avg.	AB	H	2B	3B	HR	RBI	BB	SO	OBP	Slg.
L	.250	8	2	1	0	0	1	0	1	.250	.375
R	.250	8	2	1	0	0	0	0	0	.250	.375

Year	Team (League)	W	L	Pct.	ERA	WHIP	G	GS	CG	ShO	Hld.	Sv.-Opp.	IP	H	R	ER	HR	BB-IBB	SO	Avg.
2003—	Kinston (Carol.)	2	1	.667	1.89	0.84	7	1	0	0	...	0-...	19.0	13	5	4	0	3-0	28	.191
—	Buffalo (Int'l)	0	0	...	3.86	1.43	2	0	0	0	...	0-...	7.0	6	3	3	0	4-1	6	.231
—	Akron (East.)	4	1	.800	1.24	1.06	31	0	0	0	...	3-...	72.2	62	15	10	4	15-2	78	.226
2004—	Buffalo (Int'l)	2	4	.333	5.44	1.41	12	8	0	0	...	0-...	44.2	49	28	27	9	14-0	39	.275
—	Cleveland (A.L.)	1	1	.500	4.65	1.45	14	4	0	0	0	0-0	50.1	55	30	26	6	18-0	39	.272
2005—	Cleveland (A.L.)	0	0	...	2.25	1.00	1	0	0	0	0	0-0	4.0	4	1	1	0	0-0	1	.250
—	Buffalo (Int'l)	5	5	.500	4.39	1.32	32	8	0	0	2	5-6	96.1	105	54	47	16	22-3	86	.277
Major League totals (2 years)		1	1	.500	4.47	1.42	15	4	0	0	0	0-0	54.1	59	31	27	6	18-0	40	.271

TAGUCHI, SO   OF

PERSONAL: Born July 2, 1969, in Hyogo Prefecture, Japan. ... 5-10/163. ... Bats right, throws right. ... Name pronounced: tah-gu-chee. ... High school: Nishinomiya Kita (Osaka, Japan). ... College: Kansai Gakuin (Japan).

TRANSACTIONS/CAREER NOTES: Signed as a free agent by St. Louis Cardinals (January 9, 2002).

2005 GAMES PLAYED BY POSITION (MLB): OF—131.

SCOUTING REPORT Taguchi has shortened his stroke while maintaining his bat speed. Is a good high-ball hitter who uses the whole field and is a tough out with runners in scoring position. Has surprising power when pulling the ball. Is a good defensive outfielder who can play all three positions. Has good instincts and range and is an accurate thrower. Is one of the game's best fourth outfielders. ***Grade 7***

SO TAGUCHI'S HITTING ZONE

.393	.500	.333
.295	.365	.425
.313	.256	.227

LEFTY-RIGHTY SPLITS

vs.	Avg.	AB	H	2B	3B	HR	RBI	BB	SO	OBP	Slg.
L	.276	156	43	5	2	4	25	7	28	.307	.410
R	.296	240	71	16	0	4	28	13	34	.332	.413

Year	Team (League)	Pos.	G	AB	R	H	2B	3B	HR	RBI	BB	SO	HBP	GDP	SB-CS	Avg.	OBP	SLG	OPS	E	Avg.
1992—	Orix (Jp. Pacific)	OF	47	123	...	33	...	...	1	7	...	...	...	...	5-...	.268	...	.293	...	...	...
1993—	Orix (Jp. Pacific)	OF	31	83	...	23	...	...	0	5	...	...	...	...	3-...	.277	...	.277	...	...	...
1994—	Orix (Jp. Pacific)	OF	108	329	...	101	...	...	6	43	...	...	...	...	10-...	.307	...	.362	...	...	...
1995—	Orix (Jp. Pacific)	OF	130	495	...	122	...	...	9	61	...	...	...	...	14-...	.246	...	.301	...	...	...
1996—	Orix (Jp. Pacific)	OF	128	509	...	142	...	...	7	44	...	...	...	...	10-...	.279	...	.320	...	...	...
1997—	Orix (Jp. Pacific)	OF	135	572	...	168	...	...	10	56	...	...	...	...	7-...	.294	...	.346	...	...	...
1998—	Orix (Jp. Pacific)	OF	132	497	...	135	...	...	9	41	...	...	...	...	8-...	.272	...	.326	...	...	...
1999—	Orix (Jp. Pacific)	OF	133	524	...	141	...	...	9	56	...	...	...	...	11-...	.269	...	.321	...	...	...
2000—	Orix (Jp. Pacific)	OF	129	509	...	142	...	...	8	49	...	...	...	...	9-...	.279	...	.326	...	...	...
2001—	Orix (Jp. Pacific)	OF	134	453	70	127	21	6	8	42	43	88	...	...	6-...	.280	...	.406	...	...	...
2002—	Memphis (PCL)	OF	91	304	37	75	17	0	5	36	13	44	5	5	6-3	.247	.286	.352	.638	2	.990
—	St. Louis (N.L.)	OF	19	15	4	6	0	0	0	2	2	1	0	0	1-0	.400	.471	.400	.871	1	.929
—	New Haven (East.)	OF	26	107	21	33	10	0	1	15	9	15	3	1	3-1	.308	.375	.430	.805	2	.970
2003—	Memphis (PCL)	OF-DH	90	258	31	66	8	2	2	24	22	36	2	5	14-5	.256	.318	.326	.644	1	.994
—	St. Louis (N.L.)	OF-2B	43	54	9	14	3	1	3	13	4	11	0	2	0-0	.259	.310	.519	.829	0	1.000
2004—	Memphis (PCL)	OF-DH	17	55	5	18	4	0	1	7	1	10	2	2	6-0	.327	.362	.455	.817	0	1.000
—	St. Louis (N.L.)	OF	109	179	26	52	10	2	3	25	12	23	2	6	6-3	.291	.337	.419	.756	2	.980
2005—	St. Louis (N.L.)	OF	143	396	45	114	21	2	8	53	20	62	2	11	11-2	.288	.322	.412	.734	2	.989
Major League totals (4 years)			314	644	84	186	34	5	14	93	38	97	4	19	18-5	.289	.329	.422	.751	5	.985

DIVISION SERIES RECORD

Year	Team (League)	Pos.	G	AB	R	H	2B	3B	HR	RBI	BB	SO	HBP	GDP	SB-CS	Avg.	OBP	SLG	OPS	E	Avg.
2004—	St. Louis (N.L.)	OF	1	0	0	0	0	0	0	0	0	0	0	0	0-0	...	...	...	...	0	...
2005—	St. Louis (N.L.)	OF	3	1	0	0	0	0	0	0	0	0	0	0	0-0	.000	.000	.000	.000	0	...
Division series totals (2 years)			4	1	0	0	0	0	0	0	0	0	0	0	0-0	.000	.000	.000	.000	0	...

CHAMPIONSHIP SERIES RECORD

Year	Team (League)	Pos.	G	AB	R	H	2B	3B	HR	RBI	BB	SO	HBP	GDP	SB-CS	Avg.	OBP	SLG	OPS	E	Avg.
2004—	St. Louis (N.L.)	OF	3	2	0	0	0	0	0	0	0	1	0	0	0-0	.000	.000	.000	.000	0	1.000
2005—	St. Louis (N.L.)	OF	6	6	0	0	0	0	0	0	0	3	0	0	0-0	.000	.000	.000	.000	0	1.000
Champ. series totals (2 years)			9	8	0	0	0	0	0	0	0	4	0	0	0-0	.000	.000	.000	.000	0	1.000

WORLD SERIES RECORD

Year	Team (League)	Pos.	G	AB	R	H	2B	3B	HR	RBI	BB	SO	HBP	GDP	SB-CS	Avg.	OBP	SLG	OPS	E	Avg.
2004—	St. Louis (N.L.)	DH-OF	2	4	1	1	0	0	0	1	0	2	0	0	0-0	.250	.250	.250	.500	0	1.000

TAKATSU, SHINGO   P

PERSONAL: Born November 25, 1968, in Hiroshima, Japan. ... 6-0/180. ... Throws right, bats right. ... Name pronounced: tah-kott-soo. ... High school: Hiroshima Technical (Hiroshima, Japan). ... College: Koshien University (Japan).

TRANSACTIONS/CAREER NOTES: Signed as a free agent by Chicago White Sox (January 22, 2004). ... Released by White Sox (August 1, 2005). ... Signed by New York Mets organization (August 12, 2005).

CAREER HITTING: 0-for-0 (.000), 0 R, 0 2B, 0 3B, 0 HR, 0 RBI.

SCOUTING REPORT

Throws: Takatsu has an average fastball (87-90 mph). Curve and changeup are about 25 mph slower. **Tendencies:** He creates deception with a slow windup that includes some hesitation. Is especially tough against hitters who never have seen him pitch. Fastball has some sinking action down and can bore in when up in the zone to righthanded hitters. Curve has a large, downward break. **Outlook:** The league quickly caught up with him and drove him from a closer's role. Will be a long reliever without a long major league lifespan. **Grade 4.5**

SHINGO TAKATSU'S PITCHING ZONE

.333	.500	.333
.320	.435	.280
.133	.273	.364

LEFTY-RIGHTY SPLITS

vs.	Avg.	AB	H	2B	3B	HR	RBI	BB	SO	OBP	Slg.
L	.254	59	15	1	1	6	11	11	18	.371	.610
R	.299	87	26	6	0	5	16	8	20	.354	.540

Year— Team (League)	W	L	Pct.	ERA	WHIP	G	GS	CG	ShO	Hld.	Sv.-Opp.	IP	H	R	ER	HR	BB-IBB	SO	Avg.
1991— Yakult (Jp. Cen.)	1	1	.500	4.23	1.45	13	1	1	0	...	0-...	27.2	34	15	13	4	6-...	25	...
1992— Yakult (Jp. Cen.)	5	3	.625	4.68	1.45	23	8	3	0	...	0-...	82.2	84	48	43	10	36-...	63	...
1993— Yakult (Jp. Cen.)	6	4	.600	2.30	1.19	56	1	0	0	...	20-...	78.1	69	28	20	3	24-...	72	...
1994— Yakult (Jp. Cen.)	8	4	.667	2.86	1.29	47	0	0	0	...	19-...	72.1	63	25	23	7	30-...	54	...
1995— Yakult (Jp. Cen.)	1	3	.250	2.61	1.16	39	0	0	0	...	28-...	48.1	42	14	14	2	14-...	36	...
1996— Yakult (Jp. Cen.)	2	6	.250	3.24	1.44	39	0	0	0	...	21-...	50.0	56	18	18	7	16-...	35	...
1997— Yakult (Jp. Cen.)	7	4	.636	2.04	0.95	51	3	0	0	...	7-...	79.1	55	20	18	9	20-...	68	...
1998— Yakult (Jp. Cen.)	2	3	.400	5.56	1.76	42	0	0	0	...	3-...	45.1	54	29	28	6	26-...	32	...
1999— Yakult (Jp. Cen.)	1	1	.500	2.18	0.97	40	0	0	0	...	30-...	41.1	32	11	10	6	8-...	38	...
2000— Yakult (Jp. Cen.)	0	1	.000	2.08	1.15	35	0	0	0	...	29-...	34.2	32	8	8	4	8-...	29	...
2001— Yakult (Jp. Cen.)	0	4	.000	2.61	1.20	52	0	0	0	...	37-...	51.2	49	17	15	3	13-...	39	...
2002— Yakult (Jp. Cen.)	0	2	.000	3.89	1.15	44	0	0	0	...	32-...	41.2	37	19	18	6	11-...	28	...
2003— Yakult (Jp. Cen.)	2	3	.400	3.00	1.50	44	0	0	0	...	34-...	42.0	42	18	14	7	21-...	26	...
2004— Chicago (A.L.)	6	4	.600	2.31	0.98	59	0	0	0	4	19-20	62.1	40	17	16	6	21-3	50	.182
2005— Chicago (A.L.)	1	2	.333	5.97	1.60	31	0	0	0	3	8-9	28.2	30	19	19	9	16-1	32	.270
— Norfolk (Int'l)	0	1	.000	3.38	0.88	7	1	0	0	...	0-0	8.0	6	3	3	3	1-0	10	.200
— New York (N.L.)	1	0	1.000	2.35	1.83	9	0	0	0	1	0-2	7.2	11	2	2	2	3-1	6	.314
American League totals (2 years)	7	6	.538	3.46	1.18	90	0	0	0	7	27-29	91.0	70	36	35	15	37-4	82	.211
National League totals (1 year)	1	0	1.000	2.35	1.83	9	0	0	0	1	0-2	7.2	11	2	2	2	3-1	6	.314
Major League totals (2 years)	8	6	.571	3.38	1.23	99	0	0	0	8	27-31	98.2	81	38	37	17	40-5	88	.221

TALLET, BRIAN   P

PERSONAL: Born September 21, 1977, in Midwest City, Okla. ... 6-7/208. ... Throws left, bats left. ... Full name: Brian Curtis Tallet. ... Name pronounced: tal-ETT. ... High school: Putnam City West (Bethany, Okla.). ... College: Louisiana State.

TRANSACTIONS/CAREER NOTES: Selected by Florida Marlins organization in 14th round of 1996 free-agent draft; did not sign. ... Selected by New York Yankees organization in 13th round of 1997 free-agent draft; did not sign. ... Selected by Pittsburgh Pirates organization in 19th round of 1999 free-agent draft; did not sign. ... Selected by Cleveland Indians organization in second round of 2000 free-agent draft. ... On disabled list (April 1-July 26, 2004); included rehabilitation assignments to Mahoning Valley, Lake County and Akron.

CAREER HITTING: 0-for-2 (.000), 0 R, 0 2B, 0 3B, 0 HR, 0 RBI.

LEFTY-RIGHTY SPLITS

vs.	Avg.	AB	H	2B	3B	HR	RBI	BB	SO	OBP	Slg.
L	.400	5	2	0	0	1	2	1	0	.500	1.000
R	.267	15	4	0	0	1	2	2	2	.389	.467

Year— Team (League)	W	L	Pct.	ERA	WHIP	G	GS	CG	ShO	Hld.	Sv.-Opp.	IP	H	R	ER	HR	BB-IBB	SO	Avg.
2000— Mahoning Valley (NYP)	0	0	...	1.15	0.83	6	6	0	0	...	0-...	15.2	10	2	2	0	3-0	20	.172
2001— Kinston (Carol.)	9	7	.563	3.04	1.08	27	27	2	0	...	0-...	160.0	134	62	54	12	38-0	164	.224
2002— Akron (East.)	10	1	.909	3.08	1.22	18	16	1	0	...	0-...	102.1	93	41	35	9	32-0	73	.243
— Buffalo (Int'l)	2	3	.400	3.07	1.43	8	7	0	0	...	0-...	44.0	47	17	15	1	16-0	25	.281
— Cleveland (A.L.)	1	0	1.000	1.50	1.08	2	2	0	0	0	0-0	12.0	9	3	2	0	4-0	5	.214
2003— Cleveland (A.L.)	0	2	.000	4.74	1.63	5	3	0	0	0	0-0	19.0	23	14	10	2	8-0	9	.303
— Buffalo (Int'l)	4	4	.500	5.14	1.46	15	15	0	0	...	0-...	84.0	89	50	48	10	34-1	67	.270
2004— Mahoning Valley (NYP)	0	0	...	0.00	1.13	2	1	0	0	...	0-...	2.2	3	3	0	0	0-0	2	.273
— Lake County (S.Atl.)	0	0	...	0.00	0.50	2	1	0	0	...	0-...	2.0	1	0	0	0	0-0	1	.143
— Akron (East.)	0	1	.000	5.32	1.65	14	0	0	0	...	1-...	23.2	26	15	14	0	13-1	24	.268
— Buffalo (Int'l)	0	0	...	4.15	1.15	5	0	0	0	...	0-...	8.2	7	4	4	0	3-1	7	.212
2005— Cleveland (A.L.)	0	0	...	7.71	1.93	2	0	0	0	0	0-0	4.2	6	4	4	2	3-0	2	.300
— Buffalo (Int'l)	6	5	.545	4.05	1.26	22	17	0	0	...	1-0	97.2	98	51	44	17	25-0	61	.260
Major League totals (3 years)	1	2	.333	4.04	1.49	9	5	0	0	0	0-0	35.2	38	21	16	4	15-0	16	.275

TASCHNER, JACK   P

PERSONAL: Born April 21, 1978, in Milwaukee. ... 6-3/207. ... Throws left, bats left. ... Full name: Jack Gerard Taschner. ... High school: Racine (Wis.). ... College: Wisconsin-Oshkosh.

TRANSACTIONS/CAREER NOTES: Selected by San Francisco Giants organization in second round of 1999 free-agent draft.

CAREER HITTING: 0-for-0 (.000), 0 R, 0 2B, 0 3B, 0 HR, 0 RBI.

JACK TASCHNER'S PITCHING ZONE

.400	1.000	.286
.077	.111	.444
.000	.200	.000

LEFTY-RIGHTY SPLITS

vs.	Avg.	AB	H	2B	3B	HR	RBI	BB	SO	OBP	Slg.
L	.265	34	9	3	1	0	4	3	8	.316	.412
R	.128	47	6	2	0	0	1	10	11	.281	.170

Year— Team (League)	W	L	Pct.	ERA	WHIP	G	GS	CG	ShO	Hld.	Sv.-Opp.	IP	H	R	ER	HR	BB-IBB	SO	Avg.
1999— Salem-Keizer (N'west)	3	2	.600	2.51	1.26	7	6	0	0	...	0-...	28.2	26	12	8	1	10-0	36	.241
2000— San Jose (Calif.)	2	2	.500	4.10	1.52	10	2	0	0	...	1-...	26.1	23	17	12	0	17-0	22	.237
2001— San Jose (Calif.)	4	4	.500	4.11	1.39	14	14	0	0	...	0-...	65.2	62	33	30	7	29-0	72	.244

Year Team (League)	W	L	Pct.	ERA	WHIP	G	GS	CG	ShO	Hld.	Sv.-Opp.	IP	H	R	ER	HR	BB-IBB	SO	Avg.
2003—Norwich (East.)	0	6	.000	5.71	1.63	34	12	0	0	...	0-...	75.2	78	53	48	7	45-0	46	.269
2004—Norwich (East.)	3	1	.750	2.48	1.09	14	10	0	0	...	0-...	58.0	47	17	16	5	16-0	55	.233
—Fresno (PCL)	4	7	.364	9.28	1.93	18	9	0	0	...	0-...	53.1	71	59	55	14	32-1	44	.323
2005—Fresno (PCL)	3	0	1.000	1.64	1.09	44	0	0	0	1	10-13	49.1	30	9	9	3	24-0	62	.173
—San Francisco (N.L.)	2	0	1.000	1.59	1.24	24	0	0	0	3	0-1	22.2	15	5	4	0	13-0	19	.185
Major League totals (1 year)	2	0	1.000	1.59	1.24	24	0	0	0	3	0-1	22.2	15	5	4	0	13-0	19	.185

TAVAREZ, JULIAN — P

PERSONAL: Born May 22, 1973, in Santiago, Dominican Republic. ... 6-2/195. ... Throws right, bats left. ... Name pronounced: JOOL-ee-en tah-VAR-rez. ... High school: Santiago (Dominican Republic).

TRANSACTIONS/CAREER NOTES: Signed as a non-drafted free agent by Cleveland Indians organization (March 16, 1990). ... On suspended list (June 18-21, 1996). ... Traded by Indians with 2B Jeff Kent, IF Jose Vizcaino and a player to be named to San Francisco Giants for 3B Matt Williams and a player to be named (November 13, 1996); Indians traded P Joe Roa to Giants for OF Trenidad Hubbard to complete deal (December 16, 1996). ... On disabled list (July 13-August 7, 1998); included rehabilitation assignment to Fresno. ... On suspended list (September 14-16, 1998). ... On disabled list (May 1-June 1, 1999); included rehabilitation assignment to Fresno. ... Claimed on waivers by Colorado Rockies (November 21, 1999). ... Signed as a free agent by Chicago Cubs (November 16, 2000). ... On suspended list (April 29-May 5, 2001). ... Traded by Cubs with Ps Jose Cueto and Dontrelle Willis and C Ryan Jorgensen to Florida Marlins for Ps Antonio Alfonseca and Matt Clement (March 27, 2002). ... On disabled list (April 17-May 12, 2002). ... Signed as a free agent by Pittsburgh Pirates organization (January 28, 2003). ... On suspended list (June 22-25, 2003). ... Signed as a free agent by St. Louis Cardinals (January 9, 2004). ... On suspended list (September 24-October 2, 2004).

HONORS: Named A.L. Rookie Pitcher of the Year by THE SPORTING NEWS (1995).

CAREER HITTING: 15-for-135 (.111), 8 R, 0 2B, 0 3B, 0 HR, 9 RBI.

SCOUTING REPORT

Throws: Tavarez's fastball ranges from 90-93 mph. Throws his slider at 85 and also has a split-finger fastball. ***Tendencies:*** The live-armed veteran comes at hitters with long arm action from the side and gets good sinking action on his fastball. Is not afraid to challenge hitters inside; his fastball will bore in on righthanders. Slider is sharp but occasionally flat when doesn't stay on top of it. Uses his late-diving splitter as an out pitch. Also has a little bit of a mean streak that can intimidate the hitter. ***Outlook:*** The durable Tavarez Has a resilient arm that allows him to maintain his velocity with frequent work. ***Grade 7.5***

JULIAN TAVAREZ'S PITCHING ZONE

.273	.333	.273
.237	.393	.341
.167	.429	.211

LEFTY-RIGHTY SPLITS

vs.	Avg.	AB	H	2B	3B	HR	RBI	BB	SO	OBP	Slg.
L	.294	68	20	5	1	2	8	5	17	.347	.485
R	.271	177	48	8	0	4	19	14	30	.345	.384

Year Team (League)	W	L	Pct.	ERA	WHIP	G	GS	CG	ShO	Hld.	Sv.-Opp.	IP	H	R	ER	HR	BB-IBB	SO	Avg.
1990—Dom. Indians (DSL)	5	5	.500	3.29	1.62	14	12	3	0	...	0-...	82.0	85	53	30	...	48-...	33	...
1991—Dom. Indians (DSL)	8	2	.800	2.67	1.01	19	18	1	0	...	0-...	121.1	95	41	36	...	28-...	75	...
1992—Burlington (Appal.)	6	3	.667	2.68	1.12	14	14	2	2	...	0-...	87.1	86	41	26	3	12-0	69	.250
1993—Kinston (Carol.)	11	5	.688	2.42	1.09	18	18	2	0	...	0-...	119.0	102	48	32	6	28-0	107	.228
—Cant./Akr. (Eastern)	2	1	.667	0.95	0.79	3	2	1	1	...	0-...	19.0	14	2	2	0	1-0	11	.212
—Cleveland (A.L.)	2	2	.500	6.57	1.78	8	7	0	0	0	0-0	37.0	53	29	27	7	13-2	19	.340
1994—Charlotte (Int'l)	15	6	.714	3.48	1.19	26	26	2	2	...	0-...	176.0	167	79	68	15	43-0	102	.247
—Cleveland (A.L.)	0	1	.000	21.60	4.20	1	1	0	0	0	0-0	1.2	6	8	4	1	1-1	0	.500
1995—Cleveland (A.L.)	10	2	.833	2.44	1.14	57	0	0	0	19	0-4	85.0	76	36	23	7	21-0	68	.235
1996—Cleveland (A.L.)	4	7	.364	5.36	1.52	51	4	0	0	13	0-0	80.2	101	49	48	9	22-5	46	.315
—Buffalo (A.A.)	1	0	1.000	1.29	0.93	2	2	0	0	...	0-...	14.0	10	2	2	0	3-0	10	.200
1997—San Francisco (N.L.)	6	4	.600	3.87	1.42	* 89	0	0	0	26	0-3	88.1	91	43	38	6	34-5	38	.277
1998—San Francisco (N.L.)	5	3	.625	3.80	1.55	60	0	0	0	10	1-6	85.1	96	41	36	5	36-11	52	.298
—Fresno (PCL)	0	0	...	19.29	2.57	1	0	0	0	...	0-...	2.1	6	5	5	0	0-0	1	.500
1999—San Francisco (N.L.)	2	0	1.000	5.93	1.65	47	0	0	0	5	0-2	54.2	65	38	36	7	25-3	33	.295
—Fresno (PCL)	0	0	...	2.25	0.75	4	1	0	0	...	0-...	8.0	3	2	2	1	3-0	9	.115
—San Jose (Calif.)	0	0	...	0.00	0.50	1	1	0	0	...	0-...	4.0	1	0	0	1	0-1	3	.091
2000—Colorado (N.L.)	11	5	.688	4.43	1.48	51	12	1	0	6	1-1	120.0	124	68	59	11	53-9	62	.268
2001—Chicago (N.L.)	10	9	.526	4.52	1.49	34	28	0	0	0	1-1	161.1	172	98	81	13	69-4	107	.277
2002—Florida (N.L.)	10	12	.455	5.39	1.70	29	27	0	0	0	0-1	153.2	188	100	92	9	74-7	67	.308
2003—Pittsburgh (N.L.)	3	3	.500	3.66	1.22	64	0	0	0	9	11-14	83.2	75	37	34	1	27-8	39	.244
2004—St. Louis (N.L.)	7	4	.636	2.38	1.18	77	0	0	0	19	4-6	64.1	57	21	17	1	19-0	48	.238
2005—St. Louis (N.L.)	2	3	.400	3.43	1.32	74	0	0	0	•32	4-6	65.2	68	28	25	6	19-4	47	.278
American League totals (4 years)	16	12	.571	4.49	1.43	117	12	0	0	32	0-4	204.1	236	122	102	24	57-8	133	.290
National League totals (9 years)	56	43	.566	4.29	1.47	525	67	1	0	109	21-39	877.0	936	474	418	59	356-51	493	.279
Major League totals (13 years)	72	55	.567	4.33	1.47	642	79	1	0	141	21-43	1081.1	1172	596	520	83	413-59	626	.281

DIVISION SERIES RECORD

Year Team (League)	W	L	Pct.	ERA	WHIP	G	GS	CG	ShO	Hld.	Sv.-Opp.	IP	H	R	ER	HR	BB-IBB	SO	Avg.
1995—Cleveland (A.L.)	0	0	...	6.75	1.88	3	0	0	0	1	0-1	2.2	5	2	2	1	0-0	3	.385
1996—Cleveland (A.L.)	0	0	...	0.00	2.25	2	0	0	0	0	0-0	1.1	1	0	0	0	2-0	1	.250
1997—San Francisco (N.L.)	0	1	.000	4.50	1.50	3	0	0	0	0	0-0	4.0	4	2	2	1	2-1	0	.267
2004—St. Louis (N.L.)	0	0	...	0.00	0.86	2	0	0	0	0	0-0	2.1	2	0	0	0	0-0	3	.222
2005—St. Louis (N.L.)	0	0	...	13.50	3.75	2	0	0	0	1	0-0	1.1	4	2	2	1	1-0	0	.500
Division series totals (5 years)	0	1	.000	4.63	1.80	12	0	0	0	2	0-1	11.2	16	6	6	3	5-1	7	.327

CHAMPIONSHIP SERIES RECORD

Year Team (League)	W	L	Pct.	ERA	WHIP	G	GS	CG	ShO	Hld.	Sv.-Opp.	IP	H	R	ER	HR	BB-IBB	SO	Avg.
1995—Cleveland (A.L.)	0	1	.000	2.70	1.20	4	0	0	0	0	0-0	3.1	3	1	1	0	1-1	2	.200
2004—St. Louis (N.L.)	2	1	.667	3.00	0.83	5	0	0	0	1	0-0	6.0	3	2	2	0	2-1	3	.150
2005—St. Louis (N.L.)	0	0	...	5.40	1.50	3	0	0	0	1	0-0	3.1	5	2	2	0	0-0	2	.333
Champ. series totals (3 years)	2	2	.500	3.55	1.11	12	0	0	0	2	0-0	12.2	11	5	5	2	3-2	7	.220

WORLD SERIES RECORD

Year Team (League)	W	L	Pct.	ERA	WHIP	G	GS	CG	ShO	Hld.	Sv.-Opp.	IP	H	R	ER	HR	BB-IBB	SO	Avg.
1995—Cleveland (A.L.)	0	0	...	0.00	1.15	5	0	0	0	0	0-0	4.1	3	0	0	0	2-0	1	.250
2004—St. Louis (N.L.)	0	1	.000	4.50	0.50	2	0	0	0	0	0-0	2.0	1	2	1	1	0-0	1	.125
World series totals (2 years)	0	1	.000	1.42	0.95	7	0	0	0	0	0-0	6.1	4	2	1	1	2-0	2	.200

TAVERAS, WILLY — OF

PERSONAL: Born December 25, 1981, in Tenares, Dominican Republic. ... 6-0/160. ... Bats right, throws right. ... Name pronounced: ta-VER-as.

TRANSACTIONS/CAREER NOTES: Signed as a non-drafted free agent by Cleveland Indians organization (May 27, 1999). ... Selected by Houston Astros from Indians organization in Rule 5 major league draft (December 15, 2003). ... Rights acquired by Astros as part of deal in which Astros traded P Jeriome Robertson to Indians for OF Luke Scott (March 31, 2005).

HONORS: Named N.L. Rookie of the Year by the SPORTING NEWS (2005).

2005 GAMES PLAYED BY POSITION (MLB): OF—148.

SCOUTING REPORT Offense: Taveras uses his speed very well and is a master bunter. Tends to chase the ball up and in. ***Defense:*** He can outrun his mistakes, but he takes bad angles to the ball at times. Throwing is adequate. ***Outlook:*** Expect Taveras to be a catalyst for the Astros for many years. ***Grade 8***

WILLY TAVERAS'S HITTING ZONE

.304	.150	.257
.283	.391	.305
.320	.343	.333

LEFTY-RIGHTY SPLITS

vs.	Avg.	AB	H	2B	3B	HR	RBI	BB	SO	OBP	Slg.
L	.233	159	37	6	2	1	6	8	29	.272	.314
R	.312	433	135	7	2	2	23	17	74	.344	.351

								BATTING									FIELDING	
Year Team (League)	Pos.	G	AB	R	H	2B	3B	HR	RBI	BB	SO	HBP	GDP	SB-CS	Avg.	OBP	SLG	OPS	E	Avg.
1999—Dom. Indians (DSL)	OF	68	277	57	98	19	6	3	44	32	32	10	...	26-10	.354	.435	.498	.933	0	...
2000—Burlington (Appal.)	OF	50	190	46	50	4	3	1	16	23	44	6	0	36-9	.263	.356	.332	.687	5	.961
2001—Columbus (S. Atl.)	OF	97	395	55	107	15	7	3	32	22	73	6	7	29-9	.271	.317	.367	.684	11	.952
2002—Columbus (S. Atl.)	OF	85	313	68	83	14	1	4	27	45	68	18	3	54-12	.265	.385	.355	.740	10	.944
2003—Kinston (Carol.)	OF	113	397	64	112	9	6	2	35	52	68	12	4	57-12	.282	.381	.350	.731	6	.978
2004—Round Rock (Texas)	OF-DH	103	409	76	137	13	1	2	27	38	76	9	2	55-11	.335	.402	.386	.776	6	.974
—Houston (N.L.)	OF	10	1	2	0	0	0	0	0	0	1	0	0	0-0	.000	.000	.000	.000	0	1.000
2005—Houston (N.L.)	OF	152	592	82	172	13	4	3	29	25	103	7	4	34-11	.291	.325	.341	.666	3	.991
Major League totals (2 years)		162	593	84	172	13	4	3	29	25	104	7	4	35-11	.290	.324	.341	.665	3	.991

DIVISION SERIES RECORD

																		FIELDING	
Year Team (League)	Pos.	G	AB	R	H	2B	3B	HR	RBI	BB	SO	HBP	GDP	SB-CS	Avg.	OBP	SLG	OPS	E	Avg.
2005—Houston (N.L.)	OF	4	14	2	5	1	0	0	1	1	0	0	0	0-0	.357	.400	.429	.829	0	1.000

CHAMPIONSHIP SERIES RECORD

Year Team (League)	Pos.	G	AB	R	H	2B	3B	HR	RBI	BB	SO	HBP	GDP	SB-CS	Avg.	OBP	SLG	OPS	E	Avg.
2005—Houston (N.L.)	OF	6	14	1	5	0	0	0	0	1	1	0	0	0-1	.357	.400	.357	.757	0	1.000

WORLD SERIES RECORD

Year Team (League)	Pos.	G	AB	R	H	2B	3B	HR	RBI	BB	SO	HBP	GDP	SB-CS	Avg.	OBP	SLG	OPS	E	Avg.
2005—Houston (N.L.)	OF	4	15	2	5	0	0	0	0	3	2	0	0	1-0	.333	.412	.600	1.012	0	1.000

TAYLOR, REGGIE — OF

PERSONAL: Born January 12, 1977, in Newberry, S.C. ... 6-1/178. ... Bats left, throws right. ... Full name: Reginald Tremain Taylor. ... High school: Newberry (S.C.).

TRANSACTIONS/CAREER NOTES: Selected by Philadelphia Phillies organization in first round (14th pick overall) of free-agent draft (June 1, 1995). ... On disabled list (July 23, 1998-remainder of season). ... Traded by Phillies to Cincinnati Reds for a player to be named (March 28, 2002); Phillies acquired P Hector Mercado to complete deal (March 30, 2002). ... On disabled list (August 26, 2003-remainder of season). ... Signed as a free agent by Colorado Rockies organization (December 15, 2004). ... Traded by Rockies to Tampa Bay Devil Rays for P Bobby Seay (April 8, 2005). ... Released by Devil Rays (July 20, 2005). ... Signed by St. Louis Cardinals organization (July 25, 2005).

2005 GAMES PLAYED BY POSITION (MLB): OF—10.

LEFTY-RIGHTY SPLITS

vs.	Avg.	AB	H	2B	3B	HR	RBI	BB	SO	OBP	Slg.
L	.000	2	0	0	0	0	0	1	1	.333	.000
R	.200	20	4	2	0	1	1	1	6	.238	.300

								BATTING									FIELDING	
Year Team (League)	Pos.	G	AB	R	H	2B	3B	HR	RBI	BB	SO	HBP	GDP	SB-CS	Avg.	OBP	SLG	OPS	E	Avg.
1995—Martinsville (App.)	OF-OF	64	239	36	53	4	6	2	32	23	58	6	5	18-7	.222	.301	.314	.615	8	.940
1996—Piedmont (S. Atl.)	OF-OF	128	499	68	131	20	6	0	31	29	136	3	10	36-17	.263	.305	.327	.632	•12	.961
1997—Clearwater (FSL)	OF-OF	134	545	73	133	18	6	12	47	30	130	4	3	40-23	.244	.285	.365	.650	11	.969
1998—Reading (East.)	OF-OF	79	337	49	92	14	6	5	22	12	73	2	2	22-10	.273	.300	.395	.695	10	.944
1999—Reading (East.)	OF-OF	127	526	75	140	17	10	15	61	18	79	3	11	38-22	.266	.293	.442	.715	9	.971
2000—Scran./W.B. (I.L.)	OF-OF	98	422	60	116	10	8	15	43	21	87	2	4	23-12	.275	.310	.443	.753	5	.980
—Philadelphia (N.L.)	OF	9	11	1	1	0	0	0	0	0	8	0	0	1-0	.091	.091	.091	.182	1	.750
2001—Scran./W.B. (I.L.)	OF-OF	111	464	56	122	20	9	7	50	24	94	3	10	31-15	.263	.301	.390	.691	5	.980
—Philadelphia (N.L.)	OF	5	7	1	0	0	0	0	0	1	1	0	0	0-0	.000	.125	.000	.125	0	1.000
2002—Cincinnati (N.L.)	OF	135	287	41	73	15	4	9	38	14	79	2	6	11-8	.254	.291	.429	.719	5	.973
2003—Cincinnati (N.L.)	OF	100	180	17	39	5	2	5	19	11	68	1	4	7-0	.217	.266	.350	.616	1	.990
2004—Louisville (Int'l)	OF	61	191	28	49	9	1	9	24	13	46	1	5	10-3	.257	.304	.455	.759	3	.921
—Charlotte (Int'l)	OF	58	210	34	61	14	0	11	30	21	45	2	3	11-4	.290	.357	.514	.871	3	.000
2005—Colo. Springs (PCL)	OF	1	4	0	1	0	0	1	0	0	0	0	0	0-0	.250	.250	.500	.750	0	1.000
—Tampa Bay (A.L.)	OF	11	22	2	4	2	0	1	2	2	7	0	0	2-0	.182	.250	.273	.523	0	1.000
—Durham (Int'l)	OF	67	253	30	66	10	3	7	35	24	55	3	5	12-10	.261	.332	.407	.739	12	.960
—Memphis (PCL)	OF	34	107	18	25	5	2	1	11	5	21	1	1	1-5	.234	.272	.346	.618	2	.985
American League totals (1 year)		11	22	2	4	2	0	1	2	2	7	0	0	2-0	.182	.250	.273	.523	0	1.000
National League totals (4 years)		249	485	60	113	20	6	14	57	26	156	3	10	19-8	.233	.275	.386	.660	7	.976
Major League totals (5 years)		260	507	62	117	22	6	14	58	28	163	3	10	21-8	.231	.274	.381	.654	7	.977

TEAHEN, MARK — 3B

PERSONAL: Born September 6, 1981, in Redlands, Calif. ... 6-3/210. ... Bats left, throws right. ... Full name: Mark Thomas Teahen. ... High school: Yucaipa (Calif.). ... College: St. Mary's.

TRANSACTIONS/CAREER NOTES: Selected by Oakland Athletics organization in supplemental round ("sandwich" pick between first and second rounds, 39th pick overall) of 2002 free-agent draft; pick received as part of compensation for Boston Red Sox signing Type A free agent Johnny Damon. ... Traded by Athletics with P Mike Wood to Kansas City Royals in three-team deal in which Royals acquired C John Buck from Houston Astros, Astros acquired OF Carlos Beltran from Royals and Athletics acquired P Octavio Dotel from Astros and cash from Royals (June 24, 2004). ... On disabled list (April 13-May 3, 2005); included rehabilitation assignment to Omaha.

2005 GAMES PLAYED BY POSITION (MLB): 3B—128.

SCOUTING REPORT *Offense:* His patience at the plate early in the season led to consistent contact, but indifference to driving the ball was a concern. Lacked bat speed and was content to take the ball the other way. Has become more aggressive and is using his lower body to increase bat speed. Has very good raw power but home run production will depend on his development as a hitter. Is a questionable runner but has very good instincts. *Defense:* Teahen has good agility and footwork. Charges the ball well and has a quick release from any angle. Can be a better-than-average defender with experience. *Outlook:* The Royals have something to build on with him and they will be patient with him, but his bat will be a question mark. *Grade 6.5*

MARK TEAHEN'S HITTING ZONE

.269	.308	.118
.386	.356	.275
.227	.292	.182

LEFTY-RIGHTY SPLITS

vs.	Avg.	AB	H	2B	3B	HR	RBI	BB	SO	OBP	Slg.
L	.200	120	24	7	2	2	14	9	32	.256	.342
R	.263	327	86	22	2	5	41	31	75	.328	.388

Year	Team (League)	Pos.	G	AB	R	H	2B	3B	HR	RBI	BB	SO	HBP	GDP	SB-CS	Avg.	OBP	SLG	OPS	E	Avg.
																			BATTING		FIELDING
2002—	Vancouver (N'west)	3B	13	57	10	23	5	1	0	6	5	9	0	0	4-1	.404	.444	.526	.970	4	.882
	Modesto (Calif.)	3B	59	234	25	56	9	1	1	26	21	53	2	4	1-2	.239	.307	.299	.606	4	.971
2003—	Modesto (Calif.)	3B	121	453	68	128	27	4	3	71	66	113	6	19	4-0	.283	.377	.380	.757	22	.931
2004—	Midland (Texas)	3B	53	197	31	66	15	4	6	36	29	44	1	12	0-0	.335	.419	.543	.962	5	.918
	Sacramento (PCL)	3B	20	69	9	19	8	0	0	10	11	22	1	1	0-1	.275	.383	.391	.774	1	.000
	Omaha (PCL)	3B	66	246	33	69	15	1	8	31	21	69	4	4	0-0	.280	.344	.447	.791	14	.000
2005—	Omaha (PCL)	3B-DH	8	27	4	7	2	0	0	4	7	9	0	1	0-0	.259	.412	.333	.745	1	.923
	Kansas City (A.L.)	3B	130	447	60	110	29	4	7	55	40	107	1	13	7-2	.246	.309	.376	.685	20	.947
	Major League totals (1 year)		130	447	60	110	29	4	7	55	40	107	1	13	7-2	.246	.309	.376	.685	20	.947

TEIXEIRA, MARK   1B

PERSONAL: Born April 11, 1980, in Annapolis, Md. ... 6-3/220. ... Bats both, throws right. ... Full name: Mark Charles Teixeira. ... Name pronounced: tuh-SHARE-uh. ... High school: Mount St. Joseph (Baltimore). ... College: Georgia Tech.

TRANSACTIONS/CAREER NOTES: Selected by Boston Red Sox organization in ninth round of 1998 free-agent draft; did not sign. ... Selected by Texas Rangers organization in first round (fifth pick overall) of 2001 free-agent draft. ... On disabled list (April 13-29, 2004); included rehabilitation assignment to Frisco.

HONORS: Won A.L. Gold Glove as first baseman (2005).

2005 GAMES PLAYED BY POSITION (MLB): 1B—155, DH—8.

SCOUTING REPORT *Offense:* Teixeira has a very quick, powerful bat. Most of his homers from the left side. Has become more patient. Is a good breaking-ball hitter. Will use the whole field. One of the best situational hitters with runners in scoring position. Makes adjustments at the plate. *Defense:* Teixeira has made as much defensive improvement as any first baseman has in a long time. Has improved his agility and hands, though his range is still limited. Has gone from a defensive liability to a possible Gold Glover. *Outlook:* He has become a much better all-around player and will continue to get better. Offensive production should continue to rise. Has the ability to be a Triple Crown candidate in the future. *Grade 9.7*

MARK TEIXEIRA'S HITTING ZONE

.286	.148	.391
.338	.478	.375
.290	.226	.208

LEFTY-RIGHTY SPLITS

vs.	Avg.	AB	H	2B	3B	HR	RBI	BB	SO	OBP	Slg.
L	.292	171	50	13	2	6	29	17	33	.361	.497
R	.304	473	144	28	1	37	115	55	91	.386	.603

Year	Team (League)	Pos.	G	AB	R	H	2B	3B	HR	RBI	BB	SO	HBP	GDP	SB-CS	Avg.	OBP	SLG	OPS	E	Avg.
																			BATTING		FIELDING
2001—			Did not play.																		
2002—	Charlotte (Fla. St.)	3B	38	150	32	48	10	2	9	41	21	24	3	4	2-0	.320	.411	.593	1.005	9	.902
	Tulsa (Texas)	3B	48	171	31	54	11	3	10	28	25	36	4	2	3-2	.316	.415	.591	1.006	12	.925
2003—	Texas (A.L.)	1B-OF-3B DH	146	529	66	137	29	5	26	84	44	120	14	14	1-2	.259	.331	.480	.811	12	.989
2004—	Frisco (Texas)	1B	3	1	0	0	0	0	0	0	0	1	1	0	0-0	.000	.250	.000	.250	0	1.000
	Texas (A.L.)	1B-OF-DH	145	545	101	153	34	2	38	112	68	117	10	6	4-1	.281	.370	.560	.929	10	.992
2005—	Texas (A.L.)	1B-DH	•162	644	112	194	41	3	43	144	72	124	11	18	4-0	.301	.379	.575	.954	3	.998
	Major League totals (3 years)		453	1718	279	484	104	10	107	340	184	361	35	38	9-3	.282	.362	.541	.902	25	.994

ALL-STAR GAME RECORD

	G	AB	R	H	2B	3B	HR	RBI	BB	SO	HBP	GDP	SB-CS	Avg.	OBP	SLG	OPS	E	Avg.
All-Star Game totals (1 year)	1	3	1	1	0	0	0	1	0	0	0	0	0-0	.333	.333	1.333	1.667	0	1.000

TEJADA, MIGUEL   SS

PERSONAL: Born May 25, 1976, in Bani, Dominican Republic. ... 5-9/209. ... Bats right, throws right. ... Full name: Miguel Odalis Tejada. ... Name pronounced: tay-HAH-duh.

TRANSACTIONS/CAREER NOTES: Signed as a non-drafted free agent by Oakland Athletics organization (July 17, 1993). ... On disabled list (March 22-May 20, 1998); included rehabilitation assignments to Edmonton and Huntsville. ... Signed as a free agent by Baltimore Orioles (December 18, 2003).

HONORS: Named A.L. Most Valuable Player by Baseball Writers' Association of America (2002).

2005 GAMES PLAYED BY POSITION (MLB): SS—160, DH—2.

SCOUTING REPORT *Offense:* Tejada is a terrific run producer. Has an outstanding stroke and exceptional bat speed. Shows patience early in the count. Has power to all fields. Pummels mistakes and tough pitches. Stays on the breaking ball well and rarely is fooled or off-balance. Is outstanding with runners on base. *Defense:* He has exceptional range to either side and throws hard and accurately even when on the move. Makes a lot of plays off-balance. Hands are soft and quick. Footwork is good. Gets a lot of in-between hops but reacts well. *Outlook:* Tejada has as much fun playing the game as anybody. Is an excellent team leader who continues to get better each year and has moved to the top of the list at his position. *Grade 10*

MIGUEL TEJADA'S HITTING ZONE

.214	.310	.348
.411	.426	.370
.290	.333	.314

LEFTY-RIGHTY SPLITS

vs.	Avg.	AB	H	2B	3B	HR	RBI	BB	SO	OBP	Slg.
L	.293	164	48	8	2	5	21	20	19	.371	.457
R	.308	490	151	42	3	21	77	20	64	.342	.535

Year Team (League)	Pos.	G	AB	R	H	2B	3B	HR	RBI	BB	SO	HBP	GDP	SB-CS	Avg.	OBP	SLG	OPS	E	Avg.
1994— Dom. Athletics (DSL)	2B	74	218	51	64	9	1	18	62	37	36	...	...	13-...	.294	...	.592	...	16	.927
1995— S. Oregon (N'west)	SS	74	269	45	66	15	5	8	44	41	54	2	3	19-2	.245	.346	.428	.774	26	.930
1996— Modesto (Calif.) SS-DH-3B		114	458	97	128	12	5	20	72	51	93	4	9	27-16	.279	.352	.459	.810	45	.925
1997— Huntsville (Sou.)	SS	128	502	85	138	20	3	22	97	50	99	7	9	15-11	.275	.344	.458	.802	36	.948
— Oakland (A.L.)	SS	26	99	10	20	3	2	2	10	2	22	3	3	2-0	.202	.240	.333	.574	4	.969
1998— Edmonton (PCL)	SS	1	3	0	0	0	0	0	0	1	1	0	1	0-0	.000	.250	.000	.250	0	1.000
— Huntsville (Sou.)	SS-DH	15	52	9	17	6	0	2	7	4	8	0	2	1-0	.327	.362	.558	.920	5	.922
— Oakland (A.L.)	SS	105	365	53	85	20	1	11	45	28	86	7	8	5-6	.233	.298	.384	.681	26	.951
1999— Oakland (A.L.)	SS	159	593	93	149	33	4	21	84	57	94	10	11	8-7	.251	.325	.427	.751	21	.973
2000— Oakland (A.L.)	SS	160	607	105	167	32	1	30	115	66	102	4	15	6-0	.275	.349	.479	.828	21	.972
2001— Oakland (A.L.)	SS	• 162	622	107	166	31	3	31	113	43	89	13	14	11-5	.267	.326	.476	.801	20	.973
2002— Oakland (A.L.)	SS	• 162	662	108	204	30	0	34	131	38	84	11	* 21	7-2	.308	.354	.508	.861	19	.975
2003— Oakland (A.L.)	SS	162	636	98	177	42	0	27	106	53	65	6	12	10-0	.278	.336	.472	.807	21	.972
2004— Baltimore (A.L.)	SS	162	653	107	203	40	2	34	* 150	48	73	10	• 24	4-1	.311	.360	.534	.894	24	.970
2005— Baltimore (A.L.)	SS-DH	• 162	654	89	199	* 50	5	26	98	40	83	7	• 26	5-1	.304	.349	.515	.865	22	.971
Major League totals (9 years)		1260	4891	770	1370	281	18	216	852	375	698	71	134	58-22	.280	.338	.477	.815	178	.970

DIVISION SERIES RECORD

Year Team (League)	Pos.	G	AB	R	H	2B	3B	HR	RBI	BB	SO	HBP	GDP	SB-CS	Avg.	OBP	SLG	OPS	E	Avg.
2000— Oakland (A.L.)	SS	5	20	5	7	2	0	0	1	2	2	0	0	1-0	.350	.409	.450	.859	0	1.000
2001— Oakland (A.L.)	SS	5	21	1	6	3	0	0	1	0	3	1	0	0-0	.286	.304	.429	.733	1	.958
2002— Oakland (A.L.)	SS	5	21	3	3	1	0	1	4	1	7	0	0	0-0	.143	.174	.333	.507	1	.947
2003— Oakland (A.L.)	SS	5	23	0	2	1	0	0	2	0	4	0	0	0-0	.087	.087	.130	.217	1	.957
Division series totals (4 years)		20	85	9	18	7	0	1	8	3	16	1	0	1-0	.212	.242	.329	.571	3	.966

ALL-STAR GAME RECORD

	G	AB	R	H	2B	3B	HR	RBI	BB	SO	HBP	GDP	SB-CS	Avg.	OBP	SLG	OPS	E	Avg.
All-Star Game totals (3 years)	3	6	2	2	0	0	1	2	0	0	0	0	0-0	.333	.333	.833	1.167	0	1.000

TEJEDA, ROBINSON   P

PERSONAL: Born March 24, 1982, in Bani, Dominican Republic. ... 6-3/188. ... Throws right, bats right. ... Full name: Robinson Garcia Tejeda. ... Name pronounced: tay-HEY-dah. ... High school: Liceo Club de Leones (Dominican Republic).

TRANSACTIONS/CAREER NOTES: Signed as a non-drafted free agent by Philadelphia Phillies organization (November 24, 1998).

CAREER HITTING: 2-for-20 (.100), 1 R, 0 2B, 1 3B, 0 HR, 0 RBI.

ROBINSON TEJEDA'S PITCHING ZONE

.172	.143	.241
.150	.333	.293
.250	.500	.182

LEFTY-RIGHTY SPLITS

vs.	Avg.	AB	H	2B	3B	HR	RBI	BB	SO	OBP	Slg.
L	.210	143	30	5	0	4	14	29	25	.360	.329
R	.226	164	37	10	2	1	15	22	47	.326	.329

Year Team (League)	W	L	Pct.	ERA	WHIP	G	GS	CG	ShO	Hld.	Sv.-Opp.	IP	H	R	ER	HR	BB-IBB	SO	Avg.
1999— GC Phillies (GCL)	1	3	.250	4.27	1.60	12	9	0	0	...	0-...	46.1	47	27	22	5	27-0	39	.273
2000— GC Phillies (GCL)	2	5	.286	5.54	1.44	10	6	1	1	...	0-...	39.0	44	30	24	3	12-0	22	.273
2001— Lakewood (S. Atl.)	8	9	.471	3.40	1.23	26	24	1	1	...	0-...	150.2	128	74	57	10	58-1	152	.228
2002— Clearwater (Fla. St.)	4	8	.333	3.97	1.21	17	17	1	0	...	0-...	99.2	73	48	44	14	48-0	87	.204
2003— Lakewood (S. Atl.)	0	3	.000	5.30	1.77	5	4	0	0	...	0-...	18.2	17	11	11	4	16-0	20	.246
— Clearwater (Fla. St.)	2	4	.333	3.20	1.18	11	11	1	0	...	0-...	64.2	53	25	23	4	23-0	42	.221
2004— Reading (East.)	8	14	.364	5.15	1.38	27	26	0	0	...	0-...	150.1	148	93	86	29	59-0	133	.256
2005— Scran./W.B. (Int'l)	2	0	1.000	2.22	1.20	5	5	0	0	0	0-0	28.1	21	8	7	0	13-0	28	.214
— Philadelphia (N.L.)	4	3	.571	3.57	1.38	26	13	0	0	1	0-0	85.2	67	36	34	5	51-4	72	.218
Major League totals (1 year)	4	3	.571	3.57	1.38	26	13	0	0	1	0-0	85.2	67	36	34	5	51-4	72	.218

TEJERA, MICHAEL   P

PERSONAL: Born October 18, 1976, in Havana, Cuba. ... 5-9/192. ... Throws left, bats left. ... Name pronounced: te-HAIR-ah. ... High school: Southwest (Miami).

TRANSACTIONS/CAREER NOTES: Selected by Florida Marlins organization in sixth round of 1995 free-agent draft. ... On disabled list (April 2, 2000-entire season). ... Claimed on waivers by Texas Rangers (September 10, 2004).

CAREER HITTING: 8-for-52 (.154), 5 R, 0 2B, 0 3B, 1 HR, 5 RBI.

LEFTY-RIGHTY SPLITS

vs.	Avg.	AB	H	2B	3B	HR	RBI	BB	SO	OBP	Slg.
L	.333	6	2	0	0	0	0	1	2	.500	.333
R	.600	5	3	0	0	1	3	0	0	.600	1.200

Year Team (League)	W	L	Pct.	ERA	WHIP	G	GS	CG	ShO	Hld.	Sv.-Opp.	IP	H	R	ER	HR	BB-IBB	SO	Avg.
1995— GC Marlins (GCL)	3	1	.750	2.65	1.29	11	3	0	0	...	2-...	34.0	28	13	10	2	16-1	28	.235
1996— GC Marlins (GCL)	1	0	1.000	3.60	1.20	2	0	0	0	...	0-...	5.0	6	2	2	0	0-0	2	.286
1997— Utica (N.Y.-Penn)	3	3	.500	3.76	1.10	12	12	0	0	...	0-...	69.1	65	36	29	8	11-0	67	.248
1998— Kane Co. (Midw.)	6	1	.857	2.77	1.03	10	10	0	0	...	0-...	55.1	44	20	17	3	13-0	47	.221
— Portland (East.)	9	5	.643	4.11	1.39	18	18	2	2	...	0-...	107.1	113	55	49	15	36-2	97	.268
1999— Portland (East.)	13	4	.765	2.62	1.18	25	25	0	0	...	0-...	154.2	137	55	45	13	45-1	152	.238
— Calgary (PCL)	0	2	.000	12.00	2.56	2	2	0	0	...	0-...	9.0	19	14	12	2	4-0	5	.452
— Florida (N.L.)	0	0	...	11.37	2.37	3	1	0	0	...	0-0	6.1	10	8	8	1	5-0	7	.385
2000— Florida (N.L.)			Did not play.																
2001— Portland (East.)	9	8	.529	3.57	1.30	25	25	0	0	...	0-...	141.0	143	61	56	17	41-0	131	.266
2002— Florida (N.L.)	8	8	.500	4.45	1.46	47	18	0	0	8	1-3	139.2	144	71	69	17	60-3	95	.269
2003— Florida (N.L.)	3	4	.429	4.67	1.46	50	6	0	0	5	2-2	81.0	82	44	42	6	36-3	58	.267
2004— Florida (N.L.)	0	1	.000	18.00	3.00	2	2	0	0	...	0-0	4.0	6	8	8	0	6-0	3	.375
— Jupiter (Fla. St.)	0	1	.000	0.00	1.80	1	1	0	0	...	0-0	3.1	3	1	0	0	3-0	1	.231
— Albuquerque (PCL)	0	4	.667	3.97	1.31	22	19	0	0	...	0-...	113.1	109	56	50	17	39-0	88	.253
— Texas (A.L.)	0	0	...	10.13	2.25	6	0	0	0	...	0-...	5.1	9	6	6	1	3-0	7	.360

T

Year Team (League)	W	L	Pct.	ERA	WHIP	G	GS	CG	ShO	Hld.	Sv.-Opp.	IP	H	R	ER	HR	BB-IBB	SO	Avg.
2005— Texas (A.L.)	0	0		13.50	3.00	3	0	0	0		0-0	2.0	5	3	3	1	1-0	2	.455
— Oklahoma (PCL)	3	2	.600	3.79	1.37	43	2	0	0		10	2-3	59.1	52	28	25	5	29-5	52	.239
American League totals (2 years)	0	0		11.05	2.45	9	0	0	0		0-0	7.1	14	9	9	2	4-0	9	.389
National League totals (4 years)	11	13	.458	4.95	1.51	102	27	0	0	13	3-5	231.0	242	131	127	24	107-6	163	.273
Major League totals (5 years)	11	13	.458	5.14	1.54	111	27	0	0	13	3-5	238.1	256	140	136	26	111-6	172	.278

CHAMPIONSHIP SERIES RECORD

Year Team (League)	W	L	Pct.	ERA	WHIP	G	GS	CG	ShO	Hld.	Sv.-Opp.	IP	H	R	ER	HR	BB-IBB	SO	Avg.
2003— Florida (N.L.)	0	1	.000	6.75	1.50	2	0	0	0	0	0-0	1.1	2	1	1	0	0-0	1	.333

TELEMACO, AMAURY   P

PERSONAL: Born January 19, 1974, in Higuey, Dominican Republic. ... 6-3/234. ... Throws right, bats right. ... Full name: Amaury Regalado Telemaco. ... Name pronounced: ah-MARR-ee tel-ah-MAH-ko. ... High school: Cristo Rey (La Romana, Dominican Republic).

TRANSACTIONS/CAREER NOTES: Signed as a non-drafted free agent by Chicago Cubs organization (May 23, 1991). ... On disabled list (August 20-September 4, 1996); included rehabilitation assignment to Iowa. ... Claimed on waivers by Arizona Diamondbacks (May 15, 1998). ... On disabled list (March 26-May 8, 1999); included rehabilitation assignment to Tucson. ... Claimed on waivers by Philadelphia Phillies (June 8, 1999). ... On disabled list (June 9-July 30, 2004); included rehabilitation assignment to Scranton/Wilkes-Barre.

CAREER HITTING: 14-for-116 (.121), 6 R, 4 2B, 1 3B, 0 HR, 3 RBI.

LEFTY-RIGHTY SPLITS

vs.	Avg.	AB	H	2B	3B	HR	RBI	BB	SO	OBP	Slg.
L	.150	20	3	0	0	1	3	2	4	.217	.300
R	.125	16	2	0	0	1	3	2	4	.222	.313

Year Team (League)	W	L	Pct.	ERA	WHIP	G	GS	CG	ShO	Hld.	Sv.-Opp.	IP	H	R	ER	HR	BB-IBB	SO	Avg.
1991— Dom. Cubs (DSL)	3	3	.500	3.55	1.71	15	13	0	0	...	0-...	66.0	81	43	26	...	32-...	43	...
1992— Huntington (Appal.)	3	5	.375	4.01	1.15	12	12	0	0	...	0-...	76.1	71	45	34	6	17-0	93	.240
— Peoria (Midw.)	0	1	.000	7.94	2.47	2	1	0	0	...	0-...	5.2	9	5	5	0	5-0	5	.360
1993— Peoria (Midw.)	8	11	.421	3.45	1.27	23	23	3	0	...	0-...	143.2	129	69	55	9	54-0	133	.241
1994— Daytona (Fla. St.)	7	3	.700	3.40	1.11	11	11	2	0	...	0-...	76.2	62	35	29	4	23-0	59	.221
— Orlando (Sou.)	3	5	.375	3.45	1.21	12	12	2	0	...	0-...	62.2	56	29	24	6	20-0	49	.239
1995— Orlando (Sou.)	8	8	.500	3.29	1.04	22	22	3	1	...	0-...	147.2	112	60	54	13	42-3	151	.211
1996— Iowa (A.A.)	3	1	.750	3.06	1.12	8	8	1	0	...	0-...	50.0	38	19	17	5	18-2	42	.210
— Chicago (N.L.)	5	7	.417	5.46	1.43	25	17	0	0	0	0-0	97.1	108	67	59	20	31-2	64	.281
1997— Iowa (A.A.)	5	9	.357	4.51	1.40	18	18	3	2	...	0-...	113.2	121	70	57	20	38-1	75	.267
— Chicago (N.L.)	0	3	.000	6.16	1.53	10	5	0	0	0	0-0	38.0	47	26	26	4	11-0	29	.303
— Orlando (Sou.)	1	0	1.000	2.25	1.38	1	1	0	0	...	0-...	8.0	9	2	2	0	2-0	6	.281
1998— Chicago (N.L.)	1	1	.500	3.90	1.30	14	0	0	0	1	0-0	27.2	23	12	12	5	13-0	18	.219
— Arizona (N.L.)	6	9	.400	3.94	1.32	27	18	0	0	0	0-0	121.0	127	64	53	13	33-2	60	.271
1999— Tucson (PCL)	0	3	.000	5.09	1.53	13	12	0	0	...	0-...	17.2	21	11	10	1	6-0	17	.304
— Arizona (N.L.)	1	0	1.000	7.50	2.17	5	0	0	0	0	0-0	6.0	7	5	5	2	6-1	2	.333
— Philadelphia (N.L.)	3	0	1.000	5.55	1.38	44	0	0	0	3	0-1	47.0	45	29	29	8	20-3	41	.250
2000— Philadelphia (N.L.)	1	3	.250	6.66	1.60	13	2	0	0	0	0-0	24.1	25	22	18	6	14-0	22	.275
— Scran./W.B. (Int'l)	8	3	.727	3.87	1.27	21	21	0	0	...	0-...	123.1	115	60	53	15	42-0	88	.244
2001— Philadelphia (N.L.)	5	5	.500	5.54	1.40	24	14	0	0	1	0-0	89.1	93	59	55	15	32-3	59	.274
— Scran./W.B. (Int'l)	1	2	.333	4.01	1.50	4	4	0	0	...	0-...	24.2	31	11	11	4	6-0	25	.307
2002— Scran./W.B. (Int'l)	1	0	1.000	1.80	1.00	1	1	0	0	...	0-...	5.0	5	3	1	1	0-0	3	.263
— GC Phillies (GCL)	1	0	1.000	1.64	0.55	2	2	0	0	...	0-...	11.0	4	2	2	0	2-0	5	.105
— Reading (East.)	0	0		9.00	1.00	1	1	0	0	...	0-...	1.0	1	1	1	1	0-0	1	.333
— Clearwater (FSL)	0	1	.000	1.50	1.50	3	3	0	0	...	0-...	12.0	15	5	2	0	3-0	10	.300
2003— Scran./W.B. (Int'l)	10	9	.526	3.24	0.90	25	24	3	2	...	0-...	155.1	125	59	56	15	22-1	116	.222
— Philadelphia (N.L.)	1	4	.200	3.97	1.15	8	8	0	0	0	0-0	45.1	41	22	20	5	11-2	29	.238
2004— Scran./W.B. (Int'l)	0	0		0.00	0.00	1	1	0	0	...	0-...	1.0	0	0	0	0	0-0	2	.000
— Philadelphia (N.L.)	0	2	.000	4.31	1.29	42	0	0	0	5	0-1	54.1	51	27	26	12	19-2	32	.249
2005— Scran./W.B. (Int'l)	0	1	.000	4.09	1.45	9	3	0	0	1	0-1	22.0	24	11	10	1	8-0	14	.279
— Philadelphia (N.L.)	0	1	.000	4.22	0.84	7	0	0	0	0	0-0	10.2	5	5	5	2	4-0	8	.139
Major League totals (9 years)	23	35	.397	4.94	1.37	219	64	1	0	10	0-2	561.0	572	337	308	92	194-15	364	.265

TERRERO, LUIS   OF

PERSONAL: Born May 18, 1980, in Barahona, Dominican Republic. ... 6-2/206. ... Bats right, throws right. ... Full name: Luis Enrique Terrero. ... Name pronounced: tuh-RARE-oh. ... High school: Barney Morgan (Barahona, Dominican Republic).

TRANSACTIONS/CAREER NOTES: Signed as a non-drafted free agent by Arizona Diamondbacks organization (October 15, 1997). ... On disabled list (June 8-28, 2005); included rehabilitation assignment to Tucson.

2005 GAMES PLAYED BY POSITION (MLB): OF—77.

SCOUTING REPORT He is a slasher who struggles to make offensive adjustments. Doesn't walk much and strikes out a lot. Will develop 20-home run power if he becomes more selective. Is a plus runner but has poor instincts. Doesn't get consistent jumps or take proper angles to the ball but has the speed to compensate. Has problems going back on the ball. Doesn't make good use of his strong arm. *Grade 5*

LUIS TERRERO'S HITTING ZONE

.333	.333	.364
.310	.385	.278
.050	.333	.000

LEFTY-RIGHTY SPLITS

vs.	Avg.	AB	H	2B	3B	HR	RBI	BB	SO	OBP	Slg.
L	.247	85	21	3	0	1	12	9	17	.323	.318
R	.211	76	16	3	1	3	8	5	23	.302	.395

Year Team (League)	Pos.	G	AB	R	H	2B	3B	HR	RBI	BB	SO	HBP	GDP	SB-CS	Avg.	OBP	SLG	OPS	E	Avg.
1999— Missoula (Pion.)	OF	71	272	74	78	13	7	8	40	32	91	5	2	27-10	.287	.365	.474	.839	11	.928
2000— High Desert (Calif.)	OF	19	79	10	15	3	1	0	1	3	16	1	2	5-5	.190	.229	.253	.482	3	.941
— Missoula (Pion.)	OF	68	276	48	72	10	4	8	44	10	75	8	5	23-11	.261	.305	.384	.689	5	.949
2001— South Bend (Midw.)	OF	24	89	4	14	2	0	1	8	2	29	2	2	3-0	.157	.176	.213	.389	0	1.000
— Yakima (N'west)	OF	11	41	7	13	3	2	1	0	2	8	0	0	0-3	.317	.349	.415	.763	0	1.000

T

Year	Team (League)	Pos.	G	AB	R	H	2B	3B	HR	RBI	BB	SO	HBP	GDP	SB-CS	Avg.	OBP	SLG	OPS	E	Avg.
	— Lancaster (Calif.)	OF	19	71	16	32	9	1	4	11	1	14	1	3	5-0	.451	.466	.775	1.240	1	.971
	— El Paso (Texas)	OF	34	147	29	44	13	3	3	8	4	45	3	2	9-2	.299	.331	.490	.821	5	.943
2002—	El Paso (Texas)	OF	104	360	49	103	20	6	8	54	23	89	8	9	18-22	.286	.342	.442	.784	7	.973
2003—	Arizona (N.L.)	OF	5	4	0	1	0	0	0	0	0	1	1	0	0-0	.250	.400	.250	.650	0	1.000
	— Tucson (PCL)	OF-DH	118	467	83	134	20	15	3	46	31	103	11	6	23-19	.287	.345	.413	.758	10	.968
2004—	Tucson (PCL)	OF-DH	58	217	36	68	9	6	9	35	17	48	4	7	15-3	.313	.374	.535	.909	3	.978
	— Arizona (N.L.)	OF	62	229	21	56	14	0	4	14	20	78	5	5	10-2	.245	.319	.358	.677	8	.938
2005—	Tucson (PCL)	OF	7	30	4	8	1	0	0	1	1	9	1	2	1-0	.267	.313	.300	.613	0	1.000
	— Arizona (N.L.)	OF	88	161	23	37	6	1	4	20	14	40	6	5	3-2	.230	.313	.354	.667	2	.984
	Major League totals (3 years)		155	394	44	94	20	1	8	34	34	119	12	10	13-4	.239	.317	.355	.673	10	.961

THAMES, MARCUS   OF

PERSONAL: Born March 6, 1977, in Louisville, Miss. ... 6-2/205. ... Bats right, throws right. ... Full name: Marcus Markey Thames. ... Name pronounced: timms. ... Junior college: East Central (Miss.).
TRANSACTIONS/CAREER NOTES: Selected by New York Yankees organization in 30th round of 1996 free-agent draft. ... Traded by Yankees to Texas Rangers for OF Ruben Sierra (June 6, 2003). ... Signed as a free agent by Detroit Tigers organization (December 8, 2003)
2005 GAMES PLAYED BY POSITION (MLB): OF—31, DH—4.

MARCUS THAMES'S HITTING ZONE

.000	.250	.250
.227	.182	.154
.300	.500	.000

LEFTY-RIGHTY SPLITS

vs.	Avg.	AB	H	2B	3B	HR	RBI	BB	SO	OBP	Slg.
L	.222	36	8	1	0	2	5	5	10	.317	.417
R	.183	71	13	4	0	5	11	4	28	.234	.408

Year	Team (League)	Pos.	G	AB	R	H	2B	3B	HR	RBI	BB	SO	HBP	GDP	SB-CS	Avg.	OBP	SLG	OPS	E	Avg.
1997—	GC Yankees (GCL)	OF	57	195	51	67	17	4	7	36	16	26	3	3	6-4	.344	.394	.579	.974	2	.978
	— Greensboro (S. Atl.)	OF	4	16	2	5	1	0	0	2	0	3	0	0	1-0	.313	.313	.375	.688	0	1.000
1998—	Tampa (Fla. St.)	OF	122	457	62	130	18	3	11	59	24	78	8	5	13-6	.284	.328	.409	.737	9	.970
1999—	Norwich (East.)	OF	51	182	25	41	6	2	4	26	22	40	3	2	0-1	.225	.316	.346	.662	7	.929
	— Tampa (Fla. St.)	OF	69	266	47	65	12	4	11	38	33	58	3	1	3-0	.244	.332	.444	.776	3	.974
2000—	Norwich (East.)	OF	131	474	72	114	30	2	15	79	50	89	4	13	1-5	.241	.313	.407	.721	9	.959
2001—	Norwich (East.)	OF	139	520	114	167	43	4	31	97	73	101	7	6	10-4	.321	.410	.598	1.008	8	.973
2002—	Columbus (Int'l)	OF	107	386	51	80	21	3	13	45	43	71	7	8	5-4	.207	.297	.378	.675	5	.983
	— New York (A.L.)	OF	7	13	2	3	1	0	1	2	0	4	0	0	0-0	.231	.231	.538	.769	0	1.000
2003—	Columbus (Int'l)	OF	52	194	26	54	15	2	2	28	17	48	1	4	3-4	.278	.332	.407	.739	3	.977
	— Oklahoma (PCL)	OF-DH	18	66	9	17	4	0	2	7	8	12	0	2	1-0	.258	.338	.409	.747	1	.968
	— Texas (A.L.)	OF-DH	30	73	12	15	2	0	1	4	8	18	2	2	0-1	.205	.298	.274	.572	0	1.000
2004—	Toledo (Int'l)	OF-DH	64	234	57	77	21	1	24	59	33	40	2	5	4-1	.329	.410	.735	1.145	2	.979
	— Detroit (A.L.)	OF-DH	61	165	24	42	12	0	10	33	16	42	2	3	0-1	.255	.326	.509	.835	0	1.000
2005—	Toledo (Int'l)	OF-DH	73	265	53	90	18	3	22	56	41	59	3	5	4-1	.340	.427	.679	1.106	4	.975
	— Detroit (A.L.)	OF-DH	38	107	11	21	2	0	7	16	9	38	1	1	0-0	.196	.263	.411	.674	1	.978
	Major League totals (4 years)		136	358	49	81	17	0	19	55	33	102	5	6	0-2	.226	.298	.433	.731	1	.995

THERIOT, RYAN   SS/2B

PERSONAL: Born December 7, 1979, in Baton Rouge, La. ... 5-11/175. ... Bats right, throws right. ... Full name: Ryan Stewart Theriot. ... High school: Broadmoor (Baton Rouge, La.). ... College: Louisiana State.
TRANSACTIONS/CAREER NOTES: Selected by Chicago Cubs organization in third round of 2001 free-agent draft.
2005 GAMES PLAYED BY POSITION (MLB): 2B—3.

LEFTY-RIGHTY SPLITS

vs.	Avg.	AB	H	2B	3B	HR	RBI	BB	SO	OBP	Slg.
L	.250	8	2	1	0	0	0	1	0	.333	.375
R	.000	5	0	0	0	0	0	0	2	.000	.000

Year	Team (League)	Pos.	G	AB	R	H	2B	3B	HR	RBI	BB	SO	HBP	GDP	SB-CS	Avg.	OBP	SLG	OPS	E	Avg.
2001—	Daytona (Fla. St.)	SS	30	103	20	21	5	0	0	9	21	17	1	2	2-4	.204	.341	.252	.593	7	.944
2002—	Lansing (Midw.)	2B-SS	130	489	75	123	19	4	1	37	59	77	4	3	32-8	.252	.335	.313	.648	29	.957
2003—	Lansing (Midw.)	2B-SS	58	220	29	57	8	1	1	17	31	34	1	4	21-5	.259	.353	.318	.671	12	.961
	— West Tenn (Sou.)	SS	53	178	20	42	3	0	1	9	29	21	3	6	9-8	.236	.351	.270	.621	10	.953
2004—	Daytona (Fla. St.)	SS	103	330	47	90	14	3	1	34	48	43	3	4	13-11	.273	.367	.342	.709	18	.526
2005—	West Tenn (Sou.)	2B-SS-3B	120	448	52	136	28	4	1	53	45	38	1	9	24-10	.304	.365	.391	.755	13	.975
	— Chicago (N.L.)	2B	9	13	3	2	1	0	0	0	1	2	0	0	0-0	.154	.214	.231	.445	0	1.000
	Major League totals (1 year)		9	13	3	2	1	0	0	0	1	2	0	0	0-0	.154	.214	.231	.445	0	1.000

THOMAS, CHARLES   OF

PERSONAL: Born December 26, 1978, in Fairfield, Calif. ... 6-0/190. ... Bats left, throws left. ... Full name: Charles Wesley Thomas. ... High school: Asheville (N.C.). ... College: Western Carolina.
TRANSACTIONS/CAREER NOTES: Selected by Atlanta Braves organization in 19th round of 2000 free-agent draft. ... Traded by Braves with Ps Juan Cruz and Dan Meyer to Oakland Athletics for P Tim Hudson (December 16, 2004).
2005 GAMES PLAYED BY POSITION (MLB): OF—27.

LEFTY-RIGHTY SPLITS

vs.	Avg.	AB	H	2B	3B	HR	RBI	BB	SO	OBP	Slg.
L	.143	7	1	0	0	0	1	0	0	.250	.143
R	.103	39	4	0	0	0	0	5	8	.255	.103

Year	Team (League)	Pos.	G	AB	R	H	2B	3B	HR	RBI	BB	SO	HBP	GDP	SB-CS	Avg.	OBP	SLG	OPS	E	Avg.
2000—	Jamestown (NYP)	OF	68	264	39	80	20	8	1	25	19	58	1	7	10-2	.303	.351	.451	.802	4	.974
2001—	Myrtle Beach (Carol.)	OF	12	44	4	7	1	0	0	6	3	8	0	3	1-0	.159	.208	.182	.390	0	1.000
	— Macon (S. Atl.)	OF	108	408	59	102	19	5	11	59	32	87	3	6	17-7	.250	.307	.402	.709	3	.984
2002—	Myrtle Beach (Carol.)	OF	2	7	0	2	0	0	0	0	0	2	0	0	0-0	.286	.286	.286	.571	0	1.000
	— Greenville (Sou.)	OF	71	229	40	53	9	2	0	18	28	43	4	5	5-3	.231	.322	.293	.615	2	.987
2003—	Myrtle Beach (Carol.)	OF	66	207	30	50	8	1	2	15	29	54	8	6	6-2	.242	.357	.319	.675	4	.969
	— Greenville (Sou.)	OF	47	176	29	57	14	4	0	23	18	25	1	5	5-4	.324	.396	.449	.845	2	.983

T

Year Team (League)	Pos.	G	AB	R	H	2B	3B	HR	RBI	BATTING BB	SO	HBP	GDP	SB-CS	Avg.	OBP	SLG	OPS	FIELDING E	Avg.
2004—Richmond (Int'l)	OF-DH	61	215	31	77	18	4	4	32	16	40	6	3	7-5	.358	.416	.535	.936	3	.969
—Atlanta (N.L.)	OF	83	236	35	68	8	4	7	31	21	45	9	3	3-1	.288	.368	.445	.813	1	.993
2005—Oakland (A.L.)	OF	30	46	4	5	0	0	0	1	5	8	4	0	0-1	.109	.255	.109	.363	2	.951
—Sacramento (PCL)	OF	75	277	43	63	16	3	5	33	35	56	3	7	16-4	.227	.319	.361	.680	6	.984
American League totals (1 year)		30	46	4	5	0	0	0	1	5	8	4	0	0-1	.109	.255	.109	.363	2	.951
National League totals (1 year)		83	236	35	68	8	4	7	31	21	45	9	3	3-1	.288	.368	.445	.813	1	.993
Major League totals (2 years)		113	282	39	73	8	4	7	32	26	53	13	3	3-2	.259	.349	.390	.739	3	.984

DIVISION SERIES RECORD

Year Team (League)	Pos.	G	AB	R	H	2B	3B	HR	RBI	BB	SO	HBP	GDP	SB-CS	Avg.	OBP	SLG	OPS	E	Avg.
2004—Atlanta (N.L.)	OF	5	16	1	4	0	0	0	0	2	5	1	0	1-0	.250	.368	.250	.618	0	1.000

THOMAS, FRANK   DH/1B

PERSONAL: Born May 27, 1968, in Columbus, Ga. ... 6-5/275. ... Bats right, throws right. ... Full name: Frank Edward Thomas. ... High school: Columbus (Ga.). ... College: Auburn.

TRANSACTIONS/CAREER NOTES: Selected by Chicago White Sox organization in first round (seventh pick overall) of 1989 free-agent draft. ... On disabled list (July 11-30, 1996; June 7-22, 1997; May 10, 2001-remainder of season; and July 7, 2004-remainder of season). ... On disabled list (April 2-May 30 and July 22, 2005-remainder of season); included rehabilitation assignment to Charlotte.

HONORS: Named Major League Player of the Year by THE SPORTING NEWS (1993). ... Named A.L. Most Valuable Player by Baseball Writers' Association of America (1993-94). ... Named A.L. Comeback Player of the Year by THE SPORTING NEWS (2000).

2005 GAMES PLAYED BY POSITION (MLB): DH—28.

SCOUTING REPORT **Offense:** The oft-injured Thomas is nearing the end of his career. Showed some bat speed in limited action. Can still turn on a middle-in fastball and is a good mistake hitter. Has become more of a dead pull hitter as he cheats to the fastball. **Defense:** Thomas rarely, if ever, plays in the field. Doesn't move well and has stiff hands. **Outlook:** He has problems staying healthy and his skills are leveling off, but he still is a dangerous power threat. **Grade 7.1**

FRANK THOMAS'S HITTING ZONE

.250	.143	.000
.250	.200	.333
.125	.333	.333

LEFTY-RIGHTY SPLITS

vs.	Avg.	AB	H	2B	3B	HR	RBI	BB	SO	OBP	Slg.
L	.281	32	9	1	0	4	8	6	8	.385	.688
R	.192	73	14	2	0	8	18	10	23	.282	.548

Year Team (League)	Pos.	G	AB	R	H	2B	3B	HR	RBI	BATTING BB	SO	HBP	GDP	SB-CS	Avg.	OBP	SLG	OPS	FIELDING E	Avg.
1989—GC Whi. Sox (GCL)	1B	17	52	8	19	5	0	1	11	11	3	1	0	4-0	.365	.470	.519	.989	2	.986
—Sarasota (Fla. St.)	1B	55	188	27	52	9	1	4	30	31	33	3	6	0-1	.277	.386	.399	.785	7	.985
1990—Birmingham (Sou.)	1B	109	353	85	114	27	5	18	71	112	74	5	13	7-5	.323	.487	.581	1.068	14	.987
—Chicago (A.L.)	1B-DH	60	191	39	63	11	3	7	31	44	54	2	5	0-1	.330	.454	.529	.983	5	.989
1991—Chicago (A.L.)	1B-DH	158	559	104	178	31	2	32	109	*138	112	1	20	1-2	.318	*.453	.553	1.006	2	.996
1992—Chicago (A.L.)	1B-DH	160	573	108	185	•46	2	24	115	*122	88	5	19	6-3	.323	*.439	.536	.975	13	.992
1993—Chicago (A.L.)	1B-DH	153	549	106	174	36	0	41	128	112	54	2	10	4-2	.317	.426	.607	1.033	15	.989
1994—Chicago (A.L.)	1B-DH	113	399	*106	141	34	1	38	101	*109	61	2	15	2-3	.353	*.487	*.729	1.217	7	.991
1995—Chicago (A.L.)	1B-DH	*145	493	102	152	27	0	40	111	*136	74	6	14	3-2	.308	.454	.606	1.061	7	.991
1996—Chicago (A.L.)	1B	141	527	110	184	26	0	40	134	109	70	5	25	1-1	.349	.459	.626	1.085	9	.992
1997—Chicago (A.L.)	1B-DH	146	530	110	184	35	0	35	125	109	69	3	15	1-1	*.347	*.456	.611	1.067	11	.986
1998—Chicago (A.L.)	DH-1B	160	585	109	155	35	2	29	109	110	93	6	14	7-0	.265	.381	.480	.861	2	.984
1999—Chicago (A.L.)	DH-1B	135	486	74	148	36	0	15	77	87	66	9	15	3-3	.305	.414	.471	.885	4	.983
2000—Chicago (A.L.)	DH-1B	159	582	115	191	44	0	43	143	112	94	5	13	1-3	.328	.436	.625	1.061	1	.996
2001—Chicago (A.L.)	DH-1B	20	68	8	15	3	0	4	10	10	12	0	0	0-0	.221	.316	.441	.758	1	.955
2002—Chicago (A.L.)	DH-1B	148	523	77	132	29	1	28	92	88	115	7	10	3-0	.252	.361	.472	.834	2	.955
2003—Chicago (A.L.)	DH-1B	153	546	87	146	35	0	42	105	100	115	12	11	0-0	.267	.390	.562	.952	1	.995
2004—Chicago (A.L.)	DH-1B	74	240	53	65	16	0	18	49	64	57	6	2	0-2	.271	.434	.563	.997	0	1.000
2005—Charlotte (Int'l)		11	42	3	8	1	0	1	4	4	9	0	2	0-0	.190	.261	.286	.547	0	...
—Chicago (A.L.)	DH	34	105	19	23	3	0	12	26	16	31	0	2	0-0	.219	.315	.590	.905	0	...
Major League totals (16 years)		1959	6956	1327	2136	447	11	448	1465	1466	1165	71	190	32-23	.307	.427	.568	.995	80	.991

DIVISION SERIES RECORD

Year Team (League)	Pos.	G	AB	R	H	2B	3B	HR	RBI	BB	SO	HBP	GDP	SB-CS	Avg.	OBP	SLG	OPS	E	Avg.
2000—Chicago (A.L.)	1B-DH	3	9	0	0	0	0	0	0	0	4	0	0	0-0	.000	.308	.000	.308	0	1.000

CHAMPIONSHIP SERIES RECORD

Year Team (League)	Pos.	G	AB	R	H	2B	3B	HR	RBI	BB	SO	HBP	GDP	SB-CS	Avg.	OBP	SLG	OPS	E	Avg.
1993—Chicago (A.L.)	1B-DH	6	17	2	6	0	0	1	3	10	5	0	0	0-0	.353	.593	.529	1.122	0	1.000

ALL-STAR GAME RECORD

		G	AB	R	H	2B	3B	HR	RBI	BB	SO	HBP	GDP	SB-CS	Avg.	OBP	SLG	OPS	E	Avg.
All-Star Game totals (3 years)		3	5	2	4	0	0	1	3	1	0	0	0	0-0	.800	.833	1.400	2.233	0	1.000

THOME, JIM   1B

PERSONAL: Born August 27, 1970, in Peoria, Ill. ... 6-4/244. ... Bats left, throws right. ... Full name: James Howard Thome. ... Name pronounced: TOE-mee. ... High school: Limestone (Bartonville, Ill.). ... Junior college: Illinois Central.

TRANSACTIONS/CAREER NOTES: Selected by Cleveland Indians organization in 13th round of 1989 free-agent draft. ... On disabled list (March 28-May 18 and May 20-June 15, 1992); included rehabilitation assignments to Canton/Akron. ... On disabled list (August 8-September 16, 1998). ... Signed as a free agent by Philadelphia Phillies (December 3, 2002). ... On disabled list (May 3-21 and July 1, 2005-remainder of season); included rehabilitation assignment to Clearwater.

RECORDS: Shares major league record for most strikeouts, 9-inning game (5, April 9, 2000).

2005 GAMES PLAYED BY POSITION (MLB): 1B—52, DH—5.

SCOUTING REPORT *Offense:* Thome, slowed by injuries the past two seasons, has problems catching up to good fastballs up in the zone. Power declined in 2005. Still a very patient hitter who will go deep in the count. Bat speed declined but that could come back if he's healthy. *Defense:* He's a stiff player with limited range but has good hands. Has worked hard on his defense and is better at moving around the bag to get to errant throws. *Outlook:* Thome's offensive decline is directly attributable to his forearm and back problems. When healthy can still be projected to be an outstanding run producer. Has excellent makeup. *Grade 8*

JIM THOME'S HITTING ZONE

.091	.250	.125
.160	.217	.243
.250	.400	.233

LEFTY-RIGHTY SPLITS

vs.	Avg.	AB	H	2B	3B	HR	RBI	BB	SO	OBP	Slg.
L	.164	73	12	3	0	2	11	10	22	.271	.288
R	.233	120	28	4	0	5	19	35	37	.408	.392

BATTING / FIELDING

Year	Team (League)	Pos.	G	AB	R	H	2B	3B	HR	RBI	BB	SO	HBP	GDP	SB-CS	Avg.	OBP	SLG	OPS	E	Avg.
1989—	GC Indians (GCL)	3B-SS	55	186	22	44	5	3	0	22	21	33	1	5	6-4	.237	.314	.296	.610	21	.909
1990—	Burlington (Appal.)	3B	34	118	31	44	7	1	12	34	27	18	4	2	6-3	.373	.503	.754	1.258	11	.907
—	Kinston (Carol.)	3B	33	117	19	36	4	1	4	16	24	26	1	4	4-1	.308	.427	.462	.888	8	.905
1991—	Cant./Akr. (East.)	3B	84	294	47	99	20	2	5	45	44	58	4	7	8-2	.337	.426	.469	.895	17	.924
—	Colo. Springs (PCL)	3B	41	151	20	43	7	3	2	28	12	29	0	4	0-0	.285	.331	.411	.742	6	.949
—	Cleveland (A.L.)	3B	27	98	7	25	4	2	1	9	5	16	1	4	1-1	.255	.298	.367	.665	8	.900
1992—	Colo. Springs (PCL)	3B	12	48	11	15	4	1	2	14	6	16	1	0	0-0	.313	.400	.563	.963	8	.784
—	Cleveland (A.L.)	3B	40	117	8	24	3	1	2	12	10	34	2	3	2-0	.205	.275	.299	.574	11	.882
—	Cant./Akr. (East.)	3B	30	107	16	36	9	2	1	14	24	30	1	3	0-0	.336	.462	.486	.948	4	.920
1993—	Charlotte (Int'l)	3B	115	410	85	136	21	4	25	*102	76	94	7	9	1-3	.332	.441	.585	1.026	15	.951
—	Cleveland (A.L.)	3B	47	154	28	41	11	0	7	22	29	36	4	3	2-1	.266	.385	.474	.859	6	.950
1994—	Cleveland (A.L.)	3B	98	321	58	86	20	1	20	52	46	84	0	11	3-3	.268	.359	.523	.882	15	.940
1995—	Cleveland (A.L.)	3B-DH	137	452	92	142	29	3	25	73	97	113	5	8	4-3	.314	.438	.558	.996	16	.948
1996—	Cleveland (A.L.)	3B-DH	151	505	122	157	28	5	38	116	123	141	6	13	2-2	.311	.450	.612	1.062	17	.953
1997—	Cleveland (A.L.)	1B	147	496	104	142	25	0	40	102	* 120	146	3	9	1-1	.286	.423	.579	1.001	10	.993
1998—	Cleveland (A.L.)	1B-DH	123	440	89	129	34	2	30	85	89	141	4	7	1-0	.293	.413	.584	.998	10	.991
1999—	Cleveland (A.L.)	1B-DH	146	494	101	137	27	2	33	108	* 127	* 171	4	6	0-0	.277	.426	.540	.967	6	.994
2000—	Cleveland (A.L.)	1B-DH	158	557	106	150	33	1	37	106	118	171	4	8	1-0	.269	.398	.531	.929	5	.995
2001—	Cleveland (A.L.)	1B-DH	156	526	101	153	26	1	49	124	111	* 185	4	9	0-1	.291	.416	.624	1.040	10	.992
2002—	Cleveland (A.L.)	1B-DH	147	480	101	146	19	2	52	118	* 122	139	5	5	1-2	.304	.445	* .677	1.122	10	.991
2003—	Philadelphia (N.L.)	1B-DH	159	578	111	154	30	3	* 47	131	111	* 182	4	5	0-3	.266	.385	.573	.958	5	.997
2004—	Philadelphia (N.L.)	1B-DH	143	508	97	139	28	1	42	105	104	144	2	10	0-2	.274	.396	.581	.977	7	.994
2005—	Philadelphia (N.L.)	1B-DH	59	193	26	40	7	0	7	30	45	59	2	5	0-0	.207	.360	.352	.712	0	1.000
—	Clearwater (FSL)		5	12	2	4	0	0	1	3	6	1	0	0	0-0	.333	.556	.583	1.139	0	...
American League totals (12 years)			1377	4640	917	1332	259	20	334	927	997	1377	42	86	18-14	.287	.414	.567	.982	124	.985
National League totals (3 years)			361	1279	234	333	65	4	96	266	260	385	8	20	0-5	.260	.386	.543	.928	12	.996
Major League totals (15 years)			1738	5919	1151	1665	324	24	430	1193	1257	1762	50	106	18-19	.281	.408	.562	.970	136	.988

DIVISION SERIES RECORD

Year	Team (League)	Pos.	G	AB	R	H	2B	3B	HR	RBI	BB	SO	HBP	GDP	SB-CS	Avg.	OBP	SLG	OPS	E	Avg.
1995—	Cleveland (A.L.)	3B	3	13	1	2	0	0	1	3	1	6	0	0	0-0	.154	.214	.385	.599	0	1.000
1996—	Cleveland (A.L.)	3B	4	10	1	3	0	0	0	1	1	5	1	0	0-0	.300	.417	.300	.717	0	1.000
1997—	Cleveland (A.L.)	1B	4	15	1	3	0	0	0	1	0	5	0	0	0-0	.200	.200	.200	.400	0	1.000
1998—	Cleveland (A.L.)	1B-DH	4	15	2	2	0	0	2	2	2	5	0	0	0-0	.133	.235	.533	.769	0	1.000
1999—	Cleveland (A.L.)	1B	5	17	7	6	0	0	4	10	4	5	0	0	0-0	.353	.476	1.059	1.535	0	1.000
2001—	Cleveland (A.L.)	1B	5	19	2	3	0	0	1	1	2	8	0	0	0-0	.158	.238	.316	.554	0	1.000
Division series totals (6 years)			25	89	14	19	0	0	8	17	10	34	1	0	0-0	.213	.300	.483	.783	0	1.000

CHAMPIONSHIP SERIES RECORD

Year	Team (League)	Pos.	G	AB	R	H	2B	3B	HR	RBI	BB	SO	HBP	GDP	SB-CS	Avg.	OBP	SLG	OPS	E	Avg.
1995—	Cleveland (A.L.)	3B	5	15	2	4	0	0	2	5	2	3	0	1	0-0	.267	.353	.667	1.020	1	.857
1997—	Cleveland (A.L.)	1B	6	14	3	1	0	0	0	5	4	0	0	0	0-0	.071	.316	.071	.387	0	1.000
1998—	Cleveland (A.L.)	1B-DH	6	23	4	7	0	0	4	8	1	8	1	0	0-0	.304	.360	.826	1.186	0	1.000
Champ. series totals (3 years)			17	52	9	12	0	0	6	13	8	15	1	1	0-0	.231	.344	.577	.921	1	.989

WORLD SERIES RECORD

Year	Team (League)	Pos.	G	AB	R	H	2B	3B	HR	RBI	BB	SO	HBP	GDP	SB-CS	Avg.	OBP	SLG	OPS	E	Avg.
1995—	Cleveland (A.L.)	3B	6	19	1	4	1	0	1	2	2	5	0	0	0-0	.211	.286	.421	.707	1	.889
1997—	Cleveland (A.L.)	1B	7	28	8	8	0	1	2	4	5	7	0	2	0-0	.286	.394	.571	.965	1	.984
World series totals (2 years)			13	47	9	12	1	1	3	6	7	12	0	2	0-0	.255	.352	.511	.862	2	.972

ALL-STAR GAME RECORD

	G	AB	R	H	2B	3B	HR	RBI	BB	SO	HBP	GDP	SB-CS	Avg.	OBP	SLG	OPS	E	Avg.
All-Star Game totals (4 years)	4	7	2	1	0	0	0	1	3	2	0	0	0-0	.143	.400	.143	.543	0	1.000

THOMPSON, BRAD   P

PERSONAL: Born January 31, 1982, in Las Vegas. ... 6-1/190. ... Throws right, bats right. ... Full name: Bradley Joseph Thompson. ... High school: Cimarron-Memorial (Las Vegas). ... Junior college: Dixie State (Utah).

TRANSACTIONS/CAREER NOTES: Selected by St. Louis Cardinals organization in 16th round of 2002 free-agent draft.

CAREER HITTING: 1-for-6 (.167), 0 R, 0 2B, 0 3B, 0 HR, 0 RBI.

BRAD THOMPSON'S PITCHING ZONE

.167	.000	.444
.222	.333	.306
.158	.182	.174

LEFTY-RIGHTY SPLITS

vs.	Avg.	AB	H	2B	3B	HR	RBI	BB	SO	OBP	Slg.
L	.224	76	17	2	0	3	7	4	6	.263	.368
R	.228	127	29	5	1	2	7	11	23	.310	.331

Year	Team (League)	W	L	Pct.	ERA	WHIP	G	GS	CG	ShO	Hld.	Sv.-Opp.	IP	H	R	ER	HR	BB-IBB	SO	Avg.
2003— Peoria (Midw.)	5	3	.625	2.91	1.23	30	4	0	0	...	0-...	65.0	70	23	21	2	10-2	43	.273
— Palm Beach (FSL)	1	0	1.000	0.00	0.50	2	1	0	0	...	0-...	6.0	3	0	0	0	0-0	4	.158
2004— Tennessee (Sou.)	8	2	.800	2.36	0.93	13	12	2	2	...	0-...	72.1	56	19	19	6	11-0	57	.218
— Memphis (PCL)	1	0	1.000	5.52	1.57	3	3	0	0	...	0-...	14.2	20	10	9	3	3-0	10	.333
2005— Memphis (PCL)	2	1	.667	3.29	1.39	9	0	0	0	1	0-1	13.2	12	5	5	1	7-5	11	.240
— St. Louis (N.L.)	4	0	1.000	2.95	1.11	40	0	0	0	7	1-1	55.0	46	22	18	5	15-2	29	.227
Major League totals (1 year)	4	0	1.000	2.95	1.11	40	0	0	0	7	1-1	55.0	46	22	18	5	15-2	29	.227

DIVISION SERIES RECORD

Year	Team (League)	W	L	Pct.	ERA	WHIP	G	GS	CG	ShO	Hld.	Sv.-Opp.	IP	H	R	ER	HR	BB-IBB	SO	Avg.
2005— St. Louis (N.L.)	0	0	...	13.50	2.25	2	0	0	0	0	0-...	1.1	3	2	2	1	0-0	1	.500

CHAMPIONSHIP SERIES RECORD

Year	Team (League)	W	L	Pct.	ERA	WHIP	G	GS	CG	ShO	Hld.	Sv.-Opp.	IP	H	R	ER	HR	BB-IBB	SO	Avg.
2005— St. Louis (N.L.)	0	0	...	0.00	2.00	2	0	0	0	0	0-...	1.0	2	0	0	0	0-0	0	.400

THOMPSON, DEREK — P

PERSONAL: Born January 8, 1981, in Tampa. ... 6-2/180. ... Throws left, bats left. ... Full name: Derek R. Thompson. ... High school: Land O' Lakes (Fla.). .

TRANSACTIONS/CAREER NOTES: Selected by Cleveland Indians organization in supplemental round ("sandwich pick between first and second rounds, 37th pick overall) of 2000 free-agent draft; pick received as part of compensation for Philadelphia Phillies signing Type A free agent Mike Jackson. ... Selected by Chicago Cubs from Indians organization in Rule 5 major league draft (December 16, 2002). ... Traded by Cubs to Los Angeles Dodgers for cash (December 16, 2002). ... On disabled list (March 29, 2003-entire season).

CAREER HITTING: 0-for-4 (.000), 0 R, 0 2B, 0 3B, 0 HR, 0 RBI.

DEREK THOMPSON'S PITCHING ZONE

1.000	.333	...
.333	.250	.143
.286	.500	.000

LEFTY-RIGHTY SPLITS

vs.	Avg.	AB	H	2B	3B	HR	RBI	BB	SO	OBP	Slg.
L	.231	13	3	1	0	0	4	4	3	.412	.308
R	.265	49	13	1	0	0	6	6	10	.339	.286

Year	Team (League)	W	L	Pct.	ERA	WHIP	G	GS	CG	ShO	Hld.	Sv.-Opp.	IP	H	R	ER	HR	BB-IBB	SO	Avg.
2000— Burlington (Appal.)	0	4	.000	5.82	1.48	12	12	0	0	...	0-...	43.1	50	38	28	2	14-0	40	.273
2001— Columbus (S. Atl.)	0	2	.000	9.75	1.58	2	2	0	0	...	0-...	12.0	16	13	13	2	3-0	5	.320
2002— Columbus (S. Atl.)	3	4	.429	3.42	1.33	14	14	0	0	...	0-...	73.2	71	39	28	3	27-0	50	.253
— Kinston (Carol.)	2	3	.400	3.87	1.40	13	13	0	0	...	0-...	74.1	72	36	32	1	32-1	41	.259
2003—				Did not play.															
2004— Jacksonville (Sou.)	5	7	.417	3.72	1.54	22	22	0	0	...	0-...	118.2	132	53	49	3	51-2	100	.293
2005— Los Angeles (N.L.)	0	0	...	3.50	1.44	4	3	0	0	...	0-0	18.0	16	7	7	0	10-1	13	.258
— Jacksonville (Sou.)	0	2	.000	3.89	1.54	8	8	0	0	...	0-...	41.2	45	20	18	3	19-0	43	.283
— Las Vegas (PCL)	1	2	.333	3.43	1.52	4	3	0	0	...	0-...	21.0	21	11	8	1	11-0	17	.273
Major League totals (1 year)	0	0	...	3.50	1.44	4	3	0	0	...	0-0	18.0	16	7	7	0	10-1	13	.258

THOMPSON, JUSTIN — P

PERSONAL: Born March 8, 1973, in San Antonio. ... 6-4/215. ... Throws left, bats left. ... Full name: Justin Willard Thompson. ... High school: Klein Oak (Spring, Texas).

TRANSACTIONS/CAREER NOTES: Selected by Detroit Tigers organization in supplemental round ("sandwich pick" between first and second round, 32nd pick overall) of 1991 free-agent draft; pick received as part of compensation for Minnesota Twins signing Type A free-agent P Jack Morris. ... On disabled list (April 8, 1994-entire season). ... On disabled list (June 3-August 17, 1996); included rehabilitation assignments to Fayetteville, Visalia and Toledo. ... On disabled list (July 6-21, 1997). ... On disabled list (August 16, 1999-remainder of season). ... Traded by Tigers with Ps Francisco Cordero and Alan Webb, OF Gabe Kapler, C Bill Haselman and 2B Frank Catalanotto to Texas Rangers for OF Juan Gonzalez, P Danny Patterson and C Gregg Zaun (November 2, 1999). ... On disabled list (April 1, 2000-entire season); included rehabilitation assignments to Charlotte, Tulsa and Oklahoma. ... On disabled list (March 28, 2001-entire season).

CAREER HITTING: 1-for-14 (.071), 1 R, 0 2B, 0 3B, 0 HR, 0 RBI.

LEFTY-RIGHTY SPLITS

vs.	Avg.	AB	H	2B	3B	HR	RBI	BB	SO	OBP	Slg.
L	.400	5	2	0	0	1	4	0	0	.400	1.000
R	.500	4	2	0	0	1	3	0	1	.500	1.250

Year	Team (League)	W	L	Pct.	ERA	WHIP	G	GS	CG	ShO	Hld.	Sv.-Opp.	IP	H	R	ER	HR	BB-IBB	SO	Avg.
1991— Bristol (Appal.)	2	5	.286	3.60	1.38	10	10	0	0	...	0-...	50.0	45	29	20	3	24-1	60	.238
1992— Fayetteville (SAL)	4	4	.500	2.18	1.25	20	19	0	0	...	0-...	95.0	79	32	23	6	40-0	88	.229
1993— Lakeland (Fla. St.)	4	4	.500	3.56	1.46	11	11	0	0	...	0-...	55.2	65	25	22	1	16-0	46	.294
— London (East.)	3	6	.333	4.09	1.59	14	14	1	0	...	0-...	83.2	96	51	38	9	37-0	72	.288
1994— Trenton (East.)				Did not play.															
1995— Lakeland (Fla. St.)	2	1	.667	4.88	1.58	6	6	0	0	...	0-...	24.0	30	13	13	1	8-0	20	.319
— Jacksonville (Sou.)	6	7	.462	3.73	1.20	18	18	3	0	...	0-...	123.0	110	55	51	7	38-2	98	.242
1996— Toledo (Int'l)	6	3	.667	3.42	1.19	13	13	3	1	...	0-...	84.1	74	36	32	2	26-0	69	.240
— Detroit (A.L.)	1	6	.143	4.58	1.58	11	11	0	0	...	0-...	59.0	62	35	30	7	31-...	44	.267
— Fayetteville (SAL)	0	0	...	3.00	0.33	1	1	0	0	...	0-...	3.0	1	1	1	0	0-0	5	.100
— Visalia (Calif.)	0	0	...	0.00	1.33	1	1	0	0	...	0-...	3.0	2	0	0	0	2-0	7	.182
1997— Detroit (A.L.)	15	11	.577	3.02	1.14	32	32	4	0	...	0-...	223.1	188	82	75	20	66-...	151	.233
1998— Detroit (A.L.)	11	15	.423	4.05	1.38	34	34	5	0	...	0-...	222.0	227	114	100	20	79-...	149	.267
1999— Detroit (A.L.)	9	11	.450	5.11	1.48	24	24	0	0	...	0-...	142.2	152	85	81	24	59-...	83	.270
2000— Charlotte (Fla. St.)	0	0	...	2.08	1.38	1	1	0	0	...	0-...	4.1	3	1	1	0	3-0	2	.214
— Tulsa (Texas)	1	0	1.000	4.76	1.59	1	1	0	0	...	0-...	5.2	8	3	3	1	1-0	4	.333
— Oklahoma (PCL)	0	0	...	11.12	2.47	1	1	0	0	...	0-...	5.2	10	8	7	0	4-0	4	.400
2001— Texas (A.L.)				Did not play.															
2002— GC Rangers (GCL)	0	0	...	3.00	1.33	7	7	0	0	...	0-...	15.0	19	6	5	0	1-0	11	.311
2003— Spokane (N'west)	2	0	1.000	1.24	0.79	23	0	0	0	...	0-...	29.0	15	5	4	0	8-0	21	.153
2004— Frisco (Texas)	3	2	.600	2.61	1.21	23	0	0	0	...	0-...	38.0	35	19	11	3	11-1	26	.236
2005— Frisco (Texas)	2	0	1.000	2.84	1.26	12	0	0	0	2	2-3	12.2	14	5	4	1	2-0	11	.269
— Texas (A.L.)	0	0	...	21.60	2.40	2	0	0	0	...	0-0	1.2	4	4	4	1	1-0	1	.444
— Oklahoma (PCL)	2	2	.500	4.70	1.23	25	1	0	0	...	0-0	44.0	47	24	23	3	7-3	29	.278
Major League totals (5 years)	36	43	.456	4.02	1.34	103	101	9	0	...	0-0	648.2	633	320	290	73	235-0	428	1.122

THOMSON, JOHN — P

PERSONAL: Born October 1, 1973, in Vicksburg, Miss. ... 6-3/220. ... Throws right, bats right. ... Full name: John Carl Thomson. ... Name pronounced: TOM-son. ... High school: Sulphur (La.). ... Junior college: Blinn (Texas).

TRANSACTIONS/CAREER NOTES: Selected by Colorado Rockies organization in seventh round of 1993 free-agent draft. ... On disabled list (June 16-July 26, 1998); included rehabilitation assignment to Asheville. ... On disabled list (May 19-July 19, 1999); included rehabilitation assignment to Salem. ... On disabled list (March 23, 2000-entire season); included rehabilitation assignments to AZL Rockies and Portland. ... On disabled list (March 23-May 12 and May 26-August 2, 2001); included rehabilitation assignments to Colorado Springs. ... Traded by Rockies with OF Mark Little to New York Mets for OFs Jay Payton and Robert Stratton and P Mark Corey (July 31, 2002). ... Signed as a free agent by Texas Rangers (January 3, 2002). ... Signed as a free agent by Atlanta Braves (December 10, 2003). ... On disabled list (May 17-August 13, 2005); included rehabilitation assignments to Richmond, Mississippi and Rome.
CAREER HITTING: 55-for-288 (.191), 19 R, 4 2B, 1 3B, 0 HR, 18 RBI.

SCOUTING REPORT

Throws: He has an 88-93 mph fastball, a cut fastball, a curveball and a changeup. *Tendencies:* Thomson primarily is a sinkerballer who's starting to throw his cutter with success. Curveball has good rotation. Is not overpowering. Can go up the ladder late in the count for a strikeout. Has very good arm speed and motion on a curveball that has a tight spin. Has very good command. *Outlook:* Thomson has good enough stuff to pitch in the middle of the Braves' rotation, but he also has had finger problems each of the past two seasons and could experience them again. **Grade 6.8**

JOHN THOMSON'S PITCHING ZONE

.421	.391	.320
.338	.415	.280
.232	.280	.172

LEFTY-RIGHTY SPLITS

vs.	Avg.	AB	H	2B	3B	HR	RBI	BB	SO	OBP	Slg.
L	.276	196	54	8	2	4	30	19	28	.341	.398
R	.292	195	57	17	1	2	18	9	33	.322	.421

Year—Team (League)	W	L	Pct.	ERA	WHIP	G	GS	CG	ShO	Hld.	Sv.-Opp.	IP	H	R	ER	HR	BB-IBB	SO	Avg.
1993— Ariz. Rockies (Ariz.)	3	5	.375	4.62	1.46	11	11	0	0	...	0-...	50.2	43	40	26	0	31-0	36	.225
1994—Asheville (S. Atl.)	6	6	.500	2.85	1.17	19	15	1	1	...	0-...	88.1	70	34	28	3	33-1	79	.219
—Central Valley (Caifl.)	3	1	.750	3.28	1.24	9	8	0	0	...	0-...	49.1	43	20	18	0	18-1	41	.239
1995— New Haven (East.)	7	8	.467	4.18	1.43	26	24	0	0	...	0-...	131.1	132	69	61	8	56-0	82	.261
1996— New Haven (East.)	9	4	.692	2.86	1.12	16	16	1	0	...	0-...	97.2	82	35	31	8	27-1	86	.230
—Colo. Springs (PCL)	4	7	.364	5.04	1.46	11	11	0	0	...	0-...	69.2	76	45	39	6	26-2	62	.280
1997— Colo. Springs (PCL)	4	2	.667	3.43	1.19	7	7	0	0	...	0-...	42.0	36	18	16	4	14-1	49	.235
—Colorado (N.L.)	7	9	.438	4.71	1.47	27	27	2	1	0	0-0	166.1	193	94	87	15	51-0	106	.296
1998— Colorado (N.L.)	8	11	.421	4.81	1.39	26	26	2	0	0	0-0	161.0	174	86	86	21	49-0	106	.282
—Asheville (S. Atl.)	1	0	1.000	0.00	0.67	2	2	0	0	0	0-0	9.0	5	1	0	0	1-0	12	.161
1999— Colorado (N.L.)	1	10	.091	8.04	1.93	14	13	1	0	0	0-0	62.2	85	62	56	11	36-1	34	.324
—Colo. Springs (PCL)	0	2	.000	9.45	2.20	5	5	1	0	0	0-0	20.0	36	25	21	3	8-0	19	.414
—Salem (Carol.)	0	1	.000	9.00	2.00	1	1	0	0	0	0-0	2.0	4	2	2	0	0-0	2	.400
2000— Ariz. Rockies (Ariz.)	0	1	.000	13.50	2.25	3	3	0	0	...	0-...	5.1	8	8	8	0	4-0	7	.333
—Portland (N'west)	0	0	...	2.25	1.25	1	1	0	0	...	0-...	4.0	4	1	1	0	1-0	3	.250
2001— Colo. Springs (PCL)	5	3	.625	3.31	1.28	12	12	0	0	0	0-0	68.0	74	29	25	6	13-0	52	.274
—Colorado (N.L.)	4	5	.444	4.04	1.16	14	14	1	1	0	0-0	93.2	84	46	42	15	25-3	68	.239
2002— Colorado (N.L.)	7	8	.467	4.88	1.28	21	21	0	0	0	0-0	127.1	136	77	69	21	27-6	76	.268
—New York (N.L.)	2	6	.250	4.31	1.51	9	9	0	0	0	0-0	54.1	65	39	26	7	17-3	31	.290
2003— Texas (A.L.)	13	14	.481	4.85	1.30	35	35	3	1	0	0-0	217.0	234	125	117	27	49-2	136	.276
2004— Atlanta (N.L.)	14	8	.636	3.72	1.32	33	33	0	0	0	0-0	198.1	210	93	82	20	52-5	133	.276
2005— Rome (S. Atl.)	0	0	...	0.00	0.75	1	1	0	0	0	0-0	4.0	2	0	0	0	1-0	1	.143
—Richmond (Int'l)	0	0	...	4.91	1.64	1	1	0	0	0	0-0	3.2	5	2	2	0	1-0	2	.357
—Mississippi (Sou.)	1	0	1.000	1.50	0.67	1	1	0	0	0	0-0	6.0	4	1	1	0	0-0	4	.190
—Atlanta (N.L.)	4	6	.400	4.47	1.41	17	17	1	0	0	0-0	98.2	111	52	49	6	28-2	61	.284
American League totals (1 year)	13	14	.481	4.85	1.30	35	35	3	1	0	0-0	217.0	234	125	117	27	49-2	136	.276
National League totals (7 years)	47	63	.427	4.65	1.40	161	160	7	2	0	0-0	962.1	1058	549	497	116	285-20	615	.281
Major League totals (8 years)	60	77	.438	4.69	1.38	196	195	10	3	0	0-0	1179.1	1292	674	614	143	334-22	751	.280

DIVISION SERIES RECORD

Year—Team (League)	W	L	Pct.	ERA	WHIP	G	GS	CG	ShO	Hld.	Sv.-Opp.	IP	H	R	ER	HR	BB-IBB	SO	Avg.
2004—Atlanta (N.L.)	0	0	...	0.00	6.00	1	1	0	0	0	0-0	0.1	1	0	0	0	1-0	0	.500
2005—Atlanta (N.L.)	0	0	...	0.00	0.50	1	0	0	0	0	0-0	2.0	0	0	0	0	1-0	3	.000
Division series totals (2 years)	0	0	...	0.00	1.29	2	1	0	0	0	0-0	2.1	1	0	0	0	2-0	3	.125

THORNTON, MATT   P

PERSONAL: Born September 15, 1976, in Three Rivers, Mich. ... 6-6/220. ... Throws left, bats left. ... Full name: Matthew J. Thornton. ... High school: Centreville High (Allendale,Mich.). ... College: Grand Valley State.
TRANSACTIONS/CAREER NOTES: Selected by Detroit Tigers organization in 27th round of 1995 free-agent draft; did not sign. ... Selected by Seattle Mariners organization in first round (22nd pick overall) of 1998 free-agent draft. ... On disabled list (August 15, 2003-remainder of season).
CAREER HITTING: 0-for-0 (.000), 0 R, 0 2B, 0 3B, 0 HR, 0 RBI.

MATT THORNTON'S PITCHING ZONE

.250	.167	.222
.250	.394	.262
.250	.500	.250

LEFTY-RIGHTY SPLITS

vs.	Avg.	AB	H	2B	3B	HR	RBI	BB	SO	OBP	Slg.
L	.262	103	27	2	0	7	21	18	29	.372	.485
R	.235	115	27	3	0	6	19	24	28	.364	.417

Year—Team (League)	W	L	Pct.	ERA	WHIP	G	GS	CG	ShO	Hld.	Sv.-Opp.	IP	H	R	ER	HR	BB-IBB	SO	Avg.
1998—Everett (N'west)	0	0	...	27.00	3.00	2	0	0	0	...	0-...	1.1	1	4	4	0	3-0	0	.200
1999—Wisconsin (Midw.)	0	0	...	4.91	2.18	25	1	0	0	...	1-...	29.1	39	19	16	1	25-0	34	.320
2000—Wisconsin (Midw.)	6	9	.400	4.01	1.61	26	17	0	0	...	0-...	103.1	94	59	46	2	72-1	88	.245
2001—San Bern. (Calif.)	14	7	.667	2.52	1.18	27	27	0	0	...	0-...	157.0	126	56	44	9	60-0	192	.220
2002—San Antonio (Texas)	1	5	.167	3.63	1.31	12	12	0	0	...	0-...	62.0	52	31	25	3	29-0	44	.237
2003—Inland Empire (Calif.)	0	0	...	4.00	1.44	2	2	0	0	...	0-...	9.0	9	4	4	2	4-0	14	.265
—San Antonio (Texas)	3	0	1.000	0.36	0.67	4	4	0	0	...	0-...	25.1	8	3	1	0	9-0	18	.104
—Tacoma (PCL)	0	2	.000	8.00	1.89	2	2	0	0	...	0-...	9.0	14	14	8	2	3-0	5	.359
2004—Tacoma (PCL)	7	5	.583	5.42	1.80	16	15	1	0	...	0-...	83.0	86	58	50	4	63-1	74	.273
—Seattle (A.L.)	1	2	.333	4.13	1.68	19	1	0	0	...	0-0	32.2	30	15	15	2	25-1	30	.250

Year Team (League)	W	L	Pct.	ERA	WHIP	G	GS	CG	ShO	Hld.	Sv.-Opp.	IP	H	R	ER	HR	BB-IBB	SO	Avg.
2005— Seattle (A.L.)	0	4	.000	5.21	1.68	55	0	0	0	5	0-1	57.0	54	33	33	13	42-2	57	.248
Major League totals (2 years)	1	6	.143	4.82	1.68	74	1	0	0	5	0-1	89.2	84	48	48	15	67-3	87	.249

TIFFEE, TERRY — 3B

PERSONAL: Born April 21, 1979, in North Little Rock, Ark. ... 6-3/210. ... Bats both, throws right. ... Full name: Terry R. Tiffee. ... High school: Sylvan Hills (Sherwood, Ark.). ... Junior college: Pratt (Kan.) Community College.

TRANSACTIONS/CAREER NOTES: Selected by Minnesota Twins organization in 26th round of 1999 free-agent draft.

2005 GAMES PLAYED BY POSITION (MLB): 3B—24, 1B—13, DH—10.

SCOUTING REPORT Tiffee's bat probably isn't good enough for him to play at this level. Has a long swing and poor bat speed. Is a better low-ball hitter from the left side but has a lot of holes from both sides. Doesn't handle breaking balls well. Is strong and has some power but doesn't run well. Has limited range and poor agility. Has good hands and plus arm strength. *Grade 5.0*

TERRY TIFFEE'S HITTING ZONE

.250	.200	.000
.294	.200	.320
.167	.111	.133

LEFTY-RIGHTY SPLITS

vs.	Avg.	AB	H	2B	3B	HR	RBI	BB	SO	OBP	Slg.
L	.194	36	7	3	0	0	0	5	3	.293	.278
R	.211	114	24	5	1	1	15	3	12	.229	.298

Year Team (League)	Pos.	G	AB	R	H	2B	3B	HR	RBI	BB	SO	HBP	GDP	SB-CS	Avg.	OBP	SLG	OPS	FIELDING E	FIELDING Avg.
2000— Quad City (Midw.)	3B-1B	129	493	59	125	25	0	7	60	29	73	0	14	2-0	.254	.292	.347	.639	31	.872
2001— Quad City (Midw.)	3B-1B	128	495	65	153	32	1	11	86	32	48	1	13	3-1	.309	.347	.444	.791	30	.942
2002— Fort Myers (Fla. St.)	1B-3B	126	473	47	133	31	0	8	64	25	49	2	12	0-3	.281	.316	.397	.714	14	.982
2003— New Britain (East.)	3B-1B	139	530	77	167	31	3	14	93	31	49	2	13	4-1	.315	.351	.464	.815	21	.951
2004— Rochester (Int'l) 3B-1B-DH		82	316	42	97	26	3	12	68	21	26	4	9	0-0	.307	.357	.522	.871	14	.942
— Minnesota (A.L.) 3B-1B-DH		17	44	7	12	4	0	2	8	3	3	1	2	0-0	.273	.333	.500	.833	1	.968
2005— Rochester (Int'l) 3B-1B-DH		58	229	33	61	11	1	10	39	15	24	3	9	0-1	.266	.313	.454	.768	7	.965
— Minnesota (A.L.) 3B-1B-DH		54	150	9	31	8	1	1	15	8	15	0	10	1-0	.207	.245	.293	.539	6	.962
Major League totals (2 years)		71	194	16	43	12	1	3	23	11	18	1	12	1-0	.222	.266	.340	.606	7	.963

T — TIMLIN, MIKE — P

PERSONAL: Born March 10, 1966, in Midland, Texas. ... 6-4/210. ... Throws right, bats right. ... Full name: Michael August Timlin. ... Name pronounced: TIM-lin. ... High school: Midland (Texas). ... College: Southwestern (Georgetown, Texas).

TRANSACTIONS/CAREER NOTES: Selected by Toronto Blue Jays organization in fifth round of 1987 free-agent draft. ... On disabled list (August 2-17, 1991). ... On disabled list (March 27-June 12, 1992); included rehabilitation assignments to Dunedin and Syracuse. ... On disabled list (May 25-June 9, 1994). ... On disabled list (June 22-August 18, 1995); included rehabilitation assignment to Syracuse. ... Traded by Blue Jays with P Paul Spoljaric to Seattle Mariners for OF Jose Cruz (July 31, 1997). ... Signed as a free agent by Baltimore Orioles (November 16, 1998). ... Traded by Orioles with cash to St. Louis Cardinals for 1B Chris Richard and P Mark Nussbeck (July 29, 2000). ... On disabled list (July 26-August 17, 2001). ... Traded by Cardinals with IF/OF Placido Polanco and P Bud Smith to Philadelphia Phillies for 3B Scott Rolen and P Doug Nickle (July 29, 2002). ... Signed as a free agent by Boston Red Sox (December 18, 2002).

CAREER HITTING: 0-for-7 (.000), 0 R, 0 2B, 0 3B, 0 HR, 0 RBI.

SCOUTING REPORT **Throws:** This battle-tested veteran throws a fastball that ranges from 92-95 mph and a power slider at 90. *Tendencies:* He'll cut his fastball and run it to both left-handers and righthanders. Slider is more like a cutter. Has shown a split-finger fastball on occasion but relies on his fastball. Is durable, reliable and remarkably resilient. *Outlook:* Timlin will be a key figure for the Red Sox's revamped bullpen in 2006. Has never been able to close but is one of the better setup men in the league. *Grade 8*

MIKE TIMLIN'S PITCHING ZONE

.125	.375	.211
.308	.182	.241
.375	.538	.524

LEFTY-RIGHTY SPLITS

vs.	Avg.	AB	H	2B	3B	HR	RBI	BB	SO	OBP	Slg.
L	.299	144	43	13	0	0	14	12	28	.348	.389
R	.257	167	43	11	2	2	24	8	31	.293	.383

Year Team (League)	W	L	Pct.	ERA	WHIP	G	GS	CG	ShO	Hld.	Sv.-Opp.	IP	H	R	ER	HR	BB-IBB	SO	Avg.
1987— Medicine Hat (Pio.)	4	8	.333	5.14	1.39	13	12	2	0	...	0-...	75.1	79	50	43	4	26-0	66	.271
1988— Myrtle Beach (SAL)	10	6	.625	2.86	1.30	35	22	0	0	...	0-...	151.0	119	68	48	4	77-2	106	.215
1989— Dunedin (Fla. St.)	5	8	.385	3.25	1.42	33	7	1	0	...	7-...	88.2	90	44	32	2	36-2	64	.271
1990— Dunedin (Fla. St.)	7	2	.778	1.43	1.03	42	0	0	0	...	22-...	50.1	36	11	8	0	16-2	46	.197
— Knoxville (Southern)	1	2	.333	1.73	1.04	17	0	0	0	...	8-...	26.0	20	6	5	0	7-1	21	.206
1991— Toronto (A.L.)	11	6	.647	3.16	1.33	63	3	0	0	9	3-8	108.1	94	43	38	6	50-11	85	.233
1992— Dunedin (Fla. St.)	0	0	...	0.90	1.10	6	1	0	0	...	1-...	10.0	9	2	1	0	2-0	7	.243
— Syracuse (Int'l)	0	1	.000	8.74	1.76	7	1	0	0	...	3-...	11.1	15	11	11	3	5-1	7	.333
— Toronto (A.L.)	0	2	.000	4.12	1.49	26	0	0	0	1	1-1	43.2	45	23	20	0	20-5	35	.277
1993— Toronto (A.L.)	4	2	.667	4.69	1.62	54	0	0	0	9	1-4	55.2	63	32	29	7	27-3	49	.284
— Dunedin (Fla. St.)	0	0	...	1.00	0.44	4	0	0	0	...	1-...	9.0	4	1	1	0	0-0	8	.133
1994— Toronto (A.L.)	0	1	.000	5.18	1.53	34	0	0	0	5	2-4	40.0	41	25	23	5	20-0	38	.264
1995— Toronto (A.L.)	4	3	.571	2.14	1.31	31	0	0	0	4	5-9	42.0	38	13	10	1	17-5	36	.242
— Syracuse (Int'l)	1	1	.500	1.04	0.98	8	0	0	0	...	0-...	17.1	13	6	2	2	4-0	13	.197
1996— Toronto (A.L.)	1	6	.143	3.65	1.15	59	0	0	0	2	31-38	56.2	47	25	23	4	18-4	52	.229
1997— Toronto (A.L.)	3	2	.600	2.87	1.19	38	0	0	0	2	9-13	47.0	41	17	15	6	15-4	36	.243
— Seattle (A.L.)	3	2	.600	3.86	1.29	26	0	0	0	7	1-5	25.2	28	13	11	2	5-1	9	.265
1998— Seattle (A.L.)	3	3	.500	2.95	1.18	70	0	0	0	6	19-24	79.1	78	26	26	5	16-2	60	.264
1999— Baltimore (A.L.)	3	9	.250	3.57	1.17	62	0	0	0	4	27-36	63.0	51	30	25	9	23-3	50	.221
2000— Baltimore (A.L.)	2	3	.400	4.89	1.49	37	0	0	0	1	11-15	35.0	37	22	19	6	15-3	26	.265
— St. Louis (N.L.)	3	1	.750	3.34	1.69	25	0	0	0	5	1-3	29.2	30	11	11	2	20-3	26	.265

Year	Team (League)	W	L	Pct.	ERA	WHIP	G	GS	CG	ShO	Hld.	Sv.-Opp.	IP	H	R	ER	HR	BB-IBB	SO	Avg.
2001—	St. Louis (N.L.)	4	5	.444	4.09	1.33	67	0	0	0	12	3-7	72.2	78	35	33	6	19-4	47	.277
2002—	St. Louis (N.L.)	1	3	.250	2.51	0.90	42	1	0	0	12	0-2	61.0	48	19	17	9	7-2	35	.215
—	Philadelphia (N.L.)	3	3	.500	3.79	0.95	30	0	0	0	8	0-2	35.2	27	16	15	6	7-0	15	.206
2003—	Boston (A.L.)	6	4	.600	3.55	1.03	72	0	0	0	17	2-6	83.2	77	37	33	11	9-3	65	.239
2004—	Boston (A.L.)	5	4	.556	4.13	1.23	76	0	0	0	20	1-4	76.1	75	35	35	8	19-3	56	.257
2005—	Boston (A.L.)	7	3	.700	2.24	1.32	* 81	0	0	0	24	13-20	80.1	86	23	20	2	20-5	59	.277
American League totals (13 years)		52	50	.510	3.52	1.28	729	3	0	0	107	126-187	836.2	801	364	327	72	274-52	656	.253
National League totals (3 years)		11	12	.478	3.44	1.19	164	1	0	0	37	4-14	199.0	183	81	76	23	53-9	123	.244
Major League totals (15 years)		63	62	.504	3.50	1.27	893	4	0	0	144	130-201	1035.2	984	445	403	95	327-61	779	.251

DIVISION SERIES RECORD

Year	Team (League)	W	L	Pct.	ERA	WHIP	G	GS	CG	ShO	Hld.	Sv.-Opp.	IP	H	R	ER	HR	BB-IBB	SO	Avg.
1997—	Seattle (A.L.)	0	0	...	54.00	6.00	1	0	0	0	0	0-0	0.2	3	4	4	1	1-1	1	.600
2000—	St. Louis (N.L.)	0	0	...	10.80	3.60	2	0	0	0	1	0-0	1.2	5	2	2	1	1-0	2	.500
2001—	St. Louis (N.L.)	0	0	...	0.00	0.75	1	0	0	0	0	0-0	1.1	1	0	0	0	0-0	1	.200
2003—	Boston (A.L.)	0	0	...	0.00	0.00	3	0	0	0	2	0-0	4.1	0	0	0	0	0-0	5	.000
2004—	Boston (A.L.)	0	0	...	9.00	1.33	3	0	0	0	1	0-0	3.0	3	3	3	1	1-0	5	.250
2005—	Boston (A.L.)	0	0	...	9.00	1.00	1	0	0	0	0	0-0	1.0	1	1	1	0	0-0	0	.333
Division series totals (6 years)		0	0	...	7.50	1.33	11	0	0	0	4	0-0	12.0	13	10	10	3	3-1	14	.271

CHAMPIONSHIP SERIES RECORD

Year	Team (League)	W	L	Pct.	ERA	WHIP	G	GS	CG	ShO	Hld.	Sv.-Opp.	IP	H	R	ER	HR	BB-IBB	SO	Avg.
1991—	Toronto (A.L.)	0	1	.000	3.18	1.24	4	0	0	0	0	0-1	5.2	5	4	2	1	2-1	5	.208
1992—	Toronto (A.L.)	0	0	...	6.75	3.00	2	0	0	0	1	0-0	1.1	4	1	1	0	0-0	1	.500
1993—	Toronto (A.L.)	0	0	...	3.86	1.29	1	0	0	0	0	0-0	2.1	3	1	1	0	0-0	2	.300
2000—	St. Louis (N.L.)	0	1	.000	0.00	0.90	3	0	0	0	0	0-0	3.1	1	3	0	0	2-0	0	.091
2003—	Boston (A.L.)	0	0	...	0.00	0.56	5	0	0	0	3	0-0	5.1	1	0	0	0	2-1	6	.059
2004—	Boston (A.L.)	0	0	...	4.76	2.65	5	0	0	0	0	0-1	5.2	10	3	3	0	5-0	2	.400
Champ. series totals (6 years)		0	2	.000	2.66	1.48	20	0	0	0	4	0-2	23.2	24	12	7	1	11-2	16	.253

WORLD SERIES RECORD

Year	Team (League)	W	L	Pct.	ERA	WHIP	G	GS	CG	ShO	Hld.	Sv.-Opp.	IP	H	R	ER	HR	BB-IBB	SO	Avg.
1992—	Toronto (A.L.)	0	0	...	0.00	0.00	2	0	0	0	1	1-1	1.1	0	0	0	0	0-0	0	.000
1993—	Toronto (A.L.)	0	0	...	0.00	0.86	2	0	0	0	1	0-0	2.1	2	0	0	0	1-0	4	.250
2004—	Boston (A.L.)	0	0	...	6.00	1.00	3	0	0	0	1	0-0	3.0	2	2	2	0	1-0	0	.200
World series totals (3 years)		0	0	...	2.70	0.75	7	0	0	0	1	1-1	6.2	4	2	2	0	1-0	4	.182

TOMKO, BRETT   P

PERSONAL: Born April 7, 1973, in Euclid, Ohio. ... 6-4/215. ... Throws right, bats right. ... Full name: Brett Daniel Tomko. ... Name pronounced: TOM-koh. ... High school: El Dorado (Placentia, Calif.). ... College: Florida Southern.

TRANSACTIONS/CAREER NOTES: Selected by Los Angeles Dodgers organization in 20th round of 1994 free-agent draft; did not sign. ... Selected by Cincinnati Reds organization in second round of 1995 free-agent draft. ... Traded by Reds with OF Mike Cameron, IF Antonio Perez and P Jake Meyer to Seattle Mariners for OF Ken Griffey (February 10, 2000). ... On disabled list (June 7-24, 2000). ... Traded by Mariners with C Tom Lampkin and SS Ramon Vazquez to San Diego Padres for C Ben Davis, P Wascar Serrano and SS Alex Arias (December 11, 2001). ... Traded by Padres to St. Louis Cardinals for P Luther Hackman and a player to be named (December 15, 2002); Padres acquired P Mike Wodnicki to complete deal (December 16, 2002). ... Signed as a free agent by San Francisco Giants (January 12, 2004). ... On disabled list (June 8-24, 2004); included rehabilitation assignment to Fresno.

CAREER HITTING: 68-for-394 (.173), 21 R, 9 2B, 0 3B, 0 HR, 28 RBI.

SCOUTING REPORT *Throws:* As a reliever, Tomko's fastball can hit 97 mph, up from 91-95 as a starter. Throws a slider at 84-87, a curveball and a changeup. *Tendencies:* Tomko always has had an outstanding arm but never has been consistent. Will sling the ball at times. Has overpowering velocity as a setup man with a riding, four-seam fastball. Has improved his curveball and has quick, sharp bite on his slider. Still hasn't developed a dependable changeup. *Outlook:* He has the pitches to be a good starter, but has never fulfilled his potential in that role. Could be better as a reliever because of his velocity. **Grade 7.3**

BRETT TOMKO'S PITCHING ZONE

.224	.233	.167
.301	.478	.179
.333	.357	.282

LEFTY-RIGHTY SPLITS

vs.	Avg.	AB	H	2B	3B	HR	RBI	BB	SO	OBP	Slg.
L	.282	411	116	28	6	12	49	33	53	.340	.467
R	.264	337	89	19	4	8	49	24	61	.316	.415

Year	Team (League)	W	L	Pct.	ERA	WHIP	G	GS	CG	ShO	Hld.	Sv.-Opp.	IP	H	R	ER	HR	BB-IBB	SO	Avg.
1995—	Char., W.Va. (S. Atl.)	4	2	.667	1.84	1.02	9	7	0	0	...	0-...	49.0	41	12	10	1	9-1	46	.228
1996—	Chattanooga (Sou.)	11	7	.611	3.88	1.17	27	27	0	0	...	0-...	157.2	131	73	68	20	54-4	164	.226
1997—	Indianapolis (A.A.)	6	3	.667	2.95	1.02	10	10	0	0	...	0-...	61.0	53	21	20	7	9-0	60	.232
—	Cincinnati (N.L.)	11	7	.611	3.43	1.21	22	19	0	0	0	0-0	126.0	106	50	48	14	47-4	95	.234
1998—	Cincinnati (N.L.)	13	12	.520	4.44	1.24	34	34	1	0	0	0-0	210.2	198	111	104	22	64-3	162	.247
1999—	Cincinnati (N.L.)	5	7	.417	4.92	1.37	33	26	1	0	1	0-0	172.0	175	103	94	31	60-10	132	.263
—	Indianapolis (Int'l)	2	0	1.000	4.97	1.26	2	2	0	0	...	0-...	12.2	15	7	7	1	1-0	9	.288
2000—	Tacoma (PCL)	1	0	1.000	2.84	1.42	2	2	0	0	...	0-...	12.2	13	4	4	1	5-1	8	.271
—	Seattle (A.L.)	7	5	.583	4.68	1.43	32	8	0	0	3	1-2	92.1	92	53	48	12	40-4	59	.264
2001—	Seattle (A.L.)	3	1	.750	5.19	1.64	11	4	0	0	0	0-1	34.2	42	24	20	9	15-2	22	.288
—	Tacoma (PCL)	10	6	.625	4.04	1.17	19	18	3	2	...	0-...	127.0	124	64	57	12	25-1	117	.254
2002—	San Diego (N.L.)	10	10	.500	4.49	1.33	32	32	3	0	0	0-0	204.1	212	107	102	31	60-9	126	.267
2003—	St. Louis (N.L.)	13	9	.591	5.28	1.52	33	32	2	0	0	0-0	202.2	* 252	126	• 119	35	57-2	114	.305
2004—	Fresno (PCL)	0	0	...	5.40	1.20	1	1	0	0	...	0-...	5.0	4	3	3	1	2-0	4	.211
—	San Francisco (N.L.)	11	7	.611	4.04	1.34	32	31	2	1	0	0-0	194.0	196	98	87	19	64-3	108	.260
2005—	San Francisco (N.L.)	8	15	.348	4.48	1.37	33	33	3	0	1	1-1	190.2	205	99	95	20	57-11	114	.274
American League totals (2 years)		10	6	.625	4.82	1.49	43	12	0	0	3	1-3	127.0	134	77	68	21	55-6	81	.271
National League totals (7 years)		71	67	.514	4.49	1.35	219	204	12	1	2	1-1	1300.1	1344	694	649	172	409-42	851	.267
Major League totals (9 years)		81	73	.526	4.52	1.36	262	216	12	1	5	2-4	1427.1	1478	771	717	193	464-48	932	.267

DIVISION SERIES RECORD

Year Team (League)	W	L	Pct.	ERA	WHIP	G	GS	CG	ShO	Hld.	Sv.-Opp.	IP	H	R	ER	HR	BB-IBB	SO	Avg.
2000— Seattle (A.L.)	0	0	...	0.00	0.75	1	0	0	0	0	0-0	2.2	1	0	0	0	1-0	0	.125

CHAMPIONSHIP SERIES RECORD

Year Team (League)	W	L	Pct.	ERA	WHIP	G	GS	CG	ShO	Hld.	Sv.-Opp.	IP	H	R	ER	HR	BB-IBB	SO	Avg.
2000— Seattle (A.L.)	0	0	...	7.20	1.40	2	0	0	0	0	0-0	5.0	3	4	4	0	4-1	4	.176

TORCATO, TONY   OF

PERSONAL: Born October 25, 1979, in Woodland, Calif. ... 6-1/219. ... Bats left, throws right. ... Full name: Anthony Dale Torcato. ... Name pronounced: tor-KAH-to. ... High school: Woodland (Calif.).

TRANSACTIONS/CAREER NOTES: Selected by San Francisco Giants organization in first round (19th pick overall) of 1998 free-agent draft; pick received as part of compensation for Houston Astros signing Type B free-agent P Doug Henry.

2005 GAMES PLAYED BY POSITION (MLB): OF—1.

LEFTY-RIGHTY SPLITS

vs.	Avg.	AB	H	2B	3B	HR	RBI	BB	SO	OBP	Slg.
L	.000	1	0	0	0	0	0	0	1	.000	.000
R	.300	10	3	0	0	0	0	1	1	.364	.300

								BATTING									FIELDING	
Year Team (League)	Pos.	G	AB	R	H	2B	3B	HR	RBI	BB	SO	HBP	GDP	SB-CS	Avg.	OBP	SLG	OPS	E	Avg.
1998— Salem-Keizer (N'west)	3B	59	220	31	64	15	2	3	43	14	38	3	0	4-2	.291	.333	.418	.752	17	.886
1999— Bakersfield (Calif.)	3B	110	422	50	123	25	0	4	58	30	67	3	6	2-1	.291	.338	.379	.717	28	.886
2000— San Jose (Calif.)	3B	119	490	77	159	37	2	7	88	41	62	6	2	19-4	.324	.379	.451	.830	40	.882
— Shreveport (Texas)	3B	2	8	1	4	0	0	0	2	0	1	0	0	0-0	.500	.500	.500	1.000	0	1.000
2001— San Jose (Calif.)	OF	67	258	38	88	21	2	2	47	17	40	4	5	9-3	.341	.381	.461	.842	1	.952
— Shreveport (Texas)	OF	36	147	13	43	9	1	1	23	9	15	4	6	0-1	.293	.344	.388	.731	2	.975
— Fresno (PCL)	OF	35	150	20	48	8	1	2	8	2	20	1	0	0-1	.320	.329	.427	.756	1	.985
2002— Fresno (PCL)	OF	130	490	64	142	23	3	13	64	29	65	2	6	4-6	.290	.330	.429	.758	8	.964
— San Francisco (N.L.)	OF	5	11	0	3	1	0	0	0	0	2	0	0	0-0	.273	.273	.364	.636	0	1.000
2003— Fresno (PCL) 1B-OF-3B	DH	106	423	36	125	18	2	3	48	6	33	2	18	4-0	.296	.304	.369	.672	12	.981
— San Francisco (N.L.)	OF	14	16	0	3	1	0	0	1	0	4	1	0	0-0	.188	.235	.250	.485	1	.833
2004— Fresno (PCL) OF-1B-DH	119	395	39	114	22	0	3	57	11	35	5	8	4-1	.289	.314	.367	.681	2	.993
— San Francisco (N.L.)	13	9	1	5	0	0	0	2	1	0	1	0	0-0	.556	.583	.556	1.139	0	...
2005— San Francisco (N.L.)	OF	11	11	1	3	0	0	0	0	1	2	0	2	0-0	.273	.333	.273	.606	0	1.000
— Fresno (PCL) 1B-OF-DH	105	376	41	101	15	5	10	57	21	43	4	7	3-4	.269	.310	.415	.725	8	.988
Major League totals (4 years)		43	47	2	14	2	0	0	3	2	8	2	2	0-0	.298	.346	.340	.687	1	.889

T

TORREALBA, YORVIT   C

PERSONAL: Born July 19, 1978, in Caracas, Venezuela. ... 5-11/190. ... Bats right, throws right. ... Full name: Yorvit Adolfo Torrealba. ... Name pronounced: yor-VEET tor-ee-ALL-buh. ... High school: Vincente Emilio Sojo (Venezuela).

TRANSACTIONS/CAREER NOTES: Signed as a non-drafted free agent by San Francisco Giants organization (September 14, 1994). ... Traded by Giants with P Jesse Foppert to Seattle Mariners for OF Randy Winn (July 30, 2005).

2005 GAMES PLAYED BY POSITION (MLB): C—68, DH—1.

SCOUTING REPORT He became the Mariners' No. 1 catcher after being traded by the Giants last summer. Is strong but has a long stroke and doesn't appear to make adjustments quickly. Is an overly aggressive fastball hitter who doesn't handle off-speed pitches well. Doesn't have a lot of power. Hits with a hitch that he's slow to get out of. Is a good, aggressive defensive catcher with an above-average arm and quick release. Takes charge of his pitchers. Has good hands and is mobile with above-average range to either side. ***Grade 5.3***

YORVIT TORREALBA'S HITTING ZONE

.250	.250	.556
.318	.200	.368
.125	.500	.250

LEFTY-RIGHTY SPLITS

vs.	Avg.	AB	H	2B	3B	HR	RBI	BB	SO	OBP	Slg.
L	.302	53	16	8	0	1	4	4	8	.351	.509
R	.209	148	31	4	0	2	11	12	42	.278	.277

								BATTING									FIELDING	
Year Team (League)	Pos.	G	AB	R	H	2B	3B	HR	RBI	BB	SO	HBP	GDP	SB-CS	Avg.	OBP	SLG	OPS	E	Avg.
1995— Bellingham (N'west)	C	26	71	2	11	3	0	0	8	2	14	1	1	0-1	.155	.187	.197	.384	5	.973
1996— San Jose (Calif.)	C	2	5	0	0	0	0	0	0	1	1	0	0	0-0	.000	.167	.000	.167	0	1.000
— Burlington (Midw.)	C	1	4	0	0	0	0	0	0	0	1	0	1	0-0	.000	.000	.000	.000	0	1.000
— Bellingham (N'west)	C	48	150	23	40	4	0	1	10	9	27	0	7	4-1	.267	.304	.313	.618	2	.994
1997— Bakersfield (Calif.)	C	119	446	52	122	15	3	4	40	31	58	5	8	4-2	.274	.326	.348	.673	6	.993
1998— Shreveport (Texas)	C	59	196	18	46	7	0	0	13	18	30	4	3	0-5	.235	.311	.270	.581	2	.996
— San Jose (Calif.)	C	21	70	10	20	2	0	0	10	1	4	0	0	2-2	.286	.292	.314	.606	2	.989
— Fresno (PCL)	C	4	11	1	2	1	0	0	1	1	4	0	0	0-0	.182	.250	.273	.523	0	1.000
1999— Shreveport (Texas)	C	65	217	25	53	10	1	4	19	9	34	2	6	0-2	.244	.278	.355	.633	2	.994
— Fresno (PCL)	C	17	63	9	16	2	0	2	10	4	11	2	2	0-1	.254	.319	.381	.700	2	.988
— San Jose (Calif.)	C	19	73	10	23	3	0	2	14	6	15	1	2	0-0	.315	.370	.438	.809	5	.975
2000— Shreveport (Texas)	C	108	398	50	114	21	1	4	32	34	55	6	17	2-3	.286	.350	.374	.724	8	.990
2001— Fresno (PCL)	C	115	394	56	108	23	3	8	36	19	65	4	11	2-3	.274	.313	.409	.721	9	.989
— San Francisco (N.L.)	C	3	4	0	2	0	0	0	0	0	0	0	0	0-0	.500	.500	1.000	1.500	0	1.000
2002— San Francisco (N.L.)	C	53	136	17	38	10	0	2	14	14	20	2	11	0-0	.279	.355	.397	.752	2	.993
2003— San Francisco (N.L.)	C-OF	66	200	22	52	10	2	4	29	14	39	2	3	1-0	.260	.314	.390	.702	1	.997
2004— San Francisco (N.L.)	C	64	172	19	39	7	3	6	23	17	31	2	7	2-0	.227	.302	.407	.709	2	.995
2005— San Francisco (N.L.)	C-DH	34	93	18	21	8	0	1	7	9	25	1	3	1-0	.226	.301	.344	.645	0	1.000
— Seattle (A.L.)	C	42	108	14	26	4	0	2	8	7	25	1	5	0-0	.241	.293	.333	.626	0	1.000
American League totals (1 year)		42	108	14	26	4	0	2	8	7	25	1	5	0-0	.241	.293	.333	.626	0	1.000
National League totals (5 years)		220	605	76	152	35	6	13	75	54	115	7	24	4-0	.251	.318	.393	.712	5	.996
Major League totals (5 years)		262	713	90	178	39	6	15	83	61	140	8	29	4-0	.250	.315	.384	.699	5	.997

DIVISION SERIES RECORD

Year Team (League)	Pos.	G	AB	R	H	2B	3B	HR	RBI	BB	SO	HBP	GDP	SB-CS	Avg.	OBP	SLG	OPS	E	Avg.
2003— San Francisco (N.L.)	C	2	3	0	0	0	0	0	1	0	0	0	0	0-0	.000	.000	.000	.000	1	.909

TORRES, ANDRES — OF

PERSONAL: Born January 26, 1978, in Aguada, Puerto Rico. ... 5-10/190. ... Bats both, throws right. ... Full name: Andres Vungo Torres. ... Junior college: Miami-Dade Community College North.

TRANSACTIONS/CAREER NOTES: Selected by Florida Marlins organization in 23rd round of 1997 free-agent draft; did not sign. ... Selected by Detroit Tigers organization in fourth round of 1998 free-agent draft. ... Signed as a free agent by Chicago White Sox organization (April 24, 2004). ... Signed as a free agent by Texas Rangers organization (November 19, 2004).

2005 GAMES PLAYED BY POSITION (MLB): OF—5.

LEFTY-RIGHTY SPLITS

vs.	Avg.	AB	H	2B	3B	HR	RBI	BB	SO	OBP	Slg.
L	.167	12	2	1	0	0	1	1	3	.214	.250
R	.143	7	1	0	0	0	0	0	3	.143	.143

Year Team (League)	Pos.	G	AB	R	H	2B	3B	HR	RBI	BB	SO	HBP	GDP	SB-CS	Avg.	OBP	SLG	OPS	E	Avg.
1998— Jamestown (NYP)	OF	48	192	28	45	2	6	1	21	25	50	1	1	13-2	.234	.323	.323	.646	5	.944
1999— W. Mich. (Mid.)	OF	117	407	72	96	20	5	2	34	92	116	10	2	39-18	.236	.385	.324	.710	7	.972
2000— Lakeland (Fla. St.)	OF	108	398	82	118	11	11	3	33	63	82	5	10	65-16	.296	.399	.402	.801	6	.979
— Jacksonville (Sou.)	OF	14	54	3	8	0	0	0	5	5	14	0	1	2-0	.148	.220	.148	.368	1	.971
2001— Erie (East.)	OF	64	252	54	74	16	3	1	23	36	50	5	1	19-11	.294	.391	.393	.784	1	.993
2002— Toledo (Int'l)	OF	115	462	80	123	17	8	4	42	53	116	5	3	• 42-12	.266	.345	.364	.709	10	.967
— Detroit (A.L.)	OF	19	70	7	14	1	1	0	3	6	16	1	2	2-2	.200	.266	.243	.509	1	.981
2003— Toledo (Int'l)	OF	70	271	36	69	13	3	2	16	18	61	0	1	27-11	.255	.301	.347	.648	5	.973
— Detroit (A.L.)	OF-DH	59	168	23	37	4	3	1	9	10	35	0	5	5-5	.220	.263	.298	.560	1	.991
2004— Detroit (A.L.)	DH-OF	3	0	1	0	0	0	0	0	0	0	0	0	1-0	...	...	...	...	0	...
— Bristol (Appal.)	DH-OF	6	22	8	8	0	0	1	2	3	4	1	0	5-0	.364	.462	.500	.962	0	1.000
— Charlotte (Int'l)	OF	87	322	49	95	11	4	8	26	35	74	5	3	23-7	.295	.371	.429	.799	6	.975
2005— Oklahoma (PCL)	OF	15	63	12	19	3	1	0	6	6	17	0	0	6-1	.302	.362	.381	.743	4	.900
— Texas (A.L.)	OF	8	19	2	3	1	0	0	1	1	6	0	0	1-0	.158	.190	.211	.401	0	1.000
Major League totals (4 years)		89	257	33	54	6	4	1	13	17	57	1	7	9-7	.210	.258	.276	.534	2	.988

TORRES, SALOMON — P

PERSONAL: Born March 11, 1972, in San Pedro de Macoris, Dominican Republic. ... 5-11/210. ... Throws right, bats right. ... Full name: Salomon Ramirez Torres. ... High school: Centro Academico Rogus (San Pedro de Macoris, Dominican Republic).

TRANSACTIONS/CAREER NOTES: Signed as a non-drafted free agent by San Francisco Giants organization (September 15, 1989). ... Traded by Giants to Seattle Mariners for P Shawn Estes and IF Wilson Delgado (May 21, 1995). ... Claimed on waivers by Montreal Expos (April 18, 1997). ... On voluntarily retired list (August 1, 1997-January 29, 2001). ... Released by Expos (January 29, 2001). ... Signed as a free agent by Pittsburgh Pirates organization (January 8, 2002). ... On disabled list (August 6-29, 2003); included rehabilitation assignment to Nashville (July 19-22, 2004). ... On suspended list (July 19-22, 2004).

CAREER HITTING: 14-for-97 (.144), 5 R, 1 2B, 1 3B, 0 HR, 1 RBI.

SCOUTING REPORT Throws: His fastball tops out at 94 mph. Also has a hard slider and a split-finger fastball. ***Tendencies:*** This versatile reliever has a loose arm and a plus fastball that has good finishing action. Uses it effectively up and down in the zone. Slider is has a big break and can go flat if he throws it with his hand under the ball. Uses the splitter to lefthanded and right handed hitters but is more effective with it against righthanders because of its angle. ***Outlook:*** With Torres' rubber arm and makeup, he can throw every day and work multiple innings. ***Grade 6.4***

SALOMON TORRES' PITCHING ZONE

.200	.214	.056
.143	.302	.299
.269	.143	.320

LEFTY-RIGHTY SPLITS

vs.	Avg.	AB	H	2B	3B	HR	RBI	BB	SO	OBP	Slg.
L	.272	136	37	9	2	1	14	14	27	.346	.390
R	.189	206	39	6	1	6	21	22	28	.276	.316

Year Team (League)	W	L	Pct.	ERA	WHIP	G	GS	CG	ShO	Hld.	Sv.-Opp.	IP	H	R	ER	HR	BB-IBB	SO	Avg.
1990— Dom. Giants (DSL)	11	1	.917	0.50	0.82	13	13	6	0	...	0-...	90.0	44	15	5	...	30-...	101	...
1991— Clinton (Midw.)	16	5	.762	1.41	0.93	28	28	8	3	...	0-...	210.1	148	48	33	4	47-2	214	.195
1992— Shreveport (Texas)	6	10	.375	4.21	1.24	25	25	4	2	...	0-...	162.1	167	93	76	10	34-2	151	.263
1993— Shreveport (Texas)	7	4	.636	2.70	0.95	12	12	2	1	...	0-...	83.1	67	27	25	6	12-0	67	.218
— Phoenix (PCL)	7	4	.636	3.50	1.25	14	14	4	1	...	0-...	105.1	105	43	41	5	27-0	99	.261
— San Francisco (N.L.)	3	5	.375	4.03	1.43	8	8	0	0	0	0-...	44.2	37	21	20	7	27-3	23	.231
1994— San Francisco (N.L.)	2	8	.200	5.44	1.53	16	14	1	0	0	0-...	84.1	95	55	51	10	34-2	42	.292
— Phoenix (PCL)	5	6	.455	4.22	1.47	13	13	0	0	0	0-...	79.0	85	49	37	7	31-0	64	.278
1995— San Francisco (N.L.)	0	1	.000	9.00	2.50	4	1	0	0	0	0-...	8.0	13	8	8	4	7-0	5	.394
— Phoenix (PCL)	0	0	...	0.00	1.00	1	0	0	0	0	0-...	2.0	2	0	0	0	0-0	5	.286
— Tacoma (PCL)	1	1	.500	3.21	1.18	5	4	0	0	0	0-...	28.0	20	10	10	2	13-1	19	.206
— Seattle (A.L.)	3	8	.273	6.00	1.79	16	13	1	0	0	0-...	72.0	87	53	48	12	42-3	45	.291
1996— Tacoma (PCL)	7	10	.412	5.29	1.50	22	21	3	1	...	0-...	134.1	150	87	79	16	52-1	121	.279
— Seattle (A.L.)	3	3	.500	4.59	1.37	10	7	1	1	0	0-...	49.0	44	27	25	5	23-2	36	.242
1997— Seattle (A.L.)	0	0	...	27.00	3.00	2	0	0	0	0	0-...	3.1	7	10	10	0	3-0	0	.412
— Montreal (N.L.)	0	0	...	7.25	1.66	12	0	0	0	0	0-...	22.1	25	19	18	2	12-0	11	.284
— Ottawa (Int'l)	0	0	...	5.40	1.80	2	1	0	0	0	0-...	5.0	7	5	3	0	2-0	2	.318
1998—	Did not play.																		
1999—	Did not play.																		
2000—	Did not play.																		
2001— Samsung (Kor.)	0	2	.000	...	2.00	2	...	...	...	...	0-...	5.0	...	...	...	...	10-...	5	...
2002— Nashville (PCL)	8	5	.615	3.83	1.28	26	24	2	1	...	0-...	162.1	169	78	69	12	39-2	136	.270
— Pittsburgh (N.L.)	2	1	.667	2.70	1.37	5	5	0	0	0	0-0	30.0	28	10	9	2	13-1	12	.257
2003— Nashville (PCL)	1	0	1.000	1.80	0.60	1	1	0	0	0	0-0	5.0	2	1	1	0	1-0	4	.118
— Pittsburgh (N.L.)	7	5	.583	4.76	1.40	41	16	0	0	6	2-3	121.0	128	65	64	19	42-5	84	.276
2004— Pittsburgh (N.L.)	7	7	.500	2.64	1.18	84	0	0	0	30	0-4	92.0	87	33	27	6	22-6	62	.256
2005— Pittsburgh (N.L.)	5	5	.500	2.76	1.18	78	0	0	0	8	3-3	94.2	76	34	29	7	36-7	55	.222
American League totals (3 years)	6	11	.353	6.01	1.66	28	20	2	1	0	0-0	124.1	138	90	83	17	68-5	81	.277

T

Year Team (League)	W	L	Pct.	ERA	WHIP	G	GS	CG	ShO	Hld.	Sv.-Opp.	IP	H	R	ER	HR	BB-IBB	SO	Avg.
National League totals (8 years)	26	32	.448	4.09	1.37	248	44	1	0	44	5-10	497.0	489	245	226	55	193-24	291	.263
Major League totals (9 years)	32	43	.427	4.48	1.43	276	64	3	1	44	5-10	621.1	627	335	309	72	261-29	372	.266

TOWERS, JOSH   P

PERSONAL: Born February 26, 1977, in Port Hueneme, Calif. ... 6-1/188. ... Throws right, bats right. ... Full name: Joshua Eric Towers. ... High school: Hueneme (Oxnard, Calif.). ... Junior college: Oxnard (Calif.).

TRANSACTIONS/CAREER NOTES: Selected by Baltimore Orioles organization in 15th round of 1996 free-agent draft. ... On disabled list (October 1, 2001-remainder of season). ... Signed as a free agent by Toronto Blue Jays organization (November 8, 2002).

CAREER HITTING: 0-for-10 (.000), 0 R, 0 2B, 0 3B, 0 HR, 0 RBI.

SCOUTING REPORT *Throws:* His fastball hits 86-90 mph. Also throws a slider in the upper 70s, a curveball around 75 and a changeup. *Tendencies:* He can win as long as he keeps the ball down and spots his fastball on both sides of the plate. Relies on mixing speeds. Creates deception in his delivery with long, sweeping arm action. Neither his curveball nor his slider are pitches he consistently can go to, so his changeup becomes his most effective pitch. Is a good competitor with impeccable command of all his pitches. *Outlook:* Towers had career numbers in almost every category in 2005, including his 13 victories. Has moved into the middle of the rotation and projects to get better next year with improved run support. *Grade 7.4*

JOSH TOWERS'S PITCHING ZONE

.343	.273	.273
.338	.494	.306
.173	.295	.281

LEFTY-RIGHTY SPLITS

vs.	Avg.	AB	H	2B	3B	HR	RBI	BB	SO	OBP	Slg.
L	.274	413	113	20	2	8	43	17	60	.305	.390
R	.297	418	124	24	0	16	52	12	52	.318	.469

Year Team (League)	W	L	Pct.	ERA	WHIP	G	GS	CG	ShO	Hld.	Sv.-Opp.	IP	H	R	ER	HR	BB-IBB	SO	Avg.
1996— Bluefield (Appal.)	4	1	.800	5.24	1.24	14	9	0	0	...	0-...	55.0	63	35	32	9	5-0	61	.278
1997— Delmarva (S. Atl.)	0	0		3.44	1.09	9	1	0	0	...	1-...	18.1	18	8	7	1	2-0	16	.247
— Frederick (Carol.)	6	2	.750	4.86	1.71	25	3	0	0	...	1-...	53.2	74	36	29	4	18-0	64	.323
1998— Frederick (Carol.)	8	7	.533	3.34	1.00	25	20	3	0	...	1-...	145.1	137	58	54	11	9-0	122	.247
— Bowie (East.)	2	1	.667	3.50	1.33	5	2	0	0	...	0-...	18.0	20	9	7	1	4-0	7	.270
1999— Bowie (East.)	12	7	.632	3.76	1.22	29	28	5	2	...	0-...	189.0	204	86	79	26	26-1	106	.276
2000— Rochester (Int'l)	8	6	.571	3.47	1.20	24	24	5	1	...	0-...	148.0	157	63	57	17	21-0	102	.269
2001— Rochester (Int'l)	3	1	.750	3.51	1.17	6	6	1	1	...	0-...	41.0	40	18	16	2	8-2	27	.255
— Baltimore (A.L.)	8	10	.444	4.49	1.29	24	20	1	1	0	0-0	140.1	165	74	70	21	16-0	58	.297
2002— Baltimore (A.L.)	0	3	.000	7.90	1.72	5	3	0	0	0	0-0	27.1	42	24	24	11	5-0	13	.362
— Rochester (Int'l)	0	9	.000	7.57	1.78	15	13	1	0	...	0-...	69.0	109	65	58	16	14-0	43	.353
2003— Syracuse (Int'l)	5	7	.417	3.32	1.20	21	20	1	1	...	0-...	132.2	133	55	49	10	20-1	76	.259
— Toronto (A.L.)	8	1	.889	4.48	1.15	14	8	1	0	0	1-1	64.1	67	34	32	15	7-1	42	.266
2004— Syracuse (Int'l)	3	1	.750	2.50	1.11	6	5	0	0	...	0-...	36.0	33	11	10	5	7-0	25	.246
— Toronto (A.L.)	9	9	.500	5.11	1.50	21	21	0	0	0	0-0	116.1	148	70	66	16	26-4	51	.310
2005— Toronto (A.L.)	13	12	.520	3.71	1.27	33	33	2	1	0	0-0	208.2	237	101	86	24	29-2	112	.285
Major League totals (5 years)	38	35	.521	4.49	1.33	97	85	4	2	0	1-1	557.0	659	303	278	87	83-7	276	.295

TRACHSEL, STEVE   P

PERSONAL: Born October 31, 1970, in Oxnard, Calif. ... 6-4/205. ... Throws right, bats right. ... Full name: Stephen Christopher Trachsel. ... Name pronounced: TRACKS-ul. ... High school: Troy (Fullerton, Calif.). ... College: Long Beach State.

TRANSACTIONS/CAREER NOTES: Selected by Chicago Cubs organization in eighth round of 1991 free-agent draft. ... On disabled list (July 20-August 4, 1994); included rehabilitation assignment to Iowa. ... Signed as a free agent by Tampa Bay Devil Rays (January 28, 2000). ... Traded by Devil Rays with P Mark Guthrie to Toronto Blue Jays for 2B Brent Abernathy and cash (July 31, 2000). ... Signed as a free agent by New York Mets (December 11, 2000). ... On disabled list (July 1-22, 2002); included rehabilitation assignment to Binghamton. ... On disabled list (March 30-August 23, 2005); included rehabilitation assignments to St. Lucie, Binghamton and Norfolk.

HONORS: Named N.L. Rookie Pitcher of the Year by THE SPORTING NEWS (1994).

CAREER HITTING: 98-for-589 (.166), 45 R, 16 2B, 1 3B, 2 HR, 38 RBI.

SCOUTING REPORT *Throws:* His fastball runs 87-91 mph. Also throws a split-finger fastball at 79-81, a curveball and a changeup. *Tendencies:* Trachsel, a notoriously slow worker, has improved simply by picking up the pace and using his fastball more. Is not overpowering, but his command has improved. Likes to start lefthanded hitters with a slow, big-breaking curveball that begins away. Will use a change to get back in the count. Uses the splitter as an out pitch. *Outlook:* At this point, he's better suited to pitching at the back end of the rotation. Still racks up high pitch counts. *Grade 6.8*

STEVE TRACHSEL'S PITCHING ZONE

.750	.200	.167
.300	.400	.200
.176	.333	.346

LEFTY-RIGHTY SPLITS

vs.	Avg.	AB	H	2B	3B	HR	RBI	BB	SO	OBP	Slg.
L	.288	66	19	1	1	4	14	9	9	.377	.515
R	.243	74	18	6	0	2	4	3	15	.269	.405

Year Team (League)	W	L	Pct.	ERA	WHIP	G	GS	CG	ShO	Hld.	Sv.-Opp.	IP	H	R	ER	HR	BB-IBB	SO	Avg.
1991— Geneva (NY-Penn)	1	0	1.000	1.26	1.12	2	2	0	0	...	0-...	14.1	10	2	2	0	6-0	7	.217
— Win.-Salem (Carol.)	4	4	.500	3.67	1.21	12	12	1	0	...	0-...	73.2	70	38	30	3	19-0	69	.245
1992— Charlotte (Sou.)	13	8	.619	3.06	1.13	29	29	5	2	...	0-...	191.0	180	76	65	19	35-3	135	.252
1993— Iowa (A.A.)	13	6	.684	3.96	1.26	27	26	1	1	...	0-...	170.2	170	78	75	20	45-0	135	.264
— Chicago (N.L.)	0	2	.000	4.58	0.97	3	3	0	0	0	0-0	19.2	16	10	10	4	3-0	14	.219
1994— Chicago (N.L.)	9	7	.563	3.21	1.28	22	22	1	0	0	0-0	146.0	133	57	52	19	54-4	108	.242
— Iowa (A.A.)	0	2	.000	10.00	2.00	2	2	0	0	...	0-...	9.0	11	10	10	1	7-0	8	.289
1995— Chicago (N.L.)	7	13	.350	5.15	1.56	30	29	2	0	0	0-0	160.2	174	104	92	25	76-8	117	.277
1996— Orlando (Sou.)	0	1	.000	2.77	0.85	2	2	0	0	...	0-...	13.0	11	6	4	0	0-0	12	.220
— Chicago (N.L.)	13	9	.591	3.03	1.19	31	31	3	2	0	0-0	205.0	181	82	69	30	62-3	132	.235
1997— Chicago (N.L.)	8	12	.400	4.51	1.46	34	34	0	0	0	0-0	201.1	225	110	101	* 32	69-6	160	.287
1998— Chicago (N.L.)	15	8	.652	4.46	1.38	33	33	1	0	0	0-0	208.0	204	107	103	27	84-5	149	.258
1999— Chicago (N.L.)	8	* 18	.308	5.56	1.41	34	34	4	0	0	0-0	205.2	226	133	127	32	64-4	149	.280

Year Team (League)	W	L	Pct.	ERA	WHIP	G	GS	CG	ShO	Hld.	Sv.-Opp.	IP	H	R	ER	HR	BB-IBB	SO	Avg.
2000— Tampa Bay (A.L.)	6	10	.375	4.58	1.52	23	23	3	1	0	0-0	137.2	160	76	70	16	49-1	78	.294
— Toronto (A.L.)	2	5	.286	5.29	1.54	11	11	0	0	0	0-0	63.0	72	40	37	10	25-1	32	.293
2001— New York (N.L.)	11	13	.458	4.46	1.24	28	28	1	1	0	0-0	173.2	168	90	86	28	47-7	144	.254
— Norfolk (Int'l)	2	0	1.000	2.79	0.98	3	3	1	1	...	0-...	19.1	13	6	6	0	6-0	12	.188
2002— New York (N.L.)	11	11	.500	3.37	1.38	30	30	1	1	0	0-0	173.2	170	80	65	16	69-4	105	.258
— Binghamton (East.)	1	0	1.000	0.00	1.24	1	1	0	0	...	0-...	5.2	3	1	0	0	4-0	5	.150
2003— New York (N.L.)	16	10	.615	3.78	1.31	33	33	2	2	0	0-0	204.2	204	90	86	26	65-9	111	.264
2004— New York (N.L.)	12	13	.480	4.00	1.41	33	33	0	0	0	0-0	202.2	203	104	90	25	83-9	117	.262
2005— St. Lucie (Fla. St.)	0	1	.000	1.35	0.90	2	2	0	0	0	0-0	6.2	5	2	1	0	1-0	5	.208
— Binghamton (East.)	1	0	1.000	3.00	1.00	2	2	1	0	0	0-0	12.0	8	4	4	2	4-0	7	.190
— Norfolk (Int'l)	0	1	.000	2.57	0.86	2	2	0	0	0	0-0	14.0	10	4	4	2	2-0	12	.192
— New York (N.L.)	1	4	.200	4.14	1.32	6	6	0	0	0	0-0	37.0	37	20	17	6	12-0	24	.264
American League totals (1 year)	8	15	.348	4.80	1.52	34	34	3	1	0	0-0	200.2	232	116	107	26	74-2	110	.294
National League totals (12 years)	111	120	.481	4.17	1.36	317	316	15	6	0	0-0	1938.0	1941	987	898	270	688-59	1330	.262
Major League totals (13 years)	119	135	.469	4.23	1.37	351	350	18	7	0	0-0	2138.2	2173	1103	1005	296	762-61	1440	.265

ALL-STAR GAME RECORD

	W	L	Pct.	ERA	WHIP	G	GS	CG	ShO	Hld.	Sv.-Opp.	IP	H	R	ER	HR	BB-IBB	SO	Avg.
All-Star Game totals (1 year)	0	0	...	0.00	0.00	1	0	0	0	0	0-0	1.0	0	0	0	0	0	3	.000

TRACY, CHAD — OF/1B

PERSONAL: Born May 22, 1980, in Charlotte, N.C. ... 6-2/200. ... Bats left, throws right. ... Full name: Chad Austin Tracy. ... High school: West Mecklenburg (Charlotte). ... College: East Carolina.

TRANSACTIONS/CAREER NOTES: Selected by Arizona Diamondbacks organization in seventh round of 2001 free-agent draft.

2005 GAMES PLAYED BY POSITION (MLB): 1B—80, OF—51, DH—1.

SCOUTING REPORT *Offense:* Tracy is developing power. Has an excellent stroke with good bat speed and the ability to quickly make adjustments. Is a good breaking-ball hitter who makes good contact. Has some problems with lefthanded pitchers. Has become a good hitter with runners in scoring position. *Defense:* He has played right field but is defensively challenged, doesn't get good jumps in any direction and has a lot of problems going back. Stiff hands and limited range hurt him at first. Has a lot of throwing issues in the infield and appears afraid to let the ball go. *Outlook:* Tracy has a chance to be a good power hitter and will also able to hit for average. Will probably have to play first in the N.L. as he was a defensive liability in the outfield. *Grade 7.6*

CHAD TRACY'S HITTING ZONE

.190	.400	.241
.361	.388	.350
.367	.296	.333

LEFTY-RIGHTY SPLITS

vs.	Avg.	AB	H	2B	3B	HR	RBI	BB	SO	OBP	Slg.
L	.236	89	21	4	0	4	10	9	16	.307	.416
R	.324	414	134	30	4	23	62	26	62	.370	.582

Year Team (League)	Pos.	G	AB	R	H	2B	3B	HR	RBI	BB	SO	HBP	GDP	SB-CS	Avg.	OBP	SLG	OPS	E	Avg.
2001— Yakima (N'west)	3B	10	36	2	10	1	0	0	5	3	5	1	1	1-0	.278	.350	.306	.656	0	1.000
— South Bend (Midw.)	3B-1B	54	215	43	73	11	0	4	36	19	19	2	4	3-0	.340	.393	.447	.840	17	.896
2002— El Paso (Texas)	3B-1B	129	514	80	177	39	5	8	74	38	51	4	10	2-3	.344	.389	.486	.875	26	.931
2003— Tucson (PCL)	3B	133	522	91	169	31	4	10	80	41	52	4	7	0-2	.324	.372	.456	.827	20	.951
2004— Tucson (PCL)	3B-OF	11	40	7	16	4	0	2	11	8	5	0	0	2-0	.400	.490	.650	1.140	4	.921
— Arizona (N.L.)	3B-1B-OF	143	481	45	137	29	3	8	53	45	60	0	11	2-3	.285	.343	.407	.750	26	.938
2005— Arizona (N.L.)	1B-OF-DH	145	503	73	155	34	4	27	72	35	78	8	10	3-1	.308	.359	.553	.911	5	.994
Major League totals (2 years)		288	984	118	292	63	7	35	125	80	138	8	21	5-4	.297	.351	.482	.833	31	.976

TREANOR, MATT — C

PERSONAL: Born March 3, 1976, in Garden Grove, Calif. ... 6-2/220. ... Bats right, throws right. ... Full name: Matthew Aaron Treanor. ... Name pronounced: TRAY-ner. ... High school: Mater Dei (Calif.).

TRANSACTIONS/CAREER NOTES: Selected by Kansas City Royals organization in fourth round of 1994 free-agent draft. ... Traded by Royals to Florida Marlins for P Matt Whisenant (July 29, 1997).

2005 GAMES PLAYED BY POSITION (MLB): C—55.

SCOUTING REPORT *Offense:* Treanor is a gap hitter with an long, inside-out swing and a slow bat. He swings through off-speed stuff away and cannot turn on inside heat. Bat is stiff and tentative, and he shows little knowledge of the strike zone. Is a below-average runner. *Defense:* He has average footwork, hands, and blocking and framing skills. Arm is average at best but he does have a quick release. *Outlook:* His defense will keep him in the league but he doesn' hit enough to be more than a backup. *Grade 5.6*

MATT TREANOR'S HITTING ZONE

.000	.500	.286
.267	.278	.059
.214	.364	.167

LEFTY-RIGHTY SPLITS

vs.	Avg.	AB	H	2B	3B	HR	RBI	BB	SO	OBP	Slg.
L	.148	27	4	2	0	0	6	6	8	.303	.222
R	.215	107	23	6	0	0	13	10	20	.300	.271

Year Team (League)	Pos.	G	AB	R	H	2B	3B	HR	RBI	BB	SO	HBP	GDP	SB-CS	Avg.	OBP	SLG	OPS	E	Avg.
1994— GC Royals (GCL)	C-2B-OF	46	99	17	18	5	0	1	12	14	23	3	2	1-1	.182	.299	.263	.562	6	.968
1995— Springfield (Midw.)	C	75	211	17	39	6	2	3	19	21	59	4	1	1-1	.185	.269	.275	.544	11	.976
1996— Lansing (Midw.)	C-OF	119	384	56	100	18	2	6	33	35	63	13	9	5-3	.260	.342	.365	.706	16	.978
1997— Wilmington (Caro.)	C	80	257	22	51	6	1	5	25	25	59	2	4	1-6	.198	.275	.288	.563	12	.978
— Brevard County (Fla. St.)	C	23	70	11	15	4	1	0	3	12	14	2	1	0-0	.214	.345	.300	.645	0	1.000
1998— Brevard County (Fla. St.)	C-1B-3B	80	243	24	57	8	0	3	28	38	45	5	4	3-2	.235	.346	.305	.651	4	.989
1999— Kane Co. (Midw.)	C	80	308	56	88	21	1	10	53	36	65	15	9	4-1	.286	.385	.458	.843	8	.988
2000— Brevard County (Fla. St.)	C-1B	109	350	51	86	17	0	3	37	48	65	14	6	3-3	.246	.357	.320	.677	12	.986
2001— GC Marlins (GCL)	C	11	34	10	14	4	0	1	4	7	7	0	1	3-0	.412	.512	.618	1.130	1	.968

Year	Team (League)	Pos.	G	AB	R	H	2B	3B	HR	RBI	BB	SO	HBP	GDP	SB-CS	Avg.	OBP	SLG	OPS	E	Avg.
	— Kane Co. (Midw.)	C	1	1	2	1	0	0	0	0	3	0	0	0	0-0	1.000	1.000	1.000	2.000	0	1.000
	— Portland (East.)	C-1B	35	89	7	14	2	0	2	8	13	18	9	2	1-1	.157	.324	.247	.572	1	.996
2002	— Portland (East.)	C	50	156	24	39	5	1	9	28	28	33	7	5	3-0	.250	.387	.468	.855	9	.977
	— Calgary (PCL)	C-1B	36	95	10	27	8	0	1	18	12	13	5	4	1-1	.284	.393	.400	.793	3	.984
2003	— Albuquerque (PCL)	C	98	315	45	86	18	1	11	40	39	44	17	4	9-4	.273	.380	.441	.821	11	.984
2004	— Albuquerque (PCL)	C	62	198	32	51	8	0	8	38	33	44	10	5	2-0	.258	.385	.419	.781	4	.991
	— Florida (N.L.)	C	29	55	7	13	2	0	0	1	4	13	2	3	0-0	.236	.311	.273	.584	1	.976
2005	— Florida (N.L.)	C	58	134	10	27	8	0	0	13	16	28	3	5	0-0	.201	.301	.261	.562	5	.985
	Major League totals (2 years)		87	189	17	40	10	0	0	14	20	41	5	8	0-0	.212	.304	.265	.568	8	.982

TSAO, CHIN-HUI   P

PERSONAL: Born June 2, 1981, in Hua-Lien, Taiwan. ... 6-2/177. ... Throws right, bats right. ... Full name: Chin-Hui Tsao. ... Name pronounced: chin-wee sow.
TRANSACTIONS/CAREER NOTES: Signed as a non-drafted free agent by Colorado Rockies organization (October 7, 1999). ... On disabled list (August 27-September 16, 2003). ... On disabled list (March 25-April 12 and May 12, 2005-remainder of season); included rehabilitation assignment to Colorado Springs and Modesto.
CAREER HITTING: 2-for-13 (.154), 2 R, 1 2B, 0 3B, 0 HR, 0 RBI.

LEFTY-RIGHTY SPLITS

vs.	Avg.	AB	H	2B	3B	HR	RBI	BB	SO	OBP	Slg.
L	.462	26	12	2	0	3	5	4	0	.548	.885
R	.182	22	4	2	0	0	3	1	4	.208	.273

SCOUTING REPORT ***Throws:*** Tsao uses a four-seam fastball at 93-97 mph and a changeup. Threw a slider when he was a starter but uses only the fastball and change as a reliever. ***Tendencies:*** He is a strikeout type of reliever. Fastball has overpowering riding action. Needs to improve command of it. ***Outlook:*** He has been plagued by arm problems, and his health may prevent him from reaching his potential. Might be better starting; his arm probably can't hold up to pitching every other day. ***Grade 5.5***

Year	Team (League)	W	L	Pct.	ERA	WHIP	G	GS	CG	ShO	Hld.	Sv.-Opp.	IP	H	R	ER	HR	BB-IBB	SO	Avg.
2000	— Asheville (S. Atl.)	11	8	.579	2.73	1.10	24	24	0	0		0-...	145.0	119	54	44	8	40-0	187	.220
2001	— Salem (Carol.)	0	4	.000	4.67	1.62	4	4	0	0		0-...	17.1	23	11	9	1	5-0	18	.333
2002	— Tri-Cities (N'west)	0	0	...	0.00	0.73	3	3	0	0		0-...	11.0	6	2	0	0	2-0	16	.150
	— Salem (Carol.)	4	2	.667	2.09	0.97	9	9	0	0		0-...	47.1	34	13	11	3	12-0	45	.204
2003	— Tulsa (Texas)	11	4	.733	2.46	1.01	18	18	0	0		0-...	113.1	88	34	31	7	26-0	125	.214
	— Colorado (N.L.)	3	3	.500	6.02	1.57	9	8	0	0	0	0-0	43.1	48	30	29	11	20-1	29	.284
2004	— Asheville (S. Atl.)	1	0	1.000	1.80	0.90	2	2	0	0		0-...	10.0	8	2	2	1	0-0	14	.211
	— Tulsa (Texas)	1	1	.500	2.77	1.08	2	2	0	0		0-...	13.0	12	4	4	1	2-0	10	.261
	— Colo. Springs (PCL)	1	1	.500	8.53	2.13	4	4	0	0		0-...	12.2	22	12	12	5	5-0	14	.379
	— Colorado (N.L.)	0	0	...	3.86	0.86	10	0	0	0	1	1-2	9.1	7	4	4	2	1-0	11	.200
2005	— Colo. Springs (PCL)	0	0	...	0.00	1.00	1	0	0	0	0	0-0	1.0	1	0	0	0	1-0	1	.250
	— Modesto (Calif.)	0	0	...	0.00	0.00	1	0	0	0	0	0-0	1.0	0	0	0	0	0-0	1	.000
	— Colorado (N.L.)	1	0	1.000	6.55	1.91	10	0	0	0	0	3-4	11.0	16	8	8	3	5-1	4	.333
	Major League totals (3 years)	4	3	.571	5.80	1.52	29	8	0	0,	1	4-6	63.2	71	42	41	16	26-2	44	.282

TUCKER, MICHAEL   OF

PERSONAL: Born June 25, 1971, in South Boston, Va. ... 6-2/195. ... Bats left, throws right. ... Full name: Michael Anthony Tucker. ... High school: Bluestone (Skipwith, Va.). ... College: Longwood (Va.).
TRANSACTIONS/CAREER NOTES: Selected by Kansas City Royals organization in first round (10th pick overall) of 1992 free-agent draft. ... On disabled list (June 4-21 and August 28, 1996-remainder of season); included rehabilitation assignment to Wichita. ... Traded by Royals with IF Keith Lockhart to Atlanta Braves for OF Jermaine Dye and P Jamie Walker (March 27, 1997). ... Traded by Braves with Ps Denny Neagle and Rob Bell to Cincinnati Reds for 2B Bret Boone and P Mike Remlinger (November 10, 1998). ... Traded by Reds to Chicago Cubs for Ps Chris Booker and Ben Shaffar (July 20, 2001). ... Traded by Cubs to Royals for a player to be named (December 19, 2001); Cubs acquired P Shawn Sonnier to complete deal (March 15, 2002). ... On disabled list (August 5-September 24, 2003). ... Signed as a free agent by San Francisco Giants (December 7, 2003). ... Traded by Giants to Philadelphia Phillies for P Kelvin Pichardo (August 27, 2005).
2005 GAMES PLAYED BY POSITION (MLB): OF—73, DH—4.

SCOUTING REPORT ***Offense:*** Tucker is particularly dangerous when he gets a low fastball. Has a short approach with a slight uppercut but still likes to get on top of the ball. Has problems catching up to the better high fastballs. Pitchers can change speeds on him effectively. Looks to pull the ball. Is an average runner but doesn't steal many bases. ***Defense:*** He can play all three outfield positions but is best in right, where his arm strength is an advantage. Gets good jumps but has slightly stiff hands. ***Outlook:*** Ideally a fourth outfielder, Tucker provides an experienced bat off the bench with some power. Teams always are looking to upgrade from his ability. ***Grade 6.2***

MICHAEL TUCKER'S HITTING ZONE

.200	.462	.467
.034	.387	.289
.250	.222	.152

LEFTY-RIGHTY SPLITS

vs.	Avg.	AB	H	2B	3B	HR	RBI	BB	SO	OBP	Slg.
L	.152	33	5	1	0	0	3	1	7	.189	.182
R	.251	235	59	15	1	5	33	30	45	.336	.387

Year	Team (League)	Pos.	G	AB	R	H	2B	3B	HR	RBI	BB	SO	HBP	GDP	SB-CS	Avg.	OBP	SLG	OPS	E	Avg.
1993	— Wilmington (Carol.)	2B	61	239	42	73	14	2	6	44	34	49	2	0	12-2	.305	.391	.456	.847	10	.965
	— Memphis (Sou.)	2B	72	244	38	68	7	4	9	35	42	51	6	1	12-5	.279	.392	.451	.843	13	.962
1994	— Omaha (A.A.)	OF	132	485	75	134	16	7	21	77	69	111	3	6	11-3	.276	.366	.468	.834	7	.967
1995	— Kansas City (A.L.)	OF-DH	62	177	23	46	10	4	4	17	18	51	1	3	2-3	.260	.332	.384	.716	1	.986
	— Omaha (A.A.)	OF	71	275	37	84	18	4	4	28	24	39	4	3	11-4	.305	.367	.444	.811	2	.986
1996	— Kansas City (A.L.)	OF-1B-DH	108	339	55	88	18	4	6	53	40	69	7	7	10-4	.260	.346	.442	.789	7	.980
	— Wichita (Texas)	OF-1B	6	20	4	9	1	3	0	7	5	4	0	0	0-2	.450	.538	.800	1.338	0	1.000
1997	— Atlanta (N.L.)	OF	138	499	80	141	25	7	14	56	44	116	6	7	12-7	.283	.347	.445	.792	5	.980
1998	— Atlanta (N.L.)	OF	130	414	54	101	27	3	13	46	49	112	3	4	8-3	.244	.327	.418	.745	1	.990
1999	— Cincinnati (N.L.)	OF	133	296	55	75	8	5	11	44	37	81	3	5	11-4	.253	.338	.426	.764	2	.990
2000	— Cincinnati (N.L.)	OF-2B	148	270	55	72	14	1	15	36	44	64	7	6	13-6	.267	.381	.511	.892	5	.969
2001	— Cincinnati (N.L.)	OF	86	231	31	56	10	1	7	30	23	55	1	4	12-5	.242	.308	.385	.693	3	.978

Year	Team (League)	Pos.	G	AB	R	H	2B	3B	HR	RBI	BB	SO	HBP	GDP	SB-CS	Avg.	OBP	SLG	OPS	E	Avg.
	—Chicago (N.L.)	OF-1B	63	205	31	54	9	7	5	31	23	47	1	4	4-3	.263	.339	.449	.788	3	.978
2002—	Kansas City (A.L.)	OF-DH-1B																			
		2B	144	475	65	118	27	6	12	56	56	105	3	5	23-9	.248	.330	.406	.737	4	.985
2003—	Kansas City (A.L.)	OF-DH	104	389	61	102	20	5	13	55	39	88	2	8	8-10	.262	.331	.440	.771	2	.989
2004—	San Francisco (N.L.)	OF	140	464	77	119	21	6	13	62	70	106	2	5	5-2	.256	.353	.412	.765	6	.978
2005—	San Francisco (N.L.)	OF-DH	104	250	32	60	16	1	5	33	28	48	2	6	4-0	.240	.317	.372	.689	2	.983
	—Philadelphia (N.L.)	OF	22	18	3	4	0	0	0	3	3	4	0	1	0-0	.222	.333	.222	.556	0	...
	American League totals (4 years)		418	1380	204	354	75	15	41	181	153	313	13	23	43-26	.257	.335	.422	.756	9	.988
	National League totals (7 years)		964	2647	418	682	129	34	83	341	321	633	25	42	69-30	.258	.341	.426	.767	27	.982
	Major League totals (11 years)		1382	4027	622	1036	204	49	124	522	474	946	38	65	112-56	.257	.339	.425	.763	36	.984

DIVISION SERIES RECORD

Year	Team (League)	Pos.	G	AB	R	H	2B	3B	HR	RBI	BB	SO	HBP	GDP	SB-CS	Avg.	OBP	SLG	OPS	E	Avg.
1997—	Atlanta (N.L.)	OF	2	6	0	1	0	0	0	1	0	1	0	0	0-0	.167	.167	.167	.333	0	1.000
1998—	Atlanta (N.L.)	OF	3	8	1	2	0	0	1	2	2	0	0	0	1-0	.250	.400	.625	1.025	0	1.000
	Division series totals (2 years)		5	14	1	3	0	0	1	3	2	1	0	0	1-0	.214	.313	.429	.741	0	1.000

CHAMPIONSHIP SERIES RECORD

Year	Team (League)	Pos.	G	AB	R	H	2B	3B	HR	RBI	BB	SO	HBP	GDP	SB-CS	Avg.	OBP	SLG	OPS	E	Avg.
1997—	Atlanta (N.L.)	OF	5	10	1	1	0	0	1	1	3	4	0	0	0-0	.100	.308	.400	.708	0	1.000
1998—	Atlanta (N.L.)	OF	6	13	1	5	1	0	1	5	2	5	0	0	0-0	.385	.467	.692	1.159	0	1.000
	Champ. series totals (2 years)		11	23	2	6	1	0	2	6	5	9	0	0	0-0	.261	.393	.565	.958	0	1.000

TUCKER, T.J.　　　　　　P

PERSONAL: Born August 20, 1978, in Clearwater, Fla. ... 6-3/266. ... Throws right, bats right. ... Full name: Thomas John Tucker. ... High school: River Ridge (New Port Richey, Fla.).

TRANSACTIONS/CAREER NOTES: Selected by Montreal Expos organization in supplemental round ("sandwich pick" between first and second rounds, 47th pick overall) of 1997 free-agent draft; pick received as compensation for Chicago Cubs signing free-agent P Mel Rojas. ... On disabled list (June 10, 2000-remainder of season; and August 18-September 6, 2002). ... Expos franchise transferred to Washington, D.C., and renamed Washington Nationals for 2005 season (December 3, 2004). ... On disabled list (April 20-May 26 and June 18-remainder of season, 2005); included rehabilitation assignment to New Orleans.

CAREER HITTING: 10-for-36 (.278), 4 R, 1 2B, 0 3B, 0 HR, 0 RBI.

T.J. TUCKER'S PITCHING ZONE

.500	.000	.000
.667	.333	.200
.000	.000	.500

LEFTY-RIGHTY SPLITS

vs.	Avg.	AB	H	2B	3B	HR	RBI	BB	SO	OBP	Slg.
L	.364	22	8	1	0	0	0	1	2	.391	.409
R	.375	32	12	1	0	4	9	1	3	.382	.781

Year	Team (League)	W	L	Pct.	ERA	WHIP	G	GS	CG	ShO	Hld.	Sv.-Opp.	IP	H	R	ER	HR	BB-IBB	SO	Avg.
1997—	GC Expos (GCL)	1	0	1.000	1.93	1.29	3	2	0	0	...	0-...	4.2	5	1	1	0	1-0	11	.278
1998—	GC Expos (GCL)	1	0	1.000	0.75	0.78	7	7	0	0	...	0-...	36.0	23	5	3	1	5-0	40	.178
	—Vermont (N.Y.-Penn.)	3	1	.750	2.18	1.18	6	6	0	0	...	0-...	33.0	24	9	8	0	15-0	34	.205
	—Jupiter (Fla. St.)	1	1	.500	1.00	0.56	2	1	0	0	...	0-...	9.0	5	1	1	0	1-0	10	.167
1999—	Jupiter (Fla. St.)	5	1	.833	1.23	0.91	7	7	0	0	...	0-...	44.0	24	7	6	2	16-0	35	.156
	—Harrisburg (East.)	8	5	.615	4.10	1.27	19	19	1	1	...	0-...	116.1	110	55	53	12	38-0	85	.249
2000—	Harrisburg (East.)	2	1	.667	3.60	1.11	8	8	0	0	...	0-...	45.0	33	19	18	7	17-0	24	.208
	—Montreal (N.L.)	0	1	.000	11.57	2.00	2	2	0	0	...	0-0	7.0	11	9	9	3	3-0	2	.344
2001—	Harrisburg (East.)	5	5	.500	3.73	1.39	13	13	0	0	...	0-...	82.0	77	38	34	10	37-0	57	.255
	—Ottawa (Int'l)	3	5	.375	3.11	1.20	14	14	1	0	...	0-...	84.0	68	42	29	11	33-0	63	.220
2002—	Montreal (N.L.)	6	3	.667	4.11	1.63	57	0	0	0	17	4-7	61.1	69	32	28	5	31-9	42	.290
2003—	Edmonton (PCL)	1	0	1.000	2.76	1.40	3	3	0	0	...	0-...	16.1	16	5	5	2	7-0	6	.262
	—Montreal (N.L.)	2	3	.400	4.73	1.38	45	7	0	0	3	0-2	80.0	90	49	42	8	20-1	47	.278
2004—	Edmonton (PCL)	2	0	1.000	4.86	1.86	3	3	0	0	...	0-...	16.2	26	15	9	3	5-0	3	.342
	—Montreal (N.L.)	4	2	.667	3.72	1.33	54	1	0	0	3	0-2	67.2	73	28	28	6	17-6	44	.275
2005—	New Orleans (PCL)	0	0	...	0.00	0.50	2	2	0	0	...	0-0	4.0	2	0	0	0	0-0	2	.154
	—Washington (N.L.)	1	0	1.000	6.39	1.74	13	0	0	0	...	0-0	12.2	20	9	9	4	2-0	5	.370
	Major League totals (5 years)	13	9	.591	4.57	1.47	171	10	0	0	23	4-11	228.2	263	127	116	27	73-16	140	.288

TURNBOW, DERRICK　　　　　　P

PERSONAL: Born January 25, 1978, in Union City, Tenn. ... 6-3/210. ... Throws right, bats right. ... Full name: Thomas Derrick Turnbow. ... High school: Franklin (Tenn.).

TRANSACTIONS/CAREER NOTES: Selected by Philadelphia Phillies organization in fifth round of 1997 free-agent draft. ... Selected by Anaheim Angels from Phillies organization in Rule 5 major league draft (December 13, 1999). ... On disabled list (April 20, 2001-remainder of season). ... Claimed on waivers by Milwaukee Brewers (October 14, 2004).

CAREER HITTING: 0-for-1 (.000), 0 R, 0 2B, 0 3B, 0 HR, 0 RBI.

SCOUTING REPORT **Throws:** Turnbow,s fastball ranges into the high 90s and his curveball is in the low 80s. *Tendencies:* He essentially is a two-pitch guy who will try to blow it by you. Has rough arm action and can struggle with his command. *Outlook:* After a breakout season in 2005, Turnbow is a bonafide major league closer. *Grade 8.3*

DERRICK TURNBOW'S PITCHING ZONE

.278	.313	.300
.189	.192	.233
.278	.357	.125

LEFTY-RIGHTY SPLITS

vs.	Avg.	AB	H	2B	3B	HR	RBI	BB	SO	OBP	Slg.
L	.233	120	28	4	1	1	6	12	25	.303	.308
R	.167	126	21	6	0	4	9	12	39	.245	.310

Year	Team (League)	W	L	Pct.	ERA	WHIP	G	GS	CG	ShO	Hld.	Sv.-Opp.	IP	H	R	ER	HR	BB-IBB	SO	Avg.
1997—	Martinsville (Appal.)	1	3	.250	7.40	2.05	7	7	0	0	...	0-...	24.1	34	29	20	5	16-1	7	.354
1998—	Martinsville (Appal.)	2	6	.250	5.01	1.31	13	13	1	0	...	0-...	70.0	66	44	39	7	26-1	45	.249
1999—	Piedmont (S. Atl.)	12	8	.600	3.35	1.14	26	26	•4	1	...	0-...	161.0	130	67	60	10	53-0	149	.221
2000—	Anaheim (A.L.)	0	0	...	4.74	1.89	24	1	0	0	1	0-...	38.0	36	21	20	7	36-...	25	.254
2001—	Arkansas (Texas)	0	0	...	2.57	1.21	3	3	0	0	...	0-...	14.0	12	4	4	0	5-0	11	.240
2002—	Ariz. Angels (AZL)	0	0	.000	4.50	1.00	3	3	0	0	...	0-...	8.0	5	5	4	0	3-0	12	.161
	—Rancho Cuca. (Calif.)	0	0	...	5.25	2.08	13	0	0	0	...	0-...	12.0	16	11	7	1	9-0	14	.320
2003—	Arkansas (Texas)	1	0	1.000	0.00	0.60	7	0	0	0	...	3-...	14.0	5	0	0	0	5-0	19	.087
	—Salt Lake (PCL)	1	2	.333	5.73	1.70	35	0	0	0	...	2-...	55.0	68	36	35	5	24-0	63	.300

Year	Team (League)	W	L	Pct.	ERA	WHIP	G	GS	CG	ShO	Hld.	Sv.-Opp.	IP	H	R	ER	HR	BB-IBB	SO	Avg.
— Anaheim (A.L.)		2	0	1.000	0.59	0.65	11	0	0	0	0	0-0	15.1	7	1	1	0	3-0	15	.140
2004— Anaheim (A.L.)		0	0	...	0.00	1.42	4	0	0	0	0	0-0	6.1	2	0	0	0	7-0	3	.105
— Salt Lake (PCL)		2	6	.250	5.06	1.57	46	3	0	0	...	6-...	74.2	75	46	42	8	42-0	56	.275
2005— Milwaukee (N.L.)		7	1	.875	1.74	1.08	69	0	0	0	2	39-43	67.1	49	15	13	5	24-2	64	.199
American League totals (3 years)		2	0	1.000	3.17	1.53	39	1	0	1	0	0-0	59.2	45	22	21	7	46-0	43	.213
National League totals (1 year)		7	1	.875	1.74	1.08	69	0	0	0	2	39-43	67.1	49	15	13	5	24-2	64	.199
Major League totals (4 years)		9	1	.900	2.41	1.29	108	1	0	0	3	39-43	127.0	94	37	34	12	70-2	107	.206

TYNER, JASON — OF

PERSONAL: Born April 23, 1977, in Beaumont, Texas. ... 6-1/168. ... Bats left, throws left. ... Full name: Jason Renyt Tyner. ... Name pronounced: TIE-ner. ... High school: Westbrook (Beaumont, Texas). ... College: Texas A&M.

TRANSACTIONS/CAREER NOTES: Selected by New York Mets organization in first round (21st pick overall) of 1998 free-agent draft. ... Traded by Mets with P Paul Wilson to Tampa Bay Devil Rays for P Rick White and OF Bubba Trammell (July 28, 2000). ... Signed by Atlanta Braves organization (April 27, 2004). ... Released by Braves (July 25, 2004). ... Signed by Cleveland Indians organization (July 28, 2004). ... Signed as a free agent by Minnesota Twins organization (November 10, 2004).

2005 GAMES PLAYED BY POSITION (MLB): OF—15, DH—3.

JASON TYNER'S HITTING ZONE

.750	.250	.400
.286	.167	.500
.000	1.000	.000

LEFTY-RIGHTY SPLITS

vs.	Avg.	AB	H	2B	3B	HR	RBI	BB	SO	OBP	Slg.
L	.333	12	4	0	0	0	2	1	2	.385	.333
R	.318	44	14	1	1	0	3	3	2	.362	.386

Year	Team (League)	Pos.	G	AB	R	H	2B	3B	HR	RBI	BB	SO	HBP	GDP	SB-CS	Avg.	OBP	SLG	OPS	E	Avg.
1998— St. Lucie (Fla. St.)	OF	50	201	30	61	2	3	0	16	17	20	1	3	15-11	.303	.361	.343	.704	2	.976
1999— Binghamton (East.)	OF	129	518	91	162	19	5	0	33	62	46	1	8	49-16	.313	.387	.369	.756	2	.993
— Norfolk (Int'l)	OF	3	8	0	0	0	0	0	0	0	5	0	0	0-0	.000	.000	.000	.000	0	1.000
2000— Norfolk (Int'l)	OF	84	327	54	105	5	2	0	28	30	32	2	3	33-14	.321	.380	.349	.729	1	.995
— New York (N.L.)	OF	13	41	3	8	2	0	0	5	1	4	1	1	1-1	.195	.222	.244	.466	2	.920
— Tampa Bay (A.L.)	OF-DH	37	83	6	20	2	0	0	8	4	12	1	1	6-1	.241	.281	.265	.546	0	1.000
2001— Durham (Int'l)	OF	39	157	25	49	2	1	0	12	15	10	2	1	11-5	.312	.371	.338	.709	1	1.000
— Tampa Bay (A.L.)	OF	105	396	51	111	8	5	0	21	15	42	3	6	31-6	.280	.311	.326	.637	5	.978
2002— Tampa Bay (A.L.)	OF-DH	44	168	17	36	2	1	0	9	7	19	1	1	7-1	.214	.249	.238	.487	1	.990
— Durham (Int'l)	OF	88	351	59	102	12	4	0	27	34	27	6	3	20-7	.291	.362	.348	.710	1	.994
2003— Tampa Bay (A.L.)	OF-DH	46	90	12	25	7	0	0	6	10	12	0	1	2-1	.278	.350	.356	.706	2	.962
— Durham (Int'l)	OF-DH	65	275	34	89	11	5	0	24	22	25	1	5	10-7	.324	.372	.400	.772	1	.993
2004— Richmond (Int'l)	OF	64	243	40	70	12	1	1	16	15	22	7	4	18-6	.288	.346	.358	.704	0	...
— Buffalo (Int'l)	OF	38	139	25	48	4	1	0	16	18	15	2		5-0	.345	.417	.388	.805	0	...
2005— Rochester (Int'l)	OF-DH	133	524	81	150	18	2	1	36	48	57	5	9	18-6	.286	.351	.334	.685	2	.996
— Minnesota (A.L.)	OF-DH	18	56	8	18	1	1	0	5	4	4	0	2	2-0	.321	.367	.375	.742	0	.920
American League totals (5 years)		250	793	94	210	20	7	0	49	40	89	5	11	48-9	.265	.303	.308	.611	8	.983
National League totals (1 year)		13	41	3	8	2	0	0	5	1	4	1	1	1-1	.195	.222	.244	.466	2	.920
Major League totals (5 years)		263	834	97	218	22	7	0	54	41	93	6	12	49-10	.261	.299	.305	.604	10	.980

U

URBINA, UGUETH — P

PERSONAL: Born February 15, 1974, in Caracas, Venezuela. ... 6-0/205. ... Throws right, bats right. ... Full name: Ugueth Urtain Urbina. ... Name pronounced: oo-get oor-BEE-nah. ... High school: Liceo Peres Bonalde de Miranda (Miranda, Venezuela).

TRANSACTIONS/CAREER NOTES: Signed as a non-drafted free agent by Montreal Expos organization (July 2, 1990). ... On disabled list (May 9, 2000-remainder of season). ... Traded by Expos to Boston Red Sox for Ps Tomo Ohka and Rich Rundles (July 31, 2001). ... Signed as a free agent by Texas Rangers (December 20, 2002). ... Traded by Rangers to Florida Marlins for 1B Adrian Gonzalez, P Ryan Snare and OF Will Smith (July 11, 2003). ... Signed as a free agent by Detroit Tigers (March 29, 2004). ... Traded by Tigers with 2B Ramon Martinez to Philadelphia Phillies for SS Placido Polanco (June 8, 2005).

HONORS: Named N.L. Fireman of the Year by THE SPORTING NEWS (1999).

CAREER HITTING: 5-for-53 (.094), 3 R, 0 2B, 0 3B, 0 HR, 1 RBI.

SCOUTING REPORT *Throws:* Urbina's fastball ranges from 91-95 mph. Slider is in the mid-80s. Also has a plus changeup that he throws in the low 80s. *Tendencies:* He doesn't have a loose arm but his command has improved. Throws a very heavy, boring fastball to both sides of the plate. Slider is very quick but occasionally flattens out. Has exceptional arm speed with his changeup, a pitch that sinks; it makes him very effective against lefthanded hitters. *Outlook:* Urbina is one of the highest-maintenance players in the game and has a volatile temper. Will be given an opportunity this spring to make a club and can contribute as long as he controls his emotions. Was a closer in the past but is better in a setup role now. *Grade 7*

UGUETH URBINA'S PITCHING ZONE

.217	.700	.292
.154	.364	.200
.105	.167	.125

LEFTY-RIGHTY SPLITS

vs.	Avg.	AB	H	2B	3B	HR	RBI	BB	SO	OBP	Slg.
L	.223	139	31	7	0	6	11	21	41	.325	.403
R	.167	150	25	11	0	6	21	18	56	.259	.360

Year	Team (League)	W	L	Pct.	ERA	WHIP	G	GS	CG	ShO	Hld.	Sv.-Opp.	IP	H	R	ER	HR	BB-IBB	SO	Avg.
1991— GC Expos (GCL)		3	3	.500	2.29	1.08	10	10	3	1	...	0-...	63.0	58	24	16	2	10-0	51	.244
1992— Albany (S. Atl.)		7	13	.350	3.22	1.16	24	24	5	2	...	0-...	142.1	111	68	51	14	54-0	100	.215
1993— Burlington (Midw.)		2	3	.400	4.50	1.37	10	8	0	0	...	0-...	46.0	41	31	23	7	22-1	30	.245
— Harrisburg (East.)		4	5	.444	3.99	1.40	11	11	3	1	...	0-...	70.0	66	32	31	5	32-1	45	.259
1994— Harrisburg (East.)		9	3	.750	3.28	1.14	21	21	0	0	...	0-...	120.2	95	49	44	11	43-0	86	.216
1995— W.P. Beach (FSL)		1	0	1.000	0.00	0.56	2	2	0	0	...	0-...	9.0	4	0	0	0	1-0	11	.143
— Ottawa (Int'l)		6	2	.750	3.04	1.06	13	11	2	1	...	0-...	68.0	46	26	23	1	26-0	55	.191
— Montreal (N.L.)		2	2	.500	6.17	1.71	7	4	0	0	0	0-...	23.1	26	17	16	6	14-1	15	.280
1996— W.P. Beach (FSL)		1	1	.500	1.29	1.14	3	3	0	0	...	0-...	14.0	13	3	2	0	3-0	21	.255
— Ottawa (Int'l)		2	0	1.000	2.66	0.97	5	5	0	0	...	0-...	23.2	17	9	7	2	6-0	28	.195
— Montreal (N.L.)		10	5	.667	3.71	1.28	33	17	0	0	6	0-1	114.0	102	54	47	18	44-4	108	.234
1997— Montreal (N.L.)		5	8	.385	3.78	1.26	63	0	0	0	...	27-32	64.1	52	29	27	9	29-2	84	.215

Year Team (League)	W	L	Pct.	ERA	WHIP	G	GS	CG	ShO	Hld.	Sv.-Opp.	IP	H	R	ER	HR	BB-IBB	SO	Avg.
1998— Montreal (N.L.)	6	3	.667	1.30	1.01	64	0	0	0	0	34-38	69.1	37	11	10	2	33-2	94	.157
1999— Montreal (N.L.)	6	6	.500	3.69	1.26	71	0	0	0	0	* 41-50	75.2	59	35	31	6	36-6	100	.208
2000— Montreal (N.L.)	0	1	.000	4.05	1.20	13	0	0	0	0	8-10	13.1	11	6	6	1	5-0	22	.224
2001— Montreal (N.L.)	2	1	.667	4.24	1.35	45	0	0	0	1	15-18	46.2	42	24	22	8	21-1	57	.236
— Boston (A.L.)	0	1	.000	2.25	0.95	19	0	0	0	2	9-10	20.0	16	5	5	1	3-0	32	.219
2002— Boston (A.L.)	1	6	.143	3.00	1.07	61	0	0	0	0	40-46	60.0	44	21	20	8	20-5	71	.202
2003— Texas (A.L.)	0	4	.000	4.19	1.32	39	0	0	0	0	26-30	38.2	33	19	18	6	18-2	41	.232
— Florida (N.L.)	3	0	1.000	1.41	0.94	33	0	0	0	11	6-8	38.1	23	6	6	2	13-0	37	.174
2004— Lakeland (Fla. St.)	0	0	...	0.00	1.50	2	0	0	0	0	0-...	2.0	3	3	0	0	0-1	1	.273
— Detroit (A.L.)	4	6	.400	4.50	1.30	54	0	0	0	0	21-24	54.0	38	28	27	7	32-3	56	.194
2005— Detroit (A.L.)	1	3	.250	2.63	1.28	25	0	0	0	0	9-11	27.1	21	9	8	4	14-2	31	.208
— Philadelphia (N.L.)	4	3	.571	4.13	1.15	56	0	0	0	18	1-7	52.1	35	25	24	8	25-2	66	.186
American League totals (5 years)	6	20	.231	3.51	1.20	198	0	0	0	5	105-121	200.0	152	82	78	26	87-12	231	.208
National League totals (9 years)	38	29	.567	3.42	1.22	385	21	0	0	37	132-164	497.1	387	207	189	60	220-18	583	.211
Major League totals (11 years)	44	49	.473	3.45	1.21	583	21	0	0	42	237-285	697.1	539	289	267	86	307-30	814	.210

DIVISION SERIES RECORD

Year Team (League)	W	L	Pct.	ERA	WHIP	G	GS	CG	ShO	Hld.	Sv.-Opp.	IP	H	R	ER	HR	BB-IBB	SO	Avg.
2003— Florida (N.L.)	0	0	...	3.00	1.67	3	0	0	0	0	1-1	3.0	4	1	1	0	1-1	2	.333

CHAMPIONSHIP SERIES RECORD

Year Team (League)	W	L	Pct.	ERA	WHIP	G	GS	CG	ShO	Hld.	Sv.-Opp.	IP	H	R	ER	HR	BB-IBB	SO	Avg.
2003— Florida (N.L.)	1	0	1.000	2.57	0.29	4	0	0	0	0	1-2	7.0	2	2	2	1	0-0	10	.087

WORLD SERIES RECORD

Year Team (League)	W	L	Pct.	ERA	WHIP	G	GS	CG	ShO	Hld.	Sv.-Opp.	IP	H	R	ER	HR	BB-IBB	SO	Avg.
2003— Florida (N.L.)	0	0	...	6.00	1.67	3	0	0	0	0	2-3	3.0	2	2	2	0	3-0	2	.182

ALL-STAR GAME RECORD

Year Team (League)	W	L	Pct.	ERA	WHIP	G	GS	CG	ShO	Hld.	Sv.-Opp.	IP	H	R	ER	HR	BB-IBB	SO	Avg.
All-Star Game totals (2 years)	0	1	.000	13.50	2.00	2	0	0	0	0	0-1	2.0	3	3	3	0	1-0	3	.333

URIBE, JUAN   SS

PERSONAL: Born July 22, 1979, in Bani, Dominican Republic. ... 5-11/175. ... Bats right, throws right. ... Full name: Juan C. Tena Uribe. ... Name pronounced: ohh-ree-bay. ... High school: Abel Uribe (Dominican Republic).
TRANSACTIONS/CAREER NOTES: Signed as a non-drafted free agent by Colorado Rockies organization (January 15, 1997). ... On disabled list (March 18-June 3, 2003); included rehabilitation assignments to Visalia and Tulsa. ... Traded by Rockies to Chicago White Sox for 2B Aaron Miles (December 2, 2003).
2005 GAMES PLAYED BY POSITION (MLB): SS—146.

SCOUTING REPORT **Offense:** Uribe is a highly unorthodox hitter; he carries his hands very low in his stance and away from his body. Is extremely aggressive and a dead fastball hitter. Gets out on his front foot quickly but keeps his hands back, but still has trouble laying off sliders away. Will show power on fastballs up. Is an average runner but lacks instincts. **Defense:** The World Series showed what kind of defensive player he is. Is vastly underrated and somewhat unconventional. Has very quick feet and charges the ball well. Range and hands have improved. Doesn't lay back on the ball as much. Has an outstanding arm with exceptional carry. **Outlook:** Uribe is better defensively than at any time in his career. Isn't a really good hitter but is dangerous at the bottom of the order. **Grade 7.7**

JUAN URIBE'S HITTING ZONE

.359	.320	.257
.264	.316	.222
.279	.316	.278

LEFTY-RIGHTY SPLITS

vs.	Avg.	AB	H	2B	3B	HR	RBI	BB	SO	OBP	Slg.
L	.311	122	38	8	1	5	19	9	25	.351	.516
R	.231	359	83	15	2	11	52	25	52	.284	.376

Year Team (League)	Pos.	G	AB	R	H	2B	3B	HR	RBI	BB	SO	HBP	GDP	SB-CS	Avg.	OBP	SLG	OPS	E	Avg.
1997— DSL Rockies (DSL)		65	234	32	63	12	0	0	29	31	22	...	...	7-...	.269	...	.321	...	...	...
1998— Ariz. Rockies (Ariz.)	SS	40	148	25	41	5	3	0	17	12	25	3	1	8-1	.277	.339	.351	.691	14	.927
1999— Asheville (S. Atl.)	SS	125	430	57	115	28	3	9	46	20	79	6	12	11-7	.267	.307	.409	.716	38	.938
2000— Salem (Carol.)	SS	134	485	64	124	22	7	13	65	38	100	4	11	22-5	.256	.314	.410	.724	26	.961
2001— Carolina (Southern)	SS	3	13	1	3	1	0	0	1	0	4	0	1	1-0	.231	.231	.308	.538	2	.833
— Colorado (N.L.)	SS	72	273	32	82	15	11	8	53	8	55	2	6	3-0	.300	.325	.524	.849	5	.983
— Colo. Springs (PCL)	SS	74	281	40	87	27	7	7	48	12	43	2	8	11-8	.310	.340	.530	.870	16	.960
2002— Colorado (N.L.)	SS	155	566	69	136	25	7	6	49	34	120	5	17	9-2	.240	.286	.341	.627	27	.966
2003— Visalia (Calif.)	2B-SS	2	9	4	5	1	0	0	1	1	0	0	1	0-0	.556	.600	.667	1.267	0	1.000
— Tulsa (Texas)	2B-3B-OF																			
	SS	5	20	3	5	2	0	1	4	0	2	0	0	0-0	.250	.238	.500	.738	0	1.000
— Colorado (N.L.)	SS-2B-OF	87	316	45	80	19	3	10	33	17	60	3	3	7-2	.253	.297	.427	.724	12	.974
2004— Chicago (A.L.)	2B-SS-3B DH	134	502	82	142	31	6	23	74	32	96	3	10	9-11	.283	.327	.506	.833	11	.982
2005— Chicago (A.L.)	SS	146	481	58	121	23	3	16	71	34	77	4	7	4-6	.252	.301	.412	.712	16	.977
American League totals (2 years)		280	983	140	263	54	9	39	145	66	173	7	17	13-17	.268	.314	.460	.774	27	.979
National League totals (3 years)		314	1155	146	298	59	21	24	135	59	235	10	26	19-4	.258	.298	.408	.706	44	.972
Major League totals (5 years)		594	2138	286	561	113	30	63	280	125	408	17	43	32-21	.262	.305	.432	.737	71	.975

DIVISION SERIES RECORD

Year Team (League)	Pos.	G	AB	R	H	2B	3B	HR	RBI	BB	SO	HBP	GDP	SB-CS	Avg.	OBP	SLG	OPS	E	Avg.
2005— Chicago (A.L.)	SS	3	10	4	4	1	0	1	4	0	2	0	0	0-0	.400	.400	.800	1.200	0	1.000

CHAMPIONSHIP SERIES RECORD

Year Team (League)	Pos.	G	AB	R	H	2B	3B	HR	RBI	BB	SO	HBP	GDP	SB-CS	Avg.	OBP	SLG	OPS	E	Avg.
2005— Chicago (A.L.)	SS	5	16	1	4	1	0	0	0	2	3	0	1	0-0	.250	.333	.313	.646	1	.971

WORLD SERIES RECORD

Year Team (League)	Pos.	G	AB	R	H	2B	3B	HR	RBI	BB	SO	HBP	GDP	SB-CS	Avg.	OBP	SLG	OPS	E	Avg.
2005— Chicago (A.L.)	SS	4	16	2	4	0	0	0	0	3	3	0	0	1-0	.250	.368	.438	.806	2	.923

UTLEY, CHASE   2B

PERSONAL: Born December 17, 1978, in Pasadena, Calif. ... 6-1/183. ... Bats left, throws right. ... Full name: Chase Cameron Utley. ... High school: Long Beach Poly (California). ... College: UCLA.

TRANSACTIONS/CAREER NOTES: Selected by Los Angeles Dodgers organization in second round of 1997 free-agent draft; did not sign. ... Selected by Philadelphia Phillies organization in first round (15th pick overall) of 2000 free-agent draft.

2005 GAMES PLAYED BY POSITION (MLB): 2B—135, 1B—8.

SCOUTING REPORT *Offense:* Utley's hitting makes him a future star. Has a fluid stroke with good bat speed. Has the ability to make adjustments and can hit to all fields. Is an excellent run producer and has good power for a middle infielder. Can run and will start to steal more bases. *Defense:* He will be a good infielder because his agility has improved. Gets better jumps moving to his left but is better at going to his right. Continues to improve hands and footwork. Is aggressive going out on popups and has improved his pivot. Has an average arm but has quickened his release. *Outlook:* Utley is the best offensive second baseman in the league after Jeff Kent. Is a good clutch hitter and is only going to get better. **Grade 8.2**

CHASE UTLEY'S HITTING ZONE

.182	.485	.366
.224	.400	.287
.286	.500	.286

LEFTY-RIGHTY SPLITS

vs.	Avg.	AB	H	2B	3B	HR	RBI	BB	SO	OBP	Slg.
L	.219	128	28	5	3	7	24	25	34	.348	.469
R	.313	415	130	34	3	21	81	44	75	.385	.561

										BATTING									FIELDING	
Year Team (League)	Pos.	G	AB	R	H	2B	3B	HR	RBI	BB	SO	HBP	GDP	SB-CS	Avg.	OBP	SLG	OPS	E	Avg.
2000— Batavia (NY-Penn)	2B	40	153	21	47	13	1	2	22	18	23	2	3	5-3	.307	.383	.444	.827	3	.983
2001— Clearwater (Fla. St.)	2B	122	467	65	120	25	2	16	59	37	88	12	6	19-8	.257	.324	.422	.746	17	.970
2002— Scran./W.B. (I.L.)	3B	125	464	73	122	39	1	17	70	46	89	20	5	8-3	.263	.352	.461	.813	28	.918
2003— Scran./W.B. (I.L.)	2B	113	431	80	139	26	2	18	77	41	75	11	3	10-4	.323	.390	.517	.907	13	.983
— Philadelphia (N.L.)	2B	43	134	13	32	10	1	2	21	11	22	6	3	2-0	.239	.322	.373	.696	3	.983
2004— Scran./W.B. (I.L.)	2B	33	123	23	35	8	1	6	25	18	29	0	2	4-2	.285	.368	.512	.880	5	.970
— Philadelphia (N.L.)	2B-1B	94	267	36	71	11	2	13	57	15	40	2	6	4-1	.266	.308	.468	.776	4	.988
2005— Philadelphia (N.L.)	2B-1B	147	543	93	158	39	6	28	105	69	109	9	10	16-3	.291	.376	.540	.915	16	.978
Major League totals (3 years)		284	944	142	261	60	9	43	183	95	171	17	19	22-4	.276	.350	.496	.846	23	.982

VALDEZ, ISMAEL   P

PERSONAL: Born August 21, 1973, in Ciudad Victoria, Mexico. ... 6-4/230. ... Throws right, bats right. ... Name pronounced: ees-mah-EL val-DEZ. ... High school: Mexico (Ciudad Victoria). ... Previously known as Ismael Valdes.

TRANSACTIONS/CAREER NOTES: Signed as a non-drafted free agent by Los Angeles Dodgers (June 14, 1991). ... Loaned by Dodgers organization to Mexico City Tigers of the Mexican League (April 21-June 26, 1992; and March 17-August 19, 1993). ... On disabled list (July 6-28, 1997). ... On disabled list (July 26-September 1, 1998); included rehabilitation assignments to Vero Beach and San Bernardino. ... Traded by Dodgers with 2B Eric Young to Chicago Cubs for Ps Terry Adams and Chad Ricketts and a player to be named (December 12, 1999); Dodgers acquired P Brian Stephenson to complete deal (December 16, 1999). ... On disabled list (March 20-May 4, 2000); included rehabilitation assignment to Daytona. ... Traded by Cubs to Dodgers for P Jamie Arnold, OF Jorge Piedra and cash (July 26, 2000). ... On suspended list (September 12-18, 2000). ... Signed as a free agent by Anaheim Angels (January 4, 2001). ... On disabled list (March 29-April 14 and June 15-July 4, 2001). ... Signed as a free agent by Texas Rangers (January 28, 2002). ... Traded by Rangers to Seattle Mariners for 2B Jermaine Clark and P Derrick Van Dusen (August 18, 2002). ... Signed as a free agent by Rangers (January 15, 2003). ... On disabled list (April 20-May 17 and July 24-August 18, 2003); included rehabilitation assignments to Frisco. ... Signed as a free agent by San Diego Padres (December 18, 2003). ... Traded by Padres to Florida Marlins for P Travis Chick (July 31, 2004). ... On disabled list (April 4-July 22, 2005); included rehabilitation assignments to Jupiter and Albuquerque.

CAREER HITTING: 52-for-399 (.130), 20 R, 9 2B, 0 3B, 1 HR, 17 RBI.

SCOUTING REPORT *Throws:* His fastball is 85-89 mph. Slider is 78-81. Also has a curveball and changeup. *Tendencies:* He has no room for error, especially with his fastball, which straightens out up in the strike zone. Pitch has a small, tight cut and some tailing action. Curveball is his best out pitch. Likes to use both his two-seam and four-seam fastball. Pitches more with his two-seamer and shows off his four-seamer only for effect and to get hitters to chase balls out of the zone. Is a breaking-ball guy now. *Outlook:* Valdez is at best a six-inning starter but has to have excellent command to be effective. Has a history of injuries and will have to pitch very well in the spring to earn a spot in the rotation. **Grade 6**

ISMAEL VALDEZ'S PITCHING ZONE

.333	.250	.267
.250	.529	.480
.176	.455	.357

LEFTY-RIGHTY SPLITS

vs.	Avg.	AB	H	2B	3B	HR	RBI	BB	SO	OBP	Slg.
L	.341	91	31	11	2	2	18	9	12	.408	.571
R	.292	113	33	6	1	4	15	13	15	.377	.469

Year Team (League)	W	L	Pct.	ERA	WHIP	G	GS	CG	ShO	Hld.	Sv.-Opp.	IP	H	R	ER	HR	BB-IBB	SO	Avg.
1991— GC Dodgers (GCL)	2	2	.500	2.32	1.13	10	10	0	0	...	0-...	50.1	44	15	13	0	13-0	44	.233
1992— M.C. Tigers (Mex.)	0	0	...	19.64	4.36	5	0	0	0	...	0-...	3.2	15	9	8	1	1-...	2	...
— Dom. Dodgers (DSL)	3	0	1.000	1.42	1.16	6	0	0	0	...	0-...	38.0	27	9	6	0	17-...	34	...
1993— M.C. Tigers (Mex.)	16	7	.696	3.94	1.42	26	25	11	0	...	0-...	173.2	192	87	76	16	55-...	113	...
— San Antonio (Texas)	1	0	1.000	1.38	0.92	3	2	0	0	...	0-...	13.0	12	2	2	0	0-0	11	.240
1994— San Antonio (Texas)	2	3	.400	3.38	1.18	8	8	0	0	...	0-...	53.1	54	22	20	4	9-1	55	.263
— Albuquerque (PCL)	4	1	.800	3.40	1.27	8	8	0	0	...	0-...	45.0	44	21	17	1	13-0	39	.255
— Los Angeles (N.L.)	3	1	.750	3.18	1.09	21	1	0	0	4	0-0	28.1	21	10	10	2	10-2	28	.206
1995— Los Angeles (N.L.)	13	11	.542	3.05	1.11	33	27	6	2	2	1-1	197.2	168	76	67	17	51-5	150	.228
1996— Los Angeles (N.L.)	15	7	.682	3.32	1.21	33	33	0	0	...	0-...	225.0	219	94	83	20	54-10	173	.251
1997— Los Angeles (N.L.)	10	11	.476	2.65	1.11	30	30	0	0	...	0-...	196.2	171	68	58	17	47-1	140	.234
1998— Los Angeles (N.L.)	11	10	.524	3.98	1.36	27	27	2	2	0	0-...	174.0	171	82	77	17	66-4	122	.256
— Vero Beach (FSL)	0	0	...	0.00	1.00	1	1	0	0	...	0-...	3.0	2	0	0	0	1-0	3	.200
— San Bern. (Calif.)	1	0	1.000	2.84	1.26	1	1	0	0	...	0-...	6.1	7	2	2	0	1-0	4	.280
1999— Los Angeles (N.L.)	9	14	.391	3.98	1.33	32	32	2	1	0	0-...	203.1	213	97	90	32	58-2	143	.270
2000— Daytona (Fla. St.)	1	0	1.000	1.80	1.20	1	1	0	0	...	0-...	5.0	3	2	1	0	3-0	5	.176
— Chicago (N.L.)	2	4	.333	5.37	1.46	12	12	0	0	...	0-...	67.0	71	40	40	17	27-2	45	.273
— Los Angeles (N.L.)	3	0	.000	6.08	1.65	9	8	0	0	...	0-...	40.0	53	29	27	5	13-0	29	.327
2001— Anaheim (A.L.)	9	13	.409	4.45	1.39	27	27	1	0	...	0-0	163.2	177	82	81	20	50-3	100	.277

Year — Team (League)	W	L	Pct.	ERA	WHIP	G	GS	CG	ShO	Hld.	Sv.-Opp.	IP	H	R	ER	HR	BB-IBB	SO	Avg.
2002— Texas (A.L.)	6	9	.400	3.93	1.17	23	23	0	0	0	0-0	146.2	135	65	64	19	36-1	75	.242
— Seattle (A.L.)	2	3	.400	4.93	1.42	8	8	1	0	0	0-0	49.1	59	29	27	7	11-0	27	.299
2003— Frisco (Texas)	1	2	.333	2.03	1.10	3	3	0	0	...	0-...	13.1	12	5	3	0	2-0	6	.235
— Texas (A.L.)	8	8	.500	6.10	1.54	22	22	0	0	0	0-0	115.0	148	83	78	23	29-0	47	.318
2004— San Diego (N.L.)	9	6	.600	5.53	1.51	23	20	1	1	0	0-0	114.0	141	75	70	21	31-1	37	.303
— Florida (N.L.)	5	3	.625	4.50	1.41	11	11	0	0	0	0-0	56.0	61	30	28	12	18-2	30	.277
2005— Jupiter (Fla. St.)	1	1	.500	7.88	1.13	2	2	0	0	0	0-0	8.0	7	7	7	1	2-0	5	.226
— Albuquerque (PCL)	1	0	1.000	0.00	1.17	1	1	0	0	0	0-0	6.0	3	0	0	0	4-0	4	.158
— Florida (N.L.)	2	2	.500	5.33	1.70	14	7	0	0	0	0-0	50.2	64	32	30	6	22-6	27	.314
American League totals (3 years)	25	33	.431	4.74	1.36	80	80	2	0	0	0-0	474.2	519	259	250	69	126-4	249	.279
National League totals (9 years)	79	72	.523	3.86	1.29	245	208	11	6	6	1-1	1352.2	1353	633	580	165	397-35	924	.259
Major League totals (12 years)	104	105	.498	4.09	1.31	325	288	13	6	6	1-1	1827.1	1872	892	830	234	523-39	1173	.265

DIVISION SERIES RECORD

Year — Team (League)	W	L	Pct.	ERA	WHIP	G	GS	CG	ShO	Hld.	Sv.-Opp.	IP	H	R	ER	HR	BB-IBB	SO	Avg.
1995— Los Angeles (N.L.)	0	0		0.00	0.57	1	1	0	0	0	0-0	7.0	3	2	0	1	1-0	6	.125
1996— Los Angeles (N.L.)	0	1	.000	4.26	0.79	1	1	0	0	0	0-0	6.1	5	3	3	3	0-0	5	.208
Division series totals (2 years)	0	1	.000	2.03	0.68	2	2	0	0	0	0-0	13.1	8	5	3	4	1-0	11	.167

VALDEZ, WILSON — SS

PERSONAL: Born May 20, 1978, in Nizao, Dominican Republic. ... 5-11/160. ... Bats right, throws right. ... Full name: Wilson Antonio Valdez. ... High school: Aliro Paulino (Nizao, D.R.).
TRANSACTIONS/CAREER NOTES: Signed as a non-drafted free agent by Montreal Expos organization (February 4, 1997). ... Claimed on waivers by Florida Marlins (March 29, 2002). ... Traded by Marlins to Chicago White Sox for P Billy Koch and cash (June 17, 2004). ... Claimed on waivers by New York Mets (March 29, 2005). ... Claimed on waivers by Seattle Mariners (April 1, 2005). ... Traded by Mariners to San Diego Padres for Ps Michael Bumstead and R.D. Spiehs (June 9, 2005).
2005 GAMES PLAYED BY POSITION (MLB): SS—50.

WILSON VALDEZ'S HITTING ZONE

.222	.000	.200
.261	.222	.381
.286	.091	.000

LEFTY-RIGHTY SPLITS

vs.	Avg.	AB	H	2B	3B	HR	RBI	BB	SO	OBP	Slg.
L	.143	42	6	3	0	0	1	3	11	.200	.214
R	.227	97	22	4	1	0	8	5	15	.265	.289

Year — Team (League)	Pos.	G	AB	R	H	2B	3B	HR	RBI	BB	SO	HBP	GDP	SB-CS	Avg.	OBP	SLG	OPS	E	Avg.
1999— GC Expos (GCL)	SS-2B	22	82	12	24	2	0	0	7	5	7	0	1	10-0	.293	.330	.317	.647	3	.972
— Vermont (N.Y.-Penn.)	SS-2B	36	130	19	32	7	0	1	10	7	21	0	3	4-3	.246	.283	.323	.606	4	.956
2000— Cape Fear (S. Atl.)	2B-SS	15	49	6	12	2	0	0	3	2	9	0	0	3-0	.245	.275	.286	.560	5	.921
— Vermont (N.Y.-Penn.)	SS	65	248	32	66	8	1	1	30	17	32	1	3	16-9	.266	.312	.319	.631	20	.944
2001— Clinton (Midw.)	SS	59	214	31	54	8	1	0	11	9	22	2	5	6-7	.252	.286	.299	.585	11	.966
— Jupiter (Fla. St.)	SS	64	233	34	58	13	2	2	19	10	33	2	4	7-3	.249	.286	.348	.633	8	.971
2002— Portland (East.)	SS	114	375	51	98	19	5	1	30	15	47	4	12	18-6	.261	.294	.347	.641	28	.944
2003— Carolina (Sou.)	2B-SS	37	144	28	45	6	2	0	14	15	17	0	2	16-5	.313	.373	.382	.755	4	.978
— Albuquerque (PCL)	SS-2B	90	338	45	97	12	4	0	18	19	37	1	10	33-9	.287	.326	.346	.672	11	.974
2004— Albuquerque (PCL)	SS	66	285	36	91	11	3	2	25	16	35	2	8	19-12	.319	.357	.400	.753	6	.982
— Charlotte (Int'l)	SS	70	281	37	85	7	2	2	15	12	41	3	6	13-5	.302	.338	.363	.694	6	.979
— Chicago (A.L.)	SS-2B	19	43	8	10	1	0	0	4	2	5	0	1	1-2	.233	.267	.326	.592	1	.980
2005— Seattle (A.L.)	SS	42	126	9	25	5	1	0	8	6	25	0	1	2-2	.198	.235	.254	.489	5	.973
— Tacoma (PCL)	SS	1	4	0	0	0	0	0	0	1	1	0	0	0-0	.000	.000	.000	.000	1	.833
— San Diego (N.L.)	SS	9	13	0	3	2	0	0	1	2	1	0	1	0-0	.231	.333	.385	.718	1	.944
— Portland (PCL)	SS	50	155	14	38	5	3	1	15	15	27	0	4	8-0	.245	.310	.335	.645	4	.981
American League totals (2 years)		61	169	17	35	6	1	0	12	8	30	0	2	3-4	.207	.243	.272	.515	6	.974
National League totals (1 year)		9	13	0	3	2	0	0	1	2	1	0	1	0-0	.231	.333	.385	.718	1	.944
Major League totals (2 years)		70	182	17	38	8	1	0	13	10	31	0	3	3-4	.209	.250	.280	.530	7	.972

VALENT, ERIC — 1B/OF

PERSONAL: Born April 4, 1977, in La Mirada, Calif. ... 5-11/195. ... Bats left, throws left. ... Full name: Eric Christian Valent. ... Name pronounced: va-LENT. ... High school: Canyon (Anaheim, Calif.). ... College: UCLA.
TRANSACTIONS/CAREER NOTES: Selected by Detroit Tigers organization in 26th round of 1995 free-agent draft; did not sign. ... Selected by Philadelphia Phillies organization in supplemental round ("sandwich pick" between first and second rounds, 42nd pick overall) of 1998 free-agent draft; pick received as compensation for loss of Type A free agent P J.D. Drew. ... Traded by Phillies to Cincinnati Reds (September 2, 2003), completing deal in which Reds traded C Kelly Stinnett to Phillies for a player to be named (August 31, 2003). ... Selected by New York Mets organization from Reds organization in Rule 5 minor league draft (December 15, 2003).
2005 GAMES PLAYED BY POSITION (MLB): OF—12.

LEFTY-RIGHTY SPLITS

vs.	Avg.	AB	H	2B	3B	HR	RBI	BB	SO	OBP	Slg.
L	.000	3	0	0	0	0	0	1	0	.250	.000
R	.200	40	8	3	0	1	6	17	.304	.275	

Year — Team (League)	Pos.	G	AB	R	H	2B	3B	HR	RBI	BB	SO	HBP	GDP	SB-CS	Avg.	OBP	SLG	OPS	E	Avg.
1998— Piedmont (S. Atl.)	OF	22	89	24	38	12	0	8	28	14	19	0	0	0-0	.427	.500	.831	1.331	2	.952
— Clearwater (Fla. St.)	OF	34	125	24	33	8	1	5	25	16	29	3	4	1-2	.264	.359	.464	.823	0	1.000
1999— Clearwater (Fla. St.)	OF	134	520	91	150	31	9	20	106	58	110	5	10	5-3	.288	.359	.498	.857	9	.969
2000— Reading (East.)	OF	128	469	81	121	25	5	22	90	70	89	5	7	2-3	.258	.356	.467	.823	4	.984
2001— Scran./W.B. (Int'l)	OF-1B	117	448	65	122	30	4	21	78	49	105	8	13	0-1	.272	.352	.489	.841	3	.992
— Philadelphia (N.L.)	OF-DH	22	41	3	4	2	0	0	1	4	11	1	0	0-0	.098	.196	.146	.342	0	1.000
2002— Scran./W.B. (Int'l)	OF-1B	140	546	69	137	34	2	9	84	49	94	1	13	0-2	.251	.311	.370	.681	10	.980
— Philadelphia (N.L.)	OF-1B	7	10	1	2	0	0	0	1	0	3	0	1	0-0	.200	.200	.200	.400	1	.750
2003— Scran./W.B. (Int'l)	OF-1B	134	450	62	98	27	2	12	51	60	102	1	5	0-0	.218	.308	.367	.675	8	.974
— Cincinnati (N.L.)	OF	18	42	3	9	0	0	1	2	9	0	0	0	0-0	.214	.250	.214	.464	0	1.000
2004— New York (N.L.)	OF-1B	130	270	39	72	15	2	13	34	28	61	1	10	0-1	.267	.337	.481	.818	1	.996
2005— New York (N.L.)	OF	28	43	4	8	3	0	1	1	0	7	0	0	0-0	.186	.300	.256	.556	1	.955
— Norfolk (Int'l)	OF-1B-DH	79	275	44	70	13	1	9	38	55	58	1	6	1-1	.255	.380	.407	.787	5	.985
Major League totals (5 years)		205	406	50	95	20	2	13	37	41	101	2	11	0-1	.234	.307	.389	.696	3	.992

V

VALENTIN, JAVIER — C

PERSONAL: Born September 19, 1975, in Manati, Puerto Rico. ... 5-10/192. ... Bats both, throws right. ... Full name: Jose Javier Valentin. ... Name pronounced: val-en-TEEN. ... High school: Fernando Callejo (Manati, Puerto Rico). ... Brother of Jose Valentin, infielder, Los Angeles Dodgers.

TRANSACTIONS/CAREER NOTES: Selected by Minnesota Twins organization in third round of 1993 free-agent draft. ... Traded by Twins with P Matt Kinney to Milwaukee Brewers for Ps Matt Yeatman and Gerard Oakes (November 15, 2002). ... Traded by Brewers to Tampa Bay Devil Rays for OF Jason Conti (March 24, 2003). ... Signed as a free agent by Cincinnati Reds organization (January 9, 2004).

2005 GAMES PLAYED BY POSITION (MLB): C—62, 1B—2.

SCOUTING REPORT
Valentin was one of the most productive backup catchers in either league last season. Has a slightly long stroke. Is much better from the left side. Likes the ball up and has very good carry off the bat from the left side. Hasn't shown much improvement behind the plate. Arm is very erratic and throws frequently are rushed, causing them to bounce. Doesn't have the arm strength he had showed in the past, due largely to his footwork and mechanics. Is a slightly rigid receiver but his hands are good. Range and mobility are limited. Calls a good game.
Grade 6.4

JAVIER VALENTIN'S HITTING ZONE

.231	.300	.273
.333	.609	.289
.364	.455	.269

LEFTY-RIGHTY SPLITS

vs.	Avg.	AB	H	2B	3B	HR	RBI	BB	SO	OBP	Slg.
L	.184	38	7	0	0	2	10	10	7	.354	.342
R	.301	183	55	11	0	12	40	20	30	.364	.557

										BATTING								FIELDING	
Year	Team (League)	Pos.	G	AB	R	H	2B	3B	HR	RBI	BB	SO	HBP	GDP	SB-CS	Avg.	OBP	SLG	OPS	E	Avg.
1993— GC Twins (GCL)	3B-C-DH	32	103	18	27	6	1	1	19	14	19	1	1	0-2	.262	.344	.369	.713	5	.966
— Elizabethton (Appal.)	C	9	24	3	5	1	0	0	3	4	2	1	0	0-0	.208	.345	.250	.595	2	.977
1994— Elizabethton (Appal.)	3B-C	54	210	23	44	5	0	9	27	15	44	2	9	0-1	.210	.263	.362	.625	12	.966
1995— Fort Wayne (Midw.)	3B-C	112	383	59	124	26	5	19	65	47	75	2	7	0-5	.324	.400	.567	.967	23	.974
1996— Fort Myers (Fla. St.)	C-DH-3B	87	338	34	89	26	1	7	54	32	65	4	5	1-0	.263	.330	.408	.738	4	.991
— New Britain (East.)	C-3B-DH	48	165	22	39	8	0	3	14	16	35	1	2	0-3	.236	.308	.339	.647	5	.978
1997— New Britain (East.)	C-DH-3B	102	370	41	90	17	0	8	50	30	61	1	5	2-3	.243	.297	.354	.651	6	.990
— Minnesota (A.L.)	C	4	7	1	2	0	0	0	0	0	3	0	0	0-0	.286	.286	.286	.571	0	1.000
1998— Minnesota (A.L.)	C-DH	55	162	11	32	7	1	3	18	11	30	0	7	0-0	.198	.247	.309	.556	5	.984
1999— Minnesota (A.L.)	C	78	218	22	54	12	1	5	28	22	39	1	2	0-0	.248	.313	.381	.694	1	.998
2000— Salt Lake (PCL)	C	39	140	25	50	16	2	7	35	9	27	1	1	1-0	.357	.397	.650	1.047	1	.994
2001— Edmonton (PCL)	C-3B-1B	121	431	53	121	29	2	17	71	47	108	4	14	0-1	.281	.352	.476	.827	14	.977
2002— Edmonton (PCL)	C-3B-1B	127	455	69	130	33	1	21	80	41	96	5	15	0-1	.286	.346	.501	.847	9	.984
— Minnesota (A.L.)	C	4	4	0	2	0	0	0	0	0	0	0	0	0-0	.500	.500	.500	1.000	0	1.000
2003— Tampa Bay (A.L.)	C-DH	49	135	13	30	7	1	3	15	5	31	1	7	0-0	.222	.254	.356	.609	1	1.000
2004— Cincinnati (N.L.)	C-1B	82	202	18	47	10	1	6	20	17	36	1	4	0-0	.233	.293	.381	.674	4	.989
2005— Cincinnati (N.L.)	C-1B	76	221	36	62	11	0	14	50	30	37	0	5	0-0	.281	.362	.520	.883	3	.992
American League totals (5 years)		190	526	47	120	26	3	11	61	38	103	2	16	0-0	.228	.279	.352	.631	6	.994
National League totals (2 years)		158	423	54	109	21	1	20	70	47	73	1	9	0-0	.258	.330	.454	.784	7	.991
Major League totals (7 years)		348	949	101	229	47	4	31	131	85	176	3	25	0-0	.241	.302	.397	.699	13	.993

VALENTIN, JOSE — SS/3B

PERSONAL: Born October 12, 1969, in Manati, Puerto Rico. ... 5-10/195. ... Bats left, throws right. ... Full name: Jose Antonio Valentin. ... Name pronounced: val-en-TEEN. ... High school: Fernando Callejo (Manati, Puerto Rico). ... Brother of Javier Valentin, catcher, Cincinnati Reds.

TRANSACTIONS/CAREER NOTES: Signed as a non-drafted free agent by San Diego Padres organization (October 12, 1986). ... Traded by Padres with P Ricky Bones and OF Matt Mieske to Milwaukee Brewers for 3B Gary Sheffield and P Geoff Kellogg (March 27, 1992). ... On disabled list (April 14-May 5, 1997); included rehabilitation assignment to Beloit. ... On disabled list (April 13-June 16, 1999); included rehabilitation assignment to Louisville. ... Traded by Brewers with P Cal Eldred to Chicago White Sox for Ps Jaime Navarro and John Snyder (January 12, 2000). ... On disabled list (June 8-24, 2001). ... On disabled list (April 19-May 7, 2004); included rehabilitation assignment to Charlotte. ... Signed as a free agent by Los Angeles Dodgers (December 21, 2004). ... On disabled list (May 4-July 31, 2005); included rehabilitation assignment to Las Vegas.

2005 GAMES PLAYED BY POSITION (MLB): 3B—29, OF—22, SS—1.

SCOUTING REPORT
Offense: The former switch hitter now hits only from the left side. Is impatient, chasing pitches up and out of the zone as well as breaking balls in the dirt. Has a long stroke but still has bat speed. Is a dead high-fastball hitter. Commits too quickly with his swing, making him susceptible to off-speed pitches. Best asset is power. **Defense:** Valentin is an erratic fielder. Has a plus arm but airmails many throws. Gets a better jump to his left than to his right.
Outlook: After 14 years in the majors Valentin has regressed in all phases of the game. Missed much of last season with a torn ligament in his left knee. Career is on a downward slide. May no longer be able to play every day. **Grade 5**

JOSE VALENTIN'S HITTING ZONE

.167	.333	.000
.158	.143	.135
.333	.333	.286

LEFTY-RIGHTY SPLITS

vs.	Avg.	AB	H	2B	3B	HR	RBI	BB	SO	OBP	Slg.
L	.316	19	6	0	0	1	4	3	3	.417	.474
R	.148	128	19	4	2	1	10	28	35	.313	.234

										BATTING								FIELDING	
Year	Team (League)	Pos.	G	AB	R	H	2B	3B	HR	RBI	BB	SO	HBP	GDP	SB-CS	Avg.	OBP	SLG	OPS	E	Avg.
1987— Spokane (N'west)	SS	70	244	52	61	8	2	2	24	35	38	1	4	8-5	.250	.346	.324	.670	26	.914
1988— Char., S.C. (S. Atl.)	SS	133	444	56	103	20	1	6	44	45	83	3	10	11-4	.232	.304	.322	.627	60	.911
1989— Riverside (Calif.)	SS	114	381	40	74	10	5	10	41	37	93	5	4	8-7	.194	.273	.325	.598	46	.924
— Wichita (Texas)	3B-SS	18	49	8	12	1	0	2	5	5	12	0	1	1-0	.245	.315	.388	.703	8	.899
1990— Wichita (Texas)	SS	11	36	4	10	2	0	0	2	5	7	0	1	2-1	.278	.366	.333	.699	2	.959
1991— Wichita (Texas)	SS	129	447	73	112	22	5	17	68	55	115	4	5	8-6	.251	.335	.436	.771	40	.939
1992— Denver (A.A.)	SS	139	492	78	118	19	11	3	45	53	99	5	8	9-4	.240	.317	.341	.658	38	.941
— Milwaukee (A.L.)	2B-SS	4	3	1	0	0	0	0	1	0	0	0	0	0-0	.000	.000	.000	.000	1	.667
1993— New Orleans (A.A.)	SS-1B	122	389	56	96	22	5	9	53	47	87	8	3	9-10	.247	.337	.398	.736	29	.951

| | | | | | | | | | | | BATTING | | | | | | | | | | FIELDING | |
Year	Team (League)	Pos.	G	AB	R	H	2B	3B	HR	RBI	BB	SO	HBP	GDP	SB-CS	Avg.	OBP	SLG	OPS	E	Avg.
	—Milwaukee (A.L.)	SS	19	53	10	13	1	2	1	7	7	16	1	1	1-0	.245	.344	.396	.740	6	.922
1994—	Milwaukee (A.L.)	SS-2B-3B-DH	97	285	47	68	19	0	11	46	38	75	2	1	12-3	.239	.330	.421	.751	§ 20	.961
1995—	Milwaukee (A.L.)	SS-DH-3B	112	338	62	74	23	3	11	49	37	83	0	0	16-8	.219	.293	.402	.695	15	.971
1996—	Milwaukee (A.L.)	SS	154	552	90	143	33	7	24	95	66	145	0	4	17-4	.259	.336	.475	.811	* 37	.950
1997—	Milwaukee (A.L.)	SS-DH	136	494	58	125	23	1	17	58	39	109	4	5	19-8	.253	.310	.407	.717	20	.967
	—Beloit (Midw.)	SS	2	6	3	3	1	0	0	1	2	1	0	0	0-0	.500	.625	.667	1.292	0	1.000
1998—	Milwaukee (N.L.)	SS-DH-3B	151	428	65	96	24	0	16	49	63	105	1	2	10-7	.224	.323	.393	.716	21	.963
1999—	Milwaukee (N.L.)	SS	89	256	45	58	9	5	10	38	48	52	2	3	3-2	.227	.347	.418	.765	22	.937
	—Louisville (Int'l)	SS	6	20	6	5	0	0	3	3	4	3	0	0	0-1	.250	.375	.700	1.075	0	1.000
2000—	Chicago (A.L.)	SS-OF	144	568	107	155	37	6	25	92	59	106	4	11	19-2	.273	.343	.491	.835	§ 36	.950
2001—	Chicago (A.L.)	3B-SS-OF	124	438	74	113	22	2	28	68	50	114	3	7	9-6	.258	.336	.509	.845	22	.947
2002—	Chicago (A.L.)	3B-SS-DH	135	474	70	118	26	4	25	75	43	99	2	9	3-3	.249	.311	.479	.790	19	.957
2003—	Chicago (A.L.)	3B	144	503	79	119	26	2	28	74	54	114	3	6	8-3	.237	.313	.463	.776	20	.969
2004—	Charlotte (Int'l)	DH-SS	8	31	1	2	0	0	0	2	2	15	0	1	0-0	.065	.121	.065	.186	2	.895
	—Chicago (A.L.)	SS-DH	125	450	73	97	20	3	30	70	43	139	3	5	8-6	.216	.287	.473	.760	20	.965
2005—	Las Vegas (PCL)	3B-OF-DH	12	35	8	14	0	2	5	7	7	6	1	0	1-0	.400	.512	.657	1.169	0	1.000
	2B		56	147	17	25	4	2	2	14	31	38	4	2	3-1	.170	.326	.265	.591	8	.932
	—Los Angeles (N.L.)	3B-OF-SS																			
	American League totals (11 years)		1194	4158	671	1025	230	30	200	635	436	1000	22	49	112-43	.247	.319	.461	.780	216	.959
	National League totals (3 years)		296	831	127	179	37	7	28	101	142	195	7	7	16-10	.215	.331	.378	.709	51	.951
	Major League totals (14 years)		1490	4989	798	1204	267	37	228	736	578	1195	29	56	128-53	.241	.321	.447	.768	267	.958

DIVISION SERIES RECORD

Year	Team (League)	Pos.	G	AB	R	H	2B	3B	HR	RBI	BB	SO	HBP	GDP	SB-CS	Avg.	OBP	SLG	OPS	E	Avg.
2000—	Chicago (A.L.)	SS	3	10	2	3	2	0	1	1	2	2	0	0	3-0	.300	.417	.500	.917	1	.964

VALENTINE, JOE   P

PERSONAL: Born December 24, 1979, in Las Vegas. ... 6-2/210. ... Throws right, bats right. ... Full name: Joseph John Valentine. ... High school: Deer Park (N.Y.). ... Junior college: Jefferson Davis (Ala.) Community College.

TRANSACTIONS/CAREER NOTES: Selected by Chicago White Sox organization in 26th round of 1999 free-agent draft. ... Selected by Montreal Expos from White Sox organization in Rule 5 major league draft (December 13, 2001). ... Traded by Expos to Detroit Tigers for cash (December 13, 2001). ... Returned to White Sox organization (April 1, 2002). ... Traded by White Sox with P Keith Foulke, C Mark Johnson and cash to Oakland Athletics for P Billy Koch and two players to be named (December 3, 2002); White Sox acquired P Neal Cotts and OF Daylon Holt to complete deal (December 16, 2002). ... Traded by Oakland Athletics with Ps Aaron Harang and Jeff Bruksch to Cincinnati Reds for OF Jose Guillen (July 30, 2003).

CAREER HITTING: 0-for-1 (.000), 0 R, 0 2B, 0 3B, 0 HR, 0 RBI.

SCOUTING REPORT *Throws:* His fastball ranges from 92-96 mph and his slider from 81-84. Also throws a changeup. *Tendencies:* Power is Valentine's game: The fastball is explosive and overpowering when thrown properly. Delivery is inconsistent, however, and he tends to overthrow all his pitches. Slider has a big break. Change has good sinking action. Pitching behind in the count forces him to let up at times and leaves too many pitches out over the plate. *Outlook:* He has the stuff to potentially close, but he hasn't shown much improvement since coming to the big leagues.

Grade 5.1

JOE VALENTINE'S PITCHING ZONE

.333	.400	.000
.538	.500	.308
.000	...	.333

LEFTY-RIGHTY SPLITS

vs.	Avg.	AB	H	2B	3B	HR	RBI	BB	SO	OBP	Slg.
L	.350	20	7	1	0	2	5	6	3	.481	.700
R	.268	41	11	2	1	2	7	5	6	.375	.512

Year	Team (League)	W	L	Pct.	ERA	WHIP	G	GS	CG	ShO	Hld.	Sv.-Opp.	IP	H	R	ER	HR	BB-IBB	SO	Avg.
1999—	Ariz. White Sox (AZL)	0	0	...	0.00	0.69	3	0	0	0	...	0-...	4.1	2	0	0	0	1-0	2	.154
	—Bristol (Appal.)	0	0	...	7.02	2.16	11	0	0	0	...	0-...	16.2	27	17	13	2	9-0	14	.360
2000—	Bristol (Appal.)	2	1	.667	2.88	1.04	19	0	0	0	...	7-...	25.0	14	10	8	1	12-1	30	.163
2001—	Kannapolis (S. Atl.)	2	2	.500	2.93	1.01	30	0	0	0	...	14-...	30.2	21	11	10	1	10-1	33	.194
	—Win.-Salem (Carol.)	5	1	.833	1.01	1.01	27	0	0	0	...	8-...	44.2	18	7	5	0	27-3	50	.122
2002—	Birmingham (Sou.)	4	1	.800	1.97	1.11	55	0	0	0	...	36-...	59.1	36	16	13	1	30-3	63	.173
2003—	Sacramento (PCL)	1	3	.250	4.82	1.55	40	0	0	0	...	4-...	52.1	44	33	28	5	37-3	53	.222
	—Cincinnati (N.L.)	0	0	...	18.00	3.00	2	0	0	0	0	0-0	2.0	5	4	4	1	1-0	1	.455
	—Louisville (Int'l)	1	0	1.000	0.79	0.71	9	0	0	0	0	1-...	11.1	5	1	1	0	3-0	8	.132
2004—	Louisville (Int'l)	5	5	.500	5.01	1.47	30	0	0	0	0	0-...	64.2	63	41	36	8	32-0	61	.258
	—Cincinnati (N.L.)	2	3	.400	5.22	1.64	24	1	0	0	5	4-4	29.1	23	18	17	4	25-1	29	.211
2005—	Louisville (Int'l)	0	7	.000	5.70	1.77	49	0	0	0	10	3-7	53.2	56	36	34	4	39-4	44	.272
	—Cincinnati (N.L.)	0	1	.000	8.16	2.02	16	0	0	0	2	0-1	14.1	18	15	13	4	11-0	9	.254
	Major League totals (3 years)	2	4	.333	6.70	1.82	42	1	0	0	7	4-5	45.2	46	37	34	9	37-1	39	.254

VALVERDE, JOSE   P

PERSONAL: Born July 24, 1979, in San Pedro de Macoris, Dominican Republic. ... 6-4/254. ... Throws right, bats right. ... Full name: Jose Rafael Valverde. ... Name pronounced: val-VARE-day. ... High school: Escuela San Lorenzo (El Seybo, Dominican Republic).

TRANSACTIONS/CAREER NOTES: Signed as a non-drafted free agent by Arizona Diamondbacks organization (February 6, 1997). ... On disabled list (June 14, 2004-remainder of season); included rehabilitation assignment to Tucson. ... On disabled list (March 25-May 2, 2005); included rehabilitation assignment to Tucson.

CAREER HITTING: 1-for-1 (1.000), 1 R, 1 2B, 0 3B, 0 HR, 0 RBI.

JOSE VALVERDE'S PITCHING ZONE

.154	.133	.294
.152	.296	.304
.222	.364	.158

LEFTY-RIGHTY SPLITS

vs.	Avg.	AB	H	2B	3B	HR	RBI	BB	SO	OBP	Slg.
L	.168	101	17	3	0	2	9	10	23	.248	.257
R	.241	141	34	3	0	3	14	10	52	.296	.326

SCOUTING REPORT *Throws:* Valverde features at fastball that ranges from 92-96 mph, a slider in the mid-80 and a split-finger fastball in the upper 80s. *Tendencies:* He is a strikeout pitcher who improved his command a lot. Has improved his delivery and stayed consistent with it the second half of last season. Can overpower hitters up in the zone. Has a very sharp biting slider. Splitter makes him even more effective against lefthanders; hitters can't lay off it. Can be very hyper on the mound. *Outlook:* Based on his finish in 2005, he'll be the closer in 2006. *Grade 8*

Year	Team (League)	W	L	Pct.	ERA	WHIP	G	GS	CG	ShO	Hld.	Sv.-Opp.	IP	H	R	ER	HR	BB-IBB	SO	Avg.
1997—	Dom. D'backs (DSL.)	0	0	.000	5.30	1.77	14	0	0	0	...	0-...	18.2	20	12	11	1	13-...	19	...
1998—	Dom. D'backs (DSL.)	1	3	.250	1.75	1.03	23	4	0	0	...	7-...	51.1	31	14	10	2	22-0	56	...
1999—	Ariz. D'backs (Ariz.)	1	2	.333	4.08	1.53	20	0	0	0	...	8-...	28.2	34	21	13	1	10-0	47	.274
	—South Bend (Midw.)	0	0	...	0.00	1.50	2	0	0	0	...	0-...	2.2	2	0	0	0	2-0	3	.250
2000—	South Bend (Midw.)	0	5	.000	5.40	1.77	31	0	0	0	...	14-...	31.2	31	20	19	1	25-0	39	.254
	—Missoula (Pion.)	1	0	1.000	0.00	0.60	12	0	0	0	...	4-...	11.2	3	0	0	0	4-0	24	.075
2001—	El Paso (Texas)	2	2	.500	3.92	1.52	39	0	0	0	...	13-...	41.1	36	19	18	1	27-0	72	.225
2002—	Tucson (PCL)	2	4	.333	5.85	1.43	49	0	0	0	...	5-...	47.2	45	33	31	8	23-1	65	.250
2003—	Tucson (PCL)	1	1	.500	3.10	1.38	22	0	0	0	...	5-...	29.0	26	11	10	1	14-1	26	.236
	—Arizona (N.L.)	2	1	.667	2.15	0.99	54	0	0	0	8	10-11	50.1	24	16	12	4	26-2	71	.137
2004—	Arizona (N.L.)	1	2	.333	4.25	1.35	29	0	0	0	5	8-10	29.2	23	17	14	7	17-4	38	.213
	—Tucson (PCL)	1	1	.500	4.22	1.31	10	1	0	0	...	3-...	10.2	9	5	5	0	5-0	5	.225
2005—	Tucson (PCL)	0	0	...	0.00	1.00	2	0	0	0	...	0-0	2.0	1	0	0	0	1-0	3	.143
	—Arizona (N.L.)	3	4	.429	2.44	1.07	61	0	0	0	7	15-17	66.1	51	19	18	5	20-1	75	.211
Major League totals (3 years)		**6**	**7**	**.462**	**2.71**	**1.10**	**144**	**0**	**0**	**0**	**20**	**33-38**	**146.1**	**98**	**52**	**44**	**16**	**63-7**	**184**	**.187**

VAN BUREN, JERMAINE   P

PERSONAL: Born July 2, 1980, in Laurel, Miss. ... 6-1/220. ... Throws right, bats right. ... Full name: Jermaine Russell Van Buren. ... High school: Hattiesburg (Miss.).
TRANSACTIONS/CAREER NOTES: Selected by Colorado Rockies organization in second round of 1998 free-agent draft. ... Released by Rockies (March 23, 2003). ... Signed by Fort Worth of the independent Central League (May 2003). ... Signed as a free agent by Chicago Cubs (January 24, 2004).
CAREER HITTING: 0-for-0 (.000), 0 R, 0 2B, 0 3B, 0 HR, 0 RBI.

LEFTY-RIGHTY SPLITS

vs.	Avg.	AB	H	2B	3B	HR	RBI	BB	SO	OBP	Slg.
L	.000	1	0	0	0	0	0	3	0	.750	.000
R	.125	16	2	0	0	0	0	6	3	.364	.125

Year	Team (League)	W	L	Pct.	ERA	WHIP	G	GS	CG	ShO	Hld.	Sv.-Opp.	IP	H	R	ER	HR	BB-IBB	SO	Avg.
1998—	Ariz. Rockies (Ariz.)	7	2	.778	2.22	0.98	12	11	1	1	...	0-...	65.0	42	20	16	2	22-0	92	.182
	—Portland (N'west)	0	0	...	3.60	1.40	2	2	0	0	...	0-...	10.0	7	4	4	0	7-0	9	.212
1999—	Asheville (S. Atl.)	7	10	.412	4.91	1.49	28	28	0	0	...	0-...	143.0	143	87	78	16	70-0	133	.266
2000—	Portland (N'west)	4	5	.444	2.61	1.22	13	13	0	0	...	0-...	69.0	54	27	20	1	30-0	41	.214
2001—	Casper (Pion.)	3	0	1.000	5.32	1.48	6	3	1	0	...	0-...	23.2	25	15	14	2	10-0	25	.275
	—Tri-Cities (N'west)	1	0	1.000	7.20	2.00	1	1	0	0	...	0-...	5.0	7	4	4	0	3-0	2	.304
2002—	Asheville (S. Atl.)	6	9	.400	4.96	1.49	30	17	0	0	...	0-...	107.0	115	71	59	13	44-1	88	.276
2003—	Fort Worth (Cen.)	9	4	.692	3.07	1.29	18	18	1	0	...	0-...	111.1	107	45	38	4	37-0	113	.255
2004—	Lansing (Midw.)	0	1	.000	1.80	2.20	3	0	0	0	...	0-...	5.0	6	1	1	0	5-0	7	.300
	—West Tenn (Sou.)	3	2	.600	1.87	0.89	51	0	0	0	...	21-...	53.0	23	11	11	2	24-0	64	.128
	—Iowa (PCL)	0	0	...	2.08	0.69	3	0	0	0	...	1-...	4.1	3	1	1	1	0-0	5	.188
2005—	Iowa (PCL)	2	3	.400	1.98	1.01	52	0	0	0	2	25-28	54.2	33	13	12	5	22-2	65	.181
	—Chicago (N.L.)	0	2	.000	3.00	1.83	6	0	0	0	0	0-0	6.0	2	2	2	0	9-2	3	.118
Major League totals (1 year)		**0**	**2**	**.000**	**3.00**	**1.83**	**6**	**0**	**0**	**0**	**0**	**0-0**	**6.0**	**2**	**2**	**2**	**0**	**9-2**	**3**	**.118**

VARGAS, CLAUDIO   P

PERSONAL: Born June 19, 1978, in Valverde Mao, Dominican Republic. ... 6-3/228. ... Throws right, bats right. ... Full name: Claudio Almonte Vargas.
TRANSACTIONS/CAREER NOTES: Signed as a non-drafted free agent by Florida Marlins organization (August 25, 1995). ... Traded by Florida Marlins with OF Cliff Floyd, OF/2B Wilton Guerrero and cash to Montreal Expos for Ps Carl Pavano, Graeme Lloyd and Justin Wayne, IF Mike Mordecai and a player to be named (July 11, 2002); Marlins acquired P Don Levinski to complete deal (August 6, 2002). ... On disabled list (August 6-September 15, 2003). ... Expos franchise transferred to Washington, D.C., and renamed Washington Nationals for 2005 season (December 3, 2004). ... On disabled list (March 16-May 11, 2005); included rehabilitation assignment to New Orleans. ... Claimed on waivers by Arizona Diamondbacks (June 3, 2005).
CAREER HITTING: 5-for-88 (.057), 2 R, 0 2B, 0 3B, 0 HR, 3 RBI.

SCOUTING REPORT *Throws:* Vargas' fastball ranges from 90-93 mph. Also throws a slider and a changeup. *Tendencies:* With his very loose, but long, arm action he opens up quickly and is easy to follow. Fastball's best tailing action is down and out of the zone. Pitch usually is out over the plate. Slider loops and doesn't bite sharply; it has a slower curve-like break that starts away from lefthanders. Straight change lacks deception. *Outlook:* He moved into Arizona's rotation after coming over from the Nationals, but he hasn't shown a lot of improvement. *Grade 5.7*

CLAUDIO VARGAS' PITCHING ZONE

.242	.261	.185
.243	.490	.300
.350	.294	.364

LEFTY-RIGHTY SPLITS

vs.	Avg.	AB	H	2B	3B	HR	RBI	BB	SO	OBP	Slg.
L	.268	254	68	17	2	14	31	27	44	.345	.516
R	.288	271	78	19	3	11	41	20	51	.345	.502

Year	Team (League)	W	L	Pct.	ERA	WHIP	G	GS	CG	ShO	Hld.	Sv.-Opp.	IP	H	R	ER	HR	BB-IBB	SO	Avg.
1998—	Brevard County (Fla. St.) ...	0	1	.000	4.66	1.97	2	2	0	0	...	0-...	9.2	15	5	5	1	4-0	9	.366
	—GC Marlins (GCL)	0	4	.000	4.08	1.08	5	4	0	0	...	0-...	28.2	24	15	13	1	7-0	27	.226
1999—	Kane Co. (Midw.)	5	5	.500	3.88	1.38	19	19	1	0	...	0-...	99.2	97	47	43	8	41-0	88	.255
2000—	Brevard County (Fla. St.) ...	10	5	.667	3.28	1.17	24	23	0	0	...	0-...	145.1	126	64	53	10	44-3	143	.234
	—Portland (East.)	1	1	.500	3.60	1.47	3	2	0	0	...	0-...	15.0	16	9	6	1	6-0	13	.276
2001—	Portland (East.)	8	9	.471	4.19	1.19	27	27	0	0	...	0-...	159.0	122	77	74	25	67-1	151	.211
2002—	Calgary (PCL)	4	11	.267	6.72	1.61	17	16	1	0	...	0-...	76.1	88	63	57	18	35-0	61	.291
	—Harrisburg (East.)	2	2	.500	4.64	1.42	8	8	0	0	...	0-...	33.0	38	17	17	2	9-0	34	.286
2003—	Edmonton (PCL)	0	0	...	2.79	1.24	2	2	0	0	...	0-...	9.2	7	3	3	1	5-2	12	.189
	—Harrisburg (East.)	1	0	1.000	0.75	0.83	2	2	0	0	...	0-...	12.0	7	1	1	0	3-0	13	.171
	—Montreal (N.L.)	6	8	.429	4.34	1.33	23	20	0	0	...	0-...	114.0	111	59	55	16	41-5	62	.255
2004—	Montreal (N.L.)	5	5	.500	5.25	1.55	45	14	0	0	3	0-...	118.1	120	75	69	26	64-7	89	.266
2005—	New Orleans (PCL)	2	2	.500	4.18	1.29	5	5	0	0	...	0-...	28.0	24	13	13	4	12-0	35	.231
	—Washington (N.L.)	0	3	.000	9.24	2.29	4	4	0	0	...	0-...	12.2	22	15	13	4	7-2	5	.373

V

Year Team (League)	W	L	Pct.	ERA	WHIP	G	GS	CG	ShO	Hld.	Sv.-Opp.	IP	H	R	ER	HR	BB-IBB	SO	Avg.
— Arizona (N.L.)	9	6	.600	4.81	1.37	21	19	0	0	0	0-0	119.2	124	66	64	21	40-3	90	.266
Major League totals (3 years)	20	22	.476	4.96	1.45	93	57	0	0	3	0-0	364.2	377	215	201	67	152-17	246	.267

VARGAS, JASON — P

PERSONAL: Born February 2, 1983, in Seattle. ... 6-0/215. ... Throws left, bats left. ... Full name: Jason M. Vargas. ... High school: Apple Valley (Calif.). ... College: Long Beach State.
TRANSACTIONS/CAREER NOTES: Selected by Florida Marlins organization in second round of 2004 free-agent draft.
CAREER HITTING: 8-for-26 (.308), 3 R, 2 2B, 0 3B, 0 HR, 2 RBI.

SCOUTING REPORT **Throws:** His four-seam fastball hits 94 mph, and he also has a slider and changeup. **Tendencies:** Vargas relies on a good sinking fastball and the changeup, though his slider has the potential to be his best pitch. As a rookie last year, he left too many fastballs up and had trouble commanding his changeup. Is a quick worker with a good mound presence. **Outlook:** An encouraging rookie season will keep him in the Marlins' rotation. *Grade 6.8*

JASON VARGAS'S PITCHING ZONE

.192	.267	.333
.279	.111	.302
.364	.333	.167

LEFTY-RIGHTY SPLITS

vs.	Avg.	AB	H	2B	3B	HR	RBI	BB	SO	OBP	Slg.
L	.192	73	14	3	2	0	7	5	14	.263	.288
R	.269	212	57	14	3	4	23	26	45	.353	.420

Year Team (League)	W	L	Pct.	ERA	WHIP	G	GS	CG	ShO	Hld.	Sv.-Opp.	IP	H	R	ER	HR	BB-IBB	SO	Avg.
2004— Jamestown (N.Y.-Penn.)	3	1	.750	1.96	1.16	8	8	0	0	...	0-...	41.1	35	17	9	2	13-0	41	.235
— Greensboro (S. Atl.)	2	1	.667	2.37	0.58	3	3	0	0	...	0-...	19.0	9	5	5	1	2-0	17	.143
2005— Greensboro (S. Atl.)	4	1	.800	0.80	0.77	5	5	0	0	0	0-0	33.2	16	4	3	1	10-0	33	.140
— Jupiter (Fla. St.)	2	3	.400	3.42	1.10	9	9	0	0	0	0-0	55.1	47	24	21	6	14-0	60	.225
— Carolina (Sou.)	1	0	1.000	2.84	1.05	3	3	0	0	0	0-0	19.0	13	6	6	3	7-0	25	.194
— Florida (N.L.)	5	5	.500	4.03	1.38	17	13	1	0	0	0-0	73.2	71	34	33	4	31-4	59	.249
Major League totals (1 year)	5	5	.500	4.03	1.38	17	13	1	0	0	0-0	73.2	71	34	33	4	31-4	59	.249

VARITEK, JASON — C

PERSONAL: Born April 11, 1972, in Rochester, Mich. ... 6-2/230. ... Bats both, throws right. ... Full name: Jason Andrew Varitek. ... Name pronounced: VAIR-eh-teck. ... High school: Lake Brantley (Longwood, Fla.). ... College: Georgia Tech.
TRANSACTIONS/CAREER NOTES: Selected by Minnesota Twins organization first round (21st pick overall) of 1993 free-agent draft; did not sign. ... Selected by Seattle Mariners organization in first round (14th pick overall) of 1994 free-agent draft. ... Traded by Mariners with P Derek Lowe to Boston Red Sox for P Heathcliff Slocumb (July 31, 1997). ... On disabled list (June 8, 2001-remainder of season). ... On suspended list (September 16-20, 2002).
HONORS: Won A.L. Gold Glove as catcher (2005).
2005 GAMES PLAYED BY POSITION (MLB): C—130.

SCOUTING REPORT **Offense:** Varitek, who has a long, sweeping stroke, is a better righthanded hitter despite having better bat speed from the other side. Likes to extend his arms for balls out over the plate. Is more willing to hit to the opposite field from the left side. Can drive it out of any part of the park. Strikes out chasing balls up and out of the strike zone. Is a good high-ball and mistake hitter. **Defense:** He is mobile and has good hands. Is aggressive at blocking and shifting with pitches in the dirt. Has a strong arm and has improved his release. Is one of the league's best at calling games and has instilled confidence in the pitching staff. **Outlook:** Varitek, a team leader, has improved all aspects of his game. A future major league manager. *Grade 9.5*

JASON VARITEK'S HITTING ZONE

.217	.111	.345
.292	.429	.364
.244	.444	.313

LEFTY-RIGHTY SPLITS

vs.	Avg.	AB	H	2B	3B	HR	RBI	BB	SO	OBP	Slg.
L	.320	122	39	5	0	9	27	22	24	.418	.582
R	.267	348	93	25	1	13	43	40	93	.347	.457

Year Team (League)	Pos.	G	AB	R	H	2B	3B	HR	RBI	BB	SO	HBP	GDP	SB-CS	Avg.	OBP	SLG	OPS	E	Avg.
1995— Port City (Sou.)	C	104	352	42	79	14	3	10	44	61	126	2	8	0-1	.224	.340	.366	.706	8	.988
1996— Port City (Sou.)	C-DH-3B-OF	134	503	63	132	34	1	12	67	66	93	4	14	7-6	.262	.350	.406	.756	5	.993
1997— Tacoma (PCL)	C-DH	87	307	54	78	13	0	15	48	34	71	2	13	0-1	.254	.329	.444	.772	3	.995
— Pawtucket (Int'l)	C	20	66	6	13	5	0	1	5	8	12	0	4	0-0	.197	.284	.318	.602	1	.993
— Boston (A.L.)	C	1	1	0	1	0	0	0	0	0	0	0	0	0-0	1.000	1.000	1.000	2.000	0	1.000
1998— Boston (A.L.)	C-DH	86	221	31	56	13	0	7	33	17	45	2	8	2-2	.253	.309	.407	.716	5	.988
1999— Boston (A.L.)	C-DH	144	483	70	130	39	2	20	76	46	85	2	13	1-2	.269	.330	.482	.813	* 11	.990
2000— Boston (A.L.)	C-DH	139	448	55	111	31	1	10	65	60	84	6	16	1-1	.248	.342	.388	.730	7	.992
2001— Boston (A.L.)	C	51	174	19	51	11	1	7	25	21	35	1	6	0-0	.293	.371	.489	.859	2	.996
2002— Boston (A.L.)	C-DH	132	467	58	124	27	1	10	61	41	95	7	13	4-3	.266	.332	.392	.724	8	.996
2003— Boston (A.L.)	C-DH	142	451	63	123	31	1	25	85	51	106	7	10	3-2	.273	.351	.512	.862	9	.990
2004— Boston (A.L.)	C-DH	137	463	67	137	30	1	18	73	62	126	10	11	10-3	.296	.390	.482	.872	2	.998
2005— Boston (A.L.)	C	133	470	70	132	30	1	22	70	62	117	3	10	2-0	.281	.366	.489	.856	8	.990
Major League totals (9 years)		965	3178	433	865	212	8	119	488	360	693	38	87	23-13	.272	.350	.456	.807	48	.993

DIVISION SERIES RECORD

Year Team (League)	Pos.	G	AB	R	H	2B	3B	HR	RBI	BB	SO	HBP	GDP	SB-CS	Avg.	OBP	SLG	OPS	E	Avg.
1998— Boston (A.L.)	C	1	4	0	1	0	0	0	0	0	0	0	0	0-0	.250	.250	.250	.500	0	1.000
1999— Boston (A.L.)	C	5	21	7	5	3	0	1	3	0	4	1	0	0-0	.238	.273	.524	.797	0	1.000
2003— Boston (A.L.)	C	5	14	4	4	0	0	2	2	2	0	0	0	0-0	.286	.375	.714	1.089	0	1.000
2004— Boston (A.L.)	C	3	12	3	2	0	0	1	2	2	5	1	1	0-0	.167	.333	.417	.750	0	1.000
2005— Boston (A.L.)	C	3	10	1	3	0	0	0	1	0	2	0	0	0-0	.300	.300	.300	.600	0	1.000
Division series totals (5 years)		17	61	15	15	3	0	4	9	4	14	2	1	0-0	.246	.313	.492	.805	0	1.000

V

CHAMPIONSHIP SERIES RECORD

Year Team (League)	Pos.	G	AB	R	H	2B	3B	HR	RBI	BB	SO	HBP	GDP	SB-CS	Avg.	OBP	SLG	OPS	E	Avg.
1999— Boston (A.L.)	C	5	20	1	4	1	1	1	1	1	4	0	1	0-0	.200	.238	.500	.738	1	.978
2003— Boston (A.L.)	C	6	20	4	6	2	0	2	3	1	5	0	0	0-0	.300	.333	.700	1.033	0	1.000
2004— Boston (A.L.)	C	7	28	5	9	1	0	2	7	2	6	0	0	0-0	.321	.355	.571	.926	0	1.000
Champ. series totals (3 years)		18	68	10	19	4	1	5	11	4	15	0	1	0-0	.279	.315	.588	.903	1	.993

WORLD SERIES RECORD

Year Team (League)	Pos.	G	AB	R	H	2B	3B	HR	RBI	BB	SO	HBP	GDP	SB-CS	Avg.	OBP	SLG	OPS	E	Avg.
2004— Boston (A.L.)	C	4	13	2	2	0	1	0	2	1	4	1	0	0-0	.154	.267	.308	.574	0	1.000

ALL-STAR GAME RECORD

	G	AB	R	H	2B	3B	HR	RBI	BB	SO	HBP	GDP	SB-CS	Avg.	OBP	SLG	OPS	E	Avg.
All-Star Game totals (1 year)	1	1	1	1	0	0	0	0	1	0	0	0	0-0	1.000	1.000	1.000	2.000	0	1.000

VASQUEZ, JORGE · P

PERSONAL: Born July 16, 1978, in Nagua, Dominican Republic. ... 6-1/165. ... Throws right, bats right. ... Full name: Jorge Luis Vasquez. ... Name pronounced: VAS-kez. ... High school: San Jose de Villa (Nagua, Dominican Republic).

TRANSACTIONS/CAREER NOTES: Signed as a non-drafted free agent by Kansas City Royals organization (September 1, 1998). ... Traded by Royals to Atlanta Braves for OF/C Eli Marrero and cash (December 16, 2004).

CAREER HITTING: 0-for-1 (.000), 0 R, 0 2B, 0 3B, 0 HR, 0 RBI.

LEFTY-RIGHTY SPLITS

vs.	Avg.	AB	H	2B	3B	HR	RBI	BB	SO	OBP	Slg.
L	.333	15	5	1	1	1	2	3	4	.444	.733
R	.273	22	6	2	0	1	1	2	5	.333	.500

Year Team (League)	W	L	Pct.	ERA	WHIP	G	GS	CG	ShO	Hld.	Sv.-Opp.	IP	H	R	ER	HR	BB-IBB	SO	Avg.
1999— Dom. Royals (DSL)	2	6	.250	3.09	1.70	21	10	1	0	...	2-...	75.2	105	42	26	6	24-...	78	...
2000— Dom. Royals (DSL)	2	8	.200	4.54	1.30	23	7	0	0	...	0-...	73.1	76	48	37	5	19-...	70	...
2001— GC Royals (GCL)	0	1	.000	1.13	0.69	4	2	0	0	...	0-...	16.0	10	2	2	0	1-0	19	.167
— Spokane (N'west)	1	6	.143	5.01	1.25	10	8	0	0	...	0-...	50.1	50	33	28	3	13-0	67	.259
2002— Burlington (Midw.)	2	1	.667	1.57	0.80	22	0	0	0	...	6-...	46.0	22	8	8	3	15-0	55	.141
— Wilmington (Carol.)	0	0	...	4.91	1.36	10	0	0	0	...	0-...	11.0	12	6	6	0	3-0	17	.255
2003— Wilmington (Carol.)	1	2	.333	1.96	1.43	17	0	0	0	...	7-...	23.0	19	7	5	1	14-3	31	.224
— Wichita (Texas)	3	1	.750	1.92	1.10	36	0	0	0	...	22-...	51.2	39	12	11	3	18-2	52	.212
2004— Kansas City (A.L.)	0	0	...	8.10	1.50	2	0	0	0	0	0-0	3.1	4	3	3	1	1-0	4	.267
— Wichita (Texas)	4	5	.444	4.68	1.32	49	0	0	0	0	18-...	59.2	52	34	31	3	27-1	71	.227
2005— Atlanta (N.L.)	1	0	1.000	3.00	1.78	7	0	0	0	0	0-0	9.0	11	4	3	2	5-0	9	.297
— Richmond (Int'l)	0	1	.000	10.93	1.79	14	0	0	0	0	2-2	14.0	16	17	17	1	9-1	20	.286
— Mississippi (Sou.)	2	1	.667	1.12	0.82	29	0	0	0	1	10-11	40.1	22	7	5	1	11-2	45	.163
American League totals (1 year)	0	0	...	8.10	1.50	2	0	0	0	0	0-0	3.1	4	3	3	1	1-0	4	.267
National League totals (1 year)	1	0	1.000	3.00	1.78	7	0	0	0	0	0-0	9.0	11	4	3	2	5-0	9	.297
Major League totals (2 years)	1	0	1.000	4.38	1.70	9	0	0	0	0	0-0	12.1	15	8	6	3	6-0	13	.288

VAZQUEZ, JAVIER · P

PERSONAL: Born July 25, 1976, in Ponce, Puerto Rico. ... 6-2/205. ... Throws right, bats right. ... Full name: Javier Carlos Vazquez. ... Name pronounced: VAS-kez. ... High school: Colegio de Ponce (Ponce, Puerto Rico).

TRANSACTIONS/CAREER NOTES: Selected by Montreal Expos organization in fifth round of 1994 free-agent draft. ... On suspended list (July 23-27, 1998). ... Traded by Expos to New York Yankees for 1B Nick Johnson, OF Juan Rivera and P Randy Choate (December 16, 2003). ... Traded by Yankees with P Brad Halsey, C Dioner Navarro and cash to Arizona Diamondbacks for P Randy Johnson (January 11, 2005).

CAREER HITTING: 91-for-426 (.214), 31 R, 10 2B, 2 3B, 1 HR, 24 RBI.

SCOUTING REPORT *Throws:* Vazquez throws a 91-94 mph fastball, a curveball anywhere in the 70s, a mid-80s slider and a circle changeup. *Tendencies:* He continued to have problems maintaining his release point and arm slot; when he drops down, the ball flattens out. Has a tendency to fly open when he overthrows. Has outstanding rotation on his curveball and a quick slider—when he stays on top. Throws his change with the arm speed of his fastball and gets good movement on it. *Outlook:* Vazquez's stuff has leveled off slightly over the past two season, and he needs to reestablish his release point. Is healthy and should have a better year in 2006. *Grade 7.9*

JAVIER VAZQUEZ'S PITCHING ZONE

.333	.250	.161
.324	.395	.364
.227	.222	.205

LEFTY-RIGHTY SPLITS

vs.	Avg.	AB	H	2B	3B	HR	RBI	BB	SO	OBP	Slg.
L	.244	377	92	20	2	13	37	22	78	.287	.411
R	.285	460	131	20	5	22	65	24	114	.324	.493

Year Team (League)	W	L	Pct.	ERA	WHIP	G	GS	CG	ShO	Hld.	Sv.-Opp.	IP	H	R	ER	HR	BB-IBB	SO	Avg.
1994— GC Expos (GCL)	5	2	.714	2.53	0.77	15	11	1	1	...	0-...	67.2	37	25	19	0	15-0	56	.155
1995— Albany (S. Atl.)	6	6	.500	5.08	1.52	21	21	1	0	...	0-...	102.2	109	67	58	8	47-0	87	.273
1996— Delmarva (S. Atl.)	14	3	.824	2.68	1.19	27	27	1	0	...	0-...	164.1	138	64	49	12	57-0	173	.229
1997— W.P. Beach (Fla. St.)	6	3	.667	2.16	1.12	19	19	1	0	...	0-...	112.2	98	40	27	8	28-0	100	.231
— Harrisburg (East.)	4	0	1.000	1.07	0.64	6	6	1	0	...	0-...	42.0	15	5	5	2	12-0	47	.107
1998— Montreal (N.L.)	5	15	.250	6.06	1.53	33	32	0	0	0	0-0	172.1	196	121	116	31	68-2	139	.292
1999— Montreal (N.L.)	9	8	.529	5.00	1.33	26	26	3	1	0	0-0	154.2	154	98	86	20	52-4	113	.255
— Ottawa (Int'l)	4	2	.667	4.85	1.43	7	7	0	0	0	0-...	42.2	45	24	23	7	16-0	46	.269
2000— Montreal (N.L.)	11	9	.550	4.05	1.42	33	33	2	1	0	0-0	217.2	247	104	98	24	61-10	196	.286
2001— Montreal (N.L.)	16	11	.593	3.42	1.08	32	32	5	• 3	0	0-0	223.2	197	92	85	24	44-4	208	.235
2002— Montreal (N.L.)	10	13	.435	3.91	1.27	34	34	2	0	0	0-0	230.1	* 243	111	100	28	49-6	179	.271
2003— Montreal (N.L.)	13	12	.520	3.24	1.11	34	34	4	1	0	0-0	230.2	198	93	83	28	57-5	241	.229
2004— New York (A.L.)	14	10	.583	4.91	1.29	32	32	0	0	0	0-0	198.0	195	114	108	33	60-3	150	.255
2005— Arizona (N.L.)	11	15	.423	4.42	1.25	33	33	3	1	0	0-0	215.2	223	112	106	35	46-4	192	.266
American League totals (1 year)	14	10	.583	4.91	1.29	32	32	0	0	0	0-0	198.0	195	114	108	33	60-3	150	.255
National League totals (7 years)	75	83	.475	4.20	1.27	225	224	19	7	0	0-0	1445.0	1458	731	674	190	377-35	1268	.261
Major League totals (8 years)	89	93	.489	4.28	1.27	257	256	19	7	0	0-0	1643.0	1653	845	782	223	437-38	1418	.260

DIVISION SERIES RECORD

Year Team (League)	W	L	Pct.	ERA	WHIP	G	GS	CG	ShO	Hld.	Sv.-Opp.	IP	H	R	ER	HR	BB-IBB	SO	Avg.
2004— New York (A.L.)	0	0	...	9.00	1.80	1	1	0	0	0	0-0	5.0	7	5	5	1	2-0	6	.368

CHAMPIONSHIP SERIES RECORD

Year Team (League)	W	L	Pct.	ERA	WHIP	G	GS	CG	ShO	Hld.	Sv.-Opp.	IP	H	R	ER	HR	BB-IBB	SO	Avg.
2004— New York (A.L.)	1	0	1.000	9.95	2.53	2	0	0	0	0	0-0	6.1	9	7	7	3	7-0	6	.346

ALL-STAR GAME RECORD

	W	L	Pct.	ERA	WHIP	G	GS	CG	ShO	Hld.	Sv.-Opp.	IP	H	R	ER	HR	BB-IBB	SO	Avg.
All-Star Game totals (1 year)	0	0	...	0.00	0.00	1	0	0	0	0	0-0	1.0	0	0	0	0	0-0	2	.000

VAZQUEZ, RAMON — 3B/SS

PERSONAL: Born August 21, 1976, in Aibonito, Puerto Rico. ... 5-11/170. ... Bats left, throws right. ... Full name: Ramon Luis Vazquez. ... Name pronounced: VAS-kez. ... Junior college: Indian Hills (Iowa) Community College.
TRANSACTIONS/CAREER NOTES: Selected by Seattle Mariners organization in 27th round of 1995 free-agent draft. ... Traded by Mariners with P Brett Tomko and C Tom Lampkin to San Diego Padres for C Ben Davis, P Wascar Serrano and SS Alex Arias (December 11, 2001). ... On disabled list (June 1-July 7, 2003); included rehabilitation assignment to Lake Elsinore. ... On disabled list (May 20-June 20, 2004); included rehabilitation assignment to Portland. ... Traded by Padres with OF Jay Payton and P David Pauley to Boston Red Sox for OF Dave Roberts (December 20, 2004). ... Traded by Red Sox to Cleveland Indians for SS Alex Cora (July 7, 2005).
2005 GAMES PLAYED BY POSITION (MLB): SS—14, 2B—12, 3B—8, DH—1.

SCOUTING REPORT *Offense:* He's a spray hitter who doesn't show enough patience, which is a large reason why he spent most of 2005 in the minors. Cannot turn on a good fastball. Strikes out too much for a contact hitter and doesn't walk enough. *Defense:* Vazquez is above average at second and short because of his hands and good footwork. Will be exposed at shortstop because of his sub-par range. Strong, accurate arm. *Outlook:* He signed with Indians instead of going to arbitration and goes to spring training with a solid chance of making the team as a backup because of his defense. *Grade 6.1*

RAMON VAZQUEZ'S HITTING ZONE

.000	.000	.500
.118	.143	.429
.000	.600	.000

LEFTY-RIGHTY SPLITS

vs.	Avg.	AB	H	2B	3B	HR	RBI	BB	SO	OBP	Slg.
L	.250	16	4	0	0	0	1	1	1	.294	.250
R	.203	69	14	5	0	0	4	4	16	.247	.275

									BATTING								FIELDING	
Year Team (League)	Pos.	G	AB	R	H	2B	3B	HR	RBI	BB	SO	HBP	GDP	SB-CS	Avg.	OBP	SLG	OPS	E	Avg.
1995— Ariz. Mariners (AZL) 2B-3B-SS	39	141	20	29	3	1	0	11	19	27	2	2	4-3	.206	.309	.241	.550	11	.941
1996— Everett (N'west)	SS	33	126	25	35	5	2	1	18	26	26	1	3	7-2	.278	.392	.373	.765	20	.873
— Tacoma (PCL)	2B-SS	18	49	7	11	2	1	0	4	4	12	1	2	0-0	.224	.296	.306	.602	1	.985
— Wisconsin (Midw.)	3B	3	10	1	3	1	0	0	1	2	2	0	1	0-0	.300	.417	.400	.817	2	.818
1997— Wisconsin (Midw.)	SS	131	479	79	129	25	5	8	49	78	93	3	8	16-10	.269	.373	.392	.765	35	.935
1998— Lancaster (Calif.)	SS	121	468	77	129	26	4	2	72	81	66	2	6	15-11	.276	.384	.368	.745	31	.944
1999— New Haven (East.) 2B-3B-SS	127	438	58	113	27	3	5	45	62	77	5	11	8-1	.258	.354	.368	.722	31	.942
2000— New Haven (East.)	SS	124	405	58	116	25	4	8	59	52	76	2	6	1-6	.286	.367	.427	.794	22	.961
2001— Tacoma (PCL)	SS	127	466	85	140	28	1	10	79	76	84	1	13	9-7	.300	.397	.429	.827	12	.979
— Seattle (A.L.) SS-2B-3B	17	35	5	8	0	0	0	4	5	0	3	0	0-0	.229	.222	.229	.451	1	.969
	DH																			
2002— San Diego (N.L.) 2B-SS-3B	128	423	50	116	21	5	2	32	45	79	1	6	7-2	.274	.344	.362	.706	7	.986
2003— Lake Elsinore (Calif.)	SS	5	16	3	3	0	0	1	4	3	3	1	1	0-1	.188	.350	.375	.725	1	.950
— San Diego (N.L.) SS-3B-2B	116	422	56	110	17	4	3	30	52	88	2	4	10-3	.261	.342	.341	.684	14	.968
2004— Portland (PCL) 2B-3B-SS	53	184	36	55	21	1	8	34	33	28	0	2	2-0	.299	.402	.554	.956	2	.991
— San Diego (N.L.) SS-2B-3B																				
	1B	52	115	12	27	3	2	1	13	11	24	0	2	1-1	.235	.297	.322	.619	1	.991
2005— Boston (A.L.) 3B-3B-2B																				
	DH	27	61	6	12	2	0	0	4	3	14	0	0	0-0	.197	.234	.230	.464	3	.950
— Buffalo (Int'l) SS-2B-3B	21	84	13	18	3	1	0	4	7	16	0	2	1-1	.214	.275	.274	.549	4	.959
— Cleveland (A.L.)	2B-SS	12	24	1	6	3	0	0	1	2	3	0	0	0-0	.250	.308	.375	.683	0	1.000
American League totals (2 years)		56	120	12	26	5	0	0	9	5	20	0	0	0-0	.217	.246	.258	.504	4	.968
National League totals (3 years)		296	960	118	253	41	11	6	75	108	191	3	12	18-6	.264	.338	.348	.686	22	.979
Major League totals (5 years)		352	1080	130	279	46	11	6	84	113	211	3	12	18-6	.258	.328	.338	.666	26	.978

DIVISION SERIES RECORD

Year Team (League)	Pos.	G	AB	R	H	2B	3B	HR	RBI	BB	SO	HBP	GDP	SB-CS	Avg.	OBP	SLG	OPS	E	Avg.
2001— Seattle (A.L.)		Did not play.																		

CHAMPIONSHIP SERIES RECORD

Year Team (League)	Pos.	G	AB	R	H	2B	3B	HR	RBI	BB	SO	HBP	GDP	SB-CS	Avg.	OBP	SLG	OPS	E	Avg.
2001— Seattle (A.L.)		Did not play.																		

VENTO, MIKE — OF

PERSONAL: Born May 25, 1978, in Albuquerque, N.M. ... 6-0/195. ... Bats right, throws right. ... Full name: Michael Vento. ... High school: Cibola (N.M.). ... Junior college: New Mexico.
TRANSACTIONS/CAREER NOTES: Selected by New York Yankees organization in 40th round of 1997 free-agent draft.
2005 GAMES PLAYED BY POSITION (MLB): OF—2.

LEFTY-RIGHTY SPLITS

vs.	Avg.	AB	H	2B	3B	HR	RBI	BB	SO	OBP	Slg.
L	.000	0	0	0	0	0	0	0	0	.000	.000
R	.000	2	0	0	0	0	0	0	1	.000	.000

									BATTING								FIELDING	
Year Team (League)	Pos.	G	AB	R	H	2B	3B	HR	RBI	BB	SO	HBP	GDP	SB-CS	Avg.	OBP	SLG	OPS	E	Avg.
1998— Oneonta (N.Y.-Penn.)	OF	43	148	25	45	9	3	1	23	14	28	5	1	8-3	.304	.379	.426	.805	0	1.000
1999— Tampa (Fla. St.)	OF-1B	70	255	37	66	10	1	7	28	17	69	3	1	2-3	.259	.310	.388	.698	1	.990
— Greensboro (S. Atl.)	OF	40	148	20	37	11	1	3	16	14	46	3	1	3-1	.250	.321	.399	.720	2	.938

V

Year Team (League)	Pos.	G	AB	R	H	2B	3B	HR	RBI	BB	SO	HBP	GDP	SB-CS	Avg.	OBP	SLG	OPS	E	Avg.
2000—Tampa (Fla. St.)	OF	10	30	1	5	0	0	1	4	4	12	1	0	1-0	.167	.278	.267	.545	0	1.000
—Greensboro (S. Atl.)	OF	84	318	49	83	15	2	6	52	47	66	11	11	13-8	.261	.372	.377	.749	5	.956
2001—Tampa (Fla. St.)	OF-OF	130	457	71	137	20	10	20	87	45	88	9	9	13-10	.300	.372	.519	.891	12	.945
2002—Norwich (East.)	OF-OF	64	227	29	54	16	2	4	26	25	49	1	6	3-3	.238	.314	.379	.693	3	.977
2003—Trenton (East.)	OF	81	314	46	95	19	3	9	56	22	52	5	6	4-4	.303	.354	.468	.822	5	.966
—Columbus (Int'l)	OF	51	184	28	56	14	1	5	31	14	36	3	6	1-2	.304	.363	.473	.836	1	.992
2004—Columbus (Int'l)	OF	122	451	64	124	28	1	15	72	34	77	9	8	2-3	.275	.333	.441	.774	4	.892
2005—Columbus (Int'l)	OF-DH	130	501	62	146	37	2	12	84	49	96	13	13	1-4	.291	.365	.445	.810	8	.982
—New York (A.L.)	OF	2	2	0	0	0	0	0	0	0	1	0	0	0-0	.000	.000	.000	.000	0	1.000
Major League totals (1 year)		2	2	0	0	0	0	0	0	0	1	0	0	0-0	.000	.000	.000	.000	0	1.000

VERLANDER, JUSTIN   P

PERSONAL: Born February 20, 1983, in Manakin-Sabot, Va. ... 6-5/200. ... Throws right, bats right. ... Full name: Justin Brooks Verlander. ... High school: Goochland (Va.). ... College: Old Dominion.

TRANSACTIONS/CAREER NOTES: Selected by Detroit Tigers organization in first round (second pick overall) of 2004 free-agent draft.

CAREER HITTING: 0-for-0 (.000), 0 R, 0 2B, 0 3B, 0 HR, 0 RBI.

LEFTY-RIGHTY SPLITS

vs.	Avg.	AB	H	2B	3B	HR	RBI	BB	SO	OBP	Slg.
L	.333	30	10	5	0	1	5	4	4	.429	.600
R	.278	18	5	0	0	0	3	1	3	.316	.278

Year Team (League)	W	L	Pct.	ERA	WHIP	G	GS	CG	ShO	Hld.	Sv.-Opp.	IP	H	R	ER	HR	BB-IBB	SO	Avg.
2005—Lakeland (Fla. St.)	9	2	.818	1.67	1.03	13	13	2	0	0	0-0	86.0	70	19	16	3	19-0	104	.230
—Detroit (A.L.)	0	2	.000	7.15	1.76	2	2	0	0	0	0-0	11.1	15	9	9	1	5-0	7	.313
—Erie (East.)	2	0	1.000	0.28	0.55	7	7	0	0	0	0-0	32.2	11	1	1	1	7-0	32	.103
Major League totals (1 year)	0	2	.000	7.15	1.76	2	2	0	0	0	0-0	11.1	15	9	9	1	5-0	7	.313

VICTORINO, SHANE   OF

PERSONAL: Born November 30, 1980, in Wailuku, Hawaii. ... 5-9/160. ... Bats both, throws right. ... Full name: Shane Patrick Victorino. ... High school: St. Anthony (Wailuku, Hawaii).

TRANSACTIONS/CAREER NOTES: Selected by Los Angeles Dodgers organization in sixth round of 1999 free-agent draft. ... Selected by San Diego Padres from Dodgers organization in Rule 5 major league draft (December 16, 2002). ... Claimed on waivers by Dodgers (May 28, 2003). ... Selected by Philadelphia Phillies from Dodgers organization in Rule 5 major league draft (December 13, 2004).

2005 GAMES PLAYED BY POSITION (MLB): OF—12.

LEFTY-RIGHTY SPLITS

vs.	Avg.	AB	H	2B	3B	HR	RBI	BB	SO	OBP	Slg.
L	1.000	1	1	0	0	1	3	0	0	.500	4.000
R	.250	16	4	0	0	1	5	0	3	.235	.438

Year Team (League)	Pos.	G	AB	R	H	2B	3B	HR	RBI	BB	SO	HBP	GDP	SB-CS	Avg.	OBP	SLG	OPS	E	Avg.
1999—Great Falls (Pion.)	OF	55	225	53	63	7	6	2	25	20	31	0	3	20-5	.280	.335	.391	.726	2	.986
2000—Yakima (N'west)	2B-SS	61	236	32	58	7	2	2	20	20	44	3	3	21-9	.246	.310	.318	.628	11	.964
2001—Wilmington (S. Atl.)	OF	112	435	71	123	21	9	4	32	36	61	5	3	47-13	.283	.344	.400	.744	6	.976
—Vero Beach (Fla. St.)	OF	2	6	2	1	0	0	0	0	3	1	0	0	0-0	.167	.444	.167	.611	0	1.000
2002—Jacksonville (Sou.)	OF	122	481	61	124	15	1	4	34	47	49	4	6	45-16	.258	.328	.318	.646	4	.986
2003—San Diego (N.L.)	OF	36	73	8	11	2	0	0	4	7	17	1	4	7-2	.151	.232	.178	.410	0	1.000
—Jacksonville (Sou.)	OF	66	266	37	75	9	4	2	15	21	41	3	3	16-7	.282	.340	.368	.708	4	.978
—Las Vegas (PCL)	OF-2B	11	41	6	16	1	2	1	9	1	5	0	1	0-1	.390	.395	.585	.980	1	.966
2004—Las Vegas (PCL)	OF-2B	55	200	28	47	9	1	3	20	11	37	1	3	7-2	.235	.278	.335	.613	2	.959
—Jacksonville (Sou.)	OF	75	293	70	96	13	7	16	43	20	64	5	4	9-7	.328	.375	.584	.959	2	.000
2005—Scran./W.B. (I.L.)	OF	126	494	93	153	25	16	18	70	51	74	5	4	17-9	.310	.377	.534	.912	6	.991
—Philadelphia (N.L.)	OF	21	17	5	5	0	0	2	8	0	3	0	0	0-0	.294	.263	.647	.910	0	...
Major League totals (2 years)		57	90	13	16	2	0	2	12	7	20	1	5	7-2	.178	.238	.267	.504	0	1.000

VIDRO, JOSE   2B

PERSONAL: Born August 27, 1974, in Mayaguez, Puerto Rico. ... 5-11/193. ... Bats both, throws right. ... Full name: Jose Angel Vidro. ... Name pronounced: VEE-dro. ... High school: Blanco Morales (Sabana Grande, Puerto Rico).

TRANSACTIONS/CAREER NOTES: Selected by Montreal Expos organization in sixth round of 1992 free-agent draft. ... On disabled list (May 20-June 12, 2001; and August 26, 2004-remainder of season). ... Expos franchise transferred to Washington, D.C., and renamed Washington Nationals for 2005 season (December 3, 2004). ... On disabled list (May 5-July 5, 2005); included rehabilitation assignment to Potomac.

2005 GAMES PLAYED BY POSITION (MLB): 2B—79.

SCOUTING REPORT *Offense:* Vidro missed about half of 2005 because of knee problems, and his offensive output reflected it. Was not able to hit with a firm base and lost bat speed. Is a line-drive hitter whose power numbers will continue to decline because of RFK Stadium. Is not a basestealing threat but has good baserunning instincts. *Defense:* He has good hands and footwork, but his range has declined. Is adept at pivoting and completing the double play. Has good defensive instincts. Positions himself well and takes good angles to compensate for having average speed. Throws well and can shorten up to make the pivot. *Outlook:* Vidro's production is difficult to project because of his knee problems, especially if they require further surgery. *Grade 7.5*

JOSE VIDRO'S HITTING ZONE

.263	.294	.423
.386	.294	.217
.273	.250	.268

LEFTY-RIGHTY SPLITS

vs.	Avg.	AB	H	2B	3B	HR	RBI	BB	SO	OBP	Slg.
L	.258	66	17	3	0	5	15	11	7	.354	.530
R	.280	243	68	18	2	2	17	20	23	.335	.395

Year Team (League)	Pos.	G	AB	R	H	2B	3B	HR	RBI	BB	SO	HBP	GDP	SB-CS	Avg.	OBP	SLG	OPS	E	Avg.
1992—GC Expos (GCL)	2B	54	200	29	66	6	2	4	31	16	31	0	5	10-1	.330	.376	.440	.816	4	.982
1993—Burlington (Midw.)	2B	76	287	39	69	19	0	2	34	28	54	5	7	3-2	.240	.317	.328	.644	7	.974
1994—W.P. Beach (FSL)	2B	125	465	57	124	30	2	4	49	51	56	5	5	8-2	.267	.344	.366	.709	20	.964
1995—W.P. Beach (FSL)	IF	44	163	20	53	15	2	3	24	8	21	2	5	0-1	.325	.360	.497	.857	4	.981
—Harrisburg (East.)	IF	64	246	33	64	16	2	4	38	20	37	1	5	7-7	.260	.315	.390	.705	9	.966
1996—Harrisburg (East.)	IF	126	452	57	117	25	3	18	82	29	71	2	6	3-1	.259	.300	.447	.747	15	.964

Year Team (League)	Pos.	G	AB	R	H	2B	3B	HR	RBI	BB	SO	HBP	GDP	SB-CS	Avg.	OBP	SLG	OPS	E	Avg.
1997—Ottawa (Int'l) 3B-2B-DH		73	279	40	90	17	0	13	47	22	40	1	6	2-0	.323	.370	.523	.894	8	.967
—Montreal (N.L.) 3B-2B-DH		67	169	19	42	12	1	2	17	11	20	2	1	1-0	.249	.297	.367	.664	4	.955
1998—Montreal (N.L.) 2B-3B		83	205	24	45	12	0	0	18	27	33	4	5	2-2	.220	.318	.278	.596	6	.972
—Ottawa (Int'l) 2B-3B-DH		63	235	35	68	14	2	2	32	24	25	4	4	5-2	.289	.361	.391	.752	6	.973
1999—Montreal (N.L.) 2B-1B-OF																				
3B		140	494	67	150	45	2	12	59	29	51	4	12	0-4	.304	.346	.476	.822	11	.981
2000—Montreal (N.L.)	2B	153	606	101	200	51	2	24	97	49	69	2	17	5-4	.330	.379	.540	.918	10	.986
2001—Montreal (N.L.)	2B-DH	124	486	82	155	34	1	15	59	31	49	10	18	4-1	.319	.371	.486	.856	9	.983
2002—Montreal (N.L.)	2B	152	604	103	190	43	3	19	96	60	70	3	12	2-1	.315	.378	.490	.868	11	.986
2003—Montreal (N.L.)	2B	144	509	77	158	36	0	15	65	69	50	7	16	3-2	.310	.397	.470	.866	10	.983
2004—Montreal (N.L.)	2B-DH	110	412	51	121	24	0	14	60	49	43	0	14	3-1	.294	.367	.454	.821	6	.987
2005—Potomac (Carol.)	DH-2B	5	13	3	2	1	0	0	3	4	2	0	0	0-0	.154	.353	.231	.584	0	1.000
—Washington (N.L.)	2B	87	309	38	85	21	2	7	32	31	30	1	8	0-0	.275	.339	.424	.763	5	.985
Major League totals (9 years)		1060	3794	562	1146	278	11	108	503	356	415	33	103	20-15	.302	.364	.467	.831	72	.983

ALL-STAR GAME RECORD

	G	AB	R	H	2B	3B	HR	RBI	BB	SO	HBP	GDP	SB-CS	Avg.	OBP	SLG	OPS	E	Avg.
All-Star Game totals (3 years)	3	5	0	0	0	0	0	0	0	2	0	0	0-0	.000	.000	.000	.000	1	.750

VILLARREAL, OSCAR   P

PERSONAL: Born November 22, 1981, in Nuevo Leon, Mexico. ... 6-0/205. ... Throws right, bats left. ... Full name: Oscar Eduardo Villarreal. ... Name pronounced: VEE-yuh-ray-al. ... High school: Prepa High School No. 16 (Nuevo Leon, Mexico).

TRANSACTIONS/CAREER NOTES: Signed as a non-drafted free agent by Arizona Diamondbacks organization (November 6, 1998). ... On disabled list (May 10, 2004-remainder of season); included rehabilitation assignment to Tucson. ... On disabled list (April 11-September 2, 2005); included rehabilitation assignment to Tucson.

CAREER HITTING: 0-for-3 (.000), 0 R, 0 2B, 0 3B, 0 HR, 0 RBI.

LEFTY-RIGHTY SPLITS

vs.	Avg.	AB	H	2B	3B	HR	RBI	BB	SO	OBP	Slg.
L	.207	29	6	1	0	1	4	3	2	.294	.345
R	.278	18	5	1	0	1	3	3	3	.381	.500

SCOUTING REPORT **Throws:** His fastball hits 96 mph, and his slider checks in at 83-88. Also throws a changeup. *Tendencies:* He has a plus fastball and slider but an inconsistent delivery has hurt his command. Is able to maintain consistent arm speed on his pitches, and potentially can keep hitters from sitting on his four-seamer. Does a good job of staying out of hitter's counts. *Outlook:* Villarreal missed most of last season with a rotator cuff injury but was solid after his return. If he avoids injury, he has the stuff to be a top setup man. *Grade 7.5*

Year Team (League)	W	L	Pct.	ERA	WHIP	G	GS	CG	ShO	Hld.	Sv.-Opp.	IP	H	R	ER	HR	BB-IBB	SO	Avg.
1999—Ariz. D'backs (AZL)	1	5	.167	3.78	1.38	14	11	0	0	...	0-...	64.1	64	39	27	1	25-0	51	.260
2000—Tucson (PCL)	1	0	1.000	2.08	1.85	2	0	0	0	...	0-...	4.1	6	1	1	0	2-0	4	.353
—South Bend (Midw.)	1	3	.250	4.41	1.65	13	5	0	0	...	0-...	32.2	37	19	16	0	17-3	30	.274
—Ariz. D'backs (AZL)	0	0	...	9.00	2.00	1	0	0	0	...	0-...	1.0	2	1	1	0	0-0	1	.400
—High Desert (Calif.)	0	2	.000	3.65	1.54	9	4	0	0	...	0-...	24.2	24	20	10	4	14-0	18	.253
2001—El Paso (Texas)	6	9	.400	4.41	1.54	27	27	0	0	...	0-...	140.2	154	96	69	10	63-1	108	.274
2002—El Paso (Texas)	6	3	.667	3.74	1.17	14	12	1	0	...	0-...	84.1	73	36	35	2	26-0	85	.233
—Tucson (PCL)	3	3	.500	4.36	1.41	10	10	0	0	...	0-...	64.0	68	33	31	8	22-0	40	.278
2003—Arizona (N.L.)	10	7	.588	2.57	1.29	86	1	0	0	10	0-4	98.0	80	40	28	4	46-10	80	.222
2004—Arizona (N.L.)	0	2	.000	7.00	1.78	17	0	0	0	2	0-0	18.0	25	14	14	3	7-1	17	.342
—Tucson (PCL)	0	0	.000	14.34	2.25	6	5	0	0	...	0-...	10.2	20	17	17	3	4-0	12	.385
2005—Tucson (PCL)	0	3	.000	5.19	1.33	12	8	0	0	0	0-0	17.1	19	12	10	1	4-0	8	.292
—Arizona (N.L.)	2	0	1.000	5.27	1.24	11	0	0	0	2	0-0	13.2	11	8	8	2	6-2	5	.234
Major League totals (3 years)	12	9	.571	3.47	1.35	114	1	0	0	14	0-6	129.2	116	62	50	11	59-13	102	.241

VILLONE, RON   P

PERSONAL: Born January 16, 1970, in Englewood, N.J. ... 6-3/230. ... Throws left, bats left. ... Full name: Ronald Thomas Villone. ... Name pronounced: vill-OWN. ... High school: Bergenfield (N.J.). ... College: Massachusetts.

TRANSACTIONS/CAREER NOTES: Selected by Seattle Mariners in first round (14th pick overall) of 1992 free-agent draft. ... Traded by Mariners with OF Marc Newfield to San Diego Padres for P Andy Benes and a player to be named (July 31, 1995); Mariners acquired P Greg Keagle to complete deal (September 16, 1995). ... Traded by Padres with P Bryce Florie and OF Marc Newfield to Milwaukee Brewers for OF Greg Vaughn and a player to be named (July 31, 1996); Padres acquired OF Gerald Parent to complete deal (September 16, 1996). ... Traded by Brewers with Ps Ben McDonald and Mike Fetters to Cleveland Indians for OF Marquis Grissom and P Jeff Juden (December 8, 1997). ... On disabled list (August 15-September 1, 1998); included rehabilitation assignment to Buffalo. ... Released by Indians (April 2, 1999). ... Signed by Cincinnati Reds organization (April 5, 1999). ... Traded by Reds to Colorado Rockies for two players to be named (November 8, 2000); Reds acquired Ps Jeff Taglienti and Justin Carter to complete deal (December 20, 2000). ... Traded by Rockies to Houston Astros for P Jay Powell (June 27, 2001). ... Signed as a free agent by Pittsburgh Pirates organization (February 12, 2002). ... On disabled list (August 15-September 1, 2002). ... Signed as a free agent by Arizona Diamondbacks organization (January 29, 2003). ... Released by Diamondbacks (May 15, 2003). ... Signed by Astros organization (May 19, 2003). ... Signed as a free agent by Mariners (February 10, 2004). ... Traded by Mariners to Florida Marlins for Ps Yorman Bazardo and Michael Flannery (July 31, 2005).

CAREER HITTING: 22-for-169 (.130), 7 R, 3 2B, 1 3B, 1 HR, 7 RBI.

SCOUTING REPORT **Throws:** His fastball ranges from 89-91 mph. Also throws a slider in the mid 80's and a changeup. *Tendencies:* Villone has an upright motion with short arm action and a very short stride. Has tailing action on his fastball when it's down, but it straightens out if it's up in the zone. Likes to cut his fastball in on the fists of righthanded hitters. Has very good arm speed on his change and will turn it over, giving him a pitch that he can run on the other side of the plate. Is extremely effective against lefthanders; comes sidearm when ahead in the count. *Outlook:* Villone's versatility and ability to get out righthanders allows him to pitch in roles from middle relief to situational lefty relief. Value continues to grow. *Grade 7.1*

RON VILLONE'S PITCHING ZONE

.409	.455	.167
.361	.316	.108
.231	.143	.333

LEFTY-RIGHTY SPLITS

vs.	Avg.	AB	H	2B	3B	HR	RBI	BB	SO	OBP	Slg.
L	.222	117	26	2	1	0	14	13	29	.326	.256
R	.258	120	31	6	0	4	25	22	41	.370	.408

Year Team (League)	W	L	Pct.	ERA	WHIP	G	GS	CG	ShO	Hld.	Sv.-Opp.	IP	H	R	ER	HR	BB-IBB	SO	Avg.
1993— Riverside (Calif.)	7	4	.636	4.21	1.63	16	16	0	0	...	0-...	83.1	74	47	39	5	62-0	82	.241
— Jacksonville (Sou.)	3	4	.429	4.38	1.41	11	11	0	0	...	0-...	63.2	49	34	31	6	41-3	66	.219
1994— Jacksonville (Sou.)	6	7	.462	3.86	1.56	41	5	0	0	...	8-...	79.1	56	37	34	7	68-3	94	.199
1995— Seattle (A.L.)	0	2	.000	7.91	2.22	19	0	0	0	3	0-3	19.1	20	19	17	6	23-0	26	.270
— Tacoma (PCL)	1	0	1.000	0.61	0.94	22	0	0	0	...	13-...	29.2	9	6	2	1	19-0	43	.095
— San Diego (N.L.)	2	1	.667	4.21	1.36	19	0	0	0	3	1-2	25.2	24	12	12	5	11-0	37	.242
1996— Las Vegas (PCL)	2	1	.667	1.64	1.00	23	0	0	0	...	3-...	22.0	13	5	4	0	9-0	29	.169
— San Diego (N.L.)	2	1	.500	2.95	1.31	21	0	0	0	4	0-1	18.1	17	6	6	2	7-0	19	.243
— Milwaukee (A.L.)	0	0	...	3.28	1.30	23	0	0	0	5	2-2	24.2	14	9	9	4	18-0	19	.175
1997— Milwaukee (A.L.)	1	0	1.000	3.42	1.71	50	0	0	0	8	0-2	52.2	54	23	20	4	36-2	40	.271
1998— Buffalo (Int'l)	2	2	.500	2.01	1.39	23	0	0	0	...	7-...	22.1	20	11	5	2	11-1	28	.235
— Cleveland (A.L.)	0	0	...	6.00	1.93	25	0	0	0	1	0-0	27.0	30	18	18	3	22-0	15	.297
1999— Indianapolis (Int'l)	2	0	1.000	1.42	1.16	18	0	0	0	...	1-...	19.0	9	3	3	1	13-1	23	.155
— Cincinnati (N.L.)	9	7	.563	4.23	1.31	29	22	0	0	0	2-2	142.2	114	70	67	8	73-2	97	.219
2000— Cincinnati (N.L.)	10	10	.500	5.43	1.65	35	23	2	0	1	0-0	141.0	154	95	85	22	78-3	77	.286
2001— Colorado (N.L.)	1	3	.250	6.36	1.82	22	6	0	0	2	0-0	46.2	56	35	33	6	29-4	48	.295
— Houston (N.L.)	5	7	.417	5.56	1.49	31	6	0	0	4	0-0	68.0	77	46	42	12	24-1	65	.282
2002— Pittsburgh (N.L.)	4	6	.400	5.81	1.39	45	7	0	0	0	0-1	93.0	95	63	60	8	34-3	55	.271
2003— Tucson (PCL)	1	1	.500	3.55	1.30	15	0	0	0	...	1-...	25.1	20	14	10	2	12-1	22	.233
— New Orleans (PCL)	3	1	.750	1.23	1.20	5	5	0	0	...	0-...	29.1	24	5	4	0	10-0	18	.233
— Houston (N.L.)	6	6	.500	4.13	1.30	19	19	0	0	0	0-0	106.2	91	51	49	16	48-1	91	.233
2004— Seattle (A.L.)	8	6	.571	4.08	1.42	56	10	0	0	7	0-1	117.0	102	64	53	12	64-3	86	.232
2005— Seattle (A.L.)	2	3	.400	2.45	1.39	52	0	0	0	17	1-6	40.1	33	14	11	2	23-1	41	.226
— Florida (N.L.)	3	2	.600	6.85	1.52	27	0	0	0	4	0-3	23.2	24	20	18	2	12-1	29	.264
American League totals (6 years)	**11**	**11**	**.500**	**4.10**	**1.56**	**225**	**10**	**0**	**0**	**41**	**3-14**	**281.0**	**253**	**147**	**128**	**31**	**186-6**	**227**	**.244**
National League totals (8 years)	**41**	**43**	**.488**	**5.03**	**1.45**	**248**	**83**	**2**	**0**	**18**	**3-9**	**665.2**	**652**	**398**	**372**	**81**	**316-15**	**518**	**.258**
Major League totals (11 years)	**52**	**54**	**.491**	**4.75**	**1.49**	**473**	**93**	**2**	**0**	**59**	**6-23**	**946.2**	**905**	**545**	**500**	**112**	**502-21**	**745**	**.254**

DIVISION SERIES RECORD

Year Team (League)	W	L	Pct.	ERA	WHIP	G	GS	CG	ShO	Hld.	Sv.-Opp.	IP	H	R	ER	HR	BB-IBB	SO	Avg.
2001— Houston (N.L.)	0	0	...	0.00	0.00	1	0	0	0	0	0-0	0.2	0	0	0	0	0-0	0	.000

VIZCAINO, JOSE   2B/SS

PERSONAL: Born March 26, 1968, in San Cristobal, Dominican Republic. ... 6-1/190. ... Bats both, throws right. ... Full name: Jose Luis Vizcaino. ... Name pronounced: vis-ky-ee-no. ... High school: Americo Tolentino (Palenque de San Cristobal, Dominican Republic).

TRANSACTIONS/CAREER NOTES: Signed as a non-drafted free agent by Los Angeles Dodgers organization (February 18, 1986). ... Traded by Dodgers to Chicago Cubs for IF Greg Smith (December 14, 1990). ... On disabled list (April 20-May 6 and August 26-September 16, 1992). ... Traded by Cubs to New York Mets for Ps Anthony Young and Ottis Smith (March 30, 1994). ... Traded by Mets with 2B Jeff Kent to Cleveland Indians for 2B Carlos Baerga and IF Alvaro Espinoza (July 29, 1996). ... Traded by Indians with 2B Jeff Kent, P Julian Tavarez and a player to be named to San Francisco Giants for 3B Matt Williams and a player to be named (November 13, 1996); Indians traded P Joe Roa to Giants for OF Trenidad Hubbard to complete deal (December 16, 1996). ... Signed as a free agent by Dodgers (December 8, 1997). ... On disabled list (June 22-September 9, 1998; and May 19-June 4, 1999). ... Traded by Dodgers to New York Yankees for IF/DH Jim Leyritz (June 20, 2000). ... Signed as a free agent by Houston Astros (November 20, 2000). ... On disabled list (June 25-August 21, 2003); included rehabilitation assignment to New Orleans.

2005 GAMES PLAYED BY POSITION (MLB): 2B–23, SS–17, 1B–13, 3B–8.

SCOUTING REPORT *Offense:* Vizcaino is a professional hitter, with a short stroke and very good bat control. Is more of a line-drive hitter and rarely overswings. Hits the ball to all fields. Is better from the left side. Continually makes adjustments at the plate. Goes with the pitch well. Still is an average runner but rarely steals a base. *Defense:* His range is short to either side, but he has very good hands and relies on his positioning to compensate. Arm strength has declined slightly and can be erratic when he lets up on his throws. *Outlook:* Vizcaino is a very good role player who has value coming off the bench. Can be overexposed on defense at this stage in his career. *Grade 6.3*

JOSE VIZCAINO'S HITTING ZONE

.250	.357	.100
.407	.333	.250
.154	.231	.316

LEFTY-RIGHTY SPLITS

vs.	Avg.	AB	H	2B	3B	HR	RBI	BB	SO	OBP	Slg.
L	.295	61	18	5	1	1	5	5	13	.348	.459
R	.222	126	28	5	1	0	18	10	27	.275	.278

V

Year Team (League)	Pos.	G	AB	R	H	2B	3B	HR	RBI	BB	SO	HBP	GDP	SB-CS	Avg.	OBP	SLG	OPS	E	Avg.
1987— GC Dodgers (GCL)	1B-SS	49	150	26	38	5	1	0	12	22	24	0	1	8-5	.253	.347	.300	.647	13	.933
1988— Bakersfield (Calif.)	SS	122	433	77	126	11	4	0	38	50	54	7	6	13-14	.291	.372	.335	.707	30	.946
1989— Albuquerque (PCL)	SS	129	434	60	123	10	4	1	44	33	41	1	10	16-14	.283	.333	.332	.665	30	.951
— Los Angeles (N.L.)	SS	7	10	2	2	0	0	0	0	0	1	0	0	0-0	.200	.200	.200	.400	2	.882
1990— Albuquerque (PCL)	2B-SS	81	276	46	77	10	2	2	38	30	33	0	6	13-6	.279	.346	.351	.698	14	.964
— Los Angeles (N.L.)	2B-SS	37	51	3	14	1	1	0	2	4	8	0	1	1-1	.275	.327	.333	.661	2	.962
1991— Chicago (N.L.)	2B-3B-SS	93	145	7	38	5	0	0	10	5	18	0	1	2-1	.262	.283	.297	.579	7	.960
1992— Chicago (N.L.)	SS-3B-2B	86	285	25	64	10	4	1	17	14	35	0	4	3-0	.225	.260	.298	.558	9	.970
1993— Chicago (N.L.)	SS-3B-2B	151	551	74	158	19	4	4	54	46	71	3	13	12-9	.287	.340	.358	.697	17	.974
1994— New York (N.L.)	SS	103	410	47	105	13	3	3	33	33	62	2	5	1-11	.256	.310	.324	.635	13	.970
1995— New York (N.L.)	SS-2B	135	509	66	146	21	5	3	56	35	76	1	14	8-3	.287	.332	.365	.698	10	.984
1996— New York (N.L.)	2B	96	363	47	110	12	6	1	32	28	58	3	6	9-5	.303	.356	.377	.733	6	.986
— Cleveland (A.L.)	2B-SS-DH	48	179	23	51	5	2	0	13	7	24	0	2	6-2	.285	.310	.335	.645	4	.982
1997— San Francisco (N.L.)	SS-2B	151	568	77	151	19	7	5	50	48	87	0	13	8-8	.266	.323	.350	.673	16	.976
1998— Los Angeles (N.L.)	SS	67	237	30	62	9	0	3	29	17	35	1	4	7-3	.262	.311	.338	.649	4	.985
1999— Los Angeles (N.L.)	SS-2B-3B																			
	OF	94	266	27	67	9	0	1	29	20	23	1	9	2-1	.252	.305	.297	.601	7	.976
2000— Los Angeles (N.L.)	1B-DH	40	93	9	19	2	1	0	4	10	15	1	3	1-0	.204	.288	.247	.536	2	.978
— New York (A.L.)	2B-3B-DH																			
	SS	73	174	23	48	13	1	0	12	10	33	0	3	5-7	.276	.319	.333	.652	2	.991
2001— Houston (N.L.)	SS-2B-3B	107	256	38	71	8	3	1	14	15	33	2	6	3-2	.277	.322	.344	.666	14	.939
2002— Houston (N.L.)	SS-3B-2B																			
	1B	125	406	53	123	19	2	5	37	24	40	1	5	3-5	.303	.342	.397	.738	4	.989

Year Team (League)	Pos.	G	AB	R	H	2B	3B	HR	RBI	BB	SO	HBP	GDP	SB-CS	Avg.	OBP	SLG	OPS	E	Avg.
													BATTING						FIELDING	
2003— New Orleans (PCL)	2B-SS	2	8	1	2	0	0	1	1	1	0	0	0	0-0	.250	.333	.625	.958	1	.889
—Houston (N.L.)	SS-2B-3B																			
	1B	91	189	14	47	7	3	3	26	8	22	1	5	0-1	.249	.281	.365	.646	5	.970
2004— Houston (N.L.)	SS-2B-3B																			
	1B	138	358	34	98	21	3	3	33	20	39	0	8	1-1	.274	.311	.374	.685	11	.972
2005— Houston (N.L.)	2B-SS-1B	98	187	15	46	10	2	1	23	15	40	0	2	2-0	.246	.299	.337	.636	5	.974
	3B																			
American League totals (2 years)		121	353	46	99	13	3	0	23	19	52	0	5	11-9	.280	.315	.334	.649	6	.986
National League totals (17 years)		1619	4884	568	1321	185	44	34	449	342	663	16	95	63-51	.270	.318	.347	.665	134	.975
Major League totals (17 years)		1740	5237	614	1420	198	47	34	472	361	715	16	100	74-60	.271	.318	.346	.664	140	.976

DIVISION SERIES RECORD

Year Team (League)	Pos.	G	AB	R	H	2B	3B	HR	RBI	BB	SO	HBP	GDP	SB-CS	Avg.	OBP	SLG	OPS	E	Avg.
1996— Cleveland (A.L.)	2B	3	12	1	4	2	0	0	1	1	1	0	0	0-0	.333	.385	.500	.885	1	.875
1997— San Francisco (N.L.)	SS	3	11	1	2	1	0	0	0	0	5	0	0	0-0	.182	.182	.273	.455	0	1.000
2000— New York (A.L.)	2B	1	0	1	0	0	0	0	0	0	0	0	0	0-0	...	...	...	...	0	1.000
2001— Houston (N.L.)	SS	3	6	0	1	0	0	0	0	1	0	0	0	0-0	.167	.167	.167	.333	0	1.000
2004— Houston (N.L.)	SS	5	19	2	2	0	0	0	1	1	2	0	1	0-0	.105	.143	.105	.248	0	1.000
2005— Houston (N.L.)	1B-2B-SS	2	5	0	0	0	0	0	0	0	1	0	0	0-0	.000	.000	.000	.000	1	.857
Division series totals (6 years)		17	53	5	9	3	0	0	2	2	10	0	1	0-0	.170	.196	.226	.423	2	.962

CHAMPIONSHIP SERIES RECORD

Year Team (League)	Pos.	G	AB	R	H	2B	3B	HR	RBI	BB	SO	HBP	GDP	SB-CS	Avg.	OBP	SLG	OPS	E	Avg.
2000— New York (A.L.)	2B	4	2	3	2	1	0	0	2	0	0	0	0	2-0	1.000	1.000	1.500	2.167	0	1.000
2004— Houston (N.L.)	SS-2B	7	28	1	7	1	0	0	0	0	1	0	0	0-1	.250	.250	.286	.536	1	.963
2005— Houston (N.L.)		2	2	0	0	0	0	0	0	0	0	0	0	0-0	.000	.000	.000	.000	0	...
Champ. series totals (3 years)		13	32	4	9	2	0	0	2	0	1	0	0	2-1	.281	.273	.344	.616	1	.966

WORLD SERIES RECORD

Year Team (League)	Pos.	G	AB	R	H	2B	3B	HR	RBI	BB	SO	HBP	GDP	SB-CS	Avg.	OBP	SLG	OPS	E	Avg.
2000— New York (A.L.)	2B	4	17	0	4	0	0	0	1	0	5	0	0	0-1	.235	.235	.235	.471	0	1.000
2005— Houston (N.L.)	1B-2B-SS	3	2	0	1	0	0	0	2	1	0	0	0	0-0	.500	.667	.500	1.167	0	1.000
World series totals (2 years)		7	19	0	5	0	0	0	3	1	5	0	0	0-1	.263	.300	.263	.563	0	1.000

VIZCAINO, LUIS   P

PERSONAL: Born August 6, 1974, in Bani, Dominican Republic. ... 5-11/184. ... Throws right, bats right. ... Full name: Luis Arias Vizcaino. ... Name pronounced: vis-ky-ee-no.
TRANSACTIONS/CAREER NOTES: Signed as a non-drafted free agent by Oakland Athletics organization (December 9, 1994). ... Traded by A's to Texas Rangers for P Justin Duchscherer (March 18, 2002). ... Traded by Rangers to Milwaukee Brewers for P Jesus Pena (March 24, 2002). ... Traded by Brewers with OF Scott Podsednik and a player to be named to Chicago White Sox for OF Carlos Lee (December 13, 2004).
CAREER HITTING: 0-for-2 (.000), 0 R, 0 2B, 0 3B, 0 HR, 0 RBI.

SCOUTING REPORT *Throws:* Vizcaino's fastball is in the 92-94 mph range, and his slider is at 84. Also throws a split-finger fastball. *Tendencies:* His fastball is a heavy pitch that runs and bores in on righthanded hitters. Slider is extremely quick and runs away from righties. Throws with a loose arm and low arm action; muscles the ball to achieve velocity. Lefthanders have a better view of his arm angle. Splitter was inconsistent last season. *Outlook:* Vizcaino went from setup man to nondescript middle reliever in 2005, but he has the stuff to again work in a setup role. *Grade 6.8*

LUIS VIZCAINO'S PITCHING ZONE

.273	.200	.364
.188	.160	.415
.375	.400	.393

LEFTY-RIGHTY SPLITS

vs.	Avg.	AB	H	2B	3B	HR	RBI	BB	SO	OBP	Slg.
L	.321	112	36	6	0	3	12	15	16	.402	.455
R	.242	157	38	7	0	5	28	14	27	.310	.382

Year Team (League)	W	L	Pct.	ERA	WHIP	G	GS	CG	ShO	Hld.	Sv.-Opp.	IP	H	R	ER	HR	BB-IBB	SO	Avg.
1995— Dom. Athletics (DSL)	10	2	.833	2.27	1.06	16	15	5	1	...	0-...	115.0	93	41	29	...	29-...	89	...
1996— Ariz. A's (AZL)	6	3	.667	4.07	1.37	15	10	0	0	...	1-...	59.2	58	36	27	1	24-1	52	.247
1997— Modesto (Calif.)	0	3	.000	13.19	2.58	7	0	0	0	...	0-...	14.1	24	24	21	4	13-4	15	.387
—S. Oregon (N'west)	1	6	.143	7.93	1.87	22	5	0	0	...	0-...	47.2	62	51	42	5	27-0	42	.308
1998— Modesto (Calif.)	6	3	.667	2.74	1.13	23	16	0	0	...	0-...	102.0	72	39	31	5	43-1	108	.196
—Huntsville (Sou.)	3	2	.600	4.66	1.68	7	7	0	0	...	0-...	38.2	43	27	20	8	22-0	26	.279
1999— Midland (Texas)	8	7	.533	5.85	1.61	25	19	0	0	...	0-...	104.2	120	74	68	18	48-2	88	.287
—Oakland (A.L.)	0	0	...	5.40	1.80	1	0	0	0	0	0-0	3.1	3	2	2	1	3-0	2	.231
—Vancouver (PCL)	0	1	.000	1.38	1.46	7	0	0	0	0	0-0	13.0	13	4	2	0	6-0	7	.260
2000— Oakland (A.L.)	0	1	.000	7.45	1.86	12	0	0	0	0	0-0	19.1	25	17	16	2	11-0	18	.305
—Sacramento (PCL)	6	2	.750	5.03	1.43	33	2	0	0	...	5-...	48.1	48	27	27	4	21-0	41	.276
2001— Sacramento (PCL)	2	2	.500	2.14	1.07	27	0	0	0	...	7-...	42.0	35	10	10	5	10-4	56	.220
—Oakland (A.L.)	2	1	.667	4.66	1.36	36	0	0	0	3	1-1	36.2	38	19	19	8	12-1	31	.266
2002— Milwaukee (N.L.)	5	3	.625	2.99	1.05	76	0	0	0	19	5-6	81.1	55	27	27	6	30-4	79	.194
2003— Milwaukee (N.L.)	4	3	.571	6.39	1.44	75	0	0	0	6	0-6	62.0	64	45	44	16	25-3	61	.263
2004— Milwaukee (N.L.)	4	4	.500	3.75	1.18	73	0	0	0	21	1-5	72.0	61	35	30	12	24-3	63	.228
2005— Chicago (A.L.)	6	5	.545	3.73	1.47	65	0	0	0	9	0-3	70.0	74	30	29	8	29-6	43	.275
American League totals (4 years)	8	7	.533	4.59	1.51	114	0	0	0	12	1-4	129.1	140	68	66	19	55-7	94	.275
National League totals (3 years)	13	10	.565	4.22	1.20	224	0	0	0	49	6-17	215.1	180	107	101	34	79-10	203	.226
Major League totals (7 years)	21	17	.553	4.36	1.32	338	0	0	0	61	7-21	344.2	320	175	167	53	134-17	297	.245

WORLD SERIES RECORD

Year Team (League)	W	L	Pct.	ERA	WHIP	G	GS	CG	ShO	Hld.	Sv.-Opp.	IP	H	R	ER	HR	BB-IBB	SO	Avg.
2005— Chicago (A.L.)	0	0	...	0.00	1.00	1	0	0	0	0	0-0	1.0	1	0	0	0	1-0	0	.000

PERSONAL: Born April 24, 1967, in Caracas, Venezuela. ... 5-9/175. ... Bats both, throws right. ... Full name: Omar Enrique Vizquel. ... Name pronounced: viz-KELL. ... High school: Francisco Espejo (Caracas, Venezuela).

TRANSACTIONS/CAREER NOTES: Signed as a non-drafted free agent by Seattle Mariners organization (April 1, 1984). ... On disabled list (April 7-May 13, 1990); included rehabilitation assignments to Calgary and San Bernardino. ... On disabled list (April 13-May 11, 1992); included rehabilitation assignment to Calgary. ... Traded by Mariners to Cleveland Indians for SS Felix Fermin, 1B Reggie Jefferson and cash (December 20, 1993). ... On disabled list (April 23-June 13, 1994); included rehabilitation assignment to Charlotte. ... On suspended list (September 17-18, 1998). ... On disabled list (June 12-August 26 and September 6, 2003-remainder of season); included rehabilitation assignment to Lake County. ... Signed as a free agent by San Francisco Giants (November 16, 2004).

HONORS: Won A.L. Gold Glove at shortstop (1993-2001). ... Won N.L. Gold Glove at shortstop (2005).

2005 GAMES PLAYED BY POSITION (MLB): SS—150.

SCOUTING REPORT

Offense: Vizquel has an extremely compact stroke and good bat control. Is a line-drive hitter with occasional power. Is very difficult to strike out. Has excellent overall instincts. Will bunt. Forces infielders to play shallow. *Defense:* Vizquel might have the softest hands of any shortstop in history. Is a ballet dancer in the field with his exceptional feet and lower-body agility. Range has declined some, however; relies on positioning and instincts to compensate. Throws just well enough to get runners out and is accurate. *Outlook:* Vizquel showed last year that he still can be a productive everyday player and front-line defender. Is continually making adjustments as his natural bat speed declines. **Grade 7.7**

OMAR VIZQUEL'S HITTING ZONE

.487	.250	.156
.309	.288	.284
.333	.129	.304

LEFTY-RIGHTY SPLITS

vs.	Avg.	AB	H	2B	3B	HR	RBI	BB	SO	OBP	Slg.
L	.253	146	37	11	0	1	14	9	13	.302	.349
R	.277	422	117	17	4	2	31	47	45	.354	.351

Year Team (League)	Pos.	G	AB	R	H	2B	3B	HR	RBI	BB	SO	HBP	GDP	SB-CS	Avg.	OBP	SLG	OPS	E	Avg.
1984— Butte (Pion.)	2B-SS	15	45	7	14	2	0	0	4	3	8	0	0	2-0	.311	.347	.356	.702	5	.894
1985— Bellingham (N'west)	2B-SS	50	187	24	42	9	0	5	17	12	27	0	0	4-3	.225	.270	.353	.623	19	.932
1986— Wausau (Midw.)	2B-SS	105	352	60	75	13	2	4	28	64	56	2	6	19-6	.213	.333	.295	.628	16	.968
1987— Salinas (Calif.)	2B-SS	114	407	61	107	12	8	0	38	57	55	0	5	25-19	.263	.350	.332	.682	25	.938
1988— Vermont (East.)	SS	103	374	54	95	18	2	2	35	42	44	3	6	30-11	.254	.328	.329	.657	19	.959
— Calgary (PCL)	SS	33	107	10	24	2	3	1	12	5	14	0	1	2-4	.224	.259	.327	.586	6	.957
1989— Seattle (A.L.)	SS	143	387	45	85	7	3	1	20	28	40	1	6	1-4	.220	.273	.261	.534	18	.971
— Calgary (PCL)	SS	7	28	3	6	2	0	0	3	3	4	1	1	0-2	.214	.313	.286	.598	0	1.000
1990— Calgary (PCL)	SS	48	150	18	35	6	2	0	8	13	10	2	3	4-3	.233	.299	.300	.599	6	.972
— San Bern. (Calif.)	SS	6	28	5	7	0	0	0	3	3	1	0	0	1-2	.250	.323	.250	.573	3	.914
— Seattle (A.L.)	SS	81	255	19	63	3	2	2	18	18	22	0	7	4-1	.247	.295	.298	.593	7	.980
1991— Seattle (A.L.)	2B-SS	142	426	42	98	16	4	1	41	45	37	0	8	7-2	.230	.302	.293	.595	13	.980
1992— Seattle (A.L.)	SS	136	483	49	142	20	4	0	21	32	38	2	14	15-13	.294	.340	.352	.692	7	.983
— Calgary (PCL)	SS	6	22	0	6	1	0	0	2	1	3	1	3	0-1	.273	.333	.318	.652	1	.972
1993— Seattle (A.L.)	SS-DH	158	560	68	143	14	2	2	31	50	71	4	7	12-14	.255	.319	.298	.618	15	.980
1994— Cleveland (A.L.)	SS	69	286	39	78	10	1	1	33	23	23	0	4	13-4	.273	.325	.325	.650	6	.981
— Charlotte (Int'l)	SS	7	26	3	7	1	0	0	1	2	1	0	0	1-0	.269	.321	.308	.629	1	.967
1995— Cleveland (A.L.)	SS	136	542	87	144	28	0	6	56	59	59	1	4	29-11	.266	.333	.351	.684	9	.986
1996— Cleveland (A.L.)	SS	151	542	98	161	36	1	9	64	56	42	4	10	35-9	.297	.362	.417	.779	20	.971
1997— Cleveland (A.L.)	SS	153	565	89	158	23	6	5	49	57	58	2	16	43-12	.280	.347	.368	.715	10	.985
1998— Cleveland (A.L.)	SS	151	576	86	166	30	6	2	50	62	64	4	10	37-12	.288	.358	.372	.730	5	.993
1999— Cleveland (A.L.)	SS-OF	144	574	112	191	36	4	5	66	65	50	1	8	42-9	.333	.397	.436	.833	15	.995
2000— Cleveland (A.L.)	SS	156	613	101	176	27	3	6	66	87	72	5	13	22-10	.287	.377	.375	.753	3	.995
2001— Cleveland (A.L.)	SS	155	611	84	156	26	8	2	50	61	72	2	14	13-9	.255	.323	.334	.657	7	.989
2002— Cleveland (A.L.)	SS	151	582	85	160	31	5	14	72	56	64	8	7	18-10	.275	.341	.418	.759	7	.980
2003— Lake County (S.Atl.)	SS	4	14	0	1	0	0	0	0	1	2	0	0	1-0	.071	.133	.071	.205	0	1.000
— Cleveland (A.L.)	SS	64	250	43	61	13	2	2	19	29	20	0	11	8-3	.244	.321	.336	.657	7	.978
2004— Cleveland (A.L.)	SS	148	567	82	165	28	3	7	59	57	62	1	12	19-6	.291	.353	.388	.741	11	.982
2005— San Francisco (N.L.)	SS	152	568	66	154	28	4	3	45	56	58	5	10	24-10	.271	.341	.350	.691	8	.988
American League totals (16 years)		2138	7819	1129	2147	348	54	66	715	785	794	35	151	318-129	.275	.341	.358	.699	160	.983
National League totals (1 year)		152	568	66	154	28	4	3	45	56	58	5	10	24-10	.271	.341	.350	.691	8	.988
Major League totals (17 years)		2290	8387	1195	2301	376	58	69	760	841	852	40	161	342-139	.274	.341	.358	.698	168	.984

DIVISION SERIES RECORD

Year Team (League)	Pos.	G	AB	R	H	2B	3B	HR	RBI	BB	SO	HBP	GDP	SB-CS	Avg.	OBP	SLG	OPS	E	Avg.
1995— Cleveland (A.L.)	SS	3	12	2	2	1	0	0	4	2	2	0	0	1-0	.167	.286	.250	.536	0	1.000
1996— Cleveland (A.L.)	SS	4	14	4	6	1	0	0	2	3	4	0	0	4-2	.429	.500	.500	1.000	0	1.000
1997— Cleveland (A.L.)	SS	5	18	3	9	1	0	0	1	2	1	0	0	4-0	.500	.550	.500	1.050	0	1.000
1998— Cleveland (A.L.)	SS	4	15	1	1	0	0	0	0	1	0	0	0	0-0	.067	.125	.067	.192	0	1.000
1999— Cleveland (A.L.)	SS	5	21	3	5	1	1	0	3	2	3	0	0	0-0	.238	.304	.381	.685	0	1.000
2001— Cleveland (A.L.)	SS	5	22	2	9	1	1	0	6	1	1	0	0	1-0	.409	.435	.545	.980	1	.964
Division series totals (6 years)		26	102	15	32	4	2	0	16	11	11	0	0	10-2	.314	.377	.392	.769	1	.992

CHAMPIONSHIP SERIES RECORD

Year Team (League)	Pos.	G	AB	R	H	2B	3B	HR	RBI	BB	SO	HBP	GDP	SB-CS	Avg.	OBP	SLG	OPS	E	Avg.
1995— Cleveland (A.L.)	SS	6	23	2	2	1	0	0	2	5	2	0	0	3-0	.087	.241	.130	.372	1	1.000
1997— Cleveland (A.L.)	SS	6	25	1	1	0	0	0	0	2	10	1	0	0-0	.040	.143	.040	.183	0	1.000
1998— Cleveland (A.L.)	SS	6	25	2	11	0	1	0	0	1	3	1	0	4-1	.440	.481	.520	1.001	1	.974
Champ. series totals (3 years)		18	73	5	14	1	1	0	2	8	15	2	0	7-1	.192	.286	.233	.519	2	.990

WORLD SERIES RECORD

Year Team (League)	Pos.	G	AB	R	H	2B	3B	HR	RBI	BB	SO	HBP	GDP	SB-CS	Avg.	OBP	SLG	OPS	E	Avg.
1995— Cleveland (A.L.)	SS	6	23	3	4	0	1	0	1	3	5	0	0	1-0	.174	.269	.261	.530	0	1.000
1997— Cleveland (A.L.)	SS	7	30	5	7	2	0	0	1	3	5	0	0	5-0	.233	.303	.300	.603	0	1.000
World series totals (2 years)		13	53	8	11	2	1	0	2	6	10	0	0	6-0	.208	.288	.283	.571	0	1.000

V

	G	AB	R	H	2B	3B	HR	RBI	BB	SO	HBP	GDP	SB-CS	Avg.	OBP	SLG	OPS	E	Avg.
All-Star Game totals (3 years)	3	5	0	2	0	1	0	1	1	0	0	0	0-0	.400	.500	.800	1.300	0	1.000

VOGELSONG, RYAN   P

PERSONAL: Born July 22, 1977, in Charlotte. ... 6-3/213. ... Throws right, bats right. ... Full name: Ryan Andrew Vogelsong. ... High school: Octorara Area (Atglen, Pa.). ... College: Kutztown (Pa.).
TRANSACTIONS/CAREER NOTES: Selected by San Francisco Giants organization in fifth round of 1998 free-agent draft. ... Traded by Giants with OF Armando Rios to Pittsburgh Pirates for P Jason Schmidt (July 30, 2001). ... On disabled list (March 30-August 1, 2002); included rehabilitation assignments to Lynchburg and Altoona.
CAREER HITTING: 10-for-56 (.179), 2 R, 4 2B, 0 3B, 0 HR, 3 RBI.

SCOUTING REPORT *Throws:* His fastball hits 90-92 mph, and he has a curve and slider. *Tendencies:* His fastball has life if it's down, but it's very straight when up. Varies the speed of his slider, but when he stays on top and doesn't rush it, the slider is much quicker and bites sharply. Curve is more of a slurve with a big sweeping break. *Outlook:* Vogelsong pitched in a middle relief role this past year and showed promise. Is not throwing as hard but really pitched well with runners in scoring position. Will continue in this role in 2006. ***Grade 5.2***

RYAN VOGELSONG'S PITCHING ZONE

.167	.455	.250
.220	.182	.350
.207	.444	.227

LEFTY-RIGHTY SPLITS

vs.	Avg.	AB	H	2B	3B	HR	RBI	BB	SO	OBP	Slg.
L	.275	120	33	5	2	1	18	20	22	.376	.375
R	.250	196	49	12	2	4	29	20	30	.339	.393

Year Team (League)	W	L	Pct.	ERA	WHIP	G	GS	CG	ShO	Hld.	Sv.-Opp.	IP	H	R	ER	HR	BB-IBB	SO	Avg.
1998— Salem-Keizer (N'west)	6	1	.857	1.77	0.95	10	10	0	0	...	0-...	56.0	37	15	11	5	16-0	66	.186
— San Jose (Calif.)	0	0	...	7.58	1.42	4	4	0	0	...	0-...	19.0	23	16	16	3	4-0	26	.307
1999— San Jose (Calif.)	4	4	.500	2.45	0.92	13	13	0	0	...	0-...	69.2	37	26	19	3	27-0	86	.154
— Shreveport (Texas)	0	2	.000	7.31	1.94	6	6	0	0	...	0-...	28.1	40	25	23	7	15-0	23	.336
2000— Shreveport (Texas)	6	10	.375	4.23	1.43	27	27	1	0	...	0-...	155.1	153	82	73	15	69-2 * 147		.260
— San Francisco (N.L.)	0	0	...	0.00	1.00	4	0	0	0	0	0-0	6.0	4	0	0	0	2-0	6	.182
2001— Fresno (PCL)	3	3	.500	2.79	0.91	10	10	0	0	...	0-...	58.0	35	18	18	6	18-0	53	.170
— San Francisco (N.L.)	0	3	.000	5.65	1.50	13	0	0	0	1	0-0	28.2	29	21	18	5	14-0	17	.257
— Nashville (PCL)	2	3	.400	3.98	1.29	6	6	0	0	...	0-0	31.2	26	15	14	2	15-0	33	.230
— Pittsburgh (N.L.)	0	2	.000	12.00	2.67	2	2	0	0	0	0-0	6.0	10	10	8	1	6-1	7	.357
2002— Lynchburg (Caro.)	1	1	.500	8.04	1.66	4	4	0	0	...	0-...	15.2	19	14	14	0	7-0	20	.297
— Altoona (East.)	1	5	.167	5.56	1.31	8	8	0	0	...	0-...	43.2	47	27	27	5	10-0	35	.278
2003— Nashville (PCL)	12	8	.600	4.29	1.30	26	26	1	0	...	0-...	149.0	142	75	71	12	54-5	146	.250
— Pittsburgh (N.L.)	2	2	.500	6.55	1.77	6	5	0	0	0	0-0	22.0	30	19	16	1	9-3	15	.323
2004— Pittsburgh (N.L.)	6	13	.316	6.50	1.62	31	26	0	0	0	0-0	133.0	148	97	96	22	67-7	92	.285
2005— Pittsburgh (N.L.)	2	2	.500	4.43	1.50	44	0	0	0	1	0-1	81.1	82	43	40	5	40-1	52	.259
Major League totals (5 years)	10	22	.313	5.78	1.59	100	33	0	0	2	0-1	277.0	303	190	178	34	138-12	189	.278

VOLQUEZ, EDISON   P

PERSONAL: Born July 3, 1983, in La Segunda, Dominican Republic. ... 6-1/190. ... Throws right, bats right. ... Full name: Edison Volquez.
TRANSACTIONS/CAREER NOTES: Signed as a non-drafted free agent by Texas Rangers organization (October 29, 2001).
CAREER HITTING: 0-for-0 (.000), 0 R, 0 2B, 0 3B, 0 HR, 0 RBI.

EDISON VOLQUEZ'S PITCHING ZONE

.667	.333	.667
.400	.636	.500
.167	.167	.667

LEFTY-RIGHTY SPLITS

vs.	Avg.	AB	H	2B	3B	HR	RBI	BB	SO	OBP	Slg.
L	.481	27	13	5	0	3	9	8	5	.583	.667
R	.343	35	12	2	0	3	10	2	6	.410	.657

Year Team (League)	W	L	Pct.	ERA	WHIP	G	GS	CG	ShO	Hld.	Sv.-Opp.	IP	H	R	ER	HR	BB-IBB	SO	Avg.
2002— Dom. Rangers (DSL)	1	2	.333	2.68	1.26	14	8	0	0	...	0-...	47.0	45	19	14	1	14-1	58	.254
2003— Ariz. Rangers (AZL)	2	1	.667	4.00	1.30	10	4	0	0	...	1-...	27.0	24	14	12	1	11-0	28	.245
2004— Clinton (Midw.)	4	4	.500	4.21	1.24	21	15	0	0	...	3-...	87.2	82	49	41	8	27-1	74	.246
— Stockton (Calif.)	4	1	.800	2.95	1.13	8	8	0	0	...	0-...	39.2	31	16	13	6	14-0	34	.221
2005— Bakersfield (Calif.)	5	4	.556	4.19	1.14	11	11	1	0	0	0-0	66.2	64	34	31	9	12-0	77	.252
— Ariz. Rangers (AZL)	0	0	...	0.00	1.00	1	1	0	0	0	0-0	2.0	2	0	0	0	0-0	2	.250
— Frisco (Texas)	1	5	.167	4.14	1.28	10	10	1	1	0	0-0	58.2	58	29	27	6	17-0	49	.258
— Texas (A.L.)	0	4	.000	14.21	2.76	6	3	0	0	0	0-0	12.2	25	22	20	3	10-0	11	.403
Major League totals (1 year)	0	4	.000	14.21	2.76	6	3	0	0	0	0-0	12.2	25	22	20	3	10-0	11	.403

WAECHTER, DOUG   P

PERSONAL: Born January 28, 1981, in St. Petersburg, Fla. ... 6-4/209. ... Throws right, bats right. ... Full name: Douglas Michael Waechter. ... Name pronounced: WACK-ter. ... High school: Northeast Senior (St. Petersburg, Fla.).
TRANSACTIONS/CAREER NOTES: Selected by Tampa Bay Devil Rays organization in third round of 1999 free-agent draft. ... On disabled list (June 9-September 6, 2004); included rehabilitation assignment to Durham. ... On disabled list (July 3-25, 2005); included rehabilitation assignment to Durham.
CAREER HITTING: 0-for-2 (.000), 1 R, 0 2B, 0 3B, 0 HR, 0 RBI.

DOUG WAECHTER'S PITCHING ZONE

.349	.355	.213
.344	.385	.283
.295	.256	.349

LEFTY-RIGHTY SPLITS

vs.	Avg.	AB	H	2B	3B	HR	RBI	BB	SO	OBP	Slg.
L	.310	342	106	22	3	18	59	23	38	.352	.550
R	.283	300	85	17	1	11	40	15	49	.321	.457

SCOUTING REPORT *Throws:* Waechter throws a fastball from 88-92 mph, a slider and changeup. *Tendencies:* Recurring finger problems continue to slow Waechter's progress. Fastball is sneaky because his motion is deliberate. Needs to tighten the break on his slider. His straight

W

change has some fading action. Will throw a splitter unless finger is bothering him. Pitches up in the zone too often; shouldn't be up there at all. Makes too many mistakes out over the plate and hitters become comfortable hitting against him. *Outlook:* He looks to be no better than a fifth starter who can eat innings.

Grade 5.8

Year	Team (League)	W	L	Pct.	ERA	WHIP	G	GS	CG	ShO	Hld.	Sv.-Opp.	IP	H	R	ER	HR	BB-IBB	SO	Avg.
1999— Princeton (Appal.)	0	5	.000	9.77	2.31	11	7	0	0	...	0-...	35.0	46	45	38	2	35-0	38	.317
2000— Hudson Valley (NYP)	4	4	.500	2.35	1.24	14	14	2	2	...	0-...	72.2	53	23	19	2	37-0	58	.205
2001— Char., S.C. (S. Atl.)	8	11	.421	4.34	1.42	26	26	1	0	...	0-...	153.1	179	97	74	14	38-1	107	.285
2002— Char., S.C. (S. Atl.)	3	3	.500	3.47	1.51	7	7	0	0	...	0-...	36.1	39	20	14	2	16-3	36	.277
—Bakersfield (Calif.)	6	3	.667	2.66	1.32	17	17	0	0	...	0-...	108.1	114	43	32	9	29-0	101	.267
—Orlando (Sou.)	1	3	.250	9.00	2.22	4	4	1	0	...	0-...	18.0	27	20	18	4	13-0	18	.338
2003— Char., S.C. (S. Atl.)	5	3	.625	4.13	1.22	13	12	0	0	...	0-...	76.1	74	39	35	6	19-0	45	.257
—Durham (Int'l)	3	3	.500	3.33	1.23	10	10	0	0	...	0-...	51.1	51	25	19	9	12-0	35	.262
—Tampa Bay (A.L.)	3	2	.600	3.31	1.25	6	5	1	1	0	0-0	35.1	29	13	13	4	15-0	29	.225
2004— Durham (Int'l)	0	2	.000	6.75	1.70	8	8	0	0	...	0-...	29.1	33	22	22	11	17-0	22	.277
—Tampa Bay (A.L.)	5	7	.417	6.01	1.44	14	14	0	0	0	0-0	70.1	68	54	47	20	33-1	36	.252
2005— Durham (Int'l)	0	2	.000	9.22	1.61	3	3	0	0	...	0-...	13.2	17	14	14	3	5-0	16	.304
—Tampa Bay (A.L.)	5	12	.294	5.62	1.46	29	25	0	0	0	0-0	157.0	191	109	98	29	38-5	87	.298
Major League totals (3 years)	**13**	**21**	**.382**	**5.41**	**1.42**	**49**	**44**	**1**	**1**	**0**	**0-0**	**262.2**	**288**	**176**	**158**	**53**	**86-6**	**152**	**.277**

WAGNER, BILLY   P

PERSONAL: Born July 25, 1971, in Tannersville, Va. ... 5-11/195. ... Throws left, bats left. ... Full name: William Edward Wagner. ... High school: Tazewell (Va.). ... Junior college: Ferrum (Va.).

TRANSACTIONS/CAREER NOTES: Selected by Houston Astros organization in first round (12th pick overall) of 1993 free-agent draft. ... On disabled list (August 23-September 7, 1996). ... On disabled list (July 16-August 7, 1998); included rehabilitation assignment to Jackson. ... On disabled list (June 21, 2000-remainder of season). ... On disabled list (June 4-June 19, 2001); included rehabilitation assignment to Round Rock. ... Traded by Astros to Philadelphia Phillies for Ps Brandon Duckworth, Taylor Buchholz and Ezequiel Astacio (November 3, 2003). ... On disabled list (May 8-June 8 and July 22-September 4, 2004); included rehabilitation assignment to Reading. ... On suspended list (September 17-19, 2004).

CAREER HITTING: 2-for-20 (.100), 1 R, 0 2B, 0 3B, 0 HR, 1 RBI.

SCOUTING REPORT **Throws:** The lefthander's fastball ranges from 96-100 mph, and his slider is 88-91. *Tendencies:* He is starting to throw his slider more than in the past when he feels hitters are sitting on his fastball. Fastball has excellent riding action up in the zone; few hitters can catch up. Has some deception in his delivery and arm action. Fastball explodes near the plate. Generates amazing velocity for his size (5-11, 195) and maintains it from outing to outing. *Outlook:* Wagner still is a dominant closer. Was extremely consistent pitching in a tough environment in Philadelphia. **Grade 9.6**

BILLY WAGNER'S PITCHING ZONE

.158	.091	.200
.125	.343	.154
.333	.308	.231

LEFTY-RIGHTY SPLITS

vs.	Avg.	AB	H	2B	3B	HR	RBI	BB	SO	OBP	Slg.
L	.128	47	6	0	1	0	2	2	15	.192	.170
R	.173	225	39	7	0	6	19	18	72	.237	.284

Year	Team (League)	W	L	Pct.	ERA	WHIP	G	GS	CG	ShO	Hld.	Sv.-Opp.	IP	H	R	ER	HR	BB-IBB	SO	Avg.
1993— Auburn (NY-Penn)	1	3	.250	4.08	1.74	7	7	0	0	...	0-...	28.2	25	19	13	2	25-0	31	.231
1994— Quad City (Midw.)	8	9	.471	3.29	1.24	26	26	2	0	...	0-...	153.0	99	71	56	9	91-0	204	.188
1995— Jackson (Texas)	2	2	.500	2.57	1.21	12	12	0	0	...	0-...	70.0	49	25	20	7	36-1	77	.199
—Tucson (PCL)	5	3	.625	3.18	1.34	13	13	0	0	...	0-...	76.1	70	28	27	3	32-0	80	.245
—Houston (N.L.)	0	0	...	0.00	0.00	1	0	0	0	0	0-0	0.1	0	0	0	0	0-0	0	.000
1996— Tucson (PCL)	6	2	.750	3.28	1.28	12	12	1	1	...	0-...	74.0	62	32	27	2	33-0	86	.225
—Houston (N.L.)	2	2	.500	2.44	1.12	37	0	0	0	3	9-13	51.2	28	16	14	6	30-2	67	.165
1997— Houston (N.L.)	7	8	.467	2.85	1.19	62	0	0	0	1	23-29	66.1	49	23	21	5	30-1	106	.204
1998— Houston (N.L.)	4	3	.571	2.70	1.18	58	0	0	0	1	30-35	60.0	46	19	18	6	25-1	97	.211
—Jackson (Texas)	0	0	...	0.00	0.33	3	1	0	0	...	0-...	3.0	1	0	0	0	0-0	7	.100
1999— Houston (N.L.)	4	1	.800	1.57	0.78	66	0	0	0	1	39-42	74.2	35	14	13	5	23-1	124	.135
2000— Houston (N.L.)	2	4	.333	6.18	1.66	28	0	0	0	0	6-15	27.2	28	19	19	6	18-0	28	.255
2001— Houston (N.L.)	2	5	.286	2.73	1.02	64	0	0	0	0	39-41	62.2	44	19	19	5	20-0	79	.198
—Round Rock (Texas)	0	0	...	0.00	0.00	1	1	0	0	...	0-...	1.0	0	0	0	0	0-0	2	.000
2002— Houston (N.L.)	4	2	.667	2.52	0.97	70	0	0	0	0	35-41	75.0	51	21	21	7	22-5	88	.196
2003— Houston (N.L.)	1	4	.200	1.78	0.87	78	0	0	0	0	44-47	86.0	52	18	17	8	23-5	105	.169
2004— Reading (East.)	0	0	...	0.00	1.00	1	1	0	0	0	0-...	1.0	1	0	0	0	0-0	2	.250
—Philadelphia (N.L.)	4	0	1.000	2.42	0.77	45	0	0	0	1	21-25	48.1	31	16	13	5	6-1	59	.181
2005— Philadelphia (N.L.)	4	3	.571	1.51	0.84	75	0	0	0	0	38-41	77.2	45	17	13	6	20-2	87	.165
Major League totals (11 years)	**34**	**32**	**.515**	**2.40**	**0.99**	**584**	**0**	**0**	**0**	**7**	**284-329**	**630.1**	**409**	**182**	**168**	**59**	**217-18**	**840**	**.183**

DIVISION SERIES RECORD

Year	Team (League)	W	L	Pct.	ERA	WHIP	G	GS	CG	ShO	Hld.	Sv.-Opp.	IP	H	R	ER	HR	BB-IBB	SO	Avg.
1997— Houston (N.L.)	0	0	...	18.00	3.00	1	0	0	0	0	0-0	1.0	3	2	2	0	0-0	2	.500
1998— Houston (N.L.)	1	0	1.000	18.00	4.00	1	0	0	0	0	0-1	1.0	4	2	2	1	0-0	1	.571
1999— Houston (N.L.)	0	0	...	0.00	0.00	1	0	0	0	0	0-0	1.0	0	0	0	0	0-0	1	.000
2001— Houston (N.L.)	0	0	...	5.40	0.60	2	0	0	0	0	0-0	1.2	1	1	1	1	0-0	3	.167
Division series totals (4 years)	**1**	**0**	**1.000**	**9.64**	**1.71**	**5**	**0**	**0**	**0**	**0**	**0-1**	**4.2**	**8**	**5**	**5**	**2**	**0-0**	**7**	**.364**

ALL-STAR GAME RECORD

		W	L	Pct.	ERA	WHIP	G	GS	CG	ShO	Hld.	Sv.-Opp.	IP	H	R	ER	HR	BB-IBB	SO	Avg.
All-Star Game totals (3 years)		0	0	...	4.50	0.50	3	0	0	0	1	0-0	2.0	1	1	1	1	0-0	2	.143

WAGNER, RYAN   P

PERSONAL: Born July 15, 1982, in Yoakum, Texas. ... 6-4/210. ... Throws right, bats right. ... Full name: Ryan Scott Wagner. ... High school: Yoakum (Texas). ... College: Houston.

W

TRANSACTIONS/CAREER NOTES: Selected by Cincinnati Reds organization in first round (14th pick overall) of 2003 free-agent draft. ... On bereavement list (Sept. 20-24, 2004). ... On disabled list (July 15, 2005-remainder of season).
CAREER HITTING: 0-for-1 (.000), 1 R, 0 2B, 0 3B, 0 HR, 0 RBI.

RYAN WAGNER'S PITCHING ZONE

.429	.400	.286
.405	.500	.368
.357	.200	.200

LEFTY-RIGHTY SPLITS

vs.	Avg.	AB	H	2B	3B	HR	RBI	BB	SO	OBP	Slg.
L	.311	74	23	7	0	1	11	14	15	.422	.446
R	.297	111	33	6	0	3	18	3	24	.328	.432

Year Team (League)	W	L	Pct.	ERA	WHIP	G	GS	CG	ShO	Hld.	Sv.-Opp.	IP	H	R	ER	HR	BB-IBB	SO	Avg.
2003— Chattanooga (Sou.)	1	0	1.000	0.00	0.80	5	0	0	0	...	0-...	5.0	2	1	0	0	2-0	6	.125
— Louisville (Int'l)	0	1	.000	4.50	1.25	4	0	0	0	...	0-...	4.0	5	2	2	0	4-0	4	.313
— Cincinnati (N.L.)	2	0	1.000	1.66	1.15	17	0	0	0	6	0-1	21.2	13	4	4	2	12-1	25	.173
2004— Louisville (Int'l)	1	0	1.000	2.70	1.32	15	0	0	0	...	1-...	16.2	13	5	5	0	9-0	19	.210
— Cincinnati (N.L.)	3	2	.600	4.70	1.66	49	0	0	0	8	0-3	51.2	59	31	27	7	27-2	37	.284
2005— Cincinnati (N.L.)	3	2	.600	6.11	1.60	42	0	0	0	12	0-1	45.2	56	33	31	4	17-1	39	.303
Major League totals (3 years)	**8**	**4**	**.667**	**4.69**	**1.55**	**108**	**0**	**0**	**0**	**26**	**0-5**	**119.0**	**128**	**68**	**62**	**13**	**56-4**	**101**	**.274**

WAINWRIGHT, ADAM   P

PERSONAL: Born August 30, 1981, in Brunswick, Ga. ... 6-7/205. ... Throws right, bats right. ... Full name: Adam Parrish Wainwright. ... High school: Glynn Academy (Brunswick, Ga.).
TRANSACTIONS/CAREER NOTES: Selected by Atlanta Braves organization in first round (29th pick overall) of 2000 free-agent draft. ... Traded by Braves with Ps Ray King and Jason Marquis to St. Louis Cardinals for OF J.D. Drew and OF/C Eli Marrero (December 14, 2003).
CAREER HITTING: 0-for-0 (.000), 0 R, 0 2B, 0 3B, 0 HR, 0 RBI.

LEFTY-RIGHTY SPLITS

vs.	Avg.	AB	H	2B	3B	HR	RBI	BB	SO	OBP	Slg.
L	.500	2	1	0	0	0	0	1	0	.667	.500
R	.167	6	1	0	0	1	3	0	0	.167	.667

SCOUTING REPORT **Throws:** He throws a low-90s fastball, a slider, a curveball and a changeup. All have the potential to be above-average pitches. *Tendencies:* Wainwright is a control pitcher who relies on command of his fastball. Lacks deception in his delivery and sometimes telegraphs his pitches. Is able to maintain his velocity throughout a start. Uses his height to advantage by being able to change planes with his pitches. Has tried to pitch through an arm strain in the past and remains at risk of injury. *Outlook:* He will compete for a job in the rotation this spring; if he doesn't make it, he could stick as a reliever. *Grade 7*

Year Team (League)	W	L	Pct.	ERA	WHIP	G	GS	CG	ShO	Hld.	Sv.-Opp.	IP	H	R	ER	HR	BB-IBB	SO	Avg.
2000— GC Braves (GCL)	4	0	1.000	1.13	0.78	7	5	0	0	...	0-...	32.0	15	5	4	1	10-0	42	.136
— Danville (Appal.)	2	2	.500	3.68	1.02	6	6	0	0	...	0-...	29.1	28	13	12	3	2-0	39	.252
2001— Macon (S. Atl.)	10	10	.500	3.77	1.17	28	28	1	0	...	0-...	164.2	144	89	69	9	48-1	184	.230
2002— Myrtle Beach (Carol.)	9	6	.600	3.31	1.32	28	28	1	0	...	0-...	163.1	149	67	60	7	66-0	167	.240
2003— Greenville (Sou.)	10	8	.556	3.37	1.14	27	27	1	0	...	0-...	149.2	133	59	56	9	37-0	128	.242
2004— Memphis (PCL)	4	4	.500	5.37	1.51	12	12	0	0	...	0-...	63.2	68	47	38	12	28-0	64	.280
2005— Memphis (PCL)	10	10	.500	4.40	1.40	29	29	0	0	0	0-0	182.0	204	98	89	18	51-6	147	.282
— St. Louis (N.L.)	0	0	...	13.50	1.50	2	0	0	0	0	0-0	2.0	2	3	3	1	1-0	0	.250
Major League totals (1 year)	**0**	**0**	**...**	**13.50**	**1.50**	**2**	**0**	**0**	**0**	**0**	**0-0**	**2.0**	**2**	**3**	**3**	**1**	**1-0**	**0**	**.250**

WAKEFIELD, TIM   P

PERSONAL: Born August 2, 1966, in Melbourne, Fla. ... 6-2/210. ... Throws right, bats right. ... Full name: Timothy Stephen Wakefield. ... High school: Eau Gallie (Melbourne, Fla.). ... College: Florida Tech.
TRANSACTIONS/CAREER NOTES: Selected by Pittsburgh Pirates organization in eighth round of 1988 free-agent draft. ... Played infield in Pirates organization (1988-89). ... Released by Pirates (April 20, 1995). ... Signed by Boston Red Sox organization (April 26, 1995). ... On disabled list (April 15-May 6, 1997).
HONORS: Named N.L. Rookie Pitcher of the Year by THE SPORTING NEWS (1992). ... Named A.L. Comeback Player of the Year by THE SPORTING NEWS (1995).
CAREER HITTING: 12-for-92 (.130), 4 R, 2 2B, 0 3B, 1 HR, 4 RBI.

SCOUTING REPORT **Throws:** Wakefield relies almost solely on his knuckleball. Will throw a 77-79 mph fastball and occasionally a looping curveball. *Tendencies:* His knuckleball darts and flutters, and he continually changes speeds with it. Will throw his fastball to hitters lower in the order, especially if he's falling behind with his knuckleball. *Outlook:* He is the heart of the Red Sox's staff, and his versatility is invaluable. Can work a variety of roles and eat up innings. *Grade 8.5*

TIM WAKEFIELD'S PITCHING ZONE

.329	.316	.179
.254	.378	.261
.160	.214	.326

LEFTY-RIGHTY SPLITS

vs.	Avg.	AB	H	2B	3B	HR	RBI	BB	SO	OBP	Slg.
L	.202	367	74	15	1	14	39	29	59	.264	.362
R	.278	490	136	32	1	21	60	39	92	.338	.476

Year Team (League)	W	L	Pct.	ERA	WHIP	G	GS	CG	ShO	Hld.	Sv.-Opp.	IP	H	R	ER	HR	BB-IBB	SO	Avg.
1989— Welland (NYP)	1	1	.500	3.40	1.29	36	1	0	0	...	2-...	39.2	30	17	15	1	21-0	42	.211
1990— Salem (Carol.)	10	14	.417	4.73	1.43	28	28	2	0	...	0-...	190.1	187	109	100	24	85-2	127	.261
1991— Carolina (Southern)	15	8	.652	2.90	1.13	26	25	8	1	...	0-...	183.0	155	68	59	13	51-6	120	.231
— Buffalo (A.A.)	0	1	.000	11.57	1.93	1	1	0	0	...	0-...	4.2	8	6	6	3	1-0	4	.364
1992— Buffalo (A.A.)	10	3	.769	3.06	1.28	20	20	6	1	...	0-...	135.1	122	52	46	10	51-1	71	.246
— Pittsburgh (N.L.)	8	1	.889	2.15	1.21	13	13	4	1	0	0-...	92.0	76	26	22	3	35-1	51	.232
1993— Pittsburgh (N.L.)	6	11	.353	5.61	1.71	24	20	3	2	0	0-0	128.1	145	83	80	14	75-2	59	.291
— Carolina (Southern)	3	5	.375	6.99	1.59	9	9	1	0	...	0-...	56.2	68	48	44	5	22-0	36	.293
1994— Buffalo (A.A.)	5	15	.250	5.84	1.68	30	29	4	1	...	0-...	175.2	197	127	114	27	98-0	83	.290

W

Year	Team (League)	W	L	Pct.	ERA	WHIP	G	GS	CG	ShO	Hld.	Sv.-Opp.	IP	H	R	ER	HR	BB-IBB	SO	Avg.
1995— Pawtucket (Int'l)		2	1	.667	2.52	1.28	4	4	0	0	...	0-...	25.0	23	10	7	1	9-0	14	.253
— Boston (A.L.)		16	8	.667	2.95	1.18	27	27	6	1	0	0-0	195.1	163	76	64	22	68-0	119	.227
1996— Boston (A.L.)		14	13	.519	5.14	1.55	32	32	6	0	0	0-0	211.2	238	* 151	121	38	90-0	140	.280
1997— Boston (A.L.)		12	• 15	.444	4.25	1.39	35	29	4	2	1	0-0	201.1	193	109	95	24	87-5	151	.256
1998— Boston (A.L.)		17	8	.680	4.58	1.34	36	33	2	0	0	0-0	216.0	211	123	110	30	79-1	146	.252
1999— Boston (A.L.)		6	11	.353	5.08	1.56	49	17	0	0	0	15-18	140.0	146	93	79	19	72-2	104	.266
2000— Boston (A.L.)		6	10	.375	5.48	1.47	51	17	0	0	3	0-1	159.1	170	107	97	31	65-3	102	.272
2001— Boston (A.L.)		9	12	.429	3.90	1.36	45	17	0	0	3	3-5	168.2	156	84	73	13	73-5	148	.248
2002— Boston (A.L.)		11	5	.688	2.81	1.05	45	15	0	0	5	3-5	163.1	121	57	51	15	51-2	134	.204
2003— Boston (A.L.)		11	7	.611	4.09	1.30	35	33	0	0	0	1-1	202.1	193	106	92	23	71-0	169	.246
2004— Boston (A.L.)		12	10	.545	4.87	1.38	32	30	0	0	1	0-0	188.1	197	121	102	29	63-3	116	.264
2005— Boston (A.L.)		16	12	.571	4.15	1.23	33	33	3	0	0	0-0	225.1	210	113	104	* 35	68-4	151	.245
American League totals (11 years)		130	111	.539	4.29	1.34	420	283	21	3	13	22-30	2071.2	1998	1140	988	279	787-25	1480	.252
National League totals (2 years)		14	12	.538	4.17	1.50	37	33	7	3	0	0-0	220.1	221	109	102	17	110-3	110	.268
Major League totals (13 years)		144	123	.539	4.28	1.36	457	316	28	6	13	22-30	2292.0	2219	1249	1090	296	897-28	1590	.253

DIVISION SERIES RECORD

Year	Team (League)	W	L	Pct.	ERA	WHIP	G	GS	CG	ShO	Hld.	Sv.-Opp.	IP	H	R	ER	HR	BB-IBB	SO	Avg.
1995— Boston (A.L.)		0	1	.000	11.81	1.88	1	1	0	0	0	0-0	5.1	5	7	7	1	5-0	4	.238
1998— Boston (A.L.)		0	1	.000	33.75	3.75	1	1	0	0	0	0-0	1.1	3	5	5	0	2-0	1	.500
1999— Boston (A.L.)		0	0	...	13.50	3.50	2	0	0	0	0	0-0	2.0	3	3	3	0	4-0	4	.300
2003— Boston (A.L.)		0	1	.000	3.52	1.17	2	1	0	0	0	0-0	7.2	6	5	3	1	3-0	7	.207
2005— Boston (A.L.)		0	1	.000	6.75	1.31	1	1	0	0	0	0-0	5.1	6	4	4	1	1-0	4	.300
Division series totals (5 years)		0	4	.000	9.14	1.75	7	4	0	0	0	0-0	21.2	23	24	22	2	15-0	20	.267

CHAMPIONSHIP SERIES RECORD

Year	Team (League)	W	L	Pct.	ERA	WHIP	G	GS	CG	ShO	Hld.	Sv.-Opp.	IP	H	R	ER	HR	BB-IBB	SO	Avg.
1992— Pittsburgh (N.L.)		2	0	1.000	3.00	1.06	2	2	2	0	0	0-0	18.0	14	6	6	4	5-0	7	.206
1999— Boston (A.L.)		Did not play.																		
2003— Boston (A.L.)		2	1	.667	2.57	1.00	3	2	0	0	0	0-0	14.0	8	4	4	1	6-0	10	.163
2004— Boston (A.L.)		1	0	1.000	8.59	1.64	3	0	0	0	0	0-0	7.1	9	7	7	1	3-2	6	.281
Champ. series totals (3 years)		5	1	.833	3.89	1.14	8	4	2	0	0	0-0	39.1	31	17	17	6	14-2	23	.208

WORLD SERIES RECORD

Year	Team (League)	W	L	Pct.	ERA	WHIP	G	GS	CG	ShO	Hld.	Sv.-Opp.	IP	H	R	ER	HR	BB-IBB	SO	Avg.
2004— Boston (A.L.)		0	0	...	12.27	2.18	1	1	0	0	0	0-0	3.2	3	5	5	1	5-0	2	.300

WALKER, JAMIE   P

PERSONAL: Born July 1, 1971, in McMinnville, Tenn. ... 6-2/195. ... Throws left, bats left. ... Full name: Jamie Ross Walker. ... High school: Warren County (McMinnville, Tenn.). ... College: Austin Peay.

TRANSACTIONS/CAREER NOTES: Selected by Houston Astros organization in 10th round of 1992 free-agent draft. ... Selected by Atlanta Braves from Astros organization in Rule 5 major league draft (December 9, 1996). ... Traded by Braves with OF Jermaine Dye to Kansas City Royals for OF Michael Tucker and IF Keith Lockhart (March 27, 1997). ... On disabled list (June 5-24, 1997); included rehabilitation assignment to Wichita. ... On disabled list (June 1, 1998-remainder of season). ... Released by Royals (July 27, 2000). ... Signed by Cleveland Indians organization (February 9, 2001). ... Signed as a free agent by Detroit Tigers organization (December 19, 2001).

CAREER HITTING: 0-for-0 (.000), 0 R, 0 2B, 0 3B, 0 HR, 0 RBI.

SCOUTING REPORT

Throws: Walker has very marginal stuff, with a fastball that ranges from 85-88 mph, a slurve and a changeup. **Tendencies:** His sidearm/submarine delivery is very effective against lefthanders because the ball appears to be coming from behind them. Relies on that deception and location to be effective. Sweeping slurve runs away from lefties. Improved changeup gives him a pitch against righthanders. **Outlook:** A lefthanded specialist who faces few hitters and can't be overexposed, he usually will be matched up against a team's better lefthanded hitters. **Grade 6.5**

JAMIE WALKER'S PITCHING ZONE

.375	.200	.500
.261	.211	.278
.273	.200	.304

LEFTY-RIGHTY SPLITS

vs.	Avg.	AB	H	2B	3B	HR	RBI	BB	SO	OBP	Slg.
L	.245	106	26	4	0	2	18	4	23	.286	.340
R	.271	85	23	3	0	3	8	9	7	.337	.412

Year	Team (League)	W	L	Pct.	ERA	WHIP	G	GS	CG	ShO	Hld.	Sv.-Opp.	IP	H	R	ER	HR	BB-IBB	SO	Avg.
1992— Auburn (NY-Penn)		4	6	.400	3.13	1.15	15	14	0	0	...	0-...	83.1	75	35	29	4	21-0	67	.243
1993— Quad City (Midw.)		3	11	.214	5.13	1.43	25	24	1	1	...	0-...	131.2	140	92	75	12	48-1	121	.273
1994— Quad City (Midw.)		8	10	.444	4.18	1.40	32	18	0	0	...	1-...	125.0	133	80	58	10	42-2	104	.269
1995— Jackson (Texas)		4	2	.667	4.50	1.43	50	0	0	0	...	2-...	58.0	59	29	29	6	24-5	38	.269
1996— Jackson (Texas)		5	1	.833	2.50	1.28	45	7	0	0	...	2-...	101.0	94	34	28	7	35-2	79	.249
1997— Kansas City (A.L.)		3	3	.500	5.44	1.53	50	0	0	0	3	0-1	43.0	46	28	26	6	20-3	24	.271
— Wichita (Texas)		0	1	.000	9.45	1.65	5	0	0	0	...	0-...	6.2	6	8	7	1	5-0	6	.261
1998— Omaha (PCL)		5	1	.833	2.70	1.46	7	7	0	0	...	0-...	46.2	57	15	14	3	11-1	21	.313
— Kansas City (A.L.)		0	1	.000	9.87	1.90	6	2	0	0	1	0-0	17.1	30	20	19	5	3-0	15	.380
1999— Omaha (PCL)		0	0	...	4.67	1.50	4	4	0	0	...	0-...	17.1	22	12	9	1	4-0	11	.314
— GC Royals (GCL)		1	0	1.000	3.38	1.25	2	2	0	0	...	0-...	8.0	10	3	3	1	0-0	9	.345
2000— Omaha (PCL)		3	10	.231	5.22	1.60	24	15	0	0	...	0-...	101.2	138	65	59	25	25-1	52	.336
2001— Buffalo (Int'l)		7	2	.778	3.87	1.41	38	8	0	0	...	2-...	93.0	104	44	40	12	27-1	51	.282
2002— Toledo (Int'l)		0	1	.000	1.98	0.73	10	0	0	0	...	1-...	13.2	7	3	3	2	3-0	15	.156
— Detroit (A.L.)		1	1	.500	3.71	0.94	57	0	0	0	5	1-4	43.2	32	19	18	9	9-1	40	.199
2003— Detroit (A.L.)		4	3	.571	3.32	1.20	78	0	0	0	12	3-7	65.0	61	30	24	9	17-1	45	.247
2004— Detroit (A.L.)		3	4	.429	3.20	1.25	70	0	0	0	18	1-7	64.2	69	28	23	8	12-3	53	.263
2005— Detroit (A.L.)		4	3	.571	3.70	1.27	66	0	0	0	14	0-2	48.2	49	22	20	5	13-3	30	.257
Major League totals (6 years)		15	15	.500	4.14	1.28	327	2	0	0	53	5-21	282.1	287	147	130	42	74-11	207	.259

W

WALKER, KEVIN   P

PERSONAL: Born September 20, 1976, in Irving, Texas. ... 6-4/190. ... Throws left, bats left. ... Full name: Kevin Michael Walker. ... High school: Grand Prairie (Texas).

TRANSACTIONS/CAREER NOTES: Selected by San Diego Padres organization in sixth round of 1995 free-agent draft. ... On disabled list (April 20-May 8 and May 23, 2001-remainder of season). ... On disabled list (March 27-August 8 and August 12-September 1, 2002); included rehabilitation assignments to Lake Elsinore and Portland. ... On disabled list (March 26-June 9, 2003); included rehabilitation assignment to Lake Elsinore. ... Claimed on waivers by San Francisco Giants (March 31, 2004). ... Signed as a free agent by Chicago White Sox (November 23, 2004). ... Signed as a free agent by Texas Rangers organization (November 14, 2005).

CAREER HITTING: 1-for-4 (.250), 0 R, 0 2B, 0 3B, 0 HR, 0 RBI.

LEFTY-RIGHTY SPLITS

vs.	Avg.	AB	H	2B	3B	HR	RBI	BB	SO	OBP	Slg.
L	.421	19	8	2	0	1	5	1	2	.450	.684
R	.182	11	2	0	1	0	2	4	3	.400	.364

Year—Team (League)	W	L	Pct.	ERA	WHIP	G	GS	CG	ShO	Hld.	Sv.-Opp.	IP	H	R	ER	HR	BB-IBB	SO	Avg.
1995— Ariz. Padres (Ariz.)	5	5	.500	3.01	1.20	13	12	0	0		0-...	71.2	74	34	24	1	12-0	69	.267
1996— Idaho Falls (Pio.)	1	0	1.000	3.00	1.00	1	1	0	0		0-...	6.0	4	3	2	1	2-0	4	.182
— Clinton (Midw.)	4	6	.400	4.74	1.49	13	13	0	0		0-...	76.0	80	46	40	9	33-0	43	.276
1997— Clinton (Midw.)	6	10	.375	4.88	1.54	19	19	3	1		0-...	110.2	133	80	60	9	37-0	80	.298
1998— Clinton (Midw.)	2	0	1.000	1.23	1.23	2	2	0	0		0-...	14.2	11	2	2	0	7-0	10	.216
— Rancho Cuca. (Calif.)	11	7	.611	4.15	1.40	22	22	0	0		0-...	121.1	122	62	56	10	48-0	94	.267
1999— Rancho Cuca. (Calif.)	1	1	.500	3.46	1.38	27	1	0	0		4-...	39.0	35	19	15	2	19-3	35	.243
2000— Mobile (Sou.)	0	1	.000	2.25	0.50	4	0	0	0		0-...	4.0	1	1	1	1	1-0	6	.077
— San Diego (N.L.)	7	1	.875	4.19	1.31	70	0	0	0	19	0-0	66.2	49	35	31	5	38-6	56	.206
2001— San Diego (N.L.)	0	0	...	3.00	1.08	16	0	0	0	4	0-1	12.0	5	4	4	0	8-2	17	.122
2002— Lake Elsinore (Calif.)	0	0	...	0.00	0.43	5	1	0	0		0-...	7.0	3	0	0	0	0-0	10	.136
— Portland (PCL)	0	0	...	3.00	0.33	3	0	0	0		0-...	3.0	1	1	1	1	0-0	4	.100
— San Diego (N.L.)	0	1	.000	5.63	2.13	11	0	0	0	1	0-1	8.0	12	6	5	2	5-1	11	.333
2003— Lake Elsinore (Calif.)	0	0	...	13.50	2.00	4	0	0	0		0-...	4.0	6	6	6	1	2-0	3	.333
— Portland (PCL)	3	1	.750	4.08	1.40	34	1	0	0		1-...	46.1	53	24	21	5	10-1	43	.291
— San Diego (N.L.)	0	0	...	5.40	1.50	11	0	0	0	0	0-0	6.2	5	4	4	1	5-0	5	.200
2004— San Francisco (N.L.)	0	0	...	16.20	3.00	5	0	0	0	1	0-0	1.2	3	3	3	1	2-0	1	.429
— Fresno (PCL)	1	3	.250	4.26	1.64	48	1	0	0		1-...	69.2	79	33	33	8	35-6	63	.298
2005— Chicago (A.L.)	0	1	.000	9.00	2.14	9	0	0	0	0	0-1	7.0	10	7	7	1	5-1	5	.333
— Charlotte (Int'l)	1	2	.333	5.28	1.52	51	0	0	0		5-8	46.0	49	35	27	7	21-3	52	.269
American League totals (1 year)	0	1	.000	9.00	2.14	9	0	0	0	0	0-1	7.0	10	7	7	1	5-1	5	.333
National League totals (5 years)	7	2	.778	4.45	1.39	113	0	0	0	25	0-2	95.0	74	52	47	9	58-9	90	.213
Major League totals (6 years)	7	3	.700	4.76	1.44	122	0	0	0	25	0-3	102.0	84	59	54	10	63-10	95	.223

WALKER, LARRY   OF

PERSONAL: Born December 1, 1966, in Maple Ridge, British Columbia. ... 6-3/235. ... Bats left, throws right. ... Full name: Larry Kenneth Robert Walker. ... High school: Maple Ridge (British Columbia) Senior Secondary Sc.

TRANSACTIONS/CAREER NOTES: Signed as a non-drafted free agent by Montreal Expos organization (November 14, 1984). ... On disabled list (April 4, 1988-entire season; June 28-July 13, 1991; and May 26-June 10, 1993). ... On suspended list (June 24-28, 1994). ... Signed as a free agent by Colorado Rockies (April 8, 1995). ... On disabled list (June 10-August 15, 1996); included rehabilitation assignments to Salem and Colorado Springs. ... On disabled list (June 18-July 3, 1998; March 29-April 14, 1999; May 11-June 9 and August 20, 2000-remainder of season). ... On disabled list (March 26-June 21, 2004); included rehabilitation assignment to Tulsa. ... Traded to Rockies with cash to St. Louis Cardinals for P Matt Burch and two players to be named (August 6, 2004); Rockies acquired Ps Christopher Narveson and Luis Martinez to complete deal (August 11, 2004). ... On disabled list (July 26-August 20, 2005).

HONORS: Named N.L. Most Valuable Player by Baseball Writers' Association of America (1997). ... Won N.L. Gold Glove as outfielder (1992-93, 1997-99 and 2001-02).

2005 GAMES PLAYED BY POSITION (MLB): OF—83, DH—6.

LARRY WALKER'S HITTING ZONE

.167	.421	.300
.250	.316	.394
.143	.300	.257

LEFTY-RIGHTY SPLITS

vs.	Avg.	AB	H	2B	3B	HR	RBI	BB	SO	OBP	Slg.
L	.214	56	12	1	1	3	10	7	15	.338	.429
R	.305	259	79	19	0	12	42	34	49	.395	.517

								BATTING									FIELDING	
Year—Team (League)	Pos.	G	AB	R	H	2B	3B	HR	RBI	BB	SO	HBP	GDP	SB-CS	Avg.	OBP	SLG	OPS	E	Avg.
1985—Utica (N.Y.-Penn)	1B-3B	62	215	24	48	8	2	2	26	18	57	5	1	12-6	.223	.297	.307	.604	8	.981
1986—Burlington (Midw.)	3B-OF	95	332	67	96	12	6	29	74	46	112	9	4	16-8	.289	.387	.623	1.011	10	.940
—W.P. Beach (Fla. St.)	OF	38	113	20	32	7	5	4	16	26	32	2	2	2-2	.283	.423	.540	.962	0	1.000
1987—Jacksonville (Sou.)	OF	128	474	91	136	25	7	26	83	67	120	9	6	24-3	.287	.383	.534	.917	9	.968
1988—Montreal (N.L.)					Did not play.															
1989—Indianapolis (A.A.)	OF	114	385	68	104	18	2	12	59	50	87	9	8	36-6	.270	.361	.421	.782	* 11	.959
—Montreal (N.L.)	OF	20	47	4	8	0	0	0	4	5	13	1	0	1-1	.170	.264	.170	.434	0	1.000
1990—Montreal (N.L.)	OF	133	419	59	101	18	3	19	51	49	112	5	8	21-7	.241	.326	.434	.761	4	.985
1991—Montreal (N.L.)	1B-OF	137	487	59	141	30	2	16	64	42	102	5	7	14-9	.290	.349	.458	.807	6	.990
1992—Montreal (N.L.)	OF	143	528	85	159	31	4	23	93	41	97	6	9	18-6	.301	.353	.506	.859	2	.993
1993—Montreal (N.L.)	OF-1B	138	490	85	130	24	5	22	86	80	76	6	8	29-7	.265	.371	.469	.841	6	.982
1994—Montreal (N.L.)	OF-1B	103	395	76	127	* 44	2	19	86	47	74	4	8	15-5	.322	.394	.587	.981	9	.980
1995—Colorado (N.L.)	OF	131	494	96	151	31	5	36	101	49	72	14	13	16-3	.306	.381	.607	.988	3	.988
1996—Salem (Carol.)	DH	2	8	3	4	3	0	1	1	0	1	0	1	0-0	.500	.500	1.250	1.750	...	...
—Colo. Springs (PCL)	OF	3	11	2	4	0	0	2	8	1	4	0	0	0-0	.364	.385	.909	1.294	0	1.000
—Colorado (N.L.)	OF	83	272	58	75	18	4	18	58	20	58	9	7	18-2	.276	.342	.570	.912	1	.994
1997—Colorado (N.L.)	OF-1B-DH	153	568	143	208	46	4	* 49	130	78	90	14	15	33-8	.366	* .452	* .720	1.172	2	.993
1998—Colorado (N.L.)	OF-2B-DH	130	454	113	165	46	3	23	67	64	61	4	11	14-4	* .363	.445	.630	1.075	4	.984
1999—Colorado (N.L.)	OF-DH	127	438	108	166	26	4	37	115	57	52	12	12	11-4	* .379	* .458	* .710	1.168	4	.982
2000—Colorado (N.L.)	OF-DH	87	314	64	97	21	7	9	51	46	40	9	12	5-5	.309	.409	.506	.915	1	.994
2001—Colorado (N.L.)	OF-DH	142	497	107	174	35	3	38	123	82	103	14	9	14-5	* .350	.449	.662	1.111	4	.984
2002—Colorado (N.L.)	OF-DH	136	477	95	161	40	4	26	104	65	73	7	8	6-5	.338	.421	.602	1.023	4	.984
2003—Colorado (N.L.)	OF-DH	143	454	86	129	25	7	16	79	98	87	11	9	7-4	.284	.422	.476	.898	4	.983
2004—Tulsa (Texas)	OF	5	9	3	2	0	0	1	2	2	1	1	1	0-0	.222	.462	.556	1.017	0	1.000
—Colorado (N.L.)	OF-DH	38	108	22	35	9	3	6	20	25	23	4	2	2-0	.324	.464	.630	1.093	0	1.000
—St. Louis (N.L.)	OF	44	150	29	42	7	1	11	27	24	34	4	6	4-0	.280	.393	.560	.953	1	.983
2005—St. Louis (N.L.)	OF-DH	100	315	66	91	20	1	15	52	41	64	9	9	2-1	.289	.384	.502	.886	2	.983
Major League totals (17 years)		1988	6907	1355	2160	471	62	383	1311	913	1231	138	153	230-76	.313	.400	.565	.965	57	.987

W

DIVISION SERIES RECORD

Year Team (League)	Pos.	G	AB	R	H	2B	3B	HR	RBI	BB	SO	HBP	GDP	SB-CS	Avg.	OBP	SLG	OPS	E	Avg.
1995— Colorado (N.L.)	OF	4	14	3	3	0	0	1	3	3	4	1	1	1-0	.214	.389	.429	.817	0	1.000
2004— St. Louis (N.L.)	OF	4	15	6	5	1	0	2	3	2	5	1	0	1-0	.333	.444	.800	1.244	0	1.000
2005— St. Louis (N.L.)	OF	3	9	1	0	0	0	0	0	2	5	1	0	0-0	.000	.250	.000	.250	0	1.000
Division series totals (3 years)		11	38	10	8	1	0	3	6	7	14	3	1	2-0	.211	.375	.474	.849	0	1.000

CHAMPIONSHIP SERIES RECORD

Year Team (League)	Pos.	G	AB	R	H	2B	3B	HR	RBI	BB	SO	HBP	GDP	SB-CS	Avg.	OBP	SLG	OPS	E	Avg.
2004— St. Louis (N.L.)	OF	7	29	6	7	1	1	2	5	3	8	0	0	0-0	.241	.313	.552	.864	0	1.000
2005— St. Louis (N.L.)	OF	6	19	0	3	1	0	0	1	4	4	0	0	0-0	.158	.292	.211	.502	0	1.000
Champ. series totals (2 years)		13	48	6	10	2	1	2	6	7	12	0	0	0-0	.208	.304	.417	.720	0	1.000

WORLD SERIES RECORD

Year Team (League)	Pos.	G	AB	R	H	2B	3B	HR	RBI	BB	SO	HBP	GDP	SB-CS	Avg.	OBP	SLG	OPS	E	Avg.
2004— St. Louis (N.L.)	OF	4	14	2	5	2	0	2	3	2	2	0	0	0-0	.357	.438	.929	1.366	0	1.000

ALL-STAR GAME RECORD

	G	AB	R	H	2B	3B	HR	RBI	BB	SO	HBP	GDP	SB-CS	Avg.	OBP	SLG	OPS	E	Avg.
All-Star Game totals (5 years)	5	7	1	1	0	0	0	2	1	0	0-0	.143	.333	.143	.476	0	1.000

WALKER, PETE — P

PERSONAL: Born April 8, 1969, in Beverly, Mass. ... 6-2/195. ... Throws right, bats right. ... Full name: Peter Brian Walker. ... High school: East Lyme (Conn.). ... College: Connecticut.

TRANSACTIONS/CAREER NOTES: Selected by New York Mets organization in seventh round of free-agent draft (June 4, 1990). ... Traded by Mets with P Luis Arroyo to San Diego Padres for 1B Roberto Petagine and P Scott Adair (March 17, 1996). ... Signed as a free agent by Boston Red Sox organization (June 30, 1997). ... Signed as a free agent by Colorado Rockies organization (February 8, 1999). ... Released by Rockies (November 13, 2000). ... Signed by Mets organization (December 26, 2000). ... Claimed on waivers by Toronto Blue Jays (May 3, 2002).

CAREER HITTING: 0-for-1 (.000), 0 R, 0 2B, 0 3B, 0 HR, 0 RBI.

PETE WALKER'S PITCHING ZONE

.333	.500	.286
.262	.361	.245
.190	.455	.268

LEFTY-RIGHTY SPLITS

vs.	Avg.	AB	H	2B	3B	HR	RBI	BB	SO	OBP	Slg.
L	.254	142	36	5	0	3	18	18	19	.333	.352
R	.254	177	45	8	1	7	20	15	24	.316	.429

Year Team (League)	W	L	Pct.	ERA	WHIP	G	GS	CG	ShO	Hld.	Sv.-Opp.	IP	H	R	ER	HR	BB-IBB	SO	Avg.
1990— Pittsfield (N.Y.-Penn.)	5	7	.417	4.16	1.50	16	13	1	0	...	0-...	80.0	74	43	37	1	46-0	73	.253
1991— St. Lucie (Fla. St.)	10	12	.455	3.21	1.30	26	25	1	0	...	0-...	152.0	145	77	54	9	52-2	95	.254
1992— Binghamton (East.)	7	12	.368	4.12	1.47	24	23	4	0	...	0-...	139.2	159	77	64	9	46-0	72	.289
1993— Binghamton (East.)	4	9	.308	3.44	1.35	45	10	0	0	...	19-...	100.0	89	45	38	6	46-1	89	.244
1994— St. Lucie (Fla. St.)	0	0	...	2.25	1.00	3	0	0	0	...	0-...	4.0	3	2	1	1	1-0	5	.200
— Norfolk (Int'l)	2	4	.333	3.97	1.51	37	0	0	0	...	3-...	47.2	48	22	21	3	24-2	42	.270
1995— Norfolk (Int'l)	5	2	.714	3.91	1.37	34	1	0	0	...	8-...	49.0	51	24	21	4	16-1	39	.274
— New York (N.L.)	1	0	1.000	4.58	1.64	13	0	0	0	1	0-0	17.2	24	9	9	3	5-0	5	.329
1996— Las Vegas (PCL)	5	1	.833	6.83	1.84	26	0	0	0	...	0-...	27.2	37	22	21	7	14-2	23	.336
— Ariz. Padres (AZL.)	0	1	.000	2.25	1.00	2	0	0	0	...	0-...	4.0	4	1	1	0	0-0	5	.250
— San Diego (N.L.)	0	0	...	0.00	4.50	1	0	0	0	0	0-0	0.2	0	0	0	0	3-0	1	.000
1997— GC Red Sox (GCL)	0	0	...	0.96	0.60	4	3	0	0	...	0-...	10.0	5	1	1	0	1-0	14	.147
— Trenton (East.)	0	0	...	4.05	1.50	8	0	0	0	...	3-...	14.0	14	6	6	1	7-0	13	.275
— Pawtucket (Int'l)	0	0	...	5.40	1.50	7	0	0	0	...	0-...	11.2	14	8	7	2	7-1	8	.280
1998— Pawtucket (Int'l)	1	4	.200	5.94	1.50	22	0	0	0	...	0-...	34.0	34	26	22	8	17-1	19	.272
1999— Colo. Springs (PCL)	8	4	.667	4.48	1.46	48	0	0	0	...	5-...	63.0	64	37	31	6	28-3	57	.268
2000— Colo. Springs (PCL)	7	3	.700	3.07	1.27	58	0	0	0	...	5-...	74.0	64	29	25	3	30-1	61	.231
— Colorado (N.L.)	0	0	...	17.36	3.00	3	0	0	0	0	0-0	4.2	10	9	9	1	4-0	2	.435
2001— Norfolk (Int'l)	13	4	.765	2.99	1.13	26	26	0	0	...	0-...	169.0	145	64	56	12	46-5	106	.234
— New York (N.L.)	0	0	...	2.70	0.90	2	0	0	0	0	0-0	6.2	6	2	2	0	0-0	4	.240
2002— Norfolk (Int'l)	0	0	...	3.00	1.11	2	2	0	0	...	0-...	9.0	9	3	3	1	1-0	6	.243
— New York (N.L.)	0	0	...	9.00	2.00	1	0	0	0	0	0-0	1.0	2	1	1	0	0-0	0	.400
— Toronto (A.L.)	10	5	.667	4.33	1.39	37	20	0	0	3	1-1	139.1	143	72	67	18	51-5	80	.270
2003— New Haven (East.)	0	1	.000	9.00	1.50	2	2	0	0	...	0-...	2.0	3	2	2	0	0-0	1	.375
— Syracuse (Int'l)	0	1	.000	6.75	1.29	5	5	0	0	...	0-...	14.0	15	10	10	2	3-0	8	.278
— Toronto (A.L.)	2	2	.500	4.88	1.50	23	7	0	0	2	0-0	55.1	59	31	30	11	24-2	29	.277
2004— Yokohama (Jp.)	2	4	.333	6.80	1.77	10	10	0	0	...	0-...	46.1	63	38	35	18	19-0	23	.330
2005— Toronto (A.L.)	6	6	.500	3.54	1.36	41	4	0	0	4	2-5	84.0	81	33	33	10	33-0	43	.254
American League totals (3 years)	18	13	.581	4.20	1.40	101	31	0	0	9	3-6	278.2	283	136	130	39	108-7	152	.266
National League totals (5 years)	1	0	1.000	6.16	1.76	20	0	0	0	1	0-0	30.2	42	21	21	4	12-0	12	.328
Major League totals (7 years)	19	13	.594	4.39	1.44	121	31	0	0	10	3-6	309.1	325	157	151	43	120-7	164	.273

WALKER, TODD — 2B

PERSONAL: Born May 25, 1973, in Bakersfield, Calif. ... 6-0/185. ... Bats left, throws right. ... Full name: Todd Arthur Walker. ... High school: Airline (Bossier City, La.). ... College: Louisiana State.

TRANSACTIONS/CAREER NOTES: Selected by Texas Rangers organization in 51st round of 1991 free-agent draft; did not sign. ... Selected by Minnesota Twins organization in first round (eighth pick overall) of 1994 free-agent draft. ... Traded by Twins with OF/1B Butch Huskey to Colorado Rockies for 2B Todd Sears and cash (July 16, 2000). ... Traded by Rockies with OF Robin Jennings to Cincinnati Reds for OF Alex Ochoa (July 19, 2001). ... Traded by Reds to Boston Red Sox for two players to be named (December 12, 2002); Reds acquired P Josh Thigpen and 3B Tony Blanco to complete deal (December 16, 2002). ... Signed as a free agent by Chicago Cubs (January 6, 2004). ... On disabled list (April 11-May 25, 2005); included rehabilitation assignment to Iowa.

2005 GAMES PLAYED BY POSITION (MLB): 2B—97, 1B—4, DH—2.

TODD WALKER'S HITTING ZONE

.167	.250	.333
.349	.391	.371
.429	.261	.228

LEFTY-RIGHTY SPLITS

vs.	Avg.	AB	H	2B	3B	HR	RBI	BB	SO	OBP	Slg.
L	.352	91	32	6	0	5	13	6	10	.398	.582
R	.291	306	89	19	3	7	27	25	30	.342	.441

SCOUTING REPORT **Offense:** Walker always has been a good hitter, and he has a good approach. Is a good fastball hitter who looks to pull the ball. Has deceptive power. Is streaky. Can

W

work deep counts because he makes good contact. Does not run well. *Defense:* Walker is not a good defensive second baseman. Has stiff hands and lacks agility and quick feet. Range to both sides is limited, especially to his right. Is slow turning the double play. Has a weak, erratic arm. *Outlook:* Walker is an offensive player who would be better in the American League, where he could be a DH on occasion. Will earn his keep with his bat. *Grade 6.4*

Year Team (League)	Pos.	G	AB	R	H	2B	3B	HR	RBI	BB	SO	HBP	GDP	SB-CS	Avg.	OBP	SLG	OPS	E	Avg.
1994—Fort Myers (FSL)	2B	46	171	29	52	5	2	10	34	32	15	0	4	6-3	.304	.406	.532	.938	9	.959
1995—New Britain (East.)	2B-3B	137	513	83	149	27	3	21	85	63	101	2	13	23-9	.290	.365	.478	.843	27	.955
1996—Salt Lake (PCL)	3B-2B-DH	135	551	94	187	41	9	28	111	57	91	5	17	13-8	.339	.400	.599	.999	19	.955
—Minnesota (A.L.)	3B-2B-DH	25	82	8	21	6	0	0	6	4	13	0	4	2-0	.256	.281	.329	.610	2	.965
1997—Minnesota (A.L.)	3B-2B-DH	52	156	15	37	7	1	3	16	11	30	1	5	7-0	.237	.288	.353	.641	4	.968
—Salt Lake (PCL)	3B-DH	83	322	69	111	20	1	11	53	46	49	1	10	5-5	.345	.420	.516	.936	24	.901
1998—Minnesota (A.L.)	2B-DH	143	528	85	167	41	3	12	62	47	65	2	13	19-7	.316	.374	.473	.845	13	.978
1999—Minnesota (A.L.)	2B-DH	143	531	62	148	37	4	6	46	52	83	1	15	18-10	.279	.343	.397	.740	7	.984
2000—Minnesota (A.L.)	2B-DH	23	77	14	18	1	0	2	8	7	10	0	3	3-0	.234	.287	.325	.612	4	.946
—Salt Lake (PCL)	2B	63	249	51	81	14	1	2	37	32	32	0	6	8-3	.325	.398	.414	.812	11	.964
—Colorado (N.L.)	2B	57	171	28	54	10	4	7	36	20	19	1	2	4-1	.316	.385	.544	.928	5	.975
2001—Colorado (N.L.)	2B	85	290	52	86	18	2	12	43	25	40	0	8	1-3	.297	.349	.497	.846	7	.981
—Cincinnati (N.L.)	2B-SS	66	261	41	77	17	0	5	32	26	42	1	6	0-5	.295	.361	.418	.779	4	.987
2002—Cincinnati (N.L.)	2B	155	612	79	183	42	3	11	64	50	81	3	9	8-5	.299	.353	.431	.785	8	.989
2003—Boston (A.L.)	2B-DH	144	587	92	166	38	4	13	85	48	54	1	17	1-1	.283	.333	.428	.760	16	.975
2004—Chicago (N.L.)	2B-1B-OF	129	372	60	102	19	4	15	50	43	52	4	2	0-3	.274	.352	.468	.820	7	.982
2005—Iowa (PCL)	2B	9	37	3	8	3	0	0	3	1	4	0	4	0-0	.216	.237	.297	.534	0	1.000
—Chicago (N.L.)	2B-1B-DH	110	397	50	121	25	3	12	40	31	40	1	8	1-1	.305	.355	.474	.829	6	.986
American League totals (6 years)		530	1961	276	557	130	12	36	223	169	255	5	57	50-18	.284	.339	.418	.756	46	.976
National League totals (5 years)		602	2103	310	623	131	16	62	265	195	274	10	35	14-18	.296	.356	.462	.819	37	.985
Major League totals (10 years)		1132	4064	586	1180	261	28	98	488	364	529	15	92	64-36	.290	.348	.441	.789	83	.981

DIVISION SERIES RECORD

Year Team (League)	Pos.	G	AB	R	H	2B	3B	HR	RBI	BB	SO	HBP	GDP	SB-CS	Avg.	OBP	SLG	OPS	E	Avg.
2003—Boston (A.L.)	2B	5	16	4	5	0	0	3	4	0	1	1	0	0-0	.313	.353	.875	1.228	2	.857

CHAMPIONSHIP SERIES RECORD

Year Team (League)	Pos.	G	AB	R	H	2B	3B	HR	RBI	BB	SO	HBP	GDP	SB-CS	Avg.	OBP	SLG	OPS	E	Avg.
2003—Boston (A.L.)	2B	7	27	5	10	1	1	2	2	1	2	1	0	0-0	.370	.414	.704	1.118	0	1.000

WALKER, TYLER — P

PERSONAL: Born May 15, 1976, in San Francisco. ... 6-3/255. ... Throws right, bats right. ... Full name: Tyler Lanier Walker. ... High school: University (San Francisco). ... College: California.

TRANSACTIONS/CAREER NOTES: Selected by New York Mets organization in second round of 1997 free-agent draft. ... Claimed on waivers by Detroit Tigers (April 3, 2003). ... Signed as a free agent by San Francisco Giants organization (December 6, 2003). ... On disabled list (August 21-September 7, 2005).

CAREER HITTING: 0-for-10 (.000), 0 R, 0 2B, 0 3B, 0 HR, 0 RBI.

SCOUTING REPORT *Throws:* Walker throws a mid-90s fastball and a slider. *Tendencies:* He has a herky-jerky delivery, throwing directly over the top. Loses movement on his fastball up in the zone but has good movement down. Has a late-breaking slider that sometimes moves straight down because of his release point, Has the same release point for both pitches, making it hard for hitters to lay off the slider. *Outlook:* Walker was extremely aggressive when filling in for closer Armando Benitez, but he probably is better suited as a setup man. There are concerns about his arm. *Grade 6.5*

TYLER WALKER'S PITCHING ZONE

.333	.545	.211
.342	.440	.290
.167	.417	.308

LEFTY-RIGHTY SPLITS

vs.	Avg.	AB	H	2B	3B	HR	RBI	BB	SO	OBP	Slg.
L	.284	116	33	5	1	3	17	14	25	.366	.422
R	.278	126	35	7	0	6	23	13	29	.352	.476

Year Team (League)	W	L	Pct.	ERA	WHIP	G	GS	CG	ShO	Hld.	Sv.-Opp.	IP	H	R	ER	HR	BB-IBB	SO	Avg.
1997—GC Mets (GCL)	0	0	...	1.00	1.11	5	0	0	0		3-...	9.0	8	1	1	0	2-1	9	.235
—Pittsfield (N.Y.-Penn.)	0	0	...	13.50	4.50	1	0	0	0		0-...	0.2	2	2	1	1	1-0	1	.400
1998—Capital City (S. Atl.)	5	5	.500	4.12	1.38	34	13	0	0		1-...	115.2	122	63	53	9	38-0	110	.268
1999—St. Lucie (Fla. St.)	6	5	.545	2.94	1.17	13	13	2	0		0-...	79.2	64	31	26	6	29-2	64	.219
—Binghamton (East.)	6	4	.600	6.22	1.62	13	13	0	0		0-...	68.0	78	49	47	11	32-0	59	.292
2000—Binghamton (East.)	7	6	.538	2.75	1.13	22	22	0	0		0-...	121.0	82	43	37	3	55-1	111	.191
—Norfolk (Int'l)	1	3	.250	2.39	1.44	5	5	0	0		0-...	26.1	29	7	7	0	9-0	17	.290
2001—St. Lucie (Fla. St.)	0	2	.000	8.04	1.40	4	4	0	0		0-...	15.2	19	14	14	0	3-0	11	.288
—Binghamton (East.)	1	0	1.000	0.40	0.99	4	3	0	0		0-...	22.1	9	2	1	1	13-1	13	.127
—Norfolk (Int'l)	3	2	.600	4.02	1.04	8	8	0	0		0-...	40.1	34	19	18	7	8-0	35	.230
2002—Norfolk (Int'l)	10	5	.667	3.99	1.34	28	25	1	1		1-...	142.0	152	65	63	13	38-3	109	.275
—New York (N.L.)	1	0	1.000	5.91	1.50	5	1	0	0		0-0	10.2	11	7	7	3	5-1	7	.250
2003—Toledo (Int'l)	2	9	.182	4.45	1.40	26	22	1	0		0-...	131.1	139	73	65	13	47-5	117	.270
2004—Fresno (PCL)	1	1	.500	1.72	1.15	9	1	0	0		0-...	15.2	16	5	3	1	2-0	15	.250
—San Francisco (N.L.)	5	1	.833	4.24	1.46	52	0	0	0	5	1-1	63.2	69	31	30	8	24-1	48	.288
2005—San Francisco (N.L.)	6	4	.600	4.23	1.54	67	0	0	0	7	23-28	61.2	68	31	29	9	27-6	54	.281
Major League totals (3 years)	12	5	.706	4.37	1.50	124	1	0	0	7	24-29	136.0	148	69	66	20	56-8	109	.281

WANG, CHIEN-MING — P

PERSONAL: Born March 31, 1980, in Tainan, Taiwan. ... 6-3/200. ... Throws right, bats right. ... Full name: Chien-Ming Wang. ... Name pronounced: wong. ... College: Taipei College of Physical Education.

TRANSACTIONS/CAREER NOTES: Signed as a non-drafted free agent by New York Yankees organization (May 5, 2000). ... On disabled list (July 14-September 6, 2005).

CAREER HITTING: 0-for-1 (.000), 0 R, 0 2B, 0 3B, 0 HR, 0 RBI.

W

SCOUTING REPORT *Throws:* Wang throws a fastball at 91-96 mph, a slider and a forkball. *Tendencies:* His deliberate windup and long backswing causes deception, but he also has good arm speed and a two-seam fastball that jumps on hitters. Fastball has exceptional late life; gets strikes on righthanders by starting it off the plate and running it back over. Has shortened the break on his inconsistent slider. Forkball serves as change, but arm motion slows too much, which tips pitch to hitters. *Outlook:* Wang developed into a reliable starter with a high ceiling. Is a future top-of-the-rotation guy if he can develop a more consistent off-speed pitch. *Grade 7.1*

CHIEN-MING WANG'S PITCHING ZONE

.133	.273	.258
.277	.352	.269
.310	.290	.269

LEFTY-RIGHTY SPLITS

vs.	Avg.	AB	H	2B	3B	HR	RBI	BB	SO	OBP	Slg.
L	.258	213	55	8	2	6	27	19	21	.318	.399
R	.254	228	58	9	1	3	21	13	26	.308	.342

Year Team (League)	W	L	Pct.	ERA	WHIP	G	GS	CG	ShO	Hld.	Sv.-Opp.	IP	H	R	ER	HR	BB-IBB	SO	Avg.
2000—Staten Island (N.Y.-Penn.) .	4	4	.500	2.48	1.13	14	14	2	1	...	0-...	87.0	77	34	24	2	21-1	75	.233
2001—			Did not play.																
2002—Staten Island (N.Y.-Penn.) .	6	1	.857	1.72	0.98	13	13	0	0	...	0-...	78.1	63	23	15	2	14-0	64	.219
2003—Trenton (East.)	7	6	.538	4.65	1.43	21	21	2	1	...	0-...	122.0	143	71	63	7	32-2	84	.294
—GC Yankees (GCL)	0	0	...	0.00	0.67	1	1	0	0	...	0-...	3.0	2	0	0	0	0-0	2	.182
2004—Trenton (East.)	6	5	.545	4.05	1.27	18	18	0	0	...	0-...	109.0	112	53	49	6	26-0	90	.274
—Columbus (Int'l)	5	1	.833	2.01	0.97	6	5	2	1	...	0-...	40.1	31	9	9	3	8-0	35	.215
2005—Columbus (Int'l)	2	1	.667	4.24	1.35	6	6	0	0	0	0-0	34.0	40	16	16	4	6-0	21	.301
—New York (A.L.)	8	5	.615	4.02	1.25	18	17	0	0	0	0-0	116.1	113	58	52	9	32-3	47	.256
Major League totals (1 year)	8	5	.615	4.02	1.25	18	17	0	0	0	0-0	116.1	113	58	52	9	32-3	47	.256

DIVISION SERIES RECORD

Year Team (League)	W	L	Pct.	ERA	WHIP	G	GS	CG	ShO	Hld.	Sv.-Opp.	IP	H	R	ER	HR	BB-IBB	SO	Avg.
2005—New York (A.L.)	0	1	.000	1.35	0.90	1	1	0	0	0	0-0	6.2	6	4	1	1	0-0	1	.231

WARD, DARYLE   1B/OF

PERSONAL: Born June 27, 1975, in Lynwood, Calif. ... 6-2/230. ... Bats left, throws left. ... Full name: Daryle Lamar Ward. ... High school: Brethren Christian (Riverside, Calif.). ... Junior college: Rancho Santiago (Calif.). ... Son of Gary Ward, outfielder with four major league teams (1979-90).

TRANSACTIONS/CAREER NOTES: Selected by Detroit Tigers organization in 15th round of 1994 free-agent draft. ... Traded by Tigers with C Brad Ausmus and Ps Jose Lima, C.J. Nitkowski and Trever Miller to Houston Astros for OF Brian Hunter, IF Orlando Miller, Ps Doug Brocail and Todd Jones and cash (December 10, 1996). ... Traded by Astros to Los Angeles Dodgers for P Ruddy Lugo (January 25, 2003). ... Signed as a free agent by Pittsburgh Pirates organization (December 8, 2003). ... On disabled list (June 26-August 15, 2004); included rehabilitation assignment to Nashville.

2005 GAMES PLAYED BY POSITION (MLB): 1B—109.

SCOUTING REPORT *Offense:* Ward still has a quick bat and makes good contact. Is a good low-fastball hitter who likes to pull and does not take advantage of the whole field. Has good raw power. Has an inside-out swing with a slight lift. Has really cut down on his strikeouts. *Defense:* Ward has surprising agility for his size around the bag, but he doesn't have any range. His hands are good. Has arm strength and is accurate starting the double play. *Outlook:* He must continually monitor his weight because he has the type of body that can get away from him. Needs to take advantage of his raw power to become more of a productive everyday first baseman. *Grade 6.3*

DARYLE WARD'S HITTING ZONE

.227	.294	.273
.341	.342	.282
.357	.231	.362

LEFTY-RIGHTY SPLITS

vs.	Avg.	AB	H	2B	3B	HR	RBI	BB	SO	OBP	Slg.
L	.200	105	21	5	1	0	14	7	17	.243	.267
R	.281	302	85	16	0	12	49	30	43	.343	.454

Year Team (League)	Pos.	G	AB	R	H	2B	3B	HR	RBI	BB	SO	HBP	GDP	SB-CS	Avg.	OBP	SLG	OPS	E	Avg.
1994—Bristol (Appal.)	1B	48	161	17	43	6	0	5	30	19	33	0	3	5-1	.267	.343	.398	.740	11	.968
1995—Fayetteville (S. Atl.)	1B	137	524	75	149	32	6	14	106	46	111	5	13	1-2	.284	.344	.426	.769	14	.987
1996—Lakeland (Fla. St.)	1B-DH	128	464	65	135	29	4	10	68	57	77	6	9	1-1	.291	.373	.435	.808	8	.993
—Toledo (Int'l)	1B	6	23	1	4	0	0	1	1	0	3	0	2	0-0	.174	.174	.174	.348	1	.979
1997—Jackson (Texas)	1B-DH	114	422	72	139	25	1	19	90	46	68	3	11	4-2	.329	.398	.524	.922	12	.988
—New Orleans (A.A.)	1B-DH	14	48	4	18	1	0	2	8	7	7	0	0	0-0	.375	.455	.521	.975	2	.976
1998—New Orleans (PCL)	OF-1B-DH	116	463	78	141	31	1	23	96	41	78	2	17	2-0	.305	.361	.525	.886	13	.976
—Houston (N.L.)		4	3	1	1	0	0	0	0	1	2	0	0	0-0	.333	.500	.333	.833	...	...
1999—New Orleans (PCL)	1B-OF	61	241	56	85	15	1	28	65	23	43	3	3	1-1	.353	.416	.772	1.188	5	.991
—Houston (N.L.)	OF-1B-DH	64	150	11	41	6	0	8	30	9	31	0	3	0-0	.273	.311	.473	.784	2	.973
2000—Houston (N.L.)	OF-1B-DH	119	264	36	68	10	2	20	47	15	61	0	3	0-0	.258	.295	.538	.833	1	.988
2001—Houston (N.L.)	OF-1B-DH	95	213	21	56	15	0	9	39	19	48	1	3	0-0	.263	.323	.460	.784	1	.988
2002—Houston (N.L.)	OF-DH	136	453	41	125	31	0	12	72	33	82	1	9	1-3	.276	.324	.424	.748	3	.981
2003—Jacksonville (Sou.)	1B-OF	4	16	0	2	0	0	0	1	0	3	0	0	0-0	.125	.125	.125	.250	1	.950
—Los Angeles (N.L.)	1B-OF	52	109	6	20	1	0	0	9	3	19	1	4	0-0	.183	.211	.193	.403	1	.992
—Las Vegas (PCL)	1B-DH	34	128	16	38	9	0	4	24	10	22	0	0	0-0	.297	.343	.461	.804	2	.992
2004—Nashville (PCL)	1B-DH-OF	28	96	14	27	7	0	7	17	5	16	0	1	0-0	.281	.317	.573	.890	0	1.000
—Pittsburgh (N.L.)	1B-OF	79	293	39	73	17	2	15	57	22	45	3	8	0-0	.249	.305	.474	.780	5	.992
2005—Pittsburgh (N.L.)	1B	133	407	46	106	21	1	12	63	37	60	1	18	0-2	.260	.318	.405	.723	6	.994
Major League totals (8 years)		682	1892	201	490	101	5	76	317	139	348	7	51	1-5	.259	.309	.438	.747	19	.991

DIVISION SERIES RECORD

Year Team (League)	Pos.	G	AB	R	H	2B	3B	HR	RBI	BB	SO	HBP	GDP	SB-CS	Avg.	OBP	SLG	OPS	E	Avg.
1999—Houston (N.L.)	OF	3	7	1	1	0	0	1	1	0	2	0	0	0-0	.143	.143	.714	.714	1	.750
2001—Houston (N.L.)		2	2	1	1	0	0	1	2	0	0	0	0	0-0	.500	.500	2.000	2.500	...	...
Division series totals (2 years)		5	9	2	2	0	0	2	3	0	2	0	0	0-0	.222	.222	.889	1.111	1	.750

WASDIN, JOHN   P

PERSONAL: Born August 5, 1972, in Fort Belvoir, Va. ... 6-2/190. ... Throws right, bats right. ... Full name: John Truman Wasdin. ... Name pronounced: WAAZ-din. ... High school: Amos P. Godby (Tallahassee, Fla.). ... College: Florida State.

TRANSACTIONS/CAREER NOTES: Selected by New York Yankees organization in 41st round of 1990 free-agent draft; did not sign. ... Selected by Oakland Athletics organization in first round (25th pick overall) of 1993 free-agent draft. ... Traded by A's with cash to Boston Red Sox for OF Jose Canseco (January 27, 1997). ... On disabled list (July 18-August 5, 1999); included rehabilitation assignment to GCL Red Sox. ... Traded by Red Sox with Ps Brian Rose and Jeff Taglienti and 2B Jeff Frye to Colorado Rockies for Ps Rolando Arrojo and Rick Croushore, 2B Mike Lansing and cash (July 27, 2000). ... On suspended list (September 8-10, 2000). ... Released by Rockies (June 7, 2001). ... Signed by Baltimore Orioles organization (July 18, 2001). ... Traded by Orioles to Philadelphia Phillies for P Chris Brock (December 13, 2001). ... Signed as a free agent by Yomiuri of the Japan Central League (January 9, 2002). ... Signed as a free agent by Pittsburgh Pirates organization (December 1, 2002). ... Traded by Pirates to Toronto Blue Jays for OF Rich Thompson (July 8, 2003). ... Signed as a free agent by Texas Rangers organization (October 21, 2003).
CAREER HITTING: 3-for-15 (.200), 2 R, 1 2B, 0 3B, 0 HR, 1 RBI.

SCOUTING REPORT **Throws:** His fastball is in the 89-94 mph range. Also throws a cutter, curveball and changeup. Has tried to throw knuckleballs. **Tendencies:** His loose, high three-quarters arm action causes him to drift in his delivery and elevate his fastball, but he has worked on a two-seam fastball to help keep the ball down. Cutter is very flat and he has trouble commanding its break. Curveball has tight rotation but a big downward break. Uses a straight change with some sinking action. Has improved his velocity and command. Is more effective pitching to lefthanders.
Outlook: He is a versatile pitcher who can spot start or pitch in long relief, but generally has pitched better in relief. **Grade 5.8**

JOHN WASDIN'S PITCHING ZONE

.353	.750	.100
.236	.393	.291
.200	.182	.250

LEFTY-RIGHTY SPLITS

vs.	Avg.	AB	H	2B	3B	HR	RBI	BB	SO	OBP	Slg.
L	.229	140	32	8	0	3	19	13	17	.290	.350
R	.290	155	45	10	0	6	21	7	27	.325	.471

Year — Team (League)	W	L	Pct.	ERA	WHIP	G	GS	CG	ShO	Hld.	Sv.-Opp.	IP	H	R	ER	HR	BB-IBB	SO	Avg.
1993— Ariz. A's (AZL)	0	0	...	3.00	1.00	1	1	0	0	...	0-...	3.0	3	1	1	0	0-0	1	.250
—Madison (Midw.)	2	3	.400	1.86	0.85	9	9	0	0	...	0-...	48.1	32	11	10	1	9-1	40	.186
—Modesto (Calif.)	0	3	.000	3.86	1.29	3	3	0	0	...	0-...	16.1	17	9	7	0	4-0	11	.266
1994—Modesto (Calif.)	3	1	.750	1.69	0.83	6	4	0	0	...	0-...	26.2	17	6	5	2	5-0	30	.179
—Huntsville (Sou.)	12	3	.800	3.43	1.09	21	21	0	0	...	0-...	141.2	126	61	54	13	29-2	108	.236
1995—Edmonton (PCL)	12	8	.600	5.52	1.33	29	28	2	1	...	0-...	174.1	193	117	107	26	38-3	111	.281
—Oakland (A.L.)	1	1	.500	4.67	0.98	5	2	0	0	0	0-0	17.1	14	9	9	4	3-0	6	.215
1996—Edmonton (PCL)	2	1	.667	4.14	1.38	9	9	0	0	...	0-...	50.0	52	23	23	6	17-2	30	.267
—Oakland (A.L.)	8	7	.533	5.96	1.48	25	21	1	0	0	0-1	131.1	145	96	87	24	50-5	75	.283
1997—Boston (A.L.)	4	6	.400	4.40	1.28	53	7	0	0	11	0-2	124.2	121	68	61	18	38-4	84	.251
1998—Boston (A.L.)	6	4	.600	5.25	1.44	47	8	0	0	4	0-1	96.0	111	57	56	14	27-8	59	.288
—Pawtucket (Int'l)	1	0	1.000	3.00	1.33	4	2	0	0	...	0-...	12.0	11	6	4	0	5-0	10	.239
1999—Pawtucket (Int'l)	1	1	.500	2.12	0.88	5	5	0	0	...	0-...	29.2	19	9	7	1	7-0	28	.184
—Boston (A.L.)	8	3	.727	4.12	1.13	45	0	0	0	2	2-5	74.1	66	38	34	14	18-0	57	.236
—GC Red Sox (GCL)	0	0	...	0.00	0.50	1	1	0	0	...	0-...	2.0	1	0	0	0	0-0	4	.143
2000—Boston (A.L.)	1	3	.250	5.04	1.41	25	1	0	0	0	1-2	44.2	48	25	25	8	15-1	36	.273
—Pawtucket (Int'l)	1	0	1.000	2.25	0.56	5	3	0	0	...	1-...	16.0	7	4	4	0	2-0	11	.130
—Colorado (N.L.)	0	3	.000	5.80	1.43	14	3	1	0	0	0-0	35.2	42	23	23	6	9-2	35	.302
2001—Baltimore (Int'l)	2	1	.667	7.03	1.64	18	0	0	0	0	0-3	24.1	32	19	19	7	8-2	17	.320
—Rochester (Int'l)	2	1	.667	3.98	1.57	5	3	0	0	0	0-...	20.1	27	9	9	3	5-0	20	.321
—Baltimore (A.L.)	1	1	.500	4.17	1.41	26	0	0	0	0	0-2	49.2	54	25	23	4	16-4	47	.277
2002—Yomiuri (Jp. Cen.)	1	4	.200	4.54	1.70	10	7	0	0	0	0-...	37.2	55	26	19	7	9-0	31	...
—Yomiuri (Jp. East.)	1	2	.333	1.55	1.00	7	3	0	0	0	0-...	29.0	25	12	5	4	4-0	23	...
2003—Nashville (PCL)	8	4	.667	3.04	1.10	18	18	3	1	0	0-...	112.1	101	46	38	4	24-4	116	.238
—Toronto (A.L.)	0	1	.000	23.40	4.00	3	2	0	0	0	0-0	5.0	16	13	13	2	4-0	5	.533
—Syracuse (Int'l)	2	1	.667	5.23	1.40	10	1	0	0	0	0-...	20.2	28	13	12	1	1-0	21	.318
2004—Oklahoma (PCL)	7	1	.875	3.46	1.09	18	14	2	1	...	0-...	104.0	94	43	40	10	19-0	81	.242
—Texas (A.L.)	2	4	.333	6.78	1.63	15	10	0	0	0	0-0	65.0	83	52	49	18	23-2	36	.305
2005—Oklahoma (PCL)	9	2	.818	4.93	1.48	13	11	0	0	0	0-1	73.0	84	43	40	11	24-1	57	.286
—Texas (A.L.)	3	2	.600	4.28	1.28	31	6	0	0	4	4-6	75.2	77	37	36	9	20-2	44	.261
American League totals (10 years)	34	32	.515	5.17	1.39	275	57	1	0	25	7-19	683.2	735	420	393	115	214-26	449	.273
National League totals (2 years)	2	4	.333	6.30	1.52	32	3	1	0	0	0-3	60.0	74	42	42	13	17-4	52	.310
Major League totals (10 years)	36	36	.500	5.26	1.40	307	60	2	0	25	7-22	743.2	809	462	435	128	231-30	501	.276

DIVISION SERIES RECORD

Year — Team (League)	W	L	Pct.	ERA	WHIP	G	GS	CG	ShO	Hld.	Sv.-Opp.	IP	H	R	ER	HR	BB-IBB	SO	Avg.
1998— Boston (A.L.)	0	0	...	10.80	1.80	1	0	0	0	0	0-0	1.2	2	2	2	1	1-0	2	.286
1999— Boston (A.L.)	0	0	...	27.00	3.60	2	0	0	0	0	0-0	1.2	2	5	5	1	4-0	1	.400
Division series totals (2 years)	0	0	...	18.90	2.70	3	0	0	0	0	0-0	3.1	4	7	7	2	5-0	3	.333

CHAMPIONSHIP SERIES RECORD

Year — Team (League)	W	L	Pct.	ERA	WHIP	G	GS	CG	ShO	Hld.	Sv.-Opp.	IP	H	R	ER	HR	BB-IBB	SO	Avg.
1999— Boston (A.L.)	Did not play.																		

WASHBURN, JARROD   P

PERSONAL: Born August 13, 1974, in La Crosse, Wis. ... 6-1/195. ... Throws left, bats left. ... Full name: Jarrod Michael Washburn. ... High school: Webster (Wis.). ... College: Wisconsin-Oshkosh.
TRANSACTIONS/CAREER NOTES: Selected by California Angels organization in second round of 1995 free-agent draft. ... Angels franchise renamed Anaheim Angels for 1997 season. ... On disabled list (March 25-April 9, July 22-August 7 and August 8, 2000-remainder of season); included rehabilitation assignment to Lake Elsinore. ... On disabled list (March 23-April 16, 2001); included rehabilitation assignment to Salt Lake. ... On disabled list (July 21-September 2, 2004); included rehabilitation assignment to Rancho Cucamonga. ... Angels franchise renamed Los Angeles Angels of Anaheim for 2005 season. ... On disabled list (July 25-August 12, 2005).
CAREER HITTING: 8-for-28 (.286), 2 R, 0 2B, 0 3B, 0 HR, 3 RBI.

SCOUTING REPORT **Throws:** Washburn's primary pitch is a four-seam, riding fastball that he throws at 89-92 mph. Also is throwing a two-seamer, a cut fastball, a curveball and a forkball.
Tendencies: No longer is he a one dimensional fly-ball pitcher who relies on a cut fastball. With the addition of the two-seamer, he has a pitch that he can run away from righthanders to open up the inside part of the plate. Is able to keep the ball down. Will still cut the fastball occasionally. Slider is a pitch he can run from lefthanders; it has better depth than the cutter. Uses his forkball

JARROD WASHBURN'S PITCHING ZONE

.304	.226	.220
.389	.406	.253
.309	.281	.250

LEFTY-RIGHTY SPLITS

vs.	Avg.	AB	H	2B	3B	HR	RBI	BB	SO	OBP	Slg.
L	.266	139	37	3	1	4	11	4	27	.299	.388
R	.276	532	147	28	4	15	47	47	67	.338	.429

W

as a changeup that dives from righthanders. Works quickly. ***Outlook:*** Elbow problems limited him to only 29 starts last season. Now has more pitches to get hitters out. ***Grade 7.3***

Year	Team (League)	W	L	Pct.	ERA	WHIP	G	GS	CG	ShO	Hld.	Sv.-Opp.	IP	H	R	ER	HR	BB-IBB	SO	Avg.
1995—	Boise (N'west)	3	2	.600	3.33	1.07	8	8	0	0	...	0-...	46.0	35	17	17	1	14-0	54	.208
—	Cedar Rap. (Midw.)	0	1	.000	3.44	1.31	3	3	0	0	...	0-...	18.1	17	7	7	1	7-0	20	.258
1996—	Lake Elsinore (Calif.)	6	3	.667	3.30	1.21	14	14	3	0	...	0-...	92.2	79	38	34	5	33-0	93	.229
—	Midland (Texas)	5	6	.455	4.40	1.16	13	13	1	0	...	0-...	88.0	77	44	43	11	25-0	58	.235
—	Vancouver (PCL)	0	2	.000	10.80	2.88	2	2	0	0	...	0-...	8.1	12	16	10	1	12-0	5	.333
1997—	Midland (Texas)	15	12	.556	4.80	1.46	29	29	5	1	...	0-...	189.1	211	115	101	23	65-0	146	.288
—	Vancouver (PCL)	0	0	...	3.60	1.20	1	1	0	0	...	0-...	5.0	4	2	2	0	2-0	6	.211
1998—	Vancouver (PCL)	4	5	.444	4.32	1.46	14	14	2	0	...	0-...	91.2	91	44	44	7	43-0	66	.261
—	Anaheim (A.L.)	6	3	.667	4.62	1.31	15	11	0	0	1	0-0	74.0	70	40	38	11	27-1	48	.248
—	Midland (Texas)	0	1	.000	6.23	1.73	1	1	0	0	...	0-0	8.2	13	8	6	2	2-0	8	.351
1999—	Edmonton (PCL)	1	5	.167	4.73	1.14	11	11	1	0	...	0-0	59.0	50	31	31	6	17-0	55	.226
—	Anaheim (A.L.)	4	5	.444	5.25	1.41	16	10	0	0	1	0-0	61.2	61	36	36	6	26-0	39	.261
2000—	Lake Elsinore (Calif.)	0	0	...	6.00	1.67	1	1	0	0	...	0-0	3.0	3	2	2	0	2-0	7	.250
—	Edmonton (PCL)	3	0	1.000	3.52	1.57	5	5	0	0	...	0-0	30.2	35	13	12	2	13-0	20	.299
—	Anaheim (A.L.)	7	2	.778	3.74	1.20	14	14	0	0	0	0-0	84.1	64	38	35	16	37-0	49	.215
2001—	Salt Lake (PCL)	0	1	.000	5.87	1.30	1	1	0	0	...	0-0	7.2	9	5	5	1	1-0	5	.300
—	Anaheim (A.L.)	11	10	.524	3.77	1.29	30	30	1	0	0	0-0	193.1	196	89	81	25	54-4	126	.263
2002—	Anaheim (A.L.)	18	6	.750	3.15	1.17	32	32	1	0	0	0-0	206.0	183	75	72	19	59-1	139	.235
2003—	Anaheim (A.L.)	10	15	.400	4.43	1.25	32	32	2	0	0	0-0	207.1	205	106	102	•34	54-4	118	.256
2004—	Rancho Cuca. (Calif.)	0	0	...	2.25	1.75	1	1	0	0	...	0-0	4.0	4	1	1	0	3-0	5	.250
—	Anaheim (A.L.)	11	8	.579	4.64	1.33	25	25	1	1	0	0-0	149.1	159	81	77	20	40-1	86	.269
2005—	Los Angeles (A.L.)	8	8	.500	3.20	1.33	29	29	1	1	0	0-0	177.1	184	66	63	19	51-0	94	.273
Major League totals (8 years)		**75**	**57**	**.568**	**3.93**	**1.27**	**193**	**183**	**6**	**2**	**2**	**0-0**	**1153.1**	**1122**	**531**	**504**	**150**	**348-11**	**699**	**.255**

DIVISION SERIES RECORD

Year	Team (League)	W	L	Pct.	ERA	WHIP	G	GS	CG	ShO	Hld.	Sv.-Opp.	IP	H	R	ER	HR	BB-IBB	SO	Avg.
2002—	Anaheim (A.L.)	1	0	1.000	3.75	1.25	2	2	0	0	0	0-0	12.0	12	6	5	3	3-0	4	.286
2004—	Anaheim (A.L.)	0	1	.000	10.80	2.70	2	1	0	0	0	0-0	3.1	6	8	4	2	3-0	3	.353
Division series totals (2 years)		**1**	**1**	**.500**	**5.28**	**1.57**	**4**	**3**	**0**	**0**	**0**	**0-0**	**15.1**	**18**	**14**	**9**	**5**	**6-0**	**7**	**.305**

CHAMPIONSHIP SERIES RECORD

Year	Team (League)	W	L	Pct.	ERA	WHIP	G	GS	CG	ShO	Hld.	Sv.-Opp.	IP	H	R	ER	HR	BB-IBB	SO	Avg.
2002—	Anaheim (A.L.)	0	0	...	1.29	0.86	1	1	0	0	0	0-0	7.0	6	1	1	0	0-0	7	.207
2005—	Los Angeles (A.L.)	0	0	...	0.00	1.07	1	1	0	0	0	0-0	4.2	4	1	0	0	1-0	1	.235
Champ. series totals (2 years)		**0**	**0**	**...**	**0.77**	**0.94**	**2**	**2**	**0**	**0**	**0**	**0-0**	**11.2**	**10**	**2**	**1**	**0**	**1-0**	**8**	**.217**

WORLD SERIES RECORD

Year	Team (League)	W	L	Pct.	ERA	WHIP	G	GS	CG	ShO	Hld.	Sv.-Opp.	IP	H	R	ER	HR	BB-IBB	SO	Avg.
2002—	Anaheim (A.L.)	0	2	.000	9.31	1.97	2	2	0	0	0	0-0	9.2	12	10	10	3	7-2	6	.324

WATSON, BRANDON — OF

PERSONAL: Born September 30, 1981, in Los Angeles. ... 6-1/170. ... Bats left, throws right. ... Full name: Brandon Eric Watson. ... High school: Westchester (Los Angeles).
TRANSACTIONS/CAREER NOTES: Selected by Montreal Expos organization in ninth round of 1999 free-agent draft. ... Expos franchise moved to Washington, D.C., and renamed Nationals for 2005 season (December 3, 2004).
2005 GAMES PLAYED BY POSITION (MLB): OF—13.

LEFTY-RIGHTY SPLITS

vs.	Avg.	AB	H	2B	3B	HR	RBI	BB	SO	OBP	Slg.
L	.091	11	1	0	0	0	2	0	3	.091	.091
R	.207	29	6	1	1	1	3	4	5	.303	.414

Year	Team (League)	Pos.	G	AB	R	H	2B	3B	HR	RBI	BB	SO	HBP	GDP	SB-CS	Avg.	OBP	SLG	OPS	E	Avg.
1999—	GC Expos (GCL)	OF	33	119	15	36	2	0	0	12	11	11	1	0	4-2	.303	.361	.319	.680	1	.986
2000—	Vermont (N.Y.-Penn.)	OF	69	278	53	81	9	1	0	30	25	38	3	4	26-9	.291	.354	.331	.685	7	.948
2001—	Clinton (Midw.)	OF	117	489	74	160	16	9	2	38	29	65	1	6	33-20	.327	.364	.409	.773	4	.980
2002—	Brevard County (Fla. St.)	OF	111	424	57	113	16	2	0	24	27	53	3	5	22-13	.267	.314	.314	.628	5	.983
—	Harrisburg (East.)	OF	2	6	2	2	0	0	0	1	0	0	0	0	0-0	.333	.429	.333	.762	0	1.000
2003—	Harrisburg (East.)	OF	139	565	86	180	17	6	1	39	38	60	3	9	18-17	.319	.362	.375	.737	7	.983
2004—	Edmonton (PCL)	OF	139	526	74	154	17	3	2	41	31	68	1	3	22-10	.293	.332	.348	.680	6	.870
2005—	Harrisburg (East.)	OF	34	146	13	36	1	0	0	6	7	21	2	2	7-5	.247	.290	.253	.544	4	.973
—	New Orleans (PCL)	OF-DH	88	372	69	132	15	3	1	25	28	33	1	5	31-13	.355	.400	.419	.819	6	.986
—	Washington (N.L.)	OF	25	40	8	7	1	1	1	5	4	8	0	0	0-2	.175	.250	.325	.575	1	.933
Major League totals (1 year)			**25**	**40**	**8**	**7**	**1**	**1**	**1**	**5**	**4**	**8**	**0**	**0**	**0-2**	**.175**	**.250**	**.325**	**.575**	**1**	**.933**

WATSON, MATT — OF

PERSONAL: Born November 5, 1978, in Lancaster, Pa. ... 5-11/200. ... Bats left, throws right. ... Full name: Matthew Kyle Watson. ... High school: McCaskey (Pa.). ... College: Xavier.
TRANSACTIONS/CAREER NOTES: Selected by Montreal Expos organization in 16th round of 1999 free-agent draft. ... Traded by Expos with Ps Scott Strickland and Phil Seibel to New York Mets for Ps Bruce Chen and Dicky Gonzalez, IF Luis Figueroa and a player to be named (April 5, 2002). Expos acquired P Saul Rivero to complete deal (July 14, 2002). ... Claimed on waivers by Oakland Athletics (October 9, 2003).
2005 GAMES PLAYED BY POSITION (MLB): OF—17.

LEFTY-RIGHTY SPLITS

vs.	Avg.	AB	H	2B	3B	HR	RBI	BB	SO	OBP	Slg.
L	.000	7	0	0	0	0	0	0	1	.000	.000
R	.220	41	9	3	0	0	5	2	3	.256	.293

Year	Team (League)	Pos.	G	AB	R	H	2B	3B	HR	RBI	BB	SO	HBP	GDP	SB-CS	Avg.	OBP	SLG	OPS	E	Avg.
1999—	Vermont (N.Y.-Penn.)	OF	70	284	55	108	12	3	7	47	30	27	3	6	17-7	.380	.439	.518	.957	6	.959
2000—	Jupiter (Fla. St.)	OF	40	137	10	24	5	2	0	8	18	23	1	4	4-3	.175	.276	.241	.517	2	.951
2001—	Jupiter (Fla. St.)	OF	124	446	70	147	33	4	5	74	63	45	1	6	17-9	.330	.417	.455	.872	4	.982
2002—	Harrisburg (East.)	OF	1	4	1	1	0	0	0	0	1	0	0	0	0-0	.250	.250	.250	.500	1	1.000
—	Binghamton (East.)	OF	127	437	55	122	26	4	10	67	39	52	3	14	12-8	.279	.339	.416	.755	4	.979
2003—	St. Lucie (Fla. St.)	OF	2	7	2	2	0	1	0	2	1	2	0	0	1-0	.286	.333	.571	.904	0	1.000

Year	Team (League)	Pos.	G	AB	R	H	2B	3B	HR	RBI	BB	SO	HBP	GDP	SB-CS	Avg.	OBP	SLG	OPS	E	Avg.
—Binghamton (East.)		OF-DH	8	28	6	11	3	0	1	1	2	2	1	0	1-1	.393	.452	.607	1.059	0	1.000
—Norfolk (Int'l)		OF-DH	74	254	40	75	18	1	11	55	23	23	8	4	2-2	.295	.366	.504	.870	8	.939
—Brooklyn (N.Y.-Penn.)		OF-DH	4	14	0	2	1	0	0	0	2	3	1	0	2-1	.143	.294	.214	.508	0	1.000
—New York (N.L.)		OF	15	23	0	4	2	0	0	2	1	5	0	1	0-0	.174	.208	.261	.469	2	.846
2004—Sacramento (PCL)			125	476	79	145	37	3	19	96	54	75	4	12	3-4	.305	.377	.515	.892	11	.756
2005—Oakland (A.L.)		OF	19	48	4	9	3	0	0	5	2	4	0	1	0-0	.188	.220	.250	.470	0	1.000
—Sacramento (PCL)		OF-DH	113	419	82	132	27	3	17	81	67	57	2	7	12-1	.315	.404	.516	.919	...	...
American League totals (1 year)			19	48	4	9	3	0	0	5	2	4	0	1	0-0	.188	.220	.250	.470	0	1.000
National League totals (1 year)			15	23	0	4	2	0	0	2	1	5	0	1	0-0	.174	.208	.261	.469	2	.846
Major League totals (2 years)			34	71	4	13	5	0	0	7	3	9	0	2	0-0	.183	.216	.254	.470	2	.953

WEATHERS, DAVID   P

PERSONAL: Born September 25, 1969, in Lawrenceburg, Tenn. ... 6-3/230. ... Throws right, bats right. ... Full name: John David Weathers. ... High school: Loretto (Tenn.). ... Junior college: Motlow State (Tenn.) Community College.

TRANSACTIONS/CAREER NOTES: Selected by Toronto Blue Jays organization in third round of 1988 free-agent draft. ... Selected by Florida Marlins in second round (29th pick overall) of expansion draft (November 17, 1992). ... On disabled list (June 26-July 13, 1995); included rehabilitation assignments to Brevard County and Charlotte. ... Traded by Marlins to New York Yankees for P Mark Hutton (July 31, 1996). ... Traded by Yankees to Cleveland Indians for OF Chad Curtis (June 9, 1997). ... Claimed on waivers by Cincinnati Reds (December 20, 1997). ... Claimed on waivers by Milwaukee Brewers (June 24, 1998). ... On disabled list (August 2-22, 2000). ... Traded by Brewers with P Roberto Miniel to Chicago Cubs for P Ruben Quevedo and OF Pete Zoccolillo (July 30, 2001). ... Signed as a free agent by New York Mets (December 13, 2001). ... On suspended list (September 20-22, 2002). ... Traded by Mets with P Jeremy Griffiths to Houston Astros for OF Richard Hidalgo (June 17, 2004). ... Released by Astros (September 3, 2004). ... Signed by Marlins (September 8, 2004). ... Signed as a free agent by Reds (December 15, 2004).

CAREER HITTING: 14-for-138 (.101), 7 R, 0 2B, 0 3B, 2 HR, 4 RBI.

SCOUTING REPORT *Throws:* Weathers is a sinker-slider pitcher; his fastball ranges from 87-90 mph. *Tendencies:* He gets ground balls, effectively using a sinker that bores in on righthanded hitters and runs away from lefties. Is more effective against righthanders with his slider than lefties. Is aggressive but must keep the ball down and is prone to the home run when he leaves the ball up. Never gives in and therefore goes into a lot of deep counts. *Outlook:* Weathers can pitch about 80 innings in a season as a valuable innings eater in a middle relief role. Tends to get a lot of decisions. *Grade 6.8*

DAVID WEATHERS' PITCHING ZONE

.316	.000	.000
.222	.370	.267
.278	.474	.240

LEFTY-RIGHTY SPLITS

vs.	Avg.	AB	H	2B	3B	HR	RBI	BB	SO	OBP	Slg.
L	.265	117	31	4	0	3	16	16	22	.358	.376
R	.226	177	40	8	1	4	21	13	39	.280	.350

Year	Team (League)	W	L	Pct.	ERA	WHIP	G	GS	CG	ShO	Hld.	Sv.-Opp.	IP	H	R	ER	HR	BB-IBB	SO	Avg.
1988—St. Catharines (NYP)		4	4	.500	3.02	1.34	15	12	0	0	...	0-...	62.2	58	30	21	3	26-0	36	.245
1989—Myrtle Beach (S. Atl.)		11	13	.458	3.86	1.44	31	31	2	0	...	0-...	172.2	163	99	74	3	86-2	111	.247
1990—Dunedin (Fla. St.)		10	7	.588	3.70	1.37	27	27	2	0	...	0-...	158.0	158	82	65	2	59-0	96	.266
1991—Knoxville (Sou.)		10	7	.588	2.45	1.22	24	22	5	2	...	0-...	139.1	121	51	38	3	49-1	114	.236
—Toronto (A.L.)		1	0	1.000	4.91	2.18	15	0	0	0	1	0-0	14.2	15	9	8	1	17-3	13	.263
1992—Syracuse (Int'l)		1	4	.200	4.66	1.43	12	10	0	0	...	0-...	48.1	48	29	25	3	21-2	30	.254
—Toronto (A.L.)		0	0	...	8.10	2.10	2	0	0	0	0	0-0	3.1	5	3	3	1	2-0	3	.385
1993—Edmonton (PCL)		11	4	.733	3.83	1.40	22	22	3	1	...	0-...	141.0	150	77	60	12	47-2	117	.271
—Florida (N.L.)		2	3	.400	5.12	1.53	14	6	0	0	0	0-0	45.2	57	26	26	3	13-1	34	.306
1994—Florida (N.L.)		8	12	.400	5.27	1.67	24	24	0	0	0	0-0	135.0	166	87	79	13	59-9	72	.306
1995—Florida (N.L.)		4	5	.444	5.98	1.73	28	15	0	0	1	0-0	90.1	104	68	60	8	52-3	60	.295
—Brevard County (Fla. St.) ...		0	0	...	0.00	1.25	1	1	0	0	0	0-0	4.0	4	0	0	0	1-0	3	.286
—Charlotte (Int'l)		0	1	.000	9.00	3.00	1	1	0	0	0	0-0	5.0	10	5	5	0	5-0	0	.455
1996—Florida (N.L.)		2	2	.500	4.54	1.58	31	8	0	0	0	0-...	71.1	85	41	36	7	28-4	40	.302
—Charlotte (Int'l)		0	0	...	7.71	3.43	1	1	0	0	0	0-...	2.1	5	2	2	0	3-0	5	.500
—New York (A.L.)		0	2	.000	9.35	2.13	11	4	0	0	0	0-0	17.1	23	19	18	1	14-1	13	.315
—Columbus (Int'l)		0	2	.000	5.40	1.50	3	3	0	0	0	0-...	16.2	20	13	10	1	5-0	7	.299
1997—New York (A.L.)		0	1	.000	10.00	2.44	10	0	0	0	0	0-1	9.0	15	10	10	1	7-0	4	.375
—Columbus (Int'l)		2	2	.500	3.19	1.15	5	5	1	0	0	0-...	36.2	35	18	13	3	7-0	35	.250
—Buffalo (A.A.)		4	3	.571	3.15	1.28	11	11	2	1	...	0-...	68.2	71	37	24	7	17-0	51	.266
—Cleveland (A.L.)		1	2	.333	7.56	1.86	19	1	0	0	0	0-0	16.2	23	14	14	2	8-0	14	.343
1998—Cincinnati (N.L.)		2	4	.333	6.21	1.81	16	9	0	0	0	0-0	62.1	86	47	43	3	27-2	51	.330
—Milwaukee (N.L.)		4	1	.800	3.21	1.22	28	0	0	0	3	0-1	47.2	44	22	17	3	14-1	43	.246
1999—Milwaukee (N.L.)		7	4	.636	4.65	1.51	63	0	0	0	9	2-6	93.0	102	49	48	14	38-3	74	.279
2000—Milwaukee (N.L.)		3	5	.375	3.07	1.38	69	0	0	0	14	1-7	76.1	73	29	26	7	32-8	50	.260
2001—Milwaukee (N.L.)		3	4	.429	2.03	1.08	52	0	0	0	10	4-7	57.2	37	14	13	3	25-7	46	.188
—Chicago (N.L.)		1	1	.500	3.18	1.31	28	0	0	0	6	0-3	28.1	28	10	10	3	9-1	20	.269
2002—New York (N.L.)		6	3	.667	2.91	1.36	71	0	0	0	18	0-5	77.1	69	30	25	6	36-7	61	.245
2003—New York (N.L.)		1	6	.143	3.08	1.45	77	0	0	0	26	7-9	87.2	87	33	30	6	40-6	75	.264
2004—New York (N.L.)		5	3	.625	4.28	1.66	32	0	0	0	6	0-1	33.2	41	19	16	5	15-0	25	.304
—Houston (N.L.)		1	4	.200	4.78	1.38	26	0	0	0	5	0-3	32.0	31	20	17	5	13-1	26	.261
—Florida (N.L.)		1	0	1.000	2.70	1.20	8	2	0	0	1	0-0	16.2	13	5	5	2	7-1	10	.232
2005—Cincinnati (N.L.)		7	4	.636	3.94	1.29	73	0	0	0	8	15-19	77.2	71	36	34	7	29-2	61	.241
American League totals (4 years)		2	5	.286	7.82	2.11	47	5	0	0	1	0-1	61.0	81	55	53	6	48-4	47	.324
National League totals (12 years)		57	61	.483	4.23	1.48	640	64	0	0	110	29-61	1032.2	1094	536	485	95	437-56	748	.276
Major League totals (15 years)		59	66	.472	4.43	1.52	687	69	0	0	111	29-62	1093.2	1175	591	538	101	485-60	795	.279

DIVISION SERIES RECORD

Year	Team (League)	W	L	Pct.	ERA	WHIP	G	GS	CG	ShO	Hld.	Sv.-Opp.	IP	H	R	ER	HR	BB-IBB	SO	Avg.
1996—New York (A.L.)		1	0	1.000	0.00	0.20	2	0	0	0	0	0-0	5.0	1	0	0	0	0-0	5	.071

CHAMPIONSHIP SERIES RECORD

Year	Team (League)	W	L	Pct.	ERA	WHIP	G	GS	CG	ShO	Hld.	Sv.-Opp.	IP	H	R	ER	HR	BB-IBB	SO	Avg.
1996—New York (A.L.)		1	0	1.000	0.00	1.00	2	0	0	0	0	0-0	3.0	3	0	0	0	0-0	0	.250

W

Year	Team (League)	W	L	Pct.	ERA	WHIP	G	GS	CG	ShO	Hld.	Sv.-Opp.	IP	H	R	ER	HR	BB-IBB	SO	Avg.
1996— New York (A.L.)		0	0	...	3.00	1.67	3	0	0	0	1	0-0	3.0	2	1	1	0	3-1	3	.200

WEAVER, JEFF   P

PERSONAL: Born August 22, 1976, in Northridge, Calif. ... 6-5/200. ... Throws right, bats right. ... Full name: Jeffrey Charles Weaver. ... High school: Simi Valley (Calif.). ... College: Fresno State.

TRANSACTIONS/CAREER NOTES: Selected by Chicago White Sox organziation in second round of 1997 free-agent draft; did not sign; pick received as part of compensation for Chicago Cubs signing Type A free-agent P Kevin Tapani. ... Selected by Detroit Tigers organization in first round (14th pick overall) of 1998 free-agent draft. ... Traded by Tigers to New York Yankees as part of three-team deal in which Oakland Athletics acquired Ps Ted Lilly and Jason Arnold and OF John-Ford Griffin from Yankees and Tigers acquired 1B Carlos Pena, P Franklyn German and a player to be named from A's (July 5, 2002); Tigers acquired P Jeremy Bonderman to complete deal (August 22, 2002). ... Traded by Yankees with Ps Yhency Brazoban and Brandon Wheedon and cash to Los Angeles Dodgers for P Kevin Brown (December 13, 2003).

CAREER HITTING: 35-for-159 (.220), 11 R, 5 2B, 1 3B, 0 HR, 10 RBI.

SCOUTING REPORT **Throws:** He throws his sinker at 88-92 mph, his slider in the low 80s and his curveball at 77-81. **Tendencies:** He's a slinger who has long arm action and a tendency to fly open, which causes his sinker to flatten out. Regained consistent fastball velocity last season. Curve is a looping slurve while the slider is a much sharper breaking ball that starts away from righthanded hitters. Has very good arm speed with his changeup that sinks away from left-handers. Is effective when he keeps his sinker down and uses both sides of the plate. **Outlook:** He always has had very good stuff but is very emotional on the mound. Unable to handle adversity but is maturing and could be on the verge of a big year. **Grade 7.9**

JEFF WEAVER'S PITCHING ZONE

.230	.431	.308
.212	.320	.285
.343	.180	.286

LEFTY-RIGHTY SPLITS

vs.	Avg.	AB	H	2B	3B	HR	RBI	BB	SO	OBP	Slg.
L	.297	464	138	27	3	22	62	30	73	.356	.511
R	.208	394	82	13	1	13	40	13	84	.241	.345

Year	Team (League)	W	L	Pct.	ERA	WHIP	G	GS	CG	ShO	Hld.	Sv.-Opp.	IP	H	R	ER	HR	BB-IBB	SO	Avg.
1998— Jamestown (N.Y.-Penn.) ...		1	0	1.000	1.50	0.58	3	3	0	0	...	0-...	12.0	6	4	2	0	1-0	12	.143
— W. Mich. (Midw.)		1	0	1.000	1.38	0.62	2	2	0	0	...	0-...	13.0	8	3	2	1	0-0	21	.182
1999— Jacksonville (Sou.)		0	0	...	3.00	0.83	1	1	0	0	...	0-...	6.0	5	2	2	0	0-0	6	.227
— Detroit (A.L.)		9	12	.429	5.55	1.42	30	29	0	0	0	0-...	163.2	176	104	101	27	56-2	114	.278
2000— Toledo (Int'l)		0	1	.000	3.38	1.13	1	1	0	0	0	0-...	5.1	5	2	2	1	1-0	10	.250
— Detroit (A.L.)		11	15	.423	4.32	1.29	31	30	2	0	0	0-0	200.0	205	102	96	26	52-2	136	.267
2001— Detroit (A.L.)		13	16	.448	4.08	1.32	33	33	5	0	0	0-0	229.1	235	116	104	19	68-4	152	.266
2002— Detroit (A.L.)		6	8	.429	3.18	1.19	17	17	3	‡3	0	0-0	121.2	112	50	43	4	33-1	75	.243
— New York (A.L.)		5	3	.625	4.04	1.23	15	8	0	‡0	0	2-2	78.0	81	38	35	12	15-3	57	.260
2003— New York (A.L.)		7	9	.438	5.99	1.62	32	24	0	0	1	0-0	159.1	211	113	106	16	47-2	93	.320
2004— Los Angeles (N.L.)		13	13	.500	4.01	1.30	34	34	0	0	0	0-0	220.0	219	103	98	19	67-9	153	.260
2005— Los Angeles (N.L.)		14	11	.560	4.22	1.17	34	34	3	2	0	0-0	224.0	220	111	105	35	43-1	157	.256
American League totals (5 years)		51	63	.447	4.59	1.36	158	141	10	3	1	2-2	952.0	1020	523	485	104	271-14	627	.274
National League totals (2 years)		27	24	.529	4.11	1.24	68	68	3	2	0	0-0	444.0	439	214	203	54	110-10	310	.258
Major League totals (7 years)		78	87	.473	4.44	1.32	226	209	13	5	1	2-2	1396.0	1459	737	688	158	381-24	937	.269

DIVISION SERIES RECORD

Year	Team (League)	W	L	Pct.	ERA	WHIP	G	GS	CG	ShO	Hld.	Sv.-Opp.	IP	H	R	ER	HR	BB-IBB	SO	Avg.
2002— New York (A.L.)		0	0	...	6.75	2.63	2	0	0	0	0	0-0	2.2	4	2	2	0	3-1	1	.444
2004— Los Angeles (N.L.)		0	1	.000	11.57	2.14	1	1	0	0	0	0-0	4.2	8	6	6	0	2-0	4	.381
Division series totals (2 years)		0	1	.000	9.82	2.32	3	1	0	0	0	0-0	7.1	12	8	8	0	5-1	5	.400

WORLD SERIES RECORD

Year	Team (League)	W	L	Pct.	ERA	WHIP	G	GS	CG	ShO	Hld.	Sv.-Opp.	IP	H	R	ER	HR	BB-IBB	SO	Avg.
2003— New York (A.L.)		0	1	.000	9.00	1.00	1	0	0	0	0	0-0	1.0	1	1	1	1	0-0	0	.250

WEBB, BRANDON   P

PERSONAL: Born May 9, 1979, in Ashland, Ky. ... 6-2/228. ... Throws right, bats right. ... Full name: Brandon Tyler Webb. ... High school: Ashland (Ky.). ... College: Kentucky.

TRANSACTIONS/CAREER NOTES: Selected by Arizona Diamondbacks organization in eighth round of 2000 free-agent draft.

CAREER HITTING: 17-for-176 (.097), 5 R, 1 2B, 0 3B, 0 HR, 6 RBI.

SCOUTING REPORT **Throws:** Webb features an 88-90 mph sinker, a high-70s curve, a slider and a straight changeup. **Tendencies:** He relies on the sinker, which has excellent movement, but he tries to be too fine with it at times. Has improved his command with a mechanical adjustment that makes his motion more direct to the plate. Cut his walks significantly in 2005. Needs to improve his change to lefthanders. Big-breaking curveball is difficult to command. **Outlook:** Webb could be a 20-game winner at some point, given his durability and improved command. **Grade 7.9**

BRANDON WEBB'S PITCHING ZONE

.368	.476	.200
.206	.317	.354
.244	.281	.283

LEFTY-RIGHTY SPLITS

vs.	Avg.	AB	H	2B	3B	HR	RBI	BB	SO	OBP	Slg.
L	.298	449	134	23	3	18	58	35	67	.347	.483
R	.228	416	95	18	1	3	32	24	105	.271	.298

Year	Team (League)	W	L	Pct.	ERA	WHIP	G	GS	CG	ShO	Hld.	Sv.-Opp.	IP	H	R	ER	HR	BB-IBB	SO	Avg.
2000— Ariz. D'backs (Ariz.)		0	0	...	9.00	2.00	1	1	0	0	0	0-...	1.0	2	1	1	0	0-0	3	.400
— South Bend (Midw.)		0	0	...	3.24	1.14	12	0	0	0	0	2-...	16.2	10	7	6	0	9-1	18	.172
2001— Lancaster (Calif.)		6	10	.375	3.99	1.34	29	28	0	0	0	0-...	162.1	174	90	72	9	44-0	158	.276
2002— Tucson (PCL)		0	1	.000	3.86	1.29	1	1	0	0	0	0-...	7.0	5	3	3	0	4-0	5	.200
— El Paso (Texas)		10	6	.625	3.14	1.32	26	25	1	0	0	0-...	152.0	141	66	53	4	59-1	122	.244
2003— Tucson (PCL)		1	1	.500	6.00	1.50	3	3	0	0	0	0-...	18.0	18	17	12	0	9-0	17	.257
— Arizona (N.L.)		10	9	.526	2.84	1.15	29	28	1	1	0	0-0	180.2	140	65	57	12	68-4	172	.213
2004— Arizona (N.L.)		7	* 16	.304	3.59	1.50	35	•35	1	0	0	0-0	208.0	194	111	83	17	* 119-11	164	.248

W

	W	L	Pct.	ERA	WHIP	G	GS	CG	ShO	Hld.	Sv.-Opp.	IP	H	R	ER	HR	BB-IBB	SO	Avg.
2005—Arizona (N.L.)	14	12	.538	3.54	1.26	33	33	1	0	0	0-0	229.0	229	98	90	21	59-4	172	.265
Major League totals (3 years)	31	37	.456	3.35	1.31	97	96	3	1	0	0-0	617.2	563	274	230	50	246-19	508	.244

WEBB, JOHN　　　　　　　　　P

PERSONAL: Born May 23, 1979, in Pensacola, Fla. ... 6-3/220. ... Throws right, bats right. ... Full name: John Floyd Webb. ... High school: Pensacola (Fla.). ... Junior college: Manatee (Fla.). ... College: West Florida.
TRANSACTIONS/CAREER NOTES: Selected by Chicago Cubs organization in 19th round of 1999 free-agent draft. ... Claimed on waivers by Tampa Bay Devil Rays (February 24, 2004). ... Signed as a free agent by St. Louis Cardinals organization (November 14, 2005).
CAREER HITTING: 0-for-0 (.000), 0 R, 0 2B, 0 3B, 0 HR, 0 RBI.

LEFTY-RIGHTY SPLITS

vs.	Avg.	AB	H	2B	3B	HR	RBI	BB	SO	OBP	Slg.
L	.375	8	3	1	0	0	2	2	2	.545	.500
R	.300	10	3	1	0	1	4	2	0	.417	.700

Year	Team (League)	W	L	Pct.	ERA	WHIP	G	GS	CG	ShO	Hld.	Sv.-Opp.	IP	H	R	ER	HR	BB-IBB	SO	Avg.
1999—	Ariz. Cubs (AZL)	0	0	...	3.58	1.26	18	0	0	0	...	3-...	32.2	33	20	13	0	8-0	39	.246
	Eugene (N'west)	1	0	1.000	0.00	0.50	2	0	0	0	...	1-...	4.0	1	0	0	0	1-0	3	.077
2000—	Lansing (Midw.)	7	6	.538	2.47	1.23	21	21	1	1	...	0-...	134.2	125	53	37	4	40-0	108	.250
	Daytona (Fla. St.)	1	1	.500	4.76	1.18	4	2	0	0	...	1-...	17.0	17	11	9	1	3-0	18	.250
2001—	Daytona (Fla. St.)	1	1	.500	5.40	1.50	5	4	0	0	...	0-...	20.0	23	13	12	0	7-1	20	.280
2002—	Daytona (Fla. St.)	5	3	.625	3.43	1.14	10	10	1	1	...	0-...	57.2	43	23	22	3	23-0	65	.207
	West Tenn (Sou.)	4	5	.444	4.52	1.20	11	11	0	0	...	0-...	61.2	52	33	31	5	22-0	45	.231
2003—	West Tenn (Sou.)	5	8	.385	4.50	1.42	30	22	0	0	...	1-...	132.0	135	74	66	11	52-1	85	.270
2004—	Montgomery (Sou.)	2	1	.667	4.10	1.29	9	3	0	0	...	0-...	26.1	26	12	12	3	8-0	12	.263
	Durham (Int'l)	1	3	.250	3.27	1.36	6	6	0	0	...	0-...	33.0	31	19	12	5	14-0	22	.246
	Tampa Bay (A.L.)	0	0	...	7.00	2.11	4	0	0	0	0	0-0	9.0	12	7	7	2	7-0	9	.324
2005—	Tampa Bay (A.L.)	0	1	.000	18.00	2.50	1	1	0	0	0	0-0	4.0	6	8	8	1	4-0	2	.333
	Durham (Int'l)	10	6	.625	4.85	1.44	28	27	1	0	...	0-0	163.1	175	103	88	23	61-2	86	.274
Major League totals (2 years)	0	1	.000	10.38	2.23	5	1	0	0	0	0-0	13.0	18	15	15	3	11-0	11	.327

WEBER, BEN　　　　　　　　　P

PERSONAL: Born November 17, 1969, in Port Arthur, Texas. ... 6-4/205. ... Throws right, bats right. ... Full name: Benjamin Edward Weber. ... Name pronounced: webb-er. ... High school: Port Neches-Groves (Port Neches, Texas). ... College: Houston.
TRANSACTIONS/CAREER NOTES: Selected by Toronto Blue Jays organization in 20th round of 1991 free-agent draft. ... Released by Blue Jays (March 24, 1996). ... Signed by Salinas of the independent Western League (1996). ... Signed by Taipei of the Taiwan League (1997). ... Signed by San Francisco Giants organization (October 30, 1998). ... Claimed on waivers by Anaheim Angels (August 30, 2000). ... Released by Angels (September 8, 2004). ... Signed by Cincinnati Reds (December 15, 2004). ... On disabled list (May 9-August 13, 2005); included rehabilitation assignments to Dayton and Chattanooga.
CAREER HITTING: 0-for-0 (.000), 0 R, 0 2B, 0 3B, 0 HR, 0 RBI.

BEN WEBER'S PITCHING ZONE

...	1.000	.333
.167	1.000	.375
.500	.250	.000

LEFTY-RIGHTY SPLITS

vs.	Avg.	AB	H	2B	3B	HR	RBI	BB	SO	OBP	Slg.
L	.375	16	6	2	0	0	3	3	1	.474	.500
R	.359	39	14	4	0	0	6	6	7	.447	.462

Year	Team (League)	W	L	Pct.	ERA	WHIP	G	GS	CG	ShO	Hld.	Sv.-Opp.	IP	H	R	ER	HR	BB-IBB	SO	Avg.
1991—	St. Catharines (NYP)	6	3	.667	3.24	1.33	16	14	1	0	...	0-...	97.1	105	43	35	3	24-2	60	.274
1992—	Myrtle Beach (S. Atl.)	4	7	.364	1.64	1.14	41	1	0	0	...	6-...	98.2	83	27	18	1	29-3	65	.227
1993—	Dunedin (Fla. St.)	8	3	.727	2.92	1.34	55	0	0	0	...	12-...	83.1	87	36	27	4	25-5	45	.278
1994—	Dunedin (Fla. St.)	3	2	.600	2.73	1.14	18	0	0	0	...	3-...	26.1	25	8	8	1	5-3	19	.255
	Knoxville (Sou.)	4	3	.571	3.76	1.24	25	10	0	0	...	0-...	95.2	103	49	40	8	16-0	55	.272
1995—	Syracuse (Int'l)	4	5	.444	5.40	1.51	25	15	0	0	...	1-...	91.2	111	62	55	10	27-1	38	.300
	Knoxville (Sou.)	4	1	.800	3.91	1.26	12	1	0	0	...	0-...	25.1	26	12	11	3	6-0	16	.268
1996—	Salinas (West.)	12	6	.667	3.47	1.22	22	22	2	...	...	0-...	148.0	138	68	57	11	42-1	102	.248
1997—	Taipei (Tai.)	7	3	.700	...	1.19	40	...	...	...	...	5-...	99.0	85	...	...	...	33-...	78	...
1998—	Taipei (Tai.)	12	7	.632	...	1.40	56	...	...	...	...	7-...	144.0	150	...	...	...	52-...	122	...
1999—	Fresno (PCL)	2	4	.333	3.34	1.23	51	0	0	0	...	8-...	86.1	78	34	32	6	28-2	67	.245
2000—	San Francisco (N.L.)	0	1	.000	14.63	2.50	9	0	0	0	1	0-2	8.0	16	13	13	0	4-0	6	.400
	Fresno (PCL)	4	8	.333	2.42	1.18	38	3	0	0	...	7-...	78.0	72	31	21	7	20-0	66	.245
	Erie (East.)	0	1	.000	16.20	3.00	2	0	0	0	...	0-...	1.2	3	5	3	1	2-0	2	.333
	Anaheim (A.L.)	1	0	1.000	1.84	0.95	10	0	0	0	0	0-0	14.2	12	6	3	0	2-1	8	.214
2001—	Anaheim (A.L.)	6	2	.750	3.42	1.42	56	0	0	0	6	0-1	68.1	66	28	26	4	31-8	40	.251
2002—	Anaheim (A.L.)	7	2	.778	2.54	1.18	63	0	0	0	18	7-11	78.0	70	25	22	4	22-3	43	.249
2003—	Anaheim (A.L.)	5	1	.833	2.69	1.32	62	0	0	0	11	0-2	80.1	84	26	24	7	22-7	46	.275
2004—	Anaheim (A.L.)	0	2	.000	8.06	2.33	18	0	0	0	2	0-1	22.1	37	24	20	4	15-0	11	.363
	Ariz. Angels (AZL)	0	0	...	0.00	0.00	1	0	0	0	...	0-...	1.0	0	0	0	0	0-0	2	.000
	Salt Lake (PCL)	0	2	.000	8.64	2.16	15	0	0	0	...	1-...	16.2	27	25	16	3	9-1	18	.346
2005—	Cincinnati (N.L.)	0	0	...	8.03	2.35	10	0	0	0	0	0-0	12.1	20	11	11	0	9-1	8	.364
	Dayton (Midw.)	0	0	...	0.00	0.33	2	0	0	0	1	0-0	3.0	1	0	0	0	0-0	4	.100
	Chattanooga (Sou.)	1	1	.500	2.31	1.03	9	0	0	0	3	0-0	11.2	9	3	3	2	2-0	5	.209
	Louisville (Int'l)	0	1	.000	6.43	2.00	7	0	0	0	0	0-1	7.0	8	5	5	0	6-0	5	.296
American League totals (5 years)	19	7	.731	3.24	1.37	209	0	0	0	38	7-15	263.2	269	109	95	19	92-19	148	.267
National League totals (2 years)	0	1	.000	10.62	2.41	19	0	0	0	1	0-2	20.1	36	24	24	0	13-1	14	.379
Major League totals (6 years)	19	8	.704	3.77	1.44	228	0	0	0	39	7-17	284.0	305	133	119	19	105-20	162	.277

DIVISION SERIES RECORD

Year	Team (League)	W	L	Pct.	ERA	WHIP	G	GS	CG	ShO	Hld.	Sv.-Opp.	IP	H	R	ER	HR	BB-IBB	SO	Avg.
2002—	Anaheim (A.L.)	0	1	.000	18.00	4.00	2	0	0	0	0	2	1.0	2	2	2	0	2-0	0	.400

CHAMPIONSHIP SERIES RECORD

Year	Team (League)	W	L	Pct.	ERA	WHIP	G	GS	CG	ShO	Hld.	Sv.-Opp.	IP	H	R	ER	HR	BB-IBB	SO	Avg.
2002—	Anaheim (A.L.)	0	0	...	3.38	1.13	3	0	0	0	0	0-0	2.2	1	1	1	0	0-0	3	.300

WORLD SERIES RECORD

Year	Team (League)	W	L	Pct.	ERA	WHIP	G	GS	CG	ShO	Hld.	Sv.-Opp.	IP	H	R	ER	HR	BB-IBB	SO	Avg.
2002—	Anaheim (A.L.)	0	0	...	13.50	2.57	4	0	0	0	0	0-0	4.2	10	7	7	1	2-1	5	.455

W

WEEKS, RICKIE — 2B

PERSONAL: Born September 13, 1982, in Daytona Beach, Fla. ... 6-0/195. ... Bats right, throws right. ... Full name: Rickie Darnell Weeks. ... High school: Lake Brantley (Altamonte Springs, Fla.). ... College: Southern University.

TRANSACTIONS/CAREER NOTES: Selected by Milwaukee Brewers organization in first round (second pick overall) of 2003 free-agent draft.

2005 GAMES PLAYED BY POSITION (MLB): 2B—95.

SCOUTING REPORT *Offense:* Weeks started hot start at the plate, but a thumb injury caused him to tail off at the end of the season. Is aggressive and has exceptional bat speed. Gets the bat head in the zone quickly and is going to have very good power. Pulls the ball too much. Is a good runner and will steal bases as he gets experience. *Defense:* He is extremely erratic in the field and has trouble moving to his backhand. Can be careless at times and needs a lot of work making the pivot. Has some quickness and good range to both sides. *Outlook:* Weeks is going to hit and hit for power, but he may have to change positions. Could eventually end up in center field. *Grade 6.5*

RICKIE WEEKS' HITTING ZONE

.333	.214	.318
.302	.457	.243
.179	.400	.087

LEFTY-RIGHTY SPLITS

vs.	Avg.	AB	H	2B	3B	HR	RBI	BB	SO	OBP	Slg.
L	.222	72	16	3	1	3	10	12	19	.364	.417
R	.243	288	70	10	1	10	32	28	77	.324	.389

Year	Team (League)	Pos.	G	AB	R	H	2B	3B	HR	RBI	BB	SO	HBP	GDP	SB-CS	Avg.	OBP	SLG	OPS	E	Avg.
2003—	Ariz. Brewers (Ariz.)	DH	1	4	0	2	0	0	0	4	0	2	1	0	1-0	.500	.600	.500	1.100	0	—
	— Beloit (Midw.)	2B-2B-DH	20	63	13	22	8	1	1	16	15	9	6	1	2-0	.349	.494	.556	1.050	7	.923
	— Milwaukee (N.L.)	2B	7	12	1	2	1	0	0	0	1	6	1	0	0-0	.167	.286	.250	.536	1	.667
2004—	Huntsville (Sou.)	2B	133	479	67	124	35	6	8	42	55	107	28	5	11-12	.259	.366	.407	.773	17	.795
2005—	Nashville (PCL)	2B	55	203	43	65	14	9	12	48	28	51	14	3	10-1	.320	.435	.655	1.090	10	.961
	— Milwaukee (N.L.)	2B	96	360	56	86	13	2	13	42	40	96	11	11	15-2	.239	.333	.394	.727	21	.951
	Major League totals (2 years)		103	372	57	88	14	2	13	42	41	102	12	11	15-2	.237	.331	.390	.721	22	.949

WELLEMEYER, TODD — P

PERSONAL: Born August 30, 1978, in Louisville, Ky. ... 6-3/205. ... Throws right, bats right. ... Full name: Todd Allen Wellemeyer. ... Name pronounced: WELL-my-er. ... High school: Eastern (Louisville, Ky.). ... College: Bellarmine (Ky.).

TRANSACTIONS/CAREER NOTES: Selected by Chicago Cubs organization in fourth round of 2000 free-agent draft. ... On disabled list (May 22-July 16, 2004); included rehabilitation assignment to Iowa.

CAREER HITTING: 1-for-5 (.200), 1 R, 0 2B, 0 3B, 0 HR, 0 RBI.

SCOUTING REPORT *Throws:* He has a plus fastball at 93-94 mph and throws a slider and changeup. *Tendencies:* He struggles to maintain his delivery because he rolls his wrist without allowing his arm to catch up. Fastball has good life but lacks command. Pitched on the outside too much in important situations. Slider is quick-running but inconsistent because of his arm mechanics. *Outlook:* He can be a solid reliever, and if he can harness more control and fine-tune his mechanics, he could develop into a reliable setup man. *Grade 6.2*

TODD WELLEMEYER'S PITCHING ZONE

.444	1.000	.444
.150	.333	.240
.200	.600	.111

LEFTY-RIGHTY SPLITS

vs.	Avg.	AB	H	2B	3B	HR	RBI	BB	SO	OBP	Slg.
L	.234	47	11	1	0	2	10	11	13	.373	.383
R	.284	74	21	4	0	5	13	11	19	.376	.541

Year	Team (League)	W	L	Pct.	ERA	WHIP	G	GS	CG	ShO	Hld.	Sv.-Opp.	IP	H	R	ER	HR	BB-IBB	SO	Avg.
2000—	Eugene (N'west)	4	4	.500	3.67	1.25	15	15	0	0	...	0-...	76.0	62	35	31	3	33-2	85	.225
2001—	Lansing (Midw.)	13	9	.591	4.16	1.63	27	27	1	0	...	0-...	147.0	165	85	68	14	74-0	167	.288
2002—	Daytona (Fla. St.)	2	4	.333	3.79	1.11	14	14	0	0	...	0-...	73.2	63	33	31	7	19-1	87	.230
	— West Tenn (Sou.)	3	3	.500	4.70	1.11	8	8	1	1	...	0-...	46.0	33	25	24	2	18-0	37	.204
2003—	West Tenn (Sou.)	1	1	.500	5.48	1.36	4	4	0	0	...	0-...	21.1	19	13	13	1	10-0	34	.238
	— Iowa (PCL)	5	5	.500	5.18	1.53	13	12	0	0	...	0-...	66.0	68	39	38	7	33-4	56	.272
	— Chicago (N.L.)	1	1	.500	6.51	1.59	15	0	0	0	1	1-1	27.2	25	22	20	5	19-1	30	.245
2004—	Iowa (PCL)	1	1	.500	3.91	1.57	14	4	0	0	...	0-...	23.0	24	11	10	2	12-0	23	.273
	— Chicago (N.L.)	2	1	.667	5.92	1.93	20	0	0	0	0	0-0	24.1	27	16	16	1	20-2	30	.287
2005—	Iowa (PCL)	3	2	.600	3.02	1.34	12	12	0	0	0	0-0	53.2	47	21	18	2	25-0	48	.235
	— Chicago (N.L.)	2	1	.667	6.12	1.67	22	0	0	0	3	1-1	32.1	32	23	22	7	22-1	32	.264
	Major League totals (3 years)	5	3	.625	6.19	1.72	57	0	0	0	4	2-2	84.1	84	61	58	13	61-4	92	.265

WELLS, DAVID — P

PERSONAL: Born May 20, 1963, in Torrance, Calif. ... 6-4/248. ... Throws left, bats left. ... Full name: David Lee Wells. ... High school: Point Loma (San Diego).

TRANSACTIONS/CAREER NOTES: Selected by Toronto Blue Jays organization in second round of June 1982 free-agent draft. ... Released by Blue Jays (March 30, 1993). ... Signed by Detroit Tigers (April 3, 1993). ... On disabled list (August 1-20, 1993). ... On disabled list (April 19-June 6, 1994); included rehabilitation assignment to Lakeland. ... Traded by Tigers to Cincinnati Reds for Ps C.J. Nitkowski and David Tuttle and a player to be named (July 31, 1995); Tigers acquired IF Mark Lewis to complete deal (November 16, 1995). ... Traded by Reds to Baltimore Orioles for OFs Curtis Goodwin and Trovin Valdez (December 26, 1995). ... Signed as a free agent by New York Yankees (December 24, 1996). ... Traded by Yankees with P Graeme Lloyd and 2B Homer Bush to Blue Jays for P Roger Clemens (February 18, 1999). ... Traded by Blue Jays with P Matt DeWitt to Chicago White Sox for Ps Mike Sirotka, Kevin Beirne and Mike Williams and OF Brian Simmons (January 14, 2001). ... On disabled list (July 2, 2001-remainder of season). ... Signed as a free agent by Yankees (January 17, 2002). ... Signed as a free agent by San Diego Padres (January 6, 2004). ... On disabled list (May 17-June 7, 2004). ... Signed as a free agent by Boston Red Sox (December 17, 2004). ... On disabled list (April 26-May 18, 2005). ... On suspended list (August 29-September 4, 2005).

CAREER HITTING: 14-for-120 (.117), 5 R, 1 2B, 0 3B, 0 HR, 4 RBI.

W

SCOUTING REPORT *Throws:* The ageless starter has an 89-92 mph fastball, an 83-86 cutter, a curve and a changeup. *Tendencies:* Wells has an excellent delivery with a downward plane and the ability to throw all his pitches from the same release point. Has good life down in the zone with his fastball and tight bite on his curve. Never throws consecutive pitches at the same speed and keeps hitters off-balance with impeccable command. *Outlook:* The only question about Wells is whether he can start 30 games a year. Goes deep into games and still is capable of winning 15 or more games. *Grade 8.1*

DAVID WELLS' PITCHING ZONE

.375	.467	.245
.380	.353	.269
.241	.310	.220

LEFTY-RIGHTY SPLITS

vs.	Avg.	AB	H	2B	3B	HR	RBI	BB	SO	OBP	Slg.
L	.343	169	58	6	0	5	22	7	21	.383	.467
R	.282	574	162	35	3	16	65	14	86	.302	.437

Year Team (League)	W	L	Pct.	ERA	WHIP	G	GS	CG	ShO	Hld.	Sv.-Opp.	IP	H	R	ER	HR	BB-IBB	SO	Avg.
1982—Medicine Hat (Pion.)	4	3	.571	5.18	1.60	12	12	1	0	...	0-...	64.1	71	42	37	5	32-1	53	
1983—Kinston (Carol.)	6	5	.545	3.73	1.35	25	25	5	0	...	0-...	157.0	141	81	65	13	71-2	115	.238
1984—Kinston (Carol.)	1	6	.143	4.71	1.67	7	7	0	0	...	0-...	42.0	51	29	22	1	19-1	44	.302
—Knoxville (Sou.)	3	2	.600	2.59	1.27	8	8	3	1	...	0-...	59.0	58	22	17	3	17-0	34	.262
1985—Syracuse (Int'l)			Did not play.																
1986—Florence (S. Atl.)	0	0	...	3.55	1.26	4	1	0	0	...	0-...	12.2	7	6	5	1	9-0	14	.159
—Ventura (Calif.)	2	1	.667	1.89	0.89	5	2	0	0	...	0-...	19.0	13	5	4	0	4-0	26	.200
—Knoxville (Sou.)	1	3	.250	4.05	1.50	10	7	1	0	...	0-...	40.0	42	24	18	1	18-0	32	.280
—Syracuse (Int'l)	0	1	.000	9.82	1.91	3	0	0	0	...	0-...	3.2	6	4	4	0	1-0	2	.400
1987—Syracuse (Int'l)	4	6	.400	3.87	1.23	43	12	0	0	...	6-...	109.1	102	49	47	9	32-0	106	.248
—Toronto (A.L.)	4	3	.571	3.99	1.67	18	2	0	0	2	1-2	29.1	37	14	13	0	12-0	32	.311
1988—Toronto (A.L.)	3	5	.375	4.62	1.49	41	0	0	0	8	4-6	64.1	65	36	33	12	31-9	56	.269
—Syracuse (Int'l)	0	0	...	0.00	1.59	6	0	0	0	...	3-...	5.2	7	1	0	0	2-1	8	.269
1989—Toronto (A.L.)	7	4	.636	2.40	1.09	54	0	0	0	8	2-9	86.1	66	25	23	5	28-7	78	.207
1990—Toronto (A.L.)	11	6	.647	3.14	1.11	43	25	0	0	3	3-3	189.0	165	72	66	14	45-3	115	.235
1991—Toronto (A.L.)	15	10	.600	3.72	1.19	40	28	2	0	3	1-2	198.1	188	88	82	24	49-1	106	.252
1992—Toronto (A.L.)	7	9	.438	5.40	1.45	41	14	0	0	3	2-4	120.0	138	84	72	16	36-6	62	.289
1993—Detroit (A.L.)	11	9	.550	4.19	1.20	32	30	0	0	1	0-0	187.0	183	93	87	26	42-6	139	.254
1994—Detroit (A.L.)	5	7	.417	3.96	1.23	16	16	5	1	0	0-0	111.1	113	54	49	13	24-6	71	.260
—Lakeland (Fla. St.)	0	0	...	0.00	0.83	2	2	0	0	...	0-...	6.0	5	1	0	0	0-0	3	.217
1995—Detroit (A.L.)	10	3	.769	3.04	1.20	18	18	3	0	0	0-0	130.1	120	54	44	17	37-5	83	.242
—Cincinnati (N.L.)	6	5	.545	3.59	1.24	11	11	3	0	0	0-0	72.2	74	34	29	6	16-4	50	.265
1996—Baltimore (A.L.)	11	14	.440	5.14	1.33	34	34	3	0	0	0-0	224.1	247	132	128	32	51-7	130	.285
1997—New York (A.L.)	16	10	.615	4.21	1.30	32	32	5	2	0	0-0	218.0	239	109	102	24	45-0	156	.278
1998—New York (A.L.)	18	4	.818	3.49	1.05	30	30	8	*5	0	0-0	214.1	195	86	83	29	29-0	163	.239
1999—Toronto (A.L.)	17	10	.630	4.82	1.33	34	34	*7	1	0	0-0	*231.2	*246	132	124	32	62-2	169	.271
2000—Toronto (A.L.)	•20	8	.714	4.11	1.29	35	•35	*9	1	0	0-0	229.2	*266	115	105	23	31-0	166	.289
2001—Chicago (A.L.)	5	7	.417	4.47	1.40	16	16	1	0	0	0-0	100.2	120	55	50	12	21-1	59	.297
2002—New York (A.L.)	19	7	.731	3.75	1.24	31	31	2	1	0	0-0	206.1	210	100	86	21	45-2	137	.259
2003—New York (A.L.)	15	7	.682	4.14	1.23	31	30	4	1	0	0-0	213.0	242	101	98	24	20-0	101	.286
2004—San Diego (N.L.)	12	8	.600	3.73	1.14	31	31	0	0	0	0-0	195.2	203	85	81	23	20-1	101	.266
2005—Boston (A.L.)	15	7	.682	4.45	1.31	30	30	2	0	0	0-0	184.0	220	95	91	21	21-0	107	.296
American League totals (18 years)	209	130	.617	4.09	1.26	576	405	51	12	28	13-26	2938.0	3060	1445	1336	345	629-55	1930	.268
National League totals (2 years)	18	13	.581	3.69	1.17	42	42	3	0	0	0-0	268.1	277	119	110	29	36-5	151	.266
Major League totals (19 years)	227	143	.614	4.06	1.25	618	447	54	12	28	13-26	3206.1	3337	1564	1446	374	665-60	2081	.267

DIVISION SERIES RECORD

Year Team (League)	W	L	Pct.	ERA	WHIP	G	GS	CG	ShO	Hld.	Sv.-Opp.	IP	H	R	ER	HR	BB-IBB	SO	Avg.
1995—Cincinnati (N.L.)	1	0	1.000	0.00	1.11	1	1	0	0	0	0-0	6.1	6	1	0	0	1-0	8	.231
1996—Baltimore (A.L.)	1	0	1.000	4.61	1.39	2	2	0	0	0	0-0	13.2	15	7	7	1	4-1	6	.288
1997—New York (A.L.)	1	0	1.000	1.00	0.56	1	1	1	0	0	0-0	9.0	5	1	1	0	0-0	1	.152
1998—New York (A.L.)	1	0	1.000	0.00	0.75	1	1	0	0	0	0-0	8.0	5	0	0	0	1-0	9	.172
2002—New York (A.L.)	0	1	.000	15.43	2.14	1	1	0	0	0	0-0	4.2	10	8	8	1	0-0	5	.435
2003—New York (A.L.)	1	0	1.000	1.17	1.04	1	1	0	0	0	0-0	7.2	8	1	1	0	0-0	5	.258
2005—Boston (A.L.)	0	1	.000	2.70	1.05	1	1	0	0	0	0-0	6.2	7	5	2	1	0-0	2	.269
Division series totals (7 years)	5	2	.714	3.05	1.11	8	8	1	0	0	0-0	56.0	56	23	19	3	6-1	31	.255

CHAMPIONSHIP SERIES RECORD

Year Team (League)	W	L	Pct.	ERA	WHIP	G	GS	CG	ShO	Hld.	Sv.-Opp.	IP	H	R	ER	HR	BB-IBB	SO	Avg.
1989—Toronto (A.L.)	0	0	...	0.00	2.00	1	0	0	0	0	0-0	1.0	0	1	0	0	2-0	1	.000
1991—Toronto (A.L.)	0	0	...	2.35	1.04	4	0	0	0	0	0-0	7.2	6	2	2	0	2-1	9	.207
1992—Toronto (A.L.)			Did not play.																
1995—Cincinnati (N.L.)	0	1	.000	4.50	1.67	1	1	0	0	0	0-0	6.0	8	3	3	1	2-0	3	.320
1996—Baltimore (A.L.)	1	0	1.000	4.05	1.65	1	1	0	0	0	0-0	6.2	8	3	3	0	3-0	6	.308
1998—New York (A.L.)	2	0	1.000	2.87	0.89	2	2	0	0	0	0-0	15.2	12	5	5	3	2-0	18	.218
2003—New York (A.L.)	1	0	1.000	2.35	0.91	2	1	0	0	0	0-0	7.2	5	2	2	2	2-0	5	.179
Champ. series totals (6 years)	4	1	.800	3.02	1.16	11	5	0	0	0	0-0	44.2	39	16	15	6	13-1	42	.235

WORLD SERIES RECORD

Year Team (League)	W	L	Pct.	ERA	WHIP	G	GS	CG	ShO	Hld.	Sv.-Opp.	IP	H	R	ER	HR	BB-IBB	SO	Avg.
1992—Toronto (A.L.)	0	0	...	0.00	0.69	4	0	0	0	1	0-0	4.1	1	0	0	0	2-0	3	.083
1998—New York (A.L.)	1	0	1.000	6.43	1.29	1	1	0	0	0	0-0	7.0	7	5	5	3	2-0	4	.269
2003—New York (A.L.)	0	1	.000	3.38	1.00	2	2	0	0	0	0-0	8.0	6	3	3	0	2-0	1	.222
World series totals (3 years)	1	1	.500	3.72	1.03	7	3	0	0	1	0-0	19.1	14	8	8	3	6-0	8	.215

ALL-STAR GAME RECORD

	W	L	Pct.	ERA	WHIP	G	GS	CG	ShO	Hld.	Sv.-Opp.	IP	H	R	ER	HR	BB-IBB	SO	Avg.
All-Star Game totals (3 years)	0	0	...	0.00	0.69	3	2	0	0	0	0-0	4.1	2	0	0	0	1-0	4	.143

W

WELLS, KIP — P

PERSONAL: Born April 21, 1977, in Houston. ... 6-3/200. ... Throws right, bats right. ... Full name: Robert Kip Wells. ... High school: Elkins (Fort Bend, Texas). ... College: Baylor.

TRANSACTIONS/CAREER NOTES: Selected by Milwaukee Brewers organization in 58th round of 1995 free-agent draft; did not sign. ... Selected by Chicago White Sox organization in first round (16th pick overall) of 1998 free-agent draft. ... Traded by White Sox with Ps Sean Lowe and Josh Fogg to Pittsburgh Pirates for P Todd Ritchie and C Lee Evans (December 13, 2001). ... On disabled list (August 14-September 5, 2004).

CAREER HITTING: 43-for-239 (.180), 21 R, 9 2B, 1 3B, 3 HR, 12 RBI.

SCOUTING REPORT *Throws:* His fastball is 90-94 mph, his slider is 84-87 and his curveball is 73-78. Also throws a changeup. *Tendencies:* Wells needs to be more aggressive with his fastball and learn to trust his stuff. Curve has very good rotation but is difficult to command; will vary speeds on it. Slider needs more tilt and change needs to improve. *Outlook:* An underachiever with a higher ceiling than he has shown, Wells has the ability to dial up a dominating game but rarely strings good starts together. *Grade 6.5*

KIP WELLS' PITCHING ZONE

.240	.250	.250
.339	.417	.309
.256	.159	.247

LEFTY-RIGHTY SPLITS

vs.	Avg.	AB	H	2B	3B	HR	RBI	BB	SO	OBP	Slg.
L	.288	316	91	21	1	11	54	61	62	.395	.465
R	.249	382	95	25	1	12	50	38	70	.334	.414

Year Team (League)	W	L	Pct.	ERA	WHIP	G	GS	CG	ShO	Hld.	Sv.-Opp.	IP	H	R	ER	HR	BB-IBB	SO	Avg.
1999—Win.-Salem (Carol.)	5	6	.455	3.57	1.31	14	14	0	0	...	0-...	85.2	78	39	34	4	34-1	95	.252
—Birmingham (Sou.)	8	2	.800	2.94	1.14	11	11	0	0	...	0-...	70.1	49	24	23	5	31-0	44	.198
—Chicago (A.L.)	4	1	.800	4.04	1.35	7	7	0	0	...	0-0	35.2	33	17	16	2	15-0	29	.248
2000—Chicago (A.L.)	6	9	.400	6.02	1.86	20	20	0	0	0	0-0	98.2	126	76	66	15	58-4	71	.312
—Charlotte (Int'l)	5	3	.625	5.37	1.52	12	12	2	1	0	0-...	62.0	67	38	37	10	27-1	38	.272
2001—Charlotte (Int'l)	2	1	.667	3.55	1.34	4	4	0	0	...	0-...	25.1	26	11	10	2	8-0	24	.260
—Chicago (A.L.)	10	11	.476	4.79	1.55	40	20	0	0	6	0-2	133.1	145	80	71	14	61-5	99	.281
2002—Pittsburgh (N.L.)	12	14	.462	3.58	1.35	33	33	1	1	0	0-0	198.1	197	92	79	21	71-11	134	.261
2003—Pittsburgh (N.L.)	10	9	.526	3.28	1.25	31	31	1	0	0	0-0	197.1	171	77	72	24	76-7	147	.233
2004—Pittsburgh (N.L.)	5	7	.417	4.55	1.53	24	24	0	0	0	0-0	138.1	145	71	70	14	66-4	116	.270
2005—Pittsburgh (N.L.)	8	*18	.308	5.09	1.57	33	33	1	1	0	0-0	182.0	186	116	103	23	*99-8	132	.266
American League totals (3 years)	20	21	.488	5.14	1.64	67	47	0	0	6	0-2	267.2	304	173	153	31	134-9	199	.289
National League totals (4 years)	35	48	.422	4.07	1.41	121	121	3	2	0	0-0	716.0	699	356	324	82	312-30	529	.256
Major League totals (7 years)	55	69	.444	4.36	1.47	188	168	3	2	6	0-2	983.2	1003	529	477	113	446-39	728	.265

WELLS, VERNON — OF

PERSONAL: Born December 8, 1978, in Shreveport, La. ... 6-1/225. ... Bats right, throws right. ... Full name: Vernon Wells III. ... High school: Bowie (Arlington, Texas).

TRANSACTIONS/CAREER NOTES: Selected by Toronto Blue Jays organization in first round (fifth pick overall) of 1997 free-agent draft. ... On disabled list (June 16-July 16, 2004).

HONORS: Won A.L. Gold Glove as outfielder (2004-05).

2005 GAMES PLAYED BY POSITION (MLB): OF—155, DH—2.

SCOUTING REPORT *Offense:* This five-tool player hits from an open stance but is successful when taking the ball to the opposite field. Is a good high-ball hitter but also is a patient with breaking balls. Will get into trouble when he chases pitches off the plate. Had a slow start in 2005 as a result of pulling too much. Is slow out of the box but is a plus baserunner. *Defense:* A two-time Gold Glover winner, Wells has a gliding gait and good range. Gets good jumps on the ball and takes good lateral routes to the alleys. Is accurate with a plus arm and a quick release. *Outlook:* Wells might not be as well-known as some players, but he's one of the game's best overall players. Is a good run producer and one of the few pure center fielders. *Grade 9.4*

VERNON WELLS' HITTING ZONE

.260	.379	.000
.306	.408	.217
.233	.343	.286

LEFTY-RIGHTY SPLITS

vs.	Avg.	AB	H	2B	3B	HR	RBI	BB	SO	OBP	Slg.
L	.347	147	51	8	2	12	34	16	17	.409	.673
R	.245	473	116	22	1	16	63	31	69	.292	.397

							BATTING												FIELDING	
Year Team (League)	Pos.	G	AB	R	H	2B	3B	HR	RBI	BB	SO	HBP	GDP	SB-CS	Avg.	OBP	SLG	OPS	E	Avg.
1997—St. Catharines (NYP)	OF	66	264	52	81	20	1	10	31	30	44	1	2	8-6	.307	.377	.504	.881	7	.953
1998—Hagerstown (S. Atl.)	OF	134	509	86	145	35	2	11	65	49	84	1	8	13-8	.285	.348	.426	.774	5	.980
1999—Dunedin (Fla. St.)	OF-DH	70	265	43	91	16	2	11	43	26	34	1	6	13-2	.343	.403	.543	.946	1	.993
—Knoxville (Sou.)	OF	26	106	18	36	6	2	3	17	12	15	0	0	6-2	.340	.400	.519	.919	0	1.000
—Syracuse (Int'l)	OF	33	129	20	40	8	1	4	21	10	22	1	3	5-1	.310	.357	.481	.837	2	.976
—Toronto (A.L.)	OF	24	88	8	23	5	0	1	8	4	18	0	6	1-1	.261	.293	.352	.646	0	1.000
2000—Syracuse (Int'l)	OF	127	493	76	120	31	7	16	66	48	88	4	8	23-4	.243	.313	.432	.745	3	.990
—Toronto (A.L.)	OF	3	2	0	0	0	0	0	0	0	0	0	0	0-0	.000	.000	.000	.000	0	1.000
2001—Syracuse (Int'l)	OF	107	413	57	116	27	4	12	52	29	68	4	3	15-11	.281	.333	.453	.785	5	.978
—Toronto (A.L.)	OF	30	96	14	30	8	0	1	6	5	15	1	0	5-0	.313	.350	.427	.777	2	.969
2002—Toronto (A.L.)	OF	159	608	87	167	34	4	23	100	27	85	3	15	9-4	.275	.305	.457	.762	3	.992
2003—Toronto (A.L.)	OF	161	678	118	*215	*49	5	33	117	42	80	7	21	4-1	.317	.359	.550	.909	4	.990
2004—Toronto (A.L.)	OF-DH	134	536	82	146	34	2	23	67	51	83	2	17	9-2	.272	.337	.472	.809	1	.997
2005—Toronto (A.L.)	OF-DH	156	620	78	167	30	3	28	97	47	86	3	13	8-3	.269	.320	.463	.783	0	1.000
Major League totals (7 years)		667	2628	387	748	160	14	109	395	176	367	16	72	36-11	.285	.330	.481	.811	10	.994

ALL-STAR GAME RECORD

	G	AB	R	H	2B	3B	HR	RBI	BB	SO	HBP	GDP	SB-CS	Avg.	OBP	SLG	OPS	E	Avg.
All-Star Game totals (1 year)	1	2	1	1	0	0	1	0	0	0	0	0	0-0	.500	.500	1.000	1.500	0	1.000

WERTH, JAYSON   OF

PERSONAL: Born May 20, 1979, in Springfield, Ill. ... 6-5/215. ... Bats right, throws right. ... Full name: Jayson Richard Werth. ... High school: Chatham Glenwood (Chatham, Ill.). ... Stepson of Dennis Werth, outfielder/first baseman with two major league teams (1979-82); nephew of Dick Schofield, infielder with four major league teams (1983-96); grandson of Dick Schofield, infielder/outfielder with six major league teams (1953-71).

TRANSACTIONS/CAREER NOTES: Selected by Baltimore Orioles organization in first round (22nd pick overall) of 1997 free-agent draft. ... Traded by Orioles to Toronto Blue Jays for P John Bale (December 11, 2000). ... On disabled list (March 21-April 13, 2003); included rehabilitation assignment Dunedin. ... Traded by Blue Jays to Los Angeles Dodgers for P Jason Frasor (March 29, 2004). ... On disabled list (April 6-June 4, 2004); included rehabilitation assignment to Las Vegas. ... On disabled list (April 2-May 25 and July 28-August 11, 2005); included rehabilitation assignments to Las Vegas.

2005 GAMES PLAYED BY POSITION (MLB): OF—101, DH—1.

SCOUTING REPORT
Offense: He is a strong, athletic player with good tools. Swing is on the long side, but has good power to all fields when he extends his arms. Still has problems with breaking stuff and pitches on the inner half. Is a good runner, especially for a player his size. *Defense:* Werth has played all three outfield spots but has spent the most time in left; his tools and abilities are better suited for the corners. Has a good arm with above-average carry. Range is average. *Outlook:* He has the tools to play every day but needs to stay healthy for an entire season. Is capable of hitting 25 home runs a year but must cut down his strikeouts. **Grade 6.7**

JAYSON WERTH'S HITTING ZONE

.353	.250	.200
.241	.389	.256
.143	.375	.208

LEFTY-RIGHTY SPLITS

vs.	Avg.	AB	H	2B	3B	HR	RBI	BB	SO	OBP	Slg.
L	.239	67	16	5	0	0	11	11	23	.342	.313
R	.233	270	63	17	2	7	32	37	91	.337	.389

									BATTING										FIELDING	
Year — Team (League)	Pos.	G	AB	R	H	2B	3B	HR	RBI	BB	SO	HBP	GDP	SB-CS	Avg.	OBP	SLG	OPS	E	Avg.
1997— GC Orioles (GCL)	1B-C	32	88	16	26	6	0	1	8	22	22	0	0	7-1	.295	.432	.398	.830	9	.958
1998— Delmarva (S. Atl.)	C	120	408	71	108	20	3	8	53	50	92	15	14	21-6	.265	.364	.387	.751	9	.991
— Bowie (East.)	C	5	19	2	3	2	0	0	1	2	6	0	0	1-0	.158	.238	.263	.501	0	1.000
1999— Frederick (Carol.)	C	66	236	41	72	10	1	3	30	37	37	3	4	16-3	.305	.403	.394	.797	10	.981
— Bowie (East.)	C-OF	35	121	18	33	5	1	1	11	17	26	2	1	7-1	.273	.364	.355	.719	1	.996
2000— Bowie (East.)	C-OF	85	276	47	63	16	2	5	26	54	50	4	10	9-3	.228	.361	.355	.716	7	.988
— Frederick (Carol.)	C	24	83	16	23	3	0	2	18	10	15	0	3	5-1	.277	.347	.386	.733	2	.985
2001— Dunedin (Fla. St.)	C	21	70	9	14	3	0	2	14	17	19	0	2	1-1	.200	.356	.329	.685	0	1.000
— Tennessee (Sou.)	C-1B	104	369	51	105	23	1	18	69	63	93	3	5	12-3	.285	.387	.499	.886	7	.988
2002— Syracuse (Int'l)	OF-C	127	443	65	114	25	2	18	82	67	125	4	7	24-7	.257	.354	.445	.798	5	.985
— Toronto (A.L.)	OF	15	46	4	12	2	1	0	6	6	11	0	4	1-0	.261	.340	.348	.687	0	1.000
2003— Dunedin (Fla. St.)	OF-DH	18	62	10	23	5	0	4	18	3	14	0	2	1-0	.371	.388	.645	1.033	0	1.000
— Toronto (A.L.)	OF-DH	26	48	7	10	4	0	2	10	3	22	0	0	1-0	.208	.255	.417	.672	0	1.000
— Syracuse (Int'l)	OF-DH	64	236	37	56	19	1	9	34	15	68	2	7	11-1	.237	.285	.441	.726	7	.954
2004— Las Vegas (PCL)	OF-DH	14	51	13	21	2	1	5	20	8	10	1	2	2-0	.412	.500	.784	1.284	0	1.000
— Los Angeles (N.L.)	OF-DH	89	290	56	76	11	3	16	47	30	85	4	1	4-1	.262	.338	.486	.825	4	.970
2005— Las Vegas (PCL)	OF	15	49	9	18	0	0	3	10	13	17	2	0	6-1	.367	.516	.551	1.067	2	.957
— Los Angeles (N.L.)	OF-DH	102	337	46	79	22	2	7	43	48	114	6	10	11-2	.234	.338	.374	.711	3	.987
American League totals (2 years)		41	94	11	22	6	1	2	16	9	33	0	4	2-0	.234	.298	.383	.681	0	1.000
National League totals (2 years)		191	627	102	155	33	5	23	90	78	199	10	11	15-3	.247	.338	.426	.764	7	.982
Major League totals (4 years)		232	721	113	177	39	6	25	106	87	232	10	15	17-3	.245	.333	.420	.753	7	.984

DIVISION SERIES RECORD

Year — Team (League)	Pos.	G	AB	R	H	2B	3B	HR	RBI	BB	SO	HBP	GDP	SB-CS	Avg.	OBP	SLG	OPS	E	Avg.
2004— Los Angeles (N.L.)	OF	4	14	3	4	1	0	2	3	3	4	0	0	0-0	.286	.412	.786	1.197	0	1.000

WESTBROOK, JAKE   P

PERSONAL: Born September 29, 1977, in Athens, Ga. ... 6-3/185. ... Throws right, bats right. ... Full name: Jacob Cauthen Westbrook. ... High school: Madison County (Danielsville, Ga.).

TRANSACTIONS/CAREER NOTES: Selected by Colorado Rockies organization in first round (21st pick overall) of 1996 free-agent draft. ... Traded by Rockies with P John Nicholson and OF Mark Hamlin to Montreal Expos for 2B Mike Lansing (December 16, 1997). ... Traded by Expos with two players to be named to New York Yankees for P Hideki Irabu (December 22, 1999); Yankees acquired Ps Ted Lilly (March 17, 2000) and Christian Parker (March 22, 2000) to complete deal. ... Traded by Yankees with P Zach Day to Cleveland Indians (July 25, 2000), completing deal in which Indians traded OF Dave Justice to Yankees for OF Ricky Ledee and two players to be named (June 29, 2000). ... On disabled list (September 1, 2000-remainder of season). ... On disabled list (March 30-July 11 and August 26, 2002-remainder of season); included rehabilitation assignments to Akron and Buffalo.

CAREER HITTING: 0-for-6 (.000), 0 R, 0 2B, 0 3B, 0 HR, 0 RBI.

SCOUTING REPORT
Throws: Westbrook has an outstanding sinker. Throws an 88-93 mph fastball, an 81-84 slider and a changeup. *Tendencies:* His sinker is as good as any in the league. Pounds the strike zone with it, making it difficult for hitters to elevate the ball. Has a quick, late-breaking slider that allows him to pitch to both sides of the plate. Has good arm speed on his changeup. *Outlook:* Westbrook continues to improve. Maintained his poise after a slow start in 2005 and won 15 games. **Grade 8**

JAKE WESTBROOK'S PITCHING ZONE

.211	.500	.324
.234	.427	.287
.189	.234	.290

LEFTY-RIGHTY SPLITS

vs.	Avg.	AB	H	2B	3B	HR	RBI	BB	SO	OBP	Slg.
L	.275	411	113	28	1	8	44	32	59	.330	.406
R	.255	411	105	18	1	11	66	24	60	.302	.384

Year — Team (League)	W	L	Pct.	ERA	WHIP	G	GS	CG	ShO	Hld.	Sv.-Opp.	IP	H	R	ER	HR	BB-IBB	SO	Avg.
1996— Ariz. Rockies (Ariz.)	4	2	.667	2.87	1.28	11	11	0	0	...	0-...	62.2	66	33	20	0	14-0	57	.269
— Portland (N'west)	1	1	.500	2.55	1.09	4	4	0	0	...	0-...	24.2	22	8	7	1	5-0	19	.237
1997— Asheville (S. Atl.)	14	11	.560	4.82	1.36	28	27	3	2	...	0-...	170.0	176	93	91	16	55-0	92	.269
1998— Jupiter (Fla. St.)	11	6	.647	3.26	1.34	27	27	2	0	...	0-...	171.0	169	70	62	11	60-0	79	.264

Year Team (League)	W	L	Pct.	ERA	WHIP	G	GS	CG	ShO	Hld.	Sv.-Opp.	IP	H	R	ER	HR	BB-IBB	SO	Avg.
1999— Harrisburg (East.)	11	5	.688	3.92	1.39	27	27	2	•2	...	0-...	174.2	180	88	76	14	63-1	90	.274
2000— Columbus (Int'l)	5	7	.417	4.65	1.48	16	15	2	0	...	0-...	89.0	94	53	46	3	38-0	61	.272
— New York (A.L.)	0	2	.000	13.50	2.85	3	2	0	0	0	0-0	6.2	15	10	10	1	4-1	1	.469
2001— Buffalo (Int'l)	8	1	.889	3.20	1.28	12	12	0	0	...	0-...	64.2	60	27	23	2	23-0	45	.249
— Cleveland (A.L.)	4	4	.500	5.85	1.56	23	6	0	0	5	0-0	64.2	79	43	42	6	22-4	48	.306
2002— Akron (East.)	0	1	.000	4.80	0.93	3	3	0	0	...	0-...	15.0	13	8	8	0	1-0	8	.228
— Buffalo (Int'l)	1	0	1.000	6.00	1.33	1	1	0	0	...	0-...	6.0	8	4	4	1	0-0	2	.333
— Cleveland (A.L.)	1	3	.250	5.83	1.49	11	4	0	0	1	0-2	41.2	50	30	27	6	12-1	20	.296
2003— Buffalo (Int'l)	1	0	1.000	0.40	0.40	2	2	0	0	...	0-...	10.0	0	0	0	0	4-0	7	.000
— Cleveland (A.L.)	7	10	.412	4.33	1.49	34	22	1	0	0	0-0	133.0	142	70	64	9	56-1	58	.281
2004— Cleveland (A.L.)	14	9	.609	3.38	1.25	33	30	•5	1	0	0-0	215.2	208	95	81	19	61-3	116	.255
2005— Cleveland (A.L.)	15	15	.500	4.49	1.30	34	34	2	0	0	0-0	210.2	218	121	105	19	56-3	119	.265
Major League totals (6 years)	41	43	.488	4.40	1.37	138	98	8	1	7	0-2	672.1	712	369	329	60	211-13	362	.274

WHEELER, DAN   P

PERSONAL: Born December 10, 1977, in Providence, R.I. ... 6-3/222. ... Throws right, bats right. ... Full name: Daniel Michael Wheeler. ... High school: Pilgrim (Warwick, R.I.). ... Junior college: Central Arizona.

TRANSACTIONS/CAREER NOTES: Selected by Tampa Bay Devil Rays organization in 34th round of 1996 free-agent draft. ... Released by Devil Rays (December 13, 2001). ... Signed by Atlanta Braves organization (January 10, 2002). ... Signed as a free agent by New York Mets organization (January 27, 2003). ... Traded by Mets to Houston Astros for P Adam Seuss (August 27, 2004). ... On suspended list (September 24-27, 2004).

CAREER HITTING: 1-for-7 (.143), 1 R, 0 2B, 0 3B, 0 HR, 0 RBI.

SCOUTING REPORT **Throws:** Wheeler's fastball tops out at 91 mph. Also has a curveball at 75, a slider at 81-83 and a split-finger fastball. **Tendencies:** His confidence in his fastball was renewed last season; his ability to consistently keep it down has made him more aggressive. Slider is short and quick-breaking. Splitter has good late action down in the zone; used it late in the count and made hitters chase it. **Outlook:** Wheeler's emergence as a quality setup reliever was a major development in the Astros' playoff push last year. He'll show that his 2005 success was no fluke. **Grade 7.6**

DAN WHEELER'S PITCHING ZONE

.000	.364	.375
.233	.275	.229
.154	.348	.136

LEFTY-RIGHTY SPLITS

vs.	Avg.	AB	H	2B	3B	HR	RBI	BB	SO	OBP	Slg.
L	.204	108	22	4	0	3	10	7	21	.259	.324
R	.204	152	31	9	0	4	14	12	48	.269	.342

Year Team (League)	W	L	Pct.	ERA	WHIP	G	GS	CG	ShO	Hld.	Sv.-Opp.	IP	H	R	ER	HR	BB-IBB	SO	Avg.
1997— Hudson Valley (NYP)	6	7	.462	3.00	1.10	15	15	0	0	...	0-...	84.0	75	38	28	2	17-0	81	.228
1998— Char., S.C. (S. Atl.)	12	14	.462	4.43	1.30	29	29	3	1	...	0-...	181.0	206	96	89	16	29-0	136	.290
1999— Orlando (Sou.)	3	0	1.000	3.26	1.10	9	9	0	0	...	0-...	58.0	56	27	21	7	8-0	53	.252
— Durham (Int'l)	7	5	.583	4.92	1.55	14	14	2	1	...	0-...	82.1	103	59	45	16	25-0	58	.307
— Tampa Bay (A.L.)	0	4	.000	5.87	1.57	6	6	0	0	0	0-0	30.2	35	20	20	7	13-1	32	.287
2000— Tampa Bay (A.L.)	1	1	.500	5.48	1.74	11	2	0	0	1	0-1	23.0	29	14	14	2	11-2	17	.302
— Durham (Int'l)	5	11	.313	5.63	1.50	26	26	0	0	...	0-...	150.1	183	109	94	35	42-1	91	.300
2001— Durham (Int'l)	3	5	.375	5.23	1.27	18	10	0	0	...	0-...	65.1	72	51	38	11	11-0	39	.271
— Tampa Bay (A.L.)	1	0	1.000	8.66	1.98	13	0	0	0	0	0-0	17.2	30	17	17	3	5-0	12	.375
— Orlando (Sou.)	0	2	.000	2.81	1.31	3	3	0	0	...	0-...	16.0	15	5	5	2	6-1	12	.242
2002— Richmond (Int'l)	9	6	.600	4.65	1.32	27	25	0	0	...	0-...	155.0	163	87	80	23	42-0	110	.268
2003— Norfolk (Int'l)	4	2	.667	3.94	1.40	22	5	0	0	...	4-...	45.2	48	20	20	4	16-3	44	.265
— New York (N.L.)	1	3	.250	3.71	1.29	35	0	0	0	0	2-3	51.0	49	23	21	6	17-4	35	.253
2004— Norfolk (Int'l)	1	0	1.000	2.46	1.36	5	0	0	0	...	0-...	7.1	8	2	2	0	2-0	10	.276
— New York (N.L.)	3	1	.750	4.80	1.62	32	1	0	0	3	0-0	50.2	65	29	27	9	17-2	46	.307
— Houston (N.L.)	0	0	...	2.51	0.98	14	0	0	0	2	0-0	14.1	11	4	4	1	3-0	9	.216
2005— Houston (N.L.)	2	3	.400	2.21	0.98	71	0	0	0	17	3-5	73.1	53	18	18	7	19-3	69	.204
American League totals (3 years)	2	5	.286	6.43	1.72	30	8	0	0	1	0-1	71.1	94	51	51	12	29-3	61	.315
National League totals (3 years)	6	7	.462	3.33	1.24	152	1	0	0	22	5-8	189.1	178	74	70	23	56-9	159	.248
Major League totals (6 years)	8	12	.400	4.18	1.37	182	9	0	0	23	5-9	260.2	272	125	121	35	85-12	220	.268

DIVISION SERIES RECORD

Year Team (League)	W	L	Pct.	ERA	WHIP	G	GS	CG	ShO	Hld.	Sv.-Opp.	IP	H	R	ER	HR	BB-IBB	SO	Avg.
2004— Houston (N.L.)	0	0	...	0.00	0.00	1	0	0	0	0	0-0	1.0	0	0	0	0	0-0	0	.000
2005— Houston (N.L.)	0	0	...	2.08	1.62	3	0	0	0	0	0-0	4.1	4	1	1	0	3-1	5	.235
Division series totals (2 years)	0	0	...	1.69	1.31	4	0	0	0	0	0-0	5.1	4	1	1	0	3-1	5	.190

CHAMPIONSHIP SERIES RECORD

Year Team (League)	W	L	Pct.	ERA	WHIP	G	GS	CG	ShO	Hld.	Sv.-Opp.	IP	H	R	ER	HR	BB-IBB	SO	Avg.
2004— Houston (N.L.)	1	0	1.000	0.00	0.57	4	0	0	0	0	0-0	7.0	4	0	0	0	0-0	9	.160
2005— Houston (N.L.)	0	0	...	0.00	0.75	3	0	0	0	2	0-0	2.2	2	0	0	0	0-0	2	.200
Champ. series totals (2 years)	1	0	1.000	0.00	0.62	7	0	0	0	2	0-0	9.2	6	0	0	0	0-0	11	.171

WORLD SERIES RECORD

Year Team (League)	W	L	Pct.	ERA	WHIP	G	GS	CG	ShO	Hld.	Sv.-Opp.	IP	H	R	ER	HR	BB-IBB	SO	Avg.
2005— Houston (N.L.)	0	0	...	13.50	1.50	2	0	0	0	1	0-0	2.0	2	3	3	0	1-0	1	.250

WHITE, GABE   P

PERSONAL: Born November 20, 1971, in Sebring, Fla. ... 6-2/205. ... Throws left, bats left. ... Full name: Gabriel Allen White. ... High school: Sebring (Fla.).

TRANSACTIONS/CAREER NOTES: Selected by Montreal Expos organization in supplemental round ("sandwich pick" between first and second rounds, 28th pick overall) of 1990 free-agent draft; pick received as part of compensation for California Angels signing Type A free-agent P Mark Langston. ... Traded by Expos to Cincinnati Reds for 2B Jhonny Carvajal (December 15, 1995). ... On disabled list (September 17, 1996-remainder of season). ... Traded by Reds to Colorado Rockies for P Manny Aybar (April 7, 2000). ... Traded

LEFTY-RIGHTY SPLITS

vs.	Avg.	AB	H	2B	3B	HR	RBI	BB	SO	OBP	Slg.
L	.250	12	3	1	0	0	1	0	0	.250	.333
R	.440	25	11	2	0	1	3	1	1	.462	.640

W

by Rockies with P Luke Hudson to Reds for SS Pokey Reese and P Dennys Reyes (December 18, 2001). ... On disabled list (July 12-31 and August 29, 2002-remainder of season). ... On disabled list (June 21-August 26, 2003); included rehabilitation assignments to Louisville, GCL Yankees, Tampa and Trenton. ... Traded by Reds to New York Yankees for cash (July 31, 2003). ... Traded by Yankees to Reds for P Charlie Manning, a player to be named and cash (June 18, 2004). ... Signed as a free agent by Atlanta Braves (January 7, 2005). ... Released by Braves (March 30, 2005). ... Signed by St. Louis Cardinals organization (April 24, 2005).

CAREER HITTING: 4-for-38 (.105), 1 R, 0 2B, 0 3B, 1 HR, 3 RBI.

Year	Team (League)	W	L	Pct.	ERA	WHIP	G	GS	CG	ShO	Hld.	Sv.-Opp.	IP	H	R	ER	HR	BB-IBB	SO	Avg.
1990—	GC Expos (GCL)	4	2	.667	3.14	1.08	11	11	1	0	...	0-...	57.1	50	21	20	3	12-0	41	.231
1991—	Sumter (S. Atl.)	6	9	.400	3.26	1.21	24	24	5	0	...	0-...	149.0	127	73	54	7	53-0	140	.229
1992—	Rockford (Midwest)	14	8	.636	2.84	1.12	27	27	7	0	...	0-...	187.0	148	73	59	10	61-0	176	.215
1993—	Harrisburg (East.)	7	2	.778	2.16	1.08	16	16	2	1	...	0-...	100.0	80	30	24	4	28-0	80	.221
—	Ottawa (Int'l)	2	1	.667	3.12	1.09	6	6	1	1	...	0-...	40.1	38	15	14	3	6-0	28	.242
1994—	W.P. Beach (FSL)	1	0	1.000	1.50	0.50	1	1	0	0	...	0-...	6.0	2	2	1	0	1-0	4	.105
—	Ottawa (Int'l)	8	3	.727	5.05	1.44	14	14	0	0	...	0-...	73.0	77	49	41	11	28-2	63	.270
—	Montreal (N.L.)	1	1	.500	6.08	1.48	7	5	0	0	0	1-1	23.2	24	16	16	4	11-0	17	.261
1995—	Ottawa (Int'l)	2	3	.400	3.90	1.20	12	12	0	0	...	0-...	62.1	58	31	27	10	17-0	37	.244
—	Montreal (N.L.)	1	2	.333	7.01	1.36	19	1	0	0	...	0-0	25.2	26	21	20	7	9-0	25	.260
1996—	Indianapolis (A.A.)	6	3	.667	2.77	1.14	11	11	0	0	...	0-...	68.1	69	25	21	6	9-3	51	.266
1997—	Indianapolis (A.A.)	7	4	.636	2.82	1.16	20	19	0	0	...	0-...	118.0	119	46	37	10	18-0	62	.257
—	Cincinnati (N.L.)	2	2	.500	4.39	1.15	12	6	0	0	3	1-1	41.0	39	20	20	6	8-1	25	.253
1998—	Cincinnati (N.L.)	5	5	.500	4.01	1.15	69	3	0	0	6	9-13	98.2	86	46	44	17	27-6	83	.231
1999—	Cincinnati (N.L.)	1	2	.333	4.43	1.34	50	0	0	0	3	0-1	61.0	68	31	30	13	14-1	61	.281
2000—	Cincinnati (N.L.)	0	0	...	18.00	3.00	1	0	0	0	0	0-0	1.0	2	2	2	1	1-0	2	.400
—	Colorado (N.L.)	11	2	.846	2.17	0.92	67	0	0	0	19	5-9	83.0	62	21	20	5	14-2	82	.208
2001—	Colorado (N.L.)	1	7	.125	6.25	1.42	69	0	0	0	8	0-2	67.2	70	47	47	18	26-5	47	.270
2002—	Colorado (N.L.)	6	1	.857	2.98	1.09	62	0	0	0	19	0-1	54.1	49	19	18	3	10-2	41	.239
2003—	Cincinnati (N.L.)	3	0	1.000	3.93	1.22	34	0	0	0	6	0-1	34.1	36	15	15	5	6-3	23	.275
—	Louisville (Int'l)	0	0	...	9.00	3.00	1	1	0	0	...	0-...	1.0	2	1	1	0	1-0	0	.400
—	GC Yankees (GCL)	0	0	...	0.00	1.00	1	1	0	0	...	0-...	1.0	0	0	0	0	1-0	1	.000
—	Tampa (Fla. St.)	0	0	...	0.00	1.50	1	1	0	0	...	0-...	0.2	1	0	0	0	0-0	0	.333
—	Trenton (East.)	0	0	...	7.71	1.30	2	2	0	0	...	0-...	2.1	3	2	2	1	0-0	2	.300
—	New York (A.L.)	2	1	.667	4.38	0.81	12	0	0	0	6	0-1	12.1	8	7	6	2	2-1	6	.182
2004—	New York (A.L.)	0	1	.000	8.27	1.94	24	0	0	0	3	0-2	20.2	33	19	19	2	7-4	8	.355
—	Cincinnati (N.L.)	1	2	.333	6.23	1.13	40	0	0	0	9	1-3	39.0	39	27	27	12	5-0	33	.257
2005—	Memphis (PCL)	0	0	...	0.00	0.68	8	0	0	0	1	1-1	7.1	4	0	0	0	1-0	8	.154
—	St. Louis (N.L.)	0	0	...	2.16	1.80	6	0	0	0	0	0-0	8.1	14	2	2	1	1-1	1	.378
	American League totals (2 years)	2	2	.500	6.82	1.52	36	0	0	0	9	0-3	33.0	41	26	25	4	9-5	14	.299
	National League totals (11 years)	32	24	.571	4.37	1.20	436	15	0	0	73	17-32	537.2	515	267	261	92	132-21	440	.252
	Major League totals (11 years)	34	26	.567	4.51	1.22	472	15	0	0	82	17-35	570.2	556	293	286	96	141-26	454	.255

DIVISION SERIES RECORD

Year	Team (League)	W	L	Pct.	ERA	WHIP	G	GS	CG	ShO	Hld.	Sv.-Opp.	IP	H	R	ER	HR	BB-IBB	SO	Avg.
2003—	New York (A.L.)	0	0	...	0.00	0.75	1	0	0	0	0	0-0	1.1	1	0	0	0	0-0	1	.200

CHAMPIONSHIP SERIES RECORD

Year	Team (League)	W	L	Pct.	ERA	WHIP	G	GS	CG	ShO	Hld.	Sv.-Opp.	IP	H	R	ER	HR	BB-IBB	SO	Avg.
2003—	New York (A.L.)	0	0	...	4.50	2.00	2	0	0	0	0	0-0	2.0	4	1	1	1	0-0	1	.444

WHITE, RICK   P

PERSONAL: Born December 23, 1968, in Springfield, Ohio. ... 6-4/230. ... Throws right, bats right. ... Full name: Richard Allen White. ... High school: Kenton Ridge (Springfield, Ohio). ... Junior college: Paducah (Ky.) Community College.

TRANSACTIONS/CAREER NOTES: Selected by Pittsburgh Pirates organization in 15th round of 1990 free-agent draft. ... On disabled list (April 14-May 17, 1995); included rehabilitation assignment to GCL Pirates. ... Signed as a free agent by Tampa Bay Devil Rays organization (February 4, 1997). ... Loaned by Devil Rays organization to Chicago Cubs organization (April 3-September 11, 1997). ... Traded by Devil Rays with OF Bubba Trammell to New York Mets for OF Jason Tyner and P Paul Wilson (July 28, 2000). ... On disabled list (March 31-April 21 and May 1-17, 2001). ... Signed as a free agent by Colorado Rockies (January 10, 2002). ... On disabled list (May 27-June 18, 2002); included rehabilitation assignment to Colorado Springs. ... Released by Rockies (August 12, 2002). ... Signed by St. Louis Cardinals organization (August 17, 2002). ... Signed as a free agent by Chicago White Sox (January 22, 2003). ... Released by White Sox (August 11, 2003). ... Signed by Houston Astros (August 14, 2003). ... Signed as a free agent by Los Angeles Dodgers organization (January 16, 2004). ... Traded by Dodgers to Cleveland Indians for OF Trey Dyson (April 25, 2004). ... Signed as a free agent by Pirates organization (January 27, 2005).

CAREER HITTING: 4-for-42 (.095), 1 R, 1 2B, 0 3B, 0 HR, 1 RBI.

RICK WHITE'S PITCHING ZONE

.375	.300	.389
.298	.485	.298
.344	.167	.278

LEFTY-RIGHTY SPLITS

vs.	Avg.	AB	H	2B	3B	HR	RBI	BB	SO	OBP	Slg.
L	.314	102	32	8	0	1	16	14	15	.397	.422
R	.305	190	58	8	2	2	33	15	25	.362	.400

Year	Team (League)	W	L	Pct.	ERA	WHIP	G	GS	CG	ShO	Hld.	Sv.-Opp.	IP	H	R	ER	HR	BB-IBB	SO	Avg.
1990—	GC Pirates (GCL)	3	1	.750	0.76	0.84	7	6	0	0	...	0-...	35.2	26	11	3	0	4-0	27	.194
—	Welland (N.Y.-Penn.)	1	4	.200	3.26	1.37	9	5	1	0	...	0-...	38.2	39	19	14	2	14-2	43	.265
1991—	Augusta (S. Atl.)	4	4	.500	3.00	1.37	34	0	0	0	...	6-...	63.0	68	26	21	2	18-2	52	.264
—	Salem (Carol.)	2	3	.400	4.66	1.08	13	5	1	0	...	1-...	46.1	41	27	24	2	9-3	36	.233
1992—	Salem (Carol.)	7	9	.438	3.80	1.16	18	18	3	0	...	0-...	120.2	116	58	51	15	24-1	70	.255
—	Carolina (Sou.)	1	7	.125	4.21	1.34	10	10	1	0	...	0-...	57.2	59	32	27	8	18-1	45	.265
1993—	Carolina (Sou.)	4	3	.571	3.50	1.02	12	12	1	0	...	0-...	69.1	59	29	27	5	12-0	52	.231
—	Buffalo (A.A.)	0	3	.000	3.54	1.18	7	3	0	0	...	0-...	28.0	25	13	11	1	8-0	16	.238
1994—	Pittsburgh (N.L.)	4	5	.444	3.82	1.27	43	5	0	0	6	6-9	75.1	79	35	32	9	17-3	38	.280
1995—	Pittsburgh (N.L.)	2	3	.400	4.75	1.53	15	9	0	0	0	0-0	55.0	66	33	29	3	18-0	29	.299
—	Calgary (PCL)	6	4	.600	4.20	1.35	14	11	1	0	...	0-...	79.1	97	40	37	13	10-0	56	.302
1996—	GC Pirates (GCL)	0	0	...	2.25	0.92	3	3	0	0	...	0-...	12.0	8	4	3	0	3-0	8	.205
—	Carolina (Sou.)	0	1	.000	11.37	1.58	2	1	0	0	...	0-...	6.1	9	8	8	2	1-0	7	.321
1997—	Orlando (Sou.)	5	7	.417	4.71	1.34	39	8	0	0	...	12-...	86.0	93	55	45	7	22-2	65	.275
1998—	Durham (Int'l)	4	2	.667	4.22	1.39	9	9	1	0	...	0-...	53.1	56	29	25	3	11-0	31	.294
—	Tampa Bay (A.L.)	2	6	.250	3.80	1.30	38	5	0	0	...	0-...	68.2	66	32	29	8	23-2	39	.253
1999—	Tampa Bay (A.L.)	5	3	.625	4.08	1.57	63	0	0	0	4	0-2	108.0	132	56	49	8	38-5	81	.304
2000—	Tampa Bay (A.L.)	3	6	.333	3.41	1.16	44	0	0	0	7	2-5	71.1	57	30	27	7	26-3	47	.220

W

Year	Team (League)	W	L	Pct.	ERA	WHIP	G	GS	CG	ShO	Hld.	Sv.-Opp.	IP	H	R	ER	HR	BB-IBB	SO	Avg.
—	New York (N.L.)	2	3	.400	3.81	1.34	22	0	0	0	2	1-2	28.1	26	14	12	2	12-2	20	.232
2001—	New York (N.L.)	4	5	.444	3.88	1.26	55	0	0	0	10	2-4	69.2	71	38	30	7	17-4	51	.257
2002—	Colorado (N.L.)	2	6	.250	6.20	1.65	41	0	0	0	9	0-1	40.2	49	30	28	4	18-4	27	.310
—	Memphis (PCL)	0	0	...	2.45	1.91	3	0	0	0	...	0-...	3.2	4	1	1	0	3-0	4	.286
—	St. Louis (N.L.)	3	1	.750	0.82	0.73	20	0	0	0	7	0-0	22.0	13	3	2	0	3-1	14	.169
2003—	Chicago (A.L.)	1	2	.333	6.61	1.45	34	0	0	0	3	1-1	47.2	56	39	35	11	13-2	37	.295
—	Houston (N.L.)	0	0	...	3.72	1.34	15	0	0	0	1	0-0	19.1	18	9	8	2	8-0	17	.243
2004—	Las Vegas (PCL)	0	0	...	0.00	0.43	6	0	0	0	...	2-...	11.2	4	0	0	0	1-0	14	.105
—	Cleveland (A.L.)	5	5	.500	5.29	1.49	59	0	0	0	2	1-3	78.1	88	52	46	15	29-7	44	.293
2005—	Pittsburgh (N.L.)	4	7	.364	3.72	1.59	71	0	0	0	12	2-3	75.0	90	39	31	3	29-10	40	.308
American League totals (5 years)		16	22	.421	4.48	1.41	238	4	0	0	13	4-11	374.0	399	209	186	49	129-19	248	.276
National League totals (7 years)		21	30	.412	4.02	1.39	282	14	0	0	44	11-19	385.1	412	201	172	30	122-24	236	.276
Major League totals (10 years)		37	52	.416	4.24	1.40	520	18	0	0	57	15-30	759.1	811	410	358	79	251-43	484	.276

DIVISION SERIES RECORD

Year	Team (League)	W	L	Pct.	ERA	WHIP	G	GS	CG	ShO	Hld.	Sv.-Opp.	IP	H	R	ER	HR	BB-IBB	SO	Avg.
2000—	New York (N.L.)	1	0	1.000	0.00	3.00	2	0	0	0	0	0-0	2.2	6	0	0	0	2-0	4	.429
2002—	St. Louis (N.L.)	0	0	...	0.00	1.00	2	0	0	0	1	0-1	2.0	1	1	0	0	1-0	1	.125
Division series totals (2 years)		1	0	1.000	0.00	2.14	4	0	0	0	1	0-1	4.2	7	1	0	0	3-0	5	.318

CHAMPIONSHIP SERIES RECORD

Year	Team (League)	W	L	Pct.	ERA	WHIP	G	GS	CG	ShO	Hld.	Sv.-Opp.	IP	H	R	ER	HR	BB-IBB	SO	Avg.
2000—	New York (N.L.)	0	0	...	9.00	2.00	1	0	0	0	0	0-0	3.0	5	3	3	0	1-0	1	.385
2002—	St. Louis (N.L.)	0	1	.000	4.50	1.00	3	0	0	0	1	0-1	4.0	2	2	2	1	2-1	5	.143
Champ. series totals (2 years)		0	1	.000	6.43	1.43	4	0	0	0	1	0-1	7.0	7	5	5	1	3-1	6	.259

WORLD SERIES RECORD

Year	Team (League)	W	L	Pct.	ERA	WHIP	G	GS	CG	ShO	Hld.	Sv.-Opp.	IP	H	R	ER	HR	BB-IBB	SO	Avg.
2000—	New York (N.L.)	0	0	...	6.75	1.50	1	0	0	0	0	0-0	1.1	1	1	1	0	1-1	1	.250

WHITE, RONDELL — OF

PERSONAL: Born February 23, 1972, in Milledgeville, Ga. ... 6-1/225. ... Bats right, throws right. ... Full name: Rondell Bernard White. ... High school: Jones County (Gray, Ga.).

TRANSACTIONS/CAREER NOTES: Selected by Montreal Expos organization in first round (24th pick overall) of 1990 free-agent draft; pick received as part of compensation for California Angels signing Type A free-agent P Mark Langston. ... On disabled list (April 28-July 16, 1996); included rehabilitation assignments to West Palm Beach, GCL Expos and Harrisburg. ... On disabled list (July 21, 1998-remainder of season; June 14-29 and July 2-17, 1999). ... On disabled list (July 8-August 6 and August 27, 2000-remainder of season). ... Traded by Expos to Chicago Cubs for P Scott Downs (July 31, 2000). ... On disabled list (June 26-July 12 and July 14-September 1, 2001); included rehabilitation assignment to West Tenn. ... Signed as a free agent by New York Yankees (December 21, 2001). ... Traded by Yankees to San Diego Padres for OF Bubba Trammell, P Mark Phillips and cash (March 19, 2003). ... Traded by Padres to Kansas City Royals for Ps Chris Tierney and Brian Sanches (August 26, 2003). ... Signed as a free agent by Detroit Tigers (December 19, 2003). ... On disabled list (August 15, 2005-remainder of season).

2005 GAMES PLAYED BY POSITION (MLB): OF—65, DH—30.

SCOUTING REPORT

Offense: White is an aggressive free swinger with a long hitch in his swing. Is a good fastball hitter, especially ones on the inner half. Is a line-drive hitter who will chase the breaking ball out of the zone. Has average power. Is an average runner but doesn't steal much. *Defense:* His arm is short but accurate and he has a quick release. Gets better jumps toward the line than going back; has average range but doesn't take good routes. *Outlook:* The question with White is how the shoulder injury he suffered last season will affect him. Is capable of 20 home runs when healthy. *Grade 6.4*

RONDELL WHITE'S HITTING ZONE

.435	.438	.200
.371	.333	.206
.356	.286	.100

LEFTY-RIGHTY SPLITS

vs.	Avg.	AB	H	2B	3B	HR	RBI	BB	SO	OBP	Slg.
L	.325	83	27	4	1	4	12	5	12	.363	.542
R	.309	291	90	20	2	8	41	12	36	.343	.474

Year	Team (League)	Pos.	G	AB	R	H	2B	3B	HR	RBI	BB	SO	HBP	GDP	SB-CS	Avg.	OBP	SLG	OPS	E	FIELDING Avg.
1990—	GC Expos (GCL)	OF	57	221	33	66	7	4	5	34	17	33	5	4	10-7	.299	.362	.434	.797	2	.973
1991—	Sumter (S. Atl.)	OF	123	465	80	122	23	6	13	68	57	109	8	7	50-17	.262	.351	.422	.772	3	.987
1992—	W.P. Beach (Fla. St.)	OF	111	450	80	142	10	12	4	41	46	78	5	7	42-16	.316	.384	.418	.802	3	.984
—	Harrisburg (East.)	OF	21	89	22	27	7	1	2	7	6	14	4	3	6-1	.303	.374	.472	.846	2	.938
1993—	Harrisburg (East.)	OF	90	372	72	122	16	10	12	52	22	72	5	3	21-6	.328	.371	.522	.892	1	.995
—	Ottawa (Int'l)	OF	37	150	28	57	8	2	7	32	12	20	3	4	10-1	.380	.436	.600	1.036	1	.988
—	Montreal (N.L.)	OF	23	73	9	19	3	1	2	15	7	16	0	1	1-2	.260	.321	.411	.732	0	1.000
1994—	Montreal (N.L.)	OF	40	97	16	27	10	1	2	13	9	18	3	1	1-1	.278	.358	.464	.822	2	.946
—	Ottawa (Int'l)	OF	42	169	23	46	7	0	7	18	15	17	4	5	9-2	.272	.344	.438	.782	2	.979
1995—	Montreal (N.L.)	OF	130	474	87	140	33	4	13	57	41	87	6	11	25-5	.295	.356	.464	.820	4	.986
1996—	Montreal (N.L.)	OF	88	334	35	98	19	4	6	41	22	53	2	11	14-6	.293	.340	.428	.768	2	.990
—	W.P. Beach (Fla. St.)	DH-OF	3	10	0	2	1	0	0	2	0	4	0	0	0-1	.200	.200	.300	.500	1	1.000
—	GC Expos (GCL)	OF	3	12	3	3	0	0	2	4	0	1	0	1	1-0	.250	.250	.750	1.000	0	1.000
—	Harrisburg (East.)	OF	5	20	5	7	1	0	3	6	1	1	0	1	1-1	.350	.381	.850	1.231	0	1.000
1997—	Montreal (N.L.)	OF	151	592	84	160	29	5	28	82	31	111	10	18	16-8	.270	.316	.478	.794	3	.992
1998—	Montreal (N.L.)	OF-DH	97	357	54	107	21	2	17	58	30	57	7	7	16-7	.300	.363	.513	.875	1	.966
1999—	Montreal (N.L.)	OF	138	539	83	168	26	6	22	64	32	85	11	17	10-6	.312	.359	.505	.863	11	.964
2000—	Montreal (N.L.)	OF	75	290	52	89	24	0	11	54	28	67	2	4	5-1	.307	.370	.503	.873	1	.994
—	Chicago (N.L.)	OF	19	67	7	22	4	0	2	10	5	12	2	0	0-2	.328	.392	.448	.840	0	1.000
2001—	Chicago (N.L.)	OF	95	323	43	99	19	1	17	50	26	56	7	14	1-0	.307	.371	.529	.900	3	.979
—	West Tenn (Sou.)	OF	9	28	2	4	1	0	2	3	1	8	0	0	0-0	.143	.226	.393	.619	0	1.000
2002—	New York (N.L.)	OF-DH	126	455	59	109	21	0	14	62	25	86	8	11	1-2	.240	.288	.378	.666	0	1.000
2003—	San Diego (N.L.)	OF-DH	115	413	49	115	17	3	18	66	25	71	8	11	1-4	.278	.330	.465	.795	4	.979
—	Kansas City (A.L.)	OF-DH	22	75	13	26	6	1	4	21	6	8	2	2	0-0	.347	.400	.613	1.013	1	.978

W

Year Team (League)	Pos.	G	AB	R	H	2B	3B	HR	RBI	BB	SO	HBP	GDP	SB-CS	Avg.	OBP	SLG	OPS	E	Avg.
									BATTING										FIELDING	
2004— Detroit (A.L.)	OF-DH	121	448	76	121	21	2	19	67	39	77	8	13	1-2	.270	.337	.453	.790	3	.977
2005— Detroit (A.L.)	OF-DH	97	374	49	117	24	3	12	53	17	48	5	8	1-0	.313	.348	.489	.837	0	1.000
American League totals (4 years)		366	1352	197	373	72	6	49	203	87	219	23	34	5-4	.276	.327	.447	.774	4	.993
National League totals (10 years)		971	3559	519	1044	203	27	138	507	256	633	58	96	90-42	.293	.348	.482	.830	31	.985
Major League totals (13 years)		1337	4911	716	1417	275	33	187	710	343	852	81	130	93-46	.289	.343	.472	.815	35	.986

DIVISION SERIES RECORD

Year Team (League)	Pos.	G	AB	R	H	2B	3B	HR	RBI	BB	SO	HBP	GDP	SB-CS	Avg.	OBP	SLG	OPS	E	Avg.
2002— New York (A.L.)	DH	1	3	1	1	0	0	1	1	0	0	0	0	0-0	.333	.333	1.333	1.667	0	...

ALL-STAR GAME RECORD

	G	AB	R	H	2B	3B	HR	RBI	BB	SO	HBP	GDP	SB-CS	Avg.	OBP	SLG	OPS	E	Avg.
All-Star Game totals (1 year)	1	1	0	0	0	0	0	0	0	0	0		0-0	.000	.000	.000	.000	0	...

WHITESIDE, ELI

PERSONAL: Born October 22, 1979, in New Albany, Miss. ... 6-2/208. ... Bats right, throws right. ... Full name: Dustin Eli Whiteside. ... High school: W.P. Daniel (New Albany, Miss.). ... College: Delta State.

TRANSACTIONS/CAREER NOTES: Selected by Baltimore Orioles organization in sixth round of 2001 free-agent draft.

2005 GAMES PLAYED BY POSITION (MLB): C—9.

LEFTY-RIGHTY SPLITS

vs.	Avg.	AB	H	2B	3B	HR	RBI	BB	SO	OBP	Slg.
L	.400	5	2	0	0	0	0	0	1	.400	.400
R	.143	7	1	0	0	0	1	0	1	.143	.143

Year Team (League)	Pos.	G	AB	R	H	2B	3B	HR	RBI	BB	SO	HBP	GDP	SB-CS	Avg.	OBP	SLG	OPS	E	Avg.
									BATTING										FIELDING	
2001— Delmarva (S. Atl.)	C	61	212	30	53	11	0	7	28	9	45	7	11	1-1	.250	.300	.401	.701	4	.991
2002— Frederick (Carolina)	C	80	313	34	81	19	0	8	42	14	57	4	8	0-0	.259	.296	.396	.692	15	.975
— Bowie (East.)	C	27	99	11	26	5	0	2	11	4	18	3	4	0-1	.263	.311	.374	.685	5	.972
2003— Bowie (East.)	C	81	265	21	54	13	1	1	23	5	44	4	7	0-0	.204	.230	.272	.502	6	.989
— GC Orioles (GCL)	C	1	3	0	1	1	0	0	0	1	1	0	0	0-0	.333	.500	.667	1.167	0	1.000
— Aberdeen (N.Y.-Penn.)	C	2	10	0	7	3	0	0	4	0	1	0	0	1-0	.700	.700	1.000	1.700	1	.917
2004— Bowie (East.)	C	90	297	41	75	18	0	18	60	25	65	1	3	2-2	.253	.310	.495	.805	10	.985
2005— Ottawa (Int'l)	C-DH-3B	95	317	28	74	22	1	4	27	21	65	2	1	1-3	.233	.283	.347	.630	4	.993
— Baltimore (A.L.)	C	9	12	1	3	0	0	0	1	0	2	0	1	0-0	.250	.250	.250	.500	2	.926
Major League totals (1 year)		9	12	1	3	0	0	0	1	0	2	0	1	0-0	.250	.250	.250	.500	2	.926

WHITESIDE, MATT — P

PERSONAL: Born August 8, 1967, in Charleston, Mo. ... 6-0/200. ... Throws right, bats right. ... Full name: Matthew Christopher Whiteside. ... High school: Charleston (Mo.). ... College: Arkansas State.

TRANSACTIONS/CAREER NOTES: Selected by Texas Rangers organization in 25th round of free-agent draft (June 4, 1990). ... On disabled list (May 9-25, 1995). ... Released by Rangers (March 23, 1998). ... Signed by Philadelphia Phillies (March 27, 1998). ... Signed as a free agent by San Diego Padres organization (November 23, 1998). ... Signed as a free agent by Atlanta Braves organization (January 18, 2001). ... Released by Braves (July 5, 2001). ... Signed by Colorado Rockies organization (December 7, 2001). ... Signed by Yokohama of the Japan Central League (January 9, 2003). ... Signed as a free agent by Toronto Blue Jays organization (November 11, 2004).

CAREER HITTING: 0-for-2 (.000), 0 R, 0 2B, 0 3B, 0 HR, 0 RBI.

LEFTY-RIGHTY SPLITS

vs.	Avg.	AB	H	2B	3B	HR	RBI	BB	SO	OBP	Slg.
L	.333	6	2	0	0	1	4	3	1	.600	.833
R	.364	11	4	2	0	2	4	2	4	.462	1.091

Year Team (League)	W	L	Pct.	ERA	WHIP	G	GS	CG	ShO	Hld.	Sv.-Opp.	IP	H	R	ER	HR	BB-IBB	SO	Avg.
1990— Butte (Pion.)	4	4	.500	3.45	1.41	18	5	0	0	...	2-...	58.0	57	33	22	4	25-0	45	.258
1991— Gastonia (S. Atl.)	3	1	.750	2.15	1.02	48	0	0	0	...	29-...	62.2	43	19	15	1	21-0	71	.191
1992— Tulsa (Texas)	0	1	.000	2.41	1.01	33	0	0	0	...	21-...	33.2	31	9	9	2	3-1	30	.238
— Okla. City (A.A.)	1	0	1.000	0.79	0.83	12	0	0	0	...	8-...	12.0	7	1	1	1	3-1	13	.171
— Texas (A.L.)	1	1	.500	1.93	1.32	20	0	0	0	...	4-...	28.0	26	8	6	1	11-...	13	.245
1993— Texas (A.L.)	2	1	.667	4.32	1.38	60	0	0	0	...	1-...	73.0	78	37	35	7	23-...	39	.281
— Okla. City (A.A.)	2	1	.667	5.56	2.08	8	0	0	0	...	1-...	12.0	17	7	7	1	8-0	10	.370
1994— Texas (A.L.)	2	2	.500	5.02	1.57	47	0	0	0	...	1-...	61.0	68	40	34	6	28-...	37	.286
1995— Texas (A.L.)	5	4	.556	4.08	1.26	40	0	0	0	...	3-...	53.0	48	24	24	5	19-...	46	.242
1996— Texas (A.L.)	0	1	.000	6.68	1.67	14	0	0	0	...	0-...	32.1	43	24	24	8	11-...	15	.321
— Okla. City (A.A.)	9	6	.600	3.45	1.27	36	7	0	0	...	0-...	94.0	95	41	36	8	24-2	52	.265
1997— Okla. City (A.A.)	1	1	.500	3.54	1.54	10	1	0	0	...	1-...	28.0	30	14	11	1	13-0	11	.278
— Texas (A.L.)	4	1	.800	5.08	1.53	42	1	0	0	...	1-...	72.2	85	45	41	4	26-...	44	.296
1998— Philadelphia (N.L.)	1	1	.500	8.50	1.78	10	0	0	0	...	0-...	18.0	27	18	17	6	5-...	14	.338
— Scran./W.B. (Int'l)	1	4	.200	6.48	1.59	30	1	0	0	...	5-...	34.0	47	24	24	4	7-0	21	.329
1999— Las Vegas (PCL)	9	5	.643	5.12	1.43	47	3	1	1	...	7-...	89.2	99	59	51	13	29-3	88	.274
— San Diego (N.L.)	1	0	1.000	13.91	2.18	10	0	0	0	...	0-...	11.0	19	17	17	1	5-...	9	.396
2000— Las Vegas (PCL)	2	5	.286	5.28	1.60	23	1	0	0	...	0-...	30.2	34	21	18	6	15-2	31	.279
— San Diego (N.L.)	2	3	.400	4.14	1.32	28	0	0	0	6	0-...	37.0	32	21	17	6	17-...	27	.232
2001— Richmond (Int'l)	0	0	...	0.00	0.50	9	0	0	0	...	4-...	10.0	4	0	0	0	1-1	9	.114
— Atlanta (N.L.)	0	1	.000	7.16	1.84	13	0	0	0	...	0-...	16.1	23	14	13	5	7-...	10	.319
2002— Colo. Springs (PCL)	4	7	.364	5.50	1.41	60	0	0	0	...	26-...	71.0	85	50	43	12	15-4	79	.292
2003— Yo. Bay. (Jp. Cen.)	0	2	.000	7.30	2.00	13	0	0	0	...	2-...	13.0	20	13	10	3	6-0	11	...
— Colo. Springs (PCL)	3	0	1.000	4.66	1.17	21	0	0	0	...	1-...	29.0	26	16	15	2	8-2	15	.239
2004— Richmond (Int'l)	2	4	.333	3.23	1.13	57	0	0	0	...	38-...	64.0	56	23	23	9	16-3	59	.228
2005— Toronto (A.L.)	0	0	...	19.64	3.00	2	0	0	0	0	0-0	3.2	8	8	8	3	5-0	5	.353
— Syracuse (Int'l)	4	0	.000	2.59	0.96	40	0	0	0	7	27-31	41.2	35	14	12	4	5-1	39	.226
American League totals (7 years)	14	10	.583	4.78	1.47	225	1	0	0		9-0	323.2	354	186	172	34	123-0	199	20.824
National League totals (4 years)	4	5	.444	7.00	1.64	61	0	0	0		0-...	82.1	101	70	64	18	34-...	60	.391
Major League totals (11 years)	18	15	.545	5.23	1.51	286	1	0	0	7	9-0	406.0	455	256	236	52	157-0	259	1.655

WICKMAN, BOB — P

PERSONAL: Born February 6, 1969, in Green Bay. ... 6-1/240. ... Throws right, bats right. ... Full name: Robert Joe Wickman. ... High school: Oconto Falls (Wis.). ... College: Wisconsin-Whitewater.

W

TRANSACTIONS/CAREER NOTES: Selected by Chicago White Sox organization in second round of 1990 free-agent draft. ... Traded by White Sox with Ps Melido Perez and Domingo Jean to New York Yankees for 2B Steve Sax and cash (January 10, 1992). ... Traded by Yankees with OF Gerald Williams to Milwaukee Brewers for P Graeme Lloyd and OF Pat Listach (August 23, 1996). ... Traded by Brewers with Ps Steve Woodard and Jason Bere to Cleveland Indians for 1B/OF Richie Sexson, Ps Paul Rigdon and Kane Davis and a player to be named (July 28, 2000); Brewers acquired 2B Marco Scutaro to complete deal (August 30, 2000). ... On disabled list (July 22-August 10 and August 11, 2002-remainder of season). ... On disabled list (March 29, 2003-entire season); included rehabilitation assignments to Akron and Lake County. ... On disabled list (April 2-July 6, 2004); included rehabilitation assignments to Akron and Buffalo.

CAREER HITTING: 0-for-2 (.000), 0 R, 0 2B, 0 3B, 0 HR, 0 RBI.

SCOUTING REPORT *Throws:* Wickman has two main pitches—a fastball at 91-92 mph and a slider at 83-86. *Tendencies:* Though he no longer is overpowering, his stuff has retained its effectiveness. Throws a heavy fastball that bores in on righthanded hitters and can eat them up. Slider is quick with a short, controlled break. Was impeccable in throwing his fastball away from righthanded hitters. *Outlook:* Even if he has lost a little of his stuff, Wickman still can close, and he's healthy for the first time in several years. Can close for a top-division team. *Grade 8.4*

BOB WICKMAN'S PITCHING ZONE

.308	.333	.500
.306	.571	.244
.154	.417	.167

LEFTY-RIGHTY SPLITS

vs.	Avg.	AB	H	2B	3B	HR	RBI	BB	SO	OBP	Slg.
L	.243	107	26	2	0	4	6	14	20	.331	.374
R	.250	124	31	6	0	5	12	7	21	.291	.419

Year	Team (League)	W	L	Pct.	ERA	WHIP	G	GS	CG	ShO	Hld.	Sv.-Opp.	IP	H	R	ER	HR	BB-IBB	SO	Avg.
1990— GC Whi. Sox (GCL)		2	0	1.000	2.45	0.73	2	2	0	0	...	0-...	11.0	7	4	3	0	1-0	15	.175
— Sarasota (Fla. St.)		0	1	.000	1.98	1.54	2	2	0	0	...	0-...	13.2	7	7	3	0	4-0	8	.304
— South Bend (Midw.)		7	2	.778	1.38	1.01	9	9	3	0	...	0-...	65.1	50	16	10	1	16-0	50	.212
1991— Sarasota (Fla. St.)		5	1	.833	2.05	1.23	7	7	1	1	...	0-...	44.0	43	16	10	2	11-0	32	.247
— Birmingham (Sou.)		6	10	.375	3.56	1.35	20	20	4	1	...	0-...	131.1	127	68	52	5	50-0	81	.250
1992— Columbus (Int'l)		12	5	.706	2.92	1.18	23	23	2	1	...	0-...	157.0	131	61	51	12	55-0	108	.224
— New York (A.L.)		6	1	.857	4.11	1.41	8	8	0	0	...	0-0	50.1	51	25	23	2	20-0	21	.273
1993— New York (A.L.)		14	4	.778	4.63	1.61	41	19	1	1	2	4-8	140.0	156	82	72	13	69-7	70	.284
1994— New York (A.L.)		5	4	.556	3.09	1.16	53	0	0	0	11	6-10	70.0	54	26	24	3	27-3	56	.213
1995— New York (A.L.)		2	4	.333	4.05	1.38	63	1	0	0	21	1-10	80.0	77	38	36	6	33-3	51	.253
1996— New York (A.L.)		4	1	.800	4.67	1.62	58	0	0	0	6	0-3	79.0	94	41	41	7	34-1	61	.299
— Milwaukee (A.L.)		3	0	1.000	3.24	1.32	12	0	0	0	4	0-1	16.2	12	9	6	3	10-2	14	.200
1997— Milwaukee (A.L.)		7	6	.538	2.73	1.36	74	0	0	0	* 28	1-5	95.2	89	32	29	8	41-7	78	.252
1998— Milwaukee (N.L.)		6	9	.400	3.72	1.43	72	0	0	0	9	25-32	82.1	79	38	34	5	39-2	71	.262
1999— Milwaukee (N.L.)		3	8	.273	3.39	1.52	71	0	0	0	0	37-45	74.1	75	31	28	6	38-6	60	.262
2000— Milwaukee (N.L.)		2	2	.500	2.93	1.24	43	0	0	0	0	16-20	46.0	37	18	15	1	20-2	44	.215
— Cleveland (A.L.)		1	3	.250	3.38	1.46	26	0	0	0	0	14-17	26.2	27	12	10	0	12-3	11	.270
2001— Cleveland (A.L.)		5	0	1.000	2.39	1.11	70	0	0	0	4	32-35	67.2	61	18	18	4	14-2	66	.240
2002— Cleveland (A.L.)		1	3	.250	4.46	1.51	36	0	0	0	0	20-22	34.1	42	22	17	3	10-0	36	.284
2003— Lake County (S.Atl.)		0	0	...	0.00	0.50	2	2	0	0	0	0-...	2.0	1	0	0	0	0-0	4	.143
— Akron (East.)		0	0	...	16.20	2.40	2	2	0	0	0	0-...	1.2	3	3	3	0	1-0	2	.375
2004— Akron (East.)		0	0	...	0.00	2.00	1	1	0	0	0	0-...	1.0	0	0	0	0	2-0	1	.000
— Buffalo (Int'l)		1	0	1.000	10.13	1.50	6	1	0	0	0	0-...	5.1	4	6	6	0	4-0	4	.211
— Cleveland (A.L.)		0	2	.000	4.25	1.45	30	0	0	0	4	13-14	29.2	33	14	14	4	10-0	26	.282
2005— Cleveland (A.L.)		0	4	.000	2.47	1.26	64	0	0	0	0	• 45-50	62.0	57	17	17	9	21-3	41	.247
American League totals (11 years)		48	32	.600	3.67	1.40	535	28	1	1	80	136-175	752.0	753	336	307	62	301-31	531	.262
National League totals (3 years)		11	19	.367	3.42	1.42	186	0	0	0	9	78-97	202.2	191	87	77	12	97-10	175	.252
Major League totals (13 years)		59	51	.536	3.62	1.41	721	28	1	1	89	214-272	954.2	944	423	384	74	398-41	706	.260

DIVISION SERIES RECORD

Year	Team (League)	W	L	Pct.	ERA	WHIP	G	GS	CG	ShO	Hld.	Sv.-Opp.	IP	H	R	ER	HR	BB-IBB	SO	Avg.
1995— New York (A.L.)		0	0	...	0.00	1.67	3	0	0	0	0	0-0	3.0	5	0	0	0	0-0	3	.417
2001— Cleveland (A.L.)		0	0	...	0.00	0.00	1	0	0	0	0	0-0	1.0	0	0	0	0	0-0	2	.000
Division series totals (2 years)		0	0	...	0.00	1.25	4	0	0	0	0	0-0	4.0	5	0	0	0	0-0	5	.333

ALL-STAR GAME RECORD

	W	L	Pct.	ERA	WHIP	G	GS	CG	ShO	Hld.	Sv.-Opp.	IP	H	R	ER	HR	BB-IBB	SO	Avg.
All-Star Game totals (2 years)	0	0	...	9.00	1.00	2	0	0	0	0	0-0	1.0	0	1	1	0	1-0	1	.000

WIDGER, CHRIS   C

PERSONAL: Born May 21, 1971, in Wilmington, Del. ... 6-2/210. ... Bats right, throws right. ... Full name: Christopher Jon Widger. ... High school: Pennsville (N.J.). ... College: George Mason.

TRANSACTIONS/CAREER NOTES: Selected by Seattle Mariners organization in third round of 1992 free-agent draft. ... Traded by Mariners with Ps Trey Moore and Matt Wagner to Montreal Expos for Ps Jeff Fassero and Alex Pacheco (October 29, 1996). ... On disabled list (May 25-June 9, 2000). ... Traded by Expos to Mariners for two players to be named (August 8, 2000); Expos acquired OF Sean Spencer (August 10) and OF Terrmel Sledge (September 28) to complete deal. ... On disabled list (March 31, 2001-entire season); included rehabilitation assignment to Everett. ... Signed as a free agent by New York Yankees organization (February 1, 2002). ... Released by Yankees (April 7, 2003). ... Signed by St. Louis Cardinals organization (April 12, 2003). ... On disabled list (June 10-30, 2003); included rehabilitation assignment to Memphis. ... Traded by Cardinals with IF Wilson Delgado to New York Mets for OF Roger Cedeno (April 3, 2004). ... Released by Mets (April 5, 2004). ... Signed by Camden of the independent Atlantic League (2004). ... Signed as a free agent by Chicago White Sox organization (January 19, 2005).

2005 GAMES PLAYED BY POSITION (MLB): C—42, 3B—1, DH—1, 1B—1.

SCOUTING REPORT Widger is an athletic receiver and mobile behind the plate. Tends to drop too many pitches. Arm strength is average at best; must release the ball quickly to throw out runners. Has very good range on balls in the dirt. Has a long stroke and is very aggressive as a hitter. Has a lot of holes. Sits on the fastball and likes the ball out over the plate, Is better hitter against lefthanders. *Grade 5.3*

CHRIS WIDGER'S HITTING ZONE

.167	.250	.000
.290	.313	.313
.333	.400	.167

LEFTY-RIGHTY SPLITS

vs.	Avg.	AB	H	2B	3B	HR	RBI	BB	SO	OBP	Slg.
L	.237	76	18	6	0	4	9	4	13	.284	.474
R	.246	65	16	2	0	0	2	6	9	.310	.277

W

Year Team (League)	Pos.	G	AB	R	H	2B	3B	HR	RBI	BB	SO	HBP	GDP	SB-CS	BATTING Avg.	OBP	SLG	OPS	FIELDING E	Avg.
1992—Bellingham (N'west)	C	51	166	28	43	7	2	5	30	22	36	1	4	8-1	.259	.340	.416	.756	4	.987
1993—Riverside (Calif.)	C-OF	97	360	44	95	28	2	9	58	19	64	3	8	5-4	.264	.303	.428	.731	14	.974
1994—Jacksonville (Sou.)	1B-C-OF	116	388	58	101	15	3	16	59	39	69	5	7	8-7	.260	.334	.438	.772	12	.979
1995—Tacoma (PCL)	C-DH-OF	50	174	29	48	11	1	9	21	9	29	0	4	0-0	.276	.311	.506	.817	4	.980
—Seattle (A.L.)	C-OF-DH	23	45	2	9	0	0	1	2	3	11	0	0	0-0	.200	.245	.267	.512	0	1.000
1996—Tacoma (PCL)	C-DH	97	352	42	107	20	2	13	48	27	62	2	13	7-1	.304	.355	.483	.838	8	.988
—Seattle (A.L.)	C	8	11	1	2	0	0	0	0	0	5	1	0	0-0	.182	.250	.182	.432	2	.905
1997—Montreal (N.L.)	C	91	278	30	65	20	3	7	37	22	59	1	7	2-0	.234	.290	.403	.693	*14	.983
1998—Montreal (N.L.)	C	125	417	36	97	18	1	15	53	29	85	0	5	6-1	.233	.281	.388	.670	14	.981
1999—Montreal (N.L.)	C	124	383	42	101	24	1	14	56	28	86	7	5	1-4	.264	.325	.441	.766	6	.992
2000—Montreal (N.L.)	C	86	281	31	67	17	2	12	34	29	61	1	5	1-2	.238	.311	.441	.752	8	.985
—Seattle (A.L.)	C-1B-DH-OF	10	11	1	1	0	0	1	1	1	2	0	0	0-0	.091	.167	.364	.530	0	1.000
2001—Everett (N'west)	1B	5	13	2	1	0	0	0	0	6	1	0	0	0-0	.077	.368	.077	.445	0	1.000
2002—Columbus (Int'l)	C-OF	61	217	26	53	14	1	10	39	17	31	1	3	0-3	.244	.300	.456	.756	4	.990
—New York (A.L.)	C	21	64	4	19	5	0	0	5	2	9	2	0	0-0	.297	.338	.375	.713	2	.983
2003—Memphis (PCL)	C-1B-OF	23	71	8	17	7	0	2	10	7	12	0	0	1-0	.239	.304	.423	.727	4	.968
—St. Louis (N.L.)	C-1B-OF	44	102	9	24	9	0	0	14	6	20	1	5	0-0	.235	.279	.324	.603	1	.995
2004—Camden (Atl.)	C	55	202	37	54	12	1	16	43	20	27	2	10	5-0	.267	.336	.574	.910	3	.988
2005—Chicago (A.L.)	C-1B-3B-DH	45	141	18	34	8	0	4	11	10	22	1	5	0-2	.241	.296	.383	.679	5	.982
American League totals (5 years)		107	272	26	65	13	0	6	19	16	49	4	5	0-2	.239	.290	.353	.643	9	.982
National League totals (5 years)		470	1461	148	354	88	7	48	194	114	311	10	27	10-7	.242	.300	.411	.711	40	.986
Major League totals (9 years)		577	1733	174	419	101	7	54	213	130	360	14	32	10-9	.242	.299	.402	.700	49	.985

DIVISION SERIES RECORD

Year Team (League)	Pos.	G	AB	R	H	2B	3B	HR	RBI	BB	SO	HBP	GDP	SB-CS	Avg.	OBP	SLG	OPS	E	Avg.
1995—Seattle (A.L.)	C	2	3	0	0	0	0	0	0	0	3	0	...	0-0	.000	.000	.000	.000	0	1.000
2000—Seattle (A.L.)		Did not play.																		

CHAMPIONSHIP SERIES RECORD

Year Team (League)	Pos.	G	AB	R	H	2B	3B	HR	RBI	BB	SO	HBP	GDP	SB-CS	Avg.	OBP	SLG	OPS	E	Avg.
1995—Seattle (A.L.)	C	3	1	0	0	0	0	0	0	0	1	0	...	0-0	.000	.000	.000	.000	0	1.000
2000—Seattle (A.L.)		Did not play.																		

WORLD SERIES RECORD

Year Team (League)	Pos.	G	AB	R	H	2B	3B	HR	RBI	BB	SO	HBP	GDP	SB-CS	Avg.	OBP	SLG	OPS	E	Avg.
2005—Chicago (A.L.)	C	1	1	0	0	0	0	0	0	2	1	0	0	0-0	.000	.667	.000	.667	0	1.000

WIGGINTON, TY   3B/2B

PERSONAL: Born October 11, 1977, in San Diego. ... 6-0/200. ... Bats right, throws right. ... Full name: Ty Allen Wigginton. ... High school: Chula Vista (Calif.). ... College: North Carolina-Asheville.

TRANSACTIONS/CAREER NOTES: Selected by New York Mets organization in 17th round of 1998 free-agent draft. ... On disabled list (April 21-May 7, 2004); included rehabilitation assignment to St. Lucie. ... Traded by Mets with IF Jose Bautista and P Matt Peterson to Pittsburgh Pirates for P Kris Benson and IF Jeff Keppinger (July 30, 2004).

2005 GAMES PLAYED BY POSITION (MLB): 3B—40, 1B—3, 2B—1.

SCOUTING REPORT Offense: A demotion to the minors last season hasn't helped him cut down his his long stroke. Likes the ball away. Is a patient contact hitter but doesn't have the power the club anticipated. Is a better hitter and has more power when going to the opposite field. Doesn't make too many adjustments at the plate. Bat speed has declined. Doesn't run a lot but has good instincts. Defense: He can play both third and second and has some agility despite his slightly rigid body. Hands are decent but range is limited, especially to his right. Outlook: He may never develop into a run-producing power hitter who is capable of playing regularly. Grade 6.3

TY WIGGINTON'S HITTING ZONE

.286	.000	.000
.219	.450	.389
.143	.167	.429

LEFTY-RIGHTY SPLITS

vs.	Avg.	AB	H	2B	3B	HR	RBI	BB	SO	OBP	Slg.
L	.247	73	18	3	0	5	14	8	14	.321	.493
R	.268	82	22	6	1	2	11	6	16	.326	.439

Year Team (League)	Pos.	G	AB	R	H	2B	3B	HR	RBI	BB	SO	HBP	GDP	SB-CS	BATTING Avg.	OBP	SLG	OPS	FIELDING E	Avg.
1998—Pittsfield (N.Y.-Penn.)	2B-3B-OF	70	272	39	65	14	4	8	29	16	72	1	4	11-2	.239	.284	.408	.692	14	.949
1999—St. Lucie (Fla. St.)	2B	123	456	69	133	23	5	21	73	56	82	4	5	9-12	.292	.373	.502	.875	16	.974
2000—Binghamton (East.)	2B-3B	122	453	64	129	27	3	20	77	24	107	2	4	5-5	.285	.319	.490	.809	23	.943
2001—St. Lucie (Fla. St.)	2B	3	9	1	3	1	0	0	0	4	2	1	0	0-0	.333	.571	.444	1.016	0	1.000
—Binghamton (East.)	2B-3B	8	28	5	8	3	0	0	0	5	5	0	0	1-0	.286	.394	.393	.787	3	.870
—Norfolk (Int'l)	3B-2B-1B-C-OF	78	260	29	65	12	0	7	24	27	66	2	4	3-3	.250	.323	.377	.700	17	.924
2002—Norfolk (Int'l)	3B-2B-OF-1B	104	383	49	115	26	3	6	48	43	50	1	7	5-3	.300	.366	.431	.796	11	.967
—New York (N.L.)	3B-1B-2B-OF	46	116	18	35	8	0	6	18	8	19	2	4	2-1	.302	.354	.526	.880	5	.966
2003—New York (N.L.)	3B	156	573	73	146	36	6	11	71	46	124	9	15	12-2	.255	.318	.396	.714	16	.962
2004—St. Lucie (Fla. St.)	3B	2	8	1	3	0	0	0	0	0	0	0	0	0-0	.375	.375	.375	.750	1	1.000
—New York (N.L.)	3B-2B-1B	86	312	46	89	23	2	12	42	23	48	0	11	6-1	.285	.334	.487	.822	16	.949
—Pittsburgh (N.L.)	3B	58	182	17	40	7	0	5	24	22	34	1	4	1-0	.220	.306	.341	.646	6	.955

Year Team (League)	Pos.	G	AB	R	H	2B	3B	HR	RBI	BB	SO	HBP	GDP	SB-CS	Avg.	OBP	SLG	OPS	E	Avg.
2005— Indianapolis (Int'l) 3B-1B-DH																				
	2B	72	280	53	82	18	0	14	52	45	56	1	4	8-5	.293	.390	.507	.897	7	.975
—Pittsburgh (N.L.) 3B-1B-2B		57	155	20	40	9	1	7	25	14	30	1	3	0-1	.258	.324	.465	.788	9	.921
Major League totals (4 years)		403	1338	174	350	83	9	41	180	113	255	14	37	21-5	.262	.324	.429	.753	52	.954

WILKERSON, BRAD — 1B/OF

PERSONAL: Born June 1, 1977, in Daviess, Ky. ... 6-0/206. ... Bats left, throws left. ... Full name: Stephen Bradley Wilkerson. ... High school: Apollo (Owensboro, Ky.). ... College: Florida.

TRANSACTIONS/CAREER NOTES: Selected by Los Angeles Dodgers organization in 13th round of 1995 free-agent draft; did not sign. ... Selected by Montreal Expos organization in supplemental round ("sandwich pick" between first and second rounds, 33rd pick overall) of 1998 free-agent draft; pick received as part of compensation for Toronto Blue Jays signing Type A free-agent C Darrin Fletcher. ... Expos franchise transferred to Washington, D.C., and renamed Washington Nationals for 2005 season (December 3, 2004).

HONORS: Named N.L. Rookie Player of the Year by THE SPORTING NEWS (2002).

2005 GAMES PLAYED BY POSITION (MLB): OF—129, 1B—25.

SCOUTING REPORT *Offense:* Wilkerson, an inside-out hitter with a slight loop in his swing, has good bat speed and is hitting for more power. Often is hitting behind in the count and will chase a lot of high fastballs. Is a streaky hitter with power on the ball down. Is better against left-handers than righthanders as he stays on the ball longer and doesn't open up as quickly. Has good instincts but is just an average runner. *Defense:* He gets good jumps on the ball laterally and has arm strength and accuracy. Goes back well on the ball and has good range. Charges the ball well with a quick release. *Outlook:* Wilkerson's power numbers slid with his move to a bigger park. Needs to cut down his strikeouts and should be more aggressive earlier in the count. *Grade 7.8*

BRAD WILKERSON'S HITTING ZONE

.258	.214	.171
.197	.389	.241
.302	.359	.310

LEFTY-RIGHTY SPLITS

vs.	Avg.	AB	H	2B	3B	HR	RBI	BB	SO	OBP	Slg.
L	.296	162	48	11	1	2	22	20	38	.390	.414
R	.228	403	92	31	6	9	35	64	109	.335	.402

Year Team (League)	Pos.	G	AB	R	H	2B	3B	HR	RBI	BB	SO	HBP	GDP	SB-CS	Avg.	OBP	SLG	OPS	E	Avg.
1999— Harrisburg (East.)	1B-OF	138	422	66	99	21	3	8	49	88	100	1	3	3-5	.235	.372	.355	.727	7	.972
2000— Harrisburg (East.)	1B-OF	66	229	53	77	36	2	6	44	42	38	4	4	8-4	.336	.442	.590	1.032	3	.983
—Ottawa (Int'l)	OF	63	212	40	53	11	1	12	35	45	60	3	0	5-4	.250	.387	.481	.868	6	.956
2001— Jupiter (Fla. St.)	DH	6	26	3	6	3	0	0	1	3	10	0	0	0-0	.231	.310	.346	.656	...	...
—Ottawa (Int'l)	OF	69	233	43	63	10	0	12	48	60	68	3	2	12-5	.270	.423	.468	.891	3	.973
—Montreal (N.L.)	OF	47	117	11	24	7	2	1	5	17	41	0	2	2-1	.205	.304	.325	.628	2	.970
2002— Montreal (N.L.)	OF-1B	153	507	92	135	27	8	20	59	81	161	5	5	7-8	.266	.370	.469	.840	7	.984
2003— Montreal (N.L.)	OF-1B	146	504	78	135	34	4	19	77	89	155	4	5	13-10	.268	.380	.464	.844	5	.988
2004— Montreal (N.L.)	1B-OF	160	572	112	146	39	2	32	67	106	152	4	6	13-6	.255	.374	.498	.872	7	.993
2005— Washington (N.L.)	OF-1B	148	565	76	140	42	7	11	57	84	147	7	6	8-10	.248	.351	.405	.756	6	.988
Major League totals (5 years)		654	2265	369	580	149	23	83	265	377	656	20	24	43-35	.256	.365	.452	.817	27	.989

WILLIAMS, BERNIE — OF

PERSONAL: Born September 13, 1968, in San Juan, Puerto Rico. ... 6-2/205. ... Bats both, throws right. ... Full name: Bernabe Figueroa Williams. ... High school: Escuela Libre de Musica (San Juan, Puerto Rico). ... College: University of Puerto Rico.

TRANSACTIONS/CAREER NOTES: Signed as a non-drafted free agent by New York Yankees organization (September 13, 1985). ... On disabled list (May 13-June 7, 1993; May 11-May 26, 1996; June 16-July 2 and July 15-August 1, 1997). ... On disabled list (June 11-July 18, 1998); included rehabilitation assignments to Tampa and Norwich. ... On disabled list (May 23-July 9, 2003); included rehabilitation assignment to Trenton.

RECORDS: Shares major league record for most strikeouts, 9-inning game (5, August 21, 1991).

HONORS: Won A.L. Gold Glove as outfielder (1997-2000).

2005 GAMES PLAYED BY POSITION (MLB): OF—112, DH—23.

SCOUTING REPORT *Offense:* The bat speed of this longtime Yankee continues to decline. Has problems catching up to high fastballs. Is a patient hitter, though. Is better from the left side with more power. Offensive numbers should continue to drop as his bat speed declines. Still a good runner first to third but is not a basestealer. *Defense:* He never was a prototypical center fielder and now that he no longer runs as well, balls are starting to drop too often. Has problems going back on the ball as he tends to trail it; plays the ball in front of him better. Arm strength is below average, but he has a quick release. *Outlook:* Williams is in the midst of a steady decline, and isn't even the player he was two years ago. *Grade 6*

BERNIE WILLIAMS' HITTING ZONE

.171	.333	.250
.186	.313	.309
.244	.217	.231

LEFTY-RIGHTY SPLITS

vs.	Avg.	AB	H	2B	3B	HR	RBI	BB	SO	OBP	Slg.
L	.231	182	42	7	0	1	12	20	27	.305	.286
R	.261	303	79	12	1	11	52	33	48	.330	.416

Year Team (League)	Pos.	G	AB	R	H	2B	3B	HR	RBI	BB	SO	HBP	GDP	SB-CS	Avg.	OBP	SLG	OPS	E	Avg.
1986— GC Yankees (GCL)	OF	61	230	45	62	5	3	2	25	39	40	1	3	33-12	.270	.374	.343	.717	3	.976
1987— Fort Lauderdale (Fla. St.) ..	OF	25	71	11	11	3	0	0	4	18	22	3	1	9-1	.155	.348	.197	.545	1	1.000
—Oneonta (N.Y.-Penn.)	OF	25	93	13	32	4	0	1	15	10	14	1	0	9-3	.344	.410	.387	.797	2	.952
1988— Prince William (Carol.)	OF	92	337	72	113	16	7	7	45	65	65	4	5	29-11	.335	.447	.487	.934	5	.975
1989— Columbus (Int'l)	OF	50	162	21	35	8	1	2	16	25	38	2	3	11-5	.216	.325	.315	.639	1	.991
—Alb./Colon. (East.)	OF	91	314	63	79	11	8	11	42	60	72	6	9	26-13	.252	.381	.443	.823	5	.974
1990— Alb./Colon. (East.)	OF	134	466	91	131	28	5	8	54	98	97	4	12	39-18	.281	.409	.414	.823	4	.987
1991— Columbus (Int'l)	OF	78	306	52	90	14	6	8	37	38	43	2	5	9-8	.294	.372	.458	.830	1	.994
—New York (A.L.)	OF	85	320	43	76	19	4	3	34	48	57	1	4	10-5	.238	.336	.350	.686	5	.979
1992— New York (A.L.)	OF	62	261	39	73	14	2	5	26	29	36	1	4	7-6	.280	.354	.440	.760	1	.995
—Columbus (Int'l)	OF	95	363	68	111	23	9	8	50	52	61	1	8	20-8	.306	.389	.485	.873	2	.990

W

Year Team (League)	Pos.	G	AB	R	H	2B	3B	HR	RBI	BB	SO	HBP	GDP	SB-CS	Avg.	OBP	SLG	OPS	E	Avg.
1993— New York (A.L.)	OF	139	567	67	152	31	4	12	68	53	106	4	17	9-9	.268	.333	.400	.734	4	.989
1994— New York (A.L.)	OF	108	408	80	118	29	1	12	57	61	54	3	11	16-9	.289	.384	.453	.837	3	.990
1995— New York (A.L.)	OF	144	563	93	173	29	9	18	82	75	98	5	12	8-6	.307	.392	.487	.878	•8	.982
1996— New York (A.L.)	OF-DH	143	551	108	168	26	7	29	102	82	72	0	15	17-4	.305	.391	.535	.926	5	.986
1997— New York (A.L.)	DH	129	509	107	167	35	6	21	100	73	80	1	10	15-8	.328	.408	.544	.952	2	.993
1998— New York (A.L.)	OF-DH	128	499	101	169	30	5	26	97	74	81	1	19	15-9	.339	.422	.575	.997	3	.990
— Tampa (Fla. St.)	OF	1	2	0	1	1	0	0	0	1	0	0	0	0-0	.500	.667	1.000	1.667	0	1.000
— Norwich (East.)	OF	3	11	6	6	2	0	2	5	2	1	0	1	0-0	.545	.571	1.273	1.844	0	1.000
1999— New York (A.L.)	OF-DH	158	591	116	202	28	6	25	115	100	95	1	11	9-10	.342	.435	.536	.971	5	.987
2000— New York (A.L.)	OF-DH	141	537	108	165	37	6	30	121	71	84	5	15	13-5	.307	.391	.566	.957	0	1.000
2001— New York (A.L.)	OF-DH	146	540	102	166	38	0	26	94	78	67	6	15	11-5	.307	.395	.522	.917	2	.994
2002— New York (A.L.)	OF-DH	154	612	102	204	37	2	19	102	83	97	3	19	8-4	.333	.415	.493	.908	5	.986
2003— Trenton (East.)	OF-DH	5	15	4	5	2	0	0	4	4	1	1	1	0-1	.333	.476	.467	.943	1	1.000
— New York (A.L.)	OF-DH	119	445	77	117	19	1	15	64	71	61	3	21	5-0	.263	.367	.411	.778	1	.997
2004— New York (A.L.)	OF-DH	148	561	105	147	29	1	22	70	85	96	2	19	1-5	.262	.360	.435	.795	1	.995
2005— New York (A.L.)	OF-DH	141	485	53	121	19	1	12	64	53	75	1	16	1-2	.249	.321	.367	.688	2	.991
Major League totals (15 years)		1945	7449	1301	2218	420	55	275	1196	1036	1159	37	209	145-87	.298	.384	.480	.863	47	.990

DIVISION SERIES RECORD

Year Team (League)	Pos.	G	AB	R	H	2B	3B	HR	RBI	BB	SO	HBP	GDP	SB-CS	Avg.	OBP	SLG	OPS	E	Avg.
1995— New York (A.L.)	OF	5	21	8	9	2	0	2	5	7	3	0	0	1-0	.429	.571	.810	1.381	0	1.000
1996— New York (A.L.)	OF	4	15	5	7	0	0	3	5	2	1	0	0	1-1	.467	.500	1.067	1.567	0	1.000
1997— New York (A.L.)	OF	5	17	3	2	1	0	0	1	4	3	1	1	0-0	.118	.318	.176	.495	0	1.000
1998— New York (A.L.)	OF	3	11	0	0	0	0	0	0	1	4	0	2	0-0	.000	.083	.000	.083	0	1.000
1999— New York (A.L.)	OF	3	11	2	4	1	0	1	6	1	2	1	0	0-0	.364	.462	.727	1.189	0	1.000
2000— New York (A.L.)	OF	5	20	3	5	3	0	0	1	1	4	0	0	0-1	.250	.273	.400	.673	0	1.000
2001— New York (A.L.)	OF	5	18	4	4	3	0	0	5	3	3	0	2	0-1	.222	.333	.389	.722	0	1.000
2002— New York (A.L.)	OF	4	15	4	5	1	0	1	3	3	2	0	0	0-0	.333	.444	.600	1.044	0	1.000
2003— New York (A.L.)	OF	4	15	3	6	2	0	0	3	2	2	0	0	0-0	.400	.444	.533	.978	1	.900
2004— New York (A.L.)	OF	4	18	2	5	1	0	1	3	1	2	0	0	0-0	.278	.316	.500	.816	0	1.000
2005— New York (A.L.)	OF-DH	5	19	2	4	2	0	0	1	1	3	0	0	0-0	.211	.238	.316	.554	0	1.000
Division series totals (11 years)		47	180	36	51	16	0	8	33	26	29	2	11	2-3	.283	.373	.506	.878	1	.991

CHAMPIONSHIP SERIES RECORD

Year Team (League)	Pos.	G	AB	R	H	2B	3B	HR	RBI	BB	SO	HBP	GDP	SB-CS	Avg.	OBP	SLG	OPS	E	Avg.
1996— New York (A.L.)	OF	5	19	6	9	3	0	2	6	5	4	0	0	1-0	.474	.583	.947	1.531	0	1.000
1998— New York (A.L.)	OF	6	21	4	8	1	0	0	5	7	4	0	1	1-1	.381	.536	.429	.964	0	1.000
1999— New York (A.L.)	OF	5	20	3	5	1	0	1	2	2	5	0	0	0-0	.250	.318	.450	.768	0	1.000
2000— New York (A.L.)		6	23	5	10	1	0	1	3	2	3	1	1	0-0	.435	.481	.609	1.090	0	1.000
2001— New York (A.L.)	OF	5	17	4	4	0	0	3	5	5	4	0	1	0-1	.235	.409	.765	1.174	1	.900
2003— New York (A.L.)	OF	7	26	5	5	1	0	0	2	4	3	0	0	0-0	.192	.300	.231	.531	0	1.000
2004— New York (A.L.)	OF	7	36	4	11	3	0	2	10	0	5	0	0	0-0	.306	.306	.556	.861	0	1.000
Champ. series totals (7 years)		41	162	31	52	10	0	9	33	25	28	1	3	4-2	.321	.413	.549	.962	1	.991

WORLD SERIES RECORD

Year Team (League)	Pos.	G	AB	R	H	2B	3B	HR	RBI	BB	SO	HBP	GDP	SB-CS	Avg.	OBP	SLG	OPS	E	Avg.
1996— New York (A.L.)	OF	6	24	3	4	0	0	1	4	3	6	0	1	1-0	.167	.259	.292	.551	0	1.000
1998— New York (A.L.)	OF	4	16	2	1	0	0	1	3	2	5	0	0	0-0	.063	.167	.250	.417	0	1.000
1999— New York (A.L.)	OF	4	13	2	3	0	0	0	0	4	2	0	1	1-0	.231	.412	.231	.643	0	1.000
2000— New York (A.L.)	OF	5	18	2	2	0	0	1	1	5	5	0	0	0-0	.111	.304	.278	.582	0	1.000
2001— New York (A.L.)	OF	7	24	2	5	1	0	1	4	2	6	0	0	0-0	.208	.321	.250	.571	0	1.000
2003— New York (A.L.)	OF	6	25	5	10	2	0	2	5	2	2	0	1	0-0	.400	.429	.720	1.149	0	1.000
World series totals (6 years)		32	120	16	25	3	0	5	14	20	26	0	3	2-0	.208	.319	.358	.677	0	1.000

ALL-STAR GAME RECORD

		G	AB	R	H	2B	3B	HR	RBI	BB	SO	HBP	GDP	SB-CS	Avg.	OBP	SLG	OPS	E	Avg.
All-Star Game totals (4 years)		4	5	1	0	0	0	0	0	1	1	0	0	1-0	.000	.167	.000	.167	0	1.000

WILLIAMS, DAVE   P

PERSONAL: Born March 12, 1979, in Anchorage, Alaska. ... 6-2/219. ... Throws left, bats left. ... Full name: David Aaron Williams. ... High school: Caesar Rodney (Camden, Del.). ... Junior college: Delaware Tech & Community College.

TRANSACTIONS/CAREER NOTES: Selected by Pittsburgh Pirates organization in 17th round of 1998 free-agent draft. ... On disabled list (May 28, 2002-remainder of season; March 24-June 3, 2003; and August 13-31, 2004).

CAREER HITTING: 12-for-101 (.119), 4 R, 3 2B, 0 3B, 1 HR, 9 RBI.

DAVE WILLIAMS' PITCHING ZONE

.217	.200	.314
.277	.375	.333
.333	.250	.216

LEFTY-RIGHTY SPLITS

vs.	Avg.	AB	H	2B	3B	HR	RBI	BB	SO	OBP	Slg.
L	.281	96	27	4	1	7	23	11	21	.373	.563
R	.256	429	110	29	3	13	42	47	67	.335	.429

Year Team (League)	W	L	Pct.	ERA	WHIP	G	GS	CG	ShO	Hld.	Sv.-Opp.	IP	H	R	ER	HR	BB-IBB	SO	Avg.
1998— Erie (N.Y.-Penn.)	2	2	.500	3.23	1.25	22	2	0	0	...	0-...	47.1	45	21	17	6	14-0	38	.245
1999— Will. (N.Y.-Penn.)	4	2	.667	2.56	0.96	7	7	1	1	...	0-...	45.2	33	17	13	2	11-0	47	.198
— Hickory (S. Atl.)	3	1	.750	3.20	0.90	9	9	1	1	...	0-...	59.0	42	22	21	5	11-0	46	.201
2000— Hickory (S. Atl.)	11	9	.550	2.96	1.08	24	24	1	1	...	0-...	170.0	145	66	56	14	39-2	193	.232
— Lynchburg (Carol.)	1	0	1.000	6.55	1.91	2	2	0	0	...	0-...	11.0	18	8	8	2	3-0	8	.383
2001— Altoona (East.)	5	2	.714	2.61	0.97	9	8	1	0	...	0-...	58.2	45	17	17	8	12-0	39	.211
— Nashville (PCL)	1	1	.500	3.38	1.31	2	2	0	0	...	0-...	10.2	9	5	4	3	5-0	6	.231
— Pittsburgh (N.L.)	3	7	.300	3.71	1.27	22	18	0	0	1	0-0	114.0	100	53	47	15	45-4	57	.244
2002— Pittsburgh (N.L.)	2	5	.286	4.98	1.43	9	9	0	0	0	0-0	43.1	38	26	24	9	24-2	33	.232
2003— Nashville (PCL)	7	4	.636	4.19	1.40	16	16	0	0	...	0-...	77.1	78	44	36	7	30-2	56	.260

Year	Team (League)	W	L	Pct.	ERA	WHIP	G	GS	CG	ShO	Hld.	Sv.-Opp.	IP	H	R	ER	HR	BB-IBB	SO	Avg.
2004—	Nashville (PCL)	6	2	.750	3.47	1.25	21	21	0	0	...	0-...	116.2	113	52	45	10	33-2	103	.252
	— Pittsburgh (N.L.)	2	3	.400	4.42	1.14	10	6	0	0	0	0-0	38.2	31	21	19	4	13-2	33	.217
2005—	Pittsburgh (N.L.)	10	11	.476	4.41	1.41	25	25	1	1	0	0-0	138.2	137	74	68	20	58-5	88	.261
	Major League totals (4 years)	17	26	.395	4.25	1.33	66	58	1	1	1	0-0	334.2	306	174	158	48	140-13	211	.247

WILLIAMS, GERALD — OF

PERSONAL: Born August 10, 1966, in New Orleans. ... 6-2/187. ... Bats right, throws right. ... Full name: Gerald Floyd Williams. ... High school: East St. John (Reserve, La.). ... College: Grambling State.

TRANSACTIONS/CAREER NOTES: Selected by New York Yankees organization in 14th round of 1987 free-agent draft. ... Traded by Yankees with P Bob Wickman to Milwaukee Brewers for P Graeme Lloyd and OF Pat Listach (August 23, 1996). ... Traded by Brewers to Atlanta Braves for P Chad Fox (December 11, 1997). ... Signed as a free agent by Tampa Bay Devil Rays (December 19, 1999). ... On suspended list (September 22-25, 2000). ... Released by Devil Rays (June 24, 2001). ... Signed by Yankees (June 28, 2001). ... Released by Yankees (June 5, 2002). ... Signed by St. Louis Cardinals organization (June 6, 2002). ... Released by Cardinals (July 8, 2002). ... Signed by Cincinnati Reds organization (July 11, 2002). ... Signed as a free agent by Florida Marlins organization (January 18, 2003). ... Released by Marlins (April 2, 2004). ... Signed by New York Mets organization (April 23, 2004).

2005 GAMES PLAYED BY POSITION (MLB): OF—27.

SCOUTING REPORT This veteran is in the twilight of his career. Has lost significant bat speed. Has a long swing with a big hitch and leg lift. Can be beaten with hard stuff in and has problems covering the outer half. Strikes out too much. Still can run well enough to cover ground in the outfield and play all three outfield spots. Should be a fifth outfielder. *Grade 4.7*

LEFTY-RIGHTY SPLITS

vs.	Avg.	AB	H	2B	3B	HR	RBI	BB	SO	OBP	Slg.
L	.222	9	2	0	0	0	1	0	2	.222	.222
R	.238	21	5	2	0	1	2	1	5	.273	.476

Year	Team (League)	Pos.	G	AB	R	H	2B	3B	HR	RBI	BB	SO	HBP	GDP	SB-CS	Avg.	OBP	SLG	OPS	E	Avg.
1987—	Oneonta (N.Y.-Penn.)	OF	29	115	26	42	6	2	2	29	16	18	1	3	6-2	.365	.447	.504	.951	3	.959
1988—	Prince Will. (Carol.)	OF	54	159	20	29	3	0	2	18	15	47	0	4	6-1	.182	.251	.239	.490	3	.961
	— Fort Laud. (Fla. St.)	OF	63	212	21	40	7	2	2	17	16	56	3	4	4-3	.189	.255	.269	.524	6	.965
1989—	Prince Will. (Carol.)	OF	134	454	63	104	19	6	13	69	51	120	7	7	15-10	.229	.316	.383	.699	8	.974
1990—	Fort Laud. (Fla. St.)	OF	50	204	25	59	4	5	7	43	16	52	2	1	19-5	.289	.344	.461	.805	3	.975
	— Alb./Colon. (East.)	OF	96	324	54	81	17	2	13	58	35	74	2	7	18-8	.250	.324	.435	.759	7	.969
1991—	Alb./Colon. (East.)	OF	45	175	28	50	15	0	5	32	18	26	0	5	18-3	.286	.347	.457	.804	3	.974
	— Columbus (Int'l)	OF	61	198	20	51	8	3	2	27	16	39	1	3	9-12	.258	.309	.359	.668	3	.977
1992—	Columbus (Int'l)	OF	142	547	92	156	31	6	16	86	38	98	5	12	36-14	.285	.334	.452	.786	8	.977
	— New York (A.L.)	OF	15	27	7	8	2	0	3	6	0	3	0	0	2-0	.296	.296	.704	1.000	2	.913
1993—	Columbus (Int'l)	OF	87	336	53	95	19	6	8	38	20	66	2	7	29-12	.283	.321	.446	.768	3	.985
	— New York (A.L.)	OF-DH	42	67	11	10	2	3	0	6	1	14	2	2	2-0	.149	.183	.269	.452	2	.956
1994—	New York (A.L.)	OF-DH	57	86	19	25	8	0	4	13	4	17	0	6	1-3	.291	.319	.523	.842	1	.993
1995—	New York (A.L.)	OF-DH	100	182	33	45	18	2	6	28	22	34	1	4	4-2	.247	.327	.467	.794	1	.993
1996—	New York (A.L.)	OF-DH	99	233	37	63	15	4	5	30	15	39	4	7	7-8	.270	.319	.433	.753	3	.978
	— Milwaukee (A.L.)	OF	26	92	6	19	4	0	0	4	4	18	1	1	3-1	.207	.247	.250	.497	1	.987
1997—	Milwaukee (A.L.)	OF-DH	155	566	73	143	32	2	10	41	19	90	6	9	23-9	.253	.282	.369	.651	3	.992
1998—	Atlanta (N.L.)	OF	129	266	46	81	19	2	10	44	17	48	3	5	11-5	.305	.352	.504	.856	5	.970
1999—	Atlanta (N.L.)	OF	143	422	76	116	24	1	17	68	33	67	6	8	19-11	.275	.335	.457	.792	3	.985
2000—	Tampa Bay (A.L.)	OF-DH	146	632	87	173	30	2	21	89	34	103	3	8	12-12	.274	.312	.427	.739	6	.983
2001—	Tampa Bay (A.L.)	OF	62	232	30	48	17	0	4	17	13	42	4	8	10-4	.207	.261	.332	.593	2	.989
	— New York (A.L.)	OF-DH	38	47	12	8	1	0	0	2	5	13	1	1	3-1	.170	.264	.191	.456	1	.967
2002—	New York (A.L.)	OF-DH	33	17	6	0	0	0	0	0	2	4	0	1	2-0	.000	.105	.000	.105	0	1.000
	— Memphis (PCL)	OF	21	73	11	11	3	0	1	3	3	8	1	2	2-0	.151	.195	.233	.428	0	1.000
	— Louisville (Int'l)	OF	48	205	29	54	10	3	2	12	11	36	2	4	6-4	.263	.307	.371	.678	1	.992
2003—	Albuquerque (PCL)	OF	85	327	59	99	22	5	14	50	24	45	4	2	15-11	.303	.356	.529	.885	6	.972
	— Florida (N.L.)	OF	27	31	5	4	1	0	0	3	2	5	0	0	2-0	.129	.182	.161	.343	1	.941
2004—	Norfolk (Int'l)	OF-DH	63	246	37	75	10	3	7	28	9	35	3	4	6-9	.305	.335	.455	.790	1	.993
	— New York (N.L.)	OF	57	129	17	30	8	2	4	11	8	26	0	2	2-1	.233	.277	.419	.696	1	.982
2005—	Norfolk (Int'l)	OF-DH	47	139	24	32	10	2	4	16	9	21	1	1	1-2	.230	.280	.417	.697	0	1.000
	— New York (N.L.)	OF	39	30	9	7	2	0	1	3	1	7	0	0	2-0	.233	.258	.400	.658	0	1.000
	American League totals (9 years)		773	2181	321	542	129	13	53	236	119	377	22	44	69-40	.249	.292	.392	.684	23	.984
	National League totals (5 years)		395	878	153	238	54	5	32	129	61	153	9	15	37-17	.271	.324	.453	.777	10	.978
	Major League totals (14 years)		1168	3059	474	780	183	18	85	365	180	530	31	59	106-57	.255	.301	.410	.711	33	.983

DIVISION SERIES RECORD

Year	Team (League)	Pos.	G	AB	R	H	2B	3B	HR	RBI	BB	SO	HBP	GDP	SB-CS	Avg.	OBP	SLG	OPS	E	Avg.
1995—	New York (A.L.)	OF	5	5	1	0	0	0	0	0	2	3	0	0	0-0	.000	.286	.000	.286	0	1.000
1998—	Atlanta (N.L.)	OF	2	2	1	1	0	0	0	1	0	1	0	0	0-0	.500	.500	.500	1.000	0	1.000
1999—	Atlanta (N.L.)	OF	4	18	2	7	1	0	0	3	0	3	0	0	1-0	.389	.389	.444	.833	0	1.000
	Division series totals (3 years)		11	25	4	8	1	0	0	4	2	7	0	0	1-0	.320	.370	.360	.730	0	1.000

CHAMPIONSHIP SERIES RECORD

Year	Team (League)	Pos.	G	AB	R	H	2B	3B	HR	RBI	BB	SO	HBP	GDP	SB-CS	Avg.	OBP	SLG	OPS	E	Avg.
1998—	Atlanta (N.L.)	OF	5	13	0	2	0	0	0	1	1	6	0	0	1-0	.154	.214	.154	.368	0	1.000
1999—	Atlanta (N.L.)	OF	6	28	4	5	2	0	0	1	2	2	1	0	3-1	.179	.258	.250	.508	1	.923
	Champ. series totals (2 years)		11	41	4	7	2	0	0	1	3	8	1	0	4-1	.171	.244	.220	.464	1	.938

WORLD SERIES RECORD

Year	Team (League)	Pos.	G	AB	R	H	2B	3B	HR	RBI	BB	SO	HBP	GDP	SB-CS	Avg.	OBP	SLG	OPS	E	Avg.
1999—	Atlanta (N.L.)	OF	4	17	2	3	0	1	0	0	0	4	0	1	0-0	.176	.176	.294	.471	0	1.000

W

PERSONAL: Born July 18, 1977, in Gosford, Australia. ... 6-2/195. ... Bats both, throws right. ... Full name: Glenn David Williams. ... High school: Ingleburn (Australia). ... College: None.

TRANSACTIONS/CAREER NOTES: Signed as a non-drafted free agent by Atlanta Braves organization (August 17, 1993). ... On disabled list (May 2-20, June 2-19 and July 5, 1996-remainder of season; and April 22-June 5, 1997). ... Released by Braves (March 23, 2000). ... Signed by Toronto Blue Jays organization (March 26, 2000). ... Signed as a free agent by Minnesota Twins organization (December 15, 2004). ... On disabled list (June 29, 2005-remainder of season).

2005 GAMES PLAYED BY POSITION (MLB): 3B—12.

LEFTY-RIGHTY SPLITS

vs.	Avg.	AB	H	2B	3B	HR	RBI	BB	SO	OBP	Slg.
L	.533	15	8	0	0	0	2	1	4	.563	.533
R	.360	25	9	1	0	0	1	1	3	.385	.400

Year	Team (League)	Pos.	G	AB	R	H	2B	3B	HR	RBI	BB	SO	HBP	GDP	SB-CS	Avg.	OBP	SLG	OPS	E	Avg.
1994— GC Braves (GCL)		SS	24	89	8	18	2	0	2	7	9	32	0	0	4-1	.202	.273	.292	.565	10	.906
— Danville (Appal.)		SS	24	79	11	20	2	0	1	9	8	20	3	4	2-4	.253	.344	.316	.660	10	.888
1995— Eugene (Northwest)		SS	71	268	39	60	11	4	7	36	21	71	5	4	7-4	.224	.291	.373	.664	4	.905
— Macon (S. Atl.)		SS	38	120	13	21	4	0	0	14	16	42	1	3	2-1	.175	.271	.208	.479	19	.867
1996— Macon (S. Atl.)		SS	51	181	14	35	7	3	3	18	18	47	2	3	4-2	.193	.271	.315	.586	15	.931
1997— Macon (S. Atl.)		SS	77	297	52	79	18	2	14	52	24	105	5	4	9-6	.266	.327	.481	.808	17	.944
1998— Danville (Carol.)		2B	134	470	40	101	26	1	9	44	37	132	6	5	1-3	.215	.279	.332	.611	* 26	.952
1999— Greenville (Sou.)		2B-3B	57	204	19	46	11	0	4	15	7	58	4	2	1-4	.225	.264	.338	.602	6	.977
2000— Dunedin (Fla. St.)		2B-SS-OF	107	391	53	102	26	4	13	77	33	91	6	11	4-2	.261	.323	.448	.771	17	.969
2001— Tennessee (Sou.)		3B-2B																			
		SS-1B	130	487	63	124	28	0	11	65	45	120	5	8	1-5	.255	.321	.380	.701	28	.944
2002— Syracuse (Int'l)		3B-SS-2B	94	339	49	93	18	3	15	47	20	80	2	7	2-0	.274	.319	.478	.797	21	.937
2003— Syracuse (Int'l)		3B-1B-OF																			
		2B-SS-P	59	210	27	49	10	3	3	24	12	56	1	6	2-1	.233	.277	.352	.629	4	.982
2004— Syracuse (Int'l)		3B-2B-1B	117	432	65	114	23	4	23	79	34	79	8	9	2-4	.264	.324	.495	.819	14	.867
2005— Rochester (Int'l)		3B-SS-2B																			
		DH-1B	48	175	21	53	12	1	5	22	7	35	3	3	2-0	.303	.341	.469	.809	9	.935
— Minnesota (A.L.)		3B	13	40	3	17	1	0	0	3	2	7	0	0	1-2	.425	.452	.450	.902	2	.929
Major League totals (1 year)			13	40	3	17	1	0	0	3	2	7	0	0	1-2	.425	.452	.450	.902	2	.929

PERSONAL: Born December 4, 1981, in Honolulu. ... 6-3/246. ... Throws right, bats right. ... Full name: Jerome Lee Williams. ... High school: Waipahu (Hawaii).

TRANSACTIONS/CAREER NOTES: Selected by San Francisco Giants organization in supplemental round ("sandwich" pick between first and second rounds, 39th pick overall) of 1999 free-agent draft; pick received as compensation for Seattle Mariners signing Type-A free-agent P Jose Mesa. ... On disabled list (July 31-September 16, 2004). ... Traded by Giants with P David Aardsma to Chicago Cubs for P LaTroy Hawkins (May 28, 2005).

CAREER HITTING: 12-for-107 (.112), 3 R, 2 2B, 0 3B, 0 HR, 1 RBI.

SCOUTING REPORT *Throws:* Williams delivers his four-seam fastball in the low 90s. Also has a two-seamer, curveball, slider and changeup. *Tendencies:* He is a sinkerballer who doesn't have a good breaking ball to complement that pitch. Curve rolls and the slider is often flat. Changes speeds well off his fastball and has command of it. Two-seamer is better than his four-seamer. *Outlook:* Williams has to be very fine and consistently down in the zone to win. *Grade 6*

JEROME WILLIAMS' PITCHING ZONE

.273	.118	.190
.279	.345	.305
.182	.296	.340

LEFTY-RIGHTY SPLITS

vs.	Avg.	AB	H	2B	3B	HR	RBI	BB	SO	OBP	Slg.
L	.299	187	56	15	3	4	20	31	25	.408	.476
R	.236	267	63	9	0	10	37	18	45	.292	.382

Year	Team (League)	W	L	Pct.	ERA	WHIP	G	GS	CG	ShO	Hld.	Sv.-Opp.	IP	H	R	ER	HR	BB-IBB	SO	Avg.
1999— Salem-Keizer (N'west)		1	1	.500	2.19	1.08	7	7	1	1	...	0-...	37.0	29	13	9	1	11-0	34	.213
2000— San Jose (Calif.)		7	6	.538	2.94	1.09	23	19	0	0	...	0-...	125.2	89	53	41	6	48-3	115	.201
2001— Shreveport (Texas)		9	7	.563	3.95	1.15	23	23	2	1	...	0-...	130.0	116	69	57	14	34-0	84	.235
2002— Fresno (PCL)		6	11	.353	3.59	1.18	28	28	0	0	...	0-...	160.2	140	76	64	16	50-1	130	.234
2003— Fresno (PCL)		4	2	.667	2.68	1.19	10	10	1	0	...	0-...	57.0	52	19	17	3	16-0	40	.237
— San Francisco (N.L.)		7	5	.583	3.30	1.26	21	21	2	1	0	0-0	131.0	116	54	48	10	49-3	88	.242
2004— San Francisco (N.L.)		10	7	.588	4.24	1.29	22	22	0	0	0	0-0	129.1	123	69	61	14	44-1	80	.254
2005— San Francisco (N.L.)		0	2	.000	6.48	1.50	4	3	0	0	0	0-0	16.2	11	12	12	2	4-1	11	.313
— Fresno (PCL)		1	4	.200	9.39	2.09	6	6	0	0	0	0-0	30.2	47	34	32	3	17-0	15	.364
— Iowa (PCL)		1	1	.500	2.22	1.36	4	4	0	0	0	0-0	24.1	27	10	6	2	6-0	17	.265
— Chicago (N.L.)		6	8	.429	3.91	1.35	18	17	0	0	1	0-0	106.0	98	50	46	12	45-0	59	.253
Major League totals (3 years)		23	22	.511	3.92	1.31	65	63	2	1	1	0-0	383.0	358	185	167	38	142-5	238	.252

DIVISION SERIES RECORD

Year	Team (League)	W	L	Pct.	ERA	WHIP	G	GS	CG	ShO	Hld.	Sv.-Opp.	IP	H	R	ER	HR	BB-IBB	SO	Avg.
2003— San Francisco (N.L.)		0	0	...	13.50	3.00	1	1	0	0	0	0-0	2.0	5	3	3	0	1-0	1	.455

WILLIAMS, RANDY   P

PERSONAL: Born September 18, 1975, in Harlingen, Texas. ... 6-3/195. ... Throws left, bats left. ... Full name: Randall Duane Williams. ... High school: Buna (Texas). ... College: Lamar.

TRANSACTIONS/CAREER NOTES: Selected by Chicago Cubs organization in 12th round of 1997 free-agent draft. ... Released by Cubs (March 24, 2001). ... Signed by Edinburg of the independent Texas-Lousiana League (2002). ... Signed by Seattle Mariners organization (September 30, 2002). ... Traded by Mariners to San Diego Padres for P Billy Hogan (November 19, 2004). ... Claimed on waivers by Colorado Rockies (May 11, 2005).

CAREER HITTING: 0-for-1 (.000), 0 R, 0 2B, 0 3B, 0 HR, 0 RBI.

RANDY WILLIAMS' PITCHING ZONE

.500	.333	.000
.308	.333	.375
.429	.400	.600

LEFTY-RIGHTY SPLITS

vs.	Avg.	AB	H	2B	3B	HR	RBI	BB	SO	OBP	Slg.
L	.283	53	15	3	0	4	7	3	14	.333	.566
R	.316	57	18	5	0	1	16	10	7	.412	.456

Year	Team (League)	W	L	Pct.	ERA	WHIP	G	GS	CG	ShO	Hld.	Sv.-Opp.	IP	H	R	ER	HR	BB-IBB	SO	Avg.
1997—	Ariz. Cubs (AZL)		Did not play.																
1998—	Ariz. Cubs (AZL)	1	0	1.000	0.00	0.67	2	1	0	0	...	0-...	3.0	0	0	0	0	2-0	6	.000
1999—	Daytona (Fla. St.)	3	4	.429	4.75	1.60	14	9	0	0	...	1-...	53.0	55	36	28	5	30-0	47	.266
2000—		Did not play.																		
2001—		Did not play.																		
2002—	Edinburg (Tex.-La.)	5	2	.714	1.20	0.91	42	0	0	0	...	10-...	52.2	36	8	7	1	12-...	77	...
2003—	San Antonio (Texas)	4	1	.800	1.73	0.96	29	0	0	0	...	2-...	41.2	33	9	8	2	7-0	38	.213
	—Tacoma (PCL)	2	2	.500	5.26	1.40	18	0	0	0	...	1-...	25.2	25	17	15	3	11-0	19	.253
2004—	Tacoma (PCL)	7	2	.778	3.63	1.44	50	0	0	0	...	8-...	79.1	68	37	32	6	46-0	64	.230
	—Seattle (A.L.)	0	0		5.79	1.93	6	0	0	0	1	0-0	4.2	3	3	3	0	6-0	4	.188
2005—	Portland (PCL)	1	1	.500	6.39	1.74	12	0	0	0	6	0-1	12.2	13	10	9	1	9-0	7	.271
	—San Diego (N.L.)	1	0	1.000	12.46	2.54	2	0	0	0	0	0-0	4.1	7	6	6	1	4-0	2	.350
	—Colo. Springs (PCL)	2	2	.500	3.49	0.99	26	0	0	0	4	4-5	28.1	18	14	11	1	10-0	36	.180
	—Colorado (N.L.)	2	1	.667	5.73	1.59	30	0	0	0	4	0-2	22.0	26	15	14	4	9-3	19	.289
American League totals (1 year)		0	0		5.79	1.93	6	0	0	0	1	0-0	4.2	3	3	3	0	6-0	4	.188
National League totals (1 year)		3	1	.750	6.84	1.75	32	0	0	0	4	0-2	26.1	33	21	20	5	13-3	21	.300
Major League totals (2 years)		3	1	.750	6.68	1.77	38	0	0	0	5	0-2	31.0	36	24	23	5	19-3	25	.286

WILLIAMS, TODD   P

PERSONAL: Born February 13, 1971, in Syracuse, N.Y. ... 6-3/210. ... Throws right, bats right. ... Full name: Todd Michael Williams. ... High school: Minoa (East Syracuse, N.Y.). ... Junior college: Onondaga (N.Y.) Community College.

TRANSACTIONS/CAREER NOTES: Selected by Los Angeles Dodgers organization in 54th round of 1990 free-agent draft. ... Traded by Dodgers to Oakland Athletics for P Matt McDonald (September 8, 1995). ... Released by A's (January 16, 1997). ... Signed by Cincinnati Reds organization (February 3, 1997). ... Traded by Reds to Seattle Mariners for OF Kerry Robinson (July 22, 1999). ... Released by Mariners (November 16, 2000). ... Signed by New York Yankees organization (January 3, 2001). ... On disabled list (May 27-July 18, 2001); included rehabilitation assignment to GCL Yankees. ... Signed as a free agent by Dodgers organization (December 27, 2001). ... Released by Dodgers (March 26, 2002). ... Signed by Montreal Expos organization (May 3, 2002). ... Signed as a free agent by Tampa Bay Devil Rays organization (December 23, 2002). ... Signed as a free agent by Texas Rangers organization (December 4, 2003). ... Released by Rangers (June 14, 2004). ... Signed by Baltimore Orioles organization (June 15, 2004).

CAREER HITTING: 1-for-4 (.250), 0 R, 0 2B, 0 3B, 0 HR, 0 RBI.

TODD WILLIAMS' PITCHING ZONE

.200	.333	.231
.154	.423	.400
.083	.320	.229

LEFTY-RIGHTY SPLITS

vs.	Avg.	AB	H	2B	3B	HR	RBI	BB	SO	OBP	Slg.
L	.263	114	30	2	0	1	10	9	10	.312	.307
R	.244	172	42	6	1	4	24	17	28	.320	.360

Year	Team (League)	W	L	Pct.	ERA	WHIP	G	GS	CG	ShO	Hld.	Sv.-Opp.	IP	H	R	ER	HR	BB-IBB	SO	Avg.
1991—	Great Falls (Pion.)	5	2	.714	2.72	1.40	28	0	0	0	...	8-...	53.0	50	26	16	1	24-1	59	.242
1992—	Bakersfield (Calif.)	0	0		2.30	1.15	13	0	0	0	...	9-...	15.2	11	4	4	1	7-1	11	.196
	—San Antonio (Texas)	7	4	.636	3.27	1.59	39	0	0	0	...	13-...	44.0	47	17	16	0	23-6	35	.281
1993—	Albuquerque (PCL)	5	5	.500	4.99	1.68	65	0	0	0	...	21-...	70.1	87	44	39	2	31-6	56	.302
1994—	Albuquerque (PCL)	4	2	.667	3.11	1.31	59	0	0	0	...	13-...	72.1	78	29	25	5	17-3	30	.284
1995—	Los Angeles (N.L.)	2	2	.500	5.12	1.34	16	0	0	0	0	0-1	19.1	19	11	11	3	7-2	8	.264
	—Albuquerque (PCL)	4	1	.800	3.38	1.63	25	0	0	0	...	0-...	45.1	59	21	17	4	15-4	23	.319
1996—	Edmonton (PCL)	5	3	.625	5.50	1.77	35	10	0	0	...	5-...	91.2	125	71	56	4	37-3	33	.329
1997—	Chattanooga (Sou.)	3	3	.500	2.10	1.13	48	0	0	0	...	31-...	55.2	38	16	13	1	25-2	45	.186
	—Indianapolis (A.A.)	2	0	1.000	2.13	1.34	12	0	0	0	...	2-...	12.2	11	4	3	0	6-1	11	.239
1998—	Indianapolis (Int'l)	3	0	1.000	2.31	1.34	53	0	0	0	...	26-...	58.1	54	19	15	0	24-2	35	.255
	—Cincinnati (N.L.)	0	1	.000	7.71	2.25	6	0	0	0	0	0-0	9.1	15	8	8	1	6-0	4	.341
1999—	Indianapolis (Int'l)	1	3	.250	5.10	1.20	38	0	0	0	...	24-...	42.1	38	24	24	3	13-0	35	.250
	—Tacoma (PCL)	0	0		0.00	0.60	1	0	0	0	...	1-...	1.2	1	0	0	0	0-0	0	.167
	—Seattle (A.L.)	0	0		4.66	1.86	13	0	0	0	0	0-0	9.2	11	5	5	1	7-0	7	.289
2000—	Tacoma (PCL)	2	3	.400	2.98	1.34	50	0	0	0	...	32-...	51.1	51	20	17	2	18-1	26	.268
2001—	New York (A.L.)	1	0	1.000	4.70	2.02	15	0	0	0	1	0-0	15.1	22	9	8	1	9-2	13	.324
	—GC Yankees (GCL)	0	0		0.00	0.50	1	1	0	0	...	0-...	2.0	1	0	0	0	0-0	5	.154
	—Columbus (Int'l)	0	1	.000	7.11	2.11	17	0	0	0	...	2-...	19.0	31	19	15	0	9-3	14	.352
	—Norwich (East.)	1	0	1.000	0.00	0.50	6	0	0	0	...	1-...	8.0	4	0	0	0	0-0	5	.148
2002—	Ottawa (Int'l)	3	5	.375	3.75	1.42	46	0	0	0	...	24-...	48.0	56	26	20	4	12-3	21	.298
2003—	Durham (Int'l)	3	2	.600	1.55	1.00	56	0	0	0	...	4-...	69.2	55	12	12	2	14-2	36	.215
2004—	Oklahoma (PCL)	2	2	.500	3.03	1.53	27	0	0	0	...	9-...	29.2	37	13	10	2	7-2	11	.308
	—Ottawa (Int'l)	1	1	.500	3.05	1.06	14	0	0	0	...	2-...	20.2	19	7	7	1	3-1	11	.247
	—Baltimore (A.L.)	2	0	1.000	2.87	1.12	29	0	0	0	3	0-0	31.1	26	10	10	2	9-0	13	.232
2005—	Baltimore (A.L.)	5	5	.500	3.30	1.28	72	0	0	0	18	1-3	76.1	72	34	28	6	26-4	38	.252
American League totals (4 years)		8	5	.615	3.46	1.37	129	0	0	0	22	1-3	132.2	131	58	51	9	51-6	71	.260
National League totals (2 years)		2	3	.400	5.97	1.64	22	0	0	0	0	0-1	28.2	34	19	19	4	13-2	12	.293
Major League totals (6 years)		10	8	.556	3.90	1.42	151	0	0	0	22	1-4	161.1	165	77	70	13	64-8	83	.266

W

WILLIAMS, WOODY   P

PERSONAL: Born August 19, 1966, in Houston. ... 6-0/200. ... Throws right, bats right. ... Full name: Gregory Scott Williams. ... High school: Cypress-Fairbanks (Houston). ... College: Houston.

TRANSACTIONS/CAREER NOTES: Selected by Toronto Blue Jays organization in 28th round of 1988 free-agent draft. ... On disabled list (July 17, 1995-remainder of season); included rehabilitation assignment to Syracuse. ... On disabled list (March 22-May 31 and June 11-July 26, 1996); included rehabilitation assignments to Dunedin, Syracuse and St. Catharines. ... Traded by Blue Jays with P Carlos Almanzar and OF Peter Tucci to San Diego Padres for P Joey Hamilton (December 13, 1998). ... On disabled list (May 2-July 2, 2000); included rehabilitation assignments to Rancho Cucamonga and Las Vegas. ... Traded by Padres to St. Louis Cardinals for OF Ray Lankford and cash (August 2, 2001). ... On disabled list (April 6-May 15 and July 7-August 29, 2002); included rehabilitation assignment to Memphis. ... Signed as a free agent by Padres (December 8, 2004). ... On disabled list (May 4-June 5, 2005).

CAREER HITTING: 88-for-427 (.206), 46 R, 24 2B, 1 3B, 3 HR, 37 RBI.

SCOUTING REPORT **Throws:** Williams doesn't have overpowering stuff, throwing a fastball that ranges from 86-90 mph, a slider that tops out at 86, a curveball, a cut fastball and a changeup. **Tendencies:** He must use all his pitches, mix speeds and work ahead in the count to be successful. Has a good idea what he's doing and compensates for declining velocity with excellent command. Throws a tight, downward curve to lefthanders and runs his late-biting slider away from righthanders. Fades his straight changeup with good arm speed. Is a high-ball pitcher. **Outlook:** Williams, an outstanding athlete who also swings a good bat, is more of a fifth starter because of his declining stuff. Has outstanding makeup and gets the most from his ability. *Grade 6.3*

WOODY WILLIAMS' PITCHING ZONE

.184	.323	.300
.349	.276	.345
.226	.333	.231

LEFTY-RIGHTY SPLITS

vs.	Avg.	AB	H	2B	3B	HR	RBI	BB	SO	OBP	Slg.
L	.259	274	71	18	1	9	35	31	45	.336	.431
R	.288	358	103	17	5	15	50	20	61	.326	.489

Year Team (League)	W	L	Pct.	ERA	WHIP	G	GS	CG	ShO	Hld.	Sv.-Opp.	IP	H	R	ER	HR	BB-IBB	SO	Avg.
1988— St. Catharines (NYP)	8	2	.800	1.54	0.91	12	12	2	0	...	0-...	76.0	48	22	13	1	21-0	58	.178
— Knoxville (Sou.)	2	2	.500	3.81	1.38	6	4	0	0	...	0-...	28.1	27	13	12	1	12-0	25	.250
1989— Dunedin (Fla. St.)	3	5	.375	2.32	1.11	20	9	0	0	...	3-...	81.1	63	26	21	3	27-1	60	.217
— Knoxville (Sou.)	3	5	.375	3.55	1.32	14	12	2	2	...	1-...	71.0	61	32	28	6	33-2	51	.235
1990— Knoxville (Sou.)	7	9	.438	3.14	1.19	42	12	0	0	...	5-...	126.0	111	55	44	7	39-3	74	.236
— Syracuse (Int'l)	0	1	.000	10.00	2.11	3	0	0	0	...	0-...	9.0	15	10	10	1	4-0	8	.375
1991— Knoxville (Sou.)	3	2	.600	3.59	1.31	18	1	0	0	...	3-...	42.2	42	18	17	1	14-0	37	.261
— Syracuse (Int'l)	3	4	.429	4.12	1.45	31	0	0	0	...	6-...	54.2	52	27	25	2	27-3	37	.250
1992— Syracuse (Int'l)	6	8	.429	3.13	1.29	25	16	1	0	...	1-...	120.2	115	46	42	4	41-0	81	.253
1993— Syracuse (Int'l)	1	1	.500	2.20	1.22	12	0	0	0	...	3-...	16.1	15	5	4	2	5-3	16	.246
— Toronto (A.L.)	3	1	.750	4.38	1.68	30	0	0	0	4	0-2	37.0	40	18	18	2	22-3	24	.274
— Dunedin (Fla. St.)	0	0	...	0.00	0.50	2	0	0	0	...	0-...	4.0	0	0	0	0	2-0	2	.000
1994— Toronto (A.L.)	1	3	.250	3.64	1.30	38	0	0	0	5	0-0	59.1	44	24	24	5	33-1	56	.205
— Syracuse (Int'l)	0	0	...	0.00	0.00	1	0	0	0	...	1-...	1.2	0	0	0	0	0-0	1	.000
1995— Toronto (A.L.)	1	2	.333	3.69	1.34	23	3	0	0	1	0-1	53.2	44	23	22	6	28-1	41	.220
— Syracuse (Int'l)	0	0	...	3.52	1.30	5	1	0	0	...	1-...	7.2	5	3	3	0	5-0	13	.172
1996— Dunedin (Fla. St.)	0	2	.000	8.22	1.43	2	2	0	0	...	0-...	7.2	9	7	7	1	2-0	11	.281
— Syracuse (Int'l)	3	1	.750	1.41	0.91	7	7	1	1	...	0-...	32.0	22	5	5	3	7-0	33	.191
— Toronto (A.L.)	4	5	.444	4.73	1.44	12	10	1	0	0	0-0	59.0	64	33	31	8	21-1	43	.278
— St. Catharines (NYP)	0	0	...	3.68	1.50	2	2	0	0	...	0-...	7.1	7	3	3	0	4-0	12	.269
1997— Toronto (A.L.)	9	14	.391	4.35	1.37	31	31	0	0	0	0-0	194.2	201	98	94	31	66-3	124	.269
1998— Toronto (A.L.)	10	9	.526	4.46	1.32	32	32	1	1	0	0-0	209.2	196	112	104	36	81-3	151	.245
1999— San Diego (N.L.)	12	12	.500	4.41	1.37	33	33	0	0	0	0-0	208.1	213	106	102	33	73-5	137	.268
2000— San Diego (N.L.)	10	8	.556	3.75	1.23	23	23	4	0	0	0-0	168.0	152	74	70	23	54-2	111	.239
— Rancho Cuca. (Calif.)	0	0	...	0.00	0.60	1	1	0	0	...	0-...	5.0	3	0	0	0	0-0	10	.167
— Las Vegas (PCL)	0	0	...	1.50	1.17	1	1	0	0	...	0-...	6.0	7	2	1	0	0-0	5	.292
2001— San Diego (N.L.)	8	8	.500	4.97	1.43	23	23	0	0	0	0-0	145.0	170	88	80	28	37-4	102	.296
— St. Louis (N.L.)	7	1	.875	2.28	0.97	11	11	3	1	0	0-0	75.0	54	22	19	7	19-1	52	.205
2002— St. Louis (N.L.)	9	4	.692	2.53	1.05	17	17	1	0	0	0-0	103.1	84	30	29	10	25-2	76	.222
— Memphis (PCL)	1	0	1.000	1.80	0.40	1	1	0	0	...	0-...	5.0	1	1	1	0	1-0	7	.067
2003— St. Louis (N.L.)	18	9	.667	3.87	1.25	34	33	0	0	0	0-1	220.2	220	101	95	20	55-2	153	.256
2004— St. Louis (N.L.)	11	8	.579	4.18	1.32	31	31	0	0	0	0-0	189.2	193	93	88	20	58-3	131	.262
2005— San Diego (N.L.)	9	12	.429	4.85	1.41	28	28	0	0	0	0-0	159.2	174	92	86	24	51-1	106	.275
American League totals (6 years)	28	34	.452	4.30	1.37	166	76	2	1	10	0-3	613.1	589	308	293	88	251-12	439	.252
National League totals (7 years)	84	62	.575	4.03	1.29	200	199	8	1	0	0-1	1269.2	1260	606	569	165	372-20	868	.258
Major League totals (13 years)	112	96	.538	4.12	1.31	366	275	10	2	10	0-4	1883.0	1849	914	862	253	623-32	1307	.256

DIVISION SERIES RECORD

Year Team (League)	W	L	Pct.	ERA	WHIP	G	GS	CG	ShO	Hld.	Sv.-Opp.	IP	H	R	ER	HR	BB-IBB	SO	Avg.
2001— St. Louis (N.L.)	1	0	1.000	1.29	0.71	1	1	0	0	0	0-0	7.0	4	1	1	0	1-0	9	.160
2004— St. Louis (N.L.)	1	0	1.000	3.00	1.50	1	1	0	0	0	0-0	6.0	8	2	2	0	1-0	2	.320
2005— San Diego (N.L.)	0	1	.000	27.00	4.80	1	1	0	0	0	0-0	1.2	6	5	5	1	2-1	2	.545
Division series totals (3 years)	2	1	.667	4.91	1.50	3	3	0	0	0	0-0	14.2	18	8	8	1	4-1	13	.295

CHAMPIONSHIP SERIES RECORD

Year Team (League)	W	L	Pct.	ERA	WHIP	G	GS	CG	ShO	Hld.	Sv.-Opp.	IP	H	R	ER	HR	BB-IBB	SO	Avg.
2002— St. Louis (N.L.)	0	1	.000	4.50	1.17	1	1	0	0	0	0-0	6.0	6	3	3	2	1-0	7	.261
2004— St. Louis (N.L.)	1	0	1.000	2.77	0.62	2	2	0	0	0	0-0	13.0	5	4	4	2	3-0	9	.114
Champ. series totals (2 years)	1	1	.500	3.32	0.79	3	3	0	0	0	0-0	19.0	11	7	7	4	4-0	16	.164

WORLD SERIES RECORD

Year Team (League)	W	L	Pct.	ERA	WHIP	G	GS	CG	ShO	Hld.	Sv.-Opp.	IP	H	R	ER	HR	BB-IBB	SO	Avg.
2004— St. Louis (N.L.)	0	0	...	27.00	4.71	1	1	0	0	0	0-0	2.1	8	7	7	1	3-0	1	.533

ALL-STAR GAME RECORD

Year Team (League)	W	L	Pct.	ERA	WHIP	G	GS	CG	ShO	Hld.	Sv.-Opp.	IP	H	R	ER	HR	BB-IBB	SO	Avg.
All-Star Game totals (1 year)	0	0	...	18.00	2.00	1	1	0	0	0	0-0	1.0	2	2	2	1	0-0	1	.400

WILLIAMSON, SCOTT — P

PERSONAL: Born February 17, 1976, in Fort Polk, La. ... 6-0/180. ... Throws right, bats right. ... Full name: Scott Ryan Williamson. ... High school: Friendswood (Texas). ... College: Oklahoma State.

TRANSACTIONS/CAREER NOTES: Selected by Cincinnati Reds organization in ninth round of 1997 free-agent draft. ... On disabled list (August 24-September 8, 2000; and April 4, 2001-remainder of season). ... Traded by Reds to Boston Red Sox for P Phil Dumatrait, a player to be named and cash (July 30, 2003); Reds acquired P Tyler Pelland to complete deal (August 18, 2003). ... On disabled list (May 19-June 11 and July 1-September 9, 2004); included rehabilitation assignment to Pawtucket. ... Signed as free agent by Chicago Cubs (January 18, 2005). ... On disabled list (March 30-August 5, 2005); included rehabilitation assignment to Iowa.

HONORS: Named N.L. Rookie Pitcher of the Year by THE SPORTING NEWS (1999). ... Named N.L. Rookie of the Year by Baseball Writers' Association of America (1999).

CAREER HITTING: 1-for-23 (.043), 1 R, 0 2B, 0 3B, 0 HR, 0 RBI.

SCOUTING REPORT

Throws: Williamson's four-seam fastball hits 95 mph. Also throws a slider and a split-finger fastball. **Tendencies:** Williamson's elbow injuries have turned him into a fastball-slider pitcher, and he has lost velocity off his four-seamer. Always has struggled with his release point and delivery, causing career-long command issues. Violent mechanics cause continual elbow strain, and prevent him from throwing what was once a quality out-pitch splitter. **Outlook:** The Cubs picked up Williamson's option for 2006 and will use him in the seventh and eighth innings, and hope he can stay healthy. **Grade 6.8**

SCOTT WILLIAMSON'S PITCHING ZONE

.667	...	.000
.286	.333	.429
1.000	.667	.200

LEFTY-RIGHTY SPLITS

vs.	Avg.	AB	H	2B	3B	HR	RBI	BB	SO	OBP	Slg.
L	.333	15	5	0	0	1	4	1	4	.412	.533
R	.250	40	10	1	0	2	2	5	19	.348	.425

Year — Team (League)	W	L	Pct.	ERA	WHIP	G	GS	CG	ShO	Hld.	Sv.-Opp.	IP	H	R	ER	HR	BB-IBB	SO	Avg.
1997— Billings (Pion.)	8	2	.800	1.78	1.03	13	13	2	1	...	0-...	86.0	66	25	17	5	23-0	101	.209
1998— Chattanooga (Sou.)	4	5	.444	3.78	1.31	18	18	0	0	...	0-...	100.0	85	49	42	4	46-4	105	.234
— Indianapolis (Int'l)	0	0	...	3.48	1.40	5	5	0	0	...	0-...	20.2	20	9	8	2	9-0	17	.260
1999— Cincinnati (N.L.)	12	7	.632	2.41	1.04	62	0	0	0	5	19-26	93.1	54	29	25	8	43-6	107	.171
2000— Cincinnati (N.L.)	5	8	.385	3.29	1.49	48	10	0	0	6	6-8	112.0	92	45	41	7	75-7	136	.224
2001— Cincinnati (N.L.)	0	0	...	0.00	4.50	2	0	0	0	1	0-0	0.2	1	0	0	0	2-0	0	.333
2002— Cincinnati (N.L.)	3	4	.429	2.92	1.11	63	0	0	0	8	8-12	74.0	46	27	24	5	36-5	84	.181
2003— Cincinnati (N.L.)	5	3	.625	3.19	1.39	42	0	0	0	8	21-26	42.1	34	15	15	6	25-4	53	.214
— Boston (A.L.)	0	1	.000	6.20	1.43	24	0	0	0	5	0-2	20.1	20	15	14	1	9-2	21	.253
2004— Pawtucket (Int'l)	1	0	1.000	12.27	2.45	4	1	0	0	...	0-...	3.2	3	5	5	0	6-0	6	.231
— Boston (A.L.)	0	1	.000	1.26	1.01	28	0	0	0	3	1-2	28.2	11	6	4	0	18-1	28	.115
2005— Ariz. Cubs (AZL)	0	2	.000	2.45	1.23	4	1	0	0	0	0-0	7.1	7	8	2	0	2-0	9	.250
— Iowa (PCL)	1	0	1.000	3.86	1.00	7	0	0	0	1	0-0	7.0	4	3	3	1	3-0	10	.154
— Chicago (N.L.)	1	0	...	5.65	1.47	17	0	0	0	9	0-0	14.1	15	9	9	3	6-0	23	.273
American League totals (2 years)	0	2	.000	3.31	1.18	52	0	0	0	8	1-4	49.0	31	21	18	1	27-3	49	.177
National League totals (6 years)	25	22	.532	3.05	1.27	234	10	0	0	23	54-72	336.2	242	125	114	29	187-22	403	.202
Major League totals (7 years)	25	24	.510	3.08	1.26	286	10	0	0	31	55-76	385.2	273	146	132	30	214-25	452	.199

DIVISION SERIES RECORD

Year — Team (League)	W	L	Pct.	ERA	WHIP	G	GS	CG	ShO	Hld.	Sv.-Opp.	IP	H	R	ER	HR	BB-IBB	SO	Avg.
2003— Boston (A.L.)	2	0	1.000	0.00	1.00	5	0	0	0	0	0-0	5.0	2	0	0	0	3-0	8	.125

CHAMPIONSHIP SERIES RECORD

Year — Team (League)	W	L	Pct.	ERA	WHIP	G	GS	CG	ShO	Hld.	Sv.-Opp.	IP	H	R	ER	HR	BB-IBB	SO	Avg.
2003— Boston (A.L.)	0	0	...	3.00	0.33	3	0	0	0	0	3-3	3.0	1	1	1	1	0-0	6	.100

WILLINGHAM, JOSH — C/OF

PERSONAL: Born February 17, 1979, in Florence, Ala. ... 6-1/200. ... Bats right, throws right. ... Full name: Joshua David Willingham. ... High school: Mars Hill Bible (Florence, Ala.). ... College: Northern Alabama.

TRANSACTIONS/CAREER NOTES: Selected by Florida Marlins organization in third round of 2000 free-agent draft. ... On disabled list (July 6-September 2, 2005); included rehabilitation assignment to Albuquerque.

2005 GAMES PLAYED BY POSITION (MLB): C—8, DH—1, OF—1.

LEFTY-RIGHTY SPLITS

vs.	Avg.	AB	H	2B	3B	HR	RBI	BB	SO	OBP	Slg.
L	.429	7	3	1	0	0	1	1	2	.600	.571
R	.250	16	4	0	0	0	3	1	3	.294	.250

Year — Team (League)	Pos.	G	AB	R	H	2B	3B	HR	RBI	BB	SO	HBP	GDP	SB-CS	Avg.	OBP	SLG	OPS	E	Avg.
2000— Utica (N.Y.-Penn)	OF-2B-3B-SS-1B	65	205	37	54	16	0	6	29	39	55	9	2	9-5	.263	.400	.429	.829	2	.982
2001— Kane Co. (Midw.)	3B-OF-2B	97	320	57	83	20	2	7	36	53	85	13	7	24-2	.259	.382	.400	.782	15	.945
2002— Jupiter (Fla. St.)	1B-3B-OF	107	376	72	103	21	4	17	69	63	88	13	7	18-5	.274	.394	.487	.881	9	.975
2003— Jupiter (Fla. St.)	3B	59	193	46	51	17	1	12	34	46	42	9	3	9-2	.264	.422	.549	.972	2	.994
— GC Marlins (GCL)		2	7	3	3	1	0	1	3	1	2	0	0		.429	.500	1.000	1.500	...	...
— Carolina (Sou.)	1B-C-3B-OF	22	67	15	20	1	0	5	14	13	20	3	0		.299	.434	.582	1.016	0	1.000
2004— Florida (N.L.)	C-OF	12	25	2	5	0	0	1	1	4	8	0	1	0-0	.200	.310	.320	.630	1	.955
— Carolina (Sou.)	C-1B-OF-DH-3B	112	338	81	95	24	0	24	76	91	87	18	5	6-3	.281	.449	.565	.992	5	.994
2005— Jupiter (Fla. St.)	C-3B-DH	2	9	1	2	1	0	0	1	2	1	0	0		.222	.300	.333	.633	0	1.000
— Albuquerque (PCL)	C-OF-DH	66	219	56	71	14	3	19	54	47	54	9	5	5-1	.324	.455	.676	1.131	5	.988
— Florida (N.L.)		16	23	3	7	1	0	0	4	2	5	2	1		.304	.407	.348	.755	0	1.000
Major League totals (2 years)		28	48	5	12	1	0	1	5	6	13	2	2	0-0	.250	.357	.333	.690	1	.977

W

WILLIS, DONTRELLE   P

PERSONAL: Born January 12, 1982, in Oakland. ... 6-4/239. ... Throws left, bats left. ... Full name: Dontrelle Wayne Willis. ... High school: Encinal (Alameda, Calif.).
TRANSACTIONS/CAREER NOTES: Selected by Chicago Cubs organization in eighth round of 2000 free-agent draft. ... Traded by Cubs with Ps Julian Tavarez and Jose Cueto and C Ryan Jorgensen to Florida Marlins for Ps Antonio Alfonseca and Matt Clement (March 27, 2002).
HONORS: Named N.L. Rookie Pitcher of the Year by THE SPORTING NEWS (2003). ... Named N.L. Rookie of the Year by Baseball Writers' Association of America (2003).
CAREER HITTING: 53-for-224 (.237), 21 R, 8 2B, 1 3B, 3 HR, 18 RBI.

SCOUTING REPORT Throws: His fastball tops out at 93 mph, and he also has a slider and changeup. Slider is more of a slurve. ***Tendencies:*** Willis is the league's most athletic pitcher. Throws strikes and has outstanding deception. Expands the plate laterally with his late-running fastball, which is effective against righthanded hitters. Has as much late movement with that pitch as any starter in the league; it appears to jump at the last minute Has sharp movement on his breaking ball. Throws his change with good arm speed and movement. ***Outlook:*** Willis is one of the most charismatic players in the game, a pitcher people are excited to watch. Is poised to remain a big winner because of his enthusiasm and athletic ability. ***Grade 9.3***

DONTRELLE WILLIS' PITCHING ZONE

.173	.281	.229
.267	.345	.206
.246	.333	.271

LEFTY-RIGHTY SPLITS

vs.	Avg.	AB	H	2B	3B	HR	RBI	BB	SO	OBP	Slg.
L	.222	158	35	5	2	1	14	1	51	.236	.297
R	.247	720	178	40	7	10	52	54	119	.303	.364

Year — Team (League)	W	L	Pct.	ERA	WHIP	G	GS	CG	ShO	Hld.	Sv.-Opp.	IP	H	R	ER	HR	BB-IBB	SO	Avg.
2000— Ariz. Cubs (AZL)	3	1	.750	3.86	1.21	9	1	0	0	...	0-...	28.0	26	15	12	0	8-1	22	.245
2001— Boise (N'west)	8	2	.800	2.98	1.01	15	15	0	0	...	0-...	93.2	76	36	31	1	19-0	77	.217
2002— Kane Co. (Midw.)	10	2	.833	1.83	0.88	19	19	3	2	...	0-...	127.2	91	29	26	3	21-0	101	.200
— Jupiter (Fla. St.)	2	0	1.000	1.80	0.90	5	5	0	0	...	0-...	30.0	24	7	6	2	3-0	27	.216
2003— Carolina (Sou.)	4	0	1.000	1.49	0.91	6	6	0	0	...	0-...	36.1	24	6	6	2	9-0	32	.194
— Florida (N.L.)	14	6	.700	3.30	1.28	27	27	2	2	0	0-0	160.2	148	61	59	13	58-0	142	.245
2004— Florida (N.L.)	10	11	.476	4.02	1.38	32	32	2	0	0	0-0	197.0	210	99	88	20	61-8	139	.273
2005— Florida (N.L.)	* 22	10	.688	2.63	1.13	34	34	• 7	* 5	0	0-0	236.1	213	79	69	11	55-3	170	.243
Major League totals (3 years)	46	27	.630	3.27	1.25	93	93	11	7	0	0-0	594.0	571	239	216	44	174-11	451	.254

DIVISION SERIES RECORD

Year — Team (League)	W	L	Pct.	ERA	WHIP	G	GS	CG	ShO	Hld.	Sv.-Opp.	IP	H	R	ER	HR	BB-IBB	SO	Avg.
2003— Florida (N.L.)	0	0	...	7.94	1.59	2	1	0	0	0	0-0	5.2	7	5	5	0	2-0	3	.318

CHAMPIONSHIP SERIES RECORD

Year — Team (League)	W	L	Pct.	ERA	WHIP	G	GS	CG	ShO	Hld.	Sv.-Opp.	IP	H	R	ER	HR	BB-IBB	SO	Avg.
2003— Florida (N.L.)	0	1	.000	18.90	3.00	2	1	0	0	0	0-0	3.1	4	7	7	1	6-0	4	.308

WORLD SERIES RECORD

Year — Team (League)	W	L	Pct.	ERA	WHIP	G	GS	CG	ShO	Hld.	Sv.-Opp.	IP	H	R	ER	HR	BB-IBB	SO	Avg.
2003— Florida (N.L.)	0	0	...	0.00	1.64	3	0	0	0	1	0-0	3.2	4	0	0	0	2-0	3	.267

ALL-STAR GAME RECORD

Year — Team (League)	W	L	Pct.	ERA	WHIP	G	GS	CG	ShO	Hld.	Sv.-Opp.	IP	H	R	ER	HR	BB-IBB	SO	Avg.
All-Star Game totals (1 year)	0	0	...	18.00	3.00	1	0	0	0	0	0-0	1.0	2	2	2	1	1-0	0	.500

WILSON, C.J.   P

PERSONAL: Born November 18, 1980, in Newport Beach, Calif. ... 6-2/200. ... Throws left, bats left. ... Full name: Christopher John Wilson. ... High school: Fountain Valley (Calif.). ... Junior college: Santa Ana (Calif.). ... College: Loyola Marymount.
TRANSACTIONS/CAREER NOTES: Selected by Texas Rangers organization in fifth round of 2001 free-agent draft.
CAREER HITTING: 0-for-0 (.000), 0 R, 0 2B, 0 3B, 0 HR, 0 RBI.

C.J. WILSON'S PITCHING ZONE

.381	.273	.333
.255	.448	.579
.231	.167	.333

LEFTY-RIGHTY SPLITS

vs.	Avg.	AB	H	2B	3B	HR	RBI	BB	SO	OBP	Slg.
L	.290	69	20	2	0	1	11	4	14	.329	.362
R	.339	127	43	10	0	4	22	14	16	.408	.512

Year — Team (League)	W	L	Pct.	ERA	WHIP	G	GS	CG	ShO	Hld.	Sv.-Opp.	IP	H	R	ER	HR	BB-IBB	SO	Avg.
2001— Pulaski (Appalachian)	1	0	1.000	0.96	0.88	8	8	0	0	...	0-...	37.2	24	6	4	2	9-0	49	.178
— Savannah (S. Atl.)	1	2	.333	3.18	1.15	5	5	2	0	...	0-...	34.0	30	13	12	2	9-0	26	.252
2002— Charlotte (Fla. St.)	10	2	.833	3.06	1.20	26	15	0	0	...	1-...	106.0	86	48	36	4	41-1	76	.215
— Tulsa (Texas)	1	0	1.000	1.80	1.17	5	5	0	0	...	0-...	30.0	23	6	6	0	12-0	17	.211
2003— Frisco (Texas)	6	9	.400	5.05	1.41	22	21	0	0	...	0-...	123.0	135	79	69	11	38-3	89	.276
2004—				Did not play.															
2005— Bakersfield (Calif.)	0	1	.000	3.29	1.02	4	4	0	0	0	0-0	13.2	10	5	5	2	4-0	14	.189
— Frisco (Texas)	0	4	.000	4.43	1.46	12	12	0	0	0	0-0	44.2	51	32	22	7	14-0	43	.290
— Texas (A.L.)	1	7	.125	6.94	1.69	24	6	0	0	4	1-1	48.0	63	39	37	5	18-1	30	.321
Major League totals (1 year)	1	7	.125	6.94	1.69	24	6	0	0	4	1-1	48.0	63	39	37	5	18-1	30	.321

WILSON, CRAIG   OF/1B

PERSONAL: Born November 30, 1976, in Fountain Valley, Calif. ... 6-2/220. ... Bats right, throws right. ... Full name: Craig Alan Wilson. ... High school: Marina (Huntington Beach, Calif.).
TRANSACTIONS/CAREER NOTES: Selected by Toronto Blue Jays organization in second round of 1995 free-agent draft. ... Traded by Blue Jays with SS Abraham Nunez and P Mike Halperin to Pittsburgh Pirates (December 11, 1996), completing deal in which Pirates traded 2B Carlos Garcia, 1B Orlando Merced and P Dan Plesac to Blue Jays for Ps Jose Pett and Jose Silva, SS Brandon Cromer and three players to be named (November 14, 1996). ... On disabled list (May 8-July 9 and July 17-August 28, 2005); included rehabilitation assignment to Indianapolis.
2005 GAMES PLAYED BY POSITION (MLB): OF—47, 1B—15.

SCOUTING REPORT

Offense: Prior to his injury last season, he had exceptional power to all fields. Has a fluid swing with a slight uppercut but has trouble making contact with a good fastball up in the zone. Likes the ball out over the plate and is vulnerable inside. Is not a good base runner. **Defense:** He's in the big leagues for his power, not his defense. Doesn't have a position and doesn't throw well because he doesn't get on top. Doesn't have very quick footwork around the bag but hands are good. **Outlook:** Wilson belongs in the A.L., where he can be a DH. **Grade 6.6**

CRAIG WILSON'S HITTING ZONE

.267	.091	.429
.361	.529	.267
.267	.167	.000

LEFTY-RIGHTY SPLITS

vs.	Avg.	AB	H	2B	3B	HR	RBI	BB	SO	OBP	Slg.
L	.283	53	15	4	0	1	5	12	18	.449	.415
R	.257	144	37	10	1	4	17	18	51	.361	.424

Year	Team (League)	Pos.	G	AB	R	H	2B	3B	HR	RBI	BB	SO	HBP	GDP	SB-CS	Avg.	OBP	SLG	OPS	E	Avg.
1995—	Medicine Hat (Pion.)	C	49	184	33	52	14	1	7	35	24	44	3	1	8-2	.283	.367	.484	.851	5	.982
1996—	Hagerstown (S. Atl.)	C-OF	131	495	66	129	27	5	11	70	32	120	10	12	17-11	.261	.316	.402	.718	9	.986
1997—	Lynchburg (Carol.)	C	117	401	54	106	26	1	19	69	39	98	15	3	6-5	.264	.350	.476	.826	12	.985
1998—	Lynchburg (Carol.)	1B-C	61	219	26	59	12	2	12	45	22	53	5	3	2-1	.269	.348	.507	.855	6	.986
—	Carolina (Sou.)	C	45	148	20	49	11	0	5	21	14	32	4	2	4-1	.331	.399	.507	.906	1	.995
1999—	Altoona (East.)	1B-C-OF	111	362	57	97	21	3	20	69	40	104	19	8	1-3	.268	.367	.508	.875	9	.978
2000—	Nashville (PCL)	1B-C	124	396	83	112	24	1	33	86	44	121	25	7	1-2	.283	.383	.598	.982	13	.982
2001—	Nashville (PCL)	1B-C	11	45	4	13	2	1	1	3	2	14	1	1	0-0	.289	.333	.444	.778	2	.976
—	Pittsburgh (N.L.)	1B-OF-C																			
		DH	88	158	27	49	3	1	13	32	15	53	7	4	3-1	.310	.390	.589	.979	3	.987
2002—	Pittsburgh (N.L.)	OF-1B-C																			
		DH	131	368	48	97	16	1	16	57	32	116	* 21	10	2-3	.264	.355	.443	.798	5	.988
2003—	Pittsburgh (N.L.)	OF-1B-C																			
		DH	116	309	49	81	15	4	18	48	35	89	13	6	3-1	.262	.360	.511	.872	6	.986
2004—	Pittsburgh (N.L.)	OF-1B-C																			
		DH	155	561	97	148	35	5	29	82	50	169	* 30	11	2-2	.264	.354	.499	.853	7	.990
2005—	Indianapolis (Int'l)	OF-1B-DH	7	21	4	8	1	0	3	11	3	6	1	1	1-0	.381	.480	.857	1.337	2	.920
—	Pittsburgh (N.L.)	OF-1B	59	197	23	52	14	1	5	22	30	69	10	6	3-0	.264	.387	.421	.808	2	.989
	Major League totals (5 years)		549	1593	244	427	83	12	81	241	162	496	81	37	13-7	.268	.363	.488	.851	23	.988

WILSON, DAN   C

PERSONAL: Born March 25, 1969, in Barrington, Ill. ... 6-3/215. ... Bats right, throws right. ... Full name: Daniel Allen Wilson. ... High school: Barrington (Ill.). ... College: Minnesota.

TRANSACTIONS/CAREER NOTES: Selected by New York Mets organization in 26th round of 1987 free-agent draft; did not sign. ... Selected by Cincinnati Reds organization in first round (seventh pick overall) of 1990 free-agent draft. ... Traded by Reds with P Bobby Ayala to Seattle Mariners for P Erik Hanson and 2B Bret Boone (November 2, 1993). ... On disabled list (July 21-September 1, 1998). ... On disabled list (June 15-July 14, 2000); included rehabilitation assignments to Everett and Tacoma. ... On disabled list (March 19-April 6, 2003); included rehabilitation assignment to San Antonio. ... On disabled list (May 6-September 30, 2005).

2005 GAMES PLAYED BY POSITION (MLB): C—11.

LEFTY-RIGHTY SPLITS

vs.	Avg.	AB	H	2B	3B	HR	RBI	BB	SO	OBP	Slg.
L	.000	9	0	0	0	0	0	0	4	.000	.000
R	.278	18	5	0	0	0	2	0	6	.316	.278

Year	Team (League)	Pos.	G	AB	R	H	2B	3B	HR	RBI	BB	SO	HBP	GDP	SB-CS	Avg.	OBP	SLG	OPS	E	Avg.
1990—	Char., W.Va. (S. Atl.)	C	32	113	16	28	9	1	2	17	13	17	0	1	0-0	.248	.323	.398	.721	1	.995
1991—	Char., W.Va. (S. Atl.)	C	52	197	25	62	11	1	3	29	25	21	2	6	1-1	.315	.396	.426	.822	3	.992
—	Chattanooga (Sou.)	C	81	292	32	75	19	2	2	38	21	39	2	10	2-2	.257	.303	.356	.659	4	.993
1992—	Nashville (A.A.)	C	106	366	27	92	16	1	4	34	31	58	2	7	1-4	.251	.310	.333	.644	8	.990
—	Cincinnati (N.L.)	C	12	25	2	9	1	0	0	3	3	8	0	2	0-0	.360	.429	.400	.829	0	1.000
1993—	Cincinnati (N.L.)	C	36	76	6	17	3	0	0	8	9	16	0	2	0-0	.224	.302	.263	.565	1	.994
—	Indianapolis (A.A.)	C	51	191	18	50	11	1	1	17	19	31	1	4	1-0	.262	.330	.346	.676	2	.994
1994—	Seattle (A.L.)	C	91	282	24	61	14	2	3	27	10	57	1	11	1-2	.216	.244	.312	.556	* 9	.986
1995—	Seattle (A.L.)	C	119	399	40	111	22	3	9	51	33	63	2	12	2-1	.278	.336	.416	.752	5	.996
1996—	Seattle (A.L.)	C	138	491	51	140	24	0	18	83	32	88	3	15	1-2	.285	.330	.444	.774	4	.996
1997—	Seattle (A.L.)	C	146	508	66	137	31	1	15	74	39	72	5	12	7-2	.270	.326	.423	.749	6	.995
1998—	Seattle (A.L.)	C	96	325	39	82	17	1	9	44	24	56	5	6	2-1	.252	.308	.394	.702	4	.994
1999—	Seattle (A.L.)	C-1B	123	414	46	110	23	2	7	38	29	83	2	10	5-0	.266	.315	.382	.697	4	.995
2000—	Seattle (A.L.)	C-1B-3B	90	268	31	63	12	0	5	27	22	51	0	8	1-2	.235	.291	.336	.627	5	.990
—	Everett (N'west)	C	1	2	2	1	0	0	1	1	1	0	0	0	0-0	.500	.667	2.000	2.667	0	1.000
—	Tacoma (PCL)	DH	1	4	0	1	1	0	0	0	0	1	0	0	0-0	.250	.250	.500	.750	...	...
2001—	Seattle (A.L.)	C-1B	123	377	44	100	20	1	10	42	20	69	2	6	3-2	.265	.305	.403	.708	1	.999
2002—	Seattle (A.L.)	C-1B	115	359	35	106	16	1	6	44	18	81	2	8	1-0	.295	.326	.396	.721	2	.997
2003—	San Antonio (Texas)	C	2	7	0	0	0	0	0	0	0	0	0	0	0-0	.000	.000	.000	.000	1	.941
—	Seattle (A.L.)	C	96	316	32	76	15	2	4	43	15	52	0	1	0-0	.241	.272	.339	.611	1	.998
2004—	Seattle (A.L.)	C	103	319	23	80	13	0	2	33	26	57	1	8	0-1	.251	.305	.310	.615	2	.997
2005—	Seattle (A.L.)	C	11	27	2	5	0	0	0	0	2	10	1	1	0-1	.185	.214	.185	.399	1	.975
	American League totals (12 years)		1251	4085	433	1071	207	13	88	508	268	739	24	105	23-14	.262	.309	.384	.693	44	.995
	National League totals (2 years)		48	101	8	26	4	0	0	11	12	24	0	4	0-0	.257	.333	.297	.630	1	.995
	Major League totals (14 years)		1299	4186	441	1097	211	13	88	519	280	763	24	109	23-14	.262	.309	.382	.691	45	.995

DIVISION SERIES RECORD

Year	Team (League)	Pos.	G	AB	R	H	2B	3B	HR	RBI	BB	SO	HBP	GDP	SB-CS	Avg.	OBP	SLG	OPS	E	Avg.
1995—	Seattle (A.L.)	C	5	17	0	2	0	0	0	0	2	6	0	1	0-0	.118	.211	.118	.328	0	1.000
1997—	Seattle (A.L.)	C	4	13	0	0	0	0	0	0	0	9	0	0	0-0	.000	.000	.000	.000	0	1.000
2000—	Seattle (A.L.)	C	2	3	0	0	0	0	0	1	1	2	0	0	0-0	.000	.200	.000	.200	1	.833
2001—	Seattle (A.L.)	C	5	15	0	3	1	0	0	1	0	5	0	1	0-0	.200	.200	.267	.467	0	1.000
	Division series totals (4 years)		16	48	0	5	1	0	0	2	3	22	0	2	0-0	.104	.154	.125	.279	1	.991

W

CHAMPIONSHIP SERIES RECORD

Year Team (League)	Pos.	G	AB	R	H	2B	3B	HR	RBI	BB	SO	HBP	GDP	SB-CS	Avg.	OBP	SLG	OPS	E	Avg.
1995— Seattle (A.L.)	C	6	16	0	0	0	0	0	0	0	4	0	0	0-0	.000	.000	.000	.000	1	.974
2000— Seattle (A.L.)	C	4	11	0	1	0	0	0	0	1	5	0	0	0-0	.091	.167	.091	.258	1	.960
2001— Seattle (A.L.)	C	4	13	2	2	0	0	0	0	0	1	0	0	0-0	.154	.154	.154	.308	0	1.000
Champ. series totals (3 years)		14	40	2	3	0	0	0	0	1	10	0	0	0-0	.075	.098	.075	.173	2	.977

ALL-STAR GAME RECORD

	G	AB	R	H	2B	3B	HR	RBI	BB	SO	HBP	GDP	SB-CS	Avg.	OBP	SLG	OPS	E	Avg.
All-Star Game totals (1 year)	1	1	0	0	0	0	0	0	0	0	0	0	0-0	.000	.000	.000	.000	...	...

WILSON, ENRIQUE   2B

PERSONAL: Born July 27, 1973, in Santo Domingo, Dominican Republic. ... 5-11/195. ... Bats both, throws right. ... Full name: Enrique Martes Wilson. ... High school: Liceo Ramon Amelio Jiminez (Santo Domingo, Dominican Republic).

TRANSACTIONS/CAREER NOTES: Signed as a non-drafted free agent by Minnesota Twins organization (April 15, 1992). ... Traded by Twins to Cleveland Indians (February 21, 1994), completing deal in which Twins acquired P Shawn Bryant for a player to be named (February 21, 1994). ... On disabled list (April 4-June 15, 1998); included rehabilitation assignment to Buffalo. ... On disabled list (July 14-August 1, 2000); included rehabilitation assignment to Nashville. ... Traded by Indians with OF Alex Ramirez to Pittsburgh Pirates for 1B/OF Wil Cordero (July 28, 2000). ... Traded by Pirates to New York Yankees for P Damaso Marte (June 13, 2001). ... Signed as a free agent by Baltimore Orioles organization (January 18, 2005). ... Signed as a free agent by Chicago Cubs (May 17, 2005).

2005 GAMES PLAYED BY POSITION (MLB): 2B—5, SS—3, 1B—3, 3B—1.

LEFTY-RIGHTY SPLITS

vs.	Avg.	AB	H	2B	3B	HR	RBI	BB	SO	OBP	Slg.
L	.333	3	1	1	0	0	0	1	0	.500	.667
R	.105	19	2	1	0	0	0	2	1	.190	.158

											BATTING									FIELDING	
Year Team (League)	Pos.	G	AB	R	H	2B	3B	HR	RBI	BB	SO	HBP	GDP	SB-CS	Avg.	OBP	SLG	OPS	E	Avg.
1992— GC Twins (GCL)	SS	13	44	12	15	1	0	0	8	4	4	4	0	3-0	.341	.434	.364	.798	4	.897
1993— Elizabethton (Appal.)	3B-SS	58	197	42	57	8	4	13	50	14	18	6	1	5-4	.289	.352	.569	.920	19	.909
1994— Columbus (S. Atl.)	SS	133	512	82	143	28	12	10	72	44	34	6	7	21-13	.279	.341	.439	.780	33	.947
1995— Kinston (Carol.)	2B-SS	117	464	55	124	24	7	6	52	25	38	2	10	18-19	.267	.301	.388	.689	21	.964
1996— Cant./Akr. (East.)	SS-2B	117	484	70	147	17	5	5	50	31	46	4	9	23-16	.304	.346	.391	.737	28	.949
— Buffalo (A.A.)	3B-SS	3	8	1	4	1	0	0	0	1	1	0	1	0-2	.500	.556	.625	1.181	1	.750
1997— Buffalo (A.A.)	SS-2B-3B	118	451	78	138	20	3	11	39	42	41	5	7	9-8	.306	.369	.437	.805	20	.965
— Cleveland (A.L.)	SS-2B	5	15	2	5	0	0	0	1	0	2	0	0	0-0	.333	.333	.333	.667	1	.952
1998— Cleveland (A.L.)	2B-SS-3B	32	90	13	29	6	0	2	12	4	8	1	1	2-4	.322	.354	.456	.810	2	.983
— Buffalo (Int'l)	2B-SS	56	221	40	62	13	0	4	23	19	21	0	6	8-3	.281	.335	.394	.728	6	.976
1999— Cleveland (A.L.)	3B-SS-2B																			
	DH	113	332	41	87	22	1	2	24	25	41	1	12	5-4	.262	.310	.352	.663	8	.968
2000— Cleveland (A.L.)	3B-DH-2B																			
	SS	40	117	16	38	9	0	2	12	7	11	0	2	2-1	.325	.360	.453	.813	1	.985
— Nashville (PCL)	2B-SS	2	7	0	2	0	0	0	1	0	0	0	2	0-0	.286	.286	.286	.571	1	.889
— Pittsburgh (N.L.)	3B-2B-SS	40	122	11	32	6	1	3	15	11	13	0	4	0-1	.262	.321	.402	.723	6	.942
2001— Pittsburgh (N.L.)	SS-2B-3B	46	129	7	24	3	0	1	8	3	23	0	7	0-3	.186	.203	.233	.436	4	.974
— New York (A.L.)	SS-3B-2B																			
	DH	48	99	10	24	5	1	1	12	6	14	0	3	0-2	.242	.283	.343	.626	2	.981
2002— New York (A.L.)	3B-SS-2B																			
	DH-OF	60	105	17	19	2	2	2	11	8	22	0	1	1-1	.181	.239	.295	.534	5	.955
2003— New York (A.L.)	SS-3B-2B																			
	DH	63	135	18	31	9	0	1	15	7	14	2	3	3-1	.230	.276	.363	.639	3	.979
2004— New York (A.L.)	2B-SS	93	240	19	51	9	0	6	31	15	20	0	5	1-2	.213	.254	.325	.579	8	.977
2005— Ottawa (Int'l)	SS-2B	20	61	7	17	4	0	3	8	8	5	0	1	1-0	.279	.362	.492	.854	3	.961
— Chicago (N.L.)	2B-1B-SS																			
	3B	15	22	1	3	2	0	0	0	3	1	0	0	0-0	.136	.240	.227	.467	1	.966
American League totals (8 years)		454	1133	136	284	62	4	18	118	72	132	4	28	14-15	.251	.294	.360	.654	30	.974
National League totals (3 years)		101	273	19	59	11	1	4	23	17	37	0	11	0-4	.216	.260	.308	.568	11	.961
Major League totals (9 years)		555	1406	155	343	73	5	22	141	89	169	4	39	14-19	.244	.288	.350	.638	41	.972

DIVISION SERIES RECORD

Year Team (League)	Pos.	G	AB	R	H	2B	3B	HR	RBI	BB	SO	HBP	GDP	SB-CS	Avg.	OBP	SLG	OPS	E	Avg.
1998— Cleveland (A.L.)	2B	1	2	0	0	0	0	0	0	0	0	0	0	0-0	.000	.000	.000	.000	0	1.000
1999— Cleveland (A.L.)	2B	3	2	0	0	0	0	0	0	0	0	0	0	0-0	.000	.000	.000	.000	0	1.000
2002— New York (A.L.)		1	0	0	0	0	0	0	0	0	0	0	0	0-0	...	...	...	...	0	
Division series totals (3 years)		5	4	0	0	0	0	0	0	0	0	0	0	0-0	.000	.000	.000	.000	0	1.000

CHAMPIONSHIP SERIES RECORD

Year Team (League)	Pos.	G	AB	R	H	2B	3B	HR	RBI	BB	SO	HBP	GDP	SB-CS	Avg.	OBP	SLG	OPS	E	Avg.
1998— Cleveland (A.L.)	2B	5	14	2	3	0	0	0	1	3	0	0	0	0-0	.214	.267	.214	.481	1	.960
2001— New York (A.L.)	SS	1	1	0	1	0	0	0	0	0	0	0	0	0-0	1.000	1.000	1.000	2.000	0	
2003— New York (A.L.)	3B	2	7	0	1	0	0	0	0	1	0	0	0	0-0	.143	.143	.143	.286	1	.800
Champ. series totals (3 years)		8	22	2	5	0	0	0	1	1	4	0	0	0-0	.227	.261	.227	.488	2	.933

WORLD SERIES RECORD

Year Team (League)	Pos.	G	AB	R	H	2B	3B	HR	RBI	BB	SO	HBP	GDP	SB-CS	Avg.	OBP	SLG	OPS	E	Avg.
2001— New York (A.L.)	SS	2	3	0	0	0	0	0	0	0	0	0	0	0-0	.000	.000	.000	.000	0	1.000
2003— New York (A.L.)	2B-3B	2	4	0	2	1	0	0	1	1	0	0	1	0-0	.500	.600	.750	1.350	1	.857
World series totals (2 years)		4	7	0	2	1	0	0	1	1	0	0	1	0-0	.286	.375	.429	.804	1	.875

WILSON, JACK   SS

PERSONAL: Born December 29, 1977, in Westlake Village, Calif. ... 6-0/192. ... Bats right, throws right. ... Full name: Jack Eugene Wilson. ... High school: Thousand Oaks (Calif.). ... Junior college: Oxnard (Calif.).

TRANSACTIONS/CAREER NOTES: Selected by St. Louis Cardinals organization in ninth round of 1998 free-agent draft. ... Traded by Cardinals to Pittsburgh Pirates for P Jason Christiansen (July 30, 2000).

2005 GAMES PLAYED BY POSITION (MLB): SS—157.

SCOUTING REPORT **Offense:** Wilson never returned to full strength after an offseason appendectomy. Bat speed improved as the season progressed. Has a short compact stroke and is a very good contact hitter. Hits line drives from gap to gap and has occasional power. Is a plus runner who hustles all the time. **Defense:** Wilson is one of the best defensive shortstops in the game. Has outstanding agility with very quick feet. Has exceptional range to either side. Can get to his feet after a dive as fast as anyone. Hands are very quick. hands. Has improved his throwing mechanics and accuracy. Instincts are very good. **Outlook:** A bounceback season is highly possible for Wilson in 2006 if he can stay healthy. Is a sure bet to win a Gold Glove. **Grade 7.7**

JACK WILSON'S HITTING ZONE

.298	.304	.375
.216	.276	.212
.238	.371	.192

LEFTY-RIGHTY SPLITS

vs.	Avg.	AB	H	2B	3B	HR	RBI	BB	SO	OBP	Slg.
L	.257	140	36	5	3	2	11	14	12	.325	.379
R	.257	447	115	19	4	6	41	17	46	.291	.358

Year Team (League)	Pos.	G	AB	R	H	2B	3B	HR	RBI	BB	SO	HBP	GDP	SB-CS	Avg.	OBP	SLG	OPS	E	Avg.
1998— Johnson City (Appal.)	SS	61	241	50	90	18	4	4	29	18	30	3	4	22-6	.373	.424	.531	.955	16	.940
1999— Peoria (Midw.)	SS	64	251	47	86	22	4	3	28	15	23	2	2	11-5	.343	.384	.498	.882	16	.943
— Potomac (Carol.)	SS	64	257	44	76	10	1	2	18	19	31	1	2	7-4	.296	.345	.366	.711	18	.941
2000— Potomac (Carol.)	SS	13	47	7	13	0	1	2	7	5	10	0	1	2-3	.277	.340	.447	.786	2	.967
— Arkansas (Texas)	SS	88	343	65	101	20	8	6	34	36	59	5	5	2-3	.294	.368	.452	.820	12	.971
— Altoona (East.)	SS	33	139	17	35	7	2	1	16	14	17	2	3	1-3	.252	.325	.353	.677	5	.966
2001— Pittsburgh (N.L.)	SS	108	390	44	87	17	1	3	25	16	70	1	4	1-3	.223	.255	.295	.550	16	.968
— Nashville (PCL)	SS	27	103	20	38	6	1	1	9	8	13	2	1	2-2	.369	.430	.476	.906	3	.974
2002— Pittsburgh (N.L.)	SS	147	527	77	133	22	4	4	47	37	74	4	7	5-2	.252	.306	.332	.638	15	.977
2003— Pittsburgh (N.L.)	SS	150	558	58	143	21	3	9	62	36	74	4	11	5-5	.256	.303	.353	.656	17	.975
2004— Pittsburgh (N.L.)	SS	157	652	82	201	41	•12	11	59	26	71	3	15	8-4	.308	.335	.459	.794	17	.977
2005— Pittsburgh (N.L.)	SS	158	587	60	151	24	7	8	52	31	58	6	11	7-3	.257	.299	.363	.662	14	.982
Major League totals (5 years)		720	2714	321	715	125	27	35	245	146	347	18	48	26-17	.263	.304	.368	.672	79	.977

ALL-STAR GAME RECORD

	G	AB	R	H	2B	3B	HR	RBI	BB	SO	HBP	GDP	SB-CS	Avg.	OBP	SLG	OPS	E	Avg.
All-Star Game totals (1 year)	1	2	0	0	0	0	0	0	0	0	0	0	0-0	.000	.000	.000	.000	0	1.000

WILSON, JOSH   SS/2B

PERSONAL: Born March 26, 1981, in Pittsburgh. ... 6-1/178. ... Bats right, throws right. ... Full name: Joshua Aaron Wilson. ... High school: Mt. Lebanon (Pa.).
TRANSACTIONS/CAREER NOTES: Selected by Florida Marlins organization in third round of 1999 free-agent draft.
2005 GAMES PLAYED BY POSITION (MLB): SS—6, 2B—4.

LEFTY-RIGHTY SPLITS

vs.	Avg.	AB	H	2B	3B	HR	RBI	BB	SO	OBP	Slg.
L	.000	0	0	0	0	0	0	0	0	.000	.000
R	.100	10	1	1	0	0	0	0	4	.182	.200

Year Team (League)	Pos.	G	AB	R	H	2B	3B	HR	RBI	BB	SO	HBP	GDP	SB-CS	Avg.	OBP	SLG	OPS	E	Avg.
1999— GC Marlins (GCL)	SS	53	203	29	54	9	4	0	27	24	36	5	4	14-2	.266	.352	.350	.702	19	.911
2000— Kane Co. (Midw.)	2B-SS-3B	13	52	2	14	3	1	1	6	3	14	1	2	0-0	.269	.316	.423	.739	4	.925
— Utica (N.Y.-Penn)	SS	66	259	43	89	13	6	3	43	29	47	5	6	9-8	.344	.418	.475	.893	18	.929
2001— Kane Co. (Midw.)	2B-SS-3B	123	506	65	144	28	5	4	61	28	60	4	11	17-11	.285	.325	.383	.708	30	.951
2002— Jupiter (Fla. St.)	2B-3B-SS	111	398	51	102	17	1	11	50	28	67	10	6	7-10	.256	.318	.387	.705	18	.964
— Portland (East.)	SS	12	41	5	14	3	0	2	5	2	6	0	0	0-1	.341	.372	.561	.933	2	.967
2003— Carolina (Southern)	SS-2B	118	434	53	110	30	6	3	58	27	70	2	9	6-5	.253	.294	.371	.665	22	.953
2004— Carolina (Southern)	SS-2B	81	311	63	98	21	1	10	41	42	50	1	4	8-4	.315	.396	.486	.882	16	.802
— Albuquerque (PCL)	SS-2B	56	240	32	67	12	2	5	23	19	51	2	5	6-1	.279	.337	.408	.745	8	.000
2005— Florida (N.L.)	SS-2B	11	10	2	1	1	0	0	0	0	4	1	0	0-0	.100	.182	.200	.382	0	1.000
— Albuquerque (PCL)	SS-2B	143	526	88	135	31	6	17	82	48	114	9	8	17-7	.257	.323	.435	.758		
Major League totals (1 year)		11	10	2	1	1	0	0	0	0	4	1	0	0-0	.100	.182	.200	.382	0	1.000

WILSON, PAUL   P

PERSONAL: Born March 28, 1973, in Orlando. ... 6-5/215. ... Throws right, bats right. ... Full name: Paul Anthony Wilson. ... High school: William R. Boone (Orlando). ... College: Florida State.
TRANSACTIONS/CAREER NOTES: Selected by New York Mets organization in first round (first pick overall) of 1994 free-agent draft. ... On disabled list (June 5-July 15, 1996); included rehabilitation assignments to St. Lucie and Binghamton. ... On disabled list (March 27, 1997-entire season); included rehabilitation assignments to GCL Mets and St. Lucie. ... On disabled list (March 13-August 4, 1998); included rehabilitation assignment to St. Lucie. ... On disabled list (April 8, 1999-entire season). ... Traded by Mets with OF Jason Tyner to Tampa Bay Devil Rays for OF Bubba Trammell and P Rick White (July 28, 2000). ... Signed as a free agent by Cincinnati Reds (January 11, 2003). ... On disabled list (August 14-September 1, 2004). ... On disabled list (May 25, 2005-remainder of season).
CAREER HITTING: 19-for-184 (.103), 7 R, 3 2B, 0 3B, 1 HR, 8 RBI.

SCOUTING REPORT **Throws:** He has a fastball that ranges from 86-89 mph, a low-70s curveball, a cut fastball and a split-finger fastball. **Tendencies:** Wilson, who has a history of arm problems, missed most of 2005 with rotator cuff surgery. Has lost some velocity off his fastball. Throws a slider that is more of a cut fastball. Uses his curveball as a change, but the splitter is his out pitch. **Outlook:** His durability will be questioned in 2006. Can't be counted on to start 30-35 games a year. **Grade 5.8**

PAUL WILSON'S PITCHING ZONE

.286	.455	.091
.160	.381	.469
.556	.333	.333

LEFTY-RIGHTY SPLITS

vs.	Avg.	AB	H	2B	3B	HR	RBI	BB	SO	OBP	Slg.
L	.417	84	35	7	1	5	20	9	13	.469	.702
R	.289	114	33	13	0	5	17	8	17	.347	.535

Year Team (League)	W	L	Pct.	ERA	WHIP	G	GS	CG	ShO	Hld.	Sv.-Opp.	IP	H	R	ER	HR	BB-IBB	SO	Avg.
1994— GC Mets (GCL)	0	2	.000	3.00	1.00	3	3	0	0	...	0-...	12.0	8	4	4	0	4-0	13	.190
— St. Lucie (Fla. St.)	0	5	.000	5.06	1.31	8	8	0	0	...	0-...	37.1	32	23	21	3	17-1	37	.230

W

Year	Team (League)	W	L	Pct.	ERA	WHIP	G	GS	CG	ShO	Hld.	Sv.-Opp.	IP	H	R	ER	HR	BB-IBB	SO	Avg.
1995— Binghamton (East.)	6	3	.667	2.17	0.94	16	16	4	1	...	0-...	120.1	89	34	29	5	24-2	127	.208
— Norfolk (Int'l)	5	3	.625	2.85	1.19	10	10	4	2	...	0-...	66.1	59	25	21	3	20-0	67	.242
1996— New York (N.L.)	5	12	.294	5.38	1.53	26	26	1	0	0	0-0	149.0	157	102	89	15	71-11	109	.268
— St. Lucie (Fla. St.)	0	1	.000	3.38	1.25	2	2	0	0	...	0-...	8.0	6	5	3	0	4-0	5	.194
— Binghamton (East.)	0	1	.000	7.20	2.20	1	1	0	0	...	0-...	5.0	6	4	4	0	5-0	5	.316
1997— GC Mets (GCL)	1	0	1.000	1.45	0.96	4	3	0	0	...	1-...	18.2	14	7	3	0	4-0	18	.203
— St. Lucie (Fla. St.)	0	0	...	2.57	0.86	1	1	0	0	...	0-...	7.0	6	2	2	1	0-0	6	.231
1998— St. Lucie (Fla. St.)	0	1	.000	6.38	1.47	5	5	0	0	...	0-...	18.1	23	13	13	2	4-0	16	.315
— Norfolk (Int'l)	4	1	.800	4.42	1.32	7	7	0	0	...	0-...	38.2	42	19	19	2	9-0	30	.273
1999— Norfolk (Int'l)			Did not play.																
2000— St. Lucie (Fla. St.)	2	0	1.000	1.40	1.01	5	5	0	0	...	0-...	25.2	22	9	4	0	4-0	19	.234
— Norfolk (Int'l)	5	5	.500	4.23	1.33	15	13	0	0	...	0-...	83.0	85	40	39	7	25-1	56	.266
— Tampa Bay (A.L.)	1	4	.200	3.35	1.06	11	7	0	0	1	0-0	51.0	38	20	19	1	16-2	40	.209
2001— Tampa Bay (A.L.)	8	9	.471	4.88	1.43	37	24	0	0	0	0-1	151.1	165	94	82	21	52-2	119	.278
2002— Tampa Bay (A.L.)	6	12	.333	4.83	1.48	30	30	1	0	0	0-0	193.2	219	113	104	29	67-2	111	.287
2003— Cincinnati (N.L.)	8	10	.444	4.64	1.44	28	28	0	0	0	0-0	166.2	190	97	86	24	50-5	93	.285
2004— Cincinnati (N.L.)	11	6	.647	4.36	1.39	29	29	1	0	0	0-0	183.2	192	93	89	26	63-5	117	.271
2005— Cincinnati (N.L.)	1	5	.167	7.77	1.83	9	9	0	0	0	0-0	46.1	68	41	40	10	17-1	30	.343
American League totals (3 years)	15	25	.375	4.66	1.41	78	61	1	0	1	0-1	396.0	422	227	205	51	135-6	270	.274
National League totals (4 years)	25	33	.431	5.01	1.48	92	92	2	0	0	0-0	545.2	607	333	304	75	201-22	349	.281
Major League totals (7 years)	40	58	.408	4.86	1.45	170	153	3	0	1	0-1	941.2	1029	560	509	126	336-28	619	.278

WILSON, PRESTON   OF

PERSONAL: Born July 19, 1974, in Bamberg, S.C. ... 6-2/213. ... Bats right, throws right. ... Full name: Preston James Richard Wilson. ... High school: Bamberg Erhardt (Bamberg, S.C.). ... Stepson of Mookie Wilson, outfielder with two major league teams (1980-91).

TRANSACTIONS/CAREER NOTES: Selected by Mets organization in first round (ninth pick overall) of 1992 free-agent draft. ... Traded by Mets with Ps Ed Yarnall and Geoff Goetz to Florida Marlins for C Mike Piazza (May 22, 1998). ... On disabled list (July 2-August 10, 2001); included rehabilitation assignment to Calgary. ... Traded by Marlins with C Charles Johnson, P Vic Darensbourg and 2B Pablo Ozuna to Colorado Rockies for P Mike Hampton, OF Juan Pierre and cash (November 16, 2002). ... On disabled list (April 13-June 18 and August 21, 2004-remainder of season); included rehabilitation assignment to Tulsa. ... Traded by Rockies to Washington Nationals for P Zach Day and OF J.J. Davis (July 13, 2005).

HONORS: Named N.L. Rookie Player of the Year by THE SPORTING NEWS (1999).

2005 GAMES PLAYED BY POSITION (MLB): OF—137.

SCOUTING REPORT **Offense:** Wilson is finally healthy after years of knee problems. Has a long stroke with a lot of holes. Power is an asset and can drive the ball to all fields. Contact is an issue; has problems with breaking stuff and chases lot of bad pitches when behind in the count, especially with runners on. Can run and is a good baserunner but doesn't steal bases. **Defense:** Playing in center field, Wilson was inconsistent with his reads and jumps. Doesn't run well enough to compensate for those deficiencies. Is a better corner outfielder because he doesn't take very good routes. Has a strong arm but is erratic. **Outlook:** Power is his strength but he needs to cut down on his long swing. *Grade 7.4*

PRESTON WILSON'S HITTING ZONE

.444	.444	.292
.311	.515	.203
.213	.259	.343

LEFTY-RIGHTY SPLITS

vs.	Avg.	AB	H	2B	3B	HR	RBI	BB	SO	OBP	Slg.
L	.262	126	33	9	0	10	23	13	34	.336	.571
R	.259	394	102	20	2	15	67	32	114	.322	.434

Year	Team (League)	Pos.	G	AB	R	H	2B	3B	HR	RBI	BB	SO	HBP	GDP	SB-CS	Avg.	OBP	SLG	OPS	E	Avg.
1993— Kingsport (Appal.)	3B	66	259	44	60	10	0	16	48	24	75	3	6	6-2	.232	.303	.456	.759	25	.873
— Pittsfield (N.Y.-Penn.)	3B	8	29	6	16	5	1	1	12	2	7	1	0	1-0	.552	.576	.897	1.472	6	.700
1994— Capital City (S. Atl.)	3B	131	474	55	108	17	4	14	58	20	135	3	4	10-10	.228	.262	.369	.631	47	.884
1995— Capital City (S. Atl.)	OF	111	442	70	119	26	5	20	61	19	114	9	4	20-6	.269	.311	.486	.797	8	.961
1996— St. Lucie (Fla. St.)	OF	23	85	6	15	3	0	1	7	8	21	2	3	1-1	.176	.263	.247	.510	2	.956
1997— St. Lucie (Fla. St.)	OF-DH	63	245	32	60	12	1	11	48	8	66	1	4	3-4	.245	.267	.437	.704	3	.973
— Binghamton (East.)	OF-DH-3B	70	259	37	74	12	1	19	47	21	71	2	5	7-1	.286	.340	.560	.900	6	.952
1998— Norfolk (Int'l)	OF	18	73	9	18	5	1	1	9	2	22	1	...	1-1	.247	.273	.384	.656	2	.958
— New York (N.L.)	OF	8	20	3	6	2	0	0	2	2	8	0	0	1-1	.300	.364	.400	.764	1	.909
— Charlotte (Int'l)	OF-DH	94	356	71	99	25	3	25	77	34	121	2	...	14-6	.278	.341	.576	.917	4	.979
— Florida (N.L.)	OF	14	31	4	2	0	0	1	1	4	13	1	0	0-0	.065	.194	.161	.356	0	1.000
1999— Florida (N.L.)	OF	149	482	67	135	21	4	26	71	46	156	9	15	11-4	.280	.350	.502	.852	9	.973
2000— Florida (N.L.)	OF	161	605	94	160	35	3	31	121	55 *	187	8	11	36-14	.264	.331	.486	.817	5	.988
2001— Florida (N.L.)	OF	123	468	70	128	30	2	23	71	36	107	6	14	20-8	.274	.331	.494	.825	2	.993
— Calgary (PCL)	OF	4	10	3	5	2	0	0	1	5	1	0	0	2-0	.500	.667	.700	1.367	0	1.000
2002— Florida (N.L.)	OF	141	510	80	124	22	2	23	65	58	140	4	9	20-11	.243	.329	.429	.759	6	.981
2003— Colorado (N.L.)	OF	155	600	94	169	43	1	36 *	141	54	139	4	23	14-7	.282	.343	.537	.880	7	.980
2004— Tulsa (Texas)	OF-DH	6	17	4	7	1	0	1	2	3	4	1	1	1-1	.412	.524	.647	1.171	0	1.000
— Colorado (N.L.)	OF	58	202	24	50	11	0	6	29	17	49	3	9	2-1	.248	.315	.391	.706	6	.953
2005— Colorado (N.L.)	OF	71	267	39	69	15	1	15	47	25	77	1	8	3-2	.258	.322	.491	.813	3	.979
— Washington (N.L.)	OF	68	253	34	66	14	1	10	43	20	71	6	10	3-4	.261	.329	.443	.771	0	1.000
Major League totals (8 years)		948	3438	509	909	193	14	171	591	317	947	47	107	110-52	.264	.333	.478	.811	39	.982

ALL-STAR GAME RECORD

	G	AB	R	H	2B	3B	HR	RBI	BB	SO	HBP	GDP	SB-CS	Avg.	OBP	SLG	OPS	E	Avg.
All-Star Game totals (1 year)	1	2	0	1	0	0	0	0	0	1	0	0	0-0	.500	.500	.500	1.000	0	1.000

WILSON, VANCE   C

PERSONAL: Born March 17, 1973, in Mesa, Ariz. ... 5-11/190. ... Bats right, throws right. ... Full name: Vance Allen Wilson. ... High school: Red Mountain (Mesa, Ariz.). ... Junior college: Mesa (Ariz.) Community College.

TRANSACTIONS/CAREER NOTES: Selected by New York Mets organization in 44th round of 1993 free-agent draft. ... On disabled list (September 8, 1998-remainder of season; and August 28, 1999-remainder of season). ... On disabled list (June 16-July 7 and September 14, 2004-remainder of season); included rehabilitation assignments to Binghamton and Norfolk. ... Traded by Mets to Detroit Tigers for SS Anderson Hernandez (January 6, 2005).
2005 GAMES PLAYED BY POSITION (MLB): C—60.

SCOUTING REPORT
Wilson is a good defensive catcher, with arm strength his best tool. Has a quick release and is accurate. Receives the ball well, blocks pitches in the dirt and keeps them in front. Is adept at handling a pitching staff. Is a contact hitter who will go with the pitch and speeds up his bat with pitches out over the plate. Will make adjustments in the count but doesn't have good bat speed. Has never shown enough bat to play regularly. Has good makeup and is an asset as a backup. *Grade 5*

VANCE WILSON'S HITTING ZONE

.600	.000	.286
.056	.154	.261
.222	.444	.154

LEFTY-RIGHTY SPLITS

vs.	Avg.	AB	H	2B	3B	HR	RBI	BB	SO	OBP	Slg.
L	.214	42	9	0	0	3	6	5	8	.298	.429
R	.191	110	21	4	0	0	13	6	18	.266	.227

Year	Team (League)	Pos.	G	AB	R	H	2B	3B	HR	RBI	BB	SO	HBP	GDP	SB-CS	Avg.	OBP	SLG	OPS	E	Avg.
1994—	Pittsfield (N.Y.-Penn.)	C	44	166	22	51	12	0	2	20	5	27	5	1	4-1	.307	.343	.416	.758	5	.977
1995—	Capital City (S. Atl.)	C	91	324	34	81	11	0	6	32	19	45	8	6	4-3	.250	.306	.340	.645	14	.981
1996—	St. Lucie (Fla. St.)	C	93	311	29	76	14	2	6	44	31	41	6	7	2-4	.244	.321	.360	.681	8	.987
1997—	Binghamton (East.)	C	92	322	46	89	17	0	15	40	20	46	5	6	2-5	.276	.328	.469	.797	11	.984
1998—	Norfolk (Int'l)	C	46	154	18	40	3	0	4	16	9	29	1	5	0-3	.260	.305	.357	.662	4	.990
	—GC Mets (GCL)	C	10	28	5	10	5	0	2	9	0	1	2	0	0-1	.357	.367	.750	1.117	2	.957
	—St. Lucie (Fla. St.)	C	4	16	0	1	0	0	0	0	0	5	0	0	0-0	.063	.063	.063	.125	0	1.000
1999—	Norfolk (Int'l)	C	15	53	10	14	3	0	3	5	4	8	1	4	1-0	.264	.328	.491	.818	1	.991
	—New York (N.L.)	C	1	0	0	0	0	0	0	0	0	0	0	0	0-0	...	...	...	...	0	1.000
2000—	Norfolk (Int'l)	C	111	400	47	104	23	1	16	62	24	65	12	12	11-6	.260	.319	.443	.761	3	.996
	—New York (N.L.)	C	4	4	0	0	0	0	0	0	0	2	0	0	0-0	.000	.000	.000	.000	1	1.000
2001—	Norfolk (Int'l)	C	65	228	24	56	14	0	6	31	12	34	9	7	0-1	.246	.306	.386	.692	8	.984
	—New York (N.L.)	C	32	57	3	17	3	0	0	6	2	16	2	1	0-1	.298	.339	.351	.690	1	.993
2002—	New York (N.L.)	C-1B	74	163	19	40	7	0	5	26	5	32	8	4	0-1	.245	.301	.380	.682	6	.983
2003—	New York (N.L.)	C	96	268	28	65	9	1	8	39	15	56	5	6	1-2	.243	.293	.373	.666	5	.990
2004—	Binghamton (East.)	C	1	3	2	1	0	0	1	1	0	0	1	0	0-0	.333	.500	1.333	1.833	0	1.000
	—Norfolk (Int'l)	C	1	4	1	2	0	0	1	1	0	0	0	0	0-0	.500	.500	1.250	1.750	0	1.000
	—New York (N.L.)	C	79	157	18	43	10	1	4	21	11	24	5	5	1-0	.274	.335	.427	.762	2	.993
2005—	Detroit (A.L.)	C	61	152	18	30	4	0	3	19	11	26	6	6	0-0	.197	.275	.283	.558	3	.989
American League totals (1 year)			61	152	18	30	4	0	3	19	11	26	6	6	0-0	.197	.275	.283	.558	3	.989
National League totals (6 years)			286	649	68	165	29	2	17	92	33	130	20	16	2-4	.254	.308	.384	.692	14	.989
Major League totals (7 years)			347	801	86	195	33	2	20	111	44	156	26	22	2-4	.243	.301	.365	.666	17	.989

WINN, RANDY   OF

PERSONAL: Born June 9, 1974, in Los Angeles. ... 6-2/197. ... Bats both, throws right. ... Full name: Dwight Randolph Winn. ... High school: San Ramon Valley (Danville, Calif.). ... College: Santa Clara.
TRANSACTIONS/CAREER NOTES: Selected by Florida Marlins organization in third round of 1995 free-agent draft. ... Selected by Tampa Bay Devil Rays in third round (58th pick overall) of expansion draft (November 18, 1997). ... Traded by Devil Rays to Seattle Mariners for SS Antonio Perez (October 28, 2002). ... Traded by Mariners to San Francisco Giants for C Yorvit Torrealba and P Jesse Foppert (July 30, 2005).
2005 GAMES PLAYED BY POSITION (MLB): OF—151, DH—2.

SCOUTING REPORT
Offense: Winn's speed is his best asset. Is a line-drive hitter who uses the whole field. Has a shorter stroke and more power from the left side. Is a better fastball hitter than breaking-ball hitter. Should see more fastballs in San Francisco. Likes to run but is very inconsistent with his jumps and reads. *Defense:* Winn is not a good center fielder. Gets better jumps in left. Sometimes turns routine balls into an adventure. Doesn't have good instincts, but speed helps him compensate. Arm is short and better suited for left. *Outlook:* Winn is a better offensive player now than at any time in his career and is starting to drive the ball with authority. *Grade 7.1*

RANDY WINN'S HITTING ZONE

.172	.478	.233
.380	.446	.293
.368	.333	.293

LEFTY-RIGHTY SPLITS

vs.	Avg.	AB	H	2B	3B	HR	RBI	BB	SO	OBP	Slg.
L	.269	156	42	13	2	2	14	11	21	.315	.417
R	.319	461	147	34	4	18	49	37	70	.374	.527

W

Year	Team (League)	Pos.	G	AB	R	H	2B	3B	HR	RBI	BB	SO	HBP	GDP	SB-CS	Avg.	OBP	SLG	OPS	E	Avg.
1995—	Elmira (N.Y.-Penn)	OF	51	213	38	67	7	4	0	22	15	31	3	1	19-7	.315	.365	.385	.750	5	.954
1996—	Kane Co. (Midw.)	OF	130	514	90	139	16	3	0	35	47	115	8	3	30-18	.270	.340	.313	.654	8	.970
1997—	Brevard County (Fla. St.)	OF	36	143	26	45	8	2	0	15	16	28	5	3	16-8	.315	.400	.399	.799	0	1.000
	—Portland (East.)	OF	96	384	66	112	15	6	8	36	42	92	7	4	35-20	.292	.371	.424	.795	4	.979
1998—	Durham (Int'l)	OF	29	123	25	35	5	2	1	16	15	24	0	1	10-4	.285	.362	.382	.744	2	.966
	—Tampa Bay (A.L.)	OF-DH	109	338	51	94	9	9	1	17	29	69	1	2	26-12	.278	.337	.367	.704	4	.980
1999—	Tampa Bay (A.L.)	OF	79	303	44	81	16	4	2	24	17	63	1	3	9-9	.267	.307	.366	.673	1	.995
	—Durham (Int'l)	OF	46	207	38	73	20	3	3	30	16	27	1	2	20-6	.353	.402	.522	.924	4	.966
2000—	Durham (Int'l)	OF	79	303	67	100	24	5	7	40	48	53	3	5	18-5	.330	.425	.512	.937	7	.960
	—Tampa Bay (A.L.)	OF-DH	51	159	28	40	5	0	1	16	9	23	2	0	6-7	.252	.362	.302	.664	1	.990
2001—	Tampa Bay (A.L.)	OF-DH	128	429	54	117	25	6	6	50	38	81	6	10	12-10	.273	.339	.401	.740	5	.981
2002—	Tampa Bay (A.L.)	OF-DH	152	607	87	181	39	9	14	75	55	109	6	6	27-8	.298	.360	.461	.821	3	.993
2003—	Seattle (A.L.)	OF	157	600	103	177	37	4	11	75	41	108	6	9	23-5	.295	.346	.425	.771	3	.992
2004—	Seattle (A.L.)	OF-DH	157	626	84	179	34	4	14	81	53	98	8	16	21-7	.286	.346	.427	.772	4	.991

Year—Team (League)	Pos.	G	AB	R	H	2B	3B	HR	RBI	BB	SO	HBP	GDP	SB-CS	Avg.	OBP	SLG	OPS	FIELDING E	Avg.
2005— Seattle (A.L.)	OF-DH	102	386	46	106	25	1	6	37	37	53	4	7	12-6	.275	.342	.391	.733	0	1.000
— San Francisco (N.L.)	OF	58	231	39	83	22	5	14	26	11	38	1	4	7-5	.359	.391	.680	1.071	1	.994
American League totals (8 years)		935	3448	497	975	190	39	55	375	296	606	36	58	136-64	.283	.343	.408	.752	21	.990
National League totals (1 year)		58	231	39	83	22	5	14	26	11	38	1	4	7-5	.359	.391	.680	1.071	1	.994
Major League totals (8 years)		993	3679	536	1058	212	44	69	401	307	644	37	62	143-69	.288	.346	.425	.772	22	.991

ALL-STAR GAME RECORD

	G	AB	R	H	2B	3B	HR	RBI	BB	SO	HBP	GDP	SB-CS	Avg.	OBP	SLG	OPS	E	Avg.
All-Star Game totals (1 year)	1	2	1	1	1	0	0	0	1	1	0		1-0	.500	.667	1.000	1.667	0	1.000

WISE, MATT — P

PERSONAL: Born November 18, 1975, in Montclair, Calif. ... 6-4/200. ... Throws right, bats right. ... Full name: Matthew John Wise. ... High school: Bonita (Calif.). ... College: Cal State Fullerton.

TRANSACTIONS/CAREER NOTES: Selected by Seattle Mariners organization in 54th round of 1993 free-agent draft; did not sign. ... Selected by Anaheim Angels organization in sixth round of 1997 free-agent draft. ... On disabled list (March 18, 2003-entire season). ... Released by Angels (October 6, 2003). ... Signed by Milwaukee Brewers organization (January 20, 2004). ... On disabled list (August 14-September 1, 2005).

CAREER HITTING: 1-for-5 (.200), 0 R, 0 2B, 0 3B, 0 HR, 1 RBI.

SCOUTING REPORT

Throws: He uses an 87-91 mph fastball, a big-breaking slider and a changeup. **Tendencies:** Wise has a long backswing, a deceptive windup and an unorthodox arm action. Can pitch up in the zone, where hitters have a hard time catching up to his fastball. Has excellent arm speed and good sinking action on his changeup. Has a big break in his slider, which is more of a slurve. **Outlook:** Wise is best used as a middle reliever; he has improved a lot and is effective against righthanded and lefthanded hitters. **Grade 5.8**

MATT WISE'S PITCHING ZONE

.182	.000	.200
.077	.310	.186
.125	.222	.083

LEFTY-RIGHTY SPLITS

vs.	Avg.	AB	H	2B	3B	HR	RBI	BB	SO	OBP	Slg.
L	.130	108	14	1	0	1	8	13	32	.230	.167
R	.187	123	23	7	1	5	22	12	30	.266	.382

Year—Team (League)	W	L	Pct.	ERA	WHIP	G	GS	CG	ShO	Hld.	Sv.-Opp.	IP	H	R	ER	HR	BB-IBB	SO	Avg.
1997— Boise (N'west)	9	1	.900	3.25	1.40	15	15	0	0	...	0-...	83.0	82	37	30	5	34-0	86	.269
1998— Midland (Texas)	9	10	.474	5.42	1.45	27	27	3	1	...	0-...	167.2	195	111	101	23	48-0	131	.289
1999— Erie (East.)	8	5	.615	3.77	1.29	16	16	3	0	...	0-...	98.0	102	48	41	10	24-0	72	.268
2000— Edmonton (PCL)	9	6	.600	3.69	1.19	19	19	2	1	...	0-...	124.1	122	54	51	10	26-0	82	.258
— Anaheim (A.L.)	3	3	.500	5.54	1.42	8	6	0	0	0	0-0	37.1	40	23	23	7	13-1	20	.272
2001— Anaheim (A.L.)	1	4	.200	4.38	1.32	11	9	0	0	0	0-0	49.1	47	27	24	11	18-1	50	.250
— Salt Lake (PCL)	9	9	.500	5.04	1.22	21	21	0	0	0	0-...	123.1	134	79	69	19	17-0	111	.271
2002— Anaheim (A.L.)	0	0		3.24	0.96	7	0	0	0	0	0-0	8.1	7	3	3	0	1-0	6	.233
— Salt Lake (PCL)	3	4	.429	5.42	1.50	16	16	0	0	...	0-...	78.0	102	51	47	12	15-0	76	.324
2003— Anaheim (A.L.)			Did not play.																
2004— Indianapolis (Int'l)	1	0	1.000	1.80	0.80	7	1	0	0	...	0-...	20.0	12	4	4	3	4-0	20	.176
— Milwaukee (N.L.)	1	2	.333	4.44	1.25	30	3	0	0	3	0-...	52.2	51	27	26	3	15-1	30	.252
2005— Milwaukee (N.L.)	4	4	.500	3.36	0.96	49	0	0	0	10	1-3	64.1	37	25	24	6	25-5	62	.160
American League totals (3 years)	4	7	.364	4.74	1.33	26	15	0	0	0	0-0	95.0	94	53	50	18	32-2	76	.258
National League totals (2 years)	5	6	.455	3.85	1.09	79	3	0	0	13	1-3	117.0	88	52	50	9	40-6	92	.203
Major League totals (5 years)	9	13	.409	4.25	1.20	105	18	0	0	13	1-3	212.0	182	105	100	27	72-8	168	.228

WITASICK, JAY — P

PERSONAL: Born August 28, 1972, in Baltimore. ... 6-4/235. ... Throws right, bats right. ... Full name: Gerald Alphonse Witasick. ... Name pronounced: wi-TASS-ik. ... High school: C. Milton Wright (Bel Air, Md.). ... College: Maryland-Baltimore County.

TRANSACTIONS/CAREER NOTES: Selected by St. Louis Cardinals organization in second round of 1993 free-agent draft. ... Traded by Cardinals with OF Allen Battle and Ps Bret Wagner and Carl Dale to Oakland Athletics for P Todd Stottlemyre (January 9, 1996). ... On disabled list (March 31-June 14, 1997); included rehabilitation assignment to Modesto. ... Traded by A's to Kansas City Royals for a player to be named and cash (March 30, 1999); A's acquired P Scott Chiasson to complete deal (June 10, 1999). ... Traded by Royals to San Diego Padres for P Brian Meadows (July 31, 2000). ... Traded by Padres to New York Yankees for IF D'Angelo Jimenez (June 23, 2001). ... Traded by Yankees to San Francisco Giants for OF John Vander Wal (December 13, 2001). ... On disabled list (July 27-August 15, 2002); included rehabilitation assignment to Fresno. ... Signed as a free agent by Padres (December 24, 2002). ... On disabled list (March 21-June 9, 2003); included rehabilitation assignments to Lake Elsinore and Portland. ... On disabled list (August 16-September 18, 2004); included rehabilitation assignment to Portland. ... Released by Padres (October 7, 2004). ... Signed as a free agent by Baltimore Orioles (January 18, 2005). ... Released by Orioles (April 7, 2005). ... Signed by Colorado Rockies organization (April 8, 2005). ... Traded by Rockies with P Joe Kennedy to Oakland Athletics for OF Eric Byrnes and SS Omar Quintanilla (July 13, 2005).

CAREER HITTING: 3-for-42 (.071), 0 R, 0 2B, 0 3B, 0 HR, 3 RBI.

SCOUTING REPORT

Throws: His fastball is in the low 90s. Also throws a slider, split-finger fastball and a curveball. **Tendencies:** His very long, low three-quarters arm angle and high leg lift make him easy to follow and cause him to drop his hand under a lot of pitches. Pitches can get very flat. Best fastball life is outside of the zone, running in on righthanders. Big, looping curve doesn't have good rotation. Has a big slurve break to his slider, which is frequently flat. Splitter sinks late. **Outlook:** He always has been a strikeout reliever with good stuff but his ability under pressure is suspect. **Grade 6**

JAY WITASICK'S PITCHING ZONE

.100	.333	.200
.344	.364	.265
.120	.353	.167

LEFTY-RIGHTY SPLITS

vs.	Avg.	AB	H	2B	3B	HR	RBI	BB	SO	OBP	Slg.
L	.213	108	23	7	0	2	12	20	35	.341	.333
R	.231	130	30	12	0	2	13	9	38	.306	.369

Year—Team (League)	W	L	Pct.	ERA	WHIP	G	GS	CG	ShO	Hld.	Sv.-Opp.	IP	H	R	ER	HR	BB-IBB	SO	Avg.
1993— Johnson City (Appal.)	4	3	.571	4.12	1.24	12	12	0	0	...	0-...	67.2	65	42	31	8	19-0	74	.246
— Savannah (S. Atl.)	1	0	1.000	4.50	1.50	1	1	0	0	...	0-...	6.0	7	3	3	0	2-0	8	.280
1994— Madison (Midw.)	10	4	.714	2.32	1.03	18	18	2	0	...	0-...	112.1	74	36	29	5	42-0	141	.189
1995— St. Pete. (Fla. St.)	7	7	.500	2.74	1.10	18	18	1	0	...	0-...	105.0	80	39	32	4	36-1	109	.208

Year	Team (League)	W	L	Pct.	ERA	WHIP	G	GS	CG	ShO	Hld.	Sv.-Opp.	IP	H	R	ER	HR	BB-IBB	SO	Avg.
	—Arkansas (Texas)	2	4	.333	6.88	1.82	7	7	0	0	...	0-...	34.0	46	29	26	4	16-1	26	.317
1996—	Huntsville (Sou.)	0	3	.000	2.30	1.10	25	6	0	0	...	4-...	66.2	47	21	17	3	26-2	63	.195
	—Oakland (A.L.)	1	1	.500	6.23	1.31	12	0	0	0	0	0-1	13.0	12	9	9	5	5-0	12	.245
	—Edmonton (PCL)	0	0	...	4.15	1.73	6	0	0	0	...	2-...	8.2	9	4	4	1	6-0	9	.300
1997—	Modesto (California)	0	1	.000	4.15	1.21	9	2	0	0	...	1-...	17.1	16	9	8	1	5-0	29	.232
	—Edmonton (PCL)	3	2	.600	4.28	1.46	13	1	0	0	...	0-...	27.1	25	13	13	3	15-3	17	.243
	—Oakland (A.L.)	0	0	...	5.73	1.82	8	0	0	0	1	0-0	11.0	14	7	7	2	6-0	8	.304
1998—	Edmonton (PCL)	11	7	.611	3.87	1.17	27	26	2	1	...	0-0	149.0	126	74	64	19	49-0	155	.226
	—Oakland (A.L.)	1	3	.250	6.33	1.89	7	3	0	0	0	0-0	27.0	36	24	19	9	15-1	29	.310
1999—	Kansas City (A.L.)	9	12	.429	5.57	1.73	32	28	1	1	0	0-0	158.1	191	108	98	23	83-1	102	.304
2000—	Kansas City (A.L.)	3	8	.273	5.94	1.65	22	14	2	0	0	0-0	89.1	109	65	59	15	38-0	67	.301
	—San Diego (N.L.)	3	2	.600	5.64	1.71	11	11	0	0	0	0-0	60.2	69	42	38	9	35-5	54	.284
2001—	San Diego (N.L.)	5	2	.714	1.86	1.19	31	0	0	0	5	1-3	38.2	31	14	8	3	15-3	53	.218
	—New York (A.L.)	3	0	1.000	4.69	1.61	32	0	0	0	0	0-1	40.1	47	27	21	5	18-1	53	.283
2002—	San Francisco (N.L.)	1	0	1.000	2.37	1.16	44	0	0	0	4	0-0	68.1	58	19	18	3	21-3	54	.234
	—Fresno (PCL)	0	0	...	4.50	1.00	2	2	0	0	...	0-...	2.0	1	1	1	0	1-0	2	.143
2003—	Lake Elsinore (Calif.)	0	0	...	5.79	1.30	4	0	0	0	...	0-...	4.2	6	4	3	0	1-0	7	.300
	—Portland (PCL)	0	0	...	3.00	0.80	5	0	0	0	...	1-...	6.0	4	2	2	0	1-0	8	.182
	—San Diego (N.L.)	3	7	.300	4.53	1.47	46	0	0	0	12	2-7	45.2	42	24	23	6	25-4	42	.244
2004—	San Diego (N.L.)	0	1	.000	3.21	1.35	44	0	0	0	2	1-3	61.2	57	28	22	8	26-2	57	.244
2005—	Colo. Springs (PCL)	0	0	...	3.60	1.50	8	0	0	0	2	0-1	10.0	10	5	4	0	5-0	14	.270
	—Colorado (N.L.)	0	4	.000	2.52	1.09	32	0	0	0	1	0-1	35.2	27	11	10	2	12-3	40	.209
	—Oakland (A.L.)	1	1	.500	3.25	1.55	28	0	0	0	6	1-3	27.2	26	15	10	2	17-2	33	.239
American League totals (7 years)		18	25	.419	5.47	1.68	141	45	3	1	12	1-5	366.2	435	255	223	61	182-5	304	.295
National League totals (6 years)		12	16	.429	3.45	1.35	208	11	0	0	34	4-14	310.2	284	138	119	31	134-20	300	.243
Major League totals (10 years)		30	41	.423	4.54	1.53	349	56	3	1	46	5-19	677.1	719	393	342	92	316-25	604	.272

DIVISION SERIES RECORD

Year	Team (League)	W	L	Pct.	ERA	WHIP	G	GS	CG	ShO	Hld.	Sv.-Opp.	IP	H	R	ER	HR	BB-IBB	SO	Avg.
2001—	New York (A.L.)	0	0	...	13.50	3.00	1	0	0	0	0	0-0	0.2	1	1	1	0	1-0	0	.500
2002—	San Francisco (N.L.)	0	0	...	0.00	0.00	2	0	0	0	0	0-0	2.1	0	0	0	0	0-0	1	.000
Division series totals (2 years)		0	0	...	3.00	0.67	3	0	0	0	0	0-0	3.0	1	1	1	0	1-0	1	.111

CHAMPIONSHIP SERIES RECORD

Year	Team (League)	W	L	Pct.	ERA	WHIP	G	GS	CG	ShO	Hld.	Sv.-Opp.	IP	H	R	ER	HR	BB-IBB	SO	Avg.
2001—	New York (A.L.)	0	0	...	9.00	2.00	1	0	0	0	0	0-0	3.0	6	3	3	1	0-0	2	.375
2002—	San Francisco (N.L.)	0	1	.000	9.00	1.00	1	0	0	0	0	0-0	1.0	1	1	1	1	0-0	0	.250
Champ. series totals (2 years)		0	1	.000	9.00	1.75	2	0	0	0	0	0-0	4.0	7	4	4	2	0-0	2	.350

WORLD SERIES RECORD

Year	Team (League)	W	L	Pct.	ERA	WHIP	G	GS	CG	ShO	Hld.	Sv.-Opp.	IP	H	R	ER	HR	BB-IBB	SO	Avg.
2001—	New York (A.L.)	0	0	...	54.00	7.50	1	0	0	0	0	0-0	1.1	10	9	8	0	0-0	4	.714
2002—	San Francisco (N.L.)	0	0	...	54.00	15.00	1	0	0	0	0	0-0	0.1	3	2	2	0	2-0	1	.750
World series totals (2 years)		0	0	...	54.00	9.00	3	0	0	0	0	0-0	1.2	13	11	10	0	2-0	5	.722

WOLF, RANDY   P

PERSONAL: Born August 22, 1976, in Canoga Park, Calif. ... 6-0/200. ... Throws left, bats left. ... Full name: Randall Christopher Wolf. ... High school: El Camino Real (Woodland Hills, Calif.). ... College: Pepperdine.

TRANSACTIONS/CAREER NOTES: Selected by Los Angeles Dodgers organization in 25th round of 1994 free-agent draft; did not sign. ... Selected by Philadelphia Phillies organization in second round of 1997 free-agent draft. ... On disabled list (August 2-September 1, 2001); included rehabilitation assignments to Scranton/Wilkes-Barre and Reading. ... On disabled list (March 25-April 12, 2002); included rehabilitation assignment to Clearwater. ... On disabled list (June 3-26 and August 29, 2004-remainder of season); included rehabilitation assignment to Reading. ... On disabled list (June 12, 2005-remainder of season).

CAREER HITTING: 64-for-332 (.193), 32 R, 17 2B, 0 3B, 4 HR, 30 RBI.

SCOUTING REPORT **Throws:** Wolf's stuff is just below average: He has a fastball at 87-90 mph, a curve at 70-73, a slider at 78-81 and a changeup. **Tendencies:** Intelligence and command help Wolf get hitters out. Has to spot his fastball, change speeds and hit corners to be effective. Gets a lot of swinging strikes. Big-breaking curve has good rotation. Slider is quick, short and late-breaking. Turns his straight change over with good motion. **Outlook:** Elbow surgery forced him to miss much of last season, but he will be counted on to be the fifth starter. Has to be very fine to be effective, especially in his home park. **Grade 6.5**

RANDY WOLF'S PITCHING ZONE

.148	.333	.200
.434	.241	.263
.185	.700	.172

LEFTY-RIGHTY SPLITS

vs.	Avg.	AB	H	2B	3B	HR	RBI	BB	SO	OBP	Slg.
L	.238	63	15	5	0	2	5	1	19	.273	.413
R	.293	246	72	17	0	12	32	25	42	.366	.508

W

Year	Team (League)	W	L	Pct.	ERA	WHIP	G	GS	CG	ShO	Hld.	Sv.-Opp.	IP	H	R	ER	HR	BB-IBB	SO	Avg.
1997—	Batavia (NY-Penn)	4	0	1.000	1.58	0.93	7	7	0	0	...	0-...	40.0	29	8	7	1	8-0	53	.204
1998—	Reading (East.)	2	0	1.000	1.44	0.76	4	4	0	0	...	0-...	25.0	15	4	4	0	4-0	33	.172
	—Scran./W.B. (Int'l)	9	7	.563	4.62	1.45	24	23	1	0	...	0-...	148.0	167	88	76	16	48-4	118	.285
1999—	Scran./W.B. (Int'l)	4	5	.444	3.61	1.32	12	12	0	0	...	0-...	77.1	73	36	31	8	29-1	72	.247
	—Philadelphia (N.L.)	6	9	.400	5.55	1.59	22	21	0	0	0	0-0	121.2	126	78	75	20	67-0	116	.269
2000—	Philadelphia (N.L.)	11	9	.550	4.36	1.42	32	32	1	0	0	0-0	206.1	210	107	100	25	83-2	160	.269
2001—	Philadelphia (N.L.)	10	11	.476	3.70	1.23	28	25	4	2	0	0-0	163.0	150	74	67	15	51-4	152	.248
	—Scran./W.B. (Int'l)	0	1	.000	5.00	1.67	2	2	0	0	...	0-...	9.0	10	6	5	2	5-0	7	.286
	—Reading (East.)	0	0	...	4.50	1.17	1	1	0	0	...	0-...	6.0	5	3	3	0	2-0	7	.208
2002—	Clearwater (Fla. St.)	0	0	...	0.00	0.40	1	1	0	0	...	0-...	5.0	1	0	0	0	1-0	6	.071
	—Philadelphia (N.L.)	11	9	.550	3.20	1.12	31	31	3	2	0	0-0	210.2	172	77	75	23	63-5	172	.223
2003—	Philadelphia (N.L.)	16	10	.615	4.23	1.27	33	33	2	2	0	0-0	200.0	176	101	94	27	78-4	177	.233
2004—	Reading (East.)	0	0	...	2.25	1.25	1	1	0	0	...	0-...	4.0	5	1	1	0	0-0	4	.333
	—Philadelphia (N.L.)	5	8	.385	4.28	1.32	23	23	1	1	0	0-0	136.2	145	73	65	20	36-4	89	.271

Year	Team (League)	W	L	Pct.	ERA	WHIP	G	GS	CG	ShO	Hld.	Sv.-Opp.	IP	H	R	ER	HR	BB-IBB	SO	Avg.
2005—	Philadelphia (N.L.)	6	4	.600	4.39	1.41	13	13	0	0	0	0-0	80.0	87	40	39	14	26-2	61	.282
Major League totals (7 years)		65	60	.520	4.14	1.31	182	178	11	7	0	0-0	1118.1	1066	550	515	144	404-21	927	.252

ALL-STAR GAME RECORD

	W	L	Pct.	ERA	WHIP	G	GS	CG	ShO	Hld.	Sv.-Opp.	IP	H	R	ER	HR	BB-IBB	SO	Avg.
All-Star Game totals (1 year)	0	0	...	9.00	2.00	1	0	0	0	0	0-0	1.0	1	1	1	0	1-0	2	.250

WOMACK, TONY 2B/OF

PERSONAL: Born September 25, 1969, in Danville, Va. ... 5-9/170. ... Bats left, throws right. ... Full name: Anthony Darrell Womack. ... Name pronounced: WO-mack. ... High school: Gretna (Va.). ... College: Guilford (N.C.).

TRANSACTIONS/CAREER NOTES: Selected by Pittsburgh Pirates organization in seventh round of 1991 free-agent draft. ... Traded by Pirates to Arizona Diamondbacks for OF Paul Weichard and a player to be named (February 26, 1999); Pirates acquired P Jason Boyd to complete deal (August 25, 1999). ... On disabled list (March 26-April 12, 1999); included rehabilitation assignment to Tucson. ... On disabled list (July 22-August 6, 2001); included rehabilitation assignment to Tucson. ... On disabled list (June 29-July 18, 2003); included rehabilitation assignment to El Paso. ... Traded by Diamondbacks to Colorado Rockies for P Mike Watson (July 18, 2003). ... Traded by Rockies to Chicago Cubs for P Enmanuel Ramires (August 19, 2003). ... Signed as a free agent by Boston Red Sox organization (January 24, 2004). ... Traded by Red Sox to St. Louis Cardinals for P Matt Duff (March 21, 2004). ... Signed as a free agent by New York Yankees (December 20, 2004).

2005 GAMES PLAYED BY POSITION (MLB): OF—66, 2B—24, DH—11.

SCOUTING REPORT Offense: Womack can be an offensive catalyst with exceptional speed and good instincts. Is a slap-and-run hitter who likes to hit off his front foot. Has no power but keeps the ball on the ground. Is a good baserunner, taking aggressive leads and getting good jumps. ***Defense:*** Womack played mostly in the outfield in 2005, and he did not adjust well. Had trouble tracking the ball and getting jumps going back. Has lost arm strength because of elbow problems. At second base, has plus range and good quickness but doesn't have good hands. ***Outlook:*** Womack was out of the Yankees' plans once Robinson Cano took over at second base. Puts the ball in play but is a liability defensively. ***Grade 6.4***

TONY WOMACK'S HITTING ZONE

.240	.300	.160
.227	.303	.271
.333	.294	.295

LEFTY-RIGHTY SPLITS

vs.	Avg.	AB	H	2B	3B	HR	RBI	BB	SO	OBP	Slg.
L	.254	67	17	0	0	0	2	3	15	.286	.254
R	.248	262	65	8	1	0	13	9	34	.274	.286

			BATTING																FIELDING	
Year	Team (League)	Pos.	G	AB	R	H	2B	3B	HR	RBI	BB	SO	HBP	GDP	SB-CS	Avg.	OBP	SLG	OPS	E	Avg.
1991—	Welland (N.Y.-Penn.)	2B-SS	45	166	30	46	3	0	1	8	17	39	0	1	26-5	.277	.344	.313	.658	16	.921
1992—	Augusta (S. Atl.)	2B-SS	102	380	62	93	8	3	0	18	41	59	5	2	50-25	.245	.325	.282	.606	40	.923
1993—	Salem (Carol.)	SS	72	304	41	91	11	3	2	18	13	34	2	2	28-14	.299	.331	.375	.706	28	.927
	—Carolina (Sou.)	SS	60	247	41	75	7	2	0	23	17	34	1	3	21-6	.304	.346	.348	.694	11	.961
	—Pittsburgh (N.L.)	SS	15	24	5	2	0	0	0	0	3	3	0	0	2-0	.083	.185	.083	.269	1	.971
1994—	Buffalo (A.A.)	SS-2B	106	421	40	93	9	2	0	18	19	76	0	2	41-10	.221	.253	.252	.505	22	.957
	—Pittsburgh (N.L.)	2B-SS	5	12	4	4	0	0	0	1	2	3	0	0	0-0	.333	.429	.333	.762	2	.818
1995—	Calgary (PCL)	2B-SS	30	107	12	30	3	1	0	6	12	11	0	1	7-5	.280	.353	.327	.680	5	.963
	—Carolina (Sou.)	SS-2B	82	332	52	85	9	4	1	19	19	36	2	2	27-10	.256	.300	.316	.617	18	.953
1996—	Calgary (PCL)	SS-2B-OF DH	131	506	75	151	19	11	1	47	31	79	3	3	37-12	.298	.339	.385	.725	24	.961
	—Pittsburgh (N.L.)	OF-2B	17	30	11	10	3	1	0	7	6	1	1	0	2-0	.333	.459	.500	.959	2	.905
1997—	Pittsburgh (N.L.)	2B-SS	155	641	85	178	26	9	6	50	43	109	3	6	* 60-7	.278	.326	.374	.700	§ 20	.975
1998—	Pittsburgh (N.L.)	2B-OF-SS	159	655	85	185	26	7	3	45	38	94	0	4	* 58-8	.282	.319	.357	.677	17	.978
1999—	Tucson (PCL)	OF	4	16	1	4	1	0	1	3	2	3	0	2	0-1	.250	.333	.500	.833	0	1.000
	—Arizona (N.L.)	OF-2B-SS	144	614	111	170	25	10	4	41	52	68	2	4	* 72-13	.277	.332	.370	.702	5	.987
2000—	Arizona (N.L.)	SS-OF	146	617	95	167	21	* 14	7	57	30	74	5	6	45-11	.271	.307	.384	.692	18	.970
2001—	Arizona (N.L.)	SS-OF	125	481	66	128	19	5	3	30	23	54	6	4	28-7	.266	.307	.345	.652	22	.955
	—Tucson (PCL)	SS	4	13	1	5	0	1	0	2	0	1	0	0	0-1	.385	.385	.538	.923	2	.846
2002—	Arizona (N.L.)	SS-OF	153	590	90	160	23	5	5	57	46	80	4	9	29-12	.271	.325	.353	.678	20	.964
2003—	Arizona (N.L.)	SS	61	219	30	52	10	3	2	15	8	27	2	6	8-3	.237	.270	.338	.607	7	.966
	—El Paso (Texas)	SS	4	17	3	5	0	0	0	2	2	2	0	0	3-0	.294	.368	.294	.663	1	.923
	—Colorado (N.L.)	SS-2B-OF	21	79	9	15	2	0	0	5	0	9	1	1	3-1	.190	.200	.215	.415	2	.974
	—Chicago (N.L.)	2B-SS	21	51	4	12	2	1	0	2	1	11	0	0	2-1	.235	.250	.314	.564	0	1.000
2004—	St. Louis (N.L.)	2B	145	553	91	170	22	3	5	38	36	60	3	6	26-5	.307	.350	.385	.735	15	.976
2005—	New York (A.L.)	OF-2B-DH	108	329	46	82	8	1	0	15	12	49	1	7	27-5	.249	.276	.280	.556	3	.988
American League totals (1 year)			108	329	46	82	8	1	0	15	12	49	1	7	27-5	.249	.276	.280	.556	3	.988
National League totals (11 years)			1167	4566	686	1253	179	58	35	348	288	593	27	46	335-68	.274	.319	.362	.681	131	.972
Major League totals (12 years)			1275	4895	732	1335	187	59	35	363	300	642	28	53	362-73	.273	.316	.356	.673	134	.972

DIVISION SERIES RECORD

Year	Team (League)	Pos.	G	AB	R	H	2B	3B	HR	RBI	BB	SO	HBP	GDP	SB-CS	Avg.	OBP	SLG	OPS	E	Avg.
1999—	Arizona (N.L.)	OF-SS	4	18	2	2	0	1	0	0	0	6	0	0	0-0	.111	.111	.222	.333	2	.833
2001—	Arizona (N.L.)	SS	5	17	1	5	1	0	0	1	3	2	0	0	0-1	.294	.400	.353	.753	2	.905
2002—	Arizona (N.L.)	SS	3	13	1	2	0	0	0	0	1	1	0	0	0-0	.154	.214	.154	.368	1	.941
2004—	St. Louis (N.L.)	2B	4	19	2	3	0	1	0	1	0	2	0	0	1-0	.158	.158	.263	.421	0	1.000
2005—	New York (A.L.)		2	0	0	0	0	0	0	0	0	0	0	0	0-0	...	...	...	...	0	...
Division series totals (5 years)			18	67	6	12	1	2	0	2	4	11	0	0	1-1	.179	.225	.254	.479	5	.919

CHAMPIONSHIP SERIES RECORD

Year	Team (League)	Pos.	G	AB	R	H	2B	3B	HR	RBI	BB	SO	HBP	GDP	SB-CS	Avg.	OBP	SLG	OPS	E	Avg.
2001—	Arizona (N.L.)	SS	4	20	4	4	1	0	0	0	0	2	0	0	0-1	.200	.200	.250	.450	0	1.000
2004—	St. Louis (N.L.)	2B	7	26	5	7	1	0	0	1	1	3	0	0	2-0	.269	.296	.308	.604	0	1.000
Champ. series totals (2 years)			11	46	9	11	2	0	0	1	1	5	0	0	2-1	.239	.255	.283	.538	0	1.000

WORLD SERIES RECORD

Year	Team (League)	Pos.	G	AB	R	H	2B	3B	HR	RBI	BB	SO	HBP	GDP	SB-CS	Avg.	OBP	SLG	OPS	E	Avg.
2001—	Arizona (N.L.)	SS	7	32	3	8	3	0	0	3	1	7	1	1	1-1	.250	.294	.344	.638	1	.968
2004—	St. Louis (N.L.)	2B	4	11	1	2	0	0	0	0	1	2	0	0	0-0	.182	.250	.182	.432	0	1.000
World series totals (2 years)			11	43	4	10	3	0	0	3	2	9	1	1	1-1	.233	.283	.302	.585	1	.978

	G	AB	R	H	2B	3B	HR	RBI	BB	SO	HBP	GDP	SB-CS	Avg.	OBP	SLG	OPS	E	Avg.
All-Star Game totals (1 year)	1	1	0	0	0	0	0	0	0	0	0	0	0-0	.000	.000	.000	.000	0	1.000

WOOD, KERRY — P

PERSONAL: Born June 16, 1977, in Irving, Texas. ... 6-5/225. ... Throws right, bats right. ... Full name: Kerry Lee Wood. ... High school: Grand Prairie (Texas).

TRANSACTIONS/CAREER NOTES: Selected by Chicago Cubs organization in first round (fourth pick overall) of 1995 free-agent draft. ... On disabled list (March 31, 1999-entire season). ... On disabled list (March 25-May 2 and July 30-August 22, 2000); included rehabilitation assignments to Daytona and Iowa. ... On suspended list (September 8-11, 2000). ... On disabled list (August 4-September 7, 2001). ... On suspended list (May 14-20, 2004). ... On disabled list (May 20-July 11, 2004); included rehabilitation assignment to Iowa. ... On suspended list (August 16-22, 2004). ... On disabled list (May 3-June 29, July 21-August 5 and August 30, 2005-remainder of season); included rehabilitation assignments to Iowa and Peoria.

RECORDS: Shares major league record for most strikeouts, 9-inning game (20, May 6, 1998).

HONORS: Named N.L. Rookie Pitcher of the Year by THE SPORTING NEWS (1998). ... Named N.L. Rookie of the Year by Baseball Writers' Association of America (1998).

CAREER HITTING: 56-for-338 (.166), 23 R, 5 2B, 0 3B, 7 HR, 30 RBI.

SCOUTING REPORT *Throws:* Wood throws his fastball from 95-98 mph, a slurve in the low 80s and an occasional changeup. *Tendencies:* He has a bit of a mean streak and is not afraid to knock people off the plate with his fastball. Can throw the slurve with a big, sweeping break or a shorter break more like a curveball. Has inconsistent delivery, in part because of his violent delivery. *Outlook:* Wood can't stay healthy and is coming off another surgery, and his delivery continues to be a concern. Could be one of the game's most dominant starters if he could shake arm problems. *Grade 8*

KERRY WOOD'S PITCHING ZONE

.455	.375	.067
.297	.237	.239
.188	.417	.154

LEFTY-RIGHTY SPLITS

vs.	Avg.	AB	H	2B	3B	HR	RBI	BB	SO	OBP	Slg.
L	.220	109	24	3	2	10	18	16	35	.317	.560
R	.211	133	28	7	0	4	13	10	42	.276	.353

Year	Team (League)	W	L	Pct.	ERA	WHIP	G	GS	CG	ShO	Hld.	Sv.-Opp.	IP	H	R	ER	HR	BB-IBB	SO	Avg.
1995—GC Cubs (GCL)		0	0	...	0.00	0.33	1	1	0	0	...	0-...	3.0	0	0	0	0	1-0	2	.000
—Williamsport (N.Y.-Penn.)		0	0	...	10.38	2.31	2	2	0	0	...	0-...	4.1	5	8	5	0	5-0	5	.278
1996—Daytona (Fla. St.)		10	2	.833	2.91	1.24	22	22	0	0	...	0-...	114.1	72	51	37	6	70-0	136	.179
1997—Orlando (Sou.)		6	7	.462	4.50	1.46	19	19	0	0	...	0-...	94.0	58	49	47	2	79-2	106	.181
—Iowa (A.A.)		4	2	.667	4.68	1.51	10	10	0	0	...	0-...	57.2	35	35	30	2	52-0	80	.181
1998—Iowa (PCL)		1	0	1.000	0.00	0.60	1	1	0	0	...	0-...	5.0	1	0	0	0	2-0	11	.067
—Chicago (N.L.)		13	6	.684	3.40	1.21	26	26	1	1	0	0-0	166.2	117	69	63	14	85-1	233	* .196
1999—Chicago (N.L.)				Did not play.																
2000—Daytona (Fla. St.)		2	0	1.000	1.50	0.67	2	2	0	0	...	0-...	12.0	3	2	2	0	5-0	17	.081
—Iowa (PCL)		0	0	...	2.57	1.14	1	1	0	0	...	0-...	7.0	4	2	2	0	4-0	7	.174
—Chicago (N.L.)		8	7	.533	4.80	1.45	23	23	1	0	0	0-0	137.0	112	77	73	17	87-0	132	.226
2001—Chicago (N.L.)		12	6	.667	3.36	1.26	28	28	1	0	0	0-0	174.1	127	70	65	16	92-3	217	.202
2002—Chicago (N.L.)		12	11	.522	3.66	1.24	33	33	4	1	0	0-0	213.2	169	92	87	22	97-5	217	.221
2003—Chicago (N.L.)		14	11	.560	3.20	1.19	32	32	4	2	0	0-0	211.0	152	77	75	24	100-2	* 266	.203
2004—Iowa (PCL)		1	0	1.000	0.00	0.60	1	1	0	0	...	0-...	5.0	2	0	0	0	1-0	4	.111
—Chicago (N.L.)		8	9	.471	3.72	1.27	22	22	0	0	0	0-0	140.1	127	62	58	16	51-0	144	.244
2005—Iowa (PCL)		0	0	...	2.84	1.34	3	3	0	0	0	0-0	12.2	11	4	4	1	6-0	18	.239
—Peoria (Midw.)		0	0	...	0.00	0.43	2	0	0	0	0	0-0	2.1	1	0	0	0	0-0	5	.125
—Chicago (N.L.)		3	4	.429	4.23	1.18	21	10	0	0	4	0-0	66.0	52	32	31	14	26-0	77	.215
Major League totals (7 years)		70	54	.565	3.67	1.26	185	174	11	5	4	0-0	1109.0	856	479	452	123	538-11	1286	.214

DIVISION SERIES RECORD

Year	Team (League)	W	L	Pct.	ERA	WHIP	G	GS	CG	ShO	Hld.	Sv.-Opp.	IP	H	R	ER	HR	BB-IBB	SO	Avg.
1998—Chicago (N.L.)		0	1	.000	1.80	1.40	1	1	0	0	0	0-0	5.0	3	1	1	0	4-1	5	.167
2003—Chicago (N.L.)		2	0	1.000	1.76	0.91	2	2	0	0	0	0-0	15.1	7	3	3	1	7-0	18	.132
Division series totals (2 years)		2	1	.667	1.77	1.03	3	3	0	0	0	0-0	20.1	10	4	4	1	11-1	23	.141

CHAMPIONSHIP SERIES RECORD

Year	Team (League)	W	L	Pct.	ERA	WHIP	G	GS	CG	ShO	Hld.	Sv.-Opp.	IP	H	R	ER	HR	BB-IBB	SO	Avg.
2003—Chicago (N.L.)		0	1	.000	7.30	1.70	2	2	0	0	0	0-0	12.1	14	10	10	1	7-0	13	.280

ALL-STAR GAME RECORD

Year	Team (League)	W	L	Pct.	ERA	WHIP	G	GS	CG	ShO	Hld.	Sv.-Opp.	IP	H	R	ER	HR	BB-IBB	SO	Avg.
All-Star Game totals (1 year)		0	0	...	0.00	1.00	1	0	0	0	0	0-0	1.0	1	0	0	0	0-0	2	.250

WOOD, MIKE — P

W

PERSONAL: Born April 26, 1980, in West Palm Beach, Fla. ... 6-3/210. ... Throws right, bats right. ... Full name: Michael Burton Wood. ... High school: Forest Hill Community (West Palm Beach, Fla.). ... College: North Florida.

TRANSACTIONS/CAREER NOTES: Selected by Oakland Athletics organization in 10th round of 2001 free-agent draft. ... Traded by Oakland Athletics with 3B Mark Teahen to Kansas City Royals as part of three-team deal in which Royals acquired C John Buck and cash from Houston Astros, Athletics acquired P Octavio Dotel and cash from Astros and Astros acquired OF Carlos Beltran from Royals (June 24, 2004).

CAREER HITTING: 0-for-2 (.000), 0 R, 0 2B, 0 3B, 0 HR, 0 RBI.

SCOUTING REPORT *Throws:* He has a fastball at 85-89 mph, a cut fastball at 85-86, a curveball and a slider. *Tendencies:* He has little room for error, especially with his fastball. Fastball down will sink and he occasionally cuts it. Curve is more of sweeping slurve and slider isn't very sharp. Throws a circle change with some sink but often leaves it up. Works fast. Throws across his body, which gives him some deception. *Outlook:* Wood has been used both as a starter and long reliever. Is no better than a fifth starter. *Grade 4.9*

MIKE WOOD'S PITCHING ZONE

.308	.231	.333
.302	.455	.372
.237	.080	.231

LEFTY-RIGHTY SPLITS

vs.	Avg.	AB	H	2B	3B	HR	RBI	BB	SO	OBP	Slg.
L	.295	210	62	13	3	8	32	25	27	.370	.500
R	.279	240	67	14	1	10	36	27	33	.365	.471

Year Team (League)	W	L	Pct.	ERA	WHIP	G	GS	CG	ShO	Hld.	Sv.-Opp.	IP	H	R	ER	HR	BB-IBB	SO	Avg.
2001— Vancouver (N'west)	2	0	1.000	1.25	0.97	5	2	0	0	...	0-...	21.2	17	4	3	0	4-0	24	.210
— Modesto (Calif.)	4	3	.571	3.09	0.96	10	9	0	0	...	0-...	58.1	46	22	20	6	10-3	52	.211
2002— Modesto (Calif.)	3	3	.500	3.48	1.14	7	7	0	0	...	0-...	41.1	41	17	16	4	6-0	50	.265
— Midland (Texas)	11	3	.786	3.15	1.25	17	17	0	0	...	0-...	105.2	103	41	37	8	29-0	63	.259
2003— Sacramento (PCL)	9	3	.750	3.05	1.20	16	16	0	0	...	0-...	91.1	87	34	31	8	23-1	59	.257
— Oakland (A.L.)	2	1	.667	10.54	2.27	7	1	0	0	0	0-0	13.2	24	17	16	1	7-2	15	.387
2004— Sacramento (PCL)	11	3	.786	2.80	1.19	15	15	1	0	...	0-0	90.0	83	42	28	8	24-1	66	.241
— Kansas City (A.L.)	3	8	.273	5.94	1.40	17	17	0	0	0	0-0	100.0	112	67	66	16	28-3	54	.286
2005— Omaha (PCL)	0	0	...	2.00	1.33	2	2	0	0	0	0-0	9.0	10	2	2	0	2-0	8	.286
— Kansas City (A.L.)	5	8	.385	4.46	1.57	47	10	0	0	7	2-2	115.0	129	66	57	18	52-5	60	.287
Major League totals (3 years)	10	17	.370	5.47	1.54	71	28	0	0	7	2-2	228.2	265	150	139	35	87-10	129	.293

WOODS, JAKE — P

PERSONAL: Born September 3, 1981, in Fresno, Calif. ... 6-1/190. ... Throws left, bats left. ... Full name: Jacob Thomas Woods. ... Junior college: Bakersfield (Calif.).
TRANSACTIONS/CAREER NOTES: Selected by Anaheim Angels organization in third round of 2001 free-agent draft. ... Angels franchise renamed Los Angeles Angels of Anaheim for 2005 season.
CAREER HITTING: 0-for-0 (.000), 0 R, 0 2B, 0 3B, 0 HR, 0 RBI.

JAKE WOODS'S PITCHING ZONE

.286	.250	.500
.250	.636	.333
.222	.000	.250

LEFTY-RIGHTY SPLITS

vs.	Avg.	AB	H	2B	3B	HR	RBI	BB	SO	OBP	Slg.
L	.229	48	11	0	0	2	8	3	9	.288	.354
R	.302	63	19	4	0	5	7	5	11	.362	.603

Year Team (League)	W	L	Pct.	ERA	WHIP	G	GS	CG	ShO	Hld.	Sv.-Opp.	IP	H	R	ER	HR	BB-IBB	SO	Avg.
2001— Provo (Pion.)	4	3	.571	5.29	1.53	15	14	1	1	...	0-...	64.2	70	41	38	6	29-0	84	.275
2002— Cedar Rapids (Midw.)	10	5	.667	3.05	1.19	27	27	1	0	...	0-...	153.1	128	66	52	12	54-0	121	.228
2003— Rancho Cuca. (Calif.)	12	7	.632	3.99	1.35	28	28	2	1	...	0-...	171.1	178	90	76	9	54-0	109	.270
2004— Arkansas (Texas)	9	2	.818	2.70	1.17	14	14	1	0	...	0-...	90.0	86	29	27	5	19-0	60	.259
— Salt Lake (PCL)	6	4	.600	6.07	1.80	15	14	1	0	...	0-...	83.0	107	67	56	13	42-0	60	.317
2005— Los Angeles (A.L.)	1	1	.500	4.55	1.37	28	0	0	0	2	0-0	27.2	30	18	14	7	8-0	20	.270
— Salt Lake (PCL)	3	1	.750	5.89	1.83	15	5	0	0	1	0-2	36.2	50	27	24	7	17-2	36	.314
Major League totals (1 year)	1	1	.500	4.55	1.37	28	0	0	0	2	0-0	27.2	30	18	14	7	8-0	20	.270

WOODWARD, CHRIS — SS/OF

PERSONAL: Born June 27, 1976, in Covina, Calif. ... 6-0/185. ... Bats right, throws right. ... Full name: Christopher Michael Woodward. ... High school: Northview (Covina, Calif.). ... Junior college: Mt. San Antonio (Calif.).
TRANSACTIONS/CAREER NOTES: Selected by Toronto Blue Jays organization in 54th round of 1994 free-agent draft. ... On disabled list (July 1-26, 2001); included rehabilitation assignment to Syracuse. ... On disabled list (June 21-July 11, 2002); included rehabilitation assignment to Dunedin. ... On disabled list (May 12-June 8, 2004); included rehabilitation assignment to Dunedin. ... Signed as a free agent by New York Mets organization (December 28, 2005).
2005 GAMES PLAYED BY POSITION (MLB): 1B—34, OF—23, SS—7, 3B—6, 2B—5, DH—1.

SCOUTING REPORT Woodward likes the ball out over the plate so he can extend his arms, but that makes him vulnerable to balls inside. Swing is a little long. Bat speed and power have declined. Has problems with righthanders. Loses his concentration while expanding his zone. Is a fluid infielder with soft, quick hands. Charges the ball well and has a quick release with an accurate arm. Has good range to either side. ***Grade 5.3***

CHRIS WOODWARD'S HITTING ZONE

.250	.429	.250
.298	.476	.316
.263	.250	.250

LEFTY-RIGHTY SPLITS

vs.	Avg.	AB	H	2B	3B	HR	RBI	BB	SO	OBP	Slg.
L	.260	96	25	5	0	2	6	9	22	.330	.375
R	.312	77	24	5	0	1	12	4	24	.345	.416

										BATTING							FIELDING	
Year Team (League)	Pos.	G	AB	R	H	2B	3B	HR	RBI	BB	SO	HBP	GDP	SB-CS	Avg.	OBP	SLG	OPS	E	Avg.
1995— Medicine Hat (Pion.)	SS	72	241	44	56	8	0	3	21	33	41	6	1	9-4	.232	.336	.303	.639	30	.911
1996— Hagerstown (S. Atl.)	SS	123	424	41	95	24	2	1	48	43	70	5	3	11-3	.224	.300	.297	.597	30	.951
1997— Dunedin (Fla. St.)	SS	91	314	38	92	13	4	1	38	52	52	5	3	4-8	.293	.397	.369	.767	12	.972
1998— Knoxville (Sou.)	SS	73	253	36	62	12	0	3	27	26	47	3	4	3-5	.245	.319	.328	.647	11	.971
— Syracuse (Int'l)	SS	25	85	9	17	6	0	2	6	7	20	0	4	1-1	.200	.261	.341	.602	4	.961
1999— Syracuse (Int'l)	SS-2B	75	281	46	82	20	3	1	20	38	49	1	5	4-1	.292	.378	.395	.773	11	.966
— Toronto (A.L.)	SS-3B	14	26	1	6	1	0	0	2	2	6	0	1	0-0	.231	.276	.269	.545	2	.944
2000— Toronto (A.L.) SS-3B-1B	2B	37	104	16	19	7	0	3	14	10	28	0	1	1-0	.183	.254	.337	.591	5	.963
— Syracuse (Int'l) 2B-3B-SS	37	143	23	46	13	2	5	25	11	30	0	2	2-0	.322	.370	.545	.916	2	.988
2001— Toronto (A.L.) 2B-3B-SS		1B-DH	37	63	9	12	3	2	2	5	1	14	0	1	0-1	.190	.203	.397	.600	8	.933
— Syracuse (Int'l) 3B-SS-1B	2B	51	193	29	59	14	3	11	31	16	40	1	4	0-0	.306	.360	.580	.941	9	.950
2002— Dunedin (Fla. St.)	SS	2	6	1	2	0	0	0	0	0	1	0	0	0-0	.333	.429	.333	.762	0	1.000
— Toronto (A.L.) SS-2B-1B	3B-DH	90	312	48	86	13	4	13	45	26	72	3	8	3-0	.276	.330	.468	.797	15	.964
2003— Toronto (A.L.)	SS	104	349	49	91	22	2	7	45	28	72	3	6	1-2	.261	.316	.395	.711	17	.964
2004— Dunedin (Fla. St.)	SS	6	16	2	5	2	0	1	3	1	2	0	0	0-0	.313	.333	.625	.958	0	1.000
— Toronto (A.L.)	SS-DH	69	213	21	50	13	4	1	24	14	46	1	4	1-2	.235	.283	.347	.630	5	.981

W

Year Team (League)	Pos.	G	AB	R	H	2B	3B	HR	RBI	BB	SO	HBP	GDP	SB-CS	Avg.	OBP	SLG	OPS	E	Avg.
											BATTING								FIELDING	
2005— New York (N.L.) 1B-OF-SS 3B-2B-DH		81	173	16	49	10	0	3	18	13	46	2	2	0-0	.283	.337	.393	.730	6	.979
American League totals (6 years)		351	1067	144	264	59	12	26	135	81	238	7	20	6-5	.247	.300	.398	.699	52	.964
National League totals (1 year)		81	173	16	49	10	0	3	18	13	46	2	2	0-0	.283	.337	.393	.730	6	.979
Major League totals (7 years)		432	1240	160	313	69	12	29	153	94	284	9	22	6-5	.252	.305	.398	.703	58	.967

WOODYARD, MARK   P

PERSONAL: Born December 19, 1978, in Mobile, Ala. ... 6-2/195. ... Throws right, bats right. ... Full name: Mark Anthony Woodyard. ... High school: Grand Bay (Ala.). ... College: Bethune-Cookman.

TRANSACTIONS/CAREER NOTES: Selected by Detroit Tigers organization in fourth round of 2000 free-agent draft.

CAREER HITTING: 0-for-0 (.000), 0 R, 0 2B, 0 3B, 0 HR, 0 RBI.

LEFTY-RIGHTY SPLITS

vs.	Avg.	AB	H	2B	3B	HR	RBI	BB	SO	OBP	Slg.
L	.222	9	2	0	0	0	0	0	1	.222	.222
R	.154	13	2	0	0	1	1	0	2	.154	.385

Year Team (League)	W	L	Pct.	ERA	WHIP	G	GS	CG	ShO	Hld.	Sv.-Opp.	IP	H	R	ER	HR	BB-IBB	SO	Avg.
2000— Oneonta (N.Y.-Penn.)	1	5	.167	4.59	1.71	11	9	0	0	...	0-...	51.0	48	32	26	0	39-0	38	.244
2001— W. Mich. (Midw.)	7	12	.368	4.51	1.50	25	25	2	1	...	0-...	143.2	147	81	72	5	69-2	84	.267
2002— Lakeland (Fla. St.)	2	8	.200	7.64	1.71	17	7	0	0	...	2-...	66.0	81	62	56	10	32-0	22	.302
2003— Lakeland (Fla. St.)	4	8	.333	4.53	1.59	23	23	1	0	...	0-...	117.1	133	69	59	7	53-2	84	.287
— Erie (East.)	1	0	1.000	5.56	1.68	2	2	0	0	...	0-...	11.1	14	7	7	1	5-0	6	.326
2004— Erie (East.)	6	4	.600	3.52	1.36	43	9	0	0	...	5-...	102.1	102	53	40	5	37-3	55	.264
2005— Toledo (Int'l)	5	2	.714	3.84	1.41	45	0	0	0	3	1-3	70.1	67	34	30	7	32-2	62	.251
— Detroit (A.L.)	0	0	...	1.50	0.67	3	0	0	0	0	0-0	6.0	4	1	1	1	0-0	3	.182
Major League totals (1 year)	0	0	...	1.50	0.67	3	0	0	0	0	0-0	6.0	4	1	1	1	0-0	3	.182

WOOTEN, SHAWN   1B/3B

PERSONAL: Born July 24, 1972, in Glendora, Calif. ... 5-10/220. ... Bats right, throws right. ... Full name: William Shawn Wooten. ... High school: South Hills (Covina, Calif.). ... Junior college: Mt. San Antonio (Calif.).

TRANSACTIONS/CAREER NOTES: Selected by Detroit Tigers organization in 18th round of 1993 free-agent draft. ... Released by Tigers (June 19, 1995). ... Signed by Moose Jaw of independent Prairie League (1995). ... Signed by California Angels organization (February 26, 1997). ... Angels franchise renamed Anaheim Angels for 1997 season. ... On disabled list (March 21-July 11, 2002); included rehabilitation assignments to Salt Lake and Rancho Cucamonga. ... Signed as a free agent by Philadelphia Phillies (December 23, 2003). ... Signed as a free agent to Boston Red Sox organization (February 1, 2005).

LEFTY-RIGHTY SPLITS

vs.	Avg.	AB	H	2B	3B	HR	RBI	BB	SO	OBP	Slg.
L	.000	0	0	0	0	0	0	0	0	.000	.000
R	.000	1	0	0	0	0	0	0	0	.000	.000

2005 GAMES PLAYED BY POSITION (MLB): C—1.

Year Team (League)	Pos.	G	AB	R	H	2B	3B	HR	RBI	BB	SO	HBP	GDP	SB-CS	Avg.	OBP	SLG	OPS	E	Avg.
											BATTING								FIELDING	
1993— Bristol (Appal.) 1B-3B-OF		52	177	26	62	12	2	8	39	24	20	3	7	1-2	.350	.432	.576	1.008	10	.956
— Fayetteville (SAL)	1B-3B	5	16	2	4	0	0	1	5	3	3	1	0	0-0	.250	.368	.438	.806	0	1.000
1994— Fayetteville (SAL)	1B-3B	121	439	45	118	25	4	3	61	27	84	11	11	1-3	.269	.324	.364	.689	24	.938
1995— Jacksonville (Sou.)	3B	20	70	4	9	1	0	2	7	1	17	1	3	0-0	.129	.151	.229	.379	5	.921
— Lakeland (Fla. St.)	3B	38	135	11	31	10	1	2	11	10	28	2	2	0-1	.230	.291	.363	.654	7	.942
— Moose Jaw (Prairie)		52	201	38	75	12	2	11	55	18	26	...	...	3-...	.373	...	.617	...	...	...
1996— Moose Jaw (Prairie)		77	292	44	89	17	0	12	57	18	46	2	8	2-0	.305	.348	.486	.835	...	...
1997— Cedar Rap. (Midw.)	1B-C	108	353	43	102	23	1	15	75	49	71	6	8	0-1	.289	.379	.487	.866	0	1.000
1998— Lake Elsinore (Calif.)	1B-2B-3B	105	395	56	116	31	0	16	74	38	82	3	9	0-2	.294	.357	.494	.850	1	.999
— Midland (Texas)	1B	8	28	3	9	4	0	1	6	3	4	0	0	0-0	.321	.387	.571	.959	1	.967
1999— Erie (East.) 1B-3B-C		137	518	70	151	27	1	19	88	50	102	10	12	3-1	.292	.360	.488	.818	22	.949
2000— Erie (East.)	C-3B	51	191	32	56	12	2	9	35	17	30	2	3	4-1	.293	.350	.518	.869	9	.970
— Edmonton (PCL)	C-3B-1B	66	252	43	89	21	3	11	42	18	38	3	4	0-0	.353	.401	.591	.993	7	.982
— Anaheim (A.L.)	C-1B	7	9	2	5	0	0	1	0	0	0	0	0	0-0	.556	.556	.667	1.222	0	1.000
2001— Anaheim (A.L.) DH-C-1B 3B		79	221	24	69	8	1	8	32	5	42	3	5	2-0	.312	.332	.466	.798	2	.992
2002— Anaheim (A.L.) DH-1B-C 3B		49	113	13	33	8	0	3	19	6	24	1	3	2-0	.292	.331	.442	.773	1	1.000
— Salt Lake (PCL) 1B-3B-C		10	42	2	11	2	0	0	7	0	11	1	1	0-0	.262	.279	.310	.589	1	.976
— Rancho Cuca. (Calif.)	1B	6	18	2	4	3	0	0	3	4	4	0	1	0-0	.222	.348	.389	.737	0	1.000
2003— Anaheim (A.L.) 1B-DH-C 3B		98	272	25	66	8	0	7	32	24	45	1	7	0-4	.243	.303	.349	.653	2	.994
2004— Scran./W.B. (I.L.) 3B-DH-1B		61	225	28	66	22	0	4	34	24	29	4	11	0-1	.293	.370	.444	.815	8	.941
— Philadelphia (N.L.)	1B-3B	33	53	2	9	3	0	0	2	2	9	2	4	0-0	.170	.228	.226	.454	0	1.000
2005— Boston (A.L.)	C	1	1	0	0	0	0	0	0	0	0	0	0	0-0	.000	.000	.000	.000	0	...
— Pawtucket (Int'l) .... C-1B-3B DH		114	427	45	114	20	0	17	60	35	72	9	16	0-0	.267	.329	.433	.762	9	.986
American League totals (5 years)		234	616	64	173	25	1	18	84	35	111	5	15	4-4	.281	.321	.412	.734	4	.994
National League totals (1 year)		33	53	2	9	3	0	0	2	2	9	2	4	0-0	.170	.228	.226	.454	0	1.000
Major League totals (6 years)		267	669	66	182	28	1	18	86	37	120	7	19	4-4	.272	.314	.398	.711	4	.995

DIVISION SERIES RECORD

Year Team (League)	Pos.	G	AB	R	H	2B	3B	HR	RBI	BB	SO	HBP	GDP	SB-CS	Avg.	OBP	SLG	OPS	E	Avg.
2002— Anaheim (A.L.)	DH	3	9	4	6	0	0	1	2	0	1	0	0	0-0	.667	.667	1.000	1.667	0	...

CHAMPIONSHIP SERIES RECORD

Year Team (League)	Pos.	G	AB	R	H	2B	3B	HR	RBI	BB	SO	HBP	GDP	SB-CS	Avg.	OBP	SLG	OPS	E	Avg.
2002— Anaheim (A.L.)	DH	3	8	1	2	0	0	0	0	0	3	0	0	0-0	.250	.250	.250	.500	0	...

WORLD SERIES RECORD

Year Team (League)	Pos.	G	AB	R	H	2B	3B	HR	RBI	BB	SO	HBP	GDP	SB-CS	Avg.	OBP	SLG	OPS	E	Avg.
2002— Anaheim (A.L.)	1B	3	2	0	1	0	0	0	0	0	0	0	0	0-0	.500	.500	.500	1.000	0	1.000

W

WORRELL, TIM — P

PERSONAL: Born July 5, 1967, in Pasadena, Calif. ... 6-4/230. ... Throws right, bats right. ... Full name: Timothy Howard Worrell. ... Name pronounced: wor-RELL. ... High school: Maranatha (Sierra Madre, Calif.). ... College: Biola (Calif.). ... Brother of Todd Worrell, pitcher with two major league teams (1985-97).

TRANSACTIONS/CAREER NOTES: Selected by San Diego Padres organization in 20th round of 1989 free-agent draft. ... On disabled list (April 19, 1994-remainder of season). ... On disabled list (April 24-September 1, 1995); included rehabilitation assignments to Rancho Cucamonga and Las Vegas. ... Traded by Padres with OF Trey Beamon to Detroit Tigers for Ps Dan Miceli and Donne Wall and 3B Ryan Balfe (November 19, 1997). ... Traded by Tigers with OF Dave Roberts to Cleveland Indians for OF Geronimo Berroa (June 24, 1998). ... Traded by Indians to Oakland Athletics for a player to be named (July 12, 1998); Indians acquired SS Adam Robinson to complete deal (July 27, 1998). ... On disabled list (July 20-August 8, 1999); included rehabilitation assignment to Modesto. ... Signed as a free agent by Baltimore Orioles organization (February 4, 2000). ... Released by Orioles (May 1, 2000). ... Signed by Chicago Cubs organization (May 8, 2000). ... Traded by Cubs to San Francisco Giants for 3B Bill Mueller (November 19, 2000). ... On disabled list (July 9-26, 2001); included rehabilitation assignment to AZL Giants. ... Signed as a free agent by Philadelphia Phillies (December 10, 2003). ... On disabled list (May 6-July 4, 2005); included rehabilitation assignments to Lakewood and Reading. ... Traded by Phillies to Arizona Diamondbacks for IF Matt Kata (July 21, 2005).

CAREER HITTING: 8-for-80 (.100), 6 R, 1 2B, 0 3B, 0 HR, 4 RBI.

SCOUTING REPORT **Throws:** Worrell's fastball is in the upper 80s. Also throws a slider and a changeup. **Tendencies:** He throws easily from three-quarters. Fastball doesn't have a lot of life. Can't make any mistakes up in the zone. Slider is too flat. Has good motion on and feel for his changeup, which occasionally sinks. **Outlook:** He was less effective with a decrease in velocity on his fastball; the speeds of his pitches are relatively close now. Has to have pinpoint control to be effective. Needs a strong spring to be a setup man; otherwise, he'll pitch in middle relief. ***Grade 6.3***

TIM WORRELL'S PITCHING ZONE

.533	.200	.182
.286	.435	.270
.231	.571	.286

LEFTY-RIGHTY SPLITS

vs.	Avg.	AB	H	2B	3B	HR	RBI	BB	SO	OBP	Slg.
L	.295	88	26	5	2	2	13	4	15	.330	.466
R	.303	109	33	8	1	6	25	8	24	.344	.560

Year Team (League)	W	L	Pct.	ERA	WHIP	G	GS	CG	ShO	Hld.	Sv.-Opp.	IP	H	R	ER	HR	BB-IBB	SO	Avg.
1990— Char., S.C. (S. Atl.)	5	8	.385	4.64	1.34	20	19	3	0	...	0-...	110.2	120	65	57	6	28-2	68	.272
1991— Waterloo (Midw.)	8	4	.667	3.34	1.19	14	14	3	2	...	0-...	86.1	70	36	32	5	33-0	83	.217
— High Desert (Calif.)	5	2	.714	4.24	1.54	11	11	2	0	...	0-...	63.2	65	32	30	2	33-0	70	.267
1992— Wichita (Texas)	8	6	.571	2.86	1.17	19	19	1	1	...	0-...	125.2	115	46	40	8	32-0	109	.245
— Las Vegas (PCL)	4	2	.667	4.26	1.26	10	10	1	1	...	0-...	63.1	61	32	30	4	19-0	32	.253
1993— Las Vegas (PCL)	5	6	.455	5.48	1.47	15	14	0	0	...	0-...	87.0	102	61	53	13	26-1	89	.294
— San Diego (N.L.)	2	7	.222	4.92	1.46	21	16	0	0	1	0-0	100.2	104	63	55	11	43-5	52	.269
1994— San Diego (N.L.)	0	1	.000	3.68	0.95	3	3	0	0	0	0-0	14.2	9	7	6	0	5-0	14	.170
1995— Rancho Cuca. (Calif.)	0	2	.000	5.16	1.37	9	3	0	0	...	1-...	22.2	25	17	13	2	6-1	17	.266
— Las Vegas (PCL)	0	2	.000	6.00	1.83	10	3	0	0	...	0-...	24.0	27	21	16	1	17-0	18	.273
— San Diego (N.L.)	1	0	1.000	4.73	1.65	9	0	0	0	0	0-0	13.1	16	7	7	2	6-0	13	.291
1996— San Diego (N.L.)	9	7	.563	3.05	1.22	50	11	0	0	10	1-2	121.0	109	45	41	9	39-1	99	.236
1997— San Diego (N.L.)	4	8	.333	5.16	1.56	60	10	0	0	16	3-7	106.1	116	67	61	14	50-2	81	.280
1998— Detroit (A.L.)	2	6	.250	5.98	1.38	15	9	0	0	0	0-1	61.2	66	42	41	11	19-2	47	.270
— Cleveland (A.L.)	0	0	...	5.06	1.50	3	0	0	0	0	0-0	5.1	6	3	3	0	2-0	5	.300
— Oakland (A.L.)	0	1	.000	4.00	1.17	25	0	0	0	6	0-2	36.0	34	17	16	5	8-1	33	.241
1999— Oakland (A.L.)	2	2	.500	4.15	1.49	53	0	0	0	5	0-5	69.1	69	38	32	6	34-1	62	.256
— Modesto (Calif.)	0	0	...	0.00	0.00	1	1	0	0	...	0-...	2.0	0	0	0	0	0-0	5	.000
2000— Baltimore (A.L.)	2	2	.500	7.36	2.32	5	0	0	0	0	0-0	7.1	12	6	6	3	5-3	5	.353
— Iowa (PCL)	2	0	1.000	5.06	1.31	6	0	0	0	...	0-...	10.2	9	6	6	3	5-1	7	.237
— Chicago (N.L.)	3	4	.429	2.47	1.35	54	0	0	0	12	3-6	62.0	60	20	17	7	24-8	52	.252
2001— San Francisco (N.L.)	2	5	.286	3.45	1.33	73	0	0	0	13	0-3	78.1	71	33	30	4	33-4	63	.240
— Ariz. Giants (AZL)	0	0	...	0.00	0.67	1	1	0	0	0	0-0	3.0	1	0	0	0	1-0	2	.125
2002— San Francisco (N.L.)	8	2	.800	2.25	1.18	80	0	0	0	23	0-1	72.0	55	21	18	3	30-2	55	.212
2003— San Francisco (N.L.)	4	4	.500	2.87	1.30	76	0	0	0	1	38-45	78.1	74	35	25	5	28-6	65	.246
2004— Philadelphia (N.L.)	5	6	.455	3.68	1.23	77	0	0	0	20	19-27	78.1	75	36	32	10	21-4	64	.254
2005— Lakewood (S. Atl.)	0	0	...	2.08	1.62	3	3	0	0	0	0-0	4.1	7	3	1	0	0-0	6	.350
— Reading (East.)	0	0	...	0.00	0.00	2	1	0	0	0	0-0	3.0	0	0	0	0	0-0	3	.000
— Philadelphia (N.L.)	0	1	.000	7.41	1.88	19	0	0	0	3	1-3	17.0	29	17	14	4	3-0	17	.377
— Arizona (N.L.)	1	1	.500	2.27	1.23	32	0	0	0	9	0-1	31.2	30	13	8	4	9-2	22	.250
American League totals (3 years)	6	11	.353	4.91	1.42	101	9	0	0	11	0-8	179.2	187	106	98	25	68-7	149	.264
National League totals (11 years)	39	46	.459	3.65	1.34	554	40	0	0	108	65-95	773.2	748	364	314	73	291-34	597	.253
Major League totals (13 years)	45	57	.441	3.89	1.36	655	49	0	0	119	65-103	953.1	935	470	412	98	359-41	746	.255

DIVISION SERIES RECORD

Year Team (League)	W	L	Pct.	ERA	WHIP	G	GS	CG	ShO	Hld.	Sv.-Opp.	IP	H	R	ER	HR	BB-IBB	SO	Avg.
1996— San Diego (N.L.)	0	0	...	2.45	1.36	2	0	0	0	0	0-1	3.2	4	1	1	0	1-0	5	.286
2002— San Francisco (N.L.)	0	0	...	12.00	3.00	3	0	0	0	1	0-0	3.0	7	6	4	2	2-0	3	.438
2003— San Francisco (N.L.)	0	1	.000	0.00	2.25	2	0	0	0	0	0-0	2.2	3	2	0	0	3-1	0	.273
Division series totals (3 years)	0	1	.000	4.82	2.14	7	0	0	0	1	0-1	9.1	14	9	5	2	6-1	5	.341

CHAMPIONSHIP SERIES RECORD

Year Team (League)	W	L	Pct.	ERA	WHIP	G	GS	CG	ShO	Hld.	Sv.-Opp.	IP	H	R	ER	HR	BB-IBB	SO	Avg.
2002— San Francisco (N.L.)	2	0	1.000	2.08	0.46	4	0	0	0	0	0-0	4.1	2	1	1	1	0-0	3	.133

WORLD SERIES RECORD

Year Team (League)	W	L	Pct.	ERA	WHIP	G	GS	CG	ShO	Hld.	Sv.-Opp.	IP	H	R	ER	HR	BB-IBB	SO	Avg.
2002— San Francisco (N.L.)	1	1	.500	3.18	0.88	5	0	0	0	2	0-0	5.2	4	3	2	1	1-0	4	.190

WRIGHT, DAVID — 3B

PERSONAL: Born December 20, 1982, in Norfolk, Va. ... 6-0/200. ... Bats right, throws right. ... Full name: David Allen Wright. ... High school: Hickory (Chesapeake, Va.).
TRANSACTIONS/CAREER NOTES: Selected by New York Mets organization in supplemental round ("sandwich pick" between first and second rounds, 38th pick overall) of 2001 free-agent draft; pick acquired as compensation for Colorado Rockies signing Type A free-agent P Mike Hampton.
2005 GAMES PLAYED BY POSITION (MLB): 3B—160.

W

SCOUTING REPORT *Offense:* Wright has an outstanding, short stroke with little movement. Has an extremely quick bat and is advanced in his ability to recognize pitches and take balls to the opposite field. Has power to all fields and will be a 35-plus homer, 100-RBI hitter. Is not a base-stealing threat but has good quickness and instincts on the bases. *Defense:* Wright made quick adjustments in his setup and his ability to move to the ball. Has good hands with a quick first step to both sides. Has improved his balance and agility. Has a strong but sometimes erratic throwing arm. *Outlook:* Wright will rapidly become one of the best third basemen in the game, becoming one of the most productive hitters at his position. May never be a Gold Glove winner but will be the best the Mets have had in many years. *Grade 8.4*

DAVID WRIGHT'S HITTING ZONE

.471	.323	.308
.320	.477	.313
.282	.257	.432

LEFTY-RIGHTY SPLITS

vs.	Avg.	AB	H	2B	3B	HR	RBI	BB	SO	OBP	Slg.
L	.336	128	43	7	0	9	21	15	17	.415	.602
R	.298	447	133	35	1	18	81	57	96	.380	.501

Year	Team (League)	Pos.	G	AB	R	H	2B	3B	HR	RBI	BB	SO	HBP	GDP	SB-CS	Avg.	OBP	SLG	OPS	E	Avg.
2001—Kingsport (Appal.)		3B	36	120	27	36	7	0	4	17	16	30	2	3	9-1	.300	.391	.458	.850	5	.939
2002—Capital City (S. Atl)			135	496	85	132	30	2	11	93	76	114	4	9	21-5	.266	.367	.401	.768	19	.942
2003—St. Lucie (Fla. St.)		3B	133	466	69	126	39	2	15	75	72	98	4	8	19-5	.270	.369	.459	.828	16	.951
2004—Binghamton (East.)		3B-DH	60	223	44	81	27	0	10	40	39	41	7	5	20-6	.363	.467	.619	1.072	8	.943
—Norfolk (Int'l)		3B	31	114	18	34	8	0	8	17	16	19	2	3	2-4	.298	.388	.579	.958	7	.933
—New York (N.L.)		3B	69	263	41	77	17	1	14	40	14	40	3	7	6-0	.293	.332	.525	.857	11	.942
2005—New York (N.L.)		3B	160	575	99	176	42	1	27	102	72	113	7	16	17-7	.306	.388	.523	.912	24	.948
Major League totals (2 years)			229	838	140	253	59	2	41	142	86	153	10	23	23-7	.302	.371	.524	.895	35	.946

WRIGHT, JAMEY   P

PERSONAL: Born December 24, 1974, in Oklahoma City. ... 6-6/235. ... Throws right, bats right. ... Full name: Jamey Alan Wright. ... High school: Westmoore (Moore, Okla.).
TRANSACTIONS/CAREER NOTES: Selected by Colorado Rockies organization in first round (28th pick overall) of 1993 free-agent draft. ... On disabled list (May 15-June 8, 1997); included rehabilitation assignment to Salem. ... Traded by Rockies with C Henry Blanco to Milwaukee Brewers as part of three-team deal in which Rockies acquired 3B Jeff Cirillo, P Scott Karl and cash from Brewers, Oakland Athletics acquired P Justin Miller and cash from Rockies and Brewers acquired P Jimmy Haynes from A's (December 13, 1999). ... On disabled list (March 28-May 23, 2000); included rehabilitation assignments to Huntsville and Indianapolis. ... On disabled list (May 25-June 10, 2001). ... On disabled list (April 11-May 24, 2002); included rehabilitation assignment to Indianapolis. ... Traded by Brewers with cash to St. Louis Cardinals for OF Chris Morris and a player to be named (August 29, 2002); Brewers acquired P Mike Matthews to complete deal (September 11, 2002). ... Signed as a free agent by Seattle Mariners organization (January 24, 2003). ... Released by Mariners (March 18, 2003). ... Signed by Brewers organization (March 26, 2003). ... Released by Brewers (April 28, 2003). ... Signed by Texas Rangers organization (May 7, 2003). ... Released by Rangers (June 15, 2003). ... Signed by Kansas City Royals (June 20, 2003). ... Signed as a free agent by Chicago Cubs organization (December 29, 2003). ... Signed as a free agent by Royals organization (March 27, 2004). ... Released by Royals (July 21, 2004). ... Signed by Rockies (July 22, 2004).
CAREER HITTING: 52-for-388 (.134), 22 R, 13 2B, 1 3B, 1 HR, 16 RBI.

SCOUTING REPORT *Throws:* Wright throws a consistent sinking fastball, a curve in the middle 70s, a slider in the low 80s and a change. *Tendencies:* He's an ideal pitcher for Coors Field with his ability to sink the ball, but still is inconsistent. Will throw both a two- and four-seam fastball; the latter will move away from righthanders, and he can be dominant pitching inside to them. Curve has better rotation than the slider. Has never been able to develop a feel for the change. Holds runners on well. *Outlook:* He's still an underachiever at the age of 31. Needs to learn to trust his stuff. *Grade 5.9*

JAMEY WRIGHT'S PITCHING ZONE

.259	.435	.152
.269	.436	.278
.358	.341	.303

LEFTY-RIGHTY SPLITS

vs.	Avg.	AB	H	2B	3B	HR	RBI	BB	SO	OBP	Slg.
L	.314	331	104	25	1	15	60	59	54	.419	.532
R	.279	348	97	26	2	7	43	22	47	.344	.425

Year	Team (League)	W	L	Pct.	ERA	WHIP	G	GS	CG	ShO	Hld.	Sv.-Opp.	IP	H	R	ER	HR	BB-IBB	SO	Avg.
1993—Ariz. Rockies (AZL)		1	3	.250	4.00	1.22	8	8	0	0	...	0-...	36.0	35	19	16	1	9-0	26	.243
1994—Asheville (S. Atl.)		7	14	.333	5.97	1.72	28	27	2	0	...	0-...	143.1	188	107	95	6	59-1	103	.329
1995—Salem (Carol.)		10	8	.556	2.47	1.36	26	26	2	1	...	0-...	171.0	160	74	47	7	72-3	95	.251
—New Haven (East.)		0	1	.000	9.00	3.00	1	1	0	0	...	0-...	3.0	6	6	3	0	3-0	0	.375
1996—New Haven (East.)		5	1	.833	0.81	0.87	7	7	1	1	...	0-...	44.2	27	7	4	0	12-0	54	.180
—Colo. Springs (PCL)		4	2	.667	2.72	1.26	9	9	0	0	...	0-...	59.2	53	20	18	3	22-0	40	.240
—Colorado (N.L.)		4	4	.500	4.93	1.80	16	15	0	0	1	0-0	91.1	105	60	50	8	41-1	45	.298
1997—Colorado (N.L.)		8	12	.400	6.25	1.80	26	26	1	0	0	0-0	149.2	198	113	104	19	71-3	59	.327
—Salem (Carol.)		0	1	.000	9.00	2.00	1	1	0	0	...	0-...	1.0	1	1	1	0	1-0	1	.250
—Colo. Springs (PCL)		1	0	1.000	1.64	1.27	2	2	0	0	...	0-...	11.0	9	3	2	1	5-0	11	.231
1998—Colorado (N.L.)		9	14	.391	5.67	1.60	34	34	1	0	0	0-0	206.1	235	143	130	24	95-3	86	.291
1999—Colorado (N.L.)		4	3	.571	4.87	1.74	16	16	0	0	0	0-0	94.1	110	52	51	10	54-3	49	.308
—Colo. Springs (PCL)		5	7	.417	6.46	1.70	17	16	2	0	...	0-...	100.1	133	87	72	13	38-2	75	.324
2000—Huntsville (Sou.)		2	0	1.000	0.00	0.97	2	2	0	0	...	0-...	12.1	7	0	0	0	5-0	10	.175
—Indianapolis (Int'l)		0	0	...	1.80	2.20	1	1	0	0	...	0-...	5.0	8	5	1	0	3-0	7	.364
—Milwaukee (N.L.)		7	9	.438	4.10	1.49	26	25	0	0	0	0-0	164.2	157	81	75	12	88-5	96	.261
2001—Milwaukee (N.L.)		11	12	.478	4.90	1.54	33	33	1	1	0	0-0	194.2	201	115	106	26	98-10	129	.272
2002—Indianapolis (Int'l)		1	1	.500	4.11	1.37	3	3	0	0	...	0-...	15.1	16	7	7	3	5-0	13	.271
—Milwaukee (N.L.)		5	13	.278	5.35	1.56	19	19	1	1	0	0-0	114.1	115	72	68	15	63-8	69	.270
—St. Louis (N.L.)		2	0	1.000	4.80	1.80	4	2	0	0	0	0-0	15.0	15	8	8	2	12-1	5	.263
2003—Indianapolis (Int'l)		1	3	.250	7.36	1.90	7	4	0	0	...	0-...	22.0	32	21	18	5	10-0	17	.344
—Oklahoma (PCL)		2	1	.667	4.12	1.50	7	7	2	1	...	0-...	39.1	38	18	18	1	11-0	40	.260
—Omaha (PCL)		3	5	.375	3.64	1.40	13	12	1	0	...	0-...	76.2	70	35	31	10	38-0	65	.246
—Kansas City (A.L.)		1	2	.333	4.26	1.34	4	4	2	1	0	0-0	25.1	23	14	12	1	11-0	19	.245
2004—Omaha (PCL)		8	6	.571	4.21	1.39	18	18	1	1	...	0-...	104.2	111	58	49	13	35-0	70	.266
—Colorado (N.L.)		2	3	.400	4.12	1.61	14	14	0	0	0	0-0	78.2	82	39	36	8	45-3	41	.266
2005—Colorado (N.L.)		8	16	.333	5.46	1.65	34	27	0	0	0	0-0	171.1	201	119	104	22	81-4	101	.296
American League totals (1 year)		1	2	.333	4.26	1.34	4	4	2	1	0	0-0	25.1	23	14	12	1	11-0	19	.245
National League totals (9 years)		60	86	.411	5.15	1.61	222	212	4	2	1	0-0	1280.1	1419	802	732	146	648-41	683	.288
Major League totals (10 years)		61	88	.409	5.13	1.61	226	216	6	3	2	0-0	1305.2	1442	816	744	147	659-41	702	.287

W

WRIGHT, JARET — P

PERSONAL: Born December 29, 1975, in Anaheim. ... 6-2/230. ... Throws right, bats right. ... Full name: Jaret Samuel Wright. ... High school: Katella (Anaheim). ... Son of Clyde Wright, pitcher with three major league teams (1966-75).

TRANSACTIONS/CAREER NOTES: Selected by Cleveland Indians organization in first round (10th pick overall) of 1994 free-agent draft. ... On suspended list (May 10-16, 1999). ... On disabled list (July 19-August 3 and August 9-September 10, 1999); included rehabilitation assignments to Buffalo and Akron. ... On disabled list (May 12-27 and June 3, 2000-remainder of season); included rehabilitation assignments to Buffalo and Akron. ... On disabled list (March 31-May 19 and September 1, 2001-remainder of season); included rehabilitation assignments to Buffalo and Akron. ... On disabled list (March 30-July 20, 2002); included rehabilitation assignment to Buffalo. ... Signed as a free agent by San Diego Padres (December 10, 2002). ... Claimed on waivers by Atlanta Braves (August 29, 2003). ... Signed as a free agent by New York Yankees (January 12, 2005). ... On disabled list (April 24-August 15, 2005); included rehabilitation assignments to GCL Yankees and Tampa.

CAREER HITTING: 11-for-75 (.147), 6 R, 2 2B, 0 3B, 1 HR, 5 RBI.

SCOUTING REPORT Throws: He throws a 90-93 mph fastball, a cut fastball, a curveball and a changeup. ***Tendencies:*** Wright again had problems with his shoulder during the year and missed almost half of the season. When healthy, has good riding action with his four-seamer and movement down in the zone. Will cut his fastball in on lefthanders. Curveball has a tight spin; throws it early in counts. ***Outlook:*** He needs to prove he can pitch for an entire season. ***Grade 6***

JARET WRIGHT'S PITCHING ZONE

.333	.250	.240
.400	.433	.408
.278	.250	.182

LEFTY-RIGHTY SPLITS

vs.	Avg.	AB	H	2B	3B	HR	RBI	BB	SO	OBP	Slg.
L	.273	139	38	6	0	6	23	21	19	.364	.446
R	.358	120	43	10	1	2	19	11	15	.431	.508

Year Team (League)	W	L	Pct.	ERA	WHIP	G	GS	CG	ShO	Hld.	Sv.-Opp.	IP	H	R	ER	HR	BB-IBB	SO	Avg.
1994— Burlington (Appal.)	0	1	.000	5.40	1.65	4	4	0	0	...	0-...	13.1	13	10	8	1	9-0	16	.260
1995— Columbus (S. Atl.)	5	6	.455	3.00	1.33	24	24	0	0	...	0-...	129.0	93	55	43	9	79-0	113	.205
1996— Kinston (Carol.)	7	4	.636	2.50	1.19	19	19	0	0	...	0-...	101.0	65	32	28	1	55-0	109	.190
1997— Akron (East.)	3	3	.500	3.67	1.22	8	8	1	0	...	0-...	54.0	43	26	22	4	23-2	59	.223
— Buffalo (A.A.)	4	1	.800	1.80	1.09	7	7	1	1	...	0-...	45.0	30	16	9	4	19-0	47	.185
— Cleveland (A.L.)	8	3	.727	4.38	1.38	16	16	0	0	0	0-0	90.1	81	45	44	9	35-0	63	.238
1998— Cleveland (A.L.)	12	10	.545	4.72	1.53	32	32	1	1	0	0-0	192.2	207	109	101	22	87-4	140	.277
1999— Cleveland (A.L.)	8	10	.444	6.06	1.65	26	26	0	0	0	0-0	133.2	144	99	90	18	77-1	91	.277
— Buffalo (Int'l)	0	0	...	0.00	0.00	1	1	0	0	...	0-...	3.0	0	0	0	0	0-0	4	.000
— Akron (East.)	1	0	1.000	0.00	0.80	1	1	0	0	...	0-...	5.0	3	0	0	0	1-0	6	.167
2000— Cleveland (A.L.)	3	4	.429	4.70	1.39	9	9	1	1	0	0-0	51.2	44	27	27	6	28-0	36	.235
— Buffalo (Int'l)	0	0	...	0.00	0.50	1	1	0	0	...	0-...	2.0	0	0	0	0	1-0	1	.000
— Akron (East.)	0	0	...	3.38	0.88	2	2	0	0	...	0-...	8.0	4	3	3	0	1-0	5	.133
2001— Buffalo (Int'l)	3	1	.750	4.71	1.33	7	7	0	0	...	0-...	28.2	25	18	15	3	13-0	28	.234
— Akron (East.)	0	0	...	1.29	0.29	1	1	0	0	...	0-...	7.0	2	1	1	1	0-0	4	.087
— Cleveland (A.L.)	2	2	.500	6.52	2.00	7	7	0	0	0	0-0	29.0	36	22	21	2	22-0	18	.313
2002— Cleveland (A.L.)	2	3	.400	15.71	3.22	8	6	0	0	0	0-0	18.1	40	34	32	3	19-0	12	.435
— Buffalo (Int'l)	5	3	.625	3.88	1.46	10	10	1	0	...	0-...	55.2	57	27	24	5	24-0	43	.268
2003— Portland (PCL)	2	1	.667	1.42	1.20	12	1	0	0	...	0-...	19.0	16	7	3	0	7-0	21	.222
— San Diego (N.L.)	1	5	.167	8.37	2.05	39	0	0	0	2	2-4	47.1	69	44	44	9	28-2	41	.348
— Atlanta (N.L.)	1	0	1.000	2.00	1.11	11	0	0	0	3	0-1	9.0	7	2	2	0	3-0	9	.226
2004— Atlanta (N.L.)	15	8	.652	3.28	1.28	32	32	0	0	0	0-0	186.1	168	79	68	11	70-5	159	.242
2005— GC Yankees (GCL)	0	1	.000	7.71	2.57	1	1	0	0	0	0-0	2.1	4	2	2	0	2-0	3	.364
— Tampa (Fla. St.)	1	0	1.000	1.50	1.00	2	2	0	0	0	0-0	12.0	9	2	2	0	3-0	12	.220
— New York (A.L.)	5	5	.500	6.08	1.77	13	13	0	0	0	0-0	63.2	81	51	43	8	32-1	34	.313
American League totals (7 years)	40	37	.519	5.56	1.61	111	109	2	2	0	0-0	579.1	633	387	358	68	300-6	394	.280
National League totals (2 years)	17	13	.567	4.23	1.42	82	32	0	0	4	2-5	242.2	244	125	114	20	101-7	209	.264
Major League totals (9 years)	57	50	.533	5.17	1.55	193	141	2	2	4	2-5	822.0	877	512	472	88	401-13	603	.276

DIVISION SERIES RECORD

Year Team (League)	W	L	Pct.	ERA	WHIP	G	GS	CG	ShO	Hld.	Sv.-Opp.	IP	H	R	ER	HR	BB-IBB	SO	Avg.
1997— Cleveland (A.L.)	2	0	1.000	3.97	1.59	2	2	0	0	0	0-0	11.1	11	6	5	0	7-1	10	.256
1998— Cleveland (A.L.)	0	1	.000	12.46	2.08	1	1	0	0	0	0-0	4.1	7	6	6	2	2-0	6	.350
1999— Cleveland (A.L.)	0	1	.000	22.50	2.50	1	0	0	0	0	0-0	2.0	4	5	5	1	1-0	1	.444
2003— Atlanta (N.L.)	0	0	...	0.00	0.50	4	0	0	0	1	0-0	4.0	0	0	0	0	2-0	4	.000
2004— Atlanta (N.L.)	0	2	.000	9.31	1.55	2	2	0	0	0	0-0	9.2	14	10	10	5	1-0	7	.350
Division series totals (5 years)	2	4	.333	7.47	1.56	10	5	0	0	1	0-0	31.1	36	27	26	8	13-1	28	.290

CHAMPIONSHIP SERIES RECORD

Year Team (League)	W	L	Pct.	ERA	WHIP	G	GS	CG	ShO	Hld.	Sv.-Opp.	IP	H	R	ER	HR	BB-IBB	SO	Avg.
1997— Cleveland (A.L.)	0	0	...	15.00	2.67	1	1	0	0	0	0-0	3.0	6	5	5	3	2-0	3	.400
1998— Cleveland (A.L.)	0	1	.000	8.10	2.25	2	1	0	0	0	0-0	6.2	7	6	6	1	8-0	4	.304
Champ. series totals (2 years)	0	1	.000	10.24	2.38	3	2	0	0	0	0-0	9.2	13	11	11	4	10-0	7	.342

WORLD SERIES RECORD

Year Team (League)	W	L	Pct.	ERA	WHIP	G	GS	CG	ShO	Hld.	Sv.-Opp.	IP	H	R	ER	HR	BB-IBB	SO	Avg.
1997— Cleveland (A.L.)	1	0	1.000	2.92	1.38	2	2	0	0	0	0-0	12.1	7	4	4	2	10-0	12	.167

WUERTZ, MICHAEL — P

PERSONAL: Born December 15, 1978, in Austin, Minn. ... 6-3/205. ... Throws right, bats right. ... Full name: Michael James Wuertz. ... Name pronounced: werts. ... High school: Austin (Minn.).

TRANSACTIONS/CAREER NOTES: Selected by Chicago Cubs organization in 11th round of 1997 free-agent draft.

CAREER HITTING: 0-for-3 (.000), 0 R, 0 2B, 0 3B, 0 HR, 0 RBI.

W

Throws: Wuertz uses a low-90s fastball, a tight slider and a changeup. **Tendencies:** He has one of the best sliders in the game, but Wuertz relies on it too much, especially with runners on. Occasionally throws too much over the top, leading to a smaller break on his slider. Has a straight fastball and leaves it up and out over the plate. Needs to establish better command of his fastball and use it more. Has problems keeping the ball down and has not developed a consistent changeup. **Outlook:** Wuertz needs to trust his stuff and develop better command to move into a setup role. **Grade 6.5**

MICHAEL WUERTZ'S PITCHING ZONE

.222	.167	.000
.279	.500	.355
.321	.211	.267

LEFTY-RIGHTY SPLITS

vs.	Avg.	AB	H	2B	3B	HR	RBI	BB	SO	OBP	Slg.
L	.260	96	25	4	1	2	13	18	26	.377	.385
R	.197	178	35	4	0	4	23	22	63	.282	.287

Year Team (League)	W	L	Pct.	ERA	WHIP	G	GS	CG	ShO	Hld.	Sv.-Opp.	IP	H	R	ER	HR	BB-IBB	SO	Avg.
1998—Williamsport (NYP)	7	5	.583	3.44	1.14	14	14	1	0	...	0-...	86.1	79	36	33	4	19-0	59	.236
1999—Lansing (Midw.)	11	12	.478	4.80	1.46	28	28	1	0	...	0-...	161.1	191	104	86	11	44-0	127	.290
2000—Daytona (Fla. St.)	12	7	.632	3.78	1.34	28	28	3	2	...	0-...	171.1	160	79	72	15	64-1	142	.253
2001—West Tenn (Sou.)	4	9	.308	3.99	1.36	27	27	1	1	...	0-...	160.0	160	80	71	20	58-2	135	.260
2002—Iowa (PCL)	9	5	.643	5.55	1.65	28	27	0	0	...	0-...	154.0	185	109	95	24	69-3	131	.295
2003—Iowa (PCL)	3	9	.250	4.57	1.41	43	16	0	0	...	1-...	124.0	140	70	63	16	35-8	92	.288
2004—Iowa (PCL)	1	1	.500	2.42	1.01	37	0	0	0	...	19-...	44.2	30	13	12	4	15-2	59	.186
—Chicago (N.L.)	1	0	1.000	4.34	1.34	31	0	0	0	1	1-1	29.0	22	14	14	4	17-1	30	.218
2005—Chicago (N.L.)	6	2	.750	3.81	1.32	75	0	0	0	18	0-3	75.2	60	36	32	6	40-7	89	.219
Major League totals (2 years)	7	2	.778	3.96	1.33	106	0	0	0	19	1-4	104.2	82	50	46	10	57-8	119	.219

WUNSCH, KELLY — P

PERSONAL: Born July 12, 1972, in Houston. ... 6-5/225. ... Throws left, bats left. ... Full name: Kelly Douglas Wunsch. ... Name pronounced: wunch. ... High school: Bellaire (Texas). ... College: Texas A&M.
TRANSACTIONS/CAREER NOTES: Selected by Atlanta Braves organization in 54th round of 1990 free-agent draft; did not sign. ... Selected by Milwaukee Brewers organization in first round (26th pick overall) of 1993 free-agent draft; pick received as compensation for Toronto Blue Jays signing Type-A free-agent DH Paul Molitor. ... Signed as a free agent by Chicago White Sox organization (November 15, 1999). ... On disabled list (June 18, 2001-remainder of season). ... On disabled list (March 27-May 18, 2002); included rehabilitation assignment to Charlotte. ... On disabled list (June 12-July 25, 2003); included rehabilitation assignment to Charlotte. ... On disabled list (March 31-May 9, 2004); included rehabilitation assignment to Charlotte. ... Signed as a free agent by Los Angeles Dodgers organization (December 14, 2004). ... On disabled list (July 8, 2005-remainder of season).
CAREER HITTING: 0-for-1 (.000), 0 R, 0 2B, 0 3B, 0 HR, 0 RBI.

KELLY WUNSCH'S PITCHING ZONE

.200	1.000	.000
.286	.333	.250
.000	.200	.250

LEFTY-RIGHTY SPLITS

vs.	Avg.	AB	H	2B	3B	HR	RBI	BB	SO	OBP	Slg.
L	.194	62	12	2	0	1	6	10	18	.315	.274
R	.308	26	8	2	0	1	2	4	4	.419	.500

Year Team (League)	W	L	Pct.	ERA	WHIP	G	GS	CG	ShO	Hld.	Sv.-Opp.	IP	H	R	ER	HR	BB-IBB	SO	Avg.
1993—Beloit (Midw.)	1	5	.167	4.83	1.53	12	12	0	0	...	0-...	63.1	58	39	34	5	39-1	61	.245
1994—Beloit (Midw.)	3	10	.231	6.16	1.62	17	17	0	0	...	0-...	83.1	88	69	57	11	47-1	77	.264
—Helena (Pion.)	4	2	.667	5.12	1.61	9	9	1	0	...	0-...	51.0	52	39	29	7	30-0	57	.267
1995—Beloit (Midw.)	4	7	.364	4.20	1.48	14	14	3	1	...	0-...	85.2	90	47	40	7	37-0	66	.280
—Stockton (Calif.)	5	6	.455	5.33	1.72	14	13	1	1	...	0-...	74.1	89	51	44	4	39-0	62	.303
1996—			Did not play.																
1997—Stockton (Calif.)	7	9	.438	3.46	1.42	24	22	2	2	...	0-...	143.0	141	65	55	11	62-0	98	.263
1998—El Paso (Texas)	5	6	.455	5.95	1.56	17	17	1	0	...	0-...	101.1	127	81	67	11	31-0	70	.301
—Louisville (Int'l)	3	1	.750	3.83	1.32	9	8	0	0	...	0-...	51.2	53	23	22	6	15-0	36	.264
1999—Huntsville (Sou.)	4	1	.800	1.95	1.24	22	3	0	0	...	1-...	50.2	40	13	11	1	23-1	35	.229
—Louisville (Int'l)	2	1	.667	4.75	1.58	16	2	0	0	...	0-...	41.2	52	23	22	4	14-0	20	.311
2000—Chicago (A.L.)	6	3	.667	2.93	1.29	83	0	0	0	25	1-5	61.1	50	22	20	4	29-1	51	.221
2001—Chicago (A.L.)	2	1	.667	7.66	1.34	33	0	0	0	3	0-2	22.1	21	19	19	4	9-1	16	.247
2002—Charlotte (Int'l)	1	0	1.000	2.25	1.50	10	2	0	0	...	0-...	12.0	13	3	3	0	6-0	9	.295
—Chicago (A.L.)	2	1	.667	3.41	1.42	50	0	0	0	9	0-1	31.2	26	12	12	3	19-1	22	.230
2003—Charlotte (Int'l)	0	1	.000	5.40	1.80	3	0	0	0	...	0-...	3.1	6	3	2	1	0-0	4	.429
—Chicago (A.L.)	0	0	...	2.75	1.17	43	0	0	0	5	0-0	36.0	17	13	11	4	25-4	33	.139
2004—Chicago (A.L.)	0	0	...	0.00	1.50	3	0	0	0	0	0-0	2.0	2	0	0	0	1-0	1	.286
—Charlotte (Int'l)	1	0	1.000	2.93	1.19	27	0	0	0	0	2-...	27.2	21	9	9	1	12-0	22	.216
2005—Los Angeles (N.L.)	1	1	.500	4.56	1.44	45	0	0	0	15	0-1	23.2	20	12	12	2	14-2	22	.227
American League totals (5 years)	10	5	.667	3.64	1.30	212	0	0	0	42	1-8	153.1	116	66	62	12	83-7	123	.210
National League totals (1 year)	1	1	.500	4.56	1.44	45	0	0	0	15	0-1	23.2	20	12	12	2	14-2	22	.227
Major League totals (6 years)	11	6	.647	3.76	1.32	257	0	0	0	57	1-9	177.0	136	78	74	14	97-9	145	.212

DIVISION SERIES RECORD

Year Team (League)	W	L	Pct.	ERA	WHIP	G	GS	CG	ShO	Hld.	Sv.-Opp.	IP	H	R	ER	HR	BB-IBB	SO	Avg.
2000—Chicago (A.L.)	0	1	.000	0.00	3.00	3	0	0	0	...	0-...	0.1	2	1	0	0	0-0	0	.500

YABU, KEIICHI — P

PERSONAL: Born September 28, 1968, in Mie, Japan. ... 6-1/201. ... Throws right, bats right. ... Name pronounced: KAY-ee-chee YAH-boo
TRANSACTIONS/CAREER NOTES: Played for Hanshin of the Japan Central League (1994-2004). ... Signed as a free agent by Oakland Athletics (January 12, 2005). ... Released by Athletics (October 24, 2005).
CAREER HITTING: 0-for-1 (.000), 0 R, 0 2B, 0 3B, 0 HR, 0 RBI.

KEIICHI YABU'S PITCHING ZONE

.200	.500	.286
.179	.458	.286
.316	.273	.563

LEFTY-RIGHTY SPLITS

vs.	Avg.	AB	H	2B	3B	HR	RBI	BB	SO	OBP	Slg.
L	.291	103	30	6	0	2	16	15	14	.377	.408
R	.283	120	34	6	2	4	20	11	30	.377	.467

Y

Year Team (League)	W	L	Pct.	ERA	WHIP	G	GS	CG	ShO	Hld.	Sv.-Opp.	IP	H	R	ER	HR	BB-IBB	SO	Avg.
2005—Oakland (A.L.)	4	0	1.000	4.50	1.55	40	0	0	0	1	1-2	58.0	64	34	29	6	26-3	44	.287
Major League totals (1 year)	4	0	1.000	4.50	1.55	40	0	0	0	1	1-2	58.0	64	34	29	6	26-3	44	.287

YAN, ESTEBAN   P

PERSONAL: Born June 22, 1975, in Campina del Seibo, Dominican Republic. ... 6-4/255. ... Throws right, bats right. ... Full name: Esteban Luis Yan. ... Name pronounced: YAHN. ... High school: Escuela Hicayagua (Dominican Republic).

TRANSACTIONS/CAREER NOTES: Signed as a non-drafted free agent by Atlanta Braves organization (November 21, 1990). ... Traded by Braves with OFs Roberto Kelly and Tony Tarasco to Montreal Expos for OF Marquis Grissom (April 6, 1995). ... Traded by Expos to Baltimore Orioles for cash (April 6, 1996). ... Selected by Tampa Bay Devil Rays in first round (18th pick overall) of expansion draft (November 18, 1997). ... On disabled list (June 17-July 15, 1999); included rehabilitation assignment to St. Petersburg. ... On disabled list (June 22-July 12, 2001); included rehabilitation assignment to Orlando. ... Signed as a free agent by Texas Rangers (December 26, 2002). ... Traded by Rangers to St. Louis Cardinals for OF Rick Asadoorian (May 27, 2003). ... Released by Cardinals (August 23, 2003). ... Signed by Detroit Tigers organization (January 20, 2004). ... Signed as a free agent by Anaheim Angels (December 13, 2004). ... Angels franchise renamed Los Angeles Angels of Anaheim for 2005 season.
CAREER HITTING: 2-for-2 (1.000), 1 R, 0 2B, 0 3B, 1 HR, 1 RBI.

SCOUTING REPORT **Throws:** He has a 90-94 mph fastball, a slider and a split-finger pitch that registers in the low 80s. **Tendencies:** When Yan keeps his body under control and repeats his arm slot consistently, he is much more consistent with his command. Fastball will bore in on righthanders and occasionally sink. Has good action and break on his slider, which he is better able to throw for strikes. Pitch tends to flatten out, though. **Outlook:** Yan is a journeyman middle reliever who falls apart when pitching with the game on the line. *Grade 6.4*

ESTEBAN YAN'S PITCHING ZONE

.125	.000	.250
.370	.258	.279
.200	.429	.111

LEFTY-RIGHTY SPLITS

vs.	Avg.	AB	H	2B	3B	HR	RBI	BB	SO	OBP	Slg.
L	.252	127	32	10	0	4	16	18	19	.340	.425
R	.264	129	34	9	0	4	18	12	26	.322	.426

Year	Team (League)	W	L	Pct.	ERA	WHIP	G	GS	CG	ShO	Hld.	Sv.-Opp.	IP	H	R	ER	HR	BB-IBB	SO	Avg.
1991—Dom. Braves (DSL)		4	1	.800	3.63	1.21	18	11	0	0		0-...	72.0	61	36	29		26-...	34	...
1992—Dom. Braves (DSL)		12	3	.800	1.32	0.93	16	16	7	4		0-...	115.2	85	37	17	1	23-...	86	...
1993—Danville (Appal.)		4	7	.364	3.03	1.36	14	14	0	0		0-...	71.1	73	46	24	4	24-1	50	.253
1994—Macon (S. Atl.)		11	12	.478	3.27	1.11	28	28	4	3		0-...	170.2	155	85	62	15	34-1	121	.242
1995—W.P. Beach (Fla. St.)		6	8	.429	3.07	1.25	24	21	1	0		1-...	137.2	139	63	47	3	33-0	89	.265
1996—Bowie (East.)		0	2	.000	5.63	1.63	9	1	0	0		0-...	16.0	18	12	10	2	8-0	15	.277
—Baltimore (A.L.)		0	0		5.79	1.71	4	0	0	0	0	0-0	9.1	13	7	6	3	3-1	7	.333
—Rochester (Int'l)		5	4	.556	4.27	1.30	22	10	0	0		1-...	71.2	75	37	34	6	18-0	61	.269
1997—Rochester (Int'l)		11	5	.688	3.10	1.21	34	12	0	0		2-...	119.0	107	54	41	13	37-0	131	.243
—Baltimore (A.L.)		0	1	.000	15.83	2.79	3	2	0	0	0	0-0	9.2	20	18	17	3	7-0	4	.417
1998—Tampa Bay (A.L.)		5	4	.556	3.86	1.34	64	0	0	0	8	1-5	88.2	78	41	38	11	41-2	77	.236
1999—Tampa Bay (A.L.)		3	4	.429	5.90	1.79	50	1	0	0	7	0-3	61.0	77	41	40	8	32-4	46	.326
—St. Pete. (Fla. St.)		0	0		0.00	1.00	2	2	0	0		0-...	4.0	3	1	0	0	1-0	1	.214
2000—Tampa Bay (A.L.)		7	8	.467	6.21	1.45	43	20	0	0	3	0-2	137.2	158	98	95	26	42-0	111	.285
2001—Tampa Bay (A.L.)		4	6	.400	3.90	1.20	54	0	0	0		22-31	62.1	64	34	27	7	11-1	64	.262
—Orlando (Sou.)		0	0		3.00	1.00	2	2	0	0		0-...	3.0	3	1	1	0	4-0	2	.250
2002—Tampa Bay (A.L.)		7	8	.467	4.30	1.43	55	0	0	0		19-27	69.0	70	35	33	10	29-1	53	.259
2003—Texas (A.L.)		0	1	.000	6.94	1.63	15	0	0	0	1	0-0	23.1	31	19	18	5	7-1	25	.307
—St. Louis (N.L.)		2	0	1.000	6.02	1.59	39	0	0	0	3	1-1	43.1	53	29	29	8	16-4	28	.308
2004—Detroit (A.L.)		3	6	.333	3.83	1.43	69	0	0	0	11	7-17	87.0	92	43	37	8	32-5	69	.274
2005—Los Angeles (A.L.)		1	1	.500	4.59	1.44	49	0	0	0	1	0-0	66.2	66	36	34	8	30-4	45	.258
American League totals (10 years)		30	39	.435	5.05	1.47	406	23	0	0	31	49-85	614.2	669	372	345	89	234-19	501	.277
National League totals (1 year)		2	0	1.000	6.02	1.59	39	0	0	0	3	1-1	43.1	53	29	29	8	16-4	28	.308
Major League totals (10 years)		32	39	.451	5.12	1.48	445	23	0	0	34	50-86	658.0	722	401	374	97	250-23	529	.279

CHAMPIONSHIP SERIES RECORD

Year	Team (League)	W	L	Pct.	ERA	WHIP	G	GS	CG	ShO	Hld.	Sv.-Opp.	IP	H	R	ER	HR	BB-IBB	SO	Avg.
2005—Los Angeles (A.L.)		0	0	...	9.00	2.00	1	0	0	0	0	0-0	2.0	3	2	2	0	1-0	2	.375

YOUKILIS, KEVIN   3B/1B

PERSONAL: Born March 15, 1979, in Cincinnati. ... 6-1/220. ... Bats right, throws right. ... Full name: Kevin Edmund Youkilis. ... Name pronounced: YOU-ka-lis. ... High school: Sycamore (Cincinnati). ... College: Cincinnati.

TRANSACTIONS/CAREER NOTES: Selected by Boston Red Sox organization in eighth round of 2001 free-agent draft. ... On disabled list (August 16-September 1, 2004); included rehabilitation assignment to Lowell.
2005 GAMES PLAYED BY POSITION (MLB): 3B—24, 1B—9, 2B—2.

SCOUTING REPORT **Offense:** Youkilis is a gap hitter with good bad control. Knows the strike zone. Is not afraid to work the count and hits to all fields. Has a short, compact swing and good balance. Can be jammed with better fastballs. **Defense:** His reactions and hands are only average. Has an unconventional throwing motion and is erratic because of his footwork. Is not agile and has bad balance. Is much better going to his left. **Outlook:** Youkilis will get on base, but he needs to produce more runs to be an everyday player. Could be the starter if Bill Mueller leaves. *Grade 6.0*

KEVIN YOUKILIS' HITTING ZONE

.143	.000	.500
.400	.400	.375
.300	.250	.000

LEFTY-RIGHTY SPLITS

vs.	Avg.	AB	H	2B	3B	HR	RBI	BB	SO	OBP	Slg.
L	.300	30	9	2	0	1	3	7	6	.432	.467
R	.265	49	13	5	0	0	6	7	13	.379	.367

Year	Team (League)	Pos.	G	AB	R	H	2B	3B	HR	RBI	BB	SO	HBP	GDP	SB-CS	Avg.	OBP	SLG	OPS	E	Avg.
2001— Lowell (N.Y.-Penn.)		3B	59	183	52	58	14	2	3	28	70	28	5	0	4-3	.317	.512	.464	.976	12	.936
—Augusta (S. Atl.)		3B	5	12	0	2	0	0	0	0	3	3	1	0	0-0	.167	.375	.167	.542	0	1.000
2002— Augusta (S. Atl.)		3B	15	53	5	15	5	0	0	6	13	8	1	0	0-0	.283	.433	.377	.810	4	.913
—Sarasota (Fla. St.)		1B-3B	76	268	45	79	16	0	3	48	49	37	15	5	0-2	.295	.422	.388	.810	12	.974

Y

Year	Team (League)	Pos.	G	AB	R	H	2B	3B	HR	RBI	BB	SO	HBP	GDP	SB-CS	Avg.	OBP	SLG	OPS	E	Avg.
— Trenton (East.)	3B	44	160	34	55	10	0	5	26	31	18	5	1	5-4	.344	.462	.500	.962	11	.916
2003— Portland (East.)	3B	94	312	74	102	23	1	6	37	86	40	15	7	7-0	.327	.487	.465	.952	20	.925
— Pawtucket (Int'l)	3B	32	109	9	18	3	0	2	15	18	21	3	2	0-1	.165	.295	.248	.543	4	.952
2004— Pawtucket (Int'l)	3B-1B-DH	38	154	25	41	12	0	3	18	19	28	2	1	2-0	.266	.350	.403	.745	5	.955
— Lowell (NY-Penn)	3B	2	4	1	3	1	1	0	0	2	0	1	0	0-0	.750	.857	1.500	2.333	0	1.000
— Boston (A.L.)	3B-DH	72	208	38	54	11	0	7	35	33	45	4	1	0-1	.260	.367	.413	.780	5	.968
2005— Pawtucket (Int'l)	3B-1B-2B-DH	43	152	30	49	15	1	8	27	35	29	5	0	1-2	.322	.459	.592	1.051	5	.975
— Boston (A.L.)	3B-1B-2B	44	79	11	22	7	0	1	9	14	19	2	0	0-1	.278	.400	.405	.805	0	1.000
Major League totals (2 years)		116	287	49	76	18	0	8	44	47	64	6	1	0-2	.265	.376	.411	.787	5	.980

DIVISION SERIES RECORD

Year	Team (League)	Pos.	G	AB	R	H	2B	3B	HR	RBI	BB	SO	HBP	GDP	SB-CS	Avg.	OBP	SLG	OPS	E	Avg.
2004— Boston (A.L.)	3B	1	2	0	0	0	0	0	0	0	1	0	0	0-0	.000	.000	.000	.000	0	...

YOUNG, CHRIS — P

PERSONAL: Born May 25, 1979, in Dallas. ... 6-10/250. ... Throws right, bats right. ... Full name: Christopher Ryan Young. ... High school: Highland Park (Dallas). ... College: Princeton.

TRANSACTIONS/CAREER NOTES: Selected by Pittsburgh Pirates organization in third round of 2000 free-agent draft. ... Traded by Pirates with P Jon Searles to Montreal Expos for P Matt Herges (December 20, 2002). ... Traded by Expos with OF Josh McKinley to Texas Rangers for C Einar Diaz and P Justin Echols (April 3, 2004).

CAREER HITTING: 0-for-5 (.000), 0 R, 0 2B, 0 3B, 0 HR, 0 RBI.

SCOUTING REPORT

Throws: Young has a fastball at 88-93 mph, a curveball and a changeup. **Tendencies:** One of the game's tallest pitchers, he has good coordination and angle to the plate. Fastball is sneaky as he hides the ball well. Velocity improved as last season progressed. Has an outstanding curve that he varies the break and speed on to lefthanded and righthanded batters. Has a good change. Has a good idea of how to pitch and a surprisingly good delivery. **Outlook:** A pleasant surprise in the Rangers' rotation, Young will go to spring training as the top returning starter. Has a good ceiling. Should get better as command of his fastball improves. **Grade 7.5**

CHRIS YOUNG'S PITCHING ZONE

.197	.306	.321
.261	.321	.327
.239	.222	.205

LEFTY-RIGHTY SPLITS

vs.	Avg.	AB	H	2B	3B	HR	RBI	BB	SO	OBP	Slg.
L	.281	338	95	22	2	8	36	26	77	.335	.429
R	.220	304	67	14	1	11	39	19	60	.275	.382

Year	Team (League)	W	L	Pct.	ERA	WHIP	G	GS	CG	ShO	Hld.	Sv.-Opp.	IP	H	R	ER	HR	BB-IBB	SO	Avg.
2001— Hickory (S. Atl.)	5	3	.625	4.12	1.33	12	12	2	0	...	0-...	74.1	79	39	34	6	20-0	72	.269
2002— Hickory (S. Atl.)	11	9	.550	3.11	1.11	26	26	1	0	...	0-...	144.2	127	57	50	11	34-1	136	.234
2003— Brevard County (Fla. St.)	5	2	.714	1.62	0.62	8	8	0	0	...	0-...	50.0	26	9	9	3	5-0	39	.150
— Harrisburg (East.)	4	4	.500	4.01	1.27	15	15	0	0	...	0-...	83.0	83	39	37	9	22-0	64	.259
2004— Frisco (Texas)	6	5	.545	4.48	1.42	18	18	0	0	...	0-...	88.1	94	48	44	9	31-1	75	.269
— Oklahoma (PCL)	3	0	1.000	1.48	0.96	5	5	1	0	...	0-...	30.1	20	7	5	2	9-0	34	.189
— Texas (A.L.)	3	2	.600	4.71	1.27	7	7	0	0	0	0-...	36.1	36	21	19	7	10-0	27	.250
2005— Texas (A.L.)	12	7	.632	4.26	1.26	31	31	0	0	0	0-0	164.2	162	84	78	19	45-2	137	.252
Major League totals (2 years)	15	9	.625	4.34	1.26	38	38	0	0	0	0-0	201.0	198	105	97	26	55-2	164	.252

YOUNG, DMITRI — 1B/OF

PERSONAL: Born October 11, 1973, in Vicksburg, Miss. ... 6-2/245. ... Bats both, throws right. ... Full name: Dmitri Dell Young. ... High school: Rio Mesa (Oxnard, Calif.).

TRANSACTIONS/CAREER NOTES: Selected by St. Louis Cardinals organization in first round (fourth pick overall) of 1991 free-agent draft. ... On disabled list (May 11-29, 1997); included rehabilitation assignment to Louisville. ... Traded by Cardinals to Cincinnati Reds for P Jeff Brantley (November 10, 1997). ... Selected by Tampa Bay Devil Rays in first round (16th pick overall) of expansion draft (November 18, 1997). ... Traded by Devil Rays to Reds (November 18, 1997), completing deal in which Reds traded OF Mike Kelly to Devil Rays for a player to be named (November 11, 1997). ... Traded by Reds to Detroit Tigers for OF Juan Encarnacion and P Luis Pineda (December 11, 2001). ... On disabled list (April 23-May 14 and July 6, 2002-remainder of season). ... On disabled list (April 7-May 31, 2004); included rehabilitation assignment to Toledo.

2005 GAMES PLAYED BY POSITION (MLB): DH—71, 1B—30, OF—20.

SCOUTING REPORT

Offense: He has a good stroke with good bat speed from both sides. Is a good high-ball hitter who also can handle the breaking ball. Is a better lefthanded hitter and has more power from that side. Has become more of streak hitter. Continues to have problems with his hamstrings. Is not very selective and is striking out more as he expands his zone upward. Doesn't run well. **Defense:** He basically was as a designated most of last season. Doesn't run well or cover much ground in the outfield or at first base. **Outlook:** Young is best suited to be a DH and, though his run production has dropped off due to injuries, he has value as an A.L. player. **Grade 6.1**

DMITRI YOUNG'S HITTING ZONE

.118	.522	.238
.293	.407	.309
.290	.345	.286

LEFTY-RIGHTY SPLITS

vs.	Avg.	AB	H	2B	3B	HR	RBI	BB	SO	OBP	Slg.
L	.277	119	33	8	1	4	18	2	24	.295	.462
R	.269	350	94	17	2	17	54	27	76	.334	.474

Year	Team (League)	Pos.	G	AB	R	H	2B	3B	HR	RBI	BB	SO	HBP	GDP	SB-CS	Avg.	OBP	SLG	OPS	E	Avg.
1991— Johnson City (Appal.)	3B	37	129	22	33	10	0	2	22	21	28	2	1	2-1	.256	.364	.380	.743	5	.932
1992— Springfield (Midw.)	3B	135	493	74	153	36	6	14	72	51	94	5	9	14-13	.310	.378	.493	.871	42	.879
1993— St. Petersburg (Fla. St.)	1B-3B	69	270	31	85	13	3	5	43	24	28	2	7	3-4	.315	.369	.441	.810	10	.972
— Arkansas (Texas)	1B-3B	45	166	13	41	11	2	3	21	9	29	2	4	4-4	.247	.294	.392	.685	7	.971
1994— Arkansas (Texas)	1B-OF	125	453	53	123	33	2	8	54	36	60	5	6	0-3	.272	.330	.406	.736	16	.971
1995— Arkansas (Texas)	OF-DH	97	367	54	107	18	6	10	62	30	46	3	11	2-4	.292	.347	.455	.802	9	.931
— Louisville (A.A.)	OF	2	7	3	2	0	0	0	0	1	1	0	0	0-0	.286	.375	.286	.661	1	.750
1996— Louisville (A.A.)	1B	122	459	90	153	31	8	15	64	34	67	1	5	16-5	.333	.378	.534	.912	8	.993
— St. Louis (N.L.)	1B	16	29	3	7	0	0	0	2	4	5	1	1	0-1	.241	.353	.241	.594	1	.976

Y

Year Team (League)	Pos.	G	AB	R	H	2B	3B	HR	RBI	BB	SO	HBP	GDP	SB-CS	Avg.	OBP	SLG	OPS	E	Avg.
1997—St. Louis (N.L.) 1B-OF-DH		110	333	38	86	14	3	5	34	38	63	2	8	6-5	.258	.335	.363	.698	13	.981
—Louisville (A.A.)	OF-1B	24	84	10	23	7	0	4	14	13	15	0	1	1-1	.274	.371	.500	.871	1	.985
1998—Cincinnati (N.L.)	OF-1B	144	536	81	166	48	1	14	83	47	94	2	16	2-4	.310	.364	.481	.846	12	.976
1999—Cincinnati (N.L.) OF-1B-DH		127	373	63	112	30	2	14	56	30	71	2	11	3-1	.300	.352	.504	.856	4	.982
2000—Cincinnati (N.L.) .OF-1B-DH		152	548	68	166	37	6	18	88	36	80	3	16	0-3	.303	.346	.491	.837	8	.981
2001—Cincinnati (N.L.) ...OF-1B-3B		142	540	68	163	28	3	21	69	37	77	5	22	8-5	.302	.350	.481	.832	16	.967
2002—Detroit (A.L.) ....DH-1B-3B OF		54	201	25	57	14	0	7	27	12	39	2	12	2-0	.284	.329	.458	.786	4	.972
2003—Detroit (A.L.) DH-OF-3B 1B		155	562	78	167	34	7	29	85	58	130	11	16	2-1	.297	.372	.537	.909	10	.947
2004—Toledo (Int'l)	DH	2	10	1	5	1	1	1	5	1	0	0	0	0-0	.500	.545	1.100	1.645	0	...
—Detroit (A.L.) DH-1B-OF 3B		104	389	72	106	23	2	18	60	33	71	6	8	0-1	.272	.336	.481	.816	0	1.000
2005—Detroit (A.L.) DH-1B-OF		126	469	61	127	25	3	21	72	29	100	9	16	1-0	.271	.325	.471	.796	3	.991
American League totals (4 years)		439	1621	236	457	96	12	75	244	132	340	28	52	5-2	.282	.345	.495	.839	17	.981
National League totals (6 years)		691	2359	321	700	157	15	72	332	192	390	15	74	19-19	.297	.351	.468	.818	54	.977
Major League totals (10 years)		1130	3980	557	1157	253	27	147	576	324	730	43	126	24-21	.291	.348	.479	.827	71	.978

DIVISION SERIES RECORD

Year Team (League)	Pos.	G	AB	R	H	2B	3B	HR	RBI	BB	SO	HBP	GDP	SB-CS	Avg.	OBP	SLG	OPS	E	Avg.
1996—St. Louis (N.L.)		Did not play.																		

CHAMPIONSHIP SERIES RECORD

Year Team (League)	Pos.	G	AB	R	H	2B	3B	HR	RBI	BB	SO	HBP	GDP	SB-CS	Avg.	OBP	SLG	OPS	E	Avg.
1996—St. Louis (N.L.)	1B	4	7	1	2	0	1	0	2	0	2	0	0	0-0	.286	.286	.571	.857	0	1.000

YOUNG, ERIC — OF/2B

PERSONAL: Born May 18, 1967, in New Brunswick, N.J. ... 5-8/186. ... Bats right, throws right. ... Full name: Eric Orlando Young. ... High school: New Brunswick (N.J.). ... College: Rutgers.

TRANSACTIONS/CAREER NOTES: Selected by Los Angeles Dodgers organization in 43rd round of 1989 free-agent draft. ... Selected by Colorado Rockies organization in first round (11th pick overall) of expansion draft (November 17, 1992). ... On disabled list (March 22-April 22, 1996); included rehabilitation assignments to New Haven, Salem and Colorado Springs. ... Traded by Rockies to Dodgers for P Pedro Astacio (August 19, 1997). ... On disabled list (July 13-31, 1998). ... On disabled list (July 24-August 13, 1999); included rehabilitation assignment to San Bernardino. ... Traded by Dodgers with P Ismael Valdes to Chicago Cubs for Ps Terry Adams and Chad Ricketts and a player to be named (December 12, 1999); Dodgers acquired P Brian Stephenson to complete deal (December 16, 1999). ... Signed as a free agent by Milwaukee Brewers (January 17, 2002). ... Traded by Brewers to San Francisco Giants for P Greg Bruso (August 19, 2003). ... Signed as a free agent by Texas Rangers (January 6, 2004). ... Signed as a free agent by San Diego Padres (December 9, 2004). ... On disabled list (April 8-July 2, 2005); included rehabilitation assignment to Portland.

2005 GAMES PLAYED BY POSITION (MLB): OF—25, 2B—14.

SCOUTING REPORT *Offense:* Young is a contact hitter with line-drive power. Likes the ball up. Is a good two-strike hitter. Can be fooled by breaking stuff down and away and doesn't have much power. Still can run but is not the basestealing threat he once was. *Defense:* He moved to center field to start the season and showed good range, but he still has trouble going back on the ball and he doesn't have a strong enough arm to play there. Has stiff hands and doesn't have good quickness as a second baseman. *Outlook:* Young's defense doesn't allow him to play every day, making him a role player at best. *Grade 5.3*

ERIC YOUNG'S HITTING ZONE

.333	.250	.200
.282	.278	.375
.167	.429	.000

LEFTY-RIGHTY SPLITS

vs.	Avg.	AB	H	2B	3B	HR	RBI	BB	SO	OBP	Slg.
L	.318	66	21	5	0	1	6	12	3	.423	.439
R	.237	76	18	4	0	1	6	6	9	.293	.329

Year Team (League)	Pos.	G	AB	R	H	2B	3B	HR	RBI	BB	SO	HBP	GDP	SB-CS	Avg.	OBP	SLG	OPS	E	Avg.
1989—GC Dodgers (GCL)	2B	56	197	53	65	11	5	2	22	33	16	3	1	41-10	.330	.432	.467	.899	15	.939
1990—Vero Beach (Fla. St.)	2B-OF	127	460	101	132	23	7	2	50	69	35	6	4	76-16	.287	.384	.380	.764	25	.937
1991—San Antonio (Texas)	2B-OF	127	461	82	129	17	4	3	35	67	36	2	13	70-26	.280	.373	.354	.726	13	.974
—Albuquerque (PCL)	2B	1	5	0	2	0	0	0	0	0	0	0	0	0-0	.400	.400	.400	.800	0	1.000
1992—Albuquerque (PCL)	2B	94	350	61	118	16	5	3	49	33	18	4	10	28-11	.337	.393	.437	.831	20	.961
—Los Angeles (N.L.)	2B	49	132	9	34	1	0	1	11	8	9	0	3	6-1	.258	.300	.288	.588	9	.957
1993—Colorado (N.L.)	2B-OF	144	490	82	132	16	8	3	42	63	41	4	9	42-19	.269	.355	.353	.708	18	.964
1994—Colorado (N.L.)	OF-2B	90	228	37	62	13	1	7	30	38	17	2	3	18-7	.272	.378	.430	.808	2	.981
1995—Colorado (N.L.)	2B-OF	120	366	68	116	21	•9	6	36	49	29	5	4	35-12	.317	.404	.473	.876	†11	.974
1996—New Haven (East.)	2B	3	15	0	1	0	0	0	0	0	3	0	0	0-0	.067	.067	.067	.133	0	1.000
—Salem (Carol.)	2B	3	10	2	3	0	0	0	0	3	1	0	0	2-0	.300	.462	.600	1.062	2	.875
—Colo. Springs (PCL)	2B	7	23	4	6	1	1	0	3	5	1	0	1	0-0	.261	.393	.391	.784	3	.917
—Colorado (N.L.)	2B	141	568	113	184	23	4	8	74	47	31	21	9	* 53-19	.324	.393	.421	.814	12	.985
1997—Colorado (N.L.)	2B	118	468	78	132	29	6	6	45	57	37	5	16	32-12	.282	.363	.408	.771	15	.978
—Los Angeles (N.L.)	2B	37	154	29	42	4	2	2	16	14	17	4	2	13-2	.273	.347	.364	.710	3	.979
1998—Los Angeles (N.L.)	2B-DH	117	452	78	129	24	1	8	43	45	32	5	4	42-13	.285	.355	.396	.751	13	.976
1999—Los Angeles (N.L.)	2B	119	456	73	128	24	2	2	41	63	26	5	12	51-22	.281	.371	.355	.726	9	.984
—San Bern. (Calif.)	2B	3	12	0	3	0	0	0	0	0	2	0	0	0-0	.250	.250	.250	.500	2	.833
2000—Chicago (N.L.)	2B	153	607	98	180	40	2	6	47	63	39	8	12	54-7	.297	.368	.399	.766	15	.979
2001—Chicago (N.L.)	2B	149	603	98	168	43	4	6	42	42	45	9	15	31-14	.279	.333	.393	.726	12	.981
2002—Milwaukee (N.L.) 2B-DH-OF		138	496	57	129	29	3	3	28	39	38	6	14	31-11	.260	.338	.369	.707	12	.979
2003—Milwaukee (N.L.)	2B-OF	109	404	71	105	18	1	15	31	48	34	4	9	25-7	.260	.344	.421	.764	15	.967
—San Francisco (N.L.)	2B-OF	26	71	9	14	2	0	0	3	9	10	1	3	3-5	.197	.293	.225	.518	1	.989
2004—Texas (A.L.) OF-DH-2B SS-3B		104	344	55	99	25	2	1	27	43	28	8	9	14-9	.288	.377	.381	.758	9	.952
2005—Portland (PCL)	DH-2B	5	16	3	0	0	0	0	0	6	2	0	0	0-0	.000	.273	.000	.273	0	1.000
—San Diego (N.L.)	OF-2B	56	142	22	39	9	0	2	12	18	12	0	4	7-6	.275	.356	.380	.737	3	.972
American League totals (1 year)		104	344	55	99	25	2	1	27	43	28	8	9	14-9	.288	.377	.381	.758	9	.952
National League totals (13 years)		1566	5637	921	1604	296	43	75	501	603	417	79	119	443-157	.285	.360	.392	.752	150	.977
Major League totals (14 years)		1670	5981	976	1703	321	45	76	528	646	445	87	128	457-166	.285	.361	.392	.752	159	.976

Y

DIVISION SERIES RECORD

Year Team (League)	Pos.	G	AB	R	H	2B	3B	HR	RBI	BB	SO	HBP	GDP	SB-CS	Avg.	OBP	SLG	OPS	E	Avg.
1995— Colorado (N.L.)	2B	4	16	3	7	1	0	1	2	2	2	0	0	1-0	.438	.500	.688	1.188	3	.875
2005— San Diego (N.L.)	OF	3	6	2	2	0	0	1	3	0	0	0	1	0-0	.333	.333	.833	1.167	0	
Division series totals (2 years)		7	22	5	9	1	0	2	5	2	2	0	1	1-0	.409	.458	.727	1.186	3	.875

ALL-STAR GAME RECORD

		G	AB	R	H	2B	3B	HR	RBI	BB	SO	HBP	GDP	SB-CS	Avg.	OBP	SLG	OPS	E	Avg.
All-Star Game totals (1 year)		1	1	0	0	0	0	0	0	0	0	0	0	0-0	.000	.000	.000	.000	0	1.000

YOUNG, MICHAEL   SS

PERSONAL: Born October 19, 1976, in Covina, Calif. ... 6-1/190. ... Bats right, throws right. ... Full name: Michael Brian Young. ... High school: Bishop Amat (La Puente, Calif.). ... College: UC-Santa Barbara.

TRANSACTIONS/CAREER NOTES: Selected by Baltimore Orioles organization in 25th round of 1994 free-agent draft; did not sign. ... Selected by Toronto Blue Jays organization in fifth round of 1997 free-agent draft. ... Traded by Blue Jays with P Darwin Cubillan to Texas Rangers for P Esteban Loaiza (July 19, 2000).

2005 GAMES PLAYED BY POSITION (MLB): SS—155, DH—4.

SCOUTING REPORT** Offense:* Last season's A.L. batting champ keeps getting better. Has very quick hands and can use the whole field. Stays behind the ball well and really trusts his hands. Is a very good high-ball and breaking-ball hitter. Has power, especially on pitches up. Has very good bat control. ***Defense: Young is one of the league's best shortstops. Is very fluid with quick footwork and agility to either side. Can adjust his stride very well when going after the ball. Hands are quick and soft. Has a quick release and with very good carry. Has good arm strength from the hole. ***Outlook:*** Even after leading the league in batting, Young is one of the most underrated players in the game. Is an All-Star player who continues to improve in all phases of his game. ***Grade 9.6***

MICHAEL YOUNG'S HITTING ZONE

.358	.457	.290
.298	.438	.407
.269	.324	.263

LEFTY-RIGHTY SPLITS

vs.	Avg.	AB	H	2B	3B	HR	RBI	BB	SO	OBP	Slg.
L	.340	153	52	14	1	3	16	15	15	.396	.503
R	.328	515	169	26	4	21	75	43	76	.382	.517

Year Team (League)	Pos.	G	AB	R	H	2B	3B	HR	RBI	BB	SO	HBP	GDP	SB-CS	Avg.	OBP	SLG	OPS	E	Avg.
1997— St. Catharines (NYP)	2B-SS	74	276	49	85	18	3	9	48	33	59	7	6	9-5	.308	.392	.493	.885	18	.946
1998— Hagerstown (S. Atl.)	2B-OF-SS	140	522	86	147	33	5	16	87	55	96	4	12	16-8	.282	.354	.456	.810	13	.977
1999— Dunedin (Fla. St.)	2B-SS	129	495	86	155	36	3	5	83	61	78	4	10	30-6	.313	.389	.428	.818	22	.961
2000— Tennessee (Sou.)	2B-SS	91	345	51	95	24	5	6	47	36	72	1	5	16-5	.275	.340	.426	.766	16	.965
— Tulsa (Texas)	SS	43	188	30	60	13	5	1	32	17	28	0	4	9-3	.319	.368	.457	.826	7	.965
— Texas (A.L.)	2B	2	2	0	0	0	0	0	0	0	1	0	0	0-0	.000	.000	.000	.000	0	
2001— Oklahoma (PCL)	2B-SS	47	189	28	55	8	0	8	28	20	34	1	6	3-3	.291	.358	.460	.819	6	.968
— Texas (A.L.)	2B	106	386	57	96	18	4	11	49	26	91	3	9	3-1	.249	.298	.402	.699	8	.984
2002— Texas (A.L.)	2B-SS-3B-DH	156	573	77	150	26	8	9	62	41	112	0	14	6-7	.262	.308	.382	.690	9	.988
2003— Texas (A.L.)	2B-SS	160	666	106	204	33	9	14	72	36	103	1	14	13-2	.306	.339	.446	.785	10	.987
2004— Texas (A.L.)	SS-DH	160	690	114	216	33	9	22	99	44	89	1	11	12-3	.313	.353	.483	.836	19	.972
2005— Texas (A.L.)	SS-DH	159	668	114	* 221	40	5	24	91	58	91	3	20	5-2	* .331	.385	.513	.899	18	.974
Major League totals (6 years)		743	2985	468	887	150	35	80	373	205	487	8	68	39-15	.297	.341	.451	.793	64	.981

ALL-STAR GAME RECORD

		G	AB	R	H	2B	3B	HR	RBI	BB	SO	HBP	GDP	SB-CS	Avg.	OBP	SLG	OPS	E	Avg.
All-Star Game totals (2 years)		2	3	0	1	1	0	0	0	0	0	0	0	0-0	.333	.333	.667	1.000	0	1.000

YOUNG, WALTER   1B

PERSONAL: Born February 18, 1980, in Hattiesburg, Miss. ... 6-5/322. ... Bats left, throws right. ... Full name: Walter Earnest Young. ... High school: Purvis (Miss.).

TRANSACTIONS/CAREER NOTES: Selected by Pittsburgh Pirates organization in 31st round of 1999 free-agent draft. ... Claimed on waivers by Baltimore Orioles (November 20, 2003).

2005 GAMES PLAYED BY POSITION (MLB): 1B—10, DH—3.

LEFTY-RIGHTY SPLITS

vs.	Avg.	AB	H	2B	3B	HR	RBI	BB	SO	OBP	Slg.
L	.667	3	2	0	0	0	0	0	1	.667	.667
R	.267	30	8	1	0	1	3	4	6	.353	.400

Year Team (League)	Pos.	G	AB	R	H	2B	3B	HR	RBI	BB	SO	HBP	GDP	SB-CS	Avg.	OBP	SLG	OPS	E	Avg.
1999— GC Pirates (GCL)	1B	37	130	9	30	6	2	0	15	4	34	3	4	2-2	.231	.270	.308	.578	4	.988
2000— GC Pirates (GCL)	1B	45	162	32	48	11	1	10	34	8	29	9	2	3-2	.296	.357	.562	.919	9	.975
— Williamsport (N.Y.-Penn.)...	1B	24	92	5	17	4	0	2	12	1	26	1	1	0-0	.185	.200	.293	.493	7	.955
2001— Williamsport (N.Y.-Penn.)..	1B	66	232	40	67	10	1	13	47	19	43	5	6	1-1	.289	.353	.509	.862	5	.988
2002— Hickory (S. Atl.)	1B-1B	132	492	84	164	34	2	25	103	36	102	15	11	2-6	.333	.390	.563	.953	15	.977
2003— Lynchburg (Caro.)	1B	117	431	76	120	15	2	20	87	35	88	12	10	2-4	.278	.348	.462	.810	15	.977
2004— Bowie (East.)	1B	133	486	88	133	28	1	33	98	47	145	8	11	2-3	.274	.343	.539	.882	9	.992
2005— Ottawa (Int'l)	1B-DH	123	466	48	134	29	1	13	81	30	91	5	14	1-1	.288	.334	.438	.772	10	.981
— Baltimore (A.L.)	1B-DH	14	33	2	10	1	0	1	3	4	7	0	1	0-0	.303	.378	.424	.803	0	1.000
Major League totals (1 year)		14	33	2	10	1	0	1	3	4	7	0	0	0-0	.303	.378	.424	.803	0	1.000

ZAMBRANO, CARLOS   P

PERSONAL: Born June 1, 1981, in Puerto Cabello, Venezuela. ... 6-5/255. ... Throws right, bats both. ... Full name: Carlos Alberto Zambrano. ... Name pronounced: zam-BRAH-no. ... High school: Unidad Educativa Creacion (Puerto Cabello, Venezue.

TRANSACTIONS/CAREER NOTES: Signed as a non-drafted free agent by Chicago Cubs organization (July 12, 1997). ... On disabled list (May 10-June 7, 2002); included rehabilitation assignment to Iowa. ... On suspended list (August 3-9, 2002; and August 5-11, 2004).

CAREER HITTING: 59-for-257 (.230), 25 R, 13 2B, 2 3B, 4 HR, 17 RBI.

SCOUTING REPORT *Throws:* Zambrano's fastball ranges from 92-97 mph, his slider from 84-86 and his split-finger fastball from 86-88. Also has a curveball that will clock in the low 70s. *Tendencies:* He takes advantage of his overpowering velocity and what might be the best movement in the game. Runs his fastball in on righthanders and sharply cuts it in on lefthanders. Throws a quick, short-breaking slider. Will throw his splitter as an out pitch, especially to lefthanders. Labors some with his delivery and can be erratic with his command. *Outlook:* Zambrano has terrific potential and is a determined competitor, but his hyper nature causes him to lose focus quickly, and opponents can force him to abandon his game plan. Needs to get his emotions under control. *Grade 9*

CARLOS ZAMBRANO'S PITCHING ZONE

.211	.143	.245
.286	.295	.212
.147	.275	.194

LEFTY-RIGHTY SPLITS

vs.	Avg.	AB	H	2B	3B	HR	RBI	BB	SO	OBP	Slg.
L	.212	358	76	14	0	14	43	51	75	.313	.369
R	.212	443	94	22	1	7	41	35	127	.276	.314

Year — Team (League)	W	L	Pct.	ERA	WHIP	G	GS	CG	ShO	Hld.	Sv.-Opp.	IP	H	R	ER	HR	BB-IBB	SO	Avg.
1998— Ariz. Cubs (AZL)	0	1	.000	3.15	1.60	14	2	0	0	...	1-...	40.0	39	17	14	0	25-3	36	.257
1999— Lansing (Midw.)	13	7	.650	4.17	1.38	27	24	2	1	...	0-...	153.1	150	87	71	9	62-1	98	.258
2000— West Tenn (Sou.)	3	1	.750	1.34	0.99	9	9	0	0	...	0-...	60.1	39	14	9	2	21-0	43	.181
— Iowa (PCL)	2	5	.286	3.97	1.66	34	0	0	0	...	6-...	56.2	54	30	25	3	40-2	46	.260
2001— Iowa (PCL)	10	5	.667	3.88	1.27	26	25	1	0	...	0-...	150.2	124	73	65	9	68-1	155	.226
— Chicago (N.L.)	1	2	.333	15.26	2.48	6	1	0	0	...	0-1	7.2	11	13	13	2	8-0	4	.355
2002— Iowa (PCL)	0	0	...	0.00	0.89	3	3	0	0	...	0-...	9.0	2	0	0	0	6-0	11	.069
— Chicago (N.L.)	4	8	.333	3.66	1.45	32	16	0	0	0	0-0	108.1	94	53	44	9	63-2	93	.235
2003— Chicago (N.L.)	13	11	.542	3.11	1.32	32	32	3	1	0	0-0	214.0	188	88	74	9	94-12	168	.239
2004— Chicago (N.L.)	16	8	.667	2.75	1.22	31	31	1	1	0	0-0	209.2	174	73	64	14	81-4	188	.225
2005— Chicago (N.L.)	14	6	.700	3.26	1.15	33	33	2	0	0	0-0	223.1	170	88	81	21	86-3	202	.212
Major League totals (5 years)	48	35	.578	3.26	1.27	134	113	6	2	0	0-1	763.0	637	315	276	55	332-21	655	.228

DIVISION SERIES RECORD

Year — Team (League)	W	L	Pct.	ERA	WHIP	G	GS	CG	ShO	Hld.	Sv.-Opp.	IP	H	R	ER	HR	BB-IBB	SO	Avg.
2003— Chicago (N.L.)	0	0	...	4.76	1.94	1	1	0	0	0	0-0	5.2	11	3	3	0	0-0	4	.407

CHAMPIONSHIP SERIES RECORD

Year — Team (League)	W	L	Pct.	ERA	WHIP	G	GS	CG	ShO	Hld.	Sv.-Opp.	IP	H	R	ER	HR	BB-IBB	SO	Avg.
2003— Chicago (N.L.)	0	1	.000	5.73	1.73	2	2	0	0	0	0-0	11.0	14	8	7	4	5-0	8	.311

ALL-STAR GAME RECORD

Year — Team (League)	W	L	Pct.	ERA	WHIP	G	GS	CG	ShO	Hld.	Sv.-Opp.	IP	H	R	ER	HR	BB-IBB	SO	Avg.
All-Star Game totals (1 year)	0	0	...	9.00	2.00	1	0	0	0	0	0-0	1.0	1	1	1	0	1-0	1	.250

ZAMBRANO, VICTOR   P

PERSONAL: Born August 6, 1975, in Los Teques, Venezuela. ... 6-0/203. ... Throws right, bats both. ... Full name: Victor Manuel Zambrano. ... Name pronounced: zam-BRAH-no. ... High school: Manve Maria Billolobo (Los Teques, Venezuela).
TRANSACTIONS/CAREER NOTES: Signed as a non-drafted free agent by New York Yankees organization (August 19, 1993). ... Played infield in Yankees organization (1994-95). ... Released by Yankees (February 7, 1996). ... Signed by Tampa Bay Devil Rays organization (March 14, 1996). ... Traded by Devil Rays with P Bartolome Fortunato to New York Mets for Ps Scott Kazmir and Jose Diaz (July 30, 2004). ... On disabled list (August 18, 2004-remainder of season).
CAREER HITTING: 9-for-68 (.132), 3 R, 1 2B, 1 3B, 0 HR, 3 RBI.

SCOUTING REPORT *Throws:* Zambrano has an 89-92 mph fastball, a curve, a slider in the low 80s and a changeup. *Tendencies:* His fastball has good late life, but an inability to command the pitch has prevented him from being a big winner. Is not throwing as hard now in an effort to gain command, but his fastball still has above-average life. Curve is basically a show pitch and his slider has a much quicker break. Has excellent deception with his change. Doesn't trust his stuff. *Outlook:* If he could only throw strikes—he frustrates his club because of his inability to go deep into games due to high pitch counts. *Grade 6.6*

VICTOR ZAMBRANO'S PITCHING ZONE

.222	.438	.296
.322	.351	.269
.220	.276	.303

LEFTY-RIGHTY SPLITS

vs.	Avg.	AB	H	2B	3B	HR	RBI	BB	SO	OBP	Slg.
L	.260	331	86	18	2	5	30	48	51	.354	.372
R	.268	313	84	20	2	7	39	29	61	.352	.412

Year — Team (League)	W	L	Pct.	ERA	WHIP	G	GS	CG	ShO	Hld.	Sv.-Opp.	IP	H	R	ER	HR	BB-IBB	SO	Avg.
1996— GC Devil Rays (GCL)	0	0	...	8.10	1.20	1	0	0	0	...	0-...	3.1	4	4	3	0	0-0	6	.250
1997— GC Devil Rays (GCL)	0	0	...	0.00	0.33	2	0	0	0	...	0-...	3.0	1	0	0	0	0-0	2	.100
— Princeton (Appal.)	0	2	.000	1.82	0.91	20	0	0	0	...	0-...	29.2	18	13	6	1	9-1	36	.159
1998— Char., S.C. (S. Atl.)	6	4	.600	3.38	1.19	48	2	0	0	...	0-...	77.1	72	32	29	5	20-1	89	.246
1999— St. Pete. (Fla. St.)	0	2	.000	4.00	1.67	7	0	0	0	...	0-...	9.0	10	6	4	1	5-0	15	.278
— Orlando (Sou.)	7	2	.778	4.59	1.58	40	4	0	0	...	1-...	82.1	92	55	42	5	38-2	81	.280
2000— Durham (Int'l)	0	6	.000	5.03	1.61	53	0	0	0	...	8-...	62.2	72	38	35	9	29-2	55	.285
2001— Durham (Int'l)	1	2	.333	2.08	1.25	29	0	0	0	...	12-...	30.1	26	10	7	2	12-1	29	.232
— Tampa Bay (A.L.)	6	2	.750	3.16	1.09	36	0	0	0	5	2-6	51.1	38	21	18	6	18-0	58	.201
2002— Tampa Bay (A.L.)	8	8	.500	5.53	1.65	42	11	0	0	6	1-3	114.0	120	77	70	15	68-5	73	.278
— Durham (Int'l)	0	1	.000	1.93	0.93	10	0	0	0	...	1-...	14.0	9	4	3	1	4-0	15	.180
2003— Tampa Bay (A.L.)	0	1	.000	4.50	1.50	1	1	0	0	...	0-...	4.0	4	6	2	0	2-0	6	.222
— Tampa Bay (A.L.)	12	10	.545	4.21	1.44	34	28	1	0	2	0-0	188.1	165	97	88	21	* 106-2	132	.237
2004— Tampa Bay (A.L.)	9	7	.563	4.43	1.59	23	22	0	0	1	0-0	128.0	107	68	63	13	* 96-2	109	.230
— New York (N.L.)	1	1	.000	3.86	1.29	3	3	0	0	0	0-0	14.0	12	6	6	0	6-0	14	.222
2005— New York (N.L.)	7	12	.368	4.17	1.48	31	27	0	0	0	0-0	166.1	170	85	77	12	77-2	112	.264
American League totals (4 years)	35	27	.565	4.47	1.49	135	61	1	0	14	3-9	481.2	430	263	239	55	288-9	372	.241
National League totals (2 years)	9	12	.429	4.14	1.47	34	30	0	0	0	0-0	180.1	182	94	83	12	83-2	126	.261
Major League totals (5 years)	44	39	.530	4.38	1.48	169	91	1	0	14	3-9	662.0	612	357	322	67	371-11	498	.247

Z

PERSONAL: Born April 14, 1971, in Glendale, Calif. ... 5-10/190. ... Bats both, throws right. ... Full name: Gregory Owen Zaun. ... Name pronounced: ZAHN. ... High school: St. Francis (La Canada, Calif.). ... Nephew of Rick Dempsey, coach, Baltimore Orioles, and catcher with six major league teams (1969-92).

TRANSACTIONS/CAREER NOTES: Selected by Baltimore Orioles organization in 17th round of 1989 free-agent draft. ... Traded by Orioles to Florida Marlins (August 23, 1996), completing deal in which Marlins traded P Terry Mathews to Orioles for a player to be named (August 21, 1996). ... Traded by Marlins to Texas Rangers for cash (November 23, 1998). ... Traded by Rangers with OF Juan Gonzalez and P Danny Patterson to Detroit Tigers for Ps Justin Thompson, Francisco Cordero and Alan Webb, OF Gabe Kapler, C Bill Haselman and 2B Frank Catalanotto (November 2, 1999). ... Traded by Tigers to Kansas City Royals for cash (March 7, 2000). ... On disabled list (April 15-May 29, 2000); included rehabilitation assignment to Omaha. ... On disabled list (March 31-July 23, 2001); included rehabilitation assignments to GCL Royals and Omaha. ... Signed as a free agent by Houston Astros (December 11, 2001). ... Released by Astros (August 21, 2003). ... Signed by Colorado Rockies (August 26, 2003). ... Signed as a free agent by Montreal Expos organization (January 13, 2004). ... Signed as a free agent by Toronto Blue Jays organization (April 10, 2004). ... On disabled list (May 9-24, 2005); included rehabilitation assignment to New Hampshire.

2005 GAMES PLAYED BY POSITION (MLB): C—132.

SCOUTING REPORT *Offense:* Zaun, finally an everyday player, has learned to hit. Has shortened his swing and is extremely patient. A natural righthanded hitter, he has more power and bat speed from the left side. Takes what the pitcher gives him and will use the whole field. Likes the ball up from either side of the plate. *Defense:* His arm strength is below average, but Zaun transfers the ball quickly from mitt to throwing hand and is accurate. Has good hands. Range to both sides is good . Has improved his take-charge ability. Works well with pitchers. *Outlook:* Zaun will continue as a regular in 2006 but don't look for him to increase his offensive production much. *Grade 7.3*

GREGG ZAUN'S HITTING ZONE

.240	.429	.130
.227	.378	.241
.391	.296	.298

LEFTY-RIGHTY SPLITS

vs.	Avg.	AB	H	2B	3B	HR	RBI	BB	SO	OBP	Slg.
L	.278	115	32	6	1	2	20	17	15	.366	.400
R	.241	319	77	12	0	9	41	56	55	.352	.364

											BATTING									FIELDING	
Year	Team (League)	Pos.	G	AB	R	H	2B	3B	HR	RBI	BB	SO	HBP	GDP	SB-CS	Avg.	OBP	SLG	OPS	E	Avg.
1990—	Wausau (Midw.)	C	37	100	3	13	0	1	1	7	7	17	1	2	0-0	.130	.194	.180	.374	3	.990
	—Bluefield (Appal.)	P	61	184	29	55	5	2	2	21	23	15	1	2	5-5	.299	.378	.380	.758	10	.980
1991—	Kane Co. (Midw.)	C	113	409	67	112	17	5	4	51	50	41	2	10	4-4	.274	.353	.369	.722	16	.980
1992—	Frederick (Carol.)	2B-C	108	383	54	96	18	6	6	52	42	45	3	10	3-5	.251	.324	.376	.700	18	.979
1993—	Bowie (East.)	C-P	79	258	25	79	10	0	3	38	27	26	1	7	4-7	.306	.373	.380	.753	10	.979
	—Rochester (Int'l)	C	21	78	10	20	4	2	1	11	6	11	0	1	0-0	.256	.302	.397	.700	4	.975
1994—	Rochester (Int'l)	C	123	388	61	92	16	4	7	43	56	72	4	5	4-2	.237	.337	.353	.690	9	.989
1995—	Rochester (Int'l)	C-DH	42	140	26	41	13	1	6	18	14	21	3	0	0-3	.293	.367	.529	.896	3	.989
	—Baltimore (A.L.)	C	40	104	18	27	5	0	3	14	16	14	0	2	1-1	.260	.358	.394	.753	3	.987
1996—	Baltimore (A.L.)	C	50	108	16	25	8	1	1	13	11	15	2	3	0-0	.231	.309	.352	.661	3	.987
	—Rochester (Int'l)	C-DH	14	47	11	15	2	0	0	4	11	6	0	0	0-2	.319	.441	.362	.802	2	.965
	—Florida (N.L.)	C	10	31	4	9	1	0	1	2	3	5	0	2	1-0	.290	.353	.419	.772	0	1.000
1997—	Florida (N.L.)	C-1B	58	143	21	43	10	2	2	20	26	18	2	3	1-0	.301	.415	.441	.856	3	.978
1998—	Florida (N.L.)	C-2B	106	298	19	56	12	2	5	29	35	52	1	7	5-2	.188	.274	.292	.566	8	.986
1999—	Texas (A.L.)	C-DH	43	93	12	23	2	1	1	12	10	7	0	2	1-0	.247	.314	.323	.637	3	.988
2000—	Kansas City (A.L.)	C-1B-2B	83	234	36	64	11	0	7	33	43	34	3	4	7-3	.274	.390	.410	.800	5	.988
	—Omaha (PCL)	C	9	25	7	7	3	0	0	4	4	3	0	1	1-1	.280	.379	.400	.779	0	1.000
2001—	GC Royals (GCL)	C	6	18	3	1	0	0	0	1	7	5	0	1	0-0	.056	.320	.056	.376	0	1.000
	—Omaha (PCL)	C	11	43	5	12	4	0	1	8	3	3	1	2	0-0	.279	.333	.442	.775	1	.985
	—Kansas City (A.L.)	C-DH	39	125	15	40	9	0	6	18	12	16	0	2	1-2	.320	.377	.536	.913	5	.975
2002—	Houston (N.L.)	C	76	185	18	41	7	1	3	24	12	36	2	4	1-0	.222	.275	.319	.594	5	.985
2003—	Houston (N.L.)	C	59	120	9	26	7	0	1	13	14	14	1	5	1-0	.217	.299	.300	.599	4	.976
	—Colorado (N.L.)	C	15	46	6	12	1	0	3	8	5	7	0	0	0-1	.261	.333	.478	.812	2	.973
2004—	Syracuse (Int'l)	C-DH	7	23	4	7	1	0	0	2	2	5	0	1	1-0	.304	.346	.348	.694	0	1.000
	—Toronto (A.L.)	C-DH	107	338	46	91	24	0	6	36	47	61	6	7	0-2	.269	.367	.393	.761	8	.987
2005—	New Hampshire (East.)	C-DH	2	6	1	2	1	0	0	0	2	2	0	0	0-0	.333	.500	.500	1.000	0	1.000
	—Toronto (A.L.)	C	133	434	61	109	18	1	11	61	73	70	0	11	2-3	.251	.355	.373	.729	8	.990
	American League totals (7 years)		495	1436	204	379	77	3	35	187	212	217	11	31	12-11	.264	.360	.395	.754	35	.983
	National League totals (5 years)		324	823	77	187	38	5	15	96	95	132	6	21	9-3	.227	.310	.340	.650	27	.987
	Major League totals (11 years)		819	2259	281	566	115	8	50	283	307	349	17	52	21-14	.251	.342	.375	.717	62	.985

DIVISION SERIES RECORD

Year	Team (League)	Pos.	G	AB	R	H	2B	3B	HR	RBI	BB	SO	HBP	GDP	SB-CS	Avg.	OBP	SLG	OPS	E	Avg.
1997—	Florida (N.L.)			Did not play.																	

CHAMPIONSHIP SERIES RECORD

Year	Team (League)	Pos.	G	AB	R	H	2B	3B	HR	RBI	BB	SO	HBP	GDP	SB-CS	Avg.	OBP	SLG	OPS	E	Avg.
1997—	Florida (N.L.)	C	1	0	0	0	0	0	0	0	0	0	0	0	0-0	...	...	...	...	0	1.000

WORLD SERIES RECORD

Year	Team (League)	Pos.	G	AB	R	H	2B	3B	HR	RBI	BB	SO	HBP	GDP	SB-CS	Avg.	OBP	SLG	OPS	E	Avg.
1997—	Florida (N.L.)	C	2	2	0	0	0	0	0	0	0	0	0	0	0-0	.000	.000	.000	.000	0	1.000

ZIMMERMAN, RYAN   3B

PERSONAL: Born September 28, 1984, in Washington, N.C. ... 6-3/210. ... Bats right, throws right. ... Full name: Ryan Wallace Zimmerman. ... High school: Kellam (Virginia Beach, Va.). ... College: Virginia.

TRANSACTIONS/CAREER NOTES: Selected by Washington Nationals organization in first round (fourth pick overall) of 2005 free-agent draft.

2005 GAMES PLAYED BY POSITION (MLB): 3B—14, SS—1.

SCOUTING REPORT *Offense:* Zimmerman is a free swinger who has the tools to be a gap-hitting star. Is aggressive on fastballs from the middle to out over the plate. Uses all fields. Plate discipline needs to improve so that he takes more walks and strikes out less. Makes steady contact and gets his hands through the hitting zone. Shows plus bat speed and quick hands. Shows good recognition of pitches' spin and is a good two-strike hitter. *Defense:* He has soft hands and an above-average arm with good carry on his throws. Has first-step agility and quickness for the position. At the least, he will be a steady defensive player. *Outlook:* The Nationals traded Vinny Castilla because they believe Zimmerman is ready to play every day. Is a student of the game who should be a productive player for a long time. *Grade 7.6*

RYAN ZIMMERMAN'S HITTING ZONE

1.000	1.000	.000
.500	.333	.600
.500	.250	.500

LEFTY-RIGHTY SPLITS

vs.	Avg.	AB	H	2B	3B	HR	RBI	BB	SO	OBP	Slg.
L	.400	15	6	4	0	0	1	0	3	.400	.667
R	.395	43	17	6	0	0	5	3	9	.426	.535

Year Team (League)	Pos.	G	AB	R	H	2B	3B	HR	RBI	BB	SO	HBP	GDP	SB-CS	Avg.	OBP	SLG	OPS	E	Avg.
2005— Savannah (S. Atl.)	3B	4	17	5	8	2	1	2	6	0	3	0	0	0-1	.471	.471	1.059	1.529	0	1.000
—Harrisburg (East.)	3B-SS	63	233	40	76	20	0	9	32	15	34	2	3	1-5	.326	.371	.528	.898	10	.946
—Washington (N.L.)	3B-SS	20	58	6	23	10	0	0	6	3	12	0	1	0-0	.397	.419	.569	.988	2	.951
Major League totals (1 year)		20	58	6	23	10	0	0	6	3	12	0	1	0-0	.397	.419	.569	.988	2	.951

ZITO, BARRY　　　　　　　　　　　　　　P

PERSONAL: Born May 13, 1978, in Las Vegas. ... 6-4/215. ... Throws left, bats left. ... Full name: Barry William Zito. ... Name pronounced: ZEE-toe. ... High school: University (San Diego). ... College: Southern California.
TRANSACTIONS/CAREER NOTES: Selected by Seattle Mariners organization in 59th round of 1996 free-agent draft; did not sign. ... Selected by Texas Rangers organization in third round of 1998 free-agent draft; did not sign. ... Selected by Oakland Athletics organization in first round (ninth pick overall) of 1999 free-agent draft.
HONORS: Named A.L. Pitcher of the Year by THE SPORTING NEWS (2002). ... Named A.L. Cy Young Award winner by Baseball Writers' Association of America (2002).
CAREER HITTING: 1-for-26 (.038), 0 R, 0 2B, 0 3B, 0 HR, 0 RBI.

SCOUTING REPORT *Throws:* Zito throws a low-90s fastball, a 12-6 curveball and a changeup. Added added an upper-80s two-seam fastball to be less predictable. *Tendencies:* The two-seam fastball allows Zito to pitch on both sides of the plate, making him more effective. Regained his arm speed and tight curve. Turns over his changeup and has good arm speed on it. *Outlook:* Zito showed that his arm was healthy in the second half. Increased his velocity, creating better separation with his breaking ball. Should be even better in 2006. *Grade 8.7*

BARRY ZITO'S PITCHING ZONE

.275	.158	.286
.330	.270	.206
.105	.389	.212

LEFTY-RIGHTY SPLITS

vs.	Avg.	AB	H	2B	3B	HR	RBI	BB	SO	OBP	Slg.
L	.215	191	41	8	3	3	21	20	37	.296	.335
R	.223	645	144	25	0	23	72	69	134	.306	.369

Year Team (League)	W	L	Pct.	ERA	WHIP	G	GS	CG	ShO	Hld.	Sv.-Opp.	IP	H	R	ER	HR	BB-IBB	SO	Avg.
1999— Visalia (Calif.)	3	0	1.000	2.45	1.07	8	8	0	0	...	0-...	40.1	21	13	11	3	22-0	62	.157
—Midland (Texas)	2	1	.667	4.91	1.50	4	4	0	0	...	0-...	22.0	22	15	12	1	11-0	29	.253
—Vancouver (PCL)	1	0	1.000	1.50	1.17	1	1	0	0	...	0-...	6.0	5	1	1	0	2-0	6	.227
2000— Sacramento (PCL)	8	5	.615	3.19	1.31	18	18	0	0	...	0-...	101.2	88	44	36	4	45-0	91	.230
—Oakland (A.L.)	7	4	.636	2.72	1.18	14	14	1	1	0	0-0	92.2	64	30	28	6	45-2	78	.195
2001— Oakland (A.L.)	17	8	.680	3.49	1.23	35	•35	3	2	0	0-0	214.1	184	92	83	18	80-0	205	.230
2002— Oakland (A.L.)	* 23	5	.821	2.75	1.13	35	*35	1	0	0	0-0	229.1	182	79	70	24	78-2	182	.218
2003— Oakland (A.L.)	14	12	.538	3.30	1.18	35	35	4	1	0	0-0	231.2	186	98	85	19	88-3	146	.219
2004— Oakland (A.L.)	11	11	.500	4.48	1.39	34	34	0	0	0	0-0	213.0	216	116	106	28	81-2	163	.263
2005— Oakland (A.L.)	14	13	.519	3.86	1.20	35	•35	0	0	0	0-0	228.1	185	106	98	26	89-0	171	.221
Major League totals (6 years)	86	53	.619	3.50	1.22	188	188	9	4	0	0-0	1209.1	1017	521	470	121	461-9	945	.228

DIVISION SERIES RECORD

Year Team (League)	W	L	Pct.	ERA	WHIP	G	GS	CG	ShO	Hld.	Sv.-Opp.	IP	H	R	ER	HR	BB-IBB	SO	Avg.
2000— Oakland (A.L.)	1	0	1.000	1.59	1.59	1	1	0	0	0	0-0	5.2	7	1	1	0	2-0	5	.304
2001— Oakland (A.L.)	0	1	.000	1.13	0.38	1	1	0	0	0	0-0	8.0	2	1	1	1	1-0	6	.077
2002— Oakland (A.L.)	1	0	1.000	4.50	1.50	1	1	0	0	0	0-0	6.0	5	3	3	0	4-0	8	.217
2003— Oakland (A.L.)	1	1	.500	3.46	1.00	2	2	0	0	0	0-0	13.0	9	5	5	2	4-0	13	.191
Division series totals (4 years)	3	2	.600	2.76	1.04	5	5	0	0	0	0-0	32.2	23	10	10	3	11-0	32	.193

ALL-STAR GAME RECORD

	W	L	Pct.	ERA	WHIP	G	GS	CG	ShO	Hld.	Sv.-Opp.	IP	H	R	ER	HR	BB-IBB	SO	Avg.
All-Star Game totals (1 year)	0	0	...	0.00	0.00	1	0	0	0	0	0-0	0.1	0	0	0	0	0-0	0	.000

2005 MANAGERS LIST

Year-by-year major and minor league managing statistics

Career major league playing statistics

Biographical information for all active major league managers

MAJOR LEAGUE MANAGERS

ALOU, FELIPE — GIANTS

PERSONAL: Born May 12, 1935, in Haina, Dominican Republic. ... Full name: Felipe Rojas Alou. ... College: University of Santo Domingo (Dominican Republic). ... Father of Moises Alou, outfielder, Giants; brother of Jesus Alou, outfielder with four major league teams (1965-75 and 1978-79); brother of Matty Alou, outfielder with six major league teams (1960-74). Uncle of Mel Rojas, pitcher with five major league teams (1990-1999).

RECORD AS PLAYER

	G	AB	R	H	2B	3B	HR	RBI	Avg.	BB	SO	SB	PO	A	E	Avg.
													FIELDING			
Major league totals (17 years)	2082	7339	985	2101	359	49	206	852	.286	423	706	107	6537	322	96	.986

RECORD AS MANAGER

BACKGROUND: Spring training instructor, Montreal Expos (1976). ... Coach, Expos (1979-80, 1984 and 1991-1992). ... Coach, Detroit Tigers (2002).
HONORS: Named N.L. Manager of the Year by THE SPORTING NEWS (1994). ... Named N.L. Manager of the Year by Baseball Writers' Association of America (1994).

Year Team (League)	W	L	Pct.	Pos	Year Team (League)	W	L	Pct.	Pos
1977—West Palm Beach (Fla. St.)	77	65	.542	1S	1991—West Palm Beach (Fla. St.)	33	31	.516	4E
1978—Memphis (Sou.)	30	31	.492	2W	—Second half	39	28	.582	2E
Second half	41	42	.494	2W	1992—Montreal (N.L.)	70	55	.560	2E
1981—Denver (A.A.)	76	60	.559	2W	1993—Montreal (N.L.)	94	68	.580	2E
1982—Wichita (A.A.)	70	67	.511	2W	1994—Montreal (N.L.)	74	40	.649	...
1983—Wichita (A.A.)	65	71	.478	3W	1995—Montreal (N.L.)	66	78	.458	5E
1985—Indianapolis (A.A.)	61	81	.430	4E	1996—Montreal (N.L.)	88	74	.543	2E
1986—West Palm Beach (Fla. St.)	80	55	.593	1S	1997—Montreal (N.L.)	78	84	.481	4E
1987—West Palm Beach (Fla. St.)	75	63	.543	2S	1998—Montreal (N.L.)	65	97	.401	4E
1988—West Palm Beach (Fla. St.)	41	27	.603	2E	1999—Montreal (N.L.)	68	94	.420	4E
—Second half	30	36	.455	3E	2000—Montreal (N.L.)	67	95	.414	4E
1989—West Palm Beach (Fla. St.)	39	31	.557	2E	2001—Montreal (N.L.)	21	32	.396	...
—Second half	35	33	.515	2E	2003—San Francisco (N.L.)	100	61	.621	1W
1990—West Palm Beach (Fla. St.)	49	19	.721	1E	2004—San Francisco (N.L.)	91	71	.562	2W
—Second half	43	21	.672	1E	2005—San Francisco (N.L.)	75	87	.463	3W
					Major league totals (13 years)	957	936	.519	

NOTES:
1977—Lost to St. Petersburg, 2-1, in semifinals. ... **1978**—Memphis tied one game. ... **1981**—Defeated Omaha, 4-0, in league championship. ... **1986**—Defeated Winter Haven, 2-0, in semifinals; lost to St. Petersburg, 3-1, in league championship. ... **1988**—Defeated Vero Beach, 2-0, in first round; lost to Osceola, 2-0, in semifinals. ... **1990**—Defeated Lakeland, 2-1, in semifinals; lost to Vero Beach, 2-1, in league championship. ... **1991**—Defeated Vero Beach, 2-1, in first round; defeated Lakeland, 2-0, in semifinals; defeated Clearwater, 2-0, in league championship. ... **1992**—Replaced Tom Runnells as Montreal manager with club in fourth place and record of 17-20 (May 22). ... **1994**—Montreal was in first place in N.L. East at time of season-ending strike (August 12). ... **2001**—Replaced as Montreal manager by Jeff Torborg with club in fifth place (May 31). ... **2003**—Lost to Florida, 3-1, in N.L. Division Series. ... Career major league postseason record: 1-3.

BAKER, DUSTY — CUBS

PERSONAL: Born June 15, 1949, in Riverside, Calif. ... Full name: Johnnie B. Baker Jr.. ... High school: Del Campo (Fair Oaks, Calif.). ... College: American River College (Calif.).

RECORD AS PLAYER

	G	AB	R	H	2B	3B	HR	RBI	Avg.	BB	SO	SB	PO	A	E	Avg.
													FIELDING			
Major league totals (19 years)	2039	7117	964	1981	320	23	242	1013	.278	762	926	137	4073	136	59	.986

RECORD AS MANAGER

BACKGROUND: Coach, San Francisco Giants (1988-92). ... Manager, Scottsdale Scorpions, Arizona Fall League (1992, record: 20-22, second/North).
HONORS: Named N.L. Manager of the Year by THE SPORTING NEWS (1997 and 2000). ... Named N.L. Manager of the Year by Baseball Writers' Association of America (1993, 1997 and 2000).

Year Team (League)	W	L	Pct.	Pos	Year Team (League)	W	L	Pct.	Pos
1993—San Francisco (N.L.)	103	59	.636	2W	2000—San Francisco (N.L.)	97	65	.599	1W
1994—San Francisco (N.L.)	55	60	.478	...	2001—San Francisco (N.L.)	90	72	.556	2W
1995—San Francisco (N.L.)	67	77	.465	4W	2002—San Francisco (N.L.)	95	66	.590	2W
1996—San Francisco (N.L.)	68	94	.420	4W	2003—Chicago (N.L.)	88	74	.543	1C
1997—San Francisco (N.L.)	90	72	.556	1W	2004—Chicago (N.L.)	89	73	.549	3C
1998—San Francisco (N.L.)	89	74	.546	2W	2005—Chicago (N.L.)	79	83	.488	4C
1999—San Francisco (N.L.)	86	76	.531	2W	Major league totals (13 years)	1096	945	.537	

NOTES:
1994—San Francisco was in second place in N.L. West at time of season-ending strike (August 12). ... **1997**—Lost to Florida, 3-0, in N.L. Division Series. ... **2000**—Lost to New York Mets, 3-1, in N.L. Division Series. ... **2002**—Defeated Atlanta, 3-2, in N.L. Division Series; defeated St. Louis, 4-1, N.L. Championship Series; lost to Anaheim, 4-3, in World Series. ... **2003**—Defeated Atlanta, 3-2, in N.L. Division Series; lost to Florida, 4-3, in N.L. Championship Series. ... Career postseason record: 17-19.

BELL, BUDDY — ROYALS

PERSONAL: Born August 27, 1951, in Pittsburgh. ... 6-3/200. ... Full name: David Gus Bell. ... High school: Moeller (Cincinnati). ... College: Xavier, then Miami (Ohio). Father of David Bell, third baseman, Philadelphia Phillies; and Mike Bell, third baseman with Cincinnati Reds (2000); son of Gus Bell, outfielder with four major league teams (1950-64).

RECORD AS PLAYER

	G	AB	R	H	2B	3B	HR	RBI	Avg.	BB	SO	SB	PO	A	E	Avg.
													FIELDING			
Major league totals (18 years)	2405	8995	1151	2514	425	56	201	1106	.279	836	776	55	2198	5009	262	.965

RECORD AS MANAGER

BACKGROUND: Minor league hitting instructor, Cleveland Indians (1990). ... Director of minor league instruction, Chicago White Sox (1991-93). ... Coach, Cleveland Indians (1994-95, 2002-05). ... Minor league field coordinator, Cincinnati Reds (1998-99). ... Director of player development, Reds (1999).

Year Team (League)	W	L	Pct.	Pos	Year Team (League)	W	L	Pct.	Pos
1996—Detroit (A.L.)	53	109	.327	5E	2002—Colorado (N.L.)	6	16	.273	...
1997—Detroit (A.L.)	79	83	.488	3E	2005—Kansas City (A.L.)	43	69	.384	5C
1998—Detroit (A.L.)	52	85	.380	...	American League totals (4 years)	227	346	.396	
2000—Colorado (N.L.)	82	80	.506	4W	National League totals (3 years)	161	185	.465	
2001—Colorado (N.L.)	73	89	.451	5W	Major league totals (7 years)	388	531	.477	

NOTES:
1998—Replaced as Detroit manager on interim basis by Larry Parrish with club in fifth place (September 1). ... **2002**—Replaced as Colorado manager by Clint Hurdle (April 26). ... **2005**—Replaced Kansas City manager Tony Pena (record of 8-25) and interim manager Bob Schaefer (5-12) with club in fifth place and a record of 13-37 (May 31). On suspended list (July 22-23, 2005).

BOCHY, BRUCE — PADRES

PERSONAL: Born April 16, 1955, in Landes de Boussac, France. ... Full name: Bruce Douglas Bochy. ... Name pronounced: BO-chee. ... High school: Melbourne (Fla.). ... Junior college: Brevard Community College (Fla.). ... College: Florida State.

RECORD AS PLAYER

				BATTING								FIELDING			
	G	AB	R	H	2B	3B	HR	RBI	Avg.	BB	SO	SB	PO	A	E	Avg.
Major league totals (9 years)	358	802	75	192	37	2	26	93	.239	66	170	1	1220	130	29	.979

RECORD AS MANAGER

BACKGROUND: Player/coach, Las Vegas, San Diego Padres organization (1988). ... Coach, Padres (1993-94).

HONORS: Named N.L. Manager of the Year by THE SPORTING NEWS (1996 and 1998). ... Named N.L. Manager of the Year by Baseball Writers' Association of America (1996).

Year Team (League)	W	L	Pct.	Pos	Year Team (League)	W	L	Pct.	Pos
1989—Spokane (N'west)	41	34	.547	1N	1997—San Diego (N.L.)	76	86	.469	4W
1990—Riverside (Calif.)	35	36	.493	4S	1998—San Diego (N.L.)	98	64	.605	1W
—Second half	29	42	.408	5S	1999—San Diego (N.L.)	74	88	.457	4W
1991—High Desert (Calif.)	31	37	.456	3S	2000—San Diego (N.L.)	76	86	.469	5W
—Second half	42	26	.618	1S	2001—San Diego (N.L.)	79	83	.488	4W
1992—Wichita (Texas)	39	29	.574	1W	2002—San Diego (N.L.)	66	96	.407	5W
—Second half	31	37	.456	4W	2003—San Diego (N.L.)	64	98	.395	5W
1995—San Diego (N.L.)	70	74	.486	3W	2004—San Diego (N.L.)	87	75	.537	3W
1996—San Diego (N.L.)	91	71	.562	1W	2005—San Diego (N.L.)	82	80	.506	1W
					Major league totals (11 years)	863	901	.489	

NOTES:
1989—Defeated Southern Oregon, 2-1, in league championship. ... **1991**—Defeated Bakersfield, 3-0, in semifinals; defeated Stockton, 3-2, in league championship. ... **1992**—Defeated El Paso, 2-1, in semifinals; defeated Shreveport, 4-0, in league championship. ... **1996**—Lost to St. Louis, 3-0, in N.L. Division Series. ... **1998**—Defeated Houston, 3-1, in N.L. Division Series; defeated Atlanta, 4-2, in N.L. Championship Series; lost to New York Yankees, 4-0, in World Series. ... **2005**—Lost to St. Louis, 3-0, in N.L. Division Series. ... Career major league postseason record: 7-13.

COX, BOBBY — BRAVES

PERSONAL: Born May 21, 1941, in Tulsa, Okla. ... Full name: Robert Joseph Cox. ... High school: Selma (Calif.). ... Junior college: Reedley (Calif.) JC.

RECORD AS PLAYER

				BATTING								FIELDING			
	G	AB	R	H	2B	3B	HR	RBI	Avg.	BB	SO	SB	PO	A	E	Avg.
Major league totals (2 years)	220	628	50	141	22	2	9	58	.225	75	126	3	148	426	28	.953

RECORD AS MANAGER

BACKGROUND: Minor league instructor, New York Yankees organization (1970-71). ... Player/manager, Fort Lauderdale, Yankees organization (1971). ... Coach, Yankees (1977). ... General manager, Braves (1985-90).

HONORS: Named Major League Manager of the Year by THE SPORTING NEWS (1985). ... Named N.L. Manager of the Year by THE SPORTING NEWS (1991, 1993, 1999 and 2002-05). ... Named A.L. Manager of the Year by Baseball Writers' Association of America (1985). ... Named N.L. Manager of the Year by Baseball Writers' Association of America (1991, 2004 and 2005).

Year Team (League)	W	L	Pct.	Pos	Year Team (League)	W	L	Pct.	Pos
1971—Fort Lauderdale (Fla. St.)	71	70	.504	4E	1992—Atlanta (N.L.)	98	64	.605	1W
1972—West Haven (East.)	84	56	.600	1A	1993—Atlanta (N.L.)	104	58	.642	1W
1973—Syracuse (Int'l)	76	70	.521	3A	1994—Atlanta (N.L.)	68	46	.596	...
1974—Syracuse (Int'l)	74	70	.514	2N	1995—Atlanta (N.L.)	90	54	.625	1E
1975—Syracuse (Int'l)	72	64	.529	3rd	1996—Atlanta (N.L.)	96	66	.593	1E
1976—Syracuse (Int'l)	82	57	.590	2nd	1997—Atlanta (N.L.)	101	61	.623	1E
1978—Atlanta (N.L.)	69	93	.426	6W	1998—Atlanta (N.L.)	106	56	.654	1E
1979—Atlanta (N.L.)	66	94	.413	6W	1999—Atlanta (N.L.)	103	59	.636	1E
1980—Atlanta (N.L.)	81	80	.503	4W	2000—Atlanta (N.L.)	95	67	.586	1E
1981—Atlanta (N.L.)	25	29	.463	4W	2001—Atlanta (N.L.)	88	74	.543	1E
—Second half	25	27	.481	5W	2002—Atlanta (N.L.)	101	59	.631	1E
1982—Toronto (A.L.)	78	84	.481	6E	2003—Atlanta (N.L.)	101	61	.623	1E
1983—Toronto (A.L.)	89	73	.549	4E	2004—Atlanta (N.L.)	96	66	.593	1E
1984—Toronto (A.L.)	89	73	.549	2E	2005—Atlanta (N.L.)	90	72	.556	1E
1985—Toronto (A.L.)	99	62	.615	1E	American League totals (4 years)	355	292	.549	
1990—Atlanta (N.L.)	40	57	.412	6W	National League totals (20 years)	1737	1311	.570	
1991—Atlanta (N.L.)	94	68	.580	1W	Major league totals (24 years)	2092	1603	.566	

NOTES:
1972—Defeated Three Rivers in league championship, 3-0. ... **1976**—Defeated Memphis, 3-0, in semifinals; defeated Richmond, 3-1, in league championship. ... **1985**—Lost to Kansas City, 4-3, in A.L. Championship Series. ... **1990**—Replaced Russ Nixon as Atlanta manager with club in sixth place and a record of 25-40 (June 22). ... **1991**—Defeated Pittsburgh, 4-3, in N.L. Championship Series; lost to Minnesota, 4-3, in World Series. ... **1992**—Defeated Pittsburgh, 4-3, in N.L. Championship Series; lost to Toronto, 4-2, in World Series. ... **1993**—Lost to Philadelphia, 4-2, in N.L. Championship Series. ... **1994**—Atlanta was in second place in N.L. East at time of season-ending strike (August 12). ... **1995**—Defeated Colorado, 3-1, in N.L. Division Series; defeated Cincinnati, 4-0, in N.L. Championship Series; defeated Cleveland, 4-2, in World Series. ... **1996**—Defeated Los Angeles, 3-0, in N.L. Division Series; defeated St. Louis, 4-3, in N.L. Championship Series; lost to New York Yankees, 4-2, in World Series. ... **1997**—Defeated Houston, 3-0, in N.L. Division Series; lost to Florida, 4-2, in N.L. Championship Series. ... **1998**—Defeated Chicago Cubs, 3-0, in N.L. Division Series; lost to San Diego, 4-2, in N.L. Championship Series. ... **1999**—Defeated Houston, 3-1, in N.L. Division Series; defeated New York Mets, 4-2, in N.L. Championship Series; lost to New York Yankees, 4-0, in World Series. ... **2000**—Lost to St. Louis, 3-0, in N.L. Division Series. ... **2001**—Defeated Houston, 3-0, in N.L. Division Series; lost to Arizona, 4-1, in N.L. Championship Series. ... **2002**—Lost to San Francisco, 3-2, in N.L. Division Series. ... **2003**—Lost to Chicago Cubs, 3-2, in N.L. Division Series. ... **2004**—Lost to Houston, 3-2, in N.L. Division Series. ... **2005**—Lost to Houston, 3-1, in N.L. Division Series. ... Career major league postseason record: 66-66.

FRANCONA, TERRY — RED SOX

PERSONAL: Born April 22, 1959, in Aberdeen, S.D. ... 6-1/175. ... Full name: Terry Jon Francona. ... High school: New Brighton (Pa.). ... College: Arizona. ... Son of Tito Francona, first baseman with nine major league teams (1956-70).

RECORD AS PLAYER

				BATTING									FIELDING		
	G	AB	R	H	2B	3B	HR	RBI	Avg.	BB	SO	SB	PO	A	E	Avg.
Major league totals (10 years)..........	708	1731	163	474	74	6	16	143	.274	65	119	12	2032	188	22	.990

RECORD AS MANAGER

BACKGROUND: Coach, Grand Canyon Rafters, Arizona Fall League (1992). ... Manager, Scottsdale Scorpions, Arizona Fall League (1994, record: 26-25, second/North). ... Coach, Detroit Tigers (1996). ... Special assistant to the general manager, Cleveland Indians (2001). ... Coach, Texas Rangers (2002). ... Coach, Oakland Athletics (2003).

Year Team (League)	W	L	Pct.	Pos	Year Team (League)	W	L	Pct.	Pos
1992—South Bend (Midw.)	35	33	.515	3N	1997—Philadelphia (N.L.)	68	94	.420	5E
—Second half	38	31	.551	2N	1998—Philadelphia (N.L.)	75	87	.463	3E
1993—Birmingham (Sou.)	35	36	.493	2W	1999—Philadelphia (N.L.)	77	85	.475	3E
—Second half	43	28	.606	1W	2000—Philadelphia (N.L.)	65	97	.401	5E
1994—Birmingham (Sou.)	31	38	.449	4W	2004—Boston (A.L.)	98	64	.605	2E
—Second half	34	36	.486	5W	2005—Boston (A.L.)	95	67	.586	2E
1995—Birmingham (Sou.)	33	39	.458	4W	American League totals (2 years)............	193	131	.596	
—Second half	47	25	.653	2W	National League totals (4 years).............	285	363	.440	
					Major league totals (6 years)................	478	494	.492	

NOTES:
1993—Defeated Nashville, 3-0, in semifinals; defeated Knoxville, 3-1, in league championship. ... **2004**—Defeated Anaheim, 3-0, in A.L. Division Series; defeated New York Yankees, 4-3, in A.L. Championship Series; defeated St. Louis, 4-0, in World Series. ... **2005**—On suspened list (April 29-May 2, 2005); Lost to Chicago White Sox, 3-0, in A.L. Division Series. ... Career major league postseason record: 11-6.

GARDENHIRE, RON — TWINS

PERSONAL: Born October 24, 1957, in Butzbach, West Germany. ... Full name: Ronald Clyde Gardenhire. ... High school: Okmulgee (Okla.) High School. ... Junior college: Paris (Texas). ... College: Texas.

RECORD AS PLAYER

				BATTING									FIELDING		
	G	AB	R	H	2B	3B	HR	RBI	Avg.	BB	SO	SB	PO	A	E	Avg.
Major league totals (5 years)...............	285	710	57	165	27	3	4	49	.232	46	122	13	395	665	47	.958

RECORD AS MANAGER

BACKGROUND: Coach, Minnesota Twins (1991-2001).
HONORS: Named co-A.L. Manager of the Year by THE SPORTING NEWS (2004).

Year Team (League)	W	L	Pct.	Pos	Year Team (League)	W	L	Pct.	Pos
1988—Kenosha (Midw.)	41	27	.603	1N	—Second half	43	29	.597	2E
—Second half	40	32	.556	2N	2002—Minnesota (A.L.)	94	67	.584	1C
1989—Orlando (Sou.)	40	31	.563	1E	2003—Minnesota (A.L.)	90	72	.556	1C
—Second half	39	34	.534	4E	2004—Minnesota (A.L.)	92	70	.568	1C
1990—Orlando (Sou.)	42	30	.583	1E	2005—Minnesota (A.L.)	83	79	.512	3C
					Major league totals (4 years)......................	359	288	.555	

NOTES:
1988—Defeated Rockford, 2-0, in semifinals; lost to Cedar Rapids, 3-1, in league championship. ... **1989**—Lost to Greenville, 3-1, in semifinals. ... **1990**—Defeated Jacksonville, 3-1, in semifinals; lost to Memphis, 3-2, in league championship. ... **2002**—Defeated Oakland, 3-2, in A.L. Division Series; lost to Anaheim, 4-1, in A.L. Championship Series. ... **2003**—Lost to New York Yankees, 3-1, in A.L. Division Series. ... **2004**—Lost to New York Yankees, 3-1, in A.L. Division Series. ... Career major league postseason record: 6-12.

GARNER, PHIL — ASTROS

PERSONAL: Born April 30, 1949, in Jefferson City, Tenn. ... Full name: Philip Mason Garner. ... High school: Beardon (Knoxville, Tenn.). ... College: Tennessee

RECORD AS PLAYER

				BATTING									FIELDING		
	G	AB	R	H	2B	3B	HR	RBI	Avg.	BB	SO	SB	PO	A	E	Avg.
Major league totals (16 years).............	1860	6136	780	1594	299	82	109	738	.260	564	842	225	2746	4356	259	.965

RECORD AS MANAGER

BACKGROUND: Coach, Houston Astros (1989-91).

Year Team (League)	W	L	Pct.	Pos	Year Team (League)	W	L	Pct.	Pos
1992—Milwaukee (A.L.)	92	70	.568	2E	2000—Detroit (A.L.)	79	83	.488	3C
1993—Milwaukee (A.L.)	69	93	.426	7E	2001—Detroit (A.L.)	66	96	.407	4C
1994—Milwaukee (A.L.)	53	62	.461	...	2002—Detroit (A.L.)	0	6	.000	...
1995—Milwaukee (A.L.)	65	79	.451	4C	2004—Houston (N.L.)	48	26	.649	2C
1996—Milwaukee (A.L.)	80	82	.494	3C	2005—Houston (N.L.)	89	73	.549	2C
1997—Milwaukee (A.L.)	78	83	.484	3C	American League totals (9 years)............	582	654	.471	
1998—Milwaukee (N.L.)	74	88	.457	5C	National League totals (4 years).............	263	247	.641	
1999—Milwaukee (N.L.)	52	60	.464	...	Major league totals (13 years)...............	845	901	.484	

NOTES:
1993—On suspended list (September 24-27). ... **1994**—Milwaukee was in fifth place in A.L. Central at time of season-ending strike (August 12). ... **1995**—On suspended list (July 27-31). ... **1999**—Replaced as Milwaukee manager on an interim basis by Joe Lefebvre (August 11). ... **2002**—Replaced as Detroit manager by interim manager Luis Pujols with club in fifth place (April 8). ... **2004**—Replaced Houston manager Jimy Williams on an interim basis with club in fifth place and a record of 44-44 (July 14); on suspended list (August 13); defeated Atlanta, 3-2, in N.L. Division Series; lost to St. Louis, 4-3, in N.L. Championship Series. ... **2005**—Astros tied one game; defeated Atlanta, 3-1, in N.L. Division Series; defeated St. Louis, 4-2, in N.L. Championship Series; lost to Chicago White Sox, 4-0, in World Series. ... Career major league postseason record: 13-13.

GIBBONS, JOHN — BLUE JAYS

PERSONAL: Born June 8, 1962, in Great Falls, Mont. ... Full name: John Michael Gibbons. ... High school: MacArthur (San Antonio).

RECORD AS MANAGER

BACKGROUND: Minor league instructor, New York Mets (1991-93). ... Minor league coach, Mets organization (1994). ... Coach, Toronto Blue Jays (2002-04).

Year Team (League)	W	L	Pct.	Pos	Year Team (League)	W	L	Pct.	Pos
1995—Kingsport (Appal.)	48	18	.727	1S	1999—Norfolk (Int'l)	77	63	.550	3S
1996—St. Lucie (Fla. St.)	32	34	.485	3E	2000—Norfolk (Int'l)	65	79	.451	3S
—Second half	39	28	.582	1E	2001—Norfolk (Int'l)	85	57	.599	1S
1997—St. Lucie (Fla. St.)	28	39	.418	4E	2003—Toronto (A.L.)	3	0	1.000	...
—Second half	26	42	.382	6E	2004—Toronto (A.L.)	20	30	.400	5E
1998—Binghamton (East.)	82	60	.577	2N	2005—Toronto (A.L.)	80	82	.494	3E
					Major league totals (3 years)	103	112	.479	

NOTES:
1995—Defeated Bluefield, 2-1, in league championship. ... **1996**—Defeated Vero Beach, 2-0, in semifinals; defeated Clearwater, 3-1, in league championship. ... **1998**—Lost to New Britain, 3-1, in semifinals. ... **2001**—Lost to Louisville, 3-2, in semifinals. ... **2003**—Managed Toronto on an interim basis for three games (May 2-3 and September 5). ... **2004**—Replaced Toronto manager Carlos Tosca on an interim basis with club in fifth place and a record of 47-64 (August 9).

GIRARDI, JOE — MARLINS

PERSONAL: Born October 14, 1964, in Peoria, Ill. ... 5-11/200. ... Full name: Joseph Elliott Girardi. ... Name pronounced: jeh-RAR-dee. ... High school: Spalding Institute (Peoria, Ill.). ... College: Northwestern.

RECORD AS PLAYER

					BATTING								FIELDING			
	G	AB	R	H	2B	3B	HR	RBI	Avg.	BB	SO	SB	PO	A	E	Avg.
Major league totals (15 years)	1277	4127	454	1100	186	26	36	422	.267	279	607	44	7619	605	77	.991

RECORD AS MANAGER

BACKGROUND: Broadcaster, New York Yankees (2004). ... Coach, New York Yankees (2005).

GUILLEN, OZZIE — WHITE SOX

PERSONAL: Born January 20, 1964, in Ocumare del Tuy, Miranda, Venezuela. ... 5-11/165. ... Full name: Oswaldo Jose Barrios Guillen. ... Name pronounced: GHEE-un.

RECORD AS PLAYER

					BATTING								FIELDING			
	G	AB	R	H	2B	3B	HR	RBI	Avg.	BB	SO	SB	PO	A	E	Avg.
Major league totals (16 years)	1993	6686	773	1764	275	69	28	619	.264	239	511	169	2935	5376	222	.974

RECORD AS MANAGER

BACKGROUND: Coach, Montreal Expos (2001). ... Coach, Florida Marlins (2002-03).
HONORS: Named A.L. Manager of the Year by the SPORTING NEWS (2005). ... Named A.L. Manager of the year by Baseball Writers' Association of America (2005).

Year Team (League)	W	L	Pct.	Pos
2004—Chicago (A.L.)	83	79	.512	2C
2005—Chicago (A.L.)	99	63	.611	1C
Major league totals (2 years)	182	142	.562	

NOTES:
2005—Defeated Boston, 3-0, in A.L. Division Series; Defeated Los Angeles Angels of Anaheim, 4-1, in A.L. Championship Series; Defeated Houston, 4-0, in World Series. ... Career major league postseason record: 11-1.

HARGROVE, MIKE — MARINERS

PERSONAL: Born October 26, 1949, in Perryton, Texas. ... Full name: Dudley Michael Hargrove. ... High school: Perryton (Texas). ... College: Northwestern State (Okla.).

RECORD AS PLAYER

					BATTING								FIELDING			
	G	AB	R	H	2B	3B	HR	RBI	Avg.	BB	SO	SB	PO	A	E	Avg.
Major league totals (12 years)	1666	5564	783	1614	266	28	80	686	.290	965	550	24	11603	1027	123	.990

RECORD AS MANAGER

BACKGROUND: Minor league coach, Cleveland Indians organization (1986). ... Coach, Indians (1990-91). ... Assistant to the general manager, Indians (2004).
HONORS: Named A.L. Manager of the Year by THE SPORTING NEWS (1995).

Year Team (League)	W	L	Pct.	Pos	Year Team (League)	W	L	Pct.	Pos
1987—Kinston (Carol.)	33	37	.471	T3S	1996—Cleveland (A.L.)	99	62	.615	1C
—Second half	42	28	.600	1S	1997—Cleveland (A.L.)	86	75	.534	1C
1988—Williamsport (East.)	66	73	.475	6th	1998—Cleveland (A.L.)	89	73	.549	1C
1989—Colo. Springs (PCL)	44	26	.629	1S	1999—Cleveland (A.L.)	97	65	.599	1C
—Second half	34	38	.472	3S	2000—Baltimore (A.L.)	74	88	.457	4E
1991—Cleveland (A.L.)	32	53	.376	7E	2001—Baltimore (A.L.)	63	98	.391	4E
1992—Cleveland (A.L.)	76	86	.469	4E	2002—Baltimore (A.L.)	67	95	.414	4E
1993—Cleveland (A.L.)	76	86	.469	6E	2003—Baltimore (A.L.)	71	91	.438	4E
1994—Cleveland (A.L.)	66	47	.584	...	2005—Seattle (A.L.)	69	93	.426	4W
1995—Cleveland (A.L.)	100	44	.694	1C	**Major league totals (14 years)**	1065	1056	.501	

NOTES:
1987—Defeated Winston-Salem, 2-0, in playoffs; lost to Salem, 3-1, in league championship. ... **1989**—Lost to Albuquerque, 3-2, in semifinals. ... **1991**—Replaced Cleveland manager John McNamara with club in seventh place and a record of 25-52 (July 6). ... **1994**—Cleveland was in second place in A.L. Central at time of season-ending strike (August 12). ... **1995**—Defeated Boston, 3-0, in A.L. Division Series; defeated Seattle, 4-2, in A.L. Championship Series; lost to Atlanta, 4-2, in World Series. ... **1996**—Lost to Baltimore, 3-1, in A.L. Division Series. ... **1997**—Defeated New York Yankees, 3-2, in A.L. Division Series; defeated Baltimore, 4-2, in A.L. Championship Series; lost to Florida, 4-3, in World Series. ... **1998**—Defeated Boston, 3-1, in A.L. Division Series; lost to New York Yankees, 4-2, in A.L. Championship Series. ... **1999**—Lost to Boston, 3-2, in A.L. Division Series. ... Career major league postseason record: 27-25.

HURDLE, CLINT — ROCKIES

PERSONAL: Born July 30, 1957, in Big Rapids, Mich. ... Full name: Clinton Merrick Hurdle. ... High school: Merritt Island (Fla.).

RECORD AS PLAYER

					BATTING								FIELDING			
	G	AB	R	H	2B	3B	HR	RBI	Avg.	BB	SO	SB	PO	A	E	Avg.
Major league totals (10 years)............	515	1391	162	360	81	12	32	193	.259	176	261	1	1384	96	34	.978

BACKGROUND: Roving hitting instructor, Colorado Rockies (1994-96). ... Coach, Rockies (1997-2002).

RECORD AS MANAGER

Year Team (League)	W	L	Pct.	Pos	Year Team (League)	W	L	Pct.	Pos
1988—St. Lucie (Fla. St.)	36	34	.514	4E	1992—Tidewater (Int'l)	56	86	.394	4W
—Second half	38	31	.551	1E	1993—Norfolk (Int'l)	70	71	.496	4W
1989—St. Lucie (Fla. St.)	42	28	.600	1E	2002—Colorado (N.L.)	67	73	.479	4W
—Second half	37	27	.578	1E	2003—Colorado (N.L.)	74	88	.457	4W
1990—Jackson (Texas)	35	32	.522	2E	2004—Colorado (N.L.)	68	94	.420	4W
—Second half	38	30	.559	1E	2005—Colorado (N.L.)	67	95	.414	5W
1991—Williamsport (East.)	60	79	.432	7th	Major league totals (4 years)......................	276	350	.441	

NOTES:
1988—Defeated Lakeland, 2-1, in first round; defeated Tampa, 2-0, in semifinals; defeated Osceola, 2-0, in league championship. ... **1989**—Lost to Port Charlotte, 2-1, in first round. ... **1990**—Lost to Shreveport, 2-0, in semifinals. ... **2002**—Replaced Buddy Bell as Colorado manager with club in fifth place and a record of 6-16 (April 26).

LA RUSSA, TONY   CARDINALS

PERSONAL: Born October 4, 1944, in Tampa. ... Full name: Anthony La Russa Jr.. ... High school: Jefferson (Tampa). ... College: University of Tampa, then South Florida

RECORD AS PLAYER

					BATTING								FIELDING			
	G	AB	R	H	2B	3B	HR	RBI	Avg.	BB	SO	SB	PO	A	E	Avg.
Major league totals (6 years)	132	176	15	35	5	2	0	7	.199	23	37	0	112	127	10	.960

RECORD AS MANAGER

BACKGROUND: Minor league coach, St. Louis Cardinals organization (1977). ... Coach, Chicago White Sox (1978).
HONORS: Named Major League Manager of the Year by THE SPORTING NEWS (1983). ... Named A.L. Manager of the Year by THE SPORTING NEWS (1988 and 1992). ... Named A.L. Manager of the Year by Baseball Writers' Association of America (1983, 1988 and 1992). ... Named N.L. Manager of the Year by Baseball Writers' Association of America (2002).

Year Team (League)	W	L	Pct.	Pos	Year Team (League)	W	L	Pct.	Pos
1978—Knoxville (Sou.)	49	21	.700	1st	1992—Oakland (A.L.)	96	66	.593	1W
—Second half	4	4	.500	...	1993—Oakland (A.L.)	68	94	.420	7W
1979—Iowa (A.A.)	54	52	.509	2nd	1994—Oakland (A.L.)	51	63	.447	...
—Chicago (A.L.)	27	27	.500	5W	1995—Oakland (A.L.)	67	77	.465	4W
1980—Chicago (A.L.)	70	90	.438	5W	1996—St. Louis (N.L.)	88	74	.543	1C
1981—Chicago (A.L.)	31	22	.585	3W	1997—St. Louis (N.L.)	73	89	.451	4C
—Second half	23	30	.434	6W	1998—St. Louis (N.L.)	83	79	.512	3C
1982—Chicago (A.L.)	87	75	.537	3W	1999—St. Louis (N.L.)	75	86	.466	4C
1983—Chicago (A.L.)	99	63	.611	1W	2000—St. Louis (N.L.)	95	67	.586	1C
1984—Chicago (A.L.)	74	88	.457	5W	2001—St. Louis (N.L.)	93	69	.574	2C
1985—Chicago (A.L.)	85	77	.525	3W	2002—St. Louis (N.L.)	97	65	.599	1C
1986—Chicago (A.L.)	26	38	.406	5W	2003—St. Louis (N.L.)	85	77	.525	3C
—Oakland (A.L.)	45	34	.570	3W	2004—St. Louis (N.L.)	105	57	.648	1C
1987—Oakland (A.L.)	81	81	.500	3W	2005—St. Louis (N.L.)	100	62	.617	1C
1988—Oakland (A.L.)	104	58	.642	1W	**American League totals (17 years)**	1320	1183	.527	
1989—Oakland (A.L.)	99	63	.611	1W	**National League totals (10 years)**............	894	725	.552	
1990—Oakland (A.L.)	103	59	.636	1W	**Major league totals (27 years)**.................	2214	1908	.537	
1991—Oakland (A.L.)	84	78	.519	4W					

NOTES:
1978—Became Chicago White Sox coach and replaced as Knoxville manager by Joe Jones (July 3). ... **1979**—Replaced as Iowa manager by Joe Sparks (August 3); replaced Chicago manager Don Kessinger with club in fifth place and a record of 46-60 (August 3). ... **1983**—Lost to Baltimore, 3-1, in A.L. Championship Series. ... **1985**—On suspended list (August 10-11). ... **1986**—Replaced as White Sox manager by interim manager Doug Rader (June 20); replaced Oakland manager Jackie Moore (record of 29-44) and interim manager Jeff Newman (record of 2-8) with club in seventh place and a record of 31-52 (July 7). ... **1988**—Defeated Boston, 4-0, in A.L. Championship Series; lost to Los Angeles Dodgers, 4-1, in World Series. ... **1989**—Defeated Toronto, 4-1, in A.L. Championship Series; defeated San Francisco, 4-0, in World Series. ... **1990**—Defeated Boston, 4-0, in A.L. Championship Series; lost to Cincinnati, 4-0, in World Series. ... **1992**—Lost to Toronto, 4-2, in A.L. Championship Series. ... **1993**—On suspended list (October 1-remainder of season). ... **1994**—Oakland was in second place in A.L. West at time of season-ending strike (August 12). ... **1996**—Defeated San Diego, 3-0, in N.L. Division Series; lost to Atlanta, 4-3, in N.L. Championship Series. ... **2000**—Defeated Atlanta, 3-0, in N.L. Division Series; lost to New York Mets, 4-1, in N.L. Championship Series. ... **2001**—Lost to Arizona, 3-2, in N.L. Division Series. ... **2002**—Defeated Arizona, 3-0, in N.L. Division Series; lost to San Francisco, 4-1, in N.L. Championship Series. ... **2003**—On suspended list (September 26-27). ... **2004**—Defeated Los Angeles, 3-1, in N.L. Division Series; defeated Houston, 4-3, in N.L. Championship Series; lost to Boston, 4-0, in World Series. ... **2005**—Defeated San Diego, 3-0, in N.L Division Series; Lost to Houston, 4-2, in N.L. Championship Series. ... Career major league postseason record: 48-43.

LEYLAND, JIM   TIGERS

PERSONAL: Born December 15, 1944, in Toledo, Ohio. ... Full name: James Richard Leyland. ... Name pronounced: LEE-lund. ... High school: Perrysburg (Ohio).

RECORD AS PLAYER

					BATTING								FIELDING			
	G	AB	R	H	2B	3B	HR	RBI	Avg.	BB	SO	SB	PO	A	E	Avg.
Career playing record					Did not play in major leagues.											

RECORD AS MANAGER

BACKGROUND: Minor league coach, Detroit Tigers organization (1970-71); served as player/coach (1970). ... Coach, Chicago White Sox (1982-85). ... Special assignment scout, St. Louis Cardinals (2000-2005).
HONORS: Named N.L. co-Manager of the Year by THE SPORTING NEWS (1988). Named N.L. Manager of the Year by THE SPORTING NEWS (1990 and 1992). ... Named N.L. Manager of the Year by Baseball Writers' Association of America (1990 and 1992).

Year—Team (League)	W	L	Pct.	Pos	Year—Team (League)	W	L	Pct.	Pos
1971—Bristol (Appal.)	31	35	.470	3S	1986—Pittsburgh (N.L.)	64	98	.395	6E
1972 Clinton (Midw.)	22	41	.349	5N	1987—Pittsburgh (N.L.)	80	82	.494	T4E
—Second half	27	36	.429	4N	1988—Pittsburgh (N.L.)	85	75	.531	2E
1973—Clinton (Midw.)	36	26	.581	2N	1989—Pittsburgh (N.L.)	74	88	.457	5E
—Second half	37	25	.597	1N	1990—Pittsburgh (N.L.)	95	67	.586	1E
1974—Montgomery (Sou.)	61	76	.445	3W	1991—Pittsburgh (N.L.)	98	64	.605	1E
1975—Clinton (Midw.)	29	31	.483	4S	1992—Pittsburgh (N.L.)	96	66	.593	1E
—Second half	38	30	.559	2S	1993—Pittsburgh (N.L.)	73	84	.465	5E
1976—Lakeland (Fla. St.)	74	64	.536	2N	1994—Pittsburgh (N.L.)	53	61	.465	...
1977—Lakeland (Fla. St.)	85	53	.616	1N	1995—Pittsburgh (N.L.)	58	86	.403	5C
1978—Lakeland (Fla. St.)	31	38	.449	4N	1996—Pittsburgh (N.L.)	73	89	.451	5C
—Second half	47	22	.681	1N	1997—Florida (N.L.)	92	70	.568	2E
1979—Evansville (A.A.)	78	58	.574	1E	1998—Florida (N.L.)	54	108	.333	5E
1980—Evansville (A.A.)	61	74	.452	2E	1999—Colorado (N.L.)	72	90	.444	5W
1981—Evansville (A.A.)	73	63	.537	1E	Major league totals (14 years)	1067	1128	.486	

NOTES:
1973—Lost to Wisconsin Rapids, 2-0, in division playoff. ... **1976**—Defeated Miami, 2-0, in semifinals; defeated Tampa, 2-0, in league championship. ... **1977**—Defeated Miami, 2-0, in semifinals; defeated St. Petersburg, 3-1, in league championship. ... **1978**—Defeated St. Petersburg, 1-0, in North Division playoff; lost to Miami, 2-0, in league championship. ... **1979**—Defeated Oklahoma City, 4-2, in league championship. ... **1981**—Lost to Denver, 3-1, in semifinals. ... **1990**—Lost to Cincinnati, 4-2, in N.L. Championship Series. ... **1991**—Lost to Atlanta, 4-3, in N.L. Championship Series. ... **1992**—Lost to Atlanta, 4-3, in N.L. Championship Series. ... **1993**—On suspended list (August 27-September 1). ... **1994**—Pittsburgh was tied for fourth place in N.L. Central at time of season-ending strike (August 12). ... **1997**—Defeated San Francisco, 3-0, in N.L. Division Series; defeated Atlanta, 4-2, in N.L. Championship Series; defeated Cleveland, 4-3, in World Series. ... Career major league postseason record: 19-17.

MACHA, KEN   ATHLETICS

PERSONAL: Born September 29, 1950, in Monroeville, Pa. ... Full name: Kenneth Edward Macha. ... High school: Gateway (Pittsburgh). ... College: Pittsburgh.

RECORD AS PLAYER

	G	AB	R	H	2B	3B	HR	RBI	Avg.	BB	SO	SB	PO	A	E	Avg.
Major league totals (6 years)	180	380	30	98	16	3	1	35	.258	39	68	4	237	143	13	.967

RECORD AS MANAGER

BACKGROUND: Coach, Montreal Expos (1986-91). ... Coach, California Angels (1992-94). ... Coach, Oakland Athletics (1999-2002).

Year—Team (League)	W	L	Pct.	Pos	Year—Team (League)	W	L	Pct.	Pos
1995—Trenton (East.)	73	69	.514	1S	2003—Oakland (A.L.)	96	66	.593	1W
1996—Trenton (East.)	86	56	.606	1S	2004—Oakland (A.L.)	91	71	.562	2W
1997—Pawtucket (Int'l)	81	60	.574	2E	2005—Oakland (A.L.)	88	74	.543	2W
1998—Pawtucket (Int'l)	77	64	.546	3E	Major league totals (3 years)	275	211	.566	

NOTES:
1995—Lost to Reading, 3-0, in semifinals. ... **1996**—Lost to Harrisburg, 3-2, in semifinals. ... **1997**—Lost to Rochester, 3-1, in semifinals. ... **2003**—Lost to Boston, 3-2, in A.L. Division Series. ... Career postseason record: 2-3.

MADDON, JOE   DEVIL RAYS

PERSONAL: Born February 4, 1954, in Hazelton, Pa. ... Full name: Joseph John Maddon. Name pronounced: Madden. ... High school: Hazelton (Pa.). ... College: Lafayette.

RECORD AS PLAYER

	G	AB	R	H	2B	3B	HR	RBI	Avg.	BB	SO	SB	PO	A	E	Avg.
Career playing record						Did not play in major leagues.										

RECORD AS MANAGER

BACKGROUND: Coordinator, Arizona Instructional League, California Angels (1984-93). ... Roving hitting instructor, Angels (1987-93). ... Minor league field coordinator, Angels (1992-94). ... Director of player development, Angels (1994). ... Coach, Angels (1994-2005).

Year—Team (League)	W	L	Pct.	Pos	Year—Team (League)	W	L	Pct.	Pos
1981—Idaho Falls (Pion.)	27	43	.386	3S	1986—Midland (Texas)	35	30	.538	2W
1982—Salem (N'west)	34	36	.486	1N	—Second half	27	41	.397	4W
1983—Salem (N'west)	31	39	.443	4N	1996—California (A.L.)	8	14	.364	...
1984—Peoria (Midw.)	66	73	.475	2S	1999—Anaheim (A.L.)	19	10	.655	4W
1985—Midland (Texas)	29	37	.439	4W					
—Second half	30	40	.429	3W	Major league totals (2 years)	27	24	.559	

NOTES: 1982—Defeated Medford, 2-0, in league championship. ... **1996**—Replaced California manager Marcel Lachemann (52-59) and interim manager John McNamara (5-9) on an interim basis with club in fourth place and a record of 57-68 (August 21). ... **1999**—Replaced Anaheim manager Terry Collins on an interim basis with club in fourth place and a record of 52-81 (September 3).

MANUEL, CHARLIE   PHILLIES

PERSONAL: Born January 4, 1944, in North Fork, W. Va. ... Full name: Charles Fuqua Manuel. ... High school: Parry McCluer (Buena Vista, W. Va.).

RECORD AS PLAYER

	G	AB	R	H	2B	3B	HR	RBI	Avg.	BB	SO	SB	PO	A	E	Avg.
Major league totals (6 years)	239	384	25	76	12	0	4	43	.198	40	77	1	103	6	3	.973

RECORD AS MANAGER

BACKGROUND: Scout, Minnesota Twins (1982). ... Coach, Cleveland Indians (1988-89 and 1994-99).

Year Team (League)	W	L	Pct.	Pos		Year Team (League)	W	L	Pct.	Pos
1983—Wisconsin (Midw.)	71	67	.518	2N		—Second half	42	26	.617	1S
1984—Orlando (Sou.)	34	35	.493	3E		1992—Colorado Springs (PCL)	36	33	.521	2S
—Second half	45	30	.600	2E		—Second half	48	24	.667	1S
1985—Orlando (Sou.)	29	35	.453	5E		1993—Charlotte (Int'l)	86	55	.610	1W
—Second half	43	36	.544	2E		2000—Cleveland (A.L.)	90	72	.556	2C
1986—Toledo (Int'l)	62	77	.446	6th		2001—Cleveland (A.L.)	91	71	.562	1C
1987—Portland (PCL)	20	49	.290	5N		2002—Cleveland (A.L.)	39	47	.448	...
—Second half	25	47	.347	5N		2005—Philadelphia (N.L.)	88	74	.543	2E
1990—Colo. Springs (PCL)	39	33	.541	3S		**American League totals (3 years)**	220	190	.537	
1991—Colo. Springs (PCL)	30	41	.422	5S		**National League totals (1 year)**	88	74	.543	
						Major league totals (4 years)	308	264	.538	

NOTES:
1984—Lost to Charlotte in one-game playoff. ... **1990**—Replaced Colorado Springs manager Bobby Molinaro (June 22). ... **1991**—Lost to Tuscon, 3-1, in semifinals. ... **1992**—Defeated Las Vegas, 3-2, in semifinals; lost to Vancouver, 3-0, in league championship. ... **1993**—Defeated Richmond, 3-1, in semifinals; defeated Rochester, 3-2, in league championship. ... **2001**—Lost to Seattle, 3-2, in A.L. Division Series. **2002**—Replaced as Cleveland manager on an interim basis by Joel Skinner with club in third place (July 11). ... Career major league postseason record: 2-3.

MELVIN, BOB — DIAMONDBACKS

PERSONAL: Born October 28, 1961, in Palo Alto, Calif. ... Full name: Robert Paul Melvin. ... High school: Menlo-Atherton (Menlo Park, Calif.). ... Junior college: Canada College (Calif.). ... College: California.

RECORD AS PLAYER

				BATTING										FIELDING		
	G	AB	R	H	2B	3B	HR	RBI	Avg.	BB	SO	SB	PO	A	E	Avg.
Major league totals (10 years)	692	1955	174	456	85	6	35	212	.233	98	396	4	2961	253	24	.993

RECORD AS MANAGER

BACKGROUND: Scout, Milwaukee Brewers (1996). ... Roving fielding instructor, Brewers (1997). ... Assistant to the general manager, Brewers (1998). ... Coach, Brewers (1999). ... Coach, Detroit Tigers (2000). ... Coach, Arizona Diamondbacks (2001-02).

Year Team (League)	W	L	Pct.	Pos
2003—Seattle (A.L.)	93	69	.574	2W
2004—Seattle (A.L.)	63	99	.389	4W
2005—Arizona (N.L.)	77	85	.475	2W
American League totals (2 years)	156	168	.481	
National League totals (1 year)	77	85	.475	
Major league totals (3 years)	233	253	.479	

NARRON, JERRY — REDS

PERSONAL: Born January 15, 1956, in Goldsboro, N.C. ... Full name: Jerry Austin Narron. ... High school: Goldsboro (N.C.). ... College: East Carolina. ... Nephew of Sam Narron, catcher with St. Louis Cardinals (1935, 1942-43).

RECORD AS PLAYER

				BATTING										FIELDING		
	G	AB	R	H	2B	3B	HR	RBI	Avg.	BB	SO	SB	PO	A	E	Avg.
Major league totals (8 years)	392	840	64	177	23	2	21	96	.211	67	127	0	1038	80	12	.989

RECORD AS MANAGER

BACKGROUND: Coach, Texas Rangers (1993-2001). ... Coach, Red Sox (2001-02). ... Coach, Cincinnati Reds (2003-05).

Year Team (League)	W	L	Pct.	Pos		Year Team (League)	W	L	Pct.	Pos
1989—Frederick (Carol.)	34	36	.486	2N		2002—Texas (A.L.)	72	90	.444	4W
—Second half	39	29	.574	2N		2005—Cincinnati (N.L.)	46	46	.500	5C
1990—Hagerstown (East.)	67	71	486	6th		**American League totals (2 years)**	134	162	.453	
1991—Hagerstown (East.)	81	59	.579	2nd		**National League totals (1 year)**	46	46	.500	
1992—Rochester (Int'l)	70	74	.486	3E		**Major league totals (3 years)**	180	208	.464	
2001—Texas (A.L.)	62	72	.463	4W						

NOTES:
1991—Lost to Albany, 3-0, in semifinals. ... **2001**—Replaced Texas manager Johnny Oates with club in third place and record of 11-17 (May 4). ... **2005**—Replaced Cincinnati manager Dave Miley on an interim basis with team in sixth place and a record of 27-43 (June 21); Cincinnati played one tie game.

PERLOZZO, SAM — ORIOLES

PERSONAL: Born March 4, 1951, in Cumberland, Md. ... Full name: Samuel Benedict Perlozzo. ... High school: Bishop Walsh (Cumberland, Md.) ... College: George Washington.

RECORD AS PLAYER

				BATTING										FIELDING		
	G	AB	R	H	2B	3B	HR	RBI	Avg.	BB	SO	SB	PO	A	E	Avg.
Major league totals (2 years)	12	26	6	7	0	2	0	0	.269	3	3	0	13	17	1	.968

RECORD AS MANAGER

BACKGROUND: Coach, New York Mets (1987-89); Coach, Cincinnati Reds (1990-92); Coach, Seattle Mariners (1993-95); Coach, Baltimore Orioles (1996-2005).

Year Team (League)	W	L	Pct.	Pos		Year Team (League)	W	L	Pct.	Pos
1982—Little Falls (N.Y.-Penn.)	38	38	.500	3E		1985—Jackson (Texas)	31	35	.470	3E
1983—Lynchburg (Carol.)	49	20	.710	1N		—Second half	42	28	.600	1E
—Second half	47	23	.671	1N		1986—Tidewater (Int'l)	74	66	.529	4th
1984—Jackson (Texas)	43	24	.642	1E		2005—Baltimore (A.L.)	23	32	.418	4E
—Second half	40	29	.580	1E		**Major league totals (1 year)**	23	32	.418	

NOTES: 1983—Defeated Winston-Salem, 3-0, in league championship. ... **1984**—Defeated Beaumont, 4-2, in league championship. ... **1985**—Jackson tied two games; defeated Arkansas, 2-0, in semifinals; defeated El Paso, 4-0, in league championship. ... **1986**—Lost to Richmond, 3-0, in semifinals. ... **2005**—Replaced Baltimore manager Lee Mazzilli on an interim basis with club in fourth place and a record of 51-56 (August 4).

RANDOLPH, WILLIE — METS

PERSONAL: Born July 6, 1954, in Holly Hill, S.C. ... Full name: William Larry Randolph Jr.. ... High school: Tilden (Brooklyn, N.Y.).

RECORD AS PLAYER

	G	AB	R	H	2B	3B	HR	RBI	Avg.	BB	SO	SB	PO	A	E	Avg.
					BATTING									FIELDING		
Major league totals (18 years)..........	2202	8018	1239	2210	316	65	54	687	.276	1243	675	271	4859	6339	237	.979

RECORD AS MANAGER

BACKGROUND: Assistant general manager, New York Yankees (1993). ... Coach, New York Yankees (1994-2004).

Year Team (League)	W	L	Pct.	Pos
2005— New York (N.L.)	83	79	.512	4E
Major league totals (1 year)........................	83	79	.512	

ROBINSON, FRANK — NATIONALS

PERSONAL: Born August 31, 1935, in Beaumont, Texas ... High school: McClymonds (Oakland). ... College: Xavier.

RECORD AS PLAYER

	G	AB	R	H	2B	3B	HR	RBI	Avg.	BB	SO	SB	PO	A	E	Avg.
					BATTING									FIELDING		
Major league totals (21 years).............	2808	10006	1829	2943	528	72	586	1812	.294	1420	1532	204	6346	333	106	.984

RECORD AS MANAGER

BACKGROUND: Player/manager, Indians (1975). ... Coach, California Angels (1977). ... Coach, Baltimore Orioles (1978-80 and 1985-87). ... Coach, Milwaukee Brewers (1984). ... Special assistant to the president, Orioles (1988). ... Assistant general manager, Orioles (1991-95). ... Vice president of on-field operations for Major League Baseball (1999-2001).

HONORS: Named A.L. Manager of the Year by THE SPORTING NEWS (1989).

Year Team (League)	W	L	Pct.	Pos		Year Team (League)	W	L	Pct.	Pos
1975—Cleveland (A.L.)	79	80	.497	4E		1989— Baltimore (A.L.)	87	75	.537	2E
1976—Cleveland (A.L.)	81	78	.509	4E		1990— Baltimore (A.L.)	76	85	.472	5E
1977—Cleveland (A.L.)	26	31	.456	...		1991— Baltimore (A.L.)	13	24	.351	...
1978—Rochester (Int'l)	58	64	.475	6th		2002— Montreal (N.L.)	83	79	.512	2E
1981—San Francisco (N.L.)	27	32	.458	5W		2003— Montreal (N.L.)	83	79	.512	4E
—Second half	29	23	.558	3W		2004— Montreal (N.L.)	67	95	.414	5E
1982—San Francisco (N.L.)	87	75	.537	3W		2005— Washington (N.L.)	81	81	.500	5E
1983—San Francisco (N.L.)	79	83	.488	5W		**American League totals (7 years)**................	416	474	.467	
1984—San Francisco (N.L.)	42	64	.396	...		**National League totals (8 years)**.................	578	611	.486	
1988—Baltimore (A.L.)	54	101	.348	7E		**Major league totals (15 years)**....................	994	1085	.478	

NOTES:
1977—Replaced as Cleveland manager by Jeff Torborg with club in fifth place (June 19). ... **1978**—Replaced Rochester manager Ken Boyer and interim manager Al Widmar (May 8). ... **1984**—Replaced as San Francisco manager by Jim Davenport with club in sixth place (August 4). ... **1988**—Replaced Baltimore manager Cal Ripken with club in seventh place and a record of 0-7 (April 12). ... **1991**—Replaced as Baltimore manager by Johnny Oates with club in seventh place (May 23).... **2005**—On suspended list (June 20-21, 2005).

SCIOSCIA, MIKE — ANGELS

PERSONAL: Born November 27, 1958, in Upper Darby, Pa. ... Full name: Michael Lorri Scioscia. ... Name pronounced: SO-sha. ... High school: Springfield (Pa.). ... College: Penn State.

RECORD AS PLAYER

	G	AB	R	H	2B	3B	HR	RBI	Avg.	BB	SO	SB	PO	A	E	Avg.
					BATTING									FIELDING		
Major league totals (13 years)..........	1441	4373	398	1131	198	12	68	446	.259	567	307	29	8335	737	114	.988

RECORD AS MANAGER

BACKGROUND: Minor league catching coordinator, Dodgers organization (1995-96). ... Coach, Dodgers (1997-98). ... Manager, Peoria Javelinas, Arizona Fall League (1997: record 28-17, first/North; defeated Grand Canyon, 2-1, in league championship).

HONORS: Named A.L. Manager of the Year by THE SPORTING NEWS (2002). ... Named A.L. Manager of the Year by Baseball Writers' Association of America (2002).

Year Team (League)	W	L	Pct.	Pos		Year Team (League)	W	L	Pct.	Pos
1999—Albuquerque (PCL)	65	74	.468	3C		2003—Anaheim (A.L.)	77	85	.475	3W
2000—Anaheim (A.L.)	82	80	.506	3W		2004—Anaheim (A.L.)	92	70	.568	1W
2001—Anaheim (A.L.)	75	87	.463	3W		2005—Los Angeles (A.L.)	95	67	.586	1W
2002—Anaheim (A.L.)	99	63	.611	2W		**Major league totals (6 years)**..................	520	452	.535	

NOTES:
2002—Defeated New York Yankees, 3-1, in A.L. Division Series; defeated Minnesota, 4-1, in A.L. Championship Series; defeated San Francisco, 4-3, in World Series. ... **2004**—Lost to Boston, 3-0, in A.L. Division Series. ... **2005**—Angels franchise renamed Los Angeles Angels of Anaheim for 2005 season; On suspended list (June 17-18, 2005); defeated New York Yankees, 3-2, in A.L. Division Series; Lost to Chicago White Sox, 4-1, in A.L. Championship Series. ... Career major league postseason record: 15-14.

SHOWALTER, BUCK — RANGERS

PERSONAL: Born May 23, 1956, in DeFuniak Springs, Fla. ... Full name: William Nathaniel Showalter III. ... High school: Century (Fla.). ... Junior college: Chipola Junior College (Fla.). ... College: Mississippi State.

RECORD AS PLAYER

	G	AB	R	H	2B	3B	HR	RBI	Avg.	BB	SO	SB	PO	A	E	Avg.
					BATTING									FIELDING		
Career playing record				Did not play in major leagues.												

RECORD AS MANAGER

BACKGROUND: Minor league coach, New York Yankees organization (1984). ... Coach, Yankees (1990-91).
HONORS: Named A.L. Manager of the Year by THE SPORTING NEWS (1994). ... Named A.L. co-Manager of the Year by THE SPORTING NEWS (2004). ... Named A.L. Manager of the Year by Baseball Writers' Association of America (1994 and 2004).

Year Team (League)	W	L	Pct.	Pos
1985— Oneonta (N.Y.-Penn.)	55	23	.705	1N
1986— Oneonta (N.Y.-Penn.)	59	18	.766	1Y
1987— Fort Lauderdale (Fla. St.)	85	53	.616	1S
1988— Fort Lauderdale (Fla. St.)	39	29	.574	3rd
—Second half	30	36	.455	3rd
1989— Albany (East.)	92	48	.657	1st
1992— New York (A.L.)	76	86	.469	4E
1993— New York (A.L.)	88	74	.543	2E
1994— New York (A.L.)	70	43	.619	...
1995— New York (A.L.)	79	65	.549	2E

Year Team (League)	W	L	Pct.	Pos
1998— Arizona (N.L.)	65	97	.401	5W
1999— Arizona (N.L.)	100	62	.617	1W
2000— Arizona (N.L.)	85	77	.525	3W
2003— Texas (A.L.)	71	91	.438	4W
2004— Texas (A.L.)	89	73	.549	3W
2005— Texas (A.L.)	79	83	.488	3W
American League totals (7 years)	552	515	.517	
National League totals (3 years)	250	236	.514	
Major league totals (10 years)	803	751	.517	

NOTES:
1985—Defeated Geneva, 1-0, in semifinals; defeated Auburn, 2-0, in league championship. ... **1986**—Lost to Newark, 1-0, in semifinals. ... **1987**—Defeated Lakeland, 2-0, in semifinals; defeated Osceola, 3-1, in league championship. ... **1989**—Defeated Reading, 3-1, in semifinals; defeated Harrisburg, 3-1, in league championship. ... **1994**—New York was in first place in A.L. East at time of season-ending strike (August 12). ... **1995**—Lost to Seattle, 3-2, in A.L. Division Series. ... **1999**—Lost to New York Mets, 3-1, in N.L. Division Series. ... Career major league postseason record: 3-6.

TORRE, JOE   YANKEES

PERSONAL: Born July 18, 1940, in Brooklyn, N.Y. ... Full name: Joseph Paul Torre. ... Name pronounced: TORE-ee. ... High school: St. Francis Prep (Brooklyn, N.Y.). ... Brother of Frank Torre, first baseman with two major league teams (1956-60, 1962-63).

RECORD AS PLAYER

					BATTING								FIELDING		
	G	AB	R	H	2B	3B	HR	RBI	Avg.	BB	SO	SB	PO	A	E	Avg.
Major league totals (18 years)	2209	7874	996	2342	344	59	252	1185	.297	805	1058	25	11618	1731	163	.988

RECORD AS MANAGER

BACKGROUND: Player/manager, New York Mets (May 31-June 18, 1977).

HONORS: Named Sportsman of the Year by THE SPORTING NEWS (1996). ... Named A.L. Manager of the Year by THE SPORTING NEWS (1998). ... Named co-A.L. Manager of the Year by Baseball Writers' Association of America (1996). ... ... Named A.L. Manager of the Year by Baseball Writers' Association of America (1998).

Year Team (League)	W	L	Pct.	Pos
1977— New York (N.L.)	49	68	.419	6E
1978— New York (N.L.)	66	96	.407	6E
1979— New York (N.L.)	63	99	.389	6E
1980— New York (N.L.)	67	95	.414	5E
1981— New York (N.L.)	17	34	.333	5E
—Second half	24	28	.462	4E
1982— Atlanta (N.L.)	89	73	.549	1W
1983— Atlanta (N.L.)	88	74	.543	2W
1984— Atlanta (N.L.)	80	82	.494	2W
1990— St. Louis (N.L.)	24	34	.414	6E
1991— St. Louis (N.L.)	84	78	.519	2E
1992— St. Louis (N.L.)	83	79	.512	3E
1993— St. Louis (N.L.)	87	75	.537	3E
1994— St. Louis (N.L.)	53	61	.465	...

Year Team (League)	W	L	Pct.	Pos
1995— St. Louis (N.L.)	20	27	.426	...
1996— New York (A.L.)	92	70	.568	1E
1997— New York (A.L.)	96	66	.593	2E
1998— New York (A.L.)	114	48	.704	1E
1999— New York (A.L.)	98	64	.605	1E
2000— New York (A.L.)	87	74	.540	1E
2001— New York (A.L.)	95	65	.594	1E
2002— New York (A.L.)	103	58	.640	1E
2003— New York (A.L.)	101	61	.623	1E
2004— New York (A.L.)	101	61	.623	1E
2005— New York (A.L.)	95	67	.586	1E
American League totals (10 years)	982	634	.608	
National League totals (14 years)	894	1003	.471	
Major league totals (24 years)	1876	1637	.534	

NOTES:
1977—Replaced New York Mets manager Joe Frazier with club in sixth place and record of 15-30 (May 31). ... **1982**—Lost to St. Louis, 3-0, in N.L. Championship Series. ... **1990**—Replaced St. Louis manager Whitey Herzog (33-47) and interim manager Red Schoendienst (13-11) with club in sixth place and a record of 46-58 (August 1). ... **1994**—St. Louis was tied for third place in N.L. Central at time of season-ending strike (August 12). ... **1995**—Replaced as St. Louis manager by interim manager Mike Jorgensen, with club in fourth place (June 16). ... **1996**—Defeated Texas, 3-1, in A.L. Division Series; defeated Baltimore, 4-1, in A.L. Championship Series; defeated Atlanta, 4-2, in World Series. ... **1997**—Lost to Cleveland, 3-2, in A.L. Division Series. ... **1998**—Defeated Texas, 3-0, in A.L. Division Series; defeated Cleveland, 4-2, in A.L. Championship Series; defeated San Diego, 4-0, in World Series. ... **1999**—Defeated Texas, 3-0, in A.L. Division Series; defeated Boston, 4-1, in A.L. Championship Series; defeated Atlanta, 4-0, in World Series. ... **2000**—Defeated Oakland, 3-2, in A.L. Division Series; defeated Seattle, 4-2, in A.L. Championship Series; defeated New York Mets, 4-1, in World Series. ... **2001**—Defeated Oakland, 3-2, in A.L. Division Series; defeated Seattle, 4-1, in A.L. Championship Series; lost to Arizona, 4-3, in World Series. ... **2002**—Lost to Anaheim, 3-1, in A.L. Division Series. ... **2003**—Defeated Minnesota, 3-1, in A.L. Division Series; defeated Boston, 4-3, in A.L. Championship Series; lost to Florida, 4-2, in World Series. ... **2004**—Defeated Minnesota, 3-1, in A.L. Division Series; lost to Boston, 4-3, in A.L. Championship Series ... **2005**—On suspended list (May 31-June 1, 2005); Lost to Los Angeles Angels of Anaheim, 3-2, in A.L. Division Series. ... Career major league postseason record: 74-44.

TRACY, JIM   PIRATES

PERSONAL: Born December 31, 1955, in Hamilton, Ohio. ... Full name: James Edwin Tracy. ... High school: Badin (Hamilton, Ohio). ... College: Marietta College (Ohio).

RECORD AS PLAYER

					BATTING								FIELDING		
	G	AB	R	H	2B	3B	HR	RBI	Avg.	BB	SO	SB	PO	A	E	Avg.
Major league totals (2 years)	87	185	18	46	5	4	3	14	.249	25	51	3	60	0	2	.968

RECORD AS MANAGER

BACKGROUND: Minor league field coordinator, Cincinnati Reds (1992). ... Coach, Montreal Expos (1995-98). ... Coach, Los Angeles Dodgers (1999-2000).

HONORS: Named Minor League Manager of the Year by THE SPORTING NEWS (1993).

Year Team (League)	W	L	Pct.	Pos
1987— Peoria (Midw.)	71	69	.507	2S
1988— Peoria (Midw.)	29	40	.420	6S
—Second half	41	30	.577	3S
1989— Chattanooga (Sou.)	33	38	.465	4S
—Second half	25	43	.368	5S
1990— Chattanooga (Sou.)	35	36	.493	4W
—Second half	31	42	.425	4W
1991— Chattanooga (Sou.)	35	32	.522	2W
—Second half	38	39	.494	3W
1993— Harrisburg (East.)	94	44	.681	1st
1994— Ottawa (Int'l)	70	72	.493	3W

Year Team (League)	W	L	Pct.	Pos
2001— Los Angeles (N.L.)	86	76	.531	3W
2002— Los Angeles (N.L.)	92	70	.568	3W
2003— Los Angeles (N.L.)	85	77	.525	2W
2004— Los Angeles (N.L.)	93	69	.574	1W
2005— Los Angeles (N.L.)	71	91	.438	4W
Major league totals (5 years)	427	383	.527	...

NOTES:
1993—Defeated Albany, 3-1, in semifinals; defeated Canton-Akron, 3-2, in league championship. ... **2004**—Lost to St. Louis, 3-1, in N.L. Division Series. ... Career major league postseason record: 1-3.

WEDGE, ERIC   INDIANS

PERSONAL: Born January 27, 1968, in Fort Wayne, Ind. ... Full name: Eric Michael Wedge. ... High school: Northrop (Fort Wayne, Ind.). ... College: Wichita State.

RECORD AS PLAYER

			BATTING										FIELDING			
	G	AB	R	H	2B	3B	HR	RBI	Avg.	BB	SO	SB	PO	A	E	Avg.
Major league totals (4 years)	39	86	13	20	2	0	5	12	.233	14	25	0	25	3	0	1.000

RECORD AS MANAGER

Year Team (League)	W	L	Pct.	Pos	Year Team (League)	W	L	Pct.	Pos
1998—Columbus (S. Atl.)	28	42	.400	4S	2002—Buffalo (Int'l)	87	57	.604	2N
— Second half	31	39	.443	3S	2003—Cleveland (A.L.)	68	94	.420	4C
1999—Kinston (Carol.)	37	32	.536	1S	2004—Cleveland (A.L.)	80	82	.494	3C
— Second half	42	26	.618	2S	2005—Cleveland (A.L.)	93	69	.574	2C
2000—Akron (East.)	75	68	.524	3S	**Major league totals (3 years)**	241	245	.496	
2001—Buffalo (Int'l)	91	51	.641	1N					

NOTES:
1999—Lost to Myrtle Beach, 2-1, in semifinals. ... **2001**—Lost to Scranton/Wilkes-Barre, 3-2, in semifinals. ... **2002**—Defeated Scranton/Wilkes-Barre, 3-0, in semifinals; lost to Durham, 3-0, in league championship.... **2001**—On suspended list (August 5-6, 2005).

YOST, NED   BREWERS

ERSONAL: Born August 19, 1955, in Eureka, Calif. ... Full name: Edgar Frederick Yost. ... Junior college: Chabot Junior College.

RECORD AS PLAYER

			BATTING										FIELDING			
	G	AB	R	H	2B	3B	HR	RBI	Avg.	BB	SO	SB	PO	A	E	Avg.
Major league totals (6 years)	219	605	54	128	15	4	16	64	.212	21	117	5	843	54	16	.982

RECORD AS MANAGER

BACKGROUND: Coach, Altanta Braves (1991-02).

Year Team (League)	W	L	Pct.	Pos	Year Team (League)	W	L	Pct.	Pos
1988—Sumter (S. Atl.)	29	40	.420	6S	— Second half	35	35	.500	4S
— Second half	35	33	.515	4S	2003—Milwaukee (N.L.)	68	94	.420	5C
1989—Sumter (S. Atl.)	30	40	.429	5S	2004—Milwaukee (N.L.)	67	94	.416	6C
— Second half	30	41	.423	6S	2005—Milwaukee (N.L.)	81	81	.500	3C
1990—Sumter (S. Atl.)	38	34	.528	4S	**Major league totals (3 years)**	216	269	.445	

2005 MANAGERIAL TENDENCIES

OFFENSE

	G	Att.	SB%	Pitchout Rn Mv	2nd SB-CS	3rd SB-CS	Home SB-CS	Dbl Stls	Out Percentage 0	1	2	Sac Bunts Att.	Suc. %	Fav. Inn.	Sqz.	Hit & Run Att.	Suc. %
AL Managers																	
Bell, Buddy, KC	112	48	70.8	1	32-12	2-2	0-0	0	10.4	29.2	60.4	39	82.1	7	3	54	25.9
Francona, Terry, Bos	162	57	78.9	1	42-12	3-0	0-0	0	22.8	24.6	52.6	21	85.7	3	0	37	45.9
Gardenhire, Ron, Min	162	146	69.9	4	85-39	17-4	0-1	4	30.1	35.6	34.2	60	81.7	7	5	105	39.0
Gibbons, John, Tor	162	107	67.3	1	58-32	13-2	1-1	3	14.0	41.1	44.9	30	76.7	8	4	96	37.5
Guillen, Ozzie, CWS	162	204	67.2	7	115-61	21-5	1-1	3	22.1	36.3	41.7	74	83.8	7	6	95	33.7
Hargrove, Mike, Sea	162	149	68.5	3	87-42	13-4	2-1	7	15.4	38.3	46.3	62	71.0	8	2	88	25.0
Macha, Ken, Oak	162	53	58.5	1	29-20	2-1	0-1	0	15.1	34.0	50.9	29	75.9	9	1	43	30.2
Pena, Tony, KC	33	27	48.1	1	13-12	0-1	0-1	0	25.9	33.3	40.7	15	80.0	6	1	21	19.1
Perlozzo, Sam, Bal	55	41	58.5	1	20-15	4-2	0-0	1	14.6	43.9	41.5	24	83.3	7	0	11	18.2
Piniella, Lou, TB	162	200	75.5	13	129-43	22-5	1-1	6	21.0	36.5	42.5	53	75.5	8	0	107	34.6
Schaefer, Bob, KC	17	11	54.5	0	5-5	1-0	0-0	1	18.2	54.5	27.3	3	100.0	3	0	4	0.0
Scioscia, Mike, LAA	162	218	73.9	9	149-47	12-8	0-2	5	22.0	33.5	44.5	60	80.0	8	5	125	36.8
Showalter, Buck, Tex	162	82	81.7	2	61-14	6-1	0-0	1	19.5	35.4	45.1	11	81.8	2	0	56	35.7
Torre, Joe, NYY	162	111	75.7	0	67-20	17-7	0-0	9	25.2	42.3	32.4	42	83.3	8	0	59	49.2
Trammell, Alan, Det	162	94	70.2	6	61-24	5-3	0-1	2	23.4	34.0	42.6	56	89.3	5	2	91	39.6
Wedge, Eric, Cle	162	98	63.3	5	55-30	6-5	1-1	0	18.4	41.8	39.8	54	81.5	1	0	55	21.8
NL Managers																	
Alou, Felipe, SF	162	106	67.0	1	56-30	13-2	2-3	6	17.9	38.7	43.4	110	85.5	3	9	80	36.3
Baker, Dusty, ChC	162	104	62.5	5	60-35	5-3	0-1	0	23.1	33.7	43.3	90	78.9	8	6	87	37.9
Bochy, Bruce, SD	162	143	69.2	7	94-36	4-6	1-2	2	18.9	40.6	40.6	93	87.1	5	2	80	42.5
Cox, Bobby, Atl	162	124	74.2	4	81-31	11-1	0-0	2	22.6	35.5	41.9	104	76.9	5	6	49	32.7
Garner, Phil, Hou	163	159	72.3	11	101-35	12-5	2-4	3	22.0	34.6	43.4	110	83.6	7	17	118	39.8
Hurdle, Clint, Col	162	97	67.0	2	61-26	4-5	0-1	2	12.4	29.9	57.7	118	78.0	4	6	81	28.4
La Russa, Tony, StL	162	119	69.7	3	69-28	13-4	1-4	5	13.4	32.8	53.8	101	83.2	2	22	134	47.0
Mackanin, Pete, Pit	26	19	89.5	0	17-1	0-0	0-1	0	15.8	21.1	63.2	20	65.0	5	1	14	50.0
Manuel, Charlie, Phi	162	143	81.1	1	99-26	17-1	0-0	6	20.3	35.0	44.8	87	80.5	3	1	52	40.4
McClendon, Lloyd, Pit	136	84	66.7	2	47-24	8-2	1-2	3	23.8	35.7	40.5	63	73.0	3	4	59	37.3
McKeon, Jack, Fla	162	134	71.6	7	85-36	11-1	0-1	0	32.1	24.6	43.3	110	86.4	3	3	64	46.9
Melvin, Bob, Ari	162	93	72.0	3	64-21	3-4	0-1	1	21.5	38.7	39.8	91	79.1	3	3	68	41.2
Miley, Dave, Cin	70	45	71.1	1	25-12	7-0	0-1	2	20.0	44.4	35.6	20	70.0	6	3	17	64.7
Narron, Jerry, Cin	93	50	80.0	1	36-6	4-3	0-1	1	32.0	40.0	28.0	46	71.7	5	0	27	33.3
Randolph, Willie, NYM	162	193	79.3	8	121-34	31-6	1-0	7	22.8	39.9	37.3	86	86.0	2	5	85	34.1
Robinson, Frank, Was	162	90	50.0	4	34-36	11-7	0-2	3	14.4	44.4	41.1	119	79.8	3	6	67	34.3
Tracy, Jim, LAD	162	93	62.4	1	54-33	4-2	0-0	2	21.5	34.4	44.1	79	77.2	3	7	65	33.8
Yost, Ned, Mil	162	113	69.9	6	68-30	11-3	0-1	1	24.8	28.3	46.9	92	77.2	8	9	66	39.4

DEFENSE

	G	Pitchout Total	Runners Moving	CS%	Non-PO CS%	IBB	Pct. of Situations	Fav. Score Diff.	Def Subs Total	Favorite Inning	Pos. 1	Pos. 2	Pos. 3
AL Managers													
Bell, Buddy, KC	112	26	3	66.7	43.8	13	2.8	-2	8	9	1b-3	2b-2	3b-1
Francona, Terry, Bos	162	14	3	66.7	23.9	20	2.9	-2	29	7	1b-18	2b-4	rf-4
Gardenhire, Ron, Min	162	16	1	100.0	44.3	35	6.2	-1	22	8	3b-8	2b-7	1b-4
Gibbons, John, Tor	162	45	4	75.0	24.4	22	3.7	-2	31	8	lf-14	rf-9	2b-4
Guillen, Ozzie, CWS	162	16	0	-	19.5	31	4.2	-2	18	9	1b-6	3b-3	lf-3
Hargrove, Mike, Sea	162	39	2	50.0	32.3	22	3.6	0	9	9	lf-3	ss-2	c-1
Macha, Ken, Oak	162	13	3	0.0	19.1	26	4.5	-2	7	8	lf-3	1b-1	2b-1
Pena, Tony, KC	33	4	1	100.0	23.1	11	8.7	-2	0	0	...	...	...
Perlozzo, Sam, Bal	55	8	2	50.0	18.8	2	1.0	0	23	9	c-7	1b-7	lf-4
Piniella, Lou, TB	162	19	4	25.0	40.4	34	5.2	1	47	9	rf-14	cf-9	c-8
Schaefer, Bob, KC	17	4	1	100.0	20.0	2	3.0	0	2	3	1b-1	3b-1	...
Scioscia, Mike, LAA	162	46	10	60.0	36.0	18	2.9	-2	27	7	3b-10	rf-4	c-3
Showalter, Buck, Tex	162	6	4	75.0	25.3	20	3.2	-2	8	6	lf-3	rf-2	
Torre, Joe, NYY	162	55	15	80.0	23.8	12	2.0	-2	41	9	1b-23	cf-14	rf-2
Trammell, Alan, Det	162	11	0	-	45.0	25	4.2	-2	16	9	cf-7	lf-5	ss-2
Wedge, Eric, Cle	162	9	0	-	24.3	17	2.9	-1	14	8	1b-8	rf-3	2b-1

NL Managers	G	Total	Runners Moving	CS%	Non-PO CS%	IBB	Pct. of Situations	Fav. Score Diff.	Total	Favorite Inning	Pos. 1	Pos. 2	Pos. 3
Alou, Felipe, SF	162	14	3	100.0	39.5	35	6.0	-1	21	9	1b-5	lf-4	2b-3
Baker, Dusty, ChC	162	71	10	40.0	30.0	37	6.0	-2	12	9	ss-3	lf-3	cf-2
Bochy, Bruce, SD	162	19	3	33.3	20.7	38	5.9	-1	29	8	lf-17	ss-4	cf-3
Cox, Bobby, Atl	162	12	4	25.0	28.9	37	5.8	-2	13	5	3b-5	c-3	ss-2
Garner, Phil, Hou	163	10	1	100.0	36.1	23	3.9	-1	21	9	2b-8	lf-6	c-2
Hurdle, Clint, Col	162	22	6	50.0	25.6	46	6.4	0	18	8	c-6	rf-4	cf-3
La Russa, Tony, StL	162	9	3	33.3	51.6	21	3.6	-2	26	8	3b-8	lf-8	c-2
Mackanin, Pete, Pit	26	3	1	100.0	36.4	4	3.3	0	1	5	cf-1	...	...
Manuel, Charlie, Phi	162	11	2	0.0	24.5	35	5.7	-2	9	9	cf-4	c-2	1b-2
McClendon, Lloyd, Pit	136	38	6	66.7	32.4	40	8.5	4	9	9	c-3	lf-2	cf-2
McKeon, Jack, Fla	162	16	1	100.0	23.9	43	6.9	-2	15	9	1b-4	lf-4	c-2
Melvin, Bob, Ari	162	32	8	25.0	26.5	28	4.3	-1	19	9	cf-9	ss-4	c-2
Miley, Dave, Cin	70	7	0	-	30.2	15	5.7	-2	1	3	2b-1	...	...
Narron, Jerry, Cin	93	10	3	100.0	29.2	15	4.0	-1	5	8	2b-2	lf-2	ss-1
Randolph, Willie, NYM	162	17	3	0.0	19.4	31	4.8	0	34	9	c-18	1b-5	rf-5
Robinson, Frank, Was	162	4	1	0.0	35.3	57	9.4	-1	24	7	2b-5	lf-5	1b-4
Tracy, Jim, LAD	162	19	9	55.6	18.7	25	3.6	-2	27	8	rf-8	lf-6	3b-4
Yost, Ned, Mil	162	52	5	40.0	27.8	38	5.8	-2	17	8	ss-6	1b-4	rf-3

LINEUPS

	G	Lineups Used	%LHB vs. RHSP	%RHB vs. LHSP	#PH	Percent PH Platoon	PH BA	PH HR	#PR	PR SB-CS
AL Managers										
Bell, Buddy, KC	112	93	53.3	76.0	97	72.2	.183	1	18	2-1
Francona, Terry, Bos	162	105	63.6	74.9	110	73.6	.202	1	46	0-1
Gardenhire, Ron, Min	162	135	48.2	79.6	104	72.1	.259	2	45	0-0
Gibbons, John, Tor	162	124	58.5	85.1	148	72.3	.306	3	11	0-0
Guillen, Ozzie, CWS	162	112	37.0	88.9	100	84.0	.205	2	32	5-3
Hargrove, Mike, Sea	162	97	44.3	70.3	125	89.6	.214	1	24	2-0
Macha, Ken, Oak	162	127	59.8	66.4	83	86.7	.157	0	17	0-1
Pena, Tony, KC	33	33	47.6	80.6	23	91.3	.048	0	4	1-0
Perlozzo, Sam, Bal	55	47	43.1	88.9	28	85.7	.130	0	23	2-2
Piniella, Lou, TB	162	135	43.5	77.4	127	73.2	.309	4	18	3-2
Schaefer, Bob, KC	17	15	49.1	75.6	13	69.2	.167	0	3	0-0
Scioscia, Mike, LAA	162	124	64.5	65.3	92	73.9	.234	1	37	1-2
Showalter, Buck, Tex	162	98	49.6	89.2	57	80.7	.241	3	22	1-0
Torre, Joe, NYY	162	117	63.4	64.2	94	91.5	.244	2	65	8-0
Trammell, Alan, Det	162	119	32.3	95.8	75	54.7	.266	0	26	0-0
Wedge, Eric, Cle	162	111	60.1	79.3	88	85.2	.213	0	18	0-0
NL Managers										
Alou, Felipe, SF	162	139	45.2	95.7	242	54.5	.252	3	33	2-2
Baker, Dusty, ChC	162	121	50.1	75.6	240	74.2	.195	2	21	1-1
Bochy, Bruce, SD	162	129	46.8	77.3	285	78.6	.209	4	31	4-1
Cox, Bobby, Atl	162	110	58.8	88.3	247	71.3	.226	3	54	1-2
Garner, Phil, Hou	163	101	26.9	95.1	251	74.5	.252	3	40	5-2
Hurdle, Clint, Col	162	135	48.8	81.7	273	77.3	.224	4	21	1-1
La Russa, Tony, StL	162	138	38.9	84.6	270	70.7	.226	6	25	2-1
Mackanin, Pete, Pit	26	24	38.9	76.4	54	75.9	.133	0	1	0-0
Manuel, Charlie, Phi	162	78	59.3	71.3	265	83.0	.233	4	36	1-0
McClendon, Lloyd, Pit	136	123	46.1	74.3	218	78.4	.212	1	8	1-0
McKeon, Jack, Fla	162	82	33.1	74.8	246	57.7	.273	4	24	2-0
Melvin, Bob, Ari	162	119	61.4	70.2	310	85.8	.231	9	26	1-0
Miley, Dave, Cin	70	55	53.1	71.1	104	74.0	.260	4	10	0-0
Narron, Jerry, Cin	93	72	50.6	71.4	156	75.0	.218	4	9	1-0
Randolph, Willie, NYM	162	105	55.4	82.9	222	84.7	.291	5	10	1-0
Robinson, Frank, Was	162	121	52.4	76.3	266	73.3	.199	2	48	3-2
Tracy, Jim, LAD	162	129	51.5	86.8	303	69.3	.231	4	31	0-0
Yost, Ned, Mil	162	99	31.1	81.8	259	60.6	.245	6	18	7-2

DEFENSE

	G	STARTERS					RELIEVERS					
		Slow Hooks	Quick Hooks	> 120 Pitches	> 140 Pitches	3 Days Rest	Relief App	Mid-Inning Change	Save > 1 IP	1st Batter Platoon Pct	1-Batter App	3 Pit. (<=2run)
AL Managers												
Bell, Buddy, KC	112	12	23	0	0	0	310	120	4	52.1	11	17
Francona, Terry, Bos	162	19	14	3	0	1	442	184	3	61.3	46	28
Gardenhire, Ron, Min	162	4	13	0	0	0	396	112	1	60.9	20	29
Gibbons, John, Tor	162	6	26	1	0	3	432	195	12	62.5	20	25
Guillen, Ozzie, CWS	162	15	11	3	0	0	412	198	5	68.3	41	35
Hargrove, Mike, Sea	162	20	17	1	0	1	433	192	1	64.8	44	22
Macha, Ken, Oak	162	7	15	4	0	0	410	179	13	63.7	39	38
Pena, Tony, KC	33	2	4	0	0	0	88	44	0	63.6	4	5
Perlozzo, Sam, Bal	55	5	13	0	0	2	180	84	2	67.2	21	12
Piniella, Lou, TB	162	17	21	9	0	3	401	186	10	65.3	29	20
Schaefer, Bob, KC	17	4	2	0	0	1	46	18	0	50.0	2	1
Scioscia, Mike, LAA	162	12	15	1	0	4	379	115	9	57.6	17	37
Showalter, Buck, Tex	162	15	28	2	0	0	455	209	8	65.6	24	22
Torre, Joe, NYY	162	16	16	8	0	1	418	179	7	65.7	36	24
Trammell, Alan, Det	162	19	10	0	0	2	425	170	2	70.8	46	25
Wedge, Eric, Cle	162	10	16	0	0	0	409	147	3	64.1	37	34
NL Managers												
Alou, Felipe, SF	162	8	22	7	0	0	511	201	6	59.7	62	33
Baker, Dusty, ChC	162	12	20	10	0	0	457	157	2	63.0	42	31
Bochy, Bruce, SD	162	10	20	2	0	0	456	137	1	49.3	19	35
Cox, Bobby, Atl	162	8	34	1	0	6	484	138	7	54.9	45	41
Garner, Phil, Hou	163	13	19	5	0	0	434	127	3	59.9	36	46
Hurdle, Clint, Col	162	21	21	1	0	1	459	133	2	58.4	24	28
La Russa, Tony, StL	162	14	12	1	0	1	436	182	4	66.7	67	28
Mackanin, Pete, Pit	26	1	8	0	0	1	94	38	0	55.9	4	4
Manuel, Charlie, Phi	162	9	24	3	0	0	442	108	6	48.9	22	32
McClendon, Lloyd, Pit	136	12	17	2	0	2	357	108	5	62.2	20	28
McKeon, Jack, Fla	162	10	29	4	0	1	449	138	7	54.9	23	29
Melvin, Bob, Ari	162	15	14	3	0	1	458	156	11	61.1	36	30
Miley, Dave, Cin	70	8	13	1	0	1	204	58	1	59.6	8	6
Narron, Jerry, Cin	93	6	5	1	0	1	287	96	5	63.1	26	15
Randolph, Willie, NYM	162	7	14	4	0	0	393	125	5	63.5	29	26
Robinson, Frank, Was	162	11	25	16	2	9	470	159	3	61.0	48	35
Tracy, Jim, LAD	162	5	25	6	0	0	459	141	2	54.5	48	17
Yost, Ned, Mil	162	6	17	4	0	1	395	128	2	53.4	16	33

One of the things about baseball which appeals to many of us is the game's endless opportunity for analysis. . . and few things are analyzed more than managerial decisions. Major league skippers may not have batting averages and slugging percentages to point to at the end of the season, but when it comes time to judge their performance and production, there's no reason we can't take a look at their statistics.

Which manager posted the best stolen-base success rate?

Which skippers were constantly tinkering with their lineups?

Which managers wore out a path to the pitching mound?

It's questions like these that get our second-guessing juices going, and it's questions like these that inspired the proceeding pages, which look at managerial tendencies in a number of situations. Once again, the skippers are compared based on offense, defense, lineups and pitching use. We don't rank the managers; there is plenty of room for argument on whether certain moves are good or bad. We are simply providing fodder for the discussion.

Offensively, managers have control over bunting, stealing and the timing of hit-and-runs. This section looks at the quantity, timing and success of these moves.

Defensively, this section looks at the success of pitchouts, the frequency of intentional walks, and the pattern of defensive substitutions.

Most managers spend large amounts of their time devising lineups. Here you'll find the number of lineups used, as well as the platoon percentage. The use of pinch-hitters and pinch-runners also is explored.

Finally, how does the manager use pitchers? For starters, this section shows slow and quick hooks, along with the number of times a starter was allowed to throw more than 120 and 140 pitches. For relievers, we look at the number of relief appearances, mid-inning changes and how often a pitcher gets a save going more than one inning (a rare occurrence these days).

For the purposes of this section, it is assumed that a coach filling in for his manager will make his decisions based on what the manager would do in a given situation.

The categories include:

Stolen Base Success Percentage: Stolen bases divided by attempts.

Pitchout Runners Moving: The number of times the opposition is running when a manager calls a pitchout.

Double Steals: The number of double steals attempted in 2004.

Out Percentage: The proportion of stolen bases with that number of outs.

Sacrifice Bunt Attempts: A bunt is considered a sac attempt if no runner is on third, there are no outs, or the pitcher attempts a bunt.

Sacrifice Bunt Success %: A bunt that results in a sacrifice or a hit, divided by the number of attempts.

Favorite Inning: The most common inning in which an event occurred.

Hit-and-Run Success: The hit-and-run results in baserunner advancement with no double play.

Intentional Walk Situation: Runners on base, first base open, and anyone but the pitcher up. The teams must be within two runs of each other, or the tying run must be on base, at bat or on deck.

Defensive Substitutions: Straight defensive substitutions, with the team leading by four runs or less.

Number of Lineups: Based on batting order, 1-8 for National Leaguers, 1-9 for American Leaguers.

Percent LHB vs. RHSP and RHB vs. LHSP: A measure of platooning. A batter is considered to always have the platoon advantage if he is a switch-hitter.

Percent PH platoon: Frequency the manager gets his pinch-hitter the platoon advantage. Switch-hitters always have the advantage.

Score Diff: The most common score differential on which an intentional walk is called for.

Slow and Quick Hooks: A quick hook is the removal of a pitcher who has pitched fewer than six innings and given up three runs or less. A slow hook occurs when a pitcher pitches more than nine innings, or allows seven or more runs, or whose combined innings pitched and runs allowed totals 13 or more.

Mid-Inning Change: The number of times a manager changed pitchers in the middle of an inning.

1-Batter Appearances: The number of times a pitcher was brought in to face only one batter. Called the "Tony La Russa special" because of his penchant for trying to orchestrate specific matchups for specific situations.

3 Pitchers (2 runs or less): The club gives up two runs or less in a game, but uses at least three pitchers.

2005 STATISTICAL LEADERS

2006 BASEBALL REGISTER & FANTASY HANDBOOK

2005 AMERICAN LEAGUE LEADERS

AMERICAN LEAGUE BATTING LEADERS

BATTING AVERAGE
minimum 502 PA

Player,Team	AB	H	AVG
M Young, Tex	668	221	.331
A Rodriguez, NYY	605	194	.321
V Guerrero, LAA	520	165	.317
J Damon, Bos	624	197	.316
B Roberts, Bal	561	176	.314
D Jeter, NYY	654	202	.309
V Martinez, Cle	547	167	.305
H Matsui, NYY	629	192	.305
T Hafner, Cle	486	148	.305
M Tejada, Bal	654	199	.304

ON-BASE PERCENTAGE
minimum 502 PA; * AB + BB + HBP + SF

Player,Team	*PA	OB	OBP
J Giambi, NYY	545	240	.440
A Rodriguez, NYY	715	301	.421
T Hafner, Cle	578	236	.408
D Ortiz, Bos	713	283	.397
V Guerrero, LAA	594	234	.394
D Jeter, NYY	745	290	.389
M Ramirez, Bos	650	252	.388
B Roberts, Bal	635	246	.387
M Young, Tex	732	282	.385
M Teixeira, Tex	730	277	.379

SLUGGING PERCENTAGE
minimum 502 PA

Player,Team	AB	TB	SLG
A Rodriguez, NYY	605	369	.610
D Ortiz, Bos	601	363	.604
T Hafner, Cle	486	289	.595
M Ramirez, Bos	554	329	.594
M Teixeira, Tex	644	370	.575
V Guerrero, LAA	520	294	.565
R Sexson, Sea	558	302	.541
J Giambi, NYY	417	223	.535
P Konerko, CWS	575	307	.534
J Peralta, Cle	504	262	.520

GAMES
R Ibanez, Sea	162
H Matsui, NYY	162
A Rodriguez, NYY	162
I Suzuki, Sea	162
M Teixeira, Tex	162
M Tejada, Bal	162

PLATE APPEARANCES
D Jeter, NYY	752
I Suzuki, Sea	739
M Young, Tex	732
M Teixeira, Tex	730
C Figgins, LAA	720

AT-BATS
I Suzuki, Sea	679
M Young, Tex	668
D Jeter, NYY	654
M Tejada, Bal	654
H Blalock, Tex	647

HITS
M Young, Tex	221
I Suzuki, Sea	206
D Jeter, NYY	202
M Tejada, Bal	199
J Damon, Bos	197

SINGLES
I Suzuki, Sea	158
D Jeter, NYY	153
M Young, Tex	152
J Damon, Bos	146
C Figgins, LAA	143

DOUBLES
M Tejada, Bal	50
H Matsui, NYY	45
B Roberts, Bal	45
A Soriano, Tex	43
2 tied with	42

TRIPLES
C Crawford, TB	15
I Suzuki, Sea	12
G Sizemore, Cle	11
C Figgins, LAA	10
B Inge, Det	9

HOME RUNS
A Rodriguez, NYY	48
D Ortiz, Bos	47
M Ramirez, Bos	45
M Teixeira, Tex	43
P Konerko, CWS	40

TOTAL BASES
M Teixeira, Tex	370
A Rodriguez, NYY	369
D Ortiz, Bos	363
M Young, Tex	343
M Tejada, Bal	337

RUNS SCORED
A Rodriguez, NYY	124
D Jeter, NYY	122
D Ortiz, Bos	119
J Damon, Bos	117
M Young, Tex	114

RUNS BATTED IN
D Ortiz, Bos	148
M Ramirez, Bos	144
M Teixeira, Tex	144
A Rodriguez, NYY	130
G Sheffield, NYY	123

GDP
J Kendall, Oak	26
M Tejada, Bal	26
J Cantu, TB	24
S Hatteberg, Oak	22
B Mueller, Bos	22

SACRIFICE HITS
C Crisp, Cle	13
N Logan, Det	12
T Iguchi, CWS	11
J Uribe, CWS	11
2 tied with	10

SACRIFICE FLIES
C Monroe, Det	12
C Everett, CWS	10
J Uribe, CWS	10
3 tied with	9

STOLEN BASES
C Figgins, LAA	62
S Podsednik, CWS	59
C Crawford, TB	46
J Lugo, TB	39
I Suzuki, Sea	33

CAUGHT STEALING
S Podsednik, CWS	23
C Figgins, LAA	17
J Lugo, TB	11
J Reed, Sea	11
2 tied with	10

WALKS
J Giambi, NYY	108
D Ortiz, Bos	102
A Rodriguez, NYY	91
R Sexson, Sea	89
P Konerko, CWS	81

INTENTIONAL WALKS
V Guerrero, LAA	26
I Suzuki, Sea	23
A Huff, TB	13
J Jones, Min	12
J Mauer, Min	12

HIT BY PITCH
S Hillenbrand, Tor	22
A Rowand, CWS	21
J Kendall, Oak	20
J Giambi, NYY	19
3 tied with	16

STRIKEOUTS
R Sexson, Sea	167
B Inge, Det	140
A Rodriguez, NYY	139
H Blalock, Tex	132
G Sizemore, Cle	132

SCORING POSITION AVG
minimum 100 PA

Player,Team	AB	H	AVG.
F Catalanotto, Tor	88	36	.409
M Young, Tex	136	50	.368
M Teixeira, Tex	161	59	.366
G Sheffield, NYY	162	59	.364
R White, Det	99	36	.364
M Ramirez, Bos	159	57	.358
D Ortiz, Bos	162	57	.352
M Kotsay, Oak	127	44	.346
J Kendall, Oak	128	44	.344
V Guerrero, LAA	130	44	.338

LEADOFF OBP
minimum 150 PA; * AB + BB + HBP + SF

Player,Team	PA*	OB	OBP
D Jeter, NYY	726	284	.391
B Roberts, Bal	632	243	.384
P Polanco, Det	230	88	.383
B Inge, Det	345	128	.371
J Damon, Bos	684	251	.367
J Lugo, TB	246	90	.366
R Johnson, Tor	227	83	.366
C Figgins, LAA	585	208	.356
G Sizemore, Cle	589	208	.353
D DeJesus, KC	352	124	.352

CLEANUP SLG
minimum 150 PA

Player,Team	AB	TB	SLG
M Ramirez, Bos	438	268	.612
V Guerrero, LAA	191	114	.597
T Hafner, Cle	321	189	.589
P Konerko, CWS	549	304	.554
A Rodriguez, NYY	329	182	.553
R Sexson, Sea	554	300	.542
E Chavez, Oak	409	217	.531
V Martinez, Cle	183	92	.503
M Tejada, Bal	259	124	.479
R White, Det	193	91	.472

AVG VS. LHP
minimum 125 PA

B Molina, LAA	.393
G Sheffield, NYY	.359
H Matsui, NYY	.354
I Suzuki, Sea	.352
V Wells, Tor	.347

AVG VS. RHP
minimum 377 PA

B Roberts, Bal	.332
M Young, Tex	.328
A Rodriguez, NYY	.327
C Crawford, TB	.326
C Crisp, Cle	.324

AVG AT HOME
minimum 251 PA

D Jeter, NYY	.354
A Rodriguez, NYY	.351
J Damon, Bos	.334
M Teixeira, Tex	.334
M Young, Tex	.331

AVG ON THE ROAD
minimum 251 PA

M Ellis, Oak	.335
R Cano, NYY	.335
M Young, Tex	.330
B Roberts, Bal	.325
G Sizemore, Cle	.324

OBP VS. LHP
minimum 125 PA

R Sexson, Sea	.458
G Sheffield, NYY	.436
B Molina, LAA	.430
J Giambi, NYY	.418
J Varitek, Bos	.418

OBP VS. RHP
minimum 377 PA

A Rodriguez, NYY	.423
T Hafner, Cle	.423
D Ortiz, Bos	.413
J Mauer, Min	.411
B Roberts, Bal	.404

LATE & CLOSE
minimum 50 PA

V Guerrero, LAA	.408
V Martinez, Cle	.372
M Kotsay, Oak	.360
A Kennedy, LAA	.351
2 tied with	.346

BASES LOADED
minimum 10 PA

R Johnson, Tor	.625
R Adams, Tor	.600
B Mueller, Bos	.526
R Sexson, Sea	.500
H Matsui, NYY	.474

SLG VS. LHP
minimum 125 PA

V Wells, Tor	.673
G Sheffield, NYY	.673
R Sexson, Sea	.659
B Molina, LAA	.648
M LeCroy, Min	.621

SLG VS. RHP
minimum 377 PA

D Ortiz, Bos	.641
T Hafner, Cle	.639
M Ramirez, Bos	.622
A Rodriguez, NYY	.622
M Teixeira, Tex	.603

AB PER HR
minimum 502 PA

M Ramirez, Bos	12.3
A Rodriguez, NYY	12.6
D Ortiz, Bos	12.8
J Giambi, NYY	13.0
R Sexson, Sea	14.3

TIMES ON BASE

A Rodriguez, NYY	301
D Jeter, NYY	290
D Ortiz, Bos	283
M Young, Tex	282
M Teixeira, Tex	277

PITCHES SEEN

D Jeter, NYY	2875
D Ortiz, Bos	2848
C Figgins, LAA	2813
A Rodriguez, NYY	2794
B Inge, Det	2774

PITCHES PER PA
minimum 502 PA

C Blake, Cle	4.28
G Zaun, Tor	4.25
D Dellucci, Tex	4.22
J Giambi, NYY	4.20
T Hafner, Cle	4.16

% PITCHES TAKEN
minimum 1500 pitches

J Giambi, NYY	64.9
S Hatteberg, Oak	62.8
J Kendall, Oak	62.7
S Podsednik, CWS	62.0
D Johnson, Oak	61.5

GROUND/FLY RATIO
minimum 502 PA

D Jeter, NYY	2.69
J Jones, Min	2.53
J Mauer, Min	2.11
S Podsednik, CWS	2.08
I Suzuki, Sea	2.06

GDP/GDP OPP
minimum 50 PA

B Broussard, Cle	0.04
J Damon, Bos	0.05
M Bellhorn, Bos-NYY	0.05
R Adams, Tor	0.05
I Suzuki, Sea	0.05

SB SUCCESS %
minimum 20 SB attempts

A Soriano, Tex	93.8
O Cabrera, LAA	91.3
C Crawford, TB	85.2
T Womack, NYY	84.4
A Kennedy, LAA	82.6

STEALS OF THIRD

S Podsednik, CWS	17
J Lugo, TB	12
D Jeter, NYY	9
B Roberts, Bal	9
C Crawford, TB	7

% CS BY CATCHERS
minimum 70 SB attempts

T Hall, TB	37.8
J Buck, KC	31.0
J Posada, NYY	28.0
V Martinez, Cle	20.7
A Pierzynski, CWS	20.2

†**Scoring-Position Average** denotes batting average when a runner is at second and/or third base. **Leadoff OBP** denotes OBP for a player batting in the first position of the batting order. **Cleanup Slugging** denotes slugging percentage for a player batting in the fourth position of the batting order. **Late & Close Avg.** refers to batting average when the game is in the seventh inning or later and the batting team is either leading by one run, tied, or has the potential tying run on base, at bat or on deck (a batting situation coming close to a pitcher's save situation). **Ground/Fly Ratio** denotes ground balls hit divided by fly balls hit. All batted balls except line drives and bunts are included. **GDP/GDP Opp.** denotes the ratio of times grounding into double plays per opportunities to do so (any situation with a runner on first and less than two out).

AMERICAN LEAGUE PITCHING LEADERS

EARNED RUN AVERAGE
minimum 162 IP

Player,Team	IP	ER	ERA
K Millwood, Cle	192.0	61	2.86
J Santana, Min	231.2	74	2.87
M Buehrle, CWS	236.2	82	3.12
J Washburn, LAA	177.1	63	3.20
C Silva, Min	188.1	72	3.44
J Lackey, LAA	209.0	80	3.44
K Rogers, Tex	195.1	75	3.46
B Colon, LAA	222.2	86	3.48
J Garland, CWS	221.0	86	3.50
J Blanton, Oak	201.1	79	3.53

WON-LOST PERCENTAGE
minimum 15 decisions

Pitcher,Team	W	L	Pct
C Lee, Cle	18	5	.783
R Halladay, Tor	12	4	.750
J Lackey, LAA	14	5	.737
B Colon, LAA	21	8	.724
J Crain, Min	12	5	.706
J Santana, Min	16	7	.696
M Clement, Bos	13	6	.684
J Contreras, CWS	15	7	.682
D Wells, Bos	15	7	.682
R Johnson, NYY	17	8	.680

OPPOSITION AVG
minimum 162 IP

Pitcher,Team	AB	H	AVG
J Santana, Min	856	180	.210
B Zito, Oak	836	185	.221
J Contreras, CWS	763	177	.232
J Blanton, Oak	754	178	.236
R Johnson, NYY	851	207	.243
T Wakefield, Bos	857	210	.245
B Chen, Bal	754	187	.248
S Kazmir, TB	693	172	.248
K Millwood, Cle	733	182	.248
C Sabathia, Cle	745	185	.248

GAMES
M Timlin, Bos	81
S Schoeneweis, Tor	80
T Gordon, NYY	79
B Howry, Cle	79
S Shields, LAA	78

WINS
B Colon, LAA	21
J Garland, CWS	18
C Lee, Cle	18
R Johnson, NYY	17
3 tied with	16

HITS ALLOWED
M Buehrle, CWS	240
J Towers, Tor	237
M Maroth, Det	235
Z Greinke, KC	233
J Johnson, Det	233

BATTERS FACED
M Buehrle, CWS	971
B Zito, Oak	953
F Garcia, CWS	943
T Wakefield, Bos	943
R Johnson, NYY	920

WALKS ALLOWED
S Kazmir, TB	100
B Zito, Oak	89
D Cabrera, Bal	87
J Contreras, CWS	75
G Meche, Sea	72

GAMES STARTED
R Lopez, Bal	35
B Zito, Oak	35
5 tied with	34

LOSSES
Z Greinke, KC	17
J Lima, KC	16
N Robertson, Det	16
R Franklin, Sea	15
J Westbrook, Cle	15

DOUBLES ALLOWED
J Lima, KC	58
B Arroyo, Bos	56
M Hendrickson, TB	56
R Lopez, Bal	52
Z Greinke, KC	48

INNINGS PITCHED
M Buehrle, CWS	236.2
J Santana, Min	231.2
B Zito, Oak	228.1
F Garcia, CWS	228.0
R Johnson, NYY	225.2

HIT BATSMEN
C Fossum, TB	18
M Clement, Bos	16
B Arroyo, Bos	14
3 tied with	13

COMPLETE GAMES
R Halladay, Tor	5
J Bonderman, Det	4
R Johnson, NYY	4
6 tied with	3

SAVES
F Rodriguez, LAA	45
B Wickman, Cle	45
J Nathan, Min	43
M Rivera, NYY	43
D Baez, TB	41

TRIPLES ALLOWED
B Arroyo, Bos	8
J Bonderman, Det	7
Z Greinke, KC	7
N Robertson, Det	7
5 tied with	6

RUNS ALLOWED
J Lima, KC	140
M Hendrickson, TB	126
R Lopez, Bal	126
Z Greinke, KC	125
M Maroth, Det	123

WILD PITCHES
J Contreras, CWS	20
F Garcia, CWS	20
J Lackey, LAA	18
J Johnson, Det	17
M Clement, Bos	13

GAMES FINISHED
M Rivera, NYY	67
D Baez, TB	64
M Batista, Tor	62
B Ryan, Bal	61
F Cordero, Tex	60

SHUTOUTS
J Garland, CWS	3
R Halladay, Tor	2
M Mussina, NYY	2
J Santana, Min	2
14 tied with	1

HOME RUNS ALLOWED
T Wakefield, Bos	35
B Chen, Bal	33
B Radke, Min	33
S Elarton, Cle	32
R Johnson, NYY	32

STRIKEOUTS
J Santana, Min	238
R Johnson, NYY	211
J Lackey, LAA	199
S Kazmir, TB	174
B Zito, Oak	171

BALKS
D Carrasco, KC	3
S Kline, Bal	3
9 tied with	2

SAVES

Player,Team	Saves
F Rodriguez, LAA	45
B Wickman, Cle	45
J Nathan, Min	43
M Rivera, NYY	43
D Baez, TB	41
F Cordero, Tex	37
E Guardado, Sea	36
B Ryan, Bal	36
D Hermanson, CWS	34
M Batista, Tor	31

SAVE PERCENTAGE
minimum 20 SvOp

Player,Team	OPP.	SV.	PCT.
M Rivera, NYY	47	43	91.5
B Wickman, Cle	50	45	90.0
F Rodriguez, LAA	50	45	90.0
J Nathan, Min	48	43	89.6
E Guardado, Sea	41	36	87.8
B Ryan, Bal	41	36	87.8
D Hermanson, CWS	39	34	87.2
H Street, Oak	27	23	85.2
M MacDougal, KC	25	21	84.0
D Baez, TB	49	41	83.7

RELIEF ERA
minimum 50 relief IP

Player,Team	IP	ER	ERA
M Rivera, NYY	78.1	12	1.38
H Street, Oak	78.1	15	1.72
N Cotts, CWS	60.1	13	1.94
C Politte, CWS	67.1	15	2.00
D Hermanson, CWS	57.1	13	2.04
J Duchscherer, Oak	85.2	21	2.21
M Timlin, Bos	80.1	20	2.24
B Ryan, Bal	70.1	19	2.43
J Rincon, Min	77.0	21	2.45
B Howry, Cle	73.0	20	2.47

RELIEF WINS

J Crain, Min	12
S Shields, LAA	10
B Donnelly, LAA	9
6 tied with	7

RELIEF GAMES

M Timlin, Bos	81
S Schoeneweis, Tor	80
T Gordon, NYY	79
B Howry, Cle	79
S Shields, LAA	78

OPPOSITION AVG
minimum 50 relief IP

M Rivera, NYY	177
N Cotts, CWS	179
C Politte, CWS	181
J Nathan, Min	183
F Rodriguez, LAA	184

AVG VS. LHB
minimum 50 relief IP

J Nathan, Min	158
J Speier, Tor	167
M Rivera, NYY	177
B Howry, Cle	180
C Politte, CWS	182

RELIEF LOSSES

S Shields, LAA	11
M Batista, Tor	8
T Harper, TB	6
M MacDougal, KC	6
J Rincon, Min	6

GAMES FINISHED

M Rivera, NYY	67
D Baez, TB	64
M Batista, Tor	62
B Ryan, Bal	61
F Cordero, Tex	60

OPPOSITION OBP
minimum 50 relief IP

M Rivera, NYY	235
B Howry, Cle	237
J Nathan, Min	247
C Politte, CWS	254
J Speier, Tor	254

AVG VS. RHB
minimum 50 relief IP

F Rodriguez, LAA	153
N Cotts, CWS	155
K Calero, Oak	162
H Street, Oak	172
M Rivera, NYY	176

HOLDS

T Gordon, NYY	33
S Shields, LAA	33
B Howry, Cle	29
J Rincon, Min	25
M Timlin, Bos	24

RELIEF INNINGS

S Shields, LAA	91.2
J Duchscherer, Oak	85.2
J Mateo, Sea	83.1
T Gordon, NYY	80.2
M Timlin, Bos	80.1

OPPOSITION SLG
minimum 50 relief IP

M Rivera, NYY	230
N Cotts, CWS	241
H Street, Oak	267
J Rincon, Min	274
B Howry, Cle	277

AVG RUNNERS ON
minimum 50 relief IP

B Wickman, Cle	149
C Politte, CWS	165
F Rodriguez, LAA	173
B Ryan, Bal	181
D Hermanson, CWS	183

BLOWN SAVES

D Baez, TB	8
M Batista, Tor	8
F Cordero, Tex	8
T Gordon, NYY	7
M Timlin, Bos	7

% INH RUNNERS SCORED
minimum 30 inherited runners

V Chulk, Tor	10.8
R Rincon, Oak	13.9
J Frasor, Tor	15.0
S Sauerbeck, Cle	15.6
2 tied with	18.2

1ST BATTER AVG
minimum 40 first BFP

M Rivera, NYY	092
N Cotts, CWS	119
K Farnsworth, Det	146
D Riske, Cle	151
S Sauerbeck, Cle	163

AVG ALLOWED SCPOS
minimum 50 relief IP

B Wickman, Cle	094
C Politte, CWS	154
J Nathan, Min	158
F Rodriguez, LAA	161
B Ryan, Bal	167

PITCHES PER BATTER
minimum 50 relief IP

T Mulholland, Min	3.30
J Crain, Min	3.33
M Timlin, Bos	3.42
S Schoeneweis, Tor	3.48
K Yabu, Oak	3.49

†**Holds** denote the number of times a relief pitcher enters the game in a save situation, records at least one out and leaves the game never having relinquished the lead. A pitcher cannot finish the game and receive credit for a hold, nor can he earn a hold and a save in the same game. **Blown Saves** denote the number of times a relief pitcher enters a game in a save situation and allows the tying or go-ahead run to score. **Pct. Inherited Scored** denotes the percent of inherited runners (those on base when a reliever enters the game) that score. **Avg., Runners On** denotes batting average allowed when runners are on base. **Avg., Scoring Pos.** denotes batting average allowed when a runner is at second and/or third base. **Easy Saves** denote saves in which the first batter faced doesn't represent the tying run and the reliever pitches one inning or less. **Regular Saves** denote those saves that are not Easy Saves or Tough Saves. **Tough Saves** denote saves which occur after the reliever enters with the tying run anywhere on base.

BASERUNNERS PER 9 IP
minimum 162 IP

Player,Team	IP	BR	BR/9
J Santana, Min	231.2	226	8.78
B Colon, LAA	222.2	261	10.55
R Johnson, NYY	225.2	266	10.61
C Silva, Min	188.1	224	10.70
M Buehrle, CWS	236.2	284	10.80
J Garland, CWS	221.0	266	10.83
B Radke, Min	200.2	244	10.94
C Lee, Cle	202.0	246	10.96
P Byrd, LAA	204.1	251	11.06
K Millwood, Cle	192.0	238	11.16

STRIKEOUTS PER 9 IP
minimum 162 IP

Player,Team	IP	SO	SO/9
J Santana, Min	231.2	238	9.25
J Lackey, LAA	209.0	199	8.57
S Kazmir, TB	186.0	174	8.42
R Johnson, NYY	225.2	211	8.42
C Young, Tex	164.2	137	7.49
C Sabathia, Cle	196.2	161	7.37
M Mussina, NYY	179.2	142	7.11
C Fossum, TB	162.2	128	7.08
J Bonderman, Det	189.0	145	6.90
M Clement, Bos	191.0	146	6.88

RUN SUPPORT PER 9 IP
minimum 162 IP

Player,Team	IP	R	R/9
D Wells, Bos	184.0	163	7.97
C Young, Tex	164.2	134	7.32
M Clement, Bos	191.0	146	6.88
C Lee, Cle	202.0	145	6.46
G Chacin, Tor	203.0	140	6.21
K Rogers, Tex	195.1	134	6.17
B Colon, LAA	222.2	149	6.02
F Garcia, CWS	228.0	151	5.96
M Hendrickson, TB	178.1	118	5.96
D Haren, Oak	217.0	143	5.93

OPPOSITION OBP
minimum 162 IP

J Santana, Min	.250
R Johnson, NYY	.291
B Colon, LAA	.291
M Buehrle, CWS	.295
B Radke, Min	.295

OPPOSITION SLG
minimum 162 IP

J Santana, Min	.346
B Zito, Oak	.361
J Lackey, LAA	.362
J Contreras, CWS	.372
C Sabathia, Cle	.373

HITS PER 9 IP
minimum 162 IP

J Santana, Min	6.99
B Zito, Oak	7.29
J Contreras, CWS	7.78
J Blanton, Oak	7.96
R Johnson, NYY	8.26

HOME RUNS PER 9 IP
minimum 162 IP

J Lackey, LAA	0.56
S Kazmir, TB	0.58
K Rogers, Tex	0.69
M Buehrle, CWS	0.76
J Westbrook, Cle	0.81

AVG VS. LHB
minimum 125 BFP

J Nathan, Min	.158
S Kazmir, TB	.174
M Rivera, NYY	.177
R Harden, Oak	.179
F Hernandez, Sea	.182

AVG VS. RHB
minimum 225 BFP

D Cabrera, Bal	.174
S McClung, TB	.197
J Santana, Min	.200
C Young, Tex	.220
R Harden, Oak	.221

AVG ALLOWED SCPOS
minimum 125 BFP

K Millwood, Cle	.194
F Garcia, CWS	.197
M Wood, KC	.214
J Contreras, CWS	.221
B Zito, Oak	.222

OBP LEAD OFF INNING
minimum 150 BFP

J Santana, Min	.237
J Blanton, Oak	.246
T Wakefield, Bos	.252
C Sabathia, Cle	.270
J Lackey, LAA	.278

K/BB RATIO
minimum 162 IP

C Silva, Min	7.89
J Santana, Min	5.29
D Wells, Bos	5.10
B Radke, Min	5.09
R Johnson, NYY	4.49

GRD/FLY RATIO OFF
minimum 162 IP

J Westbrook, Cle	3.13
J Johnson, Det	1.74
F Garcia, CWS	1.60
N Robertson, Det	1.59
C Silva, Min	1.55

PITCHES PER START
minimum 30 games started

B Zito, Oak	108.7
J Lackey, LAA	105.7
M Buehrle, CWS	105.4
J Garland, CWS	103.6
S Kazmir, TB	103.1

PITCHES PER BATTER
minimum 162 IP

C Silva, Min	3.06
J Towers, Tor	3.37
J Johnson, Det	3.38
N Robertson, Det	3.46
P Byrd, LAA	3.47

STEALS ALLOWED

K Millwood, Cle	33
J Contreras, CWS	28
J Moyer, Sea	27
R Johnson, NYY	23
2 tied with	22

CAUGHT STEALING OFF

R Johnson, NYY	14
M Maroth, Det	12
G Chacin, Tor	10
S Kazmir, TB	9
4 tied with	8

SB% ALLOWED
minimum 162 IP

J Washburn, LAA	0.0
M Maroth, Det	25.0
4 tied with	33.3

PICKOFFS

M Maroth, Det	11
M Buehrle, CWS	5
G Chacin, Tor	5
M Hendrickson, TB	5
5 tied with	4

PKOF THROW/RUNNER
minimum 162 IP

B Chen, Bal	0.93
J Garland, CWS	0.76
M Maroth, Det	0.75
R Lopez, Bal	0.69
N Robertson, Det	0.61

GDP INDUCED

C Silva, Min	34
M Buehrle, CWS	29
D Haren, Oak	26
5 tied with	25

GDP PER 9 IP
minimum 162 IP

C Silva, Min	1.6
J Washburn, LAA	1.2
J Pineiro, Sea	1.2
K Lohse, Min	1.2
K Rogers, Tex	1.2

QUALITY STARTS

J Santana, Min	24
6 tied with	22

†**Run Support per 9 IP** denotes the number of runs scored by a pitcher's team while he was still in the game times nine divided by his innings pitched. **Avg. Allowed Sc. Pos.** denotes batting average allowed when a runner is at second and/or third base. **Grd/Fly Ratio Off** denotes ground balls allowed divided by fly balls allowed. All batted balls except line drives and bunts are included. **PkOf Throw/Runner** denotes the number of pickoff throws made by a pitcher divided by the number of runners on first base. **Quality Starts** denote the number of outings in which a starting pitcher works at least six innings and allows three or fewer earned runs.

2005 NATIONAL LEAGUE LEADERS

NATIONAL LEAGUE BATTING LEADERS

BATTING AVERAGE
minimum 502 PA

Player,Team	AB	H	AVG
D Lee, ChC	594	199	.335
A Pujols, StL	591	195	.330
M Cabrera, Fla	613	198	.323
T Helton, Col	509	163	.320
S Casey, Cin	529	165	.312
C Tracy, Ari	503	155	.308
M Holliday, Col	479	147	.307
D Wright, NYM	575	176	.306
J Bay, Pit	599	183	.306
B Clark, Mil	599	183	.306

ON-BASE PERCENTAGE
minimum 502 PA; * AB + BB + HBP + SF

Player,Team	PA*	OB	OBP
T Helton, Col	625	278	.445
A Pujols, StL	700	301	.430
B Giles, SD	674	285	.423
D Lee, ChC	691	289	.418
L Berkman, Hou	565	232	.411
N Johnson, Was	547	223	.408
B Abreu, Phi	719	291	.405
J Bay, Pit	707	284	.402
C Delgado, Fla	616	246	.399
L Castillo, Fla	506	198	.391

SLUGGING PERCENTAGE
minimum 502 PA

Player,Team	AB	TB	SLG
D Lee, ChC	594	393	.662
A Pujols, StL	591	360	.609
C Delgado, Fla	521	303	.582
K Griffey Jr., Cin	491	283	.576
A Jones, Atl	586	337	.575
A Ramirez, ChC	463	263	.568
M Cabrera, Fla	613	344	.561
J Bay, Pit	599	335	.559
M Ensberg, Hou	526	293	.557
C Tracy, Ari	503	278	.553

GAMES

B Abreu, Phi	162
J Bay, Pit	162
C Lee, Mil	162
J Pierre, Fla	162
2 tied with	161

PLATE APPEARANCES

J Reyes, NYM	733
J Rollins, Phi	732
B Abreu, Phi	719
J Pierre, Fla	719
D Eckstein, StL	713

AT-BATS

J Reyes, NYM	696
J Rollins, Phi	677
J Pierre, Fla	656
D Eckstein, StL	630
C Lee, Mil	618

HITS

D Lee, ChC	199
M Cabrera, Fla	198
J Rollins, Phi	196
A Pujols, StL	195
J Reyes, NYM	190

SINGLES

W Taveras, Hou	152
J Pierre, Fla	147
D Eckstein, StL	144
J Reyes, NYM	142
B Clark, Mil	138

DOUBLES

D Lee, ChC	50
M Giles, Atl	45
T Helton, Col	45
J Bay, Pit	44
2 tied with	43

TRIPLES

J Reyes, NYM	17
J Pierre, Fla	13
R Furcal, Atl	11
J Rollins, Phi	11
D Roberts, SD	10

HOME RUNS

A Jones, Atl	51
D Lee, ChC	46
A Pujols, StL	41
A Dunn, Cin	40
T Glaus, Ari	37

TOTAL BASES

D Lee, ChC	393
A Pujols, StL	360
M Cabrera, Fla	344
A Jones, Atl	337
J Bay, Pit	335

RUNS SCORED

A Pujols, StL	129
D Lee, ChC	120
J Rollins, Phi	115
J Bay, Pit	110
A Dunn, Cin	107

RUNS BATTED IN

A Jones, Atl	128
P Burrell, Phi	117
A Pujols, StL	117
M Cabrera, Fla	116
C Delgado, Fla	115

GDP

S Casey, Cin	27
D Bell, Phi	24
N Perez, ChC	22
M Cabrera, Fla	20
P Feliz, SF	20

SACRIFICE HITS

O Vizquel, SF	20
L Castillo, Fla	18
A Pettitte, Hou	15
L Hernandez, Was	14
2 tied with	13

SACRIFICE FLIES

C Lee, Mil	11
J Guillen, Was	9
M Lowell, Fla	9
5 tied with	8

STOLEN BASES

J Reyes, NYM	60
J Pierre, Fla	57
R Furcal, Atl	46
J Rollins, Phi	41
R Freel, Cin	36

CAUGHT STEALING

J Pierre, Fla	17
J Reyes, NYM	15
B Clark, Mil	13
D Roberts, SD	12
W Taveras, Hou	11

WALKS

B Giles, SD	119
B Abreu, Phi	117
A Dunn, Cin	114
T Helton, Col	106
P Burrell, Phi	99

INTENTIONAL WALKS

A Pujols, StL	27
D Lee, ChC	23
T Helton, Col	22
C Delgado, Fla	20
B Abreu, Phi	15

HIT BY PITCH

J Guillen, Was	19
G Jenkins, Mil	19
B Clark, Mil	18
C Biggio, Hou	17
C Delgado, Fla	17

STRIKEOUTS

A Dunn, Cin	168
P Burrell, Phi	160
P Wilson, Col-Was	148
B Wilkerson, Was	147
T Glaus, Ari	145

SCORING POSITION AVG
minimum 100 PA

Player,Team	AB	H	AVG.
S Taguchi, StL	91	37	.407
D Eckstein, StL	126	47	.373
J Kent, LAD	134	49	.366
B Giles, SD	136	49	.360
J Bay, Pit	153	53	.346
R Aurilia, Cin	108	37	.343
O Saenz, LAD	93	31	.333
J Encarnacion, Fla	151	50	.331
D Lee, ChC	124	41	.331
O Vizquel, SF	124	41	.331

LEADOFF OBP
minimum 150 PA; * AB + BB + HBP + SF

Player,Team	PA*	OB	OBP
F Sanchez, Pit	164	64	.390
R Winn, SF	212	81	.382
B Clark, Mil	666	248	.372
R Freel, Cin	407	151	.371
M Lawton, Pit-ChC	451	165	.366
D Eckstein, StL	703	256	.364
B Wilkerson, Was	626	221	.353
D Roberts, SD	460	162	.352
C Counsell, Ari	659	231	.351
R Furcal, Atl	683	238	.348

CLEANUP SLG
minimum 150 PA

Player,Team	AB	TB	SLG
T Clark, Ari	140	97	.693
M Cabrera, Fla	291	189	.649
M Ensberg, Hou	265	159	.600
K Griffey Jr., Cin	227	135	.595
A Jones, Atl	407	238	.585
C Delgado, Fla	288	165	.573
A Ramirez, ChC	253	144	.569
J Guillen, Was	250	140	.560
M Holliday, Col	242	129	.533
N Johnson, Was	168	87	.518

AVG VS. LHP
minimum 125 PA

D Bell, Phi	.400
L Gonzalez, Col	.380
A Ramirez, ChC	.355
J Bay, Pit	.347
B Hall, Mil	.336

AVG VS. RHP
minimum 377 PA

T Helton, Col	.353
A Pujols, StL	.340
D Lee, ChC	.336
M Cabrera, Fla	.329
C Delgado, Fla	.326

AVG AT HOME
minimum 251 PA

M Holliday, Col	.357
T Helton, Col	.353
G Atkins, Col	.339
W Taveras, Hou	.330
D Lee, ChC	.328

AVG ON THE ROAD
minimum 251 PA

A Pujols, StL	.349
D Lee, ChC	.342
M Cabrera, Fla	.341
J Bay, Pit	.337
B Giles, SD	.333

OBP VS. LHP
minimum 125 PA

D Bell, Phi	.461
J Bay, Pit	.444
N Johnson, Was	.444
P Burrell, Phi	.442
D Lee, ChC	.439

OBP VS. RHP
minimum 377 PA

T Helton, Col	.480
A Pujols, StL	.432
B Giles, SD	.431
C Delgado, Fla	.431
B Abreu, Phi	.430

LATE & CLOSE
minimum 50 PA

R Hernandez, SD	.448
D Lee, ChC	.414
T Clark, Ari	.397
C Jones, Atl	.397
O Robles, LAD	.384

BASES LOADED
minimum 10 PA

J Pierre, Fla	.625
F Lopez, Cin	.600
A Nunez, StL	.600
R Church, Was	.571
J Guillen, Was	.556

SLG VS. LHP
minimum 125 PA

A Ramirez, ChC	.694
D Lee, ChC	.673
M Barrett, ChC	.624
J Bay, Pit	.620
D Wright, NYM	.602

SLG VS. RHP
minimum 377 PA

D Lee, ChC	.658
A Pujols, StL	.633
T Helton, Col	.630
C Delgado, Fla	.626
A Jones, Atl	.588

AB PER HR
minimum 502 PA

A Jones, Atl	11.5
D Lee, ChC	12.9
A Dunn, Cin	13.6
K Griffey Jr., Cin	14.0
A Pujols, StL	14.4

TIMES ON BASE

A Pujols, StL	301
B Abreu, Phi	291
D Lee, ChC	289
B Giles, SD	285
J Bay, Pit	284

PITCHES SEEN

B Abreu, Phi	3159
D Eckstein, StL	2859
P Burrell, Phi	2855
A Dunn, Cin	2848
D Lee, ChC	2786

PITCHES PER PA
minimum 502 PA

B Abreu, Phi	4.39
P Burrell, Phi	4.27
A Dunn, Cin	4.24
B Wilkerson, Was	4.21
J Edmonds, StL	4.17

% PITCHES TAKEN
minimum 1500 pitches

B Abreu, Phi	66.5
B Giles, SD	66.0
O Robles, LAD	64.9
D Roberts, SD	64.4
C Counsell, Ari	63.8

GROUND/FLY RATIO
minimum 502 PA

L Castillo, Fla	3.42
R Clayton, Ari	2.69
J Pierre, Fla	2.46
W Taveras, Hou	1.85
M Lawton, Pit-ChC	1.84

GDP/GDP OPP
minimum 50 PA

P Nevin, SD	0.03
R Langerhans, Atl	0.04
K Lofton, Phi	0.04
A Dunn, Cin	0.04
D Mohr, Col	0.04

SB SUCCESS %
minimum 20 SB attempts

J Bay, Pit	95.5
K Lofton, Phi	88.0
J Rollins, Phi	87.2
R Furcal, Atl	82.1
J Reyes, NYM	80.0

STEALS OF THIRD

J Rollins, Phi	13
J Reyes, NYM	11
R Freel, Cin	8
J Pierre, Fla	8
3 tied with	6

% CS BY CATCHERS
minimum 70 SB attempts

B Schneider, Was	37.7
M Matheny, SF	32.3
J LaRue, Cin	30.1
J Estrada, Atl	26.6
R Hernandez, SD	25.7

†**Scoring-Position Average** denotes batting average when a runner is at second and/or third base. **Leadoff OBP** denotes OBP for a player batting in the first position of the batting order. **Cleanup Slugging** denotes slugging percentage for a player batting in the fourth position of the batting order. **Late & Close Avg.** refers to batting average when the game is in the seventh inning or later and the batting team is either leading by one run, tied, or has the potential tying run on base, at bat or on deck (a batting situation coming close to a pitcher's save situation). **Ground/Fly Ratio** denotes ground balls hit divided by fly balls hit. All batted balls except line drives and bunts are included. **GDP/GDP Opp.** denotes the ratio of times grounding into double plays per opportunities to do so (any situation with a runner on first and less than two out).

EARNED RUN AVERAGE
minimum 162 IP

Player,Team	IP	ER	ERA
R Clemens, Hou	211.1	44	1.87
A Pettitte, Hou	222.1	59	2.39
D Willis, Fla	236.1	69	2.63
P Martinez, NYM	217.0	68	2.82
C Carpenter, StL	241.2	76	2.83
J Peavy, SD	203.0	65	2.88
R Oswalt, Hou	241.2	79	2.94
J Smoltz, Atl	229.2	78	3.06
J Patterson, Was	198.1	69	3.13
C Zambrano, ChC	223.1	81	3.26

WON-LOST PERCENTAGE
minimum 15 decisions

Pitcher,Team	W	L	Pct
J Sosa, Atl	13	3	.813
C Carpenter, StL	21	5	.808
C Zambrano, ChC	14	6	.700
D Willis, Fla	22	10	.688
A Eaton, SD	11	5	.688
M Mulder, StL	16	8	.667
J Smoltz, Atl	14	7	.667
A Pettitte, Hou	17	9	.654
J Beckett, Fla	15	8	.652
P Martinez, NYM	15	8	.652

OPPOSITION AVG
minimum 162 IP

Pitcher,Team	AB	H	AVG
R Clemens, Hou	761	151	.198
P Martinez, NYM	781	159	.204
C Zambrano, ChC	801	170	.212
J Peavy, SD	746	162	.217
M Prior, ChC	630	143	.227
A Pettitte, Hou	817	188	.230
C Carpenter, StL	884	204	.231
J Patterson, Was	738	172	.233
J Beckett, Fla	653	153	.234
D Davis, Mil	835	196	.235

GAMES

S Eyre, SF	86
G Majewski, Was	79
D Sanchez, LAD	79
4 tied with	78

WINS

D Willis, Fla	22
C Carpenter, StL	21
R Oswalt, Hou	20
C Capuano, Mil	18
2 tied with	17

HITS ALLOWED

L Hernandez, Was	268
R Oswalt, Hou	243
G Maddux, ChC	239
E Milton, Cin	237
B Webb, Ari	229

BATTERS FACED

L Hernandez, Was	1065
R Oswalt, Hou	1002
D Willis, Fla	960
C Carpenter, StL	953
C Capuano, Mil	949

WALKS ALLOWED

K Wells, Pit	99
D Davis, Mil	93
C Capuano, Mil	91
C Zambrano, ChC	86
J Schmidt, SF	85

GAMES STARTED

C Capuano, Mil	35
D Davis, Mil	35
L Hernandez, Was	35
J Lieber, Phi	35
D Lowe, LAD	35
G Maddux, ChC	35
R Oswalt, Hou	35

LOSSES

K Wells, Pit	18
J Wright, Col	16
7 tied with	15

DOUBLES ALLOWED

E Milton, Cin	55
A Harang, Cin	52
J Wright, Col	51
3 tied with	50

INNINGS PITCHED

L Hernandez, Was	246.1
C Carpenter, StL	241.2
R Oswalt, Hou	241.2
D Willis, Fla	236.1
J Smoltz, Atl	229.2

HIT BATSMEN

J Weaver, LAD	18
J Wright, Col	15
V Zambrano, NYM	15
B Kim, Col	14
L Hernandez, Was	13

COMPLETE GAMES

C Carpenter, StL	7
D Willis, Fla	7
A Burnett, Fla	4
P Martinez, NYM	4
R Oswalt, Hou	4

SAVES

C Cordero, Was	47
T Hoffman, SD	43
B Lidge, Hou	42
T Jones, Fla	40
2 tied with	39

TRIPLES ALLOWED

B Tomko, SF	10
D Willis, Fla	9
A Harang, Cin	8
R Ortiz, Ari	8
R Oswalt, Hou	8

RUNS ALLOWED

E Milton, Cin	141
J Francis, Col	119
J Wright, Col	119
L Hernandez, Was	116
K Wells, Pit	116

WILD PITCHES

B Webb, Ari	14
A Burnett, Fla	12
B Kim, Col	11
J Marquis, StL	10
3 tied with	9

GAMES FINISHED

B Wagner, Phi	70
B Lidge, Hou	65
C Cordero, Was	62
D Turnbow, Mil	62
2 tied with	55

SHUTOUTS

D Willis, Fla	5
C Carpenter, StL	4
J Peavy, SD	3
4 tied with	2

HOME RUNS ALLOWED

E Milton, Cin	40
J Vazquez, Ari	35
J Weaver, LAD	35
R Ortiz, Cin	34
J Lieber, Phi	33

STRIKEOUTS

J Peavy, SD	216
C Carpenter, StL	213
D Davis, Mil	208
P Martinez, NYM	208
B Myers, Phi	208

BALKS

C Capuano, Mil	4
B Myers, Phi	4
J Marquis, StL	3
M Redman, Pit	3
W Rodriguez, Hou	3

SAVES

Player,Team	Saves
C Cordero, Was	47
T Hoffman, SD	43
B Lidge, Hou	42
T Jones, Fla	40
J Isringhausen, StL	39
D Turnbow, Mil	39
B Wagner, Phi	38
R Dempster, ChC	33
B Fuentes, Col	31
B Looper, NYM	28

SAVE PERCENTAGE
minimum 20 SvOp

Player,Team	OPP.	SV.	PCT.
R Dempster, ChC	35	33	94.3
T Hoffman, SD	46	43	93.5
B Wagner, Phi	41	38	92.7
B Lidge, Hou	46	42	91.3
B Fuentes, Col	34	31	91.2
J Isringhausen, StL	43	39	90.7
D Turnbow, Mil	43	39	90.7
T Jones, Fla	45	40	88.9
C Cordero, Was	54	47	87.0
A Benitez, SF	23	19	82.6

RELIEF ERA
minimum 50 relief IP

Player,Team	IP	ER	ERA
B Wagner, Phi	77.2	13	1.51
D Turnbow, Mil	67.1	13	1.74
C Cordero, Was	74.1	15	1.82
S Linebrink, SD	73.2	15	1.83
R Dempster, ChC	58.1	12	1.85
H Carrasco, Was	61.2	14	2.04
T Jones, Fla	73.0	17	2.10
J Isringhausen, StL	59.0	14	2.14
A Reyes, StL	62.2	15	2.15
A Heilman, NYM	66.0	16	2.18

RELIEF WINS

L Ayala, Was	8
R Hernandez, NYM	8
S Linebrink, SD	8
5 tied with	7

RELIEF GAMES

S Eyre, SF	86
G Majewski, Was	79
D Sanchez, LAD	79
4 tied with	78

OPPOSITION AVG
minimum 50 relief IP

M Wise, Mil	160
B Wagner, Phi	165
A Reyes, StL	177
A Fultz, Phi	186
U Urbina, Phi	186

AVG VS. LHB
minimum 50 relief IP

B Wagner, Phi	128
M Wise, Mil	130
J Fassero, SF	149
M Gonzalez, Pit	152
C Hammond, SD	164

RELIEF LOSSES

Y Brazoban, LAD	10
L Hawkins, ChC-SF	8
D Kolb, Atl	8
J Mesa, Pit	8
A Otsuka, SD	8

GAMES FINISHED

B Wagner, Phi	70
B Lidge, Hou	65
C Cordero, Was	62
D Turnbow, Mil	62
2 tied with	55

OPPOSITION OBP
minimum 50 relief IP

B Wagner, Phi	229
C Cordero, Was	248
M Wise, Mil	249
A Reyes, StL	261
D Wheeler, Hou	265

AVG VS. RHB
minimum 50 relief IP

D Turnbow, Mil	167
A Fultz, Phi	170
A Reyes, StL	172
B Wagner, Phi	173
T Hoffman, SD	179

HOLDS

S Eyre, SF	32
R Madson, Phi	32
J Tavarez, StL	32
S Linebrink, SD	26
G Majewski, Was	24

RELIEF INNINGS

S Torres, Pit	94.2
R Madson, Phi	87.0
G Majewski, Was	86.0
D Sanchez, LAD	82.0
R Vogelsong, Pit	81.1

OPPOSITION SLG
minimum 50 relief IP

A Heilman, NYM	249
B Wagner, Phi	265
R Dempster, ChC	265
M Wise, Mil	281
T Jones, Fla	283

AVG RUNNERS ON
minimum 50 relief IP

B Wagner, Phi	147
A Reyes, StL	155
D Turnbow, Mil	165
S Eyre, SF	167
M Gonzalez, Pit	169

BLOWN SAVES

L Hawkins, ChC-SF	9
C Reitsma, Atl	9
B Looper, NYM	8
4 tied with	7

% INH RUNNERS SCORED
minimum 30 inherited runners

J Grabow, Pit	10.3
S Eyre, SF	15.4
R Cormier, Phi	15.6
K Wunsch, LAD	16.2
J Eischen, Was	16.7

1ST BATTER AVG
minimum 40 first BFP

S Eyre, SF	107
J Santana, Mil	121
A Heilman, NYM	140
U Urbina, Phi	151
B Wagner, Phi	153

AVG ALLOWED SCPOS
minimum 50 relief IP

B Fuentes, Col	128
B Wagner, Phi	130
D Turnbow, Mil	130
B Thompson, StL	139
J Isringhausen, StL	140

PITCHES PER BATTER
minimum 50 relief IP

C Qualls, Hou	3.40
B Thompson, StL	3.44
B Meadows, Pit	3.46
T Coffey, Cin	3.48
L Ayala, Was	3.48

†**Holds** denote the number of times a relief pitcher enters the game in a save situation, records at least one out and leaves the game never having relinquished the lead. A pitcher cannot finish the game and receive credit for a hold, nor can he earn a hold and a save in the same game. **Blown Saves** denote the number of times a relief pitcher enters a game in a save situation and allows the tying or go-ahead run to score. **Pct. Inherited Scored** denotes the percent of inherited runners (those on base when a reliever enters the game) that score. **Avg., Runners On** denotes batting average allowed when runners are on base. **Avg., Scoring Pos.** denotes batting average allowed when a runner is at second and/or third base. **Easy Saves** denote saves in which the first batter faced doesn't represent the tying run and the reliever pitches one inning or less. **Regular Saves** denote those saves that are not Easy Saves or Tough Saves. **Tough Saves** denote saves which occur after the reliever enters with the tying run anywhere on base.

BASERUNNERS PER 9 IP
minimum 162 IP

Player,Team	IP	BR	BR/9
P Martinez, NYM	217.0	210	8.71
R Clemens, Hou	211.1	216	9.20
A Pettitte, Hou	222.1	232	9.39
C Carpenter, StL	241.2	258	9.61
J Peavy, SD	203.0	219	9.71
J Smoltz, Atl	229.2	264	10.35
D Willis, Fla	236.1	276	10.51
C Zambrano, ChC	223.1	264	10.64
J Beckett, Fla	178.2	218	10.98
J Patterson, Was	198.1	242	10.98

STRIKEOUTS PER 9 IP
minimum 162 IP

Player,Team	IP	SO	SO/9
M Prior, ChC	166.2	188	10.15
J Peavy, SD	203.0	216	9.58
B Myers, Phi	215.1	208	8.69
J Schmidt, SF	172.0	165	8.63
P Martinez, NYM	217.0	208	8.63
A Burnett, Fla	209.0	198	8.53
D Davis, Mil	222.2	208	8.41
J Patterson, Was	198.1	185	8.39
J Beckett, Fla	178.2	166	8.36
C Zambrano, ChC	223.1	202	8.14

RUN SUPPORT PER 9 IP
minimum 162 IP

Player,Team	IP	R	R/9
J Francis, Col	183.2	130	6.37
M Morris, StL	192.2	134	6.26
J Beckett, Fla	178.2	117	5.89
B Claussen, Cin	166.2	104	5.62
K Benson, NYM	174.1	108	5.58
J Suppan, StL	194.1	120	5.56
C Lidle, Phi	184.2	114	5.56
B Myers, Phi	215.1	132	5.52
C Carpenter, StL	241.2	148	5.51
C Capuano, Mil	219.0	133	5.47

OPPOSITION OBP
minimum 162 IP

P Martinez, NYM	252
R Clemens, Hou	261
A Pettitte, Hou	268
J Peavy, SD	271
C Carpenter, StL	273

AVG VS. LHB
minimum 125 BFP

C Cordero, Was	192
R Clemens, Hou	195
S Linebrink, SD	195
A Pettitte, Hou	200
M Mulder, StL	201

K/BB RATIO
minimum 162 IP

P Martinez, NYM	4.43
J Peavy, SD	4.32
C Carpenter, StL	4.18
J Vazquez, Ari	4.17
A Pettitte, Hou	4.17

STEALS ALLOWED

G Maddux, ChC	32
J Patterson, Was	26
B Webb, Ari	26
J Wright, Col	25
V Zambrano, NYM	25

PKOF THROW/RUNNER
minimum 162 IP

C Capuano, Mil	1.17
R Clemens, Hou	0.78
D Davis, Mil	0.75
B Halsey, Ari	0.70
K Benson, NYM	0.67

OPPOSITION SLG
minimum 162 IP

R Clemens, Hou	284
P Martinez, NYM	334
A Burnett, Fla	334
C Zambrano, ChC	338
A Pettitte, Hou	348

AVG VS. RHB
minimum 225 BFP

B Wagner, Phi	173
S Torres, Pit	189
P Martinez, NYM	192
C Carpenter, StL	199
R Clemens, Hou	202

GRD/FLY RATIO OFF
minimum 162 IP

B Webb, Ari	4.34
D Lowe, LAD	2.92
M Mulder, StL	2.74
T Hudson, Atl	2.50
A Burnett, Fla	2.42

CAUGHT STEALING OFF

J Francis, Col	11
L Hernandez, Was	11
J Patterson, Was	11
3 tied with	9

GDP INDUCED

M Mulder, StL	32
H Ramirez, Atl	32
B Webb, Ari	30
J Marquis, StL	29
J Suppan, StL	29

HITS PER 9 IP
minimum 162 IP

R Clemens, Hou	6.43
P Martinez, NYM	6.59
C Zambrano, ChC	6.85
J Peavy, SD	7.18
C Carpenter, StL	7.60

AVG ALLOWED SCPOS
minimum 125 BFP

R Clemens, Hou	138
J Sosa, Atl	194
A Pettitte, Hou	203
V Padilla, Phi	205
P Martinez, NYM	209

PITCHES PER START
minimum 30 games started

L Hernandez, Was	114.6
C Zambrano, ChC	107.9
N Lowry, SF	107.5
A Harang, Cin	106.7
D Davis, Mil	106.5

SB% ALLOWED
minimum 162 IP

C Zambrano, ChC	10.0
C Carpenter, StL	16.7
D Willis, Fla	16.7
C Capuano, Mil	18.2
M Mulder, StL	20.0

GDP PER 9 IP
minimum 162 IP

H Ramirez, Atl	1.4
M Mulder, StL	1.4
J Suppan, StL	1.3
J Marquis, StL	1.3
M Redman, Pit	1.2

HOME RUNS PER 9 IP
minimum 162 IP

D Willis, Fla	0.42
R Clemens, Hou	0.47
T Glavine, NYM	0.51
A Burnett, Fla	0.52
V Zambrano, NYM	0.65

OBP LEAD OFF INNING
minimum 150 BFP

C Carpenter, StL	239
R Clemens, Hou	242
P Martinez, NYM	253
K Benson, NYM	254
A Pettitte, Hou	258

PITCHES PER BATTER
minimum 162 IP

G Maddux, ChC	3.31
J Lieber, Phi	3.43
B Lawrence, SD	3.46
M Mulder, StL	3.47
J Wright, Col	3.49

PICKOFFS

C Capuano, Mil	12
J Wright, Col	6
4 tied with	5

QUALITY STARTS

C Carpenter, StL	27
A Pettitte, Hou	27
R Clemens, Hou	26
R Oswalt, Hou	25
D Willis, Fla	25

†**Run Support per 9 IP** denotes the number of runs scored by a pitcher's team while he was still in the game times nine divided by his innings pitched. **Avg. Allowed Sc. Pos.** denotes batting average allowed when a runner is at second and/or third base. **Grd/Fly Ratio Off** denotes ground balls allowed divided by fly balls allowed. All batted balls except line drives and bunts are included. **PkOf Throw/Runner** denotes the number of pickoff throws made by a pitcher divided by the number of runners on first base. **Quality Starts** denote the number of outings in which a starting pitcher works at least six innings and allows three or fewer earned runs.

BATTING

BATTING AVERAGE
minimum 1000 PA

Rk.	Player	AB	H	AVG
1	Todd Helton	4560	1535	.337
2	Albert Pujols	2954	982	.332
3	Ichiro Suzuki	3401	1130	.332
4	Vladimir Guerrero	4895	1586	.324
5	Nomar Garciaparra	4363	1395	.320
6	Derek Jeter	6167	1936	.314
7	Manny Ramirez	6126	1922	.314
8	Larry Walker	6907	2160	.313
9	Mike Piazza	6203	1929	.311
10	Frank Thomas	6956	2136	.307
11	Alex Rodriguez	6195	1901	.307
12	Magglio Ordonez	4112	1259	.306
13	Sean Casey	4017	1225	.305
14	Juan Pierre	3411	1040	.305
15	Ivan Rodriguez	7198	2190	.304
16	Mike Sweeney	4187	1273	.304
17	Chipper Jones	5974	1811	.303
18	Bobby Abreu	4728	1432	.303
19	Jose Vidro	3794	1146	.302
20	Jason Kendall	5207	1572	.302
21	Lance Berkman	3151	951	.302
22	Moises Alou	6315	1901	.301
23	Mark Loretta	4275	1285	.301
24	Placido Polanco	3265	981	.300
25	2 tied with			.300

ON-BASE PERCENTAGE
minimum 1000 PA; * AB + BB + HBP + SF

Rk.	Player	*PA	OB	OBP
1	Barry Bonds	11632	5146	.442
2	Todd Helton	5421	2348	.433
3	Frank Thomas	8602	3673	.427
4	Albert Pujols	3427	1427	.416
5	Lance Berkman	3812	1584	.416
6	Jason Giambi	6327	2616	.413
7	Brian Giles	5656	2334	.413
8	Bobby Abreu	5677	2333	.411
9	Manny Ramirez	7223	2953	.409
10	Jim Thome	7280	2972	.408
11	Jeff Bagwell	9428	3843	.408
12	Chipper Jones	7063	2834	.401
13	Larry Walker	8023	3211	.400
14	Gary Sheffield	9385	3743	.399
15	John Olerud	9051	3602	.398
16	Carlos Delgado	6634	2608	.393
17	J.D. Drew	3163	1242	.393
18	Vladimir Guerrero	5494	2146	.391
19	Travis Hafner	1545	600	.388
20	Jason Bay	1281	496	.387
21	Derek Jeter	6939	2675	.386
22	Alex Rodriguez	7084	2729	.385
23	Jim Edmonds	6481	2490	.384
24	Bernie Williams	8580	3291	.384
25	Nick Johnson	1761	675	.383

SLUGGING PERCENTAGE
minimum 1000 PA

Rk.	Player	AB	TB	SLG
1	Albert Pujols	2954	1834	.621
2	Barry Bonds	9140	5584	.611
3	Todd Helton	4560	2769	.607
4	Manny Ramirez	6126	3668	.599
5	Vladimir Guerrero	4895	2871	.587
6	Alex Rodriguez	6195	3576	.577
7	Frank Thomas	6956	3949	.568
8	Larry Walker	6907	3904	.565
9	Jim Thome	5919	3327	.562
10	Ken Griffey Jr.	7870	4414	.561
11	Juan Gonzalez	6556	3676	.561
12	Carlos Delgado	5529	3089	.559
13	Lance Berkman	3151	1756	.557
14	Travis Hafner	1321	735	.556
15	Mike Piazza	6203	3440	.555
16	Jason Bay	1097	607	.553
17	Nomar Garciaparra	4363	2373	.544
18	Jim Edmonds	5557	3016	.543
19	Brian Giles	4656	2522	.542
20	Mark Teixeira	1718	929	.541
21	Jeff Bagwell	7797	4213	.540
22	Jason Giambi	5174	2791	.539
23	Chipper Jones	5974	3213	.538
24	Sammy Sosa	8401	4511	.537
25	David Ortiz	3108	1660	.534

HITS

Rafael Palmeiro	3020
Craig Biggio	2795
Barry Bonds	2742
Julio Franco	2521
Steve Finley	2426
Gary Sheffield	2345
B.J. Surhoff	2326
Jeff Bagwell	2314
Ken Griffey Jr.	2304
Sammy Sosa	2304
Omar Vizquel	2301
Marquis Grissom	2251
John Olerud	2239
Bernie Williams	2218
Luis Gonzalez	2214
Ivan Rodriguez	2190
Larry Walker	2160
Ruben Sierra	2147
Kenny Lofton	2142
Frank Thomas	2136

HOME RUNS

Barry Bonds	708
Sammy Sosa	588
Rafael Palmeiro	569
Ken Griffey Jr.	536
Jeff Bagwell	449
Gary Sheffield	449
Frank Thomas	448
Manny Ramirez	435
Juan Gonzalez	434
Jim Thome	430
Alex Rodriguez	429
Mike Piazza	397
Larry Walker	383
Carlos Delgado	369
Tino Martinez	339
Jim Edmonds	331
Chipper Jones	331
Jeff Kent	331
Luis Gonzalez	316
Vinny Castilla	315

RUNS BATTED IN

Barry Bonds	1853
Rafael Palmeiro	1835
Sammy Sosa	1575
Ken Griffey Jr.	1536
Jeff Bagwell	1529
Gary Sheffield	1476
Frank Thomas	1465
Manny Ramirez	1414
Juan Gonzalez	1404
Ruben Sierra	1318
Jeff Kent	1312
Larry Walker	1311
Tino Martinez	1271
Luis Gonzalez	1251
John Olerud	1230
Alex Rodriguez	1226
Mike Piazza	1223
Bernie Williams	1196
Jim Thome	1193
Carlos Delgado	1173

STOLEN BASES

Kenny Lofton	567
Barry Bonds	506
Eric Young	457
Marquis Grissom	429
Craig Biggio	407
Tony Womack	362
Omar Vizquel	342
Steve Finley	313
Reggie Sanders	297
Luis Castillo	281
Johnny Damon	281
Julio Franco	273
Juan Pierre	267
Ray Durham	248
Edgar Renteria	246
Bobby Abreu	241
Sammy Sosa	234
Larry Walker	230
Mike Cameron	229
Raul Mondesi	229

SEASONS PLAYED

Roger Clemens 22
Julio Franco 21
John Franco 21
Rafael Palmeiro 20
Barry Bonds 20
Benito Santiago 20
Greg Maddux 20
Ruben Sierra 19
Jamie Moyer 19
Terry Mulholland 19
B.J. Surhoff 19
Kevin Brown 19
David Wells 19
Tom Glavine 19
Al Leiter 19

DOUBLES

Craig Biggio 604
Rafael Palmeiro 585
Barry Bonds 564
John Olerud 500
Luis Gonzalez 495
Jeff Bagwell 488
Jeff Kent 474
Larry Walker 471
Frank Thomas 447
Ivan Rodriguez 445

TOTAL BASES

Barry Bonds 5584
Rafael Palmeiro 5388
Sammy Sosa 4511
Ken Griffey Jr. 4414
Craig Biggio 4283
Jeff Bagwell 4213
Gary Sheffield 4153
Steve Finley 3966
Frank Thomas 3949
Larry Walker 3904

STRIKEOUTS

Sammy Sosa 2194
Jim Thome 1762
Jeff Bagwell 1558
Craig Biggio 1557
Reggie Sanders 1513
Barry Bonds 1434
Ken Griffey Jr. 1416
Jim Edmonds 1411
Carlos Delgado 1363
Jose Hernandez 1351

SB SUCCESS %
minimum 100 SB attempts

Carlos Beltran 87.8
Tony Womack 83.2
Jose Reyes 82.1
Carl Crawford 81.6
Alex Rodriguez 80.1
Aaron Boone 80.0

Alfonso Soriano 79.7
Kenny Lofton 79.3
Mike Cameron 79.2
Derek Jeter 79.0

GAMES

Rafael Palmeiro 2831
Barry Bonds 2730
Craig Biggio 2564
Steve Finley 2401
Julio Franco 2377
B.J. Surhoff 2313
Omar Vizquel 2290
Sammy Sosa 2240
John Olerud 2234
Gary Sheffield 2190

TRIPLES

Steve Finley 112
Kenny Lofton 98
Johnny Damon 80
Barry Bonds 77
Jose Offerman 72
Ray Durham 70
Cristian Guzman 67
Luis Gonzalez 63
Larry Walker 62
Neifi Perez 60

WALKS

Barry Bonds 2311
Frank Thomas 1466
Jeff Bagwell 1401
Rafael Palmeiro 1353
Gary Sheffield 1280
John Olerud 1275
Jim Thome 1257
Craig Biggio 1097
Ken Griffey Jr. 1038
Bernie Williams 1036

K/BB RATIO
minimum 1000 AB

Barry Bonds 621
Eric Young 689
Brian Giles 700
Gary Sheffield 746
Frank Thomas 795
John Olerud 797
Todd Helton 805
Orlando Palmeiro 844
Albert Pujols 858
Jason Kendall 877

CAUGHT STEALING

Eric Young 166
Kenny Lofton 148
Barry Bonds 141
Omar Vizquel 139
Craig Biggio 119
Steve Finley 118
Marquis Grissom 116
Luis Castillo 114

Reggie Sanders 107
Sammy Sosa 107

AT-BATS

Rafael Palmeiro 10472
Craig Biggio 9811
Barry Bonds 9140
Steve Finley 8877
Julio Franco 8422
Sammy Sosa 8401
Omar Vizquel 8387
Marquis Grissom 8275
B.J. Surhoff 8258
Ruben Sierra 8016

AB PER HR
minimum 1000 AB

Barry Bonds 12.9
Jim Thome 13.8
Manny Ramirez 14.1
Sammy Sosa 14.3
Adam Dunn 14.4
Alex Rodriguez 14.4
Ken Griffey Jr. 14.7
Albert Pujols 14.7
Carlos Delgado 15.0
Juan Gonzalez 15.1

INTENTIONAL WALKS

Barry Bonds 607
Ken Griffey Jr. 210
Rafael Palmeiro 172
Vladimir Guerrero 170
Frank Thomas 162
John Olerud 157
Jeff Bagwell 155
Sammy Sosa 151
Carlos Delgado 148
Mike Piazza 144

SACRIFICE HITS

Omar Vizquel 205
Tom Glavine 191
Greg Maddux 159
Jose Vizcaino 105
John Smoltz 104
Royce Clayton 103
Curt Schilling 102
Rey Sanchez 93
Neifi Perez 92
Craig Biggio 89

GDP

Julio Franco 299
Ivan Rodriguez 239
John Olerud 232
Rafael Palmeiro 232
Jeff Bagwell 221
Vinny Castilla 217
Bernie Williams 209
Mike Piazza 207
Benito Santiago 204
Royce Clayton 197

RUNS SCORED

Barry Bonds 2078
Craig Biggio 1697
Rafael Palmeiro 1663
Jeff Bagwell 1517
Sammy Sosa 1422
Gary Sheffield 1411
Ken Griffey Jr. 1405
Steve Finley 1368
Kenny Lofton 1363
Larry Walker 1355

AB PER RBI
minimum 1000 AB

Manny Ramirez 4.3
Juan Gonzalez 4.7
Carlos Delgado 4.7
Frank Thomas 4.7
Albert Pujols 4.8
Richie Sexson 4.9
Barry Bonds 4.9
Jim Thome 5.0
David Ortiz 5.0
Todd Helton 5.0

HIT BY PITCH

Craig Biggio 273
Jason Kendall 197
Carlos Delgado 139
Larry Walker 138
Jeff Bagwell 128
Gary Sheffield 118
Damion Easley 115
Jason Giambi 111
Jeff Kent 105
Derek Jeter 103

SACRIFICE FLIES

Rafael Palmeiro 119
Ruben Sierra 119
Frank Thomas 109
B.J. Surhoff 104
Jeff Bagwell 102
Gary Sheffield 101
John Olerud 96
Jeff Kent 92
Jeff Conine 91
Barry Bonds 88

AB PER GDP
minimum 1000 AB

Ichiro Suzuki 136.0
Jose Reyes 132.2
Rob Mackowiak 123.4
Dave Roberts 121.8
Omar Infante 120.2
Carl Crawford 119.9
Greg Maddux 117.2
Russell Branyan 104.6
Johnny Damon 99.6
Tom Glavine 99.6

PITCHING

WINS

Roger Clemens	341
Greg Maddux	318
Tom Glavine	275
Randy Johnson	263
David Wells	227
Mike Mussina	224
Kevin Brown	211
Jamie Moyer	205
Pedro Martinez	197
Curt Schilling	192

GAMES

John Franco	1119
Mike Stanton	1027
Mike Timlin	893
Roberto Hernandez	892
Jose Mesa	887
Paul Quantrill	841
Steve Reed	833
Todd Jones	812
Jeff Nelson	792
Buddy Groom	786

COMPLETE GAMES

Roger Clemens	118
Greg Maddux	108
Randy Johnson	96
Curt Schilling	82
Kevin Brown	72
Mike Mussina	56
Tom Glavine	55
David Wells	54
Scott Erickson	51
John Smoltz	50

STRIKEOUTS

Roger Clemens	4502
Randy Johnson	4372
Greg Maddux	3052
Pedro Martinez	2861
Curt Schilling	2832
John Smoltz	2567
Mike Mussina	2400
Kevin Brown	2397
Tom Glavine	2350
David Wells	2081

LOSSES

Greg Maddux	189
Tom Glavine	184
Roger Clemens	172
Jamie Moyer	152
Kevin Brown	144
David Wells	143
Terry Mulholland	142
Scott Erickson	136
Randy Johnson	136
Steve Trachsel	135

GAMES STARTED

Roger Clemens	671
Greg Maddux	639
Tom Glavine	603
Randy Johnson	513
Jamie Moyer	485
Kevin Brown	476
David Wells	447
Mike Mussina	443
Kenny Rogers	400
John Smoltz	394

COMPLETE GAME %
minimum 100 GS

Curt Schilling	0.22
Randy Johnson	0.19
Roger Clemens	0.18
Greg Maddux	0.17
Kevin Brown	0.15
Livan Hernandez	0.15
Scott Erickson	0.14
Terry Mulholland	0.14
Mark Mulder	0.14
Pedro Martinez	0.13

WALKS ALLOWED

Roger Clemens	1520
Randy Johnson	1349
Tom Glavine	1337
Al Leiter	1163
Kenny Rogers	1017
Tom Gordon	922
Greg Maddux	907
Hideo Nomo	904
Kevin Brown	901
Tim Wakefield	897

WINNING PERCENTAGE
minimum 100 decisions

Pedro Martinez	701
Tim Hudson	688
Roy Oswalt	680
Roger Clemens	665
Mark Mulder	660
Randy Johnson	659
Andy Pettitte	654
Roy Halladay	648
Mike Mussina	638
Bartolo Colon	629

INNINGS PITCHED

Roger Clemens	4704.1
Greg Maddux	4406.1
Tom Glavine	3951.2
Randy Johnson	3593.2
Kevin Brown	3256.1
David Wells	3206.1
Jamie Moyer	3139.2
Mike Mussina	3013.0
John Smoltz	2929.1
Curt Schilling	2906.0

SHUTOUTS

Roger Clemens	46
Randy Johnson	37
Greg Maddux	35
Tom Glavine	24
Mike Mussina	23
Curt Schilling	19
Kevin Brown	17
Scott Erickson	17
Pedro Martinez	17
John Smoltz	15

STRIKEOUTS/9 IP
minimum 750 IP

Randy Johnson	10.95
Kerry Wood	10.44
Pedro Martinez	10.25
Trevor Hoffman	10.01
Jeff Nelson	9.52
Johan Santana	9.47
Arthur Rhodes	8.81
Mike Remlinger	8.77
Curt Schilling	8.77
Hideo Nomo	8.74

ERA
minimum 750 IP

Mariano Rivera	2.33
Pedro Martinez	2.72
Trevor Hoffman	2.76
John Franco	2.89
Greg Maddux	3.01
Roy Oswalt	3.07
Randy Johnson	3.11
Roger Clemens	3.12
Carlos Zambrano	3.26
John Smoltz	3.26

BATTERS FACED

Roger Clemens	19369
Greg Maddux	17925
Tom Glavine	16626
Randy Johnson	14784
Kevin Brown	13542
David Wells	13395
Jamie Moyer	13341
Kenny Rogers	12374
Mike Mussina	12314
John Smoltz	11997

QUALITY START %
minimum 100 GS

Pedro Martinez	70.7
Randy Johnson	70.0
Roy Oswalt	69.0
Greg Maddux	67.0
Curt Schilling	66.9
Carlos Zambrano	66.4
Roger Clemens	66.0
Kevin Brown	66.0
Tim Hudson	65.6
Barry Zito	64.9

WALKS PER 9 INNINGS
minimum 750 IP

Brad Radke	1.62
Jon Lieber	1.75
Greg Maddux	1.85
David Wells	1.87
Brian Anderson	1.96
Ben Sheets	2.00
Mike Mussina	2.04
Ramiro Mendoza	2.04
Curt Schilling	2.04
Mark Buehrle	2.06

K/BB RATIO
minimum 750 IP

Pedro Martinez	4.32
Curt Schilling	4.29
Trevor Hoffman	3.86
Ben Sheets	3.79
Roy Oswalt	3.78
Jon Lieber	3.71
Mike Mussina	3.51
Johan Santana	3.40
Mariano Rivera	3.39
Greg Maddux	3.36

OPPOSITION AVG
minimum 750 IP

Trevor Hoffman	208
Pedro Martinez	208
Mariano Rivera	212
Kerry Wood	214
Randy Johnson	215
Johan Santana	221
Jeff Nelson	223
Barry Zito	228
Carlos Zambrano	228
Roger Clemens	229

HIT BATSMEN

Randy Johnson	168
Roger Clemens	150
Kevin Brown	139
Tim Wakefield	136
Greg Maddux	125
Pedro Martinez	119
Al Leiter	117
Chan Ho Park	116
Pedro Astacio	110
2 tied with	108

SAVES

Trevor Hoffman	436
John Franco	424
Mariano Rivera	379
Roberto Hernandez	324
Troy Percival	324
Jose Mesa	319
Billy Wagner	284
Armando Benitez	263
Ugueth Urbina	237
Todd Jones	226

†**Quality Starts** denote the number of outings in which a starting pitcher works at least six innings and allows three or fewer earned runs.

HITS PER 9 INNINGS
minimum 750 IP

Pedro Martinez	6.82
Trevor Hoffman	6.86
Kerry Wood	6.95
Mariano Rivera	7.03
Randy Johnson	7.06
Jeff Nelson	7.25
Johan Santana	7.35
Carlos Zambrano	7.51
Barry Zito	7.57
A.J. Burnett	7.58

OPPOSITION OBP
minimum 750 IP

Trevor Hoffman	265
Mariano Rivera	269
Pedro Martinez	269
Curt Schilling	284
Johan Santana	284
Greg Maddux	289
John Smoltz	291
Roger Clemens	294
Mike Mussina	294
Randy Johnson	295

WILD PITCHES

Roger Clemens	133
John Smoltz	130
Kevin Brown	108
Hideo Nomo	108
Tom Gordon	102
David Wells	100
Matt Clement	98
Randy Johnson	98
Jason Grimsley	95
Jeff Fassero	84

SAVE %
minimum 50 SvOp

Eric Gagne	96.4
John Smoltz	91.7
Trevor Hoffman	89.5
Joe Nathan	88.0
Mariano Rivera	87.9
Billy Wagner	86.3
Jason Isringhausen	86.1
Armando Benitez	85.9
Troy Percival	85.9
Jose Mesa	85.3

BASERUNNERS PER 9 INNINGS
minimum 750 IP

Trevor Hoffman	9.53
Pedro Martinez	9.62
Mariano Rivera	9.70
Curt Schilling	10.28
Johan Santana	10.34
Greg Maddux	10.45
John Smoltz	10.63
Mike Mussina	10.76
Roger Clemens	10.84
Randy Johnson	10.86

OPPOSITION SLG
minimum 750 IP

Mariano Rivera	290
Pedro Martinez	324
Jeff Nelson	330
Trevor Hoffman	337
Roger Clemens	341
Randy Johnson	341
Carlos Zambrano	341
John Franco	343
Kevin Brown	349
A.J. Burnett	350

GDP INDUCED

Greg Maddux	375
Tom Glavine	374
Kevin Brown	328
Roger Clemens	310
Scott Erickson	308
Kenny Rogers	292
Terry Mulholland	266
Mike Hampton	262
Jamie Moyer	252
David Wells	244

GAMES FINISHED

John Franco	774
Trevor Hoffman	632
Roberto Hernandez	628
Jose Mesa	586
Mariano Rivera	541
Troy Percival	489
Billy Wagner	487
Todd Jones	472
Armando Benitez	468
Bob Wickman	416

HOME RUNS/9 IP
minimum 750 IP

Mariano Rivera	0.47
Kevin Brown	0.57
John Franco	0.59
Greg Maddux	0.61
Jeff Nelson	0.62
Carlos Zambrano	0.65
Terry Adams	0.65
Roger Clemens	0.66
Tom Glavine	0.68
Julian Tavarez	0.69

HOME RUNS ALLOWED

Jamie Moyer	381
David Wells	374
Roger Clemens	347
Randy Johnson	333
Mike Mussina	323
Brad Radke	302
Tom Glavine	300
Greg Maddux	298
Curt Schilling	298
2 tied with	296

GDP/9 IP
minimum 750 IP

Shawn Estes	1.29
Julian Tavarez	1.22
Bob Wickman	1.19
Scott Erickson	1.18
Jamey Wright	1.16
Mike Hampton	1.14
Scott Schoeneweis	1.13
Jon Garland	1.09
Mark Mulder	1.09
Danny Graves	1.09

SB % ALLOWED
minimum 750 IP

Kirk Rueter	34.3
Chris Carpenter	39.3
Terry Mulholland	41.2
Mark Buehrle	42.4
Kenny Rogers	43.1
Carlos Zambrano	45.2
Johan Santana	48.6
Brian Anderson	49.1
Tomo Ohka	50.0
Roy Oswalt	50.0

Top regular-season performances in all major categories

BATTING

TRIPLE CROWN WINNERS

Nap Lajoie, A's	1901
Ty Cobb, Tigers	1909
Heine Zimmerman, Cubs	1912
Rogers Hornsby, Cardinals	1922
Rogers Hornsby, Cardinals	1925
Jimmie Foxx, A's	1933
Chuck Klein, Phillies	1933
Lou Gehrig, Yankees	1934
Joe Medwick, Cardinals	1937
Ted Williams, Red Sox	1942
Ted Williams, Red Sox	1947
Mickey Mantle, Yankees	1956
Frank Robinson, Orioles	1966
Carl Yastrzemski, Red Sox	1967

*HIGHEST AVERAGE

1.	Nap Lajoie, A's, 1901	.426
2.	Rogers Hornsby, Cardinals, 1924	.424
3.	George Sisler, Browns, 1922	.420
	Ty Cobb, Tigers, 1911	.420
5.	Ty Cobb, Tigers, 1912	.409
6.	Joe Jackson, Indians, 1911	.408
7.	George Sisler, Browns, 1920	.407
8.	Ted Williams, Red Sox, 1941	.406
9.	Rogers Hornsby, Cardinals, 1925	.403
	Harry Heilmann, Tigers, 1923	.403
11.	Rogers Hornsby, Cardinals, 1922	.401
	Bill Terry, Giants, 1930	.401
	Ty Cobb, Tigers, 1922	.401
14.	Lefty O'Doul, Phillies, 1929	.398
	Harry Heilmann, Tigers, 1927	.398
16.	Rogers Hornsby, Cardinals, 1921	.397
17.	Joe Jackson, Indians, 1912	.395
18.	Tony Gwynn, Padres, 1994	.394
	Harry Heilmann, Tigers, 1921	.394
20.	Babe Ruth, Yankees, 1923	.393

*Based on players averaging at least 3.1 at-bats for every game played by their teams.

HIGHEST AVERAGE, ROOKIE

1.	Benny Kauff, Indianapolis F.L., 1914	.370
2.	Lloyd Waner, Pirates, 1927	.355
3.	Kiki Cuyler, Pirates, 1924	.354
4.	Hack Miller, Cubs, 1922	.352
5.	Ichiro Suzuki, Mariners, 2001	.350
6.	Dale Alexander, Tigers, 1929	.343
	Ralph Garr, Braves, 1971	.343
8.	Patsy Dougherty, Red Sox, 1902	.342
	Earle Combs, Yankees, 1925	.342
10.	Ike Boone, Red Sox, 1924	.337
11.	Paul Waner, Pirates, 1926	.336
12.	Charlie Keller, Yankees, 1939	.334
	Socks Seybold, A's, 1901	.334
14.	Richie Ashburn, Phillies, 1948	.333
15.	Earl Averill, Indians, 1929	.332
16.	Fred Lynn, Red Sox, 1975	.331
	Johnny Pesky, Red Sox, 1942	.331
18.	Rico Carty, Braves, 1964	.330
	Hal Trosky, Indians, 1934	.330
20.	Albert Pujols, Cardinals, 2001	.329

RUNS SCORED

1.	Babe Ruth, Yankees, 1921	177
2.	Lou Gehrig, Yankees, 1936	167
3.	Lou Gehrig, Yankees, 1931	163
	Babe Ruth, Yankees, 1928	163
5.	Chuck Klein, Phillies, 1930	158
	Babe Ruth, Yankees, 1920	158
	Babe Ruth, Yankees, 1927	158
8.	Rogers Hornsby, Cubs, 1929	156
9.	Kiki Cuyler, Cubs, 1930	155
10.	Jeff Bagwell, Astros, 2000	152
	Woody English, Cubs, 1930	152
	Chuck Klein, Phillies, 1932	152
	Lefty O'Doul, Phillies, 1929	152
	Al Simmons, A's, 1930	152
15.	Joe DiMaggio, Yankees, 1937	151
	Jimmie Foxx, A's, 1932	151
	Babe Ruth, Yankees, 1923	151
18.	Babe Ruth, Yankees, 1930	150
	Ted Williams, Red Sox, 1949	150
20.	Lou Gehrig, Yankees, 1927	149
	Babe Ruth, Yankees, 1931	149

HITS

1.	Ichiro Suzuki, Mariners, 2004	262
2.	George Sisler, Browns, 1920	257
3.	Lefty O'Doul, Phillies, 1929	254
	Bill Terry, Giants, 1930	254
5.	Al Simmons, A's, 1925	253
6.	Rogers Hornsby, Cardinals, 1922	250
	Chuck Klein, Phillies, 1930	250
8.	Ty Cobb, Tigers, 1911	248
9.	George Sisler, Browns, 1922	246
10.	Ichiro Suzuki, Mariners, 2001	242
11.	Babe Herman, Dodgers, 1930	241
	Heinie Manush, Browns, 1928	241
13.	Wade Boggs, Red Sox, 1985	240
	Darin Erstad, Angels, 2000	240
15.	Rod Carew, Twins, 1977	239
16.	Don Mattingly, Yankees, 1986	238
17.	Harry Heilmann, Tigers, 1921	237
	Joe Medwick, Cardinals, 1937	237
	Paul Waner, Pirates, 1927	237
20.	Jack Tobin, Browns, 1921	236

HITS, ROOKIE

1.	Ichiro Suzuki, Mariners, 2001	242
2.	Lloyd Waner, Pirates, 1927	223
3.	Ralph Garr, Braves, 1971	219
4.	Tony Oliva, Twins, 1964	217
5.	Dale Alexander, Tigers, 1929	215
6.	Benny Kauff, Indianapolis F.L., 1914	211
7.	Nomar Garciaparra, Red Sox, 1997	209
	Harvey Kuenn, Tigers, 1953	209
9.	Kevin Seitzer, Royals, 1987	207
10.	Joe DiMaggio, Yankees, 1936	206
	Johnny Frederick, Dodgers, 1929	206
	Hal Trosky, Indians, 1934	206
13.	Johnny Pesky, Red Sox, 1942	205
14.	Earle Combs, Yankees, 1925	203
15.	Dick Allen, Phillies, 1964	201
	Roy Johnson, Tigers, 1929	201
17.	Dick Wakefield, Tigers, 1943	200
18.	Earl Averill, Indians, 1929	198
19.	Buddy Hassett, Dodgers, 1936	197
20.	Carlos Beltran, Royals, 1999	194
	Albert Pujols, Cardinals, 2001	194

LONGEST HITTING STREAKS

1.	Joe DiMaggio, Yankees, 1941	56
2.	Pete Rose, Reds, 1978	44
3.	George Sisler, Browns, 1922	41
4.	Ty Cobb, Tigers, 1911	40
5.	Paul Molitor, Brewers, 1987	39
6.	Tommy Holmes, Braves, 1945	37
7.	Jimmy Rollins, Phillies, 2005	36
8.	Ty Cobb, Tigers, 1917	35
	Luis Castillo, Marlins, 2002	35
10.	George Sisler, Browns, 1925	34
	George McQuinn, Browns, 1938	34
	Dom DiMaggio, Red Sox, 1949	34
	Benito Santiago, Padres, 1987	34
14.	Hal Chase, Yankees, 1907	33
	Rogers Hornsby, Cardinals, 1922	33
	Heinie Manush, Senators, 1933	33
17.	Nap Lajoie, Indians, 1906	31
	Sam Rice, Senators, 1924	31
	Willie Davis, Dodgers, 1969	31
	Rico Carty, Braves, 1970	31
	Ken Landreaux, Twins, 1980	31
	Vladimir Guerrero, Expos, 1999	31

LONGEST HITTING STREAKS, ROOKIE

1.	Benito Santiago, Padres, 1987	34
2.	Jerome Walton, Cubs, 1989	30
	Nomar Garciaparra, Red Sox, 1997	30
4.	Jimmy Williams, Pirates, 1899	27
5.	Guy Curtright, White Sox, 1943	26
6.	Joe McEwing, Cardinals, 1999	25
7.	Chico Carrasquel, White Sox, 1950	24
8.	Richie Ashburn, Phillies, 1948	23
	Al Dark, Braves, 1948	23
	Kent Hrbek, Twins, 1982	23
	Goldie Rapp, Phillies, 1921	23
	Mike Vail, Mets, 1975	23
	Ichiro Suzuki, Mariners, 2001	23
14.	Ralph Garr, Braves NL, 1971	22
	Willie McCovey, Giants, 1959	22
	Dale Mitchell, Indians, 1947	22
	Johnny Mize, Cardinals, 1936	22
	Edgar Renteria, Marlins, 1996	22
19.	Lou Klein, Cardinals, 1943	21
	Danny Litwhiler, Phillies, 1940	21
	Jackie Robinson, Dodgers, 1947	21
	Dick Wakefield, Tigers, 1943	21
	Taffy Wright, Senators, 1938	21
	Robb Quinlan, Angels, 2004	21

CONSECUTIVE HITS

1.	Pinky Higgins, Red Sox, 1938	12
	Walt Dropo, Tigers, 1952	12
3.	Tris Speaker, Indians, 1920	11
	Johnny Pesky, Red Sox, 1946	11
	Bernie Williams, Yankees, 2002	11
6.	Jake Stenzel, Pirates, 1893	10
	Ed Delahanty, Phillies, 1897	10
	Jake Gettman, Was NL, 1897	10
	Ed Konetchy, Dodgers, 1919	10
	George Sisler, Browns, 1921	10
	Harry Heilmann, Tigers, 1922	10
	Kiki Cuyler, Pirates, 1925	10
	Harry McCurdy, White Sox, 1926	10
	Chick Hafey, Cardinals, 1929	10
	Joe Medwick, Cardinals, 1936	10
	Rip Radcliff, White Sox, 1938	10
	Buddy Hassett, Braves, 1940	10
	Woody Williams, Reds, 1943	10
	Ken Singleton, Orioles, 1981	10
	Bip Roberts, Reds, 1992	10
	Frank Thomas, White Sox, 1997	10
	Joe Randa, Royals, 1999	10

Pittsburgh's Waner brothers, Lloyd (left) and Paul, were batting terrors in their rookie years in the majors.

Frank Catalanotto, Rangers, 2000 10

PINCH HITS

1. John Vander Wal, Rockies, 1995............	28
2. Lenny Harris, Rockies-D-backs NL, 1999..	26
3. Jose Morales, Expos, 1976	25
4. Dave Philley, Orioles, 1961	24
Vic Davalillo, Cardinals, 1970	24
Rusty Staub, Mets, 1983	24
Gerald Perry, Cardinals, 1993	24
8. Greg Norton, Rockies, 2003	23
9. Sam Leslie, Giants, 1932...................	22
Peanuts Lowrey, Cardinals, 1953	22
Red Schoendienst, Cardinals, 1962......	22
Wallace Johnson, Expos, 1988	22
Mark Sweeney, Cardinals-Padres, 1997....	22
Lenny Harris, Brewers, 2002	22
15. Doc Miller, Phillies, 1913	21
Smoky Burgess, White Sox, 1966	21
Merv Rettenmund, Padres, 1977...........	21
Lenny Harris, Mets, 2001	21
19. Ed Coleman, Browns, 1936	20
Frenchy Bordagaray, Cardinals, 1938 ...	20
Joe Frazier, Cardinals, 1954................	20
Smoky Burgess, White Sox, 1965	20
Ken Boswell, Astros, 1976..................	20
Jerry Turner, Padres, 1978	20
Thad Bosley, Cubs, 1985	20
Chris Chambliss, Braves, NL, 1986	20

Dave Clark, Cubs, 1997	20
Jacob Cruz, Reds, 2005.....................	20

SINGLES

1. Ichiro Suzuki, Mariners, 2004	225
2. Lloyd Waner, Pirates, 1927	198
3. Ichiro Suzuki, Mariners, 2001	192
4. Wade Boggs, Red Sox, 1985	187
5. Juan Pierre, Marlins, 2004	184
6. Willie Wilson, Royals, 1980..............	184
7. Matty Alou, Pirates, 1969	183
8. Sam Rice, Senators, 1925	182
9. Richie Ashburn, Phillies, 1951...........	181
Jesse Burkett, Cardinals, 1901	181
Lefty O'Doul, Phillies, 1929	181
Pete Rose, Reds, 1973	181
Lloyd Waner, Pirates, 1929	181
14. Rod Carew, Twins, 1974	180
Ralph Garr, Braves, 1971..................	180
Lloyd Waner, Pirates, 1928	180
17. Jack Tobin, Browns, 1921	179
Maury Wills, Dodgers, 1962	179
19. Curt Flood, Cardinals, 1964.............	178
George Sisler, Browns, 1922	178
Paul Waner, Pirates, 1937	178

DOUBLES

1. Earl Webb, Red Sox, 1931................	67
2. George Burns, Indians, 1926..............	64

Joe Medwick, Cardinals, 1936...............	64
4. Hank Greenberg, Tigers, 1934...............	63
5. Paul Waner, Pirates, 1932	62
6. Charlie Gehringer, Tigers, 1936	60
7. Todd Helton, Rockies, 2000................	59
Chuck Klein, Phillies, 1930	59
Tris Speaker, Indians, 1923	59
10. Carlos Delgado, Blue Jays, 2000...........	57
Billy Herman, Cubs, 1935	57
Billy Herman, Cubs, 1936	57
13. Garret Anderson, Angels, 2002	56
Craig Biggio, Astros, 1999................	56
Nomar Garciaparra, Red Sox, 2002........	56
George Kell, Tigers, 1950	56
Joe Medwick, Cardinals, 1937............	56
18. Lance Berkman, Astros, 2001	55
Gee Walker, Tigers, 1936.................	55
20. Mark Grudzielanek, Expos, 1997	54
Todd Helton, Rockies, 2001................	54
Hal McRae, Royals, 1977	54
John Olerud, Blue Jays, 1993	54
Alex Rodriguez, Mariners, 1996	54

TRIPLES

1. Chief Wilson, Pirates, 1912	36
2. Sam Crawford, Tigers, 1914	26
Kiki Cuyler, Pirates, 1925.................	26
Joe Jackson, Indians, 1912...............	26
5. Sam Crawford, Tigers, 1903	25

Larry Doyle, Giants, 1911	25	Hack Wilson, Cubs, 1930	56
Tom Long, Cardinals, 1915	25	18. Ralph Kiner, Pirates, 1949	54
8. Ty Cobb, Tigers, 1911	24	Mickey Mantle, Yankees, 1961	54
Ty Cobb, Tigers, 1917	24	Babe Ruth, Yankees, 1920	54
10. Ty Cobb, Tigers, 1912	23	Babe Ruth, Yankees, 1928	54

HOME RUNS, RIGHTHANDER

1. Mark McGwire, Cardinals, 1998	70
2. Sammy Sosa, Cubs, 1998	66
3. Mark McGwire, Cardinals, 1999	65
4. Sammy Sosa, Cubs, 2001	64
5. Sammy Sosa, Cubs, 1999	63
6. Jimmie Foxx, A's, 1932	58
Hank Greenberg, Tigers, 1938	58
Mark McGwire, A's-Cardinals, 1997	58
9. Alex Rodriguez, Rangers, 2002	57
10. Hack Wilson, Cubs, 1930	56
11. Ralph Kiner, Pirates, 1949	54
12. George Foster, Reds, 1977	52
Willie Mays, Giants, 1965	52
Mark McGwire, A's, 1996	52
Alex Rodriguez, Rangers, 2001	52
16. Cecil Fielder, Tigers, 1990	51
Ralph Kiner, Pirates, 1947	51
Willie Mays, Giants, 1955	51
Andruw Jones, Braves, 2005	51
20. Albert Belle, Indians, 1995	50
Jimmie Foxx, Red Sox, 1938	50

Earle Combs, Yankees, 1927 — 23
Adam Comorosky, Pirates, 1930 — 23
Sam Crawford, Tigers, 1913 — 23
Dale Mitchell, Indians, 1949 — 23
15. many tied with 22

HOME RUNS

1. Barry Bonds, Giants, 2001	73
2. Mark McGwire, Cardinals, 1998	70
3. Sammy Sosa, Cubs, 1998	66
4. Mark McGwire, Cardinals, 1999	65
5. Sammy Sosa, Cubs, 2001	64
6. Sammy Sosa, Cubs, 1999	63
7. Roger Maris, Yankees, 1961	61
8. Babe Ruth, Yankees, 1927	60
9. Babe Ruth, Yankees, 1921	59
10. Jimmie Foxx, A's, 1932	58
Hank Greenberg, Tigers, 1938	58
Mark McGwire, A's-Cardinals, 1997	58
13. Luis Gonzalez, Diamondbacks, 2001	57
Alex Rodriguez, Rangers, 2002	57
15. Ken Griffey, Mariners, 1997	56
Ken Griffey, Mariners, 1998	56

Sammy Sosa, Cubs, 2000	50
Greg Vaughn, Padres, 1998	50

HOME RUNS, LEFTHANDER

1. Barry Bonds, Giants, 2001	73
2. Roger Maris, Yankees, 1961	61
3. Babe Ruth, Yankees, 1927	60
4. Babe Ruth, Yankees, 1921	59
5. Luis Gonzalez, Diamondbacks, 2001	57
6. Ken Griffey, Mariners, 1997	56
Ken Griffey, Mariners, 1998	56
8. Babe Ruth, Yankees, 1920	54
Babe Ruth, Yankees, 1928	54
10. Jim Thome, Indians, 2002	52
11. Johnny Mize, Giants, 1947	51
12. Brady Anderson, Orioles, 1996	50
13. Barry Bonds, Giants, 2000	49
Lou Gehrig, Yankees, 1934	49
Lou Gehrig, Yankees, 1936	49
Shawn Green, Dodgers, 2001	49
Ken Griffey, Mariners, 1996	49
Todd Helton, Rockies, 2001	49
Ted Kluszewski, Reds, 1954	49
Babe Ruth, Yankees, 1930	49
Jim Thome, Indians, 2001	49
Larry Walker, Rockies, 1997	49

Roger Maris (left), Ted Williams (center) and Mickey Mantle rate high on baseball's all-time slugging charts.

HOME RUNS, SWITCH HITTER

1. Mickey Mantle, Yankees, 1961 54
2. Mickey Mantle, Yankees, 1956 52
3. Chipper Jones, Braves, 1999 45
4. Mark Teixeira, Rangers, 2005 43
5. Lance Berkman, Astros, 2002 42
   Mickey Mantle, Yankees, 1958 42
7. Todd Hundley, Mets, 1996 41
8. Ken Caminiti, Padres, 1996 40
   Mickey Mantle, Yankees, 1960 40
10. Carlos Beltran, Royals-Astros, 2004 38
    Howard Johnson, Mets, 1991 38
    Chipper Jones, Braves, 2001 38
    Mark Teixeira, Rangers, 2004 38
14. Mickey Mantle, Yankees, 1955 37
15. Howard Johnson, Mets, 1987 36
    Howard Johnson, Mets, 1989 36
    Chipper Jones, Braves, 2000 36
18. Rip Collins, Cardinals, 1934 35
    Mickey Mantle, Yankees, 1964 35
    Ken Singleton, Orioles, 1979 35

HOME RUNS, FIRST BASEMAN

1. Mark McGwire, Cardinals, 1998 69
2. Mark McGwire, Cardinals, 1999 65
3. Hank Greenberg, Tigers, 1938 58
4. Mark McGwire, Athletics-Cardinals, 1997 .. 57
5. Jimmie Foxx, Athletics, 1932 51
   Johnny Mize, Giants, 1947 51
7. Jimmie Foxx, Red Sox, 1938 50
8. Lou Gehrig, Yankees, 1934 49
   Lou Gehrig, Yankees, 1936 49
   Ted Kluszewski, Reds, 1954 49
   Todd Helton, Rockies, 2001 49

HOME RUNS, SECOND BASEMAN

1. Rogers Hornsby, Cardinals, 1922 42
   Davey Johnson, Braves NL, 1973 42
3. Ryne Sandberg, Cubs, 1990 40
4. Rogers Hornsby, Cardinals, 1925 39
   Rogers Hornsby, Cubs, 1929 39
   Alfonso Soriano, Yankees, 2002 39
7. Jay Bell, D-backs, 1999 38
   Alfonso Soriano, Yankees, 2003 38
9. Bret Boone, Mariners, 2001 36
   Jeff Kent, Giants, 2002 36

HOME RUNS, THIRD BASEMAN

1. Mike Schmidt, Phillies, 1980 48
   Adrian Beltre, Dodgers, 2004 48
3. Eddie Mathews, Braves, 1953 47
   Alex Rodriguez, Yankees, 2005 47
5. Eddie Mathews, Braves, 1959 46
   Vinny Castilla, Rockies, 1998 46
   Troy Glaus, Angels, 2000 46
8. Mike Schmidt, Phillies, 1979 45
   Chipper Jones, Braves NL, 1999 45
10. Al Rosen, Indians, 1953 43
    Matt Williams, Giants, 1994 43

HOME RUNS, SHORTSTOP

1. Alex Rodriguez, Rangers, 2002 57
2. Alex Rodriguez, Rangers, 2001 52
3. Ernie Banks, Cubs, 1958 47
4. Alex Rodriguez, Rangers, 2003 46
5. Ernie Banks, Cubs, 1959 45
6. Ernie Banks, Cubs, 1955 44
7. Alex Rodriguez, Mariners, 1998 42
   Alex Rodriguez, Mariners, 1999 42
9. Ernie Banks, Cubs, 1960 41
   Alex Rodriguez, Mariners, 2000 41

HOME RUNS, OUTFIELDER

1. Barry Bonds, Giants, 2001 71
2. Sammy Sosa, Cubs, 1998 66
3. Sammy Sosa, Cubs, 2001 64
4. Sammy Sosa, Cubs, 1999 63
5. Roger Maris, Yankees, 1961 61
6. Babe Ruth, Yankees, 1927 60
7. Babe Ruth, Yankees, 1921 58
8. Luis Gonzalez, D-backs, 2001 57
9. Hack Wilson, Cubs, 1930 56
   Ken Griffey, Mariners, 1998 56
11. Babe Ruth, Yankees, 1920 54
    Babe Ruth, Yankees, 1928 54
    Ralph Kiner, Pirates, 1949 54
    Mickey Mantle, Yankees, 1961 54
    Ken Griffey, Mariners, 1997 54
16. Mickey Mantle, Yankees, 1956 52
    Willie Mays, Giants, 1965 52
    George Foster, Reds, 1977 52
19. Ralph Kiner, Pirates, 1947 51
    Willie Mays, Giants, 1962 51
    Andruw Jones, Braves, 2005 51

HOME RUNS, CATCHER

1. Javy Lopez, Braves NL, 2003 42
2. Todd Hundley, Mets, 1996 41
3. Roy Campanella, Dodgers, 1953 40
   Mike Piazza, Dodgers, 1997 40
   Mike Piazza, Mets, 1999 40
6. Johnny Bench, Reds, 1970 38
7. Gabby Hartnett, Cubs, 1930 36
   Mike Piazza, Dodgers, 1996 36
9. Walker Cooper, Giants, 1947 35
   Mike Piazza, Dodgers, 1993 35
   Mike Piazza, Mets, 2000 35

HOME RUNS, PITCHER

1. Wes Ferrell, Indians, 1931 9
2. Jack Stivetts, StL AA, 1890 7
   Wes Ferrell, Indians, 1933 7
   Bob Lemon, Indians, 1949 7
   Don Newcombe, Dodgers, 1955 7
   Don Drysdale, Dodgers, 1958 7
   Don Drysdale, Dodgers, 1965 7
   Earl Wilson, Tigers, 1968 7
   Mike Hampton, Rockies, 2001 7

HOME RUNS, DESIGNATED HITTER

1. David Ortiz, Red Sox, 2005 43
2. Rafael Palmeiro, Rangers, 1999 37
   Edgar Martinez, Mariners, 2000 37
4. Dave Kingman, Athletics, 1984 35
   Dave Kingman, Athletics, 1986 35
   John Jaha, Athletics, 1999 35
7. Frank Thomas, White Sox, 2003 34
8. David Ortiz, Red Sox, 2004 33
9. Greg Luzinski, White Sox, 1983 32
   Gorman Thomas, Mariners, 1985 32
   Jose Canseco, Devil Rays, 1999 32
   Brad Fullmer, Blue Jays, 2000 32
   Ellis Burks, Indians, 2002 32
   Travis Hafner, Indians, 2005 32

HOME RUNS, ROOKIE

1. Mark McGwire, A's, 1987 49
2. Wally Berger, Braves, 1930 38
   Frank Robinson, Reds, 1956 38
4. Albert Pujols, Cardinals, 2001 37
   Al Rosen, Indians, 1950 37
6. Ron Kittle, White Sox, 1983 35
   Mike Piazza, Dodgers, 1993 35
   Hal Trosky, Indians, 1934 35

9. Walt Dropo, Red Sox, 1950 34
10. Jose Canseco, A's, 1986 33
    Jimmie Hall, Twins, 1963 33
    Earl Williams, Braves, 1971 33
13. Matt Nokes, Tigers, 1987 32
    Tony Oliva, Twins, 1964 32
15. Jim Ray Hart, Giants, 1964 31
    Tim Salmon, Angels, 1993 31
    Ted Williams, Red Sox, 1939 31
18. Bob Allison, Senators, 1959 30
    Nomar Garciaparra, Red Sox, 1997 30
    Pete Incaviglia, Rangers, 1986 30
    Willie Montanez, Phillies, 1971 30

CONSECUTIVE GAMES WITH HOME RUN

1. Don Mattingly, Yankees, 1987 (10) 8
   Dale Long, Pirates, 1956 (8) 8
   Ken Griffey Jr, Mariners, 1993 (8) 8
4. Jim Thome, Indians, 2002 (7) 7
5. Frank Howard, Senators, 1968 (10) 6
   Barry Bonds, Giants, 2001 (9) 6
   George Kelly, Giants, 1924 (7) 6
   Walker Cooper, Giants, 1947 (7) 6
   Willie Mays, Giants, 1955 (7) 6
   Roger Maris, Yankees, 1961 (7) 6
   Graig Nettles, Padres, 1984 (7) 6
   Ken Williams, Browns, 1922 (6) 6
   Lou Gehrig, Yankees, 1931 (6) 6
   Roy Sievers, Senators, 1957 (6) 6
   Willie Mays, Giants, 1965 (6) 6
   Reggie Jackson, Orioles, 1976 (6) 6
   Barry Bonds, Giants, 2001 (6) 6
   Jose Cruz, Blue Jays, 2001 (6) 6
   Travis Hafner, Indians, 2005 (6) 6
20. Jim Bottomley, Cardinals, 1929 (7) 5
    Babe Ruth, Yankees, 1921 (7) 5
    Vic Wertz, Tigers, 1950 (7) 5
    Johnny Bench, Reds, 1972 (7) 5
    Mike Schmidt, Phillies, 1979 (7) 5
    Note: Number in ( ) is homer total during streak.

MOST HOMERS PER AT-BAT

1. Barry Bonds, Giants, 2001 .... .153
2. Mark McGwire, Cardinals, 1998 .... .138
3. Mark McGwire, Cardinals, 1999 .... .125
4. Mark McGwire, A's, 1996 .... .123
5. Babe Ruth, Yankees, 1920 .... .118
6. Barry Bonds, Giants, 2003 .... .115
7. Barry Bonds, Giants, 2002 .... .114
8. Babe Ruth, Yankees, 1927 .... .111
   Sammy Sosa, Cubs, 2001 .... .111
10. Babe Ruth, Yankees, 1921 .... .109
11. Jim Thome, Indians, 2002 .... .108
12. Mark McGwire, A's-Cardinals, 1997 ...... .107
13. Mickey Mantle, Yankees, 1961 .... .105
14. Hank Greenberg, Tigers, 1938 .... .104
15. Roger Maris, Yankees, 1961 .... .103
    Sammy Sosa, Cubs, 1998 .... .103
17. Barry Bonds, Giants, 2000 .... .102
18. Sammy Sosa, Cubs, 1999 .... .101
    Babe Ruth, Yankees, 1928 .... .101
20. Jimmie Foxx, A's, 1932 .... .099

PINCH-HIT HOME RUNS

1. Dave Hansen, Dodgers, 2000 7
   Craig Wilson, Pirates, 2001 7
3. Johnny Frederick, Dodgers, 1932 6
4. Joe Cronin, Red Sox, 1943 5
   Butch Nieman, Braves, 1945 5
   Gene Freese, Phillies, 1959 5
   Jerry Lynch, Reds, 1961 5
   Cliff Johnson, Astros, 1974 5

Lee Lacy, Dodgers, 1978 ... 5
Jerry Turner, Padres, 1978 ... 5
Billy Ashley, Dodgers, 1996 ... 5
David Dellucci, Diamondbacks, 2001 ... 5
Erubiel Durazo, Diamondbacks, 2001 ... 5
Mark Sweeney, Rockies, 2004 ... 5

GRAND SLAMS

1. Don Mattingly, Yankees, 1987 ... 6
2. Ernie Banks, Cubs, 1955 ... 5
   Jim Gentile, Orioles, 1961 ... 5
4. Frank Schulte, Cubs, 1911 ... 4
   Babe Ruth, Red Sox, 1919 ... 4
   Lou Gehrig, Yankees, 1934 ... 4
   Rudy York, Tigers, 1938 ... 4
   Vince DiMaggio, Phillies, 1945 ... 4
   Tommy Henrich, Yankees, 1948 ... 4
   Ralph Kiner, Pirates, 1949 ... 4
   Sid Gordon, Braves, 1950 ... 4
   Al Rosen, Indians, 1951 ... 4
   Ray Boone, Indians-Tigers, 1953 ... 4
   Jim Northrup, Tigers, 1968 ... 4
   Albert Belle, White Sox, 1997 ... 4
   Jason Giambi, Athletics, 2000 ... 4
   Edgar Martinez, Mariners, 2000 ... 4
   Phil Nevin, Padres, 2001 ... 4

TOTAL BASES

1. Babe Ruth, Yankees, 1921 ... 457
2. Rogers Hornsby, Cardinals, 1922 ... 450
3. Lou Gehrig, Yankees, 1927 ... 447
4. Chuck Klein, Phillies, 1930 ... 445
5. Jimmie Foxx, A's, 1932 ... 438
6. Stan Musial, Cardinals, 1948 ... 429
7. Sammy Sosa, Cubs, 2001 ... 425
8. Hack Wilson, Cubs, 1930 ... 423
9. Chuck Klein, Phillies, 1932 ... 420
10. Lou Gehrig, Yankees, 1930 ... 419
    Luis Gonzalez, Diamondbacks, 2001 ... 419
12. Joe DiMaggio, Yankees, 1937 ... 418
13. Babe Ruth, Yankees, 1927 ... 417
14. Babe Herman, Dodgers, 1930 ... 416
    Sammy Sosa, Cubs, 1998 ... 416
16. Barry Bonds, Giants, 2001 ... 411
17. Lou Gehrig, Yankees, 1931 ... 410
18. Lou Gehrig, Yankees, 1934 ... 409
    Rogers Hornsby, Cubs, 1929 ... 409
    Larry Walker, Rockies, 1997 ... 409

*SLUGGING PERCENTAGE

1. Barry Bonds, Giants, 2001 ... .863
2. Babe Ruth, Yankees, 1920 ... .847
3. Babe Ruth, Yankees, 1921 ... .846
4. Barry Bonds, Giants, 2002 ... .799
5. Babe Ruth, Yankees, 1927 ... .772
6. Lou Gehrig, Yankees, 1927 ... .765
7. Babe Ruth, Yankees, 1923 ... .764
8. Rogers Hornsby, Cardinals, 1925 ... .756
9. Mark McGwire, Cardinals, 1998 ... .752
10. Jeff Bagwell, Astros, 1994 ... .750
11. Barry Bonds, Giants, 2003 ... .749
    Jimmie Foxx, A's, 1932 ... .749
13. Babe Ruth, Yankees, 1924 ... .739
14. Babe Ruth, Yankees, 1926 ... .737
    Sammy Sosa, Cubs, 2001 ... .737
16. Ted Williams, Red Sox, 1941 ... .735
17. Babe Ruth, Yankees, 1930 ... .732
18. Ted Williams, Red Sox, 1957 ... .731
19. Mark McGwire, A's, 1996 ... .730
20. Frank Thomas, White Sox, 1994 ... .729

*Based on players averaging at least 3.1 at-bats for every game played by their teams.

EXTRA-BASE HITS

1. Babe Ruth, Yankees, 1921 ... 119
2. Lou Gehrig, Yankees, 1927 ... 117
3. Barry Bonds, Giants, 2001 ... 107
   Chuck Klein, Phillies, 1930 ... 107
5. Todd Helton, Rockies, 2001 ... 105
6. Albert Belle, Indians, 1995 ... 103
   Hank Greenberg, Tigers, 1937 ... 103
   Todd Helton, Rockies, 2000 ... 103
   Chuck Klein, Phillies, 1932 ... 103
   Stan Musial, Cardinals, 1948 ... 103
   Sammy Sosa, Cubs, 2001 ... 103
12. Rogers Hornsby, Cardinals, 1922 ... 102
13. Jimmie Foxx, A's, 1932 ... 100
    Lou Gehrig, Yankees, 1930 ... 100
    Luis Gonzalez, Diamondbacks, 2001 ... 100
16. Albert Belle, White Sox, 1998 ... 99
    Carlos Delgado, Blue Jays, 2000 ... 99
    Hank Greenberg, Tigers, 1940 ... 99
    Albert Pujols, Cardinals, 2004 ... 99
    Babe Ruth, Yankees, 1920 ... 99
    Babe Ruth, Yankees, 1923 ... 99
    Larry Walker, Rockies, 1997 ... 99
    Derrek Lee, Cubs, 2005 ... 99

RUNS BATTED IN

1. Hack Wilson, Cubs, 1930 ... 191
2. Lou Gehrig, Yankees, 1931 ... 184
3. Hank Greenberg, Tigers, 1937 ... 183
4. Jimmie Foxx, Red Sox, 1938 ... 175
   Lou Gehrig, Yankees, 1927 ... 175
6. Lou Gehrig, Yankees, 1930 ... 174
7. Babe Ruth, Yankees, 1921 ... 171
8. Hank Greenberg, Tigers, 1935 ... 170
   Chuck Klein, Phillies, 1930 ... 170
10. Jimmie Foxx, A's, 1932 ... 169
11. Joe DiMaggio, Yankees, 1937 ... 167
12. Lou Gehrig, Yankees, 1934 ... 165
    Manny Ramirez, Indians, 1999 ... 165
    Al Simmons, A's, 1930 ... 165
15. Babe Ruth, Yankees, 1927 ... 164
16. Jimmie Foxx, A's, 1933 ... 163
    Babe Ruth, Yankees, 1931 ... 163
18. Hal Trosky, Indians, 1936 ... 162
19. Sammy Sosa, Cubs, 2001 ... 160
20. 4 tied with 159

RBIs, RIGHTHANDER

1. Hack Wilson, Cubs, 1930 ... 191
2. Hank Greenberg, Tigers, 1937 ... 183
3. Jimmie Foxx, Red Sox, 1938 ... 175
4. Hank Greenberg, Tigers, 1935 ... 170
5. Jimmie Foxx, A's, 1932 ... 169
6. Joe DiMaggio, Yankees, 1937 ... 167
7. Manny Ramirez, Indians, 1999 ... 165
   Al Simmons, A's, 1930 ... 165
9. Jimmie Foxx, A's, 1933 ... 163
10. Sammy Sosa, Cubs, 2001 ... 160
11. Vern Stephens, Red Sox, 1949 ... 159
    Hack Wilson, Cubs, 1929 ... 159
13. Sammy Sosa, Cubs, 1998 ... 158
14. Juan Gonzalez, Rangers, 1998 ... 157
    Al Simmons, A's, 1929 ... 157
16. Jimmie Foxx, A's, 1930 ... 156
17. Joe DiMaggio, Yankees, 1948 ... 155
18. Joe Medwick, Cardinals, 1937 ... 154
19. Tommy Davis, Dodgers, 1962 ... 153
20. Albert Belle, White Sox, 1998 ... 152
    Rogers Hornsby, Cardinals, 1922 ... 152

RBIs, LEFTHANDER

1. Lou Gehrig, Yankees, 1931 ... 184
2. Lou Gehrig, Yankees, 1927 ... 175
3. Lou Gehrig, Yankees, 1930 ... 174
4. Babe Ruth, Yankees, 1921 ... 171
5. Chuck Klein, Phillies, 1930 ... 170
6. Lou Gehrig, Yankees, 1934 ... 165
7. Babe Ruth, Yankees, 1927 ... 164
8. Babe Ruth, Yankees, 1931 ... 163
9. Hal Trosky, Indians, 1936 ... 162
10. Lou Gehrig, Yankees, 1937 ... 159
    Ted Williams, Red Sox, 1949 ... 159
12. Ken Williams, Browns, 1922 ... 155
13. Babe Ruth, Yankees, 1929 ... 154
14. Babe Ruth, Yankees, 1930 ... 153
15. Lou Gehrig, Yankees, 1936 ... 152
16. Lou Gehrig, Yankees, 1932 ... 151
    Mel Ott, Giants, 1929 ... 151
18. Rafael Palmeiro, Rangers, 1999 ... 148
    David Ortiz, Red Sox, 2005 ... 148
20. Ken Griffey, Mariners, 1997 ... 147
    Todd Helton, Rockies, 2000 ... 147

RBIs, SWITCH HITTER

1. Mark Teixeira, Rangers, 2005 ... 144
2. Ken Caminiti, Padres, 1996 ... 130
   Mickey Mantle, Yankees, 1956 ... 130
4. Ripper Collins, Cardinals, 1934 ... 128
   Mickey Mantle, Yankees, 1961 ... 128
   Lance Berkman, Astros, 2002 ... 128
7. Lance Berkman, Astros, 2001 ... 126
8. Eddie Murray, Orioles, 1985 ... 124
9. Ripper Collins, Cardinals, 1935 ... 122
10. Bernie Williams, Yankees, 2000 ... 121
11. Roberto Alomar, Indians, 1999 ... 120
    Bobby Bonilla, Pirates, 1990 ... 120
13. Ruben Sierra, Rangers, 1989 ... 119
14. Tony Clark, Tigers, 1997 ... 117
    Howard Johnson, Mets, 1991 ... 117
16. Bobby Bonilla, Orioles, 1996 ... 116
    Eddie Murray, Orioles, 1980 ... 116
    Ruben Sierra, Rangers, 1991 ... 116
19. Bernie Williams, Yankees, 1999 ... 115
20. Carlos Baerga, Indians, 1993 ... 114
    Frankie Frisch, Cardinals, 1930 ... 114

RBIs, ROOKIE

1. Ted Williams, Red Sox, 1939 ... 145
2. Walt Dropo, Red Sox, 1950 ... 144
3. Hal Trosky, Indians, 1934 ... 142
4. Dale Alexander, Tigers, 1929 ... 137
5. Albert Pujols, Cardinals, 2001 ... 130
6. Joe DiMaggio, Yankees, 1936 ... 125
7. Wally Berger, Braves, 1930 ... 119
8. Mark McGwire, A's, 1987 ... 118
9. Jose Canseco, A's, 1986 ... 117
   Joe Vosmik, Indians, 1931 ... 117
11. Alvin Davis, Mariners, 1984 ... 116
    Al Rosen, Indians, 1950 ... 116
13. Smead Jolley, White Sox, 1930 ... 114
    Tony Lazzeri, Yankees, 1926 ... 114
15. Ken Keltner, Indians, 1938 ... 113
16. Ray Jablonski, Cardinals, 1953 ... 112
    Mike Piazza, Dodgers, 1993 ... 112
18. Johnny Rizzo, Pirates, 1938 ... 111
    Glenn Wright, Pirates, 1924 ... 111
20. Zeke Bonura, White Sox, 1934 ... 110

WALKS

1. Barry Bonds, Giants, 2004 ... 232
2. Barry Bonds, Giants, 2002 ... 198
3. Barry Bonds, Giants, 2001 ... 177
4. Babe Ruth, Yankees, 1923 ... 170
5. Mark McGwire, Cardinals, 1998 ... 162
   Ted Williams, Red Sox, 1947 ... 162
   Ted Williams, Red Sox, 1949 ... 162
8. Ted Williams, Red Sox, 1946 ... 156
9. Barry Bonds, Giants, 1996 ... 151
   Eddie Yost, Senators, 1956 ... 151

11.	Babe Ruth, Yankees, 1920	150
12.	Jeff Bagwell, Astros, 1999	149
	Eddie Joost, A's, 1949	149
14.	Barry Bonds, Giants, 2003	148
	Eddie Stanky, Dodgers, 1945	148
	Jimmy Wynn, Astros, 1969	148
17.	Jimmy Sheckard, Cubs, 1911	147
	Ted Williams, Red Sox, 1941	147
19.	Mickey Mantle, Yankees, 1957	146
20.	Barry Bonds, Giants, 1997	145
	Harmon Killebrew, Twins, 1969	145
	Babe Ruth, Yankees, 1921	145
	Ted Williams, Red Sox, 1942	145

INTENTIONAL WALKS

1.	Barry Bonds, Giants, 2004	120
2.	Barry Bonds, Giants, 2002	68
3.	Barry Bonds, Giants, 2003	61
4.	Willie McCovey, Giants, 1969	45
5.	Barry Bonds, Giants, 1993	43
6.	Willie McCovey, Giants, 1970	40
7.	Sammy Sosa, Cubs, 2001	37
8.	Barry Bonds, Giants, 2001	35
9.	Barry Bonds, Giants, 1997	34
10.	John Olerud, Blue Jays, 1993	33
	Ted Williams, Red Sox, 1957	33
12.	Barry Bonds, Pirates, 1992	32
	Vladimir Guerrero, Expos, 2002	32

	Kevin Mitchell, Giants, 1989	32
15.	George Brett, Royals, 1985	31
16.	Barry Bonds, Giants, 1996	30
17.	Barry Bonds, Giants, 1998	29
	Frank Howard, Senators, 1970	29
	Dale Murphy, Braves, 1987	29
	Adolfo Phillips, Cubs, 1967	29
	Frank Thomas, White Sox, 1995	29

STRIKEOUTS

1.	Adam Dunn, Reds, 2004	195
2.	Bobby Bonds, Giants, 1970	189
3.	Jose Hernandez, Brewers, 2002	188
4.	Bobby Bonds, Giants, 1969	187
	Preston Wilson, Marlins, 2000	187
6.	Rob Deer, Brewers, 1987	186
7.	Jose Hernandez, Brewers, 2001	185
	Pete Incaviglia, Rangers, 1986	185
	Jim Thome, Indians, 2001	185
10.	Cecil Fielder, Tigers, 1990	182
	Jim Thome, Phillies, 2003	182
12.	Mo Vaughn, Angels, 2000	181
13.	Mike Schmidt, Phillies, 1975	180
14.	Rob Deer, Brewers, 1986	179
15.	Richie Sexson, Brewers, 2001	178
16.	Mark Bellhorn, Red Sox, 2004	177
	Jose Hernandez, 3 clubs, 2003	177
18.	Mike Cameron, Mariners, 2002	176

19.	Jay Buhner, Mariners, 1997	175
	Jose Canseco, A's, 1986	175
	Rob Deer, Tigers, 1991	175
	Dave Nicholson, White Sox, 1963	175
	Gorman Thomas, Brewers, 1979	175

STOLEN BASES

1.	Rickey Henderson, A's, 1982	130
2.	Lou Brock, Cardinals, 1974	118
3.	Vince Coleman, Cardinals, 1985	110
4.	Vince Coleman, Cardinals, 1987	109
5.	Rickey Henderson, A's, 1983	108
6.	Vince Coleman, Cardinals, 1986	107
7.	Maury Wills, Dodgers, 1962	104
8.	Rickey Henderson, A's, 1980	100
9.	Ron LeFlore, Expos, 1980	97
10.	Ty Cobb, Tigers, 1915	96
	Omar Moreno, Pirates, 1980	96
12.	Maury Wills, Dodgers, 1965	94
13.	Rickey Henderson, Yankees, 1988	93
14.	Tim Raines Sr., Expos, 1983	90
15.	Clyde Milan, Senators, 1912	88
16.	Rickey Henderson, Yankees, 1986	87
17.	Ty Cobb, Tigers, 1911	83
	Willie Wilson, Royals, 1979	83
19.	Bob Bescher, Reds, 1911	81
	Vince Coleman, Cardinals, 1988	81
	Eddie Collins, A's, 1910	81

PITCHING

GAMES

1.	Mike Marshall, Dodgers, 1974	106
2.	Kent Tekulve, Pirates, 1979	94
3.	Mike Marshall, Expos, 1973	92
4.	Kent Tekulve, Pirates, 1978	91
5.	Wayne Granger, Reds, 1969	90
	Mike Marshall, Twins, 1979	90
	Kent Tekulve, Phillies, 1987	90
8.	Jim Brower, Giants, 2004	89
	Mark Eichhorn, Blue Jays, 1987	89
	Steve Kline, Cardinals, 2001	89
	Paul Quantrill, Dodgers, 2003	89
	Julian Tavarez, Giants, 1997	89
13.	Mike Myers, Tigers, 1997	88
	Sean Runyan, Tigers, 1998	88
	Wilbur Wood, White Sox, 1968	88
16.	Rob Murphy, Reds, 1987	87
17.	Ray King, Cardinals, 2004	86
	Paul Quantrill, Dodgers, 2002	86
	Paul Quantrill, Yankees, 2004	86
	Oscar Villarreal, Diamondbacks, 2003	86
	Scott Eyre, Giants, 2005	86

GAMES STARTED

1.	Jack Chesbro, Yankees, 1904	51
2.	Ed Walsh, White Sox, 1908	49
	Wilbur Wood, White Sox, 1972	49
4.	Joe McGinnity, Giants, 1903	48
	Wilbur Wood, White Sox, 1973	48
6.	Dave Davenport, St. Louis F.L., 1915	46
	Christy Mathewson, Giants, 1904	46
	Rube Waddell, A's, 1904	46
	Ed Walsh, White Sox, 1907	46
	Vic Willis, Braves, 1902	46
11.	Grover Alexander, Phillies, 1916	45
	Mickey Lolich, Tigers, 1971	45
	Jack Powell, Yankees, 1904	45
14.	Grover Alexander, Phillies, 1917	44
	Christy Mathewson, Giants, 1908	44
	Joe McGinnity, Giants, 1904	44
	George Mullin, Tigers, 1904	44

	Phil Niekro, Braves, 1979	44
	George Uhle, Indians, 1923	44
20.	9 tied with 43	

COMPLETE GAMES

1.	Jack Chesbro, Yankees, 1904	48
2.	Vic Willis, Braves, 1902	45
3.	Joe McGinnity, Giants, 1903	44
4.	George Mullin, Tigers, 1904	42
	Ed Walsh, White Sox, 1908	42
6.	Noodles Hahn, Reds, 1901	41
	Cy Young, Red Sox, 1902	41
	Irv Young, Braves, 1905	41
9.	Cy Young, Red Sox, 1904	40
10.	Bill Dinneen, Red Sox, 1902	39
	Joe McGinnity, Orioles, 1901	39
	Jack Taylor, Cardinals, 1904	39
	Rube Waddell, A's, 1904	39
	Vic Willis, Braves, 1904	39
15.	Grover Alexander, Phillies, 1916	38
	Walter Johnson, Senators, 1910	38
	Oscar Jones, Dodgers, 1904	38
	Joe McGinnity, Giants, 1904	38
	Jack Powell, Yankees, 1904	38
	Cy Young, Red Sox, 1901	38

INNINGS PITCHED

1.	Ed Walsh, White Sox, 1908	464.0
2.	Jack Chesbro, Yankees, 1904	454.2
3.	Joe McGinnity, Giants, 1903	434.0
4.	Ed Walsh, White Sox, 1907	422.1
5.	Vic Willis, Braves, 1902	410.0
6.	Joe McGinnity, Giants, 1904	408.0
7.	Ed Walsh, White Sox, 1912	393.0
8.	Dave Davenport, St. Louis F.L., 1915	392.2
9.	Christy Mathewson, Giants, 1908	390.2
10.	Jack Powell, Yankees, 1904	390.1
11.	Togie Pittinger, Braves, 1902	389.1
12.	Grover Alexander, Phillies, 1916	389.0
13.	Grover Alexander, Phillies, 1917	388.0
14.	Cy Young, Red Sox, 1902	384.2
15.	Rube Waddell, A's, 1904	383.0

16.	George Mullin, Tigers, 1904	382.1
17.	Joe McGinnity, Orioles, 1901	382.0
18.	Cy Young, Red Sox, 1904	380.0
19.	Irv Young, Braves, 1905	378.0
20.	Cy Falkenberg, Indianapolis F.L., 1914	377.1

CONSECUTIVE SCORELESS INNINGS

1.	Orel Hershiser, Dodgers, 1988	59
2.	Don Drysdale, Dodgers, 1968	58
3.	Walter Johnson, Senators, 1913	55.2
4.	Jack Coombs, A's, 1910	53
5.	Ed Reulbach, Cubs, 1908	*50
6.	Bob Gibson, Cardinals, 1968	47
7.	Carl Hubbell, Giants, 1933	45.1
8.	Cy Young, Red Sox, 1904	45
	Doc White, White Sox, 1904	45
	Sal Maglie, Giants, 1950	45
11.	Rube Waddell, A's, 1905	43.2
12.	Rube Foster, Red Sox, 1914	42
13.	Jack Chesbro, Pirates, 1902	41
	Grover Alexander, Phillies, 1911	41
	Art Nehf, Braves, 1917	41
	Luis Tiant, Indians, 1968	41
17.	Walter Johnson, Senators, 1918	40
	Gaylord Perry, Giants, 1967	40
	Luis Tiant, Red Sox, 1972	40
20.	Mordecai Brown, Cubs, 1908	39.2
	Billy Pierce, White Sox, 1953	39.2

* 44 in 1908; 6 in 1909.

*LOWEST ERA

1.	Dutch Leonard, Red Sox, 1914	0.96
2.	Mordecai Brown, Cubs, 1906	1.04
3.	Bob Gibson, Cardinals, 1968	1.12
4.	Christy Mathewson, Giants, 1909	1.14
	Walter Johnson, Senators, 1913	1.14
6.	Jack Pfiester, Cubs, 1907	1.15
7.	Addie Joss, Indians, 1908	1.16
8.	Carl Lundgren, Cubs, 1907	1.17
9.	Grover Alexander, Phillies, 1915	1.22
10.	Cy Young, Red Sox, 1908	1.26
11.	Ed Walsh, White Sox, 1910	1.27

All-Star Game hero Ted Williams receives a victory hug from American League manager Del Baker after the 1941 classic.

Walter Johnson, Senators, 1918	1.27
13. Christy Mathewson, Giants, 1905	1.28
14. Jack Coombs, A's, 1910	1.30
15. Mordecai Brown, Cubs, 1909	1.31
16. Jack Taylor, Cubs, 1902	1.33
17. Walter Johnson, Senators, 1910	1.36
18. Walter Johnson, Senators, 1912	1.39
Mordecai Brown, Cubs, 1907	1.39
Harry Krause, A's, 1909	1.39

*Leaders based on pitchers whose total innings equal total games played by their teams.

VICTORIES

1. Jack Chesbro, Yankees, 1904	41
2. Ed Walsh, White Sox, 1908	40
3. Christy Mathewson, Giants, 1908	37
4. Walter Johnson, Senators, 1913	36
5. Joe McGinnity, Giants, 1904	35
6. Joe Wood, Red Sox, 1912	34
7. Grover Alexander, Phillies, 1916	33
Walter Johnson, Senators, 1912	33
Christy Mathewson, Giants, 1904	33
Cy Young, Red Sox, 1901	33
11. Cy Young, Red Sox, 1902	32
12. Grover Alexander, Phillies, 1915	31
Jim Bagby, Indians, 1920	31
Jack Coombs, A's, 1910	31
Lefty Grove, A's, 1931	31
Christy Mathewson, Giants, 1905	31
Joe McGinnity, Giants, 1903	31
Denny McLain, Tigers, 1968	31
19. Grover Alexander, Phillies, 1917	30
Dizzy Dean, Cardinals, 1934	30
Christy Mathewson, Giants, 1903	30

WINNING PERCENTAGE
(Minimum 15 victories)

1. Roy Face, Pirates, 1959	.947
2. John Allen, Indians, 1937	.938
3. Greg Maddux, Braves, 1995	.905
4. Randy Johnson, Mariners, 1995	.900
5. Ron Guidry, Yankees, 1978	.893
6. Freddie Fitzsimmons, Dodgers, 1940	.889
7. Lefty Grove, A's, 1931	.886
8. Bob Stanley, Red Sox, 1978	.882
9. Preacher Roe, Dodgers, 1951	.880
10. Joe Wood, Red Sox, 1912	.872
11. Roger Clemens, Yankees, 2001	.870
12. David Cone, Mets, 1988	.870
13. Orel Hershiser, Dodgers, 1985	.864
14. Bill Donovan, Tigers, 1907	.862
Whitey Ford, Yankees, 1961	.862
16. Roger Clemens, Red Sox, 1986	.857
Dwight Gooden, Mets, 1985	.857
18. Pedro Martinez, Red Sox, 1999	.852
19. Chief Bender, A's, 1914	.850
John Smoltz, Braves, 1998	.850

CONSECUTIVE VICTORIES

1. Rube Marquard, Giants, 1912	19
2. Roy Face, Pirates, 1959	17
3. Walter Johnson, Senators, 1912	16
Joe Wood, Red Sox, 1912	16
Lefty Grove, Athletics, 1931	16
Schoolboy Rowe, Tigers, 1934	16
Carl Hubbell, Giants, 1936	16
Ewell Blackwell, Reds, 1947	16
Jack Sanford, Giants, 1962	16
Roger Clemens, Yankees, 2001	16

11. John Allen, Indians, 1937	15
Steve Carlton, Phillies, 1972	15
Alvin Crowder, Senators, 1932	15
Bob Gibson, Cardinals, 1968	15
Dave McNally, Orioles, 1969	15
Gaylord Perry, Indians, 1974	15
Dazzy Vance, Dodgers, 1924	15
Roger Clemens, Blue Jays, 1998	15
Roy Halladay, Blue Jays, 2003	15
20. Jack Chesbro, Yankees, 1904	14
Joe McGinnity, Giants, 1904	14
Ed Reulbach, Cubs, 1909	14
Walter Johnson, Senators, 1913	14
Chief Bender, Athletics, 1914	14
Lefty Grove, Athletics, 1928	14
Whitey Ford, Yankees, 1961	14
Steve Stone, Orioles, 1980	14
Rick Sutcliffe, Cubs, 1984	14
Dwight Gooden, Mets, 1985	14
Roger Clemens, Red Sox, 1986	14
John Smoltz, Braves NL, 1996	14

LOSSES

1. Vic Willis, Braves, 1905	29
2. George Bell, Dodgers, 1910	27
Paul Derringer, Cardinals-Reds, 1933	27
Dummy Taylor, Giants, 1901	27
5. Gus Dorner, Reds-Braves, 1906	26
Bob Groom, Senators, 1909	26
Happy Townsend, Senators, 1904	26
8. Ben Cantwell, Braves, 1935	25
Pete Dowling, Brewers-Indians, 1901	25
Patsy Flaherty, White Sox, 1903	25
Fred Glade, Browns, 1905	25

Walter Johnson, Senators, 1909	25
Oscar Jones, Dodgers, 1904	25
Stoney McGlynn, Cardinals, 1907	25
Harry McIntire, Dodgers, 1905	25
Scott Perry, A's, 1920	25
Bugs Raymond, Cardinals, 1908	25
Red Ruffing, Red Sox, 1928	25
Vic Willis, Braves, 1904	25
Irv Young, Braves, 1906	25

SAVES

1.	Bobby Thigpen, White Sox, 1990	57
2.	Eric Gagne, Dodgers, 2003	55
	John Smoltz, Braves, 2002	55
4.	Trevor Hoffman, Padres, 1998	53
	Randy Myers, Cubs, 1993	53
	Mariano Rivera, Yankees, 2004	53
7.	Eric Gagne, Dodgers, 2002	52
8.	Rod Beck, Cubs, 1998	51
	Dennis Eckersley, A's, 1992	51
10.	Mariano Rivera, Yankees, 2001	50
11.	Francisco Cordero, Rangers, 2004	49
12.	Rod Beck, Giants, 1993	48
	Dennis Eckersley, A's, 1990	48
	Jeff Shaw, Reds-Dodgers, 1998	48
15.	Lee Smith, Cardinals, 1991	47
	Armando Benitez, Marlins, 2004	47
	Jason Isringhausen, Cardinals, 2004	47
	Chad Cordero, Nationals, 2005	47
19.	Tom Gordon, Red Sox, 1998	46
	Bryan Harvey, Angels, 1991	46
	Jose Mesa, Indians, 1995	46
	Dave Righetti, Yankees, 1986	46
	Lee Smith, Cardinals-Yankees, 1993	46
	Mike Williams, Pirates, 2002	46

SHUTOUTS

1.	Grover Alexander, Phillies, 1916	16
2.	Jack Coombs, A's, 1910	13
	Bob Gibson, Cardinals, 1968	13
4.	Grover Alexander, Phillies, 1915	12
5.	Dean Chance, Angels, 1964	11
	Walter Johnson, Senators, 1913	11
	Sandy Koufax, Dodgers, 1963	11
	Christy Mathewson, Giants, 1908	11
	Ed Walsh, White Sox, 1908	11
10.	Mort Cooper, Cardinals, 1942	10
	Dave Davenport, St. Louis F.L., 1915	10
	Bob Feller, Indians, 1946	10
	Carl Hubbell, Giants, 1933	10
	Bob Lemon, Indians, 1948	10
	Juan Marichal, Giants, 1965	10
	Jim Palmer, Orioles, 1975	10
	John Tudor, Cardinals, 1985	10
	Ed Walsh, White Sox, 1906	10
	Joe Wood, Red Sox, 1912	10
	Cy Young, Red Sox, 1904	10

RUNS ALLOWED

1.	Snake Wiltse, A's-Orioles, 1902	226
2.	Joe McGinnity, Orioles, 1901	219
3.	Chick Fraser, A's, 1901	210
4.	Pete Dowling, Brewers-Indians, 1901	209
5.	Bobo Newsom, Browns, 1938	205
	Togie Pittinger, Braves, 1903	205
7.	Bill Carrick, Senators, 1901	198
8.	Bill Phillips, Reds, 1901	196
9.	Bill Carrick, Senators, 1902	194
10.	Dummy Taylor, Giants, 1901	193
11.	Harry Howell, Orioles, 1901	188
	Harry McIntire, Dodgers, 1905	188
13.	Sam Gray, Browns, 1931	187
14.	Case Patten, Senators, 1902	186

15.	Watty Lee, Senators, 1901	184
16.	Bill Reidy, Brewers, 1901	183
17.	Dickie Kerr, White Sox, 1921	182
18.	Ray Kremer, Pirates, 1930	181
	Al Orth, Senators, 1902	181
20.	Ray Benge, Phillies, 1930	178

HITS ALLOWED

1.	Joe McGinnity, Orioles, 1901	412
2.	Snake Wiltse, A's-Orioles, 1902	397
3.	Togie Pittinger, Braves, 1903	396
4.	Joe McGinnity, Giants, 1903	391
5.	Oscar Jones, Dodgers, 1904	387
6.	Wilbur Wood, White Sox, 1973	381
7.	George Uhle, Indians, 1923	378
8.	Dummy Taylor, Giants, 1901	377
9.	Vic Willis, Braves, 1902	372
10.	Noodles Hahn, Reds, 1901	370
11.	Bill Carrick, Senators, 1901	367
	Al Orth, Senators, 1902	367
	Case Patten, Senators, 1904	367
14.	Ray Kremer, Pirates, 1930	366
15.	Urban Shocker, Browns, 1922	365
16.	Bill Phillips, Reds, 1901	364
	Bill Reidy, Brewers, 1901	364
18.	Jack Coombs, A's, 1911	360
	Togie Pittinger, Braves, 1902	360
20.	Dickie Kerr, White Sox, 1921	357
	Vic Willis, Braves, 1904	357

STRIKEOUTS

1.	Nolan Ryan, Angels, 1973	383
2.	Sandy Koufax, Dodgers, 1965	382
3.	Randy Johnson, Diamondbacks, 2001	372
4.	Nolan Ryan, Angels, 1974	367
5.	Randy Johnson, Diamondbacks, 1999	364
6.	Rube Waddell, A's, 1904	349
7.	Bob Feller, Indians, 1946	348
8.	Randy Johnson, Diamondbacks, 2000	347
9.	Nolan Ryan, Angels, 1977	341
10.	Randy Johnson, Diamondbacks, 2002	334
11.	Randy Johnson, Mariners-Astros, 1998	329

Pete Rose

	Nolan Ryan, Angels, 1972	329
13.	Nolan Ryan, Angels, 1976	327
14.	Sam McDowell, Indians, 1965	325
15.	Curt Schilling, Phillies, 1997	319
16.	Sandy Koufax, Dodgers, 1966	317
17.	Curt Schilling, Diamondbacks, 2002	316
18.	Walter Johnson, Senators, 1910	313
	Pedro Martinez, Red Sox, 1999	313
	J.R. Richard, Astros, 1979	313

WALKS

1.	Bob Feller, Indians, 1938	208
2.	Nolan Ryan, Angels, 1977	204
3.	Nolan Ryan, Angels, 1974	202
4.	Bob Feller, Indians, 1941	194
5.	Bobo Newsom, Browns, 1938	192
6.	Sam Jones, Cubs, 1955	185
7.	Nolan Ryan, Angels, 1976	183
8.	Bob Harmon, Cardinals, 1911	181
	Bob Turley, Orioles, 1954	181
10.	Tommy Byrne, Yankees, 1949	179
11.	Bob Turley, Yankees, 1955	177
12.	Bump Hadley, White Sox-Browns, 1932	171
13.	Elmer Myers, A's, 1916	168
14.	Bobo Newsom, Senators-Red Sox, 1937	167
15.	Weldon Wyckoff, A's, 1915	165
16.	Earl Moore, Phillies, 1911	164
	Phil Niekro, Braves, 1977	164
18.	Nolan Ryan, Angels, 1973	162
	Johnny Vander Meer, Reds, 1943	162
20.	Tommy Byrne, Yankees, 1950	160

HIT BATSMEN

1.	Chick Fraser, A's, 1901	32
2.	Jack Warhop, Yankees, 1909	26
3.	Chief Bender, A's, 1903	25
4.	Otto Hess, Indians, 1906	24
	Eddie Plank, A's, 1905	24
6.	Howard Ehmke, Tigers, 1922	23
	Eddie Plank, A's, 1903	23
	Jake Weimer, Reds, 1907	23
9.	Cy Morgan, Red Sox-A's, 1909	22
10.	Jack Chesbro, Pirates, 1902	21
	Joe McGinnity, Orioles, 1901	21
	Harry McIntire, Dodgers, 1909	21
	Cy Morgan, A's, 1911	21
	Tom Murphy, Angels, 1969	21
	Doc Newton, Reds-Dodgers, 1901	21
	Henry Schmidt, Dodgers, 1903	21
	Kerry Wood, Cubs, 2003	21
18.	Many tied with 20	

WILD PITCHES

1.	Red Ames, Giants, 1905	30
2.	Tony Cloninger, Braves, 1966	27
3.	Larry Cheney, Cubs, 1914	26
	Juan Guzman, Blue Jays, 1993	26
5.	Jack Morris, Tigers, 1987	24
6.	Matt Clement, Padres, 2000	23
	Tim Leary, Yankees, 1990	23
	Christy Mathewson, Giants, 1901	23
9.	Tony Cloninger, Braves, 1965	22
	Jack Hamilton, Phillies, 1962	22
	Mike Moore, A's, 1992	22
	Bobby Witt, Rangers, 1986	22
13.	Ken Howell, Phillies, 1989	21
	Walter Johnson, Senators, 1910	21
	Joe Niekro, Astros-Yankees, 1985	21
	Nolan Ryan, Angels, 1977	21
	Scott Williamson, Reds, 2000	21
	Earl Wilson, Red Sox, 1963	21
19.	8 tied with 20	

HALL OF FAME MEMBERS

HALL OF FAME ROSTER

2006 BASEBALL REGISTER & FANTASY HANDBOOK

Members by year elected, with method of election and key statistics

HALL OF FAME MEMBERS

CLASS BY CLASS

1936

TY COBB OF
6-1, 175.　　**B:** L. **T:** R.
Born: Dec. 18, 1886.　**Died:** July 17, 1961.
Career: .366 avg., 1st on all-time list; 117 HR; 1,937 RBIs; 4,189 hits;
891 SB.
Teams: Tigers 1905-26; Athletics 1927-28.
How elected: 98.2 percent of vote.

WALTER JOHNSON P
6-1, 200.　　**B:** R. **T:** R.
Born: Nov. 6, 1887.　**Died:** Dec. 10, 1946.
Career: 417-279; 2.16 ERA; 3,509 SO.
Team: Senators 1907-27.
How elected: 83.6 percent of vote.

CHRISTY MATHEWSON P
6-1, 195.　　**B:** R. **T:** R.
Born: Aug. 12, 1880.　**Died:** Oct. 7, 1925.
Career: 373-188; 2.13 ERA; 2,502 SO.
Teams: Giants 1900-16; Reds 1916.
How elected: 90.7 percent of vote.

BABE RUTH OF
6-2, 215.　　**B:** L. **T:** L.
Born: Feb. 6, 1895.　**Died:** Aug. 16, 1948.
Career: .342 avg.; 714 HR; 2,213 RBIs.
Teams: Red Sox 1914-19; Yankees 1920-34;
Braves 1935.
How elected: 95.1 percent of vote.

HONUS WAGNER SS
5-11, 200.　　**B:** R. **T:** R.
Born: Feb. 24, 1874.　**Died:** Dec. 6, 1955.
Career: .327 avg.; 101 HR; 1,732 RBIs; 3,415 hits, 722 SB.
Teams: Louisville (Nat.) 1897-99; Pirates 1900-17.
How elected: 95.1 percent of vote.

1937

MORGAN BULKELEY EXECUTIVE
First president of N.L.
Born: Dec. 26, 1837.　**Died:** Nov. 6, 1922.
Career: Former Connecticut governor and U.S. senator; helped N.L.
organize its first league.
How elected: Centennial Commission.

BAN JOHNSON EXECUTIVE
A.L. founder/president.
Born: Jan. 5, 1864.　**Died:** March 28, 1931.
Career: A former sportswriter who revived the old Western League
and later renamed it the American League; A.L. president 1901-27.
How elected: Centennial Commission.

NAPOLEON LAJOIE 2B
6-1, 195.　　**B:** R. **T:** R.
Born: Sept. 5, 1874.　**Died:** Feb. 7, 1959.
Career: .338 avg.; 83 HR; 1,599 RBIs; 3,242 hits.
Teams: Phillies 1896-1900; Athletics 1901-02, 1915-16; Indians
1902-14.
How elected: 83.6 percent of vote.

CONNIE MACK C, MGR.
6-1, 150.　　**B:** R. **T:** R.
Born: Dec. 22, 1862.　**Died:** Feb. 8, 1956.
Managing career: 3,731-3,948, 53 years; 3 World Series champi-
onships.
Teams: Pirates 1894-96; Athletics 1901-50.
How elected: Centennial Commission.

JOHN MCGRAW IF, MGR.
5-7, 155.　　**B:** L. **T:** R.
Born: April 7, 1873.　**Died:** Feb. 25, 1934.
Playing career: .334 avg.; 13 HR; 462 RBIs.
Managing career: 2,784-1,959, 33 years; 3 World Series champi-
onships.
Teams (player): Baltimore (A.A.) 1891; Baltimore (Nat.) 1892-99;
St. Louis (Nat.) 1900; Baltimore (Amer.) 1901-02; Giants 1902-06.
Teams (manager): Baltimore (Nat.) 1899; Baltimore (Amer.) 1901-
02; Giants 1902-32.
How elected: Centennial Commission.

TRIS SPEAKER OF
5-11, 193.　　**B:** L. **T:** L.
Born: April 4, 1888.　**Died:** Dec. 8, 1958.
Career: .345 avg.; 117 HR; 1,529 RBIs; 3,514 hits.
Teams: Red Sox 1907-15; Indians 1916-26; Senators 1927;
Athletics 1928.
How elected: 82.1 percent of vote.

GEORGE WRIGHT SS
5-9, 150.　　**B:** R. **T:** R.
Born: Jan. 28, 1847.　**Died:** Aug. 21, 1937.
Career: .256 avg.; 2 HR; 132 RBIs.
Teams: Boston (Nat.) 1876-78, 1880-81; Providence (Nat.) 1879,
1882.
How elected: Centennial Commission.

CY YOUNG P
6-2, 210.　　**B:** R. **T:** R.
Born: March 29, 1867.　**Died:** Nov. 4, 1955.
Career: 511-316, 1st on all-time win list; 2.63 ERA; 2,800 SO.
Teams: Cleveland (Nat.) 1890-98; St. Louis (Nat.) 1899-1900; Red
Sox 1901-08; Indians 1909-11; Braves 1911.
How elected: 76.1 percent of vote.

1938

GROVER CLEVELAND ALEXANDER P
6-1, 185.　　**B:** R. **T:** R.
Born: Feb. 26, 1887.　**Died:** Nov. 4, 1950.
Career: 373-208; 2.56 ERA; 2,198 SO.
Teams: Phillies 1911-17, 1930; Cubs 1918-26;
Cardinals 1926-29.
How elected: 80.9 percent of vote.

ALEXANDER CARTWRIGHT ORGANIZER
Organized 1st baseball club in 1845.
Born: April 17, 1820.　**Died:** July 12, 1892.
Career: Formed the Knickerbocker Ball Club in 1845
and taught the new game to Americans from coast to coast; served
as unofficial ambassador for the game until his death.
How elected: Centennial Commission.

HENRY CHADWICK ORGANIZER
Known as "Father of Baseball."
Born: Oct. 5, 1824. **Died:** April 29, 1908.
Career: A longtime New York baseball writer and contributor to numerous statistical publications dealing with the game; longtime chairman of baseball's committee on rules and author of many significant rules changes during the game's formative years.
How elected: Centennial Commission.

1939

CAP ANSON 1B
6-1, 227. **B:** R. **T:** R.
Born: April 17, 1852. **Died:** April 14, 1922.
Career: .339 avg.; 97 HR; 1,879 RBIs, 3,081 hits.
Team: Chicago (Nat.) 1876-97.
How elected: Committee old-time players and writers.

EDDIE COLLINS 2B
5-9, 175. **B:** L. **T:** R.
Born: May 2, 1887. **Died:** March 25, 1951.
Career: .333 avg.; 47 HR; 1,300 RBIs; 3,314 hits, 743 SB.
Teams: Athletics 1906-14; White Sox 1915-26; Athletics 1927-30.
How elected: 77.7 percent of vote.

CHARLES COMISKEY 1B, MGR.,EXEC.
Founder/owner of Chicago White Sox.
6-0, 180. **B:** R. **T:** R.
Born: Aug. 15, 1859. **Died:** Oct. 26, 1931.
Playing career: .264 avg.; 29 HR; revolutionized art of playing first base by playing off the bag.
Managing career: 839-542, 12 years.
Teams: St. Louis (A.A.) 1882-89, 1891; Chicago (P.L.) 1890; Cincinnati (Nat.) 1892-94.
How elected: Committee old-time players and writers.

CANDY CUMMINGS P
5-9, 120. **B:** R. **T:** R.
Born: Oct. 17, 1848. **Died:** May 17, 1924.
Career: 21-22; 2.78 ERA; credited with throwing the first curveball.
Teams: Hartford (Nat.) 1876; Cincinnati (Nat.) 1877.
How elected: Committee old-time players and writers.

BUCK EWING C, IF, MGR.
5-10, 188. **B:** R. **T:** R.
Born: Oct. 27, 1859. **Died:** Oct. 20, 1906.
Playing career: .303 avg.; 71 HR; 883 RBIs.
Managing career: 489-395, 7 years.
Teams (player): Troy (Nat.) 1880-82; New York (Nat.) 1883-89, 1891-92; New York (P.L.) 1890; Cleveland (Nat.) 1893-94; Cincinnati (Nat.) 1895-97.
Teams (manager): New York (P.L.) 1890; Cincinnati (Nat.) 1895-99; New York (Nat.) 1900.
How elected: Committee old-time players and writers.

LOU GEHRIG 1B
6-1, 200. **B:** L. **T:** L.
Born: June 19, 1903. **Died:** June 2, 1941.
Career: .340 avg.; 493 HR; 1,995 RBIs.
Team: Yankees 1923-39.
How elected: Special election Baseball Writers.

WILLIE KEELER OF
5-4, 140. **B:** L. **T:** L.
Born: March 3, 1872. **Died:** Jan. 1, 1923.
Career: .341 avg.; 33 HR; 810 RBIs.

Teams: New York (Nat.) 1892-93, 1910; Brooklyn (Nat.) 1893, 1899-1902; Baltimore (Nat.) 1894-98; Yankees 1903-09.
How elected: 75.5 percent of vote.

HOSS RADBOURN P
5-9, 168. **B:** R. **T:** R.
Born: Dec. 9, 1853. **Died:** Feb. 5, 1897.
Career: 309-195; 2.67 ERA; 1,830 SO.
Teams: Providence (Nat.) 1881-85; Boston (Nat.) 1886-90; Cincinnati (Nat.) 1891.
How elected: Committee old-time players and writers.

GEORGE SISLER 1B
5-11, 170. **B:** L. **T:** L.
Born: March 24, 1893. **Died:** March 26, 1973.
Career: .340 avg.; 102 HR; 1,175 RBIs.
Teams: Browns 1915-27; Senators 1928; Braves 1928-30.
How elected: 85.8 percent of vote.

AL SPALDING P, MGR., OWNER
Founder A.G. Spalding & Bros. sporting goods.
6-1, 170. **B:** R. **T:** R.
Born: Sept. 2, 1850. **Died:** Sept. 9, 1915.
Career: 48-12; 1.78 ERA.
Team (player): Chicago (Nat.) 1876-77.
Team (manager): Chicago (Nat.) 1876-78.
Team (owner): Chicago (Nat.) 1882-91.
How elected: Committee old-time players and writers.

1942

ROGERS HORNSBY 2B
5-11, 200. **B:** R. **T:** R.
Born: April 27, 1896. **Died:** Jan. 5, 1963.
Career: .358 avg.; 301 HR; 1,584 RBIs.
Teams: Cardinals 1915-26, 1933; Giants 1927; Braves 1928; Cubs 1929-32; Browns 1933-37.
How elected: 78.1 percent of vote.

1944

KENESAW MOUNTAIN LANDIS EXEC.
First baseball commissioner.
Born: Nov. 20, 1866. **Died:** Nov. 25, 1944.
Career: Former U.S. District judge; became baseball's first commissioner in 1921 and served until his death.
How elected: Committee on Old-Timers.

1945

ROGER BRESNAHAN C
5-9, 190. **B:** R. **T:** R.
Born: June 11, 1879. **Died:** Dec. 4, 1944.
Career: .279 avg.; 26 HR; 530 RBIs; credited with introducing shinguards for catchers.
Teams: Washington (Nat.) 1897; Chicago (Nat.) 1900; Orioles 1901-02; Giants 1902-08; Cardinals 1909-12; Cubs 1913-15.
How elected: Committee on Old-Timers.

DAN BROUTHERS 1B
6-2, 200. **B:** L. **T:** L.
Born: May 8, 1858. **Died:** Aug. 3, 1932.
Career: .342 avg.; 106 HR; 1,296 RBIs.
Teams: Troy (Nat.) 1879-80; Buffalo (Nat.) 1881-85; Detroit (Nat.) 1886-88; Boston (Nat.) 1889; Boston (P.L.) 1890; Boston (A.A.) 1891; Brooklyn (Nat.) 1892-93; Baltimore (Nat.) 1894-95; Louisville (Nat.) 1895; Philadelphia (Nat.) 1896; Giants 1904.
How elected: Committee on Old-Timers.

FRED CLARKE OF, MGR.
5-10, 165. **B:** L. **T:** R.
Born: Oct. 3, 1872. **Died:** Aug. 14, 1960.
Playing career: .312 avg.; 67 HR; 1,015 RBIs.
Managing career: 1,602-1,181, 19 years.
Teams (player): Louisville (Nat.) 1894-99;
Pirates 1900-15.
Teams (manager): Louisville (Nat.) 1897-99;
Pirates 1900-15.
How elected: Committee on Old-Timers.

JIMMY COLLINS 3B
5-9, 178. **B:** R. **T:** R.
Born: Jan. 16, 1873. **Died:** March 6, 1943.
Career: .294 avg.; 65 HR; 983 RBIs.
Teams: Boston (Nat.) 1895, 1896-1900; Louisville 1895; Red Sox
1901-07; Athletics 1907-08.
How elected: Committee on Old-Timers.

ED DELAHANTY 1B, OF
6-1, 170. **B:** R. **T:** R.
Born: Oct. 30, 1867. **Died:** July 2, 1903.
Career: .346 avg.; 101 HR; 1,464 RBIs.
Teams: Philadelphia (Nat.) 1888-89, 1891-1901; Cleveland (P.L.)
1890; Senators 1902-03.
How elected: Committee on Old-Timers.

HUGH DUFFY OF
5-7, 168. **B:** R. **T:** R.
Born: Nov. 26, 1866. **Died:** Oct. 19, 1954.
Career: .324 avg.; 106 HR; 1,302 RBIs.
Teams: Chicago (Nat.) 1888-89; Chicago (P.L.) 1890; Boston (A.A.)
1891; Boston (Nat.) 1892-1900; Milwaukee (Amer.) 1901; Phillies
1904-06.
How elected: Committee on Old-Timers.

HUGH JENNINGS IF
5-8, 165. **B:** R. **T:** R.
Born: April 2, 1869. **Died:** Feb. 1, 1928.
Career: .311 avg.; 18 HR; 840 RBIs.
Teams: Louisville (A.A.) 1891; Louisville (Nat.) 1892-93; Baltimore
(Nat.) 1893-99; Brooklyn (Nat.) 1899-1900, 1903; Phillies 1901-02;
Tigers 1907-1909, 1912, 1918.
How elected: Committee on Old-Timers.

MIKE (KING) KELLY C, IF
5-10, 180. **B:** R. **T:** R.
Born: Dec. 31, 1857. **Died:** Nov. 8, 1894.
Career: .308 avg.; 69 HR; 950 RBIs.
Teams: Cincinnati (Nat.) 1878-79; Chicago (Nat.) 1880-86; Boston
(Nat.) 1887-90, 1891-92; Cincinnati (A.A.) 1891; New York (Nat.)
1893.
How elected: Committee on Old-Timers.

JIM O'ROURKE OF, IF
5-8, 185. **B:** R. **T:** R.
Born: Aug. 24, 1852. **Died:** Jan. 8, 1919.
Career: .310 avg.; 50 HR; 1,010 RBIs.
Teams: Boston (Nat.) 1876-78, 1880; Providence (Nat.) 1879;
Buffalo (Nat.) 1881-84; New York (Nat.) 1885-89, 1891-92, 1904;
New York (P.L.) 1890; Washington
(Nat.) 1893.
How elected: Committee on Old-Timers.

WILBERT ROBINSON C, MGR.
5-8, 215. **B:** R. **T:** R.
Born: June 2, 1864. **Died:** Aug. 8, 1934.
Playing career: .273 avg.; 18 HR; 622 RBIs.
Managing career: 1,399-1,398, 19 years.

Teams (player): Philadelphia (A.A.) 1886-90; Baltimore (A.A.)
1890-91; Baltimore (Nat.) 1892-99; St. Louis (Nat.) 1900; Baltimore
(Amer.) 1901-02.
Teams (manager): Baltimore (Amer.) 1902;
Dodgers 1914-31.
How elected: Committee on Old-Timers.

1946

JESSE BURKETT OF
5-8, 155. **B:** L. **T:** L.
Born: Dec. 4, 1868. **Died:** May 27, 1953.
Career: .338 avg.; 75 HR; 952 RBIs.
Teams: New York (Nat.) 1890; Cleveland (Nat.) 1891-98; St. Louis
(Nat.) 1899-1901; Browns 1902-04;
Red Sox 1905.
How elected: Committee on Old-Timers.

FRANK CHANCE 1B, MGR.
6-0, 190. **B:** R. **T:** R.
Born: Sept. 9, 1877. **Died:** Sept. 15, 1924.
Playing career: .296 avg.; 20 HR; 596 RBIs.
Managing career: 946-648, 11 years.
Teams (player): Cubs 1898-1912; Yankees 1913-14.
Teams (manager): Cubs 1905-12; Yankees 1913-14; Red Sox
1923.
How elected: Committee on Old-Timers.

JACK CHESBRO P
5-9, 180. **B:** R. **T:** R.
Born: June 5, 1874. **Died:** Nov. 6, 1931.
Career: 198-132; 2.68 ERA; 1,265 SO.
Teams: Pirates 1899-1902; Yankees 1903-09;
Red Sox 1909.
How elected: Committee on Old-Timers.

JOHNNY EVERS 2B
5-9, 130. **B:** R. **T:** R.
Born: July 21, 1881. **Died:** March 28, 1947.
Career: .270 avg.; 12 HR; 538 RBIs.
Teams: Cubs 1902-13; Braves 1914-17, 1929; Phillies 1917; White
Sox 1922.
How elected: Committee on Old-Timers.

CLARK GRIFFITH P, MGR., EXEC.
5-7, 156. **B:** R. **T:** R.
Born: Nov. 20, 1869. **Died:** Oct. 27, 1955.
Playing career: 237-146; 3.31 ERA; 955 SO.
Managing career: 1,491-1,367, 20 years.
Teams (player): St. Louis (A.A.) 1891; Boston (A.A.) 1891; Chicago
(Nat.) 1893-1900; White Sox 1901-02; Yankees 1903-07; Reds
1909-10; Senators 1912-14.
Teams (manager): White Sox 1901-02; Yankees 1903-08; Reds
1909-11; Senators 1912-20.
How elected: Committee on Old-Timers.

TOMMY McCARTHY OF, IF
5-7, 170. **B:** R. **T:** R.
Born: July 24, 1864 **Died:** Aug. 5, 1922.
Career: .292 avg.; 44 HR; 666 RBIs.
Teams: Boston (U.A.) 1884; Boston (Nat.) 1885; Philadelphia (Nat.)
1886-87; St. Louis (A.A.) 1888-91; Boston (Nat.) 1892-95; Brooklyn
(Nat.) 1896.
How elected: Committee on Old-Timers.

JOE McGINNITY P
5-11, 206. **B:** R. **T:** R.
Born: March 19, 1871. **Died:** Nov. 14, 1929.
Career: 246-142; 2.66 ERA; 1,068 SO.

Teams: Baltimore (Nat.) 1899; Brooklyn (Nat.) 1900; Orioles 1901-02; Giants 1902-08.
How elected: Committee on Old-Timers.

EDDIE PLANK   P
5-11, 175.   **B:** L. **T:** L.
Born: Aug. 31, 1875.   **Died:** Feb. 24, 1926.
Career: 326-194; 2.35 ERA; 2,246 SO.
Teams: Athletics 1901-14; St. Louis (Fed.) 1915; Browns 1916-17.
How elected: Committee on Old-Timers.

JOE TINKER   SS
5-9, 175.   **B:** R. **T:** R.
Born: July 27, 1880.   **Died:** July 27, 1948.
Career: .262 avg.; 31 HR; 782 RBIs.
Teams: Cubs 1902-13, 1916; Chicago (Fed.) 1914-15.
How elected: Committee on Old-Timers.

RUBE WADDELL   P
6-1, 196.   **B:** L. **T:** L.
Born: Oct. 13, 1876.   **Died:** April 1, 1914.
Career: 193-143; 2.16 ERA; 2,316 SO.
Teams: Louisville (Nat.) 1897, 1899; Pirates 1900-01; Cubs 1901; Athletics 1902-07; Browns 1908-10.
How elected: Committee on Old-Timers.

ED WALSH   P
6-1, 193.   **B:** R. **T:** R.
Born: May 14, 1881.   **Died:** May 26, 1959.
Career: 195-126; 1.82 ERA; 1,736 SO.
Teams: White Sox 1904-16; Braves 1917.
How elected: Committee on Old-Timers.

1947

MICKEY COCHRANE   C
5-10, 180.   **B:** L. **T:** R.
Born: April 6, 1903.   **Died:** June 28, 1962.
Career: .320 avg.; 119 HR; 832 RBIs.
Teams: Athletics 1925-33; Tigers 1934-37.
How elected: 79.5 percent of vote.

FRANK FRISCH   2B, MGR.
5-11, 165.   **B:** B. **T:** R.
Born: Sept. 9, 1898.   **Died:** March 12, 1973.
Playing career: .316 avg.; 105 HR; 1,244 RBIs.
Managing career: 1,138-1,078, 16 years.
Teams (player): Giants 1919-26; Cardinals 1927-37.
Teams (manager): Cardinals 1933-38; Pirates 1940-46; Cubs 1949-51.
How elected: 84.5 percent of vote.

LEFTY GROVE   P
6-3, 200.   **B:** L. **T:** L.
Born: March 6, 1900.   **Died:** May 22, 1975.
Career: 300-141; 3.06 ERA; 2,266 SO.
Teams: Athletics 1925-33; Red Sox 1934-41.
How elected: 76.4 percent of vote.

CARL HUBBELL   P
6-0, 170.   **B:** R. **T:** L.
Born: June 22, 1903.   **Died:** Nov. 21, 1988.
Career: 253-154; 2.98 ERA; 1,677 SO.
Teams: Giants 1928-43.
How elected: 87 percent of vote.

1948

HERB PENNOCK   P
6-0, 160.   **B:** B. **T:** L.

Born: Feb. 10, 1894.   **Died:** Jan. 30, 1948.
Career: 240-162; 3.60 ERA; 1,227 SO.
Teams: Athletics 1912-15; Red Sox 1915-22; Yankees 1923-33; Red Sox 1934.
How elected: 77.7 percent of vote.

PIE TRAYNOR   3B
6-0, 170.   **B:** R. **T:** R.
Born: Nov. 11, 1899.   **Died:** March 16, 1972.
Career: .320 avg.; 58 HR; 1,273 RBIs.
Team: Pirates 1920-37.
How elected: 76.9 percent of vote.

1949

MORDECAI (THREE FINGER) BROWN   P
5-10, 175.   **B:** B. **T:** R.
Born: Oct. 19, 1876.   **Died:** Feb. 14, 1948.
Career: 239-130; 2.06 ERA; 1,375 SO.
Teams: Cardinals 1903; Cubs 1904-12, 1916; Reds 1913; St. Louis (Fed.) 1914; Brooklyn (Fed.) 1914; Chicago (Fed.) 1915.
How elected: Committee on Old-Timers.

CHARLEY GEHRINGER   2B
5-11, 180.   **B:** L. **T:** R.
Born: May 11, 1903.   **Died:** Jan. 21, 1993.
Career: .320 avg.; 184 HR; 1,427 RBIs.
Team: Tigers 1924-42.
How elected: 85 percent of vote.

KID NICHOLS   P
5-10, 175.   **B:** R. **T:** R.
Born: Sept. 14, 1869.   **Died:** April 11, 1953.
Career: 361-208; 2.95 ERA; 1,868 SO.
Teams: Boston (Nat.) 1890-1901; Cardinals 1904-05; Phillies 1905-06.
How elected: Committee on Old-Timers.

1951

JIMMIE FOXX   C, 3B, 1B
6-0, 195.   **B:** R. **T:** R.
Born: Oct. 22, 1907.   **Died:** July 21, 1967.
Career: .325 avg.; 534 HR; 1,922 RBIs.
Teams: Athletics 1925-35; Red Sox 1936-42; Cubs 1942, 1944; Phillies 1945.
How elected: 79.2 percent of vote.

MEL OTT   OF
5-9, 170.   **B:** L. **T:** R.
Born: March 2, 1909.   **Died:** Nov. 21, 1958.
Career: .304 avg.; 511 HR; 1,860 RBIs.
Team: Giants 1926-47.
How elected: 87.2 percent of vote.

1952

HARRY HEILMANN   OF, 1B
6-1, 195.   **B:** R. **T:** R.
Born: Aug. 3, 1894.   **Died:** July 9, 1951.
Career: .342 avg.; 183 HR; 1,539 RBIs.
Teams: Tigers 1914-29; Reds 1930-32.
How elected: 86.8 percent of vote.

PAUL WANER   OF
5-8, 153.   **B:** L. **T:** L.
Born: April 16, 1903.   **Died:** Aug. 29, 1965.
Career: .333 avg.; 113 HR; 1,309 RBIs; 3,152 hits.
Teams: Pirates 1926-40; Dodgers 1941, 1943-44; Braves 1941-42; Yankees 1944-45.
How elected: 83.3 percent of vote.

1953

ED BARROW   **MGR., EXEC.**
Born: May 10, 1868.   **Died:** Dec. 15, 1953.
Managing career: 310-320, 5 years.
Executive career: Architect of Yankees dynasty that produced 14 A.L. pennants and 10 World Series championships as business manager and president from 1921-45; managed Red Sox to 1918 World Series title and started conversion of Babe Ruth from a pitcher to an outfielder.
How elected: Committee on Veterans.

CHIEF BENDER   **P**
6-2, 185.   **B:** R. **T:** R.
Born: May 5, 1884.   **Died:** May 22, 1954.
Career: 212-127; 2.46 ERA; 1,711 SO.
Teams: Athletics 1903-14; Baltimore (Fed.) 1915; Phillies 1916-17; White Sox 1925.
How elected: Committee on Veterans.

TOMMY CONNOLLY   **UMPIRE**
Born: Dec. 31, 1870.   **Died:** April 28, 1961.
Career: Umpired from 1901, the A.L.'s first season, until 1931; served as A.L. umpires' chief of staff until retirement in 1954; an influential member of baseball's rules committee for many years.
How elected: Committee on Veterans.

DIZZY DEAN   **P**
6-2, 200.   **B:** R. **T:** R.
Born: Jan. 16, 1911.   **Died:** July 17, 1974.
Career: 150-83; 3.03 ERA; 1,155 SO.
Teams: Cardinals 1930, 1932-37; Cubs 1938-41; Browns 1947.
How elected: 79.2 percent of vote.

BILL KLEM   **UMPIRE**
Born: Feb. 22, 1874.   **Died:** Sept. 1, 1951.
Career: Joined N.L. as an umpire in 1905 and served with distinction until 1941; called 18 World Series, more than any other umpire; served as N.L. umpires' chief of staff from 1941 until death; responsible for many umpiring innovations; generally considered the greatest arbiter of all time.
How elected: Committee on Veterans.

AL SIMMONS   **OF**
5-11, 190.   **B:** R. **T:** R.
Born: May 22, 1902.   **Died:** May 26, 1956.
Career: .334 avg.; 307 HR; 1,827 RBIs.
Teams: Athletics 1924-32, 1940-41, 1944; White Sox 1933-35; Tigers 1936; Senators 1937-38; Braves 1939; Reds 1939; Red Sox 1943.
How elected: 75.4 percent of vote.

BOBBY WALLACE   **SS**
5-8, 170.   **B:** R. **T:** R.
Born: Nov. 4, 1874.   **Died:** Nov. 3, 1960.
Career: .268 avg.; 34 HR; 1,121 RBIs.
Teams: Cleveland (Nat.) 1894-98; St. Louis (Nat.) 1899-1901, 1917-18; Browns 1902-16;
How elected: Committee on Veterans.

HARRY WRIGHT   **MANAGER**
Born: Jan. 10, 1835.   **Died:** Oct. 3, 1895.
Career: 933-660, 18 years.
Teams: Boston (Nat.) 1876-81; Providence (Nat.) 1882-83; Philadelphia (Nat.) 1884-93.
How elected: Committee on Veterans.

1954

BILL DICKEY   **C**
6-1, 185.   **B:** L. **T:** R.
Born: June 6, 1907.   **Died:** Nov. 12, 1993.
Career: .313 avg.; 202 HR; 1,210 RBIs.
Teams: Yankees 1928-43, 1946.
How elected: 80.2 percent of vote.

RABBIT MARANVILLE   **SS**
5-5, 155.   **B:** R. **T:** R.
Born: Nov. 11, 1891.   **Died:** Jan. 5, 1954.
Career: .258 avg.; 28 HR; 884 RBIs.
Teams: Braves 1912-20, 1929-35; Pirates 1921-24; Cubs 1925; Dodgers 1926; Cardinals 1927-28.
How elected: 82.9 percent of vote.

BILL TERRY   **1B, MGR.**
6-1, 200.   **B:** L. **T:** L.
Born: Oct. 30, 1898.   **Died:** Jan. 9, 1989.
Playing career: .341 avg.; 154 HR; 1,078 RBIs.
Managing career: 823-661, 10 years.
Team (player): Giants 1923-36.
Team (manager): Giants 1932-41.
How elected: 77.4 percent of vote.

1955

FRANK (HOME RUN) BAKER   **3B**
5-11, 173.   **B:** L. **T:** R.
Born: March 13, 1886.   **Died:** June 28, 1963.
Career: .307 avg.; 96 HR; 987 RBIs.
Teams: Athletics 1908-14; Yankees 1916-19, 1921-22.
How elected: Committee on Veterans.

JOE DIMAGGIO   **OF**
6-2, 193.   **B:** R. **T:** R.
Born: Nov. 25, 1914.   **Died:** March 8, 1999.
Career: .325 avg.; 361 HR; 1,537 RBIs.
Team: Yankees 1936-42, 1946-51.
How elected: 88.8 percent of vote.

GABBY HARTNETT   **C**
6-1, 200.   **B:** R. **T:** R.
Born: Dec. 20, 1900.   **Died:** Dec. 20, 1972.
Career: .297 avg.; 236 HR; 1,179 RBIs.
Teams: Cubs 1922-40; Giants 1941.
How elected: 77.7 percent of vote.

TED LYONS   **P**
5-11, 200.   **B:** B. **T:** R.
Born: Dec. 28, 1900.   **Died:** July 25, 1986.
Career: 260-230; 3.67 ERA; 1,073 SO.
Team: White Sox 1923-42, 1946.
How elected: 86.5 percent of vote.

RAY SCHALK   **C**
5-9, 165.   **B:** R. **T:** R.
Born: Aug. 12, 1892.   **Died:** May 19, 1970.
Career: .253 avg.; 11 HR; 594 RBIs.
Teams: White Sox 1912-28; Giants 1929.
How elected: Committee on Veterans.

DAZZY VANCE   **P**
6-2, 200.   **B:** R. **T:** R.
Born: March 4, 1891.   **Died:** Feb. 16, 1961.
Career: 197-140; 3.24 ERA; 2,045 SO.
Teams: Pirates 1915; Yankees 1915, 1918; Dodgers 1922-32, 1935; Cardinals 1933, 1934; Reds 1934.
How elected: 81.7 percent of vote.

1956

JOE CRONIN   IF, MGR., EXEC.
6-0, 180.   **B:** R. **T:** R.
Born: Oct. 12, 1906.   **Died:** Sept. 7, 1984.
Playing career: .301 avg.; 170 HR; 1,424 RBIs.
Managing career: 1,236-1,055, 15 years.
Teams (player): Pirates 1926-27; Senators 1928-34; Red Sox 1935-45.
Teams (manager): Senators 1933-34; Red Sox 1935-47.
Executive career: President of A.L. 1959-73.
How elected: 78.8 percent of vote.

HANK GREENBERG   1B, OF
6-3, 210.   **B:** R. **T:** R.
Born: Jan. 1, 1911.   **Died:** Sept. 4, 1986.
Career: .313 avg.; 331 HR; 1,276 RBIs.
Teams: Tigers 1930, 1933-41, 1945-46; Pirates 1947.
How elected: 85.0 percent of vote.

1957

SAM CRAWFORD   OF
6-0, 190.   **B:** L. **T:** L.
Born: April 18, 1880.   **Died:** June 15, 1968.
Career: .309 avg.; 98 HR; 1,525 RBIs.
Teams: Reds 1899-1902; Tigers 1903-17.
How elected: Committee on Veterans.

JOE McCARTHY   MANAGER
Born: April 21, 1887.   **Died:** Jan. 13, 1978.
Career: 2,125-1,333, 24 years; 7 World Series championships.
Teams: Cubs 1926-30; Yankees 1931-46; Red Sox 1948-50.
How elected: Committee on Veterans.

1959

ZACK WHEAT   OF
5-10, 170.   **B:** L. **T:** R.
Born: May 23, 1888.   **Died:** March 11, 1972.
Career: .317 avg.; 132 HR; 1,248 RBIs.
Teams: Dodgers 1909-26; Athletics 1927.
How elected: Committee on Veterans.

1961

MAX CAREY   OF
5-11, 170.   **B:** B. **T:** R.
Born: Jan. 11, 1890.   **Died:** May 30, 1976.
Career: .285 avg.; 69 HR; 800 RBIs, 738 SB.
Teams: Pirates 1910-26; Dodgers 1926-29.
How elected: Committee on Veterans.

BILLY HAMILTON   OF
5-6, 165.   **B:** L. **T:** R.
Born: Feb. 16, 1866.   **Died:** Dec. 16, 1940.
Career: .344 avg.; 40 HR; 736 RBIs; 912 SB.
Teams: Kansas City (A.A.) 1888-89; Philadelphia (Nat.) 1890-95; Boston (Nat.) 1896-1901.
How elected: Committee on Veterans.

1962

BOB FELLER   P
6-0, 185.   **B:** R. **T:** R.
Born: Nov. 3, 1918.
Career: 266-162; 3.25 ERA; 2,581 SO.
Team: Indians 1936-41, 1945-56.
How elected: 93.8 percent of vote.

BILL McKECHNIE   MANAGER
Born: Aug. 7, 1887.   **Died:** Oct. 29, 1965.
Career: 1,896-1,723, 25 years; 2 World Series championships.
Teams: Newark (Fed.) 1915; Pirates 1922-26; Cardinals 1928-29; Braves 1930-37; Reds 1938-46.
How elected: Committee on Veterans.

JACKIE ROBINSON   IF
5-11, 195.   **B:** R. **T:** R.
Born: Jan. 31, 1919.   **Died:** Oct. 24, 1972.
Career: .311 avg.; 137 HR; 734 RBIs.
Team: Dodgers 1947-56.
How elected: 77.5 percent of vote.

EDD ROUSH   OF
5-11, 170.   **B:** L. **T:** L.
Born: May 8, 1893.   **Died:** March 21, 1988.
Career: .323 avg.; 67 HR; 981 RBIs.
Teams: White Sox 1913; Indianapolis (Fed.) 1914; Newark (Fed.) 1915; Giants 1916, 1927-29; Reds 1916-26, 1931.
How elected: Committee on Veterans.

1963

JOHN CLARKSON   P
5-10, 165.   **B:** R. **T:** R.
Born: July 1, 1861.   **Died:** Feb. 4, 1909.
Career: 328-178; 2.81 ERA; 1,978 SO.
Teams: Worcester (Nat.) 1882; Chicago (Nat.) 1884-87; Boston (Nat.) 1888-92; Cleveland (Nat.) 1892-94.
How elected: Committee on Veterans.

ELMER FLICK   OF
5-9, 168.   **B:** L. **T:** R.
Born: Jan. 11, 1876.   **Died:** Jan. 9, 1971.
Career: .313 avg.; 48 HR; 756 RBIs.
Teams: Philadelphia (Nat.) 1898-1902; Indians 1902-10.
How elected: Committee on Veterans.

SAM RICE   OF
5-9, 150.   **B:** L. **T:** L.
Born: Feb. 20, 1890.   **Died:** Oct. 13, 1974.
Career: .322 avg.; 34 HR; 1,078 RBIs.
Teams: Senators 1915-33; Indians 1934.
How elected: Committee on Veterans.

EPPA RIXEY   P
6-5, 210.   **B:** R. **T:** L.
Born: May 3, 1891.   **Died:** Feb. 28, 1963.
Career: 266-251; 3.15 ERA; 1,350 SO.
Teams: Phillies 1912-1917, 1919-20; Reds 1921-33.
How elected: Committee on Veterans.

1964

LUKE APPLING   SS
5-10, 183.   **B:** R. **T:** R.
Born: April 2, 1907.   **Died:** Jan. 3, 1991.
Career: .310 avg.; 45 HR; 1,116 RBIs.
Team: White Sox 1930-43, 1945-50.
How elected: 84 percent of vote.

RED FABER   P
6-2, 180.   **B:** B. **T:** R.
Born: Sept. 6, 1888.   **Died:** Sept. 25, 1976.
Career: 254-213; 3.15 ERA; 1,471 SO.
Team: White Sox 1914-33.
How elected: Committee on Veterans.

BURLEIGH GRIMES P
5-10, 175. **B:** R. **T:** R.
Born: Aug. 18, 1893. **Died:** Dec. 6, 1985.
Career: 270-212; 3.53 ERA; 1,512 SO.
Teams: Pirates 1916-17, 1928-29, 1934; Dodgers 1918-26; Giants 1927; Braves 1930; Cardinals 1930-31, 1933-34; Cubs 1932-33; Yankees 1934.
How elected: Committee on Veterans.

MILLER HUGGINS MANAGER
Born: March 27, 1880. **Died:** Sept. 25, 1929.
Career: 1,413-1,134, 17 years.
Teams: Cardinals 1913-17; Yankees 1918-29.
How elected: Committee on Veterans.

TIM KEEFE P
5-10, 185. **B:** R. **T:** R.
Born: Jan. 1, 1857. **Died:** April 23, 1933.
Career: 342-225; 2.62 ERA; 2,527 SO.
Teams: Troy (Nat.) 1880-82; Metropolitan (A.A.) 1883-84; New York (Nat.) 1885-91; Philadelphia (Nat.) 1891-93.
How elected: Committee on Veterans.

HEINIE MANUSH OF
6-1, 200. **B:** L. **T:** L.
Born: July 20, 1901. **Died:** May 12, 1971.
Career: .330 avg.; 110 HR; 1,183 RBIs.
Teams: Tigers 1923-27; Browns 1928-30; Senators 1930-35; Red Sox 1936; Dodgers 1937-38; Pirates 1938-39.
How elected: Committee on Veterans.

JOHN MONTGOMERY WARD IF, P
5-9, 165. **B:** L. **T:** R.
Born: March 3, 1860. **Died:** March 4, 1925.
Playing career: .275 avg.; 26 HR; 867 RBIs.
Pitching career: 164-102; 2.10 ERA; 920 SO.
Teams: Providence (Nat.) 1878-82; New York (Nat.) 1883-89, 1893-94; Brooklyn 1890-92.
How elected: Committee on Veterans.

1965

PUD GALVIN P
5-8, 190. **B:** R. **T:** R.
Born: Dec. 25, 1856. **Died:** March 7, 1902.
Career: 360-308; 2.87 ERA; 1,799 SO.
Teams: Buffalo (Nat.) 1879-85; Allegheny (A.A.) 1885-86; Pittsburgh (Nat.) 1887-89, 1891-92; Pittsburgh (P.L.) 1890; St. Louis (Nat.) 1892.
How elected: Committee on Veterans.

1966

CASEY STENGEL OF, MGR.
5-11, 175. **B:** L. **T:** L.
Born: July 30, 1890. **Died:** Sept. 29, 1975.
Playing career: .284 avg.; 60 HR; 535 RBIs.
Managing career: 1,905-1,842, 25 years; 7 World Series championships.
Teams (player): Dodgers 1912-17; Pirates 1918-19; Phillies 1920-21; Giants 1921-23; Braves 1924-25.
Teams (manager): Dodgers 1934-36; Braves 1938-43; Yankees 1949-60; Mets 1962-65.
How elected: Committee on Veterans.

TED WILLIAMS OF
6-3, 205. **B:** L. **T:** R.
Born: Aug. 30, 1918. **Died:** July 5, 2002.

Career: .344 avg.; 521 HR; 1,839 RBIs.
Team: Red Sox 1939-42, 1946-60.
How elected: 93.4 percent of vote.

1967

BRANCH RICKEY EXECUTIVE
Born: Dec. 20, 1881. **Died:** Dec. 9, 1965.
Career: Began baseball association as a minor league catcher in 1903 and played briefly for the Cardinals in three seasons; advanced through the chains of the Browns, Cardinals, Dodgers and Pirates in various front-office positions; introduced concept of a farm system as a member of Cardinals organization; broke baseball's color barrier when he brought Jackie Robinson to the Dodgers in 1947.
How elected: Committee on Veterans.

RED RUFFING P
6-1, 205. **B:** R. **T:** R.
Born: May 5, 1905. **Died:** Feb. 17, 1986.
Career: 273-225; 3.80 ERA; 1,987 SO.
Teams: Red Sox 1924-30; Yankees 1930-42, 1945-46; White Sox 1947.
How elected: 86.9 percent of vote.

LLOYD WANER OF
5-9, 150. **B:** L. **T:** R.
Born: March 16, 1906. **Died:** July 22, 1982.
Career: .316 avg.; 27 HR; 598 RBIs.
Teams: Pirates 1927-41, 1944-45; Braves 1941; Reds 1941; Phillies 1942; Dodgers 1944.
How elected: Committee on Veterans.

1968

KIKI CUYLER OF
5-10, 180. **B:** R. **T:** R.
Born: Aug. 30, 1899. **Died:** Feb. 11, 1950.
Career: .321 avg.; 128 HR; 1,065 RBIs.
Teams: Pirates 1921-27; Cubs 1928-35; Reds 1935-37; Dodgers 1938.
How elected: Committee on Veterans.

GOOSE GOSLIN OF
5-11, 185. **B:** L. **T:** R.
Born: Oct. 16, 1900. **Died:** May 15, 1971.
Career: .316 avg.; 248 HR; 1,609 RBIs.
Teams: Senators 1921-30, 1933, 1938; Browns 1930-32; Tigers 1934-37.
How elected: Committee on Veterans.

JOE MEDWICK OF
5-10, 187. **B:** R. **T:** R.
Born: Nov. 24, 1911. **Died:** March 21, 1975.
Career: .324 avg.; 205 HR; 1,383 RBIs.
Teams: Cardinals 1932-40, 1947-48; Dodgers 1940-43, 1946; Giants 1943-45; Braves 1945.
How elected: 84.8 percent of vote.

1969

ROY CAMPANELLA C
5-9, 200. **B:** R. **T:** R.
Born: Nov. 19, 1921. **Died:** June 26, 1993.
Career: .276 avg.; 242 HR; 856 RBIs.
Team: Dodgers 1948-57.
How elected: 79.4 percent of vote.

STAN COVELESKI   **P**
5-11, 166.   **B:** R. **T:** R.
Born: July 13, 1890.   **Died:** March 20, 1984.
Career: 215-142; 2.89 ERA; 981 SO.
Teams: Athletics 1912; Indians 1916-24; Senators 1925-27; Yankees 1928.
How elected: Committee on Veterans.

WAITE HOYT   **P**
6-0, 180.   **B:** R. **T:** R.
Born: Sept. 9, 1899.   **Died:** Aug. 25, 1984.
Career: 237-182; 3.59 ERA; 1,206 SO.
Teams: Giants 1918, 1932; Red Sox 1919-20; Yankees 1921-30; Tigers 1930-31; Athletics 1931; Dodgers 1932, 1937-38; Pirates 1933-37.
How elected: Committee on Veterans.

STAN MUSIAL   **OF, 1B**
6-0, 175.   **B:** L. **T:** L.
Born: Nov. 21, 1920.
Career: .331 avg.; 475 HR; 1,951 RBIs; 3,630 hits.
Team: Cardinals 1941-44, 1946-63.
How elected: 93.2 percent of vote.

1970

LOU BOUDREAU   **SS, MGR.**
5-11, 185.   **B:** R. **T:** R.
Born: July 17, 1917.   **Died:** Aug. 10, 2001.
Playing career: .295 avg.; 68 HR; 789 RBIs.
Managing career: 1,162-1,224, 16 years.
Teams (player): Indians 1938-50; Red Sox 1951-52.
Teams (manager): Indians 1942-50; Red Sox 1952-54; Athletics 1955-57; Cubs 1960.
How elected: 77.3 percent of vote.

EARLE COMBS   **OF**
6-0, 185.   **B:** L. **T:** R.
Born: May 14, 1899.   **Died:** July 21, 1976.
Career: .325 avg.; 58 HR; 632 RBIs.
Team: Yankees 1924-35.
How elected: Committee on Veterans.

FORD FRICK   **EXECUTIVE**
Baseball's third commissioner.
Born: Dec. 19, 1894.   **Died:** April 8, 1978.
Career: Newspaper reporter and sportswriter; N.L. president from 1934-51; elected as baseball's third commissioner following resignation of Happy Chandler in 1951; served until retirement Dec. 14, 1965.
How elected: Committee on Veterans.

JESSE HAINES   **P**
6-0, 190.   **B:** R. **T:** R.
Born: July 22, 1893.   **Died:** Aug. 5, 1978.
Career: 210-158; 3.64 ERA; 981 SO.
Teams: Reds 1918; Cardinals 1920-37.
How elected: Committee on Veterans.

1971

DAVE BANCROFT   **SS**
5-9, 160.   **B:** B. **T:** R.
Born: April 20, 1892.   **Died:** Oct. 9, 1972.
Career: .279 avg.; 32 HR; 591 RBIs.
Teams: Phillies 1915-20; Giants 1920-23, 1930; Braves 1924-27; Dodgers 1928-29.
How elected: Committee on Veterans.

JAKE BECKLEY   **1B**
5-10, 200.   **B:** L. **T:** L.
Born: Aug. 4, 1867.   **Died:** June 25, 1918.
Career: .308 avg.; 86 HR; 1,575 RBIs.
Teams: Pittsburgh (Nat.) 1888-89, 1891-96; Pittsburgh (P.L.) 1890; New York (Nat.) 1896-97; Cincinnati (Nat.) 1897-1903; Cardinals 1904-07.
How elected: Committee on Veterans.

CHICK HAFEY   **OF**
6-0, 185.   **B:** R. **T:** R.
Born: Feb. 12, 1903.   **Died:** July 2, 1973.
Career: .317 avg.; 164 HR; 833 RBIs.
Teams: Cardinals 1924-31; Reds 1932-35, 1937.
How elected: Committee on Veterans.

HARRY HOOPER   **OF**
5-10, 168.   **B:** L. **T:** R.
Born: Aug. 24, 1887.   **Died:** Dec. 18, 1974.
Career: .281 avg.; 75 HR; 817 RBIs.
Teams: Red Sox 1909-20; White Sox 1921-25.
How elected: Committee on Veterans.

JOE KELLEY   **OF**
5-11, 190.   **B:** R. **T:** R.
Born: Dec. 9, 1871.   **Died:** Aug. 14, 1943.
Career: .317 avg.; 65 HR; 1,194 RBIs.
Teams: Boston (Nat.) 1891; Pittsburgh (Nat.) 1891-92; Baltimore (Nat.) 1892-98; Brooklyn (Nat.) 1899-1901; Orioles 1902; Reds 1902-06; Braves 1908.
How elected: Committee on Veterans.

RUBE MARQUARD   **P**
6-3, 180.   **B:** B. **T:** L.
Born: Oct. 9, 1889.   **Died:** June 1, 1980.
Career: 201-177; 3.08 ERA; 1,593 SO.
Teams: Giants 1908-15; Dodgers 1915-20; Reds 1921; Braves 1922-25.
How elected: Committee on Veterans.

SATCHEL PAIGE   **P**
6-3, 180.   **B:** R. **T:** R.
Born: July 7, 1906.   **Died:** June 8, 1982.
Career: 28-31; 3.29 ERA; 290 SO.
Teams: Indians 1948-49; Browns 1951-53; Athletics 1965.
How elected: Special Committee on Negro Leagues.

GEORGE WEISS   **EXECUTIVE**
Born: June 23, 1895.   **Died:** Aug. 13, 1972.
Career: Joined Yankees as farm director in 1932 after impressive career as minor league executive; built Yankees farm system that stocked pennant-winning machines of the 1930s, '40s and '50s; became general manager in 1948 and led Yankees to 10 pennants and seven World Series championships in 13 seasons; the man who hired Casey Stengel as manager; president of the expansion Mets from 1961-66.
How elected: Committee on Veterans.

1972

YOGI BERRA   **C**
5-8, 194.   **B:** L. **T:** R.
Born: May 12, 1925.
Career: .285 avg.; 358 HR; 1,430 RBIs.
Teams: Yankees 1946-63; Mets 1965.
How elected: 85.6 percent of vote.

JOSH GIBSON C
6-1, 215.   **B**: R. **T**: R.
Born: Dec. 21, 1911.   **Died**: Jan. 20, 1947.
Career: Negro League star; statistics not available.
How elected: Special Committee on Negro Leagues.

LEFTY GOMEZ P
6-2, 173.   **B**: L. **T**: L.
Born: Nov. 26, 1910.   **Died**: Feb. 17, 1989.
Career: 189-102; 3.34 ERA; 1,468 SO.
Teams: Yankees 1930-42; Senators 1943.
How elected: Committee on Veterans.

WILL HARRIDGE EXECUTIVE
Born: Oct. 16, 1883.   **Died**: April 9, 1971.
Career: Private secretary to A.L. President Ban Johnson; A.L. secretary after Johnson's retirement; became A.L. president when Ernest Barnard died suddenly in 1931; served with distinction until retirement in 1958.
How elected: Committee on Veterans.

SANDY KOUFAX P
6-2, 210.   **B**: R. **T**: L.
Born: Dec. 30, 1935.
Career: 165-87; 2.76 ERA; 2,396 SO.
Team: Dodgers 1955-66.
How elected: 86.9 percent of vote.

WALTER (BUCK) LEONARD 1B
5-10, 185   **B**: L. **T**: L.
Born: Sept. 8, 1907.   **Died**: Nov. 27, 1997.
Career: Negro League star; statistics not available.
How elected: Special Committee on Negro Leagues.

EARLY WYNN P
6-0, 200.   **B**: B. **T**: R.
Born: Jan. 6, 1920.   **Died**: April 4, 1999.
Career: 300-244; 3.54 ERA; 2,334 SO.
Teams: Senators 1939, 1941-44, 1946-48; Indians 1949-57, 1963; White Sox 1958-62.
How elected: 76.0 percent of vote.

ROSS YOUNGS OF
5-8, 162.   **B**: B. **T**: R.
Born: April 10, 1897.   **Died**: Oct. 22, 1927.
Career: .322 avg.; 42 HR; 592 RBIs.
Team: Giants 1917-26.
How elected: Committee on Veterans.

1973

ROBERTO CLEMENTE OF
5-11, 175.   **B**: R. **T**: R.
Born: Aug. 18, 1934.   **Died**: Dec. 31, 1972.
Career: .317 avg.; 240 HR; 1,305 RBIs; 3,000 hits; 12 gold gloves.
Team: Pirates 1955-72.
How elected: 92.7 percent of vote.

BILLY EVANS UMPIRE
Born: Feb. 10, 1884.   **Died**: Jan. 23, 1956.
Career: A.L. umpire from 1906-27; considered a master of the rules book and an expert at rules applications on tricky plays; front-office executive for the Indians, Red Sox and Tigers; president of Southern League from 1942-46.
How elected: Committee on Veterans.

MONTE IRVIN OF
6-1, 195.   **B**: R. **T**: R.
Born: Feb. 25, 1919.

Career: .293 avg.; 99 HR; 443 RBIs; Negro League statistics not available.
Teams: Giants 1949-55; Cubs 1956.
How elected: Special Committee on Negro Leagues.

GEORGE KELLY 1B
6-4, 190.   **B**: R. **T**: R.
Born: Sept. 10, 1895.   **Died**: Oct. 13, 1984.
Career: .297 avg.; 148 HR; 1,020 RBIs.
Teams: Giants 1915-17, 1919-26; Pirates 1917; Reds 1927-30; Cubs 1930; Dodgers 1932.
How elected: Committee on Veterans.

WARREN SPAHN P
6-0, 175.   **B**: L. **T**: L.
Born: April 23, 1921.   **Died**: Nov. 24, 2003.
Career: 363-245; 3.09 ERA; 2,583 SO.
Teams: Braves 1942, 1946-64; Mets 1965; Giants 1965.
How elected: 83.2 percent of vote.

MICKEY WELCH P
5-8, 160.   **B**: R. **T**: R.
Born: July 4, 1859.   **Died**: July 30, 1941.
Career: 307-210; 2.71 ERA; 1,850 SO.
Teams: Troy (Nat.) 1880-82; New York (Nat.) 1883-92.
How elected: Committee on Veterans.

1974

COOL PAPA BELL OF
6-0, 143.   **B**: B. **T**: L.
Born: May 17, 1903.   **Died**: March 7, 1991.
Career: Negro League star; statistics not available.
How elected: Special Committee on Negro Leagues.

JIM BOTTOMLEY 1B
6-0, 180.   **B**: L. **T**: L.
Born: April 23, 1900.   **Died**: Dec. 11, 1959.
Career: .310 avg.; 219 HR; 1,422 RBIs.
Teams: Cardinals 1922-32; Reds 1933-35; Browns 1936-37.
How elected: Committee on Veterans.

JOCKO CONLAN UMPIRE
Born: Dec. 6, 1899.   **Died**: April 1, 1989.
Career: N.L. umpire from 1941-64; worked 5 World Series and 6 All-Star Games; a master of the rules book known for fair and impartial decisions.
How elected: Committee on Veterans.

WHITEY FORD P
5-10, 181.   **B**: L. **T**: L.
Born: Oct. 21, 1928.
Career: 236-106; 2.75 ERA; 1,956 SO.
Team: Yankees 1950, 1953-67.
How elected: 77.8 percent of vote.

MICKEY MANTLE OF
6-0, 198.   **B**: B. **T**: R.
Born: Oct. 20, 1931.   **Died**: Aug. 13, 1995.
Career: .298 avg.; 536 HR; 1,509 RBIs.
Team: Yankees 1951-68.
How elected: 88.2 percent of vote.

SAM THOMPSON OF
6-2, 207.   **B**: L. **T**: L.
Born: March 5, 1860.   **Died**: Nov. 7, 1922.
Career: .331 avg.; 127 HR; 1,299 RBIs.
Teams: Detroit (Nat.) 1885-88; Philadelphia (Nat.) 1889-98; Tigers 1906.
How elected: Committee on Veterans.

1975

EARL AVERILL OF
5-9, 172. **B:** L. **T:** R.
Born: May 21, 1902. **Died:** Aug. 16, 1983.
Career: .318 avg.; 238 HR; 1,164 RBIs.
Teams: Indians 1929-39; Tigers 1939-40; Braves 1941.
How elected: Committee on Veterans.

BUCKY HARRIS 2B, MGR.
5-9, 156. **B:** R. **T:** R.
Born: Nov. 8, 1896. **Died:** Nov. 8, 1977.
Playing career: .274 avg.; 9 HR; 506 RBIs.
Managing career: 2,157-2,218, 29 years; 2 World Series championships.
Teams (player): Senators 1919-28; Tigers 1929, 1931.
Teams (manager): Senators 1924-28, 1935-42, 1950-54; Tigers 1929-33, 1955-56; Red Sox 1934; Phillies 1943; Yankees 1947-48.
How elected: Committee on Veterans.

BILLY HERMAN 2B
5-11, 180. **B:** R. **T:** R.
Born: July 7, 1909. **Died:** Sept. 5, 1992.
Career: .304 avg.; 47 HR; 839 RBIs.
Teams: Cubs 1931-41; Dodgers 1941-43, 1946; Braves 1946; Pirates 1947.
How elected: Committee on Veterans.

JUDY JOHNSON 3B
5-11, 150. **B:** R. **T:** R.
Born: Oct. 26, 1899. **Died:** June 14, 1989.
Career: Negro League star; statistics not available.
How elected: Special Committee on Negro Leagues.

RALPH KINER OF
6-2, 195. **B:** R. **T:** R.
Born: Oct. 27, 1922.
Career: .279 avg.; 369 HR; 1,015 RBIs.
Teams: Pirates 1946-53; Cubs 1953-54; Indians 1955.
How elected: 75.4 percent of vote.

1976

OSCAR CHARLESTON OF
5-11, 190. **B:** L. **T:** L.
Born: Oct. 14, 1896. **Died:** Oct. 5, 1954.
Career: Negro League star; statistics not available.
How elected: Special Committee on Negro Leagues.

ROGER CONNOR 1B
6-3, 220. **B:** L. **T:** L.
Born: July 1, 1857. **Died:** Jan. 4, 1931.
Career: .317 avg.; 138 HR; 1,322 RBIs.
Teams: Troy (Nat.) 1880-82; New York (Nat.) 1883-89, 1891, 1893-94; New York (P.L.) 1890; Philadelphia (Nat.) 1892; St. Louis (Nat.) 1894-97.
How elected: Committee on Veterans.

CAL HUBBARD UMPIRE
Born: Oct. 31, 1900. **Died:** Oct. 17, 1977.
Career: A.L. umpire from 1936-50; assistant to A.L. supervisor of umpires 1952-53; supervisor of umpires 1954-69; a former pro football player and a member of the National Football League Hall of Fame.
How elected: Committee on Veterans.

BOB LEMON P
6-0, 185. **B:** L. **T:** R.
Born: Sept. 22, 1920. **Died:** Jan. 11, 2000.
Career: 207-128; 3.23 ERA; 1,277 SO.
Team: Indians 1946-58.
How elected: 78.6 percent of vote.

FRED LINDSTROM 3B
5-11, 170. **B:** R. **T:** R.
Born: Nov. 21, 1905. **Died:** Oct. 4, 1981.
Career: .311 avg.; 103 HR; 779 RBIs.
Teams: Giants 1924-32; Pirates 1933-34; Cubs 1935; Dodgers 1936.
How elected: Committee on Veterans.

ROBIN ROBERTS P
6-0, 190. **B:** B. **T:** R.
Born: Sept. 30, 1926.
Career: 286-245; 3.41 ERA; 2,357 SO.
Teams: Phillies 1948-61; Orioles 1962-65; Astros 1965-66; Cubs 1966.
How elected: 86.9 percent of vote.

1977

ERNIE BANKS SS
6-1, 180. **B:** R. **T:** R.
Born: Jan. 31, 1931.
Career: .274 avg.; 512 HR; 1,636 RBIs.
Team: Cubs 1953-71.
How elected: 83.8 percent of vote.

MARTIN DIHIGO P, IF, OF
6-3, 225. **B:** R. **T:** R.
Born: May 24, 1905. **Died:** May 20, 1971.
Career: Negro League star; statistics not available.
How elected: Special Committee on Negro Leagues.

JOHN HENRY LLOYD SS
5-11, 180. **B:** L. **T:** R.
Born: April 25, 1884. **Died:** March 19, 1965.
Career: Negro League star; statistics not available.
How elected: Special Committee on Negro Leagues.

AL LOPEZ C, MGR.
5-11, 165. **B:** R. **T:** R.
Born: Aug. 20, 1908. **Died:** Oct 30, 2005.
Playing career: .261 avg.; 51 HR; 652 RBIs.
Managing career: 1,410-1,004, 17 years.
Teams (player): Dodgers 1928, 1930-35; Braves 1936-40; Pirates 1940-46; Indians 1947.
Teams (manager): Indians 1951-56; White Sox 1957-65, 1968-69.
How elected: Committee on Veterans.

AMOS RUSIE P
6-1, 200. **B:** R. **T:** R.
Born: May 30, 1871. **Died:** Dec. 6, 1942.
Career: 245-174; 3.07 ERA; 1,934 SO.
Teams: Indianapolis (Nat.) 1889; New York (Nat.) 1890-95, 1897-98; Reds 1901.
How elected: Committee on Veterans.

JOE SEWELL SS, 3B
5-7, 155. **B:** L. **T:** R.
Born: Oct. 9, 1898. **Died:** March 6, 1990.
Career: .312 avg.; 49 HR; 1,055 RBIs.
Teams: Indians 1920-30; Yankees 1931-33.
How elected: Committee on Veterans.

1978

ADDIE JOSS   **P**
6-3, 185.   **B:** R. **T:** R.
Born: April 12, 1880.   **Died:** April 14, 1911.
Career: 160-97; 1.89 ERA; 920 SO.
Team: Indians 1902-10.
How elected: Committee on Veterans.

LARRY MACPHAIL   **EXECUTIVE**
Born: Feb. 3, 1890.   **Died:** Oct. 1, 1975.
Career: A franchise builder and innovator; built
championship teams for the Reds, Dodgers and Yankees; introduced night baseball in 1935 at Cincinnati; first to use radio
broadcasts to increase revenues for his teams.
How elected: Committee on Veterans.

EDDIE MATHEWS   **3B**
6-1, 200.   **B:** L. **T:** R.
Born: Oct. 13, 1931.   **Died:** Feb. 18, 2001.
Career: .271 avg.; 512 HR; 1,453 RBIs.
Teams: Braves 1952-66; Astros 1967; Tigers 1967-68.
How elected: 79.4 percent of vote.

1979

WARREN GILES   **EXECUTIVE**
Born: May 28, 1896.   **Died:** Feb. 7, 1979.
Career: Reds general manager from 1937-47; Reds president
from 1947-52; N.L. president from 1952-69.
How elected: Committee on Veterans.

WILLIE MAYS   **OF**
5-11, 180.   **B:** R. **T:** R.
Born: May 6, 1931.
Career: .302 avg.; 660 HR; 1,903 RBIs; 3,283 hits; 12 gold gloves.
Teams: Giants 1951-52, 1954-72; Mets 1972-73.
How elected: 94.7 percent of vote.

HACK WILSON   **OF**
5-6, 190.   **B:** R. **T:** R.
Born: April 26, 1900.   **Died:** Nov. 23, 1948.
Career: .307 avg.; 244 HR; 1,062 RBIs.
Teams: Giants 1923-25; Cubs 1926-31; Dodgers 1932-34;
Phillies 1934.
How elected: Committee on Veterans.

1980

AL KALINE   **OF**
6-2, 180.   **B:** R. **T:** R.
Born: Dec. 19, 1934.
Career: .297 avg.; 399 HR; 1,583 RBIs; 3,007 hits.
Team: Tigers 1953-74.
How elected: 88.3 percent of vote.

CHUCK KLEIN   **OF**
6-0, 185.   **B:** L. **T:** R.
Born: Oct. 7, 1905.   **Died:** March 28, 1958.
Career: .320 avg.; 300 HR; 1,201 RBIs.
Teams: Phillies 1928-33, 1936-39, 1940-44; Cubs 1934-36;
Pirates 1939.
How elected: Committee on Veterans.

DUKE SNIDER   **OF**
6-0, 190.   **B:** L. **T:** R.
Born: Sept. 19, 1926.
Career: .295 avg.; 407 HR; 1,333 RBIs.
Teams: Dodgers 1947-62; Mets 1963; Giants 1964.

How elected: 86.5 percent of vote.

TOM YAWKEY   **EXECUTIVE**
Born: Feb. 21, 1903.   **Died:** July 9, 1976.
Career: Owner of Red Sox franchise from 1933 until death;
longtime champion of the A.L. and one of the most respected
figures in the game.
How elected: Committee on Veterans.

1981

RUBE FOSTER   **P, MGR., EXEC.**
6-4, 240.
Born: Sept. 17, 1879.   **Died:** Dec. 9, 1930.
Playing career: Negro League star; statistics not available.
Executive career: Founder of Negro American and Negro
National leagues; owner of Chicago-based American Giants, the
model from which all other Negro clubs were built.
How elected: Committee on Veterans.

BOB GIBSON   **P**
6-1, 195.   **B:** R. **T:** R.
Born: Nov. 9, 1935.
Career: 251-174; 2.91 ERA; 3,117 SO.
Team: Cardinals 1959-75.
How elected: 84 percent of vote.

JOHNNY MIZE   **1B**
6-2, 215.   **B:** L. **T:** R.
Born: Jan. 7, 1913.   **Died:** June 2, 1993.
Career: .312 avg.; 359 HR; 1,337 RBIs.
Teams: Cardinals 1936-41; Giants 1942, 1946-49; Yankees 1949-53.
How elected: Committee on Veterans.

1982

HANK AARON   **OF**
6-0, 180.   **B:** R. **T:** R.
Born: Feb. 5, 1934.
Career: .305 avg.; 755 HR, 1st on all-time list; 2,297 RBIs, 1st on
all-time list; 3,771 hits.
Teams: Braves 1954-74; Brewers 1975-76.
How elected: 97.8 percent of vote.

HAPPY CHANDLER   **EXECUTIVE**
Second commissioner of baseball.
Born: July 14, 1898.   **Died:** June 15, 1991.
Career: Former U.S. senator from Kentucky; was elected commis-
sioner in 1945 after the death of Kenesaw Mountain Landis; served
until his forced retirement in 1950; returned to Kentucky and won
two terms as the state's governor.
How elected: Committee on Veterans.

TRAVIS JACKSON   **SS**
5-11, 160.   **B:** R. **T:** R.
Born: Nov. 2, 1903.   **Died:** July 17, 1987.
Career: .291 avg.; 135 HR; 929 RBIs.
Team: Giants 1922-36.
How elected: Committee on Veterans.

FRANK ROBINSON   **OF**
6-1, 195.   **B:** R. **T:** R.
Born: Aug. 31, 1935.
Career: .294 avg.; 586 HR; 1,812 RBIs.
Teams: Reds 1956-65; Orioles 1966-71; Dodgers 1972; Angels
1973-74; Indians 1974-76.
How elected: 89.2 percent of vote.

1983

WALTER ALSTON   **MANAGER**
Born: Dec. 1, 1911.   **Died:** Oct. 1, 1984.
Career: 2,040-1,613, 23 years; 4 World Series championships.
Team: Dodgers 1954-76.
How elected: Committee on Veterans.

GEORGE KELL   **3B**
5-9, 175.   **B:** R. **T:** R.
Born: Aug. 23, 1922.
Career: .306 avg.; 78 HR; 870 RBIs.
Teams: Athletics 1943-46; Tigers 1946-52; Red Sox 1952-54; White Sox 1954-56; Orioles 1956-57.
How elected: Committee on Veterans.

JUAN MARICHAL   **P**
6-0, 185.   **B:** R. **T:** R.
Born: Oct. 20, 1938.
Career: 243-142; 2.89 ERA; 2,303 SO.
Teams: Giants 1960-73; Red Sox 1974; Dodgers 1975.
How elected: 83.7 percent of vote.

BROOKS ROBINSON   **3B**
6-1, 190.   **B:** R. **T:** R.
Born: May 18, 1937.
Career: .267 avg.; 268 HR; 1,357 RBIs; 16 gold gloves.
Team: Orioles 1955-77.
How elected: 92 percent of vote

1984

LUIS APARICIO   **SS**
5-9, 160.   **B:** R. **T:** R.
Born: April 29, 1934.
Career: .262 avg.; 83 HR; 791 RBIs.
Teams: White Sox 1956-62, 1968-70; Orioles 1963-67; Red Sox 1971-73.
How elected: 84.6 percent of vote.

DON DRYSDALE   **P**
6-6, 216.   **B:** R. **T:** R.
Born: July 23, 1936.   **Died:** July 3, 1993.
Career: 209-166; 2.95 ERA; 2,486 SO.
Team: Dodgers 1956-69.
How elected: 78.4 percent of vote.

RICK FERRELL   **C**
5-10, 160.   **B:** R. **T:** R.
Born: Oct. 12, 1906.   **Died:** July 27, 1995.
Career: .281 avg.; 28 HR; 734 RBIs.
Teams: Browns 1929-33, 1941-43; Red Sox 1933-37; Senators 1937-41, 1944-45, 1947.
How elected: Committee on Veterans.

HARMON KILLEBREW   **3B, 1B**
5-11, 213.   **B:** R. **T:** R.
Born: June 29, 1936.
Career: .256 avg.; 573 HR; 1,584 RBIs.
Teams: Senators 1954-60; Twins 1961-74; Royals 1975.
How elected: 83.1 percent of vote.

PEE WEE REESE   **SS**
5-10, 175.   **B:** R. **T:** R.
Born: July 23, 1918.   **Died:** August 14, 1999.
Career: .269 avg.; 126 HR; 885 RBIs.
Teams: Dodgers 1940-42, 1946-58.
How elected: Committee on Veterans.

1985

LOU BROCK   **OF**
5-11, 170.   **B:** L. **T:** L.
Born: June 18, 1939.
Career: .293 avg.; 149 HR; 900 RBIs; 3,023 hits; 938 SB.
Teams: Cubs 1961-64; Cardinals 1964-79.
How elected: 79.7 percent of vote.

ENOS SLAUGHTER   **OF**
5-9, 192.   **B:** L. **T:** R.
Born: April 27, 1916.   **Died:** Aug. 12, 2002.
Career: .300 avg.; 169 HR; 1,304 RBIs.
Teams: Cardinals 1938-42, 1946-53; Yankees 1954-55, 1956-59; Athletics 1955-56; Braves 1959.
How elected: Committee on Veterans.

ARKY VAUGHAN   **IF**
5-11, 175.   **B:** L. **T:** R.
Born: March 9, 1912.   **Died:** Aug. 30, 1952.
Career: .318 avg.; 96 HR; 926 RBIs.
Teams: Pirates 1932-41; Dodgers 1942-43, 1947-48.
How elected: Committee on Veterans.

HOYT WILHELM   **P**
6-0, 195.   **B:** R. **T:** R.
Born: July 26, 1923.   **Died:** Aug. 23, 2002.
Career: 143-122; 2.52 ERA; 1,610 SO; 1,070 games, 1st on all-time list; 227 saves.
Teams: Giants 1952-56; Cardinals 1957; Indians 1957-58; Orioles 1958-62; White Sox 1963-68; Angels 1969; Braves 1969-70, 1971; Cubs 1970; Dodgers 1971-72.
How elected: 83.8 percent of vote.

1986

BOBBY DOERR   **2B**
5-11, 175.   **B:** R. **T:** R.
Born: April 7, 1918.
Career: .288 avg.; 223 HR; 1,247 RBIs.
Team: Red Sox 1937-44, 1946-51.
How elected: Committee on Veterans.

ERNIE LOMBARDI   **C**
6-3, 230.   **B:** R. **T:** R.
Born: April 6, 1908.   **Died:** Sept. 26, 1977.
Career: .306 avg.; 190 HR; 990 RBIs.
Teams: Dodgers 1931; Reds 1932-41; Braves 1942; Giants 1943-47.
How elected: Committee on Veterans.

WILLIE McCOVEY   **1B**
6-4, 210.   **B:** L. **T:** L.
Born: Jan. 10, 1938.
Career: .270 avg.; 521 HR; 1,555 RBIs.
Teams: Giants 1959-73, 1977-80; Padres 1974-76; Athletics 1976.
How elected: 81.4 percent of vote.

1987

RAY DANDRIDGE   **3B**
5-7, 175.   **B:** R. **T:** R.
Born: Aug. 31, 1913.   **Died:** Feb. 12, 1994.
Career: Negro League star; statistics not available.
How elected: Committee on Veterans.

JIM (CATFISH) HUNTER   **P**
6-0, 195.   **B:** R. **T:** R.
Born: April 8, 1946.   **Died:** September 9, 1999.
Career: 224-166; 3.26 ERA; 2,012 SO.

Teams: Athletics 1965-74; Yankees 1975-79.
How elected: 76.3 percent of vote.

BILLY WILLIAMS OF
6-1, 175. **B:** L. **T:** R.
Born: June 15, 1938.
Career: .290 avg.; 426 HR; 1,475 RBIs.
Teams: Cubs 1959-74; Athletics 1975-76.
How elected: 85.7 percent of vote.

1988

WILLIE STARGELL OF, 1B
6-2, 225. **B:** L. **T:** L.
Born: March 6, 1940. **Died:** April 9, 2001.
Career: .282 avg.; 475 HR; 1,540 RBIs.
Team: Pirates 1962-82.
How elected: 82.4 percent of vote.

1989

AL BARLICK UMPIRE
Born: April 2, 1915. **Died:** Dec. 27, 1995.
Career: N.L. umpire from 1940-1971; worked as N.L. umpire supervisor after retirement.
How elected: Committee on Veterans.

JOHNNY BENCH C
6-1, 208. **B:** R. **T:** R.
Born: Dec. 7, 1947.
Career: .267 avg.; 389 HR; 1,376 RBIs; 10 gold gloves.
Team: Reds 1967-83.
How elected: 96.4 percent of vote.

RED SCHOENDIENST 2B
6-0, 170. **B:** B. **T:** R.
Born: Feb. 2, 1923.
Career: .289 avg.; 84 HR; 773 RBIs.
Teams: Cardinals 1945-56, 1961-63; Giants 1956-57; Braves 1957-60.
How elected: Committee on Veterans.

CARL YASTRZEMSKI OF
5-11, 182. **B:** L. **T:** R.
Born: Aug. 22, 1939.
Career: .285 avg.; 452 HR; 1,844 RBIs; 3,419 hits.
Team: Red Sox 1961-83.
How elected: 94.6 percent of vote.

1990

JOE MORGAN 2B
5-7, 160. **B:** L. **T:** R.
Born: Sept. 19, 1943.
Career: .271 avg.; 268 HR; 1,133 RBIs; 689 SB.
Teams: Astros 1963-71, 1980; Reds 1972-79; Giants 1981-82; Phillies 1983; Athletics 1984.
How elected: 81.8 percent of vote.

JIM PALMER P
6-3, 196. **B:** R. **T:** R.
Born: Oct. 15, 1945.
Career: 268-152; 2.86 ERA; 2,212 SO.
Team: Orioles 1965-67; 1969-84.
How elected: 92.6 percent of vote.

1991

ROD CAREW 2B, 1B
6-0, 182. **B:** L. **T:** R.
Born: Oct. 1, 1945.
Career: .328 avg.; 92 HR; 1,015 RBIs; 3,053 hits.
Teams: Twins 1967-78; Angels 1979-85.
How elected: 89.7 percent of vote.

FERGUSON JENKINS P
6-5, 210. **B:** R. **T:** R.
Born: Dec. 13, 1943.
Career: 284-226; 3.34 ERA; 3,192 SO.
Teams: Phillies 1965-66; Cubs 1966-73, 1982-83; Rangers 1974-75, 1978-81; Red Sox 1976-77.
How elected: 74.7 percent of vote.

TONY LAZZERI 2B
6-0, 170. **B:** R. **T:** R.
Born: Dec. 6, 1903. **Died:** Aug. 6, 1946.
Career: .292 avg.; 178 HR; 1,191 RBIs.
Teams: Yankees 1926-37; Cubs 1938; Dodgers 1939; Giants 1939.
How elected: Committee on Veterans.

GAYLORD PERRY P
6-4, 215. **B:** R. **T:** R.
Born: Sept. 15, 1938.
Career: 314-265; 3.11 ERA; 3,534 SO.
Teams: Giants 1962-71; Indians 1972-75; Rangers 1975-77, 1980; Padres 1978-79; Yankees 1980; Braves 1981; Mariners 1982-83; Royals 1983.
How elected: 76.5 percent of vote.

BILL VEECK EXECUTIVE
Born: Feb. 9, 1914. **Died:** Jan. 2, 1986.
Career: A three-time major league owner best known for his showmanship and promotional stunts; owned Indians, Browns and White Sox franchises; broke A.L. color barrier in 1947 by signing Larry Doby to an Indians contract; remembered as the man who sent a midget to the plate for the Browns in a 1951 promotional stunt.
How elected: Committee on Veterans.

1992

ROLLIE FINGERS P
6-4, 195. **B:** R. **T:** R.
Born: Aug. 25, 1946.
Career: 114-118; 2.90 ERA; 1,299 SO; 341 saves.
Teams: Athletics 1968-76; Padres 1977-80; Brewers 1981-82, 1984-85.
How elected: 81.2 percent of vote.

BILL MCGOWAN UMPIRE
Born: Jan. 18, 1896. **Died:** Dec. 9, 1954.
Career: Served as an A.L. umpire from 1925-53; worked 8 World Series and 4 All-Star Games; worked 2,541 consecutive games over a 16½-year period.
How elected: Committee on Veterans.

HAL NEWHOUSER P
6-2, 192. **B:** L. **T:** L.
Born: May 20, 1921. **Died:** Nov. 10, 1998.
Career: 207-150; 3.06 ERA; 1,796 SO.
Teams: Tigers 1939-53; Indians 1954-55.
How elected: Committee on Veterans.

TOM SEAVER P
6-1, 206. **B:** R. **T:** R.
Born: Nov. 17, 1944.
Career: 311-205; 2.86 ERA; 3,640 SO.
Teams: Mets 1967-77, 1983; Reds 1977-82; White Sox 1984-86; Red Sox 1986.
How elected: 98.8 percent of vote.

1993

REGGIE JACKSON OF
6-0, 200. **B:** L. **T:** L.
Born: May 18, 1946.
Career: .262 avg.; 563 HR; 1,702 RBIs.
Teams: Athletics 1967-75, 1987; Orioles 1976; Yankees 1977-81; Angels 1982-86.
How elected: 93.6 percent of vote.

1994

STEVE CARLTON P
6-4, 210. **B:** L. **T:** L.
Born: Dec. 22, 1944.
Career: 329-244; 3.22 ERA; 4,136 SO.
Teams: Cardinals 1965-71; Phillies 1972-86; Giants 1986; White Sox 1986; Indians 1987; Twins 1987-88.
How elected: 95.8 percent of vote.

LEO DUROCHER SS, MGR.
5-10, 160. **B:** R. **T:** R.
Born: July 27, 1905. **Died:** Oct. 7, 1991.
Playing career: .247 avg.; 24 HR; 567 RBIs.
Managing career: 2,008-1,709, 24 years; 1 World Series championship.
Teams (player): Yankees 1925, 1928-29; Reds 1930-33; Cardinals 1933-37; Dodgers 1938-41, 1943, 1945.
Teams (manager): Dodgers 1939-46, 1948; Giants 1948-55; Cubs 1966-72; Astros 1972-73.
How elected: Committee on Veterans.

PHIL RIZZUTO SS
5-6, 160. **B:** R. **T:** R.
Born: Sept. 25, 1917.
Career: .273 avg.; 38 HR; 563 RBIs.
Team: Yankees 1941-42, 1946-56.
How elected: Committee on Veterans.

1995

RICHIE ASHBURN OF
5-10, 170. **B:** L. **T:** R.
Born: March 19, 1927. **Died:** Sept. 9, 1997.
Career: .308 avg.; 29 HR; 586 RBIs.
Teams: Phillies 1948-59; Cubs 1960-61; Mets 1962.
How elected: Committee on Veterans.

LEON DAY P
5-10, 180. **B:** R. **T:** R.
Born: Oct. 30, 1916. **Died:** March 13, 1995.
Career: Negro League star; statistics not available.
How elected: Committee on Veterans.

WILLIAM HULBERT EXECUTIVE
Born: Oct. 23, 1832. **Died:** April 10, 1882.
Career: A former National Association executive and founder of the National League in 1876; served as second president of the new circuit when Morgan Bulkeley left the job after 10 months; he also is credited with hiring baseball's first umpiring staff.
How elected: Committee on Veterans.

MIKE SCHMIDT 3B
6-2, 203. **B:** R. **T:** R.
Born: Sept. 27, 1949.
Career: .267 avg.; 548 HR; 1,595 RBIs; 10 gold gloves.
Team: Phillies 1972-89.
How elected: 96.5 percent of vote.

VIC WILLIS P
6-2, 185. **B:** R. **T:** R.
Born: April 12, 1876. **Died:** Aug. 3, 1947.
Career: 249-205; 2.63 ERA; 1,651 SO.
Teams: Braves 1898-1905; Pirates 1906-09; Cardinals 1910.
How elected: Committee on Veterans.

1996

JIM BUNNING P
6-3, 195. **B:** R. **T:** R.
Born: Oct. 23, 1931.
Career: 224-184; 3.27 ERA; 2,855 SO.
Teams: Tigers 1955-63; Phillies 1964-67, 1970-71; Pirates 1968-69; Dodgers 1969.
How elected: Committee on Veterans.

BILL FOSTER P
6-1, 196. **B:** B. **T:** L.
Born: June 12, 1904. **Died:** Sept. 16, 1978.
Career: Negro League star; statistics not available.
How elected: Committee on Veterans.

NED HANLON OF, MGR.
5-10, 170. **B:** L. **T:** R.
Born: Aug. 22, 1857. **Died:** April 14, 1937.
Playing career: .260 avg.; 30 HR; 517 RBIs.
Managing career: 1,313-1,164, 19 years; 5 championships.
Teams (player): Cleveland 1880; Detroit 1881-88; Pittsburgh (N.L.) 1889, 1891; Pittsburgh (P.L.) 1890; Baltimore (N.L.) 1892.
Teams (manager): Pittsburgh (N.L.) 1889, 1891; Pittsburgh (P.L.) 1890; Baltimore (N.L.) 1892-98; Dodgers 1899-1905; Reds 1906-07.
How elected: Committee on Veterans.

EARL WEAVER MANAGER
Born: Aug. 14, 1930.
Career: 1,480-1,060, 17 years; 1 World Series championship.
Team: Orioles 1968-82, 1985-86.
How elected: Committee on Veterans.

1997

NELLIE FOX 2B
5-9,150. **B:** L. **T:** R
Born: Dec. 25, 1927. **Died:** Dec. 1, 1975.
Career: .288 avg.; 35 HR; 790 RBIs.
Teams: Athletics 1947-49; White Sox 1950-63; Astros 1964-65.
How elected: Committee on Veterans.

TOM LASORDA MANAGER
Born: September 22, 1927.
Career: 1,599-1,439, 21 years; 2 World Series championships.
Team: Dodgers 1976-96.
How elected: Committee on Veterans.

PHIL NIEKRO P
6-1,180. **B:** R. **T:** R
Born: April 1, 1939.
Career: 318-274; 3.35 ERA; 3,342 strikeouts.
Teams: Braves 1964-83, 1987; Yankees 1984-85; Indians 1986, 1987; Blue Jays 1987.
How elected: 80.3 percent of vote.

WILLIE WELLS SS, 3B, 2B, P
5-8, 160. **B:** R. **T:** R.
Born: Aug. 10, 1905. **Died:** Jan. 22, 1989.
Career: Negro League star; statistics not available.
How elected: Committee on Veterans.

1998

GEORGE DAVIS   **3B, OF, SS**
5-9, 180.   **B:** B. **T:** R.
Born: Aug. 23, 1870.   **Died:** Oct. 17, 1940.
Career: .295 avg.; 73 HR; 1,437 RBIs; 616 SB.
Teams: Cleveland N.L. 1890-92; Giants 1893-1901, 1903; White
Sox 1902, 1904-09.
How elected: Committee on Veterans.

LARRY DOBY   **OF**
6-1, 182.   **B:** L. **T:** R.
Born: Dec. 13, 1924.   **Died:** June 18, 2003.
Career: .283 avg.; 253 HR; 970 RBIs.
Teams: Indians 1947-55, 1958; White Sox 1956-57, 1959; Tigers
1959.
How elected: Committee on Veterans.

LEE MACPHAIL   **EXECUTIVE**
Born: Oct. 25, 1917.
Career: A former minor league executive, major league executive
and president of the American League (1974-83); as director of
player personnel for the New York Yankees, he helped build the
farm system that fueled seven World Series titles in 10 years; as
general manager of the Baltimore Orioles, he helped build another
championship organization; the son of Larry MacPhail, a Hall of
Fame executive and innovator who paved the way for his son's
career.
How elected: Committee on Veterans.

JOE ROGAN   **P, OF, IF**
5-7, 180.   **B:** R. **T:** R.
Born: July 28, 1889.   **Died:** March 4, 1967.
Career: Negro League star; statistics not available.
How elected: Committee on Veterans.

DON SUTTON   **P**
6-1, 185.   **B:** R. **T:** R.
Born: April 2, 1945.
Career: 324-256; 3.26 ERA; 3,574 strikeouts.
Teams: Dodgers 1966-80, 1988; Astros 1981-82; Brewers 1982-84;
Athletics 1985; Angels 1985-87.
How elected: 81.6 percent of vote.

1999

GEORGE BRETT   **3B**
6-0, 200.   **B:** L. **T:** R.
Born: May 15, 1953.
Career: .305 avg.; 317 HR; 1,595 RBIs; 3,154 hits.
Teams: Royals 1973-93.
How elected: 98.2 percent of vote.

ORLANDO CEPEDA   **1B, OF**
6-2, 210.   **B:** R. **T:** R.
Born: September 17, 1937.
Career: .297 avg.; 379 HR; 1,365 RBIs.
Teams: Giants 1958-66, Cardinals 1966-68, Braves 1969-72,
Athletics 1972, Red Sox 1973, Royals 1974.
How elected: Committee on Veterans.

NESTOR CHYLAK   **UMPIRE**
Born: May 11, 1922.   **Died:** February 17, 1982.
Career: Served as an A.L. umpire from 1954-78; worked 5 World
Series and 6 All-Star Games; known as an excellent teacher of
umpires.
How elected: Committee on Veterans.

NOLAN RYAN   **P**
6-2, 195   **B:** R. **T:** R.
Born: January 31, 1947.
Career: 324-292; 3.19 ERA; 5,714 strikeouts.
Teams: Mets 1966-71, Angels 1972-79, Astros 1980-88; Rangers
1989-93.
How elected: 98.8 percent of vote.

FRANK SELEE   **MANAGER**
Born: Oct. 26, 1859.   **Died:** July 5, 1909.
Career: 1,284-862, 16 years.
Teams: Braves 1890-1901, Cubs 1902-1905.
How elected: Committee on Veterans.

SMOKEY JOE WILLIAMS   **P, OF, 1B, MGR.**
6-4, 200.   **B:** R. **T:** R.
Born: April 6, 1885.   **Died:** March 12, 1946.
Career: Negro League star; statistics not available.
How elected: Committee on Veterans.

ROBIN YOUNT   **SS, OF**
6-0, 170.   **B:** R. **T:** R.
Born: September 16, 1955.
Career: .285 avg.; 251 HR; 1,406 RBIs; 3,142 hits.
Teams: Brewers 1974-93.
How elected: 77.5 percent of vote.

2000

SPARKY ANDERSON   **MANAGER**
Born: February 22, 1934.
Career: 2,194-1,834, 26 years; 3 World Series
championships.
Team: Reds 1970-78; Tigers 1979-95.
How elected: Committee on Veterans.

CARLTON FISK   **C**
6-2, 220.   **B:** R. **T:** R.
Born: December 26, 1947.
Career: .269 avg.; 376 HR; 1,330 RBIs.
Teams: Red Sox 1969-80; White Sox 1982-93.
How elected: 79.6 percent of vote.

JOHN (BID) MCPHEE   **2B**
5-8, 152.   **B:** R. **T:** R.
Born: Nov. 1, 1859.   **Died:** Jan. 3, 1943.
Career: .271 avg.; 53 HR; 1,067 RBIs.
Teams: Cincinnati (A.A.) 1882-89; Cincinnati (Nat.) 1890-99.
How elected: Committee on Veterans.

TONY PEREZ   **3B, 1B**
6-2, 190.   **B:** R. **T:** R.
Born: May 14, 1942.
Career: .279 avg.; 379 HR; 1,652 RBIs.
Teams: Reds 1964-76, 1984-86; Expos 1977-79; Red Sox 1980-82;
Phillies 1983.
How elected: 77.15 percent of vote.

NORMAN (TURKEY) STEARNES   **OF, 1B**
6-0, 175.   **B:** L. **T:** L.
Born: May 8, 1901.   **Died:** Sept. 4, 1979.
Career: Negro League star; statistics not available.
How elected: Committee on Veterans.

2001

BILL MAZEROSKI   **2B**
6-0, 183.   **B:** R. **T:** R.
Born: September 5, 1936.
Career: .260 avg.; 138 HR; 853 RBIs.

Teams: Pirates 1956-72.
How elected: Committee on Veterans.

KIRBY PUCKETT   OF
5-8, 210.   **B:** R. **T:** R.
Born: March 14, 1961.
Career: .318 avg.; 207 HR; 1,085 RBIs.
Teams: Twins 1984-95.
How elected: 82.1 percent of vote.

HILTON SMITH   P, OF, 1B
6-2, 180.   **B:** R. **T:** R.
Born: Feb. 27, 1912.   **Died:** Nov. 18, 1983.
Career: Negro League star; statistics not available.
How elected: Committee on Veterans.

DAVE WINFIELD   OF
6-6, 220.   **B:** R. **T:** R.
Born: October 3, 1951.
Career: .283 avg.; 465 HR; 1,833 RBIs; 3,110 hits.
Teams: Padres 1973-80; Yankees 1981-90; Angels 1990-91; Blue
Jays 1992; Twins 1993-94; Indians 1995.
How elected: 84.5 percent of vote.

2002

OZZIE SMITH   SS
5-10, 180.   **B:** B. **T:** R.
Born: December 26, 1954.
Career: .262 avg.; 28 HR; 793 RBIs; 13 gold gloves.
Teams: Padres 1978-81; Cardinals 1982-96.
How elected: 91.7 percent of vote.

2003

GARY CARTER   C
6-2, 215.   **B:** R. **T:** R.
Born: April 8, 1954.
Career: .262 avg.; 324 HR; 1225 RBIs.
Teams: Expos 1974-84, 1992; Mets 1985-89; Giants 1990; Dodgers
1991.
How elected: 78.0 percent of vote.

EDDIE MURRAY   1B
6-2, 200.   **B:** B. **T:** R.
Born: February 24, 1956.
Career: .287 avg.; 504 HR; 1917 RBIs; 3,255 hits.
Teams: Orioles 1977-88, 1996; Dodgers 1989-91, 1997; Mets
1992-93; Indians 1994-96; Angels 1997.
How elected: 85.3 percent of vote.

2004

PAUL MOLITOR   INF, OF, DH
6-0, 185.   **B:** R. **T:** R.
Born: August 22, 1956.
Career: .306 avg.; 234 HR; 1,307 RBIs; 3,319 hits.
Teams: Brewers 1978-92; Blue Jays 1993-95; Twins 1996-98.
How elected: 85.2 percent of vote.

DENNIS ECKERSLEY   P
6-2, 190.   **B:** R. **T:** R.
Born: October 3, 1954.
Career: 197-171; 3.50 ERA; 2,401 SO; 390 saves.
Teams: Indians 1975-77; Red Sox 1978-84, 1998; Cubs 1984-86;
Athletics 1987-95; Cardinals 1996-97.
How elected: 83.2 percent of vote.

2005

WADE BOGGS   3B
6-2, 197.   **B:** L. **T:** R.
Born: June 15, 1958.
Career: .328 avg.; 118 HR; 1,014 RBIs; 3,010 hits.
Teams: Red Sox 1982-92; Yankees 1993-97; Devil Rays1998-99.
How elected: 91.9 percent of vote.

RYNE SANDBERG   2B
6-2, 180.   **B:** R. **T:** R.
Born: September 18, 1959.
Career: .285 avg.; 282 HR; 1061 RBIs.
Teams: Phillies 1981; Cubs 1982-97.
How elected: 76.2 percent of vote.

2005 FANTASY BASEBALL DOLLAR VALUES

Following are final player values from the 2005 Ultimate Salary Cap Baseball game on SportingNews.com. The values shown are end-of-season salary ("Price") and season points total ("TSNP") and are ranked by the latter value. The top 425 hitters and top 425 pitchers are listed and these numbers show which players were most valuable in 2005, which is a good starting point for fantasy owners who are preparing 2006 fantasy rankings. To learn more about Ultimate Salary Cap Baseball and other fantasy baseball games from Sporting News, go to http://fantasygames.sportingnews.com.

HITTERS

Rk.	Player	Team	Price	TSNP
1.	Rodriguez, Alex	NYY	$8,350,000	2655
2.	Pujols, Albert	STL	$8,060,000	2641
3.	Lee, Derrek	CHC	$6,040,000	2606
4.	Ortiz, David	BOS	$7,940,000	2503
5.	Teixeira, Mark	TEX	$6,720,000	2395
6.	Ramirez, Manny	BOS	$8,390,000	2302
7.	Bay, Jason	PIT	$5,550,000	2264
8.	Jones, Andruw	ATL	$5,070,000	2096
9.	Abreu, Bobby	PHI	$7,420,000	2085
10.	Cabrera, Miguel	FLA	$6,080,000	2083
11.	Sheffield, Gary	NYY	$7,220,000	2074
12.	Guerrero, Vladimir	LAA	$7,780,000	2059
13.	Soriano, Alfonso	TEX	$6,040,000	2013
14.	Young, Michael	TEX	$5,560,000	1978
15.	Wright, David	NYM	$5,640,000	1971
16.	Utley, Chase	PHI	$4,120,000	1955
17.	Crawford, Carl	TB	$3,680,000	1952
18.	Matsui, Hideki	NYY	$5,620,000	1936
19.	Dunn, Adam	CIN	$6,200,000	1927
20.	Hafner, Travis	CLE	$5,660,000	1920
21.	Delgado, Carlos	FLA	$5,780,000	1913
22.	Sexson, Richie	SEA	$5,110,000	1911
23.	Kent, Jeff	LAD	$5,730,000	1859
24.	Konerko, Paul	CHW	$5,300,000	1850
25.	Roberts, Brian	BAL	$4,260,000	1847
26.	Figgins, Chone	LAA	$4,380,000	1839
27.	Giles, Brian	SD	$5,240,000	1832
28.	Ensberg, Morgan	HOU	$3,520,000	1831
29.	Helton, Todd	COL	$6,300,000	1818
30.	Sizemore, Grady	CLE	$3,370,000	1815
31.	Tejada, Miguel	BAL	$6,790,000	1813
32.	Suzuki, Ichiro	SEA	$6,430,000	1809
33.	Rollins, Jimmy	PHI	$4,070,000	1805
34.	Lee, Carlos	MIL	$5,400,000	1792
35.	Jeter, Derek	NYY	$5,770,000	1788
36.	Furcal, Rafael	ATL	$3,700,000	1749
37.	Damon, Johnny	BOS	$6,000,000	1747
38.	Floyd, Cliff	NYM	$4,370,000	1739
39.	Burrell, Pat	PHI	$4,520,000	1728
40.	Griffey, Ken	CIN	$5,160,000	1687
41.	Lopez, Felipe	CIN	$2,640,000	1676
42.	Reyes, Jose	NYM	$3,600,000	1652
43.	Glaus, Troy	ARI	$5,430,000	1640
44.	Winn, Randy	SF	$2,120,000	1627
45.	Chavez, Eric	OAK	$5,260,000	1617
46.	Edmonds, Jim	STL	$5,470,000	1613
47.	Berkman, Lance	HOU	$5,420,000	1601
48.	Giles, Marcus	ATL	$3,970,000	1591
49.	Giambi, Jason	NYY	$3,590,000	1584
50.	Cantu, Jorge	TB	$3,550,000	1583
51.	Jenkins, Geoff	MIL	$2,700,000	1570
52.	Lugo, Julio	TB	$2,620,000	1566
53.	Ibanez, Raul	SEA	$3,620,000	1551
54.	Ramirez, Aramis	CHC	$6,080,000	1547
55.	Mora, Melvin	BAL	$4,290,000	1543
56.	Gonzalez, Luis	ARI	$4,210,000	1543
57.	Wells, Vernon	TOR	$4,330,000	1533
58.	Dye, Jermaine	CHW	$3,180,000	1522
59.	Green, Shawn	ARI	$4,350,000	1521
60.	Pierre, Juan	FLA	$4,840,000	1515
61.	Biggio, Craig	HOU	$4,110,000	1504
62.	Holliday, Matt	COL	$2,400,000	1496
63.	Tracy, Chad	ARI	$2,690,000	1495
64.	Crisp, Coco	CLE	$3,300,000	1494
65.	Hillenbrand, Shea	TOR	$1,270,000	1468
66.	Peralta, Jhonny	CLE	$1,630,000	1441
67.	Dellucci, David	TEX	$3,190,000	1430
68.	Martinez, Victor	CLE	$5,160,000	1426
69.	Brown, Emil	KC	$810,000	1422
70.	Jones, Chipper	ATL	$5,350,000	1386
71.	Beltran, Carlos	NYM	$7,660,000	1374
72.	Burnitz, Jeromy	CHC	$3,270,000	1373
73.	Guillen, Jose	WAS	$4,900,000	1368
74.	Sweeney, Mike	KC	$3,990,000	1367
75.	Alou, Moises	SF	$4,270,000	1354
76.	Clark, Brady	MIL	$2,780,000	1353
77.	Hall, Bill	MIL	$1,390,000	1352
78.	Eckstein, David	STL	$3,260,000	1349
79.	Blalock, Hank	TEX	$5,740,000	1341
80.	Gibbons, Jay	BAL	$2,650,000	1340
81.	Overbay, Lyle	MIL	$4,570,000	1339
82.	Monroe, Craig	DET	$2,680,000	1334
83.	Mench, Kevin	TEX	$4,030,000	1327
84.	Johnson, Nick	WAS	$3,420,000	1320
85.	Clark, Tony	ARI	$1,220,000	1320
86.	Huff, Aubrey	TB	$4,070,000	1309
87.	Lane, Jason	HOU	$1,710,000	1309
88.	Wilson, Preston	WAS	$3,570,000	1298
89.	Renteria, Edgar	BOS	$3,440,000	1292
90.	Polanco, Placido	DET	$2,970,000	1282
91.	Iguchi, Tadahito	CHW	$3,300,000	1277
92.	Counsell, Craig	ARI	$2,250,000	1274
93.	Varitek, Jason	BOS	$4,220,000	1272
94.	Kotsay, Mark	OAK	$1,800,000	1269
95.	Jones, Jacque	MIN	$1,890,000	1252
96.	Podsednik, Scott	CHW	$4,650,000	1240
97.	Rowand, Aaron	CHW	$2,110,000	1239
98.	Anderson, Garret	LAA	$4,230,000	1236
99.	Belliard, Ronnie	CLE	$2,000,000	1228
100.	Randa, Joe	SD	$3,450,000	1213
101.	Inge, Brandon	DET	$3,380,000	1213
102.	Casey, Sean	CIN	$2,970,000	1188
103.	Atkins, Garrett	COL	$2,270,000	1188
104.	Beltre, Adrian	SEA	$4,490,000	1173
105.	Ellis, Mark	OAK	$760,000	1169
106.	Encarnacion, Juan	FLA	$3,290,000	1164
107.	Mueller, Bill	BOS	$2,800,000	1159
108.	Hinske, Eric	TOR	$2,840,000	1157
109.	Durham, Ray	SF	$1,570,000	1155
110.	Cano, Robinson	NYY	$2,020,000	1145
111.	Lawton, Matt	NYY	$3,010,000	1145
112.	Mauer, Joe	MIN	$4,510,000	1142
113.	Hunter, Torii	MIN	$5,250,000	1141
114.	Posada, Jorge	NYY	$4,510,000	1130
115.	Erstad, Darin	LAA	$3,650,000	1124
116.	Wilkerson, Brad	WAS	$2,600,000	1116
117.	Gomes, Jonny	TB	$740,000	1116
118.	Everett, Carl	CHW	$2,620,000	1113
119.	Young, Dmitri	DET	$4,810,000	1110
120.	Feliz, Pedro	SF	$4,020,000	1101
121.	DeJesus, David	KC	$1,970,000	1100
122.	Nixon, Trot	BOS	$3,760,000	1097
123.	Matthews, Gary	TEX	$630,000	1093
124.	Cabrera, Orlando	LAA	$1,610,000	1091
125.	Swisher, Nick	OAK	$2,330,000	1086
126.	Shelton, Chris	DET	$500,000	1076
127.	Roberts, Dave	SD	$1,050,000	1072
128.	Morneau, Justin	MIN	$5,180,000	1069
129.	Lofton, Kenny	PHI	$2,230,000	1063
130.	Adams, Russ	TOR	$1,700,000	1061
131.	Blake, Casey	CLE	$1,660,000	1059
132.	Sanders, Reggie	STL	$3,620,000	1046
133.	Aurilia, Rich	CIN	$750,000	1045
134.	LaRoche, Adam	ATL	$2,540,000	1044
135.	Broussard, Ben	CLE	$770,000	1041
136.	Stairs, Matt	KC	$500,000	1037
137.	Vizquel, Omar	SF	$1,910,000	1037
138.	Walker, Larry	STL	$2,150,000	1033
139.	Ford, Lew	MIN	$1,550,000	1030
140.	Freel, Ryan	CIN	$2,600,000	1025
141.	Howard, Ryan	PHI	$680,000	1013
142.	Grudzielanek, Mark	STL	$2,680,000	1012
143.	Klesko, Ryan	SD	$2,290,000	1012
144.	Catalanotto, Frank	TOR	$570,000	1012
145.	Barrett, Michael	CHC	$3,100,000	1011
146.	Taveras, Willy	HOU	$760,000	1003
147.	Hudson, Orlando	TOR	$1,030,000	1002
148.	Rodriguez, Ivan	DET	$3,890,000	996
149.	Stewart, Shannon	MIN	$3,570,000	993
150.	Kearns, Austin	CIN	$1,680,000	993
151.	Rios, Alexis	TOR	$2,950,000	988
152.	Uribe, Juan	CHW	$3,500,000	962
153.	Johnson, Dan	OAK	$1,340,000	957
154.	Crede, Joe	CHW	$590,000	952
155.	Payton, Jay	OAK	$530,000	952
156.	Castilla, Vinny	WAS	$4,030,000	950
157.	Castillo, Luis	FLA	$3,310,000	947
158.	Greene, Khalil	SD	$1,690,000	941
159.	Molina, Bengie	LAA	$2,570,000	940
160.	Kendall, Jason	OAK	$2,840,000	940
161.	White, Rondell	DET	$850,000	939
162.	Barajas, Rod	TEX	$2,000,000	934
163.	Palmeiro, Rafael	BAL	$1,770,000	930
164.	Graffanino, Tony	BOS	$590,000	925
165.	Zaun, Gregg	TOR	$2,740,000	924
166.	Boone, Aaron	CLE	$2,780,000	911
167.	Everett, Adam	HOU	$500,000	908
168.	Perez, Neifi	CHC	$590,000	906
169.	Berroa, Angel	KC	$500,000	900
170.	Walker, Todd	CHC	$2,200,000	899
171.	Mackowiak, Rob	PIT	$2,620,000	899
172.	Pierzynski, A.J.	CHW	$3,140,000	893
173.	Cruz, Jose	LAD	$760,000	888
174.	Piazza, Mike	NYM	$4,060,000	884
175.	Millar, Kevin	BOS	$3,790,000	883
176.	Lee, Travis	TB	$530,000	879
177.	Wilson, Jack	PIT	$700,000	861
178.	Kielty, Bobby	OAK	$500,000	858
179.	Cameron, Mike	NYM	$3,110,000	856
180.	Johnson, Reed	TOR	$500,000	855
181.	Crosby, Bobby	OAK	$2,350,000	852
182.	Weeks, Rickie	MIL	$2,940,000	849
183.	Taguchi, So	STL	$500,000	845
184.	Drew, J.D.	LAD	$3,690,000	838
185.	Barmes, Clint	COL	$3,610,000	837
186.	Williams, Bernie	NYY	$1,360,000	834
187.	Kennedy, Adam	LAA	$850,000	832
188.	Lowell, Mike	FLA	$2,070,000	832
189.	LaRue, Jason	CIN	$1,710,000	828
190.	Long, Terrence	KC	$500,000	828
191.	Saenz, Olmedo	LAD	$500,000	827
192.	Lo Duca, Paul	FLA	$3,890,000	825
193.	Lopez, Javy	BAL	$3,820,000	820
194.	Lieberthal, Mike	PHI	$2,190,000	820
195.	Bell, David	PHI	$700,000	819
196.	Teahen, Mark	KC	$500,000	817
197.	Ward, Daryle	PIT	$1,900,000	812

Rk.	Player	Team	Price	TSNP
198	Bradley, Milton	LAD	$3,050,000	807
199	Hernandez, Ramon	SD	$3,920,000	803
200	Reed, Jeremy	SEA	$670,000	803
201	Cuddyer, Michael	MIN	$660,000	802
202	Rivera, Juan	LAA	$500,000	800
203	Clayton, Royce	ARI	$500,000	795
204	Francoeur, Jeff	ATL	$1,890,000	782
205	Sullivan, Cory	COL	$500,000	781
206	Gonzalez, Luis A.	COL	$500,000	778
207	Sanchez, Freddy	PIT	$560,000	778
208	Matos, Luis	BAL	$1,890,000	768
209	Hatteberg, Scott	OAK	$730,000	766
210	Loretta, Mark	SD	$2,490,000	763
211	Martinez, Tino	NYY	$3,610,000	754
212	Castillo, Jose	PIT	$500,000	753
213	Nunez, Abraham O.	STL	$560,000	741
214	Valentin, Javier	CIN	$630,000	740
215	Matheny, Mike	SF	$1,550,000	737
216	Michaels, Jason	PHI	$500,000	737
217	Hollins, Damon	TB	$530,000	735
218	Pena, Wily Mo	CIN	$1,850,000	734
219	Miller, Damian	MIL	$500,000	724
220	Hardy, J.J.	MIL	$500,000	722
221	Ordonez, Magglio	DET	$3,780,000	717
222	Langerhans, Ryan	ATL	$500,000	708
223	Werth, Jayson	LAD	$720,000	707
224	Hill, Aaron	TOR	$650,000	707
225	Choi, Hee Seop	LAD	$770,000	698
226	Scutaro, Marco	OAK	$500,000	696
227	Diaz, Victor	NYM	$880,000	695
228	Church, Ryan	WAS	$500,000	695
229	Schneider, Brian	WAS	$1,730,000	692
230	LeCroy, Matthew	MIN	$2,380,000	690
231	Koskie, Corey	TOR	$1,250,000	687
232	Nady, Xavier	SD	$1,630,000	683
233	Byrnes, Eric	BAL	$1,420,000	681
234	Finley, Steve	LAA	$1,940,000	679
235	Gonzalez, Alex	FLA	$2,500,000	672
236	Conine, Jeff	FLA	$500,000	669
237	Nevin, Phil	TEX	$1,790,000	665
238	Guillen, Carlos	DET	$2,020,000	664
239	Lamb, Mike	HOU	$500,000	662
240	Hairston, Jerry	CHC	$500,000	661
241	Sweeney, Mark	SD	$500,000	660
242	Hawpe, Brad	COL	$1,440,000	659
243	Gonzalez, Alex S.	TB	$500,000	658
244	Pena, Carlos	DET	$1,930,000	632
245	Ausmus, Brad	HOU	$550,000	631
246	Cintron, Alex	ARI	$500,000	631
247	Ellison, Jason	SF	$590,000	629
248	Johnson, Kelly	ATL	$970,000	628
249	Vidro, Jose	WAS	$1,930,000	623
250	Franco, Julio	ATL	$500,000	614
251	Phillips, Jason	LAD	$1,350,000	614
252	Niekro, Lance	SF	$500,000	608
253	Hidalgo, Richard	TEX	$3,590,000	606
254	Snow, J.T.	SF	$1,080,000	601
255	Buck, John	KC	$1,050,000	601
256	Logan, Nook	DET	$500,000	596
257	Jackson, Damian	SD	$500,000	592
258	Molina, Yadier	STL	$1,490,000	589
259	Burke, Chris	HOU	$500,000	587
260	Sosa, Sammy	BAL	$2,780,000	587
261	Hall, Toby	TB	$1,880,000	583
262	Alfonzo, Edgardo	SF	$3,890,000	571
263	Infante, Omar	DET	$500,000	569
264	Easley, Damion	FLA	$500,000	567
265	Patterson, Corey	CHC	$4,670,000	561
266	Robles, Oscar	LAD	$500,000	556
267	Green, Nick	TB	$500,000	547
268	Ledee, Ricky	LAD	$500,000	547
269	Mohr, Dustan	COL	$500,000	543
270	Punto, Nick	MIN	$500,000	527
271	Izturis, Cesar	LA	$1,810,000	526
272	Mientkiewicz, Doug	NYM	$1,920,000	525
273	Tucker, Michael	PHI	$500,000	519
274	Perez, Antonio	LAD	$500,000	513
275	Branyan, Russell	MIL	$500,000	512
276	Estrada, Johnny	ATL	$3,810,000	508
277	Womack, Tony	NYY	$3,480,000	506
278	Repko, Jason	LAD	$500,000	504
279	Castro, Ramon	NYM	$560,000	501
280	Bellhorn, Mark	NYY	$3,130,000	500
281	Garciaparra, Nomar	CHC	$3,310,000	498
282	Spivey, Junior	WAS	$550,000	485
283	Betemit, Wilson	ATL	$500,000	479
284	Cirillo, Jeff	MIL	$500,000	478
285	Boone, Bret	MIN	$3,710,000	473
286	Perez, Eduardo	TB	$500,000	462
287	Miles, Aaron	COL	$1,850,000	462
288	Cota, Humberto	PIT	$500,000	462
289	Encarnacion, Edwin	CIN	$1,780,000	455
290	Doumit, Ryan	PIT	$500,000	455
291	DaVanon, Jeff	LAA	$500,000	448
292	Olerud, John	BOS	$500,000	447
293	Cairo, Miguel	NYM	$500,000	443
294	Jacobs, Mike	NYM	$2,720,000	438
295	Hollandsworth, Todd	ATL	$600,000	438
296	Gathright, Joey	TB	$500,000	433
297	Anderson, Marlon	NYM	$500,000	431
298	Wilson, Craig	PIT	$1,830,000	431
299	Sanchez, Alex	SF	$500,000	430
300	Closser, J.D.	COL	$500,000	426
301	Bloomquist, Willie	SEA	$500,000	423
302	McPherson, Dallas	LAA	$1,190,000	421
303	Palmeiro, Orlando	HOU	$500,000	417
304	Matsui, Kazuo	NYM	$500,000	416
305	Redman, Tike	PIT	$500,000	415
306	Surhoff, B.J.	BAL	$500,000	414
307	Mabry, John	STL	$500,000	413
308	Nix, Laynce	TEX	$500,000	409
309	Blum, Geoff	CHW	$500,000	408
310	Luna, Hector	STL	$500,000	408
311	Rolen, Scott	STL	$3,870,000	405
312	Olivo, Miguel	SD	$900,000	405
313	Guzman, Cristian	WAS	$500,000	405
314	Castro, Juan	MIN	$500,000	404
315	Thome, Jim	PHI	$3,650,000	396
316	Morse, Mike	SEA	$500,000	396
317	Fick, Robert	SD	$500,000	395
318	Gotay, Ruben	KC	$500,000	391
319	Thomas, Frank	CHW	$3,170,000	388
320	Byrd, Marlon	WAS	$500,000	382
321	Murton, Matt	CHC	$500,000	381
322	Carroll, Jamey	WAS	$500,000	378
323	Helms, Wes	MIL	$500,000	375
324	Piedra, Jorge	COL	$500,000	369
325	Fasano, Sal	BAL	$500,000	366
326	Gomez, Chris	BAL	$500,000	366
327	Eldred, Brad	PIT	$500,000	365
328	Wigginton, Ty	PIT	$1,740,000	365
329	DeRosa, Mark	TEX	$500,000	360
330	Newhan, David	BAL	$500,000	359
331	Bartlett, Jason	MIN	$740,000	359
332	Cora, Alex	BOS	$500,000	354
333	McCann, Brian	ATL	$500,000	351
334	Rodriguez, John	STL	$500,000	351
335	Bigbie, Larry	COL	$500,000	349
336	Granderson, Curtis	DET	$500,000	346
337	Kotchman, Casey	LAA	$500,000	345
338	Ozuna, Pablo	CHW	$500,000	343
339	Orr, Pete	ATL	$500,000	343
340	Cruz, Deivi	WAS	$500,000	340
341	Phelps, Josh	TB	$500,000	338
342	Ardoin, Danny	COL	$500,000	329
343	Rodriguez, Luis	MIN	$500,000	328
344	Lopez, Jose	SEA	$500,000	324
345	Dubois, Jason	CLE	$500,000	320
346	Young, Eric	SD	$500,000	316
347	Redmond, Mike	MIN	$500,000	314
348	Hernandez, Jose	CLE	$500,000	313
349	Jordan, Brian	ATL	$500,000	312
350	Izturis, Maicer	LAA	$500,000	312
351	Pratt, Todd	PHI	$500,000	296
352	Navarro, Dioner	LAD	$500,000	294
353	Terrero, Luis	ARI	$500,000	292
354	Bruntlett, Eric	HOU	$500,000	288
355	Blanco, Henry	CHC	$500,000	285
356	Betancourt, Yuniesky	SEA	$500,000	281
357	Torrealba, Yorvit	SEA	$500,000	281
358	Duffy, Chris	PIT	$500,000	274
359	Moeller, Chad	MIL	$500,000	273
360	Shealy, Ryan	COL	$500,000	270
361	Burroughs, Sean	SD	$500,000	270
362	Snyder, Chris	ARI	$500,000	270
363	McDonald, John	DET	$500,000	270
364	Ambres, Chip	KC	$500,000	267
365	McLouth, Nate	PIT	$500,000	267
366	Greene, Todd	COL	$500,000	265
367	Woodward, Chris	NYM	$500,000	261
368	Aybar, Willy	LAD	$500,000	260
369	Relaford, Desi	TOR	$500,000	260
370	Mirabelli, Doug	BOS	$500,000	260
371	Edwards, Mike	LAD	$500,000	260
372	Marrero, Eli	BAL	$500,000	257
373	Molina, Jose	LAA	$500,000	255
374	Sierra, Ruben	NYY	$500,000	254
375	Menechino, Frank	TOR	$500,000	253
376	McCracken, Quinton	ARI	$500,000	249
377	Vizcaino, Jose	HOU	$500,000	248
378	Baerga, Carlos	WAS	$500,000	242
379	Guiel, Aaron	KC	$500,000	238
380	Harris, Willie	CHW	$500,000	237
381	Gonzalez, Adrian	TEX	$500,000	236
382	Durazo, Erubiel	OAK	$1,980,000	234
383	Rivas, Luis	MIN	$500,000	234
384	Gerut, Jody	PIT	$500,000	231
385	Bagwell, Jeff	HOU	$1,810,000	226
386	Cruz, Jacob	CIN	$500,000	221
387	Stinnett, Kelly	ARI	$500,000	218
388	Quinlan, Robb	LAA	$500,000	212
389	Garabito, Eddy	COL	$500,000	209
390	Linden, Todd	SF	$500,000	203
391	Widger, Chris	CHW	$500,000	202
392	Valentin, Jose	LAD	$810,000	198
393	Mondesi, Raul	ATL	$500,000	197
394	Perez, Tomas	PHI	$500,000	193
395	Bonds, Barry	SF	$6,850,000	191
396	Wilson, Vance	DET	$500,000	181
397	Ross, David	SD	$500,000	181
398	Macias, Jose	CHC	$500,000	175
399	Thames, Marcus	DET	$500,000	175
400	Dobbs, Greg	SEA	$500,000	173
401	Magruder, Chris	MIL	$500,000	173
402	Johnson, Ben	SD	$500,000	172
403	Youkilis, Kevin	BOS	$500,000	170
404	Crosby, Bubba	NYY	$500,000	166
405	Chavez, Endy	PHI	$500,000	160
406	Restovich, Michael	PIT	$500,000	158
407	Martinez, Ramon	PHI	$500,000	158
408	Alomar, Sandy	TEX	$500,000	155
409	Castillo, Alberto	OAK	$500,000	154
410	Kapler, Gabe	BOS	$500,000	154
411	Cedeno, Ronny	CHC	$500,000	153
412	Offerman, Jose	NYM	$500,000	152
413	Ginter, Keith	OAK	$550,000	152
414	Hill, Bobby	PIT	$500,000	150
415	Bennett, Gary	WAS	$500,000	147
416	Harris, Lenny	FLA	$500,000	147
417	Perez, Timo	CHW	$500,000	146
418	Melhuse, Adam	OAK	$500,000	141
419	Diaz, Einar	STL	$500,000	138
420	Diaz, Matt	KC	$500,000	130
421	Gross, Gabe	TOR	$500,000	126
422	Singleton, Chris	TB	$500,000	126
423	Jimenez, D'Angelo	CIN	$500,000	122
424	Tiffee, Terry	MIN	$500,000	121
425	Hart, Corey	MIL	$500,000	120

PITCHERS

Rk.	Player	Team	Price	TSNP
1.	Carpenter, Chris	STL	$5,260,000	2877
2.	Santana, Johan	MIN	$9,610,000	2786
3.	Willis, Dontrelle	FLA	$5,190,000	2621
4.	Clemens, Roger	HOU	$7,800,000	2605
5.	Martinez, Pedro	NYM	$6,390,000	2581
6.	Pettitte, Andy	HOU	$4,790,000	2561
7.	Oswalt, Roy	HOU	$6,960,000	2424
8.	Rivera, Mariano	NYY	$6,840,000	2419
9.	Peavy, Jake	SD	$6,730,000	2347
10.	Zambrano, Carlos	CHC	$6,190,000	2344
11.	Smoltz, John	ATL	$5,570,000	2275
12.	Nathan, Joe	MIN	$5,810,000	2266
13.	Colon, Bartolo	LAA	$5,020,000	2248
14.	Johnson, Randy	NYY	$8,560,000	2246
15.	Cordero, Chad	WAS	$3,890,000	2226
16.	Wagner, Billy	PHI	$4,570,000	2217
17.	Buehrle, Mark	CHW	$6,210,000	2205
18.	Lidge, Brad	HOU	$5,500,000	2141
19.	Turnbow, Derrick	MIL	$980,000	2117
20.	Rodriguez, Francisco	LAA	$5,170,000	2097
21.	Myers, Brett	PHI	$2,940,000	2032
22.	Lackey, John	LAA	$2,570,000	1991
23.	Garland, Jon	CHW	$3,320,000	1968
24.	Webb, Brandon	ARI	$3,920,000	1963
25.	Zito, Barry	OAK	$4,310,000	1952
26.	Lee, Cliff	CLE	$3,610,000	1948
27.	Patterson, John	WAS	$1,890,000	1935
28.	Burnett, A.J.	FLA	$3,630,000	1931
29.	Contreras, Jose	CHW	$3,200,000	1920
30.	Jones, Todd	FLA	$1,130,000	1910
31.	Davis, Doug	MIL	$3,090,000	1908
32.	Baez, Danys	TB	$1,010,000	1902
33.	Beckett, Josh	FLA	$4,550,000	1878
34.	Garcia, Freddy	CHW	$5,570,000	1864
35.	Ryan, B.J.	BAL	$3,330,000	1861
36.	Dempster, Ryan	CHC	$1,580,000	1848
37.	Haren, Danny	OAK	$2,220,000	1847
38.	Capuano, Chris	MIL	$2,240,000	1834
39.	Wickman, Bob	CLE	$2,570,000	1822
40.	Wakefield, Tim	BOS	$3,110,000	1806
41.	Cordero, Francisco	TEX	$3,930,000	1790
42.	Isringhausen, Jason	STL	$5,400,000	1769
43.	Hoffman, Trevor	SD	$4,490,000	1768
44.	Lieber, Jon	PHI	$3,660,000	1764
45.	Loaiza, Esteban	WAS	$2,590,000	1759
46.	Weaver, Jeff	LAD	$2,450,000	1753
47.	Millwood, Kevin	CLE	$2,720,000	1735
48.	Sabathia, C.C.	CLE	$4,360,000	1721
49.	Lowe, Derek	LAD	$3,200,000	1718
50.	Street, Huston	OAK	$1,280,000	1717
51.	Hernandez, Livan	WAS	$5,410,000	1715
52.	Lowry, Noah	SF	$2,470,000	1707
53.	Prior, Mark	CHC	$6,710,000	1705
54.	Halladay, Roy	TOR	$5,340,000	1704
55.	Blanton, Joe	OAK	$1,080,000	1652
56.	Mulder, Mark	STL	$5,800,000	1641
57.	Harang, Aaron	CIN	$2,360,000	1637
58.	Fuentes, Brian	COL	$500,000	1636
59.	Guardado, Eddie	SEA	$3,540,000	1609
60.	Chen, Bruce	BAL	$1,300,000	1608
61.	Vazquez, Javier	ARI	$4,190,000	1588
62.	Suppan, Jeff	STL	$3,060,000	1577
63.	Hudson, Tim	ATL	$6,270,000	1568
64.	Sheets, Ben	MIL	$6,820,000	1567
65.	Hermanson, Dustin	CHW	$2,570,000	1565
66.	Maddux, Greg	CHC	$4,560,000	1564
67.	Harden, Rich	OAK	$4,780,000	1548
68.	Rogers, Kenny	TEX	$3,380,000	1533
69.	Byrd, Paul	LAA	$1,750,000	1531
70.	Towers, Josh	TOR	$1,510,000	1526
71.	Chacin, Gustavo	TOR	$1,030,000	1524
72.	Glavine, Tom	NYM	$3,480,000	1523
73.	Kazmir, Scott	TB	$2,230,000	1507
74.	Morris, Matt	STL	$3,810,000	1451
75.	Sosa, Jorge	ATL	$680,000	1428
76.	Clement, Matt	BOS	$4,300,000	1421
77.	Schmidt, Jason	SF	$7,460,000	1420
78.	Batista, Miguel	TOR	$1,240,000	1415
79.	Westbrook, Jake	CLE	$3,010,000	1413
80.	Radke, Brad	MIN	$3,370,000	1391
81.	Young, Chris	TEX	$770,000	1390
82.	Marquis, Jason	STL	$4,610,000	1383
83.	Silva, Carlos	MIN	$2,490,000	1372
84.	Bonderman, Jeremy	DET	$3,440,000	1357
85.	Mussina, Mike	NYY	$5,090,000	1354
86.	Arroyo, Bronson	BOS	$3,890,000	1351
87.	Moyer, Jamie	SEA	$2,520,000	1336
88.	Washburn, Jarrod	LAA	$2,530,000	1335
89.	Wells, David	BOS	$3,190,000	1326
90.	Farnsworth, Kyle	ATL	$570,000	1326
91.	Shields, Scot	LAA	$1,220,000	1287
92.	MacDougal, Mike	KC	$500,000	1275
93.	Benson, Kris	NYM	$2,870,000	1266
94.	Ohka, Tomo	MIL	$500,000	1265
95.	Penny, Brad	LAD	$2,780,000	1254
96.	Lopez, Rodrigo	BAL	$2,740,000	1254
97.	Heilman, Aaron	NYM	$500,000	1249
98.	Timlin, Mike	BOS	$500,000	1241
99.	Lidle, Cory	PHI	$770,000	1240
100.	Maroth, Mike	DET	$500,000	1235
101.	Duchscherer, Justin	OAK	$500,000	1232
102.	Valverde, Jose	ARI	$500,000	1199
103.	Elarton, Scott	CLE	$560,000	1192
104.	Walker, Tyler	SF	$500,000	1177
105.	Cabrera, Daniel	BAL	$1,520,000	1172
106.	Weathers, David	CIN	$500,000	1160
107.	Looper, Braden	NYM	$800,000	1160
108.	Ramirez, Horacio	ATL	$1,320,000	1153
109.	Claussen, Brandon	CIN	$500,000	1136
110.	Urbina, Ugueth	PHI	$500,000	1126
111.	Chacon, Shawn	NYY	$1,510,000	1107
112.	Johnson, Jason	DET	$1,510,000	1084
113.	Tomko, Brett	SF	$520,000	1080
114.	Robertson, Nate	DET	$650,000	1080
115.	Linebrink, Scott	SD	$500,000	1076
116.	Carrasco, Hector	WAS	$500,000	1073
117.	Bedard, Erik	BAL	$2,990,000	1049
118.	Eaton, Adam	SD	$3,070,000	1028
119.	Mesa, Jose	PIT	$1,860,000	1019
120.	Duke, Zach	PIT	$3,190,000	1014
121.	Seo, Jae Weong	NYM	$720,000	1011
122.	Santana, Ervin	LAA	$500,000	992
123.	Howry, Bob	CLE	$500,000	986
124.	Brazoban, Yhency	LAD	$2,140,000	982
125.	Politte, Cliff	CHW	$500,000	974
126.	Lohse, Kyle	MIN	$500,000	969
127.	Zambrano, Victor	NYM	$2,660,000	965
128.	Torres, Salomon	PIT	$500,000	957
129.	Gordon, Tom	NYY	$500,000	955
130.	Backe, Brandon	HOU	$1,130,000	953
131.	Lawrence, Brian	SD	$500,000	938
132.	Crain, Jesse	MIN	$500,000	938
133.	Saarloos, Kirk	OAK	$530,000	934
134.	Hernandez, Felix	SEA	$4,080,000	926
135.	Hernandez, Roberto	NYM	$500,000	923
136.	Reitsma, Chris	ATL	$500,000	919
137.	Williams, Dave	PIT	$500,000	916
138.	Williams, Woody	SD	$530,000	911
139.	Fossum, Casey	TB	$500,000	910
140.	Reyes, Al	STL	$500,000	906
141.	Wheeler, Dan	HOU	$500,000	901
142.	Rusch, Glendon	CHC	$1,490,000	896
143.	Rincon, Juan	MIN	$500,000	873
144.	Fultz, Aaron	PHI	$500,000	868
145.	Sanchez, Duaner	LAD	$500,000	866
146.	Padilla, Vicente	PHI	$500,000	858
147.	Seanez, Rudy	SD	$500,000	855
148.	Wang, Chien-Ming	NYY	$550,000	852
149.	Francis, Jeff	COL	$500,000	845
150.	Small, Aaron	NYY	$630,000	839
151.	Loe, Kameron	TEX	$500,000	831
152.	Redman, Mark	PIT	$2,580,000	819
153.	Wuertz, Michael	CHC	$500,000	812
154.	Franklin, Ryan	SEA	$500,000	807
155.	Wells, Kip	PIT	$500,000	803
156.	Betancourt, Rafael	CLE	$500,000	793
157.	Halsey, Brad	ARI	$1,400,000	787
158.	Meche, Gil	SEA	$540,000	782
159.	Schilling, Curt	BOS	$5,880,000	781
160.	Benitez, Armando	SF	$2,920,000	781
161.	Cotts, Neal	CHW	$500,000	780
162.	Benoit, Joaquin	TEX	$500,000	774
163.	Perez, Odalis	LAD	$2,120,000	763
164.	Hernandez, Orlando	CHW	$2,330,000	762
165.	Qualls, Chad	HOU	$500,000	753
166.	Park, Chan Ho	SD	$500,000	749
167.	Speier, Justin	TOR	$500,000	744
168.	Vargas, Claudio	ARI	$500,000	743
169.	Ortiz, Ramon	CIN	$500,000	739
170.	Bush, David	TOR	$500,000	739
171.	Madson, Ryan	PHI	$500,000	734
172.	Wise, Matt	MIL	$500,000	732
173.	Donnelly, Brendan	LAA	$500,000	731
174.	Moehler, Brian	FLA	$640,000	729
175.	Williams, Jerome	CHC	$500,000	728
176.	Tejeda, Robinson	PHI	$500,000	724
177.	Astacio, Pedro	SD	$500,000	722
178.	Eyre, Scott	SF	$500,000	720
179.	Majewski, Gary	WAS	$500,000	718
180.	Pineiro, Joel	SEA	$500,000	715
181.	Mateo, Julio	SEA	$500,000	714
182.	Riske, David	CLE	$500,000	712
183.	Ayala, Luis	WAS	$500,000	705
184.	Fogg, Josh	PIT	$500,000	703
185.	Kim, Byung-Hyun	COL	$500,000	700
186.	Walker, Pete	TOR	$500,000	699
187.	Hendrickson, Mark	TB	$500,000	694
188.	Lilly, Ted	TOR	$1,210,000	680
189.	Escobar, Kelvim	LAA	$1,190,000	680
190.	Rodney, Fernando	DET	$500,000	679
191.	Foulke, Keith	BOS	$4,360,000	678
192.	Downs, Scott	TOR	$500,000	678
193.	Rodriguez, Wandy	HOU	$500,000	672
194.	Estes, Shawn	ARI	$1,900,000	667
195.	Carrara, Giovanni	LAD	$500,000	666
196.	Frasor, Jason	TOR	$500,000	653
197.	Calero, Kiko	OAK	$500,000	644
198.	Wasdin, John	TEX	$500,000	639
199.	Williams, Todd	BAL	$500,000	637
200.	Santos, Victor	MIL	$500,000	637
201.	Mercker, Kent	CIN	$500,000	619
202.	Hernandez, Runelvys	KC	$500,000	618
203.	Sisco, Andy	KC	$500,000	611
204.	Houlton, D.J.	LAD	$500,000	605
205.	Cook, Aaron	COL	$500,000	603
206.	Wood, Mike	KC	$500,000	600
207.	Jenks, Bobby	CHW	$500,000	597
208.	Wood, Kerry	CHC	$3,460,000	597
209.	Fassero, Jeff	SF	$500,000	597
210.	Thompson, Brad	STL	$500,000	595
211.	Tavarez, Julian	STL	$500,000	590
212.	Witasick, Jay	OAK	$500,000	584
213.	Hennessey, Brad	SF	$500,000	584
214.	Wolf, Randy	PHI	$670,000	582
215.	Gonzalez, Mike	PIT	$500,000	578

Rk.	Player	Team	Price	TSNP
216.	Villone, Ron	FLA	$500,000	574
217.	Jennings, Jason	COL	$500,000	569
218.	Vargas, Jason	FLA	$530,000	567
219.	Putz, J.J.	SEA	$500,000	565
220.	Armas, Tony	WAS	$500,000	565
221.	Hammond, Chris	SD	$500,000	564
222.	Perez, Oliver	PIT	$3,190,000	563
223.	Thomson, John	ATL	$1,460,000	558
224.	Helling, Rick	MIL	$500,000	551
225.	Sturtze, Tanyon	NYY	$500,000	551
226.	Rhodes, Arthur	CLE	$500,000	550
227.	McCarthy, Brandon	CHW	$510,000	542
228.	Wright, Jamey	COL	$500,000	540
229.	Spurling, Chris	DET	$590,000	536
230.	Cain, Matt	SF	$2,860,000	533
231.	Kim, Sun-Woo	COL	$500,000	533
232.	Burgos, Ambiorix	KC	$500,000	532
233.	Hampton, Mike	ATL	$2,610,000	532
234.	Vizcaino, Luis	CHW	$500,000	531
235.	Waechter, Doug	TB	$500,000	528
236.	Cormier, Lance	ARI	$500,000	520
237.	Hensley, Clay	SD	$500,000	508
238.	Davies, Kyle	ATL	$500,000	501
239.	Carrasco, D.J.	KC	$500,000	501
240.	Mota, Guillermo	FLA	$840,000	501
241.	Cortes, David	COL	$500,000	495
242.	Hawkins, LaTroy	SF	$500,000	492
243.	Miller, Wade	BOS	$980,000	487
244.	Springer, Russ	HOU	$500,000	480
245.	Schoeneweis, Scott	TOR	$500,000	477
246.	Milton, Eric	CIN	$1,550,000	477
247.	Padilla, Juan	NYM	$500,000	476
248.	Belisle, Matt	CIN	$500,000	471
249.	German, Franklyn	DET	$500,000	471
250.	Romero, J.C.	MIN	$500,000	469
251.	Marte, Damaso	CHW	$500,000	469
252.	Flores, Randy	STL	$500,000	466
253.	Geary, Geoff	PHI	$500,000	464
254.	Baker, Scott	MIN	$500,000	464
255.	Meadows, Brian	PIT	$500,000	464
256.	DeJean, Mike	COL	$500,000	462
257.	Guerrier, Matt	MIN	$500,000	462
258.	White, Rick	PIT	$500,000	461
259.	Dessens, Elmer	LAD	$500,000	461
260.	Maholm, Paul	PIT	$1,820,000	458
261.	Takatsu, Shingo	NYM	$670,000	457
262.	Otsuka, Akinori	SD	$500,000	457
263.	Medders, Brandon	ARI	$500,000	452
264.	Vogelsong, Ryan	PIT	$500,000	452
265.	Chulk, Vinnie	TOR	$500,000	451
266.	Orvella, Chad	TB	$500,000	447
267.	Pavano, Carl	NYY	$3,350,000	445
268.	Douglass, Sean	DET	$500,000	445
269.	Yabu, Keiichi	OAK	$500,000	440
270.	Greinke, Zack	KC	$500,000	439
271.	Gagne, Eric	LA	$3,950,000	437
272.	Ohman, Will	CHC	$500,000	434
273.	Kennedy, Joe	OAK	$500,000	433
274.	McClung, Seth	TB	$500,000	424
275.	Kolb, Dan	ATL	$3,790,000	422
276.	Mays, Joe	MIN	$500,000	420
277.	Dominguez, Juan	TEX	$500,000	419
278.	Lyon, Brandon	ARI	$1,210,000	415
279.	Bruney, Brian	ARI	$500,000	408
280.	Boyer, Blaine	ATL	$500,000	407
281.	Walker, Jamie	DET	$500,000	405
282.	Brocail, Doug	TEX	$500,000	404
283.	Glover, Gary	MIL	$500,000	398
284.	Yan, Esteban	LAA	$500,000	390
285.	Cabrera, Fernando	CLE	$500,000	389
286.	Leiter, Al	NYY	$630,000	386
287.	Santana, Julio	MIL	$500,000	385
288.	Foster, John	ATL	$500,000	378
289.	Hasegawa, Shigetoshi	SEA	$500,000	378
290.	Ray, Chris	BAL	$500,000	377
291.	Dingman, Craig	DET	$500,000	377
292.	Myers, Mike	BOS	$500,000	373
293.	Baldwin, James	BAL	$500,000	370
294.	Ishii, Kazuhisa	NYM	$500,000	368
295.	Percival, Troy	DET	$690,000	366
296.	Miller, Matt	CLE	$500,000	365
297.	Papelbon, Jon	BOS	$500,000	362
298.	Kline, Steve	BAL	$500,000	348
299.	Eldred, Cal	STL	$500,000	347
300.	Dotel, Octavio	OAK	$1,620,000	345
301.	Schmoll, Steve	LAD	$500,000	337
302.	Julio, Jorge	BAL	$500,000	336
303.	Grabow, John	PIT	$500,000	330
304.	Stauffer, Tim	SD	$500,000	329
305.	Christiansen, Jason	LAA	$500,000	327
306.	Novoa, Roberto	CHC	$500,000	326
307.	Astacio, Ezequiel	HOU	$500,000	325
308.	Coffey, Todd	CIN	$500,000	325
309.	Munter, Scott	SF	$500,000	324
310.	Worrell, Tim	ARI	$500,000	320
311.	Shouse, Brian	TEX	$500,000	317
312.	Gregg, Kevin	LAA	$500,000	315
313.	Mecir, Jim	FLA	$500,000	311
314.	Bottalico, Ricky	BOS	$500,000	311
315.	Graves, Danny	NYM	$2,920,000	311
316.	Peralta, Joel	LAA	$500,000	308
317.	Harris, Jeff	SEA	$500,000	308
318.	Drese, Ryan	WAS	$500,000	306
319.	Eischen, Joey	WAS	$500,000	305
320.	Taschner, Jack	SF	$500,000	303
321.	Brower, Jim	ATL	$500,000	303
322.	Shackelford, Brian	CIN	$500,000	296
323.	Sele, Aaron	TEX	$500,000	296
324.	King, Ray	STL	$500,000	292
325.	Davis, Jason	CLE	$500,000	292
326.	Carter, Lance	TB	$500,000	288
327.	Correia, Kevin	SF	$500,000	282
328.	Koplove, Mike	ARI	$500,000	276
329.	Hudson, Luke	CIN	$500,000	276
330.	Sauerbeck, Scott	CLE	$500,000	275
331.	Borowski, Joe	TB	$500,000	275
332.	Carvajal, Marcos	COL	$500,000	274
333.	Nelson, Jeff	SEA	$500,000	269
334.	Miller, Trever	TB	$500,000	267
335.	Mulholland, Terry	MIN	$500,000	267
336.	Howell, J.P.	KC	$500,000	267
337.	Ponson, Sidney	BAL	$850,000	266
338.	Cormier, Rheal	PHI	$500,000	258
339.	Stanton, Mike	BOS	$500,000	256
340.	Mitre, Sergio	CHC	$500,000	253
341.	Bergmann, Jay	WAS	$500,000	249
342.	Colon, Roman	DET	$500,000	248
343.	Quantrill, Paul	FLA	$500,000	247
344.	Rincon, Ricardo	OAK	$500,000	243
345.	Rauch, Jon	WAS	$500,000	243
346.	Thornton, Matt	SEA	$500,000	240
347.	Lehr, Justin	MIL	$500,000	237
348.	Sherrill, George	SEA	$500,000	233
349.	de la Rosa, Jorge	MIL	$500,000	227
350.	Proctor, Scott	NYY	$500,000	221
351.	Colome, Jesus	TB	$500,000	219
352.	Keisler, Randy	CIN	$500,000	217
353.	Gonzalez, Jeremi	BOS	$500,000	215
354.	Wellemeyer, Todd	CHC	$500,000	210
355.	Wagner, Ryan	CIN	$500,000	209
356.	Trachsel, Steve	NYM	$500,000	203
357.	Rodriguez, Ricardo	TEX	$500,000	203
358.	Bell, Heath	NYM	$500,000	202
359.	Snell, Ian	PIT	$500,000	202
360.	Groom, Buddy	ARI	$500,000	200
361.	Bernero, Adam	ATL	$500,000	198
362.	Harville, Chad	BOS	$500,000	192
363.	Liriano, Francisco	MIN	$3,350,000	188
364.	Byrdak, Tim	BAL	$500,000	187
365.	Reyes, Dennys	NYY	$500,000	186
366.	Harper, Travis	TB	$500,000	185
367.	Wright, Jaret	NYY	$2,260,000	183
368.	Dohmann, Scott	COL	$500,000	183
369.	Gobble, Jimmy	KC	$500,000	181
370.	Halama, John	WAS	$500,000	179
371.	Affeldt, Jeremy	KC	$500,000	175
372.	Speier, Ryan	COL	$500,000	173
373.	Burns, Mike	HOU	$500,000	171
374.	Obermueller, Wes	MIL	$500,000	171
375.	Woods, Jake	LAA	$500,000	170
376.	Valdez, Ismael	FLA	$500,000	170
377.	Reyes, Anthony	STL	$2,060,000	169
378.	Davis, Kane	MIL	$500,000	168
379.	Wunsch, Kelly	LAD	$500,000	168
380.	Hancock, Josh	CIN	$500,000	167
381.	Bautista, Denny	KC	$500,000	167
382.	Darensbourg, Vic	DET	$500,000	166
383.	Lopez, Aquilino	PHI	$500,000	160
384.	Koo, Dae Sung	NYM	$500,000	159
385.	Perisho, Matt	BOS	$500,000	159
386.	Parrish, John	BAL	$500,000	159
387.	Bradford, Chad	BOS	$500,000	159
388.	Olsen, Scott	FLA	$800,000	158
389.	Accardo, Jeremy	SF	$500,000	158
390.	Osoria, Franquelis	LAD	$500,000	157
391.	Rakers, Aaron	BAL	$500,000	154
392.	Bump, Nate	FLA	$500,000	152
393.	Brito, Eude	PHI	$500,000	146
394.	Bootcheck, Chris	LAA	$500,000	142
395.	Acevedo, Jose	COL	$500,000	142
396.	Capellan, Jose	MIL	$500,000	142
397.	Gallo, Mike	HOU	$500,000	140
398.	DiNardo, Lenny	BOS	$500,000	140
399.	Standridge, Jason	CIN	$500,000	138
400.	Messenger, Randy	FLA	$500,000	137
401.	Maine, John	BAL	$500,000	137
402.	Riedling, John	FLA	$500,000	136
403.	McBride, Macay	ATL	$500,000	135
404.	Rueter, Kirk	SF	$500,000	131
405.	Breslow, Craig	SD	$500,000	130
406.	McGowan, Dustin	TOR	$1,590,000	130
407.	Alfonseca, Antonio	FLA	$500,000	130
408.	Thompson, Derek	LAD	$500,000	129
409.	Rodriguez, Felix	NYY	$500,000	128
410.	Ramirez, Erasmo	TEX	$500,000	128
411.	Adams, Mike	MIL	$500,000	127
412.	Penn, Hayden	BAL	$500,000	126
413.	DuBose, Eric	BAL	$500,000	126
414.	Williams, Randy	COL	$500,000	126
415.	Villarreal, Oscar	ARI	$500,000	124
416.	Eveland, Dana	MIL	$500,000	122
417.	Brown, Kevin	NYY	$580,000	122
418.	Grilli, Jason	DET	$500,000	122
419.	Tsao, Chin-hui	COL	$500,000	119
420.	Nomo, Hideo	NYY	$500,000	113
421.	Jensen, Ryan	KC	$500,000	112
422.	Cooper, Brian	SF	$500,000	112
423.	Aybar, Manny	NYM	$500,000	112
424.	Embree, Alan	NYY	$500,000	111
425.	Broxton, Jonathan	LAD	$500,000	107